Visio® 2003 Bible

Visio® 2003 Bible

Bonnie Biafore

Wiley Publishing, Inc.

Visio® 2003 Bible

Published by
Wiley Publishing, Inc.
10475 Crosspoint Boulevard
Indianapolis, IN 46256
www.wiley.com

Library of Congress Control Number: 2004104001

ISBN: 0-7645-5724-6

Manufactured in the United States of America

10 9 8 7 6 5 4 3 2

1Q/SQ/QU/QU/IN

For general information on our other products and services or to obtain technical support, please contact our Customer Care Department within the U.S. at (800) 762-2974, outside the U.S. at (317) 572-3993 or fax (317) 572-4002.

Wiley also publishes its books in a variety of electronic formats. Some content that appears in print may not be available in electronic books.

About the Author

Bonnie Biafore is an author as well as a project management consultant. As a consultant, she enjoys working with different clients and the diversity of projects she experiences, from CAD systems for structural steel fabrication to speech-enabled applications for telephone service field technicians and systems to manage hydro-electric power. While she's sometimes tough on her clients, she is a far worse taskmaster for herself.

Bonnie has written several books, including *Troubleshooting Microsoft Project 2002* (Microsoft Press) and *The NAIC Stock Selection Handbook* (NAIC). Since August 2000 she has been writing for *Better Investing* magazine a monthly column called *Web Watch*, which delves into the use of the World Wide Web for investing and how to develop good investing habits and smart and safe computer practices.

She is well known for her clear explanations of technical topics, whether it's the inscrutable workings of computer software or the enigma of high finance. She applies her education from MIT and Columbia University to digest technical topics and then puts her organizational skills and humor to work to present material that engages beginners and experts alike.

Her education and work experience make her the ideal author for this Visio book. With a Bachelor of Science in Architecture and a Master of Science in Structural Engineering, she is well versed in using Visio for architecture and engineering and integrating it with CAD applications. As a project manager and consultant, she constantly applies Visio to office productivity problems. As a software project manager and application developer, she has also used Visio to document databases, software systems, and networks. As an engineer, she is fascinated with both the simplicity and power of Visio and enjoys experimenting with its customization and automation features.

Credits

Senior Acquisitions Editor
Jim Minatel

Development Editor
James H. Russell

Technical Editors
Bonnie Watts
Scott Ambler

Production Editor
Eric Newman

Copy Editor
Luann Rouff

Editorial Manager
Mary Beth Wakefield

**Vice President & Executive
Group Publisher**
Richard Swadley

**Vice President and
Executive Publisher**
Bob Ipsen

Vice President and Publisher
Joseph B. Wikert

Executive Editorial Director
Mary Bednarek

Project Coordinator
Erin Smith

Graphics and Production Specialists
Beth Brooks
Carrie Foster
Lauren Goddard
Heather Pope

Quality Control Technician
Charles Spencer
Brian H. Walls

Proofreading and Indexing
TECHBOOKS Production Services

To my agent, Neil Salkind, who always believes I'm better than I am and then helps me prove him right.

Preface

Visio® 2003 Bible is a comprehensive guide to Microsoft's popular diagramming software. Covering both Visio Standard and Visio Professional, this book explains Visio fundamentals as well as advanced techniques applicable to any type of diagram. It also describes in detail how to use each of the specialized templates that Visio Standard and Visio Professional offer.

Visio 2003 includes significant changes and enhancements as well as many new features. Many templates and shapes have been improved to look and behave more consistently. Visio 2003 offers several new and improved collaboration tools, such as ink and markup, along with numerous productivity enhancements. However, several features have been discontinued, including the Forms template, the Visio Network Equipment Sampler, and a few wizards and tools. Visio 2003 Bible identifies these new features, enhancements, and changes and differentiates the capabilities available in both the Standard and Professional versions versus those available only in Visio Professional.

Visio 2003 offers a powerful combination of simple concepts and straightforward tools with far-reaching application. Whether you want to communicate basic business processes or highly specialized technical topics, Visio offers tools to simplify your work. This book strives to follow the same model. It explains Visio's concepts and basic tools in a way that helps beginners get started and more advanced users get better. In addition, the book includes dozens of chapters on specialized templates that describe how the template, tools, and shapes support the work required and simplify typical tasks.

Is This Book for You?

Visio 2003 covers a lot of ground, and this book is right there with it. If you use Visio or want to start using it, you can benefit from reading this book. Beginners can learn the basic concepts and techniques that are the foundation of Visio's power in every field and then apply those techniques to create the type of diagrams they need. Readers with some Visio experience can learn how to increase their productivity, use specialized templates and employ advanced techniques to draw more effectively or customize solutions. Advanced users can learn about new features, changes, and how to replace the features that have been discontinued in Visio 2003.

Although the book is fast paced, beginners can learn to use Visio, while more advanced users can notch up their productivity by following step-by-step instructions and applying tips and techniques. Readers in a hurry will appreciate the topic organization that makes it easy to find a solution as well as Tips and Cautions that help solve problems quickly.

Conventions Used in This Book

To help you get the most from the text and keep track of what's happening, a number of conventions are used throughout the book:

- ✦ When important terms are first introduced, they are highlighted in *italic*.
- ✦ Characters that need to be typed in are in **bold**.
- ✦ Keyboard strokes appear as follows: Ctrl+A.
- ✦ URLs, filenames, directory names, and other program elements are contrasted from regular text in a `monospaced font like this`.

Icons Used in This Book

Following is a brief description of the icons used to highlight certain types of material in this book:

 This icon highlights helpful hints, time-saving techniques, or alternative methods for accomplishing tasks.

 This icon identifies additional information about the topic being discussed.

 This icon alerts you to potential problems or methods that can impede your work if not used properly.

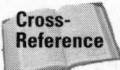 This icon points you to other chapters or books that contain additional information about a topic.

 This icon emphasizes new or significantly enhanced features in Visio 2003.

How This Book Is Organized

Visio 2003 Bible contains 41 chapters, divided into seven parts. In addition, the book is accompanied by a Web site (www.wiley.com/compbooks/biafore) that provides links to all the Web sites referenced in the book and a link to download-able sample Visio files you can use to practice what you've learned. The following sections provide an overview of each part of the book.

Part I: Understanding Visio Fundamentals

Part I introduces the features that distinguish Visio 2003 from the 2002 version as well as Visio's basic concepts and techniques. The first chapter provides an overview of Visio 2003's new features and explains concepts such as templates and stencils, drag and drop drawing, and the components of the Visio interface. Chapters 2 and 3 explain how to work with Visio files, drawing tools, drawings, and drawing pages. Chapters 4 and 5 show you how to produce diagrams by creating and editing shapes and connectors. Chapters 6 and 7 introduce techniques to improve the appearance and readability of diagrams using text and formatting.

Part II: Integrating Visio Drawings

Visio 2003 includes many new and improved integration features, as explained in this part. Chapter 8 discusses methods for linking and embedding elements in Visio or linking and embedding Visio objects into other applications. Chapter 9 describes methods for importing and exporting data to and from Visio, in addition to tech-niques for publishing Visio diagrams to the Web. Chapter 10 covers techniques and procedures for linking Visio shapes with data to dynamically update Visio drawings based on data stored in other applications.

Part III: Using Visio for Office Productivity

Part III is the first of three parts in this book that cover specialized templates. It begins with Chapter 11, which describes new and existing tools for collaborating with others, a critical element to office productivity. Chapters 12 and 13 cover tem-plates for building block diagrams and charts and graphs. Chapter 14 explains the many productivity tools, shapes, wizards, and data-sharing features for document-ing organizations in the Organization Chart template. Chapters 15 and 16 explain tools and techniques for documenting flowcharts and business processes. Chapter 17 discusses Visio's tools for documenting and scheduling projects. Chapter 18 describes the Visio Brainstorming template.

Part IV: Using Visio in Information Technology

Part IV describes the tools, wizards, and shapes that make Visio the most popular tool for documenting software systems and networks. Chapter 19 provides detailed instructions for modeling and documenting databases and database systems using a variety of notations. Chapter 20 describes how to document software systems with the Unified Modeling Language using the modeling tools available with the UML Model template and how to create different types of UML diagrams. Chapter 21 introduces several additional templates for documenting software systems. Chapter 22 describes Visio's template for mapping Web sites. Chapter 23 describes techniques for creating effective network diagrams and identifies the network features no longer available in Visio 2003.

Part V: Using Visio for Architecture and Engineering

Visio 2003 works for scaled drawings as well as it does for diagrams. Part V covers Visio's tools for scaled drawings and discusses what Visio can and can't do for architectural and engineering drawings. Chapter 24 is an introduction to the concepts that underlie scaled drawings, such as scale, units, and dimensions. Chapter 25 describes different methods for creating scaled drawings and how to use layers to manage information. Chapter 26 describes procedures for adding basic plan components, such as walls, windows, doors, and furniture, as well as how to create other types of architectural and engineering plans. Chapter 27 discusses how to use Visio's Space Plan template to plan space and manage facilities. Chapter 28 describes Visio's tools for integrating Visio and CAD drawings, which are all based on AutoCAD file formats. Chapter 29 covers Visio's Electrical Engineering, Mechanical Engineering, and Process Engineering templates.

Part VI: Customizing Templates, Stencils, and Shapes

Part VI returns to Visio concepts and techniques with a focus on customization. Chapter 30 discusses how to create and customize templates so you can start new drawings with the settings you want. Chapter 31 describes techniques for creating and customizing stencils to create custom collections of built-in shapes, shapes you've modified, or custom shapes you've developed. Chapter 32 discusses techniques for customizing shapes or creating your own and explains how to use custom properties to store data. Chapter 33 digs deeper into customizing shapes by showing you how to modify fields in Visio ShapeSheets or write custom formulas to control shape appearance and behavior. Chapter 34 explains the benefits and techniques for formatting with styles and describes how to create custom line patterns, fill patterns, and line ends. Chapter 35 describes techniques for customizing or creating your own toolbars and menus. Chapter 36 introduces the techniques available for automating Visio, including macros and writing add-ins.

Part VII: Quick Reference

Part VII includes helpful information and reference lists. Chapter 37 describes the process for installing Visio 2003. Chapter 38 provides different sources of help available for Visio 2003, both within the product and online. Chapter 39 identifies additional sources for customized and specialized templates, stencils, and Visio-based solutions. Chapter 40 is a reference to the most helpful keyboard shortcuts. Chapter 41 identifies the templates that Visio Standard and Visio Professional provide and the stencils each one opens.

Acknowledgments

Books are a collaboration of people and talents — and the final product is all the better for it.

My thanks go to my editors, Jim Minatel and James Russell, for their confidence and support; to my technical editors, Bonnie Watts and Scott Ambler, for making sure that the information in this book is not only accurate but practical; and to my copy editor, Luann Rouff, for making sure the whole ball of wax is readable. Thanks also to Teresa Stover, whose meticulous writing and readable style push me to improve.

In addition, my gratitude goes to my husband, Peter Speer, who took care of our life while I wrote this book. Finally, thanks to our dogs, Emma and Shea, who protected my feet, if not our computer cables, these many months.

Contents at a Glance

Contents

Part V: Using Visio for Architecture and Engineering   449

Chapter 24: Working with Scaled Drawings 451

Chapter 25: Creating Scaled Plan Drawings 467

Part VII: Quick Reference   687

Understanding Visio Fundamentals

Getting Started with Visio

Humans are visual creatures, so it isn't surprising that we visualize and communicate our ideas, designs, and final products graphically. In the past, high-quality graphics were the work of professional graphic artists and illustrators, but with Visio 2003, anyone can produce informative and attractive diagrams, drawings, and models. Visio is so straightforward that you can use it to capture the fast-paced output of brainstorming sessions or the frequent changes made to initial designs and models. At the same time, Visio is powerful enough to develop sophisticated models, and precise enough to document the details of existing systems.

Visio 2003 is like a good friend with expertise in dozens of fields. It jumpstarts your efforts with solutions designed specifically to produce different types of drawings. Visio templates set up your work environment with menus of specialized tools, sets of predefined shapes, and drawing settings such as page size and orientation typical for the type of drawing you want to create. Visio stencils categorize thousands of predefined symbols by industry, drawing type, and application. These Visio *SmartShapes* have built-in behaviors and properties to help you quickly assemble drawings and collect information.

Simplicity and convenience are key to Visio's power. To construct a drawing, you drag and drop predrawn shapes from stencils onto drawing pages. Defining relationships between shapes is as easy as dropping one shape onto another or dragging and dropping connectors onto shapes. Specialized tools help lay out drawings and perform typical tasks. The simplicity of integrating Visio with tools such as Microsoft Office, AutoCAD, Adobe Framemaker, and database management systems makes it easy to maintain drawings and documentation of systems.

What's New in Visio 2003?

Visio 2003 delivers brand-new templates and shapes as well as significant improvements and enhancements to many existing ones. In addition, Visio 2003 includes new and improved features to boost your productivity and enhance collaboration with others. You can send Microsoft feedback about the product or rate the usefulness of help topics and templates.

 **New Feature** Look for the New Feature icon throughout this book to learn more about what's new and improved.

New and Improved Shapes and Templates

The Visio team expands the scope of the product with every release. Visio 2003 introduces the following new templates and shapes:

✦ **Business Process templates** — New templates for event-driven process chains, fault tree analysis, and work flow, plus a new home for other business process templates

✦ **Brainstorming** — A replacement for the Mind Mapping template

✦ **Timeline** — A new template for documenting project timelines

✦ **Space Plan Startup Wizard** (Visio Professional only) — A new tool for building space plans quickly

✦ **Detailed Network Diagram** (Visio Professional only) — A replacement for the Logical Network Diagram

✦ **Rack Diagram** (Visio Professional only) — A new template for designing equipment placement in racks

✦ **Windows XP User Interface** (Visio Professional only) — A new template for designing Windows XP user interfaces

You'll appreciate the enhancements added to many existing templates and shapes, including the following:

✦ Calendar

✦ Organization Chart

✦ Basic Network Diagram

✦ Space Plan Import Data Wizard (Visio Professional only)

✦ Web Site Map (Visio Professional only)

✦ Electrical Engineering (Visio Professional only)

✦ Building Plan (Visio Professional only)

Productivity Enhancements

Visio enhances its reputation for being quick and easy with the following new features:

✦ **Task panes** — You can access many of Visio's most popular features on ten new task panes, which are docked to the right of the drawing page by default.

✦ **Shape management** — You can find shapes faster with Search for Shapes, an improved replacement for the Find Shape feature. You can organize your frequently used shapes on the Favorites stencil or add them to custom stencils, which you can store in the new My Shapes folder for easy access.

✦ **Editing tools** — Shapes now include rotation handles so you can rotate them without switching drawing tools. To select multiple shapes, you can choose from the Pointer, Lasso Select, or Multiple Select tools. It's also easier to coordinate colors if you use templates with built-in color schemes.

✦ **Getting started** — The Diagram Gallery provides an overview of Visio drawing types to help you select an appropriate template. Microsoft Office Online includes additional templates and clip art, as well as starter drawings that already contain basic content to get you going. For an introduction to Visio's features, you can use the Getting Started Tutorial on the Visio Help menu.

✦ **CAD integration** — The DWG Converter produces more accurate Visio representations of your original CAD drawings.

✦ **Help resources** — Online help from Microsoft Office Online provides up-to-the-minute help and in-depth articles about Visio and other Office applications. The Help and Template Help task panes provide access to almost all of Visio's help resources, with a few more on the Visio Help menu and online. You can pause the pointer over a shape on a stencil to view a description and access a Help link.

✦ **Customer feedback** — You can help improve future versions of Visio by choosing to participate in the Customer Experience Improvement Program, in which Microsoft collects information about your hardware configuration and how you use Microsoft Office programs. In addition, you can provide feedback about programs, the effectiveness of help topics, templates, and Microsoft Office Online content.

✦ **Features for developers** — In addition to a Visio 2003 ActiveX control for incorporating Visio into host applications, developers can increase their productivity with new ShapeSheet functions, keyboard and mouse events, and other tools. New interface elements such as ShapeStudio and the Formula Tracing window make it easier to create SmartShapes. (Visio Professional only)

Collaboration and Sharing

Collaboration and the subsequent sharing of documents are key initiatives for Microsoft today. Visio 2003 includes a number of new features to simplify collaboration with your colleagues:

✦ **Track markup** — You can propose changes to drawings and review the changes proposed by your coworkers. Each person's changes appear in a unique color on a separate overlay.

✦ **Ink** — You can add hand-drawn shapes or handwritten notes to drawings using a tablet PC or any computer with an electronic pen device. You can edit Ink shapes or add them to stencils just like other Visio shapes.

✦ **Scalable Vector Graphic format** — Visio 2003 now supports the Scalable Vector Graphics (SVG) format.

✦ **Microsoft Office Visio Viewer 2003** — People who don't have Visio can view and print your Visio drawings after downloading the Visio Viewer from the Microsoft Download Center.

✦ **Document Workspaces** — People can collaborate on documents stored in Document Workspaces, which are Microsoft Windows SharePoint Services sites. Contributors can work on the master copy in the Document Workspace or edit their own copy, which they can synchronize periodically with the master.

✦ **Language handling** — Visio 2003 supports Unicode, End User Defined Character sets, and the new Chinese character-encoding standard, GB18030. In addition, Multilingual User Interface packs simplify Visio deployment in global enterprises by displaying text for the user interface, Help, and wizards in other languages.

Features Discontinued in Visio 2003

A few templates and tools are no longer available. However, you can search Microsoft Office Online or other Web sites for replacements.

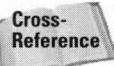
Cross-
Reference
To find other sources for Visio shapes and templates, refer to Chapter 39.

✦ **Data Flow Model Diagram Model Explorer** (Visio Professional only) — The Data Flow Model Diagram template no longer contains the Model Explorer. However, the UML template still has its Model Explorer.

✦ **Directory Services Directory Navigator** (Visio Professional only) — The Directory Services Diagram template no longer contains the Directory Navigator.

✦ **Forms** — The Forms template is no longer available. You can use Microsoft's new product, Infopath, to build forms and communicate data.

✦ **Import Flowchart Data Wizard** — You must import data into a flowchart in an earlier version of Visio and save the result in that version. You can then open the file in Visio 2003.

✦ **Organization Chart Conversion Utility** — You must convert an organization chart in an earlier version of Visio and save the result in that version. You can then open the organization chart in Visio 2003.

✦ **Visio Network Equipment Sampler** (Visio Professional only) — Shapes in the VNE Sampler are no longer available, but many equipment manufacturers provide shapes for their equipment on their Web sites.

Visio has dropped support for the following file formats and their converters:

✦ Adobe Illustrator

✦ ABC Flow Charter, versions 2.0, 3.0, and 4.0

✦ CorelDRAW!, versions 3.0 through 7.0

✦ CorelFLOW 2.0

✦ Corel Clipart

✦ Computer Graphics Metafile

✦ Microstation (DGN)

✦ MicroGrafx Designer 3.1

✦ MicroGrafx Designer 6.0 English

✦ Postscript and Encapsulated Postscript

✦ Initial Graphics Exchange Specification

✦ ZSoft PC Paintbrush (PCX)

✦ Mac Clipboard

✦ Text Files (TXT) and Comma Separated Values (CSV)

What Visio Is and Isn't

Visio can be many things to many people. Applied properly, Visio 2003 can help you produce simple diagrams or complex models. These far-reaching capabilities can be confusing if you don't understand how they differ. Even worse, you can become quite frustrated if you try to use Visio for tasks for which it wasn't designed.

Many drawings are simple diagrams with some basic connections and little or no associated data. For these drawings, you can simply drag and drop shapes and connectors in either Visio Standard or Visio Professional. The remaining chapters in Part I, Understanding Visio Fundamentals, describe the basic tools you need to diagram with Visio.

However, Visio Professional can also produce intelligent models and specialized documentation for numerous fields, including software engineering, architecture, mechanical and electrical engineering, and business process modeling. Templates for these advanced applications contain tools for performing specialized tasks. The shapes contained in the stencils for these templates have smart features —

built-in behaviors and attributes that fit the shapes to their role. For instance, intersecting walls in building plans are smart enough to clean up their overlapping lines. Cubicle shapes might contain properties that identify the people occupying the enclosed space for occupancy reports. These features are time-savers when you know how to use them, but can make Visio seem to have a mind of its own when you don't. Parts III, IV, and V of this book teach you the ins and outs of Visio's more sophisticated solutions.

You can draw precise plans to scale with Visio. Visio Standard supports only basic building plans, whereas Visio Professional supports a variety of architectural and engineering plans. Nonetheless, you'll probably want the extra power of a CAD application, such as AutoCAD, to design and document large or complex plans. Even so, Visio can be a helpful companion to your CAD application. You can create shapes faster and more easily in Visio and then import them for use in AutoCAD or other CAD applications. Team members who don't have access to AutoCAD can create their drawings in Visio using CAD drawings as a backdrop and import their work into AutoCAD if necessary. Visio also simplifies preparing presentations for large projects.

Understanding Visio Concepts

Visio enhances your drawing and modeling productivity because so many of its elements include features that incorporate industry expertise. Most of the time, you don't even think about how much Visio does for you because the templates, stencils, and shapes do just what you would expect. However, some of Visio's specialized capabilities might surprise or even confuse you at first. By understanding the concepts that make Visio so powerful, you can prevent problems and maintain your productivity.

Using Templates and Stencils

In the real world, templates are patterns you use to build something. For example, you could use a standard design for a log house to simplify the construction of your home. In Visio, templates are solutions that facilitate the construction of a specific type of drawing. Each template comprises settings, stencils, styles, and special commands to make your work on a drawing as easy as possible.

Visio stencils are categorized collections of shapes. To continue the house analogy, a Visio stencil is like a catalog of cedar logs and connecting brackets that are available from your local building supply store. To build your home, you order the components you need from the store and assemble them according to your house design. In Visio, you assemble your drawings by dragging and dropping shapes from stencils onto your drawing page.

When you create a drawing based on a template, Visio does the following things:

✦ **Opens stencils with shapes** — Visio opens stencils that contain the shapes you need for the type of drawing you are creating.

✦ **Includes styles** — Visio provides special formatting styles typical for the current drawing type. For example, a construction project created from a floor plan template includes line styles typically used to dimension architectural plans.

✦ **Automatically displays menus and toolbars** — If the template contains a special menu, Visio adds an entry for the menu to the menu bar. If the template contains a special toolbar, Visio floats the toolbar in the drawing area.

✦ **Specifies settings** — Visio specifies settings typical for the type of drawing. For basic block diagrams, Visio uses letter-size paper, portrait orientation, one-to-one scale, and inches for measurement units. For site plans, it specifies a 36" × 42" architectural drawing size in landscape orientation, a scale of 1 inch to 10 feet, and measurement units of feet and inches.

✦ **Displays rulers and grid** — To make positioning shapes easy, the rulers and grid take into account the scale and units for the drawing. For example, a block diagram shows inches on the rulers with each grid cell equal to one-quarter inch. Conversely, rulers for a site plan display feet in the rulers with each grid cell equal to ten feet.

Dragging and Dropping Shapes to Create Drawings

Visio's philosophy is elegantly simple — you construct drawings by dragging and dropping predefined shapes onto drawing pages. Although working with Visio can seem like copying clip art into a document, Visio shapes are much more powerful, quickly transforming a blank page into a professional document with a few applications of drag and drop.

What Makes Shapes Smart

Visio shapes can represent many things: ideas, processes, components of a model, and real-world objects such as people, places, and things. Visio calls them *SmartShapes* because they have built-in properties and behaviors that give them intelligence. As you work on a drawing, shape behaviors help you position the shapes and connect them appropriately to other shapes. For example, when you place a door shape in a wall, the door lines up with the wall and creates an opening into a room, as shown in Figure 1-1. That same door might contain properties to modify the shape or identify it, also shown in Figure 1-1. For example, one door property specifies whether the door is centered in the wall. Other door properties can define a door's dimensions, its catalog number, or its associated room number, so you can produce a schedule of the doors you need and where they belong in your building.

Door shapes can create openings in walls

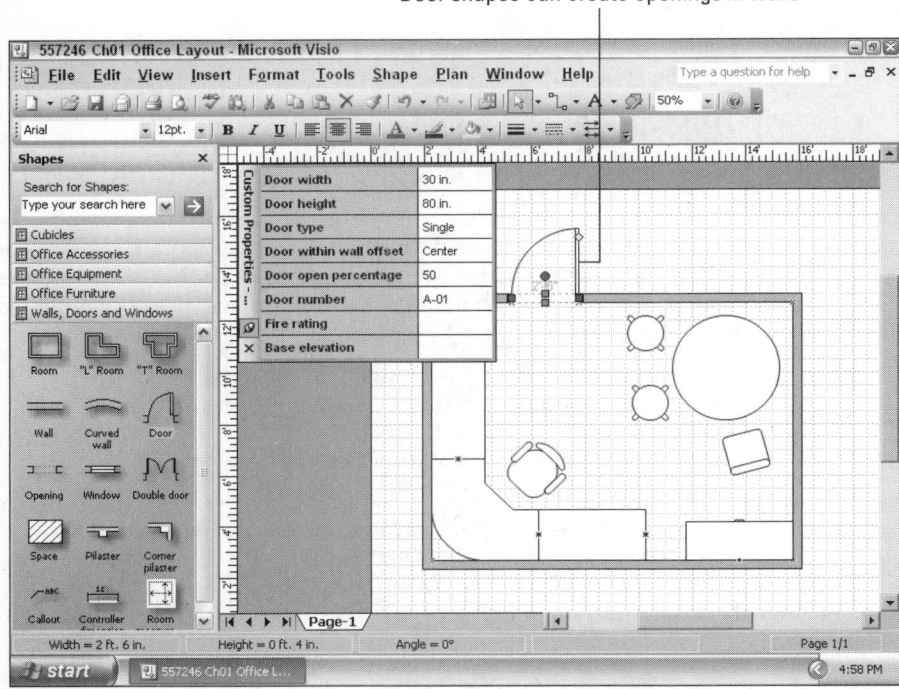

Figure 1-1: Shapes include behaviors and properties that give them intelligence.

To learn about how to define properties and behaviors for shapes, see Chapter 32.

In Visio, predrawn shapes are called *masters*, which are stored and categorized in stencils. When you drag and drop a master from a stencil onto your drawing page, you create a copy, which is called an *instance* of that master. Each instance inherits its master's behaviors, so it knows how to act when you add it to your drawing. It also inherits its master's properties, so you can assign unique values to an instance.

Using Handles to Manipulate Shapes

Shapes have other features to help you position, resize, and connect them to one another. When you select a shape, Visio marks these features with colored graphics, as illustrated in Figure 1-2. Shapes include the following types of handles:

✦ **Selection handles**—Red or green boxes appear when you select a shape. You can drag these selection handles to resize a shape or attach connectors to them.

✦ **Connection points**—Blue Xs mark locations where you can glue connectors or lines.

✦ **Rotation handle** — This is a red circle that you can drag to rotate a shape.

✦ **Control handles** — Yellow diamonds that appear on some shapes. You can drag control handles to modify a shape's appearance — for instance, to change the swing on a door.

✦ **Eccentricity handles** — Green circles that you can drag to change the shape of an arc.

Shapes can be one-dimensional or two-dimensional. Two-dimensional shapes, such as rectangles and office tables, have selection handles at each corner and the midpoints of each side, which you can drag to modify a shape's height and width. 1D shapes, such as connectors, lines, and arrows, have end points that you can drag to change the length of the shape. You can change the length of 1D shapes as well as the width of some 1D shapes, such as the 1D single arrow. However, you can't change length and width at the same time because a 1D shape doesn't have selection handles at its corners.

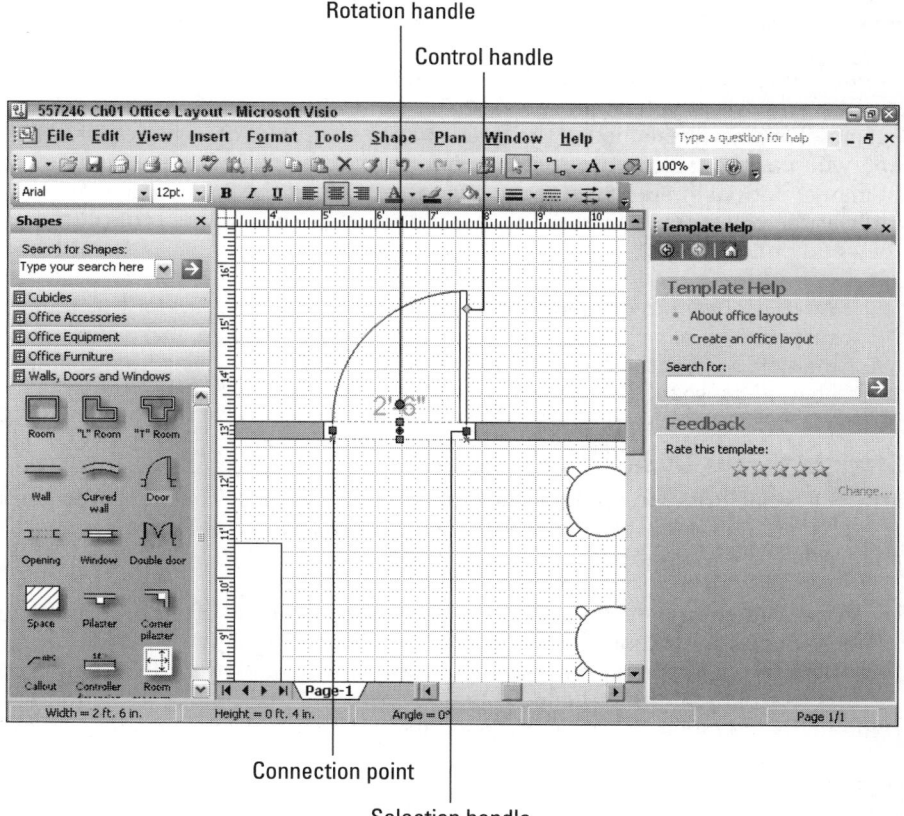

Figure 1-2: Visio uses colored marks to identify handles you can use to modify shapes.

Connecting Shapes

Relationships can convey as much information as the elements they connect. Whether you are showing who reports to a manager in an organization or defining the relationship between two database tables, connections between Visio shapes are important. In Visio, connections not only provide information about a relationship, they also help you lay out and rearrange the shapes on your drawing.

Cross-Reference To learn more about connecting shapes, see Chapter 5.

What Connectors Do

Connectors are Visio shapes that define the relationships between other shapes. In essence, connectors are lines with shapes attached to each end. When you move two connected shapes, the connector between them adjusts to maintain that connection. Likewise, connectors maintain shape connectivity when you use Visio's automatic layout tools. For example, you can change the layout of an organization chart from horizontal to vertical and the connectors alter their paths as the employee shapes take up their new locations.

Connectors have start and end points that define direction for a connection between shapes. Which end you connect to a shape can make a big difference in behavior. For example, in a database model, the table shape at the start of a connector is the ***parent***, whereas the table at the end of a connector is the ***child***. When you define a one-to-many relationship between those connected tables, the one is associated with the table at the connector's start point, and the many belongs to the table at the connector's end point.

Tip When you want to differentiate the predecessor and successor for two connected shapes, such as in a data flow diagram or project schedule, make sure you glue the start point of the connector to the shape you are connecting from and the end point to the shape you are connecting to.

Straight Versus Dynamic Connectors

Straight connectors are straight lines that connect shapes. They lengthen, shorten, and change their angle to maintain shape connectivity, but they draw straight over shapes that are in their path, as shown in Figure 1-3.

Dynamic connectors are smarter. They automatically bend, stretch, and detour around shapes instead of overlapping them. They can also jump over other connectors to make connections easier to follow on a drawing. By default, dynamic connectors use right angles to bend around shapes. You can change the path of a right-angled connector by moving any of its vertices. You can also add or move segments of a right-angled connector by dragging a midpoint of a segment. Curved connectors are dynamic as well. You can drag their control points and eccentricity handles, to modify the shape of the curve.

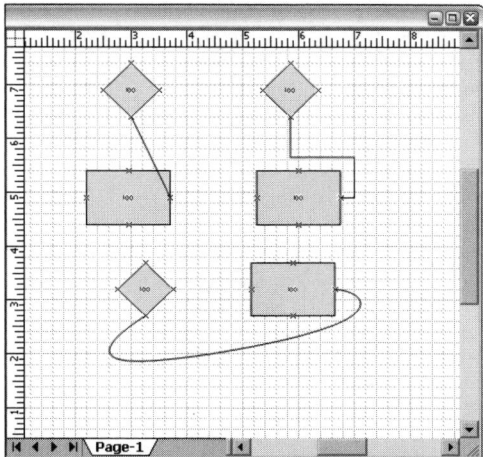

Figure 1-3: You can connect shapes with straight or dynamic connectors.

Using Glue

Just as in real life, Visio needs glue to make things stick together. Visio "glue" comes in two varieties: shape-to-shape and point-to-point. *Shape-to-shape glue,* also known as *dynamic glue,* builds dynamic connections between shapes. When you reposition shapes connected with shape-to-shape glue, the end points of the connector move to the closest available connection points, as shown in Figure 1-4. *Point-to-point glue,* also known as *static glue*, keeps the connector end points glued to the specific points you selected on the shapes, also illustrated in Figure 1-4. In addition, you can combine dynamic and static glue, gluing a connector to a shape at one end and a specific point at the other.

By default, you can glue to entire shapes, connection points, or guides. You can change glue settings to also glue to shape handles, shape vertices, or any point on a shape's geometry. As you draw a connector, a red box appears around a shape when you are connecting to that shape. If you are connecting to a point, the connection point turns red.

Dynamic glue draws shortest connection.

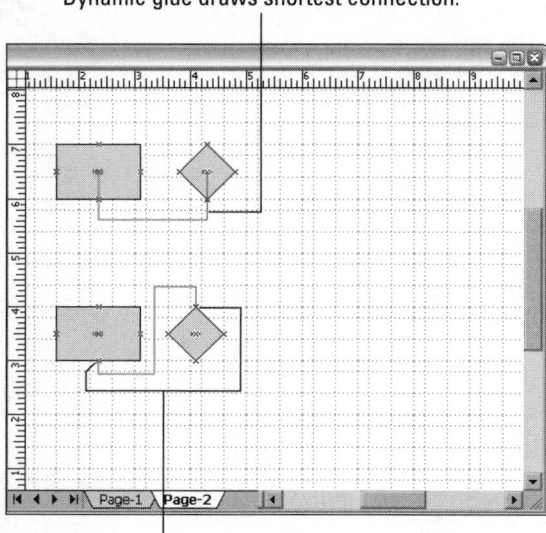

Static glue maintains the points you select.

Figure 1-4: Dynamic glue draws the shortest connectors between two shapes.

Exploring the Visio 2003 Interface

When you begin a drawing session, Visio 2003 conveniently populates the Visio desktop with features to help you work. By default, the Visio environment positions menus and toolbars across the top, the Shapes window with stencils and shapes to the left, the task pane to the right, a status bar along the bottom, and the drawing window in the center, as shown in Figure 1-5.

Menus and Toolbars

You can find most features on one of Visio's menus or toolbars. However, the fastest route to many tasks is right-clicking a shape or interface element to access a short-cut menu.

The Visio menu bar contains menus familiar to Microsoft Office users. In addition, when you work with some of the specialized templates, the Visio menu bar contains an additional entry for a specialized menu, such as Plan shown in Figure 1-5.

Shapes Window   Drawing Window

Toolbars   Menu Bar   Task Pane

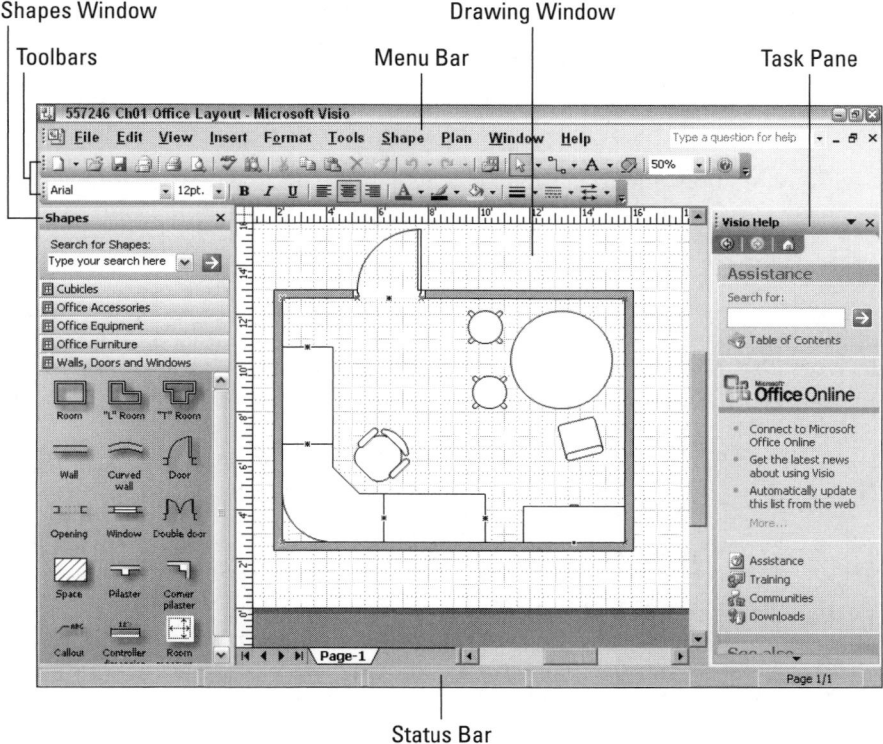

Status Bar

Figure 1-5: The Visio environment provides convenient access to tools.

Shortcuts for many tools are available on the Standard or Formatting toolbars, which appear by default. Some templates include specialized toolbars, which float in the drawing window by default. You can easily show or hide a toolbar:

✦ To display a toolbar, choose View ➪ Toolbars and choose the toolbar you want to use. A check mark appears when the toolbar is displayed. A specialized toolbar appears in the toolbar list when a drawing of its type is active.

✦ To hide a toolbar, choose View ➪ Toolbars and uncheck the checked toolbar that you want to hide.

You can dock a toolbar along the top, bottom, or sides of the Visio window. When you dock a toolbar to the left or right, the toolbar hangs vertically along the side. Toolbars are easily manipulated:

✦ To reposition a docked toolbar, drag its move handle to a new location. The move handle is a series of dots to the left of a horizontal docked toolbar and along the top of a vertical docked toolbar.

✦ To float a toolbar in the middle of the window, drag its move handle to a new position.

✦ To reposition a floating toolbar, drag its title bar to a new location.

Task Panes

Task panes provide easy access to common tasks such as creating new drawings, obtaining help, and collaborating with others. Task panes dock on the right side of the screen by default. To show or hide a task pane, choose View ➪ Task Pane. You can also display the task pane by pressing Ctrl+F1.

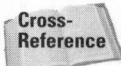

For more information about task panes and Visio help resources, see Chapter 38.

The Visio 2003 Drawing Area

The drawing window, which contains your active drawing, takes center stage in the Visio drawing area. The drawing window is visible whenever you work on a drawing. However, you can display several other windows to facilitate your work. To display one of these other windows, choose View and then the window name.

The Drawing Window

Drawing pages appear in the drawing window, where you can add shapes or modify and format the contents of your drawing. You can view different areas of a page using the horizontal and vertical scrollbars. To view another page, select the tab for that page below the drawing window.

A drawing grid and rulers make it easy to position and align shapes on a page. To display a grid in the drawing window, choose View ➪ Grid. To display rulers, choose View ➪ Rulers. The units that rulers display vary depending on the type of drawing and scale you are using. For example, the rulers for a block diagram use inches, whereas rulers for a site plan use feet.

To change the ruler units, choose Tools ➪ Options and select the Units tab. Click the Change button and choose the units you want from the Measurement Units drop-down list.

The Shapes Window

You drag and drop shapes from the Shapes window onto a drawing page. The Shapes window contains active stencils and their shapes, docked by default on the left, as shown in Figure 1-5. However, you can reposition the Shapes window or individual stencils to suit your needs. For instance, you can dock the Shapes window at the top or the bottom of the drawing area to provide more room for pages set to landscape orientation.

✦ To add another stencil to the Shapes window, choose File ⇨ Shapes, and navigate to the stencil you want.

New Feature Instead of choosing File ⇨ Stencils as in Visio 2002, you open stencils in Visio 2003 by choosing File ⇨ Shapes.

✦ To display the shapes for an open stencil in the Shapes window, click the stencil's title bar.

✦ To resize the Shapes window, drag the vertical divider between the Shapes window and the drawing window to the left or right.

✦ To change the information displayed in the Shapes window, right-click the Shapes window title bar and choose one of the options, such as Icons Only, from the shortcut menu.

Note To change the information in the Shapes window, you can also right-click a stencil title bar, choose View, and then choose the type of information you want to see.

By default, in the Shapes window you see the title bars for all open stencils, but only the shapes for the active stencil. To view multiple stencils at the same time, you can

✦ Drag a stencil out of the Shapes window and float it on the screen, as shown in Figure 1-6.

✦ Drag a stencil to the top or bottom of the Shapes window to create a second stencil pane.

Multiple stencil panes in the Shapes window   A docked stencil

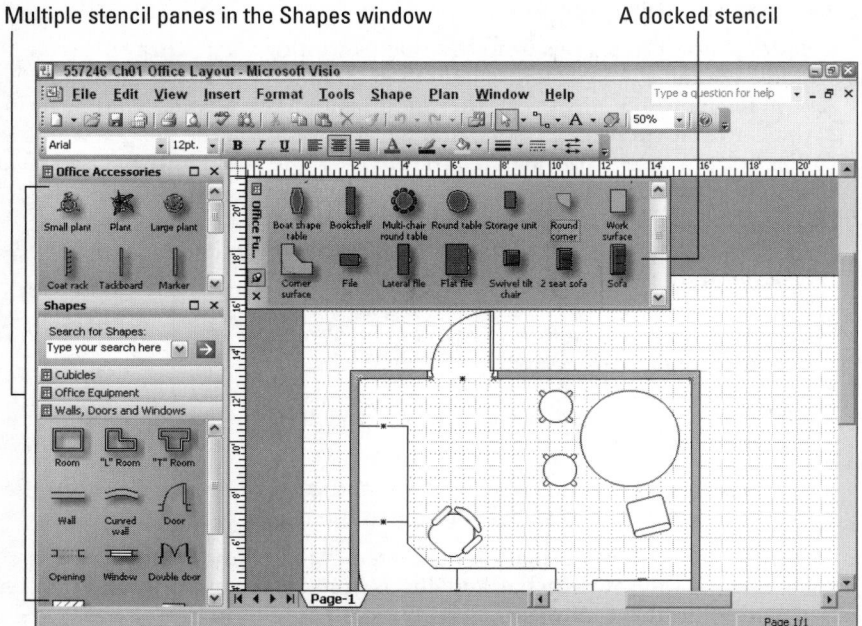

Figure 1-6: You can dock stencils in the Shapes window or float them on the screen.

The Drawing Explorer

The Drawing Explorer, shown in Figure 1-7, offers a hierarchical view of your drawing. You can use the Drawing Explorer to find, add, delete, or edit the components of your drawing, including pages, layers, shapes, masters, styles, and patterns. For example, you can select and highlight a shape on a drawing by double-clicking its name in the Drawing Explorer. To display the Drawing Explorer, choose View ➪ Drawing Explorer Window.

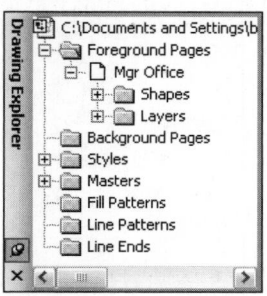

Figure 1-7: You can exploit the hierarchy of drawing components in the Drawing Explorer window.

Tip You can conserve screen real estate by docking and merging view windows. You can dock other view windows within the Shapes window or you can merge several windows into one. To dock a view window, such as Pan & Zoom, drag it into the Shapes window. To merge view windows, drag one window by its title bar into the center of another window. To switch between merged windows, select the tab for the view you want.

The Size & Position Window

The Size & Position window is particularly useful when you work on scaled drawings such as building plans, where precise measurements are important. You can use the Size & Position window to view and edit a shape's dimensions, position, or rotation.

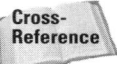

Cross-Reference To learn more about how to use the Size & Position window, see Chapter 4.

The Custom Properties Window

The Custom Properties window is the best place to modify the custom properties for a number of shapes. The window remains open until you close it and displays the values for a shape when you select that shape. To edit a property in the Custom Properties window, click the property box and enter or edit a value.

The ShapeSheet Window

You can modify any aspect of a shape in its ShapeSheet. You can display the ShapeSheet by choosing Window ➪ Show ShapeSheet.

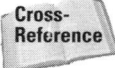

Cross-Reference To learn more about ShapeSheets, see Chapter 33.

Viewing Drawings

Examining your work is essential when you draw. As you progress from a blank page to a completed drawing, you want to view your drawing in different ways, and Visio 2003 provides the tools to do this.

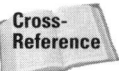

Cross-Reference People who don't have Visio installed on their computers can still view Visio drawings. To learn about using the Microsoft Visio Viewer or viewing Visio drawings on Web pages, see Chapter 11.

Panning and Zooming

Sometimes you want to see the big picture, and at other times you want detail. In Visio, you can pan and zoom in several ways to see the area and detail that you want.

Using Pan and Zoom Shortcuts

Two keyboard shortcuts provide the fastest way to zoom in and out:

✦ To zoom in, use Ctrl+Shift+left-click.

✦ To zoom out, use Ctrl+Shift+right-click.

You can change the center of the zoom area by repositioning the magnifying glass that appears when you press Ctrl+Shift.

Tip   If you want Visio to center the zoom area on the selected shape when you zoom in or out, choose Tools ➪ Options. Select the General tab and put a check in the Center Selection on Zoom check box.

Using the Pan & Zoom Window

The Pan & Zoom window shows the entire drawing page, with the zoom area outlined in red. Visio docks the Pan & Zoom window within the drawing window, but you can dock it within the Shapes window if space is at a premium. Use one of the following methods to specify the area you want to see:

✦ On the right side of the Pan & Zoom window, drag the zoom scrollbar up or down to zoom in or out, respectively.

✦ Drag a side or corner of the red outline to resize it, thereby changing the part of the drawing visible in the drawing window.

✦ Click and drag to define a new zoom area box in the Pan & Zoom window.

✦ Click a point in the Pan & Zoom window to relocate the center of the zoom area box.

Panning and Zooming from Menus and Toolbars

The View menu and the Standard toolbar both contain zoom options, but the zoom list on the Standard toolbar is faster. You can choose from several predefined zoom percentages as well as the entire page, the entire width of the page, and the last zoom used.

Tip   If you use a mouse with a scroll wheel, you can use the mouse wheel to pan and zoom. To pan up or down, roll the mouse wheel. Press the Shift key while rolling the wheel to pan from side to side. You can zoom in and out by pressing the Control key while rolling the mouse.

Working with Drawing Windows

Sometimes one window for your drawing isn't enough — for instance, when you want to copy shapes from one drawing to another or view details in two widely separated areas of the same drawing. You can create additional windows for your drawings and arrange them in several ways.

Creating New Windows

When you create a new window, Visio displays the same drawing contained in the previous window. The new window, identified by the ":2" that follows the filename in the Visio title bar, fills the drawing window.

✦ To create a new window, choose Window ➪ New Window.

Note When you create a new window, the Shapes window doesn't contain any open stencils. However, windows docked in the Shapes window are docked in the new Shapes window as well.

✦ To bring another window to the front, choose Window and then the name of the window you want to see.

Viewing Multiple Windows

You can view several drawing windows at the same time. Tiling and cascading both create panes for each open window. Tiling is helpful for viewing several areas of detail at the same time as it arranges the panes side by side in the drawing area. You can view all the windows at the same time, but each pane takes up a smaller area of the screen.

Cascading is better when you want larger panes for each window but want to switch between them quickly. Cascaded windows overlap, with each window slightly lower and to the right of the previous one. When you cascade windows, the current window appears in front.

✦ To tile the windows in the drawing area, choose Window ➪ Tile.

✦ To cascade windows, choose Window ➪ Cascade.

✦ To bring a hidden window to the forefront, click any visible part of that window.

✦ To fill the drawing area with one of the tiled or cascaded windows, click the window's Maximize button.

Summary

Visio is an essential tool for effectively communicating ideas and documenting business results. Using drag and drop drawing techniques, anyone can produce great-looking diagrams, drawings, and models. This chapter introduced you to Visio 2003.

Specifically, in this chapter you learned about the following:

✦ New and updated features in Visio 2003

✦ Features discontinued in Visio 2003

✦ The concepts that make Visio so powerful

✦ The components of Visio's interface

✦ How to view your Visio drawings

✦   ✦   ✦

Getting Started with Drawings

There's no reason to begin with a blank slate in Visio; new drawings can originate from a variety of sources, including existing Visio drawings, Visio templates on your computer, and online. Visio provides several convenient methods for creating drawings, none of which require more than a few clicks of a mouse.

After creating a drawing, you can add content quickly by dragging and dropping shapes from stencils or by using Visio's drawing tools to create your own geometry. The tools to produce lines, curves, rectangles, and ellipses are simple to use, but also pack a lot of power when you utilize all their features.

As your drawings grow in size and complexity, you can add pages to hold more content. Background pages work like watermarks, displaying company logos or repetitive background graphics for each page of your drawing. With the Page Settings menu option, you can further fine-tune how your drawings look and behave. You can create drawings of different sizes and scales, whether you want a two-inch thumbnail with shapes at their actual size or a 22-inch by 34-inch architectural plan with shapes scaled to one quarter inch equal to one foot. Layout and Routing settings influence the appearance of connections and the readability of your drawings, whereas Shadow settings add visual impact.

It's easy to work with multiple drawing pages. You can add, delete, rename, and reorder pages from a shortcut menu. In addition, you can rotate pages temporarily to easily add objects at an angle — for instance, to draw offices in a floor plan positioned at different angles.

Creating Drawings

Visio provides three places to access the features for creating drawings:

✦ **File ➪ New** — This is the quickest way to display the Choose Drawing Type pane or create a new drawing of the same type as the current one, particularly when the task pane is hidden. Choose File ➪ New ➪ Choose Drawing Type to preview and choose the available templates.

✦ **Choose Drawing Type pane** — By default, the Choose Drawing Type pane appears when you start Visio. This pane enables you to preview and choose one of Visio's templates.

Tip

If you work on existing drawings more often than you create new ones, you can turn this feature off. To do this, click Tools ➪ Options. Select the View tab and uncheck the Choose Drawing Type Pane check box.

✦ **New Drawing pane** — This pane contains links to every method for creating a new drawing. If the task pane is not visible, choose View ➪ Task Pane. Click New Drawing in the task pane drop-down list.

Creating Drawings Using Templates

Templates are incredibly convenient because they set up your drawing environment for you. Visio comes with dozens of templates, but you can also find templates on the Web or use custom templates you've built yourself or obtained from someone else.

To create a drawing from a template, follow these steps:

1. Display the Choose Drawing Type pane by choosing File ➪ Choose Drawing Type. You can also click Choose Drawing Type in the New Drawing task pane.

2. Click the category for the type of drawing you want to create. Visio displays thumbnails of each type of drawing in that category, as shown in Figure 2-1.

3. Click the picture representing the type of drawing you want.

Tip

If you're not sure that a drawing type is what you want, position the pointer over a drawing type picture to display a description of possible applications for that type. Conversely, when you know exactly which drawing type you want, it's quicker to choose File ➪ New, navigate to the category you want, and click the name of the drawing type on the submenu.

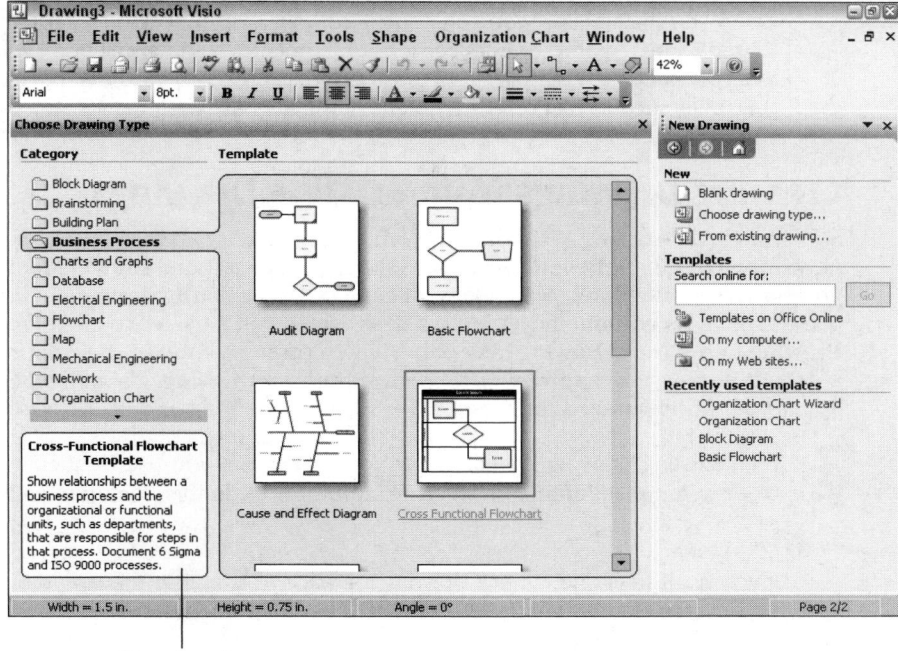

Template tip

Figure 2-1: The Choose Drawing Type pane and New Drawing task pane provide every option for creating new drawings.

The New Drawing pane offers several other options for finding templates to use for new drawings. Other links in the New Drawing pane include the following:

✦ **Search Online for**—Type keywords into this box to identify the type of template you want and click Go to search online.

✦ **Templates on Office Online**—Click this link to view templates available on the Microsoft Office Online Web site.

✦ **On My Computer**—Click this link to open the Browse Templates dialog box. Navigate to a folder on your computer, click the template you want to use, and click Open.

✦ **On My Web Sites**—Click this link to browse Web sites accessible from your My Network Places folder.

✦ **Recently Used Templates**—Click one of the templates in this section to create a new drawing based on that template.

Note When you install Visio, you can choose to install US (Microsoft's abbreviation for United States), metric, or both versions of templates. If you install both, you will see two copies of each template. US Units templates use standard U.S. page sizes and U.S. units, such as feet or inches. Metric templates use metric units and page sizes.

Creating Drawings from Existing Drawings

Sometimes, an existing Visio drawing possesses exactly the settings you want for a new drawing. It might even have some shapes you want already in place, such as your favorite title block. Although you can open an existing drawing in Visio and use the Save As command to create a new drawing, it's easier to click From Existing Drawing in the New Drawing task pane, which opens a copy of the existing file with a default name, such as Drawing1. To save the new drawing, click File ⇨ Save, specify a folder and filename, and click Save.

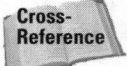

Cross-Reference If an existing drawing contains settings and content you use frequently, you can create a template of that drawing. To learn how to do this, see Chapter 30.

Note If you want to create a blank drawing, perhaps to use Visio drawing tools to mark up an image, you can create a drawing without any stencils or special settings assigned. To do this, make sure the task pane is open by choosing View ⇨ Task Pane and then display the New Drawing task pane by choosing New Drawing in the task pane drop-down list. In the New Drawing task pane, click Blank Drawing. To open stencils, choose File ⇨ Shapes, navigate to the category of shapes you want, and then choose a stencil.

Using the Fundamental Drawing Tools

You can produce most drawing content by dragging and dropping shapes and connectors. However, you can also create your own geometry to build new shapes or to annotate and mark up your drawings. Visio provides a powerful set of drawing tools. Combining these tools with drawing aids and snapping and gluing techniques, you can quickly add lines, curves, and closed shapes to any drawing.

To access the Visio drawing tools, display the Drawing toolbar by choosing View ⇨ Toolbars ⇨ Drawing.

Note The Drawing Tools icon appears to the left of the zoom box on the Standard toolbar. You can click this icon to show and hide the Drawing toolbar.

Speeding Up Drawing with Snap To Tools

Snapping helps you position lines and shapes exactly where you want by attracting a point to another shape, a ruler subdivision, a drawing guide, the drawing grid, or other elements on your drawing. You can specify which elements Visio snaps to as well as the strength of attraction for a snap. As the attraction strength increases, the pointer snaps to those elements from further away.

To select snap elements, choose Tools ➪ Snap & Glue and select the Visio components you want to snap to in the Snap To column. To specify the strength of attraction, click the Advanced tab and drag the Snap Strength scrollbars to the left or right to decrease or increase the snap strength.

Note   Although snapping is usually helpful, it can sometimes be a hindrance. When you're trying to draw freeform curves, snapping can pull the pointer to positions you don't want. To draw smoother freeform curves, choose Tools ➪ Snap & Glue and then uncheck the Snap check box in the Currently Active column. When you are finished, check the Snap check box to restore snapping.

Cross-Reference   To learn more about settings for snapping, see Chapter 4.

Drawing aids are dotted lines that indicate where to click to draw a circle, square, or a line at a particular angle. You can use them to simplify creating lines and closed shapes. When you use the Ellipse and Rectangle tools, a dotted line shows you where to click to create a circle or square, as demonstrated in Figure 2-2. When you use the Line tool, guides appear when you approach an increment of 45 degrees. When you edit a line segment, drawing aids extend at 45-degree increments as well as the line's original angle. To display drawing aids, choose Tools ➪ Snap & Glue and check the Drawing Aids check box in the Currently Active column.

Drawing aid

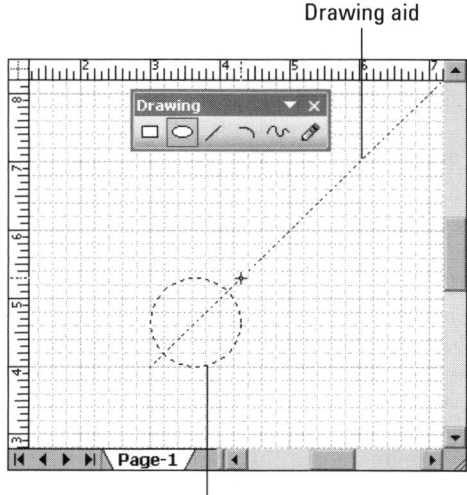

Preview of final shape

Figure 2-2: You can use drawing aids to create circles, squares, and angled lines.

Drawing Lines

Depending on how you click and drag, you can use the Line tool to create individual line segments, a series of connected line segments, or closed shapes. When the Line tool is active, the pointer changes to cross hairs with a short angled line to its right. To draw lines, follow these steps:

1. To begin a line, click the Line tool in the Drawing Tools toolbar, click the mouse button at the starting point of the line, drag to the end point of the line, and release the mouse button. Visio displays the new line segment and selects it.

Tip   To draw only orthogonal lines, hold the Shift key as you drag a line.

2. To connect another line segment to the one you just drew, click without moving the pointer from the end of the last segment, drag to the next end point, and release the mouse button.

Caution   If you click more than once before drawing a new line segment, Visio deselects the previous segment and the new line segment won't be connected to the previous one. To prevent this problem, make sure the previous segment is selected before you add the next one. To join separate line segments, Shift+click each segment and then choose Shape ➪ Operations ➪ Join.

3. To add another line segment, repeat step 2.

4. If you want to close the shape by adding another line, click and drag to the starting point of the first line segment and release the mouse button.

Note   When you create a line segment with the Line tool, Visio shows the start and end points with green squares. However, when you create a series of connected lines, Visio indicates the vertices at the ends of each line segment with green diamonds.

Note   Visio applies a solid white fill to the shape when it closes, hiding the drawing grid behind the enclosed area.

Drawing Arcs and Curves

The Arc tool draws one arc at a time, and each arc represents no more than one-fourth of an ellipse or a circle. The curve of the arc depends on the angle between the start and end points you choose and can vary between a straight line and a circular curve. Visio arcs have vertices at each end and at their midpoints and also contain control points that you can use to change their shape, as shown in Figure 2-3. To draw an arc with a deeper curve, create an arc and then change its curve by dragging its vertices or control point.

Eccentricity point changes the lean of the curve

Midpoint changes the depth of the arc

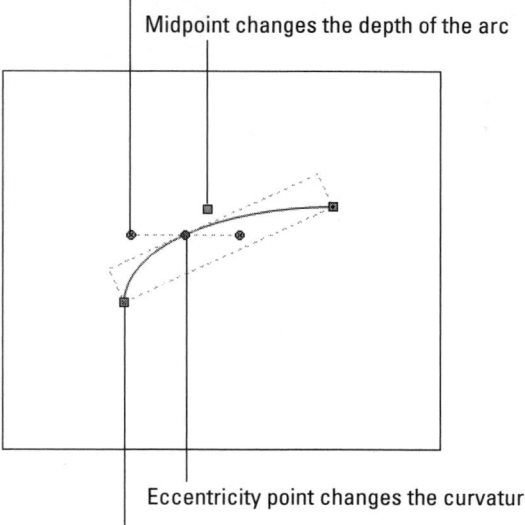

Eccentricity point changes the curvature

Vertex changes endpoints

Figure 2-3: You can drag vertices and control points to modify an arc.

Note You can't create a complete circle or ellipse with the Arc tool. You must use the Ellipse tool to draw a closed ellipse.

You can draw and modify arcs in the following ways:

✦ To draw a clockwise arc, click one point and then sweep the pointer clockwise to the next point.

✦ To draw a counterclockwise arc, click one point and then sweep the pointer counterclockwise to the next point.

Tip The direction of the arc remains fixed after the initial sweep. After the direction is set, you can drag the pointer to define the arc's curve and orientation.

✦ To move an arc, select the Pointer tool, and click the arc away from any vertices or control points. When the pointer changes to a four-headed arrow, drag the arc to a new location.

✦ To extend the arc's length, drag an end point to a new location.

Note   Depending on where you drag the end point of an arc, you can also change the shape of the arc in addition to changing its length.

✦ To change the shape of an arc, drag the control point to a new location.

✦ To modify direction or rotation, right-click an arc, click Shape on the shortcut menu, and click one of the Rotate or Flip commands.

To draw multiple arcs and splines — for instance, to mimic handwriting — you use Visio's Freeform tool. This tool senses changes in the direction of the pointer and adds vertices and control points as you draw. The result is a series of curves that you can modify section by section. To draw a freeform curve, click the Freeform tool in the Drawing toolbar and then drag the pointer slowly on the drawing page. Several factors contribute to the success of your curve drawing efforts. To improve your result, you can do the following:

✦ Take your time as you draw a freeform line. Drawing more slowly provides greater control over the curves you create, as Visio better recognizes your direction changes.

✦ Modify the freeform precision option. Precision controls how Visio switches between drawing straight lines and curved splines. To set precision, click Tools ➪ Options, click the Advanced tab, and drag the precision scrollbars to the left or right. Dragging to the left tightens the tolerance so that Visio switches to drawing splines unless you move the mouse in a very straight line. Dragging to the right loosens the tolerance, so Visio draws straight lines until you move the mouse in an obvious curve.

✦ Modify the freeform smoothness option. Smoothing controls how much Visio smoothes out your curves — in effect, how sensitive Visio is to changes in direction. Tighter settings add more control points, as shown in Figure 2-4, whereas looser settings add fewer. More control points provide greater control over the angles of arcs in a freeform curve.

✦ Disable snapping if your freeform lines are erratic. To do this, choose Tool ➪ Snap & Glue and uncheck the Snap check box in the Currently Active column.

Tip   If you change your Snap & Glue settings frequently, you can display the Snap & Glue toolbar to keep Snap & Glue commands handy. Simply choose View ➪ Toolbars ➪ Snap & Glue.

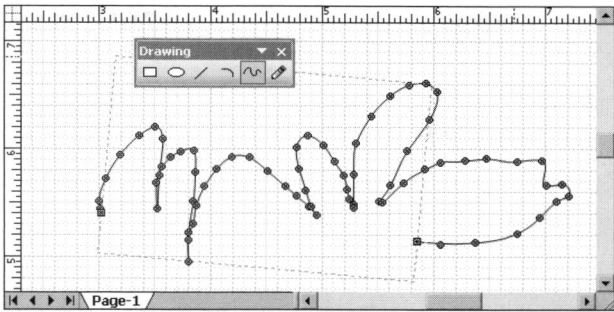

Figure 2-4: The Smoothing setting influences the number of control points added to a curve.

Drawing Closed Shapes

Although you can use the Line tool to draw closed linear shapes, ellipses and rectangles have their own Visio drawing tools. With the Ellipse and Rectangle tools, you can draw ellipses, circles, rectangles, and squares by clicking two points.

You can draw quadrilateral shapes (shapes with four sides) using the following methods:

✦ To draw a rectangle, click and drag the pointer from one position on the drawing page to another to define opposite corners of the rectangle.

✦ To draw a square, hold the Shift key while dragging from one corner to the opposite corner.

✦ To use drawing aids to draw a square, click the first corner, drag the pointer close to a 45-degree angle, and click on the drawing aid that appears to select the opposite corner.

Many diagrams use rectangles with rounded corners. To round the corners of rectangular shapes, choose one of the following methods:

✦ Right-click a shape and choose Format ➪ Line on the shortcut menu. Select the rounding you want and click OK.

Tip
You can also specify the rounding by typing a value for the radius of the corner in the Rounding box of the Format Line dialog box.

✦ Choose Format ➪ Corner Rounding. Select the rounding you want and click OK.

✦ Choose View ➪ Toolbars ➪ Format Shape. Click the Corner Rounding button on the Format Shape toolbar.

✦ To define a style with rounded corners, choose Format ➪ Define Styles and click the Line button. Select the rounding you want and then click OK.

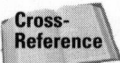

Cross-Reference
To learn more about defining styles, see Chapter 34.

You can draw ellipses and circles using the following methods:

✦ To draw an ellipse, click and drag the pointer from one corner to the opposite corner. The ellipse is circumscribed by the rectangle you defined with your two points.

✦ To draw a circle, hold the Shift key while dragging from one corner to the opposite corner.

✦ To draw a circle, click the first corner, drag close to a 45-degree angle, and click on the drawing aid that appears to select the opposite corner.

Using the Pencil Tool

The Pencil tool is quite versatile. It works as well for drawing new lines and arcs as it does for reshaping existing ones. In addition, you can use the Pencil tool to construct a polyline made up of a combination of straight lines and arcs, as demonstrated in Figure 2-5. The Pencil tool interprets your pointer movements to determine whether you want to draw a line or arc, and switches to either Line mode or Arc mode, respectively. In addition, the Pencil tool, unlike the Arc tool, can draw arcs that are almost complete circles.

To use the Pencil tool's features, use one of the following methods:

✦ To draw a straight line, drag the pointer straight in any direction. Visio indicates that it is in Line mode by changing the pointer to cross hairs with an angled line below and to the right.

✦ To draw an arc, sweep the pointer in a curve. Visio indicates that it is in Arc mode by changing the pointer to cross hairs with an arc below and to the right. You can move the pointer to define the radius of the arc, the angle that the arc circumscribes, as well as the position of the arc on the drawing page.

✦ To switch to Line mode while you are in Arc mode, move the pointer back to the starting point. When the Arc next to the cross hairs disappears, drag the pointer straight to switch to Line mode.

✦ To switch to Arc mode while you are in Line mode, move the pointer back to the starting point. When the angled line next to the cross hairs disappears, sweep the pointer to switch to Arc mode.

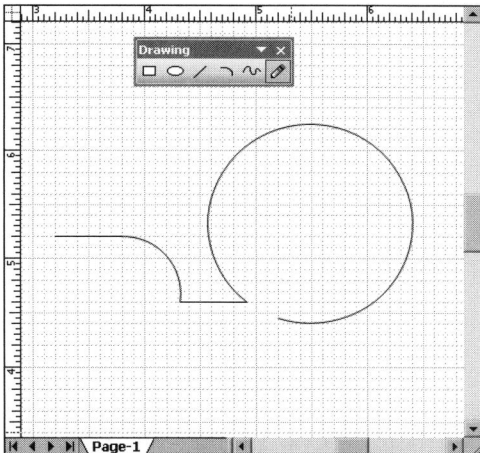

Figure 2-5: You can draw straight lines and arcs with the Pencil tool.

Working with Pages

You might add multiple pages to a drawing for several reasons. For example, the database model for an airline reservation system could require hundreds of pages to show every table. A construction project could show the entire building on one drawing page, with elevations and construction details on others. Background pages act like watermarks — for instance, displaying a company logo and standard title block for every foreground drawing. Every page you add can have its own settings for drawing size, orientation, margins, units and scale for architectural and engineering drawings, and more.

Note The settings you specify in Page Setup can differ from page to page, but the settings you specify in Print Setup affect all pages in a drawing.

The quickest way to access page commands is by right-clicking a page tab in the drawing window. From this shortcut menu, you can do all of the following:

✦ Insert new pages

✦ Delete the selected page

✦ Rename the selected page

✦ Modify the order of the pages

Creating Pages in a Drawing

A Visio drawing file contains one page by default, but you can create as many pages as you want. When you create a new page, it inherits the page settings of the active page in the drawing window. However, Visio also displays the Page Setup dialog box as part of the page creation process, so you can specify page settings at the time of creation. You can create foreground or background pages using any of the following methods:

✦ Right-click any page tab and choose Insert Page on the shortcut menu.

✦ Choose Insert ➪ New Page.

✦ In the Drawing Explorer window, right-click the Foreground or Background folder and then click Insert Page.

You can create a background page that displays the same set of shapes, such as a logo, title block, or revision block, for multiple foreground pages. To do this, you must create a background page and assign it to each foreground page. To set up a background page, follow these steps:

1. Choose Insert ➪ New Page.

2. Click the Background option and type a name for the new background page in the Name box.

3. Make any other page setting changes you want and click OK.

4. Add the shapes and text that you want on the new background page.

5. To assign the background page to a foreground page, click the page tab for the foreground page and choose File ➪ Page Setup.

6. Select the Page Properties tab, select the background page name in the Background drop-down list, and click OK.

Note   You can't delete a background page as long as at least one foreground page uses it. To remove a background page assignment, select the foreground page to which it is assigned, open the Page Setup dialog box, click None in the Background drop-down list, and then click OK. After you have removed all the background page assignments, you can delete the background page.

Setting Up Pages

Each page in a drawing can have its own unique settings. For example, a floor plan page might use a D-size sheet of paper with landscape orientation and an architectural scale. The door and window schedule for the floor plan might apply a standard letter-size sheet of paper with portrait orientation and no scale. To specify the settings for a page, click a page tab and then choose File ⇨ Page Setup to open the Page Setup dialog box.

Defining Print Settings

To specify the settings for the printer paper, select the Print Setup tab in the Page Setup dialog box. To prevent incompatibilities between drawing pages and printer paper, Visio displays a preview window that shows the current settings for both, as shown in Figure 2-6. You can resolve discrepancies by modifying settings on either of the Print Setup or Page Size tabs.

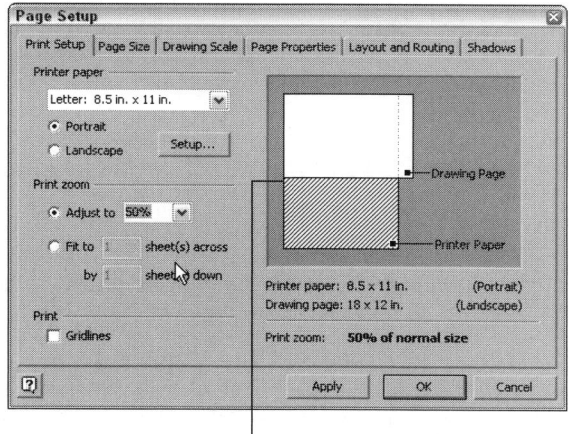

Discrepancies between Print Setup and Page Size settings

Figure 2-6: The Print Setup and Page Size tabs preview your print settings to highlight incompatibilities.

On the Print Setup tab, you can specify the following:

- ✦ **Printer Page Size** — Choose a standard paper size from the drop-down list.
- ✦ **Printer Page Orientation** — Choose the Portrait or Landscape option.
- ✦ **Page Margins** — Click the Setup button to set page margins.
- ✦ **Small Drawing Centering** — Click the Setup button and check the Center Horizontally and Center Vertically check boxes.

✦ **Print Zoom** — Specify a percentage for the print zoom or how many sheets across and down. Print Zoom enlarges or shrinks a drawing only for printing. For example, you can use Print Zoom to print a larger drawing on a letter-size sheet.

✦ **Printed Gridlines** — Check the Gridlines check box to print the drawing grid along with the contents of your drawing.

The Print Setup tab in the Page Setup dialog box controls page size and orientation for a page. Clicking the Properties button in the Print dialog box accesses page size and orientation settings for a printer. If you choose different settings in these two locations, Visio will display a warning before printing, indicating that drawing pages will print across multiple pages because they are oriented differently than the printed page. To prevent this behavior, make sure that your drawing page dimensions are compatible with printer page size and orientation.

Specifying Page Size

By default, Visio sets the drawing page size to the printer paper size. To specify a page size that is different from that of the printer paper, select the Page Size tab in the Page Setup dialog box. This tab also displays a preview window that shows the current settings for both Print Setup and Page Size. On the Page Size tab, you can specify the following:

✦ **Page Size Same As Printer Paper Size** — Visio selects this option by default.

✦ **Pre-defined Size** — Select a category of sizes, such as Standard or ANSI Architectural, and then select one of the standard sizes for that category.

✦ **Custom Page Size** — Specify the dimensions for the height and width of the custom page.

✦ **Page Size Fits Drawing Contents** — Select Size to Fit Drawing Contents to define a page size just large enough to hold the contents of the current page.

✦ **Page Orientation** — Choose Portrait or Landscape for the page. Make sure that the page orientation and printer paper orientation match.

You can also change the size of a page without opening the Page setup dialog box. To do this, click the Pointer tool, position the pointer along the edge of the page, and press and hold the Ctrl key. After the pointer changes to a double-headed arrow, drag the edge to change the dimension of the page. As you drag, the current dimension for the page appears in the status bar.

Defining Drawing Scale

When you work on scaled drawings such as construction plans, the drawing scale enables you to fit real-world objects onto sheets of paper. You can specify a drawing scale in Visio to represent real-world measurements on a drawing page. In Visio, the

No Scale option shows objects at their actual size—a one-to-one scale. On the Drawing Scale tab, you can specify the following options:

✦ **No Scale**—Objects appear at their actual size.

✦ **Pre-defined Scale**—Select a category of scales, such as Architectural or Metric, and then select one of the standard scales for that category.

The page size at the bottom of the Drawing Scale screen indicates the real-world size of your drawing page. You can modify these values to change the size of the page. If you do this, the preview window will show the relationship between your page and the printer paper.

✦ **Custom Scale**—Specify the measurement unit and the associated size in the real world to define a custom scale.

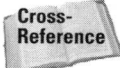

To learn more about using drawing scales, see Chapter 24.

The Title Blocks stencil includes masters that display the current drawing scale. These shapes reference a page field, so the scale in the title block updates automatically if you modify the scale for the drawing page.

Specifying Measurement Units

On the Page Properties tab, you can specify the units used for measuring objects on a page by choosing the units you want with the Measurement Units drop-down list.

The Measurement Units list includes many familiar units of distance, units of time, and a few options that you might not know. When you work on drawings that deal with time, such as graphs showing actions over time, you can specify the time units that appear on the drawing rulers. The remaining units in the list are typesetting measurements; didots and ciceros represent metric measures, and points and picas represent U.S. measures.

Setting Up Layout and Routing

The Layout and Routing tab provides options for specifying how shapes and connectors interact on a page. You can specify where connectors attach to shapes, whether connectors that share a shape overlap or not, and whether connectors use straight or curved lines. The Layout and Routing tab displays a preview of the settings you choose, so you can decide whether to apply them. On the Layout and Routing tab, you can specify the following options:

✦ **Style**—This setting specifies the appearance of connectors between shapes. For example, you can choose connectors with right angles or straight lines, or you can specify the way that Visio lays out connected shapes, such as Tree or Organization Chart.

✦ **Direction** — Only applicable to some styles, such as Tree and Organization Chart, the direction specifies the shape's layout: from top to bottom, bottom to top, left to right, or right to left.

✦ **Separate** — This specifies whether connectors that are overlapped should be separated. For example, when you choose Unrelated Lines, connectors from the same manager to multiple subordinates are related, so overlapping paths are acceptable. This setting does not affect connectors that are already separated.

✦ **Overlap** — This setting specifies whether connectors that are separated should be overlapped.

Caution   If you choose to overlap all lines, your drawing will be less cluttered, but it will be more difficult to identify relationships between shapes.

✦ **Appearance** — This specifies whether the connectors are straight or curved.

In the Page Setup menu, you can also configure the appearance of line jumps, which visually indicate that lines do not connect:

✦ **Lines That Use Line Jumps** — Choose which connectors use line jumps in the Add Line Jumps To drop-down list. For example, you can display line jumps in horizontal or vertical lines, with the first or last line displayed.

✦ **Line Jump Style** — This setting specifies the appearance of line jumps, such as arcs or gaps.

✦ **Line Jump Size** — Set the Horizontal Size to specify the width of line jumps on horizontal lines. Set the Vertical Size to specify the height of line jumps on vertical lines.

The Layout and Routing tab includes a few other settings. From here, you can also specify the following:

✦ **Move Other Shapes Away on Drop** — When this check box is checked, shapes automatically move on a page to make room for a shape that is dragged, moved, or resized on a page.

✦ **Enable Connector Splitting** — When this check box is checked, a shape dropped onto a connector splits the connector in two. The new shape automatically has connections to the two shapes that were previously connected.

✦ **Spacing** — Click this button to open the Layout and Routing Spacing dialog box. You can specify spacing between shapes, spacing between connectors, spacing between connectors and shapes, and the average shape size.

Setting Up Shadows

The Shadows tab controls the appearance of shadows associated with shapes on a page. On the Shadows tab, you can specify the following options:

✦ **Shadow Style** — This determines the angle and connection between the shadow and the shape, much like the position of a light source determines the shape of a shadow.

If you choose an oblique style, in which the shadow is oriented at an angle to the shape, you can specify the angle of rotation for the shadow.

✦ **Offset From Shape** — This setting specifies the distance between the shapes and the shadow. You can specify distances for horizontal and vertical offset or use the direction buttons.

✦ **Magnification** — Use this to specify the size of the shadow relative to the original shape.

Editing Pages

When a drawing contains several pages, it's easy to edit pages and move between them. The quickest way to navigate to a page is by clicking its page tab. If you can't see all the page tabs, you can choose Edit ➪ Go To and then click the name of the page you want to see.

Renaming Pages

When you create pages and don't name them, Visio assigns default names, such as Drawing1. If you work with multiple pages, you should assign a meaningful name to each page when you create it. This enables you to easily identify a page by the label on the page tab. Afterwards, you can rename a page with one of the following methods:

✦ Double-click a page tab and type the page's new name.

✦ Right-click a page tab, click Rename Page, and type the page's new name.

If the Page Setup dialog box is open, you can rename the current page by clicking the Page Properties tab and typing a new name in the Name box.

Deleting Pages

You can delete the current page or delete several pages at one time. To delete one page, right-click its page tab and click Delete Page. To delete several pages at once, follow these steps:

1. Choose Edit ➪ Delete Pages.

2. Ctrl+click each page you want to delete in the Delete Pages dialog box. If you are using default names and want Visio to renumber the page names, select the Update Names box. Click OK.

Reordering Pages

As you insert and delete pages, the remaining pages might need to be reordered. If you can see most of the page tabs, you can drag and drop pages into position. To do this, select the tab of the page you want to move and drag and drop the tab into a new position.

When your drawing contains many pages, it's easier to reorder them in the Drawing Explorer window. To do this, follow these steps:

1. Choose View ➪ Drawing Explorer Window.

2. Right-click either the Foreground folder or the Background folder and click Reorder Pages on the shortcut menu.

3. In the Reorder Pages dialog box, click the name of a page that you want to move and use the Move Up or Move Down buttons to move the page to its new position in the order. If you are using default names and want Visio to renumber the page names, select the Update Names box. Click OK when you have finished reordering all the pages.

Rotating Pages

You can create drawings in which different areas are at different angles without rotating each shape into position. By rotating the drawing page, you can construct each section orthogonally — that is, placing each shape at right angles to the drawing grid. Although existing shapes and guides rotate when you rotate a page, the rulers and drawing grid remain fixed. While the page is rotated, you add new shapes at right angles to the rulers and grid. When you rotate the page back to its original orientation, the shapes you added rotate with it, as illustrated in Figure 2-7.

 Note   Rotating pages does not affect print and page orientation settings. A rotated page prints as if it were not rotated.

To rotate a page, follow these steps:

1. Display the page you want to rotate in the drawing window.

2. Press Ctrl and position the pointer over a corner of the page. The pointer changes to a rotation pointer.

3. Drag the corner to the angle you want. If you want to rotate to a specific angle, release the mouse button when the rotation angle value in the status bar equals the angle you want.

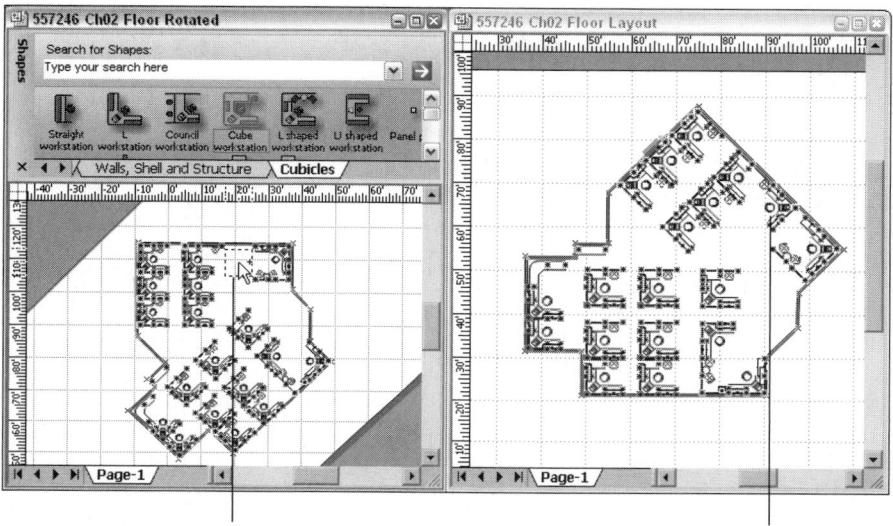

Add a shape while the page is rotated.   Shape rotates with page.

Figure 2-7: You can add a large number of shapes at an angle by rotating the page.

Summary

Visio provides a number of methods for creating drawings. By creating drawings using templates, you can get to work without worrying about settings such as page size or scale. You can also use existing drawings as a foundation for new drawings and even create your own templates if you use the same drawings repeatedly.

Although Visio provides thousands of predrawn shapes, you can add your own lines and closed shapes with Visio's drawing tools. Visio provides a number of features, such as snapping and drawing aids, that help you draw lines, arcs, and closed shapes precisely where you want.

You can add pages to a drawing to keep related information in one file or to show the detail of a large and complex model. By default, a new page inherits the settings for the previous page. However, each page in a drawing has its own unique settings, so you can modify page settings to support different types of information on each page. As you modify your drawing, you can navigate between pages — renaming, deleting, and reordering them as needed. In addition, you can easily draw shapes at different angles on a page by rotating the page and then adding shapes using the orthogonal grid.

✦   ✦   ✦

Working with Visio Files

In Visio 2003, you can open, save, and print different Visio drawing files such as drawings, stencils, and templates, and you can store these Visio file types in either binary or XML file formats. You can also work with other file formats such as AutoCAD, Scalable Vector Graphics, and Graphics Interchange Format (.gif). For many of these formats, you can open and save file formats simply by selecting the format in the File As Type list in the Open or Save As dialog boxes.

Visio provides several features that make it easy to find the files you want. Task panes include links to recently used files and templates. You can also use basic or advanced searches to locate files matching your search criteria. You can search for files in folders on your computer, your network locations, or the Internet. When you're ready to print the results of your efforts, Visio provides features for specifying which parts of your drawing to print and how to print them.

Opening Drawings

Visio 2003 uses the same Open dialog box as other Microsoft Office applications, so you can use familiar shortcuts and features to locate and open your Visio files. In addition to the Open dialog box, Visio 2003 provides several convenient methods for opening the files you want to work on. For example, several new task panes contain links to Visio files, stencils, and templates.

 **New Feature** Visio 2003 can open drawings created in earlier versions of Visio. However, Visio 2002 can't open Visio 2003 files because of changes to XML and binary file formats. You can save Visio 2003 files as Visio 2002 drawings, stencils, or templates, so you can open them in Visio 2002.

When you open a Visio file, Visio opens several elements in addition to the drawing page and stencils that you can see:

✦ The workspace list saves the files, windows, and window positions from the last work session so that Visio can reset your work environment.

✦ Visio includes styles and color palettes associated with the drawing.

✦ Visio opens a VBA project, which initially contains an empty class module: ThisDocument.

✦ Visio opens a ShapeSheet for the file, which you can use to store information about the file and the shapes within it.

Caution

If you are concerned about macros jeopardizing your computer security, you can specify security options to limit macro features. To do so, choose Tools ➪ Options and select the Security tab. To disable Visual Basic for Applications (VBA) features, clear the check boxes that relate to VBA. You can also disable Com Add-Ins and Automation Events, although this might reduce the functionality available in some drawing types. Click the Macro Security button to specify the level of macro security and macro sources you trust.

Opening Visio Drawings

The Open dialog box provides several helpful tools when you want to open a file in Visio. From this dialog box you can browse, search, access recently opened files, and open the file or files you want. To open an existing file, follow these steps:

1. Click the Open button on the Standard toolbar. Alternatively, you can choose File ➪ Open or press Ctrl+O.

2. In the Look In list, browse to the folder that contains the file you want to open. The contents of the folder appear in the dialog box.

3. Double-click a file to open it.

Tip

To select more than one file, press Ctrl and click the files you want to select. Then click Open to open all the selected files.

By default, a Visio drawing uses the units defined in the template you used to create the drawing. However, you can change the units for a drawing or specify the default units for new, blank drawings and stencils. To specify the default units for text, angles, and duration, choose Tools ➪ Options, select the Units tab, and choose the units you want. You can also specify whether Visio should offer both metric and U.S. units when you create new, blank drawings and stencils.

Working with Document Management Systems

You can open and save Visio files with a document management system (DMS) if it supports the Open Document Management Architecture (ODMA) 1.5 standard. When Visio detects an ODMA 1.5–compliant management system on your computer, it opens the DMS Open dialog box instead of Visio's Open dialog box. Likewise, when you save a file in Visio, the DMS Save dialog box appears so that you can save and store your Visio drawing within the DMS. If the DMS dialog boxes don't appear, you might need to register Visio with your DMS application. Refer to your DMS documentation for instructions.

You can't use a keyboard shortcut or a link on the File menu or Task Pane to access the DMS dialog boxes to open or save files. To open or save files with a DMS, you must choose File ⇨ Open and File ⇨ Save.

Tip   You can change the measurement units for the current drawing on the Page Properties tab in the Page Setup dialog box or by clicking the Change button on the Units tab in the Options dialog box.

Accessing Recently Used Files

Although Visio is extremely easy to use, you often need more than one work session to complete a drawing. You can quickly locate and open files you worked on recently with one of the following shortcuts:

✦ **Getting Started Task Pane** — Click a link in the Open section to open a Visio file you worked on recently.

✦ **New Drawing Task Pane** — Click a link in the Recently Used Templates section to create a new drawing based on a template you used recently.

✦ **My Recent Documents folder** — When you use the Open dialog box, click the My Recent Documents link in the Places bar to view Visio files you accessed recently. To open a file, select the file in the file list and click Open.

✦ **File menu** — Depending on the options you have chosen, a number of your recently used files appear at the bottom of the File menu. Click a file name to open that file.

Tip   You can modify the number of recently used files that appear on the File menu and in the Getting Started Task Pane. To do this, choose Tools ⇨ Options, choose the General tab, and use the Recently Used File List arrows to specify the number of entries you want to appear. By default, Visio lists four documents; but you can have it list as many as nine.

Opening Other Types of Files in Visio

In Visio 2003, you can open stencils, templates, and workspaces, as well as files in other formats. Opening a workspace opens all the files and windows for that workspace, and positions the windows as they were when the workspace was saved. You can also open stencils and templates to customize them. When you open files saved in other graphic formats, Visio opens a Visio drawing that treats the graphic file as a single shape that you can move, resize, and rotate.

To open other types of files, choose File ➭ Open to access the Open dialog box. Choose the type of file you want to open in the Files of Type drop-down list. As you navigate to the folder that contains the file you want to open. Visio displays only files of the type you specified in the file list. Select the file you want and click Open.

Tip   If you want to insert content from a type of file that Visio doesn't support, open the file using another drawing application, cut or copy a section of the image, and then paste it into a Visio drawing.

Cross-Reference   To learn more about working with other types of files, refer to Chapters 8, 9, and 28.

Finding Files

Whether you want to find a Visio drawing with a shape you customized, or locate a template for your next diagramming project, you can search for Visio files, stencils, and templates on your computer, on your network, in Microsoft Outlook, or online. Like other Microsoft Office applications, Visio 2003 provides several convenient methods for finding the files you want.

Using File Properties to Find Files

You can differentiate files by the values in their File properties, whether you use search methods or inspect the properties in the Properties dialog box. Visio automatically populates some of the file properties. Some of these are read-only, but many others are editable. In addition, you can populate other properties, such as Category or Keywords, to simplify locating the files you want in the future. When you select a file in the Open dialog box, you can click Tools ➭ Properties to view its properties before opening the file.

Visio automatically populates the properties on the General tab. These properties are read-only and provide basic identification of a file, including the type of Visio file, the folder location where the file is stored, the file size, and the template on which it is based.

Although Visio populates some of the fields on the Summary tab automatically, you can use these properties to describe and categorize your drawings and then search these fields to locate the files you want. Add or edit text in any or all of the following fields:

- ✦ **Title** — A descriptive title for the file.
- ✦ **Subject** — A description of the drawing contents.
- ✦ **Author** — Visio populates this field with the name of the person who created or last updated the file. You can enter another name.
- ✦ **Manager** — The name of the person in charge of the project or the department for which the drawing was created.
- ✦ **Company** — This can represent either the company responsible for creating the drawing or the client for which the drawing was produced.
- ✦ **Language** — Visio populates this field with the default language, but you can change the language in this field. Visio uses the language specified in this field when it checks spelling.
- ✦ **Category** — This describes the drawing type, such as a database model, block diagram, or Gantt chart.
- ✦ **Keywords** — These are words that identify the file, client, project, or other aspects of the drawing contents.
- ✦ **Description** — This option provides additional information about the file, such as purpose or revisions made.
- ✦ **Hyperlink Base** — This specifies the path used as an origin for hyperlinks for which the path is not fully defined. By default, Visio uses a path relative to the current file.
- ✦ **Save Preview Picture** — Select this check box to save a preview picture of the first page of the drawing and display the preview when you click Preview in the Views menu in the Open dialog box.

The Contents tab lists each page in the drawing and the master shapes included on them. You can use this tab to identify the names of the masters used in a drawing.

Searching for Drawing Files

You can search for files no matter which method you use for opening files. Visio provides both basic and advanced search features to help you find the file you want. To search for a file, choose one of the following methods:

- ✦ Choose File ⇨ File Search to open the Basic File Search task pane.
- ✦ Choose File ⇨ Open. Choose Tools ⇨ Search in the action bar to open the Microsoft Office Search dialog box, which includes the same features as the Basic File Search and Advanced File Search task panes, displayed using a different format.

Using Basic Search Options

With basic search options, you can look for files that contain one or more words in the body of the drawing, in keywords, or in other file properties. You can also specify where to look and the type of file you want.

> **Tip**   If your computer is configured to work with other languages and you are searching in English, French, Spanish, German, Dutch, Italian, or Swedish, you can enter one form of a word in the Search Text box and Visio will search for other forms as well. For example, you can search for "connect" and Visio will also search for "connecting" and "connected."

The basic search options include the following:

✦ **Search for text** — Type one or more words in the Search Text box that you want to find in file properties. You can use a question mark (?) as a wildcard for one character and an asterisk (*) as a wildcard for several characters.

✦ **Search in** — Click the Search In arrow and choose the locations you want to search. You can select folders and hard disks on your computer, in your network places, and in Microsoft Outlook. To browse locations, click a plus sign to expand the list. To choose a folder, select the check box next to the folder.

> **Note**   When you search your Microsoft Outlook mailbox in English, you can use natural language in your search text. For example, you can type a phrase such as "Find all the messages from engineering sent last week."

✦ **Results Should Be** — Click the Results Should Be arrow and choose the types of files you want to find. You can select Visio files, document imaging files, and Web pages.

After you have specified your search criteria, click Go to search for files. If you don't see the file you want in the Search Results task pane, click the Modify button to return to the Basic File Search task pane.

> **Tip**   To find files more quickly or to search for text in shapes and custom properties in a Visio drawing, enable fast searching on your computer. To do this, click the Search Options link in the Basic File Search task pane and select the option to enable the Indexing service. Your computer scans your files while it is idle and builds an index of file properties and contents. If the Indexing service is disabled, enabling it turns the Indexing services back on and sets its Startup Type to Automatic.

Constructing an Advanced Search

You can use the advanced search options to restrict the number of results Visio retrieves. To open the Advanced File Search task pane, shown in Figure 3-1, click the Advanced File Search link in the Basic File Search task pane or select the Advanced tab in the File Search dialog box. With advanced search options, you can do the following:

✦ Choose the text or property to search, such as Creation Date.

✦ Choose a condition that the text or property should match, such as On Or Before, for a date.

✦ Specify the value for the search criteria, such as August 27, 2003.

✦ Define several search criteria, combining them with logical Ands and Ors.

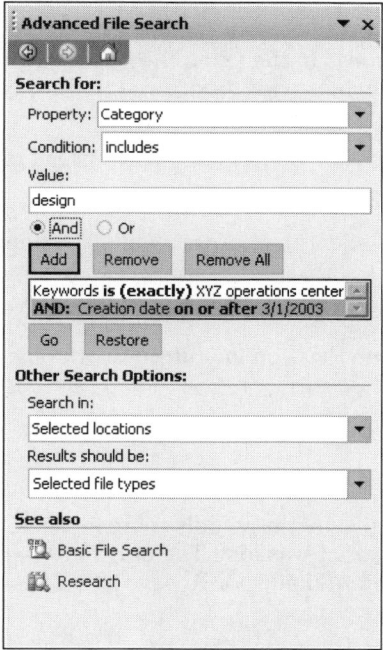

Figure 3-1: You can restrict search results with criteria defined in the Advanced File Search Task Pane.

Finding Templates and Sample Drawings

Visio provides numerous templates and sample drawings to help you get started. The Diagram Gallery introduces the different types of drawings you can create with Visio. You can also download sample drawings prepopulated with typical drawing content from Microsoft Office Online. The New Drawing Task Pane includes links to search for templates on your computer, in your network places, on Web sites, and at Microsoft Office Online. You can use the following tools to find templates and sample drawings:

✦ **Diagram Gallery** — Choose Help ➪ Diagram Gallery to identify the type of drawing you want. Click a category and a drawing type to see a description and examples of its applications. Click Next and Back to browse drawings in sequence.

✦ **New Drawing Task Pane** — To search for templates and sample files, choose View ➪ Task Pane to open the Task Pane and then choose New Drawing in the Task Pane drop-down list. Choose one of the following methods to find a template or sample drawing:

• **Search Online For** — Type words in the Open the New Drawing Task Pane and click Go. To find drawings with predrawn content, type Sample Drawings in the Search Online For box.

New Feature Sample drawings are now available at Microsoft Office Online instead of installed on your computer with Visio.

• **Templates on Office Online** — Search Microsoft Office Online for additional Visio templates.

• **On My Computer** — Browse folders on your computer for Visio templates.

• **On My Web Sites** — Browse the location in your network places.

Saving Files

Saving your work can be one of the best productivity tools there is, because nothing reduces productivity like recreating work that was lost. The only hard part about saving files in Visio is developing the habit of doing so. To save a file, choose one of the following methods:

✦ Press Ctrl+S.

✦ Click Save on the Standard toolbar.

✦ Choose File ➪ Save.

Visio includes several options to configure how and where Visio saves files. To specify save options, choose Tools ➪ Options to open the Options dialog box and then choose one or more of the following options:

✦ **User Information** — Select the General tab to specify the user name and initials you want Visio to use as the author of drawings.

✦ **Prompt for Document Properties on First Save** — Select the Save tab to select the option that prompts for document properties the first time you save a file.

✦ **Save AutoRecover Info** — Select the Save tab to specify whether Visio saves your file automatically and, if so, how many minutes elapse between automatic file saves.

✦ **Default File Type** — Select the Save tab to choose the file format to which Visio saves by default. The options are to save files as Visio 2003 drawings, Visio XML documents, or Visio 2002 drawings.

✦ **Default File Locations** — If you organize your files in specific folders, select the Advanced tab and click the File Paths button to specify the location for drawings, templates, stencils, help files, add-ons, and startup paths.

Tip You can share drawings with others by saving them to network locations, Web folders, or shared workspaces created through Windows SharePoint Services. You can access network locations and Web folders in the Places bar of the Save As dialog box. To learn more about shared workspaces, see Chapter 11.

✦ **Remove Personal Information from File Properties on Save** — Select the Security tab to remove the author name, manager name, and company name from file properties when you save a file.

When you save a drawing for the first time, Visio opens the Save As dialog box automatically. You specify a filename and location for the drawing and click Save to store the file. After the file is saved, it's quickest to press Ctrl+S to save the changes you made to your drawing.

Note When you save a file, Visio not only saves any changes you've made to pages, shapes, and properties; it also saves the position of all open windows to the drawing workspace so that your Visio environment will look the same the next time you open the file.

Saving Visio Files

You can use your drawings for different purposes by saving them as different types of Visio files. The following list identifies the types of Visio files you can save and what they represent:

✦ **Drawing** — A file that contains pages of shapes and text you use to convey information.

✦ **Stencil** — A file that contains master shapes you drag onto drawings.

✦ **Template** — A file that Visio copies to create a new drawing. Visio copies into the new drawing any settings, stencils, windows, styles, macros, and other elements you define in the template.

✦ **XML Files** — This identifies XML versions of drawings, stencils, and templates. You can work with these files as you would regular Visio files, but you can also open them in a text or XML editor and access your Visio data via XML tools.

Caution   Visio 2003 can open Visio 2002 XML files, but you can't save Visio 2003 files to Visio 2002 XML format. To do that, you must save the file as a Visio 2002 drawing and then convert it to XML in Visio 2002.

✦ **Visio 2002 Files** — You can share drawings with people who use Visio 2002 by saving a Visio 2003 file to Visio 2002 format. However, you will lose any information or formatting specific to Visio 2003.

To save a drawing as another type of Visio file, choose File ➪ Save As. Choose the type of file you want to use in the Save As Type drop-down list. Specify the file name and location and then click Save. You can also use File ➪ Save As to save Visio drawings in many other formats. These formats include the following:

✦ AutoCAD formats (.dwg, .dxf)

Cross-Reference   To learn about working with AutoCAD formats, see Chapter 28.

✦ Metafiles (.emz, .emf, .wmf)

✦ Graphics formats (.gif, .jpeg, .png, .tif, .bmp, .dib)

✦ Scalable Vector Graphics Drawing (.svg, .svgz)

New Feature   Support for Scalable Vector Graphics (SVG) format is new in Visio 2003.

✦ Web Pages (.htm, .html)

Cross-Reference   To learn more about publishing Visio drawings to the Web, see Chapter 9.

Tip   You can save a Visio drawing as a print file, which you can then print from any computer connected to the type of printer specified for the drawing, even if Visio is not installed on that computer. To do this, choose File ➪ Print and select the Print to File check box. Click OK and specify the name of the print file and where you want to save it. Then, you can use the Windows lpr command in the Command Prompt window to redirect the print file to the printer you want to use. In addition, although Visio has removed support for PostScript formats, you can save Visio to a PostScript file by choosing a PostScript printer in the Print dialog box.

Protecting Files

You can protect your files from inadvertent changes in several ways. If you save a file as a read-only version, other users can only view the drawing. If you use the Protect Document feature, you can specify which items you want to protect. If you use layers on your drawing, you can lock a layer against changes.

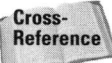

Cross-Reference

To learn how to lock a layer, see Chapter 25.

Saving a Read-Only Copy

Saving a read-only copy is not a surefire way to protect the contents of a drawing. When you open a read-only drawing, you can modify its contents all you want, but you must save the modified file with a different name. In addition, you can also remove the read-only protection in Windows Explorer. However, the warning message that appears when you try to save a read-only file is often enough to prevent someone from inadvertently changing the contents of a drawing.

To save a read-only copy of a file, choose File ➪ Save As. After specifying a file name and location for the file, click the Save drop-down arrow to display Save options. Select Read Only and then click the Save button.

Protecting Drawings

To protect specific items on a drawing, follow these steps:

1. Choose View ➪ Drawing Explorer Window.

2. Right-click the name of the drawing you want to protect and click Protect Document on the shortcut menu.

Note

If Protect Document doesn't appear on the shortcut menu, you can add the command to a Visio menu or toolbar. To do this, click the Toolbar Options arrow at the end of a toolbar, and choose Add or Remove Buttons ➪ Customize. In the Customize dialog box, select the Commands tab, select Tools in the Category list, and then drag Protect Document to a position on the toolbar.

3. Check the items you want to protect from unauthorized changes and click OK. You can protect the following elements of a Visio drawing:

   • **Styles** — Although you can still apply styles when this check box is checked, you can't create new styles or edit existing ones.

   • **Shapes** — This setting combined with the From Selection setting in the Protection dialog box prevents you from selecting shapes.

- **Preview**—This option prevents changes to a Visio file's preview image when you change the contents of a drawing page.
- **Backgrounds**—Use this to prevent the deletion or editing of background pages.
- **Master shapes**—This setting prevents the creation, editing, or deletion of masters. However, you can still create instances of masters on drawing pages.

To remove protection from a drawing, uncheck the check boxes in the Protect Document dialog box and click OK.

Previewing and Printing Drawings

Visio works hard to ensure that your drawings print as you would expect. In most templates, the drawing page and printed page settings are the same, so you don't have to adjust page settings. Visio also adjusts colors in your drawing to your printer's resources. For example, if you don't have a color printer, then colors appear in shades of gray. To get the best results the first time, it's a good idea to preview your drawing before you print. You can make sure that you set page properties such as page size and orientation properly, and define the headers and footers you want to see.

Note   Shapes that lie outside of the drawing page do not print. To include these shapes when you print your drawing, move them onto the drawing page.

Previewing Drawings

If you want to make sure that your drawing prints the way you want, you can preview your drawing before you print. Print Preview features in Visio are similar to those in other Microsoft Windows applications. To preview a drawing, choose File ➪ Print Preview or click Print Preview on the Standard toolbar. Visio shades the margins for the printer paper, so you can see how your drawing fits on it. If your drawing is larger than the paper, Visio displays shading where page breaks are located.

You can also preview the fit between your drawing page and printer paper in the Page Setup dialog box. Choose File ➪ Page Setup and select one of the Print Setup, Page Size, or Drawing Scale tabs. If the preview indicates a discrepancy, you can modify settings on these tabs to correct the problem.

Tip   The easiest way to ensure that the drawing and printer paper match is to use the Same As Printer Paper Size option. Choose File ➪ Page Setup, select the Page Size tab, and select the Same As Printer Paper Size option.

Printing Drawings

You can print entire drawings, specific elements on drawings, or specific areas of drawings. After you have previewed your drawing to confirm that it will print the way you want, it's easy to print using one of the following methods:

✦ Press Ctrl+P.

✦ Click Print on the Standard toolbar.

✦ Choose File ➪ Print.

If shapes are missing on the printed drawing, the shape might be configured as a nonprinting shape, or the layer to which it is assigned might be set not to print. To reset a nonprinting shape, follow these steps:

1. Right-click the shape and choose Format ➪ Behavior.

2. Uncheck the Non-Printing Shape check box and click OK.

To check the shape layer, follow these steps:

1. Right-click the shape and choose Format ➪ Layer.

2. Choose View ➪ Layer Properties and make sure the Print column for the layer is selected.

Note   If the shape still doesn't appear, the printer driver might have misinterpreted the shape's colors. To verify the presence of shapes, choose File ➪ Print and then select the Color As Black check box to print all lines and fills with black.

Printing Selected Parts of a Drawing

The Print dialog box contains options for specifying pages or portions of your drawing that you want to print. In addition, you can use other Visio features, such as layers and markup, to control what you print. To print selected part of a drawing, choose one of the following methods:

✦ **Selected Pages** — To specify the pages you want to print, choose File ➪ Print and choose one of the following two options:

• **Current Page** — Click this option to print the active page.

• **Pages From and To** — Type the number of the first and last page you want to print.

✦ **Printing a Portion of a Drawing** — To specify an area of the drawing you want to print, choose File ➪ Print and choose one of the following two options:

• **Selection** — If you have selected shapes on your drawing, click this option to print only the selected shapes.

• **Current View** — Click this option to print the portion of the drawing that appears in the Visio drawing window.

Tip   If you assign shapes to layers, you can control whether layers print. You can set up nonprinting layers for shapes you use as reference points, guides, or feedback. To prevent a layer from printing, choose View ➪ Layer Properties and clear the check mark in the Print column for the layer.

✦ **Printing a Background Page** — Display the background page you want to print and then choose File ➪ Print. Select the Current Page option and click OK to print the background page.

✦ **Printing Only a Foreground Page** — You must remove the background page associated with a foreground page if you want to print only the foreground page. To do this, display the foreground page and choose File ➪ Page Setup. Select the Page Properties tab, click None in the Background box, and click OK. Use the Current Page option in the Print dialog box to print the page.

✦ **Printing Drawing Markup** — Display the drawing markup and then print the drawing.

Tip   By default, guides are nonprintable objects, but you can print a guide by modifying the guide's ShapeSheet. To do this, select the guide you want to print and choose Window ➪ Show ShapeSheet. Scroll to the Miscellaneous section and type False in the NonPrinting cell.

✦ **Printing ShapeSheets** — To print a ShapeSheet, you must download the Print ShapeSheet file from the MSDN Web site (`http://msdn.microsoft.com/visio`) and install it. You can print the ShapeSheet data to a printer, copy it to the Clipboard, or save it to a text file. Currently, the MSDN Web site does not have the Print ShapeSheet tool for Visio 2003. However, Microsoft expects to have updated information by March 2004.

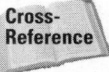

Cross-Reference   For more information about ShapeSheets, see Chapter 33.

Correcting Orientation Mismatches

Although you can specify a different size and orientation for each page in a drawing, Visio uses one set of printer settings, which can lead to page and paper discrepancies when you print an entire file. If you assign different sizes and orientations to each page, print each drawing page separately and reset the Print Setup options before you print each page.

If you try to print a Visio drawing page that uses an orientation different from the printer page, Visio displays an error message. When you click OK in response to this error, Visio prints the drawing on multiple pages. To correct the problem before printing, click Cancel and then reset either the drawing page or printer paper orientation so they match.

If your drawing contains shapes that you want to see only while you are working on the drawing, you can specify shape options to prevent them from printing. To do this, select the shape or shapes and choose Format ➪ Behavior. Select the Non-Printing Shape check box and click OK.

Printing Large Drawings

When your drawing is larger than the largest paper size that your printer can accommodate, you can choose from several solutions, depending on your needs. If you're fortunate enough to have a larger format printer available, you can add access to that printer to your computer and then print to a larger sheet of paper.

If your drawing almost fits on one sheet of paper, the easiest solution is to shrink the drawing to fit on one sheet. To do this, choose File ➪ Page Setup and select the Print Setup tab. In the Print Zoom area, click the Fit To option and type **1** in both the Across and Down boxes.

Note   You can use the Fit To option anytime you want to print a drawing to a specific number of pages. Type the number of pages you want in the horizontal direction in the Across box, and then do the same for the number of pages wanted vertically, in the Down box.

Print Zoom won't help if your drawing is much larger than your printer paper, or when you want to print your drawing to scale. You can view the relationship between your drawing size and printer paper in the Page Setup dialog box, as demonstrated in Figure 3-2. For these situations, you can tile your drawing across several sheets of paper.

Page break indicators

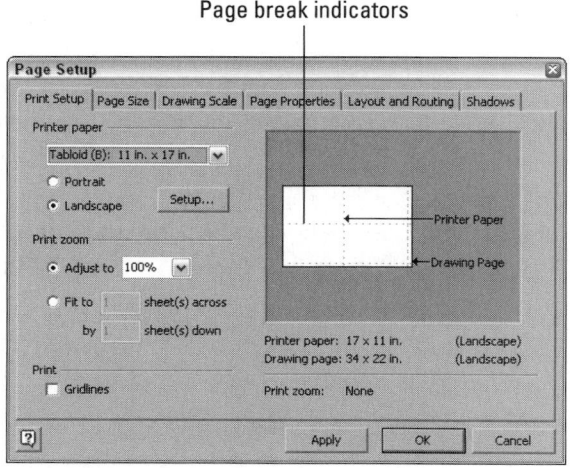

Figure 3-2: The Page Setup preview shows page breaks for tiled drawings.

When you tile a drawing, shapes that overlap the page breaks might print twice — once on each page on either side of the page break. To prevent this duplication of shapes, you can view the page breaks on your drawing and relocate any shapes that overlap them. After the overlaps are eliminated, you can print the drawing to multiple sheets. To eliminate shapes overlapping page breaks, follow these steps:

1. To view the page breaks on your drawing, choose View ⇨ Page Breaks. Visio indicates page breaks with gray shading. The thickness of the shaded lines represents the margins set for the printed page.

2. To reduce the thickness of the page breaks, choose File ⇨ Page Setup and select the Print Setup tab. Click the Setup button and specify narrower margins. Click OK in the Print Setup dialog box and then click OK in the Page Setup dialog box.

Note   Printers have minimum margins that you can't reduce. If you specify margins smaller than the minimum for the current printer, Visio sets the margins to the smallest margin that the printer can handle.

3. On the drawing page, drag any shapes that overlap the page break to one side or the other.

Printing Drawings in the Center of the Paper

Visio offers several methods for centering drawings on the printed paper. You can move the contents of a drawing to the center of the page or change the resize property of the drawing to match the size of the contents. If your drawing page and printer paper are the same size, you can center your drawing by pressing Ctrl+A to select the contents of the page and then choosing Shape ⇨ Center Drawing.

To center the contents of your drawing on a page, follow these steps:

1. Choose File ⇨ Page Setup and select the Page Size tab.

2. Click the Size to Fit Drawing Contents option. The new drawing size appears in the preview area.

3. Select the Print Setup tab and click the Setup button.

4. Select the Center Horizontally and Center Vertically check boxes to center the drawing on the printer paper and click OK. Click OK in the Page Setup dialog box.

Summary

You can work on any kind of Visio file as well as files in a number of different formats in Visio 2003, although several formats are no longer supported. Visio includes a number of shortcuts for finding and opening the files you want, including links on task panes and searching text and properties in files. When you're ready to print, you can specify how you want the drawing to print on the page as well as which portions of the drawing you want to see.

✦   ✦   ✦

Working with Shapes

Shapes are the foundation of every drawing you produce in Visio. No matter what type of diagram you want to develop, you create content for drawings by dragging and dropping shapes onto drawing pages. Known as *SmartShapes*, these predefined shapes have built-in properties and behaviors that simplify your work.

As you work, you can select the shapes you want to work on in several ways. With a combination of Visio tools and shape handles and behaviors, you can position shapes easily and as precisely as you want. After adding shapes to a drawing page, you can use several Visio tools and add-ons to move, align, and duplicate those shapes. By dragging shape handles, you can change the size and outline of shapes. To simplify work on related shapes, you can create groups of shapes that act as one.

Because many drawings convey information through text and data, Visio also provides features for annotation and data storage. Visio shapes can contain custom properties for storing data about the shapes. You can add annotation with text or property values directly to Visio shapes. You can also use Visio add-ons to label and number the shapes on your drawings.

Visio provides hundreds of built-in shapes for dozens of different types of drawings. With so many shapes to choose from, you might wonder how you would ever find the shapes you want. In addition to categorizing shapes by placing them on stencils, Visio's Search for Shapes tool helps you find shapes on your computer or the Web.

Shapes 101

If you're anxious to get started, here's what you need to know to start working with shapes. When you're ready for more detail, continue reading the remainder of this chapter.

Shape Masters and Instances

You can quickly create drawings by dragging and dropping masters from stencils onto a drawing page. Predrawn shapes, called *masters,* are stored and categorized in stencils. A master can be as simple as a single line or quite complex, with numerous graphic and text elements, custom properties, and specialized behaviors. When you drag a master from a stencil onto the drawing page, the copy or *instance* inherits its master's components, properties, and behaviors.

Although shape instances are linked to masters, you can still modify instances on drawing pages. Visio creates a special stencil that contains a copy of each master you use in a document. In fact, this document stencil is an easy way to create stencils of customized shapes by editing the instances in your document and then saving the document stencil.

Positioning Shapes

Although masters on stencils simplify your work, assembling your drawings involves more than dragging and dropping. Whether you're drawing a scaled plan in which dimensional accuracy is critical or aligning shapes to neaten the appearance of a business diagram, you can use Visio tools to snap shapes into position (a process called *snapping to*). Rulers, grids, and guides act as reference points for alignment and accurate placement. However, you can snap to many other elements in Visio, including different parts of the shapes themselves. When precision is important, you can also position shapes by specifying x and y coordinates in the Size & Position window.

In addition to the initial placement of shapes, you can choose from several methods when you want to reposition the shapes on your drawings. Visio shapes include tools and techniques for moving and flipping shapes. You can also rotate shapes by dragging their rotation handles or specifying an angle in the Size & Position window.

Modifying Shapes

Visio includes several methods for modifying and duplicating shapes. You can change shapes to suit your needs and then quickly construct your drawing by repeating existing shapes. The shapes you add to a drawing aren't always exactly what you want. After you add shapes, you can also control them in the following ways:

✦ Reposition or manipulate them

✦ Drag them to another position or use coordinates to place them precisely

✦ Rotate or mirror them to the orientation you want

✦ Change their size and even modify their shapes

✦ Change their position in the stacking order

To repeat the shapes on a page, you can stamp multiple copies of a master or copy and paste one or more shapes. For shapes positioned at regular intervals, you can create an array of shapes.

Groups of Shapes

Groups of shapes further enhance your drawing productivity. In addition to moving several shapes as one, groups can include their own behaviors and features to speed up the creation of specialized graphics, such as a bar graph or title block.

Depending on a group's properties, you can work with the group as a whole or with the individual shapes within the group. For example, when you add a title block to a drawing page, you can move the group into position, but you can also add text to the individual cells to annotate the drawing.

Finding Shapes

When you start a drawing from a template, Visio opens stencils with shapes typical for that type of drawing. However, you can add shapes already on your current drawing, from another drawing, in a stencil that isn't open, or stored somewhere on the Web. Visio 2003 includes dozens of built-in stencils with thousands of specialized shapes. However, you can also find shapes on the Web, at Microsoft Office Online, and at many vendor Web sites.

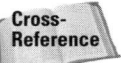

Cross-Reference For more information about shapes on the Web, including URLs for online sources, see Chapter 39.

You can search for shapes in several ways, including the Search for Shapes feature, which is a powerful tool for finding the shapes you want. If you intend to use the shapes you find frequently, you can save your search results to a custom stencil so the shapes are easy to access the next time you need them. To access Search for Shapes, open a new or existing drawing and, if the Shapes window is not open, choose View ➪ Shapes Window.

New Feature

The Search for Shapes feature is similar to the Find Shapes command available in Visio 2002, but now you can enter search criteria and search directly from the Shapes window. Instead of specifying search options in a special dialog box, you can set the Shape Search options by choosing Tools ➪ Options and selecting the Shape Search tab.

Opening Stencils

It's easy to drag shapes onto a drawing when the stencils containing the shapes you want are open. If you are working on a drawing you created without a template or the open stencils don't contain the shapes you want, you can open and close stencils to access other shapes. For example, you can open the Charting Shapes stencil to add a table of information to an organization chart.

First, open the drawing you want to work on or create a new one. Then, to open a stencil, choose File ➪ Shapes and then use one of the following methods:

✦ **Open a built-in stencil** — Point to a category and choose a stencil.

✦ **Open a custom stencil** — Point to My Shapes and choose a stencil.

✦ **Create a blank stencil** — Choose New Stencil to add shapes to create your own stencil.

✦ **Display the document stencil** — To display a stencil that contains all the shapes on the current drawing, choose Open Document Stencil.

Note

If no drawing is open in Visio and you choose File ➪ Shapes and choose a stencil to open, Visio displays stencil-related toolbars and opens the stencil in a window with very limited functionality. For example, when you right-click a master in the stencil window, you can only copy the master or add it to one of your custom stencils. To access all the stencil features, open a Visio drawing and *then* choose File ➪ Shapes to open a stencil in the Shapes window.

Finding Shapes on Drawings

The Search for Shapes feature doesn't help find shapes on your current drawing because it searches for keywords associated with shapes in stencils. For example, when a new manager assumes responsibility for a department, you might want to locate the shape for that position on a large organization chart by searching for the previous manager's name. Using the Find command, you can look for shapes in your current drawing by searching for text in shape text blocks, shape names, custom property values, and user-defined cell values in ShapeSheets. To find a shape on your drawing, follow these steps:

1. Choose Edit ➪ Find.

2. Type the words or phrase associated with the shape you are looking for. To include special characters in the search text, click Special and then choose the special character you want to include.

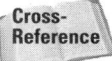

To learn more about searching for text, see Chapter 6.

3. In the Search In section, select an option to specify which pages or sections of your drawing to search.

4. To specify the shape components that you want to search, check one or more of the check boxes in the Search In section. You can search shape text, custom properties, shape names, and user-defined cells in the ShapeSheet.

5. In the Options section, check one or more of the check boxes to specify the criteria for matching text.

6. Click Find Next to begin the search. Visio highlights the first shape it finds containing the search text. If the text is not visible in the drawing, Visio displays the location of the text in the Found In text box in the Find dialog box.

Searching for Shapes

The Search for Shapes feature scans for text matching your criteria in the keywords associated with shapes. Depending on the options you choose, Visio will search built-in and custom stencils on your computer as well as stencils it finds on the Web. When you search for shapes, Visio creates a search results stencil that contains the shapes it finds. You can drag a shape from the search results stencil onto your drawing or save a shape to another stencil so it is easier to locate in the future.

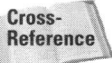

To search for shapes that you've created, you must add search keywords to the master on the custom stencil. To learn how to do this, see Chapter 32.

For the best results using Search for Shapes, specify descriptive words for your search text, such as "table" and "furniture," rather than specific shape names. You can type words as singular or plural; Visio searches for both forms. For example, typing "buttons" returns shapes with either "button" or "buttons" as a keyword. Unfortunately, you can't use wildcards in your search text. To improve your success, try the following techniques:

✦ When Visio doesn't find any matching shapes or the results aren't what you expect, try other words in your search criteria. For example, instead of "file," try "cabinet."

✦ When too many results are returned, add words or phrases to further screen the results. For example, using "table" returns a variety of database shapes in addition to furniture. Use "conference table" to locate shapes for large office tables.

Using the Search for Shapes Feature

You can search for shapes by typing keywords describing the shapes you want into the Search for Shapes box in the Shapes window and clicking the green arrow. You can enter one or more words, separating them with spaces, commas, or semicolons. Visio keeps track of the keywords you used recently so you can repeat a search by clicking the Search for Shapes down arrow, choosing the keyword entry you want to reuse, and clicking the green arrow.

Note   If the Shapes window isn't visible, choose View ⇨ Shapes Window to display it.

When you execute a search, Visio uses the current Shape Search options to determine where and how to search for shapes. If the search results don't contain the shapes you want, you can modify the Shape Search options by following these steps:

1. Right-click the Shapes window title bar or the Search for Shapes area in the Shapes window and choose Search Options on the shortcut menu.

Note   You can also access Shape Search options by choosing Tools ⇨ Options and then selecting the Shape Search tab.

2. To specify where Visio should search for stencils, check the My Computer check box in the Search Locations list to search folders on your computer. Check the Internet check box to search the Web.

Note   When you search the Web for shapes, Visio retrieves only the shapes associated with your Visio product. For example, you won't see shapes from Visio Professional if you use Visio Standard. However, Visio Professional includes all the shapes available in Visio Standard and many more.

3. To specify which keywords a shape must possess, choose the All of the Words or Any of the Words option.

4. To view the shapes found grouped by the stencil to which they belong, select the By Group option in the Results section. If you want to view the results in a new window, check the Open Results in New Window check box.

5. To prevent Visio from retrieving an overwhelming number of results, check the Warn When Results Are Greater Than check box and type a cutoff number in the box.

6. Click OK when you are finished specifying Shape Search options and click the green arrow to execute the search.

7. To specify whether Visio displays Icons, Names, or Details in the search results stencil, right-click the Shapes Window title bar and choose one of the following options:

- **Icons and Names** — Displays icons and shape names just as other stencils appear by default

- **Icons Only** — Displays only icons

- **Names Only** — Displays only names, which uses less space in the window but requires more familiarity with the shapes

- **Icons and Details** — Displays icons, names, and a brief description of the shape

Tip If you want to find more shapes similar to one that Visio retrieved, drag the shape to your drawing, right-click it, choose Shapes ➪ Find Similar Shapes. Visio uses the keywords associated with the selected shape to search for other shapes, and adds them to a search results stencil.

Speeding Up Shape Searches with the Indexing Service

If you search for shapes frequently, you can reduce search time by enabling the Indexing Service on your computer. In effect, the Indexing Service maintains an index of words associated with your shapes so that it can search a database instead of shapes or drawings.

Tip If you don't want shapes from the Web, searches are quicker if you uncheck the Internet check box on the Shape Search tab of the Options dialog box.

To enable indexing on your computer, make sure you have administrator privileges on your computer and then follow these steps:

1. Choose Tools ➪ Options and select the Shape Search tab.

2. Select Visio Local Shapes in the Search Locations list and click Properties.

3. Choose Yes, Enable Indexing Service and then click OK. Indexing might take a few minutes; the Shape Search Local Shape Properties dialog box closes when Visio finishes indexing your shapes.

Troubleshooting Shape Searches

If Visio doesn't find shapes you want and you know they exist, check for the following problems:

✦ **No Keywords Associated with Shape** — Open the custom stencil for editing and add keywords to the master.

✦ **Stencil Keywords Don't Match** — If you add keywords to a master shape and the Indexing Service is not enabled, the custom stencil in which the master is located might not have the same keywords as the master. Open the custom stencil for editing and check the keywords for the shape you created by right-clicking the master and choosing Edit Master ➪ Master Properties on the shortcut menu.

✦ **Index Being Updated** — If shapes contain keywords and the Indexing Service is enabled, Visio might be trying to search while the index is being updated. Try the search again after a minute has passed.

✦ **Custom Stencil Open for Edit** — Visio can't search stencils when they are open for editing. If the stencil icon in the stencil title bar includes a red asterisk, the stencil is open for editing. To save it so it can be searched, right-click the stencil title bar and then click Edit Stencil. When the red asterisk in the stencil title bar disappears, you can search the stencil.

✦ **Stencil Path Is Incomplete** — In addition to searching the folders that contain Visio's built-in stencils, the Search for Shapes feature searches for stencils in your stencil path. If you store stencils in several locations, make sure that your stencil path includes those locations. To modify the stencil path, choose Tools ➪ Options, select the Advanced tab, and then click File Paths. To browse folders, click the Ellipsis button to the right of the Stencils box and navigate to the folder you want. To specify more than one stencil path, type a semicolon between each path.

Saving Shape Search Results to a Stencil

Visio displays the shapes it finds in a search results stencil. To access these shapes quickly in the future, you can save individual shapes or the entire search results stencil to a custom stencil. Saving shapes to stencils on your hard drive is especially helpful when you find shapes on the Web and don't want to get online to access those shapes in the future.

New Feature   Visio 2003 automatically creates a My Shapes folder in your My Documents folder, and creates a Favorites stencil in your My Shapes folder so that you can easily access the shapes you use most frequently.

To save the search results stencil as a custom stencil, follow these steps:

1. Right-click the search results stencil title bar and choose Save As on the shortcut menu.

2. In the File Namebox, type a name for the custom stencil and then click Save. By default, Visio saves stencils in your My Shapes folder.

To save a shape in the search results stencil to a custom stencil, right-click the shape and choose Add to My Shapes ➪ Add to Existing Stencil. You can choose the Favorites stencil, other custom stencils, or click Add to New Stencil to create a new custom stencil for the shape.

Note   To access custom stencils in your My Shapes folder, choose File ➪ Shapes ➪ My Shapes and then click the stencil you want to open.

Selecting Shapes

You have to select shapes before you can edit, position, or manipulate them. Visio provides several selection methods to select individual shapes, multiple shapes, and groups.

New Feature With any drawing tool active, you can click on a line or closed shape to select that shape. If you pause the pointer, the selection handles appear, followed by control handles at line midpoints, and finally corner control handles.

Selecting Individual Shapes

You can select individual shapes whether they stand on their own or belong to a group. To select one shape, use one of the following methods:

✦ **One Shape** — Click a shape to select it and display its selection handles.

✦ **One Shape in a Group** — To subselect a shape in a group, click the shape once to select the group and then click a second time to select the shape and display its selection handles, as shown in Figure 4-1. You can also select a shape within a group by double-clicking it.

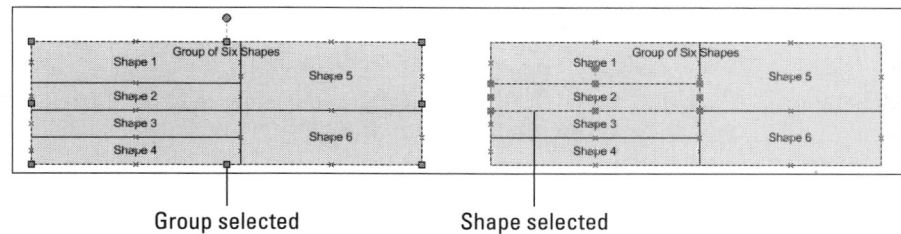

Group selected   Shape selected

Figure 4-1: Click once to select a group and a second time to select a shape in the group.

Note If clicking a shape doesn't select it, the shape might be protected against selection, or it could belong to a group. To determine whether a shape belongs to a group, click the shape and choose Format ➪ Special on the shortcut menu. If the Type field value is Group, the shape belongs to a group, and you can double-click the shape to select it. If the shape doesn't belong to a group, check for protection by clicking the shape, choosing Format ➪ Protection, and seeing whether the From Selection check box is checked. If it is, you can uncheck the box and click OK to remove this protection.

Selecting Multiple Shapes

Visio offers several ways to select multiple shapes, whether they are side by side or spread across your drawing. When you select multiple shapes, Visio highlights each selected shape with a magenta box and adds handles for the collection of selected shapes so that you can rotate and resize them all. When you want to work on several shapes at once, select them using one of the following methods:

✦ **Select Box** — To select the shapes within an area, click the Pointer tool on the Standard toolbar and drag a rectangle that completely encloses the shapes you want to select.

By default, Visio doesn't select a shape if a portion lies outside the selection rectangle. To include shapes only partially contained within the selection rectangle, choose Tools ➪ Options and select the General tab. Check the Select Shapes Partially within the Area check box and click OK.

✦ **Shift+click** — To select shapes that are scattered across your drawing, hold the Shift key and click each shape you want to select.

You can select one or more groups using the same methods you use to select shapes. To select groups, make sure you click within the group only once.

✦ **Select Tool** — Click the Pointer tool arrow on the Standard toolbar to access other multiple selection tools:

 • **Area** — Select this tool and drag a rectangle to select the shapes within an area. If you drag another rectangle while shapes are selected, the Area tool adds shapes within the new rectangle to the selections.

 • **Lasso** — Select this tool and drag the pointer around an irregular path to enclose the shapes you want to select, as illustrated in Figure 4-2.

 • **Multiple** — Select this tool and click shapes to add them to the selection. Click a selected shape to remove it from the selection.

You can draw an irregular boundary around the shapes you want to select with the Lasso tool.

✦ **Select All** — Press Ctrl+A to select all shapes on the drawing page.

✦ **Select By Type** — Choose Edit ➪ Select By Type and then select the Shape Type or Layer option. If you select by shape type, check the check boxes for each type of shape you want to select. To select layers, check the layer check boxes.

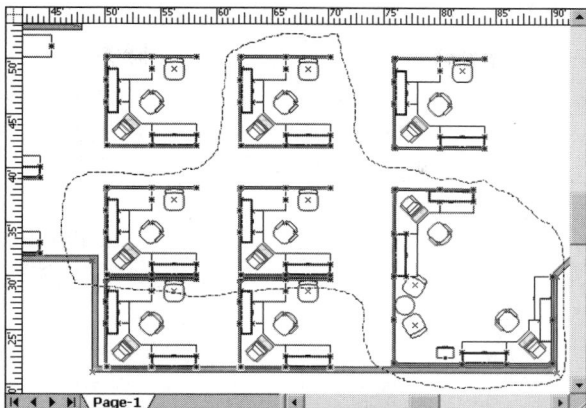

Figure 4-2: You can create an irregular selection boundary with the Lasso tool.

Positioning Shapes

With most business diagrams, you want shapes to line up so the drawing looks organized and neat, but you don't care about the exact position of the shapes. When you create scaled drawings, such as building plans, precise positions are very important. For example, a few inches in the wrong direction could place a door in the middle of a structural column. In Visio, you can align shapes or place them precisely depending on the requirements of your drawing project.

Working with Rulers, Grids, and Guides

Rulers, grids, and guides help you position shapes, whether you want them merely aligned or placed in a precise location. You can use any or all of these tools to position your shapes, as demonstrated in Figure 4-3. If you don't use these features, you can hide them from view so they don't distract you. (I tell you how in the following sections.)

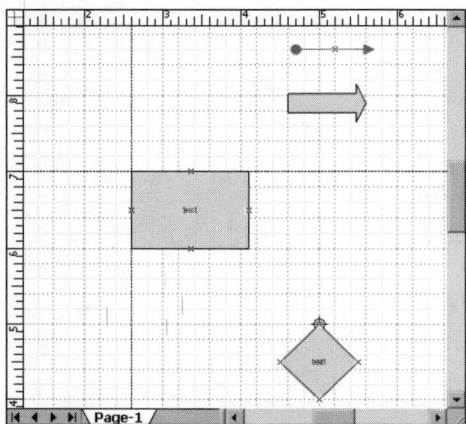

Figure 4-3: Use rulers, grids, and guides to help position shapes.

About Rulers, Grids, and Guides

Visio rulers, grids, and guides are similar to real-world tools used by drafters and graphic artists. In Visio, vertical and horizontal rulers appear along the side of the drawing window and show measurements based on the drawing scale, just like an engineering scale ruler would when you place it on a paper drawing. The Visio grid is like drawing on a sheet of grid paper. Visio drawing guides are like the light pencil lines you might sketch on a sheet of paper before you begin inking a drawing. More powerful than their real-world counterparts, rulers, grids, and guides can act as magnets, so you can quickly snap shapes into place.

Working with Rulers

Visio rulers show intervals corresponding to the measurement unit you specify on the Page Properties tab in the Page Setup dialog box. As you move the pointer on a drawing page, dotted lines on the rulers indicate the current pointer position. You can use these indicators for any editing task, including creating shapes with drawing tools, moving existing shapes, or specifying tabs in a text block. For example, you can add a wall 40 feet from the building shell by snapping to the appropriate marker on the ruler. Choose View ➪ Ruler to toggle the ruler's visibility on and off.

Note
The ruler subdivisions also determine the distance an object moves when you nudge a shape into position. When you press an arrow key with a shape selected, Visio moves the shape by one tick mark on the ruler.

You can adjust the coarseness of the ruler subdivisions and the position of the ruler origin to facilitate drawing. For example, you can reposition the ruler origin to a corner of a shape so you can easily draw other components relative to that shape.

To specify the subdivisions that appear on the rulers, use one or both of the following methods:

✦ **Set Measurement Units** — To change the units that appear on the rulers, choose File ➪ Page Setup and select the Page Properties tab. Select the units you want in the Measurement Units drop-down list.

Note

When you choose units such as Inches, or Feet and Inches, Visio sets the units based on eighths of an inch. If you choose Inches (decimal), Visio divides an inch into tenths.

✦ **Set Ruler Subdivisions** — To change how many subdivisions Visio displays, choose Tools ➪ Ruler & Grid. Select Fine, Normal, or Coarse in the Horizontal and Vertical Subdivisions boxes.

You can reposition the origin for the rulers, known as the zero point, to align with an element on your drawing. Visio also uses the zero point as the center of rotation when you rotate the drawing page. The zero point is usually located at the lower-left corner of the page. To move the zero point for the rulers, use one of the following methods:

✦ **Change the zero point on both rulers** — Hold the Ctrl key and drag from the blue cross at the intersection of the two rulers to a position on the drawing page. As you drag, Visio displays blue, dotted lines that represent the x and y axes. When you release the mouse button, Visio moves the zero point to that location.

Note

Be sure to press the Ctrl key before you click the blue cross at the ruler intersection. If you press the mouse button before you press the Ctrl key, Visio drags a guide point onto the drawing page.

✦ **Change the zero point on one ruler** — Hold the Ctrl key and drag from the ruler.

✦ **Reset the zero point to the lower-left corner** — Double-click the intersection of the two rulers.

Working with a Grid

When you display the Visio grid, horizontal and vertical lines crisscross the page to help you position shapes. Depending on the settings you choose, you can use the grid as a visual reference or you can snap shapes to the grid intersections. For example, you can quickly position structural columns every 20 feet by defining a 20 foot grid for the drawing and dropping column shapes onto grid intersections. Choose View ➪ Grid to toggle the grid on and off.

Tip

By default, the drawing grid doesn't print, but you can print it with the drawing page by choosing File ➪ Page Setup, selecting the Print Setup tab, and checking the Gridlines check box.

Most Visio drawing types use a *variable grid,* which means that Visio determines the best grid spacing based on how far you are zoomed in or out. When you zoom in, the grid intervals represent smaller distances, and switch to larger distances as you zoom out. You can also specify a fixed grid, in which the grid lines remain the same distance apart no matter how you zoom. A fixed grid is helpful when you are working with specific distances, such as drawing a ceiling grid. You can set the grid spacing to the size of the ceiling tiles so that it's easy to snap tiles into place or position HVAC components in the ceiling.

You can adjust the coarseness and origin of the grid to facilitate drawing. For example, you can reposition the grid origin to a corner of a shape so you can easily draw other components relative to that shape. To reposition the grid origin, choose Tools ➪ Ruler & Grid, type the x and y coordinates for the new grid origin, and click OK.

By default, the grid originates at the ruler zero point and moves when you move the ruler origin. However, when you specify the grid origin, it remains at that location even when you change the ruler zero point.

To specify the grid intervals, use one or both of the following methods:

✦ **Set Variable Grid Spacing** — To vary the grid spacing based on your zoom level, choose Tools ➪ Ruler & Grid. Select Fine, Normal, or Coarse in the Grid Spacing Horizontal and Vertical lists.

✦ **Set Fixed Grid Spacing** — To specify an interval for the grid spacing, choose Tools ➪ Ruler & Grid and select Fixed in the Grid Spacing Horizontal and Vertical lists. Type the distance for the grid interval in the Minimum Spacing boxes and click OK.

Working with Guides

Guides are like reference points or guidelines you can place to help you position or align shapes. For example, if a building has walls at different angles, you can add guides at those angles to help align furniture with the walls. In addition to snapping to guides, you can glue shapes to them so that you can move shapes by moving their associated guide. Choose View ➪ Guides to toggle guide visibility on and off.

By default, guides are nonprintable objects, but you can print a guide by modifying the guide's ShapeSheet. To do this, select the guide you want to print and choose Window ➪ Show ShapeSheet. Scroll to the Miscellaneous section and type False in the NonPrinting cell.

To create or modify guides, use one of the following methods:

✦ **Create a guide** — Drag a guide from the horizontal or vertical ruler onto the drawing page. Visio displays a blue dotted line for the guide.

✦ **Create a guide point** — Drag the intersection of the rulers onto the drawing page. Visio displays a blue circle with crosshairs to indicate a guide point.

✦ **Use a shape as a guide**—Any Visio shape can act as a guide, including arcs and splines. To create a guide from a shape, right-click the shape, choose Format ➪ Style on the shortcut menu, and then select Guide in the Line Style box. The shape looks and acts like a guide, but still has selection handles you can use to modify it. However, guides created in this way remain visible when you hide guides and guide points.

✦ **Delete a guide or guide point**—Select the guide or guide point and press Delete.

After defining guides for your drawing, you might want to turn off the grid so it doesn't interfere with snapping to your guides and guide points. To turn off the grid, choose View ➪ Grid.

✦ **Move a guide**—Drag a guide to a new position. You can also select a guide and type an x or y value in the Size & Position window.

✦ **Rotate a guide**—Choose View ➪ Size & Position, select the guide you want to rotate, and type an angle in the Angle box in the Size & Position window.

Moving, Rotating, and Flipping Shapes

When precision is not important, you can use shortcut commands or dragging to position and rotate shapes.

In Visio 2003, shapes include rotation handles similar to those found in other Office products. You can drag a rotation handle to rotate a shape.

To move or rotate shapes without precision, use one of the following methods:

✦ **Move by Dragging**—Position the pointer over a shape. When the pointer changes to a four-headed arrow, drag the shape to a new location.

If you try to move a shape while it is selected, you might end up resizing it instead. Before moving a shape, make sure it is not selected by clicking the page background or pressing the escape (Esc) key.

✦ **Nudging a Shape**—Select a shape and then press one of the arrow keys to nudge the shape one interval on the ruler.

✦ **Rotate by Dragging**—Select a shape and drag its rotation handle until the shape is rotated to the angle you want.

As you drag the rotation handle, you can see the rotation angle in the status bar.

✦ **Shape Menu Rotation**—Right-click a shape and choose Shape on the shortcut menu. Choose Rotate Left or Rotate Right to rotate a shape by 90 degrees. Rotate Left and Rotate Right are also available on the Action toolbar.

Sometimes you want the mirror image of an existing shape. For example, you might have an office set up for a right-handed person and want to flip the layout so the desk return is on the left instead of the right. In Visio, you can flip shapes and groups horizontally or vertically. Select the shape or group you want to flip and use one of the following methods:

✦ To mirror a shape about the vertical axis, choose Shape ➪ Rotate or Flip ➪ Flip Horizontal.

✦ To mirror a shape about the horizontal axis, choose Shape ➪ Rotate or Flip ➪ Flip Vertical.

✦ Click Flip Horizontal or Flip Vertical on the Action toolbar.

✦ Right-click the shape and choose Shape ➪ Flip Horizontal or Shape ➪ Flip Vertical from the shortcut menu.

✦ Press Ctrl+H to flip horizontally or Ctrl+J to flip vertically.

Placing Shapes with Precision

You can use several Visio tools to position shapes precisely. Snapping helps you position and align shapes by pulling shapes to elements on your drawing. For example, you can snap a desk to the walls of an office cubicle. However, you can also specify exact coordinates and angles when you know exactly where something belongs. In addition, Visio includes additional tools for specialized placement and alignment, such as distributing several shapes equidistantly.

Snapping Shapes into Position

When snapping is activated, Visio pulls the pointer to possible placement positions on the drawing page. You can easily snap one shape to another or snap a shape vertex to a position on the drawing ruler. You can specify which elements Visio snaps to as well as control the strength of attraction exerted by those elements. To activate snapping, choose Tools ➪ Snap & Glue and check the Snap check box.

Whether you are dragging an entire shape, a selection handle, a rotation handle, a vertex, or another Visio element, Visio uses the closest snap point for your editing action. As you move the pointer, Visio indicates the current pointer location with cross hairs. When the pointer nears a snap point, Visio also displays blue cross hairs at the snap point. When the pointer snaps to a connection point, Visio highlights the connection point with a red square, indicating that you can glue to that point.

You can snap to the following elements:

✦ **Ruler subdivisions** — Intervals on the horizontal and vertical rulers

✦ **Grid** — The intersections of lines on the drawing grid

✦ **Alignment box** — The dotted, green box that appears around a selected shape or group

✦ **Shape extensions** — Dotted lines or points that show how to draw a line in relation to a geometric point, such as the tangent to an arc or the midpoint of a line. You can specify which extensions Visio displays by selecting the Advanced tab and selecting the extensions you want.

✦ **Shape geometry** — The edges of a shape

✦ **Guides** — Guides and guide points you create, as described in the "Working with Guides" section earlier in this chapter

✦ **Shape intersections** — Points where two shapes intersect, shape extensions and shapes intersect, or shape edges and the grid are perpendicular

✦ **Shape handles** — Green selection handles that appear when you select a shape

✦ **Shape vertices** — Green diamonds that indicate the start and end points of line segments

✦ **Connection points** — Blue Xs that indicate points to which you can glue a shape

Cross-Reference

To see examples of shape handles, vertices, and connection points, refer to Chapter 1.

To specify the elements Visio uses for snapping and how strongly those elements attract the pointer, follow these steps:

1. Choose Tools ➪ Snap & Glue and check the Snap check box to enable snapping.

2. Check the check boxes under Snap to, to specify which elements Visio snaps to.

3. To specify the snap strength, select the Advanced tab and drag the sliders to the left or right to weaken or strengthen the attraction of an element, respectively. As you drag the slider, the number of pixels required to attract the pointer appears in the Pixels box for that element. For example, if you use one pixel for snap strength, an element doesn't attract the pointer until it is less than one-eighth of an inch away. If the snap strength is set to 40 pixels, the pointer snaps when it is about half an inch away.

Tip

Depending on what you are trying to do, snapping can become a hindrance instead of a help. For example, when you are drawing freeform curves, snapping can make curves choppy. If snapping is causing trouble, uncheck one or more check boxes in the Snap & Glue dialog box. You can also change Snap & Glue settings quickly by clicking commands on the Snap & Glue toolbar. To display this toolbar, choose View ➪ Toolbars ➪ Snap & Glue.

Using the Dynamic Grid and Drawing Aids

You can also enable the dynamic grid and drawing aids to facilitate the positioning of shapes. The dynamic grid displays horizontal or vertical, dotted lines whenever you drag the pointer to advantageous positions for shapes based on the location of other shapes on the drawing. For example, you can use the dynamic grid to drop a shape so it aligns with the top, bottom, left, right, or center of another shape on the drawing. To enable the dynamic grid, choose Tools ➪ Snap & Glue, and check the Dynamic grid check box.

Drawing aids are dotted lines that show the correct position for drawing a circle, square, or line at a specific angle. When you use the Line tool, you can snap to these aids to draw lines at a specific angle, such as 45 degrees. You can snap to drawing aids when you use the Rectangle or Ellipse tools to draw a square or circle. To enable drawing aids, choose Tools ⇨ Snap & Glue and check the Drawing aids check box. Check the Shape extensions check box in the Snap To column.

Positioning Shapes by Specifying Coordinates

When you know exactly where a shape must be placed, it's often easier to type the coordinates. The Size & Position window displays fields for specifying position and size, depending on the type of shape you select. For example, Visio draws 1D shapes based on the start point, end point, and an angle. 2D shapes include width, height, angle of rotation, and the position of the shape's pin, which is the shape's center of rotation.

The x and y coordinates that you see in the Size & Position window represent the page coordinates for the selected shape. Visio expresses page coordinates relative to the origin of the rulers and based on the drawing scale for the page. For 2D shapes, the position coordinates represent the position of the shape's pin: a green circle with cross hairs that appears when you pause the pointer over the rotation handle of a shape.

Note   Although the pin is set to the center of a shape by default, you can move the pin wherever you want by dragging it to a new position. When you rotate the shape, it will rotate around the new pin location.

Open the Size & Position window by choosing View ⇨ Size & Position window and select a shape to view its coordinates. To modify the position of a 2D shape, as shown in Figure 4-4, type values in any of the following boxes:

> ✦ **X** — Change the horizontal position of the shape's pin.

Tip   You can simplify specifying coordinates in the Size & Position window by moving the ruler zero point to a convenient position on the page. For example, if you want to move a shape four feet away from a wall, you can set the ruler zero point on the wall.

> ✦ **Y** — Change the vertical position of the shape's pin.
>
> ✦ **Width** — Although this option doesn't move the shape, it is a convenient way to specify a precise shape width.
>
> ✦ **Height** — Although this option doesn't move the shape, it is a convenient way to specify a precise shape height.
>
> ✦ **Angle** — To rotate the shape, type an angle in the Angle box. Angles start with 0 degrees pointing to the right, and increase as you move counterclockwise relative to the shape's alignment box.

✦ **Pin Pos** — To align the pin with one of the shape selection handles, select an alignment in the Pin Pos list. When you change the alignment of the pin position, Visio moves the shape so the pin is located at the existing x and y coordinates.

Shape pin position

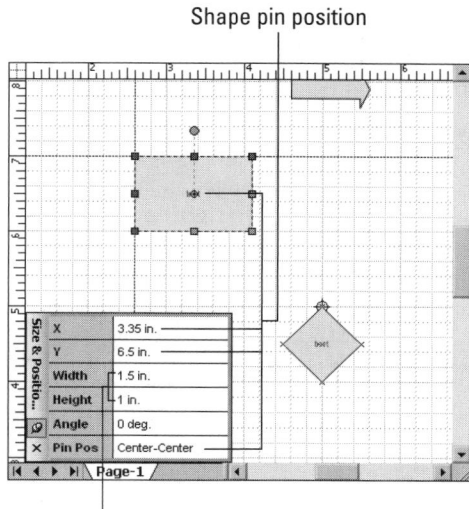

Shape dimensions

Figure 4-4: You can move or resize shapes using the Size & Position window.

The Size & Position window locks to the bottom-left corner of the drawing window by default. You can drag and dock it at the bottom of the Shapes window to keep the entire drawing area visible.

Using the Move Shapes Add-On

Visio provides another tool for moving and copying shapes. Available only in Visio Professional, the Move Shapes Add-On has several advantages over the Size & Position window. You can perform the following actions with the Move Shapes Add-On:

✦ **Specify relative distances** — Move a shape relative to its current position instead of calculating the page coordinates for the new position.

✦ **Specify polar coordinates** — Move a shape a specified distance in the direction specified by an angle. For example, you can move a shape six inches at a 45-degree angle.

✦ **Move or copy shapes** — Copy the selected shapes or move them.

To move or copy shapes with the Move Shapes Add-On, follow these steps:

1. Select the shape or shapes that you want to move or copy and then choose Tools ⇨ Add-Ons ⇨ Visio Extras ⇨ Move Shapes.

2. Select either Horizontal/Vertical or Distance/Angle. Specify the new position using one of the following sets of information:

   • **Horizontal/Vertical** — Enter the distances you want the shape to move horizontally and vertically in the Horizontal and Vertical boxes. To move a shape down or to the left, use negative numbers.

   • **Distance/Angle** — Type the radial distance (vector length) you want the shape to move into the Distance box. Type an angle to specify the direction you want to move the shape on the page, as shown in Figure 4-5. Angles start with 0 degrees pointing to the right, and increase as you move counterclockwise relative to the shape's alignment box. 90 degrees points up; 180 degrees points to the left; and 270 degrees points down.

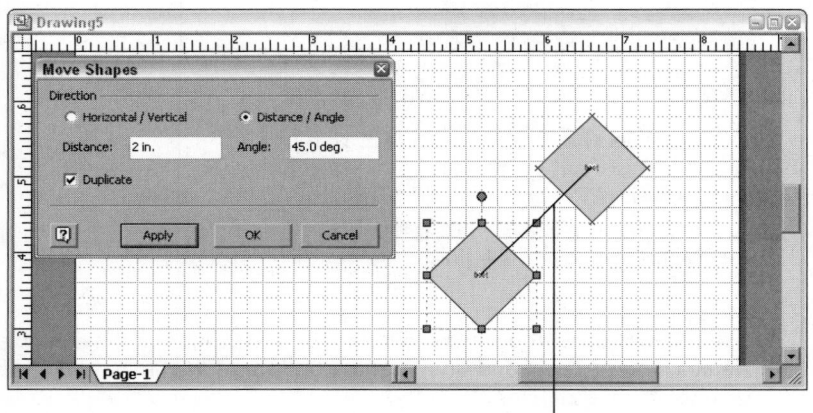

Copy positioned 2 inches away at 45 degrees

Figure 4-5: With the Move Shapes Add-On, you can specify a radial distance and angle.

3. To copy the selected shapes instead of moving them, check the Duplicate check box.

4. To preview the move or copy action, click Apply. If the results are correct, click OK. Otherwise, click Cancel.

Tip   If you click OK without previewing the results, you can press Ctrl+Z to undo the move or copy.

Aligning and Distributing Shapes

Visio provides several tools to help you arrange shapes neatly on a drawing. Although you can align shapes by snapping them into position, you can also line them up horizontally, vertically, or in both directions by using the Align Shapes command. In addition, you can distribute three or more shapes evenly using the Distribute Shapes command.

To align a shape to a guide or guide point, create the guide, as described in the "Working with Guides" section earlier in this chapter, and then drag a selection handle or end point to the guide. To facilitate the alignment of shapes with other shapes, choose Tools ➪ Snap & Glue, check the Shape Geometry, Shape Handles, or Shape Vertices check boxes, and click OK.

To use the Align Shapes command to align several shapes at once, follow these steps:

1. Select the shape to which you want to align other shapes, press Shift, and then click each shape you want to align to it. Visio outlines the primary shape with a thick magenta line.

2. Choose Shape ➪ Align Shapes and select the alignment options you want. To cancel an alignment, click the X. You can align shapes vertically to the top, center, or bottom of the primary shape. Horizontally, you can align shapes to the left, center, or right of the primary shape. Click OK to align the shapes.

To distribute shapes equally, follow these steps:

1. Select three or more shapes and then choose Shape ➪ Distribute Shapes. You can select the shapes in any order.

2. Click a distribution option. The top and bottom shapes in the selection define the distances for vertical distribution. For horizontal distribution, the shapes to the left and right define the distances. Click OK.

Caution

Distribute Shapes measures the distance between the outermost shapes and then positions the other shapes equidistantly in that space. If you want to distribute shapes at precise intervals, you can use the Offset command to create lines offset from a shape at a specific distance. You can then snap shapes to these lines. To create offset lines, select a line or curve and choose Shape ➪ Operations ➪ Offset. Type a value for the offset and click OK. Visio creates matching lines offset on either side of the original.

Moving Shapes with Guides

You can use guides to move several shapes without disrupting the arrangement of those shapes. To accomplish this, you glue the shapes to a guide and then move the guide, which drags the glued shapes along with it. For example, you can create a guide through the center of a row of equipment. By gluing the equipment shapes to the guide, you can reposition the equipment on the plant floor by moving the guide. Because the guides are nonprinting objects, they won't appear when you print your drawing unless you modify the NonPrinting cell in their ShapeSheets.

Note   You can also move several shapes at once by grouping them. When you group shapes, you can define separate settings and behaviors for the group in addition to the member shapes.

To glue shapes to a guide, follow these steps:

1. Choose Tools ➪ Snap & Glue and make sure that both the Snap and Glue check boxes are checked.

2. Check the Guides check box in the Snap To and Glue To columns and then click OK.

3. To create a guide, drag from a ruler onto the drawing page.

4. Drag a shape to the guide and drop it when Visio highlights the connection point you want with a red box.

You can also glue shapes to guides while aligning or distributing them by following these steps:

1. Select the shapes you want to glue to a guide and choose either Shape ➪ Align Shapes or Shape ➪ Distribute Shapes.

2. Select the alignment or distribution options you want, check the Create Guide and Glue Shapes To It check box (or Create Guides and Glue Shape To Them if you are distributing shapes), and click OK. Visio creates a guide or guides and glues shapes as follows:

   • **Distribute Shapes** — Visio distributes the shapes using the option you chose and creates a guide for each selected shape. You can redistribute the shapes by dragging one of the outermost guides. You can't drag an interior guide.

   • **Align Shapes** — Visio aligns the shapes using the alignment options you chose, creates one guide, and glues the shapes to it. You can move the shapes by dragging the guide to another location.

Manipulating Shapes

In addition to positioning tools, Visio provides numerous features for reproducing, resizing, and otherwise manipulating shapes on your drawings. You can copy shapes one by one or several at once. You can resize and scale shapes, group them so you can work with them as one entity, or change the order in which they appear when you stack them on top of each other. You can also add information to the custom properties for your shapes.

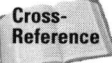

Visio 2003 introduces ink shapes that enable you to insert hand-drawn shapes into your drawings. To learn about Ink features, see Chapter 11.

When you're manipulating shapes, you can also modify Visio's display options depending on whether you want faster display or higher quality. To control how Visio displays shapes, choose Tools ➪ Options and then specify the following options:

✦ **Smooth Drawing** — Select the View tab and check this check box so your drawing doesn't flicker as you stretch a bitmap or other non-Visio object.

✦ **Higher Quality Shape Display** — Select the View tab and check this check box to draw shapes with anti-aliased lines. Anti-aliased drawing displays smooth lines even at angles but is slower than aliased drawing.

✦ **Enable Live Dynamics** — Select the General tab and check this check box to view shapes instead of only the alignment box as you transform shapes.

If you select a shape and see padlocks where you would normally see selection handles, the shape is locked to prevent you from manipulating it. To learn how to lock or unlock shapes to protect them from repositioning, resizing, formatting, deletion, and other types of editing, see Chapter 7.

Undoing Actions and Deleting Shapes

When the editing you perform makes changes you don't expect, you can delete or undo your actions using one of the following methods:

✦ **Undo one action** — If you want to undo only your last action, the quickest way is to press Ctrl+Z.

✦ **Undo recent actions** — To undo several of your most recent actions, click the arrow to the right of the Undo button on the Standard toolbar. Drag the pointer to select the actions you want to undo and release the mouse button. If you want to undo the last several actions, press Ctrl+Z multiple times.

✦ **Redo one action** — To redo one action that you undid, press Ctrl+Y.

✦ **Redo several actions** — To redo several actions, click the arrow to the right of the Redo button on the Standard toolbar. Drag the pointer to select the actions you want to redo and release the mouse button. If you want to redo the last several actions, press Ctrl+Y multiple times.

✦ **Delete shapes and other objects** — Select the shapes you want to delete and press Delete.

✦ **Cut shapes to the Clipboard** — To remove shapes from the drawing page and place them on the Clipboard, select the shapes and press Ctrl+X. To paste cut shapes, press Ctrl+V.

Note   You can also delete shapes by clicking Delete on the Standard toolbar. You can cut shapes by choosing Edit ⇨ Cut or clicking Cut on the Standard toolbar.

Duplicating Shapes

When you manipulate a shape into exactly what you want, you can avoid tedious repetition by duplicating that shape to reuse your modifications. However, if you use a shape frequently, it's easier to save the modified shape to your Favorites stencil or another custom stencil so that you can drag it onto any drawing.

Copying Shapes

In Visio, you can copy one shape or many, and you can copy the selected shapes once or multiple times. You can copy shapes in the following ways:

✦ **Copy one or more shapes on a drawing** — Select the shapes that you want to copy and press Ctrl+C to copy them to the Clipboard. Press Ctrl+V to paste them onto the drawing. You can press F4 or Ctrl+V to repeat pasting the selected shapes.

✦ **Copy shapes on a layer** — To copy shapes on one or more layers, choose Edit ⇨ Select By Type and select the Layer option. Check the check box for each layer you want to copy and click OK. Use Ctrl+C and Ctrl+V to copy and paste the selected shapes, respectively.

✦ **Copy a master** — To copy a master several times, select the Stamp tool on the Standard toolbar and follow these steps:

Note   If the Stamp tool doesn't appear on the Standard toolbar, click Toolbar Options on the Standard toolbar and choose Add or Remove Buttons ⇨ Standard ⇨ Stamp Tool.

1. On a stencil, click the master you want to duplicate.

2. Click the drawing page to add an instance of the master to the drawing. You can continue clicking to place additional instances until you select a different tool.

3. To specify the size of the shape, click and drag on the drawing page while the Stamp tool is active.

Note   The Stamp tool doesn't work with shapes on a drawing page. You must click a master in a stencil to use the Stamp tool.

Creating an Array of Shapes

The Array Shapes command duplicates a shape or shapes across a number of rows and columns, separated by the distances you specify, as illustrated in Figure 4-6.

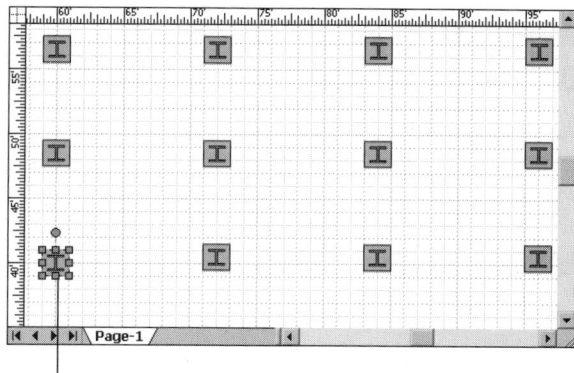

Original shape

Figure 4-6: Array Shapes creates rows and columns
of copies.

New Feature Array Shapes used to appear on the Tools menu. It is now available as a Visio Extras Add-On.

To array a shape or shapes, follow these steps:

1. Position an instance of the shape that you want to array at the bottom left of the array and choose Tools ➪ Add-Ons ➪ Visio Extras ➪ Array Shapes.

2. To specify the distance between copies in the rows and columns of the array, type the separation you want into the Rows and Column Spacing boxes.

3. To specify the number of rows and columns, type numbers in the Numbers boxes for the total number of rows and columns.

4. To specify how Visio spaces the shapes, choose a spacing option:

   • **Between Shape Centers**—Separates the centers of the shapes by the spacing distance

   • **Between Shape Edges**—Separates the edges of the shapes by the spacing distance

5. To rotate the copied shapes to match the primary shape, check the Match Primary Shape's Rotation check box.

6. Click Apply to preview the results. If they are correct, click OK. Otherwise, click Cancel.

Resizing and Reshaping Shapes

The shapes you drag from a stencil onto your drawing aren't always the right size for your purposes. Sometimes you want to enlarge a shape to emphasize it or to fit its text within the shape's boundaries. At other times, you might reduce the dimensions of a shape so you can fit more on a page. Visio provides several methods for resizing shape dimensions. You can also drag vertices and eccentricity handles to change the shape of a shape.

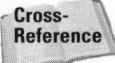 **Cross-Reference**   You can merge and decompose shapes in various ways to create more complex shapes. To learn about these capabilities, see Chapter 32.

To resize a shape, select the shape and then use one of the following methods:

✦ **Resize 1-D shapes**—Drag the selection handles at the end points to lengthen or shorten the shape. For 1D shapes with thickness, such as a 1D Single Arrow, you can also drag the selection handles at the midpoints to modify the thickness.

✦ **Resize 2-D shapes**—You can resize 2D shapes horizontally, vertically, or in both directions at once:

  • **Resize Horizontally**—Drag the selection handle at the midpoint of the left or right of the shape alignment box.

  • **Resize Vertically**— Drag the selection handle at the midpoint of the top or bottom of the shape alignment box.

  • **Resize Proportionally**—Drag a corner selection handle to change the horizontal and vertical dimensions in proportion to each other.

Note   When a shape belongs to a group, you can specify how a shape resizes when you resize the group. A shape can resize along with the group or remain the same size but reposition itself relative to the new group boundaries.

✦ **Specify Shape Dimensions**—You can use the Size & Position window to resize shapes. Refer to the "Positioning Shapes by Specifying Coordinates" section earlier in this chapter for more information.

Note   When you work on a scaled drawing, you can change the dimensions of a shape as you would on any other drawing. However, if you want shapes to appear smaller on the drawing page without changing their real-world measurements, you alter the scale of the drawing. To set the scale for a drawing page, choose File ⇨ Page Setup and select the Drawing Scale tab. Specify the scale you want and click OK.

✦ **Reshape a shape**—Pause the pointer over a shape to display its vertices and eccentricity handles. You can change the form of a shape by dragging a vertex to a new position. For example, you can stretch a corner of a rectangle. To bend the side of a shape, drag the eccentricity handle on that side.

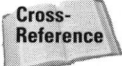

You can also change the dimensions of a shape in the ShapeSheet. To learn more about using ShapeSheets, see Chapter 33.

Reordering Overlapping Shapes

As you add or move shapes, one shape might hide a shape that you want to see. For example, if you add a 3D bar graph to a drawing and then drag the 3D axis onto the page, the axis shape hides the bar graph completely. To correct this, you can rearrange the order in which Visio overlaps shapes. Visio provides four options for reordering shapes. Bring to Front and Send to Back appear on the Action toolbar as well as in the Shape submenu on a shape's shortcut menu. To access all four reordering commands, choose Shape ➪ Order and then choose one of the following commands:

✦ **Bring to Front** — Places the selected shape in front of all other shapes

✦ **Bring Forward** — Brings the selected shape forward one layer in the stacking order

✦ **Send to Back** — Places the selected shape underneath all other shapes

✦ **Send Backward** — Sends the selected shape back one layer in the stacking order

By clicking several times where a shape is located, you can cycle through selecting the shapes stacked on top of each other even when you can't see the shapes.

Storing Data in Shapes

Shapes can contain more than the lines and text that you see on the drawing page. Custom properties associated with shapes store data similar to the way in which fields store data in a database record. You view and edit these fields in the Custom Properties dialog box. You can use them to produce reports, such as a door or window schedule for a floor plan, or display them in shape text blocks, as organization chart drawings do by showing the employee name, title, and telephone number in each organization chart shape.

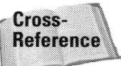

To learn how to create custom properties and associate them with shapes, see Chapter 32.

To view and store data in shapes with custom properties, follow these steps:

1. To open the Custom Properties window, choose View ➪ Custom Properties Window.

Drag the Custom Properties window into the Shapes window to dock it so that you can see shape properties and your drawing at the same time.

2. Select a shape to display its properties in the Custom Properties window. If the shape doesn't contain any custom properties, the window displays the text No Custom Properties.

3. To enter a property value, click the property you want to edit and type the value in the box. If the property includes a drop-down list, you can click a value in the list.

4. To view a prompt for a property, pause the pointer over the property label in the left-hand column of the Custom Properties window. If the property has a prompt, it will appear next to the label.

Note   You can also access a shape's custom properties in its Custom Properties dialog box. To open this dialog box, right-click the shape and choose Properties from the shortcut menu.

Grouping Shapes

Quite often, you would like several shapes to work together as if they were one shape, but you also want them to retain their individuality. For example, a table of data in Visio includes many individual boxes and text blocks. You want the table to move as a single unit, but you also want to format and resize individual table cells. The easiest way to obtain this behavior is to group shapes. Many masters in Visio stencils are actually groups, such as title blocks. You can create your own groups, ungroup and modify built-in groups, and even nest groups within other groups.

When an element on your drawing doesn't behave as you would expect, it could be a different type of object than you think it is. Groups behave differently than shapes. Merged shapes can be quite elaborate, but they are still shapes. To determine whether an element is a shape or group, select it and then choose Format ➪ Special. The Type field displays Shape or Group.

Groups are separate objects in Visio, so each group has its own text block and ShapeSheet separate from the text blocks and ShapeSheets for each shape in the group. You can add text to the group text block, configure the group's options and behaviors, and define formulas for the group. For example, you can specify how a group resizes or create a formula that adds shapes to a group based on the value of a custom property.

Caution   Think twice before ungrouping shapes; doing so eliminates the group ShapeSheet, with its associated data and formulas.

Creating and Breaking Up Groups

You can create a group out of several shapes or divide a group into its component shapes. Visio includes commands to add or remove shapes from an existing group, so you don't have to eliminate a group to add or remove shapes. Use the following methods to create, modify, or eliminate a group of shapes:

✦ **Create a group** — Select the shapes you want to group and then choose Shape ⇨ Grouping ⇨ Group.

✦ **Break up a group** — Select the group and then choose Shape ⇨ Grouping ⇨ Ungroup.

✦ **Add a shape to a group** — Select the group and the shape you want to add and then choose Shape ⇨ Grouping ⇨ Add to Group.

Note   Sometimes the group's alignment box doesn't reflect the changes you've made, particularly when you resize the shapes in a group. When the alignment box doesn't match the shape boundaries, snapping to the group might position shapes in unexpected places. To reset the alignment box, select the group and then choose Shape ⇨ Operations ⇨ Update Alignment Box.

✦ **Remove a shape from a group** — Select the shape within the group and then choose Shape ⇨ Grouping ⇨ Remove From Group.

Tip   You can select a shape within a group by double-clicking it.

You can specify the behavior of groups and some of the behaviors of the shapes that belong to them. For example, you can control how shapes within a group resize when you resize the group, the order in which you can select groups and shapes, and whether you can add shapes to groups by dropping them onto the group. To specify group behaviors, select the group and choose Format ⇨ Behavior.

Cross-Reference   To learn more about the options for controlling group and shape behaviors, see Chapter 32.

Working with Locked Groups

When you try to edit some groups, Visio warns you that shape protection prevents execution of the command. This occurs when a group is locked to prevent you from ungrouping it. Many groups in built-in stencils are locked so that you can't inadvertently reset built-in behaviors or formulas. For example, the 3-D Bar Graph on the Charting Shapes stencil is a group of bar shapes. The group has control handles so you can adjust the height of the tallest bar and the width of all the bars. If you experiment with the 3-D Bar Graph, you'll find that you can't reposition, resize, or edit the shapes in the group. You can only change them by dragging the group's control handles or by changing values in the group's custom properties.

The group is locked so you can't ungroup it and eliminate the features provided by its control handles and ShapeSheet formulas. In addition, the group is configured so that you can't reposition shapes in the group. Because the power of many grouped shapes depends on their group features, you should think twice before removing locks and other protection settings. Visio makes these settings a bit harder to change by placing them on the group ShapeSheet.

Tip   If you choose to unlock a group, consider making a copy of the group before you unlock or break it up.

To reset group protections, select the group and then choose Window ➪ Show ShapeSheet. Use one of the following options:

✦ **Unlock a group**—Scroll down until you see the LockGroup cell in the Protection section of the ShapeSheet. Click the LockGroup cell (which contains the number 1), type 0, and then press Enter.

Note   You can add or remove protections in the Protection section of the ShapeSheet by typing 1, which represents True or On, or 0, which represents False or Off, in protection cells. The Protection section of a group ShapeSheet includes special group protection settings as well as the settings available in the Protection dialog box that appears when you choose Format ➪ Protection.

✦ **Configure a group so you can reposition its shapes**—Scroll down until you see the Don'tMoveChildren cell in the Group Properties section of the ShapeSheet. Type False in this cell to enable repositioning of the shapes in the group.

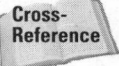

Cross-Reference   To learn more about working with ShapeSheets, see Chapter 33.

Labeling and Numbering Shapes

Drawing annotation helps your audience interpret your drawings, whether you use text shapes and callouts to display notes; label shapes with data associated with shapes; or number drawing elements for identification.

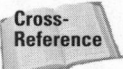

Cross-Reference   To learn how to annotate shapes with callouts and custom property values, see Chapter 6.

Many types of drawings number or label their elements for identification. For example, blueprints number the columns on a structural plan so the construction crew knows how to assemble the steel. You can use the Number Shapes Add-On to number shapes as you add them to your drawing or after all the shapes are in place. By default, Visio increments numbers moving from left to right and from top to bottom on the drawing. However, you can choose the order you want, as shown in Figure 4-7, or number shapes manually.

Shape numbering

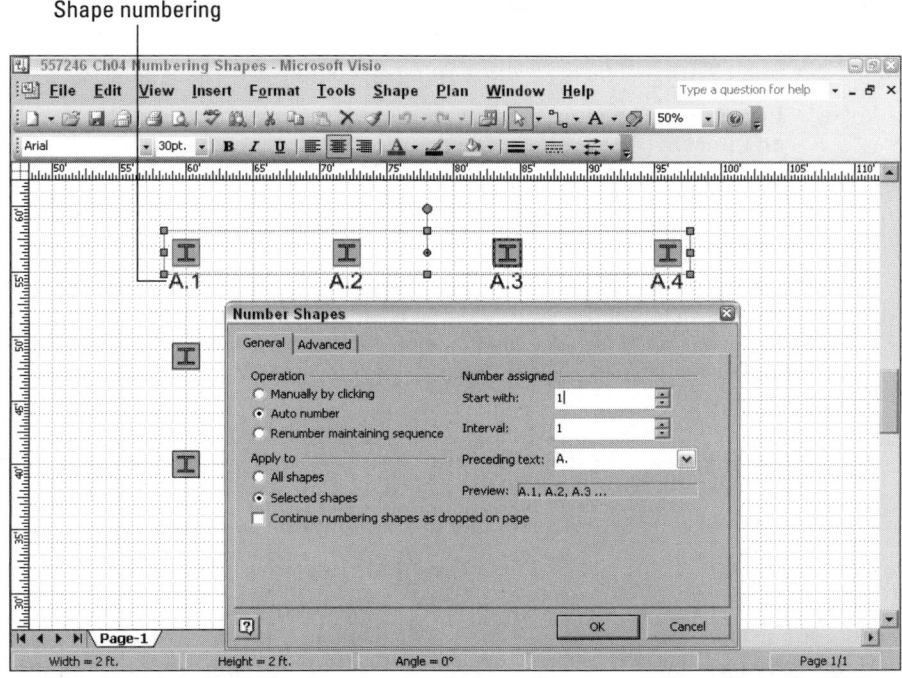

Figure 4-7: You can identify shapes on a drawing with the Number Shapes Add-On.

To number shapes on a drawing, follow these steps:

1. If you want to number specific shapes on the drawing, select them in the order you want them to be numbered.

2. Choose Tools ➪ Add-Ons ➪ Visio Extras ➪ Number Shapes.

3. Choose an Operation option to specify how you want to number the shapes:

   • **Manually By Clicking** — Adds the next number in a sequence to a shape when you click it

   • **Auto Number** — Numbers shapes based on the order you specify on the Advanced tab

Note
You can also renumber shapes by choosing Renumber Maintaining Sequence on the General tab. When you choose this option, select the Advanced tab and specify whether you want to renumber shapes with unique numbers or allow duplicates in the sequence.

4. Specify the sequence you want. The Preview field in the Number Shapes dialog box shows an example of the sequence you have specified.

- **Start With** — The first number in the sequence

- **Interval** — The gap between each number in the sequence. For example, an interval of 3 would create a sequence that begins 1, 4, 7.

- **Preceding Text** — Text that precedes the number. For example, for steps in a process, you can choose Step in the list. For columns on a floor plan, you might choose A. or a.

Tip   Sometimes you might want two numbering sequences, such as numbers for the columns and different letters to identify each row. To apply two-part numbering schemes, select each row, specify the letter for that row in the Preceding Text box, and number the shapes. Repeat this process after selecting the shapes in the next row on the page.

5. To number shapes that you add later, check the Continue Numbering Shapes As Dropped On Page check box.

6. Select the Advanced tab to specify other numbering options.

7. Select an option to specify where the number appears relative to the shape text.

8. If you are using the Auto Number option, specify the order you want. You can number from left to right and then top to bottom, top to bottom and then left to right, from back to front, or in the order that you selected the shapes.

Note   To hide the shape numbers, check the Hide Shape Numbers check box on the Advanced tab.

Summary

Drawings are made up almost entirely of shapes, so Visio provides plenty of tools for finding, adding, and manipulating the shapes on your drawings. In this chapter, you learned how to work with existing shapes in numerous ways, including the following:

✦ Finding shapes on drawings

✦ Searching for shapes in stencils

✦ Selecting the shapes you want to work with on a drawing

✦ Snapping shapes into position as well as positioning shapes precisely

✦ Aligning shapes

✦ Duplicating shapes

✦ Resizing shapes

✦ Reordering shapes when they overlap

✦ Storing data in custom properties

✦ Grouping shapes

✦ Adding numbered labels to shapes

In addition to the features you can use on existing shapes, Visio provides even more tools to help you customize and create your own shapes. See Chapters 32 and 33 to learn more about these customization tools.

✦   ✦   ✦

Connecting Shapes

Some shapes stand on their own, such as title blocks or legends, but in most diagrams the relationship between shapes constitutes a great deal of the information you're trying to convey. For example, imagine an organization chart without reporting relationships between managers and employees, or a data flow diagram without flows between processes.

In Visio, you can show the relationships between shapes with connectors. In this chapter, you'll learn how to define relationships by gluing shapes together with connectors. You can attach connectors to specific points on shapes or let Visio choose the best spot for the connection.

In fact, you can let Visio take complete control of the layout and arrangement of the shapes on your drawings. You can specify settings for the spacing between shapes, the type of shape arrangement you want, and the method for showing connectors that cross on a page. As you add or move shapes, Visio uses those settings to lay out your drawing.

Using Connectors

In Visio, you show relationships by using 1D shapes called *connectors* to join the 2D shapes on your drawings. Connectors come in all shapes and sizes, from unadorned lines to 1D shapes specialized to suit the different drawing types that Visio supports, as illustrated in Figure 5-1. No matter how fancy the formatting, connectors all boil down to lines that attach to shapes at each end.

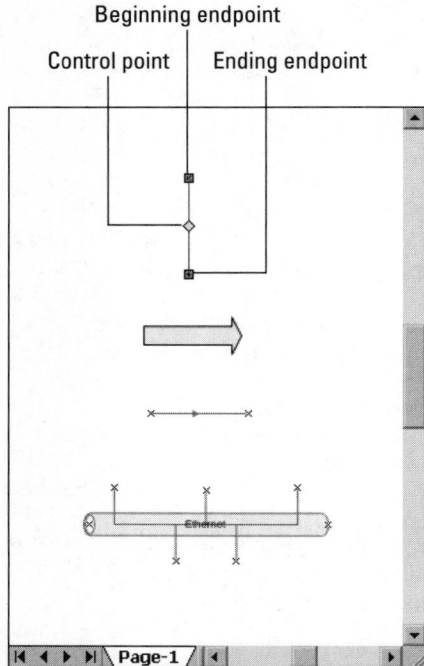

Figure 5-1: Visio includes all kinds of connectors.

The stencils associated with each drawing type usually include connectors suitable for your drawing. In addition, the Connectors stencil contains many of the most popular connectors for all drawing types.

Connectors have starting and ending points that you can use to define the predecessor and successor for two connected shapes. All connectors store direction information, whether they include visual cues, such as arrowheads, or not. For example, in an organization chart, the direction of a connector differentiates the manager and the employee. When sequence is important, you must connect the correct end of the connector to the predecessor and successor shapes. For situations in which order doesn't matter, you can connect whichever end of the connector you want.

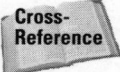 **Cross-Reference** For an overview of connection concepts, see Chapter 1.

Visio provides visual cues to show you where you can connect shapes and connectors. 2D shapes often include connection points, which are locations you're likely to use on those shapes. Visio indicates a connection point on a shape with a blue x.

Each end point on a connector looks a little different. The starting point for the connector is a green square with an x inside the square. The end point is a green square with a + inside the square, as shown (without the color, of course) in Figure 5-1.

You can also use other types of points to make connections between shapes and connectors. To learn more about specifying glue points, see the "Specifying Points for Glue" section later in this chapter.

Depending on the template you use and the shapes you want to connect, you can choose from a variety of methods for connecting shapes. With some templates, such as the Organization Chart, you can simply drop a shape onto another shape to connect them. You can also drag connectors from stencils or use the Connector tool to create connectors by dragging from shape to shape or even to create a sequence of connected shapes.

Using Stencil Connectors

Dragging connectors from stencils is probably the most popular method for connecting shapes because Visio automatically opens stencils with suitable connectors when you use templates to create drawings. It's easy to drag the connector you want onto a page and attach it to the shapes you want to connect.

Visio makes it easy to access basic connectors, such as the Dynamic connector and the Line-curve connector, by including them on many stencils. For a wide selection of connectors appropriate for numerous types of drawings, open the Connectors stencil by choosing File ➪ Shapes ➪ Visio Extras ➪ Connectors.

To connect shapes using a connector from a stencil, follow these steps:

1. Drag the connector you want from a stencil onto the page.

2. Drag one end point of the connector to a connection point on a shape.

Tip

You can create a dynamic or static connection, depending on the point you select on a shape. When you drag an end point into a shape, Visio highlights the entire shape with a red box, indicating that you're creating a dynamic, or shape-to-shape, connection. To create a static, or point-to-point, connection, drag an end point to a connection point. Visio highlights the connection point with a red box.

3. Drag the other end of the connector to a connection point on another shape.

Note

If the direction of the connection is important, drag the beginning end point of the connector to a connection point on the predecessor or superior shape. Drag the end of the connector to a connection point on the successor or subordinate shape.

Using the Connector Tool

You can also create connectors as if you were drawing lines, by dragging the pointer from the first shape to the second. It's easier to create connectors with a specific direction with this method because you naturally draw from the predecessor shape to its successor. To draw connectors with the Connector tool, activate the tool by clicking the Connector tool on the Standard toolbar and then use one of the following methods:

✦ **Static (Point to Point)** — Position the pointer over a connection point on the first shape. When Visio highlights the connection point with a red box, drag to a connection point on the second shape.

✦ **Dynamic (Shape to Shape)** — Position the pointer inside the first shape. When Visio highlights the shape with a red box, drag to a position inside the second shape.

✦ **Static-Dynamic** — Position the pointer over a connection point on the first shape. When Visio highlights the connection point with a red box, drag to a position inside the second shape.

✦ **Dynamic-Static** — Position the pointer inside the first shape. When Visio highlights the shape with a red box, drag to a connection point on the second shape.

You can also connect shapes automatically as you drop them onto a drawing page. When the Connector tool is active, Visio automatically connects each new shape you add to the previous shape with a dynamic connection.

Tip   When shapes are small or contain connection points in inconvenient locations, you can have trouble creating dynamic connections. To create a dynamic connection no matter where you position the pointer on a shape, hold the Ctrl key as you drag the end point or Connector tool over the shape.

When you use the Connector tool to draw connectors, Visio creates Dynamic connectors by default. However, you can use the Connector tool to create any kind of connector. To create another type of connector with the Connector tool, follow these steps:

1. Click the Connector tool on the Standard toolbar.

2. Click a connector master in a stencil in the Shapes window.

3. Draw a connector from the first shape to the second. Visio creates the type of connector you selected in the stencil.

Dragging Points to Connect Shapes

Specialized connectors simplify your work with behaviors and features tailored to a specific type of drawing. These connectors are actually shapes with connectors built in. You can drag control points on these shapes to attach connectors to other shapes. For example, by dragging the control point on the trunk of the Multi-Tree Sloped shape on the Blocks stencil, you can connect branches on the tree to several shapes, as shown in Figure 5-2.

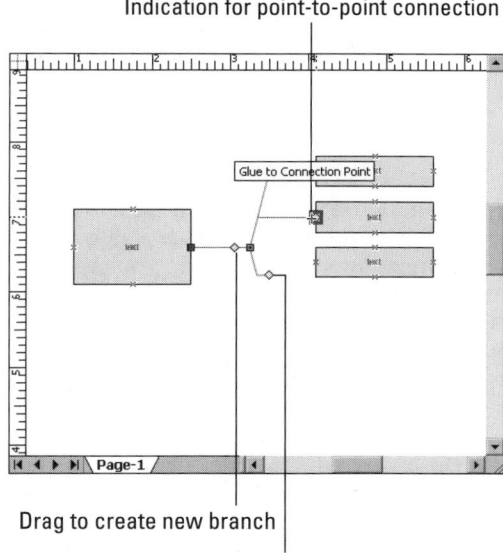

Indication for point-to-point connection

Drag to create new branch

Drag to connect branch to shape

Figure 5-2: Drag control points on connector shapes to create connections.

Tip   To find out what a control point can do, position the pointer over the control point. Visio displays a tip on the screen, as demonstrated in Figure 5-2.

Connecting a Sequence of Shapes

When you're creating a drawing with a sequence of shapes, such as the steps in a procedure, you can add the shapes to your drawing, and instruct Visio to create the dynamic connections. To connect a sequence of shapes, select the shapes in the order you want them to appear in the sequence and then choose Shape ⇨ Connect Shapes.

Organizing Connections with Glue

The paths that your connectors take depend on how you glue the connectors to shapes. Visio glue comes in two types: static and dynamic. *Static glue* (also called *point-to-point glue*) connects specific points on two connected shapes. As you move those shapes around, the connector remains attached to the points you glued, no matter how convoluted the connector path becomes. Static glue is best used when the connection point is important. For example, in a flowchart, you don't want Visio to reattach a process to a different decision when you move the process on the page. With *dynamic glue* (also called *shape-to-shape glue*), Visio changes the connection points it uses as you move shapes around, connecting the two shapes by the shortest route. Dynamic glue is helpful when you construct diagrams such as block diagrams, where the specific connection point doesn't matter.

Gluing Shapes

You can use any combination of glues when you connect two shapes. When you want to use the automatic layout tools, you must connect shapes using shape-to-shape, or dynamic, glue at both ends of the connector. However, you can also connect two shapes with one end of the connector glued with static glue and the other using dynamic glue. In this situation, the connection point that is glued dynamically can change as you move the shapes. The end point that is glued statically remains glued to the same point no matter where you position the shapes. You can also use static glue at both ends.

Tip   Use dynamic glue while you develop a diagram, so Visio automatically adjusts connections as you move shapes around. When you finalize the layout, you can change the connections between shapes to static glue to fix the connection points that Visio uses.

In some situations, glue gets in the way. For example, when you're dragging connectors onto a crowded page, it's difficult to drop a connector onto the page without gluing it to a shape. To prevent Visio from gluing connectors to shapes, choose Tools ➪ Snap & Glue, uncheck the Glue check box under Currently Active, and click OK.

Tip   The Snap & Glue toolbar includes buttons to specify which points Visio uses for snapping or gluing. If you want to switch the options for snap or glue frequently, choose View ➪ Toolbars and then choose Snap & Glue. Click one of the buttons to toggle a snap or glue option on or off.

Specifying Points for Glue

Although connection points are natural choices for gluing connectors to shapes, you can glue to other points on shapes. To specify the points that Visio uses for glue, follow these steps:

1. Choose Tools ⇨ Snap & Glue.

2. Under Glue To, select one or more of the following options:

   - **Shape Geometry** — Glues connectors anywhere on the visible edge of a shape

   - **Guides** — Glues connectors or shapes to guides

   - **Shape Handles** — Glues connectors to shape selection handles

   - **Shape Vertices** — Glues connectors to shape vertices

   - **Connection Points** — Glues connectors to shape connection points

Adding, Moving, and Deleting Connection Points

Visio adds connection points to the selected shape. Connection points don't have to reside on or within the shape to which they belong. You can position a connection point anywhere on the drawing page, although connection points too far removed from their parent shapes can lead to confusion.

You can add, move, or delete connection points only while the Connection Point tool is active. To activate the Connection Point tool, click the arrow to the right of the Connector tool button on the Standard toolbar and choose Connection Point Tool on the menu. Visio displays a green, dotted line around the selected shape. To revert to the Connector tool, click the arrow to the right of the Connection Point tool and choose Connector Tool on the menu.

Cross-Reference Visio provides three types of connection points: Inward, Outward, and Inward & Outward. Most built-in masters already contain connection points. To learn how to specify connection point types when you create your own customized shapes, see Chapter 32.

To work with connection points, activate the Connection Point tool, select a shape, and then use one of the following options:

   ✦ **Add a connection point** — Hold the Ctrl key and click the position where you want to add the connection point. Visio displays the new connection point as a small purple x, which changes to blue when you execute the next action.

Tip It's easier to add connection points when Snap & Glue is activated. To activate Snap & Glue, choose Tools ⇨ Snap & Glue, check the Snap and Glue check boxes, and click OK.

✦ **Move an existing connection point**—Drag the connection point to a new location.

✦ **Delete a connection point**—Select the connection point you want to delete and press the Delete key.

New Feature

In Visio 2002, you had to select the shape before activating the Connection Point tool because there was no way to change the selected shape while the Connection Point tool was active. In Visio 2003, you can click a shape to select it while the Connection Point tool is active.

Automatically Laying Out Shapes

When you use dynamic connectors to create shape-to-shape connections, you can take advantage of Visio's automatic layout and routing tools to arrange the shapes on your drawings. Dynamic, or shape-to-shape, connections know how to navigate around other shapes, jump over other connectors, and choose the connection points that create the best route between the connected shapes. You can harness this power and specify how you want shapes to lay out, and connectors to route and jump, by using the Layout Shapes command. Under most circumstances, automatic layout and routing perform as you would expect. By understanding how layout and routing work, you can specify options to achieve the results you want.

Caution

For automatic layout and routing to work properly, shapes must be connected with shape-to-shape connections. If connectors don't stay attached to shapes or their end points are green, they aren't glued properly. To glue connectors to shapes, drag the end point until Visio highlights the shape with a red box. An end point changes to a solid red square if it uses a shape-to-shape connection. The end point is a smaller red square with an x if it uses a point-to-point connection.

If the connections are correct, but automatic layout still doesn't work properly, verify that the connector is drawn in the right direction. To do this, make sure the connector is not selected and then drag the connector away from its shapes. The starting point for the connector is a green square with an x in it. The end point is a green square with a +. Reattach the connector end points in the correct direction.

Configuring Placement Behavior

The behaviors associated with shapes affect how those shapes react when you use the layout and routing tools. Stencil shapes for drawings that depend on connections, such as network diagrams or organization charts, are already configured to work with layout and routing. However, you can modify shape behaviors or add behaviors to shapes. For example, you can specify whether Visio lays out and routes around a shape, and, if it does, whether the shape moves during placement and how the shape interacts with other shapes and connectors.

To configure the placement behaviors for a shape, follow these steps:

1. Right-click a shape and choose Format ⇨ Behavior from the shortcut menu.

2. Select the Placement tab.

3. Specify the placement behaviors you want for the shape. You can choose the following options:

   - **Placement Behavior** — Choose Lay Out and Route Around from the drop-down list to enable the shape for automatic layout and to enable other placement options. If you choose Do Not Lay Out and Route Around, Visio won't process the shape during layout.

   - **Do Not Move During Placement** — Check this check box to prevent Visio from relocating this shape when it lays out the drawing.

   - **Allow Other Shapes to Be Placed on Top** — Check this check box to allow Visio to place other shapes on top of the shape during automatic layout. If you want every shape to be completely visible, leave this check box unchecked.

   - **Move Shapes on Drop** — Use these options to specify what shapes do when other shapes are nearby. The Move Other Shapes Away on Drop option specifies the plow behavior of the shape, which controls whether a shape plows other shapes out of the way when you drop it near other shapes. The Do Not Allow Other Shape to Move This Shape Away on Drop specifies whether other shapes can plow the selected shape out of the way. Check this check box, if you want a shape to remain where it is when you drop another shape near it.

   - **Interaction with Connectors** — Use these options to specify whether connectors can route through the shape horizontally or vertically. Leave these check boxes unchecked if you want Visio to route around the shape.

Tip   You can specify options on the Placement tab only for 2D shapes. If you select a 1D shape and then choose Format ⇨ Behavior, the Placement options are disabled.

Specifying Layout Options

The Lay Out Shapes command includes options you can use to control the arrangement of shapes on your drawing, as shown in Figure 5-3. For example, you can organize a work flow diagram horizontally or vertically. You can also specify the style, direction, and appearance of the connectors on your drawing. As you choose placement options in the Layout Shapes dialog box, Visio changes the connector options to corresponding settings. For example, when you choose a Circular layout style, Visio changes the connector style to Center To Center. Although you can choose different options for connectors, your drawings will look cleaner if you keep the placement and connector options coordinated.

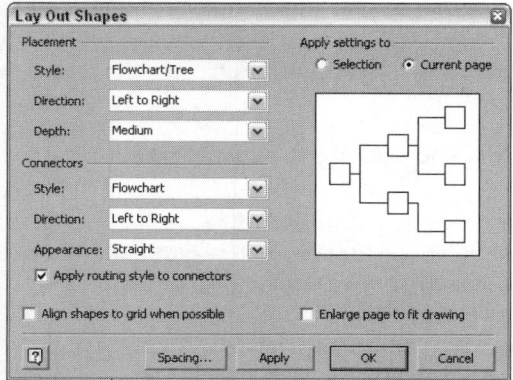

Figure 5-3: You can specify how Visio lays out and connects shapes on a drawing.

The Lay Out Shapes dialog box contains a preview window that displays a sample of the results of your chosen settings. To specify the layout and routing for a drawing, follow these steps:

1. Choose Shape ⇨ Lay Out Shapes.

2. To specify the arrangement of shapes, choose settings for the following options under the Placement heading:

   • **Style** — Select an arrangement style, such as Radial, Circular, Flowchart/Tree, or Compact Tree. Visio changes the connector options to match the placement style you select.

   • **Direction** — Select the direction you want the shapes to flow on your drawing. You can choose from Top to Bottom, Bottom to Top, Left to Right, and Right to Left.

   • **Depth** — Select a depth to specify how much space Visio places between shapes. Choosing Shallow organizes shapes well but uses more space. Choosing Deep uses less space but doesn't arrange the shapes as well. You can compromise between the two by using Medium.

3. To specify options for how connectors route in a layout, choose settings under the Connectors heading:

   • **Style** — Select a routing style, such as Right Angle, Straight, or Flowchart.

   • **Direction** — Select a direction to specify where connectors attach to shapes. For the best results, choose the same direction that you chose in Placement options.

   • **Appearance** — Select Straight or Curved connectors.

- **Apply Routing Style to Connectors** — Uncheck this check box if you want to lay out the shapes without changing the connectors.

- **Align Shapes to Grid When Possible** — Check this check box to lay out and route your drawing based on the spacing settings you specify in the Layout and Routing Spacing dialog box. (To learn how to specify the spacing for layout and routing, see the "Specifying Layout Spacing Options" section later in this chapter.)

- **Enlarge Page to Fit Drawing** — Check this check box to increase the drawing size if the optimal layout requires more room than the current drawing size provides.

4. To specify which shapes Visio lays out, choose the Selection option to lay out only the selected shapes, or the Current Page option to lay out the entire page.

5. To lay out the drawing, click Apply. If you don't like the results, go back to step 2. Otherwise, click OK.

Note To remove the new layout, press Ctrl+Z.

Tip If Visio creates an overly complicated route for a connector, you can modify its path manually by dragging the connector's green vertices to new positions. However, if you use Lay Out Shapes again, Visio overwrites your changes when it applies its layout rules.

Specifying Layout and Routing Spacing

You can adjust the spacing that Visio uses to fit more shapes on a page or to create more space around the shapes you have. To specify spacing options for a page, click the Spacing button in the Lay Out Shapes dialog box and then specify sizes for the following spaces on your drawing:

✦ **Space Between Shapes** — Specifies the horizontal and vertical space that Visio adds between shapes that it lays out

✦ **Average Shape Size** — Specifies the average size of the shapes in your drawing and sets the average shape size used by the dynamic grid

Tip If the sizes of your shapes vary significantly, try using a smaller average shape size.

✦ **Connector to Connector** — Specifies the minimum spacing between parallel connectors. For example, a horizontal spacing of one inch lays out shapes so that horizontal segments of connectors are no closer than one inch apart.

✦ **Connector to Shape** — Specifies the minimum spacing between connectors and shapes. A horizontal spacing of one inch lays out shapes so that a shape and a vertical segment of a connector are no closer than one inch apart.

Note   You can also specify spacing by choosing File ➪ Page Setup, selecting the Layout and Routing tab, and clicking the Spacing button.

Specifying Line Jump Options

When connectors frequently cross over each other, it can be difficult to follow the relationships on a drawing. You can specify the line jumps that Visio uses to clarify the paths that connectors use. You can specify line jumps for an entire drawing page or for specific connectors. To specify line jumps for a page, choose File ➪ Page Setup and then select the Layout and Routing tab. Use the following options to specify how Visio applies line jumps on the page:

✦ **Add Line Jumps To** — Choose the lines to which you want to add line jumps. For example, you can specify Horizontal or Vertical. Last Displayed Line adds line jumps to the line at the top of the stacking order.

✦ **Line Jump Style** — Choose a style for the line jump, such as Arc and Gap. You can also choose from a number of multifaceted jumps.

✦ **Horizontal Size** — Specify the size for line jumps added to horizontal lines.

✦ **Vertical Size** — Specify the size for line jumps added to vertical lines.

To specify line jumps for a connector, right-click it and choose Format ➪ Behavior from the shortcut menu and then select the Connector tab. Under Line Jumps, choose an option in the Add list to specify whether the connector conforms to the line jump options for the page or uses different options. Choose a line jump style to specify a style other than the page default.

Summary

Connections between shapes convey a great deal of information on drawings. Visio provides several methods for adding connectors to shapes, as well as dozens of different types of connectors. Some shapes, such as trees, have connectors built in. You can glue connectors to shapes using dynamic or static glue. When you use static glue, Visio keeps connectors glued to the points you selected. However, you must use dynamic glue if you want to automatically lay out and route your diagram, or you want Visio to create optimal routes between shapes.

✦   ✦   ✦

Working with Text

If you're like most people, you probably devote a significant amount of time working with text, because your drawings often contain as much text as they do graphics. Visio makes it easy to add, edit, and format text and annotations. In Visio, you can add text in a variety of ways and places. You can add text to shapes and groups or add text blocks that stand on their own.

In Visio as in other Microsoft Office applications, you can search and replace text as well as check spelling. However, in Visio you can also select and modify text and text blocks as you can other Visio shapes. For example, you can easily move and rotate text and text blocks.

In addition, Visio provides built-in shapes useful for annotating your drawings. You can add a title block shape to a drawing to identify it. You can connect callouts to shapes to include notes or comments. You can also configure text into tabular form using a built-in Table shape or by formatting the text in a text block.

Text and Visio

Every Visio shape, including connectors, has an associated text block in which you can type text to annotate your drawings. Although these text blocks belong to their parent shapes, you can relocate, rotate, and format them independently to improve the readability of your drawings. Visio also offers special shapes, such as callouts and balloons, that are dedicated to the annotation of drawings. If these shapes aren't enough, you can use the Text tool to add text-only shapes to your drawings.

In addition to the text that makes up drawing content, you often want to communicate questions and remarks to your colleagues about drawing content and changes. You can insert comments to communicate this type of information and remove them when the drawing is complete.

No matter which type of text medium you use, Visio makes it simple to add text to your drawings. In most cases, all you have to do is click a shape or text block, start typing, and press Esc when you're done. You can type without worrying about whether your text will fit. After your words are in place, you can use a variety of tools to edit or format them.

Adding Text to Drawings

Text is a major component of most drawings. Whether you're labeling a shape, tabulating details, identifying a drawing with a header or footer, or using comments to communicate with your colleagues, Visio provides simple tools and techniques to get the job done.

If you're used to working with CAD programs, Visio's text behaves differently, but is simpler to use. Text appears larger or smaller as you zoom in and out, but the Visio drawing scale has no effect on the appearance of text. Visio always displays text at its actual size relative to the printed page.

Tip   You can specify options to display aliased or antialiased text, depending on whether you prefer faster display or higher quality. To do this, choose Tools ⇨ Options and select the View tab. Select the Text Quality option you want. You can also display a wavy line in place of text when the text is smaller than a specified point size on the screen, which is known as *greeking*. If a drawing includes a lot of text, you can use this feature to improve performance while you arrange drawing components. Then, when the drawing is finished, you can display all text. Specify the point size you want in the Greek Text Under box.

Adding Text to Visio Shapes

You can add text to most shapes, including connectors, by selecting a shape and typing the text you want. By default, Visio zooms in to 100 percent so it's easier to see the text you're entering. As you type, Visio underlines spelling errors with a red, wavy line. However, the misspelling indicator disappears when the shape or text block isn't selected.

Tip   To disable automatic zooming when you edit text, choose Tools ⇨ Options ⇨ General. In the Automatically Zoom Text When Editing Under drop-down list, choose 0 for the point size. Because text point size must be greater than zero, this choice ensures that Visio never zooms text based on its point size.

Each shape includes a text block. When you select a shape with a tool other than the Text tool and begin typing, Visio replaces the text in the shape's text block with the text that you type. If you select a shape with the Text tool, Visio positions an insertion point where you click in the shape text block.

Note If you activate the Text tool and drag to define a text block, Visio creates a separate text block shape and selects it so that you can begin typing text.

To add text directly to a shape or connector, follow these steps:

1. Select a tool other than the Text tool and click a shape or connector.

2. Begin typing.

3. To complete your text entry, press Esc or click outside the text block. Pressing Enter inside the text block inserts a carriage return and moves the insertion point to the next line in the text box.

Tip When you add more text than a shape can hold, Visio simply displays the text overflowing the shape's boundaries. You can resize the shape to hold the text by selecting the shape and dragging its selection handles. If you don't want to resize the shape, you can shorten the text or apply a smaller font.

Adding Text to Groups of Shapes

Some shapes appear to include more than one text block. For example, the X-Y Axis shape on the Charting Shapes stencil includes a text block to label each of the axes. The X-Y Axis shape is actually a group of shapes. Accessing text in grouped shapes works similarly to accessing shape text, but sometimes requires a few additional clicks.

To add text to a shape in a group, click the shape you want to work with once to select the group to which it belongs and then click the shape a second time to select the shape. If you select the shape with the Text tool, Visio positions an insertion point in the text block of the shape. If you select the shape with any other tool, Visio selects the shape text block and replaces its contents when you begin typing.

Adding Text-Only Shapes

You can also add text that isn't a part of any shape on a drawing. When you use the Text tool to add text to a drawing, you create a shape that contains only text. However, you can edit and format the text in these blocks as you would any other text. To add a text-only shape to a drawing, follow these steps:

1. Click the Text tool on the Standard toolbar.

2. Drag from one point on the drawing to another to create a rectangular text block with those dimensions.

Tip   You can also add text by selecting the Text tool and clicking a point in the drawing, which creates a text block at the point you clicked using default dimensions.

3. Type the text you want in the text block.

4. To complete your text entry, press Esc or click outside the text block. By default, Visio creates a text-only shape with 8-point Arial text centered in the block.

New Feature   In previous versions of Visio, you had to copy special characters from the Character Map or use special key sequences to enter their Unicode numbers. In Visio 2003, you can insert special characters into text by choosing Insert ⇨ Symbol to open the Symbol dialog box. For the most common special characters, select the Special Characters tab, select the symbol you want, and click Insert. For other special characters, select the Symbols tab, select the symbol you want, and click Insert. If you don't see the symbol you want, choose another font from the drop-down list.

Displaying Field Information in Text

Visio stores information about shapes and documents in fields. For example, Visio fields track who created a document, the name of a page, the angle of a shape, and the values of a shape's custom properties. In addition, fields can display the results of a formula you create that uses the values from other fields. You can display this information on a drawing by inserting fields into text. For example, a Visio title block shape, shown in Figure 6-1, uses fields to automatically display information about the drawing in which it is located.

Fields that automatically display properties

557246 Ch06 Floor Plan	

REVISED	FILENAME
8/25/2003	557246 CH06 FLOOR PLAN.VSD

| SIZE | FSCM NO | | DWG NO | | REV |

DRAWN BY	SCALE	1/4" = 1'-0"	SHEET	1 OF 5
BONNIE BIAFORE				

Page-1 / Details-1 / Details-2 / Detail

Fields that automatically display properties

Figure 6-1: You can use fields to display drawing, page, shape, or custom property information in drawing text.

Visio includes several categories of fields and numerous fields within each category. You can use any of the following field types to display information in text on a drawing:

✦ **Custom Formula**—Results of a ShapeSheet formula you define in the Custom Formula box

Cross-Reference For an introduction to ShapeSheet formulas, see Chapter 33.

✦ **Date/Time**—Current date and time or the date and time that a file was created, printed, or updated

✦ **Document Info**—Information from a file's Properties box, such as creator or keywords

✦ **Geometry**—Shape width, height, or angle of rotation

✦ **Object Info**—Information from a shape's Special dialog box, such as the shape's internal ID or the master used to create it. To view these fields, right-click a shape and choose Format ⇨ Special from the shortcut menu.

✦ **Page Info**—Page settings such as the page number or number of pages in a drawing

✦ **Custom Properties**—Information from a shape's custom property fields. Custom properties vary from shape to shape.

Cross-Reference To learn more about fields and custom properties, see Chapter 32.

✦ **User-Defined Cells**—Formulas entered in the User-Defined Cells section of the ShapeSheet

You can insert a field in a text block or at a specific position in a text block. If you want to insert the field as the only text, select the shape. To insert the field within existing text, double-click the shape to open its text block and then click in the text to position the insertion point where you want to insert a field.

To insert fields in a shape text block, follow these steps:

1. With the shape selected or the insertion point in position, choose Insert ⇨ Field.

2. In the Field dialog box, select the field category you want, such as Custom Properties.

3. Select the field you want, such as Width.

4. To apply a specific format, select the format you want, and then click OK.

Note You can insert more than one field in a text block, inserting them on separate lines or within lines of text.

You can edit fields in text blocks either to change the field that is used or to modify how its value is formatted. For example, you can change the date format so that the date fits in a smaller area. To edit a field in a text block, follow these steps:

1. Select the Text tool, select a shape, and then click the field you want to modify within the text block to select it.

Note   If the text block contains only a field, clicking it selects the entire field. You can't position an insertion point within a field.

2. Choose Insert ⇨ Field. The Field dialog box appears and shows the current settings for the selected field.

3. To modify the formatting for the field, select the format you want in the Format list and click OK.

4. If you want to replace the field that is used, select the category you want, select the new field, select a format, and then click OK.

Displaying Information in Headers and Footers

Headers and footers appear only when you print your drawings, so they are useful for displaying information that isn't needed while you are working, such as the date and time that the drawing was printed. You can display this information by adding text and fields to drawing headers and footers. For example, you can automatically number the pages in your drawing by inserting the Page Number field into the drawing footer.

Tip   Although they don't appear when you view a drawing, you can see the drawing header and footer by choosing File ⇨ Print Preview.

To include text and fields in the header or footer of a drawing, follow these steps:

1. Choose View ⇨ Header and Footer.

2. To add text to a header or footer, type the text you want in the Left, Center, or Right box in the Header or Footer column.

3. To insert a field, click the list arrow to the right of one of the header or footer boxes, select the field you want to insert, and then click OK. Visio inserts a code in the box that Visio translates when you print the drawing.

4. To format the header and footer, click Choose Font, select a font, a style, a size, a color, and effects, and then click OK.

5. Click OK in the Header and Footer dialog box.

Adding Comments to Drawings

When you review a drawing, whether your own or someone else's, you can add comments about the contents of the drawing or needed changes. In many organizations, reviewers provide feedback about a drawing with *redlining* — adding text to a separate layer reserved for comments, and more often than not using the color red.

Visio provides several methods for adding feedback to a drawing. Visio 2003 includes markup features so each collaborator can add comments and drawing modifications to a separate markup layer. You can also modernize the redlining process by creating a layer to hold reviewer comments. In addition, you can insert comments directly on a page.

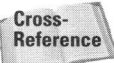 **Cross-Reference** To learn more about Visio's new markup features, see Chapter 11. To use a layer for redlining, see Chapter 25.

To add a comment to a page of a drawing, follow these steps:

1. To add a comment to the current page, choose Insert ⇨ Comment.
2. Type your comment and press Esc or click anywhere in the drawing. A comment icon appears approximately in the center of the visible drawing area.

You can view, edit, or delete comments on a page. To associate comments with an area of a page, you can move comments to other locations on the drawing page.

✦ To move a comment, drag the comment tag to another position on the page.

✦ To view the comment, click the comment tag.

✦ To edit or delete a comment, right-click the comment tag and choose Edit Comment or Delete Comment from the shortcut menu. You can also click the comment and press the Delete key.

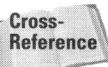 **Cross-Reference** To learn about other ways to communicate with your collaborators, see Chapter 11.

Selecting and Editing Text

You can reposition, format, and edit the contents of text blocks. You can even use the cut, copy, and paste shortcuts to process text as you do in other Microsoft Office applications. However, before you can do any of these things, you have to know how to select the text you want to work with.

Selecting Text

To replace or format the entire text block for a shape, you can select the shape and make the change you want. For example, to change the font size, you can right-click a shape, choose Format ⇨ Text, select the text format options you want, and click OK.

You can also select text and position the insertion point where you want in a text block to edit or format a portion of it. The techniques you use to do this and the results you obtain vary depending on whether you use the Pointer tool, Text tool, or Text Block tool. Choose one of the following methods to select text or position the insertion point:

✦ **Select a text block** — You can click a shape to select a text block no matter whether the Pointer, Text, Text Block or a drawing tool is active.

- **Replace the existing text** — Although there is no visual indication, typing after selecting a text block replaces the existing text.

- **Reposition, resize, or rotate a text block** — If you want to move a text block in some way, use the Text Block tool to select the text block. The text block selection handles appear.

✦ **Select the text in a text block** — You can use the following methods to select all the text in a text block. After selecting the text, you can cut, copy, and paste the text, type to replace it, or format it.

- **Shortcut key** — Click a shape to select it and press F2 to open the text block and select all the text.

- **Text tool** — Click a shape and then drag to select all the text.

✦ **Position the insertion point** — You can use the following methods to position the insertion point in a text block.

- **Text tool** — Click a shape or text block where you want to position the insertion point.

- **All other tools** — Double-click a shape to select its text. Click in the selected text to position the insertion point.

✦ **Select a portion of a text block** — You can select a word, paragraph, or any other portion of a text block. To do this, activate the Text tool or the Text Block tool and select a shape.

- **Select text** — Drag to select the text you want.

- **Select a word** — Double-click the word you want.

- **Select a paragraph** — Triple-click the paragraph you want.

Selecting Text in Groups

Sometimes, shapes and text blocks are consolidated into groups to make them easier to work with. In addition to the text blocks for each shape in a group, the group itself has a text block. You can add, edit, or format text in each shape as well as for the group as a whole. The main difference when working with text in grouped shapes is that it sometimes takes a few more clicks to select the text you want.

✦ To add text to a group, click the group to select it and begin typing.

✦ To view the text block for a group, select the group and press F2.

Note If the Text tool is active when you click a group, Visio opens the group text block and positions the insertion point in the text block.

✦ To work with text in one of the group's shapes, select the shape and then type to replace the text.

Note You can select the text in a shape within a group using the selection techniques described in the previous section. However, selecting a shape in a group with the Pointer tool could require more than one click. For example, if a shape belongs to a group that in turn belongs to a larger group, the first click selects the largest group. Clicking a second time in the same place selects the subordinate group. Clicking a third time in the same place selects the shape.

Editing Text

You can edit text in Visio using techniques similar to those used in other Microsoft Office applications. For example, you can use the Cut, Copy, and Paste commands to modify or duplicate Visio text. As with other applications, text that you cut or copy moves temporarily to the Windows Clipboard so you can paste it several times. Unlike other Microsoft Office applications, Visio zooms in to 100 percent automatically when you edit text to make the text easier to see.

Deleting Text

You can delete text in a Visio shape or a text-only shape, although deletion works differently in these two types of shapes. When you delete the text in a Visio shape, you only delete the text, not the shape's text block. You can always select the shape and type text to insert new text into the shape's text block. However, deleting all the text in a text-only shape deletes the text-only shape as well. To delete text, use one of the following methods:

✦ To delete text in a shape, select the Text tool and then click the shape to select it. Select the text you want to delete and press Delete. Press Esc to close the text block.

✦ To delete a text-only shape, select the Pointer tool, click the text block, and press Delete.

✦ To delete some of the text in a text-only shape, select the Text tool and click the text-only shape. Drag to select the text you want to delete and press Delete. Press Esc to close the text block.

Copying Text from Other Applications

If you want to copy text into Visio from another application, first create a text-only shape in your drawing and then paste the text from the other application into the text-only shape. To do this, select the text you want in an application such as Microsoft Word, and press Ctrl+C to copy it to the Windows Clipboard. In Visio, activate the Text tool and drag to create a text block in your drawing. Press Ctrl+V to paste the text into the text block.

You can also embed text from another application. To do this, copy the text from the other application and paste it directly onto the drawing page without creating a text block. When you double-click this text, Visio opens the application in which you created the text originally.

Finding, Replacing, and Correcting Text

Visio includes commands to find, replace, and check the spelling of words in drawings. These features work similarly to those in other Microsoft Office applications, although Visio offers more options for specifying the scope of its searches, as shown in Figure 6-2. When you search for text, Visio can search stencils, shapes, text-only text blocks, custom properties, and drawing properties.

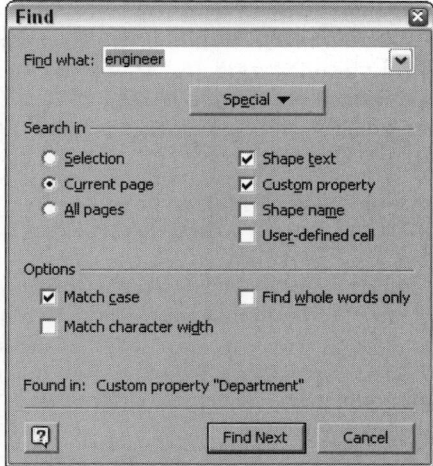

Figure 6-2: You have numerous options in Visio for specifying the scope of a text search.

Finding and Replacing Text

When you are searching for text, you can search the current selection, the current page or all pages in a drawing. In addition to specifying the pages to search, you can specify which components to search:

✦ **Shape Text** — Searches for text in shape text blocks and text-only text blocks

✦ **Custom Property** — Searches for text in custom property fields

✦ **Shape Name** — Searches for text in the Name field of shapes or masters. You can use this option to locate instances of a master in a drawing or to find a master in a stencil you are editing.

✦ **User-Defined Cell** — Searches the Value and Prompt cells in the User-Defined Cells section of ShapeSheets for all shapes in a drawing.

To find text on a drawing, follow these steps:

1. Choose Edit ➪ Find or press Ctrl+F to open the Find dialog box.

2. Type the text you want to find in the Find What box. To specify a special character, click the Special button and choose the special character.

3. Select one of the options (Selection, Current page, All pages) to specify how much of the drawing to search.

4. Check the check boxes for each of the components you want Visio to search.

5. If you want Visio to match results in a specific way, check the check boxes in the Options section.

> **Note** You can instruct Visio to return results that match the case entered in the Find What box or to return only results that match whole words, not a portion of a word. In addition, the Match Character Width check box limits the results to characters of the same width, such as searching for only wide or narrow characters in the Katakana alphabet.

6. Click Find Next to find the next occurrence of the text. Visio highlights matching text in the drawing.

7. To edit the text, close the Find dialog box and edit the text.

> **Note** If Visio finds the text in a shape name or user-defined cell, it highlights the shape on the drawing and displays the name in the Found In section of the Find dialog box, as illustrated in Figure 6-2. If you want to edit the text in a shape name, close the Find dialog box, right-click the highlighted shape, and choose Format ➪ Special to access the shape's name. To edit text in a user-defined cell, open the ShapeSheet for the highlighted shape and edit the text in the appropriate cell.

To replace text on a drawing, follow these steps:

1. Choose Edit ➪ Replace.

2. Type the text you want to find in the Find What box. To specify a special character, click the Special button and choose the special character.

3. Type the new text in the Replace With box. To specify a special character, click the Special button and choose the special character.

4. Select one of the options (Selection, Current page, All pages) to specify how much of the drawing to search.

5. If you want Visio to match results in a specific way, select the check boxes in the Options section.

6. Click Find Next to find the next occurrence.

7. Click Replace to replace the current occurrence or Replace All to replace all occurrences.

Checking Spelling

Visio can check spelling like its Office counterparts. You can perform all of the following tasks with Visio:

✦ Check spelling with the built-in dictionary.

✦ Create your own dictionary of words.

✦ Instruct Visio to correct entries automatically as you type.

✦ Add your own AutoCorrect entries.

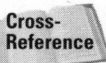

Cross-Reference   To learn how to create your own dictionary and AutoCorrect entries, refer to the Check and Correct Spelling topic in Visio Help.

To check spelling, follow these steps:

1. Choose Tools ➪ Spelling or press F7. Visio opens the Spelling dialog box for each word not found in the dictionary.

2. Click Ignore or Ignore All if the word is spelled correctly. Click Add if you want to add the unrecognized word to the spelling dictionary.

3. If the word in the Change To box is spelled correctly, click Change to replace the misspelled word with the Change To text. If it is not spelled correctly, edit the contents of the Change To box and then click Change or Change All.

Note   If you want to turn off the spell checker, choose Tools ➪ Options and select the Spelling tab. Uncheck the Check Spelling As You Type check box and click OK. You can turn spell checking back on by pressing F7.

Positioning Text

You can position text-only shapes, callouts, and other annotation shapes wherever you want on a drawing. However, in addition to moving text shapes around, you can also reposition the text within a shape. By default, a shape's text block is the same size as the shape itself and centered within it, but you can relocate or rotate a shape's text block to remove overlapping text or make your drawing more readable. For example, you can move the built-in axis label for a graph to make room for numeric labels along the axis.

Repositioning Text in a Shape

The text block in a shape is a part of the shape but doesn't have to reside in the same location on the drawing. You can move, resize, or rotate a shape's text block. To reposition text in a shape, follow these steps:

1. Click the Text Block tool on the Standard toolbar. If the Text Block tool isn't visible, click the arrow next to the Text tool and choose the Text Block tool from the menu.

2. Click a shape to select its text block and display the text block selection handles, as shown in Figure 6-3.

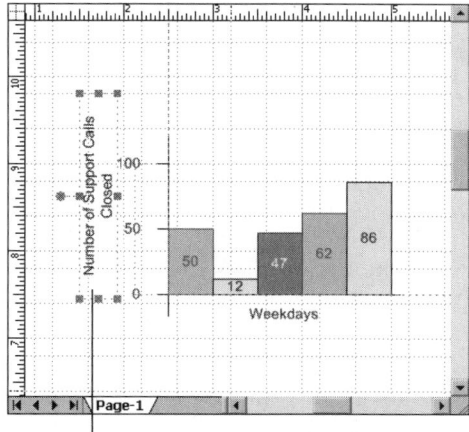

Text Block tool displays text block handles

Figure 6-3: Use the Text Block tool to select a text block and display its selection handles.

3. To move the text block to another location, position the pointer within the text block and drag to the new location.

4. To rotate the text block, drag the rotation handle until the text is rotated to the angle you want.

Tip   You can also rotate only a shape's text block by clicking the Rotate Text 90 Degrees tool on the Action toolbar.

5. To resize the text block, drag a selection handle.

Tip   You can view or modify the properties of a shape text block in the Text Transform section of a ShapeSheet. Although it's easy to modify a text block's contents and position on a drawing, you must use the ShapeSheet to perform some functions, such as preventing text from rotating.

Moving Text Shapes

To move a text-only shape or a callout shape, select the shape as you would any other and drag it to a new location on your drawing. You can also use the Size & Position window to move text to a precise position. To do this, follow these steps:

1. To open the Size & Position window, choose View ⇨ Size & Position Window.

2. Select the text shape you want to move.

3. Modify the values in the length, angle, or X and Y boxes to modify the width, rotation, and position of the shape on the drawing.

Editing Locked Shapes

Some Visio shapes and connectors are locked so that text remains right side up when you move a shape or line. When you select a locked shape with the Text Block tool, Visio indicates the protection by changing the handles to gray. To unlock a shape to modify its text block position, follow these steps:

1. Right-click the shape and choose Format ⇨ Protection from the shortcut menu.

2. To unlock the shape rotation, uncheck the Rotation check box.

3. To unlock a shape so you can resize it, uncheck the Width and Height check boxes.

4. To unlock a shape so you can move the text block, uncheck the X Position and Y Position check boxes.

5. Click OK when you are done. Select the Text Block tool, click the shape, and drag the text block handles.

Creating Special Annotations

Visio comes with predrawn shapes for displaying and emphasizing information in your drawings. Callout shapes can call attention to important information on drawings. You can use built-in title blocks to identify the drawing file and its contents or create your own custom title block to show the information you want.

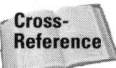 **Cross-Reference** By applying formatting, you can produce bulleted and numbered lists. To learn how to do this, see Chapter 7.

Creating Tables

The Charting Shapes stencil contains several built-in shapes for presenting tabular information. You can drag these shapes onto a drawing, select cells within the tabular shape, and type the text you want. However, if you want to show information in tabular form within one shape's text block, you must use tabs to present the text in columns.

Using Built-in Table Shapes

The tabular shapes on the Charting Shapes stencil provide several advantages over using tabs to create columns in text. These tables are groups of shapes, so you can work with each cell individually or modify the entire table. To resize the cells in a table shape, select the group and drag a selection handle. In addition, these shapes automatically assume the color scheme you apply to a drawing.

You can use the following shapes to create tables:

✦ **Grid** — Specify the number of rows and columns you want in the table.

✦ **Row Header and Column Header** — Drag these shapes and snap them into place next to a row or column in the Grid shape to label rows and columns.

✦ **Deployment Chart** — These shapes include labels for departments and phases, but you can modify the labels to represent anything you want.

✦ **Feature Comparison Chart** — This shape includes labels for products and features but you can modify the labels to represent anything you want.

To use the Grid shape to create a table, follow these steps:

1. To open the Charting Shapes stencil, choose File ➪ Shapes ➪ Charts and Graphs ➪ Charting Shapes.

2. Drag the Grid shape onto your drawing. The Custom Properties dialog box opens.

3. Select the number of rows and columns you want in the drop-down lists and click OK.

Tip   You can change the number of rows and columns later by right-clicking the Grid shape and choosing Set Grid from the shortcut menu.

4. To label a row, drag the Row Header shape and snap it to the leftmost cell in a row. With the Row Header selected, type the label text.

5. To label a column, drag the Column Header shape and snap it to the topmost cell in a column. With the Column Header selected, type the label text.

6. To add text in the table, click a table cell and type the text.

New Feature   In Visio 2003, the Grid shape replaces the Table shape. Unfortunately, the Grid shape doesn't come with the Table shape's features for inserting, deleting, or resizing columns and rows. However, you can use Ctrl+click to select several cells within a grid and rotate or resize them.

Formatting Shape Text into Columns

You can format text into columns by applying tab stops to one or more paragraphs in a text block. You can align tabs to the left, center, or right, or use a decimal tab to align columns of numbers by their decimal points.

Caution   If you resize a shape after applying tab stops, the shape margins can impinge on the text block and affect the alignment of your tabs.

The tab stop positions you specify are relative to the left edge of the text block. Because of this, it's easiest to begin your formatting by adjusting the origin of your ruler. To add tab stops to a shape, follow these steps:

1. To relocate the origin of the horizontal ruler, press the Ctrl key and drag the vertical ruler to the left edge of the shape.

2. Select the text you want to format in the text block.

3. Choose Format ➪ Text and select the Paragraph tab.

4. To set the text block alignment, select Left in the Horizontal Alignment drop-down list, and set the values in the Left, Right, and First Indentation boxes to zero.

5. To add a tab stop, select the Tabs tab. Type the distance from zero for the tab stop in the Tab Stop Position box. Select the alignment you want and click Add.

Note   You specify tab stop indentations in unscaled units even if you're working on a scaled drawing.

6. Repeat step 5 for each tab stop you want to add and click OK when you are finished.

7. To add text in columns, type a value in the text block and then press Tab to move to the next column.

Using Callouts to Highlight Information

Visio provides a variety of built-in callout shapes you can use to call attention to information on your drawings. You can drag these shapes onto a drawing, add your annotation, and point the callout line or arrow to the area you want to highlight. If you want a callout to move with the shape to which it points, you can glue the callout to a shape, as shown in Figure 6-4.

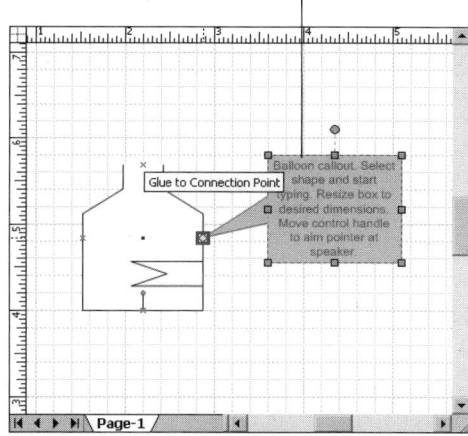

Figure 6-4: Callout shapes often include instructions as default text.

You can use callouts from any stencil regardless of which type of drawing you use. Simply open the stencil with the callout you want and drag the shape onto the drawing. Some stencils include one or two callout shapes, but you can find the widest variety of callouts on the following stencils:

✦ **Callouts** — Contains callouts, balloons, tags, notes, and other shapes for adding text to drawings. To open this stencil, choose File ⇨ Shapes ⇨ Visio Extras ⇨ Callouts.

✦ **Charting Shapes** — Contains callouts, balloons, and the annotation shape. To open this stencil, choose File ⇨ Shapes ⇨ Charts and Graphs ⇨ Charting Shapes.

✦ **Annotations** — Contains callouts in addition to other reference shapes, such as north arrows. To open this stencil, choose File ⇨ Shapes ⇨ Visio Extras ⇨ Annotations.

Adding Callouts to a Drawing

Each callout has its own special attributes, but they all function similarly. Callouts often include instructions in the text block, as illustrated in Figure 6-4. To add a call-out to a drawing, follow these steps:

1. Drag the callout from the stencil and drop it near the shape you want to annotate.

2. Click the callout shape to select it and type the annotation text.

3. To point the callout at a shape, drag the selection handle at the end of the callout line or arrow.

4. To glue the callout to a shape, drag the selection handle at the end of the call-out line or arrow to a connection point on the shape. A red box highlights the connection point when the callout and shape are connected.

Displaying Properties in Callouts

You can annotate shapes with the information stored in their custom properties, such as the person who occupies an office, their department, and their phone number. Visio provides several Custom Callout shapes in which you can specify the custom properties you want to display and how to display them.

To display custom properties in a custom callout shape, follow these steps:

1. Open the Callouts stencil.

2. Drag a Custom Callout shape onto the drawing.

3. Drag the yellow control handle on the Custom Callout to the shape with custom properties that you want to annotate. The Configure Callout dialog box appears, listing every custom property for the shape in the Shape Custom Properties box.

4. Check the check box for each property you want to display in the callout. If you select more than one property in the list, choose an option in the Separator drop-down list to indicate how you want the properties separated in the callout.

Note   To reorder the custom properties in the callout, select a custom property in the list and then click the Move Up or Move Down button.

5. To show only the custom property value and not the property name, uncheck the Show Property Name check box.

6. To move the callout when you move the shape, make sure the Move Callout with Shape check box is checked.

Using Title Blocks

Title blocks are commonly used with architectural and engineering drawings to identify and track their contents and revision history. Visio automatically opens the Borders and Titles stencil with many of the built-in templates, but you can open any stencil with title blocks and add the one you want to any type of drawing. In addition, you can create your own title block with exactly the information you want. You can open either of the following stencils to access title block shapes:

✦ **Borders and Titles** — Contains dozens of title block shapes, some of which use fields to automatically display information such as the date, scale, and page number. To open this stencil, choose File ➪ Shapes ➪ Visio Extras ➪ Borders and Titles.

✦ **Title Blocks** — Available only in Visio Professional, this stencil contains several title block and revision block shapes, along with shapes that display fields automatically. To open this stencil, choose File ➪ Shapes ➪ Visio Extras ➪ Title Blocks.

When none of the built-in title blocks suit your needs, you can use shapes on the Title Blocks stencil to create your own title block. The Title Blocks stencil contains shapes that display fields such as the current date, author of the drawing, filename, page number, and scale. You can use the Frame shape as the title block border and add these other shapes to design your custom title block. To create your own title block, follow these steps:

1. Drag the Frame shape onto your drawing and then drag other title block shapes to build the title block.

2. To group the shapes so you can move them as one, select the title block shapes and choose Shape ➪ Grouping ➪ Group.

3. To add the new title block to a stencil, open an existing stencil or create a new one.

Cross-Reference

To learn how to create custom stencils and new masters, see Chapters 31 and 32.

4. Drag the title block from the drawing into the stencil window. If Visio asks whether you want to edit the stencil to complete the operation, click Yes.

5. Right-click the new master and choose Edit Master ➪ Master Properties from the shortcut menu.

6. Enter a name and any other options and then click OK.

Formatting Title Blocks

The title blocks built into Visio are often groups of shapes, combined so that you can add the title block to your drawing in one step. In addition, some of these groups are locked to prevent you from inadvertently changing part of the group. Depending on the protection applied, you can resize, delete, format, and annotate the shapes that make up the title block.

To format a shape within a group, you must select the shape. To do this, activate the Pointer tool, click the shape once to select the group, and then click the shape a second time to select the shape. You can then use format commands to modify the shape's appearance.

If protections on a shape prevent you from modifying the title block, you can unlock the shape and then make the change you want. To do this, select the shape within the group and choose Format ⇨ Protection. Uncheck the check boxes for the type of change you want to make and click OK. You can also ungroup the shapes and then rearrange them into the configuration you want. Although Visio warns you that ungrouping the title block will break the link to its master, click OK to ungroup the shapes. If the changes you make cause problems, delete the title block from your drawing and drag a fresh one from the stencil.

Summary

You annotate drawings in a variety of ways. Every shape on a drawing has its own text block that you can use to add information. In addition, you can add text-only shapes or built-in tabular shapes to your drawings to present large amounts of textual data. Callout shapes can include notes to highlight information on a drawing or to display the values of custom properties. You can add text to title blocks or insert fields that automatically display the values of file or page properties.

✦   ✦   ✦

Formatting Visio Elements

Formatting can make the difference between dreary drawings that go unread and attractive documents that make everyone take notice. You can achieve the best formatting results in the shortest amount of time with a two-step process.

First, you can quickly obtain professional-looking results by using predefined formatting tools. These tools ensure consistency throughout each drawing and reduce the amount of time you spend choosing individual formatting options. For example, you can drag backgrounds and borders onto your drawing page to frame its contents. You can apply color schemes so that shape fills and shadows use consistent and harmonious colors. You can also use predefined styles, similar to the ones you've probably used in Microsoft Word, to apply sets of formatting options for lines, text, and fill. When you use these features, you might discover that no additional formatting is required.

However, if you do find a few shapes that need tweaking, such as those with large amounts of text or shapes that you want to emphasize, you can take a second step to apply specific formatting options to shapes, lines, or text blocks.

Applying Formats

It's much easier to apply styles than to specify several formats, but the reality is that from time to time you will end up applying specific formatting options to shapes, connectors, and text. Visio provides several methods for applying formatting to your drawing elements so that you can format just one item or several shapes at once. Whether you decide to use styles or apply formatting options individually, the options you use most frequently are available on the Formatting, Format Text, and Format Shape toolbars, shown in Figure 7-1.

Format Text toolbar

Formatting toolbar

Format Shape toolbar

Figure 7-1: The Formatting, Format Text, and Format Shape toolbars include common formatting options.

 **Note**   Most templates include the Backgrounds and Borders and Titles stencils, so you can easily add backgrounds and borders to your drawing. If you start a drawing from scratch, you can open these stencils by choosing File ⇨ Shapes ⇨ Visio Extras and then clicking the stencil name that you want. When you drag a background shape onto your foreground page, Visio automatically creates a background page for you and assigns the background page to the current foreground page.

Applying Formats to Lines

You can alter the weight, pattern, color, and end options for lines. The Formatting toolbar includes buttons to change weight, pattern, color, and ends. To select a weight, pattern, color, or end, click the option arrow and choose the format you want. If you don't see a suitable format, you can choose the More command at the bottom of any formatting list to open the associated format dialog box, such as the Line dialog box, which contains all the line formatting options. To learn how to use styles to specify formatting, see the "Formatting with Styles" section later in this chapter.

To format lines, choose one or more of the following format options:

✦ **Line Weight** — The thickness of the line, no matter what pattern you use

✦ **Pattern** — Patterns of dotted or otherwise broken lines. Visio includes 23 patterns in addition to a solid line, but you can also define your own.

 **Cross-Reference**   To learn how to define your own patterns, see Chapter 34.

 Tip   When you produce drawings for a wide audience, use patterns instead of line color so that your drawings convey all the information, even when printed on grayscale printers.

Highlighting Elements

Visio doesn't provide a highlighting feature like the one in Microsoft Word, but you can use formatting to highlight different elements of your drawings. For example, if you want to emphasize a shape on your drawing, you can change the fill color to one brighter than the ones used in the color scheme.

You can also highlight lines and connectors — for instance, to show the redundant paths in a high-availability network. To do this, click the Line tool on the Drawing toolbar. Choose Format ➪ Line, select a wide line weight and a bright color, and click OK. Draw lines using the same vertices as the paths you want to highlight. If you can't see the connectors, right-click the lines you added and choose Send to Back from the shortcut menu. If you want to be able to remove these highlight lines easily at a later time, you can add them to a separate layer and delete the entire layer to remove them. To learn more about layers, see Chapter 25.

✦ **Line Ends** — Symbols such as arrowheads that you can place at the end points of lines. The Formatting toolbar includes separate options for symbols at each end and both ends of a line. In the Line dialog box, you can specify the symbol and symbol size for each end of the line.

Tip   If an arrow points the wrong way, you can correct this problem by switching the line end to the other end of the line or by reversing the line. To reverse a line, select the line and then choose Shape ➪ Operations ➪ Reverse Ends.

✦ **Color** — The color of the line

✦ **Cap** — Only available in the Line dialog box. This option specifies whether the ends of very thick lines are squared or rounded.

Applying Formats to Text

Although Visio provides options for formatting every aspect of text on your drawings, the options you use most often are conveniently located on the Formatting and Format Text toolbars, shown in Figure 7-1. The Formatting toolbar includes familiar options for specifying font, font size, font style, horizontal alignment, and text color. The Format Text toolbar includes options to specify a text style, font size, formatting such as strikethrough and subscript, vertical alignment, indents, paragraph spacing, and bulleted lists. Visio displays the Formatting toolbar by default when you create a drawing. To display the Format Text toolbar, choose View ➪ Toolbars ➪ Format Text.

The Text dialog box is the comprehensive source for text formatting options. In addition to the text formatting options available on the toolbars, you can specify options for the language used for checking spelling, transparency of text, character spacing, paragraph spacing, indents, margins around text blocks, tabs, bullet styles, and bullet characters. You might prefer to use this dialog box for other reasons besides the abundance of formatting options. All text formatting options are available within this one dialog box. In addition, the text formatting features are grouped on tabs and, in some cases, include visual clues about the results you obtain by choosing an option. To open the Text dialog box, choose Format ⇨ Text.

Note   You can use the Text Ruler to set, modify, or remove tab stops and indents. To display the Text Ruler, double-click a shape, right-click the text, and choose Text Ruler from the shortcut menu. To create a tab stop, select the text you want to format and then click the position on the ruler where you want to place the tab. To insert a different type of tab stop, click the Tab icon until the tab stop you want appears. You can also drag tab stops to other positions or remove them by dragging them off the ruler. To adjust indents, drag the top or bottom of the hourglass on the Text Ruler to another position.

You can format different portions of text based on how you select it:

✦ **Select a shape** — Apply text formatting to all of a shape's text by selecting a shape and then choosing text formatting options.

✦ **Select text with the Text tool** — Apply text formatting to selected text by activating the Text tool, selecting the text you want to format, and choosing text formatting options.

Tip   You can also copy text formatting by using the Format Painter. Select the shape with the text formatting you want to copy with the Text tool. Select the Format Painter on the Standard toolbar and then click the shape whose text you want to format. Visio copies only the text formatting to the second shape.

Formatting Text Blocks and Paragraphs

The text blocks in many shapes contain no more than one paragraph, so it's easy to assume that formatting text blocks and paragraphs means the same thing. In reality, you can specify one set of options that apply to the text block itself and other options for each paragraph within the text block. The formatting options themselves are familiar, such as indentations, margins, and alignment.

For a text block, you can specify the vertical alignment of the text within the text block, the margins between the text and the text block boundaries, and color and transparency of the background in the text block, as illustrated in Figure 7-2. To apply text block formatting, select the shape and then choose the text block formats you want.

Text block boundary

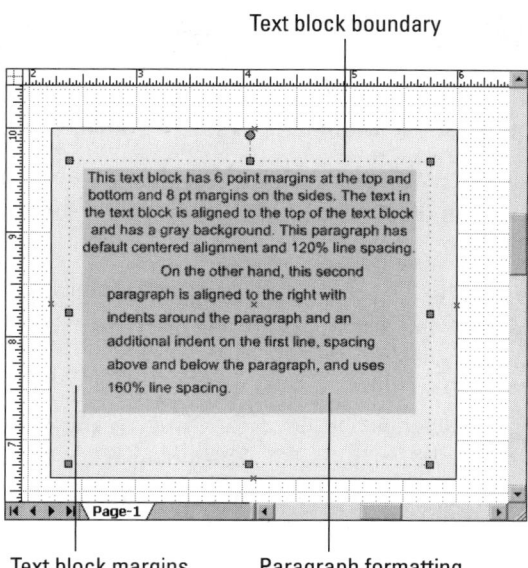

Text block margins   Paragraph formatting

Figure 7-2: Formatting options for text blocks and paragraphs are different.

Note

Most Visio shapes use a transparent background color so you can see what lies behind the text. If other elements behind your text make it unreadable, you can make the text background color opaque so that other shape components don't show through. To do this, select the shape, choose Format ⇨ Text, and select the Text Block tab. Type **0%** in the Transparency field. The opaque background only blocks out components when the shape contains text because the background color only fills the area around text.

For each paragraph within a text block, you can specify the horizontal alignment of the paragraph, the indentation for the first line of the paragraph, the indentation on each side of the paragraph, the spacing before and after the paragraph, and the spacing between the lines in the paragraph, also shown in Figure 7-2. To format a paragraph, activate the Text tool, select the paragraph you want to format, and apply the paragraph formatting you want.

Creating Bulleted and Numbered Lists

You can create bulleted lists easily by selecting a shape and then clicking Bullets on the Format Text toolbar. This applies default formatting that adds a bullet before each line that ends with a soft or hard return in the shape text block. If you want to create bullets with only some of the text in the shape, use the Text tool to select the text you want to format before you click the Bullets button.

Note You can change the font for a bulleted list without affecting the appearance of the bullet when you use Visio's built-in bullets. However, when you change font size, bullet size adjusts to match.

If you want to create a bulleted list using formatting other than the default settings, follow these steps:

1. Select the text block or the portion of the text block that you want to format as a bulleted list.

Tip If you want to build a bulleted list as you enter text, select the shape, click Bullets on the Format Text toolbar, and then type text into the shape text block.

2. Choose Format ⇨ Text and select the Bullets tab.

3. To choose a different bullet symbol, click a bullet option or type the character that you want to use as a bullet in the Custom box.

4. To adjust the font size and list spacing at the same time, increase or decrease the value in the Font Size list.

5. To change the hanging indent between the bullet and the list text, type the distance you want in the Text position box.

6. To preview the formatting you have chosen, click Apply. If the list is formatted the way you want, click OK.

You build numbered lists differently in Visio than you would in other applications, such as Word. In Visio, you have to add numbers, tabs, and indentation manually. If you plan to include a long numbered list in a Visio diagram, it might be easier to use Word to automatically create the numbered list and then create a link from your Visio drawing to the list in the Word document.

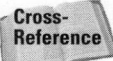

Cross-Reference To learn how to create a link to a Word document, see Chapter 8.

To create a numbered list in Visio, follow these steps:

1. Make sure that text justification is left-justified by clicking Align Left on the Formatting toolbar.

2. Double-click the shape in which you want to create the numbered list.

3. Type the number 1, press Tab, and then type the text for the first entry.

4. Repeat step 3 for each entry in the numbered list (change the number accordingly).

5. To modify the alignment of the numbered list, select all the entries and click one of the alignment options on the Formatting toolbar.

6. To align the numbers and text, first display the Text Ruler. To do this, select the text, right-click the text, and choose Text Ruler from the shortcut menu.

Tip

To display the Text Ruler when text is not selected, double-click the shape, right-click the selected text, and choose Text Ruler from the shortcut menu.

7. Drag the bottom of the hourglass in the Text Ruler to the position to which you want the text to align.

8. Drag the top of the hourglass in the Text Ruler to the position to which you want the numbers to align.

9. Press Esc or click outside the shape to close the text block.

Applying Fill Formats

When a shape is closed, you can specify its fill formatting, which is the color and pattern applied to the interior of the shape. You can choose fill colors by clicking the Fill Color button on the Standard toolbar. However, if you want to specify patterns, transparencies, or shadow formatting, select the shape you want to format and then choose Format ⇨ Fill. You can specify the following options for fill formatting:

✦ **Color** — The color for the interior of the closed shape

Caution

Colors preceded by a number in the color list are *index colors* and refer to the colors defined in the current color palette. If you choose an index color, your fill might change to another index color when you modify the color palette.

✦ **Pattern** — Visio provides 40 patterns, including cross-hatching, stippling, and gradients. You can also define your own custom patterns.

✦ **Pattern Color** — The second color used if you select a pattern other than None or Solid. This color is used for cross-hatching lines and patterns.

✦ **Transparency** — By default, fill is opaque (0%). Drag the transparency slider to the right to increase the transparency of the fill color.

Note

You can also specify fill in a shape's ShapeSheet. To do this, select the shape and then choose Window ⇨ Show ShapeSheet. Scroll to the Fill Format section and type the values for the fill you want. For more information on specifying color values in a ShapeSheet, see Chapter 33.

Formatting Shapes

You can apply different formatting options to shapes depending on what they comprise. For example, you can apply line formats to any shape containing lines whether they are open or closed shapes. When you format closed shapes, such as rectangles and circles, you can also specify the fill formatting for those shapes. If you format text-only shapes created with the Text tool or other shapes containing text, you can format the text in those shapes.

Applying Formatting to Shapes

If you want to modify the formatting on only one shape, it's easy enough to select that shape and then apply the formatting options you want from those listed in Table 7-1. However, you can easily format several shapes or groups of shapes, and you can copy formatting from one shape to another. You can remove a shape's border, but you don't use a formatting tool to accomplish this. To hide a shape's border, select the shape, click the Line Formatting arrow on the Formatting toolbar, and select No Line in the Line Style list.

Tip   If you can't apply formatting options to a shape, the shape could be protected against formatting or it could belong to a group. See the "Protecting Shapes" section later in this chapter to learn more about shape protection. To format a shape in a group, subselect the shape (click the shape within the group until Visio displays the shape's alignment box) and then apply the formatting you want.

| Table 7-1 | |
| Applying Formatting to Shapes | |
Formatting Task	*How to Accomplish It*
Format a shape	Select a shape and then choose the formatting options you want.
Format several shapes at once	Select all the shapes and then choose the formatting options you want.
Format a group of shapes	Select the group and then choose the formatting options you want.
Copy formatting from one shape to another	Select a formatted shape, click the Format Painter button on the Standard toolbar, and click the shape to which you want to copy the formatting.
Copy formatting from one shape to several others	Select a formatted shape, double-click the Format Painter button on the Standard toolbar, and click each shape to which you want to copy the formatting. To stop copying formatting, click the Format Painter button or press Esc.

For instructions on formatting only the text in shapes, refer to the "Applying Formats to Text" section earlier in this chapter.

Applying Shadows to Shapes

You can add punch to your presentations by applying shadows to your shapes. You can use Visio 3-D shapes to add shapes that already have shadows set up. Shadows are not separate shapes; they are formatting that you can apply to add shadows to any shape you want.

Note You can define a default shadow for a drawing page. To do this, display the page, choose File ➪ Page Setup, and select the Shadows tab. Specify the shadow style, offset dimensions, magnification, and direction for the shadow, and then click OK.

To format and apply shadows, follow these steps:

1. Right-click a shape and choose Format ➪ Fill from the shortcut menu or select several shapes and then choose Format ➪ Fill.

2. Choose the shadow style you want in the Style list. Each shadow style includes offset dimensions, magnification, and direction for the shadow.

Tip To use the default shadow specified in Page Setup, choose Page Default in the Style list.

3. To change the shadow color from the one assigned by the current color scheme, choose a color in the Color list.

4. To change the shadow pattern, choose the pattern you want in the Pattern list. If you choose a pattern other than None or Solid, choose a color in the Pattern Color list.

5. To specify the transparency of the shadow, drag the Transparency slider to the right. By default, the shadow is opaque.

Protecting Shapes

You can protect shapes from inadvertent changes. The Formatting menu is an unlikely place for this tool, but you can use it to protect shapes against resizing, moving, rotation, text editing, and formatting. You can also prevent someone from selecting or deleting shapes. To protect shapes, select the shapes you want to protect and choose Format ➪ Protection. The Protection dialog box enables you to protect a shape in the following ways:

✦ **Resizing** — Check the Width, Height, or Aspect Ratio check boxes to prevent users from changing the width or height of shapes or from modifying the proportions of a shape.

✦ **Moving** — Check the X Position and Y position check boxes to prevent users from moving a shape to a new location.

✦ **Rotation** — Check this check box to prevent users from rotating a shape.

✦ **Moving Endpoints** — Check the Begin Point and End Point check boxes to lock the end points of 1D shapes in place.

✦ **Editing Text** — Check the Text check box to prevent users from editing shape text.

✦ **Formatting** — Check the Format check box to prevent users from modifying the formatting of a shape.

✦ **Selection** — Check this check box to prevent users from selecting a shape.

✦ **Deletion** — Check this check box to prevent users from deleting a shape.

Tip You can quickly choose or remove protection by clicking the All or None buttons in the Protection dialog box.

Cross-Reference Some shapes are protected against changes with the GUARD function. To learn how the GUARD function works, see Chapter 33.

Formatting with Styles

When you use the same sets of formatting options repeatedly, using styles is much easier than applying each formatting option you want to each shape. Much like a style in Microsoft Word, a Visio style compiles several formatting options into one handy package. However, because Visio works with more than text, a Visio style can do much more. You can specify whether the style incorporates text, line, and fill formatting, which determines whether it appears in those style lists, and you can assign any or all formatting options to any style. This enables you to format the lines, fill, shadows, and text for a shape by applying only one style.

You can view a style's setting to determine which types of formatting it contains and which options it configures. To do this, choose Format ➪ Define Styles to open the Define Styles dialog box, shown in Figure 7-3. The check boxes in the Includes area indicate whether the style applies text, line, or fill formatting. To view the specific formatting options for the style, click the Text, Line, or Fill buttons in the Change area, but make sure you don't change any of the settings.

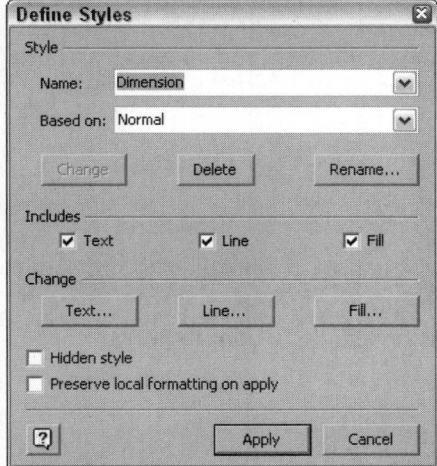

Figure 7-3: View the type of formatting a style applies in the Define Styles dialog box.

Templates for drawings often include specialized styles for the shapes they contain. For example, when you create a building plan, Visio includes line styles with end points for building dimensions, fill styles for walls, and text styles for a variety of purposes. In most cases, you don't have to think about applying styles; Visio assigns them automatically as you drag shapes onto your drawing. However, when you create a blank drawing or use drawing tools to add content, you can apply styles to format your shapes. For drawings you create without a template, Visio inserts five default styles for lines, fill, and text. Some of the default style names sound similar, so it's helpful to know what each one does:

✦ **Guide** — For a drawing guide, the line style is a dashed, blue line. Text is Arial 9-point blue. There is no fill format.

✦ **No Style** — Basic formatting options, in which the line style is a solid black line. Text is Arial 12-point black with text centered and no margins in the text block. Fill is solid white with no shadow.

✦ **None** — Removes lines and fill so a shape has no boundaries and is totally transparent. Uses default text options of Arial 12-point black but includes 4-point margins in the text block.

✦ **Normal** — By default, Normal uses the same settings as No Style. However, you can redefine normal if you want.

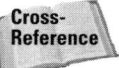

To learn how to create and modify styles, see Chapter 34.

✦ **Text Only** — Removes lines and fill. Uses Arial 12-point black but aligns the text to the top left of the text block, with no margins.

Applying Styles

Visio includes style lists on both the Format Shape and Format Text toolbars. If you choose Format ⇨ Style, Visio opens the Style dialog box, which includes three style lists for text styles, line styles, and fill styles. Styles appear on these lists based on whether their Text, Line, or Fill check boxes are checked in the Define Styles dialog box. Depending on which style list you choose from, you can control which type of formatting Visio applies to the elements you select. However, applying styles has no effect when a shape is protected against formatting. Refer to the "Protecting Shapes" section in this chapter for instructions on removing formatting protection.

When you tweak a shape's formatting options after you apply a style, it's usually to resolve a readability issue for that shape. You can retain these individual formatting options even when you apply a different style to that shape. To do this, choose Format ⇨ Style and check the Preserve Local Formatting check box.

To format using styles, select a shape or shapes and choose a style from one of the following style lists:

✦ **Text Style** — When you choose a style from the Text style list in the Format Text toolbar and the style specifies line and fill attributes, Visio asks whether you want to apply the line and fill formats. Click Yes to apply all formatting options. Click No to apply only text formatting.

✦ **Line Style** — When you choose a style from the Line style list in the Format Shape toolbar and the style specifies text and fill attributes, Visio asks whether you want to apply the text and fill formats. Click Yes to apply all formatting options. Click No to apply only line formatting.

✦ **Fill Style** — When you choose a style from the Fill style list in the Format Shape toolbar and the style specifies text and line attributes, Visio asks whether you want to apply the text and line formats. Click Yes to apply all formatting options. Click No to apply only fill formatting.

✦ **Style** — When you choose a style in the Style dialog box, Visio applies all formatting options. You can also open the Style dialog box by right-clicking a shape and choosing Format ➪ Style from the shortcut menu.

When you use styles to format shapes in a drawing, shape formatting can change when you copy the shapes to another drawing. This occurs when the destination drawing contains styles with the same names used in the source drawing but with different formatting options. To prevent your shapes from assuming the formatting in the destination drawing, rename the styles in the source drawing before copying the shapes.

Restoring Default Styles

Sometimes, you want to remove the local formatting you applied to a shape — for example, when the colors assigned locally to a shape clash with the drawing's color scheme. You can restore the default styles associated with the shape's master by selecting the shape and choosing Format ➪ Style. In any of the style lists, choose Use Master's Format, which is the first entry in the list, and click OK.

To restore the default style for a shape you created with a drawing tool, select the shape and apply the Normal style.

Working with Colors

When you're preparing presentations or illustrating complex topics, color can enhance the readability of your drawings and make them more appealing to your audience. You can choose from 16.7 million colors and 100 levels of transparency for text, lines, fill, and shadows.

You can fill shapes with transparent colors so that the colors mix when you overlap shapes. You can specify color transparency from totally transparent to completely opaque.

Although Visio provides a tempting supply of colors, drawings look more professional when you use fewer colors and coordinate them carefully. Visio provides tools to apply coherent sets of colors so you can quickly enrich the appearance of your drawings. You can select colors from a color palette or define your own custom colors. When you want to ensure that you use colors consistently throughout your drawing, you can apply a color scheme, which assigns colors to basic styles for your drawing. Any shapes or text formatted with styles based on those basic styles assume the colors from a new color scheme.

Visio displays the colors from the color palette and the current color scheme in color lists. These lists appear when you click the arrow in a Color box in any of the formatting dialog boxes. These colors also appear as color samples when you click Text Color, Line Color, or Fill Color on the Formatting toolbar.

Note You can define custom colors for text, lines, or fill by entering RGB (red, green, blue) or HSL (hue, saturation, luminosity) values in the Colors dialog box. To open the Colors dialog box, select More Colors at the bottom of any color list. When you apply custom colors to drawing elements, Visio stores the RGB or HSL values in the ShapeSheet so the colors won't change when you change the color scheme or redefine colors in the color palette.

Using the Color Palette

The color palette is a set of 24 indexed colors from which you can choose when you want to specify color for text, lines, fill, or shadows. When you apply one of these indexed colors to a shape, Visio stores in the ShapeSheet the index value of the color, such as 4 for bright blue in the default color palette. On the one hand, using indexed colors means that you can change any element that uses an indexed color by redefining that index color in the color palette. On the other hand, shapes can change color unexpectedly when someone redefines a color on the color palette or you copy shapes to a drawing that uses a different color palette.

Applying Colors from the Color Palette

You can identify indexed colors in the color list by the number from 00 to 23 that precedes the color. To apply a color from the Color Palette, follow these steps:

1. Open one of the Format dialog boxes by choosing Format ⇨ Text, Format ⇨ Line, or Format ⇨ Fill.

2. Click the arrow for one of the Color boxes in the dialog box, such as Color in the Fill dialog box.

3. Scroll to the top of the color list and click one of the colors preceded by a number.

Modifying the Color Palette

You can replace the colors in the color palette with custom colors that you define, or you can rearrange the colors in the palette so that the ones you use most frequently appear at the top of the list. For example, you can add the signature color for your company to the color palette so the company logo is the proper hue on your drawings.

Note   When you edit the color palette, your changes affect only the current file. If you want to use your modified palette for other drawings, you can save a template with that color palette or copy the color palette from the current file to another drawing.

To edit the colors in the color palette, follow these steps:

1. Choose Tools ⇨ Color Palette.

2. Click the color you want to edit and then click the Edit button to open the Edit Color dialog box.

Caution   Do not edit black (index 0) or white (index 1) in a color palette. Visio uses index 0 for the default line color and index 1 for the default fill color, so changes to index 0 or 1 can affect more than you might expect.

3. Choose a standard color or define a custom color and click OK when you are done. Define a color by using either of the following methods:

   • To use one of the colors in the hexagon of samples on the Standard tab, click the cell with the color you want.

   • To define a custom color, select the Custom tab and choose RGB or HSL in the Color Model box. Type the values in the RGB or HSL boxes, depending on which color model you selected. You can also click a color in the Colors preview area. When the color is the hue you want, you can drag the arrow up or down to lighten or darken the tint.

4. Repeat step 3 to redefine other colors, and click OK when you have finished modifying the color palette.

Copying or Restoring a Color Palette

You can replace the current color palette when you want to restore the original Visio colors or use the color palette from another source. You can copy built-in Visio color palettes or color palettes from other open Visio drawings. In addition, you can copy the default Excel Chart color palette into a Visio drawing so you can coordinate the colors when you copy your Visio drawing into an Excel spreadsheet, or vice versa.

To copy the default color palette or a color palette from another source, follow these steps:

1. To copy a color palette from one Visio file to another, open both files.

2. Select the drawing you want to change and choose Tools ⇨ Color Palette.

3. In the Copy Colors From list, choose the color palette you want to use.

- **Drawing Name** — To copy from another drawing, click the name of the open drawing whose color palette you want to copy.

- **Built-in Palette** — Click one of the entries with a .vss extension to copy a built-in color scheme.

- **Default Color Palette** — Choose Visio Default Palette to restore the color palette to Visio's default colors. Choose Excel Chart Color Palette to use the color palette for Excel charts.

4. Click OK and save your drawing.

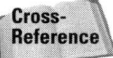

If the colors in your Visio drawing don't look the way you want when you use them in a PowerPoint presentation, see Chapter 8.

Working with Color Schemes

You can format all the shapes that support color schemes at once by applying a color scheme to your drawing. Many Visio drawing types, including most of the business diagrams, contain settings and styles that work with color schemes. Shapes in these drawing types are already formatted with styles that reference colors in the color scheme for text, lines, fill, and shadows. For example, Visio includes styles within color schemes that specify formatting for shape components such as shape faces and borders. In color schemes, you can also specify colors for the shadow for a shape, background and foreground colors in patterns, highlights, line colors, and text color. When you change the color scheme, the colors of shape components switch to the colors for the new color scheme. Although you can't edit or delete built-in color schemes, you can create your own schemes from scratch or based on an existing scheme.

Shapes that don't support color schemes won't change color when you apply a new color scheme. If you draw your own shapes or copy a shape from a drawing type that doesn't support color schemes into a drawing that does, the shape colors won't match the color scheme. However, you can apply a matching color to these shapes by selecting the shapes, opening one of the Format dialog boxes, and choosing a color scheme color in the color list. When you assign a color in this way, you must rematch the shape color manually each time you apply a new color scheme.

Applying Color Schemes

To apply a color scheme to a drawing, follow these steps:

1. Right-click the drawing page and then choose Color Schemes from the short-cut menu.

The Color Schemes command is available on the drawing page's shortcut menu only if the drawing type supports color schemes, as in templates such as Organization Chart, Calendar, and Flowchart.

2. Select the color scheme you want and click Apply to preview the new scheme.

3. If you want Visio to retain any specific color formatting you applied to shapes in the drawing, check the Preserve My Shape Color Changes check box.

4. Click OK to apply the color scheme or click Cancel to revert to the previous scheme.

Creating and Editing Color Schemes

To create or edit a custom color scheme, follow these steps:

1. Right-click the drawing page and then choose Color Schemes from the shortcut menu.

2. Click New or Edit in the Color Schemes dialog box to create a new color scheme or edit an existing scheme, respectively.

3. To change the name of the scheme, type a new name in the Name box.

4. To base a new color scheme on the color scheme in the current document, click the Use Current Document Style Colors button.

5. To modify a color scheme style, choose the style you want to change in the Style drop-down list. You can specify colors for the foreground, background, shadow, line, and text for that style. To specify one of these color settings, click the button for that setting to open the Colors dialog box. Choose a standard color or create a custom color as described in the "Modifying the Color Palette" section earlier in this chapter.

6. Repeat step 5 for each color scheme style you want to create or edit. Click OK when you are finished.

Specifying Basic Color Settings

You can specify the colors that appear by default for the drawing page, drawing page background, stencil text, stencil background, print preview background, and full-screen background. To do this, follow these steps:

1. Choose Tools ➪ Options, select the Advanced tab, and click the Color Settings button.

2. To change a color, click the arrow for the color you want to change and select a new color.

3. Repeat step 2 for each color you want to change. Click OK in the Color Settings dialog box and then click OK to close the Options dialog box.

Note The drawing window and stencil window each have two entries for background colors. With adequate screen resolution and your monitor set to display 32-bit color, Visio will grade the background from one of the colors into the other from the top to the bottom of the screen.

Color-Coding Shapes

You can color-code shapes based on the values in their custom properties. For example, you can highlight the building space occupied by different departments by color-coding space shapes by the value in the Department custom property.

To select the shapes you want to color-code, use one of the following methods:

✦ To color-code all shapes or all instances of one master, click the drawing page background to make sure nothing is selected.

✦ To color-code specific shapes, select only those shapes.

To color-code the selected shape, follow these steps:

1. Choose Tools ➪ Add-Ons ➪ Building Plan ➪ Color By Values.

2. In the Color By list, select the property by which you want to color-code the shapes.

3. In the Shape Type list, select the type of shape you want to color-code. To color-code all shapes, select <all shapes>.

4. In the Range Type list, select the type of values. Unique values apply a different color for each unique value in the custom property. Discrete values apply a different color for each range of values, such as 100 to 199. Continuous values apply colors from low to high across the range of custom property values.

5. In the Color field, select the colors you want to use.

6. To assign predefined colors to all values, click the Color arrow and select a color range. You can also click a box in the Color column to assign a new color to that box.

7. In the Value and Label fields, type the values for the color-coding and the labels you want to appear in the color legend. Click OK when you are finished.

8. To modify the color-coding in your drawing, right-click the legend on the drawing page and choose Edit Legend from the shortcut menu.

9. To update the color-coding to reflect changes to custom property values, right-click the legend and choose Refresh Legend.

Summary

Visio provides formatting tools so you can make your drawings look exactly the way you want. You can choose options to format text, lines, fill, and shadows. Color schemes and styles are the easiest way to apply consistent formatting to your drawings. By using color schemes, you can modify the formatting of all shapes that use styles associated with color schemes. You can also modify the formatting for all shapes using a specific style by modifying the formatting options of that style. Although styles appear in Text, Line, and Fill style lists, each style can include options for all three types of formatting. In addition, you can apply special formatting to specific shapes on your drawing and preserve those options as you apply the color schemes or styles.

✦   ✦   ✦

Integrating Visio Drawings

Inserting, Linking, and Embedding Objects

Your work with Microsoft Visio does not exist in a vacuum. The very point of Visio is to communicate information in a graphic way to others "out there." Sometimes, Visio drawings are the end point for the communication. Other times, they become a part of larger communications, in reports or presentations, for example.

To facilitate this kind of information sharing, you can create hyperlinks to Visio drawings. Click the hyperlink, just as you do in a Web site, and Visio and the drawing are launched. You can take this concept of linking a step further by inserting Visio drawings as links in other application files, ensuring that any edits update the links. A third method is to insert, or embed, separate copies of Visio drawings in other application files, where you can view the drawings and use Visio tools to edit them at will.

These three methods work in the other direction as well. You can create hyperlinks in Visio drawings to other applications. You can link or embed the contents of other application files and make changes to them without leaving Visio itself. One of the most common elements embedded in Visio drawings are graphics such as clip art and digital photographs.

In this chapter, I show you how to create hyperlinks to and from Visio drawings as well as how to link and embed information from one application into another. I also demonstrate the finer points of embedding graphics files in Visio, and provide tips for adding Visio drawings to PowerPoint presentations to the best effect.

Cross-Reference You can also exchange information between different applications by saving or opening files as different file formats. To learn about importing and exporting with Visio, see Chapter 9.

Understanding Linking and Embedding

The term *linking* often brings to mind hyperlinks between Web pages, and rightly so, because you can certainly create hyperlinks from Visio drawings to other files, and vice versa. In addition, you can use another type of linking that uses Object Linking and Embedding technology, or OLE. Applications that employ OLE technology, including the Microsoft Office applications, can easily swap elements with other OLE applications. Swappable objects can be entire files or items within files. For example, you can include a PowerPoint presentation or an individual PowerPoint slide within a Visio drawing.

You can swap objects between applications by either linking or embedding them. With linking, a picture of the object appears in the target, or container, application, but the object actually exists elsewhere on the computer. When that object changes in the source application, it also changes in the container application. You can access the source application's menus and tools within the container application to make changes there, and those changes also update the source file.

When an object is *embedded,* rather than linked, a separate copy of the object is inserted into the container application. The source file still exists, but separately and independently from the object in the container application. Similar to linking, you can access the source application's menus and tools within the container application and make changes there, but the changes only update the copy of the object in the container application and do not affect the source file.

Whether you're linking or embedding, you can double-click the object in the container application to make changes to it on the spot. You can also create a new object from scratch to link or embed in the container application. To decide whether you want to link or embed an object, evaluate the differences between these options in Table 8-1.

Linking Elements

When you want to create links between documents in different applications, you can choose between hyperlinks or OLE links. With hyperlinks, the container application shows an icon or a different mouse pointer. When you click a hyperlink, the application to which the hyperlink is pointing launches in a separate window, and the file or Web page opens. With an OLE link, the container application can show either a representation of the source file or just the application icon. Either way, when you double-click an OLE link, the source application and the file launch in a separate window.

Table 8-1 Linking versus Embedding		
Feature	**With Linking**	**With Embedding**
File versions	You need to deal only with one version of the object.	You have two separate and independent versions of the object.
Updating versions	When you change the object, either in the source or container application, it's updated in both locations.	Any changes to the source file do not affect the object inserted in the container file. Likewise, any changes made to the object do not affect the source.
File Size	You can maintain a smaller file size because the object is not actually within the container application — it's only a link.	The container file size can grow quite large, because it's actually storing the content of the object itself, not just the link to the source.
Time-Consuming File Launch	Larger or more complex files containing several links might take longer to open, especially across a large network. The source file is accessed and checked for changes, and those changes are updated in your target file, either manually or automatically.	Larger or more complex files containing several embedded files might take longer to open. This can be especially true if those embedded files contain graphics elements, as they take time to draw completely.
Source File Location	You must always be aware of the location of the linked file for the link to continue to work.	The container file is self-contained. You don't need to worry about the portability of the file or whether the source file has been moved.
Linking Individual Elements	You must link the entire file; you cannot link just an individual element within a file.	You can embed individual elements within a file.

Hyperlinks at Work

After you've added hyperlinks to your Visio drawing, their behavior depends on the method you choose for viewing your drawing:

✦ **Full screen mode** — If you choose View ➪ Full Screen or use a Visio drawing as a Web page, when the mouse pointer is over a shape containing a hyperlink, the pointer changes to the pointing hand icon. To follow the hyperlink, click the shape.

✦ **Normal mode** — If you are not in full-screen mode, when the mouse pointer is over a shape containing a hyperlink, the pointer changes to an arrow with the hyperlink globe icon. To follow the hyperlink, right-click the shape and then choose the link from the shortcut menu.

The Web page or file appears in its own window. If the hyperlink is designed to go to another Visio page, that page replaces the current page.

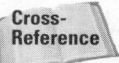

Another type of linking involves shape properties. To learn about linking shape properties to a database, see Chapter 10.

Using Hyperlinks

Add a hyperlink to a Visio drawing when you want to be able to dynamically click and launch a Web page or file from the drawing. When you have a multipage drawing, you can use hyperlinks to move from one page to another. You can also create hyperlinks from another application to a Visio drawing.

Although hyperlinks can be associated with drawing pages, they're more commonly associated with shapes, including Hyperlink buttons or circles. To use specially designed Hyperlink shapes, open the Borders and Titles stencil, drag the hyperlink shapes to the drawing page, and add hyperlinks to those shapes.

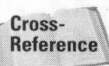

To learn more about adding hyperlink navigation shapes to your drawings, see Chapter 9.

Inserting Hyperlinks

The first step to inserting a hyperlink in a Visio drawing is to decide where to place the hyperlink. If you associate the hyperlink with a shape, when you move the mouse over the shape, the pointer changes to one of the hyperlink icons to indicate that the shape is *hot*. When you click the shape, the linked application and file or Web page launches in a separate window. You can use this approach when you use a navigation shape on a drawing or want to navigate from the last step on one page to the continuation on another.

If you do not want to associate a hyperlink with a shape in the drawing, you can make the entire page hot instead. In this case, when you move the mouse over a blank part of the page not inhabited by any shape, the mouse pointer changes to the hyperlink icon.

To insert a hyperlink in a Visio drawing, follow these steps:

1. Click the shape or page that you want to associate with the hyperlink.

2. Choose Insert ⇨ Hyperlinks.

3. In the Address box, enter the address for the hyperlink using one of the following methods:

   • **Linking to a Web page** — Type the full address starting with the protocol — for example, **http://**. You can also click the Browse button and then click Internet Address. Your Web browser launches. Navigate to the Web page to which you want your Visio hyperlink to point. Return to Visio, and you should see the full Web address in the Address box of the Hyperlinks dialog box. If not, copy the address from the Web browser and paste it into the dialog box.

   • **Linking to a file on your system** — Enter the full file path. You can also click the Browse button and then click Local File. Navigate to the location of the file to which you want your Visio hyperlink to point. Select the file and then click the Open button.

Note

If you're entering a Web address, remember to use front slashes (/) where necessary. If you're entering a file path, remember to use back slashes (\) to separate the folder names.

4. To display text when the mouse pointer pauses over the hyperlink, enter the text in the Description box. When you're finished, click OK.

Tip

By default, hyperlinks use a relative path — that is, the path relative to the location of the Visio drawing itself. If you prefer to use the absolute path, uncheck the Use Relative Path for Hyperlink check box in the Hyperlinks dialog box. Because Visio uses relative paths when creating hyperlinks, this check box is dimmed until you save the Visio file.

You can associate multiple hyperlinks with a single element — for example, to provide links to each detail drawing page for a high-level process. In the Hyperlinks dialog box, click New, enter a new hyperlink address as usual, and then click OK. When you right-click the hyperlinked shape or page, a list of hyperlinks appears and you can choose the hyperlink you want from the shortcut menu. Add multiple hyperlinks when you expect to use the drawing only in normal mode. Multiple hyperlinks are not supported in full-screen mode.

Note

When you use Internet Explorer 5.0 or later and right-click a shape with multiple hyperlinks, all the associated hyperlinks appear on the shortcut menu. For browsers or output formats such as SVG that don't support multiple hyperlinks, you see only the default hyperlink when you right-click a shape or, if there is no default hyperlink, the first hyperlink in the list.

Inserting Hyperlinks to Drill Down in a Drawing

Suppose your Visio drawing starts with an overview process and you have other pages that include detail processes for several steps in the overview. You can create hyperlinks so you can drill down to see the detailed drawings. You can also use hyperlinks to move from one page to the next in a sequence of drawing pages.

To create hyperlinks for multiple pages in a Visio drawing, follow these steps:

1. Click the shape to contain the hyperlink. If this is an overview drawing, click the shape that represents the overview of the detail drawings to come. If this is the first page of a sequence of pages, add a navigation shape that indicates a next page.

2. Choose Insert ➪ Hyperlinks.

3. Next to the Sub-address box, click the Browse button to open the Hyperlink dialog box.

4. Select the page you want in the Page drop-down list, as illustrated in Figure 8-1.

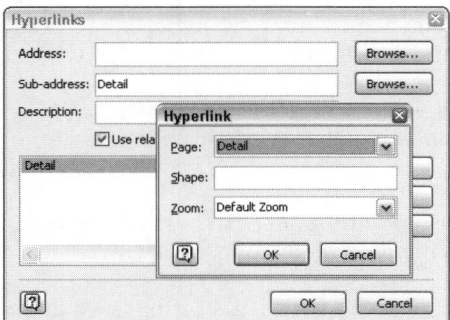

Figure 8-1: When you select the page for the hyperlink, its reference appears in the Sub-address box.

5. To focus on a specific shape on the target page, type the name of the shape in the Shape box. When you click the hyperlink, Visio centers this shape in the drawing window.

Note   To find the name of a shape, right-click the shape and choose Format ➪ Special from the shortcut menu. The shape name appears in the Name box — for example, Circle, Sheet.1, or Manager.18.

6. To change the default size of the target page, select the percentage you want in the Zoom drop-down list.

7. Click OK to return to the Hyperlinks dialog box.

8. To display text when the mouse pointer pauses over the hyperlink, enter the text in the Description box. When you're finished, click OK.

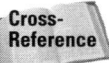
To learn about creating drill-down diagrams for network models, see Chapter 23.

Modifying Hyperlinks

If your Visio drawing is used for any length of time, it's a good idea to periodically monitor your hyperlinks to make sure their locations have not changed. This is especially important if you're pointing to Web pages or files that you don't control. Your hyperlinks can break if someone changes or removes the Web pages or moves the files to which your hyperlinks point.

However, if the location of a hyperlink target changes, you can change your hyperlink definition. To modify a hyperlink, follow these steps:

1. Click the shape or page with which the hyperlink is associated and then choose Insert ➪ Hyperlinks.

2. If there are multiple hyperlinks for the selected shape, select the name of the hyperlink you want to change in the list.

3. In the Address box, edit the Web address or path name. You can also click the Browse button and navigate to the Web page or file to automatically update the address.

4. Make any other changes you want to the hyperlink and then click OK.

Creating Hyperlinks to Visio Drawings

You can create a hyperlink in another application, such as Microsoft Excel or any application that supports hyperlinks, to launch Visio and a particular drawing. It's a similar process to creating hyperlinks in Visio. To insert a hyperlink from another application to a Visio drawing, follow these steps:

1. In the host, or container, application, click the location you want for the hyperlink.

2. Choose Insert ➪ Hyperlinks, or the equivalent command.

3. In the Text to Show box, enter a description for the hyperlink.

4. Browse through the file system to find the Visio drawing file. Select the file and then click OK.

Linking Visio Drawings with Microsoft Office Files

Insert an OLE link when you want to show part of the contents of the linked file, and when you want to just point to the file, rather than include it in its entirety. For example, suppose you want to show a Visio drawing in a Microsoft Word document. The Visio drawing is occasionally updated and you want to see those updates in the Word document. Creating a link to the drawing from Word is the perfect solution.

This works just as well in the opposite direction. You might have a Visio drawing that refers to a Microsoft Excel chart that is dynamically updated as data is entered. By linking that chart to your drawing, you can include the chart as an integral part of your Visio drawing and ensure that you're always looking at the latest version of the data.

Whether Visio is the container or the source application, you can double-click the linked object to open the source application and file in a separate window. From there, you can enlarge the window and review the entire file. You can also edit the source file to make needed changes.

Linking Visio Drawings with Other Applications

You can link Visio drawings in any application that employs OLE technology, including the Microsoft Office applications. Going in the other direction, you can link another application's files in a Visio drawing.

To link a file in one application to a file in another application, follow these steps:

1. Open the container application and the file in which you want to add the OLE link.

2. Choose Insert ➪ Object, or the equivalent command.

3. In the Object dialog box, select the Create from File tab or option and click Browse.

4. In the Browse dialog box, find and select the name of the source file you want to link to the current application's file and then click Insert. The file path is completed in the File Name box.

5. Check the Link to File check box to ensure that the object is linked, rather than embedded.

6. To show the source application's icon, rather than the file itself, in the container file, check the Display As Icon check box.

7. Click OK. At least a portion of the selected file shows in the container application, as illustrated in Figure 8-2.

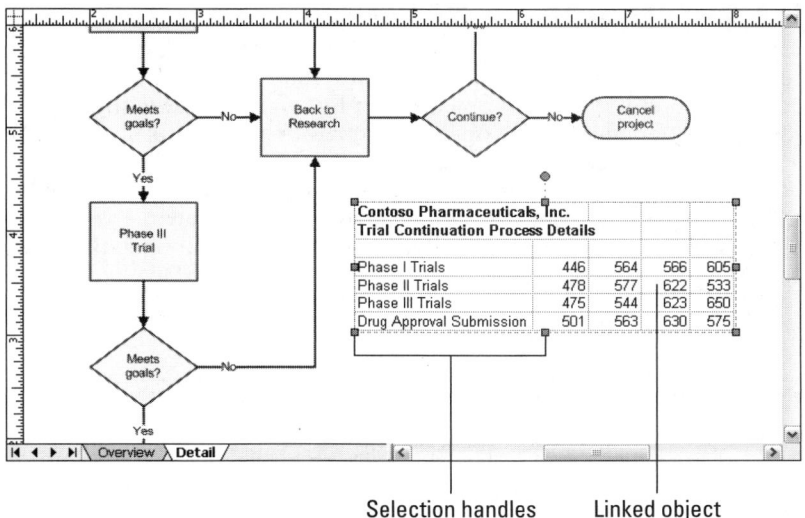

Selection handles   Linked object

Figure 8-2: The source file is linked in the container file.

Moving and Resizing Linked Objects

With the linked object in your container application, you can move and resize it at will using one of the following methods:

✦ **Select a linked object** — Click the object. A selection box similar to the selection box for a Visio shape appears around the object.

✦ **Resize the object proportionally** — Drag one of the selection handles in any of the four corners, as shown in Figure 8-2.

✦ **Stretch or condense the object along one side** — Drag one of the selection handles at the midpoint of a side.

✦ **Move the object** — Drag the middle of the object to the position you want. Take care to drag from the center of the object, and not along any of its edges.

Tip

By default, objects in Word are inserted in line with text, and you can't reposition the object. Instead, you can use line spacing to adjust the object's position. To change the object so you can drag it anywhere, right-click the object, and then choose Format Object from the shortcut menu. Select the Layout tab, click In Front of Text, and then click OK. Now you can drag the object wherever you like because it's independent of the text in the Word document.

Editing the Content of a Linked Object

You can change the content of a linked object either from within the source application or the container application. Either way, you're working with the same file. To change the content of a linked object, start by double-clicking the object. The source application and the file open in a separate window, as shown in Figure 8-3. Make whatever changes you want and then save and close the file. The source application window closes and you see the changes reflected in the object in the container application. If someone changes the source file while you're working with the linked object, you'll see the changes the next time you open the container file.

Linked object in container application

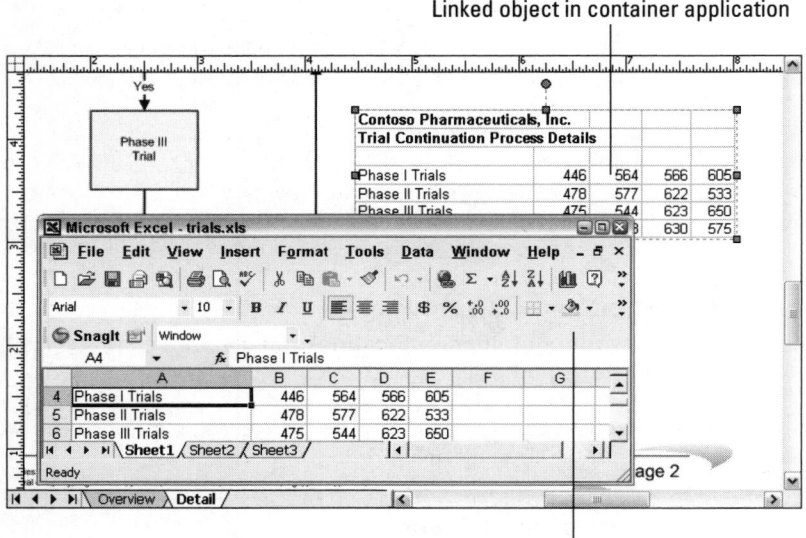

Launched source application

Figure 8-3: Double-click a linked object to open its application in a separate window.

Note   To edit the content of a linked object, you must have read-write privileges.

Managing Linked Objects

You can manage the links associated with linked objects, as well as specify how link updates are to occur. Using the Links dialog box, you can perform the following actions:

✦ Review details for all linked objects in the file.

✦ Review the path name for a linked source file and change the path if the file has moved.

✦ Specify whether you want updates from the source to be automatic or manual (they're automatic by default).

✦ Break the link between the object and source, transforming the linked object into an embedded object or a static picture.

If you link to a file that is subsequently moved or deleted, the link breaks. The next time you open the container file, instead of a picture of the linked content, an error message appears, such as "Error! Not a valid link." To change the path name for this broken link, follow these steps:

1. Choose Edit ➪ Links. The Links dialog box appears.

2. In the Links box, click the link whose path you need to edit.

3. Click the Change Source button and then browse to the new location of the source file.

4. Click the filename and then click Open.

5. When you're finished making changes in the Links dialog box, click the Close or OK button.

You can change an automatic link update to manual update. To do this, select the link in the Links dialog box, select the Manual option, and then click Close. To update the manual links in your container file, open the Links dialog box again, select the link, and then click Update Now.

Tip If you decide you no longer need a linked object at all, you can remove it from the container document by selecting the object and then pressing Delete.

Change Links to Embedded Objects or Pictures

Suppose you linked to a dynamic file that underwent ongoing changes so that you would see the most up-to-date version, but now the file is static and you would prefer to store the copy completely within the container document. You can break the link while keeping the object in the container, essentially converting a linked object to an embedded object. To do this, follow these steps:

1. In the container file, choose Edit ➪ Links, and then select the link in the Links box.

2. Click Break Link, and then click Yes in the message box that appears. The link information is removed from the Links dialog box.

3. Click Close. The object is still where it was in your container document, and looks just the same. However, it no longer is linked to the source. It becomes an independent copy existing within the container document — that is, it's now an embedded file or a static picture.

Embedding Objects

When you embed an object from another application, you're inserting an independent copy of the source file into the container application file. Like linking objects, you can access the source application's tools within the container application and make changes on the spot. However, the changes update only the copy of the object in the container, and do not affect the source. Unlike linking, you don't have to worry about the location of the source file: A copy of the file exists inside the container. Because of this, however, the size of the container file grows to accommodate that other file.

You can embed an entire source file or just a piece of it. For example, you can embed an entire Excel workbook within a Visio drawing, or just a single chart from that workbook. Likewise, you can embed all pages of a Visio drawing in a PowerPoint presentation, a single page, or even a single shape in another application.

Embedding Files and Fragments As Objects

If you're working in any OLE application, you can embed all or part of another OLE application into the container file. When embedding an entire file, you choose the Insert ⇨ Object commands. When embedding part of a file, you choose the Copy and Paste Special commands.

Embedding Entire Files

The procedure for embedding an entire file is nearly identical to linking. The difference is that you do not check the Link to File check box. To embed an entire existing source file into the container file, follow these steps:

1. Open the container application and file into which you want to embed the file from the other application.

2. Choose Insert ⇨ Object, or the equivalent command.

3. In the Object dialog box, select the Create from File tab or option and click Browse.

4. In the Browse dialog box, find and select the file you want to embed in the current application's file and then click Insert. The file path is completed in the File Name box.

Tip   If you check the Display As Icon check box in the Object dialog box, the entire file is still embedded. However, displaying just the icon saves space in your document layout while providing a visual cue that more information is present.

5. Click OK. The selected file is inserted in your container file as an embedded object. Drag the edges of the object to resize it and move it to the position you want.

Creating an Embedded Object from Scratch

If you want to create (with another application) a file whose only purpose would be to augment information in the container application file, you can create a brand-new file from within the container application.

To create a new embedded object file, follow these steps:

1. In the container application, choose Insert ⇨ Object and then select the Create New tab or option.

2. Under Object Type, select the application with which you want to create the new embedded file.

3. Click OK. A blank file is inserted in your container file, and you can start creating the new embedded file using its application's tools.

Embedding Parts of Files

You might want only a single page or portion of a Visio drawing in a Word report. Similarly, you might want to embed just a table from Word or a single PowerPoint slide in your Visio drawing, rather than the entire file. You can select and copy the portion of a file you want and embed only that much in the container file. Along with including only the necessary information, this can also help keep the size of the container file from ballooning larger than it needs to be.

To embed a part of a file in another application, follow these steps:

1. In the source application, open the file and go to the page that contains the portion you want to embed in the other application.

2. Using the application's tools, select the portion you want to embed.

Tip

If you're working in Visio, activate the Pointer tool if necessary, and then drag across the portion you want to embed. The selection area must fully enclose all elements you want to embed.

3. Choose Edit ⇨ Copy, or the equivalent commands.

Tip

If you're working with a multipage Visio drawing and you want to select the contents of a single page to embed in another application, display that page and make sure no shape is selected. Choose Edit ⇨ Copy Drawing to copy the entire page into memory so that you can paste it into the other application.

4. Switch to the container application, open the file, and go to the page in which you want to embed the object you just copied. If necessary, click the location where you want to embed the object.

5. Choose Edit ➪ Paste Special.

6. In the As box, click the type of object you've selected, such as Microsoft Visio Drawing Object or Microsoft Excel Worksheet.

7. Click OK. The copied object appears in the container file.

Note   Ordinarily, you cannot link just a fragment of a file. However, if you have a multi-page Visio drawing and you choose Edit ➪ Copy Drawing, when you choose Edit ➪ Paste Special in the container application, the Paste Link option is available to you.

If you need only a single Visio shape in the other application, you can copy and paste it. In Visio, show the shape you want in the Shapes window. Right-click the shape and then choose Copy. (If you try to copy the shape from the Shapes window using any other method, it won't work.) In the container application, select the location you want and then choose Edit ➪ Paste or click the Paste button on the Standard toolbar. You can also arrange the Visio and container applications side by side and then drag the shape from Visio to the other application.

Positioning and Formatting Embedded Objects

As soon as you insert an object into the container application, you can perform the following actions:

✦ Move it to the location you want.

✦ Resize it to the dimensions you need.

✦ Crop one or more edges of the object.

✦ Adjust the space surrounding the object.

Before you can manipulate the object, select the object by clicking it. A selection box appears around the object.

Other Object Formats

In the Paste Special dialog box, you might see other formats with which you can paste the copied object:

✦ Picture

✦ Device Independent Bitmap

✦ Picture (Enhanced Metafile)

✦ Bitmap

The options available depend on the container application. Click each item to see an explanation in the Result box.

Moving and Resizing Objects

To move an object, drag the middle of the object to the position you want. Take care to drag from the center of the object, not along any of its edges. To resize an object proportionally, drag one of the selection handles in any of the four corners. To stretch or condense the object along one side, drag one of the selection handles at the midpoint of an edge.

Cropping Objects

If you need to trim extraneous space from the edges of an object, crop the object. To crop a Visio object in another application, follow these steps:

1. In the other application, click the Visio object and then choose Format ➪ Object. The Format Object dialog box appears. Make sure the Picture tab is showing.

2. Under Crop From, enter the amount you want to crop from the Left, Right, Top, or Bottom.

3. When you're finished, click OK. You might have to repeat these steps a few times to achieve the amount of cropping you want.

To crop an object in Visio, follow these steps:

1. If it's not already showing, display the Picture toolbar by choosing View ➪ Toolbars ➪ Picture.

2. Select the object you want to crop.

3. On the Picture toolbar, click the Crop button.

4. Drag a selection handle in the object in the direction you want to crop the object.

Adjusting the Space Surrounding Objects

To adjust the space surrounding a Visio object in another application, follow these steps:

1. In the other application, double-click the Visio object to open the in-place editing window.

2. Drag one of the selection handles to change the shape surrounding the object.

3. Click in the container file outside the in-place editing window. The editing window closes, and the container file reflects the new space surrounding the object.

To adjust the space surrounding an object in Visio, follow these steps:

1. If not already showing, display the Picture toolbar by choosing View ➪ Toolbars ➪ Picture.

2. Select the object.

3. On the Picture toolbar, click the Crop button.

4. Drag a selection handle outward from the object in the direction in which you want to add space around the object.

Editing the Content of Embedded Objects

You can change the actual content of an embedded object without leaving the container application. In effect, you can work with the tools of two applications in one.

To edit an embedded object, simply double-click it. The in-place editing window appears. The menu and toolbars change from those of the container application to those of the embedded object's application, as shown in Figure 8-4. You can use them exactly as if you were working with the source application. When you're finished editing, click in the container file outside the in-place editing window. The editing window closes and the embedded object reflects your edits.

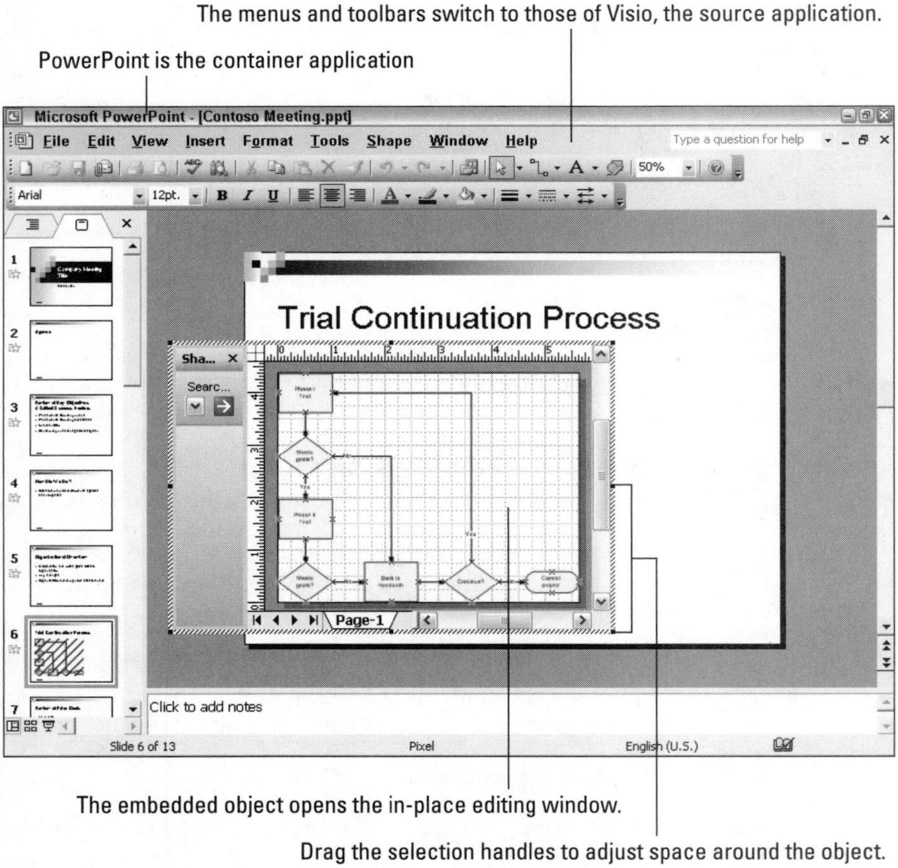

The menus and toolbars switch to those of Visio, the source application.

PowerPoint is the container application

The embedded object opens the in-place editing window.

Drag the selection handles to adjust space around the object.

Figure 8-4: Adjust the space around a drawing by dragging the selection handles in the in-place editing window.

If you prefer, you can open an object in a separate window. To do this, select the object and choose Edit, and then choose the type of object, such as Visio Object or Worksheet Object. Choose Open. The object and its source application open in a separate window where you can make the changes you want. When you're finished, choose File ➪ Update to update your changes to the container application. Close the Visio window to return to the container application. You can now see the object with your edits.

Inserting Graphics in Visio

Inserting graphics such as clip art or photographs is a specialized form of embedding. You can use the new Clip Art Task Pane in Visio 2003 to search a variety of sources for just the right piece of clip art. You can insert a graphics file you have handy, including graphics from a digital camera or scanner. Because embedding graphic files is done so frequently, Visio includes tools to make the process easy and versatile.

Inserting Graphics Files

To insert a specific graphics file you have on your hard drive or network drive into a Visio drawing, follow these steps:

1. In your Visio drawing, select the page in which you want to insert the graphic.

2. Choose Insert ➪ Picture ➪ From File. The Insert Picture dialog box appears.

3. Browse to the location of the graphic, select the file, and then click Open. The graphic appears on the page.

4. Resize, move, and crop the graphic as needed on the page.

Searching for and Inserting Clip Art

To embed a piece of clip art in Visio, follow these steps:

1. In your Visio drawing, select the page in which you want to insert the graphic.

2. Choose Insert ➪ Picture ➪ Clip Art. The Clip Art Task Pane appears.

Note
If you haven't installed the clip art feature, you'll see a prompt to do so. The CD is not required to install clip art.

3. In the Search For box, type a key word or phrase that describes the type of clip art you want.

Tip   Searches execute faster if you use specific key words or phrases. However, you can use general key words to obtain a wider selection of clip art.

4. In the Search In box, specify where you want Visio to search. You can check the check box for a particular folder on your hard drive, such as Office Collections. You can also have Visio search the Internet in a particular Web collection. Be aware that the wider the search and the larger the collections, the longer the search might take.

5. In the Results Should Be box, select the type of media you want to find, such as photographs or sounds. To further specify file formats you want, click the plus sign under the media. This can help narrow your search, especially when searching Web collections.

6. When you're finished defining your clip art search criteria, click Go. Results of your search appear in the Clip Art Task Pane as thumbnails.

7. When you find the clip art you want to use in your drawing, drag it into position in your drawing. Resize the art if necessary.

Inserting Pictures from Digital Devices

To insert a picture coming from a digital device such as a scanner or digital camera, follow these steps:

1. In your Visio drawing, select the page in which you want to insert the digital picture.

2. Choose Insert ➪ Picture ➪ From Scanner or Camera. If you have more than one digital device attached to the computer, select the one you want to use in the Device box.

3. If you're inserting a picture from a scanner, select Web Quality or Print Quality. Click Insert.

Note   If the Insert button is not available or you want to change your scanner's settings, click Custom Insert.

4. If you're inserting a picture from a digital camera, click Custom Insert. Follow the instructions for the camera until the picture is inserted.

5. Resize, move, and crop the picture as needed on the page.

Fine-Tuning Visio Drawings for PowerPoint

PowerPoint presentations and Visio drawings go together like bread and butter. Visio is great for illustrating processes, while PowerPoint provides the larger context in which to explain those processes to your audience. Embedding Visio drawings in PowerPoint adds a world of clarity to your presentations. You can apply specific techniques for size, position, color, and animation to ensure that your Visio drawings look compatible and work effectively in the presentations.

Formatting Visio Drawings in a Presentation

The text and color scheme of your Visio drawing might look great on its own, but not so great when you bring it into your PowerPoint presentation. You can adjust the drawing to coordinate its colors with PowerPoint. You can also tweak the drawing to ensure that it's appropriate for projection on a screen and for viewing at a distance by an audience. For example, you can use a smaller font size for body type and titles for a drawing in a paper report or in a Web page. However, when the drawing is being projected and viewed by a presentation audience, you need to be sure that text can be read by everyone all the way in the back of the room. Edit the text in the drawing so that it's at least two to four points larger than you typically use for reports or Web pages.

Tip   Print your drawing, place it on the floor, and stand up over it. If you can read all the text comfortably from your height, your audience will probably be able to read all the text comfortably in the presentation.

Pay attention to the contrast of letters and lines against the background. What looks snazzy on a Web site might look washed out or busy in a presentation. Use high contrast between foreground and background elements. For example, you can use combinations such as dark blue text and lines on a white background, or white text and lines on a black background.

Cross-Reference   If you're using styles in your drawing, you might be able to adjust the drawing by simply changing the text, line, and fill styles. This way, you don't have to adjust each element individually. For more information about working with styles, see Chapters 7 and 34.

Coordinating Visio Color Schemes with PowerPoint

You might find that the color scheme of your embedded Visio drawing is clashing with that of your PowerPoint presentation. You can adapt the drawing to the PowerPoint color scheme by following these steps:

1. In PowerPoint, double-click the embedded drawing to open the Visio window within PowerPoint.

2. Right-click an empty area of the Visio window and then choose Color Schemes from the shortcut menu. The Color Schemes dialog box appears.

3. To change the Visio drawing color scheme to the PowerPoint color scheme, select PowerPoint and then click OK.

4. Click outside the Visio window on the PowerPoint slide to close the Visio window.

Creating Color-Coordinated Backgrounds

You might want to retain the colors in the Visio drawing as they are, especially if the colors have special significance or if the linked drawing was created by someone else. You can make the colors work better in a presentation by simply adding a complementary background in the slide in which the drawing is linked or embedded.

To create a color-coordinated background for your Visio drawing in PowerPoint, follow these steps:

1. In PowerPoint, show the slide in which you will be linking or embedding the Visio diagram.

2. On the Drawing toolbar, click the Rectangle tool.

 Note   If the Drawing toolbar is not visible in PowerPoint, choose View ➪ Toolbars ➪ Drawing.

3. In the slide, drag the area to define the size of the rectangle. Drag any of the selection handles to further adjust the size of the rectangle.

 Note   If you have already inserted the object, it's okay to cover the object with the rectangle for now — you can bring the object to the top after you've defined the rectangle.

4. On the Drawing toolbar, choose the Fill Color tool to fill the inside of the rectangle, as shown in Figure 8-5. By doing this, you can select a color that offsets the Visio drawing well, but also works with the overall color scheme of the PowerPoint presentation.

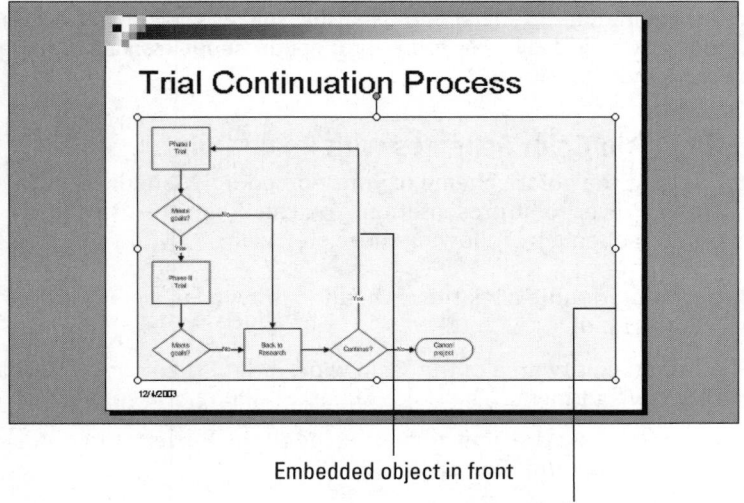

Embedded object in front

Filled rectangle in back

Figure 8-5: Place a filled rectangle behind a Visio drawing to complement the color scheme of your PowerPoint presentation.

5. On the Drawing toolbar, choose the Line Color tool to add a color to the rectangle's outline.

6. If you have not already inserted the object, do so now by choosing Insert ⇨ Object. Use the selection handles to move and resize the drawing into position within the rectangle.

7. If you have already inserted the object, you can bring it to the front of the rectangle by right-clicking the rectangle and choosing Order ⇨ Send to Back from the shortcut menu.

Building Drawings in a Presentation

Many processes are best explained by introducing a single element at a time. Not only does this break the process down into manageable chunks, it also keeps the audience focused on the current topic. When you present an entire drawing at once, many people only half-listen to the presentation while they're busy deciphering the full diagram.

You can build drawings in PowerPoint using animation in a single slide or by building a drawing incrementally across multiple slides. Either way, you can build sequential elements of the drawing with consecutive mouse clicks.

Animating a Drawing on One PowerPoint Slide

With animation on a single slide, you can control how each element enters the slide. To build multiple elements in a drawing using animation on a single PowerPoint slide, follow these steps:

1. In Visio, select the part of the drawing that makes up the first element you want on the PowerPoint slide. Either drag across the shapes or Shift+click each shape.

Note Connectors might bend in wrong directions after you separate and paste them in PowerPoint. In Visio, choose View ⇨ Toolbars ⇨ Layout & Routing. Shift+click the connectors in your drawing and then click the Never Reroute tool on the Layout & Routing toolbar.

2. Choose Edit ⇨ Copy.

3. Switch to PowerPoint and add or show the slide where you want to build the elements from the Visio drawing.

Tip The Blank or Title Only slide layouts are ideal for this purpose.

4. Choose Edit ⇨ Paste.

5. Repeat steps 1 through 4 for each succeeding element you want to build on the slide. After pasting the next element, drag the grouping into the position you want on the slide.

6. When all elements are showing in the PowerPoint slide, select the element you want to appear first in the slide show and then choose Slide Show ⇨ Custom Animation.

Note   The animation features are available in Microsoft PowerPoint 2002 and later.

7. In the Custom Animation Task Pane, choose Add Effect ⇨ Entrance, and then choose the entrance effect you want for the first element.

8. Under Modify, specify how you want the effect to behave. For example, you can specify what action triggers the effect, the direction, and the speed.

9. Repeat steps 6 through 8 for each succeeding element in the order you want to introduce them in the animation. You can choose the same or different effects for each element.

10. When you're finished, click Play at the bottom of the Custom Animation Task Pane to show the animation in the current window. You can also click Slide Show in the Custom Animation pane to show your animation in the full Slide Show screen. When you're finished, click a final time or press Esc to return to the normal window.

Tip   To remove an animation effect, right-click it in the Custom Animation Task Pane and then choose Remove.

Building Sequences of PowerPoint Slides

To build multiple elements in a drawing using multiple sequential PowerPoint slides, follow these steps:

1. In PowerPoint, click the New Slide tool on the Formatting toolbar to add a slide for each element of the drawing you want to build.

2. In the Slide Layout Task Pane, click the layout you want for each new slide. The Blank or Title Only slide layouts are ideal for this purpose.

3. In Visio, select the part of the drawing that makes up the first element you want on the PowerPoint slide, as shown in Figure 8-6. Either drag across the shapes or click each shape while pressing Ctrl or Shift, and then choose Edit ⇨ Copy.

4. Switch to PowerPoint, show the first slide of the sequence you're building, and then choose Edit ⇨ Paste, as shown in Figure 8-7.

5. Switch back to Visio again, and, with the first element still selected, Shift+ click the second element and choose Edit ⇨ Copy.

6. To paste the elements for the second slide, switch to PowerPoint, show the second slide of the sequence, and choose Edit ⇨ Paste.

7. Repeat steps 5 through 7 for each additional element you're adding to the sequence.

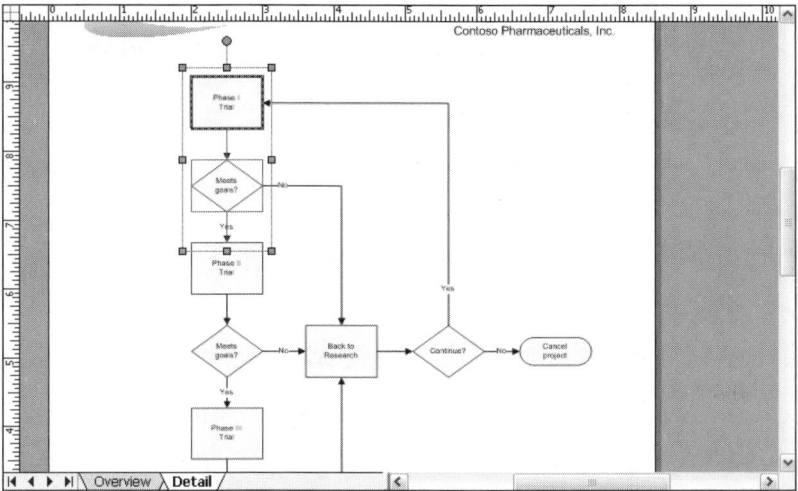

Figure 8-6: Select the part of the drawing that you want to show in the first PowerPoint slide of the sequence.

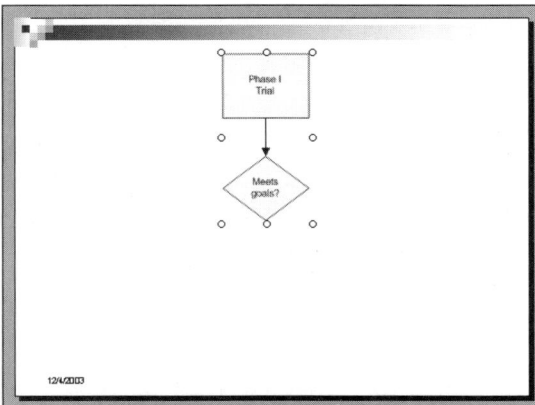

Figure 8-7: The first part of the Visio drawing is pasted in the first PowerPoint slide of the sequence.

Tip

Be sure to paste the element in the same location on each slide. Zooming into the slide and using the ruler can help position the element precisely so that the elements transition smoothly from one slide to the next.

8. When you've added all Visio drawing elements to their PowerPoint slides, choose Slide Show ➪ View Show and then click through the slides to preview the construction of the sequence.

9. After the last slide, click or press Esc to return to the normal PowerPoint view. Make any necessary adjustments to the drawing sequence.

To add a transition effect to a Visio drawing build sequence, follow these steps:

1. In PowerPoint, in the Slides pane, Shift+click to select all the slides in the drawing sequence for which you want the same transition effect.

Note   If the Slides pane is not showing, choose View ⇨ Normal (Restore Panes) and make sure the Slides tab is selected.

2. Choose Slide Show ⇨ Slide Transition.

3. In the Slide Transition Task Pane, click the effect you want when the slides move from one to the next.

4. Under Modify Transition, specify how you want the transition effect to behave. For example, you can specify how fast the effect should occur and whether any sound effect should be associated with the transition.

5. Under Advance Slide, specify the action that moves from one slide to the next.

6. Click Play at the bottom of the Slide Transition Task Pane to show the transition effect for the current slide.

7. Click Slide Show in the Slide Transition Task Pane to show the slide sequence and their transitions in the full Slide Show screen. When you're finished, click a final time or press Esc to return to the normal window.

Summary

You can integrate information between Visio and other applications in a variety of ways. You can create hyperlinks from a Visio drawing to a file in another application, and vice versa. Through the use of OLE technology, you can insert a picture from one application into another and create a dynamic link between the two so that edits instantaneously update both source and target. You can also insert an independent copy of information from another application by embedding an object. With all these integration methods, you can create and use information in the applications best suited to your task, and expect that information to behave as if it were all part of a single integrated application.

✦   ✦   ✦

Importing, Exporting, and Publishing Visio Data to the Web

◆ ◆ ◆ ◆

In This Chapter

File formats for importing and exporting

Exploring methods for importing data into Visio

Importing Outlook appointments into a Visio calendar

Exporting shapes and drawings to other formats

Choosing the right output format for Visio Web pages

Saving drawings as Web page files

Embedding Visio drawings into Web pages

Making Web page navigation easier

◆ ◆ ◆ ◆

Visio provides several ways to integrate Visio drawings with documents in other applications. Depending on your goal and the capabilities of the other applications, you can embed, link, or export data between Visio and other Office applications such as Excel, Word, and PowerPoint, as well as other applications such as databases or CAD programs. In addition, you can share Visio drawings with others who don't have Visio by publishing Visio drawings to the Web or, if you own Adobe Acrobat, by exporting them to Adobe PDF format.

Cross-Reference   To learn about linking and embedding with Visio, see Chapter 8.

Although linking and embedding documents provides more control over document appearance and the changes you can make, you can also export Visio drawings to incorporate Visio data in documents that don't use OLE or to include drawings in HTML files for publication to the Web. You can also export Visio data to store it in Excel spreadsheets, AutoCAD drawings, or ODBC-compliant databases. In many cases in which you want to transfer data in or out of Visio, such as creating organization charts from organizational data in an employee database, you can use features built into Visio templates to import and export data. In this chapter, you learn how to accomplish all these tasks.

Cross-Reference   If you want your Visio drawings to display data from other sources, you can learn how to link Visio drawings to data sources in Chapter 10.

Formats for Importing and Exporting

Visio 2003 supports numerous formats for importing and exporting data. However, this version adds support for a few new formats, while dropping support for several others, as shown in Table 9-1. In addition to a variety of graphics formats, Visio can export data to XML files, Excel spreadsheets, and ODBC-compliant databases, such as Access.

 **New Feature**   In Visio 2003, you can import and export to a new Web graphics standard format: Scalable Vector Graphics. You can also import appointments from Microsoft Outlook into Visio calendars.

Table 9-1 Import/Export Graphic Formats	
Supported Formats	**Formats No Longer Supported**
AutoCAD Drawing (.dwg)	Adobe Illustrator (.ai)
AutoCAD Interchange (.dxf)	ABC Flow Charter 2.0, 3.0, and 4.0 (.af2, .af3)
Compressed Enhanced Metafile (.emz)	CorelDRAW! 3.0 through 7.0 (.cdr)
Enhanced Metafile (.emf)	CorelFLOW (.cfl)
Graphics Interchange Format (.gif)	Computer Graphics Metafile (.cgm)
Joint Photographic Experts Group (JPEG) File Interchange Format (.jpg)	Corel Clipart Format (.CMX)
Portable Network Graphics (.png)	Bentley Microstation Drawing (.dgn)
Scalable Vector Graphics Drawing (.svg)	MicroGrafx Designer 3.1 and 6.0 (.drw, .dsf)
Scalable Vector Graphics Drawing – Compressed (.svgz)	Encapsulated Postscript (.eps)
Tag Image File Format (.tif)	Interchange Graphics Exchange Standard (.igs)
Web Page (.htm, .html)	ZSoft PC Paintbrush (.pcx)
Windows Bitmap (.bmp, .dib)	Macintosh PIST (.pct)
Windows Metafile (.wmf)	PostScript (.ps)

When you export shapes or drawings by choosing File ⇨ Save As, an Output Options dialog box might appear (depending on the export format you select) in which you can specify the settings for the exported file. In addition, the settings vary depending on the file format to which you want to export your drawing. You can find out more about the different export settings by clicking the Help button in the Output Options dialog box.

Tip   If you have Adobe Acrobat installed on your computer, you can create files in PDF format for your Visio drawings by printing them to the Adobe PDF printer.

Cross-Reference   To learn more about importing and exporting CAD drawings in Visio, see Chapter 25.

Using Template Tools to Import and Export

You can import data to create new Visio drawings or export Visio data by using database connections or wizards built into specialized templates. For example, the following templates offer tools for importing and exporting data:

✦ Project Schedules, including Gantt Chart, Timeline, and Calendar

✦ Building Plans, including Space Plan and other types of floor plans

✦ Brainstorming Diagram

✦ Organization Chart

✦ Database Model Diagram

✦ UML Model Diagram

Cross-Reference   To learn how to import data to create specialized Visio drawings, see Chapter 14 for importing organization charts, Chapter 17 for importing project information, or Chapter 19 for importing database models.

Exploring the New SVG Format

Visio 2003 supports the SVG format, albeit with some limitations, as summarized in Table 9-2.

Table 9-2	
SVG Format Features and Limitations	
SVG Support	**SVG Limitations**
Open, Insert, and Save As support for both uncompressed (SVG) and compressed (SVGZ) files.	Scripting, animation, sound, XSLT style sheets, CSS cascading rules, masking and compositing, and metadata are not supported in Visio 2003.
When you open an SVG or SVGZ file, Visio translates SVG symbols into Visio masters and transforms SVG uses and paths into Visio shapes.	SVG parameterized linear gradients map to one of four predefined linear gradients in Visio.

Continued

Table 9-2 (continued)	
SVG Support	**SVG Limitations**
Inserting SVG files as pictures inserts the SVG drawing into a Visio group.	Visio maps SVG formatting elements such as fill and line patterns, fonts, and markers to the closest corresponding Visio formats or creates custom elements.
Saving a drawing with multiple pages as a Web page in SVG format creates a separate SVG file for each page and stores the files in the folder for the Web page.	SVG filter effects are only supported for raster image elements and are limited to brightness, contrast, gamma, transparency, and blur.

Importing Data into Visio

Visio provides several methods for importing graphic files and other documents. For documents that support OLE, you can link or embed files in a Visio drawing. For some drawing types, you can import files by using the import tool located on the specialized menu for the drawing template. For other types of files, you can insert them as pictures in a Visio drawing page or save them as Visio drawings.

Importing Graphic Files into Visio

You can import files saved in other formats simply by opening them in Visio. Choose File ➪ Open, choose the file format you want to import in the Files of Type box, and choose the file you want to import. If you don't see the type of file you want to import in the Files of Type list, save the file to one of the formats that Visio supports and then import the file.

Note   If you want to import a file into an existing drawing, you can choose Insert ➪ Picture to insert the file as a picture on the current drawing page. However, this technique can change properties and set options without your intervention. For example, text boxes can end up on nonprinting layers.

Visio creates a new drawing file and adds the imported file as a picture. However, the picture acts as a shape with selection handles and a rotation handle, which you can use to resize or rotate the picture.

After you import a picture, you can crop the image to modify how much of the picture is visible on the drawing. To crop a picture, display the Picture toolbar by choosing View ➪ Toolbars ➪ Picture and then click the Crop tool. Drag a selection handle on the picture to crop it. If you want to display a different area of the picture, position the pointer over the picture and then drag the hand symbol until the area you want to display appears. When you finish cropping the picture, select another tool such as the Pointer tool.

Cropping a picture does not resize it. The cropped area is a border that reduces the amount of the picture that you see. However, the entire picture is still there. If you want to delete the areas outside the cropped border to reduce the size of the image, choose Format ➪ Picture, select the Compression tab, check the Delete Cropped Areas of Pictures check box, and then click OK.

Importing Your Outlook Appointments to a Visio Calendar

Microsoft Outlook doesn't provide an easy way to publish or distribute calendars. However, with Visio 2003 and Microsoft Outlook 2000 or later, you can import Outlook appointments into a Visio calendar, which you can then format, print, share, or publish. By using the Import Outlook Data Wizard, you can perform the following actions:

✦ Specify a date and time range.

✦ Include appointments that match a subject.

✦ Create a one-week, multiweek, or one-month calendar.

✦ Use Visio calendar tools to format and customize the calendar.

Note   You can create Visio calendars based only on the Gregorian calendar. If your Microsoft Outlook calendar format is set to Arabic, Hebrew, Chinese, Japanese, Korean, or Thai, you can change your Outlook calendar format to Gregorian, use the wizard to import your appointments into Visio, and then change your Outlook calendar format back.

To create a Visio calendar from Outlook appointments, follow these steps:

1. Choose File ➪ New ➪ Project Schedule ➪ Calendar.

2. Choose Calendar ➪ Import Outlook Data Wizard.

3. In the Import Outlook Data Wizard dialog box, select the option to specify whether you want to create a new calendar or add appointments to the selected calendar and then click Next.

Note   The Selected Calendar option is not available if you do not select a calendar before you start the wizard.

4. Specify the start and end dates and the start and end times that you want to scan for appointments.

5. To limit the appointments added to the calendar, click Filter and check the Subject Contains check box in the Filter Outlook Data dialog box. Type the subject text for the appointments you want to import, click OK, and then click Next.

6. If you choose to create a new calendar, specify the calendar type you want to create. You can specify a week, month, or multiple-week calendar, and select the day that begins the week. If you want to shade weekends, select the Yes option. If you want to display dates in a specific format, choose the language for that format in the Language list and click Next.

7. On the last wizard screen, review the calendar properties that you selected. If you want to change any properties, click Back or Cancel. To create the calendar, click Finish.

Note   If appointments overlap, you can resize the calendar or delete some appointments.

Tip   Several people can combine their schedules onto one Visio calendar. To do this, import your appointments to the calendar and then route the calendar to the next person. Each person runs the Import Outlook Data Wizard to add their appointments to the calendar.

Exporting Shapes and Drawings

Because files go through transformations during export and subsequent import into another application, exporting to other formats might alter the appearance of your Visio drawings. If you find that a special fill pattern or other format causes problems, you can apply a different format and then try exporting your drawing again.

Caution   Visio gradient fill patterns might not transfer accurately when you save them in a non-Visio graphics format. If gradient fills don't look the way you want, replace them with plain fill patterns and then export your Visio drawing.

To export Visio shapes or drawings, follow these steps:

1. Display the page you want to export in Visio. If you want to export specific shapes on a page, select them.

2. Choose File ➪ Save As and select the export format you want in the Save As Type drop-down list.

3. Type the name you want in the File Name box and click Save.

4. Depending on the type of format you chose, you might have to specify options in an Output Options or Filter Setup dialog box. After you specify the options you want, click OK. Visio exports the page and selected shapes to a file using the format you chose.

Tip

If you export Visio shapes but they don't appear in the exported file, the shapes might be metafiles, such as Visio Network Equipment shapes or some objects linked or embedded in a Visio drawing. To export metafiles, apply the Ungroup command until Visio converts all the components of the metafile to shapes, and then export the drawing.

You can specify export options for the following formats:

✦ **TIFF**—Data compression, color format, background color, color reduction, transformation, resolution, and size

✦ **JPEG**—Baseline or progressive, color format, background color, quality, transformation, resolution, and size

✦ **GIF**—Data format, background and transparency color, color reduction, transformation, resolution, and size

✦ **PNG**—Same options as GIF

Publishing to the Web

When you want to share information with a large or widely distributed audience, the Web is frequently your first choice. Fortunately, with every release, Visio makes it easier to publish Visio drawings to the Web. In Visio 2003, you can publish Visio drawings to the Web by saving Visio drawings as their own Web pages or as part of existing Web pages, saving them as graphics files that you can embed in Web pages, or saving them as Visio XML files that you can open in a Web browser.

Choosing an Output Format for a Visio Web Page

When you save a Visio drawing as a Web page, you can choose from several output formats. The best format depends on what you are trying to accomplish by publishing the Web page as well as what types of browsers your audience uses. You can use Table 9-3 to help determine which output format works best with the browsers your audience is likely to use. In addition, you can evaluate output formats based on the tasks you want to perform in the following lists.

Saving Visio drawings as Web pages is effective when you want to

✦ Export several pages of a multiple-page drawing at once

✦ Maintain navigational links in shapes when you publish to a Web page

✦ Include reports that users can view easily

Saving drawings in JPG, GIF, PNG, or SVG format is preferable when you want to

✦ Insert a Visio drawing into an existing HTML Web page

✦ Publish only a portion of a drawing

Table 9-3
Browser and Output Format Compatibility

Output Format	Earliest Browser Supported	Internet Explorer 5.0 or Later Behavior	Other Browser and Version Behavior
VML with alternate browser support	Any HTML 2.0–compliant browser that supports frames	Drawing is displayed in VML and scalable with browser window	Drawing is displayed in JPEG, GIF, or PNG, but is not scalable
		Left frame includes Go To Page, Pan and Zoom, Details, and Search Pages	Left frame shows pages as links
VML only	Internet Explorer 5.0	Drawing is displayed in VML and is scalable with browser window	Not supported
		Left frame includes Go To Page, Pan and Zoom, Details, and Search Pages	
SVG with alternate browser support	SVG Viewer and any HTML 2.0–compliant browser that supports frames	Drawing is displayed in SVG with SVG Viewer or SVG-compatible browser; otherwise, as JPEG, GIF, or PNG.	Drawing is displayed in SVG with SVG Viewer or SVG-compatible browser
		Left frame includes Go To Page, Details, and Search Pages	Left frame shows pages as links
SVG only	SVG Viewer and Internet Explorer 5	Drawing is displayed in SVG with SVG Viewer or SVG-compatible browser; otherwise, as JPEG, GIF, or PNG	Drawing is displayed in SVG with SVG Viewer or SVG-compatible browser
		Left frame includes Go To Page, Details, and Search Pages	Left frame shows pages as links

Output Format	Earliest Browser Supported	Internet Explorer 5.0 or Later Behavior	Other Browser and Version Behavior
JPEG or GIF	Internet Explorer 3.0, Netscape Navigator 3.0, and any HTML 2.0–compliant browser that supports frames	Drawing is displayed in JPEG or GIF and is not scalable.	Drawing is displayed in JPEG or GIF and is not scalable
		Left frame includes Go To Page, Details, and Search Pages	Left frame shows pages as links
PNG	Internet Explorer 4.0 or later; Netscape Navigator 6.0 or later	Drawing is displayed in PNG and is not scalable	Drawing is displayed in PNG and is not scalable
		Left frame includes Go To Page, Details, and Search Pages	Left frame shows pages as links

Saving Drawings As Web Pages

Whether your Visio drawings contain one page or several, it's easy to transform them into Web pages. When you use Microsoft Internet Explorer 5.0 or later and save Visio drawings as Web pages, you can navigate around the drawing, zoom in and out, display custom properties for shapes, search the drawing for shapes, or view reports associated with the drawing, as illustrated in Figure 9-1. When you save a Visio drawing as a Web page, by default Visio creates HTML frame pages with frames for drawing pages and controls, and generates HTML source code.

Note In order for colors to appear properly when you display a Visio drawing as a Web page, your system must have more than 256 colors. Even then, colors don't always match exactly when you display a Visio drawing on the Web.

To save a Visio drawing as a Web page, follow these steps:

1. Open the Visio drawing that you want to publish to the Web and then choose File ➪ Save As Web Page.

2. In the Save As dialog box, navigate to the folder in which you want to save the file and type the name for the Web page file in the File Name box.

3. To specify the title you want to appear in the browser title bar, click Change Title, and then, in the Page Title dialog box, type the title you want, and click OK.

4. Click Publish to specify the Web page publishing options, which are described in more detail in the next section.

5. If you didn't specify publishing options, click Save in the Save As dialog box. If you did click Publish to set additional options, click OK.

Ctrl+click shape to view custom properties

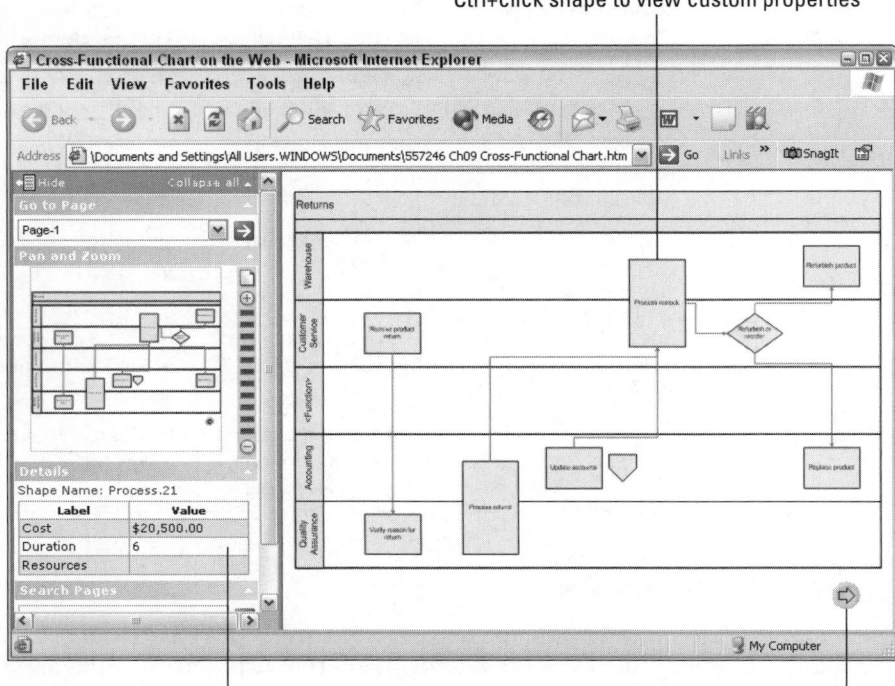

Custom properties for clicked shape   Hyperlink navigation shape

Figure 9-1: Visio includes controls and other information in the left frame of a Web page.

Specifying Web Page Publishing Options

When you save a Visio drawing as a Web page, you can specify which pages to publish, which controls appear in the left frame of the Web page, and the output format and additional display options, such as the target resolution you want. To specify Web page publishing options, click Publish in the Save As Web Page dialog box.

When you select the General tab, you can specify the following options:

✦ **Specify pages to publish** — To specify a range of pages to publish, select the Pages: From To option and type the page numbers for the first and last pages in the range.

✦ **Display search and navigation controls** — Check Go to Page and Search Pages in the Publishing Options list.

Tip   If you don't want a left frame in your browser window and don't need Go to Page to navigate between Web pages, uncheck Go to Page, Search Pages, Details, and Pan and Zoom.

✦ **Display custom properties for shapes** — If you want to display custom properties in a table on the left side of the browser window, check Details in the Publishing Options list.

Note To view custom properties in the left frame, you can Ctrl+click a shape that contains custom properties on the Web page or click the shape and then press Ctrl+Enter.

✦ **Display pan and zoom controls** — Check Pan and Zoom in the Publishing Options list. Pan and zoom controls are available only when you use the VML output format in Internet Explorer 5.0 or later.

✦ **Publish reports** — Check each report you want to publish in the Publishing Options list. Reports appear on separate pages that you can access by using the Go to Page control in the left frame of the Web page.

Note If no shapes in your drawing match the report query, Visio creates the Web page without the report.

✦ **Open Web page in browser** — To open the Web page in your browser immediately after you save it, check Automatically Open Web Page in Browser, under Additional Options.

✦ **Organize supporting files in a folder** — This option creates a subfolder for storing the supporting files for the Web page. When you move your Web page to another folder, the supporting files folder moves with it automatically.

You can specify the following options on the Advanced tab:

✦ **Specify output format** — To specify the output format for the Web page, choose the format you want in the Output Formats drop-down list. VML produces the best results for displaying controls in the left frame of the Web page. VML and SVG support scalable graphics, so the Web page output resizes if the browser window resizes.

Note Because VML and SVG require more recent browser versions, it's a good idea to specify an alternate format so that the Web page still opens in older browsers. In addition, you must install an SVG viewer to view Web pages in SVG format. If you open a Web page in SVG format without an SVG viewer, the page appears in a format such as GIF.

✦ **Specify an alternate format for older browsers** — To ensure that your Visio Web page works with a wide range of browsers, including earlier versions, check the Provide Alternate Format for Older Browsers check box and select the format you want, such as JPG or GIF.

✦ **Specify the target resolution** — If you are creating a file in JPG, GIF, or PNG format, specify the smallest resolution that you expect people to use to view your Web pages.

Note   You don't have to specify the Target Monitor resolution for scalable formats such as VML and SVG.

✦ **Embed a saved Visio Web page in another Web page** — Specify the Web page in which you want to embed the saved Web page, as described in the next section.

✦ **Specify color scheme** — If you want to apply the color scheme for your Visio drawing to the resulting Web page, select the color scheme in the Style Sheet drop-down list. This color scheme applies colors to the left frame and report pages that match the color scheme for the Visio drawing.

Caution   Visio looks for the supporting files for a Web page based on the root file's name. If you rename a root HTML file, Visio displays a warning that renaming the file will break the links to the supporting file folder. Instead of renaming a root file, open it in Visio, save it with the new name (which also creates a new subfolder), and delete the old _files folder.

Files That Visio Creates for Web Pages

Web pages require a lot of files, so it's helpful that Visio creates all the files you need for a Web page and stores them in a convenient location. However, if you publish Visio drawings as Web pages often, it's a good idea to understand what files Visio creates and where they're located.

When you save a drawing as a Web page, Visio creates a root HTML file for your Visio drawing in the folder that you specify. In addition, Visio creates a subfolder in the same location using the same name as the root HTML file but with _files appended to the end. Visio stores the files required for the Web page in the subfolder. Because of this naming convention, the subfolder moves with its root HTML file; if you delete the HTML file, the subfolder is deleted as well. However, when you move HTML files, you might have to edit them to update pointers to graphics files.

For each Visio drawing, Visio creates the following files:

✦ A root HTML file with the name you specified, such as AcmeOrg03.htm

✦ Graphics files of the output format you specified for each published page in the Visio drawing, such as vml_1.htm, and the alternate format, such as gif_1.gif, if you chose to include an alternate format for older browsers.

✦ Other files that support the publishing options you selected when you published the Web page, such as graphics (.gif) for controls, style sheet (.css), script (.js), and data files (.xml)

Embedding Visio Drawings in Web Pages

If your organization already has a Web page template, you can create a Visio Web page to embed in your company's template instead of creating one to stand on its own. If you want to distribute a drawing electronically but don't need to show custom property data or provide navigation tools, you can also embed Visio drawings as images using GIF, JPEG, or PNG format.

To embed a Visio Web page in another HTML page, you add an <IFRAME> tag to the host HTML page where you want the Visio drawing to appear, and specify the host page in the Save as Web Page dialog box. Visio provides a sample template, `Basic .htm`, in the Host in Web Page list if you need an example of how to use the `<IFRAME>` tag.

To use an existing HTML template to display a Visio Web page, follow these steps:

1. Edit your HTML template to include the following HTML tag:

   `<IFRAME src="##VIS_SAW_FILE##">`

   Note This tag embeds the Visio Web page into your HTML template. It is case-sensitive and refers to the HTML output file that Visio creates when you create a Visio Web page.

2. Choose File ⇨ Save As Web Page and specify the folder and name for the Web page in the Save As Web Page dialog box.

3. Click Publish and select the Advanced tab.

4. Under Host in Web Page, browse to the HTML template file that you want to use as the host page and click OK.

   Note Visio stores the Basic.htm template in the Visio path, usually `C:\Program Files\Microsoft Office\Visio 11\1033\`. Your customized HTML templates appear in the Host in Web Page drop-down list if you store copies of them in this same folder.

Adding Hyperlink Navigation Shapes to Drawings

Navigating between shapes and pages is easy when you add hyperlinks to the shapes on your drawings. When you create a Web page from a Visio drawing, Visio saves these hyperlinks in shapes, so people viewing the drawing on the Web can navigate to the information they want. However, Visio doesn't indicate the presence of a hyperlink until you position the pointer over a shape with a hyperlink. You can make your drawing easier to navigate by adding hyperlink navigation shapes to your drawing before you save it as a Web page. People viewing the drawing can navigate simply by clicking the navigation shapes on the Web page.

Other Ways to Reference Visio Drawings in HTML

You can include links to Visio Web pages in other Web pages or reference images of Visio drawings, if you don't need special features such as custom properties. To include a link to your Visio Web page, you can add a tag to your HTML template, such as the following:

```
<a href="##VIS_SAW_FILE##">My Drawing</a>
```

To reference a graphics file in a Web page, save your Visio drawing in JPEG, GIF, or PNG format. Then add an `<IMG>` tag to your HTML code, such as `<IMG SRC="process_flow1 .gif" >`. Visio drawings saved as graphics do not include custom properties or navigation controls, such as hyperlinks.

To keep links intact, you can print a Visio drawing to a PostScript printer to create a PostScript file. Then, you can use Acrobat Distiller to create a PDF format file of the drawing to include in the HTML file.

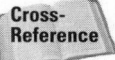
Cross-Reference

To learn about creating hyperlinks in your Visio drawings, see Chapter 8.

Although you can add hyperlinks to any shape you want, the Borders and Titles stencil includes several built-in navigation shapes, Hyperlink Button, Hyperlink Circle 1, and Hyperlink Circle 2, that automatically open the Hyperlinks dialog box when you drag them onto a page. After you add one of these hyperlink shapes to a drawing, you can change the icon that appears in the shape to indicate the function of the associated hyperlink. Table 9-4 includes the names of the icons you can use.

Table 9-4 Hyperlink Icons	
Back	Forward
Up	Down
Home	Help
Directory	Info
Search	Mail
Photo	None

To add a navigation shape to a drawing, follow these steps:

1. Drag one of the hyperlink shapes from the Borders and Titles stencil onto a drawing page.

2. In the Hyperlinks dialog box, specify the address or sub-address for the hyperlink and click OK.

3. To change the icon in the shape, right-click the hyperlink shape and choose Change Icon from the shortcut menu. Select the icon you want in the Icon Type drop-down list and click OK.

Summary

You can import and export Visio data to other formats such as Excel spreadsheets, AutoCAD drawings, ODBC-compliant databases, graphic files, and Web pages. Many of the templates that are built into Visio include tools that simplify the task of importing and exporting data to specific types of drawings. However, to import data from another source into Visio without a specialized tool, you need to select the type of file in the Open dialog box and open the file you want. To export data to another format, you use File ➪ Save As, selecting the type of format you want in the File of Type drop-down list. When you want to publish Visio drawings to the Web, the Save As Web Page command provides numerous options for specifying the contents and functionality of the resulting Web page.

✦   ✦   ✦

Linking Shapes with Data

Visio drawings are a great way to convey information. However, by linking shapes on your Visio drawings to databases, you can transform your drawings into visual and dynamic representations of the data stored in databases. For example, you might link furniture specifications from an asset database to the furniture shapes on a Visio office layout, even sizing the furniture on the plan based on the dimensions in the database. Shape-database links can be bi-directional, so you can make changes in your drawing and propagate them to the database table, or vice versa. Visio can link to any database that supports the Open Database Connectivity (ODBC) standard, which includes Oracle, Informix, Microsoft Access, and Microsoft Excel.

You can link shapes on a drawing page to database records, but it's usually more effective to link masters so that shapes are linked as soon as you drop them on a page. You can create masters that link to any record in a database table and select the record you want when you drag the master to a page. You can also create masters for each record. For example, if you have a database table, such as the computer equipment for your next client installation, you can create a stencil with a master for each component and create an equipment layout by dragging the masters onto the page. You can also export shape data to a database, including basic shape properties such as the shape's name and location on the drawing page, as well as custom properties.

No matter how you decide to use links between shapes and databases, Visio makes it easy to keep your drawings and databases synchronized. You can add commands to synchronize your data to the shortcut menus for shapes or drawing pages or specify an interval and let Visio update your shapes and linked database records automatically. In this chapter, I show you how to link your Visio drawings to database fields to synchronize your drawings with data stored in a database or to store shape information in a database.

Understanding Links Between Shapes and Databases

Databases store data in fields in records, which in turn are stored in tables. Although you view shapes on a drawing page, Visio stores shape data such as name, position, and custom properties in the cells of ShapeSheets, which look much like spreadsheets. Visio connects shapes with databases by linking cells in ShapeSheets to fields in database records.

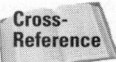

Chapter 33 explains how to use ShapeSheets to customize shapes.

You use a Data Source Name (DSN) created in the Open Database Connectivity (ODBC) Administrator to specify both the database that contains the data you want and the driver to use with it. Whether you use the Link to Database or Export to Database commands, the Database Wizard, or the Database Export Wizard, you can choose an existing DSN or create a new one.

When you link shapes to databases, each shape in a drawing corresponds to a record (or row) in a database table, and each linked field in the record corresponds to one cell in the shape's ShapeSheet, as shown in Figure 10-1. With a link between a ShapeSheet cell and a database field, you can change the value in the cell to update the field, or vice versa.

You can link Visio shapes with a database without a database application installed on your computer. However, you must have the database application installed if you want to open the database directly to edit its records.

Although you usually link custom properties to database fields, you can link other ShapeSheet cells as well. For example, you can propagate equipment dimensions in a database table to the Width and Height cells in a ShapeSheet to specify a shape's size. If the ShapeSheet doesn't have cells suitable for linking to your database fields, the Database Wizard or Link to Database command creates new cells in the Custom Properties section of the ShapeSheet.

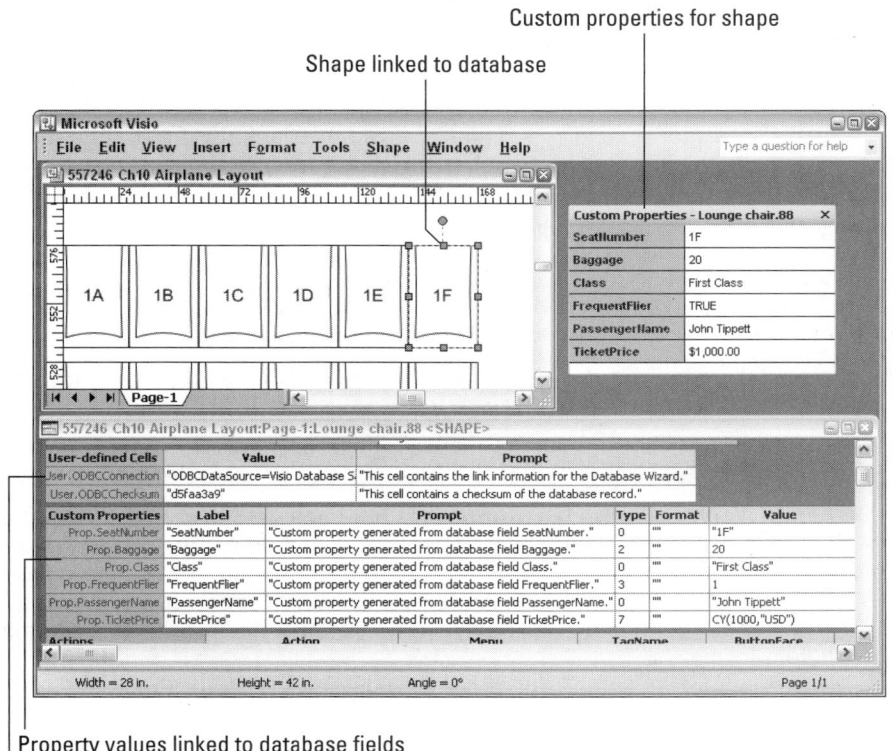

Custom properties for shape

Shape linked to database

Property values linked to database fields

Connection string for link to database

Figure 10-1: ShapeSheets cells connect to database fields.

Visio also creates a `User.ODBCConnection` cell in the User-Defined Cells section of the ShapeSheet to specify information about the connection to the database table. This cell is a concatenation of several lines of text separated by vertical bars. By separating the lines, you can see the components of the connection string:

```
ODBCDataSource=Visio Database Samples
ODBCQualifier=C:\PROGRA~1\MICROS~2\Visio11\1033\DBSAMPLE
ODBCTable=Airplane - Filled Seats
1
SeatNumber=Prop.SeatNumber
5
Baggage=Prop.Baggage=32
Class=Prop.Class=0
FrequentFlier=Prop.FrequentFlier=0
PassengerName=Prop.PassengerName=0
TicketPrice=Prop.TicketPrice=111
```

The connection string includes the following information:

✦ **ODBCDataSource=<*name*>**—The name of the data source to which the shape is linked. The example uses a sample data source installed with Visio.

✦ **ODBCQualifier=<*name*>**—If your data source includes more than one database, this parameter specifies the direct path to the database to which the shape is linked.

✦ **ODBCTable=<*name*>**—This is the name of the table to which the shape is linked.

✦ **<*number*>**—The fourth line in the example represents the number of key fields you specified. The example uses only one key field.

✦ **<*Field Name*>=<*name*>**—The fifth line in the example specifies the field and the ShapeSheet cell used to store the key.

✦ **<*number*>**—The sixth line in the example represents the number of fields linked to shape properties. In the example, five fields are linked.

✦ **<*Field Name*>=<*name*>=<*number*>**—For each field linked to a ShapeSheet cell, the connection string identifies the linked field name and the ShapeSheet cell name to which it is linked. The number at the end of the line represents the constant for the Evaluate As setting. For example, 0 represents Value, whereas 111 represents Currency. In the example, lines 7 through 11 specify field information.

Linking Drawings to Databases

By linking your Visio drawings to databases, you can transfer data between shapes and database records. You can update Visio drawings to show the current values in your databases or update your database with changes made in Visio drawings. For example, you can maintain a flowchart of a process with the estimated cost, the duration, and the assigned department from a reengineering database. Then, if you notice an error in the flowchart, you can update the database with the correction made on the Visio diagram. You can use either the Database Wizard or the Link to Database command to link drawings and databases in the following ways:

✦ Link shapes to records in databases.

✦ Create Visio drawings that represent the data in database tables.

✦ Create masters linked to database records.

Limitations of the Database Wizard

Links between Visio shapes and tables in databases have the following limitations:

✦ **String Length** — To store ODBC strings in Visio cells and fields, they must be smaller than 64K characters.

✦ **Binary Field Length** — To store ODBC binary fields in Visio cells and fields, they must be less than 32K.

✦ **Precise Numbers** — Visio stores numeric values as double floating-point numbers, truncating numbers with greater precision to 17 significant digits.

✦ **Database Key Field** — You can't use a field of the SQL_TIMESTAMP type as a primary key.

✦ **ID Replication** — You can't update replication IDs in Microsoft Access.

✦ **Timestamps** — You can't update Timestamp fields when you use an Informix database.

✦ **Row Deletion** — You can't delete rows in Excel when you use the Excel ODBC driver. The Database Wizard indicates deleted rows by setting text fields to #ROW DELETED# and numeric fields to 0. For wizard operations, such as Update, Select, and Refresh, the values 0 and #ROW DELETED# are invalid keys.

Creating Connections to Data Sources

Before you can link a Visio drawing to a database or other source of data, you must define and select an ODBC data source. By defining a data source, you specify the following:

✦ The name and location of the database you want to use

✦ The driver to use with the database

✦ The type of data source

✦ Who can access it

✦ A unique name for the data source so it's easy to find later

You can define data sources in Visio with the Export to Database and Link to Database commands and the Database wizards. You can also define data sources from the Windows Start menu by Choosing Control Panel ⇨ Administrative Tools ⇨ Data Sources (ODBC).

Each Visio database command and wizard includes similar steps for defining a data source. To define a data source using the Link to Database command, follow these steps:

1. Choose Tools ⇨ Add-ons ⇨ Visio Extras ⇨ Link to Database and then click Create. This command is not available unless a drawing is open.

2. Specify who can access the data source. In the Create New Data Source dialog box, choose one of the following options for type of data source and then click Next:

   - **File Data Source** — You can copy a file data source to other computers or network locations. Any user who can access the data source can use it.

   - **User Data Source** — This Creates a data source available only on the current computer and visible only to the current user.

   - **System Data Source** — This Creates a data source available only on the current computer but accessible to any user who logs on to the system.

3. Select the 32-bit ODBC driver you want to use in the Driver list and click Next.

4. In the driver-specific dialog box that opens, type a data source name. Because the functionality of ODBC drivers varies, it's a good idea to include the type of data source in the name, along with a brief description of the data, such as `Employees_Excel2000`. After you specify the location and name for the data source, click Next and then click Finish.

> **Note**
>
> By default, Visio creates data sources in `C:\Program Files\CommonFiles\ODBC\Data Sources`. If you create data sources in the default location, they appear in the list of available data sources. However, you can create data sources anywhere you want. If you don't see your data source in the list, click Browse and navigate to the location of your data source.

5. If you're creating an Access data source, click Select to specify an existing database for the DSN. Select the database file you want to use and click OK. For example, to use the sample database included with Microsoft Office, navigate to `C:\Program Files\Microsoft Office\Office10\Samples` in the Select Database Dialog box, select `Northwind.mdb` in the Database Name list, and click OK. The ODBC Data Source Administrator creates the data source and adds it to the list of available data sources. When you complete this step, you can continue with the Link to Database command to select and link to the data source, as described in the next section.

> **Note**
>
> If you're creating an Excel-based data source, you must specify the version of Excel and then select the Excel .xls file you want to use as the database. After you select the file to use, click Options and uncheck the Read Only check box. You can create tables in Excel files by clicking Define Table on the Choose a Database Object to Connect to screen in the Database Wizard. Visio stores tables created in Excel 5.0 or later as separate worksheets in the Excel file and creates a named range for the records.

Caution To use an Excel workbook as a data source, you must create a named range in a worksheet that includes all the rows and columns of data. Visio uses the values in the first row of the named range as table column names.

Linking Drawing Shapes to Database Records

You can use the Database Wizard or the Link to Database command to create a link between your drawing and database records. For example, if you have a furniture plan drawn, you can link the furniture shapes to records in a facilities management database that includes fields such as manufacturer, model, color, cost, department, and employee. The Database Wizard feeds you steps one at a time, whereas the Link to Database command provides the features you need to create a link in one dialog box.

To link shapes using the Link to Database command, follow these steps:

1. Select the shapes you want to link to a database and then choose Tools ➪ Add-Ons ➪ Visio Extras ➪ Link to Database.

2. Select the data source you want to use. If you select Excel Files as the data source, select the Excel file (.xls) that you want to use in the Select Workbook dialog box, uncheck the Read Only check box, and click OK.

Note If you don't see your data source in the list, click Browse, navigate to your data source folder, and select the data source. For example, to use the sample database included with Office, in the File Open dialog box, navigate to `C:\Program Files\Common Files\ODBC\Data Sources`, select the data source file you want, and click Open. You can click Create to create a new data source, as described in "Creating Connections to Data Sources" in this chapter.

3. If you can access multiple databases through your data source, select the database you want to use in the Qualifier drop-down list. To filter the list of tables to those for a specific owner, select an owner in the Owner drop-down list.

Note If you use a data source based on Excel, Access, or another application that creates single databases, the Qualifier box shows the database path and name, and the Owner box is set to All Users.

4. In the Table/View list, select the database table you want to use. For Excel data sources, the Table/View list shows the worksheets within the Excel workbook.

Note You can create a new table or worksheet in the data source by clicking New.

5. If you want to change the default mapping between database fields and ShapeSheet cells, select a field and click Modify. Select the ShapeSheet cell to which you want to link. If you want to change the data type for the field, select a type in the Evaluate As drop-down list. If you want to use a field as the primary key, select Yes in the Key drop-down list.

Note   Click Add or Delete to create new links or delete existing links between fields and cells.

6. Click OK to create the links.

7. To associate a shape on a drawing to a specific record in the table in the data source, right-click the shape and choose Select Database Record. In the Key Value list, select the record you want and click OK to insert the record values into the linked ShapeSheet cells.

The Database Wizard divides the steps in the Link to Database command into screens for each step in the process. To use the Database Wizard to link shapes to database records, follow these steps:

1. Select the shapes on a drawing that you want to link to a database.

2. Choose Tools ➪ Add-ons ➪ Visio Extras ➪ Database Wizard. Click Next on the first screen.

3. Make sure the Link Shapes to Database Records option is selected and then click Next.

4. Select the Shapes in a Drawing option and click Next.

5. By default, Visio selects the current drawing, current drawing page, and the shapes you selected in step 1. To link shapes on a different drawing, select the drawing in the drop-down list or click Browse to open the drawing file you want to link. Select the page in the Page drop-down list. You can select the shapes you want in the Shape Names and IDs list or click Select Shapes to select shapes by clicking them on the drawing. When you are finished selecting shapes, click Next.

6. Select the data source to which you want to link.

7. Select the table you want to use and click Next. Continue to step through the screens to specify the primary key, events and commands to add to shortcut menus, and field mapping. Click Finish to create the links.

8. To associate a shape to a specific record in the data source, right-click the shape and choose Select Database Record. In the Key Value list, select the record you want and click OK to insert the record values into the linked ShapeSheet cells or custom properties.

Linking Masters to Databases

Although you can link shapes on drawings to database records, you can create drawings with links to databases more effectively by using masters already configured with database links. For example, you can create office furniture masters that pull model information, such as manufacturer, model, cost, and color, from a furniture database. When you drag a master onto a page, the shape comes with custom properties pre-populated with the manufacturer, model, and cost. You can use the color from the database to specify the shape's fill color so the layout shows the color scheme for the office.

You can also create masters that link to any database record. Using an example from the Visio samples database, you can create a master for an airplane seat and link that master to a database with information about the seats in a plane. After you build a diagram of the seats for a Boeing 767, you can link each seat shape to a seat number in the database.

Generating Masters from Each Database Record

You can create a master for each record in a database table. For example, if you want to create a flowchart that shows every process in your business process reengineering database, you can generate masters for each record and then drag each master onto the drawing page to build your diagram. The shapes on the drawing are automatically linked to the appropriate record in the database. To generate masters from a database table, follow these steps:

1. Choose Tools ➪ Add-Ons ➪ Visio Extras ➪ Database Wizard. Click Next on the first screen.

2. Choose the Generate New Masters from a Database option and click Next.

3. In the Stencil box, select the stencil that contains the Visio master that you want to use as the basis for new masters. Choose the master in the Masters list and click Next.

4. Continue through the wizard to select the data source, the table, and the primary key.

5. In the Choose the Database Link and Naming Options screen, check the Keep Database Links in New Masters check box if you want to create a bi-directional link between the database and the masters. Select an option to either generate master names based on the values in the primary key field or on the original Visio master name. Click Next.

Note If the master you use doesn't show custom properties in text fields, it's easier to identify the master you want when you name the master using the primary key. For example, using the airplane seat number as the primary key, each airplane seat master would include the seat number in the name, such as Seat.2a.

6. Specify the links between ShapeSheet cells and database fields and click Next.

7. Select an option to create a new stencil or append the linked masters to an existing stencil. Click Next and then click Finish.

8. To save the stencil containing the linked masters, choose File ➪ Save, specify a folder and a stencil name, and then click Save.

9. To use the stencil, save it, close it, and then reopen it to use it on a drawing.

Linking Masters to Specific Records

When you want every instance of a master to use the same information, you can link masters to specific records in an existing database table. For example, you can link an equipment master to the database record that contains the specifications for the piece of equipment so that each instance of that master includes the specification values, such as amps, operating temperature, and BTUs. To create a master linked to a specific database record, open the master for editing. Use the Link to Database command to link the master to a data source. Then, in the master drawing window, right-click the master and choose Select Database Record to specify the record with the data for that master. Choose File ⇨ Save to save the stencil.

Note You can also create a master linked to a record by creating a link between a shape on a drawing page and a database record and then dragging the linked shape onto an editable stencil.

Creating Masters That Link to Any Database Record

You can link masters, such as furniture shapes, to database information, such as model lists, without specifying a record for the master. When you drag a master such as this onto the drawing page, you choose the database record you want the instance to represent. To create a master that can link to any record in a database table, follow these steps:

1. Choose Tools ⇨ Add-Ons ⇨ Visio Extras ⇨ Database Wizard. Click Next on the first wizard screen.

2. Select Link Shapes to Database Records and click Next.

3. Select the Master(s) on a Document Stencil option to link masters specific to a drawing, or Master(s) on a Visio Stencil to link masters that you can use on any drawing. Click Next.

4. Select a document stencil or click Browse to select a Visio stencil or one of your custom stencils. By default, Visio opens the File Open dialog box at the My Shapes folder.

5. Choose the master you want to link and click Next.

6. Continue through the Database Wizard screens to select a data source, the table to which you want to link, the primary key, events and shape shortcut menu commands, and the ShapeSheet cell that holds the primary key value.

7. On the Link ShapeSheet Cells to Database Fields screen, click a ShapeSheet cell in the Cells list, click the corresponding database field in the Database Fields list, and then click Add. Visio adds the shape-field link in the Links list. When no database fields are visible in the Database Fields list, click Next and then click Finish.

8. To save the stencil containing the linked masters, choose File ⇨ Save, specify a folder and descriptive stencil name, and click Save.

Creating Drawings from Database Records

You can use the Database Wizard to generate a Visio drawing that contains a shape for each record in an existing database table. For example, if you have a database or spreadsheet that delineates the computer equipment you're going to install at a client site, you can use the Database Wizard to create a layout drawing with shapes linked to each record. Then you can move the shapes into the layout you want.

To create a drawing based on a database table, follow these steps:

1. Follow the steps in the preceding section to create a master that links to a database table.

2. Choose Tools ➪ Add-Ons ➪ Visio Extras ➪ Database Wizard. Click Next on the first wizard screen.

3. Select the Create a Linked Drawing or Modify an Existing One option and click Next.

4. Select the Create a Drawing Which Represents a Database Table option and click Next.

5. Select the Create New Drawing option and click Next.

6. Continue through the wizard to select a drawing template, options to use to monitor the drawing, and information about the data source to use.

Note

If the database table includes data for the x and y coordinates of the shape's position, be sure to uncheck the Automatically Distribute Shape on Page check box and the Automatically Scale the Drawing Page check box.

7. When the Select a Visio Master Shape screen appears, click Browse and navigate to the stencil you saved in step 1. Select the linked master and click Finish to create a new drawing with an instance of the master for every record in the table, such as the airplane layout shown in Figure 10-2.

Shapes laid out based on positions in database table

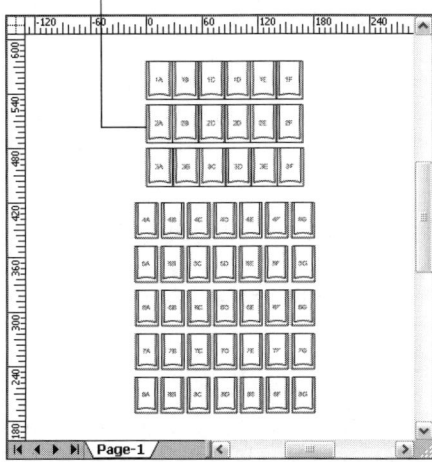

Figure 10-2: You can generate a drawing based on the records in a database table.

Exporting Shape Data to Databases

You can export shape data and custom properties to a database table using either the Database Export Wizard or the Export to Database command. In addition to stepping through the process, the Database Export Wizard includes an option to export all shapes on a layer. However, if you don't want to export by layers, you can follow a more streamlined process by choosing Tools ➪ Export to Database.

To export shape data to a database with the Database Export Wizard, follow these steps:

1. Choose Tools ➪ Add-Ons ➪ Visio Extras ➪ Database Export Wizard and click Next.

2. Select the drawing file that you want to export and then select the page you want to export and click Next.

3. Click one of the following options for the shapes you want to export and then click Next:

   - **All shapes on the page** — This option exports all shapes on the selected page.

   - **Selected shapes on the page** — This option exports any shapes you selected before you started the wizard. To select additional shapes, click Select Shapes.

   - **All shapes on one or more layers** — Select the layers you want to export in the Layers list to export all shapes on those layers.

4. For each Visio item you want to export, select the item in the Visio Cells and Fields list and click Add. Visio adds the cell or field you chose to the Cells and Fields to Export list. Click Next.

Note   Cell names for custom properties begin with Prop. followed by the custom property name. For example, the cell name for the custom property Duration is Prop.Duration.

5. Select the data source to which you want to export and click Next.

6. In the Table Name list, select the table to which you want to export the Visio data. If you want to create a new table in the data source, type the name of the table in the Table Name box.

7. To specify a key to uniquely identify each record, type a name in the Key Field box. By default, the key field is the ShapeID, which is the shape name with a sequential ID generated when you add the shape to a drawing page. To use the GUID as the unique identifier, select GUID in the Key Type drop-down list. Click Next.

Note   If the ODBC driver does not support primary keys, the Make Key Field the Primary Key for Table check box is grayed out.

8. To modify the default field mapping that Visio defines, in the Specify the Export Mapping Details screen, select an item in the Visio Data list, modify one or more of the following options, and then click Next:

- **Evaluate Data As** — Specify the data type or units for the Visio item.

- **Field Name** — Modify the field name to use in the export data source.

- **Field Type** — Modify the field type, which is a broad category such as Number.

9. If you want to re-export data by right-clicking the drawing page, make sure the Add Export Right Mouse Action to the Drawing Page check box is checked.

10. Click Next and then click Finish to export the data.

Tip When you export shape data with the Database Export Wizard, the wizard stores export-related information with the drawing page. If you want to export the data again after you have modified the drawing, right-click the drawing page and choose Database Table Export.

Keeping Drawings and Databases in Sync

Visio provides several methods for manually and automatically synchronizing the data in your linked Visio drawings and databases. When you link shapes on a Visio drawing to a database record, Visio adds four commands for maintaining database links to each shape's shortcut menu. In addition, Visio provides several add-ons that help you update many shapes at once.

To update a single shape or database record, right-click a shape and then choose one of the following commands on the shape's shortcut menu:

✦ **Select Database Record** — Specify the database record to which you want to link the shape.

✦ **Refresh Shape Properties** — Replaces the shape's properties with data from the linked database record.

✦ **Update Database Record** — Replaces the data in the database record with values from the shape's custom properties.

✦ **Delete Shape and Record** — Removes the shape on the drawing page and the linked record in the data source.

Note If you want to remove the links to a database while keeping the shape on a page, run the Database Wizard as if you were linking shapes. In the screen in which you select a drawing, a page, and shapes, select the shapes whose links you want to break and then click Remove Links.

If you want to refresh or update all the shapes on a drawing page, use one of the following add-ons:

✦ **Database Refresh** — Replaces each shape's properties with data from its linked database record

✦ **Database Update** — Replaces the data in each database record with values from the linked shape's properties

Adding Drawing Page Commands to Synchronize Shapes

When you use the Database Wizard to links shapes and databases, you can add commands to synchronize links to shape or drawing shortcut menus. In addition, you can specify what happens when you drop a shape or copy and paste one on a page. If you use the Link to Database command to link your shapes, you can use the Database Wizard later to add synchronizing commands to the drawing page.

To add shortcut commands to a drawing page, follow these steps:

1. Choose Tools ➪ Add-Ons ➪ Visio Extras ➪ Database Wizard. Click Next on the first wizard screen.

2. Click the Create a Linked Drawing or Modify an Existing One option and click Next.

3. Click the Add Database Actions and Events to a Drawing Page option and click Next.

4. Select the drawing file and page to which you want to add actions and events and then click Next. Check one or more of the following actions or events:

   • **Refresh shapes on page** — Adds a command to refresh all shapes on the page with the data from their linked database records

   • **Update shapes on page** — Adds a command to update the database records with values from the shapes on the page

   • **Refresh linked shapes on document open** — Each time you open the drawing file, Visio refreshes ShapeSheet cell values to match linked database records for all shapes in the drawing file.

   • **Periodically refresh based on NOW function** — Refreshes ShapeSheet cell values to match linked database records for all shapes in the drawing file at the interval specified by the NOW function. When you choose this option, Visio adds commands to the drawing page shortcut menu to start and stop the continuous refresh.

5. Click Next and then click Finish.

Adding Actions and Events to Shapes

When you use the Database Wizard to link shapes to databases, you can specify the commands you want to add to shape shortcut menus as well as what happens when you drop a shape on a page. If you want to add or modify those actions and events after you've linked your shapes, follow these steps:

1. After you've linked the shapes to a database, select the shapes to which you want to add actions and events.

2. Choose Tools ➪ Add-Ons ➪ Visio Extras ➪ Link to Database and click Advanced.

3. Select the actions and events you want and then click OK.

Tip By default, Visio sets Refresh Shape as the default Shape Drop Event. When you select this option and drop or paste a shape on a drawing page, Visio refreshes the values based on the database record linked to the original shape. If you want to select a different database record when you copy a shape, select the Select Record option. When you drag a master onto the page or paste a copy, Visio prompts you to select a database record.

Synchronizing Shapes and Database Records Automatically

If you would prefer to have Visio automatically refresh your drawings, you can have Visio monitor the database linked to a drawing at a regular interval and refresh the shapes in the drawing with the values from the linked database records. To refresh shapes automatically, follow these steps:

1. Choose Tools ➪ Add-Ons ➪ Visio Extras ➪ Database Settings.

2. Check the Automatically Refresh Drawing Page check box.

3. In the Refresh Drawing Interval (Secs.) box, type the number of seconds between every refresh and click OK.

If you want to keep your drawing and database up to date as you work, you can use Visio's Drawing Monitor to watch for differences between the drawing and its linked database. Whenever the Drawing Monitor finds a discrepancy, it updates the database record with the values from the shape.

In order for the Drawing Monitor to function, you must set several options:

✦ **Launch Drawing Monitor**—When you use the Database Wizard to create a drawing based on a database table, the wizard displays one screen in which you can specify options to use for the monitored drawing. In this screen, be sure to check the following check boxes:

- Launch the Drawing Monitor on Document Open
- Add 'launch monitor' Right Mouse Action to the Page
- Automatically Refresh Page Based on Global Setting

✦ **Automatically Refresh Drawing Page**—You must also choose Tools ⇨ Add-Ons ⇨ Visio Extras ⇨ Database Settings and check the Automatically Refresh Drawing Page check box and specify the interval for monitoring the database.

With these settings selected, Visio launches the Drawing Monitor every time you open the file. If you close the Drawing Monitor and want to reopen it, you can right-click the drawing page and choose Launch Database Monitor from the shortcut menu. Visio monitors the drawing and the database at the interval you specify in the Database Settings dialog box. Changes you make to shapes are reflected in the database table.

Summary

You can link the shapes on Visio drawings with data in ODBC-compliant databases. Whether you want to maintain a Visio drawing based on the data in a database, export your Visio shape data to a database, or create two-way links between shapes and database records, Visio provides wizards and commands to simplify the task. You can set up connections that link shapes on drawings or masters to database records. When you link masters to databases, you can link masters to specific records or specify the record when you add the master to a drawing page. You can also generate drawings based on the records in a database table. After you link shapes to database records, you can update values by using shortcut menu commands or by specifying a refresh interval and letting Visio update your shapes or records automatically.

✦   ✦   ✦

Using Visio for Office Productivity

Collaborating with Others

It takes a team to brainstorm, generate, and develop new ideas and processes. Together, you can all show your brilliance. Sometimes, however, you're toiling away as a team of one. Even so, you probably still need to share your Visio drawings with others, whether they are reviewers, customers, or other outside resources.

Either way, with Visio, you can use your e-mail program to distribute drawings to others, from simple attachments to a sequential routing system. You can share your drawings in a variety of situations, whether it's with non-Visio users, collaborating with team members in a shared workspace, or working with colleagues across worldwide continents and languages.

You can also exchange and review one another's Visio drawings, tracking markup to capture every important thought. Recognizing the importance of collaboration in its various forms, Visio 2003 includes many new features that facilitate collaboration with others.

In this chapter, you learn how to distribute Visio drawings through e-mail, share drawings using Visio Viewer, and collaborate using the new document workspaces. You'll learn how to work with other languages in Visio. Finally, I'll show you how to track changes in Visio and how to review and accept those changes into your drawings.

Distributing Drawings

When you send your Visio drawings via e-mail, you're efficiently getting your Visio drawings into the hands of colleagues or your target audience. Using e-mail features, you can perform the following actions:

✦ Send drawings as attachments

✦ Route them sequentially to a series of reviewers

✦ Post drawings to a public Microsoft Exchange folder for all to see

Note   Visio can distribute drawings using any e-mail program that supports the MAPI (Messaging Application Programming Interface) protocol.

Sending Drawings Using E-Mail

You can attach a Visio drawing within your e-mail program. In a new message form, choose Insert ➪ File (or the equivalent commands), and then select the drawing file. You can also create an e-mail with the Visio drawing attached from within Visio. To do this, follow these steps:

1. In Visio, open the drawing you want to send.

2. Choose File ➪ Send To ➪ Mail Recipient (As Attachment). Your e-mail program launches, if necessary, and a new e-mail message form appears with the current drawing as an attachment.

3. As appropriate, enter the recipients for the drawing in the To and Cc boxes, revise the Subject if necessary, and then type your message in the message area.

4. When you're finished, choose Send or the equivalent command.

Routing Drawings

You can send a Visio drawing to multiple recipients for their review or approval. You can route the drawing sequentially — one recipient after the other or all at once. After the recipients review or approve the drawing, the drawing routes back to the person who sent it out in the first place. To route a drawing to multiple recipients, follow these steps:

1. In the Visio drawing you want to route, choose File ➪ Send To ➪ Routing Recipient. The Routing Slip dialog box appears.

2. Under the To box, click Address. The address book for your e-mail program opens.

3. Select the e-mail addresses for the recipients of the routed drawing, and then click OK. The names are added to the To box.

4. Revise the Subject if necessary and then type your message in the Message Text box.

5. Under Route to Recipients, select One After Another to route the drawing sequentially, which is the default. To route the drawing to all recipients simultaneously, select All At Once.

Tip
Routing a drawing sequentially can be advantageous when a drawing is being reviewed and comments added. Each subsequent recipient can see the comments of the previous reviewers and add to them.

6. Check the Return When Done check box to have the routing e-mail sent back to you after it has been routed to all recipients.

7. Check the Track Status check box to monitor who has the drawing at any given time. This is helpful if you're using the One After Another routing method.

Tip
If you are routing sequentially, consider arranging the order of recipients in the To box. Select a name and click the Move Up or Move Down buttons to change the sequence.

8. When you're finished, click OK. An e-mail with the current drawing attached is sent to your routing recipients.

Distributing Drawings to Exchange Folders

Instead of sending a Visio drawing to a large number of recipients, you can simply post the drawing to a public Exchange folder. Then you can alert the recipients of the drawing's presence there so they can review it. To add a drawing to a Microsoft Exchange folder, follow these steps:

1. Open the drawing you want to add to an Exchange folder.

2. Choose File ➪ Send To ➪ Exchange Folder. The Send to Exchange Folder dialog box appears.

3. Select the folder, expanding your folders as needed. You can also create a new folder for your drawing by clicking New Folder, typing a name, and then pressing Enter.

4. Click OK.

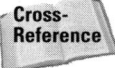

Cross-Reference
Another method for distributing drawings to others is to publish them on an intranet or Internet Web site. For more information, see Chapter 9.

Sharing Drawings

With Visio 2003, you now have powerful new capabilities for sharing drawings. Users who don't have Visio installed on their computers can download the Microsoft Office Visio Viewer 2003 to open and examine Visio documents. If your organization has set up Windows SharePoint Services as an intranet Web site, you and your team can employ Document Workspaces to share and collaborate interactively on drawings. Your drawings can more seamlessly cross language barriers through the implementation of new multiple language support.

Sharing Drawings with Colleagues Without Visio

If you're working with non-Visio users, they can now view Visio drawings on a Web page or use the Microsoft Office Visio Viewer 2003 to open and view Visio files. The Visio Viewer is an ActiveX control that displays Visio drawings in a Microsoft Internet Explorer (version 5.0 or later) window. With the Visio Viewer, a user can perform the following actions:

- ✦ View one drawing page at a time
- ✦ Navigate to another page in the drawing
- ✦ Zoom in and out
- ✦ View another area of the drawing
- ✦ Follow hyperlinks attached to shapes
- ✦ View custom properties
- ✦ Print Visio drawings

The Visio Viewer does not show stencils, rulers, guides, or guide points. Styles might not appear the same as they do in Visio. In addition, the Visio Viewer does not support rotated pages, more than one hyperlink on a shape, drawing page hyperlinks, or drawing page properties.

 **New Feature**   For Visio 2003 drawings, non-Visio users can open drawings with the Visio Viewer 2003.

The Microsoft Visio Viewer is available for download at the Microsoft Download Center (www.microsoft.com/downloads). To locate the download, type Visio Viewer in the Search box on the Microsoft Download Center site and follow the instructions for downloading and installing the Viewer.

You can use Visio Viewer 2003 to open Visio drawings (.vsd files) saved in versions 5.0, 2000, 2002, or later, or Visio XML format files (.vdx files) saved in version 2002 or later. Only the Visio Viewer 2003 can open drawings created in Visio Professional 2003. Choose one of the following methods to open a Visio file using the Visio Viewer:

✦ If you do not have Visio installed on your computer, double-click a Visio file in Windows Explorer.

✦ If you do have Visio installed on your computer, right-click a Visio file in Windows Explorer, choose Open With ➪ Internet Explorer. If Internet Explorer is not listed, choose Program, select Internet Explorer, and then click OK.

✦ In your Web browser, choose File ➪ Open and navigate to a Visio file.

Note   If you have both Visio and the Visio Viewer installed — for instance, to see how your drawings appear in the Viewer or to test Visio Viewer capabilities — opening a file in your Web browser launches Visio, rather than the Visio Viewer.

✦ Drag a Visio file from Windows Explorer into your Web browser window.

Tip   If you have trouble opening a drawing in the Visio Viewer, download the latest version from the Microsoft Download Center.

Working with Document Workspaces

If your organization is implementing Windows SharePoint Services, you have access to the new Document Workspace feature in Visio 2003. The Document Workspace is a shared area revolving around one or more drawings and hosted by the Windows SharePoint Services Web server. Using this shared workspace in either a Web browser or the Shared Workspace task pane in Visio, colleagues can perform the following tasks:

✦ Share and work on drawings

✦ Exchange information

✦ Maintain lists and related links about the drawing

✦ Assign tasks regarding the drawing

✦ Update one another about drawing and task status

When you have the appropriate permission to create a Document Workspace, you can share your drawings and invite the members you want to participate in the Document Workspace. Members work on their versions of the drawing, and update them periodically to the Web server. The other members receive updates so that all Document Workspace members can see the changes that others have saved to the drawing so far.

New Feature   You can use the new Document Workspace feature to collaborate on files created in various Office applications, including Word 2003, Excel 2003, and PowerPoint 2003.

Creating Document Workspaces

As long as you have the appropriate permissions, you can create a Document Workspace for your drawing as a subsite of the Windows SharePoint Services site. You become the administrator of any Document Workspace you create.

To create a Document Workspace for a Visio drawing using Microsoft Outlook 2003, follow these steps:

1. Choose File ➪ Send To ➪ Mail Recipient to create an e-mail with the current Visio drawing as an attachment.

2. Enter the e-mail addresses of all the individuals with whom you are collaborating on the drawing. These people become members of the Document Workspace.

3. Edit the subject and type a message as needed.

4. In the Attachment Options Task Pane, click Shared Attachments.

Note   If the Attachment Options Task Pane is not visible, click Attachment Options.

5. In the Create Document Workspace At box, enter the Web address of your Windows SharePoint Services Web site. As long as you have permission to create Document Workspaces for this Web site, the Document Workspace will be created as a subsite of the Windows SharePoint Services site, using the e-mail recipients as members.

6. Click Send.

To create a Document Workspace for a Visio drawing using the Shared Workspace Task Pane in Visio, follow these steps:

1. Choose Tools ➪ Shared Workspace. The Shared Workspace Task Pane appears.

2. Enter a descriptive name for the drawing workspace in the Document Workspace Name box.

3. In the Location for a New Workspace box, enter the Web address for the Windows SharePoint Services site, as illustrated in Figure 11-1.

Note   If you don't know the Web address, check with your system administrator.

4. Click Create.

5. Select the Members tab at the top of the Shared Workspace Task Pane and then click Add New Members.

6. Type the names of the members you want to add to your Document Workspace, separating them with semicolons. You might use e-mail addresses or Windows SharePoint Services user names, depending on how your system administrator has set up Windows SharePoint Services users.

Figure 11-1: Create a new Document Workspace using the Shared Workspace Task Pane.

To create a Document Workspace for a Visio drawing from within your Windows SharePoint Services Web site, follow these steps:

1. In your Web browser, go to the site of your Windows SharePoint Services.

2. In the navigation bar, choose Create. The Create page appears.

3. Under Web Pages, click Sites and Workspaces.

4. Type a title, description, and Web address, select a permission setting, and then click Create. The Template Selection page appears.

5. In the Template box, select Document Workspace and then click OK.

Whenever you create a Document Workspace for a drawing, that drawing is automatically added to the Windows SharePoint Services document library. Anytime a member of the Document Workspace opens a drawing stored in the document library, the Shared Workspace Task Pane opens as well.

Shared Workspace for Online Meetings

Another method for collaboration in Visio is online meetings. If your organization uses Windows SharePoint Services and MSN Messenger, you can have Visio create a shared workspace for online meetings. Choose Tools ⇨ Online Collaboration ⇨ Meet Now. The MSN Messenger Windows NetMeeting Messenger Service launches. You can call participants, allow other participants to edit the active drawing, display a chat window, and display a whiteboard.

Tip   If the drawing on which you want to collaborate is stored in your Windows SharePoint Services document library, you can create a Document Workspace from the document library. In your Web browser, go to the site of your Windows SharePoint Services and then open the document library. Point to the name of the drawing, click the Edit arrow, and then click Create Document Workspace.

Working with Drawings in a Document Workspace

When you receive a Visio drawing attached to an e-mail message that is part of a Document Workspace, follow these steps to open the drawing and begin your collaboration work with it:

1. In your e-mail program, double-click the Visio drawing attachment to open it. A message indicates that this drawing is stored in a Document Workspace.

2. To be notified whenever another member of this Document Workspace updates this drawing, click Get Updates. To check for and incorporate updates from other members manually, click Don't Update. The drawing opens in Visio, and the Shared Workspace Task Pane appears, indicating that this drawing is part of a Document Workspace.

3. In the Shared Workspace Task Pane, click Get Updates to immediately update the content of your version of the drawing. As other team members update and save their version of the drawing, the Shared Workspace Task Pane indicates that updates are available. See the "Setting Document Workspace Update Options" sidebar to learn how to receive automatic updates.

Tip   If you're working on a Document Workspace drawing but you don't see the Shared Workspace Task Pane, choose Tools ⇨ Share Workspace.

4. Make any changes you want to the drawing. If another member of the Document Workspace has specified a particular aspect of the drawing for you to work on, you might see a task assigned to you in the Shared Workspace Task Pane.

Tip   The Document Workspace administrator can establish that drawing changes should be made with Track Markup turned on. If that's the case, then the changes made by each member of the workspace are shown in a different layer. If the workspace administrator has not turned on Track Markup but you want your changes to show as markup, choose Tools ⇨ Track Markup.

5. Save the drawing periodically, as usual.

6. To share the changes you've made, first save the drawing. In the Shared Workspace Task Pane, select the Status tab and then click Update Workspace Copy. Your version of the drawing becomes the Document Workspace copy, and other team members can update their versions of the drawing with your changes.

Tip   You can also edit the shared drawing in the Windows SharePoint Services Web site for the Document Workspace if you are using Internet Explorer 6.0 or later. In the document library containing the drawing, point to the name of the document and then click the Edit arrow that appears.

Deleting Document Workspaces

When you and your team are finished collaborating on a drawing, you can delete the Document Workspace. When deleting a Document Workspace, keep the following principles in mind:

✦ Deleting a document workspace can only be done by the administrator of the Document Workspace — that is, the person who created it.

✦ It deletes all the data in the Document Workspace.

✦ It removes the associated document library, including all the documents stored there.

✦ It does not delete your own copy of documents stored on your computer.

To delete a shared workspace using the Shared Workspace Task Pane, select the title of the Document Workspace and then click Delete Workspace. To delete a shared workspace from the Windows SharePoint Services Web site, follow these steps:

1. Use your Web browser to go to the Windows SharePoint Services site and the Document Workspace.

2. In the navigation bar, choose Site Settings.

3. Under Administration, click Go to Site Administration.

4. Under Management and Statistics, click Delete This Site, and then click Delete.

You can disconnect a drawing from a Document Workspace and retain an independent copy of the drawing without affecting the other members of the Document Workspace. To do so, open the drawing, and in the Shared Workspace Task Pane, click Disconnect from Workspace. When you save and close the drawing, it is permanently disconnected from its Document Workspace.

Setting Document Workspace Update Options

You can specify that you want to receive automatic updates when you first open the shared drawing or when you click Get Updates in the Shared Workspace Task Pane. If you do not want to be notified of updated information, click Don't Get Updates when you first open the shared drawing or in the Shared Workspace Task Pane. You can still update your copy manually whenever you want by clicking Get Updates.

You can also use your e-mail program to receive notification when an update has been made to a drawing in a Document Workspace of which you're a member. In the Shared Workspace Task Pane, click E-Mail Alerts.

Managing Shared Workspace Tasks

Members of a Document Workspace can create and assign tasks associated with the shared drawing to other members. You can assign to-do items with due dates to members of the shared workspace. To assign a task to another member, follow these steps:

1. With the shared drawing open, select the Tasks tab in the Shared Workspace Task Pane and then click Add New Task.

2. Complete the fields in the Task dialog box. This includes the task title, current task status, priority, the Document Workspace member to whom you want to assign the task, any description, and the due date and time.

3. Click OK. The task is added to the Shared Workspace task pane. All members of the Shared Workspace see the task assignment and associated information.

If another member has assigned a task to you, after completing it you can check it off in the Tasks list. When other team members open the Tasks list in the Shared Workspace Task Pane, they can see that you have completed the task. To check off a completed task that has been assigned to you, follow these steps:

1. With the shared drawing open, select the Tasks tab in the Shared Workspace Task Pane. The list of all tasks assigned to all Document Workspace members appears.

2. Select the task assigned to you.

3. In the Task dialog box, change the status to indicate that it's complete. Enter any information in the Description box.

4. Click OK. The check box is checked, indicating that your task is complete.

Working with Multiple Languages

You might share your Visio drawings with colleagues or customers in other countries, such as Hungary, Greece, or Japan. Therefore, you might need to include elements of other languages and other language formats in a single drawing. You can also share and collaborate on drawings across multiple languages.

New Feature   Visio 2003 includes new support for Unicode, End User Defined Character (EUDC) sets, and GB18030. See the following sidebar, "Multilanguage Support," for details.

With the new multilanguage support, you can do all of the following:

✦ Flexibly format date, time, and number styles according to a specific region and language

✦ Type characters for Asian languages using an Input Method Editor (IME)

✦ Link fonts automatically to find needed characters in other languages. If a selected font does not include all the required characters, Visio automatically links to a second font to find the needed characters. This is particularly useful in multilingual drawings that include East Asian and right-to-left text.

✦ Create multilingual Web pages and intranet content in Visio

To work with additional languages in Visio, you might need to adjust settings in the Windows Control Panel, in Microsoft Office, and in Visio itself. Certain languages require additional resources installed to provide support.

Multilanguage Support

The new Visio 2003 multilanguage support includes the following:

✦ **Unicode** — A character encoding standard that enables almost all the written languages in the world to be represented by using a single character set. It uses more than a single byte to represent each character. Unicode makes it possible for multiple languages to appear in a single Visio drawing.

✦ **End User Defined Character (EUDC)** — A character set with which you can form Asian names and other Asian words using characters that are not available in standard screen and printer fonts.

✦ **GB18030** — A new Chinese character-encoding standard. You can use GB18030 to create Visio drawings containing Chinese characters from this character set.

Configuring Windows for Multiple Languages

Windows installs many files needed for multilanguage support. However, if the language you're using requires additional Windows support, you can adjust the appropriate settings in the Windows Control Panel. To do this, follow these steps:

1. In Windows XP or Windows 2000, click Start and choose Control Panel, and then double-click Regional and Language Options.

2. Select the Languages tab.

3. Under Supplemental Language Support, check the check boxes for the additional language support you want — for example, complex script, right-to-left languages, or East Asian languages.

4. Follow the steps in the windows that appear to install the files needed.

Note   For certain characters in certain languages, you might also need to install a particular keyboard layout. In Control Panel, double-click Text Services or Keyboard.

On the Regional Options tab within the Regional and Language Options dialog box, you can also change date, time, and number formats for other languages. In the language drop-down list, select the language whose number, currency, time, and date formats you want to change. The regional formats under Samples will all change to reflect the norm for the selected language. Click OK.

Configuring Office for Multiple Languages

To work with different languages in Visio, enable the appropriate languages to make additional language-specific options available. To do this, follow these steps:

1. In Windows XP, click Start and choose All Programs ➪ Microsoft Office Tools ➪ Microsoft Office 2003 Language Settings.

2. Select the Enabled Languages tab.

3. Under Available Languages, select the language you want to add and then click Add. The language appears in the Enabled Languages box.

4. When you're finished adding languages, click OK.

Tip   If your organization has purchased the Microsoft Office Visio 2003 Multilingual User Interface Pack, you can also change the language of the user interface and Help.

Installing IME for Asian Characters

To enter ideographic characters for Asian languages, you must use an Input Method Editor (IME). This feature is available only if support for Japanese, Simplified Chinese, Traditional Chinese, or Korean is enabled through Microsoft Office Language Settings as described above.

To install the IME, follow these steps:

1. Using your Web browser, go to the Microsoft Office Online Web site, `http://office.microsoft.com`.

2. Navigate to the page containing IME Editor downloads.

3. Click the language you want and then follow the instructions that appear.

After you have installed the IME for the language you're working with, you can access it from the Language bar that appears by default in the upper-right corner of the Visio screen.

Tip
You can make other adjustments for language settings from within Visio. Choose Tools ➪ Options and then select the Regional tab. You can also switch between metric and U.S. units in Visio. To do so, choose Tools ➪ Options, and then select the Units tab.

Tracking and Reviewing Changes

One of the most powerful means of collaborating on documents is the capability to track changes using some type of markup. With Visio 2003, you can now track and review changes using separate colored overlays for each reviewer. When track markup mode is turned on, reviewers can add text comments, shapes, or use Ink to create freehand markups on a drawing. After the reviewers have finished their work, the originator can review all the comments and other markup, and incorporate the changes as appropriate.

New
Feature
The Reviewing Task Pane and Reviewing toolbar, with their markup features in separate colored overlays, are all new in Visio 2003.

Turning Markup On or Off

When track markup mode is on, reviewers can add their comments and other markup. Each reviewer's markup is kept separate from the original and all other reviewers' markups. To turn on track markup mode, follow these steps:

1. Open the drawing for which you want to turn on track markup mode.

2. Choose Tools ➪ Track Markup. A colored band appears around the drawing workspace, the Reviewing Task Pane appears, and the Reviewing toolbar appears, as illustrated in Figure 11-2.

Caution
You can edit your markup overlay only when track markup mode is turned on. To edit the original drawing, you must turn track markup mode off.

Colored band

Reviewing taskbar

Reviewing Task Pane

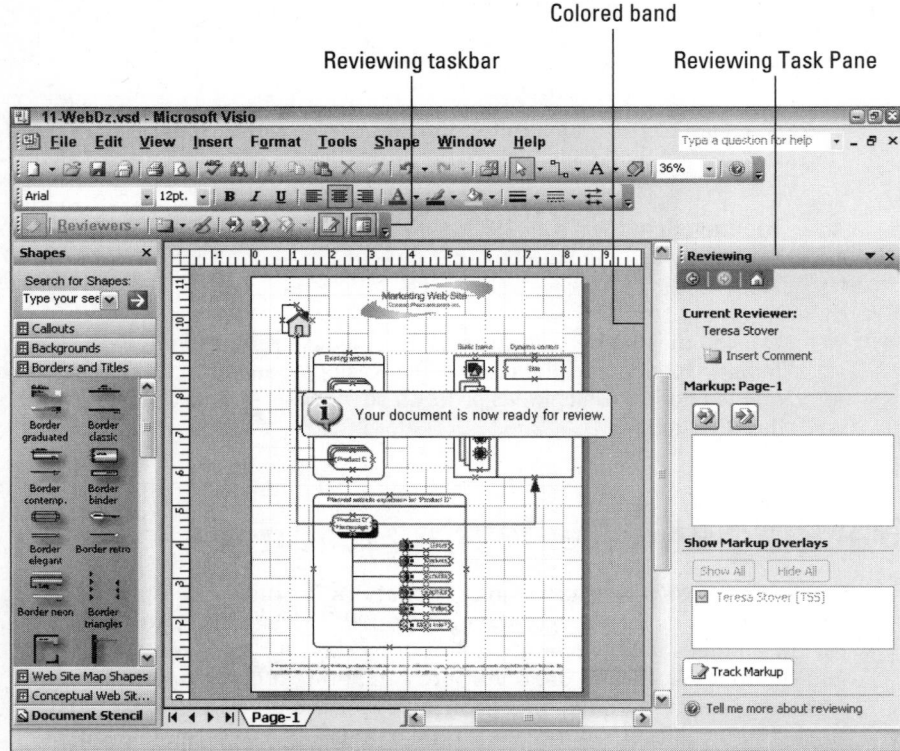

Figure 11-2: Visual cues, including the Reviewing Task Pane, indicate that track markup mode is on.

To turn track markup mode off, click Track Markup at the bottom of the Reviewing Task Pane. You can also choose Tools ➪ Track Markup, which acts as an on/off toggle. When markups exist and track markup mode is turned off, tabs appear on the right side of the drawing window, showing the original drawing, and the overlays of each reviewer's comments, each one in a different color.

Caution   To print a drawing without your markup and comments showing, be sure to turn off track markup mode.

Marking Up Drawings

When you're marking up a Visio drawing with track markup mode turned on, Visio assigns you an overlay in a particular color. You can add your markup to your overlay without affecting the original drawing or other reviewers' markup. You can create three types of markup: comments, shapes, and Ink.

 **Caution** Markup appears only in the reviewer's assigned color. Although the reviewer can apply colors to shapes and Ink, the colors are not visible until the shape is copied or moved onto the original drawing.

 **New Feature** In Visio 2003, you can use the new Ink features to mark up a drawing, creating free-form shapes and handwriting with a tablet computer stylus or a regular computer mouse. Visio automatically converts the handdrawing into shapes that can be added to a custom stencil.

Inserting Comments

To add a text comment as drawing markup, follow these steps:

1. Make sure that track markup mode is on for the drawing.

2. If your comment is associated with a particular page in a multipage drawing, click the page.

3. In the Reviewing Task Pane, click Insert Comment. A comment bubble appears in the drawing.

4. Type your comment. When finished, click off the comment. The bubble disappears, but the comment marker with your initials remains, associated with the current page. A list of your comments builds in the Reviewing Task Pane.

Inserting Shapes

To add a shape to a drawing, simply drag it from the stencil into place. The shape appears in the color of your markup, and "Shape added" appears with your initials in the Reviewing Task Pane.

Although you can review other reviewers' markup, you can change or remove only your own. To remove a markup, select it in the drawing or in the Reviewing Task Pane and then press Delete.

Adding Freehand Markup Using Ink

Ink is the name of the freehand method of annotating a drawing in track markup mode. With Ink, you can draw shapes and add handwritten notes. You can work with these shapes like any other shape. You can even add them to custom stencils if they're shapes you want to reuse. While Ink facilitates tablet computer input with a stylus, you can use your mouse on a desktop or notebook computer to draw freehand markup. To use Ink to mark up a drawing, follow these steps:

1. Make sure that track markup mode is on for the drawing.

2. If you're adding Ink on a particular page in a multipage drawing, click the page.

3. On the Reviewing toolbar, choose the Ink tool. The Ink toolbar appears, showing different Ink colors, an Eraser tool, a Color tool, and a Line-width tool, as shown in Figure 11-3.

Note The Reviewing toolbar appears as soon as a drawing enters track markup mode. If the Reviewing toolbar is not showing, choose View ➪ Toolbars ➪ Reviewing.

Shape drawn with Ink   Handwriting with Ink

Ink tool   Ink pointer   Ink toolbar

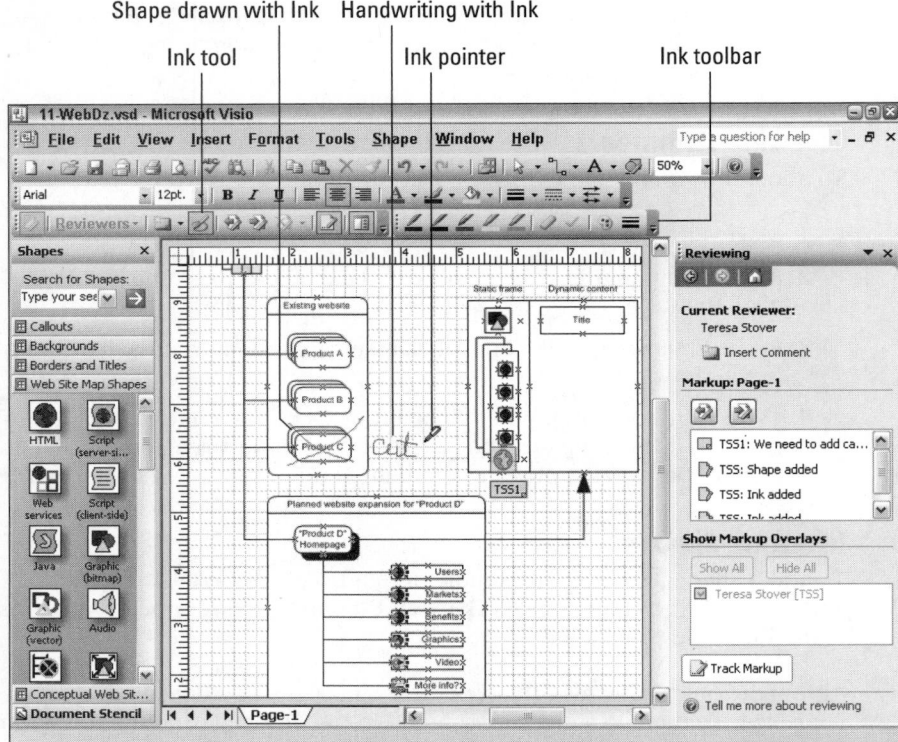

Figure 11-3: Use Ink to add freehand shapes and handwritten comments to a Visio drawing.

4. Choose the tools on the Ink toolbar to set up the markup you're adding.

5. Use your computer's pointing device (such as the mouse or stylus) to draw the markup shape or use handwriting to mark up the drawing. After you finish a shape, it is converted to a shape that can be manipulated as a unit like any other Visio shape. The message "Ink added" appears with your initials in the Reviewing Task Pane.

6. When you're finished using Ink, choose the Pointer tool on the Standard toolbar.

Tip You can set the speed of your Ink entry conversion to a shape. Choose Tools ➪ Options and then select the Advanced tab. Under Ink Tool, drag the slider in the direction you want to indicate how fast or slow you want an Ink entry to be transformed into a Visio shape.

Reviewing Markup

By default, all markup in a drawing is displayed. Each reviewer's markup appears in a different color, and each reviewer's overlay can be seen by selecting the tab containing the reviewer's initials on the right edge of the drawing. To see the original drawing containing all reviewers' markups, select the Original tab.

To hide all markup, click Hide All in the Reviewing Task Pane. To show all markup again, click Show All.

To hide just the markup of selected reviewers, uncheck the check boxes for those reviewers under Show Markup Overlays in the Reviewing Task Pane. To specify which reviewers' markup should show, check the check boxes for those reviewers.

Updating Drawings with Markup Changes

To incorporate markups into the original drawings, you first must turn off track markup mode. Then you can review markups and copy elements into the original drawing. To do this, follow these steps:

1. In the Reviewing Task Pane, click Track Markup to turn track markup mode off.
2. Select the tab for the reviewer whose markup you want to incorporate into the original drawing.
3. Select the shape(s), and then click the Copy tool on the Standard toolbar.
4. Select the Original tab at the lower-right edge of the drawing.
5. Click the Paste tool on the Standard toolbar. The copied shapes appear at the center of the drawing.
6. Drag the shape(s) to move them into place, using the markup overlay as a guide.

To move from one markup to the next, choose the Next Markup tool in the Reviewing Task Pane or the Reviewing toolbar. To delete a markup, select it, and then choose the Delete Markup tool in the Reviewing Task Pane or the Reviewing toolbar.

Summary

With Visio 2003, you can work as closely as you need to with colleagues, whether they're right next door or on the other side of the globe. Using e-mail, a Windows SharePoint Services site on your intranet, or sophisticated layers of markup, you can discuss, experiment, and hammer out the most innovative ideas and processes. You can then effectively capture those ideas and processes in your Visio drawings.

✦   ✦   ✦

Building Block Diagrams

Visio Block Diagrams are versatile and yet quite easy to use, so you can employ them to communicate an astounding variety of ideas. They can illustrate the structure and relationships between ideas, concepts, designs, or real-world objects, or show the flow within processes.

You can create simple diagrams using basic shapes or spruce up a diagram for a presentation with 3D shapes that show perspective. In addition, Visio's Blocks stencil includes shapes to develop more specialized arrangements, such as hierarchical trees or onion diagrams. In this chapter, you'll learn how to create different types of Visio Block Diagrams and configure your Block Diagram shapes.

Exploring the Block Diagram Templates

The Visio Block Diagram templates are some of the most popular templates because workers from any field can use the Visio techniques they already know, such as dragging, dropping, editing, and formatting, to communicate their ideas to their colleagues. Many of the Block Diagram shapes and connectors include powerful but simple to use features that speed up common diagramming tasks. For example, you can connect branches on one of Visio's Tree shapes to boxes on a drawing to construct a hierarchical tree.

Block Diagram shapes are so simple that the Block Diagram templates don't contain any specialized menus, toolbars, or add-ons. You can build diagrams that satisfy many different requirements by dragging and dropping shapes from Visio's Block Diagram stencils. You can modify and tweak Block Diagram shapes by dragging selection handles or control handles. Annotation is as easy as selecting a shape and typing.

Choosing the Right Template

The descriptions that accompany the three Block Diagram templates in Visio sound quite similar — you can document structure, hierarchy, and flow using a combination of 2D or 3D shapes. However, the many solutions that you can create with Block Diagrams boil down to three fundamental formats: blocks, trees, and onions, as illustrated in Figure 12-1. *Block diagrams* communicate relationships between concepts or steps in a process and use geometric shapes such as rectangles and circles connected with arrows. For example, you can show the processes in the life-cycle of a project. *Tree diagrams* present hierarchical information, such as the descendants and ancestors in a family tree or the progress of teams in tournament play-offs. *Onion diagrams* illustrate relationships that build from a core. For example, an onion diagram is the best way to show the layers that make up the earth from its core to the crust.

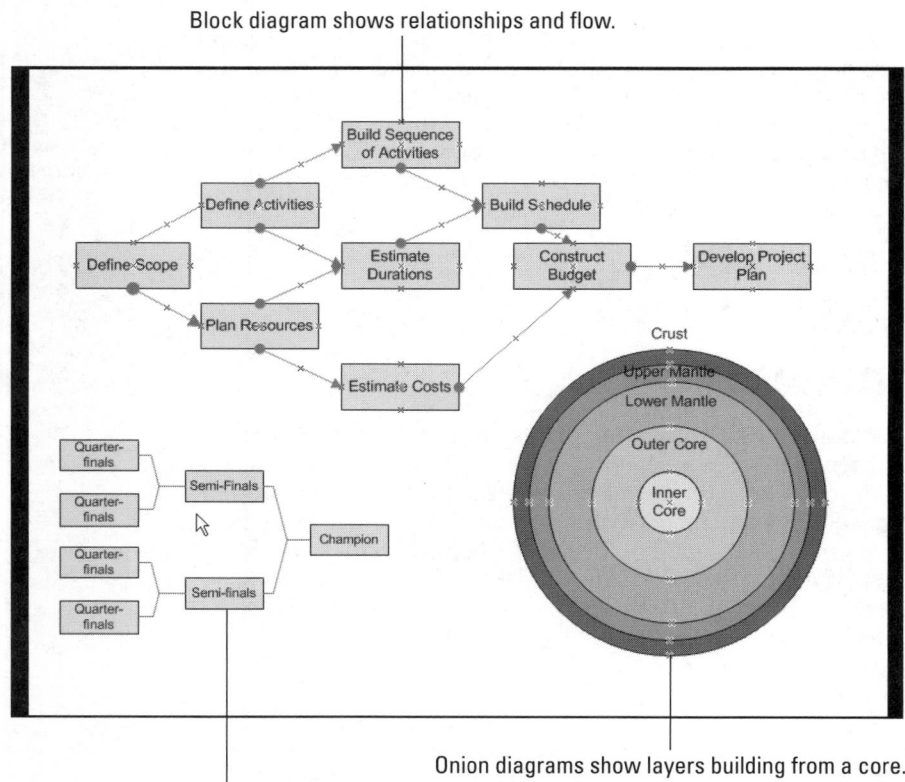

Block diagram shows relationships and flow.

Onion diagrams show layers building from a core.

Tree diagrams present hierarchies such as family trees or tournament results.

Figure 12-1: Block diagrams can show flow, hierarchical structure, or concentric layers.

The three types of block diagrams don't correspond directly to the three templates that Visio provides. Use Table 12-1 to choose the template that contains the shapes you need for the diagram you want to create. Each Block Diagram template automatically sets the page to a letter-size sheet with portrait orientation, and uses inches drawn at one-to-one scale.

<table>
<tr><td colspan="3" align="center">Table 12-1
Templates for Block Diagrams</td></tr>
<tr><td>*Diagram Type*</td><td>*Template*</td><td>*Features*</td></tr>
<tr><td>Basic Blocks</td><td>Basic Diagram</td><td>Opens the Basic Shapes, Borders and Titles, and Backgrounds stencils.</td></tr>
<tr><td>Blocks with Style</td><td>Block Diagram</td><td>Opens the Blocks, Raised Blocks, Borders and Titles, and Backgrounds stencils.</td></tr>
<tr><td>Tree</td><td>Block Diagram</td><td>Opens the Blocks, Raised Blocks, Borders and Titles, and Backgrounds stencils. Tree shapes show hierarchy.</td></tr>
<tr><td>Onion</td><td>Block Diagram</td><td>Opens the Blocks, Raised Blocks, Borders and Titles, and Backgrounds stencils. Concentric and Partial Layer shapes build onion diagrams.</td></tr>
<tr><td>High-Impact Blocks</td><td>Block Diagram with Perspective</td><td>Opens the Blocks with Perspective, Borders and Titles, and Backgrounds stencils. 3D and Vanishing Point shapes show perspective.</td></tr>
</table>

Exploring Block Diagram Shapes

Every Block Diagram template sets up the same basic environment, so you can use Block Diagram templates almost interchangeably. However, each Block Diagram stencil offers some specialized shapes that help create specific types of diagrams. By understanding the shapes available on each stencil, you can open the stencils as you need them, regardless of the Block Diagram template you start with.

Basic Shapes

The Basic Shapes stencil is a workhorse for simple block diagrams. It offers basic geometric shapes, arrow-like shapes that can act as connectors, as well as the standard Dynamic connector and Line-curve connector.

✦ **Geometric Shapes** — Drag and drop geometric shapes such as Rectangles, Circles, Stars, Rounded rectangles, Shadowed or 3D boxes, and shapes for polygons from Triangles to Octagons.

✦ **Arrows** — Drag and drop Arrow shapes onto a drawing to connect the geometric shapes. Choose from arrows with different arrowheads and tails.

✦ **Flexi-Arrows** — You can drag control points on the Flexi-arrow shapes to customize the angles and length of arrowheads and tails.

Blocks

The Blocks stencil is the most versatile, with shapes for block, tree, and onion diagrams. It contains connectors with dozens of different end styles as well as Tree shapes for building hierarchies. You can choose from a variety of shapes, with behaviors that help show relationships and flow.

✦ **Geometric Shapes** — Drag and drop Box, Diamond, and Circle shapes.

✦ **Auto-sizing Boxes** — The Auto-height Box increases or decreases its height to accommodate the text you enter. The Auto-size Box increases its height and width.

✦ **Open/Close Shapes** — The Open/close Bar and the Open/close Arrow shapes can display borders to represent a boundary, or hide borders so shapes appear to flow together.

✦ **Arrow Box** — This shape combines a box and an arrow to show both a process and the flow to the next step.

✦ **Arrows** — Drag the control points on the Curved Arrow shape to change the direction of the arrowhead and the curvature of the bend.

✦ **Onion Shapes** — Concentric Layer and Partial Layer shapes drop on top of each other to show relationships around a central core.

✦ **Tree Shapes** — Tree shapes show hierarchies with two to six branches.

✦ **Connectors** — In addition to the Dynamic connector and the Line-curve connector, the Blocks stencil includes several connectors with specialized styles, such as dots and arrows, at the end or midpoint.

Blocks Raised

The Blocks Raised stencil contains geometric shapes and arrows that appear three-dimensional. However, the height and orientation of the third dimension are fixed. Although these shapes appear to be three-dimensional, they do not change as you move a *vanishing point*, which is a Block Diagram feature with which you can add perspective to a drawing.

Blocks with Perspective

The Blocks with Perspective stencil contains geometric shapes and arrows that change their perspective in relation to a vanishing point. You can adjust the depth and angle of perspective by moving the Vanishing Point shape on the drawing.

✦ **Geometric Shapes** — Drag Block, Circle, Arrow, and Elbow shapes that adjust to the position of a Vanishing Point shape.

✦ **Holes** — Drag a Hole shape onto another shape to create the appearance of a hole.

✦ **Wireframe Blocks** — These shapes are three-dimensional boxes in which the edges are visible and the sides are transparent.

✦ **Vanishing Point** — Drag a second Vanishing Point shape onto a drawing to add more impact to diagrams.

Showing Structure and Flow

Block diagrams work equally well to represent static structural relationships or the flow between processes or steps. In a structural diagram, boxes and other geometric shapes represent components, and arrows or connectors indicate order or hierarchy. For processes and procedures, geometric shapes signify each process or step, while arrows show the dependencies and sequence between them. No matter which type of relationship you're trying to communicate, you can use the same basic steps to create your diagram.

Creating Block Diagrams

You can use basic Visio techniques to create your Visio Block Diagrams. You begin by dragging shapes onto a drawing and typing the text you want to appear in each shape. You can connect shapes as you go or attach arrows and connectors after the shapes are in place. If necessary, you can rearrange the shapes and format them. To create a block diagram, follow these steps:

1. Choose File ➪ New ➪ Block Diagram ➪ Block Diagram.

Tip

To access other Block Diagram shapes, click the Shapes icon on the Standard toolbar and choose Block Diagram ➪ Basic Shapes.

2. Drag shapes onto the drawing from the Basic Shapes, Blocks, or Blocks Raised stencils.

3. Select a shape and type any text you want to appear in the shape.

4. Connect shapes by dragging an Arrow shape from one of the stencils and gluing it to a shape on the drawing. A red square highlights a shape connection point when the Arrow shape connects to another shape. After one end of the Arrow is connected to a shape, drag the end point at the other end and glue it to another shape.

Tip   To connect shapes automatically, click the Connector tool before you drag shapes onto a drawing. Each shape automatically connects to the previous shape.

Modifying Block Diagrams

Block Diagrams don't include any specialized formatting or layout tools. You can use basic techniques to rearrange the shapes on a drawing or apply predefined backgrounds and color schemes to enhance its appearance. To adjust the overall appearance of a diagram, use any of the following techniques:

✦ **Rearrange Shapes** — Rearrange shapes in a diagram by dragging them to new locations.

✦ **Adjust Shape Location** — To make minor adjustments to the position of a shape, select it and then press one of the arrow keys to nudge it in that direction.

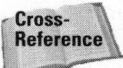

Cross-Reference   To learn about other ways to modify the location of a shape, see Chapter 4.

✦ **Apply Color Schemes** — To use a specific color scheme, right-click an empty area of the drawing page and choose Color Schemes from the shortcut menu. Select a color scheme and click OK.

Modifying Block Diagram Shapes

Some Block Diagram shapes exhibit special behaviors. However, you still use basic Visio techniques to modify all the shapes available in the Block Diagram stencils. Use any of the following techniques to modify shapes on a Block Diagram:

✦ **Add Text** — To add or modify text for an existing shape, select the shape and begin typing. You can also double-click a shape to edit its existing text.

Note   When you type text in a shape, Visio zooms in to make the text more legible.

✦ **Modify Relationships** — Select a connector or Arrow shape. Drag one of its end points and glue it to another shape or another connection point on the same shape.

✦ **Resize Shapes** — Select a shape and drag one of its square, green selection handles to resize it. Drag a corner to modify height and width proportionately. Drag a mid-point selection handle to change just one dimension.

✦ **Reshape Shapes** — Activate the Line, Arc, Pencil, or Freeform tool on the Drawing toolbar and select a shape. Drag a vertex (a green diamond) to reshape.

✦ **Bend Shape Segments** — Activate the Line, Arc, Pencil, or Freeform tool on the Drawing toolbar and select a shape. Drag an eccentricity handle (a green circle) to bend one segment of the shape.

✦ **Reorder Overlapping Shapes** — To change a shape's position in the stacking order, right-click it and choose Shape ➪ Bring to Front of Shape ➪ Send to Back.

✦ **Format Shapes** — To apply formatting to a shape, right-click it, choose Format from the shortcut menu, and then choose one of the Format commands.

✦ **Specify Shadow Colors** — To set the shadow colors for Raised Blocks and Blocks with Perspective, right-click a shape and choose one of the shadow color options from the shortcut menu. You can choose from three options:

   • **Automatic Shadow** — Sets the shadow color based on the shape's fill color. This is the default setting.

   • **Manual Shadow** — Displays the shadow color you specified for the shape. To specify shadow color, select a shape, choose Format ➪ Fill or Format ➪ Shadow, and select the color you want from the Color drop-down list.

   • **Color Scheme Shadow** — This option sets the shadow color based on the color scheme you apply.

Using Special Editing Techniques for Boxes

You can use special behaviors, control handles, and shortcut menu options that come with some of the Block Diagram Boxes to modify their appearance. If you use these shapes, take advantage of the following editing shortcuts:

✦ **3-D Box** — Drag the control point on a 3D Box to modify the amount and orientation of the box depth.

✦ **Auto-height Box** — Type text in an Auto-height Box, and the height of the box changes automatically to accommodate the text you enter. To adjust the width of the box, drag one of the side selection handles.

✦ **Auto-size Box** — Type text in an Auto-size Box, and the height and width of the box changes to fit your text. Press Enter to start a new line. The box width is set by the longest line of text.

Modifying Block Diagram Arrows

You can use special behaviors, control handles, and shortcut menu options that come with some of the Block Diagram Arrows to modify their appearance. If you use these shapes, take advantage of the following editing shortcuts:

✦ **Arrow Box** — Drag the control point on the arrowhead to adjust its width. Drag the control point at the intersection of the arrow and the box to change the height of the box and the length of the arrow.

✦ **Flexi-arrows** — Drag the control points on the arrowhead to change the width and shape of the arrowhead and the width of the arrow tail, as shown in Figure 12-2.

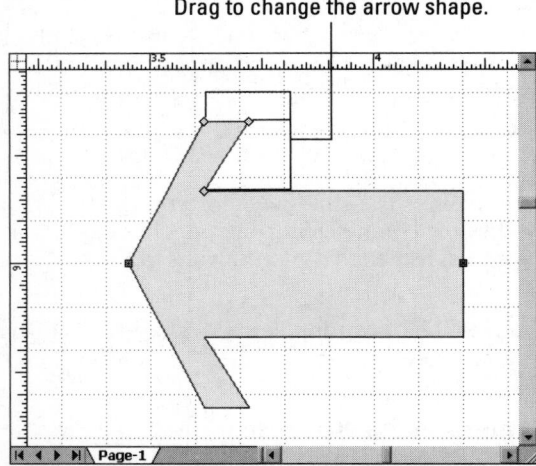

Drag to change the arrow shape.

Figure 12-2: You can reshape the arrowhead and arrow tail of the Flexi-arrow shapes.

✦ **Curved Arrow** — Drag the control point on the arrowhead to reposition the arrowhead. Drag the control point at the curve to change the curvature.

Emphasizing Flow Between Shapes

Flow is easier to see on a diagram when there are no boundaries between shapes. Several Block Diagram shapes hide or show boundaries to emphasize flow. In the Blocks stencil, these shapes include the 1-D Single Arrow, 2-D Single Arrow, and Open/closed Bar shapes. In the Blocks Raised stencil, you can open and close Right

Arrows, Up Arrows, Left Arrows, and Down Arrows, Horizontal Bars, Vertical Bars, and Elbow shapes. To open and close these shapes, follow these steps:

1. Drag a shape from a stencil and drop it onto the drawing.

2. To open the end of an arrow, right-click the shape and choose Open Tail from the shortcut menu.

3. Drag the open end of the arrow to the flat side of a box or other block shape.

4. To close the end of an arrow, right-click the shape and choose Close Tail from the shortcut menu.

5. To open or close Bar shapes from the Blocks or Blocks Raised stencil, right-click the bar and choose one of the following commands:

   • Open Left End Only

   • Open Right End Only

   • Open Both Ends

   • Close Both Ends

Note For vertical bars, the commands on the shortcut menu change to Open Top End Only and Open Bottom End Only.

Creating Hierarchical Trees

You can use tree diagrams to show hierarchies such as play-off standings or genealogy. As with other Block Diagrams, you can drag, arrange, and format shapes using basic Visio tools. Tree connectors include control points to help build your hierarchy. To build a hierarchical tree, follow these steps:

1. Choose File ⇨ New ⇨ Block Diagram ⇨ Block Diagram.

2. Drag boxes from the Blocks stencil.

3. Drag one of the four Tree shapes from the Blocks stencil onto the drawing.

Note You can choose from Trees with square or sloped branches. The Double-tree Sloped and Double-tree Square shapes provide only two branches. With the Multi-tree Sloped and Multi-tree Square shapes, you can draw from two to six branches.

4. For vertical Tree shapes, drag one of the green selection handles to rotate the shape.

Tip Press Ctrl+L to rotate a Tree by 90 degrees. With horizontal Trees, you can also press Ctrl+H to flip the Tree from right to left.

5. To connect a branch to a shape, drag the control handle at the end of a branch to a connection point on the shape. A red square highlights the connection point when the branch and the shape are connected.

6. To add text to the trunk of a tree, select the Tree and type the text you want.

Note   You can add text to trunks only, not the branches of a tree.

Modifying Tree Shapes

You can use basic Visio techniques to modify and format the blocks and text in tree diagrams. You can use control points and built-in behaviors to modify tree trunks and branches. Use the following methods to modify trees:

✦ **Add a Branch** — Drag the control handle on the trunk of a Multi-tree shape to a position. The distance perpendicular to the trunk controls the width of the branch, whereas the distance parallel to the trunk determines the length of the branch, as illustrated in Figure 12-3.

Drag to control the branch width and length.

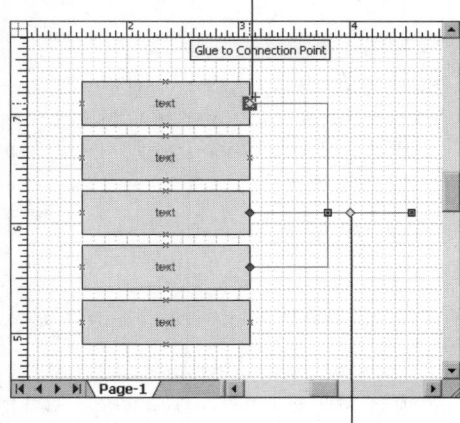

Drag to add a branch.

Figure 12-3: Drag a Multi-Tree control handle to add a branch to the tree.

✦ **Remove a Branch** — Drag the control handle at the end of the branch on top of any other control handle on the tree.

✦ **Adjust Branch Position** — Drag the control handle at the end of a branch to a new position.

✦ **Modify Distance Between Branches** — Move the boxes attached to the branches to new positions. You can move these boxes by dragging them or applying the Align Shapes or Distribute Shapes commands on the Shape menu.

✦ **Move a Tree Trunk** — Select the Tree and press an arrow key to move the trunk in that direction.

Caution   When you move the shape connected to a tree trunk, the tree trunk rotates. One end of the trunk moves with the shape while the other end of the trunk stays fixed. To keep the trunk and branches of a tree orthogonal, select the tree and all the shapes connected to it and drag them all to a new position.

Adding Impact with 3D Block Diagrams

3D block diagrams are visually appealing, so they're perfect for presentations. Although they look like they require hours of effort, they're just as easy to construct as regular block diagrams. When you create a block diagram using the Block Diagrams with Perspective template, the drawing includes a vanishing point that defines the perspective for the three-dimensional shapes. You can adjust the depth and orientation of the shape shadows by moving the Vanishing Point shape on the drawing.

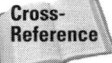

Cross-Reference   To learn how to change the color of the shadows for 3D shapes, see the "Modifying Block Diagram Shapes" section earlier in this chapter.

Note   Only shapes from the Blocks with Perspective stencil adjust to the position of the Vanishing Point shape. Shapes from the Blocks Raised stencil might look three-dimensional, but their depth and orientation remain fixed.

To create a 3D block diagram, choose File ➪ New ➪ Block Diagram ➪ Block Diagram with Perspective to open a drawing that contains a Vanishing Point shape. Drag 3D shapes from the Blocks with Perspective stencil onto the drawing. You can drag, arrange, align, and format 3D block shapes with basic Visio tools.

The depth and orientation of a 3D shape changes as you move the Vanishing Point on a drawing. To add impact or emphasize specific parts of a diagram, you can change the perspective on the diagram, change the depth of a 3D shape, or disconnect a 3D shape from the Vanishing Point.

Note   If a shape on the drawing doesn't adjust its perspective as you move the Vanishing Point, it might not be a shape with perspective, such as a Box on the Blocks Raised stencil. It also might be disconnected from the Vanishing Point.

Modifying Perspective

Use the following methods to modify the perspective of a 3D block diagram:

✦ **Change the Diagram Perspective** — Make sure no shapes are selected and then drag the Vanishing Point to another location.

✦ **Change a Shape's Perspective** — To change the perspective for one shape, select the shape and then drag the red control handle on the Vanishing Point to another location. The Vanishing Point's control handle that you move turns yellow, indicating that it and the selected shape are no longer connected to the Vanishing Point. However, when you select the Vanishing Point again, a red control handle still appears for the rest of the shapes connected to the Vanishing Point.

✦ **Connect a Shape to the Vanishing Point** — Select the shape. Drag the yellow control handle that appears on the drawing page and glue it to the connection point on the Vanishing Point shape.

✦ **Change a Shape's Depth** — Right-click a shape and choose Set Depth from the shortcut menu. Select a smaller percentage for a shallower shape, a larger percentage for a deeper shape.

Tip

You can hide the Vanishing Point shape — for instance, to print the diagram or use it in a presentation. To hide the Vanishing Point for printing, click View ⇨ Layer Properties and uncheck the check mark in the Print column of the Vanishing Point row. To hide the Vanishing Point on the drawing, uncheck the check mark in the Visible column of the Vanishing Point row.

Using Multiple Vanishing Points

You can create even more dramatic diagrams by adding additional Vanishing Point shapes to a diagram and associating shapes to those Vanishing Points. Visio doesn't support true two-point perspective. Although each shape connects to only one Vanishing Point, adding a second Vanishing Point can spice up your presentation graphics. To work with an additional Vanishing Point, follow these steps:

1. Drag a Vanishing Point from the Block with Perspective stencil onto the drawing.

2. To associate a shape to the new Vanishing Point, first select the shape. If the shape is associated with another Vanishing Point, drag the red control handle that appears in the first Vanishing Point and glue it to the connection point on the new Vanishing Point. A red square highlights the Vanishing Point, indicating that the shapes are connected. If the shape is not associated with a Vanishing Point shape, drag the yellow control handle that appears on the

drawing page when you select the shape, and glue it to the connection point on the new Vanishing Point.

Note　When you add new shapes, they associate automatically with the first Vanishing Point, which Visio adds by default to each block diagram that you create with the Block Diagram with Perspective template. You must change the connection for each shape you want connected to the other Vanishing Point.

Working with Onion Diagrams

Onion diagrams use concentric rings to illustrate concepts or elements that build up from a core, such as the layers that make up our planet. Although the objects represented on an onion diagram grow from the center, you construct an onion diagram from the outside in.

Creating Onion Diagrams

The Blocks stencil contains Concentric Layer and Partial Layer shapes that you can use out of the box for up to four layers of an onion. If you require more than four layers, you can resize the largest layer and add additional rings. To create an onion diagram, follow these steps:

1. Choose File ➪ New ➪ Block Diagram ➪ Block Diagram.

2. To establish the outer layer of the onion, drag the Concentric Layer 1 shape onto the drawing page.

3. To add the next layer of the onion, drag the Concentric Layer 2 shape onto the drawing and drop it onto the center of the first concentric shape.

4. To add the third layer of the onion, drag the Concentric Layer 3 shape onto the drawing and drop it onto the center of the other concentric shapes.

5. To add the core of the onion, drag the Concentric Center shape onto the drawing and drop it onto the center of the other concentric shapes.

6. To add text to a ring, select the shape and type the text you want.

Modifying Onion Diagram Shapes

Whether you need additional layers or want to change a layer's size or thickness, you'll probably modify the standard concentric rings after you add them to your drawing.

Adjusting Layer Dimensions

You can resize Concentric Layer shapes or change their radius and thickness. You must realign the shapes after you make these adjustments. Use one of the following methods to adjust Concentric Layer shapes:

✦ To resize a Concentric Layer shape, drag one of the selection handles to change the radius of the circle. The opposite selection handle remains fixed on the drawing, as demonstrated in Figure 12-4.

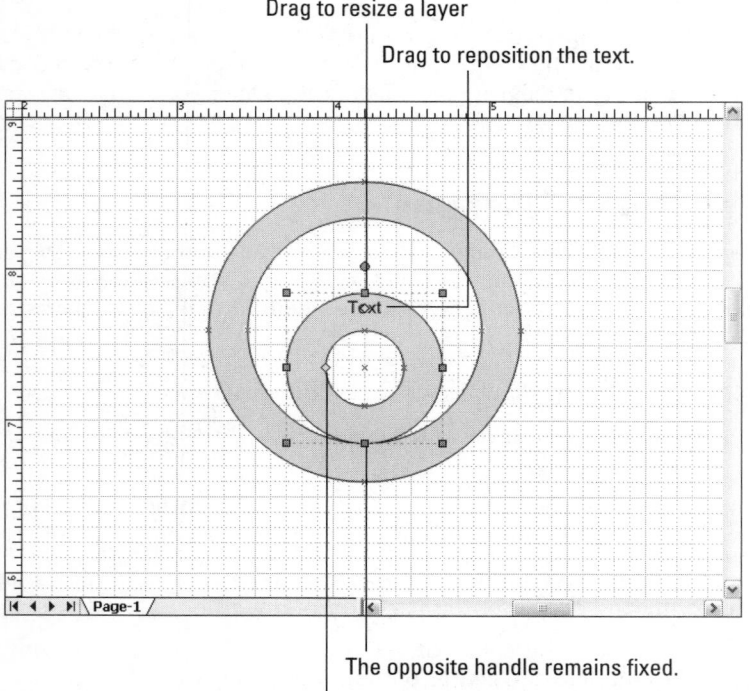

Figure 12-4: You can change the radius, thickness, and text position of a Concentric Layer shape.

✦ To change the thickness of a ring, drag the yellow control handle on the inside edge of the shape.

Tip To realign concentric rings after you modify their size or thickness, select all the Concentric Layer shapes and choose Shape ⇨ Align Shapes. Select the centered vertical alignment option, select the centered horizontal alignment option, and then click OK.

✦ To fit a smaller ring inside a larger ring, drag the selection handle on the left outside edge of the smaller ring and snap it to the connection point on the left inside edge of the larger ring. Then, drag the selection handle on the right outside edge of the smaller ring and snap it to the connection point on the right inside edge of the larger ring.

Dividing a Concentric Layer into Sections

You can divide a Concentric Layer shape into sections to show several components. The Partial Layer shapes on the Blocks stencil fit the Concentric Layer shapes. When you drop a Partial Layer shape onto a Concentric Layer shape, they connect and act as one, so you can drag a Concentric Layer shape's selection handles to resize it and its associated Partial Layer shapes. To divide a Concentric Layer into sections, follow these steps:

1. Drag a Partial Layer shape that matches the size of the Concentric Layer onto the drawing.

2. To rotate a Partial Layer, select it after dropping it onto the page and then press Ctrl+L as many times as necessary to rotate the shape into the correct quadrant.

3. If necessary, use the editing techniques described in the previous section to adjust the radius or thickness of the partial layer.

4. Drag the Partial Layer over the Concentric Layer you want to divide. When the Partial Layer snaps to the Concentric Layer, the red squares highlight the outside connection point and the center of the Concentric Layer shape to indicate that the shapes are glued, as shown in Figure 12-5.

Working with Text in Onion Diagrams

Text can be difficult to work with in onion diagrams because the shapes are curved and the text is straight. You have a few options when a long text string doesn't fit within a concentric ring. For text that almost fits, you can apply a smaller font or try a narrower font such as Arial Narrow. For long text, you can position the text outside the shape by dragging the control handle in the middle of the Concentric Layer to a position outside the shape. You can also annotate an onion diagram using Callout shapes. To open a stencil of Callout shapes, choose File ⇨ Shapes ⇨ Visio Extras ⇨ Callouts.

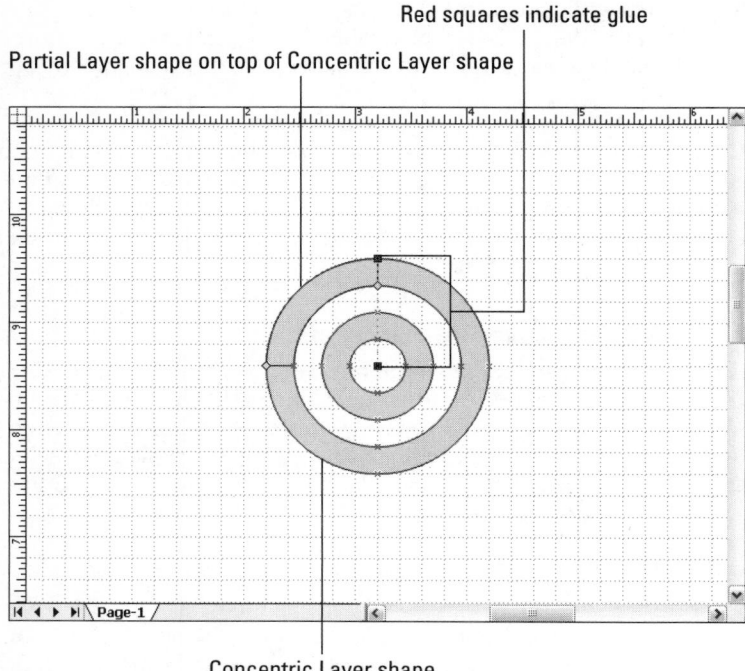

Figure 12-5: You can subdivide Concentric Layers by gluing Partial Layer shapes to them.

5. To modify the length of the arc for a Partial Layer, drag the yellow control handle on the Partial Layer's outside edge.

6. To rotate a Partial Layer within the Concentric Layer, drag the red selection handle.

Summary

The templates and shapes for Block Diagrams are easy to use and include many helpful features. Using basic Visio techniques, you can document structure and flow or communicate hierarchy or concepts revolving around a central idea. Visio Block shapes can be as simple as one-dimensional arrows and two-dimensional geometric shapes, but you can also produce impressive diagrams for presentations by using shadows or shapes with perspective.

✦   ✦   ✦

Constructing Charts and Graphs

Charts and graphs illustrate scientific results, financial performance, marketing analysis, and many other types of quantitative data. Microsoft Visio and Microsoft Excel both offer features for constructing charts and graphs.

If the data you want to present is already stored in a Microsoft Excel spreadsheet, you can use the Insert Chart command in Excel to create different types of charts or graphs based on your spreadsheet data. In Excel, you can format every component of an Excel chart to achieve the look you want. In most cases, Excel is better than Visio for developing and formatting charts.

However, if you're developing a presentation that summarizes data from a variety of sources, it might be easier to build a chart or graph in Visio. The charts and graphs in the Visio Charts and Graphs template don't work with data stored in other sources, so you have to drag Visio shapes onto a drawing and type the values you want into the shape text blocks.

The Visio Charts and Graphs template includes shapes for common chart and graph styles, such as bar graphs, line graphs, pie charts, distribution curves, feature comparison tables, and any kind of tabular information. In addition, you can use Visio's marketing shapes to analyze and communicate sales and marketing information, such as sales prospects, market analysis, market share, and marketing mix.

> **Note** The Forms template is no longer available in Visio 2003, having been replaced by the form-building features in Microsoft's new product, InfoPath.

Exploring the Chart and Graph Templates

Chart and graph shapes are simple enough that the Chart and Graph templates don't contain any specialized menus, toolbars, or add-ons. You can create charts and graphs by dragging and dropping shapes from Visio's stencils and adding text and numbers to components in the shapes. You can modify charts and graphs by dragging shape handles or by applying colors and formatting.

Choosing the Right Template

Visio offers two templates for charts and graphs, both of which contain shapes you can use for general purposes or specialized marketing presentations. Both templates automatically set the page to a letter-size sheet with portrait orientation, use inches drawn at a one-to-one scale, and open the Backgrounds and Borders and Titles stencils.

The Charts and Graphs template supports more generic charting applications, such as basic bar and line graphs, pie charts, and generic grids to show tabular information. However, if you're not sure what kind of chart and graph shapes you want, just use the Marketing Charts and Diagrams template, which opens all three chart and graph stencils: Charting Shapes, Marketing Shapes, and Marketing Diagrams.

Note   The Forms template and Forms stencil are not available in Visio 2003. Beginning with Office 2003, you can use Microsoft InfoPath to design and construct forms. These forms are based on XML so you can use them to collect data for XML-compatible databases and back-end business systems.

Exploring Visio Chart and Graph Shapes

Chart and Graph shapes are simple to use. You can drag selection handles or control handles to resize them or modify their components. In tabular shapes, such as the Grid shape and the Feature Comparison chart, you can select and edit individual cells. Chart shapes that include custom properties for configuring the shape display a dialog box after you drop the shape onto a drawing. You can specify how many data points or other elements you want and click OK to complete the addition of the shape. To configure one of these shapes after you add it to a drawing, right-click it and choose a configuration command from the shortcut menu.

New Feature   The Grid shape on the Charting Shapes stencil replaces the Table shape available in previous versions of Visio. When you open a drawing that contains a Table shape in Visio 2003, the Table retains its formatting, but the formatting commands aren't available to modify the table formatting further. If you want to format the table, you must recreate your table by dragging a Grid shape onto the drawing page and reentering the table values.

Charting Shapes

The Charting Shapes stencil, shown in Figure 13-1, provides the basic shapes to create standard charts and graphs. You can drag the shapes you want onto the drawing and add text to the shapes or in separate annotation shapes. Some of these shapes include control handles you can drag to modify the appearance of the chart and graph components.

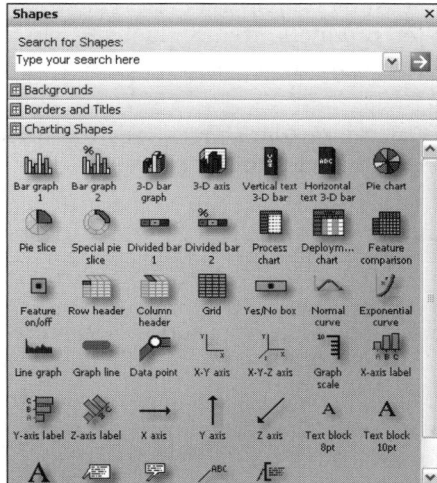

Figure 13-1: The Charting Shapes stencil provides shapes for commonly used charts and graphs.

✦ **Bar Graphs** — The Bar Graph 1 shape shows numerical values, whereas Bar Graph 2 is set up to show percentages. You can use the X-Y axis, Graph Scale, and axis label shapes to add axes to your bar graphs.

✦ **3-D Bar Graphs** — The 3-D Bar Graph and 3-D Axis shapes work together to document three-dimensional bar graphs. You can construct your own 3-D graph using the 3-D bar shapes, the X-Y-Z axis shape, and the shapes that label the x, y, and z axes.

✦ **Pie Charts** — The Pie Chart shape creates a whole pie with up to ten slices. To create a pie with more slices, you can use Pie Slice shapes. The Special Pie Slice shape shows a concentric ring that you can place on top of a pie slice. It is similar to the Partial Layer shape for onion diagrams available in the Block Diagram template.

✦ **Divided Bars** — The Divided Bar 1 shape shows numerical values, whereas the Divided Bar 2 shape is set up to show percentages. You can add text to the divided bars or use the X-axis and axis label shapes to annotate the divided bars.

✦ **Tabular Charts** — The Process Chart shape includes up to ten steps, with symbols to document the activities within each step. The Deployment Chart is a table for tracking the rollout of systems in an organization. It can show up to six departments implemented over five phases.

✦ **Feature Comparison Charts** — The Feature Comparison Chart shape can compare up to ten features across up to ten products. You can indicate whether a product supports a feature completely, partially, or not at all by adding Feature On/Off shapes in each grid cell.

✦ **Grids** — The Grid, Row Header, and Column Header shapes create generic tables. The Yes/No Box can display a filled circle, hollow circle, or text.

✦ **Distribution and Exponential Graphs** — The Normal Curve shape displays a distribution curve. Control points change the shape and skew of the distribution. You can change the height and width of the Exponential Curve, but not its shape.

✦ **Line Graph Shapes** — The Line Graph shape displays a series of data points with the area under the graph filled. You can highlight lines on a graph with the Graph Line and Data Point shapes.

✦ **Annotation Shapes** — You can annotate your chart or graph with labels, text blocks with different font sizes, balloons, callouts, or annotation shapes.

Marketing Shapes

Most of the shapes in the Marketing Shapes stencil look like clip art and are useful for developing sales and marketing presentations. A few of the shapes are extendable, such as People and Variable Building. When you drag the selection handle on the side of the People shape, it will add up to four people. Dragging the selection handle on the top of the Variable building shape adds up to ten floors to a skyscraper.

Marketing Charts and Diagrams

The Marketing Diagrams stencil, shown in Figure 13-2, provides shapes to create charts and graphs typically used for marketing, such as market share, circle-spoke, or marketing mix. However, you can take advantage of these shapes to illustrate any kind of data.

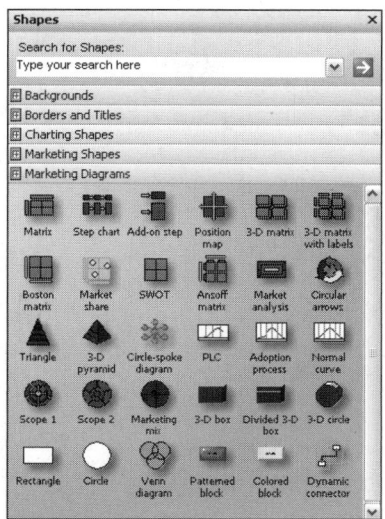

Figure 13-2: The Marketing Diagrams stencil provides shapes for a variety of marketing-oriented charts.

Constructing Basic Charts and Graphs

Visio provides shapes for commonly drawn charts, such as 3-D bar graphs, but also includes shapes so you can assemble your own chart from scratch. If you find that a predefined chart won't illustrate your data the way you want, you can build a graph with individual shapes.

Constructing Bar Graphs

In Visio 2003, you can create 2-D or 3-D bar graphs. Visio provides predefined 2-D shapes that can display up to ten bars. The 3-D bar graph shape includes up to five 3-D bars.

Creating 2-D Bar Graphs

You can construct a 2-D bar graph by dropping one of the bar graph shapes onto a drawing. To annotate the bar graph, you can add axes and axis labels as well as a variety of annotation shapes. To create a 2-D bar graph, follow these steps:

1. Drag a Bar Graph shape onto your drawing, choose the number of bars from the drop-down list, and click OK.

2. To set the height for the tallest bar in the graph, drag the yellow control handle at the top left of the Bar Graph shape until the tallest bar is the height you want for the largest Y-value, or 100% for graphs showing percentages, as demonstrated in Figure 13-3.

Drag to set the height of the tallest bar.

Drag to resize the entire graph.

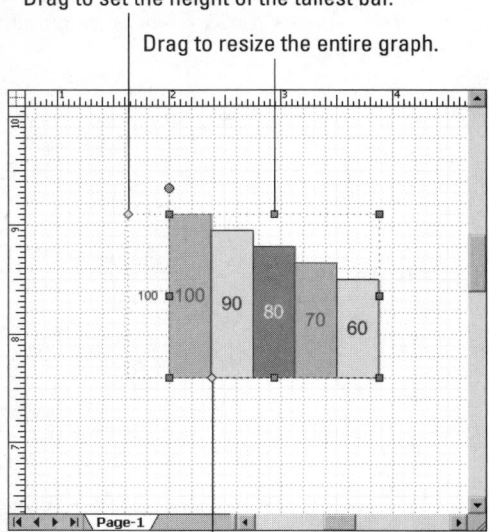

Drag to change the width of the bars.

Figure 13-3: Drag selection and control handles to adjust the size of a bar graph.

3. To set the width of all the bars, drag the yellow control handle at the bottom right of the first bar and drag it until the bars are the width you want.

4. To specify the value for a bar, click the graph, click the bar to select it, and type the value for that bar.

Caution

Although the Bar Graph 2 shape is set up to show percentages, you must type **%** after the number when you enter a value for a bar. If you don't end a number with %, Visio converts the number to a percentage by multiplying by 100 and sets the bar to the resulting height. For example, typing **1** will create a bar the same height as 100%.

5. To change the number of bars in a graph, right-click the Bar Graph shape, choose Set Number of Bars from the shortcut menu, select the number of bars you want, and click OK.

Note

To access the shortcut menu for the Bar Graph shape, make sure that none of the individual bars are selected and then right-click anywhere on the bar graph. Right-clicking a selected bar displays the shortcut menu for that bar. If a bar is selected, you can select the Bar Graph shape by right-clicking the dotted, green boundary line of the shape.

6. To change the color for a bar, first select the bar, then right-click it, and choose Format ⇨ Fill from the shortcut menu. Select the fill options you want and click OK.

7. To add the x and y axes to a 2-D bar graph, drag the X-Y axis shape until the origin snaps to the bottom-left corner of the first bar in the graph.

8. To label the units for the axes, click the X-axis or Y-axis text blocks and type the label you want.

Creating 3-D Bar Graphs

To create a 3-D bar graph, follow these steps:

1. Drag the 3-D Axis shape onto your drawing.

Note   You can drag the control handles on the 3-D Axis shape to reposition the labels, change the number of grid lines, change the thickness of the wall, or change the depth of the third dimension.

2. Drag the 3-D Bar Graph shape onto your drawing and drop it on the origin of the 3-D Axis shape. In the Custom Properties dialog box that appears automatically, select the number of bars from the drop-down list. You can also specify the values and colors for each of the bars. Click OK when you are finished.

Tip   If you drag the 3-D Bar Graph shape onto your drawing before the 3-D Axis shape, the axis shape hides the bar graph. To change the stacking order of these shapes, right-click the 3-D Axis shape and choose Shape ⇨ Send to Back from the shortcut menu.

3. To change the height of the graph, drag the green selection handle at the top or bottom of the shape.

4. To set the width of all the bars, drag the yellow control handle at the bottom right of the first bar and drag it until the bars are the width you want.

5. To specify the value or color for a bar, right-click the 3-D Bar Graph shape, choose Bar Properties from the shortcut menu, and edit the values in the Custom Properties dialog box. Click OK when you are finished.

6. To change the number of bars in a graph, right-click the 3-D Bar Graph shape and choose Bar Count and Range from the shortcut menu. Select the number of bars you want in the Bar Count drop-down list and click OK.

7. To change the height of bars in relation to the overall shape, right-click the 3-D Bar Graph shape and choose Bar Count and Range from the shortcut menu. In the Range box, type the value represented by the top of the y axis. For example, if you change the range from 4 to 8, the bars in the graph shorten by half.

Constructing Line Graphs

Unlike Microsoft Excel, Visio provides only one type of line graph. If you want to graph two lines or choose from different markers for data points, it's easier to add data to a spreadsheet and use Insert Chart in Excel. If you want to create a simple line graph in Visio, follow these steps:

1. Drag the Line Graph shape onto a drawing. In the Custom Properties dialog box that appears automatically, select the number of data points you want, and click OK.

Tip To change the number of data points after adding the shape to a drawing, right-click the line graph, choose Set Number of Data Points, pick a number, and click OK.

2. To change the length of the x or y axis, drag the control handle at the end of the axis to the length you want.

3. To change the value of a data point, drag the control handle for that data point to the appropriate value on the y axis.

4. To emphasize data points on a line graph, drag a Data Point shape onto the drawing and snap it to the control handle for a data point. To emphasize the lines between data points, drag a Graph Line shape onto the drawing. Glue each end to a pair of consecutive data points.

Labeling Axes

The axis shapes include text blocks that you can edit to show the units for an axis, such as the number of support calls handled on the y axis versus days of the week on the x axis. In addition to the text blocks in the axis shapes, you can add axis label shapes to show numeric values along each axis. To add axis labels to bar graphs or line graphs, follow these steps:

1. Drag the Y-axis Label shape onto the drawing so that its horizontal line is aligned with the x axis.

Tip If you want to zoom in to make it easier to add labels, press and hold Ctrl+Shift and click the graph.

2. To copy the Y-axis label, select the Y-axis shape and then press Ctrl+D. Drag the second label so its horizontal line is even with the highest value you want to label.

3. Repeat step 2 to create labels for intermediate values along the y axis.

4. Repeat steps 1 through 3 with X-axis Label shapes to add labels along the x axis.

5. Select each label shape and type the value or name corresponding to the label position.

Tip You can use Distribute Shapes to space labels evenly along an axis. Select all the labels along an axis and choose Shape ➪ Distribute Shapes, select the first option for Vertical Distribution for Y-axis labels, select the first option for Horizontal Distribution for X-axis labels, and then click OK.

Working with Pie Charts

In most cases, it's easier to use Microsoft Excel for pie charts, but if you decide to create a pie chart in Visio, follow these steps:

1. Drag the Pie Chart shape onto the drawing, select the number of slices you want, and click OK.

2. To specify the size of each slice, right-click the pie chart and choose Set Slice Sizes from the shortcut menu. Type the percentage for each slice in the Custom Properties dialog box and then click OK.

Note If the values you enter for the slices don't total 100 percent, part of the pie will be empty.

The Pie Chart shape is a single shape that can represent up to ten slices. If you want to create a pie chart with more than ten slices or emphasize one or more of the slices, you can use Pie Slice shapes, which represent individual slices of pie to build a pie chart. To do this, follow these steps:

1. Drag the first Pie Slice shape onto the drawing.

2. To change the radius of the slice, drag the green selection handle at the outside edge of the slice.

3. Drag another Pie Slice shape and drop it close to the first slice.

4. Drag the green selection handle at the bottom right of the second slice to the vertex at the top left of the first slice, as shown in Figure 13-4. Drag the green selection handle at the center of the second slice to the vertex at the bottom left of the first slice. When you are done, the radius of the second slice will match that of the first slice.

5. To modify the percentage of a slice, select the slice and drag the yellow control handle until the percentage shown in the slice is the value you want.

Tip To increase the size of a slice by 1 percent, right-click the slice and choose Add 1% from the shortcut menu.

6. To change the color of a slice, right-click it and choose Format ➪ Fill from the shortcut menu. Select the fill options you want and click OK.

7. Repeat steps 3 and 4 to add additional slices, always adding slices counterclockwise around the pie.

This handle has been dragged into position.

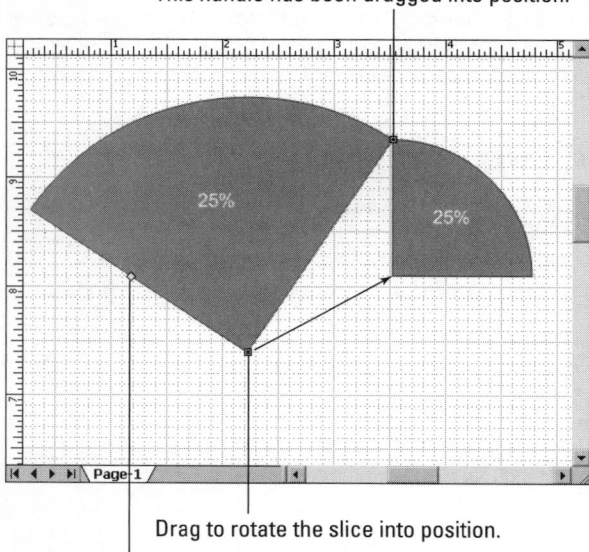

Drag to rotate the slice into position.

Drag to modify the slice percentage.

Figure 13-4: Drag selection handles to build a pie chart from pie slice shapes.

If you create a pie chart with individual slices, you can emphasize a slice by dragging the slice away from the center of the pie. If the slice tends to snap to another shape, choose Tools ➪ Snap & Glue. Uncheck some of the check boxes, such as Shape Geometry, in the Snap To column, click OK, and then try to move the slice again.

Creating Feature Comparison Charts

Feature comparison charts illustrate the features that products possess so that you can choose the product that best fits your requirements. The Feature On/Off shape includes three status options:

+ **Blank** — Indicates that the feature doesn't exist for that product

+ **A filled circle** — Indicates that the product provides the feature

+ **A hollow circle** — Can indicate that the product provides the feature with some limitations

To create a feature comparison table, follow these steps:

1. Drag the Feature Comparison shape onto the drawing. Select the number of features and number of products to compare and click OK.

2. To enter a feature description, click a row header cell and type the name of the feature. To add a product name, click a column header cell and type the name of the product.

3. To add a status, drag the Feature On/Off shape onto a cell in the comparison chart, select the status option you want, and click OK. Repeat this step for each cell in the chart.

4. To change the number of features or products, right-click the chart and choose Set Fields from the shortcut menu.

Working with Marketing Diagrams

You can create marketing diagrams by dragging shapes from the Marketing Diagram stencil and specifying options for those shapes. Many of the marketing shapes include shortcut menu commands to modify the shape configuration. For example, you can specify the number of arrows in a Circular Arrows shape when you first add the shape, or you can specify the number later using the Set Number of Arrows command on the shape's shortcut menu. Some shapes also include control handles that you can drag to make other adjustments. This section describes some of the special features on marketing diagrams.

Building Circle-Spoke Drawings

Circle-spoke diagrams include up to eight circles arranged on spokes around a center circle. To create a circle-spoke diagram, follow these steps:

1. Drag the Circle-spoke shape onto the drawing. Select the number of circles desired and click OK. You can change the number of circles later by right-clicking the shape and choosing Set Number of Circles from the shortcut menu.

2. To relocate or rearrange the outer circles, drag the yellow control handle in the middle of a circle to a new location, as shown in Figure 13-5.

3. To resize the diagram, drag a selection handle.

Note   When you resize a diagram, Visio resets outer circles to be equally spaced from one another and at the same distance from the center.

Drag to resize the circle-spoke diagram.

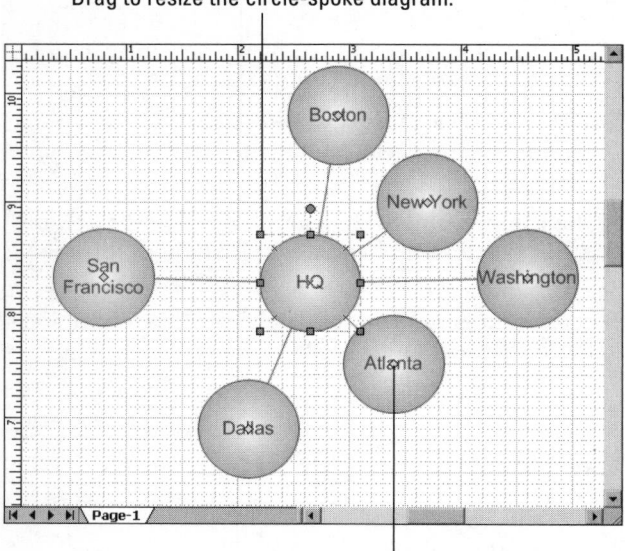

Drag to reposition a circle.

Figure 13-5: You can reposition and rearrange the circles in a circle-spoke diagram.

Constructing Triangles and Pyramids

You can create triangular charts and 3-D pyramids to show hierarchical relationships. To create a triangular chart, follow these steps:

1. Drag a Triangle shape onto the drawing. Select the number of levels wanted and click OK.

2. To specify an offset that defines the gap between each layer of the triangle, right-click the shape and choose Set Offset from the shortcut menu. Type the number of inches between the layers and click OK.

3. To switch between a flat triangle and a three-dimensional triangle, right-click the triangle shape on the drawing and choose either 2-Dimensional or 3-Dimensional from the shortcut menu.

4. To change the number of levels after you have added the shape to the drawing, right-click the shape and choose Set Number of Levels from the shortcut menu.

When you add a 3-D pyramid to a drawing, you can specify up to six levels in the pyramid and can choose one color for the entire pyramid. To change these settings later, right-click the pyramid and choose Set Number of Levels or Set Pyramid Color from the shortcut menu.

Adding Text to Charts and Graphs

Depending on the chart and graph shapes you use, you can select a shape, a cell, or a text block within a shape and add text simply by typing. For example, you can select the text block on the left side of a Bar Graph shape to label the y axis. You can also select each bar in the Bar Graph shape to specify the height of the bar. If you select the entire Bar Graph shape and begin typing, Visio adds a text block below the x axis.

In addition to the text within shapes, the Visio Chart and Graph templates open stencils with title and callout shapes you can use to annotate your drawing. To add a title to your drawings, you can use the Text Block shapes from the Charting Shapes stencil or choose one of the title block shapes from the Borders and Titles stencil.

You can add other types of annotation to a chart or graph. To add a word balloon to a drawing, follow these steps:

1. Drag a 1-D or 2-D Word Balloon shape onto the drawing.
2. With the word balloon shape selected, type the text you want in the word balloon.
3. To change the size of the word balloon, drag a green selection handle to a new position.
4. To aim the pointer, drag the yellow control handle to a new position. The pointer automatically protrudes from the side of the balloon closest to the end of the pointer.

To add other annotation to a drawing, follow these steps:

1. Drag a Horizontal Callout or Annotation shape onto the drawing.
2. With the shape selected, type the text you want. The height of the shape adjusts to display the text you type.
3. To change the width of the annotation, drag a green selection handle to a new position.

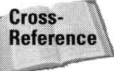 To learn more about annotating drawings, refer to Chapter 6.

Using Stackable and Extendable Shapes

You can easily modify marketing shapes that are stackable or extendable. When you stretch stackable shapes, they stack additional shapes vertically or horizontally — for example, showing additional people to represent population. Extendable shapes stretch without distorting parts of the shape.

To work with stackable shapes in a chart or graph, follow these steps:

1. Drag a stackable shape, such as the People shape or the Variable Building shape, from the Marketing Shapes stencil onto the drawing.

2. To extend the shape, drag a selection handle. Additional repeating elements will appear.

3. To create a longer series, press Ctrl+D to copy the stackable shape and align it end to end with the first shape.

To work with extendable shapes in a chart or graph, follow these steps:

1. Drag an extendable shape, such as the Pencil shape, from the Marketing Shapes stencil onto the drawing.

2. To change the length of the extendable shape, drag a green selection handle.

Summary

Visio chart and graph templates provide shapes to produce a wide variety of charts, graphs, and marketing diagrams. However, if you want to create commonly used charts and graphs from numeric data stored in a spreadsheet, the Insert Chart command in Microsoft Excel is easier and more flexible. The Visio Marketing Shapes stencil includes clip art shapes for sales presentations. If you want to communicate the results of marketing efforts, you can use marketing-oriented shapes, such as feature comparison charts or marketing mix shapes in the Charting Shapes and Marketing Diagrams stencils.

✦　　✦　　✦

Working with Organization Charts

Organizations come in many shapes and sizes, with both formal and informal reporting structures. In strictly hierarchical enterprises, authority and communication travels up and down lines of command. Alternatively, companies that perform large multidisciplinary projects often use a strong matrix structure whereby workers report to project managers for the projects they work on in addition to a functional manager for other assignments and administrative issues.

Organization charts document the formal structure and relationships within an enterprise, including business units, functional areas, teams, and individuals. It's sad but typically true that the unofficial relationships that propel progress remain undocumented even with an easy-to-use tool like Visio 2003.

When you use the Organization Chart template to create organization charts in Visio 2003, your diagrams are inherently hierarchical diagrams because even the strongest matrix organization has a hierarchy at its core. You can use the Visio 2003 organization chart features just as easily for other hierarchical diagrams, such as the genealogy of a family tree. In this chapter, you learn how to create organization charts from scratch or by importing organization data from other sources.

Exploring the Organization Chart Template

The Organization Chart template includes a stencil of Organization Chart shapes, a menu of specialized Organization Chart commands, a toolbar with layout and positioning tools, and a wizard to help build organization charts. The following sections describe the basics of these features.

Exploring the Organization Chart Tools

The Organization Chart menu contains commands to create, layout, format, modify, and update Visio organization charts. As you can see in Figure 14-1, when you open an existing Visio organization chart or create a new organization chart drawing, an Organization Chart stencil and toolbar appear and the Visio menu bar picks up an Organization Chart entry that you can choose to access the Organization Chart menu.

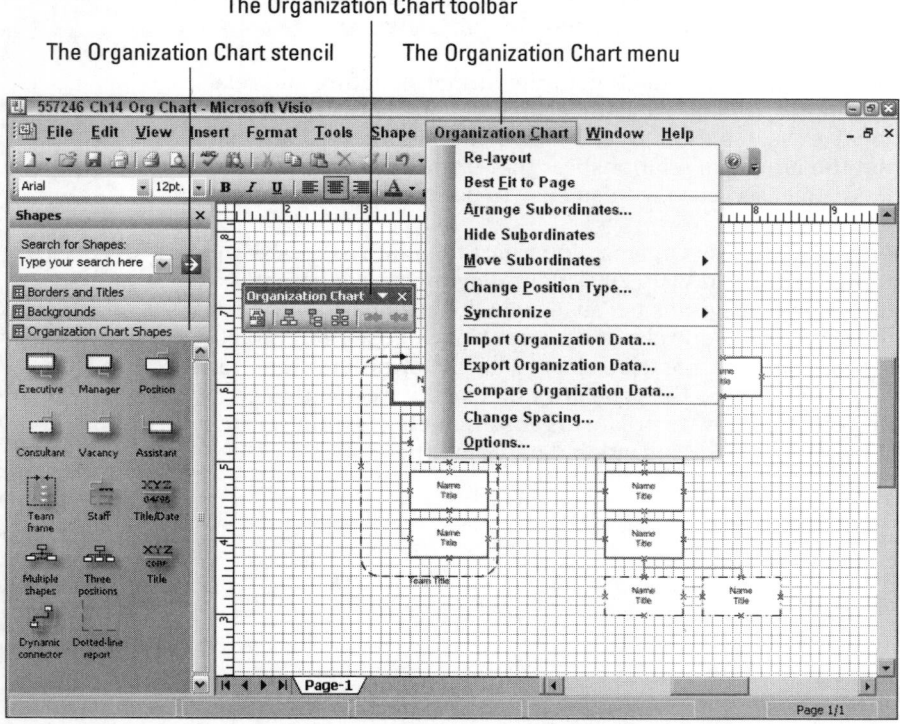

Figure 14-1: The Organization Chart template includes a menu, toolbar, and stencil.

Tip   Many of the Organization Chart commands are also available on a shortcut menu when you right-click a shape on a drawing page.

You can construct a hierarchical drawing manually by dragging and dropping shapes from the Organization Chart stencil onto the drawing page. When you drop an employee shape on top of another shape, Visio adds a connector between the shapes, which creates a reporting relationship from an employee to his or her manager. Standard Visio tools and techniques work for rearranging shapes or modifying an organization chart's content and format. However, it's much easier to use the template's layout and editing tools to arrange and format the shapes on your organization chart.

Exploring Visio's Organization Chart Shapes

The Organization Chart stencil includes shapes with formats that denote levels in a hierarchy or special conditions such as assistants, outside consultants, and vacancies. However, any employee shape in the stencil can act as either superior or subordinate. The Organization Chart stencil also includes a few shapes to speed up frequently used groupings, such as several resources reporting to a superior. For example, the appearance of the following employee shapes helps show levels in an organization chart:

+ Executive

+ Manager

+ Position

+ Staff position

The appearance of the following shapes indicate special situations, such as a dotted-line boundary for a vacancy, but these shapes can still act as superiors or subordinates:

+ Consultant

+ Assistant

+ Vacancy

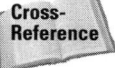

Cross-Reference   To learn how to change the appearance of Organization Chart shapes by applying a design theme, refer to the "Setting Organization Chart Options" section later in this chapter.

The following shapes simplify working with groups of employees in an organization chart:

✦ **Multiple Shapes** — Adds the number of positions and connectors that you specify to the superior shape on which you drop it

✦ **Three Positions** — Adds three positions as subordinates to the superior shape on which you drop it

✦ **Team Frame** — Indicates graphically that the employees within the frame are members of a team

New Feature The Dotted Line Report connector is a dynamic connector new in Visio 2003. An employee can have only one primary reporting relationship. To show an employee reporting to an additional manager, you can drop the dotted line report connector onto an additional shape that represents a superior and drag the other end to the shape that represents the employee.

Creating Organization Charts Manually

When you're documenting a large organization, it's easier to import data into Visio. If you don't have an existing source of organization data or you're building an organization chart for a small group, it's just as easy to create an organization chart manually. Starting at the top of the hierarchy — with a company president or the manager of a group, for example — you drag and drop shapes representing employees from the Organization Chart stencil onto the drawing page. By dropping a subordinate shape onto a superior, you can define the connection and reporting relationship as you add employees to the chart, as demonstrated in Figure 14-2.

Visio creates a connector and arranges the shapes.

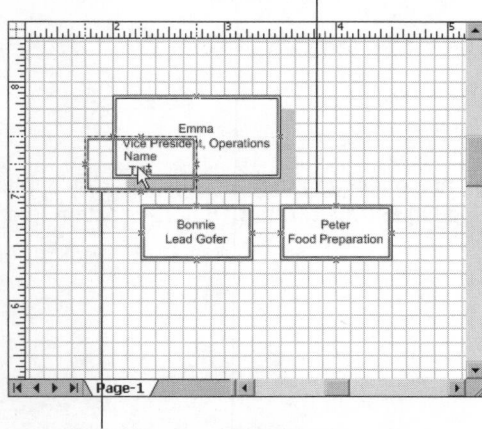

Figure 14-2: Organization chart shapes are smart enough to create connections and reporting relationships when you drop them on other shapes.

Drag a shape onto the shape it reports to.

To create an organization chart manually, follow these steps:

1. Choose File ➪ New ➪ Organization Chart ➪ Organization Chart.

2. Drag an Executive shape onto the drawing page.

Note When you begin your first organization chart, Visio displays a message box that demonstrates how to connect shapes. To hide this reminder in the future, check the Don't Show This Message Again check box and click OK.

3. Because the Executive shape is selected immediately after you add it, type the employee's name, press Enter, and then type the employee's title.

4. To add a manager reporting to the executive, drag and drop a Manager shape from the stencil onto the Executive shape. Visio adds a connector between the shapes and assigns the manager as a subordinate to the executive. Visio also arranges the shapes based on the current layout.

5. Drag and drop additional shapes from the stencil onto their superiors on the drawing page.

Note You can assign a name and title to each shape as you add it or add all the shapes to the chart and then select each one and assign its values.

6. Select a shape and type the employee's name and title as you did in step 3. To conclude your text entry, click the drawing page, press Esc, or drag a shape from the stencil.

Tip If the shapes you add overlap each other, click Re-layout on the Organization Chart toolbar to rearrange them.

7. To modify the layout of a group of subordinates, select the superior shape to which the group reports, click a layout option in the Organization Chart toolbar, and select a layout configuration.

8. To add additional information such as department or telephone number, right-click a shape and choose Properties from the shortcut menu. Type values in custom property boxes and click OK when you are finished.

Tip If your organization chart is cluttered or doesn't look the way you want, see the "Formatting Organization Chart Appearance" section later in this chapter.

Creating Organization Charts Using the Organization Chart Wizard

The Organization Chart Wizard guides you through the steps of creating an organization chart whether you have organization data ready or not. It's easy to build an organization chart if you already have personnel data in an ODBC-compliant database, a Microsoft Exchange Server, or even a spreadsheet or text file.

If you store personnel data in another type of system, you can still use that data to construct an organization chart by exporting it into a spreadsheet or comma-delimited file. In the worst case, when the personnel data is still in your head, the Organization Chart Wizard will create a file or spreadsheet for you to fill out.

You can use one of the following methods to access the Organization Chart Wizard to create an organization chart:

✦ Choose File ➪ New ➪ Organization Chart folder ➪ Organization Chart Wizard.

✦ Choose Tools ➪ Add-Ons ➪ Organization Chart ➪ Organization Chart Wizard

✦ If the Organization Chart template is active, choose Organization Chart ➪ Import Organization Data.

Building a File for Organization Data Using the Organization Chart Wizard

Follow the steps in this section to construct an organization chart data file using a template in the wizard:

Note   With this option, you can only work with data entered in the default columns. If you want to import additional data into boxes and custom properties in an organization chart, you must create your organization chart data file before you start the wizard. Then, when you start the wizard, select the Information That's Already Stored in a File or Database option.

1. To create the organization chart by entering data into a new file, select the Information That I Enter Using The Wizard option and click Next.

2. Select the Microsoft Excel option to enter data in a spreadsheet, or the Delimited Text option to create a text file. To specify the name and folder for the new data file, click Browse.

3. Navigate to the folder you want to use, type the name for the data file into the File Name box, and then click Save. Click Next to open the file.

4. After reading the instructions for creating the data file, click OK. A template file opens in Excel for a spreadsheet, as shown in Figure 14-3; or a text editor opens for a delimited file. The file contains three sample entries that demonstrate how to define top-level and subordinate entries in the organization chart. Replace the sample text with your data and enter additional rows of data for each position in your organization chart.

5. After you have completed your data entry, choose File ➪ Exit to save the file and return to the Organization Chart Wizard. Next, skip to the "Finalizing Your Chart" section later in this chapter and follow the steps outlined there to finish creating your organization chart.

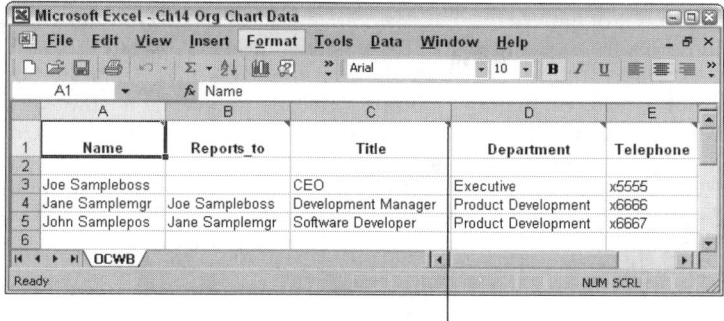

Click to view additional instructions.

Figure 14-3: Excel's Organization Chart Data template includes sample entries and instructions for entering data.

Using Existing Organization Data

Follow the steps in this section to build an organization chart using data from an existing file.

1. To create an organization chart from existing data, select the Information That's Already Stored in a File or Database option and click Next.

2. Select the option for the type of data file you want to use and click Next.

3. For the type of data file you chose, specify the information required to identify the data file you want to use. Your options are as follows:

   - **Spreadsheet or delimited text file** — Click Browse to specify the folder and filename.

   - **Microsoft Exchange Directory** — You do not have to provide any information for this option.

   - **ODBC-compliant data source** — If you have already defined a data source for your organization data, click the name of the data source in the list. If you select a generic type of ODBC-compliant data source, such as Microsoft Access Database or Excel Files, you must also specify the folder and filename of the database. After specifying the data source, you must also select the table in the database that contains your organization data.

Tip   One advantage to using an ODBC-compliant data source is that you can link database records to shapes so that shape values change when the data source is updated.

Note   If the ODBC-compliant data source list doesn't contain the type of data source you are using, click Create Data Source. To create a data source, you must specify whether the data source applies only to the current machine or is machine-independent. You also must choose the driver for the data source and the file that contains your organization data as the file to which this data source should be connected.

4. After defining the data source, click Next to associate the columns or fields in the data file to the data in the Visio organization chart.

5. To specify the field that contains employee names, select an entry in the Name drop-down list, as shown in Figure 14-4. The entries correspond to the column headings in a spreadsheet or delimited file, or to the field names in an ODBC-compliant database. Optionally, you can associate a field or column heading with the First Name drop-down list.

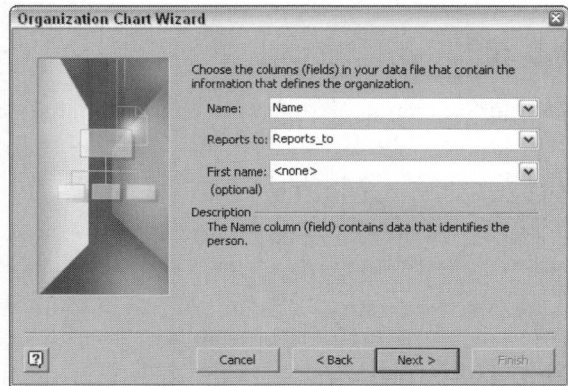

Figure 14-4: You can define your organization structure by associating fields in your data source to Organization Chart properties.

6. To specify a field that contains reporting relationships in a data source, select an entry in the Reports To drop-down list and click Next.

7. Select the fields that you want to appear in each box on the organization chart. You can use the Add or Remove buttons to build the list of fields, and the Up and Down buttons to define the order in which the fields appear. Click Next.

Note   Organization Chart shapes contain four default properties: department, telephone, name, and title. If you remove these properties from the field lists in the wizard, the custom properties still appear but the wizard will not transfer the values from your data file to the Visio diagram.

8. Select the fields whose data you want stored in custom properties associated with each box on the organization chart. You can use the Add or Remove buttons to build the list of fields. Click Next.

Linking Database Records to Shapes

When you link database records to shapes, you can control how these links operate by clicking the Settings button in the wizard. You can specify which database-related commands to include on a shortcut menu that appears when you right-click a linked shape.

✦ **Select database record** — Selects a database record to link to a shape.

✦ **Refresh shape's custom properties** — Updates a shape's custom properties to match the values in the linked data source.

✦ **Update database record** — Updates the linked database record to match the values in the shape's custom properties.

✦ **Delete shape and database record** — Removes the shape in the organization chart and the linked record in the data source.

You can also control when updates occur; update shape custom properties and database records each time you display a page; and refresh custom properties either when you open a Visio document or periodically by using the NOW function.

Tip

Displaying a field in a box on the organization chart automatically includes that field as a custom property for each shape. By associating a field with a custom property without displaying it in Organization Chart shapes, you can reduce clutter while providing access to the data. To view custom properties for a shape, right-click a shape and choose Properties from the shortcut menu.

9. Execute this step only if you are using an ODBC-compliant data file. Select either the Copy Database Records to Shapes or Link Database Records to Shapes option. If you link database records to shapes, the values in the organization chart will change when the database values change. Click Next.

Finalizing the Chart

You can control the placement of organization chart boxes across multiple pages in a Visio diagram. For example, you can produce summary pages for large organizations or show employees for different departments on separate pages. The steps to accomplish this are common to every type of data file, either existing or created using the wizard:

1. To create a hyperlink between shapes that represent the same employee on more than one page of your organization chart, check the Hyperlink Employee Shapes Across Pages check box. With this option, you can follow a hyperlink to a copy of an employee by right-clicking the shape and choosing the hyperlink from the shortcut menu.

2. To synchronize all shapes that represent the same employee so that changes made to one copy propagate to all other copies, check the Synchronize Employee Shapes Across Pages check box.

3. (Optional) If you want Visio to choose the breakpoints between pages, select the I Want The Wizard to Automatically Break My Organization Chart Across Pages option. After choosing this option, click Finish to create the organization chart and skip the rest of the steps in this list.

4. To specify how to distribute your organization across multiple pages, select the I Want to Specify How Much of My Organization to Display on Each Page option.

5. To specify the levels that you want to display on the first page, shown in Figure 14-5, click Modify Page. To use the first page as an executive summary, select the number of levels that you want to appear in the Number of Additional Levels box. Type a name for the page in the Page Name box and then click OK to return to the wizard screen.

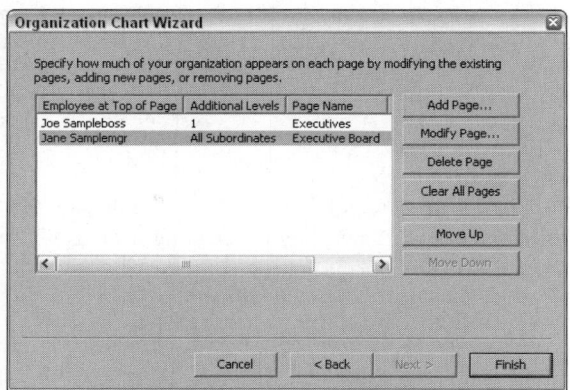

Figure 14-5: You can modify the number of organization chart pages and how many levels appear on each one.

6. To add additional pages to the organization chart — for example, to create a page for a lower level department — click Add Page. When you create additional pages, you can specify their contents and then click OK to return to the wizard screen:

   • To choose the name that appears at the first level on this new page, select a name in the Name at Top of Page list. For example, select the name of a manager shown at the lowest level of the executive summary page.

   • To show all subordinates who report to the person at the top-level of the page, select All Subordinates in the Additional Levels list.

- To show a number of levels below the top-level on this page, select that number in the Additional Levels list.

- Type a name for the page in the Page Name box.

7. When you have finished defining the pages for your chart, click Finish.

Formatting Organization Chart Appearance

The Organization Chart template includes tools and options to help you build attractive and easy-to-read organization charts. With Visio's organization chart layout options, you should rarely have to resort to laying out shapes manually. Visio's organization chart options enable you to fashion just the look you want for shapes and text. You can even apply a design theme, which applies consistent shape and text style formatting to your entire chart.

Laying Out the Organization

Visio provides numerous layout options that you can use to arrange subordinates reporting to a superior. Although Visio arranges subordinate shapes horizontally by default, you can specify different layout options for each person with *direct reports*. If you have synchronized copies of shapes on multiple pages of a chart, you can apply a different layout to each synchronized copy.

Tip　Although each shape with direct reports can use a different layout, your organization chart will be more readable if you choose one or two layouts only.

You can layout the direct reports for one or more managers or ask Visio to layout all the shapes on the active drawing page. To layout shapes on an organization chart, choose one of the following methods:

✦ **Layout a group** — Select the superior to whom the group reports, click one of the layout options on the Organization Chart toolbar, and click the configuration you want.

✦ **Layout multiple groups** — Select the superior for every group you want to layout by clicking the first superior and then Shift+clicking the others. Click one of the layout options on the Organization Chart toolbar and click the configuration you want.

Note　To see examples of each layout option, as shown in Figure 14-6, choose Organization Chart ➪ Arrange Subordinates. Click the layout you want and then click OK.

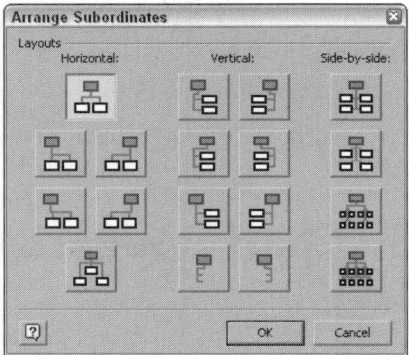

Figure 14-6: You can preview layouts before applying them.

✦ **Optimize your layouts** — You can optimize the location of the shapes on the drawing page using the layouts you chose by clicking Re-layout on the Organization Chart menu or toolbar. Visio moves the shapes on the page but maintains the layout options you selected for each superior.

✦ **Optimize overall layout** — To have Visio select the best layout options for you, choose Organization Chart ➪ Best Fit to Page.

Caution

If your Organization Chart shapes explode over your drawing page when you apply a layout, the connections between shapes could be broken. This can occur if you or an earlier author positioned shapes manually and inadvertently broke the connections between shapes. You can continue to position shapes manually. However, to correct this chaotic behavior, reconnect shapes, ideally with shape-to-shape glue. To connect shapes with shape-to-shape glue, select a connector and drag each end point to the center of a shape, or drag the predecessor shape over the supervisor shape.

Setting Organization Chart Options

You can customize many aspects of an organization chart's appearance by choosing Organization Chart ➪ Options to specify the settings you want. These options manipulate the appearance of Organization Chart shapes and text and determine which fields of information appear in the shapes. You can restore default settings by clicking Restore Defaults in the Options dialog box.

New
Feature

You can display employee photos in organization charts created with Visio 2003. To attach a picture to a shape, right-click a shape and choose Insert Picture from the shortcut menu. Specify the folder and filename for the picture and click Open. To display pictures, choose Organization Chart ➪ Options. Select the Options tab and then check the Show Pictures check box. If a picture doesn't appear in a shape, it might be too large. Crop the picture to a smaller size.

Setting Shape Options

Select the Options tab to customize shapes in the following ways:

✦ Set the height and width for all employee shapes.

✦ Apply a design theme, which sets shape and text styles for each type of organization chart shape.

✦ Show or hide employee pictures that have been inserted into shapes.

✦ Show or hide the divider line between the first and second line of text in shapes.

✦ Show drawing tips.

✦ Use the organization chart options that you choose for all new organization charts and for all Organization Chart shapes used on other types of drawings.

Note Visio 2002 included an option to move shapes into position automatically when possible. Although this option is no longer available in Visio 2003, you can use Re-layout or Best Fit to Page to optimize shape layout.

Specifying the Fields to Display in Shapes

Organization Chart shapes can display the values for custom properties in five locations within their boundaries. The center of a shape can show one or more fields. Each corner of a shape can show the value for one field.

By selecting the Fields tab, you can perform the following actions:

✦ Select the fields that appear in the center of a shape.

✦ Rearrange the order for the fields in the center of a shape.

✦ Select the fields that appear at each corner of a shape.

Setting Text Options

By selecting the Text tab, you can customize the appearance of organization chart text in the following ways:

✦ Choose the field whose text style you want to set.

✦ Specify the font to use for a field.

✦ Specify the font size to use for a field.

✦ Specify whether a field's text should be bolded or italicized.

Improving Chart Readability

Sometimes, organization charts require more tweaking than choosing layouts and options can provide. If your chart is still hard to read, you can adjust the spacing between shapes or hide some subordinates.

To modify the spacing between shapes, choose Organization Chart ➪ Change Spacing. You can adjust the spacing between shapes in the following ways:

✦ **Make qualitative changes** — Select the Tighter or Looser option to decrease or increase the current spacing.

✦ **Define specific spacing** — Select the Custom option and click Value to define values for spacing. For each layout type, you can specify the spacing between subordinates, the spacing between superiors and subordinates or assistants, and the justification spacing for layouts aligned to the left or right.

✦ **Apply Spacing to Shapes** — Select an option to apply the spacing changes to the selected shape, all shapes on the current drawing page, or all shapes in the file.

Tip

You can also improve readability by distributing a large or complex chart across multiple pages. To learn how to do this, see the "Working with Multiple Page Organization Charts" section later in this chapter.

In addition, you can improve a chart's readability by hiding some of the subordinate shapes temporarily. To hide the subordinates for a shape, select a shape and choose Organization Chart ➪ Hide Subordinates. When subordinates are hidden, the entry on the menu changes to Show Subordinates, which you can choose to restore the subordinates to the view.

Caution

The Re-layout and Best Fit to Page functions optimize the layout of your chart based on the shapes that aren't hidden. When you show the subordinates, you might have to apply Re-layout or Best Fit to Page again.

Working with Organization Charts

Organizational structure can be quite fluid, with people getting promoted or reassigned and even business units being reorganized, acquired, or divested. You can keep your organization chart up to date and still have time for other work by using Organization Chart tools to rearrange and update shapes.

Moving and Deleting Organization Chart Shapes

Visio includes standard commands to move and delete shapes, but these tools can sometimes cause problems when you use them in organization charts. The following sections identify the safest methods for moving and deleting shapes.

In most cases, it's easiest to use the Organization Chart layout tools, such as Arrange Subordinates, Re-layout, or Best Fit to Page to arrange the shapes in a chart. If you drag Organization Chart shapes to relocate them, those changes disappear when you subsequently use a layout tool. In addition, you could inadvertently break the connections between shapes by moving them manually.

Reordering Subordinates

When you add a subordinate to a chart, Visio inserts the subordinate to the right of existing subordinates in a horizontal layout or below existing subordinates in a vertical layout. To change the order of subordinates, select the subordinate shape you want to move, choose Organization Chart ➪ Move Subordinates, and then click Left/Up or Right/Down. Visio moves the selected shape to the left or right in a horizontal layout, and up or down in a vertical layout.

Deleting Organization Chart Shapes

You can use Cut to delete a shape as long as the shape is not linked to a database record. To delete a shape that isn't linked to a database, right-click the shape and choose Cut, or select the shape and press Ctrl+X.

When a shape is linked to a database record, cutting that shape does not delete the linked record in the database. When you want to delete a shape and its linked database record, right-click the shape and choose Delete Shape and Record from the shortcut menu.

Editing Organization Chart Shapes

Organization Chart shapes are still Visio shapes, so you can edit them as you would other types of shapes. For example, you can resize a regular shape by dragging its selection handles. However, because these shapes are so specialized, you'll use Organization Chart tools or modify custom properties to perform most editing tasks. For example, if shapes aren't large enough to display the information you want, it's easiest to specify larger shape dimensions in the organization chart Options dialog box.

To learn more about organization chart options, see the "Setting Organization Chart Options" section earlier in this chapter.

Editing Shape Text and Custom Properties

The text that appears in Organization Chart shapes is actually data stored in custom properties associated with each shape. By default, the values for the Name and Title custom properties appear in the center of a shape. (To learn how to select the fields that appear in shapes, see the "Specifying the Fields to Display in Shapes" section earlier in this chapter.)

You can modify organization chart custom property values in two ways: by editing the text in the shape or by editing the values in custom properties. When shapes are linked to database records, you can send updates from the database to Visio shapes, or vice versa. To edit shape values, choose one of the following methods:

✦ Select a shape and begin typing to edit the name and title.

✦ Right-click a shape and choose Properties from the shortcut menu. Click a custom property box and enter the new value.

✦ To update a shape's properties from a linked database record, right-click the shape and choose Refresh Shape Properties from the shortcut menu.

✦ To update a database record from the values associated with a linked shape, right-click a shape and choose Update Database Record from the shortcut menu.

Changing the Type of Organization Chart Shape

Sometimes, the type of shape you dragged onto a drawing is no longer appropriate — for instance, when a person in the organization is promoted or a position becomes vacant. When this occurs, you can change the type of shape for a position by selecting a shape and choosing Organization Chart ⇨ Change Position Type. Select the new position type and click OK. Because each Organization Chart shape has the same custom properties and behaviors, you don't have to make any other adjustments.

Working with Multiple-Page Organization Charts

For large organizations, it's often clearer to present portions of the organization on different pages. For example, you can show top-level executives on a summary page and include additional pages to display the organization that each executive leads. When you do this, the same employee appears on more than one page. By creating synchronized copies of these shapes, you can ensure that any text, custom properties, or subordinates that you add to a shape on one page apply to the copies on other pages.

Note   Adding, deleting, or moving a shape, or modifying a shape's associated layout, does not affect its synchronized copies.

To create a synchronized copy of a group or department, follow these steps:

1. Select a shape to which a group reports and choose Organization Chart ⇨ Synchronize ⇨ Create Synchronized Copy.

2. To create a copy on a new page, select the New Page option. To create a copy on an existing page, select the Existing Page option and choose the page from the drop-down list.

3. If you don't want to see the subordinates on the original page after you create a synchronized copy, check the Hide Subordinates on Original Page check box.

4. Click OK to create a synchronized copy. If you create a copy on a new page, double-click the tab for the new page to rename the page.

If you add subordinates to a synchronized copy, those subordinates are initially visible only on that page. To update another synchronized copy to show the new subordinates, select that synchronized copy and choose Organization Chart ⇨ Synchronize ⇨ Expand Subordinates. Expanding subordinates applies to one level of subordinates for a shape, so you must expand each level that you added to a synchronized copy.

Creating Hyperlinks Between Copies

You can add hyperlinks to synchronized shapes so you can navigate more easily between them. Follow these steps to add hyperlinks to shapes:

1. Select a shape and choose Insert ➪ Hyperlink.

2. Click the Browse button next to the Sub-Address box and choose the page that contains a synchronized copy of the shape.

3. To create a hyperlink so Visio pans and zooms into a specific shape, type the shape ID into the Shape box and click OK. Visio displays the page and shape ID as a link in a shape's shortcut menu.

Note   The shape ID is a unique name that Visio assigns. To find a shape ID, right-click a shape and choose Format ➪ Special from the shortcut menu. The shape ID appears in the Name box.

Comparing Versions of Organization Charts

When you build organization charts from imported data, you can end up with more than one version of an organization chart. You can compare versions of an organization chart and view a report of changes and then save the report. Follow these steps to compare two versions:

1. Open one of the versions of an organization chart and choose Organization Chart ➪ Compare Organization Data. If you would rather update the older version to maintain the layout and settings you have applied, open the older version.

2. Specify the file that contains the other version in the Drawing to Compare It With box. To compare only values from specific fields, click the Advanced button, delete the fields you don't want to compare, and click OK.

3. If the version you opened is older, select the My Drawing Is Older option and click OK. Otherwise, select the My Drawing Is Newer option.

4. Review the Comparison Report that Visio displays in your browser and save it if you want to use it later.

Sharing Organization Chart Data

If your Visio organization chart is your source for information about an organization, you can share that data with others through reports or by exchanging data files. For example, you can produce a report showing employees along with other information stored in shape custom properties. If you want to provide organization chart data that someone can use in another application, you can export the data to other file formats.

To produce a report for an organization chart, follow these steps:

1. Choose Tools ➪ Reports and select Organization Chart Report in the report list.

2. If you want to modify the report definition, click Modify and make your changes. You can choose options to specify the shapes you want to report on or define criteria that limits the report.

3. Click Run, choose the report format you want, and then click OK.

Note   You can produce reports in Excel, HTML, Visio shapes, or XML.

You can also export organization chart data to Excel spreadsheets, text files, or comma-delimited files. To do this, choose Organization Chart ➪ Export Organization Data. Specify the folder and filename for the export file. Choose a file format in the Save As Type box and click Save. Visio exports the values stored in custom properties. It also exports the shape ID and the master shape designation so that you can use the exported file to build a Visio organization chart.

Summary

With the features available in the Organization Chart template, you can build and easily maintain documentation for an organization. Organization Chart shapes are smart enough to create reporting relationships when you drop one shape on top of another. However, if you already have organization chart data in another data source, you can build and update Visio organization charts automatically from that data.

To satisfy different documentation requirements, you can modify the appearance of organization charts in several ways:

✦ Specify the layout for subordinates in a group or instruct Visio to optimize layout for you.

✦ Specify the information fields that appear in organization chart shapes.

✦ Format the shapes and text styles in a chart.

✦ Distribute portions of an organization across multiple pages.

You can also share the information in your Visio organization charts by producing organization reports or data files based on Visio organization chart data.

✦   ✦   ✦

Working with Flowcharts

Many business endeavors result in diagrams documenting the flow of information or material through an enterprise. Whether you are describing the steps in a procedure, analyzing the flow of data in a business process, or showing how departments interact, Visio provides templates and tools for producing the flowcharts that describe these efforts. Flowcharts show both connections and flow between elements.

Whether you create basic flowcharts to document a procedure or develop specialized flowcharts using specific notation, in this chapter, you'll learn how to create the types of flowcharts Visio offers. In addition, this chapter shows you how to modify flowchart contents and format them to look exactly the way you want. Because flowcharts are often quite complex, you'll learn how to continue flowcharts onto additional pages.

Exploring Flowchart Templates

Current business practices use many specialized flowcharts for business process analysis, quality management, risk management, and other initiatives, and Visio includes templates to support many of these approaches. In fact, Flowchart templates are available within several of Visio's template categories. In addition to the Flowchart category, you can find Flowchart templates within the Business Process, Process Engineering, and Software template categories. Even organization charts and project schedules incorporate characteristics of flowcharts.

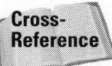

Cross-Reference   To learn more about business process flowcharts such as Cause and Effect Diagrams, Fault Tree Analysis Diagrams, and Work Flow Diagrams, see Chapter 16.

Constructing flowcharts in Visio is quite simple. By creating your drawing with one of the Visio Flowchart templates, you can create professional-looking flowcharts using basic Visio techniques, such as dragging and dropping, connecting shapes, editing shape text, and formatting Visio elements.

Flowchart templates don't include specialized menus, toolbars, or add-ons. You can create flowcharts by dragging and dropping shapes from stencils, connecting those shapes, and annotating and formatting your diagram.

Note   Visio 2003 does not offer the Import Flowchart Data Wizard, which was available in Visio 2002. To import data into a flowchart in Visio 2003, you must open the file in Visio 2002, use the Import Flowchart Data Wizard in that version, save the diagram as a Visio 2002 file, and then open the flowchart in Visio 2003.

Choosing the Right Template

Visio includes several templates for flowcharts within the Flowchart template category. These templates automatically set the page to a letter-size sheet and use inches drawn at a one-to-one scale. Visio sets the orientation depending on the template or diagram orientation that you choose. Visio 2003 has recategorized many of the Flowchart templates. Table 15-1 shows the Flowchart templates available in Visio 2003, including what they do, the template category Visio 2002 used, and the current template category for Visio 2003.

Tip   If you don't find the template you want under Flowcharts, look for the template in the Business Process category.

Table 15-1
Visio Flowchart Templates

Flowchart	Purpose	Visio 2002 Category	Visio 2003 Category
Basic Flowchart	Describe processes, document procedures, show work and/or information flow, track cost and efficiency, or document process improvements and process management in projects that use Six Sigma techniques.	Flowchart	Flowchart, Business Process
Cross-Functional Flowchart	Show how departments interact while executing a process.	Flowchart	Flowchart, Business Process

Flowchart	Purpose	Visio 2002 Category	Visio 2003 Category
Data Flow Diagram[a]	Document the logical flow of data through processes or procedures.	Flowchart	Flowchart, Business Process
IDEF0 Diagram	Model decisions, actions, and activities based on the Structured Analysis and Design Technique (SADT). See nearby note for a definition of IDEF.	Flowchart	Flowchart
SDL Diagram[a]	Document event-driven systems such as communication and telecommunication systems and networks using the Specification and Description Language (SDL).	Flowchart	Flowchart
Audit Diagram	Create auditing diagrams for accounting, inventory, financial and money management, tracking fiscal information, and decision-making.	Flowchart	Business Process
Cause and Effect Diagram	Categorize the sources of problems and their effects on a process to help identify solutions to problems.	Flowchart	Business Process
EPC Diagram	Use EPC (Event-driven Process Chain) from the SAP R/3 methodology to engineer business processes as chains of functions and events.	Did not exist	Business Process
Fault Tree Analysis Diagram	Document events that can lead to failure to help prevent potential failures. Fault tree analysis is commonly used in Six Sigma processes.	Did not exist	Business Process
TQM Diagram	Document business process reengineering, continuous improvement, and quality solutions.	Flowchart	Business Process
Work Flow Diagram	Show the flow of information or work in processes for business process reengineering and business process automation.	Flowchart	Business Process
Brainstorming (previously Mind Mapping Diagram)	Documents the ideas and concepts identified during brainstorming sessions.	Flowchart	Brainstorming

[a]Available in Visio Professional only.

 **Note** Visio provides shapes for methodologies such as SDL and IDEF0, but it doesn't provide tools to ensure that you have constructed your flowcharts in accordance with the rules of those methodologies.

 Note IDEF is an acronym of an acronym. IDEF originates from the acronym I-CAM Definition Methods. I-CAM is the acronym for Integrated Computer-Aided Manufacturing. The U.S. Air Force initiated the I-CAM project to develop methods for improving manufacturing productivity through a systematic application of rules enabled by computer technology.

Exploring Flowchart Shapes

Many Flowchart shapes are simple shapes. They have connection points so you can connect them to other shapes, but they lack control points, custom properties, or special behaviors other than working with the automatic layout tools. However, some Flowchart shapes include additional features, several of which are described in Table 15-2.

Table 15-2		
Flowchart Shapes with Special Features		
Stencil	*Shape*	*Special Features*
Basic Flowchart Shapes	Flowchart Shapes	Can transform into a Process, Decision, Document, or Data shape when you right-click the shape on the page and choose the type of shape you want from the shortcut menu
Cross-Functional Flowchart Shapes (Horizontal and Vertical stencils)	Functional Band	Grouped shape with text blocks for the Process name and Function name
Data Flow Diagram Shapes	Oval Process	Contains a control point in the center of the oval that you can drag to create data flows to other shapes
IDEF0 Shapes	Activity Box	Contains custom properties for Process Name, Process ID, and Sub-Diagram ID

Understanding Flowchart Basics

Whether you want to create a basic flowchart or a specialized diagram, you can use familiar Visio techniques to build much of your diagram. Flowchart shapes work with Visio's automatic layout tools, so you can add and connect shapes and then let Visio arrange them for you. You can also use Visio's annotation and formatting tools to enhance the appearance of your diagrams.

To create a flowchart, choose File ➪ New ➪ Flowchart and then choose one of the templates from the submenu, such as Basic Flowchart, Data Flow Diagram, or SDL Diagram.

Adding and Connecting Flowchart Shapes

The best method for adding and connecting shapes depends on the type of flowchart you create and the type of shapes you want to add. Because flowcharts indicate order or flow, you must take extra care to connect shapes in the proper order.

Visio Flowchart templates enable the dynamic grid by default to make it easy to position shapes relative to shapes already on your diagram. When the dynamic grid is active, Visio displays dotted lines as you drag a shape around to indicate positions that align the shape with other shapes already on the page. To align a shape, drag it and snap it to one of the horizontal or vertical dotted lines on the dynamic grid.

Tip

If you have trouble positioning shapes because of the dynamic grid, you can turn it off by choosing Tools ➪ Snap & Glue and unchecking Dynamic Grid under the Currently Active heading.

Adding Flowchart Shapes in a Sequence

For sequential processes, you can create a sequence by dragging the shapes onto the page in order, or you can specify the sequence after you add shapes to the diagram. Create a sequence of shapes using one of the following methods:

✦ **Dragging** — When you already know the sequence of steps, the Connector tool is the easiest way to define that sequence. Click the Connector tool on the Standard toolbar. As you drag shapes onto the page, Visio connects the new shape to the shape you added previously with a shape-to-shape connection.

Cross-Reference

To learn more about all the methods for connecting shapes, refer to Chapter 5.

✦ **Selecting a Sequence** — If you plan to work out the sequence by analyzing the shapes on your diagram, you can add shapes to the page and then use the

Connect Shapes command to create a sequence. Follow these steps to create a sequence out of shapes already on the page:

1. Drag all the shapes in the sequence onto the page.

2. After you determine the correct sequence, select each shape in order and then choose Shapes ⇨ Connect Shapes. Visio connects the shapes in order using shape-to-shape connections. Visio does not rearrange the shapes when it connects them.

3. If the layout is difficult to read, rearrange the layout by choosing Shapes ⇨ Lay Out Shapes, specifying the layout options you want, and clicking OK.

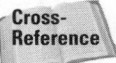

Cross-Reference

If your flowchart shapes don't contain numbering, you can use the Number Shapes command to add numbering. To learn how to use this tool, see Chapter 7.

Connecting Nonsequential Shapes

For processes that don't flow directly from start to finish, it's easier to drag shapes onto the drawing page, and then use the Connector tool to connect them. For example, Decision shapes connect to one other shape for each possible outcome of a decision. You don't want Visio to automatically connect Decision shapes with shape-to-shape connections because switching connection points can modify the decision.

To create a nonsequential flowchart, use the following methods to connect shapes:

✦ **Processes**—Connect process shapes or other shapes for which the connection points don't matter using shape-to-shape connections. Click the Connector tool on the Standard toolbar and position the pointer within the predecessor process. When Visio highlights the shape with a red box, drag to a position within the successor process.

Tip

If process shapes are small, Visio highlights connection points instead of an entire process box. In this case, you can also create shape-to-shape connections by pressing the Ctrl key while using the Connector tool.

✦ **Decisions**—Use the following steps to connect a decision shape to its potential outcomes, as illustrated in Figure 15-1.

1. With the Connector tool active, drag from a connection point on the Decision shape to a position within the process that represents one outcome. When Visio highlights the process with a red box, release the mouse button.

2. Double-click the connector to edit the text box for that line and type a description or reference for the decision that leads to that outcome.

3. Repeat steps 1 and 2 for each additional outcome.

Decision

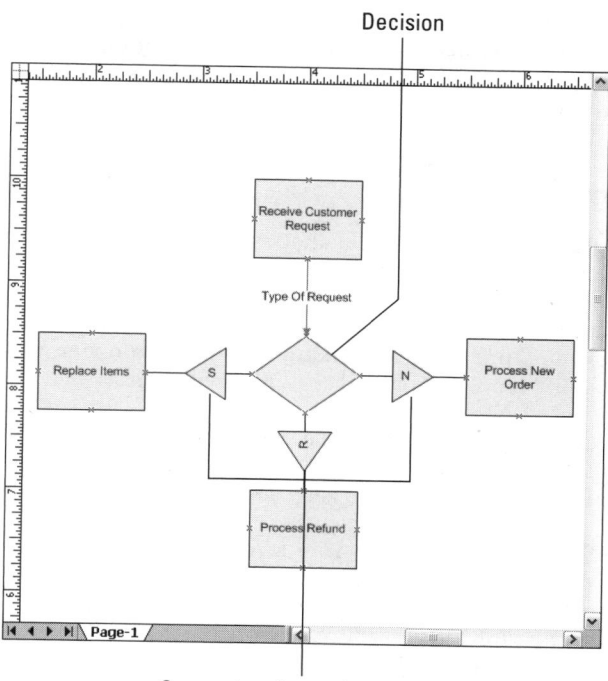

Connectors for each outcome

Figure 15-1: Decision shapes connect to one shape for each possible outcome.

Modifying Flowcharts

You don't need special techniques to modify flowcharts. You can rearrange, annotate, and format your diagrams with any of the following methods:

✦ **Annotate Shapes and Connectors** — To add descriptive text to your steps, select a shape or connector and type the text you want.

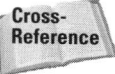

To learn about other ways to annotate diagrams, see Chapter 6.

✦ **Rearrange Shapes** — You can manually rearrange individual shapes and connectors or use Visio's automatic layout tools:

  • **Move Individual Elements** — To manually rearrange shapes, drag shapes you want to move to new locations. To manually modify connector paths, drag green vertices on connectors to new locations.

  • **Automatically Layout Shapes** — To use Visio's layout tools to automatically lay out your diagram, choose Shapes ➪ Lay Out Shapes and select the options you want. Note that using automatic layout overwrites any manual arrangement you have performed.

✦ **Reverse Direction of Flow** — To change the direction of flow between two steps, select the connector between the steps and choose Shape ➪ Rotate or Flip. Choose Flip Horizontal for a horizontal connector, or Flip Vertical for a vertical connector.

Formatting Flowcharts

You can modify the appearance of individual shapes and connectors or your entire diagram using the following formatting tools:

✦ **Format Shapes and Connectors** — You can modify the formatting for individual shapes and connectors by right-clicking a shape or connector, choosing Format, and choosing Line, Fill, or Text from the shortcut menu.

Many of the shapes on Flowchart stencils use predefined styles. You can apply formatting to individual shapes and connectors to emphasize specific steps, but you should use special formatting sparingly to keep your diagrams neat and consistent.

✦ **Apply Styles to Shapes and Connectors** — Modify line, text, and fill formatting consistently by applying styles to shapes and connectors. To do so, right-click a shape or connector and choose Format ➪ Style from the shortcut menu. To redefine the formatting for a style, choose Format ➪ Define Styles, select the style you want to change, and select new formatting options.

✦ **Add a Background** — To add a background to a flowchart page, drag a background shape from the Backgrounds stencil onto the page. Visio automatically creates a new page for the background and associates it with the current foreground page.

If the Flowchart template you're using doesn't open the Backgrounds stencil, choose File ➪ Shapes ➪ Visio Extras ➪ Backgrounds.

✦ **Apply a Color Scheme** — To apply a consistent and coordinated set of colors to the shapes on your drawing, right-click the drawing page and choose Color Schemes from the shortcut menu.

✦ **Add a Border and Title** — To add a border or title to identify your diagram, drag a border or title shape from the Borders and Titles stencil.

To learn about applying formatting, using styles, and applying color schemes, see Chapter 7. To learn about borders and titles, see Chapter 6. For more about working with background pages, see Chapter 2.

Creating Multiple Page Flowcharts

Complex processes typically require multiple pages to show all their steps. Flowcharts can also include a process summary on one page and show detailed steps for each high-level process on other pages. For these situations, you can use

On-page and Off-page reference shapes to indicate that your flowchart continues elsewhere on the diagram.

> **Note**
>
> The Data Flow Diagram and IDEF0 Diagram templates do not contain On-page and Off-page reference shapes. To add these shapes to those drawing types, choose File ⇨ Shapes ⇨ Flowchart ⇨ Basic Flowchart Shapes and drag the shapes onto the page.

The On-page reference shape creates a visual link between two steps on the same page. To create on-page references, follow these steps:

1. Drag an On-page reference shape onto the drawing page near the end of the main procedure.

2. Select the On-page shape and type a number or letter to label the reference.

3. Press Ctrl+C to copy the on-page reference to the Windows Clipboard.

4. Press Ctrl+V to paste a copy on the drawing page.

5. Drag the copy to the position where the procedure continues on the page.

> **Tip**
>
> To connect an on-page reference to the Flowchart shape to which it refers, click the Connector tool on the Standard toolbar and then drag between connection points on the on-page reference and the Flowchart shape.

When you want to continue your flowchart on another page, you can create a reference to a new or existing page with an Off-page reference shape. You can add an off-page reference to the second page, synchronize the text on both reference shapes, or add hyperlinks so you can easily switch from one page to the next, as shown in Figure 15-2.

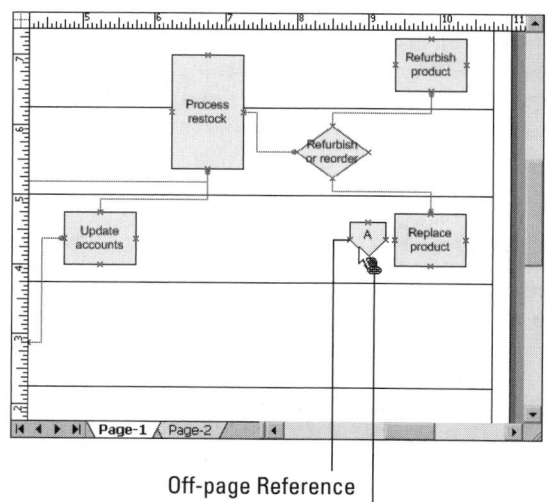

Off-page Reference

Hyperlink to process continuation

Figure 15-2: Synchronize off-page references or add hyperlinks to simplify navigating between them.

To create off-page references, follow these steps:

1. Drag the Off-page reference shape from the stencil onto the page near the last shape on that page. Visio displays the Off-page Reference dialog box and selects the New Page option by default.

2. To add off-page references to both the current page and a new page, make sure the New Page option is selected. You can rename the new page by typing a new name in the Name field. To create the off-page reference on an existing page, select the Existing Page option and then choose the page on the drop-down list.

Tip   You can convey information about a reference by changing the shape of an off-page reference. To change the reference's appearance, right-click the off-page reference and choose Outgoing, Incoming, Circle, or Arrow from the shortcut menu.

3. If you don't want Visio to create an off-page reference on the other page, uncheck the Drop Off-Page Reference Shape on Page check box in the dialog box that appears after your reference is dragged over.

4. To synchronize the labels on corresponding off-page references, check the Keep Shape Text Synchronized check box.

5. To create a hyperlink between the two Off-page references, check the Insert Hyperlinks on Shape(s) check box.

Tip   To navigate between the pages of the flowchart, double-click an Off-page reference shape with a hyperlink to another off-page reference.

Working with Cross-Functional Flowcharts

Cross-functional flowcharts show the steps in a process along with the departments that contribute to the execution of those steps. The flowchart includes steps, just as a basic flowchart does, but you denote the participation of departments by stretching a shape that represents a process across horizontal bands on the diagram that represent each participating department.

Setting Up Cross-Functional Flowcharts

When you create a new cross-functional flowchart, you can choose between a horizontal or vertical orientation. The Cross-Functional dialog box provides for only five functional bands, but you can create as many as you want after you create the initial diagram. To create a cross-functional flowchart, follow these steps:

1. Choose File ➪ New ➪ Flowchart ➪ Cross-Functional Flowchart. Visio displays the Cross-Functional Flowchart dialog box, which contains options for setting up the diagram.

2. Select Horizontal or Vertical to specify the orientation and then type a number from 1 to 5 to specify the number of departments. If you choose the horizontal orientation, Visio changes the page orientation to landscape.

Caution You can't change the cross-functional flowchart orientation once you have selected one.

3. To include a title bar for the diagram, check the Include Title Bar check box.

4. Click OK to create the diagram. Visio adds the number of bands you specified to the diagram and opens the Arrow Shapes stencil, the Basic Flowchart Shapes stencil, and the Cross-Functional Flowchart Shapes stencil for the orientation you chose.

5. To label the flowchart or any of the bands, select the shape you want to label and type the label text.

Adding Processes to Cross-Functional Flowcharts

Creating steps for a process in a cross-functional flowchart is no different than creating a basic flowchart. You drag and connect shapes to represent the process steps. To indicate that a step crosses departments or functions, resize the shape for that step so that it spans the participating departments. Use the following methods to add processes and steps to a cross-functional flowchart:

✦ **Add Process Steps** — Drag Flowchart shapes from the stencil onto the page as you would for a basic flowchart. Use any of the basic methods for connecting those shapes to define your process.

✦ **Label Process Steps** — Select a shape and type the process description.

✦ **Associate Departments with Steps** — Drag a selection handle on a shape for a process until it spans the departments that participate in the process, as shown in Figure 15-3.

Tip You can't split a process into multiple pieces to associate it with departments whose functional bands are not coincident in the diagram. However, you can show functional bands in a different order on each page. If several steps in a process relate to the same departments, you can show those steps on another page and rearrange the functional bands to co-locate those departments.

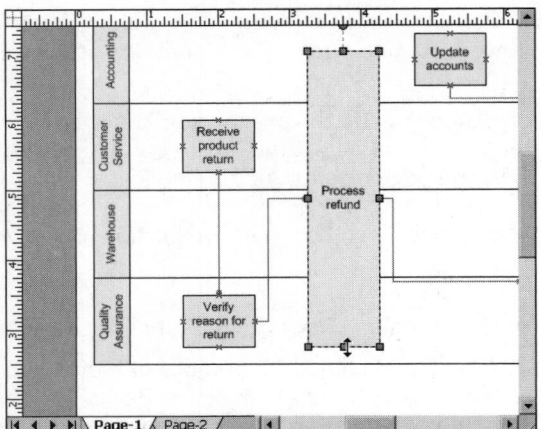

Figure 15-3: Processes can span multiple departments.

Working with Functional Bands

You can add, remove, edit, or rearrange the functional bands on a cross-functional flowchart. When you move or reorder the bands on a diagram, Visio moves the steps along with the bands, which can result in messy connections. You can drag the green vertices on connectors to reorganize the paths between steps. Use the following methods to modify the functional bands in a cross-functional flowchart:

✦ **Add a Functional Band** — Drag a functional band shape from the stencil to an approximate vertical position on the page. Visio snaps the functional band into place, aligning the band horizontally with the other bands. To add a functional band above another band, position the pointer within or slightly above the existing band. To label the band, select the label text and type the department or function name.

Note   If you insert a functional band between two shapes that share a step, Visio resizes the step to span all three bands.

✦ **Remove a Functional Band** — Select the label of a functional band and then press Delete.

Caution   When you delete a functional band, Visio also deletes any shapes within that band, without requesting a confirmation. If you inadvertently delete shapes you want to keep, press Ctrl+Z to undo the deletion. Move the shapes to other bands and then delete the functional band.

✦ **Resize a Functional Band** — To resize a band, select the band and then drag one of the selection handles until the band is the width you want. For example, to change the width of a vertical band, drag a selection handle on either side. To change the height of a horizontal band, drag the top or bottom selection handle.

✦ **Change the Length of All Bands** — Select the border or title of the cross-functional flowchart to display the selection handles for the chart group. Drag a selection handle until the bands are the length you want.

✦ **Move a Band** — To change the order of bands, select a band and drag it to a new location. Visio moves or resizes any shapes wholly or partially contained within the band.

✦ **Move a Shape to Another Band** — Drag the shape to another band. If you want to associate a shape with multiple bands, drag a selection handle on the shape until it spans all the bands to which it relates.

Identifying Process Phases

You can specify phases in a process with a Separator shape. When you add a separator to a flowchart, Visio associates the steps that follow the separator with that phase. On vertical cross-functional flowcharts, separators are horizontal; for horizontal flowcharts, they are vertical.

To add a separator to a flowchart, drag the Separator shape from the stencil onto the page. Select the separator and type a description for the phase. When you move a separator, Visio moves all the steps in that phase. To move a separator without moving the steps, delete the separator and add a new one in the new location.

Creating Other Types of Flowcharts

Visio provides templates for data flow diagrams, IDEF0 diagrams, and SDL flowcharts. Although the Visio stencils contain shapes for these methodologies, Visio does not verify that your diagrams follow the rules underlying the Gane and Sarson data flow diagram, IDEF0, and SDL methodologies.

Creating Data Flow Diagrams

You can create flowcharts that document the flow of data between processes and data stores using two different templates:

✦ **Basic Data Flow Diagram** — Choose File ➪ New ➪ Flowcharts ➪ Data Flow Diagram. Visio opens the Data Flow Diagram Shapes stencil, which contains shapes for processes, entities, states, and data stores.

✦ **Data Flow Model Diagram** — To create a data flow model based on the Gane and Sarson symbology, choose Data Flow Model Diagram within the Software template category. Visio opens the Gane and Sarson stencil.

Note   Visio 2002 displayed a data flow model in the Model Explorer and indicated syntactic errors in the Output window. The Model Explorer and Output window are no longer available in Visio 2003.

Adding Data Flow Shapes

Drag the following types of shapes onto your diagram to document the elements of your process:

- ✦ **External Interactor** — An external source or destination for data
- ✦ **Process** — A process that transforms data in some way
- ✦ **State** — A state achieved during a process
- ✦ **Data Store** — A source or destination for data that is internal to the process
- ✦ **Entity** — An entity that performs a process
- ✦ **Entity Relationship** — A shape that indicates the relationship between entities
- ✦ **Oval Process** — A Process shape that contains a control point you can use to create multiple data flows from the process

Showing Flow Between Shapes

You indicate flow on a data flow diagram with Center to Center shapes. To create a data flow, follow these steps:

1. Drag a Center to Center shape onto the page near the two shapes between which data flows.

2. To change the direction of the flow, choose Shape ⇨ Rotate or Flip, and then choose Flip Horizontal or Flip Vertical.

3. Glue the end points of the Center to Center shape to the connection points at the center of each of the other shapes. Visio highlights the end points with red squares when the shapes are connected.

4. To change the curvature of the data flow arrow, drag the green selection handle in the middle of the arc to a new location. To change the location of arrows, drag one of the control handles.

Showing a Data Loop

To indicate a loop in the process, follow these steps:

1. Drag a Loop on Center shape onto the page until Visio displays a red square around the connection point on the process that loops.

2. To change the size or position of the loop, drag the end point. To change the location of the ends of the loop, drag the control handle and the selection handle.

Creating IDEF0 Diagrams

The IDEF0 communication methodology uses context diagrams, parent/child diagrams, and node trees to model business and organizational processes. Context diagrams are high-level diagrams that show activities and external interfaces. IDEF0 node trees show an entire decomposition in one diagram. Parent/child diagrams illustrate the relationships between processes.

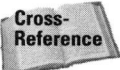

Cross-Reference

To learn about the IDEF0 methodology, navigate to `www.idef.com`.

Creating Context Diagrams

Context diagrams show the relationships between activities. To create a context diagram, drag activity boxes onto the page and type the process name and process ID in their corresponding fields in the Custom Properties dialog box. If the process is a decomposition, also type the ID for the decomposition diagram in the Sub-diagram ID field. You use the 1-legged Connector shape to connect activities to external interfaces. To add purpose and viewpoint statements to the diagram, drag 8 Pt Text Block shapes onto the page and type the text you want.

Creating Parent/Child Diagrams

Parent/child diagrams also show activities and connections. On these diagrams, you can use the IDEF0 connector to create a variety of connections between processes. After adding parent and child processes, choose one of the following methods to connect the process on your diagram:

✦ **Joined Arrows**—Drag one IDEF0 connector between connection points on two activity boxes. Drag a second IDEF0 connector onto the page and glue one end to a connection point on another activity box. Drag the free end of this connector so its arrowhead overlaps the first connector's arrow.

✦ **Forked Arrows**—Drag one IDEF0 connector between connection points on two activity boxes. Drag a second IDEF0 connector onto the page and overlap its start point with the start point of the first connector. Glue the other end of the second connector to another activity box.

✦ **Branching Arrows**—Drag one IDEF0 connector between connection points on two activity boxes. Select the connector, press Ctrl, and drag a copy of the connector to create a branch. Press F4 to create additional branches. Connect the end points of the branches to the appropriate activity boxes.

Tip

To align the branches, connect the beginning points of all the branches. You can drag the control handle on each branch to reposition the middle leg of each branch.

Creating a Node Tree

To create a node tree, follow these steps:

1. Drag a node onto the page and type the node number or name of the node for the root of the tree in the Custom Properties dialog box.

2. Drag a Solid Connector shape onto the page and glue an end point to the connection point at the center of the node. Drag the other end point until the connector is the length and direction you want.

3. Repeat step 2 until you have created the branches you need to connect nodes to the top node.

4. Drag Node shapes onto the page and glue their centers to the open ends of the branches.

5. Repeat steps 2, 3, and 4 for each level of the tree.

Tip   Add a hyperlink between a node and the page that contains process details when you want to quickly view the details associated with a node.

Creating SDL Flowcharts

SDL flowcharts use shapes and connectors based on International Telecommunications Union standards to illustrate communications and telecommunications systems networks. These shapes are similar to other types of flowchart shapes, including procedures and decisions. Some include control points that you can use to modify the position of dividers within the shapes.

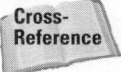

Cross-Reference   To review the SDL specifications, navigate to `http://iis-web.coloradotech.edu/bsanden/CS670/SDL.pdf`.

Summary

You can create any type of Visio flowchart by dragging shapes onto the page and then connecting them. Although many flowchart shapes contain only selection handles for resizing, several include control points that you can use to modify the shapes or create additional connectors. You can use standard techniques to annotate and format flowcharts. For multiple-page diagrams, you can continue processes on other pages by adding Off-page reference shapes. You can quickly jump from the main process to the continuation by adding hyperlinks between the reference shapes.

Cross-functional flowcharts have a few additional behaviors. On these flowcharts, you can associate processes with one or more departments or functional bands. As you add, move, or delete functional bands, Visio modifies the processes to maintain the connection between the steps and departments.

✦   ✦   ✦

Documenting Business Processes

Most organizations today look to business process improvement methodologies, such as Total Quality Management and Six Sigma, to improve results such as quality, customer satisfaction, profits, and competitive edge. These business methodologies model processes in different ways to highlight potential problems or opportunities for improvement.

Whether you're documenting and analyzing current processes or engineering process improvements, this chapter will show you how you can use specialized shapes in Visio's Business Process templates to construct the diagrams you need. Although you have to know how to represent your business process information in a specific type of diagram before you begin your Visio session, you can still use standard Visio techniques to produce your documentation.

Working with Business Process Templates

Business Process templates don't include specialized menus, toolbars, or add-ons. You can create business process flowcharts as you do any flowchart, but you use specialized Business Process shapes to create different types of diagrams. Business Process templates automatically set the page to a letter-size sheet, with the orientation depending on the template you choose. As with other flowcharts, Visio uses inches drawn at a one-to-one scale. The templates open the Backgrounds and Borders and Titles stencils so you can annotate and format your diagrams.

CHAPTER 16

✦ ✦ ✦ ✦

In This Chapter

Working with the Audit Diagram template

Creating Cause and Effect diagrams

Working with EPC diagrams

Creating Fault Tree Analysis diagrams

Understanding TQM diagrams

Using Work Flow diagrams

Adding data to Flowchart shapes

Adding custom properties to Flowchart shapes

Generating custom property reports

✦ ✦ ✦ ✦

To learn about basic techniques for building flowcharts as well as more information about basic flowcharts, data flow diagrams, and cross-functional flowcharts, see Chapter 15.

Basic Flowchart, Data Flow Diagram, and Cross-Functional Flowchart templates appear in both the Flowchart and Business Process template categories, but they are identical, no matter which category you select when you create your drawing.

Audit Diagrams

Audit diagrams document processes, including accounting, bookkeeping, inventory, and other types of financial transactions. For example, you can model the process for an online stock trade to ensure that checks and balances are in place to satisfy the Securities and Exchange Commission.

The Audit Diagram template opens several stencils, including the Audit Diagram Shapes stencil, with shapes for processes, operations, documents, and data repositories, as well as basic flowchart shapes such as On-page and Off-page references and connectors. You can use Tagged Process and Tagged Document shapes to mark the process elements that you want to research further. After adding Tagged shapes to the page, right-click a Tagged shape and choose Tagged or Untagged from the shortcut menu to toggle the Tagged setting.

Cause and Effect Diagrams

Cause and effect diagrams document potential and real factors that produce an effect. By arranging these factors or causes by their level of importance or detail, cause and effect diagrams can help you identify root causes or problem areas, and can show the priority of different causes that lead to an effect. These diagrams are also called *fishbone diagrams* because they resemble a fish's skeleton, with main causes shown as the bones that attach to the "spine" of the fish. They are also called *Ishikawa diagrams,* after their creator, Dr. Kaori Ishikawa, who initiated a well-known approach to quality management in the Kawasaki shipyards.

In quality management, you typically create a cause and effect diagram after investigating the problems associated with a product or service and ranking them in a *Pareto chart* (also known as an *80-20 chart*). You use the effect ranked highest in the Pareto chart as the starting point for your cause and effect diagram. For example, when you determine that the most frequent customer complaint is late delivery, you can construct a cause and effect diagram to explore the reasons for this.

When you create a new drawing with the Visio Cause and Effect Diagram template, Visio opens a new page and automatically adds an Effect shape for the effect you are studying, and four Category boxes to classify the causes on your drawing. The template also includes shapes for primary and secondary causes, which you can use to add more detail.

Note Causes are frequently grouped into four major categories. You can choose your own categories to suit your study or choose one of two sets: Manufacturing, including manpower, methods, materials, and machinery, or Service, including equipment, policies, procedures, and people.

To create a cause and effect diagram, follow these steps:

1. Choose File ➪ New ➪ Business Process ➪ Cause and Effect Diagram.

2. To specify the effect you're studying, select the horizontal arrow on the page and type text describing the effect or problem.

3. To create the cause categories you want, use one of the following methods:

   • **Add a category** — Drag a Category 1 or Category 2 shape onto the page and position it so the arrowhead touches the horizontal arrow of the Effect shape. Visio automatically glues the Category shape to the geometry of the Effect shape.

   • **Delete a category** — Select a Category shape and press the Delete key.

   • **Move a category** — Drag a Category shape to the new location until it snaps to the geometry of the Effect shape.

4. For each Category shape on the page, select the shape, and type the name of the cause category that you want to appear as text in the shape box.

5. To show major causes in a category, drag Primary Cause shapes onto the page until the arrowheads snap to category lines, as shown in Figure 16-1.

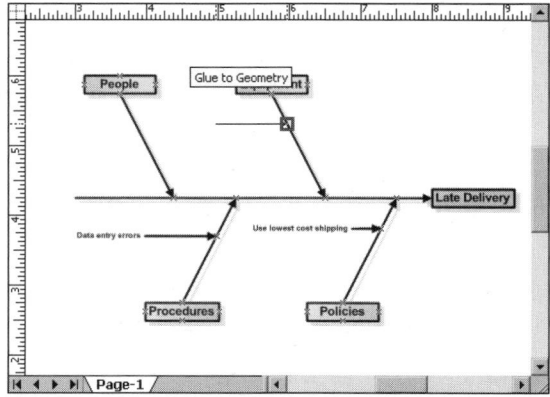

Figure 16-1: Cause and Effect shapes snap anywhere on shape geometry.

Note The only differences between the two versions of primary and secondary cause shapes are the direction of the line and the location of the text relative to the line.

6. To illustrate secondary causes that contribute to primary causes, drag Secondary Cause shapes onto the page until the arrowheads snap to primary cause lines.

7. For each cause, select the shape, and type a description of the cause.

Tip

If text in Cause shapes overlaps on the page, click Align Left or Align Right on the Formatting toolbar to reposition the text in the text boxes within Cause shapes. You can also distribute the text over several lines by adding line breaks. To do this, select the Text tool, click the text, and press Ctrl+Enter.

Event Process Chain (EPC) Diagrams

EPC diagrams are part of the SAP R/3 modeling methodology for business engineering. EPC diagrams illustrate business process work flows by showing the transfer of control in processes as a chain of events and functions, as demonstrated in Figure 16-2.

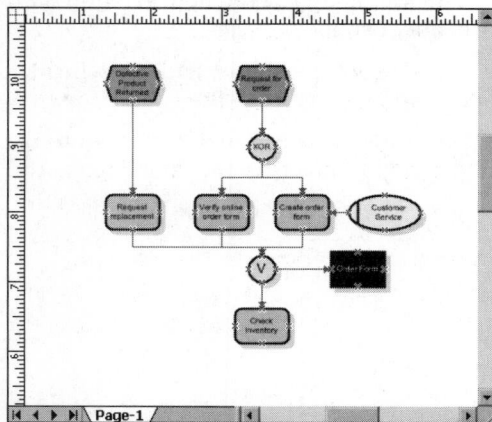

Figure 16-2: EPC diagrams use events and functions to show flow.

You can use the following types of shapes to produce an EPC diagram:

✦ **Functions** — Represent processes or activities, such as creating forms or checking inventory

✦ **Events** — Trigger functions or are the result of functions. In EPC modeling, events also represent process states, such as Order Form Created.

✦ **Organizational Units** — Indicate the part of the organization responsible for a process or activity

✦ **Information/Material**—Represent data elements such as forms or data records

✦ **Logical Operators**—Specify how events and functions interact. For example, the AND operator indicates that both events must occur to trigger a function, whereas the exclusive OR (XOR) operator specifies that the occurrence of only one of the events triggers the function. An OR operator indicates that the occurrence of any or all of the events triggers the function.

✦ **Connectors**—Show the relationships between the components on the diagram

Fault Tree Analysis Diagrams

Fault tree analysis studies the events that can lead to failure in an effort to prevent failures from occurring. Fault tree analysis diagrams are frequently used in the Analyze phase of the Six Sigma business improvement process. Fault tree diagrams use a top-down structure to represent the routes within a system that can lead to a failure, as shown in Figure 16-3. You can use logical operators to interconnect events or conditions that contribute to a failure. By analyzing the factors that lead to failure, you can prevent failures by eliminating their causes.

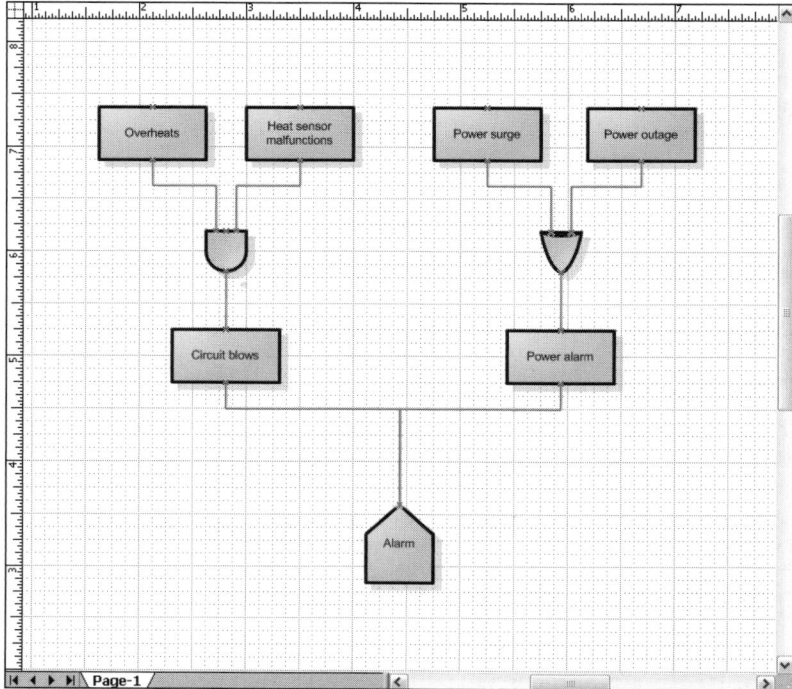

Figure 16-3: Fault Tree Analysis diagrams show the events that can lead to failure.

Note   Bell Telephone Laboratories developed fault tree analysis in 1962 for the U.S. Air Force so they could analyze the Minuteman system.

To create a fault tree diagram, follow these steps:

1. Choose File ⇨ New ⇨ Business Process ⇨ Fault Tree Analysis Diagram.

2. From the Fault Tree Analysis Shapes stencil, drag the Event shape to the top of the drawing page. With the shape selected, type the description of the failure.

3. Drag a Gate shape, such as the AND or OR gate, onto the page directly below the top event.

4. Drag additional Event and Gate shapes onto the page and position them from the top down to identify potential causes of the failure represented by the top-level event.

5. Connect the shapes using the Connector tool.

TQM Diagrams

TQM is a structured approach to business process improvement that focuses on building quality into products and services from the beginning. All employees and departments participate, from top-level management on down. The TQM Diagram template includes shapes and connectors for creating flowcharts for Total Quality Management projects.

Six Sigma Templates

Six Sigma projects include phases for defining, measuring, analyzing, improving, and controlling processes. You can use a Visio DMAIC Flowchart template, available on Microsoft Office Online, to document requirements and steps for a Six Sigma project. When you create Visio diagrams or other documents as part of your project, you can link these documents directly to the DMAIC diagram to keep your project information organized.

The DMAIC Flowchart template includes an overview page and two additional pages for drilling down. Each page includes shapes to get you started. The quickest way to find the DMAIC template is by using the Search drop-down list on Microsoft Office Online; from this list choose Templates and then type **DMAIC** in the Search For box. Click the button with the green arrow. Click the link for the DMAIC flowchart with the units you want and then click the Download Now button. After downloading and opening the template, learn how to use it by clicking the Using This Template link in the Template Help Task Pane.

Work Flow

Work flow diagrams are high-level flowcharts that show the interactions and flow of control for business processes. The Workflow Diagram Shapes stencil includes shapes that represent different departments and personnel. For example, it includes shapes such as Accounting, Information Systems, and Shipping. It also includes shapes for generic employees, such as Person 1, and specific roles, such as Treasurer. You can use basic Visio techniques to develop these diagrams.

Estimating and Reporting with Flowcharts

In addition to graphically depicting business processes, Visio flowcharts can also store data about the processes they represent. Many flowchart shapes contain custom properties for cost, duration, and resources. By adding data to these fields for each step in a process, you can produce reports or compute estimates or results automatically. For example, when you add cost, duration, and resources involved for each step in your organization's current and proposed procurement processes, you can produce reports that show the potential cost and time savings from implementing the new process.

Adding Data to Flowcharts

Many flowchart shapes include predefined custom properties for Cost, Duration, and Resources. You can view and enter data in these fields as you would for any other custom property. You can also add custom fields to Flowchart shapes to support additional requirements for a special project.

To add data to Flowchart shapes, follow these steps:

1. Choose View ➪ Custom Properties Window.

2. Select a shape to which you want to add data.

3. In the Custom Properties window, click a field and type the data for that field for the selected shape. Repeat this step for each field you want to analyze or track.

Note   If a shape has no custom properties, the words "No Custom Properties" appear in the Custom Properties window. You can also access custom properties by right-clicking a shape and choosing Properties from the shortcut menu.

4. To add data to other shapes, repeat steps 2 and 3 for each shape.

5. After adding data to the shapes you want, close the Custom Properties window by clicking the Close button.

Adding Custom Properties to Shapes

You can add custom properties to shapes to track other types of data or to add custom properties to shapes that don't include them, such as Cause and Effect shapes. For example, if you're evaluating outsourcing opportunities, you can track the number of employees with general skills involved in each step of a process.

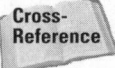

Cross-Reference   To learn more about creating custom properties, see Chapter 32.

To add custom properties to an existing flowchart master, follow these steps:

1. With the flowchart open, choose File ➪ Shapes ➪ Show Document Stencil. Visio opens the Document stencil, which contains master versions of the shapes you have used in your diagram. By adding custom properties to these masters, you can add the custom properties to all corresponding shapes in your drawing.

2. To add custom properties to a shape, right-click it in the Document stencil and choose Edit Master ➪ Edit Master Shape. Visio opens the master window and zooms into the shape so it's easier to edit.

3. Right-click the master in the master drawing window and choose Properties from the shortcut menu. In the Custom Properties dialog box, click Define.

4. Click New. In the Define Custom Properties dialog box, specify the fields and options you want for the new custom property. To add another custom property, click New again.

5. When you're finished adding custom properties, click OK. Your new properties appear in the Custom Properties dialog box. Click OK again.

6. Click the Close button for the master drawing window to return to the flowchart. When prompted to update the master and all of its instances, click Yes.

7. Repeat steps 2 through 6 for each master to which you want to add new property fields.

8. When you're finished adding custom properties to masters, right-click the title bar of the Document stencil, choose Close, and save the flowchart.

Generating Reports with Custom Property Data

After you add data to your Flowchart shapes, you can produce inventories or lists, such as the types of job skills used in a process. You can also generate reports that calculate process statistics or total values so you can estimate costs or durations.

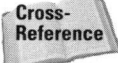

To learn more about producing reports using custom properties, see Chapter 32.

You can use the Database Export Wizard to transfer the data stored in your flowchart into a database. To learn more about exporting data to a database, see Chapter 10.

Summary

Visio's Business Process templates help you construct diagrams based on several popular methodologies for business process improvement, such as Six Sigma. You need to know how to document business processes using the different types of diagrams, such as Cause and Effect or Fault Tree Analysis, but you can use standard Visio techniques to produce your drawings. The Basic Flowchart, Data Flow Diagram, and Cross-Functional Flowchart templates appear in both the Business Process and Flowchart categories, but they are identical.

You can create, edit, annotate, and format business process flowcharts as you do their more generic cousins. For multiple-page diagrams, you can continue processes on other pages by adding Off-page reference shapes or by adding hyperlinks between reference shapes to navigate between the main process and continuations. By using the custom properties associated with many Flowchart shapes, you can also estimate costs, durations, and other measures for your organization's processes.

✦   ✦   ✦

Scheduling Projects with Visio

Projects are endeavors that have a definite beginning and ending—typically, special initiatives that are distinct from routine operations of an organization. Projects don't just happen on their own; they take conscientious planning and tracking. Project managers monitor and control tasks, schedules, resources, and budgets to ensure that projects achieve their goals. Typically, project managers use software such as Microsoft Project to build and track project plans, maintain the database of project information, and perform calculations.

Although Visio is not a project management tool, you can develop project-related diagrams with it to communicate project plans and status. You can also use the Timeline, Gantt Chart, and PERT Chart templates to build and report on very simple projects. Whether you're managing a project or creating a calendar to track your kids' school activities, the Calendar template provides shapes to construct calendars that span one day to several years.

In addition to building project management diagrams by dragging and dropping shapes, you can also import data from Microsoft Project or other applications into Visio diagrams. If you develop a prototype schedule in Visio, you can also jumpstart projects by exporting your schedules to Microsoft Project.

In this chapter you learn how to work with the Visio Calendar, Timeline, Gantt Charts, and PERT Chart templates to effectively represent your projects and other time-sensitive information.

Exploring the Project Scheduling Templates

In Visio 2003, four project-related templates present project and date-related information in distinct ways. Each template automatically sets the page to a letter-size sheet with landscape orientation, and uses inches drawn at a one-to-one scale. Use the template that corresponds with the type of information you want to convey:

✦ **Calendar** — Create calendars for projects as well as other purposes showing days, weeks, months, or years. Add reminders, meetings, special events, milestones, and more. The template includes the Calendar Shapes stencil and the Calendar menu.

✦ **Timeline** — Provides a set of dated timeline shapes that show events along a horizontal or vertical timeline. There are also shapes for milestones and intervals. The Timeline template includes the Timeline Shapes, Background, and Borders and Titles stencils, along with the Timeline menu.

✦ **Gantt Chart** — Drag shapes onto a page to create Gantt charts and import data from Microsoft Outlook or Microsoft Project. The Gantt Chart template includes the Gantt Chart Shapes, Background, and Borders and Titles stencils, along with the Gantt Chart menu and toolbar.

✦ **PERT Chart** — Provides a pair of PERT (Program Evaluation and Review Technique) Chart boxes, or *nodes*, to show the interdependencies between tasks without taking timing into account. There are shapes for node connectors, callouts, and legends. The PERT Chart template includes the PERT Chart Shapes, Background, and Borders and Titles stencils.

To create a drawing using one of the project scheduling templates, choose File ➪ New ➪ Project Schedule and then choose Calendar, Gantt Chart, PERT Chart, or Timeline. To use one of the project scheduling stencils in a different template, choose File ➪ Shapes ➪ Project Schedule and then choose the stencil you want. Visio adds the appropriate menu to the Visio menu bar when you drag a shape from one of the template stencils onto the drawing page.

Constructing Calendars

Use the Calendar template to create daily, weekly, monthly, or yearly calendars. You can add appointments, events, or project tasks to calendar days, which are then associated with the calendar dates. With calendar art, you can highlight special dates. You can create calendars by creating a new Visio drawing using the Calendar template or by opening the Calendar Shapes stencil. By specifying a language for the calendar, you set the date formats for your calendars.

New Feature   With Visio 2003, you can now import appointments and other schedule information from your Microsoft Outlook Calendar (see the "Importing Outlook Calendar Data into Visio" section later in this chapter).

Creating Daily Calendars

You can create a calendar consisting of a single day or multiple nonconsecutive days. You could create a calendar of nonconsecutive days to show meetings or events that always occur on Tuesdays and Thursdays, for example. To create a calendar of selected days, follow these steps:

1. Drag the Day shape onto the drawing. The Configure dialog box appears.

2. Enter the date and the date format (if necessary) and then click OK. You can also change the date format by choosing another language. For example, if you choose French (Canadian), the date format changes to yyyy-mm-dd.

3. Repeat steps 1 and 2 for each day you want in your calendar.

4. Resize and move the Day shapes into the size and position you want. To change the date or date format in a Day shape after you've created it, select the shape and then choose Calendar ➪ Configure.

Creating Weekly Calendars

To create a weekly calendar, follow these steps:

1. Drag the Week shape onto the drawing. The Configure dialog box appears.

2. In the Start Date box, enter the date for the beginning of the week.

3. In the End Date drop-down list, select the number of days for the week and the resulting end date.

4. Specify the date format, language, whether you want the weekend to be shaded, and whether you want to show the title of the week (for example, "Week of July 12, 2004").

5. To add additional weeks, repeat steps 1 through 4.

6. Resize and move the week shapes into the size and position you want.

Tip   Rather than add multiple individual weeks, you can create a multiweek calendar for consecutive weeks. Drag the Multiple Week shape onto the drawing. In the Configure dialog box, specify the start and end dates and any other calendar formatting options, and then click OK.

Creating Monthly Calendars

You can create a single-month or multimonth calendar. To create a monthly calendar, follow these steps:

1. Drag the Month shape onto the drawing. The Configure dialog box appears.

2. Enter the month and year for the calendar.

3. Select the day on which the weeks should begin in the Begin Week On drop-down list.

4. Specify the language if necessary, whether you want the weekends to be shaded, and whether you want to show the title of the month (for example, "August 04").

5. If necessary, resize and move the Month shape into the size and position you want. By default, it fills the page.

Tip You can add previous and next month thumbnails to a Month calendar. Drag the Thumbnail Month shape to the position you want in your Month calendar. In the Custom Properties dialog box, enter the month and year and then click OK.

6. To add additional months, add a new page by choosing Insert ➪ New Page and then clicking OK in the Page Setup dialog box. Repeat steps 1 through 5 to set up the month on the new page.

Tip To show the phases of the moon, drag the Moon Phases shape onto a day of the month. Right-click the shape and choose New Moon, First Quarter, Last Quarter, or Full Moon.

Creating Yearly Calendars

You can create a yearly calendar on a single page, or a multiyear calendar across multiple pages in your drawing. To create a yearly calendar, follow these steps:

1. Drag the Year shape onto the drawing. The Custom Properties dialog box appears.

2. Enter the calendar's year, the day on which the weeks should begin (that is, Sunday or Monday), the language if necessary, and then click OK.

3. If necessary, resize and move the Year shape into the size and position you want. By default, it fills the page.

4. To add another year to the drawing, add a new page by choosing Insert ➪ New Page and then clicking OK. Repeat steps 1 through 3 to set up the year on the new page.

Tip You might find the Year shape better suited to a portrait page orientation than the default landscape orientation. Choose File ➪ Page Setup and then select the Print Setup tab. Under Printer Paper, select Portrait and then click OK.

Exploring Calendar Art Shapes

The Calendar Shapes stencil includes a number of shapes, or *calendar art*, that you can use to enhance or visually categorize appointments and events. You can use shapes such as Clock or Meeting to flag appointments and events by category. Shapes such as Important, Idea, and To Do can emphasize calendar items. You can also highlight travel days with shapes, such as with Travel-Air. Shapes such as Birthday or Sports can enhance the appearance of your calendar in addition to reminding you of these types of activities. You can also add shapes, such as Milestone or Completion, for example, to make important project dates stand out.

Note   Calendar art is associated with the day, but not the date, to which you add it. This means if you change the date, the calendar art does not move to the new date.

Working with Calendars

After you've created a calendar, you can modify it in various ways:

✦ **Change dates or format settings** — Select a calendar and choose Calendar ➪ Configure.

✦ **Change colors** — You can change the color of a Calendar shape — for example, an individual day in a monthly calendar or the title area of a weekly calendar. Right-click the area whose color or pattern you want to change and choose Format ➪ Fill from the shortcut menu.

✦ **Change the color scheme** — To change a calendar's entire combination of color, right-click an empty area of the drawing page outside the Calendar shape itself. From the shortcut menu, choose Color Schemes, select the color scheme you want, and click Apply or OK.

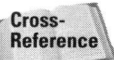

Cross-Reference   To learn more about working with color schemes, see Chapter 7.

✦ **Change the calendar title** — Double-click the calendar's title and then type the text you want. When you're finished, press Esc. To change the title for a year calendar, right-click the calendar and then choose Configure from the shortcut menu. Enter a year in the Year box and then click OK.

Working with Appointments and Events

After you've created a calendar, you can add appointments, such as meetings or classes, and events, such as conferences, as shown in Figure 17-1. Appointments and events are associated with the calendar dates you specify, so they move to the new dates automatically if you change the dates on which they occur.

✦ **Add an appointment** — Drag the Appointment shape onto a calendar day. In the Configure dialog box, enter the start and end times and the subject and location of the meeting, or the name of a one-day project task. You can specify the time and date format displayed as well. Click OK.

✦ **Add a multiple-day event** — Drag the Multi-Day Event shape onto your calendar. In the Configure dialog box, enter the subject and location of the event or project task as well as the start and end dates. Click OK.

✦ **Add text** — Double-click the day in which you want to add text, type the text you want, and press Esc. The text box and day box are grouped so that you can move and resize them as one. You can use standard techniques to edit and delete text in calendars.

Caution   Text added to a day box is associated with the day box, but not the actual day, as are appointments and events. To move the text to another day, you can cut and paste it from one day box to another.

Multi-day event   Project milestone

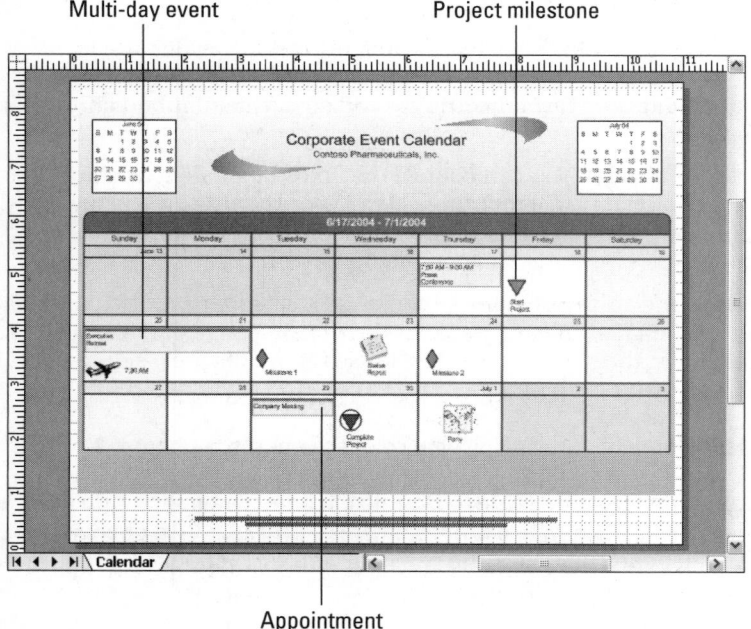

Appointment

Figure 17-1: Create a calendar to show appointments, events, or project tasks.

✦ **Revise an appointment or event** — Right-click it and choose Configure from the shortcut menu.

✦ **Delete an appointment or event** — Right-click it and choose Cut from the shortcut menu.

Consolidating Schedules for Several Individuals

You can import appointments from multiple individuals into a single Visio calendar to compare or combine the schedules of team members on a project. To combine appointments from different people, follow these steps:

1. Import your own appointments into a new or existing Visio calendar.

2. When you're finished, choose File ⇨ Send To ⇨ Routing Recipient.

3. In the Routing Slip dialog box, enter the e-mail addresses for the people whose appointments you want to import.

4. In the Message Text box, instruct the recipients on how to run the Import Outlook Data Wizard on the calendar.

5. Under Route to Recipients, select One After Another. Be sure that the Return When Done check box is checked and then click OK.

Each recipient in turn runs the Import Outlook Data Wizard on the calendar to add his or her appointments. When the last recipient finishes, the calendar returns to you, complete with everyone's imported appointments.

Importing Outlook Calendar Data into Visio

In Visio 2003, you can create, format, and share calendar appointments from Microsoft Outlook 2002 and later. To import Outlook calendar appointments into a Visio calendar, follow these steps:

1. Choose File ⇨ New ⇨ Project Schedule ⇨ Calendar or open an existing calendar drawing into which you want to import Outlook appointments.

2. Choose Calendar ⇨ Import Outlook Data Wizard.

Note If the Choose Profile dialog box appears, select the profile you want to use in the Profile Name drop-down list.

3. In the first wizard page, select whether you want to import Outlook appointments into a new or existing Visio calendar and then click Next. The Selected Visio Calendar option is available only if you have already selected an existing Visio calendar on the drawing page.

4. In the second wizard page, specify the range of dates and times that contain the appointments you want to import and then click Next.

Tip You can filter the appointments to import based on words in their Subject. Click Filter to open the Filter Outlook Data dialog box. Check the Subject Contains check box, type in the word or phrase for which you want to filter, and click OK.

5. In the third wizard page, which appears only if you import appointments into a new Visio calendar, specify the calendar type and properties and click Next.

6. In the last wizard page, review the import properties you specified. To change any of the import properties, click Back to open and edit the appropriate wizard page. When all import properties are set the way you want, click Finish.

Note

If there are too many appointments to fit in a single day in your calendar, they stack on top of each other. Resize the calendar to show all the appointments.

Documenting Project Timelines

Use the Timeline template to show milestones, intervals, tasks, or phases along a horizontal or vertical bar. A timeline drawing, as illustrated in Figure 17-2, can help you communicate dates and show progress toward a deadline.

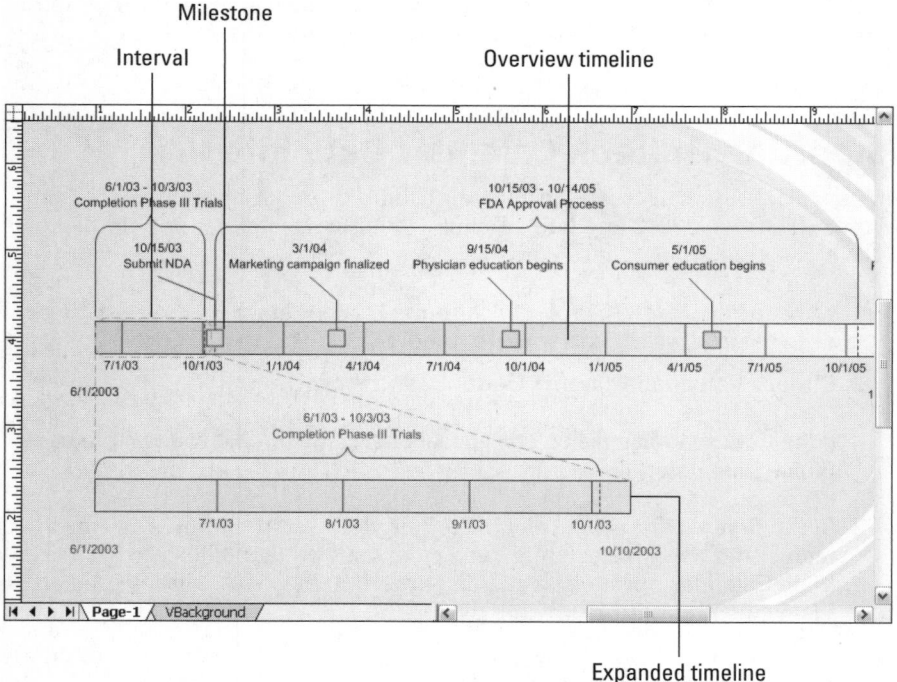

Figure 17-2: Create horizontal or vertical timelines and summary and expanded timelines to show project milestones and intervals.

New Feature In Visio 2003, you can create vertical as well as horizontal timelines. You can also create a detailed view of a segment in an overview timeline.

With the Timeline template, you can take advantage of the following options:

✦ **Timeline shapes** — Specify the look and style of the timeline by selecting a particular Timeline shape.

✦ **Milestones** — Add one of several Milestone shapes to highlight and describe important dates along the timeline and to synchronize milestones across multiple timelines.

✦ **Intervals** — Define and annotate intervals in the timeline and synchronize intervals across multiple timelines on a single page.

✦ **Markers** — Annotate the timeline to show the current day or elapsed time. The Today Marker automatically moves to the current date as set in your computer system clock. You can also add the Elapsed Time shape to show the duration of a project up to the current date.

✦ **Expanded timeline** — Add an Expanded Timeline shape to show a detailed view of a segment in an overview timeline.

✦ **Data exchange with Project** — Import data from Microsoft Project into your Visio Timeline or export Visio Timelines to Microsoft Project.

Creating Timelines

You can construct a timeline showing important beginning or ending dates (milestones) or phases of time (intervals). To create a new timeline drawing, follow these steps:

1. Choose File ⇨ New ⇨ Project Schedule ⇨ Timeline.

2. From the Timeline Shapes stencil, drag one of the Timeline shapes, such as Block Timeline or Cylindrical Timeline, onto the drawing.

3. In the Configure Timeline dialog box, under Time Period, specify the start and finish dates and times for the timeline.

4. Under Scale, specify the timescale properties you want in the Time Scale and Start Weeks On drop-down lists. If you select Quarters in the Time Scale drop-down list, you can also specify the Start Fiscal Year On date. Click OK.

New Feature In Visio 2003, you can now divide your timeline by seconds, minutes, hours, or quarters of the fiscal year.

5. Drag the new timeline to the position you want on the drawing.

Tip   If you don't see dates or times on your timeline, select it and choose Timeline ⇨ Configure Timeline. Select the Time Format tab and check the check boxes for the dates you want to show in the timeline.

To add a Milestone shape to your timeline to show an event on a particular date, such as the kickoff date of a phase or the due date of a major deliverable, follow these steps:

1. From the Timeline Shapes stencil, drag one of the Milestone shapes, such as Diamond Milestone or Pin Milestone, onto the timeline.

2. In the Configure Milestone dialog box, specify the date in the Milestone Date box. If the time is important, specify it in the Milestone Time box.

3. In the Description box, type the text for the milestone.

4. To change the date format, select a format from the Date Format drop-down list.

5. Click OK. The Milestone shape moves to the specified date in the timeline, and the date and description appear above or below the timeline itself as the milestone's label.

Tip   If part of the Milestone shape is not visible, right-click any visible part of it and then choose Shape ⇨ Bring to Front from the shortcut menu.

To add an Interval shape to your timeline to show work over a period of time, such as the duration of the research phase of a project, follow these steps:

1. From the Timeline Shapes stencil, drag one of the Interval shapes, such as Block Interval or Cylindrical Interval, onto the timeline.

2. In the Configure Interval dialog box, specify the start and finish dates for the interval. If the time is also important, specify the start and finish times as well.

3. In the Description box, type the text you want to appear with the interval in the timeline.

4. Change the date format if necessary and click OK. The Interval shape appears at the specified dates in the timeline with the dates and description as labels in the Interval shape.

Expanding Timelines

In Visio 2003, you can use the Expanded Timeline shape to create a more detailed view of a segment of an overview timeline. For example, you can create an overview timeline that shows the phases for a project as a whole. Then you can expand one part of the timeline to show the detailed tasks for just one phase. You expand timelines to several levels. You can expand one timeline from an overview timeline. Then, you can create a second expanded timeline to show additional detail for the first expanded timeline. You can also have more than one expanded timeline for a single overview timeline. To add an expanded timeline shape to your drawing, follow these steps:

1. Draw and configure the overview timeline.

2. From the Timeline Shapes stencil, drag the Expanded Timeline shape onto the drawing.

3. In the Configure Timeline dialog box, specify the start and finish dates for the expanded timeline. If the time is also important, specify the start and finish times as well.

Note The dates in the expanded timeline must be within the date range of the overview timeline.

4. In the Time Scale box, select the detailed timescale. For example, if the overview timeline has a timescale of months, consider using a timescale of weeks in the expanded timeline.

5. Click OK to configure the expanded timeline. Any milestones, intervals, and date markers drawn on the overview timeline for the expansion time period also appear in the expanded timeline. As illustrated in Figure 17-2, gray, dashed lines correlate the start and finish dates on the expanded timeline and the overview timeline.

6. Draw any additional milestones or intervals on the expanded timeline.

Note Milestones and intervals added to the expanded timeline do not appear on the overview timeline. However, if you add a milestone or interval to the overview timeline within the date range of an expanded timeline, it appears on the expanded timeline as well. Visio synchronizes changes to milestones or intervals with the associated timelines.

You can use the mouse to change the expanded timeline in the following ways:

✦ **Move** — Drag the expanded timeline to the location you want on the drawing. The expanded timeline's association with the overview timeline is maintained even when you move it.

✦ **Resize** — Select the expanded timeline and drag any of the four selection handles to the size you want. This only resizes the timeline, and does not change the dates.

✦ **Change the start or end date** — Select the expanded timeline. On the overview timeline, drag the yellow control handles to the new date.

Synchronizing Milestones and Intervals

Just as Visio synchronizes milestones and intervals in overview and expanded time-lines, you can synchronize milestones and intervals across multiple timelines on a page. You can synchronize existing milestones or intervals or you can create the synchronization using the Synchronized Milestone and Synchronized Interval shapes.

New Feature In Visio 2003, you can synchronize milestones and intervals across multiple time-lines on a page and see visual cues as to which items are synchronized.

To synchronize a milestone or interval with another, follow these steps:

1. Use one of the following methods to select a milestone or interval:

   • **Existing shapes** — Select the milestone or interval you want to synchronize.

   • **New shapes** — From the Timeline Shapes stencil, drag the Synchronized Milestone or Synchronized Interval shape onto the timeline.

2. Choose Timeline ➪ Synchronize Milestone or Timeline ➪ Synchronize Interval.

3. In the Synchronize With drop-down list, select the milestone or interval with which the selected shape should be synchronized.

4. Select the date format if necessary and click OK. A gray, dotted line appears, showing the synchronization between the milestones or intervals.

Note Deleting the gray, dotted line does not remove the association between synchro-nized milestones or intervals. To break the link between synchronized milestones or intervals, delete one of the synchronized shapes. You can then add it back as a regular unsynchronized shape.

Modifying Timelines

For existing timelines, you can modify dates and times as well as the overall look of a timeline. To change date or time information and formats, select the timeline and choose Timeline ➪ Configure Timeline. In the Configure Timeline dialog box, use one or more of the following methods:

✦ **Start and end dates** — Select the Time Period tab if necessary. Under Time Period, change the start or finish dates.

✦ **Timescale** — Select the Time Period tab if necessary. In the Time Scale drop-down list, select the timescale you want, such as Months or Weeks. The timescale specifies the tick marks and interim dates that show on the timescale.

✦ **Date or time format** — Select the Time Format tab. Under Show Start and Finish Dates on Timeline, select the date format you want in the Date Format drop-down list. To change the date format for interim dates, select the format under Show Interim Time Scale Markings on Timeline.

✦ **Timescale date and markings** — Select the Time Format tab. Uncheck the Show Interim Time Scale Markings on Timeline check box if you don't want any tick marks or dates between the start and finish dates. Uncheck the Show Dates on Interim Time Scale Markings check box if you don't want interim dates to show. Your start and finish dates, as well as any milestone and interval dates, still appear.

✦ **Revise dates automatically** — Select the Time Format tab. Check the Automatically Update Dates When Markers Are Moved check box when you want dates to dynamically change as you move milestones or intervals along the timeline (this is the default). Uncheck this check box if you do not want dates to update automatically.

New Feature

In Visio 2003, you can edit all date and time formatting for different elements in a timeline. Select the timeline and then choose Timeline ➪ Change Date and Time Formats. Change the date format for the elements you want, such as the start and finish dates or the milestone dates.

You can change the look of your timeline in the following ways:

✦ **Change the timeline orientation** — Select the timeline and drag the selection handles to move the timeline to a vertical orientation.

✦ **Change the type of timeline** — Right-click the timeline and choose Set Timeline Type from the shortcut menu. In the Timeline Type drop-down list, select the type of timeline you want.

✦ **Show arrowheads** — Right-click the timeline and then choose Show Start Arrowhead or Show Finish Arrowhead.

Note

To delete a timeline, select it and press Delete. All milestones, intervals, and any other shapes associated with the timeline are deleted as well.

Importing and Exporting Timeline Data

You can import and export timeline data between Visio and Microsoft Project if Microsoft Project 2000 or later is installed on your computer along with Visio.

Note

In Visio 2003, you can no longer import Microsoft Excel data, .txt, or .mpx files into a timeline or convert data between a timeline and a Gantt chart. However, you can import Excel data, .txt, and .mpx files into a Visio Gantt Chart. If you export that data to Microsoft Project, you can use the Import Timeline Data wizard to import the new Microsoft Project data as a timeline or convert a timeline to a Gantt Chart in Visio.

Importing Microsoft Project Data into a Timeline

Bring information from Microsoft Project into Visio when you want to create a timeline based on existing project management information. This is particularly useful for presenting or reporting project status. You can import all tasks in the project or just the top-level tasks, the summary tasks, the milestones, or any combination of these. To import information from Microsoft Project into a Visio Timeline, follow these steps:

1. In Visio, open an existing Timeline drawing or create a new one.

2. Choose Timeline ➪ Import Timeline Data.

Note If you don't see Import Timeline Data on the Timeline menu, you don't have Microsoft Project 2000 or later installed on your computer.

3. In the wizard page, click Browse. Navigate to the Microsoft Project file that contains the information you want to import into Visio. Select the file, click Open, and click Next.

Caution To successfully import project data, make sure that the Microsoft Project file that you're importing is not currently open.

4. In the next wizard page, select the type of tasks you want to import from Microsoft Project to Visio and click Next.

5. In the next wizard page, select the Timeline, Milestone, and Interval shapes for the Microsoft Project information being imported and click Next.

Note Any Microsoft Project tasks with 0 duration are imported as milestones. Tasks with durations are imported as intervals, showing their start dates, finish dates, and durations. Any tasks designated as milestones but containing duration are imported as intervals, not milestones.

6. In the final wizard page, review the import properties you specified. To change any of the import properties, click Back.

7. When all import properties are set the way you want, click Finish. Visio imports the selected tasks. If you imported into an existing Timeline drawing, Visio creates the imported timeline on a new page.

Exporting Visio Timelines to Microsoft Project

Suppose you built a simple project as a Visio Timeline, perhaps as a proposal or to gather input from team members. Now it's time to initiate the project and you want to transform the Visio Timeline into a Microsoft Project plan so you can take full advantage of scheduling, resource allocation, and budget tracking features. You can export milestones and intervals from your Visio Timeline. In Microsoft Project, intervals become tasks with start dates, finish dates, and durations. To export information from a Visio Timeline to Microsoft Project, follow these steps:

1. In Visio, open and select the timeline.

2. Choose Timeline ➪ Export Timeline Data.

Note If you select a timeline that's associated with expanded timelines, a prompt asks if you want to export markers on the expanded timelines. Click Yes or No.

3. In the browser window that appears, navigate to the folder in which you want to save the exported project file.

4. In the File Name box, type a name for the project file. Be sure that Microsoft Project File (*.mpp) is selected in the Save As Type box, and then click Save.

5. In the wizard page again, click Next. A message will appear saying that the project has been successfully exported. Click OK.

6. Open Microsoft Project and review the project file you just created with the exported timeline data.

Scheduling Projects Using Gantt Charts

The Gantt chart is one of the most popular diagrams for showing project task information. With a Gantt Chart, you can list tasks next to charts of task bars, milestone markers, and other symbols along a horizontal timescale. Using the Gantt Chart template to draw a Gantt chart in Visio can be helpful in the initial planning stages of a project when you're developing a broad outline of project phases and milestones. A Visio Gantt Chart, shown in Figure 17-3, can also be helpful during project execution when you're preparing presentations or progress reports.

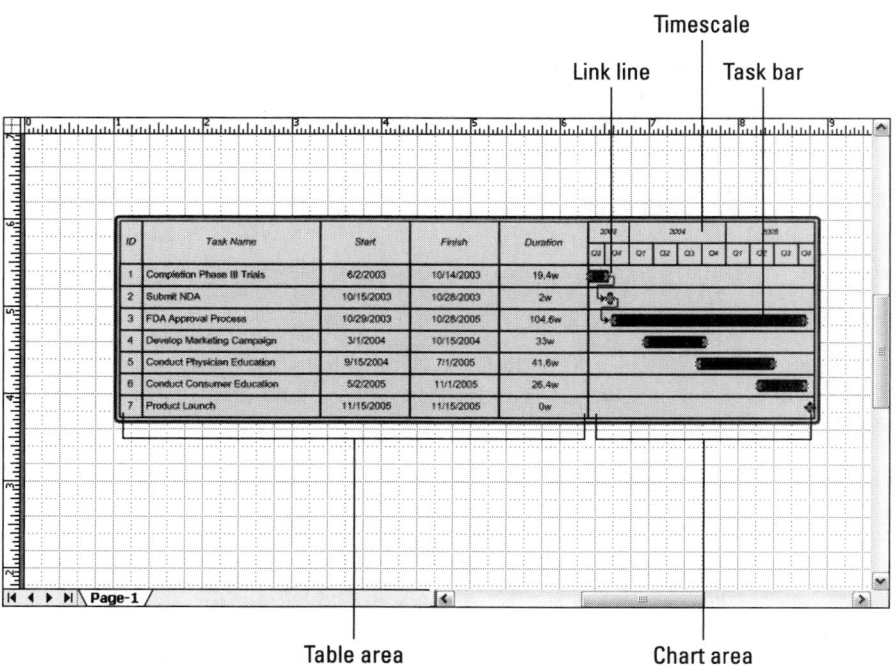

Figure 17-3: Create a Gantt chart in Visio to gain consensus on a proposed project plan or to report ongoing progress.

With the Gantt Chart template, you can perform the following actions:

✦ **Draw a Gantt Chart** — Use the Gantt Chart Frame, Column, and Row shapes to define the Gantt Chart drawing.

✦ **Draw task bars and milestones** — Indicate the scheduling of tasks with the Task Bar shape, and the major accomplishments with the Milestone shapes.

✦ **Create a hierarchy of project tasks** — Indent and outdent tasks to create summary tasks and subtasks.

✦ **Link tasks** — Show dependencies between predecessor and successor tasks using the Link Lines shape.

✦ **Specify working time** — Indicate the normal working days and hours for your project team.

✦ **Explain the Gantt Chart to others** — Use the Title, Legend, Text Block, and Horizontal Callout shapes to add clarification to the Gantt Chart.

✦ **Add columns** — Insert predefined or custom project fields, such as Resource Names or % Complete, in the table area of the Gantt Chart.

✦ **Format the Gantt Chart** — Specify the look of the task bars, milestones, summary task bars, and text.

✦ **Exchange project data** — Import and export project information with Microsoft Project.

Note   The Visio Gantt Chart is primarily a visual representation of a project. It uses SmartShapes technology and can perform basic calculations among start dates, finish dates, and durations. However, the Visio Gantt Chart does not calculate resource allocation, budget estimates, and other typical project management information. To perform such project management activities, use a software tool such as Microsoft Project.

Creating Gantt Charts

Start a new Gantt Chart drawing by setting up the overall parameters of the project. Next, specify the details for individual tasks. Add milestones, organize the tasks into a hierarchical outline or work breakdown structure, and link tasks together to show task dependencies.

To create a new Gantt Chart in Visio, follow these steps:

1. Choose File ➪ New ➪ Project Schedule ➪ Gantt Chart. A new drawing with the Gantt Chart Shapes stencil, the Gantt Chart toolbar, and the Gantt Chart menu appears, along with the Gantt Chart Options dialog box.

Note   To add a Gantt Chart to an existing drawing, choose File ➪ Shapes ➪ Project Schedule ➪ Gantt Chart Shapes. From the Gantt Chart Shapes stencil, drag the Gantt Chart Frame shape onto the drawing.

2. In the Gantt Chart Options dialog box, specify the number of tasks you want to define, the major and minor timescale units, the duration time units you prefer, the anticipated start and finish date for the project, and so on.

Caution Under Time Units, don't make your timescale too detailed for the timescale date range you specify. For example, if your timescale range is a year, and you set the time units for days within months, your chart will be much larger than what can fit on a standard page.

3. When you're finished, click OK to build and display the Gantt Chart.

To enter task details in the table area of your Gantt Chart, follow these steps:

1. Zoom into the Gantt Chart if necessary to see text in the columns.

2. In the Task Name column, double-click Task 1 in the first row and change Task 1 to the first task name in your project. When you're finished, double-click Task 2 and repeat the process. Repeat this for each task in your project.

3. In the Start and Finish columns, double-click a date and change it to the date for the corresponding task. When you're finished, click outside the field.

4. In the same way, change the Duration field to the duration you want for the corresponding task.

Although you can specify the start date, finish date, and duration for tasks by typing in their table columns, you can also specify this information by dragging task bars under the dates indicated on the timescale of the Gantt Chart. When you select a task bar, selection handles and control handles appear, which you can use to define task information. Specify task details in the chart area of the Gantt Chart as follows:

✦ **Change the start date** — Drag the left green selection handle to the left or right until it's under the start date you want. The date in the Start Date column for the task changes as well.

✦ **Change the finish date** — Drag the right green selection handle to the left or right until it's under the finish date you want. The date in the Finish Date column for the task changes as well.

✦ **Change the task duration** — Drag either green selection handle until the task bar spans the number of days you want. The amount in the Duration column for the task changes as well.

✦ **Indicate progress in the task bar** — Drag the left yellow control handle toward the right in the task bar to display a pink progress bar.

Navigating in Gantt Charts

Tools on the Gantt Chart toolbar, illustrated in Figure 17-4, help you scroll to task bars or dates in your Gantt Chart. Use the following tools to scroll the chart area within your Gantt Chart.

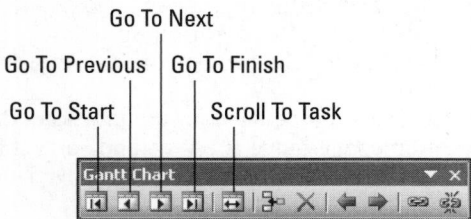

Figure 17-4: The Gantt Chart toolbar provides tools for navigating to tasks.

✦ **Go To Start** — Shows the first task bar in the project

✦ **Go To Previous** — Shows the time period just before the period currently showing

✦ **Go To Next** — Shows the time period just after the first period currently showing

✦ **Go To Finish** — Shows the last task bar in the project

✦ **Scroll To Task** — Shows the task bar for the currently selected task

Adding Milestones

To add a milestone to your Gantt Chart, follow these steps:

1. From the Gantt Chart Shapes stencil, drag the Milestone shape onto the task above which you want to insert a new milestone task. Visio inserts a new task above that point and the milestone marker appears in the chart area.

2. Double-click New Task in the Task Name column and then change the placeholder name to the milestone name.

3. Change the Start Date field to the milestone date. In Visio, milestones must have a duration of 0, so as soon as you enter the start date, Visio updates the finish date to the same date. You can also drag the milestone marker in the chart area to the date you want. Visio updates the fields in the Start and Finish columns automatically.

Note   Leave the duration for the milestone task at 0. If you add a duration, the milestone marker changes to a Task Bar shape in the chart area. Likewise, if you change a task duration to 0, its task bar changes to a milestone marker.

Organizing Tasks

You can set up the tasks in your Gantt Chart as an outline of summary tasks and subtasks. This is helpful for setting up individual tasks within phases or for subdividing tasks with larger scope into their component tasks, as in a work breakdown structure. To arrange tasks into a hierarchy of summary tasks and subtasks, follow these steps:

1. Add all the summary tasks and subtasks in the proper order for the hierarchy.

Tip To move a task, select the entire task row by clicking the task's ID. Drag the row to the location you want.

2. Select the task you want to transform into a subtask of the task above it.

3. Click the Indent tool on the Gantt Chart toolbar or choose Gantt Chart ⇨ Indent, which makes the following changes:

   • Visio indents the selected task to show that it's a subtask of the task above it.

   • Visio bolds the font for the task above, indicating that it's now a summary task of the indented tasks below it.

   • The summary task information calculates rolled up values for all its subtasks.

   • The task bar for the summary task is marked with triangular end points, and represents the start, finish, and duration for all subtasks.

Linking Tasks

Many tasks cannot start until other tasks are completed, a condition which is known as a *task dependency,* or *task link.* To link tasks to show their dependencies, follow these steps:

1. Select the first task or the predecessor you want to link. Then Shift+click or Ctrl+click the second task, or successor. Click as many tasks as you want in the order that you want them linked.

Note Shift+clicking selects one task at a time, rather than a series of consecutive tasks.

2. On the Gantt Chart toolbar, click the Link Tasks tool. Visio links the selected tasks in a finish-to-start relationship, as shown by link lines in the chart area of the Gantt Chart. Start and finish dates might be recalculated to reflect the scheduling changes caused by the new task links.

Note Tasks are linked in a finish-to-start relationship only. There is no way to represent start-to-start, finish-to-finish, or start-to-finish task links in a Visio Gantt Chart.

Setting the Project Working Time

By setting a project's working time, you can show the days and times in which work occurs on the project — for example, Monday through Friday 8:00 A.M. through 5:00 P.M. If a project is behind schedule and Saturdays are workdays, you can specify that as well.

To specify working days and times for the project, choose Gantt Chart ➪ Configure Working Time. Under Working Days, check the check boxes for the days of the week designated as workdays and uncheck the check boxes for days off. Under Working Time, enter the start and finish times for the working days. Working time is reflected with different colors in the chart area of the Gantt Chart and can affect task finish dates.

Annotating Gantt Charts

You can polish up Gantt Charts by adding annotations. From the Gantt Chart Shapes stencil, drag one or more of the following shapes to the Gantt Chart drawing:

✦ Title

✦ Legend

✦ Text Block (8-point, 10-point, or 12-point text)

✦ Horizontal Callout or Right-Angle Horizontal (callout)

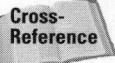
Cross-Reference   For information on annotation techniques, see Chapter 6.

Modifying the Content in Gantt Charts

After you've built your Gantt Chart, you can modify it to make necessary adjustments or add detail. You can add and delete tasks or show and hide columns in the table area of the Gantt Chart. Use one or more of the following methods to modify the content of your Gantt Chart:

✦ **Add a new task** — Click the task above which you want to add a new task. On the Gantt Chart toolbar, click New Task. You can also choose Gantt Chart ➪ New Task or drag the Row shape from the Gantt Bar Shapes stencil onto the Gantt Chart. Type the name of the new task along with the start date, finish date, duration, and any other task information.

✦ **Delete a task** — Select the task you want to delete. On the Gantt Chart toolbar, choose Delete Task, or choose Gantt Chart ➪ Delete Task.

✦ **Rename a task** — Double-click the task name, edit the name, and press Esc.

✦ **Add a column to the table** — Click the column heading to the left of where you want the new column. Choose Gantt Chart ➪ Insert Column or drag the Column shape from the Gantt Chart Shapes stencil onto the Gantt Chart. In the Column Type drop-down list, select the field you want to add, such as % Complete or Actual Duration. To add a custom column, select one of the User Defined fields, such as User Defined Duration. Click OK.

✦ **Remove a column from the table** — Click anywhere in the column you want to delete. Choose Gantt Chart ⇨ Hide Column.

Formatting Gantt Charts

To clarify a Gantt Chart, you can format how Visio displays time-based information. You can also change the appearance of chart area elements to make a Gantt Chart more compelling. Format your Gantt Chart in the following ways:

✦ **Change timescale dates and units** — Choose Gantt Chart ⇨ Options and then select the Date tab if necessary. Under Time Units, specify the major and minor time periods for the timescale in the chart area of the Gantt Chart. Under Duration Options, specify the time unit for duration. Under Timescale Range, specify the start and finish dates for the project.

✦ **Change the look of task bars and milestones** — Choose Gantt Chart ⇨ Options and then select the Format tab. Specify the shapes on the ends of task bars and summary bars (the type of text appearing in or around the task bars) and the shape of milestones.

✦ **Change text formatting in the table area** — Select the text you want to format and then choose Format ⇨ Text.

✦ **Change colors in the Gantt Chart** — Select the item whose color you want to change and choose Format ⇨ Fill.

Importing and Exporting Gantt Chart Data

You can import and export Gantt Chart data between Visio and Microsoft Project. When Microsoft Project 2000 or later is installed on your computer with Visio, the Import and Export commands appear on the Visio Gantt Chart menu.

Importing Project Data into Visio Gantt Charts

Bring information from Microsoft Project into Visio when you want to create a Gantt Chart based on existing project management information.

New Feature The Import Project Data Wizard creates only Gantt Charts, not Timelines, now that Visio 2003 includes the Import Timeline Wizard.

To import Microsoft Project data into a Visio Gantt Chart, follow these steps:

1. In Visio, choose File ⇨ New ⇨ Project Schedule ⇨ Gantt Chart or open an existing Gantt Chart drawing. Choose Gantt Chart ⇨ Import.

2. Select Information That's Already Stored in a File and then click Next.

3. In the next wizard page, select Microsoft Office Project File and click Next.

Tip In this wizard page, you can also choose to import project information from existing Excel spreadsheets (.xls files) or text files (.txt or .csv files).

4. In the third wizard page, click Browse and navigate to the Microsoft Project file that contains the information you want to import as a Visio Gantt Chart. Select the file and click Open. Click Next.

5. In the fourth wizard page, specify the major and minor timescale units, as well as the duration time units to be used. Click Next.

6. In the fifth wizard page, select the type of tasks you want to import from Microsoft Project to Visio. Click Next.

Note Any Microsoft Project tasks with 0 duration are imported as milestones. Any tasks designated as milestones but containing a duration, such as one day, are imported as a milestone with a 0 duration.

7. In the final wizard page, review the import properties you specified. To change any of the import properties, click Back. When all import properties are set the way you want, click Finish. The selected task information is built as a Gantt Chart in Visio. If you are importing into an existing drawing, Visio creates the imported Gantt Chart on a new page.

Entering Gantt Chart Data via an Excel or Text File

You might find it more efficient to enter large amounts of project data in an Excel (.xls) file or a text (.txt or .csv) file and then import that file into Visio. You can create these data files directly in Excel or an application that produces text files, or create the spreadsheets or text files within Visio. To import data from a spreadsheet or text file, follow these steps:

1. In Visio, choose File ⇨ New ⇨ Project Schedule ⇨ Gantt Chart or open an existing Gantt Chart drawing.

2. Choose Gantt Chart ⇨ Import. The Import Project Data Wizard appears.

3. Select Information That I Enter Using the Wizard and then click Next.

4. In the second wizard page, select Microsoft Excel or Delimited Text and then click Next. If you select Microsoft Excel, an Excel spreadsheet opens. If you select Delimited Text, a text file opens. Either option provides preset column headings to help you quickly enter project information for your Visio Gantt Chart.

5. Under the New Filename box, click Browse. Navigate to the folder in which you want to store the new file. Type a name for the file in the File Name box. Make sure that Microsoft Office Excel Workbooks (*.xls) or Text Files (*.txt; *.csv) is selected in the Save As Type box and then click Save.

6. Click Next. Microsoft Excel or Notepad will appear, with a page containing project-related headings that contribute to your Gantt Chart in Visio, such as Task Name, Duration, and Start Date. In a Notepad text file, the information for the different columns is separated by commas.

7. Replace the sample data under the headings with your own project data.

8. When you're finished, save and close the file. For best results, close Microsoft Excel or Notepad as well.

9. Back in Visio, continue to work through the remaining wizard pages to import the information from the file you just created.

10. Check the information in the final wizard page and then click Finish. Visio creates a Gantt Chart using the selected task information from your data file.

Exporting Visio Gantt Charts to Microsoft Project

To export project information from your Visio Gantt Chart into Microsoft Project, follow these steps:

1. In Visio, open and select the Gantt Chart and then choose Gantt Chart ⇨ Export.

2. Select Microsoft Office Project File and then click Next.

3. In the browser window that appears, navigate to the folder in which you want to save the exported project file.

4. In the File Name box, type a name for the new project. Be sure that Microsoft Project File (*.mpp) is selected in the Save As Type box. Click Save. In the wizard page again, click Next.

5. In the next wizard page, review the export properties you specified and click Back to change any properties. When all export properties are set the way you want, click Finish. A message indicates that the project has been successfully exported. Click OK.

6. Open Microsoft Project and the project file you just created with the exported Visio Gantt Chart data.

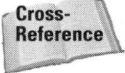 **Cross-Reference** To learn more about importing and exporting information between Visio and other applications, see Chapter 9.

Building PERT Charts

Like Gantt charts, Program Evaluation and Review Technique (PERT) charts are also popular for displaying project task information in a network diagram layout. Each task is represented by a box, or *node*, which is connected to other nodes in the PERT chart via their task links in a manner similar to a flowchart. Each node contains task information such as task duration, start date, and finish date. Use Visio to create PERT charts showing the relationship between tasks in your project, as shown in Figure 17-5.

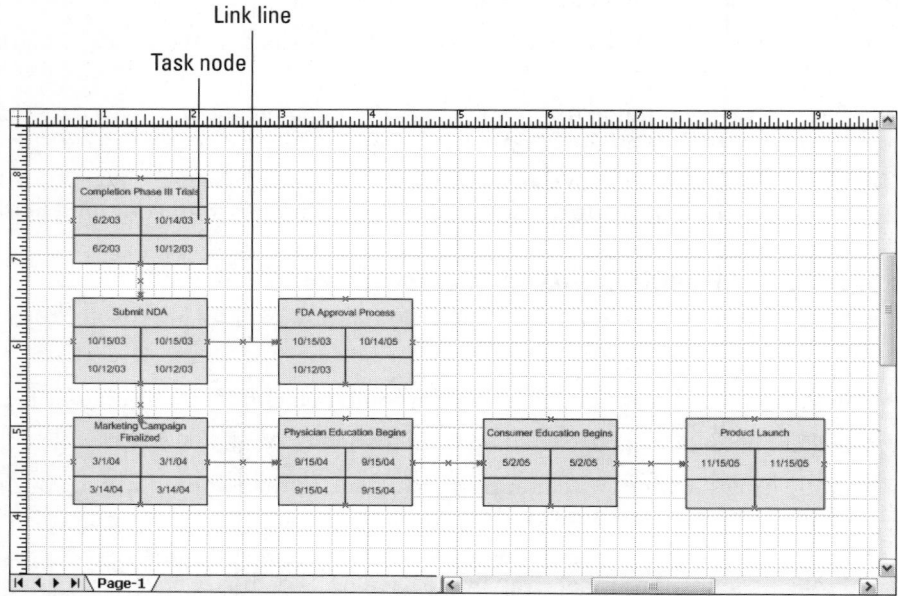

Figure 17-5: Draw a PERT chart to show project tasks in a network diagram layout.

 **Caution** Unlike Visio Gantt Charts and Timelines, the Visio PERT Chart does not calculate start dates, finish dates, or durations. Use the PERT Chart strictly as a visual representation of your project tasks.

Creating PERT Charts

To create a new PERT Chart in Visio, follow these steps:

1. Choose File ➪ New ➪ Project Schedule ➪ PERT Chart. A new drawing containing the PERT Chart Shapes stencil appears.

 **Tip** To add a PERT Chart to an existing drawing, choose File ➪ Shapes ➪ Project Schedule ➪ PERT Chart Shapes.

2. From the PERT Chart Shapes stencil, drag the PERT 1 or PERT 2 shape onto the drawing. The PERT 1 shape creates a task node containing the task name, with six boxes in which to enter task details. The PERT 2 shape contains four additional boxes for task details.

Note Both the PERT 1 and PERT 2 task node shapes contain placeholder project information, including duration, early start, slack, scheduled finish, and more. You can replace the placeholders with any type or format of information you want.

3. Drag a PERT node shape onto the drawing for each project task you want to show. It's best to use the same type of PERT shape for all tasks.

4. To enter a task name, select a node and then type the task name. When you're finished, press Esc.

5. To enter other task information in the node, first select the node, select a text box, type the information, and then press Esc.

Tip To empty a text box, select it, press the spacebar, and then press Esc.

6. To show a task dependency from one node to another, click the Connector tool on the Standard toolbar, click the Line Connector, Line-curve Connector, or Dynamic Connector in the PERT Chart Shapes stencil, and then drag from the predecessor to the successor node.

7. To add a legend or callouts, drag the Legend shape onto the drawing and update the text to help others understand the information in your task nodes, or drag the Horizontal Callout or Right-Angle Horizontal shape onto the drawing.

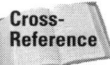

Cross-Reference If you want to show specific information, you can create your own PERT task node shape. To learn more about customizing shapes, see Chapter 32.

Summarizing Projects on PERT Charts

You can use the PERT Chart's Summarization Structure shape to create a high-level graphical overview of a project. To do this, follow these steps:

1. Choose File ➪ New ➪ Project Schedule ➪ PERT Chart. A new drawing containing the PERT Chart Shapes stencil appears. To add a PERT Chart to an existing drawing, choose File ➪ Shapes ➪ Project Schedule ➪ PERT Chart Shapes.

2. From the PERT Chart Shapes stencil, drag the Summarize Structure shape onto the drawing.

3. Type the text you want in the box. The drawing instantly zooms when you begin typing. When you're finished, press Esc, and the drawing zooms out.

4. Repeat steps 2 and 3 for the additional shapes in your project summary.

5. To show links among the summary structures, as shown in Figure 17-6, drag the yellow control handle in a structure lower in the hierarchy to the connection point on the bottom of the related structure above it.

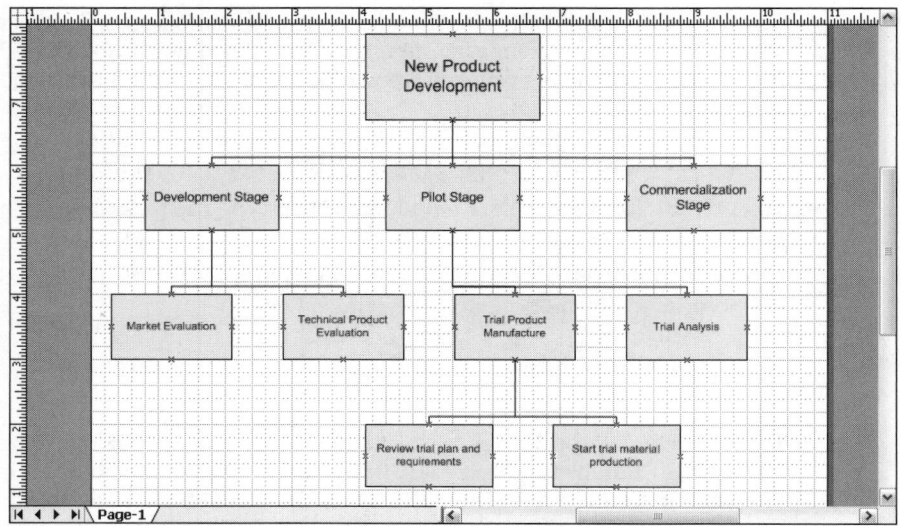

Figure 17-6: Use the Summarization Structure shapes to draw a project overview or work breakdown structure.

Tip

You can also use the Summarization Structure shape to add notes or other additional text under PERT Chart task nodes. With the PERT Chart drawing open, drag the Summarization Structure shape under the node. Drag the yellow handle to the node to connect them. Type the text you want and press Esc when you're finished.

Summary

In Visio 2003, you can create Calendars, Timelines, Gantt Charts, and PERT Charts to help plan and communicate project information. Calendars and PERT Charts strictly reflect the information you provide. By contrast, Timelines and Gantt Charts calculate start dates, finish dates, and durations, to assist with basic project scheduling.

Visio's project scheduling tools are designed to exchange information easily with other programs. You can import appointments from your Microsoft Outlook calendar and exchange timeline information with Microsoft Project. You can import and export Gantt Chart information with Microsoft Project, Microsoft Excel, and text files.

✦　　　✦　　　✦

Documenting Brainstorming Sessions

Brainstorming is an effective way to get people to think outside the box to generate new ideas and creative solutions to challenging problems. During brainstorming sessions, participants express any idea that comes to mind. By giving people's minds free rein and withholding criticism, you can expand your options or identify innovative solutions. Brainstorming can help you flesh out ideas for any purpose, including business strategy, research, new applications for existing products, and even the plot of a novel.

In this chapter, you'll learn how to create brainstorming diagrams to show the relationships between topics and numerous levels of subtopics. You'll also learn how to rearrange topics on diagrams and format them to enhance their appearance. Finally, I will show you how to add a legend to a diagram to identify the symbols used.

Exploring the Brainstorming Template

The Visio Brainstorming template includes shapes and tools to help you document the results of brainstorming sessions. For brainstorming that progresses in an organized fashion, you can begin with a main topic and outline subtopics to generate a hierarchy of ideas. However, when participants think at full throttle, it's hard to keep up with the volume of information. In these situations, you can use Visio Brainstorming tools to capture ideas as quickly as your team generates them and later analyze, organize, and refine the results.

The Visio Brainstorming template is simple yet powerful. You can quickly create brainstorming diagrams by adding, connecting, and arranging topics. Later, you can reorganize topics, emphasize ideas by formatting the diagram, and annotate the results with symbols and a legend. By default, the Outline window opens to show brainstorming topics hierarchically so that you can analyze and refine the results of a session before sharing them with your colleagues.

New Feature

The Brainstorming template in Visio 2003 replaces the Mind Mapping template in Visio 2002.

Accessing Visio Brainstorming Tools

Brainstorming is frequently fast-paced, so Visio provides Brainstorming commands in several places. You can access most Brainstorming tools on the Brainstorming menu on the Visio menu bar as well as the shortcut menus that appear when you right-click a Brainstorming diagram or shape. The Brainstorming toolbar, which you can dock or float as you prefer, includes several commonly used Brainstorming commands. When you open or create a Brainstorming diagram using the Brainstorming template, Visio opens several stencils, floats the Brainstorming toolbar in the drawing window, and adds the Brainstorming menu to the Visio menu bar, as demonstrated in Figure 18-1.

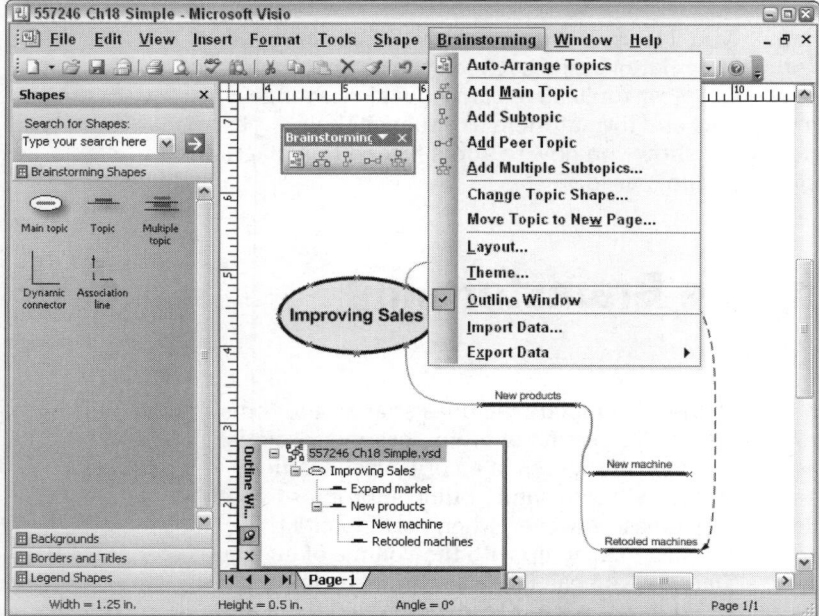

Figure 18-1: The Brainstorming template includes menus, a toolbar, and stencils.

You can document ideas by dragging and dropping different types of topic shapes from the Brainstorming Shapes stencil onto the drawing page or by using the topic commands on the Brainstorming menus. As you work, you can quickly attach Legend shapes to topics to convey shorthand messages, such as order of priority or ideas that need more work. Whenever you have time during or after your session, you can create a legend, modify the topic and connector styles, or use Visio's Auto-Arrange feature to optimize the layout of the topics on the page.

Note If you don't see the Brainstorming toolbar when you open a Brainstorming diagram, choose View ⇨ Toolbars and choose Brainstorming from the submenu. To display the Outline window when it is hidden, choose Brainstorming ⇨ Outline Window.

Exploring the Brainstorming Outline Features

The Outline window, which displays topics on a brainstorming diagram hierarchically, offers a convenient way to work with Visio Brainstorming topics, particularly when your diagram covers several pages. You can rearrange topics in the outline without affecting the appearance of your diagram and without navigating between pages. You can reposition the Outline window, dock it along the side of the drawing area or within the Shapes window, or hide it when you want to work directly on the diagram. Within the Outline window, you can add, delete, or reorder topics in the hierarchy, change topic text, or navigate to a specific topic on the diagram.

You can also export a Brainstorming diagram to Microsoft Word and use its Outline view to fine-tune the results. The topic order you define in the Visio Outline window reappears in the exported Word document.

Exploring Visio's Brainstorming Shapes

A Brainstorming diagram shows a hierarchy of topics with one or more main topics and as many levels of subtopics as you want. In addition, you can illustrate isolated ideas by dropping Topic shapes onto a drawing without connecting them to other topics. The Brainstorming Shapes stencil contains three Topic shapes and two connectors. Although you can drag shapes from the Brainstorming stencil onto a drawing page, the commands on the Brainstorming menus or toolbar are easier because they create and connect Topic shapes at the same time. The following shapes are the basic components for brainstorming diagrams:

✦ **Main Topic** — Represents a central theme or idea. You can add more than one Main Topic to a diagram.

✦ **Topic** — Represents ideas or topics. Although Visio provides only one Topic shape, you can use it to create peer-level or subordinate topics.

Tip   When you work with several hierarchical levels in a diagram, you can modify Topic shapes to differentiate levels in the hierarchy. To do this, right-click the shape and choose Change Topic Shape on the shortcut menu. Select the type of shape you want in the Change Topic dialog box and click OK.

✦ **Multiple Topics** — Opens a dialog box in which you can type the text for multiple topics. Visio adds separate Topic shapes for each line you type in the dialog box.

✦ **Dynamic Connector** — This option connects topics when you glue each end to shapes representing topics on the drawing page.

✦ **Association Line** — Choose this to shows an ancillary relationship between two topics.

The Legend Shapes stencil opens when you use the Brainstorming template. It contains the Legend shape itself as well as symbol shapes that you can glue to Topic shapes to include shorthand reminders. The Brainstorming template also opens the Backgrounds stencil and the Borders and Titles stencil.

Creating Brainstorming Diagrams

The easiest way to create a Brainstorming diagram is to create a new file using the Brainstorming template and then use Brainstorming commands to add topics to the page. To create a Brainstorming diagram, choose File ➪ New ➪ Brainstorming, ➪ Brainstorming Diagram.

Adding and Connecting Topics

Visio doesn't automatically connect Topic shapes when you drag them from the Brainstorming stencil, but connections between Topic shapes are important, particularly when you want to use the Outline window to rearrange topics and their subordinates. It's easier to use commands on the Brainstorming menus or within the Outline window to create shapes and automatically connect them to other shapes. To add text to a Topic shape, select it and type the text you want.

Topics that are not connected using shape-to-shape connections appear in the Outline window as standalone topics. To add or correct the connections between topics, drag an end point of a connector to the center of the first Topic shape. When the shapes are connected shape-to-shape, Visio highlights the topic with a red box, which appears gray in Figure 18-2. Drag the other end point of the connector to the center of the second Topic shape. Solid red squares at the connector end points indicate that the shapes are connected correctly, also illustrated in gray Figure 18-2.

Connector eccentricity handle

Highlighted box indicates topic to be glued with connection.

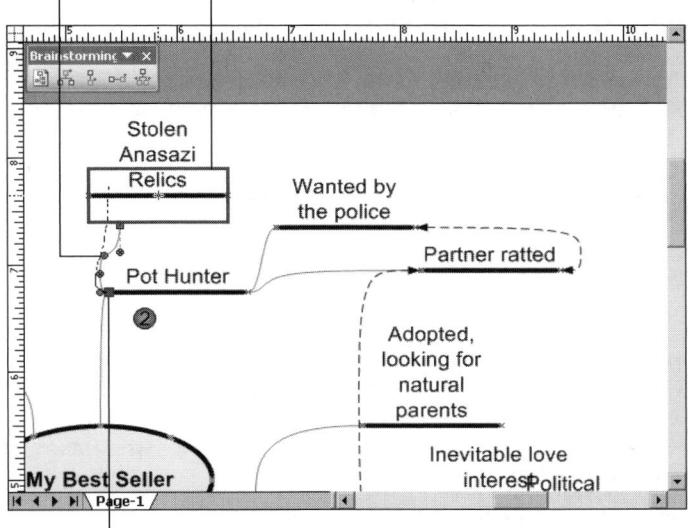

Highlighted connection point indicates topic end point is glued.

Figure18-2: Visio highlights topics to be glued and end points that are glued shape-to-shape.

Adding Main Topics

A Brainstorming diagram doesn't have to contain only one Main Topic, although it's easier to maintain your focus when you ration your main ideas. To create a Main Topic, choose your favorite from the following methods:

✦ **Drag and Drop** — Drag the Main Topic shape onto the drawing page.

✦ **Menu or Toolbar** — Choose Add Main Topic from the Brainstorming menu or the Brainstorming toolbar.

✦ **Shortcut Menu** — Right-click the drawing page and choose Add Main Topic from the shortcut menu.

✦ **Outline Window** — Right-click the diagram filename in the Outline window and choose Add Main Topic.

Adding Subtopics

You can create as many levels of subtopics as you want in a Brainstorming diagram. To create and automatically connect a topic as a subordinate to a superior topic at a higher level, use one of the following methods:

✦ **Menu or Toolbar** — Select a Main Topic or Topic shape on the diagram and choose Add Subtopic from the Brainstorming menu or the Brainstorming toolbar.

✦ **Shortcut Menu** — Right-click a topic on the drawing page and choose Add Subtopic from the shortcut menu.

✦ **Outline Window** — Right-click a topic in the Outline window and choose Add Subtopic.

Tip

You can reference documents containing additional information by adding hyperlinks to topics. To add a hyperlink, select a topic and choose Insert ➪ Hyperlinks. In the Address box, click Browse, and then click Local File. If necessary, choose the type of file you want to link to in the Save As Type list. Navigate to the file you want and click Open. To name the hyperlink, type the name you want in the Description box in the Hyperlinks dialog box and click OK.

To view the document connected by a hyperlink, right-click a topic and choose the hyperlink name from the shortcut menu.

Adding Topics at the Same Level

Peer topics are topics at the same level as another topic in the hierarchy. Create a peer topic using one of the following methods:

✦ **Menu or Toolbar** — Select a Topic shape at the same level as the topic you want to create and choose Add Peer Topic from the Brainstorming menu or the Brainstorming toolbar.

✦ **Shortcut Menu** — Right-click a topic on the drawing page and choose Add Peer Topic from the shortcut menu.

✦ **Outline Window** — Right-click a topic in the Outline window and choose Add Peer Topic.

Adding Multiple Topics at Once

The Add Multiple Subtopics command enables you to add several subtopics to the same superior topic. To add multiple subtopics, follow these steps:

1. Select a Topic shape and choose Add Multiple Subtopics from the Brainstorming menu or the Brainstorming toolbar.

Note

You can also initiate the Add Multiple Subtopics command by right-clicking a topic on the drawing page and choosing Add Multiple Subtopics from the shortcut menu or by right-clicking a topic in the Outline window and choosing Add Multiple Subtopics.

2. In the dialog box, type text for each topic and press Enter to continue with the next topic.

3. When you have added all the topics you want, click OK.

Connecting Topics Manually

You can manually connect topics on a brainstorming diagram or add ancillary relationships between topics. If you added topics by dragging Topic shapes onto the page or want to connect Topic shapes that you inadvertently disconnected, create a shape-to-shape connection by following these steps:

1. Drag the Dynamic connector from the Brainstorming stencil and drop it near the first Topic shape you want to connect.

2. Drag an end point of the connector to the center of the first Topic shape until Visio highlights the Topic shape with a red box.

3. Drag the other end point of the connector to the center of the second Topic shape. Solid red squares at end points indicate that the shapes are connected correctly.

Note Each subordinate shape can only connect to one superior shape. *Association lines* are connectors on the Brainstorming stencil that visually indicate connections to more than one superior topic, or relationships between topics at the same level. However, Topic shapes connected by Association connectors do not appear connected in the Outline window or when you export the diagram.

Laying Out Brainstorming Diagrams

Brainstorming diagrams are meant to capture and present ideas unearthed during brainstorming sessions, which often results in an arrangement of topics as hectic as the discussion that brought it to light. After collecting everyone's thoughts, the next step is cleaning up the clutter to present those ideas for review and further refinement. In Visio, you can rearrange Topic shapes manually or automatically, or modify the layout style to present ideas more clearly. If you would rather keep a large diagram on one page, you can resize the drawing to match your diagram.

Tip You can use the Outline window to quickly locate and select a specific topic on a large brainstorming diagram. In the Outline window, navigate the hierarchy until you find the topic you want and then double-click the topic name. Visio displays the page on which the corresponding Topic shape is located, selects the shape, and centers it in the drawing area.

Moving and Reordering Topics

Visio offers several methods for moving Topics in a Brainstorming diagram. You can relocate Topics within a page or change their level in the diagram hierarchy. For large or complex diagrams, you can move Topics, with or without their subordinates, to other pages in the diagram. Table 18-1 describes methods you can use to move and reorder brainstorming topics.

Table 18-1	
Methods for Moving and Reordering Topics	
Method	*Steps*
Move a topic on the same page	Select the Topic shape and drag it to a new position on the page. Visio moves any subordinate Topic shapes and automatically repositions their connectors.
Move a topic and its subordinates to another page	Select the top-level topic that you want to move on the drawing page or in the Outline window and then choose Brainstorming ➪ Move Topic to New Page. In the Move Topics dialog box, click the New Page or Existing Page option. To move the topic and its subordinates to a new page, type the name you want for the new page. To move them to an existing page, select the page name from the Existing Page list. Click OK to close the dialog box and move the topic.
Copy a topic without its subordinates to another page	Right-click the Topic shape you want to copy on the drawing page and choose Copy from the shortcut menu. Navigate to the page onto which you want to copy the shape, right-click the page, and choose Paste from the shortcut menu.
	You can copy several Topic shapes without their subordinates by holding the Shift key and selecting all the Topic shapes you want. After selecting them, right-click one of the selected shapes and choose Copy from the shortcut menu.
Change a topic's level in the hierarchy	In the Outline window, drag the topic whose level you want to change and drop it on top of the topic you want to be superior. Visio moves the topic and all its subordinates underneath the superior topic and changes connections on the diagram.
Rearrange topics automatically	Choose Auto-Arrange Topics on the Brainstorming menu or toolbar. As long as the Topic shapes on your diagram are connected using shape-to-shape connections, Visio automatically rearranges the Topic shapes for you.

Note When you move a Topic shape and its subordinates, the top-level Topic shape remains on the original drawing page with an arrow symbol that indicates that the topic appears on another page. To navigate to the corresponding Topic shape on the other page, right-click the Topic shape and choose Go to Sub Page from the shortcut menu. To navigate back to the original page, right-click the moved Topic shape and choose Go to Page Containing Parent.

Changing Layout and Connector Styles

The *layout style* governs how Visio positions Topic shapes on the drawing page, whereas the *connector style* specifies whether the connectors are straight or curved. By default, Visio uses curved connectors, and positions the Main Topic shape in the center of the page with shapes for subtopics radiating outward. Follow these steps to change the layout or connector style:

1. Choose Brainstorming ⇨ Layout and select the layout or connector style in the Layout dialog box.

2. To view the selected layout without committing your change, click Apply. If the results are acceptable, click OK.

Note The layout you select applies to the current drawing page and to any Topic shapes you add to that page. The connector style applies only to the current drawing page.

Resizing the Page to Fit the Diagram

If your colleagues are on a roll but you've run out of room on the drawing page, you can add Topic shapes beyond the borders of the page. Later, when you have time, you can resize the page to fit your diagram using one of the following methods:

✦ **Dragging the page borders** — To display the page borders, right-click the page and choose View ⇨ Whole Page. Press the Ctrl key and position the pointer on a page border. When the pointer changes to a two-headed arrow, drag the pointer to resize the page. The status bar displays the current height and width as you drag the border.

Note You can change either the height or width by positioning the pointer near the middle of a border. To change both height and width, position the pointer near but not on the corner of the page. When you position the pointer on a corner, the Rotation tool appears, enabling you to rotate the entire page.

✦ **Using Page Setup** — Choose File ⇨ Page Setup and select the Page Size tab. Specify the new page size and click OK.

Enhancing Brainstorming Diagram Appearance

Visio includes tools to help you refine the relationships between topics or craft a professional appearance for your diagrams. You can change the shape of Topic shapes to emphasize specific ideas, reshape connections to clarify relationships, or apply themes and color schemes to create a presentation. Use one of the following methods to enhance your diagrams:

✦ **Change topic shape** — Select one or more Topic shapes and then choose Brainstorming ➪ Change Topic Shape. In the New Shape box, select the type of shape you want to apply and click OK.

✦ **Reshape connections** — Drag a green eccentricity handle to change the curvature of a curved connector or Association connector. Drag a green diamond vertex to modify the angle of a straight connector.

✦ **Applying a theme** — To apply a theme to the current drawing page, choose Brainstorming ➪ Theme and then select the theme you want in the Theme dialog box. To preview the theme's appearance, click Apply. If the theme is acceptable, click OK. Visio changes the appearance of Topic shapes up to four levels in the hierarchy. Visio uses the shape type of the fourth-level for any additional levels.

Note   You should apply a theme only after you're sure the diagram is finished. If you add new Topic shapes or move Topic shapes to different levels in the hierarchy, you must reapply the theme.

✦ **Apply a color scheme** — To specify a set of coordinated colors for all pages in your diagram, right-click the drawing page, choose Color Schemes from the shortcut menu, and select the color scheme you want. To preview the appearance of the selected color scheme, click Apply. If the color scheme is what you want, click OK.

Working with Legends

You can attach symbol shapes, such as Attention, Note, or Priority 1, to Topic shapes to quickly annotate your diagram. For example, you can prioritize ideas by associating Priority 1 shapes with your top priority Topic shapes, or indicate Topic shapes that include additional information or need additional work with Note or To Do shapes. When you move a Topic shape, any symbol shapes attached to it move with it.

Creating New Symbol Shapes

If the symbols on the Legend Shapes stencil aren't sufficient, you can transform any Visio shape into a symbol shape as long as your drawing page contains a Legend shape. For example, instead of using the Note shape on the Legend Shapes stencil, you might want to convert a built-in Note shape to a customized Note shape with a custom property that contains the note text.

You can use shapes on a Brainstorming diagram or from other stencils and drawing types. To turn a shape into a symbol, drag the shape you want to use as a symbol onto the Legend shape on the drawing page. When Visio asks whether you want to convert the shape into a symbol and add it to the legend, click Yes. You can drag the control handle in a custom symbol shape to connect it to a Topic shape, as shown in the following figure.

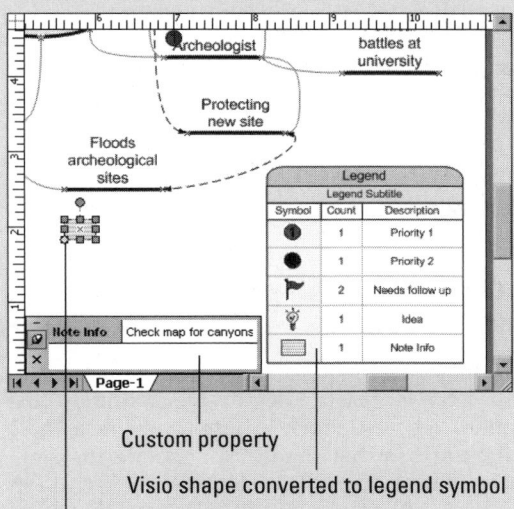

Custom property

Visio shape converted to legend symbol

Control handle for connecting to a topic

Visio adds a row for the symbol in the Legend shape and adds a control handle to the shape. Whenever you add another instance of that shape to the drawing by dragging it from a stencil or copying an instance on the drawing, you can drag its control handle to a Topic shape's connection point to connect them.

A Legend shape displays the symbol shapes included on a page, the symbol descriptions, and the number of times each one appears on that page. The Legend shape on the page updates automatically as you add symbol shapes to the page, so you can choose whether to add the Legend shape or symbol shapes first.

Tip   Although the Legend Shapes stencil opens automatically for only the Brainstorming, Network Diagram, and Building Plan templates, you can use it with any type of Visio drawing.

Adding Symbols to Topics

You can attach each instance of a symbol shape to only one Topic shape. To add a symbol shape to a Topic shape, follow these steps:

1. To display the Legend Shapes stencil, click the Legend Shapes stencil title bar to display it in the Shapes window. If the Legend Shapes stencil isn't open, choose File ⇨ Shapes ⇨ Brainstorming ⇨ Legend Shapes.

2. Drag a symbol shape from the Legend Shapes stencil and drop it near the Topic shape with which you want to associate it.

Note   As soon as you drop a symbol shape on a drawing page that contains a Legend shape, the symbol appears in the legend with its description and an updated count of the number of occurrences on the page.

3. To connect the symbol to a topic, drag the yellow control handle from the symbol shape to a blue connection point on the Topic shape. The control handle turns red when it's attached.

Note   To detach a symbol from a topic, select the symbol shape and drag the red square away from the Topic shape. To delete a symbol, select it and press Delete.

Tip   Symbols are simple shapes with little room for text in their text blocks and no custom properties for storing information. You can attach a Note shape to a Topic shape, but you can't include the note text in that shape. To annotate the Note shape with a reference to the associated note text, type an alphanumeric ID, such as A1, as text into the Note shape and then add a text block to the drawing with the Text tool to add the identifier and note text.

Creating and Configuring Legends

You can catalog the symbols on a drawing page by adding a legend to the page. However, a Legend shape shows the symbols only for the drawing page on which it is located, not the entire diagram. If you want to differentiate symbols, you can add more than one Legend shape to a page and configure each one to display the symbols you want. For example, you can use one Legend shape to show topic priority and another to highlight actions needed, such as To-dos, tasks, or topics that need follow-up.

Creating Legends

To create a legend on a page, follow these steps:

1. Drag the Legend shape from the Legend Shapes stencil onto the drawing page. If the page contains symbol shapes, the legend automatically displays them.

2. To add a title and subtitle, double-click the Title or Subtitle text and type the titles you want.

Configuring Legends

Each Legend shape can have its own unique configuration and formatting. You can configure Legend shapes using the Configure Legend command or by editing and formatting text directly in the Legend shape. Right-click the Legend shape you want to configure and choose Configure Legend from the shortcut menu to specify its appearance and formatting:

✦ **Show or hide the subtitle** — Check or uncheck the Show Subtitle check box to show or hide the legend subtitle.

✦ **Show or hide the quantity column** — Check or uncheck the Show Count check box to show or hide the Quantity column.

✦ **Show or hide the column names** — Check or uncheck the Show Column Names check box to show or hide the column names.

✦ **Show or hide specific symbols** — To hide symbols in a Legend shape, uncheck the check boxes in the Visible column. By default, Visio displays all the symbols on the page.

✦ **Change the sort order for symbols in the Legend shape** — Select a row in the Legend shape for the symbol you want to move and click Move Up or Move Down to reposition it in the list.

Note

Visio retains sort order changes only for symbols that are set to Visible. Before you rearrange the sort order, check the check boxes in the Visible column for each symbol you want to sort and then use the Move Up and Move Down buttons to re-sort the symbols.

✦ **Modify the width of theLegend shape** — Drag a selection handle on one of the sides of the Legend shape to the width you want.

✦ **Edit Legend text** — Subselect the text you want to edit by clicking the Legend shape and then clicking the text you want to edit. Type the text you want. You can edit the title, subtitle, or text in any column except the Count column.

✦ **Format Legend text** — Subselect the text you want to format and choose Format ⇨ Text. Choose the formatting options you want and then click OK.

Note

To delete a legend, select it and press Delete. Visio deletes only the Legend shape, not the symbol shapes associated with Topic shapes, on the drawing page.

Importing and Exporting Brainstorming Data

You can export brainstorming data if you want to refine or expand your ideas using Microsoft Word 2003 or Excel 2003. Visio also exports brainstorming data to XML format if you plan to edit the data using other applications. Visio structures exported topics based on the hierarchy that appears in the Outline window. The export file includes topic text, custom properties, hyperlink data, and topic associations, but not symbols associated with topics.

 Note   You must have Microsoft Word 2003 or Excel 2003 installed in order to export Visio Brainstorming diagrams to those applications' formats.

To export brainstorming data from a Visio drawing, follow these steps:

1. Choose Brainstorming ➪ Export Data and then choose To Microsoft Word, To Microsoft Excel, or To XML.

2. In the File Save dialog box, navigate to the folder in which you want to save the export file, type a name in the File Name box, and click Save. If you export to Word or Excel, that application launches automatically and displays the exported data. If you export to XML, Visio saves the data in an XML file.

3. If you exported your diagram to Word, choose View ➪ Outline in Word to work with the data in a hierarchical view.

If you have XML files that contain brainstorming topics and subtopics, you can import them into Visio brainstorming diagrams. To do this, choose Brainstorming ➪ Import Data. Select XML files (*.xml) in the Files of Type list, navigate to the folder that contains the XML file you want to import, and double-click the file.

Summary

Brainstorming diagrams can seem quite complex, but they contain only a few different Visio shapes. You can drag Brainstorming shapes from the Brainstorming stencil, but you must then connect those Topic shapes to their superiors or peers. It's much faster to use the commands on the Brainstorming menu or toolbar because these commands add and connect Topic shapes at the same time. You can neaten up a first draft by moving Topic shapes or selecting different layouts and connector types. You can easily create a professional-looking brainstorming diagram by applying a theme or color scheme.

Symbol shapes act as shortcuts for annotating your diagram, whether you want to prioritize your ideas or identify topics that need more refinement. The Legend Shapes stencil includes a number of symbols you can use, but you can also create your own by dragging any Visio shape onto a Legend shape on a drawing page.

You can export diagrams to Word 2003 or Excel 2003 if you would prefer to use those applications to further develop your ideas. You can also import and export to XML files.

✦　　✦　　✦

Using Visio in Information Technology

◆   ◆   ◆   ◆

Modeling and Documenting Databases

Database models and diagrams help you design databases that better satisfy requirements. In addition, database maintenance is much easier when you can refer to accurate and up-to-date documentation.

If you don't have commonly used data modeling tools such as ERwin or Oracle Designer, you can use the Database Model Diagram template in Visio to design and document logical database models for both relational and object-relational databases as long as you have a working knowledge of database concepts and database management practices. Whether you want to build a diagram from scratch, import a model from another application, or reverse-engineer an existing database, the Database Model Diagram template offers commands and wizards to simplify the process. You can add to or modify objects in your database model, including tables, columns, parent-child relationships, indexes, and code.

Although Visio provides templates for Object Role Modeling diagrams and Express-G diagrams, these templates produce only diagrams, not models.

In this chapter, you learn how to create database models from scratch, as well as how to import models from other applications or reverse engineer models from existing databases. You'll learn how to set database options and preferences in Visio and work with elements in Visio database model diagrams.

Note Database templates are available only in Visio Professional and the Visio Studio .NET Enterprise Architect.

Exploring the Database Model Templates

Visio 2003 Professional includes three templates to help you produce database documentation. The Express-G and ORM templates include shapes that conform to these special notations. The Database Model Diagram is useful for both logical data modeling and physical database modeling. ORM diagrams show the objects in a model, the relationships between them, the roles that the objects play in those relationships, and any constraints within the domain. These diagrams are useful in presenting conceptual domain models and also provide an effective way to communicate the details of relationships between business objects to project stakeholders. Express-G diagrams help database designers visualize large information models by showing relationships between objects and other components within a data model. You build Express-G and ORM drawings with basic Visio techniques, dragging shapes onto the page, connecting them, and adding custom property data to document and annotate your diagrams. Express-G and ORM templates don't include the Database menu, so you can't reverse engineer an existing database into diagrams using these notations. However, the shapes in the Express-G and ORM stencils include custom properties that make it easy to create diagrams with the proper notation.

Note   In earlier versions of Visio, you could create a physical database from a Visio model. Now this capability is part of Visio for Enterprise Architects, which is part of Visual Studio .NET Enterprise, *not* Visio Professional. You can import logical database models from Visio Professional into Visio for Enterprise Architects, and then use that tool to transform them into physical database schemas or DDL scripts. To learn more about Visio for Enterprise Architects, search `http://msdn.microsoft.com/vstudio` for Visio-based database modeling.

With the Database Model Diagram template, you can do more than diagram databases; you can do logical as well as physical data modeling. With physical data modeling, you can model tables, views, relationships, stored procedures, and other elements, using either relational or IDEF1X notation. The Database Model Diagram template adds the Database menu to the Visio menu bar and provides several specialized windows for viewing and modifying database properties. In this template, the Reverse Engineer Wizard takes an existing database and builds a Visio database model for you.

If you're fairly new to data modeling and database design, trying to learn what you need to do might be a bit overwhelming. In reality, you probably want to learn more about data and databases so that you can decide whether Visio 2003 has the tools you need. With this knowledge, you can more easily choose the right Visio template and build the diagram you want. The following are some educational resources to help you learn more about data modeling and database models:

✦ *Data and Databases: Concepts in Practice* by J. Celko (San Francisco: Morgan Kaufmann, 1999) is a good introductory book to database technology.

✦ *An Introduction to Database Systems*, *Seventh Edition*, by C. J. Date (Boston: Addison-Wesley, Inc., 2003) describes the fundamentals of data theory.

✦ Just because documentation is helpful, you don't necessarily need a lot of it. To learn how to produce just the right amount of database documentation, read *Agile Modeling* by Scott Ambler (Indianapolis: Wiley, 2002).

✦ *Agile Database Techniques* (Indianapolis: Wiley, 2003) by Scott Ambler and one of Scott Ambler's Web sites, www.ambysoft.com/agileDatabaseTechniques.html, both introduce the process of data modeling and also discuss database refactoring.

✦ To learn more about what you need to model physical databases, see www.agiledata.org/essays/umlDataModelingProfile.html.

✦ *Information Modeling and Relational Databases: From Conceptual Analysis to Logical Design* by T. A. Halpin (San Francisco: Morgan Kaufmann, 2001) is *the* book about ORM diagramming.

Caution

If Visio encounters an unexpected error from either an internal or external source, your template-specific menus, such as the Database menu, can disappear. If Visio shuts down unexpectedly, restart it and then choose Tools ➪ Options. Select the Advanced tab, check the Enable Automation Events check box, and click OK. Save any open drawings, exit and restart Visio, and then reopen your database model diagram.

Exploring Database Model Shapes

When you create a new database model diagram, Visio opens the Entity Relationship stencil and Object Relational stencil. Although relational and object-relational notations both use entities, columns, views, and relationships, the shapes on each stencil appear and behave according to the rules of their respective database modeling methods.

The Entity Relationship stencil includes an Entity shape to represent tables, a View shape to show combinations of columns assembled from other tables, and a Relationship connector to shows parent-child relationships. In addition, you can use the Category shape to relate multiple child tables to a parent table. Parent to Category and Category to Child connectors link tables to categories and create foreign keys within parent tables.

The Object Relational stencil includes all of the shapes from the Entity Relationship stencil plus a few specific to object-relational modeling. The Table Inheritance and Type Inheritance connectors configure child tables or types to inherit the attributes of a parent automatically. You can nest object-relational tables in a model by using the Type shape to define a type and then assigning it as the data type for a column in another table.

Updating Database Shapes

In Visio releases, the Database Model Diagram template frequently, and automatically, implements new shape behaviors. When you open a database model diagram, Visio opens the Update Shapes dialog box if it finds older versions of Database

Model shapes. Microsoft recommends that you keep shapes up to date, but you don't have to do so. However, if you choose not to update shapes, they continue to behave as they did in the earlier version of Visio and include the same shortcut menus as they had in the earlier version.

Note   If you don't update shapes when you open a diagram, you can update them later by choosing Tools ⇨ Add-Ons ⇨ Visio Extras ⇨ Update Shapes.

Creating Database Models

You can create database models in Visio in three different ways. If you want to document an existing database, you can use the Reverse Engineer Wizard to create a model by extracting information from the database. You can also import database models that you developed in other applications. If you're starting from scratch, you can build a diagram by dragging and dropping shapes and connectors onto the drawing page.

Building Database Models from Scratch

To create a database model and specify the modeling options you want to use, follow these steps:

1. Choose File ⇨ New ⇨ Database ⇨ Database Model Diagram. Visio creates a new drawing file with a blank page and adds the Database menu to the Visio menu bar.

2. To specify the modeling options you want to use, choose Database ⇨ Options ⇨ Document.

3. To specify the symbols you want to use and the names that appear on the diagram, follow these steps:

    a. In the Database Document Options dialog box, select the General tab.

    b. Select the symbol set you want to use (IDEF1X or Relational).

    c. Select the names you want to see on the diagram.

4. Select the Table tab and check the check boxes for the attributes you want to display for tables. Choose options to specify the order in which keys appear and which data types to show.

5. Select the Relationship tab and specify the notation you want to use and how to display relationship names.

6. Click OK to apply the settings.

Tip   You can save the current settings as the default for all new database models or restore other settings by clicking Defaults and then choosing a command from the list.

Importing Database Models from Other Applications

If you modeled a database using ERwin or Visio Modeler, you can import those model files into Visio and continue your work there. To import an ERwin .erx or Visio Modeler file, follow these steps:

1. Choose File ➪ New ➪ Database ➪ Database Model Diagram.

2. Choose Database ➪ Import and then choose either Import ERwin ERX File or Import Visio Modeler .IMD File.

3. Type the path and filename for the file you want to import, or click Browse and navigate to the file, and then click Open. Click OK in the Import dialog box. Visio imports the file and displays import progress in the Output window. After the import is complete, Visio shows the imported tables in the Tables and Views window.

Reverse Engineering an Existing Database

It's easy to build a model of an existing database by using the Reverse Engineer Wizard in Visio Professional. When you run the Reverse Engineer Wizard, Visio enables options if they match features provided by the target database management system. In addition to walking you through the steps to extract information from your database, the wizard analyzes your database schema and reports any problems it finds in the Output window.

Setting Up Data Sources

You can use existing database drivers and data sources or configure them in the Reverse Engineer Wizard. If you want to keep your reverse engineering process as simple as possible, you can set up database drivers from the Database menu and define data sources using the Data Sources (ODBC) administrative tool in the Windows Control Panel.

 Note   To define data sources with Windows Control Panel tools, choose Start ➪ Settings ➪ Control Panel ➪ Administrative Tools ➪ Data Sources (ODBC).

Visio provides several default database drivers that work specifically with the Database Model Diagram template. You can use the following drivers or combine one of the generic drivers with an ODBC driver provided by your database vendor:

✦ Generic OLE DB Provider

✦ IBM DB2 Universal Database

✦ INFORMIX Online/SE Server

✦ Microsoft Access

✦ Microsoft SQL Server

✦ ODBC Generic Driver

✦ Oracle Server

✦ Sybase Adaptive Service Enterprise

To set up a default Visio driver to work with the database management system you use, follow these steps:

1. Choose Database ➭ Options ➭ Drivers and select the default driver you want to use.

2. If you want to associate a vendor's ODBC driver with the selected Visio driver, click Setup. Check the check box for the ODBC driver you want to use. To specify other settings, such as the comment style or semicolons at the end of SQL statements, select the Preferred Settings tab. Click OK when you're done.

3. To specify the default property values for the portable data types used in a database, select the Default Mapping tab. For each category in the Category list, choose attributes such as type, size, length, and scale.

4. To specify the type of category you want to use for new columns in tables, in the Default Category Type for Column Creation list, select a category in the drop-down list.

5. Click OK.

Using the Reverse Engineer Wizard

You can specify the information you want to extract from your database and whether you want Visio to create a diagram for you. To reverse engineer a database, follow these steps:

1. Choose File ➭ New ➭ Database ➭ Database Model Diagram to create a new database model diagram file.

2. Choose Database ➭ Reverse Engineer.

3. On the first Reverse Engineer Wizard screen, use one of the following methods to set up or connect to a data source and then click Next:

   • **Set up a database driver and data source** — Click Setup if you want to configure a database driver to work with the database management system for the database you want to reverse engineer. If the data source you want doesn't exist, click New to define it.

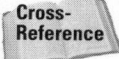
Cross-Reference

To learn about configuring database drivers and defining data sources, see Chapter 10.

   • **Use an existing driver and data source** — Select the Visio driver appropriate for the database you want to reverse engineer. For example, to reverse engineer a Microsoft Access database, select Microsoft Access in the Installed Visio Drivers list. Select the data source you want to use in the Data Source list.

Note If you create a new data source in the Reverse Engineer Wizard, you can select its name in the Data Sources list.

4. If a driver-specific dialog box appears, such as the Connect Data Source dialog box, follow its instructions. For example, type a user name and password in the Connect Data Source dialog box and then click OK.

5. In the Select Object Types to Reverse Engineer screen, uncheck the check boxes for any objects you don't want to extract from the database. Click Next.

6. Check the check boxes for the tables and views you want to extract. You can also click Select All to extract all tables and views. Click Next.

7. If you checked the Stored Procedures check box in step 5, check the check boxes for the procedures that you want to extract, or click Select All to extract them all. Click Next.

8. To automatically create a diagram of the reverse engineered database, select Yes, Add the Shapes to the Current Page option and click Next.

Note If you select No, I Will Add the Shapes Later, you can drag objects from the Tables and Views window onto the drawing page.

9. On the final screen, review the tables and catalog information that Visio will reverse engineer. To change any selections, click Back. To extract the information shown, click Finish.

Caution The Reverse Engineer Wizard does not handle hyperlink fields in Access databases properly; nor does it reverse engineer default values and primary key names in Sybase databases. If you want to flag Access hyperlink fields so you can correct them in Visio, add a comment to the field in Access and reverse engineer the database. In Visio's Database Properties window, look for the Access comments, which appear as notes in the Columns category.

Viewing Reverse-Engineered Information

Visio shows the information extracted from the database in the Tables and Views window. Every table and view in a database model shows up in this window, even if they don't appear on the drawing page. If you did not choose to add shapes to your drawing during the reverse-engineering process, you can drag objects from the Tables and Views window onto the drawing page.

Tip After you drag a table onto the drawing page, you can display tables related to it by right-clicking it on the drawing page and choosing Show Related Tables from the shortcut menu.

The Output window displays progress and summarizes the tasks accomplished during the reverse engineering process. You can check the objects that the process extracted, including tables, attributes, and code. When Visio validates the model, it displays any errors or problems, such as conflicting names, in the Output window.

If you want to copy the messages in the Output window to another application so you can refer to them while you correct the identified problems, right-click the Output window and choose Copy Message or Copy All Messages.

Updating Reverse-Engineered Database Models

After you reverse engineer a database, you can update your Visio model with changes made to the physical database. The Refresh Model command starts a wizard that compares your diagram to the current physical schema and enables you to update your model and diagram if you want to.

Caution   The Refresh Model Wizard doesn't detect new tables in a database. To add new tables to your model, rerun the Reverse Engineer Wizard and choose Select All. The wizard adds only the new tables to your model.

To refresh a model, choose Database ➪ Refresh Model. You can choose individual discrepancies that you want to resolve or select an entire category of discrepancies. To ignore an issue, select the No Change option. To update the diagram to match the database schema, select the Refresh Model option.

Note   The Update Database option under the Resolution heading provides compatibility with Visual Studio .Net Enterprise Edition and is always disabled in the Refresh Model Wizard.

Working with Database Models

In Visio Professional, you can create and edit objects in your database models. You can work with tables, columns, views, and relationships, modifying attributes such as data type, primary and foreign keys, cardinality and referential integrity, and indexes and extended attributes.

Note   If you change the schema of a database in Visio, you also must update the data in your database.

Working in the Database Windows

The Database Model Diagram template includes several windows that make it easy to view and modify database objects and to navigate to any table or view in your database model. Although some of these windows appear automatically when you use the Reverse Engineer Wizard, you can open them by choosing Database ➪ View and then choosing the window you want.

By default, Visio anchors the Tables and Views window, Types window, and Code window at the bottom of the Shapes window. When more than one window is open at a time, Visio adds tabs for each window so you can navigate between them. You can also float each of these windows individually by right-clicking its tab and choosing Float Window from the shortcut menu. If you want to float the entire window that contains the docked database window, drag the window title bar to a new location, as shown in Figure 19-1.

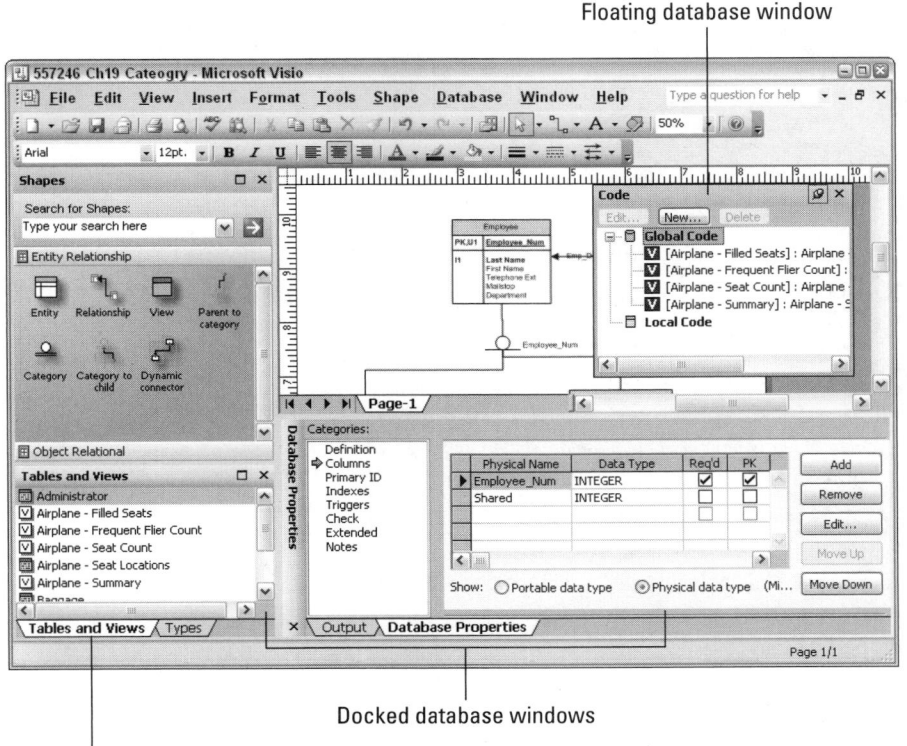

Floating database window

Docked database windows

Tabs to navigate between docked windows

Figure 19-1: You can dock or float the database windows.

The Output window docks in the same window as the Database Properties window by default. You can float either of these windows by right-clicking their tabs and choosing Float Window from the shortcut menu.

As you work on database model diagrams, you'll find yourself frequently using the Database Properties window, in which you can view and modify properties associated with objects in your database model. When you select an object, such as a table, the categories of table properties that you can specify appear in the Database Properties window, as shown in Figure 19-2.

Selected table on drawing page

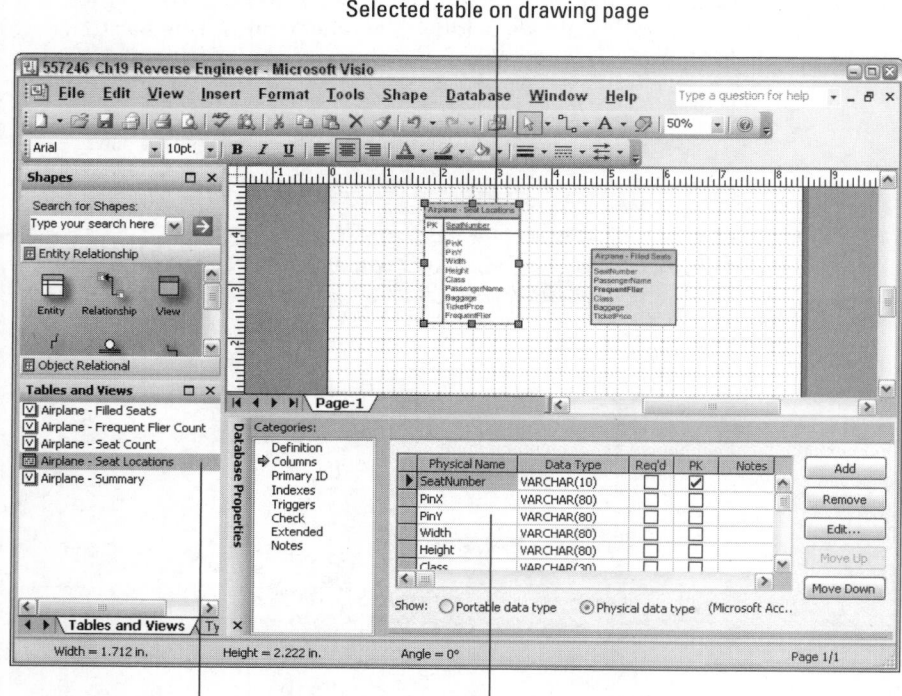

Selected table in model Properties for selected table

Figure 19-2: You can modify properties for any database object in the Database Properties window.

The Database Properties window displays different categories depending on the object you select in the Tables and Views window or on the drawing page. You can view or edit the following properties for the following objects:

✦ **Table categories**—The following categories appear when you select a table in the Tables and Views window or an Entity shape on the drawing page:

- **Definition**—Specify physical and conceptual names and whether you want to synchronize the two as you type. You can use name spaces to distinguish similarly named tables in a model. Owner and Source Database specify the owner and path for the source database. You can create typed tables using the composite data types in the Defining Type field.

- **Columns** — Add, remove, edit, or change the order of columns in a table. You can specify column data types, primary and foreign keys, required fields, and whether to show physical or portable data types.

- **Primary ID** — Edit or remove primary keys from the columns in a table. You can specify whether to create an index using the primary key.

- **Indexes** — Create, edit, rename, or delete indexes. You can also specify the type of index you want to create, or extended attributes if your database management system supports them.

- **Triggers** — Add, edit, or remove triggers associated with a table. The Code Editor window opens when you click Add or Edit.

- **Check** — Add, edit, or remove check clauses associated with a table. The Code Editor window opens when you click Add or Edit.

- **Extended** — If your database supports extended attributes, set them in this tab.

- **Notes** — Add notes about a table.

✦ **View categories** — The following categories appear when you select a view in the Tables and Views window or a View shape on the drawing page:

- **Definition** — The properties are the same as for tables.

- **Columns** — Add, remove, edit, or change the order of columns in a view. They are the same properties as for tables.

- **Join Criteria** — Add or edit the columns to join for a view and any criteria for the join.

- **SQL** — Create or edit the SQL statements that create a view.

- **Extended** — Same as for tables

- **Notes** — Same as for tables

✦ **Relationship categories** — The following categories appear when you select a Relationship connector on the drawing page:

- **Definition** — Specify the parent, child, and foreign key for a relationship.

- **Name** — Specify the verb phrases to use to describe the relationship, the physical name of the foreign key, and any notes.

- **Miscellaneous** — Specify or modify the cardinality, relationship type, and whether a child table must have a parent.

- **Referential Action** — Specify the action to take to check referential integrity when a parent is updated or deleted.

To access the properties for an object, choose one of the following methods:

✦ **Database Properties window closed** — Double-click the shape on the drawing page.

✦ **Database Properties window open** — Select the object in the model or on the drawing page.

✦ **Database Properties window hidden** — Select the object in the model or on the drawing page and then move the pointer over the Database Properties title bar.

Tip   When the Database Properties window is floating and you want it to remain open, click the Push Pin in the title bar to turn off AutoHide.

Working with Tables and Columns

Tables in a Visio model appear as Entity shapes on a database model diagram. When you add an Entity shape to a drawing page, Visio displays the shape based on the stencil from which you dragged the shape and the modeling and display options you've chosen.

To add a table to your drawing, follow these steps:

1. Drag an Entity shape from the Entity Relationship or Object Relational stencil onto the drawing page.

2. In the Database Properties window, type a name in the Physical Name box. If the Sync Names When Typing check box is checked, Visio updates the Conceptual Name automatically.

To remove a table from your drawing, follow these steps:

1. Select the table you want to remove on the drawing page and press Delete.

2. In the Delete Object dialog box, click Yes to remove the table from the model. Click No to remove the table only from the drawing page.

Note   If the Delete Object dialog box doesn't appear when you delete an object from the drawing, choose Database ➪ Options ➪ Modeling and select the Logical Diagram tab in the Database Modeling Preferences dialog box. Select the Ask User What to Do option under the When Removing an Object from the Diagram heading.

Categorizing Tables

To simplify the creation of several tables of the same type or tables that share the same attributes, you can create categories that include the common columns, the primary key, and the discriminator, which is the column that Visio uses to determine the category to which a table belongs. For example, an Employee table can contain all the columns common to every employee in a company, and a discriminator that uses the Job_Category column. Category tables such as administrator, executive, and engineer can include columns specific to those job categories.

The Category shape represents a category table on the drawing page. You associate category tables to parent tables using the Parent to Category connector. The Category to Child connector associates a category table with the children. Complete categories include all possible subtypes and are indicated by double lines in the Category shapes. Categories that don't include all possible subtypes use single lines.

To define a category, follow these steps:

1. Drag a Category shape onto the drawing page.

2. To link a parent table (the table with the common attributes) to a category, click the Connector tool on the Standard toolbar, click the Parent to Category shape in one of the Database Model Diagram stencils, and then drag from the parent Entity shape to the Category shape.

3. To link the category to the child tables, with the Connector tool still selected, click the Category to Child connector in one of the Database Model Diagram stencils and drag from the Category shape to a child Entity shape. Repeat this step for each child table that uses that category.

4. To specify the properties for the Category, double-click the Category shape on the drawing page. Check the Category Is Complete check box if the category represents all subtypes. To specify the column that acts as the discriminator for child tables, select the This Attribute option and choose the column in the list.

Adding Columns to Tables

You can add columns to any table in your model, whether it appears on the drawing page or not or has been reverse engineered from an existing database. When you use *relational notation,* Visio shows *keys,* which specify uniqueness in tables, as shown in Figure 19-3.

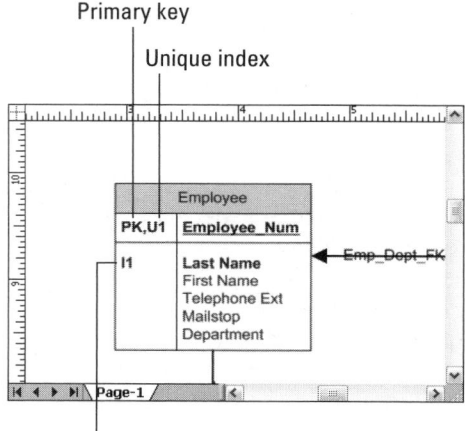

Figure 19-3: Relational notation shows keys in tables.

Understanding Keys

A *key* is one or more data attributes that uniquely identify an entity. A key that is made up of more than one attribute is called a *composite key*. A key defined by attributes that already exist in the real world is called a *natural key*. For example, U.S. citizens receive a Social Security Number (SSN) that is unique to them. For a project limited to the U.S., the SSN could be used as a natural key for a Person entity, assuming privacy laws allow it. In a logical data model, an entity type has zero or more *candidate keys*, also referred to as *unique identifiers*. For example, for American citizens, the SSN is one candidate key for the Person data entity, and a unique combination of name and phone number is potentially a second candidate key. In a physical data model, candidate keys can act as the *primary key* or an *alternate key* (also known as a *secondary key*), or not act as a key at all. A primary key is the preferred key for an entity type.

There are two strategies for assigning keys to tables. The first is to simply use a natural key, one or more existing data attributes that are unique to a business concept. For example, in a Customer table with two candidate keys, such as `CustomerNumber` and `SocialSecurityNumber`, you could use either candidate key. The second strategy is to introduce a new column to act as a key, which is called a *surrogate key* because it has no business meaning. For example, an AddressID column in an Address table is useful as a surrogate key, because addresses don't have an "easy" natural key. You would need all of the columns of the Address table to form a key for itself, so a surrogate key is a much better option. The primary advantage of natural keys is that they exist already, so you don't need to introduce a new "unnatural" value to your data schema. However, because they have business meaning, they might change if your business requirements change. If you decide to use surrogate keys, you can use one of the following strategies:

✦ **Key values assigned by the database** — Most leading database vendors, such as Oracle, Sybase, and Informix, implement a surrogate key strategy called *incremental keys*. Although each strategy uses a similar concept, some assign values uniquely across all tables, whereas others assign values that are unique only within a single table.

✦ **MAX() + 1** — A common strategy is to use an integer column, starting the first record at 1, and then using the SQL `MAX` function to set the value for a new row to the maximum value in this column plus one.

✦ **Universally unique identifiers (UUIDs)** — UUIDs are 128-bit values that are created from a hash of the ID of your Ethernet card or an equivalent software representation, and the current date and time of your computer system. The algorithm for doing this is defined by the Open Software Foundation (`www.opengroup.org`).

✦ **Globally unique identifiers (GUIDs)** — GUIDs are a Microsoft standard that extend UUIDs, if an Ethernet card exists. If one doesn't, GUIDs hash a software ID and the current date and time to produce a value that is guaranteed to be unique to the machine that creates it.

✦ **High-low strategy** — With this approach, your key value, often called a *persistent object identifier* (*POID*) or an object identified (*OID*), comprises a unique HIGH value that you obtain from a defined source and an *n*-digit LOW value that your application assigns itself. Each time that the application obtains a HIGH value, the LOW value is set to zero and begins to increment. An implementation of a HIGH-LOW generator can be found at www.theserverside.com.

To add columns to a table, follow these steps:

1. Double-click the Entity shape that represents the table to which you want to add a column on the drawing page.

2. In the Database Properties window, click Columns in the Categories list, and then use one of the following methods to add the column:

   • Click the Physical Name field in a blank line and type the name you want for the column. To add additional columns, press Enter or the Down Arrow key and type the next column name.

   • Click Add. Visio generates a default name for the column using the naming conventions you specified in the Database Modeling Preferences dialog box. If you want to change the name, double-click the physical name and type a new one.

3. Select the Portable Data Type or Physical Data Type option to specify the data types you want to use. Portable Data Types are generic data types you can use in any database. Physical Data Types correspond to the data types supported by the database management system you're using.

4. To designate a column as a primary key for the table, check the PK check box for the column you want to act as the primary key.

Note

If you want the primary keys to appear at the top of the table, choose Database ➪ Options ➪ Document, select the Table tab, and then select the Primary Keys at Top option. To display a separator line between the primary keys and other columns, check the Draw Separator Line check box.

5. To specify or change the data type for a column, click the column's Data Type field and select the data type from the list.

Note

You can also change the data type when you click Edit to access other column properties.

6. To require values for the column, select its Req'd check box.

7. To edit the properties of the column, click Edit and select the following tabs to specify column properties:

- **Definition** — Specify physical and conceptual names and whether you want to synchronize the two as you type. You can specify a default value and whether the default value is a literal or an expression. For optional columns, check the Allow NULL Values check box.

- **Data Type** — Specify the data type you want in the Data Type box and choose whether you want to use portable or physical data types.

- **Collection** — Specify whether the column contains a single value, a set of values, an ordered list of values, or values that can include duplicates.

- **Check** — Specify check clauses for the column.

- **Extended** — If your database supports extended attributes, set them in this tab.

- **Notes** — Add notes about the column.

Creating Additional Data Types

Each column in a table has an associated data type that determines the kind of information you can store in that column. When you choose the Portable Data Types option in the Database Properties window, you can select from data types that are independent of the specific database management system you're using. If you are building a diagram for a specific type of database or have reverse-engineered a database, you can choose the Physical Data Type option to use the data types for that database.

Note   You can view the field types you use in the Types window. It lists built-in logical data types for your target database, composite types, and portable data types you create within the User Defined Data Types dialog box.

In addition, you can define your own data types, including composite data types. Composite data types can contain sets of several data types. Although they appear as distinct elements in a diagram, you can optimize the performance of your database by storing several values as one element. You can also use composite data types to create typed tables and views.

To create a user-defined data type, follow these steps:

1. Choose Database ➪ User Defined Types and click Add in the User Defined Types dialog box.

2. In the Add New User Defined Type window, type the name for the new data type. If you want to base the new type on an existing user-defined data type, check the Copy From check box and then select the data type in the list. Click OK.

3. Specify the data type category, data type, size, length, and scale as necessary. If you want to add a description of the data type, type text in the Description box. Click OK when you're done.

To create a composite data type, follow these steps:

1. Drag a Type shape from the Object Relational stencil onto the drawing page.

2. Double-click the Type shape and then click Definition in the Categories list in the Database Properties window.

3. Type the name you want for the composite data type in the Name box and choose one of the Composite Type options.

4. To specify other properties for the composite type, click a category in the Database Properties window and specify the properties and settings you want.

Reordering Columns

If the columns in a table don't appear in the order you want, you can reorder them. For example, after you define the primary key and index columns, you can reorder the columns so that the primary keys appear first. To reorder columns in a table, double-click the Entity shape that represents the table that you want to reorder and click Columns in the Categories list in the Database Properties window. Click the column you want to move and then click Move Up or Move Down.

Tip   You can move several columns at once by Shift+clicking the first and last column in a group of contiguous columns and then dragging the columns to a new location in the column list.

Defining Database Views

Database views provide more than a pretty picture of your data. By using views, you can assemble information from several tables without modifying the structure of your underlying database. You can also use views to manipulate data and control access to information, or to encapsulate access to database tables, as described in *Agile Database Techniques* by Scott Ambler (Indianapolis: Wiley, 2003). In Visio, you can create views by dragging View shapes from the Entity Relationship or Object-Relational stencils onto the drawing page. When you do this, Visio automatically creates the SQL code to define the view.

To create a view, follow these steps:

1. Drag a View shape onto the drawing page.

2. If the Database Properties window isn't open, double-click the View shape and then type the view name in the Physical Name box.

3. Click Columns in the Categories list and then use one of the following methods to add columns to the view:

- Click the Physical Name field in a blank line and type the name you want for the column. To add additional columns, press Enter or the Down Arrow key and type the next column name.

- Click Add. Visio generates a default name for the column using the naming conventions you specified in the Database Modeling Preferences dialog box. If you want to change the name, double-click the physical name and type a new name.

4. To specify the source for the column, click the name of the column and then click Edit.

5. In the View Column Properties dialog box, select the Source tab, click the Known Column in Another Table or View option, and then click Change.

6. In the Pick a Column dialog box, select a column from the list of tables and views in your database model and click OK.

Note   You can also choose the Derivation Rule option and then specify how to derive the information you want to display in the column.

7. Modify any of the other settings you want in the View Column Properties dialog box and then click OK. Repeat steps 4 through 6 to edit each column added in step 3.

Creating Relationships Between Tables

When you create a relationship between two tables, the child table is assigned the foreign key attributes of the parent. In Visio, you use the Relationship connector to create parent-child relationships. By specifying properties for a Relationship connector, you can define the parent and child in the relationship, the key you want to use to join the tables (in case the primary key isn't what you want), the referential integrity rules, and the optionality and cardinality of the relationship.

To add a relationship between two tables and specify the relationship's properties, follow these steps:

1. Click the Connector tool on the Standard toolbar.

2. Position the Connector tool over the parent Entity shape. When Visio outlines the parent Entity shape in red, drag to the center of the child Entity shape and release the mouse button when the child Entity shape is outlined in red. Visio changes the Relationship connector end points to red and displays the primary keys for the parent Entity shape as foreign keys in the child Entity shape.

3. To specify the properties for the relationship, double-click the Relationship connector on the drawing page.

4. To specify the cardinality of the relationship, in the Database Properties window, click Miscellaneous in the Categories list. Choose one of the cardinality options.

Tip

If the Database Properties window is not open, double-click a shape on the drawing to open the window.

5. To specify the referential integrity actions, click Referential Action in the Categories list and then select options to specify the actions to perform when a parent is updated or when a parent is deleted. You can choose from No Action, Cascade, Set NULL, Set Default, and Do Not Enforce.

Creating and Editing Indexes

Database management systems use indexes to speed up searching and sorting the records in databases. You can significantly improve the performance of a database by defining indexes for columns you plan to search frequently. In the Database Properties window, you can create and edit indexes for columns or modify indexes extracted during the reverse engineering process.

Note

When Visio extracts indexes during reverse engineering, it automatically applies uniqueness constraints to primary keys, unique indexes to alternate keys in an IDEF1X model, and non-unique indexes for inversion entries in an IDEF1X model.

To create a new index for a table, follow these steps:

1. Double-click an Entity shape that represents the table to which you want to add an index.

2. In the Database Properties window, click Indexes in the Categories list and then click New.

3. In the Create Index dialog box, type a name for the index and click OK.

4. To specify the type of index, such as Unique Index Only, select a type in the Index Type drop-down list.

5. In the Available Columns list, select each column you want to include in the index and click Add.

Note

You can Shift+click or Ctrl+click to select multiple columns for the index.

6. In the Indexed Columns list, uncheck the ASC check box if you want the index to use descending sort order. The Disp. Name field represents the index notation that Visio displays on the database model diagram.

Note

If you want to specify extended attributes for a database management system that supports them, click Options.

Editing Database Code

The Code window lists the code that is associated with your model, including code extracted during reverse engineering of a database. From the Code window, you can view the code for your model, write new code, and edit or delete existing code. Check clauses and triggers for tables are also available when you click the Check category and Triggers categories, respectively, in the Database Properties window.

When you write or edit code in Visio, it's a good idea to use a mirror file to store your code. A *mirror file* is a separate file that you can save, access outside of Visio, and manage using your source code control application. To specify a mirror file for code, select the Properties tab in the Code Editor window and type the path and filename in the Mirror File File Name box.

Code listed in the Global Code category includes stored procedures, functions, and other platform-specific types of data definition language code. Local code includes triggers and check clauses specific to a table or column in a model. Entries in the Code window include the name of the table or view that uses the code. You can work with the following types of database code:

✦ **Check clauses** — To define check clauses for a table, double-click the Entity shape that represents the table and then click the Check category in the Database Properties window. Click Add to open the Code Editor. You can specify the check clause name on the Properties tab and type the SQL statements in the box on the Body tab. Check clauses appear in the Local Code list in the Code window.

✦ **Stored procedures** — To create a stored procedure, click Global Code in the Code window and then click New to open the Code Editor. Type the name of the stored procedure on the Properties tab. Select one of the Stored Proc, Function, or Raw DDL options. Type the SQL statements on the Body tab.

Note   If the Code window isn't open, choose Database ➪ View ➪ Code.

✦ **Triggers** — To create a trigger, double-click the Entity shape that represents the table to which you want to apply a trigger and then click the Triggers category in the Database Properties window. Click Add to open the Code Editor. You can specify the trigger name on the Properties tab and type the SQL statements in the box on the Body tab. Triggers appear in the Local Code list in the Code window.

✦ **View SQL Code** — Double-click the View shape whose SQL code you want to edit and click the SQL category in the Database Properties window. Uncheck the Auto-Generated check box and edit the code.

The Code Editor provides several tools and shortcuts to help you edit your database code, which are described in Table 19-1. To specify settings for editing code, click the Window Properties icon in the Code Editor toolbar to open the Window Properties dialog box.

Table 19-1
Code Editing Tools in the Code Editor Window

Editing Task	Visio Method
Insert code skeleton	To insert a skeleton for the type of code you are editing, click the Insert Code Skeleton icon on the Code Editor toolbar.
Print the code for an item	Click the Print icon in the Code Editor toolbar.
Change code keyword colors	To highlight code keywords in different colors, click the Window Properties icon in the Code Editor toolbar, select the Color/Font tab, select Keywords in the Item list, and select the color you want to use. You can specify colors and font styles for several other code elements, such as line numbers and comments.
Automatically indent lines	To specify how the Code Editor indents lines, click the Window Properties icon in the Code Editor toolbar, select the Language/Tabs tab. Select the Follow Language Scoping option and select the language to which the scoping rules should be applied. Select Copy from Previous Line to use the same indentation as the previous line.
Assign keyboard shortcuts	To define keyboard shortcuts for frequently used commands, click the Window Properties icon in the Code Editor toolbar, select the Keyboard tab, select a command, and assign a keyboard shortcut.
Number lines automatically	Click the Window Properties icon in the Code Editor toolbar, select the Misc tab, select the Numbering style you want to use in the Style drop-down list, and type the starting line number in the Start At box.

Setting Database Options and Preferences

You can specify settings and preferences to control how shapes look and behave in your Visio model and database model diagram. For example, modeling preferences include options for deleting an object from a model and diagram. Database document options control the type of notation you use as well as other display options. For the database management systems that support them, extended attributes enable you to fine-tune object definitions in your model.

By default, Visio applies default options stored in the Database Model Diagram template to new diagrams you create. However, you can change these settings and use them for future diagrams.

Setting Modeling Preferences

You can use database modeling preferences to control shape behavior and naming in your database model. Visio uses the settings you choose for each new database model diagram you create until you change the settings again. To specify modeling preferences, choose Database ➪ Options ➪ Modeling. In the Database Modeling Preferences dialog box, select the Logical Diagram tab to specify the following preferences:

✦ **When Removing an Object from the Diagram** — You can choose to remove objects from the model as well as the drawing page, remove objects from the drawing page only, or ask the user what to do.

✦ **Show Relationships After Adding Table to Diagram** — Check this check box to show relationships for new tables you add to a diagram.

✦ **Show Relationships After Adding Type to Diagram** — Check this check box to show relationships for new types you add to a diagram.

✦ **Sync Conceptual and Physical Name in New Tables and Columns When Typing** — Check this check box if you want the changes you make to a name in one field in the Database Properties window to propagate automatically to the other field.

Select the Logical Misc tab to specify the following preferences:

✦ **FK Propagation** — Check Propagate on Add if you want Visio to create a foreign key relationship between parent and child tables when you connect them with a Relationship connector. Check Propagate on Delete if you want Visio to remove a foreign key relationship when you delete a Relationship connector.

✦ **Name Conflict Resolution** — Select the action you want Visio to take when you add a foreign key that uses the same name as a column in the child table.

✦ **Default Name Prefixes** — Specify the prefix you want to use in the default conceptual name for objects in a database model.

✦ **Default Name Suffixes** — Specify the suffix you want to add to the default prefix of the default conceptual name for objects in a database model.

✦ **FK Name Generation Option** — Specify the objects to use when automatically generating foreign key names. In the FK Name Generation Option list entries, the object, Suffix, inserts the text you typed in the Foreign Key box under Default Name Suffixes into the generated FK name.

Specifying Notation and Other Display Options

You can control the appearance of shapes in a database model diagram by specifying the database notation type. For example, IDEF1X notation shows a table as a rectangle with the conceptual name above the rectangle. Relational notation shows the conceptual name in a shaded section at the top of the table rectangle. You can also specify other display options, such as the level of detail you want to show and whether you use crow's feet to show relationships. Choose Database ➪ Options ➪ Document and then use one of the following methods to specify notation and display options:

✦ **Notation** — To specify IDEF1X or relational notation, select the General tab, select either IDEF1X or Relational under the Symbol Set heading, and click OK.

Tip

You can switch between IDEF1X and relational notation whenever you want. If you collaborate with someone who prefers a different notation, you can change the notation each time you receive a copy of the file.

✦ **Crow's Feet** — To specify how relationships are shown, select the Relationship tab. To use crow's feet to show relationships such as one-to-many, check the Crow's Feet check box.

✦ **Cardinality** — When the Crow's Feet check box is unchecked, you can check this check box to display cardinality notation on Relationship connectors.

✦ **Referential Integrity** — Select the Relationship tab and check this check box to display symbols on Relationship connectors to indicate referential integrity constraints.

✦ **Level of Detail** — Select the Table tab and check or uncheck check boxes to specify the information you want to display on your diagram. For example, you can show keys, indexes, annotations, data types, and IDEF1X optionality.

Creating Express-G and ORM Diagrams

Express-G and ORM are notations designed to convey special types of information. For example, with Express-G notation, you can create entity-level and schema-level diagrams to document product data so it can be interpreted and exchanged via computer. Object Role Modeling captures business rules and describes them in terms of real-world objects and the roles they play in processes. ORM diagrams provide documentation for these rules so you can design databases to support them.

Note   You can build ORM models that you can engineer into databases using Visio for Enterprise Architects, which is a part of the Visual Studio .Net Enterprise product.

Using Express-G to Create Entity-Level and Schema-Level Diagrams

The Express-G stencil contains shapes and connectors to represent entities and relationships for Express-G diagrams. You can construct an Express-G diagram by dragging shapes from the Express-G stencil to the drawing page. To build an Express-G diagram, follow these steps:

1. Choose File ⇨ New ⇨ Database ⇨ Express-G. Visio creates a new letter-size drawing and opens the Express-G stencil.

2. To add an entity or data type to the drawing, drag an Entity shape or one of the following data shapes from the Express-G stencil onto the drawing page:

    • **Base types**—Uses a custom property to specify the data type as Binary, Boolean, Integer, Logical, Number, Real, or String.

    • **Enumerated type**—Type the data type you want in the Data Type custom property.

    • **Defined type**—Type the data type you want in the Data Type custom property.

    • **Select type**—Type the data type you want in the Data Type custom property.

3. To change an entity name or data type, use one of these methods:

    • **Entity**—Right-click the Entity shape, choose Set Entity Name from the shortcut menu, and type a new name or entity type.

    • **Data type**—Right-click the data shape, choose Set Data Type from the shortcut menu, and type a new data type.

Note   If your diagram is larger than one page, you can use To-page reference shapes and From-page reference shapes to indicate that the diagram continues on another drawing page. You can connect these reference shapes to Entity shapes and data shapes and add hyperlinks to make it easy to navigate between pages.

4. To reference foreign schemas, drag a USED Entity or REFERENCED Entity shape onto the drawing page. You can specify the schema details at any time by right-clicking the shape and choosing Set Schema Details from the shortcut menu.

5. To show relationships on the diagram, drag one of the following connectors onto the page. You can specify or change the type of relationship by right-clicking the connector, choosing Set Attributes from the shortcut menu, and typing or selecting values in the custom property fields:

- Cardinality

- Inverse cardinality

- Normal r'ship

- Subtype/supertype

6. To include schemas and boundaries, drag Schema and Boundary shapes onto the page.

Note   If you want to view only entities and data shapes on an Express-G diagram, you can assign your Express-G entities and relationships to different layers and then turn off the visibility of the relationship layer. To assign shapes to a layer, select the shapes you want, choose Format ➪ Layer, check the layer to which you want to assign the shapes, and then click OK.

Creating Object Role Model Diagrams

To create an ORM diagram in Visio, choose File ➪ New ➪ Database ➪ ORM Diagram. After Visio creates a new drawing and opens the ORM Diagram stencil, you can drag shapes and connectors onto the page to document the components of your diagram:

Note   To learn more about the uses and benefits of ORM diagrams, see the books and online resources provided in the "Exploring the Database Model Templates" section earlier in this chapter.

✦ **Entity types**—To represent a real-world object, drag an Entity shape onto the drawing page. While the shape is selected, type the entity type's name. To include the entity reference, press Enter and type the reference mode in brackets, such as <Serial Number>.

Note   Entity types are also referred to as *facts*.

✦ **Values**—To represent a value that is stored in the database, drag a Value shape onto the drawing page and type the name for the value type. Press Esc to end your text entry.

Note Value types are also referred to as *references*.

✦ **Subtypes** — To indicate that one entity type is a subtype of another, glue a Subtype connector to the two Entity shapes, with the arrowhead on the connector pointing to the subtype Entity shape.

✦ **Relationships, roles, or facts** — In ORM, predicates containing one or more roles indicate relationships between entity types or between entity types and value types. To show relationships and roles, drag a Predicate shape with enough role boxes to relate all the associated entity types on the drawing and then glue Role connectors between each Entity shape and a role box on the Predicate shape:

  • **Unary** — Includes only one role.

  • **Binary** — The most commonly used predicate indicates relationships or roles between two entity types or between an entity and a value.

  • **Vertical Binary** — This predicate shows a binary relationship but is oriented vertically.

  • **Ternary** — Indicates relationships between three entities.

  • **Quarternary** — Indicates relationships between four entities.

Note To add the names for the roles that an entity type plays, double-click the Predicate shape, place the insertion point between the ellipsis in the text block, and type the name for the role.

✦ **Nested entities** — To indicate nested entities in an ORM diagram, use the Rectangle tool to draw a rectangle around the Predicate shape you want to designate as an objectified predicate. Select the rectangle, choose Format ⇨ Corner Rounding, click the third rounding option in the top row, and click OK.

✦ **Mandatory roles** — Mandatory roles mean that every member of an entity type must play that role, so null values are invalid in the relationship. To indicate that a role is mandatory, glue the Mandatory Role connector to the Entity shape and the Predicate shape.

✦ **Uniqueness** — To show that a role is unique, drag the Uniqueness Constraint shape onto the drawing page and place it directly above or below the Predicate shape you want to constrain.

Note The Uniqueness shape is sized so that it can be glued to the connection points above a role in a Predicate shape.

✦ **Frequency** — To show that each instance of a role occurs a specific number of times, drag the Frequency Constraint shape onto the drawing page and place it near the Predicate shape you want to constrain. With the Frequency Constraint shape selected, type the number of times the role occurs.

✦ **Subset or Equality constraints** — To indicate a subset or equality constraint, drag the Subset Constraint or Equality Constraint shape onto the drawing page and place it between the Predicate shapes whose roles you want to constrain. Glue one end point of the Constraint shape to a role box on one Predicate shape. Glue the other end point of the Constraint shape to the corresponding role box on the other Predicate shape.

✦ **Ring constraints** — To show that an entity type plays two roles in a predicate, drag a Ring Constraint shape onto the drawing page near the Predicate shape with the two roles you want to constrain. Depending on whether the Predicate shape includes two or more roles, use one of the following methods to indicate a ring constraint:

- **Two roles** — For a binary predicate, you show only the constraint type with no line between the roles. Right-click the Ring Constraint shape and choose Format ➪ Line from the shortcut menu. Click None in the Pattern drop-down list and click OK.

- **Three or more roles** — Glue the end points of the Ring Constraint shape to the roles you want to constrain in a Predicate shape.

Note
To designate the type of ring constraint, double-click the Ring Constraint shape and type a two-letter abbreviation. Use "ir" to indicate an irreflexive constraint or "as" to indicate an asymmetric constraint.

✦ **External constraints** — To show an external constraint, drag one of the External Constraint shapes (Ext. Freq., Ext. P, Ext. Mand., or Ext. Uniq.) onto the drawing page near the Predicate shape whose roles you want to constrain. Glue a Constraint connector to the role box on the Predicate shape and a connection point on the External Constraint shape.

Summary

Database templates are available only in Visio Professional. You can draw Express-G and ORM database diagrams using basic Visio techniques. If you use the Database Model Diagram template, you can create both a diagram and model for your database. You can also reverse engineer existing databases into Visio models. In a Visio model, you can create additional objects, modify the properties of objects, and update the physical database with those changes.

✦   ✦   ✦

Building UML Models

Developing an overall architecture and design before you begin to write code helps you produce a software system that meets requirements and is easier to develop and maintain in the long run. As you model a software system, you progressively develop the detail of that system, alternately decomposing high-level objectives and broad requirements into manageable pieces, and then assembling software components into packages and eventually a complete run-time system. Models and diagrams make it easier to visualize both high-level architecture and low-level components, so you can make the most of design opportunities or spot potential problems before you write code.

The Unified Modeling Language (UML) defines diagrams and the semantics behind them for modeling software systems through each phase of the software development life cycle, as specified by the Object Management Group (www.omg.org), which is the not-for-profit consortium that produces and maintains specifications for interoperable enterprise applications. In Visio Professional, you can build object-oriented models using the UML Model Diagram template, which contains stencils and shapes that use the UML notation and support the different types of diagrams used with UML. One Visio drawing file can contain all the models and diagrams for one software system. You can build and work on models in the hierarchical view provided by the UML Model Explorer window or on diagram drawing pages. In addition, the UML Model Explorer window is a handy tool for navigating to the diagram or component you want.

In addition to constructing models for new software systems, the UML Model Diagram template can help you model existing systems. You can reverse engineer projects created in several Microsoft programming languages and generate UML static structure models for those projects.

Note   The UML Model Diagram template is available only in Visio Professional and Visio Studio .NET Enterprise Architect.

In this chapter, you are introduced to the templates and stencils that Visio offers for UML, and you learn how to use the modeling tools that Visio provides for building UML models. In addition, you will learn how to work with each type of UML diagram that Visio offers, and examine the differences between Visio's UML shapes and terminology and those used in the current UML 2.0 specification.

Exploring the UML Model Diagram Template

Large or complex software systems require a coordinated development approach in which teams can collaborate on analysis and design for each phase of a system life cycle. The UML methodology and Visio Professional's UML Model Diagram template provide tools to model and document each phase of system design and development.

The UML Model Diagram template includes stencils for several types of UML diagrams you create during a development project. Although this chapter describes only the basic approach for specifying properties, you can specify dozens of properties for most of the shapes on the UML stencils to represent the different attributes and conditions that UML supports. You can double-click any shape on a drawing page or an element in the Model Explorer window to open its UML Properties dialog box. If you're not sure what a property does, click the Help button in the lower-left corner of the dialog box.

Caution   Visio 2003 is far from a perfect solution for producing UML models, Its UML templates do not fully support the entire UML notation and in some cases, its support for UML notation does not match the current UML specification. Visio 2003 still uses nomenclature from earlier UML specifications for UML diagrams and doesn't support Composite Structure diagrams, Interaction Overview diagrams, Object diagrams, and Timing diagrams for the UML 2 specification. However, in many cases, these discrepancies won't prevent you from performing your work.

Cross-Reference   As the industry-standard language for specifying, constructing, and documenting software systems, UML covers a lot of ground. To learn more about this methodology and its notation, search for UML at http://msdn.microsoft.com or go to the Object Management Group's Web site, www.omg.org. For more information about UML diagrams, see www.agilemodeling.com/essays/umlDiagrams.htm.

If you are new to UML and don't know which Visio diagram you should use, consider the following resources to increase your knowledge:

✦ *The Object Primer, 3rd Edition: Agile Model Driven Development with UML 2.0* by Scott Ambler (New York: Cambridge University Press, 2001). This book is a distillation of software development practices and provides a comprehensive description of all 13 UML diagrams in addition to other critical models.

✦ *UML Distilled,* Third Edition, by M. Fowler (Boston: Addison Wesley Longman, 2003). This book provides a very good overview of UML, along with good descriptions of the most common UML diagrams.

✦ *Applying UML and Patterns: An Introduction to Object-Oriented Analysis and Design and the Unified Process* by C. Larman (Upper Saddle River, N.J.: Prentice-Hall, 2001). This book uses UML in great detail to describe object-oriented analysis and design.

✦ www.agilemodeling.com/essays/umlDiagrams.htm provides a good overview of the UML 2.0 diagrams. Think of it as a free, online version of *UML Distilled.*

Choosing the Right UML Diagram

Within the Software template category, Visio Professional provides only one template for UML: the UML Model Diagram template. When you create a new drawing file with this template, Visio opens stencils for each type of UML diagram you can create. As you proceed through phases in your project, you can create different UML diagrams using the stencils listed in Table 20-1.

Table 20-1
UML Diagrams and Visio UML Stencils

UML Diagram	Stencil	Description
Use Case Diagram	UML Use Case	Shows use cases, actors, and their interrelationships. Used to present an overview of usage requirements and/or the analysis model for your system.
Class Diagram (the Visio 2003 stencil is misnamed)	UML Static Structure	Shows the classes of a system, including their operations, attributes, and inter-relationships. Typically used for several purposes, including the exploration of domain concepts in the form of a domain model, the analysis of requirements, or the presentation of the detailed design of object-oriented software.
Package Diagram	UML Static Structure UML Use Case	Shows how related elements in a software system are grouped into packages. Commonly used to group classes or use cases.

Continued

Table 20-1 *(continued)*

UML Diagram	Stencil	Description
Activity Diagram	UML Activity	Similar to flowcharts and data flow diagrams in structured development, these diagrams are often used to show high-level business processes, including data flow, or to model complex logic within a system.
Statechart Diagram (called a State Machine Diagram in UML 2)	UML Statechart	Shows the dynamic behavior of entities in response to events based on their current state. Used to explore complex behavior of classes, actors, subsystems, or components. Also used for modeling hardware and real-time systems.
Sequence Diagram	UML Sequence	Shows the classifiers, such as classes, objects, components, and use cases, that participate in an interaction, and the sequence and timing of events that they generate. Used to explore potential usage of a system, to determine the complexity of classes, and to detect potential bottlenecks in an object-oriented system.
Collaboration Diagram (called a Communication Diagram in UML 2)	UML Collaboration	Shows instances of classes, their interrelationships, and messages exchanged during an interaction. Typically depicts the organization of objects that send and receive messages.
Component Diagram	UML Component	Documents the components within an application, system, or enterprise, as well as component interrelationships, interactions, and public interfaces. Also used as a high-level architecture model.
Deployment Diagram	UML Deployment	Shows the structure of deployed systems and the configuration and deployment of hardware and software components. Also used as a high-level architecture model.

Tip

If you would like to see examples of each of the UML diagram types, you can download a sample file from the Downloads section of Microsoft Office Online. Choose Help ⇨ Microsoft Office Online. On the Microsoft Office Online Web site, select Download in the Search drop-down list. Type **Visio 2003 sample** in the Search text box and click the green arrow. To download an executable file with 20 sample diagrams of different types, click Visio 2003 Sample: 20 Sample Diagrams in the Search Results list and follow the instructions for downloading and installing the file on your computer. After you extract the sample .vsd files, you can open them as you would any Visio drawing file.

For UML style guidelines that help you develop readable, high-quality diagrams, visit www.modelingstyle.info.

Exploring the UML Menu

When you use the UML Model Diagram template to create a new Visio drawing file, the UML menu appears on the Visio menu bar. Unlike the Database menu, which appears when you create a database model diagram using the Visio Database Model Diagram template, the UML menu doesn't include any wizards. However, you can use it to create, view, or modify system elements such as models, packages, stereotypes, and events. You can also display or hide the UML windows and specify options for the appearance and behavior of elements in your models and diagrams. Choose UML on the menu bar and then choose the following commands on the UML menu:

✦ **Models** — Opens the UML Models dialog box, in which you can create or modify models for your system.

✦ **Stereotypes** — Opens the UML Stereotypes dialog box, in which you can create or modify stereotypes to extend UML functionality.

✦ **Packages** — Opens the UML Packages dialog box, in which you can create or modify packages for your system. This dialog box lists the packages for the different data types within your system, not packages that you create within models.

✦ **Events** — Opens the UML Events dialog box, in which you can create or modify events within any of the packages in your system. This dialog box lists all packages in your system in the Packages list box. To add an event, select the package to which you want to add the event and then click New.

✦ **View** — Choose Model Explorer, Properties, or Documentation from the View submenu to toggle between hiding and displaying those windows.

✦ **Options** — Opens the Options dialog box, in which you can specify options for default behavior for shapes, packages, object names, and more in the UML Model Diagram template.

Caution   If Visio encounters an unexpected error from either an internal or external source, your template-specific menus, such as the UML menu, can disappear. If Visio shuts down unexpectedly, restart it and then choose Tools ⇨ Options. Select the Advanced tab, check the Enable Automation Events check box, and click OK. Save any open drawings, exit and restart Visio, and then reopen your UML model drawing file.

Updating UML Shapes

In Visio releases, the UML Model Diagram template frequently implements new shape behaviors. When you open a UML model drawing file, Visio opens the Update Shapes dialog box if it finds older versions of UML shapes. Microsoft recommends that you keep shapes up to date, but you don't have to. However, if you choose not to update shapes, they continue to behave as they did in the earlier version of Visio, and include the same shortcut menus they had in the earlier version.

Note   If you don't update shapes when you open a diagram, you can update them later by choosing Tools ⇨ Add-Ons ⇨ Visio Extras ⇨ Update Shapes.

Working with UML Models

In Visio Professional, you can build UML models that act like blueprints for the system you want to develop. Whether you work in the Model Explorer window or with diagrams on drawing pages, you can use UML models and diagrams to develop your system from requirements through deployment.

Working with the Model Explorer

You can represent an entire software system within one Visio drawing file, although that file typically contains multiple models and diagrams. The Model Explorer window displays the elements of a system as a hierarchy, including models and packages that you use to organize the system as well as diagrams that present different views of the system. In addition to viewing and navigating an entire system, you can also use the UML Model Explorer to create diagrams, add elements, or apply properties to elements.

When you create a UML drawing file, Visio adds several elements by default. As you work, you can create additional elements or organize them within the model hierarchy, as shown in Figure 20-1.

System being modeled

One model of system

Add new diagram or element by right-clicking in Model Explorer window.

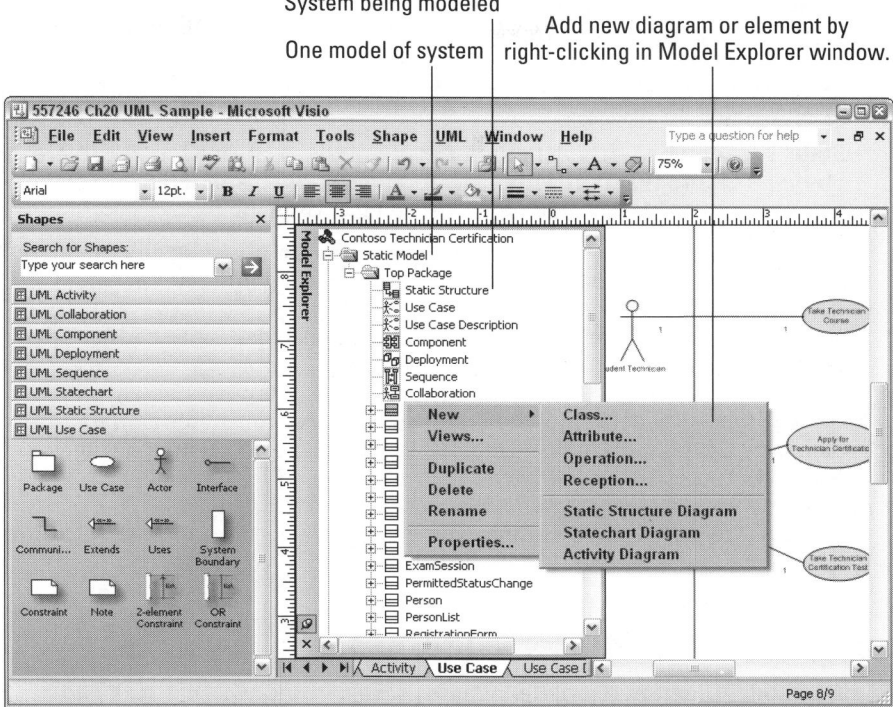

Figure 20-1: You can view, navigate, and modify system elements in the Model Explorer window.

The hierarchy in the Model Explorer window includes the following elements:

✦ **System** — The top node of the hierarchy represents the system you're designing or documenting.

✦ **Static Model** — By default, Visio creates a static model, which contains all the packages, elements, and diagrams for a software system model.

✦ **Top Package** — By default, for every static model in the system, Visio creates a top package, which contains all the elements and diagrams for that model. By right-clicking the top package, you can display a shortcut menu with commands for adding new elements to the package, renaming the package, or specifying its properties.

✦ **Package** — You can create additional packages within a model to organize your model elements, including subpackages nested underneath higher-level packages. The shortcut menu for packages includes commands for adding new elements to the package, duplicating, renaming, or deleting the package, or specifying its properties.

✦ **Static Structure-n** — By default, for each model in the system, Visio creates a Static Structure diagram within the top package. This diagram corresponds to a drawing page of the same name in the Visio drawing file.

✦ **Elements** — Within a package, you can create additional elements, including subsystems, classes, interfaces, data types, actors, and use cases.

Note The shortcut menu for every diagram in a model includes commands to open the diagram, rename it, or delete it from the model.

✦ **Data Types** — By default, Visio includes packages for common data types, including C#, C++, IDL, and Visual Basic. You can also create packages for your own data types.

Note You can't delete the built-in Data Type packages, because the UML Add-on tool uses them.

Using the UML Model Windows

The UML Model Diagram template includes several windows that make it easy to view and modify UML model elements and to navigate within the models and diagrams for your system:

✦ **The Model Explorer window** — Shows all the elements in a software system in a hierarchical tree. You can add elements or access their properties from this window.

Tip To navigate to the drawing page for a diagram, double-click the diagram name in the Model Explorer window. If you want to display the drawing page that contains an element such as an actor, right-click the element, choose Views from the shortcut menu, select the diagram in the UML Diagram list, and then click OK.

✦ **The Properties window** — Shows the main properties associated with the selected element. The properties are for reference only. To edit element properties, right-click the element in the Model Explorer window and choose Properties from the shortcut menu. Although this window does not appear by default, you can open it by choosing UML ➪ View ➪ Properties.

✦ **The Documentation window** — Displays the documentation tagged value of the element you select on the drawing page or in the Model Explorer window. You can add documentation to the selected element by typing text in this window. Although this window does not appear by default, you can open it by choosing UML ➪ View ➪ Documentation.

When you open a new UML drawing file, the Model Explorer window appears by default and docks on the left side of the screen. You can hide or show each of the UML windows by choosing UML ➪ View and then choosing the name of the window you want to hide or display. Although the Properties and Documentation windows don't appear by default, Visio anchors them within the Model Explorer window when you display them. When more than one window is open at a time, Visio adds tabs for each window so you can switch among them.

You can also float each window individually by right-clicking its tab and choosing Float Window from the shortcut menu. If you want to float the entire window with all the UML windows in it, drag the window title bar to a new location.

Organizing Models with Packages

For large or complex software models, you can subdivide your models and diagrams into more manageable pieces by using packages in the Visio Model Explorer. Each model you create includes a top package, which contains all the elements, packages, and diagrams you create within that model. The top package in a model is like a big suitcase you pack for a trip. You can create additional packages within the top package to organize elements into smaller groups, as you might pack your travel toiletries in a smaller container within your suitcase. For more information about when to use Package diagrams and how to make the most of the Package diagrams you develop, see www.agilemodeling.com/artifacts/packageDiagram.htm.

Each element in a model belongs to only one package. However, you can add any kind of model element to a package, including other packages, so you can partition the elements in your model any way you want. You can even use packages to partition diagrams when they become unwieldy. Use the following methods to package the contents of your model:

+ **Create a package in a model** — Right-click a package in the Model Explorer window and choose New ➪ Package from the shortcut menu. Visio adds a package icon to the model.

+ **Add a package to a diagram** — Display the diagram drawing page you want to package. Drag the Package shape from the UML Static Structure, UML Use Case, UML Component, or UML Deployment stencil onto the drawing page. Visio adds a package icon to the model, with the diagram within the package.

+ **Create a diagram from a package** — To automatically create a new diagram when you add a package to your model, choose UML ➪ Options and select the UML Add-on tab. Make sure the Create a Diagram Page When a Package or Subsystem Shape Is Added to a Document check box is checked.

+ **Show package contents on a diagram** — In the Model Explorer window, right-click the package whose contents you want to show on a diagram and choose the type of diagram you want from the shortcut menu. Visio displays the stencil for that type of diagram and opens a blank drawing page. Drag shapes for the elements you want to include in the package onto the drawing page.

✦ **Partition a diagram**—In the Model Explorer window, create multiple diagrams within one package. You can drag the elements you want to include onto as many of the diagrams in the package as you want. Each instance refers to the same element in the UML model. To view all the references to an element on diagrams, right-click the element in the Model Explorer window and choose Views from the shortcut menu.

Working with Shapes and Model Elements

You can work on a UML model through shapes on diagram drawing pages or directly in the model using the Model Explorer window. In addition to adding and removing elements in a model, you can modify their properties to match the characteristics of your system. On UML diagrams, you can specify the element property values that appear on shapes.

Adding and Removing Elements in a Model

As you build or modify your UML model, the additions, changes, and deletions you make appear in the hierarchy shown in the Model Explorer window. When you drag shapes from stencils onto a diagram drawing page, Visio adds the elements that those shapes represent to the UML model. However, diagrams are merely views of a model, and you can choose what you want to display on them. This means that you can add elements to a model without adding them to a diagram, or drag an element in the Model Explorer window onto several drawing pages, creating multiple views of the same element.

You can use the following methods to add elements to a model:

✦ In the Model Explorer window, right-click a package or subsystem, choose New from the shortcut menu, and then choose the type of element you want to add to the model.

✦ Drag a shape that represents the element you want to add onto a drawing page.

Note   Elements added in the Model Explorer window do not appear on diagrams by default. After you add an element to a model in the Model Explorer window, you can add it to a diagram by dragging its icon from the Model Explorer window onto a drawing page.

If you want to remove an element from a model, right-click it in the Model Explorer window and then choose Delete from the shortcut menu. Visio deletes the element from the model as well as all UML diagrams.

Caution   If you delete a shape from a diagram, Visio deletes only the view of the element that the shape represents. The element remains in the model in the Model Explorer window.

Displaying Information in UML Shapes

The shapes on the UML stencils represent each element in the UML notation, and the behaviors for these shapes conform to UML rules. Although you don't have to customize the appearance or behavior of UML shapes, you can change the values that appear on shapes in a diagram to show the information you want.

To specify the values that appear in UML shapes, right-click a shape in a UML diagram and choose Shape Display Options from the shortcut menu. Visio opens the UML Shape Display Options dialog box. You can specify values that you want to show or suppress in the following categories:

- ✦ **General options** — You can display the name, visibility, stereotype, operation parameters, properties, and realization links on a shape.

- ✦ **Attribute** — You can show attribute types, the initial value for attributes, and attribute multiplicity.

- ✦ **End Options** — For connectors, you can specify whether to show end names, multiplicity, navigability, and visibility.

- ✦ **Suppress** — Check these check boxes to suppress the display of attributes, operations, and template parameters. For connectors, you can suppress information at each end of the connector.

You can also choose whether to apply shape display options to other shapes. To apply the shape display options you selected to other shapes of the same type on the current drawing page, check the Apply to the Same Selected UML Shapes in the Current Drawing Window Page check box. To apply the options to new shapes you drop on the page, check the Apply to Subsequently Dropped UML Shapes of the Same Type in the Current Drawing Window Page check box.

Specifying Element Properties

The elements you add to a UML model include numerous built-in properties that support UML notation and behavior. To configure an element in a model, double-click the element in the Model Explorer window or the shape that represents it on a drawing page. Visio opens a properties dialog box for that element, such as the UML Class Properties dialog box for a class or the UML Use Case Properties dialog box for a use case. In the dialog box, you can select the category of properties you want to edit and then specify the properties you want, as shown in Figure 20-2.

Note You can use stereotypes, constraints, and tagged values in a UML <element> Properties dialog box to extend the behavior of elements in a system. To specify a stereotype for an element, select Class in the Categories list and then select the stereotype you want in the Stereotype drop-down list. To specify constraints, select Constraints in the Category list and then define the constraints you want. To add tagged values to an element, select Tagged Values in the Category list, select the tag you want, and then type the value in the Tag Value box.

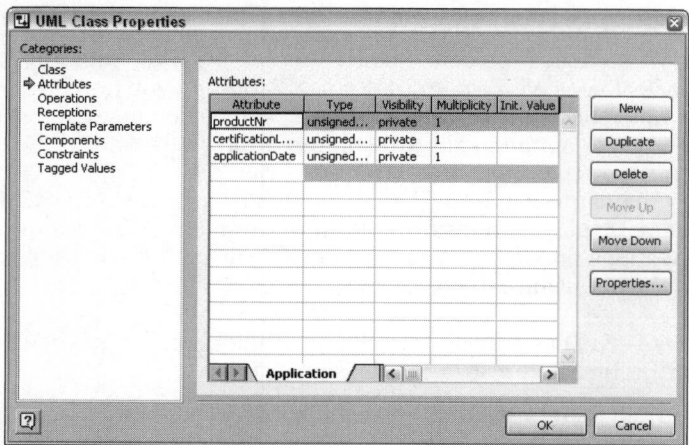

Figure 20-2: You can specify numerous properties for a model element in a properties dialog box, such as the UML Class Properties dialog box.

Specifying UML Options

You can specify options to control the behavior of the UML Model Diagram template. For example, you can choose whether to use the lollipop or classlike version of an Interface shape, or whether to prompt before deleting a model element when you delete a shape on a drawing page. To specify the options for the UML Model Diagram template, choose UML ➪ Options to open the UML Options dialog box. Select the UML Add-on tab and then specify one or more of the following options:

✦ **Shape Ctrl-Drag Behavior** — To duplicate the UML element the shape represents, select Copy Object in the drop-down list. To create a view of the element the shape represents so that you can drag the shape to another package or diagram, choose Copy Object View in the drop-down list.

✦ **Create a Diagram Page When a Package or Subsystem Shape Is Added to a Document** — Check this check box to create a diagram page for every package or subsystem shape you add to a model.

✦ **Create Watermark on Drawing Page** — Check this check box to display a watermark that identifies the type of diagram the drawing page represents.

✦ **Prompt for Model Element(s) Delete on Delete of Shape(s)** — Check this check box if you want Visio to ask you if you want to delete the model element that a shape represents when you delete the shape on a drawing page.

✦ **Delete Connectors When Deleting Shapes** — Check this check box to delete the connectors glued to a shape when you delete the shape.

✦ **On Drop of an Interface from the Model Explorer** — Select an option to specify the default style you want to use for Interface shapes. If you want to show attributes on an Interface shape, select the Class-Like Interface Shape option.

✦ **Auto Assign Name to Newly Created UML Model Element** — Check this check box if you want Visio to generate names for elements you create. You can rename the elements after you create them.

Creating UML Models

When you create a new Visio drawing file with the UML Model Diagram template, Visio opens the stencils for each type of UML diagram, docks the Model Explorer window on the left side of the screen, and adds the UML menu to the Visio menu bar. In addition, the UML Model Diagram template creates several default model elements, including the Static Structure-1 diagram and a corresponding drawing page by the same name. UML diagrams use a letter-size drawing page with portrait orientation and no drawing scale. To create a new UML drawing file, choose File ➪ New ➪ Software ➪ UML Model Diagram.

You can create more than one model for a software system. To create a new model within the Visio drawing file, follow these steps:

1. Choose UML ➪ Models.
2. In the UML Models dialog box, click a blank cell in the model column and type the name of the model.
3. To specify the properties for the model, click Properties in the UML Models dialog box. Select a category and specify the properties within that category. Click OK when you're done.

Note You can also access the properties for a model by right-clicking it in the Model Explorer window and then choosing Properties from the shortcut menu.

4. To add a diagram to the model, right-click a package in the Model Explorer window, choose New from the shortcut menu, and then choose the type of UML diagram you want to add. You can also right-click a drawing page and choose Insert UML diagram from the shortcut menu. Visio performs the following actions:

   • Creates a blank page named *<diagram>-n*, where *<diagram>* is the name of the type of diagram you are creating and *n* is the next number in the sequence of that type of diagram in the drawing file
   • Displays the new page in the drawing window
   • Brings the UML stencil for that type of diagram to the front in the Shapes window
   • Adds an icon for the diagram to the element to which you added it in the Model Explorer window

Note If you right-click a class or use case in the Model Explorer window and choose New from the shortcut menu, you can create diagrams appropriate for the selected element. You can choose from Static Structure Diagram, Activity Diagram, and Statechart Diagram for classes; and Activity Diagram and Statechart Diagram for use cases.

5. To add an element to the model, in the Model Explorer window, right-click a package, choose New from the shortcut menu, and then choose the element you want to add. You can also add subclasses to an existing class by right-clicking the class and choosing New ➪ Class from the shortcut menu.

Working with Static Structure Diagrams (UML 2 Class Diagrams)

Early in the development life cycle, you create conceptual class diagrams to show the real-world objects represented by your system and the relationships between them. These diagrams help clarify the terminology used within the context of the system, and the classes of a system, including their operations, attributes, and interrelationships. You can use class diagrams to explore the domain concepts, to analyze system requirements, and to present the detailed design of object-oriented software. As you progress in the development cycle, class diagrams show the software classes that the system implements and how they relate to each other, as shown in Figure 20-3. Class diagrams specify attributes, associations, operations, methods, interfaces, and dependencies for the classes in a system.

Creating Static Structure Diagrams

To create a static structure diagram in an existing model, follow these steps:

1. In the Model Explorer window, right-click the package to which you want to add the static structure diagram and choose New ➪ Static Structure Diagram from the shortcut menu.

2. Drag Object or Class shapes onto the drawing page to represent real-world objects or the software classes that implement them in your system.

3. To specify properties for an object or class, double-click the object or class in the Model Explorer window or its corresponding shape on the drawing page. In the UML Object Properties dialog box, you can specify attributes, constraints, and tagged values for objects; in the UML Class Properties dialog box, you can specify attributes, operations, receptions, template parameters, components, constraints, and tagged values for a class. Click OK when you're done.

Note When you select the Tagged Values category in the UML Object Properties or UML Class Properties dialog box, Visio displays default tags for the selected element. To add a value to a tag, select the tag you want to modify in the Tags list and type text in the Tag <tag> Value box. You can also add additional tags by clicking New.

Class

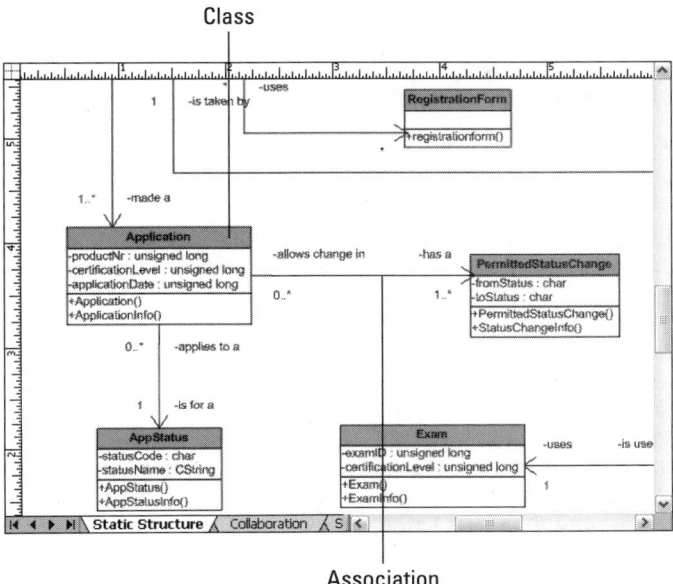

Association

Figure 20-3: Class static structure diagrams show information about a system's software classes.

4. To specify the information you want to display or suppress on shapes, right-click each object or class shape and choose Shape Display Options from the shortcut menu.

5. To show relationships between objects and classes, drag Association, Link, Dependency, Generalization, or Composition shapes onto the drawing page and glue them to the related objects or classes.

6. To specify properties for a relationship, double-click its relationship shape on the drawing page to open the UML <relationship> Properties dialog box, specify the properties you want, and click OK.

Troubleshooting UML Relationships

Relationship shapes have a few idiosyncrasies that might make them behave in ways you don't expect or don't want. For example, unlike other model elements, relationships appear only on drawing pages, not in the Model Explorer window. You must work on the drawing page to view, add, modify, or delete relationship shapes. Other behaviors that you might observe include the following:

✦ **Qualifier associations do not appear on diagrams**—The UML specification indicates that qualifier associations appear in UML diagrams, with attributes listed inside a box shape. In Visio, attributes of qualifiers are stored in the properties pages for association ends. To view qualifier attributes, follow these steps:

1. Double-click an Association shape with a qualified association, which Visio indicates with a small box at one end.

2. In the UML Association Properties dialog box, under Association Ends, select the End Name that has the attributes you want to view and click Properties.

3. In the UML Association End Properties dialog box, select Qualifier Attributes under Categories to view the details of the qualifier association.

✦ **Relationships persist after you delete them** — If you delete an Association shape on one drawing page, the relationship it represents persists if shapes representing the associated elements exist on other pages. To remove a relationship from a model, you must delete all views of an Association shape.

Tip

You can find all the views of an association by right-clicking the Association shape and choosing Views from the shortcut menu. In the UML Diagram dialog box, select a view in the list and then click OK.

✦ **Association shape labels don't appear near the right shape** — When several lines connect to the same shape, you might not be able to distinguish the shape to which a label applies. However, you can unlock and move text labels for Association shapes to make diagrams more legible by following these steps:

1. Select the Association shape whose label you want to move.

2. Choose Window ⇨ Show ShapeSheet.

3. In the Protection section of the ShapeSheet, in the LockTextEdit cell, change the value from 1 to 0 and press Enter.

4. To move the label for the Association shape, click the Text Block tool on the Standard toolbar, select the label you want to move, and then drag it to a new location.

✦ **Relationship lines appear for every instance of the same class** — If you create more than one instance of a class, Visio displays relationship lines between every instance of the class and the other classes to which it relates. Although Visio is designed to do this, the multiple relationships lines can make your diagrams difficult to decipher. You can turn off the automatic display of additional relationship lines and then use the Show Relationships command from a shape's shortcut menu to view its relationship lines. To turn off the automatic display of additional relationships lines, follow these steps:

1. Use the registry editor to access HKEY_CURRENT_USER\Software\ Microsoft\Office\11.0\Visio\Solution\UML Solution.

2. Right-click the Automatic Instance UML Relationships registry entry, choose Modify from the shortcut menu, and change the value in the Value Data box from 1 to 0.

Creating Use Case Diagrams

In early stages of development, use case diagrams present an overview of how users (called *actors*) interact with and generate events in a system. Use case diagrams begin by showing the use cases in context within the system, highlighting the interaction of processes, rather than individual steps. As you progress, you can refine the diagrams to show more detail.

To create a use case diagram, in the Model Explorer window, right-click the package or subsystem to which you want to add the use case diagram and choose New ➪ Use Case Diagram from the shortcut menu. You can drag shapes from the UML Use Case stencil onto the drawing page to construct a use case diagram. After you have added a shape to the diagram, you can double-click it to open its UML <element> Properties dialog box and define any properties you want. Use the following shapes to show the actors, use cases, and interactions between them:

◆ **System Boundary** — Although few people use this symbol, you can drag this shape onto the drawing page to indicate the boundary of the system.

You can move a system boundary and all the use cases it contains by dragging a selection rectangle around the System Boundary shape and then dragging it to a new location.

◆ **Use Case** — Drag this shape onto the drawing page for each use case in the system and place it inside the system boundary.

◆ **Actor** — Drag this shape onto the drawing page for each actor in the system and place it outside the system boundary.

Because an actor represents a role played by an external object, one physical object might be represented by more than one actor, and vice versa.

◆ **Communicates** — To indicate a relationship between an actor and a use case, click the Connector tool on the Standard toolbar, click the Communicates connector in the UML Use Case stencil, and then drag from the Actor shape to the Use Case shape.

To show the actor who initiates an interaction of the primary actor in a use case, double-click the Communicates shape. In the UML Association Properties dialog box in the Association category, check the IsNavigable check box for the end to which you want to add an arrow and click OK.

◆ **Extends** — To extend the behavior of one use case to another, click the Connector tool on the Standard toolbar, click the Extends connector in the UML Use Case stencil, and then drag from the Use Case shape with the behavior you want to extend to the Use Case shape that includes that behavior.

✦ **Uses** — To show that one use case uses the behavior of another, click the Connector tool on the Standard toolbar, click the Uses connector in the UML Use Case stencil, and then drag from the Use Case shape that contains the used behavior to the Use Case shape that uses that behavior. Visio draws an arrowhead at the end of the connector glued to the Use Case shape that uses the behavior.

Note   In the UML 2 specification, the term "uses" has been replaced with "include."

Creating Activity Diagrams

Similar in many ways to data flow diagrams used in structured development, UML activity diagrams model business and software processes and can be used to depict logic for complex business rules and operations. They represent flows driven by internally generated actions, whereas statechart diagrams show flow in response to external events. Because activity diagrams emphasize parallel and concurrent activities, you can use them to model workflow, analyze use cases, and make sure that multithreaded applications perform properly.

To create an activity diagram in an existing UML model, follow these steps:

1. In the Model Explorer window, right-click the subsystem, package, class, use case, or operation to which you want to add the activity diagram and choose New ⇨ Activity Diagram from the shortcut menu.

2. To indicate responsibility for activities, drag Swimlane shapes from the UML Activity stencil onto the drawing page for each class, person, or organizational unit you want to represent. You can double-click Swimlane shapes to add names and other property values or drag side selection handles to resize the lanes.

3. Drag Action State or State shapes onto the drawing page for each state you want to represent. Use the Initial State and Final State shapes for the first and last states.

4. To show the flow of control as one state changes to another, connect Control Flow shapes to Action State or State shapes. Click the Connector tool on the Standard toolbar, click the Control Flow shape in the UML Activity stencil, and then drag from the shape that represents the source state to the shape representing the state to which it changes.

Note   If you want to further define the transition between states, double-click the Control Flow shape on the drawing page and specify events, guard conditions, action expressions, and other information in the UML Transition Properties dialog box.

5. Double-click any shape to open its UML <element> Properties dialog box, specify the properties you want, and click OK.

Showing Complex Transitions

When one state forks into multiple parallel states, or several states synchronize into one state, you can use Transition shapes with Transition (Fork) and Transition (Join) shapes to show the transition. To represent a complex transition, follow these steps:

1. Drag a Transition (Fork) or Transition (Join) shape from the UML Activity stencil onto the drawing page.

2. Drag a Transition shape from the UML Statechart stencil onto the drawing page and glue it to the source State shape and the Transition (Fork) or Transition (Join) shape. When several states synchronize into one, repeat this step to add transitions from each of the original State shapes into the Transition (Join) shape.

3. Drag a Transition shape from the UML Statechart stencil onto the drawing page and glue it to the Transition (Fork) or Transition (Join) shape, as shown in the following figure. When one state forks into multiple parallel states, repeat this step to add transitions from the Transition (Fork) shapes to each forked State shape.

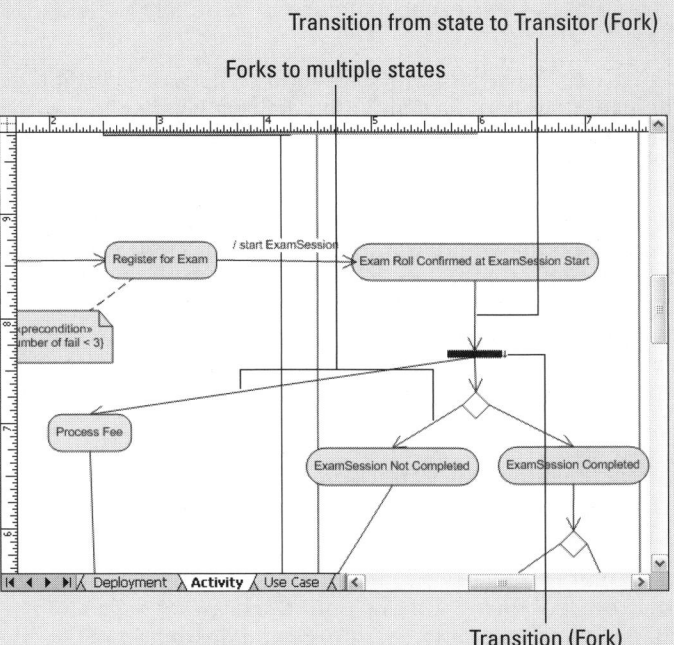

Transition from state to Transitor (Fork)

Forks to multiple states

Transition (Fork)

4. To use signal icons instead of transition strings with signal icons, drag Signal Send and Signal Receipt shapes onto the drawing page to represent the signals. Glue the control handles on these shapes to the source and destination Action State shapes.

Creating State Machine Diagrams

A *state machine*, which is attached to a class or use case, shows the dynamic behavior of an object in response to events, showing the responses to events based on the object's current state. In Visio Professional, a statechart diagram represents a state machine. If you want to represent flow driven by internally generated actions, rather than external events, use an activity diagram instead.

To create a statechart diagram in an existing UML model, follow these steps:

1. In the Model Explorer window, right-click the class or use case that you want to document in the statechart diagram and choose New ⇨ Statechart Diagram from the shortcut menu.

2. To show the states on the diagram, drag the following shapes onto the drawing page:

   - **State** — Represents the sequence of states through which an object passes

   - **Composite State** — Represents concurrent, mutually exclusive, or nested substates

   Note   Visio creates a new statechart drawing page for a composite state. You can click the tab for the new statechart diagram in the drawing window to navigate to it. Drag State, Transition, Shallow History, or Deep History indicators and other shapes onto the drawing page to show the substates within the composite state.

3. To show transitions from one state to another in response to an event, click the Connector tool on the Standard toolbar, click the Transition shape in the UML Statechart stencil, and then drag from the first State shape to the next.

   Note   You can show a state forking into multiple states or several states synchronizing into one by connecting Transition shapes to Transition (Fork) and Transition (Join) shapes, as described in the "Showing Complex Transactions" sidebar earlier in this chapter.

4. To show that an object remains in the same state in response to an event, drag the arc-shaped Transition shape onto the drawing page and glue both ends to the same State shape.

5. To show that an object resumes a state it held last within a region, drag a Shallow History or Deep History shape onto the drawing page and use Transition shapes to connect it to the source and destination State shapes.

6. Double-click any shape to open its UML <element> Properties dialog box, specify the properties you want, and click OK.

Creating Sequence Diagrams

Sequence diagrams are used to model the dynamic logic within classes and to show the time sequence of events generated by actors participating in an interaction. For example, you can use a sequence diagram to show the messages generated in a real-time transaction. In a sequence diagram, the horizontal dimension shows the actors or objects and the vertical dimension represents time. UML sequence diagrams are typically used to do the following:

✦ Expand and validate the logic for potential usage of a system.

✦ Walk through the invocation of the operations defined by your classes.

✦ Detect bottlenecks generated by messages being sent to objects within an object-oriented design. By examining the messages sent to objects and the time it takes to run an invoked method, you can identify design changes to better distribute the load within your system.

✦ Identify the classes in an application that are going to be complex, which therefore might benefit from the development of state machine (statechart) diagrams.

To create a sequence diagram in an existing UML model, follow these steps:

1. In the Model Explorer window, right-click the package or subsystem to which you want to add a sequence diagram, and choose New ➪ Sequence Diagram from the shortcut menu.

2. For each actor involved in the interaction, drag an Object Lifeline shape onto the drawing page and then drag the Object Lifeline control handle to define the length of the actor's life in the interaction.

3. To indicate that the actor or object is destroyed during the interaction, right-click the Object Lifeline shape, choose Shape Display Options on the shortcut menu, and select Destruction Marker. Visio adds a black X at the end of the object's lifeline.

Note To apply this change only to the selected actor, in the UML Shape Display Options dialog box, make sure that the Apply to the Same Selected UML shapes in the Current Drawing Window Page check box is unchecked.

4. To define the classifier associated with an Object Lifeline shape, double-click the Object Lifeline shape to display the UML Classifier Role Properties dialog box. In the Classifier Role category, select the classifier that the actor represents in the Classifier drop-down list. Visio changes the appearance of the Object LifeLine shape to reflect the classifier you choose.

Tip

You can define your own classifiers by clicking New, specifying the properties for the class, and clicking OK.

5. To indicate when an actor performs an action, drag an Activation shape onto the drawing page and glue it to the actor's Object Lifeline shape. Drag the end points of the Activation shape to correspond to the period during which the actor performs the action.

6. To indicate communication between actors, drag a Message shape onto the drawing page and glue it from the Actor shape sending the message to the Actor shape receiving the message.

Note

You can indicate transition times on a sequence diagram. For example, you can show how long a transition takes as well as any constraints on the time it takes to send a message. Use the Text tool to add a name that represents the time a message is sent. The convention is to show the name, usually a letter, in the left margin, aligned with the message to which it applies. If a message does not arrive instantaneously, slant the message line and name each end of the line. For the message received name, you can use the message sent name with a prime appended to it. For example, if the time a message is sent is a, the message receipt time is a'. You can indicate a constraint for the message time, such as b − a < 1 sec by dragging a Constraint shape onto the drawing page near the message name, double-clicking the Constraint, and adding text in the Body text box.

7. Double-click any shape to open its UML <element> Properties dialog box, specify the properties you want, and click OK.

Creating Collaboration Diagrams

Collaboration diagrams are now called *communication diagrams* in the UML 2 specification. Like sequence diagrams, these diagrams show the exchange of messages between objects in response to system events, and imply the relationships between classes. Unlike sequence diagrams, collaboration diagrams do not show the sequence of messages by their position on the diagram. Instead, they use numbers associated with messages to indicate sequence. You can use communication diagrams to accomplish the following:

✦ Provide an overview of collaborating objects, particularly within a real-time environment.

✦ Allocate functionality to classes based on the behaviors within a system.

✦ Model the logic of complex operations, particularly those that interact with many other objects.

✦ Analyze the roles that objects play within a system, and the relationships associated with those roles.

To create a collaboration diagram in an existing UML model, follow these steps:

1. In the Model Explorer window, right-click the package in which you want to add a collaboration diagram, and choose New ⇨ Collaboration Diagram from the shortcut menu.

2. For each actor or object role that collaborates in the interaction, drag a Classifier Role shape from the UML Collaboration stencil onto the drawing page.

3. To name the classifier role or specify other properties, double-click a Classifier Role shape. In the UML Classifier Role Properties dialog box, type the name in the Name box or select other properties for the role and then click OK.

4. To represent a set of objects, drag a Multi-Object shape onto the drawing page.

Note   A multi-object shows operations that affect an entire set of objects as a unit, rather than a single object within the set. To indicate an operation on each object in the set, use a single message with an iteration and include a many indicator (*) in the target role name.

5. To show links between objects, glue Association Role shapes to the Classifier Role or Multi-Object shapes. Double-click an Association Role shape to specify its name, message flow, message label, multiplicity, and other property values.

6. Double-click any shape to open its UML <element> Properties dialog box, specify the properties you want, and click OK.

Creating Component Diagrams

UML component diagrams are typically used as architecture-level artifacts, to model the business software architecture and the technical software architecture for systems. You can enhance your architectural work by iterating between component diagrams for business and technical software architecture and UML deployment diagrams or network diagrams for the physical architecture.

Component diagrams help distribute development across large teams. Initially, your architectural modeling focuses on modeling the high-level software components and the interfaces to those components. After the team defines and agrees to the interfaces for the system, it's much easier to assign development among smaller teams. As work progresses and you identify new requirements or needed changes, you can negotiate changes between teams and implement the modified interfaces. You can also use component diagrams to partition a system into components and use dependencies to indicate the relationships between components.

To create a component diagram in an existing UML model, follow these steps:

1. In the Model Explorer window, right-click the subsystem or package in which you want to add a component diagram and choose New ➪ Component Diagram from the shortcut menu.

2. For each component, drag a Component shape from the UML Component stencil onto the drawing page.

3. To add an interface to a component, drag an Interface shape from the UML Component stencil onto the drawing page and glue the end point without the circle to a connection point on the Component shape.

Tip If you want to list the operations for an interface, right-click the Interface shape and choose Show As Class-like Interface from the shortcut menu. The operations you specify in the Operations category in the UML Interface Properties dialog box appear in the lower half of the rectangular Interface shape.

4. To show relationships between components or between a component and another component's interface, click the Connector tool on the Standard toolbar, click the Dependency shape on the UML Component stencil, and then drag from one Component shape to the Component shape that depends on it.

5. Double-click any shape to open its UML <element> Properties dialog box, specify the properties you want, and click OK.

Creating Deployment Diagrams

Deployment diagrams, like component diagrams, provide a view of your system implementation. These diagrams illustrate the structure of the run-time system as well as the configuration and deployment of hardware and software. In deployment diagrams, nodes represent processing resources such as computers, mechanical processing devices, or human resources who perform processing activities. Components represent physical modules of code or business documents. You can use deployment diagrams to accomplish the following:

✦ Identify installation issues for your system.

✦ Identify the dependencies between your system and other current or planned production systems.

✦ Document the deployment configuration of a business application.

✦ Configure the hardware and software for an embedded system.

✦ Represent the network and hardware infrastructure of an organization.

To create a deployment diagram in an existing UML model, follow these steps:

1. In the Model Explorer window, right-click the subsystem or package in which you want to add a deployment diagram and choose New ⇨ Deployment Diagram from the shortcut menu.

2. For each node in your system, drag a Node shape from the UML Deployment stencil onto the drawing page.

3. Drag Component and Object shapes into the Node shape to which they belong.

 Tip   If you want to resize a Node shape, drag one of its selection handles.

4. To add an interface to a component, drag an Interface shape from the UML Deployment stencil onto the drawing page and glue the end point without the circle to a connection point on the Component shape.

5. To show relationships between nodes, click the Connector tool on the Standard toolbar, click the Communicates shape on the UML Deployment stencil, and then drag from one Node shape to another.

6. To show relationships between components or between a component and another component's interface, click the Connector tool on the Standard toolbar, click the Dependency shape on the UML Deployment stencil, and then drag from one Component shape to the Component shape that depends on it.

7. Double-click any shape to open its UML <element> Properties dialog box, specify the properties you want, and click OK.

Reverse Engineering Code into UML Models

If you develop projects using Microsoft Visual C++, Microsoft Visual Basic, or Microsoft Visual C#, you can use Visual Studio to reverse engineer your source code into UML and generate a UML diagram in Visio from your project's class definitions. For example, if you're maintaining a legacy system, you can build a UML model to better understand the system and make software maintenance easier.

Visio includes Visio UML Add-Ins for Visual Basic and Visual C++, which provide toolbars you can use to reverse engineer source code to create a UML static structure model in Visio. The reverse-engineered code elements appear in the Visio Model Explorer window. Then, to create a UML static structure diagram, you can drag the elements from the model onto the drawing page.

Note You can't use the Visio 2003 UML reverse engineering add-ins for Visual Basic 6.0 and Visual C++ 6.0 simultaneously on the same machine.

Depending on the language you use, you can reverse engineer different aspects of a project. Visio reverse engineers the following elements:

✦ **Visual C++ 6.0** — Classes, user-defined types, enumerated types, member functions, member variables, and method parameters

✦ **Visual C++ 7.0** — Namespaces, classes, enums, structs, unions, member operations, member variables, method parameters, typedefs, template definitions, Inline function specifier, cv qualifier, conversion-function ID, and operator-function ID.

✦ **Visual Basic 6.0** — Classes, modules, and forms, functions and subroutines, parameters, constants, member variables, properties, events, and user defined types

✦ **Visual Basic .NET and Visual Studio .NET** — Namespaces, classes, interfaces, enumerated types, structures, properties, delegates, member operations, member variables, method parameters, events, and constants

✦ **Visual C#** — Namespaces, classes, interfaces, enumerated types, structs, properties, delegates, member operations, member variables, method parameters, and constants

 **Note** To prepare to use the Visio 2003 add-ins, shut down all instances of Visio and Visual Studio 6.0 that are running and then run and close Visio 2003 once.

Reverse Engineering Visual C++ Code

Before you can reverse engineer a Visual C++ project, you must customize Visual C++ with the Visio UML Add-In, and you must generate a Browse Information file, which the UML Add-In uses to generate a UML model from the source code in your project.

To customize Visual C++ so you can reverse engineer code, follow these steps:

1. In Visual C++, choose Tools ⇨ Customize.

2. In the Customize dialog box, select the Add-Ins and Macro Files tab, select the Visio UML Add-In in the Add-Ins and Macro files list, and click Close. The Visio UML Add-In toolbar appears.

3. To generate a Browse Information file in Visual C++, open the project you want to reverse engineer and choose Project ⇨ Settings.

4. In the Project Settings dialog box, choose the type of build configuration you want, select the C/C++ tab, and then click Generate Browse Info.

5. Select the Browse Info tab to specify the name and location of the Browse Information file, click Build Browse Info File, and then click OK.

To reverse engineer a Visual C++ project, follow these steps:

1. Build the project in Visual C++.

 Note If you modify a Visual C++ project after you reverse engineer it, you must rebuild the project and reverse engineer it into Visio again to see the changes.

2. In Visual C++, click the Reverse Engineer UML Model button on the Visio UML Add-In toolbar. After the reverse engineering process is complete, Visio opens a blank static structure diagram drawing page. The Model Explorer includes elements for the class definitions from your project's source code.

 **Note** If more than one project exists in the Visual C++ workspace, in the Select Project dialog box, select the project you want to reverse engineer and click OK. If more than one Browse Information file exists in the project hierarchy, in the Select Browse File dialog box, select the file you want and then click OK.

3. To create a static structure diagram, drag elements from the Model Explorer window onto the drawing page.

 Caution The Browse Information file API contains a bug that sometimes corrupts class names and class method names. When you reverse engineer a project with corrupted names, the elements with corrupted names are usually not added to the UML model. However, if the reverse engineering process doesn't detect the name corruption, the corrupted names are added to the model. Visio creates a log file that lists the errors detected during the reverse engineering process. By default, the file is written to `C:\Temp\project.txt`.

Reverse Engineering Visual Basic Code

Before you can reverse engineer a Visual Basic project, you must customize Visual Basic with the Visio UML Add-In.

To reverse engineer Visual Basic code, follow these steps:

1. To customize Visual Basic, in Visual Basic, choose Add-Ins ⇨ Add-In Manager. In the Add-In Manager dialog box, select Visio UML Add-In. For Load Behavior, select Loaded/Unloaded and Load on Startup and click OK. The Visio UML Add-In toolbar appears.

2. Open the project that you want to reverse engineer.

3. In Visual Basic, click the Reverse Engineer UML Model button on the Visio UML Add-In toolbar. Visio opens a blank static structure diagram drawing page and populates the Model Explorer window with the elements that represent the class definitions in the source code.

4. To create a static structure diagram, drag elements from the Model Explorer window onto the drawing page.

Summary

The UML Model Diagram template is available only in Visio Professional and Visio Studio .NET Enterprise Architect. To model a software system, you can create a single Visio drawing file and create the multiple models and diagrams of your system within that file. You can work on the model of your system in the Model Explorer window or by modifying shapes on drawing pages. However, the shapes on drawing pages represent views of the elements in your model. You can add elements to a model without displaying them on diagrams or you can add views of elements to more than one diagram. You can also reverse engineer existing source code into Visio models.

✦   ✦   ✦

Building Software Development Diagrams

Whether or not you use the Unified Modeling Language
to model a software system, other types of software
diagrams can help you design and document software architecture, program structure, and memory management. Visio
makes it easy to visualize your software system with several
additional software templates for other software development
methodologies. The diagrams you produce can help identify
problems or communicate designs to your development team.

You can create software diagrams using basic Visio techniques
and the shapes on Visio's software stencils. For example, after
you drag and drop shapes onto the drawing page, you can
glue them together with connectors, drag control handles to
change their configuration, or right-click them to choose special configuration commands from their shortcut menus. You
can also format them using Line, Text, or Fill formatting tools.
If you want to produce reports about the elements on a diagram, you can add custom properties to the software shapes.

This chapter describes how to apply each software template
that Visio offers. You'll also learn how to create different types
of software diagrams. For prototyping user interfaces, you will
learn how to develop diagrams for application windows, wizards, dialog boxes, menus, and toolbars.

Choosing the Right Software Template

The Visio template you should choose depends on what you want to model, as well as the methodology you use, and the phase of development you're in. In addition to the UML Modeling template, Visio provides seven other software templates for producing diagrams of software systems.

Note   To learn more about other types of software diagrams, read *Agile Modeling* by Scott Ambler (Indianapolis: Wiley, 2002) and *The Object Primer, 3rd Edition: Agile Model Driven Development with UML 2.0* by Scott Ambler (New York: Cambridge University Press, 2001).

In the templates that support the construction of software diagrams, many of the shapes conform to standard software modeling notations. However, in these templates, Visio does not verify that your diagrams conform to the rules and syntax of the methodology associated with the diagram. These templates don't include specialized menus or toolbars. New diagrams based on these templates open with a new letter-size drawing page using portrait orientation and no drawing scale.

In the Software category, Visio provides the following software diagram templates:

✦ **COM and OLE** — Create diagrams that show the structure of Component Object Model (COM) and Object Linking and Embedding (OLE) components for an application and the interfaces between them.

✦ **Data Flow Model Diagram** — Design software by modeling the flow and transformation of data with process, interface, data store, and data flow shapes from the Gane-Sarson notation.

Note   To learn about data flow diagrams (DFDs) and structured analysis, read *Structured Systems Analysis: Tools and Techniques* by Chris Gane and T. Sarson (Prentice-Hall, 1977) or go to www.agilemodeling.com/artifacts/dataFlowDiagram.htm.

✦ **Enterprise Application** — When you're building large enterprise-wide applications, use this template to create logical and physical diagrams for systems. Logical diagrams document processes, components, interfaces, and boundaries. You can document the physical architecture of an application with mainframes, servers, workstations, laptops, interfaces, and communication links.

✦ **Jackson** — Document design from system analysis through physical design using the Jackson software design method, which focuses on the system activities that affect data. You can develop data structure diagrams, system network diagrams, and program structure diagrams using the Jackson notation, as described in *Problem Frames: Analyzing and Structuring Software Development Problems* by Michael Jackson (Addison-Wesley, 2000).

✦ **Program Structure** — Document program architecture, structure, and memory management with shapes that represent language elements such as functions and subroutines; and memory objects, such as stacks, pointers, and bytes.

✦ **ROOM** — Create diagrams of real-time systems using object-oriented concepts and real-time software techniques to show the structure of system components and the system's response to events.

✦ **Windows XP User Interface** — Create prototypes of Windows XP interfaces — from individual buttons and message boxes to tabbed dialog boxes and application windows.

Constructing COM and OLE Diagrams

COM is a Microsoft standard that supports the structured development of application software, in which software components can be written in more than one language and communicate through object interfaces. OLE is a subset of COM functionality. With COM and OLE diagrams, you can show the software components associated with processes and how those software components relate to each other through interfaces.

Understanding the Elements of COM

COM controls the identification, structure, and interaction of software components. Com specifications regulate the following:

✦ The structure of component interfaces

✦ Communication between components, including communication across process and network boundaries

✦ Shared memory management

✦ The dynamic loading of components

✦ Error and state reporting

✦ Unique identification of components and interfaces

Client applications and component objects interact through interfaces that define the behavior and responsibilities of the component objects. *Interfaces* are collections of functions that component objects make available to client components or applications. All component objects must implement the IUnknown interface, which counts references to determine component lifetime, and enables clients to determine whether an object supports a required interface and to connect pointers to object interfaces.

Each component object and interface receives a globally unique identifier, or GUID, which is a 128-bit integer that is unique across space and time. By uniquely identifying component objects and interfaces, you can prevent component objects from connecting to the wrong components or interfaces. For computers with Ethernet cards, GUID integers are based on the computer used to create the component or interface and the date and time at which the component or interface was created. If a computer doesn't have an Ethernet card, the GUID is only guaranteed to be unique on that computer.

By using Vtables, you can write component objects in any language that uses pointers to call functions, such as C, C++, or Microsoft Visual Basic. COM specifies the layout of Vtables in computer memory and a standard method for calling functions through Vtables.

Creating COM and OLE Diagrams

When you create a new COM and OLE diagram, Visio opens only the COM and OLE stencil. Depending on the shapes you drag from the COM and OLE stencil, you can use custom properties, control handles, and commands on the shape shortcut menus to configure your diagram. To create a COM and OLE diagram, follow these steps:

1. Choose File ➪ New ➪ Software ➪ COM and OLE. Visio creates a new drawing file with one drawing page.

2. To create a COM object, drag a COM Object shape from the COM and OLE stencil onto the drawing page. COM objects include the IUnknown interface by default. To name the COM Object shape, select it, type the name you want, and press Esc.

3. To add an interface to the COM Object shape, drag the control handle in the center of the shape in the direction you want the interface to point. To name the new interface, subselect it, type the name for the interface, and then press Esc.

4. To change the style of a COM Object shape, right-click it and choose the COM Style command from the shortcut menu. This command toggles between COM Style 1 and COM Style 2.

5. To add Vtables to your diagram, drag a Vtable shape onto the drawing page. In the Custom Properties dialog box, specify the number of cells you want and click OK. To add text to table cells, subselect a cell and type the text you want. You can drag Vtables into COM Object shapes.

Note   To specify the number of cells in a Vtable at a later time, right-click the table and choose Set Number of Cells from the shortcut menu.

6. To create relationships between COM objects, Vtables, and interfaces, drag Reference or Weak Reference connectors onto the drawing page and glue them to shapes or interfaces.

Note To change the angle of the bend in a Reference connector, drag its control handle to a new location.

Creating Data Flow Diagrams

The Gane-Sarson methodology represents software systems and business processes with data flow diagrams (DFDs) that show the data stores that hold data, the processes that transform data, and the data flows that processes generate. This approach to designing software begins by defining top-level processes and then decomposes those processes into lower-level processes, as shown in Figure 21-1.

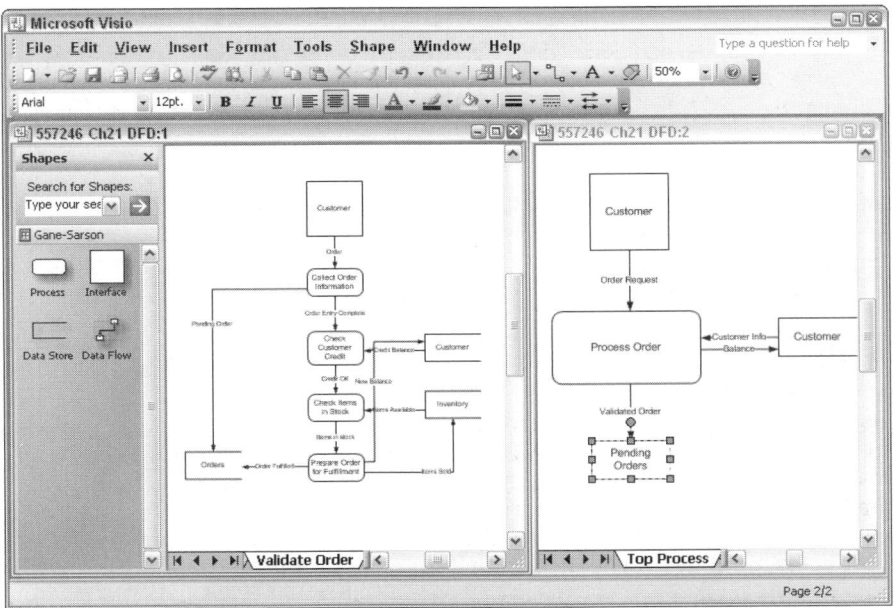

Figure 21-1: Drag and connect shapes to show processes, data, and data flows.

Note In Visio 2003, the Model Explorer and DFD menu are no longer available.

To create a data flow diagram, follow these steps:

1. Choose File ➪ New ➪ Software ➪ Data Flow Model Diagram. Visio creates a new drawing file containing the Top Process drawing page and opens the Gane-Sarson stencil.

2. Define the top-level process by dragging Interface and Process shapes from the Gane-Sarson stencil onto the drawing page.

3. To show data repositories for your system, drag Data Store shapes onto the drawing page.

4. To indicate data flows between processes or to and from data stores, click the Connector tool on the Standard toolbar, click the Data Flow connector in the Gane-Sarson stencil, and then drag from the source to the destination of the data flow.

5. To define a lower-level process, create a new drawing page for the subprocess. Drag and connect Interface, Process, and Data Store shapes to define the lower-level process.

You can create additional drawing pages to define additional levels of subprocesses in your system until you have described the entire data flow model in sufficient detail.

Creating Software Diagrams with Jackson Notation

The Jackson software design methodology encompasses the software system life cycle from analysis to physical design. With this methodology, you analyze the effect of system actions on input and output data streams, not functional tasks. The Jackson design method uses system network diagrams to show the interactions between processes at the top-level of a software system. Each data stream shown on the system network diagram is described in detail by a data structure diagram. Each program is described by a program structure diagram. It's important to note that the Jackson methodology has been overshadowed by UML-based object techniques in recent years, although it is still a common technique within traditional development circles.

Creating System Network Diagrams

To create system network diagrams, you use drawing tools to create circles that represent data streams, rectangles that represent programs, and arrows for the flow of data streams in and out of programs. When you create Jackson system network diagrams, use arrows to connect data stream circles to program rectangles.

Note In the Jackson methodology, you should not connect two circles or two rectangles. In addition, each circle can have only one arrow pointing into the data stream and one arrow flowing out.

To create a system network diagram, follow these steps:

1. Choose File ⇨ New ⇨ Software ⇨ Jackson. Visio creates a new drawing file with one drawing page and opens the Jackson stencil.

2. Click the Drawing Tools button on the Standard toolbar to display the Drawing Tools toolbar.

3. To create data streams, click the Ellipse tool and drag the pointer to draw circles.

Note When you use the Ellipse tool, Visio displays drawing aids that show you where to click to create a circle.

4. To represent programs on the diagram, click the Rectangle tool and drag the pointer to define opposite corners of the rectangle.

5. To add the program or data stream name, select a rectangle or circle that you drew and type the name or other annotation you want. Press Esc to complete the text entry in a shape.

6. To show flow of data, click the Connector tool on the Standard toolbar and drag from a rectangle representing a program to a circle representing a data stream.

Creating Jackson Data or Program Structure Diagrams

The Jackson template includes shapes for creating tree diagrams to document data structure or program structure. Tree structure diagrams comprise four basic components: sequence, elementary, selection, and iteration. Elementary components are the lowest components in a tree structure. Other components consist of component parts as follows:

✦ **Elementary** — Contains no structure or parts of its own and is represented by a rectangle with no notation in the top-right corner.

✦ **Sequence** — Contains elementary component parts in sequence from left to right with the leftmost component part occurring first and the rightmost occurring last.

✦ **Selection** — Contains two or more component parts, but only one of the component parts occurs for the component. Indicated by a circle in the top-right corner of the shape.

✦ **Iteration** — Contains one component that can occur once, many times, or not at all. Indicated by an asterisk in the top-right corner of the shape.

As you build tree structure diagrams, you must comply with the following rules:

✦ Don't connect a component part to a component on a different level.

✦ Don't include different types of component parts in the same component. For example, do not include a sequence, iteration, and elementary component part for the same component type.

✦ Don't include more than one component part for an iteration component.

To create a tree structure diagram to represent data structure or program structure, follow these steps:

1. Choose File ➪ New ➪ Software ➪ Jackson.

2. Drag a Process, Procedure, or Procedure 2 shape from the Jackson stencil onto the drawing page. With the shape selected, type the name of the component and then press Esc to end your text entry.

3. To specify the component type, right-click the shape and choose one of the following commands from the shortcut menu:

   • **No Symbol** — Represents a sequence or elementary component

   • **Show Asterisk** — Represents an iteration

   • **Show Circle** — Represents a selection

4. To annotate the process or procedure using the text block within the shape, subselect the text below the shape and type the text you want. To hide the additional text, right-click the shape and choose Hide Note from the shortcut menu.

Tip   If you want to create reports about the processes and procedures in your diagram, customize the Jackson stencil shapes by adding custom properties. You can then store your annotation in the custom properties and produce reports using them. To learn how to create and assign custom properties to shapes, see Chapter 32.

5. Repeat steps 2 through 4 to create additional processes or procedures.

6. To connect processes or procedures, drag the Tree Connector shape onto the drawing page and follow these steps to connect shapes:

   a. Glue the trunk of the tree to a connection point on a Process, Procedure, or Procedure 2 shape.

   b. Drag the control handles at the ends of the branches to glue branches to connection points on other shapes.

   c. To add additional branches, drag the control handle on the trunk of the tree and glue the new branch to a shape.

   d. To include text with the connector, select it and type the text you want. To reposition the text, drag the control handle in the center of the text to a new location.

Modeling Large-Scale Application Architectures

Enterprise architecture diagrams present logical and physical views of the architecture of a large-scale or enterprise system. During analysis, you can use these diagrams to show the system architecture at a conceptual level. During design and development, you can add physical details to the architecture diagram. Later in the system life cycle, you can use these diagrams to design test platforms and plan delivery and support services.

The shapes on the Enterprise Architecture stencil don't have any extra bells and whistles. However, you can drag and drop them onto the drawing page, glue them together with connectors, add text to them, format them, or add custom properties to them as you would any standard Visio shape. To create an enterprise architecture diagram, choose File ➪ New ➪ Software ➪ Enterprise Application. Drag shapes that represent logical or physical components from the Enterprise Application stencil onto the drawing page and connect them as needed.

Creating Program Structure Diagrams

In addition to the program structure diagrams within the Jackson template, Visio offers another template for program structure that you can use to show memory management and language-level functions within structured/procedural computer programs. Although both types of program structure diagrams depict the same information, the symbols for Jackson notation differ from those in the Program Structure template. To document program structure or memory management using non-Jackson symbology, choose File ➪ New ➪ Software ➪ Program Structure and then use shapes from the following stencils:

✦ Language Level Shapes

- To show program structure, drag Function/Subroutine, Function w/Invocation, Switch, and other shapes from the Language Level Shapes stencil onto the drawing page.

- To reposition connections on shapes, drag control handles on the Function w/Invocation or Switch shapes. You can add additional switches by dragging the control handle on the vertical line in a switch to a new location.

✦ Memory Objects

- To represent memory management, drag shapes from the Memory Objects stencil onto the drawing page.

- To connect pointers to memory cells, drag end points or control handles from Pointer shapes and glue them to connection points on shapes representing memory objects, such as Array.

Modeling Real Time Systems with ROOM Diagrams

The Real-Time Object-Oriented Modeling (ROOM) language is a combination of real-time and object-oriented software techniques that you can use to show the structure of system components and a system's response to events. The Visio ROOM template includes shapes for building ROOM structure and behavior diagrams.

Note   To learn more about using ROOM to model software, read *Real-Time Object-Oriented Modeling* by Bran Selic (Wiley, 1994).

To create a new ROOM diagram, choose File ➪ New ➪ Software ➪ ROOM and then use the following shapes:

✦ ROOM Structure diagrams

  • Drag an Actor Class shape onto the drawing page. With the shape selected, type its name.

  • Drag an Actor Reference or a Modified Actor Ref. shape inside an Actor Class shape. To change the Modified Actor Ref. object type, right-click the shape, and then choose Select Actor Reference Type from the shortcut menu.

  • Drag one of the Port shapes onto the drawing page and connect it to an Actor shape. To change the port type, right-click the shape and choose Select Reference Port or Select Relay Port from the shortcut menu.

  • To represent a communication path between ports, drag a Binding shape onto the drawing page and connect it to Port shapes.

  • To show ROOM layers for your diagram, drag Layer/Export Connection shapes onto the drawing page to connect different layers.

✦ ROOM Behavior diagrams

  • Drag a State Context shape onto the drawing page and type its name.

  • Drag a State shape inside a State Context shape.

  • Drag a Transition Points shape onto the drawing page, select the type of transition point in the Custom Properties dialog box and click OK. Connect it to a State shape. To change the transition point type, right-click the shape and then choose Select Transition Point Type from the shortcut menu.

  • Drag Transition, Group Transition, Internal Self-transition, and Transition To History shapes onto the drawing page and connect them to State shapes.

Note To create multiple paths for a transition, drag a Choicepoint shape onto the drawing page and glue the beginning end points of each diverging Transition shape to it.

Prototyping User Interfaces

By creating a prototype interface, you can design the menus, toolbars, dialog boxes, and controls for your application. You can then walk through the interface with end users to obtain feedback on its usability before you create the interface. In most cases, development resources use prototyping tools or Visual Basic to develop user interface prototypes. However, if don't have access to tools such as these and want to experiment with interface elements, you can use Visio Professional's Windows XP User Interface template.

New Feature Visio 2003 replaces the Windows User Interface and Office User Interface stencils with the Windows XP User Interface template and several stencils with standard user interface components.

Exploring the Windows XP User Interface Template

The Windows XP User Interface template doesn't contain specialized menus, toolbars, or commands. You can use basic Visio techniques to compose an interface for your application. Many of the interface shapes include shortcut commands you can use to configure the shape. For example, you can show the interface element as enabled or disabled or specify the type of button. To create a new user interface drawing, choose File ➪ New ➪ Software ➪ Windows XP User Interface. When you create a new user interface diagram, Visio opens the following stencils:

✦ **Windows and Dialogs** — Contains shapes for forms, panels, tab controls, group boxes, status bars, buttons and icons

✦ **Wizards** — Contains shapes for simple and advanced wizard windows, including welcome screens, completion screens, and interior screens for all the steps in between

✦ **Toolbars and Menus** — Contains shapes for menu bars, top-level menu items, drop-down menu items, toolbars, toolbar buttons, and other toolbar icons

✦ **Icons** — Includes commonly used interface icons such as the Recycle Bin, My Documents, Help, and Folder

✦ **Common Controls** — Includes shapes for frequently used controls, such as command buttons, option buttons, check boxes, scroll bars, list boxes, combo boxes, tree nodes, and sliders

Creating an Application Window

You can prototype the entire user interface for an application by starting with an application window. You begin with a blank form and add the user interface elements you want, as shown in Figure 21-2. To create a mock-up of an application interface, follow these steps:

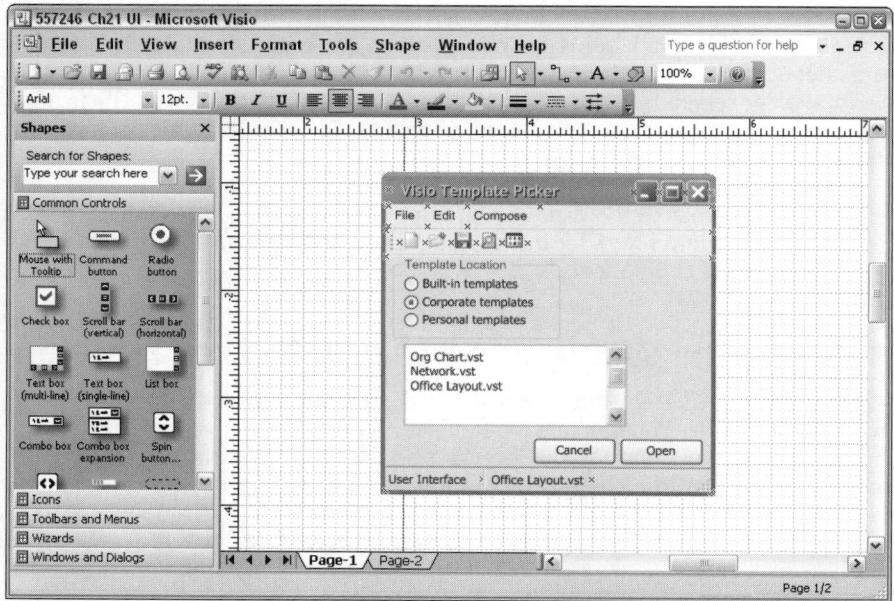

Figure 21-2: You can mock up a Windows XP user interface before writing code.

1. Drag a Blank Form shape from the Windows and Dialogs stencil onto the drawing page. With the shape selected, type the title for the application window.

2. If you want to add an icon to the left of the text in the title bar, right-click the Blank Form shape and check the Room for Icon check box on the shortcut menu.

Note   You can also specify the background color for the Blank Form shape by right-clicking it and choosing White Background, Gray Background, or Custom Background from the shortcut menu. To change the appearance of the Blank Form shape to that of an inactive window, uncheck Active window on the shortcut menu.

3. To add buttons to the title bar of the form, drag a Windows Buttons shape onto the right end of the title bar area of the Blank Form shape and select the type of button you want. The typical arrangement of buttons for a form is the Minimize button, the Maximize button, and the Close button from left to right, respectively.

4. Drag a Status Bar shape from the Windows and Dialogs stencil and glue it to the bottom edge of the Blank Form shape. To add a divider to the status bar, drag a Status Bar Divider shape onto the page and glue it to the control handle for the Status Bar shape or another Status Bar Divider shape. To add text to the Status Bar or Status Bar Divider, select the shape and type the text you want.

Note If the Status Bar Divider shape disappears when you glue it to a Status Bar shape, right-click the Status Bar shape and choose Shape ➪ Send to Back from the shortcut menu.

5. To indicate that the window is resizable, drag a Window Resize shape from the Windows and Dialogs stencil and glue it to the connection point at the bottom right of the Status Bar shape.

6. Drag Scroll Bar shapes (horizontal and vertical) from the Common Controls stencil onto the bottom and right edges of the Blank Form shape, respectively. To specify how far the window scrolls, right-click the Scroll Bar shapes and choose Set Thumb Size from the shortcut menu.

Note To indicate that only a small portion of the document is visible, make the thumb size small. To indicate that most of the document is visible, make the thumb size large.

You can continue to drag shapes from the Windows XP User Interface stencils to add menus, toolbars, icons, and common controls to the form.

Prototyping Wizards

The Wizards stencil includes shapes for the different types of screens you see in wizards. You can use the Simple-Single Page shape to create one-page wizards. For wizards with two or three pages, use the Simple Wizard shapes. Use the Advanced Wizard shapes for wizards with more than three pages.

Creating Wizards with One to Three Pages

1. Drag a Simple-Single Page or Simple-Welcome shape from the Wizards stencil onto the drawing page. With the Wizard shape still selected, type the name of the wizard.

2. To add a graphic to the panel on the right side of the screen, subselect the box within the right panel and then choose Insert ➪ Picture to specify the graphic file to use.

3. To add the wizard instructions, select the Wizard Text text block in the main panel of the Wizard shape and type the instructions for your wizard.

4. To construct the interface elements of the wizard, drag shapes from the Common Control stencil onto the main panel of the Wizard shape.

Because each Wizard shape includes the navigational buttons appropriate for that wizard page, you can't edit them.

5. For each remaining wizard page, create a new drawing page and repeat steps 1 through 4.

Creating Wizards with More Than Three Pages

Wizards with more than three pages include a welcome page, a completion page, and two or more interior pages. You define the contents of each page as you would for a simpler wizard by dragging shapes from the Common Controls stencil onto the corresponding Wizard shape. To create the pages for an advanced wizard, follow these steps:

1. Drag an Advanced-Welcome shape from the Wizards stencil onto the drawing page. With the Wizard shape still selected, type the name of the wizard.

2. To create interior pages for a wizard, create new drawing pages and then drag an Advanced-Interior shape onto each drawing page. It's common practice to include a graphic related to the one on the Welcome page at the right edge of the Wizard Text box.

3. To create a completion page, create a new drawing page and then drag an Advanced-Completion shape onto the drawing page.

Simulating Wizard Navigation

You can simulate the navigation through a wizard to test its usability before you write the code to implement it. To simulate wizard navigation, you must place the shapes for each wizard page on a separate drawing page and save the drawing file. To configure wizard diagrams so that you can simulate their behavior, follow these steps:

1. Navigate to the drawing page that contains the first page for the wizard.

2. To modify the drawing size to fit the wizard page exactly, choose File ➪ Page Setup and select the Page Size tab. Under Page Size, select the Size to Fit Drawing Contents option.

3. To add navigation to the Navigation buttons on the Wizard shape, follow these steps:

   a. Draw an invisible rectangle around each button using the Rectangle tool on the Drawing toolbar.

   b. Right-click the rectangle and choose Format ➪ Line. In the Pattern drop-down list, select 00: None and then click OK.

c. Right-click the rectangle and choose Format ⇨ Fill. In the Pattern drop-down list, select 00: None and then click OK.

d. With the rectangle selected, choose Insert ⇨ Hyperlinks. Click the Browse button to the right of the Address box and choose Local File.

e. In the Link to File dialog box, double-click the drawing you are working on.

f. Click the Browse button to the right of the Sub-address box.

g. In the Hyperlink dialog box, in the Page box, select the Visio drawing page that contains the wizard page to which the button should take you and click OK. In the Hyperlinks dialog box, click OK.

4. To run the simulation, choose View ⇨ Full Screen and click the Next or Back buttons to navigate from page to page.

Building Menus and Toolbars

In the Windows XP User Interface template, you can mock up menu bars, drop-down menus, and toolbars. You can create menus and toolbars on their own on a drawing page or attach them to a blank form.

Creating Menu Bars

To create a menu bar, follow these steps:

1. Drag a Menu Bar shape from the Toolbars and Menus stencil onto the drawing page. To add the menu bar to a blank form, glue the Menu Bar shape to the connection points on the bottom edge of the title bar area in the Blank Form shape.

2. To display the gripper dots at the left edge of the menu bar that indicate that you can move the menu bar around, right-click the Menu Bar shape and uncheck the Lock Menu bar check box.

Note You can add an icon at the beginning of a menu bar, similar to the menu bar in Visio and other Microsoft Office programs. Drag an Icon shape from the Icons stencil and glue it to the left edge of the Menu Bar shape. To learn how to import a graphic file of an icon into a Visio shape that you can add to the menu bar, refer to Chapter 9.

3. To add a menu item to the menu bar, drag a Top-level Menu Item shape from the stencil and glue it to the connection point at the top-right corner of the Menu Bar shape. With the shape selected, type the menu name.

If the menu item has an associated keyboard shortcut, underline the appropriate letter in the menu name.

4. Repeat step 3 to glue additional Top-level Menu Item shapes to the right edge of the previous Top-level Menu Item.

Creating Drop-Down Menus

In most cases, you create drop-down menus associated with the top-level menu items in a menu bar. However, you can also build standalone versions. To create a drop-down menu, follow these steps:

1. Drag a Top-level Menu Item shape from the Toolbars and Menus stencil onto the drawing page. With the shape selected, type the name for the menu item, underlining the appropriate letter in the name if the menu item has a keyboard shortcut associated with it.

To add the top-level item to a menu bar, glue the Top-level Menu Item shape to the connection point at the top-right corner of the Menu Bar shape or to the connection point at the top-left corner of the previous Top-level Menu Item shape.

2. Drag a Drop-down Menu Item from the Toolbars and Menus stencil and glue it to the bottom of the Top-level Menu Item shape. Type the name of the drop-down menu item.

3. To add additional drop-down menu items, drag the Drop-down Menu Item shape and glue it to the bottom of the previous Drop-down Menu Item shape.

4. To resize all the drop-down menu items to the width of the widest menu entry, drag from the vertical ruler and glue the blue guide line to the connection point at the bottom right of the widest entry. Then, select each Drop-down Menu Item shape and glue its green end point to the guide line.

5. To specify options for drop-down menu items, right-click each shape and choose Menu Item Properties from the shortcut menu. You can choose an entry in the Menu Item Style drop-down list to change the menu item to Checked, Radio, Cascading, or Separator. The Menu Item Position option sets the justification and width of the menu item, depending on whether it is the top, bottom, or a middle entry in the menu.

Building Toolbars

You can build toolbars within a blank form or on their own on the drawing page. To create a toolbar, follow these steps:

1. Drag a Toolbar shape from the Toolbars and Menus stencil onto the drawing page. To add the toolbar to a blank form, glue the Toolbar shape to connection points for shapes within the blank form, such as the connection points on the bottom of a Menu Bar shape.

2. To display the gripper dots at the left edge of the toolbar that indicate that you can float the toolbar, right-click the Toolbar shape and uncheck the Lock Toolbar check box.

3. To add buttons to the toolbar, drag a Toolbar Buttons shape or an XP Toolbar Buttons shape from the Toolbars and Menus stencil and glue it to the left edge of the Toolbar shape. In the Custom Properties dialog box, choose the type of button you want.

Note   To change the type of button later, right-click the button and choose Set Button Type from the shortcut menu.

4. To add a separator between buttons, drag a Toolbar Separator shape from the stencil and glue it to the right edge of the previous Toolbar Buttons shape.

5. Repeat steps 3 and 4 to add buttons and separators to the toolbar.

Note   You can also add shapes to indicate a toolbar drop-down menu or the Overflow Chevron.

Designing Dialog Boxes

The Windows and Dialogs stencil includes shapes you can use to design basic dialog boxes or dialog boxes with tabs. After you create a dialog box, you can use shapes from the Icons and Common Controls stencils to add interface elements to the dialog box.

To create a basic dialog box, follow these steps:

1. Drag a Blank Form shape onto the drawing page and type a title for the dialog box.

2. To add buttons to the dialog box title bar, drag a Windows Button shape, glue it to the right end of the title bar area in the Blank Form shape and select the button type. You can choose to add Restore, Minimize, Maximize, Close, or Help buttons to the title bar area.

3. To add command buttons, such as OK, Cancel, or Apply to the dialog box, drag a Command Button shape from the Common Controls stencil into the Blank Form shape and type the command name.

Note   If you add your own text blocks to the Blank Form shape with the Text tool, use Tahoma 8-point text to match the text in the user interface shapes.

4. Add other interface elements by dragging shapes from the Common Controls stencil onto the Blank Form shape.

Tip

To align user interface shapes, drag guide lines from the horizontal and vertical rulers onto the drawing page and glue Interface shapes to the guide lines.

5. To assemble interface elements into logical groups, drag a Group Box or Group Line shape onto the Blank Form shape. Group Box shapes include boundary line and heading text to identify the group. Group Line shapes include a horizontal line and heading text.

To add tab controls to a dialog box, follow these steps:

1. Drag a Blank Form shape onto the drawing page, and type a title for the dialog box.

2. To add a tab control to the dialog box, drag a Tab Control (Body) shape from the Windows and Dialogs stencil onto the Blank Form shape. Drag the Tab Control (Body) selection handles to resize the shape to fit inside the Blank Form shape with room along the top for tabs.

3. Drag a Tab Control (Tabs) shape from the Windows and Dialogs stencil and glue it to the top edge of the Tab Control (Body) shape. With the Tab Control (Tabs) shape selected, type the tab name.

4. Repeat step 3 for each tab, gluing the new tab to the connection point at the bottom right of the previous tab.

5. To display a tab as the front tab, right-click the tab you want in front and choose Foreground Tab from the shortcut menu.

Note

By default, tabs are set to Background Tab. If you end up with more than one foreground tab, right-click the tab you want to send to the background and choose Background Tab from the shortcut menu.

6. Add other interface elements by dragging shapes from the Common Controls and Windows and Dialogs stencils onto the Blank Form shape.

Summary

You can choose from seven Visio software templates in addition to the UML template. Unlike the UML template, which provides a modeling environment, the other software templates provide only diagramming tools. They don't validate your diagrams to make sure you correctly apply the rules of the selected methodology. You can use basic Visio techniques such as drag and drop, formatting, control handles, and custom properties to build your diagrams.

✦   ✦   ✦

Mapping Web Sites

Whether a Web site is simple or complex, it requires careful planning during the development stage. After a site is up and running, it requires conscientious maintenance to ensure that it serves the needs of the organization and its customers.

Visio 2003 assists with tools for both stages of Web site work. With the Conceptual Web Site template, you can lay out the concept, structure, and elements for new or revamped Web sites. The Web Site Map template includes tools to generate maps of existing Web sites. With a site map, it's easier to maintain a Web site because you can see its current content and organization as well as detect broken links. This chapter shows you how to use Visio to create and fine-tune conceptual Web diagrams. You'll also learn how to generate and work with Web site maps for existing Web sites.

Exploring the Web Diagram Templates

Visio Professional includes the following two Web diagram templates:

✦ **Conceptual Web Site** — Draft the structure and elements for a planned Web site or application. Show Web pages, groups, pop-ups, forms, jumps, and other items to graphically describe the behavior and appearance of a proposed Web site. The template includes the Conceptual Web Site Shapes stencil, Web Site Map Shapes stencil, and Callouts, Backgrounds, and Borders and Titles stencils. The Conceptual Web Site Shapes stencil contains shapes for entire pages, objects and elements on pages, site map nodes, and jumps and connectors.

✦ **Web Site Map** — Generate a map of a Web site to review the structure and find any broken links or other problems. Generate the map to the number of levels you want. The template includes the Web Site Map Shapes stencil, the Web Site Map menu, the List window, and the Filter window.

To create a drawing using one of the Web diagram templates, choose File ⇨ New ⇨ Web Diagram, and then choose Conceptual Web Site or Web Site Map. To use one of the Web diagram stencils in a different template, choose File ⇨ Shapes ⇨ Web Diagram and then choose the stencil you want.

Planning Web Sites

As the Webmaster for an organization's Internet or intranet Web site, you might start your Web site development with a laundry list of items that should be included in the Web site, which might have been identified during a brainstorming session documented with a Visio brainstorming diagram. When you're ready to organize that list into a structure, use the Conceptual Web Site template. This helps you and others on your Web development team visualize how you want to organize the elements in the Web site, as shown in Figure 22-1. As new ideas arise, you can easily change the drawing before any programming is performed for the site. When the concept is complete and approved by the powers that be, you're ready to transform that conceptual Web design into a living, breathing Web site that serves its target audience well.

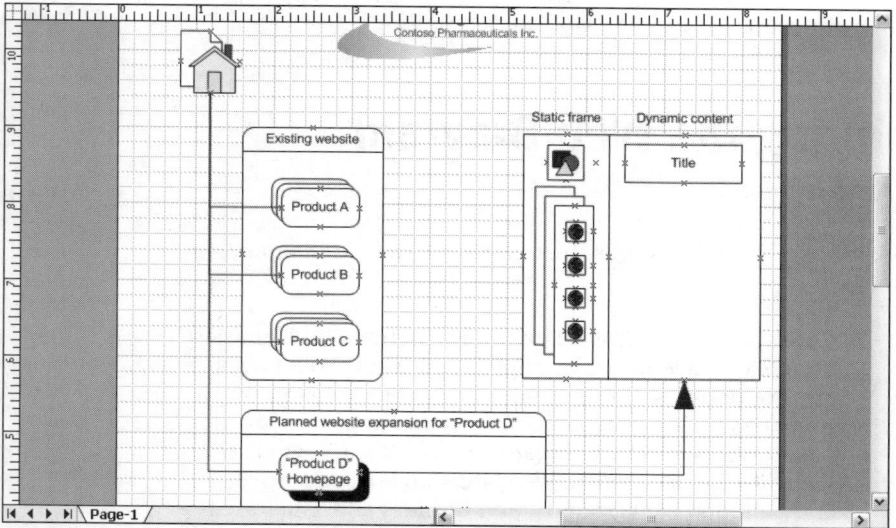

Figure 22-1: Use the Conceptual Web Site template to plan the content, organization, and interactions of a new Web site.

Creating Conceptual Web Diagrams

Because of the hierarchical nature of most Web sites, you might find it useful to create an overview page that shows all the major groups of pages. Then you can create pages to show detail for each of the major groups. If you want, you can take it down another level of detail and use provided shapes to show the elements on each page. For a simpler Web site, you might draw an overview of the Web site structure as a whole and then add pages for detail for each individual Web page you want to create.

Tip   You don't need to restrict the use of this template to Web sites. You can also use it for planning user interfaces in general. For example, use the Conceptual Web Site template to plan the screens in a Visual Basic application.

Either way, with a high-level overview page, you can set up the big picture of your Web site (or application) before tackling the details of the individual elements on the individual pages. With the conceptual Web diagram, you can create a storyboard or flow diagram, showing major features and the relationships among them. Using this diagram, you can do the following:

✦ Develop and examine the interactions in your proposed Web site.

✦ Create and refine the navigation flow throughout the site.

✦ Determine whether any elements or connections are missing or superfluous.

✦ Determine whether the Web site is too complex.

To create a new conceptual Web diagram, follow these steps:

1. Choose File ➪ New ➪ Web Diagram ➪ Conceptual Web Site.

2. From the Conceptual Web Site Shapes stencil, drag the first shape you want onto the drawing.

3. Label the shape by selecting it and then typing its label.

4. Repeat steps 2 and 3 for each shape you want in your drawing.

5. Resize and move the conceptual Web site shapes into the size and position you want.

6. Drag connector shapes — for example, the 2-Way Data Connection connector or Dynamic connector — onto the drawing. Position the connector to show links among the different shapes on the drawing.

Tip   When you're creating conceptual Web diagrams to include detail about groups of pages of the Web site, you might want to add shapes from the Web Site Map Shapes stencil. This stencil contains more page-specific shapes, such as Presentation, Database, FTP, and Search.

You can create a hyperlink from a node in the overview diagram to a page that contains the detail for that node. Hyperlinks can help others navigate as they review the Web site conceptual diagram. To create a hyperlink from one page in your diagram to another, follow these steps:

1. Select the node in the overview page and then choose Insert ➪ Hyperlinks.

2. Click Browse, next to the Sub-Address box.

3. In the Page drop-down list, select the page that contains the detail drawing for the selected node.

4. Click OK and then click OK again.

To move from a shape on the overview page to the detailed diagram for that shape, right-click the shape and then choose the name of the page on which the link resides.

For more information about working with hyperlinks, see Chapter 8.

Fine-tuning Conceptual Web Diagrams

You can refine your conceptual Web diagram by formatting, aligning shapes, and adding callouts.

Formatting Web Diagrams

You can change the font, line style, and fill color of the shapes on your drawing. If necessary, activate the Pointer tool on the Standard toolbar and then select the shapes whose formatting you want to change by either dragging across the shapes or Shift+clicking or Ctrl+clicking them.

✦ **Change the font style** — Choose Format ➪ Text. Select the Font tab if necessary and then make the font changes you want for the selected shapes.

✦ **Change the line style** — Choose Format ➪ Line. Specify the changes you want to the line, the line ends, and the corners. The changes you make affect shape outlines and connectors in the current selection.

✦ **Change the fill style** — Choose Format ➪ Fill. Specify the changes you want to make to the insides of shapes, including the color, patterns, and shadow.

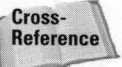

To learn more about formatting, see Chapter 7.

Arranging Shapes in Web Diagrams

You can have Visio arrange the shapes on your drawing according to a pattern you select. Using Visio's tools for arranging shapes automatically, you can focus on the content of your Web diagram and let Visio worry about the alignment and spacing.

✦ **Align Shapes** — Select the shapes you want to align to one of the shapes. Choose Shape ⇨ Align Shapes. Select the vertical or horizontal alignment you want. Select the red X button to deselect an option.

✦ **Distribute Shapes** — Select three or more shapes you want distributed at regular intervals on the page. Choose Shape ⇨ Distribute Shapes. When you select a vertical distribution, the selected shapes are arranged at equal intervals along a horizontal axis. When you select a horizontal distribution, the selected shapes are arranged along a vertical axis.

✦ **Center Drawing** — Choose Shape ⇨ Center Drawing. The entire drawing is positioned to the center of the drawing page.

To learn more about aligning and distributing shapes, see Chapter 4.

Annotating Web Diagrams

You can explain elements in your Web diagram using shapes from the Callouts stencil. This stencil, which is part of the Conceptual Web Site template, contains shapes for line callouts, bracketed text, boxes, balloons, starbursts, and other shapes designed to annotate elements in your diagram.

To annotate your Web diagram, select the Callouts stencil in the Shapes window. Drag the Callout shape you want to use onto your Web diagram. With the shape still selected, type the text for the callout. When finished, press Esc. Resize and move the shape as needed.

For best results, use a consistent style of callouts throughout your Web diagram. Use different types of callouts for different types of information.

To learn more about text and methods of annotating diagrams, see Chapter 6.

Working with Web Site Maps

If you're maintaining or revamping an existing Web site, you can use Visio to generate and work with a site map. Not only does this site map "discover" and show the structure and elements contained in the hierarchy of the Web site, but it can also find changes since the last time you generated the site map, including any broken links.

Use the Web site map as the starting point for reorganizing existing content, adding new elements, and merging or deleting duplicated pages. By keeping an eye on the overall Web site structure, you can ensure that the Web site is meeting the organization's needs as well as those of the target audience.

Keeping Your Web Site Up to Date

Use the Visio Web Site Map to regularly check your Web site and keep it up to date. This is a very important aspect of Web site maintenance. An excellent process to achieve this is to work iteratively with the Web site, as follows:

1. Generate the map of the Web site using the Visio Web Site Map template.

2. Review the map to detect any broken links and other problems or potential problems with the site.

3. Model the repairs to the broken links and other issues in the Web site map. You might find it helpful to track markup in the Web site map, as described in Chapter 11, so you have a clear guide to what needs changing in the actual Web pages.

4. Open the source files for the Web pages that need updating. Use your changes in the Visio Web site map as your "punch list" for the required changes.

5. In Visio, generate the Web site map again to confirm that your changes work the way you expect.

Repeat this process at a frequency appropriate to the nature and expected usage of your Web site. For generally static Web sites, a monthly check might be sufficient. For sites whose content is constantly changing, a daily check might be required.

Note

The generated Web site map is a visual representation of the elements in a specified Web site. Although you can add and remove shapes representing Web page elements and repair broken links on the drawing, these actions don't change the Web site itself. For best results, keep track of the changes you're making on the site map. When you're finished modeling your changes in the Visio Web site map, make those changes to the Web site itself.

The Web Site Map template consists of the Web Site Map Shapes stencil, the Web Site Map menu, the List window, and the Filter window. The stencil includes shapes that represent various page elements. These include HTML or XML content, scripts, graphics, audio, and video. Content-related shapes represent documents created with Microsoft Word, Excel, or PowerPoint. Shapes for protocols such as FTP, Mailto, Newsgroup, and Telnet are also included. The stencil provides two types of connectors.

New Feature

In Visio 2003, the Web Site Map template has been updated for more compact layouts, increased speed, editable shape text, and new shapes for Web technology.

Generating Maps of Existing Web Sites

When you use Visio to create a Web site map, you can specify how many levels of the site's hierarchy that you want Visio to discover. To generate a Web site map, follow these steps:

1. Choose File ⇨ New ⇨ Web Diagram ⇨ Web Site Map. The Generate Site Map dialog box appears.

2. In the Address box, type the address for the Web site you want to map. Enter the full path, including the protocol and the name of the individual page—for example, `http://www.microsoft.com/default.asp`.

Tip   You can also map an HTML file, ASP page, or Internet shortcut stored on your local computer. In the Generate Site Map dialog box, click Browse. Navigate through your computer's filing system to find and select the file. Click Open. This can be particularly helpful if you're analyzing a Web site offline.

3. Review the discovery and diagramming settings. To learn about specifying the settings for discovery, see the next section. When you're ready to generate the site map, click OK. Visio finds and scans the Web site or Web documents, verifies their links, searches the specified levels of the hierarchy, and then finally displays the Web structure and elements as a site map on the drawing page.

The site map appears as a series of shapes linked in a hierarchy, as illustrated in Figure 22-2.

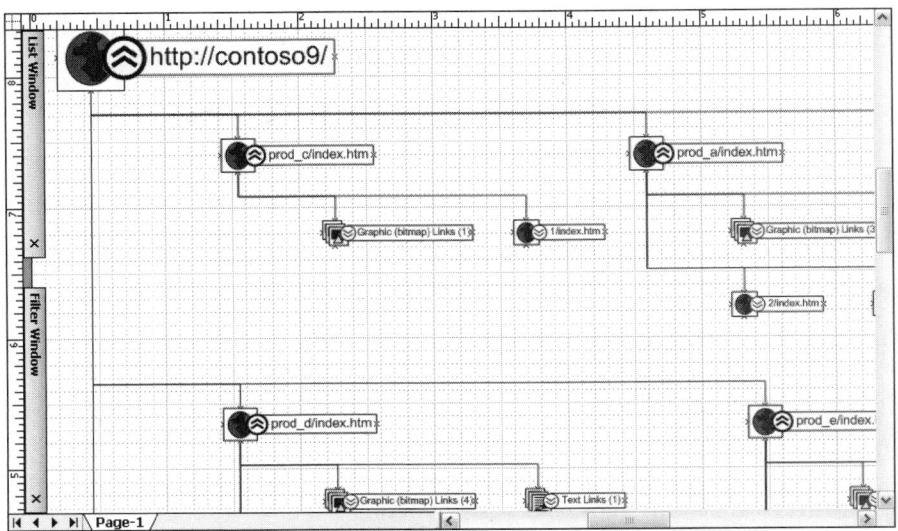

Figure 22-2: Visio shapes represent each site map element; connectors show the hierarchical relationship between the levels.

Caution   When Visio 2003 is discovering the levels and links in a Web site, a page with pop-up windows and scripts might display incorrectly or even generate errors. Because there is no workaround for now, if Visio asks you if you want to debug the current page, click No.

Configuring the Content and Format of Site Maps

Use the Web Site Map Settings dialog box to specify how you want Visio to discover, generate, and diagram the Web site map. Choose Web Site Map ⇨ Generate Site Map, enter the Web address, and then click Settings.

Note   When you change any of the Web site map settings, generate the site map again to see the results of your changes.

You can use settings in the following areas on the Layout tab to control the level of detail and layout arrangement of a diagram:

✦ **Discover**—Enter the number of levels you want Visio to discover. Although the default is three levels, you can specify from one to twelve levels. Also enter the number of elements or links you want Visio to discover. The default is 300 links, and you can specify a maximum of 5,000. If you enter a number of levels or links greater than those contained in the Web site, Visio will discover all levels and links.

✦ **Layout Style** — Select the placement and routing styles Visio uses on the site map. To change these styles, click Modify Layout. Specify the styles you want under Placement and Connectors.

✦ **Shape Text**—Specify the default text to include in the shape, such as Relative URL (the default), Absolute URL, Filename Only, HTML Title, and No Text.

Tip   You can also change shape text after a site map is generated. Choose Web Site Map ⇨ Modify Shape Text.

✦ **Shape Size** — You can control the size of shapes at each level, which provides an instant visual cue as to which level you're looking at on the drawing. By default, the root level is displayed at 200 percent, level 1 at 100 percent, level 2 at 75 percent, and level 3 at 50 percent.

The Extensions, Protocols, and Attributes tabs on the Web Site Map Settings dialog box include lists of items that Visio can discover and represent with a shape in your Web site map. By default, Visio selects all the listed elements. Uncheck the check box for any elements you want to exclude from the site map. Click Add if there are other elements you want that are not currently represented in the list. The following list describes the options available on the tabs on the Web Site Map Settings dialog box:

✦ **Extensions tab** — Specify the types of programs, files, and scripts that you want to display or hide when Visio generates the Web site map. The Shape column shows the shape Visio uses to represent the file type on the site map.

✦ **Protocols tab** — Review or change the Internet protocols that Visio is able to discover when generating a Web site map. Examples include FTP, File, Mailto, Newsgroups, Search, and so on. The Shape column shows the shape Visio uses to represent the protocol on the site map.

✦ **Attributes tab** — Indicate the HTML attributes that Visio should include in its discovery and generation of Web site maps. Examples include Code, SRC, and HREF.

When you finish specifying site map settings, click OK in the dialog box. In the Generate Site Map dialog box, click OK to generate the site map according to your new parameters.

Viewing Site Maps

Visio generates a Web site map in a new drawing. Each shape represents a page, a link, or other element in the Web site. Connectors between shapes indicate the relationships between elements on the site.

The different shapes also delineate the type of page or element. You can compare the shapes on the drawing with the shapes in the Web Site Map Shapes stencil to learn more about the element. For example, you can see whether an element is an HTML page, a graphic image, a style sheet, or JavaScript.

Collapsing and Expanding Site Map Shapes

When your Web site map is first generated, it might only display a single large shape, which shows the name of the Web site you mapped. To reveal the levels or child links beneath this page, double-click the shape. You can also right-click the shape and then choose Expand Hyperlink from the shortcut menu.

Continue to double-click any shapes whose child links you want to see on the drawing. To see all child links beneath a shape, right-click the shape and then choose Select All Hyperlinks Beneath from the shortcut menu. Shapes that are collapsed and can be expanded include the down arrow icon.

You can also hide child links of a shape. Again, just double-click the shape, or right-click the shape and then choose Collapse Hyperlink from the shortcut menu. Shapes that are expanded and can be collapsed include the up arrow icon.

Note   You can expand or collapse only shapes that already contain links.

Finding Shapes in Web Site Maps

Suppose you're searching for a particular shape or link in your Web site map—for example, a plug-in on the second level of the hierarchy. You can find shapes by searching for shape names, text, custom properties, and so on. To find a shape in your Web site map, follow these steps:

1. Choose Edit ➪ Find. The Find dialog box appears.

2. In the Find What box, type the text associated with the shape you're looking for, such as the name of a Web page you are removing from the site.

3. Under Search In, select an option to specify whether you want Visio to search the current selection, the current page, or all pages on the drawing.

4. Under Search In, check the check boxes that indicate the element you want to search on. This element should correspond with the text you entered in the Find What box. For example, because Web page names appear in shape text, check the Shape Text check box to find a Web page name. You can check multiple check boxes.

5. Under Options, check the check boxes for any additional search parameters you want to use.

6. Click Find Next. Visio finds and highlights the first shape that meets your search criteria. Click Find Next to find the next shape that meets your criteria.

Mapping Protected Areas on Web Sites

In the Web site map, you might see areas that are not filled in or that are covered with a red X. These might be protected areas that require you to click a link or enter a password to continue the site map discovery process. In other words, you need to interact with the Web site itself to enable the site map discovery process to move forward.

To allow mapping of protected areas in a Web site, follow these steps:

1. On the drawing page, find the shape representing a link to the Web page that requires you to click a link or enter a password.

2. Right-click the link and choose Interactive Hyperlink Selection from the shortcut menu. The Interactive Discovery dialog box appears and loads the selected Web page.

3. Work with the Web page as needed and then click Close. The links you navigated to are added to your site map.

Working with the Web Site Map Memory Model

When you generate a Web site map, Visio creates a memory model that becomes an integral part of the site map drawing file. This memory model contains information about every Web element discovered and how they relate to each other. Through the use of this memory model, Visio is able to lay out the Web site map.

The List window and the Filter window show the contents of the memory model, as illustrated in Figure 22-3. These windows are part of the Web Site Map template, and list every element in the Web site map, whether or not those elements actually appear on the drawing. In fact, you can delete a shape from the drawing, but the element represented by that shape still remains in the List window and Filter window. You can easily add the element back into the drawing by dragging it from either of these windows onto a drawing page.

Expanded List window

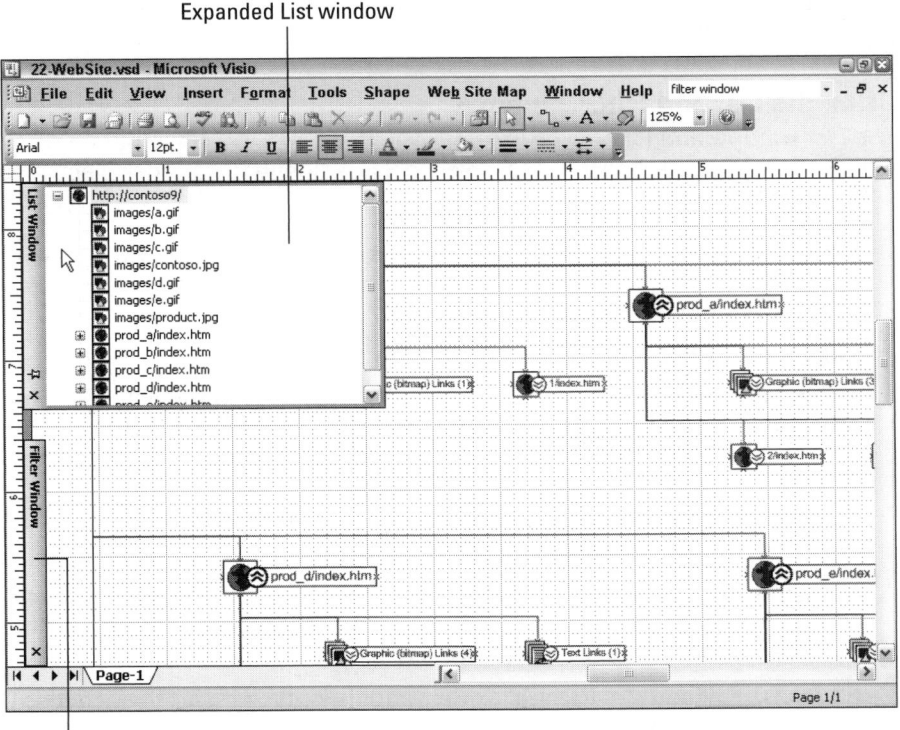

Collapsed Filter window

Figure 22-3: The List window and Filter window contain all elements in the memory model, which in turn builds the Web site map.

Using Web Site Maps Across Different Visio Versions

Although you can open a Web site map generated in Visio 2000, it's best to just regenerate the Web site map in Visio 2003. Previous versions do not contain the memory model. When you open those old Web site maps in Visio 2003, Visio creates a memory model based on the contents of the site map. However, if you open and save a 2003 Web site map in Visio 2000, the memory model is deleted.

However, if you delete an element from the List window or Filter window, the element is deleted from the windows as well as every shape representing that element on drawing pages.

Note   Remember that any changes you make to the Web site map and the memory model only affect the drawing itself. These changes do not update the actual Web site itself.

Using the List and Filter windows

The List window and Filter window appear in the Web Site Map template by default. The List window lists every Web page element in alphabetical order. The Filter window lists the Web page elements by file type.

- ✦ **Show the window** — Choose Web Site Map ➪ Windows ➪ List Window or Web Site Map ➪ Windows ➪ Filter Window. The windows appear as title bars in the left edge of the drawing.

- ✦ **Expand the window** — Click the window's title bar.

- ✦ **Collapse the window** — Click outside the expanded window. The window collapses as long as the window is in AutoHide mode. To turn AutoHide mode on or off, right-click the window's title bar and then choose AutoHide.

- ✦ **Float the window** — Right-click the anchored window's title bar and then choose Float Window. The title bar becomes the top edge of the window and you can drag it anywhere you want on your screen.

- ✦ **Anchor the window** — Right-click the floating window's title bar and choose Anchor Window. The title bar becomes the left edge of the window, which is docked at the left edge of the drawing.

- ✦ **Close the window** — Right-click the window's title bar and then choose Close.

Adding Shapes from the Memory Model

You can add any Web site elements cataloged in the List window or Filter window to the Web site map drawing. Even if you delete corresponding shapes from the drawing, they're still in the Web site map's memory model. To add an element listed in the memory model as a shape in the Web site map drawing, follow these steps:

1. Click the title bar of the List window or Filter window to expand the window.

2. Drag the element you want onto the drawing. The Web Site Map template redraws the site map to incorporate the new shape.

Deleting Elements from the Memory Model

If you delete a shape from the drawing, the element still exists in the memory model. However, if you delete an element from the memory model, it's completely removed from the Web site map. To delete an element shape from the memory model, follow these steps:

1. Click the title bar of the List window or Filter window to expand the window.

2. Right-click the Web site element and then choose Delete from the shortcut menu. Visio deletes the element from the window and from all drawing pages. Any child links off that element are deleted as well.

Comparing Map Versions

You can compare one version of a Web site map with another version. This can be useful when you want to discern the changes made to a Web site — since last month, for example. To compare a Web site map with another version of the same Web site, follow these steps:

1. Have the current Web site map open.

2. Choose Web Site Map ⇨ Compare to Previous Document. The File Open dialog box appears.

3. Navigate to the location of the earlier version of the Web site map you saved. Select the drawing and click Open. The Visio drawing you open must contain a Web site map. Visio compares the memory models of the two drawings and finds instances where a shape or link appears in only one of the models. For shapes or links that appear in both versions, Visio compares error status, file titles, file sizes, and file modification dates. Visio then generates an HTML file displaying the results.

Formatting Web Site Maps

To change the layout of your Web site map, you need to select the layout you want in the Web Site Map Settings dialog box and then generate the site map again. However, there are a few ways you can modify the look of the site map without having to regenerate the site map. You can switch between a hierarchical view and a page-centric view. You can move portions of the site map to other pages, with page connectors between them.

 **Tip** You can change the text displayed in site map shapes. To do so, choose Web Site Map ➭ Modify Shape Text. Select the option for the text you want to display as the title of the shape(s) and click OK.

Displaying Links to and from a Single Shape

By default, Visio displays your Web site map in the hierarchical view, which displays all the shapes in your Web site map in a top-down scheme according to the layout pattern you've chosen — for example, flowchart or circular. The hierarchical view provides a complete big picture of the Web site to the level of detail you have specified.

However, you can also create the page-centric view, which is shown in Figure 22-4. In the page-centric view, you select a single shape, which becomes the center of the page. Links to the shape appear above the central shape. Links from the shape appear below that shape. The page-centric view is great for focusing on the surrounding relationships of one particular element in a Web site.

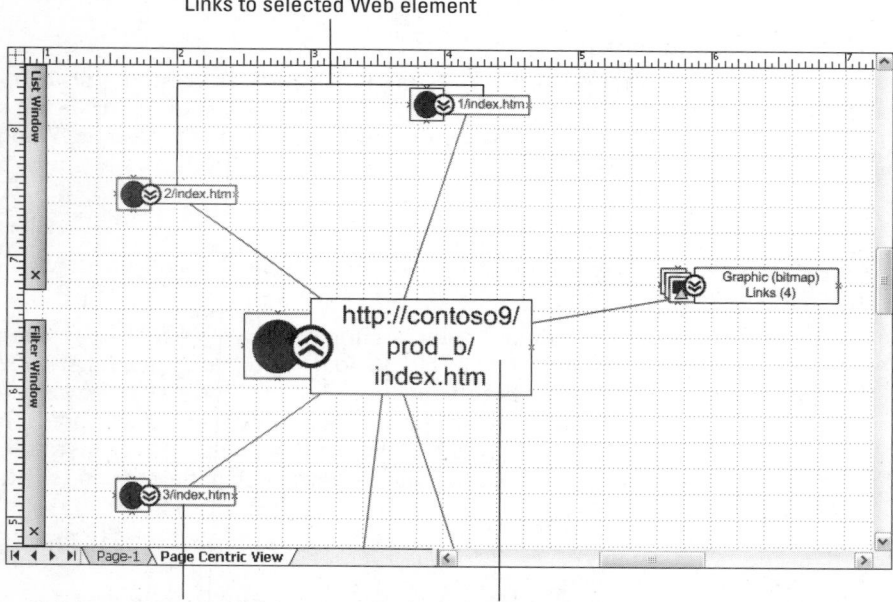

Figure 22-4: The page-centric view shows the links to and from a single selected shape.

To create the page-centric view from your hierarchical site map, choose Web Site Map ➭ View ➭ Page Centric. Visio adds only one page to the drawing file for the page-centric view. If you select another shape for the page-centric view, the new shape replaces the previous shape in the one page–centric viewing page.

Panning Duplicate Links to the Original

Many Web sites have duplicate links throughout the site or even on the same page. For example, a Web page might contain a link to contact information in the midst of a paragraph of content, in a navigation pane, and in a standard menu across the bottom of the page. Duplicate links are grayed out in your Web site map. If you would rather not show duplicate links in your Web site map, you can remove them by right-clicking the duplicate link and choosing Jump to Original from the shortcut menu.

Displaying Site Maps Across Multiple Pages

You might find it advantageous to divide your Web site map across additional pages. This can help you separate categories and help others understand the structure of the site map.

To move a selected portion of a site map onto a separate page, right-click the shape with the child links you want to move to a separate page and choose Make Subpage from the shortcut menu. The Make Subpage command creates a new page, moves the child links to the new page, and creates an Off-Page Connector shape on both pages.

To move between pages, double-click the Off-Page Connector shape. You can also right-click the Off-Page Connector shape and choose the name of the hyperlink from the shortcut menu.

Identifying Web Site Problems

Shapes in a Web site map drawing covered by a red X indicate a link or element that is either broken or that Visio could not discover. Finding these broken links can help you determine whether you have a problem with the Web site itself, or just with the process of generating the site map. Once you find the broken links, you can determine the reasons and then resolve the problems. You can also run reports that summarize problems with the Web site map.

Finding Broken Links

If you're a Webmaster responsible for maintaining a Web site, periodically generate the Web site map specifically to find broken links. You can then go straight to the problems in the Web site itself and, with a little luck, fix them before your users find them.

You can easily see broken links, either on the drawing page or in the List window or Filter window. If you see a broken link in one of the windows and you don't see the element in your drawing, right-click the link in the window and choose Show on Page from the shortcut menu.

Getting information about the broken link is your first step toward fixing the problem. Position your mouse pointer over the broken link on the drawing to show the shape tag button. Click that button and read the information it provides. Broken links can be caused by the following errors:

✦ File Not Found (incorrect file name, incorrect file location, or missing file)

✦ Site Not Found

✦ Access Denied

✦ Password Required

✦ Site Timed Out

Try these strategies to fix a broken link in your Web site map:

✦ **Check the Web address** — Make sure you entered every part of the address — from the protocol (`http://` or `ftp://`, for example) through to the page (`home.htm` or `default.asp`, for example), and that there are no typographical errors. If you entered a file path to an HTML file, make sure the path is typed accurately, and that the file is actually where you say it is.

✦ **Refresh the link** — If a broken link is caused by a timeout error, refreshing the link or the parent of the link should resolve the error. To do so, right-click the link and choose either Refresh or Refresh Parent.

✦ **Enter required information** — If a link connects to an area of the Web site that requires user entry, such as a password or a click, use the Interactive Discovery dialog box. To summon the dialog box, right-click the broken link and choose Interactive Hyperlink Selection from the shortcut menu. The Web page appears in the dialog box. Make the required entry and then click Close.

✦ **Fix the link on the Web site** — If the link is still displayed as broken, fix the link on your Web site or report the broken link to your Webmaster. After you fix the link, update the shape representing the link on your drawing. Right-click the link and then choose Refresh Parent. Visio regenerates the parent HTML or ASP page and the first level of links from that page.

Running Web Site Map Reports

You can generate reports of site links, including broken links. Visio provides three built-in reports. You can modify these reports to suit your requirements or create entirely new reports. To generate a Web site map report, follow these steps:

1. Choose Web Site Map ⇨ Reports. The Reports dialog box appears, listing the three built-in reports: Inventory, Web Site Map All Links, Web Site Map Links with Errors.

2. Select the report you want and then click Run.

3. In the Run Report dialog box, select the report format — for example, Excel or XML. Visio Shape is the default, which displays the report as a shape in the current drawing page.

4. Specify whether you want to save the report with a copy of the report definition or a link to the report definition and then click OK. Visio generates the report according to your specifications.

Summary

You can use the Web diagramming tools in Visio 2003 to assist with your Web site development and maintenance efforts. The Conceptual Web Site template provides resources for brainstorming, organizing, and prototyping a new Web site or application interface. The Web Site Map template includes sophisticated functionality for generating a Web site map, including all elements and links, and representing them as shapes in a drawing. You can then examine the map for broken links or other problems. You can also use the site map to help plan improvements to your Web site.

✦   ✦   ✦

Creating Network Diagrams

With people collaborating throughout organizations as well as over the Internet, computer networks have become the backbone of organizations large and small. Just like buildings and software, networks need to be designed well to satisfy requirements and adjust to changing needs. In addition, they must be regularly maintained to keep things humming. Whether you're just starting to design a network or you're trying to reverse engineer a network that has evolved, Visio network diagrams provide an easy way to represent the equipment in your network and how it interconnects.

With Visio Standard, you can create network diagrams using basic network equipment shapes. If you use Visio Professional, you can produce detailed logical or physical network diagrams, document directory services, or lay out network equipment in racks.

You can integrate your Visio network diagrams with other applications to store network information in databases, track equipment in spreadsheets, or present network designs in PowerPoint presentations. You can store network information in network shape custom properties, update your diagrams based on the information stored in a database, and produce reports, such as inventories for your network equipment.

This chapter explains the changes to network diagrams in Visio 2003. You'll learn how to create logical and physical network diagrams as well as diagrams that drill down to lower levels of detail. You will also learn how to use Visio templates to create directory services diagrams and diagrams that show the placement of equipment in racks. Finally, you will learn how to store information in network shapes as well as how to label, number, and color-code your diagrams.

Exploring Network Templates

Visio 2003 includes templates for producing several types of network diagrams. You can use Visio Network templates to document high-level network designs, detailed logical and physical network designs, and the arrangement of network equipment in equipment racks. In addition, you can use them as architecture-level artifacts and as an alternative to UML deployment diagrams. Network tools for Visio 2003 have changed quite a bit. Many network shapes look better and behave more consistently. However, several features are no longer available. The following sections outline the changes made to Visio 2003.

What's New in the Network Templates?

In Visio Standard and Visio Professional, the shapes in the Basic Network Diagram template have an enhanced look and feel that produces presentation-quality diagrams. In Visio Professional, the Detailed Network Diagram template replaces the Logical Network Diagram template in Visio 2002. You can use the Detailed Network Diagram to document logical and physical network topology.

The appearance of the shapes in these templates has been enhanced and their behavior is more consistent. In addition, network shapes include a consistent set of custom properties that you can use in conjunction with three new predefined reports (Network Device, Network Equipment, and PC Report) to extract data from your network diagrams.

New
Feature

The Rack Diagram template is new in Visio Professional and provides shapes in standard industry sizes that you can use to determine rack space requirements for new equipment. The shapes in this template fit together precisely so you can stack equipment and accurately estimate the rack space you need.

What's Missing?

Visio 2003 does not offer several networking features that were available in previous versions, including the following:

✦ Visio's AutoDiscovery features are no longer available.

✦ In Visio 2003, you can't use SNMP to discover the network resources in a local or wide area network and create a diagram of your existing network.

✦ You can't import directory services information, such as an existing Active Directory structure.

Using Visio with Large Networks

If you are designing or managing a large network with thousands of nodes, you can still use Visio Professional to produce high-level network diagrams. For example, you might produce diagrams that show all the routers on your network or the service providers that support your network in different geographical areas. However, you probably won't want to spend the time required to draw diagrams that show every end node.

When you manage large networks, you can use products such as HP OpenView Network Node Manager, MicroMuse Precision, or What's Up Gold to automatically generate maps of your network topology. Even with advanced discovery and mapping tools such as these, the maps they generate might require editing to represent your network the way you want.

✦ The Directory Services Diagram templates no longer include the Directory Navigator.

✦ The Visio Network Equipment Sampler is no longer available in Visio 2003. However, you can still download network shapes from equipment manufacturers' Web sites.

If you want to use Visio to map your network, you can check out third-party products, such as the Optiview Console (formerly Network Inspector) and LAN MapShot products from Fluke Networks, which use Visio to generate diagrams of discovered network devices. An article about Fluke Networks' network tools is available at the following URL:

```
http://www.microsoft.com/resources/casestudies/casestudy.asp?ca
sestudyid=11908
```

Choosing the Right Template

The Network templates available in Visio 2003 do not include network-specific menus, toolbars, or add-ons. When you create a new network diagram, Visio creates a letter-size page using portrait orientation and no drawing scale, and opens stencils appropriate for the type of network diagram. The Basic Network Diagram template is available in both Visio Standard and Visio Professional. The other templates are available only in Visio Professional. In Visio 2003, you can choose from the Network templates described in Table 23-1.

Table 23-1
Visio 2003 Network Templates

Network Template	Description	Associated Stencils
Basic Network Diagram	Design and document simple networks or produce presentation graphics for high-level networks.	• Backgrounds • Borders and Titles • Computers and Monitors • Network and Peripherals
Detailed Network Diagram	Design and document logical network connections or the layout and physical connections for network equipment at specific sites. Produce drill-down diagrams showing progressive levels of network detail.	• Annotations • Borders and Titles • Callouts • Computers and Monitors • Detailed Network Diagram • Network and Peripherals • Network Locations • Network Symbols • Servers
Active Directory	Design and document directory services for sites using Microsoft Active Directory.	• Active Directory Objects • Active Directory Sites and Services • Exchange Objects
LDAP Directory	Design and document directory services for sites using Lightweight Directory Access Protocol (LDAP.)	• LDAP Objects
Novell Directory Services	Design and document directory services for sites using Novell Directory Services.	• NDS Additional Objects • NDS GroupWise • NDS Objects • NDS Partitions • NDS ZenWorks
Rack Diagram	Optimize the use of space in equipment racks and document the configuration of equipment in racks.	• Annotations • Callouts • Free-standing Rack equipment • Network Room Elements • Rack-mounted Equipment

Creating Logical and Physical Network Diagrams

You can use standard Visio techniques to create network diagrams that show the logical or physical design of your network. You add network devices to diagrams by dragging and dropping the shapes you want from Network stencils. You can represent network topology by gluing the connectors on Ring Network or Ethernet shapes to connection points on shapes that represent network equipment. You can show additional information on your network diagrams by using text for labels or numbers, showing notes in annotation shapes, storing data in custom properties, or formatting shapes based on the values in shape properties.

Setting Up Network Diagrams

Although network diagrams might show different types of equipment and different levels of detail, you use the same techniques to construct them whether you use the Basic or Detailed Network Diagram templates. To create a network diagram to design or document a logical or physical network, choose File ➪ New ➪ Network and then choose either Basic Network Diagram (in Visio Standard and Visio Professional) or Detailed Network Diagram (in Visio Professional only).

Depending on the scope of your network or the detail you want to include, you can change the drawing size by choosing File ➪ Page Setup, selecting the Page Size tab, and specifying the page size you want. To change the page orientation, under Page Orientation, select the Portrait or Landscape option.

Cross-Reference

When you draw a wide area network (WAN), you can create a background for your network diagram by importing a map (see Chapters 9 and 28), inserting a graphic image (see Chapters 8 and 9), or dragging a shape from the Backgrounds stencil.

Adding Nodes and Network Topology

Whether you want to document a small network for a home-based business or a wide area network for a global corporation, you start by dragging topology shapes and equipment shapes onto the drawing page. Topology shapes, such as the Ethernet shape, have control handles that you drag and glue to the shapes that represent nodes and devices in your network.

New Feature   In previous versions of Visio, network shapes often detached from each other when you moved them. For example, if you glued servers to an Ethernet shape, and then moved the Ethernet shape, the connections to servers were lost. The updated network shapes in Visio 2003 remain attached no matter which shapes you move.

To add topology and nodes, follow these steps:

1. From the Network and Peripherals stencil, drag a Ring Network shape or Ethernet shape onto the drawing page.

Note   You can also use the Cloud shape on the Network Locations stencil to show high-level connectivity.

2. To change the length of an Ethernet shape or the size of a Ring Network shape, drag a selection handle to a new location.

3. From stencils such as Computers and Monitors, Network and Peripherals, or Detailed Network Diagram, drag shapes that represent network devices onto the drawing page.

4. Select a topology shape, such as an Ethernet shape. Visio displays yellow control handles that you can use to connect the shape to shapes that represent network devices. Drag a control handle and glue it to a connection point on a device shape. When the device shape is glued to the topology shape, its connection point turns red.

5. If you use all the connectors that appear on a topology shape by default, add additional connectors by dragging one of the control handles within the topology shape, as shown in Figure 23-1.

Tip   You can hide an unused connector by dragging its control handle back to the interior of the Ethernet or Ring Network shape.

6. To add text to a topology shape or device shape, select the shape, type the label you want, and press Esc. You can move text on device shapes by dragging the yellow control handle at the center of the text block.

Note   You can also show communication connections, such as satellite or microwave links, by gluing a Comm-Link shape, which looks like a lightning bolt, to shapes on a network diagram.

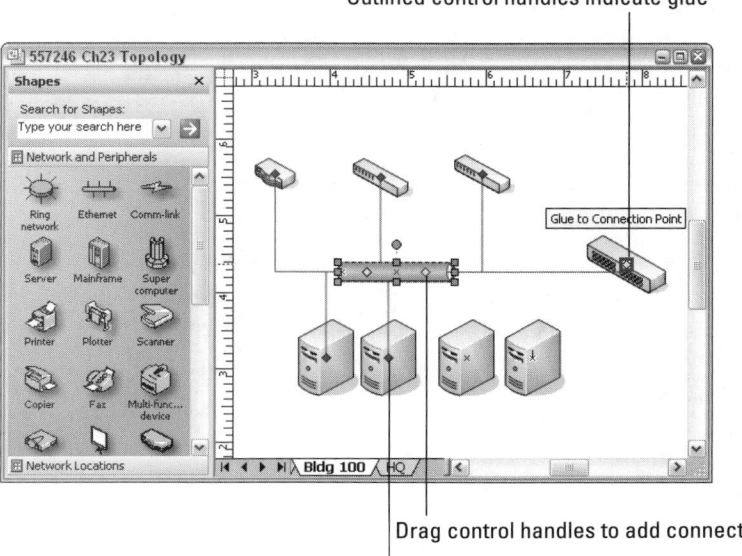

Outlined control handles indicate glue

Drag control handles to add connectors

Glued control handles are red

Figure 23-1: Add more connectors to a topology shape by dragging control handles.

Creating Drill-down Diagrams

When you want to document a large or complex network, you can create *drill-down diagrams* to show the high-level view of your network on one page, with detail on additional pages. For example, you can use Cloud and Building shapes from the Network Locations stencil to show the campus buildings that your network supports. Then, you can show the network equipment within each building on other drawing pages, as shown in Figure 23-2. If necessary, you can create additional drawing pages for details such as the network equipment within a computer room in one of the buildings. To use hyperlinks to create a drill-down diagram, follow these steps:

1. Draw a high-level view on the first drawing page in your Visio drawing file.

2. To create additional pages for detailed diagrams of your network, choose Insert ➪ New Page. Type the name of the network diagram for that drawing page and click OK.

Note   You can create detailed diagrams in the same file or in separate Visio drawing files. You can create the additional drawing files or pages all at once or create them as you realize they're needed.

Detail appears on other pages

Right-click a shape and choose the hyperlink to navigate to the detail page

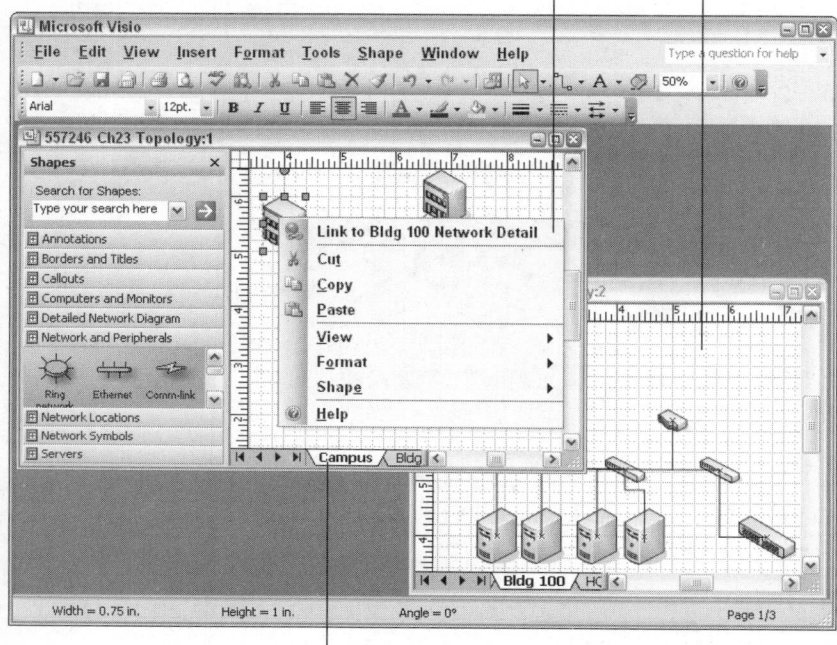

High-level information appears on a summary page

Figure 23-2: Drill-down diagrams show additional detail on other drawing pages.

3. Select a topology or device shape on the page that shows a higher-level view of your network. For example, select a Building shape on the campus view of your network.

4. Choose Insert ➪ Hyperlinks.

5. If your detailed diagram is in another Visio drawing file, click Browse in the Address box, and then click Local File. In the Link to File dialog box, navigate to the file with the detailed diagram and click Open.

6. To link to a specific drawing page, click Browse in the Sub-address box. In the Hyperlinks dialog box, select the drawing page in the Page drop-down list and then click OK.

7. In the Hyperlinks dialog box, type the text you want to use to identify the hyperlink in the Description box and click OK.

Note   When you position the pointer over a shape that includes a hyperlink, the Hyperlink icon appears, followed by the Hyperlink description you provided.

8. To navigate to the diagram associated with the hyperlink, right-click the shape and then choose the Hyperlink description from the shortcut menu.

Documenting Directory Services

Visio Professional provides templates for documenting directory services, whether you use Active Directory, LDAP Directory Services, or Novell Directory Services. You can develop directory services diagrams to design new directories, redesign existing directories, or plan the migration of your current network directory. You can also use Visio's Directory Services templates to plan network resources and set network policies.

Note   The Novell Directory Services template is available only in the English and French language versions of the product.

The procedure for creating directory services diagrams is the same no matter which type of directory service you want to document:

1. Choose File ➪ New ➪ Network and then choose the template for the type of directory services diagram you want to create. Visio creates a drawing file with one drawing page and opens the stencils associated with the Directory Services template you chose.

2. To add objects to the diagram, drag shapes from any of the Directory Services stencils onto the drawing page.

3. To create a parent-child relationship between directory services objects, click the Connector tool on the Standard toolbar, click the Directory connector in one of the stencils (such as LDAP Objects), and then, on the drawing page, drag from the shape that represents the parent object to the shape that represents the child object.

Showing Relationships in Active Directory Diagrams

You can use shapes on the Active Directory Sites and Services stencil to plan networks and directories or to show how information is distributed and replicated to servers in your network. The following shapes show relationships between network domains, sites, and services:

✦ **Site shapes** — Represent regions for network connectivity, whether by geography or function, and can show one or more LANs and their interconnections.

✦ **Domain shapes** — Define security and administrative boundaries in a network. These shapes exist within a site or sites and move along with the shape that represents a site. A domain might have one or more domain controllers. Sites can also have one or more domain controllers.

✦ **Site link shapes** — Represent the transport links that communicate information between sites. The Site-Link Bridge 3D shape delineates a set of site links joined to form a larger link or bridge.

✦ **Replication connection shape** — Represents intersite replication between two domain controllers.

Laying Out Equipment Racks

Rack diagrams are helpful as installation guides for the people installing equipment in racks. The shapes in the stencils for rack diagrams conform to industry-standard sizes, so they fit together precisely. Connection points are positioned on equipment shapes, so they snap to racks and other rack-mounted equipment. Rack-mounted equipment glues together so your rack configurations stay connected even when you move them.

When you create a rack diagram in Visio Professional, the following stencils open along with your new drawing:

✦ **Annotations** — Add labels, notes, and reference symbols to your rack layouts.

✦ **Callouts** — Add labels and notes to your rack layouts.

✦ **Free-standing Rack Equipment** — Include equipment that doesn't attach directly to racks, such as monitors, printers, and laptops.

✦ **Network Room Elements** — Include shapes for elevation views of doors, windows, chairs, and tables.

✦ **Rack-mounted Equipment** — This is useful for network equipment that attaches directly to racks, such as routers, switches, patch panels, shelves, and servers.

Tip   If you want to use the Rack shape in other types of Visio drawings, open the Rack-mounted Equipment stencil with another drawing open by choosing File ➪ Shapes ➪ Network ➪ Rack-mounted Equipment.

To create a rack diagram, follow these steps:

1. Choose File ➪ New ➪ Network ➪ Rack Diagram.

2. From the Rack-mounted Equipment stencil, drag the Rack shape or Cabinet shape onto the drawing page. The Rack shape has open sides, whereas the Cabinet shape has sides that enclose the equipment.

3. To change the height of the rack or cabinet, choose one of the following methods:
   - Select the Rack or Cabinet shape and then drag a selection handle at the top or bottom of the shape to a new location.
   - Right-click the shape, choose Properties from the shortcut menu, and type a new distance in the Height field in the Custom Properties window.

4. To change the width between rack holes, right-click the Rack or Cabinet shape, choose Properties from the shortcut menu, and select the width you want in the Width Between Holes field in the Custom Properties window.

5. To add equipment to a rack or cabinet, drag equipment shapes from the Rack-mounted Equipment stencil and glue them to the Rack or Cabinet shape. Connection points at the lower corners of the equipment shape glue to the connection points on the Rack or Cabinet shape, as shown in Figure 23-3, and turn red to indicate that they are glued.

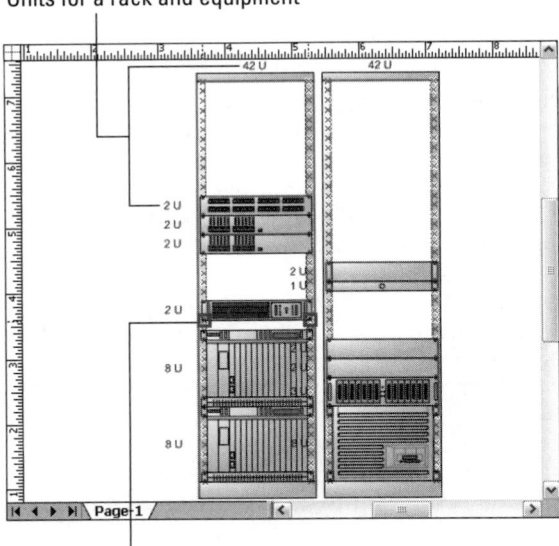

Figure 23-3: Equipment shapes glue to the connection points on Rack and Cabinet shapes.

Note The U height is the number of units a rack holds or a piece of equipment uses. By default, the U height appears above Rack and Cabinet shapes and to the left of Rack-mounted equipment shapes. To hide the U height, right-click a shape and choose Hide U Sizes from the shortcut menu. To show U height, right-click a shape and choose Show U Sizes.

Enhancing Network Diagrams

Many techniques that increase the usefulness of other types of Visio drawings work equally well on network drawings. You can use text-oriented techniques to label and annotate your network diagrams, as described in Chapter 6, and formatting techniques to change the graphic appearance of shapes on your diagrams, as described in Chapter 7. You can also store additional information in custom properties within network shapes, or link those custom properties to data in a database. With data stored in custom properties, you can generate reports about your network, add dynamic labels to network shapes on drawings, and color-code shapes based on the custom property values.

Storing Network Information in Visio Shapes

The shapes in the Visio 2003 network diagram templates include a consistent set of custom properties that you can use to store information about the network devices they represent. By adding data to the custom properties associated with network device shapes, you can view information about devices in the Custom Properties window or in predefined or customized reports.

New Feature In Visio 2003, the custom properties associated with shapes in the Network stencils are more consistent from shape to shape. Network equipment shapes provided by equipment manufacturers also include numerous custom properties, many of them identical to the ones that Visio provides. However, if the predefined properties aren't sufficient, you can modify Visio's network shapes to add your own properties, as described in Chapter 32.

Most network shapes include a handful of custom properties, such as Asset Number, Serial Number, and Building, that you can use to identify the device and its location. Network devices, such as Routers and Switches, include additional properties, such as IP Address and Number of Ports, to identify specific network information.

To add data to a shape within Visio, right-click the shape and choose Properties from the shortcut menu. In the Custom Properties window, click the cell next to the Property name and type the value you want to add. To move to the next property in the list, press Enter. You can also choose View ➪ Custom Properties Window to open the Custom Properties window. As you select shapes, you can view and edit their custom property values in the Custom Properties window.

Tip If you want to add the same value to a custom property for many shapes on a drawing, select all of the shapes first, open the Custom Properties window, and then type the value in the cell for the property.

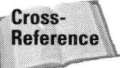

Cross-Reference To learn how to create dynamic links between custom properties and fields in a database, see Chapter 10.

Generating Equipment Reports

Visio 2003 includes several new predefined reports you can use to present information about your network. The Inventory report has been available in several previous versions of Visio. Network Device, Network Equipment, and the PC Report are new report definitions in Visio 2003. If these reports don't quite fit your needs, you can modify them or create your own.

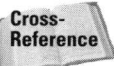

Cross-Reference To learn how to create or modify reports, see Chapter 32.

When the shapes on your diagram include data in their custom properties, you can generate reports by following these steps:

1. Choose Tools ➪ Reports.

2. In the Reports list, select the name of the report you want to use.

Tip If the report definition you want doesn't appear in the list, uncheck the Show Only Drawing-specific Reports check box. If the report still doesn't appear, click Browse, navigate to the folder that contains the report definition, select the report definition (.vrd) file, and click Open.

3. In the Reports dialog box, click Run.

4. In the Run Report dialog box, select the report format you want. You can create the report as an Excel spreadsheet, a Web page using HTML, a Visio shape, or an XML file.

Note Excel must be installed on your computer to create a report as an Excel spreadsheet or as a Visio shape. When you create a report as a Visio shape, Visio saves the report as an Excel spreadsheet embedded in a shape on the drawing page.

5. Perform one of the following steps based on the report format you choose:

- **HTML**—Specify the path and filename for the HTML file.

- **Visio shape**—If you want others to be able to see the report, save a copy of the report definition with the Visio shape by selecting the Copy of Report Definition option. Otherwise, Visio saves the report as part of your Visio installation and does not transmit it when you send the drawing to others.

- **XML**—Specify the path and filename for the XML file.

6. Click OK to generate the report. If you chose the Visio shape format, Visio adds the report shape to the current drawing page.

Labeling and Numbering Network Diagrams

Visio add-ons include two tools that are helpful for annotating your network diagrams: the Number Shapes add-on and the Label Shapes add-on.

The Number Shapes add-on can number shapes either in sequence as you add them to your diagram or after all the shapes are in place. By default, the add-on increments numbers from left to right and from top to bottom on the drawing, but you can specify the sequence order you want. To number network shapes in your diagram, choose Tools ➪ Add-Ons ➪ Visio Extras ➪ Number Shapes.

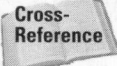
To learn how to use the Number Shapes add-on, refer to Chapter 4.

The Label Shapes add-on was originally developed for the Visio building plan templates, but works with any type of drawing in which shapes include custom properties. Using the Label Shapes add-on, you can specify which custom properties you want to display in four label text blocks that you can apply to shapes. You can label all shapes, selected shapes, or specific types of shapes on your diagram. You can also specify a data source from which to import data into the labels. To add labels to network shapes, choose Tools ➪ Add-Ons ➪ Building Plan ➪ Label Shapes.

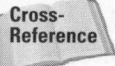
To learn how to use the Label Shapes add-on, refer to Chapter 26.

Color-Coding Network Diagrams

Network diagrams can contain a lot of information, much of which might be stored in custom properties associated with shapes. Displaying custom property values is one way to show information, but doing so can clutter your diagrams and make them harder to read. Another approach for showing information is color-coding shapes based on custom property values. For example, you can color-code equipment based on the LAN to which it belongs.

When Color Isn't Enough

Not everyone has access to a color printer and some people are color-blind, so you might want to use patterns instead of or in conjunction with colors. To assign a pattern when you use the Color By Values add-on, in the Color By Values dialog box, click the color that you want to change in the Colors list. In the Change Color dialog box, choose a pattern in the Pattern drop-down list. You can also choose a color for the pattern in the Pattern Color drop-down list.

If you use Dynamic connectors to show network connections, you can also use patterns in line formatting to designate different types of cables. For example, you might use dashed lines to indicate multi-mode fiber, dotted lines for gigabit Ethernet, and solid lines for Cat-5 cable. You can apply this formatting by choosing Format ➪ Line and selecting a line pattern. If these connection types are used throughout your organization, you might want to build a custom stencil with multiple versions of the Dynamic connector predefined with the patterns you want.

The Color by Values add-on is another tool originally targeted for building plans that you can use on other types of Visio drawings, including network diagrams. In the Color by Value add-on, you can specify the custom property whose values control the color-coding and the shapes you want to color-code. You can color-code all shapes, selected shapes, or specific types of shapes on your diagram. If the custom property includes a set of unique values, you can assign a color to each value. For custom properties that can cover a range of numbers, you can assign a color to a range of values. After you color-code shapes, the add-on places a legend on the drawing page. You can change colors and patterns in the diagram by right-clicking the Legend shape and then choosing Edit Legend from the shortcut menu. To color-code network shapes, choose Tools ➪ Add-Ons ➪ Building Plan ➪ Color By Values.

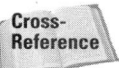

Cross-Reference

To learn how to use the Label Shapes add-on, see Chapter 26.

Summary

The tools in the network templates have changed a great deal with the release of Visio 2003. The Visio Network Equipment Sampler, AutoDiscovery, and the Directory Navigator have all been discontinued. Although the Network templates are now primarily drag and drop tools, the shapes have been enhanced so they look better, connect consistently, and behave more reliably. In Visio Standard, you can create basic network diagrams. With Visio Professional, you can create basic and detailed network diagrams for logical and physical networks, directory services diagrams, and rack layouts. In addition to dragging, dropping, and connecting network shapes, you can use custom properties to label, color-code, and report on the devices in your network.

✦   ✦   ✦

Using Visio for Architecture and Engineering

Working with Scaled Drawings

If you've ever experimented with a new office layout by moving your office furniture around, you understand the value of scaled drawings. You can design real-world objects on paper before beginning construction, and you can work on your plan at a size that fits on a piece of paper. By scaling real-world objects up or down, you can work on them at a manageable size, manipulate them into the results you want, and easily share them with colleagues. In addition, you can draw real-world objects at different scales depending on the level of detail you want to show; for example, you could show either the layout of a floor or the connection details between a steel column and a floor joist.

When you work on technical drawings such as architectural plans, accuracy is essential. To ensure that components such as structural steel or modular furniture fit together when assembled in the field, you must draw them accurately and position them precisely.

Although Visio isn't meant to replace a computer-aided design (CAD) application, you can use it to draw detailed plans that are both precise and accurate. Visio includes shapes that are designed to work on scaled drawings and adjust to the scale you're using. In addition, many architectural and engineering shapes include behaviors that help you lay out components on your plans. In this chapter, you'll learn which Visio templates produce scaled drawings, how to use scale and units to your advantage, and how to indicate dimensions on your scaled drawings.

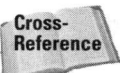
Cross-Reference

To learn about methods for positioning shapes precisely, see Chapter 4.

Exploring Scaled Drawing Templates

Visio 2003 provides several drawing templates that are designed to produce scaled drawings. Visio automatically sets the units and drawing scale to those common for the type of drawing. Scaled shapes on the associated stencils resize to the scale of the drawing as long as the drawing and shapes scales aren't too disparate. However, if these templates don't suit your needs, you can specify the drawing scale for any drawing and create shapes to work at that scale.

Choosing the Right Scaled Drawing Template

If you use Visio Standard, the Office Layout template works not only for office layouts but for scaled building plans as well. In fact, it's your only choice because the Office Layout template is the only Visio Standard template with shapes for walls. With Visio Professional, you can choose Building Plan templates suited to the type of plan you want to create. Although the Office Layout template is available, the Floor Plan template is better because it creates a standard architectural size page and opens stencils with more shapes for walls, doors, windows, and other common building components. Most of the Building Plan templates use an architectural page size of 36 inches by 24 inches and a drawing scale of ¼" = 1' or an A4 page using a drawing scale of 1:50 and millimeters for metric units. In addition, in the Mechanical Engineering category, the Parts and Assembly template uses mechanical engineering page size and scale. Table 24-1 includes the templates available for scaled drawings.

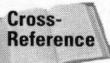 **Cross-Reference**   For a complete list of the stencils that open with templates, see Chapter 41.

Table 24-1 Scaled Drawings Templates			
Template	*Default U.S. Page Size*	*Default U.S. Drawing Scale*	*Metric Page Size and Scale*
Office Layout (Visio Standard and Professional)	Letter Landscape	Architectural ½" = 1' 0"	A4 at 1:25
Electric and Telecom Plan (Professional only)	ANSI Architectural 36" × 24"	Architectural ¼" = 1' 0"	A4 at 1:50
Floor Plan (Professional only)	ANSI Architectural 36" × 24"	Architectural ¼" = 1' 0"	A4 at 1:50

Template	Default U.S. Page Size	Default U.S. Drawing Scale	Metric Page Size and Scale
Home Plan (Professional only)	ANSI Architectural 36" × 24"	Architectural ¼" = 1' 0"	A4 at 1:50
HVAC Control Logic Diagram Plan (Professional only)	ANSI Architectural 36" × 24"	No scale (one to one)	A4 and no scale
HVAC Plan (Professional only)	ANSI Architectural 36" × 24"	Architectural ¼" = 1' 0"	A4 at 1:50
Plant Layout Plan (Professional only)	ANSI Architectural 36" × 24"	Architectural ¼" = 1' 0"	A4 at 1:50
Plumbing and Piping Plan (Professional only)	ANSI Architectural 36" × 24"	Architectural ¼" = 1' 0"	A4 at 1:50
Reflected Ceiling Plan (Professional only)	ANSI Architectural 36" × 24"	Architectural ¼" = 1' 0"	A4 at 1:50
Security and Access Plan (Professional only)	ANSI Architectural 36" × 24"	Architectural ¼" = 1' 0"	A4 at 1:50
Site Plan (Professional only)	ANSI Architectural 36" × 24"	Civil Engineering 1" = 10' 0"	A4 at 1:200
Space Plan (Professional only)	Letter Landscape	Architectural ⅛" = 1' 0"	A4 at 1:100
Parts and Assembly (Professional only Mechanical Engineering category)	ANSI Engineering B:17" × 11"	Mechanical Engineering ¼:1	A4 at 1:10

Working with U.S. and Metric Templates

Visio templates are available in both U.S. and metric units. When you install the English language version of Visio, the installation procedure checks the settings on your computer and installs the templates that match. If you use both types of units in your work, you can install both sets of templates on your computer. With both sets of templates installed, you can choose which type of template you want to use when you create a new drawing.

To install both sets of templates after Visio is already installed, follow these steps:

1. If Visio is running, save your work and then choose File ➪ Exit.

2. Click the Start button and choose Settings ➪ Control Panel ➪ Add or Remove Programs.

3. In the Currently Installed Programs list, select Microsoft Office Visio and then click Change.

4. On the first wizard page, select the Add or Remove Features option and then click Next.

5. In the Advanced Customization box, click the plus sign next to Microsoft Office Visio. For each category of template that you want to install that is preceded by a red X, including Solutions (US units), Solutions (Metric units), Add-ons (US units), and Add-ons (Metric units), click the arrow to the right of the red X and then choose Run from My Computer from the shortcut menu.

6. Click Update.

After you have both U.S. and metric unit templates installed, when you create a new drawing Visio displays two options for each built-in template. When you choose File ➪ New and point to the template category, you'll see one template with (US units) after the template name (Visio doesn't use the periods for U.S.), and the other followed by (Metric). When you select the template that uses the units you want, Visio sets up the drawing with the appropriate measurement units and drawing scale.

Caution   When you work with both types of templates and open a stencil after starting a drawing, make sure you open the version of the stencil whose units match the template you're working with. Mixing U.S. units and metric units in the same drawing can cause shapes to align improperly.

Working with Scale and Units

When you use templates for scaled drawings, Visio automatically sets up your drawing with appropriate units and scale to show real-world objects at a manageable yet accurate size. As you add shapes associated with scaled drawing stencils to the drawing page, the shapes resize to match the drawing scale you're using. In addition, as you modify or reposition shapes, the dynamic grid, rulers, and other Visio drawing aids help you place shapes precisely, based on the current units and scale. When you glue dimensioning shapes to shapes on a scaled drawing, the distances shown are based on the units and drawing scale. If Visio doesn't set up the drawing page with the units and scale that you want, you can choose the units and drawing scale you want to work with.

Working with Scale

A drawing scale represents how a distance on a piece of paper corresponds to a distance in the real world. Whether you use architectural or engineering formats, you can choose the scale that makes your drawing readable on the drawing page. For example, the typical U.S. architectural scale of ¼" = 1' 0" means that ¼ inch on a piece of paper is the equivalent of one foot in the real world, which is useful for most building plans. However, you might use ⅛" = 1' 0" for a large building. Conversely, you might use a scale of 1" = 1' 0" to show welds and connection details for a steel column. For site plans that show the configuration of buildings, roads, parking lots, and more, you might use 1" = 10' 0".

Note   Sometimes, scales show only the ratio between paper size and real-world size. For example, the metric scale of ⅛:1 means that the drawing on paper is one eighth of actual size. In Visio, metric scales are represented as ratios, such as 1:50, which indicates that one meter on paper represents 50 meters actual size.

The smaller the drawing scale, the more you can show on the same size piece of paper. Table 24-2 shows the real-world distances you can show on a 36" × 24" architectural page at different scales.

Caution   Because the drawing scale you choose affects the size at which a shape appears on the drawing page, you should set the drawing scale before you add shapes to the drawing page. In addition, if you change the drawing scale after you've added shapes to the page, they might not resize properly. For example, the text blocks in title block shapes might not fit properly in their designated boxes.

Table 24-2
Distances You Can Represent on Scaled Drawings

Drawing Scale	*Real-world Dimensions*
1" = 10' 0"	360 feet × 240 feet
⅛" = 1' 0"	288 feet × 192 feet
¼" = 1' 0"	144 feet × 96 feet
1" = 1' 0"	36 feet × 24 feet
1:50	45.72 meters × 30.48 meters

The shapes on the stencils that open when you use a scaled template are designed to work with scaled drawings. When you drag one of these shapes onto a scaled drawing page, the shape resizes to match the drawing scale, as shown in Figure 24-1.

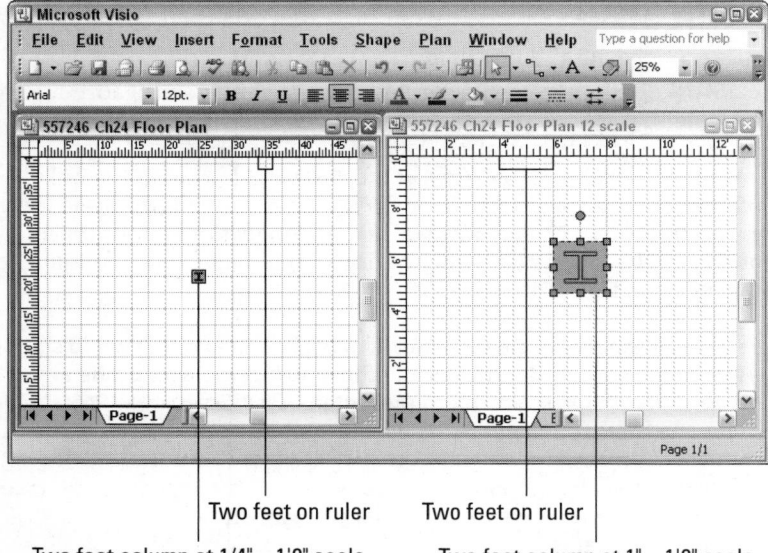

Two feet on ruler   Two feet on ruler

Two foot column at 1/4" = 1'0" scale   Two foot column at 1" = 1'0" scale

Figure 24-1: Scaled shapes resize to match the scale of your drawing.

Note

A shape won't resize if its scale is more than eight times larger or smaller than the scale of the drawing page. If shapes don't resize, make sure that you are using scaled shapes from stencils designed to work with the type of drawing you're using. Visio compares the scale of the drawing on which the master resides to the scale of the drawing on which you drop shapes. You can create masters that work at a specific scale by setting the scale on your master drawing before you create the master shapes.

Setting Drawing Scale

Each drawing page in a drawing file can use a different drawing scale. This is handy when you want to show the layout of a floor on one page but need a larger scale drawing of a construction detail on another page. To specify the drawing scale for a drawing page, follow these steps:

1. Display the page whose drawing scale you want to set.

2. Choose File ➪ Page Setup and select the Drawing Scale tab.

3. To specify one of the scales predefined in Visio, select the Pre-defined scale option and select one of the following types of predefined scales:

- **Architectural** — Relates a number of inches or a fraction of an inch on paper to one foot in the real world

- **Civil Engineering** — Relates one inch on paper to a number of feet in the real world

- **Metric** — Relates meters on paper to a number of meters in the real world

- **Mechanical Engineering** — Relates a fraction of a unit to one unit in the real world in order to scale objects down to fit on the page. Relates multiple units on paper to one unit in the real world in order to scale objects up so they're legible on paper.

Note You can also create your own drawing scale by selecting the Custom Scale option and specifying the paper distance and its corresponding real-world distance.

4. Choose the predefined scale you want in the Scale drop-down list. The values in the Page Size boxes change to indicate how many measurement units fit on the page at the scale you've selected.

5. Click Apply to save the drawing scale with the drawing page. Although the shapes on the drawing resize to match the new drawing scale, and the distances shown in the rulers adjust to the new scale, the real-world dimensions of the shapes on the drawing page remain the same.

6. If you use background pages with your scaled drawings, display the background page and then repeat steps 2 through 4 to apply the same drawing scale to it.

Showing Scale on Drawings

When you work with scaled drawings, it's a good idea to indicate the drawing scale somewhere on the drawing page. In that way, anyone viewing a hard copy of the drawing knows what the scale is and can measure objects on it correctly. Visio provides several shapes that automatically display the drawing scale for you. Table 24-3 lists some of the shapes you can use to show drawing scale. To use one of these shapes, simply open the stencil on which the master is located and drag it onto the drawing page. By default, each shape shows the drawing scale differently, as outlined in Table 24-3 and shown in Figure 24-2. However, if you use the Drawing Scale shape from the Annotations stencil, you can change the scale type by right-clicking the shape and then choosing one of the scale styles from the shortcut menu.

Table 24-3 Shapes That Show Drawing Scale		
Shapes	**Stencil**	**Scale Style**
Drawing Scale	Annotations	Mechanical Engineering $\frac{1}{48}$:1
Scale Symbol	Annotations	Graphical display of scaled distances
Scale	Title Blocks	Decimal format 1:48
Title Block Large	Title Blocks	Maintains drawing scale format specified
Title Block Small	Title Blocks	Maintains drawing scale format specified

Title Block shape uses the format for selected scale

Format for Scale shape is fixed

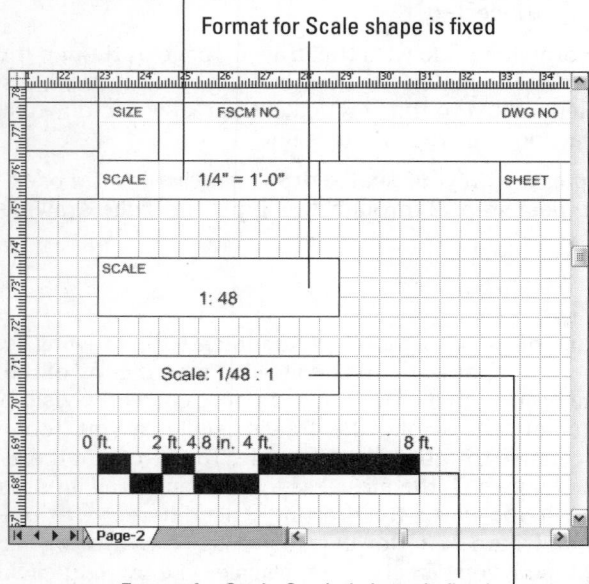

Format for Scale Symbol shape is fixed

Right-click Drawing Scale shape to change format

Figure 24-2: Shapes that automatically display drawing scale use different scale formats.

Specifying Measurement Units

When you work with scaled drawings, two types of units are important: page units and measurement units. Page units represent the distances or units on the printer page or piece of paper you print. Measurement units represent real-world distances or the units for the actual sizes of the objects you're drawing. For example, in the architectural scale of ¼" = 1', the page units are inches and the measurement units are feet.

If you use one of Visio's scaled drawing templates, Visio automatically sets both the drawing scale and measurement units for you. If you use both types of scaled templates, you can specify the units you want by choosing a U.S. units template or a Metric template when you create a new drawing. In addition, because drawing scales specify the relationship between page distances and real-world distances, Visio sets the measurement units and page units for you when you choose a drawing scale.

Setting Default Units

If you don't use Visio's templates to create scaled drawings or you use shapes you've created yourself, you can specify the units you want to use. To specify either U.S. or metric units, choose Tools ➪ Options and select the Units tab. Under Default Units, check the Always Offer 'Metric' and 'US Units' for New Blank Drawings and Stencils check box. If you want to change the units for the current page, click Change and then choose the new units in the Measurement Units drop-down list.

Tip   The list of measurement units includes units such as days and weeks. You can choose these units if you want to produce schedules in which one inch represents one week or some other length of time.

Specifying Measurement Units for a Page

You can set or change the measurement units for a drawing page. For example, you can specify whether the rulers and drawing grid use inches, meters, or even miles. In addition, when you want to make sure that the plan you're drawing fits on the page, you can specify the page size in measurements units. For example, if you want to draw a building that is 60 feet long and 30 feet wide, you can set your drawing page to 70 feet by 40 feet in measurement units. To specify measurement units, use one of the following methods:

   ✦ **Specify measurement units** — Choose File ➪ Page Setup and select the Page Properties tab. Choose the units you want from the Measurement Units drop-down list and then click Apply. Visio changes the distances you see on the rulers and adjusts the grid to match the new units.

✦ **Specify the page size in measurement units**—Choose File ↪ Page Setup and select the Drawing Scale tab. In the Page Size (In Measurement Units) boxes, type the distances you want to represent on the page. For example, to create a page that represents 70 feet by 40 feet, type **70 ft.** in the first box and type **40 ft.** in the second box. Click Apply to change the page size. Visio shows the size of the drawing page and the printer paper in the preview pane, as shown in Figure 24-3.

Preview of drawing page versus printer paper

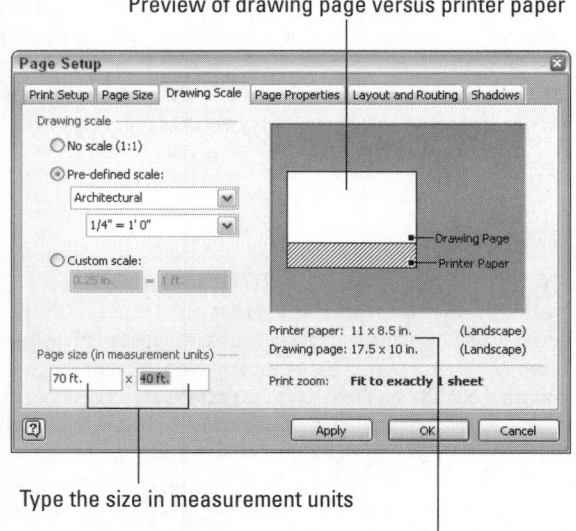

Type the size in measurement units

Printer paper and drawing page in page unit

Figure 24-3: You can set the page size so your plan fits.

Dimensioning Scaled Drawings

Measuring a hard copy of a scaled drawing to determine the sizes of scaled objects isn't always possible. Only the most hard-core architects and engineers walk around with scales in their pockets. Typically, scaled drawings include dimensions to show sizes, offsets, and distances from reference points. Visio Professional provides stencils with shapes you can use to dimension linear, radial, and angular distances.

In Visio Standard, the Room Measurement shape and the Controller Dimension shape on the Walls, Doors, and Windows stencil are the only way you can add dimensions to a scaled drawing.

Visio Professional provides two stencils with shapes specifically designed to glue to scaled shapes and show their dimensions. Although the shapes on each of these stencils share the same names and work the same way, they display dimensions in different formats. Depending on the type of drawing you are creating, you can open a dimensioning stencil by choosing File ➪ Shapes ➪ Visio Extras and then choosing either of the following stencils:

✦ **Dimensioning–Architectural** — For linear dimensions, architectural dimension shapes display the dimension value above the dimension line and use slashes at the ends of the dimension line.

✦ **Dimensioning–Engineering** — For linear dimensions, engineering dimension shapes display the dimension value in the middle of the dimension line and use arrowheads at the ends of the dimension line.

Adding Dimensions

Some scaled shapes, such as Room and Wall shapes, display dimensions automatically when you select them. However, to annotate your drawings so that dimensions appear whether shapes are selected or not, you can use dimension shapes. Although the Dimensioning stencils include numerous dimension shapes, they all behave similarly. You drag a dimension shape onto the drawing page and glue its dimension lines to the shapes you want to measure. The dimension shape displays the dimension and recalculates the dimension automatically when you resize the shape.

Dimension shapes include control handles you drag to define the distance to measure as well as the location of the dimension lines. The control handles that appear depend on the dimension shape you choose. For example, you can add linear dimensions from a vertical baseline by following these steps:

1. Drag the Horizontal Baseline shape onto the page and position it at the bottom and to the left of the distances you want to dimension.

2. Drag the lower green end point and glue it to a geometry point that defines the baseline for all your dimensions, such as the corner of an exterior wall.

3. Drag the other green end point and glue it to a geometry point that defines the end of the first distance you want to dimension, such as the lower edge of a window.

4. To reposition the text and vertical dimension line for the first dimension, drag the yellow control handle on the first dimension line to the left or right.

5. To define the next dimension, drag the yellow control handle between the dimension shape's selection handles to a position above the first dimension. Another yellow control handle appears at the end of the horizontal reference line. Drag this control handle and glue it to a point that defines the second distance you want to dimension, as illustrated in Figure 24-4.

Define dimension and position of extension line

Reposition first dimension to left or right | Refine dimension

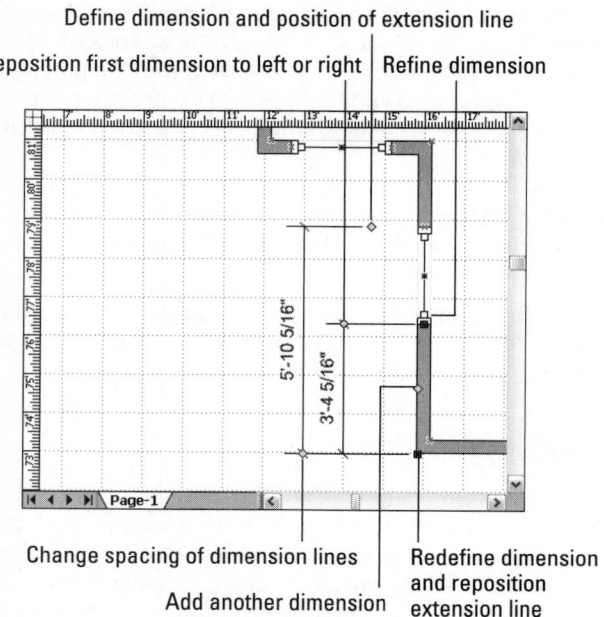

Change spacing of dimension lines | Redefine dimension and reposition extension line

Add another dimension

Figure 24-4: Drag control handles to define multiple dimensions.

6. Repeat step 3 until you have added the dimensions you want.

7. To change the spacing between the vertical dimension lines, drag the yellow control handle at the bottom of the dimension shape to the left or right.

8. To change a dimension, drag a control handle or selection handle at the end of the horizontal reference lines up or down.

Shapes for dimensioning angles include selection and control handles you can drag to configure the angular dimension. For example, you can dimension a radius with the Radius shape by following these steps:

1. Drag the Radius shape onto the drawing and glue it to a point at the center of the radius you want to dimension.

2. Drag the yellow control handle onto the arc you want to dimension.

3. To position the radial dimension text, drag the green selection handle to a new location.

Tip

To find out what a control handle does, position the pointer over the control handle to display a screen tip.

For example, you can dimension an angle by following these steps:

1. Drag the Angle Even shape onto the drawing page and glue it to the origin of the angle you want to dimension.

2. To change the lower edge of the angular dimension, drag the selection handle on the Angle Even shape to a new location.

3. To change the top edge of the angular dimension, drag the yellow control handle at the top of the Angle Even shape to a new location, as shown in Figure 24-5.

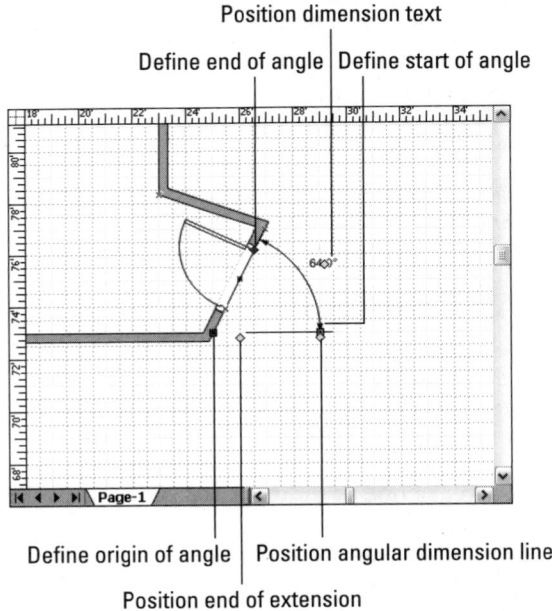

Figure 24-5: Drag control handles to define an angular dimension.

Note
You can also drag control handles on any of the Angle shapes to change the length of the extension line, the position of the angular dimension line, and the position of the dimension text.

Specifying Precision and Units for Dimensions

The dimensions that you add to a drawing show distances based on the measurement units you've chosen for that drawing page. However, you can specify precision and units for a dimension that differ from the ones that apply to the drawing page. To change precision and units for a dimension, follow these steps:

1. Right-click a dimension shape, such as Vertical, Radius Outside, or Angle Center, and choose Precision & Units from the shortcut menu. The Custom Properties window appears.

2. To specify the number of decimal points of precision for the dimension shape, select an entry from the Precision drop-down list.

3. To specify the units you want to use, select an entry from the Units drop-down list.

4. In the Units Display list, select an entry to specify whether or not to show the units.

5. To change the angle of the dimension, type an angle in the Angle box.

6. Click OK.

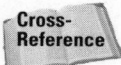 You can also show a shape's dimensions by inserting a geometry field in the shape's text block. To learn how to do this, see Chapter 32.

Calculating Area and Perimeter

Visio Professional also includes tools you can use to automatically measure the area and perimeter of any closed shape. For example, you can calculate the area within the floor of a building to determine the number of sprinkler heads you need for fire protection, or the perimeter of a parking lot to order fencing.

To measure the area and perimeter of one or more shapes, choose Tools ➪ Add-Ons ➪ Visio Extras ➪ Shape Area and Perimeter. The Shape Area and Perimeter dialog box opens, displaying the area in square inches and the perimeter in inches by default. You can keep the Shape Area and Perimeter dialog box open as you issue other commands. If no shapes are selected, the Total Area and Total Perimeter boxes display the words "No Selection." As you select shapes, their area and perimeter values appear in the boxes.

If you select more than one shape, the Total Area and Total Perimeter values reflect the values of all the individual shapes combined. For example, to measure the square footage of several separate rooms, Shift+click each room shape. The Shape Area and Perimeter values reflect the total area and total perimeter of all the rooms combined.

To calculate the area and perimeter of the boundary for several shapes, such as the footprint of a building, use the Pencil or Line tool to trace the boundary you want to measure. To calculate the area and perimeter of the boundary, select the boundary you drew.

Measuring Areas with Holes

In many situations, you want to calculate the area for a space but want to ignore some space within it. Suppose you want to calculate the area of a space with a hole in it. For example, to calculate the rentable space within a building floor, you might want to calculate the area of the building boundary without the area for the building core, which contains stairs and elevators. You can use a Visio shape operation to help perform this calculation for you by following these steps:

1. Click the Line tool or Pencil tool on the Drawing toolbar.

2. Draw a shape around the building perimeter and then draw another shape around the building core.

3. With no other shapes selected, Shift+click the two shapes you just drew and then choose Shape ⇨ Operations ⇨ Combine. The Combine command creates a hole in the floor using the shape you drew around the building core.

4. Select the combined shape and choose Tools ⇨ Add-Ons ⇨ Visio Extras ⇨ Area Shape and Perimeter. The Total Area and Total Perimeter represent the values for the entire floor minus the values for the hole.

Summary

Scaled drawings make it easy to communicate plans in which accuracy and precision are important. In Visio, you can specify drawing scales and measurement units so your plan fits on the drawing page. Visio includes shapes designed to work with scaled drawings. These shapes resize based on the scale you've set for the drawing page. Each drawing page can use a difference drawing scale and measurement unit, so you can show a site plan on one drawing page, a floor plan on another, and a detail of a structural connection on yet another page.

Because accuracy is important, you can add dimensions to your scaled drawings to show the real-world sizes of the objects. Visio provides two stencils for dimensions, which display dimensions in either architectural or engineering formats. Dimension shapes include control handles and selection handles you can drag to define and configure dimensions.

✦　　✦　　✦

Creating Scaled Plan Drawings

Although Visio isn't meant to replace or compete with CAD programs, there are plenty of reasons to use Visio as a complement to a CAD program. Visio building plan templates are ideal for fast prototyping. You can drag and drop Visio shapes to quickly experiment with different layouts. When you're ready to produce CAD drawings, you can export your Visio shapes into your CAD application. Visio is also a good choice when you want to enhance drawings created in other applications for presentations. You can insert CAD drawings into Visio drawings and use Visio tools to add presentation details.

For folks who don't have access to a CAD program, Visio is an adequate substitute for reviewing CAD drawings or for producing smaller plan drawings from scratch. Visio Professional stencils offer numerous shapes for a variety of building plans. Displaying CAD drawings as backgrounds in Visio is a great way to jumpstart new plans.

Like CAD programs, Visio provides the capability to organize the contents of plans by using layers. Although Visio layers differ from their CAD cousins, you can use layers to control shape behavior, such as whether shapes are visible on the screen or when printed or whether they are editable or not. Each shape can belong to multiple layers so that you can manage shapes to suit your needs. By assigning masters to layers, you can ensure that Visio automatically assigns the shapes to the proper layers as you drag them onto your drawings. In addition, when you drop shapes with layer assignments onto a page, Visio automatically creates that layer for the page.

This chapter shows you how to create plan drawings by using Visio plan templates, either by starting with an existing CAD drawing or by using an existing Visio plan drawing. You will also learn the ways in which you can use layers to control the behavior of shapes, and how to make the assignment of shapes to layers as easy as possible.

Creating Plan Drawings

Every once in a while, you do have to create a scaled plan drawing from scratch, but more often than not, there's a floor plan kicking around that you can use to get started. For example, you might have a CAD drawing of a basic floor plan that you want to use as a reference as you try out different furniture layouts. You might also want to use Visio to review and add comments to a CAD drawing produced by someone else. In these cases, you can insert CAD drawings into Visio drawings and use them as backgrounds onto which you drag and drop Visio shapes.

Conversely, if you have a Visio drawing with some of the information you want, such as a building shell and core, you can use that as a basis for additional plans, such as electrical, telecom or HVAC plans. With Visio plan drawings, you can copy and paste just the shapes you want or the entire drawing into a new plan drawing. If you paste the existing Visio floor plan onto a background page, you can display it in every foreground page you create. If you want to make sure that your underlying floor plan doesn't change, you can lock its layers so that the shapes on them can't be edited.

Setting Up Plan Drawings

Whether you're going to create a plan drawing from scratch or want to set up a Visio drawing file to hold an existing plan, follow these steps to prepare your Visio drawing file:

1. Choose File ➪ New ➪ Building Plan and then choose the template you want to use.

2. To make changes to the default drawing scale or units, choose File ➪ Page Setup, and use one or more of the following methods:

   - **Change the drawing scale** — To use a different drawing scale — for instance, to match the scale of an underlying CAD drawing — select the Drawing Scale tab, select the Pre-defined Scale option, and select the type of scale and the specific scale you want to use from the drop-down lists.

   - **Change the page size** — To adjust the page size to match the contents of a CAD or Visio plan drawing, select the Page Size tab, select the Pre-defined Size option, and select the type of page size and the specific page size you want from the drop-down lists.

   - **Change the printer paper size** — To change the size of the printer paper, select the Print Setup tab and select the paper size you want in the Printer Paper drop-down list.

Note   The Printer Paper list includes paper sizes for the current printer. If you want to print to a different printer or plotter, choose File ➪ Print and then select the printer or plotter you want to use. Then, click Close in the Print dialog box and reopen the Page Setup dialog box to select a paper size for the new printer.

Using Existing CAD Floor Plans

If you have an existing CAD drawing, you can insert it into a Visio drawing file by following these steps:

1. Open the Visio drawing page into which you want to insert the CAD drawing.

2. Choose Insert ➪ CAD Drawing. By default, Visio sets the entry in the Files of Type box to AutoCAD Drawing (*.dwg, *.dxf).

3. Navigate to the folder with the CAD drawing you want to use, select the CAD file, and click Open. Visio opens the CAD Drawing Properties dialog box, populated with CAD drawing units and a custom drawing scale that fits the drawing to the page. In addition, Visio checks the Lock Size and Position check box, Lock Against Deletion, and View Extents check boxes by default so that the CAD drawing can't be moved, resized, or deleted in Visio.

4. Click OK to insert the CAD drawing on the Visio drawing page.

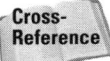

Cross-Reference To learn more about options and methods for importing CAD drawings into Visio, see Chapter 28.

5. If you want to use the inserted CAD drawing as a background for Visio drawing pages, choose File ➪ Page Setup and then select the Page Properties tab. Select the Background option, type the name you want for the background page, and click OK.

Using Existing Visio Plan Drawings

Sometimes, several plans share information, such as the basic building shell for multiple building service plans or the same basic floor plan elements for several floors in a high-rise building. If you already have these shared elements in a Visio drawing, you can copy and paste them into other Visio drawing pages so you can reuse the common shapes.

Caution When you paste shapes from a scaled drawing, Visio resizes the shapes using the drawing scale for the destination drawing page. If the drawing scales in the source and destination drawing pages are more than a factor of eight apart—for example, 1:12 and 1:200—the pasted shapes might look very large or too small. If this occurs, you can change the scale of the destination drawing page to match the scale of the source page.

To copy an existing Visio plan into another drawing, follow these steps:

1. Open both the existing Visio plan drawing (the source) and the Visio drawing file into which you want to paste the existing Visio plan (the destination.)

2. To display both drawing windows, choose Window ➪ Cascade or Window ➪ Tile.

3. Click the title bar for the source drawing, select the shapes you want to copy, and then press Ctrl+C. If you want to copy the entire drawing page, choose Edit ➪ Copy Drawing.

4. Click the title bar for the destination drawing and press Ctrl+V to paste the copied shapes onto the drawing page.

Managing Plan Drawing Files

When you work with plan drawings that contain numerous types of information, you can create or store that information in drawing files in different ways to satisfy different requirements. For example, by placing the data for each building service in a different file and using OLE links to link those drawings in Visio background pages, you can assemble a compiled plan in one Visio drawing file while ensuring that different resources can edit each building service plan simultaneously when necessary.

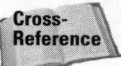 **Cross-Reference**   For information about linking and embedding files or portions of files, see Chapter 8.

Conversely, if you're working on your own, you can add all your shapes to the same drawing page and use layers to specify which shapes you see and whether they are editable. If you want to add additional flexibility to your solo environment, you can also place information on separate drawing pages, using some as background pages so they are available to several different foregrounds.

Although these techniques are more typical in a sophisticated CAD environment, it's worthwhile to plan your Visio drawing files, drawing pages, and layers before you create your plan drawings.

Managing Shapes with Layers

If you're familiar with CAD programs, you know that layers help you organize and manage the information on your drawings. In Visio, you can use layers to accomplish the following:

✦ Selectively view objects or shapes

✦ Selectively print objects or shapes

✦ Display categories of objects or shapes in different colors

✦ Lock categories of objects or shapes against editing

✦ Control whether you can snap or glue to shapes on a layer

CAD Layers Versus Visio Layers

Although Visio layers share many characteristics with the layers in CAD programs, they also differ from CAD layers in several key ways. Visio layers don't determine the order in which shapes appear on the drawing. To specify whether a shape appears in front or in back of other shapes, you right-click the shapes and choose Shape ➪ Bring to Front or Shape ➪ Send to Back from the shortcut menu.

In Visio, shapes can belong to no layer at all or multiple layers. In addition, each Visio drawing can have no layers or multiple layers, and the layers for each drawing page can be different. Finally, you can't group Visio layers.

For example, in a building plan, you can assign the structural components to one layer; walls, doors, and windows to another layer; furniture to a third layer; and electrical outlets to a fourth. When you want to work on the furniture layout for the building, you can lock the other layers so you don't move building components inadvertently. If you want to evaluate whether the electrical outlets are sufficient, you can turn off the display of the structural and furniture layers to focus on electrical components. In addition, you might assign review comments to a layer so that you can print the plan with or without those comments. By turning off snap and glue for layers, you can make sure that new shapes don't snap or glue to inappropriate shapes. For example, when you want to add electrical outlets to a plan, you can turn off snapping and gluing to all layers except the ones for walls.

You can create layers to organize shapes in the categories you want and then assign shapes on drawing pages to those layers. Many shapes in Visio stencils already contain layer assignments. You can use those assignments or create your own versions of those masters with the layer assignments you want. Each shape can belong to multiple layers or no layers at all. If you drag a master with a layer assignment onto a drawing page, Visio automatically adds the layer associated with the shape to the drawing page, if it doesn't already exist.

Creating Layers

You can create layers using several methods. No matter which method you choose, you must create the layers you want for each drawing page, because new layers are added only to the current page and new drawing pages don't inherit the layers associated with existing pages. Every page in a drawing can have a different set of layers.

If you use shapes with layer assignments, you don't have to create layers at all. Visio creates layers for the drawing page automatically when you drop or copy a shape with a layer assignment onto the page. If the page already contains a layer with the same name, Visio adds the shape to the existing layer.

Caution
If you use shape layer assignments to create your layers, you might end up with layers you don't want if you copy the wrong type of shapes onto the page. If you end up with layers you didn't expect, you can uncheck the visibility of all layers except the ones that concern you to see which shapes are the culprits. Then, you can reassign those shapes to other layers by following the instructions in the "Removing Layers" section later in this chapter.

To create a layer for a drawing page, follow these steps:

1. Choose View ⇨ Layer Properties and then click New.

2. In the New Layer dialog box, type a name for the layer and then click OK. Visio creates the layer for the current page.

3. In the Layer Properties dialog box, click the cells in the column for each property you want to apply to the layer, if they are not already checked, as shown in Figure 25-1.

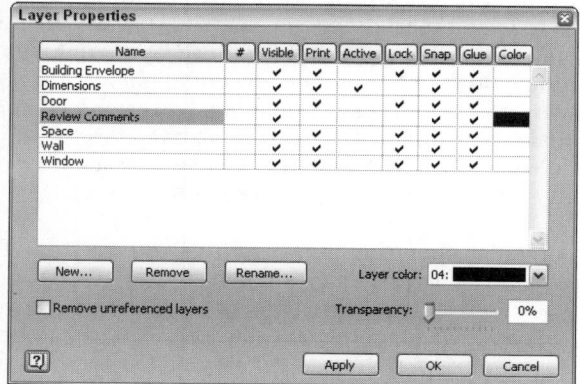

Figure 25-1: The Layer Properties dialog box contains all the commands you need to work with layers.

Tip
To avoid the repetition of creating the same layers for each plan drawing you develop, create a Visio drawing file with the drawing pages you want and the layers you want associated with those drawing pages. Save the file as a Visio template, as described in Chapter 3, and use that template as the basis for new plans.

Renaming Layers

You can rename existing layers for the current drawing page. The shapes on the layer remain the same. To rename a layer, choose View ⇨ Layer Properties, select the layer you want to rename, and click Rename. In the Rename Layer dialog box, type a new name and click OK.

You should only rename layers that you create. Although you can rename the pre-defined layers for shapes on Visio built-in stencils, Visio creates a new layer with the original layer name as soon as you add another shape with that layer assignment. For example, if you rename the Building Envelope layer to Building Outline and then add another Exterior Wall shape, you'll end up with a Building Envelope and Building Outline layer.

Activating Layers

When you drag a shape without a pre-defined layer assignment onto the page, Visio assigns it to the active layer. If no layers are active, Visio adds the shapes to the drawing page without assigning them to a layer. You can select the shapes after adding them and assign them to a layer. However, it's much easier to assign shapes to a layer as you add them. To do this, activate the layer to which you want to assign the shapes by choosing View ➪ Layer Properties and then clicking the cell to add a check mark in the Active column for the layer you want to make active. Visio makes the layer you choose active for the current page.

You can use this approach to assign shapes to multiple layers by choosing more than one active layer. Shapes you add to the page are automatically assigned to all of the active layers.

Make sure you reset the active layer as you work so that the shapes you add are assigned to the correct layer. However, if you use built-in Visio shapes, you don't have to use an active layer because the shapes already have the proper layer assignments built in.

Removing Layers

Removing layers associated with a drawing page is easy. However, removing a layer also deletes any shapes assigned to it, so you should reassign any shapes you want to keep to other layers before deleting layers. To remove a layer, follow these steps:

1. Choose View ➪ Layer Properties.
2. To display the number of shapes assigned to each layer, click the # button along the top of the Layer Properties table.
3. If the layer you want to remove has shapes on it, reassign them to a different layer by following these steps:

   a. To make it easier to see the shapes you want to reassign, uncheck the Visible cells for every layer except the one you want to remove.
   b. Click OK to close the Layer Properties dialog box.
   c. Select the shapes you want to reassign and choose Format ➪ Layer.
   d. In the Layer dialog box, uncheck any layers that are checked and check only the layer to which you want to assign the shapes. Click OK. If all other layers are invisible, the reassigned shapes disappear from the screen.

4. In the Layer Properties dialog box, select the layer you want to delete and then click Remove.

5. Check the Visible cell for every layer you want to see on the page.

Tip   If your list layers have gotten out of hand, it's easy to delete all unused layers. To do this, in the Layer Properties dialog box, check the Remove Unreferenced Layers check box and then click OK.

Putting Layers to Work

To put layers to work for you, you can specify layer properties to control the behavior of shapes as a group. Layer properties specify whether you can see shapes on the screen or when you print the drawing, whether you can edit shapes or snap and glue to them, and the color in which shapes appear. In the Layer Properties dialog box, you can specify the properties for any layer in the current drawing page. If you want the same properties for layers on other pages, you must apply those properties to each of those pages.

To specify properties, choose View ⇨ Layer Properties. Click a cell in the column for a property you want to apply and the row for the layer to which you want to apply it. Click an empty cell to add a check mark and activate the property. Click a cell with a check mark to deactivate the property. You can specify the following properties for layers:

✦ **Visible** — Check this property to display the shapes on the layer on the screen. To temporarily hide shapes on a layer, uncheck the layer.

✦ **Print** — Check this property to print the shapes on the layer when you print the drawing. To prevent shapes from printing, such as construction lines when you're printing final drawings, uncheck this property.

✦ **Active** — Check this property to assign shapes dropped on the page automatically to this layer.

✦ **Lock** — When this property is checked, you can't select, move, edit, or add shapes to the layer. In addition, you can't make the layer active.

Note   Although you can't select, move, edit, or add shapes to a locked layer, you can change the color of shapes on a locked layer by setting the color in the Color column of the Layer Properties dialog box.

✦ **Snap** — Check this property if you want to snap to shapes assigned to the layer. When you uncheck this property, you can't snap to shapes on the layer, although the shapes on the layer can snap to other shapes on snappable layers.

Using Layers on Background Pages

Although you can't share layers between drawing pages, you can achieve the same result by assigning layers to background pages. For example, you can put the basic building plan on a background page with different types of building components assigned to different layers. If you want to hide the furniture shapes for all the drawing pages in your file, you only have to hide the furniture layer on the background page. However, with this approach, the layer properties you specify on the background page apply to every foreground page.

✦ **Glue** — Check this property if you want to glue to shapes assigned to the layer. When you uncheck this property, you can't glue to shapes on the layer, although the shapes on the layer can glue to other shapes.

Note

If shapes are assigned to multiple layers, you must uncheck the Snap or Glue properties for every layer to which the shape is assigned.

✦ **Color** — Check this property to assign a color to the shapes on the layer. Each layer can use a different color, which overrides any color associated with graphic components of shapes on the layer. Shapes assigned to multiple layers appear in their original colors.

Assigning Color to a Layer

You can assign different colors to each layer for a drawing page. You can make colors opaque or transparent. For example, if you use filled rectangles to show areas on a plan, you can make the layer for those rectangles transparent so that you can still see the furniture and building components. To assign a color for a layer on the current page, follow these steps:

1. Choose View ➪ Layer Properties.

2. Click the cell in the Color column to add a check mark for the layer you want to color.

3. Click the arrow next to the Layer Color box and then select a color in the Layer Color list.

4. To change the transparency for the color, drag the Transparency slider to the value you want: 100 percent makes the layer totally invisible; 0 percent makes the layer completely opaque. To make a color visible but transparent, choose a value between 0 and 100.

Layer color overrides any color and transparency level associated with graphic components of shapes on the layer. However, shapes assigned to multiple layers appear in their original colors.

Selecting Shapes Using Layers

In addition to selecting shapes by dragging or clicking shapes on the drawing page, you can select groups of shapes by taking advantage of layers. To select shapes based on the layers to which they are assigned, choose Edit ➪ Select by Type, and then use one of the following methods:

✦ **Select shapes on a specific layer** — Select the Layer option and then check the check box for the layer that contains the shapes you want. To select more than one layer, Ctrl+click each layer you want to select.

✦ **Select shapes without layer assignments** — Select the Layer option and then check the {No Layer} check box.

Assigning Shapes to Layers

Many shapes that come with Visio already have layer assignments. When you add these shapes to drawing pages, Visio creates the appropriate layer if it doesn't already exist and assigns the shape to that layer. If a shape doesn't have a pre-defined layer assignment, you can assign it to layers as you add it to the drawing page by specifying an active layer. Visio assigns any shapes you add without specific layer assignments to the active layer. You might have to change the active layer to ensure that new shapes are added to the appropriate layer.

You can use other methods to assign shapes to layers. You can assign shapes to layers after you've added them to a drawing. If you plan to use layers frequently, it's more effective to assign masters to layers so Visio adds your shapes to their assigned layers automatically.

You can assign shapes to more than one layer to achieve more flexibility. For example, you can assign office furniture to both the Furniture layer as well as the Office Equipment layer. Then, the shapes for office furniture appear whenever either of those layers is visible.

Assigning Individual Shapes to Layers

To assign shapes that you've added to a drawing page to a layer, follow these steps:

1. Select the shape or shapes you want to assign and choose Format ➪ Layer.

2. In the Layer dialog box, check the check box for the layer to which you want to assign the selected shapes. To select more than one layer, Ctrl+click each check box, as illustrated in Figure 25-2.

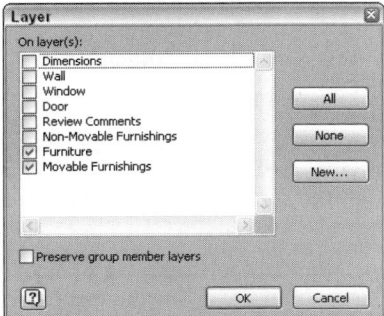

Figure 25-2: Select layer check boxes to assign shapes to one or more layers.

Assigning Masters to Layers

It's more effective to use masters with predefined layer assignments, because Visio adds them to the correct layer automatically. You can add layer assignments to shapes you create or to built-in masters. However, because Visio built-in stencils are copyrighted as well as read-only, you should make a copy of the masters you want to change in a custom stencil of your Favorites stencil and edit them there. You can also edit the layer assignments for masters on a drawing's Document stencil and then save it as a new stencil to use in the future.

Note   If you edit the layer assignment for a master and then drag it onto the drawing page, the instance you create uses the new layer assignment. However, any shapes you added prior to the layer change still use the previous layer assignment. You can change the assignment for those shapes by selecting them and choosing Format ➪ Layer.

If you want to assign a Visio master to a layer or change its current layer assignment, copy the Visio master to your Favorites stencil or another custom stencil. To do this, right-click the master in the Visio stencil and then choose Add to My Shapes from the shortcut menu. Choose one of the custom stencils on the submenu or choose Add to New Stencil or Add to Existing Stencil.

To assign a master to a layer or to change its layer assignment, open a Visio drawing so that the Shapes window appears, and then follow these steps:

1. Open the stencil that contains the master you want to assign to a layer. If the stencil is read-only, right-click the stencil title bar and choose Edit Stencil from the shortcut menu.

2. Right-click the master you want to edit and choose Edit Master ➪ Edit Master Shape from the shortcut menu.

3. In the master drawing window, select the master.

4. Choose Format ⇨ Layer.

5. Use one of the following methods to create a layer assignment:

   • If the master is not assigned to a layer, in the New Layer dialog box, type the name of the layer to which you want to assign it in the Layer Name box and click OK. You can assign the master to additional layers by clicking New and typing the name for the next layer.

   • To change the layer assignment, uncheck a layer's check box to remove an assignment and then click New to create a new layer assignment.

6. To close the master drawing window, click the Close button for the master drawing window. When Visio prompts you to update the master, click Yes.

7. To save your changes, right-click the stencil's title bar and click Save.

8. To change the stencil to read-only, right-click the stencil title bar and choose Edit Stencil.

Assigning Groups to Layers

Groups of shapes can also have layer assignments. By default, when you select a group and choose Format ⇨ Layer to assign the group to a layer, all of the shapes in the group become members of the new layer, losing their previous layer assignments. However, if you want individual shapes in a group to retain their current layer assignments, you can check the Preserve Group Member Layers check box in the Layer dialog box. For example, if you build groups of shapes to represent standard office configurations that include office furniture as well as computer equipment, you can assign the shapes for furniture to the Furniture layer and shapes for computer equipment to the Electronics layer before grouping them. If you assign the group to the Office Equipment layer, the furniture and computer equipment retain their previous layer assignments but also include assignments to the Office Equipment layer.

Caution   If you can see shapes on the drawing page, but can't select them, the layer might be locked. However, if you open the Layer Properties dialog box and find that the layer isn't locked, group layer assignments could be the culprit. The problem can occur when you assign individual shapes to one layer, and the group to which they belong to another layer. If you also turn off the visibility of the group's layer but not the visibility of the individual shape's layer, you can see the shapes because of their layer assignment, but you won't be able to select or edit them.

Summary

You can use Visio plan templates to create blank plan drawings. If you have other plans available, either CAD drawings or Visio plan drawings, you can insert them in background pages to quickly create foundations for new plans. To manage the content of plan drawings, you can create layers to categorize the shapes on your drawings. You can assign shapes to one or more layers. By specifying whether layers are visible on the screen, appear when you print your drawing, and are active or locked, you can control both the appearance of shapes and access to shapes.

✦　　✦　　✦

Laying Out Architectural and Engineering Plans

Whether you're creating a plan of your house to try out remodeling ideas or designing your company's new manufacturing facility, Visio provides tools to make your job easier. Although Visio Standard provides only a few shapes for laying out office space, Visio Professional includes numerous stencils and shapes for creating a variety of architectural and engineering plans.

With Visio Professional plan templates, you can develop plans beginning with the shell of a building and gradually add walls, doors, windows, and furnishings. You can create additional plans for building services, such as electrical service, plumbing, and HVAC. To complete your plan package, you can expand outdoors and develop site and landscaping plans or draw maps.

Unlike CAD programs, which come with tons of drafting commands, Visio provides its architectural and engineering capabilities through shapes on stencils. The Visio shapes for plan drawings are easy to drag, drop, and configure using basic Visio techniques along with control handles and custom properties to implement special behaviors. Of course, Visio Building Plan templates provide the tools you need to draw plans, but not the specialized skills needed to determine what the plans should contain. You'll have to read other books to learn about that.

Note   Many of the techniques described in this chapter work equally well for basic office plans you can create in Visio Standard and more specialized architectural and engineering plans available only in Visio Professional. Content specific to Visio Professional is identified as such throughout this chapter.

To learn about the different types of Visio Building Plan templates and how to create a Visio plan drawing, see Chapter 24.

Working with Walls

Visio provides shapes that represent different types of walls, such as exterior, interior, curtain, or window walls. Built-in shapes for walls are available on both the Walls, Shell, and Structure stencil and the Walls, Doors, and Windows stencil. These shapes come with built-in behaviors that make it easy to draw connecting walls the way you want, and contain custom properties to specify attributes such as wall thickness and fire rating. Additionally, you can create your own custom wall shapes, with, for instance, a hatched fill to show walls to be demolished.

You can create walls by dragging and dropping shapes, such as Wall, Exterior Wall, or Curved Wall, onto the drawing page, by using the Connector tool, or, if you've started your design with Space shapes, by converting Space shapes into walls.

Converting Spaces into Walls

When you begin with a space plan, you can easily transform those spaces into walls with the Convert to Walls command. You can specify the type of wall you want to use, as well as whether to display dimension lines or add guides to the walls created. In addition, you can delete the original Space shapes or keep them for further use. For example, if you want to show the square footage of spaces on the drawing or you intend to track space in your building, keep the Space shapes for those purposes.

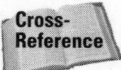

To learn more about Space shapes and other methods for laying out spaces and rooms, see Chapter 27.

To convert Space shapes into walls, follow these steps:

1. Select the Space shape or shapes you want to convert and initiate the Convert to Walls command using one of these methods:

   • Right-click a shape and then choose Convert to Walls from the shortcut menu.

   • Select the shapes you want to convert using any selection method and then choose Plan ⇨ Convert to Walls.

2. In the Convert to Walls dialog box, in the Wall Shape list, select the type of Wall shape you want to use.

The Wall Shape list includes only the Wall shapes available on open stencils. If you don't see the Wall shape you want, click Cancel, open the stencil with the desired Wall shape, and begin again with step 1.

3. To automatically add dimensions to each segment of a wall that is created, check the Add Dimensions check box.

Note The dimensions that Visio adds automatically might not dimension the segments you want and often produce redundant dimensions. If you are converting multiple shapes, you might prefer to add dimensions yourself.

4. To glue guides to each vertical and horizontal wall segment, check the Add Guides check box. You can reposition wall segments while maintaining their connection to other wall segments by dragging these guides.

5. To keep the Space shapes after you convert them to Wall shapes, select the Retain option. If you are converting some other type of geometry to Wall shapes, select the Convert to Space shape to turn the geometry into Space shapes.

6. Click OK to convert the Space shapes into Wall shapes and add any additional elements you specified, as illustrated in Figure 26-1. Visio creates a separate Wall shape for each wall segment in the building. Because the Wall shapes are glued together, the intersections between Wall shapes are cleaned up.

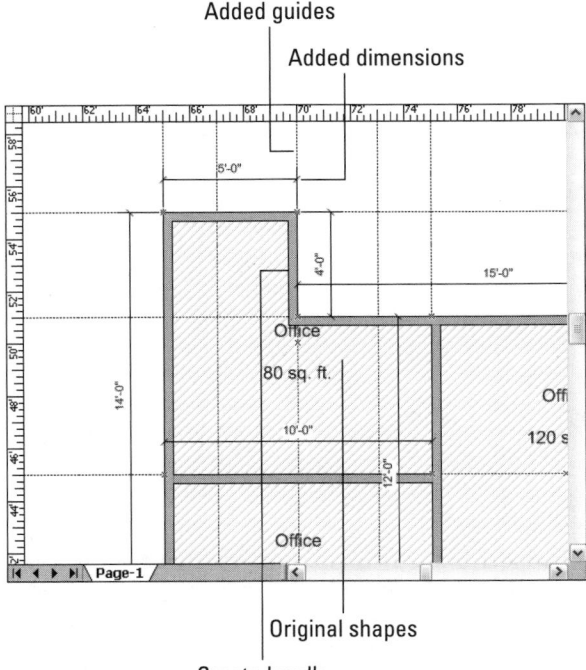

Figure 26-1: The Convert to Walls command can use Space shapes or other geometry to create walls, dimensions, and guides.

7. To reposition a Wall shape, drag the guide glued to it. Wall shapes glued to the guide resize, but the original Space shapes remain the same.

Tip

If you want to resize a Space shape to match the new wall configuration, right-click the Space shape and choose Auto Size from the shortcut menu.

Creating Walls

When you want to add walls from scratch, standard techniques such as dragging and dropping, drawing connectors, and dragging handles work effectively with Wall shapes. You can choose the technique you like or switch between techniques depending on the circumstances. For example, if you want to draw all the wall segments for a building shell, using the Connector tool with the Exterior Wall shape is convenient. Conversely, when you add bits and pieces of interior walls as you modify a floor plan, dragging and dropping the Wall shape might be more effective. As you add Wall shapes to the page and glue them together, Visio cleans up the intersections so you see lines only for wall surfaces, as shown in Figure 26-2.

Original wall segments

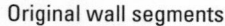

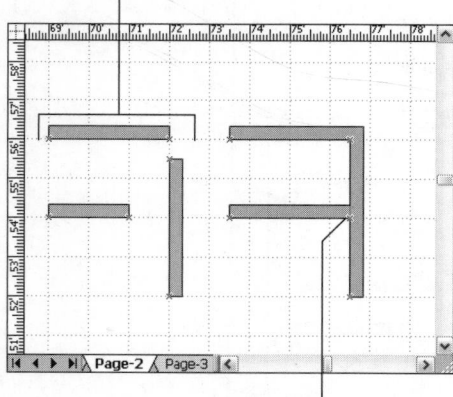

Glued walls with intersections cleaned up

Figure 26-2: Visio cleans up wall intersections.

Note

For Wall shapes to connect properly, snap and glue must both be turned on. Choose Tools ⇨ Snap & Glue. In the Snap & Glue dialog box, make sure that both the Snap check box and the Glue check box are checked under the Currently Active heading. In addition, make sure that the Connection Points and Shape Geometry check boxes are checked under both the Snap To and Glue To headings.

To create new walls on a drawing, use one of the following methods:

✦ **Drag and drop Wall shapes** — To add walls one at a time, drag the Wall shape you want onto the drawing page. To glue the new Wall shape to Wall shapes already on the page, glue its end points to connection points or shape geometry on existing Wall shapes. Visio highlights the connection points or shape geometry with a red square to indicate that the shapes are glued.

✦ **Use the Connector tool** — To add several connected walls, click the Connector tool on the Standard toolbar, click the master for the type of wall you want to add on a stencil, and then follow these steps:

1. For the first wall, drag between two points to define the beginning and end of the Wall shape. As soon as you complete this Wall shape, the pointer changes to the four-headed arrow, indicating that you can move the current point to a new location.

2. To add another Wall shape that starts where the first Wall shape ends, move the pointer away from the end point and then move it back, but not quite over the end point, until the pointer changes to the Connector icon (a plus sign with a small connector next to it).

3. Drag from the current point to the end of the next Wall shape.

4. Repeat steps 2 and 3 to create the Wall shapes for each wall segment you want.

Note
When you add Exterior Wall shapes to a plan, you want the selection handles to appear on the interior surface of the building wall. If an Exterior Wall shape's selection handles are on the edge that represents the exterior of the building, right-click the shape and choose Flip Wall on Reference Line from the shortcut menu.

Connecting and Resizing Walls

When you glue Wall shapes together, Visio cleans up the corners and other intersections. However, this glue only goes so far. If you drag a Wall shape to another position, it separates from its friends and the corners fill in again. You can use guides to move multiple Wall shapes and lengthen, shorten, or otherwise resize connecting Wall shapes. It's easy to glue Wall shapes to guides as you construct your plan using one of the following methods:

✦ **Gluing to existing guides** — In many cases, you begin a floor plan by dragging guides onto the drawing page to use as reference. If you drag a Wall shape onto a page and drag its end points to guides, Visio glues the shape to the guide automatically.

✦ **Creating guides with the Convert to Walls command** — If you convert Space shapes to Wall shapes as discussed in the section "Converting Spaces to Walls," you can create guides glued to the Wall shapes created during the conversion.

✦ **Right-clicking a wall shape** — To add a guide to an existing Wall shape, right-click the shape and then choose Add a Guide from the shortcut menu.

When you drag a guide that is glued to a Wall shape, the Wall shape moves with the guide and any Wall shapes that adjoin that Wall shape stretch or contract.

Modifying a Wall's Properties and Appearance

Wall shapes include custom properties and options that you can use to change the appearance of the walls on your plan. For example, you can configure every dimension of a wall, including length, thickness, and height, by specifying values for custom properties. You can also change the number of lines Visio uses to display walls.

Changing Wall Thickness and Other Properties

Visio Wall shapes include several custom properties, some of which modify the configuration of the shape itself, while others store data for reference or reports. For example, the Wall Length and Wall Thickness properties change the length and thickness of the shape, respectively. The Wall Justification property controls the alignment of the Wall shape, such as Centered or Edge. Conversely, the Wall Height and Base Elevation properties won't change the shape outline. However, you can produce legends, quantity take-offs, or bills of material based on these values. To change a custom property value, right-click a Wall shape and choose Properties from the shortcut menu. Type or select a value from a field's drop-down list and click OK when you're done.

Note   If you modify custom properties frequently, it's easier to dock the Custom Properties window by choosing View ⇨ Custom Properties Window. The field boxes display the values for the selected shape. To change or enter a value, select the property you want to edit and type or select a value.

Changing the Way Walls Are Shown

By default, Visio shows walls as double lines, one line for each wall surface, although you might have to zoom in to see them. However, you can also display walls as single lines to streamline a crowded drawing, or show walls as double lines with a reference so that the centerline of the wall is easy to spot. If you want to change how Visio displays walls, right-click any Wall shape on a drawing page and choose Set Display Options from the shortcut menu (available only in Visio Professional). Make sure the Walls tab is selected and then choose the option you want.

Note   Changing the display options for walls affects all the Wall shapes on the current drawing page but not Wall shapes on other pages in the file.

Changing Wall Color and Line Style

In addition to the number of lines that represent walls, you can easily change the color and line style for the Wall shapes on a drawing. Wall shapes such as Wall, Exterior Wall, and Curved Wall use the Wall line and fill styles. To change color or line style, select a Wall shape and then choose Format ⇨ Define Styles. The Define Styles dialog box opens, pre-populated with the information for the Wall style.

To change the line style, click Line, select the pattern, weight, color, or other properties for the line style, and then click OK. To change the fill style, click Fill, specify color, pattern, and transparency for the fill style, and click OK. In the Define Styles dialog box, click Apply to change the line style for the Wall shapes on all drawing pages in the drawing file.

Adding Doors, Windows, and Other Openings

Doors, windows, and openings in walls are important, because rooms aren't very useful if you can't enter them. Visio shapes for openings make it easy to add openings to walls. For example, when you add one of these shapes, it automatically rotates to match the angle of the Wall shape, glues itself to the Wall shape, adjusts its width to match that of the Wall shape, and cleans up the Wall shape where the opening is located.

After adding these shapes to your drawing, it's easy to change the configuration of the shape, such as reversing the direction in which a door opens or whether the door opens to the left or right. These configuration features are available whether you use Door, Window, or Opening shapes on the Walls, Doors, and Windows stencil available for Visio Standard or the Walls, Shell, and Structure stencil available only in Visio Professional.

Adding Openings to Walls

To insert a door, window, or other type of opening into a wall, drag a Door, Window, or Opening shape from the stencil onto a Wall shape. When you drop the shape on the Wall shape, the shape rotates into position in the Wall shape, glues itself to the Wall shape, and changes its thickness to match the Wall shape, as shown in Figure 26-3.

Note   If a shape for a door, window, or other opening, doesn't rotate to match the direction of the Wall shape, the shape isn't glued to the Wall shape. Drag the shape over the Wall shape until you see the red square indicating that the shape is glued and that it has been rotated to match the Wall shape, and then release the mouse button.

Change openings between outside and inside

Drag to change swing angle

Change width of opening

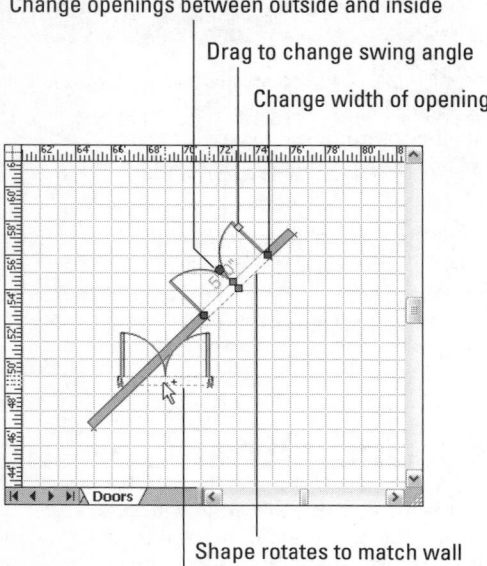

Shape rotates to match wall

Position an opening near a wall

Figure 26-3: Openings change to match the wall thickness and orientation.

Modifying Doors, Windows, and Openings

Shapes for doors, windows, and other openings include custom properties and shortcut menu commands that modify the configuration of the shapes. For example, you can change the direction that a door swings (in or out) or the width of openings. In addition, you can use Display Options to change how doors, windows, and openings appear on each drawing page. Use one of the following methods to change door, window, and opening shapes:

✦ **Reverse direction** — Right-click a Door, Window, or Opening shape, and then choose Reverse In/Out Opening from the shortcut menu.

✦ **Reverse swing** — Right-click a Door, Window, or Opening shape, and then choose Reverse Left/Right Opening from the shortcut menu.

✦ **Reposition opening** — Drag the shape to a new position in the Wall shape. Visio heals the opening in the Wall shape at the original position and cleans up the Wall shape at the new location.

Creating Door and Window Schedules

For architectural projects, door and window schedules identify each door and window in a set of architectural plans and specify the dimensions and other attributes for these components, so that the right components are installed in the right places. In Visio Professional, you can use reports to create door and window schedules that automatically report information for the Door and Window shapes on your drawing. For example, the default Door Schedule report shows door number, door size, door type, and thickness. The default Window Schedule report includes window number, size, and type. You can run the predefined report as is or modify the report definition to include other custom properties or to specify which shapes to include in the report.

An easy way to produce a door or window schedule is to drag a Door Schedule or Window Schedule shape from the Walls, Shell and Structure stencil onto the drawing page. These tabular shapes use the existing schedule report definition to show information on the drawing page.

✦ **Modify dimensions and other attributes** — Open the Custom Properties window and then select the shape whose properties you want to change. Type or select the new value from a property drop-down list. For example, with the Double-Door shape, you can specify the width of the door, its height, the type of door, the percentage that the door is open on the page, its number, its fire rating, and its base elevation.

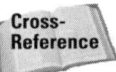

Cross-Reference   If you track information about building components in a database, you can import that data into the custom properties for Visio Building Plan shapes, as described in Chapter 10.

✦ **Change the door and window components that appear** — You can specify which components you want Visio to display for Door and Window shapes. For example, Visio displays the window frame and sash by default, but you can also show the header and sill. To change the components you see, right-click any Door or Window shape on a drawing page and choose Set Display Options from the shortcut menu. On the Doors or Windows tab, check the check boxes for the components you want to see and then click OK. Changing the display options for Door or Window shapes affects the shapes only on the current drawing page, so you must repeat this step for each drawing page you want to change.

✦ **Set default configurations** — When you use standard sizes, you can specify default properties for doors and windows. For example, you can specify the width of the door frame and the door panel so that every Door shape you add uses those dimensions. To do so, right-click a Door or Window shape, and choose Set Display Options from the shortcut menu. On the Doors or Windows tab, click Properties. In the Set Door Component Properties or Set Window

Component Properties dialog box, specify the default properties you want and then click OK. These settings affect only the current drawing page, so you must redefine these defaults for every page to which you want to apply them.

Note   Set Display Options is available only in Visio Professional.

Cross-Reference   To learn how to modify and run report definitions, see Chapter 32.

Adding Cubicles and Furniture

Both Visio Standard and Visio Professional include shapes for laying out furniture for an office building. If you use Visio Standard, the Office Layout template is the only Building Plan template available to you. However, it includes the most frequently used shapes, including basic building components, office furniture, office equipment, office accessories, and cubicles. If you use Visio Professional, you can create a more detailed floor plan using the Floor Plan template. Then, you can open the Cubicles, Office Accessories, Office Equipment, and Office Furniture stencils to lay out your office within that floor plan.

Adding Cubicles to an Office Layout

Visio includes masters on the Cubicles stencil that are preconfigured with cubicle walls, furniture, and equipment. It's easy to build an office layout by dragging these ready-made Workstation shapes onto the drawing page. If the built-in Workstation shapes don't conform to the standards for your organization, you can create your own custom Workstation shapes.

You can also construct cubicles piece by piece with Panel shapes, Panel Post shapes, and shapes for work surfaces and storage units from the Cubicles stencil. You can create a cubicle configured the way you want, group its shapes, and then copy the group to lay out the rest of the office. In addition to cubicle components, you can add free-standing pieces such as Round Table and Stool shapes from the Office Furniture stencil to your custom Workstation shapes.

To create a cubicle from components, follow these steps:

1. Drag Panel or Curved Panel shapes from the Cubicles stencil onto the drawing page. To resize panels, drag selection handles on the shapes.

2. To connect panels, follow these steps:

a. Drag a Panel Post shape onto the page and glue it to one end of a Panel shape. Visio highlights the connection point in red to indicate that the two shapes are glued.

b. Drag a connection point from another Panel shape and glue it to a connection point on the Panel Post shape. The Panel Post shape rotates into position based on the connection point you choose. For example, if you position the pointer over the connection point on the right side of the Panel Post shape, the Panel shape will rotate to horizontal.

3. To add furniture and equipment to a cubicle, drag one or more of the following shapes into the cubicle:

- **Modular work surfaces** — Drag shapes such as Work Surface or Corner Surface from the Cubicles stencil and position them along Panel shapes. You can use the shape's rotation handles or the Rotate or Flip commands on the Shape menu to orient the shapes properly.

- **Modular storage units** — Drag shapes such as Storage Unit from the Cubicles stencil and position them along Panel shapes.

- **Suspended shelves and lateral files** — Drag shapes such as Susp Open Shelf or Suspended Lateral File from the Cubicles stencil on top of shapes for modular work surfaces.

- **Chairs and other free-standing furniture** — Drag shapes from the Office Furniture and Office Accessories stencils into the Workstation shape.

- **Computers and other equipment** — Drag shapes from the Office Equipment stencil into the Workstation shape.

Connecting Modular Furniture

The shapes on the Office Furniture stencil are designed with inward/outward connection points that make it easy to connect furniture components. Similar to Door and Wall shapes, shapes that represent modular furniture glue and rotate to match the Furniture shapes to which you glue them.

To connect modular furniture, follow these steps:

1. Drag a modular Office Furniture shape, such as 45 Deg Table, onto the drawing page.

2. Drag a connection point on a second modular Office Furniture shape and position the pointer over a connection point on the first shape. When Visio highlights the connection points with a red square and rotates the second shape into the proper position, release the mouse button.

Laying Out Plant Floors

In addition to laying out offices and cubicles on an office floor plan, you can also lay out machinery and equipment for manufacturing plants and distribution centers. As with other types of floor plans, you can start by creating a drawing with the Plant Layout template, or by laying out shapes over an existing Visio or CAD plan drawing. When you create a new plant layout by choosing File ➪ New ➪ Building Plan ➪ Plant Layout, Visio Professional opens some stencils shared with other plan templates and a few specific to plant layout, including the following:

✦ **Shop Floor–Machines and Equipment** — Includes shapes for machines such as lathes, saws, and other equipment

✦ **Shop Floor–Storage and Distribution** — Includes shapes for equipment such as forklifts, cranes, shelves, and racks

✦ **Vehicles** — Includes shapes for cars, trucks, buses, and shapes that show turning radii for vehicles

✦ **Warehouse–Shipping and Receiving** — Includes shapes for shipping doors, containers, and other equipment

The shapes on these stencils include selection and rotation handles you can use to position them. A few also include control handles for repositioning parts of the shape. However, these shapes are meant to be standalone and don't include connection points for gluing the shapes together. Many of the shapes include custom properties you can use to specify the size of equipment, the department to which it is assigned, or asset number.

Modifying Cubicles

Predefined cubicles make it easy to lay out an office. By dragging Workstation shapes into place, you can add cubicle walls, work surfaces, office equipment, and other furniture in one step. If Visio's built-in Workstation shapes aren't set up the way you want, you can modify one of them and use it to populate your plan. You can also create a custom stencil of Workstation shapes configured to your organization's standards.

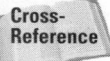 **Cross-Reference** To learn how to create custom masters, see Chapter 32.

To modify a cubicle, follow these steps:

1. Drag one of the Workstation shapes, such as an L workstation, from the Cubicles stencil onto the drawing page.

2. To change the size of the cubicle, drag the Workstation shape's selection handles. Shapes such as Panels and Work Surfaces resize automatically to match the new cubicle size.

3. To move, delete, or format an individual component within the cubicle, select the Workstation shape and then subselect the individual shape inside it. Drag the shape to move it, press Delete to delete it, or choose format commands to reformat it.

4. To add additional furniture of equipment to the cubicle, drag a shape, such as Telephone, from the Office Equipment stencil, onto the Workstation shape. With the Workstation shape selected, Shift+click the new Furniture or Equipment shape, and then choose Shape ➪ Grouping ➪ Add to Group.

5. To copy the Workstation shape, press Ctrl+D to create a duplicate and then drag it into position.

 **Tip**   If the office layout is laid out on a grid, you can also use the Array Shapes command to create Workstation shapes at regular intervals both vertically and horizontally. For information on using Array shapes, see Chapter 4.

Creating Building Services Plans

Documenting the equipment and services that keep a building running requires a lot more than just building walls and openings. If you use Visio Professional, you can create plans for each building service, including electrical, plumbing, HVAC, and security systems. Most of the shapes on stencils for building services include shortcut commands and custom properties that you can use to select a type of component, specify component dimensions, or configure shapes in numerous ways. In addition, these shapes include layer assignments so that it's easy to use layers to control the behavior of building services shapes.

Adding HVAC Services

If you've ever worked in your office building on the weekend when the air conditioning is turned off, you know how important HVAC service is to people's comfort. In Visio Professional, you can create two types of HVAC plans. An HVAC Plan shows the ductwork, registers, and diffusers that deliver and remove air. An HVAC Control Logic diagram represents the sensors and control equipment that control the delivery of air, such as quantity and temperature.

Separating Building Services from the Basic Building

Typically, you draw each building services plan over the exterior walls, structural elements, the building core, the interior walls, and, in some cases, the cubicles. You can use the same basic plan as a foundation for each building services plan by placing the basic building on a background page. You can associate the background page with each foreground page you create for different building services plans. In addition to sharing the same building plan for all your building services plans, a background page also prevents you from inadvertently modifying the basic building plan.

If you add all the building shapes to the same drawing page, layers on the drawing page act as separators. You can turn off the layers you don't want to see for a specific plan; for example, you could turn off the HVAC layer when you're documenting the electrical service plan. In addition, if you want to protect the basic building components, you can lock layers, such as Building Envelope, Wall, and Stair, so you can't edit them as you work on Plumbing shapes.

If you've imported a CAD drawing as a backdrop, you also lock that drawing against editing. To do so, right-click the drawing and then choose CAD Drawing Object ⇨ Properties from the shortcut menu. In the CAD Drawing Properties dialog box, on the General tab, make sure both the Lock Size and Position check box and the Lock Against Deletion check box are checked.

 **Cross-Reference**   To learn more about using background pages, see Chapter 2. Chapter 25 describes how to use layers to control shapes. Chapter 28 discusses the use of CAD drawings within Visio drawings.

Drawing HVAC Plans

If you start an HVAC plan with the HVAC Plan template, Visio Professional opens the stencils with HVAC equipment and ductwork for you. If you are adding an HVAC plan in an existing drawing, you can open the same stencils by choosing File ⇨ Shapes ⇨ Building Plan and then selecting the following stencils:

✦ **HVAC Equipment**—Includes pumps, condensers, fans, and other types of HVAC equipment

✦ **HVAC Ductwork**—Includes numerous types of ducts shapes

✦ **Registers, Grills and Diffusers**—Includes shapes for openings that deliver, remove, or diffuse air

✦ **Drawing Tool Shapes**—Includes shapes for creating geometric shapes useful in duct layout

To lay out HVAC ductwork and equipment, follow these steps:

1. Open the drawing page on which you want to create your HVAC plan, whether it's an existing floor plan page, a page with an imported CAD drawing, or a new page.

2. To simplify changing shape properties, open the Custom Properties window by choosing View ➪ Custom Properties Window.

3. Drag shapes that represent ductwork from the HVAC Ductwork stencil onto the drawing page.

4. To change the dimensions of a Ductwork shape, such as Straight Duct or Y Junction, use one of the following methods:

   • **Selection handles** — Drag selection handles to change the length or width of ducts.

   • **Control handles** — Drag control handles to change the angle of branches on ducts.

   • **Enter dimensions** — If the Custom Properties window is open, select the Ductwork shape and then type the new length or width in the Duct Length or Duct Width box.

5. To connect Ductwork shapes on the drawing page, drag a connection point on the second Ductwork shape to a connection point on the first Ductwork shape. For example, drag from a Branch Duct shape to the shape that represents the main duct. Visio highlights the connection points with a red square to indicate they're glued, and rotates the second Ductwork shape to match the orientation of the first.

Note   If you drag a Ductwork shape from a stencil, position one of its connection points over a connection point on a Ductwork shape on the page to connect them.

6. To change other attributes for some ductwork shapes, right-click a shape and choose a command from the shortcut menu. For example, you can choose between Rectangular Duct and Circular Duct or specify whether the ends are open or closed.

7. To label ducts, use one of the following methods:

   • **Show duct size** — Right-click a Ductwork shape and choose Show Duct Size from the shortcut menu. Shapes that represent rectangular ducts show the duct width and depth. Shapes that represent circular ducts show the diameter followed by the diameter symbol.

   • **Add a text label** — As with other standard shapes, you can select a shape and type the label text you want. You can reposition the label text by dragging the control handle on the text block.

8. To add registers, grills, diffusers, and other types of HVAC equipment, drag shapes from either the Registers, Grills, and Diffusers or HVAC Equipment stencils and drop them on top of Ductwork shapes. These shapes don't glue to Ductwork shapes or rotate to match the orientation of Ductwork shapes. However, you can use the rotation handles on these shapes to rotate them.

Drawing HVAC Control Logic Diagrams

HVAC Control Logic diagrams show the sensors, equipment, and wiring that control the HVAC system drawn on an HVAC plan. However, unlike the HVAC Plan template, the HVAC Control Logic Diagram template creates unscaled schematic drawings by default. These HVAC control logic schematics are single-line or double-line drawings that represent ducts, sensors, and mechanical equipment to control the HVAC system. The built-in shapes for sensors and equipment match the width of the Ductwork shapes so they snap into position when you drag them onto a Ductwork shape as shown in Figure 26-4.

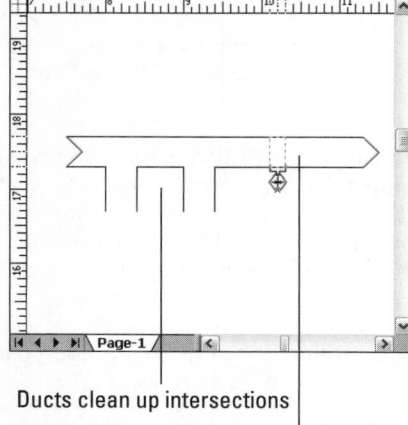

Ducts clean up intersections

Device alignment boxes match duct width so they snap into place

Figure 26-4: Ducts and sensor shapes include features to simplify building a control diagram.

In addition, many of the shapes for HVAC controls include custom properties you can use to select the exact configuration you want. For example, after you add a Control shape such as Voltage or Smoke to the page, you can select custom property values to specify whether the shape is a controller or a sensor, the type of controller or sensor, and the limit switch and reset switch settings.

To create an HVAC Control Logic diagram, follow these steps:

1. Start your diagram with one of the following methods:

    • **Use the HVAC Control Logic Diagram template** — To start a diagram from scratch, choose File ⇨ New ⇨ Building Plan ⇨ HVAC Control Logic Diagram.

    • **Add to an existing plan drawing** — Open the drawing page you want to use and then open the HVAC Control and HVAC Control Equipment stencils.

2. If you are starting from scratch, drag guides from the horizontal and vertical rulers to provide reference points for adding ducts to the diagram.

3. To add ducts to the diagram, drag Duct shapes, such as Duct, Return Duct, or Supply Duct, from the HVAC Controls Equipment stencil onto the drawing page and glue them to guides. By default, Visio draws Duct shapes with double lines. To represent ducts with single lines, right-click a Duct shape and choose Single Line Ducts from the shortcut menu.

 Tip

By adding guides to the page and gluing Duct shapes to them, you can easily move Duct shapes and their associated Control shapes as one by dragging the guide to which they are glued. Glue horizontal Duct shapes to horizontal guides, and vertical Duct shapes to vertical guides.

 Note

When you show ducts as double lines, position a Duct shape that is perpendicular to another by positioning an end point of the perpendicular Duct shape at the centerline of the existing Duct shape. If the connection doesn't show an opening between the Duct shapes, as shown in Figure 26-4, right-click the Duct shape you are adding and choose Shape ➪ Bring to Front.

4. To resize Duct shapes, drag their end points. If you want to constrain the Duct shape to its current rotation, press Shift as you drag its end point.

5. Drag Equipment shapes, such as Centrifugal Fan or Humidifier, from the HVAC Controls Equipment stencil onto the drawing page and place them on top of Duct shapes.

6. Drag Sensor shapes, such as Timer or Light, from the HVAC Controls stencil onto Duct shapes on the drawing page. The alignment boxes for these shapes match the width of Duct shapes so they snap into place, as illustrated in Figure 26-4.

 Note

If a Duct shape is glued to a guide, dragging Equipment and Sensor shapes onto the Duct shape also glues those shapes to the guide. To reposition the Duct shape and all of its associated Equipment and Sensor shapes, drag the guide to a new location.

7. To configure some Equipment and Sensor shapes, in the Custom Properties window, change the values for the custom properties. If the Custom Properties window isn't open, you can also right-click a shape and choose Properties from the shortcut menu.

Creating Reflected Ceiling Plans

The Reflected Ceiling Plan template doesn't actually include a tool to automate the creation of a reflected ceiling plan, so you can start with any building plan template you want. You can create the ceiling grid itself using drawing tools, guides, and the Array Shapes command. After the grid is constructed, open the Electrical and

Telecom stencil and the Registers, Grills, and Diffusers stencil if they aren't open already and drag shapes for light fixtures, air diffusers, and smoke detectors onto the plan.

Ceiling grids often repeat the same pattern of tiles and devices throughout most of a building. Because of this, you can draw a portion of the grid with shapes for ceiling tiles and ceiling-mounted equipment and then use the Array Shapes command to repeat that pattern in the rest of the building. To create a ceiling grid, follow these steps:

1. Drag guides onto the page to define reference points for one or more ceiling tiles.

2. Use the Line tool or Rectangle tool to draw one or more ceiling tiles.

3. If the ceiling-mounted equipment is located at regular intervals in the grid, drag shapes for lighting from the Electrical and Telecom stencil on the drawing. Drag Diffuser shapes from the Registers, Grills, and Diffuser stencil onto the drawing.

4. Select the shapes for the ceiling tiles and ceiling-mounted equipment that you want to repeat.

5. Choose Tools ➪ Add-Ons ➪ Visio Extras ➪ Array Shapes.

6. To copy the shapes as a grid, in the Array Shapes dialog box, set the Spacing for Rows and Columns to zero, select the Between Shape Edges option, and then click OK.

7. If the ceiling-mounted equipment is not located at regular intervals or some rooms have special equipment, place equipment by dragging shapes from the Electrical and Telecom or Registers, Grills, and Diffusers stencils onto the drawing page.

Adding Electrical and Telecom Services

The Electrical and Telecomm stencil includes shapes you can use to show lighting fixtures, electrical switches and outlets, and other electrical devices on plans for a home, building, or manufacturing plant. You can start a diagram from scratch by choosing File ➪ New ➪ Building Plan ➪ Electrical and Telecom, but it's often easier to open the Electrical and Telecom stencil while you work on an existing floor plan.

Most of the shapes on the Electrical and Telecom stencil include custom properties with multiple values for specifying different types of electrical devices. For example, the Switch Type property for the Switches shape can change the switch between Single Pole, 3 Way, 4 Way, Timer, and Weatherproof switches. Although the basic shape might stay the same, the shape displays other graphics to indicate which type of component it is. In addition, some shapes include shortcut menu commands for reconfiguring shapes. For example, you can use a shortcut command to flip the orientation of the Switches shape.

Tip If you don't see a shape for the device you want, drag one of the shapes onto the drawing page and then right-click it to display the shortcut menu. Look for configuration commands on the shortcut menu or choose Properties to look for custom properties that show different device types.

Although switches and outlets connect to walls on a floor plan, shapes for switches and outlets don't rotate into position as Door and Window shapes do. You can use the rotation handle on the shape to rotate the shape into position. You can also rotate a shape to the left or right by ninety degrees by selecting the shape and then pressing Ctrl+L or Ctrl+R.

Visio doesn't offer a tool to draw wiring between electrical devices. You can use the Freeform tool or Pencil tool to draw connections between devices. To add wiring between two shapes, select the Freeform tool, drag from a connection point on the first shape, and drag slowly to the connection point where the wire ends.

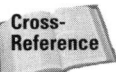

Cross-Reference To learn about the Freeform tool, see Chapter 2.

Adding Plumbing

The Plumbing and Piping Plan template creates a new scaled drawing and opens stencils with shapes you can use to show pipes, valves, and fixtures for water supply or wastewater disposal systems. You can start a diagram from scratch by choosing File ➪ New ➪ Building Plan ➪ Plumbing and Piping Plan, but you can also open the following stencils while you work on an existing floor plan:

✦ **Pipes and Valves–Pipes 1 and 2** — These two stencils include dozens of linear shapes that represent pipelines and pipeline devices.

✦ **Pipes and Valves–Valves 1 and 2** — These two stencils include numerous valves you can glue to the ends of pipeline shapes.

✦ **Plumbing** — This stencil offers standard plumbing shapes, including Boiler, Radiator, Toilet, and Bath. Bathroom shapes include both top view and side view shapes so you can show how fixtures are connected in a plan or cutaway view.

To create a plumbing and piping plan, follow these steps:

1. Drag Plumbing fixtures onto the drawing page.

2. Drag shapes for pipelines onto the page and glue each end to connection points on shapes for fixtures or plumbing equipment. You can resize shapes for pipelines by dragging their end points.

3. Drag Valve shapes onto the drawing. Glue Valve shapes to the ends of shapes for pipelines.

4. For shapes that include shortcut commands or custom properties, such as the In-line Valve shape, right-click the shape and choose a configuration command from its shortcut menu or select a value in a custom property field.

Adding Security and Access Systems

Unfortunately, good security becomes more important every day. Whether you're designing a state-of-the-art security system for a top-secret development facility or setting up electronic access for an office building, you can use the Security and Access Plan template to draw a security plan. You can start a diagram from scratch by choosing File ➪ New ➪ Building Plan ➪ Security and Access Plan, but you can also open the following stencils while you work on an existing floor plan:

✦ **Alarm and Access Control** — Includes shapes for card readers, keypads, cameras, and other access devices

✦ **Initiation and Annunciation** — Includes shapes for paging and alarms

✦ **Video Surveillance** — Includes shapes for motion detectors, cameras, and other video equipment

Most of the shapes on the Security and Access stencils include custom properties with multiple values for specifying different device configurations. For example, the Mount Type property, which is associated with numerous shapes, specifies whether the device is mounted on the ceiling, on the wall, flush, hidden, or in other ways. The shape label changes to reflect the type of mounting, the type of technology, and the function type.

Creating Site and Landscaping Plans

Site plans come in two flavors, depending on the type of site information you want to show. Landscaping plans can be as small as a garden in the backyard of a town home, showing plants, fences, irrigation equipment, and recreational elements for the site. Conversely, site plans usually represent a much larger area and show landscaping, irrigation, parking, driveways, and traffic management features.

 **Note**   Site plans are available only in Visio Professional.

For smaller sites, you can use an existing building plan as a foundation and add site details around the building. For larger sites, you'll probably need a separate site plan that uses a smaller scale to fit the larger area onto the drawing page. To create

a site plan from scratch, choose File ➪ New ➪ Building Plan ➪ Site Plan. Visio creates a new drawing using a civil engineering scale of 1" = 10' 0". This scale fits a site 360 feet by 240 feet on the architectural drawing page. If your site is larger than that, you can choose predefined civil engineering scales up to 1" = 100' 0" or you can specify a custom scale.

If you use an existing building plan, your buildings are already on the drawing page. However, when you start a new site plan with the Site Plan template, you must draw building outlines using drawing tools such as Line, Rectangle, or Pencil.

Adding Landscaping Elements

Several stencils provide shapes to show the plantings and constructed features for a landscape. These shapes work equally well for commercial landscaping and home garden layouts. Drag shapes from the following stencils to add landscaping elements to the site plan:

✦ **Garden Accessories** — Includes shapes for fences, posts, and gates; and shapes for surfaces, such as flagstone, brick pathways, concrete, driveways, and patios

✦ **Irrigation** — Includes shapes for irrigation lines, spray heads, valves, and other devices. These shapes include custom properties you can use to specify different types of irrigation devices.

✦ **Planting** — Includes shapes for different types of trees, shrubs, hedges, and potted plants. You can use the Plant Callout shape to label plants with both common names and plant descriptions.

✦ **Sport Fields and Recreation** — Includes shapes for recreational equipment, such as pools, swing sets, and different types of sports fields

Many of the Landscaping shapes end up positioned at regular intervals, whether you are planting a grid of palm trees or placing a series of brick pathway shapes to represent a brick sidewalk. To create and arrange shapes at regular intervals vertically and horizontally, use the Array Shapes command.

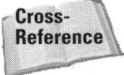 **Cross-Reference** To learn how to apply the Array Shapes command, see Chapter 4.

Working with Roads and Parking Lots

The Site Plan template opens both the Parking and Road stencil and the Vehicles stencil. You can use shapes on the Parking and Road stencil to add roads, driveways, parking stalls and lots, sidewalk ramps, and traffic islands. By adding shapes from the Vehicles stencil to the plan, you can make sure that differently sized vehicles can navigate the site.

Creating Roads and Parking Lots

To create roads and parking lots, follow these steps:

1. Drag guides onto the drawing page to mark reference points for the perimeter of the site, roads, and parking stalls.

2. Drag Curb and Driveway shapes onto the drawing page. To connect Curb and Driveway shapes, use the Line tool to draw lines between the shapes.

3. To add parking strips, stalls, and islands, drag shapes from the Parking and Roads stencil onto the drawing page. Glue their end points to guides on the page to simplify repositioning them.

4. To glue Parking and Road shapes, glue the end points or control points of Island and Driveway shapes to connection points on Parking Stall or other parking shapes.

5. If you drag individual Parking Stall shapes onto the page and glue them to a guide, you can reposition all the Parking Stall shapes at once by dragging the guide to which they are glued.

6. Drag shapes from the Vehicles, Site Accessories, and Planting stencils, to show vehicles, parking lot components, drains, outdoor furniture, and plants. Glue shape end points to guides.

Modifying Parking and Road Shapes

Parking and Road shapes include selection and control handles you can use to modify the configuration of the shape. Some shapes, such as the Parking Strip shape, are extendable shapes, and add additional parking stalls as you drag the selection handle at either end of the shape. Other shapes include control handles that modify the shape. For example, the control handle on the Radial Strip shape changes the number of stalls as you drag it, as shown in Figure 26-5.

Tip   To find out what a control handle does, position the pointer over the control handle until the screen tip appears.

Some shapes include custom properties that can modify the shape configuration. For example, the Parking Strip and Parking Stall shapes include a Stall Angle custom property. By default, parking stalls in the shape are oriented at seventy degrees. To create straight parking stalls, right-click a Parking Strip or Parking Stall shape on the drawing page and choose Properties from the shortcut menu. Type **90deg.** in the Stall Angle box and click OK. You can also type new values for the Stall Width and Stall Length properties to change the size of the parking stall. Shapes with curves, such as Curbs, include a Radius property that controls the radius of the curve on the shape.

Drag to change the number of stalls

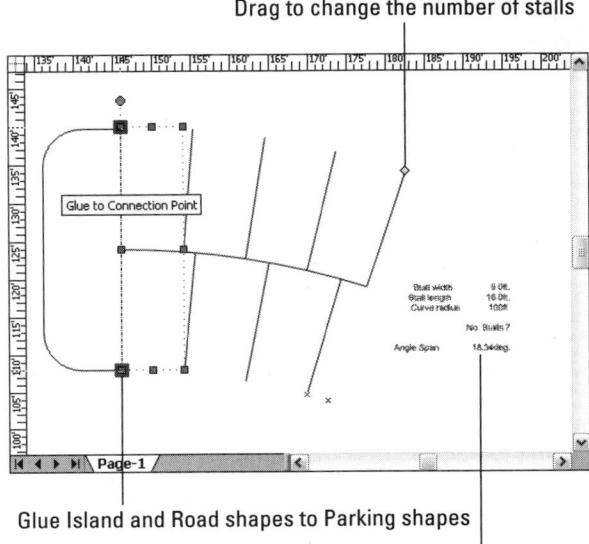

Glue to Connection Point

Stall width   9.0ft.
Stall length   18.0ft.
Curve radius   100ft

No. Stalls 7

Angle Span   18.34deg.

Glue Island and Road shapes to Parking shapes

Text block showing properties for the Parking Strip shape

Figure 26-5: Drag control handles to change the number of parking stalls, and glue islands and road shapes to parking shapes.

Some Parking shapes include shortcut commands to reconfigure the shape. For example, with the Radial Strip shape, you can choose Stalls Inside or Stalls Outside from the shortcut menu to change whether the stalls face the inside radius or outside radius for the shape.

Drawing Directional Maps

Another type of Visio drawing that covers an even larger area than that of site plans is the *directional map*. With the Directional Map template, you can create road maps that show how to drive to your destination, or metro maps that help users navigate the transportation system in a city. These maps can include roads, transportation lines, and landmarks. In Visio, three-dimensional Directional Map shapes make it easy to render small geographic areas, such as villages or towns, with appealing and colorful three-dimensional shapes. By default, Visio creates maps without scale, but you can indicate an approximate scale by adding text to a Scale shape.

Note   The Directional Map templates are available in both Visio Standard and Visio Professional.

Creating Road and Metro Maps

To create a directional map, follow these steps:

1. Choose File ⇨ New ⇨ Map ⇨ Directional Map.

2. To add roads to the map, drag a shape, such as Road Square, Curve 2, or Railroad from the Road Shapes stencil onto the drawing page. You can resize Road shapes by dragging their end points.

3. To specify the thickness of a Road shape, right-click the shape and choose Thin, Standard, Thick, or Custom from the shortcut menu. If you choose Custom, drag the control handle to specify the thickness you want.

Tip

To change the direction of a Road shape, right-click the shape and choose one of the Rotate or Flip commands. You can also click Rotate or Flip buttons on the Action toolbar or use keyboard shortcuts such as Ctrl+L and Ctrl+R to rotate a shape ninety degrees to the left or right.

4. To simplify moving multiple road segments at once, glue Road shapes to guides and then drag the guides to reposition the shapes.

5. Drag 3-Way, 4-Way, Roundabout, and Interchange shapes onto the drawing page to represent intersections. Glue end points for Road shapes to connection points on the shapes that represent intersections.

6. Identify numbered roadways, such as interstates, by dragging shapes, such as Interstate and State Route, onto the page near the Roadshape you want to identify.

7. To draw metro or subway systems, use shapes on the Metro Shapes stencil. These shapes work similarly to Road shapes, but also include shapes to show stations and stops.

8. To indicate landmarks such as lakes, rivers, airports, malls, schools, and hospitals, drag the appropriate shapes onto the map. You can drag selection handles to resize Landmark shapes in one direction or proportionally.

9. To add transportation signs, such as one-way street signs or freeway exits, drag shapes from the Transportation Shapes stencil.

10. To indicate the location of recreational areas, drag shapes from the Recreation Shapes stencil.

Modifying Roads and Intersections

Visio Road shapes are quite simple, but you can combine straight, curved, and flexible Road shapes to adequately represent roads for a directional map. Road shapes include control handles and custom properties that you can use to change the width of the roadways or the length of intersection components. Use one or more of the following methods to modify the roads and intersections on your map:

✦ **Road thickness** — Make sure no shapes are selected and then right-click the drawing page and choose Shape ➪ Custom Properties. Type values in the Road Width and Metro Width fields to specify the thickness for Thin Road and Metro Line shapes. Standard and Thick Road and Metro Line shapes are multiples of these values.

✦ **3-way and 4-way intersections and interchanges** — To change the thickness of intersection roadways, right-click the shape and choose the thickness you want from the shortcut menu. All arms of the shape change to the same thickness. To change the length of vertical or horizontal intersection arms, drag the selection handles on the sides or the top and bottom of the shape. To lengthen all the arms, drag one of the corner selection handles.

✦ **Flexible roads or flexible metros** — To change the thickness of intersection roadways, right-click the shape and choose the thickness you want from the shortcut menu. Use one or more of the following methods to modify a flexible shape:

- **Change a curve** — Click the Pencil tool on the Drawing toolbar. Drag a vertex or selection handle to reposition the points or redefine the curves.

- **Add a vertex** — Click the Pencil tool on the Drawing toolbar. Press Ctrl and click the shape where you want to add the vertex.

Using 3-D Map Shapes

Three-dimensional directional maps are perfect for producing illustrated maps or tourist guides. These maps aren't to scale, but show buildings, roads, and landmarks in an isometric three-dimensional view. To create a three-dimensional map, you choose File ➪ New ➪ Map ➪ Directional Map 3D and then drag and drop shapes from the Directional Map Shapes 3D stencil onto the drawing page. You use standard Visio techniques to work with these shapes, including the following:

✦ Dragging selection handles to resize the shapes

✦ Using Ctrl+D to quickly duplicate shapes, such as road segments

✦ Using rotation handles to rotate shapes

✦ Grouping shapes so you can move them as one

✦ Adding text to shapes by selecting the shape and typing

Labeling and Numbering Plans

Building plans are like other types of drawings when it comes to annotation. You can use a variety of means to add textual detail to your drawings. For example, you can use text blocks, Callout shapes, and the text blocks within shapes themselves to show notes and comments. You can number shapes on the drawing in sequence or display custom properties and other shape fields in shape text blocks. Because building plans are scaled drawings, you can also add Dimension shapes to show the distances represented on the plan.

Cross-Reference   To learn how to use the Number Shapes add-on to number shapes in sequence, see Chapter 4. For more information on annotating drawings, see Chapter 6. Chapter 32 describes how to include custom properties and fields in text blocks.

In addition to these techniques, the Label Shapes add-on was developed specifically for building plans, although you can use it to label shapes on other types of drawings as well. With the Label Shapes add-on, you can display up to four custom properties in labels on the shapes. You can also import data into the labels from other data sources.

To use the Label Shapes add-on, follow these steps:

1. Choose Tools ➪ Add-Ons ➪ Building Plan ➪ Label Shapes.

2. To specify which shapes you want to label, select an entry in the Shape Type drop-down list. You can label all shapes on the page, all selected shapes on the page, or specify a shape name.

3. For each of the Label boxes, select the custom property that you want to appear in that label. The drop-down list contains all the custom properties associated with the shapes you've selected to label.

4. To import data from another data source into the labels, click Import Data, which initiates the Import Data Wizard. In the Import Data Wizard, you specify the data source and the data in it that you want to use, the property that uniquely identifies your shapes, and the column in the data source that matches the unique property. The Import Data Wizard then imports the data from the source into Custom Properties associated with the shapes.

5. Click OK to label the shapes.

You can use basic Visio annotation techniques to add notes to your directional maps. The Landmark Shapes stencil includes several Text Block shapes for adding text at different font sizes to the drawing page. You can use the Callout shape to add text and point it to an element on the map.

You can also use shapes on the Landmark Shapes stencil to indicate scale and direction for your map. Although maps are unscaled by default, you can drag the Scale shape onto the drawing page to indicate the approximate scale of the map. Select the Scale shape and type the total distance that the shape represents. To indicate direction, drag either the Direction or North shape onto the drawing page. Drag the rotation handles on either of these shapes so that north is pointing in the right direction.

Summary

Visio Professional includes templates for numerous types of architectural and engineering plans, as well as directional maps. You can create the basics for your scaled plans by adding shapes for walls, openings, and building core elements. By placing these shapes on a background page, you can use them as the foundation for other types of plans, such as building services. Most of the shapes for architectural and engineering plans include shortcut menu commands, control handles, and custom properties that you can use to modify a shape's configuration. In addition, you can use custom properties to create component schedules and other types of reports.

Directional maps show larger areas than building or site plans. Although they are unscaled in Visio by default, they still represent real-world distances. You can drag and glue shapes together to depict roads, metros, and landmarks for road and city maps.

✦   ✦   ✦

Planning Space and Managing Facilities

Space plans provide value from the very beginning of building design to the ongoing management of facilities. Early on, space plans are essential tools for determining the optimal arrangement of building space to meet organizational needs. Then, when buildings are occupied, space plans help track the use of space by departments and the location of resources, and help manage the space and resources within facilities.

Visio Standard and Visio Professional both include Space and Room shapes on Building Plan stencils that simplify the initial layout of space on floors. You drag and drop the shapes onto the page, move them around, and resize them until you're satisfied with the layout.

When it's time to document who and what goes where in your facilities, only the Space Plan template in Visio Professional can help. This template helps you build a model of space, assets, and resources, whether you build it from scratch or import data to do so. In addition, whether you work with model elements in the Explorer windows or on the drawing page, Visio propagates your changes in the model and on the drawing.

New Feature Visio 2003 includes a new Space Plan Startup Wizard and additional enhancements to simplify what was once a painstaking process in previous versions of Visio.

Because space and facilities management plans require significant amounts of data, the Space Plan template also provides tools to emphasize data on space plan drawings. You can label or color-code space plan shapes with values from custom properties.

This chapter begins by showing you how to create space plans using the Space Plan Startup Wizard, either by importing spaces using the Import Data Wizard or by adding shapes directly to drawings. You will then learn how to assign resources, such as people, furniture, and equipment to space plans. Finally, you will learn how to use these space plans to manage facilities.

Understanding Space Planning and Facilities Management Using Visio

Space planning typically involves laying out space within a building in a way that provides groups of people with the space they need and arranges space so business processes can operate efficiently. High-level space planning can begin as no more than hand-drawn ovals on a napkin, but eventually space planning requires laying out detailed spaces within a building shell.

You can perform both high-level and detailed space planning in both Visio Standard and Visio Professional. Depending on the stage of planning, you can use the following Visio features to produce space plans:

✦ **Conceptual planning** — Use the Ink tool or the Ellipse tool to draw rough outlines of space on a drawing page. Select the Ink or Ellipse shapes and type the name of the area. You can draw arrows between shapes to show spaces that should be located near each other.

✦ **Detailed conceptual planning** — When you have an existing floor plan for the building you're planning or you know the amount of space each department needs, you can use Visio Space shapes to plan. Space shapes appear on the Walls, Doors, and Windows stencil and the Walls, Shell, and Structure stencil. Drag Space shapes onto the page and resize them until the value for the area that appears in the shape matches a department's allocation. You can also drag Space shapes onto an existing Visio drawing or on top of an imported CAD drawing.

✦ **Detailed space planning** — When you're planning space within a fully constructed building, you can drag Space shapes onto the page and resize them to meet a department allocation and fit within the Wall shapes that represent constructed walls. You can choose Auto-Fit from a Space shape's shortcut menu to fit the space to existing shapes on the floor plan.

No matter which type of space planning you want to do, Boundary and Space shapes help you focus on abstract spaces. With custom properties associated with these shapes, you can keep track of the intended use for a space (such as office or conference room), the name of the space, the department using it, its occupancy, and more. You can enter these properties manually or by importing facilities data.

To help you size and lay out spaces properly, the Space and Boundary shapes automatically calculate and display the area they enclose. You can change the color and fill pattern of Space shapes to help in the space planning process. Later, you can convert Space shapes to Wall shapes and begin a detailed building plan.

Facilities management typically means relocating and tracking people, computers, equipment, and furniture to respond to reorganizations and office moves. For small facilities, management can be as simple as relocating Visio shapes on a drawing page. However, for larger facilities or more systematic tracking and management, Visio Professional offers tools to track space and assets accurately, and can use external data to show your facilities and automatically refresh plans with data changes. With Visio Professional space planning tools, you can perform the following tasks:

✦ Develop space plans that reflect the physical spaces you manage.

✦ Populate areas and offices with people and assets, such as equipment and furniture, by importing data from a spreadsheet or database.

✦ Allocate unassigned people and assets to spaces in the plan.

✦ Reassign people and assets by dragging shapes from one space to another in the Space Plan model or on drawing pages.

✦ Automatically update the space plan when data in the spreadsheet or database changes.

Accomplishing these objectives using the Visio Space Plan template requires a few steps. However, the new Visio Space Plan Startup Wizard has simplified these steps considerably. Before you can track and manage resources in a space plan, you must do the following:

✦ Prepare your facilities data in your external source.

✦ Import your facilities data into a space plan using the Space Plan Startup Wizard or the Import Data Wizard.

✦ Set up your space plan to refresh when the data in your external source changes.

✦ Make sure that all spaces are placed in your space plan using the Space Explorer window.

✦ Assign people and resources to the correct categories and spaces using the Space or Category Explorer window.

✦ Make sure that unassigned people and resources are assigned to spaces using the Space or Category Explorer window.

New Feature The Space Plan Startup Wizard is new in Visio Professional 2003.

Exploring the Space Plan Template

Available only in Visio Professional, the Space Plan template includes numerous tools to simplify both space planning and facilities management, including several features that are new or enhanced with this release. When you create a new drawing using the Space Plan template, Visio opens a letter-size drawing using landscape orientation and a scale of $\frac{1}{8}$" = 1' 0". In addition, the template adds the Plan menu to the Visio menu bar and opens stencils associated with space planning and facilities management. Because space planning and facilities management are data-intensive processes, the Space Plan template uses both the new Space Plan Startup Wizard and an improved Import Data Wizard to set up space plans, import data, and manage the facilities represented by plans.

Menus and Stencils

The Plan menu that appears when you use the Space Plan template is beefier than its architectural and engineering plan counterpart. In addition to the Convert to Walls and Set Display Options commands, the Plan menu for the Space Plan template includes commands for importing and refreshing facilities data, assigning shapes to categories, opening the Space Explorer and Category Explorer windows, and labeling and coloring shapes based on custom property values.

When you use the Space Plan template to create a new space plan, Visio opens the Resources stencil, which includes Space and Boundary shapes for delineating departments, offices, and other areas in a building. The Resources stencil also includes shapes that represent resources, such as Person, Computer, and Asset for identifying the resources associated with spaces. You can create space facilities management reports quickly and easily by dragging Report shapes onto a drawing page.

Using the Space and Category Explorers

Because a Visio space plan is also a model of your facilities, you can use the Space and Category Explorers to easily view and modify the spaces and resources in your entire model, not just those on a drawing page. The Space Explorer displays a hierarchy of boundaries, shapes, and resources, where boundaries represent larger areas such as departments, shapes represent offices or rooms, and resources represent people, computers, or other assets associated with spaces. For example, you can associate people and equipment to offices, and offices to departments. In the Space Explorer, you can see which resources are located in which spaces, as shown in Figure 27-1, regardless of which drawing page shows them. The Category Explorer groups elements in the space plan by category, such as Person, Computer, or Space.

Space and assigned person on page   Boundary

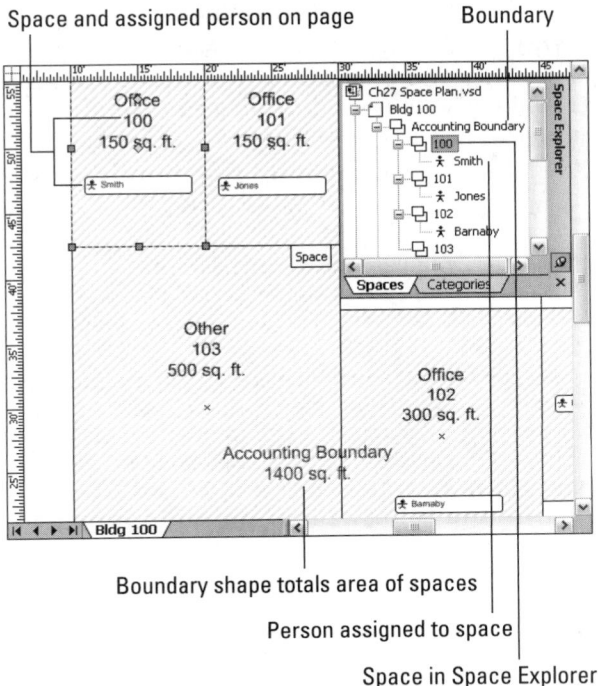

Boundary shape totals area of spaces

Person assigned to space

Space in Space Explorer

Figure 27-1: The Space and Category Explorers dock in the same window, showing spaces and the resources assigned to them.

Using the Space Explorer and the Category Explorer, you can perform the following tasks:

✦ **Locate and select spaces and resources on a drawing page** — In an Explorer window, right-click a space or resource and choose Show from the shortcut menu. Visio displays the drawing page on which the corresponding Space or Resource shape is located and selects the shape on the page.

✦ **Easily move resources between drawing pages** — Instead of cutting a shape from one page and pasting it onto another, you can move resources by dragging the person or asset from one space to another in the Space Explorer. The corresponding shape moves on the drawing as well.

✦ **Enter resource information** — Right-click a resource in an Explorer window and choose Properties from the shortcut menu. In the Custom Properties dialog box, click a custom property field and type or select a value. The value you type in the Name custom property appears by default on the shape and in the Explorer windows.

✦ **Rename resources** — Right-click a resource in an Explorer window and choose Rename from the shortcut menu.

✦ **Assign resources to spaces** — If resources haven't been assigned to spaces, expand Unplaced Data in either Explorer window. Drag a resource from the Unplaced Data area to a Space shape on a drawing page.

✦ **Delete resources** — To delete a resource both in the model and on the drawing page, select a resource in an Explorer window and press Delete.

Note   The drawing pages in your space plan might not include all Space and Resource shapes for your space plan. You can see spaces and resources that don't exist on drawing pages within the Unplaced Data folder in either Explorer window.

When you open a new space plan, by default the Space and Category Explorer windows appear in one docked window, with tabs for each window. You can hide or show both of the Explorer windows by choosing Plan ➪ Explorer. You can also float each window individually by right-clicking its tab and choosing Float Window from the shortcut menu. If you want to float the entire window with both Explorer windows in it, drag the window title bar to a new location.

Creating Space Plans

The amount of detail in space plans depends on their purpose. Space plans for prototyping the arrangement of departments and offices can be quite spare. Space plans used to manage the assets, personnel, and space in a facility are often loaded with detailed data and kept up to date with facility changes. Because of the tools that the Space Plan template provides, it's a good idea to start a space plan by choosing File ➪ New ➪ Building Plan ➪ Space Plan to create your Visio drawing. After the file is open, the method you use to create your space plan depends on the purpose of your plan:

✦ **Preliminary layouts** — For prototyping, you don't need detailed building outlines or floor plans. You can start by using drawing tools on the Drawing toolbar to sketch the outline of floors. Alternatively, you can just start dragging Space shapes onto the page.

✦ **Tracking plans** — When you plan to track resources on a space plan, you want accurate and detailed information. When you create a space plan with the Space Plan template, the Space Plan Startup Wizard opens, in which you can add a background floor plan and add Space shapes based on a list of room numbers and names. The shapes added by the wizard appear on the drawing page and in the Explorer windows. You still must add other spaces not in the original list, add resources, and associate them with spaces.

Using the Space Plan Startup Wizard

The Space Plan Startup Wizard doesn't do everything for you, but it makes setting up a new space plan a little easier. You can specify a floor plan to use as a background for your space plan and select a data source with information about spaces in your plan.

Preparing Your Space Plan Data

Whether you want to import spaces or more detailed facilities data, you can import information from a variety of sources, including Excel spreadsheets, Microsoft Active Directory directory services, Microsoft Exchange, and any ODBC-compliant data source, such as a Microsoft Access database or a spreadsheet. To import data into your space plan properly, follow these guidelines to set up your data:

✦ Include a field or column in the data source that uniquely identifies the resources or assets you want to add to your space plan. A key field, such as employee number or asset tag number, is necessary if you want to automatically update the space plan when data in your data source changes.

✦ For resources and assets assigned to specific spaces, include a field in the data source for room numbers. Room numbers in the data source must match the room numbers for spaces in your space plan. Leave the room field blank if the resource or asset isn't assigned to a space.

✦ Use the same room number for each asset or resource assigned to a space.

✦ For data sources that include data for more than one building, include a field that contains the building name or number and specify this field when you import the data.

✦ Include fields for other attributes you want to import, such as asset tag numbers, serial numbers, or maintenance dates. You can import this data into custom property fields associated with shapes.

Creating Space Plans Using the Wizard

To use the Space Plan Startup Wizard to create a space plan, follow these steps:

1. Choose File ➪ New ➪ Building Plan ➪ Space Plan.

2. On the first page of the Space Plan Startup Wizard, select the type of image or drawing you want to use as a background for your space plan. You can use a graphics file, a Visio drawing, a CAD drawing, or no background. Click Next.

3. If you chose to use a graphics file or a drawing, navigate to the file you want and click Open.

4. On the next wizard page, select an option for the source of spaces you want to add to your space plan. You can use an existing spreadsheet, create a new spreadsheet, or type the room number manually. Click Next.

Tip It's best to create a spreadsheet of rooms before you start the wizard, so you don't have to recreate your data in case something goes wrong during the wizard process.

5. If you use an existing spreadsheet, click Browse on the next wizard page and open the spreadsheet that contains your room data. If the workbook includes more than one worksheet or multiple columns, specify the worksheet and column that contain the room numbers. Click Next.

6. On the final wizard page, click Finish. Visio adds the spaces to the Category and Space Explorers. If Visio finds a shape on a drawing page with a matching room number, it lists the space under that drawing page in the Space Explorer hierarchy. Otherwise, it shows the spaces under the Unplaced heading.

7. For spaces that the wizard doesn't place on a drawing page, drag an unplaced space from the Unplaced Data folder in the Space or Category Explorer window onto the drawing page, making sure not to overlap Space shapes. To resize a Space shape, drag one of its selection handles.

Adding Spaces Using the Import Data Wizard

When you store data about spaces in a data source, you can add spaces to your space plan using the Import Data Wizard. With this approach, you can add spaces to your model and associate more information than a room number with those spaces.

1. Choose Plan ➪ Import Data.

2. On the first wizard page, choose the Store Them in the Explorer Window Under Unplaced Data option. Click Next.

3. On subsequent wizard pages, specify the source of the data and where the fields and values are stored.

4. When the wizard asks what kind of shape you want to add to your drawing, select the Space shape. Click Next.

5. Choose the field you want to use to label the spaces in the Explorer window. For example, use the room or space number. Click Next.

6. Specify the key field that uniquely identifies the space data, such as the room number. Click Next and then click Finish.

Using Shapes to Create Space Plans

It's easy to add broader boundaries and new spaces to your space plan model. If these new areas and spaces exist in your facilities data, you can use the Import

Data Wizard to update your plan. However, you can also add these elements by dragging shapes onto drawing pages. In the Resources stencil, the Boundary shape can depict larger areas such as departments or divisions. The Space shape acts as a container for the resources assigned to a specific space or office.

Caution To ensure that spaces are assigned to boundaries, and resources are assigned to spaces, add Boundary shapes to your drawing page first, followed by Space shapes, and finally Resource shapes. If you don't add these elements in this order, you can correct assignments by dragging spaces or resources to the proper boundary or space in an Explorer window.

Manually Creating Spaces

You can create Space shapes manually using either of the following methods:

✦ Drag Space shapes from the Resources stencil onto a drawing page. Visio adds a 100-square-foot square space by default. You can drag the shape's selection handles to resize it, at which point Visio updates the square footage that appears within the shape when you select it, as shown in Figure 27-2.

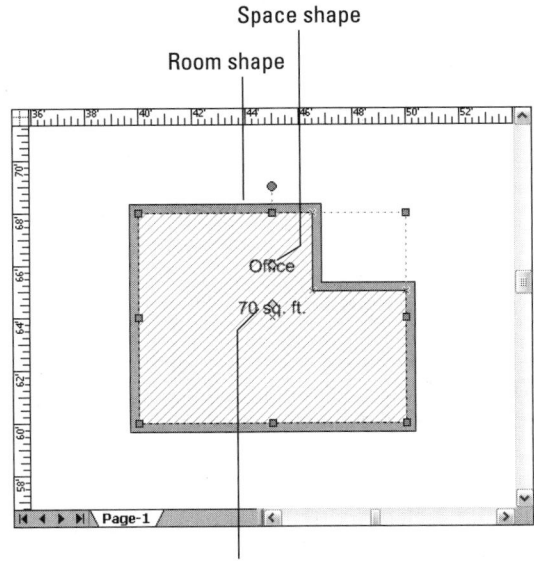

Figure 27-2: Space shapes automatically display the area that they enclose.

Tip When you drag a Space shape onto an existing floor plan with Wall or Room shapes, you can automatically adjust the shape to fit the area. Right-click the Space shape and choose Auto-Fit from the shortcut menu. Visio changes the outline of the Space shape to match the perimeter defined by the Wall shapes on the floor plan and displays the new enclosed area in the Space shape text block.

✦ Use drawing tools to outline spaces and then convert the drawing shapes to Space shapes by choosing Plan ➪ Assign Category. In the Assign Category dialog box, select Space in the Category drop-down list and click OK.

✦ Drag Boundary shapes onto the drawing page to designate larger areas, such as departments. You can place Space shapes within a Boundary shape to assign specific offices to a department. However, you can't assign people or assets to boundaries. The Boundary shape displays the area it encloses, so you can use it to show the area of multiple Space shapes.

Caution To ensure that you are tracking the area of your space plan properly, do not overlap Space shapes. When Space shapes overlap, the Space shapes include calculated area, but the overall total of space area won't match the area assigned within your building.

When you intend to import facilities data from a spreadsheet or database, spaces you add must include a value in their Name field, so you can match the space with a record in your data source. The value you specify must match a unique identifier in the spreadsheet or database. For example, if the office room number in the spreadsheet is 301, type **301** in the Space shape's Name field. To do this, follow these steps:

1. If the Custom Properties window is not open, choose View ➪ Custom Properties Window.

2. Select the Space shape on the drawing page.

3. In the Custom Properties window, click the Name field and type the value that matches the identifier in the data source.

Tip You can also specify the intended purpose of a Boundary or Space shape by clicking the Space Use field in the Custom Properties window and typing the purpose for the Space shape or selecting one of the predefined purposes in the drop-down list.

Modifying Boundary and Space Outlines

Although the Space and Boundary shapes on the Resources stencil are 100-square-foot squares by default, you don't have to stick to rectangular areas in your space plan. You can resize and reshape Boundary and Space shapes with basic Visio tools. No matter how you change the outline or size of these shapes, Visio displays the new total for the enclosed area within the shape. You can make the following modifications to Boundary and Space shapes:

✦ **Resize a Space or Boundary shape** — Drag any selection handle on one of these shapes to resize it as you would any other type of shape.

✦ **Reshape a Space or Boundary shape** — To reshape a space or boundary, right-click it and then choose Edit from the shortcut menu, or click the Pencil tool on the Drawing toolbar, and then choose from the following methods:

• Add a new vertex by Ctrl+clicking the outline of the shape.

• Move a vertex by positioning the pointer directly over it. When the pointer changes to a four-headed arrow and the vertex turns magenta, drag the vertex to a new location.

Tip
To select more than one vertex to move, Shift+click each vertex and then drag to a new location.

✦ **Auto-size a shape** — If the Wall shapes that surround a Space shape change, you can fit the shape to the new wall configuration by right-clicking the Space shape and choosing Auto-Size from the shortcut menu.

Assigning Resources to Space Plans

To track and manage the people, equipment, furniture, and other assets that occupy your facilities, you assign them to categories and then to spaces in your space plan. When you use the Visio Space Plan template, these resources are grouped into six categories, each with its own set of predefined custom properties:

✦ **Boundary** — A location category that represents larger areas such as departments or functional uses

✦ **Space** — A location category that represents specific spaces such as offices or rooms and can contain other resources, such as people or assets

✦ **Person** — Represents the human resources assigned to spaces

✦ **Computer** — An asset category that represents computer equipment that you track

✦ **Printer** — An asset category that represents printers that you track

✦ **Asset** — A generic asset category for tracking any other kind of asset

By categorizing the resources in a space plan, you can standardize the data associated with resources, view the resources in your plan for each category, and produce facilities reports by category. The Space Explorer displays a hierarchy of your facilities that shows the boundaries in a space plan, with spaces underneath the boundaries to which they belong, and resources underneath the spaces to which they are assigned. The Category Explorer shows all the resources for each category in your space plan.

Placing Unassigned Resources

When you import resources into your space plan, the Import Data Wizard places resources within spaces when it can match a space identifier in the resource record with a space identifier in your space plan model. If a person or asset is not yet assigned to a space or the wizard can't make a match, it places the people or assets in the Unplaced Data folder in the Space and Category Explorer windows.

To assign an unplaced resource in the Space Explorer window, click the plus sign to expand the Unplaced Data folder for the drawing page that contains the spaces to which you want to assign resources. Drag an unassigned person or asset from the Unplaced Data folder onto the icon that represents the space to which you want to assign it. Visio adds a shape for the person or asset to the Space shape on the drawing page as well. You can also drag an unassigned resource from the Unplaced Data folder onto a Space shape on the drawing page. In addition to adding the Resource shape to the drawing, Visio also moves the resource from the Unplaced Data folder to the icon that represents the space containing the resource.

Note   You can't rename the built-in categories or define your own.

It's easy to add resources to space plans, because the Resources stencil includes a shape for each type of resource. You can create resources automatically assigned to a category by dragging these shapes onto a drawing page. In addition, the Import Data Wizard and Explorer windows use these masters to add shapes.

Tip   If you want to use shapes other than those on the Resources stencil, you can assign any shape to a category, as described in the section "Assigning Categories to Resources" later in this chapter. For example, you might want to use custom shapes to represent different types of computers, or assign different shapes for furniture to the Asset category.

Adding Resources to Space Plans

To track resources, they must be part of your space plan model. As with spaces, you can add resources to your model manually or by importing resource data. You can use either of the following methods to add resources to your model:

✦ **Add resources manually** — To add new resources to your space plan, drag one of the Resource shapes from the Resources stencil onto the appropriate Space shape on the drawing page. Visio adds the shape to the drawing page and assigns the resource to the space and to the appropriate category based on the shape you chose. In the Custom Properties window, type the name of the resource in the Name field.

✦ **Import resources** — Choose Plan ➪ Import Data and use the Import Data Wizard to create resources and Resource shapes, and to associate data with the custom properties for the Resource shape. For instructions on how to use the Import Data Wizard, see the section "Importing Facilities Data into Space Plans" later in this chapter.

Note Resource shapes on the Resources stencil include layer assignments, so shapes on the drawing page are assigned to a layer of the same name as its resource category, such as Space, Person, and Computer. You can hide or lock shapes on the drawing page by choosing View ➪ Layer Properties.

Assigning Categories to Resources

The shapes for resources on the Resources stencil are generic. You might have dozens of different pieces of furniture and equipment in an office, but by default, they'll all use either an Asset, a Computer, or a Printer shape. If you want to use other shapes so the resources on your space plan drawing are more meaningful, you can assign categories to any Visio shape. For example, you can assign categories to the shapes from stencils, such as Office Equipment or Office Furniture. When these shapes are assigned to categories, you get the best of both worlds — not only do the shapes on the drawing page depict the resource they represent, but they also take on the custom properties for the category and appear in the appropriate category in the Category Explorer window.

To assign a category to a shape, follow these steps:

1. Select all the shapes on the drawing page that you want to assign to the same category.

2. Choose Plan ➪ Assign Category.

3. In the Category drop-down list, select the category to which you want to assign the shapes.

4. If the shapes you selected have custom properties associated with them, you can associate these properties with predefined space plan properties by following these steps:

    a. In the Assign Categories dialog box, click Properties. The Properties dialog box will appear.

    b. Under Properties, select the shape custom property you want to associate with a predefined property for the category.

    c. Under Category Properties, select the predefined category property, and then click Add to associate the two properties, as shown in Figure 27-3.

Correspondence between the two

Custom properties on shapes

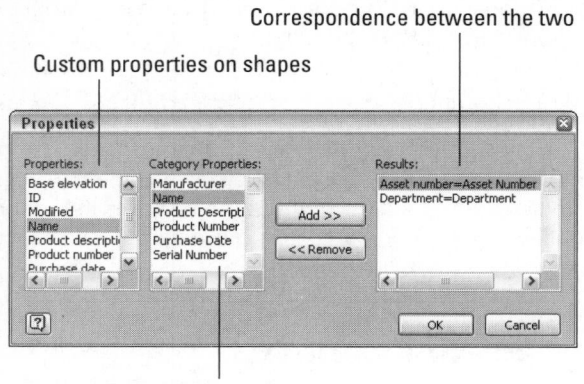

Properties for category

Figure 27-3: You can associate shape custom properties with the properties for a Resource category.

5. Repeat steps 2 and 3 for each custom property that you want to associate with a predefined space plan property. Click OK when you're done.

Note   Shape properties that you don't assign to predefined space plan properties remain associated with shapes so you don't lose any existing data.

6. Click OK to finish assigning the category to the selected shapes.

Using Visio Space Plans to Manage Facilities

You can use space plans to keep track of people, computers, equipment, and furniture as they relocate in response to reorganizations and office moves. Whether you add facilities data by hand or import it from external sources, you can display that data on your Visio space plan so you have a graphic map of the resources you manage. You can also produce facilities reports for executives or financial groups or to show departments the space and resources they have.

Importing Facilities Data into Space Plans

The Import Data Wizard makes it easy to import data into space plans. The wizard can handle data from Excel spreadsheets, Exchange Server Address Books, an Active Directory server, or tables in any ODBC-compliant database. The wizard can create new entities for the data it imports, either cascading shapes that represent the entities onto the drawing page or storing the entities as unplaced data in the Space and Category Explorer windows for later placement.

If you already have shapes on your drawing, the wizard can add the imported data to custom properties for those shapes or add the data as new shapes. For example, if you want to import data such as Space Use for Space shapes, you can import the data into custom properties in existing Space shapes on the drawing page. However, if you import data about people and assets, you can use the wizard to add Resource shapes to the Space shapes on your drawing. Even with these Resource shapes, the wizard associates other imported fields with custom properties on the Resource shapes.

Preparing Your Resource Data for Import

To produce the results you want when you import resource data, it's a good idea to review your data. It's also helpful to understand how the Import Data Wizard uses data to create and update shapes on space plans. The Import Data Wizard uses data in the following ways:

✦ **Assigning resources to spaces** — For each person or asset assigned to a space or room number in your data source, Visio places a Resource shape within the corresponding Space shape on the drawing page. You choose the type of Resource shape you want Visio to place for the imported data.

✦ **Assigning resources to spaces that don't exist** — When a resource is assigned to a space number that doesn't exist in the space plan, Visio places the resource in the Unplaced Data folder in the Explorer windows. You can create the spaces, if necessary, and manually place the resources in the appropriate spaces.

✦ **Assigning multiple resources to one space** — You can assign multiple resources to the same space by using the same space number in each resource record. For example, you can assign a person, several pieces of computer equipment, a printer, and several pieces of office furniture to the same room. Visio stacks the shapes for all these resources within the same Space shape. If you want to see all the shapes on the drawing page, drag each shape away from the shapes underneath while keeping them within the Space shape.

✦ **Refreshing data in shapes** — The Import Data Wizard uses unique identifiers in your source data when it refreshes the data associated with shapes on the drawing page. When you import data, the wizard matches the identifier in the source data with a value in a custom property for a shape. Before you import data, make sure that the field in your data source contains unique identifiers. For example, for spaces, the identifier might be the room number. For personnel, you might be able to use an employee name, but you can be assured of unique identifiers when you use an employee ID instead.

Using the Import Data Wizard

To import resource data and create new shapes within Space shapes on the drawing page, follow these steps:

1. If you want the wizard to automatically assign resources to spaces, make sure your spreadsheet or database includes a field for room or space numbers.

2. Make sure each Space shape in your drawing includes a room or space number in the Name field.

Tip   The easiest way to check for room numbers is to inspect the spaces in the Space Explorer window. If any space is named Space, you know that its Name property is blank.

3. Choose Plan ➪ Import Data. The first wizard page opens.

4. To create shapes as you import data, select the Into Shapes That Are Already on My Drawing option, and then, underneath that option, select the Add As New Shapes on Top of Existing Shapes option. Click Next.

5. In the wizard screen for the data source, select the type of data source that contains your facilities data. For an Excel spreadsheet, specify the path and filename for the file. Click Next.

6. In the next wizard screen, depending on which type of data source you chose, specify the location of the data you want to import in the data source. For example, for a spreadsheet, specify the worksheet. Click Next.

7. In the wizard screen for the shape to use, select the stencil that contains the shape you want, which is the Resources stencil by default. Then, click the shape you want in the window. Click Next.

8. On the next screen, you can specify a custom property for labeling or color-coding the new shapes. Click Next.

9. On the next screen, specify the field in your data source with unique identities, such as employee ID. Visio adds these values to a custom property associated with the new shapes and uses those values to update data when you use the Refresh Data command. Click Next.

10. On the next wizard screen, specify the shapes on which you want to place new shapes. When you're adding shapes for resources, choose the Space shape.

Tip   If you're using the Import Data Wizard to add spaces, you can choose the Boundary shape.

11. On the next wizard page, specify the custom property, which uniquely identifies the shapes already on the drawing, such as Name. Click Next.

12. On the next wizard page, specify the field in the data source that corresponds to the shape's custom property that you specified in step 11, such as room number. Click Next.

Note   The wizard places new shapes on existing shapes only when the values in the shape's property and the field in the data record match. For example, to place personnel within spaces, select the Name property for the Space shapes on the drawing, and a field, such as Room Number, in your data source.

13. On the final wizard page, click the Import Data Report link to view the results of importing your data. When you're done reviewing the results, click Finish. Visio adds the new shapes to the Space shapes on the drawing page and adds any unassigned resources to the Unplaced Data folder.

Note   Just as you can with other shapes, you can manually add or change data in Resource shapes by typing or selecting values in the Custom Properties window. However, changing the data in your drawing does not change the corresponding data in your spreadsheet or database. Visio does not export data from your drawing back to your source data.

Refreshing Space Plan Data

When you import information into a space plan, you can create a connection between the data in the data source and the shapes on your space plan. After that connection is established, you can keep your space plan drawing current, reflecting any changes in your data source. For example, if employees move to other offices and the data source contains the new office numbers, you can update the drawing to show the employees in their new spaces. When assets are sold or recycled and deleted from the data source, Visio can remove them from the space plan as well. In addition, when the data source includes a new field such as maintenance data, the data for that field is added to the shapes on drawing when you refresh data.

To refresh the data in a space plan, follow these steps:

1. Make sure that the data source hasn't been deleted or moved.

2. If you haven't done so already, use the Import Data Wizard and specify the field in your spreadsheet or database that contains unique identifiers.

3. Choose Plan ➪ Refresh Data. After the Refresh Data command processes the data, click the Import Data Report link to see a log of the changes the command made. Click OK.

Labeling Facilities Shapes

You can find spaces and resources more easily by adding labels to the shapes on your space plan. Labels are particularly helpful if you use the shapes from the Resources stencil, because they are so similar in appearance. The Plan menu in the Space Plan template includes the Label Shapes command, which runs the Label Shapes add-on. To label Space and Resource shapes, follow these steps:

1. Select the shape or shapes you want to label and then choose Plan ➪ Label Shapes.

2. In the Label Shapes dialog box, make sure the Shape Type box is set to `<all selected shapes>`. If you want to choose other shapes, select the type of shape you want to label.

3. In the Label 1 box, select the custom property you want to use as the first line of the shape's label, as shown in Figure 27-4.

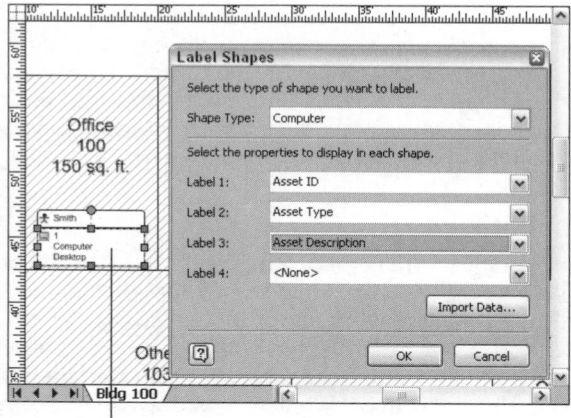

Each line represents a label

Figure 27-4: You can add up to four labels to a shape with the Label Shapes command.

4. If you want to display additional properties as labels, select the properties you want for Label 2, Label 3, and Label 4.

5. Click OK.

Controlling the Display of Spaces

Space shapes on space plans include display options similar to those for Wall, Door, and Window shapes on floor plans. You can control the appearance of Space shapes for a drawing page by setting the display options on that page. Right-click any Space shape and choose Set Display Options from the shortcut menu. In the Set Display Options dialog box, on the Spaces tab, you can perform the following tasks:

✦ Specify the custom properties that appear in Labels 1 through 4 on Space shapes.

✦ Choose options to auto size Space shapes to Wall shapes or to wall reference lines.

✦ Choose the units to use for the area of the shape.

✦ Specify the precision of the total area calculation.

Color-Coding Space Plans

Color-coding makes it easy to spot shapes on your drawing. For example, you can color-code Space shapes by assigned departments so that you can easily identify which spaces belong to which departments. If you see the same color scattered throughout a building, you might consider an office move to co-locate all the people in that department.

You use the Color By Values add-on to color-code shapes. When you create your drawing using the Space Plan template, you can choose Plan ➪ Color By Values to color-code shapes.

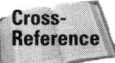

Cross-Reference To learn how to use the Color By Values add-on, see Chapter 7.

Finding and Moving Resources

The life of a facility manager is never boring with people quitting, new people being hired, and regular reorganizations thrown in for good measure. Naturally, as the location of people and assets constantly changes in a facility, so, therefore, will your space plan. You can move people or assets in the Explorer window or move the corresponding shape on the drawing page. In addition, when you manage a large number of resources, you can use tools in Visio to quickly locate the resource you want.

To find resources in a space plan, use one of the following methods:

✦ **Using the Explorer windows** — In the Space or Category window, expand a space or category, right-click the resource you want to locate and choose Show from the shortcut menu. Visio displays the drawing page that contains the corresponding shape, selects the shape on the drawing page, and centers it in the drawing window.

✦ **Using the Find command** — If there are so many resources that it's hard to find the one you want even in the Explorer window, choose Edit ➪ Find. In the Find What box, type text that is associated with the shape you're looking for, such as its name. You can use text that appears on a shape, in a custom property, or the shape name itself. Under Search In, click the locations you want to search and then click Find Next. The Find command finds the first shape containing the text you specified and highlights text within a shape or selects the shape if the text is found in a custom property, shape name, or cell.

To move resources in a space plan, use one of the following methods:

✦ **Using the Explorer windows** — In the Space Explorer window, expand pages and space until you find the resource you want to move. Drag the icon for the resource onto a different space icon.

✦ **On the drawing page** — Select the shape that represents the resource you want to move and drag it into a different Space shape on the drawing page.

Finding and Installing a Printer from a Space Plan

You can use Visio space plans to locate printers. In addition, if Smart Tags are turned on, you can install that printer on computers right from the Visio plan. To set up a space plan to do this, follow these steps:

1. To turn Smart Tags on, choose Tools ➪ Options, select the View tab and make sure the Smart Tags check box is checked.

2. Drag a Printer shape from the Resources stencil onto the space plan.

3. Position the pointer over the Printer shape. When the Smart Tag appears, click Configure Printer on the Smart Tag.

4. Choose either Find a Printer in the Directory if you use an Active directory or Browse for Printer to find the printer on the network.

5. Select a printer, click OK, and then save the space plan drawing.

When others open the drawing, they can locate a printer that's convenient. To set the printer as their default printer, they position the pointer over the Printer shape, click the Printer Smart Tag button and then choose Set As Default Printer from the shortcut menu. If they want to see the documents in the printer's queue, they choose Open Print Queue from the shortcut menu.

Generating Facilities Reports

Similar to other management callings, facilities management has its fair share of reports. Visio Professional includes several predefined reports, such as Door and Window Schedules, that are useful to facilities management. In addition, the Space Plan template includes three specialized reports for space planning and facilities management:

✦ **Asset Report**—For each asset in a space plan, this report shows the asset type, its name, its manufacturer, and to whom it belongs. You can use this report as part of a facilities audit to ensure that resources are located where they should be or that the proper group has responsibility for the assets under their control.

✦ **Move Report**—This report shows where people are located.

✦ **Space Report**—This report shows the department, room number, space use, and area for each space in a plan.

The easiest way to create one of these facilities management reports is to drag a Report shape from the Resources stencil onto a drawing page. The shape uses the current report definition and displays the results in a shape on a page. To display other information, just modify the report definition before adding the shape to the page.

Cross-Reference To learn how to run or modify reports, see Chapter 23.

Summary

You can use Visio to plan space to varying levels of accuracy and then, after construction, manage facilities and the resources within them. For high-level space planning, you can use Ink or the Space shapes available in both Visio Standard and Visio Professional. As you become more precise about the location and areas you're planning, the Space Plan template provides specialized shapes and tools to help you. This chapter introduced you to the following features:

✦ **Space Plan Startup Wizard** — Gets a space plan started by setting up a background drawing or image and imports spaces into a plan

✦ **Import Data Wizard** — Imports space and resource data into new or existing shapes on a drawing

✦ **Refresh Data command** — Updates the data in a space plan from data in an external source

✦ **Space and Category Explorer windows** — Simplifies viewing, assigning, reorganizing, and selecting spaces or resources

✦ **Label Shapes and Color By Values** — Simplifies the display of facilities data by adding labels or color-coding based on values in custom properties

✦ ✦ ✦

Integrating CAD and Visio

Visio was never meant to be a substitute for a CAD program, such as AutoCAD. If you're producing hard-core architectural or engineering drawings for large or complex projects, you'll need every bit of functionality that the CAD application can provide — and even then, there are things you'll wish it did, but doesn't.

However, although Visio doesn't replace CAD, it can complement it. By integrating Visio and CAD, you can do things that aren't possible with either program alone. For example, if you're designing part of a building and an architectural or engineering plan already exists, there's no need to recreate that CAD drawing in Visio. You can insert CAD drawings as backgrounds in Visio and use them as a reference as you work with Visio shapes.

Visio also works well as a review tool. If you don't have a CAD application or don't know how to use the one you have, you can review CAD drawings by opening them in Visio. In addition, you can use Visio shapes and Ink to quickly mark up and add comments about CAD drawings to a separate layer.

If it turns out that you want to edit CAD drawings in Visio, you can convert their contents into Visio shapes. Although this solution has its faults, including slow redraw, it's invaluable if you must edit a CAD drawing and no longer have access to the CAD program that created it.

 **New Feature** Visio 2003 supports only .dwg and .dxf file formats. However, competitive CAD programs can produce these formats, so you can still integrate Visio with most commercial CAD packages. If you have a Microstation .dgn file that you want to insert, open it in Visio 2002 and convert it to Visio shapes. Then, open it in Visio 2003.

Understanding CAD and Visio Integration

Visio provides several methods for integrating CAD and Visio drawings, whether you want to bring CAD drawings into Visio, or vice versa. The following methods are available in both Visio Standard and Visio Professional:

✦ **Insert CAD drawings into Visio** — This method is typically the best approach for bringing a CAD drawing into Visio. Inserted drawings are OLE objects that offer the following benefits:

- You can view, but not edit, inserted CAD drawings, so that you can use the CAD drawing as a reference without worrying about it being changed inadvertently.

- You can snap Visio shapes to the geometry in an inserted CAD drawing just as you snap to other Visio shapes, rulers, grids, and guides in Visio.

- You can crop CAD drawings to show details for part of a Visio drawing.

- Inserted CAD drawings provide better visual results and faster opens and redraws.

✦ **Convert CAD drawings to Visio shapes** — If you must edit a CAD drawing and don't have access to the program that created it, you can convert the drawing into Visio shapes and continue your work in Visio. Keep in mind the following when using this approach:

- CAD blocks and entities are mapped to the closest Visio shapes.

- Converted CAD drawings don't look as good as inserted CAD drawings; as with any conversion, accuracy and some details are lost.

- File opens, redraws, and editing can be slow because of the number of shapes that the conversion process creates.

✦ **Convert CAD symbol libraries to Visio masters on a stencil** — You can take advantage of predefined CAD objects by converting libraries of CAD blocks into Visio shapes on a custom stencil. Then, drawing in Visio is as simple as dragging and dropping your new masters onto the drawing page.

Caution   When you convert a CAD drawing to Visio, advanced features available only in the originating CAD program are discarded. If you subsequently reconvert the Visio drawing back into CAD, you might lose additional information. For the best results, Microsoft recommends that you perform conversions in only one direction.

✦ **Export Visio drawings to CAD format** — If you sketch up a plan in Visio, you can export your Visio drawing to CAD format when it's time to get serious about drawing. You can save Visio drawings as .dwg or .dxf files.

Tip   You can export Visio drawings to CAD format for CAD users who want to review Visio drawings. However, an easier solution for reviewing is for the CAD users to download the Visio Viewer 2003 from http://office.microsoft.com.

If you're familiar with CAD programs, Visio might leave you hungry for more. Conversely, as a Visio user, you might be frustrated by the complexity of most CAD programs. However, by understanding and appreciating their differences and similarities, you'll know when to use which tool. Table 28-1 compares Visio and CAD features.

Table 28-1
A Comparison of Visio and CAD Features

Feature	Visio	CAD
Coordinate Systems	Coordinates are based on the size and scale of the Visio drawing page. For example, for a drawing page using feet for measurement units and a scale of 1:12, one inch on paper equals one foot in real-world measurements. To specify drawing size and scale, choose File ⇨ Page Setup and select the Page Size and Drawing Scale tabs.	CAD programs often include two types of coordinate systems. Model space represents the true size of the objects in the model. Paper space applies a scale to the model so you can print or plot the model on paper. You can create multiple paper spaces from the same model space.
Units	Measurement units are the units you choose on the Page Properties tab in the Page Setup dialog box. You can select from U.S. units, metric units, publishing units, and even time-based units.	Units represent the real-world units for the model coordinate system, but aren't set to specific units such as feet or meters.
Scale	Drawing scale is the ratio of real-world measurements on the drawing page to the measurements on the printer paper. Every shape on a drawing page is drawn at the same scale. When you insert or convert a CAD drawing, Visio sets a custom drawing scale that fits the CAD drawing to the Visio drawing page.	In paper space, CAD creates views of your model in which each view can use a different scale. You can use one scale for an entire floor plan and another for a construction detail. Unlike Visio, you can compose a print or plot with multiple views, each using a different scale.
Layers	Visio layers separate shapes into categories, but don't specify stacking order. You can specify attributes such as color, visibility, printability, and whether shapes are editable.	CAD layers also separate shapes into categories that you can use to control attributes. However, unlike Visio, CAD layers can also control the order in which CAD objects appear.
Objects	Shapes	Blocks

Displaying CAD Drawings in Visio

Visio is ideal as a viewing tool for CAD drawings. It's easy to use and includes tools, such as markup and Ink, that even the most sophisticated CAD programs might not offer. For viewing CAD drawings, inserting them into Visio is the way to go. Your CAD drawings look better, Visio responds faster; and you can still control many aspects of inserted drawings. Using inserted CAD drawings, you can perform the following tasks:

✦ Use Visio to review CAD drawings produced by someone else, adding comments with Visio shapes, text, Ink, or markup on a separate Visio layer.

✦ Insert CAD drawings as backgrounds for Visio drawings. For example, if you want to use Visio to quickly prototype different office layouts, you can insert a CAD floor plan into your drawing as a reference and add Visio Furniture and Equipment shapes over it. As you work in Visio, you can snap to the geometry within the CAD drawing.

✦ Insert CAD drawings as details. For example, you can insert a CAD drawing that shows a highly detailed structural connection on a Visio drawing of an entire floor.

Inserting CAD Drawings into Visio

When inserting a CAD drawing from a .dwg or .dxf file into Visio, the Visio drawing assumes the last saved spatial view of the CAD drawing, either in model space or paper space. By using a CAD drawing saved in model space, you have more control over the CAD drawing after it's inserted into Visio. For example, with CAD drawings saved in model space, you can change the CAD drawing's scale in Visio. In addition, panning and resizing in Visio is faster when you use model space drawings. To insert a CAD drawing into a Visio drawing, follow these steps:

1. Open the Visio drawing file and the page that you want to contain the CAD drawing.

2. Choose Insert ➪ CAD Drawing. In the Insert AutoCAD Drawing dialog box, navigate to the .dwg or .dxf file you want to insert and click Open.

3. In the CAD Drawing Properties dialog box, Visio automatically chooses CAD drawing settings designed to produce the best results. For example, Visio sets the drawing scale to ensure that the CAD drawing fits on the current Visio drawing page. However, if you have specific requirements, choose the settings you want, as described in other sections of this chapter.

4. When you've specified the settings that you want, click OK.

Displaying CAD Layers in Visio

Although CAD drawings typically contain a number of layers, each inserted CAD drawing is assigned one Visio layer that is named CAD Drawing. However, within that inserted CAD drawing, you can specify which CAD layers are visible, along with the color and line weight for the objects on each layer. You can specify these settings when you insert the CAD drawing or at any time afterward by right-clicking the CAD drawing on the Visio drawing page and choosing CAD Drawing Object ➪ Properties from the shortcut menu. Select the Layer tab and then use one of the following methods:

✦ **Visibility** — To toggle the visibility of a layer, select the layer and then click the Visible field for the layer you want to toggle.

✦ **Color** — To specify the color of a layer, select the layer and then click Set Color. Click a color cell on the Standard tab or select the Custom tab and specify the color you want. Click OK.

✦ **Line Weight** — To specify the line weight for lines on a layer, select the layer and then click Set Line Weight. Type the line weight in points and then click OK.

Reviewing CAD Drawings in Visio

If you want only to view a CAD drawing and don't plan to add Visio shapes or even markup on top of it, you don't have to insert the CAD drawing into a Visio drawing. You can open the CAD drawing directly by following these steps:

1. Choose File ➪ Open.

2. In the Files of Type box, select AutoCAD Drawing (*.dwg, *.dxf).

3. Navigate to the folder that contains the file you want to open, select the file, and click Open. Visio creates a drawing page, inserts the CAD drawing onto the page, and sets the Visio measurement units and drawing scale to the units and scale of the CAD drawing.

4. To see when the CAD drawing was last updated, right-click the inserted CAD drawing and choose Shape ➪ Custom Properties from the shortcut menu. The Last Updated box shows the latest modification data, and the CAD File Name property shows the path and filename of the CAD drawing.

5. After you open the drawing, you can crop, resize, rescale, or reposition the drawing, as well as hide or show its layers and change layer colors, as described in other sections in this chapter.

Note Image files embedded in .dwg files don't appear when you insert the CAD drawing into Visio. However, they will appear if you convert the drawing to Visio shapes. If you have no reason to convert the CAD drawing to Visio, you can embed the image files in the Visio drawing directly using the methods described in Chapter 8.

Working with External File References

When you insert or convert a CAD drawing that references external files, Visio tries to open any external linked files as well. Visio looks for external reference files in a folder with the same path as the one used when the file was originally linked or in the same folder as the Visio drawing. Before you insert a CAD drawing or when you receive a message that Visio can't find the externally linked files, be sure to place any external files in the same folder as your Visio drawing or create a folder structure that mirrors the original used by the CAD drawing.

Modifying Inserted CAD Drawings

Although you can't edit the CAD drawings you insert into Visio, you can modify them in several ways. If you plan to add Visio shapes over the top of an inserted CAD drawing, you can change its units and scale so that CAD objects and Visio shapes are sized in the same way. If you want to show specific portions of an inserted CAD drawing, you can crop, pan, move, or modify the visibility of layers in the CAD drawing. You can drop Visio shapes on top of the CAD drawing and even position Visio shapes by snapping to the geometry of the inserted drawing.

Note   If you want to edit or delete individual objects in an inserted CAD drawing, convert only the layers containing those objects to Visio shapes and then make the changes you want.

Modifying Units and Scale

To achieve the results you want, it's important to coordinate the units and scale you use in both your inserted CAD drawings and the Visio drawings that hold them. If the CAD units and Visio measurement units don't match when you insert a CAD drawing into a Visio drawing, you might see a blank rectangle or only a portion of the CAD drawing.

When you insert a CAD drawing into a Visio drawing, Visio sets the Visio drawing scale so that the CAD drawing fits on the Visio drawing page. For very large drawings inserted onto small Visio drawing pages, the result can be totally unreadable. In addition, when you drag Visio shapes on top of an inserted CAD drawing, your Visio shapes might appear too small or large, as illustrated in Figure 28-1. This occurs when the CAD drawing scale and the Visio drawing scale are set differently. Even when you match the drawing scales when you insert a CAD drawing, you can change the CAD drawing scale by dragging the border of the inserted drawing.

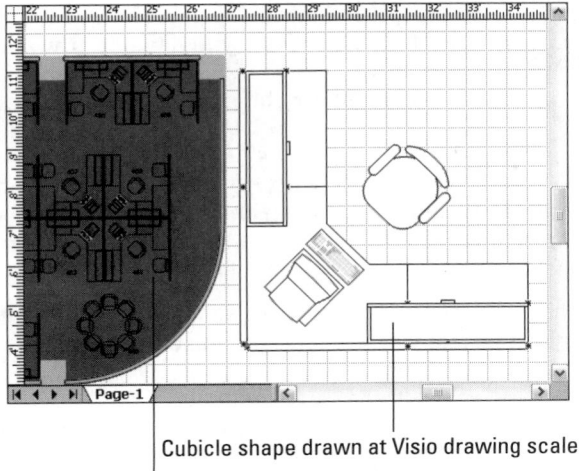

Cubicle shape drawn at Visio drawing scale

Cubicle drawn at scale of inserted CAD drawing

Figure 28-1: Visio shapes can appear too large or small when CAD and Visio drawing scales don't match.

Coordinating CAD Units with Visio Measurement Units

CAD drawings don't use pre-set drawing units. In the CAD world, a drawing unit can represent any unit — from a centimeter to an inch, or even a mile. When you insert a CAD drawing into a Visio drawing, Visio interprets CAD drawing units as Visio measurement units, which might be incorrect, especially if you insert a metric CAD drawing into a Visio drawing based on U.S. drawing units. To change the measurement unit for a CAD drawing, follow these steps:

1. To check the measurement units for the drawing page in which the CAD drawing is inserted, select the drawing page tab and then choose File ➪ Page Setup.

2. Select the Page Properties tab and check the value in the Measurement Units box. Click OK. If you prefer to change Visio units, change the value for Measurement Units here.

3. On the Visio drawing page, right-click the inserted CAD drawing and choose CAD Drawing Object ➪ Properties from the shortcut menu. On the General tab, select units to match the Visio measurement units in the CAD Drawing Units drop-down list. For example, if the Visio drawing uses feet and inches, select Feet in the CAD Drawing Units list. Click OK.

Modifying Drawing Scales

CAD drawings can represent very large areas, such as the architectural plans for a shopping mall. When you insert CAD drawings like this into Visio drawings, they might appear at a very small scale to fit on the Visio drawing page. You can change the CAD drawing scale to match the Visio drawing scale. If you haven't drawn any Visio shapes yet, you can even change the drawing page size and then change both the CAD and Visio scales to improve the readability of the plan. To change drawing scales, follow these steps:

1. If you want to change the Visio drawing scale, choose File ➪ Page Setup and select the Drawing Scale tab. For example, you can change the Visio drawing scale to match the custom scale that Visio used to fit the CAD drawing on the Visio drawing page.

2. To use a standard architectural or engineering scale, select the Pre-Defined Scale option, select the type of scale you want, and then select the scale you want to use. Click OK.

Note   If you want to use a custom scale, select the Custom Scale option and then enter a paper dimension in the first box and the real-world distance it represents in the second box.

3. To change the drawing scale for the inserted CAD drawing, right-click the inserted CAD drawing and choose CAD Drawing Object ➪ Properties from the shortcut menu.

4. Select the General tab, and select the scale using one of the following methods:

   • **Match CAD and Visio scale** — If you want the Visio shapes that you drop on top of a CAD drawing to match the scale of the CAD drawing, select the Pre-defined Scale option and then select Page Scale in the drop-down list. This sets the CAD drawing to the same scale as the Visio drawing scale.

   • **Use industry-standard scale** — If you are only reviewing an inserted drawing and won't add Visio shapes on top of it, select the Pre-defined Scale option, select the type of scale you want to use, and then the specific scale.

   • **Define a custom scale** — Select the Custom Scale option and then enter a paper dimension in the first box and the real-world distance it represents in the second box.

5. Click Apply and then make sure that the CAD drawing still fits on the Visio drawing page by looking at the extent of the CAD drawing compared with the extent of the Visio drawing, as demonstrated in Figure 28-2. If the CAD drawing doesn't fit, either change the Visio drawing size or specify a smaller CAD drawing scale. When the inserted drawing is scaled the way you want, click OK.

Note   You can't change the scale of an inserted DWG drawing saved in paper space.

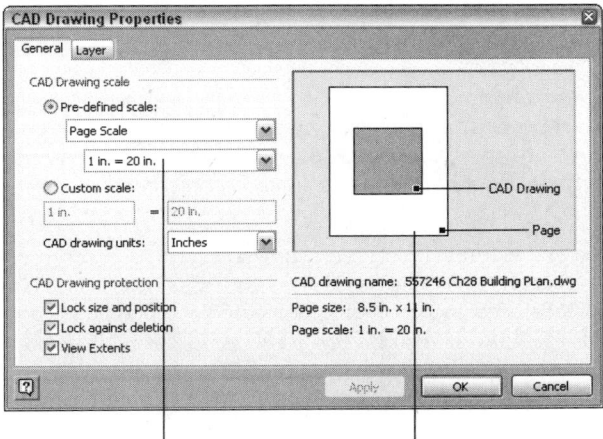

Drawing scale for inserted CAD drawing

Preview of CAD drawing extent on Visio page based on current CAD drawing scale

Figure 28-2: Compare the CAD and Visio drawing extents in the preview pane.

Protecting Inserted CAD Drawings

By default, Visio protects CAD drawings you insert from deletion, resizing, and repositioning. When a CAD drawing is locked, you can't inadvertently move it, reposition it, or delete it as you work on Visio shapes overlaid on top of it. However, when you do want to reposition the CAD drawing or change it in other ways, you can unlock the drawing from within the CAD Drawing Properties dialog box. To unlock an inserted CAD drawing, follow these steps:

1. Right-click the inserted CAD drawing and choose CAD Drawing Object ➪ Properties from the shortcut menu.

2. Select the General tab and uncheck the Lock Size and Position check box and the Lock Against Deletion check box.

3. Click OK.

Tip Unlock an inserted CAD drawing only when you want to make a change. Then, after you've completed the change, lock the CAD drawing again.

In addition to the locking you can do with CAD Drawing Properties, you can also lock the Visio layer on which the CAD drawing is inserted. Although this technique mainly duplicates the efforts of CAD Drawing Properties locking, it also prevents the drawing from moving when you pan using the Crop tool.

Finding the Invisible CAD Drawing

Placing an object far from the main drawing is an all-too-common error in CAD. It's easy to apply a CAD command incorrectly or specify the wrong dimension. When you don't see the object where you expect it, you might just add it again. By doing this, you end up with one object where it's supposed to be, but another out in space somewhere.

If you can't see the contents of your CAD drawing in Visio, go back to the original CAD application and zoom to the drawing extents. If you see a tiny speck of color off in one corner, chances are good that the drawing has some wayward objects. Visio scales an inserted drawing to fit everything, including wayward objects, onto the Visio drawing page, resulting in a tiny drawing scale and an all but invisible CAD drawing. To correct this issue both in your CAD drawing and in Visio, open the drawing in the CAD program, locate and delete the objects that are misplaced, and resave the drawing.

Positioning and Resizing Inserted CAD Drawings

Visio provides several techniques for positioning and resizing CAD drawings inserted in a Visio drawing. The result you obtain depends on the tool you use, as described in Table 28-2. You can reposition or resize the entire CAD drawing. You can also crop the CAD drawing, reducing the CAD drawing border so that only a portion of the drawing appears. You can pan within a cropped border to display the portion of the CAD drawing that you want to see, as shown in Figure 28-3.

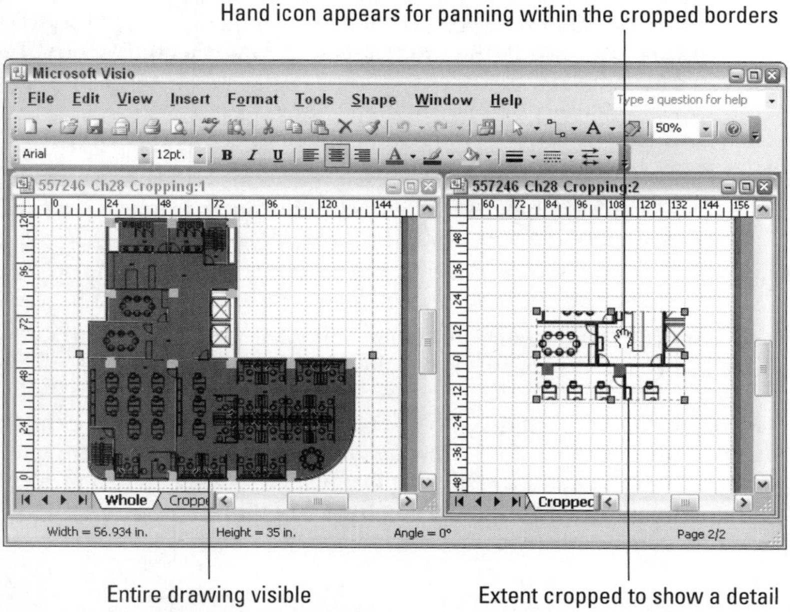

Hand icon appears for panning within the cropped borders

Entire drawing visible   Extent cropped to show a detail

Figure 28-3: Crop a CAD drawing and pan to view the portion you want.

Before you attempt to reposition or resize an inserted CAD drawing, make sure that the drawing is unlocked. To confirm that it is unlocked in the CAD Drawing Properties dialog box, right-click the drawing, choose CAD Drawing Object ⇨ Properties from the shortcut menu, and then uncheck the Lock Size and Position check box and the Lock Against Deletion check box. To confirm that the Visio layer into which the CAD drawing is inserted is also unlocked, choose View ⇨ Layer Properties and make sure that the Lock field for the CAD Drawing layer is unchecked.

Tip When you've completed repositioning and resizing, lock the drawing so that you don't accidentally move or resize it as you continue your work.

Table 28-2
Tools for Positioning and Resizing CAD Drawings

Visio Tool	Positioning	Resizing
Pointer Tool	Drag the inserted CAD drawing to move the entire drawing to a new location.	Drag a selection handle to change the size of the CAD drawing on the Visio drawing page. This also changes the CAD drawing scale.
Crop Tool	To pan the area of the CAD drawing that appears within the CAD drawing border, click the Crop tool on the Picture toolbar, click inside the CAD drawing border, and drag the Hand icon to a new location.	To crop the CAD drawing border so only a portion of the CAD drawing appears, right-click the CAD drawing, click the Crop tool on the Picture toolbar, and then drag a selection handle on the CAD drawing border until it's the size you want. Click the Pointer tool to turn off the Crop tool.
Drawing Scale	Does not apply	You can change the size of a CAD drawing by specifying a different scale in the CAD Drawing Properties dialog box. This is more precise than dragging the inserted CAD drawing's selection handles.

Converting CAD Drawings to Visio Format

If you want to edit or delete CAD objects in an inserted CAD drawing, you can convert the inserted drawing into Visio shapes. For example, if you have a CAD drawing that you received from an architect and absolutely must make changes to it before a presentation Monday morning, you can convert the drawing to Visio shapes and use Visio tools to modify the contents the way you want.

Caution   If you do convert a drawing to make changes, don't convert the modified drawing back into the CAD format. This two-way conversion can reduce the quality of the drawing. Instead, ask the originator of the drawing to use the CAD program to make the same changes you did.

The Disadvantages of CAD Conversion

CAD and Visio formats differ significantly, and converting a CAD drawing into Visio format highlights those differences. CAD drawings can contain thousands, even hundreds of thousands, of objects, each of which belongs to a layer. When you convert a CAD drawing into Visio shapes, Visio converts those CAD objects into Visio shapes and assigns them to layers using the layer names contained in the source CAD drawing. Even with an improved .dwg converter, Visio 2003 isn't able to recognize that all objects that represent the same item, such as an office chair, should convert into the same Visio shape. Therefore, a converted CAD drawing uses thousands of different shapes, each stored separately in the Visio drawing file. This glut of unique Visio shapes raises two issues with converted CAD drawings:

✦ **Slow response time** — Visio must sort through thousands of shapes and perform tremendous amounts of processing for the simplest actions, such as selecting all the shapes and repositioning them. Even relatively small converted drawings generate a noticeable delay in redraws or completion of commands.

✦ **Large file size** — When you use Visio masters, Visio stores the definition of the master only once and uses instances of the master to show shapes on the drawing page. When you convert CAD objects into unique shapes, Visio stores each shape definition separately, which greatly increases the Visio file size. For example, a .dwg file that consumes 850 kilobytes of space might require 10 megabytes of space after it's converted into Visio shapes.

New Feature   In Visio 2003, the .dwg converter can convert CAD objects into Visio shapes. Earlier Visio conversion tools converted CAD objects into separate shapes for each vector in the CAD objects.

When you convert a CAD drawing, you convert the last saved view of that drawing, which might have been saved in model space or paper space. Converting a drawing saved in model space converts all the objects and text on the layers you select into Visio shapes. However, when you convert a drawing saved in paper space, Visio converts only the objects wholly contained within the paper space viewport into Visio shapes, converting anything partially contained in the viewport into lines.

Converting CAD Drawings to Visio Format

You can convert CAD drawings into Visio shapes. Because of the quantity of data often contained in CAD drawings, the Visio conversion tool enables you to specify the CAD layers you want to convert. Even so, it's a good idea to eliminate unused layers, blocks, linetypes, and other types of CAD objects from the CAD drawing before you begin conversion. To convert a CAD drawing into Visio shapes, follow these steps:

1. Make sure the CAD drawing is cleaned up and contains no extraneous elements.

2. Insert the CAD drawing into Visio as described in the section "Inserting CAD Drawings into Visio," earlier in this chapter.

3. Right-click the CAD drawing and choose CAD Drawing Object ➪ Convert from the shortcut menu.

4. In the Convert CAD Object dialog box, click Unselect All to ensure that no layers are selected. This is a precautionary measure so that your converted drawing displays as fast as possible and is as small as possible.

5. Check only the check boxes for the layers you want to convert to Visio shapes.

6. To specify additional options for the conversion, click Advanced.

7. In the Convert CAD Object dialog box, shown in Figure 28-4, choose one of the following options to specify the action you want Visio to take with the original CAD layers:

Check only the layers you want to convert

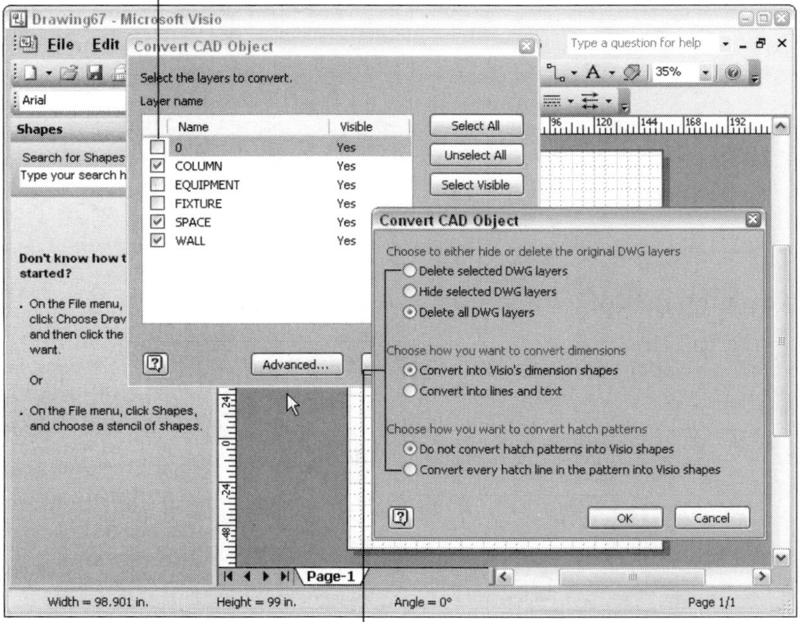

Specify options for how to convert layers

Figure 28-4: You can specify the layers you want to convert and how to convert their contents.

- **Delete Selected DWG Layers** — For each layer you select for conversion, Visio deletes the layers from the original inserted CAD drawing. Unconverted layers remain as part of the display-only inserted CAD drawing.

- **Hide Selected DWG Layers** — For each layer you select for conversion, Visio hides the original CAD layers so they don't duplicate the portion of the drawing not represented by Visio shapes.

- **Delete All DWG Layers** — Visio converts the selected layers into Visio shapes and then deletes the entire inserted CAD drawing.

8. In the Convert CAD Object dialog box, specify whether you want any dimensions on the CAD layers converted into Visio dimension shapes or lines and text.

9. In the Convert CAD Object dialog box, specify whether you want to convert hatch patterns into Visio lines or not.

10. Click OK to close the Convert CAD Object dialog box and then click OK to convert the CAD drawing into Visio shapes. Depending on the size and detail in your CAD drawing, this process can take some time. A progress bar shows you how much of the conversion process is complete.

11. After you've converted the layers you want, be sure to lock the remainder of the inserted CAD drawing, as described earlier in this chapter.

12. Save the Visio drawing.

Tip   When blocks in a CAD drawing overlap, the resulting Visio shapes in the converted drawing overlap as well, but they might not appear in the correct order. To correct the stacking order in which converted Visio shapes appear, choose Shape, and then choose either Bring to Front, Bring Forward, Send to Back, or Send Backward.

Converting Multiple CAD Drawings

If you want to convert several CAD drawings, you can use the Convert CAD Drawings add-on. However, this add-on converts each CAD drawing into a separate Visio drawing file and converts every layer in each CAD drawing. If you need more control over the conversion process, convert each drawing separately using the Convert command. To use the Convert CAD Drawings add-on, follow these steps:

1. Copy or move all the files you want to convert into one folder.

2. Choose Tools ➪ Add-Ons ➪ Visio Extras ➪ Convert CAD Drawings.

3. In the Convert CAD Drawings dialog box, navigate to the folder that contains the drawings you want to convert, select all the files you want to convert, and then click Open.

4. After Visio converts the CAD files into Visio drawing files, save each of the converted files by choosing File ▷ Save. Although Visio opens the Save As dialog box, the Save As Type option is set to Drawing (*.vsd) for a Visio drawing file. Type the name for the new file and click Save.

Creating Stencils from CAD Libraries

When you work in Visio, you don't have to forego the symbols you store in symbol libraries with your CAD application. Symbol libraries are nothing more than .dwg files that contain blocks that act as library objects. You can convert the symbols in those .dwg files into Visio masters and store them on a stencil to drag and drop as you would any other Visio shape. When you convert a symbol library, each block becomes a Visio master and is named based on the name of the original block used to create it. Block attributes are converted into Visio custom properties and are stored with the master on the stencil. No matter how many symbol libraries you convert at once, Visio places the new masters on one new stencil. Block attributes become Visio custom properties stored in the master on the stencil.

To convert CAD libraries to a Visio stencil, follow these steps:

1. Choose Tools ▷ Add-Ons ▷ Visio Extras ▷ Convert CAD Library.

2. In the Convert CAD Library dialog box, select all the .dwg files for the libraries you want to convert and then click Open. The add-on converts each block in the selected .dwg files to a master and places them on a new stencil.

3. To save the stencil, right-click its title bar and then click Save As from the shortcut menu. In the Save As dialog box, type a name for the stencil and then click Save.

Converting Visio Drawings to CAD Format

In some circumstances, you might want to save a Visio drawing to CAD format. For example, suppose you've prototyped a plan in Visio and don't want to redraw it in your CAD application. It's easy to save Visio files as .dwg or .dxf files. You simply choose File ▷ Save As, select either AutoCAD Drawing (*.dwg) or AutoCAD Interchange (*.dxf) in the Save as Type drop-down list, and then click Save. However, you must save each page in a multipage Visio file separately. Metafiles, such as Ink objects, inserted in Visio files are not supported when you save a Visio file as an AutoCAD drawing.

New Feature The Save functionality in Visio 2003 has been enhanced to map Visio entities to the most representative entity in .dwg or .dxf file formats.

Visio drawings are saved as .dwg or .dxf files with fills and hatches turned off. You can turn fills and hatches back on in AutoCAD by setting the `FILLMODE` system variable to 1 and then using the `REGEN` command to regenerate the drawing.

New Feature When you save Visio files as CAD drawings or convert CAD drawings, Visio records any mapping errors and warnings that occur during file conversion to a common log file, located by default in `D:\Documents and Settings\`*`<username>`*`\ Local Settings\Application Data\Microsoft\Visio\Temp`, but continues the conversion.

Summary

You can integrate CAD drawings and Visio drawings in several ways. When you don't need to edit CAD drawings, you can insert CAD drawings as OLE objects into Visio drawings, move and resize them, and modify settings such as scale and visibility. If you do want to edit the CAD drawings in Visio, you can convert them along with CAD symbol libraries to Visio drawings and stencils. You can also convert Visio drawings to CAD format using Save As, and one of the AutoCAD file formats.

✦   ✦   ✦

Working with Engineering Drawings

Although engineering drawings can be complex, building them doesn't have to be. The templates that Visio provides for engineering disciplines include many of the shapes and symbols you need to prepare mechanical, electrical, and process engineering drawings, diagrams, and schematics.

What's more, you can use basic Visio techniques, such as drag and drop, shape text blocks, snap and glue, and custom properties, to construct and fine-tune your engineering drawings. You can drag shapes from Electrical Engineering, Mechanical Engineering, and Process Engineering stencils onto a drawing page, using basic Visio tools to position shapes to the precise tolerances required in parts and assembly diagrams. You can use connectors and glue to define the relationships conveyed in process flow diagrams. Engineering stencils include hundreds of configurable shapes that make it easy to produce the documents you want.

In addition, the Process Engineering template includes tools that help you build a process engineering model. You can create components to track the elements of your model and view your model on a Visio drawing or in outline form.

This chapter shows you how to create mechanical engineering drawings and electrical engineering diagrams and schematics. It also describes how to build process engineering models and create process engineering diagrams. In addition, you will learn how to use components to add data to the shapes on your engineering drawings, tag and number components, and generate component lists and bills of materials.

Exploring Visio's Engineering Templates

Visio provides templates for mechanical, electrical, and process engineering drawings and schematics. The Mechanical Engineering and Electrical Engineering templates include stencils of shapes that make it easy to assemble drawings. In addition to SmartShapes, the Process Engineering templates include tools to build a model and manage components. Each engineering discipline has its own category for templates. You can choose from the following categories and templates when you select File ➪ New or use the Choose Drawing Type pane:

✦ **Mechanical Engineering**

- **Fluid Power**—Document designs for hydraulic or pneumatic controls, assemblies, and systems, such as assembly-line machinery or robotic equipment.

- **Part and Assembly Drawing**—Design or produce specifications for mechanical parts or devices, or to show how to assemble equipment.

✦ **Electrical Engineering**

- **Basic Electrical**—Produce wiring diagrams, electrical schematics, or one-line diagrams.

- **Circuits and Logic**—Document integrated circuit designs, printed circuit boards, or digital or analog transmission paths.

- **Industrial Control Systems**—Design industrial control systems, assembly lines, and power systems.

- **Systems**—Represent components and relationships between electrical devices, particularly for large-scale systems such as utility infrastructure.

✦ **Process Engineering**

- **Piping and Instrumentation Diagram**—Design and document industrial process equipment and pipelines.

- **Process Flow Diagram**—Represent piping and distribution systems and processes.

Tip

If you want to see an example of a diagram to help you decide which template is most appropriate, choose Help ➪ Diagram Gallery and then browse the templates in the engineering categories. Some templates provide more detailed examples. If Visio displays an orange border around the image of the diagram when you position the pointer over it, click the image to open a window containing a more detailed example.

Using Basic Visio Techniques in Engineering Drawings

In many cases, you can produce complex engineering drawings simply by employing basic Visio tools. You can use the following Visio tools to build a large portion of the contents of your engineering drawings:

✦ **Drag and drop** — Drag shapes from Engineering stencils onto drawing pages.

✦ **Connectors and the Connector tool** — Drag connectors onto a page and glue the ends to Engineering shapes. You can also use the Connector tool to draw the connector you want between shapes.

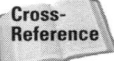
Cross-Reference

Refer to Chapter 5 for detailed instructions on using connectors and connection points.

✦ **Drawing precision** — Use snap and glue settings, shape extension lines, and the Size & Position window to draw and position shapes to the tolerances you want.

Cross-Reference

Refer to Chapter 4 for more information about positioning shapes precisely.

✦ **Shape operations** — Use Visio drawing tools and Shape Operation commands to draw unique parts.

✦ **Custom properties and custom property sets** — Associate custom properties to shapes and add data to custom properties to configure shapes or include real-world information about the components that the shapes represent.

Cross-Reference

To learn how to use drawing tools, Shape Operation commands, custom properties, and custom property sets, see Chapter 32.

✦ **Text features** — Label shapes by editing shape text blocks or adding callouts and other annotation shapes.

Cross-Reference

Refer to Chapter 6 for more information about using text and annotation tools.

✦ **Background pages** — Include title blocks on background pages to identify the contents of engineering drawings.

Cross-Reference

Refer to Chapter 2 for more information on background pages.

Working with Mechanical Engineering Drawings

You can use the Parts and Assembly Drawing template to create detailed specifications of parts or to show how pieces of equipment fit together in an assembly. The Fluid Power template helps you document hydraulic or pneumatic power systems, flow control, and fluid power schematics and assemblies. These templates don't include specialized menus or toolbars, but they open several stencils with specialized shapes. Many of the Mechanical Engineering shapes include control handles or shortcut commands you can use to specify different shapes and sizes.

Drawing Parts and Assemblies

To manufacture mechanical parts, you need drawings that specify every dimension, edge, plane, and curve for a part. To assemble separate parts into a functional whole, you need instructions that show how the parts fit together. The Visio Parts and Assembly Drawing template includes masters that help you construct the geometric shapes found frequently on part and assembly drawings.

To create a part and assembly drawing, choose File ⇨ New ⇨ Mechanical Engineering ⇨ Part and Assembly Drawing. If you use the US Units template, Visio creates a new ANSI B-size (17 inches by 11 inches) drawing in landscape orientation using a mechanical engineering one-quarter scale (shapes appear on the page at one fourth of their actual size). In addition, the following stencils open:

✦ Stencils in the Mechanical Engineering stencil category:

- **Fasteners 1** — Nuts and bolts

- **Fasteners 2** — Rivets and washers

- **Geometric Dimensioning and Tolerances** — Symbols used to show dimensioning origins and tolerances

- **Springs and Bearings** — Shapes for springs and different types of bearing conditions

- **Welding Symbols** — Standard shapes that indicate different types of welds

✦ Stencils in the Visio Extras stencil category:

- **Annotations** — Annotation shapes for callouts, text blocks, north arrows, reference and section indicators, and drawing scale symbols

- **Drawing Tool Shapes** — Geometric shapes often used for parts and assemblies, including circle tangents, perpendicular lines, triangles, and rounded rectangles. These shapes might save you the trouble of using Shape Operations to create some geometries.

- **Dimensioning-Engineering** — Dimensioning shapes for linear and radial dimensions drawn using standard mechanical engineering dimension styles

- **Title Blocks** — Frames, tables, title blocks, and revision blocks

Using Geometric Shortcuts

The Drawing Tool Shapes stencil provides shapes that help you create geometric constructions more easily than you can with Visio drawing tools or Shape Operation commands. Drawing tools provide one way to construct rectangles and ellipses. The Drawing Tool Shapes stencil includes shapes that enable you to define geometry in other ways. For example, you can use shapes to create circles by specifying the circle diameter, the circle radius, and one point on the circumference, or by using three points on the circumference. In addition to handles that you can drag, some shapes have shortcut menus with commands that you can use to display other constructions. For example, the Sector-graphical shape shortcut menu includes the Show Complementary Sector command, which changes a pie slice to the rest of the pie.

You can use the following special geometric constructions or explore other shapes on the Drawing Tool Shapes stencil:

✦ **Measure shapes** — The icons for these masters look like measuring tapes. Drag a shape, such as Measure Tool, Horizontal Measure, or Vertical Measure, onto a page and glue it to the shape from which you want to measure. As you drag the green selection handle around, the text block shows the distance from the glued point in the set measurement units.

✦ **Circle Tangents and Arc Tangents** — Use these shapes to draw belt systems. The control handles on the Arc Tangent shape adjust the radius at the corresponding end of the shape. The yellow control handle on the Circle Tangent shape enables you to change the length of the tangent line and keep the line tangent to the circle.

Note You can use Arc Tangent shapes to create linkages for belt systems. For example, to connect one mechanical cam to another, add an Arc Tangents shape to the drawing page to represent the first cam, then drag another Arc Tangents shape onto the page and glue one of its connection points to the Arc Tangents shape.

✦ **Rounded Rectangle** — Use this shape to quickly draw process storage tanks. Change the roundness of the corners by dragging the control handle.

Note The Equipment–Vessels stencil in the Process Engineering Piping and Instrumentation Diagram template includes several tank shapes.

✦ **Sector-graphical and Arc-graphical** — The Sector-graphical shape is a pie slice with selection handles for changing the radius, origin, and rotation of the slice, and a control handle that modifies the angle circumscribed by the slice. The Arc-graphical shape is an arc shape that works the same way as the Sector-graphical shape.

✦ **Sector-numeric and Arc-numeric** — The selection handles and control handles determine the radius and origin for the sector or arc. Type a number while the shape is selected to change the angle circumscribed by the slice or arc.

✦ **Triangle shapes** — Use these shapes to construct triangles in different ways. You can adjust the angles in the Right Triangle: Angle, Hypotenuse shape by typing the angle you want while the shape is selected.

✦ **Multigon shapes** — Drag one of these shapes onto the drawing page, right-click the shape, and then choose the polygon you want from the shortcut menu.

Creating Springs, Bearings, and Fasteners

Springs, bearings, and fasteners come in many standard shapes and sizes — too many to include one of each on the Mechanical Engineering stencils. Many of these shapes include custom properties that control shape dimensions. When you modify the value in a custom property, the size of the shape adjusts accordingly. You can specify one dimension and let Visio adjust the other dimensions based on industry standards or you can specify all dimensions. Although these shapes are locked so you can't resize them inadvertently, you can unlock and display the shape handles so you can use them to resize the shapes. The following list includes some of the commands that appear on shape shortcut menus, depending on which shape you right-click:

✦ **Set Standard Sizes** — Modify the thread diameter in the Custom Properties dialog box. Visio adjusts the other dimensions for the shape to industry-standard lengths.

✦ **Set Dimensions** — Modify one or more of the dimensions in the Custom Properties dialog box to configure the shape the way you want.

✦ **Resize with Handles** — Display the selection handles on a shape so you can resize it by dragging.

✦ **Hatched** — Display cross-hatching on the shape. Choosing Unhatched from the shortcut menu removes the cross-hatching.

✦ **Simplified** — Show a simplified version of the shape with some lines removed. When the simplified version appears, the command on the shortcut menu changes to Detailed.

✦ **Alternate Symbol** — Alter the appearance of the shape slightly, such as changing an X to a plus within a shape.

Creating Welding Symbols

You can use the symbols on the Welding Symbols stencil to show the locations and types of welds on a drawing. To add a weld to a drawing, follow these steps:

1. Drag one of the Arrow shapes onto the drawing page and position it so that the leader on the arrow points to the weld joint.

2. To specify additional weld information, right-click the arrow shape and choose Show All Around Circle and/or Show Tail from the shortcut menu.

3. To add symbols to specify the type of weld, follow these steps:

   a. Double-click the Arrow shape on the drawing page to open the group window.

Tip   If you can't see the Shapes window while the group window is open, choose Window ⇨ Tile to display all the windows side by side.

   b. Drag symbols that represent different types of welds, such as V-groove, onto the Arrow shape in the group window.

   c. To annotate the weld, drag Annotation shapes into the group window and edit the text. You can glue Welding Symbol shapes and Annotation shapes to the guides in the group window to keep symbols positioned correctly when you resize the Arrow shape.

4. To return to the drawing page, click the Close button in the group window.

Annotating Dimensions and Tolerances

Part and assembly drawings usually include numerous dimensions. You can add dimensions and datum points using shapes from the Dimensioning-Engineering stencil and Geometric Dimensioning and Tolerancing stencil.

Dimension shapes include control handles you can drag to define the distance to measure as well as the location of the dimension lines, as illustrated in Figure 29-1. The control handles that appear depend on the dimension shape you choose. As an example, you can add dimensions from a vertical baseline by following these steps:

1. Drag the Vertical Baseline shape onto the page near the bottom of the part you want to dimension. Drag the green end points to both position the ends of the horizontal reference lines and define the distance for the first dimension.

2. To position the text and vertical dimension lines for the first dimension, drag the yellow control handle on the first dimension line.

3. Drag the yellow control handle both equidistant from the base reference line and the first horizontal reference line and between the green selection handles up and to the left to define another vertical dimension line.

4. After you have added the dimensions you want, you can drag the control handles at the top of each dimension up or down to change the height of the dimension. When you drag these yellow control handles to the left or right, Visio repositions the horizontal reference line.

5. To change the spacing between the vertical dimension lines, drag the yellow control handle at the bottom of the Vertical Baseline shape.

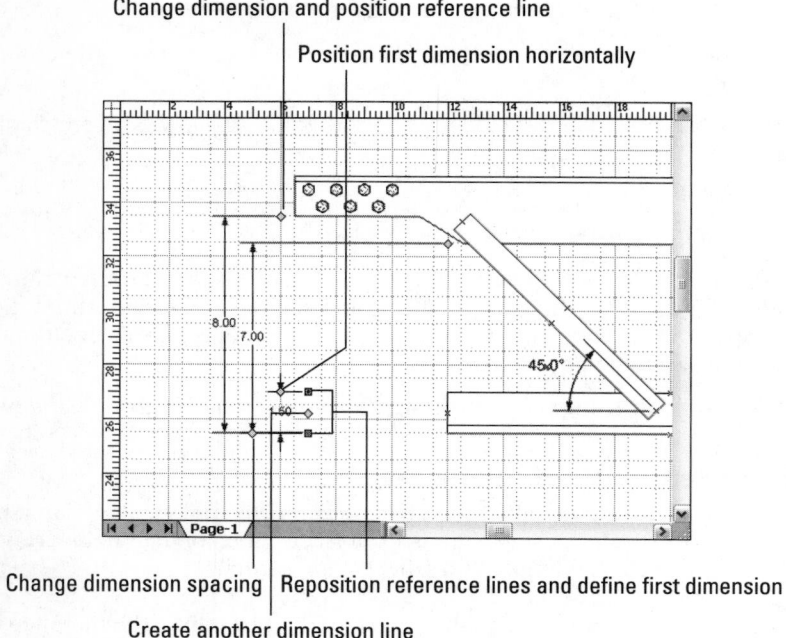

Change dimension and position reference line

Position first dimension horizontally

Change dimension spacing | Reposition reference lines and define first dimension

Create another dimension line

Figure 29-1: You can modify dimensions by dragging control handles.

You can also add datum points and datum frames to specify origins and geometric characteristics. Datum points delineate positions that you can use to align shapes on different pages or drawings. To add these symbols, use one of the following methods:

✦ **Datum shapes** — Drag a Datum shape, such as Datum Symbol or Datum (New), from the Geometric Dimensioning and Tolerancing stencil onto the drawing page and, while the shape is selected, type the text you want in the symbol. Press Esc to complete your text entry.

✦ **Datum Frame** — Drag a Datum Frame shape, such as 1 Datum Frame or 2 Datum Frame, onto the drawing page, and then double-click it to open the group window. To denote geometric characteristics, drag shapes, such as Cylindricity, into the box on the left end of the Datum Frame shape. To add text to the other boxes in the shape, double-click the box and type the text you want. When you have finished editing the Datum Frame shape, click the Close button for the group window to return to the drawing window.

Constructing Fluid Power Diagrams

To document pipes and equipment for fluid power diagrams, you can use the Visio Fluid Power template. To create a fluid power drawing, choose File ⇨ New ⇨

Mechanical Engineering ⇨ Fluid Power. Visio creates a new letter-size drawing in landscape orientation with no scale and opens the following stencils:

✦ The following stencils are in the Mechanical Engineering stencil category and open automatically when you use the Fluid Power template:

- **Fluid Power-Equipment** — Pumps, compressors, gauges, meters, and other types of equipment

- **Fluid Power-Valve Assembly** — Shapes that represent valves and other types of equipment

- **Fluid Power-Valves** — Different types of valves

✦ The following stencils are in the Visio Extras stencil category:

- **Annotations** — Annotation shapes for callouts, text blocks, north arrows, reference and section indicators, and scale symbols

- **Connectors** — Different types of generic connectors

Putting together fluid power diagrams requires nothing more than basic Visio techniques. Use the following steps to construct a fluid power diagram:

1. Drag shapes from Fluid Power stencils onto the drawing page.

2. To change the configuration or version of a shape, right-click the shape and choose a command from the shortcut menu. For example, you can configure the Pump/motor (Simple) shape to be hydraulic or pneumatic, bi-directional or uni-directional, variable, or compensated. You can also configure the Pump/motor (Simple) shape to represent a pump, a motor, or a combination of the two.

Note Most but not all shapes on Fluid Power stencils include configuration commands on their shortcut menus.

3. Add text to shapes by selecting a shape and typing the text you want. After you add text, most shapes include a control handle you can drag to reposition the text if it overlaps graphics on the drawing.

4. To connect equipment on the drawing, use the Connector tool to draw connectors between connection points, by following these steps:

   a. Click the Connector tool on the Standard toolbar.

   b. On the Connectors stencil, click, but don't drag, the connector master that you want to use.

   c. On the drawing page, drag with the Connector tool from a connection point on one Fluid Power-Equipment shape to a connection point on another. Visio draws a connection between the shapes using the connector master you chose. The end points of the connector turn red when it is glued to the shape connection points.

Note   Some shapes on Fluid Power stencils include control handles that you can use to connect them to other shapes. To find out what a control handle does, position the pointer over the control handle to see a screen tip.

Working with Electrical Engineering Drawings

The Electrical Engineering templates include stencils with shapes you can drag and connect to assemble electrical engineering drawings and schematics. You can create the following types of electrical engineering diagrams:

✦ **Basic electrical diagrams** — Produce wiring diagrams, electrical schematics, or one-line diagrams.

✦ **Circuits and logic diagrams** — Document integrated circuit designs, printed circuit boards, or digital or analog transmission paths.

✦ **Industrial control systems diagrams** — Design industrial control systems, assembly lines, power systems.

✦ **Systems** — Represent components and relationships between electrical devices, particularly for large-scale systems such as utility infrastructure.

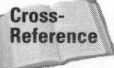

Cross-Reference   Visio 2003 includes enhancements to some Electrical Engineering shapes so that they connect more cleanly than in Visio 2002.

To create an electrical engineering drawing, choose File ⇨ New ⇨ Electrical Engineering and then choose the template for the type of drawing you want. Visio creates a new letter-size drawing in portrait orientation and no scale. You can use basic Visio techniques to add shapes to the page and connect them. As with mechanical engineering drawings, the Connector tool is the best way to connect specific points on your Electrical Engineering shapes.

Use the following basic steps to construct an electrical engineering drawing:

1. Drag shapes onto the drawing page.

2. To change the configuration or version of a shape, right-click the shape and choose a command from the shortcut menu. For example, when you use the Indicator shape on the Fundamental Items stencil, you can choose Configure Indicator from the shortcut menu to choose from 16 different types of indicators.

3. Add text to shapes by selecting a shape and typing the text you want. After you add text, most shapes include a control handle you can drag to reposition the text if it overlaps graphics on the drawing.

4. To connect the equipment on the drawing, use the Connector tool to draw connectors between connection points, by following these steps:

    a. Click the Connector tool on the Standard toolbar.

    b. On a stencil that contains connectors, click, but don't drag, the connector master that you want to use. For example, you can click the Transmission Path connector on the Transmission Paths stencil to connect two shapes that represent devices.

    c. On the drawing page, drag with the Connector tool from a connection point on one Fluid Power-Equipment shape to a connection point on another. Visio draws a connection between the shapes using the connector master you chose. The end points of the connector turn red when it is glued to the shape connection points.

Caution

Because Electrical Engineering shapes include connection points that are not interchangeable, such as the positive or negative terminals on a battery, you usually want to glue to specific connection points. rather than use shape-to-shape glue. When you glue connectors to Electrical Engineering shapes, make sure that Visio highlights only the connection points in red, not the entire shape.

Building Process Engineering Models

With the Visio Process Engineering template, it's easy to draw piping and instrumentation diagrams (P&IDs) and process flow diagrams (PFDs). You can drag shapes from Process Engineering Equipment stencils onto your drawing page, connect them with Pipeline shapes, and then add shapes to represent components, such as valves. Process engineering models use components, which represent physical objects, such as pipelines or pieces of equipment. In addition to the graphical view of your process engineering diagram, you can use the Component Explorer and Connectivity Explorer windows to view components and connections hierarchically.

You can add information to components through their custom properties and use those properties to produce reports or equipment lists. In addition, tags identify and track the components on your drawings. By default, Visio adds tags to components when you drag them onto the drawing page. Tags appear in component text blocks by default, but you can choose whether to hide or show them to improve the readability of a drawing. Visio provides predefined tag formats, but you can also create your own. If you construct different views that contain the same component, such as an overall plan and a detail, you can assign the same tag to multiple shapes, so you can accurately track components.

New
Feature

In Visio 2002, custom property sets were available only through the Custom Property Manager in the Process Engineering template. In Visio 2003, custom property sets are available in all templates.

Using Process Engineering Views

In addition to viewing diagrams, you can use the Component Explorer and Connectivity Explorer windows to see an outline of the components and connections in your process engineering model. You can also easily view data associated with components as you work by opening the Custom Properties window. The Processing Engineering templates provide the following windows for viewing and working on your process engineering models and drawings:

✦ **Drawing window** — Shows the equipment and how it is connected. You can create process engineering diagrams across multiple pages or create detailed views of portions of a model. When you select a shape in the drawing window, Visio highlights the corresponding component in the Component Explorer window.

✦ **Component Explorer window** — Presents a hierarchical view of components in a model, grouped by category, such as Equipment, Pipelines, Valve, or Instrument. In the Component Explorer window, the component tag numbers appear in the outline. For each component, you can expand the outline to see the shapes that belong to it.

✦ **Connectivity Explorer window** — Shows a hierarchical view of the pipelines that connect components in your model. Pipelines appear at the top level of the hierarchy, identified by their tag numbers. For each pipeline, the components connected to the pipeline are listed by tag number.

✦ **Custom Properties window** — Whether you select a shape in one of the Explorer windows or on the drawing page, you can view the custom property values for the shape in the Custom Properties window. Process Engineering shapes come with several properties predefined. For example, Pipeline shapes include properties for line size, material, design pressure, design temperature, and more.

You can open and close Explorer windows or switch between Explorers, depending on what you want to see. To open an Explorer window, choose Process Engineering ➪ Component Explorer or Process Engineering ➪ Connectivity Explorer.

Tip   When both Explorer windows are open, you can switch between Explorers by selecting the Components or Connectivity tab at the bottom of the window.

The outline format of the Explorer windows provides an easy and familiar way to see your entire model even if it spans several drawing pages. You can also use the Expand and Collapse icons to filter the components you see, as shown in Figure 29-2. In the Explorer windows, you can create new components, rearrange them in the outline, and rename them. If you are trying to find a component on a complex drawing, you can quickly zoom into the shape that represents the component using the Select Shapes command. Choose from the methods in Table 29-1 to work with components within the Explorer windows.

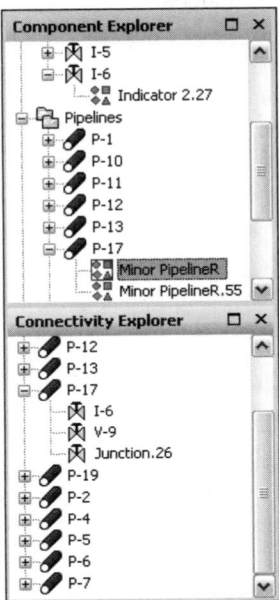

Figure 29-2: You can manage components and connections in the Explorer windows.

Table 29-1
What You Can Do in the Explorer Windows

Task	Description	Explorer
Expand or collapse hierarchy levels	Click the plus icon to expand the outline to show the next lower level in the hierarchy. Click the minus icon to hide the lower level.	Both
Select components	Double-click a component or right-click a component and then choose Select Shapes from the shortcut menu. Visio zooms in and centers the shape that represents the selected component on the drawing page.	Both
Create components	Create a new component by right-clicking the category to which you want to add a component and then choose New Component from the shortcut menu.	Component Explorer only
Rename components	Right-click a component in an Explorer window and choose Rename from the shortcut menu. Type the new name and press Esc when you're done. Visio renames the component in the Explorer windows and the drawing.	Both

Continued

Table 29-1 *(continued)*		
What You Can Do in the Explorer Windows		
Task	*Description*	*Explorer*
Associate shapes with other components	To change the component to which a shape belongs, in the Components Explorer window, drag a shape from one component to another component in the same category.	Component Explorer only

Updating Process Engineering Projects from Visio 2000

Visio's approach to process engineering drawings changed drastically between Visio 2000 and Visio 2002. If you want to take advantage of all the features in the Visio 2003 Process Engineering solution, you must update models built in Visio 2000. To do this, you should first migrate your Visio 2000 Process Engineering project to Visio 2002 and then open it in Visio Professional 2003.

In the Visio 2000 Process Engineering template, projects contained all the drawings and documents for a model, including PFDs, P&IDs, and other files. Projects could contain multiple drawings, each in its own Visio drawing file, so you used the Project Explorer to open and view your documents. In Visio 2003, process engineering drawings work like other types of drawings. There is no need to use separate functionality to manage project files, project databases, or other files. Data for components is stored in custom properties, not project databases, so it's easier to manage, in addition to being more portable.

The migration process converts each drawing in a Visio 2000 project to a separate Visio 2002 process engineering drawing. In moving to Visio 2003, you can include several process engineering drawings in the same Visio drawing file by adding each drawing as a separate page.

After you migrate a Visio 2000 project to Visio 2002, you'll see the following changes:

✦ All masters and shapes function as Visio 2002 and Visio 2003 shapes.

✦ All pipelines function as Visio 2002 and Visio 2003 pipelines.

✦ Information in datasheets migrates from the project database into custom properties associated with components.

✦ Datasheet field definitions become custom property sets, which Visio applies to the appropriate shapes.

✦ Tags are still applied to the same shapes as they were in Visio 2000.

✦ Automatic Label shapes become Callout shapes from the Process Annotations stencil.

> **Note** The migration process doesn't affect the Visio 2000 files in any way. All files associated with the Visio 2000 Process Engineering project are preserved. You can even migrate your files within the same folder, because Visio uses slightly different names for the migrated drawing files to prevent the files from being overwritten.

To migrate a Visio 2000 Process Engineering project to Visio 2003, follow these steps:

1. To save the migrated files in a new folder, create a destination folder using Windows Explorer.

2. Open the Visio 2000 Process Engineering project (.vsd) in Visio 2002. When Visio prompts you, click Enable Macros to begin the migration. When Visio prompts you to migrate all drawings, click Yes to convert all the drawings in the Visio 2000 project to Visio 2002 drawings.

> **Note** If you click No, Visio does not migrate the drawings. However, you can still open them as read-only drawings in Visio.

3. In the Browse for Folder dialog box, select the destination folder you created in step 1 and then select a filename. Visio begins to migrate the files into the new format.

> **Caution** The migration process might take some time, particularly if you are migrating a large Visio 2000 project. To avoid tying up your computer, you can start the migration and let it run on its own.

4. After the migration is complete, click OK. Visio presents a summary of the names and paths of the migrated files. Review the summary and then open the migrated files in Visio 2003.

Creating P&ID and PFD Drawings

The approach to creating process engineering drawings isn't much different than creating other types of engineering drawings, although Visio provides some additional tools to simplify some tasks, such as adding valves to pipelines. The steps in this section provide an overview of the basic sequence for creating a process engineering drawing. You can then obtain more detailed instructions in other sections in this chapter.

To create a process engineering drawing, choose File ➪ New ➪ Process Engineering and then choose the template for the type of drawing you want. Visio creates a new ANSI B-size (17 inches by 11 inches) drawing in landscape orientation and with no scale. For either template, Visio opens the following stencils from the Process Engineering category:

- ✦ Equipment-General
- ✦ Equipment-Heat Exchangers
- ✦ Equipment-Pumps
- ✦ Equipment-Vessels
- ✦ Instruments
- ✦ Pipelines
- ✦ Process Annotations
- ✦ Valves and Fittings

To quickly assemble a process engineering drawing, follow these basic steps:

1. Drag shapes for major equipment, from the Equipment-Vessels, Equipment-Pumps, Equipment-Heat Exchangers, and Equipment-General stencils onto your drawing. As you drop them onto the page, Visio adds tags that identify each piece of equipment as a component.

2. Use Pipeline shapes to connect the shapes for major equipment. The easiest way to connect Equipment shapes using Pipeline shapes is to click the Connector tool on the Standard toolbar, click the Pipeline connector master you want to use in the Pipelines stencil, and then drag the mouse pointer from one shape representing a component to another on the drawing page.

Tip   To change to a different type of pipeline, click another Pipeline connector master in the Pipelines stencil and then continue to draw between Equipment shapes on the drawing page.

Note   You can modify the direction of a pipeline or the type of pipeline by changing the line style of the Pipeline shape, as described in the next section.

3. Drag Valve shapes from the Valves and Fittings stencil onto Pipeline shapes on the drawing page. When a red square appears on the Pipeline shape and the Valve shape rotates to the orientation of the Pipeline shape, release the mouse button to glue them. Visio automatically splits the Pipeline shape into two pieces, both of which are glued to the Valve shape.

4. Drag Instrument shapes from the Instruments stencil onto the drawing page near the Pipeline shapes, Valve shapes, or shapes for the equipment that the instruments monitor. If the Instrument shape includes a control handle, you can drag it to glue the Instrument shape to the shape for the component it monitors.

5. Drag shapes, such as Callouts or Text, from the Process Annotations stencil onto the drawing page and edit their text blocks to annotate the drawing.

6. Add data to components. Choose View ➪ Custom Properties Window. Select a shape, click a custom property field, and then type or select a value.

Building Pipelines

In Visio process engineering drawings, pipelines are components that connect equipment, such as vessels or centrifuges. However, as you connect Pipeline shapes to one another or add shapes for other equipment components to them, Visio splits the Pipeline shapes into separate shapes. Although a pipeline in the model might comprise several separate shapes on the drawing page, each one belongs to the same component and shares the same tag and custom properties.

Specifying Pipeline Behavior

To specify how pipelines behave when you add valves or connect other pipelines, choose Process Engineering ➪ Diagram Options and then specify the following options:

✦ To split Pipeline shapes when you drop Valve and Fitting shapes onto them, check the Split Pipelines Around Components check box.

✦ To split Pipeline shapes when you connect other Pipeline shapes to them, check the Split Pipelines When Branches Are Created check box.

✦ To repair Pipeline shapes when you delete components or other Pipeline shapes, check the Repair Split Pipelines check box.

Note If you want Pipeline shapes to split, you must also be sure to glue to shape geometry. Choose Tools ➪ Snap & Glue and check the Shape Geometry check box under the Glue To heading.

Specifying Pipeline Type

Although you can specify attributes such as design pressure in custom properties associated with a pipeline component, the type of pipeline is determined by the line style you apply to a Pipeline shape. To change the line style for a Pipeline shape, right-click it and then choose Format ➪ Style from the shortcut menu. Select the type of Pipeline style you want in the Line Style drop-down list and click OK.

You can also use line styles to show the direction of flow in a pipeline. To show the flow direction of a Pipeline shape, select the shape and then select a style from the Line Style list on the toolbar. For example, the P&ID Minor Pipe-> line style shows flow from the starting point to the ending point of a pipeline shape. P&ID Minor Pipe<- indicates flow from the end back to the beginning.

Adding Components to Pipelines

When you drop a Valve shape onto a Pipeline shape, Visio splits the Pipeline shape into two pieces, with the ends of the two segments glued to the component you inserted, as shown in Figure 29-3. The two shapes still belong to the same component and share the same tag and properties as the original Pipeline shape.

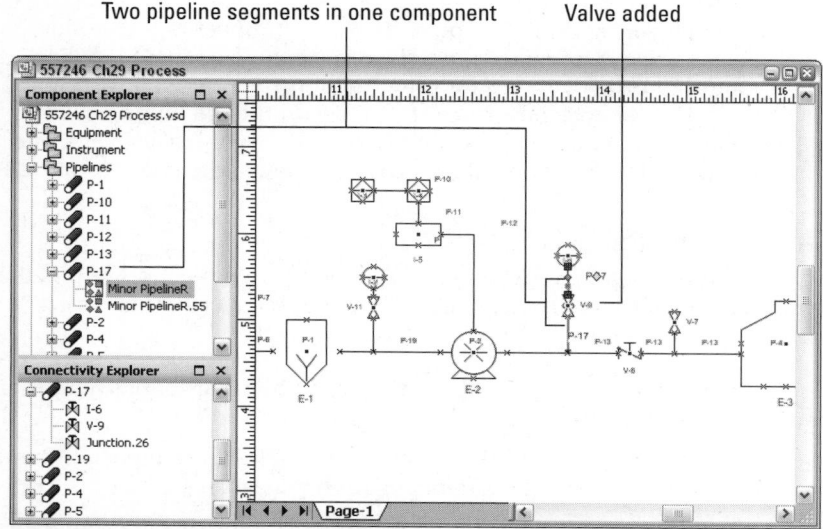

Figure 29-3: When pipelines split, the shapes still belong to the same component.

When you connect one pipeline to another, the original Pipeline shape also splits into two pieces. Visio adds a Junction shape at the point where the three Pipeline shapes intersect. Although you don't see Junction shapes on the drawing page, they do appear in the Connectivity Explorer window.

Tip   If you want to display Junction shapes—for example, to validate your drawing— choose Process Engineering ⇨ Diagram Options, check the Split Pipelines When Branches Are Created check box, and then select Junction in the drop-down list.

To add a valve or fitting to a pipeline, follow these steps:

1. Drag a Valve or Fitting shape from the Valves and Fittings stencil and position it on top of a Pipeline shape.

2. Release the mouse button when Visio displays a red square on the shape indicating that the shapes are glued. Visio rotates the Valve or Fitting shape to match the orientation of the Pipeline shape.

Note   When you delete a valve or other component that splits a pipeline into two pieces, the pipeline heals into a single shape. However, if you delete a component between two different pipeline components, the pipelines remain separate components. If pipelines that belong to the same component don't repair themselves when you delete a component, choose Process Engineering ⇨ Diagram Options and check the Repair Split Pipelines check box.

Continuing Pipelines on Other Pages

In some circumstance, you might want to continue the same pipeline on different pages. For example, if a pipeline spans a distance that doesn't fit on the drawing page you're using, you can add shapes that show that the pipeline continues on another page. Clicking those shapes navigates to the continuation of the pipeline.

To continue a pipeline on another page, follow these steps:

1. Drag one of the Off-Sheet Label shapes from the Process Annotations stencil onto one of the end points of a Pipeline shape. When a red square appears, indicating that the Pipeline shape is glued to the Off-Sheet Label shape, release the mouse button.

2. In the Off-Page Reference dialog box, select either the New Page or Existing Page option. If you choose to refer to a new page, type the name of the page in the Name box. If you choose to jump to an existing page, select the name of the existing page in the drop-down list. Click OK. Visio displays the other page and adds an Off-Page Reference shape to it.

3. From the Pipelines stencil, drag a Pipeline shape onto the Off-Sheet Label shape on the new page. When a red square appears, indicating that the shape is glued to the Off-Sheet Label shape, release the mouse button.

4. To specify that the Pipeline shape on the new page is a continuation of the original, double-click the Pipeline shape and type the tag for the original Pipeline shape and press Esc. Visio associates the Pipeline shape with the original component and moves the entry for the Pipeline shape into the original component in the Component Explorer window.

 Note   To navigate between pages, right-click an Off-Sheet Label shape and then choose Off-page Reference.

Working with Components

Components represent individual real-world objects such as valves, pumps, or pipelines. In Visio process engineering drawings, components might be made up of one or more Visio shapes. For example, a main pipeline with several intersecting branches requires a separate Visio shape for each segment, but to you, it's still one component. Each component includes properties, such as pressure, temperature, or material, that apply to all the shapes in it.

You can categorize components in a process engineering model so that it's easier to track and report on different types of components. Visio includes several categories that correspond to the shapes on the Process Engineering stencils: Equipment, Instrument, Pipelines, and Valve. You can also create your own categories.

Caution   Only shapes from the Process Engineering stencils appear automatically in the Component and Connectivity Explorer windows. If you add shapes from other stencils or draw your own, they won't appear as components. However, you can convert these shapes so that they will work with Visio Process Engineering features by following the steps outlined in the section "Converting Shapes into Components."

Associating Shapes with Components

When you add Process Engineering shapes to drawings, Visio automatically creates components for you. Each shape you place on the drawing page receives a tag number that identifies the component to which the shape belongs. However, you can associate more than one shape with the same component or move a shape from one component to another.

Use one of the following methods to associate a shape with a component:

✦ In the Component Explorer window, drag an entry from one component to another component in the same category.

✦ On the drawing page, select a shape and type the tag for the component to which you want the shape to belong.

Note   If you want to remove a component association completely, you must delete the shape on the drawing page.

Working with Component Data

To accurately model and engineer processes, your drawings must include information about the components in the process, such as the operating temperature range for a piece of equipment or the design pressure of a pipeline. Visio uses custom properties to store process engineering data so that you can view component properties in the Custom Property window or display data directly on your drawings. In addition, Visio provides some custom properties to configure shapes — for example, displaying different versions of the shape depending on the type of instrument you choose.

Process Engineering shapes come with several custom properties by default, as shown in Table 29-2. Visio uses custom property sets to associate groups of custom properties to each category of component. You can use these properties and property sets or modify them to suit your organization's needs. Although you can add data to components individually in the Custom Properties window, you might want to use Visio's Database wizards to import and link data from engineering databases.

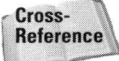

Cross-Reference
To learn how to create your own custom properties and custom property sets and apply them to Visio shapes, see Chapter 32.

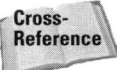

Cross-Reference
To learn how to import data from databases or link Visio shapes to database records, see Chapter 10.

Table 29-2
Default Custom Properties for Component Categories

Equipment	Instruments	Pipelines	Valves and Fittings
Description	Description	Description	Description
Material	Connection Size	Line Size	Line Size
Manufacturer	Service	Schedule	Valve Class
Model	Manufacturer	Material	Manufacturer
	Model	Design Pressure	Model
	Instrument Type	Design Temperature	Valve Type
	Local/remote		

Adding Data to Components

You can add data to component properties by using the Custom Properties window or by employing Visio's Database wizards and commands to link shapes to engineering databases. To enter custom property values in the Custom Properties window, follow these steps:

1. Choose View ⇨ Custom Properties Window to open the window.

2. Select a component in the Component Explorer window or the Connectivity Explorer window, or select the corresponding shape on the drawing page.

3. In the Custom Properties window, click the custom property you want to enter and either type a value or select a value from a drop-down list.

Displaying Component Data

Visio displays the component tag in the text block of each Process Engineering shape by default. You can choose whether to show or hide component tags by right-clicking shapes on the drawing page and choosing Hide Tag or Show Tag from the shortcut menu. In addition, you can display other component data on the drawing page. For example, Callout shapes from the Process Annotations stencil can show key design attributes on the drawing, such as temperature or pressure.

To display component data using Callout shapes, follow these steps:

1. Drag one of the Callout shapes from the Process Annotations stencil onto the drawing page near the shape whose properties you want to display.

2. Drag the control handle from the Callout shape to any point on the shape that you want to annotate.

3. In the Configure Callout dialog box, check the check boxes for the custom properties you want to display in the Callout shape. With the Callout shape linked to the custom properties, changes to the custom property fields appear in the Callout shape automatically. If you select more than one property, be sure to specify a separator, so you can distinguish individual values in the Callout shape.

Note   If you want to change the order in which custom properties appear in the Callout shape, select a property and then click Move Up or Move Down to reposition it in the order.

4. To show the property name in addition to the value, check the Show Property Name check box.

5. Click OK. The properties appear in the Callout shape.

6. If you want to change the properties that appear, or you want to change whether the property name is shown after you add the Callout shape to the drawing page, right-click the Callout shape and choose Configure Callout from the shortcut menu. You can also choose Show Leader to draw a leader from the Callout shape to its associated shape.

Tagging and Numbering Components

Visio identifies the components in your process engineering model with a tag. In Process Engineering shapes, the tag appears in the shape's text block. By default, Visio formats tags as *<tag name>-<tag counter>*. The tag name is the first letter of the component category and the tag counter is a number that increments by one every time you add a component from that category to the drawing. If you want to number components in a specific way, you can define your own custom tag format.

Note   If you don't want Visio to automatically number components as you add them, choose Process Engineering ➪ Diagram Options and uncheck the Number Components When They Are Added to the Drawing check box.

Applying Tag Formats to Shapes

You can change the tag format associated with shapes on the drawing page. If you want to change the tag format for all instances of a shape, you can change the tag format for a master on a stencil. To use a different tag format for shapes already on a drawing, follow these steps:

1. Select the shape or shapes you want to change on the drawing page and then choose Process Engineering ⇨ Apply Tag Format.

2. In the Apply Tag Format dialog box, select the tag format you want in the Tag Format drop-down list, click the Apply to Shapes Selected in Drawing option, and click OK.

To change the tag format for masters in a stencil, follow these steps:

1. Open the stencil that contains the masters whose tag formats you want to change and then choose Process Engineering ⇨ Apply Tag Format.

2. In the Apply Tag Format dialog box, select the tag format you want in the Tag Format drop-down list.

3. Click the Apply to Shapes in a Stencil option and then click Choose Shapes.

4. In the Choose Shapes dialog box, select the stencil you want to modify from the Document drop-down list, which includes all open stencils.

Note If you want to choose masters on the Document stencil, select the drawing name in the Document drop-down list.

5. Check the check boxes for the masters whose tag formats you want to change and click OK. In the Apply Tag Format dialog box, click OK to apply the new tag format to the selected masters.

6. Right-click the stencil title bar in the Shapes window and choose Save from the shortcut menu.

Defining Tag Formats

Visio includes a default tag format for each category of components in the Process Engineering templates. You can modify these existing formats to fit your organization's standards or you can create formats of your own. Tag formats can include text, punctuation, the values of custom properties, and numeric sequences, and can span more than one line.

To create a new tag format, follow these steps:

1. Choose Process Engineering ⇨ Edit Tag Formats and click Add.

2. Type the name for the new tag format in the Name box.

3. Use one of the following options to specify the basis for the new format:

- **Create a New Format** — Choose this option to create a brand-new format based on the default tag format, `<tag format name>-[Counter]`.

- **Create from an Existing Format** — Choose this option to use an existing format as the basis for the new tag format. Select the drawing or stencil that contains the format you want to use in the Document drop-down list. Then, from the Format drop-down list, select the tag format you want to use.

4. Click OK. Visio adds the new name to the Tag Format list.

To specify a new format you just created or to edit an existing one, follow these steps:

1. In the Edit Tag Formats dialog box, select the tag format you want to modify and click Modify. Visio opens the Tag Format Properties dialog box and selects the text in the Tag Expression box.

You can preview the results of the current tag expression in the Sample Tag Value box.

2. To insert text in the tag expression, position the insertion point in the tag expression and type the text you want.

You can add punctuation marks such as hyphens to the tag expression text to separate fields.

3. To replace text in the tag expression, select the text and type the new text you want.

4. To create a multi-line tag, position the insertion point where you want to start a new line in the tag expression and press Enter.

5. To add a custom property to the tag expression, position the insertion point where you want to insert the property, select a custom property in the Available Custom Properties list, and then click Insert Property.

6. To insert a sequential counter to the tag expression, position the insertion point where you want to insert the counter and then click Insert Counter.

You can specify the number of digits that the counter occupies by selecting an entry in the Format drop-down list. Visio adds leading zeroes to the counter. For values larger than the number of digits specified, Visio simply adds more digits to the counter.

7. When you have completed the tag expression, click OK. The tag expression appears in the Expression column of the Edit Tag Formats dialog box.

 **Note** You can also rename or delete tag formats in the Edit Tag Formats dialog box by clicking Rename or Delete.

Renumbering Components

As you add components to your model, Visio numbers them using a numeric sequence in their tags. For example, the tag for the first piece of equipment you add is E-1, followed by E-2, and so on. However, as you work on a model, you might want to clean up the tag sequence. For example, if you delete components or reassign shapes from one component to another, you can end up with sequence numbers that are no longer used. You can renumber components to reuse those numbers, specifying the starting value you want to use and the increment between each tag.

To renumber the components in a model, follow these steps:

1. Choose Process Engineering ⇨ Renumber Components.

2. To specify which components you want to renumber, click one of the following options:

    • **Document**—Renumbers all the components in the current drawing file

    • **Page**—Renumbers all the components on the current drawing page

    • **Selection**—Renumbers the selected components

3. Uncheck the check boxes for any tag format you don't want to renumber. By default, all the tag formats are checked.

4. To specify how to renumber components that use a tag format, select a tag format in the Include Tag Formats list. Type the starting value in the Starting Value box and type the increment between numbers in the Interval box. Repeat these steps for each tag format.

5. Click OK to renumber the components.

 Note After Visio renumbers the components, the tags for new components begin where the last renumbered components left off. In addition, new tags use the settings from the renumbering you applied. For example, if you renumber pipelines starting at 100 using an interval of 2 and the pipelines in the model are tagged from 100 to 128, the next pipeline you add will start at 130.

Generating Component Lists and Bills of Material

You can generate reports about components in your model from the values in custom properties. Visio includes a predefined report for each category of components, which lists specific information about each component. You can use these reports as provided or use Visio's report features to define your own reports. Even if you don't add values to custom properties, you can still run these built-in reports to see a list of components by tag number, because Visio adds tag numbers automatically.

Visio provides the following predefined reports:

✦ **Equipment List**—Includes tag number, description, manufacturer, material, and model

✦ **Instrument List**—Includes tag number, description, connection size, service, manufacturer, and model

✦ **Pipeline List**—Includes tag number, description, line size, schedule, design pressure, and design temperature

✦ **Valve List**—Includes tag number, description, line size, valve class, manufacturer, and model

✦ **Inventory**—Shows the number of shapes on the page grouped by shape name

To run one of these reports, select it in the Report list and then click Run.

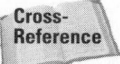

To learn more about creating, modifying, and running reports, see Chapter 32.

Converting Shapes and Symbols into Components

In order to work with Visio Process Engineering features, shapes must belong to a component category and have a tag format assigned to them. Without these, you won't see the shapes in the Component Explorer or Connectivity window and they won't function as other Process Engineering shapes do. However, you can convert shapes or objects from other sources into Process Engineering shapes using the Shape Conversion command. You can convert the following elements:

✦ Shapes you draw with Visio drawing tools

✦ Existing shapes on a drawing page

✦ Shapes from stencils other than the Process Engineering stencils

✦ Symbols created in AutoCAD

Process Engineering shapes can lose their attributes when you perform some actions—for example, ungrouping a grouped Process Engineering shape or applying Shape Operation commands to them. When this happens, you can use the Shape Conversion command to reassign a category and tag format.

To transform shapes or symbols into Process Engineering shapes, follow these steps:

1. If you want to convert shapes on the drawing page, select the shapes you want to convert.

2. Choose Process Engineering ➪ Shape Conversion. Then, under the Source heading, choose one of the following options:

- **Selected Shapes** — Converts the shapes you selected on the drawing page
- **Shapes in a Visio Stencil** — Converts masters on a Visio stencil. Click Choose Shapes, select the stencil in the Document list, check the check boxes for the masters you want to convert, and click OK.

Tip   To convert masters on the current drawing's Document stencil, in the Choose Shapes dialog box, select the drawing name in the Document list. By doing this, you can convert all the shapes in the current drawing file.

- **Symbols in a CAD File** — Converts symbols in a CAD file. Click Browse and then locate and select the CAD file containing the symbols you want to convert. To set the drawing scale in Visio, enter a positive value for the number of Visio measurement units that equals one CAD unit and select the units you want to use in the Units drop-down list.

3. Select or type the name of a category in the Category box to assign it to the converted shapes.

Note   If you type a category name that doesn't exist, Visio creates a new category for you.

4. In the Tag Format list, select a tag format to assign it to the converted shapes.

New Feature   In Visio 2002, you could also specify a custom property set for the shape conversion. In Visio 2003, you apply custom property sets to the shapes outside of the Shape Conversion command. For more information, see Chapter 32.

5. Click OK to convert the shapes. If you converted CAD symbols, Visio creates a new stencil that contains the shapes you converted. To save the stencil, right-click the stencil title bar and choose Save from the shortcut menu.

Summary

Visio provides templates for mechanical, electrical, and process engineering drawings. You can use basic Visio techniques such as drag and drop to perform much of the work for creating drawings. Visio uses custom properties not only to add engineering information to shapes, but also to configure shapes to show different varieties of equipment.

The Process Engineering solution includes additional tools to help you build a model. Visio uses components with identifying tags to track and report on the objects in a process engineering model. The Component and Connectivity Explorer windows present your model as an outline. You can create, delete, rename, and move components around on the drawing page or in these windows.

✦   ✦   ✦

Customizing Templates, Stencils, and Shapes

Creating and Customizing Templates

Visio Standard 2003 provides 25 built-in templates, while Visio Professional 2003 includes over 60. You can obtain additional Visio templates from online sources listed in Chapter 39. Even with all these templates at your disposal, you might want to customize a built-in template or create your own.

Templates increase your productivity by setting up an environment appropriate for a type of drawing or conforming to your organization's standards. You can automatically configure page settings, open stencils, position windows, add drawing pages, including backgrounds, and even pre-populate a page with shapes, such as your company logo, just by creating a drawing based on a template.

If a built-in Visio template offers most of what you need, it's simpler to customize a built-in template. However, you can quickly create your own templates by saving an existing drawing as a template. In addition to regular Visio templates that create new Visio drawings, you can also create XML templates to create new Visio drawings as XML drawings. In this chapter, you'll learn how to create your own templates. You'll also learn to add stencils and styles to the templates you create, and how to configure page settings for the pages in your templates.

Reasons to Customize Templates

Developing your own set of templates makes sense for a number of reasons, even if many of the settings in a built-in template are exactly what you want. Customized templates can save you time if you

- ✦ Use specific page settings for different types of drawings.
- ✦ Create drawings using unusual page sizes.
- ✦ Draw plans using unusual drawing scales.
- ✦ Apply special formatting, such as color palettes, to different types of drawings.
- ✦ Use backgrounds on your drawings.
- ✦ Use stencils other than the ones that a built-in Visio template opens.
- ✦ Use different stencils to produce the same type of drawing for different departments.
- ✦ Drag shapes from custom stencils to create different types of drawings.
- ✦ Include the same shapes on all your drawings, such as company logos or title blocks.
- ✦ Prefer specific positions for Visio windows.

Note   Even when you have an existing drawing that is similar to the one you want to create, it's better to create your new drawing from a template with the settings you want. When you open a template, Visio automatically creates a copy of the template for your new drawing. If you use an existing drawing and forget to use the Save As command, you overwrite your original drawing instead of creating a new one. In addition, you must remove or revise the content on an existing drawing.

Customizing Templates

It's easy to build your own templates, whether you want to customize one of the built-in Visio templates or create your own from an existing drawing. In short, you set up a drawing with the content, settings, and stencils you want, and then save it as a template or XML template.

Creating and Saving Customized Templates

You can create templates from existing Visio drawings, built-in Visio templates, or other customized templates. If you want to customize a built-in template, it's better to create a new template based on the built-in template. You can use your customized template and still have a copy of the original if you need it.

When you save a file as a template, you assemble the file's page settings, print settings, snap and glue options, drawing pages with any existing shapes, layers, styles, color palette, macros, and window sizes and positions into a reusable package. Make sure you set the file up exactly the way you want before you save it as a template, because every new drawing based on the template will inherit the same settings.

To create a template, follow these steps:

1. Open an existing Visio drawing (.vsd file) or create a new drawing based on the template you want to customize.

2. Set up the file with the content and settings that you want. For more information on making these changes, see the next section.

3. Choose File ➪ Save As, and, in the Save as Type list, select either Template or XML Template. Type the name for your template in the File Name box.

4. Click the Save arrow and, if necessary, check Workspace. Click Save. Visio saves your workspace to a .vst file if you chose a template, or to a .vtx file if you chose an XML template.

Note You can use Visio drawings to create XML templates without losing any of the drawing's information. You can also create Visio XML templates by importing XML files created in other applications as long as they comply with the XML for Visio Schema and Visio's internal rules.

Setting Up a File for Use as a Template

You can specify as many or as few settings as you want, and pre-populate the file with pages and shapes if you want. You can apply these changes in any order as long as you make all the changes before you save the file as a new template. Use any of the following methods to set up your template:

✦ **Open Stencils** — To open a set of stencils when you use the template, open the stencils that you want Visio to open automatically and close any stencils that you don't want Visio to open.

Caution If you make changes to a stencil as you are setting up your template, be sure to save the stencil file as well as the template file. Otherwise, your stencil changes will be lost even though Visio opens the stencil as part of the template.

✦ **Pre-populate Pages** — To define pages that you want Visio to create automatically in a new drawing, insert the number of pages you want and specify the page settings you want for each page.

Tip   You can add a background page to a template to display your company logo, or a standard title block for every new drawing based on that template. To do this, create the background page, add the shapes you want to it, and assign it to foreground pages before you save the template.

✦ **Pre-define Layers**—If you want drawings to use a standard set of layers, create the layers you want for each page in the drawing.

✦ **Pre-populate Shapes**—To begin drawings with a standard set of shapes, add the shapes you want to a drawing page (and layer, if you use them.)

✦ **Pre-define Print Settings**—Choose File ➪ Page Setup, select the Print Setup tab, and specify the print settings you want, such as the size of the printer paper.

✦ **Pre-define Page Settings**—Choose File ➪ Page Setup, select other Page Setup tabs, and specify the settings you want, such as page orientation, drawing scale, line jump settings, and shadow settings.

✦ **Pre-define Snap and Glue Options**—Choose Tools ➪ Snap & Glue and select the options you want.

✦ **Pre-define a Color Palette**—Choose Tools ➪ Color Palette and select the color palette or colors that you want.

✦ **Pre-assign a Color Scheme**—Right-click a page and choose Color Schemes from the shortcut menu.

Caution   When you customize both the stencils and colors in a template, make sure that the styles and colors for the template and stencil files are compatible. The style and color settings for the template file override the settings in the stencil file, which can lead to strange results when they conflict.

✦ **Make Styles Available**—Custom styles are associated with the drawing that's open when the styles are created. To make a custom style available for future drawings, modify or create the styles you want before saving the template.

✦ **Set Up Visio Windows**—To open and position windows automatically when you create a new drawing, open the windows you want and position them where you want.

Note   You can also specify where stencils appear in the Visio window and whether they are docked or floating. Position the stencils where you want them to appear when Visio opens them.

✦ **Include Macros**—Create any macros that you want to use.

Accessing Customized Templates

By default, Visio installs its built-in templates in category folders within C:\Program Files\Microsoft Office\Visio11\1033\Solutions. If you save your customized template files in one of these Solutions folders, Visio lists your templates along with built-in templates when you choose File ➪ New and then choose the category of template you want.

However, you might want to keep your customized templates separate from Visio's built-in templates. Not only does that make it easier to differentiate customized and built-in templates, but you can ensure that your customized files are backed up. To store and retrieve your customized templates from other locations, follow these steps:

1. To keep your templates organized, save them in a folder dedicated to your customized templates, such as My Documents\My Visio Templates.

 Tip You can categorize your templates just as Visio categorizes its built-in templates by creating subfolders underneath your main folder, such as My Documents\My Visio Templates\Scaled Drawings.

2. To specify the file path for your templates, choose Tools ➪ Options and select the Advanced tab. Click the File Paths button and type the file path in which you store your templates in the Templates box. Click OK to close the Advanced dialog box. Click OK again to close the Options dialog box.

 Note You can save your templates on your own computer or on a network device.

3. To create a drawing using one of your templates, open the New Drawing Task Pane and click On My Computer under the Templates heading. Visio opens the Browse Templates dialog box, which displays the files within your template file path, as shown in Figure 30-1. Select a template name and click Open.

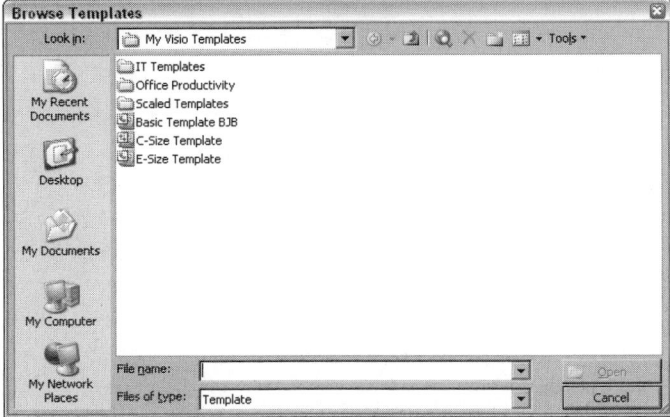

Figure 30-1: Choose a template in your template file path.

Summary

Whenever you create several drawings that use the same settings or configuration, you can simplify your work by creating a template with those settings. Every time you want to create a drawing with those settings, you simply create a new drawing based on that template. Visio automatically sets up the new drawing with all the settings, configurations, and content you added to the template. You can specify a variety of settings with templates, including page settings, style definitions, color palettes and schemes, drawing pages, and common shapes, such as company logos. You can store your customized templates along with Visio's built-in templates or keep them in a separate location.

✦   ✦   ✦

Creating and Customizing Stencils

When you create a drawing based on a template, Visio opens one or more stencils that include *shape masters* you can use to construct your diagram. You can access other masters by opening other stencils. When you want to consolidate the masters you use frequently, you can copy them to a custom stencil. In addition, you can create custom stencils to store custom shapes that you create. When you create your own stencils, you can store them in your My Shapes folder or keep them with the Visio built-in stencils. Either way, they're easy to open.

In this chapter, you learn how to create custom stencils for the shapes you use frequently, whether they are built-in Visio masters or custom masters you create. You'll also learn how to add masters to the Favorites stencil. Finally, you will learn how to modify the shape information that appears in stencils, and how masters are arranged.

Note Microsoft has copyrighted the masters on the stencils that Visio installs. You can copy and modify masters to suit your requirements and distribute drawings that contain copyrighted shapes. However, you can't sell or distribute original or modified Visio masters.

Creating and Saving Stencils

New stencils come in handy if you want to consolidate your favorite Visio masters from several built-in stencils or access custom shapes you create. You can use existing stencils as a foundation for your custom stencils or create them from scratch. In addition, Visio 2003 provides several shortcuts for quickly storing your favorite shapes. When you create your own stencils, you can prevent others from editing them by saving them as read-only. Although Visio saves custom stencils in the My Shapes folder by default, you can save your stencils wherever you want, including the Solutions folder Visio uses for its built-in stencils.

Note   You can use shapes from stencils other than the ones that a template opens by default. Visio includes many useful stencils in the Visio Extras category. To open one of these stencils, choose File ➪ Shapes ➪ Visio Extras and then choose the stencil you want. Visio Extras stencils include masters for annotations, backgrounds, borders and titles, callouts, connectors, patterns, dimensioning, symbols, title blocks, and more.

Creating a Stencil from an Existing Stencil

If an existing stencil contains most of the shapes you want, you can use it as the basis for a custom stencil. To create a new stencil from an existing one, follow these steps:

1. Open a new or existing drawing so the Shapes window opens and then choose File ➪ Shapes ➪ Open Stencil. In the Open Stencil dialog box, Visio displays the contents of the My Shapes folder by default.

2. If you want to create a stencil from one of your custom stencils stored within the My Shapes folder, navigate to the folder within the My Shapes folder that contains the existing stencil you want to use and select the stencil name. On the other hand, if you want to use a built-in Visio stencil, navigate to `C:\Program Files\Microsoft Office\Visio11\1033` and select one of the stencil names.

3. Instead of clicking Open immediately, click the drop-down arrow on the Open button and choose Copy from the drop-down menu. Visio opens a copy of the stencil in the Shapes window using a default name, such as Stencil1. The icon in the stencil title bar includes an asterisk, indicating that the stencil is editable.

4. Add, remove, or rearrange masters on the stencil, as described in later sections in this chapter.

5. To save the new stencil, right-click the stencil title bar and choose Save from the shortcut menu. In the Save As dialog box, type a name for your stencil and then click Save.

Note   If the stencil you want to copy is already open, you can right-click the stencil's title bar and choose Save As from the shortcut menu. In the Save As dialog box, type the name for the new stencil and click Save.

Creating Stencils from Shape Search Results

When you search for shapes by typing keywords in the Search for Shapes box in the Shapes window, Visio displays the shapes it finds in a search results stencil. You can save individual shapes or the entire search results stencil to a custom stencil if you want to access those shapes in the future without performing another search. In addition, adding the shapes you find online to stencils stored on your hard drive saves you from going online to access those shapes in the future.

To save the search results stencil as a custom stencil, follow these steps:

1. Right-click the title bar of the search results stencil and choose Save As from the shortcut menu.

2. In the File Name box, type a name for the custom stencil and then click Save. By default, Visio saves stencils in your My Shapes folder.

See the section "Adding Shapes from Other Stencils" later in this chapter to learn how to save individual shapes in the search results stencil to another stencil.

Creating Stencils from Scratch

If you want to create your own stencils to hold the custom shapes you create, you can begin with a new, blank stencil and add your shapes as you create them. To create a new stencil, choose File ➪ Shapes ➪ New Stencil. When you have finished adding masters to the stencil, right-click the stencil's title bar and choose Save from the shortcut menu. In the Save As dialog box, type a name for the stencil and click Save.

Creating a Custom Stencil from a Document Stencil

If you use only a few shapes from each of the stencils that Visio opens by default for a specific type of drawing, you might prefer to open one stencil that contains only the shapes you use. After you complete a drawing, you can use its Document stencil to create a stencil that contains masters for only the shapes you added to your drawing.

Creating a new stencil from the Document stencil in a drawing requires a few steps, which aren't intuitive. First, you open the Document stencil and edit it so that it contains the masters that you want in the order you want. Then, you delete all the shapes and drawing pages within the Visio file and save the drawing file as a stencil file.

Caution Because you delete all the drawing file contents except the Document stencil, you must be careful to use the Save As command to prevent overwriting your drawing file.

Understanding the Document Stencil

For each drawing you create, Visio creates a Document stencil specific to that file, and stores a master for each shape you add to the drawing. Whether you create shapes with drawing tools or drag them from stencils or shape search results, Visio places a master for each unique shape on the Document stencil.

The Document stencil is a component of a Visio drawing file, not a separate file. You can use it to see which shapes you've used in a drawing or to make changes to every instance of a master across all pages in a drawing file. For example, if you want to make the Manager boxes in an organization chart smaller, you can modify the Manager master on the Document stencil. Every instance of the Manager shape in your drawing resizes to match that master. If you create a shape that you will use only in the current drawing, you can add it to the Document stencil so it's easier to copy.

To create a new stencil from the Document stencil, follow these steps:

1. To prevent overwriting your drawing file, save the Visio drawing file that contains the Document stencil you want to work with.

2. To display the drawing file's Document stencil, choose File ⇨ Shapes ⇨ Show Document Stencil.

3. If necessary, add or remove masters in the Document stencil, so that the Document stencil contains the master you want in the new stencil. If you want the masters in a different order, drag them into the sequence you want. You can also edit the master properties or rename the masters.

4. Delete all the shapes on all the pages in the drawing. The fastest way to delete all the shapes on a page is to press Ctrl+A and then press Delete.

Caution   It's very important that you delete the shapes on the drawing pages before saving the file as a stencil. If you don't, the shapes on the pages remain in the file and take up disk space even though they aren't visible.

5. To save the Visio drawing file as a new stencil, choose File ⇨ Save As. In the Save as Type list, choose Stencil. In the Save As dialog box, type the name for the stencil and click Save.

Quickly Storing Your Favorite Shapes

When you want to set aside favorite shapes without interrupting your work on a diagram, new tools in Visio 2003 come to the rescue. You can add shapes that you use often or want to access quickly to the Favorites stencil, which Visio creates automatically during installation and stores in the My Shapes folder under My

Documents. As you work with Visio and develop an abundant supply of favorite and customized shapes, you can create additional custom stencils and store them in your My Shapes folder for easy access.

 **New Feature** During installation, Visio 2003 automatically creates a My Shapes folder in your My Documents folder to store your custom stencils and creates a Favorites stencil in your My Shapes folder so that you can easily store the shapes you use most frequently.

To store and retrieve favorite shapes, use one of the following methods:

✦ **Store a favorite shape** — To store a shape in your Favorites stencil, right-click the shape you want in the Shapes window and choose Add to My Shapes ➪ Favorites from the shortcut menu.

✦ **Open your Favorites stencil** — To access masters in your Favorites stencil, choose File ➪ Shapes ➪ My Shapes ➪ Favorites.

✦ **Open other custom stencils** — If you created other custom stencils in your My Shapes folder, choose File ➪ Shapes ➪ My Shapes and then choose the custom stencil you want.

Saving Stencils

As with other types of Visio files, you can apply the Save command to stencils in several ways. Because stencils contain masters that are the basis for the shapes you add to drawings, you can maintain consistency on drawings by specifying a stencil as read-only so others can't edit the masters.

When you choose File ➪ Shapes, Visio displays a list of stencil categories. When you choose a category, Visio displays the stencils in that category and you can choose the stencil you want to open. If you want to see your custom stencils in Visio's stencil category list, you can save your custom stencils in subfolders within the Visio Solutions folder. By default, Visio installs stencils in `C:\Program Files\Microsoft Office\Visio11\1033\Solutions`.

You can also create a separate folder for your stencils on your computer or network and categorize your stencils by creating subfolders for each stencil category. You can easily access your custom stencils by setting Visio's default stencil path to the top-level stencil folder you create. To specify the default path for your stencils, choose Tools ➪ Options and select the Advanced tab. Click File Paths and type your stencil path in the Stencils box.

To save a stencil, use one of the following methods:

✦ **Save a docked stencil** — To save a stencil docked in the Shapes window or elsewhere in the Visio window, right-click the stencil title bar and choose Save from the shortcut menu.

✦ **Save a floating stencil** — Click the icon in the stencil title bar and then choose Save from the shortcut menu.

✦ **Copy a stencil** — To save a stencil as a new stencil, right-click the stencil title bar and then choose Save As from the shortcut menu.

✦ **Prevent others from editing your stencil** — To prevent others from opening your stencil and editing the masters, set the Read Only option in the Save As dialog box by clicking the Save arrow and then choosing Read Only.

Tip

Workspaces save the current arrangement of windows and stencils open in the Visio window as well as a few other items, so the next time you open your drawing, your Visio environment is just as you left it. By default, Visio saves the drawing workspace when you save a file. If you want to save the changes you've made to drawing pages without saving the window arrangement, click the Save arrow in the Save As dialog box and uncheck the Workspace check box in the drop-down list.

Adding Shapes to Stencils

In most cases, you create or customize stencils because you want quick access to the shapes you use frequently. You can turn any shape on a drawing page into a master by adding it to a stencil, whether you create it with Visio drawing tools or modify an existing shape. You can also add shapes from other stencils to the current editable stencil. To make a stencil editable, follow these steps:

1. Open the stencil you want to edit by using one of the following methods:

   • **Create a new stencil** — Choose File ➪ Shapes ➪ New Stencil.

   • **Open your Favorites stencil** — Choose File ➪ Shapes ➪ My Shapes ➪ Favorites.

   • **Open another custom stencil** — Choose File ➪ Shapes ➪ My Shapes and choose the custom stencil you want.

Note

If you store your custom stencils in subfolders within the Visio Solutions folder choose File ➪ Shapes, choose the category for the stencil, and then choose the stencil you want.

2. To make the stencil editable, right-click the stencil title bar and choose Edit Stencil from the shortcut menu. The icon in the stencil title bar changes to include an asterisk, indicating that the stencil is editable, as shown in Figure 31-1.

Open but not editable

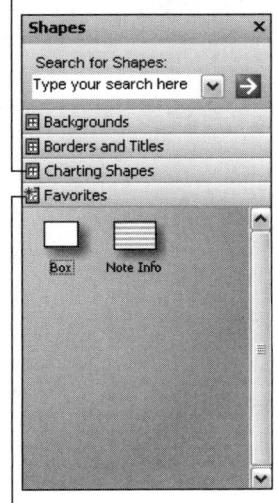

Open and editable stencil

Figure 31-1: Visio shows whether a stencil is editable or not.

 Note By default, Visio opens stencils as read-only, but allows you to open them for editing when you use the Edit Stencil command. This behavior protects the contents of a stencil from inadvertent modifications. However, when you save a stencil as read-only to prevent others from changing your masters, Visio sets the Windows Read-Only flag on the stencil file. If you try to use Edit Stencil on this type of Read-Only file, Visio displays a message that the stencil can't be edited at this time. If you want to edit a Read-Only file—perhaps to update the masters with new company standards—you can reset the Read-Only flag on the file. To do this, locate the file in Windows Explorer, right-click it, and choose Properties on the shortcut menu. In the Properties dialog box, select the General tab, uncheck the Read-Only check box, and click OK.

Adding Shapes from Drawing Pages

To add a shape from a drawing page to a stencil, follow these steps:

1. Make sure the stencil is open and editable.
2. On the drawing page, select the shape you want to add to the stencil.

3. Add the shape to the stencil by using one of the following methods:

- **Move the shape** — Drag the shape from the drawing page to the stencil.
- **Copy the shape** — Hold the Ctrl key as you drag the shape to the stencil.

Note When you add a shape to a stencil, it becomes a master. The master appears as an icon in the stencil with a label, Master.*x*, where *x* is a number.

4. To rename the master with a more descriptive name, right-click the master icon in the stencil and choose Rename Master from the shortcut menu. Type the new name in the icon label and press Enter when you're finished.

5. When you have finished adding shapes to the stencil, save the stencil file. See the "Saving Stencils" section in this chapter for more information about the different ways you can save a stencil.

Note To remove a master in a stencil, select the master and then press Delete.

Adding Shapes from Other Stencils

You can also add a shape from one stencil to another by using the Add to My Shapes command.

New Feature In Visio 2003, the Add to My Shapes command appears on the shortcut menu when you right-click a master in a stencil. You can use it to quickly copy a master to another stencil.

To add a shape from another stencil, follow these steps:

1. To make it easy to see the shapes you copy to a stencil, open both the stencil containing the master you want to copy and the stencil to which you want to copy it.

Copying and Pasting Masters Between Stencils

You can also use the Copy and Paste commands to add masters to other stencils. To do so, right-click the master you want to copy and choose Copy from the shortcut menu. Then right-click in the stencil to which you want to copy the master and choose Paste on the shortcut menu. If the destination stencil is editable, Visio copies the master. If the destination stencil is not editable, Visio asks you whether you want to open the stencil for editing so you can complete the paste operation. You can also use Ctrl+C and Ctrl+V to copy and paste masters, respectively.

If you try to paste a master into a built-in stencil, Visio displays a message that you can't edit the stencil and provides instructions for adding the master to a custom stencil.

If you don't open the stencil to which you copy a shape, Visio still copies the shape but doesn't open the stencil so that you can confirm that the copy worked.

2. In the stencil that contains the master you want to copy, right-click the master, choose Add to My Shapes, and then choose one of the following options:

- **Favorites** — Adds the master to your Favorites stencil

- **A Custom Stencil** — Adds the master to the custom stencil you choose on the shortcut menu. Visio adds the master to the stencil without opening the stencil and saves the stencil automatically.

- **Add to New Stencil** — Creates a new stencil and then adds the master to it

- **Add to Existing Stencil** — Opens the Open stencil dialog box so you can choose the stencil to which you want to copy the master

Modifying Stencil Appearance

Depending on the size of your screen or the amount of space your drawing window takes up, you might want to modify the appearance of your stencil windows to minimize the space they use. You can minimize the space needed for a stencil window by displaying only icons for masters. If you need as much information about a master as possible, you can display icons, master names, and details about each master. As a compromise between the two, you can display icons and names, which is the default setting, and specify how much text appears in the master labels. You can also rearrange the shapes in the stencil or use different background colors to make the stencils easier to read.

Displaying Master Information

To specify the amount of information that Visio displays for each master in a stencil, right-click the Shapes window title bar and choose one of the following options:

- ✦ **Icons and Names** — Displays icons and master names

- ✦ **Icons Only** — Displays only icons

- ✦ **Names Only** — Displays only names, which uses less space in the window but requires more familiarity with the masters

- ✦ **Icons and Details** — Displays icons, names, and a brief description of the master

You can also right-click the title bar of a stencil and choose View to specify the information that Visio displays. Visio changes the information that appears in every stencil you open.

Changing Spacing and Color Settings

If you recognize shapes visually, you can reduce the space required for a stencil window by limiting the text displayed with each master. You can also use the amount of text displayed in labels to increase or decrease the spacing between master icons. In addition, you can change the background color for stencils to make them easier to read. Use any of the following methods to change the appearance of stencils:

✦ **Characters per line** — To specify how many characters of text appear in each line of a master label, choose Tools ⇨ Options and select the View tab. Type the number of characters you want in the Characters Per Line box underneath the Stencil Spacing label. By specifying more characters per line, you increase the horizontal space between masters, in addition to providing more room for the master name.

✦ **Lines per master** — To specify the number of lines of text for each master label, choose Tools ⇨ Options and select the View tab. Type the number of lines you want in the Lines Per Master box underneath the Stencil Spacing label. By increasing the number of lines, you increase the vertical space between masters, in addition to providing more room for the master name.

✦ **Background color** — To change the background color for stencils, choose Tools ⇨ Options and select the Advanced tab. Click Color Settings and specify any of the following colors:

• **Text Color** — Specify the color for master labels.

• **Background Color 1** — Specify the background color for a stencil.

• **Background Color 2** — If your monitor is set to 32-bit color, the stencil background grades smoothly from the first background color to the second.

Rearranging Shapes in Stencils

You can rearrange shapes in stencils by dragging the shapes to different positions in the stencil. Open the stencil you want to rearrange. If it isn't editable, right-click the stencil title bar and choose Edit Stencil from the shortcut menu. Be sure to save the stencil after you have moved the masters into the positions you want.

Summary

Custom stencils are handy for a variety of reasons. You can use them to consolidate the built-in Visio shapes that you use most frequently onto a smaller number of stencils. You can use them to store your custom shapes. You can copy built-in Visio stencils to custom stencils so you can modify the shapes to suit your requirements. Visio provides several easy ways to create custom stencils. In addition to creating blank stencils or copying existing ones, you can use search results stencils or Document stencils as the foundation for new custom stencils. After creating a stencil, you can add, remove, or rearrange masters. You can also modify the information that appears in stencils to provide more detail or minimize the space the stencil requires.

✦   ✦   ✦

Creating and Customizing Shapes

Whether you only use shapes from the built-in Visio stencils or craft highly specialized shapes used by your entire organization, you can modify many characteristics of the shapes on your drawings. You can change the appearance of any shape on a drawing, modify how it acts, edit the data associated with it, and define special behaviors for it.

When you plan to use a customized shape frequently or on more than one drawing, you can create a master of the shape that you can reuse by dragging it from a stencil onto a drawing page. If you're creating customized shapes, you can use Visio drawing tools and Shape Operation commands to build just the shape you want, whether it is an open path or an enclosed area, a shape that acts like a line or a box with two dimensions. You can create masters by drawing geometry with Visio's drawing tools, but it's often easier to begin with existing shapes or objects from other applications as the basis for customized masters. In addition, masters offer an easy way to make changes to every copy of a shape on a drawing.

This chapter explains the difference between shapes and masters as well as the features that make shapes smart. You will learn how to create and modify masters and how to customize the graphic elements that comprise shapes and the behaviors that shapes exhibit. Finally, you will learn how to create and apply custom properties to shapes as well as how to create reports of custom property values.

Understanding Shapes and Shape Properties

If you plan to do more than drag shapes from an existing stencil onto a drawing page, it's helpful to understand what makes shapes tick. Visio shapes are highly customizable, and they do what they're told. By understanding the different types of shapes, and their components, behaviors, and properties, you can build custom shapes that do exactly what you want. Conversely, if a shape doesn't behave as you would expect, you can more easily troubleshoot the problem by analyzing the shape's configuration.

What Makes Shapes Smart?

Built-in Visio shapes are preprogrammed to perform their tasks. Modular furniture shapes snap together as they do in real life. Electrical components connect to represent the wiring for a building. Organization charts show information about employees and their position in the organization's reporting structure.

Visio shapes have several features you can exploit to make the shapes behave the way you want for different situations. Whether you want to tweak the behavior of a built-in shape or develop your own custom shape behaviors, you can take advantage of the following smart features:

✦ **Shape behaviors**—Use the options in the Behavior dialog box to control shape selection, editing, positioning, and connections. For example, when you select a box in a title block, you can add text to the box to identify the drawing, whereas when you select a piece of equipment, you can add text to identify the equipment, not its components. See the section "Customizing Shape Behavior" later in this chapter to learn more.

✦ **Custom properties**—If data is an important part of a diagram, such as the department and employee associated with an office on a facilities plan, you can store additional information in custom properties associated with shapes. You can display custom property values in shape text, use them in calculations, or present them in reports. See the section "Working with Custom Properties" later in this chapter to learn more.

✦ **ShapeSheets**—The ShapeSheet for a shape contains fields that control every aspect of that shape. You can change shape behaviors and properties in the ShapeSheet, as well as define customized formulas for advanced performance.

Although you can specify a great deal about a shape by modifying it on a drawing page or in the master drawing window, you can learn how to program more advanced behaviors with a ShapeSheet in Chapter 33.

Understanding Shapes and Masters

Inheritance can be a powerful influence, whether it comes from a rich aunt or a Visio master. In Visio, you can easily construct drawings by adding shapes with behaviors and properties predefined. Visio uses the concept of masters to make drawing smart shapes fast and easy. A Visio master is a lot like the plate that Uncle Sam uses to produce money. It's an original from which you can make as many copies as you want, with each copy initially possessing the same appearance, behavior, and properties as the original. By using masters to create the shapes on your drawings, you can do the following:

✦ Configure a shape once and reuse it again and again.

✦ Ensure consistency on all your drawings.

✦ Share shapes with other Visio users.

✦ Set up standard shapes for your entire organization.

When you drag a master onto a drawing page, you create an instance of the master. Initially, the instance is an exact duplicate of the master and is linked to the master so that changes made to the master propagate to every instance in the active drawing file. You can edit the instances of masters in any way you want, but some modifications break the link between an instance and its shape master. For example, if you ungroup a shape created from a grouped master, you'll see the message "This action will sever the object's link to its master." The warning sounds ominous, but the only consequence is that the instance no longer inherits changes made to the master on the Document stencil. The instance remains on the page and you can continue to edit it.

Understanding Shape Geometry

Shape geometry isn't that important if you simply drag built-in shapes onto a drawing and use them as is. However, when you begin to modify the appearance of existing shapes or create your own, understanding the building blocks of shapes is an important step for success. By learning shape terminology as well as the features and benefits of different shape elements, you can produce shapes that look and behave the way you want.

Exploring Shape Components

No matter how simple or complex shapes are, they are composed of line segments, arcs, and the occasional text block. Each line segment and arc has a start point and an end point. If you draw a single line segment or arc, you can identify the start point with a green square with an X inside it, and the end point by a green square with a plus symbol inside it. In addition, line segments and arcs include control points, indicated by a small green circle, at their midpoints. You can change the curvature or symmetry of a line or arc by selecting the Pencil tool and dragging the control point to a new location.

When you create a connected string of line segments and arcs, a diamond-shaped vertex appears at each intersection. You can change the length of lines and arcs or reposition them by dragging their end points or vertices. By assembling line segments and arcs to create shapes, you can access additional points to help you position, resize, and connect shapes. When you select a shape, Visio marks these points, called *handles,* so you know where to drag on a shape to make the changes you want. Shapes include the following types of handles:

✦ **Selection handles** — When you select a shape, red or green boxes appear, which you can drag to resize the shape.

✦ **Control points** — When you select a shape with the Pencil tool, small green circles appear, which you can drag to change the curve or symmetry of a line or arc, or to adjust the angle and magnitude of the eccentricity of an arc.

✦ **Connection points** — Blue Xs mark locations where you can glue connectors or other shapes.

✦ **Rotation handles** — For 2-D shapes, you can drag the red circle to rotate a shape.

✦ **Control handles** — You can drag the yellow diamonds that appear on some shapes to modify the shape's appearance. For example, you can use a control handle to change the swing on a door or to change the width of all the bars in a bar graph.

Understanding 1-D and 2-D Behavior

Visio shapes are either 1-D or 2-D, but the distinction has nothing to do with the way the shape looks. You can tell the difference between 1-D and 2-D shapes by the way they behave.

One-dimensional shapes don't have to look like thin lines. You can transform a Fancy Arrow or Road shape into a 1-D shape, as described in the section "Switching Between 1-D and 2-D Behavior" later in this chapter. One distinguishing characteristic of 1-D shapes is that you can rotate and change the length of a 1-D shape in one step by moving one of its end points. Because 1-D shapes include start points and end points, you can use them to specify direction. One-dimensional shapes can include line ends, such as arrowheads, which you can use to differentiate the start and end of a line.

With 1-D shapes, you can change the relative proportion of the shape, as shown in Figure 32-1. For example, you can increase the length of a Fancy Arrow shape by dragging an end point, but the width of the arrowhead and tail remain the same. However, when you drag the selection handles on the sides of a Fancy Arrow shape, the proportions of the arrowhead change to fit the new width, even though the length remains the same. Even if you want to, you can't change the length and width of a 1-D shape at the same time, because 1-D shapes don't have selection handles at their corners.

Drag to change the length of a 1-D shape

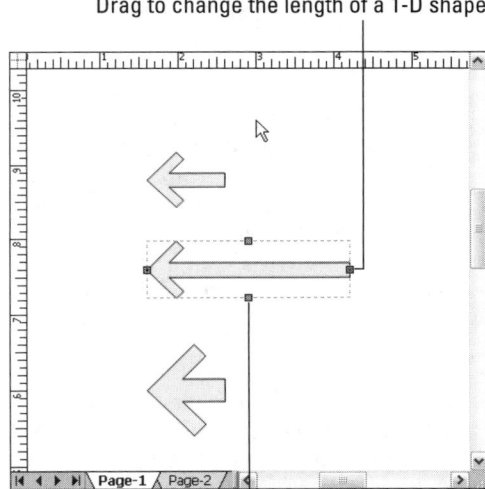

Drag to change the width as shown in the bottom shape

Figure 32-1: You can change the proportion of a 1-D shape.

Two-dimensional shapes include up to eight selection handles for resizing. You can drag selection handles on the edges of 2-D shapes to change their height or width independently. However, dragging selection handles at shape corners to resize the shape proportionately is a behavior unique to 2-D shapes.

Note   The distinction between 1-D and 2-D shapes is merely a behavioral difference that you set by choosing an Interaction Style option in the Behavior dialog box. For example, by default, a line segment is a 1-D shape with start and end points that you can drag to lengthen or shorten the line or to change its orientation. You can transform a single line segment into a 2-D shape by right-clicking the shape, choosing Format ➪ Behavior, and selecting the Box (2-dimensional) option on the Behavior tab. When you do so, you can drag selection handles at the midpoint of the line to transform the line into a box.

In addition to 1-D and 2-D shapes, it's important to recognize the difference between *open shapes* and *closed shapes*. You create an open shape when you draw a series of connected line segments that zigzag across the page. Because open shapes don't enclose an area, you can format the lines and text, but you can't apply fill formatting to them. Conversely, you create a closed shape when you connect a path back to its starting point. Visio indicates that a shape is closed by applying a default fill format to it. However, you can apply a different fill format if you choose.

Creating and Editing Masters

Although Visio provides hundreds of built-in shapes, with thousands more available from other sources, you can create your own custom masters to exactly match your requirements. For example, if you design and sell custom furniture, you can create Visio masters for each of your designs so you can help clients lay out their furniture. You can create masters by drawing them with Visio's drawing tools or by copying and editing existing shapes. You can even generate masters using converted CAD objects or data in a database. If your needs change, you can modify the appearance, behaviors, and properties of your custom masters, and apply those changes to the instances on your drawings.

 Note   Access to Stencil commands varies depending on whether you have a drawing open or not. To create and edit masters, you must first open a drawing so that the Shapes window opens. Otherwise, you won't be able to access commands to make stencils editable or edit masters.

Creating Masters

Although Visio's drawing tools are easy to use, you don't have to apply them every time you want to create a custom master. You can create your own masters using any of the following methods:

✦ **Build a master with drawing tools** — Create a master and add graphics to it with Visio's drawing tools and Shape Operation commands.

✦ **Use an existing shape** — Drag an existing shape from a drawing page to a stencil.

✦ **Create a master from an object from another application** — Convert an object from another application, such as Microsoft PowerPoint or AutoCAD, into a Visio master.

✦ **Copy an existing master** — Save an existing master on a stencil as a new custom master and modify it to suit your needs.

✦ **Build a master from database information** — Generate new masters by combining data from a database table with existing masters in stencils.

Drawing Masters

To create a new master in a stencil, follow these steps:

1. If you want to edit a built-in stencil, first save it as a custom stencil as discussed in Chapter 31.

2. Open any Visio drawing and then open the custom stencil in which you want to create a master by choosing File ➪ Shapes and then choosing the category and stencil you want. If the stencil is not editable, right-click the stencil title bar and choose Edit Stencil from the shortcut menu.

3. Right-click inside the stencil window and choose New Master.

4. In the New Master dialog box, specify the properties for the master. See the section "Modifying Master Properties" in this chapter to learn more. Click OK when you are done. In the stencil, Visio adds a blank master icon with the master name as a label.

Note If you want to locate your master using the Search for Shapes command, add keywords separated by commas to the Keywords property in the Master Properties dialog box.

5. Right-click the new master and choose Edit Master ➪ Edit Master Shape.

6. In the master drawing window, create the graphics for the master. You can use any of the following methods:

   - **Draw components** — Use Visio drawing tools or Shape Operation commands to create the master graphics that you want.

   - **Use an existing shape or master** — Drag a shape from a drawing page or drag a master from a stencil into the master drawing window.

   - **Paste an object from another application** — Copy an object from another application such as AutoCAD and paste the object in the master drawing window.

Tip You can also import an AutoCAD drawing into Visio, converting the AutoCAD objects into Visio shapes. You can then drag these shapes into an editable stencil to create new masters.

7. Choose File ➪ Close to close the master drawing window. When Visio prompts you to update the master, click Yes.

8. To save your changes, right-click the stencil title bar and choose Save Stencil from the shortcut menu.

Saving Existing Shapes as Masters

If you customize a shape on one of your drawings and want to use it on other drawings, you can save it as a master on a stencil. To save a shape on a drawing page as a master, follow these steps:

1. Open a drawing file so that the Shapes window opens and then open the stencil in which you want to save a master by choosing File ⇨ Shapes. Choose the category and stencil you want. If the stencil is not editable, right-click the stencil's title bar and choose Edit Stencil from the shortcut menu.

2. Drag the shape from the drawing page into the stencil. Visio adds an icon to the stencil with a generic name such as Master.x, where x is a number.

3. Click the icon label. When the master name is highlighted, type the name you want for the master and then press Enter.

4. If you want to specify other properties for the master, such as search keywords, right-click the new master, choose Edit Master ⇨ Master Properties from the shortcut menu, and then define the properties you want.

5. Choose File ⇨ Close to close the master drawing window. When Visio prompts you to update the master, click Yes.

6. To save your changes, right-click the stencil's title bar and choose Save Stencil on the shortcut menu.

Creating Masters from Database Information

You can also build new masters based on an existing master and data within a database. For example, if you have a master for an office cubicle and store data about the cubicle's color and components in a table in a database, you can create masters for each cubicle configuration in the database. When you drag a master to a drawing page, the instance shows the data for the associated record in the database. To create masters in this way, use the Database Wizard to create a stencil containing a master for each record in a database table.

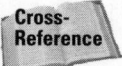 To learn how to use the Database Wizard, see Chapter 10.

Modifying Masters

You can edit your masters to adapt them to your requirements, whether it's to correct errors you find or to adjust them to meet changing requirements. For example, if your company decides to show which department owns each piece of furniture in an office plan, you can modify your furniture masters to do so.

You can configure the appearance and behavior of masters as you create them or revise them later. To modify an existing master, open any Visio drawing file so that the Shapes window opens and then open the stencil that contains the master. If the stencil is not editable, right-click the stencil's title bar and choose Edit Stencil from the shortcut menu. After the stencil is open and editable, you can perform the following actions:

✦ **Delete a master** — Right-click the master you want to delete and then choose Delete Master from the shortcut menu.

✦ **Rename a master** — Right-click the master you want to rename, choose Rename Master from the shortcut menu, type the new name in the master label, and press Enter.

✦ **Modify master graphics** — You can edit the drawing components for a master, including lines, arcs, text, and connection points. See the next section in this chapter to learn more.

✦ **Modify master properties** — You can specify properties for a master, such as Name, Icon Size, and Keywords for shape searches. See the section "Modifying Master Properties" later in this chapter to learn more.

✦ **Change the icon image** — You can revise the icon that represents the master in a stencil. See the section "Displaying Master Icons" later in this chapter to learn how.

✦ **Add or edit custom properties** — You can associate custom properties with a master. See section "Working with Custom Properties" in this chapter to learn more.

When you finish modifying masters on an editable stencil, be sure to save your changes by saving the stencil.

Editing Master Graphics

You can modify the appearance of a master by editing a shape on a drawing and then saving the shape as a master. However, you can also edit a master's drawing elements in the master drawing window. Working in the master drawing window is much like working on a Visio drawing. You can use Visio drawing tools to edit existing graphics or add other shapes and objects to the master by dragging them into the window. However, unlike working in a Visio drawing, Visio prompts you to update the master shape when you close the master drawing window.

To edit a master in the master drawing window, first open any Visio drawing file so that the Shapes window opens, and then follow these steps:

1. In an editable stencil, right-click the master you want to edit and choose Edit Master ▷ Edit Master Shape. Visio opens the master drawing window with the master in the middle of the master drawing area.

2. Make any of the following changes you want to the master's graphics:

   • **Edit drawing elements** — Use Visio drawing techniques to modify the lines, closed shapes, and text in a master. See the section "Operating on Shapes" later in this chapter to learn how to perform more sophisticated editing operations.

   • **Format drawing elements** — Use Visio formatting commands to change colors, line styles, text styles, and fills.

   • **Modify connection points** — See the section "Adding Connection Points to Shapes" later in this chapter to learn how to add or modify connection points on shapes and masters.

3. When you have finished editing the master graphics, choose File ⇨ Close to close the master drawing window. When Visio prompts you to update the master, click Yes. On all the drawing pages in the active drawing file, Visio updates all the instances of the master with your changes.

4. If you want to continue editing masters, click Cancel when Visio prompts you to save changes to the stencil containing the master you edited. Repeat steps 1 through 3 to edit another master.

5. When you finish modifying masters, save the changes you made by right-clicking the stencil's title bar and choosing Save from the shortcut menu.

Note   The Document stencil in each Visio drawing file stores a copy of each master used on the drawing. When you open a Visio drawing that uses a master that you've changed on a stencil, you won't see those changes by default because the drawing file references the copy of the master on the Document stencil. If you want the drawing file to use the master that you modified on a custom stencil, copy the modified master to the Document stencil.

Modifying Master Icons

If you drag a shape onto a stencil to create a master, Visio uses a miniature version of the shape as the icon you see in the stencil. However, you can modify the icon to better represent the master. For example, for complex shapes, you can simplify the icon to make it more readable. Editing a master icon in the icon editing window is a bit different from editing master graphics. You modify icons pixel by pixel, by pressing a mouse button and dragging the mouse over the pixels you want to change. Visio applies the color that you assigned to the mouse button. For larger changes, you can move or delete groups of pixels. The changes you make to a master icon apply only to the icon. They don't affect the appearance of the master.

You can change the icon you see in a stencil by following these steps:

1. In an editable stencil, right-click the master you want to edit and choose Edit Master ⇨ Edit Icon Image. Visio opens the icon editing window, displays the icon in the window, and displays two toolbars containing icon editing tools, as shown in Figure 32-2.

Caution   If you make changes to an icon manually, be sure to uncheck the Generate Icon Automatically from Shape Data check box in the Master Properties dialog box. Otherwise, Visio will replace the icon with the revised master when you modify the master in the master drawing window.

Icon editing window

Asterisk indicates editable stencil   Icon editing toolbars

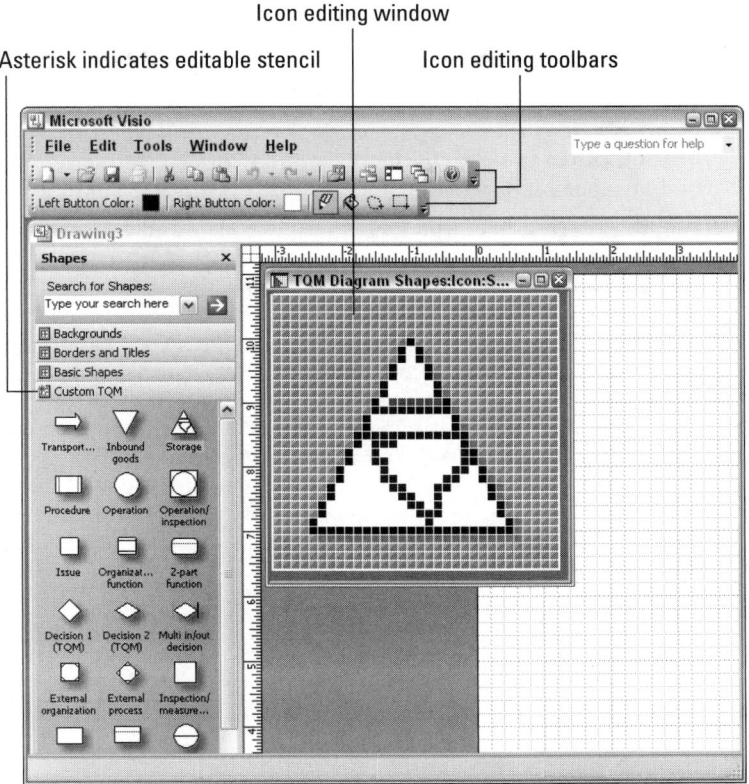

Figure 32-2: Edit a master icon in the icon editing window.

2. While the icon editing window is open, you can use the following methods to change the appearance of the master icon:

- **Select colors** — To assign colors to the left and right mouse buttons, click the Left Button Color or Right Button Color box and click the color you want to apply with that mouse button.

Note

If you want the background to show through the icon, click Transparent for a mouse button color.

- **Change single pixel colors** — Click the Pencil tool on the Icon Tools toolbar and then click the pixel you want to change with the mouse button assigned the color you want.

- **Change the color of an area**—Click the Bucket tool on the Icon Tools toolbar and then click a pixel in the area you want to change with the mouse button assigned the color you want. Visio changes the color of all contiguous pixels of the same color as the pixel you clicked.

- **Move pixels**—Click the Lasso tool or Selection Net tool on the Icon Tools toolbar and drag around the area you want to move. When Visio displays a selection box around the pixels, drag them to a new location.

- **Delete pixels**—Click the Lasso tool or Selection Net tool on the Icon Tools toolbar and drag around the area you want to delete. When Visio displays a selection box around the pixels, press Delete.

 When you move or delete pixels in a master icon, the stencil background color appears in the area from which you moved or deleted pixels.

3. When you have finished modifying the master icon, choose File ➪ Close to close the icon editing window. The changes you made to the icon appear in the stencil. If you want to continue modifying masters, click Cancel when Visio prompts you to save the stencil containing the master you edited. Otherwise, save your changes by right-clicking the stencil's title bar and choosing Save from the shortcut menu.

 You can undo changes you make to an icon while the icon editing window is open by choosing Edit ➪ Undo. However, after you close the icon editing window, you can't use the Undo command to reverse the changes you made. You must edit the icon and use the icon tools to return the icon to its original appearance.

Modifying Master Properties

In addition to the graphic elements of a master, you can modify other aspects of a master, such as its name, the prompt that appears when you point to a shape in a stencil, the icon size, or the keywords you can use to search for the master. To modify a master's properties, right-click a master in an editable stencil and choose Edit Master ➪ Master Properties. In the Master Properties dialog box, modify the properties you want and then click OK to close the dialog box when you're done. To save the changes to the master, save the stencil that contains it. You can modify the following properties in the Master Properties dialog box:

- ✦ **Name**—The label that appears under the master icon in a stencil can be up to 31 characters. Visio might truncate the name you see depending on the number of characters per line and the number of lines per master you specify on the View tab of the Options dialog box.

- ✦ **Prompt**—If you create a prompt for a master, it appears in a balloon when you point to a master in a stencil. You can use the Prompt property to provide a description of the shape, its purpose, or hints about how to use it.

✦ **Icon Size** — The size of the icon for a master in a stencil can be Normal, Wide, Tall, or Double. By default, icons are Normal, which is 32 by 32 pixels.

✦ **Align Master Name** — You can align the master name to the left, center, or right of the master icon in the stencil.

✦ **Keywords** — The Search for Shapes command uses the words in this property to locate the master. When you enter more than one keyword, separate the keywords with commas. This field is only available when the master drawing page contains at least one shape.

✦ **Match Master by Name on Drop** — When you drag a master onto a page, you can specify whether Visio uses the version of the master stored on the Document stencil or the version stored on the shape stencil. When you check this check box, Visio looks for a master by the same name in the Document stencil. If it finds a match, it copies the master from the Document stencil to the drawing page. Use this setting to use a master that you modified in your drawing file instead of the default master on the shape stencil. If you uncheck this box, Visio copies the master from the shape stencil, so that you always use the original version of the master.

✦ **Generate Icon Automatically from Shape Data** — Check this check box when you want Visio to update the master icon every time you edit the master graphics. Uncheck this check box if you edit the icon manually and want to retain those changes.

Creating Shortcuts to Masters

If you want to include a master on more than one stencil, you can create a shortcut to the master so that you can modify the master on one stencil and propagate the changes automatically to the other stencils. For example, if you want to add a master for a custom-built desk to the stencils for different lines of furniture, you can add the master to the first stencil and then copy shortcuts to the other stencils. To create a master shortcut, follow these steps:

1. Open both the stencil that contains the master you want to copy and the custom stencil to which you want to add the shortcut. If the destination stencil is not editable, right-click its title bar and choose Edit Stencil from the shortcut menu.

2. In the stencil that contains the master, right-click the master and choose Copy from the shortcut menu.

3. Right-click the destination stencil window and choose Paste Shortcut from the shortcut menu.

4. To save your changes, right-click the editable stencil's title bar and choose Save Stencil from the shortcut menu. When you edit the master in any of the stencils, Visio changes the master in every stencil linked with a shortcut.

Drawing Shapes and Masters

No matter how many stencils and masters Visio provides, sooner or later you'll want to create a new shape or master or make changes to existing ones. For example, you might create or revise shapes to do the following:

✦ Draw a shape directly on a drawing when you plan to use it only once.

✦ Modify the line and fill styles for shapes to show status.

✦ Create masters for specific configurations of furniture that your organization uses for office cubicles to simplify the construction of office layouts.

✦ Create new masters by modifying existing Organization Chart masters to show each level of management in an organization chart with a different shape.

Whether you want to create a new shape or modify an existing one, you can use Visio's drawing tools and Shape Operation commands to achieve the look you want. Even with the most specialized shapes, you can usually get a head start by modifying an existing shape. Drawing tools and Shape Operation commands work whether you are drawing a shape directly on a page or drawing a master in the master drawing window. In addition, if you draw a shape on a page and decide you want to make it a master, you can do so simply by dragging the shape onto an editable stencil.

Visio provides tools and drawing aids to simplify the construction of lines and curves. You can draw straight lines with the Line tool or the Pencil tool. For curves, you can use the Pencil tool, Arc tool, or Freeform tool. If you change your mind, you can even use the Pencil tool to convert arcs to lines, and vice versa. By using drawing aids and shape extension lines, you can snap your lines and curves to define the geometry you want. For example, you can use drawing aids or shape extension lines to draw lines at 45 degrees, create a line perpendicular to another, or draw a line tangent to a circle.

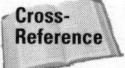 For additional instructions on drawing lines, curves, and closed shapes, see Chapter 2.

Drawing Line Segments and Paths

It's easy to draw a single line. Click the Line tool on the Drawing Tool toolbar and then drag between two points on the drawing page. However, to produce a connected path or a closed shape, you have to draw a series of connected line segments. When line segments are connected, you can move or format them as a single entity, but you can also reposition each vertex to modify the path or shape. To create connected line segments, follow these steps:

1. Select the Line tool or the Pencil tool.

2. Drag the pointer from point to point to define the first line segment and release the mouse button without moving the mouse.

3. With the pointer still positioned over the second point, drag from point to point to create the next line segment.

Tip

If you draw a line segment incorrectly or in the wrong place, simply continue to create line segments until the path is complete. You can then use the Pencil tool to edit the line segments in the path.

4. Repeat step 3 until you have drawn all the line segments you want. If you want to close the shape, make sure that the last point in the drawing path overlaps the very first point in the path.

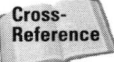
Cross-Reference

You can use drawing tools to create construction lines that you can use to align shapes on drawings. Although the Visio guide lines that you drag from a ruler onto a page perform the same function, they are a special type of drawing element and don't print by default. To learn how to convert regular lines into infinite lines that you can use as a reference, see Chapter 33.

Creating Closed Shapes

You can use the Rectangle or Ellipse drawing tools to quickly create closed shapes. To draw a closed shape with one of these tools, click the tool you want on the Drawing toolbar and then drag between two points on the drawing page. Visio creates the closed shape and applies a default fill style so you can see that the shape is closed.

If you use the Line, Pencil, Arc, or Freeform tool, you must be sure to close the drawing path if you want to apply a fill pattern or color to the shape. To close a drawing path, position the last point in the same position as the first point on the path, as shown in Figure 32-3. When you successfully close a shape, Visio applies a default fill to the shape so you can see that the shape is closed.

Note

If you can still see the drawing grid behind your shape after you've completed the entire path, the shape is not closed. See the section "Creating and Editing Shapes with the Pencil Tool" later in this chapter to learn how to close an open shape.

Click here to close the shape

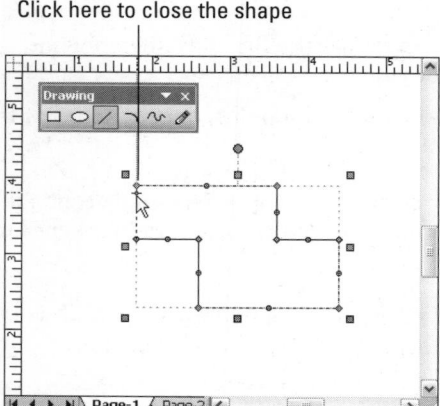

Figure 32-3: Overlap the first and last points to close a shape.

Drawing Graphics Precisely

When you create your own shapes, you often want to position lines and curves precisely in relation to other shapes on your drawing. For example, to construct HVAC or plumbing plans, you might want to draw ducts and pipes perpendicular to other lines or at specific angles. Visio drawing aids and shape extensions are guides to help you create a variety of precise geometric constructions, such as tangent lines.

Note   You can also specify precise coordinates for the end points of lines in the Size & Position window.

Drawing aids are temporary dotted lines that show you where to click to draw squares, circles, and angled or perpendicular lines. Shape extensions function similarly to drawing aids, but enable snapping to additional geometry, as shown in Figure 32-4. For example, you can use drawing aids or shape extensions to perform the following tasks:

✦ **Drawing circles and squares** — When you use the Ellipse or Rectangle tools, drawing aids show you where to click to create a circle or square.

✦ **Drawing lines** — When you use the Line tool or Pencil tool, drawing aids appear when the line you are constructing approaches an increment of 45 degrees. Depending on the shape extensions you enable, shape extensions show you where to click to draw lines such as tangents to a curve or perpendicular to other lines.

✦ **Editing lines** — When you edit a line segment, drawing aids extend at 45-degree increments as well as at the line's original angle.

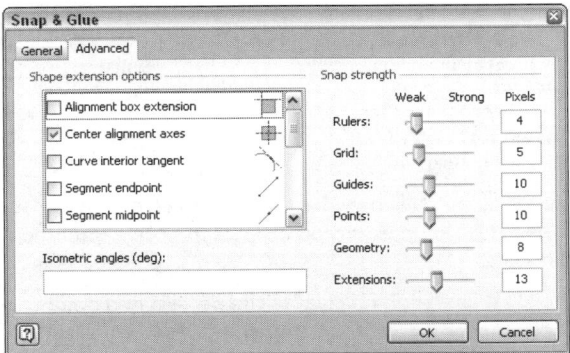

Figure 32-4: Shape extensions facilitate the creation of precise geometry.

To display drawing aids, choose Tools ➪ Snap & Glue and check the Drawing Aids check box in the Currently Active column. To enable snapping to shape extensions, check the Shape Extensions check box in the Snap To column, select the Advanced tab, and check the check box for each shape extension option you want to enable. Table 32-1 describes the shape extensions you can use to draw geometry.

Note You can adjust the attraction that shape extensions exert on the mouse pointer by dragging the Extensions slider to the left or right. As you drag the slider, the proximity of the pointer, in pixels, required to activate snapping appears in the Pixels box.

Table 32-1
Shape Extension Options

Option	Function
Alignment Box Extension	Extends lines from a shape's alignment box so you can snap to the edges of a shape
Center Alignment Axes	Extends a line from the center of a shape's alignment box so you can snap to the center of a shape
Curve Interior Tangent	Displays an extension line tangent to a curve. To draw a tangent to a curve, drag the pointer from the edge of the curve until the tangent extension line appears, and then drag the pointer along the extension line until the extension line turns red. As you continue to move the pointer, Visio shows a tangent line from the current pointer position to the curve.
Segment Endpoint	Highlights and snaps to the end point of a line segment or arc
Segment Midpoint	Highlights and snaps to the midpoint of a line segment or arc

Continued

Table 32-1 *(continued)*	
Option	**Function**
Linear Extension	Displays an extension of a line beyond its end point so you can extend the current line
Curved Extension	Extends an arc to show where to click to create an ellipse. For splines, this shape extension extends the curve from the nearest end point.
Endpoint Perpendicular	Displays a line perpendicular to the nearest end point of a line or arc so you can create a line perpendicular to an existing line or arc
Midpoint Perpendicular	Displays a perpendicular line from the midpoint of a line or arc so you can create a perpendicular line that bisects a line or arc
Horizontal Line at Endpoint	Displays a horizontal line from the end point of a line or arc so you can create a horizontal line starting at the end of an existing line
Vertical Line at Endpoint	Displays a vertical line from the end point of a line or arc so you can create a vertical line starting at the end of an existing line
Ellipse Center Point	Highlights and snaps to the center of an ellipse
Isometric Angles	Displays extension lines at isometric angles to simplify the construction of isometric diagrams

Creating and Editing Shapes with the Pencil Tool

With the Pencil tool, you can edit existing lines and arcs or create new ones. You can use it to correct crooked lines, reposition vertices and end points, switch between straight lines and circular arcs, or close open shapes. Click the Pencil tool on the Drawing Tool toolbar and then use one of the following methods to create or edit lines and arcs:

✦ **Draw a straight line** — Click a point on the drawing page and then drag the pointer straight in any direction. Visio indicates that it is in Line mode by changing the pointer to crosshairs, with an angled line below and to the right.

✦ **Draw an arc** — Click a point on the drawing page and then sweep the pointer in a curve. Visio indicates that it is in Arc mode by changing the pointer to crosshairs, with an arc below and to the right. By moving the pointer, you can adjust the radius of the arc as well as the angle it circumscribes.

✦ **Switch between Line and Arc mode** — Move the pointer back to the starting point. When the pointer changes to crosshairs only, drag or sweep the pointer to switch to Line mode or Arc mode.

✦ **Correct a crooked line** — If you created line segments that aren't orthogonal, straighten them by selecting the shape to display its vertices and then dragging an end point or vertex to a new location.

✦ **Change an arc into a straight line** — Select the shape to display its handles. Drag the green eccentricity handle at the midpoint of an arc until the line is straight.

✦ **Change a straight line into an arc** — Select the shape to display its handles. Drag the green eccentricity handle at the midpoint of a line until the arc is the radius you want.

✦ **Close an open shape** — Select the shape to display its vertices. You can close a shape using one of the following methods:

- Drag a vertex to the starting point of the first segment in the shape.

- Draw a line from the last vertex in the existing path to the first.

Transforming Shapes into New Ones

The Visio Operations menu includes specialized commands you can use to assemble simple shapes into more complex shapes, deconstruct shapes into more elementary components, or tweak shape geometry into exactly what you want. Some shapes, such as those with holes or cutouts, are feasible only by splicing several shapes into one. Even complex shapes that you can construct with repeated use of the Pencil and Group commands are often easier to build with Shape Operation commands, and the resulting Visio files are more compact. If you've worked with CAD programs, you're probably familiar with many of these functions. If not, the best approach is to experiment with these commands to find the combination that works.

To use Shape Operation commands, select the shapes you want to transform, choose Shape ⇨ Operations, and then choose the command you want.

Note   For Shape Operation commands, the order in which you select shapes is important for several reasons. For some commands, such as Subtract, Visio modifies the first shape selected using additional selected shapes, so the results vary depending on which shape you select first. In addition, Visio formats the resulting shape with the formatting from the first shape you select.

Assembling and Disassembling 2-D Shapes

Some Shape Operation commands transform several shapes into one. Conversely, the Fragment command divides shapes into smaller pieces. In some instances, you can achieve the same results using different Shape Operation commands. For other results, there's only one solution. If one command doesn't produce the results you want, try another command or experiment with a combination of them.

Updating the Alignment Box

You can use a shape's alignment box to align it to the drawing grid or other shapes. If shapes don't end up where you expect when you snap to a shape, the shape's alignment box could be out of whack. To reset an alignment box to match the boundaries of a shape or group, select the shape or group and then choose Shape ➪ Operations ➪ Update Alignment Box.

Caution   The 2-D Shape Operation commands delete your original shapes, so it's a good idea to make a copy of your shapes before you start. If a command doesn't produce the results you expect, you can also reverse the changes by immediately choosing Edit ➪ Undo.

Creating a Union from Shapes

The Union command produces a new shape that encloses the area of the original shapes. When you apply the Union command to overlapping shapes, it creates a new shape that includes the total area occupied by the original shapes and deletes the original shapes. For example, you can produce a single shape that looks like a mountain range from a collection of triangles. To create results similar to those shown in Figure 32-5, first select the shape whose format you want to apply to the resulting shape, Shift+click the other shapes you want to merge, and then choose Shape ➪ Operations ➪ Union.

Additional shapes for union

First shape for formatting

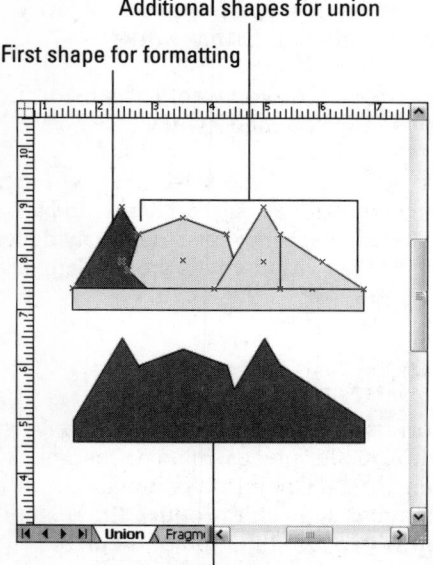

Figure 32-5: You can create one shape that encloses the area of several.

Result of Union command

Tip You can create a single shape from several shapes that don't overlap with the Union command. However, by creating a group out of several shapes by using the Group command, you can specify how the shapes in the group behave.

Combining Shapes

You can use the Combine command to produce a shape with holes, such as the frame of a window. The Combine command makes the overlapping areas of the selected shapes transparent so they look like holes, as demonstrated in Figure 32-6. It formats the shape based on the formatting of the first shape you select and deletes the original shapes when it's done. To combine shapes, select the shape with the format you want for the resulting shape, Shift+click the other shapes you want to process, and then choose Shape ➪ Operations ➪ Combine.

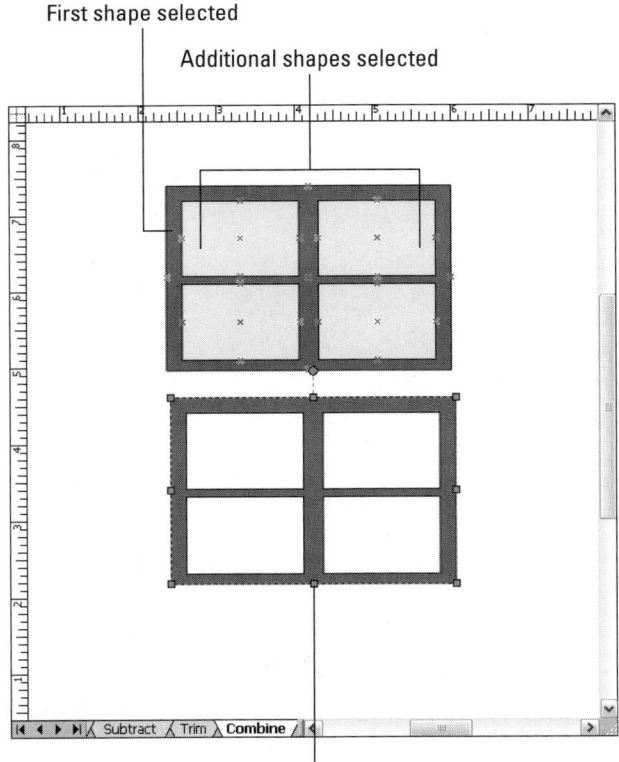

Figure 32-6: Combine shapes to create a shape with holes.

Breaking Shapes into Smaller Pieces

You can break overlapping shapes into smaller pieces by using the Fragment command. When you fragment two or more shapes, any areas that overlap become new 2-D shapes and the remaining areas that don't overlap also become 2-D shapes, as shown in Figure 32-7. In addition, you can draw lines through a 2-D shape to show where you want to break it. For example, by drawing lines through the center of a circle, you can break it into pie-shaped slices. To fragment shapes, select the shape with the format you want for the resulting shape, Shift+click the other shapes you want to process and any lines you want to use as breaks, and then choose Shape ➪ Operations ➪ Fragment.

First shape for formatting

Lines to show breakpoints   Another shape for Fragment

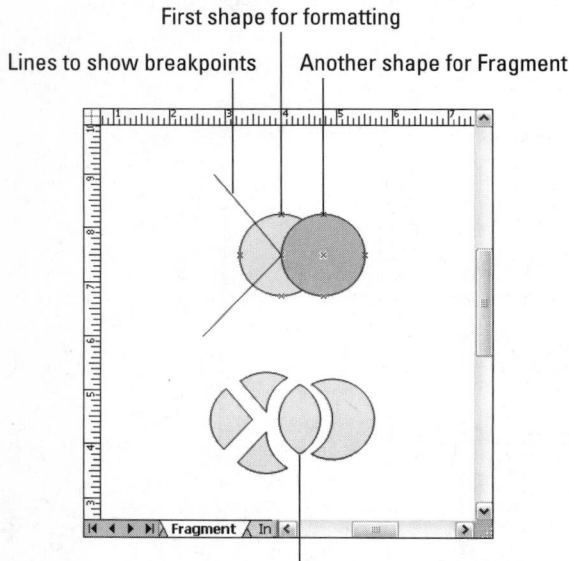

Results of Fragment command, separated for emphasis

Figure 32-7: You can use the Fragment command to break shapes into smaller pieces.

Removing Areas That Don't Overlap

The Intersect command produces one shape that includes only the overlapping areas of the shapes you select. For example, you can intersect two ellipses to produce an irregularly shaped island for a traffic intersection, as shown in Figure 32-8. The Intersect command deletes the original shapes and formats the resulting shape like the first shape you select. To intersect shapes, select the shape with the format you want for the resulting shape, Shift+click the other shapes you want to process, and then choose Shape ➪ Operations ➪ Intersect.

Original shapes

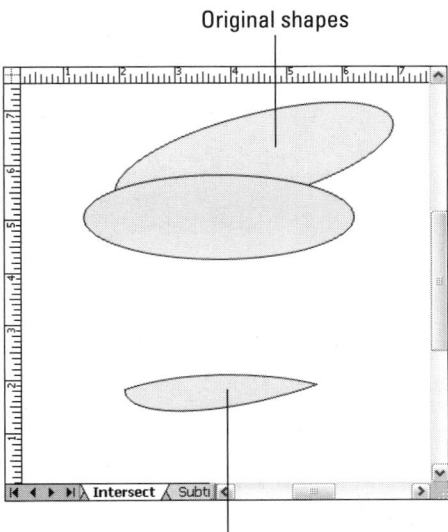

Result of Intersect command

Figure 32-8: You can create a shape from the overlapping area of other shapes.

Caution   Because shapes that don't overlap don't have any intersecting areas, applying the Intersect command to non-overlapping shapes or individual shapes simply deletes the original shapes.

Creating Cutouts

You can create shapes with areas cut out. The Subtract command creates a new shape that looks like the first shape you select minus the overlapping areas from additional shapes. The order in which you select shapes is particularly important for the Subtract command because it affects both the resulting shape and the formatting that Visio applies, as illustrated in Figure 32-9. To cut shapes out of another shape, select the shape from which you want to cut out areas, Shift+click the other shapes you want to use as cutouts, and choose Shape ➪ Operations ➪ Subtract.

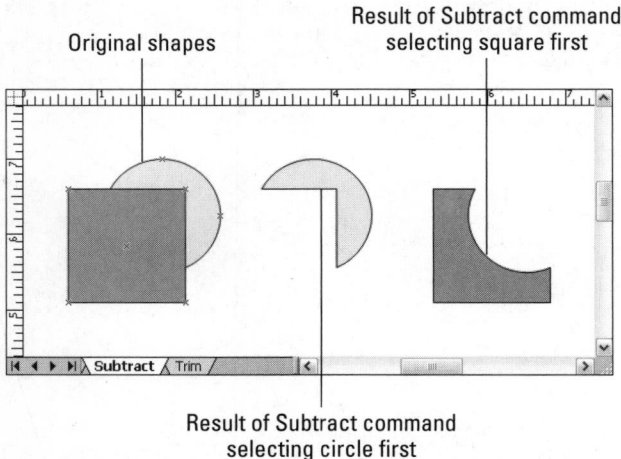

Figure 32-9: The order in which you select shapes is important for the Subtract command.

Manipulating Lines

Visio includes several Shape Operation commands specifically for creating and manipulating 1-D shapes on your drawings. For example, you can produce a set of parallel lines with the Offset command or use the Join command to create 2-D shapes from lines and arcs.

Joining Lines into Paths

The Join command and the Combine command have a lot in common. Just as Combine produces a single 2-D shape from several separate shapes, the Join command turns the 1-D lines and arcs you select into a single 2-D shape. For example, you can use the Join command to connect individual line segments into a single path. Although the Join command produces a 2-D shape, it only applies text and line formatting, not fill formatting, to the resulting shape. To join several lines and arcs, select the 1-D shape with the format you want to apply to the resulting shape, Shift+click the other shapes you want to join, and then choose Shape ⇨ Operations ⇨ Join.

Breaking Shapes into Lines and Arcs

The Trim command breaks shapes into separate lines and arcs. You can use lines to denote break points for the Trim command just as you can for the Fragment command. Visio converts shapes and lines into separate pieces wherever the lines intersect. For example, if you want to turn a long free-form curve into several shorter pieces, you can draw lines through the curve where you want to split it and then use the Trim command to break it into separate curves. Select the shape with the format you want to apply to the resulting shape, Shift+click the other shapes you want to trim, and then choose Shape ➪ Operations ➪ Trim.

Creating Parallel Lines and Curves

You can quickly create parallel lines, grids, cross-hatching, concentric circles, or other repeating patterns with the Offset command. When you use the Offset command, it creates a set of parallel lines or curves at the distance you specify on both sides of the original shape, as shown in Figure 32-10. Unlike other shape operations, Offset does not delete the original shape. For example, if you use Offset on a single line, you end up with three equally spaced lines, the original in the middle and the two new ones on either side. To create parallel lines or curves, follow these steps:

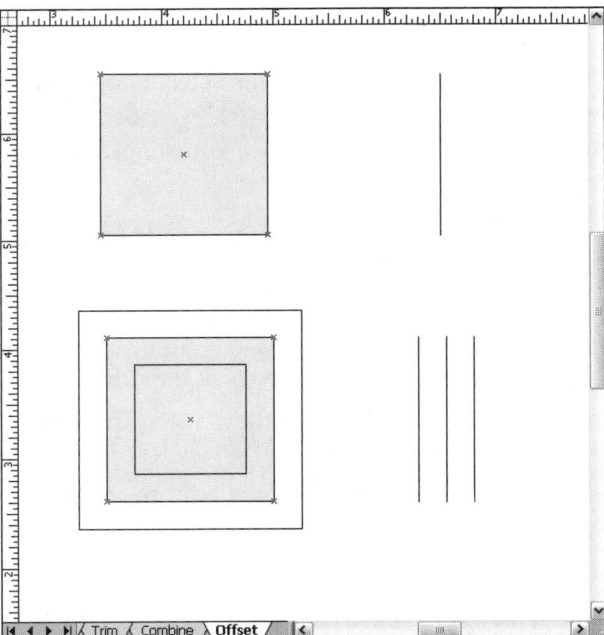

Figure 32-10: Offset creates new shapes on either side of the original shape.

1. Select a shape and choose Shape ➪ Operations ➪ Offset.

2. In the Offset dialog box, type the offset distance and click OK. Visio creates the additional lines on either side of the original.

Reversing Line Ends

Sometimes, you draw a line in the wrong direction, such as lines with arrowheads. If the line direction is important, as in data flow diagrams, you can correct your error without recreating the line. To switch the start and end points of a line, select the line and then choose Shape ⇨ Operations ⇨ Reverse Ends.

Creating Curves from Lines

The Fit Curve command transforms lines with multiple segments into curves. Unfortunately, this command can produce very different results depending on the settings and error tolerance you choose. The only solution is trial and error. If you don't like the results you obtain, press Ctrl+Z to undo those changes and try different settings. To create a free-form curve from a connected series of line segments, follow these steps:

1. Select the path that you want to convert to a curve and choose Shape ⇨ Operations ⇨ Fit Curve.

2. To create a curve that exactly fits the vertices of the selected path, use the default settings in the Fit Curve dialog box and click OK.

3. If you want to produce a simpler curve with fewer points, type a larger value in the Error Tolerance box and then click OK.

You can specify how Visio transforms a path into a combination of lines, arcs, and splines by setting the following curve parameters:

✦ **Periodic splines**—Check this check box to create a seamless spline from a closed and smooth shape. If the original shape is not smooth, uncheck the Cusps and Bumps check box to smooth sharp angles in the original shape.

✦ **Circular arcs**—Check this check box to replace the vertices in a path with either circular arcs or line segments.

✦ **Cusps and bumps**—Check this check box when you want to preserve sharp angles in the original shape.

Customizing Connection Points

Connection points identify locations on shapes where you can easily glue connectors and other shapes. If you want to glue to other positions, you can add connection points to any shape, regardless of whether it's a built-in Visio shape or a custom one you created. You can also move connection points to other positions on a shape.

Connection points are available in different types. By specifying the connection point type, you can control how shapes connect. For example, you can use connection point types to ensure that the wiring on an electrical plan connects to electrical outlets the way it should in the real world.

Adding, Moving, and Deleting Connection Points

You can add, move, or delete connection points on any shape on a drawing. If you want to modify the connection points on a built-in Visio master, create a custom copy of the master and then edit the connection points the way you want.

To select the Connection Point tool, click the arrow next to the Connector tool on the Standard toolbar and then choose Connection Point Tool. To work with connection points, use one of the following methods:

✦ **Add a connection point** — Select a shape and click the Connection Point tool. Ctrl+click the selected shape at the position where you want the new connection point. As soon as you press Ctrl, Visio changes the pointer to blue crosshairs so that it's easier to position the connection point.

Note   Make sure that the shape you want to edit is selected before adding a connection point. Visio creates connection points only for the selected shape, even if you click a position on a different shape.

✦ **Delete a connection point** — Click the Connection Point tool and select a connection point on a shape. When the connection point turns magenta, indicating it is selected, press Delete.

✦ **Move a connection point** — Click the Connection Point tool and select a connection point on a shape. When the connection point turns magenta, indicating it is selected, drag it to a new location.

Working with Types of Connection Points

For some drawing types, such as electrical plans or piping and instrumentation diagrams, you glue shapes to each other instead of connecting them with linear connectors. In the systems that these diagrams represent, components connect in specific ways. For example, it's important that you connect the wiring to an electrical outlet the correct way or sparks will fly. Visio provides different types of connection points so you can control how shapes glue together.

Understanding Types of Connection Points

Visio provides three types of connection points to model the way components connect in the real world. Built-in Visio shapes already include the types of connection points needed to glue them properly. However, if you're creating your own shapes and solutions, it's important to understand how the three types work so that you can choose the right ones for your shapes:

✦ **Inward connection point**—Connects to end points of 1-D shapes (such as connectors), Outward connection points, and Inward & Outward connection points. It is the default connection point type used almost exclusively on drawings in which connectors connect shapes, such as organization charts. Visio indicates Inward connection points with a blue X. If you position a shape with an Inward connection point over another Inward connection point, the shapes won't glue together.

✦ **Outward connection point**—Connects to Inward connection points, Inward & Outward connection points, shape geometry, and 1-D endpoints. For example, the Work Peninsula shape on the Cubicles stencil includes an Outward connection point. You can glue a Work Peninsula shape to the connection points on Work Surface or Corner Surface shapes, but you can't glue two Work Peninsula shapes together, because in real life, the resulting cubicle arrangement wouldn't stand up. Visio indicates Outward connection points with a blue square.

✦ **Inward & Outward connection point**—Connects to all types of connection points. For example, modular furniture on the Office Furniture stencil include Inward & Outward connection points so you can glue the components together in any order. The indicator for Inward & Outward connection points appropriately looks like a combination of the blue X of an Inward connection point and the blue square of an Outward connection point.

If shapes don't glue the way you would expect, you might be trying to glue the wrong connection points together. Refer to Table 32-2 for a quick reference of valid connection points.

Table 32-2
Valid Connections for Connection Points

	Inward connection points	Outward connection points	Inward and Outward connection points	Shape geometry points	1-D shape end points
Inward connection point	No	Yes	Yes	No	Yes
Outward connection point	Yes	No	Yes	Yes	Yes
Inward and Outward connection point	Yes	Yes	Yes	Yes	Yes

Changing the Type of Connection Point

By default, Visio adds Inward connection points when you use the Connection Point tool. However, you can modify the type of connection point so your shape glues to the points you want. You can change connection points on shapes on drawings or on masters in custom stencils. If you want to change the type of connection point for a built-in shape, create a custom version of the shape and then change the connection point. To change the type of connection points, follow these steps:

1. Click the Connection Point tool on the Standard toolbar.

 If the Connection Point tool is not visible, select it by clicking the arrow next to the Connector tool on the Standard toolbar and then choosing Connection Point tool.

2. Right-click the connection point you want to modify. After it turns magenta, choose the type of connection point you want from the shortcut menu.

 In Visio 2002, you could also specify an angle for a connection point, to glue shapes at a specific angle. In Visio 2003, this feature is no longer available.

Customizing Shape Behavior

In addition to the visible components of a shape that appear on a drawing page and the connection points that control how shapes connect to each other, you can customize dozens of behaviors exhibited by shapes. For example, you specify what Visio highlights when you select a shape, whether a shape prints, how you can resize a shape, what happens when you double-click it, or how you can place it on a drawing. You can customize the behavior of any shape on your drawings or the masters in your custom stencils. If you want to customize the behavior for a built-in shape, create a custom version of the shape and then specify the behaviors you want.

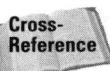 You can define more advanced behaviors for shapes by modifying formulas in a shape's ShapeSheet, as described in Chapter 33.

Specifying Double-Click Behavior for Shapes

By default, when you double-click a shape, Visio opens the shape's text block so you can edit its text. However, you can choose from several other actions if you want the shape to perform another action when you double-click it. You can direct a shape to perform more complex actions by running a macro when you double-click the shape. To specify the action that occurs when you double-click a shape, follow these steps:

1. Right-click the shape you want to customize and choose Format ⇨ Behavior from the shortcut menu.

2. Select the Double-Click tab and choose one of the Double-Click options, described in Table 32-3.

3. Click OK. Confirm that the behavior works the way you want by double-clicking the shape.

Table 32-3
Double-Click Behaviors for Shapes

Double-Click Option	Resulting Behavior
Perform Default Action	Performs the default double-click action defined for the shape
Perform No Action	Does nothing when you double-click the shape
Edit Shape's Text	Opens the shape's text block so you can edit its text
Open Group in New Window	When you select a group, this option opens the group in the group editing window so that you can modify the group. This option is not available if you select a shape.
Open Shape's ShapeSheet	Opens the ShapeSheet for the shape
Custom	If you define a custom behavior in the EventDblClick cell in the Events section of the shape's ShapeSheet, this option is selected. However, the option is always dimmed.
Display Help	Displays a help topic for the shape. To specify a help topic, enter either *FILENAME!keyword* or *FILENAME!#number*, where *FILENAME* is the name of a .hlp or .chm Windows help file, *keyword* is a term associated with the help topic, and *number* is an ID referenced in the MAP section of the help project file.
OLE Verb	When you select a linked or embedded object, this option activates an OLE command, such as Open. This option is not available when you select a Visio shape.
Run Macro	Runs the macro or add-on that you select in the drop-down list. The list box includes your custom macros as well as built-in Visio tools, such as Database Update.
Go to Page	Jumps to the page number specified in the drop-down list. To open the page in a new window, check the Open in New Window check box.

Note   If you define a custom formula for a shape in its ShapeSheet, you can overwrite the custom behavior by choosing a double-click behavior other than Custom. However, if you protect the custom formula with the `Guard` function, Visio ignores the double-click option you choose and uses the custom formula instead.

Specifying Placement Behavior

You can specify how a 2-D shape reacts when you use the Layout and Routing tools. For drawings in which connections are key components that convey critical information, such as database models, built-in shapes are already configured to behave the way you would expect. However, you can specify whether Visio lays out and routes around a shape, and, if it does, what happens when you place the shape on a drawing page.

Note   Because Placement options apply only to 2-D shapes, they are not available in the Behavior dialog box when you select a 1-D shape.

To specify Placement behaviors for a shape, follow these steps:

1. Right-click a shape and choose Format ➪ Behavior from the shortcut menu.
2. Select the Placement tab and specify the Placement options you want for the shape. Table 32-4 describes the options.
3. Click OK.

Table 32-4
Placement Options for Shapes

Placement Option	*Description*
Placement Behavior	Specifies whether Visio always lays out and routes around a shape, ignores the shape during layout, or decides what to do based on the type of connector you glue to the shape. If you choose Let Visio Decide, Visio lays out the shape when you glue a Dynamic connector to it.
Do Not Move During Placement	Prevents Visio from moving the shape during automatic layout.
Allow Other Shape to Be Placed on Top	Allows Visio to place other shapes on top of the shape during automatic layout. To ensure that every shape on a page is visible, uncheck this check box.

Continued

Table 32-4 *(continued)*	
Placement Option	**Description**
Move Shapes Away on Drop	Specifies whether the shape moves other shapes out of the way when you reposition it on the page. You can choose to keep other shapes where they are, always move other shapes away, or use the option specified in the Page Setup dialog box. This option overrides the Move Other Shapes Away on Drop option on the Layout and Routing tab in the Page Setup dialog box.
Do Not Allow Other Shapes to Move This Shape Away on Drop	Specifies whether the shape remains where it is when other shapes are dropped onto the page, regardless of which Move Other Shapes Away on Drop option you choose.
Route Through Horizontally	Specifies whether connectors can route through the shape horizontally. Uncheck this check box if you want Visio to route around the shape.
Route Through Vertically	Specifies whether connectors can route through the shape vertically. Uncheck this check box if you want Visio to route around the shape.

Modifying Other Shape Behaviors

In addition to Double-Click and Placement behaviors, you can specify a variety of other behaviors for shapes on the Behavior tab of the Behavior dialog box. For example, you can specify the following:

- ✦ Whether a shape acts like a line or a 2-D shape
- ✦ Whether connectors split when you drop shapes on them
- ✦ Which elements are highlighted when you select a shape
- ✦ How you can resize a shape
- ✦ How groups behave

Preventing Shapes from Printing

If you want to add reference shapes to a drawing, such as construction lines or notes to colleagues, you can view them while you work on the drawing but prevent them from printing. To prevent a shape from printing, right-click the shape, choose Format ➪ Behavior, and select the Behavior tab. Check the Non-printing Shape check box under the Miscellaneous heading and click OK.

Switching Between 1-D and 2-D Behavior

No matter what a shape looks like, you can make it behave like a 1-D line or a 2-D shape. For example, if you define a line as a 2-D shape, you drag its selection handles to turn it into a rectangle. Conversely, you can create a shape with 2-D graphics, such as the Fancy Arrow shape on the Basic Shapes stencil, and make it act like a line. You can change the thickness of the Fancy Arrow shape by dragging its side selection points, but you can glue only to its start and end points.

To specify whether a shape behaves like a 1-D or 2-D shape, follow these steps:

1. Right-click the shape you want to switch, choose Format ➪ Behavior, and select the Behavior tab.

2. Under Interaction Style, select the Line (1-dimensional) or Box (2-dimensional) option, and then click OK.

Caution

Switching a shape's behavior from 1-D to 2-D or vice versa can produce unexpected results, because this option changes the contents of the shape's ShapeSheet. For example, it can break customized formulas you define in the ShapeSheet or glued connections between the shape and other shapes.

Showing That a Shape Is Selected

You can specify the elements that Visio highlights when you select a shape. To highlight different shape elements, right-click the shape and choose Format ➪ Behavior from the shortcut menu. Select the Behavior tab and then specify one or more of the following options under the Selection Highlighting heading:

✦ **Show Shape Handles**—Check this check box to display the shape's selection handles.

Caution

If you uncheck Show Shape Handles, you can move the shape but won't be able to resize it. If you uncheck Show Control Handles, you can activate the editing features that the control handles provide, but you must know where the control handles are without seeing them.

✦ **Show Control Handles**—Check this check box to display the shape's control handles.

✦ **Show Alignment Box**—Check this check box to see the alignment box for the shape.

Note

If you uncheck all the Selection Highlighting options, Visio provides no visual indication that the shape is selected.

Controlling the Splitting of Connectors

If you work on a data flow diagram and realize that you've missed a process, the easiest solution is to drop a shape onto the connector where you want to insert the process, have Visio split the connector, and glue the two connector pieces to the new shape. You can specify exactly that behavior with the following options under the Connector Splitting heading in the Behavior dialog box:

✦ **Connector Can Be Split By Shapes** — When you select a connector, you can check this check box so that Visio splits the connector in two when you drop a shape that splits connectors onto it.

✦ **Shape Can Split Connectors** — When you select a shape, you can check this check box so that Visio splits a connector that can be split when you drop the shape onto it.

> **Note**   For these splitting options to work, you must also check the Enable Connector Splitting option on the Layout and Routing tab of the Page Setup dialog box and on the General tab of the Options dialog box.

Controlling Group-related Behaviors

Although groups are comprised of shapes, the groups are entities with properties and behaviors of their own. For shapes that belong to a group, you can control how a shape resizes. For groups, you can also specify how you add shapes to groups, select groups, and display group text and data.

To specify group-related behaviors, right-click the shape or group and choose Format ➪ Behavior from the shortcut menu. Select the Behavior tab and then choose one or more of the following behaviors:

✦ **Resizing shapes in groups** — In a predefined office cubicle, you don't want to change the size of the work surfaces or partitions, because they represent the actual size of the furniture that the manufacturer delivers. Conversely, if you create a group of cells to create a tabular form, you might want the cells to change size as you increase or decrease the size of the table. To control how a shape resizes when it belongs to a group, choose one of the following options under the Resize Behavior heading:

- **Scale with Group** — Select this option to have the shape resize proportionally when you resize the group. This is helpful when the shapes don't represent real-world dimensions.

- **Reposition Only** — Select this option to have the shape remain the same size when you resize the group. For example, if you create a group to represent a kitchen, you can set the appliances to Reposition Only so you can rearrange them within the kitchen, but not change their dimensions.

- **Use Group's Setting** — Select this option to have the shape resized based on the Resize behavior defined for the group.

✦ **Adding shapes to groups** — You can always add shapes to groups by selecting the shape and group and choosing Shape ⇨ Grouping ⇨ Group. However, you can also choose whether to use a drag and drop shortcut for adding shapes to groups. To control the methods you can use to add shapes to groups, use the following options:

   • **Add Shape to Groups on Drop** — Check this check box under the Miscellaneous heading to add a shape to a group that accepts dropped shapes. To ensure that a shape remains separate no matter what option is set for a group, uncheck this check box.

   • **Accept Dropped Shapes** — Check this check box under the Group Behavior heading if you want a group to absorb a dropped shape whose Add Shape to Groups on Drop check box is checked. For self-contained groups, such as factory-configured equipment, uncheck this check box if you want to prevent shapes from joining the group.

✦ **Selecting shapes and groups** — In some groups, such as office workstations, the group is the important element. You're more likely to select the group so you can arrange your office space. For other groups, such as a title block, you usually want to select the shapes within the group to add the text to identify your drawing. To specify whether clicking selects the group or a shape within the group, choose one of the following options in the Selection drop-down list:

   • **Group Only** — Select this option to prevent the selection of shapes within a group. By doing so, you can only edit the shapes within the group when you ungroup them.

   • **Group First** — Select this option to select the group the first time you click and then subselect the shape within the group upon subsequent clicks.

   • **Members First** — Select this option to select the shape within a group the first time you click and then select the group with the next click.

✦ **Snapping in groups** — If you want to snap and glue to shapes in a group, such as connecting cables to the Equipment shapes within a Cubicle group, check the Snap to Member Shapes check box under the Group Behavior heading.

✦ **Displaying and editing text** — To specify the display and editing of group text, choose one of the following:

   • **Edit Text of Group** — Check this check box under the Group Behavior heading if you want to add text for the group. For example, you can use the group text box to show the model number for an office workstation.

   • **Hide** — Select this option in the Group Data drop-down list to hide the group text box.

   • **Behind Member Shapes** — Select this option in the Group Data drop-down list to display the group text behind the shape text.

   • **In Front of Member Shapes** — Select this option in the Group Data drop-down list to display the group text in front of the shape text.

Adding Screen Tips to Shapes

If you're creating shapes for others to use or want to show additional information about a shape on a page, you can customize shapes with ScreenTips that appear when you position the pointer over the shapes. Use one of the following methods to add or edit ScreenTips:

✦ **Add a ScreenTip** — Select the shape to which you want to add a ScreenTip and then choose Insert ➪ Shape ScreenTip. Type the text for the ScreenTip and click OK.

✦ **Edit a ScreenTip** — Select the shape and choose Insert ➪ Edit Shape ScreenTip. Edit the text the way you want and then click OK.

✦ **Delete a ScreenTip** — Select the shape and choose Insert ➪ Edit Shape ScreenTip. Delete the text in the Shape ScreenTip dialog box and click OK.

Working with Custom Properties

You can store data along with the graphics in your drawings by associating custom properties with shapes. With data attached to shapes on your drawings, you can search for shapes based on values in custom properties, review shape property values as you work, annotate your shapes by displaying properties in shape text blocks, and produce reports from shape data.

You can also use custom properties to configure the appearance of a shape. For example, by specifying a value for the Slices custom property associated with a Pie Chart shape, you can create or modify a Pie Chart shape to contain that number of slices. Configuring shapes with custom properties requires that both custom properties and programming be defined in a shape's ShapeSheet. To learn how to configure a shape using custom properties and the ShapeSheet, see Chapter 33.

If you want to add the same set of properties to several masters or shapes, you can reuse custom properties and apply them in groups by creating custom property sets. For example, many of the shapes in the Business Process stencils include Duration, Cost, and Resources properties so you can track process statistics. In the Custom Property Set window, you can create, rename, or delete custom property sets and assign custom properties to those sets. You can also apply the properties in custom property sets to all the shapes you want at one time.

In Visio 2002, custom property sets were a feature of the Edit Custom Property Set add-on. In Visio 2003, Custom Property Sets is a command on the Tools menu. In addition, you can now apply more than one custom property set to shapes.

To store data in custom properties after they are associated with shapes, follow these steps:

1. Open the Custom Properties window by choosing View ⇨ Custom Properties Window.

2. Select a shape to display its properties in the Custom Properties window. If the shape doesn't contain any custom properties, the window displays the text No Custom Properties.

Note   For some shapes, you can open the Custom Properties dialog box by right-clicking the shape and choosing Properties from the shortcut menu. After the dialog box is open, you can enter or edit values and click OK when you are finished.

3. To enter a value, click the property you want to edit and type the value in the box or click a value in a drop-down list.

Tip   If you aren't sure what a custom property represents or what format you should enter, you can display the prompt for a property by pointing to the property label in the Custom Properties window.

Creating and Editing Custom Properties

Whether you want to store data in shapes or annotate shapes with custom property values, you must first create custom properties and associate them with your masters or shapes. Although you can add custom properties to individual shapes on a drawing, it's easier to apply custom properties to masters so that the instances you create on drawings already contain the properties you want.

When you add or edit custom properties for masters, you can control the scope of your changes by choosing the stencil in which you make your changes. If you want every instance you create in the future to incorporate your changes, edit the master in the Visio stencil. However, if you only want to change the instances on your current drawing, edit the master in the Document stencil for that drawing.

Defining Custom Properties

Whether you create individual properties or define them through custom property sets, the real work of defining a custom property occurs in the Define Custom Properties dialog box. You can define new properties for shapes and masters by specifying options, as described in Table 32-5. When you select a shape that already contains custom properties, the Define Custom Properties dialog box displays those properties at the bottom of the dialog box. You can modify the options for these properties or delete them from the shape or master.

New Feature   In Visio 2003, you can specify the language used to format a date as well as the calendar to use.

Table 32-5
Custom Property Options

Option	Description
Label	Consisting of alphanumeric characters and underscore characters, the label is the name of the custom property and appears next to the field in which you enter the property value.
Type	The data type for the property, including String, Number, Fixed List, Variable List, Boolean, Currency, Date, and Duration
Language	Specifies the language to correctly format the date and time when you create a Date property. For example, English (U.S.) uses mm/dd/yy, whereas English (U.K.) uses dd/mm/yy.
Calendar	Specifies whether to use the Arabic Hijri (Islamic), Hebrew Lunar (Jewish), Saka Era (Hindu), or Western (Gregorian) calendar to convert a date entered in a Date property
Format	The format for the data type. The options available depend on the Type and Calendar options selected. You can select from lists of predefined formats when you define data types such as String, Number, Fixed List, Variable List, Currency, Boolean, Date, and Duration. To specify fixed lists or variable lists, type each item in the list separated by semicolons. For example, you can create a color list by entering **red;white;blue**. If you create a fixed list, you can only select one of the entries on the list. With variable lists, you can enter another value, such as **green**.
Value	Specifies the initial value for the property. For existing properties, this box shows the current value. Omit this value if you want the property to be blank initially.
Prompt	Specifies text that appears when you select the property in the Custom Properties dialog box or pause the pointer over the custom property label in the Custom Properties window. You can use the prompt to see a description of the property or instructions on its use.
Properties	Displays the existing custom properties for a shape. When you select a property in the list and modify it, Visio applies the changes you make to its definition immediately.
New	Creates a new custom property
Delete	Deletes the custom property selected in the Properties list

Note   In Developer mode, you can also do the following: specify the order in which custom properties appear in the Custom Properties dialog box and Custom Properties window, hide the property, or prompt users to enter custom property information when they create, duplicate, or copy shapes.

To define, edit, or delete custom properties for a shape or master, follow these steps:

1. Select the shape or master to which you want to add a property by using one of the following methods:

   - **Add to shape** — Select the shape on the drawing page.

   - **Add to master** — Right-click the custom stencil's title bar and click Edit Stencil. Right-click the master and choose Edit Master ➪ Edit Master Shape. Select the shape in the master drawing window.

Note You can edit a master in a stencil to modify all future instances of the master. To modify existing instances in the current drawing, edit a master on the Document stencil.

   - **Add to page** — Click any blank area of the page to ensure that nothing is selected.

2. Choose Shape ➪ Custom Properties. If Visio asks if you want to define custom properties, click Yes. If the shape already contains custom properties and the Custom Properties dialog box appears, click Define.

3. Choose one of the following tasks:

   - **Create a property** — If the shape has no custom properties assigned, you can begin specifying the property options for the default property, Property1. If the shape already has at least one custom property, click New.

Note When you define custom properties in the Define Custom Properties dialog box, you can't copy properties from one shape to another. To reuse custom properties, add them to custom property sets and apply those sets to your shapes and masters.

   - **Edit a property** — Select the property you want to edit in the Properties list and make the changes you want to the Label, Type, Language, Format, Calendar, Value, and Prompt options.

   - **Delete a property** — Select the property you want to delete in the Properties list and click Delete.

Caution If a shape has predefined custom properties, deleting them might affect the shape's behavior.

4. When you have finished working with the custom properties, click OK.

5. If you worked with properties for a shape, you're finished. If you added, edited, or deleted custom properties for a master, click the Close button in the master drawing window. When Visio prompts to update the master, click Yes and then save the stencil.

Note If you edit a master in the Document stencil, Visio will update the master as well as all the shapes in the drawing file based on that master.

Displaying Custom Properties in Shape Text

To annotate shapes with custom properties, you can include in the shape's text block a field that references the custom property. Text blocks can contain as many fields as you want and you can format the fields just as you can format text. For example, you can display multiple custom properties, such as an employee's name and telephone extension. To display a custom property in a shape's text block, follow these steps:

1. Select a shape on a drawing or a master in an editable stencil to which you want to add a text field and choose Insert ➪ Field.

2. In the Category list, select Custom Properties.

3. In the Field list, select the custom property you want to display in the text block.

4. In the Format list, select the format you want to apply to the custom property value.

To add more than one property to a shape or master's text box, as demonstrated in Figure 32-11, follow these steps:

Field in shape text block

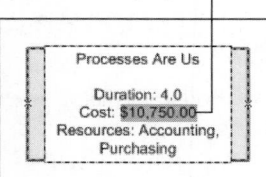

Figure 32-11: You can display more than one custom property in a shape's text block.

1. Double-click the shape or master to open its text block. Position the insertion point in the text where you want to insert the field for the property.

2. Choose Insert ➪ Field, select Custom Properties in the Category list, select the property you want to insert, select the format you want to apply, and click OK.

3. Position the insertion point in the shape's text block where you want to insert text or another custom property field. Type the text or repeat step 2 to add another field.

Using Custom Property Sets

Custom property sets provide an easy way to define or modify a group of custom properties and apply them to multiple shapes. After you create and name a custom property set, you can add the properties you want to it or modify the definitions of its properties. When you have configured the custom property set the way you want, you can apply the collection of properties in the set to the selected shapes on a drawing page, the Document stencil, or any open editable stencil.

Custom property sets also simplify adding custom properties to shapes that weren't created by dragging masters from stencils. For example, built-in Workstation shapes on the Cubicles stencil include a dozen different custom properties. You can create a custom property set from the properties associated with a built-in Workstation shape. If you import additional Workstation shapes or create you own, you can easily associate those custom properties to your new shapes by applying the custom property set to your selected Workstation shapes or masters.

Creating Custom Property Sets

You can create custom property sets from scratch, but it's often easier to create them from the properties associated with a shape, or to expand on a custom property set that already exists. For example, you can create a new custom property set based on the properties assigned to TQM shapes: Cost, Duration, and Resources. You might add Work and Department properties and then apply the new custom property set to all the masters in your custom TQM Shapes stencil.

To create a new custom property set, follow these steps:

1. If you intend to create a custom property set based on the properties associated with a shape or master, select the shape on a drawing page or a master in an editable stencil.

2. Choose Tools ➪ Custom Property Sets and click Add in the Custom Property Sets window.

3. Type the name for the set in the Name box, choose one of the following options, and then click OK:

   • **Create a New Set**—Creates a custom property set with the name you specify and no properties in it initially

   • **Create a New Set From the Shape Selected in Visio**—Creates a custom property set with the name you specify and all of the properties associated with the shape or master you selected in step 1

   • **Create a New Set From an Existing Set**—When you select this option, you can choose an existing custom property set from a drop-down list that contains the custom property sets available in every open drawing

Visio creates the custom property set and stores it in the current drawing or stencil. To add properties to a set, modify properties in a set, or apply a set to shapes, see the following sections.

Editing Custom Property Sets

Within the Custom Property Sets window, shown in Figure 32-12, you can add or modify the properties in a custom property set, as well as rename or delete existing custom property sets. To make changes to custom property sets, use one of the following methods:

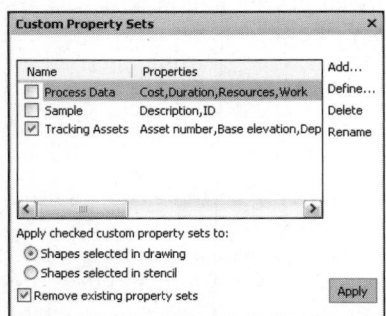

Figure 32-12: Work with groups of custom properties in the Custom Property Sets window.

✦ **Rename a custom property set**—In the Custom Property Sets window, select the set you want to rename in the list and click Rename. Type the new name and press Enter.

✦ **Delete a custom property set**—In the Custom Property Sets window, select the set you want to delete in the list and click Delete.

✦ **Modify the properties in a custom property set**—In the Custom Property Sets window, select the set whose properties you want to modify and click Define. In the Define Custom Properties dialog box, create new properties, modify existing property definitions, or delete properties, as described in the section "Defining Custom Properties" earlier in this chapter. Click OK when you're done.

Applying Custom Property Sets to Shapes and Masters

You can apply custom property sets to different shapes and masters depending on where you save the custom property sets. When you create a custom property set in a drawing, the set is saved in the drawing file and you can apply the set to shapes on the drawing pages or to masters in the Document stencil. However, if you create a custom property set in a stencil, you can only apply the custom property set to the masters in the stencil.

New Feature

In Visio 2002, you applied custom property sets using the Apply Custom Property Sets add-on, and you could only apply one custom property set at a time to a shape or master. If you applied a new set, Visio automatically removed the previous custom property set. In Visio 2003, you apply custom property sets within the Custom Property Sets window and you can add as many sets as you want. You can also specify whether to remove existing sets when you add new ones.

To apply custom property sets to shapes or masters, follow these steps:

1. Select the shape or master to which you want to apply the custom property set using one of these methods:

   - **Select shapes** — On a drawing page, select the shape you want.
   - **Select masters** — In an editable stencil, select the master you want.

Tip

   To select additional shapes or masters, Shift+click the other shapes or masters you want to add to the selection.

2. Choose Tools ➪ Custom Property Sets and then check the check boxes for all of the custom property sets that you want to apply in the list.

3. Choose an option to either apply the set to selected shapes or selected masters. If you want to remove the existing custom property sets from the selected shapes or masters, make sure the Remove Existing Property Sets check box is checked.

4. Click Apply.

Producing Reports with Custom Property Data

Several Visio templates include predefined reports that you can run to view and analyze the data stored with the shapes in your drawings. However, you can also define and format your own reports. Although you can create new reports from scratch, you can also modify existing reports to match your requirements and then save the modified report with a new name.

Defining Custom Reports

When you want to work on reports, choose Tools ➪ Reports. By default, Visio displays the reports specific to the type of drawing that is active. If you want to start with an existing report from another type of drawing, uncheck the Show Only Drawing-specific Reports check box to view all of Visio's built-in reports. To create a new custom report, click New in the Reports dialog box. If you want to base your report on an existing report, select the report you want to base your new report on in the Report list and click Modify. Either way, the Report Definition Wizard steps you through the process of defining a report. When you have completed the report definition, Visio saves your report where you specify and adds it to the list of available reports. As you step through the Report Definition Wizard, you specify the following features of your report:

✦ The objects on which you want to report

✦ The properties you want to display in the columns of the report and any criteria you want to use to limit the results shown in the report

✦ The format for the report, including how the contents are grouped and sorted and how numbers are formatted

✦ The Save options for the report, including the report definition name, a description, and where Visio saves the report

The following sections describe how to use the features in each step of the wizard.

Selecting Shapes on Which to Report

The first step to defining a report is to choose the shape to scan for data. You can report on every shape in your drawing file, the shapes on the current page, or only selected shapes. You can also specify criteria to further limit the shapes that Visio scans by clicking Advanced. In the Advanced dialog box, you can define multiple criteria that shapes must meet for inclusion in the report. For example, to produce a report of the furniture for the Accounting department, you can specify that the Department property in shapes on the Furniture layer must equal Accounting.

You can limit the shapes used in one of the following ways:

✦ **Shapes on a layer**—Select the <Layer Name> property. You can include or exclude a layer from a report by selecting = or <> in the Condition box.

✦ **Shapes by name or ID**—You can use the <Master Name>, <Shape Name>, or <Shape ID> properties to specify the named shapes you want.

✦ **Shapes with specific custom properties**—Select the custom property, select Exists in the Condition list, and then select TRUE in the Value list.

✦ **Shapes with specific values in custom properties**—Select the custom property and then specify the condition and value for the property. For example, you can select Duration, >, and 5 to report on all processes whose duration is longer than five weeks.

✦ **AutoDiscovery shapes**—Select the <Autodiscovery Shape> property to report on shapes that result from using AutoDiscovery.

Note

The conditions and values you can choose depend on the property that you select. However, Visio offers a limited number of conditional operators, such as =, <>, and >=.

To add an additional criterion, define the criterion and then click Add. To delete a criterion, select it in the Defined Criteria list and then click Delete. You can delete all the defined criteria by clicking Clear.

After you define criteria, click OK to close the Advanced dialog box and then click Next to continue selecting the properties for the report columns.

If Visio's report capabilities are too limited, you can export shape data to another format and use an application with more robust reporting tools to produce your report. To learn how to export data, see Chapter 9. You can also store data in a database so that you can produce reports from the database application but display the data in Visio by linking the data to shapes. To learn more about linking shapes to databases, see Chapter 10.

Choosing Report Columns

In the screen for choosing properties, Visio displays default shape properties, such as <Master Name> and <Height>, in addition to custom properties and user-defined properties from the ShapeSheet User-Defined Cells section. Default shape properties appear within angled brackets in the list. To see user-defined properties from the ShapeSheet, check the Show All Properties check box.

Check the check box for each property you want to use as a column in the report. Click Next to continue grouping, sorting, and formatting your report.

Grouping, Sorting, and Formatting Report Contents

You can group, sort, and format report results in several ways. For example, you can produce a report that groups the office furniture by department, calculating the number of desks for each department, and sorting the report by the average furniture cost per department.

To group the results of your report and calculate group values, click Subtotals. Choose the property you want to use to group your results in the Group By drop-down list, which contains the properties you specified as columns for your report. You can also specify which rows appear in your report by clicking Options. For example, you can show all values, only unique values, only subtotals, or grand totals. You can also prevent duplicate rows from appearing in your report.

If you want to perform a calculation for your report, for each property in the Properties list, check the check boxes for the calculations you want. Count is available for any type of custom property, but the other calculations only work with numerical properties. If a calculation isn't valid for a property, the check box is dimmed. When you perform a calculation, it calculates the value for each group in the report. If you create an ungrouped report, the calculation represents all entries. You can choose from the following calculations:

✦ **Count** — Calculates the number of shapes with the same value in a custom property. For example, if there are 16 shapes with the value "Accounting" in the Department property, Count returns 16.

✦ **Total** — Sums the value of all the entries in a group or all entries for an ungrouped report

✦ **Avg** — Calculates the average of property values in a group or the entire report

✦ **Max**—Returns the largest number from the list of property values

✦ **Min**—Returns the smallest number from the list of property values

✦ **Median**—Calculates the median for a list of property values. In a group of numbers, the median is the number with an equal number of values greater and less than it.

You can arrange the order of the columns in your report as well as specify the sort order for rows by clicking Sort. To rearrange the columns in your report, select a column in the Column Order list and then click Move Up or Move Down to change its position in the column order.

You can sort the rows in a report with up to three properties. Choose the custom properties for the first sort in the Sort By list and select the Ascending or Descending option. You can specify one or two more sort properties in the two Then By lists, also specifying ascending or descending order. For example, you can sort a report of office furniture first by department, then by employee name, and finally by Shape Name if it indicates the type of furniture.

For custom properties with numeric values, you can specify the number of decimals in numbers and whether to show units. Click Format and then choose the number of places to the right of the decimal point in the Precision box. To show units, check the Show Units check box.

Note After you specify any grouping, subtotals, sorting, and formatting you want, click Next to continue to saving the report.

Saving Custom Reports

When you save a custom report, you name the report and choose a location in which to save the report definition file. To save a report, follow these steps:

1. Type the name that you want to appear in the Reports dialog box. Use a brief but descriptive name for each report so you can choose the report you want more easily. To further identify the report, type a detailed description in the Description box. This description appears in the Description box in the Reports dialog box.

2. Choose an option to either save the report in the current drawing file or to a .vrd file in a folder on your computer. If you save the report in the current drawing file, you can access the report whenever the drawing file is open.

Note Saving a report to a .vrd file enables you to run the report for any Visio drawing file.

3. Click Finish. Visio adds the report to the Report list in the Reports dialog box.

Note The final step in the save process only saves the report. You must click Run in the Reports dialog box to run a report and view the results.

Running Reports with Custom Property Data

When you run a report, you can specify how to format the results: as an Excel spreadsheet, as an HTML file to display as a Web page, as an XML file, or within a Visio shape. To run an existing report or one you defined, follow these steps:

1. Open the drawing on which you want to report and choose Tools ⇨ Reports.

2. Select the report you want to use. If you don't see the report in the list, uncheck the Show Only Drawing-specific Reports check box.

3. Click Run.

Summary

You can customize shapes on your drawings in numerous ways or create brand-new shapes using Visio drawing tools and Shape Operation commands. To reuse customized shapes, you can save them as masters on custom stencils so you can drag masters onto drawing pages to create drawing shapes. In this chapter, you learned the concepts that make shapes and masters so smart. You also learned how to perform the following actions:

✦ Create masters

✦ Modify master graphics and properties

✦ Modify master icons

✦ Use drawing tools and Shape Operation commands to create or edit shapes and masters

✦ Configure connection points to control how shapes glue together

✦ Specify shape behavior, including what shapes do when you double-click them, how layout and routing lays them out, and whether shapes act like 1-D or 2-D shapes

✦ Create and apply custom properties to shapes and masters

In the next chapter, you learn how to further customize your shapes by modifying properties and creating formulas in ShapeSheets.

✦   ✦   ✦

Customizing Shapes Using ShapeSheets

Throughout this book, you'll run across tips and techniques that talk about making changes to a shape's ShapeSheet when there's no way to make a shape do what you want from a drawing page. In reality, a shape on a drawing page is merely the graphical representation of the Visio shape. You can use Visio commands and dialog boxes to control and modify many aspects of a Visio shape through its graphical representation. However, a *ShapeSheet* in Visio is a spreadsheetlike view that includes fields that control every shape feature. Each field includes values or formulas that specify the graphic elements of a shape, how the shape looks, and how it behaves.

A shape on a drawing page and the set of values and formulas in a ShapeSheet are two views of the same Visio shape. When you modify a shape on a drawing page, Visio changes the appropriate values in the shape's ShapeSheet. Conversely, when you modify fields in a ShapeSheet, Visio changes the appearance or behavior of the shape on the drawing page.

Of course, not every shape requires a value for every field. For example, if a shape doesn't use connection points, the ShapeSheet doesn't waste space by filling in fields with connection point attributes. Even so, shapes require numerous fields to completely define their appearance and behavior. The ShapeSheet is organized in tabular sections so that you can target the section you want to modify and locate the field you want to change. For example, the Shape Transform section specifies attributes for the location, size, and rotation for a shape, whereas the Fill Format section specifies attributes for filled areas.

This chapter explains the different sections of the ShapeSheet and shows you how to create a ShapeSheet formula.

Viewing ShapeSheets

Because a ShapeSheet is another view of a shape, it opens in a separate window. You can open every ShapeSheet in the same ShapeSheet window or open a new window for every ShapeSheet you want to see. You can focus on the changes you want to make by specifying which sections of the ShapeSheet appear in the window. If you want to add functionality to a shape, you can insert sections that are applicable to the type of shape but not currently used.

Opening ShapeSheets

Each element in a Visio drawing has a ShapeSheet associated with it, as illustrated in Figure 33-1. To open the ShapeSheet for an element, select the element and then choose Window ➪ Show ShapeSheet. The title bar for the ShapeSheet window shows the Visio drawing file, the drawing page, and the shape represented in the window. To select a Visio element so you can open its ShapeSheet, use one of the following methods:

✦ **Shape, group, guide, guidepoint, or OLE object** — Click the element to select it and then choose Window ➪ Show ShapeSheet.

✦ **Shape in a group** — Subselect the shape by clicking once to select the group, clicking again to select the shape, and choosing Window ➪ Show ShapeSheet.

✦ **Master** — Open the master's stencil for editing by right-clicking the stencil's title bar and choosing Edit Stencil from the shortcut menu. Right-click the master and choose Edit Master from the shortcut menu. Select the master in the master drawing window and choose Window ➪ Show ShapeSheet.

✦ **Page** — To show a page ShapeSheet, click an empty area of the drawing page to make sure no shapes are selected and then choose Window ➪ Show ShapeSheet.

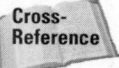
Cross-
Reference

For more information about selecting shapes, see Chapter 4.

You can specify whether every ShapeSheet opens in the same window or a new window opens for each. If you want to compare values for more than one shape, the option for opening new windows enables you to view multiple ShapeSheets side by side. However, if you work on each ShapeSheet independently, one ShapeSheet window requires less of the screen. To specify ShapeSheet window options, follow these steps:

1. Choose Tools ➪ Options and select the Advanced tab.

2. To use only one ShapeSheet window, check the Open Each ShapeSheet in the Same Window check box. Leaving this check box unchecked opens a new window for each ShapeSheet you view.

ShapeSheet view of shape

Graphical representation of shape

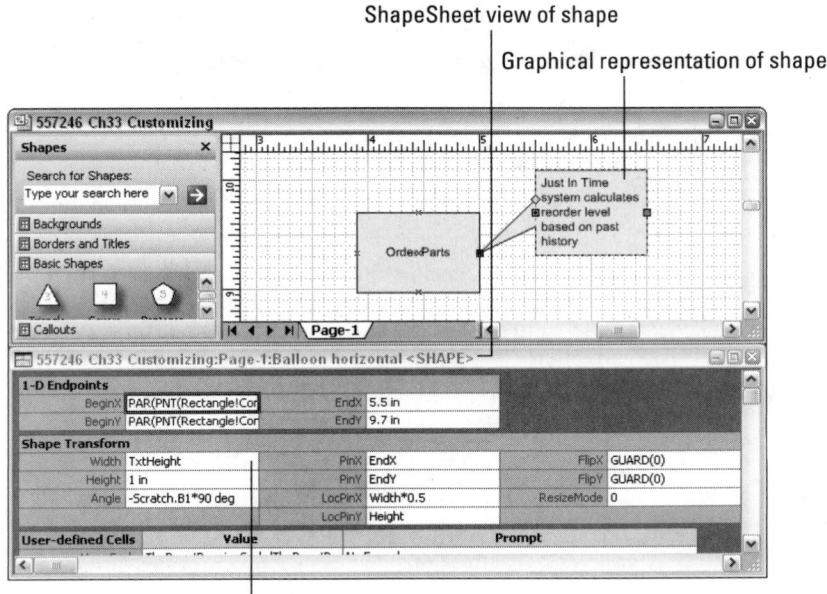

Cells specify shape appearance and behavior

Figure 33-1: A shape on a drawing is a graphical view of shape attributes in a ShapeSheet.

 Tip

If you access ShapeSheets frequently, you can display the Show ShapeSheet command automatically on every shape's shortcut menu (shown by right-clicking the shape) by choosing Tools ⇨ Options, selecting the Advanced tab, and checking the Run in Developer Mode check box.

Viewing and Adding ShapeSheet Sections

When you consider all the things you can do with Visio shapes, it should come as no surprise that Visio ShapeSheets can include numerous sections. In fact, there are thirty different sections that a shape might use, depending on its configuration and features. For example, one-dimensional shapes include the 1-D Endpoints section, whereas only shapes with control points use the Controls section. Visio adds the sections required to construct a shape to its ShapeSheet. However, you can show or hide those sections or add others. Table 33-1 shows some of the more commonly used ShapeSheet sections.

Table 33-1
Commonly Used ShapeSheet Sections

Section	Purpose
1-D Endpoints	Specifies the coordinates of each end point on a 1-D shape
Shape Transform	Specifies shape extent, the coordinates of its position on the drawing page, rotation, pin position, and more
User-defined Cells	Includes custom values or formulas, such as the Visio version, keywords used for searching shapes, and scaling formulas. For example, formulas and attributes for employee pictures in Organization Chart shapes are stored in this section.
Custom Properties	Includes the labels and values for the custom properties associated with a shape
Geometry	Each path in a shape has its own Geometry section. Each Geometry section contains coordinates for each vertex in a path and specifies attributes such as whether shapes can be filled.
Protection	Specifies lock settings that you can set by choosing Format ⇨ Protection, as well as a few locking options available only in the ShapeSheet, such as LockGroup
Miscellaneous	Includes fields for controlling various shape behaviors, some of which are available by choosing Format ⇨ Behavior
Group Properties	Specifies group behaviors, such as whether a group accepts a dropped shape
Line Format	Includes settings for lines and line ends
Fill Format	Includes settings for fill formats
Paragraph	Specifies paragraph formatting as defined on the Paragraph tab after choosing Format ⇨ Text
Text Block Format	Specifies text block formatting as defined on the Text Block tab after choosing Format ⇨ Text
Text Transform	Specifies size and position of a shape's text block
Events	Defines behavior in response to specific events, such as double-clicking or dropping the shape onto the drawing page
Shape Layout	Specifies settings for layout features as defined on the Layout and Routing tab of the Page Setup dialog box, as well as Placement Behavior settings

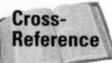

Cross-Reference To learn how to print ShapeSheet sections, see Chapter 3.

To hide or show the sections in a ShapeSheet, right-click the ShapeSheet window and choose View Sections from the shortcut menu. Check a Section check box to show the section; uncheck a Section check box to hide it, as demonstrated in Figure 33-2. To quickly modify the sections that appear, click All or None and then check and uncheck sections you want or don't want.

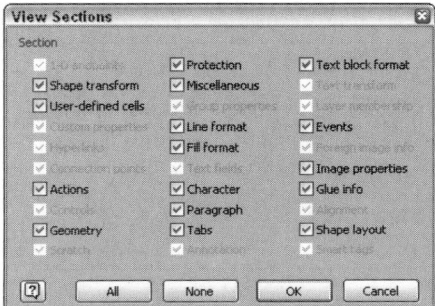

Figure 33-2: Check or uncheck Section check boxes to hide or show ShapeSheet sections.

In the View Sections dialog box, the check boxes and labels for sections not currently in use appear dimmed. For example, the Scratch section is useful for adding custom formulas without affecting built-in features. It won't appear in the ShapeSheet unless you add it. To insert a section that isn't in use, right-click the ShapeSheet window and choose Insert Section from the shortcut menu. The Insert Section dialog box opens, showing the sections you can insert. Sections that don't apply to the shape are dimmed. Check the check box for each section you want to insert and then click OK.

Exploring ShapeSheet Sections

The Visio ShapeSheet is a powerful tool that you can use to control every aspect of a shape. With thirty different ShapeSheet sections and numerous cells within each section, this part of the chapter highlights cells that are particularly useful and provides examples of their use. For a complete reference to the purpose of each section and cell, choose Help ⇨ Developers Reference. In the Visio Help Table of Contents, expand Microsoft Office Visio ShapeSheet Reference and then expand Sections to learn about ShapeSheet sections. Expand Cells to learn what each cell can do.

Tip   You can also learn a lot about ShapeSheet cells and formulas by looking at the settings for some of the built-in Visio shapes. Select a built-in shape that you have dragged onto the drawing page and open its ShapeSheet.

Here are some examples of ShapeSheet cells and what you might do with them:

✦ **Shape Transform** — Controls the position and orientation of a shape:

- **Width** — Use a formula to set a shape's width based on the size of the picture it contains, as in the User.Width cell for an Organization Chart shape.

- **Height** — Link this cell to a database field to define a shape's height with a dimension stored in a parts database.

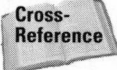

To learn about linking ShapeSheet cells to fields in external data sources, see Chapter 10.

- **LocPinX and LocPinY** — Use formulas to position the center of rotation of a shape based on the shape's width and height. By default, the pin is located at the center of a shape, but you can position it wherever you want.

- **Angle** — Use a formula to constrain a shape's rotation to multiples of ninety degrees, as the Balloon Vertical Callout shape does.

✦ **Geometry** — Each path in a shape has its own Geometry section, which contains coordinates for each vertex in the path, and attributes that control the path's appearance:

- **MoveTo** — Use a reference to the ShapeSheet cells for control handle coordinates to start a line at the location of a control handle, similar to the behavior of Dimensioning shapes.

- **LineTo** — Use a reference to other cells in the Geometry section to intersect one line with another, also illustrated by Dimensioning shapes.

- **EllipticalArcTo** — If you draw several lines and arcs with the Pencil tool and accidentally create an arc when you intended to draw a straight line, you can correct the mistake in the ShapeSheet. In the Geometry section for the Pencil tool path, it's easy to spot arcs even if they look like straight lines on the screen, as shown in Figure 33-3. Click an EllipticalArcTo cell to highlight the vertex on the drawing page. When the correct vertex is highlighted, right-click the EllipticalArcTo cell and choose Change Row Type on the shortcut menu. Select LineTo to draw a straight line instead.

- **Infinite Line** — You can convert a line drawn on the drawing page to an infinite line, which acts like a true construction line. In the Geometry section, right-click the LineTo cell for the line and then choose Change Row Type from the shortcut menu. Select Infinite Line to create a construction line.

- **Geometry.NoFill** — By default, Visio changes the NoFill value from TRUE to FALSE when you close a path so that you can apply a fill format to closed shapes. If you use Shape Operation commands to create compound shapes, you can set the NoFill fields for each Geometry section to

TRUE or FALSE, depending on whether you want that geometry to accept fill formatting when you apply it. For example, if you transform a checkerboard of squares into one shape, you can set alternating squares to NoFill = TRUE. When you apply fill formatting to the shape, half the squares apply the fill format.

Select row type to change to

Vertex selected on drawing page   Current row type

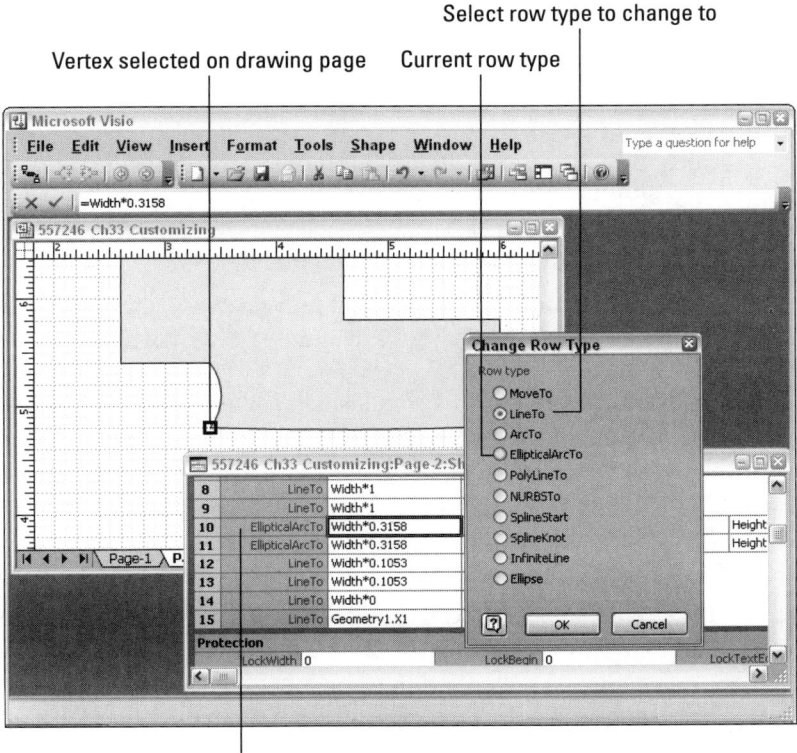

Vertex selected in ShapeSheet

Figure 33-3: You can highlight a vertex and change the kind of line segment it defines from the ShapeSheet.

✦ **Miscellaneous** — This section provides cells to set various attributes, including handle selection and visibility. Many of these attributes can be modified by choosing options on the Behavior tab in the Behavior dialog box:

- **NoObjHandles** — To ensure that a shape is not resized, hide its selection handles by setting this field to TRUE.

- **Comment** — Use logical functions in formulas along with cell references to custom properties to display different comments, depending on the values in custom properties.

- **NonPrinting** — Use logical functions and cell references so that a shape that includes an infinite line doesn't print.

- **NoAlignBox** — To prevent someone from snapping to a shape's alignment box, hide the alignment box by setting NoAlignBox to TRUE.

- **DropOnPageScale** — Use formulas to specify scaling factors based on the scale for the drawing page.

✦ **Fill Format** — This section specifies fill formatting and shadows:

- **FillForegnd** — Link this cell to a database field — for example, to show a Chair shape in the color specified by a catalog database.

- **FillBkgnd** — Use the RGB function to specify the exact color you want, such as FillBkgnd = RGB(250,150,100) to create a sepia tone for a pattern background.

✦ **Group Properties** — This section specifies behaviors and other attributes for groups, not the individual shapes within them:

- **DontMoveChildren** — If you can't move a shape that you subselect within a group, change the value in this cell in the group's ShapeSheet to FALSE.

- **IsTextEditTarget** — Use formulas and cell references to make the group's text block editable when the grouped shapes already include text.

✦ **Protection** — This section includes cells for locking different aspects of shapes, including some that can only be modified in the ShapeSheet, including the following:

- **LockCustProp** — Locks custom properties so they can't be edited

- **LockCrop** — Locks an OLE object to prevent it from being cropped with the Crop tool

- **LockGroup** — Locks a group so it can't be ungrouped. If you drop a built-in master onto a drawing page and can't move a shape within it, change this cell value to 1 in the group's ShapeSheet to unlock the group.

- **LockCalcWH** — Locks a shape's selection rectangle so it doesn't change when vertices are edited

- **LockVtxEdit** — Locks shape vertices so you can't edit them with drawing tools

✦ **Actions** — This section defines menu items on a shape's shortcut menu or a shape's SmartTags.

- **Action** — Type the formula to execute when a user chooses the command from the shortcut or SmartTag menu, as demonstrated in Figure 33-4.

- **Menu** — Specify the name of a menu item on a shortcut or SmartTag menu.

- **Checked** — Indicates whether an item is checked

- **Disabled** — Indicates whether an item is dimmed

Command on shortcut menu

Result of command

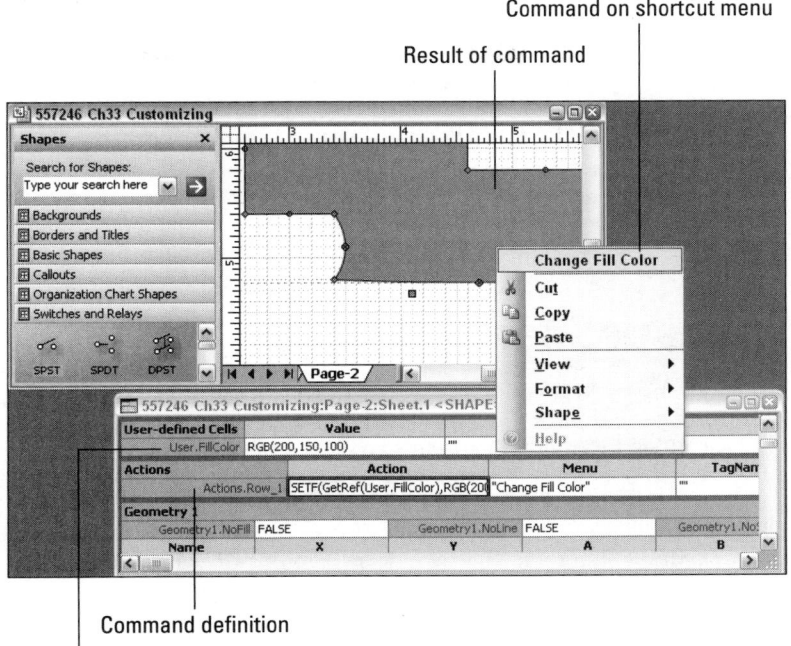

Command definition

User-defined cell used in formula

Figure 33-4: Add shortcut commands in the ShapeSheet.

✦ **Events** — This section specifics the actions to take when events occur:

- **EventDblClick** — Specify a formula to execute when a user double-clicks a shape, such as editing the shape text block, as most shapes do by default.

- **EventDrop** — Specify a formula to execute when a user drops a shape onto the drawing page.

✦ **Custom Properties** — This section defines the custom properties associated with a shape, as well as attributes about each property, such as language or sort order:

- **Ask** — If you want Visio to query the user to enter custom properties when an instance is created, set this cell to TRUE.

- **SortKey** — Influences the order in which items are listed in the Custom Properties window and dialog box

- **Type** — Specifies the data type for the property

✦ **User-defined cells** — You can specify formulas that you can reference from other cells. You can name the cells in this section so that references to them are meaningful. The cells in the Scratch section can also contain user-defined formulas, but you can't name Scratch cells.

- **Prompt** — Specify the prompt for the User-defined cell.
- **Value** — Specify a formula. For example, Visio Organization Shapes include User-defined cells to specify employee photo attributes. Built-in scaled objects often include an anti-scaling User-defined field.

Writing ShapeSheet Formulas

To Visio, anything you type in a ShapeSheet cell is a formula, whether it's a numeric value, a reference to another cell, or a formula with functions and operators. You can write formulas for ShapeSheet cells to define the shape behavior you want. For example, you can specify that the height of a shape is always half its width by writing a formula in the Height cell in the Shape Transform section. Visio evaluates a formula and shows the results in units appropriate for the cell. You can display cell contents in a ShapeSheet window as either formulas or values.

Visio creates many formulas by default when you create a shape. For example, Visio positions a shape's pin at the shape's center by default. If you look in a ShapeSheet, you'll see the following formulas:

```
LocPinX = Width*0.5
LocPinY = Height*0.5
```

To conserve file space and simplify the propagation of changes from masters to instances, Visio instances inherit formulas from masters whenever possible. Shape instances inherit formulas from their masters on the Document stencil and inherit formatting from style definitions stored with the drawing. However, you can write local formulas in any cell for an instance. A local formula replaces the formula inherited from the master and is shown in blue text in the ShapeSheet window. If you change the formula for that cell in the master, the local formula in the instance's cell prohibits the inheritance of the master's formula.

Note   When a cell contains a local formula, the formula appears as blue text.

Visio automatically updates some cells when you change a shape. When you apply a style to a shape, Visio deletes local formulas in the related cells unless you check the Preserve Local Formatting check box in the Style dialog box. If you want to prevent local formatting formulas from being overwritten, you can use the GUARD function.

Learning More About Programming Shapes

Programming shapes and automating Visio provides enough material to produce a second volume to this book. However, if you want to learn more about how to use ShapeSheets to program shapes, you can find resources on the Microsoft Developer Network Web site at `http://msdn.microsoft.com/visio`. This site includes articles about Visio shape programming, Visio developers' documentation, plus links to books, training resources, and much more. To find specific information, enter keywords in the Search For box on the site.

Exploring the Elements of Formulas

Visio formulas are similar to Excel formulas. They always start with an equals sign, although Visio inserts the equals sign automatically. A formula can comprise any of the following elements:

✦ Numbers

✦ Coordinates

✦ Boolean values

✦ Operators

✦ Functions

✦ Strings

✦ Cell references

✦ Units of measure

Note The ShapeSheet Reference explains how each element works and how to include it in formulas. To learn more about these elements, choose Help ➪ Developer Reference. In the Visio Help Table of Contents, expand Microsoft Office Visio ShapeSheet Reference and then expand Concepts. To learn how to insert elements into formulas, expand Procedures.

Creating Formulas

If you're familiar with creating formulas in an Excel spreadsheet, you'll find that ShapeSheet formulas work much the same way. You can select a cell and type a formula or double-click a cell to display the insertion point so that you can edit the formula. However, if you are developing a long formula, it's easiest to select the cell and then edit the formula in the formula bar.

To create or edit a formula in the formula bar, follow these steps:

1. In the ShapeSheet window, click a cell to select it and display the formula in the formula bar.

2. Type the formula, for example to calculate the position of a shape's pin, as shown here.

   ```
   LocPinX = GUARD(Width*0.5)
   ```

3. To include a reference to another cell in the formula, type the name of the cell, such as Width in the LocPinX formula.

4. To include a function, type the function name and then type its parameters in parentheses, as in the GUARD function in the LocPinX formula. To choose the function you want from a list, position the insertion point where you want to insert the function in the formula and then choose Insert ⇨ Function. Select the function you want and click OK.

Tip   The GUARD function is used frequently to prevent a formula from being modified by actions performed on the drawing page, such as moving or resizing. Cells often affected by moving and resizing are Width, Height, PinX, and PinY.

5. To accept the formula, click the Accept button to the left of the formula bar or press Enter.

6. If the formula contains an error, Visio displays an error message box. Click OK in the message box. Visio highlights the area, if not the exact location, of the error in the formula.

7. After you correct the error, click Accept or press Enter.

Tip   If you want to add shapes to a scaled drawing but don't want the shapes to scale, you can define a formula in the ShapeSheet to prevent the shape from scaling. You can read an article about scaling formulas at http://msdn.microsoft .com/library/default.asp?url=/library/en-us/devref/HTML/ DVS_12_Scaled_Shapes_and_Measured_Drawings_487.asp. Type **Formula Scale Visio** in the Search For box on the MSDN Web site to find other topics about controlling scaling with the ShapeSheet.

Summary

ShapeSheets and shapes on drawing pages are just different views of the same Visio element. You can create and modify many aspects of Visio shapes by working on the drawing page. However, some shape settings are available only on a shape's ShapeSheet. You can open each ShapeSheet in a separate window to compare values between ShapeSheets or open each ShapeSheet in the same window to save screen space.

You can also define formulas in a shape's ShapeSheet to specify how a shape appears or behaves based on shape settings, values in other ShapeSheet cells, or even values in an external database. Formulas in ShapeSheets are powerful, as demonstrated by the behaviors exhibited by built-in Visio shapes. You can learn about customizing ShapeSheets in the Visio ShapeSheet Reference by choosing Help ➪ Developers Reference. You can also study the ShapeSheets for built-in shapes to see how they use formulas to produce specific behaviors.

✦   ✦   ✦

Formatting with Styles

If you're like most people, you choose a formatting command when you want to change the way lines, text, and fill look on your Visio shapes. There's nothing wrong with that technique if you're changing the appearance of one or two shapes. However, when you want to apply the same formatting to several shapes or to all the shapes of the same type, applying styles is faster and produces more consistent results.

Built-in Visio shapes practically format themselves when you drag them onto a drawing page. Shapes associated with a template often have a coordinated appearance and automatically conform to the color schemes you apply. When you use Visio templates and built-in stencils, the shapes you add usually have styles that specify the formatting they use. Styles can control the formatting for lines, text, and fill; and they include a variety of options, such as line ends, patterns, color, and fonts.

It's easy to apply the same formatting to shapes by applying the same style to them. In addition, to change the formatting for all the shapes that use the same style, you redefine the style, rather than reset the formatting on every shape. Although Visio templates offer sets of styles designed to work together, you can customize styles and define new line, fill, and line end patterns to fit your needs.

This chapter shows you how to work with existing styles as well as create and edit styles. You'll also learn how to define line patterns, such as dots and dashes, fill patterns for hatch patterns, and line end patterns for the marks at the ends of lines.

Working with Styles

If you've used styles in Microsoft Word, you'll find the concepts for Visio styles to be similar. However, in Visio, styles involve formatting more than just text — a style represents a named collection of format settings, including line, text, and fill formats that you can apply to text blocks and shapes. Because a style defines the formatting for lines, text, and fill, you can format every aspect of a shape's appearance by applying one style.

Cross-Reference   For more information about applying styles to shapes, see Chapter 7.

When you apply a style to a shape, the style definition specifies the formatting for the lines, text, and fill for that shape. By using styles, you can ensure that the appearance of similar shapes is consistent. However, you can also apply shape-specific formatting to override the style formatting. For example, you can change the fill color for Organization Chart shapes that represent vacant positions that are about to be filled. This formatting that you apply manually with Format Text, Format Line, or Format Fill commands is known as *local formatting* because Visio stores the formatting locally with the shape. When you manually format shapes and then apply a style to those shapes, the styles overwrite the formatting settings for those shapes by default, removing your local formatting. You must check the Preserve Local Formatting check box in the Format Style dialog box if you want Visio to retain any manual formatting you've applied.

Note   Visio does not apply colors for a color scheme to shapes with local formatting, because color schemes function by redefining the colors associated with styles. Because local formatting overrides style formatting, your locally formatted shapes keep the color you assign. However, if you restore the original styles to shapes, they automatically conform to the current color scheme.

Assigning Default Styles to Drawings

Every Visio template includes a few basic predefined styles as well as styles specific to the template. For example, every template includes Guide, No Style, None, Normal, and Text Only styles. The Guide style applies formatting so that guide lines appear as dotted, blue lines, by default. The None style, as you would expect, formats elements by removing lines and fills and applying a basic text formatting to text. When you create your own templates by saving Visio drawing files, the styles in the drawing file are available automatically for every new drawing file you create using the template.

In addition, you can specify the default styles Visio applies when you draw shapes with drawing tools. Click an empty area on the drawing page to make sure that no shapes are selected. Choose Format ⇨ Style, select the styles you want to use as defaults in the Text Style, Line Style, and Fill Style drop-down lists, and then click OK.

Style lists control which types of style formatting you apply. You can apply a specific type of formatting for a style, such as line formatting, or apply each type of formatting that the style specifies. When you work with styles but want manual formatting to remain, you can specify options to preserve your local formatting. In addition, you can protect your shapes in various ways so that formatting won't change. If all else fails, you can start over by restoring the default styles for a shape. Use one or more of the following methods to apply styles to your shapes:

✦ **Apply specific types of formatting** — Choose a style from the style lists on the Format Shape or Format Text toolbars to apply text formatting, line formatting, or fill formatting. If the style you choose includes other types of formatting as well, Visio asks whether you want to apply those formats.

✦ **Apply all types of formatting** — Choose Format ⇨ Style to select a style for each type of formatting.

Tip

If the formatting you apply isn't what you want, press Ctrl+Z to undo the formatting.

✦ **Preserve local formatting** — If you want to apply styles to shapes without resetting any local formatting that you've applied, choose Format ⇨ Style, select the styles you want to apply, check the Preserve Local Formatting check box, and click OK.

✦ **Formatting locked shapes** — Shapes can be locked in two different ways, but you can remove these locks if you want to format the shapes in question. When you see an error message about shape protection preventing the execution of your command, that means the shape is locked against formatting. To remove this formatting lock, right-click the shape, choose Format ⇨ Protection from the shortcut menu, and then uncheck the Format check box. If a shape doesn't accept your formatting but you don't see an error message, the formatting settings in the ShapeSheet are guarded, which prevents you from changing the value in the formatting cell. To remove the guard, select the shape and choose Window ⇨ Show ShapeSheet. In the ShapeSheet, find the cell for the formatting you want to change and remove the GUARD function in that cell.

Caution

Typically, shapes include the GUARD function or formatting locks when the shapes' formatting is key to the proper behavior or appearance of those shapes. Although you can remove formatting locks and guards, be aware that shapes might behave differently or change their appearance in unexpected ways.

✦ **Restoring default styles for shapes** — If you want to remove local formatting so shapes revert to using style formatting, choose Format ⇨ Style. For each type of style, select Use Master's Format from the drop-down list.

Note

Selecting Use Master's Format resets styles only for shapes dragged from a stencil. Shapes that you draw directly on the page don't have masters, so there are no master's formats to apply.

Creating and Editing Styles

If you don't like the formatting used in existing styles, you can edit them to specify the line, text, and fill formatting you want. If you frequently create your own custom shapes, you might want to create your own styles to accompany them. You can use style names that indicate the association between the shapes and styles. In addition, you can rename styles, delete styles no longer used, or copy styles between Visio drawings. No matter how you want to create or edit your styles, the Define Styles dialog box provides all the commands you need. You can create or modify multiple styles in one editing session. By using the Apply button in the Define Styles dialog box, you can apply the styles you've created or edited to selected shapes.

Creating Styles

Like styles in Microsoft Word, Visio styles can be based on other styles, inheriting formatting settings from the parent style. For example, if you want a set of styles to use the same color fills and fonts, but apply progressively thicker line weights, you can create a base style with the colors, fill formatting, text formatting, and line patterns you want. Then, you can base each style on the original, changing only the line weight. However, basing a unique style on another style might just mean more work. If you want to create a style from scratch, you can base it on the No Style style that is built into every Visio file by default.

If you're a visual person and want to see the formatting before you create a style, you can format a shape with the settings you want. When the shape looks the way you want, you can save those settings as a style.

Creating Styles Based on Shape Formatting

You can create styles that include all the formatting applied to a shape. In addition to creating styles more quickly, you can preview the appearance of the formatting before you save the style. To create a style based on a shape's formatting, follow these steps:

1. Select a shape that includes most, if not all, of the formatting you want. If you want to make any formatting changes, choose Format ➪ Text, Format ➪ Line, or Format ➪ Fill and select additional format options.

2. When the shape is formatted the way you want, choose Define ➪ Styles.

3. In the Name box, select <New Style> at the top of the drop-down list. Visio fills in the settings to match those of the selected shape.

4. Type the name you want for the style in the Name box and click Add to save the style to the drawing file. You can continue to define or edit other styles or click Close to end the style session.

Creating Styles from Scratch

To create a style from scratch, follow these steps:

1. Click an empty area on the drawing page to ensure that no shapes are selected and then choose Format ⇨ Define Styles.

2. In the Name box, type the name you want for the new style.

3. In the Based On list, select an existing style that uses the formatting settings you want in the new style. If you don't want to base the style on another style, select No Style from the drop-down list.

4. Under the Includes heading, check the check box for each type of formatting you want the style to apply. For example, to define a style for connectors, which don't use fill, you can check the Text and Line check boxes, leaving the Fill check box unchecked.

Note
Checking the Includes check boxes also determines which toolbar style lists include the style.

5. To edit the formatting settings for the style, click the buttons in the Change area to open the dialog box for that type of formatting. For example, if you click Line, the Line dialog box opens, as shown in Figure 34-1. Specify the formatting you want and click OK to close the formatting dialog box. Repeat this step to edit formatting options for each type of formatting you want the style to apply.

Tip
You can prevent a style from appearing in the style lists — for example, when styles are designed for specific masters and you don't want others to use those styles for anything else. To hide a style so it doesn't appear on the style lists, check the Hidden Style check box before you save the style. Hidden styles still appear in the Name list in the Define Styles dialog box and in the Drawing Explorer window.

6. To save the style in the current drawing file, click Add.

7. Use one of the following methods to close the dialog box:

   - If shapes are selected and you want to apply the style to those shapes, click Apply and then click Close.

   - If you don't want to apply the style to the selected shapes, click Close.

   - If no shapes are selected, click OK.

Types of formatting included

Style name

Line formatting options

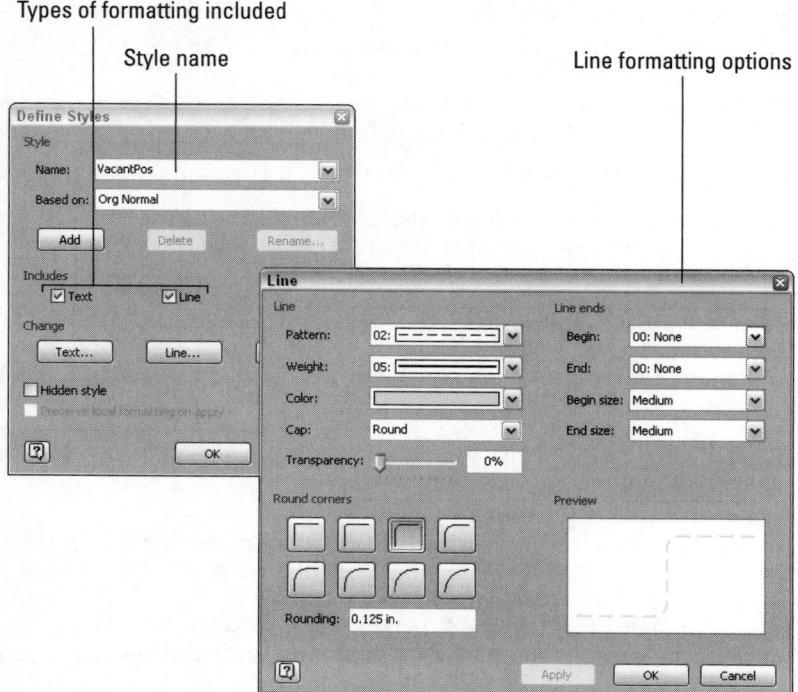

Figure 34-1: Specify the formatting options you want for a style within the Define Styles dialog box.

Editing Styles

You can edit the formatting in a style definition at any time. When you modify a style, any shapes in the drawing file formatted with that style reflect the changes to the style. To edit a style, follow these steps:

1. Choose Format ➪ Define Styles.

2. In the Name box, select the style you want to edit in the drop-down list.

3. For each type of formatting you want to edit, click the corresponding button in the Change area. In the formatting dialog box that opens, make the changes you want and click OK.

4. Under the Style heading, click the Change button to update the style definition and all shapes formatted with the style.

5. Repeat steps 2 through 4 to edit another style. Click Close when you're finished.

Copying Styles Between Files

You can copy styles you create to other drawing files. If you intend to use the styles you create in many drawing files, the easiest approach is to save the drawing file containing the styles as a template. When you create new drawing files based on that template, they automatically contain the styles you want.

However, you can also copy styles from one drawing file to another drawing file that already exists by copying shapes formatted with those styles. When you paste shapes into a destination file, Visio copies any styles associated with the shapes. The styles remain in the destination file even if you delete the pasted shapes. If you want to copy several styles, you can create a new drawing page and paste all the shapes with the styles you want to copy onto that drawing page. After the styles are copied, you can delete the drawing page to easily remove the shapes.

If the destination drawing file already includes styles with the same names as the ones you want to paste, Visio doesn't copy the styles from the source. Instead, it applies the style with the same name to the pasted shapes. To copy styles in this situation, you must rename the styles in the source before you copy the shapes to which they are applied.

You can also delete and rename styles in the Define Styles dialog box. For example, if you want to create a template, it's a good idea to clean up the file by removing any unused styles before you save it. When you copy styles between drawing files, the styles you copy can't use the same names as styles in the destination file. You can rename the styles in the source drawing file so that the styles copy correctly.

To delete a style, select the name of the style you want to delete and then click Delete. To rename a style, select the name of the style you want to rename and then click Rename. In the Rename Style dialog box, type the new name and click OK.

Creating Custom Patterns

Visio comes with numerous built-in line, line end, and fill patterns that you can apply to lines and shapes directly or associate with styles. However, you can also create your own patterns. Whether you want to create a line, line end, or fill pattern, you start by creating a *pattern shape*, which represents one copy of the pattern. Pattern shapes can be Visio shapes and fills or bitmaps you import from another application. You can use a pattern shape as a line pattern, a line end, or a fill pattern, as demonstrated in Figure 34-2.

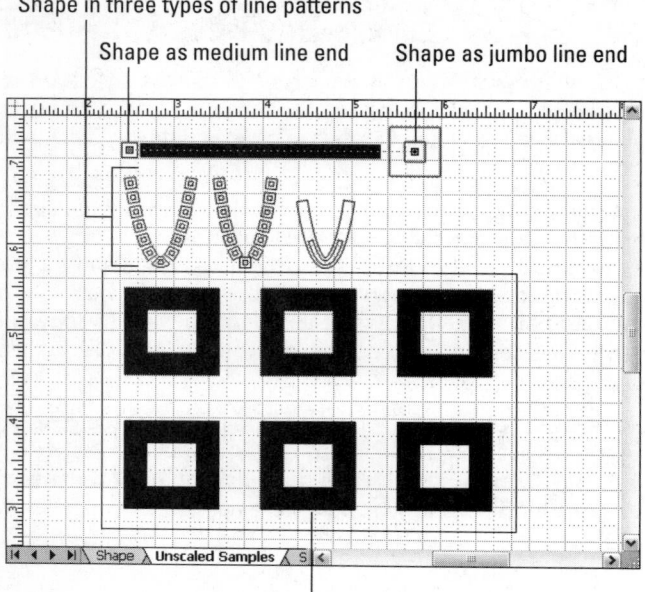

Shape in three types of line patterns

Shape as medium line end   Shape as jumbo line end

Unscaled shape in tiled fill pattern

Figure 34-2: You can use a pattern shape for line patterns, for fill patterns, or as line ends.

You can also specify how the pattern shape behaves under different circumstances, such as with straight or curved lines, or when closed shapes are resized. In addition, you can specify whether the pattern should be adjusted along with the drawing scale or maintained at a constant size.

After you define patterns, you can apply them to shapes as you would with any built-in pattern. Visio lists custom fill and line patterns at the bottom of the Pattern drop-down list in the Fill and Line dialog boxes. Custom line ends appear at the bottom of the Begin and End drop-down lists in the Line dialog box.

Note   When you create custom patterns, you can't use text, metafiles such as Visio Ink shapes, or gradient fills, rendered as solid fills.

Designing Pattern Shapes

Pattern shape design is the foundation of the patterns you create. Decisions you make while drawing a pattern shape can produce significantly different results in the patterns you create. Visio uses the following attributes of a pattern shape to determine the position and appearance of the shape in patterns:

✦ **Pin position** — Visio aligns a pattern shape in a pattern by the shape's pin or center of rotation. If the pin is in the center of the pattern shape, a line pattern using the shape displays the shape centered along the line. However, if the pin is at the top of the shape, the pattern shape is offset below the line in the line pattern.

✦ **Alignment box** — When you tile a pattern shape in a pattern, Visio positions the alignment boxes for the pattern shape side by side. You can create the appearance of spaces between pattern shapes by making the alignment box larger than the pattern shape. If you make the alignment box smaller than the shape, the shapes overlap in the pattern.

Tip

To change the alignment box of a shape, use the Rectangle tool to draw a rectangle of the size you want and located where you want the alignment box to be. Select both the rectangle and the pattern shape and press Shift+Ctrl+G to group them. With the group selected, choose Edit ➪ Open Group to open the group window. In the group window, delete the rectangle and close the group window. The result is the pattern shape with an alignment box of the size and position of the deleted rectangle.

✦ **Color** — After you apply a pattern to a shape, you can change the color of any black areas in the pattern by changing the color of the line or fill. Areas created in any other color remain that color. When you design a pattern shape, be sure to draw elements in black if you want them to change color.

✦ **Line weight** — If you draw your own dash patterns, draw the line segments with lines of zero weight. The line segments inherit the line weight of the shape to which the pattern is applied.

Note

When you use a bitmap for a pattern shape, transparent areas on the bitmap aren't transparent in the pattern. When you use a Visio shape as a pattern shape, the background shows through.

Designing Line Patterns

When you use shapes in line patterns, it's important to take into account how your pattern shape will accommodate straight and curved lines and lines of varying widths. Visio line patterns use the following behavior options to specify how Visio applies your pattern shape under different circumstances, as shown in Figure 34-3.

Line pattern in Drawing Explorer window

Tiled and distorted line pattern in use

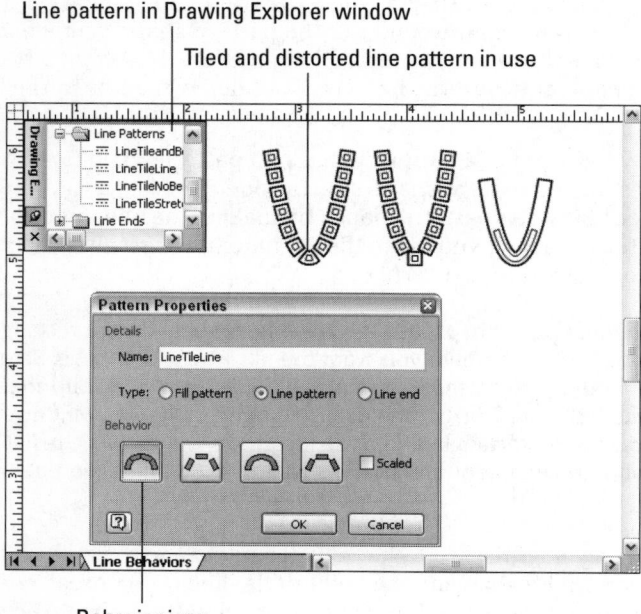

Behavior icon

Figure 34-3: Visio can arrange pattern shapes in several ways to create different line patterns.

✦ **Tile and bend** — Visio tiles the pattern along the path of the line. If the path is not straight, Visio also distorts the pattern to conform to the path. For example, you can define a line pattern that includes all the painted lines for a highway. When you apply that style to a curved line, you want each of the painted lines to bend with the curves in the road, and you want the dashes for the passing line to stay the same length.

✦ **Tile without distortion** — Visio tiles the pattern along the path of the line, but doesn't distort the pattern to account for curves. For example, engineering plans often indicate pipelines with lines interspersed with letters that identify the type of pipeline. In this case, you want the line to bend with the curves, but you don't want the letters to distort.

✦ **Stretch** — Visio stretches a single copy of the pattern over the length of the line. You might use this behavior to create an arrow whose head and tail stretch to fit the length of the line.

✦ **Tile over line** — Visio tiles the pattern without distortion but retains the original line formatting as well. You might use this behavior to draw a line pattern that looks like barbed wire, with a solid line that follows the curve but undistorted shapes at regular intervals along it.

 **Note** Line patterns can have no more than 1,000 instances of the pattern shape along a line.

Designing Line End Patterns

Line end patterns are simply pattern shapes attached to the ends of lines, so they have fewer options than line and fill patterns. You can add pattern shapes to the ends of lines in two ways:

✦ **Oriented with the line** — Visio rotates the pattern shape so it is aligned with the line. For example, arrowheads are typically oriented with the line.

✦ **Always upright** — The pattern shape is always upright with respect to the drawing page no matter what the orientation of the line is. If you use a symbol with letters in it, use this behavior to ensure that the letters are always right side up.

When you use a pattern shape as a line end, Visio positions the pin of the pattern shape at the end point of a line. However, if you want to simulate the behavior of Visio's built-in arrowheads, move the pin to the side of the shape that you want to attach to the line and orient the shape with the line.

 **Tip** If a line end implies direction, such as the arrowheads on connectors on an organization chart, draw your pattern shape so it points to the right. By doing this, Visio points the line end in the right direction whether you apply it to the start point or end point of a line.

Designing Fill Patterns

Visio uses fill patterns to fill in closed shapes. Although fill patterns are often solid colors, you can create fill patterns with Visio shapes or bitmaps. If you've ever used a picture as a Windows background, the options for applying a shape or bitmap to a fill pattern should be familiar. You can use one of the following three techniques to apply a shape or image as fill, as shown in Figure 34-4:

✦ **Tile** — Visio copies the shape or image over a grid, as you would place tiles on a floor.

✦ **Center** — Visio positions one copy of the shape or image at the center of the closed area.

✦ **Stretch** — Visio stretches a single copy of the shape or image to fill the closed area.

Centered fill pattern

Tiled fill pattern

Stretched fill pattern

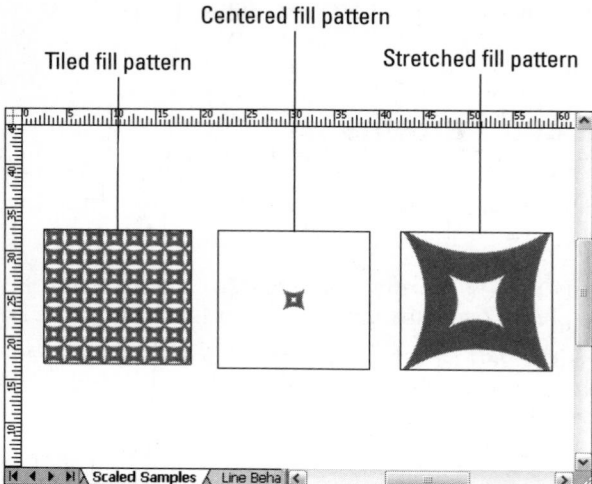

Figure 34-4: You can apply images to fill patterns in three ways.

For the best results, design separate fill patterns for scaled and unscaled drawings. Unscaled fill patterns appear at the size you created them. If the fill pattern uses a shape that is one inch square, the fill pattern uses a one-inch square no matter what scale the drawing uses. When you apply an unscaled fill pattern to a scaled drawing, the pattern might look as if it's a solid black fill.

Note   Scale and pattern size don't affect fill pattern when you use the option that stretches the image to fill the area.

Scaling Line Ends

You can specify whether line ends are scaled or unscaled, which affects the size of the line ends when you apply them to lines. If you choose to apply an unscaled line end, the line end appears the same height as the weight of the line. If you use a very thin line, you won't be able to see the line end. To increase the size of the line end, change the weight of the line, such as increasing it to .25 inches.

Conversely, when you create a line pattern that includes a shape that represents a real-world object, you can specify a scaled pattern shape. When you apply a scaled line end to a line, the line end resizes to match the scale of the drawing. In this situation, changing the weight of the line or selecting a size in the Begin Size or End Size drop-down list has no effect on the line end.

In addition to tiling and scaling, you can also control the transparency of fill patterns. Fill patterns that use shapes show the area between the repeated shapes as transparent. For example, if you tile a circle over an area, the pattern looks like colored polka dots over a transparent background.

Note Fill patterns are limited to 40,000 instances of a pattern shape or a grid of 200 by 200 shapes.

Creating New Custom Patterns

When the pattern shapes that you want to use exist, you can create any type of custom pattern using similar steps. Depending on where you want to save the pattern, use one of the following methods:

✦ **In current drawing** — Choose View ➭ Drawing Explorer Window.

✦ **In an existing stencil** — Choose File ➭ Shapes ➭ My Shapes and then choose the stencil in which you want to save the pattern. Right-click the stencil's title bar and choose Edit Stencil. Right-click the title bar a second time and choose Drawing Explorer Window.

✦ **In a new stencil** — Choose File ➭ Shapes ➭ New Stencil. Right-click the title bar for the new stencil and choose Drawing Explorer Window.

Note If the Drawing Explorer Window option doesn't appear on the stencil shortcut menu, choose Tools ➭ Options, select the Advanced tab, and check the Run in Developer Mode check box.

Creating a New Pattern

To create a line pattern, line end pattern, or fill pattern, follow these steps:

1. In the Drawing Explorer window, depending on the type of pattern you want to create, right-click Fill Patterns, Line Patterns, or Line Ends, and then choose New Pattern from the shortcut menu.

2. In the New Pattern dialog box, type the name for the pattern in the Name box.

3. If necessary, select the option for the type of pattern you want to create. By default, Visio selects the option based on which Drawing Explorer folder you right-clicked.

4. Click the icon for the behavior you want for the pattern. Visio displays icons that show each behavior for the type of pattern you are creating.

5. To adjust the pattern as the drawing scale changes, check the Scaled check box.

6. Click OK. Visio adds the new pattern to the appropriate folder in the Drawing Explorer window.

7. In the Drawing Explorer window, right-click the new pattern and choose Edit Pattern.

8. In the drawing page for the pattern, draw the pattern shape you want or copy a shape from another drawing page and paste it onto the pattern drawing page. You can also insert a bitmap onto the drawing page. Be sure to cover the entire drawing page with the fill pattern so that the pattern fills shapes completely.

9. Click the Close button at the top-right corner of the pattern shape drawing window and click Yes to update the pattern.

Sizing Line Ends

If you have added line ends, follow these steps to make the line ends appear at the size you want:

1. Draw or select a line on the drawing page and choose Format ➪ Line.

2. Click the arrow next to the Begin or End list and scroll down until you see the line end pattern you want. Select the line end in the drop-down list.

3. Click Apply.

4. If the line ends don't appear at the size you want, click the arrow in the Weight box and choose Custom.

5. Type a heavier line weight, such as .25 in. Check the appearance of the line end in the preview window. Repeat this step until the line end is the size you want.

6. Click OK. To simplify the application of the pattern, save the current settings as a line style.

Summary

Formatting shapes with styles makes it easy to coordinate the appearance of shapes and quickly modify the appearance of many shapes at once. Although Visio includes quite a few built-in styles, you can define your own. You can create styles based on the formatting applied to a shape on a drawing page or specify options within the Define Styles dialog box.

You can also define your own patterns for lines, fills, or line ends. Line, line end, and fill patterns all use pattern shapes to define their patterns. Designing pattern shapes requires some care, as the pin position, alignment box, color, and line weights within a pattern shape can produce drastically different patterns. When you create patterns, you can specify how Visio applies the pattern shape to create the pattern and whether the pattern scales with the drawing page scale.

✦   ✦   ✦

Customizing Toolbars and Menus

Like the user interface for other Microsoft Office applications, Visio menus, toolbars, and keyboard shortcuts provide easy access to commonly used commands. By default, Visio displays the commands you use most frequently and hides the ones you don't. However, if you prefer, you can show full menus at all times.

You can also customize or create Visio menus and toolbars to display the commands you want in the order you want. If you prefer to use the keyboard, you can assign keyboard shortcuts so you can execute commands without switching between keyboard and mouse.

This chapter shows you how to customize menus and toolbars to include the commands you use frequently. You will learn how to modify button images on toolbars and specify menu and toolbar options. In addition, you'll learn how to create keyboard shortcuts to increase your productivity.

Customizing Toolbars and Menus

Whether you use menus or toolbars, you don't want to take screen space away from your drawings by displaying commands you don't use. You can minimize the space that toolbars and menus consume by customizing existing toolbars and menus or creating your own.

Note It's easy to customize the Visio interface, but the changes you make to menus and toolbars appear for every drawing you open. If you don't want to change Visio's built-in toolbars and menus or you want specialized menus for specific tasks, you can create new menus and toolbars that contain only the commands you want.

Using Personalized Menus

By default, Visio personalizes toolbars and menus by displaying frequently used commands. Initially, menus and toolbars contain commands popular with most users. As you work, Visio adds the commands you choose to the menu and hides the commands you rarely use. To display the full menu of commands, click the chevron at the bottom of the menu.

If you would rather see full menus all the time, right-click any menu and choose Customize from the shortcut menu. In the Customize dialog box, select the Options tab and check the Always Show Full Menus check box. If you like personalized menus but your recent work has skewed the contents of your personalized menus, you can reset them to Visio's default selections by clicking Reset Menu and Toolbar Usage Data on the Options tab.

Customizing Toolbars

You can add, remove, and rearrange buttons on toolbars. You can also specify the appearance of buttons, or create your own icons. To open a toolbar so you can customize it, follow these steps:

1. If the toolbar you want to customize is not visible, choose View ➪ Toolbars and then choose the toolbar you want.

2. Choose Tools ➪ Customize ➪ Toolbars. Visio displays the Customize dialog box.

Tip
You can reduce the area that toolbars take up by displaying the Standard and Formatting toolbars on one line. Right-click any toolbar and then choose Customize on the menu. Select the Options tab and uncheck the Show Standard and Formatting Toolbars on Two Rows check box. If a command you want doesn't appear when these toolbars share a row, click the Toolbar Options arrow on the right end of the toolbar and choose the toolbar button you want.

To modify the contents or order of a toolbar, choose one of the following methods:

✦ **Add a button** — To add a button to a toolbar, follow these steps:

1. In the Customize dialog box, select the Commands tab. In the dialog box, Visio displays categories of commands on the left side and the commands within the selected category on the right side.

2. Choose the category of the command you want to add.

3. Drag the command you want from the Commands list to the toolbar until the I-beam (which resembles a standard cursor but looks more like a bolded, uppercase I) is where you want to add the command and release the mouse button.

✦ **Remove a button** — To remove a button from a toolbar, open the Customize dialog box, right-click the button you want to remove on the toolbar, and choose Delete in the shortcut menu.

Note

If the Customize dialog box isn't open, you can remove a button from a toolbar by pressing and holding the Alt key as you drag the button you want to remove off the toolbar. When an X appears below and to the right of the button, release the Alt key and the mouse button.

✦ **Rearrange buttons** — To move a button to another position on a toolbar, open the Customize dialog box and drag the button on the toolbar until the I-beam is positioned where you want to place the command, as illustrated in Figure 35-1, and then release the mouse button.

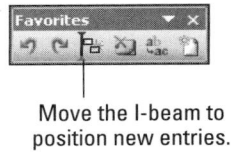

Move the I-beam to
position new entries.

Figure 35-1: Use the I-beam to position buttons on a toolbar.

You can hide or display buttons without using the Customize dialog box. To do this, click the Toolbar Options button at the end of the toolbar, choose Add or Remove Buttons, and choose the name of the toolbar you want to customize. Visio displays a list of all the buttons associated with the toolbar. Check a command to display it or uncheck a command to hide it.

Note

Although you can hide or display toolbar buttons using Toolbar Options, you can add buttons to or remove buttons from toolbars only when the Customize dialog box is open.

Adding Menus to Toolbars

To add a menu to a toolbar, open the Customize dialog box and select the Commands tab. To add a built-in menu to a toolbar, select the Built-In Menus category and drag the menu you want from the Commands list onto the toolbar.

To add a custom menu to a toolbar, select New Menu in the Categories box and drag New Menu from the Commands list to the toolbar. Right-click the new menu on the toolbar, type a name in the Name box on the shortcut menu, and press Enter. You can add commands or menus to the new menu by dragging the commands or menus you want from the Customize dialog box to the pull-down area below the new menu name. To modify a menu entry, right-click it.

Customizing Menus

Just like toolbars, menus can contain commands or other menus. Although menus use more space than toolbars, they can include descriptions of commands and sub-menus that help you choose the right feature. In addition to adding, removing, or rearranging commands and submenus on a menu, you can change the appearance of menu buttons and even specify whether the menu displays buttons or text, as shown in Figure 35-2.

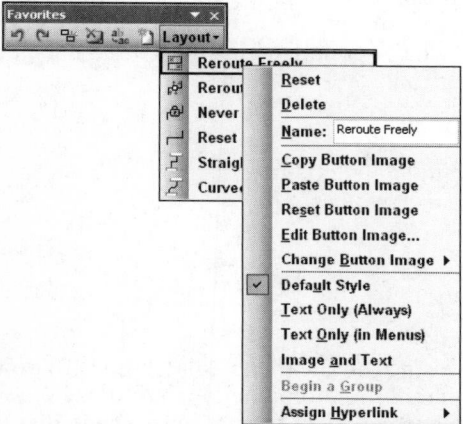

Figure 35-2: Edit commands or submenus on pull-down menus.

To customize a menu, open the Customize dialog box by choosing Tools ➪ Customize ➪ Toolbars and then using one of the following methods:

✦ **Add a command** — Select the Commands tab in the Customize dialog box, choose the category for the command you want to add, and drag the command from the Commands list to the position you want on the menu.

✦ **Add a menu** — Select the Commands tab in the Customize dialog box and choose the New Menu or Built-In Menus category. To create a new menu, drag the New Menu command from the Commands list to the desired position on the menu. To add a built-in menu to another menu, drag the menu from the Commands list to the menu.

✦ **Remove a command from a pull-down menu** — To remove an entry from a menu, with the Customize dialog box open, navigate to the command you want to remove, right-click it, and then choose Delete from the shortcut menu.

✦ **Rearrange commands** — To move a command or submenu to another position on a menu, with the Customize dialog box open, drag the command in the menu until the I-beam is positioned where you want to place the command and then release the mouse button.

✦ **Remove a menu from the menu bar** — With the Customize dialog box open, right-click the menu you want to remove from the menu bar and choose Delete from the shortcut menu.

Note If you want to reset menus you have customized to the commands Visio provides by default, choose View ➪ Toolbars ➪ Customize. Select the Toolbars tab and click Reset. When Visio prompts you, click OK to reset your menus.

Creating Toolbars and Menus

When you frequently use a small number of commands from several built-in toolbars or menus, you can create a toolbar or menu of your favorites.

To create a new toolbar, open the Customize dialog box and then follow these steps:

1. Select the Toolbars tab and click New.

2. In the New Toolbar dialog box, type the name of the toolbar and click OK. Visio adds the toolbar name to the Toolbars list and displays the empty toolbar on the screen.

3. Follow the instructions in the section "Customizing Toolbars" earlier in this chapter to create the contents of the toolbar.

You can create new menus in the process of customizing a toolbar or another menu. To create a new menu on a toolbar or menu, select the Commands tab in the Customize dialog box, choose the New Menu category, and drag the New Menu command from the Commands list to the position you want on the menu. Name the menu and drag the commands you want onto the new menu.

Note When you create a new menu, it is available only on the toolbar or menu on which you place it. Visio doesn't maintain a list of user-defined menus that you can use to add customized menus to other toolbars or menus.

You can only delete toolbars that you create. To delete a user-defined toolbar, open the Customize dialog box, select the Toolbars tab, choose the user-defined toolbar you want to delete, and choose Delete from the shortcut menu. When prompted, click OK to confirm the deletion.

Although you can't delete built-in toolbars, you can reset them to their original configuration. When you select a built-in toolbar in the Customize dialog box, the Delete button is dimmed. To reset a built-in toolbar, select the Toolbars tab, select the toolbar in the Toolbars list, and then click Reset. When prompted, click OK.

Caution   Resetting a toolbar removes any custom buttons you created. To save custom buttons, copy them to another toolbar before you reset the current one.

Modifying Toolbars and Menus

You can rename toolbars and menus and group the commands on them. You can also modify button images and specify whether Visio displays a button, text, or both.

Renaming Toolbars and Menus

You can rename both user-defined and built-in menus, but you can only rename user-defined toolbars. Visio uses the menu name as the text that appears in a menu or toolbar, so it's best to keep menu names short and descriptive. To rename toolbars and menus, open the Customize dialog box and then use one of the following methods:

✦ **Rename a user-defined toolbar**—Select the Toolbars tab, choose the toolbar you want to rename, and click Rename. In the Rename Toolbar dialog box, type the new name and click OK.

✦ **Rename a menu**—Right-click the menu, type the new name in the Name box on the shortcut menu, and press Enter.

Note   To add a keyboard shortcut to access a menu, when you type the menu name in the Name box on the shortcut menu, type an ampersand (&) in front of the letter you want to use as the shortcut.

Grouping Commands and Menus

To group buttons on a toolbar or menu, right-click the button you want as the first in the group and choose Begin Group on the shortcut menu. To remove a separator, drag the two buttons or commands on either side of the separator closer together.

Changing the Width of a Drop-down List

To change the width of a drop-down list in a toolbar, follow these steps:

1. Open the Customize dialog box and select the drop-down list in the toolbar whose width you want to change.

2. Position the pointer over either end of the drop-down list and drag the pointer until the drop-down list is the width you want.

Modifying the Appearance of an Entry

When you right-click a menu or toolbar entry while the Customize dialog box is open, a shortcut menu appears with commands for changing the appearance of the entry. The commands on this shortcut menu include the following:

- ✦ **Reset** — Restores the original button, associated command, and settings for the button on a built-in toolbar

- ✦ **Delete** — Removes the button

- ✦ **Name** — Displays a box in which you can type the ToolTip for the button

- ✦ **Copy Button Image** — Copies the selected button image to the Clipboard so you can paste it to another button

- ✦ **Paste Button Image** — Pastes the image on the Clipboard to the selected button. You can copy graphics or images from other applications or buttons.

- ✦ **Reset Button Image** — Restores the default button image

- ✦ **Edit Button Image** — Opens the Button Editor dialog box so that you can edit the image

- ✦ **Change Button Image** — Displays a selection of images from which you can choose a new image

- ✦ **Default Style** — Displays only a button image on a toolbar and the button image and text on a menu

- ✦ **Text Only (Always)** — Displays only text in both toolbars and menus

- ✦ **Text Only (In Menus)** — Displays a button image on a toolbar and only text on menus

- ✦ **Image and Text** — Displays a button image and text in toolbars and menus

- ✦ **Begin a Group** — Adds a divider to the toolbar or menu

- ✦ **Assign Macro** — Opens the Customize Tool dialog box so you can designate a macro for the button

Modifying Button Images

You can modify the button images on a toolbar. For example, if you have different Print buttons for each printer you use, you can modify button images to indicate the associated printer.

To modify a button image, follow these steps:

1. Open the Customize dialog box, right-click the button you want to edit, and then click Edit Button Image. The Button Editor dialog box appears.

2. To modify the image, choose a color in the Colors section of the dialog box. To erase colored boxes in the image, click the Erase box.

3. In the Picture section, click individual cells or drag the mouse pointer over cells to change their color. You can see what the image looks like in the Preview section of the dialog box.

4. To move the image within the Picture section, click a directional arrow in the Move section of the dialog box. When the image fills the Picture section in one or more directions, Visio dims the appropriate directional arrows.

Creating Keyboard Shortcuts

If you prefer to use the keyboard more than the mouse, you can assign keyboard shortcuts to any command on any menu. To use a keyboard shortcut, press and hold the Alt key, press the shortcut letter for the menu, and then press the shortcut letter for the command. For example, to save a file, you can press Alt+F+S.

To create a keyboard shortcut, follow these steps:

1. Open the Customize dialog box and right-click the menu or command for which you want to define a keyboard shortcut.

2. In the Name box on the shortcut menu, type an ampersand (&) before the letter you want to use as the shortcut. In the menu, Visio underlines the shortcut letter for the command.

Note   Use a different letter for each keyboard shortcut. If you choose a letter that is already in use by another menu entry, you might have to press the letter more than once to select the command you want.

Sharing Customized Toolbars and Menus

When you customize toolbars and menus, they are associated with your Visio application, not a drawing file. To share a customized toolbar with someone else, you must copy it to a drawing file and send that file to your colleague. To share a customized toolbar or menu, follow these steps:

1. Choose View ➪ Toolbars ➪ Customize.

2. Select the Toolbars tab and then click Attach.

3. In the Custom Toolbars list, select a toolbar that you want to share and click Copy. Click OK after all the toolbars you want to share appear in the Toolbars in Drawing list.

4. Save the drawing file with the toolbars by pressing Ctrl+S.

Summary

You can customize built-in toolbars and menus to include only the commands you want. You can also create new toolbars and menus to consolidate your favorite commands from several built-in menus or to create specialized menus for the tasks you perform most often. Whether you customize or create menus and toolbars, you can add, remove, or rearrange entries. In addition, you can specify whether Visio displays a button image, a text description of the entry, or both. You can also customize or create button images to better represent the commands they represent.

✦   ✦   ✦

Automating Visio

If you're not a programmer, you might think that it's difficult to automate Visio procedures, but you would be wrong. In Visio 2003, you can use a macro recorder to save the steps required to accomplish a task. You can save the macro as is or modify it using Visual Basic for Applications (VBA) to make it more flexible.

If you are a programmer, or can at least find your way around a programming language such as Visual Basic, you can write code to develop more complex automated solutions. You can automate any feature you want by writing code that controls Visio documents, windows, drawing pages, shapes, and ShapeSheet cells. To extend Visio's capabilities, you write code to create Component Object Model (COM) add-ins, similar to the add-ons that are packaged with Visio, such as the Number Shapes add-on. You can then run these add-ins from menus, from shape shortcut menus, or in response to events.

In addition to macros and COM add-ins, you can use the Visio ActiveX control to integrate Visio into an external application. With this ActiveX control, you have complete access to the Visio object model and user interface. For example, you could develop an application that helps an engineer design a sound system for a customer and, when the design is complete, scan the resulting diagram to produce a parts list, an estimate, and a purchase order.

This chapter provides you with an overview of the development features that Visio offers and identifies resources for learning more both within Visio Help and online.

What's New for Developers in Visio 2003

Visio 2003 includes several new features for developers, including a few significant additions, such as the macro recorder and the Visio Drawing control. If you've been using Visio automation features already, here are some of the new features in this release:

✦ **Microsoft Office Visio Drawing Control 2003** — Available with both Visio Standard and Visio Professional, this ActiveX control provides complete access to the Visio object model and user interface so you can fully integrate Visio into an external application.

✦ **Formula tracing window** — To identify interdependencies between ShapeSheet cells, this window shows cells that use or reference a ShapeSheet cell.

✦ **Keyboard and mouse events** — New events to handle mouse and keyboard events, such as mouse movements, mouse clicks, and keyboard actions.

✦ **Macro recorder** — Records the actions you perform within the Visio application. You can save these macros as is or edit them with VBA to add functionality or flexibility.

✦ **Primary interop assemblies (PIAs)** — Access the Visio object model from applications that use the common language runtime (CLR) 1.1.

✦ **ShapeStudio** — Available with the Visio 2003 Software Developers Kit (SDK), this add-on provides a development environment for creating Visio shapes.

✦ **SmartTags** — Add SmartTags to shapes to display drop-down menus and make shape actions and settings easier to find.

✦ **Publishing add-ons** — Instead of specifying file paths for Visio add-ons, you can publish add-ons using a Microsoft Windows Installer package to take advantage of Microsoft Office System application features such as language switching, installation on demand, and repair.

✦ **XML Web Service support** — Integrate XML Web Service into diagrams by selecting Web Service references from a dialog box.

Working with Macros

Macros are the simplest way to automate smaller tasks within Visio. If you're still learning your way around VBA, you can generate the basic code for a procedure by using the macro recorder. You execute the commands and steps you want and Visio stores the code for those actions in a macro. You can edit the macro to add more functionality or prompts for input from the user. You can also write macros directly using VBA in the Visio environment.

To record a macro, follow these steps:

1. Choose Tools ➪ Macros ➪ Record New Macro.

2. Type the name of the macro, select the location in which you want to store the macro, and click OK.

3. Execute the commands and actions you want to automate.

4. When you're done with the steps in your procedure, click Stop on the Stop Recording toolbar or choose Tools ➪ Macros ➪ Stop Recording.

To edit a macro using VBA, follow these steps:

1. Choose Tools ➪ Macros ➪ Macros.

2. In the Macros dialog box, select the macro you want to edit and click Edit.

Note If the macro you want to edit doesn't appear, select the location in which the macro is stored in the Macros In drop-down list.

3. In the Microsoft Visual Basic Editor window, make the changes you want to the VBA code, as shown in Figure 36-1.

4. When you're finished editing, choose File ➪ Close and Return to Visio.

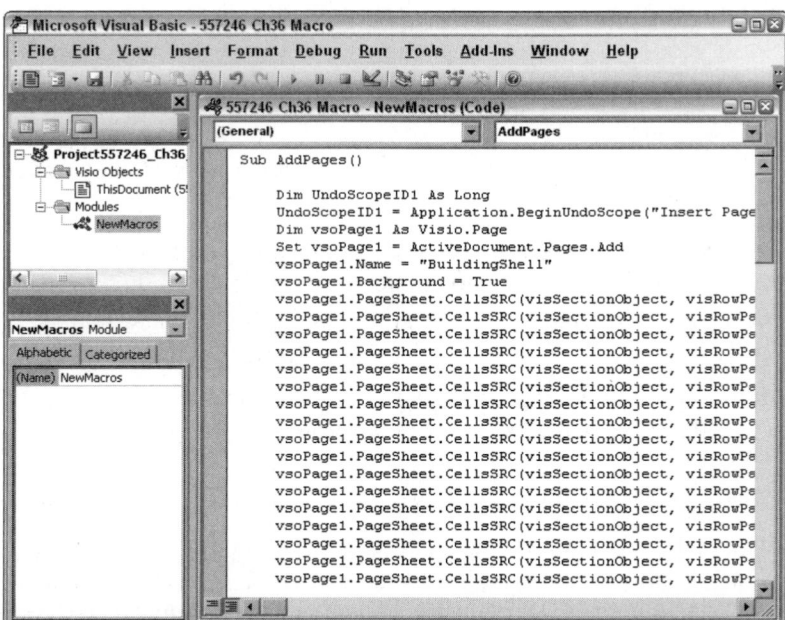

Figure 36-1: You can write macros or complete VBA programs in the Visual Basic Editor window.

You can run macros in several ways, with the following representing the most common methods:

✦ Choose Tools ➪ Macros ➪ Macros. Select the macro and click Run.

✦ Double-click a shape whose double-click behavior is set to run a macro.

Note To specify a macro for a shape's double-click behavior, select the shape and choose Format ➪ Behavior. Select the Double-Click tab and select the Run Macro option. Select the macro to run in the Run Macro drop-down list and click OK.

✦ Right-click a shape and choose a menu item that runs a macro. To add a shortcut command to run a macro, add the menu item in the Actions section of the ShapeSheet window as described in Chapter 33.

Writing Add-Ins to Automate Visio

You can automate Visio with programs written in VBA, Microsoft Visual Basic, C++, or any programming language that supports Automation, a proprietary Microsoft development environment. You can use COM add-ins the same way you do in other Microsoft Office System applications. In fact, if written appropriately, COM add-ins can work in more than one application. You can create COM add-ins using Microsoft Visual Basic 5.0 and later, Microsoft C++, Microsoft Office 2000 Developer Edition and later, or any of the Microsoft Visual Studio .NET applications.

With Automation, programs control Visio elements by accessing and using the Visio object model — Visio objects and their properties, methods, and events. Visio includes a type library that defines the objects, properties, methods, events, and constants that Visio exposes to Automation clients. Automation components include the following:

✦ **Objects** — Elements within the Visio application, such as documents, drawing pages, windows, shapes, and ShapeSheet cells containing formulas

✦ **Properties** — Attributes that determine the appearance or behavior of objects, much like the custom properties associated with shapes

✦ **Methods** — Actions that an object provides. For example, applying the Delete method to the Page object deletes a Page object and can renumber the remaining pages.

✦ **Events** — Occurrences that trigger the execution of code or programs

To use the Visio type library, a development environment must reference it. VBA projects in a Visio document reference the Visio type library automatically. If you use other development environments, you must use the appropriate commands or steps to reference the library. When you use the Visio type library, you can use an *object browser,* such as the one in VBA, to view descriptions of objects supplied by an Automation server. The object browser displays the syntax of a Visio property, method, or event, and might include code you can paste into your program. In addition, by using the type library, the development environment you use can bind your code to Automation server code at compile time, which can result in faster program execution. For example, you can use objects such as Visio.Shape instead of the generic Object.

Note   If you write your add-ins using VBA, you can access the Visual Basic Editor from within Visio. To open the Visual Basic Editor window, choose Tool ➪ Macros ➪ Visual Basic Editor.

Using the Visio Drawing Control

New to Visio 2003 is the Microsoft Office Visio Drawing Control 2003, an ActiveX control that enables you to integrate the Visio drawing surface into applications you develop. The Visio Drawing control provides full access to the Visio object model and user interface so you can interact through the Visio user interface and automate Visio procedures from within your applications.

Note   The Visio Drawing control is installed when you install Visio, even if you choose the Minimal Install.

You can embed the Visio Drawing control in Visual Basic 6.0, Visual C++ 6.0, Visual Studio 7.1, and other ActiveX control containers. However, you can't use the Visio Drawing control if you are developing a solution in VBA in Visio. You can insert more than one instance of the Visio Drawing control in your application, but each instance displays only one drawing window and one Visio drawing file.

By default, the Visio Drawing control opens a blank Visio drawing, but you can specify that the control open an existing Visio document, either at design time or at run time. The control doesn't display the Visio startup screen, the Choose Drawing Type pane, or a docked Shapes window on startup. However, if you load an existing drawing that already displays a docked Shapes window, the window appears in the Visio Drawing control window. You can also display the Shapes window in a blank drawing by using the `Document.OpenStencilWindow` method from the Visio object model. You can use other methods to display menus and toolbars.

Note   The Visio Drawing control does not expose the ShapeSheet in the user interface. However, you can use methods and properties in Automation to access ShapeSheet cells.

Learning More About Automating Visio

This chapter acts only as an introduction to programming features available in Visio 2003. Depending on which programming language you use or whether you're developing macros within Visio with VBA or using the Visio Active X control, you can find dozens of books devoted to writing code in each language or environment. You can use the following Visio Help and Microsoft's Web resources to obtain a great deal of material about developing solutions with Visio:

✦ **Visio Help** — Choose Help ⇨ Developer Reference to access the Visio Automation Reference and the Visio ShapeSheet Reference. You can read about the Visio object model, Visio programming concepts, and obtain detailed information about objects, interfaces, methods, properties, events, and enumerations.

✦ **VBA Help** — When you're working in the VBA window, choose Help ⇨ Microsoft Visual Basic Help to read about generic Visual Basic topics and obtain assistance with VBA editing tools.

✦ **MSDN** — At `http://msdn.microsoft.com/visio`, you can access Microsoft's documentation for Visio development as well as technical articles about development topics.

✦ **Other online resources** — At `www.mvps.org/visio`, you can download code contributed by Visio developers and find other sites with downloads or development information.

Summary

Visio 2003 introduces numerous enhancements and significant new features for developers. For less experienced programmers, Visio 2003 offers the macro recorder, which transforms the actions you perform in Visio into VBA code. For more advanced automation assignments, you can use any programming language that supports Automation, such as Visual Basic or Visual C++, to write COM add-ins with access to the entire Visio object model. In addition, the new Visio Drawing control is an ActiveX control that enables you to include the Visio interface and Visio functionality in external applications you develop.

✦   ✦   ✦

Quick Reference

◆   ◆   ◆   ◆

In This Part

Chapter 37
Installing Visio 2003

Chapter 38
Visio 2003 Help
Resources

Chapter 39
Additional Resources
for Templates and
Stencils

Chapter 40
Keyboard Shortcuts

Chapter 41
Template and
Stencil Reference

◆   ◆   ◆   ◆

Installing Visio 2003

If you have installed other Microsoft products on your computer, the Visio installation should be quite familiar. Visio's Setup program and the Microsoft Windows Installer use procedures similar to those for other Microsoft Office applications. This chapter describes how to install Visio 2003 from a CD or use other methods designed for deploying it in large organizations. You'll learn how to install multiple versions of Visio on your computer, which is helpful if you use some of the features discontinued in Visio 2003 or previous versions. Although the installation procedure includes default options, this chapter will show you how to choose where to install Visio as well as which components you want to install.

To verify that you are installing a legal copy of the software, Microsoft requires that you activate your copy after installation. If you don't, you can only run Visio a few times and can only use some of Visio's features during those sessions.

Exploring Visio Installation Methods

If you are installing Visio on your home computer or a business computer that is not attached to a network, it's easy to install Visio 2003 from the Visio 2003 CD. However, Microsoft Office 2003 offers additional installation methods when you want to deploy programs throughout an organization and allow users to easily maintain the software on their computers.

Cross-Reference
To learn more about the advanced deployment features of Microsoft Office 2003, review the Office Review Kit on Microsoft's Web site at www.microsoft.com/office/ork/2003/.

Using a Local Installation Source

When you install Microsoft Office 2003 applications from a CD or from a compressed CD image on the network, the Setup program copies any required installation files to a hidden folder on the local computer. Windows Installer uses this local installation source to install Office. In addition, you can use this local source later to repair, reinstall, or update your Office programs. The local source also makes it easy to install features on demand or run the Setup program in Maintenance mode to add features you didn't install initially.

With the local installation source, you can do the following:

✦ **Add features easily** — Users with slow or intermittent network connections can install features on demand or add new features without accessing the installation source on the network or CD.

✦ **Distribute smaller updates** — Administrators can distribute smaller client patches and users can apply them without access to the original installation source.

✦ **Use less disk space** — By using compressed cabinet files, the local installation source requires far less hard disk space than an entire uncompressed administrative image.

Deploying with an Administrative Installation Point

For large deployments, you can use an administrative installation point to customize Microsoft Office 2003 client installations and deploy them to users throughout your organization. The administrative installation point resides on a network server from which you can run Setup. When you use an administrative installation point, updates and maintenance originate from the administrative installation point on the network. Setup can't create a local installation source for local updates and repairs. However, an administrative installation point provides the following benefits:

✦ **Centralized management** — You can manage one set of Office files located in a central location. You can also apply patches to a single administrative image and update all installations from that image.

✦ **Standardized installations** — You can create standard Office configurations suited to the needs of groups of users.

✦ **Flexible installation options** — You can specify whether features are installed on first use or run over the network. You can also use other deployment tools, such as Microsoft Systems Management Server to install software.

Using a Compressed CD Image

If you want the benefits of an administrative installation point but also want a local installation source, a compressed CD image for installing Office applications is an alternative. To create a compressed CD image, you simply copy the compressed files from the Visio 2003 CD or Office 2003 CD to a network share. With a compressed CD image, you can perform the following actions:

✦ **Create multiple configurations** — You can modify Setup.ini to customize Office and create multiple configurations from the same compressed CD image.

✦ **Set features for install on demand** — You can set features to be installed on demand, but you can't run Office applications over the network.

✦ **Create chained packages** — You can attach additional packages to the Office installation to install standalone products such as Microsoft Office Publisher 2003 or Microsoft Office Project 2003.

✦ **Use software deployment tools** — You can use deployment tools such as Microsoft Systems Management Server to install Office on users' computers.

Installing Visio on Your Computer

If you want to install Visio from a CD onto your computer, the Visio Setup program walks you through the steps for the installation. To start your Visio installation, follow these steps:

1. Close any programs that are running — including your virus protection software — and insert the Visio 2003 CD into your computer.

Note   If the Setup program doesn't start automatically, click Start to open the Windows Start menu and choose Run. Type **D:\Setup** and click OK. If your CD drive uses a different drive letter, replace D with the CD drive letter on your computer.

2. Type the product key in the boxes in the first screen of the Microsoft Visio Setup dialog box and click Next.

3. Type your name, initials, and organization in the next screen and click Next.

4. Review the license agreement, select the I Accept the Terms in the License Agreement check box at the bottom of the screen, and click Next.

If a previous version of Visio is installed on your computer, continue with the following section. For a new installation, skip ahead to the section "Using the Microsoft Windows Installer."

Installing When a Previous Version Is Present

By default, the Visio 2003 Setup program removes installations of Visio 2002 and Visio 2000. If it finds previous versions of Visio, it displays them in the Previous Versions screen. To keep your Visio 2000 or Visio 2002 installations, follow these steps:

1. Select the Custom Install option in the Type of Installation dialog box and click Next.

2. In the Previous Versions screen, select the Keep All Previous Versions option and click Next.

Tip If you plan to work with multiple versions and you don't keep the installation source files on your computer, make sure that your Visio CD for each version you want to use is handy. You will need your CD every time the Auto-repair program runs.

Note When you use multiple versions of Visio on the same computer, Visio might display a dialog box when you start Visio. Wait while the Visio Auto-repair process sets up the files properly for the version you want to run and then work with Visio as you would normally.

Using the Microsoft Windows Installer

When you install Visio, you can specify the type of installation you want and where you want to install the program files on your computer. By default, the Setup program automatically selects the Typical Install option, which installs the most commonly used components. However, you can also choose to install every feature, only the required features, or only the features you want.

To continue with your Visio installation, follow these steps:

1. Select the type of installation you want from the following options:

   • **Typical Install** — Installs the most commonly used features and components. You can add or remove components later using the Setup program Maintenance mode.

   • **Complete Install** — Installs all Visio components and features

   • **Minimal Install** — Installs only the required components, which is helpful when disk space is at a premium

   • **Custom Install** — Installs the features you specify

2. To install Visio in a location other than the default path, `C:\Program Files\ Microsoft Office\`, click the Browse button, navigate to the installation path you want, and click OK. Click Next.

3. If you chose the Custom Install option, in the Advanced Customization screen, choose the features you want to install and how you want to run them with the following steps:

   a. Navigate to the feature you want to install by clicking the + in front of a category and then clicking the icon that precedes the feature you want, as shown in Figure 37-1.

   b. For the selected feature, choose one of the following installation methods:

      • **Run From My Computer** — Installs the selected feature on your computer

      • **Run All From My Computer** — Installs the selected features and all its options on your computer

      • **Installed on First Use** — Does not install the feature as part of the current installation. Visio will prompt you to install it the first time you try to use it. You will need your Visio CD handy or access to the installation files on your computer or the network.

      • **Not Available** — Does not install the selected feature

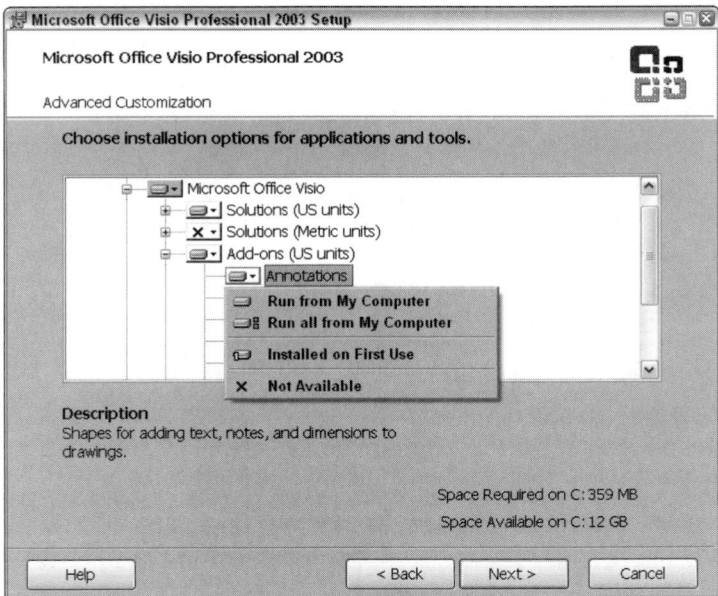

Figure 37-1: Choose features to install and also how to run them.

4. Repeat steps a and b for each feature you want to customize. Click Next when you have specified how you want to install the features you want.

Installation Option Icons

The Setup program uses the following icons to indicate how features will be installed:

✦ A white box with a drive icon indicates that features and options will be installed as you've specified.

✦ A gray box with a drive icon means some options for a feature won't be installed.

✦ A white box with a red X mean the features and its options won't be installed.

✦ A white box with a drive icon and the number one means the feature will be installed the first time you use it.

Note   Visio provides two versions of each template and add-on: one version using U.S. units and the other using metric units. By default, the Setup program selects the version to install based on the locale and configuration on your computer. If you want to include both versions, you must perform a custom install and specify that you want to install the following: Solutions (US units), Solutions (Metric Units), Add-ons (US units), and Add-ons (Metric units).

5. Click Install to proceed with the installation. If you notice a problem after the installation begins, you can stop the installation by clicking the Cancel button. If you do this, the Setup program terminates. After you correct the problem, you must run the Setup program again and start from the beginning.

6. After Setup is complete, check for updates to Visio by checking the Check the Web for Updates and Additional Downloads check box.

7. If you don't want to keep the Visio installation files on your computer for repairs or updates to your installation, check the Delete Installation Files check box. Deleting these files saves approximately 184MB of disk space. However, without these files, you will need your Visio CD to repair your installation or add components in the future.

8. Click Finish to complete the installation.

Activating a New Visio Installation

Activation is a technique that Microsoft uses to ensure that you've installed a legal copy of a Microsoft product. If you run Visio without activating it, the product runs in Reduced Functionality mode, which enables you to evaluate Visio's features, but limits your ability to perform meaningful work. In addition, after you run Visio several times without activating, you won't be able to run the program again until you reinstall and activate it.

When you activate Visio, Microsoft requires that you indicate your country or region, not personal information. The Microsoft Office Visio Activation Wizard creates a unique hardware identifier that identifies only the configuration of your computer solely for the purpose of activating Visio. You don't have to reactivate your copy of Visio for minor upgrades, although you might have to reactivate if you completely rebuild your computer. During activation, you can also register your copy of Visio. The Activation Wizard starts automatically when you run Visio for the first time. However, you can also start the wizard by choosing Help ⇨ Activate Product.

Although registration requires personal information such as your name and contact information, rest assured that Microsoft employs a privacy policy and uses security mechanisms to protect your personal information and privacy.

If you have trouble activating Visio, your Internet connection might be disconnected. To activate Microsoft Office Visio by telephone, start the Microsoft Office Visio Activation Wizard and follow the instructions.

If you do not activate Microsoft Office Visio after you install it, Visio starts in Reduced Functionality mode. You can open, close, and print existing drawings in Reduced Functionality mode, but you can't perform the following tasks:

✦ Create new files

✦ Save changes to existing files

✦ Display anchored windows, such as Pan & Zoom, Size & Position, and Custom Properties

✦ Display built-in or custom stencils or drag shapes from stencils

✦ Cut, copy, or paste content. This includes the Paste Special command and placing content on the Clipboard.

✦ Access or assign shape properties or custom properties

✦ Import or export data

✦ Use Microsoft Visual Basic for Applications (VBA) and the Visio object model

✦ Enable existing macros or create new macros

✦ Access the ShapeSheet window

Maintaining and Repairing Visio

After your initial installation of Visio, you can uninstall Visio, add or remove Visio-specific features, or reinstall features that aren't working properly. You can also instruct Visio to look for installation problems, such as missing or damaged files, and repair them.

Adding and Removing Components

You use the Visio Setup program when you want to install features that you omitted during your initial installation or remove features you don't use, to recover disk space. You can also uninstall Visio using this program. When you run the Visio Setup program, you can choose from the following options:

✦ **Add or Remove Features** — Install or remove specific Visio features

✦ **Reinstall or Repair** — Reinstall or repair installed features when there is a problem with your Visio installation and you can't run Visio or access Detect and Repair on Visio's Help menu.

✦ **Uninstall** — Removes the Visio 2003 installation from your computer

To add or remove specific Visio features, follow these steps:

1. Click Start and choose Settings ➪ Control Panel ➪ Add/Remove Programs. If you're using an earlier version of the Windows operating system or have configured Windows to not have the Control Panel as a menu, use the commands necessary to open the Control Panel window and then choose Add/Remove Programs.

2. Choose the version of Visio that you are using in the Currently Installed Programs list (Microsoft Office Visio Professional 2003 or Microsoft Office Visio Standard 2003).

3. To enter Maintenance mode, click Change.

4. Choose Add or Remove Features and click Next.

5. Expand the tree of features until you can see the feature you want to change. Click the feature and then select an option to remove it or run it. For more information about the update options that are available, refer to the section "Installing Visio on Your Computer" earlier in this chapter.

6. After you have made all your changes, click Update.

Repairing Your Visio Installation

You can find and correct problems with your Visio installation, such as missing files and registry settings. The Visio Detect and Repair command does not detect or repair problems with other Microsoft Office applications or fix problems with personal files, such as drawings.

Tip   If running Detect and Repair does not fix the problem, try reinstalling Visio.

To repair your Visio installation, follow these steps:

1. Choose Help ➪ Detect and Repair.

2. To restore the program shortcuts to the Microsoft Windows Start menu, check the Restore My Shortcuts While Repairing check box.

3. If your customized settings are hopelessly compromised, as a last resort you can restore default settings by checking the Discard My Customized Settings and Restore Default Settings check box.

Caution Discarding your customized settings affects all Microsoft Office System applications, including Word and Excel. Checking the Discard My Customized Settings and Restore Default Settings check box resets the following: the application window's size, menu and toolbar positions and customizations, the security level, view settings, the list of recently used files, and your user name and initials.

If you still choose to discard your settings, you will have to reenter your user name and initials and then reset your environment when you restart Visio.

4. Click Start. Visio analyzes your installation and repairs any problems it finds.

Learning More About Your Version of Visio

To learn about last-minute changes to Visio 2003, read the Microsoft Office Visio 2003 README file by following these steps:

1. Click Start ➪ My Computer. Double-click the drive on which you installed the Microsoft Office System. For earlier versions of the Windows operating system, open the Windows Explorer window and navigate to the drive that contains your Office installation.

Note You can also open the My Computer window by double-clicking My Computer on your desktop.

2. Double-click Program Files, double-click Microsoft Office, and then double-click Visio11.

3. Double-click the folder corresponding to your language. For example, double-click 1033 for English or 1041 for Japanese.

4. Double-click `VIREADME.htm`.

When you're connected to the Internet, you can also access the most up-to-date Help information by downloading Help topics from Microsoft Office Online. To change your Help settings, in the Help task pane, click the Online Content Settings link and make sure that the Show Content and Links from Microsoft Office Online check box and the Search Online Content When Connected check box are checked.

Summary

Whether you want to install Visio on one computer or hundreds, you can choose a method that makes installation easy. When you install Visio on your own computer, you can keep a copy of the installation on your hard disk so you can easily repair or reconfigure your installation without having to find your Visio CD. You can also use the Visio Setup program to add or remove Visio features, repair your Visio installation, or reinstall or uninstall the software.

In addition to the installation process, you must activate your copy of the software to use all its features. Activation doesn't require any personal information; it is required solely to verify that you are installing a legal copy of the software.

✦   ✦   ✦

Visio 2003 Help Resources

Although many of its features are intuitive, Visio 2003 is a powerful tool with plenty of productivity shortcuts and special features. You can quickly increase your Visio expertise with the tools described in this quick reference.

The Getting Started Tutorial

The Getting Started Tutorial for Visio 2003 is a quick introduction to Visio's basics. You can learn about basic concepts such as templates, stencils and shapes, components of the Visio interface, and how to obtain help.

The tutorial uses animations that demonstrate how to accomplish common tasks such as creating a drawing using a template. To start the tutorial, click Help ⇨ Getting Started Tutorial. To watch an animation of the steps, expand a top-level topic, such as Create Diagrams, select a lesson, and then click Play (a green triangle) in the tutorial window. After watching the animation, you can minimize the tutorial window and duplicate the steps in Visio to perform the task on your own.

The tutorial covers creating drawings and adding shapes, connections, and text to those drawings. It shows how to format drawing contents and share drawings with others. Topics also include creating shapes, stencils, and templates. To familiarize you with working with specialized templates, the tutorial demonstrates how to create block diagrams, organization charts, and office layouts for scaled drawings.

Finding Help About Visio

When you are offline, Visio 2003 searches help topics stored on your computer. However, you can access help at Microsoft Office Online (http://office. microsoft.com/home/) when you are connected to the Internet. Microsoft Office Online provides more up-to-date help. You can read in-depth articles about Visio and other Office applications, study online training courses, and download templates and clip art.

To access specific pages of the Microsoft Office Online Web site in your browser, click one of the following links in the Help Task Pane:

> ✦ **Assistance** — Find help for any application in the Microsoft Office suite covering Office 97, Office 2000, Office XP, and Office 2003.

 **Tip**
To view any new Visio content on Microsoft Office Online, click New on the Web on the Visio Assistance page.

> ✦ **Training** — Take online training courses for any application in the Microsoft Office suite.
>
> ✦ **Communities** — Ask questions and obtain answers from other users through the Microsoft Office newsgroups.
>
> ✦ **Downloads** — Obtain additional tools, such as the Visio Viewer.

To open the Microsoft Office Online home page, choose one of the following methods:

> ✦ Choose Help ➪ Microsoft Office Online.
>
> ✦ Click Connect to Microsoft Office Online in the Getting Started or Help task pane.

You can access additional resources at Microsoft Office Online:

> ✦ **Templates** — Download additional templates and starter drawings. To locate Visio templates, type **Visio** in the Search box on the Templates page. You can also access Microsoft Office Online templates by clicking Templates on Office Online in the New Drawing Task Pane.
>
> ✦ **Clip Art and Media** — Download clip art and sounds.
>
> ✦ **Office Marketplace** — To increase your Visio productivity, obtain products from other companies or find a solution provider to help you customize Visio.

Viewing Visio Help Topics

Most people don't read help files for fun. When you need assistance, you're usually looking for help on a specific topic. To find help for a Visio topic, you can type a question or enter one or more keywords in the following locations:

✦ The Search For box in the Help Task Pane

✦ The Search box in the Search Results Task Pane

✦ The Ask a Question box in the top-right corner of the Visio interface

 **New Feature** By default, Visio displays help topics from Microsoft Office Online when you are connected to the Internet. When you are not connected to the Internet, Visio searches Offline Help.

If you want information about a broad topic, such as connecting shapes, the Visio table of contents is more useful. The table of contents pulls information from Microsoft Office Online if you are online; otherwise, it uses Microsoft Offline help. Follow these steps to quickly locate information for the topic you want in the Help table of contents:

1. Display the Help Task Pane by choosing View ➪ Task Pane. Click the down arrow in the task pane's title bar and choose Help from the drop-down list.

2. Type a question or enter one or more keywords in the Search For box and click the green right arrow to start searching.

3. Look for a result that fits your keywords but is more general than specific, as demonstrated in Figure 38-1.

4. Click the table of contents heading, which is a gray link below the search result, as shown in Figure 38-1.

Configuring Your Help Settings

You can specify where Visio should look for help and what content it should display. To change your Online Content Settings, follow these steps:

1. Display the Help Task Pane by choosing View ➪ Task Pane, and then click the down arrow in the task pane's title bar and choose Help from the drop-down list.

2. Click Online Content Settings under the See Also heading.

3. To use offline help, uncheck the Search Online Content When Connected check box.

4. To specify the online content you want to see, check one or more of the following check boxes:

   • **Search Online Content When Connected** — Displays online content when you are online

   • **Show Template Help When Available** — Displays help topics for the current template in the Template Help Task Pane

   • **Show Microsoft Office Online Featured Links** — Includes links to features at Microsoft Office Online in task panes

5. Click OK.

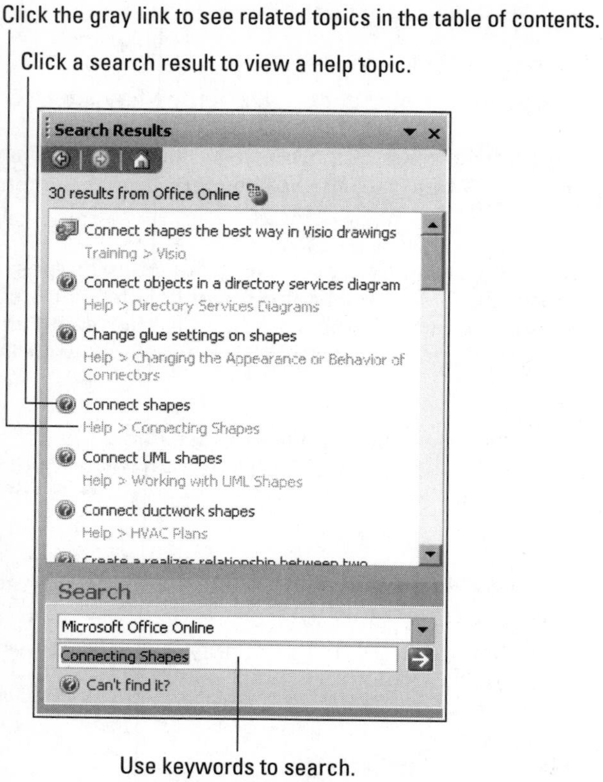

Click the gray link to see related topics in the table of contents.

Click a search result to view a help topic.

Use keywords to search.

Figure 38-1: You can click links to access help topics or the table of contents.

Searching the Microsoft Knowledge Base

The Microsoft Knowledge Base is a comprehensive database of support articles for every Microsoft product. No matter what keywords you enter, the Knowledge Base usually has some answers. To search the Microsoft Knowledge Base, follow these steps:

1. Navigate to `http://support.microsoft.com` in your browser window.

2. Click Search the Knowledge Base.

3. Choose your version of Visio in the Select a Microsoft Product drop-down list.

4. Type keywords in the Search For box.

Tip
To maximize the relevance of your results, type words you would expect to find in an answer to your problem. Don't use words that could apply to any answer, such as **how**, **why**, and **is**. To find help on errors, copy an error message in the Search For box.

5. Select options to specify how to use your keywords to search and how far back to look and then click the green arrow or click Go.

Working with Visio Task Panes

Task panes organize the features that are helpful for the most common tasks in Visio. The task pane docks on the right side of the screen by default. It is easy to work with task panes:

✦ To display the task pane in the drawing area, click View ➪ Task Pane.

✦ To choose a task pane, click the name of the task pane you want in the Task Pane drop-down list.

 **Tip**
If you close the Visio task pane to display more of your Visio drawing, you can quickly display it again by clicking Ctrl+F1.

Visio 2003 includes several new task panes. The Help Task Pane includes links to the Microsoft Office Online Web site and a Search box in which you can enter questions or keywords. The Template Help Task Pane displays links to help topics for the template associated with the current drawing.

 New Feature
In addition to the Help and Template Task Panes, Visio includes several new task panes for collaboration, including Shared Workspace, Document Updates, and Reviewing.

Accessing Help Quickly

If you need only a hint about a shape or a toolbar command, ScreenTips are faster than help topics. To display ScreenTips, use one of the following methods:

✦ For a shape ScreenTip, pause the pointer over a master in a stencil. To obtain more information about the master, click More in the ScreenTip dialog box.

✦ For a toolbar ScreenTip, pause the pointer over the toolbar icon.

If you want help for a dialog box, click the question mark in the dialog box to display a help topic about the options in the dialog box.

Other Helpful Resources

Microsoft Office Online includes links to several additional Web sites with helpful resources. To navigate to these sites, click a link under the Related Web Sites heading:

✦ **Product Support** — Search the Knowledge Base, download software, work with Microsoft support technicians, or post a request to a community newsgroup at the Microsoft Support Web sit.

✦ **Office Worldwide** — Navigate to the Microsoft Office Online Web site, which offers specialized content for a region or country.

✦ **Office Community** — Access Microsoft Office newsgroups.

✦ **Office Developer Center** — Navigate to the MSDN Web site to obtain Visio development resources and information.

✦ **Office Resource Kit** — Obtain tools to facilitate deploying Visio and other Office applications in your organization.

✦ **MS Press** — Find books and interactive training materials produced by Microsoft Press.

✦ **Microsoft.com** — Navigate to Microsoft's home page.

✦ **Windows Update** — Review and install updates to your computer's operating system, software, and hardware.

✦ **bCentral** — Obtain Office resources targeted for small businesses at Microsoft's `bcentral.com` Web site (`www.bcentral.com`).

✦ **MSN** — This link takes you to MSN.com, Microsoft's Web portal to all sorts of Internet content.

Summary

Visio offers a number of features you can use to learn about Visio. You can start with the Getting Started Tutorial. As you work, you can use the Visio Help Task Pane to find help on different topics or to select a topic from the Help table of contents. In addition, you can use numerous online help resources offered by Microsoft and many third parties.

✦   ✦   ✦

Additional Resources for Templates and Stencils

Visio comes with dozens of templates and thousands of shapes. You can view thumbnails of diagram types in Visio to help you identify the one you want. You can also download additional templates and sample files from Microsoft Office Online.

Even with all of Microsoft's Visio resources, you might not find what you need if you are producing highly specialized diagrams, such as detailed wiring diagrams for Juniper Networks equipment or a dog agility course. Fortunately, many companies provide additional templates and stencils for these applications. For example, you can obtain Visio stencils for some equipment when you purchase it from the manufacturer. Other companies sell third-party templates for a variety of applications. This chapter shows you how to find the templates and stencils that Visio offers, and templates, stencils, and other solutions from third-party resources and Web sites.

Using the Diagram Gallery

When you want to create a new drawing, Visio can help you select the right template for your drawing. When you select a category in the Choose Drawing Type Task Pane, Visio displays a simple example for each type of drawing in that category. If you position the pointer over an example, a description of the uses for that drawing type appears in the lower-left corner of the window. If these hints aren't enough, you can browse through the Diagram Gallery to see more detailed examples and potential uses for each type of diagram.

To open the Diagram Gallery, choose Help ➪ Diagram Gallery. You can browse through all the examples in the gallery by clicking Next or Back. Visio displays an example of the diagram, a description, and several potential uses, as shown in Figure 39-1. For example, when you choose a Floor Plan diagram, Visio specifies that a floor plan shows doors, windows, electrical outlets, and floor layout in a building. It describes how architects, general contractors, and facilities managers can use a floor plan to perform their work.

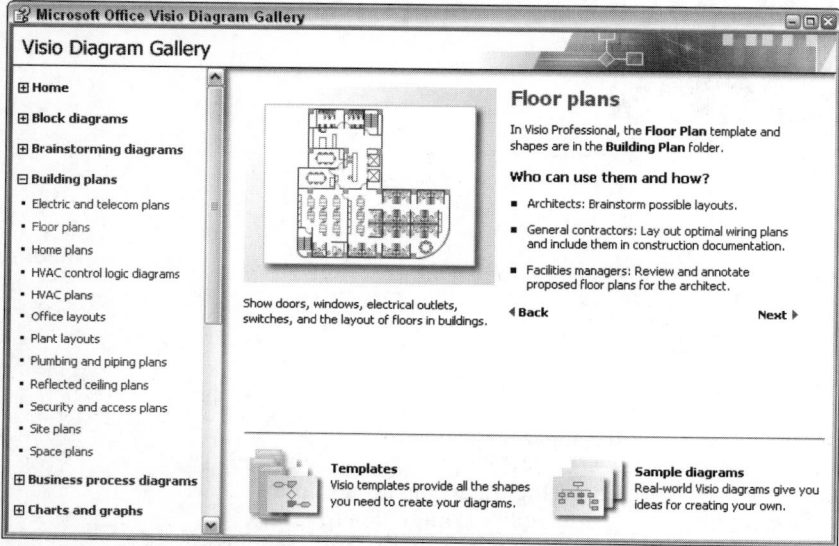

Figure 39-1: Browse the Diagram Gallery to find the right template.

Tip   The Diagram Gallery also provides links to templates and sample drawings on Microsoft Office Online. To find additional templates, click Templates in the Diagram Gallery to navigate to the Templates page at Microsoft Office Online. To download sample files, click Samples Diagrams to navigate to the Downloads page at Microsoft Office Online.

Exploring the Visio Extras Stencils

No matter what type of drawing you're creating, you can use shapes from stencils other than the ones the template opens by default. Visio includes many of the most useful stencils in the Visio Extras category. To open one of these stencils, choose File ➪ Shapes ➪ Visio Extras and choose the stencil you want. Visio Extras stencils include shapes for annotations, backgrounds, borders and titles, callouts, connectors, patterns, dimensioning, symbols, title blocks, and more.

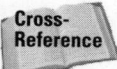

Cross-Reference   For a complete list of Visio Extras stencils, see Chapter 41.

Finding Templates and Samples at Microsoft Office Online

Microsoft Office Online provides additional templates as well as Visio files that contain sample content to get you started. For example, Microsoft Office Online includes 2004 calendars, localized network diagrams, and a DMAIC Flowchart for Six Sigma projects. To obtain templates online at the Templates page on Microsoft Office Online, follow these steps:

1. In the New Drawing Task Pane, click Templates on Office Online.

2. Type **Visio** in the Search box and click the green arrow to initiate the search. The search results include links to download templates and a rating for the template based on user opinion.

3. To download a template, click the name of the template. The download page shows a large example of a diagram for the template, the download size, and the version of Visio required to use the template.

4. Click Download Now. Visio opens a new drawing based on the downloaded template and displays help topics for the template in the Template Help Task Pane.

To download Visio files that contain sample diagrams that help you understand how to use those types of drawings, open the Downloads page at Microsoft Office Online by clicking Downloads in the Help Task Pane. To find Visio 2003 sample files, type **Visio 2003** in the Search box. For example, you can download Visio 2003 Sample:20 Sample Diagrams file, which contains 20 diagrams with shapes already added, including a floor plan, flowchart, network diagram, calendar, electrical engineering control diagram, and a UML model. Use steps 3 and 4 above to download the file you want.

Finding Third-party Visio Templates and Stencils

Many equipment vendors offer Visio templates and stencils with shapes that represent the equipment they sell. For example, you can build accurate equipment layouts and network diagrams that show exactly where cables connect by downloading and using Visio templates from companies such as Dell, Cisco, and Hewlett-Packard. These templates include shapes that look just like their real-world components and contain connection points where network cables plug into the devices in real life.

In addition, third-party vendors and many service companies sell Visio templates for a variety of applications. If you are looking for a particular kind of template, enter keywords, such as "Visio," "template," and "networking" in your favorite search engine.

The following are a few online resources for finding, downloading, and purchasing templates and stencils:

✦ **An overall Visio resource site** — www.mvps.org/visio/ offers all kinds of helpful Visio resources, including the following:

- Information about using Visio

- The newsgroups that Microsoft created for Visio

- Links to other informational Web sites

- Links to Web sites with stencils and templates for download or purchase. Click Download Sites to open a page that lists categories in alphabetical order on the left, and links to sites for templates and stencils on the right. The list includes companies under each category of template that they offer.

- Examples of VBA code for Visio tasks

✦ **Visio Network Equipment** — If you obtained Visio Enterprise Network Tools before it was discontinued on June 30, 2003, you can download network shapes from www.microsoft.com/office/visio/networkcenter/.

✦ **Visimation.com** — This site sells stencils for numerous applications such as manufacturing, firefighting, restaurant management, and biology.

✦ **Templatesnext.com** — This site sells thousands of templates for categories such as agriculture, dating, jewelry, medical, and transportation.

✦ **Altimatech.com** — This site sells Visio stencils for over 1,300 IT equipment manufacturers, such as Cisco, Sun, Hewlett-Packard, Dell, Texas Instruments, and StorageTek.

✦ **Wireless Templates** — Orinoco offers Visio templates for wireless networks at www.orinocowireless.com/about/imagebank/.

✦ **Home-grown Sun Visio Templates** — Bruce Pullig offers the templates he created for Sun equipment at www.visio.pullig.com.

Summary

You can find many templates and stencils within Visio or within Microsoft's online resources. In addition, thousands of third-party vendors sell additional templates and stencils for a variety of specialized applications. You can also find templates and stencils that individuals or companies offer at no charge by searching the Internet.

✦   ✦   ✦

Keyboard Shortcuts

You can use keyboard shortcuts to increase your pro-
ductivity and reduce fatigue. With keyboard shortcuts,
you can keep your hands on the keyboard, saving the time it
takes to switch between keyboard and mouse or to move the
pointer to choose a command. Keyboard shortcuts can save
significant time when you edit or format text, such as applying
bold. They are equally effective for executing frequently used
commands, such as Save. In addition, you can switch between
using keyboard shortcuts and the mouse to give your fingers
and muscles a break during long work sessions.

This chapter explains how to use keyboard shortcuts and
identifies some of the more useful keyboard shortcuts built
into Visio.

Using Keyboard Shortcuts

Many commands and tasks have their own keyboard shortcuts, whether it's a function key, such as F4 to repeat your last
action, or some combination of Ctrl, Shift, and letters of the
alphabet, such as Ctrl+S to save. When a command has an
associated keyboard shortcut, any menu entry for that command shows the keyboard shortcut after the command name.

Note   Keyboard shortcuts in Help topics, menus, and dialog boxes
refer to the U.S. keyboard layout. If the language for the
keyboard layout you are using and the one you chose for
Microsoft Office Visio or Visio Help are different, you might
have to use different keys for your keyboard shortcuts.

In addition, you can easily access commands on menus and
submenus by holding the Alt key while you press the letter
underlined in a menu entry. For example, on the menu bar, the
F in File is underlined. You can open the File menu by pressing
Alt+F. While the File menu is open and you are still holding
the Alt key, you can save your file by pressing S.

 **Note**   You can't use Alt and a key for a second-level menu item unless the top-level menu is open. For example, Alt+S works only after you press Alt+F to open the File menu.

Handy Keyboard Shortcuts

Visio provides keyboard shortcuts for almost every command and menu entry. You can work on Visio drawings almost exclusively with the keyboard. However, if you can't remember all those combinations of Ctrl, Shift, and Alt, memorize the keyboard shortcuts associated with the commands you use most frequently. This section includes a sampling of the more useful keyboard shortcuts. For a thorough list of keyboard shortcuts, type **keyboard shortcuts** in the Search box in the Help Task Pane and click the Help>Shortcut Keys link that appears.

File Shortcuts

File shortcuts make it easy to issue file-related commands, such as Open, New, Save, and Close.

Ctrl+N	Open a new drawing based on the open drawing (File Í New Í New Drawing).
Ctrl+O	Open the Open dialog box (File Í Open).
Ctrl+S	Save the active drawing (File ⇨ Save).
Ctrl+P	Open the Print dialog box (File ⇨ Print).
Ctrl+F4	Close the active drawing window (File ⇨ Close).

Action Shortcuts

You can quickly undo, redo, or repeat your actions with the following shortcuts.

Ctrl+Z	Undo the last action you performed (Edit ⇨ Undo).
Ctrl+Y	Redo the action undone by the Undo command (Edit ⇨ Redo).
F4	Repeat the previous action. For example, if you just pasted a shape onto the page, you can paste another copy by pressing F4.

Editing and Formatting Shortcuts

Editing and formatting go much more quickly if you memorize and use the following keyboard shortcuts.

Ctrl+X	Cut the selection from the active drawing and place it on the Clipboard (Edit ➪ Cut).
Ctrl+C	Copy the selection to the Clipboard (Edit ➪ Copy).
Ctrl+V	Paste the contents of the Clipboard to the active drawing page (Edit ➪ Paste).
Delete	Delete the selection (Edit ➪ Clear).
Ctrl+A	Select all the shapes on the active page (Edit ➪ Select All).
Ctrl+D	Copy the selection to the active drawing (Edit ➪ Duplicate).
	Note: You can copy a shape or text to the active drawing page by selecting it and then pressing Ctrl+D. You can make additional copies by pressing Ctrl+D again. To copy selected shapes or text to another drawing page or another application, use Ctrl+C to copy the selection to the Clipboard. After switching to the other page or application, press Ctrl+V to paste the contents of the Clipboard.
Ctrl+F	Open the Find dialog box (Edit ➪ Find).
Ctrl+Shift+P	Toggle the Format Painter tool on or off.
Ctrl+B	Toggle bold on or off.
Ctrl+I	Toggle italic on or off.
Ctrl+U	Toggle underline on or off.

Window and Viewing Shortcuts

It's easy to access different views or display different areas of a drawing with the following keyboard shortcuts.

Ctrl+F1	Toggle the task pane (View ➪ Task Pane).
Ctrl+Shift+I	Zoom to 100 percent magnification (View ➪ Zoom ➪ 100%).
Ctrl+W	Zoom to show the whole page (View ➪ Zoom ➪ WholePage).
Alt+F10	Maximize the Visio program window.
Alt+F5	Restore the Visio program window to its previous size after maximizing it.
Alt+Tab	Switch to the next program window.
Alt+Shift+Tab	Switch to the previous program window.
Ctrl+Tab	Make the next open drawing the active drawing.
Ctrl+F10	Maximize the active drawing window.

Continued

Ctrl+F5	Restore the active drawing window size after maximizing it.
F6	Cycle focus through all open stencils, anchored windows, the task pane, and the drawing window.
Print Screen	Copy a picture of the screen to the Clipboard.
Alt+Print Screen	Copy a picture of the selected window to the Clipboard.

Zoom Shortcuts

The easiest way to zoom in or out is with the following keyboard shortcuts.

Alt+F6	Zoom in.
Alt+Shift+F6	Zoom out.

Tool Shortcuts

You can check spelling or access macros with the following keyboard shortcuts.

F7	Check the spelling on the active drawing (Tools ➪ Spelling).
Alt+F8	Open the Macros dialog box (Tools ➪ Macros ➪ Macros).

Shape Shortcuts

As you work on drawings, use the following shortcuts to work with and edit shapes.

Ctrl+G	Group the selected shapes (Shape ➪ Grouping ➪ Group).
Ctrl+L	Rotate the selected shape to the left (Shape ➪ Rotate or Flip ➪ Rotate Left).
Ctrl+R	Rotate the selected shape to the right (Shape ➪ Rotate or Flip ➪ Rotate Right).
Ctrl+H	Flip the selected shape horizontally (Shape ➪ Rotate or Flip ➪ Flip Horizontal).
Ctrl+J	Flip the selected shape vertically (Shape ➪ Rotate or Flip ➪ Flip Vertical).
F2	Toggle between Text Edit and Shape Selection mode on a selected shape.
Tab	Change focus from shape to shape on the drawing page. Visio displays a dotted box around the shape with focus.

Shift+Tab	Change focus from current shape to previous shape on the drawing page.
Enter	Select a shape that has focus.
	Note: To select multiple shapes, hold down Shift while you press Tab to cycle focus to another shape. When the shape you want has focus, press Enter to add that shape to the selection. Repeat for each shape you want to select.
Escape	Clear selection of or focus on a shape.
Arrow Keys	Nudge a selected shape.

Dialog Box Shortcuts

When a dialog box is open, you can use the following keyboard shortcuts to move to the option or tab you want.

Tab	Move to the next option or option group.
Shift+Tab	Move to the previous option or option group.
Ctrl+Tab	Switch to the next tab in a dialog box.
Ctrl+Shift+Tab	Switch to the previous tab in a dialog box.
Arrow Keys	Move between options in an open drop-down list or between options in a group of options.
Spacebar	Perform the action assigned to the selected button; check or uncheck the selected check box.

Edit Box Shortcuts

An edit box is a field in a dialog box in which you type an entry, such as the name of a new page. The following keyboard shortcuts help you move and select edit box contents.

Home	Move to the beginning of the entry.
End	Move to the end of the entry.
Left Arrow	Move one character to the left.
Right Arrow	Move one character to the right.
Ctrl+Left Arrow	Move one word to the left.
Ctrl+Right Arrow	Move one word to the right.
Shift+Home	Select everything from the insertion point to the beginning of the entry.
Shift+End	Select everything from the insertion point to the end of the entry.

Menu and Toolbar Shortcuts

Even when you use menus and toolbars, the following keyboard shortcuts can help you open and close menus or select the command you want.

F10 or Alt	Select the menu bar or close an open menu and submenu at the same time.
Tab	When a toolbar or menu bar is selected, select the next button or menu.
Shift+Tab	When a toolbar or menu bar is selected, select the previous button or menu.
Down Arrow	When a menu or submenu is open, select the next command. Pressing the Up Arrow key selects the previous command.
Enter	Open the selected menu or perform the action for the selected button or command.
Escape	Close an open menu. When a submenu is open, close only the submenu.

Help Shortcuts

The Task Pane is a window within the Visio program window that provides access to all Visio help. The Help window is a separate window that displays topics and other Help content.

F1	Display the Help Task Pane from a Visio window, or a context-sensitive topic from a Visio dialog box.
F6	Switch between the Help Task Pane and the active application.
Tab	Select the next item in the Help Task Pane or the next hidden text or hyperlink in the Help window.
Shift+Tab	Select the previous item in the Help Task Pane or the next hidden text or hyperlink in the Help window.
Enter	Perform the action for the selected item.
Down Arrow	In a table of contents, select the next item. Pressing the Up Arrow key selects the previous item. In the Help window, the Down Arrow key scrolls down a small amount within the currently displayed Help topic. The Up Arrow key scrolls up in the Help topic.
Right Arrow	In a table of contents, expand the selected item. The Left Arrow key collapses the selected item.
Page Down	Scroll down one page within the currently displayed Help topic. The Page Up key scrolls one page up.

Summary

Keyboard shortcuts can save you time and reduce the finger and arm fatigue that ensues when you hold your hands over the mouse or keyboard for extended periods. Visio provides keyboard shortcuts for almost every command it offers, but you can increase your productivity by memorizing even a small subset of the available shortcuts. Even if you don't know the function key or keyboard sequence for a command, you can select it from a menu or submenu by using the Alt key with the letters underlined in menu entries.

✦　✦　✦

Template and Stencil Reference

Visio comes with dozens of templates that you can use to create diagrams for work or play. Visio Standard 2003 provides templates for common diagramming tasks, such as building block diagrams, documenting business processes, or creating charts and graphs. You can also create basic diagrams for some architecture, engineering, and information technology tasks, such as laying out office space or creating a basic network diagram. Only a few of the architectural and engineering templates are available in the Standard version. The Basic Network Diagram template is the only informational technology template available in Visio Standard 2003.

When you want to create a variety of specialized diagrams, you'll want to use Visio Professional 2003. With the Professional version, you can create most of the common building plan diagrams, including electrical, HVAC, and mechanical plans. For information technology, you can create diagrams to document databases, networks, software, and Web sites using many of the popular modeling methodologies.

When you create a drawing with a template, Visio automatically opens stencils with the shapes typically used on that type of drawing. However, you can open additional stencils if you need other shapes. This chapter identifies the templates in each Visio category, the stencils these templates use, and the chapter of the book that describes how to use them. In addition, this chapter provides a list of the stencils available in the Visio Extras stencil category.

Templates for Office Productivity

Visio templates for office productivity run from the mundane block diagram to specialized diagrams for business process improvement methodologies such as Total Quality Management. Table 41-1 shows the templates for office productivity and business process improvement.

 **Note**   The Data Flow Diagram template is the only template that appears in an office productivity category that is available only with Visio Professional 2003. Several Flowchart templates, such as Basic Flowchart and Cross-functional Flowchart, are available in both the Flowchart and Business Process categories.

Table 41-1
Office Productivity Templates and Stencils

Category	Template	Stencils	Chapter
Block Diagram	Basic Diagram	Backgrounds, Borders and Titles, Basic Shapes	12
	Block Diagram	Backgrounds, Borders and Titles, Blocks Raised, Blocks	12
	Block Diagram with Perspective	Backgrounds, Borders and Titles, Blocks with Perspective	12
Brainstorming Diagram	Brainstorming Diagram	Backgrounds, Borders and Titles, Brainstorming Shapes, Legend Shapes	18
Business Process	Audit Diagram	Backgrounds, Borders and Titles, Arrow Shapes, Audit Diagram Shape	16
	Cause and Effect Diagram	Backgrounds, Borders and Titles, Arrow Shapes, Cause and Effect Diagram Shapes	16
	EPC Diagram	Backgrounds, Borders and Titles, Arrow Shapes, Callouts, EPC Diagram Shapes	16
	Fault Tree Analysis Diagram	Backgrounds, Borders and Titles, Arrow Shapes, Fault Tree Analysis Shapes	16

Category	Template	Stencils	Chapter
Business Process (continued)	TQM Diagram	Backgrounds, Borders and Titles, Arrow Shapes, TQM Diagram Shapes	16
	Work Flow Diagram	Backgrounds, Borders and Titles, Arrow Shapes, Work Flow Diagram Shapes	16
Charts and Graphs	Charts and Graphs	Backgrounds, Borders and Titles, Charting Shapes	13
	Marketing Charts and Diagrams	Backgrounds, Borders and Titles, Charting Shapes, Marketing Shapes, Marketing Diagrams	13
Flowchart	Basic Flowchart	Backgrounds, Borders and Titles, Arrow Shapes, Basic Flowchart Shapes	15
	Cross Functional Flowchart	Arrow Shapes, Basic Flowchart Shapes, Cross Functional Flowchart Shapes (horizontal/vertical)	15
	Data Flow Diagram (Professional only)	Backgrounds, Borders and Titles, Arrow Shapes, Data Flow Diagram Shapes	15
	IDEF0 Diagram	IDEF0 Diagram Shapes	15
	SDL Diagram	Backgrounds, Borders and Titles, SDL Diagram Shapes	15
Organization Chart	Organization Chart	Backgrounds, Borders and Titles, Organization Chart Shapes	14
Project Schedule	Calendar	Calendar Shapes	17
	Gantt Chart	Backgrounds, Borders and Titles, Gantt Chart Shapes	17
	PERT Chart	Backgrounds, Borders and Titles, PERT Chart Shapes	17
	Timeline	Backgrounds, Borders and Titles, Timeline Shapes	17

Templates for Information Technology

You can use Visio information technology templates to document, design, and model your IT infrastructure and services. Whether you are working on software, hardware, or networks, you can find Visio templates to assist you. Table 41-2 shows the templates for information technology.

If you are using Visio Standard 2003, you can access the Basic Network Diagram only.

Table 41-2			
Information Technology Templates and Stencils			
Category	*Template*	*Stencils*	*Chapter*
Database	Database Model Diagram (Professional only)	Entity Relationship, Object Relational	19
	Express-G (Professional only)	Express-G	19
	ORM Diagram (Professional only)	ORM Diagram	19
Network	Basic Network Diagram	Backgrounds, Borders and Titles, Computers and Monitors, Network and Peripherals	23
	Active Directory (Professional only)	Active Directory Objects, Active Directory Sites and Services, Exchange Objects	23
	Detailed Network Diagram (Professional only)	Borders and Titles, Annotations, Callouts, Computers and Monitors, Network and Peripherals, Detailed Network Diagram, Network Locations, Network Symbols, Servers	23
	LDAP Directory Diagram (Professional only)	LDAP Objects	23

Category	Template	Stencils	Chapter
Network *(continued)*	Novell Directory Services Diagram (Professional only)	NDS Additional Objects, NDS GroupWise, NDS Objects, NDS Partitions, NDS ZenWorks	23
	Rack Diagram (Professional only)	Annotations, Callouts, Free-standing Rack Equipment, Network Room Elements, Rack-Mounted Equipment	23
Software	COM and OLE (Professional only)	COM and OLE	21
	Data Flow Model Diagram (Professional only)	Gane-Sarson	21
	Enterprise Application (Professional only)	Enterprise Application	21
	Jackson (Professional only)	Jackson	21
	Program Structure (Professional only)	Memory Structure, Language Level Shapes	21
	ROOM (Professional only)	ROOM	21
	UML Model Diagram (Professional only)	UML Activity, UML Collaboration, UML Component, UML Deployment, UML Sequence, UML Statechart, UML Static Structure, UML Use Case	20
	Windows XP User Interface (Professional only)	Common Controls, Icons, Toolbars and Menus, Wizards, Windows and Dialogs	21
Web Diagram	Conceptual Web Site (Professional only)	Backgrounds, Borders and Titles, Annotations, Callouts, Web Site Map Shapes, Conceptual Web Site Shapes	22
	Web Site Map (Professional only)	Web Site Map Shapes	22

Templates for Architecture and Engineering

Visio Professional 2003 provides templates for numerous architecture and engineering plans. You can build plans with Visio shapes or convert the contents of existing CAD drawings into Visio shapes. Table 41-3 shows the architecture and engineering templates. A few stencils for architecture and engineering don't open automatically for any templates. You can access these stencils by choosing File ➪ Shapes, choosing the category you want, and then the stencil you want.

If you are using Visio Standard 2003, you can only access the Office Layout, Directional Map, and Directional Map 3D templates.

Table 41-3
Visio Templates and Stencils

Category	Template	Stencils	Chapter(s)
Building Plan	Office Layout	Cubicles, Office Accessories, Office Equipment, Office Furniture, Walls, Doors, and Windows	25, 26
	Electric and Telecom Plan (Professional only)	Annotations, Drawing Tool Shapes, Electrical and Telecom, Walls, Shell and Structure	26
	Floor Plan (Professional only)	Annotations, Building Core, Dimensioning-Architectural, Drawing Tool Shapes, Electrical and Telecom, Points of Interest, Walls, Shell and Structure	25, 26
	Home Plan (Professional only)	Annotations, Appliances, Bath and Kitchen Plan, Building Core, Cabinets, Dimensioning-Architectural, Drawing Tool Shapes, Electrical and Telecom, Furniture, Garden Accessories, Walls, Shell and Structure	25, 26
	HVAC Control Logic Diagram Plan (Professional only)	Annotations, HVAC Controls, HVAC Controls Equipment	26

Category	Template	Stencils	Chapter(s)
Building Plan (continued)	HVAC Plan (Professional only)	Annotations, Building Core, Drawing Tool Shapes, HVAC Ductwork, HVAC Equipment, Registers Grills and Diffusers, Walls, Shell and Structure	26
	Plant Layout Plan (Professional only)	Annotations, Building Core, Dimensioning-Architectural, Drawing Tool Shapes, Electrical and Telecom, Shop Floor-Machines and Equipment, Shop Floor-Storage and Distribution, Vehicles, Walls, Shell and Structure, Warehouse-Shipping And Receiving	25
	Plumbing and Piping Plan (Professional only)	Annotations, Drawing Tool Shapes, Pipes and Valves–Pipes 1, Pipes and Valves–Pipes2, Pipes and Valves–Valves 1, Pipes and Valves–Valves 2, Plumbing, Walls, Shell and Structure	26
	Reflected Ceiling Plan (Professional only)	Annotations, Building Core, Drawing Tool Shapes, Electrical and Telecom, Registers Grills and Diffusers, Walls, Shell and Structure	26
	Security and Access Plan (Professional only)	Annotations, Alarm and Access Control, Initiation and Annunciation, Video Surveillance, Walls, Shell and Structure	26
	Site Plan (Professional only)	Annotations, Dimensioning-Architectural, Drawing Tool Shapes, Garden Accessories, Irrigation, Parking and Roads, Planting, Points of Interest, Site Accessories, Sport Fields and Recreation, Vehicles	26

Table 41-3 *(continued)*

Category	Template	Stencils	Chapter(s)
Electrical Engineering	Basic Electrical Diagram (Professional only)	Fundamental Items, Qualifying Symbols, Semiconductors and Electron Tubes, Switches and Relays, Transmission Paths	29
	Circuits and Logic Diagram (Professional only)	Analog and Digital Logic, Integrated Circuit Components, Terminals and Connectors, Transmission Paths	29
	Industrial Control Systems (Professional only)	Fundamental Items, Rotating Equip and Mech Functions, Switches and Relays, Terminals and Connectors, Transformers and Windings, Transmission Paths	29
	Systems (Professional only)	Composite Assemblies, Maintenance Symbols, Maps and Charts, Switches and Relays, Telecom Switch and Peripheral Equip, Terminals and Connectors, Transformers and Windings, Transmission Paths, VHF-UHF-SHF	29
Map	Directional Map	Landmark Shapes, Metro Shapes, Recreation Shapes, Transportation Shapes, Road Shapes	26
	Directional Map 3D	Directional Map Shapes 3D	26
Mechanical Engineering	Fluid Power Diagram (Professional only)	Annotations, Fluid Power–Equipment, Fluid Power–Valve Assembly, Fluid Power–Valves, Connectors	29
	Part and Assembly Diagram (Professional only)	Annotations, Dimensioning–Engineering, Drawing Tool Shapes, Fasteners 1, Fasteners 2, Geometric Dimensioning and Tolerancing, Springs and Bearings, Title Blocks, Welding Symbols	29

Category	Template	Stencils	Chapter(s)
Process Engineering	Piping and Instrumentation Diagram (Professional only)	Equipment–General, Equipment–Heat Exchangers, Equipment–Pumps, Equipment–Vessels, Instruments, Pipelines, Process Annotations, Valves and Fittings	29
	Process Flow Diagram (Professional only)	Equipment–General, Equipment–Heat Exchangers, Equipment–Pumps, Equipment–Vessels, Instruments, Pipelines, Process Annotations, Valves and Fittings	29

Visio Extras Stencils

Several handy stencils are grouped within the Visio Extras category. Many templates open the following stencils, but you can use them to annotate and embellish any type of drawing:

✦ Annotations

✦ Backgrounds

✦ Borders and Titles

✦ Callouts

✦ Connectors

✦ Custom Line Patterns

✦ Custom Patterns–Scaled

✦ Custom Patterns–Unscaled

✦ Dimensioning–Architectural

✦ Dimensioning–Engineering

✦ Drawing Tool Shapes

✦ Embellishments

✦ Symbols

✦ Title Blocks

Summary

Visio Standard 2003 provides templates for basic diagramming tasks, but you'll want to use Visio Professional if you create specialized diagrams. Visio automatically opens stencils when you use a template to create a drawing, but you can open other stencils if you need different shapes.

✦   ✦   ✦

Index

Continued

Continued

Continued

Continued

Continued

Continued

Continued

Continued

Continued

Continued

Continued

Directory of
Special Libraries and
Information Centers

Directory of
Special Libraries and
Information Centers

8th Edition

A Guide to Special Libraries, Research Libraries,
Information Centers, Archives, and Data Centers Maintained by
Government Agencies, Business, Industry, Newspapers, Educational
Institutions, Nonprofit Organizations, and Societies in the
Fields of Science and Technology, Medicine, Law, Art, Religion,
the Social Sciences, and Humanistic Studies.

BRIGITTE T. DARNAY
Editor

SHARON L. STANTON
Associate Editor

VOLUME 1
Descriptive Listings
A-N

GALE RESEARCH COMPANY • BOOK TOWER • DETROIT, MICHIGAN 48226

Holly M.G. Leighton, John Nimchuk, Catharina Slautterback, Carol Southward, *Assistant Editors*

Henrietta Krohn, *Editorial Assistant*

Carol Blanchard, *Production Supervisor*

Arthur Chartow, *Cover Design*

Lois Lenroot-Ernt, *Contributing Editor*

Directory of Special Libraries and Information Centers
Eighth Edition, in Three Volumes

Volume 1—Directory of Special Libraries and Information Centers
in the United States and Canada

Volume 2—Geographic and Personnel Indexes

Volume 3—New Special Libraries (a periodic supplement to Volume 1)

Computerized photocomposition by
Computer Composition Corporation,
Madision Heights, Michigan

ISBN 0-8103-0357-4
Library of Congress Catalog Card Number 82-6068 (set)
ISSN 0731-633X

Contents

Introduction

The eighth edition of the *Directory of Special Libraries and Information Centers,* like its predecessors, is a comprehensive guide to information centers, archives, and special and research libraries. Facilities maintained by business, nonprofit organizations, educational institutions, governmental agencies, and other types of organizations are included.

For such facilities, the directory is a source of information about subject interests, materials held, journal and newspaper subscriptions, computer-based services offered, network or consortia memberships, staff size, library publications, and more. (A simulated listing, followed by explanations of the various items in an entry, is shown on page ix.)

Reflecting the dramatic growth of specialized information centers in the last twenty years, the eighth edition of the directory lists more than 16,000 entries, up from 10,000 in its first edition.

Preparation of This Edition

Questionnaires were mailed to all libraries listed in the seventh edition. More than eighty percent of those contacted responded to our inquiries. A dagger (†) next to an entry indicates that no reply was received but that the library's existence was verified in current secondary sources. An asterisk (*) denotes a library that failed to answer our three requests for updated information but which the editors are reasonably certain still exists. A small number of facilities was omitted because their librarians asked not to be listed. Nearly 1,000 new libraries have been added since the last edition.

Scope of the Directory

As defined for purposes of this directory, special libraries are libraries built around a special collection limited by subject matter or form; functionally, these libraries (which may also have collections of a general nature) operate in support of a special mission or activity chosen by their sponsoring organizations.

The libraries in this directory are grouped under one of five major categories:

1) Subject divisions, departmental collections, and professional libraries in colleges and universities.

2) Branches, divisions, departments, and special collections in large public library systems, which concentrate exclusively upon one particular subject or group of subjects.

3) Company libraries which operate within the framework of a business or industry producing goods, services, or information for profit.

4) Governmental libraries—including those serving city departments, bureaus, and boards; state legislative reference libraries as well as those in departments, divisions, and ministries of state or province government; and federal libraries within federal departments and agencies, the military establishment, and divisions of the national libraries.

5) Libraries supported by nonprofit organizations, associations, and institutions, including those of scientific, technical, and learned societies; civic, social, and religious organizations; historical societies, bar associations, museums, and hospitals; business and trade associations; and significant private collections available for research use.

These categories also apply to the information centers listed in this directory. Information centers are also characterized by limitations in subject matter, area of research, or field of inquiry. In addition, however, the information center concept usually implies a narrow subject field with greater depth of analysis and control than a special library, and a wide variety of records, including raw data. Information centers also provide more advanced informational services such as evaluation, syntheses, review, and manipulation of both raw data and published material. Greater use is made of subject specialists and less of professional librarians. In some cases, a library unit may be part of an information center.

Certain categories of libraries, occasionally found in other lists of special libraries, were omitted. Among these are collections of purely recreational reading material found in hospitals and prisons. Inclusion in this directory should not be construed as "recognition" of any organization, nor does omission imply lack of importance.

Arrangement of Entries

More than 16,500 libraries and information centers are described in the following pages. United States and Canadian libraries now appear in one alphabetical sequence. With a few exceptions, the ALA filing rules were used as a guide to determine entry order. All libraries associated with a company, institution, agency, or association are grouped under the official name of the parent organization.

Examples of exceptions to a purely alphabetic arrangement follow:

Administration libraries are subarranged geographically; Federal Archives and Records Centers as well as some other governmental information units are listed numerically by region; some state supreme courts are arranged numerically by judicial district. Libraries within one university system with more than one campus are grouped alphabetically by campus. For instance, the University of Wisconsin, Madison libraries file together before libraries situated at the University of Wisconsin, Milwaukee.

More than 6,000 cross references are interfiled with the libraries and information centers to direct the user. They are supplied for libraries with multiple sponsors or memorial names, libraries using bilingual names, libraries of subsidiaries of large corporations, and for many government agencies. Libraries with potentially variant names, e.g., George Washington University which some users might seek under Washington (George) University, are assigned additional cross references to lead the user to the main entry.

Subject Index

The subject index identifies major fields of interest of each reporting unit. While the index is based on terms provided by librarians describing their collections' subject interests, considerable selection and interpretation were exercised by the editors to arrive at standard headings; cross references are used from synonyms and related terms. The *Library of Congress Subject Headings* was used as a professional guide but was not followed in all cases. There are nearly 3,000 subject headings and cross references.

Acknowledgments

The editors are grateful for the cooperation given by the large numbers of conscientious librarians and information specialists who took the time and effort to respond to our questionnaires and who supplied the information which represents the substance of the directory.

Special thanks go to the competent and dedicated staff whose hard work made the publication of the directory possible.

We are most grateful to the production staff of Gale Research Company who helped us to prepare this edition.

New Special Libraries

A periodic supplement to the directory, *New Special Libraries,* provides the user with information between editions.

Comments and Suggestions

We invite comments and suggestions for improvements from the users of the directory. To make this book a more inclusive and better reference tool, we solicit the submission of names and addresses of libraries and information centers not yet listed.

Description of Listings

A simulated listing is shown below. Each numbered item is explained in the descriptive paragraph bearing the same number.

---

(1) ECONOMIC ANALYSTS' RESEARCH LABORATORY, INC. (2) INFORMATION CENTER (3) (Bus-Fin; Soc Sci)

(4) Box 5995
Washington, DC 21112

(5) Phone: (202) 999-1100
(6) Justine Comstock, Dir.

(7) Founded: 1975. **(8) Staff:** Prof 3; Other 5. **(9) Subjects:** Economics; monetary, credit and fiscal policy; political science; international relations. **(10) Special Collections:** Economic Growth Center Collection (focuses on national economies of developing countries, their development, plans, budgets, and statistics; 12,000 volumes, 3000 microforms); U.S. census data, 1900 to present (3000 items); Department of Commerce publications (20,000). **(11) Holdings:** 25,000 books; 10,000 bound periodical volumes; 20,000 reports on microfiche; 1000 staff reports; 500 computer tapes; 100 VF drawers of government documents. **(12) Subscriptions:** 300 journals and other serials; 25 newspapers. **(13) Services:** Interlibrary loans (limited); copying; SDI; center open to public by appointment. **(14) Computerized Information Services:** SDC, NEXIS, full-text or KWIC form; Earlyon (internal database); computerized cataloging, acquisitions, and serials. **(15) Networks/Consortia:** Member of ECONET. **(16) Publications:** EARLI Warning (review of journals received), biweekly—for internal distribution only. **(17) Special Catalogs:** Catalog of staff reports and publications (card). **(18) Special Indexes:** Index to government publications received by the center (computer printout). **(19) Remarks:** The center is located at 6200 Keynes Ave., N.W., Washington, DC 21114. **(20) Formerly:** Economic Researchers, Inc. **(21) Also Known As:** EARL, Inc. **(22)** Formed by the Merger of: Its Professional Library and Government Documents Department. **(23) Staff:** A.A. Smith, Supv. Libn.; R.J. Johnson, Ref. Libn.; Dolly Brown, Online Supv.

---

(1) NAME OF ORGANIZATION. Name of parent organization, society, or agency which sponsors or is served by the library or information center. Independent libraries and centers and those commonly known by a distinctive name are entered directly under the library's name. Cross-references are included in the body of the work for those entries to which there may be multiple approaches.

(2) NAME OF LIBRARY OR INFORMATION CENTER. Descriptive and memorial names are given as reported. Otherwise the appropriate generic term is used, e.g., library, archives, collection, information center. In many cases the generic term has been supplied by the editors and the inclusion of the term library does not indicate the existence of a formal library.

(3) PRINCIPAL SUBJECT KEYWORD. The major subject or type of material represented by the collection as a whole. When there are two areas of equal importance both are indicated. When collections have more than three major subjects or are general in scope no keyword is used. The keywords offer a classification by broad subject category only; each library's more specialized interests are mentioned in the body of each listing. Both the general keywords and specialized interests are used as entry words in the subject index. The following keywords are employed in the eighth edition.

Agri	- agriculture	Law	- law
Area-Ethnic	- area ethnic	Med	- medicine
Art	- art	Mil	- military
Aud-Vis	- audio visual	Mus	- mus
Bus-Fin	- business and finance	Pict	- picture
Educ	- education	Plan	- planning
Energy	- energy	Publ	- publishing
Env-Cons	- environment and conservation	Rare Book	- rare book
		Rec	- rec
Food-Bev	- food sciences and beverage	Rel-Theol	- religion and theology
Geog-Map	- geography-map	Sci-Tech	- science - technology
Hist	- history	Soc Sci	- social sciences
Hum	- humanities	Theater	- theater
Info Sci	- information science	Trans	- transportation

(4) MAILING ADDRESS. The permanent mailing address of library or center. In some instances this will differ from the headquarters address of the parent organization and the physical location of the library. When there is a separate location address, it is given under "Remarks" (see item 19).

(5) TELEPHONE NUMBER. Area code and telephone number. When more than one telephone number is supplied, alternate ones are listed under "Remarks" (see item 19). Extensions are not provided, since they are subject to frequent change.

(6) HEAD OF LIBRARY OR INFORMATION CENTER. Name and title of the person directly in charge of library or information center. Where no librarian has been identified or where there is no position as such, the name of the administrative officer may be given.

(7) FOUNDING DATE. Year when library or information center was established, either formally or informally.

(8) NUMBER OF STAFF. Number of individuals directly engaged in the operation of the library or center on a regular basis. Part-time employees are included but student assistants and other occasional help generally are not. Professional staff includes librarians, bibliographers, subject specialists, information specialists, and other related specialists. Semi-professionals and clerical assistants are grouped in the second category. Distinction between professional and non-professional staff was made by the respondents. Where the differentiation was not made, the total number of staff is listed.

(9) SUBJECTS. Terms specifically designating the most important subjects represented in the collection as a whole. This section of the listing, obtained from submitted questionnaires, was ordinarily used as the basis of the subject index.

(10) SPECIAL COLLECTIONS. Separately grouped collections of unusual or notable interest that are identifiable either by subject, form, name of donor or distinctive name.

(11) HOLDINGS. Quantitative data concerning collections. Numbers of books, bound periodical volumes, pamphlets, and technical reports are given separately when supplied by respondents. When the term "volumes" is used, it generally indicates bound units or collections of bound and unbound items which have been accessioned and cataloged. Unbound material is indicated either by unit count, number of vertical file drawers, linear shelf feet or cubic storage space. Estimates rather than exact statistics have frequently been given. Holdings of non-book materials are also indicated whenever of significant size and importance.

(12) SUBSCRIPTIONS. Figures generally represent the number of journal and serial titles, not separate copies, received by paid subscription, gift, and exchange. Newspaper subscriptions are given separately when numerically significant.

(13) SERVICES. Most special libraries provide bibliographic or reference services primarily for their own organizations. For these, an appropriate statement of service limitations is given. When the

library or center provides some form of access to outside clientele, it is so indicated. When services offered are of an unusual nature they are noted and indication is given whether such services are for internal or external use. Entries for libraries which honor interlibrary loan requests include the appropriate information, as do those for libraries with copying or reproducing facilities. Normally, copying services to outside users are on a fee basis. Some libraries now charge for interlibrary loans and this information is included when supplied by respondent.

(14)   COMPUTERIZED INFORMATION SERVICES. This item indicates a special library's access to online information systems, such as MEDLINE, SDC or LEXIS, etc. Also included here are computer applications to other library processes including cataloging, acquisitions, serials, and circulation.

(15)   NETWORKS/CONSORTIA. Here is listed the special library's membership in formal or informal groups involved in cooperative sharing on the local, regional, or national level. Acronyms are used for networks and consortia which are familiar to the library profession (e.g., OCLC). Appendix A lists geographically the names, acronyms, and addresses of the networks and consortia reported by the special libraries in this directory. An alphabetical index follows.

(16)   PUBLICATIONS. Periodical, serial, and other publications issued or prepared by the library or information center are included. Title, frequency, and basis of distribution are indicated when known.

(17)   SPECIAL CATALOGS. Unique and unusual catalogs which are locally prepared and maintained, including card, book, computer printout, and other forms.

(18)   SPECIAL INDEXES. Unique and unusual catalogs which are locally prepared and maintained.

(19)   REMARKS. Additional information not adaptable to the standard form of entry, including historical data, explanatory notes, and descriptions of unusual activities. Corporate affiliations are often noted here. Also included is the address of a special library's location when it differs from the mailing address in item 4.

(20)   FORMERLY. Former names and/or locations of a special library or its parent organization when there is a recent change of names under which they were formerly listed. Cross-references are generally supplied from the former names.

(21)   ALSO KNOWN AS. Variant names of a special library or its parent organization. Cross-references from these are provided when needed.

(22)   MERGED LIBRARIES. When the special library has been recently created by the merger of two or more separate libraries previously listed separately, the names of the components are identified here. Mergers of parent organizations which affect the special library are also noted here.

(23)   STAFF NAMES. Names and titles of professional and supervisory personnel in the special library or information center. Only principal members of the professional staff are listed for large operations.

Abbreviations

AB	— Alberta		Clghse.	— Clearinghouse
Acq.	— Acquisitions		CO	— Colorado
Act.	— Acting		Co.	— Company
Adm.	— Administration, Administrative, Administrator		Coll.	— Collection, College
			COM	— Computer Output Microfilm
Adv.	— Advisor		Comm.	— Committee
Aff.	— Affairs		Commn.	— Commission
Agri.	— Agriculture		Commnr.	— Commissioner
AK	— Alaska		Commun.	— Communications
AL	— Alabama		Comp.	— Computer, Computing
Amer.	— American		Cons.	— Consultant, Conservation, Conservator
Anl.	— Analysis, Analyst		CONSER	— Conservation of Serials
APO	— Army Post Office		Coop.	— Cooperative
AR	— Arkansas		Coord.	— Coordinator
Arch.	— Architect, Architecture		Corp.	— Corporate, Corporation
Archeo.	— Archeologist, Archeology		Coun.	— Council
Archv.	— Archives, Archivist		Couns.	— Counsel
AS	— American Samoa		CRL	— Center for Research Libraries
Assn.	— Association		CT	— Connecticut
Assoc.	— Associate		Ct.	— Court
Asst.	— Assistant		Ctr.	— Center
ASTED	— Association pour l'Avancement des Sciences et des Techniques de la Documentation		Ctrl.	— Central
			CUNY	— City University of New York
			Cur.	— Curator
Att.	— Attorney		Curric.	— Curriculum
Aud.	— Audio		Cus.	— Custodian
AV	— Audiovisual		DC	— District of Columbia
Ave.	— Avenue		DE	— Delaware
AZ	— Arizona		Dept.	— Department
BADADUQ	— Banque de Donnes a Acces Direct de l'Universite du Quebec		Dev.	— Development
			Dir.	— Director
BC	— British Columbia		Distr.	— Distribution
Bd.	— Board		Div.	— Division, Divisional
Bev.	— Beverages		DOBIS	— Dortmunder Bibliothekssystem
Bibliog.	— Bibliographical, Bibliographer		Doc.	— Document, Documentation
Biomed.	— Biomedical		DOE	— U.S. Department of Energy
Bk.	— Book		DOE/RECON	— U.S. Department of Energy Online Information Retrieval System
Bldg.	— Building			
Blvd.	— Boulevard		Dp.	— Deputy
Br.	— Branch		Dr.	— Drive
Bro.	— Brother		DTIC	— Defense Technical Information Center
BRS	— Bibliographic Retrieval Services, Inc.		E.	— East
Bur.	— Bureau		Econ.	— Economics
Bus.	— Business		Ed.	— Editor, Editorial
CA	— California		Educ.	— Education
CALICO	— Columbus Area Library and Information Council of Ohio		Engr.	— Engineer, Engineering
			Env.	— Environment, Environmental
CALINET	— California Library Network		ERIC	— Educational Resources Information Center
CAPCON	— Capitol Consortium Network		Exch.	— Exchange
Cart.	— Cartographic, Cartography		Exec.	— Executive
Cat.	— Catalog(er), Cataloging		Ext.	— Extension
CCLC	— Cooperative College Library Center		FAUL	— Five Associated University Libraries
Ch.	— Child, Children		Fed.	— Federal, Federation
Chem.	— Chemical, Chemist, Chemistry		FEDLINK	— Federal Library and Information Network
Chf.	— Chief		Fin.	— Finance
Chm.	— Chairman		FL	— Florida
CIN	— Cooperative Information Network		Fl.	— Floor
Circ.	— Circulation		Fld.	— Field
Ck.	— Clerk		Found.	— Foundation
CLASS	— California Library Authority for Systems and Services		Fr.	— Father
			Ft.	— Fort
CLENE, Inc.	— Continuing Library Education Network and Exchange		Fwy.	— Freeway
			GA	— Georgia

Gen.	— General		Musm.	— Museum
Geog.	— Geographer, Geography		Myth.	— Mythology
Govt.	— Government		N.	— North
GU	— Guam		NASA	— National Aeronautics and Space Administration
Hd.	— Head		Natl.	— National
HI	— Hawaii		NB	— New Brunswick
Hist.	— Historian, History		NC	— North Carolina
Hon.	— Honorable, Honorary		ND	— North Dakota
Hosp.	— Hospital		NE	— Nebraska
HQ	— Headquarters		NELINET	— New England Library Information Network
Hum.	— Humanities		NEOMAL	— Northeastern Ohio Major Academic Libraries
Hwy.	— Highway		NF	— Newfoundland
IA	— Iowa		NH	— New Hampshire
ID	— Idaho		NJ	— New Jersey
IL	— Illinois		NLM	— National Library of Medicine
ILL	— Interlibrary Loan		NM	— New Mexico
ILLINET	— Illinois Library & Information Network		No.	— Number
Illus.	— Illustration, Illustrative, Illustrator		NS	— Nova Scotia
IN	— Indiana		NT	— Northwest Territories
INCOLSA	— Indiana Cooperative Library Services Authority		NTIS	— National Technical Information Service
Indiv.	— Individual		NV	— Nevada
Info.	— Information, Informational		NY	— New York
Inst.	— Institute, Institutional		OCLC	— Online Computer Library Center
Instr.	— Instruction, Instructional, Instructor		Off.	— Office, Officer
Int.	— Internal		OH	— Ohio
Interp.	— Interpreter, Interpretive, Interpretation		OHIONET	— Ohio Library Network
Intl.	— International		OK	— Oklahoma
Jnl.	— Journal		ON	— Ontario
Jr.	— Junior		Oper.	— Operator, Operations
JURIS	— Justice, Retrieval & Inquiry System		OR	— Oregon
Kpr.	— Keeper		PA	— Pennsylvania
KS	— Kansas		PALINET	— Pennsylvania Area Library Network
KWIC	— Keyword in Context		PE	— Prince Edward Island
KWOC	— Keyword out of Context		Per.	— Periodicals
KY	— Kentucky		Perf.	— Perform, Performing
LA	— Louisiana		PHILSOM	— Periodical Holdings in Libraries of Schools of Medicine
Lab.	— Laboratory		Photodup.	— Photoduplication
Lang.	— Language		PHUY	— Princeton, Harvard, Union, and Yale Network
Lat.	— Latin		Pict.	— Picture
LATCH	— Literature Attached to the Chart (Medical)		Pk.	— Park
LCDR	— Lieutenant Commander		Pkwy.	— Parkway
Ldr.	— Leader		Pl.	— Place
Leg.	— Legislative		Plan.	— Planning
Lib., Libs.	— Library, Libraries		PQ	— Quebec
Libn.	— Librarian		P.R.	— Public Relations
Lit.	— Literature		PR	— Puerto Rico
Ln.	— Lane		Pres.	— President
LRC	— Learning Resources Center		Prin.	— Principal
Lrng. Rsrcs.	— Learning Resources		Proc.	— Process, Processing, Processor
MA	— Massachusetts		Prod.	— Production
Mag.	— Magazine		Prof.	— Professional, Professor
MB	— Manitoba		Prog.	— Program, Programmer
MD	— Maryland		Proj.	— Project
ME	— Maine		Prov.	— Provincial
Med.	— Medical, Medicine		Psych.	— Psychology
METRO	— New York Metropolitan Reference & Research Library Agency		Pub.	— Public
Mfg.	— Manufacturer, Manufacturing		Publ.	— Published, Publisher, Publishing
Mgr.	— Manager		Pubn.	— Publication
Mgt.	— Management		R&D	— Research and Development
MI	— Michigan		Rd.	— Reader, Road
MIDLNET	— Midwest Regional Library Network		Rec.	— Records, Recreation
Mil.	— Military		Ref.	— Reference
MINITEX	— Minnesota Interlibrary Telecommunications Exchange		Rel.	— Relations, Religion, Religious
Mktg.	— Marketing		Rep.	— Representative
MN	— Minnesota		Res.	— Research, Researcher
Mng.	— Managing		Ret.	— Retrieval
MO	— Missouri		Rev.	— Reverend
MS	— Mississippi		RI	— Rhode Island
Mss.	— Manuscripts		RIBLIN	— Reseau Informatise de Bibliotheques Library Information Networks
MT	— Montana		RLG	— Research Libraries Group, Inc.
Mtls.	— Materials			
Mus.	— Music			

RLIN	— Research Libraries Information Network	Techn.	— Technician
Rm.	— Room	Theol.	— Theology
Rpt.	— Report	TN	— Tennessee
Rsrcs.	— Resources	Tpke.	— Turnpike
Rte.	— Route	TRALINET	— U.S. Army Training & Doctrine Command Library & Information Network
S.	— South		
SC	— South Carolina	Trans.	— Transportation
Sch.	— School	Transl.	— Translation, Translator
Sci.	— Science, Sciences, Scientist	Treas.	— Treasurer
SD	— South Dakota	Trng.	— Training
SDC	— System Development Corporation	TX	— Texas
SDI	— Selective Dissemination of Information	U.N.	— United Nations
Sec.	— Secretary	Univ.	— University
Sect.	— Section	Unpubl.	— Unpublished
Ser.	— Serials	U.S.	— United States
Serv.	— Services	UT	— Utah
SK	— Saskatchewan	UTLAS Inc.	— University of Toronto Library Automation Systems
SLA	— Special Libraries Association		
Soc.	— Social, Society	VA	— Virginia
SOLINET	— Southeastern Library Network	VALNET	— Veterans Administration Library Network
Spec.	— Special, Specialist, Specialized	VI	— Virgin Islands
Sq.	— Square	VILINET	— Virgin Islands Library & Information Network
Sr.	— Senior, Sister		
St.	— Saint, Street	Vis.	— Visual
Sta.	— Station	Vols.	— Volumes
Stat.	— Statistics	V.P.	— Vice President
Ste.	— Sainte	VT	— Vermont
Sts.	— Saints, Streets	W.	— West
Stud.	— Students, Studies, Study	WA	— Washington
SUNY	— State University of New York	WEBNET	— Western Pennsylvania Buhl Network
Sup.	— Support	WELEXACOL	— Wellesley-Lexington Area Cooperating Libraries
Supt.	— Superintendent		
Supv.	— Supervising, Supervisor	WI	— Wisconsin
Sys.	— Systems	WICHE	— Western Interstate Commission for Higher Education
TALINET	— Telefax Library Information Network		
TALON	— South Central Regional Medical Library Program (Texas, Arkansas, Louisiana, Oklahoma, New Mexico)	WLN	— Washington Library Network
		WV	— West Virginia
		WY	— Wyoming
Tchg.	— Teaching	YT	— Yukon Territory
Tech.	— Technical, Technology		

Directory of
Special Libraries and
Information Centers

A

A.B. DICK COMPANY
See: Dick (A.B.) Company

A.E.M.C. ALUMNI LIBRARY
See: Einstein (Albert) Medical Center - School of Nursing Library

AAA
See: American Automobile Association

AAAA CONTACT CENTER
See: Contact, Inc.

★1★
AACA LIBRARY & RESEARCH CENTER, INC. (Rec)
501 W. Governor Rd.
Box 417　　　　　Phone: (717) 534-1910
Hershey, PA 17033　　　　　Kim M. Miller, Libn.
Founded: 1972. **Staff:** Prof 1. **Subjects:** Automobiles, trucks, motorcycles, recreational vehicles. **Holdings:** 5200 books; 700 unbound periodical volumes; 225 shop manuals; 75 VF drawers of advertisements and sales literature; 10 volumes on exterior color information. **Subscriptions:** 165 journals and other serials. **Services:** Copying; library open to AACA members; to others by special permission of librarian only. **Special Catalogs:** Automobile make index (card). **Formerly:** Antique Automobile Club of America - AACA Automobile Reference Collection.

★2★
AAI CORPORATION - TECHNICAL LIBRARY (Sci-Tech; Energy)
Box 6767　　　　　Phone: (301) 628-3193
Baltimore, MD 21204　　　　　Joyce F. Peacock, Libn.
Founded: 1957. **Staff:** Prof 1. **Subjects:** Electronics, training and simulation; automatic test equipment; weapons and munitions; ordnance vehicles; industrial, aviation and marine materials handling equipment; hydraulic systems; solar energy systems. **Holdings:** 2900 books; 40 bound periodical volumes; 4 VF drawers; NASA microfiche; 10,000 reports. **Subscriptions:** 100 journals and other serials. **Services:** Interlibrary loans; copying; library open to industrial research and development librarians. **Remarks:** Library is located at Industry Lane, Cockeysville, MD 21030.

AARON (A.H.) MEDICAL LIBRARY
See: Buffalo General Hospital, Inc. - A.H. Aaron Medical Library

★3★
AB BOOKMAN PUBLICATIONS, INC. - LIBRARY (Publ)†
Box AB　　　　　Phone: (201) 772-0020
Clifton, NJ 07015　　　　　Ellen Chernofsky, Libn.
Founded: 1948. **Staff:** Prof 1. **Subjects:** Bibliography, book trade history, printing history, book production arts, literary biography, censorship. **Holdings:** 5500 books; 1200 bound periodical volumes. **Subscriptions:** 45 journals and other serials. **Services:** Library open to qualified researchers by written request only. **Remarks:** Publishes AB Bookman's Weekly.

★4★
ABAM ENGINEERS, INC. - TECHNICAL LIBRARY (Sci-Tech)
500 S. 336th, Suite 200
Federal Way　　　　　Phone: (206) 952-6100
Tacoma, WA 98003　　　　　Patricia Williams, Tech.Libn.
Founded: 1976. **Staff:** Prof 1. **Subjects:** Engineering. **Holdings:** 700 books; 1300 other cataloged items. **Subscriptions:** 124 journals and other serials. **Services:** Interlibrary loans; library not open to public.

ABBELL (Maxwell) LIBRARY
See: North Suburban Synagogue Beth El - Maxwell Abbell Library

★5★
ABBEY OF REGINA LAUDIS, ORDER OF ST. BENEDICT - LIBRARY (Rel-Theol)
　　　　　Phone: (203) 266-7727
Bethlehem, CT 06751　　　　　Mother Agnes, O.S.B., Libn.
Founded: 1947. **Staff:** Prof 1; Other 1. **Subjects:** Patrology, scripture, theology, ecclesiastical history, social sciences, art, musicology, New England history, natural sciences, literature. **Special Collections:** Patristic writings through the Middle Ages; Newman's writings; medieval mystics. **Holdings:** 21,000 books; 100 bound periodical volumes; 100 manuscripts on monasticism; 1600 pamphlets; 50 reels of microfilm of medieval and monastic history; 500 reels of magnetic tape of theology; 3000 slides of New England themes. **Subscriptions:** 34 journals and other serials; 8 newspapers. **Services:** Interlibrary loans; copying; collection available to serious researchers with prior permission. **Networks/Consortia:** Member of Region One Cooperating Libraries Service Unit for Northwestern Connecticut.

★6★
ABBOTT LABORATORIES - ABBOTT INFORMATION SERVICES (Sci-Tech)†
1400 Sheridan Rd.　　　　　Phone: (312) 688-2513
North Chicago, IL 60064　　　　　Dr. R.G. Wiegand
Founded: 1888. **Staff:** Prof 11; Other 14. **Subjects:** Chemistry, pharmacology, medicine, pharmacy, microbiology. **Special Collections:** Abbott archives. **Holdings:** 30,000 volumes. **Subscriptions:** 1000 journals and other serials. **Services:** Interlibrary loans; use of library may be requested. **Publications:** Science Information Index, weekly; Abbott Abstracts, weekly; New Books, biweekly; Abbott Authors, annual. **Remarks:** Also maintains Business Information Services and Legal-Tax Library.

★7★
ABBOTT LABORATORIES, LTD. - COMPANY LIBRARY (Sci-Tech; Med)
Sta. A, P.O. Box 6150　　　　　Phone: (514) 341-6880
Montreal, PQ, Canada H3C 3K6　　　　　Genevieve Heroux, Lib.Techn.
Founded: 1944. **Staff:** Prof 1. **Subjects:** Chemistry, medicine, nutrition, pharmacology. **Holdings:** 1500 books and bound periodical volumes. **Subscriptions:** 140 journals and other serials. **Services:** Interlibrary loans; copying; library not open to public.

★8★
ABBOTT-NORTHWESTERN HOSPITAL CORPORATION - HEALTH SCIENCES RESOURCE CENTER (Med)
800 E. 28th St.　　　　　Phone: (612) 874-4312
Minneapolis, MN 55407　　　　　Donna Johnson, Resource Ctr.Dir.
Founded: 1970. **Staff:** Prof 5; Other 5. **Subjects:** Medicine, nursing. **Holdings:** 4500 books; 15,000 bound periodical volumes; 2 VF drawers of clippings and pamphlets; 140 filmstrips/records; 250 videotapes. **Subscriptions:** 750 journals and other serials. **Services:** Interlibrary loans; copying; SDI; library open to public for reference use only with librarian's permission. **Computerized Information Services:** BRS, NLM. **Networks/Consortia:** Member of Twin Cities Biomedical Consortium (TCBC). **Remarks:** Includes some of the holdings of the Sister Kenny Institute. **Staff:** Guntis Kupers, AV Spec.; Marianne Kelley, Ref.Libn.; Sharon Charles, Circuit Libn.; Howard Epstein, Mgr., Health Info.

★9★
ABBY ALDRICH ROCKEFELLER FOLK ART CENTER - LIBRARY (Art)
307 S. England St.
Drawer C　　　　　Phone: (804) 229-1000
Williamsburg, VA 23185　　　　　Anne Watkins, Registrar/Libn.
Founded: 1939. **Staff:** 1. **Subjects:** Folk art. **Holdings:** 2500 volumes; manuscripts and photographs. **Services:** Copying; library open to public by appointment.

ABC
See: American Broadcasting Companies, Inc.

★10★
ABCOR, INC. - LIBRARY (Sci-Tech; Env-Cons)†
850 Main St.　　　　　Phone: (617) 657-4250
Wilmington, MA 01887　　　　　Kathleen Morton, Libn.
Staff: Prof 1; Other 1. **Subjects:** Chemical engineering, polymer science, water pollution, biochemical technology. **Holdings:** 2500 books; 2000 government documents. **Subscriptions:** 100 journals and other serials. **Services:** Interlibrary loans; copying; SDI; library open to public with restrictions. **Computerized Information Services:** DIALOG, SDC. **Publications:** Library Acquisitions, irregular - for internal distribution only.

★11★
ABELL (A.S.) PUBLISHING COMPANY INC. - BALTIMORE SUNPAPERS - LIBRARY (Publ)
501 N. Calvert　　　　　Phone: (301) 332-6253
Baltimore, MD 21202　　　　　Clement G. Vitek, Chf.Libn.
Founded: 1906. **Staff:** Prof 3; Other 17. **Subjects:** General and current topics, Marylandia, Baltimoriana. **Special Collections:** Reports and studies dealing with Maryland and city of Baltimore. **Holdings:** 5002 books; 110 telephone books; 20 million newspaper clippings (18 million in 350,000 microfilm jackets); 1 million glossy photographs; 3082 reels of microfilmed newspapers; 29 reels of microfilm; 10 VF cabinets; pamphlets; maps; charts.

Subscriptions: 50 journals and other serials. Services: Interlibrary loans; copying (limited); library open to public with restrictions. Special Indexes: Sunpapers card index, 1891-1951 (174 reels of microfilm). Remarks: Library serves staff of The Sun, The Evening Sun, The Sunday Sun, The Howard Sun and The Arundel Sun. Staff: Mary Agnes Schultz, Asst.Libn.; Yeon Jean Hugh, Chf. Indexer.

★12★
ABELSON-FRANKEL - RESEARCH LIBRARY (Bus-Fin)
111 E. Wacker Dr.   Phone: (312) 938-1900
Chicago, IL 60601   Lynn Fitzgerald, Res.Libn.
Staff: Prof 1; Other 1. Subjects: Sales promotion, advertising, fast food, consumer packaging, consumer durables. Holdings: 150 books; 4 VF drawers of subject files; 500 primary research reports. Subscriptions: 103 journals and other serials. Services: Library not open to public. Computerized Information Services: DIALOG, New York Times Information Service.

ABERCROMBIE (Lelia) HISTORICAL LIBRARY
See: Pensacola Historical Society - Lelia Abercrombie Historical Library

ABERDEEN PROVING GROUND
See: U.S. Army - Chemical Systems Laboratory; U.S. Army Medical Research Institute of Chemical Defense; U.S. Army - Environmental Hygiene Agency; U.S. Army Ordnance Center & School

ABERNATHY SALMON CULTURAL DEVELOPMENT CENTER
See: U.S. Fish & Wildlife Service

★13★
ABILENE REPORTER-NEWS - LIBRARY (Publ)†
Box 30   Phone: (915) 673-4271
Abilene, TX 79604   Anne Bell, Libn.
Founded: 1940. Staff: Prof 2; Other 2. Subjects: Newspaper reference material. Holdings: Microfilm. Services: Library open to public with restrictions.

★14★
ABILENE STATE SCHOOL - SPECIAL LIBRARY (Soc Sci)
Box 451   Phone: (915) 692-4053
Abilene, TX 79604   Peggy G. Allen, Libn.
Founded: 1971. Staff: Prof 1. Subjects: Mental retardation, psychology, education, behavior modification, social services, special education and child development. Holdings: 2869 books; 322 bound periodical volumes; 300 pamphlets; 6 VF drawers of dissertations, reports and government documents. Subscriptions: 28 journals and other serials. Services: Interlibrary loans; copying; library open to public with restrictions. Staff: William N. Fryer, Chf., Psych.Serv.

ABINGTON LIBRARY SOCIETY
See: Jenkintown Library

★15★
ABINGTON MEMORIAL HOSPITAL - WILMER MEMORIAL MEDICAL LIBRARY (Med)
    Phone: (215) 885-4000
Abington, PA 19001   Marion C. Chayes, Libn.
Staff: Prof 1. Subjects: Medicine, surgery. Holdings: 2000 books; 5000 bound periodical volumes; 568 tapes; 30 self-learning programs. Subscriptions: 200 journals and other serials. Services: Interlibrary loans; copying; library open to public by appointment only. Networks/Consortia: Member of Mideastern Regional Medical Library Service (MERMLS); Delaware Valley Information Consortium (DEVIC).

★16★
ABITIBI-PRICE INC. - RESEARCH CENTRE LIBRARY (Sci-Tech)
Sheridan Park   Phone: (416) 822-4770
Mississauga, ON, Canada L5K 1A9   Joy A. Armstrong, Libn.
Founded: 1947. Staff: Prof 2. Subjects: Pulp, paper, board, graphic arts. Holdings: 4800 books; 2475 bound periodical volumes; 48 VF drawers. Subscriptions: 165 journals and other serials. Services: Interlibrary loans; copying; library open to other libraries only. Computerized Information Services: SDC, DIALOG, INFOLINE, PATSEARCH. Staff: May L. Isaac, Asst.Libn.

ABNEY (James Madison) LIBRARY
See: Tompkins (D.A.) Memorial Library

★17★
ABRAHAM BALDWIN AGRICULTURAL COLLEGE - LIBRARY (Agri)
ABAC Station   Phone: (912) 386-3223
Tifton, GA 31794   Mary Emma Henderson, Libn.
Founded: 1933. Staff: Prof 4; Other 6. Subjects: Agriculture, home economics, business, computer science, liberal arts. Holdings: 56,000 books; 1800 bound periodical volumes. Subscriptions: 788 journals and other serials; 12 newspapers. Services: Interlibrary loans; copying; library open to public on a limited basis. Computerized Information Services: Computerized cataloging. Networks/Consortia: Member of OCLC through SOLINET; Georgia Library Information Network; South Georgia Associated Libraries. Staff: Harriett E. Mayo, Asst.Libn.; Brenda A. Sellers, Asst.Libn.; Mark A. Alley, Instr. Media Spec.

★18★
ABT ASSOCIATES INC. - LIBRARY (Soc Sci)
55 Wheeler St.   Phone: (617) 492-7100
Cambridge, MA 02138   Nancy Dvorin, Libn.
Founded: 1974. Staff: Prof 1; Other 1. Subjects: Social sciences. Special Collections: Company reports. Holdings: 6000 books. Subscriptions: 250 journals and other serials; 8 newspapers. Services: Interlibrary loans; copying; library open to public with restrictions. Computerized Information Services: DIALOG, SDC, New York Times Information Service, MEDLARS.

★19★
ABUNDANT LIFE SEED FOUNDATION - LIBRARY (Agri)
1029 Lawrence   Phone: (206) 385-5660
Port Townsend, WA 98368   Forest Roth-Shomer, Dir.
Founded: 1977. Staff: 1. Subjects: Gardening, seed growing, native plants. Special Collections: British Columbia Department of Agriculture - Seed Production Series (15 in series). Holdings: 100 books; 14 bound periodical volumes. Subscriptions: 24 journals and other serials; 8 newspapers. Services: Library open to public for reference use only.

AC SPARK PLUG DIVISION
See: General Motors Corporation

★20★
ACACIA MUTUAL LIFE INSURANCE COMPANY - LIBRARY (Bus-Fin)
51 Louisiana Ave., N.W.   Phone: (202) 628-4506
Washington, DC 20001   Dorothy Bockler, Libn.
Staff: 3. Subjects: Life insurance. Holdings: 6500 books; 1000 pamphlets. Subscriptions: 120 journals and other serials. Services: Library not open to public.

★21★
ACADEMY OF AERONAUTICS - LIBRARY (Sci-Tech)
LaGuardia Airport Sta.   Phone: (212) 429-6600
Flushing, NY 11371   JoAnn Jayne, Hd.Libn.
Founded: 1955. Staff: Prof 3; Other 1. Subjects: Aeronautics, engineering, physical science, mathematics. Special Collections: NASA Reports, SAE Reports, Aircraft Maintenance Manuals (24,991). Holdings: 28,102 books; 1787 bound periodical volumes; 57,194 microforms; 456 AV materials. Subscriptions: 381 journals and other serials; 12 newspapers. Services: Interlibrary loans; copying; library open to public by appointment. Staff: Hilary Gold, Cat./Asst.Libn.; William Assad, Govt.Doc.Libn.

★22★
ACADEMY OF AMERICAN FRANCISCAN HISTORY - LIBRARY (Hist)
Box 34440   Phone: (301) 365-1763
Washington, DC 20034   Jesse Joseph Torres, Libn.
Founded: 1944. Staff: Prof 1. Subjects: Latin American history and culture, history of the Catholic Church in Latin America, history of the Franciscan Order in Latin America. Special Collections: Mary Coleman Powell Collection (700 volumes on American Southwest history). Holdings: 11,360 books; 1656 bound periodical volumes; 150 reels of microfilm; 130 volumes of bound microprints. Subscriptions: 60 journals and other serials. Services: Library open to public by arrangement. Publications: The Americas: A Quarterly Review of Inter-American Cultural History - by subscription. Special Catalogs: Catalog of Franciscan-related documents in the Archives of the Indies at Seville (Spain) and in the Archivo Historico Nacional de Mejico; catalog of academy library holdings in multilith. Remarks: "The Academy maintains a close relationship with institutions of higher learning in Spain, Portugal, and Latin America...it seeks to convey a better understanding of the colonial background of the South and West which were once part of the Spanish Empire.... It seeks to make available the letters and other writings of the Franciscan missionaries of pioneer days." Library is located at 9901 Carmelita Dr., Potomac, MD 20854.

★23★
ACADEMY FOR EDUCATIONAL DEVELOPMENT, INC. - EDUCATIONAL FACILITIES LABORATORIES DIVISION - LIBRARY (Educ; Art)
680 Fifth Ave.   Phone: (212) 397-0040
New York, NY 10019   S. De Camp, Prog.Dir.
Subjects: Educational and community facilities, institutional planning, design and construction, energy management. **Holdings:** Figures not available for books; technical reports; photographs and journals. **Services:** Library not open to public. **Publications:** List of publications - available on request.

ACADEMY OF FOOD MARKETING
See: St. Joseph's University

ACADEMY HALL MUSEUM
See: Rocky Hill Historical Society

ACADEMY OF HEALTH SCIENCES
See: U.S. Army - Academy of Health Sciences

ACADEMY FOR INTERSCIENCE METHODOLOGIES
See: Merriam Center Library

★24★
ACADEMY OF MEDICINE OF THE COUNTY OF QUEENS, INC. - CARL M. BOETTIGER MEMORIAL LIBRARY (Med)†
112-25 Queens Blvd., 4th Fl.   Phone: (212) 268-7300
Forest Hills, NY 11375   Ella M. Abney, Libn.
Staff: Prof 2. **Subjects:** Medicine and related subjects. **Holdings:** 16,000 books; 23,929 bound periodical volumes; 3 VF drawers. **Subscriptions:** 465 journals and other serials. **Services:** Interlibrary loans; copying; reference searches for members; library open to students and researchers. **Staff:** Vivian Moore, Lib.Asst.

★25★
ACADEMY OF MEDICINE, TORONTO - WILLIAM BOYD LIBRARY (Med)
288 Bloor St., W.   Phone: (416) 964-7088
Toronto, ON, Canada M5S 1V8   Sheila Swanson, Libn.
Staff: Prof 3; Other 2. **Subjects:** Clinical medicine; history of medicine. **Special Collections:** T.G.H. Drake Collection (pediatrics); Klotz Collection (pathology); W.S. Stanbury Collection (hematology); J.W. Graham Collection (rheumatology). **Holdings:** 40,000 books; 40,000 bound periodical volumes; 10,000 pamphlets, reports and reprints. **Subscriptions:** 600 journals and other serials. **Services:** Interlibrary loans; copying; special services to hospitals without adequate collections; library open to public for reference use only.

★26★
ACADEMY OF MOTION PICTURE ARTS AND SCIENCES - MARGARET HERRICK LIBRARY (Theater)
8949 Wilshire Blvd.   Phone: (213) 278-4313
Beverly Hills, CA 90211   Linda H. Mehr, Lib.Adm.
Founded: 1927. **Staff:** Prof 5; Other 21. **Subjects:** Motion picture history, biography and production. **Special Collections:** George Stevens; John Huston; George Cukor; Mack Sennett; William Selig; Mary Pickford; Pete Smith; Jules White; U.S. and British patents; Scrapbook Collection (Richard Barthelmess, Jean Hersholt, Louella Parsons, Hedda Hopper, Irene, Henry Grace); Lux Radio Theatre scripts; Paramount Collection (scripts; stills); RKO Collection (stills); MGM Collection (stills); Cecil B. DeMille Collection (stills); Thomas Ince Collection (stills). **Holdings:** 15,000 books; 2500 bound periodical volumes; 905 VF drawers of clippings and stills; 4500 scripts. **Subscriptions:** 225 journals and other serials; 12 newspapers. **Services:** Copying; photographic reproduction; library open to public for reference use only; special collections open to public by appointment. **Publications:** Annual Index to Motion Picture Credits. **Special Indexes:** Periodical Index (card); script index (card). **Staff:** Susan Oka, Asst.Libn.; Robert Cushman, Photographic Serv.; Sam Gill, Archv.; Lisa Mosher, Asst.Libn.; Susan Umpleby, Asst.Libn.

★27★
ACADEMY OF NATURAL SCIENCES - LIBRARY (Sci-Tech; Env-Cons)
19th & The Parkway   Phone: (215) 299-1040
Philadelphia, PA 19103   Sylva Baker, Hd.Libn.
Founded: 1812. **Staff:** Prof 5; Other 7. **Subjects:** Ecology, biosystematics, marine biology, geology-paleontology, history of science, museology. **Special Collections:** Library of the American Entomological Society; Pre-Linnean collection (pre-1750 imprints; 900 volumes); manuscript collection (250,000). **Holdings:** 190,000 books and bound periodical volumes. **Subscriptions:** 3317 journals and other serials. **Services:** Interlibrary loans; copying; library open to public. **Computerized Information Services:** DIALOG; computerized cataloging. **Networks/Consortia:** Member of OCLC.

Publications: Serial Titles in The Academy of Natural Sciences and Franklin Institute Libraries, semiannual - for sale. **Special Catalogs:** Guide to the Manuscript Collection of the Academy of Natural Sciences (book); Catalog of the Wolf Room Collection (book); Catalog of the Library of the Academy of Natural Sciences of Philadelphia, 1972 (book). **Staff:** Janet Evans, Asst.Libn.; Carol Spawn, Mss.Libn.; Barbara Weir, Cat.Supv.

★28★
ACADEMY OF THE NEW CHURCH - LIBRARY (Rel-Theol)
2815 Huntingdon Pike
Box 278-68   Phone: (215) 947-0203
Bryn Athyn, PA 19009   Mary Alice Carswell, Dir.
Founded: 1876. **Staff:** Prof 3; Other 2. **Subjects:** Religion, literature, history, arts, sciences, philosophy, education, language, biography and travel. **Special Collections:** Swedenborgiana (Emanuel Swedenborg's works in original translations and 16th to 18th century works studied and referred to by Swedenborg; 5212 volumes). **Holdings:** 102,000 books and bound periodical volumes; 75 VF drawers of pamphlets, pictures and recordings; 560 reels of microfilm. **Subscriptions:** 356 journals and other serials; 11 newspapers. **Services:** Interlibrary loans; copying; library open to public with borrowing through interlibrary loan. **Staff:** Patricia Hay, Cat.

ACADEMY OF PHARMACY LIBRARY
See: Pharmaceutical Society of the State of New York

ACADEMY OF THE STREET OF PUERTO RICAN CONGRESS
See: Puerto Rican Congress of Music & Art

ACADEMY OF TELEVISION ARTS & SCIENCES
See: University of California, Los Angeles

★29★
ACADIA UNIVERSITY - SCIENCE LIBRARY (Sci-Tech)
Huggins Science Hall
Box 70   Phone: (902) 542-2201
Wolfville, NS, Canada B0P 1X0   Dr. Nirmal K. Jain, Hd., Sci.Lib.
Founded: 1970. **Staff:** Prof 3; Other 10. **Subjects:** Geology, mathematics, chemistry, computer science, home economics, physics, information science, technology, biology. **Holdings:** 20,807 books; 6005 bound periodical volumes; 200 reports; 1202 government documents; 110 boxes of Bell System Technical Reports; 20 boxes of reprints; 76 reels of microfilm; 1800 microfiche. **Subscriptions:** 500 journals and other serials. **Services:** Interlibrary loans; copying; library open to public. **Computerized Information Services:** CAN/OLE, SDC, DIALOG, QL Systems, MEDLARS, Info Globe, New York Times Information Service. **Networks/Consortia:** Member of Nova Scotia On-Line Consortium. **Remarks:** Since 1970, the university's departmental libraries in the area of science have been merged into one centralized Science Library, including its Biology Library. **Staff:** Enid Davison, ILL.

★30★
ACADIAN GENEALOGICAL & HISTORICAL ASSOCIATION OF NEW ENGLAND - LIBRARY (Hist)
Box 668   Phone: (603) 623-1781
Manchester, NH 03105   Jean L. Pellerin, Assoc.Libn.
Staff: 12. **Subjects:** Local history, genealogy. **Special Collections:** Acadian Genealogical & Historical Association publications. **Holdings:** 100 books; 100 bound periodical volumes. **Subscriptions:** 12 journals and other serials; 5 newspapers. **Services:** Copying (limited); library open to public for reference use only. **Publications:** L'Etoile d'Acadie, quarterly.

ACCREDITING COMMISSION ON EDUCATION FOR HEALTH SERVICES ADMINISTRATION
See: Association of University Programs in Health Administration

ACCREDITING COMMISSION ON POSTSECONDARY EDUCATION
See: Natl. Association of Private, Nontraditional Schools & Colleges - Accrediting Commission on Postsecondary Educ.

★31★
ACCURAY CORPORATION - ENGINEERING LIBRARY (Bus-Fin; Sci-Tech)
650 Ackerman Rd.   Phone: (614) 261-2000
Columbus, OH 43202   Patricia Daley, Libn.
Founded: 1981. **Staff:** 1. **Subjects:** Process control technology, computer science. **Special Collections:** Pulp and paper technology (100 volumes). **Holdings:** 800 books; 20 bound periodical volumes; 300 technical reports. **Subscriptions:** 34 journals and other serials. **Services:** Interlibrary loans; copying; library open to public for reference use only. **Computerized Information Services:** MULTICS (internal database); computerized cataloging.

Publications: The Source, monthly - for internal distribution only.

ACDA
See: U.S. Arms Control and Disarmament Agency

ACHENBACH FOUNDATION FOR GRAPHIC ARTS REFERENCE LIBRARY
See: Fine Arts Museums of San Francisco

★32★
ACHESON INDUSTRIES, INC. - CORPORATE INFORMATION CENTER (Sci-Tech)
315 Peoples Bank Bldg.
Box 8   Phone: (313) 984-5583
Port Huron, MI 48060   Myles T. Musgrave, Asst. to V.P.
Founded: 1957. **Staff:** Prof 1; Other 1. **Subjects:** Colloid chemistry, lubrication, graphite, carbon chemistry, engineering. **Special Collections:** Archives of Dr. E.G. Acheson. **Holdings:** Figures not available. **Services:** Interlibrary loans; copying; library open to public with restrictions. **Publications:** Library and Patent Acquisitions Lists - for internal distribution only. **Remarks:** Library also serves Acheson Colloids Company and Acheson Industries Ltd. (Europe) divisions.

★33★
ACKERMAN INSTITUTE FOR FAMILY THERAPY, INC. - LIBRARY (Soc Sci)
149 E. 78th St.   Phone: (212) 879-4900
New York, NY 10021   Ruth Perl
Founded: 1960. **Subjects:** Psychiatry, family psychotherapy, family studies, couples therapy. **Holdings:** 750 books; journals, monographs (cataloged). **Subscriptions:** 25 journals and other serials. **Services:** Library not open to public.

ACKERMAN (Louise S.) FINE ARTS LIBRARY
See: San Francisco Museum of Modern Art - Louise S. Ackerman Fine Arts Library

ACKERSON (Justice Henry) LIBRARY OF LAW & CRIMINAL JUSTICE
See: Rutgers University, The State University of New Jersey - Justice Henry Ackerson Lib. of Law & Criminal Justice

ACKLEY (David B.) MEDICAL LIBRARY
See: Mercer Medical Center - David B. Ackley Medical Library

ACOUSTIC RESEARCH CENTER LIBRARY
See: System Development Corporation

★34★
ACRES AMERICAN INC. - LIBRARY (Env-Cons; Sci-Tech)
900 Liberty Bank Bldg.   Phone: (716) 853-7525
Buffalo, NY 14202   Susan C. Doughtie, Libn.
Staff: Prof 1; Other 1. **Subjects:** Wastewater treatment, hydropower, geotechnology, air and water pollution, environment. **Holdings:** 3600 books and bound periodical volumes; in-house reports; product catalogs; topographic maps. **Subscriptions:** 60 journals and other serials. **Services:** Interlibrary loans; copying; library open to public by appointment. **Computerized Information Services:** DIALOG, SDC. **Networks/Consortia:** Member of Western New York Library Resources Council (WNYLRC).

★35★
ACRES CONSULTING SERVICES, LTD. - LIBRARY (Sci-Tech)
5259 Dorchester Rd.
Box 1001   Phone: (416) 354-3831
Niagara Falls, ON, Canada L2E 6W1   Mrs. A. McKay, Libn.
Staff: Prof 1; Other 2. **Subjects:** Engineering - civil, mechanical, hydraulic, environmental, electrical, geotechnical, thermal; architecture. **Holdings:** 8000 books. **Subscriptions:** 300 journals and other serials. **Services:** Interlibrary loans; library open to public with restrictions. **Computerized Information Services:** SDC, QL Systems, DIALOG.

★36★
ACRES CONSULTING SERVICES, LTD. - TORONTO LIBRARY (Sci-Tech)
480 University Ave.   Phone: (416) 595-2000
Toronto, ON, Canada M5G 1V2
Founded: 1967. **Subjects:** Engineering, economics, transportation, urban and regional planning, natural resources. **Holdings:** 3000 books; 700 standards; 150 maps; 500 catalogs. **Subscriptions:** 273 journals and other serials. **Services:** Interlibrary loans; copying; library open to public by appointment, for reference use. **Computerized Information Services:** DIALOG; computerized serials. **Publications:** Library Lines, bimonthly.

ACTION
See: U.S. Peace Corps

★37★
ACTION FOR CHILDREN'S TELEVISION - ACT RESOURCE LIBRARY (Educ)
46 Austin St.   Phone: (617) 527-7870
Newtonville, MA 02160   Paula Rohrlick, Rsrcs.Dir.
Founded: 1972. **Staff:** Prof 1. **Subjects:** Children's TV programs, broadcasting, TV advertising, early childhood education, consumer education, media curricula. **Special Collections:** ACT Archives (8 volumes of clippings). **Holdings:** 750 books; 250 research reports (cataloged); 15 boxes of testimony and petitions (FCC and FTC); 30 VF drawers of pamphlets and clippings. **Subscriptions:** 100 journals and other serials. **Services:** Library not open to public. **Publications:** Children and Television: An ACT Bibliography; ACT Materials: A Resource List; reference lists on topics in children's television. **Special Indexes:** Subject Headings in Children's Television Programming.

★38★
ACTION-HOUSING, INC. - LIBRARY & HOUSING INFORMATION CENTER (Soc Sci)
2 Gateway Ctr.   Phone: (412) 281-2102
Pittsburgh, PA 15222   Terri F. Gould, Dir. of Educ.
Staff: 1. **Subjects:** Housing, urban renewal, community services. **Holdings:** 4000 volumes; housing information packages. **Subscriptions:** 40 journals and other serials. **Services:** Library open to public; housing information referral service.

ACTRON TECHNICAL LIBRARY
See: Mc Donnell Douglas Corporation

★39★
ACUREX CORPORATION - CORPORATE LIBRARY (Energy)
485 Clyde Ave.   Phone: (415) 964-3200
Mountain View, CA 94042   Cindy Hill, Chf.Libn.
Founded: 1972. **Staff:** Prof 2; Other 2. **Subjects:** Aerospace, alternate energy sources, environmental sciences. **Holdings:** 4000 books; 100 bound periodical volumes; 47,000 technical reports; 5000 in-house reports. **Subscriptions:** 350 journals and other serials. **Services:** Interlibrary loans; copying; library not open to public. **Computerized Information Services:** DIALOG, SDC, DOE/RECON, BRS, NASA/RECON, DTIC, Dun & Bradstreet, Inc.; computerized cataloging, acquisitions and serials. **Networks/Consortia:** Member of CIN; CLASS; Government-Industry Data Exchange Program (GIDEP); South Bay Area Reference Network. **Staff:** Paul North, Libn.

★40★
ADAMS ADVERTISING AGENCY, INC. - LIBRARY (Bus-Fin)
111 N. Canal St.   Phone: (312) 922-0856
Chicago, IL 60606   George Lewis, Libn.
Staff: Prof 2; Other 1. **Subjects:** Advertising, sales promotion, psychology. **Holdings:** 75,000 books. **Subscriptions:** 400 journals and other serials; 75 newspapers. **Services:** Copying; library open to public with restrictions. **Staff:** A.A. Hibbs, Jr., Mgr.

★41★
ADAMS COUNTY HISTORICAL SOCIETY - ARCHIVES (Hist)
1330 N. Burlington Ave.
Box 102   Phone: (402) 463-5838
Hastings, NE 68901
Founded: 1965. **Staff:** Prof 1; Other 5. **Subjects:** Local history, the Great Plains. **Holdings:** 200 books; 250 bound periodical volumes; 500 reels of newspapers on microfilm; 500 cassette tapes; 25 AV tapes; 58 document cases of church records; 8 linear feet of school records; 150 maps; 100 document cases of other archival materials; inventory of county and city records, 1873 to present. **Subscriptions:** 10 journals and other serials. **Services:** Copying; library open to public. **Publications:** Historical News, monthly. **Special Indexes:** Index to Burton and Lewis, Past and Present of Adams County, Nebraska, published 1916; index to Goodspeed's Biographical and Historical Memoirs of Adams, Clay, Hall and Hamilton Counties, 1890-Adams County portion.

★42★
ADAMS COUNTY HISTORICAL SOCIETY - LIBRARY (Hist)
Drawer A, Schmucker Hall
Seminary Campus   Phone: (717) 334-4723
Gettysburg, PA 17325   Dr. Charles Glatfelter, Dir.
Subjects: Adams County history. **Holdings:** 1000 volumes; 172 VF drawers of records, manuscripts, clippings, newspapers and genealogical files. **Services:** Library and museum open to public.

★43★
ADAMS COUNTY LAW LIBRARY (Law)
Courthouse, Rm. 207   Phone: (513) 544-5155
West Union, OH 45693   Roy E. Gabbert, Libn.
Staff: 1. **Subjects:** Law. **Holdings:** 4000 books; 50 bound periodicals. **Services:** Library open to public. **Remarks:** Library maintained by Adams County Law Library Association.

★44★
ADAMS COUNTY LAW LIBRARY (Law)†
Court House   Phone: (717) 334-6781
Gettysburg, PA 17325   Mr. C. Weaver, Law Libn.
Subjects: Law. **Holdings:** 10,000 volumes.

★45★
ADAMS, DUQUE & HAZELTINE - LIBRARY (Law)
523 W. 6th St.   Phone: (213) 620-1240
Los Angeles, CA 90014   Randall J. Gray, Hd. Law Libn.
Staff: Prof 1; Other 2. **Subjects:** Law - California, federal, civil, insurance, products liability, corporate, real estate, tax. **Holdings:** 18,000 volumes. **Subscriptions:** 240 journals and other serials; 15 newspapers. **Services:** Interlibrary loans; copying; library not open to public. **Computerized Information Services:** Mead Data Central, New York Times Information Service. **Special Catalogs:** Book catalog of legal memoranda (computer produced).

★46★
ADAMS EXPRESS COMPANY - LIBRARY (Bus-Fin)
201 N. Charles St.   Phone: (301) 752-5900
Baltimore, MD 21201   Dorothy Marvel, Libn.
Founded: 1930. **Staff:** Prof 1; Other 1. **Subjects:** Business, finance, economics. **Holdings:** 1100 books; 140 bound periodical volumes; 135 VF drawers of corporate and industrial files; 10K, 10Q and SEC reports for 150 corporations on microfiche; 30 Investment Titles/Services. **Subscriptions:** 65 journals and other serials; 15 newspapers. **Services:** Library not open to public.

ADAMS (Hunter M.) ARCHITECTURE LIBRARY
See: University of Kentucky - Hunter M. Adams Architecture Library

★47★
ADAMS-PRATT OAKLAND COUNTY LAW LIBRARY (Law)
1200 N. Telegraph Rd.   Phone: (313) 858-0011
Pontiac, MI 48054   Richard L. Beer, Law Libn.
Founded: 1925. **Staff:** Prof 2; Other 3. **Subjects:** U.S. law, criminal justice, legal medicine. **Special Collections:** Michigan Supreme Court Records and Briefs, 1927-1929 and 1933 to present; House and Senate Bills of Michigan legislature, 1973 to present. **Holdings:** 39,600 books and bound periodical volumes; Michigan Attorney General Reports, 1838 to present; Michigan House and Senate Journals, 1929 to present. **Subscriptions:** 1077 journals and other serials; 10 newspapers. **Services:** Interlibrary loans; copying; library open to public for reference use only. **Computerized Information Services:** WESTLAW, LEXIS; computerized cataloging. **Networks/Consortia:** Member of Michigan Library Consortium; OCLC. **Also Known As:** Clark J. Adams-Philip Pratt, Oakland County Law Library. **Staff:** Lane E. Fichtenau, Asst.Libn.; Kristin Major, Comp.Res.Spec.

★48★
ADAMS STATE COLLEGE - LIBRARY - SPECIAL COLLECTIONS (Educ)
    Phone: (303) 589-7781
Alamosa, CO 81102   Nellie N. Hasfjord, Dir.
Founded: 1925. **Special Collections:** Children's Collection; Colorado history; law library; San Luis Valley history; Chicano Collection. **Holdings:** Figures not available. **Services:** Interlibrary loans; copying; library open to public. **Networks/Consortia:** Member of Bibliographical Center for Research, Rocky Mountain Region, Inc. (BCR). **Publications:** Handbook. **Special Catalogs:** Bibliographies or Pathfinders (mimeos). **Staff:** Christine Moeny, Spec.Coll.

★49★
ADATH JESHURUN CONGREGATION - JENNY GROSS MEMORIAL LIBRARY (Rel-Theol)
3400 Dupont, S.   Phone: (612) 824-2685
Minneapolis, MN 55408   Naomi Goldberg Honor, Libn.
Founded: 1931. **Staff:** Prof 1. **Subjects:** Zionism, Bible, theology, Jewish history, liturgy, law and literature, modern Israel. **Special Collections:** Children's Book Collection. **Holdings:** 5000 books. **Subscriptions:** 10 journals and other serials. **Services:** Library open to public.

ADDICTION RESEARCH FOUNDATION
See: Alcoholism and Drug Addiction Research Foundation

★50★
ADDISON GALLERY OF AMERICAN ART - LIBRARY (Art)
Phillips Academy   Phone: (617) 475-3706
Andover, MA 01810
Subjects: American art. **Holdings:** Books, slides and art films. **Services:** Library open to public for reference use only. **Remarks:** Art books shelved at Oliver Wendell Holmes Library on campus of Phillips Academy, with exception of those books dealing with individual American artists.

★51★
ADDISON-WESLEY PUBLISHING COMPANY - LIBRARY (Publ)
Jacob Way   Phone: (617) 944-3700
Reading, MA 01867   Patricia Musto, Info. & Commun.Mgr.
Founded: 1967. **Staff:** Prof 1; Other 1. **Subjects:** Physics, mathematics, engineering science, business and economics, biological sciences, sociology, health and physical education, psychology, anthropology. **Special Collections:** Company archives (copies of all company publications). **Holdings:** 25,000 books; reports and pamphlets. **Subscriptions:** 500 journals and other serials; 10 newspapers. **Services:** Library not open to public.

★52★
ADDISON-WESLEY PUBLISHING COMPANY - SCHOOL DIVISION LIBRARY (Publ)
2725 Sand Hill Rd.   Phone: (415) 854-0300
Menlo Park, CA 94025   Elede Toppy Hall, Libn.
Staff: Prof 1. **Subjects:** Archive collection of School Division publications; reference. **Special Collections:** Company archives (articles about company). **Holdings:** 2500 volumes. **Subscriptions:** 103 journals and other serials. **Services:** Interlibrary loans; copying; library open to public by appointment. **Computerized Information Services:** DIALOG, BRS. **Networks/Consortia:** Member of CIN; CLASS; Bay Area Reference Center (BARC). **Publications:** Acquisition list and periodical holding list - to staff.

ADELBERG (Peter) ARCHIVE
See: European Art Color - Peter Adelberg Archive

★53★
ADELPHI UNIVERSITY - FINE ARTS LIBRARY - SPECIAL COLLECTIONS - ARCHIVES (Art; Hist)
South Ave.   Phone: (516) 663-1042
Garden City, NY 11530   Erica Doctorow, Hd.
Staff: Prof 2; Other 2. **Subjects:** Art, rare books, music. **Special Collections:** William Cobbett; Americana; William Blake; Gerhart Hauptmann; Small Presses; Expatriate Writers; university archives. **Holdings:** 22,643 books; 1756 manuscripts and clippings; 10,000 slides; 8000 sound recordings; 120 slide kits. **Subscriptions:** 130 journals and other serials. **Services:** Interlibrary loans; copying; library open to public for reference use only. **Computerized Information Services:** DIALOG, New York Times Information Service. **Networks/Consortia:** Member of Long Island Library Resources Council (LILRC). **Publications:** Exhibition catalogs, irregular. **Staff:** Gary Cantrell, Music Libn.

★54★
ADELPHI UNIVERSITY - SCIENCE LIBRARY (Sci-Tech)
    Phone: (516) 663-1043
Garden City, NY 11530   Liselotte Matzka, Hd., Sci.Lib.
Founded: 1959. **Staff:** Prof 1; Other 3. **Subjects:** Physics, chemistry, biology. **Special Collections:** Henry Drysdale Dakin Memorial Collection (organic chemistry). **Holdings:** 22,000 books; 23,000 bound periodical volumes; 14,500 microforms. **Subscriptions:** 500 journals and other serials. **Services:** Interlibrary loans; copying; library open to public for reference use only. **Computerized Information Services:** DIALOG, SDC, NLM, New York Times Information Service. **Networks/Consortia:** Member of Long Island Library Resources Council (LILRC).

★55★
ADELPHI UNIVERSITY - SOCIAL WORK LIBRARY (Soc Sci)
    Phone: (516) 560-8040
Garden City, NY 11530   Rita Edwards, Hd.
Founded: 1977. **Staff:** Prof 7; Other 5. **Subjects:** Social work, social welfare, psychiatry and mental health, social policy administration. **Special Collections:** Sophie Robison Archives. **Holdings:** 15,000 books; 730 bound periodical volumes; 80 Princeton files. **Subscriptions:** 138 journals and other serials. **Services:** Copying; library open to public with restrictions. **Publications:** Social Work Bibliographic Bulletin, irregular. **Staff:** Mary Ann Trocchia, Sr.Asst.

★56★

ADIRONDACK HISTORICAL ASSOCIATION - ADIRONDACK MUSEUM - RESEARCH LIBRARY (Hist)

Phone: (518) 352-7311

Blue Mountain Lake, NY 12812   Craig Gilborn, Dir.

Founded: 1957. **Staff:** Prof 1; Other 1. **Subjects:** Adirondack Mountains - history, geography, natural history, economic history, recreation, art. **Special Collections:** E.Z.C. Judson (Ned Buntline) writings and memorabilia; Association for the Protection of the Adirondacks papers; McIntyre Iron Mine papers; Northern New York newspapers on microfilm (700 reels). **Holdings:** 6000 volumes; 50,000 photographs and postcards; 1000 maps; 650 linear feet of manuscripts; 1200 reels of microfilm; 46 VF drawers. **Subscriptions:** 120 journals and other serials. **Services:** Interlibrary loans; copying; library open to outside users by appointment. **Networks/Consortia:** Member of North Country Reference and Research Resources Council (NCRRRC). **Staff:** Jerold Pepper, Libn.

ADIRONDACK MUSEUM - RESEARCH LIBRARY
See: Adirondack Historical Association

★57★

ADISTRA CORPORATION - R & D LIBRARY (Bus-Fin)

101 Union St.   Phone: (313) 425-2600

Plymouth, MI 48170   John H. Dillon, Mgr.

Founded: 1965. **Staff:** Prof 1. **Subjects:** Marketing, distribution, business management. **Holdings:** 200 books; 5 bound periodical volumes. **Subscriptions:** 25 journals and other serials. **Services:** Library serves staff and clients only.

★58★

ADLER (Alfred) INSTITUTE - LIBRARY (Soc Sci)

159 N. Dearborn St.   Phone: (312) 346-3458

Chicago, IL 60601   Eugene McClory, Pres.

Founded: 1964. **Staff:** 1. **Subjects:** Psychology, psychiatry, education, counseling, guidance. **Special Collections:** Adlerian Psychology (200 books). **Holdings:** 4700 volumes; 1500 articles and reprints; 2500 journals and periodicals; 40 films and videotapes; 1500 cassettes and audiotapes. **Subscriptions:** 50 journals and other serials. **Services:** Interlibrary loans; library open to public for reference use only. **Staff:** Miriam Tabachnik, Libn.

★59★

ADLER BARISH DANIELS LEVIN & CRESKOFF - LIBRARY

Rohm & Haas Bldg., 2nd Fl.

Philadelphia, PA 19106

Defunct

★60★

ADLER CENTER - LIBRARY

2204 Griffith Dr.

Champaign, IL 61820

Defunct

★61★

ADLER PLANETARIUM - LIBRARY (Sci-Tech)

1300 S. Lake Shore Dr.   Phone: (312) 322-0304

Chicago, IL 60605   James Seevers, Adm.

Staff: Prof 1; Other 1. **Subjects:** Astronomy, history of astronomy, astronomical instrumentation, space sciences. **Special Collections:** Rare books on astronomy, 1400-1800; atlases, 1482 to present. **Holdings:** 6000 books; 630 bound periodical volumes; 50 early prints on antique instruments; 50 celestial charts and maps. **Subscriptions:** 15 journals and other serials. **Services:** Astronomical information service by telephone and letter; library open to public by appointment. **Special Indexes:** Photograph and data file on museum's antique instrument collection. **Staff:** Il Byun, Libn.

★62★

ADLER POLLOCK & SHEEHAN, INC. - LAW LIBRARY (Law)

One Hospital Trust Plaza   Phone: (401) 274-7200

Providence, RI 02903   Dolores E. O'Rourke, Law Libn.

Staff: Prof 1; Other 1. **Subjects:** Law - business, corporate, commercial, labor, tax, securities; estate planning. **Holdings:** 5000 books; 1000 bound periodical volumes; 500 legal memorandum. **Subscriptions:** 54 journals and other serials. **Services:** Interlibrary loans; library open to public with restrictions.

★63★

ADP NETWORK SERVICES - MARKETING SERVICES LIBRARY (Sci-Tech)

175 Jackson Plaza   Phone: (313) 769-6800

Ann Arbor, MI 48106   Brenda Larison, Corp.Libn.

Staff: Prof 1; Other 1. **Subjects:** Computers, data processing, marketing. **Holdings:** 400 books; 250 bound periodical volumes; 300 manuals; 14 VF drawers of company documents and clippings; 5 VF drawers of unbound reports; 3 VF drawers of microfilm and magnetic tapes. **Subscriptions:** 60 journals and other serials; 25 newspapers. **Services:** Copying; SDI; library not open to public. **Computerized Information Services:** DIALOG, New York Times Information Service, BRS; internal databases; computerized cataloging. **Publications:** Acquisitions lists, monthly; competitive bulletins, quarterly - both for internal distribution only.

★64★

ADVANCED MICRO DEVICES, INC. - TECHNICAL LIBRARY (Sci-Tech)

901 Thompson Pl., M/S 1   Phone: (408) 749-2260

Sunnyvale, CA 94086   Pamela McCoy, Tech.Libn.

Founded: 1971. **Staff:** Prof 1. **Subjects:** Semiconductor technology. **Holdings:** 2500 books; 500 bound periodical volumes; 10 VF drawers of military specifications and standards; patents. **Subscriptions:** 200 journals and other serials. **Services:** Interlibrary loans; copying; SDI; library not open to public. **Computerized Information Services:** DIALOG. **Networks/Consortia:** Member of CIN. **Publications:** Acquisitions List, monthly - for internal distribution only. **Special Catalogs:** Semiconductor subject catalog (card).

★65★

ADVERTISING RESEARCH FOUNDATION - LIBRARY (Bus-Fin)

3 E. 54th St.   Phone: (212) 751-5656

New York, NY 10022   Elisabeth R. Proudfit, Mgr., Info.Ctr.

Founded: 1952. **Staff:** Prof 2. **Subjects:** Market research; advertising; research methods; media research. **Special Collections:** Foundation publications. **Holdings:** 3000 books and bound periodical volumes; 2000 vertical files of clippings, reports, surveys. **Subscriptions:** 110 journals and other serials. **Services:** Library open to members and qualified graduate students for reference use only. **Publications:** List of publications - free upon request. **Staff:** John Lovari, Libn.

ADVISORY COMMISSION ON INTERGOVERNMENTAL RELATIONS
See: U.S. Advisory Commission on Intergovernmental Relations

★66★

ADVISORY GROUP ON ELECTRON DEVICES - LIBRARY (Sci-Tech)

201 Varick St., 11th Fl.   Phone: (212) 620-3374

New York, NY 10014   David Slater, Sec.

Subjects: Electron devices. **Holdings:** 9000 technical reports. **Subscriptions:** 15 journals and other serials. **Services:** Specialized informational services to government agencies and government contractors on research and development in the field of electron devices; library not open to public.

THE ADVOCATE - LIBRARY
See: Connecticut Newspapers Inc.

★67★

AERIAL PHENOMENA RESEARCH ORGANIZATION, INC. - LIBRARY INFORMATION SERVICES (Sci-Tech)†

3910 E. Kleindale Rd.   Phone: (602) 323-1825

Tucson, AZ 85712   Coral Lorenzo, Libn.

Founded: 1975. **Staff:** Prof 1; Other 1. **Subjects:** Unidentified flying objects. **Holdings:** 637 books; 34,000 documents; 64 VF drawers; AV materials. **Subscriptions:** 213 journals and other serials. **Services:** Interlibrary loans; copying; SDI; library open to serious UFO researchers only. **Computerized Information Services:** Computerized cataloging. **Publications:** APRO Bulletin.

★68★

AEROJET-CHEMICAL CORPORATION - AEROJET TACTICAL PROPULSION COMPANY - TECHNICAL INFORMATION CENTER (Sci-Tech)†

Box 13400   Phone: (916) 355-4076

Sacramento, CA 95813   Rimma Mironeullo, Tech.Libn.

Staff: Prof 1. **Subjects:** Chemistry, aerospace. **Holdings:** 10,000 books; 10,000 bound periodical volumes. **Subscriptions:** 125 journals and other serials. **Services:** Library not open to public.

★69★

AEROJET ORDNANCE COMPANY - TECHNICAL LIBRARY (Sci-Tech)

9236 E. Hall Rd.   Phone: (213) 923-7511

Downey, CA 90241   Fran Nimmo, Libn.

Founded: 1953. **Staff:** Prof 1. **Subjects:** Ordnance, physics, chemistry, mathematics, weapons systems, aerospace. **Holdings:** 6000 books; 1100 bound periodical volumes; 25,000 technical reports; 80,000 technical reports in microform. **Services:** Interlibrary loans; copying; Termatrex retrieval system; library not open to public. **Publications:** Acquisition List.

AEROJET TACTICAL PROPULSION COMPANY
See: Aerojet-Chemical Corporation

AEROMEDICAL RESEARCH LABORATORY
See: U.S. Army - Aeromedical Research Laboratory

★70★
AEROPHILATELIC FEDERATION OF THE AMERICAS - LIBRARY (Hist)
Box 269   Phone: (312) 485-1109
Brookfield, IL 60513   Earl H. Wellman, Libn.
Staff: 1. **Subjects:** Aero-philatelic history, astro-philatelic history, philatelic history of the Americas, aviation records, aviation philatelic publications. **Special Collections:** Schedules of airlines, 1929 to present. **Holdings:** 3000 books; 200 bound periodical volumes; contemporary material issued on long-gone air services; manuscripts; clippings; early data on pilots. **Subscriptions:** 50 journals and other serials. **Services:** Copying; library open to researchers by request. **Publications:** AFA News, quarterly - for sale; Jack Knight Air Log, quarterly - by subscription. **Special Catalogs:** Air Transport Label Catalog of the World (5 volumes); rocket mail catalog; American air mail catalog.

★71★
AEROSPACE CORPORATION - CHARLES C. LAURITSEN LIBRARY (Sci-Tech; Energy)
Sta. M1-199, Box 92957   Phone: (213) 648-6738
Los Angeles, CA 90009   Edythe Moore, Mgr., Lib.Serv.
Founded: 1960. **Staff:** Prof 13; Other 20. **Subjects:** Aerospace management and technology, systems engineering, satellite systems, weapon systems, reentry vehicles, space physics, computer science, energy and energy systems. **Special Collections:** Aerospace Corporation Authors Collection. **Holdings:** 66,000 books; 33,000 bound periodical volumes; 162,000 technical reports; 350 pamphlets; 240,500 microforms; 1500 maps and charts; 12,000 specifications and standards. **Subscriptions:** 900 journals and other serials; 10 newspapers. **Services:** Interlibrary loans; library open to public by appointment. **Computerized Information Services:** DIALOG, SDC, BRS, CIS, DOE/RECON, NASA/RECON, DTIC, Source Telecomputing Corporation, ONTYME; computerized circulation, bibliographic and subject retrieval and file maintenance. **Networks/Consortia:** Member of CLASS. **Publications:** Library Services Announcements; Serials and Journals Currently Received; Reprints of Professional Papers. **Special Indexes:** Index of reports and publications of the Aerospace Corporation. **Staff:** Robert Anthony, Lit.Res.Anl.; Theodore Cheron, Lit.Res.Anl.; Susan Crowe, Supv., Tech.Serv.; Virginia Ford, Lit.Res.Anl.; Stanley Larson, Ref.Libn.; Ruby Oshiro, Supv., User Serv.; Karen Olds, Ref.Libn.; Thelma Louie, Subject Anl.; Shirley McElroy, Subject Anl.; Maureen Miller, Subject Anl.; Michael Toman, Subject Anl.; Beverly Ware, Subject Anl.

★72★
AEROSPACE CORPORATION - GERMANTOWN LIBRARY
20030 Century Blvd.
Germantown, MD 20767
Defunct. Holdings absorbed by Aerospace Corporation - Washington Library.

★73★
AEROSPACE CORPORATION - WASHINGTON LIBRARY (Sci-Tech; Energy)
955 L'Enfant Plaza, S.W., Suite 4000   Phone: (202) 488-6154
Washington, DC 20024   Patricia W. Green, Libn.
Founded: 1974. **Staff:** Prof 1; Other 2. **Subjects:** Petroleum reserves, alternate energy sources, environment, electric vehicles, telecommunications. **Holdings:** 5000 books; 7000 technical reports; 5000 DOE reports on microfiche. **Subscriptions:** 303 journals and other serials. **Services:** Interlibrary loans; copying; SDI; library open to public with restrictions. **Computerized Information Services:** DIALOG, SDC, New York Times Information Service, DOE/RECON, DTIC, Alternative Fuels Data Bank; ASKLIBR (internal database); computerized cataloging and circulation. **Networks/Consortia:** Member of Interlibrary Users Association; Metropolitan Washington Library Council. **Publications:** New Acquisitions List, monthly - free upon request. **Remarks:** Contains the holdings of the former Aerospace Corporation - Germantown Library.

★74★
AEROSPACE INDUSTRIES ASSOCIATION OF AMERICA - LIBRARY (Sci-Tech)
1725 DeSales St., N.W.   Phone: (203) 429-4653
Washington, DC 20036   Mrs. Billie Ann Perry, Libn.
Founded: 1962. **Staff:** Prof 1; Other 1. **Subjects:** Aeronautics, astronautics,

aircraft industries, spacecraft, rockets and missiles, business economics, procurement, exports and imports. **Special Collections:** Annual reports, directories, government documents and newspapers. **Holdings:** 2300 books; 204 unbound periodical volumes; 77 VF drawers of documents; 690 reels of microfilm. **Subscriptions:** 200 journals and other serials; 5 newspapers. **Services:** Interlibrary loans; library open to member companies and scholars. **Staff:** Sharon Powell, Asst.Libn.

AEROSPACE MEDICAL ASSOCIATION ARCHIVES
See: Wright State University - Health Sciences Library

AEROSPACE RESEARCH APPLICATIONS CENTER
See: Indianapolis Center for Advanced Research - ARAC

AEROSPACE STRUCTURES INFORMATION AND ANALYSIS CENTER
See: U.S. Air Force - Wright Aeronautical Laboratories

★75★
AESTHETIC REALISM FOUNDATION, INC. - LIBRARY (Hum)
141 Greene St.   Phone: (212) 777-4490
New York, NY 10012   Richard Palumbo
Founded: 1964. **Staff:** Prof 1; Other 1. **Subjects:** Literature, drama, poetry, psychology, sociology, art and aesthetics. **Special Collections:** Published poems and philosophic essays by the late Eli Siegel, founder of Aesthetic Realism (25); selections from Eli Siegel's personal library (2000 books). **Holdings:** 1000 volumes; unpublished lectures. **Services:** Library open to public with restrictions. **Publications:** TRO, weekly. **Special Catalogs:** Index to Eli Siegel's lectures (card); TRO index, issues 1-410.

★76★
AETNA LIFE & CASUALTY COMPANY - CORPORATE INFORMATION CENTER (Bus-Fin)
151 Farmington Ave.   Phone: (203) 273-2946
Hartford, CT 06156   Kathryn W. Porter, Libn.
Founded: 1931. **Staff:** Prof 2; Other 3. **Subjects:** Business, insurance, management, communications. **Holdings:** 9000 books. **Subscriptions:** 300 journals and other serials. **Services:** Interlibrary loans; library open to public for reference use on request. **Publications:** On-line Info; New at the Corporate Information Center. **Staff:** Beth Steinhardt, Asst.Libn.

★77★
AETNA LIFE & CASUALTY COMPANY - ENGINEERING LIBRARY (Sci-Tech)
151 Farmington Ave.   Phone: (203) 683-3648
Hartford, CT 06156   Melissa Pierce, Libn.
Staff: Prof 2. **Subjects:** Engineering - safety, chemical, construction, electrical, transportation; products liability. **Holdings:** 1500 books; 3 bound periodical volumes; 150 NIOSH documents; 180 VF drawers. **Subscriptions:** 62 journals and other serials. **Services:** Interlibrary loans; copying; library open to public by appointment. **Computerized Information Services:** DIALOG. **Staff:** Nancy Harney, Asst.Libn.

★78★
AETNA LIFE & CASUALTY COMPANY - FINANCIAL LIBRARY (Bus-Fin)
Bond Investment Dept.
151 Farmington Ave.   Phone: (203) 273-0974
Hartford, CT 06156   Anne G. Johnson, Info.Spec.
Founded: 1982. **Staff:** Prof 1; Other 3. **Subjects:** Finance, investment analysis, corporate information. **Holdings:** Figures not available. **Subscriptions:** 70 journals and other serials; 5 newspapers. **Services:** Interlibrary loans; copying; library open to public by appointment. **Computerized Information Services:** DIALOG. **Networks/Consortia:** Member of Capitol Region Library Council.

★79★
AETNA LIFE & CASUALTY COMPANY - LAW LIBRARY (Law)
151 Farmington Ave.   Phone: (203) 273-8183
Hartford, CT 06156   Patricia Sechrist, Law Libn.
Staff: Prof 6; Other 1. **Subjects:** Law. **Holdings:** 15,000 books. **Subscriptions:** 1200 journals and other serials; 5 newspapers. **Services:** Interlibrary loans; copying; library open to public with restrictions. **Computerized Information Services:** WESTLAW. **Publications:** Law Library Liaison, monthly - for internal distribution only. **Staff:** Frances Bertelli, Tech.Serv.Libn.; Betty I. Nork, Circ./Ref.Libn.

AFFAIRES DES ANCIENS COMBATTANTS CANADA
See: Canada - Veterans Affairs Canada

AFFAIRES EXTERIEURES CANADA
See: Canada - External Affairs Canada

AFFAIRES INDIENNES ET DU NORD CANADA
See: Canada - Indian & Northern Affairs Canada

AFL-CIO
See: Amalgamated Clothing & Textile Workers Union

AFL-CIO
See: American Federation of Labor and Congress of Industrial Organizations

AFL-CIO
See: American Federation of State, County and Municipal Employees, AFL-CIO (AFSCME)

AFL-CIO, UNITED FARM WORKERS OF AMERICA
See: United Farm Workers of America, AFL-CIO

★80★
AFRAM ASSOCIATES, INC. - AFRAMAILIBRARY (Soc Sci)*
Beatrice Lewis Bldg.
68-72 E. 131st St.   Phone: (212) 281-6000
Harlem, NY 10037   Mr. Westcott, Dir.
Founded: 1968. Staff: 4. Subjects: Education, community action, human development, Afrikan history, economic development. Holdings: Black directories, position statements, educational models, training materials, workbooks (organizations, subjects, serial publications), AV materials. Subscriptions: 35 journals and other serials. Services: Mail orders; telephone response; film rentals; research. Publications: Directory: National Black Organizations; AFRAM DRUM; subscriptions; AFRAMonographs; AFRAM reprints; public service documents. Special Catalogs: AFRAMaterials Katalog - for sale. Remarks: Maintains Afrikan Reference Library which is open to public.

★81★
AFRICAN-AMERICAN INSTITUTE - LIBRARY (Area-Ethnic)
833 United Nations Plaza   Phone: (212) 949-5666
New York, NY 10017
Subjects: Africa. Holdings: 1000 books; 200 bound periodical volumes; magazines; news clippings; conference reports; Africa Report (a complete set of the institute's publication). Services: Copying; library open to public.

★82★
AFRICAN-AMERICAN LABOR CENTER (AALC) - LIBRARY (Soc Sci)
1125 Fifteenth St., N.W.   Phone: (202) 293-3603
Washington, DC 20005   John T. Sarr, Pubn.Off.
Staff: Prof 1. Subjects: American and African trade unions. Holdings: 8000 volumes; newspaper clippings, brochures and newsletters. Subscriptions: 50 journals and other serials; 14 newspapers. Services: Library not open to public. Publications: AALC Reporter, bimonthly newsletter - free upon request. Special Indexes: Index to AALC Reporter.

★83★
AFRICAN BIBLIOGRAPHIC CENTER - STAFF RESOURCE LIBRARY (Area-Ethnic)
1346 Connecticut Ave., N.W., Rm. 901   Phone: (202) 223-1392
Washington, DC 20036   Linda Fink Matthews, Adm.Dir.
Staff: Prof 9. Subjects: Africana and black studies. Special Collections: Current Africana. Holdings: 8000 books and bound periodical volumes. Subscriptions: 100 journals and other serials. Services: Research and analysis surveys; multimedia consultation; conference and library development. Publications: Habari Transcript Series, weekly or quarterly; Current Reading List Series, irregular; A Current Bibliography on African Affairs, quarterly; SADEX, The Southern Africa Development Information/Documentation Exchange, bimonthly; Special Bibliographic Series, irregular; Multimedia Series; AMA: Women in African and American Worlds - An Outlook. Special Catalogs: Subject and geographic catalogs in card form in all fields of African studies.

★84★
AFRICAN LITERATURE ASSOCIATION - SECRETARIAT LIBRARY (Area-Ethnic)
University of Alberta
Dept. of Comparative Literature   Phone: (403) 432-5535
Edmonton, AB, Canada T6G 2E6   Stephen H. Arnold, Sec.-Treas., Ed.
Staff: Prof 1. Subjects: African literature. Holdings: 15 VF drawers of business and editorial archives. Services: Copying; library open to public by

written request. Publications: Newsletter, quarterly; Directory, annual; Annual Selected Conference Papers.

AFRICAN STUDIES ASSOCIATION
See: Northwestern University - Melville J. Herskovits Library of African Studies

AFRICANA STUDIES AND RESEARCH CENTER LIBRARY
See: Cornell University

AFRIKAN REFERENCE LIBRARY
See: AFRAM Associates, Inc. - AFRAMAIlibrary

★85★
AFRO-AMERICAN CULTURAL AND HISTORICAL SOCIETY MUSEUM - LIBRARY (Area-Ethnic)†
1839 E. 81st St.   Phone: (216) 231-2131
Cleveland, OH 44103   Icabod Flewellen, Dir.
Founded: 1953. Staff: Prof 3; Other 2. Subjects: Afro-American history and culture. Special Collections: Afro-American music; blacks in aviation; black theology; black church in Cleveland. Holdings: 200 books; 200 bound periodical volumes; 10,000 negatives; 100 paintings; 100,000 news clippings; 500 slides; 100 oral tapes; 50 pieces of art; 15 proclamations; 3 Reconstruction maps. Services: Library open to public with restrictions.

AFRO-AMERICAN LEARNING RESOURCE CENTER
See: Indiana University

AFRRI
See: U.S. Armed Forces Radiobiology Research Institute (AFRRI)

AFSCME
See: American Federation of State, County and Municipal Employees, AFL-CIO

AGA KHAN PROGRAM IN ISLAMIC ARCHITECTURE - DOCUMENTATION CENTER
See: Harvard University - Fine Arts Library

★86★
AGBABIAN ASSOCIATES - LIBRARY (Sci-Tech)†
250 N. Nash St.   Phone: (213) 640-0576
El Segundo, CA 90245   Elizabeth Tucker, Info.Dir.
Staff: Prof 1. Subjects: Structural analysis, applied mathematics, physics, engineering, geology, computer sciences, automotive research. Holdings: 1080 books; 30 bound periodical volumes; 25,000 technical documents (cataloged); 2000 microfiche. Subscriptions: 55 journals and other serials. Services: Interlibrary loans; copying; library open to public by appointment.

AGEE (Rucker) CARTOGRAPHICAL COLLECTION
See: Birmingham Public and Jefferson County Free Library - Rucker Agee Cartographical Collection

AGENCE CANADIENNE DE DEVELOPPEMENT INTERNATIONAL
See: Canada - Canadian International Development Agency

★87★
AGENCY FOR INSTRUCTIONAL TELEVISION (AIT) - RESEARCH LIBRARY (Educ; Aud-Vis)
1111 W. 17th St.
Box A   Phone: (812) 339-2203
Bloomington, IN 47402   Saul Rockman, Dir. of Res.
Founded: 1978. Staff: Prof 1; Other 1. Subjects: Instructional television, education, public broadcasting, instructional design, educational measurement, curriculum development. Holdings: 4000 books; 360 bound periodical volumes; 3 VF drawers of station ITV program schedules; 15 VF drawers of agency publications; 5 VF drawers of reprints and clippings; 200 titles of instructional films and videotapes. Subscriptions: 205 journals and other serials. Services: Copying; SDI; library open to qualified researchers for reference use only. Computerized Information Services: Online systems. Networks/Consortia: Member of Stone Hills Area Library Services Authority. Publications: Acquisitions list, monthly; subject bibliographies; Survey of Library Facilities at Telecommunications and Educational Research Organizations, 1978. Remarks: AIT is a nonprofit American-Canadian organization established to strengthen education through television and other technologies. It develops joint program projects involving state and provincial agencies.

AGENCY FOR INTERNATIONAL DEVELOPMENT
See: U.S. Agency for International Development

AGNEWS RESIDENTIAL FACILITY
See: California State Department of Developmental Services - Residents Library

AGOOS (Lassor) LIBRARY
See: Beth Israel Hospital - Lassor Agoos Library

AGRI-SILVICULTURE INSTITUTE LIBRARY
See: Youth Resources, Inc.

AGRICULTURAL AND TECHNICAL COLLEGE AT...
See: SUNY

AGRICULTURE CANADA
See: Canada - Agriculture Canada

★88★
AGUDAS ACHIM CONGREGATION - STEIN MEMORIAL LIBRARY (Rel-Theol)†
2767 E. Broad St.   Phone: (614) 237-2747
Columbus, OH 43209   Mrs. William Goldsmith, Libn.
Founded: 1962. Staff: 1. Subjects: Judaica. Holdings: 3238 volumes. Services: Library not open to public.

★89★
AGUDATH ISRAEL CONGREGATION - MALCA PASS MEMORIAL LIBRARY (Rel-Theol)
1400 Coldrey Ave.
Ottawa, ON, Canada K1Z 7P9   Frieda Lauterman, Libn.
Founded: 1960. Staff: Prof 1. Subjects: Judaica (for adults and children); Canadian Judaica. Special Collections: Judaic and general art. Holdings: 6145 books. Services: Library open to members.

★90★
AGWAY, INC. - CORPORATE LIBRARY (Agri; Sci-Tech)
Box 4766   Phone: (315) 477-6408
Syracuse, NY 13221   Ron Herrgesell, Libn.
Staff: Prof 1; Other 1. Subjects: Animal husbandry, crop production, farm management, agricultural statistics, pest control, feeds, fertilizers, soils, agricultural engineering. Special Collections: Agricultural cooperatives. Holdings: 2000 books; 1500 bound periodical volumes; 3500 government agricultural experiment station bulletins; 60 dissertations; archival materials. Subscriptions: 450 journals and other serials; 10 newspapers. Services: Interlibrary loans; copying; library open to public with permission of librarian. Computerized Information Services: DIALOG. Networks/Consortia: Member of Central New York Library Resources Council.

★91★
AHMADIYYA MOVEMENT IN ISLAM - MUSLIM LIBRARY (Rel-Theol; Area-Ethnic)
2141 Leroy Place, N.W.   Phone: (202) 232-3737
Washington, DC 20008   Ata Ullah Kaleem, Info.Dir.
Staff: Prof 2; Other 1. Subjects: Islamic theology; history of different countries and religions; politics. Special Collections: Work of Hazrat Ahmad the Promised Messiah on Islam and other religions. Holdings: 2040 books; 500 bound periodical volumes; 5000 other cataloged items; 10 drawers of newspapers and periodicals. Subscriptions: 16 journals and other serials; 5 newspapers. Services: Copying; library open to public for reference use only. Publications: Muslim Sunrise, quarterly; Ahmadiyya Gazette, monthly; Annoor, bimonthly. Staff: Mr. Munawwar Saeed, Mgr.; Inamul Haq Kausar, Asst.

AICU INTERNATIONAL EDUCATION LIBRARY
See: Association of International Colleges & Universities

AID
See: U.S. Agency for International Development

★92★
AID ASSOCIATION FOR LUTHERANS - CORPORATE LIBRARY (Bus-Fin)
4321 N. Ballard Rd.   Phone: (414) 734-5721
Appleton, WI 54919   Ordelle Aaker, Libn.
Founded: 1968. Staff: 5. Subjects: Life and health insurance, actuarial science, business management, fraternal benefit societies. Special Collections: Ziegler collection of the history of fraternal benefit societies (250 volumes). Holdings: 10,000 books; 1000 bound periodical volumes; 25 VF drawers of subject files. Subscriptions: 294 journals and other serials; 6 newspapers. Services: Interlibrary loans; copying; library open to public for reference use only by permission. Computerized Information Services: DIALOG. Networks/Consortia: Member of Fox Valley Library Council, Inc. Publications: Acquisition list, monthly - for internal distribution only; periodical holdings list, annual. Staff: Yvonne Rohm, Asst.Libn.

AIDS INFORMATION SERVICE
See: Forest Products Research Society

★93★
AIR CANADA - LIBRARY (Trans)
1 Place Ville Marie, 38th Fl.   Phone: (514) 874-4841
Montreal, PQ, Canada H3B 3P7   Iris L. Land, Mgr., Lib.Serv.
Founded: 1944. Staff: Prof 1; Other 5. Subjects: Air transportation, management, statistics, travel, computer sciences, aeronautical engineering. Holdings: 30,000 books; 2500 bound periodical volumes; 4 VF drawers of annual reports and pamphlets. Subscriptions: 700 journals and other serials. Services: Interlibrary loans; copying; library open to public for reference use only. Computerized Information Services: DIALOG, BRS, Info Globe, CAN/OLE; computerized cataloging, serials and circulation. Publications: Library Bulletin, monthly.

AIR FORCE ACADEMY
See: U.S. Air Force Academy

AIR FORCE ARMAMENT LIBRARY
See: U.S. Air Force - Armament Division, Air Force Armament Laboratory

★94★
AIR FORCE ASSOCIATION - RESEARCH LIBRARY (Mil)
1750 Pennsylvania Ave., N.W.   Phone: (202) 637-3300
Washington, DC 20006
Founded: 1956. Staff: Prof 1. Subjects: Military aviation, military history, military budget. Holdings: 2000 books; congressional hearings on military budget. Services: Library open to public for reference use only on request.

AIR FORCE GEOPHYSICS LABORATORY
See: U.S. Air Force - Air Force Systems Command - Air Force Geophysics Laboratory

AIR FORCE MANPOWER AND PERSONNEL CENTER
See: U.S. Air Force - Air Force Manpower and Personnel Center

AIR FORCE SYSTEMS COMMAND
See: U.S. Air Force - Air Force Systems Command

★95★
AIR FRANCE - PUBLIC RELATIONS DEPARTMENT - LIBRARY (Trans)
1350 Ave. of the Americas, 16th Fl.   Phone: (212) 841-7300
New York, NY 10019   Annie Fellenberg, Stud. & Doc.Adm.
Founded: 1933. Subjects: Air France, French aviation. Holdings: Pamphlets and brochures; photographs; slides. Services: Press releases, brochures and photographs are available on request, without charge; library open only upon written request and appointment with staff.

AIR LIQUIDE CANADA LTEE.
See: Canadian Liquid Air, Ltd.

★96★
AIR POLLUTION CONTROL ASSOCIATION - LIBRARY (Env-Cons)
Box 2861   Phone: (412) 621-1090
Pittsburgh, PA 15230
Founded: 1950. Subjects: Air pollution. Holdings: 1000 books. Services: Copying; library open to members of the association.

★97★
AIR PRODUCTS AND CHEMICALS, INC. - BUSINESS LIBRARY (Bus-Fin)
Box 538   Phone: (215) 481-7442
Allentown, PA 18105   Michelle A. Burylo, Libn.
Staff: Prof 1; Other 1. Subjects: Chemical marketing, business and industry statistics, international business and marketing. Holdings: 4000 books; 210 shelf feet of vertical files; 3000 microfiche; 60 reels of microfilm. Subscriptions: 192 journals and other serials; 8 newspapers. Services: Interlibrary loans; copying; SDI; library open to public by appointment. Computerized Information Services: DIALOG, SDC, BRS, New York Times Information Service, Dow Jones News Retrieval, NLM, DOE/RECON, Conference Board, Inc., Control Data Corporation; computerized serials. Networks/Consortia: Member of OCLC through PALINET and Union Library Catalogue of Pennsylvania. Publications: LibraryLetter, bimonthly - for

internal distribution only.

★98★
AIR PRODUCTS AND CHEMICALS, INC. - CRSD INFORMATION SERVICES
(Sci-Tech)
Box 538   Phone: (215) 481-7292
Allentown, PA 18105   Valerie K. Tucci, Mgr., Info.Serv.
Founded: 1959. **Staff:** 15. **Subjects:** Chemical engineering, cryogenics, chemistry, physics, catalysis, refrigeration, gas technology. **Holdings:** 25,000 books; 8000 bound periodical volumes; 225 VF drawers of reports, manuscripts, documents and translations; 200 reels of microfilm. **Subscriptions:** 500 journals and other serials. **Services:** Interlibrary loans (limited); copying; library open to public by special permission. **Computerized Information Services:** DIALOG, SDC, BRS, NLM, New York Times Information Service, DTIC, DOE/RECON, NASA/RECON, Dow Jones News Retrieval, LEXIS, NEXIS; research report retrieval system; computerized journal routing. **Networks/Consortia:** Member of OCLC through PALINET & Union Library Catalogue of Pennsylvania. **Publications:** Library Letter. **Formerly:** Its Trexlertown Library. **Staff:** R.B. Smith, Supv., Database Serv.; L. Dragotta, Supv., Lib.Serv.; M. Bongiorno, Supv., Spec.Serv.

★99★
AIR PRODUCTS AND CHEMICALS, INC. - HOUDRY LABORATORIES - INFORMATION SERVICES
Box 427
Marcus Hook, PA 19061
Founded: 1942. **Subjects:** Chemistry; chemical engineering; catalysis; petroleum and polymer chemistry. **Holdings:** 7000 books; 3500 bound periodical volumes. **Remarks:** Presently inactive.

★100★
AIR TRANSPORT ASSOCIATION OF AMERICA - LIBRARY (Trans)
1709 New York Ave., N.W.   Phone: (202) 626-4184
Washington, DC 20006   Mrs. Marion Mistrik, Libn.
Founded: 1936. **Staff:** Prof 1; Other 1. **Subjects:** Scheduled air carrier financial and travel statistics; air transportation; public utility regulation; law, general and air; aeronautics. **Special Collections:** Official airline guide from 1929; legislative histories of Air Commerce Act, 1926, and Civil Aeronautics Act, 1938. **Holdings:** 17,000 books and bound periodical volumes; 11 VF drawers of pamphlets and annual reports; 350 reels of microfilm; 1800 report files. **Subscriptions:** 225 journals and other serials; 9 newspapers. **Services:** Interlibrary loans; copying; library open to public for reference use only.

AIR UNIVERSITY
See: U.S. Air Force

★101★
AIRCO CARBON - RESEARCH AND DEVELOPMENT LIBRARY (Sci-Tech)†
800 Theresa St.   Phone: (814) 834-2801
St. Marys, PA 15857   Rebecca Mattivi, Libn.
Founded: 1935. **Staff:** 2. **Subjects:** Carbon and graphite, electronic components, chemistry, metallurgy. **Holdings:** 2251 books; 1678 bound periodical volumes; 2561 technical reports. **Subscriptions:** 81 journals and other serials. **Services:** Interlibrary loans; copying; library not open to public.

★102★
AIRCO CARBON - RESEARCH LIBRARY (Sci-Tech)
Packard Rd. & 47th St.   Phone: (716) 285-9381
Niagara Falls, NY 14302   Rita Smith, Res.Libn.
Founded: 1960. **Staff:** 1. **Subjects:** Carbon, graphite, electrodes. **Holdings:** 5000 books; 6100 bound periodical volumes; 8600 technical reports; 4600 reprints; microfilm and microcards. **Subscriptions:** 80 journals and other serials. **Services:** Interlibrary loans; copying; library open to public for reference use only on request.

★103★
AIRCO, INC. - CENTRAL RESEARCH LABORATORIES - INFORMATION CENTER (Sci-Tech)
                                        Phone: (201) 464-8100
Murray Hill, NJ 07974   Loretta J. Kiersky, Mgr.
Founded: 1947. **Staff:** Prof 4; Other 4. **Subjects:** Chemical engineering, cryogenics, metallurgy, engineering, welding, anesthesiology, industrial gases. **Holdings:** 25,000 volumes; 4000 volumes on microfilm; AV materials. **Subscriptions:** 600 journals and other serials. **Services:** Interlibrary loans; copying; SDI; library open to public for reference use only by special arrangement. **Computerized Information Services:** DIALOG. **Publications:** Table of Contents Bulletin, weekly; Translations, quarterly; Papers-Talks-Patents, annual. **Special Indexes:** Welding bibliography on oxyfuel flame cutting; food bibliography on controlled atmospheres; Airco Research Reports

and Laboratory Notebooks. **Remarks:** Acquired by BOC International. **Staff:** Katherine Faber, Sr.Info.Spec..; Katharine Alig, Sr.Info.Spec.; Doris Wang, Jr.Info.Spec.

★104★
AIRCRAFT TECHNICAL PUBLISHERS - LIBRARY (Sci-Tech)
101 South Hill Dr.   Phone: (800) 227-4610
Brisbane, CA 94005   Dorothy Lunsford, Lib.Mgr.
Founded: 1973. **Staff:** Prof 9; Other 40. **Subjects:** Aviation, avionics. **Special Collections:** General aviation maintenance related publications, including Federal Aviation Administration, U.S. Civil Registry and military specifications. **Holdings:** 4500 books; 7000 microfiche; 60,000 Service Information serials; manuals; catalogs; diagrams; price lists. **Subscriptions:** 15 journals and other serials. **Services:** Micropublishing; Microfiche Library Systems and revision service; copying; library not open to public. **Computerized Information Services:** AVCOM (internal database); computerized cataloging, acquisitions, serials and indexing. **Publications:** Aircraft Maintenance Information. **Special Indexes:** Service Information and Department of Transportation indexes generated by computer and published on microfiche. **Staff:** Doug Tapscott, Acq.

★105★
AIRD & BERLIS - LIBRARY (Law)
145 King St., W., 15th Fl.   Phone: (416) 364-1241
Toronto, ON, Canada M5H 2J3   Carol Malcolm, Libn.
Staff: 2. **Subjects:** Corporate law, tax law, real estate, litigation. **Holdings:** 6000 books; 200 bound periodical volumes. **Subscriptions:** 70 journals and other serials. **Services:** Interlibrary loans; library open to public with restrictions.

AIRESEARCH MANUFACTURING COMPANY
See: Garrett Corporation

★106★
AIRPORT OPERATORS COUNCIL INTERNATIONAL - LIBRARY (Trans)
1700 K St., N.W.   Phone: (202) 296-3270
Washington, DC 20006   Deborah E. Lunn, Dir., Pub.Rel.
Staff: Prof 1. **Subjects:** Airports, aviation. **Holdings:** Figures not available. **Services:** Library open to public. **Publications:** Airport Highlights, weekly newsletter; legal newsletter, monthly; surveys on various airport subjects.

★107★
AIRPOWER MUSEUM - LIBRARY (Trans)
Antique Airfield
Rte. 2, Box 172
Ottumwa, IA 52501   David J. Sutton, Musm. Trustee
Subjects: Historical and current aviation. **Special Collections:** Early airframe drawings, 1920-1945 (750). **Holdings:** 500 books; 20,000 periodical volumes. **Services:** Library open to public with restrictions. **Publications:** APM Bulletin, quarterly - to members. **Special Indexes:** Index to back issues of Antique Airplane Association publications. **Remarks:** Affiliated with the Antique Airplane Association.

★108★
AKIBA HEBREW ACADEMY - JOSEPH M. FIRST LIBRARY (Educ)
N. Highland Ave. & Old Lancaster Rd.
Merion, PA 19066   Jane Schofer, Libn.
Staff: Prof 2. **Subjects:** Education and pedagogy; Hebraica and Judaica. **Holdings:** 12,000 volumes. **Services:** Copying; library open to public for reference use only. **Computerized Information Services:** Computerized circulation.

★109★
AKIN, GUMP, STRAUSS, HAUER & FELD LAW LIBRARY (Law)
2800 Republic National Bank Bldg.   Phone: (214) 655-2800
Dallas, TX 75201   Joan Hass, Hd.Libn.
Subjects: Law - civil procedure, corporate, securities, tax, real estate, labor. **Holdings:** 20,000 volumes. **Subscriptions:** 50 journals and other serials. **Services:** Interlibrary loans. **Computerized Information Services:** LEXIS. **Staff:** Edgar Bone; Marla Sweet .

★110★
AKIN HALL ASSOCIATION - AKIN FREE LIBRARY (Hist)
Quaker Hill   Phone: (914) 855-5099
Pawling, NY 12564   James Mandracchia, Libn.
Staff: Prof 1. **Subjects:** Quakers, local authors, genealogy. **Special Collections:** Quaker Hill Historical Series. **Holdings:** 10,000 volumes; ledgers, 1769-1825. **Services:** Library open to public.

AKINS LIBRARY
See: Nova Scotia - Public Archives of Nova Scotia

★111★
AKRON ART MUSEUM - LIBRARY (Art)
70 E. Market St.   Phone: (216) 376-9185
Akron, OH 44308   Marcianne Herr, Cur. of Educ.
Staff: Prof 1; Other 5. **Subjects:** Art history and criticism, museology. **Special Collections:** Edwin Shaw Archives. **Holdings:** 2400 books; exhibition catalogs; art periodicals; artist monographs. **Subscriptions:** 50 journals and other serials. **Services:** Library open to members only. **Publications:** Exhibition catalogs and annual reports.

★112★
AKRON BEACON JOURNAL - REFERENCE LIBRARY (Publ)
44 E. Exchange St.   Phone: (216) 375-8514
Akron, OH 44328   Catherine M. Tierney, Chf.Libn.
Staff: Prof 1; Other 6. **Subjects:** Newspaper reference topics. **Special Collections:** Microfilmed clippings of the Kent State University student shootings from May 1970 to April 1971; Akron-built dirigibles. **Holdings:** 2000 books; newspapers on microfilm from 1839; clipping and picture files. **Services:** Library open to public with permission of executive editor or managing editors. **Special Indexes:** Typed topic index (for marking paper). **Staff:** Margaret Davis, Asst.Libn.

★113★
AKRON CITY HEALTH DEPARTMENT - PUBLIC HEALTH LIBRARY (Med)
177 S. Broadway   Phone: (216) 375-2960
Akron, OH 44308   Dr. C. William Keck, Dir. of Health
Staff: 1. **Subjects:** Public health, medicine, nursing. **Holdings:** 675 books; 80 reference file boxes; 33 films and filmstrips; pamphlets. **Subscriptions:** 60 journals and other serials; 135 newsletters. **Services:** Interlibrary loans; copying; library open to public.

★114★
AKRON CITY HOSPITAL - MEDICAL LIBRARY (Med)
525 E. Market St.   Phone: (216) 375-3360
Akron, OH 44309   Marilee S. Creelan, Dir. of Hosp.Libs.
Staff: Prof 3; Other 3. **Subjects:** Medicine, nursing, allied health science, social sciences, hospital administration. **Holdings:** 7000 books; 15,000 bound periodical volumes; 100 AV items; 750 Audio-Digests and cassettes. **Subscriptions:** 311 journals and other serials. **Services:** Interlibrary loans; copying; library open to public with director's approval. **Computerized Information Services:** BRS; computerized cataloging. **Networks/Consortia:** Member of Northeastern Ohio Universities College of Medicine (NEOUCOM). **Staff:** E. Chekouras, Ref.Libn.; V. Haren, Ref.Libn.

★115★
AKRON - DEPARTMENT OF PLANNING AND URBAN RENEWAL AND METROPOLITAN AREA TRANSPORTATION STUDY - LIBRARY (Plan)
403 Municipal Bldg.   Phone: (216) 375-2091
Akron, OH 44308   Louise A. Morris, Libn.
Founded: 1960. **Staff:** Prof 2. **Subjects:** Planning, transportation, economics, recreation, urban renewal, housing, census. **Holdings:** 2000 books; maps (cataloged). **Subscriptions:** 50 journals and other serials. **Services:** Interlibrary loans; copying; library open to public with restrictions. **Computerized Information Services:** DIALOG. **Staff:** Corliss C. Davis, Asst.Libn.

★116★
AKRON GENERAL MEDICAL CENTER - J.D. SMITH MEMORIAL LIBRARY (Med)
400 Wabash Ave.   Phone: (216) 384-6242
Akron, OH 44307   Lois Arnold, Med.Libn.
Founded: 1947. **Staff:** Prof 1; Other 1. **Subjects:** Medicine and related subjects. **Holdings:** 1500 books; 7000 bound periodical volumes; audiotapes. **Subscriptions:** 170 journals and other serials. **Services:** Interlibrary loans; copying; library open to university students. **Computerized Information Services:** BRS. **Networks/Consortia:** Member of Northeastern Ohio Universities College of Medicine (NEOUCOM). **Staff:** Lynn M. Chapman, Lib.Techn.

★117★
AKRON LAW LIBRARY (Law)
Summit County Court House
Akron, OH 44308   Phone: (216) 379-5734
     Rosemarie Chrisant, Lib.Dir.
Staff: Prof 2; Other 4. **Subjects:** Law. **Holdings:** 67,000 volumes. **Services:** Interlibrary loans; copying; library not open to public. **Staff:** Rosmarie T. Fox, Asst.Libn.

★118★
AKRON-SUMMIT COUNTY PUBLIC LIBRARY - BUSINESS, LABOR AND GOVERNMENT DIVISION (Bus-Fin)
55 S. Main St.   Phone: (216) 762-7621
Akron, OH 44326   William G. Johnson, Div.Hd.
Staff: Prof 5; Other 5. **Subjects:** Investments, business, law, transportation, economics, government. **Special Collections:** Trucking history; mail order catalogs; telephone directories (2000). **Holdings:** 27,801 books. **Subscriptions:** 972 journals and other serials; 30 newspapers. **Services:** Interlibrary loans; library open to public. **Computerized Information Services:** Online systems; computerized cataloging. **Networks/Consortia:** Member of OCLC.

★119★
AKRON-SUMMIT COUNTY PUBLIC LIBRARY - SCIENCE AND TECHNOLOGY DIVISION (Sci-Tech)
55 S. Main St.   Phone: (216) 762-7621
Akron, OH 44326   Joyce McKnight, Div.Hd.
Staff: Prof 6; Other 1. **Subjects:** Science and technology. **Special Collections:** Rubber and plastics; lighter-than-air; radio and television schematics. **Holdings:** 49,000 volumes; 50,000 pamphlets and clippings; depository for government documents. **Subscriptions:** 575 journals and other serials. **Services:** Interlibrary loans; library open to public. **Computerized Information Services:** Online systems; computerized cataloging. **Networks/Consortia:** Member of OCLC. **Special Catalogs:** Lighter-Than-Air Collection catalog (pamphlet). **Special Indexes:** Science Fair Project Index (card file and published index).

★120★
AKWESASNE LIBRARY CULTURAL CENTER (Area-Ethnic)
     Phone: (518) 358-2240
Hogansburg, NY 13655   Margaret M. Jacobs, Dir.
Staff: 3. **Special Collections:** American Indian collection (1000 items). **Holdings:** AV materials; pamphlets; framed pictures. **Subscriptions:** 71 journals and other serials. **Services:** Interlibrary loans; copying; library open to public. **Networks/Consortia:** Member of Clinton Essex Franklin Library System; North Country Reference Research Resources Council. **Publications:** Ka-Ri-Wen-Ha-Wi Newsletter, bimonthly - free upon request. **Staff:** Beatrice Cole, Libn.; Carol White, Libn.

AKZO, NV, HOLLAND - AMERICAN ENKA COMPANY
See: American Enka Company

ALA
See: American Library Association

★121★
ALABAMA A & M UNIVERSITY - JOSEPH F. DRAKE MEMORIAL LEARNING RESOURCES CENTER (Educ)
     Phone: (205) 859-7309
Normal, AL 35762   Dr. Birdie O. Weir, Dir.
Founded: 1904. **Staff:** Prof 10; Other 12. **Subjects:** Education, business, agriculture, the sciences, computer science, economics, literature, library science. **Special Collections:** Black Collection; Archival Collection (1806 items); Curriculum Collection (4790 items); Schomburg Collection; Carnegie-Mydral Collection; J.F. Kennedy Memorial Collection; ERIC Collection (315,707 microfiche); International Studies Collection; Professional Collection (10,380 items). **Holdings:** 130,866 books; 16,678 bound periodical volumes; 73,916 volumes in microform; 4528 nonprint materials (cataloged); 79,228 government documents; 10,119 periodicals on microfilm; 215 maps; 1682 college catalogs; 647 telephone directories; 30 VF drawers (9696 items). **Subscriptions:** 1124 journals and other serials; 76 newspapers. **Services:** Interlibrary loans; copying; videotaping; library open to public; courtesy card must be purchased for check out of materials by persons not enrolled at the university or at one of the cooperating institutions. **Computerized Information Services:** DIALOG. **Networks/Consortia:** Member of Alabama Center for Higher Education (ACHE). **Publications:** Mixed Media, annual newsletter; LRC News; brochures. **Special Catalogs:** The Bibliotheca, semiannual. **Also Known As:** Alabama Agricultural and Mechanical University. **Staff:** Mamie G. Browne, Univ.Archv.; Prudence W. Bryant, Libn./Hd., Rd.Serv.; Patricia D. Ford, Asst. to Dir./Acq.Libn.; Gloria B. Evans, Ser./Ref.Libn.; Larry N. Saunders, Hd., Media Serv.; Frances S. Stewart, Tech.Serv.Libn.; Kathryn B. Neal, Ref./Govt.Doc.Libn.; Joyce J. Vann, Cat.; Barbara P. Rooks, Acq.Asst.

ALABAMA BAPTIST STATE CONVENTION ARCHIVES
See: Samford University - Baptist Historical Collection

★122★
ALABAMA INSTITUTE FOR THE DEAF AND BLIND - LIBRARY FOR THE BLIND AND PHYSICALLY HANDICAPPED (Aud-Vis)
525 North Court St.　　　　　　　　Phone: (205) 362-1050
Talladega, AL 35160　　　　　　　Gloria S. Lemaster, Libn.
Founded: 1965. **Staff:** Prof 2; Other 4. **Subjects:** General interest materials. **Holdings:** 22,000 books. **Subscriptions:** 35 journals and other serials. **Services:** Interlibrary loans; copying; library open to the blind and physically handicapped only. **Publications:** Newsletter, irregular. **Remarks:** Maintained by Alabama Department of Education; serves Talladega, Coosa and St. Clair Counties, Alabama School for the Blind and E.H. Gentry Technical Facility. **Staff:** Charles J. Delong, Dir.

ALABAMA LAW REVIEW - LIBRARY
See: University of Alabama - School of Law

★123★
ALABAMA LEAGUE OF MUNICIPALITIES - LIBRARY (Soc Sci)
Box 1270　　　　　　　　　　Phone: (205) 262-2566
Montgomery, AL 36102　　　　　John F. Watkins, Exec.Dir.
Staff: Prof 1. **Subjects:** Municipal law and ordinances; intergovernmental relations, census data. **Holdings:** 1200 books; 250 bound periodical volumes; Alabama newspaper clippings; municipal subject files; state and federal agency publications. **Subscriptions:** 85 journals and other serials; 20 newspapers. **Services:** Copying; library open to member municipalities only. **Special Indexes:** Index to Alabama Municipal Journal (in preparation). **Staff:** Julianne Sinclair, Libn.

ALABAMA MARINE RESOURCES LABORATORY
See: Alabama State Department of Conservation & Natural Resources

ALABAMA MUSEUM OF THE HEALTH SCIENCES
See: University of Alabama in Birmingham - Lister Hill Library of the Health Sciences

ALABAMA MUSEUM OF NATURAL HISTORY
See: University of Alabama - Science Library

★124★
ALABAMA POWER COMPANY - LIBRARY (Energy)
600 N. 18th St.
Box 2641　　　　　　　　　　Phone: (205) 250-2180
Birmingham, AL 35291　　　　　Carol S. Johnson, Libn.
Founded: 1936. **Staff:** Prof 1. **Subjects:** Electric utilities, engineering, management. **Holdings:** 2000 books; 1500 bound periodical volumes; 15 filing cabinets of clippings and company archival materials. **Subscriptions:** 400 journals and other serials. **Services:** Interlibrary loans; library open to public for reference use only. **Computerized Information Services:** DIALOG, Electric Power Research Institute (EPRI), DOE/RECON.

★125★
ALABAMA REGIONAL LIBRARY FOR THE BLIND AND PHYSICALLY HANDICAPPED (Aud-Vis)
Alabama Public Library Service
6030 Monticello Dr.　　　　　　Phone: (205) 277-7330
Montgomery, AL 36130　　　　　Hulen E. Bivins, Hd.
Staff: Prof 6; Other 9. **Subjects:** Recorded and braille fiction and nonfiction. **Special Collections:** Locally recorded materials (100 titles). **Holdings:** 169,000 books. **Subscriptions:** 41 journals and other serials. **Services:** Interlibrary loans; copying; library open to public. **Computerized Information Services:** Computerized cataloging and circulation. **Publications:** WhAT'S LINE, quarterly - to mailing list. **Staff:** Kenneth E. Zaleski, Asst.Hd.; Hilda Dent, Rd.Adv.; Annette Cates, Rd.Adv.; James Gibson, Braille Libn.; Frazine Taylor, Volunteer Coord.

★126★
ALABAMA STATE DEPARTMENT OF ARCHIVES AND HISTORY (Hist)
624 Washington Ave.　　　　　　Phone: (205) 832-6510
Montgomery, AL 36130　　　　　Edwin C. Bridges, Dir.
Founded: 1901. **Staff:** Prof 12; Other 10. **Subjects:** Alabama - government records, history. **Holdings:** Figures not available. **Subscriptions:** 90 journals and other serials. **Services:** Copying; library open to public with restrictions, upon registration. **Networks/Consortia:** Member of OCLC through SOLINET. **Publications:** Alabama Historical Quarterly; Official and Statistical Register, quadrennial. **Staff:** Albert K. Craig, Libn.; Eugenia Rankin, Libn.; Miriam C. Jones, Archv.; D. Floyd Watson, Archv.; Genene Nelson, Archv.

★127★
ALABAMA STATE DEPARTMENT OF CONSERVATION & NATURAL RESOURCES - ALABAMA MARINE RESOURCES LAB. - LIBRARY
Box 189
Dauphin Island, AL 36528
Founded: 1962. **Subjects:** Marine biology, oceanography, aquatic life, aquaculture. **Holdings:** 486 books; 11,000 bound periodical volumes; 1500 reprints and 637 leaflets (cataloged). **Publications:** Alabama Marine Resources Bulletin. **Remarks:** Presently inactive.

ALABAMA STATE DEPARTMENT OF EDUCATION - ALABAMA INSTITUTE FOR THE DEAF AND BLIND
See: Alabama Institute for the Deaf and Blind

★128★
ALABAMA STATE DEPARTMENT OF PUBLIC HEALTH - REFERENCE LIBRARY (Med)
206 State Office Bldg.　　　　　Phone: (205) 832-3194
Montgomery, AL 36130　　　　　Fran Edwards, Lib.Techn.
Staff: 2. **Subjects:** Medicine, public health. **Special Collections:** Transactions and roster of the Alabama State Medical Association, 1852 to present; Alabama legislation. **Holdings:** 700 books; 1102 bound periodical volumes; 64 pamphlets; 800 films. **Subscriptions:** 140 journals and other serials. **Services:** Interlibrary loans; copying; library open to public. **Publications:** Annual Reports of the Health Department, 1900 to present - free upon request to libraries; Alabama's Health, monthly - free upon request to county health departments, schools and others who are interested.

★129★
ALABAMA STATE DEVELOPMENT OFFICE - PLANNING DIVISION - PLANNING REFERENCE SERVICE (Plan)
135 S. Union St.　　　　　　　Phone: (205) 832-6400
Montgomery, AL 36130　　　　　John P. Worsham, Jr., Adm.
Staff: 1. **Subjects:** Alabama - development and planning. **Holdings:** 500 books and documents; 6000 state and local documents on Alabama. **Subscriptions:** 150 journals and other serials. **Services:** Interlibrary loans; copying; bibliographies on call; current awareness; SDI; automatic mailing list; service open to public for reference use only. **Publications:** List of publications - available on request.

ALABAMA STATE GEOLOGICAL SURVEY
See: Geological Survey of Alabama

ALABAMA STATE MEDICAL ASSOCIATION
See: Alabama State Department of Public Health

★130★
ALABAMA STATE SUPREME COURT - SUPREME COURT AND STATE LAW LIBRARY (Law)
Judicial Bldg., 445 Dexter Ave.　　Phone: (205) 832-6410
Montgomery, AL 36130　　　　　William C. Younger, Dir.
Founded: 1828. **Staff:** Prof 5; Other 5. **Subjects:** Law. **Holdings:** 144,000 volumes. **Subscriptions:** 708 legal periodicals. **Services:** Interlibrary loans; copying; library open to public. **Computerized Information Services:** WESTLAW. **Networks/Consortia:** Member of OCLC through SOLINET. **Publications:** Alabama Appellate Courts Brochure, 6th edition, 1981. **Staff:** Cherry L. Thomas, Rd.Serv.Libn.; Sarah L. Frins, Tech.Serv.Libn.; Lynn D. Boyd, Govt.Doc.Libn.

★131★
ALABAMA STATE WATER IMPROVEMENT COMMISSION - LIBRARY
State Office Bldg.
Montgomery, AL 36130
Defunct

★132★
ALADDIN INDUSTRIES INC. - LIBRARY (Bus-Fin)
703 Murfreesboro Rd.　　　　　Phone: (615) 748-3427
Nashville, TN 37210　　　　　　Nancy S. Rumsey, Info.Spec.
Founded: 1970. **Staff:** Prof 1. **Subjects:** Management, business. **Holdings:** 3500 books and bound periodical volumes; 100 annual reports. **Subscriptions:** 75 journals and other serials. **Services:** Copying; library open to public with restrictions. **Computerized Information Services:** DIALOG.

★133★
ALAMANCE COUNTY PLANNING DEPARTMENT - LIBRARY
124 W. Elm St.
Graham, NC 27253
Subjects: Codes and ordinances; population and social analyses; community

facilities and services; land development and use. **Special Collections:** Alamance County Historic Site Inventory and other county history records. **Holdings:** 1000 books; 25 VF drawers of pamphlets, reports, newspaper clippings; 500 slides. **Remarks:** Presently inactive.

★134★
ALAMEDA-CONTRA COSTA MEDICAL ASSOCIATION - LIBRARY (Med)
1411 E. 31st St.   Phone: (415) 534-8055
Oakland, CA 94602   Julia T. Duboczy, Med.Libn.
Founded: 1915. **Staff:** Prof 1; Other 2. **Subjects:** Medicine, surgery, orthopedics. **Special Collections:** Association history. **Holdings:** 4550 books; 16,000 bound periodical volumes; 750 cassettes. **Subscriptions:** 325 journals and other serials; 10 newspapers. **Services:** Interlibrary loans; copying; library is open only to medical and paramedical personnel. **Computerized Information Services:** MEDLINE. **Networks/Consortia:** Member of Pacific Southwest Regional Medical Library Service (PSRMLS).

★135★
ALAMEDA COUNTY LAW LIBRARY (Law)
South County Branch
224 W. Winton Ave.   Phone: (415) 881-6380
Hayward, CA 94544   Cossette T. Sun, Law Lib.Dir.
Founded: 1967. **Staff:** Prof 1; Other 1. **Subjects:** Law. **Holdings:** 18,396 volumes; cassette tapes. **Subscriptions:** 346 journals and other serials. **Services:** Interlibrary loans; copying; library open to public. **Networks/Consortia:** Member of LAWNET. **Publications:** Acquisitions list.

★136★
ALAMEDA COUNTY LAW LIBRARY (Law)
1225 Fallon St.   Phone: (415) 874-5823
Oakland, CA 94612   Cossette T. Sun, Law Lib.Dir.
Founded: 1891. **Staff:** Prof 5; Other 6. **Subjects:** Law. **Special Collections:** California briefs. **Holdings:** 115,000 volumes. **Subscriptions:** 858 journals and other serials; 6 newspapers. **Services:** Interlibrary loans; library open to public. **Computerized Information Services:** WESTLAW; computerized cataloging. **Networks/Consortia:** Member of LAWNET. **Publications:** Acquisitions list. **Staff:** Louis E. Von Gunten, Asst.Libn.; Ronald C. Lomax, Ref.Libn.; Gary K. Kitajo, Ref.Libn.; Roberta A. Walters, Tech.Serv.Libn.

★137★
ALAMEDA COUNTY LIBRARY - BUSINESS & GOVERNMENT LIBRARY (Bus-Fin; Soc Sci)
2201 Broadway   Phone: (415) 874-5178
Oakland, CA 94612-3044   David Lewallen, Mgr.
Founded: 1968. **Staff:** Prof 4; Other 5. **Subjects:** Business (how to start and manage), investments, city and county government, real estate, insurance, accounting, economics, management and personnel, San Francisco Bay area. **Special Collections:** Alameda County employment information. **Holdings:** 12,000 books; 42 VF drawers of pamphlets. **Subscriptions:** 450 journals and other serials; 30 newspapers. **Services:** Interlibrary loans; copying; library open to public. **Computerized Information Services:** Computerized circulation. **Networks/Consortia:** Member of Bay Area Library and Information System (BALIS). **Publications:** New Books Received, irregular - free upon request; subject bibliographies, irregular. **Special Indexes:** Analytical index to representative subject material in books, documents, clippings, reports (cards); directory holdings by subject (visifile cards). **Staff:** Lillian Nurmela, Libn.; David Weber, Libn.; Joan Galvez, Libn.; Maureen Madsen, Adm.Supv.

★138★
ALAMEDA COUNTY OFFICE OF EDUCATION - TEACHERS' PROFESSIONAL LIBRARY (Educ)
685 A St.   Phone: (415) 881-6372
Hayward, CA 94541   Loretta M. Chin, Lib./Media Spec.
Founded: 1945. **Staff:** Prof 1; Other 2. **Subjects:** Education. **Special Collections:** State Instructional Materials - Print/Non-Print Display Center. **Holdings:** 9500 books and bound periodical volumes; 450 curriculum materials. **Subscriptions:** 75 journals and other serials. **Services:** Library open to public for reference use only. **Computerized Information Services:** San Mateo Educational Resource Center.

★139★
ALAMEDA COUNTY PLANNING DEPARTMENT - STAFF LIBRARY (Plan)†
399 Elmhurst St.   Phone: (415) 881-6401
Hayward, CA 94544
Staff: Prof 1; Other 1. **Subjects:** Planning, land use, resources, economics, population. **Special Collections:** General plans of Alameda County cities and places. **Holdings:** 4000 volumes; pamphlets. **Subscriptions:** 50 journals and other serials; 6 newspapers. **Services:** Library not open to public.

ALASKA AGRICULTURAL EXPERIMENT STATION
See: University of Alaska

★140★
ALASKA AIR NATIONAL GUARD - 176TH TACTICAL CLINIC MEDICAL LIBRARY (Med)
Kulis Air Natl. Guard Base
6000 Air Guard Rd.   Phone: (907) 266-1276
Anchorage, AK 99506   Billi L. Baird, Med.Libn.
Staff: 1. **Subjects:** Emergency medicine, dentistry, pharmacy, veterinary medicine, nursing. **Holdings:** 56 books. **Services:** Library not open to public.

ALASKA COURT LIBRARIES
See: Alaska State Court System

ALASKA FIELD OPERATIONS CENTER LIBRARY
See: U.S. Bureau of Mines

ALASKA GEOPHYSICAL INSTITUTE LIBRARY
See: University of Alaska - Geophysical Institute Library

★141★
ALASKA HEALTH SCIENCES LIBRARY (Med)
3211 Providence Dr.   Phone: (907) 263-1870
Anchorage, AK 99508   Stanley Truelson, Dir.
Founded: 1968. **Staff:** Prof 3; Other 6. **Subjects:** Medicine and related health sciences. **Services:** Interlibrary loans; copying; SDI; Table of Contents; library open to public with restrictions on services. **Computerized Information Services:** MEDLINE; computerized cataloging. **Networks/Consortia:** Member of WLN. **Remarks:** Administered by Alaska State Division of State Libraries & Museums. Collections merged into University of Alaska, Anchorage Library. **Staff:** Patricia A. Yenney, Libn. I; Loretta Andress, Libn. I.

ALASKA INSTITUTE OF MARINE SCIENCE
See: University of Alaska - Institute of Marine Science

ALASKA NATIVE HEALTH SERVICE
See: U.S. Public Health Service

ALASKA NATIVE LANGUAGE CENTER
See: University of Alaska

ALASKA PIPELINE COMMISSION
See: Alaska State Department of Commerce and Economic Development

ALASKA POWER ADMINISTRATION
See: U.S. Dept. of Energy

ALASKA RESOURCES LIBRARY
See: U.S. Dept. of the Interior

★142★
ALASKA STATE COURT SYSTEM - ALASKA COURT LIBRARIES (Law)
303 K St.   Phone: (907) 264-0585
Anchorage, AK 99501   Aimee Ruzicka, State Law Libn.
Founded: 1960. **Staff:** Prof 3; Other 3. **Subjects:** Law. **Holdings:** 115,000 books. **Subscriptions:** 375 journals and other serials. **Services:** Interlibrary loans; library open to public for reference use only. **Computerized Information Services:** WESTLAW; computerized cataloging. **Networks/Consortia:** Member of WLN. **Remarks:** Totals above include the holdings of the 14 branch libraries located in Bethel, Dillingham, Fairbanks, Homer, Juneau, Kenai, Ketchikan, Kodiak, Kotzebue, Nome, Palmer, Sitka, Valdez and Wrangell. **Staff:** John Akins, Ref.Libn.; Cynthia Fellows, Ref.Libn.

★143★
ALASKA STATE COURT SYSTEM - KETCHIKAN LAW LIBRARY (Law)
State Office Bldg.
415 Main St., Rm. 403   Phone: (907) 225-3196
Ketchikan, AK 99901   Berniece Cleveland, Act.Libn.
Staff: 1. **Subjects:** Law. **Holdings:** 14,000 volumes. **Subscriptions:** 20 journals and other serials. **Services:** Library open to public for reference use only.

★144★
ALASKA STATE COURT SYSTEM - VALDEZ LAW LIBRARY (Law)
Box 127   Phone: (907) 835-2266
Valdez, AK 99686   Aimee Ruzicka
Founded: 1975. **Subjects:** Law. **Holdings:** 1000 volumes. **Subscriptions:** 25 journals and other serials. **Services:** Library open to public.

★145★

ALASKA STATE DEPARTMENT OF ADMINISTRATION - STATE ARCHIVES
(Hist)
Pouch C   Phone: (907) 465-2275
Juneau, AK 99811   John M. Kinney, State Archv.
Founded: 1971. Staff: Prof 2; Other 1. Subjects: Alaska state government
records. Special Collections: Alaska Territorial Records. Holdings: 2000
cubic feet of state government records. Services: Copying; library open to
public. Special Catalogs: Microfilm index (card); finding aids to records.
Remarks: The archives are the official repository for all permanently valuable
records of the executive branch of Alaska's state government.

★146★

ALASKA STATE DEPARTMENT OF COMMERCE AND ECONOMIC
DEVELOPMENT - ALASKA PIPELINE COMMISSION - LIBRARY (Energy)*
338 Denali
McKay Bldg., 12th Fl.   Phone: (907) 279-0583
Anchorage, AK 99502   Eric Hansen, Res.Anl.
Founded: 1974. Staff: 3. Subjects: Oil and gas - pipeline transportation, law,
development. Holdings: 250 books and bound periodical volumes; 180
volumes of transcripts from pipeline hearings; 45 unbound reports; clippings.
Subscriptions: 10 journals and other serials. Services: Copying; library open
to public for reference use only. Publications: Alaska Pipeline Commission
Report to the Legislature, annual, 1974-1978 - issued to governor and
legislators; copies available to the public.

★147★

ALASKA STATE DEPARTMENT OF FISH AND GAME - LIBRARY (Env-Cons)
Box 3-2000   Phone: (907) 465-4119
Juneau, AK 99802   Sondra Stanway, Libn.
Founded: 1954. Staff: Prof 1; Other 1. Subjects: Fisheries management,
aquaculture, aquatic life, oceanography. Holdings: 300 volumes; 2000
microfiche; 100 dissertations. Subscriptions: 30 journals and other serials;
10 newspapers. Services: Interlibrary loans; copying; library open to public
with restrictions. Computerized Information Services: DIALOG.

ALASKA STATE DEPARTMENT OF HEALTH AND SOCIAL SERVICES -
LIBRARY
See: Alaska State Division of State Libraries & Museums - State Library

★148★

ALASKA STATE DEPARTMENT OF LAW - ATTORNEY GENERAL'S LIBRARY
(Law)†
Pouch K, State Capitol Bldg.   Phone: (907) 465-3600
Juneau, AK 99811
Staff: 1. Subjects: Law. Special Collections: Alaska Session Laws and Alaska
Senate and House Journals. Holdings: 3025 volumes. Subscriptions: 10
journals and other serials; 20 newspapers. Services: Copying; library open to
state residents.

★149★

ALASKA STATE DEPARTMENT OF NATURAL RESOURCES - DIVISION OF
GEOLOGICAL SURVEY - INFORMATION CENTER (Sci-Tech)†
415 Main St.
Box 7438   Phone: (907) 225-4181
Ketchikan, AK 99901   Geraldine Zartman, Mining Info.Spec.
Subjects: Mining, lands, state parks. Holdings: Figures not available.
Services: Library open to public. Publications: Monthly Bulletin; Annual;
information circulars on mining - free upon request; microfiche on statewide
claims, updated monthly - library use only; state geology and geochemical
reports - available for sale.

★150★

ALASKA STATE DEPARTMENT OF TRANSPORTATION & PUBLIC
FACILITIES - TECHNICAL LIBRARY (Trans)
Box 1467   Phone: (907) 465-2461
Juneau, AK 99802   Carol Ottesen, Libn.
Staff: Prof 1. Subjects: Highways, transportation, engineering. Holdings:
10,000 books. Subscriptions: 40 journals and other serials; 5 newspapers.
Services: Interlibrary loans; library not open to public.

ALASKA STATE DIVISION OF STATE LIBRARIES & MUSEUMS - ALASKA
HEALTH SCIENCES LIBRARY
See: Alaska Health Sciences Library

★151★

ALASKA STATE DIVISION OF STATE LIBRARIES & MUSEUMS -
HISTORICAL LIBRARY (Hist)
Pouch G   Phone: (907) 465-2925
Juneau, AK 99811   Phyllis J. DeMuth, Libn.
Founded: 1900. Staff: Prof 2; Other 1. Subjects: Alaska history, Arctic.
Special Collections: James Wickersham Collection; Dolgopolov Russian
History and Culture Collection. Holdings: 29,000 volumes including
manuscripts, tapes, video cassettes and maps; 85,000 photographs;
microfilm. Services: Noncirculating collection open to public for research; mail
or telephone reference and copying services. Networks/Consortia: Member
of Washington Library Network. Publications: Some Books About Alaska
Received, annual; Northern Libraries Bulletin, irregular. Special Indexes:
Historical monograph series includes guides and bibliographies.

★152★

ALASKA STATE DIVISION OF STATE LIBRARIES & MUSEUMS - STATE
LIBRARY (Info Sci)
Pouch G, State Office Bldg.   Phone: (907) 465-2910
Juneau, AK 99811   Richard B. Engen, Dir., Lib. & Musm.Div.
Staff: Prof 18; Other 31. Subjects: Alaska, Arctic, government and
legislative reference, planning. Holdings: 100,000 volumes; 527,000
microfiche; 84,000 reels of microfilm; manuscripts, clippings, archives,
pamphlets and documents. Subscriptions: 650 journals and other serials; 48
newspapers. Services: Interlibrary loans; copying; library open to public
through interlibrary loan. Computerized Information Services: DIALOG, SDC;
computerized cataloging. Networks/Consortia: Member of Washington
Library Network; University of Washington Libraries Resource Sharing
Program (UWRSP); Alaska Health Sciences Library; Alaska Statewide Library
Network. Publications: Alaska Blue Book. Special Catalogs: Film, record and
cassette catalogs. Special Indexes: Alaska Directory Index. Remarks:
Includes regional offices in Anchorage and Fairbanks, film libraries in
Anchorage and Juneau, Blind and Physically Handicapped, Institutions Services
in Anchorage, and the State Department of Health and Social Services Library
in Juneau. Staff: Margaret Leibowitz, Dp.Dir.

★153★

ALASKA STATE LEGISLATURE/LEGISLATIVE AFFAIRS AGENCY -
REFERENCE LIBRARY (Law)
Pouch Y, State Capitol   Phone: (907) 465-3808
Juneau, AK 99811   Jean B. Henry, Co-Libn.
Staff: Prof 2; Other 1. Subjects: State law. Special Collections: Alaska law;
Alaska Constitutional Convention papers (4 file drawers, 2 boxes); audiotapes
and files of Alaska legislative committees (30 file drawers); publications of
Legislative Affairs Agency (17 file drawers). Holdings: 1000 books; states'
current session laws on microfiche; 32 reels of microfilmed bills introduced to
Alaska legislature. Subscriptions: 180 journals and other serials. Services:
Interlibrary loans; copying; library open to public for reference use only.
Computerized Information Services: Legislative Computer Systems (internal
database). Staff: Kathryn H. Shelton, Co-Libn.

★154★

ALBANY BUSINESS COLLEGE - LIBRARY (Bus-Fin)
130 Washington Ave.   Phone: (518) 449-7163
Albany, NY 12210   Richard C. Matturro, Libn.
Founded: 1961. Staff: Prof 1. Subjects: Economics, secretarial practice,
accounting, data processing, marketing, business management. Holdings:
4900 books; 350 bound periodical volumes. Subscriptions: 49 journals and
other serials. Services: Library open to public with restrictions. Networks/
Consortia: Member of Capital District Library Council for Reference &
Research Resources.

ALBANY COLLEGE OF PHARMACY
See: Union University

★155★

ALBANY INSTITUTE OF HISTORY AND ART - MC KINNEY LIBRARY (Hist;
Art)
125 Washington Ave.   Phone: (518) 463-4478
Albany, NY 12210   James R. Hobin, Libn.
Staff: Prof 2; Other 1. Subjects: Albany and Upper Hudson region history;
American painting and decorative art reference; Hudson River School of Art.
Special Collections: Papers of Thomas Cole, 1801-1848 (395 items);
Erastus Corning, 1794-1872 (40,000 items); Erastus Dow Palmer, 1817-
1904 (361 items); John Q.A. Ward, 1830-1910 (700 items); Albany
imprints, directories, almanacs; broadsides, including the DeWitt Clinton
Collection; manuscripts, including papers of the Dutch in the Upper Hudson
Valley, 17th and 18th centuries; Albany social, political and business history,
18th and 19th centuries; American painters and sculptors. Holdings: 10,000

books; 700 bound periodical volumes; 2200 exhibition catalogs (cataloged); 500,000 manuscripts; 7000 photographs; 6 VF drawers; maps; 2000 deeds and indentures. **Subscriptions:** 55 journals and other serials. **Services:** Interlibrary loans (restricted); copying; library open to public. **Staff:** Suzanne Roberson, Asst.Libn.; Daryl Severson, Mss.Libn.

ALBANY LAW SCHOOL
See: Union University

ALBANY MEDICAL COLLEGE
See: Union University

ALBANY MEDICAL COLLEGE - CAPITAL DISTRICT PSYCHIATRIC CENTER
See: Capital District Psychiatric Center

★156★
ALBERTA ALCOHOLISM AND DRUG ABUSE COMMISSION - LIBRARY (Soc Sci)
3rd Fl., 1177 11th Ave., S.W.   Phone: (403) 244-2727
Calgary, AB, Canada T2R 0G5   Molly Taylor, Lib.Techn.
Subjects: Alcoholism, drug abuse, psychology, psychiatry. **Holdings:** 1800 books; 3000 reprints; 90 audio cassettes. **Subscriptions:** 90 journals and other serials. **Services:** Interlibrary loans; copying; library open to public. **Computerized Information Services:** Computerized cataloging. **Publications:** Acquisitions list, monthly - distributed to Commission branches and others in the addictions field.

★157★
ALBERTA ALCOHOLISM AND DRUG ABUSE COMMISSION - LIBRARY (Soc Sci)
10909 Jasper Ave., 7th Fl.   Phone: (403) 427-7303
Edmonton, AB, Canada T5J 3M9   Bette Reimer, Libn.
Founded: 1974. **Staff:** Prof 1; Other 3. **Subjects:** Alcoholism, drug dependence, counseling. **Special Collections:** Classified Abstract Archive of the Alcohol Literature (CAAAL) on microfiche (3000 documents). **Holdings:** 4000 books; 170 bound periodical volumes; 6000 reprints; 6 linear feet of news clippings. **Subscriptions:** 150 journals and other serials; 15 newspapers. **Services:** Interlibrary loans; copying; SDI; library open to public. **Computerized Information Services:** DIALOG, Info Globe, QL Systems, BRS, SDC. **Networks/Consortia:** Member of Alberta Government Libraries' Council; OCLC. **Publications:** Acquisitions list, monthly; Current Awareness, weekly - both to staff and outside professionals. **Special Indexes:** Printout KWOC index to reprints held by library; printout KWOC index to addiction articles contained in library serials collection.

★158★
ALBERTA ASSOCIATION OF REGISTERED NURSES - LIBRARY (Med)
10256 112th St.   Phone: (403) 426-0160
Edmonton, AB, Canada T5K 1M6   Lloanne G. Walker, Libn.
Founded: 1958. **Staff:** Prof 1; Other 1. **Subjects:** Nursing. **Holdings:** 2000 books. **Subscriptions:** 36 journals and other serials. **Services:** Interlibrary loans; copying; library open to related professional groups and students. **Publications:** AARN Documents.

ALBERTA ATTORNEY GENERAL
See: Alberta - Department of the Attorney General

ALBERTA COLLEGE OF ART BRANCH
See: Southern Alberta Institute of Technology - Learning Resources Centre

★159★
ALBERTA - DEPARTMENT OF ADVANCED EDUCATION AND MANPOWER - LIBRARY (Soc Sci)
9th Fl., East Tower
11160 Jasper Ave.
Edmonton, AB, Canada T5K 0L1   Phone: (403) 427-5590
          Noeline H. Bridge, Hd.Libn.
Staff: Prof 2; Other 3. **Subjects:** Manpower, higher education, immigration, career counselling, learning systems, adult education; Statistics Canada publications. **Holdings:** 9000 books; 300 pamphlets; 10 VF drawers of clippings; microforms; Alberta legislative materials. **Subscriptions:** 320 journals and other serials; 7 newspapers. **Services:** Interlibrary loans; copying; library open to public with restrictions on borrowing. **Computerized Information Services:** DIALOG, SDC. **Publications:** Library Acquisitions, monthly - for internal distribution only; Table of Contents; library brochure. **Remarks:** Includes the holdings of its Manpower Division Library.

★160★
ALBERTA - DEPARTMENT OF THE ATTORNEY GENERAL - ATTORNEY GENERAL LAW LIBRARY (Law)
4th Fl., N. Wing
9833 109th St.
Edmonton, AB, Canada T5K 2E8   Phone: (403) 427-5021
          Andrew Balazs, Dept.Libn.
Founded: 1912. **Staff:** Prof 1; Other 2. **Subjects:** Canadian civil, criminal and constitutional law. **Special Collections:** 19th century English law texts and reports (25 volumes). **Holdings:** 3440 books; 7200 bound law reports; 900 government documents; 110 audiotapes (Criminal Law Audio Series); 950 reasons and memoranda of judgements. **Subscriptions:** 240 journals and other serials; 1000 research digests. **Services:** Copying; library not open to public. **Publications:** Recent Acquisitions in the Alberta Attorney General Law Library, monthly - to all solicitors.

★161★
ALBERTA - DEPARTMENT OF THE ATTORNEY GENERAL - JUDGES' LAW LIBRARY (Law)
611 4th St., S.W.   Phone: (403) 261-7475
Calgary, AB, Canada T2P 1T5   Melody M. Hainsworth, Libn.
Staff: Prof 1; Other 4. **Subjects:** Law. **Special Collections:** Biographical information for all federal judges in Alberta. **Holdings:** 6571 volumes; 2 drawers of unreported decisions of Alberta and federal supreme courts. **Subscriptions:** 124 journals and other serials. **Services:** Interlibrary loans; copying; library not open to public. **Remarks:** Housed with Law Society of Alberta - Calgary Library.

★162★
ALBERTA - DEPARTMENT OF THE ATTORNEY GENERAL - LAW SOCIETY LIBRARY (Law)
Court House   Phone: (403) 329-3266
Lethbridge, AB, Canada T1J 0P5   Mrs. J. Kiprick, Libn.
Staff: 1. **Subjects:** Law. **Holdings:** 11,000 books; 1500 bound periodical volumes. **Subscriptions:** 50 journals and other serials. **Services:** Library not open to public.

★163★
ALBERTA - DEPARTMENT OF CONSUMER AND CORPORATE AFFAIRS - RESOURCE CENTRE (Bus-Fin)
Main Fl., 11044 82nd Ave.   Phone: (403) 427-5215
Edmonton, AB, Canada T6G 0T2   Linda Giffen, Oper.Mgr.
Staff: Prof 3; Other 3. **Subjects:** Consumer education, corporation information, insurance, real estate, credit unions, cooperatives. **Holdings:** 7000 books, bound periodical volumes and kits; 50 films; 4000 pamphlets. **Subscriptions:** 260 journals and other serials; 50 newspapers. **Services:** Interlibrary loans; copying; library open to public, with borrowing privileges to educators. **Computerized Information Services:** DIALOG, Info Globe; computerized cataloging, serials and circulation. **Networks/Consortia:** Member of Alberta Government Libraries' Council. **Publications:** Annotated Consumer Education Bibliography, annual - distributed to all schools and libraries in Alberta. **Special Indexes:** KWOC index to magazine collection; KWOC index to pamphlet collection.

★164★
ALBERTA - DEPARTMENT OF CULTURE - DEPARTMENTAL LIBRARY (Art)
CN Tower, 11th Fl.
10004 104th Ave.   Phone: (403) 427-2571
Edmonton, AB, Canada T5J 0K5   Lucy M. Pana, Dept.Libn.
Founded: 1972. **Staff:** Prof 1; Other 2. **Subjects:** Performing arts, fine arts, librarianship. **Special Collections:** Plays (one-act, full-length, collections; 6000 items); sheet music (instrumental and choral; 5000 items). **Holdings:** 4500 books; 1000 cataloged pamphlets; 15 VF drawers of uncataloged pamphlets. **Subscriptions:** 200 journals and other serials; 50 newspapers. **Services:** Interlibrary loans; copying; library open to public with restrictions.

★165★
ALBERTA - DEPARTMENT OF CULTURE - HISTORICAL RESOURCES LIBRARY (Hist)
12845 102nd Ave.   Phone: (403) 452-2150
Edmonton, AB, Canada T5N 0M6   Mrs. J. Toon, Libn.
Founded: 1967. **Staff:** Prof 1; Other 2. **Subjects:** Alberta history and natural history; Indians of Alberta; museum and archive techniques; antiques; historic preservation. **Special Collections:** Alberta local histories. **Holdings:** 20,000 books; 1000 bound periodical volumes; 1000 pamphlets. **Subscriptions:** 350 journals and other serials. **Services:** Interlibrary loans; copying; library open to public for reference use only. **Special Catalogs:** List of Alberta local histories in library (loose-leaf); periodical holdings (book).

★166★
ALBERTA - DEPARTMENT OF ECONOMIC DEVELOPMENT - LIBRARY (Bus-Fin; Plan)
11th Fl., Pacific Plaza
10909 Jasper Ave.   Phone: (403) 427-4957
Edmonton, AB, Canada T5J 3M8   Donna M. Gordon, Libn.
Founded: 1979. Staff: Prof 1; Other 2. Subjects: International trade, marketing, planning, transportation, economics, administration. Special Collections: Statistics Canada publications, 1979 to present (27 shelves); annual reports from 700 companies (8 drawers). Holdings: 3000 books. Subscriptions: 300 journals and other serials; 15 newspapers. Services: Interlibrary loans; copying; SDI; library open to public for reference use only. Computerized Information Services: DIALOG, Info Globe, INFOMART, CAN/OLE, CANSIM.

★167★
ALBERTA - DEPARTMENT OF EDUCATION - LIBRARY (Educ)
4th Fl., Devonian Bldg.
11160 Jasper Ave.   Phone: (403) 427-2985
Edmonton, AB, Canada T5K 0L2   Helen Skirrow, Adm., Lib.Serv.
Staff: Prof 6; Other 29. Subjects: Education - reference and research, trends, preschool, intercultural, administration, supervision, evaluation, curriculum building. Special Collections: Archives Collection of Alberta Education; curriculum guides; ERIC documents on microfiche; master and student copies of braille books, large print books and tapes (3000 titles). Holdings: 8000 books; 800 bound periodical volumes; 2000 government reports and documents; 3000 microforms; 2000 archives; 1000 pamphlets. Subscriptions: 500 journals and other serials. Services: Interlibrary loans; copying; library open to teachers, civil servants and public. Computerized Information Services: DIALOG, SDC; computerized cataloging. Networks/Consortia: Member of UTLAS. Publications: Library News & Acquisitions; Content Pages. Special Indexes: KWOC index of curriculum materials for regional offices; KWOC index to special format textbooks (online). Staff: Marie Matiaszow, Mtls.Rsrcs.Ctr./N.; Darlene Taylor, Mtls.Rsrcs.Ctr./S.; Shirley Wolodko, Libn., Ctrl.Lib.; David Ruston, Libn./Cat., Ctrl.Lib.; Louise Grady, Libn./Cat.; Dixie Anderson, Lib.Asst.-Ref.

★168★
ALBERTA - DEPARTMENT OF ENERGY AND NATURAL RESOURCES - LIBRARY (Energy)
9th Fl., South Tower, Petroleum Plaza
9915 108th St.   Phone: (403) 427-7425
Edmonton, AB, Canada T5K 2C9   Peter K. Mutchler, Chf.Libn.
Founded: 1977. Staff: Prof 2; Other 6. Subjects: Energy resources, forestry, mineral resources, public lands, reclamation, energy conservation, fish and wildlife. Special Collections: Herbarium of Alberta forage plants (6 cabinets). Holdings: 15,000 books; 200 bound periodical volumes; 810 folders of clipping files; 381 folders in VF drawers; 150 microfiche. Subscriptions: 450 journals and other serials; 15 newspapers. Services: Interlibrary loans; copying; SDI; library open to public. Computerized Information Services: DIALOG, QL Systems, Info Globe, SDC, CISTI. Networks/Consortia: Member of Alberta Government Libraries' Council. Publications: New Books, bimonthly; Current Magazine Articles, weekly - both for internal distribution only. Special Indexes: Energy and Natural Resources KWOC Indexes.

★169★
ALBERTA - DEPARTMENT OF ENERGY AND NATURAL RESOURCES - MAP & AIR PHOTO REFERENCE LIBRARY (Geog-Map; Pict)
2nd Fl. W., North Tower, Petroleum Plaza
9945 108th St.   Phone: (403) 427-7417
Edmonton, AB, Canada T5K 2G6   Alice S. Chen, Supv.
Founded: 1950. Staff: 2. Subjects: Alberta - aerial photography and maps. Holdings: 150 books; 600,000 air photos; 6000 maps; 900 microfilm cassettes. Services: Copying; library open to public. Publications: Aerial Photography & Mosaics Brochure, annual; Map Catalogue, annual - both distributed on request; Distribution Services Newsletter, annual. Special Catalogs: Map Catalogue. Special Indexes: Aerial photography index maps. Staff: B. Pike, Technologist.

ALBERTA - DEPT. OF ENERGY AND NATURAL RESOURCES - SOLAR & WIND ENERGY RESEARCH PROGRAM INFO. CENTRE
See: Alberta Research Council - Solar & Wind Energy Research Program (SWERP) Information Centre

★170★
ALBERTA - DEPARTMENT OF THE ENVIRONMENT - LIBRARY (Env-Cons)
14th Fl., Oxbridge Place
9820 106th St.   Phone: (403) 427-6132
Edmonton, AB, Canada T5K 2J6   Ione Hooper, Libn.
Founded: 1971. Staff: Prof 2; Other 7. Subjects: Water resources; land use planning; environmental conservation; pollution - air, water, odor, noise. Holdings: 25,000 books; 475 bound periodical volumes; 6 drawers of maps; 4 cabinets of microfiche. Subscriptions: 600 journals and other serials; 25 newspapers. Services: Interlibrary loans; copying; library open to public. Computerized Information Services: DIALOG, SDC, QL Systems, SPIRES. Publications: Acquisition list, monthly; periodical list, semimonthly; Athabasca Oil Sands Bibliography. Special Indexes: KWIC index of periodical titles held by library. Staff: Betty Rost, Cat.; J. Thomas, ILL.

★171★
ALBERTA - DEPARTMENT OF FEDERAL AND INTERGOVERNMENTAL AFFAIRS - LIBRARY (Soc Sci)
14th Fl., South Tower
10030 107th St.   Phone: (403) 427-2611
Edmonton, AB, Canada T5J 3E4   Anita E. Duncan, Lib.Techn.
Staff: Prof 2. Subjects: Intergovernmental affairs, political science. Holdings: 2347 federal and provincial government publications and documents; 250 Alberta and federal annual reports; 6 VF drawers of newspaper clippings; 4 VF drawers of intergovernmental agreements. Subscriptions: 155 journals and other serials; 10 newspapers. Services: Interlibrary loans; copying; library open to public for reference use only. Publications: Acquisitions lists, monthly.

★172★
ALBERTA - DEPARTMENT OF HOSPITALS AND MEDICAL CARE - HOSPITAL SERVICES LIBRARY (Med)
11010 101st St., 5th Fl.
Box 2222   Phone: (403) 427-8720
Edmonton, AB, Canada T5J 2P4   Margaret Bradfield, Lib.Techn.
Staff: 2. Subjects: Hospital administration, nursing and pharmacy. Holdings: 6000 books; 211 bound periodical volumes; 60 AV items. Subscriptions: 247 journals and other serials; 6 newspapers. Services: Interlibrary loans; copying; library open to public with restrictions. Publications: Book acquisitions, monthly; table of contents pages of journals, semimonthly.

★173★
ALBERTA - DEPARTMENT OF HOUSING AND PUBLIC WORKS - HOUSING LIBRARY (Soc Sci)†
10050 112th St., 4th Fl.   Phone: (403) 427-8144
Edmonton, AB, Canada T5K 1L9   Dolores Ogilvie, Libn.
Founded: 1970. Staff: 1. Subjects: Housing, land development, neighbourhood improvement, urban development, loans and mortgages. Holdings: 4500 books; 5 boxes of acts and regulations; Canada information; 26 binders of Alberta Hansard and Gazette. Subscriptions: 111 journals and other serials; 21 newspapers. Services: Interlibrary loans; library open to public by appointment.

★174★
ALBERTA - DEPARTMENT OF LABOUR - BUILDING STANDARDS BRANCH RESOURCE CENTRE (Sci-Tech)
10808 99th Ave., Rm. 707   Phone: (403) 427-8265
Edmonton, AB, Canada T5K 0G2
Founded: 1976. Subjects: Building standards, construction, engineering. Holdings: 350 books; 4000 standards; 300 manufacturers catalogs; 4 VF drawers of clippings. Subscriptions: 64 journals and other serials. Services: Library open to public for reference use only.

★175★
ALBERTA - DEPARTMENT OF LABOUR - LABOUR LIBRARY (Bus-Fin)
10808 99th Ave., Rm. 501   Phone: (403) 427-8531
Edmonton, AB, Canada T5K 0G2   Wendy Kinsella, Hd.Libn.
Founded: 1975. Staff: Prof 2; Other 4. Subjects: Labour law, human rights, building standards, inspection services, industrial relations, management. Holdings: 6000 books; 300 bound periodical volumes; 220 microforms; 2550 pamphlets. Subscriptions: 350 journals and other serials; 5 newspapers. Services: Interlibrary loans; copying; library open to public for reference use only. Computerized Information Services: DIALOG, SDC, Info Globe, CAN/OLE. Publications: Compendium, bimonthly; Directory of Industrial Relations Libraries in Canada, annual; Bibliography Series, irregular. Special Indexes: Alberta Board of Industrial Relations Decisions Index (book). Remarks: Contains the holdings of the former Alberta Human Rights Commission - Library. Staff: Alison O'Sullivan, Pub.Serv.Libn.

★176★
ALBERTA - DEPARTMENT OF MUNICIPAL AFFAIRS - LIBRARY (Plan)
9925 107th St., 9th Fl.   Phone: (403) 427-4829
Edmonton, AB, Canada T5K 2H9   Bettie Bayrak, Libn.
Founded: 1975. **Staff:** Prof 1; Other 3. **Subjects:** Urban and regional planning; municipal government and finance. **Holdings:** 14,000 books. **Subscriptions:** 250 journals and other serials; 50 newspapers. **Services:** Interlibrary loans; copying; library open to public for reference use only. **Publications:** Urban & Regional Studies in Alberta, annual; Alberta Municipal Affairs Publications, annual - both to mailing list and by request.

★177★
ALBERTA - DEPARTMENT OF RECREATION & PARKS - LIBRARY (Rec)
Standard Life Centre, 8th Fl.
10405 Jasper Ave.   Phone: (403) 427-7638
Edmonton, AB, Canada T5J 3N4   Michael N. Aston, Dept.Libn.
Staff: Prof 2. **Subjects:** Parks - planning, design; wilderness areas; outdoor recreation; recreation administration; leisure; natural history; sports. **Holdings:** 7000 books; 200 cassettes; 500 microforms. **Subscriptions:** 202 journals and other serials. **Services:** Interlibrary loans; copying; library open to public with borrowing only through ILL. **Computerized Information Services:** Computerized cataloging, serials and circulation. **Publications:** Library Bulletin, monthly - for internal distribution only. **Special Indexes:** Index of periodical articles in select periodicals (computer printout).

ALBERTA - DEPARTMENT OF SOCIAL SERVICES AND COMMUNITY HEALTH - ALBERTA HOSPITAL PONOKA
See: Alberta Hospital Ponoka

ALBERTA - DEPARTMENT OF SOCIAL SERVICES AND COMMUNITY HEALTH - ALBERTA MENTAL HEALTH SERVICES
See: Alberta Mental Health Services

★178★
ALBERTA - DEPARTMENT OF SOCIAL SERVICES & COMMUNITY HEALTH - LIBRARY (Soc Sci)
6th Fl., Seventh St. Plaza
10030 107th St.   Phone: (403) 427-7272
Edmonton, AB, Canada T5J 3E4   Pauline Howatt, Dept.Libn.
Founded: 1972. **Staff:** Prof 2; Other 4. **Subjects:** Social services, public health, mental health, handicapped. **Holdings:** 15,000 books; 1500 bound periodical volumes; 8 VF drawers; 25 shelves of Statistics Canada publications. **Subscriptions:** 455 journals and other serials; 7 newspapers. **Services:** Interlibrary loans; copying; library open to public with restrictions. **Computerized Information Services:** DIALOG, MEDLINE. **Networks/Consortia:** Member of Alberta Government Libraries' Council. **Publications:** New Books, monthly - for internal distribution only. **Staff:** Teresa Bendall, Asst.Libn.

★179★
ALBERTA - DEPARTMENT OF THE SOLICITOR GENERAL - LIBRARY (Law)
Melton Bldg., 5th Fl.
10310 Jasper Ave.   Phone: (403) 427-3421
Edmonton, AB, Canada T5J 2W4   Aileen Wright, Dept.Libn.
Staff: Prof 4; Other 2. **Subjects:** Criminal justice and corrections, law enforcement, crime prevention, administration, transportation. **Special Collections:** Crime prevention films (55 titles). **Holdings:** 4000 books; 2000 documents; 400 microfiche. **Subscriptions:** 200 journals and other serials; 6 newspapers. **Services:** Interlibrary loans; copying; library open to public at discretion of librarian. **Computerized Information Services:** DIALOG. **Networks/Consortia:** Member of Alberta Government Libraries' Council. **Publications:** Selective List of Periodicals, monthly; Acquisition List, quarterly. **Special Catalogs:** Crime Prevention Film Catalogue. **Staff:** Kathryn Ribeiro, Regional Libn. (North); Marcia Ducharme, Regional Libn. (South); Eunice Cutting, Lib.Asst.

★180★
ALBERTA - DEPARTMENT OF TOURISM AND SMALL BUSINESS - LIBRARY (Bus-Fin)
15th Fl., Capitol Sq.
10065 Jasper Ave.   Phone: (403) 427-3294
Edmonton, AB, Canada T5J 0H4   Glenna Winter, Libn.
Founded: 1979. **Staff:** 2. **Subjects:** Business, economics, industrial studies, regional business development, tourism. **Holdings:** 5000 books. **Subscriptions:** 250 journals and other serials; 14 newspapers. **Services:** Interlibrary loans; library open to public with restrictions.

★181★
ALBERTA - DEPARTMENT OF TRANSPORTATION - LIBRARY (Trans)
9630 106th St.   Phone: (403) 427-8802
Edmonton, AB, Canada T5K 2B8   D.L. Smith, Dept.Libn.
Founded: 1975. **Staff:** Prof 1; Other 3. **Subjects:** Highway planning, construction and maintenance; urban transportation; transportation safety. **Special Collections:** Transportation Research Board reports; Transport and Road Research Laboratory reports. **Holdings:** 7500 books and cataloged reports; 4500 technical reports; 6 VF drawers of pamphlets and miscellaneous reports; 15 films; 500 microfiche. **Subscriptions:** 350 journals and other serials. **Services:** Interlibrary loans; copying; library open to public for reference use only. **Computerized Information Services:** DIALOG, CAN/OLE. **Networks/Consortia:** Member of Alberta Government Libraries' Council. **Publications:** Library Bulletin, monthly - for internal distribution only.

★182★
ALBERTA - DEPARTMENT OF TREASURY - BUREAU OF STATISTICS LIBRARY (Bus-Fin)
7th Fl., Sir Frederick W. Haultain Bldg.
9811 109th St.   Phone: (403) 427-3058
Edmonton, AB, Canada T5K 0C8   Christine Minailo, Lib.Techn.
Founded: 1955. **Staff:** Prof 1. **Subjects:** Statistics, economics, census of Canada. **Special Collections:** Statistics Canada publications (1500 items). **Holdings:** 4600 books and bound periodical volumes; maps; microforms. **Services:** Interlibrary loans; library open to public with restrictions on borrowing. **Computerized Information Services:** Computerized serials. **Special Catalogs:** Statistics catalog. **Special Indexes:** Index of library's microforms.

★183★
ALBERTA - DEPARTMENT OF TREASURY - CORPORATE TAX ADMINISTRATION LIBRARY (Bus-Fin; Law)
Sir Fredrick Haultain Bldg., 5th Fl.
9811 109th St.   Phone: (403) 427-9425
Edmonton, AB, Canada T5K 0C8   Helen Harness
Founded: 1981. **Staff:** Prof 1. **Subjects:** Taxation, law, auditing, business. **Holdings:** 300 books; 25 bound periodical volumes; 30 boxes of government documents; 1 file drawer of clippings. **Subscriptions:** 56 journals and other serials. **Services:** Interlibrary loans; copying; library open to public with restrictions.

★184★
ALBERTA - DEPARTMENT OF TREASURY - LIBRARY SERVICES (Bus-Fin)
404 Terrace Bldg.
9515 107th St.   Phone: (403) 427-7595
Edmonton, AB, Canada T5K 2C3   J. Robin Brown, Dept.Libn.
Founded: 1974. **Staff:** Prof 3. **Subjects:** Economics, banking, taxation, statistics. **Holdings:** 8000 books. **Subscriptions:** 310 journals and other serials; 10 newspapers. **Services:** Interlibrary loans; library open to public with special permission. **Publications:** Library Bulletin, bimonthly; Table of Contents, weekly.

★185★
ALBERTA - ENERGY RESOURCES CONSERVATION BOARD - LIBRARY (Energy)
640 5th Ave., S.W.   Phone: (403) 261-8242
Calgary, AB, Canada T2P 3G4   Liz Johnson, Libn.
Founded: 1964. **Staff:** Prof 1; Other 2. **Subjects:** Oil, gas, coal, hydro and electric power, pipelines, geology, energy economics. **Holdings:** 4000 books; 5000 government documents (cataloged). **Subscriptions:** 400 journals and other serials; 12 newspapers. **Services:** Interlibrary loans; copying; library open to public by permission. **Computerized Information Services:** Online systems; computerized cataloging. **Publications:** Accessions List - distributed on request.

★186★
ALBERTA - ENVIRONMENT COUNCIL - INFORMATION CENTRE (Env-Cons)†
2100 College Plaza, Tower 3
8215 112th St.   Phone: (403) 427-5792
Edmonton, AB, Canada T6G 2M4   Colleen MacLachlan, Libn.
Founded: 1971. **Staff:** Prof 1; Other 1. **Subjects:** Conservation, energy, land use, renewable and nonrenewable resources, pollution, urbanization. **Special Collections:** Mackenzie Valley Pipeline Inquiry Transcripts (281 volumes). **Holdings:** 5000 books and government reports; ECA reports and recommendations, proceedings and summaries of public hearings; 3 VF drawers of pamphlets; 8 VF drawers of clippings. **Subscriptions:** 140 journals and other serials; 10 newspapers. **Services:** Interlibrary loans; copying; library open to public with restrictions on borrowing. **Publications:** List of ECA publications - distributed on request.

★187★
ALBERTA - GOVERNMENT SERVICES - INFORMATION SERVICES DIVISION LIBRARY (Bus-Fin)
9515 107th St., Rm. 259
Edmonton, AB, Canada T5K 2C4
Phone: (403) 427-2353
Danielle Bugeaud, Libn.
Founded: 1977. **Staff:** Prof 2; Other 2. **Subjects:** Data processing, management. **Holdings:** 2000 books; 200 reports. **Subscriptions:** 250 journals and other serials; 9 newspapers. **Services:** Interlibrary loans; copying; reference/research; library not open to public. **Publications:** New Books List. **Special Indexes:** Keyword Index to Periodical Articles.

★188★
ALBERTA HEART FOUNDATION - LIBRARY (Med)
2011 10th Ave., S.W.
Calgary, AB, Canada T3C 0K4
Phone: (403) 244-0786
Emily Alstad, Educ.Coord.
Staff: Prof 1; Other 2. **Subjects:** Cardiovascular health and disease, stress, smoking, nutrition and heart health. **Holdings:** 600 books and pamphlets; 54 films; 12 slide-tape presentations. **Subscriptions:** 7 journals and other serials. **Services:** Interlibrary loans; copying; library open to public with restrictions. **Publications:** Coronary Care Newsletter, quarterly.

★189★
ALBERTA HOSPITAL ASSOCIATION - RESOURCE CENTRE (Med)
10025 108th St., 6th Fl.
Edmonton, AB, Canada T5J 1K9
Phone: (403) 423-1776
Patricia Baxter, Libn.
Staff: 1. **Subjects:** Health care management and research; systems development. **Holdings:** 1000 books; 50 bound periodical volumes; 400 briefs and studies (cataloged). **Subscriptions:** 60 journals and other serials. **Services:** Interlibrary loans; copying; library open to public at librarian's discretion.

★190★
ALBERTA HOSPITAL - LIBRARY (Med)†
Box 307
Edmonton, AB, Canada T5J 2J7
Phone: (403) 973-2268
Margaret Pierre, Lib.Techn. (Supv.)
Subjects: Psychiatry, psychiatric nursing, psychology, neuropsychology, social service, occupational and recreational therapy, gerontology, forensic psychiatry, hospital administration, rehabilitation. **Holdings:** 3000 books; 100 periodicals. **Services:** Interlibrary loans; library not open to public. **Networks/Consortia:** Member of Alberta Government Libraries' Council.

★191★
ALBERTA HOSPITAL PONOKA - STAFF LIBRARY (Med)
P.O. Box 1000
Ponoka, AB, Canada T0C 2H0
Phone: (403) 783-3351
Peter Managhan, Staff Libn.
Staff: Prof 1; Other 1. **Subjects:** Psychiatry and psychiatric nursing, psychology, social work, geriatrics, medicine, nursing. **Holdings:** 4000 books; VF material; cassette tapes. **Subscriptions:** 97 journals and other serials. **Services:** Interlibrary loans; copying; library open to public. **Remarks:** Maintained by the Alberta Department of Social Services and Community Health.

★192★
ALBERTA HUMAN RIGHTS COMMISSION - LIBRARY
10053 111th St., Rm. 501
Edmonton, AB, Canada T5K 2H8
Defunct. Holdings absorbed by Alberta - Department of Labour - Labour Library.

ALBERTA LAW SOCIETY
See: Law Society of Alberta

★193★
ALBERTA - LEGISLATIVE ASSEMBLY OF ALBERTA - LEGISLATURE LIBRARY (Law)
216 Legislature Bldg.
Edmonton, AB, Canada T5K 2B6
Phone: (403) 427-2473
D.B. McDougall, Leg.Libn.
Founded: 1906. **Staff:** Prof 6; Other 22. **Subjects:** Political science, law, economics, sociology, Canadian history. **Special Collections:** Most provincial weekly newspapers since 1907. **Holdings:** 131,557 volumes; Alberta and federal government documents. **Subscriptions:** 466 journals and other serials; 135 newspapers. **Services:** Interlibrary loans; copying; library open to public with restrictions. **Computerized Information Services:** CAN/OLE, DIALOG, Info Globe, INFOMART, SDC, New York Times Information Service, Library Information Services, QL Systems, SPIRES, Cooperative Documents Network Project (CODOC); computerized cataloging, serials and indexing of government publications. **Networks/Consortia:** Member of Alberta Government Libraries' Council. **Publications:** Annual Report; New Books in the Library, 11/year; Selected Periodical Articles List, 11/year; Alberta

Government Libraries' Newsletter, 11/year; Directory of Alberta Government Libraries, semiannual; Library Handbook, biennial. **Special Catalogs:** Alberta Government Libraries' Union Catalog; Union List of Serials in Alberta Government Libraries. **Staff:** L.R. Buhr, Hd., Info. & Ref.Serv.; K.L. Powell, Coord., Coop.Govt.Serv.

★194★
ALBERTA MENTAL HEALTH SERVICES - CLINIC LIBRARY (Med)†
5th Fl., 9942 108th St.
Edmonton, AB, Canada T5K 2J5
Founded: 1948. **Staff:** 1. **Subjects:** Psychiatry, psychology, nursing, occupational therapy, social work, domestic science. **Holdings:** 1290 books. **Subscriptions:** 38 journals and other serials. **Services:** Library not open to public. **Remarks:** Maintained by Alberta Department of Social Services and Community Health.

★195★
ALBERTA MENTAL HEALTH SERVICES - LIBRARY (Soc Sci)
Zapotec Bldg., 2nd Fl.
1000 8th Ave., S.W.
Calgary, AB, Canada T2P 3M7
Phone: (403) 261-7483
K.L. Walsh, Chm., Lib.Comm.
Founded: 1955. **Staff:** Prof 2. **Subjects:** Emotional disturbance in children, psychiatry, social work, psychology, community organization, social planning. **Holdings:** 511 books. **Subscriptions:** 28 journals and other serials. **Services:** Interlibrary loans; library open to public. **Remarks:** Maintained by Alberta Department of Social Services and Community Health.

★196★
ALBERTA - OFFICE OF THE OMBUDSMAN - OMBUDSMAN'S LIBRARY (Soc Sci)†
1630 Phipps-McKinnon Bldg.
10020 101A Ave.
Edmonton, AB, Canada T5J 3G2
Phone: (403) 427-2756
Ms. D. Harry, Supv.
Subjects: Government information, law. **Holdings:** 300 books; 80 bound periodical volumes; 70 pamphlets; 14 maps; government reports and statutes; Ombudsman annual reports from around the world; special reports of the Ombudsman, Province of Alberta. **Services:** Interlibrary loans (restricted); library not open to public.

ALBERTA OIL SANDS INFORMATION CENTRE
See: Alberta Research Council

★197★
ALBERTA - PERSONNEL ADMINISTRATION OFFICE - LIBRARY (Bus-Fin)
Jarvis Bldg., 12th Fl.
9925 107th St.
Edmonton, AB, Canada T5K 2H9
Phone: (403) 427-7897
Jasveer Jhass, Lib.Techn.
Staff: Prof 1. **Subjects:** Management, personnel, training, women, retirement. **Holdings:** 1141 books. **Subscriptions:** 89 journals and other serials; 5 newspapers. **Services:** Interlibrary loans; copying; library open to public with restrictions.

★198★
ALBERTA PETROLEUM MARKETING COMMISSION - LIBRARY (Energy; Bus-Fin)
250 6th Ave., S.W., No. 1900
Calgary, AB, Canada T2P 3H7
Phone: (403) 262-8808
T. Armanious, Libn.
Staff: Prof 1; Other 2. **Subjects:** Petroleum. **Holdings:** 2200 books; periodicals. **Subscriptions:** 500 journals and other serials; 5 newspapers. **Services:** Interlibrary loans; copying; library open to other libraries only. **Computerized Information Services:** Infomart, SDC, Info Globe; computerized cataloging and serials. **Publications:** New books list, irregular - for internal distribution only.

★199★
ALBERTA - PUBLIC UTILITIES BOARD - LIBRARY (Bus-Fin; Energy)
Manulife House, 11th Floor
10055 106th St.
Edmonton, AB, Canada T5J 2Y2
Phone: (403) 427-4901
James E. McKee, Lib.Techn.
Founded: 1915. **Staff:** 2. **Subjects:** Public utilities, law, accounting, engineering, business, statistics. **Holdings:** 2800 books; 200 reports and government documents. **Subscriptions:** 100 journals and other serials. **Services:** Library not open to public. **Remarks:** This library also operates an extension library in Calgary.

★200★

ALBERTA RESEARCH COUNCIL - ALBERTA OIL SANDS INFORMATION CENTRE (Sci-Tech)
6th Fl., Highfield Pl.
10010 106th St.   Phone: (403) 427-8382
Edmonton, AB, Canada T5J 3L8   Helga Radvanyi, Mgr.
Founded: 1975. **Staff:** Prof 3; Other 7. **Subjects:** Oil sands, heavy oil, enhanced recovery. **Holdings:** 8200 volumes. **Services:** Copying; library open to public. **Computerized Information Services:** SPIRES, CAN/OLE; computerized acquisitions and circulation. **Publications:** TAR Paper (newsletter), bimonthly; Oil Sands Researchers' Projects, annual. **Special Indexes:** Alberta Oil Sands Index; Heavy Oil/Enhanced Recovery Index (both hard copy and computerized).

★201★

ALBERTA RESEARCH COUNCIL - LIBRARY SERVICES (Sci-Tech)
Terrace Plaza
4445 Calgary Trail, S.   Phone: (403) 438-1810
Edmonton, AB, Canada T6H 5R7   Sharon M. Gee, Mgr.
Founded: 1921. **Staff:** Prof 4; Other 6. **Subjects:** Geology, groundwater, soils, atmospheric sciences, forest products, engineering, chemistry, frontier sciences, computing, transportation and surface engineering, chemical processing, electricity, energy. **Holdings:** 42,000 books; 15,000 reports; 2000 maps. **Subscriptions:** 750 journals and other serials; 20 newspapers. **Services:** Interlibrary loans; copying; SDI; library open to public. **Computerized Information Services:** DIALOG, SDC, CAN/OLE, QL Systems, SPIRES; SCITECH (internal database); computerized cataloging and serials. **Networks/Consortia:** Member of SCITECH. **Remarks:** Maintains 2 branch libraries. **Staff:** Karen Fletcher, Sys./Cat.; Jennifer Fuller, Ref.; Barbara Storms, Cat.

★202★

ALBERTA RESEARCH COUNCIL - SOLAR & WIND ENERGY RESEARCH PROGRAM (SWERP) INFORMATION CENTRE (Energy)
5th Fl., Terrace Plaza
4445 Calgary Trail, S.   Phone: (403) 438-1808
Edmonton, AB, Canada T6H 5R7   Karen D. Beliveau, Coord.
Founded: 1977. **Staff:** Prof 1; Other 1. **Subjects:** Passive and active solar heating, solar technology, photovoltaics, wind energy, solar cooling. **Holdings:** 2500 books; 1536 bound periodical volumes; 1000 government documents; 3000 unbound reports. **Subscriptions:** 47 journals and other serials. **Services:** Interlibrary loans; copying; library open to public. **Computerized Information Services:** Online systems; computerized cataloging. **Publications:** Monthly Accessions List. **Special Indexes:** SWERP Index (4 volumes), annual, with supplement. **Remarks:** The Centre is administered by the Alberta Department of Energy and Natural Resources.

★203★

ALBERTA SCHOOL FOR THE DEAF - L.A. BROUGHTON LIBRARY (Educ)
6240 113th St.   Phone: (403) 434-1481
Edmonton, AB, Canada T6H 3L2   Charmaine Muise, Teacher/Libn.
Staff: Prof 1. **Subjects:** Deafness - teaching, psychology, research, educational technology. **Holdings:** 1500 books; tapes; 50 journals and annuals. **Subscriptions:** 25 journals and other serials. **Services:** Interlibrary loans; library not open to public.

★204★

ALBERTA SOCIETY FOR AUTISTIC CHILDREN - LIBRARY (Soc Sci)
Edmonton School for Autistic Children
7330 113th St.   Phone: (403) 435-0161
Edmonton, AB, Canada T6G 1L6   Rheva Frank, Prog.Dir.
Subjects: Behavior analysis, autism. **Holdings:** Figures not available. **Subscriptions:** 18 journals and other serials. **Services:** Library open to public by appointment.

★205★

ALBERTA TEACHERS' ASSOCIATION - LIBRARY (Educ)
11010 142nd St., Barnett House
Edmonton, AB, Canada T5N 2R1   Phone: (403) 453-2411
                                                          Maria Loranger, Libn.
Founded: 1935. **Staff:** Prof 1; Other 1. **Subjects:** Instructional methods, philosophy, psychology, educational research, sociology, history of education, administration. **Special Collections:** ATA publications. **Holdings:** 6000 volumes. **Subscriptions:** 120 journals and other serials. **Services:** Library open to public for reference use only. **Publications:** Bibliographies on selected subjects.

★206★

ALBERTA - WORKERS' HEALTH SAFETY & COMPENSATION - OCCUPATIONAL HEALTH & SAFETY LIBRARY (Med)
5th Fl., 10709 Jasper Ave.   Phone: (403) 427-4671
Edmonton, AB, Canada T5J 3N3   W. Keith McLaughlin, Libn.
Founded: 1977. **Staff:** Prof 6; Other 2. **Subjects:** Occupational medicine, industrial safety, chemical toxicology, radiation. **Special Collections:** U.S. NIOSH Recommended Standards...(600 volumes); U.S. Bureau of Mines Reports of Investigations (400 volumes). **Holdings:** 8000 books; 1000 bound periodical volumes; 350 films; 22,000 pamphlets and reprints. **Subscriptions:** 500 journals and other serials; 15 newspapers. **Services:** Interlibrary loans; library open to public with restrictions. **Computerized Information Services:** DIALOG. **Networks/Consortia:** Member of OCLC. **Publications:** Recent Acquisitions, monthly; Film Catalog - both available on request. **Staff:** Helene Wickins; Ann Chung .

★207★

ALBERTO-CULVER COMPANY - RESEARCH LIBRARY (Sci-Tech)
2525 Armitage Ave.   Phone: (312) 450-3313
Melrose Park, IL 60160   Ellen P. Gunther, Res.Libn.
Staff: Prof 1; Other 1. **Subjects:** Toiletries, household and grocery products. **Holdings:** 2000 books; 2000 bound periodical volumes; 12 VF drawers of pamphlets. **Subscriptions:** 195 journals and other serials. **Services:** Interlibrary loans; copying; library not open to public. **Computerized Information Services:** DIALOG, SDC. **Networks/Consortia:** Member of Suburban Library System.

ALBERTSON (James H.) CENTER FOR LEARNING RESOURCES
See: University of Wisconsin, Stevens Point - James H. Albertson Center for Learning Resources

★208★

ALBRIGHT-KNOX ART GALLERY - ART REFERENCE LIBRARY (Art)
1285 Elmwood Ave.   Phone: (716) 882-8700
Buffalo, NY 14222   Annette Masling, Libn.
Founded: 1905. **Staff:** Prof 2; Other 3. **Subjects:** Contemporary and modern art. **Holdings:** 17,000 books; 2000 bound periodical volumes; 10,000 VF including folders on artists, dealers and museums throughout the world; 200 artists' books; archives; microfiche; videotapes. **Subscriptions:** 350 journals and other serials. **Services:** Interlibrary loans; copying; library open to public for scholarly research projects. **Networks/Consortia:** Member of Western New York Library Resources Council (WNYLRC). **Staff:** Mary Bell, Asst.Libn.; Nancy Lucow, Cat.

★209★

ALBUQUERQUE MUNICIPAL REFERENCE LIBRARY
Albuquerque Public Library
501 Copper N.W.
Albuquerque, NM 87103
Defunct

★210★

ALBUQUERQUE MUSEUM OF ART, HISTORY & SCIENCE - LIBRARY (Hist)†
2000 Mountain Rd.
Box 1293   Phone: (505) 766-7878
Albuquerque, NM 87103   James C. Moore, Dir.
Founded: 1974. **Staff:** 1. **Subjects:** History of the Southwest, art, photography, aviation, anthropology, archeology. **Special Collections:** Clark Speakman Collection - Aviation History of Albuquerque. **Holdings:** 1000 books; 200 bound periodical volumes. **Subscriptions:** 10 journals and other serials. **Services:** Library open to public for reference use only. **Publications:** Newsletter, monthly. **Remarks:** Maintained by City of Albuquerque.

★211★

ALCAN ALUMINUM CORPORATION - CORPORATE LIBRARY (Bus-Fin)
100 Erieview Plaza   Phone: (216) 523-6860
Cleveland, OH 44114   Winifred B. Bowes, Libn.
Staff: Prof 2; Other 1. **Subjects:** Aluminum industry, business, finance, law. **Holdings:** 8000 books; 100 bound periodical volumes; 2000 reports and pamphlets; 8 VF drawers of clippings. **Subscriptions:** 283 journals and other serials; 9 newspapers. **Services:** Interlibrary loans; library open to public by appointment only. **Computerized Information Services:** DIALOG. **Publications:** New Publications Received in Library, bimonthly; From the Clipping File, weekly. **Staff:** Mary Ann Cofta, Asst.Libn.

★212★
ALCAN ALUMINUM, LTD. - GROUP INFORMATION CENTRE (Sci-Tech)
One Place Ville Marie
Box 6090
Montreal, PQ, Canada H3C 3H2
Phone: (514) 877-2610
Ellen A. Johnston, Chf.Libn.
Founded: 1945. **Staff:** Prof 4; Other 9. **Subjects:** Aluminum, business management, commerce, finance, industrial medicine, law, metallurgy, personnel management, power. **Holdings:** 5000 books; 130 VF drawers. **Subscriptions:** 1800 journals and other serials; 25 newspapers. **Services:** Interlibrary loans; library open to public by request. **Computerized Information Services:** DIALOG, SDC, QL Systems, BRS, TEXTLINE, Informatech France-Quebec; BASIS (internal database).

★213★
ALCAN INTERNATIONAL LTD. - KINGSTON LABORATORIES - LIBRARY (Sci-Tech)
P.O. Box 8400
Kingston, ON, Canada K7L 4Z4
Phone: (613) 549-4500
Miss E.M. Vanags, Hd.
Founded: 1941. **Staff:** Prof 6; Other 5. **Subjects:** Metallurgy of light metals; aluminum smelting, fabrication and production. **Holdings:** 10,000 books and bound periodical volumes; 25,000 reports (cataloged); 6000 patents (cataloged); 150,000 pamphlets (cataloged); 450 reels of microfilm; 49 VF drawers of correspondence; 5000 slides. **Subscriptions:** 500 journals and other serials. **Services:** Interlibrary loans; copying; library open to public by request. **Computerized Information Services:** DIALOG, SDC; BASIS (internal database). **Publications:** Accessions List, monthly - for internal distribution only.

★214★
ALCAN INTERNATIONAL, LTD. - TECHNICAL INFORMATION CENTRE (Sci-Tech)
P.O. Box 1250
Arvida, PQ, Canada G7S 4K8
Phone: (418) 548-1121
Ms. P. Leclerc, Chf.Libn.
Founded: 1950. **Staff:** Prof 4; Other 7. **Subjects:** Aluminum technology, chemistry, metallurgy, engineering. **Holdings:** 10,000 books; 3000 bound periodical volumes; technical reports; patents; correspondence; microfilm. **Subscriptions:** 400 journals and other serials. **Services:** Interlibrary loans; library not open to public. **Computerized Information Services:** DIALOG, Infomart, CAN/OLE, QL Systems; BASIS (internal database); computerized cataloging and serials. **Staff:** Marion Jefferies, Ref.Spec.

ALCOA
See: **Aluminum Company of America**

★215★
ALCOHOL AND DRUG CONCERNS, INC. - AUDIOVISUAL LIBRARY (Aud-Vis)
15 Gervais Dr., Rm. 603
Don Mills, ON, Canada M3C 1Y8
Phone: (416) 449-4933
Rev. Karl N. Burden, Exec.Dir.
Subjects: Alcohol and drugs. **Holdings:** Figures not available.

ALCOHOL AND DRUG EDUCATION SERVICE (Manitoba) INC.
See: **Alcoholism Foundation of Manitoba**

ALCOHOLISM CENTER
See: **Comprehensive Health Council of Metropolitan Chicago**

ALCOHOLISM COMMISSION OF SASKATCHEWAN
See: **Saskatchewan Alcoholism Commission**

★216★
ALCOHOLISM AND DRUG ADDICTION RESEARCH FOUNDATION - LIBRARY (Med; Soc Sci)
33 Russell St.
Toronto, ON, Canada M5S 2S1
Phone: (416) 595-6144
R.J. Hall, Hd., Info.& Promotion
Founded: 1958. **Staff:** Prof 3; Other 7. **Subjects:** Alcoholism and drug abuse. **Special Collections:** Dr. E.M. Jellinek Collection; Rev. Ben Spense Temperance Collection; Nathan B. Eddy Collections; Dr. Robert J. Gibbens Memorial (psychology); R.J. Linton Temperance Collection. **Holdings:** 7355 books; 2056 bound periodical volumes; 177 theses; 40,000 reprints; 6 VF drawers of pamphlets; 100 newsletters; 1045 foundation reports; 300 government statistical reports; 50 boxes of control acts and regulations; 240 films; 150 audio and video cassettes. **Subscriptions:** 355 journals and other serials. **Services:** Interlibrary loans (in Canada only); copying; SDI; library open to qualified users. **Networks/Consortia:** Member of Librarians and Information Specialists in Addictions (LISA). **Publications:** Acquisitions List, monthly - free upon request; bibliographies and microfiche articles - for sale through Marketing Services. **Also Known As:** Addiction Research Foundation. **Staff:** Mrs. B. Merritt, Film & ILL Libn.; Ms. B. Boucher, Documentalist.

★217★
ALCOHOLISM FOUNDATION OF MANITOBA - WILLIAM POTOROKA MEMORIAL LIBRARY (Soc Sci)
1580 Dublin Ave.
Winnipeg, MB, Canada R3B 0L4
Phone: (204) 775-8601
Diana Ringstrom, Libn.
Staff: Prof 1; Other 1. **Subjects:** Alcohol and drug use and abuse, psychology, sociology, education, counselling, values clarification. **Holdings:** 3200 books; 19 pamphlet titles; 323 16mm films; 78 filmstrips. **Subscriptions:** 45 journals and other serials. **Services:** Interlibrary loans; copying; library open to public. **Special Catalogs:** Subject file for journal holdings (card). **Remarks:** Contains the holding of the former Alcohol and Drug Education Service (Manitoba) Inc.

★218★
ALCOLAC, INC. - RESEARCH LIBRARY (Sci-Tech)
3440 Fairfield Rd.
Baltimore, MD 21226
Phone: (301) 355-2600
Lydia Beyerlein, Res.Libn.
Founded: 1971. **Staff:** Prof 2; Other 1. **Subjects:** Chemistry - organic, analytical; government regulations. **Holdings:** 1200 books; 1000 bound periodical volumes; 840 reels of microfilm; 6000 patents; 7100 item product file. **Subscriptions:** 210 journals and other serials. **Services:** Interlibrary loans; copying; library not open to public. **Computerized Information Services:** DIALOG, BRS, Chemical Abstracts Service (CAS). **Special Indexes:** Patent index; subject index for internal documents and reports.

★219★
ALCON LABORATORIES, INC. - RESEARCH & DEVELOPMENT LIBRARY (Med)
6201 S. Fwy.
Box 1959
Fort Worth, TX 76101
Phone: (817) 293-0450
Darlene Fleming, Sci.Libn.
Founded: 1959. **Staff:** Prof 2; Other 1. **Subjects:** Ophthalmology, dermatology, lens care, surgery, pharmaceutics. **Special Collections:** Ophthalmology (library holds most English language books and complete sets of periodicals). **Holdings:** 5500 books; 10,000 bound periodical volumes; 1000 patents. **Subscriptions:** 200 journals and other serials. **Services:** Interlibrary loans; bibliographic and reference services for members of the association; will answer brief inquiries and make referrals; library open to public for reference use only on request. **Computerized Information Services:** DIALOG, SDC, MEDLARS, Chemical Abstracts Service (CAS). **Networks/Consortia:** Member of Dallas-Tarrant County Consortium of Health Science Libraries. **Special Catalogs:** Union List of Periodicals. **Staff:** Marlin Rogers, Mgr., Sci.Info.

★220★
ALCORN STATE UNIVERSITY - JOHN DEWEY BOYD LIBRARY (Hist)
Box 539
Lorman, MS 39096
Phone: (601) 877-6350
Ms. Epsy Y. Hendricks, Lib.Dir.
Special Collections: Archives (75,683 government documents (cataloged)). **Services:** Interlibrary loans (fee); copying; library open to public for reference use only. **Publications:** Booklist, irregular; bibliographies. **Staff:** Jessie Arnold, Dir.,Pub.Serv./Doc.

ALDEN (George I.) LIBRARY
See: **Worcester Vocational Schools - George I. Alden Library**

ALDEN LIBRARY
See: **Ohio University**

ALDERMAN LIBRARY
See: **University of Virginia**

★221★
ALDERSGATE COLLEGE - WILSON MEMORIAL LIBRARY (Rel-Theol)
Box 460
Moose Jaw, SK, Canada S6H 4P1
Phone: (306) 692-1816
Ruth Huston, Dir.
Staff: Prof 1; Other 12. **Subjects:** Theology, Wesleyan studies. **Special Collections:** Wesleyana (200 volumes). **Holdings:** 12,150 books; 160 bound periodical volumes; 325 volumes in microform; 69 tapes and cassettes. **Subscriptions:** 120 journals and other serials. **Services:** Interlibrary loans; copying; library open to public for reference use only.

ALDRICH LIBRARY OF MUSIC
See: **Aldrich (Mariska) Memorial Foundation, Inc.**

★222★

ALDRICH (Mariska) MEMORIAL FOUNDATION, INC. - ALDRICH LIBRARY OF MUSIC (Mus)
8451-8491 Swarthout Canyon Rd.
Box 369   Phone: (619) 249-6751
Wrightwood, CA 92397-0369   Dr. Ric Anderson, Chm./Chf.Exec.Off.
Founded: 1973. **Staff:** Prof 1; Other 3. **Subjects:** Music, musicians. **Holdings:** 2500 books; 21,000 phonograph records; 8000 historical 78 rpm phonograph records; 2000 audiotapes; 1600 piano rolls; scores and sheet music; music and recording periodicals. **Subscriptions:** 11 journals and other serials. **Services:** Copying; library open to public. **Computerized Information Services:** Computerized cataloging. **Formerly:** Its Library of Rare Music located in Pearl City, HI. **Staff:** Anna Mary Anderson, Pres./Cur.

ALDRICH MUSEUM OF CONTEMPORARY ART
See: Soho Center for Visual Artists

★223★

ALEXANDER & ALEXANDER, INC. - NATIONAL PRODUCTION INFORMATION CENTER (Bus-Fin)
4205 Lancaster Ln.   Phone: (612) 559-3284
Minneapolis, MN 55441   Laura E. Dirks, Libn.
Staff: Prof 1. **Subjects:** Group insurance, mass marketing. **Holdings:** 500 books; 5000 brochures on mass merchandised insurance plans. **Subscriptions:** 118 journals and other serials. **Services:** Interlibrary loans; copying; center open to public with permission of librarian. **Networks/Consortia:** Member of METRONET. **Publications:** A&A InfoGram, monthly bulletin - for internal distribution only; A&A Profiles, quarterly - for internal distribution only.

ALEXANDER (Franz) LIBRARY
See: Southern California Psychoanalytic Institute - Franz Alexander Library

★224★

ALEXANDER GRAHAM BELL ASSOCIATION FOR THE DEAF - VOLTA BUREAU LIBRARY (Sci-Tech; Med)
3417 Volta Place, N.W.   Phone: (202) 337-5220
Washington, DC 20007   Suzanne Pickering Neel, Dir., Prof.Prog./Serv.
Founded: 1893. **Staff:** 1. **Subjects:** Deafness, hearing, speech. **Special Collections:** Rare and out-of-print books on hearing and deafness; letters and books of Alexander Graham Bell, Alexander Melville Bell, John Hitz and Helen Keller. **Holdings:** 28,000 books; 2500 bound periodical volumes; photographs; 640 shelf feet of pamphlets, reports of schools for the deaf; 30 VF drawers of clippings and reprints. **Subscriptions:** 190 journals and other serials. **Services:** Copying; SDI; library open to public by appointment.

ALEXANDER LIBRARY
See: Rutgers University, The State University of New Jersey

★225★

ALEXANDRIA CITY PUBLIC SCHOOLS - EDUCATIONAL MEDIA CENTER - NICHOLS PROFESSIONAL LIBRARY (Educ)
3801 W. Braddock Rd.   Phone: (703) 998-9045
Alexandria, VA 22302   Dale W. Brown, Supv., Lib. & Media Serv.
Founded: 1968. **Staff:** Prof 1; Other 1. **Subjects:** Education. **Holdings:** 9000 books; 229,301 microfiche of ERIC documents. **Subscriptions:** 200 journals and other serials. **Services:** Interlibrary loans; copying; SDI; library open to public for reference and limited circulation. **Networks/Consortia:** Member of Northern Virginia Library Consortium; Metropolitan Washington Library Council.

★226★

ALEXANDRIA GAZETTE - LIBRARY
Box 119
Alexandria, VA 22313
Subjects: Newspaper reference topics. **Holdings:** Clipping files; newspapers on microfilm. **Remarks:** Presently inactive.

★227★

ALEXANDRIA HOSPITAL - HEALTH SCIENCES LIBRARY (Med)
4320 Seminary Rd.   Phone: (703) 379-3126
Alexandria, VA 22304   Libby Hamilton, Libn.
Staff: Prof 1; Other 1. **Subjects:** Medicine, nursing and nursing education, health sciences. **Holdings:** 2800 books; 800 bound periodical volumes. **Subscriptions:** 165 journals and other serials. **Services:** Interlibrary loans; copying; SDI; library open to public on request. **Computerized Information Services:** MEDLINE.

★228★

ALEXANDRIA LIBRARY - LLOYD HOUSE (Hist)
220 N. Washington St.   Phone: (703) 838-4577
Alexandria, VA 22314   Jeanne G. Plitt, Dir.
Founded: 1794. **Staff:** Prof 2; Other 1. **Subjects:** History - Virginia, American, Alexandria; genealogy; American manuscripts. **Special Collections:** Virginia Collection; Manuscript Collection; Sweeney Papers (social history of Alexandria City; 3000 pieces); McKnight Papers (25 pieces); Rare Book Collection (3500). **Holdings:** 10,618 books; 580 bound periodical volumes; 10,851 pamphlets and 62 manuscripts (cataloged); 8187 microforms; 5 boxes of diaries and pamphlets on microfilm; personal recollections; 4 boxes of early city records. **Subscriptions:** 15 journals and other serials. **Services:** Interlibrary loans; copying; library open to public, original material may not circulate. **Computerized Information Services:** Computerized circulation. **Networks/Consortia:** Member of Metropolitan Washington Library Council; Washington Consortium; OCLC through SOLINET. **Special Indexes:** Alexandria special indexes to uncataloged manuscripts, annual reports; 1860 U.S. Census index. **Staff:** Allan W. Robbins, Hd.Libn.

★229★

ALEXIAN BROTHERS MEDICAL CENTER - MEDICAL LIBRARY (Med)
800 W. Biesterfield Rd.   Phone: (312) 437-5500
Elk Grove Village, IL 60007   Jocelyn A. Bernholdt, Med.Libn.
Founded: 1967. **Staff:** Prof 2; Other 1. **Subjects:** Medicine, nursing, and allied health sciences. **Holdings:** 2450 books; 3875 bound periodical volumes; 6 VF drawers of pamphlets; 70 videotapes; 470 audiotapes; 47 slide/tape kits. **Subscriptions:** 205 journals and other serials. **Services:** Interlibrary loans; copying; literature searches; library open to nursing and paramedical students. **Computerized Information Services:** MEDLARS. **Networks/Consortia:** Member of Illinois Health Libraries Consortium; Regional Medical Library - Region 3. **Publications:** Monthly New Books List. **Staff:** On-Sook Lee, Asst.Libn.

★230★

ALFORD HOUSE/ANDERSON FINE ARTS CENTER - ART REFERENCE LIBRARY (Art)
226 W. 8th St.   Phone: (317) 649-1248
Anderson, IN 46016   Judith Dillingham, Asst. to Dir.
Founded: 1967. **Staff:** 1. **Subjects:** Art history, artists. **Holdings:** 400 books; 200 other cataloged items; 1500 unbound periodicals; 500 exhibition catalogs. **Subscriptions:** 16 journals and other serials; 4 newspapers. **Services:** Library open to public for reference use only.

★231★

ALFRED UNIVERSITY - HERRICK MEMORIAL LIBRARY - OPENHYM COLLECTION (Hum)
                                    Phone: (607) 871-2184
Alfred, NY 14802   Norma Higgins, Spec.Coll.Tech.Spec.
Staff: 2. **Subjects:** British literature and social history. **Holdings:** 5000 books; 4 VF drawers of letters, autographs and photographs. **Services:** Interlibrary loans; copying; SDI; library open to public. **Networks/Consortia:** Member of OCLC; South Central Research Libraries Council (SCRLC). **Publications:** Bibliography of the Openhym Collection of Modern British Literature and Social History, 1980. **Special Catalogs:** Author/subject catalog.

ALFRED UNIVERSITY - NEW YORK STATE COLLEGE OF CERAMICS
See: New York State College of Ceramics at Alfred University

★232★

ALGONQUIN COLLEGE OF APPLIED ARTS & TECHNOLOGY - RESOURCE CENTRES (Bus-Fin; Sci-Tech)†
1385 Woodroffe Ave.   Phone: (613) 725-7301
Ottawa, ON, Canada K2G 1V8   James Feeley, Dir.
Founded: 1967. **Staff:** Prof 17; Other 66. **Subjects:** Business, trades and technology, social sciences, nursing and allied health sciences. **Holdings:** 125,206 volumes; AV materials. **Subscriptions:** 2297 journals and other serials. **Services:** Centres open to public. **Remarks:** Above data encompasses libraries from 8 campuses of the college located in Ottawa, Hawkesbury, Pembroke, and Perth, ON.

★233★

ALGONQUIN PARK MUSEUM - LIBRARY & ARCHIVES (Env-Cons; Hist)*
Box 219   Phone: (705) 633-5592
Whitney, ON, Canada K0J 2M0   Ronald G. Tozer, Interp.Serv.Supv.
Founded: 1953. **Subjects:** Algonquin Park ecology and history. **Special Collections:** Historical Photograph Archives (early logging; 5500 photographs). **Holdings:** 350 books; 3000 unbound reprints, reports, manuscripts; 2000 newspaper clippings; 100 oral history tapes. **Services:**

Library open to public with prior notification and approval. **Remarks:** Maintained by Ontario Ministry of Natural Resources.

★234★
ALIVE FELLOWSHIP OF HARMONIOUS LIVING - LIBRARY
Star Route Box 86
Olga, WA 98279
Defunct

★235★
ALL SAINTS EPISCOPAL HOSPITAL - F.M. CORSELIUS LIBRARY (Med)†
1400 Enderly Pl.
Box 31   Phone: (817) 926-2544
Fort Worth, TX 76101   Alma Enis, Libn.
Founded: 1965. **Staff:** Prof 1. **Subjects:** Medicine, nursing, hospital administration. **Holdings:** 1707 books; 1952 bound periodical volumes; 350 pamphlets; 2 drawers of clippings. **Subscriptions:** 150 journals and other serials. **Services:** Interlibrary loans; copying; library not open to public. **Networks/Consortia:** Member of Dallas-Tarrant County Consortium of Health Science Libraries.

★236★
ALL SOULS UNITARIAN CHURCH - E. BURDETTE BACKUS LIBRARY (Rel-Theol)
5805 E. 56th St.   Phone: (317) 545-6005
Indianapolis, IN 46226   Marcia Blumenthal, Chm., Lib.Comm.
Subjects: General nonfiction. **Special Collections:** Unitarian-Universalist publications. **Holdings:** 1500 books; 200 tapes (cataloged). **Services:** Library open to friends and members of the church.

ALLAN MEMORIAL INSTITUTE OF PSYCHIATRY
See: Mc Gill University

★237★
ALLEGANY COUNTY CIRCUIT COURT - LIBRARY (Law)
Court House, Washington St.   Phone: (301) 722-5633
Cumberland, MD 21502   Wanda Keller, Libn.
Staff: Prof 1. **Subjects:** Law. **Holdings:** 15,000 volumes. **Services:** Library open to public with restrictions.

★238★
ALLEGANY COUNTY MUSEUM - LIBRARY (Hist)
Court House   Phone: (716) 268-7612
Belmont, NY 14813   Bill Greene, Hist.
Staff: Prof 1; Other 1. **Subjects:** Local history and genealogy. **Special Collections:** John Barker Church Land Tract Records. **Holdings:** 1000 books; 150 volumes of local newspaper on microfilm. **Services:** Copying; library open to public. **Publications:** Ye Olde Alleganian, 6/year. **Special Indexes:** Indexes to 1810-1855 county census.

★239★
ALLEGHENY COLLEGE - WALTER M. SMALL GEOLOGY LIBRARY (Sci-Tech)
Alden Hall
Meadville, PA 16335   Phone: (814) 724-2350
                                             Margaret L. Moser, Libn.
Staff: Prof 1; Other 1. **Subjects:** General geology, marine geology. **Special Collections:** Catalog of fossil spores and pollen. **Holdings:** 700 books; 400 bound periodical volumes; 200 quadrangle maps; 4500 U.S. Bureau of Mines Information Circulars; 3225 Geological Society of America bulletins and professional papers; 725 State Geological Survey publications; 4 VF drawers of student projects. **Subscriptions:** 20 journals and other serials. **Services:** Interlibrary loans; library open to public except high school students.

★240★
ALLEGHENY COUNTY - DEPARTMENT OF PLANNING - LIBRARY (Plan)
429 Forbes Ave., 12th Fl.   Phone: (412) 355-4353
Pittsburgh, PA 15219   Patricia M. Carle, Libn.Cons.
Founded: 1960. **Subjects:** Physical planning, local government documents. **Special Collections:** Zoning and subdivision ordinances of Allegheny County municipalities. **Holdings:** 2000 books. **Subscriptions:** 31 journals and other serials. **Services:** Interlibrary loans; library open to public. **Computerized Information Services:** Computerized cataloging.

★241★
ALLEGHENY COUNTY HEALTH DEPARTMENT - LIBRARY (Med)
40th St. & Penn Ave.   Phone: (412) 578-8028
Pittsburgh, PA 15224   Carol Schmitt, Libn.
Staff: Prof 1; Other 1. **Subjects:** Public health. **Holdings:** 1282 books. **Subscriptions:** 78 journals and other serials. **Services:** Interlibrary loans; copying; library open to public for reference use only. **Publications:** Timely

Topics, monthly - for internal distribution only.

★242★
ALLEGHENY COUNTY LAW LIBRARY (Law)
921 City-County Bldg.   Phone: (412) 355-5353
Pittsburgh, PA 15219   Joel Fishman, Law Libn.
Founded: 1867. **Staff:** Prof 4; Other 5. **Subjects:** Law. **Special Collections:** Original papers and briefs of the Alaskan Boundary Dispute with Great Britain; original records and briefs of U.S. Supreme Court (1912 to present); U.S. Government Depository Library. **Holdings:** 124,000 books; 26,000 bound periodical volumes; 1069 reels of microfilm; 38,700 microfiche. **Subscriptions:** 350 journals and other serials. **Services:** Interlibrary loans; copying; library open to public. **Networks/Consortia:** Member of Pittsburgh Regional Library Center.

★243★
ALLEGHENY GENERAL HOSPITAL - HEALTH SCIENCES LIBRARY (Med)
320 E. North Ave.   Phone: (412) 237-3041
Pittsburgh, PA 15212   Jennifer J. Angier, Hd.
Founded: 1936. **Staff:** Prof 1; Other 3. **Subjects:** Medicine, surgery, oral surgery and related subjects. **Holdings:** 2650 books; 5500 bound periodical volumes; 400 audiotapes. **Subscriptions:** 350 journals and other serials. **Services:** Interlibrary loans; copying; library open to public by request. **Computerized Information Services:** MEDLARS, DIALOG.

ALLEGHENY LUDLUM INDUSTRIES, INC. - SPECIAL METALS CORPORATION
See: Special Metals Corporation

★244★
ALLEGHENY LUDLUM STEEL CORPORATION - RESEARCH CENTER TECHNICAL LIBRARY (Sci-Tech)
Alabama & Pacific Aves.
Brackenridge, PA 15014   Eileen W. Gallagher, Libn.
Founded: 1952. **Staff:** 2. **Subjects:** Metallurgy, chemistry, physics. **Special Collections:** Brutcher Translations (microfiche). **Holdings:** 3340 books; 2500 bound periodical volumes; 7 VF drawers of United States patents; 2 VF drawers of foreign patents; 2500 slides; 4000 technical translations. **Subscriptions:** 252 journals and other serials. **Services:** Interlibrary loans; library not open to public. **Staff:** Leona Sikorski, Supv., Tech.Info.

ALLEGHENY OBSERVATORY
See: University of Pittsburgh

ALLEGHENY PORTAGE RAILROAD NATL. HISTORIC SITE
See: U.S. Natl. Park Service

★245★
ALLEN-BRADLEY COMPANY - CORPORATE LIBRARY (Sci-Tech)
1201 S. 2nd St.
Box 2086   Phone: (414) 671-2000
Milwaukee, WI 53201   Agnes G. Rice, Libn.
Founded: 1942. **Staff:** Prof 1; Other 2. **Subjects:** Electrical engineering, electronic engineering, metallurgy, physics, chemistry, mathematics, management. **Holdings:** 8000 books; 9000 bound periodical volumes. **Subscriptions:** 400 journals and other serials. **Services:** Interlibrary loans; copying; SDI; library not open to public. **Computerized Information Services:** DIALOG; computerized circulation. **Publications:** Book lists - for internal distribution only.

ALLEN (Charlotte Whitney) LIBRARY
See: University of Rochester - Charlotte Whitney Allen Library

★246★
ALLEN COUNTY-FORT WAYNE HISTORICAL SOCIETY - LIBRARY AND MANUSCRIPT COLLECTIONS (Hist)
302 E. Berry St.   Phone: (219) 426-2882
Fort Wayne, IN 46802   Doris Perry, Registrar
Founded: 1950. **Staff:** Prof 1. **Subjects:** Allen County and Fort Wayne history, local politics, architecture, business. **Special Collections:** Reports of county commissioners; Nickle Plate Railroad (13 manuscript boxes); Allen Hamilton Papers, 1831-1875; Brentwood Tolan architectural renderings; Samuel Hanna business papers, 1840-1880; Ivan Lebamoff mayoral papers, 1971-1975. **Holdings:** 10,000 books; 40 bound periodical volumes; 8 VF drawers of architectural drawings; 19 VF drawers of maps and prints; 200 reels of microfilmed letters to Secretary of War. **Services:** Copying; library open to public for reference use only. **Publications:** Old Fort News, quarterly - to members.

★247★
ALLEN COUNTY HISTORICAL SOCIETY - ELIZABETH M. MAC DONELL MEMORIAL LIBRARY (Hist)
620 W. Market St.   Phone: (419) 222-9426
Lima, OH 45801   Anna B. Selfridge, Asst.Cur./Mss., Archv.
Founded: 1908. **Staff:** Prof 1. **Subjects:** Local history and genealogy, Ohio history, railroading, American Indian. **Special Collections:** John H. Keller Railroad Collection; Interurban and Street Railway Collection; Lima Locomotive Works Collection; Railroad Labor History Collection (30 cubic feet). **Holdings:** 6000 books; 585 bound periodical volumes; file of Lima, Ohio newspapers, 1840s to present; Lima directories, 1878 to present; 1280 reels of microfilmed newspapers and census records. **Subscriptions:** 38 journals and other serials. **Services:** Copying; library open to public. **Publications:** Allen County Reporter, quarterly - to members. **Remarks:** Library is part of Allen County Museum.

★248★
ALLEN COUNTY LAW LIBRARY (Law)
Court House, 4th Fl.
Lima, OH 45801   Ruth Laudahn, Act.Libn.
Staff: 3. **Subjects:** Law. **Holdings:** 23,000 volumes. **Services:** Copying; library open to public for reference use only. **Remarks:** Maintained by Allen County Law Library Association. **Staff:** Gregory M. Novak, Attorney/Libn.

★249★
ALLEN COUNTY LAW LIBRARY ASSOCIATION, INC. (Law)
Courthouse, Rm. 105   Phone: (219) 423-7638
Fort Wayne, IN 46802   Virginia B. Howell, Law Libn.
Founded: 1900. **Staff:** Prof 1. **Subjects:** Law. **Holdings:** 17,000 books; 15,000 bound periodical volumes. **Subscriptions:** 20 journals and other serials. **Services:** Copying; library not open to public. **Computerized Information Services:** Computerized acquisitions.

★250★
ALLEN COUNTY PUBLIC LIBRARY - BUSINESS AND TECHNOLOGY DEPARTMENT (Bus-Fin; Sci-Tech)
900 Webster St.   Phone: (219) 424-7241
Fort Wayne, IN 46802   Wesley Avins, Mgr.
Founded: 1900. **Staff:** Prof 2; Other 1. **Subjects:** Business, physical science, auto service, agriculture, engineering, investments. **Special Collections:** Hunter Collection (handicapped children); foreign trade. **Holdings:** 80,000 books; 22,000 bound periodical volumes; auto service manuals; business and tax loose-leaf services; telephone directories. **Subscriptions:** 400 journals and other serials; 54 newspapers. **Services:** Interlibrary loans; copying. **Formerly:** Public Library of Fort Wayne and Allen County, Indiana. **Staff:** Charles Eckman, Libn.

★251★
ALLEN COUNTY PUBLIC LIBRARY - INDIANA COLLECTION (Hist)
900 Webster St.   Phone: (219) 424-7241
Fort Wayne, IN 46802   Helen Colchin, Ref.Dept.Mgr.
Staff: Prof 4; Other 1. **Subjects:** Indiana history and authors. **Holdings:** 12,556 books; 1521 bound periodical volumes; 133,100 clippings; 17,816 pamphlets; 21,933 pictures. **Subscriptions:** 77 journals and other serials. **Services:** Copying; library open to public. **Networks/Consortia:** Member of TRI-ALSA.

ALLEN (David F.) MEMORIAL LEARNING RESOURCES CENTER
See: Indiana Law Enforcement Academy - David F. Allen Memorial Learning Resources Center

ALLEN (Fanny) HOSPITAL
See: Fanny Allen Hospital

ALLEN (Ivan, Jr.) DEPARTMENT OF SCIENCE, INDUSTRY AND GOVERNMENT
See: Atlanta Public Library - Ivan Allen, Jr. Department of Science, Industry and Government

★252★
ALLEN (J.C.) AND SON, INC. - LIBRARY (Pict; Agri)
Box 2061   Phone: (317) 463-9614
West Lafayette, IN 47906
Founded: 1912. **Staff:** 2. **Subjects:** Agriculture, farms, livestock, flowers. **Holdings:** 77,000 black/white negatives and 20,000 color transparencies showing agricultural activities in the Corn Belt states.

★253★
ALLEN (John E.), INC. - MOTION PICTURE ARCHIVES (Aud-Vis)
116 North Ave.   Phone: (201) 391-3464
Park Ridge, NJ 07656   Robert A. Summers, Archv.
Staff: Prof 2; Other 1. **Subjects:** Motion pictures. **Special Collections:** Kinogram Newsreel Company, 1915-1930; Telenews Company, 1947-1953; Primitive Motion Pictures, 1896 to present; Silent Motion Pictures, pre-1930. **Holdings:** 20 million feet of 35mm film; 1 million motion picture still photographs, 1910-1960; trade publications. **Services:** Copying; library open to public on payment of research fee. **Staff:** Martha Allen, Archv.

ALLEN LIBRARY
See: First United Methodist Church

ALLEN MEMORIAL LIBRARY (Cleveland, OH)
See: Cleveland Health Sciences Library

ALLEN MEMORIAL LIBRARY (West Hartford, CT)
See: University of Hartford - Hartt School of Music

ALLEN (Warren D.) MUSIC LIBRARY
See: Florida State University - Warren D. Allen Music Library

★254★
ALLENDALE MUTUAL INSURANCE COMPANY - LIBRARY (Bus-Fin)
Allendale Park
Box 7500   Phone: (401) 275-4500
Johnston, RI 02919   Carol Emby, Libn.
Staff: Prof 1. **Subjects:** Insurance, fire and fire protection, engineering, business, management. **Holdings:** 2000 books; 100 audio cassette programs; 100 films. **Subscriptions:** 100 journals and other serials. **Services:** Interlibrary loans; library not open to public. **Publications:** Acquisitions list, monthly - to employees.

★255★
ALLENTOWN ART MUSEUM - RESEARCH LIBRARY (Art)
5th & Court Sts.
Box 117   Phone: (215) 432-4333
Allentown, PA 18105   Peter F. Blume, Cur.
Founded: 1957. **Staff:** Prof 4; Other 8. **Subjects:** Art history. **Holdings:** 7000 books; 400 bound periodical volumes; 1000 pamphlets (cataloged); 16 VF drawers of clippings; museum catalogs. **Subscriptions:** 68 journals and other serials. **Services:** Copying; library open to public by appointment. **Staff:** Richard N. Gregg, Dir.

★256★
ALLENTOWN CALL-CHRONICLE - NEWSPAPER LIBRARY (Publ)
6th & Linden Sts.
Box 1260   Phone: (215) 820-6523
Allentown, PA 18105   Lois A. Doncevic, Dir. of Lib.Serv.
Founded: 1932. **Staff:** Prof 1; Other 10. **Subjects:** Newspaper reference topics. **Holdings:** 1000 books; pamphlets; VF drawers; microfiche. **Subscriptions:** 100 journals and other serials; 32 newspapers. **Services:** Interlibrary loans; copying; library open to public with restrictions. **Computerized Information Services:** New York Times Information Service, IN/FORM Data Services; Info-Ky News Storage and Retrieval System (internal database).

★257★
ALLENTOWN HOSPITAL ASSOCIATION - HEALTH SCIENCES LIBRARY (Med)
17th & Chew Sts.   Phone: (215) 821-2263
Allentown, PA 18102   Barbara J. Iobst, Libn.
Founded: 1940. **Staff:** Prof 1; Other 1. **Subjects:** Medicine, surgery, basic sciences, obstetrics, gynecology, psychiatry. **Holdings:** 5000 books; 6000 bound periodical volumes; 600 AV items. **Subscriptions:** 250 journals and other serials. **Services:** Interlibrary loans; copying; bibliographic and reference services for members of the hospital staff; library open to public with restrictions. **Computerized Information Services:** MEDLINE. **Networks/Consortia:** Member of Cooperating Hospital Libraries of the Lehigh Valley Area.

★258★
ALLENTOWN & SACRED HEART HOSPITAL CENTER - HEALTH SCIENCES LIBRARY (Med)
1200 S. Cedar Crest Blvd.   Phone: (215) 821-3148
Allentown, PA 18105   Carolyn Nippert, Dir.
Staff: Prof 1; Other 2. **Subjects:** Burn care, open heart surgery, trauma and neurosurgery. **Holdings:** 1475 books; 3416 bound periodical volumes.

Subscriptions: 312 journals and other serials. **Services:** Interlibrary loans; copying; SDI; library open to public for reference use only. **Computerized Information Services:** MEDLINE. **Networks/Consortia:** Member of Mideastern Regional Medical Library Service (MERMLS); Cooperating Hospital Libraries of the Lehigh Valley Area. **Publications:** Library Acquisitions List, monthly; Educational Resource Manual.

★259★
ALLENTOWN STATE HOSPITAL - HEIM MEMORIAL LIBRARY (Med)
1600 Hanover Ave.   Phone: (215) 821-6265
Allentown, PA 18103   Margaret M. Caffrey, Libn.
Founded: 1959. **Staff:** Prof 1. **Subjects:** Psychiatry, psychology, social work, pastoral counseling, community mental health, gerontology. **Special Collections:** Psychoanalysis (600 volumes); archival materials on Allentown State Hospital (6 boxes). **Holdings:** 3000 books; 600 unbound periodical volumes; 150 audiotapes. **Subscriptions:** 163 journals and other serials. **Services:** Interlibrary loans; copying; library open to students with recommendation of staff member. **Networks/Consortia:** Member of Cooperating Hospital Libraries of the Lehigh Valley Area. **Publications:** Union journal list, annual - to area libraries. **Special Catalogs:** Union catalog of books in consortium (card).

★260★
ALLERGAN PHARMACEUTICALS, INC. - PROFESSIONAL INFORMATION SERVICES (Med)
2525 Dupont Dr.   Phone: (714) 752-4500
Irvine, CA 92713   Carolyn Henderson, Mgr.
Founded: 1964. **Staff:** Prof 18; Other 3. **Subjects:** Ophthalmology, dermatology, pharmacology, management, general medical reference. **Holdings:** 3500 books; 2000 bound periodical volumes; 1000 market reports and 20,000 reprints (cataloged); 300 technical reports; 300 patents; 50 lecture series; 300 pamphlets; 70 binders of bulletins; 300 cassette tapes. **Subscriptions:** 450 journals and other serials; 10 newspapers. **Services:** Interlibrary loans; copying; SDI; library open to public with previous permission. **Computerized Information Services:** MEDLINE, DIALOG, SDC; Allergan Literature File Index, Laboratory Notebook Index (internal databases); computerized cataloging. **Networks/Consortia:** Member of Pacific Southwest Regional Medical Library Service (PSRMLS); CLASS. **Publications:** Current Awareness Bulletin, bimonthly - for internal distribution only. **Special Indexes:** Index to Allergan Lecture Series; index to technical report series; index to patents held. **Staff:** Jake Jaramillo, Info.Anl.; Evelyn Ware, Info.Anl.; Heidemarie B. Wierzba, Sect.Supv.; Paul Nowacki, Sr.Info.Anl.; Linda Cusimano, Info.Anl.; Susan Pool, Sr.Info.Anl.; Loyd Law, Info.Anl.; Cathy Tuthill, Sr.Info.Assoc.; Annette Gilbert, Info.Anl.; Suzanne Bustamante, Sr.Info.Assoc.; Jennifer Brown, Sr.Info.Assoc.; Ed Hauser, Sr.Info.Anl.; Julia Petrauskas, Sect.Supv.; Michelle Vivirito, Tech. Writer; Judy Simon, Tech. Writer; Jolynn Valoff, Tech. Writer; Kathy Pape, Tech. Writer II.

ALLERTON (Robert) LIBRARY
See: Honolulu Academy of Arts - Robert Allerton Library

ALLHANDS (James L.) MEMORIAL LIBRARY
See: Associated General Contractors of America - James L. Allhands Memorial Library

ALLIANCE FRANCAISE
See: French Institute/Alliance Francaise

★261★
ALLIANCE TO SAVE ENERGY - LIBRARY (Energy)
1925 K St., N.W., Suite 507   Phone: (202) 857-0668
Washington, DC 20006   Robin Miller, Res.Assoc.
Staff: Prof 18. **Subjects:** Energy policy and conservation. **Special Collections:** U.S. Code (complete); code of federal regulations. **Holdings:** 3440 books; 350 reports. **Subscriptions:** 21 journals and other serials. **Services:** Copying; SDI; library open to public with permission of librarian. **Publications:** Newsletter, monthly - to members.

ALLIED CHEMICAL CORPORATION - UNION TEXAS PETROLEUM CORPORATION
See: Union Texas Petroleum Corporation

★262★
ALLIED CORPORATION - ALLIED CHEMICAL - LIBRARY (Sci-Tech)
20 Peabody St.   Phone: (716) 827-6229
Buffalo, NY 14210   Dr. J. Northcott, Supv.
Founded: 1879. **Staff:** Prof 1; Other 1. **Subjects:** Organic chemicals, polymers, organofluoro chemicals, electronic chemicals, synthetic resins and intermediates. **Holdings:** 10,000 books; 17,000 bound periodical volumes;

23,000 internal reports; 2.5 million foreign and U.S. patents; microforms. **Subscriptions:** 230 journals and other serials. **Services:** Interlibrary loans; copying; library open to public by appointment.

★263★
ALLIED CORPORATION - ALLIED CHEMICAL - SYRACUSE RESEARCH LABORATORY - LIBRARY (Sci-Tech)
Box 6   Phone: (315) 487-4151
Solvay, NY 13209   Betty L. Emery, Libn.
Founded: 1900. **Staff:** Prof 1; Other 1. **Subjects:** Applied technology, inorganic chemistry, chemical engineering, agriculture. **Special Collections:** Historical material on the alkali industry. **Holdings:** 5300 books; 8800 bound periodical volumes; 3400 government publications; 14 VF drawers of reprints and photostats (cataloged); 19 VF drawers of U.S. patents; 15 VF drawers of foreign patents; 21 VF drawers of pamphlets, specifications, house organs. **Subscriptions:** 430 journals and other serials. **Services:** Interlibrary loans (local only); copying; library open to public for reference use, by appointment only. **Networks/Consortia:** Member of Central New York Library Resources Council (CENTRO). **Publications:** Library Briefs, irregular - for internal distribution only.

★264★
ALLIED CORPORATION - BUSINESS LIBRARY
Box 1021 R
Morristown, NJ 07960
Defunct. Holdings absorbed by Allied Corporation - Library and Information Services.

★265★
ALLIED CORPORATION - CORPORATE MEDICAL AFFAIRS LIBRARY
Columbia Rd.
Box 1021R
Morristown, NJ 07960
Defunct. Holdings absorbed by Allied Corporation - Library and Information Services.

★266★
ALLIED CORPORATION - FIBERS & PLASTICS COMPANY - TECHNICAL CENTER LIBRARY (Sci-Tech)
Box 31   Phone: (804) 520-3617
Petersburg, VA 23804   Mrs. R.P. Murphy, Libn.
Staff: Prof 2; Other 2. **Subjects:** Polymer science, textile chemistry, organic chemistry. **Holdings:** 4000 books; 300 bound periodical volumes. **Subscriptions:** 125 journals and other serials. **Services:** Interlibrary loans; copying (limited); library open to public by appointment. **Computerized Information Services:** DIALOG, SDC.

★267★
ALLIED CORPORATION - LAW LIBRARY (Law)
Box 2245R   Phone: (201) 455-4445
Morristown, NJ 07960   Jeanne C. Seigle, Law Libn.
Staff: Prof 1; Other 1. **Subjects:** Law. **Holdings:** 8500 books; 500 bound periodical volumes. **Subscriptions:** 105 journals and other serials. **Services:** Interlibrary loans; copying; SDI; library not open to public. **Computerized Information Services:** LEXIS, NEXIS, Dow Jones News Retrieval, New York Times Information Service, DIALOG, Legi-Slate.

★268★
ALLIED CORPORATION - LIBRARY & INFORMATION SERVICES (Sci-Tech)
Box 1021R   Phone: (201) 455-3014
Morristown, NJ 07960   Linnea Ditchey, Mgr.
Staff: Prof 7; Other 5. **Subjects:** Polymers, chemistry, materials science. **Special Collections:** Toxicology; Regulations; Business; Health Sciences. **Holdings:** 20,000 books; 25,000 bound periodical volumes; U.S. patents, 1960 to present, on microfilm. **Subscriptions:** 1167 journals and other serials. **Services:** Interlibrary loans; copying; library open to public with restrictions. **Computerized Information Services:** SDC, DIALOG, NLM; computerized cataloging. **Publications:** New Book list - for internal distribution only. **Formed by the Merger of:** Allied Corporation - Corporate Medical Affairs Library, Business Library and Technical Information Service. **Staff:** Dr. Marianne Kriman, Lit. Searcher; Loretta Massari, Bus.Info.Spec.; Emma Gergely, Health Sci.Info.Spec.; Maryanne Novak, Env./Regulatory Info.Spec; Rosemary Diverio, Tech.Info.Spec.; Deborah Flanner, Acq./Abstracting Spec.

★269★
ALLIED HEALTH SCIENCES LIBRARY (Med)
707 E. 14th St.   Phone: (512) 474-2001
Austin, TX 78701   Margaret Peloquin, Med.Libn.
Staff: Prof 1; Other 4. **Subjects:** Medicine, surgery, nursing, public health,

hospitals. **Special Collections:** History of nursing and nursing education (220 volumes). **Holdings:** 7500 books; 300 bound periodical volumes; 600 AV items; 8 VF drawers of reprints, pamphlets and other medical care material. **Subscriptions:** 175 journals and other serials. **Services:** Copying; library open to public with restrictions. **Computerized Information Services:** NLM, DIALOG, BRS. **Remarks:** Library is maintained by Austin Community College.

ALLIOTT (Hector) MEMORIAL LIBRARY OF ARCHAEOLOGY
See: Southwest Museum - Research Library

★270★
ALLIS-CHALMERS CORPORATION - ADVANCED TECHNOLOGY CENTER - LIBRARY (Sci-Tech)
Box 512   Phone: (414) 475-2102
Milwaukee, WI 53201   R.A. Schlueter, Libn.
Founded: 1943. **Staff:** Prof 2. **Subjects:** Mathematics, engineering, physics, chemistry, metals and materials, metallurgy. **Holdings:** 14,000 books; 5200 bound periodical volumes; 600 other cataloged items. **Subscriptions:** 500 journals and other serials; 30 newspapers. **Services:** Interlibrary loans; library not open to public. **Staff:** Eartha Walters, Asst.Libn.

★271★
ALLIS-CHALMERS CORPORATION - AMERICAN AIR FILTER DIVISION - TECHNICAL LIBRARY (Sci-Tech)
215 Central Ave.
Box 35260   Phone: (502) 637-0251
Louisville, KY 40232   Richard D. Rivers, Mgr. of Res.
Founded: 1964. **Staff:** 1. **Subjects:** Air pollution, scientific and technical engineering, air conditioning, heating and ventilation. **Holdings:** 1300 books; 29 titles on microfilm (cataloged); 15,000 technical articles; 365 articles on microfilm; abstracts and serials. **Services:** Copying; library open to public on application. **Formerly:** American Air Filter Company, Inc.

ALLOY DATA CENTER
See: U.S. Natl. Bureau of Standards

★272★
ALLSTATE INSURANCE COMPANY - LAW LIBRARY (Law)
Allstate Plaza, Bldg. E5   Phone: (312) 291-5407
Northbrook, IL 60062   Alice Bruemner, Lib.Serv.Supv.
Founded: 1974. **Staff:** Prof 3; Other 8. **Subjects:** Law, insurance. **Holdings:** 30,000 books; 4000 microfiche. **Subscriptions:** 300 journals and other serials; 7 newspapers. **Services:** Interlibrary loans; copying; library open to public with restrictions. **Computerized Information Services:** DIALOG, SDC, WESTLAW; computerized cataloging. **Networks/Consortia:** Member of ILLINET; RLIN. **Publications:** New Book List, monthly - for internal distribution only.

★273★
ALLY AND GARGANO, INC. - INFORMATION CENTER (Bus-Fin)
805 3rd Ave.   Phone: (212) 688-5300
New York, NY 10022   Marsha Cohen, Mgr., Info.Serv.
Founded: 1968. **Staff:** Prof 2; Other 1. **Subjects:** Advertising, marketing. **Holdings:** 800 books; 35 VF drawers. **Subscriptions:** 110 journals and other serials; 10 newspapers. **Services:** Interlibrary loans; copying; library open to SLA members. **Staff:** Yvonne Gloede, Info.Spec.

ALLYN (Edna) ROOM
See: Hawaii State Library - Edna Allyn Room

★274★
ALLYN (Lyman) MUSEUM - LIBRARY (Art)
625 Williams St.   Phone: (203) 443-2345
New London, CT 06320   Marianne S. Dinsmore, Libn.
Staff: Prof 1; Other 2. **Subjects:** Furniture and decorative arts, American art, fine arts. **Holdings:** 14,000 books; exhibition catalogs, museum reports, and drawings. **Subscriptions:** 24 journals and other serials. **Services:** Copying; library open to public.

★275★
ALPENA COUNTY LAW LIBRARY (Law)
Courthouse   Phone: (517) 356-0395
Alpena, MI 49707   Joyce D. McLain, Law Libn.
Staff: Prof 1. **Subjects:** Law. **Holdings:** Figures not available. **Services:** Library open to public for reference use only.

ALPHIN (Albert) MUSIC LIBRARY
See: Boston Conservatory of Music - Albert Alphin Music Library

★276★
ALPINE CLUB OF CANADA - LIBRARY (Rec)
Box 160   Phone: (403) 762-2291
Banff, AB, Canada T0L 0C0   A.M. Daffern, Club Libn.
Founded: 1906. **Staff:** Prof 1. **Subjects:** Mountaineering, mountains, rock climbing, glaciology. **Holdings:** 2344 books and pamphlets; 473 bound periodical volumes; 2000 photographs; 20 boxes of Alpine Club of Canada Archives (restricted). **Subscriptions:** 69 journals and other serials. **Services:** Copying; library open to public with restrictions. **Remarks:** The Alpine Club of Canada Library is administered by the Archives of the Canadian Rockies.

★277★
ALPINE COUNTY LAW LIBRARY (Law)
Box 158   Phone: (916) 694-2281
Markleeville, CA 96120   Joan G. Chacon, Alpine County Ck.
Staff: 2. **Subjects:** Law. **Holdings:** 4000 books. **Services:** Library open to public by appointment.

ALSON (Jacob) MEMORIAL LIBRARY
See: Anti-Defamation League of B'nai B'rith - Jacob Alson Memorial Library

★278★
ALSTON & BIRD - LIBRARY (Law)
35 Broad St., Suite 1200   Phone: (404) 586-1508
Atlanta, GA 30335   Anne H. Butler, Libn.
Founded: 1911. **Staff:** Prof 5; Other 2. **Subjects:** Law - corporate/securities, tax, antitrust, labor, health; litigation. **Holdings:** 40,000 books and bound periodical volumes; 10 VF drawers of pamphlets; 2000 volumes in microform. **Subscriptions:** 500 journals and other serials; 10 newspapers. **Services:** Interlibrary loans; copying; library not open to public. **Computerized Information Services:** Dow Jones News Retrieval, DIALOG, LEXIS, WESTLAW, New York Times Information Service. **Publications:** Library Newsletter, monthly - for internal distribution only. **Special Catalogs:** Memoranda of Law. **Formed by the Merger of:** Alston, Miller and Gaines and Jones, Bird & Howell. **Staff:** Claudia Drum, Asst.Libn.; Cheryl Mckenzie, Asst.Libn.; Eliza Campbell, Asst.Libn.; Stephanie Kirkes, Asst.Libn.

★279★
ALTA BATES HOSPITAL - STUART MEMORIAL LIBRARY (Med)
3001 Colby at Ashby   Phone: (415) 845-7110
Berkeley, CA 94705   Kay Kammerer, Health Sci.Libn.
Founded: 1975. **Staff:** Prof 2. **Subjects:** Medicine. **Holdings:** 1800 books; 2500 bound periodical volumes; 500 reprints. **Subscriptions:** 200 journals and other serials. **Services:** Interlibrary loans; copying; library open to health science professionals for reference use. **Computerized Information Services:** MEDLINE, DIALOG.

★280★
ALTERNATIVE ENERGY RESOURCES ORGANIZATION (AERO) - LIBRARY (Energy)
424 Stapleton Bldg.   Phone: (406) 259-1958
Billings, MT 59101   Joy Coombs, Adm.
Founded: 1974. **Staff:** Prof 1. **Subjects:** Solar energy and architecture; wind and water power; biofuels. **Holdings:** 400 books. **Subscriptions:** 50 journals and other serials. **Services:** Library open to public for reference use only. **Publications:** AERO Sun-Times, monthly - distributed to members.

★281★
ALTERNATIVE PRESS CENTER - LIBRARY (Soc Sci)
Box 7229   Phone: (301) 243-2471
Baltimore, MD 21218   Peggy D'Adamo, Pres.
Founded: 1969. **Staff:** Prof 10. **Subjects:** Liberation - women's, gay, black; Third World movement; ecology; alternative life styles. **Holdings:** 420 volumes. **Subscriptions:** 120 journals and other serials; 180 newspapers. **Services:** Interlibrary loans; library open to public. **Publications:** Alternative Press Index, quarterly. **Remarks:** The Alternative Press Center began in 1969 as the Radical Research Center, Carleton College in Northfield, Minnesota. Its goal was to index and collect the alternative periodicals of the U.S. and Canadian left. The center was established with the aid of a small grant and is now run on income from subscriptions alone. In 1972, the center was moved to Rochdale College, Toronto, Canada. In 1975, it moved to its present location in Baltimore, Maryland. **Staff:** Tim Ford; Betsy Getaz; Laura Glass; Greta Pollard; Jeff Jones; Roger Hansen; Liz Reiley; Irene Reville; Ruth Kifer.

★282★

ALTERNATIVE SOURCES OF ENERGY, INC. - LIBRARY AND REFERRAL SERVICE (Energy)
107 S. Central Ave.   Phone: (612) 983-6892
Milaca, MN 56353   Donald Marier, Dir.
Founded: 1971. **Staff:** Prof 4. **Subjects:** Agriculture; energy - wind, conversion, conservation, water, nonrenewable; architecture; solar transportation. **Holdings:** 900 books; 350 bound periodical volumes; files of 5000 energy companies and organizations; 400 reports and pamphlets. **Subscriptions:** 250 journals and other serials; 30 newspapers. **Services:** Copying (limited); information searches; bibliographies; library not open to public. **Computerized Information Services:** DIALOG. **Publications:** Alternative Sources of Energy Magazine, bimonthly; Wind Industry News Digest (WIND), monthly - both by subscription. **Formerly:** Its Energy Information Referral Service (EIRS). **Staff:** Nancy A. Eggert, Adm.Asst.; Linda Day, Adm.Asst.

★283★

ALTOBELLO (Henry D.) CHILDREN AND YOUTH CENTER - PROFESSIONAL COLLECTION (Soc Sci)†
Undercliff Rd.   Phone: (203) 238-6085
Meriden, CT 06450   Joetta Poppalardo, Dir. of Prof.Ed.
Founded: 1979. **Staff:** Prof 2. **Subjects:** Adolescent care, psychiatric treatment, growth and development, psychiatric nursing, parenting skills, adolescent crisis and intervention. **Holdings:** 250 books. **Services:** Interlibrary loans; library open to other Department of Children and Youth Service programs. **Remarks:** The Collection is maintained by the Department of Children and Youth Service. **Staff:** Ann Juknis, Staff Libn.

★284★

ALTON MEMORIAL HOSPITAL - HEALTH SCIENCES LIBRARY (Med)
One Memorial Dr.   Phone: (618) 463-7343
Alton, IL 62002   Betty Jameson, Libn.
Staff: Prof 1. **Subjects:** Medicine, nursing. **Holdings:** 1500 books; 200 bound periodical volumes; 6 VF drawers. **Subscriptions:** 125 journals and other serials. **Services:** Interlibrary loans; copying; library open to public with restrictions. **Computerized Information Services:** BRS. **Networks/Consortia:** Member of Areawide Hospital Library Consortium of Southwestern Illinois (AHLC); ILLINET.

★285★

ALTON MENTAL HEALTH CENTER - PROFESSIONAL LIBRARY (Med)
4500 College Ave.   Phone: (618) 465-5593
Alton, IL 62002   Thomas M. McConahey, Dir., Dev. & Training
Founded: 1941. **Subjects:** Psychiatry, psychology, nursing, activity therapy, social work, mental retardation, medicine. **Holdings:** 1832 books; 463 bound periodical volumes. **Subscriptions:** 58 journals and other serials. **Services:** Interlibrary loans; copying; library open to students and consortium members.

★286★

ALTON OCHSNER MEDICAL FOUNDATION - MEDICAL LIBRARY (Med)
1516 Jefferson Hwy.   Phone: (504) 838-3760
New Orleans, LA 70121   Joan M. Marcotte, Med.Libn.
Founded: 1942. **Staff:** Prof 1; Other 4. **Subjects:** Medicine, nursing, allied health sciences. **Holdings:** 3000 books; 15,000 bound periodical volumes. **Subscriptions:** 450 journals and other serials. **Services:** Interlibrary loans; copying; library open to nonaffiliated health professionals for reference use only. **Computerized Information Services:** BRS, NLM.

★287★

ALTON TELEGRAPH PRINTING COMPANY - LIBRARY (Publ)†
111 E. Broadway   Phone: (618) 463-2573
Alton, IL 62002   Charlene Heard, Libn.
Staff: Prof 1. **Subjects:** Newspaper reference topics. **Holdings:** 9 file cabinets and 60 archive boxes of clippings; 419 reels of microfilm of early Alton newspapers and Alton Telegraph. **Services:** Copying; library open to public with supervision. **Special Indexes:** Newspaper index, 1836-1936.

★288★

ALTOONA AREA PUBLIC LIBRARY & DISTRICT CENTER - PENNSYLVANIA ROOM (Hist)
1600 Fifth Ave.   Phone: (814) 946-0417
Altoona, PA 16602   Alberta Y. Haught, Ref.Libn.
Staff: Prof 1; Other 2. **Subjects:** State and local history, genealogy, biography, fiction by Pennsylvania authors, railroads, travel, folklore. **Special Collections:** Negatives and glass plates from the test plant of the Pennsylvania Railroad (13,000 items). **Holdings:** Figures not available for books; 17 drawers of clippings and unbound reports. **Services:** Interlibrary loans; copying. **Networks/Consortia:** Member of OCLC.

★289★

ALTOONA HOSPITAL - GLOVER MEMORIAL MEDICAL AND NURSING LIBRARY (Med)
Howard Ave. & 7th St.   Phone: (814) 946-2318
Altoona, PA 16603   Mary Lou Himes, Chf. of Lib.Serv.
Founded: 1940. **Staff:** Prof 2; Other 3. **Subjects:** Medicine and the medical specialties, health science, nursing. **Holdings:** 7480 books; 403 bound periodical volumes; 8 VF drawers; 2 VF drawers of college catalogs; 31 films; 1590 slides; 138 filmstrips; 23 film loops; 67 sound film loops; 31 microfiche; 32 models; 500 audiotapes; 179 video cassettes; 72 phonograph records; 166 posters; 89 Viewmaster slides. **Subscriptions:** 210 journals and other serials. **Services:** Interlibrary loans; copying; library open to public for reference use only. **Computerized Information Services:** NLM; internal database; computerized cataloging, acquisitions, serials and circulation. **Networks/Consortia:** Member of Central Pennsylvania Health Science Library Association (CPHSLA); Mideastern Regional Medical Library Service (MERMLS). **Publications:** New Book List and Film List, monthly - for internal distribution only; Glover Memorial Library Newsletter, quarterly - for internal use and to some hospitals on request. **Special Indexes:** Index to Nursing Service Manuals (book). **Staff:** Bonnie Lantz, Libn.

★290★

ALTOONA MIRROR - LIBRARY (Publ)†
1000 Green Ave.
Box 2008
Altoona, PA 16603   Phone: (814) 946-7457
                                      Esther Barnes, Libn.
Founded: 1929. **Staff:** 2. **Subjects:** Newspaper reference topics. **Holdings:** Figures not available. **Services:** Copying; library open to public by permission. **Staff:** John Timothy Doyle, Asst.Libn.

ALTSCHUL MEDICAL LIBRARY
See: Monmouth Medical Center

ALTUS AIR FORCE BASE (OK)
See: U.S. Air Force Base - Altus Base Library

★291★

ALUMINUM ASSOCIATION - INFORMATION CENTER (Sci-Tech)
818 Connecticut Ave., N.W.   Phone: (202) 862-5100
Washington, DC 20006   Ellen J. Levin, Mgr., Info.Ctr.
Founded: 1980. **Staff:** Prof 1; Other 1. **Subjects:** Aluminum and aluminum products. **Holdings:** 4000 books. **Subscriptions:** 195 journals and other serials; 5 newspapers. **Services:** Interlibrary loans; copying; library open to public by appointment. **Computerized Information Services:** DIALOG, New York Times Information Service, Warner-Eddison Associates, Inc. (INMAGIC). **Networks/Consortia:** Member of Metropolitan Washington Library Council.

★292★

ALUMINUM COMPANY OF AMERICA - ALCOA TECHNICAL CENTER - INFORMATION DEPARTMENT (Sci-Tech)
                                      Phone: (412) 337-2283
Alcoa Center, PA 15069   P.W. Morton, Mgr., Info.Dept.
Founded: 1960. **Staff:** Prof 4; Other 8. **Subjects:** Aluminum, nonferrous metals. **Holdings:** 17,000 volumes; 180 VF drawers of company reports; 175 VF drawers of company correspondence; 1 million documents on microfilm. **Subscriptions:** 900 journals and other serials. **Services:** Interlibrary loans; copying; library open to public by special arrangement only. **Computerized Information Services:** DIALOG, SDC, New York Times Information Service, New England Research Application Center (NERAC); in-house report retrieval system; computerized serials and circulation. **Staff:** V.J. Sapp, Lib.Supv.; John F. Kane, Coord., Info.Serv.; A. Dacko, Rpt.Supv.

★293★

ALUMINUM COMPANY OF AMERICA - CORPORATE LIBRARY (Bus-Fin)
325 Alcoa Bldg.   Phone: (412) 553-4482
Pittsburgh, PA 15219   Nancy J. Furlan, Info.Serv.Adm.
Founded: 1949. **Subjects:** Management, industry, nonferrous metallurgy. **Special Collections:** Aluminum industry history. **Holdings:** 100,000 books and bound periodical volumes; 35 VF drawers. **Subscriptions:** 400 journals and other serials; 7 newspapers. **Services:** Interlibrary loans; copying; translations; library open to public with manager's permission. **Computerized Information Services:** DIALOG, SDC, New York Times Information Service, NLM, ADP Network Services Inc., BRS, Dow Jones News Retrieval; Budget (internal database). **Publications:** Acquisitions List, monthly; featured publications; Guide to the Library.

★294★
ALVERNO COLLEGE - RESEARCH CENTER ON WOMEN (Soc Sci)†
3401 S. 39th St.   Phone: (414) 671-5400
Milwaukee, WI 53215   Lola Stuller, Libn.
Staff: Prof 1; Other 1. **Subjects:** Women - careers/professions, education, religion, life styles, employment; women's movement. **Holdings:** 2300 books; 50 bound periodical volumes; 113 microfiche; 12 VF drawers of clippings and pamphlets; 80 AV items. **Subscriptions:** 104 journals and other serials. **Services:** Interlibrary loans; library open to public. **Networks/Consortia:** Member of OCLC.

★295★
ALZA CORPORATION - RESEARCH LIBRARY (Sci-Tech; Med)
950 Page Mill Rd.   Phone: (415) 494-5215
Palo Alto, CA 94304   Mary Susan Laird, Mgr., Lib.Serv.
Founded: 1968. **Staff:** Prof 1; Other 2. **Subjects:** Pharmacology, biochemistry, medicine, organic chemistry, physiology, polymer science, analytical chemistry, chemical engineering. **Holdings:** 16,000 books; 20,000 bound periodical volumes; 5000 reels of microfilm; 500 microfiche; 20 VF drawers. **Subscriptions:** 400 journals and other serials; 6 newspapers. **Services:** Interlibrary loans; copying; library open to public by appointment.

AMA
See: American Medical Association

★296★
AMALGAMATED CLOTHING & TEXTILE WORKERS UNION, AFL-CIO - RESEARCH DEPARTMENT LIBRARY (Soc Sci)
15 Union Sq.   Phone: (212) 255-7800
New York, NY 10003
Founded: 1954. **Subjects:** Labor economics; industry data on male apparel, textiles and shoes in the U.S. and Canada; collective bargaining; minimum wages; trade unions; labor statistics; wages and hours. **Holdings:** 4500 books; 33 VF drawers of government reports, documents and hearings. **Subscriptions:** 363 journals and other serials. **Services:** Interlibrary loans; library open to graduate students and others doing special work by permission.

AMARILLO BAR ASSOCIATION
See: Texas State - Court of Appeals - 7th Supreme Judicial District and Potter County - Law Library

★297★
AMARILLO COLLEGE - LEARNING RESOURCE CENTER - SPECIAL COLLECTIONS (Hist)
Box 447   Phone: (806) 376-5111
Amarillo, TX 79178   George E. Huffman, Dir.
Founded: 1929. **Special Collections:** Southwest Americana Collection (575 books). **Services:** Interlibrary loans; library open to public with restrictions. **Computerized Information Services:** Computerized cataloging and circulation. **Networks/Consortia:** Member of OCLC through AMIGOS Bibliographic Council, Inc. **Publications:** Media Alert, monthly - for internal use; Faculty and Student Handbook.

★298★
AMARILLO GENEALOGICAL SOCIETY - LIBRARY (Hist)
Amarillo Public Library
Box 2171   Phone: (806) 378-3054
Amarillo, TX 79189   Mary Kay Snell, Hd.Libn.
Subjects: Family histories. **Holdings:** 2316 books; 767 bound periodical volumes; 1650 reels of microfilm; county resource material. **Subscriptions:** 60 journals and other serials. **Services:** Interlibrary loans; copying; library open to public. **Special Catalogs:** Catalog of genealogical material in the Amarillo Public Library (book). **Staff:** Judith Brown, Hd.Ref.Libn.

★299★
AMARILLO GLOBE-NEWS LIBRARY (Publ)
9th & Harrison Sts.   Phone: (806) 376-4488
Amarillo, TX 79166   Bobbie Fortenberry, Libn.
Founded: 1950. **Staff:** Prof 1; Other 3. **Special Collections:** History of the Texas Panhandle (material published in the Globe-News papers). **Holdings:** 150 books; 1600 bound periodical volumes; 472 VF drawers of clippings, pamphlets and documents; 4 VF drawers of photographs. **Services:** Copying; library open to public for reference use only.

AMARILLO HOSPITAL DISTRICT - HEALTH SCIENCES LIBRARY
See: Texas Tech University - Health Sciences Centers - Harrington Library of the Health Sciences

AMARILLO PUBLIC LIBRARY - AMARILLO GENEALOGICAL SOCIETY
See: Amarillo Genealogical Society

★300★
AMARILLO PUBLIC LIBRARY - LOCAL HISTORY COLLECTION (Hist)
413 E. 4th
Box 2171   Phone: (806) 378-3050
Amarillo, TX 79189   Alice Green, Libn.
Subjects: Southwestern history, Indian tribes and customs, religion. **Special Collections:** Bush/FitzSimon Collection of Books on the Southwest; John L. McCarty Papers (4030). **Holdings:** 5078 books; 765 unbound periodicals; 219 maps. **Services:** Copying; library open to public with restrictions. **Computerized Information Services:** Computerized cataloging. **Networks/Consortia:** Member of OCLC. **Special Indexes:** Bibliography of the Bush/FitzSimon/McCarty Southern Collections. **Staff:** Mary Kay Snell, Asst.Libn.; Mark Hanna, Ref.Libn.

★301★
AMATEUR ASTRONOMERS ASSOCIATION - JANE H. DOUGLAS MEMORIAL LIBRARY (Sci-Tech)
1010 Park Ave.
New York, NY 10028   Salomea Brainin, Libn.
Founded: 1930. **Staff:** Prof 2. **Subjects:** Amateur astronomy, general astronomy, history of astronomy, observational astronomy. **Special Collections:** Historical archives of New York area astronomy. **Holdings:** 1500 books; 6 VF drawers of clippings, articles and papers relating to amateur and career astronomy in New York City. **Staff:** John Pazmino, Asst.Libn.

★302★
AMATEUR SOFTBALL ASSOCIATION - ASA RESEARCH CENTER AND LIBRARY (Rec)
2801 N.E. 50th St.   Phone: (405) 424-5266
Oklahoma City, OK 73136   Bill Plummer, III, Comm.Dir.
Staff: 1. **Subjects:** Softball - history, skills analysis/tests, teaching methods, biomechanics, kinesiology, psychology. **Holdings:** 57 books; 67 bound periodical volumes. **Subscriptions:** 24 journals and other serials and newspapers. **Services:** Library open to public for reference use only. **Publications:** Newspaper, monthly; Hall of Fame brochure, biennial; Hall of Fame newsletter, quarterly.

★303★
AMAX, INC. - CLIMAX MOLYBDENUM COMPANY OF MICHIGAN - LIBRARY (Sci-Tech)
1600 Huron Parkway   Phone: (313) 761-2300
Ann Arbor, MI 48105   Eva Maria Di Giulio, Libn.
Founded: 1938. **Staff:** Prof 1. **Subjects:** Molybdenum metallurgy, chemistry, lubrication, pigments, corrosion. **Holdings:** 2800 books; 3300 bound periodical volumes; 6 VF drawers of patents; 17 VF drawers of internal reports; 40 VF drawers of external reports; complete set of Climax reprints. **Subscriptions:** 100 journals and other serials. **Services:** Interlibrary loans; copying; library not open to public. **Computerized Information Services:** DIALOG, Termatrex Information Retrieval System.

★304★
AMAX, INC. - CLIMAX MOLYBDENUM COMPANY - TECHNICAL INFORMATION DEPARTMENT (Sci-Tech)†
1 Greenwich Plaza   Phone: (203) 622-3587
Greenwich, CT 06830   Ellen Jones, Supv., Info.Serv.
Founded: 1947. **Staff:** Prof 5; Other 4. **Subjects:** Molybdenum, molybdenum alloys, tungsten, tungsten alloys, physical metallurgy, properties, applications. **Holdings:** 1500 books; 300 bound periodical volumes; 500 NASA publications; 400 Defense Metals Information Center (DMIC) reports; 450 Air Force reports; 300 other company reports; 20 VF drawers of articles, documents, brochures; 500 company reports, brochures, proceedings. **Subscriptions:** 150 journals and other serials. **Services:** Optical coincidence searching system for company use; limited reference service for outside inquiries; center not open to public. **Computerized Information Services:** DIALOG. **Publications:** Molysulfide Newsletter; Mosaic; Tungsten News, all quarterly - distributed to mailing lists free upon request. **Special Catalogs:** Catalyst bibliography, every 2 years (book).

★305★
AMAX, INC. - CLIMAX MOLYBDENUM COMPANY - TECHNICAL LIBRARY (Sci-Tech)
                    Phone: (303) 486-2150
Climax, CO 80429   Howard Hallman, Jr., Indus.Engr.
Founded: 1955. **Subjects:** Mining methods and engineering; metallurgical-physical and mineral beneficiation; industrial relations; geology; medicine; finance; law; ventilation; civil and safety engineering; electrical and mechanical

engineering. **Holdings:** 4201 books; 6 VF drawers of pamphlets; 2 VF drawers of annual reports; 615 government technical publications; 27,000 original engineering drawings. **Subscriptions:** 148 journals and other serials. **Services:** Library not open to public.

★306★
AMAX EXPLORATION, INC. - SCIENCE LIBRARY (Sci-Tech)
1707 Cole Blvd.   Phone: (303) 231-0647
Golden, CO 80401   Laura A. Christensen, Supv. of Lib.Serv.
Staff: Prof 1; Other 1. **Subjects:** Minerals and metals, mining engineering, geology, geophysics, geochemistry, environmental science, geothermal energy. **Special Collections:** U.S. Bureau of Mines and U.S. Geological Survey Bulletins; professional papers and monographs. **Holdings:** 2500 books; 100 bound periodical volumes; 7000 government documents; 3000 maps. **Subscriptions:** 200 journals and other serials; 6 newspapers. **Services:** Interlibrary loans; copying; SDI; library open to public with management approval. **Computerized Information Services:** DIALOG, SDC. **Remarks:** Subsidiary of AMAX, Inc.

★307★
AMAX EXTRACTIVE RESEARCH & DEVELOPMENT, INC. - TECHNICAL INFORMATION CENTER (Sci-Tech)
5950 McIntyre St.   Phone: (303) 279-7636
Golden, CO 80401   James W. Carter, Supv.
Founded: 1974. **Staff:** Prof 2; Other 2. **Subjects:** Metallurgy, chemistry. **Holdings:** 2200 books; 2000 bound periodical volumes; 7500 patents; 18,000 internal reports. **Subscriptions:** 125 journals and other serials. **Services:** Interlibrary loans; copying; SDI; library open to public with restrictions. **Computerized Information Services:** Online systems; computerized cataloging, serials and circulation. **Staff:** Donna A. Atkins, Libn.

★308★
AMAX, INC. - LAW LIBRARY (Law)
AMAX Center   Phone: (203) 622-3021
Greenwich, CT 06830   Virginia S. Grayson, Libn.
Subjects: Law. **Holdings:** 3038 volumes; 500 other items. **Services:** Library not open to public.

★309★
AMAX, INC. - LIBRARY (Bus-Fin; Sci-Tech)
AMAX Center   Phone: (203) 629-6022
Greenwich, CT 06836   Virginia S. Grayson, Libn.
Founded: 1951. **Staff:** Prof 2; Other 1. **Subjects:** Metallurgy, mining, geology, business and finance, law, economic statistics, management. **Holdings:** 10,000 books; 2000 bound periodical volumes; company reports (cataloged); 600 annual reports. **Subscriptions:** 700 journals and other serials; 32 newspapers. **Services:** Interlibrary loans; copying; library open to SLA members by appointment. **Computerized Information Services:** DIALOG, SDC, New York Times Information Service, Dow Jones News Retrieval. **Staff:** Charry D. Boris, Asst.Libn.

★310★
AMBASSADOR COLLEGE - LIBRARY - SPECIAL COLLECTIONS (Agri; Rare Book)
Box 111
Big Sandy, TX 75755   Luren E. Dickinson, Dir.
Special Collections: Woodburn Agricultural Collection (2400 volumes); rare book collection (religion and history; 750 volumes). **Holdings:** 38,500 books; 2100 bound periodical volumes; 3763 microforms; 12,474 ultrafiche; 8 VF drawers of material. **Subscriptions:** 210 journals and other serials; 14 newspapers. **Services:** Interlibrary loans; copying; SDI; library open to public. **Computerized Information Services:** Computerized cataloging. **Networks/Consortia:** Member of OCLC. **Publications:** Library Leads, monthly; Guidebook for Church Libraries, annual. **Remarks:** Ambassador College is sponsored by the Worldwide Church of God.

★311★
AMC CANCER RESEARCH CENTER AND HOSPITAL - GRACE & PHILIP LICHTENSTEIN SCIENTIFIC LIBRARY (Med)
6401 W. Colfax Ave.   Phone: (303) 233-6501
Lakewood, CO 80214   Eleanor Krakauer, Libn.
Staff: Prof 1; Other 1. **Subjects:** Cancer research. **Holdings:** 1400 books; 2000 bound periodical volumes; 8 VF drawers of pamphlets. **Subscriptions:** 114 journals and other serials. **Services:** Interlibrary loans; copying; library open to those with valid reason for use. **Computerized Information Services:** BRS, NLM, SDC; computerized cataloging. **Networks/Consortia:** Member of Denver Area Health Sciences Library Consortium.

★312★
AMDAHL CORPORATION - CORPORATE LIBRARY (Sci-Tech)
1250 E. Arques Ave.   Phone: (408) 746-6376
Sunnyvale, CA 94086   Lourdes (Ludy) Dorilag, Mgr.
Founded: 1978. **Staff:** Prof 3; Other 2. **Subjects:** Computers, electronics, engineering, data processing, science and technology. **Holdings:** 3500 books; 2500 bound periodical volumes. **Subscriptions:** 200 journals and other serials. **Services:** Interlibrary loans; copying; SDI; library not open to public. **Computerized Information Services:** Computerized cataloging. **Networks/Consortia:** Member of CIN; CLASS. **Remarks:** The library contains the holdings of the now defunct Friden Division of the Singer Company. **Staff:** Jessie Shangkuan, Info.Spec.; Gloria Curtis, Info.Spec.

★313★
AME ENGINEERING LTD. - LIBRARY (Sci-Tech)
700-10160 112th St.   Phone: (403) 425-1710
Edmonton, AB, Canada T5K 1M3   Darlene Elias, Lib.Supv.
Staff: Prof 3. **Subjects:** Electrical engineering, business, codes and standards, mechanical engineering. **Holdings:** 400 books; 20 bound periodical volumes; 500 product catalogs; 175 codes and standards. **Subscriptions:** 70 journals and other serials; 6 newspapers. **Services:** Interlibrary loans; library not open to public. **Computerized Information Services:** DIALOG. **Staff:** Patti Hryniw, Lib.Techn.; Suzanne Dubois, Lib.Techn.

★314★
AMELIA HISTORICAL LIBRARY - JACKSON MEMORIAL LIBRARY (Hist)
Box 113
Amelia, VA 23002   W. Cary McConnaughey, Chm.
Founded: 1957. **Subjects:** Amelia County and Virginia history and genealogy. **Special Collections:** Gemstones historical collection. **Holdings:** Figures not available. **Services:** Library open to public with restrictions.

★315★
AMERICAN ACADEMY OF ASIAN STUDIES - LIBRARY
2842 Buchanan
San Francisco, CA 94110
Subjects: Asia and North Africa. **Holdings:** 10,000 books; 2800 bound periodical volumes. **Remarks:** Presently inactive.

★316★
AMERICAN ACADEMY OF DRAMATIC ARTS - LIBRARY (Theater)
120 Madison Ave.   Phone: (212) 686-9244
New York, NY 10016   John Barrow, Libn.
Staff: Prof 2; Other 1. **Subjects:** Theater. **Holdings:** 3900 books; 420 audiotapes; 35 videotapes. **Subscriptions:** 18 journals and other serials. **Services:** Interlibrary loans; copying; library open to public with referral from another library. **Networks/Consortia:** Member of METRO.

★317★
AMERICAN ACADEMY OF FAMILY PHYSICIANS - INFORMATION RESOURCE DEPARTMENT (Med)
1740 W. 92nd St.   Phone: (816) 333-9700
Kansas City, MO 64114   Karen R. Carter, Mgr., Info.Rsrcs.Dept.
Staff: Prof 1; Other 2. **Subjects:** Medicine. **Holdings:** Figures not available. **Subscriptions:** 250 journals and other serials; 10 newspapers. **Services:** Department open to public for reference use only.

★318★
AMERICAN ACADEMY AND INSTITUTE OF ARTS AND LETTERS - LIBRARY (Hum)
633 W. 155th St.   Phone: (212) 368-5900
New York, NY 10032   Casindania P. Eaton, Libn.
Founded: 1904. **Staff:** Prof 1. **Subjects:** Works by and about members of the American Academy and Institute of Arts and Letters; art; music. **Special Collections:** Archives (correspondence, manuscripts, memorabilia, clippings). **Holdings:** 17,300 books; letters; 500 phonograph records. **Services:** Interlibrary loans; library open to accredited scholars by appointment.

★319★
AMERICAN ACADEMY OF OPTOMETRY - LIBRARY (Med)
5530 Wisconsin Ave., N.E., Suite 950
Washington, DC 20815   Dr. John N. Schoen, Sec.-Tres.
Subjects: Optometry, physiological optics, ocular pathology. **Holdings:** Figures not available. **Subscriptions:** 12 journals and other serials. **Services:** Library not open to public. **Formerly:** Located in Owatonna, MN.

★320★
AMERICAN ACADEMY OF PEDIATRICS - LIBRARY (Med)
1801 Hinman Ave.
Box 1034   Phone: (312) 869-4255
Evanston, IL 60204   Frances Curry, Libn.
Subjects: Pediatrics, health and medical education, manpower, accident prevention. **Holdings:** 750 books; 330 bound periodical volumes; pamphlets and monographs. **Subscriptions:** 33 journals and other serials. **Services:** Interlibrary loans (fee); copying (limited); library open to public for reference use only.

★321★
AMERICAN ACADEMY OF PHYSICIAN ASSISTANTS - INFORMATION CENTER (Med)
2341 Jefferson Davis Hwy., No. 700   Phone: (703) 920-5730
Arlington, VA 22202   Susan M. Anderson, Info.Spec.
Staff: Prof 1. **Subjects:** Physicians' assistants, health manpower. **Holdings:** 100 books; 750 journal articles and bibliography research materials. **Subscriptions:** 51 journals and other serials. **Services:** Copying; center open to public by appointment. **Remarks:** Includes the holdings of the Association of Physician Assistant Programs.

★322★
AMERICAN ACADEMY OF PSYCHOTHERAPISTS - AAP TAPE LIBRARY (Med)
2400 86th St., Suite 30   Phone: (515) 278-8741
Des Moines, IA 50322   Dr. Herbert S. Roth, Dir.
Founded: 1957. **Staff:** Prof 1; Other 1. **Subjects:** Psychotherapy, psychotherapists. **Special Collections:** Psychotherapeutic interviews with real patients; biographical and psychotherapeutic interviews from the Division of Psychotherapy of the American Psychological Association; tapes on hypnosis from the Society for Clinical and Experimental Hypnosis. **Holdings:** 110 cassette tapes, most accompanied by verbatim transcript. **Services:** Library open to mental health and educational personnel only; tapes and scripts are available for sale to qualified institutions and individuals. **Publications:** AAP Tape Library Catalog, irregular - sent to mailing list plus previous users. **Staff:** Linda L. Howe, Adm.Asst.

AMERICAN AIR FILTER COMPANY, INC.
See: Allis-Chalmers Corporation - American Air Filter Division

★323★
AMERICAN AIRLINES, INC. - CORPORATE LIBRARY (Bus-Fin)
Box 61616   Phone: (817) 355-1464
Dallas-Fort Worth Airport, TX 75261   Carla Martindell Felsted, Corp.Libn.
Founded: 1940. **Staff:** Prof 1. **Subjects:** Airline and transportation statistics, aviation history, economics, finance, business statistics. **Holdings:** 4150 books; 520 bound periodical volumes; 126 VF drawers of pamphlets and reports. **Subscriptions:** 140 journals and other serials. **Services:** Interlibrary loans; copying; library open to aviation researchers by appointment. **Publications:** Library newsletter.

★324★
AMERICAN AIRLINES, INC. - ENGINEERING LIBRARY (Sci-Tech)
3800 N. Mingo Rd.   Phone: (918) 832-2821
Tulsa, OK 74151   Amy Dodson, Rec.Libn.
Staff: Prof 1; Other 1. **Subjects:** General aviation, aerospace. **Holdings:** 5000 books; 1000 standards and specifications; 1000 catalogs and vendor data; 6000 vendor catalogs on microfiche; technical reports. **Subscriptions:** 11 journals and other serials. **Services:** Interlibrary loans; copying; SDI; library not open to public. **Publications:** Engineering Library Bulletin, bimonthly.

★325★
AMERICAN ALLIANCE FOR HEALTH, PHYSICAL EDUCATION, RECREATION & DANCE - INFORMATION CENTER FOR THE HANDICAPPED (Med)
1900 Association Dr.   Phone: (202) 833-5547
Reston, VA 22091   Mary Coscarelli, Dir.
Staff: 2. **Subjects:** Activities and therapeutic areas for impaired, disabled and handicapped persons - adapted physical education; recreation; therapeutic recreation; physical education; sports; athletics; camping; outdoor education; aquatics; swimming; rhythms; dance; perception-motor functions. **Holdings:** Figures not available. **Subscriptions:** 300 journals and other serials. **Services:** Copying; dissemination/distribution referral system; library open to public for reference use only. **Publications:** Guides, information sheets, bibliographies on subjects of priority need - to personnel in the field. **Also Known As:** American Alliance for Health, Physical Education, Recreation & Dance - Information & Research Utilization Center in Physical Education and Recreation for the Handicapped.

AMERICAN ALLIANCE FOR HEALTH, PHYSICAL EDUCATION, RECREATION & DANCE - NASPE
See: National Association for Sport & Physical Education

★326★
AMERICAN ALPINE CLUB - LIBRARY (Rec)
113 E. 90th St.   Phone: (212) 722-1628
New York, NY 10028   Horst Von Henning, Chm., Lib.Comm.
Founded: 1913. **Staff:** Prof 2. **Subjects:** Mountaineering. **Holdings:** 10,000 books and bound periodical volumes; maps, photographs, and slides. **Services:** Copying; library open to public by appointment. **Staff:** P.A. Fletcher, Libn.

★327★
AMERICAN AMBULANCE ASSOCIATION - INFORMATION CENTER (Med)*
1919 Market St.   Phone: (216) 744-4161
Youngstown, OH 44507   Daniel Becker
Founded: 1975. **Staff:** Prof 1; Other 1. **Subjects:** AMSAA services and membership information; legislation - E.M.S.; emergency medical services; ambulance services; paramedical training. **Subscriptions:** 30 journals and other serials. **Services:** Copying; center open to public. **Publications:** AMSAA Paramedical News Review, quarterly; AMSAA Newsletter, 8/year - to membership; Directory of Ambulance Service (book).

★328★
AMERICAN ANTIQUARIAN SOCIETY - LIBRARY (Hist)
185 Salisbury St.   Phone: (617) 755-5221
Worcester, MA 01609   Marcus A. McCorison, Dir.
Founded: 1812. **Staff:** Prof 17; Other 18. **Subjects:** American history and culture at all levels - national, regional, state, town, family. **Special Collections:** Early American newspapers, imprints, almanacs, directories, children's books; material printed in the area of the present United States before 1877. **Holdings:** 600,000 books; 135,000 bound periodical volumes; 1500 boxes and 3400 volumes of manuscripts. **Subscriptions:** 550 journals and other serials. **Services:** Copying; library open to qualified adults. **Computerized Information Services:** Computerized cataloging. **Networks/Consortia:** Member of Worcester Area Cooperating Libraries (WACL); OCLC through NELINET; RLG. **Publications:** Proceedings, 2/year. **Staff:** Frederick E. Bauer, Jr., Assoc.Libn.

★329★
AMERICAN APPRAISAL COMPANY - LIBRARY (Bus-Fin)
525 E. Michigan St.   Phone: (414) 271-7240
Milwaukee, WI 53201   Stella Lorenz, Libn.
Staff: 2. **Subjects:** Real estate, appraising, depreciation, engineering, taxation. **Holdings:** 5200 books and bound periodical volumes; 40 drawers of clippings and pamphlets; 62 drawers of annual reports. **Subscriptions:** 348 journals and other serials. **Services:** Interlibrary loans; copying; library not open to public. **Publications:** Memo of new books and periodicals, monthly.

★330★
AMERICAN ARBITRATION ASSOCIATION - EASTMAN ARBITRATION LIBRARY (Soc Sci)
140 W. 51st St.   Phone: (212) 484-4127
New York, NY 10020   Laura Ferris Brown, Chf.Libn.
Founded: 1954. **Staff:** Prof 3; Other 1. **Subjects:** Arbitration, mediation and other forms of voluntary dispute settlement - general, commercial, international, labor, environmental, compulsory, maritime, uninsured motorist, no-fault, medical and health, public employment. **Special Collections:** Archival collection of early history and development of arbitration in the U.S.; arbitration rules of trade associations, chambers of commerce and arbitral institutions throughout the world; arbitration statutes. **Holdings:** 16,000 books and bound periodical volumes; arbitration awards; 159 microfiche. **Subscriptions:** 240 journals and other serials. **Services:** Interlibrary loans; copying; fee-based research service; library open to public. **Publications:** The Library: Recent Acquisitions, quarterly - published in The Arbitration Journal; bibliographies - for sale. **Special Catalogs:** Paul Felix Warburg Union Catalog of Arbitration. **Staff:** Paula Merritt, Tech.Serv.Libn.; Diane T. Olsson, Ref.Libn.

AMERICAN ARCHIVE OF ENCYCLOPAEDIA CINEMATOGRAPHICA
See: Pennsylvania State University - Audiovisual Services

AMERICAN ARCHIVES OF THE FACTUAL FILM
See: Iowa State University - Library - Special Collections

AMERICAN ARRIAGA ARCHIVE
See: University of Wisconsin, Milwaukee - Music Collection

★331★
AMERICAN ASSOCIATION FOR THE ADVANCEMENT OF SCIENCE -
    LIBRARY (Sci-Tech)
1515 Massachusetts Ave., N.W.   Phone: (202) 467-4428
Washington, DC 20005   Janet Kegg, Libn.
Staff: 1. Special Collections: Publications of the association. Holdings:
3000 books and bound periodical volumes. Subscriptions: 50 journals and
other serials. Services: Interlibrary loans; library open to public by
appointment.

AMERICAN ASSOCIATION OF ADVERTISING AGENCIES - LITERACY
    CLEARINGHOUSE
See: Contact, Inc.

★332★
AMERICAN ASSOCIATION OF ADVERTISING AGENCIES - MEMBER
    INFORMATION SERVICE (Bus-Fin)
666 3rd Ave.   Phone: (212) 682-2500
New York, NY 10017   Marilyn M. Bockman, V.P.
Founded: 1938. Staff: Prof 9; Other 7. Subjects: Advertising, marketing.
Holdings: 2000 books; 185 VF drawers of clippings, reports and pamphlets.
Subscriptions: 350 journals and other serials. Services: Interlibrary loans;
copying; library primarily serves association members. Computerized
Information Services: DIALOG, SDC, New York Times Information Service.
Staff: Marsha Appel, Staff Exec.; Marge Morris, Asst.Mgr.; Mary Ann Emma,
Info.Spec.; Edith Ziffer, Info.Spec.; Elaine Rothman, Info.Spec.; Virginia
Gregory, Info.Spec.; Julie-Ann Zilavy, Info.Spec.; Amy Mills, Info.Spec.; Gail
Levinson, Info.Spec.

★333★
AMERICAN ASSOCIATION OF BIOANALYSTS - SLIDE LIBRARY (Sci-Tech)†
81 Olive, Suite 918   Phone: (314) 241-1445
St. Louis, MO 63101   Mary E. Wood, Cur.
Founded: 1960. Staff: Prof 1; Other 1. Subjects: Parasitology, hematology,
bacteriology, mycology. Holdings: Prepared and stained microscopic slides;
11 boxes of other cataloged items. Services: Material available with payment
of deposit. Formerly: Located in Redwood City, CA.

AMERICAN ASSOCIATION OF COLLEGES FOR TEACHER EDUCATION - ERIC
    CLEARINGHOUSE ON TEACHER EDUCATION
See: ERIC Clearinghouse on Teacher Education

★334★
AMERICAN ASSOCIATION OF CORRECTIONAL OFFICERS - LIBRARY (Law)
2309 State St., North Office   Phone: (517) 799-8208
Saginaw, MI 48602   Herbert Van Dusen, Libn.
Founded: 1977. Staff: 2. Subjects: Criminal rehabilitation, law enforcement.
Special Collections: Supreme Court decisions. Holdings: 205 volumes; 63
unbound reports; 54 manuscripts. Subscriptions: 10 journals and other
serials. Services: Interlibrary loans; copying; library open to public with
restrictions. Publications: Library Guide.

★335★
AMERICAN ASSOCIATION OF COST ENGINEERS - LIBRARY (Sci-Tech)
308 Monongahela Bldg.   Phone: (304) 296-8444
Morgantown, WV 26505   Kenneth K. Humphreys, Exec.Dir.
Founded: 1956. Staff: Prof 3; Other 7. Subjects: Cost engineering, cost
estimation, business planning, management science, construction costs,
engineering economy. Holdings: 2000 volumes. Subscriptions: 30 journals
and other serials. Services: Interlibrary loans; copying; library not open to
public. Publications: Cost engineering, bimonthly - by subscription; AACE
Transactions, annual; Cost Engineers Notebook, irregular. Special Indexes:
KWIC Index of cost engineering papers.

★336★
AMERICAN ASSOCIATION OF CRIMEAN TURKS, INC. - ISMAIL GASPIRALI
    LIBRARY (Area-Ethnic)†
4509 New Utrecht Ave.   Phone: (212) 438-9567
Brooklyn, NY 11219   Halim Saylik, Mgr.
Founded: 1965. Staff: 3. Subjects: Crimean Turks - history, culture,
literature. Holdings: 200 books. Services: Library open to public.

★337★
AMERICAN ASSOCIATION FOR THE INTERNATIONAL COMMISSION OF
    JURISTS, INC. - LIBRARY (Soc Sci; Law)
777 United Nations Plaza   Phone: (212) 972-0883
New York, NY 10017   Denise Jessum, Adm.Asst.
Staff: 1. Subjects: Human rights, international law and organizations,
refugees. Special Collections: United Nations documents. Holdings: 400

books. Services: Copying; library open to public. Publications: Newsletter, 3/
year - free upon request and by subscription. Special Indexes: Indexes to all
articles published by the International Commission of Jurists, all United
Nations documents and all United Nations human rights covenants.

AMERICAN ASSOCIATION FOR JEWISH EDUCATION
See: Jewish Education Service of North America, Inc.

AMERICAN ASSOCIATION OF LAW LIBRARIES
See: University of Illinois - Law Library

★338★
AMERICAN ASSOCIATION OF MEDICO-LEGAL CONSULTANTS - LIBRARY
    (Med; Law)
Park Towne Pl., N-105
2200 Benjamin Franklin Pkwy.   Phone: (215) 561-2121
Philadelphia, PA 19130   Arlene Goldman, Libn.
Staff: Prof 2. Subjects: Medicine, law, pharmacology, malpractice, medico-
legal subjects. Holdings: 350 books; Clin-Alert, Medical Letter, Citation.
Subscriptions: 20 journals and other serials. Services: Interlibrary loans;
copying; library open to public by request. Staff: Evelyn M. Goldstein, Dir.

★339★
AMERICAN ASSOCIATION OF MUSEUMS - MUSEUM RESOURCES AND
    INFORMATION SERVICE (Hum; Art)
1055 Thomas Jefferson St., N.W.
Washington, DC 20007   Sybil Walker, Ed.Asst.
Founded: 1906. Subjects: Museology, museum related topics. Holdings:
1100 books; 300 bound periodical volumes. Subscriptions: 100 journals and
other serials.

★340★
AMERICAN ASSOCIATION OF OCCUPATIONAL HEALTH NURSES - LIBRARY
    (Med)
3500 Piedmont Rd., N.E.   Phone: (404) 262-1162
Atlanta, GA 30305   Ricki Herrling, Libn.
Founded: 1965. Staff: 1. Subjects: Occupational health nursing,
occupational medicine. Holdings: 700 books; 22 bound periodical volumes;
1050 pamphlets; 70 file folders of pamphlets. Subscriptions: 54 journals and
other serials; 12 newspapers. Services: Interlibrary loans; copying; library
open to public with restrictions. Publications: Occupational Health Nursing,
monthly; American Association of Occupational Health Nurses, monthly - both
to members. Formerly: Located in New York, NY.

★341★
AMERICAN ASSOCIATION OF PETROLEUM GEOLOGISTS - LIBRARY (Sci-
    Tech)
1444 S. Boulder
Box 979   Phone: (918) 584-2555
Tulsa, OK 74101   Kathy Shanks, Libn.
Founded: 1965. Staff: Prof 1. Subjects: Petroleum geology, geology.
Special Collections: Publications of the AAPG and its affiliated societies.
Holdings: 600 books; 64 bound periodical volumes; 600 reports and state
geological surveys. Subscriptions: 75 journals and other serials; 8
newspapers. Services: Interlibrary loans; copying (fee); library open to public
with restrictions.

★342★
AMERICAN ASSOCIATION OF RETIRED PERSONS - NATIONAL
    GERONTOLOGY RESOURCE CENTER (Soc Sci)
1909 K St., N.W.   Phone: (202) 728-4700
Washington, DC 20049   Paula M. Lovas, Hd.
Staff: Prof 7; Other 4. Subjects: Social gerontology, retirement, pre-
retirement planning, social welfare, voluntarism, adult education and
association management. Holdings: 6000 books; 150 bound periodical
volumes; 250 1961 and 1971 White House Conference on Aging reports;
1000 archival items; 500 pamphlet files. Subscriptions: 450 journals and
other serials; 150 newsletters; 6 newspapers. Services: Interlibrary loans;
center open to public for reference use only. Computerized Information
Services: DIALOG, New York Times Information Service, SDC, MEDLARS.
Publications: Monthly accessions list; Weekly Table of Contents - free upon
request. Special Indexes: Subject indexes to association journals: Modern
Maturity, NRTA Journal, Dynamic Maturity. Formerly: National Retired
Teachers Association/American Association of Retired Persons. Staff: Mary
Power, Coord., Ref.Serv.; Eve Rafferty, Acq.Libn.; Lynne Masterson, Cat.

★343★

AMERICAN ASSOCIATION OF TEXTILE CHEMISTS AND COLORISTS - LIBRARY (Sci-Tech)

Box 12215   Phone: (919) 549-8141
Research Triangle Park, NC 27709   George J. Mandikos, Tech.Dir.
Subjects: Textile test methods for wet processing. **Holdings:** Figures not available. **Services:** Copying; library open to public.

★344★

AMERICAN ASSOCIATION OF UNIVERSITY WOMEN - EDUCATIONAL FOUNDATION LIBRARY AND ARCHIVES (Educ)

2401 Virginia Ave., N.W.   Phone: (202) 785-7763
Washington, DC 20037   Mary K. Jordan, Libn./Archv.
Founded: 1960. **Staff:** Prof 1; Other 1. **Subjects:** Education and higher education; women's activities and achievements; status of women; college and university trends and histories. **Special Collections:** Graduate Woman (formerly AAUW Journal), complete bound collection since its beginning in 1898 as ACA Journal (also on microfilm). **Holdings:** 4500 books, pamphlets (cataloged); copies of association publications; 400 archival and records boxes relating to history and formation of the association; work done on research education projects; study topics and issues; bound volumes of board meetings for both association and foundation; biennial reports for association from 1933 and foundation from 1958; 158 reels of microfilm of archives, 1881-1976. **Subscriptions:** 150 journals and other serials; 5 newspapers. **Services:** Interlibrary loans; copying (both limited); library open to graduate students in education or related fields and to others with related interest or need, by prior appointment.

★345★

AMERICAN ASSOCIATION OF VARIABLE STAR OBSERVERS - MC ATEER LIBRARY (Sci-Tech)

187 Concord Ave.   Phone: (617) 354-0484
Cambridge, MA 02138   Janet A. Mattei, Dir.
Subjects: Astronomy, mathematics. **Holdings:** Figures not available. **Subscriptions:** 75 journals and other serials. **Services:** Copying; library not open to public.

★346★

AMERICAN AUTOMOBILE ASSOCIATION - LIBRARY (Trans)

8111 Gatehouse Rd.   Phone: (703) 222-6466
Falls Church, VA 22047   Sue Williams, Libn.
Founded: 1955. **Staff:** Prof 2; Other 2. **Subjects:** Travel guide books; market studies; highway and traffic safety; driver education; auto history, statistics and insurance; business management. **Special Collections:** AAA Tour Books and road maps; official Automobile Blue Books from 1910; rare guide books. **Holdings:** 14,000 books; 120 bound periodical volumes; 20 VF drawers of miscellaneous pamphlets, reports and articles. **Subscriptions:** 600 journals and other serials. **Services:** Interlibrary loans; library open to researchers with permission. **Computerized Information Services:** SDC, New York Times Information Service, DIALOG, Source Telecomputing Corporation. **Publications:** Infoscan, bimonthly - for internal distribution only. **Staff:** Janice Sherman, Res.Libn.

★347★

AMERICAN AVIATION HISTORICAL SOCIETY - AAHS REFERENCE LIBRARY (Hist; Mil)

2333 Otis   Phone: (714) 549-4818
Santa Ana, CA 92704   Jacqueline M. Sweaza, Off.Mgr.
Founded: 1975. **Staff:** 1. **Subjects:** Aviation - history, personalities, manufacture; military aviation. **Holdings:** 5500 books; 700 unbound periodical volumes; 12,100 negatives and aircraft photos; 2000 slides; 25 VF drawers of clippings, drawings and reference data. **Subscriptions:** 12 journals and other serials. **Services:** Interlibrary loans; copying; library open for validated research projects. **Publications:** American Aviation Historical Society Journal, quarterly; AAHS Newsletter, quarterly - to membership. **Special Catalogs:** Negatives Lending Library Catalog; yearly index of journal and newsletter with cumulative index published each ten years.

AMERICAN BANDMASTER ASSOCIATION RESEARCH CENTER
See: University of Maryland, College Park - Libraries - Music Library

★348★

AMERICAN BANKER, INC. - LIBRARY (Bus-Fin)

One State St. Plaza   Phone: (212) 943-4844
New York, NY 10004   Patricia Y. Bluestein, Hd.Libn.
Founded: 1968. **Staff:** Prof 3; Other 2. **Subjects:** Banking and banks; municipal finance, bonds and notes. **Special Collections:** Archives; American Banker, original volumes to present (not complete); Daily and Weekly Bond Buyer (complete). **Holdings:** 1600 books; 350,000 clippings, 1964 to present; 24 VF drawers of pamphlets; 28 VF drawers of annual reports; microfilm, 1945 to present. **Subscriptions:** 100 journals and other serials. **Services:** Interlibrary loans; copying; library not open to public. **Computerized Information Services:** NEXIS. **Publications:** American Banker Index - monthly, annual; reprints of special features; American Banker's Directory of U.S. Bank Executives; Directory of Municipal Bond Dealers. **Special Indexes:** American Banker Index (book); Bond Buyer cumulative index, quarterly. **Staff:** Lou Levanthal, Asst.Libn.; Martha A. Monte, Asst.Libn.

★349★

AMERICAN BANKERS ASSOCIATION - LIBRARY & INFORMATION SERVICES (Bus-Fin; Law)

1120 Connecticut Ave., N.W.   Phone: (202) 467-4180
Washington, DC 20036   Joan Gervino, Dir.
Founded: 1911. **Staff:** Prof 5; Other 6. **Subjects:** Law, banking and finance, legislative documents, economics. **Special Collections:** Stonier Graduate School of Banking and National Graduate Trust School theses. **Holdings:** 41,000 books and bound periodical volumes; legislative documents on microfiche; 20 VF drawers. **Subscriptions:** 600 journals and other serials. **Services:** Interlibrary loans; copying; library open to public with permission. **Computerized Information Services:** DIALOG, SDC, New York Times Information Service; computerized circulation and routing. **Special Indexes:** The Banking Literature Index (computer generated). **Staff:** Kathryn Kupstas, Hd., Tech.Serv.; Carol Penne, Asst.Dir.; Linda Wengel, Ref.Libn.; Charles Sabella, Ref.Libn.

★350★

AMERICAN BAPTIST CHURCHES IN THE U.S.A. - BOARD OF EDUCATIONAL MINISTRIES - EDITORIAL LIBRARY (Rel-Theol; Publ)

                                          Phone: (215) 768-2378
Valley Forge, PA 19481   Dorothy A. Martin, Libn.
Founded: 1923. **Subjects:** Theology, Christian education, Bible, church history. **Special Collections:** Judson Press Historical Collection, comprised of all the books and material printed and published by the American Baptist Publication Society, including curriculum and Sunday School materials (2000 volumes); current books of Judson Press. **Holdings:** 3000 books; 500 bound periodical volumes; 100 minutes of ABPS and ABBEP; 200 pamphlets; 200 archives. **Subscriptions:** 65 journals and other serials. **Services:** Interlibrary loans; copying; library open to public for reference use in consultation with librarian.

★351★

AMERICAN BAPTIST CHURCHES IN THE U.S.A. - BOARD OF INTERNATIONAL MINISTRIES - LIBRARY AND CENTRAL FILES (Rel-Theol)

                                          Phone: (215) 768-2365
Valley Forge, PA 19481   Priscilla B. Shaw, Libn.
Staff: 2. **Subjects:** Mission material - historical, biographical and ethnological. **Special Collections:** Biographical material on Adoniram Judson and his wives. **Holdings:** 4333 books; 720 bound periodical volumes; 1727 other cataloged items; 571 reels of microfilm; 4 VF drawers of maps; 224 VF drawers of reports, clippings, pamphlets; 38 VF drawers of biographical files; 28 VF drawers of property files; 31 VF drawers of candidate files. **Subscriptions:** 115 journals and other serials. **Services:** Library open to public with permission of Overseas Secretary.

★352★

AMERICAN BAPTIST CHURCHES IN THE U.S.A. - BOARD OF NATIONAL MINISTRIES - RECORDS MANAGEMENT & CENTRAL FILES (Rel-Theol)

                                          Phone: (215) 768-2383
Valley Forge, PA 19481   Mrs. Henrene George, Supv.
Founded: 1832. **Staff:** Prof 1. **Subjects:** Missions. **Special Collections:** Historical and current records of Board of National Ministries. **Holdings:** 45 volumes of minutes of the American Baptist Home Mission Societies; 55 file cabinets of unbound material; 680 reels of microfilmed records. **Subscriptions:** 19 journals and other serials. **Services:** Library open to public for reference use only but clearance must be obtained from the Board of National Ministries.

AMERICAN BAPTIST HISTORICAL SOCIETY - DANISH BAPTIST GENERAL CONFERENCE OF AMERICA
See: Danish Baptist General Conference of America

★353★

AMERICAN BAPTIST HISTORICAL SOCIETY - SAMUEL COLGATE BAPTIST HISTORICAL LIBRARY (Hist; Rel-Theol)

1106 S. Goodman St.   Phone: (716) 473-1740
Rochester, NY 14620   William H. Brackney, Exec.Dir.
Staff: Prof 2; Other 4. **Subjects:** Baptist history, theology and authors. **Special Collections:** Henry Sweetser Burrage collection of 17th and 18th

century English Baptist materials; Walter Rauschenbusch papers; American Baptist Archives repository. **Holdings:** 50,000 books; 15,000 bound periodical volumes; 250,000 annual reports and pamphlets; 6000 manuscripts; clippings, photographs and microfilm. **Subscriptions:** 300 journals and other serials. **Services:** Interlibrary loans (limited); library open to qualified research students. **Publications:** Baptist Bibliography, volumes 1-25 published. **Remarks:** Maintains Danish Baptist General Conference of America - Archives.

AMERICAN BAPTIST SEMINARY OF THE WEST
See: Graduate Theological Union

★354★
AMERICAN BAPTIST THEOLOGICAL SEMINARY - T.L. HOLCOMB LIBRARY (Rel-Theol)
1800 White's Creek Pike   Phone: (615) 262-1369
Nashville, TN 37207   Dorothy B. Lucas, Libn.
Staff: Prof 1; Other 3. **Subjects:** Bible, religion, theology, black studies. **Holdings:** 19,500 books; 1350 vertical file items (cataloged). **Subscriptions:** 147 journals and other serials. **Services:** Interlibrary loans; library open to public with restrictions.

AMERICAN BAR ASSOCIATION COMMITTEE ON CONTINUING PROFESSIONAL EDUCATION
See: American Law Institute

★355★
AMERICAN BAR ASSOCIATION - WASHINGTON OFFICE - INFORMATION SERVICES (Law)
1800 M St., N.W., 2nd Fl.   Phone: (202) 331-2207
Washington, DC 20036   Peggy A. Richter, Staff Dir.
Staff: Prof 2; Other 3. **Subjects:** Legal profession, ethics and education. **Special Collections:** State and local bar journal collection (82 titles). **Holdings:** 2200 books; 800 bound periodical volumes; American Bar Association Reports to the House of Delegates, 1881 to present. **Subscriptions:** 131 journals and other serials. **Services:** Interlibrary loans; copying; SDI; library open to public by appointment. **Publications:** Washington Summary, weekly when Congress is in session; Washington Letter, monthly - both by subscription. **Staff:** Laura Speer, Cat.

★356★
AMERICAN BAR FOUNDATION - WILLIAM NELSON CROMWELL LIBRARY (Law)
1155 E. 60th St.   Phone: (312) 667-4700
Chicago, IL 60637   Olavi Maru, Libn.
Founded: 1954. **Staff:** Prof 2; Other 2. **Subjects:** Law. **Special Collections:** Bar association materials with special emphasis on the American Bar Association (800 feet of shelving). **Holdings:** 65,000 volumes. **Subscriptions:** 1000 journals and other serials. **Services:** Interlibrary loans; library open to public on a limited basis.

★357★
AMERICAN BIBLE SOCIETY - LIBRARY (Rel-Theol)
1865 Broadway   Phone: (212) 581-7400
New York, NY 10023   Dr. Louis O. Dorn, Supv.Off.
Founded: 1816. **Staff:** 9. **Subjects:** A collection of over 40,000 copies of the Bible or its parts in more than 1640 languages and dialects; related information about science of linguistics and language location, translations of the Bible, Bible printing, use and influence of the Bible. **Special Collections:** 6662 reference works about the Bible and the society; holdings of the Chicago Bible Society (605 volumes). **Holdings:** 39,500 books; 67 bound periodical volumes; 111 VF drawers; 7534 microforms; 8924 archives. **Subscriptions:** 400 journals and other serials. **Services:** Interlibrary loans (limited); copying; library open to public for special research. **Publications:** Historical Catalog of Printed Bibles, English 1525-1961 (with British & Foreign Bible Society, London); The English Bible in America, 1777-1957 (with New York Public Library); The Book of a Thousand Tongues, 2nd revision, 1972 - 3rd revision in process; Scriptures of the World, 1981. **Staff:** Virginia Carew, Ref.Libn.; Andrew Kuo, Bible Cat.; Erroll Rhodes, Sr.Res.; Janice Pearson, Archv.

★358★
AMERICAN BIBLIOGRAPHICAL CENTER - CLIO PRESS - THE INGE BOEHM LIBRARY (Hist)
2040 Alameda Padre Serra   Phone: (805) 963-4221
Santa Barbara, CA 93103   Hope Smith, Libn.
Founded: 1967. **Staff:** Prof 1; Other 4. **Subjects:** History, political science, social sciences, humanities. **Holdings:** 1000 books; 2000 periodical volumes. **Services:** Copying; library open to public with special permission.

★359★
AMERICAN BLAKE FOUNDATION - RESEARCH LIBRARY (Rare Book; Hum)
Memphis State University
Dept. Of English   Phone: (901) 454-2653
Memphis, TN 38152   Dr. Roger R. Easson, Exec.Dir.
Founded: 1970. **Staff:** Prof 2; Other 1. **Subjects:** Blake - his art, editions of his works, biography, bibliography, original engravings, his followers, auction catalogs, poetry criticism. **Holdings:** 780 books; 1500 pages of unpublished essays and catalogs; 2000 prints and slides. **Subscriptions:** 15 journals and other serials. **Services:** Copying; library open to public with written permission. **Publications:** Blake Studies, semiannual; William Blake: Book Illustrator, 3 volumes. **Remarks:** This is a public research library consisting mainly of rare materials. Persons wishing to use the library should direct their inquiries in writing to the American Blake Foundation. **Staff:** Dr. Kay P. Easson, Exec.Dir.

★360★
AMERICAN BRAHMAN BREEDERS ASSOCIATION - LIBRARY (Agri)
1313 La Concha Ln.   Phone: (713) 795-4444
Houston, TX 77054   Cecilia Cowart, Dir., Commun.
Staff: Prof 6; Other 12. **Subjects:** Registered Brahman cattle, other cattle, crossbreeding, animal science. **Holdings:** 5000 books. **Subscriptions:** 125 journals and other serials. **Services:** Copying; library open to public for reference use only. **Publications:** The Brahman Handbook; The American Brahman; The Brahman Hybrid; The History of the American Brahman - for sale.

★361★
AMERICAN BRANDS, INC. - AMERICAN TOBACCO COMPANY - DEPARTMENT OF RESEARCH & DEVELOPMENT LIBRARY (Sci-Tech; Agri)
Box 899   Phone: (804) 748-4561
Hopewell, VA 23860   Dorothy D. Robben, Supv., Lib. & Rec.
Founded: 1936. **Staff:** Prof 2; Other 2. **Subjects:** Tobacco, engineering, mathematics, physics, plant physiology, quality control, ecology. **Holdings:** 3701 books; 4390 bound periodical volumes; 24,600 patents, technical articles and translations; 2289 microforms. **Subscriptions:** 169 journals and other serials; 5 newspapers. **Services:** Interlibrary loans; copying; library open to public by request. **Publications:** Library Accessions, monthly - for internal distribution only. **Special Catalogs:** Annual Tobacco Titles (generated from magnetic cards).

★362★
AMERICAN BROADCASTING COMPANIES, INC. - ABC NEWS INFORMATION CENTER (Info Sci)
1926 Broadway   Phone: (212) 887-3796
New York, NY 10023   Madeline Cohen, Mgr., Lib.Serv.
Founded: 1945. **Staff:** Prof 2; Other 4. **Subjects:** Current and background news; radio and television. **Holdings:** 4500 books and bound periodical volumes; 50 VF drawers of current and background news clippings; microfilm of newspapers and selected periodicals. **Subscriptions:** 100 journals and other serials. **Services:** Interlibrary loans; copying; library open to public with restrictions. **Computerized Information Services:** New York Times Information Service, DIALOG, SDC, Mead Data Central; internal database. **Publications:** Source, monthly - for internal distribution only.

AMERICAN BROADCASTING COMPANIES, INC. - CHILTON COMPANY
See: Chilton Company

★363★
AMERICAN BUSINESS PRESS, INC. - LIBRARY (Publ)
205 E. 42nd St.   Phone: (212) 661-6360
New York, NY 10017   Evelyn G. French, Dir. of Info.Sys.
Staff: 1. **Subjects:** Business publications. **Holdings:** 503 books; 30 VF drawers of unbound materials. **Services:** Library open to public for reference use only.

★364★
AMERICAN CAMELLIA SOCIETY - LIBRARY (Sci-Tech)
Box 1217   Phone: (912) 967-2358
Fort Valley, GA 31030   Milton H. Brown, Exec.Sec.
Staff: 4. **Subjects:** Camellias. **Holdings:** 2000 books; 150 bound periodical volumes; color slides of camellias (cataloged). **Subscriptions:** 15 journals and other serials. **Services:** Library open to public.

★365★
AMERICAN CAMPING ASSOCIATION - LIBRARY (Rec)
Bradford Woods   Phone: (317) 342-8456
Martinsville, IN 46151
Founded: 1910. **Subjects:** Organized camping, recreation, education, nature, camp administration. **Holdings:** 5000 volumes; 1000 pamphlets and reprints. **Services:** Copying; library open to qualified students for reference.

★366★
AMERICAN CAN COMPANY - BARRINGTON TECHNICAL CENTER - TECHNICAL INFORMATION CENTER (Sci-Tech)
433 N. Northwest Hwy.   Phone: (312) 381-1900
Barrington, IL 60010   Mary T. Gormley, Supv.
Staff: Prof 1; Other 2. **Subjects:** Basic sciences, materials science, engineering, metallurgy, plastics, packaging, canning and preserving, food technology. **Holdings:** 1500 books; 3000 bound periodical volumes; pamphlets; reprints; patents; microfilm. **Subscriptions:** 450 journals and other serials. **Services:** Interlibrary loans; library not open to public. **Computerized Information Services:** DIALOG, SDC. **Networks/Consortia:** Member of North Suburban Library System.

★367★
AMERICAN CAN COMPANY - BUSINESS INFORMATION CENTER (Bus-Fin)
American Ln. - 1B8   Phone: (203) 552-3137
Greenwich, CT 06830   Estelle C. Adler, Mgr.
Founded: 1968. **Staff:** Prof 3; Other 2. **Subjects:** Business; marketing; economics; packaging; plastics; technical, insurance, financial services. **Special Collections:** Corporation annual reports and 10Ks. **Holdings:** 5000 books and bound periodical volumes; 150 VF drawers; 20 drawers of microforms of back periodicals and newspapers. **Subscriptions:** 600 journals and other serials; 10 newspapers. **Services:** Interlibrary loans; copying; library open to other librarians. **Computerized Information Services:** DIALOG, SDC, New York Times Information Service, BRS, MEDLINE, TEXTLINE, Spectrum Data Base. **Networks/Consortia:** Member of Southwestern Connecticut Library Council. **Publications:** Business Information Bulletin, semimonthly; Periodicals List, annual. **Remarks:** Center contains the holdings of the former Marketing Information Library and the Technical Information Center. **Staff:** Ruth Gruettner, Info.Spec.; Debra R. Kaufman, Info.Spec.

★368★
AMERICAN CAN COMPANY - BUTTERICK FASHION MARKETING COMPANY - BUTTERICK ARCHIVES/LIBRARY (Hist)
161 Ave. of the Americas   Phone: (212) 620-2555
New York, NY 10013   Jenny Oparski, Archv.Ck.
Founded: 1863. **Staff:** 1. **Subjects:** Costume history, marketing history. **Special Collections:** Archives of Butterick and Vogue Patterns; Butterick Fashion Marketing Company. **Holdings:** 500 books; 1500 bound periodical volumes; 1300 cubic feet of archives; 100 cubic feet of pictures, clippings and posters. **Subscriptions:** 10 journals and other serials. **Services:** Copying; will answer brief inquiries by mail.

★369★
AMERICAN CAN COMPANY - MARKETING INFORMATION LIBRARY
American Ln.
Greenwich, CT 06830
Defunct. Merged with American Can Company - Technical Information Center to form the Business Information Center.

AMERICAN CAN COMPANY - NEENAH TECHNICAL CENTER
See: James River Corporation - Neenah Technical Center

★370★
AMERICAN CAN COMPANY - PRINCETON RESEARCH INFORMATION CENTER (Sci-Tech)†
Box 50   Phone: (609) 921-2510
Princeton, NJ 08540   Kathleen A. Giovannini, Info.Sci.
Founded: 1964. **Staff:** Prof 1; Other 1. **Subjects:** Chemistry - organic, polymer; resource recovery; chemical engineering; pulp and paper. **Holdings:** 3000 books; 3000 bound periodical volumes; 5 VF drawers of patents; 30 VF drawers of government documents. **Subscriptions:** 250 journals and other serials. **Services:** Interlibrary loans; copying; SDI; library open to public by appointment. **Computerized Information Services:** Online systems.

★371★
AMERICAN CAN COMPANY - RESEARCH AND DEVELOPMENT LIBRARY (Sci-Tech)
                                  Phone: (715) 359-6544
Rothschild, WI 54474   Marion B. Haase, Libn.
Founded: 1949. **Staff:** 1. **Subjects:** Wood, paper, paper chemicals.

Holdings: 1300 books; 850 bound periodical volumes; 800 other volumes. **Subscriptions:** 70 journals and other serials. **Services:** Library open to public with permission.

★372★
AMERICAN CAN COMPANY - TECHNICAL INFORMATION CENTER
American Lane, Mail Code 2B2
Greenwich, CT 06830
Defunct. Merged with American Can Company - Marketing Information Center to form the Business Information Center.

★373★
AMERICAN-CANADIAN GENEALOGICAL SOCIETY - FATHER LEO E. BEGIN CHAPTER - LIBRARY (Hist)
Box 2125
Lewiston, ME 04240   Bernadette Tardif, Libn.
Founded: 1980. **Subjects:** Genealogical marriage repertories, history, genealogy. **Holdings:** 181 books. **Services:** Library open to public with donation.

★374★
AMERICAN-CANADIAN GENEALOGICAL SOCIETY - LIBRARY (Hist)
Box 668   Phone: (603) 623-1781
Manchester, NH 03105   Richard Gagnon, Libn.
Staff: Prof 1; Other 12. **Subjects:** Genealogy, history. **Special Collections:** Loisell Index of Quebec Marriages (microfilm); Lambert Collection of Genealogies and Local Histories. **Holdings:** 600 books; 5000 bound periodical volumes; family histories. **Subscriptions:** 100 journals and other serials; 22 newspapers. **Services:** Copying (limited); library open to public for reference use only. **Publications:** The Genealogist, semiannual - available upon request. **Special Indexes:** Surname research index; Marriage Index of Franklin, NH; index of French genealogical resources from the Church of Jesus Christ of Latter-Day Saints. **Remarks:** The library is located at 52 Concord St., Manchester, NH 03101.

★375★
AMERICAN CANCER SOCIETY - AUDIO VISUAL LIBRARIES (Med; Aud-Vis)
777 Third Ave.   Phone: (212) 371-2900
New York, NY 10017   Stefan Bodnariuk, Supv. Film Ed.
Staff: Prof 1; Other 1. **Subjects:** Cancer - diagnosis, treatment, rehabilitation, prevention and protection. **Holdings:** Figures not available for 16mm and super 8mm films, video cassettes, filmstrips, slide sets, audio cassettes. **Services:** Library open to public with restrictions. **Remarks:** All AV programs are available for distribution through local chapters of the American Cancer Society.

★376★
AMERICAN CANCER SOCIETY - HAWAII DIVISION - LIBRARY (Med)
200 N. Vineyard Blvd.   Phone: (808) 531-1662
Honolulu, HI 96817   Dotty Morgan, Pub.Educ.Dir.
Founded: 1959. **Staff:** 2. **Subjects:** Cancer and cancer education. **Holdings:** 200 books; 150 films; 25,000 leaflets on cancer; 5000 leaflets on specific cancer sites; 500 leaflets on the American Cancer Society. **Subscriptions:** 400 journals and other serials. **Services:** Interlibrary loans; public and professional education; library open to public.

★377★
AMERICAN CANCER SOCIETY - MEDICAL LIBRARY (Med)
4 W. 35th St.   Phone: (212) 736-3030
New York, NY 10001   Dr. Sourya Henderson, Med.Libn.
Founded: 1947. **Staff:** Prof 4; Other 4. **Subjects:** Oncology, biochemistry, cytology, public health, radiobiology, general medicine. **Holdings:** 13,000 books; 6200 bound periodical volumes; 30 file holders of reports from foundations, institutes, and laboratories. **Subscriptions:** 706 journals and other serials. **Services:** Interlibrary loans; selected bibliographies on specific subjects in answer to requests from researchers, doctors and investigators; package lending service available; library serves all state and local divisions of the society in the United States; library open to public by appointment. **Staff:** Julia Chai, Asst.Libn.; Alice Wou, Bibliog.; Flora Seruya, Cat.

★378★
AMERICAN CAST IRON PIPE COMPANY - TECHNICAL LIBRARY (Sci-Tech)
2930 N. 16th St.
Box 2727   Phone: (205) 325-7886
Birmingham, AL 35202   Lela Turner, Tech.Libn.
Staff: Prof 1. **Subjects:** Foundry practices, engineering, corrosion, hydraulics, metallurgy. **Holdings:** Figures not available. **Subscriptions:** 78 journals and other serials. **Services:** Interlibrary loans; copying; library not open to public.

★379★
AMERICAN CERAMIC SOCIETY - LIBRARY (Sci-Tech; Art)
65 Ceramic Dr.   Phone: (614) 268-8645
Columbus, OH 43214   Joanna Dobson, Libn.
Subjects: Science and technology of ceramics. **Special Collections:** Ross Coffin Purdy Museum of Ceramics. **Holdings:** 1750 books; 2900 bound periodical volumes; 400 pamphlets. **Subscriptions:** 260 journals and other serials. **Services:** Copying; library open to public with restrictions.

AMERICAN CERAMIC SOCIETY - PHASE DIAGRAMS FOR CERAMISTS
See: U.S. Natl. Bureau of Standards - Phase Diagrams for Ceramists

★380★
AMERICAN CETACEAN SOCIETY - NATIONAL LIBRARY (Env-Cons)
Box 4416   Phone: (213) 548-6279
San Pedro, CA 90731   Virginia C. Callahan, Libn.
Founded: 1980. **Staff:** Prof 1. **Subjects:** Whales, marine mammals. **Special Collections:** International Whaling Commission reports. **Holdings:** 125 books; 500 reports and reprints. **Services:** Copying; library open to public by appointment.

AMERICAN CHEMICAL SOCIETY - CENTER FOR THE HISTORY OF CHEMISTRY
See: University of Pennsylvania - Center for the History of Chemistry

AMERICAN CHEMICAL SOCIETY, INC. - CHEMICAL ABSTRACTS SERVICE
See: Chemical Abstracts Service

★381★
AMERICAN CHEMICAL SOCIETY, INC. - LIBRARY (Sci-Tech)
1155 16th St., N.W.   Phone: (202) 872-4509
Washington, DC 20036   Barbara A. Gallagher, Hd., Lib.Serv.
Staff: Prof 4; Other 2. **Subjects:** Chemistry, chemical engineering and related subjects. **Holdings:** 7000 books; 6000 bound ACS periodical volumes; 300 bound volumes of non-ACS publications; American Chemical Society publications and other periodicals on microfilm. **Subscriptions:** 600 journals and other serials; 10 newspapers. **Services:** Interlibrary loans; copying (through interlibrary loans only); library open to public for reference use only. **Computerized Information Services:** DIALOG, SDC. **Publications:** ACS Library Acquisitions List, monthly. **Special Indexes:** Chemical and Engineering News Index. **Staff:** Clarita H. Flores, Libn.; Ruby G. Alvarado, Cat.; Nancy Gleboff, Indexer.

★382★
AMERICAN CHEMICAL SOCIETY, INC. - RUBBER DIVISION - JOHN H. GIFFORD MEMORIAL LIBRARY & INFORMATION CTR. (Sci-Tech)
Bierce Library, University of Akron   Phone: (216) 375-7197
Akron, OH 44325   Ruth Murray, Info.Spec.
Staff: Prof 1; Other 1. **Subjects:** Rubber and polymer chemistry and technology; rubber manufacture and processing; rubber history. **Special Collections:** Rubber Reserve Reports; reprints of the Rubber Division, ACS meetings; publications of the Center for Information Services, University of Akron. **Holdings:** Books, periodicals, symposia, catalogs. **Services:** Interlibrary loans (limited); copying; bibliographies; custom literature search; borrowing limited to members. **Computerized Information Services:** DIALOG, BRS. **Networks/Consortia:** Member of OCLC. **Publications:** List of Bibliographies - available on request. **Remarks:** The Library and Information Service for Rubber (LISFORR) shares the holdings held by the Science and Technology Library of the University of Akron and it draws upon resources of cooperating research libraries. This combined listing makes available practically all literature in the rubber and polymer field. Services are available to all of the rubber industry, with special rates and privileges for members and affiliates of the Rubber Division and to subscribers of Rubber Chemistry and Technology.

AMERICAN CHORAL FOUNDATION - LIBRARY
See: Free Library of Philadelphia - Music Department - Drinker Library of Choral Music

★383★
AMERICAN CIVIL LIBERTIES UNION - LIBRARY/ARCHIVES (Law)†
132 W. 43rd St.   Phone: (212) 944-9800
New York, NY 10036   Barbara J. Eichman, Libn.
Founded: 1920. **Staff:** Prof 1. **Subjects:** Civil liberties, law. **Holdings:** 5000 books; 50 files of ACLU mimeographs (cataloged); 1 VF drawer of manuscripts; board and committee annual reports; ACLU pamphlets and newsletters. **Subscriptions:** 45 journals and other serials. **Services:** Copying; library open to public for research only. **Remarks:** Archives housed at Princeton University.

★384★
AMERICAN CLASSICAL COLLEGE - LIBRARY (Art)
Box 4526   Phone: (505) 843-7749
Albuquerque, NM 87106   Dr. C.M. Flumiani, Dir.
Founded: 1960. **Staff:** Prof 1. **Subjects:** Art, psychology, business, Italian. **Special Collections:** Art. **Holdings:** 11,256 volumes; art items. **Subscriptions:** 25 journals and other serials. **Services:** Copying; library open to members. **Publications:** The American Idea. **Remarks:** Library is located at 614 Indian School Rd., Albuquerque, NM 87102.

★385★
AMERICAN CLASSICAL COLLEGE - STOCK MARKET LIBRARY (Bus-Fin)
Box 4526   Phone: (505) 843-7749
Albuquerque, NM 87106   Dr. C.M. Flumiani, Dir.
Staff: Prof 1. **Subjects:** Stock market, Wall Street. **Holdings:** 3000 books; papers and reports. **Services:** Copying; library not open to public. **Publications:** Monthly reports. **Remarks:** Library is located at 614 Indian School Rd., Albuquerque, NM 87102.

★386★
AMERICAN CLOCK AND WATCH MUSEUM - EDWARD INGRAHAM LIBRARY (Rec)
100 Maple St.   Phone: (203) 583-6070
Bristol, CT 06010   Mr. Chris H. Bailey, Mng.Dir.
Staff: 1. **Subjects:** Horology - its history, mechanics, and genealogy. **Special Collections:** Largest known collection of American Clock trade catalogs. **Holdings:** 1500 books; 600 bound periodical volumes; 1200 horological trade catalogs; 5000 horological photographs; 25 original patents; 32 VF drawers of horological pamphlets; 50 volumes of account books and materials. **Subscriptions:** 6 journals and other serials. **Services:** Library open to serious horological researchers, preferably members. **Publications:** Annual reproduction trade catalogs.

★387★
AMERICAN COLLECTORS ASSOCIATION, INC. - ACA MEMORIAL LIBRARY (Bus-Fin)
4040 W. 70th St.   Phone: (612) 926-6547
Minneapolis, MN 55435   Debra J. Ciskey, Libn.
Staff: 1. **Subjects:** Debt collection. **Special Collections:** State collection agency laws (50 volumes); state assignment laws (50 volumes); ACA State Units bylaws and constitutions (50 volumes). **Holdings:** 125 books; 22 bound periodical volumes; 127 notebooks. **Subscriptions:** 60 journals and other serials. **Services:** Library open to members of ACA only.

★388★
AMERICAN COLLEGE OF HERALDRY - LIBRARY (Hist)
Drawer CG
University, AL 35486   Dr. David P. Johnson
Subjects: Heraldry, genealogy, names, flags. **Holdings:** 368 bound periodical volumes. **Subscriptions:** 5 journals and other serials. **Services:** Library not open to public.

★389★
AMERICAN COLLEGE OF HOSPITAL ADMINISTRATORS - RAY E. BROWN MANAGEMENT COLLECTION (Bus-Fin)
840 N. Lakeshore Dr.   Phone: (312) 943-0544
Chicago, IL 60611   Diana Brown, Coord.
Founded: 1970. **Subjects:** General management. **Holdings:** 600 books. **Services:** Interlibrary loans; copying; collection open to public. **Publications:** Annual bibliography - available upon request. **Remarks:** The American College of Hospital Administrators supports and develops the collection while space and service are provided by the Asa Bacon Library of the American Hospital Association.

★390★
AMERICAN COLLEGE OF NATURAL THERAPEUTICS & ARIZONA COLLEGE OF NATUROPATHIC MEDICINE - LIBRARY (Med)†
Box 1406   Phone: (602) 969-5293
Mesa, AZ 85201   Zona P. Dial, Libn.
Founded: 1968. **Staff:** Prof 1; Other 1. **Subjects:** Natural healing, naturopathy, massage and manipulation, homeopathy, hydrotherapy, nutrition. **Holdings:** 1200 books. **Services:** Copying; library not open to public.

★391★
AMERICAN COLLEGE OF NURSING HOME ADMINISTRATORS - LIBRARY (Med)
Box 5890   Phone: (301) 652-8384
Bethesda, MD 20814   Helene Zubkoff, Serv.Spec.
Staff: Prof 2; Other 1. **Subjects:** Long term care administration, gerontology.

Holdings: 1500 books. Subscriptions: 60 journals and other serials. Services: Interlibrary loans; copying; library open to public by appointment. Staff: Joan Sugarman, Ref./Info.

★392★
AMERICAN COLLEGE OF OBSTETRICIANS AND GYNECOLOGISTS - RESOURCE CENTER (Med)
600 Maryland Ave., S.W., Suite 300
Washington, DC 20024
Phone: (202) 638-5577
Pamela Van Hine, Libn.
Founded: 1970. Staff: Prof 3; Other 2. Subjects: Obstetrics, gynecology, medical socioeconomics, medical education, women's health care. Special Collections: Archives. Holdings: 2500 books; 175 bound periodical volumes; reprints; literature on abortion, contraception, venereal disease, sex education and patient education. Subscriptions: 200 journals and other serials. Services: Interlibrary loans; copying; center open to public by appointment. Special Indexes: Educational Materials for Obstetrics and Gynecology. Staff: Paula Olson, Asst.Libn.; Patricia Broida, Asst.Libn.

★393★
AMERICAN COLLEGE OF ORGONOMY, INC. - LIBRARY
Ansonia Sta., Box 565
New York, NY 10028
Defunct

★394★
AMERICAN COLLEGE OF SURGEONS - LIBRARY (Med)
55 E. Erie St.
Chicago, IL 60611
Phone: (312) 664-4050
Mrs. Jeri A. Ryan, Libn.
Founded: 1921. Staff: Prof 1; Other 2. Subjects: History of medicine. Holdings: 25,000 books; 3300 bound periodical volumes; 500 pamphlets on the history of medicine and surgery; 10 filing cabinets of archival material. Subscriptions: 300 journals and other serials. Services: Interlibrary loans; copying; library open to persons in allied medical fields. Networks/Consortia: Member of Chicago Library System. Publications: A Bibliography of the Operating Room Environment; A Bibliography of Hospital Emergency Departments and Trauma Units - Organization and Management, both semiannual - available upon request.

★395★
AMERICAN COLLEGE TESTING PROGRAM - LIBRARY (Educ)
Box 168
Iowa City, IA 52243
Phone: (319) 337-1165
Lois Renter, Hd.Libn.
Founded: 1968. Staff: Prof 1; Other 1. Subjects: Education, psychology, psychometrics, educational sociology. Special Collections: Complete ERIC file on microfiche. Holdings: 21,000 books; 1200 bound periodical volumes; 950 technical reports; 12 VF drawers of documents; 6 VF drawers of archives; 350 reels of microfilm. Subscriptions: 325 journals and other serials; 6 newspapers. Services: Interlibrary loans; copying; library open to qualified researchers in education. Computerized Information Services: DIALOG. Publications: Selected New Book List, monthly - to staff members.

★396★
AMERICAN COLLEGE - VANE B. LUCAS MEMORIAL LIBRARY (Bus-Fin)
270 S. Bryn Mawr Ave.
Bryn Mawr, PA 19010
Phone: (215) 896-4507
Judith L. Hill, Libn.
Founded: 1960. Staff: Prof 2; Other 2. Subjects: Insurance, taxation, financial planning, adult learning, testing. Holdings: 12,500 books; 350 bound periodical volumes; 100 microforms (cataloged); 50 AV materials; 22 VF drawers; 1000 microfiche (collection in education, primarily ERIC); 40 films. Subscriptions: 600 journals and other serials; 20 newspapers. Services: Interlibrary loans; copying; SDI; library open to public for reference use only. Computerized Information Services: DIALOG, SDC, BRS; computerized cataloging and serials. Networks/Consortia: Member of OCLC through PALINET and Union Library Catalogue of Pennsylvania. Publications: Library Bulletin, monthly. Staff: Jane M. Dawson, Asst.Libn.

★397★
AMERICAN COLLEGE - VANE B. LUCAS MEMORIAL LIBRARY - ORAL HISTORY CENTER & ARCHIVES (Hist)
270 Bryn Mawr Ave.
Bryn Mawr, PA 19010
Phone: (215) 525-9500
Marjorie Amos Fletcher, Dir.
Founded: 1977. Staff: Prof 1; Other 1. Subjects: History - American College, life insurance business and education, women in life insurance as a profession. Special Collections: S.S. Huebner Archives (1800 cubic feet); S.S. Huebner writings translated into Japanese and Chinese; Edward A. Woods Ivory Collection; Oral History Interviews (100); photographs (200 cubic feet). Services: Copying; library open to public. Special Indexes: Index for each oral history interview.

★398★
AMERICAN COLOR AND CHEMICAL CORPORATION, INC. - LIBRARY (Sci-Tech)†
Mt. Vernon St.
Lock Haven, PA 17745
Phone: (717) 748-6747
Founded: 1957. Staff: 1. Subjects: Dyes, organic chemistry, chemical technology, industrial chemistry. Holdings: 1350 books; 500 bound periodical volumes; 22,000 U.S. patents; 1 VF drawer of technical literature; 6 shelves of product books. Subscriptions: 16 journals and other serials. Services: Copying; library open to chemistry students of Lock Haven State College.

★399★
AMERICAN CONCRETE INSTITUTE - LIBRARY (Sci-Tech)
Box 19150
Detroit, MI 48219
Phone: (313) 532-2600
Betty Borschell, Libn.
Subjects: Concrete materials and structural design; concrete construction. Holdings: 1550 books; 450 bound periodical volumes; 3000 technical reports. Subscriptions: 238 journals and other serials. Services: Interlibrary loans; copying; library open to public for reference use only.

★400★
AMERICAN CONGREGATIONAL ASSOCIATION - CONGREGATIONAL LIBRARY (Rel-Theol)
14 Beacon St.
Boston, MA 02108
Phone: (617) 523-0470
Rev.Dr. Harold F. Worthley, Libn.
Founded: 1853. Staff: Prof 3; Other 4. Subjects: Congregationalism; 16th, 17th and 18th century religion and theology; modern writings in the field of religion and theology. Special Collections: Congregational Councils; church architecture; hymnals; town histories; local church histories; works of Richard, Increase, Cotton and the Minor Mathers. Holdings: 100,000 books; 100,000 pamphlets and periodicals (cataloged). Subscriptions: 80 journals and other serials. Services: Interlibrary loans; copying; direct mail service available to individuals in the U.S.; library open to public. Publications: Bulletin of the Congregational Library, 3/year - for sale.

★401★
AMERICAN CONSERVATORY OF MUSIC - LIBRARY (Mus)
116 S. Michigan Ave.
Chicago, IL 60603
Phone: (312) 263-4161
Lauren Dennhardt, Hd.Libn.
Founded: 1886. Staff: Prof 1; Other 1. Subjects: Music. Special Collections: Complete Bach Gesellschaft (Edwards); Beethoven (Edwards); Neue Ausgabe Samtlicher Werke von J.S. Bach; Neue Ausgabe Samtlicher Werke von Mozart; Werke von Haydn. Holdings: 6200 books; piano scores; organ scores; pieces of Japanese music; miniature scores and chamber music; song collections; libretti; operas; oratorios; 1500 phonograph records; 375 audiotapes. Subscriptions: 21 journals and other serials. Services: Interlibrary loans; library open to public with approval of librarian.

★402★
AMERICAN CONTRACT BRIDGE LEAGUE - ALBERT H. MOREHEAD MEMORIAL LIBRARY (Rec)
2200 Democrat Rd.
Memphis, TN 38116
Phone: (901) 332-5586
Edith Simon, Libn.
Founded: 1927. Staff: Prof 1. Subjects: Bridge, chess, whist and other allied games. Special Collections: Publications about bridge from all over the world. Holdings: 1400 books; 250 bound periodical volumes; pamphlet material (cataloged). Subscriptions: 50 journals and other serials. Services: Interlibrary loans with restrictions; library open to public for research. Publications: Contract Bridge Bulletin, monthly; Official Encyclopedia of Bridge; annual report of World Championships.

★403★
AMERICAN CORRECTIONAL ASSOCIATION - LIBRARY (Law)
4321 Hartwick Rd., Suite L-208
College Park, MD 20740
Phone: (301) 699-7600
Diana Travisono, Res.
Founded: 1973. Staff: Prof 1. Subjects: Corrections, correctional institutions, offenders, criminal justice. Special Collections: Corrections Photograph Collection (2000 prints); American Correctional Association Congresses (proceedings from 1870). Holdings: 3700 books; 1 VF drawer of photographs and clippings. Subscriptions: 50 journals and other serials. Services: Copying (limited); SDI; library open to public for reference use only. Special Indexes: Index to Corrections Photograph Collection.

★404★
AMERICAN COUNCIL FOR THE ARTS - LIBRARY (Art; Bus-Fin)
570 Seventh Ave.
New York, NY 10018
Phone: (212) 354-6655
Robert Porter, Mgr., Info.Serv.
Staff: Prof 2. Subjects: Arts - management, economics, councils, organizations; cultural policy; funding and support. Holdings: 800 books; 30

VF drawers of reports, clippings, pamphlets, archives. **Subscriptions:** 85 journals and other serials. **Services:** Copying; library open to public. **Staff:** Will Linden, Libn.

★405★

AMERICAN COUNCIL ON EDUCATION - NATIONAL CENTER FOR HIGHER EDUCATION (NCHE) - LIBRARY (Educ)
One Dupont Circle, Suite 640   Phone: (202) 833-4690
Washington, DC 20036   Judith A. Pfeiffer, Dir.
Founded: 1952. **Subjects:** Higher education policy and administration. **Special Collections:** Complete holdings of the publications of the American Council on Education including special newsletters and research reports. **Holdings:** 5000 books; college catalogs on microfiche. **Subscriptions:** 154 journals and other serials. **Services:** Interlibrary loans; copying; library open to public. **Networks/Consortia:** Member of Metropolitan Washington Library Council.

★406★

AMERICAN COUNCIL OF THE INTERNATIONAL INSTITUTE OF WELDING - LIBRARY
2501 N.W. 7th St.
Miami, FL 33125
Subjects: Welding and allied processes. **Holdings:** Figures not available. **Remarks:** Presently inactive.

★407★

AMERICAN COUNCIL OF LIFE INSURANCE - LIBRARY (Bus-Fin)
1850 K St., N.W.   Phone: (202) 862-4050
Washington, DC 20006   Marjorie Gordon, Libn.
Founded: 1976. **Staff:** Prof 3. **Subjects:** Life and health insurance statistics and consumer information, personal family money management, economics and vital statistics. **Holdings:** 10,000 books and bound periodical volumes; 1200 volumes of proceedings; 125 VF drawers of pamphlets and clippings; 35 VF drawers of archives. **Subscriptions:** 400 journals and other serials. **Services:** Interlibrary loans; copying; library open to public. **Publications:** Catalog of publications - available upon request. **Remarks:** Library also serves the Health Insurance Association of America, a central source of information to the public on health insurance which is located at the same address. **Staff:** Mary Jane Bowman, Tech.Serv.; Kori Calvert, Ref.Libn.

★408★

AMERICAN COUNCIL FOR NATIONALITIES SERVICE - LIBRARY AND INFORMATION CENTER (Soc Sci)
20 W. 40th St.   Phone: (212) 398-9142
New York, NY 10018   Wells C. Klein, Exec.Dir.
Subjects: Immigration, naturalization. **Holdings:** Figures not available. **Services:** Library not open to public. **Publications:** How to Become a Citizen of the U.S. - for sale; Interpreter Releases (technical information service on immigration and naturalization) - by subscription.

AMERICAN COUNCIL FOR NATIONALITIES SERVICE - UNITED STATES COMMITTEE FOR REFUGEES
See: United States Committee for Refugees

★409★

AMERICAN COUNCIL OF VOLUNTARY AGENCIES FOR FOREIGN SERVICE, INC. - TECH. ASSISTANCE INFO. CLEARING HOUSE (Soc Sci)
200 Park Ave. S., 11th Fl.   Phone: (212) 777-8210
New York, NY 10003   Mary Ellen Burgess, Exec.Sec.
Staff: Prof 6; Other 5. **Subjects:** U.S. nonprofit organizations and their development assistance programs; materials on organizations, categories of development assistance and countries. **Holdings:** 2000 books; annual reports of 200 agencies (cataloged); VF on 1500 organizations involved in overseas development assistance including U.S. nonprofit organizations, foreign government and nonprofit organizations and intergovernmental organizations; VF on categories, or kinds, of development assistance; VF on countries. **Subscriptions:** 580 journals and other serials. **Services:** Copying (limited); clearing house open to public by appointment. **Computerized Information Services:** Internal database. **Publications:** List of publications - available upon request. **Also Known As:** TAICH. **Staff:** Jane Morgan-Meskill, Info. & Res.Assoc.; Frederick W. Haight, Sys.Mgr.; Roger McClanahan, Ed.; Wynta Boynes, Mng.Ed.; Florence Lowenstein, Ed.

★410★

AMERICAN CRAFT COUNCIL - LIBRARY (Art)
44 W. 53rd Fl., 2nd Fl.   Phone: (212) 397-0638
New York, NY 10019   Joanne Polster, Libn.
Founded: 1956. **Staff:** Prof 1. **Subjects:** Crafts - contemporary by media: fiber, clay, metal, wood, glass, enamel, plastics. **Special Collections:** Portfolio

files of biographical and visual data on contemporary American craftsmen (over 2000); Photo Archives of the American Craft Museum; Archives of the American Craft Museum; Your Portable Museum (35mm slide kits, filmstrips and 16mm film available for purchase or study); Archives of the American Craft Council. **Holdings:** 3500 books; 124 bound periodical volumes; 1500 exhibition catalogs (cataloged); craft suppliers' catalogs, craft course brochures; craft organizations' newsletters; 10 VF drawers of clippings; 4 VF drawers of announcements, invitations, posters; 55 VF drawers of archives; 300 slide study sets. **Subscriptions:** 40 journals and other serials. **Services:** Library open to members only. **Publications:** List of American Craft Council publications and AV catalogs - free upon request.

★411★

AMERICAN CRITICAL CARE - INFORMATION CENTER (Sci-Tech)
1600 Waukegan Rd.   Phone: (312) 473-3000
McGaw Park, IL 60085   Marlene Galante Kozak, Mgr.
Founded: 1978. **Staff:** Prof 6; Other 3. **Subjects:** Pharmacology, biomedicine, chemistry, computer science, information science, business. **Holdings:** 1600 books; 2500 bound periodical volumes. **Subscriptions:** 325 journals and other serials. **Services:** Interlibrary loans; copying; SDI; library not open to public. **Computerized Information Services:** SDC, DIALOG, BRS, NLM; computerized cataloging, circulation and records management. **Networks/Consortia:** Member of Lake County Consortium; North Suburban Library System; American Hospital Supply Corporation Information Services Network. **Remarks:** This is a division of the American Hospital Supply Corporation. **Staff:** Nancy Leipzig, Info.Anl.; Kathy Syverson, Info.Anl.; Kathy Vick, Assoc.Info.Anl.; Anne Gregg, Info.Anl.; Joanne Decker, Doc.Coord.

★412★

AMERICAN CYANAMID COMPANY - AGRICULTURAL RESEARCH DIVISION - TECHNICAL INFORMATION SERVICES (Sci-Tech; Agri)
Box 400   Phone: (609) 799-0400
Princeton, NJ 08540   Judith C. Leondar, Mgr.
Founded: 1947. **Staff:** Prof 6; Other 6. **Subjects:** Agronomy, entomology, veterinary medicine, agricultural chemicals. **Special Collections:** U.S.D.A. and Agricultural Experiment Stations publications. **Holdings:** 15,000 books; 40,000 bound periodical volumes; 50 VF drawers of patents; 300 dissertations; 16 VF drawers of pamphlets. **Subscriptions:** 550 journals and other serials. **Services:** Interlibrary loans; copying (limited); library not open to public. **Computerized Information Services:** DIALOG, SDC, NLM; computerized cataloging and serials. **Publications:** Library Accessions Bulletin, monthly - limited distribution; patent bulletins - limited distribution. **Staff:** John Arthur, Info.Sci.; Bea Kolmes, Info.Sci.; June Grosse, Info.Sci.; Mary Anna Reeves, Info.Sci.; Lila MacKinnon, Info.Sci./Libn.

★413★

AMERICAN CYANAMID COMPANY - BUSINESS INFORMATION CENTER (Bus-Fin)
Berdan Ave.   Phone: (201) 831-3592
Wayne, NJ 07470   Claudia A. Gentner, Mgr.
Founded: 1951. **Staff:** Prof 1; Other 1. **Subjects:** Business, finance, management, marketing, economics. **Holdings:** 2000 books; 1000 special reports; 1000 company annual reports. **Subscriptions:** 440 journals and other serials; 15 newspapers. **Services:** Interlibrary loans; copying; library open to public by appointment. **Computerized Information Services:** DIALOG, SDC, New York Times Information Service, Mead Data Central, Dun and Bradstreet, Inc., Dow Jones News Retrieval. **Publications:** Serials holdings list, annual.

★414★

AMERICAN CYANAMID COMPANY - CHEMICAL RESEARCH DIVISION - LIBRARY (Sci-Tech)
2 West Main St.   Phone: (201) 356-2000
Bound Brook, NJ 08805   Joan L. Gallagher, Mgr.Tech.Info.
Founded: 1916. **Staff:** Prof 4; Other 3. **Subjects:** Dyes, plastics, pigments, rubber chemicals, textile chemicals. **Holdings:** 6000 books; 8500 bound periodical volumes; 1000 volumes of company reports; 100 VF drawers of patents; 3000 reels of microfilm. **Subscriptions:** 250 journals and other serials. **Services:** Interlibrary loans; SDI. **Computerized Information Services:** DIALOG, SDC, NLM; internal databases. **Networks/Consortia:** Member of OCLC. **Publications:** Patent Abstracts Bulletin, weekly; Library Bulletin, irregular; Accessions Bulletin, biweekly.

★415★

AMERICAN CYANAMID COMPANY - CONSUMERS PRODUCTS RESEARCH DIVISION - LIBRARY (Sci-Tech)
697 Rte. 46   Phone: (201) 365-6148
Clifton, NJ 07015   Linda Willett, Mgr.
Staff: Prof 2; Other 1. **Subjects:** Organic chemistry, pharmacology,

cosmetology, perfumery, dermatology, microbiology, biochemistry, dyes, essential oils. **Holdings:** 3000 books; 2000 bound periodical volumes; 24 file boxes of British and U.S. patents. **Subscriptions:** 275 journals and other serials. **Services:** Interlibrary loans; copying; library open to public by appointment. **Computerized Information Services:** SDC, NLM, DIALOG, Derwent Publications, Inc. **Publications:** Library Bulletin - for internal distribution only. **Formerly:** Shulton, Inc. - Research and Development Library.

★416★
AMERICAN CYANAMID COMPANY - ENVIRONMENTAL HEALTH LIBRARY (Med)
One Cyanamid Plaza   Phone: (201) 831-4379
Wayne, NJ 07470   Kaarin Kolbre, Supv.
Founded: 1952. **Staff:** Prof 2; Other 1. **Subjects:** Toxicology, occupational medicine, industrial hygiene and safety, clinical medicine, environmental protection, loss prevention. **Holdings:** 2000 books; 350 bound periodical volumes; 2000 pamphlets (cataloged); 12 VF drawers of reprints. **Subscriptions:** 132 journals and other serials. **Services:** Interlibrary loans; library open to public with restrictions. **Computerized Information Services:** DIALOG, SDC, NLM, NIH-EPA Chemical Information System (CIS), Federal-State Reports, Inc. **Networks/Consortia:** Member of OCLC. **Publications:** Items of current interest and acquisitions, bimonthly - to physicians and technical personnel of the plants. **Formerly:** Its Environmental Services Division Library. **Staff:** Frances Scholten, Libn.

AMERICAN CYANAMID COMPANY - IRC FIBERS COMPANY - LIBRARY
See: American Cyanamid Company - Stamford Research Center Library

★417★
AMERICAN CYANAMID COMPANY - LEDERLE LABORATORIES DIVISION - SUBBAROW MEMORIAL LIBRARY (Med)
N. Middletown Rd.   Phone: (914) 735-5000
Pearl River, NY 10965   Dr. M.G. Howell, Hd., Tech.Info.Serv.
Founded: 1930. **Staff:** Prof 12; Other 6. **Subjects:** Biomedical sciences, pharmacology, organic chemistry, management. **Holdings:** 71,000 volumes; 8000 reels of microfilm; 150 AV items. **Subscriptions:** 950 journals and other serials. **Services:** Interlibrary loans; SDI; library open to public with restrictions. **Computerized Information Services:** DIALOG, SDC, BRS, NLM, RLIN, NIH-EPA Chemical Information System, Chemical Abstracts Service, Telesystemes (QUESTEL); computerized cataloging, acquisitions and serials. **Networks/Consortia:** Member of OCLC; Health Information Libraries of Westchester (HILOW); Medical Library Center of New York (MLCNY); Southeastern New York Library Resources Council (SENYLRC); SUNY/OCLC Library Network. **Staff:** Tom A. Wainwright, Libn.; Frances M. Stratton, Leader, Ref. Group; Stanley E. DeVoe, Mgr., Lit.Serv.

★418★
AMERICAN CYANAMID COMPANY - SANTA ROSA PLANT - LIBRARY (Sci-Tech)
    Phone: (904) 994-5311
Milton, FL 32570   Dee Rogers, Libn.
Founded: 1958. **Staff:** Prof 1. **Subjects:** Chemistry - organic, inorganic; textiles; management; statistics; computers; safety. **Holdings:** 2000 books; 1000 bound periodical volumes; 4 VF drawers of patents; 25 VF drawers of technical project reports. **Subscriptions:** 72 journals and other serials. **Services:** Library not open to public.

★419★
AMERICAN CYANAMID COMPANY - STAMFORD RESEARCH CENTER LIBRARY (Sci-Tech)
Box 60   Phone: (203) 348-7331
Stamford, CT 06904   Barbara Potter, Libn.
Founded: 1936. **Staff:** Prof 4; Other 5. **Subjects:** Chemistry, physics, physical chemistry, polymer chemistry. **Holdings:** 15,000 books; 20,000 bound periodical volumes. **Subscriptions:** 350 journals and other serials. **Services:** Library not open to public. **Remarks:** Library contains the holdings of the American Cyanamid Company - IRC Fibers Company.

★420★
AMERICAN DENTAL ASSOCIATION - BUREAU OF LIBRARY SERVICES (Med)
211 E. Chicago Ave.   Phone: (312) 440-2653
Chicago, IL 60611   Aletha A. Kowitz, Dir.
Founded: 1927. **Staff:** Prof 9; Other 10. **Subjects:** All phases of dentistry. **Special Collections:** Association archives; photographs. **Holdings:** 20,000 books; 15,000 bound periodical volumes; 3500 package libraries on 2200 topics. **Subscriptions:** 975 journals and other serials. **Services:** Interlibrary loans; copying; library use is a privilege of membership but is generally open to all dental auxiliary personnel, physicians, nurses and graduate students; all others on an individual basis. **Computerized Information Services:** BRS.

Networks/Consortia: Member of OCLC; Chicago Library System. **Publications:** Books and Package Libraries for Dentists, annual - free; Index to Dental Literature, quarterly cumulative indexing service - subscription basis or by annual volume. **Staff:** Ruth Schultz, Asst.Dir.

AMERICAN DENTAL SOCIETY OF ANESTHESIOLOGY ARCHIVES
See: Loma Linda University - Niels Bjorn Jorgensen Memorial Library

★421★
AMERICAN DIETETIC ASSOCIATION - LULU G. GRAVES MEMORIAL LIBRARY
430 N. Michigan Ave.
Chicago, IL 60611
Founded: 1950. **Subjects:** Nutrition; diet therapy; organization and management of institutional food service; foods and food values; food chemistry. **Special Collections:** Early nutrition texts; recipe books. **Holdings:** 1500 books; 10 VF drawers of reprints and pamphlets. **Remarks:** Presently inactive.

★422★
AMERICAN DONKEY AND MULE SOCIETY - INFORMATION OFFICE (Rec)
Rte. 5, Box 65   Phone: (817) 382-6845
Denton, TX 76201   Betsy Hutchins, Info.Off.
Staff: 2. **Subjects:** Donkeys, mules. **Holdings:** 300 books; 900 unbound periodicals. **Subscriptions:** 14 newsletters. **Services:** Copying; library open to public by appointment. **Publications:** List of publications - available on request. **Remarks:** This is a private collection in a private home. Visitors and researchers are welcome.

★423★
AMERICAN DRUGGIST MAGAZINE LIBRARY
224 W. 57th St.
New York, NY 10019
Founded: 1944. **Subjects:** Medicine, retailing, drug trade, pharmaceuticals. **Holdings:** 150 books; 135 bound periodical volumes; 2500 journals (cataloged). **Remarks:** Presently inactive.

★424★
AMERICAN DRY MILK INSTITUTE - LIBRARY (Food-Bev)
130 N. Franklin St.   Phone: (312) 782-4888
Chicago, IL 60606   Warren S. Clark, Jr., Exec.Dir.
Subjects: Dry milk. **Holdings:** Figures not available.

★425★
AMERICAN ECONOMIC DEVELOPMENT COUNCIL - AEDC LIBRARY
Chicago O'Hare Aerospace Ctr.
4849 N. Scott St., Suite 1C
Chicago, IL 60176
Subjects: Industrial and economic development. **Holdings:** 979 books; 100 bound periodical volumes; 610 dissertations, theses and tapes; brochures, reprints of articles and speeches. **Special Catalogs:** Annotated Bibliography; Journal Index. **Remarks:** Presently inactive. **Formerly:** Located in Kansas City, MO.

★426★
AMERICAN ELECTRIC POWER SERVICE CORP. - LIBRARY (Energy; Sci-Tech)
2 Broadway   Phone: (212) 440-9000
New York, NY 10004   Janet T. Bulger, Act.Libn.
Staff: 3. **Subjects:** Engineering, electric utilities, energy, nuclear power, heating and air conditioning, business mangement. **Special Collections:** IEEE Transactions on power apparatus and systems, formerly AIEE Transactions (1900 to present). **Holdings:** 3000 books; 500 bound periodical volumes; 56 VF drawers of technical reports and pamphlets. **Subscriptions:** 355 journals and other serials. **Services:** Interlibrary loans; library open to SLA members. **Staff:** Cathy Smit, Res.Asst.; Cathleen Roberts, Res.Asst.

★427★
AMERICAN ENKA COMPANY - BUSINESS AND TECHNICAL LIBRARY (Sci-Tech; Bus-Fin)
    Phone: (704) 667-6936
Enka, NC 28728   Ruth H. Easter, Libn.
Founded: 1951. **Staff:** Prof 1; Other 1. **Subjects:** Textiles, polymer chemistry, chemistry, engineering, business management, physics. **Holdings:** 5000 books; 1500 bound periodical volumes; 8 VF drawers of pamphlets; 28 VF drawers of reports; 1450 boxes of microfilm; 400 annual company reports. **Subscriptions:** 303 journals and other serials. **Services:** Interlibrary loans; copying; library open to public by appointment. **Computerized Information Services:** DIALOG, SDC. **Publications:** Monthly Accession List;

Weekly Reading List; Patent Abstracts; Annual Report - all for internal distribution only. **Remarks:** Company is a division of AKZO, NV, Holland.

★428★
AMERICAN ENTERPRISE INSTITUTE FOR PUBLIC POLICY RESEARCH - LIBRARY (Soc Sci)
1150 17th St., N.W.   Phone: (202) 862-5831
Washington, DC 20036   Evelyn B. Caldwell, Libn.
Founded: 1972. **Staff:** Prof 1; Other 1. **Subjects:** Economics, political science, international relations, law. **Holdings:** 10,000 books; pamphlet files. **Subscriptions:** 300 journals and other serials; 4 newspapers. **Services:** Interlibrary loans; copying (fee); library open to public with librarian's permission.

AMERICAN ENTOMOLOGICAL SOCIETY - LIBRARY
See: Academy of Natural Sciences

★429★
AMERICAN EXPRESS COMPANY - CARD DIVISION - LIBRARY (Bus-Fin)
125 Broad St., 17th Fl.   Phone: (212) 323-4961
New York, NY 10004   Sarika Mahant, Supv., Info.Sys.Adm
Staff: Prof 1; Other 1. **Subjects:** Data processing, computers, business, management. **Holdings:** 500 books; 5000 IBM manuals; 350 technical reports. **Subscriptions:** 180 journals and other serials. **Services:** Interlibrary loans; copying; library open to Special Libraries Association members only. **Computerized Information Services:** DIALOG, SDC, New York Times Information Service; computerized circulation. **Networks/Consortia:** Member of American Express Company Library Consortium. **Publications:** Recent Acquisitions List - for internal distribution only.

★430★
AMERICAN EXPRESS COMPANY - CARD DIVISION - WESTERN REGION OPERATIONS CENTER - SYSTEMS LIBRARY (Bus-Fin)*
2423 E. Lincoln Dr.   Phone: (602) 248-3914
Phoenix, AZ 85016   Judith Kettner, Sys.Libn.
Founded: 1978. **Staff:** 2. **Subjects:** Computer science, systems analysis, data processing, database management, banking. **Special Collections:** IBM technical manuals. **Holdings:** 525 volumes; reports on microfiche. **Subscriptions:** 30 journals and other serials. **Services:** Library not open to public.

★431★
AMERICAN EXPRESS COMPANY - CARD INFORMATION CENTER (Bus-Fin)
American Express Plaza   Phone: (212) 323-4146
New York, NY 10004   Joan B. Lurye, Mgr.
Founded: 1978. **Staff:** Prof 1; Other 1. **Subjects:** Marketing, marketing research, travel. **Holdings:** 325 books; 2000 corporate annual reports; 10 VF drawers of market research reports. **Subscriptions:** 125 journals and other serials. **Services:** Interlibrary loans; library not open to public. **Networks/Consortia:** Member of American Express Company Library Consortium.

★432★
AMERICAN EXPRESS COMPANY - CORPORATE SYSTEMS & TELECOMMUNICATIONS INFORMATION CENTER (Bus-Fin)
125 Broad St., 11th Fl.   Phone: (212) 323-4063
New York, NY 10004   Stephanie Morrell, Corp.Tech.Libn.
Founded: 1977. **Staff:** Prof 1; Other 1. **Subjects:** Communications, telecommunications, computers and data processing, business, management. **Holdings:** 250 books; IBM manuals; 300 corporate annual reports and 10Ks; VF drawers. **Subscriptions:** 110 journals and other serials. **Services:** Interlibrary loans; copying; library open to SLA members by request. **Computerized Information Services:** DIALOG. **Networks/Consortia:** Member of American Express Company Library Consortium.

★433★
AMERICAN EXPRESS COMPANY - SYSTEMS LIBRARY (Bus-Fin)
4780 N. State Rd. 7   Phone: (305) 474-6084
Lauderhill, FL 33319   Marva Blair, Asst.Libn.
Founded: 1975. **Staff:** Prof 1. **Subjects:** Data processing industry, management, credit cards. **Special Collections:** IBM System 370 Manuals (200); American Express Internal Standards Manuals (20); Center for Human Potential (management; 50 volumes). **Holdings:** 500 books; 2000 technical reports on microfiche; 16 VF drawers of internal documents. **Subscriptions:** 28 journals and other serials. **Services:** SDI; library not open to public. **Computerized Information Services:** Access to AMEXCO Internal System Libraries via TSO - for internal use only. **Networks/Consortia:** Member of American Express Company Library Consortium. **Special Indexes:** AMEXCO Internal Document Identifier Index; IBM Manuals Inventory (both are online and hard copy). **Formerly:** Located in Fort Lauderdale, FL.

★434★
AMERICAN EXPRESS COMPANY - TRAVELERS CHEQUE DIVISION - T/C SYSTEMS LIBRARY (Bus-Fin)
4315 S. 2700 W.   Phone: (801) 965-5000
Salt Lake City, UT 84184   Louise Pollard, Sys.Libn.
Staff: 1. **Subjects:** Computer science. **Holdings:** 250 books; 300 IBM manuals; 5 VF drawers of historical materials; 10 VF drawers of program documentation. **Subscriptions:** 38 journals and other serials. **Services:** Library not open to public. **Computerized Information Services:** Computerized cataloging. **Networks/Consortia:** Member of American Express Company Library Consortium. **Publications:** Library Newsletter, monthly - for internal distribution only. **Special Catalogs:** IBM Manual Catalog and distribution list (automated). **Formerly:** Its Travelers Check Systems and Data Processing Library, located in New York, NY.

★435★
AMERICAN FEDERATION OF ASTROLOGERS, INC. - LIBRARY (Rec)
6535 S. Rural Rd.
Box 22040   Phone: (602) 838-1751
Tempe, AZ 85282   Robert W. Cooper, Exec.Sec.
Staff: Prof 3; Other 7. **Subjects:** Astrology. **Holdings:** 2000 books; 7500 bound periodical volumes; 50,000 data cards (cataloged) on various incidents, used for research purposes. **Services:** Library not open to public. **Publications:** AFA Monthly Bulletin - issued to members only. **Staff:** Sara E. Cooper, Chf.Libn.

AMERICAN FEDERATION OF LABOR AND CONGRESS OF INDUSTRIAL ORGANIZATIONS - AMALGAMATED CLOTHING & TEXTILE WORKERS UNION
See: Amalgamated Clothing & Textile Workers Union

★436★
AMERICAN FEDERATION OF LABOR AND CONGRESS OF INDUSTRIAL ORGANIZATIONS - LIBRARY (Soc Sci)
815 16th St., N.W.   Phone: (202) 637-5297
Washington, DC 20006   Dora Kelenson, Libn.
Founded: 1916. **Staff:** Prof 1; Other 2. **Subjects:** Labor, labor economics, trade unions, industrial relations. **Holdings:** 20,000 books and bound periodical volumes; 75 VF drawers of pamphlets and clippings. **Subscriptions:** 325 journals and other serials; 64 newspapers. **Services:** Interlibrary loans; library open to public. **Computerized Information Services:** DIALOG. **Publications:** Acquisitions List, monthly; Booklist, irregular. **Also Known As:** AFL-CIO.

AMERICAN FEDERATION OF LABOR AND CONGRESS OF INDUSTRIAL ORGANIZATIONS - UNITED FARM WORKERS OF AMERICA
See: United Farm Workers of America, AFL-CIO

★437★
AMERICAN FEDERATION OF POLICE RESEARCH CENTER AND LIBRARY (Soc Sci)
1100 N.E. 125th St.   Phone: (305) 891-1700
North Miami, FL 33161   Sgt. James Gordon, Res. & Trng.Asst.
Staff: Prof 1; Other 2. **Subjects:** Law enforcement, crime and crime prevention. **Holdings:** 2000 books; 50 police films. **Subscriptions:** 10 journals and other serials. **Services:** Library not open to public. **Publications:** Police Command and Police Times, monthly - to law enforcement officers.

★438★
AMERICAN FEDERATION OF SMALL BUSINESS - INFORMATION CENTER (Bus-Fin)†
407 S. Dearborn St., Rm. 980   Phone: (312) 427-0206
Chicago, IL 60605   Ira H. Latimer, Exec. V.P.
Staff: Prof 3; Other 4. **Subjects:** Small business, economic education, Congressional and state legislation, labor law. **Special Collections:** Union Power vs. The Right to Work. **Holdings:** 3000 volumes; 50 pamphlets; 100 position papers. **Subscriptions:** 10 journals and other serials; 5 newspapers. **Services:** Copying; library open to public with restrictions.

★439★
AMERICAN FEDERATION OF STATE, COUNTY AND MUNICIPAL EMPLOYEES, AFL-CIO (AFSCME) - DC37 RESEARCH LIBRARY (Soc Sci)
140 Park Place   Phone: (212) 766-1032
New York, NY 10007   Evelyn Seinfeld, Libn.
Founded: 1974. **Staff:** Prof 1; Other 3. **Subjects:** Labor-management relations, collective bargaining in New York City, labor unions, U.S. economy, urban crisis. **Special Collections:** Contracts between New York City and District Council 37; New York City fiscal crisis; Public Sector Productivity. **Holdings:** 50 bound periodical volumes; 10,000 government documents;

contracts, local documents, newspaper clippings file. **Subscriptions:** 150 journals and other serials; 20 newspapers. **Services:** Library open to public by appointment. **Publications:** Acquisitions list.

★440★
AMERICAN FEDERATION OF STATE, COUNTY AND MUNICIPAL EMPLOYEES, AFL-CIO (AFSCME) - INFORMATION CENTER (Soc Sci)
1625 L St., N.W.   Phone: (202) 452-4882
Washington, DC 20036   Jodie Fine, Mgr.
Staff: Prof 1; Other 3. **Subjects:** Public sector labor relations. **Holdings:** 4500 books; 5 VF drawers of subject files; AFSCME Union proceedings, 1934 to present. **Subscriptions:** 800 journals and other serials. **Services:** Interlibrary loans; library open to public with restrictions. **Computerized Information Services:** Online systems. **Publications:** Serials Listing, annual - to headquarters staff.

★441★
AMERICAN FILM INSTITUTE - LOUIS B. MAYER LIBRARY (Aud-Vis)
2021 N. Western Ave.
Box 27999   Phone: (213) 856-7655
Los Angeles, CA 90027   Anne G. Schlosser, Lib.Dir.
Founded: 1969. **Staff:** Prof 2; Other 5. **Subjects:** Moving pictures, television, video, cable, satellite. **Special Collections:** Mitchell Leisen Collection; George B. Seitz Collection; RKO RADIO FLASH, 1932-1955 (18 volumes); Buster Keaton Scrapbook (1902-1909); Henry Hathaway Script Collection; Darryl F. Zanuck Script Collection. **Holdings:** 5200 books; 738 bound periodical volumes; 2000 moving picture and television scripts (cataloged); 44 oral history transcripts; 535 seminar transcripts; 2 file drawers of Film Festival information; 14,136 files of clippings; 62 reels of microfilm. **Subscriptions:** 207 journals and other serials; 5 newspapers. **Services:** Interlibrary loans; copying; library open to qualified scholars. **Special Indexes:** Writer, director and subject index to Script Collections (card); FIAF Periodical Card Indexing Service. **Formerly:** Its Center for Advanced Film Studies - Charles K. Feldman Library, located in Beverly Hills, CA.

★442★
AMERICAN FILM INSTITUTE - RESOURCE CENTER (Aud-Vis)
JFK Center for the Performing Arts   Phone: (202) 828-4088
Washington, DC 20566   Deborah Davidson Boutchard, Libn.
Founded: 1975. **Staff:** Prof 1. **Subjects:** Motion pictures, television, video. **Holdings:** 2500 books; 36 VF drawers of clippings; 34 VF drawers of motion picture stills; files on media organizations and film/video festivals. **Subscriptions:** 60 journals and other serials. **Services:** Copying; library open to public by appointment. **Publications:** Factfile series (13 titles).

AMERICAN FIRST DAY COVER SOCIETY ARCHIVES
See: American Philatelic Research Library

AMERICAN FOLKLIFE CENTER
See: Library of Congress

★443★
AMERICAN FORESTRY ASSOCIATION - LIBRARY (Env-Con)
1319 18th St., N.W.   Phone: (202) 467-5810
Washington, DC 20036
Subjects: Forestry and related subjects of soil, water, wildlife and recreation. **Holdings:** 2000 books and bound periodical volumes. **Services:** Library not open to public.

★444★
AMERICAN FOUNDATION FOR THE BLIND - M.C. MIGEL MEMORIAL LIBRARY (Soc Sci)
15 W. 16th St.   Phone: (212) 620-2161
New York, NY 10011   Judith M. Kaplan, Hd.Libn.
Founded: 1926. **Staff:** Prof 1; Other 3. **Subjects:** Blindness - education, psychology, rehabilitation. **Holdings:** 35,000 volumes. **Subscriptions:** 125 journals and other serials. **Services:** Interlibrary loans; copying; library open to public on a limited schedule. **Staff:** Robin Tannenbaum, Info.Spec.

AMERICAN FOUNDATION FOR MANAGEMENT RESEARCH
See: American Management Associations - D.W. Mitchell Memorial Library

★445★
AMERICAN FOUNDRYMEN'S SOCIETY - TECHNICAL INFORMATION CENTER (Sci-Tech)
Golf & Wolf Rds.   Phone: (312) 824-0181
Des Plaines, IL 60016   Ann V. Duggan, Mgr., Lib.Serv.
Staff: Prof 2; Other 1. **Subjects:** Cast metals, safety, foundry practice,

hygiene, air pollution control. **Holdings:** 3500 volumes. **Subscriptions:** 200 journals and other serials. **Services:** Literature searches; library open to public. **Networks/Consortia:** Member of North Suburban Library System. **Publications:** Current Awareness Service, monthly Newsletter - by subscription; Film Directory, annual - free upon request.

AMERICAN FRIENDS OF LAFAYETTE COLLECTION
See: Lafayette College

AMERICAN FRIENDS SERVICE COMMITTEE INC.
See: Society of Friends - Philadelphia Yearly Meeting

AMERICAN FRIENDS SERVICE COMMITTEE INC. - NATIONAL ACTION/ RESEARCH ON THE MILITARY-INDUSTRIAL COMPLEX
See: National Action/Research on the Military-Industrial Complex

★446★
AMERICAN GAS ASSOCIATION - LIBRARY (Bus-Fin; Energy)†
1515 Wilson Blvd.   Phone: (703) 841-8415
Arlington, VA 22209   Steven J. Dorner, Mgr., Lib.Serv.
Founded: 1919. **Staff:** Prof 2; Other 3. **Subjects:** Natural gas, gas utility industry, gas pipeline industry, gas research and technology, utility regulation, gas appliances, synthetic natural gas, liquified natural gas. **Special Collections:** History of the Gas Industry in the U.S., 19th century to present - Proceedings of predecessor associations; gas company annual reports. **Holdings:** 21,400 books; 960 bound periodical volumes; 670 reels of microfilm (cataloged); 150 VF drawers of clippings, pamphlets and archives. **Subscriptions:** 677 journals and other serials; 8 newspapers. **Services:** Interlibrary loans; copying; library open to public by appointment only. **Computerized Information Services:** DIALOG, DOE/RECON. **Publications:** New in the Library, fortnightly - to Association staff and member company libraries. **Staff:** L. Cate, Asst.Libn.

★447★
AMERICAN GEAR MANUFACTURERS ASSOCIATION - LIBRARY (Sci-Tech)
1901 N. Fort Myer Dr., Suite 1000   Phone: (703) 525-1600
Arlington, VA 22209
Founded: 1916. **Subjects:** General gear data. **Holdings:** Figures not available. **Publications:** AGMA Standards and Technical Publications Index - free upon request.

★448★
AMERICAN GENERAL CAPITAL MANAGEMENT, INC. - RESEARCH LIBRARY (Bus-Fin)
Box 3121   Phone: (713) 522-1111
Houston, TX 77001   Betty J. Mohrman, Libn.
Founded: 1928. **Staff:** Prof 2; Other 2. **Subjects:** Business, finance and industry; mutual funds and securities. **Holdings:** 763 books; 116 lateral file drawers of research and financial files on corporations; 37 VF drawers of research material on industry; 10 shelves of government statistical material; 25 shelves of periodical reference material; 9 shelves of newspapers; 26 microfiche drawers of 10K, 10Q and N1R reports. **Subscriptions:** 49 journals and other serials; 27 newspapers; 186 statistical or special services. **Services:** Copying; library open to researchers with restrictions. **Remarks:** Library is located in the Riviana Bldg., 10th Fl., 2777 Allen Parkway, Houston, TX 77019. **Staff:** Glenda J. Lanphier, Asst.Libn.

★449★
AMERICAN GEOGRAPHICAL SOCIETY COLLECTION OF THE UNIVERSITY OF WISCONSIN, MILWAUKEE - GOLDA MEIR LIBRARY (Geog-Map)
Box 399   Phone: (414) 963-6282
Milwaukee, WI 53201   Roman Drazniowsky, Cur.
Founded: 1852. **Staff:** Prof 6; Other 12. **Subjects:** Geography, exploration, cartography, earth sciences, social sciences, history. **Holdings:** 196,800 books and bound periodical volumes; 374,910 maps; 6394 atlases; 45,900 photographs; 33,700 pamphlets; 71 globes; 98,000 Landsat Images. **Subscriptions:** 2000 journals and other serials. **Services:** Interlibrary loans; library open to public with Infopass. **Publications:** Current Geographical Publications, monthly (except July and August) - available by subscription. **Special Catalogs:** Research Catalog (book), 1962; First Supplement, 1972-73; Regional Section, 1974; Second Supplement, Regional and Topical, 1978. **Special Indexes:** Index to Maps in Books and Periodicals, 1968; First Supplement, 1971; Second Supplement, 1975. **Remarks:** Collection was transferred to UWM Library on July 26, 1978. **Staff:** Susan Ewart Peschel, Cat./Ref.Libn.; Christopher M. Baruth, Map Cat./Ref.Libn.; Howard A. Deller, Lit.Anl.; Jovanka Ristic, Map Cat./Ref.Libn.; Ellen M. Murphy, Map/Gift Cat.

★450★

AMERICAN GEOLOGICAL INSTITUTE - GEOREF INFORMATION SYSTEM (Sci-Tech)
One Skyline Pl.
5205 Leesburg Pike　　　　　　　Phone: (703) 379-2480
Falls Church, VA 22041　　　　　　John Mulvihill, Dir.
Staff: Prof 13; Other 12. **Subjects:** Earth sciences, geology, geophysics, hydrology, paleontology, environmental geology. **Special Collections:** GeoRef: a worldwide, computer-searchable, Earth Science, bibliographic database of 700,000 citations, 1961 to present. **Services:** SDI and retrospective searches; open to public. **Special Catalogs:** List of serials in GeoRef (microfiche); GeoRef Thesaurus and Guide to Indexing; Bibliography and Index of Geology, monthly with annual cumulation - for sale. **Formerly:** Its GEO-REF Retrospective Search Service. **Staff:** Dr. G.N. Rassam, Chf.Ed.; Sharon Tahirkheli, Sr.Ed.

★451★

AMERICAN GRADUATE SCHOOL OF INTERNATIONAL MANAGEMENT - LIBRARY (Bus-Fin)
Thunderbird Campus　　　　　　　Phone: (602) 938-7620
Glendale, AZ 85306　　　　　　　Lora Jeanne Wheeler, Libn.
Founded: 1946. **Staff:** Prof 3; Other 2. **Subjects:** Economic conditions, geography, politics and government, international commerce, books in Spanish, Portuguese and French. **Holdings:** 79,000 books; 3822 bound periodical volumes; 264 maps (cataloged). **Subscriptions:** 915 journals and other serials; 58 newspapers. **Services:** Interlibrary loans; copying; library open to public for reference use only; materials circulate to students and faculty only. **Computerized Information Services:** DIALOG. **Staff:** Jeanie Welch, Asst.Libn.; Russell L. Sears, Acq.Libn.

★452★

AMERICAN HARDWARE MUTUAL INSURANCE COMPANY - LIBRARY (Bus-Fin)
3033 Excelsior Blvd.　　　　　　　Phone: (612) 920-1400
Minneapolis, MN 55416　　　　　　Sylvia Kamrud, Libn.
Founded: 1938. **Staff:** 1. **Subjects:** Insurance, office management, advertising, marketing, statistics, safety engineering. **Holdings:** 1280 volumes; 58 VF drawers of correspondence files; 7 VF drawers of clippings and pamphlets; 6 VF drawers of bureau bulletins. **Subscriptions:** 50 journals and other serials. **Services:** Interlibrary loans; library not open to public. **Publications:** Library Bulletin, irregular - for supervisory employees and officers.

★453★

AMERICAN HARP SOCIETY REPOSITORY (Mus)
c/o School of Music, Ohio University　　Phone: (614) 594-5587
Athens, OH 45701　　　　　　　Lucile H. Jennings, Proj.Dir.
Founded: 1980. **Staff:** 1. **Subjects:** All aspects of the harp. **Holdings:** Figures not available for manuscripts, letters, autograph scores, historic sound recordings, microfilm, scrapbooks. **Services:** Copying (limited); library open to serious scholars, harpists and composers. **Remarks:** This is a new special collection located in the Music Division of the Library of Congress, Washington, DC. It is known as the Repository of the American Harp Society and is being funded for three years through 1983 by a grant from the National Endowment for the Humanities. Inquiries should be directed to the project director.

★454★

AMERICAN HEART ASSOCIATION - LIBRARY/RECORDS CENTER (Med)
7320 Greenville Ave.　　　　　　Phone: (214) 750-5408
Dallas, TX 75231　　　　　　　Barbara Arie Lightfoot, Mgr.
Founded: 1954. **Staff:** Prof 3; Other 2. **Subjects:** Cardiovascular and cerebrovascular diseases. **Special Collections:** American Heart Association publications. **Holdings:** 4000 books; 1000 bound periodical volumes; 110 VF drawers of clippings, archives, pamphlets, reprints, tearsheets; microforms. **Subscriptions:** 225 journals and other serials. **Services:** Interlibrary loans; copying; SDI; library open to public. **Networks/Consortia:** Member of Metroplex Council of Health Science Librarians; Dallas Health Science Consortium. **Staff:** Katherine Trickey, Libn.; Teresa Blodgett, Asst.Libn./Rec.Anl.

★455★

AMERICAN HELICOPTER SOCIETY - TECHNICAL INFORMATION (Sci-Tech)
1325 18th St., N.W., Suite 103　　　Phone: (202) 659-9524
Washington, DC 20036　　　　　　John F. Zugschwert, Exec.Dir.
Founded: 1943. **Staff:** 4. **Subjects:** History of the helicopter - acoustics, aerodynamics, structures, dynamics, propulsion, operations, design, maintenance, stability and control, navigation. **Holdings:** Figures not available. **Services:** Copying. **Special Catalogs:** Publications catalog (book).

★456★

AMERICAN HEMEROCALLIS SOCIETY - LIBRARY (Sci-Tech)*
c/o Joan D. Senior
Rt.2, Box 360
DeQueen, AR 71832　　　　　　Ned Irish, Chm., Pubn.Comm.
Founded: 1946. **Subjects:** Gardening. **Holdings:** Figures not available. **Publications:** Hemerocallis Journal, quarterly; Cultivar Checklist, annual; Beginners' Handbook of Daylilies.

★457★

AMERICAN HERITAGE PUBLISHING COMPANY, INC. - LIBRARY (Publ)
10 Rockefeller Plaza　　　　　　Phone: (212) 399-8931
New York, NY 10020　　　　　　Patrick Bunyan, Libn.
Founded: 1956. **Staff:** Prof 1; Other 1. **Subjects:** American history and art. **Special Collections:** Pictures (250,000). **Holdings:** 11,000 books; 150 bound periodical volumes. **Subscriptions:** 90 journals and other serials. **Services:** Interlibrary loans; library open to public by appointment.

AMERICAN HISTORICAL SOCIETY OF GERMANS FROM RUSSIA - GREELEY PUBLIC LIBRARY
See: Greeley Public Library - Special Collections

★458★

AMERICAN HOECHST - FILMS DIVISION - TECHNICAL INFORMATION CENTER (Sci-Tech)
Box 1400　　　　　　　　　Phone: (803) 877-8471
Greer, SC 29651　　　　　　　Judith Duffie, Info.Spec.
Founded: 1970. **Staff:** Prof 1; Other 1. **Subjects:** Polymer chemistry, FDA regulations, plastics patents. **Holdings:** 900 books; 100 bound periodical volumes; 290 reels of microfilm; 1200 reports. **Subscriptions:** 153 journals and other serials. **Services:** Interlibrary loans; copying; library open to public with restrictions. **Computerized Information Services:** DIALOG; internal database; computerized serials and circulation. **Special Indexes:** Index to Patents; computer index to internal documents.

★459★

AMERICAN HOIST & DERRICK CO. - ENGINEERING STANDARDS LIBRARY*
63 S. Robert St.
St. Paul, MN 55107
Subjects: Standards, vendor data, specifications. **Also Known As:** Amhoist. **Remarks:** Presently inactive.

★460★

AMERICAN HOME ECONOMICS ASSOCIATION - LIBRARY
2010 Massachusetts Ave., N.W.
Washington, DC 20036
Founded: 1970. **Subjects:** Home economics, American Home Economics Association. **Special Collections:** American Home Economics Association publications; early home economics books (historical collection); Ellen H. Richards Collection. **Remarks:** The library is presently inactive. Persons interested in using the historical collections should contact Dr. Gladys Gary Vaughan, Director of Research.

★461★

AMERICAN HOME PRODUCTS CORPORATION - WYETH LABORATORIES DIVISION - ANTIBIOTICS LABORATORIES LIBRARY (Med)
611 E. Nield St.　　　　　　　Phone: (215) 696-3100
West Chester, PA 19380　　　　　Beverly L. Cantor, Tech.Libn.
Founded: 1950. **Staff:** Prof 1; Other 1. **Subjects:** Antibiotics, microbiology, organic chemistry. **Holdings:** 2784 books; 4447 bound periodical volumes; 2 VF drawers of reprints. **Subscriptions:** 113 journals and other serials. **Services:** Interlibrary loans; copying; library open to qualified users.

★462★

AMERICAN HOME PRODUCTS CORPORATION - WYETH LABORATORIES DIVISION LIBRARY (Med)
Box 8299　　　　　　　　　Phone: (215) 688-4400
Philadelphia, PA 19101　　　　　Larry D. Taylor, Supv., Lib.Serv.
Founded: 1945. **Staff:** Prof 4; Other 6. **Subjects:** Pharmacy, medicine, analytical and organic chemistry, biochemistry, patents (pharmaceutical). **Holdings:** 27,500 books; 33,000 bound periodical volumes; 3550 reports; 12,350 microforms. **Subscriptions:** 1100 journals and other serials. **Services:** Interlibrary loans; copying; library open to public with restrictions. **Computerized Information Services:** DIALOG, SDC, MEDLINE. **Networks/Consortia:** Member of PALINET and Union Library Catalogue of Pennsylvania. **Publications:** Acquisitions List, quarterly. **Special Catalogs:** Book catalog. **Remarks:** Library located at King of Prussia Rd. & Lancaster Pike, Radnor, PA 19087. **Staff:** Judith Knott, Asst.Libn.; Linda Becker, Jnl.Libn.; Beverly Cantor, Br.Libn.

★463★

AMERICAN HORTICULTURAL SOCIETY - HAROLD B. TUKEY MEMORIAL LIBRARY (Sci-Tech)

Natl. Center for American Horticulture   Phone: (703) 768-5700
Mount Vernon, VA 22121   Jane Steffey, Horticultural Adv.
Subjects: Horticulture. **Holdings:** 5000 books. **Services:** Library open to society members. **Publications:** Directory of American Horticulture. **Special Indexes:** Horticultural Film Index.

★464★

AMERICAN HOSPITAL ASSOCIATION - ASA S. BACON MEMORIAL LIBRARY (Med; Bus-Fin)

840 N. Lake Shore Dr.   Phone: (312) 280-6263
Chicago, IL 60611   Eloise C. Foster, Dir.
Founded: 1929. **Staff:** Prof 12; Other 12. **Subjects:** Administration, planning and financing of health care facilities; administrative aspects of medical, nursing, paramedical and prepayment fields. **Special Collections:** Rare books on hospital administration and related fields; Ray E. Brown Collection (management). **Holdings:** 35,000 books; 2500 bound periodical volumes; 5500 pamphlets; 15,000 microfiche; 2 VF drawers of hospital annual reports; 114 cassettes. **Subscriptions:** 1000 journals and other serials. **Services:** Interlibrary loans (fee); copying; literature searches; open for room use to anyone with legitimate interest. **Computerized Information Services:** DIALOG, SDC, NLM. **Networks/Consortia:** Member of Regional Medical Library - Region 3; OCLC. **Publications:** Hospital Literature Index, quarterly with annual cumulation - by subscription; Administrator's Collection, irregular; Cumulative Index of Hospital Literature, multiannual cumulations of Hospital Literature Index from 1945-1977. **Remarks:** The Ray E. Brown Collection is developed by the American College of Hospital Administrators.

★465★

AMERICAN HOSPITAL ASSOCIATION - CLEARINGHOUSE FOR HOSPITAL MANAGEMENT ENGINEERING (Bus-Fin)

840 N. Lake Shore Dr.   Phone: (312) 280-6023
Chicago, IL 60611   Richard P. Covert, Dir.
Founded: 1974. **Subjects:** Hospital management engineering, productivity. **Holdings:** 1200 reports and papers. **Services:** Copying; open to public with restrictions.

AMERICAN HOSPITAL SUPPLY CORPORATION - AMERICAN CRITICAL CARE - INFORMATION CENTER

See: American Critical Care - Information Center

★466★

AMERICAN HOSPITAL SUPPLY CORPORATION - CORPORATE INFORMATION CENTER (Bus-Fin; Law)

One American Plaza   Phone: (312) 866-4586
Evanston, IL 60201   Sharon I. Meyer, Mgr.
Staff: Prof 3; Other 2. **Subjects:** Domestic and international business, law. **Holdings:** 6000 books; 6 VF drawers of economic files; 6 VF drawers of health care files. **Subscriptions:** 610 journals and other serials; 5 newspapers. **Services:** Interlibrary loans; copying; library open to public with restrictions. **Computerized Information Services:** DIALOG, SDC, BRS, CACI, Inc. (SITE, SITE II), TEXTLINE, Dow Jones News Retrieval, Value Line Data Services. **Networks/Consortia:** Member of Metropolitan Chicago Library Assembly; North Suburban Library System; OCLC. **Publications:** American Info, monthly newsletter. **Staff:** Mary Ann Berragry, Info.Anl.; Soon-Ho Lee, Libn.

★467★

AMERICAN HOSPITAL SUPPLY CORPORATION - DADE DIVISION LIBRARY (Med)

1851 Delaware Pkwy.
Box 520672
Miami, FL 33152   Phone: (305) 633-6461
     Patsy A. Bentley, Sr.Med.Libn.
Staff: Prof 1. **Subjects:** Clinical chemistry, chemical abstracts, biochemistry, immunology, medicine, pathology. **Holdings:** 2800 books; 1200 bound periodical volumes; 2000 unbound journals; 45 file boxes of newsletters and bulletins; 24 VF drawers of scientific reprints; 37 directories; 2000 patents; 75 journal titles on microfilm. **Subscriptions:** 140 journals and other serials. **Services:** Interlibrary loans; library not open to public. **Computerized Information Services:** BRS. **Networks/Consortia:** Member of Miami Health Sciences Library Consortium. **Publications:** Newsletter/Acquisitions, monthly - for internal distribution only.

★468★

AMERICAN HUMANE EDUCATION SOCIETY - HUMANE EDUCATION LIBRARY (Env-Cons)

450 Salem End Rd.   Phone: (617) 879-5345
Framingham, MA 01701   Marshall McKee, Libn./Cur. Designer
Founded: 1963. **Staff:** Prof 1. **Subjects:** Conservation, zoology, pet care, humane education, animal welfare. **Special Collections:** George T. Angell papers (founder of the MSPCA; 5 linear feet). **Holdings:** 1500 volumes; curricula packets; 4000 slides; AV materials. **Subscriptions:** 20 journals and other serials. **Services:** Library open to public by appointment.

★469★

AMERICAN HUNGARIAN LIBRARY AND HISTORICAL SOCIETY (Area-Ethnic)†

215 E. 82nd St.   Phone: (212) 744-5298
New York, NY 10028
Founded: 1955. **Subjects:** Hungaricana. **Holdings:** 3000 volumes. **Publications:** Studies on Hungarian culture, irregular. **Remarks:** Society promotes research and study in the contribution of Hungarian culture to that of the United States.

★470★

AMERICAN HYPNOTISTS' ASSOCIATION - HYPNOSIS TECHNICAL CENTER (Med)

Glanworth Bldg., Suite 6
1159 Green St.   Phone: (415) 775-6130
San Francisco, CA 94109   Dr. Angela Bertuccelli, Libn.
Founded: 1959. **Staff:** Prof 1. **Subjects:** Hypnosis - medical, psychological and surgical; methods of hypnotism; history and practice of hypnosis. **Special Collections:** Historical publications (worldwide). **Holdings:** 3800 books; 304 bound periodical volumes; International Association of Hypnotists' reports. **Services:** Interlibrary loans; library open to members only. **Publications:** Hypnosis News - to membership.

★471★

AMERICAN INDIAN ARCHAEOLOGICAL INSTITUTE, INC. - LIBRARY (Area-Ethnic)

Box 260   Phone: (203) 868-0518
Washington, CT 06793   Dr. Roger Moeller, Dir. of Res.
Subjects: American archeology - prehistoric, historic; American Indian - literature, history, crafts; ethnobotany. **Holdings:** Figures not available for books. **Services:** Copying; library open to public by appointment. **Publications:** List of publications - available on request. **Staff:** Stephen Post, Dir. of Educ.

★472★

AMERICAN INDIAN BIBLE INSTITUTE - DOROTHY CUMMINGS MEMORIAL LIBRARY (Rel-Theol; Soc Sci)

10020 N. 15th Ave.   Phone: (602) 944-3335
Phoenix, AZ 85021   Dorothy Skipp, Act.Libn.
Staff: Prof 1; Other 5. **Subjects:** Christian education, business management, nursing, sociology, music. **Special Collections:** Books about different Indian tribes (319 volumes). **Holdings:** 11,509 books; 16 VF drawers of maps, booklets and clippings; 186 boxed periodicals; 7 shelves of filmstrips and cassettes; 300 other cataloged items. **Subscriptions:** 23 journals and other serials; 6 newspapers. **Services:** Copying; library open to ministers for reference use only. **Publications:** A.I.B.I. Thunderer.

★473★

AMERICAN INDIAN HISTORICAL SOCIETY - LIBRARY (Area-Ethnic)†

1451 Masonic Ave.   Phone: (415) 626-5235
San Francisco, CA 94117   Dr. Jeanette Henry
Founded: 1964. **Staff:** 1. **Subjects:** The American Indian - history, anthropology, arts, law, education, archaeology, ethnology, sociology, language texts. **Special Collections:** Archives Collection - Indians of North America (400 bound volumes, including rare, obscure early works on the American Indian). **Holdings:** 4000 books; 100 bound periodical volumes; pamphlets; 20 maps; 100 tapes containing oral histories; 500 slides. **Subscriptions:** 35 journals and other serials; 150 newspapers. **Services:** Library open to those who send written application. **Special Indexes:** Index to Literature on the American Indian - published by the Indian Historian Press which is supported by the Society.

★474★

AMERICAN INDIAN REFUGEES - NATIVE LIBRARY

6701 S.W. 62nd Ave., No. 604
Miami, FL 33143
Defunct

★475★

AMERICAN INDIAN RESEARCH PROJECT - LIBRARY (Hist; Area-Ethnic)*
University of South Dakota
16 Dakota Hall   Phone: (605) 677-5208
Vermillion, SD 57069   Dr. Richmond L. Clow, Dir.
Founded: 1966. Staff: Prof 2; Other 1. Subjects: History - South Dakota, Indian. Special Collections: Jurrens Collection of Native American music (36 tapes); South Dakota Folk Music (22 tapes). Holdings: 3102 audiotapes (cataloged). Services: Copying; SDI; library open for scholarly research. Publications: Oyate Iyechinka Woglakapi (Indian collection catalog, 4 volumes); The South Dakota Experience (5 volumes, continuing); American Indian Research Project Index - all distributed on request; list of additional publications - available upon request. Special Indexes: Subject index to American Indian collection. Staff: Suzanne Julin, Res.Asst.

AMERICAN INDIAN STUDIES CENTER
See: University of California, Los Angeles

AMERICAN INDUSTRIAL ARTS ASSOCIATION ARCHIVES
See: Millersville State College - Helen A. Ganser Library - Special Collections

★476★

AMERICAN INSTITUTE OF AERONAUTICS AND ASTRONAUTICS - LIBRARY (Sci-Tech)
9841 Airport Blvd., Suite 800   Phone: (213) 641-4100
Los Angeles, CA 90045   Donald M. Stone, Dir.
Staff: Prof 2; Other 2. Subjects: Astronautics, aeronautics. Holdings: 25 books; 50 bound periodical volumes; 25 astronautics and aeronautics monographs (cataloged). Subscriptions: 7 journals and other serials. Services: Library open to members.

AMERICAN INSTITUTE OF AERONAUTICS AND ASTRONAUTICS - PACIFIC AEROSPACE LIBRARY
See: Northrop University - Alumni Library - Special Collections

★477★

AMERICAN INSTITUTE OF AERONAUTICS AND ASTRONAUTICS - TECHNICAL INFORMATION SERVICE (Sci-Tech)
555 W. 57th St.   Phone: (212) 247-6500
New York, NY 10019   E.H. Seymour, Adm.
Founded: 1936. Staff: Prof 3; Other 7. Subjects: Aerospace, space sciences, physics, chemistry, earth sciences, engineering. Holdings: 26,000 books; 1000 bound periodical volumes; 27,500 conference papers (cataloged); 200,000 microfiche of IAA and STAR items. Subscriptions: 1600 journals and other serials. Services: Copying; SDI; service open to public. Computerized Information Services: DIALOG, SDC, NASA/RECON. Networks/Consortia: Member of National Aeronautics and Space Administration Library Network (NALNET). Publications: IAA, semimonthly; selected bibliographies. Special Indexes: IAA cumulated indexes, annual. Staff: Patricia Marshall, Dir., Lib.Rsrcs.

★478★

AMERICAN INSTITUTE OF ARCHITECTS - LIBRARY (Art; Plan)
1735 New York Ave., N.W.   Phone: (202) 626-7493
Washington, DC 20006   Stephanie C. Byrnes, Libn.
Staff: Prof 6; Other 1. Subjects: Architecture, building, urban planning. Special Collections: Richard Morris Hunt Collection. Holdings: 22,000 volumes; 20 VF drawers of pamphlets and clippings; 15,000 slides. Subscriptions: 400 journals and other serials. Services: Interlibrary loans; copying; library open to public for reference use only. Publications: Accession List, bimonthly. Staff: Faith Vosburgh, Asst.Libn./Ref.; Sally Hanford, Asst.Libn./Tech.Serv.; Sheryl Romeo, Asst.Libn./AV; Tony Wrenn, Archv.; Michelle Jones, Asst.Mgr./AV.

★479★

AMERICAN INSTITUTE OF ARCHITECTS - PORTLAND CHAPTER - LIBRARY (Art)
519 S.W. Third, Suite 200   Phone: (503) 223-8757
Portland, OR 97201   Joan Vance, Adm.Asst.
Subjects: Architecture, design, technology. Holdings: 2000 books. Services: Copying; library open to public by appointment.

★480★

AMERICAN INSTITUTE OF BAKING - LIBRARY (Food-Bev)
1213 Bakers Way   Phone: (913) 537-4750
Manhattan, KS 66502   Ruth Emerson, Libn.
Founded: 1925. Staff: Prof 1; Other 1. Subjects: Baking science and technology, food chemistry, nutrition. Holdings: 5200 books; 3500 bound periodical volumes; 96 VF drawers of unbound material on baking and nutrition. Subscriptions: 134 journals and other serials. Services: Interlibrary loans; copying; library open to accredited inquirers. Computerized Information Services: DIALOG. Special Indexes: Index of journal articles, pamphlets, reprints, patents (card).

★481★

AMERICAN INSTITUTE OF CERTIFIED PUBLIC ACCOUNTANTS - LIBRARY SERVICES (Bus-Fin)
1211 Ave. of the Americas   Phone: (800) 223-4155
New York, NY 10036   Karen Hegge Simmons, Chf.Libn.
Founded: 1918. Staff: Prof 10; Other 9. Subjects: Accounting, auditing, taxation, finance, management. Special Collections: Old accounting texts. Holdings: 16,300 books; 3131 bound periodical volumes; 57,000 pamphlets (cataloged); all NYSE, AMEX and OTC annual reports, 1977 to present, on microfiche; 120 titles of tax and business loose-leaf services. Subscriptions: 300 journals and other serials. Services: Interlibrary loans; copying; library open to public but only AICPA members may borrow. Computerized Information Services: Source of input for Accountants' Index and database available through SDC. Publications: Accountants' Index, quarterly with annual cumulation - by subscription; AICPA Library Acquisitions List, monthly - on request to AICPA and SLA members. Remarks: Toll-free number for New York residents is 800-522-5434. Staff: Lillian Rosenfeld, Ref.Libn.; Linda Pierce, Index Ed.

★482★

AMERICAN INSTITUTE FOR ECONOMIC RESEARCH - E.C. HARWOOD LIBRARY (Soc Sci)
Division St.   Phone: (413) 528-1216
Great Barrington, MA 01230   Laura Tucker, Libn.
Founded: 1934. Staff: Prof 10; Other 25. Subjects: Economics and related fields. Holdings: 10,000 volumes. Subscriptions: 70 journals and other serials; 7 newspapers. Services: Copying; library open to public. Publications: Research Reports, weekly; Economic Education Bulletins, monthly.

★483★

AMERICAN INSTITUTE OF FAMILY RELATIONS - ROSWELL H. JOHNSON RESEARCH LIBRARY (Soc Sci)†
5287 Sunset Blvd.   Phone: (213) 465-5131
Los Angeles, CA 90027   Dr. Edward Peacock, Exec.Dir.
Founded: 1930. Staff: 5. Subjects: Heredity, sex, love, marriage, parenthood. Special Collections: Psychotherapy; preparation for childbirth; Christopher Ruess collection on maturity and old age. Holdings: 12,000 books; 40 VF drawers. Subscriptions: 125 journals and other serials. Services: Library open to public for reference use only.

AMERICAN INSTITUTE OF THE HISTORY OF PHARMACY
See: State Historical Society of Wisconsin - Archives Division

★484★

AMERICAN INSTITUTE OF INDUSTRIAL ENGINEERS, INC. - FRANK & LILIAN GILBRETH MEMORIAL LIBRARY (Sci-Tech)
25 Technology Park/Atlanta   Phone: (404) 449-0460
Norcross, GA 30092   Gregory Balestrero, Mgr., Tech.Serv.
Staff: Prof 1; Other 1. Subjects: Industrial engineering, management, engineering technology. Special Collections: Complete bound sets of Industrial Engineering magazine (31 volumes), IIE Transactions (12 volumes) The Engineering Economist (25 volumes); Industrial Management. Holdings: 2400 books; 80 bound periodical volumes; 50 conference proceedings; 100 government reports. Subscriptions: 60 journals and other serials; 5 newspapers. Services: Copying (limited); library open to public by appointment.

★485★

AMERICAN INSTITUTE OF ISLAMIC STUDIES - MUSLIM BIBLIOGRAPHIC CENTER (Rel-Theol; Area-Ethnic)
Box 10398   Phone: (303) 936-0108
Denver, CO 80210   C.L. Geddes, Dir.
Founded: 1965. Staff: Prof 1; Other 1. Subjects: Islamic, Muslim culture; North African, Southeast Asian and Near Eastern bibliography. Holdings: 7500 books and bound periodical volumes; 150 reels of microfilm in bibliographic collection. Subscriptions: 32 journals and other serials. Services: Interlibrary loans; copying; center open to public by appointment. Publications: Bibliographic series, irregular - sold through bookstores.

★486★

AMERICAN INSTITUTE OF MANAGEMENT - LIBRARY (Bus-Fin)
607 Boylston St.   Phone: (617) 536-2503
Boston, MA 02116   D. Ellis, Libn.
Subjects: Business management and allied subjects. **Holdings:** Figures not available. **Services:** Library not open to public. **Publications:** The Presidents Journal, monthly; The Executive Counsellor, monthly; The Associates Digest, monthly; National Biographic, irregular.

★487★

AMERICAN INSTITUTE FOR MARXIST STUDIES - LIBRARY (Soc Sci)
20 E. 30th St.   Phone: (212) 689-4530
New York, NY 10016   Henry Klein, Libn.
Staff: Prof 1. **Subjects:** Marxism, general philosophy, general history, political economy. **Holdings:** 8000 books; 250 bound periodical volumes; clipping files; tapes; photographs. **Subscriptions:** 25 journals and other serials; 5 newspapers. **Services:** Library open to public. **Publications:** AIMS Newsletter, bimonthly; monographs; occasional papers; bibliographies.

★488★

AMERICAN INSTITUTE OF PARLIAMENTARIANS - LIBRARY (Soc Sci)
229 Army Post Rd., Suite B   Phone: (515) 287-5154
Des Moines, IA 50315   Lester L. Dahms, Exec.Dir.
Founded: 1958. **Staff:** Prof 1. **Subjects:** Parliamentary procedure. **Holdings:** 500 volumes. **Services:** Library not open to public. **Publications:** Parliamentary Directory, annual; Parliamentary Bibliography (about every 5 years); Parliamentary Journals, quarterly.

★489★

AMERICAN INSTITUTE OF PHYSICS - CENTER FOR HISTORY OF PHYSICS - NIELS BOHR LIBRARY (Sci-Tech)
335 E. 45th St.   Phone: (212) 661-9404
New York, NY 10017-3483   John C. Aubry, Archv./Libn.
Founded: 1962. **Staff:** Prof 3; Other 4. **Subjects:** History and philosophy of physics; physics; history and philosophy of science. **Holdings:** 15,600 books; 3320 bound periodical volumes; manuscripts, notebooks, photographs, autobiographies, oral history materials, dissertations, microfilm, and other archival materials documenting 19th and 20th century physics history. **Subscriptions:** 60 journals and other serials. **Services:** Interlibrary loans; copying; access to archival materials only upon application. **Publications:** Newsletter, biennial. **Special Catalogs:** Catalog of Sources for History of Physics (card index locating collections of manuscript source materials). **Staff:** Spencer Weart, Mgr.; Joan Warnow, Asst.Mgr.

★490★

AMERICAN INSTITUTE FOR PROPERTY & LIABILITY UNDERWRITERS - INSURANCE INSTITUTE OF AMERICA - LIBRARY (Bus-Fin)
Providence & Sugartown Rds.   Phone: (215) 644-2100
Malvern, PA 19355   Kim Holston, Libn.
Founded: 1978. **Staff:** Prof 1. **Subjects:** Insurance, risk management, economics, management, accounting, continuing education. **Special Collections:** O.D. Dickerson Memorial Library (insurance, mathematics; 500 volumes). **Holdings:** 3000 books. **Subscriptions:** 90 journals and other serials. **Services:** Copying; library open to public.

AMERICAN INSTITUTE FOR PSYCHOANALYSIS
See: Ivimey (Muriel) Library

★491★

AMERICAN INSTITUTE OF TIMBER CONSTRUCTION - LIBRARY (Sci-Tech)
333 W. Hampden Ave.   Phone: (303) 761-3212
Englewood, CO 80110   Paul T. Nicholas, Dir. of Engr.Serv.
Subjects: Engineering and building construction, timber. **Holdings:** 250 books; 12 VF drawers. **Subscriptions:** 10 journals and other serials. **Services:** Library not open to public.

★492★

AMERICAN INSTITUTES FOR RESEARCH - LIBRARY (Soc Sci)
1791 Arastradero Rd.
Box 1113
Palo Alto, CA 94302   Phone: (415) 493-3550
                                          Nancy Hull, Libn.
Founded: 1967. **Staff:** Prof 1. **Subjects:** Education, psychology. **Special Collections:** AIR technical reports (1900 titles). **Holdings:** 3000 books; 1050 bound periodical volumes; 7000 internal and external reports; 10 VF drawers of pamphlets; 4 VF drawers of tests (internal use only). **Subscriptions:** 275 journals and other serials. **Services:** Interlibrary loans; copying; library open to public for reference use only by advance arrangement.

★493★

AMERICAN INSTITUTES FOR RESEARCH - LIBRARY (Soc Sci)†
1055 Thomas Jefferson St., N.W.   Phone: (202) 342-5000
Washington, DC 20007   Lily Griner, Libn.
Staff: Prof 1. **Subjects:** Psychology, sociology, criminal justice, aging, management. **Holdings:** 8000 books; 25 bound periodical volumes; 6 VF drawers; 200 technical reports. **Subscriptions:** 73 journals and other serials. **Services:** Interlibrary loans; copying; library open to public by appointment. **Computerized Information Services:** DIALOG. **Special Catalogs:** AIR reports. **Remarks:** The AIR library supports the research staff in proposal and report preparation. A branch library is maintained in Palo Alto, CA.

★494★

AMERICAN INSTITUTES FOR RESEARCH - PROJECT TALENT DATA BANK (Educ; Soc Sci)
Box 1113   Phone: (415) 493-3550
Palo Alto, CA 94302   Lauri Steel, Dir., Data Bank
Staff: Prof 1. **Subjects:** Education, psychology, testing, measurement, statistics, students, schools. **Holdings:** Longitudinal data spanning 15 years (ages 14-29) on 400,000 students and their (circa 1000) high schools; 150 final reports, dissertations and journal articles based on Project TALENT Data Bank studies. **Services:** Data analysis and worktape preparation for outside users (fee); 4000 case Public Use File. **Publications:** Research reports; Project TALENT Data Bank Handbook. **Special Indexes:** Annotated bibliography.

★495★

AMERICAN INSURANCE ASSOCIATION - ENGINEERING & SAFETY DEPARTMENT LIBRARY (Bus-Fin)
85 John St.   Phone: (212) 433-5667
New York, NY 10038   Lynne Wizowski, Libn.
Founded: 1975. **Staff:** Prof 1. **Subjects:** Fire protection, loss control, safety engineering. **Holdings:** 1010 books; 100 VF drawers. **Subscriptions:** 72 journals and other serials. **Services:** Library open to public with restrictions.

★496★

AMERICAN INSURANCE ASSOCIATION - LAW LIBRARY (Law)†
85 John St.   Phone: (212) 433-4400
New York, NY 10038   Lorna L. Beasley, Libn.
Staff: Prof 1; Other 1. **Subjects:** Insurance, law. **Holdings:** 15,500 volumes; 70 VF drawers. **Services:** Library open to public by appointment.

★497★

AMERICAN IRISH HISTORICAL SOCIETY - LIBRARY (Area-Ethnic)
991 Fifth Ave.   Phone: (212) 288-2263
New York, NY 10028   Dr. William Griffin, Libn./Archv.
Staff: Prof 1. **Subjects:** Irish in the American colonies and the United States. **Holdings:** 25,000 books; 200 linear feet of archives and manuscripts. **Services:** Library open to public. **Publications:** Recorder, annual - to members.

AMERICAN JEWISH ARCHIVES
See: Hebrew Union College - Jewish Institute of Religion

★498★

AMERICAN JEWISH COMMITTEE - BLAUSTEIN LIBRARY (Area-Ethnic)
165 E. 56th St.   Phone: (212) 751-4000
New York, NY 10022   Cyma M. Horowitz, Lib.Dir.
Founded: 1939. **Staff:** Prof 3; Other 2. **Subjects:** Intergroup relations; Jewish community organization; contemporary Jewish problems; civil rights and liberties; ethnic groups; interreligious relations. **Holdings:** 30,000 books and pamphlets; 60 VF drawers; 1450 reels of microfilm. **Subscriptions:** 625 journals and other serials; 85 newspapers. **Services:** Library open to qualified scholars for reference only. **Publications:** Recent Additions to the Library, quarterly; Articles of Interest in Current Periodicals, 6/year - free to libraries on request. **Staff:** Phyllis Flynn, Asst.Libn.; Michele Anish, Asst.Libn.

★499★

AMERICAN JEWISH COMMITTEE - WILLIAM E. WIENER ORAL HISTORY LIBRARY (Area-Ethnic)
165 E. 56th St.   Phone: (212) 751-4000
New York, NY 10022   Irma Kopp Krents, Dir.
Founded: 1969. **Staff:** Prof 3. **Subjects:** All aspects of the ''American Jewish Experience in the 20th Century.'' **Special Collections:** Oral memoirs, including the Jacob Blaustein Oral History Collection; Irving M. Engel Oral History Collection on Civil Rights; Lautenberg Collection on East European Jewish Communities; The Politics of American Jews: The Election of 1972; A Study in American Pluralism Through Oral Histories of Holocaust Survivors; Oral Histories of Recent Soviet Emigres in America; American Jewish Women

of Achievement. **Holdings:** Over 1000 taped interviews and transcripts. **Services:** Library open to researchers by appointment. **Staff:** Will Sandy, Lib.Coord.; Milton E. Krents, Sr.Cons.

★500★

AMERICAN JEWISH CONGRESS - CHARLES AND BERTIE G. SCHWARTZ JUDAICA READING ROOM & LIBRARY
Martin Steinberg Ctr. for Jewish Artists
15 E. 84th St.
New York, NY 10028
Founded: 1970. **Subjects:** Art and music, Bible, Talmud, prayers, history, philosophy, biography, Holocaust literature, Yiddish and Hebrew literature, Jewish-Christian relations, Judaism, sociology, Israel and Zionism, marriage and family, Hassidism. **Special Collections:** Collection of Jewish records and tapes. **Holdings:** 1500 books; back copies of Judaica Book News. **Remarks:** Presently inactive.

★501★

AMERICAN JEWISH CONGRESS-COMMISSION ON LAW, SOCIAL ACTION & URBAN AFFAIRS - SHAD POLIER MEMORIAL LIBRARY (Soc Sci)
15 E. 84th St.　　　　　　　　　Phone: (212) 879-4500
New York, NY 10028　　　　　　Laraine C. Spector, Libn.
Founded: 1978. **Subjects:** Civil rights, constitutional law, civil liberties, history of discrimination, church-state relations, social and economic affairs. **Special Collections:** Commission archives (120 VF drawers); U.S. Supreme Court briefs (850); American-Jewish Congress historical material; commission reports. **Holdings:** 3000 books; 600 pamphlets. **Services:** Library open to public by appointment. **Publications:** Guide to the Shad Polier Library. **Special Indexes:** Index to Commission Archives; Index to CLSA distribution material.

★502★

AMERICAN JEWISH HISTORICAL SOCIETY - LIBRARY (Area-Ethnic)
2 Thornton Rd.　　　　　　　　Phone: (617) 891-8110
Waltham, MA 02154　　　　　　Nathan M. Kaganoff, Libn.
Founded: 1892. **Staff:** Prof 3; Other 2. **Subjects:** American Jewish history. **Holdings:** 68,000 books; 500,000 unbound periodicals; 6 million pieces of manuscript; 500 Yiddish theatre posters; 2000 pieces of Yiddish sheet music; 75,000 synagogue and other Jewish institutional items. **Subscriptions:** 250 journals and other serials; 300 newspapers. **Services:** Interlibrary loans; copying; library open to public with restrictions. **Publications:** American Jewish History; Newsletter. **Special Catalogs:** 2 catalogs of manuscript collections; 1 catalog of theatre posters; catalog of art treasures and daguerreotypes. **Staff:** Donald Altshiller, Asst.Libn.; Leibl Scheiner, Asst.Libn.

★503★

AMERICAN JEWISH JOINT DISTRIBUTION COMMITTEE - ARCHIVES (Area-Ethnic)
60 E. 42nd St., Suite 1914　　　　Phone: (212) 687-6200
New York, NY 10645　　　　　　Rose Klepfisz, Dir., Archv.
Founded: 1914. **Staff:** Prof 4. **Subjects:** Committee archives. **Holdings:** 1200 feet of archival material. **Services:** Archives open to accredited scholars and students.

★504★

AMERICAN JEWISH JOINT DISTRIBUTION COMMITTEE - LIBRARY (Area-Ethnic)
60 E. 42nd St., Suite 1914　　　　Phone: (212) 687-6200
New York, NY 10645　　　　　　Micha F. Oppenheim, Libn.
Founded: 1979. **Staff:** Prof 1; Other 1. **Subjects:** Refugees, Holocaust, Israel/Palestine, Jews in other countries. **Holdings:** 3000 books. **Also Known As:** Joint Distribution Committee.

AMERICAN JEWISH PERIODICAL CENTER
See: Hebrew Union College - Jewish Institute of Religion

★505★

AMERICAN JOURNAL OF NURSING COMPANY - SOPHIA F. PALMER LIBRARY (Med)
555 W. 57th St.　　　　　　　　Phone: (212) 582-8820
New York, NY 10019　　　　　　Frederick W. Pattison, Libn.
Founded: 1928. **Staff:** Prof 1; Other 2. **Subjects:** Nursing and related fields. **Special Collections:** Early nursing books and history of nursing. **Holdings:** 9000 books and bound periodical volumes. **Subscriptions:** 500 journals and other serials. **Services:** Interlibrary loans; library open to graduate students and researchers by appointment only. **Networks/Consortia:** Member of Manhattan-Bronx Health Sciences Library Group; New York & New Jersey Regional Medical Library Program. **Publications:** International Nursing Index, quarterly - by subscription.

★506★

AMERICAN JUDICATURE SOCIETY - RESEARCH LIBRARY (Law)
200 W. Monroe St., Suite 1606　　Phone: (312) 558-6900
Chicago, IL 60606　　　　　　　Timothy Pyne, Libn.
Founded: 1913. **Staff:** 1. **Subjects:** Judicial administration. **Special Collections:** 300 court studies. **Holdings:** 5000 books; 12 file drawers of articles (cataloged). **Subscriptions:** 75 journals and other serials. **Services:** Interlibrary loans; copying; library open to public by appointment.

★507★

AMERICAN JUSTICE INSTITUTE - LIBRARY (Law; Soc Sci)
725 University Ave.　　　　　　Phone: (916) 924-3700
Sacramento, CA 95825-6793　　　Deborah Scowcroft, Adm.Asst.
Staff: Prof 1. **Subjects:** Criminal justice, police, courts, corrections, juvenile justice. **Special Collections:** American Justice Institute publications (332 titles). **Holdings:** 3895 books; juvenile justice system research reports. **Subscriptions:** 32 journals and other serials. **Services:** Interlibrary loans; copying (fee); library open to public with restrictions.

★508★

AMERICAN KENNEL CLUB - LIBRARY (Rec)
51 Madison Ave.　　　　　　　Phone: (212) 481-9245
New York, NY 10010　　　　　　Roberta A. Vesley, Lib.Dir.
Founded: 1935. **Staff:** Prof 2; Other 2. **Subjects:** Dogs - breeding, training, health, literature, art, sports. **Special Collections:** Domestic and foreign stud books; collections of prominent past and present dog-fanciers including John W. Cross, Shearer and Rosenberg. **Holdings:** 15,000 volumes; 10 VF drawers of clippings; 16 VF drawers of pictures and photographs of dogs; 10 VF drawers of pamphlets (uncataloged); 45 VF drawers of periodicals (uncataloged). **Subscriptions:** 300 journals and other serials. **Services:** Copying; library open to public. **Staff:** Aida Ferrer, Asst.Libn.

★509★

AMERICAN LAW INSTITUTE - LIBRARY (Law)
4025 Chestnut St.　　　　　　　Phone: (215) 243-1658
Philadelphia, PA 19104　　　　Loretta U. McConnell, Libn.
Founded: 1965. **Staff:** Prof 1; Other 1. **Subjects:** Law, legal education. **Special Collections:** American Law Institute publications (Restatement of the Law, Uniform Commercial Code, Model Penal Code and other special projects); American Law Institute-American Bar Association Committee on Continuing Professional Education publications; continuing legal education publications of various bar associations. **Holdings:** 10,400 books; 850 pamphlets; 1020 audiotapes and cassette tapes; 28 volumes of clippings; 2 file drawers of Continuing Legal Education course brochures. **Subscriptions:** 214 journals and other serials. **Services:** Interlibrary loans (limited); library open to public with permission of librarian. **Remarks:** Library also serves the American Law Institute-American Bar Association Committee on Continuing Professional Education.

★510★

AMERICAN LAWN BOWLS ASSOCIATION - LIBRARY (Rec)
1524 Lake Shore Dr.　　　　　　Phone: (305) 896-2178
Orlando, FL 32853　　　　　　　Harold L. Esch, Hist.
Staff: 1. **Subjects:** Lawn bowling. **Holdings:** 500 volumes; magazines, club histories, organizational records, minutes, yearbooks, photographs and drawings.

★511★

AMERICAN LEGION - FILM LIBRARY
Box 1055
Indianapolis, IN 46206
Defunct

★512★

AMERICAN LEGION - NATIONAL HEADQUARTERS - LIBRARY (Rec)
700 N. Pennsylvania St.
Box 1055　　　　　　　　　　Phone: (317) 635-8411
Indianapolis, IN 46206　　　　Thomas V. Hull, Dir.
Founded: 1923. **Staff:** Prof 1; Other 4. **Subjects:** U.S. veteran affairs, children and youth, U.S. national defense, patriotism, American Legion. **Special Collections:** Archives of the American Legion, including national and state organizations and posts; unit histories for WWI, WWII, Korean and Vietnam wars. **Holdings:** 8500 volumes; 300 periodicals; 1140 VF drawers of pamphlets, reports, manuscripts, correspondence and other archival material. **Services:** Interlibrary loans; copying; library open to public for reference use only by appointment.

★513★

AMERICAN LIBRARY ASSOCIATION - HEADQUARTERS LIBRARY (Info Sci)
50 E. Huron St.   Phone: (312) 944-6780
Chicago, IL 60611   Joel M. Lee, Libn.
Founded: 1924. **Staff:** Prof 3; Other 3. **Subjects:** Library science, library associations, library architecture. **Special Collections:** Materials selection policy statements; library building programs, plans, pictures and slides; public relations materials; IFLA Conference Papers; library staff personnel and procedure manuals; library surveys; handbooks of instruction in library use; materials produced, published or sponsored by ALA. **Holdings:** 20,199 books and bound periodical volumes; 200 linear feet of pamphlets; 220 reels of microfilm; 4 drawers of microfiche. **Subscriptions:** 900 journals and other serials. **Services:** Interlibrary loans; copying; library open to public with reference needs. **Computerized Information Services:** DIALOG, New York Times Information Service; computerized cataloging. **Networks/Consortia:** Member of Metropolitan Chicago Library Assembly; Chicago Library System; OCLC through ILLINET. **Special Catalogs:** Checklist of materials - free upon request; ALA Publications Checklist, annual. **Staff:** Celeste Lavelli, Asst.Libn.; Gail Gradowski, Asst.Libn.

AMERICAN LIBRARY ASSOCIATION - OFFICE OF LIBRARY SERVICES - FELETI PACIFIC LIBRARY
See: Feleti Pacific Library

★514★

AMERICAN LIBRARY ASSOCIATION - WASHINGTON OFFICE (Info Sci)
110 Maryland Ave., N.E.
Box 54   Phone: (202) 547-4440
Washington, DC 20002   Eileen D. Cooke, Dir.
Founded: 1945. **Staff:** Prof 3; Other 4. **Subjects:** Library legislation, development and services. **Holdings:** VF materials on legislation with library implications; American Library Association publications. **Subscriptions:** 67 journals and other serials. **Services:** Library open to public by appointment. **Publications:** ALA Washington Newsletter, irregular (12/year minimum).

★515★

AMERICAN LIBRARY OF RAILWAY AND TRACTION HISTORY (Trans)
455-A Riverside Dr.   Phone: (213) 846-6098
Burbank, CA 91506   Brian C. Smith, Dir.
Staff: Prof 1. **Subjects:** Interurban electric railways, railroads, rapid transit, street railways, subways, urban transit. **Holdings:** 1348 books; 75 reels of microfilm; 17 films; 11 VF drawers of railroad information. **Subscriptions:** 15 journals and other serials. **Services:** Interlibrary loans; copying; library open to public with restrictions. **Remarks:** Telephone reference services are available on a 24-hour basis.

★516★

AMERICAN LIFE FOUNDATION - PRANG-MARK SOCIETY - LIBRARY (Art)
Old Irelandville   Phone: (607) 535-4004
Watkins Glen, NY 14891   L. M. Goodman, Coord.
Staff: Prof 1; Other 3. **Subjects:** Printing, early greeting cards, tradecards. **Special Collections:** Original Prang Prints. **Holdings:** 7000 books. **Services:** Library open to public by appointment only, June 1 through September 1. **Publications:** Prang-Mark Society Newsletter, irregular - for internal distribution only.

★517★

AMERICAN LIFE FOUNDATION AND STUDY INSTITUTE - AMERICANA RESEARCH LIBRARY (Art)
Old Irelandville
Box 349   Phone: (607) 535-4737
Watkins Glen, NY 14891   John Crosby Freeman, Dir.
Staff: Prof 3; Other 2. **Subjects:** Decorative arts, architecture, art, history, agriculture, landscape architecture, city planning. **Special Collections:** Ruth S. Freeman Collection of Children's Picture Books; Victorian Periodical Library; Larry Freeman Decorative Arts Library. **Holdings:** 5000 books; 2500 bound periodical volumes; 5000 art and architecture slides; 30 drawers of posters and broadsides; 3000 pamphlets. **Subscriptions:** 25 journals and other serials. **Services:** Library open to qualified scholars with an advance letter of introduction and statement of purpose. **Staff:** Ruth Freeman, Cur., Pict.Bk.Coll.; Larry Freeman, Cur., Dec. Arts Lib.

AMERICAN LIFESAVING EMERGENCY RESPONSE TEAM (A.L.E.R.T.)
See: United States Lifesaving Association - Library & Information Center

★518★

AMERICAN LUNG ASSOCIATION OF HAWAII - LEARNING CENTER FOR LUNG HEALTH (Med)
245 N. Kukui St.   Phone: (808) 537-5966
Honolulu, HI 96817   Catherine C. Tamura, Learning Ctr.Coord.
Founded: 1981. **Staff:** Prof 1. **Subjects:** Lung health, asthma education, smoking prevention, air pollution, adult patient health care. **Holdings:** 100 books; 40 bound periodical volumes; 100 items of air pollution material; 50 items of smoking prevention education; 25 marijuana and health education materials. **Services:** Interlibrary loans; center open to public.

★519★

AMERICAN LUNG ASSOCIATION OF KANSAS - INFORMATION CENTER (Med)
Box 4426   Phone: (913) 272-9290
Topeka, KS 66604   Darrel Walton, Exec.Dir.
Founded: 1908. **Subjects:** Lung diseases - emphysema, tuberculosis, asthma, air pollution, smoking and health. **Holdings:** Books; pamphlets; filmstrips; films. **Services:** Publications available; films and filmstrips loaned on request.

★520★

AMERICAN LUTHERAN CHURCH - ARCHIVES (Rel-Theol)
Wartburg Theological Seminary   Phone: (319) 556-8151
Dubuque, IA 52001   Robert C. Wiederaenders, Archv.
Subjects: Archives of the American Lutheran Church and its antecedent church bodies. **Holdings:** 3500 books; 3000 bound periodical volumes; 5000 synodical reports (cataloged); manuscripts and correspondence of leading churchmen; 500 audiotapes of church meetings and theological lectures; 950 reels of 35mm microfilm of congregation records; 100,000 pages of minutes and reports on microfiche; 2200 shelf feet of records relating to the American Lutheran Church. **Subscriptions:** 10 journals and other serials; 5 newspapers. **Services:** Interlibrary loans; copying; limited translation; archives open to public with restrictions. **Computerized Information Services:** Internal database. **Publications:** Annual Report. **Special Catalogs:** Finding Aids and Inventories in the ALC Archives, 1982. **Special Indexes:** Index to over 3000 congregation records on microfilm. **Remarks:** Norwegian antecedent records and collections of the ALC are housed in the Luther-Northwestern Theological Seminary, St. Paul, MN. All records relating to publishing and all publications of the ALC and its antecedents are housed in the Augsburg Publishing House, Minneapolis, MN.

AMERICAN LUTHERAN CHURCH - SOUTH DAKOTA DISTRICT - ARCHIVES
See: Augustana College - Center for Western Studies

★521★

AMERICAN MC GAW - TECHNICAL INFORMATION CENTER (Med)
Box 11887   Phone: (714) 754-2066
Santa Ana, CA 92711   Carol DeLape, Sci.Info.Coord.
Founded: 1934. **Staff:** Prof 1; Other 2. **Subjects:** Medicine, biochemistry, chemistry, nutrition, pharmacology. **Holdings:** 4000 books; 3000 bound periodical volumes. **Subscriptions:** 400 journals and other serials. **Services:** Interlibrary loans; copying; SDI; library open to public on request. **Computerized Information Services:** DIALOG, SDC, BRS, NLM; internal databases. **Networks/Consortia:** Member of Libraries of Orange County Network (LOCNET). **Publications:** Current Awareness Bulletin.

★522★

AMERICAN MANAGEMENT ASSOCIATIONS - D.W. MITCHELL MEMORIAL LIBRARY (Bus-Fin)
Box 88   Phone: (315\ 824-2000
Hamilton, NY 13346   Madge Snyder, Libn.
Founded: 1964. **Staff:** Prof 1. **Subjects:** Management - educational, business, health care, associations; planning. **Holdings:** 5000 books; 120 bound periodical volumes; 25 VF drawers of management references; 2 VF drawers of annual reports. **Subscriptions:** 77 journals and other serials. **Services:** Interlibrary loans; copying; library open to public by appointment. **Networks/Consortia:** Member of Central New York Library Resources Council (CENTRO). **Remarks:** Includes the holdings of the American Foundation for Management Research Library, which was absorbed in 1973.

★523★

AMERICAN MANAGEMENT ASSOCIATIONS - LIBRARY (Bus-Fin)†
135 W. 50th St.   Phone: (212) 586-8100
New York, NY 10020   Claire A. Lambkin, Chf.Libn.
Founded: 1923. **Staff:** Prof 4; Other 3. **Subjects:** Management, personnel, marketing, finance, production, international operations. **Holdings:** 12,000 books; 175 file drawers of clippings, pamphlets and company documents. **Subscriptions:** 321 journals and other serials. **Services:** Library open to

members only. **Publications:** File Headings, biennial - for internal distribution and upon request to libraries and members. **Staff:** Anne Jones, Libn.; Virginia Varnum, Libn.; Tung-Fen Lin, Libn.

★524★
AMERICAN MARKETING ASSOCIATION - INFORMATION CENTER (Bus-Fin)
250 S. Wacker Dr.   Phone: (312) 648-0536
Chicago, IL 60606   Lorraine Caliendo, Dir.
Founded: 1977. **Staff:** Prof 1; Other 2. **Subjects:** Marketing. **Special Collections:** Complete collection of all association publications, including Journal of Marketing, Journal of Marketing Research, Marketing News and conference proceedings. **Holdings:** 3000 books; 128 bound periodical volumes; 24 VF drawers of pamphlets. **Subscriptions:** 50 journals and other serials. **Services:** Interlibrary loans; library open to public by appointment.

★525★
AMERICAN MEDICAL ASSOCIATION - DIVISION OF LIBRARY AND ARCHIVAL SERVICES (Med)
535 N. Dearborn St.   Phone: (312) 751-6000
Chicago, IL 60610   Arthur W. Hafner, Ph.D., Dir.
Founded: 1911. **Staff:** Prof 13; Other 15. **Subjects:** Clinical medicine, medical socioeconomics, U.S. medical history, international health. **Special Collections:** Archive of American Medical Association and of Organized Medicine; sociology and economics of medicine, complete world coverage since 1962. **Holdings:** 110,000 bound volumes; medical socioeconomics file (75,000 items); 150,000 documents and artifacts; 150 linear feet of general medical and pamphlet material; 350 linear feet of biographical data in Physician File. **Subscriptions:** 2605 journals and other serials. **Services:** Interlibrary loans (fee); copying; records management; current awareness service; library open to AMA members and allied health organizations. **Computerized Information Services:** MEDLINE, BRS, DIALOG, New York Times Information Service, AMA Policy Computerized Data Bank; internal database; computerized cataloging. **Networks/Consortia:** Member of OCLC; NLM; MIDLNET. **Publications:** Proceedings of the A.M.A. House of Delegates, semiannual; Digest of A.M.A. Official Actions, quinquennial; Index to A.M.A. News, annual; Index to Journal of the American Medical Association, semiannual; indexes to nine AMA Specialty Journals, annual; Medical Socioeconomics Current Awareness, monthly; Medical Socioeconomic Research Sources, online; monthly list of AMA councils, committees and sponsored national meetings; Books Received by AMA Division of Library and Archival Services; American Association of Medical Society Executives - Management Resources Guide. **Special Indexes:** Index to Proceedings of AMA House of Delegates, semiannual; Index to Medical Socioeconomic Literature, 1962-1970. **Staff:** Terry Austin, Dir., Spec.Coll.; Ann C. Weller, Hd. Clinical Med.; Phyllis H. O'Donnell, AMA Pubn. Indexing; Susan K. Roberts, Dir. Automation/Tech.Serv; Mary Moules, Hd.Tech.Serv.

★526★
AMERICAN MEDICAL ASSOCIATION - WASHINGTON OFFICE LIBRARY (Med)
1101 Vermont Ave., N.W.   Phone: (202) 857-1338
Washington, DC 20005   James H. Jackson, Dir.
Staff: Prof 1; Other 1. **Subjects:** Health economics, statistics, association affairs. **Holdings:** 10,000 books; 1400 bound periodical volumes; 30 drawers of VF material. **Subscriptions:** 250 journals and other serials. **Services:** Interlibrary loans; copying; library open to public. **Computerized Information Services:** DIALOG, BRS; computerized cataloging. **Networks/Consortia:** Member of OCLC.

★527★
AMERICAN MEDICAL RECORD ASSOCIATION - FORE RESOURCE CENTER (Med)
875 N. Michigan Ave., Suite 1850   Phone: (312) 787-2672
Chicago, IL 60611   Mary Kay Siebert, Libn.
Founded: 1965. **Staff:** Prof 1; Other 1. **Subjects:** Medical record materials. **Holdings:** 2500 books. **Subscriptions:** 125 journals and other serials. **Services:** Interlibrary loans; copying; library open to public. **Remarks:** FORE is an acronym for Foundation of Record Education.

★528★
AMERICAN MERCHANT MARINE LIBRARY ASSOCIATION - PUBLIC LIBRARY OF THE HIGH SEAS (Hum)
One World Trade Center, Suite 2601   Phone: (212) 775-1038
New York, NY 10048   Sally-Ann Coash, Dir.
Founded: 1921. **Staff:** 4. **Special Collections:** William Bollman collection (biography, history, travel). **Holdings:** 3500 volumes. **Services:** Library open to public for reference use only. **Remarks:** Association solicits books from the public and prepares boxed libraries for placement aboard American-flag vessels. Merged with United Seaman's Service.

★529★
AMERICAN METEOROLOGICAL SOCIETY - ABSTRACTS PROJECT - LIBRARY (Sci-Tech)†
45 Beacon St.   Phone: (617) 227-2425
Boston, MA 02108   Kenneth C. Spengler, Exec.Dir.
Founded: 1949. **Staff:** Prof 11; Other 2. **Subjects:** Meteorology, geophysics, astrophysics, hydrology, oceanography, atmospheric sciences, environmental sciences. **Special Collections:** Russian language serials and monographs in atmospheric sciences (large collection). **Holdings:** 2600 books; 300 bound periodical volumes; 25,000 unbound periodical issues (cataloged). **Subscriptions:** 100 journals and other serials. **Services:** Copying; library not open to public. **Computerized Information Services:** Online systems. **Publications:** Journal of Meteorological & Geostrophical Abstracts, monthly. **Special Indexes:** Annual indexes in card and book form.

★530★
AMERICAN METEOROLOGICAL SOCIETY - BROOKS LIBRARY
45 Beacon St.
Boston, MA 02108
Founded: 1965. **Subjects:** Meteorology, history of meteorology. **Special Collections:** Papers and letters of Charles F. Brooks and A. Lawrence Rotch. **Holdings:** 6000 books; 350 bound periodical volumes. **Remarks:** Historical library for headquarters use only. Presently inactive.

★531★
AMERICAN MICROSYSTEMS, INC. - INFORMATION CENTER (Sci-Tech)
3800 Homestead Rd., Bldg. 800   Phone: (408) 246-0330
Santa Clara, CA 95051   Nancy Kay Walton, Info./Rec.Ctr.Mgr.
Staff: Prof 2; Other 2. **Subjects:** Semiconductors, electronics, microelectronics, business, computers, management. **Holdings:** 4700 books; 70 bound periodical volumes; 14,500 pamphlets and reprints; 5000 reports; 500 microforms. **Subscriptions:** 175 journals and other serials; 25 newspapers. **Services:** Interlibrary loans; copying; library open to public with permission. **Computerized Information Services:** DIALOG. **Networks/Consortia:** Member of CLASS; CIN; South Bay Area Reference Network. **Publications:** I C Bulletin, weekly - available to employees. **Special Indexes:** KWOC index to pamphlet collection (computer printout).

★532★
AMERICAN MIME, INC. - LIBRARY (Theater)
61 4th Ave.   Phone: (212) 677-9276
New York, NY 10003   Paul J. Curtis, Dir.
Founded: 1970. **Subjects:** History of the American Mime Theatre. **Holdings:** Course syllabi; picture files; scrapbooks, clippings; American Mime scripts; bibliography of mime works. **Services:** Library open to public for reference use only with permission of the Director. **Staff:** Jean Barbour, P.R.

AMERICAN MUSEUM OF IMMIGRATION
See: U.S. Natl. Park Service - Statue of Liberty Natl. Monument

★533★
AMERICAN MUSEUM OF MAGIC - LIBRARY (Rec)
107 E. Michigan   Phone: (616) 781-7666
Marshall, MI 49068   Robert Lund, Owner
Staff: 1. **Subjects:** Conjuring, confidence games, superstition. **Special Collections:** Irving Desfor collection of photographs of magicians (50,000). **Holdings:** 9000 books; 25,000 magazines; 150,000 letters, newspaper clippings, programs, photographs, films, posters, manuscripts. **Subscriptions:** 25 journals and other serials. **Services:** Library open to public with restrictions. **Publications:** American Museum of Magic Newsletter, irregular.

★534★
AMERICAN MUSEUM OF NATURAL HISTORY - DEPARTMENT OF ICHTHYOLOGY - DEAN MEMORIAL LIBRARY (Sci-Tech)
Central Park W. at 79th St.   Phone: (212) 873-1300
New York, NY 10024   Dr. Gareth Nelson, Cur.
Staff: Prof 2; Other 3. **Subjects:** Fish - anatomy, physiology, classification, distribution. **Holdings:** 1700 books and bound periodical volumes; 7000 pamphlets. **Subscriptions:** 10 journals and other serials. **Services:** Copying; library open to qualified users by appointment.

★535★
AMERICAN MUSEUM OF NATURAL HISTORY - HAYDEN PLANETARIUM - RICHARD S. PERKIN LIBRARY (Sci-Tech)
Central Park W. at 81st St.   Phone: (212) 873-1300
New York, NY 10024   Sandra Kitt, Libn.
Founded: 1958. **Staff:** Prof 1. **Subjects:** Astronomy, astronautics, radio astronomy, planetariums, space flight, meteorology, navigation. **Holdings:** 9000 books; 200 bound periodical volumes; 15,000 photographs; 300

pamphlets (cataloged); 150 astronomical films; 100 maps and charts; slides; 5000 reprints from observatories and planetariums; 3 boxes of archives. **Subscriptions:** 82 journals and other serials. **Services:** Interlibrary loans; copying; library open to public for reference use only by appointment.

★536★
AMERICAN MUSEUM OF NATURAL HISTORY - LIBRARY (Sci-Tech)
Central Park W. at 79th St.   Phone: (212) 873-1300
New York, NY 10024   Nina J. Root, Chairperson
Founded: 1869. **Staff:** Prof 10; Other 18. **Subjects:** Anthropology, archaeology, paleontology, entomology, mammalogy, ornithology, ichthyology, malacology, herpetology, mineralogy, geology, museology, zoology, travels and voyages, natural history. **Special Collections:** Rare books, manuscripts, museum archives, memorabilia, rare films, photographic collection (800,000 items). **Holdings:** 145,000 books; 230,000 bound periodical volumes; maps. **Subscriptions:** 6000 journals and other serials. **Services:** Interlibrary loans; copying; photo rights and reproduction; library open to public. **Computerized Information Services:** Computerized cataloging. **Networks/Consortia:** Member of OCLC; New York State Interlibrary Loan Network. **Publications:** Catalog of the Special Film Collection - for sale; Recent Publications in Natural History, quarterly (in Curator). **Special Catalogs:** Research Catalogs of the AMNH Library; slide catalog. **Special Indexes:** Index to Natural History (card). **Staff:** Miriam Tam, Asst.Libn., Tech.Serv.; Pamela Haas, Asst.Libn., Photo Coll.; Mary Genett, Asst.Libn., Ref.Serv.

★537★
AMERICAN MUSEUM OF NATURAL HISTORY - OSBORN LIBRARY OF VERTEBRATE PALEONTOLOGY (Sci-Tech)
Central Park W. at 79th St.   Phone: (212) 873-1300
New York, NY 10024   Charlotte Holton, Libn.
Founded: 1908. **Staff:** 1. **Subjects:** Vertebrate paleontology. **Holdings:** 10,000 books and pamphlets; 15,000 reprints. **Services:** Library not open to public.

★538★
AMERICAN MUSIC CENTER - LIBRARY (Mus)
250 W. 54th St., Rm. 300   Phone: (212) 265-8190
New York, NY 10019   Candice Feldt, Libn.
Founded: 1940. **Staff:** Prof 2; Other 1. **Subjects:** Works of contemporary American composers. **Holdings:** 17,000 published and unpublished scores; 1000 phonograph records; tapes; 1500 biographical files of composer members. **Subscriptions:** 75 journals and other serials. **Services:** Interlibrary loans; library open to public. **Computerized Information Services:** Computerized cataloging. **Networks/Consortia:** Member of RLG. **Publications:** Library Additions, semiannual - to mailing list; AMC Newsletter, quarterly - to subscribers. **Special Indexes:** AMC Library catalogs (book): volume 1 Choral and vocal works; volume 2 Chamber music; volume 3 Orchestra and band music; volume 4 Opera and theater music (in preparation). **Staff:** Leroy Richmond, Cat.

★539★
AMERICAN MUSIC RESEARCH CENTER - LIBRARY (Mus)
Dominican College   Phone: (415) 457-4440
San Rafael, CA 94901   Sr. Mary Dominic Ray, Founder-Dir.
Founded: 1968. **Staff:** Prof 5. **Subjects:** Music - 18th century comic opera, California Mission; early New England singing schools. **Special Collections:** Tunebooks (18th & 19th century; 115); color microfilm of all music in Santa Barbara Mission Archives; comic operas (200); psalters with music (16th-19th century); Moravian music (recordings and sheet music); National Tune Index (microfiche). **Holdings:** 600 books; 4000 albums of music and sheet music; 725 disc recordings, cassettes, reels; 2000 slides; 35 reels of microfilm; 200 8x10 photographs of California mission music; early playbills, maps, charts and programs. **Services:** Copying; library open to public by appointment only. **Publications:** Lists of rare items and of comic opera collection - available on request. **Remarks:** The American Music Research Center is a specialized reference library, and also offers lectures on and off campus, and consultation.

★540★
AMERICAN NAME SOCIETY - PLACE NAME SURVEY OF THE UNITED STATES - LIBRARY (Geog-Map)
James Gilliam Gee Library
East Texas State University
Commerce, TX 75428   Phone: (214) 886-5251
    Dr. Fred Tarpley, Natl.Dir.
Founded: 1889. **Subjects:** U.S. geographical names. **Holdings:** 305 books; 300 bound periodical volumes; 75,000 Texas place names on cards (cataloged); 30 theses and dissertations on place names.

★541★
AMERICAN NATIONAL BUILDING - JOINT VENTURE LAW LIBRARY (Law)
818 17th St., Suite 730   Phone: (303) 623-3467
Denver, CO 80202   Frances Ellis
Founded: 1979. **Staff:** Prof 1. **Subjects:** Law. **Holdings:** 9000 volumes. **Services:** Library not open to public.

★542★
AMERICAN NATIONAL METRIC COUNCIL - LIBRARY (Sci-Tech)
5410 Grosvenor Lane   Phone: (301) 530-8333
Bethesda, MD 20814   Lou Anne Wheeler, Ed.
Staff: 1. **Subjects:** Metric system. **Holdings:** Figures not available. **Services:** Copying; library open to public. **Publications:** Metric Reporter, monthly - by subscription. **Special Indexes:** Annual Index - by subscription and upon request.

AMERICAN NATIONAL RED CROSS
See: American Red Cross

★543★
AMERICAN NATURAL RESOURCE COMPANY - SYSTEM ECONOMIC LIBRARY
One Woodward Ave., 26th Fl.
Detroit, MI 48226
Defunct

★544★
AMERICAN-NEPAL EDUCATION FOUNDATION - WOOD NEPAL LIBRARY (Area-Ethnic)
Box ANEF   Phone: (503) 842-4024
Oceanside, OR 97134   Hugh B. Wood, Libn.
Founded: 1959. **Staff:** Prof 1. **Subjects:** Nepal, education, social sciences. **Special Collections:** Archives of the University of Oregon/Nepal/USAID Project 1954-1959. **Holdings:** 900 books; 10 bound periodical volumes; 400 photocopies of periodical materials; 22 dissertations; 60 reports; 2000 slides; 2 16mm films. **Services:** Interlibrary loans; copying; library open to researchers by appointment only. **Special Catalogs:** Nepal Bibliography, 1959 (now out of print).

★545★
AMERICAN NEWSPAPER PUBLISHERS ASSOCIATION - LIBRARY (Publ)†
The Newspaper Center
11600 Sunrise Valley Dr.   Phone: (703) 620-9500
Reston, VA 22091   Yvonne L. Egertson, Libn.
Founded: 1952. **Staff:** Prof 1; Other 2. **Subjects:** Newspaper publishing; journalism; freedom of the press. **Holdings:** 5000 books; 700 bound periodical volumes; 2 VF drawers of ANPA Archives; 4 VF drawers of pamphlets on newspaper publishing; bulletins of state press associations (current 3 months); microfilm of Editor & Publisher and other journals. **Subscriptions:** 386 journals and other serials; 4 newspapers. **Services:** Interlibrary loans; copying; library open to public with restrictions. **Publications:** ANPA Library Memo, irregular, aimed at newspaper librarians - on request. **Staff:** J. Curtis Loughin, Mgr., Info.Serv.

AMERICAN NEWSPAPER PUBLISHERS ASSOCIATION RESEARCH INSTITUTE
See: ANPA Research Institute

★546★
AMERICAN NUCLEAR INSURERS - INFORMATION RECORDS CENTER (Sci-Tech)
The Exchange, Bldg. 3
245 Farmington Ave.   Phone: (203) 677-7305
Farmington, CT 06032   Dottie Sherman, Dir., Lib./Info.Ctr.
Founded: 1974. **Staff:** Prof 1; Other 3. **Subjects:** Nuclear power plants, nuclear engineering, health physics, nuclear law. **Special Collections:** Nuclear power plant facility information (500,000 microfiche); nuclear standards; nuclear insurance. **Holdings:** 3000 books; 4500 technical reports. **Subscriptions:** 303 journals and newsletters. **Services:** Interlibrary loans; copying; library open to public by appointment. **Computerized Information Services:** DIALOG, SDC, Nuclear Safety Information Center (NSIC). **Networks/Consortia:** Member of Capitol Region Library Council. **Publications:** Acquisitions List, monthly; newsletter.

★547★
AMERICAN NUCLEAR SOCIETY - LIBRARY (Energy)
555 N. Kensington Ave.   Phone: (312) 352-6611
La Grange Park, IL 60525   Lois S. Webster, Libn.
Founded: 1973. **Staff:** 1. **Subjects:** Nuclear engineering and physics;

business management; science biographies. **Holdings:** 2500 books. **Services:** Library open to public with restrictions. **Computerized Information Services:** DIALOG, NEXIS. **Networks/Consortia:** Member of Suburban Library System (SLS).

★548★
AMERICAN NUMISMATIC ASSOCIATION - LIBRARY (Rec)
818 N. Cascade   Phone: (303) 632-2646
Colorado Springs, CO 80903   Nancy Green, Libn.
Founded: 1891. **Staff:** Prof 1; Other 2. **Subjects:** Coins, medals, currency, tokens, check collecting, banks and banking. **Holdings:** 10,000 books; 5000 bound periodical volumes; 20,000 auction catalogs (cataloged); 4 VF drawers of pamphlets and articles; 35mm slide programs. **Subscriptions:** 140 journals and other serials. **Services:** Copying; library open to public for reference use only; circulation restricted to members. **Publications:** Library Catalog - for sale. **Special Indexes:** Index to The Numismatist.

★549★
AMERICAN NUMISMATIC SOCIETY - LIBRARY (Rec)
Broadway at 155th St.   Phone: (212) 234-3130
New York, NY 10032   Francis D. Campbell, Jr., Libn.
Founded: 1858. **Staff:** Prof 2; Other 1. **Subjects:** Numismatics. **Holdings:** 30,000 books and bound periodical volumes; 52 VF drawers of pamphlets; 42 VF drawers of auction catalogs; 23 VF drawers of fixed price lists; 200 reels of microfilm. **Subscriptions:** 100 journals and other serials. **Services:** Interlibrary loans; copying; library open to public for reference use only. **Staff:** Margaret D'Ambrosio, Assoc.Libn.

AMERICAN NURSES' ASSOCIATION ARCHIVES
See: University of Missouri, Kansas City - Health Sciences Library

★550★
AMERICAN OCCUPATIONAL MEDICAL ASSOCIATION - LIBRARY
150 N. Wacker Dr.
Chicago, IL 60606
Defunct

★551★
AMERICAN OCCUPATIONAL THERAPY ASSOCIATION - REFERENCE LIBRARY (Med)
1383 Piccard Dr.   Phone: (301) 948-9626
Rockville, MD 20850   Amy R. Bridgman, Libn.
Staff: Prof 1; Other 1. **Subjects:** Occupational therapy - physical and psychosocial disabilities, perceptual motor disabilities, child development, geriatrics, leisure time, work and rehabilitation. **Special Collections:** AOTA archives; journals since 1922; theses. **Holdings:** 2500 books; 100 bound periodical volumes; 2 VF drawers of pamphlets. **Subscriptions:** 63 journals and other serials; 14 newsletters. **Services:** Interlibrary loans; copying; library open to faculty and students of occupational therapy and practicing occupational therapists. **Publications:** Library manual, annual.

AMERICAN OIL COMPANY
See: AMOCO

★552★
AMERICAN OLD TIME FIDDLERS ASSOCIATION - ARCHIVES
6141 Morrill Ave.
Lincoln, NE 68507
Defunct

★553★
AMERICAN OPTICAL CORPORATION - RESEARCH CENTER LIBRARY (Sci-Tech)†
14 Mechanic St.   Phone: (617) 765-9711
Southbridge, MA 01550   C. Hermas Swope, Lib.Adm.
Founded: 1954. **Staff:** 2. **Subjects:** Physics, optics, microscopy, ophthalmology and optometry, glass technology. **Holdings:** 5600 books; 2450 bound periodical volumes. **Subscriptions:** 170 journals and other serials. **Services:** Interlibrary loans; copying; library open to public by special arrangement. **Staff:** Aileen A. Carlson, Libn.

AMERICAN ORIENTAL SOCIETY LIBRARY
See: Yale University

★554★
AMERICAN ORTHOTIC AND PROSTHETIC ASSOCIATION - LIBRARY (Med)
717 Pendleton St.   Phone: (703) 836-7114
Alexandria, VA 22314   William L. McCulloch, Exec.Dir.
Subjects: Prosthetics and orthotics. **Holdings:** 200 books. **Subscriptions:** 10

journals and other serials.

★555★
AMERICAN OSTEOPATHIC ASSOCIATION - ANDREW TAYLOR STILL MEMORIAL LIBRARY (Med)†
212 E. Ohio St.   Phone: (312) 944-2713
Chicago, IL 60611   Barbara E. Peterson, Libn.
Founded: 1930. **Staff:** Prof 1; Other 1. **Subjects:** Medicine, osteopathic medicine. **Holdings:** 5000 books; 1000 bound periodical volumes. **Subscriptions:** 100 journals and other serials. **Services:** Interlibrary loans (limited); copying (limited); library not open to public.

★556★
AMERICAN OTOLOGICAL SOCIETY, INC. - LIBRARY (Med)
734 Lavergne   Phone: (312) 938-4327
Wilmette, IL 60091   Jack D. Clemis, M.D., Ed.-Libn.
Holdings: 114 books; Transactions of the American Otological Society. **Services:** Interlibrary loans; copying; library open to public.

★557★
AMERICAN PAPER INSTITUTE - LIBRARY (Bus-Fin)
260 Madison Ave.   Phone: (212) 340-0612
New York, NY 10016   Barbara L. Wolf, Libn.
Staff: Prof 1. **Subjects:** Paper - manufacturing, history and products; management; business; finance. **Holdings:** 500 books; 10 VF drawers. **Subscriptions:** 250 journals and other serials. **Services:** Interlibrary loans; copying; library open to public by appointment.

★558★
AMERICAN PATENT LAW ASSOCIATION - PATENT LAW LIBRARY (Law)
2001 Jefferson Davis Hwy., Suite 203   Phone: (703) 521-1680
Arlington, VA 22202   Gail D. Durant, Dir. of Adm.
Staff: 5. **Subjects:** Patents, trademarks, copyright. **Holdings:** Figures not available. **Services:** Library open to public for reference use only.

★559★
AMERICAN PERSONNEL AND GUIDANCE ASSOCIATION - HEADQUARTERS OFFICE LIBRARY (Soc Sci)
5203 Leesburg Pike   Phone: (703) 820-4700
Falls Church, VA 22041   Sylvia Nisenoff, Prof.Info.Spec.
Founded: 1952. **Staff:** Prof 1; Other 1. **Subjects:** Guidance and counseling, student personnel work, rehabilitation, vocational information, educational information, psychology, exceptional children, delinquency, tests and testing. **Holdings:** 2500 volumes; 10,000 pamphlets, reports, articles, speeches, booklets, and newsletters; 21 VF drawers of archives. **Subscriptions:** 15 journals and other serials. **Services:** Interlibrary loans; copying; library open to public for research purposes only.

★560★
AMERICAN PETROLEUM INSTITUTE - CENTRAL ABSTRACTING & INDEXING SERVICE
156 William St.
New York, NY 10038
Defunct

★561★
AMERICAN PETROLEUM INSTITUTE - LIBRARY (Sci-Tech; Energy)
2101 L St., N.W.   Phone: (202) 457-7269
Washington, DC 20037   Gladys E. Siegel, Libn.
Founded: 1932. **Staff:** Prof 5; Other 2. **Subjects:** Petroleum, natural gas and energy; environmental affairs; economics and statistics; legislative development; historical development. **Holdings:** 10,000 books; 1300 bound or microfilmed periodical volumes; 20,000 reports and papers (cataloged); API publications and proceedings. **Subscriptions:** 300 journals and other serials. **Services:** Interlibrary loans; copying; library open to public. **Computerized Information Services:** DIALOG, NLM, SDC, New York Times Information Service; computerized cataloging and acquisitions. **Networks/Consortia:** Member of OCLC through CAPCON. **Publications:** Monthly Acquisitions List; Petropubs, monthly - limited distribution. **Staff:** Lois J. Schuermann, Asst.Libn; Danuta Kuhl, Acq.Libn.; Lori Hauser, Cat.; Gail Kouril, Info.Spec.

★562★
AMERICAN PHARMACEUTICAL ASSOCIATION - FOUNDATION LIBRARY (Med)
2215 Constitution Ave., N.W.   Phone: (202) 628-4410
Washington, DC 20037   Colleen Pritchard, Libn.
Founded: 1934. **Staff:** Prof 1; Other 1. **Subjects:** Pharmaceuticals, health, pharmacy, medicine, pharmacology. **Special Collections:** History of

pharmacy. **Holdings:** 6000 books; 2000 bound periodical volumes; 1000 unbound periodicals; 45 VF drawers of Pharmacy Intelligence Center materials. **Subscriptions:** 200 journals and other serials. **Services:** Interlibrary loans; copying; identification of new drugs; library open to public. **Special Catalogs:** Drug compendiums.

★563★
AMERICAN PHILATELIC RESEARCH LIBRARY (Rec)
Box 8338   Phone: (814) 237-3803
State College, PA 16801   Steven A. Pla, Libn.
Founded: 1968. **Staff:** Prof 4; Other 5. **Subjects:** Stamp collecting, postal history, U.S. postal records, stamp production. **Special Collections:** American First Day Cover Society Archives; Postal History Society Library. **Holdings:** 8000 books; 4000 bound periodical volumes. **Subscriptions:** 450 journals and other serials; 6 newspapers. **Services:** Interlibrary loans; copying; library open to public but nonmembers must borrow by interlibrary loan. **Publications:** Philatelic Literature Review, quarterly - distributed to members. **Special Catalogs:** Manual of Philatelic Headings, American Philatelic Periodicals. **Staff:** Gladys C. Hoffman, Cat.; Joanne Mast, Asst.Libn., Tech.Serv.; Martha Micuda, Asst.Libn., Pub.Serv.

★564★
AMERICAN PHILOSOPHICAL SOCIETY - LIBRARY (Sci-Tech; Hist)
105 S. Fifth St.   Phone: (215) 627-0706
Philadelphia, PA 19106   Dr. Edward C. Carter, II, Libn.
Founded: 1743. **Staff:** Prof 10; Other 4. **Subjects:** History of American science including important European background material; Americana (early imprints, travels). **Special Collections:** Papers of Benjamin Franklin, Charles Darwin, Charles Willson Peale; Lewis and Clark Journals; American Indian linguistics; Thomas Paine; Simon Flexner; genetics; Stephen Girard papers; Franz Boaz Collection; society's archives, rich in material for the history of American science, are analysed from beginning through 1908; history of quantum physics. **Holdings:** 159,300 volumes; over 5 million manuscripts; microfilm; maps; prints, particularly of Philadelphia and Frankliniana. **Subscriptions:** 950 journals and other serials. **Services:** Interlibrary loans; copying; library open to public for reference use only. **Publications:** Annual Report of the Committee on Library - distributed free to libraries. **Special Catalogs:** Catalog of Manuscripts; Guide to Archives and Manuscript Collection; Guide to Manuscripts relating to the American Indian; Sources for the History of Quantum Physics; Calendar of the Papers of Benjamin Franklin; Calendar of the Correspondence of George Weedon, Richard Henry Lee, Hon. Arthur Lee, and Nathanael Green relating to the American Revolution; The Thomas Paine Collection of Richard Gimbel in the Library; Electricity, Magnetism and Animal Magnetism: a Checklist; An Annotated Calendar of the Letters of Charles Darwin in the Library; Catalog of Portraits; Catalog of Instruments and Models. **Staff:** Murphy D. Smith, Assoc. Libn.; Hildegard G. Stephans, Asst.Libn. & Cat.; Roy E. Goodman, Reading Rm.Libn.; Stephen Catlett, Mss.Libn.

AMERICAN PLANNING ASSOCIATION
See: Merriam Center Library

★565★
AMERICAN PLAYERS THEATRE, INC. (APT) - LIBRARY (Theater)
Route 3   Phone: (608) 588-7401
Spring Green, WI 53588   Margaret L. Hayes, Libn.
Founded: 1977. **Staff:** Prof 2. **Subjects:** Shakespeare; drama - English, French, German, Greek, Russian; language and languages; theater and theaters; religion and philosophy. **Holdings:** 6502 books and bound periodical volumes; 5 boxes of scripts; 4 boxes of playbills and theater programs; 2 boxes of theater reviews; 2 drawers of archives; memorabilia; architectural drawings. **Subscriptions:** 10 journals and other serials. **Services:** Interlibrary loans; copying; SDI; library open to public for reference use only. **Staff:** Kathleen Jakel, Libn.

★566★
AMERICAN PLYWOOD ASSOCIATION - INFORMATION CENTER (Sci-Tech)
Box 11700   Phone: (206) 565-6600
Tacoma, WA 98411   June Packer, Rec.Mgr.
Founded: 1968. **Staff:** Prof 1. **Subjects:** Forestry, plywood, plywood statistics, business. **Special Collections:** Plywood Historical Monographs. **Holdings:** 500 books and bound periodical volumes; 150 forest products laboratory reports; 20 VF drawers of U.S. Government material; 100 boxes of association material. **Subscriptions:** 250 journals and other serials; 5 newspapers. **Services:** Interlibrary loans; copying; literature searching; library open to public with restrictions. **Publications:** New Acquisitions, irregular.

★567★
AMERICAN PODIATRY ASSOCIATION - WILLIAM J. STICKEL MEMORIAL LIBRARY (Med)†
20 Chevy Chase Circle, N.W.   Phone: (202) 537-4900
Washington, DC 20015   Roberta McVeigh, Libn.
Subjects: Podiatry. **Holdings:** 500 books; 40 VF drawers; films, filmstrips and slides. **Subscriptions:** 50 journals and other serials.

AMERICAN POLITICAL SCIENCE ASSOCIATION ARCHIVES
See: Georgetown University - Special Collection Division

★568★
AMERICAN POWER JET COMPANY - LIBRARY (Sci-Tech)
705 Grand Ave.   Phone: (201) 945-8203
Ridgefield, NJ 07657   Harriet Wolf, Libn.
Staff: Prof 1. **Subjects:** Applied science, mathematics, statistics. **Holdings:** 17,000 items. **Subscriptions:** 31 journals and other serials. **Services:** Library not open to public.

★569★
AMERICAN PSYCHIATRIC MUSEUM ASSOCIATION - LIBRARY AND ARCHIVES (Med)
1700 18th St., N.W.   Phone: (202) 232-7878
Washington, DC 20009   Zing Jung, Dir.
Founded: 1961. **Staff:** Prof 3; Other 2. **Subjects:** Psychiatry, history of American psychiatry, psychoanalysis, community and social psychiatry, psychosomatic medicine, child and adolescent psychiatry. **Special Collections:** Rare Book Collection; APA Archives. **Holdings:** 17,000 books; 5000 bound periodical volumes. **Subscriptions:** 200 journals and other serials; 2 newspapers. **Services:** Interlibrary loans; copying; current awareness; library open to public with permission of librarian. **Computerized Information Services:** BRS, MEDLARS.

★570★
AMERICAN PSYCHOLOGICAL ASSOCIATION - ARTHUR W. MELTON LIBRARY (Soc Sci)
1400 N. Uhle St.   Phone: (202) 833-7590
Arlington, VA 22201   Elizabeth B. Lawton, Libn.
Founded: 1971. **Staff:** Prof 2. **Subjects:** Psychology and related disciplines. **Special Collections:** APA central office, division and state association journals and publications, 1894 to present; Journal Supplement Abstracts Service manuscripts on microfiche. **Holdings:** 4400 books and journals. **Services:** Interlibrary loans; copying; library open to qualified researchers by appointment. **Computerized Information Services:** PsychINFO Data Base Search and Retrieval (computerized literature search). **Special Indexes:** Index to Psychological Abstracts. **Remarks:** The library also manages the American Psychological Association Archives. **Staff:** Peggy Mechanic, Asst.Libn.

★571★
AMERICAN PSYCHOTHERAPY ASSOCIATION - LIBRARY (Soc Sci)
Box 2436
West Palm Beach, FL 33402   Sandra Simonds, Dir.
Founded: 1974. **Staff:** Prof 1. **Subjects:** Religion, psychology, psychotherapy, behavioral sciences. **Holdings:** 1100 books. **Services:** Copying; library not open to public.

★572★
AMERICAN PUBLIC HEALTH ASSOCIATION - INTERNATIONAL HEALTH PROGRAMS - RESOURCE CENTER (Med; Soc Sci)
1015 15th St., N.W.   Phone: (202) 789-5710
Washington, DC 20005   Maria Emma McMurtry, Mgr.
Staff: Prof 1; Other 1. **Subjects:** Developing countries - health delivery systems, nutrition, development, water and sanitation, family planning, maternal and child health. **Special Collections:** Association reports (400); primary health care collection. **Holdings:** 1000 books; 130 newsletters; 120 pamphlet boxes; reports, monographs. **Subscriptions:** 110 journals and other serials. **Services:** Interlibrary loans; copying; library open to public with restrictions. **Computerized Information Services:** DIALOG, NTIS. **Publications:** Information packets, bimonthly.

★573★
AMERICAN PUBLIC POWER ASSOCIATION - LIBRARY (Energy)
2301 M St., N.W.   Phone: (202) 342-7200
Washington, DC 20037   Deborah Nuttall, Libn.
Staff: Prof 2. **Subjects:** Electric utilities, energy, environment. **Holdings:** 1500 books; 60 bound periodical volumes; 2000 volumes of technical reports; 1000 volumes of congressional documents; 82 VF drawers. **Subscriptions:** 123 journals and other serials. **Services:** Interlibrary loans; copying; library open to public by appointment. **Special Indexes:** Public Power,

Public Power Weekly Newsletter and APPA Conference and Workshop papers. **Staff:** Anne Darlington, Asst.Libn.

★574★

AMERICAN PUBLIC TRANSIT ASSOCIATION - LIBRARY (Trans)
1225 Connecticut Ave., N.W., Suite 200   Phone: (202) 828-2843
Washington, DC 20036   Tandy L. Stevens, Mgr.
Staff: Prof 1; Other 1. **Subjects:** Mass transit, rail rapid transit, transit systems, transit operations and equipment. **Holdings:** 500 books; 50 bound periodical volumes; 150 VF drawers of reports and newspaper clippings. **Subscriptions:** 80 journals and other serials. **Services:** Library open to public with restrictions. **Staff:** Rose M. Gandee, Asst.Libn.

★575★

AMERICAN PUBLIC WORKS ASSOCIATION - INFORMATION SERVICE (Trans; Plan)
1313 E. 60th St.   Phone: (312) 667-2200
Chicago, IL 60637   Mary K. Simon, Dir. of Info.
Staff: Prof 2; Other 1. **Subjects:** Public works, buildings and grounds management, transportation, solid waste, equipment services, water resources. **Special Collections:** Public Works Historical Society Collection; University of Wyoming American Heritage Center Archives. **Holdings:** 5000 volumes. **Subscriptions:** 350 journals and other serials; 15 newspapers. **Services:** Interlibrary loans; copying; library open to public with restrictions. **Computerized Information Services:** DIALOG. **Networks/Consortia:** Member of Metropolitan Chicago Library Assembly. **Publications:** Access to Information; Public Works History Archives; monthly column in APWA magazine, The Reporter. **Staff:** Mary Beth Sasso, Libn./Info.Spec.

★576★

AMERICAN RAILWAY CAR INSTITUTE - LIBRARY (Trans)
303 E. Wacker Dr.
Chicago, IL 60601   Elwyn T. Ahnquist, Pres.
Subjects: Transportation, railroad cars. **Holdings:** Figures not available.

★577★

AMERICAN RED CROSS - NATIONAL HEADQUARTERS LIBRARY (Soc Sci)
17th & D Sts., N.W.   Phone: (202) 857-3491
Washington, DC 20006   Roberta F. Biles, Lib.Dir.
Founded: 1910. **Staff:** Prof 4; Other 2. **Subjects:** Red Cross (American, other national and international societies); voluntary agencies; disaster relief; medicine; nursing; social work. **Special Collections:** U.S. Sanitary Commission documents; American Red Cross historical monographs; Henry P. Davison Red Cross papers. **Holdings:** 16,000 books and bound periodical volumes; 330 VF drawers of pamphlets, agency material, clippings and reprints; 380 reels of microfilm. **Subscriptions:** 450 journals and other serials. **Services:** Interlibrary loans; copying; reference and limited research services are provided in areas of American Red Cross bibliographical, statistical and historical materials; library open to qualified persons for reference use. **Publications:** Acquisitions list - for internal distribution only. **Staff:** Meyer Mathis, Dir., Off.Gen.Adm.; Leon Gilbert, Translator; Rudolf A. Clemen, Jr., Info.Res.Spec.

★578★

AMERICAN RIVER HOSPITAL - ERLE M. BLUNDEN MEMORIAL LIBRARY (Med)
4747 Engle Rd.   Phone: (916) 486-2128
Carmichael, CA 95608   Carolyn Kopper, Health Sci.Libn.
Founded: 1965. **Staff:** 1. **Subjects:** Medicine, nursing, psychiatry, hospital administration. **Holdings:** 500 books. **Subscriptions:** 100 journals and other serials. **Services:** Interlibrary loans; library open to hospital staff. **Also Known As:** Eskaton American River Hospital.

★579★

AMERICAN ROSE SOCIETY - LIBRARY (Sci-Tech)
Box 30,000   Phone: (318) 938-5402
Shreveport, LA 71130   Harold S. Goldstein, Exec.Dir.
Founded: 1899. **Subjects:** Roses and rose culture, horticulture, landscape design. **Special Collections:** Old and rare volumes on roses. **Holdings:** 7200 books and bound periodical volumes; 100 boxes of manuscripts, articles, and research data; 1200 slides. **Subscriptions:** 142 journals. **Services:** Library open to public for special reference or research; mail rental of materials for members only.

AMERICAN SADDLE HORSE MUSEUM LIBRARY
See: Audrain County Historical Society - Ross House Library/American Saddle Horse Museum Library

★580★

AMERICAN-SCANDINAVIAN FOUNDATION - WILLIAM HENRY SCHOFIELD MEMORIAL LIBRARY
127 E. 73rd St.
New York, NY 10021
Subjects: Books in English and in the Scandinavian languages on the history, art, geography and description of the Scandinavian countries - Denmark, Finland, Iceland, Norway, Sweden; Scandinavian fiction in the original languages; Scandinavian fiction in English translation. **Holdings:** 4000 volumes; manuscripts, letters and clippings. **Remarks:** Presently inactive.

★581★

AMERICAN SCIENCE FICTION ASSOCIATION - ASFA LIBRARY (Rec)
Box 10   Phone: (702) 361-4703
Port Neches, TX 77651   P.G. Silvers, Hd., Lib.Serv.
Staff: Prof 4; Other 4. **Subjects:** Science fiction, fantasy. **Special Collections:** SF Gold Medal Books (48 volumes). **Holdings:** 6400 books; 1120 bound periodical volumes; 7200 manuscripts; 4000 dissertations. **Subscriptions:** 16 journals and other serials. **Services:** Copying; library open to public with restrictions. **Computerized Information Services:** Computerized cataloging and circulation. **Publications:** Cross Reference Catalog, annual update. **Special Catalogs:** Science Fiction and Fantasy Combined Catalog; Cross Reference Catalog. **Remarks:** The library's executive office address is 421 E. Carson St., Suite 95, Las Vegas, NV 89119.

★582★

AMERICAN-SCOTTISH FOUNDATION, INC. - SCOTTISH RESEARCH LIBRARY (Area-Ethnic)†
Lenox Hill Sta., Box 537   Phone: (212) 249-5556
New York, NY 10021   Lady Malcolm Douglas-Hamilton, Pres.
Founded: 1976. **Staff:** 4. **Subjects:** Scotland - clans, history, traditions, literature, genealogy, travel. **Holdings:** Figures not available. **Subscriptions:** 150 journals and other serials; 4 Scottish newspapers. **Services:** Library open to public. **Publications:** Newsletter of American-Scottish Foundation: Calling All Scots. **Remarks:** Library is located at 174 E. 74th St., New York, NY 10021.

★583★

AMERICAN SECURITY COUNCIL EDUCATION FOUNDATION - SOL FEINSTONE LIBRARY (Mil)†
                                              Phone: (703) 825-1776
Boston, VA 22713   John M. Fisher, Pres.
Founded: 1973. **Staff:** Prof 4. **Subjects:** National defense, international affairs. **Holdings:** 16,000 books; 3000 government hearings; 3500 vertical files. **Subscriptions:** 390 journals and other serials; 30 newspapers. **Services:** Copying; library not open to public. **Computerized Information Services:** Computerized cataloging and acquisitions. **Special Indexes:** Special indexes for internal use. **Remarks:** The library receives almost every English language defense publication from around the world. It receives all relevant Congressional hearings and nonclassified U.S. Dept. of Defense and CIA reports on national defense, and receives many foreign radio broadcast summaries. **Also Known As:** Sol Feinstone Library for the Survival of Freedom.

★584★

AMERICAN SEED TRADE ASSOCIATION - LIBRARY (Agri)
Suite 964 Executive Bldg.
1030 15th St., N.W.
Washington, DC 20005
Founded: 1883. **Staff:** Prof 4; Other 4. **Subjects:** Seed raising, development, conditioning and marketing. **Special Collections:** Proceedings of the Corn & Sorghum Industry Research Conferences, the Soybean Seed Research Conferences and the Farm Seed Research Conferences. **Holdings:** 500 books; 20 bound periodical volumes. **Services:** Library not open to public. **Special Catalogs:** Vegetable variety listing (card).

★585★

AMERICAN SHORT LINE RAILROAD ASSOCIATION - LIBRARY (Trans)
2000 Massachusetts Ave., N.W.   Phone: (202) 785-2250
Washington, DC 20036   P.H. Croft, Pres.
Founded: 1913. **Subjects:** Transportation and railroads. **Special Collections:** Legislative histories and legal records relating to railroads and railway labor organizations. **Holdings:** Figures not available. **Services:** Library is open to public for research only with prior approval.

AMERICAN SMELTING AND REFINING COMPANY
See: ASARCO Inc.

★586★

AMERICAN SOCIETY OF ABDOMINAL SURGEONS - DONALD COLLINS MEMORIAL LIBRARY (Med)
675 Main St.   Phone: (617) 665-6102
Melrose, MA 02176   Dr. Blaise F. Alfano, Hd.Libn.
Staff: Prof 2. **Subjects:** Surgery, medicine. **Holdings:** 900 books; 45 bound periodical volumes. **Subscriptions:** 52 journals and other serials; 10 newspapers. **Services:** Interlibrary loans; library open to public on request. **Staff:** Priscilla Maher, Asst.Libn.

★587★

AMERICAN SOCIETY FOR AEROSPACE EDUCATION (Educ; Sci-Tech)†
1750 Pennsylvania Ave. N.W., Suite 1303   Phone: (202) 347-5187
Washington, DC 20006   Julie Bettenberg, Rsrcs.Ed.
Subjects: Aeronautics, astronautics, aerospace education, meteorology, astronomy. **Holdings:** 1000 books; teacher guides, curricula, directories, career information. **Subscriptions:** 100 journals and other serials. **Services:** Library not open to public. **Publications:** Aviation/Space, the Journal of Aerospace Education, bimonthly - by subscription; Directory of Aerospace Education, biennial - free with subscription; Book of Aerospace Education.

★588★

AMERICAN SOCIETY OF AGRONOMY - INFORMATION CENTER (Agri)
677 S. Segoe Rd.   Phone: (608) 274-1212
Madison, WI 53711
Subjects: Agronomy, crops, soils. **Holdings:** Figures not available. **Services:** Library not open to public. **Publications:** List of publications - available upon request. **Remarks:** Affiliated with Soil Science Society of America and Crop Science Society of America.

★589★

AMERICAN SOCIETY OF ANCIENT INSTRUMENTS - LIBRARY (Mus)
1205 Blythe Ave.   Phone: (215) 789-1205
Drexel Hill, PA 19026   Frederick Stad, V.P.
Founded: 1929. **Staff:** Prof 1. **Subjects:** Renaissance and Baroque instrumental and vocal music. **Holdings:** 60 books; 2940 pieces of sheet music; 150 tape recordings; 200 records; 8 reels of microfilmed facsimile music; archives (uncataloged). **Services:** Library not open to public.

★590★

AMERICAN SOCIETY OF ANESTHESIOLOGISTS - WOOD LIBRARY-MUSEUM OF ANESTHESIOLOGY (Med)
515 Busse Hwy.   Phone: (312) 825-5586
Park Ridge, IL 60068   Patrick Sim, Libn.
Founded: 1929. **Staff:** Prof 1. **Subjects:** Anesthesiology, resuscitation, shock, hypnotism (medical application), inhalation therapy, history of medicine. **Special Collections:** Museum of anesthesiological equipment and apparatus. **Holdings:** 8000 books; 1000 bound periodical volumes; 40 VF drawers of pamphlets, photographs, clippings; 20 shelf feet of manuscripts. **Subscriptions:** 65 journals and other serials. **Services:** Interlibrary loans; copying; library open to public. **Networks/Consortia:** Supplementary resource library of Regional Medical Library - Region 3. **Publications:** Anesthesiology Bibliography, quarterly; Residents Reading List; History of Anesthesiology Reprints Series, annual; Self-Evaluation Program Reference Manual for Anesthesiologists.

★591★

AMERICAN SOCIETY OF APPRAISERS - INTERNATIONAL VALUATION SCIENCES CENTRE LIBRARY (Bus-Fin; Law)†
Dulles Intl. Airport
Box 17265   Phone: (703) 620-3838
Washington, DC 20041   Suzann Allen, Hd.Libn.
Founded: 1977. **Staff:** 1. **Subjects:** Appraisal of real estate, personal property, natural resources; eminent domain. **Special Collections:** Masters theses. **Holdings:** 1100 books and bound periodical volumes; 100 papers and pamphlets. **Subscriptions:** 31 journals and other serials. **Services:** Copying; library open to public with restrictions. **Publications:** ASA Valuation, annual; ASA Monographs, irregular. **Special Catalogs:** Bibliography of appraisal literature, with about 10,000 references, also for sale.

★592★

AMERICAN SOCIETY OF ARTISTS, INC. - RESOURCE CENTER (Art)
1297 Merchandise Mart Plaza   Phone: (312) 751-2500
Chicago, IL 60654   Donald Metcoff, Libn.
Founded: 1978. **Staff:** Prof 1. **Subjects:** Art, crafts, supplies. **Special Collections:** Foreign art catalogs and journals; slide and photo files of arts and crafts by members of the society. **Holdings:** 25 volumes; 43 VF drawers. **Subscriptions:** 11 journals and other serials. **Services:** Lectures, demonstrations and workshops are available; center open to public with restrictions. **Publications:** Lecture and Demonstration Service Guide; Art Lovers Bulletin, quarterly; ASA Bulletin, quarterly - to members. **Special Catalogs:** Arts and crafts supply catalogs. **Remarks:** The society has a national membership of professional artists and craftspeople.

★593★

AMERICAN SOCIETY OF ASSOCIATION EXECUTIVES - INFORMATION CENTRAL (Bus-Fin)†
1575 Eye St., N.W., 12th Fl.   Phone: (202) 626-2723
Washington, DC 20005   Elissa Matulis Myers, Dir., Res. & Info.
Founded: 1954. **Staff:** Prof 4; Other 4. **Subjects:** All phases of association management. **Special Collections:** Bound volumes of Association Management, the official ASAE monthly publication. **Holdings:** 1500 books and research publications; 40,000 (105 VF drawers) cataloged loan items; hotel evaluation file; speaker evaluation file. **Subscriptions:** 34 journals and other serials. **Services:** Distributive literature available for purchase; loan material available to members and nonmembers. **Publications:** ASAE Information Central Catalog, annual list of publications available from ASAE.

★594★

AMERICAN SOCIETY OF BAKERY ENGINEERS - INFORMATION SERVICE AND LIBRARY (Food-Bev)†
2 N. Riverside Plaza, Rm. 1921   Phone: (312) 332-2246
Chicago, IL 60606   Robert A. Fischer, Sec.-Treas.
Subjects: Baking and related subjects. **Holdings:** 10,000 references.

★595★

AMERICAN SOCIETY OF CIVIL ENGINEERS - INFORMATION SERVICES (Sci-Tech)
345 E. 47th St.   Phone: (212) 705-7520
New York, NY 10017   Melanie G. Edwards, Mgr., Tech.Info.Serv.
Staff: Prof 1; Other 1. **Subjects:** Civil engineering. **Special Collections:** ASCE Transactions (all volumes); ASCE Proceedings (all volumes); journals of various divisions of the society. **Holdings:** Figures not available. **Subscriptions:** 16 journals and other serials. **Services:** Services open to public. **Computerized Information Services:** Computerized circulation and typesetting for information services. **Publications:** ASCE Publications Abstracts, bimonthly; ASCE Combined Index, annual; ASCE Cumulative Index, irregular; ASCE Transactions, annual; ASCE Directory, biennial; Index to Civil Engineering magazine, annual.

★596★

AMERICAN SOCIETY OF DOWSERS, INC. - LIBRARY (Rec)
                                          Phone: (802) 684-3417
Danville, VT 05828   Paul J. Sevigny, Pres.
Staff: 1. **Subjects:** Dowsing - history, theory and practice. **Holdings:** 300 books; 25 bound periodical volumes; 8 scrapbooks. **Services:** Library open to public by appointment.

★597★

AMERICAN SOCIETY FOR INFORMATION SCIENCE - INFORMATION CENTER (Info Sci)
1010 Sixteenth St., N.W.   Phone: (202) 659-3644
Washington, DC 20036
Founded: 1937. **Staff:** Prof 3; Other 3. **Subjects:** Information systems and technology - design, management, use. **Holdings:** Figures not available. **Services:** Library open to public for reference use only. **Publications:** Bulletin and Journal of ASIS, both bimonthly - by subscription.

★598★

AMERICAN SOCIETY OF INTERNATIONAL LAW - LIBRARY (Law)
2223 Massachusetts Ave., N.W.   Phone: (202) 265-4313
Washington, DC 20008   Helen S. Philos, Libn.
Subjects: International law and related subjects. **Holdings:** 8000 books; 3000 bound periodical volumes; 6500 pamphlets, documents and reprints (cataloged). **Subscriptions:** 350 journals and other serials. **Services:** Interlibrary loans; copying; library open to public.

★599★

AMERICAN SOCIETY OF LAW & MEDICINE - ELLIOT L. AND ANNETTE Y. SAGALL LIBRARY (Law; Med)
765 Commonwealth Ave., 16th Fl.   Phone: (617) 262-4990
Boston, MA 02215   Kim Simmons, Libn.
Founded: 1979. **Staff:** Prof 1. **Subjects:** Medicolegal relations, health law, medical malpractice, forensic medicine. **Holdings:** 3500 books; 4000 VF items covering journal articles and court cases. **Subscriptions:** 300 journals and other serials. **Services:** Interlibrary loans; copying; library open to public.

★600★

AMERICAN SOCIETY FOR MEDICAL TECHNOLOGY - LIBRARY (Med)†
330 Meadowfern Dr.   Phone: (713) 893-7072
Houston, TX 77067
Subjects: Cytology, histology, microbiology, hematology, biochemistry.
Holdings: Films and filmstrips.

★601★

AMERICAN SOCIETY FOR METALS - METALS INFORMATION (Sci-Tech)
                                             Phone: (216) 338-5151
Metals Park, OH 44073   William A. Weida, Libn.
Founded: 1960. **Staff:** Prof 1; Other 3. **Subjects:** Technical information
related to all aspects of metals and metallurgy - extraction and refining,
fabrication, properties, applications, and including areas of mechanical
engineering, electrical engineering, electronics, solid state physics, and
inorganic chemistry. **Special Collections:** Eisenmann Rare Book Collection (54
titles dating from 1534 to 1893); Henry Brutcher Technical Translations.
Holdings: 9000 books; reports, reprints, pamphlets, microfilm.
Subscriptions: 1200 journals and other serials. **Services:** Interlibrary loans;
copying; information searching services, retrospective and current awareness
(SDI); translation distribution service; bibliography series; library open to
public. **Computerized Information Services:** METADEX (tape lease program);
DIALOG. **Publications:** Metals Abstracts; Digest series; World Aluminum
Abstracts, monthly - by subscription; ASM Translations Index, quarterly;
Source Journals in Metallurgy, irregular. **Staff:** Betty A. Bryan, Asst.Dir.;
Joseph Davis, Mgr., Info. Retrieval.

★602★

AMERICAN SOCIETY OF MILITARY HISTORY - LIBRARY (Mil)*
1816 S. Figueroa St.   Phone: (213) 746-1776
Los Angeles, CA 90015   Donald Michelson, Exec.Dir.
Staff: Prof 1; Other 3. **Subjects:** Military history. **Holdings:** 10,000 books;
7000 bound periodical volumes; 5000 defense department papers. **Services:**
Library open to public.

★603★

**AMERICAN SOCIETY FOR NONDESTRUCTIVE TESTING - LIBRARY AND
   INFORMATION CENTER** (Sci-Tech)
Caller 28518   Phone: (614) 274-6003
Columbus, OH 43228   Michael P. Walcoff, Mgr.
Subjects: Nondestructive testing - industrial radiography, eddy currents,
magnetic particles, penetrants, ultrasonics. **Holdings:** 332 volumes; 1500
technical reports; manuscripts, microfilms, slides, films, and tapes. **Services:**
Copying; library serves members primarily.

★604★

AMERICAN SOCIETY OF NOTARIES - LIBRARY (Law)
810 18th St., N.W.   Phone: (202) 347-7303
Washington, DC 20006   Eugene E. Hines, Exec.Dir.
Founded: 1965. **Staff:** Prof 1. **Subjects:** Law of notary public; commercial
law; trade associations. **Holdings:** 400 books; 500 ancient notarized
documents, deeds and other memorabilia of the office of notary public.
Services: Interlibrary loans; copying; library open to public with restrictions.

★605★

AMERICAN SOCIETY OF PHOTOGRAMMETRY - HEINZ GRUNER LIBRARY
   (Geog-Map)
210 Little Falls St.   Phone: (703) 534-6617
Falls Church, VA 22046   William D. French, Exec.Dir.
Founded: 1979. **Subjects:** Photogrammetry, remote sensing, mapping,
photography. **Holdings:** 1000 books; 45 bound periodical volumes;
proceedings of technical meetings; 4 shelves of technical reports.
Subscriptions: 57 journals and other serials. **Services:** Interlibrary loans;
library open to public for reference use only. **Publications:** Photogrammetric
Engineering and Remote Sensing, monthly - to society members and
subscribers. **Special Indexes:** Complete Index to Photogrammetric
Engineering and Remote Sensing, 1934-1979 (book).

★606★

AMERICAN SOCIETY FOR PSYCHICAL RESEARCH - LIBRARY (Sci-Tech)
5 W. 73rd St.   Phone: (212) 799-5050
New York, NY 10023   Laura F. Knipe, Exec.Sec.
Founded: 1885. **Staff:** Prof 1; Other 5. **Subjects:** Parapsychology, psychical
research, spiritualism, philosophy, psychology, religion. **Special Collections:**
Shaker materials; Mediumistic sittings; archive materials. **Holdings:** 6000
books; 400 bound periodical volumes. **Subscriptions:** 32 journals and other
serials. **Services:** Interlibrary loans; copying; library open to public with
restrictions. **Publications:** Journal of the American Society for Psychical
Research; ASPR newsletter, both quarterly - to members only. **Special**

Indexes: Index for Journal from 1885 to present. **Staff:** Rhea A. White,
Cons.

★607★

AMERICAN SOCIETY FOR QUALITY CONTROL - LIBRARY (Sci-Tech)
230 W. Wells St.   Phone: (414) 272-8575
Milwaukee, WI 53203   Debra Owens, Dir., Tech.Serv.
Staff: Prof 1; Other 1. **Subjects:** Quality assurance, quality control, statistical
quality control and quality management in: consumer products, fabrication
industries, health and process industries, standards activities, quality
methodologies and technologies. **Special Collections:** ASQC publications.
Holdings: Figures not available. **Services:** Copying; library open to public for
reference use only with prior appointment. **Staff:** Patricia Y. Vosteen, Mgr.,
Div. & Tech.Comm.

★608★

**AMERICAN SOCIETY OF SAFETY ENGINEERS - TECHNICAL INFORMATION
   CENTER** (Sci-Tech)
850 Busse Hwy.   Phone: (312) 692-4121
Park Ridge, IL 60068   T.H. Honn, Dir., Educ.
Founded: 1911. **Staff:** Prof 10. **Subjects:** Safety, fire, occupational health,
loss prevention. **Services:** Copying (limited); library not open to public.
Publications: Professional Safety Magazine, monthly. **Staff:** Dwight B. Esau,
Dir., Tech.Pubn.

★609★

AMERICAN SOCIETY OF SUGAR BEET TECHNOLOGISTS - LIBRARY (Agri;
   Sci-Tech)
Box 1546   Phone: (303) 482-8250
Fort Collins, CO 80522   James H. Fischer, Sec.-Treas.
Subjects: Agronomy, entomology, plant pathology, agricultural engineering,
sugar beet chemistry, sugar beet production. **Holdings:** Journals, reports,
foreign literature and data exchange from European countries. **Also Known
As:** Beet Sugar Development Foundation.

★610★

**AMERICAN SOCIETY FOR TESTING AND MATERIALS - INFORMATION
   CENTER** (Sci-Tech)
1916 Race St.   Phone: (215) 299-5474
Philadelphia, PA 19103   Dolores G. Collyer, Adm.
Founded: 1960. **Staff:** 1. **Subjects:** Standards, materials science. **Holdings:**
3400 books; 13,000 unbound standards. **Subscriptions:** 270 journals and
other serials. **Services:** Center open to public for reference use only.

★611★

AMERICAN SOCIETY OF TRAVEL AGENTS - LIBRARY (Bus-Fin)†
711 Fifth Ave.   Phone: (212) 486-0700
New York, NY 10022   Arthur Schiff, Staff V.P.
Subjects: Travel and tourism. **Holdings:** Biographical archives.

★612★

**AMERICAN SOKOL EDUCATION AND PHYSICAL CULTURE ORGANIZATION
   - LIBRARY** (Rec)
6424 W. Cermak Rd.   Phone: (312) 795-6671
Berwyn, IL 60402
Founded: 1976. **Staff:** 1. **Subjects:** Athletics, gymnastics, physical fitness,
Czech and Sokol history. **Holdings:** 1000 books; 250 bound periodical
volumes. **Subscriptions:** 16 journals and other serials. **Services:** Copying;
library open to members of the organization for reference use only.

★613★

AMERICAN SOYBEAN ASSOCIATION - LIBRARY (Agri; Food-Bev)
777 Craig Rd.
Box 27300   Phone: (314) 432-1600
St. Louis, MO 63141
Founded: 1977. **Staff:** Prof 1. **Subjects:** Agriculture, economics, nutrition,
food processing. **Special Collections:** Technical papers on soy production and
utilization. **Holdings:** 3000 books. **Subscriptions:** 502 journals and other
serials. **Services:** Interlibrary loans; copying; library open to public with
restrictions. **Networks/Consortia:** Member of St. Louis Regional Library
Network. **Publications:** Soybean Digest; Soybean Update; Animal Nutrition
Highlights; bibliographies on current research.

★614★

AMERICAN STANDARDS TESTING BUREAU, INC. - SAM TOUR LIBRARY
   (Sci-Tech)
40 Water St.   Phone: (212) 943-3157
New York, NY 10004   Mr. C. Chavis, Libn.
Staff: Prof 2. **Subjects:** Standards and specifications - chemistry, metallurgy,

applied physics, applied mechanics. **Holdings:** 15,000 books. **Subscriptions:** 100 journals and other serials. **Services:** Interlibrary loans; library open to public with restrictions.

★615★
AMERICAN STATES INSURANCE COMPANY - LIBRARY (Bus-Fin)
500 N. Meridian St.
Box 1636   Phone: (317) 262-6560
Indianapolis, IN 46207   Sue Overstreet, Libn.
Founded: 1973. **Staff:** Prof 1. **Subjects:** Law, insurance, management, psychology, accounting. **Holdings:** 8500 books; 20 bound periodical volumes; 300 cassette tapes. **Subscriptions:** 150 journals and other serials. **Services:** Interlibrary loans; copying; library open to public on request. **Computerized Information Services:** Mechanized services.

★616★
AMERICAN STERILIZER COMPANY - LIBRARY (Sci-Tech; Med)
2424 W. 23rd St.   Phone: (814) 452-3100
Erie, PA 16512   Janis M. Ruben, Info.Spec.
Founded: 1959. **Staff:** Prof 1; Other 1. **Subjects:** Bacteriology, medicine, microbiology, engineering, industrial design, marketing, management. **Holdings:** 3500 books; 300 bound periodical volumes; 13 drawers of reprints; microforms; 8 drawers of patents. **Subscriptions:** 350 journals and other serials. **Services:** Interlibrary loans; library open to public with identification. **Computerized Information Services:** DIALOG; internal database. **Networks/Consortia:** Member of Erie Health Information Library Cooperative; Northwest Interlibrary Cooperative of Pennsylvania.

★617★
AMERICAN STOCK EXCHANGE - MARTIN J. KEENA MEMORIAL LIBRARY (Bus-Fin)
86 Trinity Pl.   Phone: (212) 938-2280
New York, NY 10006   Karen E. Buchanan, Hd.Libn.
Founded: 1966. **Staff:** 5. **Subjects:** Corporation records (U.S. annual reports, prospectuses, proxies), government regulations, stock exchanges. **Special Collections:** Prices of all stocks listed on AMEX, 1930 to present. **Holdings:** 300 books; 100 bound periodical volumes; corporate reports of 1000 listed companies; 5000 reels of microfilm; 125,000 microfiche. **Subscriptions:** 100 journals and other serials. **Services:** Interlibrary loans; library open to public.

★618★
AMERICAN SUFFOLK HORSE ASSOCIATION (ASHA) - LIBRARY (Rec)†
15 B Roden   Phone: (817) 855-6998
Wichita Falls, TX 76311   Mary Margaret M. Read, Sec.
Staff: 1. **Subjects:** Most complete collection of Suffolk horse material in North America. **Holdings:** Figures not available.

★619★
AMERICAN SURVIVAL ASSOCIATION - REFERENCE LIBRARY (Sci-Tech)
Box 213   Phone: (801) 635-4671
La Verkin, UT 84745   Donald R. Spradling, V.P.
Founded: 1980. **Staff:** 1. **Subjects:** Survival, homesteading. **Holdings:** 500 books; 600 newsletters. **Subscriptions:** 50 journals and other serials. **Services:** Library open to public. **Publications:** American Survivalist Newsletter.

★620★
AMERICAN SWEDISH HISTORICAL MUSEUM - NORD LIBRARY (Hist; Area-Ethnic)
1900 Pattison Ave.   Phone: (215) 389-1776
Philadelphia, PA 19145   Ann-Kristin Bohlin, Cur.
Founded: 1926. **Staff:** 1. **Subjects:** Books by and about Swedish Americans; Swedish colonization of the Delaware Valley; religion (Swedish contributions to religious life in the U.S.); reference works pertaining to Sweden, Swedish culture, literature, handcrafts. **Special Collections:** John Ericsson, Jenny Lind and Fredrika Bremer collections; diaries, letters, other memoirs of Swedish immigrants. **Holdings:** 14,000 books and bound periodical volumes; manuscripts, clippings, pamphlets, dissertations, documents, slides, maps, prints, and pictures. **Subscriptions:** 19 journals and other serials. **Services:** Interlibrary loans; copying; inquiries answered; libraries open to students and scholars for research. **Publications:** Newsletter, 6/year - distributed to members and consulates.

★621★
AMERICAN SWEDISH INSTITUTE - LIBRARY (Area-Ethnic)
2600 Park Ave., S.   Phone: (612) 871-4907
Minneapolis, MN 55407   Dagmar Getz, Archv./Libn.
Staff: Prof 2. **Subjects:** Swedish history and culture, Swedish immigration

history. **Holdings:** 13,000 books; 212 reels of microfilm. **Subscriptions:** 10 journals and other serials; 7 newspapers. **Services:** Library open to public by appointment only. **Staff:** Susan Larson-Fleming, Archv./Libn.

★622★
AMERICAN SYMPHONY ORCHESTRA LEAGUE - LIBRARY (Mus)
Box 669   Phone: (703) 281-1230
Vienna, VA 22180   Joy A. Hulse, Adm.Asst.
Founded: 1942. **Subjects:** Orchestra management, performance issues, non-profit organizations. **Holdings:** Books; programs and brochures; operational and financial data; orchestra files; music publications. **Subscriptions:** 22 journals and other serials. **Services:** Library not open to public. **Publications:** Symphony Magazine, bimonthly - to league members. **Remarks:** League archives containing clippings, programs, brochures and correspondence are located at George Mason University, Fairfax, VA 22030.

★623★
AMERICAN TEILHARD ASSOCIATION FOR THE FUTURE OF MAN - LIBRARY (Rel-Theol)†
Box 67   Phone: (212) 920-0114
White Plains, NY 10604   Donald P. Gray
Founded: 1968. **Subjects:** Jesuit theologian-scientist Teilhard de Chardin. **Holdings:** 670 books; 2 VF drawers of manuscript material and dissertations; writings by Teilhard de Chardin in French and English; scholarly criticisms; related works. **Services:** Library open to members and others by permission. **Publications:** Newsletter; Teilhard Studies, semiannual - sent to members and subscribers. **Remarks:** The library is located at Manhattan College, 4513 Manhattan College Pkwy., Bronx, NY 10471.

★624★
AMERICAN TELEPHONE & TELEGRAPH COMPANY - BUSINESS SERVICES EDUCATION - LEARNING RESOURCE CENTER (Sci-Tech)
4765 Oakland St.   Phone: (303) 370-8746
Denver, CO 80239   Kathy L. Weimer, Asst.Mgr.
Founded: 1980. **Staff:** Prof 1; Other 1. **Subjects:** Telecommunication, private branch exchanges, engineering, computer science, instructional design. **Special Collections:** Bell System Dimension PBX materials. **Holdings:** 226 books; 286 other cataloged items; 21,000 Bell System technical documents; 3000 microfiche; 1200 reels of microfilm. **Subscriptions:** 49 journals and other serials. **Services:** Copying; SDI; center not open to public. **Computerized Information Services:** DIALOG; internal database. **Publications:** Information Update, quarterly - for internal distribution only; Advance Printing list, monthly - to instructors and course developers. **Special Indexes:** Engineering letters index (book); documents cross reference lists (book).

★625★
AMERICAN TELEPHONE & TELEGRAPH COMPANY - BUSINESS & TECHNICAL RESOURCE CENTER (Bus-Fin)
444 Hoes Ln., Rm. 10-4 A1000   Phone: (201) 699-2169
Piscataway, NJ 08854   Betty J. Kauffman, Hd.Libn.
Founded: 1976. **Staff:** Prof 2; Other 5. **Subjects:** Computers, management, training, psychology, economics, statistics, mathematics, telecommunications. **Holdings:** 10,000 books; 1750 bound periodical volumes; 1150 reels of microfilm of periodical holdings; 680 microfiche; 2595 documents and pamphlets in information file. **Subscriptions:** 790 journals and other serials; 10 newspapers. **Services:** Interlibrary loans; copying; library open to public by appointment. **Computerized Information Services:** DIALOG. **Networks/Consortia:** Member of OCLC; AT&T Corporate Library Network. **Publications:** Technical Bulletin, bimonthly; Management Bulletin, monthly - both 'or internal distribution only. **Also Known As:** AT&T. **Staff:** Donna Lowich, Asst.Libn.

★626★
AMERICAN TELEPHONE & TELEGRAPH COMPANY - CORPORATE LIBRARY (Bus-Fin)
295 N. Maple Ave., Rm. 4430C1   Phone: (201) 221-4143
Basking Ridge, NJ 07920   Anne Garty, Chf.Libn.
Founded: 1975. **Staff:** Prof 3; Other 5. **Subjects:** Management, business, telecommunications, marketing, mathematics and statistics. **Holdings:** 9000 books; 2500 bound periodical volumes; 2500 annual reports; 4000 government documents. **Subscriptions:** 978 journals and other serials. **Services:** Interlibrary loans; copying; library open to public by appointment. **Computerized Information Services:** Online systems. **Networks/Consortia:** Member of AT&T Corporate Library Network. **Publications:** Library Network serials catalog, semiannual; Library Bulletin, monthly; Marketing Alert, bimonthly. **Staff:** Constance Williams, Ref.Libn.

★627★

AMERICAN TELEPHONE & TELEGRAPH COMPANY - CORPORATE RESEARCH LIBRARY (Bus-Fin)
195 Broadway, Rm. 850   Phone: (212) 393-3714
New York, NY 10007   Marianne V. Benjamin, Chf.Libn.
Founded: 1910. **Staff:** Prof 2; Other 4. **Subjects:** Telecommunications policy and history, regulation, management, public affairs, biography, forecasting. **Special Collections:** Annual reports of all Bell companies (complete set); Bell System periodicals. **Holdings:** 12,000 books; 3000 bound periodical volumes; 1000 pamphlets (cataloged); 3500 reels of microfilm; 30,000 microfiche. **Subscriptions:** 700 journals and other serials. **Services:** Interlibrary loans; copying; library open to public by appointment. **Computerized Information Services:** Online systems. **Networks/Consortia:** Member of AT&T Corporate Library Network. **Staff:** Carol Griffin, Ref.Libn.

★628★

AMERICAN TELEPHONE & TELEGRAPH COMPANY - EDITORIAL RESEARCH CENTER (Bus-Fin)
195 Broadway, Rm. 412   Phone: (212) 393-4955
New York, NY 10007   Barry Campbell, Dist.Mgr.
Founded: 1970. **Staff:** 6. **Subjects:** Public relations. **Holdings:** 100 volumes; 30,000 clippings, news releases, biographies, public talks, Bell System publications, audiovisual productions. **Subscriptions:** 150 journals and other serials; 10 newspapers. **Services:** Interlibrary loans; library not open to public. **Computerized Information Services:** New York Times Information Service, DIALOG; Public Relations Information Retrieval System (internal database); computerized cataloging and acquisitions. **Publications:** PR-IRS Brochure. **Staff:** Tony Sano, P.R.Supv.

★629★

AMERICAN TELEPHONE & TELEGRAPH COMPANY - LAW LIBRARY (Law)
195 Broadway, Rm. 2511   Phone: (212) 393-3652
New York, NY 10007   C.M. Ortega, Law Libn.
Founded: 1911. **Staff:** 3. **Subjects:** Law. **Special Collections:** Telecommunications; public utility and regulatory, ICC, FCC, FPC and state codes and session laws; opinions. **Holdings:** 39,000 volumes. **Subscriptions:** 98 journals and other serials; 4 newspapers. **Services:** Interlibrary loans; library not open to public.

★630★

AMERICAN TELEPHONE & TELEGRAPH COMPANY - LONG LINES DEPARTMENT - GOVERNMENT COMMUNICATIONS LIBRARY (Bus-Fin)
1120 20th St., N.W., 5th Fl.   Phone: (202) 457-3028
Washington, DC 20036   Mary B. Freeman, Staff Supv.-Lib.
Founded: 1973. **Staff:** Prof 1; Other 2. **Subjects:** Telecommunications, government, business. **Holdings:** 4000 books; 100 bound periodical volumes; 15 VF drawers; 175 audio cassettes; 100 video cassettes. **Subscriptions:** 253 journals and other serials. **Services:** Interlibrary loans; copying; library not open to public. **Computerized Information Services:** DIALOG, NEXIS; computerized cataloging. **Networks/Consortia:** Member of OCLC through CAPCON. **Publications:** Library Bulletin, monthly; News Clips, daily - both for internal distribution only.

★631★

AMERICAN TELEPHONE & TELEGRAPH COMPANY - LONG LINES DEPARTMENT - INFORMATION RESEARCH CENTER (Bus-Fin)
Rm. 3B100   Phone: (201) 234-3280
Bedminster, NJ 07921   Jack Borbely, Mgr.
Founded: 1976. **Staff:** Prof 22; Other 10. **Subjects:** Communications, business management and administration, U.S. industries, international affairs, economics, marketing. **Holdings:** 10,000 books; 100 tapes. **Subscriptions:** 1000 journals and other serials; 50 newspapers. **Services:** Interlibrary loans; copying; SDI; library not open to public. **Computerized Information Services:** DIALOG, SDC, New York Times Information Service, Dow Jones News Retrieval, Data Resources, Inc., Chase Econometrics, I.P. Sharp Associates; internal database; computerized cataloging and acquisitions. **Networks/Consortia:** Member of OCLC through PALINET & Union Library Catalogue of Pennsylvania. **Publications:** Tele-SCOPE, weekly; International Monitor, biweekly - both for internal distribution only. **Staff:** Nancy Audino, Tech.Sys.Supv.

★632★

AMERICAN TELEPHONE & TELEGRAPH COMPANY - MORRISTOWN HUMAN RESOURCES LIBRARY (Bus-Fin)
1776 On The Green   Phone: (201) 540-6439
Morristown, NJ 07960   Alfred Giraldi, Ref.Libn.
Founded: 1976. **Staff:** Prof 1; Other 1. **Subjects:** Corporate education and training, labor relations, management, occupational health and safety, personnel administration, psychology, sociology. **Holdings:** 2000 books.

Subscriptions: 350 journals and other serials; 15 newspapers. **Services:** Interlibrary loans; copying; library open to public. **Computerized Information Services:** DIALOG. **Networks/Consortia:** Member of AT&T Corporate Library Network. **Publications:** Management Bulletin, monthly - for internal distribution only. **Formerly:** Its Morristown Corporate Marketing Library. **Staff:** Betty Kauffman, Supv.Libn.

★633★

AMERICAN TEXTILE MANUFACTURERS INSTITUTE (ATMI) - LIBRARY (Sci-Tech)
1101 Connecticut Ave., N.W., No. 300   Phone: (202) 862-0573
Washington, DC 20036   Mabry R. McCloud, Libn.
Staff: Prof 1; Other 1. **Subjects:** Textile fiber, fabric and history; international trade; chemicals, safety and health. **Holdings:** 1200 books; 600 ATMI historical records. **Subscriptions:** 70 journals and other serials; 15 newspapers. **Services:** Interlibrary loans; copying (limited); library open to public by appointment.

★634★

AMERICAN THEATRE ORGAN SOCIETY - ARCHIVES (Mus)
Elon College Library   Phone: (919) 228-0254
Elon College, NC 27244
Subjects: The theatre organ as an art form. **Holdings:** Figures not available for pictures, recordings, music, player rolls; society meeting minutes; complete catalog of Theatre Organ Magazine.

AMERICAN TOBACCO COMPANY
See: American Brands, Inc.

★635★

AMERICAN TRUCK HISTORICAL SOCIETY - LIBRARY (Trans)
201 Office Park Dr.   Phone: (205) 879-2131
Birmingham, AL 35223   Zoe S. James, Exec.Dir.
Founded: 1971. **Staff:** 2. **Subjects:** Trucks, truck companies, people in trucking. **Holdings:** 100 books; 100 bound periodical volumes; 100 biographies; 100 company histories; 16 VF drawers of unbound periodicals; 25 films; 200 slides; 3 VF drawers of photographs. **Subscriptions:** 15 journals and other serials. **Services:** Copying; library open to public. **Publications:** Wheels of Time, bimonthly - to members.

★636★

AMERICAN TRUCKING ASSOCIATIONS, INC. - LIBRARY (Trans)
1616 P St., N.W.   Phone: (202) 797-5291
Washington, DC 20036   Linda Rothbart, Libn.
Staff: Prof 1; Other 1. **Subjects:** Economic and financial analysis of trucking industry, trucking regulation, highway legislation, truck engineering and safety, freight transportation. **Holdings:** 30,000 volumes. **Subscriptions:** 475 journals and other serials. **Services:** Interlibrary loans; library open to public. **Computerized Information Services:** SDC, New York Times Information Service; computerized CG and serials. **Publications:** Information Carrier.

★637★

AMERICAN TYPE CULTURE COLLECTION - DONOVICK LIBRARY (Sci-Tech)
12301 Parklawn Dr.   Phone: (301) 881-2600
Rockville, MD 20852   Mary Jane Gantt, Info.Sci.
Founded: 1965. **Staff:** Prof 1; Other 1. **Subjects:** Microbiology, bacteriology, protozoology, virology, tissue culture, mycology. **Holdings:** 2100 books; 2500 bound periodical volumes. **Subscriptions:** 145 journals and other serials. **Services:** Interlibrary loans; copying; library open to public with restrictions.

★638★

AMERICAN UNIVERSITY - FOREIGN AREA STUDIES LIBRARY (Soc Sci)
5010 Wisconsin Ave., N.W.   Phone: (202) 686-2740
Washington, DC 20016   Gilda Nimer, Libn.
Staff: Prof 1. **Subjects:** Foreign area studies. **Special Collections:** J.P.R.S. (Joint Publications Research Service) Documents (68 feet of shelving). **Holdings:** 5400 books; 1000 bound periodical volumes; 96 reels of microfilmed dissertations (cataloged); 20 VF drawers of foreign area documentation. **Subscriptions:** 200 journals and other serials. **Services:** Interlibrary loans; copying; library open to public with consent of librarian. **Publications:** Area handbooks of foreign countries.

★639★

AMERICAN UNIVERSITY - WASHINGTON COLLEGE OF LAW - LIBRARY (Law)
4400 Massachusetts Ave., N.W.   Phone: (202) 686-2625
Washington, DC 20016   Patrick E. Kehoe, Dir.
Staff: Prof 6; Other 7. **Subjects:** Law, international law. **Holdings:** 190,000

volumes. **Subscriptions:** 1906 journals and other serials. **Services:** Interlibrary loans; copying; library open to students, alumni and other qualified users. **Computerized Information Services:** LEXIS. **Networks/Consortia:** Member of OCLC through CAPCON.

★640★
AMERICAN VETERINARY MEDICAL ASSOCIATION - LIBRARY (Med)
930 N. Meacham Rd.   Phone: (312) 885-8070
Schaumburg, IL 60196   Janice Johnson, Libn.
Founded: 1945. **Staff:** Prof 1. **Subjects:** Veterinary medicine and related fields. **Holdings:** 5000 books; 300 bound periodical volumes. **Subscriptions:** 35 journals and other serials; 185 exchanges. **Services:** Copying (limited); library open to public for reference use only.

★641★
AMERICAN WATCHMAKERS INSTITUTE - LIBRARY (Rec)
3700 Harrison Ave.   Phone: (513) 661-3838
Cincinnati, OH 45211   Mrs. Michael Danner, Libn.
Founded: 1960. **Staff:** Prof 2; Other 2. **Subjects:** Horology. **Services:** Interlibrary loans; copying; library open to public with permission. **Staff:** Milton C. Stevens, Dir./AWI Elm Trust.

★642★
AMERICAN WATER WORKS ASSOCIATION - TECHNICAL LIBRARY AND INFORMATION CENTER (Sci-Tech)
6666 W. Quincy   Phone: (303) 794-7711
Denver, CO 80235   Kurt M. Keeley, Tech.Info.Serv.Mgr.
Founded: 1977. **Staff:** Prof 2; Other 1. **Subjects:** Water - public supply systems and utilities; potable water technology and reuse. **Holdings:** 2000 books; 200 bound periodical volumes; 100 AV items; 1500 technical reports. **Subscriptions:** 175 journals and other serials. **Services:** Interlibrary loans; copying; library open to public by appointment. **Computerized Information Services:** SDC, DIALOG; computerized cataloging. **Networks/Consortia:** Member of Bibliographical Center for Research, Rocky Mountain Region Inc. (BCR). **Publications:** AV Catalog, annual; topical bibliographies, monthly. **Special Indexes:** Annual book index. **Staff:** Janette L. Kavanagh, Lib.Asst.

★643★
AMERICAN WATERWAYS OPERATORS, INC. - LIBRARY (Trans)
1600 Wilson Blvd., Suite 1101   Phone: (703) 841-9300
Arlington, VA 22209   Neil D. Schuster, V.P., Res.
Staff: Prof 1. **Subjects:** Shallow-draft water carriers; inland river navigation; Corps of Engineers; transportation safety; energy efficiency. **Special Collections:** Waterborne commerce of the U.S. (Corps of Engineers, 23 volumes). **Holdings:** 500 books; 25 bound periodical volumes; Congressional Record; Federal Register; Traffic World; Coast Guard reports; maps, internal publications; Transportation Lines (Corps of Engineers); miscellaneous government publications. **Subscriptions:** 50 journals and other serials; 5 newspapers. **Services:** Library open to public with permission. **Publications:** Inland Waterborne Commerce Statistics, annual; Big Load Afloat, irregular.

★644★
AMERICAN WORK HORSE MUSEUM - LIBRARY (Hist)
    Phone: (703) 338-6290
Paeonian Springs, VA 22129   Frank Joy Hopkins, Chf.Libn.
Founded: 1971. **Staff:** Prof 1; Other 1. **Subjects:** Work horse - in agriculture, in the military, in industry; history. **Holdings:** 785 books; 15 bound periodical volumes; 25 cataloged pamphlets; 100 slides. **Subscriptions:** 5 journals and other serials; 2 newspapers. **Services:** Library open to public for reference use only. **Staff:** Dr. Henry L. Buckardt, Pres.

AMERICANA RESEARCH LIBRARY
See: American Life Foundation and Study Institute

★645★
AMERICANS UNITED FOR LIFE - AUL LEGAL DEFENSE FUND - INFORMATION CENTER (Soc Sci)
230 N. Michigan Ave., Suite 915   Phone: (312) 263-5029
Chicago, IL 60601   Melinda Delahoyde, Dir. of Educ.
Subjects: Abortion, euthanasia, infanticide, invitro fertilization. **Holdings:** Figures not available. **Services:** Copying; library open to public with advance telephone call. **Publications:** AUL Studies in Law and Medicine - list of titles available on request; Lex Vitae, legal newsletter; AUL Educational Newsletter.

★646★
AMERICANS UNITED FOR SEPARATION OF CHURCH AND STATE - ARCHIVES (Soc Sci)†
8120 Fenton St.   Phone: (301) 589-3707
Silver Spring, MD 20910   Morgan Dukes, Dir., Gen.Serv.
Founded: 1948. **Staff:** Prof 1. **Subjects:** Church-state separation and

clericalism. **Special Collections:** Primary source documents on anti-Catholicism, persecution of Protestants in Columbia and Spain, Vatican ambassadorship question. **Holdings:** 1200 books; 50 bound periodical volumes; 125 boxes of papers, documents; minutes of AUSCS staff and board meetings. **Subscriptions:** 10 journals and other serials. **Services:** Copying; library open to serious scholars.

★647★
AMERIFIRST FEDERAL SAVINGS & LOAN - LIBRARY (Bus-Fin)†
One S.E. Third Ave.   Phone: (305) 577-6397
Miami, FL 33131   Emerita M. Cuesta, Res.Libn.
Founded: 1943. **Staff:** Prof 1. **Subjects:** Savings and loans, local economy and information management. **Holdings:** 1400 books; 500 pamphlets; 15 statistics files; maps; 95 shelves of unbound journals; 20 cabinet shelves of newspapers. **Subscriptions:** 350 journals and other serials; 20 newspapers. **Services:** Interlibrary loans (limited); library open to public by appointment.

★648★
AMERIND FOUNDATION, INC. - FULTON-HAYDEN MEMORIAL LIBRARY (Area-Ethnic; Soc Sci)
    Phone: (602) 586-3003
Dragoon, AZ 85609   Mario N. Klimiades, Libn.
Founded: 1937. **Staff:** Prof 1; Other 1. **Subjects:** Archeology, anthropology, Greater American Southwest, ethnology and history. **Special Collections:** Parral Archives, complete in microfilm; facsimile editions of major American codices. **Holdings:** 15,500 books; 1000 bound periodical volumes; 1700 pamphlets and reprints; 370 manuscripts; 250 maps; 1300 slides and photographs; 2 VF drawers of clippings and translations. **Subscriptions:** 150 journals and other serials; 5 newspapers. **Services:** Copying; library open to serious researchers by appointment only and with written statement of intent. **Networks/Consortia:** Member of Intermountain Union List of Serials. **Publications:** Recent Additions - in-house and sent to individuals allied with the Foundation.

★649★
AMES (A.E.) AND COMPANY, LTD. - LIBRARY (Bus-Fin)†
320 Bay St.   Phone: (416) 867-4058
Toronto, ON, Canada M5H 2P7   Wilberta M. Malcom, Libn.
Founded: 1955. **Staff:** 4. **Subjects:** Canadian corporations, industry, and statistics. **Holdings:** 1500 books; 250 bound periodical volumes; 65 vertical files of corporation clippings, reports, and legal documents. **Subscriptions:** 250 journals and other serials; 15 newspapers. **Services:** Interlibrary loans; library open to clients, and to others for reference use by request.

★650★
AMES LABORATORY - DOCUMENT LIBRARY (Energy)
Iowa State University   Phone: (515) 294-1856
Ames, IA 50011   Burton J. Gleason, Hd., Office of Info.
Founded: 1942. **Staff:** Prof 2; Other 2. **Subjects:** Energy-related research, materials and metallurgy, chemistry, physics, fossil energy. **Holdings:** 3000 books; 50,000 documents, 3000 dissertations. **Subscriptions:** 100 journals and other serials. **Services:** Copying; library open to public. **Computerized Information Services:** DIALOG, DOE/RECON. **Remarks:** The Ames Laboratory operates under contract to the U.S. Department of Energy. **Staff:** Dianne A. Borgen, Info.Spec.

AMES LIBRARY OF SOUTH ASIA
See: University of Minnesota

AMES (Oakes) LIBRARY OF ECONOMIC BOTANY
See: Harvard University - Economic Botany Library

AMES (Oakes) ORCHID LIBRARY
See: Harvard University - Oakes Ames Orchid Library

AMES RESEARCH CENTER
See: U.S. NASA

★651★
AMES RUBBER CORPORATION - TECHNICAL INFORMATION CENTER
2347 Ames Blvd.
Hamburg, NJ 07419
Defunct

AMF/HARLEY-DAVIDSON MOTOR CO.
See: Harley-Davidson Motor Co.

★652★

AMF, INC. - TECHNICAL INFORMATION CENTER (Sci-Tech)
689 Hope St.   Phone: (203) 325-2211
Stamford, CT 06907   Maria Jacobson, Tech.Libn.
Staff: Prof 2. **Subjects:** Chemical engineering, plastics and rubber, analytical chemistry, polymer science, tobacco, water and wastes engineering/pollution, sports equipment. **Holdings:** 9000 books; 2000 bound periodical volumes; 1000 NTIS reports; 30 VF drawers of patents; 50 VF drawers of technical reports; 15 VF drawers of pamphlets; archival proprietary technical reports. **Subscriptions:** 267 journals and other serials. **Services:** Interlibrary loans; SDI; library open to public with restrictions. **Computerized Information Services:** DIALOG, SDC. **Networks/Consortia:** Member of Southwestern Connecticut Library Council. **Publications:** Library News, monthly - for internal distribution only; Current Acquisitions, monthly - for internal distribution only. **Staff:** Charlotte Mason, Asst.

★653★

AMHERST COLLEGE - SCIENCE LIBRARY (Sci-Tech)
                                      Phone: (413) 542-2076
Amherst, MA 01002   Eleanor T. Brown, Hd.
Founded: 1968. **Subjects:** Astronomy, chemistry, physics. **Holdings:** 7600 books; 9000 bound periodical volumes. **Subscriptions:** 150 journals and other serials. **Services:** Interlibrary loans; library open to public for reference use only. **Computerized Information Services:** DIALOG. **Networks/Consortia:** Member of OCLC through SUNY. **Remarks:** The collection of books on astronomy has existed since the 19th century.

★654★

AMHERST COLLEGE - SPECIAL COLLECTIONS DEPARTMENT AND ARCHIVES (Hum)
                                      Phone: (413) 542-2299
Amherst, MA 01002   John Lancaster, Libn. & Archv.
Founded: 1821. **Staff:** Prof 1; Other 3. **Subjects:** American poetry and theater, English literature and theater, Amherst College history. **Special Collections:** Louise Bogan papers (15 linear feet); Richard Wilbur papers (18 linear feet); Dwight Morrow papers (80 VF drawers); Clyde Fitch collection (1000 volumes and 5 linear feet); Emily Dickinson papers (15 linear feet); Robert Frost collection (5 linear feet and 750 volumes); Joseph Eastman papers (40 linear feet); Rolfe Humphries papers (10 linear feet); George Bellows papers (3 linear feet); Marshall Bloom/LNS underground newspapers (150 linear feet); college history collection (1000 linear feet of historical manuscripts, 400 linear feet of honors and masters' theses, 500 VF drawers of official college records, 2000 linear feet of other bound manuscripts and printed college history sources). **Holdings:** 30,000 books; 30,000 acting editions of English and American plays. **Subscriptions:** 7 journals and other serials. **Services:** Copying; library open to public. **Computerized Information Services:** Computerized cataloging. **Networks/Consortia:** Member of OCLC through NELINET; HILC, Inc. **Staff:** Joanne Dougherty, Asst.Libn. & Archv.

★655★

AMISTAD RESEARCH CENTER - LIBRARY (Soc Sci)
400 Esplanade Ave.   Phone: (504) 944-0239
New Orleans, LA 70116   Clifton H. Johnson, Exec.Dir.
Staff: Prof 5; Other 3. **Subjects:** Ethnic minorities of America; Negro education; abolitionism; civil rights; Negro churches; Indian missions; Oriental American churches; Western frontier life; Africa . **Special Collections:** Manuscripts (eight million). **Holdings:** 30,000 books; 1600 bound periodical volumes; 300,000 pamphlets (cataloged); 2100 reels of microfilm; 500,000 newspaper clippings. **Subscriptions:** 334 journals and other serials; 24 newspapers. **Services:** Interlibrary loans; copying; library open to public. **Staff:** Florence E. Borders, Sr.Archv.; Lester Sullivan, Archv.; Gracia Hardacre, Archv.; Frank Miele, Archv.; Harold Handy, Archv.

★656★

AMOCO CANADA PETROLEUM COMPANY, LTD. - LIBRARY/INFORMATION CENTER (Energy)
Amoco Canada Bldg.
444 7th Ave., S.W., Rm. 1012   Phone: (403) 233-1963
Calgary, AB, Canada T2P 0Y2   Frances M. Drummond, Supv.
Founded: 1965. **Staff:** 4. **Subjects:** Geology, petroleum engineering, petroleum economics, geophysics. **Holdings:** 18,000 books; 3000 confidential reports; 2500 pamphlets (cataloged). **Subscriptions:** 275 journals and other serials; 8 newspapers. **Services:** Interlibrary loans; copying; library open to public with restrictions. **Computerized Information Services:** SDC, Info Globe, Dow Jones News Retrieval, CAN/OLE, New York Times Information Service; computerized acquisitions, serials and circulation. **Staff:** J. Nasser, Info.Spec.; S. Pascual, Info.Spec.

★657★

AMOCO PRODUCTION COMPANY INTERNATIONAL - LIBRARY INFORMATION CENTER (Sci-Tech; Energy)
16825 Northchase Dr.   Phone: (713) 931-2584
Houston, TX 77060   Eloise F. Martinez, Supv.
Founded: 1980. **Staff:** Prof 5; Other 5. **Subjects:** Geology, petroleum, geophysics, chemical engineering, geoscience, business, management, law. **Special Collections:** Foreign scouting service documents. **Holdings:** 5500 books; 150 bound periodical volumes; 55 slides and cassettes; 8500 maps; 42 well logs; 500 titles on microfiche; 10 films; 200 annual reports. **Subscriptions:** 400 journals and other serials; 15 newspapers. **Services:** Interlibrary loans; copying; SDI; library open to public with restrictions. **Computerized Information Services:** DIALOG, SDC, BRS, RLIN, Middle East Database (MEDAB); SOCON Corporate Libraries Network (internal database); computerized cataloging, acquisitions, serials and circulation. **Networks/Consortia:** Member of RLG. **Publications:** New Acquisitions in LIC; New Periodicals List; Newsletter. **Special Indexes:** Index to technical reports (computer printout). **Remarks:** Amoco Production Company International is a subsidiary of Standard Oil Company of Indiana. **Staff:** Jan B. Heagy, Circ.-Ref.; Linda Delaney, Tech.Serv.Asst.; Brenda Bolenbaucher, Cat.Asst.; Barbara Wesley, Circ.Asst.

★658★

AMOCO PRODUCTION COMPANY - LAW DEPARTMENT LIBRARY (Law)
Box 591   Phone: (918) 581-3523
Tulsa, OK 74102   Sally Shipley, Libn.
Staff: 1. **Subjects:** Law. **Holdings:** Figures not available. **Services:** Interlibrary loans (limited); library open to local residents through a corporation attorney.

★659★

AMOCO PRODUCTION COMPANY - NEW ORLEANS REGION - LIBRARY INFORMATION CENTER (Sci-Tech; Energy)
Box 50879   Phone: (504) 586-6572
New Orleans, LA 70150   Louise M. Seidler, Supv.
Staff: 3. **Subjects:** Geology, geophysics, paleontology, computer science, engineering, management, economics. **Holdings:** 6550 volumes. **Subscriptions:** 175 journals and other serials. **Services:** Interlibrary loans; copying; library not open to public. **Computerized Information Services:** SDC, DIALOG; internal database; computerized circulation.

★660★

AMOCO PRODUCTION COMPANY - RESEARCH CENTER LIBRARY (Energy)
Box 591   Phone: (918) 664-3238
Tulsa, OK 74102   Carolyn Beson, Supv., Tech.Info.Serv.
Founded: 1943. **Staff:** 7. **Subjects:** Petroleum exploration and production, mathematics, physics, geology, chemistry, electronics, computer science. **Special Collections:** State and U.S. Geological Survey publications. **Holdings:** 40,000 books and bound periodical volumes; 1600 maps; 800 reels of microfilm. **Subscriptions:** 450 journals and other serials. **Services:** Interlibrary loans; copying; library open by prior appointment; reference and literature searching. **Computerized Information Services:** Online systems; computerized cataloging and serials.

AMOCO RESEARCH CENTER - STANDARD OIL COMPANY OF INDIANA - CENTRAL RESEARCH LIBRARY
See: Standard Oil Company of Indiana - Central Research Library

★661★

AMP, INC. - TECHNICAL INFORMATION CENTER (Sci-Tech)
Box 3608, Res. Div.   Phone: (717) 780-8131
Harrisburg, PA 17105   Kay Birula, Mgr.
Founded: 1956. **Staff:** Prof 3; Other 4. **Subjects:** Engineering - electrical, electronic, mechanical; plastics technology; business; metallurgy; electroplating. **Holdings:** 10,000 books; 700 journals; 10,000 volumes of back files; audio and video cassettes (cataloged). **Subscriptions:** 400 journals and other serials. **Services:** SDI; library not open to public. **Computerized Information Services:** Online systems; mechanized storage and retrieval of company technical documents; computerized serials. **Publications:** Monthly Library Additions; SDI Service; selected bibliographies.

★662★

AMPEX CORPORATION - TECHNICAL INFORMATION SERVICES (Sci-Tech)
401 Broadway   Phone: (415) 367-3368
Redwood City, CA 94063   Gwyneth Heynes Mallinson, Mgr.Tech.Info.Serv.
Founded: 1959. **Staff:** Prof 4; Other 4. **Subjects:** Magnetism, magnetic materials, solid state electronics, physics, chemistry, mathematics, economics, business, management. **Special Collections:** Collection of books, articles, and reports on magnetic recording and magnetic tape recording,

1888 to present (5000 items). **Holdings:** 9000 books; 8000 bound periodical volumes; 2050 literature searches. **Subscriptions:** 350 journals and other serials; 11 newspapers. **Services:** Interlibrary loans; copying; SDI; library not open to public. **Computerized Information Services:** DIALOG, SDC; computerized cataloging. **Networks/Consortia:** Member of CIN. **Publications:** Current literature checklist, monthly. **Special Catalogs:** Magnetic Recording Bibliography (KWIC). **Staff:** Mary Garbarino; Marjorie Wilbur .

AMPHIBIOUS WARFARE RESEARCH FACILITY
See: U.S. Marine Corps - Education Center - James Carson Breckinridge Library

★663★
AMSTAR CORPORATION - RESEARCH AND DEVELOPMENT LIBRARY (Food-Bev)†
266 Kent Ave. Phone: (212) 387-6800
Brooklyn, NY 11211 Joseph X. Cavano, Info.Spec.
Founded: 1948. **Staff:** Prof 1. **Subjects:** Sugar technology, analytical chemistry, food technology, chemical engineering. **Holdings:** 2000 books; 100 bound periodical volumes; 20 VF drawers of pamphlets; 100 reels of microfilm; 40 VF drawers of internal reports. **Subscriptions:** 100 journals and other serials. **Services:** Interlibrary loans; copying; library not open to public. **Publications:** Bibliographies - for internal distribution only.

★664★
AMUNDSON ASSOCIATES - PLANNING REFERENCE LIBRARY (Plan)
Box F Phone: (503) 746-8231
Springfield, OR 97477 John M. Amundson, Prin.
Founded: 1955. **Staff:** 2. **Subjects:** Building design, technical planning, Construction Specification Institute (CSI). **Holdings:** 600 books; 10,000 articles, papers; 5000 reports; 3000 slides. **Subscriptions:** 10 journals and other serials. **Services:** Copying; library open to public with restrictions.

AMX LIBRARY
See: Classic AMX Club, International

ANACONDA...
See: Atlantic-Richfield Company...

ANACONDA COPPER COMPANY
See: Atlantic-Richfield Company

★665★
ANAHEIM MEMORIAL HOSPITAL - MEDICAL LIBRARY (Med)
1111 W. LaPalma Ave. Phone: (714) 999-6020
Anaheim, CA 92801 Hilary J. Brover, Med.Libn.
Staff: Prof 1; Other 1. **Subjects:** Medicine. **Holdings:** 1200 books. **Subscriptions:** 136 journals and other serials. **Services:** Interlibrary loans; copying; SDI; library not open to public. **Computerized Information Services:** MEDLINE, DIALOG; computerized cataloging. **Networks/Consortia:** Member of Pacific Southwest Regional Medical Library Service (PSRMLS).

★666★
ANALYTIC SCIENCES CORPORATION - LIBRARY (Sci-Tech)
1 Jacob Way Phone: (617) 944-6850
Reading, MA 01867 Lynne E. Fabrizio, Dir.
Staff: Prof 1; Other 2. **Subjects:** Control systems, navigation, mathematical modeling, electrical engineering, waste management, computer programming. **Holdings:** 3500 books; 16,000 technical reports; 8000 reports on microfiche. **Subscriptions:** 320 journals and other serials. **Services:** Library not open to public. **Computerized Information Services:** DIALOG, SDC, DOE/RECON, NASA/RECON, DTIC. **Publications:** Library Bulletin, monthly.

ANALYTIC SERVICES, INC.
See: ANSER

★667★
ANALYTICAL PSYCHOLOGY CLUB OF NEW YORK - KRISTINE MANN LIBRARY (Soc Sci)
28 E. 39th St. Phone: (212) 697-7877
New York, NY 10016 Peggy Brooks, Lib.Chm.
Founded: 1945. **Subjects:** Carl Gustav Jung; analytical psychology. **Special Collections:** Jung Press Archive (clippings from newspapers and periodicals in the United States and abroad, 1905 to present, about C.G. Jung and/or analytical psychology; about 2500 items, in addition to clipped articles listed below). **Holdings:** 7100 books; 400 bound periodical volumes; 2600 clipped articles, separately mounted. **Subscriptions:** 8 journals and other serials. **Services:** Library open to public with restrictions. **Special Catalogs:** Book

catalog published in 1978. **Remarks:** The collection includes everything published by Jung, for the most part in all editions in German and English; all the works of other specialists in the field of analytical psychology; books and articles by others about analytical psychology; related material in mythology, religions, alchemy, art, anthropology. **Staff:** Doris Albrecht, Libn.

★668★
ANALYTICAL SYSTEMS ENGINEERING CORPORATION - LIBRARY (Sci-Tech)
5 Old Concord Rd. Phone: (617) 272-7910
Burlington, MA 01803 Rayna Lee Caplan, Libn.
Staff: Prof 1. **Subjects:** Communication, marine and urban transportation, navigation systems, environmental engineering. **Holdings:** 500 books; 3000 technical reports. **Subscriptions:** 50 journals and other serials. **Services:** Interlibrary loans; copying; library open to public with restrictions. **Publications:** Library Accessions List, monthly - for internal distribution only.

★669★
ANATEC BIOLOGICAL LABORATORIES, INC. - LIBRARY (Sci-Tech)
435 Tesconi Circle, No. 14 Phone: (707) 526-7200
Santa Rosa, CA 95401 Dalene Ried, Libn.
Founded: 1979. **Staff:** 1. **Subjects:** Marine biology, oceanography. **Special Collections:** Reprints on marine biology. **Holdings:** 5000 books; 3000 bound periodical volumes. **Subscriptions:** 100 journals and other serials. **Services:** Interlibrary loans; copying; library not open to public.

★670★
ANCESTRAL ROUTES - COMPUTERIZED GENEALOGY LIBRARY (Hist)
57 W. South Temple, Suite 553 Phone: (801) 355-9141
Salt Lake City, UT 84101 David Barrs, Dir.
Founded: 1979. **Staff:** Prof 1; Other 1. **Subjects:** Genealogy, pedigrees. **Holdings:** 300 books; 36 cubic feet of manuscripts; 4 VF drawers of travel materials. **Subscriptions:** 150 journals and other serials; 5 newspapers. **Services:** Interlibrary loans; copying; library open to public. **Computerized Information Services:** Internal database containing 300,000 lineage-linked names. **Publications:** Genealogy Digest, monthly - by subscription. **Special Indexes:** Pedigree Archive. **Formerly:** Who Am I - Library.

★671★
ANCHOR FOUNDATION - LIBRARY OF SOCIAL HISTORY (Soc Sci)†
410 West St. Phone: (212) 255-1767
New York, NY 10014 Barbara West, Dir.
Founded: 1972. **Staff:** Prof 1. **Subjects:** U.S. socialist movements and labor history. **Holdings:** Figures not available. **Services:** Copying; library open to public by appointment.

★672★
ANCHOR HOCKING CORPORATION - CORPORATE LIBRARY (Sci-Tech)
2980 W. Fair Ave. Phone: (614) 687-2403
Lancaster, OH 43130 Peggy J. Myers, Corp.Libn.
Founded: 1971. **Staff:** Prof 2. **Subjects:** Glass manufacture and technology, mechanical and chemical engineering, business and finance, management, physics, chemistry, microwave, polymers. **Special Collections:** W.A. Weyl Collection - glass and ceramic technology and research (100 texts). **Holdings:** 5000 books; 60 bound periodical volumes; 200 research reports; 35 VF drawers of pamphlets; 30,000 patents on microfilm; 200 films; 200 cassettes and videotapes; 185 literature and patent searches. **Subscriptions:** 275 journals and other serials. **Services:** Interlibrary loans; library open to public by appointment. **Computerized Information Services:** SDC, Derwent Publications, Ltd.; mechanized retrieval of patents and internal searches. **Networks/Consortia:** Member of Library Council of Fairfield County; CALICO; OHIONET. **Publications:** New Books and Literature Bulletin, semiannual - for internal distribution only. **Special Indexes:** U.S., Canadian and international patents indexed by number, inventor, assignee and patent classification number (computer programmed and produced); cassette and film indexes. **Staff:** Judy Sowers, Lib.Techn.

★673★
ANCHORAGE HISTORICAL AND FINE ARTS MUSEUM - ARCHIVES (Hist; Art)
121 W. Seventh Ave. Phone: (907) 264-4326
Anchorage, AK 99501 M. Diane Brenner, Musm.Archv.
Founded: 1968. **Staff:** Prof 1; Other 1. **Subjects:** Alaskana (prehistoric, native, Russian, Gold Rush, current); fine arts. **Special Collections:** Arthur Eide photographs (400 items); Valdez photographs, 1900-1910 (12 albums); Alaska Railroad historical photographs (3000 items). **Holdings:** 3000 books; 10,000 photographs; 16 boxes of archives (Alaskana); 5000 slides of contemporary Alaskan art; 8 VF drawers (Alaska); 8 drawers of historical photographs; 200 maps. **Subscriptions:** 15 journals and other serials. **Services:** Interlibrary loans (limited); copying; archives open to public.

★674★

ANCIENT AND HONORABLE ARTILLERY COMPANY OF MASSACHUSETTS - LIBRARY (Hist; Mil)
Faneuil Hall   Phone: (617) 227-1638
Boston, MA 02109   Lt.Col. Charles F. Hoar, Exec.Sec.
Staff: 1. **Subjects:** Military history; colonial and provincial history. **Holdings:** 2000 books; Company records. **Services:** Copying; library open to researchers for reference use only.

★675★

ANCLOTE PSYCHIATRIC CENTER - MEDICAL LIBRARY (Med)†
Box 1224   Phone: (813) 937-4211
Tarpon Springs, FL 33589   Carol Lynn, Med.Libn.
Founded: 1966. **Staff:** Prof 1. **Subjects:** Psychiatry, sociology, neurology, medicine, nursing. **Special Collections:** Psychotherapy. **Holdings:** 2316 books; 1200 bound periodical volumes; 2 VF drawers of pamphlets; 1 VF drawer of manuscripts. **Subscriptions:** 74 journals and other serials. **Services:** Interlibrary loans; copying; library open to public with approval of the staff. **Publications:** Library Notes, monthly - distributed to hospital staff and mailing list.

★676★

ANCORA PSYCHIATRIC HOSPITAL - HEALTH SCIENCES LIBRARY (Med)
    Phone: (609) 561-1700
Hammonton, NJ 08037   Norman T. Karchmer, Libn.
Founded: 1955. **Staff:** Prof 1. **Subjects:** Psychiatry, neurology, medicine, surgery, social services, nursing. **Special Collections:** Psychiatry and psychology collections. **Holdings:** 8588 books; 135 bound periodical volumes; 289 audio cassettes; 24 video cassettes; 16 films. **Subscriptions:** 35 journals and other serials; 5 newspapers. **Services:** Interlibrary loans; copying; library open to public for reference use only with permission.

ANDERSEN (Arthur) & CO. ...
See: Arthur Andersen & Co. ...

ANDERSEN (Elmer L. & Eleanor J.) HORTICULTURAL LIBRARY
See: University of Minnesota - Landscape Arboretum - Elmer L. & Eleanor J. Andersen Horticultural Library

★677★

ANDERSEN LABORATORIES, INC. - LIBRARY (Sci-Tech)
1280 Blue Hills Ave.   Phone: (203) 242-0761
Bloomfield, CT 06002   Fran Feldman, Libn.
Founded: 1964. **Staff:** 2. **Subjects:** Electronics, microwave, television. **Holdings:** 632 books. **Subscriptions:** 23 journals and other serials. **Services:** Library not open to public.

★678★

ANDERSON CLAYTON FOODS - W.L. CLAYTON RESEARCH CENTER (Food-Bev)
3333 N. Central Expy.   Phone: (214) 231-6121
Richardson, TX 75080   Irmgarde Martin, Libn.
Founded: 1967. **Staff:** Prof 1; Other 1. **Subjects:** Edible fats and oils, food processing, food chemistry, analytical chemistry, packaging, quality control. **Holdings:** 3100 books; 2250 bound periodical volumes; 250 pamphlets (cataloged); 2200 patents; company correspondence, files; technical reports. **Subscriptions:** 223 journals and other serials. **Services:** Interlibrary loans (restricted); copying; SDI; library open to public with special permission. **Computerized Information Services:** DIALOG, SDC.

★679★

ANDERSON COLLEGE - SCHOOL OF THEOLOGY - BYRD MEMORIAL LIBRARY (Rel-Theol)
    Phone: (317) 649-9071
Anderson, IN 46012   Delena Goodman, Libn.
Founded: 1950. **Staff:** Prof 1; Other 2. **Subjects:** Bible, theology, church history, pastoral psychology, Christian education, preaching. **Special Collections:** Church of God Archives. **Holdings:** 56,314 books and bound periodical volumes; 10,389 pamphlets; 2614 tracts; 224 reels of microfilm; 2439 AV items; 17 manuscripts. **Subscriptions:** 362 journals and other serials. **Services:** Interlibrary loans; copying; library open to city ministers. **Computerized Information Services:** Computerized cataloging and ILL. **Networks/Consortia:** Member of Chicago Area Theological Library Association (CATLA); OCLC through INCOLSA.

ANDERSON (Dwight) MEMORIAL MUSIC LIBRARY
See: University of Louisville - Dwight Anderson Memorial Music Library

ANDERSON FINE ARTS CENTER
See: Alford House/Anderson Fine Arts Center

ANDERSON HOUSE LIBRARY AND MUSEUM
See: Society of the Cincinnati

ANDERSON (I.C.) MEMORIAL LIBRARY & MEDIA CENTER
See: First Baptist Church - I.C. Anderson Memorial Library & Media Center

ANDERSON LIBRARY
See: Georgia State Department of Natural Resources - Coastal Resources Division

ANDERSON (M.D.) HOSPITAL AND TUMOR INSTITUTE
See: University of Texas - M.D. Anderson Hospital and Tumor Institute

ANDERSON RESOURCE CENTRE
See: Loyalist College of Applied Arts & Technology

ANDERSON SCHOOL OF MANAGEMENT
See: University of New Mexico - Bureau of Business & Economic Research Data Bank

★680★

ANDOVER COLLEGE - LIBRARY (Bus-Fin)
335 Forest Ave.   Phone: (207) 774-6126
Portland, ME 04101   Irene H. Tuttle, Libn.
Staff: Prof 2; Other 1. **Subjects:** Business, accounting, management, secretarial science, data processing. **Holdings:** 5000 books. **Subscriptions:** 48 journals and other serials. **Services:** Interlibrary loans; copying; library open to public by appointment. **Remarks:** Andover College is an accredited 2-year college, granting degrees in data processing, management, accounting, and secretarial sciences. **Staff:** Frances Marcus, Asst.Libn.

ANDOVER-HARVARD THEOLOGICAL LIBRARY
See: Harvard University - Divinity School

★681★

ANDOVER HISTORICAL SOCIETY - CAROLINE M. UNDERHILL RESEARCH LIBRARY (Hist)
97 Main St.   Phone: (617) 475-2236
Andover, MA 01810   Marsha Rooney, Dir./Cur.
Staff: 2. **Subjects:** Local history. **Special Collections:** Andover imprints (200 volumes). **Holdings:** 2000 books; 12 VF drawers; 5 VF drawers of historical photographs; 50 boxes of archival materials. **Services:** Copying; library open to public on a limited schedule.

★682★

ANDOVER NEWTON THEOLOGICAL SCHOOL - TRASK LIBRARY (Rel-Theol)
169 Herrick Rd.   Phone: (617) 964-1100
Newton Centre, MA 02159   Ellis E. O'Neal, Jr., Libn.
Founded: 1807. **Staff:** Prof 3; Other 4. **Subjects:** Religion, theology. **Special Collections:** Papers of Isaac Backus (15 pamphlet boxes and 4 microfilms); papers of Jonathan Edwards (3 packets and 10 microfilms); records of New England Baptist Library Association (21 feet of records). **Holdings:** 197,866 books and bound periodical volumes; 5000 pamphlets; 1191 microforms. **Subscriptions:** 523 journals and other serials. **Services:** Interlibrary loans; copying; library open to public at graduate level only upon request. **Computerized Information Services:** Computerized cataloging. **Networks/Consortia:** Member of Boston Theological Institute - Library Development Program; OCLC through NELINET. **Staff:** Linda P. Lerman, Tech.Serv.Libn.; Diana Yount, Spec.Coll.Libn.

ANDREWS AIR FORCE BASE (Washington, DC)
See: U.S. Air Force Base - Andrews Base Library; U.S. Air Force Hospital - Malcolm Grow Medical Center

★683★

ANDREWS UNIVERSITY - JAMES WHITE LIBRARY (Rel-Theol)
    Phone: (616) 471-3264
Berrien Springs, MI 49104   Marley H. Soper, Dir.
Founded: 1962. **Staff:** Prof 12; Other 16. **Subjects:** Religion and theology; education; liberal arts; science; technology; social sciences; Seventh-day Adventist history. **Special Collections:** Heritage Room: Holds research material on the history and development of the Adventist Movement and of the Seventh-day Adventist Church before and since 1844, such as personal papers, letters, manuscripts, photographs (475 linear feet); 24,951 books, special collections and theses; 5660 S.D.A. denominational and Millerite

periodicals; 9097 pamphlets. Teaching Materials Center: 17,003 pamphlets; 1364 curriculum guides; 8315 textbooks; 1302 teaching devices; 7904 recordings; 10,537 filmstrips, filmloops, slide sets; entire ERIC microfiche collection located here. Music Materials Center: 3715 phonograph records and tapes; 4741 scores; 941 reference books. **Holdings:** 421,804 books and bound periodical volumes; 236,461 microforms; 28,565 maps (cataloged). **Subscriptions:** 3394 journals and other serials; 40 newspapers. **Services:** Interlibrary loans; copying; library open to public. **Computerized Information Services:** BRS, DIALOG; computerized cataloging. **Networks/Consortia:** Member of OCLC; Michigan Library Consortium; Berrien Library Consortium. **Remarks:** Houses E.G. White Research Center. **Staff:** Elaine Mutale, Ref.Libn.; Harvey Brenneise, Assoc.Ref.Libn.; Esther Tyler, Supv., Tech.Serv.; Carol Crider, Cat.; Nancy Vhymeister, Semy.Libn.; Richard Powell, Supv., Tchg.Mtls.Ctr.; Catherine B. Watts, Per. & Maps; Jessie Oliver, Asst., Tchg.Mtls.Ctr.; Elaine Waller, Supv., Music Mtls.Ctr.; Thelma Gilbert, Acq.Libn.; Louise Dederen, Cur., Heritage Rm.

★684★
ANDROSCOGGIN COUNTY LAW LIBRARY (Law)
County Bldg.
Auburn, ME 04210
Phone: (207) 782-3121
Hon. Thomas E. Delahanty, Libn.
Subjects: Law. **Holdings:** 14,000 volumes. **Staff:** Wendy Rau, Asst.Libn.

★685★
ANDROSCOGGIN HISTORICAL SOCIETY - CLARENCE E. MARCH LIBRARY (Hist)
2 Turner St., County Bldg.
Auburn, ME 04210
Phone: (207) 784-0586
Leon M. Norris, Exec.Sec. & Cur.
Staff: 3. **Subjects:** History of Androscoggin County and Maine. **Special Collections:** 500 early photographs of local people and places. **Holdings:** 5000 books; 50 bound periodical volumes; 2000 historical papers; 1000 records; 70 maps; 400 documents; 5000 pages on microfilm. **Services:** Library open to public for reference use only.

★686★
ANDROSCOGGIN VALLEY HOSPITAL - MEDICAL LIBRARY (Med)
Page Hill Rd.
Berlin, NH 03570
Phone: (603) 752-2200
Clarisse Legere, Med.Rec.
Staff: 1. **Subjects:** Medicine. **Holdings:** 640 volumes. **Subscriptions:** 44 journals and other serials. **Services:** Interlibrary loans; copying; library open to public with restrictions. **Networks/Consortia:** Member of Hospital Library Development Services.

ANDRUS (Ethel Percy) GERONTOLOGY CENTER
See: University of Southern California - Ethel Percy Andrus Gerontology Center

ANDRUSS (Harvey A.) LIBRARY
See: Bloomsburg State College - Harvey A. Andruss Library

ANGELL (Katharine) LIBRARY
See: Culinary Institute of America - Katharine Angell Library

ANGERT (Richard W.) MEMORIAL LIBRARY
See: Deaconess Hospital - School of Nursing - Richard W. Angert Memorial Library

★687★
ANGLICAN CHURCH OF CANADA - CHURCH HOUSE LIBRARY (Rel-Theol)
600 Jarvis St.
Toronto, ON, Canada M4Y 2J6
Phone: (416) 924-9192
Alice Marie Hedderick, Libn.
Founded: 1965. **Staff:** Prof 1. **Subjects:** Anglican Communion; social conditions; missions; Christian education. **Holdings:** 2000 books; 70 unbound periodicals (retained); 27 VF drawers; 16 drawers of photographs. **Subscriptions:** 200 journals and other serials. **Services:** Interlibrary loans; copying; library open to public, but with priority to internal clientele. **Also Known As:** Chancellor R.V. Harris Memorial Library.

★688★
ANGLICAN CHURCH OF CANADA - DIOCESE OF CALGARY - ANGLICAN ARCHIVES (Rel-Theol; Hist)
Special Collections Library
University of Calgary
Calgary, AB, Canada T2N 1N4
Phone: (403) 269-1905
John W. Carter, Archv.
Founded: 1945. **Subjects:** History of the Anglican Church in Calgary. **Holdings:** 100 volumes; correspondence and records, 1883 to present. **Services:** Archives open to public with permission of archivist.

★689★
ANGLICAN CHURCH OF CANADA - DIOCESE OF MONTREAL - ARCHIVES (Rel-Theol; Hist)
Synod Office, 1444 Union Ave.
Montreal, PQ, Canada H3A 2B8
Phone: (514) 845-6211
Rev. Canon M.A. Hughes, Adm.Off.
Founded: 1950. **Staff:** Prof 2; Other 6. **Subjects:** History of the Diocese of Montreal, Ecclesiastical Province of Canada, and General Synod of the Anglican Church of Canada. **Holdings:** Registers of marriages, births and deaths; old parish and other records; Episcopal and other letters. **Services:** Archives open to accredited researchers. **Also Known As:** Montreal Diocesan Archives. **Staff:** Mrs. A.R. Lebans, Archv.

★690★
ANGLICAN CHURCH OF CANADA - DIOCESE OF TORONTO - DIOCESAN LIBRARY & RESOURCE CENTRE (Rel-Theol)†
135 Adelaide St., E.
Toronto, ON, Canada M5C 1L8
Phone: (416) 924-9121
Anne Tanner, Diocesan Libn.
Staff: Prof 1; Other 1. **Subjects:** Theology, Bible, doctrine, prayer, spiritual life, Christian education and ethics, pastoral theology, psychology, social concerns, biography, history. **Holdings:** 7000 books; 72 AV items; 8 VF drawers of clippings. **Subscriptions:** 14 journals and other serials. **Services:** Library open to public at librarian's discretion.

★691★
ANGLICAN CHURCH OF CANADA - ECCLESIASTICAL PROV. OF BRITISH COLUMBIA & DIOCESE OF NEW WESTMINSTER - ARCHV. (Rel-Theol)
6050 Chancellor Blvd.
Vancouver, BC, Canada V6T 1X3
Phone: (604) 228-9031
R. Garth Walker, Archv.
Founded: 1956. **Staff:** Prof 1. **Subjects:** History and official records of the Anglican Church in British Columbia and the Yukon. **Special Collections:** Diary of Bishop George Hills, 1838-1895 (39 volumes); British Columbia and Yukon Church Aid Society Collection; Alan Greene Collection (Columbia Coast Mission). **Holdings:** 1100 books; 121 bound periodical volumes; 50 linear feet of parish documents; 64 reels of microfilm; 100 maps; 42 manuscripts. **Subscriptions:** 11 journals and other serials; 7 newspapers. **Services:** Copying; archives open to public. **Networks/Consortia:** Member of Association of British Columbia Archivists; Association of Canadian Archivists.

ANGLICAN CHURCH OF CANADA - ECCLESIASTICAL PROVINCE OF RUPERT'S LAND - ARCHIVES
See: Manitoba - Provincial Archives of Manitoba

★692★
ANGLICAN CHURCH OF CANADA - GENERAL SYNOD ARCHIVES (Rel-Theol; Hist)
600 Jarvis St.
Toronto, ON, Canada M4Y 2J6
Phone: (416) 924-9192
Mrs. Terry Thompson, Archv.
Founded: 1955. **Staff:** Prof 2; Other 1. **Subjects:** General Synod of the Anglican Church of Canada and its Departments; Canadian Anglican history. **Special Collections:** Archival collections relating to the Canadian Anglican Dioceses of the Arctic and Moosonee; church newspapers, printed and microfilmed. **Holdings:** Synod journals; reports of English Missionary Societies relating to Canada; parish histories; sermons; Episcopal charges; religious literature printed in native languages; biographies. **Subscriptions:** 26 Canadian Anglican newspapers and periodicals. **Services:** Archives open to serious researchers. **Staff:** Dorothy Kealey, Asst.Archv.

★693★
ANHEUSER-BUSCH COMPANIES, INC. - CORPORATE LIBRARY (Food-Bev)
One Busch Pl.
St. Louis, MO 63118
Phone: (314) 577-2669
Ann Hunter, Corp.Libn.
Founded: 1933. **Staff:** Prof 2; Other 1. **Subjects:** Brewing chemistry, fermentation technology, food and beverage industries, alcohol and alcoholism, yeast, business and industrial management. **Special Collections:** History of beer and brewing industry. **Holdings:** 9000 books; 17,000 bound periodical volumes; 100 pamphlet boxes of annual reports; 25 VF drawers of U.S. and foreign patents; 70 pamphlet boxes of clippings. **Subscriptions:** 550 journals and other serials. **Services:** Interlibrary loans; copying; library open to public by appointment. **Computerized Information Services:** DIALOG, SDC, New York Times Information Service, Dow Jones News Retrieval; computerized cataloging and ILL. **Networks/Consortia:** Member of St. Louis Regional Library Network. **Publications:** New acquisitions list, bimonthly - distributed to department heads and assistants, and by request; Annual Periodical Holdings List.

ANIMAL DISEASES RESEARCH INSTITUTE LIBRARY
See: Canada - Agriculture Canada

★694★
ANIMAL LIBERATION, INC. - LIBRARY (Food-Bev)
319 W. 74th St.   Phone: (212) 874-1792
New York, NY 10023   Dudley Giehl, Pres.
Subjects: Vegetarianism, animal welfare, factory farming, ecology. **Special Collections:** Bound collection of magazine articles dating from 1908; collection of tapes of radio and television programs dealing with vegetarianism. **Holdings:** 200 books; 7 legal file cases of news clippings; reports and correspondence from foreign countries. **Services:** Copying; library open to public with restrictions.

★695★
ANIMAL MEDICAL CENTER - LIBRARY (Med)
510 E. 62nd St.   Phone: (212) 838-8100
New York, NY 10021   A. Christine MacMurray, Ed./Libn.
Staff: Prof 1. **Subjects:** Veterinary medicine, medicine. **Holdings:** 1500 books; 1500 bound periodical volumes. **Subscriptions:** 50 journals and other serials. **Services:** Interlibrary loans; library not open to public.

ANIMAL RESEARCH CENTRE LIBRARY
See: Canada - Agriculture Canada

★696★
ANN ARBOR NEWS - LIBRARY (Publ)
340 E. Huron St.   Phone: (313) 994-6953
Ann Arbor, MI 48106   Mary Meernik, Libn.
Founded: 1938. **Staff:** Prof 1; Other 1. **Special Collections:** Notebooks on specific events or activities; Washtenaw County newspapers on microfilm from 1829. **Holdings:** Reference books; clippings; picture negatives. **Subscriptions:** 20 journals and other serials; 20 newspapers. **Services:** Interlibrary loans; copying; library not open to public.

★697★
ANNE ARUNDEL COUNTY CIRCUIT COURT - LAW LIBRARY (Law)
Court House, Church Circle   Phone: (301) 224-1387
Annapolis, MD 21401   Joan B. Simison, Libn.
Staff: Prof 1. **Subjects:** Law. **Holdings:** 10,920 books; 80 bound periodical volumes. **Subscriptions:** 87 journals and other serials. **Services:** Copying; library open to public with permission of librarian.

★698★
ANNE ARUNDEL COUNTY OFFICE OF PLANNING AND ZONING - LIBRARY (Plan)
Arundel Center   Phone: (301) 224-1880
Annapolis, MD 21404   Alexander D. Speer, Planner
Staff: Prof 1. **Subjects:** Planning, land use, housing, population, zoning. **Holdings:** 1000 books; 30 bound periodical volumes; 4000 unbound reports. **Subscriptions:** 8 journals and other serials. **Services:** Interlibrary loans; copying; library open to public with restrictions. **Publications:** Acquisition List, irregular; office memorandum - to state and regional planning libraries.

★699★
ANNE ARUNDEL GENERAL HOSPITAL - MEMORIAL LIBRARY (Med)
Franklin & Cathedral Sts.   Phone: (301) 267-1562
Annapolis, MD 21401   Joyce Richmond, Libn.
Staff: Prof 1; Other 1. **Subjects:** Medicine, nursing. **Holdings:** 1076 books; 1060 bound periodical volumes; 142 AV items. **Subscriptions:** 248 journals and other serials; 6 newspapers. **Services:** Interlibrary loans; copying; library open to public for reference use only. **Networks/Consortia:** Member of Mid-Atlantic Regional Medical Library Program (MARLIN); Baltimore Consortium for Resource Sharing; Maryland Association of Health Science Librarians. **Staff:** James Kopelke, Dir., Educ.Serv.

ANNENBERG SCHOOL OF COMMUNICATIONS
See: University of Pennsylvania

★700★
ANOKA AREA VOCATIONAL TECHNICAL INSTITUTE - MEDIA CENTER (Sci-Tech)
1355 W. Main St.   Phone: (612) 427-1880
Anoka, MN 55303   Deborah J. Brude, Hd.Libn.
Founded: 1971. **Staff:** Prof 3; Other 4. **Subjects:** Nursing and other health-related fields; electronics, business, horticulture. **Holdings:** 17,000 books; 580 bound periodical volumes; 807 AV items. **Subscriptions:** 480 journals and other serials; 10 newspapers. **Services:** Library open to public for reference use only. **Computerized Information Services:** DIALOG. **Networks/Consortia:** Member of MINITEX; METRONET. **Publications:** Mediations, quarterly - for internal distribution only. **Staff:** Jeanne Stevens, Asst.Libn; Bruce Anderson, AV Prod.

★701★
ANOKA COUNTY HISTORICAL GENEALOGICAL SOCIETY - LIBRARY (Hist)
1900 3rd Ave. S.   Phone: (612) 421-0600
Anoka, MN 55303   Pat Schwappach, Musm.Dir.
Founded: 1934. **Staff:** 2. **Subjects:** Anoka County history. **Holdings:** 3 VF drawers of manuscripts; newspapers and clippings; 60 reels of microfilm; 25 oral history tapes and maps; county records. **Subscriptions:** 5 journals and other serials. **Services:** Interlibrary loans (microfilm only); copying; library open to public. **Publications:** Historical and genealogical newsletters.

★702★
ANOKA STATE HOSPITAL - LIBRARY (Med)
3300 4th Ave., N.   Phone: (612) 422-4150
Anoka, MN 55303   Harriet Moore, Libn.
Founded: 1951. **Staff:** Prof 1. **Subjects:** Medicine, psychiatry, psychology, social science, nursing. **Holdings:** 3300 books. **Subscriptions:** 46 journals and other serials. **Services:** Interlibrary loans; copying; library open to public. **Networks/Consortia:** Member of Minnesota Department of Public Welfare Library Consortium.

★703★
ANPA RESEARCH INSTITUTE - LIBRARY (Publ)
1350 Sullivan Trail
Box 598   Phone: (215) 253-6155
Easton, PA 18042   Erwin Jaffe, Dir., Res.Ctr.
Subjects: Printing, paper, ink, graphic arts. **Holdings:** 3000 books. **Also Known As:** American Newspaper Publishers Association Research Institute.

★704★
ANSER - TECHNICAL LIBRARY (Sci-Tech)
400 Army-Navy Dr.   Phone: (703) 979-0700
Arlington, VA 22202   Francie G. Binion, Mgr.
Staff: Prof 5; Other 2. **Subjects:** Military science, operations research, health services, mathematics, physics. **Holdings:** 5000 books; 30,000 government and contractor documents. **Subscriptions:** 200 journals and other serials. **Services:** Interlibrary loans; copying; library not open to public. **Publications:** ANSER Library Accession List, monthly - to ANSER clients. **Formerly:** Analytic Services, Inc. **Staff:** Andrea Hutchins, Dp.Mgr.; Claire Leifer, Libn.; Sandy Seh, Libn.

★705★
ANSHE HESED TEMPLE - LIBRARY (Rel-Theol)*
10th & Liberty Sts.   Phone: (814) 454-2426
Erie, PA 16502   Rose Tanner, Chm.
Founded: 1945. **Staff:** 4. **Subjects:** Jewish fiction, literature, biography and history; Bible and Talmud; religion; art. **Holdings:** 3000 books. **Services:** Library open to public.

★706★
ANTA CORPORATION - LIBRARY (Bus-Fin)
101 N. Robinson, Suite 1400   Phone: (405) 272-9321
Oklahoma City, OK 73102   Virginia Milam, Res.Asst.
Staff: Prof 1; Other 1. **Subjects:** Aluminum, plastics, nursing home care, oil, business. **Holdings:** 2500 books; 1500 unbound reports; 8 VF drawers of annual reports. **Subscriptions:** 125 journals and other serials; 25 newspapers. **Services:** Library not open to public. **Computerized Information Services:** Merrill Lynch Econometrics.

★707★
ANTAEUS RESEARCH INSTITUTE - LIBRARY (Med; Hum)*
2470 Gregg Ave.   Phone: (501) 443-3050
Fayetteville, AR 72701   Larry Horn, Libn.
Founded: 1959. **Subjects:** Medicine, humanities. **Holdings:** 5000 books; 2000 bound periodical volumes; 5000 slides. **Subscriptions:** 30 journals and other serials. **Services:** Library open to medical personnel only.

★708★
ANTHOLOGY FILM ARCHIVES - LIBRARY (Aud-Vis)
491 Broadway   Phone: (212) 226-0010
New York, NY 10012
Staff: Prof 1; Other 5. **Subjects:** History of cinema, avant-garde film, video, performance art. **Special Collections:** Biographical files on individual film-makers, video-makers and critics (1642); original manuscripts; Joseph Cornell Collection (52 folders). **Holdings:** 2800 books; 225 bound periodical volumes; 650 magnetic tapes; 525 stills files (arranged by director); 450 film and video organization files; audiotapes of lectures; international publications and periodicals. **Subscriptions:** 125 journals and other serials. **Services:** Copying; archives open to public by appointment. **Publications:** Film Culture Magazine. **Special Catalogs:** Catalog of books and articles on avant-garde

film (card). **Remarks:** Includes the holdings of Film Culture Non-Profit Corporation.

ANTHON (Harold S.) MEMORIAL LIBRARY
See: Chicago Transit Authority - Harold S. Anthon Memorial Library

★709★
ANTHROPOLOGY RESOURCE CENTER (ARC) - CITIZENS INFORMATION CENTER (Soc Sci)
59 Temple Place, Suite 444   Phone: (617) 426-9286
Boston, MA 02111   Michael De Petrillo, Libn.
Staff: Prof 4. **Subjects:** Public interest anthropology - indigenous peoples, international development, energy, education, United States and New England. **Holdings:** 2000 books; 240 bound periodical volumes; 50 VF drawers of clippings, reports, manuscripts, dissertations, government and foreign documents. **Subscriptions:** 250 journals and other serials; 20 newspapers. **Services:** Copying; library open to public for reference use only. **Publications:** ARC Newsletter, quarterly - to members and subscribers; ARC bulletins, bimonthly; list of publications - available upon request. All reports and newsletters are available in bulk for classroom use. **Special Catalogs:** Periodicals, clippings and book catalogs. **Staff:** Sally Swenson, Pubn.Coord.; Luisa Marques, Intern/Libn.

★710★
ANTHROPOSOPHICAL SOCIETY IN CANADA - RUDOLPH STEINER LIBRARY (Rel-Theol)†
81 Lawton Blvd.   Phone: (416) 488-2886
Toronto, ON, Canada M4V 1Z6   Barbara Gunther, Libn.
Founded: 1953. **Staff:** Prof 2; Other 2. **Subjects:** Anthroposophy; spiritual science in religion, art and philosophy. **Special Collections:** Rudolph Steiner's writings and printed lectures on spiritual research on the history and evolution of man. **Holdings:** 5500 books (half in German); 200 bound periodical volumes. **Subscriptions:** 10 journals and other serials. **Services:** Interlibrary loans; library open to public; mail service to out of town patrons. **Special Catalogs:** Lists of holdings in English and in German. **Staff:** Isabel Grieve, Libn.

★711★
ANTI-DEFAMATION LEAGUE OF B'NAI B'RITH - JACOB ALSON MEMORIAL LIBRARY (Soc Sci)
823 United Nations Plaza   Phone: (212) 689-7400
New York, NY 10017   Florence Lummer, Libn.
Founded: 1939. **Staff:** Prof 1; Other 3. **Subjects:** Human relations, discrimination, civil rights, intergroup relations, anti-Semitism, political extremism. **Special Collections:** Anti-Semitic periodicals. **Holdings:** 5000 books; 10,000 pamphlets (cataloged); 8 VF drawers of pamphlets (uncataloged); 300 reels of microfilm. **Subscriptions:** 300 journals and other serials; 30 newspapers. **Services:** Interlibrary loans; copying; library open to public by appointment. **Remarks:** Library is one section of Anti-Defamation League's Department of Research and Evaluation.

ANTI-DEFAMATION LEAGUE OF MINNESOTA-DAKOTAS
See: Jewish Community Relations Council

ANTIETAM NATL. BATTLEFIELD
See: U.S. Natl. Park Service

★712★
ANTIOCH SCHOOL OF LAW - LIBRARY (Law)†
1624 Crescent Place, N.W.   Phone: (202) 265-9500
Washington, DC 20009   William P. Statsky, Libn.
Founded: 1972. **Staff:** Prof 4; Other 5. **Subjects:** Law. **Special Collections:** Judge E. Barrett Prettyman Collection (2411 items). **Holdings:** 13,450 books; 39,975 bound periodical volumes. **Subscriptions:** 110 journals and other serials; 10 newspapers. **Services:** Interlibrary loans; copying; library open to public upon request.

ANTIOCH UNIVERSITY - GLEN HELEN ASSOCIATION
See: Glen Helen Association

★713★
ANTIOCH UNIVERSITY - RESOURCE CENTER (Educ)
401 N. Broad   Phone: (215) 629-1370
Philadelphia, PA 19108   William B. Saunders, Libn./External Coord.
Staff: Prof 1; Other 3. **Subjects:** Behavioral sciences, black studies, humanities, social sciences. **Holdings:** 4300 books; 2 file cabinets of Antioch archives (Philadelphia Center). **Subscriptions:** 169 journals and other serials. **Services:** Interlibrary loans; library open to public with special permission. **Networks/Consortia:** Member of Tri-State College Library Cooperative

(TCLC). **Publications:** Imprints (literary magazine), biennial. **Staff:** Joanna DiPaolo, Internal Coord.; Tyrone Long, Media Spec.; Joann Ford, Cat.

ANTIQUARIAN AND NUMISMATIC SOCIETY OF MONTREAL
See: Societe d'Archeologie et de Numismatique de Montreal

ANTIQUE AIRPLANE ASSOCIATION
See: Airpower Museum

ANTIQUE AUTOMOBILE CLUB OF AMERICA
See: AACA Library & Research Center, Inc.

★714★
ANTIQUE AND CLASSIC CAR CLUB OF CANADA - LIBRARY (Rec)
27 Queen St., E., Suite 404   Phone: (416) 621-9743
Toronto, ON, Canada M5C 2M6   Peter Weatherhead, Pubn.Chm.
Founded: 1955. **Staff:** 1. **Subjects:** Automobiles - antique, classic, veteran, vintage, post-war thoroughbred. **Holdings:** 1000 books; original brochures, photographs. **Services:** Library open to members with restrictions.

★715★
ANTIQUE AND HISTORIC GLASS FOUNDATION - LIBRARY (Art)
Box 7413   Phone: (419) 531-5679
Toledo, OH 43615   Carl U. Fauster, Dir.
Subjects: American glass, New England Glass Company, Libbey Glass Company. **Special Collections:** Libbey Glass (200 pieces). **Holdings:** 200 books; Libbey catalogs, booklets, advertisments, documents, photographs. **Publications:** Amberina Glass, New England Glass Works, 1884; Libbey Cut Glass, 1896, (both reprints); Libbey Glass since 1818.

★716★
ANTIQUE PHONOGRAPH MONTHLY - APM LIBRARY OF RECORDED SOUND (Aud-Vis; Mus)
502 E. 17th St.   Phone: (212) 941-6835
Brooklyn, NY 11226   Allen Koenigsberg, Dir.
Founded: 1968. **Staff:** Prof 2; Other 1. **Subjects:** History of recorded sound; discography; antique phonograph repair. **Special Collections:** Early history of sound recording on cylinder records (5000 cylinders dating from 1892 to 1929). **Holdings:** 500 books; 12 bound periodical volumes; 2000 phonograph patents; 200 trade catalogs; 75 antique phonographs dated 1878-1913. **Subscriptions:** 15 journals and other serials. **Services:** Copying; library open to public by appointment. **Computerized Information Services:** Computerized cataloging; computerized phototypesetting from an internal database. **Publications:** Antique Phonograph Monthly - by subscription. **Special Catalogs:** Edison Cylinder Records, 1889-1912 (book); A Collector's Guide to the Columbia Graphophone (book); Victor Record Index, 1900-1909 (book); Edison Blue Amberol Recordings, 1912-1929; Columbia Cylinder Records, 1890-1909 (cards). **Staff:** Robert Feinstein, Archv.

★717★
ANTIQUE WIRELESS ASSOCIATION, INC. - LIBRARY (Hist; Sci-Tech)†
Main St. (East Bloomfield)   Phone: (716) 657-7489
Holcomb, NY 14469   Bruce Kelley, Dir./Cur.
Staff: 2. **Subjects:** History of radio, television, telegraph; electricity; communication. **Holdings:** 2000 books; 5000 radio/electronic magazines. **Subscriptions:** 10 journals and other serials. **Services:** Library open to public by appointment. **Publications:** Old Timers Bulletin, quarterly journal.

APA ARCHIVES
See: American Psychiatric Museum Association

APLIC INTERNATIONAL
See: Association for Population/Family Planning Libraries & Information Centers International

APM LIBRARY OF RECORDED SOUND
See: Antique Phonograph Monthly

★718★
APPALACHIA EDUCATIONAL LABORATORY - RESEARCH & INFORMATION CENTER (Educ)
Box 1348   Phone: (304) 347-0428
Charleston, WV 25325   Louise Kinzy, Libn.
Staff: Prof 1. **Subjects:** Education. **Special Collections:** ERIC microfiche (complete set). **Holdings:** 8000 books; 100 titles of unbound and microfilmed periodicals. **Subscriptions:** 105 journals and other serials. **Services:** Interlibrary loans; copying; library open to public for reference use only.

★719★
APPALACHIAN BIBLE COLLEGE - LIBRARY (Rel-Theol)
Bradley, WV 25818
Phone: (304) 877-6428
John Van Puffelen, Libn.
Founded: 1950. **Staff:** Prof 2; Other 2. **Subjects:** Religion, theology, Bible. **Special Collections:** Patterson Collection of Judaica (425 items). **Holdings:** 30,000 books. **Subscriptions:** 175 journals and other serials. **Services:** Interlibrary loans; copying; library open to area ministers. **Staff:** Sharon Lucas, Asst.Libn.

★720★
APPALACHIAN MOUNTAIN CLUB - LIBRARY (Geog-Map; Rec)
5 Joy St.
Boston, MA 02108
Phone: (617) 523-0636
C. Francis Belcher, Archv./Cons.
Subjects: Mountains, mountaineering, exploration, history of mountain areas. **Special Collections:** Journals of mountain clubs around the world; White Mountains. **Holdings:** 6000 books, periodicals, and pamphlets. **Services:** Interlibrary loans; library open to public for reference use only.

APPALACHIAN ORAL HISTORY PROJECT
See: Lloyd (Alice) College

★721★
APPALACHIAN REGIONAL COMMISSION - LIBRARY (Plan)
1666 Connecticut Ave., N.W.
Washington, DC 20235
Phone: (202) 673-7845
Linda M. Harrison, Libn.
Founded: 1966. **Staff:** 1. **Subjects:** Appalachia, regional planning, energy policy. **Holdings:** 15,000 books and reports. **Subscriptions:** 433 journals and other serials. **Services:** Interlibrary loans; library open to public. **Networks/Consortia:** Member of Metropolitan Washington Library Council. **Publications:** Periodical holdings list, annual.

★722★
APPALACHIAN REGIONAL HOSPITAL - MEDICAL LIBRARY (Med)
306 Stanaford Rd.
Beckley, WV 25801
Phone: (304) 255-3261
Thelma Wilson, Dir. of Educ.
Staff: 1. **Subjects:** Internal medicine, surgery, pediatrics, nursing, psychiatry and behavioral science, allied health sciences. **Holdings:** 2000 books; 600 bound periodical volumes. **Subscriptions:** 80 journals and other serials; 5 newspapers. **Services:** Interlibrary loans; copying; library open to public for reference use only. **Computerized Information Services:** Online systems. **Networks/Consortia:** Member of Huntington Health Science Library Consortium.

★723★
APPALACHIAN STATE UNIVERSITY - BELK LIBRARY - SPECIAL COLLECTIONS (Educ; Hist)
Boone, NC 28608
Phone: (704) 262-2186
Richard T. Barker, Univ.Libn.
Founded: 1903. **Special Collections:** Instructional Materials Center; Appalachian Regional Collection. **Holdings:** Figures not available for books; 100,000 government documents. **Services:** Interlibrary loans; copying; library open to public. **Computerized Information Services:** DIALOG, ERIC; computerized cataloging. **Networks/Consortia:** Member of OCLC through SOLINET. **Publications:** Belk Library News.

★724★
APPALACHIAN STATE UNIVERSITY - MUSIC LIBRARY (Mus)
I.G. Greer Music Bldg.
Boone, NC 28608
Phone: (704) 262-2292
Joan O. Falconer, Music Libn.
Founded: 1952. **Staff:** Prof 1; Other 1. **Subjects:** Music and music education. **Holdings:** 9000 books and music scores; 6500 phonograph records and tapes (cataloged); 2257 volumes of ensemble music. **Services:** Library open to Boone residents for in-house use. **Publications:** Bibliography of new materials, quarterly. **Remarks:** All music periodicals and other music books are housed in the Belk Library.

★725★
APPLIED TECHNOLOGY CORPORATION - LIBRARY (Sci-Tech)
Box FF
Norman, OK 73070
Phone: (405) 364-5431
Founded: 1977. **Subjects:** Chemical engineering, liquefied natural and petroleum gases, fire safety. **Holdings:** 1500 volumes; 75 dissertations; 6 VF drawers of reports and clippings; 200 reports on microfiche. **Subscriptions:** 35 journals and other serials. **Services:** Copying; SDI; library not open to public. **Computerized Information Services:** Online systems.

APPOMATTOX COURT HOUSE NATL. HISTORICAL PARK
See: U.S. Natl. Park Service

APPSST
See: Association Paritaire de Prevention pour la Sante et la Securite du Travail du Quebec

★726★
AQUATIC RESEARCH INSTITUTE - AQUATIC SCIENCES & TECHNOLOGY ARCHIVE (Sci-Tech)
2242 Davis Court
Hayward, CA 94545
Phone: (415) 785-2216
V. Parker, Archv.
Founded: 1962. **Subjects:** Aquatic sciences; limnology; oceanology; marine, freshwater and estuarine biology; water quality; aquaculture and mariculture; fisheries; ocean engineering and mining; submersibles; undersea military; aquarium technology. **Special Collections:** Rare books on fish and fisheries. **Holdings:** 40,000 biological specimens; 45,000 volumes; 1000 journals; 5000 photographs; 3000 slides; 1000 maps and charts; 1100 abstracts and indexes; 1500 technical reports; 150,000 pamphlets; 1000 microforms. **Services:** Interlibrary loans; copying (limited); identifies aquatic organisms; library open to public in presence of librarian. A fee may be charged for services, depending on the nature and extent of the service requested. **Publications:** Aquatica journal; special reports.

AQUINAS MEDICAL LIBRARY
See: St. Michael Medical Center

ARAB INFORMATION CENTER
See: League of Arab States

★727★
ARABIAN HORSE OWNERS FOUNDATION - W.R. BROWN MEMORIAL LIBRARY (Rec)
4633 E. Broadway, Suite 131
Tucson, AZ 85711
Phone: (602) 326-1515
Sharon Byford, Exec.Sec.
Founded: 1957. **Subjects:** Arabian horses - history, breeding, use; horse in general - use, care, training, literature, history. **Special Collections:** Correspondence and farm records for Maynesboro Stud, owned by W.R. Brown. **Holdings:** 800 books; 20 bound periodical volumes; films and photographs; Arabian show and sale programs. **Services:** Copying; limited research for individuals by correspondence; library open to public for reference use only by appointment. **Publications:** Reprints of historical books and pamphlets, irregular.

★728★
ARABIAN HORSE TRUST - LIBRARY (Rec)
8751 E. Hampden, Suite B-8
Denver, CO 80231
Phone: (303) 750-5689
William M. Riley, Jr., Exec.Dir.
Founded: 1974. **Staff:** 5. **Subjects:** Arabian horses - breeding, history; horsemanship. **Special Collections:** James Lewis Collection; Preston Dyer Collection; Randolph Huntington Collection; John Rogers Collection. **Holdings:** 400 books; 150 bound periodical volumes; over 3000 horse photographs; 20,000 pictures of Arabian horses. **Services:** Copying; library open to public with restrictions. **Publications:** Arabian Horse Trust Newsletter. **Special Catalogs:** Complete bibliography of all Arabian horse related publications (in preparation); catalog of Arabian horse pictures by registration number; 30 Year Breeder Scrapbook Program. **Formerly:** Arabian Horse Registry Trust of America.

ARAS (Archive For Research In Archetypal Symbolism)
See: Jung (C.G) Institute of Los Angeles, Inc.

★729★
ARCAIR COMPANY - LIBRARY (Sci-Tech)
Box 406
Lancaster, OH 43130
Phone: (614) 653-5618
Dottie Young, Libn.
Founded: 1974. **Staff:** Prof 1; Other 1. **Subjects:** Welding, management. **Special Collections:** Air carbon ARC cutting reports; underwater cutting and welding (175 books and reports). **Holdings:** 1000 books; 30 bound periodical volumes; 500 specifications and standards; 10 VF drawers of technical reports and engineering design catalogs; 1500 patents. **Subscriptions:** 190 journals and other serials. **Services:** Interlibrary loans; copying; library open to public by appointment. **Computerized Information Services:** DIALOG; internal database. **Networks/Consortia:** Member of Library Council of Fairfield County.

★730★
ARCANE ORDER - LIBRARY (Rel-Theol)
Studio of Contemplation
2904 Rosemary Lane
Falls Church, VA 22042 Jennifer E. O'Neill, Cur.
Founded: 1950. **Staff:** 4. **Subjects:** Psychology, parapsychology, mysticism, biography, art, history. **Special Collections:** Archives of publications of the Arcane Order. **Holdings:** 1500 books; 25 bound periodical volumes; 30 art works (cataloged); 2 cases of correspondence with members; 30 other items. **Subscriptions:** 25 journals and other serials; 5 newspapers. **Services:** Library not open to public. **Publications:** Academic Research Cenotaph, serial publication - to members; Second Intellectual List of Leaders Yearbook, irregular. **Special Catalogs:** Catalog of membership (1010 cards). **Staff:** Randel Dean Drake, Kpr./Ephemera; Leonard J. Mather, Kpr./Memorabilia.

★731★
ARCHAEOLOGICAL SOCIETY OF NEW JERSEY - LIBRARY (Soc Sci)*
Rm. 8, Humanities Bldg.
Seton Hall University Phone: (201) 762-6680
South Orange, NJ 07079 Joan E. Kraft, Chm., Lib.Comm.
Founded: 1931. **Staff:** 1. **Subjects:** Archeology - prehistoric, historic; American Indian ethnology. **Special Collections:** Reports and references dealing with New Jersey prehistory. **Holdings:** 300 books; 200 periodicals (cataloged). **Subscriptions:** 20 journals and other serials. **Services:** Interlibrary loans; copying; library open to public with restrictions and by appointment.

ARCHBISHOP BERGAN MERCY HOSPITAL
See: Bergan Mercy Hospital

ARCHBISHOP CORRIGAN MEMORIAL LIBRARY
See: St. Joseph's Seminary

★732★
ARCHBOLD BIOLOGICAL STATION - LIBRARY (Sci-Tech)
Rte. 2, Box 180 Phone: (813) 465-2571
Lake Placid, FL 33852 Fred E. Lohrer, Libn.
Founded: 1941. **Staff:** Prof 1. **Subjects:** Ecology, behavior and evolution of vertebrates and terrestrial arthropods; plant ecology; general biology; Florida natural history. **Special Collections:** Hymenopteran taxonomic literature (65 books, 1200 cataloged reprints); Results of the Archbold Expeditions - Numbers 1-86 (Zoology, 9 bound volumes; Botany, 4 bound volumes); Physiological Ecology of Vertebrates (3 VF drawers of reprints). **Holdings:** 2600 books; 2700 bound periodical volumes; 7625 color transparencies of Florida natural history (cataloged); 1400 U.S. Geological Survey quadrangle maps of Florida; 1940, 1944, 1958, 1966, 1971 and 1980 series of U.S. Department of Agriculture aerial photographs of Highlands County; 17,000 reprints on vertebrate ecology; 8 VF drawers of archives of Archbold Biological Station and Expeditions. **Subscriptions:** 290 journals and other serials. **Services:** Interlibrary loans; copying; library open to public by appointment. **Publications:** List of Recent Publications of the Archbold Biological Station, irregular - by exchange. **Special Catalogs:** Bibliography of the Archbold Biological Station (card).

ARCHBOLD (Charles J. and Anna N.) MEMORIAL LIBRARY
See: St. John and West Shore Hospital - Media Center

★733★
ARCHBOLD (John D.) MEMORIAL HOSPITAL - RALPH PERKINS MEMORIAL LIBRARY (Med)
Gordon & Mimosa Sts.
Box 1018 Phone: (912) 226-4121
Thomasville, GA 31792 Susan Danner, Med.Libn.
Staff: Prof 1. **Subjects:** Medicine and related subjects. **Holdings:** 200 books; 2000 bound periodical volumes; 40 video cassettes. **Subscriptions:** 50 journals and other serials. **Services:** Interlibrary loans; copying; library open to public for reference use only. **Computerized Information Services:** NLM. **Networks/Consortia:** Member of Southwest Georgia Health Science Library Consortium.

★734★
ARCHDIOCESE OF CINCINNATI - ARCHIVES (Rel-Theol)
6616 Beechmont Ave.
Cincinnati, OH 45230 Phone: (513) 731-9229
Fr. M. Edmund Hussey, Archv.
Staff: Prof 2; Other 1. **Special Collections:** History of the Archdiocese of Cincinnati (manuscripts); Cincinnati Archdiocesan Records, 1813-1928 (25 linear feet); Mt. St. Mary of the West Seminary, Cincinnati, Ohio, 1850-1948, (25 linear feet); papers and correspondence of: Archbishop John Baptist Purcell, 1818-1883 (15 linear feet); Archbishop William Henry Elder,

1824-1904 (41 linear feet); Archbishop Henry Moeller, 1875-1924 (50 linear feet); Archbishop John Timothy McNicholas, 1900-1950 (14 linear feet). **Holdings:** Figures not available for books. **Services:** Archives open to public by appointment. **Staff:** Gerard P. Hiland, Asst.Archv.

ARCHDIOCESE OF CINCINNATI - ATHENAEUM OF OHIO - MOUNT ST. MARY'S SEMINARY OF THE WEST
See: Mount St. Mary's Seminary of the West

★735★
ARCHDIOCESE OF HARTFORD - CATHOLIC LIBRARY & INFORMATION CENTER (Rel-Theol)
125 Market St. Phone: (203) 522-0602
Hartford, CT 06103 Rev. Edward J. McLean, Exec.Dir.
Founded: 1935. **Staff:** Prof 1; Other 6. **Subjects:** Theology, church history, scripture, biography. **Special Collections:** Georges Rouault Art Collection. **Holdings:** 10,000 books. **Subscriptions:** 8 newspapers. **Services:** Interlibrary loans; library open to public with restrictions.

ARCHDIOCESE OF NEWARK - ARCHIVES
See: Seton Hall University - University Archives

★736★
ARCHDIOCESE OF PHILADELPHIA - CATHOLIC INFORMATION CENTER (Rel-Theol)
936 Market St. Phone: (215) 587-3520
Philadelphia, PA 19107 Rev. Paul F. Curran, Dir.
Founded: 1953. **Staff:** Prof 1; Other 3. **Subjects:** Catechetics, Biblical exegesis, biography, prayer and meditation, moral theology, religion and the arts. **Holdings:** 1800 books; 10 racks of pamphlets and educational materials. **Subscriptions:** 25 journals and other serials; 7 newspapers. **Services:** Interlibrary loans; copying; SDI; center open to public. **Publications:** On Center, monthly. **Staff:** Rev. Francis J. Renz, S.J., Mgr.

★737★
ARCHDIOCESE OF SAN FRANCISCO - CHANCERY ARCHIVES (Rel-Theol)
Box 1799 Phone: (415) 994-5211
Colma, CA 94014 James Abajian, Archv.
Staff: Prof 1. **Subjects:** Catholic Church in Northern California, California missions and history, charitable organizations. **Special Collections:** Alexander S. Taylor collection of manuscripts relating to California missions, 1772-1849 (2550 items). **Holdings:** 800 books; 154 VF drawers of correspondence, miscellaneous reports (1850-1952); San Francisco Catholic newspapers (1867-1981), both original and on microfilm. **Subscriptions:** 7 journals and other serials. **Services:** Copying; library open to public with restrictions.

★738★
ARCHER DANIELS MIDLAND COMPANY - LIBRARY (Food-Bev)
4666 Faries Pkwy. Phone: (217) 424-5397
Decatur, IL 62526 Richard E. Wallace, Mgr., Info.Serv.
Founded: 1969. **Staff:** Prof 2; Other 3. **Subjects:** Foods, fats and oils, grains, agricultural economics, nutrition, organic chemistry. **Holdings:** 6500 books; 500 bound periodical volumes; 9000 U.S. and foreign patents; 6500 reports, reprints; 1500 reels of serials on microfilm; 7000 microfiche; 1300 slides; 19 VF drawers. **Subscriptions:** 908 journals and other serials. **Services:** Interlibrary loans; copying; library open to public by appointment. **Computerized Information Services:** DIALOG, SDC, Dow Jones News Retrieval, New York Times Information Service, BRS. **Networks/Consortia:** Member of Rolling Prairie Library System.

ARCHIBALD FOUNDATION LIBRARY
See: Canadian Bible College/Canadian Theological Seminary

ARCHIBALD LIBRARY
See: Briercrest Bible College

ARCHIBALD MAC LEISH COLLECTION
See: Greenfield Community College Foundation

★739★
ARCHITECTS COLLABORATIVE - LIBRARY (Art; Plan)
46 Brattle St. Phone: (617) 868-4200
Cambridge, MA 02138 Anne Hartmere, Libn.
Founded: 1956. **Staff:** Prof 1; Other 2. **Subjects:** Architecture, building, planning. **Special Collections:** Manufacturer's catalogs (2000). **Holdings:** 2000 books; 220 bound periodical volumes; 250 firm reports (cataloged); 70,000 slides of firm's work; 50,000 construction drawings, 1946 to present; 150 reels of microfilmed working drawings. **Subscriptions:** 137 journals and other serials. **Services:** Library open to public with restrictions.

Publications: Acquisitions list; Guide to the Library.

★740★

ARCHITECTURAL WOODWORK INSTITUTE - LIBRARY (Art)
2310 S. Walter Reed Dr.   Phone: (703) 671-9100
Arlington, VA 22206
Subjects: Architectural woodwork and woodwork practice. **Holdings:** Books, reports, photographs, and data. **Services:** Library open to qualified users.

ARCHIVE OF FOLK CULTURE
See: Library of Congress - American Folklife Center

ARCHIVE FOR NEW POETRY
See: University of California, San Diego - University Libraries

ARCHIVE OF PACIFIC NORTHWEST ARCHAEOLOGY
See: University of Idaho

ARCHIVE OF POPULAR AMERICAN MUSIC
See: University of California, Los Angeles - Music Library

ARCHIVE OF POPULAR CULTURE
See: University of Pittsburgh - Special Collections Department

ARCHIVE FOR RESEARCH IN ARCHETYPAL SYMBOLISM
See: Jung (C.G.) Institute of Los Angeles, Inc.

★741★

ARCHIVES OF AMERICAN ART/SMITHSONIAN INSTITUTION - NATIONAL HEADQUARTERS (Art)
41 E. 65th St.   Phone: (212) 826-5722
New York, NY 10021   W.E. Woolfenden, Dir.
Founded: 1954. **Staff:** Prof 31; Other 8. **Subjects:** American art; history of American visual arts; general American history. **Holdings:** Manuscripts (8 million items in over 3000 collections); 1700 oral history interviews; 15,000 catalogs of art auctions and exhibitions; official records of galleries and art institutions (all material is on microfilm). **Services:** Interlibrary loans; depository of manuscripts and papers related to American art, and art in America, of all sources; archives open to scholars. **Publications:** Archives of American Art Journal, quarterly; Arts in America: A Bibliography (4 volumes). **Special Catalogs:** Card Catalog of the Manuscript Collection of the Archives of American Art (10 volumes). **Remarks:** The archives maintains 6 research centers and the microfilm holdings are available in all centers. The 6 centers are located as follows: New York Area - 41 E. 65th St., New York, NY 10021 (for research purposes); New England Area - 87 Mount Vernon St., Boston, MA 02108; Washington Area - Fine Arts & Portrait Gallery Bldg., 8th & F Sts., N.W., Washington, DC 20560; Midwest Area - Detroit Institute of Arts, 5200 Woodward Ave., Detroit, MI 48202; West Coast Area - Fine Arts Museums of San Francisco, M.H. de Young Memorial Museum, Golden Gate Park, San Francisco, CA 94118; Texas Area - Museum of Fine Arts, Box 6826, Houston, TX 77005.

ARCHIVES OF APPALACHIA
See: East Tennessee State University

★742★

ARCHIVES OF CALIFORNIA ART (Art)
Oakland Museum
1000 Oak St.   Phone: (415) 273-3005
Oakland, CA 94607   Christine Doran, Libn.
Staff: Prof 1. **Subjects:** Historical and contemporary California art, American art, Western Americana, Gold Rush Period, Mission Days, Rancho Period. **Holdings:** 2500 books; 40 scrapbooks; 2000 catalogs, including those of Western museums; archival material on 15,000 artists, craftsmen and photographers. **Subscriptions:** 20 journals and other serials. **Services:** Archives open to public by appointment.

★743★

ARCHIVES OF THE CANADIAN ROCKIES (Hist)
Box 160   Phone: (403) 762-2291
Banff, AB, Canada T0L 0C0   Edward J. Hart, Adm.
Founded: 1965. **Staff:** Prof 4; Other 1. **Subjects:** History, peoples and geology of Western Canada and the Canadian Rockies. **Holdings:** 3990 books and pamphlets; 141 bound periodical volumes; 400 manuscripts; 60,000 photographs; 40,000 negatives, tapes and artifacts. **Subscriptions:** 39 journals and other serials; 7 newspapers. **Services:** Archives open to public for reference use only. **Publications:** The CAIRN Quarterly; Friends of the Peter and Catharine Whyte Foundation. **Remarks:** Maintained by the Peter and Catharine Whyte Foundation, the Archives of the Canadian Rockies also

administers the Alpine Club of Canada Library. **Staff:** Mary Andrews, Libn.

ARCHIVES OF THE CANADIAN ROCKIES - ALPINE CLUB OF CANADA
See: Alpine Club of Canada

ARCHIVES OF THE HISTORY OF AMERICAN PSYCHOLOGY
See: University of Akron

ARCHIVES OF THE MENNONITE CHURCH
See: Historical Committee of the Mennonite Church

ARCHIVES PUBLIQUES DU CANADA
See: Canada - Public Archives of Canada

ARCHIVES AND SPECIAL COLLECTIONS ON WOMEN IN MEDICINE
See: Medical College of Pennsylvania

ARCHIVES DES URSULINES DE QUEBEC
See: Monastere des Ursulines

ARCHIVO GENERAL DE INDIAS OF SEVILLE
See: Tulane University of Louisiana - Latin American Library

ARCHIVO GENERAL DE LA NACION OF MEXICO
See: Tulane University of Louisiana - Latin American Library

ARCHIVO GENERAL DE PUERTO RICO
See: Puerto Rico - Institute of Puerto Rican Culture

ARCO
See: Atlantic-Richfield Company

ARCTIC BIOLOGICAL STATION LIBRARY
See: Canada - Fisheries & Oceans - R&D Directorate

ARCTIC ENVIRONMENTAL INFORMATION AND DATA CENTER
See: University of Alaska, Anchorage

★744★

ARCTIC INSTITUTE OF NORTH AMERICA - LIBRARY (Area-Ethnic; Sci-Tech)
University Of Calgary Library
2500 University Dr., N.W.   Phone: (403) 284-5966
Calgary, AB, Canada T2N 1N4   Hazel Fry, Northern Stud.Libn.
Founded: 1945. **Subjects:** Arctic and Antarctic regions - geology, geography, meteorology, oceanography, glaciology, zoology, botany; snow, ice and permafrost studies; history of exploration; native studies; economic and social development; energy resources. **Holdings:** 16,000 books and bound periodical volumes; 30,000 reprints and pamphlets; 50 boxes of manuscripts and field reports. **Subscriptions:** 650 journals and other serials; 21 newspapers. **Services:** Interlibrary loans; copying; library open to public. **Computerized Information Services:** DIALOG, QL Systems, SDC, CAN/OLE (through University of Calgary Library). **Special Catalogs:** Catalogue of the Arctic Institute of North America, 1968 (4 volumes and 3 supplements).

★745★

AREA COOPERATIVE EDUCATIONAL SERVICES - TEACHER LIBRARY (Educ)
295 Mill Rd.   Phone: (203) 234-0130
North Haven, CT 06473   Virginia Evitts, Libn.
Founded: 1971. **Staff:** Prof 1. **Subjects:** Education. **Holdings:** 975 books; 750 newsletters and research papers. **Subscriptions:** 125 journals and other serials. **Services:** Copying; SDI; library open to public. **Special Catalogs:** Card catalog of literature searches performed.

★746★

AREA COUNCIL FOR ECONOMIC EDUCATION (ACEE) - LIBRARY (Bus-Fin)†
254 Suburban Sta. Bldg.
1617 John F. Kennedy Blvd.   Phone: (215) 564-3504
Philadelphia, PA 19103
Founded: 1949. **Staff:** Prof 4; Other 2. **Subjects:** Economics, free enterprise, American business, economic education in high schools, people and profits, productivity. **Holdings:** 150 books; 50 bound periodical volumes; 300 pamphlets (cataloged); 5 volumes of newspaper clippings; 2 VF drawers of brochures (by other economic organizations); 1500 brochures (by ACES); 5 series films. **Subscriptions:** 15 journals and other serials; 8 newspapers. **Services:** Interlibrary loans; library open to public by referral. **Publications:** ACEE Newsletter, bimonthly.

ARECIBO OBSERVATORY
See: Cornell University

ARENSBERG ARCHIVES
See: Francis Bacon Foundation

★747★
ARENT, FOX, KINTNER, PLOTKIN & KAHN - LIBRARY (Law)
1815 H St., N.W.   Phone: (202) 857-6296
Washington, DC 20006   Mark P. Shaw, Libn.
Staff: Prof 4; Other 2. Subjects: Law. Special Collections: Federal and District of Columbia legislative histories. Holdings: 22,000 books. Subscriptions: 16 newspapers. Services: Interlibrary loans; copying; SDI; library not open to public. Computerized Information Services: DIALOG, New York Times Information Service, LEXIS; computerized serials. Staff: Robert Dickey, Asst.Libn.; Katherine King, Fed.Leg.Libn.; Darlene Weingarth, D.C. Leg.Libn.

ARENTS COLLECTION OF BOOKS IN PARTS
See: New York Public Library - Arents Collection of Books in Parts and Associated Materials

ARENTS (George) RESEARCH LIBRARY FOR SPECIAL COLLECTIONS
See: Syracuse University - George Arents Research Library for Special Collections

ARENTS TOBACCO COLLECTION
See: New York Public Library

★748★
ARGENTINE INFORMATION SERVICE CENTER
60 E. 42nd St.
New York, NY 10017
Defunct

★749★
ARGONNE NATIONAL LABORATORY - ARGONNE-WEST TECHNICAL LIBRARY (Energy)
Box 2528   Phone: (208) 526-7237
Idaho Falls, ID 83401   Barbara J. Swanson, Libn.
Staff: Prof 1; Other 1. Subjects: Chemistry, physics, mathematics, nuclear and mechanical engineering. Special Collections: Liquid metal fast breeder reactor and sodium technology materials. Holdings: 5000 books; 100,000 microfiche; 13,000 unbound reports. Subscriptions: 80 journals and other serials. Services: Interlibrary loans; copying; library open to public on a need to know basis, limited access to some material. Computerized Information Services: DOE/RECON. Remarks: The Argonne National Laboratory operates under contract to the U.S. Department of Energy.

★750★
ARGONNE NATIONAL LABORATORY - NATIONAL ENERGY SOFTWARE CENTER (Info Sci; Energy)
9700 S. Cass Ave.   Phone: (312) 972-7250
Argonne, IL 60439   Margaret K. Butler, Dir.
Staff: Prof 11; Other 6. Subjects: Computer software in energy research and development areas, mathematical software. Holdings: 900 computer software packages. Services: Library open to public with restrictions. Computerized Information Services: DOE/RECON; computerized cataloging, acquisitions and circulation. Publications: ANL-7411 Revised, ANL-8040; frequent notes, bulletins and newsletters. Remarks: The Argonne National Laboratory operates under contract to the U.S. Department of Energy.

★751★
ARGONNE NATIONAL LABORATORY - TECHNICAL INFORMATION SERVICES DEPARTMENT (Energy)
9700 S. Cass Ave., Bldg. 203-C110   Phone: (312) 972-4221
Argonne, IL 60439   Hillis L. Griffin, Dir.
Founded: 1946. Staff: Prof 13; Other 15. Subjects: Nuclear science and engineering, physics, mathematics, chemistry, biological sciences, materials science, energy and environmental sciences. Special Collections: DOE, AEC and foreign reports on topics of programmatic interest. Holdings: 155,000 volumes; 800,000 unclassified reports. Subscriptions: 2200 journals. Services: Interlibrary loans; library open to public upon application. Computerized Information Services: DOE/RECON, DIALOG, SDC, BRS, New York Times Information Service, MEDLINE, RLIN; computerized cataloging, acquisitions, serials and technical reports. Networks/Consortia: Member of OCLC. Publications: Additions to the Library, weekly; List of Serial Holdings, quarterly; AV materials, irregular. Remarks: The Argonne National Laboratory operates under contract to the U.S. Department of Energy.

★752★
ARGUS ARCHIVES, INC. (Sci-Tech)
228 E. 49th St.   Phone: (212) 355-6140
New York, NY 10017   Jean Stewart, Res.Assoc.
Staff: 1. Subjects: Animal welfare, humane education. Holdings: 280 books; 12 VF drawers of reports, clippings, state and federal documents. Subscriptions: 50 journals and other serials. Services: Copying; library open to researchers and writers by appointment. Publications: List of publications - available upon request; Alternatives to Pain in Experiments on Animals; Films for Humane Education; Traps and Trapping; Furs and Fashion.

★753★
ARGUS RESEARCH CORPORATION - LIBRARY (Bus-Fin)
42 Broadway   Phone: (212) 425-7500
New York, NY 10004   Laurie Wiehle, Libn.
Staff: 1. Subjects: Business and industry. Holdings: Company and industry files; government publications. Subscriptions: 50 journals and other serials; 12 newspapers. Services: Interlibrary loans for clients; library open to clients only.

★754★
ARICA INSTITUTE, INC. - LIBRARY AND ARCHIVES (Soc Sci)
235 Park Ave., S.
New York, NY 10003   David J. Johnson, Libn./Archv.
Founded: 1975. Subjects: Psychology, medicine, creativity and organization. Holdings: Figures not available. Services: Library not open to public.

ARID LANDS INFORMATION CENTER
See: University of Arizona

ARIEL ARCHIVES
See: University of Calgary - Special Collections Division

★755★
ARINC RESEARCH CORPORATION - TECHNICAL LIBRARY (Info Sci)
1075 Camino del Rio, S.
Box 85130   Phone: (714) 299-7561
San Diego, CA 92138-9179   Hope E. Anderson, Libn.
Founded: 1979. Staff: Prof 1. Subjects: Computer systems - reliability, availability, maintainability; naval weapon systems. Special Collections: ARINC publications (2000 volumes). Holdings: 200 books; 400 technical reports. Subscriptions: 91 journals and other serials. Services: Interlibrary loans; copying; library open to public by special arrangement. Computerized Information Services: DIALOG, DTIC.

★756★
ARINC RESEARCH CORPORATION - TECHNICAL LIBRARY (Sci-Tech)
2551 Riva Rd.   Phone: (301) 224-4000
Annapolis, MD 21401   William O. Lively, Libn.
Staff: 1. Subjects: Reliability, maintainability, cost analysis, systems architecture, systems analysis. Holdings: 3000 books; 5000 Defense Documentation Center reports; 450 NASA reports; 20,000 specifications, standards and handbooks; 8000 DDC and NASA reports on microfiche. Subscriptions: 105 journals and other serials. Services: Interlibrary loans; library not open to public.

ARIZONA BUREAU OF GEOLOGY & MINERAL TECHNOLOGY LIBRARY
See: University of Arizona

ARIZONA COLLEGE OF NATUROPATHIC MEDICINE
See: American College of Natural Therapeutics & Arizona College of Naturopathic Medicine

ARIZONA COOPERATIVE WILDLIFE RESEARCH UNIT
See: University of Arizona

★757★
ARIZONA DAILY STAR - LIBRARY (Publ)
4850 S. Park Ave.
Box 26807   Phone: (602) 294-4433
Tucson, AZ 85726   Elaine Y. Raines, Chf.Libn.
Founded: 1950. Staff: Prof 2; Other 13. Subjects: Tucson subjects from 1939 to present. Special Collections: Tucson telephone directories from 1937 to present; Tucson city directories from 1918 to present. Holdings: 1200 books; back issues of Daily Star, 1877 to present on microfilm; newspaper clippings with emphasis on Tucson, 1939 to present; 200,000 photographs; 9000 pamphlets. Subscriptions: 40 journals and other serials; 17 newspapers. Services: Copying; hourly research fee. Staff: Michele R. Canney, Libn.

ARIZONA HEALTH SCIENCES CENTER LIBRARY
See: University of Arizona

★758★
ARIZONA HISTORICAL FOUNDATION - HAYDEN LIBRARY (Hist)
Arizona State University   Phone: (602) 966-8331
Tempe, AZ 85287   Susie S. Sato, Act.Hd./Archv.
Founded: 1959. **Staff:** Prof 1. **Subjects:** Arizona and American
Southwestern history. **Special Collections:** Papers of Senator Barry
Goldwater and Senator Paul Fannin; collections of Goldwater family, B. Sacks,
Thomas Maddock, Roscoe Willson and Grace Sparkes; Richard Schaus Arizona
Cattle Growers Association Collection (books, biographies, photographs and
negatives; 135 cubic feet); Fred Eldean/John H. Page Land Company Papers
(200 reels of microfilm and index). **Holdings:** 3500 books; 300 bound
periodical volumes; 1130 linear feet of manuscripts; 120 linear feet of
photographs and negatives; 1000 reels of microfilm; 700 maps. **Services:**
Selective copying; historical consultants; library open to public. **Special
Catalogs:** Information (card); photograph (card); manuscript (guide and
calendars).

★759★
ARIZONA HISTORICAL SOCIETY - LIBRARY (Hist)
949 E. Second St.   Phone: (602) 882-5774
Tucson, AZ 85719   Margaret S. Bret-Harte, Hd.Libn.
Founded: 1884. **Staff:** Prof 7. **Subjects:** Southwestern Americana - Arizona
territorial and state government, mining, Mexican history, Spanish North
American colonial history, military history, ranching, Southwestern Indians.
Special Collections: W.J. Holliday books and manuscripts (6113 items);
Charles B. Gatewood military collection; Byron Cummings ethnological and
archaeological collection; Frederick S. Dellenbaugh Colorado River collection;
Aguiar collection of early 19th century Mexican documents; Carl Hayden
biographical files of 1854-1864 Arizonans; Will C. Barnes ranching and
forestry papers; 1120 manuscript collections. **Holdings:** 48,000 books;
5000 bound periodical volumes; 10,000 pamphlets; 5000 maps; 250,000
photographs; 500 manuscripts; 750 linear feet of documents. **Subscriptions:**
25 journals and other serials; 33 newspapers. **Services:** Copying; library open
to public for reference use only. **Publications:** Journal of Arizona History,
quarterly. **Staff:** Lori Davisson, Res.Spec.

★760★
ARIZONA PHOTOGRAPHIC ASSOCIATES, INC. - LIBRARY (Pict)
2344 W. Holly   Phone: (602) 258-6551
Phoenix, AZ 85009   Dorothy McLaughlin, Dir.
Founded: 1945. **Staff:** Prof 1. **Subjects:** Arizona and Southwestern United
States. **Special Collections:** Historical photographs, including Phoenix
metropolitan area, dating back to 1860s (13,000). **Holdings:** 350,000
photographs, prints, negatives and transparencies. **Services:** Copying; library
open to public by appointment. **Publications:** Phoenix, 1870-1970 - book
containing 800 photographs.

★761★
ARIZONA-SONORA DESERT MUSEUM - LIBRARY (Env-Cons)
Rte. 9, Box 900   Phone: (602) 883-1380
Tucson, AZ 85743   Janice Hunter, Lib.Supv.
Founded: 1952. **Staff:** Prof 1; Other 6. **Subjects:** Deserts, conservation,
earth sciences, Sonora Desert region, zoo animals, Southwestern plants.
Special Collections: Carr Collection - The West (100 items). **Holdings:** 5000
books; 400 bound periodical volumes; 500 unbound sets; 450 unbound
monographs and bulletins; 21,000 photographs; 3000 separates and
pamphlets. **Subscriptions:** 100 journals and other serials. **Services:**
Interlibrary loans; copying; library open to museum members only.

★762★
**ARIZONA STATE DEPARTMENT OF HEALTH SERVICES - PUBLIC HEALTH
LIBRARY** (Med)
1740 W. Adams   Phone: (602) 255-1013
Phoenix, AZ 85007   Charles L. Nelson, Sr.Libn.
Founded: 1975. **Staff:** Prof 1; Other 5. **Subjects:** Public health,
environmental health, statistics, consumer health, management, medicine.
Holdings: 11,500 books and government publications; 350 bound periodical
volumes. **Subscriptions:** 212 journals and other serials. **Services:** Interlibrary
loans; copying; library open to public for reference use only. **Computerized
Information Services:** MEDLARS, BRS. **Networks/Consortia:** Member of
Channelled Arizona Information Network (CHAIN).

★763★
**ARIZONA STATE DEPARTMENT OF LIBRARY, ARCHIVES & PUBLIC
RECORDS** (Soc Sci)
State Capitol, 3rd Fl.   Phone: (602) 255-5240
Phoenix, AZ 85007   Sharon G. Womack, Dir.
Founded: 1864. **Staff:** Prof 34; Other 69. **Subjects:** Arizona and Southwest
history, law, political science, biography. **Special Collections:** State Archives.
Holdings: 1.1 million volumes; federal and state documents. **Subscriptions:**
2500 journals and other serials; 125 newspapers. **Services:** Interlibrary
loans; copying; library open to public with restrictions. **Computerized
Information Services:** Readers Advisory - computerized circulation system
for blind and physically handicapped.

★764★
ARIZONA STATE DEPARTMENT OF MINERAL RESOURCES - LIBRARY (Sci-
Tech)
State Fairgrounds   Phone: (602) 255-3791
Phoenix, AZ 85007   John H. Jett, Dir.
Founded: 1939. **Staff:** 12. **Subjects:** Mining and geology in Arizona.
Holdings: Figures not available. **Services:** Library open to public.
Publications: Directories; mineral reports; information circulars.

★765★
ARIZONA STATE ENERGY INFORMATION CENTER (Energy)
1700 W. Washington, 5th Fl.   Phone: (602) 255-3303
Phoenix, AZ 85007   Mary Mize, Info.Spec.
Staff: 2. **Subjects:** Energy. **Special Collections:** 1977 Arizona Energy Flow;
1981 Arizona Energy Inventory; 1979 final report, Governor's Conference on
Energy Policy. **Holdings:** Figures not available. **Subscriptions:** 25 journals and
other serials. **Services:** Energy hotline for Arizona residents. **Computerized
Information Services:** DOE/RECON, New York Times Information Service,
DIALOG, Source Telecomputing Corporation; internal database. **Networks/
Consortia:** Member of Western Information Network on Energy.
Publications: Brochures on energy-related subjects - free upon request.
Remarks: The toll free number for state residents is 1-800-352-5499.
Staff: Mary Silva, Libn.

★766★
ARIZONA STATE HIGHWAY DEPARTMENT - LIBRARY
206 S. 17th Ave.
Phoenix, AZ 85007
Defunct

★767★
ARIZONA STATE HOSPITAL - MEDICAL LIBRARY (Med)
2500 E. Van Buren   Phone: (602) 244-1331
Phoenix, AZ 85008   Marguerite Cooper, Med.Libn.
Founded: 1954. **Staff:** Prof 1; Other 1. **Subjects:** Psychiatry, psychiatric
nursing, psychology (including psychotherapy and psychoanalysis), social case
work, child psychiatry, addictive behaviors. **Holdings:** 8930 books; 2977
bound periodical volumes; 20 VF drawers of pamphlets and mental health
reports; 650 cassettes and tapes. **Subscriptions:** 125 journals and other
serials. **Services:** Interlibrary loans; copying; library open to public for
reference use only. **Computerized Information Services:** BRS. **Networks/
Consortia:** Member of Maricopa Biomedical Library Association.

ARIZONA STATE MUSEUM LIBRARY
See: University of Arizona

★768★
**ARIZONA STATE OFFICE OF ECONOMIC PLANNING AND DEVELOPMENT -
RESEARCH LIBRARY** (Plan)
1700 W. Washington, Rm. 400   Phone: (602) 255-5725
Phoenix, AZ 85007   Mary Silva, Libn.
Staff: Prof 1; Other 1. **Subjects:** Arizona economy, state and community
planning and development, energy conservation. **Special Collections:** Arizona
community documents, including those of Indian tribes (2500 volumes).
Holdings: 7500 books; 36 reels of microfilm; 2 drawers of microfiche; 1
case of maps; computer printouts. **Subscriptions:** 340 journals and other
serials; 10 newspapers. **Services:** Interlibrary loans; copying; SDI; library
open to public. **Computerized Information Services:** DIALOG, DOE/RECON,
New York Times Information Service. **Publications:** Arizona Office of
Economic Planning and Development Publication List, irregular - by request.

★769★
**ARIZONA STATE REGIONAL LIBRARY FOR THE BLIND AND PHYSICALLY
HANDICAPPED** (Aud-Vis)
3120 E. Roosevelt   Phone: (602) 255-5578
Phoenix, AZ 85008   Richard C. Peel, Adm.Libn.
Staff: Prof 6; Other 10. **Subjects:** Fiction, nonfiction, blindness, physical

handicaps. **Special Collections:** Arizona and Southwest U.S. recorded books; Spanish recorded books. **Holdings:** 120,000 talking books. **Subscriptions:** 30 journals and other serials. **Services:** Interlibrary loans; library open to eligible public. **Computerized Information Services:** Computerized cataloging, acquisitions, serials and circulation. **Networks/Consortia:** Member of Library of Congress - National Library Service for the Blind and Physically Handicapped. **Publications:** Newsletter, bimonthly. **Staff:** Betty Waznis, Asst.Libn.; Margaret Wilkinson, Volunteer Coord.; Glenore Cole, Tech.Serv.

★770★
ARIZONA STATE UNIVERSITY - ARIZONA COLLECTIONS (Hist)
Hayden Library   Phone: (602) 965-3145
Tempe, AZ 85287   Dr. Geoffrey P. Mawn, Cur.
Founded: 1943. **Staff:** Prof 1; Other 5. **Subjects:** Arizona and Southwestern United States history, politics, water, land use, peoples. **Special Collections:** Senator Carl T. Hayden Papers; Congressman John J. Rhodes Papers; Governor George W.P. Hunt Papers; William J. Murphy Collection; Hayden Pioneer Biographical Files; The Collection of Arizona Photography. **Holdings:** 10,000 books; 1000 bound periodical volumes; 4500 linear feet of manuscripts; 150 linear feet of photographs and negatives; 1700 microfilms; 1200 maps; biographical and general information files on Arizona history. **Subscriptions:** 27 journals and other serials. **Services:** Copying (limited); collection open to public. **Computerized Information Services:** Computerized cataloging, acquisitions and serials. **Publications:** Manuscript guide and calendars. **Special Indexes:** Index to information and newspapers (card); index to photographs (card).

★771★
ARIZONA STATE UNIVERSITY - CENTER FOR METEORITE STUDIES - LIBRARY (Sci-Tech)
                                        Phone: (602) 965-6511
Tempe, AZ 85281   Carleton B. Moore, Dir.
Founded: 1961. **Staff:** 4. **Subjects:** Meteorites. **Special Collections:** Meteorite articles. **Holdings:** 3000 items on microfilm. **Services:** Interlibrary loans; copying; literature searching by meteorite name; center open to public. **Publications:** Publications of the Center for Meteorite Studies, irregular. **Staff:** John F. Larimer, Assoc.Dir.; Charles F. Lewis, Assoc.Cur.

★772★
ARIZONA STATE UNIVERSITY - CHICANO STUDIES COLLECTION (Area-Ethnic)
Hayden Library   Phone: (602) 965-2594
Tempe, AZ 85287   Christine N. Marin, Chicano Bibliog.
Founded: 1970. **Staff:** 1. **Subjects:** Mexican-American literature, history and activism; bilingual education; political science; Chicano movement leaders. **Special Collections:** Chicano newspapers, manuscripts; Mexican-American biographies (50); Chicano Movement literature; student activism reports. **Holdings:** 1500 books; 25 bound periodical volumes; 100 unbound reports; 2000 newspaper clippings; 100 ephemeral items. **Subscriptions:** 20 journals and other serials. **Services:** Interlibrary loans (limited); copying (limited); collection open to public. **Computerized Information Services:** Computerized cataloging, acquisitions and serials.

★773★
ARIZONA STATE UNIVERSITY - COLLEGE OF LAW - LIBRARY (Law)
Armstrong Hall   Phone: (602) 966-6141
Tempe, AZ 85282   Richard L. Brown, Dir.
Founded: 1967. **Staff:** Prof 6; Other 7. **Subjects:** Law - American, English, foreign. **Holdings:** 174,064 books and bound periodical volumes; 1651 reels of microfilm; 139,075 microfiche. **Subscriptions:** 2371 journals and other serials; 8 newspapers. **Services:** Interlibrary loans; copying; library open to public for legal research. **Computerized Information Services:** LEXIS; computerized cataloging. **Publications:** Monthly Acquisitions - for internal distribution only. **Staff:** Richard M. Nash, Assoc. Law Libn.; Jeannette Chin Chun Au, Hd., Tech.Serv.; Sharon Firestone, Acq. & Ser.Libn.; Marianne Alcorn, Circ. & Ref.Libn.

★774★
ARIZONA STATE UNIVERSITY - DANIEL E. NOBLE SCIENCE AND ENGINEERING LIBRARY (Sci-Tech)
                                        Phone: (602) 965-7607
Tempe, AZ 85287   Vladimir T. Borovansky, Hd.
Founded: 1983. **Staff:** Prof 8; Other 30. **Subjects:** Engineering; physical, life and health sciences; mathematics; agriculture; geography. **Special Collections:** Solar energy (11,000 archival items); patent depository library (1.1 million U.S. patents in microform). **Holdings:** 160,000 books; 60,000 bound periodical volumes; 110,000 maps. **Subscriptions:** 4500 journals and other serials. **Services:** Interlibrary loans; copying; SDI; library open to public. **Computerized Information Services:** DIALOG, SDC, BRS, New York Times

Information Service, NASA/RECON, DOE/RECON, CASSIS; computerized circulation. **Networks/Consortia:** Member of OCLC through AMIGOS Bibliographic Council, Inc. **Special Indexes:** KWOC index on solar energy (book). **Staff:** Mara Pinckard, Hd., Sci.Ref.; George Machovec, Solar Energy Libn.; Connie Wick, Physical Sci.Ref.Libn.; Sheila Walters, Health Sci.Libn.; Rosanna Miller, Hd., Map Coll.; Phyllis Cox McClara, Supv., Circ.; Dorothy Saunders, Supv., Per./Microforms.

ARIZONA STATE UNIVERSITY - HAYDEN LIBRARY
See: Arizona Historical Foundation

★775★
ARIZONA STATE UNIVERSITY - HOWE ARCHITECTURE LIBRARY (Art)
College of Architecture   Phone: (602) 965-6400
Tempe, AZ 85287   Katherine M. Weir, Hd.
Founded: 1960. **Staff:** 4. **Subjects:** Architecture, city planning, landscape architecture, interior design. **Special Collections:** Paolo Soleri Archives. **Holdings:** 16,784 volumes; 106 tape recordings; 360 reels of microfilm. **Subscriptions:** 139 journals and other serials. **Services:** Interlibrary loans; copying; library open to public. **Special Indexes:** Index to Paolo Soleri Archives.

★776★
ARIZONA STATE UNIVERSITY - LLOYD BIMSON MEMORIAL LIBRARY (Bus-Fin)
College of Business Administration   Phone: (602) 965-6138
Tempe, AZ 85287   Robert F. Rose, Hd.Bus.Lib.
Founded: 1969. **Staff:** Prof 1; Other 4. **Subjects:** Business administration, taxation. **Special Collections:** Arthur Young Tax Library (1000 volumes). **Holdings:** 1500 books; 1350 annual reports; 246 unbound periodical titles; 300 business college catalogs; 8 drawers of pamphlets. **Subscriptions:** 225 journals and other serials; 6 newspapers. **Services:** Copying; library open to public for reference use only. **Computerized Information Services:** DIALOG, SDC, BRS. **Publications:** Bimson Report, irregular - distributed to college faculty.

★777★
ARIZONA STATE UNIVERSITY - MAP COLLECTION (Geog-Map)
University Library   Phone: (602) 965-3582
Tempe, AZ 85287   Rosanna Miller, Hd.
Staff: Prof 1; Other 2. **Subjects:** Topography, geology, transportation, mines and mineral resources, hydrography, economics. **Holdings:** 1284 books; 101,384 sheet maps. **Services:** Interlibrary loans; copying; library open to public. **Computerized Information Services:** Computerized map index. **Special Indexes:** Map index.

★778★
ARIZONA STATE UNIVERSITY - MUSIC LIBRARY (Mus)
                                        Phone: (602) 965-3513
Tempe, AZ 85287   Arlys L. McDonald, Music Libn.
Staff: Prof 1; Other 5. **Subjects:** Music. **Special Collections:** International Percussion Reference Library (3500 items); Pablo Casals International Cello Library; Wayne King Collection of Popular Music (5300 items, including television films); sheet music collection (5500 items). **Holdings:** 30,000 books and scores; 1500 microforms; 13,000 recordings. **Subscriptions:** 140 journals and other serials. **Services:** Interlibrary loans (Hayden Library, 965-3282); copying; library open to public for reference use only. **Computerized Information Services:** DIALOG, BRS, SDC; computerized cataloging. **Networks/Consortia:** Member of OCLC through AMIGOS Bibliographic Council, Inc. **Publications:** International Percussion Reference Library catalog, irregular.

★779★
ARIZONA STATE UNIVERSITY - SPACE PHOTOGRAPHY LABORATORY (Sci-Tech)
Department of Geology   Phone: (602) 965-7029
Tempe, AZ 85281   Ronald Greeley, Professor
Staff: 1. **Subjects:** Space images. **Holdings:** 500,000 images. **Services:** Library not open to public. **Computerized Information Services:** SPACEL BIRP (internal database). **Networks/Consortia:** Member of National Planetary Image Libraries.

★780★
ARIZONA STATE UNIVERSITY - SPECIAL COLLECTIONS (Hum)
University Library   Phone: (602) 965-6519
Tempe, AZ 85287   Marilyn Wurzburger, Hd., Spec.Coll.
Staff: Prof 1; Other 1. **Subjects:** Pre-Raphaelite brotherhood, Victorian literature and illustrators, book arts, nineteenth and twentieth century first editions. **Special Collections:** Kelmscott Press; Mosher Press; George Moore;

film history; Rubaiyat of Omar Khayyam; Children's Theatre Archive (50 linear feet); Glendon Swarthout Archive (15 linear feet); Elleston Trevor Archive (18 linear feet); Edwin Bliss Hill Archive (14 linear feet); Ted Schwarz Archive (30 linear feet). **Holdings:** 17,000 books. **Services:** Copying; collections open to public. **Computerized Information Services:** Computerized cataloging. **Networks/Consortia:** Member of OCLC through AMIGOS Bibliographic Council, Inc. **Publications:** Brochure. **Special Catalogs:** Chronological and printer files of rare books (COM and card).

★781★
ARIZONA STATE UNIVERSITY - UNIVERSITY ARCHIVES (Hist; Educ)
University Archives Bldg.   Phone: (602) 965-7645
Tempe, AZ 85287   Alfred Thomas, Jr., Univ.Archv.
Founded: 1972. **Staff:** Prof 1; Other 2. **Subjects:** Arizona State University. **Special Collections:** University records; student records; faculty and student publications, 1885-1975; board of regents and faculty senate minutes; presidential correspondence; theses and dissertations, 1885-1981; Samuel Burkhard Collection (188 articles, books and monographs); James John Jelinek Collection (184 articles, books and monographs); Agnes Smedley Collection (56 bound volumes, 1900-1980); Jeannette Veatch Collection (109 cassettes); Paula Kloster Wasser Collection (14 bound volumes); C. Gilbert Wrenn Collection (208 articles, books and monographs). **Holdings:** 10,838 volumes; 1973 reels of microfilm; 233 films; 205 cassettes; 11,858 photographic prints; 40,000 negatives; 20,561 news clippings; 3822 slides; 54,015 folders and box material items, 1885 to present. **Subscriptions:** 115 journals and other serials. **Services:** Interlibrary loans (limited); copying; archives open to public with restrictions. **Publications:** List of publications - available upon request. **Special Catalogs:** Publications of the Faculty, biennial.

★782★
ARKANSAS ARTS CENTER - ELIZABETH PREWITT TAYLOR MEMORIAL LIBRARY (Art; Mus)†
MacArthur Park, Box 2137   Phone: (501) 372-4000
Little Rock, AR 72203   Evelyn McCoy, Libn.
Founded: 1963. **Staff:** Prof 1; Other 2. **Subjects:** Art, drama, early American jazz. **Special Collections:** John D. Reid Collection of early American Jazz (4000 phonograph records, 70 books, pamphlet files of unbound catalogs, photographs and other memorabilia - all cataloged). **Holdings:** 6000 books; 450 bound periodical volumes; 16 VF drawers of pamphlets; 1940 AV items. **Subscriptions:** 126 journals and other serials. **Services:** Interlibrary loans; library open to public with limited circulation. **Networks/Consortia:** Member of OCLC through AMIGOS Bibliographic Council, Inc. **Special Catalogs:** Catalog of John Reid Jazz Collection (book and card).

★783★
ARKANSAS GAZETTE - NEWS LIBRARY (Publ)
Box 1821   Phone: (501) 371-3740
Little Rock, AR 72203   Alfred M. Thomas, Hd.Libn.
Staff: Prof 5. **Subjects:** Arkansas persons and subjects; newspaper reference topics. **Holdings:** 2000 books; clippings and picture files; microfilm of the Gazette from 1819 to the present. **Subscriptions:** 82 newspapers. **Services:** Interlibrary loans; library not open to public except to noncompeting media and other libraries.

★784★
ARKANSAS STATE DEPARTMENT OF POLLUTION CONTROL AND ECOLOGY - LIBRARY (Env-Cons)
8001 National Dr.
Box 9583   Phone: (501) 562-7444
Little Rock, AR 72209   Becky Hooten, Libn.
Founded: 1949. **Staff:** Prof 2; Other 1. **Subjects:** Pollution - water, air; solid waste; environmental preservation; geology; engineering. **Special Collections:** Basin Surveys (250 publications). **Holdings:** 700 books; 450 bound periodical volumes; 5000 paperbacks (cataloged); 12 films; slide presentations. **Subscriptions:** 45 journals and other serials; 10 newspapers. **Services:** Interlibrary loans; copying; library open to public for reference use only. **Computerized Information Services:** Computerized cataloging, acquisitions, serials and circulation. **Publications:** Annual report; Monitor (newsletter); Legislative Summary; News releases; Acts of Arkansas. **Special Catalogs:** Public Hearing Transcripts.

★785★
ARKANSAS STATE ENERGY OFFICE LIBRARY (Energy)
One Capitol Mall   Phone: (501) 371-1370
Little Rock, AR 72201   Nancy C. Lewis, Libn.
Founded: 1977. **Staff:** Prof 1; Other 1. **Subjects:** Energy - policy and legislation, conservation and management, resources, data. **Holdings:** 3500 books and reports; maps; slides. **Subscriptions:** 37 journals and other serials. **Services:** Interlibrary loans with restrictions; copying; library open to public

for reference use only; state employees may borrow.

★786★
ARKANSAS (State) HISTORY COMMISSION - ARCHIVES (Hist)
One Capitol Mall   Phone: (501) 371-2141
Little Rock, AR 72201   Dr. John L. Ferguson, State Hist.
Founded: 1909. **Staff:** Prof 8; Other 13. **Subjects:** Arkansas history; genealogy; Arkansas government. **Holdings:** 25,000 books; 6000 bound periodical volumes; 15,000 reels of microfilm; 600 maps; 4000 photographs and paintings; 400 document boxes containing manuscript materials; 100 VF drawers of pamphlets, clippings, cards. **Subscriptions:** 30 journals and other serials; 200 newspapers. **Services:** Copying; archives open to public. **Staff:** Russell P. Baker, Archv.; Mary Nell Shaw, Rec.Mgr.; Robert D. Devan, Consrv.; Lynn Ewbank, Archv.; Frances Valescu, Libn.

★787★
ARKANSAS STATE HOSPITAL - MEDICAL LIBRARY (Med)
4313 W. Markham St.   Phone: (501) 664-4500
Little Rock, AR 72201   Bernadine Zerr, Asst.Med.Libn.
Founded: 1950. **Staff:** Prof 1. **Subjects:** Psychiatry, nursing, psychology, sociology, medicine, clinical sciences, forensic medicine, social work, pediatrics. **Holdings:** 5089 books; 1683 bound periodical volumes; 420 cassettes. **Subscriptions:** 108 journals and other serials. **Services:** Interlibrary loans; copying; library open to public for reference use only. **Publications:** Bibliographies - for internal distribution only.

★788★
ARKANSAS STATE LIBRARY (Info Sci)†
One Capitol Mall   Phone: (501) 371-1524
Little Rock, AR 72201   Frances Nix, Assoc.Dir.
Founded: 1935. **Staff:** Prof 12; Other 35. **Special Collections:** Arkansas material. **Holdings:** 144,278 volumes; 24 VF drawers. **Subscriptions:** 285 journals and other serials. **Services:** Library open to public. **Networks/Consortia:** Member of OCLC through AMIGOS Bibliographic Council, Inc.

★789★
ARKANSAS STATE SUPREME COURT LIBRARY (Law)
Justice Bldg.   Phone: (501) 374-2512
Little Rock, AR 72201
Founded: 1850. **Staff:** Prof 2. **Subjects:** Law. **Special Collections:** Annual state statutes; English law. **Holdings:** 70,000 volumes. **Subscriptions:** 30 journals and other serials. **Services:** Library open to public for reference use only.

★790★
ARKANSAS STATE UNIVERSITY - DEAN B. ELLIS LIBRARY - SPECIAL COLLECTIONS (Educ; Hum)
Box 2040   Phone: (501) 972-3078
State University, AR 72467   William Hansard, Lib.Dir.
Special Collections: Lois Lenski Collection; Arkansas Authors of Childrens Books; Cass S. Hough Aeronautical Collection; Curriculum Laboratory Library; government documents (221,705); ERIC microfiche (complete collection). **Services:** Interlibrary loans; copying; library open to public. **Computerized Information Services:** BRS; computerized cataloging, acquisitions, serials and circulation. **Networks/Consortia:** Member of OCLC through AMIGOS Bibliographic Council, Inc. **Publications:** Lois Lenski Collection in Dean B. Ellis Library: A Bibliography, Arkansas State University, 1972.

★791★
ARKANSAS STATE UNIVERSITY MUSEUM - HISTORICAL LIBRARY (Hist)
Box 490   Phone: (501) 972-2074
State University, AR 72467   Mary Coles, Musm. Registrar
Founded: 1936. **Staff:** Prof 2; Other 1. **Subjects:** History - Indian, American military, Arkansas, the States, American and European; old textbooks; religion; children's rare books; minerals and fossils. **Special Collections:** Rare newspapers, 1750-1900 (1500); letter collections (50); sheet music, 1840-1950 (1050); Sharp County, Arkansas Courthouse Ledgers. **Holdings:** 5000 books; 6500 other cataloged items. **Subscriptions:** 10 journals and other serials. **Services:** Interlibrary loans; library open to public for reference use only.

★792★
ARKANSAS TECH UNIVERSITY - TOMLINSON LIBRARY - SPECIAL COLLECTIONS (Soc Sci)
                    Phone: (501) 968-0304
Russellville, AR 72801   W.A. Vaughn, Lib.Dir.
Special Collections: Recreation and Parks (6000 items); government documents (50,000). **Services:** Interlibrary loans; copying; library open to public. **Computerized Information Services:** DIALOG, BRS; computerized

cataloging and acquisitions. **Networks/Consortia:** Member of OCLC through AMIGOS Bibliographic Council, Inc. **Special Indexes:** Recreation, Parks and Leisure.

★793★
ARKANSAS TERRITORIAL RESTORATION - LIBRARY (Hist)
Third & Scott   Phone: (501) 371-2348
Little Rock, AR 72201   Karen Norman, Educ.Coord.
Founded: 1941. **Staff:** Prof 4. **Subjects:** Arkansas history, decorative arts, conservation, historic preservation, gardens. **Special Collections:** Territorial and early statehood documents. **Holdings:** 500 books; 100 archival items; 200 documents; 25 maps. **Subscriptions:** 24 journals and other serials. **Services:** Library open to qualified researchers.

★794★
ARLINGTON BAPTIST COLLEGE - EARL K. OLDHAM LIBRARY (Rel-Theol)
3001 W. Division   Phone: (817) 461-8741
Arlington, TX 76012   Sandra H. Tanner, Libn.
Staff: Prof 1; Other 1. **Subjects:** Religion. **Holdings:** 25,000 books and bound periodical volumes; 1000 theses and tracts. **Subscriptions:** 221 journals and other serials. **Services:** Interlibrary loans; copying; library open to public with restrictions.

★795★
ARLINGTON COUNTY CENTRAL LIBRARY - VIRGINIANA COLLECTION (Hist)
1015 N. Quincy St.   Phone: (703) 527-4777
Arlington, VA 22201   Sara Collins, Virginiana Libn.
Founded: 1961. **Staff:** Prof 1. **Subjects:** History of Arlington County, Virginia; metropolitan Washington. **Special Collections:** Library-Zonta Oral History Collection (50 transcribed interviews); community archives (100 linear feet). **Holdings:** 6661 books and bound periodical volumes; 477 unbound reports and documents; 25 VF drawers of clippings and ephemera; 100 linear feet of manuscripts; 800 photographs; 2 drawers of Cavilir Solinet union list on microfiche; 750 maps. **Subscriptions:** 282 journals and other serials; 6 newspapers. **Services:** Interlibrary loans; copying; library open to public for reference use only. **Computerized Information Services:** DIALOG; computerized cataloging, acquisitions and circulation. **Networks/Consortia:** Member of Consortium for Continuing Higher Education in Northern Virginia - Library Networking Committee. **Special Indexes:** Indexes to local newspapers, clippings, maps, Arlingtoniana in periodicals, current documents.

★796★
ARLINGTON COUNTY CENTRAL LIBRARY - ZONTA ORAL HISTORY COLLECTION
1015 N. Quincy St.
Arlington, VA 22201
Defunct. Collection included in the library's Virginiana Collection.

★797★
ARLINGTON DEVELOPMENTAL CENTER - PROFESSIONAL LIBRARY (Med)
11293 Memphis-Arlington Rd.   Phone: (901) 867-2921
Arlington, TN 38002   Christine B. Gavin, Instr. Media Spec.
Founded: 1969. **Staff:** 1. **Subjects:** Medicine, psychology, special education, social work, speech pathology, mental retardation, developmental disabilities. **Holdings:** 2300 books; 26 bound periodical volumes. **Subscriptions:** 26 journals and other serials. **Services:** Interlibrary loans; copying; library open to public with restrictions. **Networks/Consortia:** Member of Association of Memphis Area Health Sciences Libraries.

★798★
ARLINGTON HISTORICAL SOCIETY - ARCHIVES (Hist)*
Box 402
Arlington, VA 22210   Ruth M. Ward, Archv.
Staff: 1. **Subjects:** History of Arlington County and northern Virginia. **Holdings:** Figures not available; papers, county board minutes, clippings, theses, pictures.

★799★
ARLINGTON HOSPITAL - DOCTORS' LIBRARY (Med)†
1701 N. George Mason Dr.   Phone: (703) 558-6524
Arlington, VA 22205   Olga Taylor, Libn.
Founded: 1954. **Staff:** 1. **Subjects:** Medicine. **Holdings:** 650 books; 2725 bound periodical volumes; 960 audiotapes; 130 video cassettes; 386 unbound volumes of journals. **Subscriptions:** 115 journals and other serials. **Services:** Interlibrary loans (fee); copying; bibliographies; literature searches; AV programs in continuing medical education; library open to public by special permission only. **Networks/Consortia:** Member of Northern Virginia Hospital Libraries; Hospital Council of the National Capital Area, Inc.

ARLINGTON HOUSE, THE ROBERT E. LEE MEMORIAL
See: U.S. Natl. Park Service

★800★
ARLINGTON PUBLIC SCHOOLS - PROFESSIONAL LIBRARY (Educ)
1426 N. Quincy St.   Phone: (703) 558-2836
Arlington, VA 22207   Luke Yaeger, Supv., School Lib.Serv.
Staff: Prof 1; Other 1. **Subjects:** Education. **Holdings:** 7000 books; ERIC microfiche. **Subscriptions:** 160 journals and other serials. **Services:** Interlibrary loans; copying; library open to teachers and residents of Arlington. **Networks/Consortia:** Member of Consortium for Continuing Higher Education in Northern Virginia - Librarians Networking Committee.

★801★
ARMAK COMPANY - RESEARCH LIBRARY (Sci-Tech)
8401 W. 47th St.   Phone: (312) 442-7100
McCook, IL 60525   Robyn Petry, Hd.Libn.
Founded: 1926. **Staff:** Prof 2; Other 1. **Subjects:** Organic chemistry, fatty acid chemistry. **Holdings:** 2500 books; 5000 bound periodical volumes; 20,000 patents; 10 file boxes of company reprints; 7000 internal reports; microfilmed chemical patents. **Subscriptions:** 180 journals and other serials. **Services:** Interlibrary loans; library open to public with restrictions. **Computerized Information Services:** DIALOG, SDC, NLM, Chemical Abstracts Service Online. **Networks/Consortia:** Member of Suburban Library System; Metropolitan Chicago Library Assembly. **Publications:** Monthly Literature Accession List; Monthly Patent Accession List; Newsnotes. **Staff:** Karen Pacetti, Asst.Libn.

ARMAMENT DIVISION, AIR FORCE ARMAMENT LABORATORY
See: U.S. Air Force

ARMAMENT MATERIEL READINESS COMMAND
See: U.S. Army - Armament Materiel Readiness Command

ARMAMENT RESEARCH & DEVELOPMENT COMMAND
See: U.S. Army

ARMCO, INC. - HITCO - TECHNICAL LIBRARY
See: Hitco

★802★
ARMCO, INC. - TECHNICAL INFORMATION CENTER (Bus-Fin; Sci-Tech)
703 Curtis St.   Phone: (513) 425-2596
Middletown, OH 45043   David C. Heckard, Mgr.
Staff: Prof 2; Other 3. **Subjects:** Ferrous metallurgy, physical and analytical chemistry, instrumentation, composite materials, business management, commercial research. **Holdings:** 7500 books and bound periodical volumes; 10,000 government reports; 2500 translations; 1500 corporate annual reports; 1500 volumes of journals on microfilm. **Subscriptions:** 420 journals and other serials. **Services:** Interlibrary loans; copying; library open to public by appointment. **Computerized Information Services:** DIALOG, SDC, New York Times Information Service. **Publications:** Alerting Bulletin, semimonthly - for internal distribution only.

★803★
ARMED FORCES COMMUNICATIONS AND ELECTRONICS ASSOCIATION - C3I LIBRARY (Sci-Tech)
5205 Leesburg Pike, Suite 300   Phone: (703) 820-5028
Falls Church, VA 22041   M.L. Peterson
Subjects: Command and control communications and intelligence (C3I), electronics, imagery, computer sciences. **Subscriptions:** 38 journals and other serials. **Services:** Most services are for association members, subscribers and C3I professionals. **Publications:** Signal, 11/year; Symposia Proceedings, semiannual. **Special Indexes:** Articles in Signal (card index).

ARMED FORCES INSTITUTE OF PATHOLOGY
See: U.S. Armed Forces Institute of Pathology

ARMED FORCES PEST MANAGEMENT BOARD
See: U.S. Army

ARMED FORCES RADIOBIOLOGY RESEARCH INSTITUTE
See: U.S. Armed Forces Radiobiology Research Institute (AFRRI)

★804★
ARMENIAN ASSEMBLY CHARITABLE TRUST - LIBRARY AND INFORMATION CENTER (Area-Ethnic)†
1420 N St., N.W.   Phone: (202) 332-3434
Washington, DC 20005   Ross Vartian, Adm.Dir.
Founded: 1972. **Staff:** 5. **Subjects:** Armenian history, culture, genocide,

political evolution. **Holdings:** 140 volumes; 50 pamphlets (cataloged); 1 VF drawer of clippings; AV material. **Subscriptions:** 19 journals and other serials. **Services:** Copying; library open to public with permission of director. **Publications:** Directory of Armenian Scholars; Participation in the Democratic Process; Newsletter, quarterly.

★805★
ARMENIAN LIBRARY AND MUSEUM OF AMERICA (Area-Ethnic)
Box 147
Belmont, MA 02178   Dr. Lucy Der Manuelian, Board Member
Staff: 1. **Subjects:** Armenia - history, art, literature, language. **Holdings:** 5000 volumes; archival materials; oral history tapes. **Subscriptions:** 10 journals and other serials. **Services:** Library not open to public.

★806★
ARMOUR PHARMACEUTICAL COMPANY - LIBRARY (Med)†
Rte. 50 N., Box 511   Phone: (815) 932-6771
Kankakee, IL 60901   Shirley Wells, Libn.
Staff: 1. **Subjects:** Chemistry, biology, medicine, pharmacy. **Holdings:** 2000 books; 4000 bound periodical volumes; 40 VF drawers of reprints, pamphlets and manuscripts. **Subscriptions:** 400 journals and other serials. **Services:** Interlibrary loans; copying; library open to public by special request.

★807★
ARMOUR RESEARCH CENTER - LIBRARY (Food-Bev; Sci-Tech)
15101 N. Scottsdale Rd.   Phone: (602) 998-6120
Scottsdale, AZ 85260   Lorraine Nesvig, Libn.
Founded: 1976. **Staff:** 3. **Subjects:** Food sciences, meat, dairy, poultry, microbiology, nutrition, chemistry, soaps, detergents, cosmetics, personal care products, transportation, energy. **Special Collections:** Cookbooks from the 1800s (330). **Holdings:** 6800 books; 7700 bound periodical volumes; 10,000 pamphlets. **Subscriptions:** 360 journals and other serials. **Services:** Interlibrary loans; copying; library open to public by appointment. **Computerized Information Services:** DIALOG, SDC, BRS, New York Times Information Service, DOE/RECON, NIH/EPA Chemical Information System, MEDLINE, RLIN, Dow Jones News Retrieval, NLM, ISI; computerized cataloging. **Networks/Consortia:** Member of OCLC through AMIGOS; IMULS. **Publications:** Accession Bulletin, bimonthly; list of serials and journals, annual. **Remarks:** Library serves both Armour & Co. and Greyhound Corp. **Staff:** Linda Monroe, Info.Spec.

ARMS CONTROL AND DISARMAMENT AGENCY
See: U.S. Arms Control and Disarmament Agency

ARMSTRONG BROWNING LIBRARY
See: Baylor University

★808★
ARMSTRONG COLLEGE - LIBRARY (Bus-Fin)
2222 Harold Way   Phone: (415) 848-2500
Berkeley, CA 94704   Egon A. Selge, Coll.Libn.
Founded: 1918. **Staff:** Prof 1; Other 2. **Subjects:** Business administration, accounting, advertising, economics, law, transportation. **Special Collections:** Annual reports of top thousand companies in Fortune Magazine; biographies (700 volumes). **Holdings:** 17,500 books; 150 reels of microfilm; 11 boxes of archival material; 52 student theses and papers. **Subscriptions:** 260 journals and other serials; 6 newspapers. **Services:** Library open to public for reference use only.

ARMSTRONG (Ruth) MEMORIAL MEDICAL LIBRARY
See: Butler County Memorial Hospital - Ruth Armstrong Memorial Medical Library

★809★
ARMSTRONG WORLD INDUSTRIES, INC. - MANAGEMENT REFERENCE SERVICES (Bus-Fin)
Liberty & Charlotte Sts.
Box 3001
Lancaster, PA 17604   Phone: (717) 397-0611
                                            Margaret B. Boyer, Libn.
Founded: 1926. **Staff:** 2. **Subjects:** Business management, factory management, manufacturing methods, manufacturing processes, economics, statistics, accounting, finance. **Holdings:** 1820 books; 50 VF drawers of pamphlets; 130 VF drawers of archival material. **Subscriptions:** 346 journals and other serials. **Services:** Interlibrary loans; copying; library open to public for reference use only by request. **Publications:** Resource Readings, monthly - for internal distribution only. **Staff:** Jean L. Immel, Archv.

★810★
ARMSTRONG WORLD INDUSTRIES, INC. - TECHNICAL CENTER - TECHNICAL INFORMATION SERVICES (Sci-Tech)
2500 Columbia Ave.   Phone: (717) 397-0611
Lancaster, PA 17604   Dr. Joseph M. Judge, Mgr.
Founded: 1926. **Staff:** Prof 4; Other 6. **Subjects:** Chemistry, polymer science, chemical engineering, physics, mathematics. **Holdings:** 10,000 books and bound periodical volumes; 9500 research reports; U.S. patents on microfilm; microforms. **Subscriptions:** 350 journals and other serials. **Services:** Interlibrary loans; copying; SDI; library open to public for reference use on request. **Computerized Information Services:** DIALOG, NIH/EPA Chemical Information System, SDC, Chemical Abstracts Service Online; computerized circulation. **Publications:** Current Awareness Bulletin, monthly; Technical Information Bulletin, monthly - both for internal distribution only. **Special Catalogs:** Catalog of corporate holdings (book). **Staff:** J. Philip Franze, Info.Ret.; Cloyd R. Smith, Tech.Libn.; Susan I. Wood, Asst.Libn.

ARMY AVIATION TRAINING LIBRARY
See: U.S. Army Aviation Training Library

ARMY COMBAT DEVELOPMENTS EXPERIMENTATION COMMAND
See: U.S. Army Combat Developments Experimentation Command

ARMY LIBRARY
See: U.S. Army

ARMY MOBILITY EQUIPMENT RESEARCH & DEVELOPMENT COMMAND
See: U.S. Army

★811★
ARMY AND NAVY CLUB - LIBRARY (Mil)†
Farragut Sq. & I St., N.W.   Phone: (202) 628-8400
Washington, DC 20006   John S. Mayfield, Libn.
Staff: 2. **Subjects:** Military doctrines, social sciences, natural sciences, history, geography, languages, biography. **Holdings:** 17,886 volumes. **Services:** Library open to public upon request of a club member.

ARNESON LIBRARY
See: St. Louis Park Medical Center-Research Foundation

ARNETT (Trevor) LIBRARY
See: Atlanta University Center - Robert W. Woodruff Library

ARNETT (Trevor) LIBRARY OF BLACK CULTURE
See: University of District of Columbia - Harvard Street Library

★812★
ARNHOLD AND S. BLEICHROEDER, INC. - LIBRARY (Bus-Fin)
30 Broad St.   Phone: (212) 943-9200
New York, NY 10004
Staff: Prof 1. **Subjects:** Corporate finance, industry. **Holdings:** Figures not available for books; 100 VF drawers of corporate and industry reports. **Subscriptions:** 15 journals and other serials; 10 newspapers. **Services:** Library open to public with restrictions.

ARNOLD ARBORETUM & GRAY HERBARIUM
See: Harvard University

★813★
ARNOLD ENGINEERING DEVELOPMENT CENTER TECHNICAL LIBRARY (Sci-Tech)
Mail Stop 100   Phone: (615) 455-2611
Arnold Air Force Sta., TN 37389   Gay D. Goethert, Lib.Supv.
Founded: 1952. **Staff:** Prof 3; Other 5. **Subjects:** Aerospace sciences, aerodynamics, mathematics, physics, astronomy, aircraft propulsion, pollution, chemistry, optics. **Special Collections:** NACA and NASA reports, complete sets; American Institute of Aeronautics and Astronautics papers on microfiche, 1963-1977. **Holdings:** 15,642 books; 14,694 bound periodical volumes; 266,361 technical reports and documents; 117,732 microforms; 2 VF drawers of standards and specifications. **Subscriptions:** 700 journals and other serials. **Services:** Interlibrary loans; copying; library not open to public. **Computerized Information Services:** DIALOG, NASA/RECON, DTIC; computerized cataloging. **Networks/Consortia:** Member of OCLC through SOLINET. **Publications:** Periodicals Holdings List, irregular; Accession Lists of Books and Reports, monthly. **Remarks:** The center is operated by Pan Am World Services, Inc. for the U.S. Air Force. **Staff:** Della C. Burch, Tech.Libn., Lib.Div.; Effie W. Boyd, Tech.Libn., Doc.Div.

ARNOLD LIBRARY
See: Straub Clinic & Hospital, Inc.

ARNOLD LIBRARY OF AGRICULTURAL CREDIT
See: Ohio State University - Agriculture Library

★814★
ARNOLD AND PORTER - LIBRARY (Law)
1200 New Hampshire Ave., N.W.   Phone: (202) 872-3994
Washington, DC 20036   James W. Shelar, Libn.
Staff: Prof 6; Other 5. **Subjects:** Law. **Special Collections:** Congressional
documents: hearings, reports, committee prints (10,000 items). **Holdings:**
50,000 books; 2000 bound periodical volumes. **Subscriptions:** 80 journals
and other serials; 8 newspapers. **Services:** Interlibrary loans only with special
permission of librarian; library not open to public. **Computerized Information
Services:** LEXIS, New York Times Information Service, SDC, DIALOG, Dow
Jones News Retrieval, WESTLAW, NEWSNET. **Networks/Consortia:**
Member of OCLC.

★815★
ARNOLD SCHOENBERG INSTITUTE - ARCHIVES (Hist; Mus)
University of Southern California
University Park - MC 1101   Phone: (213) 743-5393
Los Angeles, CA 90089-1101   Jerry McBride, Asst.Archv.
Founded: 1975. **Staff:** Prof 2; Other 1. **Subjects:** Arnold Schoenberg.
Holdings: 2200 books; 6000 pages of manuscripts; 230 audiotapes; 730
phonograph records; 200 microfiche; 60 reels of microfilm; 15 boxes of
concert programs, news clippings; 2500 photographs. **Services:** Copying;
library open to public by appointment. **Computerized Information Services:**
RLIN; computerized cataloging. **Networks/Consortia:** Member of CLASS;
RLG. **Publications:** Journal of the Arnold Schoenberg Institute, biennial - by
subscription. **Remarks:** The Institute is maintained and supported by the
University of Southern California; California State University, Los Angeles and
California Institute of the Arts.

★816★
ARNOLD, WHITE & DURKEE - LIBRARY (Law)
Box 4433   Phone: (713) 621-9100
Houston, TX 77210   Sharan L. Zwick, Libn.
Staff: Prof 1. **Subjects:** Law - patent, trademark, copyright, antitrust,
franchise. **Special Collections:** Official Gazette of Patents; Official Gazette of
Trademarks. **Holdings:** 7900 books; 320 bound periodical volumes.
Subscriptions: 34 journals and other serials. **Services:** Interlibrary loans;
copying; library open to public by appointment. **Computerized Information
Services:** Online systems.

★817★
ARNOT-OGDEN MEMORIAL HOSPITAL - WEY MEMORIAL LIBRARY (Med)
Roe Ave. at Grove St.   Phone: (607) 737-4101
Elmira, NY 14901   Katherine F. Mekos, Med.Libn.
Founded: 1934. **Staff:** Prof 1; Other 2. **Subjects:** Medicine, nursing.
Holdings: 3200 books; 6400 bound periodical volumes; 28 VF drawers; 278
cataloged items in historical collection; 550 items of AV software.
Subscriptions: 288 journals and other serials. **Services:** Interlibrary loans;
copying; library open to health professionals and students. **Computerized
Information Services:** NLM.

★818★
**AROOSTOOK MEDICAL CENTER - A.R. GOULD DIVISION - HEALTH
    SCIENCES LIBRARY (Med)**
151 Academy St.   Phone: (207) 769-2511
Presque Isle, ME 04769   Marilyn W. Dean, Lib.Supv.
Staff: Prof 1. **Subjects:** Medicine, surgery, nursing. **Holdings:** 250 books; 75
periodicals. **Services:** Interlibrary loans; copying; library open to public with
restrictions. **Computerized Information Services:** MEDLINE. **Networks/
Consortia:** Member of Health Science Library and Information Cooperative of
Maine; Aroostook Health Information and Resource Consortium.

★819★
**ART CENTER COLLEGE OF DESIGN - JAMES LEMONT FOGG MEMORIAL
    LIBRARY (Art)**
1700 Lida St.   Phone: (213) 577-1700
Pasadena, CA 91103   Elizabeth Galloway, Lib.Dir.
Founded: 1930. **Staff:** Prof 2; Other 4. **Subjects:** Fine arts, communications
design, industrial design, illustration, photography and film. **Holdings:** 22,721
book titles; 750 bound periodical volumes; 1000 exhibition catalogs; 8 VF
drawers; 700 annual reports; 42,140 slides; 90 films. **Subscriptions:** 310
journals and other serials; 10 newspapers. **Services:** Copying; library not open
to public. **Networks/Consortia:** Member of Art Libraries Society/North

America. **Special Indexes:** Index to visual file and slides. **Staff:** Alison Holt,
Asst.Libn./Cat.; Marie Jordan, Slide Libn.; Margaret Rose, Acq.Libn.; Steven
Takata, Circ.Supv.

★820★
ART CENTER, INC. - LIBRARY (Art)
120 S. St. Joseph St.   Phone: (219) 284-9102
South Bend, IN 46601   Judy Oberhausen, Act.Dir./Cur.
Founded: 1947. **Subjects:** Visual arts. **Special Collections:** Collection of
Carlotta Murray Banta (306 volumes). **Holdings:** 1205 volumes; 1300
catalogs. **Subscriptions:** 25 journals and other serials. **Services:** Library open
to public for reference use only.

★821★
ART GALLERY OF GREATER VICTORIA - LIBRARY (Art)
1040 Moss St.   Phone: (604) 384-4101
Victoria, BC, Canada V8V 4P1   Susan Vial, Libn.
Founded: 1951. **Staff:** Prof 1. **Subjects:** Canadian and Oriental art.
Holdings: 3000 books; 3000 exhibition catalogs; 2000 artist files; 2000
pamphlets. **Subscriptions:** 50 journals and other serials. **Services:** Interlibrary
loans; library open to public for reference use only.

★822★
ART GALLERY OF HAMILTON - MURIEL ISABEL BOSTWICK LIBRARY (Art)†
123 King St., W.   Phone: (416) 527-6610
Hamilton, ON, Canada L8P 4S8   Andrew J. Oko, Cur., Hist.Coll.
Founded: 1966. **Staff:** Prof 2. **Subjects:** Fine art. **Holdings:** 2000 books and
bound periodical volumes; 500 exhibition catalogs; 3 VF drawers of gallery
archives; 6 VF drawers of annual reports; 8 VF drawers of artists reference
files. **Services:** Interlibrary loans; copying; library open to public for reference
use only.

★823★
**ART GALLERY OF ONTARIO - EDWARD P. TAYLOR AUDIO-VISUAL CENTRE
    (Art)**
317 Dundas St., W.   Phone: (416) 977-0414
Toronto, ON, Canada M5T 1G4   Catherine Jonasson, Hd.
Founded: 1927. **Staff:** Prof 3; Other 2. **Subjects:** Art - Canadian, European,
American. **Special Collections:** Henry Moore Archives (slides and films).
Holdings: 70,000 circulating slides; 15,000 archival slides; 180 films; 49
videotapes; 225 audiotapes; 50 media kits. **Services:** Library open to
Canadian residents. **Publications:** Catalog, published every three years. **Staff:**
Margaret Brennan, Sr.Cat.; Lynne Burry, Res.-Cat.

★824★
**ART GALLERY OF ONTARIO - EDWARD P. TAYLOR REFERENCE LIBRARY
    (Art)**
317 Dundas St. W.   Phone: (416) 361-0414
Toronto, ON, Canada M5T 1G4   Karen McKenzie, Chf.Libn.
Founded: 1933. **Staff:** Prof 3; Other 2. **Subjects:** Western art and history of
art. **Special Collections:** Allan Garrow Collection (English book illustration,
1855-1875); manuscripts and printed material on Canadian artists; Canadian
book illustration. **Holdings:** 38,000 volumes; 22,000 auction catalogs;
10,500 artists files (clippings, reproductions, photographs). **Subscriptions:**
150 journals and other serials. **Services:** Interlibrary loans (limited); copying;
library open to nonstaff with restrictions. **Publications:** Selected Acquisitions,
quarterly. **Special Indexes:** The Art Gallery of Ontario; 60 years of
exhibitions, 1906-1966; Exhibitors Finding Aid (card). **Staff:** Larry Pfaff,
Dp.Libn./Ref.Libn.; Carol Lowrey, Tech.Serv.Libn.

★825★
ART INFORMATION CENTER, INC. (Art)
280 Broadway, Suite 412   Phone: (212) 725-0335
New York, NY 10007   Betty Chamberlain, Dir.
Founded: 1959. **Staff:** Prof 2; Other 1. **Subjects:** Contemporary art by living
visual artists. **Services:** Helps artists to find New York outlets for their work,
by appointment. Supplies information by phone or mail if return postage is
supplied, regarding living artists and where they exhibit - 50,000 on file;
information on special skills studies. **Remarks:** Center is a free clearinghouse
of information on contemporary fine arts.

★826★
ART INSTITUTE OF BOSTON - LIBRARY (Art)
700 Beacon St.   Phone: (617) 262-1223
Boston, MA 02215   Susan M. Eisen, Libn.
Founded: 1970. **Staff:** Prof 1; Other 6. **Subjects:** Art history, photography,
graphics, design, humanities. **Holdings:** 4508 books and bound periodical
volumes; 14,000 slides; 7 VF drawers of picture reference files; 4 VF
drawers of exhibition catalogs; 1 VF drawer of pamphlets. **Subscriptions:** 68

journals and other serials. **Services:** Interlibrary loans; copying; library open to public for reference use only. **Special Catalogs:** Card cross reference catalog for picture collection.

★827★
ART INSTITUTE OF CHICAGO - RYERSON AND BURNHAM LIBRARIES (Art)
Michigan Ave. at Adams St.   Phone: (312) 443-3671
Chicago, IL 60603   Daphne C. Roloff, Dir.
Founded: 1901. **Staff:** Prof 7; Other 10. **Subjects:** Fine arts, architecture. **Special Collections:** Mary Reynolds Collection on Surrealism and its affinities; Percier and Fontaine Collection (architecture and decorative arts); Ryerson Collection of Japanese and Chinese Illustrated Books; Burnham Library Archives (letters and manuscripts relating to Chicago architects). **Holdings:** 135,400 books and bound periodical volumes; 60,000 pamphlets and exhibition catalogs; 256,000 slides; 5000 photographs; 1398 reels of microfilm. **Subscriptions:** 862 journals and other serials. **Services:** Interlibrary loans; copying; library open to members and visiting curators. **Computerized Information Services:** SCIPIO (internal database); computerized cataloging. **Networks/Consortia:** Member of Metropolitan Chicago Library Assembly; RLG. **Publications:** Ryerson Index to Art Periodicals, volumes 1-11, First Supplement, 1975; Architectural Records in Chicago, 1981. **Special Indexes:** Burnham Index to Architectural Periodicals, 1919 to 1963 (card index); Chicago Art and Artists Scrapbook, 1890 to present (Chicago newspaper clippings). **Staff:** Karen Muller, Hd., Tech.Serv.; Nancy Kirkpatrick, Hd., Slide Dept.; Rosemary Lopiano, Ref./ILL Libn.; Janice Kraus, Cat./Ref.Libn.; Carol Terry, Ser.Libn.

★828★
ART INSTITUTE OF CHICAGO - SCHOOL OF THE ART INSTITUTE OF CHICAGO - LIBRARY (Art)
280 S. Columbus Dr.
Chicago, IL 60603   Nadene Byrne, Dir.
Staff: Prof 3; Other 1. **Subjects:** Art, photography, film, humanities, education, music. **Special Collections:** Artists' Video Interview Series (400 videotapes); artists' books (200); Erens Film Scripts Collection; Film Study Collection (270). **Holdings:** 16,500 books; 500 bound periodical volumes; 16 VF drawers of pictures; 500 pamphlets; 700 audiotapes. **Subscriptions:** 165 journals and other serials; 5 newspapers. **Services:** Interlibrary loans; copying; library open to public for reference use only. **Computerized Information Services:** Computerized cataloging. **Networks/Consortia:** Member of ILLINET; OCLC; Metropolitan Chicago Library Assembly; Union of Independent Colleges of Art (UICA). **Staff:** Fred Hillbruner, Hd. of Tech.Serv.; Roland Hansen, Hd. of Rd.Serv.

★829★
ART MUSEUM OF SOUTH TEXAS - LIBRARY (Art)★
1902 N. Shoreline   Phone: (512) 884-3844
Corpus Christi, TX 78401   Susan Walker-Atchison, Cur.
Staff: Prof 1. **Subjects:** Art (general, contemporary, American). **Holdings:** 2100 books; 155 bound periodical volumes; 8 VF drawers of clippings; 4 VF drawers of exhibition catalogs. **Subscriptions:** 33 journals and other serials. **Services:** Interlibrary loans; copying (limited); library open to public for reference use only. **Remarks:** Maintained by the Corpus Christi Art Foundation.

★830★
ART REFERENCE BUREAU, INC. (Pict)
Box 1324   Phone: (413) 443-4365
Pittsfield, MA 01202   Polly-Ann Duff, Hd. of Res.
Staff: Prof 4. **Subjects:** Painting, sculpture, architecture, and minor arts. **Holdings:** Photographs. **Services:** Pictorial research for the publishing trade; facilities not open to public. **Formerly:** Located in Ancram, NY.

★831★
ART STUDENTS LEAGUE OF NEW YORK - LIBRARY (Art)
215 W. 57th St.   Phone: (212) 247-4510
New York, NY 10019   Rosina A. Florio, Exec.Dir.
Subjects: Art. **Holdings:** 2000 books; 17 VF drawers.

★832★
ARTESIA HISTORICAL MUSEUM AND ART CENTER - LIBRARY (Hist)†
505 W. Richardson   Phone: (505) 748-2390
Artesia, NM 88210   Frances W. Collins, Dir. of Musm.
Staff: Prof 2; Other 1. **Subjects:** Area history, farming, ranching, water basins. **Special Collections:** Terrill Book Collection, 1796-1897 (12 volumes). **Holdings:** 284 books; 378 bound periodical volumes; pioneer diaries, 1908-1929; photographs; newspapers, 1903-1974; 28 oral history tapes of pioneer life; pamphlets; genealogies; 56 school annuals. **Services:** Copying (limited); library open to public with restrictions.

ARTHRITIS CENTER LIBRARY
See: Medical University of South Carolina

★833★
ARTHRITIS INFORMATION CLEARINGHOUSE (Med)
Herner and Company
Box 9782   Phone: (703) 558-8250
Arlington, VA 22209   Lois Lunin, Project Dir.
Founded: 1978. **Staff:** Prof 2; Other 1. **Subjects:** Arthritis, rheumatic diseases, musculoskeletal diseases, education. **Special Collections:** Documents and information in professional and patient education areas, community demonstration programs and federal programs designed for rheumatic diseases. **Holdings:** 2700 database items. **Services:** Clearinghouse serves health professionals. **Computerized Information Services:** Online systems; internal database; computerized cataloging, acquisitions and serials. **Publications:** List of publications - available on request. **Remarks:** The clearinghouse is operated by the U.S. Department of Health and Human Services, the National Institutes of Health, and the National Institute of Arthritis, Diabetes, Digestive and Kidney Diseases. **Staff:** Lee S. Bernstein, Info.Spec.

★834★
ARTHRITIS SOCIETY - NATIONAL OFFICE LIBRARY (Med)
920 Yonge St., Suite 420   Phone: (416) 967-1414
Toronto, ON, Canada M4W 3J7   Joan-Mary Attwood, Libn.
Staff: Prof 1. **Subjects:** Arthritis and related diseases and their care; voluntary organizations and their management; health organizations and research. **Holdings:** 1000 books; 8 drawers of pamphlets and related material. **Subscriptions:** 35 journals and other serials. **Services:** Interlibrary loans; library open to public for reference use only by appointment.

★835★
ARTHUR ANDERSEN & CO. - BUSINESS LIBRARY (Bus-Fin)
711 Louisiana, Suite 700   Phone: (713) 237-2718
Houston, TX 77338   Ann Ghist, Libn.
Founded: 1941. **Staff:** Prof 3; Other 3. **Subjects:** Taxation, international taxes, accounting, auditing. **Holdings:** 5000 books; 350 bound periodical volumes; 800 reels of microfilm; 400 ultrafiche. **Subscriptions:** 250 journals and other serials; 5 newspapers. **Services:** Copying; library open to public with restrictions. **Computerized Information Services:** LEXIS. **Special Catalogs:** Taxation, auditing, international taxes (all on card). **Staff:** Patricia A. Edwards, Asst.Libn.; Cindy Kehoe, Lib.Asst., Intl.

★836★
ARTHUR ANDERSEN & CO. - GENERAL LIBRARY (Bus-Fin)
33 W. Monroe St.   Phone: (312) 580-0033
Chicago, IL 60603   Marilyn R. Murray, Libn.
Staff: Prof 2; Other 4. **Subjects:** Accounting. **Holdings:** 16,000 books; 900 bound periodical volumes; binders of annual reports of 3000 companies; 50 VF drawers; 100,000 items on microfilm; U.S. Securities and Exchange Commission (SEC) materials on microfiche, 1969 to present; Wall Street Journal market sections on microfiche, 1969 to present. **Subscriptions:** 300 journals and other serials. **Services:** Interlibrary loans; library open to public by special arrangement. **Computerized Information Services:** DIALOG, New York Times Information Service, LEXIS. **Staff:** Kathleen McGrath, Asst.Libn.

★837★
ARTHUR ANDERSEN & CO. - LIBRARY (Bus-Fin; Law)
Box 7757   Phone: (415) 856-8485
San Francisco, CA 94120   Joanna S. Beyer, Libn.
Staff: Prof 1; Other 1. **Subjects:** Tax law, accounting, management consulting, auditing, business. **Holdings:** 1000 books; 30 bound periodical volumes; 300 annual reports; releases of the Financial Accounting Standards Board and the American Institute of Certified Public Accountants; 50 loose-leaf services. **Subscriptions:** 47 journals and other serials; 8 newspapers. **Services:** Library open to public with approval of company partner. **Computerized Information Services:** Mead Data Central, National Automated Accounting Research System (NAARS), Disclosure, Inc. **Networks/Consortia:** Member of Private Law Library Association of San Francisco.

★838★
ARTHUR ANDERSEN & CO. - LIBRARY (Bus-Fin)
One Financial Plaza   Phone: (203) 522-2600
Hartford, CT 06103   Jenifer M. Berman, Libn.
Founded: 1962. **Staff:** Prof 1. **Subjects:** Accounting, taxation. **Special Collections:** Management Information Consulting Library (800 volumes); Tax Services (30 volumes). **Holdings:** 8000 books; 50 VF drawers of audit and tax subject files; 12 VF drawers of annual reports; 2 VF drawers of

prospectuses. **Subscriptions:** 40 journals and other serials; 6 newspapers. **Services:** Interlibrary loans; copying; library open to public with restrictions. **Computerized Information Services:** LEXIS.

★839★
ARTHUR ANDERSEN & CO. - LIBRARY (Bus-Fin; Law)
100 Federal St.   Phone: (617) 423-1400
Boston, MA 02110   Jean Fisher, Libn.
Staff: Prof 1; Other 2. **Subjects:** Tax law and legislation, accounting and auditing, management consulting, business, computer applications, statistics. **Holdings:** 6000 books; 250 bound periodical volumes; 1300 annual reports; 600 reels of microfilm; 52 VF drawers of company reports; 500 pamphlets. **Subscriptions:** 200 journals, newsletters and other serials; 10 newspapers. **Services:** Interlibrary loans; copying; library open to public with restrictions on some materials. **Computerized Information Services:** LEXIS, New York Times Information Service, DIALOG, SDC. **Remarks:** Library is currently in three parts: Tax Library, Audit Library, Administrative Services Library.

★840★
ARTHUR ANDERSEN & CO. - LIBRARY (Bus-Fin)†
1345 Ave. of the Americas   Phone: (212) 956-2815
New York, NY 10019   Louise Wagner, Libn.
Founded: 1921. **Staff:** Prof 1; Other 2. **Subjects:** Accounting. **Holdings:** 5000 volumes; 250 VF drawers. **Subscriptions:** 460 journals and other serials; 5 newspapers. **Services:** Interlibrary loans; copying.

★841★
ARTHUR ANDERSEN & CO. - LIBRARY (Bus-Fin)
Toronto Dominion Ctr.
Box 29   Phone: (416) 863-1540
Toronto, ON, Canada M5K 1B9   Mary O'Neill, Libn.
Founded: 1960. **Staff:** Prof 1; Other 1. **Subjects:** Accounting, auditing, taxation, management consulting. **Holdings:** 2000 books; 20 bound periodical volumes; 100,000 subject files on microfilm; 350 Arthur Andersen & Co. publications. **Subscriptions:** 100 journals and other serials; 6 newspapers. **Services:** Interlibrary loans; copying. **Computerized Information Services:** Info Globe. **Publications:** Canadian Tax and Trade Brief, irregular - to clients and interested parties.

★842★
ARTHUR ANDERSEN & CO. - TAX LIBRARY (Bus-Fin; Law)
33 W. Monroe   Phone: (312) 580-0033
Chicago, IL 60603   Caroline Basciani, Tax Libn.
Staff: Prof 1; Other 2. **Subjects:** Tax law. **Holdings:** 5500 books; 300 bound periodical volumes; 6 VF drawers; pamphlets. **Subscriptions:** 200 journals and other serials; 6 newspapers. **Services:** Copying; library open to public by appointment. **Computerized Information Services:** LEXIS.

★843★
ARTHUR D. LITTLE, INC. - BURLINGTON LIBRARY (Info Sci; Sci-Tech)
17 Acorn Park   Phone: (617) 864-5770
Cambridge, MA 02140   Marcia J. Kindzerske, Libn.
Founded: 1979. **Staff:** Prof 1; Other 1. **Subjects:** Information systems, telecommunications, computer engineering, computer application. **Holdings:** 650 books; 200 volumes of computer system manuals. **Subscriptions:** 223 journals and other serials. **Services:** Interlibrary loans; library not open to public. **Computerized Information Services:** DIALOG, BRS, SDC, NEXIS, New York Times Information Service; computerized cataloging. **Networks/Consortia:** Member of OCLC through NELINET. **Publications:** Periodicals currently received, 2/year - for internal distribution only.

★844★
ARTHUR D. LITTLE, INC. - LIFE SCIENCES LIBRARY (Sci-Tech)
Acorn Park   Phone: (617) 864-5770
Cambridge, MA 02140   Margaret A. Miller, Hd.
Founded: 1954. **Staff:** Prof 2; Other 1. **Subjects:** Biomedical sciences, toxicology, carcinogenesis, environmental health, bioassay. **Holdings:** 700 books; 1135 bound periodical volumes. **Subscriptions:** 154 journals and other serials. **Services:** Interlibrary loans; SDI; library open to public by appointment. **Computerized Information Services:** DIALOG, NLM, BRS, CAS Online, NEXIS, SDC, NIH-EPA Chemical Information System; computerized cataloging. **Special Indexes:** Index of In Vitro bioassays (card). **Remarks:** Library is located at 30 Memorial Dr., Cambridge, MA. **Staff:** Marie C. Dellovo, Info.Spec.

★845★
ARTHUR D. LITTLE, INC. - MANAGEMENT LIBRARY (Bus-Fin; Soc Sci)
35 Acorn Pk.   Phone: (617) 864-5770
Cambridge, MA 02140   Edith B. Mintz, Hd.Libn.
Founded: 1975. **Staff:** Prof 2; Other 3. **Subjects:** Management, administrative and statistical resources in: operations research, health care, marketing, chemical industries, social systems, education. **Special Collections:** 10K Reports of companies listed on the New York, American and Over-the-Counter Stock Exchanges (microfiche). **Holdings:** 4000 books; 575 bound periodical volumes; 7000 company annual reports; 1500 reels of microfilm of periodicals and newspapers; 300 microfiche. **Subscriptions:** 800 journals and other serials; 6 newspapers. **Services:** Interlibrary loans; copying; library not open to public. **Computerized Information Services:** DIALOG, SDC, Dow Jones News Retrieval, New York Times Information Service, BRS; computerized cataloging. **Networks/Consortia:** Member of OCLC. **Staff:** Cynthia Hibberd, Info.Spec.

★846★
ARTHUR D. LITTLE, INC. - RESEARCH LIBRARY (Sci-Tech)
25 Acorn Pk.   Phone: (617) 864-5770
Cambridge, MA 02140   Ann J. Wolpert, Hd.
Founded: 1886. **Staff:** Prof 2; Other 3. **Subjects:** Chemistry, physics, electrical and mechanical engineering, electronics, food and agriculture, research administration. **Holdings:** 22,000 books; 3000 bound periodical volumes; 3 file cabinets of microfiche reports. **Subscriptions:** 1200 journals and other serials. **Services:** Interlibrary loans; copying; SDI; library open to public by appointment. **Computerized Information Services:** DIALOG, SDC, BRS, NLM, New York Times Information Service, DOE/RECON, CAS Online, NEXIS; computerized cataloging and serials. **Networks/Consortia:** Member of OCLC through NELINET. **Publications:** Accessions List, quarterly - for internal distribution only; Union List of Serials, annual with quarterly supplement - to section heads, foreign offices, and libraries in the area. **Staff:** Ethel M. Salonen, Asst.Hd.Libn./Info.Spec.

★847★
ARTHUR YOUNG & COMPANY - LIBRARY (Bus-Fin)
One IBM Plaza
Chicago, IL 60611   Helen Facto, Libn.
Staff: Prof 1; Other 2. **Subjects:** Accounting, taxation. **Holdings:** 1200 books; 1500 annual reports. **Subscriptions:** 400 journals and other serials; 20 newspapers. **Services:** Interlibrary loans; copying; SDI; library not open to public. **Computerized Information Services:** LEXIS, New York Times Information Service, DIALOG, SDC.

★848★
ARTHUR YOUNG & COMPANY - LIBRARY (Bus-Fin)
277 Park Ave.   Phone: (212) 922-4880
New York, NY 10172   Jeanne F. Mellon, Libn.
Founded: 1953. **Staff:** Prof 3; Other 7. **Subjects:** Accounting and auditing; management consulting; taxation. **Holdings:** 5500 books; 115,000 microfiche. **Subscriptions:** 350 journals and other serials. **Services:** Interlibrary loans; library open to clients and librarians by appointment. **Computerized Information Services:** New York Times Information Service, SDC. **Staff:** John D. Midgley, Asst.Libn.; Carol Christiansen, Asst.Libn.

ARTHUR YOUNG TAX LIBRARY
See: Arizona State University - Lloyd Bimson Memorial Library

ARTHUR YOUNG TAX RESEARCH LIBRARY
See: San Diego State University - Bureau of Business & Economic Research Library

★849★
ARTISTS SPACE - COMMITTEE FOR THE VISUAL ARTS - UNAFFILIATED ARTISTS FILE (Art)
105 Hudson St.   Phone: (212) 226-3970
New York, NY 10013   Linda Shearer, Dir.
Founded: 1973. **Staff:** 4. **Subjects:** Artists. **Holdings:** Slide files of 1800 New York State artists not represented by commercial or cooperative galleries, including resumes, photos, slide sheets and descriptive material. **Services:** The Registry is open to public. **Special Catalogs:** Exhibition catalogs for Artists Space; gallery program of the Committee for the Visual Arts. **Staff:** Susan Wyatt, Asst.Dir.

ARUNDEL (Anne) GENERAL HOSPITAL
See: Anne Arundel General Hospital

ASAMI LIBRARY OF YI DYNASTY
See: University of California, Berkeley - East Asiatic Library

★850★
ASARCO INC. - LIBRARY (Sci-Tech)†
Central Research Dept.
901 Oak Tree Rd.   Phone: (201) 756-4800
South Plainfield, NJ 07080   Betty E. Hurlbert, Libn.
Founded: 1938. **Staff:** Prof 1; Other 1. **Subjects:** Nonferrous metallurgy, minerals research. **Holdings:** 5000 books; 6200 bound periodical volumes; 112 VF drawers of patents, pamphlets, unbound reports, dissertations, papers, articles; 14 drawers and 1 carousel of microforms. **Subscriptions:** 284 journals and other serials; 5 newspapers. **Services:** Interlibrary loans. **Publications:** Library Acquisitions Bulletin, monthly - for internal distribution only. **Also Known As:** American Smelting and Refining Company.

★851★
ASBESTOS CORPORATION, LTD. - PRODUCT RESEARCH & DEVELOPMENT LIBRARY (Sci-Tech)
835 Mooney St.
P.O. Box 9   Phone: (418) 335-9171
Thetford Mines, PQ, Canada G6G 5S1   Yves Demers, Dir. de la Qualite
Staff: 1. **Subjects:** Asbestos - characteristics, fiber applications, mining and milling, industry hygiene, testing standards, government specifications; plastics; engineering. **Holdings:** 597 books and reports; 1000 patents of asbestos fiber processing and uses (Canadian, U.S. and other). **Subscriptions:** 23 journals and other serials. **Services:** Interlibrary loans; copying (both limited); library open to staff, customers and representatives only.

★852★
ASBESTOS INFORMATION ASSOCIATION/NORTH AMERICA - TECHNICAL AND MEDICAL FILES (Med; Sci-Tech)
1745 Jefferson Davis Hwy., Suite 509   Phone: (703) 979-1150
Arlington, VA 22202   B.J. Pigg, Exec.Dir.
Staff: 4. **Subjects:** Health and asbestos, asbestos regulation. **Special Collections:** Asbestos information - technical, medical and regulatory. **Holdings:** 300 books; 10 VF drawers of clippings and medical files. **Subscriptions:** 18 journals and other serials. **Services:** Library open to public by appointment. **Publications:** News and Notes, monthly; other educational and informational materials.

★853★
ASBURY THEOLOGICAL SEMINARY - B.L. FISHER LIBRARY (Rel-Theol)
                                           Phone: (606) 858-3581
Wilmore, KY 40390   D. William Faupel, Dir., Lib. Serv.
Founded: 1939. **Staff:** Prof 5; Other 9. **Subjects:** Bible, religion, theology, Methodism, Middle Eastern languages, philosophy, history, psychology, pastoral service, Christian education, sociology. **Special Collections:** World Council of Churches Faith and Order Documents; Alfred W. Price Collection on Divine Healing; Christian Holiness Association Collection on Perfectionism. **Holdings:** 129,000 books and bound periodical volumes; 2900 microforms; 100 filmstrips; 2000 sound recordings; 1700 slides; 100 linear feet of archival material; 80 kits. **Subscriptions:** 610 journals and other serials. **Services:** Interlibrary loans; copying; library open to local residents and ministers. **Computerized Information Services:** Computerized cataloging. **Networks/Consortia:** Member of OCLC through SOLINET; Theological Education Association of Mid-America (TEAM-A). **Publications:** Accessions list, quarterly - to faculty, students and mailed on request. **Staff:** John A. Seery, Pub.Serv.; Kenneth A. Boyd, Media Serv.; Michael P. Boddy, Acq.; Donald A. Butterworth, Tech.Serv.; Sandra Abernathy, Circ.Supv.

★854★
ASBURY UNITED METHODIST CHURCH - LIBRARY (Rel-Theol)
5601 S. Puget Sound
Box 9448   Phone: (206) 472-4239
Tacoma, WA 98409   Crystal M. Parks, Libn.
Staff: 2. **Subjects:** Religious education, hymns, missionary biographies. **Special Collections:** Dr. H.W. Michener Collection - Puget Sound Conference, 1884-1981 (Methodist Annual Conference Journals). **Holdings:** 1800 books; 50 bound periodical volumes; maps. **Services:** Interlibrary loans; library open to public with restrictions.

★855★
ASCENSION LUTHERAN CHURCH - LIBRARY (Rel-Theol)
1236 S. Layton Blvd.   Phone: (414) 671-5066
Milwaukee, WI 53215   Lorraine H. Pike, Libn.
Founded: 1954. **Staff:** Prof 3; Other 14. **Subjects:** Religion and related subjects. **Special Collections:** Memorial Organ Music Collection (4 file drawers, cataloged). **Holdings:** 9000 books and bound periodical volumes;

100 books in Spanish; 4 VF drawers; 2 drawers of teaching pictures; 1 drawer of flannelgraphs; 52 religious pictures; 600 phonograph records; 70 audio cassettes; 120 filmstrips. **Subscriptions:** 40 journals and other serials. **Services:** Interlibrary loans (limited); library open to public. **Staff:** Grace Fiedler, Asst.Libn.; Shirley Pritzlaff, Cat.

★856★
ASGROW SEED COMPANY - RESEARCH CENTER (Sci-Tech)
Box 1235   Phone: (208) 326-4321
Twin Falls, ID 83301   Leland R. Schweitzer, Mgr. of Res.Lab.
Founded: 1953. **Staff:** 3. **Subjects:** Seed technology and physiology, horticulture. **Holdings:** 500 books; 5500 journal clippings and reprints. **Subscriptions:** 74 journals and other serials. **Services:** Library not open to public. **Remarks:** Subsidiary of The Upjohn Company.

ASH LIBRARY
See: U.S. Armed Forces Institute of Pathology

ASHER (Norman and Helen) LIBRARY
See: Spertus College of Judaica - Norman and Helen Asher Library

★857★
ASHFORD MEMORIAL COMMUNITY HOSPITAL - MEDICAL LIBRARY (Med)†
1451 Ashford Ave.
Box 32   Phone: (809) 721-2160
San Juan, PR 00902
Staff: 2. **Subjects:** Medicine, clinical disciplines, basic sciences, surgery, hospital administration. **Holdings:** 600 books; 100 bound periodical volumes; films; tapes; video cassettes. **Subscriptions:** 35 journals and other serials. **Services:** Interlibrary loans; bibliographies; center open to public for reference use only.

★858★
ASHLAND CHEMICAL COMPANY - TECHNICAL INFORMATION CENTER (Sci-Tech)
Box 2219   Phone: (614) 889-3281
Columbus, OH 43216   Priscilla Ratliff, Supv.
Founded: 1970. **Staff:** Prof 3; Other 3. **Subjects:** Chemistry - organic, polymer, catalysis and surface, analytical; carbon black. **Special Collections:** Chemical Abstracts, 1907 to present (complete). **Holdings:** 7000 books; 5525 bound periodical volumes; 33,500 U.S. patents; 20,700 foreign patents; U.S. chemical patents on microfilm, 1960 to present. **Subscriptions:** 550 journals and other serials. **Services:** Interlibrary loans; copying; library open to public by appointment. **Computerized Information Services:** DIALOG, SDC, NLM, NIH/EPA Chemical Information System. **Networks/Consortia:** Member of OHIONET. **Staff:** Evelyn Donohue, Lib.Techn.; Kay Landis, Lit.Chem.; David Anderson, Lit.Chem.

★859★
ASHLAND HISTORICAL SOCIETY - LIBRARY
Box 321
Ashland, MA 01721
Subjects: Local history and genealogy. **Holdings:** 300 books and pamphlets; VF drawers of manuscripts, clippings and ephemera; microfilm of local newspapers from 1869; photographs and portraits of town officials from 1850-1900; 400 slides. **Remarks:** Presently inactive.

★860★
ASHLAND OIL, INC. - TECHNICAL INFORMATION CENTER (Sci-Tech; Energy)
Box 391   Phone: (606) 739-4166
Ashland, KY 41101   L.H. Workman, Libn.
Staff: Prof 2. **Subjects:** Petroleum technology, organic chemistry, mathematics, engineering, analytical chemistry. **Holdings:** 1900 books; 1800 bound periodical volumes; 8000 U.S. and foreign patents. **Subscriptions:** 53 journals and other serials. **Services:** Library not open to public. **Staff:** Sherry Payne, Libn.

★861★
ASHLAND THEOLOGICAL SEMINARY - ROGER DARLING MEMORIAL LIBRARY (Rel-Theol)
910 Center St.   Phone: (419) 289-4126
Ashland, OH 44805   Rev. Bradley E. Weidenhamer, Libn.
Founded: 1963. **Staff:** Prof 1; Other 2. **Subjects:** Biblical and textual commentaries, Anabaptist and pietistic works, Biblical archaely. **Special Collections:** J. Allen Miller Collection; Sauer Bibles; Darling Debate Collection; Mary Queen of Scots Collection; Robert H. Smith Archaeological Collection; Charles F. Pfeiffer Collection. **Holdings:** 56,003 volumes; 3137 bound periodical volumes; 10 cartons and 43 unbound volumes of Brethren Church

Archives. **Subscriptions:** 342 journals and other serials. **Services:** Interlibrary loans; copying; library open to qualified persons.

ASHTONBEE CAMPUS RESOURCE CENTRE
See: Centennial College of Applied Arts & Technology

★862★
ASIA SOCIETY - LIBRARY (Area-Ethnic)†
725 Park Ave.
New York, NY 10021
Phone: (212) 751-4210
Mary Anne Cartelli, Lib.Asst.
Founded: 1956. **Subjects:** Literature, religion, politics, geography and other aspects of Asia. **Special Collections:** Teacher-oriented reference and resource collection. **Holdings:** 6000 books.

ASIAN AMERICAN STUDIES CENTER READING ROOM
See: University of California, Los Angeles

★863★
ASIAN ART MUSEUM OF SAN FRANCISCO - LIBRARY (Art)
Golden Gate Pk.
San Francisco, CA 94118
Phone: (415) 558-2993
Fred A. Cline, Jr., Libn.
Founded: 1967. **Staff:** Prof 1; Other 1. **Subjects:** Oriental art. **Holdings:** 15,558 books; 1000 bound periodical volumes; 960 microfiche; 40 reels of microfilm; 1000 items in pamphlet file. **Subscriptions:** 140 journals and other serials. **Services:** Copying; library open to public. **Special Indexes:** Index to sales catalogs; Indexes to Chinese and Japanese painters and other artists. **Formerly:** Its Avery Brundage Collection. **Remarks:** Museum is now responsible for all Oriental art owned by the City of San Francisco.

ASIAN LIBRARY
See: Oakland Public Library

★864★
ASIAN STUDIES NEWSLETTER ARCHIVES (Area-Ethnic)
McKeldin Library
University of Maryland
College Park, MD 20742
Phone: (301) 454-2819
Frank Joseph Shulman, Dir.
Staff: Prof 1. **Subjects:** Asian studies, China, Southeast Asia, Japan. **Holdings:** 40 linear feet of newsletters and bulletins (450 titles). **Subscriptions:** 450 newsletters. **Services:** Copying; archives open to public by appointment. **Remarks:** The collection of newsletters is undertaken by Frank Joseph Shulman on a private basis. He will answer mail requests for xerox copies whenever possible at cost.

ASIS
See: American Society for Information Science

"ASK NSP" TAPE LIBRARY
See: Northern States Power Company

ASKEW (Sarah Byrd) LIBRARY
See: William Paterson College of New Jersey - Sarah Byrd Askew Library

★865★
ASOCIACION NACIONAL PRO PERSONAS MAYORES - LIBRARY (Soc Sci; Area-Ethnic)
1730 W. Olympic Blvd., Suite 401
Los Angeles, CA 90015
Phone: (213) 487-1922
Carmela G. Lacayo, Natl.Exec.Dir.
Founded: 1975. **Staff:** Prof 2; Other 1. **Subjects:** Minority aging; Hispanic aging and elderly; Hispanic affairs. **Holdings:** 1000 volumes; 6 VF drawers. **Services:** Training seminars and conferences; library open to public. **Publications:** Legislative bulletin and newsletter, quarterly. **Also Known As:** National Association for Hispanic Elderly. **Staff:** Peggy Smith, Adm.Coord.

★866★
ASPEN HISTORICAL SOCIETY - LIBRARY (Hist)
620 W. Bleeker
Aspen, CO 81611
Phone: (303) 925-3721
Staff: Prof 1. **Subjects:** Aspen area history, Colorado state. **Holdings:** 500 books; 200 bound periodical volumes; 4000 photographs; manuscripts; clippings; newspapers on microfilm; 200 cassette and reel tapes.

★867★
ASPEN INSTITUTE FOR HUMANISTIC STUDIES - DAVID MAYER LIBRARY
1000 N. 3rd St.
Aspen, CO 81611
Founded: 1962. **Subjects:** Humanities. **Special Collections:** Aspen Scholars Collection which consists of works by participants of Aspen Institute Programs (250 books). **Holdings:** 3100 books. **Remarks:** Presently inactive.

★868★
ASPEN SYSTEMS CORPORATION - LAW LIBRARY & INFORMATION CENTER (Law)†
1600 Research Blvd.
Rockville, MD 20850
Phone: (301) 251-5000
Judy Meadows, Info.Mgr.
Founded: 1962. **Staff:** Prof 1; Other 2. **Subjects:** Law, information science, environment, health management, copyright. **Special Collections:** Hazardous waste information (1000 volumes). **Holdings:** 16,000 books; 12 VF drawers. **Subscriptions:** 250 journals and other serials. **Services:** Interlibrary loans; copying (fee); library admission by special arrangement. **Computerized Information Services:** WESTLAW, SDC.

★869★
ASPEN SYSTEMS CORPORATION - PROJECT SHARE (Soc Sci)
Box 2309
Rockville, MD 20852
Phone: (301) 251-5170
Eileen Wolff, Project Off.
Staff: Prof 3. **Subjects:** Human services. **Holdings:** 7226 books; 101 bound periodical volumes. **Subscriptions:** 50 journals and other serials. **Services:** Copying; SDI; library open to public for reference use only during business hours. **Computerized Information Services:** Project SHARE (internal database); computerized acquisitions. **Publications:** Journal of Human Services Abstracts, quarterly; Bibliography Series, 10/year; Monograph Series, 10/year; SHARING, bimonthly. **Remarks:** Operated under contract to U.S. Dept. of Health and Human Services - Office of the Assistant Secretary for Planning & Evaluation. **Staff:** Deborah Ferrara, Ref.Supv.; Vivian Workman, Ref.Spec.; Deborah Smyth, Ref.Spec.

★870★
ASPHALT INSTITUTE - RESEARCH LIBRARY (Sci-Tech)
Asphalt Institute Bldg.
College Park, MD 20740
Phone: (301) 927-0422
Charles A. Mayer, Lib.Cons.
Founded: 1919. **Subjects:** Asphalt - technology, history, industry. **Holdings:** 1000 volumes; 288 boxes of fugitive literature. **Subscriptions:** 20 journals and other serials. **Services:** Library open to serious students by advance application.

ASSATEAGUE ISLAND NATL. SEASHORE
See: U.S. Natl. Park Service

★871★
ASSELIN, BENOIT, BOUCHER, DUCHARME, LAPOINTE, INC. - LIBRARY DEPARTMENT (Sci-Tech)
85 W. Ste. Catherine
Montreal, PQ, Canada H2X 3P4
Phone: (514) 287-8546
Diane Mercier, Libn.
Founded: 1975. **Staff:** Prof 2. **Subjects:** Engineering - hydraulic, nuclear; construction; electronics. **Holdings:** 6000 books; 1500 bound periodical volumes; 150 annual reports; standards and Canadian government specifications. **Subscriptions:** 280 journals and other serials; 8 newspapers. **Services:** Interlibrary loans; copying; library not open to public. **Computerized Information Services:** SDC, CAN/OLE, QL Systems, QUESTEL; computerized cataloging, acquisitions, serials and circulation. **Publications:** Liste des nouveautes; liste des periodiques, both monthly. **Staff:** Micheline Picard, Asst.Libn.

★872★
ASSEMBLIES OF GOD GRADUATE SCHOOL - CORDAS C. BURNETT LIBRARY (Rel-Theol)
1445 Boonville Ave.
Springfield, MO 65802
Phone: (417) 862-2781
Larry L. Haight, Libn.
Founded: 1973. **Staff:** Prof 1; Other 11. **Subjects:** Bible, theology, Holy Spirit, missions, anthropology, communications, philosophy and psychology, sociology, Assemblies of God. **Holdings:** 42,597 books and bound periodical volumes; 2503 reels of microfilm; 33,377 microfiche; 1818 cassette tapes; 80 dissertations and theses. **Subscriptions:** 460 journals and other serials. **Services:** Interlibrary loans; copying; library open to public with restrictions. **Computerized Information Services:** DIALOG; computerized cataloging. **Networks/Consortia:** Member of Southwest Missouri Academic Libraries Cooperative; Assemblies of God Library Consortium; Southwest Missouri Library Network. **Staff:** Joseph Marics, Hd. of Circ.; Joyce Stuart, Coord. of Tech.Serv.

ASSEMBLIES OF GOD NORTHWEST COLLEGE
See: Northwest College of the Assemblies of God

ASSOCIATED COLLEGES OF UPPER NEW YORK ARCHIVES
See: SUNY at Binghamton - Special Collections

★873★
ASSOCIATED COLLEGIATE PRESS/NATIONAL SCHOLASTIC PRESS
   ASSOCIATION - INFORMATION CENTER (Publ)
720 Washington Ave., S.E., Suite 205
University of Minnesota   Phone: (612) 373-3180
Minneapolis, MN 55414   Tom Rolnicki, Exec.Dir.
Founded: 1921. Staff: Prof 4; Other 9. Subjects: Educational services
concerning publishing and production of student publications. Special
Collections: American college and high school yearbooks, magazines and
newspapers. Holdings: Figures not available. Services: Interlibrary loans
(fee); center open to public with restrictions. Publications: Scholastic Editor's
Trends in Publications, 8/school year - by subscription.

★874★
ASSOCIATED ENGINEERING SERVICES, LTD. - INFORMATION CENTRE (Sci-
   Tech)
13140 St. Albert Trail   Phone: (403) 453-8111
Edmonton, AB, Canada T5L 4R8   M. Davidson, Libn.
Founded: 1960. Staff: 3. Subjects: Engineering - civil, mechanical,
structural, electrical, petrochemical and industrial. Special Collections:
Northern collection (Yukon, Northwest Territories and other permafrost areas,
with special attention to water and sewerage in the North; 750 titles).
Holdings: 2000 books; 150 bound periodical volumes; 2000 trade catalogs.
Subscriptions: 60 journals and other serials; 15 newspapers. Services:
Interlibrary loans (by special request). Computerized Information Services:
Computerized cataloging.

★875★
ASSOCIATED GENERAL CONTRACTORS OF AMERICA - INFORMATION
   CENTER (Sci-Tech)
8100 Schaefer Hwy.   Phone: (313) 342-5100
Detroit, MI 48235   Joan Boram, Libn.
Founded: 1981. Staff: Prof 1. Subjects: Construction labor relations, history
of Detroit construction industry, construction literature (general), construction
site safety. Holdings: 500 books; slide shows on construction safety.
Subscriptions: 25 journals and other serials; 5 newspapers. Services:
Interlibrary loans; copying; center open to public by appointment.

★876★
ASSOCIATED GENERAL CONTRACTORS OF AMERICA - JAMES L.
   ALLHANDS MEMORIAL LIBRARY (Hist)
1957 E St., N.W.   Phone: (202) 393-2040
Washington, DC 20006   John C. Ellis, Dir.
Founded: 1963. Staff: 2. Subjects: History of construction industry.
Holdings: 250 books. Services: Interlibrary loans; library open to public by
appointment only.

★877★
ASSOCIATED GRANTMAKERS OF MASSACHUSETTS, INC. - RESOURCE
   CENTER FOR PHILANTHROPY (Soc Sci)
294 Washington St., Suite 501   Phone: (617) 426-2608
Boston, MA 02108   Philip Conley, Libn.
Founded: 1971. Staff: Prof 1; Other 1. Subjects: Foundations, corporate
philanthropy, fund raising, technical assistance. Special Collections: Tax
return forms filed with Internal Revenue Service (IRS) by Massachusetts
private foundations (microfilm); Gardiner Howland Shaw Foundation Collection
(criminal justice management). Holdings: 500 books and bound periodical
volumes; 450 annual reports of national foundations; 4 VF drawers of
pamphlets; Grantsmanship Center News, August, 1973 to present; Foundation
News, 1960 to present. Subscriptions: 20 journals and other serials.
Services: Copying; library open to public by appointment. Networks/
Consortia: Member of Consortium of Foundation Libraries.

★878★
ASSOCIATED MENNONITE BIBLICAL SEMINARIES - MENNONITE BIBLICAL
   SEMINARY - LIBRARY (Rel-Theol)
3003 Benham Ave.   Phone: (219) 295-3726
Elkhart, IN 46514   Paul Roten, Libn.
Founded: 1945. Staff: Prof 2; Other 6. Subjects: Biblical studies, theology,
missions, church history, Christian education, psychology, ethics. Special
Collections: Studer Bible Collection; Mennonitica. Holdings: 85,500 books;
3500 bound periodical volumes. Subscriptions: 440 journals and other
serials. Services: Interlibrary loans; copying; library open to public. Staff: Lois
Longenecker, Asst.Libn.

★879★
ASSOCIATED PRESS - NEWSPHOTO LIBRARY (Pict)
50 Rockefeller Plaza   Phone: (212) 621-1913
New York, NY 10020   Grant Lamos, III, Dir.
Founded: 1927. Staff: Prof 18. Subjects: General. Holdings: 7 million
negatives and prints (photographs of personalities and subject matter).
Services: Library open to public through application to Wide World Photos,
Inc.

★880★
ASSOCIATED SPRING BARNES GROUP, INC. - CORPORATE LIBRARY (Sci-
   Tech)
18 Main St.   Phone: (203) 583-1331
Bristol, CT 06010   Jackie A. Ives, Libn.
Founded: 1957. Staff: Prof 1; Other 1. Subjects: Springs, metallurgy,
business management. Special Collections: Barnes Archives. Holdings: 2000
books; 44 VF drawers of documents, reports, patents and vendors catalogs.
Subscriptions: 130 journals and other serials. Services: Interlibrary loans;
copying; library open to public with permission of Technical Center Director.
Networks/Consortia: Member of Capitol Region Library Council.
Publications: Library Bulletin, 4/year; Monthly Summary of Library
Acquisitions - both for internal distribution only.

★881★
ASSOCIATED TECHNICAL SERVICES, INC. - RESEARCH LIBRARY (Sci-Tech)
855 Bloomfield Ave.   Phone: (201) 748-5673
Glen Ridge, NJ 07028   Leon Jacolev, Lib.Dir.
Founded: 1949. Staff: Prof 1; Other 1. Subjects: Chemistry, chemical
engineering, petroleum production and refining, earth sciences, palynology,
linguistics, biosciences, bibliography. Special Collections: 3500 dictionaries
and glossaries in 55 languages covering the entire spectrum of science and
technology; 17,000 translations in science and technology; collection of
Russian technical journals. Holdings: 3000 books; 1300 pamphlets
(cataloged); 15 filing cabinets of clippings, catalogs, tear sheets, and
translations. Subscriptions: 35 journals and other serials. Services: Copying;
translation; technical literature research; worldwide photocopy service for
technical documents and patents; current awareness services monitoring
Russian and Japanese technical literature; library open to scholars by request.
Publications: Russian Oil and Gas Bulletin (covers prospecting, production,
research), bimonthly - publications are in English and are available by
subscription. Comprehensive dictionary catalog is published irregularly and is
for sale; current catalog lists 1300 titles. Remarks: The library is unique in
having one of the most extensive technical dictionary and glossary collections
in existence; inquiries from scholars and lexicographers are welcome. Staff:
Ruth E. Leffler, Tech.Libn.

ASSOCIATION FOR THE ADVANCEMENT OF PSYCHOANALYSIS
See: Ivimey (Muriel) Library

ASSOCIATION OF AMERICAN GEOGRAPHERS ARCHIVES
See: Smithsonian Institution - National Anthropological Archives

★882★
ASSOCIATION OF AMERICAN MEDICAL COLLEGES - ARCHIVES (Med)
One DuPont Circle, N.W.   Phone: (202) 828-0400
Washington, DC 20008   Mary H. Littlemeyer, Archv.
Staff: Prof 1. Subjects: Medical education. Special Collections: History of
the AAMC since 1876. Holdings: Figures not available for books;
manuscripts, governance and program records, microfilm, magnetic tapes.
Services: Copying; archives open to public with restrictions. Special Indexes:
Index of AAMC Executive Council actions since 1960; finding aid.

★883★
ASSOCIATION OF AMERICAN PUBLISHERS - PUBLISHING EDUCATION
   INFORMATION SERVICE - STEPHEN GREENE MEMORIAL LIBRARY (Publ)
One Park Ave.   Phone: (212) 689-8920
New York, NY 10016   Sandra Math, Libn.
Founded: 1970. Staff: Prof 1. Subjects: Book publishing. Holdings: Reports
and data. Services: Collection primarily for member use.

★884★
ASSOCIATION OF AMERICAN RAILROADS - ECONOMICS AND FINANCE
   DEPARTMENT - RAIL INFORMATION CENTER (Trans)
American Railroads Bldg., Rm. 523
1920 L St., N.W.   Phone: (202) 835-9387
Washington, DC 20036   Helen M. Rowland, Supv., Lib.Serv.
Founded: 1910. Staff: Prof 1; Other 1. Subjects: Transportation economics
and history, railroad history and statistics, finance, labor relations, taxation,
international transport, valuation, management, public relations. Special

Collections: Source material on railroads from 1808; annual reports (7300); engineers' surveys and reports; congressional materials; proceedings of railroad associations and clubs. **Holdings:** 14,000 books; 2200 bound periodical volumes. **Subscriptions:** 139 journals and other serials. **Services:** Interlibrary loans; copying; library open to public with restrictions; subject bibliographies prepared on special request.

ASSOCIATION ARCHIVES
See: Gale Research Company - Library

★885★
ASSOCIATION OF AVERAGE ADJUSTERS OF THE UNITED STATES - LIBRARY (Bus-Fin)
College of Insurance
123 William St.   Phone: (212) 962-4111
New York, NY 10038   Donald E. Carson, Libn.
Founded: 1879. **Staff:** 5. **Subjects:** Admiralty and insurance laws. **Holdings:** 591 books. **Services:** Library open to public.

★886★
ASSOCIATION OF AVIATION & SPACE MUSEUMS - INFORMATION CENTER (Sci-Tech)
6203 Yellowstone Dr.   Phone: (703) 941-4724
Alexandria, VA 22312   Douglas Campbell, Dir.
Staff: Prof 2; Other 5. **Subjects:** Air and space museums, aviation, aeronautics. **Special Collections:** Listings of over 500 air and space museums throughout the world and their holdings. **Holdings:** 220 books; 12 feet of information packets; 6 feet on aerial photography; 2000 slides of military aircraft. **Subscriptions:** 20 journals and other serials. **Services:** Library not open to public. **Publications:** Windsock, quarterly. **Special Indexes:** Indexes of U.S. military aircraft and aerial photographs; index of aircraft and space items on display around the world.

★887★
ASSOCIATION OF BALLOON & AIRSHIP CONSTRUCTORS - TECHNICAL LIBRARY (Trans)
Box 7
Rosemead, CA 91770   Donald E. Woodward, Pres.
Founded: 1974. **Staff:** Prof 1; Other 4. **Subjects:** Airship design, balloon technology, hot-air balloon construction. **Holdings:** 90 books; 1500 reports; article and clippings file. **Services:** Copying; library open to public with restrictions. **Publications:** Lighter Than Air (LTA) books and publication checklist in Aerostation Journal, quarterly - limited circulation. **Special Catalogs:** Bibliography papers on selected Lighter Than Air technology subjects for technical society meetings. **Staff:** George E. Wright, Jr., Archv.

★888★
ASSOCIATION OF THE BAR OF THE CITY OF NEW YORK - LIBRARY (Law)†
42 W. 44th St.   Phone: (212) 840-3550
New York, NY 10036   Anthony P. Grech, Libn.
Founded: 1870. **Staff:** Prof 11; Other 34. **Subjects:** Law - Anglo-American, foreign and international. **Special Collections:** Appellate Court briefs and records. **Holdings:** 396,524 volumes. **Services:** Library not open to public.

ASSOCIATION OF BAY AREA GOVERNMENTS
See: Metropolitan Transportation Commission

★889★
ASSOCIATION OF BOOK PUBLISHERS OF BRITISH COLUMBIA - LIBRARY (Publ)
1622 W. 7th Ave.   Phone: (604) 734-1611
Vancouver, BC, Canada V6J 1S5   Susan P. Hutchinson, Project Coord.
Staff: 1. **Subjects:** Book publishing in British Columbia. **Holdings:** 500 books; 60 catalogs; 4 VF drawers of archives. **Services:** Copying; library open to public for reference use only. **Publications:** Signature, quarterly - to industry, media and government. **Special Catalogs:** Books from British Columbia (magazine).

ASSOCIATION CANADIENNE D'EDUCATION
See: Canadian Education Association

ASSOCIATION CANADIENNE D'ETUDES FISCALES
See: Canadian Tax Foundation

ASSOCIATION CANADIENNE D'EXPORTATION
See: Canadian Export Association

ASSOCIATION CANADIENNE DE NORMALISATION
See: Canadian Standards Association

ASSOCIATION CANADIENNE POUR LA SANTE MENTALE
See: Canadian Mental Health Association

★890★
ASSOCIATION CANADO-AMERICAINE - INSTITUT CANADO-AMERICAIN (Area-Ethnic)
Box 989   Phone: (603) 625-8577
Manchester, NH 03105   Robert A. Beaudoin, Chm., Archv.Comm.
Subjects: Franco-Americans in New England, Acadians and Cajuns, Quebecois, French in the United States and in France. **Special Collections:** Sculptures by Alfred Laliberte of Montreal (50); paintings by Lorenzo de Nevers (15); manuscripts of Henri D'Arles (14). **Holdings:** 40,000 volumes; old newspapers in French (250 reels of microfilm); photographs; 189 VF drawers of miscellaneous materials. **Subscriptions:** 20 journals and other serials. **Services:** Copying; library open to public for reference use only. **Remarks:** The library of L'Association Canado-Americaine, called L'Institut Canado-Americain, is supported and housed by the ACA, a Franco-American fraternal life insurance society.

★891★
ASSOCIATION FOR CHILDHOOD EDUCATION INTERNATIONAL - LIBRARY
3615 Wisconsin Ave., N.W.
Washington, DC 20016
Defunct

★892★
ASSOCIATION OF CONSULTING MANAGEMENT ENGINEERS - LIBRARY (Bus-Fin)
230 Park Ave.   Phone: (212) 697-9693
New York, NY 10169   Joseph J. Brady, Pres.
Subjects: Management and consulting. **Holdings:** 1300 volumes. **Services:** Library not open to public. **Publications:** List of publications - available upon request.

★893★
ASSOCIATION FOR EXPERIENTIAL EDUCATION - LIBRARY (Educ)
7200 E. Dry Creek Rd., Suite F203   Phone: (313) 779-0519
Englewood, CO 80112   Stephanie Takis, Exec.Off.
Subjects: Experiential education. **Holdings:** 200 books; 4 VF drawers of program reports; 1000 copies of newsletters and journals published by the AEE; 6 tapes of speeches. **Publications:** Journal of Experiential Education, 3/year with membership or by subscription; Jobs Clearing House, monthly - by subscription. **Remarks:** AEE places its materials into circulation through the ERIC Clearinghouse.

★894★
ASSOCIATION FOR GERONTOLOGY IN HIGHER EDUCATION - RESOURCE LIBRARY (Soc Sci)
600 Maryland Ave., S.W., West Wing 204   Phone: (202) 484-7505
Washington, DC 20024   Elizabeth Douglass, Exec.Dir.
Staff: 3. **Subjects:** Aging - education, training programs and courses. **Holdings:** Brochures and information for over 200 schools offering programs and courses in aging. **Services:** Library open to public with restrictions. **Publications:** National Directory of Educational Programs in Gerontology, 3rd edition, 1982. **Staff:** Joy Lobenstine, Adm.Asst.

★895★
ASSOCIATION OF GOVERNING BOARDS OF UNIVERSITIES AND COLLEGES - TRUSTEE INFORMATION CENTER (Soc Sci)
One Dupont Circle, Suite 400   Phone: (202) 296-8400
Washington, DC 20036   Linda E. Henderson, Info.Ctr.Coord.
Founded: 1974. **Staff:** Prof 1. **Subjects:** Higher education issues - governance, trusteeship, trustee role and responsibility, board organization. **Holdings:** 800 books; 200 clippings. **Subscriptions:** 14 journals and other serials. **Services:** Copying; library open to public with restrictions. **Publications:** Bibliographies; briefing papers; informational kits.

ASSOCIATION DES HOPITAUX DU CANADA
See: Canadian Hospital Association

★896★
ASSOCIATION OF IDAHO CITIES - LIBRARY
3314 Grace
Boise, ID 83706
Subjects: Model ordinances, city planning, construction standards. **Special Collections:** City Codes. **Holdings:** 700 volumes; 32 VF drawers; manuals,

directories and specifications. **Remarks:** Presently inactive.

★897★
ASSOCIATION OF INTERNATIONAL COLLEGES & UNIVERSITIES - AICU INTERNATIONAL EDUCATION LIBRARY (Educ)
1301 S. Noland Rd. Phone: (816) 931-6374
Independence, MO 64055 John W. Johnston, Dir.
Founded: 1973. **Staff:** Prof 1; Other 2. **Subjects:** Education - comparative, international, transcultural. **Holdings:** 625 books; 125 bound periodical volumes; 82 manuscripts; 45 dissertations; 54 unbound reports; 4200 clippings. **Subscriptions:** 15 journals and other serials. **Services:** Copying; library open to public with restrictions. **Publications:** AICU Report, monthly - by subscription.

★898★
ASSOCIATION OF JUNIOR LEAGUES - RESOURCE CENTER (Soc Sci)
825 Third Ave. Phone: (212) 355-4380
New York, NY 10022 Thomas Littler, Libn.
Founded: 1971. **Staff:** 1. **Subjects:** Voluntarism, community projects, Junior League. **Holdings:** 400 volumes; 50 bound periodical volumes; 15 VF drawers of subject files. **Subscriptions:** 240 journals and other serials. **Services:** Copying; SDI; center not open to public.

★899★
ASSOCIATION DES MEDECINS DE LANGUE FRANCAISE DU CANADA - UNION MEDICALE DU CANADA - RESEARCH LIBRARY
1440 St. Catherine St. W., Suite 510
Montreal, PQ, Canada H3G 2P9
Founded: 1872. **Subjects:** Medicine. **Holdings:** 2000 books. **Subscriptions:** 145 journals and other serials. **Remarks:** Presently inactive.

ASSOCIATION DE MONTREAL POUR LES DEFICIENTS MENTAUX
See: Montreal Association for the Mentally Retarded

★900★
ASSOCIATION OF NATIONAL ADVERTISERS - LIBRARY (Bus-Fin)
155 E. 44th St. Phone: (212) 697-5950
New York, NY 10017 Rosemary Collins, Mgr.
Staff: Prof 1; Other 2. **Subjects:** Advertising, marketing. **Holdings:** 1500 books; 150 VF drawers of pamphlets and clippings. **Subscriptions:** 150 journals and other serials. **Services:** Interlibrary loans; library open to association members.

★901★
ASSOCIATION OF NORTH AMERICAN DIRECTORY PUBLISHERS - PRICE & LEE COMPANY DIRECTORY LIBRARY (Publ)
Box 317
Bellows Falls, VT 05101 Pat Lentocha
Founded: 1912. **Staff:** 1. **Special Collections:** All city, county and telephone directories published by association members in the U.S. and Canada. **Holdings:** 1500 volumes. **Services:** Library open for academic research only.

★902★
ASSOCIATION OF OPERATING ROOM NURSES - LIBRARY (Med)
10170 E. Mississippi Ave. Phone: (303) 755-6300
Denver, CO 80231 Sara Katsh, Libn.
Founded: 1972. **Staff:** Prof 1; Other 1. **Subjects:** Nursing, surgery. **Holdings:** 2000 books; 1200 bound periodical volumes. **Subscriptions:** 100 journals and other serials. **Services:** Interlibrary loans; SDI; library open to Denver area health professionals with limited services. **Computerized Information Services:** NLM. **Networks/Consortia:** Member of Denver Area Health Sciences Library Consortium.

★903★
ASSOCIATION DE PARALYSIE CEREBRALE DU QUEBEC, INC. - CENTRE DE DOCUMENTATION (Med)
525 Boul. Hamel Est, Suite A-50 Phone: (418) 529-5371
Quebec, PQ, Canada G1M 2S8
Staff: Prof 1; Other 1. **Subjects:** Cerebral palsy, handicaps, treatment methods. **Holdings:** Figures not available. **Subscriptions:** 40 journals and other serials. **Services:** Interlibrary loans; copying; library open to members and rehabilitation staff.

★904★
ASSOCIATION PARITAIRE DE PREVENTION POUR LA SANTE ET LA SECURITE DU TRAVAIL DU QUEBEC - TECH.INFO. CENTER (Sci-Tech)
1016 St. Alexandre Phone: (514) 866-1871
Montreal, PQ, Canada H2P 1P5 Lise Locas, Doc. Recherchiste
Staff: Prof 1; Other 1. **Subjects:** Accident prevention, regulation, education

and training; occupational health and safety; fire prevention; safety research. **Holdings:** 600 books; 1000 pamphlets (cataloged). **Subscriptions:** 15 journals and other serials; 10 newspapers. **Services:** Copying; center open to public for reference use only on request. **Publications:** Prevention, monthly - distributed to members. **Formerly:** Industrial Accident Prevention Association. **Also Known As:** APPSST.

ASSOCIATION OF PARTIALLY OR WHOLLY FRENCH LANGUAGE UNIVERSITIES
See: Association des Universites Partiellement ou Entierement de Langue Francaise

★905★
ASSOCIATION OF PHILIPPINE COCONUT DESICCATORS - LIBRARY (Food-Bev)†
Times Sq. Sta., Box 787 Phone: (212) 929-0104
New York, NY 10036 Conrado A. Escudero, U.S. Rep.
Founded: 1970. **Staff:** 1. **Subjects:** Philippine desiccated coconut - cuts, nutritional analysis, recipes and formulas, uses. **Services:** Information service to association members. **Publications:** Newsletter; annual report.

ASSOCIATION OF PHYSICIAN ASSISTANT PROGRAMS
See: American Academy of Physician Assistants

★906★
ASSOCIATION FOR POPULATION/FAMILY PLANNING LIBRARIES & INFORMATION CENTERS INTERNATIONAL (Soc Sci)
c/o Carolina Population Center Library
University Square - East 300A
Chapel Hill, NC 27514 Doreen S. Goyer, Pres.
Subjects: Population and family planning. **Publications:** Proceedings of Conferences, annual - 1968 to present; Newsletter (APLICommunicator); special publications; monograph: Union List of Population/Family Planning Periodicals. **Remarks:** APLIC is a cooperative and collaborative association of 175 individual members representing organizations throughout the world concerned with identifying, collecting and disseminating information relevant to population and family planning. Its objectives include the professional development of effective documentation and information systems and services in the field of population and family planning, the worldwide exchange of population information, an international cooperative network of population documentation, information and library centers and continuing education programs for the professional development of population documentalists, librarians and information specialists. For additional information contact Susan Robbins, APLIC Publicity Officer, c/o The Population Council, One Dag Hammarskjold Plaza, New York, NY 10017. **Also Known As:** APLIC International.

★907★
ASSOCIATION FOR RESEARCH AND ENLIGHTENMENT - ARE BRAILLE LIBRARY (Rel-Theol; Aud-Vis)†
215 67th St.
Box 595 Phone: (804) 428-3588
Virginia Beach, VA 23451 Alma Crovatt, Libn.
Founded: 1969. **Staff:** Prof 1; Other 2. **Subjects:** Parapsychology, metaphysics, psychology, health. **Special Collections:** Clairvoyant readings of Edgar Cayce (in braille and on tape). **Holdings:** 100 braille books (161 volumes); 65 open-reel tape books; 30 lecture tapes; 80 cassette books; 150 cassette lectures; 24 large-print books. **Services:** Interlibrary loans; copying; library open to blind and handicapped. **Remarks:** This is a free-loan library to any blind or physically handicapped person in the world. It is one of the largest libraries for this type of material in the U.S. and one of the few equipped to thermoform books. **Staff:** Louise Rothrock, Proofreader; Josephine Peebles, Proofreader.

★908★
ASSOCIATION FOR RESEARCH AND ENLIGHTENMENT - EDGAR CAYCE FOUNDATION - LIBRARY (Rel-Theol)
Box 595 Phone: (804) 428-3588
Virginia Beach, VA 23451 Stephen Jordan, Lib.Mgr.
Founded: 1931. **Staff:** Prof 4; Other 8. **Subjects:** Psychic phenomena; religious thought; health - physical, mental and spiritual; Bible and related subjects; psychology; metaphysical thought; dreams. **Special Collections:** Psychic Readings of Edgar Cayce (typescripts of 14,256 discourses and answers given by Edgar Cayce in response to questions while in a trance state, 643 volumes); Andrew Jackson Davis Collection; Egerton Sykes Collection on Atlantis (3000 volumes). **Holdings:** 36,000 books; 600 bound periodical volumes; 2500 other cataloged items; 700 cassettes; 15 VF drawers. **Subscriptions:** 178 journals and other serials; 10 newspapers. **Services:** Interlibrary loans; Braille translations; library open to public for

reference use only; Association members may borrow materials. **Publications:** A.R.E. Journal, bimonthly; A.R.E. News, monthly; booklets, 4/ year - to members; A.R.E. Library Booklist with 3 supplements. **Special Indexes:** Index to the Cayce "readings" by subject (card); special supplemental indexes. **Staff:** Charlotte Schoen, Tech.Serv.; Alma Crovatt, Circ.Supv.

★909★
ASSOCIATION OF SCIENCE/TECHNOLOGY CENTERS - LIBRARY (Sci-Tech)
1016 16th St., N.W.   Phone: (202) 452-0655
Washington, DC 20036   Bonnie VanDorn, Exec.Dir.
Staff: Prof 1. **Subjects:** Science, technology, museums. **Holdings:** 50 books; 500 magazines and pamphlets. **Services:** Library open to public by appointment.

★910★
ASSOCIATION OF STUDENT INTERNATIONAL LAW SOCIETIES - INFORMATION CENTER (Law)
2223 Massachusetts Ave., N.W.   Phone: (202) 387-8467
Washington, DC 20008   Elizabeth L. Rodgers, Exec.Sec.
Staff: 1. **Subjects:** International law and legal education. **Special Collections:** Philip C. Jessup International Law Moot Court Competition (past problems and judges' memoranda). **Holdings:** Figures not available. **Services:** Copying; library open to public for reference use only.

★911★
ASSOCIATION FOR THE STUDY OF AFRO-AMERICAN LIFE AND HISTORY, INC. - CARTER G. WOODSON LIBRARY (Area-Ethnic)
1401 14th St., N.W.   Phone: (202) 667-2822
Washington, DC 20005   Sr. Anthony Scally, Chf.Libn.
Founded: 1976. **Staff:** 1. **Subjects:** Afro-American history. **Special Collections:** Rare books on black involvement in America prior to 1865 (200 books). **Holdings:** 4200 books; 88 bound periodical volumes. **Services:** Library open to public for reference use only.

★912★
ASSOCIATION OF TRIAL LAWYERS OF AMERICA - ATLA LIBRARY (Law)
1050 31st St., N.W.   Phone: (202) 965-3500
Washington, DC 20007   Keith Searls, Libn.
Staff: Prof 1; Other 1. **Subjects:** Trial advocacy; products liability; law - tort, criminal, medical, federal. **Holdings:** 10,000 volumes. **Subscriptions:** 200 law reviews, journals and other serials. **Services:** Interlibrary loans; copying; library open to public with restrictions. **Computerized Information Services:** WESTLAW, DIALOG.

★913★
ASSOCIATION DES UNIVERSITES PARTIELLEMENT OU ENTIEREMENT DE LANGUE FRANCAISE - BIBLIOTHEQUE (Educ)
Universite de Montreal
B.P. 6128   Phone: (514) 343-6630
Montreal, PQ, Canada H3C 3J7   Francoise Sorieul
Founded: 1961. **Staff:** Prof 1; Other 1. **Subjects:** Higher education, interuniversity cooperation, French studies, pedagogical innovation, information science, technology transfer. **Holdings:** 3000 books. **Subscriptions:** 280 journals and other serials. **Services:** Interlibrary loans; copying; SDI; library open to public. **Publications:** Liste des publications recues, monthly - for internal distribution only. **Also Known As:** Association of Partially or Wholly French Language Universities.

★914★
ASSOCIATION OF UNIVERSITIES AND COLLEGES OF CANADA - DOCUMENTATION CENTRE (Educ)
151 Slater St.   Phone: (613) 563-1236
Ottawa, ON, Canada K1P 5N1   Hazel J. Roberts, Mgr.
Founded: 1957. **Staff:** Prof 2; Other 4. **Subjects:** Higher education (Canadian, British, U.S.). **Special Collections:** Canadian universities documents (174 linear feet). **Holdings:** 8000 books; 8 VF drawers of newspapers clippings; 15 VF drawers of pamphlets. **Subscriptions:** 350 journals and other serials; 13 newspapers. **Services:** Interlibrary loans; copying; library open to public for reference use only. **Special Catalogs:** Academic collective bargaining, university financing, status of women academics, university organizations (each on cards).

ASSOCIATION OF UNIVERSITIES FOR RESEARCH IN ASTRONOMY (AURA, Inc.)
See: Kitt Peak National Observatory

ASSOCIATION OF UNIVERSITIES FOR RESEARCH IN ASTRONOMY - SACRAMENTO PEAK NATIONAL OBSERVATORY
See: Sacramento Peak National Observatory

★915★
ASSOCIATION OF UNIVERSITY PROGRAMS IN HEALTH ADMINISTRATION - RESOURCE CTR. FOR HEALTH SERVICES ADM. EDUCATION (Educ)
1911 N. Fort Myer Dr., Suite 503   Phone: (703) 524-5500
Arlington, VA 22209   Lydia S. Clary, Coord.
Founded: 1977. **Staff:** Prof 1. **Subjects:** Health services administration, health services administration education, long term care administration, international health, hospital administration, higher education, medical care, medical economics and public health. **Special Collections:** U.S. and Canadian accreditation surveys of health administration programs (40). **Holdings:** 1500 books; 150 program information files; 50 accreditation self-survey reports; 75 geographic files; 200 files for related organizations. **Subscriptions:** 100 journals and other serials. **Services:** Interlibrary loans; copying; library open to public by appointment. **Computerized Information Services:** Internal databases. **Publications:** Descriptive flyer. **Also Known As:** The Michael M. Davis Reading Room. **Remarks:** The Resource Center is jointly maintained by the Association of University Programs in Health Administration and the Accrediting Commision on Education for Health Services Administration. The commission's phone number is (703) 524-0511. **Formerly:** Located in Washington, DC.

★916★
ASSUMPTION ABBEY - LIBRARY (Rel-Theol)
          Phone: (701) 974-3315
Richardton, ND 58652   Bro. Paul Nyquist, Hd.Libn.
Staff: Prof 1; Other 1. **Subjects:** Theology, scripture, Benedictines, monasteries, religion, history (especially North Dakota). **Holdings:** 80,000 books; 2000 bound periodical volumes. **Subscriptions:** 125 journals and other serials; 5 newspapers. **Services:** Interlibrary loans; copying; library open to public with restrictions. **Staff:** Bro. Aaron Jensen, Asst.Libn.

ASSUMPTION FRIARY LIBRARY
See: Franciscan Friars

★917★
ASSUMPTION SEMINARY - LIBRARY (Rel-Theol)†
2600 W. Woodlawn   Phone: (512) 734-5137
San Antonio, TX 78284   John R. McGrath, Libn.
Founded: 1952. **Staff:** 2. **Subjects:** Theology, Mexican-American literature, psychology, family relationships. **Holdings:** 20,000 books; 500 bound periodical volumes; 1000 pamphlets. **Subscriptions:** 200 journals and other serials; 20 newspapers. **Services:** Interlibrary loans; library open to public with special permission.

AST (Birdie Goldsmith) RESOURCE COLLECTION
See: Barnard College Women's Center - Birdie Goldsmith Ast Resource Collection

★918★
ASTOR HOME FOR CHILDREN - PROFESSIONAL LIBRARY (Soc Sci)
36 Mill St.   Phone: (914) 876-4081
Rhinebeck, NY 12572   William J. Nichols, Libn.
Staff: Prof 1. **Subjects:** Child psychology and allied fields; residential treatment centers; foster child care; adoption. **Holdings:** 2618 books; 637 bound periodical volumes; 2 VF drawers of staff papers and theses. **Subscriptions:** 36 journals and other serials. **Services:** Interlibrary loans; copying; library open to public with restrictions. **Networks/Consortia:** Member of Southwestern New York Library Resources Council.

ASTOR (Samuel & Rebecca) JUDAICA LIBRARY
See: Jewish Community Center - Samuel & Rebecca Astor Judaica Library

ATAS/UCLA TELEVISION ARCHIVES
See: University of California, Los Angeles - Academy of Television Arts and Sciences.

★919★
ATASCADERO STATE HOSPITAL - PROFESSIONAL LIBRARY (Med)
Box A   Phone: (805) 461-2491
Atascadero, CA 93423   Marie V. Logan, Sr.Libn.
Founded: 1957. **Staff:** Prof 1; Other 3. **Subjects:** Sex pathology, forensic psychiatry, criminal insanity, psychotherapy, nursing and nursing education, medicine. **Holdings:** 9000 books; 4000 bound periodical volumes; 950 AV items; 5 VF drawers. **Subscriptions:** 125 journals and other serials. **Services:**

Interlibrary loans; copying; library open to public for reference use only upon request. **Networks/Consortia:** Member of Total Interlibrary Exchange (TIE).

★920★
ATE MANAGEMENT AND SERVICE COMPANY, INC. - RESOURCE CENTER (Trans)
617 Vine St., Suite 800   Phone: (513) 381-7424
Cincinnati, OH 45202   Jean M. Lucas, Libn.
Staff: Prof 1; Other 1. **Subjects:** Mass transit, motor buses, transit marketing, business, paratransit/ridesharing. **Special Collections:** U.S. Dept. of Transportation - Urban Mass Transportation Administration depository. **Holdings:** 400 books; 2500 government technical reports; 1000 internal reports; 7 VF drawers of catalogs, specifications, marketing samples and forms. **Subscriptions:** 35 journals and other serials. **Services:** Interlibrary loans; copying; library open to public by appointment. **Computerized Information Services:** Computerized cataloging. **Networks/Consortia:** Member of OCLC through OHIONET.

ATENEO PUERTORRIQUENO
See: Puerto Rico - Ateneo Puertorriqueno

★921★
ATHEARN, CHANDLER AND HOFFMAN - LIBRARY (Law)
111 Sutter St.   Phone: (415) 421-5484
San Francisco, CA 94104
Subjects: Law. **Holdings:** Figures not available. **Services:** Library not open to public.

ATHENAEUM OF OHIO - MOUNT ST. MARY'S SEMINARY OF THE WEST
See: Mount St. Mary's Seminary of the West

★922★
ATHENAEUM OF PHILADELPHIA (Hum; Hist)
219 S. Sixth St.   Phone: (215) 925-2688
Philadelphia, PA 19106   Dr. Roger W. Moss, Jr., Exec.Dir.
Founded: 1814. **Staff:** Prof 5; Other 6. **Subjects:** 19th century America - fiction, architecture, decorative arts, biographies, periodicals; early travel and exploration; western Americana; early 19th century French culture; Philadelphia French Language Imprints. **Holdings:** 100,000 volumes; microfilm; photographic archives (architectural materials); manuscript collections (literary and historical); 20,000 architectural photographs; 1 million architectural manuscripts. **Subscriptions:** 40 journals and other serials. **Services:** Interlibrary loans; restrictions on all books printed prior to 1900; copying; library open to public for reference use only. **Computerized Information Services:** Computerized cataloging. **Networks/Consortia:** Member of OCLC. **Publications:** Annual Report; Athenaeum Library of the Nineteenth Century (reprint series), 2-3/year; Athenaeum Annotations, quarterly. **Staff:** Sandra Tatman, Arch.Libn.; Keith A. Kamm, Bibliog.; Ellen Batty, Circ.Libn.; Eileen Magee, Prog.Coord.

★923★
ATHENS COUNTY LAW LIBRARY (Law)
Courthouse, 3rd Fl.   Phone: (614) 594-2234
Athens, OH 45701   Fran Ridge, Libn.
Founded: 1898. **Staff:** 3. **Subjects:** Law. **Holdings:** 9500 books. **Services:** Library not open to public.

★924★
ATHENS MENTAL HEALTH CENTER - STAFF LIBRARY (Med)
Richland Ave.   Phone: (614) 592-3031
Athens, OH 45701   Judy McGinn, Staff Libn.
Staff: Prof 1. **Subjects:** Psychology, psychiatry, medicine, nursing, sociology. **Holdings:** 2300 books; 675 bound periodical volumes; 150 indexes, directories, reference tools (cataloged); 6 VF drawers of pamphlets and clippings; 105 audio cassette tapes. **Subscriptions:** 87 journals and other serials. **Services:** Copying; library open to public with restrictions.

★925★
ATKINS (Gordon) AND ASSOCIATES ARCHITECTS LTD. - LIBRARY (Art)
1909 17th Ave., S.W.   Phone: (403) 245-4545
Calgary, AB, Canada T2T 0E9   Robert Wenton, Libn.
Founded: 1961. **Subjects:** Architectural, graphic, industrial and landscape design; photography; planning; art. **Holdings:** 350 books; 2000 bound periodical volumes; 600 product specification manuals; drawings for 50 architectural projects; 10,000 photograph negatives. **Subscriptions:** 11 journals and other serials. **Services:** Library open to public on request.

ATKINS MUSEUM
See: Nelson Gallery-Atkins Museum

★926★
ATLANTA BUREAU OF PLANNING - LIBRARY (Plan; Trans)
10 Pryor St., S.W., Suite 200   Phone: (404) 658-6400
Atlanta, GA 30303   John Wright Heath, Dir./Lib. & Info.Serv.
Staff: Prof 3; Other 2. **Subjects:** Planning, transportation, economic development, land use, rapid transit, citizen participation. **Special Collections:** Virginia B. Slaughter Parks & Recreation Planning Collection (121 volumes); S.D. Hood Transportation Collection (850 volumes). **Holdings:** 2000 books; 100 bound periodical volumes. **Subscriptions:** 21 journals and other serials; 5 newspapers. **Services:** Library open to public by appointment. **Publications:** Neighborhood development plans and the city's Comprehensive Development Plan, annual. **Staff:** Allan J. Miles, Asst. to Dir.; Caroline Kitchens, Pub.Info.Off.

★927★
ATLANTA COLLEGE OF ART - LIBRARY (Art)
1280 Peachtree St.   Phone: (404) 892-3600
Atlanta, GA 30309   Jo Anne Paschall, Hd.Libn.
Founded: 1928. **Staff:** Prof 3; Other 6. **Subjects:** Visual arts, including video, film and photography. **Special Collections:** Artists' books (300). **Holdings:** 12,000 books; 1139 bound periodical volumes; 250 exhibition catalogs; 45,000 slides; 500 sound recordings; 56 art catalogs on microfiche; 14 drawers of miscellaneous bulletins and clipping file; 80 videotapes. **Subscriptions:** 214 journals and other serials. **Services:** Interlibrary loans; copying; library open to public for reference use only. **Computerized Information Services:** Computerized cataloging. **Networks/Consortia:** Member of University Center in Georgia, Inc.; CCLC; Union of Independent Colleges of Art (UICA). **Publications:** Video Documentation of ACA Visiting Artists Series. **Staff:** Jan Avgikos, Visual Coll.Cur.; Carol Harlow, Circ./Per.Libn.

★928★
ATLANTA HISTORICAL SOCIETY - ARCHIVES (Hist)
3101 Andrews Dr., N.W.   Phone: (404) 261-1837
Atlanta, GA 30305   Nancy J. Bryant, Sr.Archv.
Founded: 1926. **Staff:** 31. **Subjects:** History of Atlanta and its environs, personalities, organizations, businesses; Civil War history. **Special Collections:** Official City and County Records (1143 cubic feet); Atlanta maps and plats (500); 931 cataloged private collections (1930 cubic feet); architectural drawings (12,000); ephemera (90 cubic feet); Official Records of the Union and Confederate Armies - War of the Rebellion (complete set); Coca-Cola Company Cook Book Collection, (471 volumes); Cherokee Garden Club Library (1747 volumes; periodicals and archives). **Holdings:** 10,000 books; 545 bound periodical volumes; 152 newspaper titles; 203 periodical titles; 40,000 indexed photographs; 10,000 slides; 172 cubic feet of vertical files. **Subscriptions:** 31 journals and other serials; 7 newspapers. **Services:** Copying; library open to public. **Publications:** Atlanta Historical Journal, quarterly; Newsletter, bimonthly. **Special Indexes:** Descriptive inventories (card); Guide to Manuscript Collections, 1976. **Staff:** John Kerwood, Dir.; Eugene Craig, Libn.; Nancy Wight, Res.Asst.

★929★
ATLANTA LAW SCHOOL - LIBRARY (Law)
56 Tenth St., N.E.   Phone: (404) 872-0990
Atlanta, GA 30309   Sharon I. Pierce, Law Libn.
Founded: 1890. **Staff:** Prof 1; Other 4. **Subjects:** Law. **Holdings:** 19,000 books and bound periodical volumes; 860 volumes of periodicals on microfilm. **Subscriptions:** 43 journals and other serials. **Services:** Copying; library open to students, faculty and alumni.

★930★
ATLANTA NEWSPAPERS - REFERENCE LIBRARY (Publ)
72 Marietta St., N.W.   Phone: (404) 526-5420
Atlanta, GA 30303   Diane C. Hunter, Mgr., Lib.Serv.
Founded: 1950. **Staff:** Prof 5; Other 6. **Subjects:** Newspaper reference topics; Atlanta and Georgia history. **Holdings:** 1500 books; 100 bound periodical volumes; 11 million newspaper clippings; 2.5 million photographs, maps and graphics. **Subscriptions:** 60 journals and other serials; 40 newspapers. **Services:** Interlibrary loans; library open to members of the media only. **Computerized Information Services:** DIALOG, SDC, Dow Jones News Retrieval, New York Times Information Service; internal database; computerized cataloging. **Publications:** Information Update, irregular - for internal distribution only. **Staff:** Carl Moody, Ref.Libn.; Mary Civille, Text Libn.; Valerie Lyons, Photo Libn.; Peter Kent, Sys.Libn.

★931★

ATLANTA PUBLIC LIBRARY - IVAN ALLEN, JR. DEPARTMENT OF SCIENCE, INDUSTRY AND GOVERNMENT (Bus-Fin; Sci-Tech)

1 Margaret Mitchell Sq.   Phone: (404) 688-4636
Atlanta, GA 30303   Claudia Schmitt, Hd.
Founded: 1950. **Staff:** Prof 8; Other 7. **Subjects:** Industry and finance, business and management, social science, law, government, pure and applied science. **Special Collections:** Atlanta city documents and plat maps; federal document depository (partial). **Holdings:** 65,500 volumes; annual and 10K reports on microfiche for 11,000 corporations from 1976 to present; Georgia Laws, 1787 to present; Georgia House and Senate Journals, 1820-1950; 1500 VF folders; subject directories. **Subscriptions:** 1350 journals and other serials; 15 newspapers. **Services:** Interlibrary loans; copying; library open to public. **Computerized Information Services:** DIALOG; computerized cataloging, acquisitions, serials and circulation. **Networks/Consortia:** Member of OCLC through SOLINET. **Publications:** I.A.D. Annotated Booklist, irregular - free upon request. **Staff:** Debora Mack, Asst.Hd.; Wanda Jolly, Libn.; Yaramakala Manjula, Libn.; Fern Pachter, Libn.; Anne Haywood, Libn.; Sherry Petry, Libn.

★932★

ATLANTA PUBLIC LIBRARY - IVAN ALLEN, JR. DEPT. OF SCIENCE, INDUSTRY & GOVERNMENT - FOUNDATION COLLECTION (Soc Sci)

1 Margaret Mitchell Sq.   Phone: (404) 688-4636
Atlanta, GA 30303   Claudia Schmitt, Hd., Ivan Allen Dept.
Founded: 1962. **Subjects:** Grantsmanship, philanthropy, proposal writing, foundations in the Southeast, fund raising. **Special Collections:** Internal revenue forms (990-AR and 990-PF) for all private foundations in Georgia, South Carolina, Florida, Tennessee, Alabama. **Holdings:** 120 books; 13 bound periodical volumes; 18 file boxes of annual reports; 13 boxes of microforms; 3 loose leaf notebooks of foundation newsletters. **Services:** Copying; library open to public. **Networks/Consortia:** Member of Foundation Center, New York. **Publications:** Georgia Foundation Directory, irregular. **Remarks:** The Foundation Collection is a regional cooperating collection of the Foundation Center in New York City.

★933★

ATLANTA PUBLIC LIBRARY - SPECIAL COLLECTIONS DEPARTMENT (Area-Ethnic; Hist)

1 Margaret Mitchell Sq.   Phone: (404) 688-4636
Atlanta, GA 30303   Janice White Sikes, Cur.
Staff: Prof 8; Other 1. **Subjects:** Genealogy, oral history, Atlanta Public Library history, Afro-American studies, Georgia history, literature written by Georgians. **Special Collections:** Hattie Wilson High Memorial Genealogical Collection (6500 books; 1000 bound periodical volumes; 350 reels of microfilm of U.S. Census); Atlanta Public Library Archives; Samuel Williams Collection of materials by and about Afro-Americans (6110 items); Georgia Collection (3930 items); Margaret Mitchell Collection (primarily display exhibit of 1481 items); rare books; oral history. **Holdings:** 15,000 books; 1000 bound periodical volumes; 1400 vertical file folders; 571 reels of microfilm and 490 microforms of old newspapers; 112 cassettes. **Subscriptions:** 120 journals and other serials; 10 newspapers. **Services:** Copying (fee basis); department open to public for reference use only. **Computerized Information Services:** Computerized acquisitions. **Publications:** Genealogy Handbook (1970); Black Genealogy: A Source Guide, 1978 (update in process). **Special Indexes:** Indexes to black periodicals, biography, vertical file, poetry, book reviews, biographical project central file, quotations (all on cards); literary criticism; hard knots. **Remarks:** Frequent workshops are conducted for the public. **Staff:** Joyce Jelks, Libn.; Debra Perry, Libn.; Sarah Alexander, Libn.

★934★

ATLANTA UNIVERSITY CENTER - ROBERT W. WOODRUFF LIBRARY (Area-Ethnic)

111 Chestnut St., S.W.   Phone: (404) 223-5378
Atlanta, GA 30314   Minnie H. Clayton, Div.Hd.
Founded: 1982. **Staff:** Prof 5; Other 2. **Subjects:** The Afro-American experience; Afro-Americana in the southeastern United States; materials by and about peoples of African descent. **Special Collections:** Thayer-Lincoln Collection (125 manuscripts, pictures and artifacts recording the career of Abraham Lincoln); manuscript collections representing outstanding persons in Afro-American history including John Brown, Thomas Clarkson, Henry O. Tanner, C. Eric Lincoln, George A. Towns, Grace Towns Hamilton, Arthur Ashe, Eslanda G. Robson, Rose McLendon and Andrew Young; Cullen-Jackman Collection (black artists and writers); Henry G. Slaughter Collection (19th century Abolitionists); archival holdings for academic institutions in the Atlanta University Center consortium (Atlanta University, Clark College, Morris Brown College and some schools of the Inter-denominational Theological Center) and from race relations and socioeconomic organizations in the South including the Neighborhood Union in Atlanta, Commission on Interracial Cooperation,

Association of Southern Women for the Prevention of Lynching, Southern Regional Council and Southern Conference for Human Welfare (manuscripts and archives total approximately 2000 cubic feet); Carl Van Vechten Photograph Collection of internationally known persons of African descent; George Washington Carver Papers; Paul Laurence Dunbar Papers; American Missionary Association Papers; Freedmen's Bureau correspondence. **Holdings:** 20,000 books; 953 bound periodical volumes; 313 college and university catalogs; 94 VF drawers of subject files; 59 audiotapes; 76 microfiche; dissertations on Negros, 1931-1966 (microfilm); Atlanta University graduate theses and dissertations; pamphlets. **Services:** Copying (limited); library open to public for reference use only for a fee. **Computerized Information Services:** DIALOG. **Networks/Consortia:** Member of CCLC; University Center in Georgia, Inc. **Publications:** Graduate Theses of Atlanta University; Guide to Manuscripts and Archives in the Negro Collection of Trevor Arnett Library. **Special Catalogs:** Finding aids for archival and manuscript collections. **Formed by the Merger of:** The libraries of the schools in the Atlanta University Center Consortium and the Trevor Arnett Library. **Staff:** Mrs. Lee G. Alexander, Archv.; Gloria J. Mims, Spec.Coll.Libn.; Mrs. Jessie B. Ebanks, Archv.Libn.; Mrs. Dovie T. Patrick, Archv.Libn.

★935★

ATLANTA UNIVERSITY - SCHOOL OF LIBRARY & INFORMATION STUDIES - LIBRARY (Info Sci)

223 Chestnut St., S.W.   Phone: (404) 681-0251
Atlanta, GA 30314   Chih Wang, Libn.
Founded: 1941. **Staff:** Prof 1; Other 5. **Subjects:** Library and information sciences. **Special Collections:** Children's books; Afro-American studies; ethnic studies. **Holdings:** 21,629 books; 3521 bound periodical volumes; 12 VF drawers; microfilms; microcards; filmstrips; motion pictures; tapes and phonograph records. **Subscriptions:** 122 journals and other serials. **Services:** Interlibrary loans; library open to public with restrictions.

★936★

ATLANTIC CITY MEDICAL CENTER - MEDICAL LIBRARY (Med)

1925 Pacific Ave.   Phone: (609) 344-4081
Atlantic City, NJ 08401   John P. Doesburgh, Med.Libn.
Founded: 1930. **Subjects:** Medicine, nursing and allied health sciences. **Holdings:** 1125 books; 686 bound periodical volumes; Audio-Digest tapes in surgery and internal medicine. **Subscriptions:** 143 journals and other serials. **Services:** Interlibrary loans; copying; library open to public with restrictions. **Computerized Information Services:** MEDLINE. **Networks/Consortia:** Member of Southwest New Jersey Consortium for Health Information Services; New Jersey Health Sciences Network.

★937★

ATLANTIC COUNCIL OF THE UNITED STATES, INC. - LIBRARY (Soc Sci)

1616 H St., N.W.   Phone: (202) 347-9353
Washington, DC 20006   June Haley, Libn.
Staff: Prof 1; Other 1. **Subjects:** Atlantic community, NATO, Atlantic-international relations, world politics, intergovernmental organizations, international communism, international law, economics, defense strategy. **Special Collections:** International organization publications such as OECD, IMF, EEC, EFTA, GATT and UN. **Holdings:** 2000 books; 75 bound periodical volumes; 250 special studies (cataloged); 2 VF drawers of North Atlantic Council documents; 1 VF drawer of Atlantic Treaty Association documents; 4 VF drawers of newsletters and publications from NATO countries; 1000 Congressional documents. **Subscriptions:** 60 journals and other serials. **Services:** Interlibrary loans; copying; library open to public for reference use only. **Special Catalogs:** Atlantic Bibliography published in Atlantic Community Quarterly.

★938★

ATLANTIC COUNTY HISTORICAL SOCIETY - LIBRARY (Hist)

907 Shore Rd.
Box 301
Somers Point, NJ 08244   Phone: (609) 927-5218
                                                  Elaine Abrahamson, Libn.
Subjects: History, genealogy and maritime history of Atlantic County and Southern New Jersey; Civil War. **Holdings:** 2000 books and bound periodical volumes; 15 VF drawers; 35 manuscript books; 100 family Bibles; 132 maps; microfilm of Atlantic County census data; photographs; lantern slides; postcards; deeds; letters; diaries; ship logs; oral history tapes. **Subscriptions:** 14 journals and other serials. **Services:** Copying; library open to public. **Publications:** Year Book; Absegami Yesteryear (book); Railroading in Atlantic County, New Jersey; pamphlets on Atlantic County history. **Special Indexes:** Indexes of manuscript and picture collections.

★939★
ATLANTIC INSTITUTE OF EDUCATION - LIBRARY (Educ)
5244 South St.   Phone: (902) 425-5430
Halifax, NS, Canada B3J 1A4   Diane Brooks, Libn.
Staff: 1. **Subjects:** Teacher education, curriculum development, educational research. **Holdings:** 3000 books and bound periodical volumes; 2 VF drawers of archival material, documents and clippings. **Subscriptions:** 100 journals and other serials. **Services:** Interlibrary loans; copying; library open to public with restrictions.

★940★
ATLANTIC PROVINCES ECONOMIC COUNCIL - LIBRARY (Bus-Fin)
5121 Sackville St., Suite 500   Phone: (902) 422-6516
Halifax, NS, Canada B3J 1K1   L. Duffy, Adm.Asst.
Subjects: Economy of the Atlantic Provinces, statistics. **Holdings:** Books, government reports, pamphlets, clippings. **Subscriptions:** 15 journals and other serials; 10 newspapers. **Services:** Interlibrary loans; library open to public by special permission.

★941★
ATLANTIC RESEARCH CORPORATION - LIBRARY (Sci-Tech)
5390 Cherokee Ave.   Phone: (703) 642-4178
Alexandria, VA 22314   Ellen Levin, Libn.
Staff: 1. **Subjects:** Chemistry, electronics, aerospace. **Holdings:** 5000 books; 10,000 bound periodical volumes; archival holdings of technical journals and proceedings. **Subscriptions:** 360 journals and other serials. **Services:** Interlibrary loans; copying; library open to public with permission of librarian and security. **Computerized Information Services:** DIALOG. **Networks/Consortia:** Member of Interlibrary Users Association.

ATLANTIC RESEARCH LABORATORY
See: Canada - National Research Council

★942★
ATLANTIC-RICHFIELD COMPANY - ANACONDA ALUMINUM COMPANY - COLUMBIA FALLS REDUCTION DIVISION - LIBRARY (Sci-Tech)
Box 10   Phone: (406) 892-3261
Columbia Falls, MT 59912   Hilda Parry, Libn.
Founded: 1955. **Staff:** Prof 2. **Subjects:** Chemistry - inorganic, metals and metallurgy, environmental control, raw materials data; technical analytical data; management; technological writing. **Special Collections:** Aluminum and aluminum casting and principles; environmental control. **Holdings:** 1000 books; 50 bound periodical volumes; 5 drawers of prints and negatives (cataloged); 1700 pamphlets and patents; 200 trade catalogs. **Subscriptions:** 30 journals and other serials. **Services:** Interlibrary loans; copying; library open to public by request. **Special Catalogs:** Patent and document catalog; library catalog (book). **Staff:** Donald F. Ryan, Tech.Supt.

★943★
ATLANTIC-RICHFIELD COMPANY - ANACONDA COPPER COMPANY - LIBRARY (Sci-Tech)
Interstate 10 E. and Kolb Rd.
Box 27007   Phone: (602) 889-5361
Tucson, AZ 85726   Mary A. Forrest, Libn.
Staff: Prof 1. **Subjects:** Metallurgy, geology, mining, engineering. **Holdings:** 4167 books; 1124 bound periodical volumes; 200 reports on microfiche; 8 VF drawers of U.S. and foreign patents; 35 VF drawers of reprints; 25 VF drawers of U.S. Bureau of Mines reports, IC - RI; 1088 bound volumes of U.S. Geological Survey reports. **Subscriptions:** 91 journals and other serials; 6 newspapers. **Services:** Interlibrary loans; copying; library open to public by appointment.

★944★
ATLANTIC-RICHFIELD COMPANY - ANACONDA INDUSTRIES - RESEARCH AND TECHNICAL CENTER LIBRARY
245 Freight St.
Box 747
Waterbury, CT 06720
Defunct. Holdings merged with Atlantic-Richfield Company - ARCO Metals Company - Technical Information Center.

★945★
ATLANTIC-RICHFIELD COMPANY - ARCO CHEMICAL COMPANY - LYONDELL PLANT LIBRARY (Energy)
Box 777   Phone: (713) 452-8147
Channelview, TX 77530   Virginia Wood, Lib.Supv.
Founded: 1956. **Staff:** Prof 4. **Subjects:** Chemical engineering, environmental affairs, safety, chemistry, management. **Holdings:** 6000 books; 1000 bound periodical volumes. **Subscriptions:** 150 journals and

other serials. **Services:** Interlibrary loans; copying; library not open to public. **Computerized Information Services:** SDC; computerized serials.

★946★
ATLANTIC-RICHFIELD COMPANY - ARCO CHEMICAL COMPANY - RESEARCH & ENGINEERING TECHNICAL INFORMATION CENTER (Energy)†
3801 West Chester Pike   Phone: (215) 359-2000
Newton Square, PA 19073   Anthony J. Costanzo, Tech.Info.Supv.
Founded: 1924. **Staff:** Prof 5; Other 1. **Subjects:** Chemistry, chemical engineering and economics, petroleum and petroleum technology, mathematics, physics. **Special Collections:** Technical Oil Mission Reels. **Holdings:** 7000 books; 9000 bound periodical volumes; technical reports and memoranda; reprints. **Subscriptions:** 500 journals and other serials. **Services:** Interlibrary loans; copying; SDI; center open to public by appointment. **Computerized Information Services:** DIALOG; SDC; NLM. **Publications:** R&D Library Bulletin, bimonthly; R&D Search, monthly. **Staff:** Christy McSwain, Libn.; Donna Mendenhall, Info.Spec.; Irene Frese, Lib. Aide; Cassandra Burcham, Info.Spec.

★947★
ATLANTIC-RICHFIELD COMPANY - ARCO METALS COMPANY - TECHNICAL INFORMATION CENTER (Sci-Tech)
3205 N. Frontage Rd.
Box 3010   Phone: (312) 577-5527
Arlington Heights, IL 60006   Donna M. Mendenhall, Supv., Tech.Info.
Founded: 1982. **Subjects:** Metallurgy, engineering, aluminum, copper, brass, metal working. **Holdings:** 3000 books; 250 vertical files. **Subscriptions:** 100 journals and other serials. **Services:** Interlibrary loans; copying; SDI; library open to public with restrictions. **Computerized Information Services:** DIALOG, SDC. **Remarks:** Formed by the merger of Anaconda Aluminum and Anaconda Industries.

★948★
ATLANTIC-RICHFIELD COMPANY - ARCO OIL AND GAS COMPANY - RESEARCH & DEVELOPMENT TECHNICAL INFORMATION CENTER (Energy)
Box 2819   Phone: (214) 422-6965
Dallas, TX 75221   Inge Loncaric, Supv.
Founded: 1942. **Staff:** Prof 3; Other 5. **Subjects:** Chemistry, economics and planning, electrical engineering, electronics, civil and mechanical engineering, geology, geophysics, mathematics, petroleum exploration and production, paleontology, oceanography, remote sensing in earth sciences, synthetic fuels. **Holdings:** 15,000 books; 10,000 bound periodical volumes. **Subscriptions:** 400 journals and other serials. **Services:** Center not open to public. **Computerized Information Services:** DIALOG, SDC.

★949★
ATLANTIC-RICHFIELD COMPANY - DEPARTMENT OF LAW - LIBRARY
600 Anaconda Bldg.
Box 689
Butte, MT 59703
Defunct

★950★
ATLANTIC-RICHFIELD COMPANY - GOVERNMENT RESOURCE CENTER (Law)
515 S. Flower St., Rm. 4010   Phone: (213) 486-0777
Los Angeles, CA 90071   Esther Eastman, Coord.
Staff: Prof 1; Other 2. **Subjects:** Federal and state legislation and regulations; congressional monitors. **Special Collections:** Federal legislative bill service and state legislation for Alaska, Arizona, California, Idaho, Nevada, Oregon, Montana, Texas, Pennsylvania and Washington. **Holdings:** 1000 books; 50 bound periodical volumes; company situation reports and position papers. **Subscriptions:** 150 journals and other serials; 5 newspapers. **Services:** Copying; SDI; library not open to public. **Computerized Information Services:** Internal databases. **Publications:** New Publications, weekly - for divisions of Government Relations, Corporate Library and other departments upon request.

★951★
ATLANTIC-RICHFIELD COMPANY - INFORMATION RESEARCH CENTER (Energy; Bus-Fin)
Terminal Annex, Box 2679   Phone: (213) 486-2400
Los Angeles, CA 90051   Meryl H. Swanigan, Mgr.
Founded: 1972. **Staff:** Prof 5; Other 4. **Subjects:** Economics, petroleum and petroleum refining, chemistry, geology and geophysics, management, foreign affairs. **Holdings:** 15,000 books; 1500 bound periodical volumes; 500 unbound periodicals; 3800 annual reports; 200 reels of microfilmed

newspapers and journals; microfiche; databases of API Refining literature and patents and Tulsa University Petroleum Abstracts. **Subscriptions:** 2000 journals and other serials; 20 newspapers. **Services:** Interlibrary loans; copying (both limited); library open to public by appointment. **Computerized Information Services:** SDC, I.P. Sharp Associates Limited, DIALOG, Dow Jones News Retrieval, New York Times Information Service, ISI, BRS; computerized cataloging, acquisitions and circulation. **Networks/Consortia:** Member of CLASS. **Publications:** INFOACCESS, biweekly newsletter; special bibliographies. **Special Catalogs:** Library Administrative System, COM catalog, updated monthly; joint journal holdings list. **Remarks:** The library is located at 515 S. Flower St., Los Angeles, CA 90051. **Staff:** T.G. White, Supv., Tech.Serv.; L. Ecklund, Tech.Info.Spec.; F.A. Bowman, Supv., Ref.Serv.; C.A. Alexander, Tech.Info.Spec.

★952★
ATLANTIC-RICHFIELD COMPANY - PHOTOGRAPHY COLLECTION (Pict)
515 S. Flower St., Rm. 16103   Phone: (213) 486-3386
Los Angeles, CA 90071   Mildred Simpson, Libn.
Staff: Prof 1; Other 1. **Subjects:** Oil and gas-petroleum industry, coal mining, aluminum industry, metals, solar energy. **Holdings:** Figures not available for original negatives and transparencies. **Services:** Copying; library not open to public. **Computerized Information Services:** PMIS (Photographic Management Information System; internal database); computerized cataloging. **Publications:** New Photography, bimonthly - for internal distribution only.

★953★
ATLANTIC-RICHFIELD COMPANY - TECHNICAL INFORMATION CENTER (Sci-Tech)
555 17th St.
Anaconda Tower   Phone: (303) 575-4425
Denver, CO 80202   Marlene Bundy, Supv.
Founded: 1981. **Staff:** Prof 2; Other 1. **Subjects:** Geology, mining engineering. **Special Collections:** Department of Energy open file reports; U.S. Geological Survey open file reports. **Holdings:** 5000 books; 130 bound periodical volumes; 150 guide books; 15,000 state and foreign documents; 5000 annual reports; 460 shelving feet of unbound journals. **Subscriptions:** 160 journals and other serials; 12 newspapers. **Services:** Interlibrary loans; library use requires special permission of the librarian and manager of office services. **Computerized Information Services:** SDC, Computerized Resources Information Bank, New York Times Information Service, Dow Jones News Retrieval, DIALOG; computerized cataloging.

★954★
ATLANTIC SCHOOL OF THEOLOGY - LIBRARY (Rel-Theol)†
640 Francklyn St.   Phone: (902) 423-7986
Halifax, NS, Canada B3H 3B5   Alice W. Harrison, Libn.
Founded: 1971. **Staff:** Prof 3; Other 1. **Subjects:** Theology and related subjects. **Special Collections:** Rare books; historical records of Nova Scotia churches. **Holdings:** 60,000 books; 5470 bound periodical volumes; 250 graduate theses in theology. **Subscriptions:** 275 journals and other serials. **Services:** Interlibrary loans; copying; library open to students and faculty of local universities and clergy of the Atlantic provinces. **Special Catalogs:** Bibliographies (pamphlet form). **Staff:** Sr. Margaret Flahiff, Per.Libn.; Lloyd J. Melanson, Tech.Serv.Libn.

ATLAS LIBRARY
See: ICI Americas, Inc.

★955★
ATLAS POWDER COMPANY - RESEARCH & DEVELOPMENT LABORATORY - LIBRARY (Sci-Tech)
Box 271   Phone: (717) 386-4121
Tamaqua, PA 18252   Charlotte D. Fisler, Libn.
Staff: 1. **Subjects:** Explosives, mining, chemistry, chemical engineering, patents (U.S. and foreign). **Special Collections:** Complete collection of Chemical Abstracts. **Holdings:** 2200 books; 3600 bound periodical volumes; 12 file drawers of patents; 20 file drawers of Bureau of Mines reports; 3 file drawers of Department of Defense - Index of Federal Specifications and Standards. **Subscriptions:** 66 journals and other serials. **Services:** Interlibrary loans; copying; library not open to public. **Computerized Information Services:** DIALOG, SDC; internal database. **Publications:** Library Bulletin, quarterly.

★956★
ATLAS TRAFFIC CONSULTANTS CORPORATION - TARIFF DEPARTMENT LIBRARY (Trans)
18-42 College Point Blvd.   Phone: (212) 461-0556
Flushing, NY 11356   Diana Otero, Tariff Libn.
Staff: Prof 1. **Subjects:** Freight tariffs. **Special Collections:** Interstate

Commerce Commission reports. **Holdings:** 10,000 books. **Services:** Library not open to public.

★957★
ATLAS TRAVEL, INC. - LIBRARY (Geog-Map)
3411 Montrose   Phone: (713) 527-4555
Houston, TX 77006   William C. Morrison, Libn.
Staff: Prof 1. **Subjects:** Travel, tourism and geography. **Special Collections:** Travel and tour publications. **Holdings:** 294 books; maps; brochures. **Subscriptions:** 54 journals and other serials. **Services:** Copying; SDI; library open to public by appointment. **Publications:** Atlas Travel Notes. **Special Indexes:** Special Events Index.

★958★
ATMANIKETAN ASHRAM - LIBRARY (Rel-Theol)
1291 Weber St.   Phone: (714) 629-8255
Pomona, CA 91768   Michael Zucker, Libn.
Founded: 1973. **Staff:** Prof 1; Other 3. **Subjects:** Sri Aurobindo, Indian spirituality, Vedanta, Sanskrit studies, Vedic-Upanishadic texts, education. **Special Collections:** Sri Aurobindo Birth Centenary Library (30 volumes); Collected Works of the Mother (15 volumes); Mahabharata (12 volume English translation); Cultural Heritage of India (5 volume set); Sacred Books of the East (50 volume set); Rigveda Samhita (6 volume set). **Holdings:** 2000 books; 60 bound periodical volumes; 100 papers and reprints (cataloged); complete back issue sets of annual, monthly and quarterly journals of Sri Aurobindo Ashram. **Subscriptions:** 8 journals and other serials. **Services:** Library open to public by appointment. **Publications:** Purna Yoga magazine, annual - available on request. **Also Known As:** Auromere.

ATMOSPHERIC ENVIRONMENT SERVICE
See: Canada - Atmospheric Environment Service

ATOMIC COLLISION CROSS SECTION DATA CENTER
See: University of Colorado, Boulder - Joint Institute for Laboratory Astrophysics - Data Center

★959★
ATOMIC ENERGY OF CANADA, LTD. - COMMERCIAL PRODUCTS LIBRARY (Sci-Tech)
Sta. J, P.O. Box 6300   Phone: (613) 592-2790
Ottawa, ON, Canada K2A 3W3   Herb Fletcher, Libn.
Staff: 1. **Subjects:** Radionuclides. **Holdings:** 5000 books and bound periodical volumes; 8000 other cataloged items. **Subscriptions:** 150 journals and other serials. **Services:** Interlibrary loans; copying; library not open to public.

★960★
ATOMIC ENERGY OF CANADA, LTD. - ENGINEERING COMPANY LIBRARY (Sci-Tech)
Sheridan Park Research Community   Phone: (416) 823-9040
Mississauga, ON, Canada L5K 1B2   Christine C. Byrne, Hd.
Staff: Prof 2; Other 6. **Subjects:** Nuclear power, nuclear reactors, reactor design, design engineering. **Holdings:** 12,000 books; 20,000 hardcopy reports; 76,000 microfiche reports. **Subscriptions:** 500 journals and other serials. **Services:** Interlibrary loans; library not open to public. **Computerized Information Services:** DIALOG, CAN/OLE.

★961★
ATOMIC ENERGY OF CANADA, LTD. - ENGINEERING COMPANY LIBRARY (Sci-Tech)
1600 Dorchester Blvd. W.   Phone: (514) 934-4811
Montreal, PQ, Canada H3H 1P9   Susan Nish, Techn.
Founded: 1977. **Staff:** 1. **Subjects:** Nuclear power, nuclear reactors, design engineering. **Holdings:** 1000 books; 1000 standards; 1000 reports. **Subscriptions:** 80 journals and other serials. **Services:** Interlibrary loans; copying; library not open to public.

★962★
ATOMIC ENERGY OF CANADA, LTD. - TECHNICAL INFORMATION BRANCH - MAIN LIBRARY (Sci-Tech)
Chalk River Nuclear Labs.   Phone: (613) 687-5581
Chalk River, ON, Canada K0J 1J0   H. Greenshields, Chf.Libn.
Founded: 1944. **Staff:** Prof 3; Other 18. **Subjects:** Nuclear science, engineering, physics, chemistry, metallurgy, electronics, materials, mathematics, biology. **Holdings:** 73,208 books and pamphlets; 50,270 bound periodical volumes; 7313 paper copy translations and 25,302 microform translations; 143,164 paper copy reports and 330,042 microform reports (non-AECL); 1532 microfilm cartridges (periodicals and abstracts). **Subscriptions:** 1732 journals and other serials; 8 newspapers. **Services:**

Interlibrary loans (inquiries by mail preferred); copying; publication and distribution of AECL technical reports; SDI; library open to public by arrangement. **Computerized Information Services:** CAN/SDI, CAN/OLE, SDC, DIALOG, INFOMART; computerized serials and circulation. **Publications:** Library Accessions, weekly; AECL List of Publications, annual (with supplements); Serial Holdings. **Special Indexes:** Computer generated indexes for technical reports, translations, patents in nuclear and related subjects (card). **Staff:** Jill Williams, Cat.; T.P. Alburger, Acq.Libn.

★963★
ATOMIC ENERGY OF CANADA, LTD. - WNRE LIBRARY (Sci-Tech)
Whiteshell Nuclear Research Establishment   Phone: (204) 753-2311
Pinawa, MB, Canada R0E 1L0   Gladys Gibson, Chf.Libn.
Founded: 1963. **Staff:** Prof 1; Other 11. **Subjects:** Nuclear science, nuclear waste management, chemistry, medical biophysics. **Holdings:** 50,000 books; 200,000 microfiche. **Subscriptions:** 700 journals and other serials. **Services:** Interlibrary loans; copying; library open to public with permission. **Computerized Information Services:** DIALOG, SDC, CAN/OLE; computerized acquisitions, serials and circulation. **Special Indexes:** KWIC Index to WNRE Reports; KWIC Index to Foreign Waste Management Reports; Canadian Waste Management Reports Index.

★964★
ATOMIC ENERGY CONTROL BOARD - LIBRARY (Sci-Tech; Energy)
P.O. Box 1046   Phone: (613) 995-1359
Ottawa, ON, Canada K1P 5S9   Helen T. Booth, Chf., Lib.Serv.
Founded: 1976. **Staff:** Prof 2; Other 1. **Subjects:** Nuclear science, radiation dosimetry, reactors, safeguards, regulatory bodies. **Holdings:** 35,000 books; 500 NTIS microfiche; complete set of Atomic Energy of Canada, Ltd. reports; complete INIS ATOMINDEX. **Subscriptions:** 100 journals and other serials; 5 newspapers. **Services:** Interlibrary loans; copying; SDI; library open to public. **Computerized Information Services:** DOBIS; computerized cataloging. **Publications:** Accessions List, monthly - available upon request; current contents of periodicals - for internal distribution only. **Staff:** Margot L. Beckwith, Acq. & Cat.Libn.

ATOMIC ENERGY LEVELS DATA CENTER
See: U.S. Natl. Bureau of Standards

★965★
ATOMIC INDUSTRIAL FORUM - LIBRARY (Energy)
7101 Wisconsin Ave.   Phone: (301) 654-9260
Bethesda, MD 20814   Melinda Renner, Libn.
Founded: 1954. **Staff:** Prof 1. **Subjects:** Energy - atomic and other forms; environment; waste management; nuclear regulation. **Special Collections:** AEC technical reports, 1954-1961 (250,000 microfiche); hearings from Atomic Energy Act, 1954; speeches by prominent persons in the field of nuclear energy. **Holdings:** 8000 books; 300 bound periodical volumes; 6000 technical reports; 17,000 pamphlets and clippings. **Subscriptions:** 300 journals and other serials; 5 newspapers. **Services:** Interlibrary loans; library not open to public. **Publications:** New Materials Bulletin, monthly; Periodical Holdings, annual.

ATONEMENT SEMINARY LIBRARY
See: Franciscan Friars of the Atonement

AT&T
See: American Telephone & Telegraph Company

ATWATER LIBRARY
See: Mechanics' Institute of Montreal

AUBREY (Will) MEMORIAL LIBRARY
See: Press Club of San Francisco - Will Aubrey Memorial Library

AUBURN AUTOMOTIVE HERITAGE, INC.
See: Auburn-Cord-Duesenberg Museum

★966★
AUBURN-CORD-DUESENBERG MUSEUM - TRI-KAPPA COLLECTION OF AUBURN AUTOMOTIVE LITERATURE (Trans)
1600 S. Wayne St.
Box 271
Auburn, IN 46706   Phone: (219) 925-1444
Gregg Buttermore, Archv.
Founded: 1971. **Staff:** Prof 1; Other 1. **Subjects:** Automotive literature and photographs; transportation. **Special Collections:** The Auburn Built Automobiles; manufacturing concerns in Auburn. **Holdings:** 500 books; 4000 pamphlets (cataloged); 3400 photographs; 3900 magazines; 450 blueprints; 10 films. **Subscriptions:** 25 journals and other serials. **Services:** Copying;

library open to public. **Remarks:** Maintained by the Auburn Automotive Heritage, Inc.

★967★
AUBURN MEMORIAL HOSPITAL - LIBRARY/RESOURCE CENTER (Med)
5-19 Lansing St.   Phone: (315) 255-7231
Auburn, NY 13021   Anne Costello Tomlin, Dir.
Founded: 1951. **Staff:** 1. **Subjects:** Medicine, nursing and allied fields. **Special Collections:** Hospital archives (15 drawers). **Holdings:** 2620 books; 3500 bound periodical volumes; 12 VF drawers of pamphlets (uncataloged). **Subscriptions:** 283 journals and other serials. **Services:** Interlibrary loans; reference service; media management; copying; library open to public by appointment or referral. **Networks/Consortia:** Member of Central New York Health Resources Council; New York and New Jersey Regional Medical Library Program. **Special Catalogs:** Printed list of journals currently received.

★968★
AUBURN UNIVERSITY - ARCHITECTURE AND FINE ARTS LIBRARY (Art)
Dudley Hall   Phone: (205) 826-4510
Auburn, AL 36830   Mary K. Dudman, Libn.
Staff: Prof 1; Other 2. **Subjects:** Architecture and allied subjects. **Holdings:** 20,814 bound volumes; 10,544 slides. **Subscriptions:** 103 journals and other serials. **Services:** Interlibrary loans; copying; library open to public for reference use only. **Networks/Consortia:** Member of OCLC through SOLINET.

★969★
AUBURN UNIVERSITY - ARCHIVES (Hist)
Ralph B. Draughon Library   Phone: (205) 826-4465
Auburn, AL 36849   Dr. Allen W. Jones, Archv.
Founded: 1964. **Staff:** Prof 3; Other 1. **Subjects:** Politics, agriculture, religion, military, American history, architecture, Auburn University history. **Special Collections:** Congressman George Andrews Collection (100 linear feet); Dr. George Petrie Collection (15 linear feet); Congressman Bill Nichols Collection (130 linear feet); Alabama League of Women Voters (25 linear feet); Fred Allison Papers (15 linear feet); James H. Lane Papers (4 linear feet); Alabama Farm Bureau Federation Records (31 linear feet); Alabama Republican Party Records (30 linear feet). **Holdings:** 2000 pamphlets (cataloged); 650 manuscripts and record collections; 1000 taped recordings; 900 reels of microfilm; 60,000 photographs (cataloged); 3200 films and videotapes. **Services:** Copying; archives open to public. **Publications:** Descriptive brochure. **Special Catalogs:** Selected subject guides to holdings. **Staff:** David J. Rosenblatt, Rec.Mgr.; Bill Sumners, Asst.Archv.

★970★
AUBURN UNIVERSITY - DEPARTMENT OF SPECIAL COLLECTIONS (Rare Book)
University Libraries   Phone: (205) 826-4500
Auburn, AL 36830   Gene Geiger, Spec.Coll.Libn.
Founded: 1963. **Staff:** Prof 1; Other 3. **Subjects:** Alabama, history, genealogy. **Special Collections:** Treasure Collection (rare books); Petrie Memorial Collection (history and religion); genealogy; Streit Collection (sports); Alabama Collection; Dobbins Collections (Alabamiana); Oxmore House Collection; Special Collection of semi-rare and fragile books; theses and dissertations; maps (92,923). **Holdings:** 39,000 volumes. **Subscriptions:** 605 journals and other serials. **Services:** Interlibrary loans; copying; library open to public.

★971★
AUBURN UNIVERSITY - INTERNATIONAL CENTER FOR AQUACULTURE - LIBRARY (Env-Cons)
Swingle Hall   Phone: (205) 826-4786
Auburn University, AL 36849   Dr. E.W. Shell, Dir.
Staff: Prof 1; Other 1. **Subjects:** Aquacultures - fresh, brackish and marine water; aquatic plants management; nutrition and feeds; parasites and disease; limnology; aquaculture waste disposal; aquatic biochemistry. **Holdings:** 2500 books; annual reports of the Fisheries Resources Unit, 1936 to present; 10,000 slides and pictures; 130 dissertations; 300 theses. **Services:** Copying; library open to public with supervision by librarian. **Publications:** Abstracts, Articles and Reprints from the International Center for Aquacultures; newsletter, quarterly; list of other publications - available upon request.

★972★
AUBURN UNIVERSITY - LEARNING RESOURCES CENTER (Aud-Vis)
Haley Center   Phone: (205) 826-4420
Auburn, AL 36830   Dr. C.D. Wright, Dir.
Staff: Prof 3; Other 9. **Subjects:** Curricula subjects in Schools of Education and Arts & Sciences. **Holdings:** 10,000 books; 7500 nonprint materials

(cataloged); 2000 unbound reports. **Subscriptions:** 80 journals and other serials. **Services:** Copying; center open to public for reference use only. **Computerized Information Services:** Computerized cataloging and circulation. **Special Catalogs:** Alphabetical and subject lists of 16mm films (computerized). **Staff:** Judith Lechner, Libn.; Bill Scales, Media Serv.Supv.

★973★
AUBURN UNIVERSITY - OFFICE OF PUBLIC SERVICE & RESEARCH - RESOURCE CENTER (Bus-Fin)
2232 Haley Center   Phone: (205) 826-4781
Auburn, AL 36849   Joanne S. Patton, Res. & Media Asst.
Staff: Prof 1; Other 2. **Subjects:** Public administration and finance; government - local, state, federal; personnel management; legislation. **Holdings:** 1900 books. **Subscriptions:** 125 journals and other serials. **Services:** Copying; library open to public officials. **Networks/Consortia:** Member of Inter-University Consortium for Political and Social Research (ICPSR). **Publications:** List of publications - free upon request.

★974★
AUBURN UNIVERSITY - VETERINARY MEDICAL LIBRARY (Med; Sci-Tech)
Veterinary Medical Complex   Phone: (205) 826-4780
Auburn University, AL 36849   Atha Louise Henley, Libn.
Staff: Prof 1; Other 1. **Subjects:** Veterinary medicine, microbiology, clinical medicine, anatomy, physiology, medicine, neurology. **Holdings:** 26,710 volumes; 253 reels of microfilm and 3 filmstrips of periodicals (cataloged); 60 slide/tape productions; 20 videotapes; 14 microfiche. **Subscriptions:** 552 journals and other serials. **Services:** Interlibrary loans; library open to public for reference use only. **Computerized Information Services:** Online systems. **Networks/Consortia:** Member of OCLC through SOLINET. **Publications:** Library guides and lists.

★975★
AUBURN UNIVERSITY - WATER RESOURCES RESEARCH INSTITUTE - INFORMATION CENTER (Env-Cons)
202 Hargis Hall   Phone: (205) 826-5075
Auburn University, AL 36849   James C. Warman, Dir.
Staff: 3. **Subjects:** All aspects of water resources. **Services:** Center open to public on limited basis. **Publications:** Technical bulletins; Proceedings, quarterly newsletter; annual report.

★976★
AUDRAIN COUNTY HISTORICAL SOCIETY - ROSS HOUSE LIBRARY/ AMERICAN SADDLE HORSE MUSEUM LIBRARY (Hist)
501 South Muldrow   Phone: (314) 581-3910
Mexico, MO 65265   Clara Kaiser, Libn./Genealogist
Subjects: County history, saddle horses. **Holdings:** 400 books; magazines; newspapers; breeder manuals; genealogical records; cemetery records. **Services:** Copying; library open to public for reference use only on a limited schedule.

★977★
AUDUBON HOSPITAL - MEDICAL LIBRARY (Med)
One Audubon Plaza   Phone: (502) 636-7296
Louisville, KY 40217   Elizabeth Fischer, Libn.
Staff: Prof 1. **Subjects:** Medicine and nursing. **Holdings:** 1100 books; 2700 bound periodical volumes; 500 Audio-Digest tapes. **Subscriptions:** 100 journals and other serials. **Services:** Interlibrary loans; copying; library open to students.

★978★
AUDUBON NATURALIST SOCIETY OF THE CENTRAL ATLANTIC STATES, INC. - LIBRARY (Env-Cons)
8940 Jones Mill Rd.   Phone: (301) 652-9188
Chevy Chase, MD 20815   Kathryn K. Rushing, Ed.
Staff: 1. **Subjects:** Ornithology, natural history, environmental conservation, ecology. **Holdings:** 2000 books; 50 bound periodical volumes; 200 monographs, 1500 unbound periodicals; 4 VF drawers of pamphlets. **Subscriptions:** 87 journals and other serials. **Services:** Library open to public with restrictions. **Publications:** Audubon Naturalist News, 10/year; Atlantic Naturalist, annual - both to members or on an exchange basis with other publications. **Special Indexes:** Author and Subject Index to Atlantic Naturalist and the Wood Thrush, 1946-1976.

AUDUBON SOCIETY OF MICHIGAN
See: Michigan Audubon Society

★979★
AUDUBON SOCIETY OF RHODE ISLAND - HARRY S. HATHAWAY LIBRARY OF NATURAL HISTORY AND CONSERVATION (Env-Cons)
40 Bowen St.   Phone: (401) 521-1670
Providence, RI 02903   Tim Rumage, Libn.
Founded: 1950. **Staff:** Prof 1. **Subjects:** Animals, plants, geology - regional and state; environmental problems and management; ecology. **Special Collections:** Complete Elephant Folio (Audubon's Mammals and other old books on birds and animals). **Holdings:** 1000 books; 200 bound periodical volumes; 300 pamphlets (cataloged). **Subscriptions:** 25 journals and other serials. **Services:** Interlibrary loans; library open to public.

AUERBACH ART LIBRARY
See: Wadsworth Atheneum

★980★
AUGLAIZE COUNTY LAW LIBRARY (Law)†
Court House   Phone: (419) 738-2961
Wapakoneta, OH 45895   Ron Miller, Att.
Founded: 1895. **Staff:** 2. **Subjects:** Law. **Holdings:** 15,000 volumes. **Services:** Library not open to public.

★981★
AUGSBURG COLLEGE - GEORGE SVERDRUP LIBRARY AND MEDIA CENTER (Rel-Theol; Hum)
731 21st Ave., S.   Phone: (612) 330-1017
Minneapolis, MN 55454   Margaret J. Anderson, Hd.Libn.
Founded: 1869. **Staff:** Prof 6; Other 2. **Subjects:** Theology, education, American and English literature, urban studies. **Special Collections:** Manuscript collection of George Sverdrup and Sven Oftedal; Scandinavian music. **Holdings:** 133,520 books; 12,904 bound periodical volumes; 8052 records, scores, tapes, filmstrips (cataloged); college archives; theses in theology. **Subscriptions:** 633 journals and other serials; 15 newspapers. **Services:** Interlibrary loans; copying; library open to public with deposit. **Computerized Information Services:** Computerized cataloging. **Networks/ Consortia:** Member of Cooperating Libraries in Consortium (CLIC); MINITEX. **Staff:** Marjorie H. Sibley, Ref.Libn.; Boyd Koehler, Rd.Serv. & Ref.Libn.; Irene Schilling, Cat.Libn.; Grace K. Sulerud, Acq. & Ref.Libn.; James Olson, AV Libn.

AUGSBURG PUBLISHING HOUSE - AMERICAN LUTHERAN CHURCH - ARCHIVES
See: American Lutheran Church - Archives

★982★
AUGUSTA CHRONICLE-HERALD NEWS - LIBRARY (Publ)
Box 1928(13)   Phone: (404) 724-0851
Augusta, GA 30913   P. Craig Morris, Libn.
Staff: Prof 1; Other 2. **Holdings:** 166 drawers of news clippings; 10 drawers of microfilm of newspapers, 1786 to present; 93 drawers of pictures. **Services:** Copying (limited); library open to public with restrictions. **Remarks:** This newspaper is owned by the Southeastern Newspapers Corporation.

★983★
AUGUSTANA COLLEGE - CENTER FOR WESTERN STUDIES (Hist; Area-Ethnic)
29th & Summit Sts.   Phone: (605) 336-4007
Sioux Falls, SD 57102   Sven Froiland, Dir.
Founded: 1970. **Subjects:** Upper Middle West - history (including Canada before 1900), literature; Indians of the Upper Middle West and west of the Mississippi; Norwegians (before 1900). **Special Collections:** Krause Collection (history and literature of the Upper Middle West, birds, Africa; 10,000 items); Dakota Collection; Archives of the Episcopal Diocese of South Dakota; Archives of the South Dakota District of the American Lutheran Church; Augustana College archives; Donald Parker papers. **Holdings:** 18,000 books; 100 bound periodical volumes; manuscripts and letters of Herbert Krause; 300 photographs of Sioux Falls and of South Dakota. **Subscriptions:** 10 journals and other serials. **Services:** Copying; Norwegian translation; center open to public for reference use only. **Publications:** Bibliography of Krause Collection; list of other publications - available on request.

AUGUSTANA COLLEGE - CENTER FOR WESTERN STUDIES - ARCHIVES OF THE EPISCOPAL DIOCESE OF SOUTH DAKOTA
See: Protestant Episcopal Church - Episcopal Diocese of South Dakota - Archives

★984★

AUGUSTANA COLLEGE - DENKMANN MEMORIAL LIBRARY (Hum)
3520 7th Ave.   Phone: (309) 794-7266
Rock Island, IL 61201   John Caldwell, Dir.
Founded: 1860. **Staff:** Prof 8; Other 6. **Special Collections:** Scandinaviana; Swedish immigration; Upper Mississippiana; English literature, 17th to 19th century; Swedish-American newspapers. **Holdings:** 252,039 books and bound periodical volumes; 28,895 microforms; 1448 phonograph records and cassettes. **Subscriptions:** 1494 journals; 19 newspapers. **Services:** Interlibrary loans; copying; library open to public. **Computerized Information Services:** DIALOG, SDC; computerized cataloging. **Networks/Consortia:** Member of OCLC through ILLINET; Bi-State Academic Libraries. **Publications:** Augustana College Library Occasional Papers.

★985★

AUGUSTANA HOSPITAL AND HEALTH CARE CENTER - CARL A. HEDBERG HEALTH SCIENCE LIBRARY (Med)
411 W. Dickens Ave.   Phone: (312) 975-5109
Chicago, IL 60614   Elizabeth Clausen, Chf.Libn.
Founded: 1970. **Staff:** Prof 1; Other 1. **Subjects:** Medicine, biomedicine, nursing, hospitals, allied health sciences, hospital administration. **Holdings:** 4995 books; 4800 bound periodical volumes; 350 cassettes; 8 VF drawers of pamphlets, reports, clippings and reprints. **Subscriptions:** 130 journals and other serials. **Services:** Interlibrary loans; copying; SDI; library open to public for reference use only. **Computerized Information Services:** MEDLINE. **Networks/Consortia:** Member of Metropolitan Consortium; Regional Medical Library - Region 3; OCLC through ILLINET.

★986★

AUGUSTANA LUTHERAN CHURCH - LIBRARY (Rel-Theol)†
5000 E. Alameda Ave.   Phone: (303) 388-4678
Denver, CO 80222   Ellen Swanson, Chm., Lib.Comm.
Founded: 1963. **Staff:** 4. **Subjects:** Religion. **Holdings:** 5300 books; phonograph records (cataloged); 3 drawers of pamphlets, maps and charts; 20 cassettes. **Services:** Library open to members of Denver Lutheran churches.

AUGUSTINE LIBRARY
See: St. Norbert Abbey

★987★

AUGUSTINIAN HISTORICAL INSTITUTE - LIBRARY (Rel-Theol)
Villanova University, Falvey Hall   Phone: (215) 645-7590
Villanova, PA 19085   Marcese W. Downey, Libn.
Founded: 1972. **Staff:** Prof 1. **Subjects:** Theology, philosophy, missiology, biography. **Special Collections:** History of the Augustinian Order. **Holdings:** 3000 books; 740 bound periodical volumes; 8 VF drawers of pamphlets, pictures and clippings; 200 reels of microfilmed books; 250 manuscripts; journals (cataloged). **Subscriptions:** 25 journals and other serials. **Services:** Copying; library open to public with approval of director. **Staff:** Rev. Joseph C. Schnaubelt, O.S.A., Dir.

★988★

AULLWOOD AUDUBON CENTER AND FARM - LIBRARY (Env-Cons)†
1000 Aullwood Rd.   Phone: (513) 890-7360
Dayton, OH 45414   Evelyn Pereny, Libn.
Founded: 1957. **Staff:** Prof 5. **Subjects:** Nature and the environment, natural history. **Holdings:** 2000 books. **Subscriptions:** 10 journals and other serials. **Services:** Copying; library open to public with permission.

★989★

AULTMAN HOSPITAL - MEDICAL LIBRARY (Med)
2600 6th St., S.W.   Phone: (216) 452-9911
Canton, OH 44710   Leah R. Lloyd, Libn.
Staff: 1. **Subjects:** Medicine. **Holdings:** 1119 books; 4022 bound periodical volumes; 90 AV items. **Subscriptions:** 165 journals and other serials. **Services:** Interlibrary loans; copying; library not open to public. **Computerized Information Services:** BRS; computerized cataloging. **Networks/Consortia:** Member of Northeastern Ohio Universities College of Medicine. **Special Catalogs:** Medical Periodicals in Northeast Ohio (notebook).

★990★

AULTMAN HOSPITAL - SCHOOL OF NURSING LIBRARY (Med)
2614 6th St., S.W.   Phone: (216) 452-9911
Canton, OH 44710   Violet E. Russell, Libn.
Founded: 1954. **Staff:** 2. **Subjects:** Nursing, medicine, education. **Special Collections:** History of medicine and nursing. **Holdings:** 5613 books; 455 bound periodical volumes; 6 VF drawers of pamphlets and clippings. **Subscriptions:** 94 journals and other serials. **Services:** Interlibrary loans (area hospital schools only); copying (limited); library open to public for reference

use only with permission. **Special Catalogs:** Medical and Nursing Periodicals List in Northeast Ohio (notebook). **Publications:** Door to Knowledge, monthly - school and hospital personnel only. **Remarks:** AV materials have been moved to Hospital Media Center.

AUROBINDO (Sri) BIRTH CENTENARY LIBRARY
See: Atmaniketan Ashram

AUROMERE
See: Atmaniketan Ashram

★991★

AURORA COLLEGE - JENKS MEMORIAL COLLECTION OF ADVENTUAL MATERIALS (Rel-Theol)
347 S. Gladstone   Phone: (312) 892-6431
Aurora, IL 60507   Moses C. Crouse, Cur.
Founded: 1920. **Staff:** Prof 1. **Subjects:** Second Advent (theology); Adventists, 1845-1900; Advent Christian Church, 1860 to present; The Life and Advent Union. **Special Collections:** Millerite Movement, including the papers of William Miller and the Millerite Movement from 1814-1849; correspondence of missionaries in China and India, 1880 to present. **Holdings:** 1150 books; 580 bound periodical volumes; 1800 volumes of tracts; manuscript sermons; clippings; pictures; 300 research papers; 25 theses and dissertations; 76 reels of microfilm; 60 audiotapes; 7 linear feet of diaries, scrapbooks, prophetic charts, manuscripts and correspondence of the Advent Christian Church; 3 1/2 linear feet of materials of the American Advent Mission Society; 10 linear feet of Church School curriculum materials; 12 linear feet of records of defunct churches and societies; 6 linear feet of photographs. **Subscriptions:** 17 journals and other serials. **Services:** Interlibrary loans (limited); copying (limited); library open to public upon application by advance notice. **Computerized Information Services:** Computerized cataloging. **Networks/Consortia:** Member of OCLC; LIBRAS; DuPage Library System. **Staff:** Mary M. Howrey, Lib.Dir.

★992★

AURORA HISTORICAL SOCIETY - ELBERT HUBBARD LIBRARY AND MUSEUM (Hist)
Main & Pine Sts.
East Aurora, NY 14052   Genevieve M. Steffen, Cur.
Founded: 1962. **Staff:** 1. **Subjects:** Books authored by Elbert and Alice Hubbard, biographies of Elbert Hubbard, books by other authors printed and bound by Roycrofters. **Special Collections:** Furniture, copper, silver and leather items manufactured by Roycrofters. **Holdings:** 1000 books; 100 bound periodical volumes; 2 VF drawers of clippings; 6 VF drawers of pictures; manuscripts; Hubbard magazines. **Services:** Interlibrary loans; copying; library open to public.

★993★

AURORA HISTORICAL SOCIETY - MUSEUM LIBRARY (Hist)
305 Cedar St.   Phone: (312) 897-9029
Aurora, IL 60507   Fred B. Graham, Jr., Cur.
Founded: 1906. **Staff:** 1. **Subjects:** History - Aurora, Kane County, Illinois; local industry; local educational groups. **Special Collections:** City and county directories since 1857; local geology and natural history; Indian artifacts. **Holdings:** 500 volumes; letters and manuscripts. **Services:** Library open to society members; open to others on payment of fee.

★994★

AURORA PUBLIC SCHOOLS - PROFESSIONAL LIBRARY (Educ)
Peoria Center, 875 Peoria St.   Phone: (303) 344-8060
Aurora, CO 80011   Bill Murray, Dir.
Founded: 1960. **Staff:** Prof 1; Other 2. **Subjects:** Education, psychology, management, communications. **Holdings:** 3000 books; 275 kits. **Subscriptions:** 242 journals and other serials. **Services:** Copying; library open to public. **Computerized Information Services:** Online systems; computerized cataloging. **Networks/Consortia:** Member of Central Colorado Regional Library System.

★995★

AUSTEN (Jane) SOCIETY OF NORTH AMERICA - ARCHIVES (Hum)
Box 621   Phone: (914) 425-9548
Nanuet, NY 10954   Joseph J. Costa, Pres.
Founded: 1979. **Staff:** 1. **Subjects:** Jane Austen - criticism, biography; Austeniana. **Special Collections:** Copies of periodicals; rare critical information. **Holdings:** 1000 books; periodical articles, recordings, tapes, slides, postcards, memorabilia, dramatizations. **Services:** Library open to public by correspondence. **Special Indexes:** Bibliography (card). **Formerly:** Located in New York, NY.

★996★
AUSTIN AMERICAN STATESMAN - LIBRARY (Publ)
Box 670   Phone: (512) 445-3676
Austin, TX 78767   Karen Anderson, Hd.Libn.
Staff: Prof 1; Other 2. **Subjects:** Austin, Texas. **Holdings:** 250 books; 1750 reels of microfilm; 20,000 clipping files; 30,000 photograph files; 10,000 sports and byline files. **Subscriptions:** 25 journals and other serials. **Services:** Copying; library open to public. **Special Indexes:** Index to Austin American Statesman (card).

AUSTIN COMMUNITY COLLEGE - ALLIED HEALTH SCIENCES LIBRARY
See: Allied Health Sciences Library

AUSTIN (Ethel L.) LIBRARY
See: South Congregational Church - Ethel L. Austin Library

★997★
AUSTIN PRESBYTERIAN THEOLOGICAL SEMINARY - STITT LIBRARY (Rel-Theol)
106 W. 27th St.   Phone: (512) 472-6736
Austin, TX 78705   Calvin Klemt, Libn.
Founded: 1902. **Staff:** Prof 2; Other 2. **Subjects:** Bible, theology, Christianity, Presbyterianism, Biblical archeology. **Special Collections:** Presbyterian and Reformed Churches of the World. **Holdings:** 114,000 books; 8800 bound periodical volumes; archives; curriculum materials; microfilm. **Subscriptions:** 320 journals and other serials. **Services:** Interlibrary loans; copying; library open to public with restrictions.

★998★
AUSTIN PUBLIC LIBRARY - AUSTIN-TRAVIS COUNTY COLLECTION (Hist)
810 Guadalupe   Phone: (512) 472-5433
Austin, TX 78701   Audray Bateman, Cur.
Staff: Prof 7; Other 2. **Subjects:** Austin history, women's suffrage, country western and current music, 19th century architecture. **Special Collections:** Travis county documents; Pease Collection (Texas Governor, 1853-1857). **Holdings:** 5769 books; 429 bound periodical volumes; 89,018 manuscripts; 730 maps; 61,475 printed items; 41,775 photographs (prints and negatives); 90,431 clippings; 8333 slides; 333 taped interviews; 200 boxes of scrapbooks, bills, biography files. **Subscriptions:** 75 journals and other serials; 15 newspapers. **Services:** Copying; library open to public for reference use only. **Computerized Information Services:** Computerized cataloging (books only). **Networks/Consortia:** Member of OCLC. **Publications:** Waterloo Press (7 hardbound books, 6 softbound); 1887 map reproduction; postcards. **Special Indexes:** Data processed newspaper and photograph indexes; index of archival papers; index to clubs and organizations; index to vertical file materials and periodical analytics (all card). **Remarks:** The Austin-Travis County Collection is the local history depository and the official depository for noncurrent documents of Travis County. **Staff:** Kathleen Sykes, Sr. Staff Libn.; Nancy Byrd, Govt.Doc.Spec.; Frances Moore, Asst.Cur.; Mary Jo Cooper, Asst.Cur.; Linda Zezulka, Asst.Cur.; Karen Warren, Asst.Cur.; Sharmyn Lumsden, Photo Cur.

★999★
AUSTIN STATE HOSPITAL - STAFF LIBRARY (Med)
4110 Guadalupe St.   Phone: (512) 452-0381
Austin, TX 78751   Nancy H. Dobson, Libn.
Founded: 1980. **Staff:** Prof 1; Other 1. **Subjects:** Psychiatry, neurology, community mental health. **Holdings:** 8000 books; 3000 bound periodical volumes; 10,000 reprints; 450 tape recordings. **Subscriptions:** 130 journals and other serials. **Services:** Interlibrary loans; copying; library open to public with restrictions. **Networks/Consortia:** Member of TALON.

AUSTIN (Stephen F.) STATE UNIVERSITY
See: Stephen F. Austin State University

★1000★
AUSTINE SCHOOL - LIBRARY (Educ)
120 Maple St.   Phone: (802) 254-4571
Brattleboro, VT 05301   John I. Enola, Libn.
Founded: 1912. **Staff:** 1. **Subjects:** Education of the deaf. **Holdings:** 10,000 books; 315 bound periodical volumes. **Subscriptions:** 65 journals and other serials. **Services:** Library open to students interested in education of the deaf.

AUSTRALIAN CONSULATE-GENERAL
See: Australian Information Service

★1001★
AUSTRALIAN EMBASSY - LIBRARY (Area-Ethnic)
1601 Massachusetts Ave.   Phone: (202) 797-3166
Washington, DC 20036   Patricia Kay, Libn.
Staff: Prof 1; Other 1. **Subjects:** Australian reference material. **Holdings:** 10,000 books; 950 bound periodical volumes; annual reports of 27 Australian government departments and statutory corporations; 3 VF drawers of press releases of Australian government departments; 6000 Parliamentary papers; 700 Australian state statutes; 10 VF drawers of Australian press clippings. **Subscriptions:** 504 journals and other serials; 15 newspapers. **Services:** Interlibrary loans; library open to public.

★1002★
AUSTRALIAN INFORMATION SERVICE - REFERENCE LIBRARY/INFORMATION SERVICE (Area-Ethnic)
636 5th Ave.   Phone: (212) 245-4000
New York, NY 10020   G. Dixon, Dp. Consul-General/Info.
Founded: 1945. **Staff:** 2. **Subjects:** Australia - economics, Aboriginals, law, history, geography, arts, industry and resources, literature, sport, transport, flora and fauna, education, politics and government, science. **Special Collections:** Australian films, photographs, slides, maps; extensive anthropological and sociological holdings on the Australian Aboriginals. **Holdings:** 10,000 books; 750 bound periodical volumes; 43 octavo books of pamphlets; 3 drawers of biographical files; 20 drawers of statistical publications; 30 folders of ministerial press releases; 1300 vertical files of newspaper and magazine clippings and parliamentary papers; 71 octavo boxes of Australian Standards. **Subscriptions:** 140 journals and other serials; 10 newspapers. **Services:** Interlibrary loans; library open to public. **Publications:** Business Week, bimonthly; Australia Handbook, annual; Australia in Brief, annual; fact sheets and reference papers, irregular - all free upon request. **Special Indexes:** Card index of news items in daily Radio Australia broadcast. **Remarks:** The library is located within the Australian Consulate-General. **Staff:** Jill Hutchison, Res.Off.; Lois Karner, Lib.Asst.

★1003★
AUSTRIAN PRESS AND INFORMATION SERVICE (Area-Ethnic)
31 E. 69th St.   Phone: (212) 737-6400
New York, NY 10021   Peter C. Marboe, Dir.
Founded: 1948. **Subjects:** Austrian affairs. **Holdings:** 300 volumes; current Austrian newspapers and periodicals. **Services:** General educational and cultural information supplied; service not open to public. **Remarks:** Merged with library of the Austrian Institute, 11 E. 52nd St., New York, NY 10022.

★1004★
AUTHENTICATED NEWS INTERNATIONAL - PHOTO LIBRARY (Pict)†
29 Katohah Ave.   Phone: (914) 232-7726
Katonah, NY 10536   Sidney Polinsky, Mng.Ed.
Staff: Prof 4. **Subjects:** All subjects, including personality file. **Holdings:** 1.5 million photographs. **Staff:** Helga Brink Polinsky, Exec.Ed.

★1005★
AUTO CLUB OF MISSOURI - INFORMATION RESOURCE CENTER (Trans)
Box 14611   Phone: (314) 576-7350
St. Louis, MO 63178   Muriel Lindsay, Libn.
Founded: 1966. **Staff:** Prof 1; Other 1. **Subjects:** Transportation, travel, automobiles, traffic safety. **Special Collections:** Transportation Research Board publications. **Holdings:** 4600 books; 20 VF drawers of annual reports, pamphlets and bibliographies. **Subscriptions:** 300 journals and other serials. **Services:** Copying; library open to public with restrictions. **Publications:** Shortcut to Information, bimonthly - for internal distribution only. **Remarks:** Center is located at 12901 North Forty Dr., St. Louis, MO 63141.

★1006★
AUTOMATED LOGISTIC MANAGEMENT SYSTEMS AGENCY - LIBRARY (Bus-Fin)
210 N. 12th St., Rm. 1232a   Phone: (314) 263-5955
St. Louis, MO 63101   Oneta M. Welch, Lib.Techn.
Staff: 1. **Subjects:** Automatic data processing. **Holdings:** 500 books; 100 periodical volumes; 1000 Regulations. **Subscriptions:** 75 journals and other serials. **Services:** Interlibrary loans; library open to government employees only. **Remarks:** This agency is administered by the U.S. Army - Materiel Development & Readiness Command.

★1007★
AUTOMATIC SPRINKLER COMPANY - INTERSTATE ELECTRONICS DIVISION - LIBRARY (Sci-Tech)
1001 E. Ball Rd., Dept. 2540
Box 3117   Phone: (714) 635-7210
Anaheim, CA 92803   Frances P. Zuehlsdorf, Libn.
Founded: 1956. **Staff:** 1. **Subjects:** Electronics. **Holdings:** 1200 books;

1500 manufacturers' brochures; 1500 reports and reprints; 2500 Armed Services Technical Information Agency (ASTIA) documents; 2000 military specifications. **Subscriptions:** 250 journals and other serials. **Services:** Interlibrary loans; copying; library not open to public.

★1008★
AUTOMATIC SWITCH COMPANY - ASCO LIBRARY (Sci-Tech)
50 Hanover Rd.   Phone: (201) 966-2479
Florham Park, NJ 07932   Nancy G. Garvey, Libn.
Founded: 1956. **Staff:** Prof 1; Other 1. **Subjects:** Engineering - electrical, electronic, hydraulic; business. **Holdings:** 2000 books; 55 VF drawers; 10 VF drawers of standards (ANSI, UL, NEMA, IEEE); complete microfilm set of military specifications and standards. **Subscriptions:** 325 journals and other serials. **Services:** Interlibrary loans; copying; library open to public with restrictions. **Computerized Information Services:** DIALOG. **Publications:** Abstract Bulletin - home and field offices.

★1009★
AUTOMATION INDUSTRIES, INC. - VITRO LABORATORIES DIVISION - ADMINISTRATIVE SUPPORT DEPARTMENT LIBRARY (Sci-Tech)
14000 Georgia Ave.   Phone: (301) 871-4258
Silver Spring, MD 20910   James R. Griffin, Dept.Hd.
Founded: 1948. **Staff:** Prof 5; Other 19. **Subjects:** Missiles and spacecraft, systems engineering, management, data processing, electronic engineering, ships, underwater acoustics, antisubmarine warfare. **Holdings:** 13,964 books; 1135 bound periodical volumes; 87,960 technical manuals and reports; 19,790 technical correspondence; 1,262,000 engineering drawings (1mm microfilm); Standards and Specifications (650,000 hard copy and on microfilm); 270 nautical charts. **Subscriptions:** 625 journals and other serials; 15 newspapers. **Services:** Interlibrary loans; copying; library open to public by appointment. **Computerized Information Services:** SDC; computerized cataloging and circulation. **Networks/Consortia:** Member of Interlibrary Users Association (Washington DC - Baltimore MD area); Metropolitan Washington Library Council. **Publications:** List of new drawings and technical correspondence, daily - for internal distribution only; list of new technical reports, weekly - for internal distribution only; list of new books, monthly - for internal distribution only. **Special Indexes:** Indexes to drawings of ballistic missiles, guided missiles, missile engineering; technical correspondence index; books, technical reports and manuals index on COM (internal distribution only). **Staff:** Mary Ann Foohey, Supv., Info.Proc. Group; Jay D. Tebo, Supv., Info.Ctr. Group; Eileen F. Cole, Ref.Libn.; Joan E. Halpin, Ref.Libn.; Mary C. Wardlow, Cat.

★1010★
AUTOMOBILE CLUB OF SOUTHERN CALIFORNIA - HIGHWAY ENGINEERING DEPARTMENT LIBRARY (Trans)
2601 S. Figueroa St.   Phone: (213) 741-4490
Los Angeles, CA 90007   Donnalee L. Simmons, Libn./Info.Spec.
Founded: 1974. **Staff:** Prof 1; Other 1. **Subjects:** Highway engineering, transportation planning and legislation. **Holdings:** 9000 books; 170 bound periodical volumes; 8000 reports; 1200 folders of VF material. **Subscriptions:** 100 journals and other serials. **Services:** Library open to public with restrictions. **Computerized Information Services:** DIALOG. **Publications:** Recent Acquisitions, monthly.

★1011★
AUTOMOTIVE HALL OF FAME, INC. - LIBRARY (Hist; Trans)
3225 Cook Rd.
Box 1742
Midland, MI 48640   Phone: (517) 631-5760
                                 Dorothy M. Ross, Pres.
Subjects: History of automobiles, biography. **Services:** Library open to public.
Formerly: Automotive Organization Team, Inc.

★1012★
AUTOMOTIVE INFORMATION COUNCIL - LIBRARY (Trans)
28333 Telegraph Rd.   Phone: (313) 358-0290
Southfield, MI 48034   Peggy Pentecost, Info.Coord.
Founded: 1972. **Staff:** Prof 1. **Subjects:** Motor vehicles - manufacture, maintenance and repair; environment; consumerism; safety. **Special Collections:** Periodicals dealing with all facets of the automotive industry. **Holdings:** 100 books; 4000 newspaper clippings; 150 subject files of reports, manuscripts and pamphlets. **Subscriptions:** 75 journals and other serials. **Services:** Copying (fee); library open to public by appointment. **Publications:** You and Your Car, weekly; Callahan Column, bimonthly; Radio and TV Public Service Spots; Newsletter, 9/year; Action Report, 3/year. **Special Indexes:** Index of information in automotive journals not indexed elsewhere.

AUTOMOTIVE ORGANIZATION TEAM, INC.
See: Automotive Hall of Fame, Inc.

★1013★
AVANTEK, INC. - TECHNICAL INFORMATION SERVICE (Sci-Tech)
3175 Bowers Ave.   Phone: (408) 727-0700
Santa Clara, CA 95051   Sarah P. Morrison, Corp.Libn.
Founded: 1970. **Staff:** Prof 1. **Subjects:** Electronic circuits, microwave technology, communications, manufacturing processes, solid state devices, metallurgy, telecommunication, cable television, semiconductors. **Special Collections:** FCC rules and regulations (updated); military specification collection (microfilm). **Holdings:** 350 books; 200 pamphlets; 1000 government/industry technical reports; 300 patents; 25 microfiche. **Subscriptions:** 130 journals and other serials. **Services:** Interlibrary loans; copying; library not open to public. **Computerized Information Services:** DIALOG. **Networks/Consortia:** Member of CIN. **Publications:** Union List, annual. **Formerly:** Its Corporate Services Library.

★1014★
AVCO CORPORATION - AEROSTRUCTURES DIVISION - ENGINEERING LIBRARY (Sci-Tech)†
Box 210   Phone: (615) 361-2472
Nashville, TN 38102   Martha G. Hardee, Libn.
Staff: Prof 1. **Subjects:** Engineering, aircraft, aeronautics, chemistry, metallurgy. **Holdings:** 1242 books; 3100 pamphlets (cataloged); 2591 shelves of NASA reports; 6 VF drawers and 400 shelves of catalogs. **Subscriptions:** 35 journals and other serials. **Services:** Interlibrary loans (to local libraries); library not open to public. **Publications:** Library Bulletin, monthly - for internal distribution only.

★1015★
AVCO CORPORATION - AVCO-EVERETT RESEARCH LABORATORY - LIBRARY (Sci-Tech)†
2385 Revere Beach Pkwy.   Phone: (617) 389-3000
Everett, MA 02149   Lorraine T. Nazzaro, Libn.
Founded: 1955. **Staff:** Prof 3; Other 4. **Subjects:** Gas dynamics, magnetohydrodynamics, laser technology, superconductivity, physics, plasma physics, chemistry, cardiovascular research. **Special Collections:** Magnetohydrodynamic power generation; Dr. Arthur Kantrowitz Collection (3000 items). **Holdings:** 20,000 books; 7500 bound periodical volumes; 33,000 technical reports (cataloged); 315,500 reports on microfiche; 8 VF drawers of pamphlets; 13 VF drawers of reprints. **Subscriptions:** 636 journals and other serials. **Services:** Interlibrary loans; translation; SDI; library open to public by appointment. **Computerized Information Services:** DIALOG, BRS, DOE/RECON. **Networks/Consortia:** Member of OCLC. **Publications:** Accession List, semimonthly. **Staff:** Joanne Campbell, Asst.Libn.-Cat.; Paul Cote, Asst.Libn.-Ref.; Patricia Cardello, Automated Serv.Libn.

★1016★
AVCO CORPORATION - LYCOMING DIVISION - LIBRARY & INFORMATION CENTER (Sci-Tech)
550 S. Main St.   Phone: (202) 385-2547
Stratford, CT 06497   Lorraine Wallace, Engr.Libn.
Founded: 1955. **Staff:** Prof 2; Other 1. **Subjects:** Engineering - aerospace, mechanical and management; gas turbine engines; fluid mechanics; dynamics; systems analysis. **Special Collections:** Papers of Dr. A. Franz (a pioneer in gas turbines) and papers on the JUMO 004B (the first turbine engine). **Holdings:** 3000 books; 50 bound periodical volumes; 70,000 internal reports and memos; 5000 NACA, NASA reports; 5500 ASME papers (1956 to present); SAE papers (1955 to present); AIAA, AHS technical papers. **Subscriptions:** 86 journals and other serials. **Services:** Interlibrary loans; library not open to public. **Computerized Information Services:** DIALOG, DTIC, SDC, NASA/RECON; internal databases; computerized cataloging, acquisitions, serials and circulation. **Networks/Consortia:** Member of Southwestern Connecticut Library Council (SWLC). **Publications:** Periodicals List, annual; accessions list, monthly - for internal distribution only. **Staff:** Lee Russell, Sr.Libn.

★1017★
AVCO CORPORATION - SYSTEMS DIVISION - RESEARCH LIBRARY (Sci-Tech)
201 Lowell St.   Phone: (617) 657-2632
Wilmington, MA 01887   Elizabeth M. Howard, Libn.
Staff: Prof 3; Other 2. **Subjects:** Aerodynamics, chemistry, metallurgy, space technology, physics, geophysics, instrumentation, electronics, missile technology, plasma physics, re-entry physics. **Holdings:** 15,000 books; 8000 bound periodical volumes; 125,000 technical reports and documents including 100,000 microfiche documents. **Subscriptions:** 150 journals and other serials. **Services:** Interlibrary loans; library not open to public. **Computerized**

Information Services: DIALOG, SDC. **Special Indexes:** KWOC system for internal and external documents.

AVERY ARCHITECTURAL AND FINE ARTS LIBRARY
See: Columbia University

★1018★
AVERY, HODES, COSTELLO & BURMAN - LIBRARY (Law)
180 N. LaSalle St., Suite 3800   Phone: (312) 855-5000
Chicago, IL 60601   Judith Hansel, Libn.
Staff: Prof 1; Other 1. **Subjects:** Law. **Holdings:** 6000 books; 20 bound periodical volumes. **Subscriptions:** 200 journals and other serials; 10 newspapers. **Services:** Interlibrary loans; copying; SDI; library not open to public. **Computerized Information Services:** LEXIS. **Networks/Consortia:** Member of Chicago Library System. **Publications:** Library Guide; List of New Acquisitions, irregular - for internal distribution only.

★1019★
AVERY INTERNATIONAL CORPORATION - RESEARCH CENTER LIBRARY (Sci-Tech)
325 N. Altadena Dr.   Phone: (213) 799-0881
Pasadena, CA 91107   Joanne McKinney, Info.Spec.
Founded: 1968. **Staff:** Prof 1; Other 2. **Subjects:** Adhesives, polymer chemistry, process and control engineering. **Holdings:** 1500 books; 110 bound periodical volumes; 5000 patents (cataloged). **Subscriptions:** 175 journals and other serials. **Services:** Interlibrary loans (limited); SDI; library not open to public. **Computerized Information Services:** DIALOG, SDC; internal database; computerized serials. **Publications:** Current Awareness Bulletin, bimonthly - distributed to company executives, technical staff and marketing departments.

★1020★
AVIATION ELECTRIC, LTD. - TECHNICAL DATA SECTION LIBRARY (Sci-Tech)
St. Laurent
P.O. Box 2140   Phone: (514) 744-2811
Montreal, PQ, Canada H4L 4X8   R. Warrick, Mgr., Tech.Serv.
Staff: 2. **Subjects:** Aircraft instruments and accessories technical literature. **Holdings:** 12,000 volumes. **Subscriptions:** 150 journals and other serials. **Services:** Interlibrary loans; copying; library not open to public. **Remarks:** Library is located at 200 Laurentien Blvd., Montreal, PQ, H4M 2L5. **Staff:** A. Frenette, Libn.

★1021★
AVIATION SAFETY INSTITUTE - ASI TECHNICAL LABS. - LIBRARY (Trans)
893 High St., Suite J
Box 304   Phone: (614) 885-4242
Worthington, OH 43085   John B. Galipault, Pres.
Founded: 1973. **Staff:** 2. **Subjects:** Aviation accidents, incidents and hazards; flight attendant and pilot fatigue and stress studies. **Holdings:** 53 books and bound periodical volumes; reports; microfiche; periodicals; flight recorder archives. **Services:** Copying; library open to public by prior arrangement.

AVIATION TECHNOLOGY LIBRARY
See: Purdue University

★1022★
AVON PRODUCTS, INC. - CENTRAL LIBRARY (Bus-Fin)†
9 W. 57th St.   Phone: (212) 593-5375
New York, NY 10019   Regina Gottesman, Lib.Coord.
Founded: 1972. **Staff:** 2. **Subjects:** Business, marketing, design. **Special Collections:** Company archives (450 bound volumes). **Holdings:** 700 books; 5 VF drawers of current information; 25 VF drawers of archival material; 60 reels of microfilm; annual reports. **Subscriptions:** 120 journals and other serials. **Services:** Interlibrary loans (limited); library not open to public.

★1023★
AVON PRODUCTS, INC. - TECHNICAL INFORMATION CENTER LIBRARY (Sci-Tech)
Division St.   Phone: (914) 357-2000
Suffern, NY 10901   Rosa K. Conlon, Sect.Mgr.
Founded: 1934. **Staff:** Prof 3; Other 1. **Subjects:** Cosmetics, packaging, dermatology, analytical chemistry, medicine. **Holdings:** 6500 books; 3500 bound periodical volumes; 5500 U.S. and foreign patents; 5000 U.S. and foreign reprints; 250 periodicals on microfilm. **Subscriptions:** 250 journals and other serials. **Services:** Interlibrary loans; library open to public for reference use only on request. **Computerized Information Services:** DIALOG, SDC, MEDLINE, New York Times Information Service. **Networks/**

Consortia: Member of Southeastern Libraries Bibliographic Center through NYSILL. **Special Catalogs:** List of serials received by library. **Staff:** Sarah Boroson, Tech.Libn.

AXE (Leonard H.) LIBRARY
See: Pittsburg State University - Leonard H. Axe Library

★1024★
AYER (NW) INCORPORATED - AYER INFORMATION CENTER (AIC) (Publ)
1345 Ave. of the Americas   Phone: (212) 708-5178
New York, NY 10105   Holly J. Bussey, Mgr. of AIC
Subjects: Advertising, general business, merchandising, sales, statistics, trade directories. **Holdings:** 2500 volumes; 100 VF drawers. **Subscriptions:** 700 journals and other serials; 10 newspapers. **Services:** Interlibrary loans; copying; SDI; information center not open to public. **Computerized Information Services:** New York Times Information Service, DIALOG, SDC, Mead Data Central.

AYER ORNITHOLOGY LIBRARY
See: Field Museum of Natural History

★1025★
AYERST LABORATORIES - INFORMATION CENTER (Med)
685 Third Ave.   Phone: (212) 878-5970
New York, NY 10017   George A. Laszlo, Mgr.
Staff: Prof 3; Other 4. **Subjects:** Pharmacology, medicine, cardiology, business. **Special Collections:** Complete literature files on Ayerst products. **Holdings:** 6000 books; 3400 bound periodical volumes; 50,000 reports on microfiche. **Subscriptions:** 340 journals and other serials. **Services:** Interlibrary loans; copying; SDI; library open to public by appointment. **Computerized Information Services:** NLM, SDC, DIALOG, QUESTEL, Source Telecomputing Corporation, Control Data Corporation; Ayerst Laboratories System (ALPHALIT; internal database); computerized cataloging and serials. **Networks/Consortia:** Member of Manhattan-Bronx Health Sciences Library Group; Medical Library Center of New York. **Publications:** Current Drug Literature, bimonthly - for internal distribution only. **Staff:** Ursula Jung, Ref.Asst.; Ed Bury, ILL & Acq.

★1026★
AYERST LABORATORIES, INC. - INFORMATION CENTER (Sci-Tech)
Maple St.   Phone: (518) 297-6611
Rouses Point, NY 12979   Christina Ransom, Mgr.Info.Ctr.
Staff: Prof 1; Other 3. **Subjects:** Chemistry - analytical, pharmaceutical; chromatography; quality control. **Holdings:** 4100 books; 4000 bound periodical volumes; chemical patents on microfilm, 1974 to present; 4 drawers of chemical patents prior to 1974; 400 volumes on microfilm; 60 cassette programs. **Subscriptions:** 513 journals and other serials. **Services:** Interlibrary loans; copying; library open to public by appointment. **Computerized Information Services:** DIALOG, BRS. **Networks/Consortia:** Member of North Country Reference & Research Council; New York State Interlibrary Loan Network; Northern New York Health Information Cooperative. **Publications:** Chromatography bibliographies; monthly bulletin - for internal distribution only. **Special Indexes:** 25 file-drawer subject index.

★1027★
AYERST LABORATORIES - RESEARCH LIBRARY (Sci-Tech; Med)†
Box 6115   Phone: (514) 744-6771
Montreal, PQ, Canada H3C 3J1   Nicole Barrette-Pilon, Libn.
Founded: 1940. **Staff:** Prof 2; Other 2. **Subjects:** Biochemistry, endocrinology, organic chemistry, medicine, pharmacology. **Holdings:** 4600 books; 32,000 bound periodical volumes; 2000 patents; 2000 microforms. **Subscriptions:** 311 journals and other serials. **Services:** Interlibrary loans; copying; library open to public with restrictions. **Computerized Information Services:** CAN/OLE, DIALOG, SDC, Derwent Publications Ltd., MEDLINE. **Remarks:** Library is located at 1025 Laurentian Blvd., Montreal, PQ, H4R 1J6.

AZTEC RUINS NATL. MONUMENT
See: U.S. Natl. Park Service

B

★1028★
B.C. HYDRO - ENGINEERING LIBRARY (Sci-Tech)
555 W. Hastings St.
Box 12121   Phone: (604) 663-2894
Vancouver, BC, Canada V6B 4T6   Judith Bradshaw, Asst.Libn.
Founded: 1960. **Staff:** Prof 1; Other 3. **Subjects:** Hydroelectric and steam power plants; hydrology. **Special Collections:** Engineering standards (20 drawers). **Holdings:** 3000 books. **Subscriptions:** 280 journals and other serials. **Services:** Interlibrary loans; copying; SDI; library open to public with limited circulation of materials. **Computerized Information Services:** DIALOG, SDC; computerized serials. **Publications:** Engineering Library Bulletin - distributed on request. **Special Indexes:** KWOC index to technical reports, selected articles from literature (maintained online on disc storage). **Formerly:** British Columbia Hydro & Power Authority.

★1029★
B.C. HYDRO - LIBRARY (Energy)
970 Burrard St.   Phone: (604) 663-2416
Vancouver, BC, Canada V6Z 1Y3   Elizabeth Preston, Libn.
Founded: 1957. **Staff:** Prof 4; Other 7. **Subjects:** Public utilities, electrical engineering, industrial development, natural gas industry, statistics, transportation. **Holdings:** 4000 books; 750 bound periodical volumes; 2000 pamphlets (cataloged); 18 VF drawers of annual reports; 26 VF drawers of government documents; 5 VF drawers of clippings. **Subscriptions:** 700 journals and other serials. **Services:** Interlibrary loans; copying; library open to public for reference use only, by request. **Computerized Information Services:** DIALOG, SDC, CAN/OLE; computerized serials. **Publications:** Library Bulletin, irregular. **Formerly:** British Columbia Hydro & Power Authority.

★1030★
B.E.A. ASSOCIATES, INC. - LIBRARY (Bus-Fin)
153 E. 53rd St.   Phone: (212) 832-2626
New York, NY 10022   Anita B. Collins, Info.Mgr./Libn.
Staff: Prof 1; Other 1. **Subjects:** Companies, bonds. **Holdings:** 100 books; 500 company files; 600 bond files. **Subscriptions:** 74 journals and other serials. **Services:** Library not open to public. **Computerized Information Services:** Computerized cataloging.

B.O.T.I. SPECIAL RESEARCH COLLECTION
See: M.P.K. Omega Company

★1031★
BA INVESTMENT MANAGEMENT CORPORATION - LIBRARY (Bus-Fin)
555 California St.   Phone: (415) 622-6883
San Francisco, CA 94104   Lee Stocks, Lib.Serv.Mgr.
Founded: 1969. **Staff:** Prof 2; Other 3. **Subjects:** Investment, economics and business. **Special Collections:** Disclosure (formerly Leasco) SEC Filings (corporate reports, 200,000 fiche). **Holdings:** 7000 volumes; corporate and industry files; Wall Street Journal on microfilm since 1950, Barron's since 1973. **Subscriptions:** 600 journals and other serials; 20 newspapers. **Services:** Interlibrary loans; library not open to public. **Computerized Information Services:** Online systems; computerized cataloging and serials. **Publications:** Library Newsletter - for internal distribution only. **Remarks:** BA Investment Management Corporation is a subsidiary of BankAmerica Corporation. **Staff:** Ruth Girill, Ref.Libn.

BABBAGE (Charles) INSTITUTE
See: University of Minnesota - Charles Babbage Institute

BABCOCK GRADUATE SCHOOL OF MANAGEMENT
See: Wake Forest University

BABCOCK (Wealthy) MATHEMATICS LIBRARY
See: University of Kansas - Wealthy Babcock Mathematics Library

★1032★
BABCOCK AND WILCOX COMPANY - FOSSIL POWER GENERATION DIVISION - TECHNICAL LIBRARY (Sci-Tech)†
20 S. Van Buren Ave.   Phone: (216) 753-4511
Barberton, OH 44203   Gloria H. Broaddus, Libn.
Founded: 1960. **Staff:** Prof 1; Other 1. **Subjects:** Engineering, management, heat transfer, data processing, welding. **Special Collections:** Engineering Journal, 1935 to present; Welding Journal, 1931 to present; American Society for Testing and Materials standards, 1914 to present; U.S. Bureau of

Mines Reports, 1911 to present. **Holdings:** 9000 books; 4000 bound periodical volumes; 120 VF drawers. **Subscriptions:** 300 journals and other serials; 10 newspapers. **Services:** Interlibrary loans; copying; translations; library not open to public. **Publications:** Bimonthly Abstract List and List of Acquisitions - for internal distribution only. **Special Indexes:** Uniterm Index. **Remarks:** Babcock and Wilcox is a subsidiary of McDermott Inc.

★1033★
BABCOCK AND WILCOX COMPANY - NUCLEAR POWER GENERATION DIVISION - LIBRARY (Energy)
3315 Old Forest Rd.   Phone: (804) 385-2475
Lynchburg, VA 24501   Ruth H. Johnson, Hd.Libn.
Founded: 1955. **Staff:** Prof 2; Other 2. **Subjects:** Nuclear technology, physics, materials, computer technology, chemistry. **Holdings:** 20,000 books; 3000 bound periodical volumes; 40,000 technical reports; 400,000 technical reports on microfiche; 13 VF drawers of standards and conference papers. **Subscriptions:** 300 journals and other serials; 20 newspapers. **Services:** Interlibrary loans; copying; library open to public by appointment. **Computerized Information Services:** DIALOG, BRS, DOE/RECON. **Publications:** Information Services Digest, weekly - to company engineers. **Remarks:** Babcock and Wilcox is a subsidiary of McDermott Inc. **Staff:** Gordon E. Jessee, Asst.Libn.

★1034★
BABCOCK AND WILCOX COMPANY - RESEARCH CENTER LIBRARY (Energy)
Box 835   Phone: (216) 821-9110
Alliance, OH 44601   Elmer H. Fisher, Mgr., Info.Serv.
Founded: 1947. **Staff:** Prof 4; Other 3. **Subjects:** Mechanics, chemical engineering, fuels engineering, heat transfer, chemistry, metallurgy, welding, electronics, nuclear science and technology. **Holdings:** 15,000 books; 1500 reels of microfilmed back files of periodicals; 100,000 government and company reports on microfiche. **Subscriptions:** 900 journals and other serials. **Services:** Interlibrary loans; copying; library open to public. **Computerized Information Services:** DIALOG, SDC, DOE/RECON, BRS; internal database. **Remarks:** Babcock and Wilcox is a subsidiary of McDermott Inc. **Staff:** Judy Birmingham, Info.Spec.; Victor Zoller, Info.Spec.; Rena Baker, Info.Spec.

★1035★
BABSON COLLEGE - HORN LIBRARY - SPECIAL COLLECTIONS (Sci-Tech)
                                             Phone: (617) 235-1200
Babson Park, MA 02157   Elizabeth DiBartolomeis, Spec.Coll.Cur.
Founded: 1919. **Subjects:** Sir Isaac Newton, Roger W. Babson. **Holdings:** 2000 items including important editions, commentaries, autograph manuscripts and memorabilia; Babson Giant Relief Model of United States. **Services:** Interlibrary loans; copying; media services and technical instruction; library open to public with librarian's approval. **Computerized Information Services:** DIALOG; internal database; computerized cataloging. **Special Catalogs:** Isaac Newton Catalog. **Remarks:** Library is said to contain world's largest revolving globe. **Formerly:** Sir Isaac Newton Library.

BABSON LIBRARY
See: Springfield College

BABSON (Paul Talbot) MEMORIAL LIBRARY
See: Newton-Wellesley Hospital - Paul Talbot Babson Memorial Library

BACCHUS WORKS INFORMATION SERVICES
See: Hercules, Inc.

BACH LIBRARY
See: Baldwin-Wallace College - Riemenschneider Bach Institute

BACHE HALSEY STUART SHIELDS
See: Prudential-Bache Securities Inc.

BACKUS (E. Burdette) LIBRARY
See: All Souls Unitarian Church - E. Burdette Backus Library

★1036★
BACKUS (William W.) HOSPITAL - MEDICAL/NURSING LIBRARY (Med)
326 Washington St.   Phone: (203) 889-8331
Norwich, CT 06360   Florence Lamoureux, Med.Libn.
Staff: Prof 1. **Subjects:** Anesthesiology, surgery, obstetrics, gynecology, internal medicine, pediatrics. **Holdings:** 2000 books; 1700 bound periodical volumes. **Subscriptions:** 100 journals and other serials. **Services:** Interlibrary loans; copying; library not open to public.

BACON (Asa S.) MEMORIAL LIBRARY
See: American Hospital Association - Asa S. Bacon Memorial Library

BACON COLLECTION
See: Dalhousie University

BACON (Francis) FOUNDATION
See: Francis Bacon Foundation

BACON (Governor) HEALTH CENTER
See: Governor Bacon Health Center

BACON (Howard E.) MEMORIAL LIBRARY
See: Metropolitan Toronto Association for the Mentally Retarded - Howard E. Bacon Memorial Library

★1037★
BACONE COLLEGE - LIBRARY - SPECIAL COLLECTIONS (Area-Ethnic)
East Shawnee   Phone: (918) 683-4581
Muskogee, OK 74401   Frances A. Donelson, Lib.Dir.
Subjects: North American Indians. **Holdings:** 4000 volumes. **Services:** Interlibrary loans; copying; library open to public with restrictions.
Publications: Acquisition lists of new books - for internal use or on request.

BADGER AMERICA, INC.
See: Raytheon Company

★1038★
BADISCHE CORPORATION - LIBRARY (Sci-Tech)
Drawer D   Phone: (804) 887-6335
Williamsburg, VA 23187   Carmalita J. Beasley, Libn.
Founded: 1958. **Staff:** Prof 1. **Subjects:** Synthetic fibers, textile technology, chemistry, physics, engineering. **Holdings:** 7500 books; 3400 bound periodical volumes; company reports; theses, reprints, translations, miscellaneous publications. **Subscriptions:** 106 journals and other serials. **Services:** Interlibrary loans; copying; library not open to public.

BADLANDS NATL. MONUMENT
See: U.S. Natl. Park Service

★1039★
BAECK (Leo) INSTITUTE - LIBRARY (Area-Ethnic)
129 E. 73rd St.   Phone: (212) 744-6400
New York, NY 10021   Stephanie Stern, Libn.
Founded: 1955. **Staff:** Prof 7; Other 7. **Subjects:** History and literature of German-speaking Jewry in Central Europe. **Holdings:** 50,000 books; 10,000 bound periodical volumes; 1200 linear feet of archival matter; 1700 reels of microfilm; 590 unpublished memoirs, manuscripts and typescripts; 385 other manuscripts. **Subscriptions:** 96 journals and other serials. **Services:** Interlibrary loans; copying; library open to public. **Publications:** Leo Baeck Institute Library & Archives News, 3-4/year - distributed to libraries, scholars, and institutions. **Special Catalogs:** Katalog: LBI New York "Bibliothek und Archiv," Volume I, 1970; unpublished inventories. **Staff:** Fred Bogin, Ref./Acq.Libn.; Dr. Sybil Milton, Chf.Archv.; Jonathan Sperber, Asst.Archv.; Ilse Turnheim, Archv.

BAETJER MEMORIAL LIBRARY
See: Johns Hopkins University - School of Medicine - Department of Pediatrics

BAGSHAW (Marguerite G.) COLLECTION
See: Toronto Public Library - Marguerite G. Bagshaw Collection

★1040★
BAHAI REFERENCE LIBRARY OF PEORIA (Rel-Theol)†
5209 N. University   Phone: (309) 692-7597
Peoria, IL 61614   Carolyn Henderer, Libn.
Founded: 1928. **Staff:** Prof 1. **Subjects:** Bahai, comparative religions, world order administration, philosophy, sociology, spirituality of man, education. **Special Collections:** Star of the West (30 volumes); Bahai News (complete); Bahai World (complete set). **Holdings:** 1000 books; 50 bound periodical volumes; 1200 pamphlets (cataloged); music; 125 tapes (cassettes and reel); 25 filmstrips and slides. **Services:** Library open to public by request. **Remarks:** Maintained by Peoria Bahai Assembly.

BAHAN (Tom and Mae) LIBRARY
See: Sherman College of Straight Chiropractic - Tom and Mae Bahan Library

BAILEY HORTORIUM LIBRARY
See: Cornell University

BAILEY/HOWE LIBRARY
See: University of Vermont - Wilbur Collection of Vermontiana

BAILEY (Jean) MEMORIAL LIBRARY
See: Burnaby School Board - Teachers' Professional Library

★1041★
BAIRD CORPORATION - TECHNICAL LIBRARY (Sci-Tech)†
125 Middlesex Tpke.   Phone: (617) 276-6390
Bedford, MA 01730   Frances G. Greene, Libn.
Founded: 1950. **Staff:** Prof 1; Other 1. **Subjects:** Optics, analytical chemistry, nuclear medicine. **Holdings:** 2270 books and bound periodical volumes; 44 VF drawers of technical reports, reprints and patents. **Subscriptions:** 226 journals and other serials. **Services:** Interlibrary loans; library open to public for reference use only on request. **Publications:** Acquisition List, monthly.

★1042★
BAIRD HOLM MC EACHEN PEDERSEN & HAMANN LAW OFFICES - LIBRARY (Law)
1500 Woodmen Tower   Phone: (402) 344-0500
Omaha, NE 68102   Patricia Carstens, Libn.
Staff: Prof 1; Other 1. **Subjects:** Law - taxation, securities, school, hospital, labor. **Holdings:** 9500 books; 150 bound periodical volumes. **Subscriptions:** 125 journals and other serials. **Services:** Copying; library open to public with restrictions on borrowing. **Computerized Information Services:** LEXIS.

BAIZERMAN (Eugenie Silverman) ARCHIVE
See: University of North Carolina, Greensboro - Eugenie Silverman Baizerman Archive

BAIZERMAN (Saul) ARCHIVE
See: University of North Carolina, Greensboro - Saul Baizerman Archive

BAKER (Blanche M.) MEMORIAL LIBRARY
See: ONE, Inc. - Blanche M. Baker Memorial Library

★1043★
BAKER & BOTTS - LAW LIBRARY (Law)
3000 One Shell Plaza   Phone: (713) 229-1412
Houston, TX 77002   Melissa Colbert, Libn.
Staff: Prof 4; Other 6. **Subjects:** Law - tax, patent, public utilities, labor, railroad, corporate. **Holdings:** 60,000 books; 900 bound periodical volumes. **Subscriptions:** 45 journals and other serials. **Services:** Interlibrary loans; copying; library open to attorneys. **Computerized Information Services:** DIALOG, SDC, LEXIS. **Publications:** Library Notes, monthly - to all attorneys. **Special Indexes:** Index to Texas legal periodicals (card). **Staff:** Emily Clement, Assoc.Libn.; Fleeta Gorrell, Asst.Libn.; Odell Dehart, Cat.

★1044★
BAKER CENTRE - SERVICES FOR THE HANDICAPPED - LIBRARY (Soc Sci)
P.O. Box 72   Phone: (403) 261-7506
Calgary, AB, Canada T2P 2H2   Clement Blakeslee, Spec. Projects Coord.
Staff: 2. **Subjects:** Mental retardation, behavior modification, deinstitutionalization. **Holdings:** 500 books; 1 VF drawer of clippings. **Subscriptions:** 16 journals and other serials. **Services:** Interlibrary loans; library open to public for reference use only. **Special Catalogs:** Complete annotated bibliography of all materials in the library.

★1045★
BAKER & DANIELS - LAW LIBRARY (Law)
810 Fletcher Trust Bldg.   Phone: (317) 636-4535
Indianapolis, IN 46204   Paula Schmidt, Libn.
Staff: Prof 1; Other 1. **Subjects:** Law. **Holdings:** 19,000 books; 2000 bound periodical volumes; 4300 microfiche; 12 drawers of pamphlets. **Subscriptions:** 250 journals and other serials; 8 newspapers. **Services:** Interlibrary loans; library not open to public. **Computerized Information Services:** LEXIS; computerized cataloging. **Networks/Consortia:** Member of Indianapolis Legal Cataloging Consortia. **Publications:** Newsletter, monthly.

★1046★
BAKER (H.M.) ASSOCIATES - RESEARCH COLLECTION (Hist; Bus-Fin)
266 E. Dudley Ave.
Westfield, NJ 07090   Helen M.B. Cushman, Dir.
Founded: 1958. **Staff:** Prof 1. **Subjects:** Product and business history, advertising history. **Holdings:** 5000 books and bound periodical volumes; 100

cubic feet of pictorial materials. **Subscriptions:** 40 journals and other serials. **Services:** Copying; bibliographic, reference, and searching service available on a fee basis; library open to clients of Baker Associates. **Publications:** Newsletters, irregular; Business Anniversaries Manual.

BAKER (Herman M., M.D.) MEMORIAL LIBRARY
See: St. Mary's Medical Center - Herman M. Baker, M.D. Memorial Library

★1047★
BAKER AND HOSTETLER - LIBRARY (Law)
3200 National City Ctr.   Phone: (216) 621-0200
Cleveland, OH 44114   Alvin M. Podboy, Libn.
Staff: Prof 2; Other 2. **Subjects:** Law. **Holdings:** 40,000 volumes. **Services:** Library open to clients and outside counsel associated with the firm. **Computerized Information Services:** LEXIS. **Staff:** Susan Miljenovic, Asst.Libn.

★1048★
BAKER (J.T.) CHEMICAL COMPANY - RESEARCH LIBRARY (Sci-Tech)
    Phone: (201) 859-2151
Phillipsburg, NJ 08865   Frances E. Steele, Tech.Libn.
Founded: 1945. **Staff:** Prof 1. **Subjects:** Chemistry - analytical, organic, clinical, inorganic. **Holdings:** 13,000 books; 13,000 bound periodical volumes; 10 VF drawers of patents; 24 VF drawers and 60 boxes of microfilm cartridges; 4 VF drawers of AEC and government reports on microfiche. **Subscriptions:** 261 journals and other serials. **Services:** Interlibrary loans; copying; library open to qualified technologists and researchers on request. **Computerized Information Services:** New England Research Application Center (NERAC). **Publications:** Library Lantern, irregular.

BAKER (K.M.) MEMORIAL LIBRARY
See: Lansing General Hospital - Osteopathic - K.M. Baker Memorial Library

BAKER LIBRARY
See: Dartmouth College

BAKER LIBRARY
See: Harvard University - Graduate School of Business Administration

BAKER LIBRARY
See: U.S. Air Force Base - Castle Base

★1049★
BAKER, LOVICK, LTD. - INFORMATION RETRIEVAL CENTRE
60 Bloor St., W.
Toronto, ON, Canada M4W 3B8
Founded: 1970. **Subjects:** Advertising, marketing. **Holdings:** 200 books; 8 drawers of Statistics Canada material. **Remarks:** Presently inactive.

★1050★
BAKER & MC KENZIE - LAW LIBRARY (Law)
375 Park Ave.   Phone: (212) 751-5700
New York, NY 10022   Janet S. Zagorin, Libn.
Founded: 1971. **Staff:** Prof 1; Other 3. **Subjects:** Law, foreign law. **Holdings:** 10,000 volumes. **Subscriptions:** 25 journals and other serials. **Services:** Interlibrary loans; library not open to public.

★1051★
BAKER & MC KENZIE - LIBRARY (Law)
Box 7258   Phone: (415) 433-7600
San Francisco, CA 94131   Manuel J. Koff
Staff: Prof 1; Other 1. **Subjects:** Law. **Holdings:** 3000 books; 100 bound periodical volumes; 1000 pamphlets and other materials. **Subscriptions:** Interlibrary loans; copying; library not open to public. **Computerized Information Services:** LEXIS.

★1052★
BAKER & MC KENZIE - LIBRARY (Law)
2800 Prudential Plaza   Phone: (312) 861-2915
Chicago, IL 60601   Frank Lukes, Law Libn.
Founded: 1950. **Staff:** Prof 4; Other 5. **Subjects:** U.S. taxation, corporations, foreign trade and investment, Illinois law, foreign taxation, foreign industrial property laws, securities, products liability, medical malpractice. **Special Collections:** Complete tax library in original languages on Germany, Switzerland, Netherlands, France, Italy, British Commonwealth of Nations; substantial holdings on Latin American, European, Asian and Middle Eastern countries of interest to American corporations. **Holdings:** 35,000 volumes. **Subscriptions:** 400 journals and other serials; 700 loose-leaf

services. **Services:** Interlibrary loans; use of library for reference may be requested. **Computerized Information Services:** LEXIS; internal database. **Publications:** Monthly Bulletin - for internal distribution only.

★1053★
BAKER (Michael, Jr.), INC. - LIBRARY (Plan)
4301 Dutch Ridge Rd.
Box 280   Phone: (412) 495-7711
Beaver, PA 15009   Ruth J. Williams, Libn.
Staff: Prof 1. **Subjects:** Civil engineering, urban planning, environmental planning, business, transportation. **Special Collections:** Company planning reports (300 bound volumes). **Holdings:** 3000 books; 12 VF drawers of pamphlets. **Subscriptions:** 250 journals and other serials; 5 newspapers. **Services:** Interlibrary loans; library not open to public. **Computerized Information Services:** DIALOG, ISI.

BAKER (Solomon R.) LIBRARY
See: Bentley College - Solomon R. Baker Library

★1054★
BAKER UNIVERSITY - ARCHIVES AND HISTORICAL LIBRARY (Rel-Theol)
Collins Library   Phone: (913) 594-6451
Baldwin City, KS 66006   Harold Kolling, Univ.Cur.
Staff: 1. **Subjects:** United Methodism, Kansas, Abraham Lincoln. **Special Collections:** Baker Archives. **Holdings:** 10,000 books and bound periodical volumes; 50 file drawers of manuscripts and photographs; church histories and records; clippings; missionary artifacts; Baker University memorabilia. **Services:** Copying (limited); library open to public. **Computerized Information Services:** Computerized cataloging. **Remarks:** Maintained also by Commission on Archives and History of the Kansas East Conference of the United Methodist Church.

★1055★
BAKER UNIVERSITY - QUAYLE RARE BIBLE COLLECTION (Rel-Theol)
Baker University Library, Eighth St.   Phone: (913) 594-3422
Baldwin City, KS 66006   Dr. John M. Forbes, Dir. of Libs.
Staff: Prof 1; Other 1. **Subjects:** Rare Bibles and religious works. **Special Collections:** Bishop William Alfred Quayle Collection of Rare Bibles (275). **Holdings:** 450 books; 4 clay tablets and hieroglyphic fragment (cataloged). **Services:** Copying (limited); collection open to public by appointment. **Special Catalogs:** Catalog of the Quayle Rare Bible Collection - for sale.

BAKHMETEFF ARCHIVE OF RUSSIAN AND EAST EUROPEAN HISTORY AND CULTURE
See: Columbia University - Rare Book and Manuscript Library

BAKKEN (Lavola) MEMORIAL LIBRARY
See: Douglas County Museum - Lavola Bakken Memorial Library

★1056★
BALCH, BINGHAM, BAKER, HAWTHORNE, WILLIAMS & WARD - LIBRARY (Law)†
600 N. 18th St.
Box 306   Phone: (205) 251-8100
Birmingham, AL 35201   Joanna Chen, Libn.
Founded: 1920. **Staff:** 1. **Subjects:** Law. **Holdings:** 18,000 volumes. **Subscriptions:** 75 journals and other serials. **Services:** Library not open to public.

★1057★
BALCH INSTITUTE FOR ETHNIC STUDIES - LIBRARY (Soc Sci)
18 S. 7th St.
Philadelphia, PA 19106   R. Joseph Anderson, Lib.Dir.
Founded: 1971. **Staff:** Prof 5; Other 3. **Subjects:** North American immigration and ethnic history, labor movement, radicalism. **Holdings:** 50,000 books and other printed items; 100 manuscript collections; 200 sound recordings; 1000 photographs; 500 broadsides; 5000 reels of microfilm. **Subscriptions:** 130 journals and other serials. **Services:** Interlibrary loans; copying; library open to public for reference use only. **Computerized Information Services:** Computerized cataloging. **Networks/Consortia:** Member of OCLC through PALINET and Union Library Catalogue of Pennsylvania. **Publications:** New Dimensions, 3/year; A Selected List of Newspaper and Manuscript Holdings, 1980; ethnic reading lists, irregular. **Staff:** Patricia Proscino, Ref./Acq.; Sheila Walker, Cat.; Frances Sinclair, Cat.; Judith Felsten, Archv.

BALCONES RESEARCH CENTER
See: Texas State Bureau of Economic Geology - Well Sample and Core Library

BALDWIN (Abraham) AGRICULTURAL COLLEGE
See: Abraham Baldwin Agricultural College

BALDWIN LIBRARY
See: University of Florida

★1058★
BALDWIN-WALLACE COLLEGE - CHEMISTRY LIBRARY (Sci-Tech)
Berea, OH 44017
Subjects: Chemistry. **Holdings:** Figures not available.

★1059★
BALDWIN-WALLACE COLLEGE - RIEMENSCHNEIDER BACH INSTITUTE -
  BACH LIBRARY (Mus)
Merner-Pfeiffer Hall
49 Seminary St.   Phone: (216) 826-2207
Berea, OH 44017   Dr. Elinore Barber, Dir., Bach Inst.
Staff: Prof 5; Other 3. **Subjects:** Music - Baroque and other periods; Baroque musical treatises; music literature. **Special Collections:** Rare first editions and manuscripts including the Riemenschneider, Emmy Martin and Hans David Collections (circa 700 vault items). **Holdings:** 9000 volumes. **Services:** Copying (limited); library open to public by appointment. **Computerized Information Services:** Computerized cataloging. **Networks/Consortia:** Member of OCLC. **Publications:** BACH, The Quarterly Journal of the Riemenschneider Bach Institute. **Special Catalogs:** Catalog of the Riemenschneider Collection (book); catalogs of the Martin and David Collections and later acquisitions (mimeograph). **Staff:** Lois Claspy, Music Libn.

★1060★
BALL AEROSPACE SYSTEMS DIVISION - TECHNICAL LIBRARY (Sci-Tech)
Boulder Industrial Park
Box 1062   Phone: (303) 441-4436
Boulder, CO 80306   Judy Dayhoff, Tech.Libn.
Founded: 1960. **Staff:** 1. **Subjects:** Physics, electronics, engineering, optics, space sciences, astronomy and astrophysics. **Holdings:** 2500 books; NASA documents and government reports - 56 bookshelves (paper copy) and 12 double file drawers of microfiche. **Subscriptions:** 121 journals and other serials. **Services:** Interlibrary loans; copying; library not open to public.

★1061★
BALL CORPORATION - CORPORATE INFORMATION CENTER AND LAW
  LIBRARY (Bus-Fin; Law)
345 S. High St.   Phone: (317) 747-6420
Muncie, IN 47302   Peg Nelson, Corp.Libn.
Founded: 1974. **Staff:** Prof 1; Other 1. **Subjects:** Management, marketing, law, patents. **Holdings:** 5000 books; 900 annual reports. **Subscriptions:** 230 journals and other serials; 20 newspapers. **Services:** Interlibrary loans; copying; library open to public with permission. **Computerized Information Services:** New York Times Information Service, DIALOG, SDC, BRS.

★1062★
BALL CORPORATION - RESEARCH LIBRARY (Sci-Tech)
1509 S. Macedonia   Phone: (317) 747-6707
Muncie, IN 47302   Julia Mertens, Tech.Libn.
Staff: Prof 1. **Subjects:** Chemistry, environmental science, metallurgy, engineering, electronics. **Holdings:** 5000 books; 800 bound periodical volumes; microfiche; 5 filing drawers of patents; 8 file cabinets of engineering information. **Subscriptions:** 161 journals and other serials. **Services:** Interlibrary loans; copying; SDI; library not open to public. **Computerized Information Services:** DIALOG.

★1063★
BALL MEMORIAL HOSPITAL - HEALTH SCIENCE LIBRARY (Med)
2401 University Ave.   Phone: (317) 747-3204
Muncie, IN 47303   Betty J. Daugherty, Dir. of Lib.Serv.
Staff: Prof 2; Other 2. **Subjects:** Surgery, internal medicine, family practice, nursing and practical nursing, hospital administration, patient education. **Holdings:** 2500 books; 5500 bound periodical volumes; 15 files of subject headings; VF drawers. **Subscriptions:** 523 journals and other serials. **Services:** Interlibrary loans; copying; SDI; library not open to public. **Computerized Information Services:** DIALOG, MEDLINE, BRS. **Networks/Consortia:** Member of Health Science Library Consortium of East Central Indiana. **Publications:** Know-Know, quarterly newsletter. **Staff:** Melisa Day, Asst.Dir.; Kay McKibben, Coord., Consortium; Dana Fine, ILL; Margaret Hill, Ser.Libn.

★1064★
BALL STATE UNIVERSITY - ALTHEA L. STOECKEL DELAWARE COUNTY
  ARCHIVES & LOCAL HISTORY COLLECTION (Hist)
Bracken Library   Phone: (317) 285-7800
Muncie, IN 47306   David C. Tambo, Cur./Ref.Libn.
Founded: 1972. **Staff:** Prof 1; Other 1. **Subjects:** Local history, Middletown studies. **Special Collections:** County and municipal records (1000 linear feet); local historical maps (850 items); local photographs (5000 prints and negatives); oral history (150 reels and cassettes); manuscript collection (Muncie and Delaware County businesses, labor, religious groups, organizations, individuals and families; 250 linear feet); Middletown studies project research papers (5 linear feet); Muncie as Middletown study materials (10 linear feet). **Services:** Copying; library open to public. **Special Catalogs:** Internal guides to larger collections (loose-leaf); name indexes to most collections (card).

★1065★
BALL STATE UNIVERSITY - BRACKEN LIBRARY - SPECIAL COLLECTIONS
  (Hum)
Bracken Library, Rm. 210   Phone: (317) 285-5078
Muncie, IN 47306   Juanita J. Smith, Spec.Coll.Libn.
Founded: 1972. **Staff:** Prof 1. **Subjects:** Humanities. **Special Collections:** Sir Norman Angell Papers (54 VF drawers and 28 storage boxes); John Steinbeck Collection (900 volumes; 5 VF drawers; 12 storage boxes); Aldous Huxley Collection (115 volumes); Ku Klux Klan Collection (81 volumes); Nazi Collection (557 volumes); contemporary poetry collection; volleyball archives. **Services:** Copying; library open to public for reference use only. **Computerized Information Services:** Computerized cataloging. **Networks/Consortia:** Member of OCLC through INCOLSA.

★1066★
BALL STATE UNIVERSITY - COLLEGE OF ARCHITECTURE & PLANNING -
  LIBRARY (Art; Plan)
                                                    Phone: (317) 285-4760
Muncie, IN 47306   Marjorie Joyner, Arch.Libn.
Founded: 1966. **Staff:** Prof 1; Other 2. **Subjects:** Architecture, urban planning, regional development, design, landscape architecture. **Holdings:** 19,874 books; 3400 bound periodical volumes; 35 VF drawers; 50,000 35mm slides; 640 manufacturers' product catalogs. **Subscriptions:** 174 journals and other serials. **Services:** Interlibrary loans; copying; permission to check out materials may be obtained from the director. **Computerized Information Services:** Computerized cataloging. **Networks/Consortia:** Member of OCLC. **Publications:** Monthly acquisitions list - for internal distribution only. **Special Catalogs:** Student theses; product catalogs (both on cards); construction documents (on microfilm and cards).

★1067★
BALL STATE UNIVERSITY - DEPARTMENT OF LIBRARY SERVICE - MAP
  COLLECTION (Geog-Map)
Bracken Library, Rm. 218   Phone: (317) 285-4077
Muncie, IN 47306   Paul W. Stout, Map Libn.
Staff: Prof 1; Other 1. **Subjects:** Maps - topographic, Indiana and city. **Holdings:** 90,000 maps. **Services:** Interlibrary loans; copying; library open to public.

★1068★
BALL STATE UNIVERSITY - MUSIC LIBRARY (Mus)
                                                    Phone: (317) 285-7356
Muncie, IN 47306   Dr. Nyal Williams, Music Libn.
Founded: 1975. **Staff:** Prof 1; Other 2. **Subjects:** Music. **Special Collections:** Tubists Universal Brotherhood Association (TUBA) Resource Library (300 scores for tuba); International Horn Society Archives (correspondence files, papers, and recordings of speeches and performances of the International Workshops; 20 linear feet); Cecil Leeson Archival Saxophone Collection (17 historical instruments, 10 boxes of manuscripts); archives of Buescher and Conn instrument makers. **Services:** Interlibrary loans; copying; library open to public for reference use only. **Computerized Information Services:** Computerized cataloging. **Networks/Consortia:** Member of OCLC through INCOLSA.

BALLARD (Frances Hall) LIBRARY
See: Manhattan School of Music - Frances Hall Ballard Library

★1069★
BALLARD, SPAHR, ANDREWS AND INGERSOLL - LAW LIBRARY (Law)
30 S. 17th St., 20th Fl.   Phone: (215) 564-1800
Philadelphia, PA 19103   Shari Y. Liu, Libn.
Subjects: Law. **Holdings:** 11,500 volumes.

BALLISTIC MISSILE RADIATION ANALYSIS CENTER
See: Environmental Research Institute of Michigan - Infrared Information and Analysis Center

BALLOU (L.E. & E.L.) LIBRARY
See: Buena Vista College - L.E. & E.L. Ballou Library

BALTIMORE BAR LIBRARY COMPANY
See: Library Company of the Baltimore Bar

★1070★
BALTIMORE BRIEFING CENTER - LIBRARY (Bus-Fin)
36 S. Charles St.   Phone: (301) 837-6068
Baltimore, MD 21201
Staff: 2. Subjects: Industrial and economic development, demographics. Holdings: 500 books. Subscriptions: 65 journals and other serials; 7 newspapers. Services: Copying; library open to public by appointment. Formerly: Baltimore Economic Development Corporation.

★1071★
BALTIMORE CITY DEPARTMENT OF HOUSING AND COMMUNITY DEVELOPMENT - RESEARCH LIBRARY (Soc Sci)
222 E. Saratoga St., Rm. 450   Phone: (301) 396-4248
Baltimore, MD 21202   Mrs. Shifra Cohen, Res.Anl.
Founded: 1955. Staff: 1. Subjects: Baltimore and U.S. housing, planning, census, urban renewal, relocation, building costs, aging, poverty. Holdings: 5300 books; 2 VF drawers of pamphlets; 80 computer printouts listing vacant houses, assessments, multiple family dwellings, etc. in Baltimore. Subscriptions: 40 journals and other serials. Services: Library open to public for reference use only.

★1072★
BALTIMORE CITY DEPARTMENT OF PLANNING - LIBRARY (Plan)†
222 E. Saratoga St., 8th Fl.   Phone: (301) 396-4332
Baltimore, MD 21202   Charles Newton, Libn.
Founded: 1958. Staff: 1. Subjects: City planning, urban renewal, housing, architecture, transportation and land use, energy, statistical materials. Holdings: 3000 books; 450 bound periodical volumes; 6 VF drawers of pamphlets; 10,000 slides. Subscriptions: 95 journals and other serials. Services: Interlibrary loans; library open to public with restrictions. Publications: Baltimore Plans - free upon request to libraries and planning departments; Baltimore Development Program.

★1073★
BALTIMORE CITY HOSPITALS - HAROLD E. HARRISON LIBRARY (Med)†
4940 Eastern Ave.   Phone: (301) 396-9030
Baltimore, MD 21224   Edlea Jones, Libn.
Founded: 1935. Staff: Prof 1; Other 3. Subjects: Medicine, dentistry. Holdings: 3503 books; 13,202 bound periodical volumes. Subscriptions: 377 journals and other serials. Services: Interlibrary loans; copying; SDI; library open to medical and paramedical personnel only.

★1074★
BALTIMORE CITY PUBLIC SCHOOLS - PROFESSIONAL MEDIA CENTER (Educ)†
181 North Bend Rd.   Phone: (301) 396-5348
Baltimore, MD 21229   Jacqueline M. Merchant, Libn.
Staff: Prof 1. Subjects: Education. Holdings: 7000 books; 14 VF drawers. Subscriptions: 250 journals and other serials; 70 on microfilm. Services: Interlibrary loans; copying; SDI; library open to public for reference use only.

★1075★
BALTIMORE COUNTY CIRCUIT COURT - LAW DEPARTMENT LIBRARY (Law)†
401 Bosley Ave.   Phone: (301) 494-2621
Towson, MD 21204   Douglas T. Skeen, Ct.Libn.
Subjects: Law. Holdings: 20,000 volumes. Subscriptions: 32 journals and other serials. Services: Copying; library not open to public.

★1076★
BALTIMORE COUNTY GENERAL HOSPITAL - HEALTH SCIENCES LIBRARY (Med)
5401 Old Court Rd.   Phone: (301) 521-2200
Randallstown, MD 21133   Bettie S. Holmes, Libn.
Founded: 1969. Staff: Prof 2; Other 1. Subjects: Medicine, surgery, nursing, management, oncology. Holdings: 1000 books; 500 bound periodical volumes: 3 shelves of college catalogs and miscellanea. Subscriptions: 125 journals and other serials. Services: Interlibrary loans; copying; LATCH; literature searches; library open to public with permission. Networks/

Consortia: Member of Maryland Health Care Systems, Inc. Publications: Newsletter, monthly - to physicians and nurses.

★1077★
BALTIMORE - DEPARTMENT OF LEGISLATIVE REFERENCE - LIBRARY (Soc Sci)†
90 State Circle   Phone: (301) 396-4733
Baltimore, MD 21401   Bernard F. Murphy, Dir.
Founded: 1907. Staff: Prof 5; Other 5. Subjects: Baltimore ordinances, ordinances of other cities, state and municipal codes, municipal planning, welfare, social services, housing, community development. Holdings: 23,940 books; 1715 bound periodical volumes; 35 drawers of clippings on local items, elections and referenda; 10 drawers of biographies; 125 drawers of municipal documents and reports; 85 drawers of proceedings, ordinances and resolutions. Subscriptions: 104 journals and other serials; 8 newspapers. Services: Copying. Publications: Bulletin, bimonthly; Municipal Handbook; Annual Report. Special Catalogs: Catalog of City Charter, City Code, Ordinances and Resolutions (card). Staff: Barry E. Boston, Principal Libn.

BALTIMORE ECONOMIC DEVELOPMENT CORPORATION
See: Baltimore Briefing Center

★1078★
BALTIMORE GAS AND ELECTRIC COMPANY - LIBRARY (Energy)
2nd Fl., Monument St. Warehouse
Box 1475
Baltimore, MD 21203   Phone: (301) 234-6292
                         Agnes M. Lindemon, Libn.
Staff: Prof 1; Other 2. Subjects: Public utilities. Special Collections: Maryland Geological Survey Bulletins; annual reports of utilities and other companies. Holdings: 3100 books; 328 bound periodical volumes; 60 VF drawers of technical reports, pamphlets and clippings. Subscriptions: 134 journals and other serials. Services: Library not open to public. Computerized Information Services: DIALOG. Staff: Joan S. Bonomolo, Asst.Libn.

★1079★
BALTIMORE HEBREW COLLEGE - JOSEPH MEYERHOFF LIBRARY (Rel-Theol)
5800 Park Heights Ave.   Phone: (301) 466-7900
Baltimore, MD 21215   Dr. Jesse Mashbaum, Dir.
Founded: 1919. Staff: Prof 2; Other 3. Subjects: Jewish studies, modern Middle East, religion. Special Collections: Rare book collection (600 volumes). Holdings: 40,000 books; 5000 bound periodical volumes; 3000 microforms; 8 VF drawers. Subscriptions: 240 journals and other serials; 20 newspapers. Services: Interlibrary loans; copying; library open to public. Staff: Elaine Mael, Asst.Libn.

BALTIMORE MEDICAL CENTER
See: Greater Baltimore Medical Center

BALTIMORE MUNICIPAL MUSEUM
See: Peale Museum

★1080★
BALTIMORE MUSEUM OF ART - REFERENCE LIBRARY (Art)
Art Museum Dr.   Phone: (301) 396-6317
Baltimore, MD 21218   Anita Gilden, Libn.
Founded: 1930. Staff: Prof 2; Other 1. Subjects: History of art, 19th and 20th century painting and sculpture, American decorative arts, graphic arts. Holdings: 25,000 books; 2000 bound periodical volumes; 160 drawers of exhibition catalogs, annual reports, bulletins. Subscriptions: 90 journals and other serials. Services: Interlibrary loans; copying; library open to public by appointment. Staff: Pat Lynagh, Asst.Libn.

★1081★
BALTIMORE NEWS AMERICAN LIBRARY (Publ)
Lombard & South Sts.   Phone: (301) 752-1212
Baltimore, MD 21203   Clark F. Ickes, Hd.Libn.
Founded: 1902. Staff: 2. Subjects: Newspaper reference topics. Special Collections: Chronology of Maryland historic events. Holdings: 2038 books; 3.5 million newspaper clippings and biographical sketches; 2000 reports and pamphlets; photographs and microfilm. Subscriptions: 10 journals and other serials. Services: Library open to public for serious research by appointment.

BALTIMORE REGION INSTITUTIONAL STUDIES CENTER
See: University of Baltimore

BALTIMORE SUNPAPERS
See: Abell (A.S.) Publishing Company Inc.

★1082★
BALTIMORE ZOO - ARTHUR R. WATSON LIBRARY (Sci-Tech)
Druid Hill Pk.   Phone: (301) 396-7102
Baltimore, MD 21217   Ethel R. Hardee, Libn.
Founded: 1980. **Staff:** Prof 1; Other 3. **Subjects:** General zoology,
ornithology, herpetology, mammalogy, ecology, natural history. **Holdings:**
1000 volumes; 4 VF drawers of journal reprints, dissertations, clippings and
pamphlets; 2 VF drawers of photographs, clippings and other graphic materials
of animals. **Subscriptions:** 120 journals and other serials. **Services:** Copying;
library open to public for reference use only. **Publications:** Serials holding list -
free upon request.

★1083★
BALZEKAS MUSEUM OF LITHUANIAN CULTURE - RESEARCH LIBRARY
   (Area-Ethnic)
4012 Archer Ave.   Phone: (312) 847-2441
Chicago, IL 60632   Jurgis Kasakaitis, Hd.Libn.
Founded: 1966. **Staff:** Prof 1. **Subjects:** Eastern European history,
Lithuanian culture, numismatics, philately, fiction. **Special Collections:**
Eastern European genealogy and heraldry; rare books on Eastern European
history dating back to the 16th century; rare maps of Eastern Europe.
Holdings: 20,000 books; 1500 bound periodical volumes; 800 catalogs; 200
maps; 25 reels of microfilm. **Subscriptions:** 30 journals and other serials; 10
newspapers. **Services:** Interlibrary loans; library open to members only.
Computerized Information Services: Computerized cataloging.
Publications: Lithuanian Museum Review, bimonthly - to members and
donors; Bibliography of Lithuanian Folk Art and Customs. **Special Catalogs:**
Lithuanian Artists. **Remarks:** Museum includes a children's museum. **Staff:**
Stanley Balzekas, Jr., Pres.

★1084★
BANCROFT, AVERY AND MC ALISTER - LAW LIBRARY (Law)
601 Montgomery St., Suite 900   Phone: (415) 788-8855
San Francisco, CA 94111   Diane Huijgen, Dir., Lib.Serv.
Staff: Prof 3; Other 1. **Subjects:** Law - U.S., California, estate planning, tax,
business. **Holdings:** 33,000 books; 720 bound periodical volumes; 600 tapes
(cataloged). **Subscriptions:** 530 journals and other serials; 5 newspapers.
Services: Interlibrary loans; library open to public with special permission.
Staff: Michaele Lee Huygen, Ref.Libn.; Barbara Ahrens, Res.Libn.

BANCROFT LIBRARY
See: University of California, Berkeley

BANCROFT PRE-RAPHAELITE LIBRARY
See: Delaware Art Museum

★1085★
BANCROFT-WHITNEY COMPANY - EDITORIAL LIBRARY (Publ)
301 Brannan St.   Phone: (415) 986-4410
San Francisco, CA 94107   Phyllis M. Ross, Libn.
Founded: 1855. **Staff:** 7. **Subjects:** Law, state laws and medico-legal
material. **Holdings:** 175,000 books; 2000 bound periodical volumes.
Subscriptions: 100 journals and other serials; 10 newspapers.

BANDELIER NATL. MONUMENT
See: U.S. Natl. Park Service

★1086★
BANFF CENTRE FOR CONTINUING EDUCATION - SCHOOL OF FINE ARTS -
   LIBRARY (Art)
Box 1020   Phone: (403) 762-6265
Banff, AB, Canada T0L 0C0   Bob Foley, Libn.
Founded: 1980. **Staff:** Prof 2; Other 6. **Subjects:** Music, visual arts,
performing arts, theatre crafts and design. **Holdings:** 12,000 books and
scores; 150 bound periodical volumes; 10,000 slides; 1000 audiotapes;
2000 phonograph records. **Subscriptions:** 223 journals and other serials.
Services: Interlibrary loans; copying; library open to public with restrictions.

★1087★
BANGOR MENTAL HEALTH INSTITUTE - HEALTH SCIENCES MEDIA
   CENTER (Med)
Box 926   Phone: (207) 947-6981
Bangor, ME 04401   Wendy E. Troiano, Libn.
Staff: Prof 1; Other 1. **Subjects:** Psychiatry, psychology, mental health
services, medicine. **Holdings:** 1500 books; 8 drawers of pamphlets; 150 AV
items. **Subscriptions:** 80 journals and other serials. **Services:** Interlibrary
loans; copying; library open to public with restrictions. **Computerized
Information Services:** DIALOG. **Networks/Consortia:** Member of Health
Sciences Library and Information Cooperative of Maine (HSLIC); New England

Regional Medical Library Service (NERMLS); Five County Hospital Consortium.
Remarks: Bangor Mental Health Institute is a state psychiatric hospital.

★1088★
BANGOR THEOLOGICAL SEMINARY - MOULTON LIBRARY (Rel-Theol)
300 Union St.   Phone: (207) 942-6781
Bangor, ME 04401   Clifton Davis, Libn.
Staff: 2. **Subjects:** Maine church history, church history, biblical literature,
theology, philosophy. **Special Collections:** Rare theological volumes (350).
Holdings: 62,442 books; 8800 bound periodical volumes; 3000 manuscripts,
archives, and pamphlets. **Subscriptions:** 410 journals and other serials.
Services: Interlibrary loans; library open to public. **Staff:** S.A. Kaubris-
Kowalzyk, Asst.Libn.

★1089★
BANK OF AMERICA, NT & SA - LAW LIBRARY (Law)
Dept. 3220
Box 37000   Phone: (415) 622-6040
San Francisco, CA 94137   Sharon K. French, Libn.
Staff: Prof 2; Other 3. **Subjects:** Law. **Holdings:** 20,000 volumes.
Subscriptions: 200 journals and other serials; 5 newspapers. **Services:**
Interlibrary loans; SDI; library not open to public. **Computerized Information
Services:** Mead Data Central, New York Times Information Service;
computerized cataloging, acquisitions and serials. **Publications:** Daily Notes -
for internal distribution only. **Special Catalogs:** Online catalog.

★1090★
BANK OF AMERICA, NT & SA - REFERENCE LIBRARY (Bus-Fin)
555 California St.
Box 37000   Phone: (415) 622-2068
San Francisco, CA 94137   Marydee Ojala, Lib.Mgr.
Founded: 1921. **Staff:** Prof 4; Other 4. **Subjects:** Banking, economics,
foreign trade, international business, agriculture. **Special Collections:** Foreign
government and bank reports. **Holdings:** 6500 books; 286 bound periodical
volumes; 19,000 pamphlets (cataloged). **Subscriptions:** 1300 journals and
other serials; 24 newspapers. **Services:** Interlibrary loans; copying; library
open to public with restrictions. **Computerized Information Services:**
DIALOG, SDC, New York Times Information Service, Dow Jones News
Retrieval. **Publications:** Selected Additions to the Reference Library, monthly
- available on request to libraries. **Staff:** Janet Baker, Libn.; Jay Smith, Libn.;
Patricia Wong, Libn.

★1091★
BANK OF AMERICA - SOUTHERN CALIFORNIA HEADQUARTERS - LAW
   LIBRARY NO. 4017 (Law)
555 S. Flower St.   Phone: (213) 683-3101
Los Angeles, CA 90071   Kathleen G. Slattery, Law Libn.
Staff: Prof 1; Other 1. **Subjects:** Banking law, California law. **Holdings:**
18,000 books; 1000 bound periodical volumes; 100 audio cassettes.
Subscriptions: 100 journals and other serials; 5 newspapers. **Services:**
Interlibrary loans; copying; SDI. **Computerized Information Services:** LEXIS;
New York Times Information Service; computerized cataloging and serials.

★1092★
BANK OF AMERICA - SYSTEMS LIBRARY - 3099 B (Sci-Tech)
1455 Market St., 18th Fl.   Phone: (415) 953-2375
San Francisco, CA 94137   Jeannette E. Glynn, Supv.
Staff: Prof 2; Other 2. **Subjects:** Data processing, software engineering,
telecommunications, programming, systems analysis. **Holdings:** 600 books;
800 vendor manuals; 100 videotapes. **Subscriptions:** 80 journals and other
serials. **Services:** Interlibrary loans; SDI; library not open to public. **Staff:** Paul
Reist, Coll.Dev.Libn.

★1093★
BANK OF CALIFORNIA - BUSINESS RESEARCH LIBRARY
400 California St.
San Francisco, CA 94145
Defunct

★1094★
BANK OF CANADA - LIBRARY (Bus-Fin)
245 Sparks St.   Phone: (613) 563-8201
Ottawa, ON, Canada K1A 0G9   Jane E. King, Chf.Libn.
Founded: 1935. **Staff:** Prof 7; Other 19. **Subjects:** Banking, finance,
economic conditions, international finance. **Holdings:** Figures not available.
Subscriptions: 2000 journals and other serials; 50 newspapers. **Services:**
Interlibrary loans; library open to public for reference use only. **Computerized
Information Services:** DIALOG, SDC, Info Globe, QL Systems, CAN/OLE;
computerized serials. **Staff:** Jacqueline Woods, Dp.Chf.Libn.

★1095★

BANK OF HAWAII - INFORMATION CENTER (Bus-Fin)
Financial Plaza Tower Bldg., 20th Fl.
Box 2900   Phone: (808) 537-8375
Honolulu, HI 96846   Sally Campbell, Info.Mgr.
Founded: 1968. **Staff:** Prof 2. **Subjects:** Economics, business statistics, finance and banking, visitor industry, construction, demography, domestic and foreign trade. **Special Collections:** Business and economic development surveys of Hawaii, Pacific Islands. **Holdings:** 1500 books and pamphlets; 24 VF drawers of newspaper clippings. **Subscriptions:** 550 journals and other serials. **Services:** Interlibrary loans; copying; library open to public for reference use only. **Computerized Information Services:** Computerized serials. **Publications:** What's New in the Information Center, bimonthly - for internal distribution only. **Staff:** Elaine Schultz, Info.Spec.

★1096★

BANK MARKETING ASSOCIATION - INFORMATION CENTER (Bus-Fin)
309 W. Washington St.   Phone: (312) 782-1442
Chicago, IL 60606   Bonnie Wang, V.P./Dir., Info.Serv.
Staff: Prof 4; Other 4. **Subjects:** Banking, marketing, sales, training, advertising. **Special Collections:** Golden Coin Competition Entries (750); School of Bank Marketing project reports (1200). **Holdings:** 4000 books; 1300 theses (cataloged); 1000 subject files of clippings and advertisements (cataloged). **Subscriptions:** 225 journals and other serials. **Services:** Interlibrary loans (limited); copying; library open to BMA members only. **Computerized Information Services:** DIALOG, SDC; computerized cataloging. **Networks/Consortia:** Member of OCLC. **Publications:** IC News, bimonthly - to all members of BMA. **Staff:** Cynthia Porter, V.P., Info.Serv.

★1097★

BANK OF MONTREAL - HEAD OFFICE LIBRARY (Bus-Fin)
Postal Sta. A., P.O. Box 6002   Phone: (514) 877-6890
Montreal, PQ, Canada H3C 3B1   Nancy C. Leclerc, Mgr./Chf.Libn.
Staff: Prof 3; Other 6. **Subjects:** Management, management education, human resources, banks and banking, economics, finance. **Special Collections:** Annual reports (internal use only). **Holdings:** 22,000 volumes; 72 VF drawers of clippings and reports. **Subscriptions:** 1400 journals and other serials; 31 newspapers. **Services:** Interlibrary loans; library open to public for reference use only. **Computerized Information Services:** DIALOG, SDC, QL Systems, Info Globe, FRI Information Services Ltd., Textline; computerized serials. **Publications:** Accession list, monthly; listing of corporate information and annual reports, semiannual. **Remarks:** Library located at 129 St. James St., W., Montreal, PQ H2Y 1L6. **Staff:** Richard Orlando, Res.Libn.; Mary McPhaden, Circ. & ILL; Ruth Ludwig, Per.Asst.; Rosalie Kaushansky, Cat./Sys.Libn..

★1098★

BANK OF MONTREAL - OPERATIONS & SYSTEMS LIBRARY (Bus-Fin)
Box 6002   Phone: (514) 877-8235
Montreal, PQ, Canada H3C 3B1   Sylvia E.A. Piggott, Tech.Libn.
Staff: 3. **Subjects:** Computer and data processing. **Holdings:** 500 books. **Subscriptions:** 69 journals and other serials. **Services:** Interlibrary loans; copying; library not open to public.

★1099★

BANK OF MONTREAL - TECHNICAL INFORMATION CENTRE (Bus-Fin)
Box 7000   Phone: (416) 498-8800
Scarborough, ON, Canada M1S 4M5   Carol M. Diakun, Mgr., Tech.Info.Serv.
Staff: Prof 3; Other 5. **Subjects:** Data processing, management, office automation, banking, communications. **Holdings:** 1000 books; 25 bound periodical volumes; 1500 technical reports and articles; 2500 IBM manuals; 500 hardware and software manuals; 1000 systems documentation items; internal bank project documents. **Subscriptions:** 210 journals and other serials; 5 newspapers. **Services:** Interlibrary loans; SDI (both limited); centre not open to public. **Computerized Information Services:** SDC; computerized cataloging. **Publications:** Newsletter, monthly. **Staff:** Janice Reynolds, Tech.Libn.; Sylvia Piggott, Tech.Libn.

★1100★

BANK OF MONTREAL - TECHNICAL INFORMATION CENTRE (Bus-Fin)
245 Consumers Rd.   Phone: (416) 493-2440
Willowdale, ON, Canada M2J 1S2   Janice Reynolds, Tech.Libn.
Staff: Prof 1; Other 2. **Subjects:** Computer operations, online banking, performance measurement and evaluation. **Special Collections:** Banking Online System Technical Specifications (1300 unbound reports). **Holdings:** 400 books; 1300 IBM manuals; 24 VF drawers of technical specifications. **Subscriptions:** 113 journals and other serials; 5 newspapers. **Services:** Interlibrary loans; SDI; library not open to public. **Computerized Information Services:** SDC; computerized indexing. **Publications:** Technical Information

Centre Newsletter, monthly. **Special Indexes:** KWOC index to IBM manuals, books, Bank of Montreal manuals, VF material, technical reports.

★1101★

BANK OF NEW ENGLAND - LIBRARY (Bus-Fin)
128 State St.   Phone: (617) 742-4000
Boston, MA 02106   Helen Mazareas, Libn.
Founded: 1965. **Staff:** Prof 1; Other 1. **Subjects:** Banking, management, business, marketing, economic conditions. **Special Collections:** Theses from Stonier Graduate School of Banking and Pacific Coast Banking School. **Holdings:** 3500 books; 14 VF drawers of industry related clippings; 12 VF drawers of business subject clippings; statistical newsletters and microfiche; 250 theses. **Subscriptions:** 200 journals and other serials; 8 newspapers. **Services:** Interlibrary loans; copying; library open to public. **Publications:** Recent Acquisitions List, monthly; Tuesday Sheet, weekly - both for internal distribution only. **Formerly:** New England Merchants National Bank.

★1102★

BANK OF NOVA SCOTIA - LIBRARY (Bus-Fin)
44 King St., W.   Phone: (416) 866-6257
Toronto, ON, Canada M5H 1H1   Beverley Kent, Chf.Libn.
Founded: 1951. **Staff:** Prof 3; Other 4. **Subjects:** Banking, finance, economics, business, Canadian industry. **Special Collections:** Foreign bank publications; Statistics Canada publications. **Holdings:** 12,000 books; 200 subject files. **Subscriptions:** 1000 journals and other serials; 40 newspapers. **Services:** Interlibrary loans; copying; library open to public by appointment for unique material only. **Computerized Information Services:** SDC, Info Globe, New York Times Information Service. **Publications:** Library bulletin, irregular - for internal distribution only. **Special Indexes:** Index of selected periodical articles (card). **Staff:** Hilary Meredith, Ref.Libn.; Barbara Neumann, Cat.

★1103★

BANK OF NOVA SCOTIA - OPERATIONS LIBRARY (Bus-Fin)
10 Gateway Blvd.   Phone: (416) 424-3551
Don Mills, ON, Canada M3C 3A1   Cathy Kealey, Sys.Libn.
Founded: 1972. **Staff:** Prof 1; Other 1. **Subjects:** Data processing, computers, banking. **Holdings:** 1000 books; 800 IBM reference manuals. **Subscriptions:** 105 journals and other serials; 10 newspapers. **Services:** Interlibrary loans; copying; library open to public by appointment. **Computerized Information Services:** Computerized acquisitions, serials and circulation.

★1104★

BANK STREET COLLEGE OF EDUCATION - LIBRARY (Educ)
610 W. 112 St.   Phone: (212) 663-7200
New York, NY 10025   Eleanor Kulleseid, Lib.Dir.
Founded: 1915. **Staff:** Prof 7; Other 3. **Subjects:** Child development, early childhood education, elementary education, elementary and secondary guidance, psychology, sociology, children's literature, elementary curriculum materials. **Holdings:** 92,000 books; 165,000 research reports on microfiche. **Subscriptions:** 700 journals and other serials. **Services:** Interlibrary loans; copying; library open to public for reference or by payment of fee for full privileges. **Networks/Consortia:** Member of METRO. **Staff:** Lelita Jaspal, Ref.Libn.

BANKAMERICA CORPORATION - BA INVESTMENT MANAGEMENT CORPORATION
See: BA Investment Management Corporation

★1105★

BANKERS LIFE & CASUALTY COMPANY - MARKETING INFORMATION DEPARTMENT - LIBRARY (Bus-Fin)
4444 W. Lawrence Ave.   Phone: (312) 777-7000
Chicago, IL 60630   William B. Grow, Marketing Anl.
Staff: Prof 1. **Subjects:** Health insurance. **Special Collections:** Internal reports (microfiche). **Holdings:** 600 books; 2600 marketing surveys and projects; 200 competitive company comparisons. **Subscriptions:** 41 journals and other serials. **Services:** Library open to public. **Computerized Information Services:** Internal database; computerized cataloging. **Special Indexes:** Health Insurance Research Data Bank; Competitive Companies Information File.

BANKS AFRO-AMERICAN HERITAGE COLLECTION
See: Bishop College - Zale Library

BANKS (Daniel T.) HEALTH SCIENCE LIBRARY
See: St. Vincent's Medical Center - Daniel T. Banks Health Science Library

BANKS (W.R.) LIBRARY
See: Prairie View A & M College of Texas - W.R. Banks Library

BANNON HEALTH SCIENCE LIBRARY
See: St. Elizabeth Hospital Medical Center

BANQUE DU CANADA
See: Bank of Canada

BANQUE DE MONTREAL
See: Bank of Montreal

★1106★
BANTAM BOOKS, INC. - LIBRARY
666 Fifth Ave.
New York, NY 10019
Defunct

★1107★
BAPTIST BIBLE COLLEGE OF PENNSYLVANIA - RICHARD J. MURPHY MEMORIAL LIBRARY (Rel-Theol)
538 Venard Rd.   Phone: (717) 587-1172
Clarks Summit, PA 18411   David C. McClain, Hd.Libn.
Founded: 1932. Staff: Prof 3; Other 10. Subjects: Bible and theology; Christian education; church history; church ministries; music. Holdings: 68,169 books; 2479 bound periodical volumes; 39 VF drawers of pamphlets and clippings; 3100 microforms; 3206 phonograph records and cassette tapes; 1319 filmstrips; 686 music scores; 6412 pictures; 661 transparencies. Subscriptions: 469 journals and other serials. Services: Interlibrary loans; copying; SDI; library open to public with special permission. Staff: Margaretta Grosjean, Cat.Libn.; Richard Erickson, Dir. of IMC.

★1108★
BAPTIST BIBLE COLLEGE - VICK MEMORIAL LIBRARY (Rel-Theol)
628 E. Kearney St.   Phone: (417) 869-4130
Springfield, MO 65802   Ronald L. Walker, Dir.
Staff: Prof 1; Other 15. Subjects: Bible, theology. Holdings: 29,875 books; 938 bound periodical volumes; 2328 theses; 27,574 nonbook items. Services: Interlibrary loans; copying; library open to public. Computerized Information Services: Computerized cataloging. Networks/Consortia: Member of Bibliographical Center for Research, Rocky Mountain Region, Inc. (BCR).

★1109★
BAPTIST BIBLE INSTITUTE - IDA J. MC MILLAN LIBRARY (Rel-Theol)
1306 College Dr.   Phone: (904) 263-3261
Graceville, FL 32440   Professor William D, Jones, Libn.
Founded: 1968. Staff: Prof 1; Other 8. Subjects: Religion, Christian education, church music, marriage, ethics, philosophy. Holdings: 33,450 books; 1374 bound periodical volumes. Subscriptions: 291 journals and other serials. Services: Interlibrary loans; copying; library open to public.

★1110★
BAPTIST CONVENTION OF ONTARIO AND QUEBEC - CANADIAN BAPTIST ARCHIVES (Rel-Theol)
McMaster Divinity College   Phone: (416) 525-9140
Hamilton, ON, Canada L8S 4K1   Judith Colwell, Libn.
Founded: 1865. Staff: Prof 2. Subjects: Canadian Baptists in Ontario, Quebec and Western Canada. Special Collections: Plymouth Brethren; French Canadian Protestants; biographical material for prominent Canadian Baptists (29 shelves); McMaster University Archives (to 1957). Holdings: 208 shelves of books and bound periodical volumes; 700 shelves of church and denominational records; 125 shelves of Canadian Baptist educational records; 20 shelves of pamphlets; 46 VF drawers of clippings, photographs and historical sketches. Subscriptions: 35 journals and other serials. Services: Copying; library open to public with restrictions. Staff: Kim Hanville, Asst.Libn.

★1111★
BAPTIST GENERAL CONFERENCE - ARCHIVES (Rel-Theol)
3949 Bethel Dr.   Phone: (612) 638-6282
St. Paul, MN 55112   G. David Guston, Archv.
Staff: Prof 1. Subjects: Archives of Baptist General Conference and its antecedent, Swedish Baptist General Conference; Bethel College and Seminary Archives. Holdings: 1000 books; 425 bound periodical volumes; 48 VF drawers of correspondence; 40 VF drawers of biography and history; 200 reels of audiotapes; 75 reels of microfilm; pictures and slides. Services: Copying; archives open to public. Remarks: Housed in the Bethel Theological Seminary Library. An alternate telephone number is (612) 638-6184.

★1112★
BAPTIST HOSPITAL - LIBRARY (Med)
2000 Church St.   Phone: (615) 329-5373
Nashville, TN 37236   Vickie A. Overstreet, Med.Libn.
Staff: Prof 1. Subjects: Medicine, nursing, allied health sciences. Holdings: 4598 books; 3883 bound periodical volumes; 1543 cataloged pamphlets; clippings; anatomy charts and models; 464 tapes and slides. Subscriptions: 154 journals and other serials. Services: Interlibrary loans (fee); copying; library open to public for reference use only. Computerized Information Services: Internal database. Networks/Consortia: Member of Mid-Tennessee Health Science Librarians. Publications: Newsletter. quarterly - for internal distribution only.

★1113★
BAPTIST HOSPITAL - MEDICAL LIBRARY (Med)
1000 W. Moreno   Phone: (904) 434-4877
Pensacola, FL 32501   Ellen Richbourg, Libn.
Founded: 1959. Staff: Prof 1. Subjects: Medicine. Special Collections: Merle Wilkins Education Resource Center (190 volumes). Holdings: 500 books; 4000 bound periodical volumes; 260 video cassettes. Subscriptions: 85 journals and other serials. Services: Interlibrary loans; copying; library open to public with restrictions. Networks/Consortia: Member of Southeastern Regional Medical Library Program (SERMLP); Coordinated Services Program (CSP).

★1114★
BAPTIST HOSPITAL OF MIAMI - HEALTH SCIENCES LIBRARY (Med)
8900 S.W. 88th St.   Phone: (305) 596-1960
Miami, FL 33176   Diane F. Ream, Dir.,Health Sci.Lib.Serv.
Founded: 1965. Staff: Prof 1; Other 3. Subjects: Medicine, nursing and allied health sciences, hospital administration, consumer health. Holdings: 550 books; 1800 bound periodical volumes; 2 VF drawers of pamphlets, reprints, and clippings; 5500 slides; 500 audio cassettes. Subscriptions: 117 journals and other serials. Services: Interlibrary loans; copying; library open to nursing students. Computerized Information Services: BRS; internal database; computerized cataloging and circulation. Networks/Consortia: Member of Miami Health Sciences Library Consortium; SOLINET. Publications: Library Letter, semiannual.

★1115★
BAPTIST HOSPITAL OF SOUTHEAST TEXAS - MEDICAL LIBRARY (Med)
Box 1591   Phone: (713) 839-5160
Beaumont, TX 77704   Deloris Blake, Med.Libn.
Founded: 1962. Staff: Prof 1. Subjects: Nursing, health administration, medicine, surgery, obstetrics, pediatrics. Holdings: 5539 books; 1296 bound periodical volumes; 2 VF drawers of pamphlets; 569 Audio-Digest tapes; 13 films; 101 files of clippings. Subscriptions: 80 journals and other serials. Services: Interlibrary loans; copying (fee); library open to public with restrictions.

★1116★
BAPTIST MEDICAL CENTER - AMELIA WHITE PITTS MEMORIAL LIBRARY (Med)
Taylor at Marion St.   Phone: (803) 771-5281
Columbia, SC 29220   Lois W. Smith, Libn.
Founded: 1954. Staff: Prof 1. Subjects: Nursing, medicine, pharmacology, pastoral care, respiratory therapy, hospital administration. Holdings: 4000 books; 100 bound periodical volumes; 20 VF drawers of clippings and pamphlets; masters' theses. Subscriptions: 115 journals and other serials. Services: Interlibrary loans; copying; library open to public with restrictions; reference assistance and orientation to nursing and allied health students. Networks/Consortia: Member of Columbia Area Medical Library Association.

★1117★
BAPTIST MEDICAL CENTER - MEDICAL LIBRARY (Med)
701 Princeton Ave., S.W.   Phone: (205) 783-3078
Birmingham, AL 35211   Romilda F. Cook, Med.Libn.
Founded: 1942. Staff: Prof 1; Other 2. Subjects: Medicine and allied health sciences; hospital administration. Holdings: 2014 books; 5800 bound periodical volumes; 300 tapes. Subscriptions: 137 journals and other serials. Services: Interlibrary loans; copying; library open to public with administrative approval. Networks/Consortia: Member of Southeastern Regional Medical Library Program (SERMLP); Alabama Health Libraries Association. Also Known As: Clyde L. Sibley Medical Library.

★1118★
BAPTIST MEDICAL CENTER - MEDICAL LIBRARY (Med)†
2105 East South Blvd.   Phone: (205) 288-2100
Montgomery, AL 36198   Ruth Steffen, Libn.
Staff: Prof 1. **Subjects:** Medicine, nursing and allied health sciences. **Holdings:** 941 books; 522 bound periodical volumes. **Subscriptions:** 73 journals and other serials. **Services:** Interlibrary loans; copying; library open to public for reference use only. **Computerized Information Services:** MEDLINE.

★1119★
BAPTIST MEDICAL CENTER SYSTEM - CENTRAL BAPTIST HOSPITAL LIBRARY (Med)
12th & Marshall   Phone: (501) 227-3235
Little Rock, AR 72202   Mrs. Theo H. Storey, Libn.
Staff: 3. **Subjects:** Medicine, nursing, physical and occupational therapy, education, religion. **Holdings:** 7600 books; 600 bound periodical volumes. **Subscriptions:** 213 journals and other serials. **Services:** Interlibrary loans; copying; library open to public for reference use only.

★1120★
BAPTIST MEDICAL CENTER SYSTEM - MARGARET CLARK GILBREATH MEMORIAL LIBRARY (Med)
9600 W. 12th St.   Phone: (501) 227-2671
Little Rock, AR 72201   Auburn Steward, Libn.
Founded: 1974. **Staff:** Prof 1; Other 1. **Subjects:** Nursing, medicine. **Holdings:** 1350 books; 2400 bound periodical volumes. **Subscriptions:** 241 journals and other serials. **Services:** Interlibrary loans; library open to nursing students of the University of Central Arkansas, Harding College, Henderson State College and medical students from the University of Arkansas Medical Sciences Campus.

★1121★
BAPTIST MEDICAL CENTER - WANN LANGSTON MEMORIAL LIBRARY (Med)
3300 Northwest Expy.   Phone: (405) 949-3766
Oklahoma City, OK 73112   Phyllis Bennett, Dir., Med.Lib.
Founded: 1968. **Staff:** Prof 1; Other 2. **Subjects:** Medicine, nursing, hospital management. **Holdings:** 2200 books; 2580 bound periodical volumes; 1000 audiotapes. **Subscriptions:** 184 journals and other serials. **Services:** Interlibrary loans; copying; library open to public with permission of librarian. **Computerized Information Services:** MEDLINE. **Networks/Consortia:** Member of GOAL Consortium.

★1122★
BAPTIST MEDICAL CENTERS-SAMFORD UNIVERSITY - IDA V. MOFFETT SCHOOL OF NURSING - L.R. JORDAN LIBRARY (Med)
820 Montclair Rd.   Phone: (205) 591-2371
Birmingham, AL 35213   Jewell Alexander Carter, Lib.Dir.
Founded: 1922. **Staff:** Prof 2; Other 8. **Subjects:** Nursing; allied health sciences. **Special Collections:** Nursing Historical Collection. **Holdings:** 7073 books; 1533 bound periodical volumes; 420 VF folders; 200 unbound reports; 1342 AV items. **Subscriptions:** 115 journals and other serials. **Services:** Interlibrary loans; copying; library open to public for reference use only. **Staff:** Patty P. Grissett, Tech.Serv.Libn.

★1123★
BAPTIST MEMORIAL HOSPITAL - JOHN L. MC GEHEE LIBRARY (Med)
899 Madison Ave.   Phone: (901) 522-5140
Memphis, TN 38146   Donna L. Davis, Med.Libn.
Staff: Prof 1; Other 3. **Subjects:** Medicine. **Holdings:** 1000 books; 4500 bound periodical volumes; 535 volumes of journals on microfiche; 1500 Audio-Digest tapes. **Subscriptions:** 167 journals and other serials. **Services:** Interlibrary loans; copying; library not open to public. **Computerized Information Services:** MEDLINE. **Networks/Consortia:** Member of Association of Memphis Area Health Science Libraries; Tennessee Health Science Library Association.

★1124★
BAPTIST MEMORIAL HOSPITAL - LEARNING RESOURCES CENTER (Med)
6601 Rockhill Road   Phone: (816) 361-3500
Kansas City, MO 64131   Barbara Seiglar, Dir.
Staff: Prof 1; Other 3. **Subjects:** Health sciences. **Holdings:** 6500 books; 3500 bound periodical volumes; 10 VF drawers of pamphlets. **Subscriptions:** 270 journals and other serials; 10 newspapers. **Services:** Interlibrary loans; copying; library open to public with restrictions. **Computerized Information Services:** DIALOG, NLM. **Networks/Consortia:** Member of Kansas City Library Network, Inc.

★1125★
BAPTIST MEMORIAL HOSPITAL - MEDICAL LIBRARY (Med)
1007 Goodyear Ave.   Phone: (205) 492-1240
Gadsden, AL 35903   Rebecca S. Buckner, Med.Libn.
Staff: Prof 1; Other 1. **Subjects:** Medicine, nursing, surgery, obstetrics and gynecology. **Holdings:** 1350 books; 712 bound periodical volumes. **Subscriptions:** 100 journals and other serials. **Services:** Library not open to public.

★1126★
BAPTIST MEMORIAL HOSPITAL - SCHOOL OF NURSING - LIBRARY (Med)
999 Monroe   Phone: (901) 522-4309
Memphis, TN 38104   Sherry Young, Libn.
Founded: 1920. **Staff:** Prof 1. **Subjects:** Nursing and related medical sciences. **Special Collections:** First editions. **Holdings:** 4950 books; 269 bound periodical volumes; 1 VF drawer of clippings and pamphlets; 45 anatomical maps and charts; 225 slides. **Subscriptions:** 42 journals and other serials. **Services:** Interlibrary loans; copying; library open to public for reference use only. **Networks/Consortia:** Member of Memphis Area Health Science Libraries. **Staff:** Kathleen Meier, Libn.

★1127★
BAPTIST MEMORIAL HOSPITAL SYSTEM - BRUCE A. GARRETT MEMORIAL LIBRARY & MEDIA CENTER (Med)
111 Dallas St.   Phone: (512) 222-8431
San Antonio, TX 78286   Martha E. Knott, Chf.Libn.
Founded: 1968. **Staff:** Prof 1; Other 4. **Subjects:** Nursing and general medicine. **Holdings:** 3120 books; 376 bound periodical volumes. **Subscriptions:** 100 journals and other serials. **Services:** Interlibrary loans; copying; library open to public for reference use only. **Networks/Consortia:** Member of Health Oriented Libraries of San Antonio; TALON.

★1128★
BAPTIST MISSIONARY ASSOCIATION THEOLOGICAL SEMINARY - KELLAR LIBRARY (Rel-Theol)
1410 E. Pine St.
Box 1797   Phone: (214) 586-2501
Jacksonville, TX 75766   James C. Blaylock, Libn.
Founded: 1957. **Staff:** 4. **Subjects:** Religion, Bible and theology. **Special Collections:** Association and convention minutes (6710); Baptist history. **Holdings:** 27,227 books; 3892 bound periodical volumes; 235 reels of microfilm; 334 titles on microfiche; 1814 cassette tapes. **Subscriptions:** 916 journals and other serials. **Services:** Interlibrary loans; copying; library open to public.

BAPTIST SUNDAY SCHOOL BOARD - DARGAN-CARVER LIBRARY
See: Dargan-Carver Library

★1129★
BAR ASSOCIATION OF THE DISTRICT OF COLUMBIA - LIBRARY (Law)
3518 U.S. Court House Bldg.   Phone: (202) 535-3573
Washington, DC 22101   Elizabeth K. Van Horn, Libn.
Founded: 1875. **Staff:** Prof 3; Other 3. **Subjects:** Law. **Special Collections:** Briefs and records of the U.S. Court of Appeals, D.C. Circuit; publications of the D.C. Bar Association. **Holdings:** 50,000 volumes; 3600 bound periodical volumes; 6 VF drawers of pamphlets; 14 stacks of American Bar Association publications; legislative histories; codes and statutes; legal treaties. **Subscriptions:** 200 journals and other serials. **Services:** Copying; library open to public with restrictions. **Publications:** District of Columbia Bar Association Newsletter, monthly. **Staff:** Warren Juggins, Asst.Libn.

BAR OF MONTREAL
See: Barreau de Montreal

★1130★
BARBEAU, MC KERCHER, COLLINGWOOD & HANNA, BARRISTERS & SOLICITORS - LIBRARY (Law)
1106-1170 Harwood St.   Phone: (604) 688-9411
Vancouver, BC, Canada V6E 3X1   Johanna Sigurdson, Libn.
Staff: Prof 1; Other 1. **Subjects:** Law - corporate, tax, estate and trust, securities; litigation; business. **Holdings:** 200 books; 2000 bound periodical volumes; 55 loose-leaf services. **Subscriptions:** 78 journals and other serials. **Services:** Copying; SDI; library open to clients only. **Computerized Information Services:** QL Systems. **Publications:** Accessions list, bimonthly - for internal distribution only.

★1131★
BARBER (Richard J.) ASSOCIATES, INC. - LIBRARY (Trans)
1828 L St., N.W., Suite 406
Washington, DC 20036   Phone: (202) 785-0597
  Elizabeth Schomer, Chf.Libn.
Founded: 1972. **Staff:** Prof 9; Other 5. **Subjects:** Rail and other transportation, antitrust law, energy, urban affairs. **Holdings:** 2700 books; 75 bound periodical volumes; 60 other cataloged items. **Subscriptions:** 60 journals and other serials; 6 newspapers. **Services:** Interlibrary loans; copying; library not open to public. **Remarks:** Provides consultative services to Congress, other government agencies, and business.

★1132★
BARBERTON CITIZENS HOSPITAL - MEDICAL LIBRARY (Med)†
Tuscora Pk.   Phone: (216) 745-1611
Barberton, OH 44203   Helen Young, Adm.Coord.
Staff: 2. **Subjects:** Medicine. **Services:** Copying; library not open to public. **Remarks:** Alliance with Cleveland Health Sciences Library of Case Western Reserve University through services of circuit librarian.

BARBOUR (Clifford E.) LIBRARY
See: Pittsburgh Theological Seminary - Clifford E. Barbour Library

BARD LIBRARY
See: Community College of Baltimore

★1133★
BARIUM AND CHEMICALS, INC. - RESEARCH LIBRARY (Sci-Tech)†
County Rd. 44
Box 218
Steubenville, OH 43952   Phone: (614) 282-9776
  Eleanor R. Naylor, Libn.
Founded: 1947. **Staff:** 1. **Subjects:** Inorganic and organic chemicals, ores and mining, chemical engineering. **Holdings:** 1000 books; 3000 bound periodical volumes; 16 VF drawers of research reports, pamphlets and patents concerning alkaline earth compounds. **Services:** Library open to public with permission of management.

BARKER ENGINEERING LIBRARY
See: Massachusetts Institute of Technology

BARKER (Eugene C.) TEXAS HISTORY CENTER
See: University of Texas, Austin - Eugene C. Barker Texas History Center

BARKSDALE AIR FORCE BASE (LA)
See: U.S. Air Force Base - Barksdale Base Library

BARKSDALE MEDICAL LIBRARY AND SCHOOL OF NURSING LIBRARY
See: Virginia Baptist Hospital

★1134★
BARLOW HOSPITAL - ELKS LIBRARY (Med)
2000 Stadium Way   Phone: (213) 628-4165
Los Angeles, CA 90026   Rose Thompson, Libn.
Founded: 1946. **Staff:** Prof 1. **Subjects:** Tuberculosis and diseases of the chest. **Holdings:** 3000 volumes; 12,000 medical reprints. **Subscriptions:** 70 journals and other serials. **Services:** Interlibrary loans; library open to health professionals and students.

★1135★
BARNARD COLLEGE WOMEN'S CENTER - BIRDIE GOLDSMITH AST RESOURCE COLLECTION (Soc Sci)
100 Barnard Hall
3001 Broadway   Phone: (212) 280-2067
New York, NY 10027   Jane S. Gould, Dir., Women's Ctr.
Founded: 1971. **Staff:** Prof 3. **Subjects:** Sex roles and sex differences, women's movement, education, employment, legal status, health, violence and sexual exploitation. **Holdings:** 1000 volumes; 5000 journal articles, reports, clippings, fact sheets, pamphlets, conference proceedings, unpublished papers, government documents (in file boxes); bibliographies, handbooks, directories, special issues of journals. **Subscriptions:** 80 periodicals, newspapers and newsletters. **Services:** Collection open to public for reference use only. **Publications:** List of publications - available on request. **Staff:** Janie Kritzman, Assoc.Dir.; Maria La Sala, Asst.

BARNARD (Joseph F.) MEMORIAL LAW LIBRARY ASSOCIATION
See: New York State Supreme Court - 9th Judicial District - Joseph F. Barnard Memorial Law Library Association

BARNES ARCHIVES
See: Associated Spring Barnes Group, Inc.

★1136★
BARNES ENGINEERING COMPANY - LIBRARY (Sci-Tech)
30 Commerce Rd.   Phone: (203) 348-5381
Stamford, CT 06904   Belle B. Shipe, Libn.
Founded: 1959. **Staff:** 1. **Subjects:** Electro-optical instruments, physics, electronics, infrared components. **Holdings:** 2100 books; 225 bound periodical volumes; 1900 technical reports. **Subscriptions:** 35 journals and other serials. **Services:** Interlibrary loans (limited); copying; library open to public subject to security regulations. **Publications:** Library bulletin, monthly.

★1137★
BARNES HOSPITAL - SCHOOL OF NURSING LIBRARY & INSTRUCTIONAL RESOURCE LABORATORY (Med)
416 S. Kingshighway Blvd.   Phone: (314) 454-2554
St. Louis, MO 63110   Rosemary Buhr, Libn.
Founded: 1955. **Staff:** Prof 1; Other 3. **Subjects:** Nursing. **Holdings:** 4000 books; 300 bound periodical volumes; AV material (cataloged); 12 VF drawers. **Subscriptions:** 60 journals and other serials. **Services:** Copying; library not open to public. **Special Indexes:** Subject index of journals received that are not picked up in Current Index to Nursing Literature.

BARNETT-BRIGGS LIBRARY
See: San Francisco General Hospital Medical Center

BARNETT-HALL LIBRARY
See: Palo Alto Medical Foundation

BARON-FORNESS LIBRARY
See: Edinboro State College

★1138★
BAROQUE STRINGS OF VANCOUVER - LIBRARY (Mus)
104-1425 Esquimalt Ave.   Phone: (604) 922-4849
West Vancouver, BC, Canada V7T 1L1   Ronald L. Milne, Libn.
Staff: Prof 1. **Subjects:** Music. **Holdings:** 120 scores. **Services:** Library not open to public; some loans to educational institutions.

BARR (C.W.) PLANNING AND DESIGN LIBRARY
See: Michigan State University - C.W. Barr Planning and Design Library

★1139★
BARR ENGINEERING COMPANY - LIBRARY (Env-Cons)
6800 France Ave. S.   Phone: (612) 920-0655
Minneapolis, MN 55435   Francine Creme, Tech.Libn.
Founded: 1962. **Staff:** Prof 1. **Subjects:** Water resources, hydrology, hydraulics, soil mechanics, solid waste, environmental engineering. **Special Collections:** Company reports. **Holdings:** 2000 books; 115 bound periodical volumes; 400 government reports. **Subscriptions:** 85 journals and other serials. **Services:** Interlibrary loans; library not open to public. **Publications:** Library Bulletin, monthly.

BARR LIBRARY
See: Mary Holmes College

BARR (Robert N.) PUBLIC HEALTH LIBRARY
See: Minnesota State Department of Health - Robert N. Barr Public Health Library

★1140★
BARREAU DE MONTREAL - BIBLIOTHEQUE (Law)
Palais de Justice   Phone: (514) 873-3083
Montreal, PQ, Canada H2Y 1B6   Arthur Perrault, Libn.
Staff: Prof 2; Other 5. **Subjects:** Law. **Special Collections:** Canadiana. **Holdings:** 87,278 volumes. **Services:** Interlibrary loans; copying; library open to members of the Bar and judges. **Also Known As:** Bar of Montreal. **Staff:** Richard Dubuc, Assoc.Libn.

BARRETT-BYAM HOMESTEAD LIBRARY
See: Chelmsford Historical Society

BARRETT (Clifton Waller) LIBRARY
See: University of Virginia - Clifton Waller Barrett Library

BARRETT (Kim) MEMORIAL LIBRARY
See: Hospital for Special Surgery - Kim Barrett Memorial Library

★1141★
BARRETT SMITH SCHAPIRO SIMON & ARMSTRONG - LIBRARY (Law)
26 Broadway   Phone: (212) 422-8180
New York, NY 10004   Alice Arant-Cousins, Dir.
Staff: Prof 3; Other 2. **Subjects:** Law - commodities, aviation, tax. **Holdings:** 20,000 volumes. **Subscriptions:** 52 journals and other serials; 14 newspapers. **Services:** Interlibrary loans; copying; library open to SLA members by appointment. **Computerized Information Services:** LEXIS, New York Times Information Service. **Staff:** Virginia Anne Lewis, Ref.Libn.; Robert Winger, Tech.Serv.Libn.

★1142★
BARRINGTON COLLEGE - LIBRARY (Rel-Theol)†
Middle Hwy.   Phone: (401) 246-1200
Barrington, RI 02806   Eleanor C. Wilson, Libn.
Founded: 1900. **Staff:** Prof 2; Other 1. **Subjects:** Bible, theology, missions, music, social sciences, natural sciences, humanities, education. **Holdings:** 65,000 books; 1100 bound periodical volumes; Biblical slides. **Subscriptions:** 300 journals and other serials. **Services:** Interlibrary loans; copying; library open to public. **Publications:** Acquisitions List. **Staff:** Barbara Briggs, Ref.Libn. & Cat.

★1143★
BARRISTERS' SOCIETY OF NEW BRUNSWICK - LAW LIBRARY (Law)
Justice Bldg., Queen St.   Phone: (506) 453-2500
Fredericton, NB, Canada E3B 5C2   Diane Hanson, Prov. Law Libn.
Founded: 1846. **Staff:** Prof 1; Other 1. **Subjects:** Law. **Holdings:** 22,000 books and bound periodical volumes. **Subscriptions:** 100 journals and other serials. **Services:** Interlibrary loans; copying; library open to public for reference use only. **Special Indexes:** Index to Maritime Provinces Reports cases. **Remarks:** The Barristers' Society of New Brunswick also administers law libraries in Bathurst, Edmundston, Newcastle, Campbellton, St. Stephen and Woodstock. **Staff:** Margaret McKinney .

BARRY (Edith Cleaves) LIBRARY
See: Brick Store Museum - Edith Cleaves Barry Library

★1144★
BARTHOLOMEW COUNTY HISTORICAL SOCIETY LIBRARY (Hist)
524 Third St.   Phone: (812) 372-3541
Columbus, IN 47201   Renee Henry, Musm.Dir.
Staff: Prof 1. **Subjects:** Local and state history, antiques, genealogy. **Special Collections:** George Pence Manuscript Collection (12 cubic feet). **Holdings:** 500 books; 500 bound periodical volumes; 12 cubic feet of clippings, ephemera; 300 volumes of City of Columbus records. **Services:** Copying; library open to public by appointment.

★1145★
BARTHOLOMEW (Harland) AND ASSOCIATES, INC. - LIBRARY (Trans)
2701 Union Extended   Phone: (901) 527-3521
Memphis, TN 38112   Jennifer B. Fox, Libn.
Founded: 1970. **Staff:** Prof 1. **Subjects:** Traffic and transportation engineering, planning, highway design, environmental services, structural engineering, landscape architecture. **Holdings:** 1500 books; 2800 company reports (cataloged). **Subscriptions:** 90 journals and other serials. **Services:** Copying; library not open to public.

BARTHOLOMEW (Robbie) MEMORIAL LIBRARY
See: Tongass Historical Society, Inc. - Robbie Bartholomew Memorial Library

BARTLE (Glenn G.) LIBRARY
See: SUNY at Binghamton - Special Collections

BARTLESVILLE ENERGY TECHNOLOGY CENTER LIBRARY
See: U.S. Dept. of Energy

★1146★
BARTLESVILLE PUBLIC LIBRARY - HISTORY ROOM (Hist)
6th & Johnstone   Phone: (918) 336-2133
Bartlesville, OK 74003   Herbert E. Winn, Libn.
Founded: 1913. **Staff:** Prof 3; Other 13. **Subjects:** Delaware Indians, local and Oklahoma history. **Holdings:** 3800 books; 75 bound periodical volumes; Washington County newspapers on microfilm, 1895 to present. **Services:** Interlibrary loans; copying; library open to public.

BARTLETT HISTORICAL LIBRARY
See: Beloit Historical Society

BARTOK (Bela) ARCHIVE
See: New York Bartok Archive

★1147★
BARTON-ASCHMAN ASSOCIATES, INC. - PLANNING LIBRARY
820 Davis St.
Evanston, IL 60201
Defunct

★1148★
BARTON-ASCHMAN ASSOCIATES, INC. - RESOURCE CENTER (Plan)
10 Cedar Square West
1610 S. Sixth St.   Phone: (612) 332-0421
Minneapolis, MN 55454   Janet L. Fabio, Resource Ctr.Mgr.
Founded: 1975. **Staff:** 1. **Subjects:** Transportation, urban planning, environment. **Holdings:** 300 books; 3000 reports and documents. **Subscriptions:** 100 journals and other serials; 10 newspapers. **Services:** Copying; library not open to public. **Computerized Information Services:** DIALOG.

BARTON (Bruce) MEMORIAL LIBRARY
See: International Center for the Disabled (ICD) - Bruce Barton Memorial Library

★1149★
BARTON MUSEUM OF WHISKEY HISTORY - LIBRARY (Hist; Food-Bev)
Bardstown, KY 40004   Oscar Getz, Founder
Founded: 1957. **Subjects:** History of whiskey prior to 1919. **Holdings:** Books, catalogs, memorabilia, advertisements, photographs. **Services:** Library not open to public; may be consulted by liquor industry representatives, writers and researchers.

BARTON (Sarah C.) LIBRARY
See: Erlanger Medical Center - School of Nursing - Sarah C. Barton Library

BARTUNEK (Joseph W., III) LAW LIBRARY
See: Cleveland State University - Joseph W. Bartunek III Law Library

★1150★
BARUCH (Belle W.) INSTITUTE FOR MARINE BIOLOGY AND COASTAL RESEARCH - LIBRARY (Sci-Tech)†
University of South Carolina   Phone: (803) 777-5288
Columbia, SC 29208   Ms. V. Smith, Adm.Asst.
Subjects: Marine biology, marine geology, physical and chemical oceanography, ecosystem studies. **Holdings:** Figures not available. **Also Known As:** Belle W. Baruch Library in Marine Science.

★1151★
BARUCH (Bernard M.) COLLEGE OF THE CITY UNIVERSITY OF NEW YORK - LIBRARY (Bus-Fin)
156 E. 25th St.   Phone: (212) 725-3112
New York, NY 10010   Harold Eiberson, Chf.Libn.
Staff: Prof 21; Other 24. **Subjects:** Business; economics and finance; social studies; history. **Holdings:** 265,000 books; 28,000 bound periodical volumes; 7000 reels of microfilm; 20 VF drawers of pamphlets; SEC 10K reports; 80 business, labor, and tax services maintained. **Subscriptions:** 1900 journals and other serials; 10 newspapers. **Services:** Interlibrary loans; library open to public for reference use only. **Computerized Information Services:** DIALOG, BRS, SDC, New York Times Information Service, Dow Jones News Retrieval; computerized cataloging. **Networks/Consortia:** Member of OCLC. **Staff:** Alan Weiner, Chf., Ref.; Minja Lee, Tech.Serv.Libn.; John B. Jones, Ser.Libn.; Thomas Atkins, Hd., Instr.Serv.

BASCOM PALMER EYE INSTITUTE
See: University of Miami - School of Medicine

★1152★
BASF WYANDOTTE CORPORATION - DEVELOPMENT LABORATORY - LIBRARY (Sci-Tech)†
36 Riverside Ave.   Phone: (518) 465-4511
Rensselaer, NY 12144
Subjects: Chemistry, dyestuffs. **Holdings:** 8100 books and bound periodical volumes; patents; microfilmed PB reports. **Subscriptions:** 60 journals and other serials. **Services:** Interlibrary loans (limited); copying; library not open to public.

★1153★
BASF WYANDOTTE CORPORATION - PIGMENTS LIBRARY (Sci-Tech)
491 Columbia Ave.   Phone: (616) 392-2391
Holland, MI 49423   Janice A. Wierenga, Libn.
Staff: Prof 1; Other 1. Subjects: Pigments, inks, paint, chemistry, physics, printing, resins, lacquers, emulsions. Holdings: 2000 books; 3500 bound periodical volumes; 10,000 patents. Subscriptions: 150 journals and other serials. Services: Interlibrary loans; copying; library not open to public. Computerized Information Services: Internal database. Networks/Consortia: Member of Lakeland Area Library Network. Publications: Acquisitions Bulletin - for internal distribution only.

★1154★
BASF WYANDOTTE CORPORATION - RESEARCH LIBRARY (Sci-Tech)
Box 111   Phone: (313) 282-3300
Wyandotte, MI 48192   Janice B. Spector, Res.Libn.
Founded: 1939. Staff: Prof 2; Other 3. Subjects: Organic and inorganic chemistry, agricultural chemicals, dyes, alkalies, cleaning compounds, surfactants, urethanes. Holdings: 25,000 books; bound periodical volumes. Subscriptions: 320 journals and other serials. Services: Library not open to public. Computerized Information Services: DIALOG, SDC, BRS, Chemical Abstracts Serice, Pergamon-Infoline. Formerly: Its Corporate Library. Staff: William Conger, Tech.Info.Spec.

BASILEIAD LIBRARY
See: Manor Junior College

BASLOE (Rose) LIBRARY
See: Temple Beth Joseph - Rose Basloe Library

BASS (Harry W.) COLLECTION IN BUSINESS HISTORY
See: University of Oklahoma - Harry W. Bass Collection in Business History

BASS (Sophie Frye) LIBRARY OF NORTHWEST AMERICANA
See: Seattle & King County Historical Society - Sophie Frye Bass Library of Northwest Americana

BASSETT ARMY HOSPITAL
See: U.S. Army Hospitals

★1155★
BASSETT (Mary Imogene) HOSPITAL - MEDICAL LIBRARY (Med)
Atwell Rd.   Phone: (607) 547-3115
Cooperstown, NY 13326   Wendy E. Rice, Med.Libn.
Staff: Prof 1; Other 2. Subjects: Clinical medicine, surgery. Holdings: 5000 books; 25,000 bound periodical volumes. Subscriptions: 527 journals and other serials. Services: Interlibrary loans; copying; library open to public for reference use only. Computerized Information Services: MEDLARS. Networks/Consortia: Member of Albany Area Health Library Association; South Central Research Library Council (SCRLC); Health Resources Council of Central New York. Publications: Medical Library Bulletin, monthly - for internal distribution only. Special Indexes: Bibliographies of staff's published materials, annual.

★1156★
BASSIST COLLEGE - LIBRARY (Art)
2000 S.W. Fifth Ave.   Phone: (503) 228-6528
Portland, OR 97201   Norma H. Bassist, Libn.
Founded: 1963. Staff: Prof 2; Other 6. Subjects: Fashion and costume history, interior decoration, furniture history, world history, textiles, clothing and fashion industry, retailing and marketing. Special Collections: Peterson's magazine; Godey's magazine; fashion history, including rare volumes. Holdings: 7500 books; 110 bound periodical volumes; 85 VF drawers of clippings; 150 carousel slide trays. Subscriptions: 102 journals and other serials; 5 newspapers. Services: Copying; library open to professionals in the field. Staff: Jarka Posik, Asst.Libn.

BATCHELDER (Alice Coleman) MUSIC LIBRARY
See: Pasadena Public Library - Alice Coleman Batchelder Music Library

★1157★
BATEMAN EICHLER, HILL RICHARDS, INC. - RESEARCH LIBRARY (Bus-Fin)
700 S. Flower St.   Phone: (213) 625-3545
Los Angeles, CA 90013   Paula DeMaria, Libn.
Staff: Prof 1; Other 2. Subjects: Business, financial services, economics. Special Collections: Financial information dating back to 1926. Holdings: 481 books; 1781 bound periodical volumes; 1200 company files; 2400 research reports in archive collection. Subscriptions: 130 journals and other

serials; 27 newspapers. Services: Interlibrary loans; copying; library not open to public.

BATES (Bruce Everett) MEMORIAL LIBRARY
See: Museum of Arts and Sciences - Bruce Everett Bates Memorial Library

★1158★
BATES COLLEGE - LIBRARY - SPECIAL COLLECTIONS (Hum)†
                                           Phone: (207) 784-2949
Lewiston, ME 04240   Joseph J. Derbyshire, Libn.
Founded: 1863. Special Collections: Free Will Baptists (425 volumes); Batesiana (3892 volumes); Stanton Natural History (325 volumes); William Lyon Phelps collection of signed first editions (155 volumes); Marsden Hartley (100 volumes); Maine Small Press Publications (95 volumes). Services: Interlibrary loans; copying; library open to public for reference use only. Computerized Information Services: Computerized cataloging. Networks/Consortia: Member of OCLC through NELINET. Staff: Mary Riley, Spec.Coll.Libn.

★1159★
BATES (Ted) AND COMPANY - LIBRARY (Bus-Fin)
1515 Broadway   Phone: (212) 869-3131
New York, NY 10036   Ms. Bert Schachter, Lib.Supv.
Founded: 1940. Staff: Prof 1; Other 2; Subjects: Advertising, marketing. Special Collections: Competitive advertising; pictures; annual reports. Holdings: 3500 volumes; 305 VF drawers. Subscriptions: 300 journals and other serials. Services: Interlibrary loans; copying; library open to SLA members by appointment. Computerized Information Services: DIALOG, New York Times Information Service, BRS, Dow Jones News Retrieval.

★1160★
BATH MEMORIAL HOSPITAL - HEALTH SCIENCES LIBRARY (Med)
23 Winship St.   Phone: (207) 443-5524
Bath, ME 04530   Ellen Johnstone, Health Sci.Libn.
Staff: Prof 1. Subjects: Medicine and related health sciences. Holdings: 420 books and bound periodical volumes. Subscriptions: 27 journals and other serials. Services: Interlibrary loans; copying; library open to public with restrictions. Computerized Information Services: MEDLINE.†

★1161★
BATON ROUGE STATE-TIMES & MORNING ADVOCATE NEWSPAPERS - LIBRARY (Publ)
525 Lafayette St.   Phone: (504) 383-1111
Baton Rouge, LA 70821   Mrs. Lou Thomas, Lib.Dir.
Staff: Prof 5; Other 5. Subjects: Local and state news, government, politics, biographies, state statutes. Holdings: 1200 books; photograph files; clipping files. Subscriptions: 75 journals and other serials; 50 newspapers. Services: Library not open to public; assistance provided to libraries. Computerized Information Services: Internal database. Staff: Anne Legett, Asst.Lib.Dir.; Sallie Honeychurch, Libn.; Thelma Berg, Libn.; Frances Thomas, Libn.

★1162★
BATTELLE-COLUMBUS LABORATORIES - COPPER DATA CENTER (Sci-Tech)
505 King Ave.   Phone: (614) 424-7679
Columbus, OH 43201   Ross A. Gubiotti, Project Mgr.
Founded: 1965. Staff: Prof 1; Other 4. Subjects: Copper and copper-base alloy technology. Holdings: 30,000 reports, articles, patents. Subscriptions: 40 journals and other serials, plus access to more in Battelle Library, through the Metals Society and Japanese CDA. Services: Library open to public. Computerized Information Services: Tymshare, Inc., BASIS. Publications: Extracts of documents on copper technology (75 volumes). Special Indexes: Thesaurus (book), biennial.

★1163★
BATTELLE-COLUMBUS LABORATORIES - DIVER EQUIPMENT INFORMATION CENTER
505 King Ave.
Columbus, OH 43201
Defunct

★1164★
BATTELLE-COLUMBUS LABORATORIES - LIBRARY (Sci-Tech)
505 King Ave.   Phone: (614) 424-6424
Columbus, OH 43201   Carol A. Feltes, Mgr., Lib.Serv.
Founded: 1929. Staff: Prof 10; Other 10. Subjects: Engineering, chemistry, physics, biosciences, economics. Special Collections: Slavic science and technology; economics. Holdings: 150,000 books and bound periodical volumes; 80,000 technical reports; 40 VF drawers of microfilm and

microcards. **Subscriptions:** 3000 journals and other serials; 75 newspapers. **Services:** Interlibrary loans (limited); copying; library open to public. **Computerized Information Services:** DIALOG, BRS, DTIC, SDC; computerized cataloging and ILL. **Networks/Consortia:** Member of OCLC. **Publications:** Main Library Bulletin, monthly - for internal distribution only. **Staff:** Virginia Lyons, ILL Libn.; William Buckel, Ref.Libn.; Esther Hall, Order Libn.; Bobbie Jean Powell, Circ.Libn.

★1165★
BATTELLE-COLUMBUS LABORATORIES - MECHANICAL PROPERTIES DATA CENTER
505 King Ave.
Columbus, OH 43201
Defunct. Merged with Battelle-Columbus Laboratories - Metals and Ceramics Information Center.

★1166★
BATTELLE-COLUMBUS LABORATORIES - METALS AND CERAMICS INFORMATION CENTER (Sci-Tech)
505 King Ave.   Phone: (614) 424-5000
Columbus, OH 43201   Harold Mindlin, Prog.Mgr.
Founded: 1958. **Staff:** Prof 10; Other 10. **Subjects:** Properties, processing, behavior and applications of special metals important to defense systems, such as light metals, refractory metals, superalloys, high-strength steels, ceramics and composites. **Holdings:** 130,000 extracts or abstracts of reports, journal articles, and other documents, reproduced and filed for rapid retrieval. **Services:** Center open to public on a cost-incurred basis. **Computerized Information Services:** Metals and Ceramics Information Center Database on the Defense RDT&E On-Line System (internal database). **Publications:** MCIC Current Awareness Bulletin (MCIC publications also available from NTIS); Critical Reviews; State-of-the-Art Surveys; handbooks; databooks; proceedings of conferences; bibliographies; Aerospace Structural Metals Handbook; Structural Alloys Handbook. **Remarks:** Includes holdings of the former Battelle-Columbus Laboratories - Mechanical Properties Data Center. **Staff:** Helen Pestel, Mgr., MCIC Info.Serv.

★1167★
BATTELLE-COLUMBUS LABORATORIES - RAPIDLY SOLIDIFIED MATERIALS (RaSoMat) - RESOURCE CENTER (Sci-Tech)
505 King Ave.   Phone: (614) 424-4324
Columbus, OH 43201   Dr. R.S. Carbonara, Assoc.Mgr.
Staff: Prof 3; Other 1. **Subjects:** Alloy development, process research and development, properties, new applications. **Holdings:** 5000 articles on Rapidly Solidified Materials. **Services:** Library not open to public. **Staff:** Dr. R.V. Raman .

★1168★
BATTELLE-COLUMBUS LABORATORIES - STACK GAS EMISSION CONTROL COORDINATION CENTER - LIBRARY (Env-Cons; Energy)
505 King Ave.   Phone: (614) 424-7885
Columbus, OH 43201   Joseph H. Oxley, Mgr.
Subjects: Scrubbers, fuel gas desulfurization, clean fuels. **Holdings:** Figures not available. **Services:** Information available on a quick response basis for an annual fee. **Publications:** Bimonthly reports.

★1169★
BATTELLE-COLUMBUS LABORATORIES - TACTICAL TECHNOLOGY CENTER (Sci-Tech)
505 King Ave.   Phone: (614) 424-5047
Columbus, OH 43201   J.T. Brown, Mgr.
Founded: 1963. **Staff:** Prof 4; Other 4. **Subjects:** Tactical warfare. **Holdings:** 3000 books; 50,000 reports (cataloged). **Subscriptions:** 50 journals and other serials. **Services:** Interlibrary loans; library open to U.S. Department of Defense agencies or others by permission of Defense Advanced Research Projects Agency. **Computerized Information Services:** DIALOG, SDC; computerized cataloging. **Publications:** Reports and responses to users, irregular. **Remarks:** The Tactical Technology Center is sponsored by the Defense Advanced Research Projects Agency. **Staff:** E.E. Westbrook, Info.Ctr.Mgr.

★1170★
BATTELLE NEW ENGLAND RESEARCH LABORATORY - WILLIAM F. CLAPP LABORATORIES, INC. - LIBRARY (Sci-Tech)†
Washington St.   Phone: (617) 934-5682
Duxbury, MA 02332   Lawrence W. Martin, Libn.
Founded: 1934. **Staff:** Prof 1. **Subjects:** Marine biology, oceanography. **Holdings:** 2508 volumes. **Subscriptions:** 25 journals and other serials. **Services:** Interlibrary loans; library not open to public.

★1171★
BATTELLE-NORTHWEST - PACIFIC NORTHWEST LABORATORY - TECHNICAL INFORMATION LIBRARY (Sci-Tech; Energy)
Box 999   Phone: (509) 376-5451
Richland, WA 99352   W.A. Snyder, Mgr., Tech.Info.
Staff: Prof 8; Other 23. **Subjects:** Energy technology, nuclear science, engineering, physics, chemistry, mathematics, metallurgy, radiological sciences. **Holdings:** 50,000 books; 50,000 bound periodical volumes; 100,000 technical reports; 450,000 technical reports in microform. **Subscriptions:** 1800 journals and other serials. **Services:** Interlibrary loans; translation; library open to public with restrictions. **Computerized Information Services:** DIALOG, SDC, New York Times Information Service, Derwent Patents Documentation Services, DOE/RECON, NASA/RECON, MEDLARS, DTIC; computerized cataloging, acquisitions, serials and circulation. **Networks/Consortia:** Member of WLN. **Publications:** List of Additions to Files, weekly - for internal distribution only. **Remarks:** Battelle-Northwest operates under contract to the U.S. Department of Energy. **Staff:** Lois A. Holmes, Supv., Lib. & File; E.L. Daniel, Cat.; N.G. Carter, Ref.Spec.; S.P. Gydesen, Ref.Spec.; R.A. Bush, Ref.Spec.; C.A. Sample, Ref.Spec.; S. Edmunds, Ref.Spec.

★1172★
BATTEN, BARTON, DURSTINE, OSBORN, INC. - INFORMATION RETRIEVAL CENTER (Bus-Fin)†
383 Madison Ave.   Phone: (212) 355-5800
New York, NY 10017   Paula Brown, Mgr.
Founded: 1964. **Staff:** Prof 9; Other 4. **Subjects:** Advertising, marketing, general business. **Special Collections:** Competitive advertising; collection of television and print advertising. **Holdings:** 3500 books; 20,000 marketing and research reports; 5000 corporate/product/subject files. **Subscriptions:** 400 journals; 6 newspapers. **Computerized Information Services:** DIALOG, New York Times Information Service; internal database. **Publications:** Newsletter, monthly - for internal distribution only. **Staff:** Suzanne Hayes, Ref.Libn.; Karen Walsh, Ref.Libn.; Kathleen Dowling, Ref.Supv.; Hannah Hofmann, Ref.Libn.; Susan Friedman, Tech.Serv.Libn.; Lee Boylan, Ref.Libn.; Viki Goldman, Ref.Libn.

BATTISTA (O.A.) RESEARCH INSTITUTE
See: Research Services Corporation - The O.A. Battista Research Institute

★1173★
BATTLE CREEK ADVENTIST HOSPITAL - MEDICAL LIBRARY (Med)
165 N. Washington Ave.   Phone: (616) 964-7121
Battle Creek, MI 49016   Joni Wildman, Dir.
Founded: 1914. **Staff:** Prof 1; Other 2. **Subjects:** Psychiatry, surgery, medicine, nursing. **Holdings:** 371 books; 253 AV items. **Subscriptions:** 36 journals and other serials. **Services:** Interlibrary loans; library open to public with restrictions. **Formerly:** Battle Creek Sanitarium Hospital. **Staff:** Sheri Angus, Ref.Libn.

★1174★
BATTLE CREEK ART CENTER - MICHIGAN ART ARCHIVES (Art)
265 E. Emmett   Phone: (616) 963-1219
Battle Creek, MI 49017   Linda Poirier, Cur. of Coll./Exhibitions
Staff: Prof 1. **Subjects:** Michigan art. **Special Collections:** Bibliographies and information on Michigan art and artists. **Holdings:** 300 books; 600 files of clippings and archives. **Services:** Copying; library open to public. **Computerized Information Services:** Detroit Artist Registration and Information System (DARIS).

★1175★
BATTLEFORD NATIONAL HISTORIC PARK - CAMPBELL INNES MEMORIAL LIBRARY (Hist)
Box 70   Phone: (306) 937-2621
Battleford, SK, Canada S0M 0E0   Mrs. M.A. Simpson, Supt.
Founded: 1971. **Staff:** 1. **Subjects:** History of the Canadian Northwest, especially the Battleford area; history of the North-West Mounted Police; Indians of North America; social sciences; biography. **Special Collections:** Personal diaries and letterbooks; Saskatchewan Herald (1878-1938; on microfilm); bound volumes of the Battleford Press (1906-1949). **Holdings:** 1797 books; 78 bound periodical volumes; 2000 newspaper clippings; 829 volumes of pamphlets (cataloged); 2 VF drawers of documents; 10 drawers of maps and plans. **Services:** Copying (restricted); library open to public for reference use only, on request. **Remarks:** Maintained by Parks Canada.

★1176★
BAUDER FASHION COLLEGE - LIBRARY (Art)
508 S. Center St.   Phone: (817) 277-6666
Arlington, TX 76010   Jane Kennedy, Libn.
Founded: 1967. **Staff:** 1. **Subjects:** Fashion, history of costume, art, interior design, merchandising. **Holdings:** 2000 books. **Subscriptions:** 75 journals and other serials. **Services:** Copying; library not open to public. **Staff:** Lyn Silver, Adm.Dir.

★1177★
BAUSCH & LOMB, INC. - LIBRARY RESOURCE CENTER (Sci-Tech)
1400 N. Goodman St.   Phone: (716) 338-6053
Rochester, NY 14692   Delsa I. Benz, Corp.Libn.
Founded: 1916. **Staff:** Prof 2. **Subjects:** Ophthalmology, glass technology, optics, physics, business, management, contact lenses. **Holdings:** 5750 books; 1780 bound periodical volumes. **Subscriptions:** 300 journals and other serials. **Services:** Interlibrary loans; copying; library open to public by appointment. **Publications:** Lists of new material, bimonthly - for internal distribution only. **Remarks:** Contains holdings of the former Bausch & Lomb, Inc. - Soflens Division - Soflens Technical Information Center. **Formerly:** Its Corporate Library. **Staff:** Mary J. Brunette, Asst.Corp.Libn.

★1178★
BAUSCH & LOMB, INC. - SOFLENS DIVISION - SOFLENS TECHNICAL INFORMATION CENTER
1400 N. Goodman St.
Rochester, NY 14602
Defunct. Merged with Bausch & Lomb, Inc. - Corporate Library to form its Library Resource Center.

BAVER MEMORIAL LIBRARY
See: Pennsylvania Dutch Folk Culture Society, Inc.

BAXTER (L.C.) MEDICAL LIBRARY
See: Oklahoma Osteopathic Hospital - L.C. Baxter Medical Library

BAXTER (Matthew A.) SCHOOL OF LIBRARY & INFORMATION SCIENCE
See: Case Western Reserve University - Matthew A. Baxter School of Library & Information Science

★1179★
BAXTER TRAVENOL LABORATORIES, INC. - BUSINESS AND LAW LIBRARY/INFORMATION CENTER (Law)
2-2W, One Baxter Pkwy.   Phone: (312) 948-3881
Deerfield, IL 60015   Frank J. Locker, Supv.
Founded: 1972. **Staff:** Prof 2; Other 1. **Subjects:** Law - corporate, patent, tax; management - business, personnel, sales, production, financial. **Holdings:** 12,000 books; 25 VF drawers. **Subscriptions:** 360 journals and other serials; 10 newspapers. **Services:** Interlibrary loans; SDI; library open to public by prior arrangement with supervisor or associate librarian. **Computerized Information Services:** DIALOG, SDC, NLM. **Networks/Consortia:** Member of North Suburban Library System; Lake County Consortia. **Staff:** Margaret Gardner, Assoc.Libn.

★1180★
BAY AREA COUNCIL ON SOVIET JEWRY - ARCHIVES (Area-Ethnic)†
106 Baden St.   Phone: (415) 585-1400
San Francisco, CA 94131   Natasha Kats, Exec.Sec.
Founded: 1968. **Staff:** Prof 1. **Subjects:** USSR - Jewish emigration, prisoners of conscience, human rights movements, psychiatric abuse; U.S. activist movement for Soviet Jewish emigration. **Holdings:** 40 VF drawers of articles, reports, manuscripts, documents and newsletters. **Subscriptions:** 30 journals and other serials; 5 newspapers. **Services:** Copying; library open to public by mail request only. **Publications:** Outcry, monthly newsletter - distributed to members and by subscription.

BAY AREA ELECTRIC RAILROAD ASSOCIATION - CALIFORNIA RAILWAY MUSEUM
See: California Railway Museum

★1181★
BAY COUNTY HISTORICAL SOCIETY - LIBRARY (Hist)
1700 Center Ave.   Phone: (517) 893-5733
Bay City, MI 48706   Kathleen Krueger, Cur. of Coll.
Founded: 1932. **Staff:** Prof 3; Other 2. **Subjects:** History - Bay County, Michigan, U.S.; Great Lakes shipping, especially Lake Huron; lumbering. **Special Collections:** Bay City directories, 1866-1973; Michigan Pioneer & Historical Collection, volumes 1-40; Michigan Manual, 1899-1962; Public Acts of Michigan, 1872-1954. **Holdings:** 1500 books; periodicals; 70 diaries; 90 scrapbooks; 3500 photographs (50 albums); 50 linear feet of archival materials; 8 file drawers of pamphlets and clippings; 5 map drawers of maps. **Subscriptions:** 15 journals and other serials. **Services:** Copying; research; library open to public but staff member must be present. **Formerly:** Its Museum of the Great Lakes - Library. **Staff:** Gay McInerney, Musm.Dir.; Eurdine Ringwelski, Res.

★1182★
BAY HARBOR HOSPITAL - MEDICAL LIBRARY (Med)
1437 W. Lomita Blvd.   Phone: (213) 325-1221
Harbor City, CA 90710   Lily Yang, Med.Libn.
Founded: 1970. **Staff:** Prof 1. **Subjects:** Medicine and allied sciences, nursing, hospital administration. **Holdings:** 1000 books; Audio-Digest tapes. **Subscriptions:** 61 journals. **Services:** Interlibrary loans; copying; SDI; library not open to public. **Computerized Information Services:** MEDLINE.

★1183★
BAY MEDICAL CENTER - HEALTH SCIENCES LIBRARY (Med)
1900 Columbus Ave.   Phone: (517) 894-3782
Bay City, MI 48706   Barbara Kormelink, Med.Libn.
Founded: 1958. **Staff:** Prof 1; Other 1. **Subjects:** Medicine, nursing, hospital administration, allied health sciences. **Holdings:** 2200 books; 3420 bound periodical volumes; 175 sets of slides; 74 titles on microfilm; 355 AV items; 12 VF drawers of pamphlets. **Subscriptions:** 290 journals and other serials. **Services:** Interlibrary loans; copying; library open to public. **Computerized Information Services:** MEDLINE, BRS. **Networks/Consortia:** Member of Michigan Area Serials Holdings (MASH); Valley Regional Health Science Librarians (VRHSL).

BAY VIEW HOSPITAL - CHARLES J. AND ANNA N. ARCHBOLD MEMORIAL LIBRARY
See: St. John and West Shore Hospital - Media Center

★1184★
BAYFRONT MEDICAL CENTER, INC. - HEALTH SCIENCES LIBRARY (Med)
701 6th St.,S.   Phone: (813) 823-1234
St. Petersburg, FL 33701   Polly Jean Duffey, Health Sci.Libn.
Founded: 1945. **Staff:** 2. **Subjects:** Medicine, geriatrics, nursing, oncology. **Holdings:** 1000 books; 2800 bound periodical volumes; 100 pamphlets; 1000 Audio-Digest tapes; 1000 videotapes. **Subscriptions:** 215 journals and other serials. **Services:** Interlibrary loans; copying; library not open to public. **Computerized Information Services:** MEDLARS; computerized cataloging. **Networks/Consortia:** Member of Tampa Bay Medical Library Network.

★1185★
BAYLEY SETON HOSPITAL - CHARLES FERGUSON MEDICAL LIBRARY (Med)
Bay St. & Vanderbilt Ave.   Phone: (212) 447-3010
Staten Island, NY 10304   Marie A. Sheldon, Med.Lib.Asst.
Founded: 1950. **Staff:** 1. **Subjects:** Medicine, surgery, radiology, urology, dermatology, pediatrics, dentistry, nursing. **Holdings:** 5100 books; 7900 bound periodical volumes; 408 audiotapes; 126 cassette tapes; 92 video cassettes; 107 slide and cassette programs; 10 VF drawers. **Subscriptions:** 464 journals and other serials. **Services:** Interlibrary loans; copying (for staff only); library open to students in the health care field. **Networks/Consortia:** Member of Brooklyn-Queens-Staten Island Health Sciences Librarians (BQSI); METRO. **Formerly:** U.S. Public Health Service Hospital.

★1186★
BAYLOR UNIVERSITY - ARMSTRONG BROWNING LIBRARY (Hum)
Box 6336   Phone: (817) 755-3566
Waco, TX 76706   Dr. Jack W. Herring, Dir.
Founded: 1912. **Staff:** Prof 4; Other 12. **Special Collections:** Robert Browning; Elizabeth Barrett Browning; Browning Family (750 items); Edward Dowden (183 items); Browning-Milsand (88 items); Edward Robert Bulwer Lytton; A. Joseph Armstrong (350 items); Meynell; Hagedorn; Shields; Gibbs (60 items); Arthur A. Houghton, Jr. Collection (160 items); John Forster (400 items). **Holdings:** 12,500 books; 2675 periodicals (cataloged); 21 volumes of clippings; 133 reels of microfilm; 3000 manuscripts and letters; 500 slides and taped lectures; 35 phonograph records. **Subscriptions:** 10 journals and other serials. **Services:** Interlibrary loans; copying; consultation and research; library open to public for reference use only. **Publications:** Studies in Browning and His Circle, biannual; Baylor Browning Interests, irregular; Armstrong Browning Library Newsletter, biannual. **Special Catalogs:** Music catalog (book); catalog of literary manuscripts. **Staff:** Betty A. Coley, Libn.; Rita S. Humphrey, Adm.Asst.; Nancy Dobbins, Spec.Actv.Coord.

★1187★

BAYLOR UNIVERSITY - CONGRESSIONAL COLLECTION (Soc Sci)
Box 245																		Phone: (817) 755-3530
Waco, TX 76798																James Rogers, Dir.
Founded: 1979. **Staff:** Prof 2. **Subjects:** Federal and state government. **Special Collections:** Congressional papers of former congressmen W.R. Poage, O.C. Fisher, John Dowdy and Alan Steelman. **Holdings:** 1136 books; 2000 linear feet of personal and legislative papers and other documents. **Services:** Copying; collection open to public with restrictions. **Staff:** Phillip Thompson, Archv.

★1188★

BAYLOR UNIVERSITY - CROUCH MUSIC LIBRARY (Mus)
Moody Memorial Library
Box 6307																		Phone: (817) 755-1366
Waco, TX 76706																Dr. Avery T. Sharp, Music Libn.
Founded: 1929. **Staff:** Prof 2; Other 3. **Subjects:** Musicology, music theory, church music, instrumental and orchestral music, historical sets (collected), music education, vocal music, editions and monuments of music. **Special Collections:** Mrs. J.W. Jennings Collection (medieval music manuscripts and early printed music); Mr. and Mrs. Travis Johnson Collection (early American song books); Francis G. Spencer Collection of American Printed Music; David W. Guion Collection (manuscripts); eighteenth century editions of ensemble music; eighteenth and nineteenth century American hardbacks. **Holdings:** 9954 books; 3356 bound periodical volumes; 696 microforms; 51,573 music items; 19,153 phonograph records; 5121 tapes; 810 orchestrations. **Subscriptions:** 105 journals and other serials. **Services:** Library open to public. **Computerized Information Services:** Computerized circulation. **Staff:** Miriam Griffis, Audio Supv.

★1189★

BAYLOR UNIVERSITY - DEPARTMENT OF GEOLOGY - FERDINAND ROEMER GEOLOGICAL LIBRARY (Sci-Tech)
Moody Library																	Phone: (817) 755-2361
Waco, TX 76703																H.H. Beaver, Chm.
Founded: 1952. **Staff:** 9. **Subjects:** Geology, earth sciences. **Special Collections:** Student papers and theses (2000). **Holdings:** 3500 books; 9000 bound periodical volumes; 3500 maps; 100,000 well logs; 3200 aerial photographs. **Subscriptions:** 60 journals and other serials. **Services:** Interlibrary loans; library open to public for reference use only. **Publications:** Baylor Geological Studies, semiannual.

★1190★

BAYLOR UNIVERSITY - J.M. DAWSON CHURCH-STATE RESEARCH CENTER - LIBRARY (Rel-Theol)
Box 380																		Phone: (817) 755-1519
Waco, TX 76798																Julie Sams, Libn.
Founded: 1968. **Staff:** Prof 3; Other 1. **Subjects:** Church-state relations. **Holdings:** 4300 books; 500 bound periodical volumes; 16 VF drawers of pamphlets, archives, reports and clippings; 30 bound volumes of theses and dissertations; 70 reels of microfilm; 65 tapes. **Subscriptions:** 154 journals and other serials. **Services:** Copying; library open to public for reference use only. **Publications:** Journal of Church and State, 3/year - by subscription.

★1191★

BAYLOR UNIVERSITY - LAW LIBRARY (Law)
Box 6342																		Phone: (817) 755-2168
Waco, TX 76706																Della M. Geyer, Law Libn.
Staff: Prof 2; Other 1. **Subjects:** Law. **Holdings:** 131,423 volumes. **Subscriptions:** 300 journals and other serials. **Services:** Interlibrary loans; copying; library open to public for reference use only.

★1192★

BAYLOR UNIVERSITY - STRECKER MUSEUM LIBRARY (Sci-Tech)
Richardson Bldg.																Phone: (817) 755-1110
Waco, TX 76798																Dr. Bryce C. Brown, Musm.Dir.
Founded: 1893. **Subjects:** Natural history, anthropology, archeology. **Holdings:** 1547 books; 53 bound periodical volumes; 4400 natural history reprints. **Subscriptions:** 22 journals and other serials. **Services:** Interlibrary loans; library open to public by request.

★1193★

BAYLOR UNIVERSITY - TEXAS COLLECTION (Hist)
Carroll Library Bldg.
Box 6396																		Phone: (817) 755-1268
Waco, TX 76706																Kent Keeth, Dir.
Founded: 1923. **Staff:** Prof 4; Other 12. **Subjects:** Texana, Baylor University. **Special Collections:** Gildersleeve Photograph Collection (4000); Connally-Dobie Collection. **Holdings:** 80,000 books; 6300 bound periodical volumes; 4700 Baylor theses and dissertations; 250 transcribed oral history memoirs with tapes; 120 VF drawers of subject files; 1400 maps; 1650 collections of historical manuscripts; Baylor University archives; 40 VF drawers of photographs; microfilm; Texas newspapers; depository for records of 11 central Texas counties of Texas State Library's Regional Historical Resource Depository program. **Subscriptions:** 375 journals and other serials; 15 newspapers. **Services:** Interlibrary loans; copying; library open to public with restrictions. **Publications:** A Treasure of Maps, 1975; The Connally-Dobie Gift, 1974; occasional publications. **Special Indexes:** Biographical reference file (punched card); index to census reports published in quarterlies (book); checklist of oral history memoirs, picture file (card); registers and calendars of selected manuscript and archival holdings (book); indexes to selected nonself-indexed periodicals (book). **Staff:** Ellen K. Brown, Hd.,Archv./Hist.Mss.; Virginia H. Ming, Hd.,Ser. & Pub.Serv.; William L. Ming, Hd.,Acq. & Bibliog.; Dr. Thomas L. Charlton, Chm.,Texas Coll.Comm.

★1194★

BAYLOR UNIVERSITY, DALLAS - LIBRARY (Med)
3402 Gaston Ave.															Phone: (214) 820-2372
Dallas, TX 75246															Marcel C. Carol, Libn.
Founded: 1940. **Staff:** Prof 3; Other 3. **Subjects:** Medicine, dentistry, nursing. **Special Collections:** Lyle Sellers Medical Collection (early medicine). **Holdings:** 17,000 books; 35,000 bound periodical volumes; 126 reels of microfilm; 2 VF drawers of microfiche; 12 VF drawers. **Subscriptions:** 740 journals and other serials. **Services:** Interlibrary loans; copying; library open to public for reference use only. **Computerized Information Services:** MEDLINE. **Networks/Consortia:** Member of Dallas-Tarrant County Consortium of Health Science Libraries. **Staff:** Betty Freeman, Asst.Libn.; Barbara Downey, Asst.Libn.

★1195★

BAYSTATE MEDICAL CENTER - LIBRARY (Med)
759 Chestnut St.															Phone: (413) 787-4293
Springfield, MA 01107												Jean Scougall, Dir.
Staff: Prof 3; Other 5. **Subjects:** Medicine, nursing, allied health sciences, health care administration. **Holdings:** 20,000 books and bound periodical volumes; 6 VF drawers. **Subscriptions:** 500 journals and other serials. **Services:** Interlibrary loans; copying; library open to public. **Computerized Information Services:** MEDLINE. **Networks/Consortia:** Member of Cooperating Libraries of Greater Springfield; Western Massachusetts Health Information Consortium. **Publications:** FOCUS (newsletter), quarterly. **Staff:** Lily Peng, Info./Circ.Libn.; Diane Mazur, Cat.; Shirley Kolby, Coord./Acq.; Carolyn Gove, Coord./Ser.

★1196★

BAYVET - LIBRARY (Med)
12707 W. 63rd St.															Phone: (913) 631-4800
Shawnee, KS 66201													Cindy Stacy, Res.Data Coord.
Founded: 1974. **Staff:** Prof 1. **Subjects:** Veterinary medicine, animal health, pharmaceuticals. **Holdings:** 1000 books; 5000 bound periodical volumes; 12,000 hard copy technical reports; 100 company brochures; 50 annual reports. **Subscriptions:** 81 journals and other serials. **Services:** Interlibrary loans; copying; library not open to public. **Remarks:** BAYVET is a division of Cutter Laboratories, Inc.

BAZZINI (Dr. Massimo) MEMORIAL LIBRARY
See: Cabrini Medical Center - Dr. Massimo Bazzini Memorial Library

BBDO ADVERTISING/TRACY-LOCKE
See: Tracy-Locke/BBDO Advertising

★1197★

BBDO CHICAGO - INFORMATION CENTER (Bus-Fin)
410 N. Michigan Ave.													Phone: (312) 337-7860
Chicago, IL 60611														Ann Hullihan, Res.Libn.
Staff: Prof 1; Other 1. **Subjects:** Advertising, marketing. **Holdings:** 615 books; 13 VF drawers; 4 drawers of pictures; 106 research reports. **Subscriptions:** 74 journals and other serials. **Services:** Interlibrary loans; library not open to public. **Computerized Information Services:** DIALOG, New York Times Information Service. **Publications:** It's New at the BBDO Chicago Information Center, monthly. **Special Indexes:** Vertical file index (card and book).

BCR
See: Bibliographical Center for Research

★1198★
BDM CORPORATION - CORPORATE LIBRARY (Energy; Mil)
7915 Jones Branch Dr.   Phone: (703) 821-5181
McLean, VA 22102   Dana D. Mallett, Corp.Libn.
Founded: 1976. **Staff:** Prof 1; Other 3. **Subjects:** Defense, transportation, communications, environment, energy, advanced technology. **Holdings:** 6000 books; 25,000 hard copy technical reports. **Subscriptions:** 350 journals and other serials; 16 newspapers. **Services:** Interlibrary loans; copying; library not open to public. **Computerized Information Services:** DTIC, SDC, DIALOG; internal databases; computerized cataloging, acquisitions and circulation. **Special Catalogs:** Technical Reports Catalog (computer printouts).

BEACOM (Goldey) COLLEGE
See: Goldey Beacom College

★1199★
BEAK CONSULTANTS LTD. - LIBRARY (Env-Cons)
6870 Goreway Dr.   Phone: (416) 671-2600
Mississauga, ON, Canada L4V 1P1   R.K. Suri, Libn.
Founded: 1978. **Staff:** Prof 1. **Subjects:** Pollution control, aquatic biology, toxicology, ecological modelling, land use. **Special Collections:** Consultants' and private industry reports. **Holdings:** 350 books; 4000 government documents; 2000 reprints; 600 engineering catalogs; 1000 internal reports. **Subscriptions:** 98 journals and other serials. **Services:** Interlibrary loans; copying (fee); library open to public with restrictions. **Computerized Information Services:** DIALOG, QL Systems, INFOMART. **Special Catalogs:** Catalogue of reports and proposals (card).

★1200★
BEAL COLLEGE - LIBRARY (Bus-Fin)
629 Main St.   Phone: (207) 947-4591
Bangor, ME 04401   Jean Elston, Libn.
Staff: Prof 1. **Subjects:** Business management, economics, tax accounting, data processing, medical assisting, travel and airline careers. **Holdings:** 7000 books; 59 bound periodical volumes; 4 scrapbooks of clippings concerning the college; Maine Revised Statutes Annotated; 1 file drawer of pamphlets. **Subscriptions:** 51 journals and other serials. **Services:** Interlibrary loans; copying; library open to public.

BEAL LIBRARY
See: Macomb Intermediate School District

BEAL-MALTBIE SHELL MUSEUM
See: Rollins College

BEALE AIR FORCE BASE (CA)
See: U.S. Air Force Base - Beale Base Library

★1201★
BEAR MOUNTAIN TRAILSIDE MUSEUMS - LIBRARY (Hist)
Bear Mountain State Park   Phone: (914) 786-2701
Bear Mountain, NY 10911   John H. Mead, Musm.Dir.
Subjects: History, natural history. **Special Collections:** Daniel Carter Beard material. **Holdings:** 5000 books. **Services:** Library open to public by appointment only.

BEARDSLEE LIBRARY
See: Western Theological Seminary

BEATON INSTITUTE ARCHIVES
See: College of Cape Breton

★1202★
BEATRICE FOODS CO. - RESEARCH CENTER LIBRARY (Food-Bev)†
1526 South State St.   Phone: (312) 791-8292
Chicago, IL 60605   Carol Berger, Mgr., Lib./Info.Serv.
Founded: 1969. **Staff:** 4. **Subjects:** Organic chemistry, industrial microbiology, dairy science, nutrition, food science. **Holdings:** 4000 books; 9000 U.S. patents; 1600 foreign patents; 150 food and food related corporate reports; 11 VF drawers of pamphlets. **Subscriptions:** 305 journals and other serials. **Services:** Interlibrary loans; SDI; limited patent searching; library open to public with restrictions. **Computerized Information Services:** DIALOG, SDC. **Networks/Consortia:** Member of Metropolitan Chicago Library Assembly; Regional Medical Library - Region 3; RLG. **Publications:** Interface, monthly; Serials Holdings List, biennial. **Staff:** Muriel McKune, Asst.Libn.

★1203★
BEAUCHEMIN-BEATON-LAPOINTE, INC. - BBL LIBRARY (Art; Plan)
1134 Ste-Catherine St., W.   Phone: (514) 871-9555
Montreal, PQ, Canada H3B 1H4   Danielle Dallaire, Documentalist
Staff: 1. **Subjects:** Architecture; city planning; construction (buildings, roads, municipal facilities, airports); environment and pollution control; projects management. **Special Collections:** Urban development in the North. **Holdings:** 2000 books; 350 bound periodical volumes; 1500 government publications and pamphlets; 1000 company reports. **Services:** Interlibrary loans; copying; library not open to public.

★1204★
BEAUMONT ART MUSEUM - LIBRARY (Art)
1111 9th St.   Phone: (713) 832-3432
Beaumont, TX 77702   Julie Redding, Asst.Cur. of Educ.
Staff: Prof 1; Other 9. **Subjects:** Art, architecture, history. **Holdings:** 1600 volumes; 1575 exhibition catalogs; 8700 art color slides. **Subscriptions:** 17 journals and other serials. **Services:** Library open to public by appointment for reference use.

★1205★
BEAUMONT ENTERPRISE & JOURNAL - LIBRARY (Publ)
380 Walnut
Box 3071   Phone: (713) 833-3311
Beaumont, TX 77704   Jeanne E. Houston, Libn.
Founded: 1953. **Staff:** Prof 1; Other 1. **Subjects:** Newspaper reference topics. **Holdings:** Clippings, photographs, microfilms. **Subscriptions:** 15 newspapers. **Services:** Library not open to public.

★1206★
BEAUMONT PUBLIC LIBRARY SYSTEM - TYRRELL HISTORICAL LIBRARY (Hist)
695 Pearl St.
Box 3827   Phone: (713) 838-0780
Beaumont, TX 77704   Mabel Leyda, Libn.
Staff: 2. **Subjects:** Texas history, genealogy. **Holdings:** 8786 books; 227 bound periodical volumes. **Subscriptions:** 47 journals and other serials. **Services:** Copying; library open to public.

BEAUMONT (William) ARMY MEDICAL CENTER
See: U.S. Army Hospitals - William Beaumont Army Medical Center

★1207★
BEAUMONT (William) HOSPITAL - MEDICAL LIBRARY (Med)
3601 W. Thirteen Mile Rd.   Phone: (313) 288-8340
Royal Oak, MI 48072   Joan M.B. Smith, Med.Libn.
Staff: Prof 3; Other 6. **Subjects:** Medicine, nursing. **Holdings:** 6000 books; 8500 bound periodical volumes. **Subscriptions:** 720 journals and other serials. **Services:** Interlibrary loans; copying; SDI. **Computerized Information Services:** MEDLINE, TOXLINE, DIALOG. **Networks/Consortia:** Member of Detroit MEDLINE Consortium; Detroit Cooperative Cataloging Center. **Staff:** Virginia A. Crossley, Asst.Med.Libn.

★1208★
BEAVER COUNTY BAR ASSOCIATION - LAW LIBRARY (Law)
Court House   Phone: (412) 728-5700
Beaver, PA 15009   Jean Watson, Libn.
Staff: 1. **Subjects:** Law. **Holdings:** 16,831 books; 85 pamphlet boxes of county law journals. **Subscriptions:** 70 journals and other serials. **Services:** Copying; library open to public.

BEAVER COUNTY - RESOURCE & RESEARCH CENTER
See: Resource & Research Center for Beaver County & Local History

★1209★
BEAVER COUNTY TIMES - LIBRARY (Publ)
400 Fair Ave.
Box 400   Phone: (412) 775-3200
Beaver, PA 15009   Dorothy L. Basar, Hd.Libn.
Founded: 1957. **Staff:** Prof 2; Other 1. **Subjects:** Newspaper reference material. **Holdings:** One million newspaper clippings in 80,000 envelopes; Beaver County Times and its predecessors (from 1900) on microfilm; Beaver Falls News Tribune (1903-1979) on microfilm. **Subscriptions:** 8 journals and other serials; 8 newspapers. **Services:** Copying (including clippings); library open to public by appointment. **Remarks:** Maintained by Beaver Newspapers, Inc. **Staff:** Zola Chysh, Asst.Libn.

THE BEAVER DEFENDERS
See: Unexpected Wildlife Refuge

BEAVER (R. Pierce) MISSIONS LIBRARY
See: Memphis Theological Seminary - Library

★1210★
BECHTEL - AUDIO-VISUAL LIBRARY (Aud-Vis)
Box 3965   Phone: (415) 768-5799
San Francisco, CA 94119   Leslie Holmes, Supv.
Staff: 3. **Subjects:** Bechtel Power Corporation. **Holdings:** 500,000 photographs, slides and transparencies; 300 films. **Services:** Reproduction of material in any form (prints, slides, transparencies, enlargements, framings, mounted displays); viewing rooms; free loan of films; library not open to public.

★1211★
BECHTEL CANADA LIMITED - ENGINEERING CONSULTANTS - LIBRARY (Sci-Tech)
250 Bloor St., E., 15th Fl.   Phone: (416) 928-1671
Toronto, ON, Canada M4W 3K5   Irene Cairns, Libn.
Founded: 1960. **Staff:** 1. **Subjects:** Engineering - mining, metallurgical, civil, mechanical, electrical; instrumentation. **Holdings:** 1000 books; 700 engineering standards; 4 VF drawers; 75 Canadian government documents; 500 vendor catalogs. **Subscriptions:** 100 journals and other serials. **Services:** Interlibrary loans; copying; library not open to public. **Publications:** Library Bulletin, monthly.

★1212★
BECHTEL - CENTRAL LIBRARY (Sci-Tech; Bus-Fin)
50 Beale St.   Phone: (415) 768-5306
San Francisco, CA 94119   Betty Jo Hardison, Chf.Libn.
Founded: 1951. **Staff:** Prof 4; Other 7. **Subjects:** Engineering, construction, business. **Holdings:** 20,000 books; 950 unbound periodical titles; 2200 government documents; 2000 miscellaneous reports and pamphlets; 1000 codes and standards. **Subscriptions:** 750 journals and other serials; 7 newspapers. **Services:** Interlibrary loans; library not open to public. **Computerized Information Services:** DIALOG, SDC, New York Times Information Service, Info Globe, LEXIS, NEXIS, Technet. **Networks/Consortia:** Member of The Bechtel Information Network. **Publications:** New Information Sources, monthly. **Staff:** Doris Lanctot, Libn.; Jeffery Mah, Cat.; Ellen Reinheimer, Asst.Chf.Libn.

★1213★
BECHTEL CIVIL & MINERALS, INC. - MINING & METALS BUSINESS DEVELOPMENT LIBRARY (Bus-Fin)
Box 3965   Phone: (415) 768-7294
San Francisco, CA 94119   O. Paul Oraha, Libn.
Staff: Prof 1. **Subjects:** Mining and metals industry market data. **Holdings:** 200 volumes; 38 filing cabinets of VF material. **Subscriptions:** 21 journals and other serials. **Services:** Interlibrary loans; copying. **Computerized Information Services:** Computerized cataloging, acquisitions, serials and circulation.

★1214★
BECHTEL - DATA PROCESSING LIBRARY (Sci-Tech)
Box 3965   Phone: (415) 768-9015
San Francisco, CA 94119   Mercedes Dumlao, Libn.
Staff: Prof 3; Other 4. **Subjects:** Data processing. **Holdings:** Documentation, listings and files of Bechtel's production engineering and business programs; bibliographic guides to computer programs; data processing standards, periodicals and monographs. **Services:** Interlibrary loans; ordering and routing of periodicals; distribution of program changes to Bechtel's production computer programs and information on Bechtel's computers. **Computerized Information Services:** Computerized reports, distribution lists. **Networks/Consortia:** Member of Bechtel Information Network. **Publications:** Bechtel Computer Programs Catalog. **Staff:** Sherry Cook, Libn.; Maria Szabo, Libn.

★1215★
BECHTEL - FINANCE LIBRARY (Bus-Fin)
Box 3965   Phone: (415) 768-5166
San Francisco, CA 94119   Phyllis S. Morales, Finance Libn.
Founded: 1978. **Staff:** Prof 1; Other 1. **Subjects:** Business and finance, project financing, economic and statistical information, domestic and foreign banks, country and regional information. **Holdings:** Directories, periodicals, statistical yearbooks, vertical file materials, reports and surveys. **Subscriptions:** 275 journals and other serials; 7 newspapers. **Services:** Interlibrary loans; research; reference; circulation. **Remarks:** An additional telephone number is (415) 768-5122.

★1216★
BECHTEL - GEOLOGY LIBRARY (Sci-Tech)
Box 3965   Phone: (415) 786-5353
San Francisco, CA 94119   Gail Sorrough, Libn.
Staff: 1. **Subjects:** Geology, geotechnical engineering. **Holdings:** 850 books; 4000 reports, documents and manuscripts; maps. **Services:** Library not open to public. **Computerized Information Services:** DIALOG.

★1217★
BECHTEL - LEGAL DEPARTMENT LIBRARY (Law)
Box 3965   Phone: (415) 768-5545
San Francisco, CA 94119   Patricia Boyd, Law Libn.
Staff: Prof 1; Other 1. **Subjects:** Law - labor, environmental, government contracts, construction contracts, foreign, nuclear regulation. **Holdings:** Figures not available for books, periodicals, legal forms. **Services:** Interlibrary loans; research; routing; library not open to public. **Publications:** New books list.

★1218★
BECHTEL PETROLEUM INC. - LIBRARY (Sci-Tech)
Box 3965   Phone: (415) 882-2621
San Francisco, CA 94119   Gary Cohn, Libn.
Founded: 1981. **Staff:** Prof 3. **Subjects:** Engineering, petroleum, pipelines, arctic regions, data processing. **Special Collections:** Arctic reference collection (1200 volumes); computer services library (3000 volumes). **Holdings:** 10,000 books; 1 drawer of arctic engineering microfilm; 12 pipeline computer program tapes. **Services:** Interlibrary loans; copying; library not open to public. **Computerized Information Services:** Computerized cataloging and circulation. **Publications:** B.P.I. Library Bulletin, monthly - to mailing list. **Special Catalogs:** Arctic reference collection catalog (book and online); vendor catalogs (book and punched card). **Staff:** Tatiana Petroff, Standards Libn.; Albert Jones, Asst.Libn.

★1219★
BECHTEL POWER CORPORATION - LIBRARY (Sci-Tech)
12400 E. Imperial Hwy.
Box 60860, Terminal Annex   Phone: (213) 864-6011
Los Angeles, CA 90060   Jean Gregory, Chf.Libn.
Staff: 6. **Subjects:** Technology - engineering, nuclear, environmental; management. **Holdings:** Figures not available for U.S. and foreign standards and codes (microform); vendor catalogs; foreign language textbooks; government documents. **Services:** Interlibrary loans; routing. **Computerized Information Services:** Online literature searches; computerized cataloging. **Publications:** Library news, weekly. **Also Known As:** L.A. Power Corporation Library.

★1220★
BECHTEL POWER CORPORATION - LIBRARY (Sci-Tech; Energy)
Box 3965   Phone: (415) 768-1152
San Francisco, CA 94119   Stacia Kato, Hd.Libn.
Staff: Prof 2; Other 2. **Subjects:** Engineering and construction of nuclear and fossil power plants; electric power industry. **Special Collections:** U.S. Nuclear Regulatory Commission Docket information (250,000 microfiche). **Holdings:** 10,500 books; 500 bound periodical volumes; vendor catalogs (400 hard copy and 18,000 on microfilm); industry standards and codes (hard copy and microfilm); U.S.D.O.E., E.P.A. and NRC reports and regulations; Bechtel company documents; technical reports. **Subscriptions:** 100 journals and other serials. **Services:** Interlibrary loans; copying; library open to public with restrictions. **Computerized Information Services:** Computerized periodicals routing program. **Staff:** Bok Ng, Asst.Libn.

★1221★
BECHTEL POWER CORPORATION - LIBRARY (Sci-Tech)
15740 Shady Grove Rd.   Phone: (301) 258-3000
Gaithersburg, MD 20877   Carol A. Bell, Hd.Libn.
Founded: 1962. **Staff:** Prof 1; Other 1. **Subjects:** Engineering, nuclear engineering. **Holdings:** 3500 books; 18 VF drawers of pamphlets, documents, codes and standards; 12 VF drawers of Bechtel Corporation monthly reports and publications. **Subscriptions:** 50 journals and other serials. **Services:** Interlibrary loans; copying; library open to public by appointment.

★1222★
BECHTEL POWER CORPORATION - LIBRARY (Sci-Tech)
Box 2166   Phone: (713) 850-2365
Houston, TX 77001   Jean Adams, Libn.
Founded: 1966. **Staff:** Prof 1; Other 1. **Subjects:** Thermal power plant engineering/construction; electric power industry; environment. **Holdings:** 4000 books; 2000 standards; 2000 government and technical reports. **Subscriptions:** 100 journals and other serials. **Services:** Interlibrary loans;

copying; library open to public for reference use only by request. **Special Indexes:** Government documents and Bechtel material. **Also Known As:** Houston Power Library.

★1223★
BECHTEL POWER CORPORATION - TRUST & THRIFT INVESTMENTS CENTER (Bus-Fin)
Box 3965   Phone: (415) 768-6301
San Francisco, CA 94119   Marsha Edwards, Adm.Sec.
Staff: 2. **Subjects:** Investment analysis, economic trends and forecasts, corporate retirement plans. **Holdings:** Figures not available for books; VF drawers of company annual reports; periodicals. **Services:** Interlibrary loans; research; routing; library not open to public. **Publications:** Periodical listing.

BECHTEL (Stephen D.) ENGINEERING CENTER
See: University of California, Berkeley - Sebastian S. Kresge Engineering Library

BECK (Ira M.) MEMORIAL LIBRARY
See: Rocky Mountain Jewish Historical Society - Ira M. Beck Memorial Library

★1224★
BECK (R.W.) & ASSOCIATES - LIBRARY (Energy)
Tower Bldg., 7th Ave. at Olive Way   Phone: (206) 622-5000
Seattle, WA 98101   Enid Miller Slivka, Libn.
Staff: Prof 1; Other 2. **Subjects:** Public utilities, engineering and economics. **Holdings:** 4000 books; 7500 technical reports. **Subscriptions:** 250 journals and other serials; 15 newspapers. **Services:** Interlibrary loans; copying; SDI; library open to public with restrictions. **Computerized Information Services:** DIALOG, SDC, BRS, DOE/RECON.

★1225★
BECKER COUNTY HISTORICAL SOCIETY - WALTER D. BIRD MEMORIAL HISTORICAL LIBRARY (Hist)
915 Lake Ave.   Phone: (218) 847-2938
Detroit Lakes, MN 56501   Merry J. Coleman, Dir.
Staff: Prof 2. **Subjects:** History - Northwest Area, Minnesota, Becker County. **Holdings:** 2312 volumes; 15 VF drawers of letters, manuscripts and clippings; 18 linear feet of township and school records; 8 VF drawers of photographs; 125,000 cards of county vital statistics records. **Services:** Copying; library open to public. **Networks/Consortia:** Member of Northern Lights Library Network. **Staff:** Otto F. Zeck, Cur.

★1226★
BECKMAN INSTRUMENTS, INC. - RESEARCH LIBRARY (Sci-Tech)
2500 Harbor Blvd.   Phone: (714) 773-8906
Fullerton, CA 92634   Jean R. Miller, Chf.Libn.
Founded: 1954. **Staff:** Prof 2; Other 5. **Subjects:** Electrochemistry, scientific instrumentation, spectroscopy, physics, chemistry, chromatography, medical electronics, clinical chemistry. **Holdings:** 6500 books; 7000 bound periodical volumes; 1200 reports, papers and pamphlets (cataloged); 10 VF drawers of pamphlets (uncataloged); 1200 reels of microfilm; 3500 microfiche. **Subscriptions:** 350 journals and other serials. **Services:** Interlibrary loans; copying; library open to public with referral from outside library. **Computerized Information Services:** DIALOG, SDC, MEDLINE; computer indexing of company reports. **Networks/Consortia:** Member of CLASS. **Publications:** Monthly accessions list; Periodical Holdings list, annual. **Staff:** Colleen Alcott, Asst.Libn.

★1227★
BECKMAN INSTRUMENTS, INC. - SPINCO DIVISION - TECHNICAL LIBRARY (Sci-Tech)
1050 Page Mill Rd.   Phone: (415) 857-1150
Palo Alto, CA 94304   Phyllis M. Browning, Sci.Info.Mgr.
Founded: 1958. **Staff:** Prof 3; Other 2. **Subjects:** Biochemistry, molecular biology, engineering. **Holdings:** 5300 books; 4500 bound periodical volumes; 30 VF drawers of reprints, reports and theses. **Subscriptions:** 178 journals and other serials. **Services:** Interlibrary loans; copying; library open to public by appointment. **Computerized Information Services:** DIALOG. **Networks/Consortia:** Member of CIN. **Publications:** Current Literature Checklist, monthly - for internal distribution only; Accession List, bimonthly - for internal distribution only. **Special Indexes:** Extensive index to ultracentrifuge and amino acid analyzer applications published in the periodical literature since 1958 (card). **Staff:** Linda Frank, Asst.Libn.

★1228★
BECTON, DICKINSON & COMPANY - CORPORATE INFORMATION CENTER (Med)
Mack Centre Dr.   Phone: (201) 967-3928
Paramus, NJ 07652   Barbara L. Swan, Mgr.
Staff: Prof 2; Other 1. **Subjects:** Medicine, science and technology, business. **Holdings:** 1100 books; 202 bound periodical volumes. **Subscriptions:** 133 journals and other serials. **Services:** Interlibrary loans; copying; SDI; library open to public by telephone or written appointment. **Computerized Information Services:** DIALOG, MEDLINE, Dow Jones News Retrieval, New York Times Information Service; computerized cataloging. **Networks/Consortia:** Member of OCLC. **Staff:** Crystel Kurtzberg, Corp.Libn.

★1229★
BECTON, DICKINSON & COMPANY - RESEARCH CENTER LIBRARY (Med)
Box 12016   Phone: (919) 549-8641
Research Triangle Park, NC 27709   Dora Zia, Res.Libn.
Founded: 1973. **Staff:** Prof 1. **Subjects:** Biomedicine, bioengineering, polymer chemistry, microbiology and immunology, materials science, business. **Holdings:** 1500 books; 150 bound periodical volumes; 350 microfiche; pamphlets. **Subscriptions:** 150 journals and other serials. **Services:** Interlibrary loans; copying; library open to public with restrictions. **Computerized Information Services:** MEDLARS, DIALOG. **Publications:** Acquisitions List, quarterly - for internal distribution only.

★1230★
BECTON, DICKINSON IMMUNODIAGNOSTICS - TECHNICAL RESEARCH AND DEVELOPMENT LIBRARY (Sci-Tech)†
Mountain View Ave.   Phone: (914) 359-2700
Orangeburg, NY 10962   Olga Mancebo, Libn.
Staff: 1. **Subjects:** Immunochemistry, radioimmunoassay. **Holdings:** 1200 books; 3000 bound periodical volumes. **Subscriptions:** 56 journals and other serials. **Services:** Interlibrary loans; copying; translations; abstracts; literature searches; library open to public with restrictions.

BEDELL (Arthur J.) MEMORIAL LIBRARY
See: Wills Eye Hospital and Research Institute - Arthur J. Bedell Memorial Library

★1231★
BEDFORD HISTORICAL SOCIETY - LIBRARY (Hist)
30 S. Park St.
Box 282   Phone: (216) 232-3925
Bedford, OH 44146   Richard J. Squire, Dir.
Founded: 1955. **Subjects:** Ohio and local history, Americana, 1876 Centennial, Lincoln and Civil War, railroads and electric traction. **Holdings:** 6000 books; periodicals; pamphlets and documents. **Subscriptions:** 8 journals and other serials. **Services:** Library and museum open to public.

★1232★
BEDFORD INSTITUTE OF OCEANOGRAPHY - LIBRARY (Sci-Tech)
Box 1006   Phone: (902) 426-3675
Dartmouth, NS, Canada B2Y 4A2   J. Elizabeth Sutherland, Hd., Lib.Serv.
Founded: 1962. **Staff:** Prof 4; Other 5. **Subjects:** Physical and chemical oceanography; marine biology, ecology, geology and geophysics; fisheries research; ocean engineering; hydrographic surveys and charting. **Special Collections:** Atlantic and Arctic Canada environmental assessment documents; **Holdings:** 13,000 books; 3000 reports; 13,000 reports on microfiche; 10,000 maps and charts. **Subscriptions:** 1450 journals and other serials. **Services:** Interlibrary loans; copying; SDI; library open to public. **Computerized Information Services:** CAN/OLE, QL Systems, DIALOG, SDC; computerized serials list. **Networks/Consortia:** Member of Nova Scotia On-Line Consortium. **Publications:** BIO Review, annual - selected distribution. **Special Indexes:** KWIC indexes to reports and map/chart collections. **Staff:** N.C. Sabowitz, Systems Libn.; Ms. S. Svetlik, Ref.Libn.; Ms. J. Charest, Tech.Serv.Supv.; Ms. A. Mazeral, Lib.Info.Off.

★1233★
BEECHAM, INC. - BEECHAM LABORATORIES - MEDICAL LIBRARY (Med)
501 5th St.   Phone: (615) 764-5141
Bristol, TN 37620   Peggy Rutsis, Med.Libn.
Founded: 1945. **Staff:** Prof 1. **Subjects:** Medicine, veterinary medicine, chemistry, biology, business. **Holdings:** 2000 books; 6660 bound periodical volumes; 2.5 VF drawers of patents (Class 424). **Subscriptions:** 145 journals and other serials. **Services:** Library open to area physicians and college students.

★1234★
BEECHAM PRODUCTS - WESTERN HEMISPHERE RESEARCH - LIBRARY
(Sci-Tech)
1500 Littleton Rd.   Phone: (201) 267-1200
Parsippany, NJ 07504   Caroline Perkons, Info.Serv.Spec.
Founded: 1978. **Staff:** Prof 1; Other 1. **Subjects:** Household products, cosmetics, toiletries, proprietary drugs. **Holdings:** 900 books; 150 titles of periodicals on microfilm. **Subscriptions:** 153 journals and other serials. **Services:** Interlibrary loans; copying; SDI; library not open to public. **Computerized Information Services:** DIALOG, SDC, NLM. **Networks/Consortia:** Member of New York & New Jersey Regional Medical Library Program. **Publications:** Table of Contents Bulletin, weekly - for internal distribution only.

BEEKMAN DOWNTOWN HOSPITAL
See: New York Infirmary Beekman Downtown Hospital

BEERS (Clifford) MEMORIAL LIBRARY
See: National Mental Health Association - Clifford Beers Memorial Library

BEESON LIBRARY
See: Blackford County Historical Society - Museum and Beeson Library

BEET SUGAR DEVELOPMENT FOUNDATION
See: American Society of Sugar Beet Technologists

BEGIN (Father Leo E.) CHAPTER - LIBRARY
See: American-Canadian Genealogical Society - Father Leo E. Begin Chapter - Library

BEHAN HEALTH SCIENCE LIBRARY
See: South Hills Health System

★1235★
BEIHOFF MUSIC CORPORATION - SHEET MUSIC DEPARTMENT (Mus)
5040 W. North Ave.   Phone: (414) 442-3920
Milwaukee, WI 53208   Robert F. Loomer, Mgr.
Staff: Prof 2; Other 9. **Subjects:** Music - band, orchestra, choral; instrumental and vocal solos and ensembles; popular instrumental and vocal collections and sheets. **Holdings:** Figures not available. **Subscriptions:** 15 journals and other serials. **Services:** Department open to public; saleable music from publishers available to schools, churches, civic organizations and general public. **Staff:** Rodney Rahn, Asst.

BEINECKE RARE BOOK AND MANUSCRIPT LIBRARY
See: Yale University

BEINECKE (Richard S.) MEDICAL LIBRARY
See: Good Samaritan Hospital - Richard S. Beinecke Medical Library

★1236★
BELDING HEMINWAY COMPANY - BELDING CORTICELLI RESEARCH CENTER - LIBRARY (Sci-Tech)
                                           Phone: (203) 928-2784
Putnam, CT 06260   E.J. Page, Chf. Chemist
Subjects: Textile science, polymer science. **Holdings:** 1800 books; 1350 bound periodical volumes. **Subscriptions:** 40 journals and other serials. **Services:** Interlibrary loans; copying.

★1237★
BELGIAN CONSULATE GENERAL - LIBRARY (Area-Ethnic)
50 Rockefeller Plaza   Phone: (212) 586-5110
New York, NY 10020   Moureau Lorette
Staff: 1. **Subjects:** Belgian history, art, culture, and other aspects of Belgian life; Belgian literature in French, Dutch, and English translation. **Holdings:** 6000 volumes; reports; documents; pamphlets; photographs. **Subscriptions:** 15 journals and other serials. **Services:** Library open to public for reference use only.

BELK LIBRARY
See: Appalachian State University

BELKNAP COLLECTION FOR THE PERFORMING ARTS
See: University of Florida

BELKNAP (Waldron P.) RESEARCH LIBRARY OF AMERICAN PAINTING
See: Du Pont (Henry Francis) Winterthur Museum

BELL AEROSPACE TEXTRON - DALMO VICTOR OPERATIONS
See: Textron, Inc.

★1238★
BELL AEROSPACE TEXTRON - LAWRENCE D. BELL MEMORIAL LIBRARY
(Sci-Tech)
Box 1   Phone: (716) 297-1000
Buffalo, NY 14240   Lester M. Breslauer, Chf.Libn.
Founded: 1943. **Staff:** Prof 2. **Subjects:** Aeronautics, mathematics, aircraft, propulsion, chemistry, management, spaceflight, physics, electronics, lasers, materials and processes, air cushion vehicles, coal gasification. **Holdings:** 9500 books; 9600 bound periodical volumes; 80,000 government and contractor reports; 50,000 reports on microfiche. **Subscriptions:** 450 journals and other serials; 5 newspapers. **Services:** Interlibrary loans; copying; SDI; use of library by application through security office. **Computerized Information Services:** DIALOG, DTIC, NASA/RECON, DOE/RECON; microfiche duplication; uniterm technical reports from internal database. **Networks/Consortia:** Member of Western New York Library Resources Council (WNYLRC). **Publications:** Accession List, monthly.

BELL (Alexander Graham) ASSOCIATION FOR THE DEAF
See: Alexander Graham Bell Association for the Deaf

★1239★
BELL CANADA - INFORMATION RESOURCE CENTRE (Bus-Fin)
1050 Beaver Hall Hill, 1st Fl.   Phone: (514) 870-8500
Montreal, PQ, Canada H3C 3G4   B. Eskelson, Sect.Mgr.
Founded: 1926. **Staff:** Prof 5; Other 7. **Subjects:** Telecommunications, business and management, technology, economics, labour relations, telephony, personnel management, finance. **Holdings:** 13,000 books; 1500 bound periodical volumes; 2000 other cataloged items. **Subscriptions:** 950 journals and other serials; 10 newspapers. **Services:** Interlibrary loans; copying; SDI; library not open to public. **Computerized Information Services:** DIALOG, SDC, QL Systems, Informatech France-Quebec, New York Times Information Service, CAN/OLE, Info Globe; computerized cataloging and periodicals routing. **Publications:** Information Resource Centre Bulletin, monthly - for internal distribution only. **Staff:** Rhonda Greenfeld, Ref.Libn.; Pierre Dion, Cat.Libn.; Elinor Bartlett, SDI Libn.; Stephanie Boyd, Tech.Serv.Libn.

★1240★
BELL CANADA - LAW LIBRARY (Law)
1050 Beaver Hall Hill, Rm. 1500   Phone: (514) 861-6550
Montreal, PQ, Canada H2Z 1S4   Patricia M. Young, Law Libn.
Founded: 1924. **Staff:** Prof 1; Other 2. **Subjects:** Telephony; law - civil, communications, common. **Holdings:** 5000 books; 4000 bound periodical volumes. **Subscriptions:** 100 journals and other serials. **Services:** Library not open to public.

★1241★
BELL CANADA - O.R. INFORMATION RESOURCE CENTRE (Bus-Fin; Sci-Tech)
393 University Ave., 6th Fl.   Phone: (416) 599-7096
Toronto, ON, Canada M5G 1W9   Vivian Lung, Libn.
Founded: 1954. **Staff:** Prof 2; Other 3. **Subjects:** Business, telecommunications, engineering, management, training methods. **Special Collections:** Telephony. **Holdings:** 6000 books; 50 bound periodical volumes; 40 VF drawers of pamphlets and clippings. **Subscriptions:** 400 journals and other serials. **Services:** Interlibrary loans; copying; library open to public upon special request. **Computerized Information Services:** Info Globe, New York Times Information Service, DIALOG, SDC; computerized serials. **Publications:** Periodical checklist; periodical holdings list; IRC Bulletin. **Special Indexes:** Subject index to vertical file material.

★1242★
BELL CANADA - TELEPHONE HISTORICAL COLLECTION (Hist)
1050 Beaver Hall Hill, Rm. 820   Phone: (514) 870-5214
Montreal, PQ, Canada H2Z 1S4   Miss E.M.L. Geraghty, Hist.
Founded: 1936. **Staff:** 17. **Subjects:** History of Bell Canada, history of telephone in Canada, Alexander Graham Bell, telecommunications, Canadian telephone companies. **Special Collections:** Telephone equipment, photos, maps, directories, documents, letters, from 1870s to present. **Holdings:** 50,000 pictures and documents. **Services:** Collection open to public with restrictions. **Staff:** S. Sykes, Sect.Mgr.

★1243★
BELL HELICOPTER TEXTRON, INC. - ENGINEERING TECHNICAL LIBRARY
(Sci-Tech)
Box 482   Phone: (817) 280-3608
Fort Worth, TX 76101   Carol A. Barrett, Libn.
Founded: 1952. **Staff:** Prof 1. **Subjects:** Aerospace, aeronautics, management, engineering, computer science, mathematics. **Special Collections:** Aerospace technology/helicopters; reference data on BHC Model Helicopters; Bell Helicopter files/archives. **Holdings:** 8000 books; 500 bound periodical volumes; 10,000 technical reports; visual search microfilm files of military specifications; 10 maps; 100 AV items. **Subscriptions:** 150 journals and other serials. **Services:** Interlibrary loans; copying; SDI; library not open to public. **Computerized Information Services:** SDC, DIALOG, DTIC; computerized cataloging. **Publications:** Monthly accession list. **Formerly:** Textron, Inc. - Bell Helicopter Company - Technical Library.

★1244★
BELL & HOWELL COMPANY - LIBRARY/TECHNICAL INFORMATION SERVICES (Sci-Tech)
360 Sierra Madre Villa   Phone: (213) 796-9381
Pasadena, CA 91109   Beverly V. Busenbark, Mgr., Lib.Serv.
Founded: 1953. **Staff:** 1. **Subjects:** Chemistry, physics, electronics, photography, business, instrumentation, recording methods, mathematics. **Holdings:** 8000 books; 200 bound periodical volumes; 8000 technical reports. **Subscriptions:** 202 journals and other serials. **Services:** Interlibrary loans; copying; library open to public for limited use on request.

★1245★
BELL & HOWELL COMPANY - MICRO PHOTO DIVISION - MICROFORMS ARCHIVE (Publ)
Old Mansfield Rd.   Phone: (216) 264-6666
Wooster, OH 44691
Founded: 1946. **Staff:** 370. **Special Collections:** All on microfilm or microfiche - Underground Press Collection, American Revolutionary and Civil War Collections, Dow Jones Publications, telephone directories. **Holdings:** Periodicals on microfiche; microfilm of editions of 5500 newspapers; 130 million feet of microfilm negatives. **Services:** Copying; indexing; systems microfilming; micropublishing; library materials available for sale. **Computerized Information Services:** Career and occupational information system (COIN; internal database; materials also available on microfiche). **Publications:** Publications on Microfilm; Publications on Microfiche, annual; hardware and equipment catalogs. **Special Indexes:** Newspaper indexes to 10 daily newspapers; indexes to the American Banker, Christian Science Monitor and black newspapers; TRANSDEX Index; COIN Index. **Staff:** Dwain H. Pearce, V.P., Gen.Mgr.; Pam Myers, Advertising; Jean Austin, Supv., Indexing; Audette Karan, Supv., Spec.Coll.

★1246★
BELL & HOWELL EDUCATION GROUP - DE VRY INSTITUTE OF TECHNOLOGY - LEARNING RESOURCE CENTER (Sci-Tech)
3300 N. Campbell Ave.   Phone: (312) 929-8500
Chicago, IL 60618   Gary A. Meszaros, Libn.
Staff: Prof 1; Other 3. **Subjects:** Electronics, computer science. **Special Collections:** Sams Photofact Service (1946 to present); electronic manufacturers' catalogs; data books and specifications manuals. **Holdings:** 6234 volumes; 1 VF drawer of pamphlets; 460 senior seminar project reports. **Subscriptions:** 184 journals and other serials; 20 newspapers. **Services:** Interlibrary loans; copying; library open to public for reference use only. **Networks/Consortia:** Member of Chicago Library System; ILLINET; Metropolitan Chicago Library Assembly. **Special Catalogs:** Senior Seminar Project Reports (book).

BELL (James Ford) LIBRARY
See: University of Minnesota - James Ford Bell Library

BELL (James Ford) TECHNICAL CENTER
See: General Mills, Inc. - James Ford Bell Technical Center

BELL (Lawrence D.) MEMORIAL LIBRARY
See: Bell Aerospace Textron - Lawrence D. Bell Memorial Library

BELL-MARSH MEMORIAL LIBRARY
See: Medical Center Hospital

BELL MUSEUM OF NATURAL HISTORY
See: University of Minnesota

BELL-NORTHERN RESEARCH INC.
See: BNR Inc.

★1247★
BELL-NORTHERN RESEARCH LTD. - TECHNICAL INFORMATION CENTRE
(Sci-Tech)†
P.O. Box 3511, Station C   Phone: (613) 596-2467
Ottawa, ON, Canada K1Y 4H7   Maureen Towaij, Mgr.
Founded: 1971. **Staff:** Prof 11; Other 18. **Subjects:** Telecommunications, computer science, electronics, systems engineering, business. **Special Collections:** Standards and regulator information. **Holdings:** 30,000 books; 3000 bound periodical volumes; 18,000 technical reports (8000 hard copy; 10,000 on microfiche); 118 VF drawers containing annual reports, patents, in-house confidential reports, microforms, dissertations, technical and engineering letters, pamphlets and other documents. **Subscriptions:** 750 journals and other serials; 10 newspapers. **Services:** Interlibrary loans; copying; SDI; centre open to public by permission only. **Computerized Information Services:** DIALOG, SDC, BRS, CAN/OLE; computerized cataloging. **Publications:** "Neo" (blue, red, green), semimonthly; Upcoming Conferences, bimonthly. **Special Catalogs:** ALIRT Union Catalogue (COM), semiannual with monthly cumulative updates; Union List of Serials, semiannual. **Special Indexes:** KWOC indexes (book); Internal Document Index, quarterly - for internal distribution only; KWIC/KWOC Index to reports. **Remarks:** The information given above includes the five information centres within the Company: 3 located in Ottawa, one in Montreal, PQ and one in Toronto. **Staff:** Mrs. J. Carkner, ILL; Grant Birks, Mgr.; Mrs. C. Dimsdale, Mgr.

★1248★
BELL-NORTHERN RESEARCH LTD. - TECHNICAL INFORMATION CENTRE
(Sci-Tech)
522 University Ave.   Phone: (416) 598-0196
Toronto, ON, Canada M5G 1W7   D. Masseau, Lib.Techn.
Founded: 1976. **Subjects:** Computer science, information systems, office of the future, software development, information management, telecommunications. **Holdings:** 500 books; 500 bound periodical volumes; 100 technical reports. **Subscriptions:** 125 journals and other serials; 10 newspapers. **Services:** Interlibrary loans; copying; SDI; library not open to public. **Computerized Information Services:** DIALOG, SDC; computerized cataloging.

★1249★
BELL-NORTHERN RESEARCH LTD. - TECHNICAL INFORMATION CENTRE
(Sci-Tech)
3 Place du Commerce, Suite 500   Phone: (514) 761-5831
Verdun, PQ, Canada H3E 1H6   Ghislaine Gauthier, Info.Spec.
Founded: 1975. **Staff:** 3. **Subjects:** Telecommunications, computer communications, fiber optic communications, telephony. **Holdings:** 1300 books; 500 bound periodical volumes; 400 other cataloged items. **Subscriptions:** 200 journals and other serials; 12 newspapers. **Services:** Interlibrary loans; copying; library open to public with permission. **Computerized Information Services:** Online systems. **Remarks:** This is a branch of the Bell-Northern Technical Information Centre in Ottawa.

BELL (Ralph Pickard) LIBRARY
See: Mount Allison University - Winthrop P. Bell Collection of Acadiana

★1250★
BELL SYSTEM CENTER FOR TECHNICAL EDUCATION - LEARNING RESOURCE CENTER (Sci-Tech; Educ)
6200 Rt. 53   Phone: (312) 960-6080
Lisle, IL 60532   Mary M. Williams, Asst.Supv.
Staff: Prof 1; Other 5. **Subjects:** Telecommunications, technical training, management, instructional design. **Holdings:** 1025 books; 150 bound periodical volumes; 320 technical reference materials; 1400 binders of internal publications (for employees only); 800 videotapes; 141 audiotapes; 250 directories and catalogs; 2 drawers of microfilm. **Subscriptions:** 140 journals and other serials; 7 newspapers. **Services:** Interlibrary loans; copying; library not open to public. **Computerized Information Services:** DIALOG; computerized cataloging, acquisitions, serials and circulation. **Networks/Consortia:** Member of Suburban Library System (SLS). **Publications:** Book Lists, quarterly; Journal and Videotape Lists, annual - both for internal distribution only. **Special Catalogs:** Technical Reports (card); Monographs (card). **Remarks:** "The Bell System Center provides technical management training to the Bell System Management Force."

★1251★
BELL TELEPHONE LABORATORIES, INC. - LIBRARIES AND INFORMATION SYSTEMS CENTER (Sci-Tech; Info Sci)
600 Mountain Ave.   Phone: (201) 582-2854
Murray Hill, NJ 07974   R.A. Kennedy, Dir.
Staff: Prof 75; Other 117. **Computerized Information Services:** DIALOG, SDC, NLM, New York Times Information Service;numeric information retrieval systems, MERCURY (internal documents); computerized cataloging, acquisitions, serials and circulation. **Networks/Consortia:** Member of Bell Laboratories Library Network, serving Bell Laboratories and Western Electric personnel; OCLC through PALINET & Union Library Catalogue of Pennsylvania. **Publications:** Current Telecommunications Information, monthly; Current Management Literature, monthly; Current Technical Papers, semimonthly; Current Technical Reports, semimonthly; Bell Laboratories Talks and Papers, monthly, annual cumulation; Library Bulletin, monthly; Technical Memoranda Index, monthly, annual cumulation; Life Sciences Bulletin, monthly; Computing Information Bulletin, monthly; bibliographies, translations and book and serial catalogs - all for internal distribution only. **Remarks:** The Bell Telephone Laboratories library system comprises the principal libraries whose listings follow. A number of these are jointly managed by Bell Laboratories and Western Electric. Centralized system activities, not shown in the unit library listings are: Systems Design and Programming, Library Network Support, Technical Reports Service, Internal Technical Information Services, Information Retrieval and Alerting Services, and the Computing Information Libraries. Total staff figures above include supervisory personnel in all units listed. **Staff:** W.S. Brown, Hd., Info.Sys.Dept.; F.H. Spaulding, Hd., Lib.Oper.Dept.; V.J. Fortney, Hd., Info.Serv.Dept.; R.O. Stanton, Hd., Internal Tech.Info.; C.C. Mims, Int.Tech.Doc.Serv.Supv.; L.M. Cole, Tech.Info.Serv.Supv.; G.E. Grant, Lib. Network Sup.Supv.; A. Wang, Tech. Reports Supv.; A.F. French, Comp.Info.Supv.; D.T. Hawkins, Info.Ret./Alerting Serv.; I.C. Ross, Sys. Design Prog.Supv.

★1252★
BELL TELEPHONE LABORATORIES, INC. - TECHNICAL LIBRARY (Sci-Tech; Info Sci)
                                     Phone: (312) 690-2550
Naperville, IL 60540   Robert E. Furlong, Lib. Group Supv.
Founded: 1966. **Staff:** Prof 4; Other 8. **Subjects:** Electrical engineering, computer sciences, electronics, telecommunications, mathematics. **Holdings:** 23,000 books; 7900 bound periodical volumes; 1800 standards. **Subscriptions:** 700 journals and other serials. **Services:** Interlibrary loans; copying (both limited); library not open to public. **Publications:** Read Out. **Special Catalogs:** Visual Search Microfile. **Staff:** David D. Smith, Ref.Libn.; Kathy Romano, Ref.Libn.; Ruby Chapman, Ref.Libn.

★1253★
BELL TELEPHONE LABORATORIES, INC. - TECHNICAL LIBRARY (Sci-Tech; Info Sci)
                                     Phone: (201) 949-5236
Holmdel, NJ 07733   John E. Cooper, Lib. Group Supv.
Founded: 1962. **Staff:** Prof 4; Other 9. **Subjects:** Electronics, statistics, systems engineering, mathematics, physics, computer technology, telecommunications. **Special Collections:** BTL-authored book collection. **Holdings:** 28,300 books; 18,600 bound periodical volumes; 5400 reels of microfilm; 3800 standards; 600 AV items. **Subscriptions:** 725 journals and other serials. **Services:** Interlibrary loans; copying (both limited); library not open to public. **Special Catalogs:** Visual Search Microfile. **Remarks:** Satellite libraries are located at Crawford Hill, Holmdel, NJ 07733 and West Long Branch, NJ 07764. **Staff:** Elisabeth K. Zimmerman, Ref.Libn.; Susan Wong, Ref.Libn.; Wing Chan, Ref.Libn.; Thomas Marsden, Comp.Ref.Libn.

★1254★
BELL TELEPHONE LABORATORIES, INC. - TECHNICAL LIBRARY (Sci-Tech; Info Sci)
Middletown-Lincroft Rd.   Phone: (201) 576-2186
Lincroft, NJ 07738   Joseph A. Canose, Lib. Group Supv.
Staff: Prof 2; Other 2. **Subjects:** Electronics, statistics, competitive analysis, computer technology, software engineering, telecommunications. **Holdings:** 1500 books; 1000 bound periodical volumes. **Subscriptions:** 350 journals and other serials. **Services:** Interlibrary loans; copying; library not open to public. **Staff:** Melissa Young, Ref.Libn.

★1255★
BELL TELEPHONE LABORATORIES, INC. - TECHNICAL LIBRARY (Sci-Tech; Info Sci)
                                     Phone: (201) 582-4612
Murray Hill, NJ 07974   Ann W. Talcott, Lib. Group Supv.
Founded: 1925. **Staff:** Prof 4; Other 9. **Subjects:** Telecommunications, physics, mathematics, electronic engineering, chemistry, computers,

psychology, management, metallurgy, materials. **Holdings:** 44,900 books; 51,400 bound periodical volumes; 5100 reels of microfilm; 350 AV items. **Subscriptions:** 1150 journals and other serials. **Services:** Interlibrary loans; copying (both limited); library not open to public. **Special Catalogs:** Visual Search Microfile. **Staff:** Audrey M. Jackson, Circ.Supv.; Martha Broad, Computer Ref.Libn.; William F. Wright, Ref.Libn.; Leslie M. Lunas, Ref.Libn.

★1256★
BELL TELEPHONE LABORATORIES, INC. - TECHNICAL LIBRARY (Sci-Tech; Info Sci)
6 Corporate Pl.   Phone: (201) 981-6500
Piscataway, NJ 08854   Don T. Ho, Lib. Group Supv.
Founded: 1972. **Staff:** Prof 3; Other 4. **Subjects:** Computers, data processing, business information systems, management, software engineering, human factors, psychology, telecommunications. **Holdings:** 11,500 books; 5000 bound periodical volumes; 5500 reels of microfilm; 1500 computer documents; 285 AV tapes. **Subscriptions:** 350 journals and other serials. **Services:** Interlibrary loans; copying (both limited); library not open to public. **Special Catalogs:** Metropolitan telephone directories. **Remarks:** A satellite library is located in South Plainfield, NJ 07080. **Staff:** Marianne Purzycki, Ref.Libn.; Connie Carlson, Ref.Libn.

★1257★
BELL TELEPHONE LABORATORIES, INC. - TECHNICAL LIBRARY (Sci-Tech)
150 J.F. Kennedy Parkway
Short Hills, NJ 07078   Margaret L. McSpiritt, Lib.Supv.
Founded: 1981. **Staff:** Prof 2; Other 2. **Subjects:** Telecommunications, economics, statistics, technical writing, management, marketing. **Holdings:** 4000 books; 1000 bound periodical volumes. **Subscriptions:** 250 journals and other serials. **Services:** Interlibrary loans; copying (both limited).

★1258★
BELL TELEPHONE LABORATORIES, INC. - TECHNICAL LIBRARY (Sci-Tech)
50 Cragwood Wood   Phone: (201) 561-2587
South Plainfield, NJ 07080   Melissa L. Young, Info.Libn.
Founded: 1980. **Staff:** Prof 1; Other 1. **Subjects:** Electronics, statistics, systems engineering, telecommunications, computer technology, mathematics. **Holdings:** 1750 books; 500 bound periodical volumes. **Subscriptions:** 167 journals and other serials. **Services:** Interlibrary loans; copying (both limited).

★1259★
BELL TELEPHONE LABORATORIES, INC. - TECHNICAL LIBRARY (Sci-Tech)
185 Monmouth Parkway   Phone: (201) 870-7823
West Long Branch, NJ 07764   Elizabeth K. Zimmerman, Info.Libn.
Staff: Prof 1; Other 1. **Subjects:** Electronics, statistics, systems engineering, computer technology, telecommunications. **Holdings:** 3000 books; 2300 bound periodical volumes; 1000 computing documents. **Subscriptions:** 161 journals and other serials. **Services:** Interlibrary loans; copying (both limited); library not open to public.

★1260★
BELL TELEPHONE LABORATORIES, INC. - TECHNICAL LIBRARY (Sci-Tech; Info Sci)
                                     Phone: (201) 386-2604
Whippany, NJ 07981   Mary Jane Miller, Lib. Group Supv.
Founded: 1940. **Staff:** Prof 2; Other 5. **Subjects:** Mathematics, systems engineering, statistics, electronics, physics, solar energy, underwater technology, telecommunications. **Holdings:** 20,000 books; 17,800 bound periodical volumes; 1500 reels of microfilm; 175 AV tapes. **Subscriptions:** 700 journals and other serials. **Services:** Interlibrary loans; copying (both limited); library not open to public. **Special Catalogs:** Visual Search Microfile. **Staff:** Kathy Belyea, Ref.Libn.

★1261★
BELL TELEPHONE LABORATORIES, INC. & WESTERN ELECTRIC, INC. - TECHNICAL LIBRARY (Sci-Tech)
11900 Pecos St.   Phone: (303) 451-4275
Denver, CO 80234   James H. Varner, Lib. Group Supv.
Founded: 1969. **Staff:** Prof 1; Other 3. **Subjects:** Electronics, electrical engineering, computer science. **Holdings:** 8600 books; 1300 bound periodical volumes; 3100 technical reports. **Subscriptions:** 350 journals and other serials. **Services:** Interlibrary loans; copying (both limited); library not open to public. **Publications:** Library Bulletin; Business Communications Headlines; PBX Literature Notes. **Special Catalogs:** Visual Search Microfile.

★1262★
BELL TELEPHONE LABORATORIES, INC. & WESTERN ELECTRIC, INC. - TECHNICAL LIBRARY (Sci-Tech)
2000 Northeast Expy.   Phone: (404) 447-2803
Norcross, GA 30071   John T. Shaw, Lib. Group Supv.
Founded: 1972. **Staff:** Prof 2; Other 1. **Subjects:** Electronics, telecommunications, polymer science, fiber optics, plastics, metals and metallurgy, materials science. **Holdings:** 7000 books; 1600 bound periodical volumes; 5800 technical reports. **Subscriptions:** 300 journals and other serials. **Services:** Interlibrary loans; copying; (both limited); library not open to public. **Publications:** Library Bulletin. **Special Catalogs:** Georgia Institute of Technology card catalog on microfiche; Visual Search Microfile. **Staff:** K. Woodworth, Ref.Libn.

★1263★
BELL TELEPHONE LABORATORIES, INC. & WESTERN ELECTRIC, INC. - TECHNICAL LIBRARY (Sci-Tech)
2525 Shadeland Ave.   Phone: (317) 352-3347
Indianapolis, IN 46206   Bernard L. English, Lib. Group Supv.
Founded: 1962. **Staff:** Prof 2; Other 2. **Subjects:** Acoustics, electrical and mechanical engineering, industrial management, plastics, materials, telecommunications, physics, mathematics. **Holdings:** 6000 books; 1800 bound periodical volumes; 100 technical reports. **Subscriptions:** 500 journals and other serials. **Services:** Interlibrary loans; copying (both limited); library not open to public. **Publications:** New Directions in Research; Library Bulletin. **Special Catalogs:** Visual Search Microfile. **Staff:** Irene Cain, Ref.Libn.

★1264★
BELL TELEPHONE LABORATORIES, INC. & WESTERN ELECTRIC, INC. - TECHNICAL LIBRARY (Sci-Tech)
1600 Osgood St.   Phone: (617) 681-6752
North Andover, MA 01845   Mary E. Sexton, Lib. Group Supv.
Founded: 1957. **Staff:** Prof 2; Other 1. **Subjects:** Electronics, electrical engineering, telecommunications, computer sciences. **Holdings:** 7200 books; 2100 bound periodical volumes; 7500 technical reports. **Subscriptions:** 350 journals and other serials. **Services:** Interlibrary loans; copying (both limited); library not open to public. **Publications:** TIPS (Technical Information Publications Service). **Special Catalogs:** Visual Search Microfile. **Staff:** Natasha Glendon, Ref.Libn.

★1265★
BELL TELEPHONE LABORATORIES, INC. & WESTERN ELECTRIC, INC. - TECHNICAL LIBRARY (Sci-Tech)
6200 E. Broad St.   Phone: (614) 868-3696
Columbus, OH 43213   Beverly A. Kaushagen, Lib. Group Supv.
Founded: 1959. **Staff:** Prof 1; Other 4. **Subjects:** Electronics, engineering, physics, chemistry, computer science, mathematics, telecommunications, metallurgy. **Holdings:** 8900 books; 2450 bound periodical volumes; 7800 technical reports (microfiche). **Subscriptions:** 350 journals and other serials. **Services:** Interlibrary loans; copying (both limited); library not open to public. **Publications:** Library Bulletin. **Special Catalogs:** Visual Search Microfile.

★1266★
BELL TELEPHONE LABORATORIES, INC. & WESTERN ELECTRIC, INC. - TECHNICAL LIBRARY (Sci-Tech)
555 Union Blvd.   Phone: (215) 439-7648
Allentown, PA 18103   Mary L. Coakley, Lib. Group Supv.
Founded: 1957. **Staff:** Prof 2; Other 2. **Subjects:** Materials, electronics, chemistry, telecommunications, solid state physics. **Holdings:** 6900 books; 3400 bound periodical volumes; 10,500 technical reports. **Subscriptions:** 350 journals and other serials. **Services:** Interlibrary loans; copying (both limited); library not open to public. **Publications:** Library News; Special Catalogs: Visual. **Staff:** C.L. Dane, Ref.Libn.

★1267★
BELL TELEPHONE LABORATORIES, INC. & WESTERN ELECTRIC, INC. - TECHNICAL LIBRARY (Sci-Tech)
2525 N. 11th St.   Phone: (215) 929-7990
Reading, PA 19603   Ann M. Buck, Lib. Group Supv.
Founded: 1961. **Staff:** Prof 2; Other 1. **Subjects:** Physics, chemistry, mathematics, electronics. **Holdings:** 6100 books; 3100 bound periodical volumes. **Subscriptions:** 260 journals and other serials. **Services:** Interlibrary loans; copying (both limited); library not open to public. **Publications:** Library News. **Special Catalogs:** Visual Search Microfile. **Staff:** Genevieve L. Johnson

BELL (Winthrop P.) COLLECTION OF ACADIANA
See: Mount Allison University - Winthrop P. Bell Collection of Acadiana

BELLAIRE RESEARCH CENTER LIBRARY
See: Shell Development Company

★1268★
BELLARMINE COLLEGE - THOMAS MERTON STUDIES CENTER (Rel-Theol; Soc Sci)
Newburg Rd.   Phone: (502) 452-8187
Louisville, KY 40205   Robert E. Daggy, Cur.
Staff: Prof 1. **Subjects:** Thomas Merton, monasticism, spirituality, peace and peace movements, literary criticism, civil rights. **Holdings:** 1708 books; 16,104 journals and pieces of correspondence; 1122 typescripts and other manuscripts; 3469 photographs and drawings; 518 tapes. **Services:** Copying; library open to public with restrictions. **Publications:** The Merton SEASONAL of Bellarmine College (occasional newsletter); The Ark: An Ecumenical Newsletter.

★1269★
BELLET (Samuel) LIBRARY OF LAW, MEDICINE AND BEHAVIORAL SCIENCE (Soc Sci)
201E Piersol Bldg. H.U.P.   Phone: (215) 662-2848
Philadelphia, PA 19104
Founded: 1974. **Staff:** Prof 1. **Subjects:** Forensic psychiatry. **Holdings:** 600 books; 54 bound periodical volumes; 95 cassette tapes (cataloged); VF drawers. **Subscriptions:** 41 journals and other serials. **Services:** Interlibrary loans; copying; library open to public by appointment. **Publications:** New Acquisitions List, quarterly - available to interested patrons; Recent Publications in Forensic Psychiatry, quarterly. **Remarks:** Affiliated with the University of Pennsylvania Hospital.

★1270★
BELLEVUE HOSPITAL - MEDICAL LIBRARY (Med)
1st Ave. at 27th St.   Phone: (212) 561-6535
New York, NY 10016   Paul Barth, Dir.
Staff: Prof 1; Other 1. **Subjects:** Clinical medicine. **Holdings:** 2000 books; 10,000 bound periodical volumes. **Subscriptions:** 225 journals and other serials. **Services:** Copying; library open to public.

★1271★
BELLIN MEMORIAL HOSPITAL - HEALTH SCIENCES LIBRARY (Med)
744 S. Webster Ave.
Box 1700   Phone: (414) 468-3693
Green Bay, WI 54305   Cynthia Reinl, Health Sci.Libn.
Founded: 1909. **Staff:** Prof 1; Other 7. **Subjects:** Nursing, medicine. **Holdings:** 2700 books; 1055 bound periodical volumes; 400 video cassettes; 400 filmstrip programs; 15 motion pictures; 6 VF drawers of pamphlets and clippings. **Subscriptions:** 190 journals and other serials. **Services:** Interlibrary loans; copying; library open to public for reference use only. **Computerized Information Services:** DIALOG, MEDLINE. **Networks/Consortia:** Member of Fox River Valley Area Library Cooperative; Northeast Wisconsin Intertype Libraries; Regional Medical Library - Region 3. **Publications:** List of acquisitions, monthly - for internal distribution only.

BELLIS MEDICAL LIBRARY
See: St. Mary Medical Center

BELLMAN (Russell) LIBRARY
See: St. Joseph's Hospital - Russell Bellman Library

★1272★
BELMONT ABBEY COLLEGE - ABBOT VINCENT TAYLOR LIBRARY - SPECIAL COLLECTIONS (Hum)
       Phone: (704) 825-3711
Belmont, NC 28012   Marjorie McDermott, Dir., Lrng.Rsrcs.
Founded: 1941. **Special Collections:** Benedictine Monasticism (1230 volumes); Caroliniana (819 volumes); rare books (10,020 volumes). **Services:** Interlibrary loans; copying; library open to public with restrictions. **Networks/Consortia:** Member of Charlotte Area Educational Consortium.

★1273★
BELMONT COUNTY LAW LIBRARY (Law)†
Court House   Phone: (614) 695-2121
St. Clairsville, OH 43950   John W. Greenlee, Libn.
Subjects: Law. **Holdings:** 22,000 volumes.

BELMONT REGIONAL LIBRARY
See: New York Public Library

★1274★
BELOIT COLLEGE - HERBERT V. KOHLER SCIENCE LIBRARY (Sci-Tech)
Phone: (608) 365-3391
Beloit, WI 53511   Glenn Remelts, Hd., Pub.Serv./Br.Lib.
Founded: 1931. **Staff:** Prof 1; Other 1. **Subjects:** Physics, chemistry, geology, biology, mathematics. **Holdings:** 17,000 books; 10,000 bound periodical volumes; depository for U.S. government documents. **Subscriptions:** 150 journals and other serials. **Services:** Interlibrary loans; copying; library open to public for reference use only. **Computerized Information Services:** BRS. **Networks/Consortia:** Member of Wisconsin Library Consortium; OCLC.

★1275★
BELOIT COLLEGE - LOGAN MUSEUM OF ANTHROPOLOGY - LIBRARY (Soc Sci)
Phone: (608) 365-3391
Beloit, WI 53511   Dr. J. Edson Way, Dir.
Staff: Prof 4. **Subjects:** Ethnography, archeology, physical anthropology. **Special Collections:** French and North African Paleolithic Collection; A.G. Heath Collection; North American Indian materials. **Holdings:** Figures not available for books. **Subscriptions:** 10 journals and other serials. **Services:** Interlibrary loans; copying; library open to public. **Publications:** Bulletin series, occasional papers - both irregular.

★1276★
BELOIT HISTORICAL SOCIETY - BARTLETT HISTORICAL LIBRARY (Hist)
2149 St. Lawrence Ave.   Phone: (608) 365-3811
Beloit, WI 53511   Ivy P. Knibbs, Exec.Sec.
Founded: 1910. **Subjects:** Local history, politics, education, religion, industry, home and family. **Special Collections:** Farm and garden tools; Service Doll Collections; furniture. **Holdings:** 1200 books and bound periodical volumes; 175 clippings **Subscriptions:** 200 journals and other serials. **Services:** Library open to public for reference use only.

BELT (Elmer) LIBRARY OF VINCIANA
See: University of California, Los Angeles - Art Library - Elmer Belt Library of Vinciana

BEMIDJI STATE UNIVERSITY - NORTH CENTRAL MINNESOTA HISTORICAL CENTER
See: North Central Minnesota Historical Center

BENDER (John H.) LIBRARY OF PRINTS AND DRAWINGS
See: Nelson Gallery-Atkins Museum - Spencer Art Reference Library

BENDER (Lauretta) STAFF LIBRARY
See: Queens Children's Psychiatric Center - Lauretta Bender Staff Library

★1277★
BENDER (Matthew) AND COMPANY, INC. - LIBRARY (Law)
235 E. 45th St.   Phone: (212) 661-5050
New York, NY 10017   Rudolph Caughman, Chf.Libn.
Staff: Prof 2; Other 1. **Subjects:** Law. **Holdings:** 55,000 books. **Services:** Library not open to public.

★1278★
BENDIX CORPORATION - ADVANCED TECHNOLOGY CENTER LIBRARY (Sci-Tech)
9140 Old Annapolis Rd., Rte. 108   Phone: (301) 992-6680
Columbia, MD 21045   T.A. Rupprecht, Supv. of Lib.Serv.
Founded: 1981. **Staff:** Prof 1. **Subjects:** Physics, acoustics, composites, signal processing, friction, semi-conductor materials. **Holdings:** 2000 books; 1500 bound periodical volumes. **Subscriptions:** 103 journals and other serials. **Services:** Interlibrary loans; library open to public by appointment. **Computerized Information Services:** DIALOG, SDC, New York Times Information Service; internal database; computerized circulation. **Networks/Consortia:** Member of OCLC.

★1279★
BENDIX CORPORATION - BENDIX AVIONICS DIVISION - LIBRARY (Sci-Tech)
2100 N.W. 62nd St.
Box 9414
Fort Lauderdale, FL 33310   Phone: (305) 776-4100
                                   Patricia Ferguson, Libn.
Staff: 1. **Subjects:** Avionics engineering. **Holdings:** 1000 books; 100 unbound periodical volumes; 8 VF drawers of DDC/NTIS documents and 2500 microforms of documents; Government Reports Announcements, 1968 to present. **Subscriptions:** 125 journals and other serials. **Services:** Interlibrary loans (within corporation); library not open to public. **Publications:** Library News, quarterly.

★1280★
BENDIX CORPORATION - BENDIX ENERGY CONTROLS DIVISION - ENGINEERING LIBRARY (Sci-Tech)
717 Bendix Dr.   Phone: (219) 237-5976
South Bend, IN 46620   Mary Jane Brayfield, Libn.
Founded: 1935. **Staff:** 1. **Subjects:** Aeronautical engineering, strength of materials and structures, propulsion, energy absorption, fuel controls. **Holdings:** 2300 books; 1800 bound periodical volumes; 10,000 technical reports. **Subscriptions:** 300 journals and other serials. **Services:** Interlibrary loans.

★1281★
BENDIX CORPORATION - COMMUNICATIONS DIVISION - ENGINEERING LIBRARY (Sci-Tech)
1300 E. Joppa Rd.   Phone: (301) 853-4383
Baltimore, MD 21204   Phyllis Davis, Libn.
Founded: 1950. **Staff:** 2. **Subjects:** Technology - electrical, electronics; physics; mathematics; business. **Holdings:** 2200 books; 717 bound periodical volumes; 24 file drawers of transactions; 35 feet of shelf space of conference proceedings; 4 VF drawers. **Subscriptions:** 153 journals and other serials. **Services:** Interlibrary loans; copying; library open to public with restrictions. **Publications:** Bulletin - for internal distribution only. **Staff:** Alice Tribull, Asst.Libn.

★1282★
BENDIX CORPORATION - ELECTRICAL COMPONENTS DIVISION - ENGINEERING LIBRARY (Sci-Tech)
Phone: (607) 563-5605
Sidney, NY 13838   Betty L. Burnham, Libn.
Founded: 1942. **Staff:** Prof 1; Other 1. **Subjects:** Electrical engineering, physics, ignition systems and devices, materials engineering, electronic components, mathematics, microelectronics, fuel injection. **Holdings:** 2300 books; 10 VF drawers of internal reports; 750 microfiche; 1000 government reports; 1100 pamphlets; 65 shelves of unbound periodicals. **Subscriptions:** 80 journals and other serials. **Services:** Interlibrary loans (limited); library not open to public. **Computerized Information Services:** Computerized cataloging and serials.

★1283★
BENDIX CORPORATION - ENGINEERING REFERENCE LIBRARY (Sci-Tech)
Phone: (201) 288-2000
Teterboro, NJ 07608   Beth Charnley Owen, Libn.
Founded: 1940. **Staff:** Prof 1; Other 1. **Subjects:** Aeronautics, astronautics, mathematics, computer sciences, electronics, flight instruments, physics, chemistry. **Holdings:** 35,000 books; government reports; military and NASA specifications and standards. **Subscriptions:** 100 journals and other serials. **Services:** Interlibrary loans; library not open to public.

★1284★
BENDIX CORPORATION - INDUSTRIAL GROUP - RESEARCH DIVISION LIBRARY (Sci-Tech)
28999 Aurora Rd.   Phone: (216) 432-6144
Solon, OH 44139   Carla S. Newsome, Libn.
Founded: 1952. **Staff:** Prof 1. **Subjects:** Engineering, machine tools, materials, management. **Holdings:** 3000 books; 100 bound periodical volumes; 8000 microfiche; 2000 NTIS Reports. **Subscriptions:** 175 journals and other serials. **Services:** Interlibrary loans; copying; library open to public with permission of librarian. **Computerized Information Services:** DIALOG, SDC; computerized cataloging. **Networks/Consortia:** Member of OCLC; OHIONET. **Publications:** Research Division Library Newsletter, monthly - for internal distribution only. **Formerly:** Warner & Swasey Company - Research Division Library.

★1285★
BENDIX CORPORATION - INFORMATION CENTER (Sci-Tech)
Box 5060   Phone: (313) 827-5618
Southfield, MI 48037   Mary C. Blaschak, Sr.Libn.
Founded: 1950. **Staff:** Prof 1; Other 1. **Subjects:** Business information. **Holdings:** 500 books. **Subscriptions:** 50 journals and other serials. **Services:** Interlibrary loans; copying; library open to public by permission of the librarian. **Computerized Information Services:** DIALOG, New York Times Information Service, SDC. **Networks/Consortia:** Member of OCLC; Michigan Library Consortium. **Staff:** E. Giancott, Acq.

★1286★
BENDIX CORPORATION - INSTRUMENTS & LIFE SUPPORT DIVISION - ENGINEERING LIBRARY (Sci-Tech)*
2734 Hickory Grove Rd.   Phone: (319) 383-6387
Davenport, IA 52808   Kathryn Nitz, Tech.Libn.
Staff: Prof 1. **Subjects:** Mechanical and electrical engineering, cryogenics,

medical sciences, physics, chemistry, mathematics, business management. **Holdings:** 1000 books; 3200 bound periodical volumes; 3000 pamphlets (indexed); 38 VF drawers of unbound technical journals; patents, 1948 to present. **Subscriptions:** 80 journals and other serials. **Services:** Interlibrary loans; copying; SDI; library not open to public. **Networks/Consortia:** Member of Quad City Biomedical Consortium; River Bend Library System.

★1287★
BENDIX CORPORATION - KANSAS CITY DIVISION - TECHNICAL INFORMATION CENTER (Sci-Tech)
2000 E. 95th St.
Box 1159   Phone: (816) 997-2694
Kansas City, MO 64141   Lucile Stratton, Libn.
Founded: 1970. **Staff:** Prof 2. **Subjects:** Materials, processing. **Holdings:** 9000 books; military and federal specifications and standards; technical reports; vendor catalogs. **Subscriptions:** 275 journals and other serials; 30 newspapers. **Services:** Interlibrary loans; center not open to public. **Computerized Information Services:** Online system.

★1288★
BENDIX FIELD ENGINEERING CORPORATION - GRAND JUNCTION OFFICE - TECHNICAL LIBRARY (Energy)
Box 1569   Phone: (303) 242-8621
Grand Junction, CO 81502-1569   Sara L. Murphy, Sr.Libn.
Founded: 1947. **Staff:** Prof 3; Other 2. **Subjects:** Geology, chemistry, mining, geophysics, uranium, physics, geoscience. **Special Collections:** Law (100 titles); U.S. Geological Survey publications (complete set). **Holdings:** 14,000 books; 1000 bound periodical volumes; 13,000 unbound journals and reports; 10,000 microfiche; 50,000 drill logs; 25,000 maps. **Subscriptions:** 350 journals and other serials. **Services:** Interlibrary loans; copying; library open to public. **Remarks:** The Bendix Field Engineering Corporation operates under contract to the U.S. Department of Energy. **Staff:** Kristin Graves, Libn.; William C. Graham, Libn.

BENEDICTINE SISTERS OF COVINGTON, KENTUCKY - ST. WALBURG CONVENT
See: St. Walburg Convent of Benedictine Sisters of Covington, Kentucky

★1289★
BENEFICIAL MANAGEMENT CORPORATION - LIBRARY (Bus-Fin)†
Beneficial Bldg.   Phone: (201) 455-7000
Morristown, NJ 07208   Patricia A. Moffat, Libn.
Founded: 1955. **Staff:** 1. **Subjects:** Consumer finance. **Holdings:** 2000 books. **Subscriptions:** 150 journals and other serials. **Services:** Library not open to public.

BENET LIBRARY
See: St. Benedict's Abbey

BENET WEAPONS LABORATORY
See: U.S. Army - Armament Research & Development Command

BENGER LABORATORY
See: Du Pont de Nemours (E.I.) & Company, Inc.

★1290★
BENHAM GROUP - INFORMATION RESOURCE CENTER (Art; Sci-Tech)
1200 N.W. 63rd
Box 20400   Phone: (405) 848-6631
Oklahoma City, OK 73156   Nevine Butcher, Mgr.
Founded: 1980. **Staff:** Prof 2; Other 3. **Subjects:** Architecture; engineering - mechanical, civil, electrical; power; environmental services. **Special Collections:** Webster L. Benham Engineering Collection. **Holdings:** 3000 books; 175 bound periodical volumes; 50,000 slides; 60 reels of microfilm; 300 microfiche. **Subscriptions:** 175 journals and other serials; 12 newspapers. **Services:** Copying; SDI; library not open to public. **Computerized Information Services:** SDC, DIALOG; computerized cataloging. **Staff:** Julie Wickens, Info.Spec.; Susan Fulkerson, Info.Spec.

BENNER SPRING FISH RESEARCH STATION
See: Pennsylvania State Fish Commission Library

BENNETT (Charles A.) COLLECTION
See: Bradley University - Virginius H. Chase Special Collections Center - Charles A. Bennett Collection

★1291★
BENNETT COLLEGE - THOMAS F. HOLGATE LIBRARY - SPECIAL COLLECTIONS (Area-Ethnic)
                                      Phone: (919) 273-4431
Greensboro, NC 27420   Ednita W. Bullock, Hd.Libn.
Staff: Prof 3; Other 4. **Special Collections:** Afro-American Women's Collection (386 books and 2 VF drawers); Norris Wright Cuney Papers (manuscripts and newspaper clippings); College Archives (51 boxes, 3 file cabinets, 1 bookcase). **Services:** Interlibrary loans; copying; library open to public. **Networks/Consortia:** Member of Cooperative College Library Center (CCLC). **Staff:** Doris Davis, Tech.Serv.Libn.; Montez Byers, Rd.Serv.Libn.

★1292★
BENNETT JONES - LIBRARY (Law)
3200 Shell Centre
400 4th Ave., S.W.   Phone: (403) 267-3226
Calgary, AB, Canada T2P 0X9   Jennifer Martison, Libn.
Staff: Prof 1; Other 1. **Subjects:** Law. **Holdings:** 10,000 books. **Subscriptions:** 200 journal titles. **Services:** Interlibrary loans; copying; SDI; library open to public with restrictions. **Special Indexes:** Legal memoranda (in-house).

★1293★
BENNINGTON MUSEUM - GENEALOGICAL LIBRARY (Hist)
W. Main St.   Phone: (802) 442-2180
Bennington, VT 05201   P.N. Kennedy, Libn.
Staff: Prof 1. **Subjects:** Genealogy, regional history. **Holdings:** 4000 books; manuscripts; bound newspaper files; Vermont atlases. **Services:** Copying (limited); library open to public by appointment March through November.

BENSCHOTER (Agnes & Clarence) MEMORIAL LIBRARY
See: Sheridan County Historical Society, Inc. - Agnes & Clarence Benschoter Memorial Library

BENSON LATIN AMERICAN COLLECTION
See: University of Texas, Austin

★1294★
BENTLEY COLLEGE - SOLOMON R. BAKER LIBRARY (Bus-Fin)
Beaver & Forest Sts.   Phone: (617) 891-2231
Waltham, MA 02154   Joyce A. Bennett, Dir.
Founded: 1959. **Staff:** Prof 11; Other 13. **Subjects:** Accounting, auditing, taxation, finance, economic and business conditions. **Special Collections:** Bowles Collection; Historical Accounting Collection; business history (McConnell); rare accounting; business works; archives. **Holdings:** 109,771 books; 4327 bound periodical volumes; 7442 reels of microfilm; 10,000 slides; 600 cassettes; 301 filmstrips; 58,526 microfiche; 150 videotapes; 75 films. **Services:** Interlibrary loans; copying; library open to public with registration and fee. **Computerized Information Services:** DIALOG; internal database; computerized cataloging, serials and acquisitions. **Networks/Consortia:** Member of WELEXACOL. **Publications:** Library Newsletter; journal listing; Accessions Lists. **Staff:** Index of Archives Materials. **Staff:** Tjalda Belastock, Hd., Rd.Serv.; Karen Kahn, ILL, Ref.Libn.; Ruth Horwitz, Media Spec.; Stephanie Griffin, Cat.; John Cathcart, Hd., Tech.Serv.; Sheila Ekman, Ref.Libn.; Karen Delorey, Ref.Libn.; Lauren Muffs, Ref.Libn.; Marcia Ladd, Bibliog.Instr.; Colleen Murphy, Hd., Media Serv.

BENTLEY HISTORICAL LIBRARY
See: University of Michigan - Michigan Historical Collections

★1295★
BENTON AND BOWLES, INC. - LIBRARY (Bus-Fin)
909 3rd Ave.   Phone: (212) 758-6200
New York, NY 10022   Lois Burke, Libn.
Founded: 1932. **Staff:** Prof 3; Other 2. **Subjects:** Advertising, marketing and promotion, industries, products and services. **Holdings:** 6000 books; 1100 bound periodical volumes; 9800 unbound periodicals; 260 reels of microfilm; 10 years of advertising tearsheets. **Subscriptions:** 600 journals and other serials. **Computerized Information Services:** DIALOG, New York Times Information Service, Mead Data Central; computerized circulation.

★1296★
BENTON COUNTY HISTORICAL SOCIETY - MUSEUM & LIBRARY/ARCHIVES (Hist)
Box 355   Phone: (501) 524-3217
Siloam Springs, AR 72761   J. Roger Huff, Sec./Ed.
Founded: 1954. **Staff:** Prof 1. **Subjects:** Local history and genealogy. **Holdings:** 116 books and bound periodical volumes; 200 other cataloged items; photographs. **Subscriptions:** 25 journals and other serials. **Services:**

Library open to public by appointment. **Publications:** Benton County Pioneer, quarterly - to members.

★1297★
BENTON SERVICES CENTER - MEDICAL LIBRARY (Med)
Phone: (501) 778-1111
Benton, AR 72015   Wilma Umberson, Lib.Techn.
Founded: 1964. **Staff:** 1. **Subjects:** Psychiatry, geriatrics, psychology, medicine, nursing, social work. **Holdings:** 3873 books; 604 bound periodical volumes; 86 article files on mental health; 200 pamphlets and documents (uncataloged). **Subscriptions:** 50 journals and other serials. **Services:** Interlibrary loans; copying; library open to public for reference use only.

BENZ LIBRARY
See: 3M - 236 Library

★1298★
BEREA COLLEGE - HUTCHINS LIBRARY - SPECIAL COLLECTIONS (Hum; Hist)
Phone: (606) 986-9341
Berea, KY 40404   Gerald F. Roberts, Spec.Coll.Libn.
Staff: Prof 1; Other 1. **Subjects:** Appalachia, Berea, Lincoln. **Special Collections:** Weatherford-Hammond Appalachian Collection (8145 volumes); Berea Collection (1430 volumes); Lincoln Collection (1541 volumes); rare books (9469 volumes); Southern Appalachian Archives (350 linear feet); college archives (350 linear feet). **Holdings:** 20,585 books; 821 bound periodical volumes. **Subscriptions:** 50 journals and other serials; 11 newspapers. **Services:** Interlibrary loans; copying; library open to public with restrictions. **Computerized Information Services:** Computerized cataloging. **Networks/Consortia:** Member of OCLC through SOLINET.

★1299★
BEREAN BIBLE COLLEGE - LIBRARY (Rel-Theol)
460 31st Ave., N.W.
Box 3900, Postal Station B   Phone: (403) 230-3424
Calgary, AB, Canada T2M 4N2   J. Ray Doerksen, Dir. of Lib.Serv.
Founded: 1948. **Staff:** Prof 1; Other 1. **Subjects:** Theological doctrine, missions, science, history, Christian education, apologetics, homiletics, evangelism. **Holdings:** 6400 books; 84 bound periodical volumes; 200 unbound periodicals; 500 AV programs; 500 clipping files; 200 cassettes and tapes; 500 microfiche. **Subscriptions:** 70 journals and other serials. **Services:** Library open to public by arrangement.

★1300★
BEREAN INSTITUTE - LIBRARY (Bus-Fin; Sci-Tech)
1901 W. Girard Ave.   Phone: (215) 763-4833
Philadelphia, PA 19130   Pamela Theus, Hd.Libn.
Staff: Prof 1; Other 1. **Subjects:** Business administration, secretarial science, electronics, cosmetology, data processing. **Special Collections:** Edyth Ingraham (black history and education; 300 volumes). **Holdings:** 2000 books; 1000 unbound periodicals; 200 cassette tapes; 25 filmstrips; 100 transparencies. **Subscriptions:** 49 journals and other serials. **Services:** Interlibrary loans; copying; library open to public for reference use only. **Publications:** Suggested reading list.

BERENS (Conrad) LIBRARY
See: National Society to Prevent Blindness - Conrad Berens Library

BERENSON ARCHIVE
See: Columbia University - Department of Art History & Archaeology - Photograph Collection

BERG COLLECTION
See: New York Public Library

★1301★
BERGAN MERCY HOSPITAL - MEDICAL LIBRARY (Med)
7500 Mercy Rd.   Phone: (402) 398-6092
Omaha, NE 68124   Ken Oyer, Libn.
Staff: Prof 1; Other 1. **Subjects:** Obstetrics, gynecology, medicine, nursing, health care administration. **Holdings:** 2800 books; 2600 bound periodical volumes; 500 folders of reprints; 6124 microfiche; 234 reels of microfilm; 650 AV items. **Subscriptions:** 179 journals and other serials. **Services:** Interlibrary loans; copying; lending AV materials; AV production (in-house); library not open to public. **Networks/Consortia:** Member of Midcontinental Regional Medical Library Program. **Formerly:** Archbishop Bergan Mercy Hospital.

★1302★
BERGEN COUNTY HISTORICAL SOCIETY - JOHNSON LIBRARY (Hist)
274 Main St.
Hackensack, NJ 07601   Richard Goerner, Libn.
Founded: 1902. **Staff:** Prof 1. **Subjects:** State and local history, genealogy. **Special Collections:** Colonial and early American manuscripts of local importance; historical atlases and maps (original editions and facsimiles). **Holdings:** 2900 books; 30 VF drawers of pamphlets; 5 VF drawers of maps; 49 reels of microfilmed manuscripts; 68 reels of microfilmed newspapers. **Subscriptions:** 43 journals and other serials. **Services:** Copying; library open to public. **Networks/Consortia:** Member of New Jersey Library Network Services; Bergen County Cooperative Library System. **Special Catalogs:** Union List of Periodicals, Manuscripts on Microfilm (Hackensack-Ridgewood Local History Service).

★1303★
BERGEN COUNTY LAW LIBRARY (Law)
Administrative Bldg.   Phone: (201) 646-2056
Hackensack, NJ 07601   Edna M. Oakley, Libn.
Subjects: Law. **Holdings:** 11,000 volumes. **Services:** Copying.

★1304★
BERGEN PINES COUNTY HOSPITAL - MEDICAL LIBRARY (Med)
E. Ridgewood Ave.   Phone: (201) 967-4000
Paramus, NJ 07652   Victoria Gonzalez, Med.Libn.
Staff: 1. **Subjects:** Medicine. **Holdings:** 1200 books; 1824 bound periodical volumes. **Subscriptions:** 160 journals and other serials. **Services:** Library not open to public. **Networks/Consortia:** Member of Bergen/Passaic Health Sciences Library Consortium.

BERGER BAND LIBRARY
See: University of Minnesota - Music Library

BERGQUIST (Ehrling) REGIONAL HOSPITAL
See: U.S. Air Force Hospital - Ehrling Bergquist Regional Hospital

BERGSTROM AIR FORCE BASE (TX)
See: U.S. Air Force Base - Bergstrom Base Library

★1305★
BERGSTROM-MAHLER MUSEUM - REFERENCE LIBRARY
165 N. Park Ave.
Neenah, WI 54956
Founded: 1964. **Subjects:** Glass paperweights, glass, art - American, Italian, French, Far and Near Eastern, Spanish and German. **Special Collections:** Glass paperweights; antique Bibles (5). **Holdings:** 1450 books; 70 bound periodical volumes. **Remarks:** Presently inactive.

★1306★
BERKELEY PUBLIC LIBRARY - ART AND MUSIC DEPARTMENT (Art; Mus)
2090 Kittredge St.   Phone: (415) 644-6785
Berkeley, CA 94704   Anne C. Nutting, Supv.Prog.Libn./Hd.
Founded: 1960. **Staff:** Prof 3; Other 7. **Subjects:** Art, music. **Holdings:** 20,582 books; 2909 music scores (cataloged); 9168 phonograph records; 13,267 art slides; 464 framed reproductions; 378 miniature scores; 865 cassettes. **Subscriptions:** 120 journals and other serials. **Services:** Interlibrary loans; copying; library open to public. **Networks/Consortia:** Member of Bay Area Library & Information System. **Staff:** Heo Park, Sr.Libn.; Lynn Murdock, Libn.

★1307★
BERKELEY UNIFIED SCHOOL DISTRICT - CURRICULUM LIBRARY (Educ)★
1720 Oregon St.   Phone: (415) 644-6260
Berkeley, CA 94703   Scott McFarland, Prog.Supv.
Subjects: Education. **Holdings:** Figures not available. **Services:** Library not open to public.

BERKENMEYER (Wilhelm C.) COLONIAL PARISH LIBRARY
See: Wittenberg University - Thomas Library

★1308★
BERKLEE COLLEGE OF MUSIC - LIBRARY (Mus)
1140 Boylston St.   Phone: (617) 266-1400
Boston, MA 02215   John Voigt, Libn.
Founded: 1945. **Staff:** Prof 2; Other 12. **Subjects:** Core music, jazz, core humanities, commercial music. **Special Collections:** Jazz; Woody Herman Archives. **Holdings:** 16,000 books; 189 bound periodical volumes; 5537 records and tapes; 10,798 musical scores. **Subscriptions:** 70 journals and

other serials. **Services:** Library open to public by specific request. **Staff:** Gary Haggerty, Asst.Libn.

★1309★
BERKS COUNTY LAW LIBRARY (Law)
Court House
Reading, PA 19601
Phone: (215) 375-6121
Linda Fuerle Fisk, Libn.
Founded: 1859. **Staff:** Prof 1. **Subjects:** Law. **Holdings:** 23,000 books and bound periodical volumes. **Subscriptions:** 185 journals and other serials. **Services:** Interlibrary loans; copying; library open to public for reference use only; librarian must be present.

★1310★
BERKSHIRE ATHENAEUM - MUSIC AND ARTS DEPARTMENT (Art; Mus)
One Wendell Ave.
Pittsfield, MA 01201
Phone: (413) 442-1559
Jean Bousquet, Supv., Music & Art
Staff: Prof 1; Other 3. **Subjects:** Music, art, crafts, antiques, dance, photography. **Special Collections:** Morgan Room Collection - books, prints, programs and photographs on the dance (1000 items). **Holdings:** 5000 books; 12,000 phonograph records; 2500 scores; 1600 pieces of early sheet music; 1000 cassettes (all cataloged); 3000 art prints. **Subscriptions:** 28 journals and other serials. **Services:** Interlibrary loans; library open to public.

★1311★
BERKSHIRE CHRISTIAN COLLEGE - DR. LINDEN J. CARTER LIBRARY (Rel-Theol)
200 Stockbridge Rd.
Lenox, MA 01240
Phone: (413) 637-0838
Lois W. Jones, Dir. of Lib.
Founded: 1897. **Staff:** Prof 2; Other 1. **Subjects:** Bible, theology, religion, social sciences, philosophy, psychology, history, literature, fine arts, languages. **Special Collections:** History and doctrine of 19th century Adventist movement; archives of Advent Christian Church. **Holdings:** 40,000 books and bound periodical volumes. **Subscriptions:** 400 journals and other serials; 5 newspapers. **Services:** Interlibrary loans; copying; library open to public.

BERKSHIRE EAGLE
See: Eagle Publishing Company

★1312★
BERKSHIRE MEDICAL CENTER - MEDICAL LIBRARY (Med)
725 North St.
Pittsfield, MA 01201
Phone: (413) 499-4161
Jutta Luhde, Libn.
Founded: 1964. **Staff:** Prof 1; Other 3. **Subjects:** Medicine, nursing, allied health sciences. **Holdings:** 8500 books; 5000 bound periodical volumes; 12 VF drawers. **Subscriptions:** 260 journals and other serials. **Services:** Interlibrary loans; copying; library open to professionals in the health fields and students. **Networks/Consortia:** Member of Western Massachusetts Health Information Consortium.

BERKSHIRE SANCTUARIES
See: Massachusetts Audubon Society

BERLACK, ISRAELS AND LIBERMAN
See: Debevoise & Liberman

★1313★
BERLEX LABORATORIES, INC. - RESEARCH AND DEVELOPMENT DIVISION LIBRARY (Med)
110 E. Hanover Ave.
Cedar Knolls, NJ 07927
Phone: (201) 540-8700
Lorene Lingelbach, Libn.
Staff: Prof 1; Other 2. **Subjects:** Pharmacology and the pharmaceutical industry; chemistry; internal medicine. **Holdings:** 3500 books; 5000 bound periodical volumes; 350 reels of microfilm of periodicals; 225 reels of patents on microfilm. **Subscriptions:** 575 journals and other serials. **Services:** Interlibrary loans; copying; SDI; library not open to public. **Computerized Information Services:** DIALOG, BRS, SDC, NLM. **Publications:** Berlex Library News, quarterly; Berlex Library Serials, annual. **Staff:** Kathleen Millington, Asst.Libn.

BERMAN (Buddy) MEMORIAL LIBRARY
See: Temple Beth El - Buddy Berman Memorial Library

★1314★
BERNALILLO COUNTY - DISTRICT COURT LAW LIBRARY (Law)
415 Tijeras, N.W.
Box 488
Albuquerque, NM 87103
Phone: (505) 242-2961
Donna Ruvolo, Asst.Libn.
Staff: Prof 1. **Subjects:** Law. **Special Collections:** New Mexico reports from 1852 to present. **Holdings:** 20,100 volumes; 500 other items (cataloged). **Services:** Copying; library open to public.

BERNARD (David) MEMORIAL AVIATION LAW LIBRARY
See: University of California, Los Angeles - Law Library

BERNER (Gertrude C.) MEMORIAL LIBRARY OF SPIRITUAL SCIENCES
See: Sanatana Dharma Foundation - Gertrude C. Berner Memorial Library of Spiritual Sciences

★1315★
BERNHARD (Arnold) AND COMPANY, INC. - BUSINESS LIBRARY (Bus-Fin)
711 Third Ave.
New York, NY 10017
Phone: (212) 687-3965
Gloria Napoli, Chf.Libn.
Staff: Prof 1; Other 3. **Subjects:** Finance and economics. **Holdings:** Figures not available. **Subscriptions:** 54 journals and other serials. **Services:** Interlibrary loans; copying; library open to public with restrictions. **Computerized Information Services:** Computerized circulation. **Publications:** Business Library, daily.

BERNHARD (Dorothy L.) LIBRARY
See: Child Welfare League of America, Inc. - Informational Resource Services - Dorothy L. Bernhard Library

BERNHARD (Richard J.) MEMORIAL LIBRARY
See: Federation Employment & Guidance Service - Richard J. Bernhard Memorial Library

★1316★
BERNSTEIN (Sanford C.) & COMPANY, INC. - RESEARCH LIBRARY (Bus-Fin)
767 5th Ave.
New York, NY 10153
Phone: (212) 486-5899
Marcia Alexis Hylton, Corp.Libn.
Founded: 1967. **Staff:** Prof 1; Other 1. **Subjects:** Investments. **Holdings:** 100 bound periodical volumes; Wall Street Journal (1971 to present); Stock Guides and Bond Guides (1970 to present). **Subscriptions:** 350 journals and other serials; 10 newspapers. **Services:** Interlibrary loans; copying; library open to SLA members only. **Computerized Information Services:** Computerized acquisitions and circulation.

BERRY (E.Y.) LIBRARY-LEARNING CENTER
See: Black Hills State College - E.Y. Berry Library-Learning Center

BERTRAND (Ellen Clarke) LIBRARY
See: Bucknell University - Ellen Clarke Bertrand Library

★1317★
BERTRAND RUSSELL SOCIETY, INC. - LIBRARY (Hum)
4461 23rd St.
San Francisco, CA 94114
Jack Ragsdale, Libn.
Founded: 1975. **Staff:** 2. **Subjects:** Bertrand Russell. **Holdings:** 100 books; 8 films; 5 video cassettes; 20 audio cassettes; Archives of the Bertrand Russell Society. **Services:** Copying; library open to public with restrictions. **Formerly:** Located in Chicago, IL. **Also Known As:** BRS Library. **Staff:** Donald W. Jackanicz, Pres.

★1318★
BESSEMER TRUST COMPANY, N.A. - INVESTMENT LIBRARY (Bus-Fin)
630 Fifth Ave.
New York, NY 10111
Phone: (212) 708-9184
Merrill H. Lishan, Libn.
Staff: Prof 1; Other 1. **Subjects:** Corporate records, finance, banking, industry files. **Special Collections:** International financial and corporate information. **Holdings:** 300 books; 120 bound periodical volumes; 52 VF drawers of corporate records and subject files; 200 microfiche. **Subscriptions:** 110 journals and other serials; 7 newspapers. **Services:** Interlibrary loans; library open to members of SLA by appointment. **Computerized Information Services:** Online systems.

★1319★
BESSER (Jesse) MUSEUM - LIBRARY (Hist; Art)
491 Johnson St.
Alpena, MI 49707
Phone: (517) 356-2202
Dennis R. Bodem, Dir.
Staff: Prof 2. **Subjects:** Local and regional history; art - American, 19th and 20th centuries; American antiques and collectibles; museum administration. **Holdings:** 900 books; 2400 archival items; 3000 photographs. **Subscriptions:** 15 journals and other serials. **Services:** Copying; library open to public for reference use only. **Staff:** Eugene A. Jenneman, Interpretation Chf.

BEST FOODS RESEARCH CENTER
See: CPC International

BETANCES (Ramon Emeterio) MEDICAL LIBRARY
See: Puerto Rico Department of Health - Ramon Emeterio Betances
Medical Library

★1320★
BETH ABRAHAM HOSPITAL - PATIENT LIBRARY (Area-Ethnic)
612 Allerton Ave.   Phone: (212) 920-5856
Bronx, NY 10467   Pamela S. George, Social Worker
Founded: 1961. **Staff:** Prof 1. **Subjects:** Judaica, fiction, biographies, nonfiction. **Special Collections:** Jewish history. **Holdings:** 3038 books; The Jewish Weekly and The Jewish Press, current copies; talking books; large print books. **Services:** Interlibrary loans; library serves staff, volunteers, patients and their relatives. **Computerized Information Services:** Computerized cataloging, acquisitions and circulation. **Publications:** Between the Bookends, 9/year - for patients, staff and relatives.

★1321★
BETH DAVID CONGREGATION - HARRY SIMONS LIBRARY (Rel-Theol)
2625 S.W. Third Ave.
Box 561718
Miami, FL 33156   Phone: (305) 854-3911
Founded: 1962. **Staff:** Prof 1; Other 3. **Subjects:** Judaica. **Holdings:** 9000 books. **Services:** Library not open to public.

★1322★
BETH DAVID REFORM CONGREGATION - JEWEL K. MARKOWITZ LIBRARY
 (Rel-Theol)
5220 Wynnefield Ave.   Phone: (215) 473-8438
Philadelphia, PA 19131   Mrs. Jerome Apfel, Chm.
Founded: 1951. **Staff:** 10. **Subjects:** Judaica. **Holdings:** 3400 books. **Subscriptions:** 10 journals and other serials. **Services:** Interlibrary loans; library not open to public. **Publications:** Synagogue Bulletin.

BETH-EL SCHOOL OF NURSING
See: Memorial Hospital and Beth-El School of Nursing

★1323★
BETH EL SYNAGOGUE - MAX SHAPIRO LIBRARY (Rel-Theol)
5224 W. 26th St.   Phone: (612) 920-3512
St. Louis Park, MN 55416
Staff: 1. **Subjects:** Judaica, Jewish literature, religion, philosophy. **Holdings:** 2580 books. **Subscriptions:** 19 journals and other serials. **Services:** Library open to public. **Staff:** Rabbi Kassel Abelson, Supv.

★1324★
BETH EL TEMPLE CENTER - CARL KALES MEMORIAL LIBRARY (Rel-Theol)†
2 Concord Ave.   Phone: (617) 484-6668
Belmont, MA 02178
Staff: 2. **Subjects:** Israel, Judaism, religion, philosophy, Bible, history, theology, customs. **Holdings:** 2370 books; 500 bound periodical volumes. **Subscriptions:** 9 journals and other serials. **Services:** Interlibrary loans; library open to public for reference use only.

★1325★
BETH EMET, THE FREE SYNAGOGUE - BRUCE GORDON MEMORIAL
 LIBRARY (Rel-Theol)
1224 Dempster   Phone: (312) 869-4230
Evanston, IL 60202   Myrtle Gordon, Libn.
Founded: 1950. **Staff:** Prof 1; Other 4. **Subjects:** Judaica and religion. **Holdings:** 5000 volumes. **Subscriptions:** 12 journals and other serials. **Services:** Interlibrary loans; copying; library open to public.

★1326★
BETH ISRAEL CONGREGATION - LIBRARY (Rel-Theol)
1015 E. Park Ave.   Phone: (609) 691-0852
Vineland, NJ 08360   Mrs. Newton Greenblatt, Dir.
Founded: 1926. **Staff:** Prof 2; Other 1. **Subjects:** Judaica - religion, history, literature, biography. **Holdings:** 4000 books; 2 VF drawers of pamphlets; 115 recordings. **Subscriptions:** 14 journals and other serials. **Services:** Interlibrary loans; library open to public with restrictions. **Staff:** Mrs. Hartley Tucker, Asst.Libn.; Mrs. Irving Zislin, Cat.

★1327★
BETH ISRAEL HOSPITAL & GERIATRIC CENTER - HEALTH SCIENCE
 LIBRARY (Med)
1601 Lowell Blvd.   Phone: (303) 825-2190
Denver, CO 80204   Bunny Braunger, Health Sci.Libn.
Founded: 1970. **Staff:** Prof 1; Other 1. **Subjects:** Medicine, geriatrics, gerontology, nursing, long-term care. **Holdings:** 700 books; 1000 bound periodical volumes; 225 AV items. **Subscriptions:** 127 journals and other serials. **Services:** Interlibrary loans; copying; library open to public with restrictions. **Computerized Information Services:** MEDLINE; computerized cataloging. **Networks/Consortia:** Member of Denver Area Health Sciences Library Consortium; Colorado Council of Medical Libraries.

★1328★
BETH ISRAEL HOSPITAL - LASSOR AGOOS LIBRARY (Med)
330 Brookline Ave.   Phone: (617) 735-4225
Boston, MA 02215   Martha F. Cole, Med.Libn.
Founded: 1928. **Staff:** Prof 2; Other 1. **Subjects:** Medicine and related fields. **Holdings:** 4256 books; 3171 bound periodical volumes. **Subscriptions:** 209 journals and other serials. **Services:** Interlibrary loans; copying (fee); library open to public with restrictions. **Computerized Information Services:** Internal database.

★1329★
BETH ISRAEL MEDICAL CTR. - HOSPITAL FOR JOINT DISEASES
 ORTHOPAEDIC INST. - SEYMOUR J. PHILLIPS HEALTH SCI.LIB. (Med)
10 Nathan D. Perlman Pl.   Phone: (212) 420-2168
New York, NY 10003   Arlene L. Freedman, Dir. of Lib.Serv.
Founded: 1952. **Staff:** Prof 3; Other 6. **Subjects:** Medicine, nursing, allied health sciences, social work, substance addiction. **Holdings:** 6000 books; 6500 bound periodical volumes. **Subscriptions:** 600 journals and other serials. **Services:** Interlibrary loans; copying; library not open to public. **Computerized Information Services:** MEDLARS, BRS; computerized cataloging. **Networks/Consortia:** Member of OCLC; Medical Library Center of New York; Manhattan-Bronx Health Sciences Library Group; New York and New Jersey Regional Medical Library Program. **Remarks:** Contains holdings of the School of Nursing Library and the Department of Psychiatry Library. **Staff:** Sharon K. Butler, Sr.Libn., User Serv.; Linda Mininni, Libn., Tech.Serv.

★1330★
BETH JACOB SYNAGOGUE - LIBRARY (Rel-Theol)
400 New London Tpke.   Phone: (203) 886-2459
Norwich, CT 06360
Founded: 1950. **Staff:** 1. **Subjects:** Jewish history, theology and related topics. **Holdings:** 1150 books; magazines and newspapers. **Subscriptions:** 8 journals and other serials. **Services:** Library open to public with restrictions.

★1331★
BETH SHALOM CONGREGATION - BLANCHE AND IRA ROSENBLUM
 MEMORIAL LIBRARY (Rel-Theol)
9400 Wornall Rd.   Phone: (816) 363-3331
Kansas City, MO 64114   Frances Wolf, Libn.
Staff: 1. **Subjects:** Judaica. **Holdings:** 9000 books; 300 phonograph records; 150 filmstrips. **Subscriptions:** 32 journals and other serials. **Services:** Library open to public with restrictions.

★1332★
BETH SHOLOM CONGREGATION - JOSEPH & ELIZABETH SCHWARTZ
 LIBRARY (Rel-Theol)†
Foxcroft & Old York Rd.   Phone: (215) 887-1342
Elkins Park, PA 19117   David J. Salaman, Libn.
Founded: 1959. **Staff:** Prof 1; Other 10. **Subjects:** Jewish music and Judaica. **Special Collections:** Jewish music and art. **Holdings:** 5500 volumes; 300 phonograph recordings. **Services:** Library open to public with permission of Congregation Executive Director.

★1333★
BETH TZEDEC SYNAGOGUE - CONGREGATIONAL LIBRARY (Rel-Theol)
1700 Bathurst St.   Phone: (416) 781-5658
Toronto, ON, Canada M5P 3K3   Samuel Simchovitch, Libn.
Founded: 1956. **Staff:** Prof 1. **Subjects:** Judaica, Hebraica. **Holdings:** 10,000 books; VF drawers of pamphlets, documents. **Subscriptions:** 22 journals and other serials. **Services:** Interlibrary loans; library open to public for reference use only.

★1334★
BETHANY BIBLE COLLEGE - LIBRARY (Rel-Theol)
800 Bethany Dr.   Phone: (408) 438-3800
Scotts Valley, CA 95066   Arnold McLellan, Hd.Libn.
Founded: 1919. **Staff:** Prof 2; Other 5. **Subjects:** Religion, liberal arts, Bible, theology. **Special Collections:** Pentecostalism (500 books). **Holdings:** 49,288 books; 824 bound periodical volumes; 545 reels of microfilm (cataloged). **Subscriptions:** 390 journals and other serials; 8 newspapers. **Services:** Interlibrary loans; copying; library open to public. **Networks/Consortia:** Member of CIN. **Staff:** Edward A. Koetitz, Ref.Libn.

★1335★
BETHANY COLLEGE - CHEMISTRY LIBRARY (Sci-Tech)
Richardson Hall of Science   Phone: (304) 829-7711
Bethany, WV 26032   Rosalie S. Draper, Ck.
Founded: 1956. **Staff:** 1. **Subjects:** All branches of chemistry. **Holdings:** 2500 books; 2268 bound periodical volumes; 6 VF drawers of pamphlets, technical literature, clippings and reprints; 1 journal on microcards (1949-1956). **Subscriptions:** 35 journals and other serials. **Services:** Interlibrary loans; copying; library open to public with permission from librarian.

★1336★
BETHANY LUTHERAN THEOLOGICAL SEMINARY - LIBRARY (Rel-Theol)
447 N. Division St.   Phone: (507) 625-2977
Mankato, MN 56001   Milton H. Otto, Act.Libn.
Staff: Prof 1; Other 1. **Subjects:** Bible, religion, history, theology, hymnology, catechism. **Special Collections:** Hymnal Collection (705 volumes); Catechism Collection (604 volumes); rare theological books (922). **Holdings:** 8392 books; 998 bound periodical volumes; 1658 monographs and booklets. **Subscriptions:** 116 journals and other serials. **Services:** Interlibrary loans; copying; library open to public with librarian's permission. **Networks/Consortia:** Member of OCLC; MINITEX; South Central Minnesota Interlibrary Exchange (SMILE).

★1337★
BETHANY MEDICAL CENTER - W.W. SUMMERVILLE MEDICAL LIBRARY (Med)
51 N. 12th St.   Phone: (913) 281-8770
Kansas City, KS 66102   Barbara Shannon, Libn.
Staff: Prof 1; Other 2. **Subjects:** Medicine, nursing and allied health sciences. **Holdings:** 1500 books; 2100 bound periodical volumes. **Subscriptions:** 322 journals and other serials. **Services:** Interlibrary loans; copying; library open to public. **Computerized Information Services:** MEDLINE. **Networks/Consortia:** Member of Health Sciences Library Group of Greater Kansas City.

★1338★
BETHANY AND NORTHERN BAPTIST THEOLOGICAL SEMINARIES - LIBRARY (Rel-Theol)
Butterfield & Meyers Rds.   Phone: (312) 620-2214
Oak Brook, IL 60521   Murray L. Wagner, Hd.Libn.
Staff: Prof 3; Other 5. **Subjects:** Baptist history, Church of the Brethren history, pacifism, missions, intentional and Utopian communities. **Special Collections:** Cassel Collection (religion and history of the 16th-19th centuries; 11,420 volumes); Huston Bible Collection (300 Bibles in English language). **Holdings:** 130,000 books and bound periodical volumes. **Subscriptions:** 684 journals and other serials. **Services:** Interlibrary loans; copying (limited); library open to public for reference use only. **Networks/Consortia:** Member of Chicago Cluster of Theological Schools. **Staff:** Kenneth M. Shaffer, Jr., Asst.Libn.; Gwen Vandon, Circ. & Ser.Libn.; Hedda Durnbaugh, Cat./Spec.Coll.

★1339★
BETHANY UNITED METHODIST CHURCH - LIBRARY (Rel-Theol)
7265 W. Center St.   Phone: (414) 258-2868
Wauwatosa, WI 53210   Barbara A. Jones, Libn.
Staff: Prof 7; Other 1. **Subjects:** Philosophy, religion. **Holdings:** 250 books. **Services:** Library not open to public.

★1340★
BETHEL COLLEGE - MENNONITE LIBRARY AND ARCHIVES (Rel-Theol)
                                               Phone: (316) 283-2500
North Newton, KS 67117   Robert Kreider, Dir.
Founded: 1935. **Staff:** Prof 3; Other 1. **Subjects:** Anabaptists; Mennonites in Europe, America, Latin America and Asia; peace; Kansas. **Special Collections:** Manuscript collection (400 shelf feet); General Conference Church Archives (500 shelf feet); oral history of World War I and II conscientious objectors; rare Anabaptist books; H.R. Voth manuscript and photograph collection on Hopi Indians; Rudolph Petter manuscript collection on Cheyenne Indians; H.P. Krehbiel manuscript collection on peace; Mennonite hymnbooks (2000); Mennonite art collection including 17th century Dutch art. **Holdings:** 23,300

books; 3200 bound periodical volumes; 550 reels of microfilm (cataloged); 1000 reels of audiotape (cataloged); 150 maps. **Subscriptions:** 300 journals and other serials; 80 newspapers. **Services:** Interlibrary loans; copying; translation; library open to public. **Computerized Information Services:** Internal database; computerized cataloging. **Networks/Consortia:** Member of Associated Colleges of Central Kansas (ACCK). **Publications:** Mennonite Life, quarterly; Gleanings from the Threshing Floor, quarterly newsletter - free subscription; Guide to Mennonite Library and Archives, 1981. **Staff:** David A. Haury, Archv.; Laurie Wolfe, Libn.

BETHEL THEOLOGICAL SEMINARY - BAPTIST GENERAL CONFERENCE - ARCHIVES
See: Baptist General Conference

★1341★
BETHEL THEOLOGICAL SEMINARY - RESOURCE CENTER (Rel-Theol)
3949 Bethel Dr.   Phone: (612) 641-6184
St. Paul, MN 55112   Norris Magnuson, Dir.
Founded: 1871. **Staff:** Prof 2; Other 4. **Subjects:** Biblical studies, theology, church history, practical theology. **Special Collections:** Skarstedt Collection of Pietistic literature; Archives of the Baptist General Conference (formerly Swedish Baptist General Conference). **Holdings:** 102,000 books; 8674 bound periodical volumes. **Subscriptions:** 1000 journals and other serials. **Services:** Interlibrary loans; copying; library open to public. **Computerized Information Services:** Computerized cataloging, acquisitions and serials. **Networks/Consortia:** Member of Consortium of Minnesota Seminary Libraries. **Publications:** Booklist, irregular. **Staff:** Pam Jervis, Cat.Libn.; Betty Kleinschmidt, Asst.Libn.

★1342★
BETHESDA HOSPITAL - CHILDBIRTH EDUCATION LIBRARY (Med)
2951 Maple Ave.
Zanesville, OH 43701
Defunct

★1343★
BETHESDA HOSPITAL - INFORMATION RESOURCE CENTER (Med)†
619 Oak St.   Phone: (513) 559-6337
Cincinnati, OH 45206   Margaret Gomien, Libn.
Staff: Prof 2; Other 12. **Subjects:** Obstetrics, gynecology, medicine, nursing. **Holdings:** 10,000 books; 500 bound periodical volumes. **Subscriptions:** 350 journals and other serials. **Services:** Interlibrary loans; copying; SDI; library not open to public. **Computerized Information Services:** BRS, MEDLINE. **Networks/Consortia:** Member of Cincinnati Area Health Sciences Library Association.

★1344★
BETHESDA HOSPITAL - LIBRARY AND EDUCATION SERVICES (Med)
2951 Maple Ave.   Phone: (614) 454-4220
Zanesville, OH 43701   Patty Y. Hartley, Dir.
Founded: 1952. **Staff:** Prof 1; Other 1. **Subjects:** Internal medicine, cardiology, surgery, pediatrics, oncology, psychiatry. **Special Collections:** Rare medical books (65). **Holdings:** 1591 volumes; 632 bound periodical volumes; pamphlets. **Subscriptions:** 116 journals and other serials. **Services:** Interlibrary loans; copying; library open to public with recommendation by a physician. **Computerized Information Services:** MEDLINE; computerized cataloging and acquisitions. **Networks/Consortia:** Member of Kentucky-Ohio-Michigan Regional Medical Library Program (KOMRML). **Publications:** Periodical List, annual.

★1345★
BETHESDA HOSPITAL - PROFESSIONAL LIBRARY (Med)
4400 E. Iliff Ave.   Phone: (303) 758-1514
Denver, CO 80222   Dolores Leone, Educ.Dir.
Founded: 1960. **Staff:** 2. **Subjects:** Psychiatry, psychology, psychiatric nursing. **Holdings:** 400 books. **Subscriptions:** 15 journals and other serials. **Services:** Interlibrary loans (fee); library open to professionals and students with approval of library committee.

★1346★
BETHESDA LUTHERAN MEDICAL CENTER - MEDICAL-NURSING LIBRARY (Med)
570 Capitol Blvd.   Phone: (612) 221-2291
St. Paul, MN 55103   Eileen M. Erlandson, Hd.Libn.
Staff: Prof 2. **Subjects:** Nursing, medicine, hospital administration, allied health fields. **Holdings:** 3850 books; 135 bound periodical volumes; VF drawers of pamphlets and brochures. **Subscriptions:** 196 journals and other serials. **Services:** Interlibrary loans and copying for local libraries only; library open to staff, students, other medical personnel and local consortium users.

Computerized Information Services: MEDLINE. Networks/Consortia: Member of Twin Cities Biomedical Consortium (TCBC). Also Known As: Sister Esther Porter Medical-Nursing Library. Staff: Carole L. Topp, Asst.Libn.

★1347★
BETHESDA MEMORIAL HOSPITAL - MEDICAL LIBRARY (Med)
2815 S. Seacrest Blvd.   Phone: (305) 737-7733
Boynton Beach, FL 33435   Carol S. Ploch, Med.Libn.
Founded: 1967. Staff: Prof 1; Other 1. Subjects: Medicine, nursing, hospital administration, related health fields. Holdings: 1425 books; 3218 bound periodical volumes; 253 unbound volumes (cataloged); 6 VF drawers of clippings and pamphlets; 75 video cassettes; 217 cassettes. Subscriptions: 143 journals and other serials. Services: Interlibrary loans; copying; bibliographies prepared; SDI; translations; library open to public with permission of librarian. Computerized Information Services: MEDLINE. Networks/Consortia: Member of Palm Beach County Health Science Libraries Consortium.

★1348★
BETHLEHEM LUTHERAN CHURCH - LIBRARY (Rel-Theol)
215 Fourth Ave., S.E.   Phone: (605) 225-9740
Aberdeen, SD 57401   Bernice Theeler
Staff: 16. Subjects: Lutheran Church. Holdings: 4000 books. Services: Library open to public.

★1349★
BETHLEHEM STEEL CORPORATION - BERNARD D. BROEKER LAW LIBRARY (Law)
Martin Tower Bldg., Rm. 2027   Phone: (215) 694-5002
Bethlehem, PA 18016   David D. Hendley, Law Libn.
Founded: 1954. Staff: Prof 1; Other 1. Subjects: Law - corporate, antitrust, real property. Holdings: 20,000 volumes. Subscriptions: 75 journals and other serials. Services: Library open to attorneys only. Computerized Information Services: LEXIS.

★1350★
BETHLEHEM STEEL CORPORATION - SCHWAB MEMORIAL LIBRARY (Bus-Fin; Sci-Tech)
Martin Tower   Phone: (215) 694-3325
Bethlehem, PA 18016   Darla L.W. Lucas, Dir. of Lib.Serv.
Staff: Prof 1; Other 5. Subjects: Steelmaking economics and technology, metallurgy, business and economics, engineering. Special Collections: C.M. Schwab material. Holdings: 45,000 volumes; 167 VF drawers of pamphlets, annual reports and specifications; 28 drawers of newspapers and reports on microfilm. Subscriptions: 225 journals. Services: Interlibrary loans. Computerized Information Services: DIALOG, Dow Jones News Retrieval. Publications: Acquisitions List, monthly - for internal distribution only.

★1351★
BETHLEHEM STEEL CORPORATION - TECHNICAL INFORMATION (Sci-Tech)
Homer Research Laboratories   Phone: (215) 694-6938
Bethlehem, PA 18016   W.M. Perry, Supv., Tech.Info.
Founded: 1938. Staff: Prof 4; Other 4. Subjects: Metallurgy, ceramics, engineering, chemistry, physics, mechanics. Holdings: 14,000 books; 5000 bound periodical volumes. Subscriptions: 480 journals and other serials. Services: Library open to public.

★1352★
BETTERLEY CONSULTING GROUP - TECHNICAL INFORMATION CENTER (Bus-Fin)
200 Clarendon St.   Phone: (617) 267-4300
Boston, MA 02116   Kathleen J. Berggren, Libn.
Founded: 1978. Staff: Prof 1; Other 1. Subjects: Risk management, insurance. Holdings: 300 books; 15 VF drawers of clippings. Subscriptions: 52 journals and other serials. Services: Interlibrary loans; copying; library not open to public. Publications: IN-SIGHTS, monthly - for internal distribution only.

BETTIS ATOMIC POWER LABORATORY
See: Westinghouse Electric Corporation

★1353★
BETTMANN ARCHIVE, INC. (Pict)
136 E. 57th St.   Phone: (212) 758-0362
New York, NY 10022   Melvin Gray, Pres.
Subjects: History, culture, daily life, science, sport. Special Collections: Movie stills (1920 to present); historical and current exclusive news coverage from World War II to present; Underwood and Underwood News Photos, Inc., 1890-1940 (several million photographs). Holdings: 5 million black/white

pictures; 1 million color pictures. Services: Photographs available for loan; research by staff; library not open to public. Publications: Bettman Portable Archive; Bettman Picture History of the World - both for sale.

★1354★
BETZ LABORATORIES, INC. - RESEARCH LIBRARY (Sci-Tech)
4636 Somerton Rd.   Phone: (215) 355-3300
Trevose, PA 19047   Joan E. Goldberg, Tech.Libn.
Founded: 1925. Staff: Prof 2; Other 1. Subjects: Waste treatment - industrial and municipal; water treatment; air pollution control. Holdings: 2500 books; 3000 bound periodical volumes; 12 VF drawers of patents; 2000 documents on microfiche. Subscriptions: 200 journals and other serials. Services: Interlibrary loans; SDI; library open to public by appointment. Computerized Information Services: DIALOG, SDC, NLM, Chemical Abstracts Service, Chemical Information Systems, Inc. Networks/Consortia: Member of PALINET & Union Library Catalogue of Pennsylvania. Special Indexes: Internal Reports Index (Uniterm cards). Staff: Wendy Hamilton, Asst.Libn.

★1355★
BEVERLY HILLS PUBLIC LIBRARY - FINE ARTS DIVISION (Art)
444 N. Rexford Dr.   Phone: (213) 550-4720
Beverly Hills, CA 90210   Nick Cellini, Libn.
Founded: 1970. Staff: Prof 1; Other 1. Subjects: Art, film, theatre, photography. Special Collections: Dorathi Bock Pierre Dance Collection (500 items); American and European auction catalogs. Holdings: 7500 books; 3000 exhibition catalogs; 4500 slides on 20th century artists. Subscriptions: 90 journals and other serials. Services: Interlibrary loans; copying; library open to public for reference use only.

★1356★
BEVERLY HISTORICAL SOCIETY - LIBRARY AND ARCHIVES (Hist)
Cabot House, 117 Cabot St.   Phone: (617) 922-1186
Beverly, MA 01915   John C. MacLean, Dir.
Founded: 1891. Staff: Prof 1; Other 12. Subjects: Americana; history - local, general, maritime; genealogy. Special Collections: Charles William Galloupe Library. Holdings: 5000 books; 500 bound periodical volumes; 20,000 manuscripts. Services: Copying; library open to public with restrictions.

★1357★
BEVERLY HOSPITAL - LIBRARY (Med)
Herrick St.   Phone: (617) 922-3000
Beverly, MA 01915   Margaret A. Firth, Libn.
Staff: Prof 1. Subjects: Medicine. Holdings: 6000 books and bound periodical volumes. Subscriptions: 125 journals and other serials. Services: Interlibrary loans; copying; library open to public by appointment. Networks/Consortia: Member of Northeast Consortium for Health Information (NECHI).

BEVIER ENGINEERING LIBRARY
See: University of Pittsburgh

BEXAR ARCHIVES
See: University of Texas, Austin - Eugene C. Barker Texas History Center

★1358★
BEXAR COUNTY LAW LIBRARY (Law)
Court House, 5th Fl.   Phone: (512) 227-8822
San Antonio, TX 78205   Jimmy Alleson, Libn.
Subjects: Law. Holdings: 35,000 volumes. Services: Library open to public.

★1359★
BEXAR COUNTY MEDICAL LIBRARY ASSOCIATION (Med)
202 W. French Place
Box 12678   Phone: (512) 734-6691
San Antonio, TX 78212   Laura Haning, Libn.
Founded: 1912. Staff: Prof 1. Subjects: Medicine. Holdings: 7000 books; 150 bound periodical volumes; 10 VF drawers of clippings. Subscriptions: 17 journals and other serials. Services: Interlibrary loans (limited to University of Texas); copying; library open to public.

BEXLEY HALL
See: Colgate Rochester/Bexley Hall/Crozer Theological Seminaries

★1360★
BEYOND BAROQUE FOUNDATION - LIBRARY (Publ)
Old Venice City Hall
681 Venice Blvd.   Phone: (213) 822-3006
Venice, CA 90291   Amy Gerstler, Lib.Dir.
Founded: 1973. Staff: Prof 1; Other 1. Subjects: Poetry, fiction, arts.

Special Collections: Small press literary books and magazines. **Holdings:** 20,000 volumes. **Subscriptions:** 7000 journals and other serials. **Services:** Interlibrary loans; copying; library open to public. **Networks/Consortia:** Member of Southern California Answering Network (SCAN). **Publications:** Poetry News, monthly - by subscription. **Special Indexes:** Author index to little magazines (card).

BHUBANESHWAR ARCHIVE ON MODERN ORISSA
See: University of Chicago - South Asia Collection

★1361★
BIBB COUNTY LAW LIBRARY (Law)
Bibb County Court House
New Annex, Rm. A500   Phone: (912) 745-6871
Macon, GA 31207   Lucille Waldron, Libn.
Staff: 1. **Subjects:** Law. **Holdings:** 10,000 volumes. **Services:** Library open to public.

BIBBY (Basil G.) LIBRARY
See: Eastman Dental Center - Basil G. Bibby Library

★1362★
BIBLE SCIENCE ASSOCIATION - RESEARCH CENTER (Rel-Theol)
2911 E. 42nd St.   Phone: (612) 724-1883
Minneapolis, MN 55406   Rev. Walter Lang, Exec.Dir.
Staff: 1. **Subjects:** Creation, model of origins. **Holdings:** 500 books and pamphlets; 200 periodicals; tracts, AV materials. **Subscriptions:** 10 journals and other serials. **Services:** Copying; library open to public. **Remarks:** Associated with Genesis Institute, a study and research group located at the same address.

★1363★
BIBLICAL THEOLOGICAL SEMINARY - LIBRARY (Rel-Theol)
200 N. Main St.
Box 9   Phone: (215) 368-5000
Hatfield, PA 19440   James C. Pakala, Libn.
Founded: 1971. **Staff:** Prof 2; Other 7. **Subjects:** Bible, theology, Christian education, church history. **Special Collections:** Biblical Seminary in New York thesis collection. **Holdings:** 35,000 books; 2300 bound periodical volumes; 1072 pamphlets; 2000 microforms. **Subscriptions:** 118 journals and other serials. **Services:** Interlibrary loans; copying; library open to public. **Networks/Consortia:** Member of Southeastern Pennsylvania Theological Libraries Association; Delaware Valley Information Consortium. **Staff:** John C. Pickard, Asst.Libn.

★1364★
BIBLIOGRAPHIC RESEARCH LIBRARY (Info Sci)
964 Chapel Hill Way   Phone: (408) 247-2810
San Jose, CA 95122   Robert B. Harmon, Res.Bibliog.
Staff: Prof 2. **Subjects:** Bibliography, political science, library science. **Special Collections:** John Steinbeck Collection; Ernest Hemingway Collection. **Holdings:** 704 books; 20 bound periodical volumes; 5 reels of microfilm. **Subscriptions:** 15 journals and other serials. **Services:** Interlibrary loans; copying; library not open to public. **Publications:** The Checklist, irregular; The Steinbeck Collector, irregular. **Staff:** Merlynn S. Harmon, Res.Libn.

★1365★
BIBLIOGRAPHIC SERVICE
4912 Wallbank Ave.
Downers Grove, IL 60515
Staff: Prof 1. **Subjects:** General science, chemistry, botany, medicine, technology, applied sciences. **Holdings:** Figures not available. **Remarks:** Presently inactive.

★1366★
BIBLIOGRAPHICAL CENTER FOR RESEARCH - ROCKY MOUNTAIN REGION, INC. (Info Sci)
245 Columbine, Suite 212   Phone: (303) 388-9261
Denver, CO 80206   JoAn S. Segal, Exec.Dir.
Founded: 1935. **Staff:** Prof 9; Other 6. **Special Collections:** Professional collection of library and networking materials (500 volumes). **Subscriptions:** 50 journals and other serials. **Services:** Interlibrary loans; center open by referral from member libraries. **Computerized Information Services:** DIALOG, SDC, BRS, New York Times Information Service, Ontyme II; computerized cataloging, acquisitions, serials and ILL. **Networks/Consortia:** Bibliographical Center for Research (BCR) is a library network headquarters; member of OCLC. **Publications:** Action for Libraries, monthly. **Staff:** Dennis Reynolds, Hd., OCLC Serv.; James Maloney, Hd., Info.Ret.Serv.; Joyce Coyne, Hd., Adm.Serv.

BIBLIOTHECA CRAWFORDIANA
See: Crawford (F. Marion) Memorial Society

BIBLIOTHECA NEUROLOGICA COURVILLE
See: University of California, Irvine - Biomedical Library

BIBLIOTHEQUE MALLET
See: Union Saint-Jean Baptiste - Mallet Library

BIBLIOTHEQUE NATIONALE DU QUEBEC
See: Quebec Province

★1367★
BIBLIOTHEQUE DE LA VILLE DE MONTREAL - CINEMATHEQUE (Aud-Vis)
880 Roy St. E., Suite 200   Phone: (514) 872-3680
Montreal, PQ, Canada H2L 1E6   Lise Depatie-Bourassa, Coord., AV Serv.
Founded: 1947. **Staff:** Prof 2; Other 9. **Subjects:** Arts, children's films, geography, social sciences. **Holdings:** 5601 16mm films; 20,738 slides; 1480 filmstrips; 125 8mm films; 700 video cassettes. **Special Catalogs:** Film and slide catalogs (each in book form).

★1368★
BIBLIOTHEQUE DE LA VILLE DE MONTREAL - COLLECTION GAGNON (Hist; Hum)
1210 Sherbrooke St., E.   Phone: (514) 872-5923
Montreal, PQ, Canada H2L 1L9   Carmen Catelli, Hd.
Founded: 1902. **Staff:** Prof 2; Other 4. **Subjects:** Canadian history, French Canadian genealogy, French and English Canadian literature, Canadian geography, French Canadian heritage, Americana. **Special Collections:** Manuscripts and maps of Old Canada; original editions. **Holdings:** 41,742 books; 3000 bound periodical volumes; 10,500 pamphlets (cataloged); 23,000 photographs and portraits; 37,000 microcards (Americana); 1550 maps, plans and surveys; 1200 engravings and illustrations; 875 cartons of archives; 1200 slides (New France); 1500 rare books. **Subscriptions:** 90 journals and other serials. **Services:** Interlibrary loans; copying; reference by telephone and mail; library open to public. **Also Known As:** Montreal City Library - Gagnon Collection. **Staff:** Jacques Panneton, Consrv.; Daniel Olivier, Dept.Hd.; Pierre Paquin, Ref.Libn.

★1369★
BIBLIOTHEQUE DE LA VILLE DE MONTREAL - SONOTHEQUE (Aud-Vis)
880 Roy St., E., Suite 300   Phone: (514) 872-3680
Montreal, PQ, Canada H2L 1E6
Founded: 1982. **Staff:** Prof 1; Other 4. **Holdings:** 4200 cassettes; 2800 phonograph records.

BICKERS (Alice J.) LIBRARY
See: Nutley Historical Society Museum - Alice J. Bickers Library

BIDDLE LAW LIBRARY
See: University of Pennsylvania

BIG HOLE NATL. BATTLEFIELD
See: U.S. Natl. Park Service

BIG TIMBERS MUSEUM
See: Prowers County Historical Society

BIGELOW LABORATORY FOR OCEAN SCIENCES
See: Maine State Department of Marine Resources

★1370★
BIGHAM, ENGLAR, JONES AND HOUSTON - LIBRARY (Law)
14 Wall St.   Phone: (212) 732-4646
New York, NY 10005   Sharon M. Kallop, Libn.
Staff: Prof 1; Other 1. **Subjects:** Law. **Special Collections:** Admiralty law. **Holdings:** 10,000 volumes. **Services:** Interlibrary loans (limited); library not open to public.

BIGHORN CANYON NATL. RECREATION AREA
See: U.S. Natl. Park Service

★1371★
BIKELIBRARY (Rec)
Box 276   Phone: (316) 343-1961
Emporia, KS 66801   Larry S. Bonura, Dir.
Founded: 1978. **Staff:** Prof 1. **Subjects:** Bicycles and bicycling. **Holdings:** 412 books; 35 bound periodical volumes; 12 VF drawers of magazine and newspaper clippings; 700 newsletters. **Subscriptions:** 97 journals and other

serials. **Services:** Copying; library open to public. **Publications:** bicyclio, bimonthly - by exchange and subscription; bikecards - for sale; bikes and books, bicycle books reviewed, annual - by subscription.

BILLINGS (Dr. Frank) LIBRARY
See: University of Chicago - Dr. Frank Billings Library

★1372★
BILLINGS GAZETTE - NEWS LIBRARY (Publ)
401 N. Broadway
Box 2507   Phone: (406) 657-1271
Billings, MT 59103   Odelta A. Thomsen, Libn.
Founded: 1970. **Staff:** Prof 1. **Subjects:** Newspaper reference topics. **Special Collections:** Microfilm of newspaper from 1882 to present. **Holdings:** Figures not available. **Services:** Library open to other journalists.

★1373★
BILLINGS PUBLIC SCHOOLS - INSTRUCTIONAL MATERIALS CENTER (Aud-Vis)
504 North 29th St.   Phone: (406) 259-0291
Billings, MT 59101   W. Marshall Jones, Dir.
Staff: Prof 3; Other 11. **Subjects:** Mathematics, biological science, history, social studies, health, physical education, literature, physical science. **Holdings:** 1200 16mm films; 6000 filmstrips; 10,000 transparency masters; 50 boxes of pictures. **Services:** Center open to public with restrictions. **Publications:** Instructional Materials Newsletter - distributed to school libraries. **Special Catalogs:** Film, filmstrip and teaching materials catalogs. **Staff:** Pat Allen, Instr.Techn.

★1374★
BILLINGTON, FOX & ELLIS - RESEARCH DEPARTMENT - LIBRARY (Bus-Fin)†
20 N. Wacker Drive   Phone: (312) 236-5000
Chicago, IL 60606
Staff: 4. **Subjects:** Business. **Holdings:** 500 books; 1500 linear feet of vertical files. **Subscriptions:** 10 journals and other serials. **Services:** Interlibrary loans; copying; library not open to public.

BILOXI SUN AND HERALD LIBRARY
See: Gulf Publishing Co., Inc. - Editorial Library

BIMSON (Lloyd) MEMORIAL LIBRARY
See: Arizona State University - Lloyd Bimson Memorial Library

★1375★
BINGHAM, DANA AND GOULD - LAW LIBRARY (Law)
100 Federal St.   Phone: (617) 357-9300
Boston, MA 02110   Filippa Elizabeth Marullo, Hd.Libn.
Staff: Prof 3; Other 2. **Subjects:** Law - banking, corporate, admiralty. **Holdings:** 15,000 books. **Services:** Interlibrary loans; library not open to public. **Computerized Information Services:** LEXIS. **Special Catalogs:** Opinion file; memoranda file of in-house research.

★1376★
BINGHAMTON GENERAL HOSPITAL - STUART B. BLAKELY MEMORIAL LIBRARY (Med)
Mitchell Ave.   Phone: (607) 771-2200
Binghamton, NY 13903   Maryanne Mattimore, Med.Libn.
Founded: 1940. **Staff:** Prof 1; Other 3. **Subjects:** Medicine and nursing. **Holdings:** 11,000 volumes; 400 audiotapes; 200 videotapes; 10 films; 500 slides; 10 VF drawers of pamphlets. **Subscriptions:** 208 journals and other serials. **Services:** Interlibrary loans; copying; library open to medical professionals. **Networks/Consortia:** Member of New York and New Jersey Regional Medical Library Program.

★1377★
BINGHAMTON PRESS AND SUN BULLETIN - LIBRARY (Publ)
Vestal Pkwy., E.   Phone: (607) 798-1159
Binghamton, NY 13901   Annamary Allen, Libn.
Founded: 1942. **Staff:** Prof 1; Other 3. **Subjects:** Newspaper reference topics. **Holdings:** 250 books; 20 bound periodical volumes; maps (cataloged); 6 cabinets of microfilm; 50 cabinets of clippings; 50 cabinets of pictures. **Services:** Library open to public by appointment. **Remarks:** This paper is operated by Gannett Newspapers.

★1378★
BINGHAMTON PSYCHIATRIC CENTER - PROFESSIONAL LIBRARY (Med)
425 Robinson St.   Phone: (607) 724-1391
Binghamton, NY 13901   Martha A. Mason, Sr.Libn.
Staff: Prof 2. **Subjects:** Psychiatry, child psychiatry, community mental health, psychology, child psychology, group psychotherapy, mental illness, general medicine, psychoanalysis, social services. **Holdings:** 8864 books, bound periodicals and pamphlets; 270 cassette tapes. **Subscriptions:** 67 journals and other serials. **Services:** Interlibrary loans; library open to public for reference or research. **Networks/Consortia:** Member of Health Resources Council of Central New York. **Special Catalogs:** Catalog of Psychiatric Institute holdings - New York City. **Staff:** Nancy L. Helmer, Asst.Libn.

★1379★
BIO-ENERGY COUNCIL - LIBRARY (Energy)
1625 Eye St., N.W.   Phone: (202) 833-5656
Washington, DC 20006   Dr. Paul F. Bente, Jr., Exec.Dir.
Founded: 1977. **Staff:** Prof 2; Other 2. **Subjects:** Bio-energy - resources, microbial conversions, thermal conversions, appraisals. **Holdings:** Figures not available. **Services:** Library open to public by appointment. **Publications:** Bio-Energy Directory; Bio-Energy Conference Proceedings; reports of research funded by grants; briefs on perspectives of bio-energy.

★1380★
BIOLA UNIVERSITY - LIBRARY (Rel-Theol)
13800 Biola Ave.   Phone: (213) 944-0351
La Mirada, CA 90639   Gerald L. Gooden, Dir.
Founded: 1907. **Staff:** Prof 4; Other 12. **Subjects:** Bible versions, eschatology, United States history and presidents, Civil War, psychology. **Holdings:** 175,000 books; 23,500 bound periodical volumes; 4800 reels of microfilm; 2 VF drawers of maps and charts; 30 VF drawers of pamphlets and clippings; 2 VF drawers of microcards. **Subscriptions:** 1200 journals and other serials; 10 newspapers. **Services:** Interlibrary loans; copying; library open to public with payment of annual fee. **Computerized Information Services:** DIALOG; computerized cataloging. **Networks/Consortia:** Member of CLASS. **Special Indexes:** Sermon files; Subject Index (sermons and speech illustrative material); Hymn Index (all three on cards). **Remarks:** Includes the holdings of Rosemead Graduate School of Professional Psychology - Library. **Staff:** Stella P. Kim, Hd., Tech.Proc.; Robert Bamattre, Hd., Pub.Serv.; Sue Whitehead, Hd., Per.; Lawrance Marshburn, Graduate Ref.Libn.

BIOLOGICAL ABSTRACTS - LIBRARY
See: Biosciences Information Service

★1381★
BIOMEDICAL COMPUTING TECHNOLOGY INFORMATION CENTER (Med; Info Sci)
R-1302
Vanderbilt Medical Center   Phone: (615) 322-2385
Nashville, TN 37232
Staff: Prof 3; Other 2. **Subjects:** Biomedical computing - computer technology, computer codes and programs, algorithms, interface design. **Holdings:** Card decks; paper and magnetic tapes; engineering drawings; computer output listings. **Services:** SDI. **Computerized Information Services:** Online systems; computerized cataloging. **Publications:** Newsletter, bimonthly. **Remarks:** The Biomedical Computing Technology Information Center operates under contract to the U.S. Department of Energy. **Staff:** Jon Erickson, Co-Dir.; Ronald R. Price, Co-Dir.

BIO-RAD LABORATORIES, INC. - SADTLER RESEARCH LABORATORIES, INC.
See: Sadtler Research Laboratories, Inc.

★1382★
BIO-SCIENCE LABORATORIES - LIBRARY (Med)
7600 Tyrone Ave.   Phone: (213) 989-2520
Van Nuys, CA 91405   Dr. R. Beardslee, Asst.Dir., Res.
Founded: 1948. **Staff:** Prof 1. **Subjects:** Clinical chemistry, microbiology, endocrinology and immunology, business management. **Holdings:** 2000 books; 5000 bound periodical volumes; 200 doctors' papers written at laboratories. **Subscriptions:** 175 journals and other serials. **Services:** Interlibrary loans; copying; library open to cooperating libraries. **Publications:** Reprints of doctors' papers - free. **Staff:** Lois M. Mackey, Libn.

★1383★
BIOSCIENCES INFORMATION SERVICE - BIOLOGICAL ABSTRACTS - LIBRARY (Sci-Tech)
2100 Arch St.   Phone: (215) 568-4016
Philadelphia, PA 19103   Janet M. Sherr, Group Ldr.
Founded: 1969. **Staff:** Prof 2; Other 1. **Subjects:** Life sciences. **Holdings:** 15,000 books; 847 bound periodical volumes; 475 sample abstracting and indexing periodicals (cataloged). **Subscriptions:** 263 journals and other serials. **Services:** Interlibrary loans; library open to public for reference use only with permission. **Staff:** Deborah Willis, Asst.Libn.

★1384★
BIOSPHERICS INC. - LIBRARY (Med)
4928 Wyaconda Rd.   Phone: (301) 770-7700
Rockville, MD 20852   Frances Lederer, Chf.Libn.
Staff: Prof 3; Other 1. **Subjects:** Cancer, environmental health, sewage treatment, space exploration. **Holdings:** 1000 books; 200 bound periodical volumes; 2000 unbound reports; 25 VF drawers. **Subscriptions:** 75 journals and other serials. **Services:** Interlibrary loans; copying; library not open to public. **Computerized Information Services:** Online systems. **Staff:** Diane E.P. Johnson, Info.Rsrcs.Mgr.; Lucie C. Chen, Env.Libn.

BIOSYSTEMATICS RESEARCH INSTITUTE
See: Canada - Agriculture Canada - Plant Research Library

★1385★
BIOVIVAN RESEARCH INSTITUTE - LIBRARY (Sci-Tech)
9 S. Eighth St.   Phone: (609) 692-1499
Vineland, NJ 08360   Herbert Schwartz, Res.Coord.
Founded: 1964. **Staff:** 2. **Subjects:** Chemistry, biochemistry, pesticides, medicine, biology. **Holdings:** 1000 books; 200 bound periodical volumes; 250 U.S. patents; 50 Dutch dissertations. **Subscriptions:** 50 journals and other serials. **Services:** Library not open to public. **Remarks:** Translating service available for foreign language papers or articles in library, or if copies are provided. Quotations on request.

BIRD (E.S.) LIBRARY
See: Syracuse University - E.S. Bird Library

★1386★
BIRD MACHINE COMPANY, INC. - LIBRARY (Sci-Tech)
Neponset St.   Phone: (617) 668-0400
South Walpole, MA 02071   Barbara E. Mangion, Libn.
Founded: 1973. **Staff:** Prof 1. **Subjects:** Engineering - mechanical, chemical, sanitary; pulp and paper technology. **Holdings:** 1400 books. **Subscriptions:** 200 journals and other serials. **Services:** Interlibrary loans; copying; library not open to public.

BIRD S. COLER HOSPITAL
See: Coler Memorial Hospital

BIRD (Walter D.) MEMORIAL HISTORICAL LIBRARY
See: Becker County Historical Society - Walter D. Bird Memorial Historical Library

BIRKHOFF (George David) LIBRARY
See: Harvard University - Mathematical Library

★1387★
BIRMINGHAM BOTANICAL GARDENS - HORACE HAMMOND MEMORIAL LIBRARY (Sci-Tech)
2612 Lane Park Rd.   Phone: (205) 879-1227
Birmingham, AL 35223   Gary G. Gerlach, Dir.
Founded: 1971. **Staff:** Prof 2; Other 1. **Subjects:** Horticulture, botany, landscape architecture, flower arranging, gardens of the world, herbaceous and woody plants. **Special Collections:** Complete set of Richenbachia (4 volumes). **Holdings:** 2000 books; 50 bound periodical volumes; 500 pamphlets (cataloged); 4 VF drawers of newspaper clippings, magazine articles and garden club program materials (cataloged). **Subscriptions:** 32 journals and other serials. **Services:** Interlibrary loans; copying; library open to public. **Publications:** Botanical Society Newsletter, bimonthly. **Staff:** Mrs. D.J. Burns, Libn.

★1388★
BIRMINGHAM MUSEUM OF ART - REFERENCE LIBRARY (Art)
2000 Eighth Ave., N.   Phone: (205) 254-2565
Birmingham, AL 35203   Richard N. Murray, Dir.
Founded: 1959. **Staff:** Prof 2; Other 1. **Subjects:** History of art. **Holdings:** 10,000 volumes. **Subscriptions:** 10 journals and other serials. **Services:**

Library open to public by appointment.

★1389★
BIRMINGHAM NEWS - REFERENCE LIBRARY (Publ)
2200 Fourth Ave., N.   Phone: (205) 325-2409
Birmingham, AL 35203   Laurie Orr, Hd., Ref.Lib.
Founded: 1950. **Staff:** Prof 1; Other 2. **Subjects:** Newspaper reference topics. **Special Collections:** Historical pictures. **Holdings:** 1500 books; clipping files, photographs, microfilm. **Services:** Library not open to public.

★1390★
BIRMINGHAM PUBLIC AND JEFFERSON COUNTY FREE LIBRARY - ART AND MUSIC DEPARTMENT (Art; Mus)
2020 Park Place   Phone: (205) 254-2538
Birmingham, AL 35203   Jane F. Greene, Dept.Hd.
Staff: Prof 2; Other 3. **Subjects:** Music, art, architecture, arts and crafts, photography, costume, landscape architecture. **Holdings:** 28,200 books; 2454 bound periodical volumes; 18,820 phonograph records; 8 VF drawers of pamphlets; 22 VF drawers of clippings; 27 VF drawers of pictures; 825 audio cassettes; 520 art slides; 38 framed pictures. **Subscriptions:** 65 journals and other serials. **Services:** Interlibrary loans; piano practice room; listening facilities for records and cassettes (for members only); circulating mounted picture file; copying; library open to public. **Computerized Information Services:** DIALOG; internal database; computerized cataloging, acquisitions and serials. **Networks/Consortia:** Member of OCLC through SOLINET. **Staff:** Patsy Sweeney, Libn.

★1391★
BIRMINGHAM PUBLIC AND JEFFERSON COUNTY FREE LIBRARY - COLLINS COLLECTION OF THE DANCE (Art)
2020 Park Place   Phone: (205) 254-2538
Birmingham, AL 35203   Lois A. Eady, Cur.
Founded: 1967. **Staff:** 1. **Subjects:** Dance. **Holdings:** 1985 books; 39 bound periodical volumes. **Services:** Copying; library open to public.

★1392★
BIRMINGHAM PUBLIC AND JEFFERSON COUNTY FREE LIBRARY - DEPARTMENT OF ARCHIVES AND MANUSCRIPTS (Hist)
2020 Park Place   Phone: (205) 254-2698
Birmingham, AL 35203   Marvin Y. Whiting, Archv./Cur., Mss.
Staff: Prof 2; Other 2. **Subjects:** Birmingham, Alabama - history, civil rights, real estate development, politics and government, private utilities, photographic history. **Special Collections:** Birmingham Municipal Records (300 linear feet); Civil Rights in Alabama (75 linear feet and microforms); Robert Jemison, Jr. papers (250 linear feet); Birmingham Water Works Company Records (300 linear feet). **Holdings:** 500 books; 200 bound periodical volumes; 7500 linear feet of archives and manuscripts; 500 reels of microfilmed newspapers, archives and manuscripts; 600 oral history cassette tapes; 110,000 photographic prints and negatives. **Subscriptions:** 12 journals and other serials; 20 newspapers. **Services:** Interlibrary loans; copying; library open to public for reference use only. **Computerized Information Services:** Computerized acquisitions. **Publications:** The Journal of the Birmingham Historical Society, 2/year - by subscription. **Special Indexes:** Subject file index to photographic collections (card). **Special Catalogs:** Preliminary and Descriptive Inventories for Manuscript Collections and Archival Records Groups, Sub-groups, & Series. **Staff:** Robert G. Corley, Asst.Archv.

★1393★
BIRMINGHAM PUBLIC AND JEFFERSON COUNTY FREE LIBRARY - GOVERNMENT DOCUMENTS DEPARTMENT (Info Sci)
2020 Park Place   Phone: (205) 254-2555
Birmingham, AL 35203   Rebecca Scarborough, Hd., Govt.Doc.Dept.
Founded: 1895. **Staff:** Prof 2; Other 2. **Subjects:** Federal government documents. **Special Collections:** ASI microfiche collection; U.S. Patent Depository, 1976 to present (complete patents); CIS full microfiche collection, 1970 to present (pre-1970 reports, prints, serial set); SRI microfiche collection, January 1981 to present. **Holdings:** 160,000 volumes; 2000 shelves of federal documents. **Services:** Interlibrary loans; copying; SDI; library open to public. **Computerized Information Services:** DIALOG, BRS, WESTLAW. **Publications:** List of new documents and subject bibliographies, irregular - for library departments, branches and patrons. **Staff:** Barbara Clotfelter, Libn.

★1394★
BIRMINGHAM PUBLIC AND JEFFERSON COUNTY FREE LIBRARY - J. HUBERT SCRUGGS, JR. COLLECTION OF PHILATELY (Rec)
2020 Park Place   Phone: (205) 254-2698
Birmingham, AL 35203   Marvin Y. Whiting, Cur.
Founded: 1975. **Subjects:** Philately, Alabama and Confederate history.

Holdings: 400 books; 75 bound periodical volumes; 425 unbound periodicals; auction catalogs; early Alabama stampless covers; Alabama steamboat covers and bills of lading; Alabama legal documents with revenue stamps; philatelic exhibits; Confederate States of America stamped covers and manuscripts; Confederate money; Alabama land grants; U.S. postal stamps, blocks and plates, 1847-1950; first day covers; 30,000 miscellaneous items and manuscripts; Alabama newspapers. **Services:** Collection open to public by appointment.

★1395★
BIRMINGHAM PUBLIC AND JEFFERSON COUNTY FREE LIBRARY - RUCKER AGEE CARTOGRAPHICAL COLLECTION (Geog-Map)
2020 Park Place
Birmingham, AL 35203
Phone: (205) 254-2534
Ruth S. Spence, Map Cur.
Founded: 1964. **Staff:** Prof 1. **Subjects:** Alabama, Southeast, historical cartography, discovery and exploration, Civil War. **Special Collections:** Rucker Agee Collection; Joseph H. Woodward, II, Collection. **Holdings:** 2300 books and bound periodical volumes; 3500 maps (cataloged); 675 atlases (cataloged). **Subscriptions:** 8 journals and other serials. **Services:** Copying; collection open to public by appointment. **Computerized Information Services:** DIALOG; computerized cataloging, acquisitions and serials. **Networks/Consortia:** Member of OCLC through SOLINET. **Publications:** A List of Nineteenth Century Maps of the State of Alabama (1973); List of Maps of Birmingham (1978); A List of 16th, 17th, and 18th Century Material in the Rucker Agee Map Collection (1978).

★1396★
BIRMINGHAM PUBLIC AND JEFFERSON COUNTY FREE LIBRARY - TUTWILER COLLECTION OF SOUTHERN HISTORY AND LITERATURE (Hist)
2020 Park Place
Birmingham, AL 35203
Phone: (205) 254-2534
Virginia Scott, Hd.Libn.
Founded: 1927. **Staff:** Prof 3; Other 5. **Subjects:** Birmingham and Alabama history and literature; Southeastern genealogy; Civil War and Reconstruction history; slave history. **Special Collections:** State, county and municipal documents. **Holdings:** 48,000 books; 6900 bound periodical volumes; 9975 reels of microfilm (cataloged); 1500 pamphlets (cataloged); 6000 microforms; 154 VF drawers. **Subscriptions:** 171 journals and other serials; 38 newspapers. **Services:** Copying; library open to public for reference use only. **Computerized Information Services:** DIALOG; computerized cataloging, acquisitions and serials. **Networks/Consortia:** Member of OCLC through SOLINET. **Publications:** George B. Ward: Birmingham's Urban Statesman - on request; Research in Black History; Genealogical Research in the Tutwiler Collection. **Special Catalogs:** Bibliography of Birmingham, Alabama, 1872-1972 (book) - distributed on request. **Special Indexes:** Index to the Birmingham News-Birmingham Post Herald (microfiche computer printout). **Staff:** Yvonne Crumpler, Libn.; Anne Knight, Libn.

★1397★
BIRMINGHAM PUBLIC AND JEFFERSON COUNTY FREE LIBRARY - YOUTH DEPARTMENT (Hum)
2020 Park Place
Birmingham, AL 35203
Phone: (205) 254-2530
Eva Yates, Hd.
Founded: 1948. **Staff:** Prof 2; Other 1. **Subjects:** 19th century children's books. **Special Collections:** Grace Hardie Collection of Children's Books. **Holdings:** 427 books; 76 bound periodical volumes. **Services:** Interlibrary loans (limited); copying (limited); library open to public for reference use only. **Computerized Information Services:** Computerized cataloging and acquisitions. **Special Indexes:** Hardie Collection catalog (card).

★1398★
BIRMINGHAM-SOUTHERN COLLEGE - CHARLES ANDREW RUSH LEARNING CENTER/LIBRARY - SPECIAL COLLECTIONS (Rel-Theol; Hist)
800 8th Ave., W.
Birmingham, AL 35254
Phone: (205) 328-5250
Barbara G. Scott, Dir.
Founded: 1859. **Special Collections:** Methodism (880 volumes); Americana (1920 items); Alabama History and Authors (1314 volumes); Branscomb Collection For, By, About Women (189 volumes). **Services:** Interlibrary loans (fee); copying (fee); library open to public. **Computerized Information Services:** EBSCO Subscription Services; computerized acquisitions. **Networks/Consortia:** Member of Southern College-University Union Library Group.

★1399★
BIRMINGHAM TEMPLE - LIBRARY (Rel-Theol)†
28611 W. Twelve Mile Rd.
Farmington, MI 48024
Phone: (313) 477-0177
Founded: 1971. **Staff:** Prof 1. **Subjects:** Humanism, Judaism. **Holdings:** 2000 books. **Subscriptions:** 20 journals and other serials. **Services:**

Interlibrary loans; library open to public by special request. **Publications:** Jewish Humanist (a publication of the Birmingham Temple), monthly; Humanistic Judaism (a publication of the Society for Humanistic Judaism), quarterly - both by subscription; High Holy Days for Humanists; Meditation Services for Humanistic Judaism; What is Humanist Judaism? - available for sale.

★1400★
BISHOP BARAGA ASSOCIATION - ARCHIVES (Hist)
444 S. Fourth St.
Marquette, MI 49855
Fr. N. Daniel Rupp, Archv.
Staff: Prof 2; Other 1. **Subjects:** Bishop Baraga. **Special Collections:** Baraga's books, diaries and letters, 1830-1868; microfilm of the Office of Indian Affairs, early 1800s. **Holdings:** 1000 books; 3 bound periodical volumes; microfilm. **Services:** Library open to accredited historians. **Publications:** Bishop Baraga Bulletin. **Remarks:** The office of the association is located at 239 Baraga Ave. in Marquette. **Staff:** Linda Panian, Res.Asst.

★1401★
BISHOP (Bernice P.) MUSEUM - LIBRARY (Sci-Tech)
1525 Bernice St.
Box 19000-A
Honolulu, HI 96819
Phone: (808) 847-3511
Cynthia Timberlake, Libn.
Founded: 1889. **Staff:** Prof 4; Other 5. **Subjects:** Anthropology, entomology, botany, malacology, marine biology, Hawaiiana, exploration, history, linguistics, geology. **Special Collections:** Fuller Collection of Pacific Books (anthropology, 2500 volumes); 19th century Hawaiian language newspapers; Carter Collection of Hawaiiana (1500 volumes). **Holdings:** 85,000 books and bound periodical volumes; 42 microfiche and 315 reels of microfilm (cataloged); 22,600 pamphlets; 275 feet of manuscripts; 300,000 photographs and negatives. **Subscriptions:** 1404 journals and other serials. **Services:** Copying; library open to public. **Publications:** Additions to the Catalog, irregular - distributed to the staff, the University of Hawaii and other Pacific libraries. **Special Catalogs:** Book catalog published (111 volumes). **Staff:** Lynn Davis, Photo Libn.; Janet Short, Cat.; Marguerite K. Ashford, Ref.Libn.

BISHOP (Bernice P.) MUSEUM - PACIFIC SCIENTIFIC INFORMATION CENTER
See: Pacific Scientific Information Center

★1402★
BISHOP CLARKSON MEMORIAL HOSPITAL - PATHOLOGY/MEDICAL STAFF LIBRARY (Med)
Box 3328
Omaha, NE 68103
Phone: (402) 559-2058
Barbara McReynolds, Libn.
Staff: Prof 1. **Subjects:** Medicine, pathology, laboratory diagnosis. **Holdings:** 450 books; 1200 bound periodical volumes; 50 cassette tapes. **Subscriptions:** 115 journals and other serials. **Services:** Interlibrary loans; copying; SDI; library not open to public.

★1403★
BISHOP COLLEGE - ZALE LIBRARY - BANKS AFRO-AMERICAN HERITAGE COLLECTION (Hist)
3837 Simpson-Stuart Rd.
Dallas, TX 75241
Phone: (214) 372-8734
Dennis M. Hawkins, Pub.Serv.Libn.
Founded: 1976. **Staff:** Prof 1; Other 4. **Subjects:** Black history, black church history, black authors, accomplishments of blacks. **Holdings:** 25,000 books; 150 bound periodical volumes; 500 files of VF material. **Subscriptions:** 50 journals and other serials; 15 newspapers. **Services:** Copying; library open to public. **Networks/Consortia:** Member of Association for Higher Education of North Texas - Library Committee.

★1404★
BISHOP & MC KENZIE, BARRISTERS & SOLICITORS - LIBRARY (Law)
Canadian Commercial Bank Bldg.
Edmonton, AB, Canada T5J 1V3
Phone: (403) 426-5550
Katherine McKenney, Libn.
Staff: Prof 1. **Subjects:** Law. **Holdings:** 4000 volumes. **Subscriptions:** 81 journals and other serials. **Services:** Copying; SDI; library not open to public. **Computerized Information Services:** QL Systems.

BISHOP MEMORIAL LIBRARY
See: Wyoming Historical and Geological Society

★1405★
BISHOP'S MILL HISTORICAL INSTITUTE - SOL FEINSTONE LIBRARY (Hist)
Ridley Creek State Park
Edgemont, PA 19028
Phone: (215) 353-1777
Marie A. Martin, Exec.Sec.
Staff: Prof 1; Other 3. **Subjects:** Pennsylvania colonial history. **Holdings:**

1500 books; 500 bound periodical volumes; 125 reels of microfilm of county records; 25 local maps; 25 local architectural drawings. **Subscriptions:** 20 journals and other serials; 5 newspapers. **Services:** Library open to public with restrictions.

★1406★
BISMARCK TRIBUNE - NEWS LIBRARY (Publ)
707 E. Front Ave.
Box 1498   Phone: (701) 223-2500
Bismarck, ND 58502   Elizabeth A. Simes, Libn.
Staff: Prof 1; Other 1. **Subjects:** Newspaper reference topics. **Holdings:** 125 books; 8 binders of Tribune special sections; cuts, mats, clippings, pictures. **Services:** Library not open to public. **Special Indexes:** Index to subject files (binder).

★1407★
BISSELL (Emily P.) HOSPITAL - MEDICAL LIBRARY (Med)
3000 Newport Gap Pike   Phone: (302) 995-8400
Wilmington, DE 19808   Lucille M. Reilly, Med.Serv.Sec.
Subjects: Pulmonary tuberculosis, medicine, geriatrics. **Holdings:** 250 books. **Services:** Library not open to public.

★1408★
BITTER ROOT VALLEY HISTORICAL SOCIETY - RAVALLI COUNTY MUSEUM (Hist)
205 Bedford Ave.   Phone: (406) 363-3338
Hamilton, MT 59840   Erma Owings, Dir.
Staff: Prof 1; Other 2. **Subjects:** Pioneer and Indian history. **Special Collections:** Indian Collection; Granville Stuart Collection; Miles Romney Memorial Library. **Holdings:** Figures not available for books; Western News Files, 1890-1977. **Services:** Library open to public.

★1409★
BITUMINOUS COAL RESEARCH, INC. - LIBRARY (Energy)†
350 Hochberg Rd.
Box 278   Phone: (412) 327-1600
Monroeville, PA 15146   Mary Ann Sakoian, Libn.
Founded: 1936. **Staff:** Prof 1; Other 2. **Subjects:** Coal - combustion, carbonization, gasification, mining, preparation; environmental improvement. **Holdings:** 1800 books; 325 bound periodical volumes; 5000 technical publications; 15,000 technical abstracts on cards. **Subscriptions:** 150 journals and other serials. **Services:** Library open to those interested in coal and related matters.

★1410★
BITUMINOUS PIPE INSTITUTE - LIBRARY (Sci-Tech)*
221 N. La Salle St.
Chicago, IL 60601
Subjects: Hydraulics, sanitation, buried piping. **Holdings:** Figures not available.

★1411★
BIXBY (Emma L.) HOSPITAL - PATMOS MEMORIAL LIBRARY (Med)
818 Riverside Ave.   Phone: (517) 263-0711
Adrian, MI 49221   Cinda Walton, Dir. of Med.Rec.
Staff: 1. **Subjects:** Medicine, surgery, obstetrics-gynecology, pediatrics. **Holdings:** 500 books; 150 bound periodical volumes. **Subscriptions:** 11 journals and other serials. **Services:** Interlibrary loans (limited); library not open to public.

★1412★
BLACK ECONOMIC RESEARCH CENTER - REFERENCE LIBRARY
112 W. 120th St.
New York, NY 10027
Defunct. Holdings absorbed by Clark College - Southern Center for Studies in Public Policy - Research Library.

★1413★
BLACK HAWK COLLEGE - LEARNING RESOURCES CENTER (Area-Ethnic)
6600 34th Ave.   Phone: (309) 796-1311
Moline, IL 61265   Donald C. Rowland, Dir.
Founded: 1946. **Staff:** Prof 4; Other 3. **Special Collections:** Belgian history and culture. **Holdings:** 800 books; 250 music tapes (cataloged). **Services:** Interlibrary loans; copying; library open to public with restrictions.

★1414★
BLACK HILLS STATE COLLEGE - CURRICULUM LIBRARY (Educ)
Berry Library-Learning Ctr.
University St.   Phone: (605) 642-6833
Spearfish, SD 57783   Vicki Kapust, Libn.
Founded: 1968. **Staff:** Prof 1. **Subjects:** Instructional materials for kindergarten through 12th grade; special education. **Holdings:** 8500 books; 953 kits (cataloged); filmstrips; phonograph records; curriculum guides; teachers' guides; textbooks; tests; workbooks; publishers catalogs. **Services:** Library open to public for reference use only.

★1415★
BLACK HILLS STATE COLLEGE - E.Y. BERRY LIBRARY-LEARNING CENTER - SPECIAL COLLECTIONS (Educ; Hist)†
   Phone: (605) 642-6833
Spearfish, SD 57783   Dora Jones, Spec.Coll.
Founded: 1925. **Special Collections:** E.Y. Berry Collection (164 boxes of manuscripts dealing with his 20 years of service in the U.S. House of Representatives from 1951-1971, plus photographs, color slides, tape recordings, and motion picture films, also related to that period); Case Library for Western Historical Studies. **Services:** Interlibrary loans; copying; library open to public.

BLACK ROCK FOREST LIBRARY
See: Harvard University - Harvard Black Rock Forest Library

BLACK SPARROW PRESS ARCHIVES
See: University of Alberta - Special Collections

★1416★
BLACK & VEATCH CONSULTING ENGINEERS - CENTRAL LIBRARY (Sci-Tech)
1500 Meadow Lake Pkwy.
Box 8405   Phone: (913) 967-2223
Kansas City, MO 64114   Leo M. Hack, Libn.
Staff: Prof 1; Other 1. **Subjects:** Engineering. **Holdings:** 3000 books; 100 bound periodical volumes. **Subscriptions:** 150 journals and other serials. **Services:** Interlibrary loans. **Computerized Information Services:** SDC.

BLACKADER LIBRARY
See: Canadian Hospital Association

BLACKADER LIBRARY OF ARCHITECTURE/LAUTERMAN LIBRARY OF ART
See: Mc Gill University

BLACKER/WOOD LIBRARY OF ZOOLOGY AND ORNITHOLOGY
See: Mc Gill University

★1417★
BLACKFORD COUNTY HISTORICAL SOCIETY - MUSEUM AND BEESON LIBRARY (Hist)*
321 N. High St.
Box 264   Phone: (317) 348-1905
Hartford City, IN 47348   Dwight Mikkelson, Pres.
Founded: 1956. **Staff:** 1. **Subjects:** Local history, genealogy. **Special Collections:** Local newspapers, 1890-1963 (100 bound volumes). **Holdings:** 200 books; 100 bound periodical volumes; 100 Quaker records and 40 county records on microfilm; 20 genealogies. **Services:** Copying; library open to public with restrictions.

★1418★
BLACKHAWK GENEALOGICAL SOCIETY - LIBRARY (Hist)
Box 912
Rock Island, IL 61201   Mrs. F.A. Moseley, Lib.Chm.
Subjects: Genealogy, history. **Holdings:** 250 books; 950 unbound periodicals; pamphlets; U.S. Locality Microfilm Collection of Church of Jesus Christ of Latter-Day Saints Genealogical Library (51 reels of microfilm). **Subscriptions:** 28 journals and other serials. **Services:** Copying; library open to public with restrictions. **Remarks:** Collection processed by society committee, then placed in Moline Public Library, 5th Ave. and 17th St., Moline, IL 61265. Collection may be used by society members and the public.

★1419★
BLACKHAWK TECHNICAL INSTITUTE, JANESVILLE - LEARNING MATERIALS CENTER (Sci-Tech)
Prairie Ave., Rte. 3   Phone: (608) 756-4121
Janesville, WI 53545   Grace Sweeney, Libn.
Founded: 1965. **Staff:** Prof 2; Other 2. **Subjects:** Health, electronics, avionics, marketing, agriculture, machine shop. **Special Collections:** Transactions of American Foundrymen's Association from 1915-1972. **Holdings:** 25,000 books; 1000 items of AV material. **Services:** Interlibrary loans; copying; library open to public with restrictions. **Networks/Consortia:** Member of Midwest Health Science Library Network. **Remarks:** The Beloit Library, located at 1149 4th St., Beloit, WI 54511, is part of the Janesville Campus. **Staff:** Roger Dray, AV Spec.

★1420★
BLACKMER (Samuel H.) MEMORIAL LIBRARY (Law)†
County Court House
207 South St.
Bennington, VT 05201   Phone: (802) 442-8528
Founded: 1952. **Subjects:** Law. **Special Collections:** Old Vermont statutes. **Holdings:** 2000 volumes. **Services:** Use of library for reference will be granted on request.

BLACKWELL LIBRARY
See: Salisbury State College

★1421★
BLACKWELL, WALKER, GRAY, POWERS, FLICK & HOEHL - LAW LIBRARY
(Law)
2400 Amerifirst Bldg.
One S.E. Third Ave.
Miami, FL 33131   Phone: (305) 358-8880
                              Dr. Cesar J. Armstrong, Res.Libn.
Staff: Prof 1; Other 2. **Subjects:** Law - business, tax, medical. **Holdings:** 28,000 volumes. **Subscriptions:** 35 journals and other serials. **Services:** Library not open to public.

★1422★
BLACKWELL (William) - PRIVATE LIBRARY
Box 184
Hastings, MN 55033
Defunct

BLAIR (Allan) MEMORIAL CLINIC
See: Saskatchewan Cancer Foundation - Allan Blair Memorial Clinic

★1423★
BLAIR COUNTY LAW LIBRARY (Law)
County Court House
Hollidaysburg, PA 16648   Phone: (814) 695-5541
                              June C. Ringdal, Law Libn.
Subjects: Law, tax. **Holdings:** Figures not available. **Services:** Library open to public with self service.

BLAIR-LIPPINCOTT LIBRARY
See: Eye and Ear Hospital of Pittsburgh

★1424★
BLAISDELL INSTITUTE FOR ADVANCED STUDY IN WORLD CULTURES AND
RELIGIONS - LIBRARY (Rel-Theol)
143 E. 10th St.
Claremont, CA 91711   Phone: (714) 626-0521
Subjects: Major world religions and cultures. **Holdings:** 1000 volumes. **Remarks:** Associated with Claremont University Center.

★1425★
BLAKE, CASSELS & GRAYDON - LIBRARY (Law)
Commerce Court West
P.O. Box 25
Toronto, ON, Canada M5L 1A9   Phone: (416) 863-2650
                              Judith A. Douglas, Libn.
Founded: 1864. **Staff:** Prof 2; Other 1. **Subjects:** Law - corporate, securities, Canada, Great Britain; Canadian statues. **Holdings:** 3700 books; 500 bound periodical volumes; 15,500 bound volumes of reports. **Subscriptions:** 60 journals and other serials. **Services:** Interlibrary loans; copying; library open to public by written request. **Computerized Information Services:** QL Systems, Info Globe. **Publications:** Acquisitions list, weekly. **Staff:** Jane Wilson; Maria Lechicky .

BLAKELY (Stuart B.) MEMORIAL LIBRARY
See: Binghamton General Hospital - Stuart B. Blakely Memorial Library

BLANCHFIELD ARMY COMMUNITY HOSPITAL
See: U.S. Army Hospitals

BLAND (Schuyler Otis) MEMORIAL LIBRARY
See: U.S. Merchant Marine Academy - Schuyler Otis Bland Memorial
Library

BLANDY EXPERIMENTAL FARM LIBRARY
See: University of Virginia

★1426★
BLANEY, PASTERNAK, SMELA & WATSON - LAW LIBRARY (Law)
20 Queen St. W., Suite 1400   Phone: (416) 364-9421
Toronto, ON, Canada M5H 2V3   Rowan J. Amott, Libn.
Staff: Prof 1. **Subjects:** Law. **Holdings:** 4000 volumes. **Subscriptions:** 85 journals and other serials. **Services:** Interlibrary loans; copying; SDI to lawyers; library not open to public. **Special Indexes:** Memo of Law index.

BLANKENBUEHLER (John H.) MEMORIAL LIBRARY
See: Hobart Brothers Technical Center - John H. Blankenbuehler
Memorial Library

BLAU (Helen) MEMORIAL LIBRARY
See: Central Synagogue of Nassau County - Helen Blau Memorial Library

BLAUSTEIN LIBRARY
See: American Jewish Committee

BLAXTER MEMORIAL LIBRARY
See: Children's Hospital of Pittsburgh

BLEICHROEDER (Arnhold and S.), INC.
See: Arnhold and S. Bleichroeder, Inc.

★1427★
BLESSED SACRAMENT SEMINARY - LIBRARY (Rel-Theol)*
5384 Wilson Mills Rd.
Highland Heights, OH 44143   Phone: (216) 442-3410
Staff: 1. **Subjects:** Theology, philosophy, humanities, religion, biblical studies. **Special Collections:** Migne's Patrologia Graeca, Latina (386 volumes). **Holdings:** 25,000 books; 3500 bound periodical volumes; 16 VF drawers of pamphlets and documents. **Subscriptions:** 155 journals and other serials; 5 newspapers. **Services:** Library open to professors and students only. **Publications:** Recent Acquisitions, semiannual; Bibliography of Current Trends, semiannual.

BLISS ARMY HOSPITAL
See: U.S. Army Hospitals

★1428★
BLISS (Malcolm) MENTAL HEALTH CENTER - ROBERT J. BROCKMAN
MEMORIAL LIBRARY (Med)
1420 Grattan St.   Phone: (314) 241-7600
St. Louis, MO 63104   William G. Heigold, Med.Libn.
Founded: 1956. **Staff:** Prof 1; Other 1. **Subjects:** Psychiatry, psychology, psychiatric nursing, community mental health, social work. **Holdings:** 4600 books and bound periodical volumes; 90 National Institute of Mental Health Reports; 4 VF drawers of special bibliographies. **Subscriptions:** 93 journals and other serials. **Services:** Interlibrary loans; copying; SDI; library open to qualified users with approval of hospital superintendent.

BLISS MEMORIAL LIBRARY
See: First Methodist Church

★1429★
BLOCH (Ernest) SOCIETY - ARCHIVES (Mus)
Star Route 2   Phone: (707) 884-3473
Gualala, CA 95445   Lucienne Bloch Dimitroff, Supv.
Founded: 1969. **Staff:** 1. **Subjects:** Ernest Bloch - biography, music, bibliography. **Special Collections:** Ernest Bloch Letters (300); notes on Bloch's pedagogy. **Holdings:** 60 scores; 130 Ernest Bloch recordings, 20 concert tapes; 50 books on science and philosophy annotated by Ernest Bloch; 100 photographs; 200 programs and clippings; 30 articles on Bloch. **Services:** Archives open to members by appointment. **Publications:** Ernest Bloch Society Bulletin, annual - to members and libraries. **Remarks:** The music departments of the Library of Congress and of the University of California in Berkeley, CA, have music and letters by Ernest Bloch. The Center for Creative Photography, University of Arizona at Tucson has E. Bloch's photograph collection in its archives.

★1430★
BLODGETT MEMORIAL MEDICAL CENTER - RICHARD ROOT SMITH
LIBRARY (Med)
1840 Wealthy St., S.E.   Phone: (616) 774-7624
Grand Rapids, MI 49506   Brian Simmons, Med.Libn.
Staff: Prof 2. **Subjects:** Medicine, surgery and supporting subjects. **Holdings:** 1800 books; 7100 bound periodical volumes; 500 cassette audiotapes; 3000 anatomical slides; 3000 unbound periodicals. **Subscriptions:** 200 journals and other serials. **Services:** Interlibrary loans; copying; SDI; library

open to public. **Computerized Information Services:** MEDLINE. **Networks/Consortia:** Member of Michigan Area Serial Holdings Consortium (MASH). **Staff:** Sara Anne Hook, Asst.Libn.

★1431★
BLOMMEL HISTORIC AUTOMOTIVE DATA COLLECTION - LIBRARY AND INFORMATION CENTER (Hist)
Rte. 5   Phone: (317) 825-9259
Connersville, IN 47331   Henry H. Blommel, Collector-Dir.
Founded: 1928. **Subjects:** History of Connersville, Fayette County and Indiana; history of U.S. and Indiana automotive industry; history of U.S. Army and its vehicles. **Special Collections:** Connersville industrial history and "Little Detroit" era of Indiana and U.S. automotive makers; Cord Corporation automobiles. **Holdings:** 650 books; 1500 bound periodical volumes; 500 other items (cataloged); collections of former craftsmen. **Subscriptions:** 25 journals and other serials; 10 newspapers. **Services:** Library open to public with restrictions.

BLOMMER SCIENCE LIBRARY
See: Georgetown University

★1432★
BLOOMFIELD COLLEGE - GEORGE TALBOT HALL LIBRARY - SPECIAL COLLECTIONS (Hist)
467 Franklin St.   Phone: (201) 748-9000
Bloomfield, NJ 07003   Dr. Painan R. Wu, Chf.Libn.
Special Collections: Presbyterian Church History; Abraham Lincoln. **Services:** Interlibrary loans; copying; library open to public for reference use only. **Computerized Information Services:** Computerized cataloging. **Networks/Consortia:** Member of OCLC through PALINET & Union Library Catalogue of Pennsylvania. **Publications:** Library Notes, quarterly - to faculty, administration, students.

★1433★
BLOOMINGTON-NORMAL DAILY PANTAGRAPH - NEWSPAPER LIBRARY (Publ)
301 W. Washington St.   Phone: (309) 829-9411
Bloomington, IL 61701   Diane Miller, Lib.Dir.
Staff: Prof 2; Other 2. **Subjects:** Newspaper reference topics. **Special Collections:** Adlai Stevenson II (news articles and pictures). **Holdings:** 500 books; clippings; 6000 photographs; 80,000 microfiche. **Subscriptions:** 15 journals and other serials; 22 newspapers. **Services:** Library not open to public. **Staff:** Sandy Stroud, Asst.Libn.

★1434★
BLOOMSBURG STATE COLLEGE - HARVEY A. ANDRUSS LIBRARY - SPECIAL COLLECTIONS (Educ)
                                Phone: (717) 389-2900
Bloomsburg, PA 17815   William V. Ryan, Dir., Lib.Serv.
Founded: 1839. **Special Collections:** Juvenile literature (12,691 volumes); government documents (Pennsylvania depository); Harvey A. Andruss Collection (business education). **Services:** Interlibrary loans; copying; library open to public. **Computerized Information Services:** Computerized cataloging and serials.

BLOUGH (Glenn O.) LIBRARY
See: National Science Teachers Association - Glenn O. Blough Library

★1435★
BLOUNT MEMORIAL HOSPITAL - LESLIE R. LINGEMAN MEMORIAL MEDICAL LIBRARY (Med)
New Walland Highway   Phone: (615) 983-7211
Maryville, TN 37801   Miriam B. Williamson, Libn.
Founded: 1947. **Staff:** Prof 1. **Subjects:** Cardiology, oncology, internal medicine, gastroenterology, psychiatry, surgery. **Holdings:** 594 books; 1270 bound periodical volumes; 135 audiotapes and 19 audio records; 6 VF drawers of pamphlets. **Subscriptions:** 65 journals and other serials. **Services:** Interlibrary loans; copying; library open to public for reference use only by request. **Computerized Information Services:** MEDLINE. **Networks/Consortia:** Member of Knoxville Area Health Science Library Consortium. **Publications:** Library Notes, bimonthly newsletter - for internal distribution only.

★1436★
BLUE CLOUD ABBEY - LIBRARY (Rel-Theol)
                                Phone: (605) 432-5528
Marvin, SD 57251   Rev. John David McMullen, O.S.B., Hd.Libn.
Staff: Prof 1; Other 4. **Subjects:** Scripture; monastic theology, patristics, church history, general theology; Indian history. **Special Collections:** Bureau

of American Ethnology publications (complete set). **Holdings:** 40,000 books. **Subscriptions:** 140 journals and other serials; 8 newspapers. **Services:** Interlibrary loans; copying; library open to public with restrictions.

★1437★
BLUE CROSS AND BLUE SHIELD ASSOCIATION - LIBRARY (Med; Bus-Fin)
676 N. St. Clair   Phone: (312) 440-6147
Chicago, IL 60611   Mary T. Drazba, Sr.Dir.
Founded: 1965. **Staff:** Prof 1. **Subjects:** Hospital and medical economics, health planning. **Holdings:** 20,000 books; 3000 congressional documents; 10 VF drawers of pamphlets and clippings; 4 VF drawers of NTIS health planning microfiche; Federal Register on microfilm, 1965 to present; 39 other serial titles on microfilm. **Subscriptions:** 180 journals and other serials. **Services:** Interlibrary loans; copying; library open to other libraries and organizations; open to public by request. **Computerized Information Services:** DIALOG. **Networks/Consortia:** Member of Chicago Library System; Metropolitan Chicago Library Assembly; Regional Medical Library - Region 3. **Remarks:** Merged with the Blue Shield Association in 1982.

★1438★
BLUE CROSS/BLUE SHIELD OF GREATER NEW YORK - REFERENCE LIBRARY (Med)
3 Park Ave.   Phone: (212) 481-2384
New York, NY 10016   Iona Prilop, Libn.
Staff: Prof 2; Other 1. **Subjects:** Health care, medical economics. **Holdings:** 5000 books; 3000 clippings (indexed); 399 reels of microfilm. **Subscriptions:** 350 journals and other serials; 15 newspapers. **Services:** Interlibrary loans; library open to public by request. **Publications:** Acquisitions List, monthly. **Staff:** Melba Howson, Dept.Hd.; Annie Miller, Asst.Libn.

★1439★
BLUE CROSS AND BLUE SHIELD OF NORTH CAROLINA - INFORMATION CENTER (Med)
5901 Chapel Hill-Durham Blvd.   Phone: (919) 489-7431
Chapel Hill, NC 27514   Tera B. White, Mgr., Corp.Info.Serv.
Founded: 1970. **Staff:** Prof 2; Other 2. **Subjects:** Health economics, health insurance, management, computer science. **Holdings:** 4500 books; 150 bound periodical volumes; 50,000 reports; 6500 microfiche; microfilm. **Subscriptions:** 180 journals and other serials; 7 newspapers. **Services:** Interlibrary loans; SDI; library open to public by appointment. **Computerized Information Services:** DIALOG, SDC; computerized cataloging and serials. **Publications:** For Your Information, monthly - to management. **Special Indexes:** Index to BCBSNC'S filings with North Carolina Department of Insurance. **Staff:** Sara U. Ensor, Libn.

★1440★
BLUE CROSS AND BLUE SHIELD OF VIRGINIA - PLANS LIBRARY (Med)
2015 Staples Mill Rd.
Box 27401   Phone: (804) 359-7177
Richmond, VA 23279   Frank Johns, Libn.
Staff: Prof 1. **Subjects:** Health insurance, management. **Holdings:** 1500 books. **Subscriptions:** 42 journals and other serials. **Services:** Interlibrary loans; library open to public by appointment.

★1441★
BLUE CROSS OF CALIFORNIA - LIBRARY (Med)
Box 70,000   Phone: (213) 703-3160
Van Nuys, CA 91470   Frances Baur Linke, Hd.Libn.
Founded: 1982. **Staff:** Prof 2; Other 1. **Subjects:** Law; economics - medical, hospital; management; government publications. **Special Collections:** Hospital cost containment studies. **Holdings:** 8000 books; 395 bound periodical volumes; 30 vertical files; 50 films; 250 audio cassettes; 900 microfiche. **Subscriptions:** 298 journals and other serials. **Services:** Interlibrary loans; copying (limited); library not open to public. **Networks/Consortia:** Member of Southern California Answering Network (SCAN). **Publications:** Library Newsletter, monthly. **Remarks:** Library located at 21555 Oxnard St., Woodland Hills, CA 91367. **Staff:** Eliza C. Chu, Asst.Libn.

★1442★
BLUE CROSS OF GREATER PHILADELPHIA - E.A. VAN STEENWYK MEMORIAL LIBRARY (Med)
1333 Chestnut St.
16th Fl., Widener Bldg.   Phone: (215) 448-5400
Philadelphia, PA 19107   Judith Delbaum, Libn.
Founded: 1965. **Staff:** Prof 1. **Subjects:** Medical economics, health insurance, health education, hospitals. **Special Collections:** Medicare, health insurance. **Holdings:** 2500 books and bound periodical volumes; 15 VF drawers of pamphlets and clippings. **Subscriptions:** 150 journals and other serials. **Services:** Interlibrary loans; copying; library open to public by

appointment.

★1443★

BLUE CROSS HOSPITAL SERVICE, INC. - LIBRARY (Med)
4444 Forest Park Blvd.   Phone: (314) 658-4774
St. Louis, MO 63108   Mary Hebert, Lbn.
Founded: 1970. **Staff:** Prof 1. **Subjects:** Health care, insurance, economics, business. **Holdings:** 2000 books; 175 bound periodical volumes; 4 VF drawers of pamphlets and clippings; 1 VF drawer of speeches and reports. **Subscriptions:** 220 journals and other serials; 8 newspapers. **Services:** Interlibrary loans; SDI; library open to public by appointment. **Networks/Consortia:** Member of Midcontinental Regional Medical Library Network; St. Louis Regional Library Network. **Publications:** Library Bulletin, monthly - for internal distribution only.

★1444★

BLUE CROSS OF WESTERN PENNSYLVANIA - IN-HOUSE BUSINESS LIBRARY (Med)
1 Smithfield St.   Phone: (412) 255-8220
Pittsburgh, PA 15222   Connie Ferguson, Lbn.
Founded: 1945. **Staff:** 2. **Subjects:** Health care, related general business management. **Holdings:** 2000 books; 1000 pamphlets. **Subscriptions:** 88 journals and other serials. **Services:** Library not open to public.

★1445★

BLUE EARTH COUNTY HISTORICAL SOCIETY - MUSEUM ARCHIVES (Hist)
606 S. Broad St.   Phone: (507) 345-4154
Mankato, MN 56001   Audrey K. Hicks, Staff Archv.
Founded: 1916. **Staff:** 2. **Subjects:** Blue Earth County history - agriculture, Indians, industries, prominent families, organizations. **Special Collections:** Papers of Thomas Hughes, R. Dean Hubbard, J. A. Willard family, Franklin H. Waite, and Anna Wiecking. **Holdings:** 500 books; 2500 other cataloged items; 250 daybooks, diaries, programs; 1000 letters, newspaper clippings, scrapbooks, atlases, maps; 500 photographs; 54 bound newspaper volumes. **Services:** Copying; archives open to public for reference use only. **Special Indexes:** Index to old newspapers (card); index to obituaries (card and book); index to photographs (card); index to vertical file (card). **Formerly:** Its Hubbard House Museum Archives.

★1446★

BLUE MOUNTAIN COLLEGE - MUSIC LIBRARY (Mus)
                                          Phone: (601) 685-5711
Blue Mountain, MS 38610   Carolyn Mounce, Lbn.
Subjects: Music. **Holdings:** 1805 books and scores; 1605 recordings (cataloged); 190 unbound periodical volumes. **Subscriptions:** 7 journals and other serials. **Services:** Interlibrary loans; copying; library open to public with permission.

BLUE RIDGE INSTITUTE FOR SOUTHERN COMMUNITY SERVICE EXECUTIVES
See: Florida State University - Special Collections

BLUE SHIELD OF PENNSYLVANIA
See: Pennsylvania Blue Shield

★1447★

BLUE SPRINGS HISTORICAL SOCIETY - LIBRARY (Hist)
3929 Milton Dr.   Phone: (816) 373-5309
Independence, MO 64055   Larry Wiebusch, Musm.Chm.
Founded: 1976. **Subjects:** Local history. **Holdings:** 50 books; 5 oral histories. **Services:** Library not open to public. **Publications:** Newsletters, irregular; Cook Book; Blue Springs History. **Staff:** Robert L. Grover, Chm.

★1448★

BLUEFIELD DAILY TELEGRAPH - LIBRARY (Publ)
412 Bland St.   Phone: (304) 327-6171
Bluefield, WV 24701   Karen Kaplan, Lbn.
Staff: Prof 1. **Subjects:** Newspaper reference topics. **Holdings:** Bluefield Daily Telegraph, 1893 to present. **Subscriptions:** 10 journals and other serials. **Services:** Copying; library open to public with restrictions.

★1449★

BLUFFTON COLLEGE - MENNONITE HISTORICAL LIBRARY (Hist; Rel-Theol)
                                          Phone: (419) 358-8015
Bluffton, OH 45817   Delbert L. Gratz, Lbn.
Founded: 1937. **Staff:** 1. **Subjects:** Mennonite history, Amish history, Anabaptist history, Hutterian Brethren history, Apostolic Christian history, genealogy, peace. **Holdings:** 7000 books; 500 bound periodical volumes; 30 boxes of letters and manuscripts; 200 reels of microfilm; 1000 theses,

dissertations, pictures, maps and miscellaneous papers. **Subscriptions:** 300 journals and other serials; 10 newspapers. **Services:** Interlibrary loans; copying; library open to public by appointment. **Computerized Information Services:** Computerized cataloging and ILL. **Networks/Consortia:** Member of OCLC. **Special Indexes:** Index to family histories relating to Mennonite and Amish families (slip file); index to periodical articles in non-Mennonite periodicals relating to the Amish and Mennonites.

BLUFORD (F.D.) LIBRARY
See: North Carolina Agricultural & Technical State University - F.D. Bluford Library

BLUNDEN (Erle M.) MEMORIAL LIBRARY
See: American River Hospital - Erle M. Blunden Memorial Library

BLYTHEVILLE AIR FORCE BASE (AR)
See: U.S. Air Force Base - Blytheville Base Library

★1450★

B'NAI B'RITH CAREER & COUNSELING SERVICES - LIBRARY
7818 Liberty Rd.
Baltimore, MD 21207
Defunct

★1451★

B'NAI B'RITH CAREER & COUNSELING SERVICES - LIBRARY (Educ)
1405 Locust St.   Phone: (215) 545-1455
Philadelphia, PA 19102   Julius S. Romanoff, Exec.Dir.
Staff: 2. **Subjects:** Counseling psychology, career information, psychological testing. **Holdings:** 500 books; 300 college catalogs; 50 items of vocational and technical information; 20 boxes of career information. **Subscriptions:** 13 journals and other serials. **Services:** Copying; library open to public for reference use only.

★1452★

B'NAI BRITH HILLEL FOUNDATION AT MC GILL UNIVERSITY - LIBRARY (Area-Ethnic)
3460 Stanley St.   Phone: (514) 845-9171
Montreal, PQ, Canada H3A 1R8
Founded: 1950. **Staff:** Prof 1. **Subjects:** Philosophy and religion of Judaism; Jewish law; contemporary Jewish problems; Jewish art, music and drama; Jewish history; Israel; Zionism. **Holdings:** 6000 books; 400 bound periodical volumes; 700 pamphlets. **Subscriptions:** 100 journals and other serials; 15 newspapers. **Services:** Library open to public for reference use only.

★1453★

B'NAI JESHURUN TEMPLE ON THE HEIGHTS - JACK JACOBSON MEMORIAL LIBRARY (Rel-Theol)
27501 Fairmount Blvd.   Phone: (216) 831-6555
Pepper Pike, OH 44124
Founded: 1928. **Staff:** Prof 1. **Subjects:** Judaica, Holocaust, juvenile Judaica, Israel. **Holdings:** 9000 volumes. **Subscriptions:** 25 journals and other serials; 15 newspapers. **Services:** Library open to public.

★1454★

B'NAI ZION TEMPLE - MEMORIAL LIBRARY (Area-Ethnic)
Box 5172   Phone: (318) 861-2122
Shreveport, LA 71105   Jean Stein, Adm. & Hd.
Staff: Prof 1; Other 3. **Subjects:** Judaica - reference and teaching, history, philosophy, literature, language, arts, music. **Holdings:** 3699 books; 86 bound periodical volumes. **Subscriptions:** 11 journals and other serials. **Services:** Library open to public.

★1455★

BNR INC. - INFORMATION RESOURCE CENTER (Sci-Tech)
685A E. Middlefield Rd.   Phone: (415) 969-9170
Mountain View, CA 94043   Ms. L.S. Menashian, Mgr.
Founded: 1978. **Staff:** Prof 2; Other 1. **Subjects:** Telecommunications, communications, computers. **Holdings:** 1200 books; 1000 bound periodical volumes; 1000 technical reports. **Subscriptions:** 200 journals and other serials and newspapers. **Services:** Interlibrary loans; copying; library not open to public. **Computerized Information Services:** DIALOG; online catalog and statistics database; computerized acquisitions and circulation. **Networks/Consortia:** Member of CLASS; CIN. **Also Known As:** Bell-Northern Research Inc. **Staff:** Susan Fujiwara, Info.Spec.

★1456★
BOARD OF COOPERATIVE EDUCATIONAL SERVICES OF NASSAU COUNTY (BOCES) - NASSAU EDUC. RSRCS. CTR. (NERC) (Educ)
111 Cantiague Rock Rd.   Phone: (516) 931-8121
Westbury, NY 11590
Founded: 1971. **Staff:** Prof 3; Other 3. **Subjects:** Education. **Special Collections:** Occupational and career education; special education; bilingual education. **Holdings:** 23,000 books; 550 unbound periodical volumes; 5400 pamphlets (cataloged); 2500 curriculum guides; microfiche of ERIC documents (complete); 14,000 AV items; 300 16mm films, filmstrips, tapes. **Subscriptions:** 125 journals and other serials. **Services:** Interlibrary loans (limited); copying; library open to public, material loaned only to Nassau County school personnel. **Computerized Information Services:** BRS. **Networks/ Consortia:** Member of Long Island Library Resources Council. **Publications:** Learning packages; bibliographies on current educational topics. **Staff:** Rita Weinroth, Ref.Libn./Occup.Info; Nava Krieger, Ref.Libn./Spec.Educ.; .

★1457★
BOARD OF JEWISH EDUCATION OF GREATER NEW YORK - EDUCATIONAL RESOURCE LIBRARY (Educ; Rel-Theol)
426 W. 58th St.   Phone: (212) 245-8200
New York, NY 10019   Benjamin Miller, Media Libn.
Staff: Prof 1; Other 1. **Subjects:** Jewish education, Judaica, general education. **Special Collections:** Resources - Holocaust, Israel, teacher. **Holdings:** 18,000 books; 100 bound periodical volumes; 1100 AV materials; 100 Princeton files of Jewish education material. **Subscriptions:** 45 journals and other serials. **Services:** Copying; library open to public. **Networks/ Consortia:** Member of Association of Jewish Libraries. **Staff:** Dr. Israel Lerner, Judaic Spec.

★1458★
BOARD OF TRADE OF METROPOLITAN TORONTO - RESOURCE CENTRE (Plan; Bus-Fin)
3 First Canadian Pl.
Box 60   Phone: (416) 366-6811
Toronto, ON, Canada M5X 1C1   Janis Campbell, Res.Libn.
Founded: 1977. **Staff:** Prof 1; Other 1. **Subjects:** Urban planning, international trade, business and finance. **Special Collections:** Board of Trade Council Minutes and Metropolitan Toronto Business Journal (both on microfilm). **Holdings:** 2500 books; 50 bound periodical volumes; 2 VF drawers of prints and slides; 50 reels of microfilm. **Subscriptions:** 200 journals and other serials; 22 newspapers. **Services:** Interlibrary loans; copying; library open to public by appointment. **Publications:** Resource Centre Newsletter, irregular.

BOATWRIGHT LIBRARY
See: University of Richmond

★1459★
BOB JONES UNIVERSITY - CHURCH MINISTRIES RESOURCE LAB (Rel-Theol)
     Phone: (803) 242-5100
Greenville, SC 29614   Mrs. James Berg, Supv.
Founded: 1957. **Staff:** Prof 5; Other 11. **Subjects:** Church ministries, denominational and nondenominational curriculums, youth programs, children's materials, adult materials. **Holdings:** 1500 books; 29 VF drawers of clippings and articles; 200 filmstrips and phonograph records; 50 tapes; 1050 cassettes. **Subscriptions:** 25 journals and other serials. **Services:** Library not open to public. **Staff:** Mrs. Daniel Boone; Mrs. Nelson McGeoch; Mrs. Tony Miller; Mrs. Charles Smith .

★1460★
BOB JONES UNIVERSITY - MUSIC LIBRARY (Mus)
     Phone: (803) 242-5100
Greenville, SC 29614   Dr. Karen S. Wilson, Music Libn.
Staff: Prof 1; Other 2. **Subjects:** Music. **Holdings:** 3323 books; 681 folders of piano books and sheet music; 374 folders of sheet music; 6352 music recordings; 295 speech recordings; 286 cassette tapes; 21 masters' projects; 380 opera vocal scores; 4629 oratorio and opera chorus scores. **Services:** Interlibrary loans; copying; library open to public with restrictions.

★1461★
BOB JONES UNIVERSITY - SCHOOL OF EDUCATION - MEDIA CENTER (Educ; Aud-Vis)
     Phone: (803) 242-5100
Greenville, SC 29614   Bill Yost, Supv.
Founded: 1953. **Staff:** Prof 1; Other 4. **Subjects:** Children's literature, school administration, guidance, psychology. **Holdings:** 1500 books; 10 bound periodical volumes; 400 media catalogs; 50 VF drawers; master's

theses and prospectuses; sample textbooks. **Services:** Copying; library not open to public.

BOBST (Elmer Holmes) LIBRARY
See: New York University - Elmer Holmes Bobst Library

BOC INTERNATIONAL - AIRCO, INC.
See: Airco, Inc. - Central Research Laboratories

★1462★
BOCA RATON COMMUNITY HOSPITAL - HEALTH SCIENCES LIBRARY (Med)
800 Meadows Rd.   Phone: (305) 395-7100
Boca Raton, FL 33432   Judy Andrews, Adm.Libn.
Staff: Prof 1; Other 1. **Subjects:** Medicine, nursing. **Holdings:** 850 books; 2300 bound periodical volumes; 1 VF drawer of medical material. **Subscriptions:** 210 journals and other serials. **Services:** Interlibrary loans; copying; library open to students for reference use only, with permission. **Computerized Information Services:** MEDLARS. **Networks/Consortia:** Member of Palm Beach County Health Sciences Library Consortium.

★1463★
BOCES - ORLEANS-NIAGARA EDUCATIONAL COMMUNICATIONS CENTER (Educ)
4124 Saunders Settlement Rd.
Niagara East - Box 310D   Phone: (716) 731-4146
Sanborn, NY 14132   Douglas David, Supv.,Instr.Serv.
Staff: 9. **Holdings:** 10,703 AV materials (cataloged). **Remarks:** Maintained by the Orleans-Niagara BOCES (Orleans-Niagara Board of Cooperative Educational Services).

★1464★
BOCKUS RESEARCH INSTITUTE - LIBRARY (Med)†
19th & Lombard Sts.   Phone: (215) 893-2372
Philadelphia, PA 19146   Marta Lee Bussard, Adm.
Founded: 1962. **Staff:** 1. **Subjects:** Cardiovascular research, cardiology, physiology. **Holdings:** 360 books; 500 bound periodical volumes. **Subscriptions:** 35 journals and other serials. **Services:** Library open to graduates and hospital staff.

★1465★
BODINE ELECTRIC COMPANY - LIBRARY (Sci-Tech)
2500 W. Bradley Pl.   Phone: (312) 478-3515
Chicago, IL 60618
Staff: 1. **Subjects:** Microprocessors, electrical engineering, mechanical engineering, business administration. **Holdings:** 1610 books and bound periodical volumes; 551 manufacturers' catalogs; 238 engineering project reports; 27 VF drawers. **Subscriptions:** 119 journals and other serials. **Services:** Interlibrary loans; library not open to public.

BOECKMANN LIBRARY
See: Ramsey County Medical Society

BOEHM (Inge) LIBRARY
See: American Bibliographical Center - Clio Press - The Inge Boehm Library

★1466★
BOEHRINGER INGELHEIM LTD. - RESEARCH LIBRARY (Sci-Tech)
90 E. Ridge   Phone: (203) 748-4200
Ridgefield, CT 06877   Margaret Norman, Hd.Libn.
Staff: Prof 3; Other 4. **Subjects:** Pharmacology, chemistry, biochemistry. **Holdings:** 4000 books; 12,000 bound periodical volumes; 15,000 items in product files. **Subscriptions:** 508 journals and other serials. **Services:** Interlibrary loans; copying; SDI; library open to public by appointment. **Computerized Information Services:** BRS, SDC, NLM, DIALOG; computerized circulation. **Networks/Consortia:** Member of Connecticut Association of Health Sciences Libraries (CAHSL); Southwestern Connecticut Library Council (SCLC). **Staff:** Ms. R. Kenny Fryer, Pub.Serv.Libn.; Katherine Simon, Tech.Serv.Libn.

★1467★
BOEHRINGER MANNHEIM CORPORATION - BMC INFORMATION CENTER (Sci-Tech; Med)†
8021 Knue Rd.
Box 50528   Phone: (317) 849-6635
Indianapolis, IN 46250   George L. Curran, III, Supv./Libn.
Founded: 1966. **Staff:** Prof 1; Other 2. **Subjects:** Laboratory instrumentation and technology, orthopedic and dental prosthetics and implants, analytical and

clinical chemistry, bioengineering, biochemistry, health and corporate law. **Holdings:** 1250 books; 350 bound periodical volumes. **Subscriptions:** 138 journals and other serials. **Services:** Interlibrary loans; copying; SDI. **Computerized Information Services:** DIALOG, SDC, MEDLINE; computerized cataloging, serials and acquisitions. **Networks/Consortia:** Member of OCLC through INCOLSA; Central Indiana Area Library Services Authority; Central Indiana Health Sciences Consortium; Regional Medical Library - Region 3; MIDLNET. **Special Catalogs:** Catalog to classified collection (book).

★1468★
BOEING COMPANY - SEATTLE SERVICES DIVISION - HISTORICAL SERVICES AND ARCHIVES
Box 3707
Seattle, WA 98124
Defunct. Merged with Boeing Company - Seattle Services Division - Kent Technical Library and Renton Library to form Boeing Company - Seattle Services Division - Technical Libraries.

★1469★
BOEING COMPANY - SEATTLE SERVICES DIVISION - KENT TECHNICAL LIBRARY
Box 3707, M/S 8K-38
Seattle, WA 98124
Defunct. Merged with Historical Services and Archives and Renton Library to form Boeing Company - Seattle Services Division - Technical Libraries.

★1470★
BOEING COMPANY - SEATTLE SERVICES DIVISION - RENTON LIBRARY
Box 3707, Mail Stop 74-60
Seattle, WA 98124
Defunct. Merged with Kent Technical Library and Historical Services and Archives to form Boeing Company - Seattle Services Division - Technical Libraries.

★1471★
BOEING COMPANY - SEATTLE SERVICES DIVISION - TECHNICAL LIBRARIES (Sci-Tech)
Box 3707, MS 74-60   Phone: (206) 237-8314
Seattle, WA 98124   Diana K. Carey, Mgr.
Staff: Prof 14; Other 23. **Subjects:** Aeronautics, astronautics, engineering, electronics, transportation, business, management. **Special Collections:** International Data Bank; Historical Archives (3000 cubic feet of records; 150,000 photographs). **Holdings:** 63,000 books; 18,000 bound periodical volumes; 107,000 reports; one million reports on microfiche; 27,000 company documents; 5000 maps. **Subscriptions:** 3200 journals and other serials. **Services:** Interlibrary loans; copying; SDI; library not open to public. **Computerized Information Services:** DIALOG, SDC, BRS, New York Times Information Service, Dow Jones News Retrieval, NASA/RECON, DOE/RECON, DTIC, Dun & Bradstreet, Inc., Data Resources, Inc. (DRI); internal databases; computerized cataloging, serials and circulation. **Networks/Consortia:** Member of Washington Library Network; Seattle Area Hospital Library Consortium; University of Washington Resource Sharing Program. **Publications:** Technical Libraries Accession Bulletin, monthly; Boeing Documents Announcement Bulletin, monthly; custom literature searches and information surveys. **Special Catalogs:** Computer generated catalogs of holdings and Boeing documents (microfiche); Union List of Serials (hard copy and microfiche). **Remarks:** Collections include holdings of the former Historical Services and Archives, Kent Technical Library and Renton Library. **Staff:** Nancy L. Wilson, Serv.Supv.; Solange V. McIntyre, Renton Lib.Res. Lead; Julia Phillips, Kent Lib.Res. Lead; Geneva St.Clair, Acq. Lead; Patricia A. Johnston, Cat. Lead.

★1472★
BOEING COMPUTER SERVICES COMPANY - TECHNICAL LIBRARY (Sci-Tech)
7980 Gallows Ct.   Phone: (703) 821-6062
Vienna, VA 22180   Cheryl Gore, Lib.Mgr.
Founded: 1976. **Staff:** Prof 1; Other 2. **Subjects:** Data processing, computer technology, electronics, management, business. **Holdings:** 1000 books; 1000 technical reports; 3000 technical documents. **Subscriptions:** 225 journals and other serials. **Services:** Interlibrary loans; copying; library not open to public. **Computerized Information Services:** DIALOG; computerized cataloging and serials. **Publications:** BCS Access - for internal distribution only.

★1473★
BOEING MILITARY AIRPLANE COMPANY - LIBRARY (Sci-Tech)
3801 S. Oliver   Phone: (316) 526-3801
Wichita, KS 67210   C.H. Jones, Lib.Supv.
Staff: 4. **Subjects:** Aerodynamics, electronics, management, chemical engineering, chemistry, metallurgy, mechanical engineering, electricity, computer technology, plastics. **Holdings:** 6200 books and bound periodical volumes; 53,000 technical reports. **Subscriptions:** 400 journals and other serials. **Services:** Interlibrary loans; copying; research; library not open to public. **Staff:** Juanita Stovall, Acq.; Jack Robertson, Cat.; Mary Yeager, Circ.; Darline Shaw, Circ.

BOEING SERVICES INTERNATIONAL
See: U.S. Bureau of Mines - Boeing Services International

★1474★
BOEING VERTOL COMPANY - LYDIA RANKIN TECHNICAL LIBRARY (Sci-Tech)
Box 16858   Phone: (215) 522-2536
Philadelphia, PA 19142   Bethany Evanson, Libn.
Founded: 1945. **Staff:** Prof 1; Other 1. **Subjects:** Aeronautics, aerodynamics, engineering, propulsion, metallurgy, management. **Special Collections:** Peterson Memorial Collection (helicopter and V/STOL technology; 200 books). **Holdings:** 3000 books; 50 bound periodical volumes; 5000 reports (cataloged); 32,000 technical reports; 250 VF drawers of military specifications; 200 reels of microfilm; 40 drawers of microfiche. **Subscriptions:** 200 journals and other serials. **Services:** Interlibrary loans; library not open to public. **Computerized Information Services:** Computerized cataloging. **Publications:** Monthly Bulletin - for internal distribution only. **Special Catalogs:** Total Boeing holdings (computer-output microfiche).

BOETTIGER (Carl M.) MEMORIAL LIBRARY
See: Academy of Medicine of the County of Queens, Inc. - Carl M. Boettiger Memorial Library

BOHR (Niels) LIBRARY
See: American Institute of Physics - Center for History of Physics - Niels Bohr Library

★1475★
BOISE BIBLE COLLEGE - LIBRARY (Rel-Theol)
8695 Marigold   Phone: (208) 376-7731
Boise, ID 83704   Zella Chamberlain, Libn.
Founded: 1946. **Staff:** Prof 2; Other 2. **Subjects:** Bible, missions, Greek, speech, psychology, archeology, Hebrew history. **Special Collections:** U.S. Restoration history (300 volumes). **Holdings:** 14,000 books; 178 bound periodical volumes; 10 VF drawers of reports, pamphlets, documents; 324 cassettes; 920 volumes on microfiche. **Subscriptions:** 52 journals and other serials. **Services:** Interlibrary loans; library open to students and by arrangement. **Publications:** Boise Bible College Newsletter, monthly - free upon request.

★1476★
BOISE CASCADE CORPORATION - PULP & PAPER RESEARCH LIBRARY (Sci-Tech)
909 W. Seventh St.   Phone: (206) 695-4477
Vancouver, WA 98660   Vernon N. Gagnon, Libn.
Founded: 1947. **Staff:** Prof 1. **Subjects:** Pulp and paper technology, chemistry, chemical engineering. **Holdings:** 1000 books; 3300 bound periodical volumes; 28 VF drawers of special reports, reprints, proceedings, and patents. **Subscriptions:** 70 journals and other serials. **Services:** Interlibrary loans; copying; library open to public. **Publications:** Current Awareness Bulletin, biweekly. **Special Catalogs:** Unbound special reports and translations; subject index of current literature; bibliographies and literature searches by subject (all on cards).

★1477★
BOISE GALLERY OF ART - LIBRARY (Art)
670 S. Julia Davis Dr.   Phone: (208) 345-8330
Boise, ID 83701   Sandy Harthorn, Registrar
Subjects: Art. **Holdings:** 1200 books; 800 exhibition catalogs (national and international). **Subscriptions:** 21 journals and other serials. **Services:** Library open to public with permission.

BOISEN (Anton) PROFESSIONAL LIBRARY
See: Elgin Mental Health Center - Anton Boisen Professional Library

BOLEY (Paul L.) LAW LIBRARY
See: Lewis and Clark Law School - Northwestern School of Law - Paul L. Boley Law Library

BOLLING AIR FORCE BASE (Washington, DC)
See: U.S. Air Force Base - Bolling Base Library

BOLLING (Richard Walker) MEMORIAL MEDICAL LIBRARY
See: St. Luke's Hospital Center - Richard Walker Bolling Memorial Medical Library

★1478★
BOLT BERANEK AND NEWMAN, INC. - LIBRARY (Sci-Tech)
10 Moulton St.   Phone: (617) 491-1850
Cambridge, MA 02138   Margaret H. Troy, Hd.Libn.
Staff: Prof 3; Other 1. **Subjects:** Technology - architectural, environmental, noise control, underwater; information sciences; computer systems. **Holdings:** 6000 books; 1600 bound periodical volumes; 2000 government reports. **Subscriptions:** 375 journals and other serials. **Services:** Interlibrary loans; library not open to public. **Computerized Information Services:** DIALOG; computerized serials. **Staff:** Barbara Smith, Asst.Libn.; Jeanne Ross, Asst.Libn.

★1479★
BON SECOURS HOSPITAL - HEALTH SCIENCE LIBRARY (Med)
468 Cadieux Rd.   Phone: (313) 343-1619
Grosse Pointe, MI 48230   Sr. M. Bernita, S.S.J., Lib.Dir.
Founded: 1971. **Staff:** Prof 2; Other 2. **Subjects:** Medicine, nursing, hospital administration, pharmacology. **Holdings:** 2550 books; 2100 bound periodical volumes; 18 volumes and 140 sets of slide tapes (cataloged); 70 videotapes; 628 AV items; 200 government documents; 8 VF drawers of clippings, pamphlets, newspaper articles. **Subscriptions:** 315 journals and other serials; 5 newspapers. **Services:** Interlibrary loans; copying; library open to public only by referral. **Computerized Information Services:** MEDLINE. **Networks/Consortia:** Member of Metropolitan Detroit Medical Library Group (MDMLG); DGP Consortium (Detroit, Grosse Pointe); NLM.

★1480★
BON SECOURS HOSPITAL - HEALTH SCIENCES LIBRARY (Med)
2000 W. Baltimore St.   Phone: (301) 233-7100
Baltimore, MD 21223   Rosemary Pool, Med.Libn.
Founded: 1970. **Staff:** Prof 1. **Subjects:** Medicine, surgery, obstetrics and gynecology, cardiovascular diseases, pathology, nursing. **Holdings:** 1908 books; 1876 bound periodical volumes; 12 VF drawers of pamphlets and clippings (cataloged); 1053 Audio-Digest tapes. **Subscriptions:** 81 journals and other serials; 6 newspapers. **Services:** Interlibrary loans; copying; library open to public with restrictions. **Networks/Consortia:** Member of Maryland Association of Health Sciences Librarians.

★1481★
BON SECOURS HOSPITAL - MEDICAL HEALTH SCIENCE LIBRARY (Med)
70 East St.   Phone: (617) 687-0151
Methuen, MA 01844   Chin-Soon Han, Hd.Libn.
Founded: 1950. **Staff:** Prof 1; Other 2. **Subjects:** Medicine, psychiatry, pastoral care. **Special Collections:** Oncology. **Holdings:** 800 books; 1200 bound periodical volumes; 10 volumes of hospital archives; 22 boxes of pamphlets on specific diseases; 1 VF drawer of medical career materials; 4 VF drawers of abstracts and bibliographies. **Subscriptions:** 138 journals and other serials. **Services:** Interlibrary loans; copying; library not open to public. **Networks/Consortia:** Member of Northeastern Consortium for Health Information (NECHI). **Publications:** Weekly paper and Quarterly Bulletin - for internal distribution only. **Special Catalogs:** Computerized serials and AV software holdings list.

BONCOMPAGNI (Baldassare) ARCHIVES
See: Cornell University - History of Science Collections

★1482★
BONNER COUNTY HISTORICAL SOCIETY, INC. - RESEARCH LIBRARY (Hist)
Lakeside Pk.
Box 1063   Phone: (208) 263-2344
Sandpoint, ID 83864   Eunice L. Perks
Staff: 1. **Subjects:** Local history, biography. **Holdings:** 300 books; 2500 photographs (cataloged); 50 maps; 3000 newspaper clippings; 50 oral history tapes; 3000 memorabilia. **Services:** Copying; library open to public for reference use only on request. **Special Catalogs:** Photographs and books (card); oral history tapes (book); newspapers by subject (card).

★1483★
BONNER & MOORE ASSOCIATES, INC. - LIBRARY (Energy)
2727 Allen Pkwy., 17th Fl.   Phone: (713) 522-6800
Houston, TX 77019   J. Lawton, Libn./Info.Spec.
Founded: 1977. **Staff:** Prof 1; Other 1. **Subjects:** Energy economics, refining, computer software, coal, environmental information. **Special Collections:** Department of Energy "Energy Information" series. **Holdings:** 2000 volumes; 8 VF drawers of government documents; 7 VF drawers of unbound reports, clippings, documents; 5 VF drawers of annual company reports; 1 file drawer of company archives. **Subscriptions:** 60 journals and other serials; 8 newspapers. **Services:** Interlibrary loans; copying; library open to other libraries. **Computerized Information Services:** SDC; internal database; computerized cataloging. **Publications:** Monthly publication. **Special Catalogs:** Computerized listing of all company reports (disc tape).

BONNEVILLE POWER ADMINISTRATION
See: U.S. Dept. of Energy

★1484★
BOOK CLUB OF CALIFORNIA - LIBRARY (Publ)
312 Sutter St.   Phone: (415) 781-7532
San Francisco, CA 94108
Founded: 1912. **Staff:** 2. **Subjects:** Printing, bookbinding, typography, books, paper making, private presses, history of printing and printing methods. **Holdings:** 2000 books; ephemera from private presses. **Services:** Library open to public. **Publications:** Quarterly News-Letter; Keepsakes, fine press books.

BOOKS ACROSS THE SEA LIBRARY
See: English-Speaking Union of the U.S.A.

BOOKS BY MAIL
See: Public Library of Cincinnati and Hamilton County - Institutions/Books by Mail

★1485★
BOONE COUNTY GENEALOGICAL SOCIETY - LIBRARY (Hist)
Box 10   Phone: (304) 369-4675
Hewett, WV 25108   Sue Roberts, Sec.
Founded: 1974. **Subjects:** Genealogy. **Special Collections:** Boone County records from 1847 to present; family genealogies (30 complete). **Holdings:** 250 books; microfilm. **Subscriptions:** 30 journals and other serials. **Services:** Copying; library open to public. **Publications:** Kith and Kin of Boone County West Virginia, semiannual; Quarterly. **Remarks:** The genealogical collection is housed at the Boone-Madison Public Library, 375 Main St., Madison, WV 25130.

BOONE (Dr. Henry) MEMORIAL LIBRARY
See: De Paul Hospital - Dr. Henry Boone Memorial Library

BOONE-MADISON PUBLIC LIBRARY - BOONE COUNTY GENEALOGICAL SOCIETY - LIBRARY
See: Boone County Genealogical Society - Library

BOOTH (Mrs. Arthur W.) LIBRARY
See: Chemung County Historical Society, Inc. - Mrs. Arthur W. Booth Library

BOOTH (Edwin) THEATER COLLECTION AND LIBRARY
See: Walter Hampden - Edwin Booth Theater Collection and Library

★1486★
BOOTH MEMORIAL MEDICAL CENTER - HEALTH EDUCATION LIBRARY (Med)
Main St. at Booth Memorial Ave.   Phone: (212) 670-1118
Flushing, NY 11355   Rita S. Maier, Lib.Dir.
Founded: 1961. **Staff:** Prof 1; Other 4. **Subjects:** Medicine, surgery, pediatrics and pediatric surgery, ophthalmology, pathology, nursing, otolaryngology, dentistry, physical therapy, hematology. **Holdings:** 4294 books; 6451 bound periodical volumes. **Subscriptions:** 363 journals and other serials. **Services:** Interlibrary loans; copying; bibliographies compiled; library open to public with director's approval. **Publications:** Library Acquisitions, 6/year. **Remarks:** Medical Center is a Salvation Army Service. **Staff:** Nina Fedoroff, Asst.Libn.

★1487★
BOOTHBAY THEATRE MUSEUM (Theater)
Corey Ln.   Phone: (207) 633-4536
Boothbay, ME 04537   Franklyn Lenthall, Cur.
Founded: 1957. **Staff:** Prof 1. **Subjects:** Theatre memorabilia, 18th century to present. **Holdings:** 5000 books; playbills, broadsides and posters; autographs and holograph material; stage jewelry; photographs, lithographs, properties, costumes, model theatres, figurines, sculpture. **Services:** Open to outside users by written request. **Remarks:** Open mid-June to mid-September for tours - conducted daily, except Sunday. Appointment necessary.

★1488★
BOOTHE, PRICHARD & DUDLEY - LAW LIBRARY (Law)
4103 Chain Bridge Rd.
Box 338
Fairfax, VA 22030   Phone: (703) 273-4600
                                                     Peyton L. Moncure, Libn.
Staff: 1. **Subjects:** Taxation, business, real estate. **Holdings:** 8000 books; 1000 bound periodical volumes. **Subscriptions:** 200 journals and other serials; 30 newspapers. **Services:** Interlibrary loans; copying; library open to public by appointment with librarian's approval. **Computerized Information Services:** LEXIS.

★1489★
BOOZ ALLEN & HAMILTON, INC. - FOSTER D. SNELL DIVISION - INFORMATION CENTER
66 Hanover Rd.
Florham Park, NJ 07932
Defunct

★1490★
BOOZ, ALLEN & HAMILTON, INC. - LIBRARY (Bus-Fin)
Three First National Plaza   Phone: (312) 346-1900
Chicago, IL 60602   Christine Entman, Mgr.
Staff: Prof 1; Other 1. **Subjects:** Business, finance, management, marketing. **Holdings:** 1000 books; client reports; 80 shelves of annual reports. **Subscriptions:** 175 journals and other serials; 5 newspapers. **Services:** Interlibrary loans; copying; library not open to public. **Computerized Information Services:** DIALOG, NEXIS, COMPUSTAT Services, Inc., Value Line Data Services, New York Times Information Service.

★1491★
BOOZ, ALLEN & HAMILTON, INC. - LIBRARY (Sci-Tech)
4330 East-West Hwy.   Phone: (301) 951-2786
Bethesda, MD 20814   Linda Dodson, Libn.
Founded: 1955. **Staff:** Prof 3; Other 1. **Subjects:** Mathematics, economics and finance, physics, management engineering, electronics, transportation systems, energy, environmental science. **Holdings:** 3700 volumes. **Subscriptions:** 300 journals and other serials. **Services:** Interlibrary loans; copying; library open to public with librarian's permission. **Computerized Information Services:** DIALOG, SDC, DOE/RECON, New York Times Information Service, COMPUSTAT Services, Inc. **Formerly:** Booz, Allen Applied Research, Inc. **Staff:** Dona Mennella, Libn.; Katherine Schiff, Libn.

★1492★
BOOZ, ALLEN & HAMILTON, INC. - RESEARCH SERVICE (Bus-Fin)
101 Park Ave.   Phone: (212) 697-1900
New York, NY 10178   Ellen L. Miller, Mgr.,Res.Serv.
Founded: 1945. **Staff:** Prof 5; Other 6. **Subjects:** Business organization; industrial and consumer marketing; executive compensation; production; finance; mergers and acquisitions. **Holdings:** 3350 books; 300 VF drawers; 1135 reels of microfilmed periodicals; 36,250 corporate documents on microfiche. **Subscriptions:** 375 journals and other serials; 10 newspapers. **Services:** Interlibrary loans; copying; library not open to public. **Computerized Information Services:** DIALOG, SDC, New York Times Information Service, Control Data Corporation, COMPUSTAT Services, Inc., BRS, NEXIS, Info Globe, Dun & Bradstreet, Inc., TEXTLINE; internal database; computerized acquisitions. **Staff:** Marilyn Lukas, Res.; Jessica Frankel, Res.; Robin Jaffe, Res.

★1493★
BORDEN INC. - RESEARCH CENTRE - LIBRARY (Food-Bev)
600 N. Franklin St.   Phone: (315) 474-8526
Syracuse, NY 13204   Carol Lenz Taylor, Libn.
Staff: Prof 1. **Subjects:** Food science and technology. **Holdings:** 1400 books; 1500 bound periodical volumes; 14 VF drawers of pamphlets and reprints; 7000 patents. **Subscriptions:** 130 journals and other serials. **Services:** Interlibrary loans; copying; library open to public. **Computerized Information Services:** DIALOG.

BOREAL INSTITUTE FOR NORTHERN STUDIES
See: University of Alberta

★1494★
BORG-WARNER CHEMICALS, INC. - LIBRARY (Sci-Tech)
Box 68   Phone: (304) 863-7335
Washington, WV 26181   Sharon D. Watson, Libn.
Founded: 1960. **Staff:** Prof 1; Other 3. **Subjects:** Polymers, organic chemistry, plastics, rubber, management, adhesives, chemical engineering, petrochemicals. **Holdings:** 25,000 books and bound periodical volumes; 32 VF drawers of pamphlets (cataloged); 24 VF drawers of U.S. patents (paper copies); 13 drawers of U.S. patents (microfiche copies); 12 VF drawers of foreign patents; 10 drawers of government reports (AD and PB reports on microfiche). **Subscriptions:** 500 journals and other serials; 5 newspapers. **Services:** Interlibrary loans; copying; SDI; library not open to public. **Computerized Information Services:** DIALOG, SDC, NLM, Dow Jones News Retrieval, Chemical Abstracts Service; internal database; computerized serials and circulation. **Publications:** Patent Abstract Bulletins, weekly; New Library Materials, monthly; Current Content Bulletins, weekly. **Formerly:** Borg-Warner Corporation - Chemicals Library.

BORG-WARNER CORPORATION - CHEMICALS LIBRARY
See: Borg-Warner Chemicals, Inc. - Library

★1495★
BORG-WARNER CORPORATION - ROY C. INGERSOLL RESEARCH CENTER - LIBRARY (Sci-Tech)
Wolf & Algonquin Sts.   Phone: (312) 827-3131
Des Plaines, IL 60018   Roberta B.. Seefeldt, Mgr., Info.Serv.
Staff: Prof 2; Other 3. **Subjects:** Chemistry, engineering, thermoelectricity, automotive engineering, metallurgy, physics. **Holdings:** 11,000 books; 3000 bound periodical volumes; 600 cartridges of microforms of journals. **Subscriptions:** 600 journals and other serials. **Services:** Interlibrary loans; copying (limited); library open to public by appointment. **Computerized Information Services:** Online systems; computerized cataloging and serials. **Networks/Consortia:** Member of OCLC through ILLINET; North Suburban Library System; Midwest Health Science Library Network (MHSLN). **Publications:** Information Survey. **Special Indexes:** Index of internal reports (magnetic tape); periodical holdings (magnetic tape). **Staff:** Loretto M. Wellman, Info.Spec.

★1496★
BORG-WARNER CORPORATION - YORK DIVISION - ENGINEERING LIBRARY (Sci-Tech)
Box 1592   Phone: (717) 846-7890
York, PA 17405   Doris Dellinger, Libn.
Founded: 1942. **Staff:** 1. **Subjects:** Refrigeration, air conditioning, engineering, metallurgy, heating, acoustics. **Holdings:** 2960 books; 1496 bound periodical volumes; 32 VF drawers of pamphlets (cataloged); 2043 articles on microfilm; 6 VF drawers of standards and codes; 2 VF drawers of translations. **Subscriptions:** 90 journals and other serials. **Services:** Interlibrary loans; copying; library open to public by special arrangement. **Publications:** Current Awareness Bulletin, quarterly - for internal distribution only.

★1497★
BORGESS MEDICAL CENTER - MEDICAL LIBRARY (Med)
1521 Gull Rd.   Phone: (616) 383-4868
Kalamazoo, MI 49001   Sheila Hofstetter, Dir.
Founded: 1946. **Staff:** Prof 2; Other 1. **Subjects:** Medicine, nursing, pharmacology, allied health sciences. **Holdings:** 2050 books; 6500 bound periodical volumes; AV materials; models; 8 drawers of pamphlets and information files; 35 drawers of audiotapes. **Subscriptions:** 403 journals and other serials. **Services:** Interlibrary loans; copying; LATCH; current awareness; library not open to public. **Computerized Information Services:** DIALOG, NLM. **Networks/Consortia:** Member of Kalamazoo Et Al (KETAL); Southwest Michigan Library Cooperative. **Publications:** Inhouse Acquisition List, bimonthly. **Staff:** Jackie Mardikian, Ref.Libn.

★1498★
BORICUA COLLEGE - LIBRARY (Educ; Area-Ethnic)
3755 Broadway   Phone: (212) 865-9000
New York, NY 10032   Aurora Gomez, Libn.
Founded: 1973. **Staff:** Prof 3. **Subjects:** Education, civil rights, census, Puerto Ricans in United States, Puerto Rican children's books. **Special Collections:** Collection on Puerto Rico. **Holdings:** 2000 books; VF drawers; filmstrips; slides; microfiche. **Services:** Copying (limited); library open to public for reference use only. **Publications:** Noticiero, newsletter - distributed to Puerto Ricans throughout the U.S. and the island as well as people concerned

with Puerto Rico. **Remarks:** A branch library is located at 9 Grand Ave., Brooklyn, NY 11206. **Formerly:** Universidad Boricua - Puerto Rican Research & Resources Center, Inc. - Reference Library.

BORLAND HEALTH SCIENCES LIBRARY
See: Jacksonville Health Education Programs, Inc.

BORN (Sidney) TECHNICAL LIBRARY
See: University of Tulsa - Sidney Born Technical Library

BORROWMAN (G.L.) ASTRONAUTICS LIBRARY
See: United States Space Education Association - G.L. Borrowman Astronautics Library

BORSODI (Ralph) MEMORIAL LIBRARY
See: School of Living - Ralph Borsodi Memorial Library

★1499★
BOSTON ARCHITECTURAL CENTER - ALFRED SHAW AND EDWARD DURELL STONE LIBRARY (Art; Energy)
320 Newbury St. Phone: (617) 536-9018
Boston, MA 02115 Susan Lewis, Hd.Libn.
Founded: 1966. **Staff:** Prof 3; Other 3. **Subjects:** Architectural design and history, building technology, urban planning, urban design, landscape architecture, photography, interior design, energy conservation, solar energy. **Special Collections:** 19th and early 20th century architectural books and journals (1500 volumes, separately housed). **Holdings:** 12,000 books; 500 other cataloged items; 280 student theses; 30,000 slides; 500 pamphlets, government documents, reports. **Subscriptions:** 130 journals and other serials. **Services:** Copying; library open to public for reference use only. **Publications:** Recent Acquisitions, bimonthly - free on request to libraries, students and faculty. **Staff:** Margaret Bartley, Asst.Libn.; Julia Selz, Slide Libn.; Jim Kosinsky, AV Spec.

★1500★
BOSTON ATHENAEUM LIBRARY (Hist; Hum)
10 1/2 Beacon St. Phone: (617) 227-0270
Boston, MA 02108 Rodney Armstrong, Dir. & Libn.
Founded: 1807. **Staff:** Prof 35; Other 6. **Subjects:** History; fine and decorative arts; belles lettres; biography. **Special Collections:** Confederate States imprints; books owned by George Washington and General Henry Knox; King's Chapel Library, 1698; early U.S. documents; books owned by Adams Family; gypsy literature; Charles E. Mason print collection; 19th century tracts; early photographs and daguerrotypes. **Holdings:** 650,000 volumes; 15,000 pamphlets (cataloged); maps, manuscripts; 2200 reels of microfilm; archives; 1000 broadsides. **Subscriptions:** 450 journals and other serials; 20 newspapers. **Services:** Interlibrary loans; copying; library open to scholars and persons seeking information that is unique to the Boston Athenaeum. **Computerized Information Services:** Computerized cataloging. **Networks/Consortia:** Member of OCLC through NELINET; Boston Metropolitan Cultural Alliance. **Publications:** Readers Guide to the Boston Athenaeum; monographs, irregular; exhibition catalogs, irregular - free to members, for sale to nonmembers. **Special Indexes:** Print and Photograph Collection Index by Charles E. Mason; Portrait File; Views of Boston houses; Shipwrecks (card); Provenance (card); bookplate file; Obituary Index to Boston Transcript, 1830-1874. **Staff:** Norman P. Tucker, Res. & Prog.Off.; John P. Harrison, Hd.Cat.; Cynthia English, Hd.Ref.Libn.; John Lannon, Hd., Acq.; Sally Pierce, Cur., Prints/Photographs; Stephen Nonack, ILL; Stanley E. Cushing, Consrv.; Jack Jackson, Art Res.; Donald Kelly, Art Gallery; Jonathan Harding, Photodup./Archv.

★1501★
BOSTON CITY HOSPITAL - MEDICAL LIBRARY (Med)
818 Harrison Ave. Phone: (617) 424-4198
Boston, MA 02118 Margie Dempsey, Sr.Med.Libn.
Founded: 1864. **Staff:** Prof 1; Other 3. **Subjects:** Medicine, health sciences, Boston medical history. **Special Collections:** Anthony Michelidakis Memorial Collection - a history of medicine collection as well as a history of Boston City Hospital and Boston medicine (131 volumes). **Holdings:** 3239 books; 13,353 bound periodical volumes; 2400 pamphlets (cataloged); 504 pictures; 123 microforms; 592 audiotapes; 16 slide sets. **Subscriptions:** 198 journals and other serials. **Services:** Interlibrary loans; copying (limited); library open to students and researchers. **Networks/Consortia:** Member of New England Regional Medical Library Service (NERMLS); Boston Biomedical Library Consortium. **Publications:** Guide to the Medical Library, annual. **Remarks:** Maintained by Department of Health and Hospitals, City of Boston.

★1502★
BOSTON CITY HOSPITAL - NURSING - MORSE-SLANGER LIBRARY (Med)
35 Northampton St. Phone: (617) 424-4771
Boston, MA 02118 Jane Keating Latus, Hd.Libn.
Founded: 1878. **Staff:** Prof 2; Other 5. **Subjects:** Nursing - medical, surgical, maternal, infant; pediatrics; paramedicine; psychology; sociology. **Special Collections:** Historical nursing literature (438 volumes, 325 titles). **Holdings:** 5390 books; 593 bound periodical volumes; 21 VF drawers of pamphlets. **Subscriptions:** 102 journals and other serials. **Services:** Interlibrary loans; copying; library not open to public. **Networks/Consortia:** Member of Libraries for Nursing Consortium (LINC); Massachusetts Health Science Library Network (MAHSLIN). **Publications:** Library Newsletter.

★1503★
BOSTON COLLEGE - GRADUATE SCHOOL OF SOCIAL WORK LIBRARY (Soc Sci)
McGuinn Hall Phone: (617) 969-0100
Chestnut Hill, MA 02167 Harriet Nemiccolo, Chf.Libn.
Founded: 1936. **Staff:** Prof 2; Other 5. **Subjects:** Case work, including social work/social welfare; child welfare; family welfare; crime and corrections; community organization and social planning; research methodology; administration-human services. **Holdings:** 25,000 books; 4700 bound periodical volumes; 1000 pamphlets; 840 masters' theses; doctoral dissertations in social work (microfiche); government documents (cataloged). **Subscriptions:** 394 journals and other serials. **Services:** Interlibrary loans; copying; library open to public with restrictions, reserve materials circulate to social work students only. **Computerized Information Services:** Online systems; computerized cataloging and serials. **Networks/Consortia:** Member of Boston Library Consortium; Northeast Academic Science Information Center (NASIC); New England On-line Users Group; NELINET. **Publications:** Periodic acquisitions list; subject bibliographies. **Staff:** Vivian Moreau, Ref.Libn.

★1504★
BOSTON COLLEGE - LAW SCHOOL LIBRARY (Law)
885 Centre St. Phone: (617) 969-0100
Newton Centre, MA 02159 Sharon Hamby, Dir.
Founded: 1929. **Staff:** Prof 5; Other 8. **Subjects:** Anglo-American law, international law and relations, foreign and comparative law, Common Market materials. **Special Collections:** Moreana (St. Thomas More collection); Massachusetts Supreme Judicial Court papers and briefs, 1935 to present; U.S. Supreme Court Papers and Briefs, 1946 to present (microform). **Holdings:** 130,000 books; 11,500 volumes in microform. **Subscriptions:** 1715 journals and other serials. **Services:** Interlibrary loans; copying; library open to public with restrictions. **Computerized Information Services:** LEXIS; computerized cataloging. **Networks/Consortia:** Member of Boston Library Consortium. **Publications:** Library Guide, annual - to entering students. **Staff:** Gyorgy Lang, Ref.Libn.; Catherine Fitzgerald, Cat.; Jane Gionfriddo, Circ.; Darcy Kirk, Tech.Serv.

★1505★
BOSTON COLLEGE - SCHOOL OF MANAGEMENT LIBRARY (Bus-Fin)
Fulton Hall Phone: (617) 969-0100
Chestnut Hill, MA 02167 Rhoda K. Channing, Chf.Libn.
Founded: 1938. **Staff:** Prof 3; Other 8. **Subjects:** Business, economics, computer science. **Holdings:** 53,600 books; 8678 bound periodical volumes; 28,942 microforms; 1200 annual and interim reports of major corporations; SEC (10K) reports of all companies on Fortune list (microfiche). **Subscriptions:** 1345 journals and other serials. **Services:** Interlibrary loans; copying; library open to public with restrictions. **Computerized Information Services:** DIALOG, BRS, SDC. **Networks/Consortia:** Member of Boston Library Consortium. **Staff:** Pearl L. Alberts, Ref.Libn.; Barbara Mento, Ref.Libn.

★1506★
BOSTON COLLEGE - SCHOOL OF NURSING LIBRARY (Med)
Cushing Hall Phone: (617) 969-0100
Chestnut Hill, MA 02167 Mary L. Pekarski, Asst.Univ.Libn.
Founded: 1948. **Staff:** Prof 2; Other 6. **Subjects:** Nursing, medicine, comprehensive health planning and delivery. **Special Collections:** Boston College - Guild of St. Luke Bioethics Collection; Rita P. Kelleher Nursing Collection. **Holdings:** 26,559 books and bound periodical volumes; 1658 AV items; 849 dissertations (nursing); 28,916 microforms; 72 VF drawers of government documents relating to health. **Subscriptions:** 860 journals and other serials. **Services:** Interlibrary loans; copying; library open to public for reference use only. **Computerized Information Services:** DIALOG, SDC, BRS, MEDLARS; computerized cataloging and acquisitions. **Networks/Consortia:** Member of Boston Library Consortium; OCLC; New England Regional Medical Library Service (NERMLS). **Publications:** Recent Acquisitions, bimonthly - for internal distribution only; Keys to the Literature

(selected subjects). **Staff:** Anne Lippman, Ref.Libn.

★1507★
BOSTON COLLEGE - SCIENCE LIBRARY (Sci-Tech)
Devlin Hall   Phone: (617) 969-0100
Chestnut Hill, MA 02167   F. Clifford McElroy, Sci.Libn.
Founded: 1954. **Staff:** Prof 2; Other 5. **Subjects:** Biology, chemistry,
geology and geophysics, mathematics, physics. **Special Collections:**
Government depository on selective basis. **Holdings:** 56,335 books and
bound periodical volumes; 20,000 reports and documents; 40,000
microforms. **Subscriptions:** 550 journals and other serials. **Services:**
Interlibrary loans; copying; library open to public for reference use only.
Networks/Consortia: Member of Boston Library Consortium. **Staff:** Marilyn
A. Grant, Ref.Libn.

★1508★
BOSTON COLLEGE - SPECIAL COLLECTIONS DEPARTMENT (Hist; Hum)
St. Thomas More Hall, Rm. 216   Phone: (617) 969-0100
Chestnut Hill MA 02167   Ralph Coffman, Hd., Spec.Coll.
Staff: Prof 4; Other 1. **Special Collections:** Abbey Theater, Ireland, 20th
century (manuscripts and plays on microfilm); N.M. Williams Collection of
Africana, 17th-19th century (books and manuscripts); Catholic Americana,
1729-1925 (books, pamphlets and manuscripts); antislavery, 1790-1865
(books; pamphlets); Maurice Baring, 1874-1945 (books and manuscripts);
Hilaire Belloc, 1870-1953 (books; manuscripts; maps; photographs; drawings;
paintings); Bostoniana, 1630 to present (includes Brehaut Collection, W.J.
Gannon Collection and F. Daly Collection; books; manuscripts; maps;
photographs; drawings); Calligraphy, 15th-20th century (includes Trenholm
Collection, Catalan and Castilian Collection; books and manuscripts); N.M.
Williams Collection of Caribbeana, 17th-19th century (books and
manuscripts); Catholic Life, Liturgy and Art, 1925-1980 (books; pamphlets;
manuscripts; maps; photographs; drawings; paintings; religious artifacts and
vestments); Catholic literature, 17th-20th century; Catholic theology, 2nd-
20th century; G.K. Chesterton, 1874-1936 (books; manuscripts;
photographs; drawings); David Goldstein Collection of Christian Socialism,
1890-1950; Desegregation of Secondary Schools/Boston City-wide
Coordinating Committee, 1974-1976; Robert F. Drinan, S.J., 1970-1980;
Eire Society of Boston, Massachusetts, 1937 to present (serials; books;
manuscripts; photographs); Eric Gill, 1882-1940; David Goldstein, 1870-
1958; Free Masonry, 18th-19th century; Graham Greene, 1904 to present;
Irish History, Literature and Art, 9th-20th century; J.W. Morrissey Memorial
Collection of Japanese Art, 18th-19th century; David Jones, 1895-1974;
Ronald Knox, 1888-1957; Peter Levi, 1931 to present; 18th-19th century
maps; Thomas Merton, 1915-1968; Alice Meynell, 1847-1922; music,
1900-1950; Oxford Movement, 19th century; Coventry Patmore, 1823-
1896; G.F. Trenholm Collection of 20th Century Printing; Burns and Oates
Collection of Publishing History of British Catholicism, 1840-1960; Rare Book
Collection, 14th-20th century (incunabula; books; manuscripts); Rex Stout,
1886-1975; Library of First Church of Christ, Salem, Massachusetts, 1629-
1900; School Texts and Primers, 18th-19th century; 20th Century Small
Presses (Franklin Library, Golden Cockerel, Heritage, Oriole, Peppercanister,
Stanbrook Abbey); Society of Jesus, 1540 to present (includes J.S. Shaw
Collection, Society of Jesus Collection); theater, 19th-20th century; Francis
Thompson, 1859-1907; George Francis Trenholm, 1886-1958;
Ultramontane Movement, 18th-19th century; Evelyn Waugh, 1903-1966;
World War II - Cold War Era, 1930-1950. **Holdings:** 39,000 books.
Services: Copying; library open to researchers with a serious need for using
this collection and with identification. **Computerized Information Services:**
DIALOG, BRS, SDC. **Networks/Consortia:** Member of Boston Library
Consortium; OCLC. **Staff:** H. Lawrence Durant, Cat.; Frank J. Seegraber,
Libn.; Rev. William Leonard, S.J., Liturgical Coll.Cur.

★1509★
BOSTON COLLEGE - WESTON OBSERVATORY - CATHERINE B. O'CONNOR
    LIBRARY (Sci-Tech)
                                                      Phone: (617) 899-0950
Weston, MA 02193   F. Clifford McElroy, Sci.Libn.
Founded: 1961. **Staff:** Prof 1; Other 2. **Subjects:** Geophysics, seismology,
geomagnetism, meteorology, geology, glaciology. **Special Collections:** Energy
research. **Holdings:** 11,000 books; 7300 bound periodical volumes; 15,000
government documents. **Subscriptions:** 117 journals and other serials.
Services: Interlibrary loans; copying; library open to public for reference use
only. **Networks/Consortia:** Member of Boston Library Consortium.

★1510★
BOSTON CONSERVATORY OF MUSIC - ALBERT ALPHIN MUSIC LIBRARY
    (Mus)
8 The Fenway   Phone: (617) 536-6340
Boston, MA 02215   Cathy S. Balshone, Hd.Libn.
Founded: 1867. **Staff:** Prof 3; Other 1. **Subjects:** Music, music education,

drama, musical theater, dance, opera, humanities. **Special Collections:** Jan
Veen - Katrine Amory Hooper Memorial Dance and Art Collection; Joan
Katherine Rossi Memorial Music Education Collection. **Holdings:** 12,000
books; 800 tapes; 6000 phonograph records; 16,000 scores. **Subscriptions:**
80 journals and other serials. **Services:** Interlibrary loans; library open to
public for reference use only by appointment. **Publications:** Trichordon
(Boston Conservatory of Music journal and newsletter), quarterly. **Staff:**
Reginald Didham, Tech.Proc.; Lynn Loring, Circ., Per.; Robert Cunningham,
Ref.

BOSTON DEPARTMENT OF HEALTH AND HOSPITALS - BOSTON CITY
    HOSPITAL
See: Boston City Hospital - Medical Library

★1511★
BOSTON GLOBE NEWSPAPER COMPANY - LIBRARY
135 Morrissey Blvd.
Boston, MA 02107
Founded: 1872. **Subjects:** News, photographs. **Special Collections:** News
clippings (10 million); photographs (1 million). **Holdings:** 10,000 books; 200
bound periodical volumes; 1000 pamphlets (cataloged); 9 VF drawers of
statistical reports; 30 VF drawers of pamphlets; 500 maps; 4000 reels of
microfilm. **Computerized Information Services:** New York Times
Information Service, CompuServe, Inc., Source Telecomputing Corporation;
internal database. **Remarks:** Presently inactive.

★1512★
BOSTON HERALD AMERICAN - REFERENCE LIBRARY (Publ)†
300 Harrison Ave.   Phone: (617) 426-3000
Boston, MA 02106   John Cronin, Chf.Libn.
Staff: Prof 1; Other 4. **Subjects:** Newspaper reference topics. **Holdings:**
1000 books. **Subscriptions:** 10 journals and other serials; 30 newspapers.
Services: Interlibrary loans; copying; library open to public with restrictions.
Special Indexes: Indexes to photo and clipping collections.

BOSTON INSURANCE LIBRARY ASSOCIATION
See: Insurance Library Association of Boston

BOSTON & MAINE RAILROAD HISTORICAL SOCIETY COLLECTION
See: University of Lowell, North Campus - University Libraries - Special
    Collections

BOSTON MEDICAL LIBRARY
See: Harvard University - Schools of Medicine, Dental Med. & Public
    Health, Boston Medical Library

★1513★
(Boston) METROPOLITAN DISTRICT COMMISSION - LIBRARY (Plan)
20 Somerset St.   Phone: (617) 727-5218
Boston, MA 02108   Albert A. Swanson, Archv.
Founded: 1972. **Staff:** Prof 1. **Subjects:** Development of the Metropolitan
District Commission, including water, sewer, park. **Holdings:** 1000
photographs of construction; 500 slides. **Services:** Library open to public for
reference use only.

★1514★
BOSTON MUNICIPAL RESEARCH BUREAU - LIBRARY (Soc Sci)
294 Washington St.   Phone: (617) 482-3626
Boston, MA 02108   Harry M. Durning, Exec.Dir.
Founded: 1932. **Staff:** 4. **Subjects:** Municipal government organization, law,
personnel, education, public finance, economic conditions. **Special
Collections:** Boston and Massachusetts material. **Holdings:** 5000 books; 500
reports and pamphlets; 10 boxes of clippings. **Subscriptions:** 20 journals and
other serials. **Services:** Library open to public by request. **Publications:**
Special Report, monthly - to contributors and City of Boston officials. **Staff:**
Samuel R. Tyler, Assoc.Exec.Dir.

★1515★
BOSTON PUBLIC LIBRARY - FINE ARTS DEPARTMENT (Art)
Copley Sq.
Box 286
Boston, MA 02117   Phone: (617) 536-5400
                                                      Theresa Cederholm, Cur.
Staff: Prof 4; Other 3. **Subjects:** Fine arts, architecture, sculpture, painting,
graphic arts, industrial arts, decorative arts. **Special Collections:** Ephemera
on New England artists and art galleries; Ball collection of ephemera on
American artists; photographs and postcards of Boston architecture;
photographs and reproductions of works of art. **Holdings:** 130,000 titles.
Subscriptions: 280 journals and other serials. **Services:** Interlibrary loans;
copying; library open to public with a courtesy card. **Networks/Consortia:**

Member of Boston Library Consortium. **Special Catalogs:** Afro-American Artists by Theresa Cederholm (book); Department Description (pamphlet); Society of Arts & Crafts, Boston, 1897-1927; Exhibition Record and History by Karen Ulehla (book); Childs Gallery, Boston: Exhibition Chronology and Publications by Gladys Dratch (book). **Special Indexes:** Boston Architecture (cards); index to exhibitors of Boston Society of Arts and Crafts (card); Exhibition Record of Boston Society of Independent Artists (card); Exhibition Record of Boston Art Club (card); Index to Boston Building Inspector's Reports, 1879-1900 (card). **Staff:** Janice H. Chadbourne, Ref.Libn.

★1516★
BOSTON PUBLIC LIBRARY - GOVERNMENT DOCUMENTS, MICROTEXT, NEWSPAPERS (Info Sci)
Copley Sq.
Box 286　　　　　　　　　　　Phone: (617) 536-5400
Boston, MA 02117　　　　　V. Lloyd Jameson, Div.Coord.
Staff: Prof 6; Other 7. **Subjects:** The Government Documents Section serves as a depository for United Nations, General Agreement on Tariffs and Trade (GATT), Colombo Plan, Danube Commission, European Community, U.S. Government Printing Office (1859 and regional since 1971), U.S. Arms Control and Disarmament Agency, U.S. Employment and Training Administration, U.S. Air Quality Control Commission, U.S. Geological Survey, U.S. Patent Office. Special strengths include U.S. Congressional publications, censuses, Massachusetts newspapers, publications of many international organizations, Current Urban Documents, 19th and early 20th century foreign and state publications, federal and Massachusetts laws and regulations, court decisions, Massachusetts and Boston documents, 18th-20th century British documents, indexing services; member of Documents Expediting Project. The Microtext Section includes Early American Imprints; Books Printed in English Before 1640; English and American Plays 1516-1900; Tax and Valuation Lists of Massachusetts Towns Before 1776; U.S. Census schedules for New England through 1910; Social and Economic Development Plans of the World; Historic American Buildings Survey; Index of American Design; Anti-Slavery Propaganda Collection; U.S. National Historical Publications Commission microforms; Early American Directories; Presidential papers; Landmarks of Science; ERIC documents; Transportation Master File; Boston passenger lists; Securities and Exchange Commission Releases; Internal Revenue Service Foundation Tax Returns (Massachusetts); Massachusetts newspapers; German Foreign Ministry Archives 1920-1945. The Newspaper Section includes Boston and Massachusetts newspapers; 260 newspapers currently received from around the world. **Holdings:** Figures not available. **Services:** Interlibrary loans; copying; open to public. **Networks/Consortia:** Member of Center for Massachusetts Data. **Publications:** CMD Newsletter, irregular; Government Publications on Microform in the Boston Public Library; Newspapers on Microform in the Boston Public Library. **Special Indexes:** Boston and Massachusetts documents (card); obituary index (card). **Staff:** Charles Longley, Cur.; Marilyn McLean, Ref.Libn.; George Cumming, Ref.Libn.

★1517★
BOSTON PUBLIC LIBRARY - HUMANITIES REFERENCE (Hum)
Copley Sq.
Box 286　　　　　　　　　　　Phone: (617) 536-5400
Boston, MA 02117　　　　　Raymond B. Agler, Coord.
Staff: Prof 6; Other 1. **Subjects:** Philosophy, psychology, religion, language, literature, bibliography. **Services:** Copying.

★1518★
BOSTON PUBLIC LIBRARY - KIRSTEIN BUSINESS BRANCH (Bus-Fin)
20 City Hall Ave.　　　　　　Phone: (617) 523-0860
Boston, MA 02108　　　　　Joseph E. Walsh, Bus.Br.Libn.
Founded: 1930. **Staff:** Prof 4; Other 5. **Subjects:** Business administration, retailing, advertising, international finance, marketing, real estate, insurance, banking, taxation, accounting, investments, economics, business law, small business. **Special Collections:** Moody's Manuals, 1920 to present; Commercial and Financial Chronicle (latest 30 years); Bank and Quotation Record, 1928 to present; Standard and Poor's Daily Stock Price Record: NYSE and ASE, 1962 to present; OTC, 1968 to present; trade directories (domestic and foreign); city directories (major cities in the U.S. and Canada); telephone directories (New England and U.S. cities over 50,000 plus major foreign cities); New York and American Stock Exchange companies annual and 10K reports on microfiche (latest 10 years); Wall Street Journal on microfilm (latest 10 years); Wall Street Transcript on microfilm (latest 5 years); D-U-N-S Account Identification Service (1966 to present). **Services:** Copying.

★1519★
BOSTON PUBLIC LIBRARY - MUSIC DEPARTMENT (Mus)
Copley Sq.
Box 286　　　　　　　　　　　Phone: (617) 536-5400
Boston, MA 02117　　　　　Ruth M. Bleecker, Cur. of Music
Founded: 1852. **Staff:** Prof 4. **Subjects:** Music - scores and theory; music

literature; dance. **Special Collections:** Allen A. Brown Music Collection of music scores and reference works (40,000); Koudelka Collection of early theoretical works; Koussevitzky Collection - scores, scrapbooks, memorabilia (2000); Walter Piston Collection; Handel and Haydn Society Collection. **Holdings:** 100,000 books, scores and bound periodical volumes; 300 scrapbooks, letters, unbound sheet music. **Subscriptions:** 400 journals and other serials. **Services:** Interlibrary loans and copying (both restricted); library open to public with restrictions. **Networks/Consortia:** Member of Boston Library Consortium. **Publications:** Catalog of the Allen A. Brown Music Collection; Dictionary Catalog of the Music Collection (24 volumes, 1972-1976). **Special Catalogs:** Song index; first performances; obituary file; vertical file. **Staff:** Diane Ota, First Asst.

★1520★
BOSTON PUBLIC LIBRARY - PRINTS (Art)
Copley Sq.
Box 286　　　　　　　　　　　Phone: (617) 536-5400
Boston, MA 02117　　　　　Sinclair H. Hitchings, Kpr. of Prints
Founded: 1941. **Staff:** Prof 2; Other 2. **Subjects:** Old Master prints and drawings; 19th Century French, British and American prints and drawings; Boston Pictorial Archive of prints, drawings and photographs; American 19th Century photographs by Bell, O'Sullivan and W.H. Jackson. **Special Collections:** Rowlandson, Goya, Daumier, Toulouse-Lautrec, Fantin-Latour, Forain, George Bellows, Charlet, Gavarni, Meryon, Jacques Villon, Charles Shannon, John Copley, Prints after Homer and Nast, Whistler, Pennell, Hassam. **Services:** Copying (limited, by special arrangement); library open to public. **Special Indexes:** Card index of Boston pictorial collection.

★1521★
BOSTON PUBLIC LIBRARY - RARE BOOKS AND MANUSCRIPTS (Rare Book)
Copley Sq.
Box 286　　　　　　　　　　　Phone: (617) 536-5400
Boston, MA 02117　　　　　Dr. Laura V. Monti, Kpr.
Staff: Prof 5; Other 3. **Subjects:** American history and literature; English literature; Spanish and Portuguese civilization; landscape architecture; early astronomy; mathematics and navigation; graphic arts; theatre history; antislavery movement; the Caribbean; French-American culture; juvenile literature. **Special Collections:** Prince Collection of Americana; Barton Collection of English Literature; Ticknor Collection of Spanish Literature; Benton Collection of Book of Common Prayer; Allen A. Brown Dramatic Collection; Chamberlain Collection of Manuscripts; 20th Regiment Collection of Civil War Material; Bowditch Collection of Astronomy and Mathematics; Sabatier Collection of Franciscana; Bentley Collection of early books on accounting; Feer Collection of World Fairs of North America; William A. Dwiggins Collection; Library of the Browning Society; Library of the Boston Authors Club; Trent Collection of Defoe and Defoeniana; Chamberlain Collection of autographs; Felicani Collection of Sacco-Vanzetti Papers; Fred Allen Collection; Wilfrid Beaulieu Papers on Franco-American subjects; Codman Collection of Landscape Architecture; Galatea Collection of History of Women (5200 volumes). **Holdings:** 460,000 books; bound periodical volumes. **Services:** Copying (limited, by special arrangement); open to qualified researchers. **Special Catalogs:** Catalogs to most of the collections. **Staff:** Ellen Oldham, Asst.Kpr./Rare Books; Bertha Zonghi, Jr.Cat.

★1522★
BOSTON PUBLIC LIBRARY - SCIENCE REFERENCE (Sci-Tech)
Copley Sq.
Box 286　　　　　　　　　　　Phone: (617) 536-5400
Boston, MA 02117　　　　　Suzanne K. Gray, Coord.
Staff: Prof 5; Other 2. **Subjects:** Science and technology, U.S. and British patents, German patents to 1938. **Special Collections:** Inventor Information Resource Center. **Services:** Copying; library open to public. **Computerized Information Services:** BRS, DIALOG, New York Times Information Service, Pergamon-InfoLine Ltd.

★1523★
BOSTON PUBLIC LIBRARY - SOCIAL SCIENCES (Soc Sci)
Copley Sq.
Box 286　　　　　　　　　　　Phone: (617) 536-5400
Boston, MA 02117　　　　　William R. Lewis, Coord.
Staff: Prof 5. **Subjects:** History; business and economics; education; financial reporting services; geography and maps; genealogy and heraldry; political science; sports and games. **Special Collections:** College catalogs; city street maps - U.S., Canada, and major foreign cities. **Services:** Copying. **Special Catalogs:** American families' coat-of-arms.

★1524★
BOSTON REDEVELOPMENT AUTHORITY - STAFF LIBRARY (Plan)
City Hall, 9th Fl.
One City Hall Sq.   Phone: (617) 722-4300
Boston, MA 02201   Rita M. Smith, Lib.Dir.
Founded: 1966. **Staff:** Prof 1. **Subjects:** Urban renewal, planning, housing, zoning, urban economics, transportation planning. **Special Collections:** City of Boston planning and renewal reports. **Holdings:** 10,000 volumes; 1000 color slides; 50 maps; 200 transcripts; 18 VF drawers of pamphlets; 8 VF drawers of newspaper clippings. **Subscriptions:** 45 journals and other serials; 17 newspapers. **Services:** Interlibrary loans; copying; library is open to serious researchers for reference use only. **Publications:** Recent Acquisition Bulletin, monthly - distributed outside the department on request.

★1525★
BOSTON SCHOOL COMMITTEE OF THE CITY OF BOSTON - ADMINISTRATION LIBRARY (Educ)
26 Court St.   Phone: (617) 726-6449
Boston, MA 02108   Elizabeth F. Scannell, Adm.Libn.
Founded: 1923. **Staff:** Prof 1; Other 1. **Subjects:** Education. **Special Collections:** Documents of the Boston School Committee; textbooks on current authorized list for Boston schools. **Holdings:** 12,911 books and pamphlets. **Subscriptions:** 98 journals and other serials. **Services:** Interlibrary loans; library serves public occasionally when need is established.

BOSTON SOCIETY OF NATURAL HISTORY
See: Museum of Science - Library

★1526★
BOSTON STATE HOSPITAL - MEDICAL LIBRARY (Med)
591 Morton St.   Phone: (617) 436-6000
Boston, MA 02124   John B. Picott, Libn.
Founded: 1864. **Staff:** Prof 1. **Subjects:** Psychiatry, neurology, community mental health, psychiatric nursing, social service. **Holdings:** 1800 books; 1000 unbound and bound periodical volumes. **Subscriptions:** 65 journals and other serials. **Services:** Interlibrary loans; copying; library not open to public.

★1527★
BOSTON UNIVERSITY - AFRICAN STUDIES LIBRARY (Area-Ethnic)
771 Commonwealth Ave.   Phone: (617) 353-3726
Boston, MA 02215   Gretchen Walsh, Hd.
Founded: 1953. **Staff:** Prof 2; Other 2. **Subjects:** Africana - political science, history, economics, anthropology, languages, linguistics, literature. **Special Collections:** African government documents (40,000 volumes). **Holdings:** 45,000 books; 500 maps; pamphlet and political ephemera file (2500 items); 4500 microforms. **Subscriptions:** 600 journals and other serials; 30 newspapers. **Services:** Interlibrary loans; library open to public. **Networks/Consortia:** Member of Boston Library Consortium. **Publications:** Catalog of African Government Documents and Area Index, 3rd edition, 1976; Africana Libraries Newsletter, bimonthly. **Staff:** Victoria Evalds, Libn.

★1528★
BOSTON UNIVERSITY - DEPARTMENT OF SPECIAL COLLECTIONS - NURSING ARCHIVES (Med)
771 Commonwealth Ave.   Phone: (617) 353-3696
Boston, MA 02215   Dr. Nancy L. Noel, Cur.
Founded: 1966. **Staff:** Prof 2; Other 1. **Subjects:** History - nursing education, nursing organizations, individual nurses. **Special Collections:** Over 130 manuscript collections of papers of individuals and organizations including records of the American Nurses' Association and the American Journal of Nursing Company, Inc. (2750 manuscript boxes). **Holdings:** 1500 volumes. **Services:** Copying; library open to public with letter of request. **Publications:** Brochures and books describing the Nursing Archives and documenting the contributions of nursing leaders; Nursing Archives Newsletter, semiannual - to donors and members of Nursing Archives Associates. **Special Indexes:** Each collection has its own index. **Staff:** Helen Sherwin, Archv.

★1529★
BOSTON UNIVERSITY - GERONTOLOGY RESOURCE CENTER (Soc Sci)
730 Commonwealth Ave., 4th Fl.   Phone: (617) 738-1004
Boston, MA 02215   Gretchen Batra, Plan./Coord., Educ.
Staff: Prof 3. **Subjects:** Aging - health, housing, training, education, policy, House and Senate hearings, international aspects. **Holdings:** 300 books; 5000 published and unpublished reports, papers, directories, articles, newsletters and national conference notices. **Subscriptions:** 15 journals and other serials. **Services:** Center open to public for reference use only. **Special Catalogs:** Listing of staff publications (booklet). **Staff:** Elizabeth Markson, Dir. for Soc.Res.; Ellen Kane, Res.

★1530★
BOSTON UNIVERSITY - KRASKER MEMORIAL FILM LIBRARY (Aud-Vis)
765 Commonwealth Ave.   Phone: (617) 353-3272
Boston, MA 02215   Earl E. Adreani, Dir.
Staff: Prof 2; Other 10. **Holdings:** 10,000 16mm films. **Services:** Library open to public for fee. **Publications:** Catalogue of 16mm Films - free upon request.

★1531★
BOSTON UNIVERSITY MEDICAL CENTER - ALUMNI MEDICAL LIBRARY (Med)
80 E. Concord St.   Phone: (617) 247-6187
Boston, MA 02118   Irene Christopher, Chf.Libn.
Founded: 1873. **Staff:** Prof 6; Other 9. **Subjects:** Medicine, dentistry, public health. **Holdings:** 86,127 volumes. **Subscriptions:** 1546 journals and other serials. **Services:** Interlibrary loans; copying; library not open to public. **Computerized Information Services:** NLM, BRS; computerized cataloging and serials. **Networks/Consortia:** Member of Boston Library Consortium; New England Regional Medical Library Service (NERMLS); OCLC. **Staff:** Emily L. Beattie, Hd., Tech.Serv.; Nancy J. Golden, Hd., Pub.Serv.; Velda E. Hatcher, Ref.Libn.

★1532★
BOSTON UNIVERSITY - PAPPAS LAW LIBRARY (Law)
765 Commonwealth Ave.   Phone: (617) 353-3151
Boston, MA 02215   Virginia J. Wise, Dir./Assoc. Professor
Staff: Prof 11; Other 12. **Subjects:** Law and related disciplines. **Special Collections:** Taxation, banking law, law and medicine. **Holdings:** 181,000 books; 20,000 bound periodical volumes. **Subscriptions:** 2400 journals and other serials; 10 newspapers. **Services:** Interlibrary loans; copying. **Computerized Information Services:** LEXIS; computerized cataloging. **Networks/Consortia:** Member of RLG; Boston Library Consortium. **Staff:** Catherine Tierney, Hd., Tech.Serv.; L. Kurt Adamson, Hd., Pub.Serv.

★1533★
BOSTON UNIVERSITY - SCHOOL OF THEOLOGY LIBRARY (Rel-Theol)
745 Commonwealth Ave.   Phone: (617) 353-3034
Boston, MA 02215   William E. Zimpfer, Libn.
Founded: 1839. **Staff:** Prof 4; Other 4. **Subjects:** Bible, theology, church history, social ethics, psychology of religion, pastoral care. **Special Collections:** Metcalf-Nutter Hymnal Collection; Massachusetts Bible Society Library; Kimball Bible Collection; Archives of Southern New England Conference of United Methodist Church. **Holdings:** 116,530 books and bound periodical volumes; 30 VF drawers of packets of New England Methodist history. **Subscriptions:** 675 journals and other serials; 6 newspapers. **Services:** Interlibrary loans; copying; library open to public with proper credentials. **Computerized Information Services:** Computerized cataloging. **Networks/Consortia:** Member of Boston Theological Institute - Library Development Program.

BOSTON UNIVERSITY - SCHOOL OF THEOLOGY - UNITED METHODIST CHURCH - SOUTHERN NEW ENGLAND CONFERENCE
See: United Methodist Church - Southern New England Conference

★1534★
BOSTON UNIVERSITY - WOMEN'S CENTER (Soc Sci)
775 Commonwealth Ave., North Tower   Phone: (617) 353-4240
Boston, MA 02216   Beth Williams, Programmer
Staff: 10. **Subjects:** Women's studies, sociology, health, fiction, poetry. **Holdings:** 150 books; 300 unbound periodicals; 200 issues of MS. Magazine, 1970s; 3 drawers of clippings and archives. **Subscriptions:** 16 journals and other serials. **Services:** Center open to public. **Publications:** The Rising River, annual - available on campus and through mailing list.

★1535★
BOSTONIAN SOCIETY - LIBRARY (Hist)
Old State House, 206 Washington St.   Phone: (617) 242-5614
Boston, MA 02109   Thomas W. Parker, Dir.
Founded: 1881. **Staff:** Prof 3. **Subjects:** Boston history, antiquities, marine history. **Special Collections:** Colburn collection of autographs; Boston directories. **Holdings:** 5000 books; 300 bound periodical volumes; 60 volumes of clippings; 20 boxes of documents and manuscripts; 10 drawers of maps of Boston; 10,000 photographs and negatives; 1100 prints and lithographs; 100 broadsides. **Subscriptions:** 6 journals and other serials. **Services:** Copying; library open to public. **Publications:** Proceedings. **Remarks:** The library is located at 15 State Street, 3rd floor, Boston, MA 02109. **Staff:** Mary Leen, Libn.

★1536★
BOSTON'S MUSEUM OF TRANSPORTATION - LIBRARY
Museum Wharf
300 Congress St.
Boston, MA 02210
Subjects: Transportation, automobiles and automobile industry, care and repair of vehicles, people and transportation, bicycles, carriages, wagons, coaches, horses, trains, planes, boats. **Holdings:** 1000 books; 4000 slides; 250 photographs; 7 VF drawers of pamphlets, clippings, advertising. **Remarks:** The collection is part of "Boston/A City in Transit," a major permanent exhibit which traces the history of Boston from 1630 to the present day, focusing on developing transportation technologies. "Crossroads" is a hands-on activity area for all ages where visitors learn about transportation by actually trying out various devices from the museum's collection. Presently inactive.

BOSTROM DIVISION - ENGINEERING LIBRARY
See: UOP Inc. - Bostrom Division - Engineering Library

BOSTWICK (Muriel Isabel) LIBRARY
See: Art Gallery of Hamilton - Muriel Isabel Bostwick Library

BOSWELL (Thomas E.) MEMORIAL LIBRARY
See: First Presbyterian Church - Thomas E. Boswell Memorial Library

BOSWORTH MEMORIAL LIBRARY
See: Lexington Theological Seminary

★1537★
BOTEIN, HAYS, SKLAR & HERZBERG - LIBRARY (Law)
200 Park Ave., Suite 3014   Phone: (212) 867-5500
New York, NY 10166   Donald Wecht, Libn.
Founded: 1872. **Staff:** Prof 1; Other 1. **Subjects:** Law, tax, accounting, trade and securities regulation, public utility. **Holdings:** 17,000 volumes. **Services:** Interlibrary loans; copying; library open to profession by appointment. **Computerized Information Services:** LEXIS.

BOTHIN AMERICAN ART LIBRARY COLLECTION
See: Fine Arts Museums of San Francisco

★1538★
BOTSFORD GENERAL HOSPITAL, OSTEOPATHIC - HOSPITAL LIBRARY AND MEDIA CENTER (Med)
28050 Grand River Ave.   Phone: (313) 476-7600
Farmington, MI 48024   Deborah L. Adams, Dir.
Staff: Prof 1; Other 4. **Subjects:** Medicine, nursing. **Holdings:** 2000 books; AV material (cataloged); 120 journal titles (microfilm). **Subscriptions:** 200 journals and other serials. **Services:** Interlibrary loans; copying; SDI; library open to public for reference use only. **Computerized Information Services:** MEDLARS, DIALOG. **Networks/Consortia:** Member of Detroit Osteopathic Hospital Consortium; Metropolitan Detroit Medical Library Group (MDMLG); Wayne Oakland Region of Interlibrary Cooperation.

BOTTINEAU BRANCH AND INSTITUTE OF FORESTRY
See: North Dakota State University

★1539★
BOULDER HISTORICAL SOCIETY - DOCUMENTARY COLLECTIONS DEPARTMENT (Hist)
1019 Spruce St.   Phone: (303) 449-3464
Boulder, CO 80302   Ellen D. Wagner, Cur., Doc.Coll.
Founded: 1944. **Staff:** Prof 1; Other 2. **Subjects:** Local and state history, 1858 to present. **Special Collections:** Colorado Chautauqua Association Collection, 1898-1960 (15 linear feet); Sturtevant Photograph Collection, 1880-1920 (50 linear feet); A.A. "Gov" Paddock Collection, 1858 to present; Ed Tangen Photograph Collection, 1905-1935 (35 linear feet). **Holdings:** 2000 books; 200 bound periodical volumes; 200 manuscript collections; 80,000 photographs. **Services:** Copying; library open to public. **Formerly:** Its Pioneer Museum - Library.

★1540★
BOULDER PUBLIC LIBRARY - MUNICIPAL GOVERNMENT REFERENCE CENTER (Soc Sci)
1000 Canyon Blvd.
P.O. Drawer H   Phone: (303) 441-3100
Boulder, CO 80306   Virginia Braddock, Hd., MGRC
Founded: 1965. **Staff:** 3. **Subjects:** Boulder government and politics; municipal government; city and town planning; transportation; personnel management; municipal finance; police and law enforcement; parks and recreation; housing. **Special Collections:** National Technical Information Service (1800 microfiche). **Holdings:** 8000 books; 600 boxes of uncataloged pamphlets; 25 VF drawers of clippings. **Subscriptions:** 200 journals and other serials; 5 newspapers. **Services:** Interlibrary loans; copying; center open to public. **Computerized Information Services:** Computerized cataloging and circulation. **Publications:** MGRC Newsletter, quarterly - for sale. **Special Catalogs:** Municipal Government Reference Center Catalog (book form - for sale).

★1541★
BOULDER VALLEY MEDICAL LIBRARY (Med)
Boulder Community Hospital
1100 Balsam Ave.   Phone: (303) 442-8190
Boulder, CO 80302   Carol M. Boyer, Med.Libn.
Founded: 1922. **Staff:** Prof 1. **Subjects:** Medical reference topics and nursing. **Holdings:** 285 books; 80 bound periodical volumes. **Subscriptions:** 22 journals and other serials. **Services:** Interlibrary loans; library open to health professionals. **Remarks:** Maintained by the United Medical Staff of Boulder.

★1542★
BOULDER VALLEY PUBLIC SCHOOLS, REGION 2 - PROFESSIONAL LIBRARY (Educ)
6500 E. Arapahoe Ave.   Phone: (303) 447-1010
Boulder, CO 80302   Carol Newman, Libn.
Staff: Prof 1; Other 1. **Subjects:** Education and special education. **Special Collections:** George Reavis Library (Phi Delta Kappa); Talented and Gifted Collection (TAG). **Holdings:** 5200 books; 300 microfiche; 150 boxes of VF materials; sample texts. **Subscriptions:** 251 journals and other serials. **Services:** Interlibrary loans; copying; library open to public for teaching purposes only. **Computerized Information Services:** Online systems. **Networks/Consortia:** Member of OCLC; Central Colorado Library System.

BOUNTY (H.M.S.) SOCIETY, INTERNATIONAL
See: H.M.S. Bounty Society, International

BOUQUET (Henry) ROOM
See: Fort Ligonier Memorial Foundation - Henry Bouquet Room

BOWDITCH (Ingersoll) LIBRARY
See: Faulkner Hospital - Ingersoll Bowditch Library

★1543★
BOWDOIN COLLEGE - LIBRARY - SPECIAL COLLECTIONS (Hist; Hum)
                                   Phone: (201) 725-8731
Brunswick, ME 04011   Dianne M. Gutscher, Cur.
Staff: 2. **Subjects:** Bowdoin College history, Maine authors and history, graphic arts, Brunswick history. **Special Collections:** Abbott Memorial Collection (25,000 books and manuscripts); American Imprints (2500 books and pamphlets printed in the United States and the English colonies before 1821); Anthoensen Press Collection (1200 books and pamphlets; 200 brochures and bookplates); Atlantic and St. Lawrence Railroad Archives, 1844-1889 (800 items); Robert A. Bartlett Papers (15,000 manuscripts, photographs and clippings); Beston Collection (150 volumes; 10,000 pieces of correspondence); Susan Dwight Bliss Collection (1200 volumes); Vance Bourjaily Papers (manuscripts and correspondence); Bowdoin Collection (2700 volumes; 1000 pamphlets); Horatio Bridge Papers (100 items); Charles Brockden Brown Papers (159 letters and manuscripts); Thomas Carlyle Collection (1500 volumes); Joshua L. Chamberlain Papers (1900 manuscripts); Chase-Johnson Papers (8000 items relating to the history of Brunswick and Bowdoin College); Parker Cleaveland Papers (1600 items); Robert P.T. Coffin Collection (1000 items); Cuala Press Collection (73 volumes); Fessenden Family Papers (4000 items); Nathaniel Hawthorne Collection (759 volumes; 170 letters); Oliver Otis Howard Papers (150,000 items); Hubbard Family Papers (12,000 items); Elijah Kellogg Collection (80 volumes; 1500 other items); Henry Wadsworth Longfellow Collection (1200 volumes; 160 manuscripts; 665 pieces of sheet music); McArthur Family Papers (8000 items); Donald B. MacMillan Collection (arctic exploration; clippings, scrapbooks, journals, photographs, maps and other records); Maine Collection (books and pamphlets printed in Maine before 1836); Mellen Papers (New England history; 5000 items); Mosher Press Collection (500 volumes); Pickard Collection (500 volumes); Franklin Pierce Collection (29 manuscripts and letters); Thomas Brackett Reed Papers (200 items); Charles Asbury Stephens Collection (40 volumes; 2350 manuscripts); Thomas C. Upham Collection (65 volumes); Kate Douglas Wiggin Collection (450 volumes; scrapbooks; correspondence); William Willis Papers (355 items); Marguerite Yourcenar Collection (100 volumes). **Holdings:** 30,000 books; 600 bound periodical volumes; 400,000 manuscripts; 650 boxes of archives; 600 honors theses. **Services:** Copying; library open to public. **Computerized**

Information Services: Computerized cataloging. **Networks/Consortia:** Member of OCLC through NELINET. **Special Catalogs:** Chronological and alphabetical lists of manuscript collections (binders). **Staff:** Susan B. Ravdin, Asst. to Cur.

★1544★
BOWERS (Charles W.) MEMORIAL MUSEUM - LIBRARY AND ARCHIVES
2002 N. Main St.
Santa Ana, CA 92706
Founded: 1936. **Subjects:** California and the Southwest; Orange County history; Southwestern Indians. **Holdings:** 1500 books. **Remarks:** Presently inactive.

★1545★
BOWKER (R.R.) COMPANY - FREDERIC G. MELCHER LIBRARY (Publ)
1180 Ave. of the Americas   Phone: (212) 764-5126
New York, NY 10036   Margaret Spier, Libn.
Founded: 1963. **Staff:** Prof 1; Other 1. **Subjects:** Book industries and trade; library science. **Special Collections:** Frederic G. Melcher Library of books about books; Adolf Growoll scrapbooks on book trade history. **Holdings:** 10,000 books; 650 bound periodical volumes; 85 VF drawers and 31 boxes of pamphlets organized by subject. **Subscriptions:** 500 journals and other serials. **Services:** Interlibrary loans; library open to public for reference use only on request. **Computerized Information Services:** BRS, DIALOG. **Remarks:** This is a Xerox Education Company.

★1546★
BOWLING GREEN STATE UNIVERSITY - CENTER FOR ARCHIVAL COLLECTIONS (Hist)
Library, 5th Fl.   Phone: (419) 372-2411
Bowling Green, OH 43403   Dr. Richard J. Wright, Dir.
Founded: 1968. **Staff:** Prof 10; Other 3. **Subjects:** State and local history; Great Lakes maritime history; university archives; historic preservation. **Special Collections:** State and local government records; manuscripts (3000 cubic feet); newspapers (2000 cubic feet); published materials; archives (3000 cubic feet); Ohio Labor History (300 cubic feet); Women's History (100 cubic feet); Ray Bradbury Collection (100 volumes); Franklin D. Roosevelt Collection (1000 volumes; 1000 items of ephemera). **Holdings:** 10,000 volumes; 3500 other cataloged items; 2500 volumes of newspapers of 19 counties of northwest Ohio; 16,000 marine engineer drawings and tracings; 5000 volumes of local government records; 18,000 microforms; 125,000 photographs. **Subscriptions:** 220 journals and other serials; 50 newspapers. **Services:** Photocopying, photography, microphotography; document conservation; center open to public. **Networks/Consortia:** Member of Ohio Network of American History Research Centers. **Publications:** Lake Log Chips, weekly - by subscription; Northwest Ohio Quarterly; Archival Chronicle, quarterly - free upon request. **Special Catalogs:** Wood County Historical Church Records Survey; Guide to Newspaper Holdings; Guide to Local Government Records at the Center for Archival Collections. **Staff:** Paul D. Yon, Assoc.Dir.; Ann M. Bowers, Univ.Archv./Cur.; Ron Burdick, Hist. Preservation Coord.; Claudia Morchesky, Off.Mgr.; Nancy Steen, Rare Books Libn.; Regina K. Lemaster, Microfilm Spec.; Marilyn I. Levinson, Cat.

★1547★
BOWLING GREEN STATE UNIVERSITY - POPULAR CULTURE LIBRARY (Hum)
                                   Phone: (419) 372-2450
Bowling Green, OH 43403   Evron Collins, Hd.Libn.
Founded: 1969. **Staff:** Prof 1; Other 13. **Subjects:** Popular culture, 19th and 20th century American fiction, performing arts, comic art, juvenile culture, sports. **Special Collections:** Utah Gospel Mission Collection (anti-Mormon). **Holdings:** 50,000 books; 500 bound periodical volumes; comic books, manuscripts, paperback fiction, scrapbooks, posters, trading cards, Big Little Books, dime novels, sales catalogs, alternate press publications, pennants, postcards, greeting cards. **Subscriptions:** 25 journals and other serials. **Services:** Interlibrary loans (limited); copying; library open to public; not all portions of the collection are completely available for public use.

★1548★
BOY SCOUTS OF AMERICA - LIBRARY (Rec)
1325 Walnut Hill Ln.   Phone: (214) 659-2280
Irving, TX 75062   Ann L. McVicar, Libn.
Founded: 1950. **Staff:** Prof 1; Other 1. **Subjects:** Youth, psychology, leadership training, camping, recreation, nature and conservation, education, handicrafts, health and safety, American Indians. **Special Collections:** Early and current books on the history of scouting: books by Baden-Powell, Ernest T. Seton and William D. Boyce. **Holdings:** 8600 books; 300 bound periodical volumes; 3000 other cataloged items; 450 theses. **Subscriptions:** 125 journals and other serials. **Services:** Interlibrary loans; copying; library open to

public by request.

BOY SCOUTS OF AMERICA - SETON MEMORIAL LIBRARY & MUSEUM
See: Seton Memorial Library & Museum

★1549★
BOY SCOUTS OF CANADA - MUSEUM & ARCHIVES OF CANADIAN SCOUTING (Hist; Rec)
1345 Base Line Rd.
Sta. F, Box 5151   Phone: (613) 224-5131
Ottawa, ON, Canada K2C 3G7   Melanie E. Crampton, Cur./Libn.
Founded: 1951. **Staff:** Prof 1. **Subjects:** Lord Baden-Powell; early days in the Canadian scouting movement; national and world Boy Scout Jamborees and other scouting events. **Special Collections:** Siege of Mafeking, South African War, where Baden-Powell was commanding officer; South African Constabulary, also founded by Baden-Powell. **Holdings:** Historical records, photographs, memorabilia, documents (figures not available). **Services:** Museum open to public.

★1550★
BOY SCOUTS OF CANADA - NATIONAL LIBRARY (Rec)
1345 Base Line Rd.
Sta. F, Box 5151   Phone: (613) 224-5131
Ottawa, ON, Canada K2C 3G7   Melanie Crampton, Libn.
Staff: Prof 1. **Subjects:** Scouting, child study, Canadiana. **Special Collections:** Works of Lord Baden-Powell. **Holdings:** 3500 books; 150 bound periodical volumes; 540 pamphlets and clippings. **Services:** Library not open to public.

BOYCE (James P.) CENTENNIAL LIBRARY
See: Southern Baptist Theological Seminary - James P. Boyce Centennial Library

BOYD (John Dewey) LIBRARY
See: Alcorn State University - John Dewey Boyd Library

BOYD (William) LIBRARY
See: Academy of Medicine, Toronto - William Boyd Library

BOYER (Beryl L.) LIBRARY
See: National Foundation of Funeral Service - Beryl L. Boyer Library

BOYS TOWN SEARCH SERVICE
See: Father Flanagan's Boys' Home

★1551★
BOZELL & JACOBS, INC. - CORPORATE INFORMATION CENTER (Bus-Fin)
444 N. Michigan Ave.   Phone: (312) 644-9800
Chicago, IL 60611   Laura M. Johnson, Mgr.
Founded: 1977. **Staff:** Prof 1. **Subjects:** Advertising, marketing. **Holdings:** 300 books; 22 VF drawers of reports, clippings and pamphlets. **Subscriptions:** 128 journals and other serials. **Services:** Interlibrary loans; copying; SDI; library not open to public. **Computerized Information Services:** Online systems; computerized cataloging. **Networks/Consortia:** Member of OCLC through ILLINET.

BRACE RESEARCH INSTITUTE
See: Mc Gill University - Macdonald Campus

★1552★
BRACEWELL & PATTERSON - LAW LIBRARY (Law)
2900 South Tower, Pennzoil Place   Phone: (713) 221-1129
Houston, TX 77002   Susan Mims Yancey, Libn.
Staff: Prof 1; Other 4. **Subjects:** Law. **Holdings:** 16,000 books; 2000 bound periodical volumes. **Subscriptions:** 250 journals and other serials; 8 newspapers. **Services:** Interlibrary loans; copying; SDI; library open to public with restrictions. **Computerized Information Services:** LEXIS.

BRACKEN LIBRARY
See: Ball State University

BRACKEN LIBRARY
See: Queen's University at Kingston

BRACKETT (Frank P.) OBSERVATORY - LIBRARY
See: Claremont Colleges - Library

★1553★
BRADFORD HOSPITAL - HUFF MEMORIAL LIBRARY (Med)
Interstate Pkwy.   Phone: (814) 368-4761
Bradford, PA 16701   Genevieve R. Killen, Dir., Med.Rec.
Staff: 1. **Subjects:** Medicine. **Holdings:** 440 books; 712 bound periodical volumes. **Subscriptions:** 37 journals and other serials. **Services:** Interlibrary loans; copying; library open to public with restrictions.

BRADFORD MEMORIAL LIBRARY
See: Presbyterian Denver Hospital

★1554★
BRADFORD NATIONAL CORPORATION - LIBRARY
100 Church St., 12th Fl.
New York, NY 10007
Defunct

BRADFORD (Samuel James) MEMORIAL LIBRARY
See: Denver Theological Seminary/Bible Institute - Samuel James Bradford Memorial Library

★1555★
BRADLEY (Emma Pendleton) HOSPITAL - AUSTIN T. AND JUNE ROCKWELL LEVY LIBRARY (Med)
1011 Veterans Memorial Pkwy.   Phone: (401) 434-3400
Riverside, RI 02915   Carolyn A. Waller, Med.Libn.
Founded: 1932. **Staff:** Prof 1; Other 1. **Subjects:** Child psychiatry, child psychology, social work, special education, child neurology, pediatrics. **Holdings:** 1500 books; 1500 bound periodical volumes; 300 archives; 200 pamphlets; 350 audiotape cassettes; 25 dissertations. **Subscriptions:** 173 journals and other serials. **Services:** Interlibrary loans; copying; library open to medical professionals and staff. **Networks/Consortia:** Member of Association of Rhode Island Health Sciences Libraries.

BRADLEY LAW LIBRARY
See: Rutgers University, The State University of New Jersey - Justice Henry Ackerson Lib. of Law & Criminal Justice

BRADLEY (Sydney Wood) MEMORIAL LIBRARY
See: Canadian Dental Association - Sydney Wood Bradley Memorial Library

BRADLEY UNIVERSITY - CULLOM-DAVIS LIBRARY - PEORIA HISTORICAL SOCIETY
See: Peoria Historical Society - Harry L. Spooner Memorial Library

★1556★
BRADLEY UNIVERSITY - VIRGINIUS H. CHASE SPECIAL COLLECTIONS CENTER - CHARLES A. BENNETT COLLECTION (Sci-Tech)
Cullom-Davis Library   Phone: (309) 676-7611
Peoria, IL 61625   Charles J. Frey, Spec.Coll.Libn.
Founded: 1939. **Subjects:** Industrial education and industrial arts. **Special Collections:** Wahlstrom Collection; Manual Arts Press Collection (2250 books). **Holdings:** 1140 books; 6692 pamphlets. **Services:** Copying; collection open to public for reference use only.

★1557★
BRADLEY UNIVERSITY - VIRGINIUS H. CHASE SPECIAL COLLECTIONS CENTER - CHASE COLLECTION (Hist)
Cullom-Davis Library   Phone: (309) 676-7611
Peoria, IL 61625   Charles J. Frey, Spec.Coll.Libn.
Founded: 1979. **Subjects:** Bishop Philander Chase, Jubilee College, Kenyon College, Protestant Episcopal Church, history of Illinois. **Special Collections:** Charles Scully Collection; Robert Herschel Collection; Library of the Citizens Committee to Preserve Jubilee College. **Holdings:** 200 books and pamphlets; 1400 manuscript letters. **Services:** Copying (limited); collection open to public for reference use only. **Special Indexes:** Name and date index to letters.

★1558★
BRADLEY UNIVERSITY - VIRGINIUS H. CHASE SPECIAL COLLECTIONS CENTER - LINCOLN COLLECTIONS (Hist)
Cullom-Davis Library   Phone: (309) 676-7611
Peoria, IL 61625   Charles J. Frey, Spec.Coll.Libn.
Founded: 1949. **Subjects:** Abraham Lincoln, Civil War. **Special Collections:** Houser collection; Stone collection; microfilm collection. **Holdings:** 1800 items. **Services:** Copying; collections open to public for reference use only. **Publications:** The Lincoln Collections of Bradley University, composed by Robert M. Lightfoot, Jr. (an inventory with subject index).

★1559★
BRADLEY UNIVERSITY - VIRGINIUS H. CHASE SPECIAL COLLECTIONS CENTER - PEORIA HISTORICAL SOCIETY COLLECTIONS (Hist)
Cullom-Davis Library   Phone: (309) 676-7611
Peoria, IL 61625   Charles J. Frey, Spec.Coll.Libn.
Founded: 1963. **Subjects:** Peoria history, Old Northwest, Illinois, Civil War. **Special Collections:** Harry L. Spooner Library; A. Wilson Oakford Collection; Ernest E. East Collection. **Holdings:** 1500 books; 20 VF drawers of pamphlets and clippings; extensive file of photographs and negatives. **Services:** Copying; collection open to public for reference use only. **Special Indexes:** Thesaurus of vertical file descriptors.

★1560★
BRADWELL (David) & ASSOCIATES, INC. - LIBRARY (Plan)
2227 Lombard St.   Phone: (415) 567-9800
San Francisco, CA 94123   David Bradwell, Pres.
Staff: 1. **Subjects:** Bay Area planning. **Holdings:** 1000 books; 1200 bound periodical volumes; 1980 California census data on microfiche; 80 diskettes of survey data; planning reports. **Services:** Interlibrary loans; library open to public by appointment. **Computerized Information Services:** Internal database. **Publications:** Ad hoc reports.

BRADY/GREEN EDUCATIONAL RESOURCES CENTER
See: University of Texas Health Science Center, San Antonio

★1561★
BRAILLE CIRCULATING LIBRARY, INC. (Rel-Theol; Aud-Vis)
2700 Stuart Ave.   Phone: (804) 359-3743
Richmond, VA 23220   Robert N. Gordon, Exec.Dir.
Founded: 1925. **Staff:** Prof 12. **Subjects:** Bible, Christian biographies, fiction, Bible studies, missionary messages, sermons. **Holdings:** 5500 braille books; talking book records, cassettes and reel tapes. **Services:** Interlibrary loans; copying; library open to public by appointment. **Publications:** Thermoform copies of library's braille books. **Special Catalogs:** Ink-print catalog of all departments; catalog of braille and talking books and cassette tapes (braille).

★1562★
BRAILLE INSTITUTE OF AMERICA - LIBRARY (Aud-Vis)
741 N. Vermont Ave.   Phone: (213) 660-3880
Los Angeles, CA 90029   Phyllis Cairns, Lib.Dir.
Founded: 1934. **Staff:** Prof 3; Other 27. **Subjects:** General collection of books for the blind and physically handicapped. **Holdings:** 21,422 Braille volumes; 121,540 talking books; 6949 open-reel tapes; 198,176 cassette tapes. **Subscriptions:** 45 talking book periodicals; 36 braille periodicals. **Services:** Library not open to public. **Staff:** Catherine Englund, Ref.Libn.; Paula Dacker, Fld.Serv.Libn.; Henry Hayden, Asst.Lib.Dir.

BRAIN INFORMATION SERVICE
See: University of California, Los Angeles

★1563★
BRAINERD STATE HOSPITAL - LIBRARY (Med)
East Oak St.   Phone: (218) 835-2357
Brainerd, MN 56401   David C. Bauer, Libn.
Founded: 1961. **Staff:** Prof 1. **Subjects:** Mental retardation, psychiatry and psychotherapy, alcoholism. **Holdings:** 2560 volumes. **Subscriptions:** 52 journals and other serials. **Services:** Interlibrary loans; library not open to public. **Computerized Information Services:** Online systems. **Networks/Consortia:** Member of Regional Medical Library - Region 3.

★1564★
BRAINTREE HISTORICAL SOCIETY, INC. - LIBRARY (Hist)
786 Washington St.   Phone: (617) 848-1640
Braintree, MA 02184   Mrs. Donald G. Maxham, Libn.
Founded: 1930. **Staff:** Prof 1; Other 3. **Subjects:** Local history and genealogy. **Special Collections:** Rev. Dr. George Penniman Genealogical Library (300 volumes). **Holdings:** 2500 volumes. **Services:** Copying; library open to public by appointment. **Publications:** Thayer genealogy of 1874 (reprints); The Penniman Family, 1631-1900. **Remarks:** The society also maintains the General Sylvanus Thayer Birthplace (National Register), a barn/library/museum and a school program for all 5th grades in Braintree featuring historic living.

★1565★
BRAKELEY, JOHN PRICE JONES, INC. - LIBRARY (Bus-Fin)
1600 Summer St.   Phone: (203) 348-8100
Stamford, CT 06905   Rose M. Price, Libn.
Founded: 1919. **Staff:** 1. **Subjects:** Fund-raising, philanthropy and public

relations. **Holdings:** 3000 books; 150 VF drawers of clippings, pamphlets, and foundation annual reports. **Subscriptions:** 28 journals and other serials. **Services:** Library open to public with special permission. **Formerly:** Located in New York, NY.

BRALLEY MEMORIAL LIBRARY
See: Texas Woman's University - Special Collections

BRAND LIBRARY
See: Glendale Public Library

★1566★
BRANDEIS-BARDIN INSTITUTE - HOUSE OF THE BOOK (Rel-Theol)
Phone: (213) 348-7201
Brandeis, CA 93064   Hannah R. Kuhn, Spec.Libn.
Founded: 1973. **Staff:** Prof 1. **Subjects:** Judaica, Bible, Talmud, Jewish history and literature, Israel and Zionism. **Special Collections:** Hebrew collection (3000 items). **Holdings:** 10,000 books; 50 bound periodical volumes. **Subscriptions:** 50 journals and other serials. **Services:** Copying; library not open to public. **Publications:** Torah at Brandeis Institute.

★1567★
BRANDEIS UNIVERSITY - GERSTENZANG SCIENCE LIBRARY (Sci-Tech)
415 South St.   Phone: (617) 647-2534
Waltham, MA 02254   Elizabeth Fitzpayne, Assoc.Sci.Libn.
Founded: 1965. **Staff:** Prof 3; Other 5. **Subjects:** Biochemistry, chemistry, biology, physics, mathematics, computer science. **Holdings:** 100,000 books and bound periodical volumes. **Subscriptions:** 900 journals and other serials. **Services:** Interlibrary loans; copying; contact librarian for information about use of library; membership program for industry. **Computerized Information Services:** DIALOG, NLM, BRS; computerized cataloging. **Networks/Consortia:** Member of Boston Library Consortium. **Publications:** Serials and Journals of Gerstenzang Science Library, annual - for sale. **Staff:** Linda Gelb, Rd.Serv.Libn.

BRANDES MEMORIAL LIBRARY
See: Willmar State Hospital - Library

★1568★
BRANDON GENERAL HOSPITAL - LIBRARY SERVICES (Med)
150 McTavish Ave., E.   Phone: (204) 728-3321
Brandon, MB, Canada R7A 2B3   Kathy Eagleton, Dir.
Founded: 1955. **Staff:** Prof 1; Other 2. **Subjects:** Medicine, nursing, allied health sciences, hospital administration. **Holdings:** 5000 books; AV programs. **Subscriptions:** 350 journals and other serials. **Services:** Interlibrary loans; copying; library open to public for reference use only, on request.

★1569★
BRANDON MENTAL HEALTH CENTRE - REFERENCE AND LENDING LIBRARY (Med)
Box 420   Phone: (204) 728-7110
Brandon, MB, Canada R7A 5Z5   Marjorie G. McKinnon, Lib.Techn.
Founded: 1963. **Staff:** Prof 1; Other 2. **Subjects:** Psychiatry, psychiatric treatment services, psychology, social service, hospital administration. **Special Collections:** Early psychiatric texts. **Holdings:** 5723 books; 209 bound periodical volumes; 954 tapes; 5 drawers of pamphlets; 23,053 journals. **Subscriptions:** 213 journals and other serials. **Services:** Interlibrary loans; copying; library open to public with restrictions. **Computerized Information Services:** Computerized cataloging, acquisitions, serials and circulation. **Networks/Consortia:** Member of Manitoba Health Libraries Association. **Special Indexes:** Subject index cards.

★1570★
BRANDON TRAINING SCHOOL - LIBRARY (Educ)
Phone: (802) 247-5711
Brandon, VT 05733   Lorna Z. Whitehorne, Libn.
Founded: 1968. **Staff:** Prof 1; Other 1. **Subjects:** Mental retardation, education, psychology. **Holdings:** 1600 books; 60 bound periodical volumes; 80 AV materials. **Subscriptions:** 65 journals and other serials. **Services:** Interlibrary loans; copying; library open to public.

★1571★
BRANDON UNIVERSITY - CHRISTIE EDUCATION LIBRARY (Educ)
Eighteenth St.   Phone: (204) 728-9520
Brandon, MB, Canada R7A 6A9   Mrs. M. Nichols, Libn.
Founded: 1967. **Staff:** Prof 1; Other 3. **Subjects:** Education development, curriculum. **Holdings:** 35,000 books; 110,000 ERIC microfiche; 2000 AV items. **Subscriptions:** 600 journals and other serials. **Services:** Interlibrary loans; copying; library open to public with restrictions. **Computerized**

Information Services: Online systems; computerized cataloging, acquisitions and serials.

★1572★
BRANDON UNIVERSITY - MUSIC LIBRARY (Mus)
Music Bldg.   Phone: (204) 728-9520
Brandon, MB, Canada R7A 6A9   June D. Jones, Music Libn.
Founded: 1963. **Staff:** Prof 1; Other 2. **Subjects:** Music history, theory and criticism. **Holdings:** 4000 books; 1000 bound periodical volumes; 5500 scores (cataloged); 2600 phonograph records; 3000 tapes. **Subscriptions:** 102 journals and other serials. **Services:** Interlibrary loans; library open to public with restrictions.

★1573★
BRANDYWINE RIVER MUSEUM LIBRARY (Art; Hist)
Box 141   Phone: (215) 388-7601
Chadds Ford, PA 19317   Ruth Bassett, Libn.
Founded: 1971. **Staff:** Prof 1; Other 2. **Subjects:** American art, Brandywine Valley artists, Howard Pyle, N.C. Wyeth, Andrew Wyeth, James Wyeth, Pyle students, American illustration. **Special Collections:** N.C. Wyeth collection (material collected by the family, including proofs and photographs). **Holdings:** 1150 books; 370 bound periodical volumes; 35 prints; 18 posters; 21 calendars; 450 exhibition catalogs. **Subscriptions:** 33 journals and other serials. **Services:** Copying; SDI; library open to public by appointment. **Special Indexes:** Index of titles and locations of illustrations of easel paintings by the Wyeth family, Pyle students and American illustrators.

BRANNER EARTH SCIENCES LIBRARY
See: Stanford University

BRANNER (Dr. Robert) LIBRARY
See: University of Maryland, College Park - Libraries - Architecture Library

★1574★
BRANT COUNTY MUSEUM - LIBRARY (Hist)
57 Charlotte St.   Phone: (519) 752-2483
Brantford, ON, Canada N3T 2W6   William R. Robbins
Staff: Prof 1; Other 1. **Subjects:** Local history including social, religious, transportation. **Holdings:** 500 books; 200 pamphlets; 200 documents; 2000 pictures; 400 files of clippings; 17 binders of historical articles. **Services:** Library open to public. **Remarks:** Maintained by Brant Historical Society.

★1575★
BRANT (Joseph) MEMORIAL HOSPITAL - HOSPITAL LIBRARY (Med)
1230 Northshore Blvd.   Phone: (416) 632-3730
Burlington, ON, Canada L7R 4C4   Janice McMillan, Hosp.Libn.
Staff: Prof 1. **Subjects:** Medicine, nursing, administration, paramedicine. **Holdings:** 700 books; videotapes; slide-tape programs. **Subscriptions:** 60 journals and other serials. **Services:** Interlibrary loans; copying; library not open to public. **Computerized Information Services:** Online systems. **Networks/Consortia:** Member of Hamilton/Wentworth District Health Library Network.

BRANTIGAN (Otto C.) MEDICAL LIBRARY
See: St. Joseph Hospital - Otto C. Brantigan Medical Library

BRASSERIES MOLSON DU CANADA, LTEE.
See: Molson Breweries of Canada, Ltd.

★1576★
BRATTLEBORO MEMORIAL HOSPITAL - MEDICAL LIBRARY (Med)
9 Belmont Ave.   Phone: (802) 257-0341
Brattleboro, VT 05301   Martha J. Fenn, Libn.
Founded: 1970. **Staff:** Prof 1. **Subjects:** Medicine, nursing, hospitals, health. **Holdings:** 1100 books; 100 cassette tapes; 100 pamphlets and clippings. **Subscriptions:** 40 journals and other serials. **Services:** Interlibrary loans; copying; library open to public by permission.

★1577★
BRATTLEBORO RETREAT - MEDICAL LIBRARY (Med)
75 Linden St.   Phone: (802) 257-7785
Brattleboro, VT 05301   Jane Rand, Dir. of Lib.Serv.
Staff: 3. **Subjects:** Psychiatry, psychoanalysis, psychology. **Holdings:** 2100 books; 643 bound periodical volumes. **Subscriptions:** 44 journals and other serials. **Services:** Interlibrary loans; copying; library open to professionals and students.

BRAUDE (William G.) LIBRARY
See: Temple Beth-El - William G. Braude Library

★1578★
BRAUN (C.F.) COMPANY - MURRAY HILL DIVISION - ENGINEERING LIBRARY (Sci-Tech)
Diamond Hill Rd.   Phone: (201) 464-9000
Murray Hill, NJ 07974   Marion C. Bale, Libn.
Founded: 1960. **Staff:** Prof 1; Other 1. **Subjects:** Engineering. **Holdings:** Figures not available.

★1579★
BRAUN (C.F.) COMPANY - REFERENCE LIBRARY (Sci-Tech; Energy)
1000 S. Fremont Ave.   Phone: (213) 570-2233
Alhambra, CA 91802   Beverly Muller, Lib.Mgr.
Founded: 1935. **Staff:** Prof 1; Other 3. **Subjects:** Petrochemicals; engineering - civil, chemical, electrical, mechanical; nuclear power; solar energy. **Holdings:** 22,000 books; 3500 bound periodical volumes; 5000 microfiche; language tapes. **Subscriptions:** 400 journals and other serials. **Services:** Interlibrary loans; copying. **Computerized Information Services:** DIALOG, DOE/RECON. **Publications:** Library Bulletin, monthly - for internal distribution only. **Remarks:** Company is a subsidiary of Santa Fe International.

BRAVER (Alfred T.) LIBRARY
See: University of North Carolina, Chapel Hill - Alfred T. Braver Library

BRAY LIBRARY
See: Library Company of Philadelphia

★1580★
BRAZILIAN-AMERICAN CULTURAL INSTITUTE, INC. - HAROLD E. WIBBERLEY, JR. LIBRARY (Area-Ethnic)
4201 Connecticut Ave., N.W., Suite 211   Phone: (202) 362-8334
Washington, DC 20008   Paulo Costa, Libn.
Staff: Prof 2. **Subjects:** Brazilian history, literature and arts, anthropology, cultural history. **Special Collections:** 19th and 20th century Brasiliana. **Holdings:** 3800 books; 1050 bound periodical volumes; 3000 slides, cassettes and films. **Subscriptions:** 18 journals and other serials. **Services:** Interlibrary loans; copying; library open to public with restrictions. **Staff:** Dr. Jose Neistein, Exec.Dir.

★1581★
BRAZOSPORT MUSEUM OF NATURAL SCIENCE - LIBRARY (Sci-Tech)
400 College Dr.   Phone: (713) 265-7831
Brazosport, TX 77566
Subjects: Malacology, mineralogy, paleontology, marine science, insects, reptiles, archeology. **Holdings:** 200 books; 25 bound periodical volumes. **Services:** Library open to public for reference use only.

BRECKINRIDGE (James Carson) LIBRARY
See: U.S. Marine Corps - Education Center - James Carson Breckinridge Library

★1582★
BREED, ABBOTT & MORGAN - LIBRARY (Law)
153 E. 53rd St.   Phone: (212) 888-0800
New York, NY 10022   Carol H. Barra, Hd.Libn.
Founded: 1898. **Staff:** Prof 2; Other 5. **Subjects:** Law. **Holdings:** 20,000 volumes. **Subscriptions:** 96 journals and other serials. **Services:** Interlibrary loans; library not open to public. **Computerized Information Services:** LEXIS, New York Times Information Service. **Staff:** Shelley Markowitz, Asst.Libn.

BREIDENBACH (Andrew W.) ENVIRONMENTAL RESEARCH CENTER, CINCINNATI
See: Environmental Protection Agency - Andrew W. Breidenbach Environmental Research Center, Cincinnati

BREMER (Anne) MEMORIAL LIBRARY
See: College of the San Francisco Art Institute - Anne Bremer Memorial Library

BRENAU COLLEGE
See: Northeast Georgia Medical Center and Hall School of Nursing

BRENDLE (Thomas R.) MEMORIAL LIBRARY & MUSEUM
See: Historic Schaefferstown, Inc. - Thomas R. Brendle Memorial Library & Museum

BRENGLE MEMORIAL LIBRARY
See: Salvation Army School for Officers Training

BRENNEMANN (Joseph) LIBRARY
See: Children's Memorial Hospital - Joseph Brennemann Library

★1583★
BRETHREN IN CHRIST CHURCH AND MESSIAH COLLEGE - ARCHIVES (Rel-Theol)
Messiah College   Phone: (717) 766-2511
Grantham, PA 17027   Dr. E. Morris Sider, Archv.
Founded: 1952. **Staff:** Prof 1; Other 1. **Subjects:** History and life of the Brethren in Christ Church and related subjects. **Holdings:** 120 books; 240 bound periodical volumes; 600 boxes of historical manuscripts; council records; tapes; films; pamphlets; photographs; 150 museum items. **Services:** Copying; library open to public with restrictions on use of some material. **Publications:** Brethren in Christ History and Life, semiannual - by subscription. **Special Indexes:** Index to minutes of the General Conference of the Brethren in Christ (1871-1960).

★1584★
BREVARD COLLEGE - JAMES A. JONES LIBRARY - FINE ARTS DIVISION (Mus)
    Phone: (704) 883-8292
Brevard, NC 28712   Mary Margaret Houk, Dir.
Subjects: Music. **Holdings:** 2900 recordings and 800 scores (cataloged). **Services:** Interlibrary loans; copying; library open to public with restrictions. **Networks/Consortia:** Member of Smoky Mountain Consortium; North Carolina Center for Independent Higher Education Inc. Consortium. **Staff:** Michael M. McCabe, Libn.

★1585★
BREVARD COUNTY BAR ASSOCIATION - A. MAX BREWER MEMORIAL LAW LIBRARY (Law)
County Courthouse, Fl. 4
400 South St.   Phone: (305) 269-8197
Titusville, FL 32780   Mrs. George McFarland, Law Libn.
Staff: Prof 1. **Subjects:** Law. **Holdings:** 20,000 books and bound periodical volumes. **Services:** Copying; library open to public for reference use only.

BREWER (A. Max) MEMORIAL LAW LIBRARY
See: Brevard County Bar Association - A. Max Brewer Memorial Law Library

★1586★
BREWERS ASSOCIATION OF CANADA - LIBRARY (Food-Bev)
151 Sparks St., Suite 805   Phone: (613) 232-9601
Ottawa, ON, Canada K1P 5E3   Mary Jane Maffin, Libn.
Founded: 1970. **Staff:** Prof 1. **Subjects:** Alcoholic beverages and their abuse; history of the brewing industry; taverns and inns. **Holdings:** 500 books; 500 papers on use and abuse of alcohol. **Subscriptions:** 60 journals and other serials; 19 newspapers. **Services:** Interlibrary loans; library open to public by appointment only. **Computerized Information Services:** CAN/OLE, MEDLARS, Info Globe. **Publications:** Press Clipping Survey, weekly - for internal distribution only.

BRIARCLIFF LIBRARY
See: Pace University, Pleasantville/Briarcliff - Library

★1587★
BRICK STORE MUSEUM - EDITH CLEAVES BARRY LIBRARY (Hist)
117 Main St.
Box 117   Phone: (207) 985-4802
Kennebunk, ME 04043   Sandra S. Armentrout, Dir.
Founded: 1936. **Subjects:** Maine and local history, antiques, maritime history, genealogy. **Special Collections:** Local documents (5000); William Lord papers (450). **Holdings:** 2200 books; 100 bound periodical volumes; 500 pamphlets (cataloged); 2 file drawers of handwritten genealogical information. **Subscriptions:** 10 journals and other serials. **Services:** Copying; library open to public for reference use only.

★1588★
BRIDGEPORT HOSPITAL - REEVES MEMORIAL LIBRARY (Med)
267 Grant St.   Phone: (203) 384-3254
Bridgeport, CT 06602   Violet Rigia, Dir. of Lib.Serv.
Founded: 1948. **Staff:** Prof 1; Other 4. **Subjects:** Medicine and related subjects. **Holdings:** 3675 books; 4513 bound periodical volumes; 872 AV items (cataloged). **Subscriptions:** 233 journals and other serials. **Services:** Interlibrary loans; copying; library open to public for reference use only.

Networks/Consortia: Member of Southwestern Connecticut Health Science Library Consortium.

★1589★

BRIDGEPORT PUBLIC LIBRARY - HISTORICAL COLLECTIONS (Hist)
925 Broad St.   Phone: (203) 576-7417
Bridgeport, CT 06604   David W. Palmquist, Hd., Hist.Coll.
Staff: Prof 1; Other 3. **Subjects:** Local history, genealogy, circus, P.T. Barnum, labor and business history. **Special Collections:** Circus and P.T. Barnum Collection (1100 items); Calliopean Society Library, pre-1855 (1200 volumes); Bridgeport city government archives and documents. **Holdings:** 12,500 books; 670 bound periodical volumes; 870 linear feet of manuscripts and archives; 420 linear feet of newspaper clipping files; 2500 photographs; 1000 bound volumes of newspapers; 5070 reels of microfilm; 240 maps. **Subscriptions:** 250 journals and other serials. **Services:** Copying; library open to public. **Computerized Information Services:** DIALOG; computerized cataloging and circulation. **Networks/Consortia:** Member of Southwestern Connecticut Library Council; NELINET. **Publications:** Notes on the Historical Collections of the Bridgeport Public Library - free upon request. **Special Catalogs:** Manuscript and archival registers.

★1590★

BRIDGEPORT PUBLIC LIBRARY - TECHNOLOGY AND BUSINESS DEPARTMENT (Bus-Fin; Sci-Tech)
925 Broad St.   Phone: (203) 576-7406
Bridgeport, CT 06604   E. Paul Jones, Hd.
Staff: Prof 2; Other 3. **Subjects:** Technology, business, physical sciences. **Holdings:** 63,577 books and bound periodical volumes; 4 VF drawers of vocational pamphlets; topographic maps; government documents. **Subscriptions:** 400 journals and other serials. **Services:** Interlibrary loans; copying (limited); library open to public. **Computerized Information Services:** DIALOG; computerized cataloging. **Staff:** Gloria Wollnar, ILL Libn.; Douglas G. Reid, Hd.Libn.

★1591★

BRIDGETON HOSPITAL - HEALTH SCIENCES LIBRARY (Med)
Irving & Manheim Aves.   Phone: (609) 451-6600
Bridgeton, NJ 08302   Jeanne Garrison, Health Sci.Libn.
Founded: 1975. **Staff:** Prof 1. **Subjects:** Medicine, nursing. **Holdings:** 736 books; AV catalogs; 237 AV programs; 7 VF drawers of articles and pamphlets. **Subscriptions:** 51 journals and other serials. **Services:** Interlibrary loans; copying; library open to public with restrictions. **Networks/Consortia:** Member of Southwest New Jersey Consortium for Health Information Services.

★1592★

BRIDGEWATER COLLEGE - ALEXANDER MACK MEMORIAL LIBRARY - SPECIAL COLLECTIONS (Rel-Theol)
                                                Phone: (703) 828-2501
Bridgewater, VA 22812   Orland (Jack) Wages, Libn.
Founded: 1880. **Staff:** Prof 3; Other 3. **Special Collections:** Church of the Brethren; old Bibles; broadsides; manuscripts; U.S. government documents (44,301). **Services:** Interlibrary loans; copying; library open to public with restrictions. **Networks/Consortia:** Member of Shenandoah Valley Independent Colleges Library Cooperative; SOLINET. **Staff:** Dr. Buu Duong, Ref.Serv.; Lizabeth Chabot, Cat.; Sean Barnett, Cat.

★1593★

BRIDGEWATER COURIER-NEWS - LIBRARY (Publ)
1201 Route 22
Box 6600
Bridgewater, NJ 08807   Phone: (201) 722-8800
                                                Linda H. Crow, Libn.
Staff: Prof 1. **Subjects:** Local history, newspaper reference topics. **Holdings:** 200 volumes; 240 VF drawers of clippings; 22 VF drawers of microfilm; 9 VF drawers of photographs; 2 VF drawers of maps. **Subscriptions:** 7 newspapers. **Services:** Copying; library open to public. **Remarks:** The Courier-News is a Gannett newspaper.

★1594★

BRIDGEWATER STATE COLLEGE - CLEMENT C. MAXWELL LIBRARY (Educ)
Shaw Rd.   Phone: (617) 697-8321
Bridgewater, MA 02434   Owen T.P. McGowan, Ph.D., Lib.Dir.
Founded: 1840. **Staff:** Prof 14; Other 24. **Subjects:** Education. **Special Collections:** Theodore Roosevelt Collection; Charles Dickens; early American textbooks; ERIC documents. **Holdings:** 205,714 books and bound periodical volumes; 263,735 ERIC and other microfiche; 6200 reels of microfilm; 16,700 ultrafiche. **Subscriptions:** 1441 journals and other serials; 20 newspapers. **Services:** Interlibrary loans; copying; library open to public. **Computerized Information Services:** Computerized cataloging. **Networks/**

Consortia: Member of Southeastern Massachusetts Cooperating Libraries (SMCL); OCLC through NELINET. **Publications:** Library Notes, monthly - to faculty. **Staff:** Mabell S. Bates, Spec.Coll.Libn.; Barbara S. Britton, Per.Asst.; Susan Pfister, Cat.Libn.; Joyce Leung, Ref.Libn.; Shirley E. Libby, Lib.Sec.; Joyce Marcus, Ref.Asst.; Mary Myers, Per.Libn.; Robert M. Simmons, Curric.Libn.; Emily G. Stone, Cat.Asst.; Carol J. Neubauer, Circ.Libn.; Adeline Ziino, Cat.Asst.; Alan Howell, Acq.Libn.

BRIDWELL LIBRARY
See: Southern Methodist University

BRIDWELL (Margaret M.) ART LIBRARY
See: University of Louisville - Allen R. Hite Art Institute - Margaret M. Bridwell Art Library

★1595★

BRIERCREST BIBLE COLLEGE - ARCHIBALD LIBRARY (Rel-Theol)
                                                Phone: (306) 756-2321
Caronport, SK, Canada S0H 0S0   Allan R. Johnson, Lib.Dir.
Founded: 1974. **Staff:** Prof 3; Other 5. **Subjects:** Christian education. **Holdings:** 33,000 books; 2500 bound periodical volumes; 500 archival files; 123,000 microforms; 2500 slides and cassettes. **Subscriptions:** 450 journals and other serials; 5 newspapers. **Services:** Interlibrary loans; copying; library open to public with restrictions. **Computerized Information Services:** Computerized acquisitions. **Staff:** Laura Klassen, Asst. to Dir.

★1596★

BRIGER & ASSOCIATES - LIBRARY (Law)
299 Park Ave.   Phone: (212) 758-4000
New York, NY 10017   Jacqueline Granek, Libn.
Staff: Prof 1. **Subjects:** Tax law, international law. **Holdings:** 4000 books. **Services:** Interlibrary loans; copying.

★1597★

BRIGGS ENGINEERING & TESTING COMPANY, INC. - LIBRARY (Sci-Tech)
164 Washington St.   Phone: (617) 773-2780
Norwell, MA 02061   R. Wayne Crandlemere, Dir.
Subjects: Construction materials, cement and concrete, bituminous materials, roofing. **Holdings:** 1000 books; 1000 technical reports. **Subscriptions:** 50 journals and other serials. **Services:** Copying; fee-based literature searches; library not open to public.

BRIGGS (Hilton M.) LIBRARY
See: South Dakota State University - Hilton M. Briggs Library

BRIGHAM (Carl Campbell) LIBRARY
See: Educational Testing Service - Carl Campbell Brigham Library

★1598★

BRIGHAM AND WOMEN'S HOSPITAL - ABRAMSON CENTER FOR INSTRUCTIONAL MEDIA
75 Francis St.
Boston, MA 02115
Defunct

★1599★

BRIGHAM AND WOMEN'S HOSPITAL - PETER BENT BRIGHAM SCHOOL OF NURSING - LIBRARY (Med)
300 Brookline Ave.   Phone: (617) 732-5922
Boston, MA 02115   Ann B. Snyder, Libn.
Founded: 1912. **Staff:** Prof 1; Other 2. **Subjects:** Nursing, medicine, behavioral sciences, related natural sciences. **Special Collections:** Historical collection relating to school and parent institution. **Holdings:** 3000 books; 925 bound periodical volumes; 8 VF drawers of pamphlets and reprints; AV materials. **Subscriptions:** 126 journals and other serials. **Services:** Interlibrary loans (limited); copying; library open with permission of director of School of Nursing. **Networks/Consortia:** Member of Libraries for Nursing Consortium (LINC). **Publications:** Recent Acquisitions, semiannual - for internal distribution and to consortium members.

★1600★

BRIGHAM YOUNG UNIVERSITY - HUMANITIES AND ARTS DIVISION LIBRARY (Hum)
University Library   Phone: (801) 378-4005
Provo, UT 84602   Blaine H. Hall, Div.Coord.
Staff: Prof 2; Other 6. **Subjects:** Literature, music, art, languages, speech, drama, theater arts, cinematic arts, library science. **Holdings:** Figures not available. **Services:** Interlibrary loans; copying; library open to public. **Computerized Information Services:** DIALOG, SDC, BRS, New York Times

Information Service; computerized cataloging, serials and circulation. **Networks/Consortia:** Member of RLG; Utah College Library Council.

★1601★
BRIGHAM YOUNG UNIVERSITY - J. REUBEN CLARK LAW SCHOOL LIBRARY (Law)
B.Y.U.   Phone: (801) 378-3593
Provo, UT 84602   David A. Thomas, Law Libn.
Founded: 1972. **Staff:** Prof 7; Other 40. **Subjects:** Law - American and British Commonwealth. **Holdings:** 215,000 books; 124,000 bound periodical volumes; 58,000 monographs, 40,000 government documents and 1300 other items; 64,000 volumes in microform. **Subscriptions:** 3875 journals and other serials; 38 newspapers. **Services:** Interlibrary loans; copying; library open to public for legal research use only. **Computerized Information Services:** LEXIS, WESTLAW. **Networks/Consortia:** Member of Utah College Library Council; RLG. **Publications:** Foreign Law Classification Schedule, Class K, 2nd edition; Abstracts of Book Reviews in Current Legal Periodicals, semimonthly; LC Subject Headings - KF: Cross-References. **Staff:** Larry Hood, Ref.Libn.; Heinz Peter Mueller, Assoc. Law Libn.; Joanne Hillam, Circ.Libn.; Louisa Hurtado, Doc.Libn.; Gary Grott, Acq.Libn.; Curt Conklin, Cat.Libn.; Karen Haroldsen, Ser.Libn.

★1602★
BRIGHAM YOUNG UNIVERSITY - MUSEUM OF PEOPLES AND CULTURES LIBRARY (Sci-Tech)
Allen Hall   Phone: (801) 378-6112
Provo, UT 84602   Dale L. Berge, Dir.
Staff: Prof 1; Other 1. **Subjects:** Archeology - Mesoamerican, Southwestern, historical. **Holdings:** 4000 books; 1500 bound periodical volumes. **Services:** SDI; library open to public. **Publications:** Publications in Archaeology, annual.

★1603★
BRIGHAM YOUNG UNIVERSITY - RELIGION AND HISTORY DIVISION LIBRARY (Hist; Rel-Theol)
University Library   Phone: (801) 378-6198
Provo, UT 84602   Donald H. Howard, Div.Coord.
Staff: Prof 2; Other 7. **Subjects:** History, religion, biography, philosophy, geography, anthropology, archeology. **Holdings:** Figures not available. **Services:** Interlibrary loans; copying; library open to public. **Computerized Information Services:** DIALOG, SDC, BRS, New York Times Information Service; computerized cataloging, serials and circulation. **Networks/Consortia:** Member of RLG; Utah College Library Council.

★1604★
BRIGHAM YOUNG UNIVERSITY - SCIENCE DIVISION LIBRARY (Sci-Tech)
University Library   Phone: (801) 378-2986
Provo, UT 84602   Carol T. Smith, Div.Coord.
Staff: Prof 3; Other 7. **Subjects:** Science and technology. **Holdings:** Figures not available. **Services:** Interlibrary loans; copying; library open to public. **Computerized Information Services:** DIALOG, SDC, BRS, New York Times Information Service, MEDLINE; computerized cataloging, serials and circulation. **Networks/Consortia:** Member of RLG; Utah College Library Council.

★1605★
BRIGHAM YOUNG UNIVERSITY - SOCIAL SCIENCE DIVISION LIBRARY (Soc Sci)
University Library   Phone: (801) 378-3809
Provo, UT 84602   Susan Fales, Div.Coord.
Staff: Prof 5; Other 9. **Subjects:** Business, economics, education, sociology, government, psychology, government documents, maps. **Special Collections:** Asian Collection. **Holdings:** Figures not available. **Services:** Interlibrary loans; copying; library open to public. **Computerized Information Services:** DIALOG, SDC, BRS, New York Times Information Service; computerized cataloging, serials and circulation. **Networks/Consortia:** Member of RLG; Utah College Library Council.

★1606★
BRIGHAM YOUNG UNIVERSITY - SPECIAL COLLECTIONS (Rel-Theol)
University Library   Phone: (801) 378-2932
Provo, UT 84602   Chad Flake, Cur.
Founded: 1956. **Staff:** Prof 7; Other 3. **Subjects:** Renaissance and Reformation; history of printing; Mormonism; Utah and Western history; 19th century American and English literature; typography; 17th century astronomy; 16th century European diplomatics. **Special Collections:** LeRoy Hafen Collection of Western American History; J. Reuben Clark Collection of Law and Religion; Mormon Americana; Victorian book collection; Tyrus Hillway Collection of Herman Melville; Marco Heidner collection of 15th and 16th century printing. **Holdings:** 157,002 books and bound periodical volumes;

20,912 pamphlets (cataloged); 3960 linear feet of manuscripts. **Services:** Interlibrary loans; copying; collections open to public. **Computerized Information Services:** DIALOG, SDC, BRS, New York Times Information Service; computerized cataloging, serials and circulation. **Networks/Consortia:** Member of RLG; Utah College Library Council. **Publications:** Mormon Americana. **Staff:** Scott Duvall, Asst.Cur./Bks.; Dennis Rowley, Asst.Cur./Mss. & Archv.

★1607★
BRIGHAM YOUNG UNIVERSITY - UTAH VALLEY BRANCH GENEALOGICAL LIBRARY (Hist)
Harold B. Lee Library, Rm. 4385   Phone: (801) 378-3934
Provo, UT 84602   Roger C. Flick, Libn.
Founded: 1964. **Staff:** Prof 2; Other 1. **Subjects:** Church of Jesus Christ of Latter-Day Saints - genealogy and history. **Holdings:** 400,000 volumes in microform. **Services:** Interlibrary loans; copying; library open to public. **Computerized Information Services:** DIALOG, SDC, BRS, New York Times Information Service; computerized cataloging, serials and circulation. **Networks/Consortia:** Member of RLG; Utah College Library Council. **Publications:** Utah Valley Branch Genealogical Library Bulletin. **Special Indexes:** Name Index to DAR Revolutionary War Burial Lists. Contains 63,000 names taken from tombstone inscriptions. **Remarks:** This library is a branch of the genealogical society located in Salt Lake City and has access to their collection on a loan basis.

★1608★
BRIGHAM YOUNG UNIVERSITY, HAWAII CAMPUS - JOSEPH F. SMITH LIBRARY AND MEDIA CENTER - SPECIAL COLLECTION (Educ)
55-220 Kulanui St.   Phone: (808) 293-3850
Laie, HI 96762   Richard C. Pearson, Dir.
Founded: 1955. **Special Collections:** Pacific Islands (8500 books); Mormonism (3850 books); children's collection (2050 books); government documents (37,500); archives. **Services:** Interlibrary loans; copying; library open to public on payment of annual fee. **Computerized Information Services:** DIALOG; computerized cataloging, acquisitions and circulation. **Networks/Consortia:** Member of OCLC. **Special Catalogs:** Periodical Index for Pacific Islands; Mormons in the Pacific: An Annotated Bibliography. **Staff:** Marynelle DeVore, Ref./Govt.Doc.; Rex Frandsen, Archv.

BRILL (Abraham A.) LIBRARY
See: New York Psychoanalytic Institute - Abraham A. Brill Library

BRILL SCIENCE LIBRARY
See: Miami University

BRIMLEY (H.H.) MEMORIAL LIBRARY
See: North Carolina State Museum of Natural History - H.H. Brimley Memorial Library

★1609★
BRINCO LIMITED - LIBRARY (Sci-Tech)
20 King St. W., 10th Fl.   Phone: (416) 868-6970
Toronto, ON, Canada M5H 1C4   Deborah M. Kelly, Corp.Libn.
Founded: 1970. **Staff:** Prof 1. **Subjects:** Geology, law, nuclear engineering, finance, Newfoundland history. **Holdings:** 2000 books; 60 bound periodical volumes; 10,000 geological maps on microfilm; 4000 geological reports (mostly on Newfoundland). **Subscriptions:** 100 journals and other serials; 18 newspapers. **Services:** Interlibrary loans; copying; library not open to public. **Special Indexes:** Computer index to geological reports.

BRISTOL COUNTY BAR ASSOCIATION
See: Fall River Law Library

★1610★
BRISTOL COUNTY LAW LIBRARY (Law)
Superior Court House   Phone: (617) 824-7632
Taunton, MA 02780   Carol A. Francis, Libn.
Founded: 1858. **Staff:** Prof 1. **Subjects:** Law. **Holdings:** 28,654 volumes. **Services:** Library open to public for reference use only. **Remarks:** Maintained by Massachusetts State - Trial Court.

★1611★
BRISTOL HISTORICAL AND PRESERVATION SOCIETY - LIBRARY (Hist)
48 Court St.   Phone: (401) 253-8825
Bristol, RI 02809   Helene L. Tessler, Cur.-Libn.
Founded: 1936. **Staff:** 1. **Subjects:** Genealogy and local history. **Special Collections:** Ships - logs, journals, crew lists. **Holdings:** 4 VF drawers of shipping papers; 12 VF drawers of local area clippings, obituaries, deeds and correspondence. **Services:** Copying; library open to public with fee to

nonmembers.

★1612★
BRISTOL-MYERS COMPANY - BRISTOL LABORATORIES - LIBRARY AND INFORMATION SERVICES (Sci-Tech)
Box 657   Phone: (315) 432-2232
Syracuse, NY 13201   Dr. John E. MacNintch, Dir.
Founded: 1946. **Staff:** Prof 7; Other 6. **Subjects:** Pharmacology, pharmacy, organic chemistry, microbiology, medicine; engineering. **Holdings:** 16,500 books; 23,000 bound periodical volumes; 16 VF drawers; 65 VF drawers of reprints; 2500 microfilm cartridges. **Subscriptions:** 805 journals and other serials; 27 newspapers. **Services:** Interlibrary loans; copying; SDI; library open to public by appointment. **Computerized Information Services:** DIALOG, SDC. **Networks/Consortia:** Member of Central New York Library Resources Council (CENTRO). **Publications:** Pharmaceutical Information Digest; Patent Bulletin, biweekly; Library Report, bimonthly - all for internal distribution only. **Special Catalogs:** Product bibliographies. **Staff:** Dr. Kenneth A. Kerridge, Hd., Lit.Sect.; John S. Silvin, Hd., Lib.Serv.; Dr. William B. Wheatley, Chem.Doc.

BRISTOL-MYERS COMPANY - DRACKETT DIVISION
See: Drackett Company

★1613★
BRISTOL-MYERS COMPANY - PHARMACEUTICAL RESEARCH & DEVELOPMENT DIVISION - RESEARCH LIBRARY - EVANSVILLE (Med)
                                      Phone: (812) 426-6546
Evansville, IN 47721   Alice Weisling, Libn.
Founded: 1951. **Staff:** Prof 3; Other 5. **Subjects:** Pharmacology, chemistry, biochemistry, pharmacy, nutrition, medicine, pediatrics. **Holdings:** 35,000 books; 20,000 bound periodical volumes; 8 VF drawers of patents; 4 VF drawers of pamphlets; 2000 reels of microfilm of journals and patents. **Subscriptions:** 800 journals and other serials. **Services:** Interlibrary loans; copying (company personnel only); translations; bibliography preparation; library open to public by special permission. **Computerized Information Services:** MEDLINE, DIALOG, SDC; computerized cataloging. **Networks/Consortia:** Member of Evansville Area Health Science Library Consortium; OCLC. **Publications:** Weekly list of current journal articles; annual product bibliographies. **Special Indexes:** Computer-produced index to bibliographies on magnetic tape. **Formerly:** Mead Johnson and Company - Mead Johnson Research Center - Library.

★1614★
BRISTOL-MYERS PRODUCTS - TECHNICAL INFORMATION CENTER (Sci-Tech)
225 Long Ave.   Phone: (201) 926-6691
Hillside, NJ 07207   Mary F. Bondarovich, Mgr., Tech.Info.Ctr.
Founded: 1946. **Staff:** Prof 3; Other 2. **Subjects:** Biology, pharmacology, chemistry, microbiology, pharmaceutical science, toiletries. **Holdings:** 10,000 books; 10,000 bound periodical volumes; 3000 reels of journals on microfilm; 6500 microfiche (reports and documents). **Subscriptions:** 550 journals and other serials; 5 newspapers. **Services:** Interlibrary loans; copying; SDI; library open to public by appointment. **Computerized Information Services:** SDC, DIALOG, NLM. **Publications:** Recent Acquisitions Bulletin, weekly; Subject Profiles, weekly. **Staff:** Helen Dyer, Res.Libn.; Anne C. Swist, Lit.Anl.

BRITE DIVINITY SCHOOL COLLECTION
See: Texas Christian University - Mary Couts Burnett Library

★1615★
BRITISH COLUMBIA ALCOHOL AND DRUG PROGRAMS - LIBRARY (Med)
1755 W. Broadway, 2nd Fl.   Phone: (604) 731-9121
Vancouver, BC, Canada V6J 4S5   W. Holmes, Lib.Techn.
Founded: 1974. **Staff:** Prof 1; Other 1. **Subjects:** Alcohol and other drugs; counseling techniques. **Holdings:** 5200 books; 103 titles of unbound periodicals; 3 drawers of clippings; 1 bookcase of archives; 1000 vertical file items. **Subscriptions:** 107 journals and other serials. **Services:** Interlibrary loans; copying; library open to public for reference use only. **Remarks:** Alcohol and Drug Programs are under the jurisdiction of the British Columbia Ministry of Health.

BRITISH COLUMBIA CANCER INSTITUTE
See: Cancer Control Agency of British Columbia

★1616★
BRITISH COLUMBIA CENTRAL CREDIT UNION - RESOURCE CENTRE (Bus-Fin; Hist)
P.O. Box 2038   Phone: (604) 734-2511
Vancouver, BC, Canada V6B 3R9   Valerie Redston, Libn.
Staff: Prof 1; Other 1. **Subjects:** Credit unions and cooperatives and their

history; finance. **Holdings:** 1250 books; 300 annual reports; 125 cubic feet of credit union records; 35 oral history tapes; 2000 photographs; clippings. **Subscriptions:** 336 journals and other serials. **Services:** Interlibrary loans; copying; library open to public with restrictions.

★1617★
BRITISH COLUMBIA - COUNCIL OF FOREST INDUSTRIES OF BRITISH COLUMBIA - LIBRARY (Env-Cons)†
1055 W. Hastings St., Suite 1800   Phone: (604) 684-0211
Vancouver, BC, Canada V6E 2H1   Sheila Foley, Libn.
Staff: 1. **Subjects:** Forest industry - economics and trade; environmental issues; transportation. **Holdings:** 4000 books; 100 Statistics Canada titles; Canadian, U.S. and foreign government documents. **Subscriptions:** 155 journals and other serials. **Services:** Interlibrary loans; copying; library open to public with restrictions.

BRITISH COLUMBIA - DEPARTMENT OF ...
See: British Columbia - Ministry of ...

★1618★
BRITISH COLUMBIA GENEALOGICAL SOCIETY - REFERENCE LIBRARY (Hist)†
Box 94371   Phone: (604) 274-3659
Richmond, BC, Canada V7C 1J3   Alice Marwood, Libn.
Founded: 1971. **Staff:** 15. **Subjects:** Genealogy, local history, related subjects. **Special Collections:** British Columbia Research File (100,000 3x5 cards of vital statistics from church records and newspapers). **Holdings:** 500 books; 100 bound periodical volumes. **Subscriptions:** 80 journals and other serials. **Services:** Copying; library open to public for reference use only.

★1619★
BRITISH COLUMBIA HEALTH ASSOCIATION (BCHA) - LIBRARY (Med)
440 Cambie St.   Phone: (604) 683-7421
Vancouver, BC, Canada V6B 2N6   Carolyn Hall, Lib.Techn.
Founded: 1974. **Staff:** 2. **Subjects:** Hospital and health care administration. **Holdings:** 2000 books; 4000 unbound periodicals; hospital annual reports; 101 films and videotapes; 200 pamphlets. **Subscriptions:** 39 journals and other serials. **Services:** Interlibrary loans; copying; library not open to public. **Publications:** BCHA Reports, semimonthly - to members. **Special Catalogs:** Bibliography of materials published by the association. **Staff:** Marta Umblia, Lib.Asst.

BRITISH COLUMBIA HYDRO & POWER AUTHORITY
See: B.C. Hydro

★1620★
BRITISH COLUMBIA INSTITUTE OF TECHNOLOGY - LIBRARY SERVICES DIVISION (Bus-Fin; Sci-Tech)†
3700 Willingdon Ave.   Phone: (604) 434-5734
Burnaby, BC, Canada V5G 3H2   Joseph E. Carver, Dean of Lib.Serv.
Founded: 1964. **Staff:** Prof 12; Other 41. **Subjects:** Business; management - administrative, operations, financial; computer programming; hospitality and tourism; mechanical, civil and structural engineering; forest resources; electricity and electronics; building; chemistry and metallurgy; natural gas and petroleum; health technologies (including nursing). **Holdings:** 80,740 books, government publications and bound periodical volumes; 1427 films (cataloged); 5470 reels of microfilm; 1920 audiotapes; 170 filmloops; 25,000 pamphlets and forestry reprints; 125,000 volumes on microfiche. **Subscriptions:** 4200 journals and other serials; 25 newspapers. **Services:** Interlibrary loans (fee); copying; library open to public with restrictions. **Computerized Information Services:** DIALOG, SDC, QL Systems, CAN/OLE; computerized cataloging and circulation. **Networks/Consortia:** Member of UTLAS, Inc.; British Columbia Union Catalogue. **Publications:** Current awareness alert services. **Special Indexes:** Computerized keyword index to pamphlets, reports, films and other AV materials. **Staff:** Robert Roy, Dept.Hd.; Sheila Ferry, Ref.Coord.; Margot Allingham, Engr.Libn.; Marj McLeod, Health Libn.; Robert Young, Adm. & Core Libn.; Gerry Weeks, Forestry Libn.; Frank Knor, Sys.Libn.; Trish Labonte, Sys.Libn.; Paula Pick, Hd.Cat.; Merilee MacKianon, Cat.Libn.; Anthony Kelly, Bus.Libn.

★1621★
BRITISH COLUMBIA - JUDGES' LIBRARY - SUPERIOR & COUNTY COURTS (Law)
Law Courts, 800 Smithe St.   Phone: (604) 668-2799
Vancouver, BC, Canada V6Z 2E1   A. Rector, Libn.
Founded: 1945. **Staff:** 2. **Subjects:** Law and related subjects. **Holdings:** 9000 books. **Services:** Interlibrary loans; library not open to public. **Publications:** Digests of Judgments of the Court of Appeal.

★1622★
BRITISH COLUMBIA - JUDGES' LIBRARY - SUPERIOR & COUNTY COURTS (Law)†
Law Courts, 850 Burdett Ave.
Victoria, BC, Canada V8W 1B4
Subjects: Law and related subjects. **Holdings:** 5500 books. **Remarks:** Administered by the Vancouver Judges' Library staff.

★1623★
BRITISH COLUMBIA LAW LIBRARY FOUNDATION - KAMLOOPS COURTHOUSE LIBRARY (Law)
Court Annex
1165 Battle St.   Phone: (604) 374-7415
Kamloops, BC, Canada V2C 2N4   Denise Caldwell, Area Libn.
Staff: 1. **Subjects:** Statute law - federal, British Columbia, Western Provinces, Ontario; case law - English, Canadian. **Special Collections:** British Columbia Gazette, part II, regulations. **Holdings:** 8000 books; 300 bound periodical volumes; 210 gazettes. **Subscriptions:** 110 journals and other serials. **Services:** Interlibrary loans; copying; library open to public for reference use only. **Computerized Information Services:** QL Systems; computerized cataloging. **Networks/Consortia:** Member of British Columbia Law Library Foundation. **Special Indexes:** Case table index reporting service.

★1624★
BRITISH COLUMBIA LAW LIBRARY FOUNDATION - VANCOUVER COURTHOUSE LIBRARY (Law)
800 Smithe St.   Phone: (604) 689-7295
Vancouver, BC, Canada V6Z 2E1   Maureen B. McCormick, Exec.Dir.
Founded: 1888. **Staff:** Prof 4; Other 8. **Subjects:** Law. **Holdings:** 31,000 volumes. **Subscriptions:** 400 journals and other serials. **Services:** Interlibrary loans; copying; library open to public. **Computerized Information Services:** QL Systems; computerized cataloging. **Remarks:** Vancouver Library is the centre of a system of 28 courthouse law libraries. **Staff:** Joan L. Honeywell, Libn.; Eve Porter, Ref.Libn.

★1625★
BRITISH COLUMBIA - LEGISLATIVE LIBRARY (Law; Soc Sci)
Parliament Bldgs.   Phone: (604) 387-6510
Victoria, BC, Canada V8V 1X4   J.G. Mitchell, Leg.Libn.
Founded: 1863. **Staff:** Prof 16; Other 18. **Subjects:** Government, political science, constitutional law. **Special Collections:** Panama Canal; sessional clipping books. **Holdings:** 250,000 books; 60,000 bound periodical volumes; 350,000 government documents; 10,000 reels of microfilm. **Subscriptions:** 1500 journals and other serials; 270 newspapers. **Services:** Interlibrary loans; copying; library open to referrals from other libraries only. **Computerized Information Services:** DIALOG, Infomart, New York Times Information Service, QL Systems, CAN/OLE, Globe & Mail. **Special Indexes:** British Columbia newspaper index (card); government document index (card). **Staff:** Margaret Hastings, Asst.Libn.; Joan Barton, Hd., Ref.

★1626★
BRITISH COLUMBIA LIONS SOCIETY FOR CRIPPLED CHILDREN - LIBRARY
177 W. 7th
Vancouver, BC, Canada V5Y 1L8
Defunct

BRITISH COLUMBIA MEDICAL LIBRARY SERVICE
See: College of Physicians and Surgeons of British Columbia

★1627★
BRITISH COLUMBIA - MINISTRY OF EDUCATION - LIBRARY (Educ)
835 Humboldt St.   Phone: (604) 387-6279
Victoria, BC, Canada V8V 2M4   Norma Lofthouse, Libn.
Staff: Prof 1; Other 2. **Subjects:** Education - finance, administration. **Holdings:** 5000 books and government documents. **Subscriptions:** 400 journals and other serials. **Services:** Library open to public by appointment only. **Computerized Information Services:** DIALOG; computerized cataloging. **Networks/Consortia:** Member of British Columbia Union Catalogue Project. **Publications:** List of Acquisitions - for internal distribution only.

★1628★
BRITISH COLUMBIA - MINISTRY OF EDUCATION - PROVINCIAL EDUCATIONAL MEDIA CENTRE (Aud-Vis)
7351 Elmbridge Way   Phone: (604) 278-4961
Richmond, BC, Canada V6X 1B8   B.A. Black, Dir.
Founded: 1946. **Staff:** Prof 10; Other 30. **Subjects:** School subjects. **Holdings:** 7000 films; 2500 videotape programs. **Services:** Materials circulate to British Columbia schools, colleges and universities; videotape and audiotape dubbing centers; production center; centre not open to public. **Computerized Information Services:** Computerized circulation. **Special Catalogs:** Film, audiotape and videotape catalogs; radio and television guidebooks.

★1629★
BRITISH COLUMBIA - MINISTRY OF ENERGY, MINES AND PETROLEUM RESOURCES - LIBRARY (Energy)
Douglas Bldg., Rm. 430   Phone: (604) 387-6407
Victoria, BC, Canada V8V 1X4   S.E. Ferris, Libn.
Founded: 1896. **Staff:** 2. **Subjects:** Geology, chemistry, mining, economic geology, mining engineering, petroleum engineering, energy. **Holdings:** 5000 books; 3000 bound periodical volumes; 12,000 papers. **Subscriptions:** 127 journals and other serials. **Services:** Library open to public for reference use only. **Computerized Information Services:** SDC; computerized cataloging and serials. **Publications:** Annual Reports: Geology, Exploration and Mining in British Columbia; bulletins. **Special Indexes:** Index of annual reports and bulletins.

★1630★
BRITISH COLUMBIA - MINISTRY OF ENVIRONMENT - LIBRARY (Env-Cons)
780 Blanshard   Phone: (604) 387-5194
Victoria, BC, Canada V8W 2H1   Marg Palmer, Ministry Libn.
Staff: Prof 2; Other 2. **Subjects:** Pollution management, fish and wildlife management, marine resources, water management. **Special Collections:** Wildlife original reports; Water Treaty documents. **Holdings:** 20,000 books; 250 bound periodical volumes; water treaty theses; archives. **Subscriptions:** 740 journals and other serials; 10 newspapers. **Services:** Interlibrary loans; library open to public with restrictions. **Computerized Information Services:** DIALOG, Infomart, CISTI, QL Systems; computerized cataloging. **Networks/Consortia:** Member of Government Libraries Association of British Columbia; Federated Information Network (FIN); International Association of Marine Science Libraries and Information Centers. **Publications:** Current awareness table of contents, weekly - for internal distribution only. **Staff:** Carol Smith; Nadine Bigelow; Tony Markle.

★1631★
BRITISH COLUMBIA - MINISTRY OF ENVIRONMENT - MAPS-B.C. (Geog-Map)
Parliament Bldgs.   Phone: (604) 387-1441
Victoria, BC, Canada V8V 1X5   G.H. Harris, Supv.
Staff: 6. **Holdings:** Published provincial maps, departmental maps, air photographs, air photograph indexes. **Services:** Copying; library open to public. **Publications:** Key maps - distributed on request. **Special Catalogs:** Map & Air Photo Catalog. **Remarks:** MAPS is an acronym for Map and Air Photo Sales.

★1632★
BRITISH COLUMBIA - MINISTRY OF FORESTS - LIBRARY (Sci-Tech)
Parliament Bldgs.
1450 Government St.   Phone: (604) 387-3628
Victoria, BC, Canada V8W 3E7   S.E. Barker, Mgr.
Staff: 2. **Subjects:** Forests, ecology, business, range management, land use planning. **Holdings:** 23,000 books, serials and government documents; 2000 bound periodical volumes. **Subscriptions:** 356 journals and other serials. **Services:** Interlibrary loans; copying; library open to public for reference use only. **Computerized Information Services:** DIALOG, QL Systems, INFOMART; computerized catalog. **Publications:** New Books Lists; bibliographies. **Special Catalogs:** Union catalog of the Ministry of Forests six regional libraries, located in Kamloops, Vancouver, Williams Lake, Prince George, Smithers and Nelson. **Staff:** Roxanne Smith, Lib.Techn.

★1633★
BRITISH COLUMBIA - MINISTRY OF FORESTS - NELSON FOREST REGION LIBRARY (Sci-Tech)
518 Lake St.   Phone: (604) 354-4181
Nelson, BC, Canada V1L 4C6   Marianne Abraham, Regional Rsrcs.Info.Ck.
Founded: 1956. **Staff:** Prof 1. **Subjects:** Forestry, natural resources. **Holdings:** 2000 books; 400 bound periodical volumes; 2500 research papers; 4 VF drawers of pamphlets and clippings; 300 government documents. **Subscriptions:** 50 journals and other serials. **Services:** Interlibrary loans; library open to public with restrictions. **Computerized Information Services:** Computerized cataloging, acquisitions and serials. **Publications:** Accession List, monthly - for internal distribution only. **Special Catalogs:** Selected Bibliography of Canadian Forest Literature, 1917-1946.

BRITISH COLUMBIA - MINISTRY OF HEALTH - ALCOHOL AND DRUG PROGRAMS
See: British Columbia Alcohol and Drug Programs

★1634★

BRITISH COLUMBIA - MINISTRY OF HEALTH - LIBRARY (Med)
1515 Blanshard St., 5th Fl.   Phone: (604) 386-3166
Victoria, BC, Canada V8W 3C8   Elizabeth M. Woodworth, Libn.
Founded: 1946. **Staff:** 4. **Subjects:** Public health, medicine, hospital administration, nursing, mental health, nutrition, geriatrics, health education. **Special Collections:** Provincial Board of Health Annual Reports. **Holdings:** 10,000 books and bound periodical volumes; 8 VF drawers of pamphlets. **Subscriptions:** 500 journals and other serials. **Services:** Interlibrary loans; copying; bibliographic searches; library open to health professionals. **Computerized Information Services:** MEDLINE, SDC; computerized cataloging. **Publications:** Accessions list, semimonthly; serials list, annual.

BRITISH COLUMBIA - MINISTRY OF HEALTH - MENTAL HEALTH PROGRAMS - STAFF REFERENCE LIBRARY
See: Riverview Hospital - Staff Reference Library

★1635★

BRITISH COLUMBIA - MINISTRY OF HEALTH - MENTAL HEALTH SERVICES LIBRARY (Med)
3405 Willingdon Ave.   Phone: (604) 434-4247
Burnaby, BC, Canada V5G 3H4   Joy Fourchalk, Libn.
Founded: 1957. **Staff:** 1. **Subjects:** Psychiatry, psychology, social sciences, special education. **Holdings:** 3045 books; 1200 bound periodical volumes; 216 Audio-Digest tapes. **Subscriptions:** 87 journals and other serials. **Services:** Interlibrary loans; copying; library not open to public.

★1636★

BRITISH COLUMBIA - MINISTRY OF HUMAN RESOURCES - LIBRARY (Soc Sci)
800 Cassiar St.   Phone: (604) 387-6415
Vancouver, BC, Canada V8W 2Z2   M.J. Love, Libn.
Founded: 1974. **Staff:** 4. **Subjects:** Social welfare, social work, sociology, psychology, child welfare, management. **Holdings:** 10,000 books; 1000 AV items; 75 archive items. **Subscriptions:** 180 journals and other serials. **Services:** Interlibrary loans; copying; SDI; library not open to public. **Computerized Information Services:** Computerized cataloging. **Networks/Consortia:** Member of Government Libraries Association of British Columbia. **Publications:** Accessions List, bimonthly. **Special Catalogs:** Media Catalog.

★1637★

BRITISH COLUMBIA - MINISTRY OF INDUSTRY & SMALL BUSINESS DEVELOPMENT - LIBRARY (Bus-Fin)
Legislative Bldgs.   Phone: (604) 387-3765
Victoria, BC, Canada V8V 1X4   Helen G. Bruce, Libn.
Staff: Prof 2; Other 5. **Subjects:** Statistics, regional economics, energy, resource economics, trade and commerce. **Special Collections:** N.E. Coal studies. **Holdings:** 40,000 volumes, including Statistics Canada publications; 10 drawers of pamphlets; 12 drawers of corporation annual reports; 5 drawers of clippings; 5 drawers of economics vertical files; 744 microforms; directories; Statistics Canada publications. **Subscriptions:** 1200 journals and other serials; 20 newspapers. **Services:** Interlibrary loans; copying; library open to public with restrictions. **Computerized Information Services:** Online systems. **Publications:** Accession List, monthly; Periodicals List, irregular. **Special Indexes:** MICOM.

★1638★

BRITISH COLUMBIA - MINISTRY OF LANDS, PARKS AND HOUSING - PARKS LIBRARY (Env-Cons)
Parliament Bldgs.   Phone: (604) 387-5044
Victoria, BC, Canada V8V 1X4   Shirley Desrosiers, Libn.
Founded: 1971. **Staff:** 1. **Subjects:** Park and wilderness management, outdoor recreation, tourism and travel research, conservation, administration. **Holdings:** 5500 books; 1350 items in vertical file. **Subscriptions:** 143 journals and other serials. **Services:** Interlibrary loans; copying; library open to public. **Computerized Information Services:** Computerized cataloging. **Networks/Consortia:** Member of Government Libraries Association of British Columbia; Federated Information Network (FIN). **Publications:** Accessions List, irregular; Journals: Tables of Contents, monthly - both for internal distribution only. **Special Indexes:** Index to reprint and journal literature in parks and outdoor recreation. **Remarks:** Includes holdings of the former British Columbia - Ministry of Tourism - Library.

★1639★

BRITISH COLUMBIA - MINISTRY OF PROVINCIAL SEC. & GOVERNMENT SERV. - HERITAGE CONSRV. BR. - RESOURCE INFO. CTR. (Plan)
Parliament Bldgs.   Phone: (604) 387-6956
Victoria, BC, Canada V8V 1X4   Anne Morgan, Br.Libn.
Staff: Prof 1; Other 1. **Subjects:** Historic preservation, archeology, architecture, zoning, planning, ethnology. **Special Collections:** Archeological permit reports - investigations, site surveys and excavations carried out by the branch (350). **Holdings:** 3800 books; 18 films; 15 slide/tape kits; newspaper clippings. **Subscriptions:** 151 journals and other serials. **Services:** Interlibrary loans; copying; SDI; center open to public. **Computerized Information Services:** DIALOG, NTIS; computerized cataloging. **Publications:** Resource Information Center: Resources and Services. **Special Indexes:** Index to archeological permit reports (computer printout and microfiche). **Remarks:** Center is located at 1016 Langley St.

BRITISH COLUMBIA - MINISTRY OF TOURISM - LIBRARY
See: British Columbia - Ministry of Lands, Parks and Housing - Parks Library

★1640★

BRITISH COLUMBIA - MINISTRY OF TOURISM - PHOTOGRAPHIC LIBRARY (Aud-Vis)
1117 Wharf St., 3rd Fl.   Phone: (604) 387-6490
Victoria, BC, Canada V8W 2Z2   K.L. Gibbs, Act.Dir.
Founded: 1950. **Staff:** Prof 10; Other 4. **Subjects:** Travel and recreation; movie making; still photography. **Holdings:** 150 motion picture prints; 50,000 negatives. **Services:** Library open to public. **Publications:** Beautiful British Columbia magazine, quarterly - by subscription. **Remarks:** Motion pictures are also available through National Film Board of Canada offices in Canada, or in Canadian Government Office of Travel in the United States.

★1641★

BRITISH COLUMBIA - PROVINCIAL ARCHIVES (Hist)
Parliament Bldgs.   Phone: (604) 387-5885
Victoria, BC, Canada V8V 1X4   John A. Bovey, Prov.Archv.
Staff: Prof 19; Other 25. **Subjects:** Pacific Northwest history; British Columbia history. **Holdings:** 37,000 books and bound periodical volumes; 19,000 pamphlets; 100,000 photographs; 30,000 maps; 16,000 audiotapes. **Services:** Interlibrary loans; copying; archives open to public. **Publications:** Sound Heritage; Provincial Archives Memoir Series, irregular. **Remarks:** The archives are administered by the Library & Maps Section. **Staff:** David B. Mason, Archv. & Lib.Prog.; Kent M. Haworth, AV Rec.Prog.

★1642★

BRITISH COLUMBIA - PROVINCIAL ARCHIVES - LIBRARY & MAPS SECTION - MAP COLLECTION (Geog-Map)
Parliament Bldgs.   Phone: (604) 387-6516
Victoria, BC, Canada V8V 1X4   David R. Chamberlin, Hd., Lib. & Maps Sect.
Staff: Prof 2; Other 1. **Subjects:** British Columbia and Yukon maps concerning gold mining, roads, railroads, trails, townsites; hydrographic charts. **Special Collections:** F.M. Rattenbury architectural plans (70 items); A.F. Buckham Collection of British Columbia mining engineering maps and plans (4 drawers). **Holdings:** 600 books; 200 atlases; 30,000 maps and plans; 2500 35mm aperture cards; 14,000 105mm negatives; 1000 slides; 75 geological and mining reports. **Subscriptions:** 32 journals and other serials. **Services:** Copying; library open to public. **Staff:** Geoffrey Castle, Archv.

BRITISH COLUMBIA - PROVINCIAL EDUCATIONAL MEDIA CENTRE
See: British Columbia - Ministry of Education

BRITISH COLUMBIA REGISTERED NURSES' ASSOCIATION
See: Registered Nurses' Association of British Columbia

★1643★

BRITISH COLUMBIA RESEARCH COUNCIL - LIBRARY (Sci-Tech)
3650 Wesbrook Mall   Phone: (604) 224-4331
Vancouver, BC, Canada V6S 2L2   Viona Coates, Libn.
Founded: 1946. **Staff:** Prof 1; Other 3. **Subjects:** Waste treatment, water and air pollution, ocean engineering, corrosion, mineral studies, applied chemistry, wood preservation, offshore technology, electro-luminescence, management services, marine biology, applied engineering, biotechnology. **Special Collections:** Traffic safety; computer-aided design/computer-aided manufacturing. **Holdings:** 14,500 books; 4000 bound periodical volumes; 15,000 separates (cataloged). **Subscriptions:** 400 journals and other serials; 5 newspapers. **Services:** Interlibrary loans; copying; SDI; library open to outside users in a professional capacity. **Publications:** Accessions list, bimonthly.

★1644★

BRITISH COLUMBIA RESEARCH COUNCIL - URANIUM INFORMATION CENTRE (Sci-Tech)
3650 Wesbrook Mall   Phone: (604) 224-4331
Vancouver, BC, Canada V6S 2L2   Viona Coates, Res.Libn.
Staff: Prof 1; Other 1. **Subjects:** Uranium - environmental impact,

exploration, waste disposal, mining and milling, occupational health and safety. **Special Collections:** Royal Commission of Inquiry into Health and Environmental Protection in Uranium Mining. **Holdings:** 2800 books; 49 bound periodical volumes; 533 exhibits; 15 video cassettes; 74 transcripts; 300 microfiche. **Subscriptions:** 20 journals and other serials. **Services:** Interlibrary loans; copying; library open to public. **Computerized Information Services:** DIALOG, SDC, CAN/OLE, QL Systems. **Publications:** Accessions List, quarterly. **Special Indexes:** Uranium Index.

★1645★
BRITISH COLUMBIA RESOURCES INVESTMENT CORPORATION - CORPORATE INFORMATION CENTER (Energy; Bus-Fin)
2600-1177 W. Hastings St.   Phone: (604) 687-2600
Vancouver, BC, Canada V6E 4B9   Abha Goomar, Corp.Info.Asst.
Staff: 1. **Subjects:** Coal, energy, management. **Holdings:** 400 books; 100 bound periodical volumes; 500 company files; information for 200 companies on microfiche. **Subscriptions:** 110 journals and other serials; 10 newspapers. **Services:** Interlibrary loans; copying; library not open to public. **Computerized Information Services:** Info Globe, Dow Jones News Retrieval, SDC, DIALOG, QL Systems, CAN/OLE.

★1646★
BRITISH COLUMBIA TEACHERS' FEDERATION - RESOURCES CENTRE (Educ)
2235 Burrard St.   Phone: (604) 731-8121
Vancouver, BC, Canada V6J 3H9   Teresa M. Murphy, Libn.
Founded: 1966. **Staff:** Prof 2; Other 2. **Subjects:** Education, labour, law, psychology. **Holdings:** 9000 books; 700 unbound periodicals; films; tapes; kits. **Subscriptions:** 704 journals and other serials. **Services:** Interlibrary loans; copying; centre open to members of Central Vancouver Library Group. **Networks/Consortia:** Member of Central Vancouver Library Group. **Special Catalogs:** AV catalogs, annual. **Staff:** Alice Wong, Libn.

★1647★
BRITISH COLUMBIA TELEPHONE COMPANY - BUSINESS LIBRARY (Bus-Fin; Sci-Tech)
3777 Kingsway, 5th Fl.   Phone: (604) 432-2671
Burnaby, BC, Canada V5H 3Z7   Elizabeth B. Murray, Libn.
Founded: 1948. **Staff:** 4. **Subjects:** Telephony, electronics, public relations, business. **Holdings:** 2000 books and bound periodical volumes; 20 VF drawers of clippings; 22,360 pamphlets. **Subscriptions:** 200 journals and other serials; 20 newspapers. **Services:** Interlibrary loans; library not open to public. **Computerized Information Services:** DIALOG, SDC; computerized cataloging. **Networks/Consortia:** Member of British Columbia Union Catalogue Project; Vancouver On-Line Users Group. **Special Catalogs:** COM Book Catalogue. **Special Indexes:** COM Pamphlet Index; British Columbia Telephone News Index. **Staff:** Myron B. Patterson, Lib.Res.

★1648★
BRITISH COLUMBIA UTILITIES COMMISSION - LIBRARY (Energy)
2100-1177 W. Hastings St.   Phone: (604) 689-1831
Vancouver, BC, Canada V6E 2L3   C. Brian Tu, Mgr., Info.Serv.
Founded: 1973. **Staff:** Prof 1; Other 1. **Subjects:** Energy, economics, accounting, engineering, regulation, utilities. **Holdings:** 2000 books; 1000 vertical files (cataloged); hearing documents. **Subscriptions:** 175 journals and other serials. **Services:** Interlibrary loans; copying; library open to public for reference use only. **Networks/Consortia:** Member of Central Vancouver Librarians Group. **Publications:** Accessions list; duplication list; periodical list. **Special Indexes:** Index to selected hearing transcripts.

★1649★
BRITISH COLUMBIA - WORKER'S COMPENSATION BOARD - LIBRARY (Med; Law)
5255 Heather St.   Phone: (604) 266-0211
Vancouver, BC, Canada V5Z 3L8   Barbara L. Sanderson, Libn.
Staff: Prof 2; Other 3. **Subjects:** Industrial hygiene and medicine; worker's compensation law; accident prevention; first aid and safety training; rehabilitation of the industrially injured. **Holdings:** 11,000 books; 600 bound periodical volumes; 1500 government publications. **Subscriptions:** 950 journals and other serials; 8 newspapers. **Services:** Interlibrary loans; copying; library open to public for bona fide research only.

★1650★
BRITISH COLUMBIA AND YUKON CHAMBER OF MINES - LIBRARY (Sci-Tech; Bus-Fin)
840 W. Hastings St.   Phone: (604) 681-5328
Vancouver, BC, Canada V6C 1C8   Jack M. Patterson, Mgr.
Staff: 1. **Subjects:** Geology and economics of British Columbia and Yukon Territory; geology of Alaska; minerals and markets. **Holdings:** 3000 volumes

of bound and unbound periodicals, journals and government publications; company, mineral and map files. **Subscriptions:** 19 journals and other serials. **Services:** Copying; library open to public. **Remarks:** Library maintained primarily for prospectors and interested public.

★1651★
BRITISH CONSULATE-GENERAL - LIBRARY (Area-Ethnic)
120 Montgomery St.   Phone: (415) 981-3030
San Francisco, CA 94104   Teresa Perrett, Libn.
Founded: 1946. **Staff:** Prof 2. **Subjects:** British education, government, politics, economy, journals, social services, trade statistics, newspapers and history. **Holdings:** 200 books; 50 reference pamphlets; Government Command Papers. **Services:** Library open to public for reference use only.

★1652★
BRITISH INFORMATION SERVICES - LIBRARY (Area-Ethnic)
845 Third Ave.   Phone: (212) 752-8400
New York, NY 10022   Margaret J. Gale, Libn.
Founded: 1942. **Subjects:** British affairs - economics, education, foreign affairs, industry and trade, social services. **Holdings:** 2000 books; 10,000 British government documents; 2000 clipping files. **Services:** Interlibrary loans; copying; library not open to public.

BRITTAIN LIBRARY
See: First United Presbyterian Church of the Covenant

BRITTINGHAM (Harold H.) MEMORIAL LIBRARY
See: Cleveland Metropolitan General Hospital - Harold H. Brittingham Memorial Library

BROAD (Robert) MEDICAL LIBRARY
See: Tompkins Community Hospital - Robert Broad Medical Library

BROADCAST FOUNDATION OF AMERICA
See: Syracuse University - E.S. Bird Library - Media Services Department

★1653★
BROADCAST PIONEERS LIBRARY (Hist)
1771 N St., N.W.   Phone: (202) 223-0088
Washington, DC 20036   Catharine Heinz, Dir.
Founded: 1971. **Staff:** Prof 1; Other 1. **Subjects:** Radio and television broadcasting history. **Special Collections:** William S. Hedges Collection (12,000 items); Elmo Neale Pickerill Collection (1610 items); Federal Communications Bar Association Archive (343 items); Mrs. Alois Havrilla Photo Collection; St. Louis Post-Dispatch Photo Collection; Phillips Carlin scrapbooks; John Fitzgerald scrapbooks; Joseph E. Baudino Collection (480 items); Rod Phillips Children's Books Collection (193 volumes); Group W Collection (Washington News Bureau Archive; 2300 items). **Holdings:** 4500 books; 1300 bound periodical volumes; 215 VF drawers and boxes of archives, clippings, research studies, scripts, scrapbooks, documents and correspondence; 1463 AV tapes; 700 oral histories; 850 audiotapes; 20,000 photographs; 1500 subject files. **Subscriptions:** 24 journals and other serials. **Services:** Copying; microfilm information retrieval system; library open to public by appointment. **Publications:** Newsletter, irregular. **Special Catalogs:** Radio and Television Program Sources. **Staff:** Diana Hanson, Asst. to Dir.

BROADHURST (William) LIBRARY
See: Nazarene Theological Seminary - William Broadhurst Library

★1654★
BROADLAWNS MEDICAL CENTER - HEALTH SCIENCES LIBRARY (Med)
18th & Hickman Rd.   Phone: (515) 282-2200
Des Moines, IA 50314   Charles Z. Hughes, Libn.
Staff: Prof 1. **Subjects:** Medicine, nursing. **Holdings:** 800 books. **Subscriptions:** 90 journals and other serials. **Services:** Interlibrary loans; copying; library not open to public. **Networks/Consortia:** Member of Polk County Biomedical Consortium; Midwest Health Science Library Network (MHSLN).

★1655★
BROADVIEW DEVELOPMENTAL CENTER - REGIONAL STAFF LIBRARY (Med)
9543 Broadview Rd.   Phone: (216) 526-5000
Broadview Heights, OH 44147   Noreen M. Kenney, Regional Staff Libn.
Staff: Prof 1. **Subjects:** Mental retardation, special education, rehabilitation, infant development. **Holdings:** 1600 books. **Subscriptions:** 10 journals and other serials. **Services:** Interlibrary loans (limited); copying; library open to public with prior approval from superintendent.

★1656★
BROBECK, PHLEGER & HARRISON - LIBRARY (Bus-Fin; Law)
1 Market Plaza
Spear St. Tower   Phone: (415) 442-1054
San Francisco, CA 94105   Alice McKenzie, Libn.
Staff: Prof 2; Other 2. **Subjects:** Law and business. **Holdings:** 30,000 books;
2000 bound periodical volumes; 4 VF drawers. **Subscriptions:** 80 journals
and other serials; 12 newspapers. **Services:** Interlibrary loans (limited); library
not open to public. **Computerized Information Services:** DIALOG, New York
Times Information Service, LEXIS, NEXIS, RLIN. **Networks/Consortia:**
Member of San Francisco Law Librarians; CLASS. **Publications:** Library
newsletter, monthly. **Staff:** Alan R. MacDougall, Asst.Libn.

BROCK (Benjamin L.) MEDICAL LIBRARY
See: Holley (A.G.) State Hospital - Benjamin L. Brock Medical Library

★1657★
BROCK UNIVERSITY - DEPARTMENT OF GEOGRAPHY - MAP LIBRARY
   (Geog-Map)
Decew Campus   Phone: (416) 688-5550
St. Catharines, ON, Canada L2S 3A1   Olga Slachta, Map Libn.
Founded: 1965. **Staff:** 1. **Subjects:** Topography, cartography, aerial
photography, geography. **Holdings:** 40,000 maps; 14,000 aerial photographs;
300 atlases. **Subscriptions:** 30 journals and other serials. **Services:**
Interlibrary loans; copying; library open to public.

BROCKENBROUGH (Eleanor S.) LIBRARY
See: Confederate Memorial Literary Society - Museum of the
   Confederacy - Eleanor S. Brockenbrough Library

BROCKMAN (Robert J.) MEMORIAL LIBRARY
See: Bliss (Malcolm) Mental Health Center - Robert J. Brockman Memorial
   Library

★1658★
BROCKTON ART MUSEUM - FULLER MEMORIAL LIBRARY (Art)
Oak St. on Upper Porters Pond   Phone: (617) 588-6000
Brockton, MA 02140   Andrea C. DesJardins, Lib.Cons.
Staff: Prof 1. **Subjects:** American art. **Holdings:** 1600 books; 6 VF drawers
of annual reports, pamphlets, clippings, artist file. **Subscriptions:** 8 journals
and other serials. **Services:** Library open to members and staff.

★1659★
BROCKTON DAILY ENTERPRISE AND BROCKTON TIMES-ENTERPRISE -
   LIBRARY (Publ)†
60 Main St.   Phone: (617) 586-6200
Brockton, MA 02401   Bernice W. Johnson, Hd.Libn.
Founded: 1880. **Staff:** Prof 1; Other 1. **Subjects:** History of Brockton and
southeastern Massachusetts. **Holdings:** 316 VF drawers of clippings;
microfilm. **Services:** Library not open to public.

★1660★
BROCKTON HOSPITAL - LIBRARY (Med)
680 Centre St.   Phone: (617) 586-2600
Brockton, MA 02402   Lovisa Kamenoff, Mgr., Lib.Serv.
Staff: Prof 1; Other 4. **Subjects:** Medicine, nursing, hospital administration.
Holdings: 2222 books; 4499 bound periodical volumes; 13 VF drawers of
medical bibliographies. **Subscriptions:** 259 journals and other serials.
Services: Interlibrary loans; copying; literature searching; library open to
public for reference use only. **Networks/Consortia:** Member of Southeast
Massachusetts Consortium of Health Science Libraries (SEMCO);
Massachusetts Health Sciences Library Network (MAHSLIN). **Staff:** Diane
Wallace, Asst.Libn.

BROCKTON LAW LIBRARY
See: Plymouth County Law Library Association

★1661★
BROCKWAY GLASS COMPANY, INC. - ENGINEERING AND RESEARCH
   CENTER LIBRARY (Sci-Tech)
Engineering & Research Ctr.   Phone: (814) 261-5275
Brockway, PA 15824   Ed McKinley
Subjects: Glass and plastic technology, engineering, chemistry, physics,
mathematics. **Holdings:** 2200 books; 350 bound periodical volumes;
pamphlets and patents (cataloged). **Subscriptions:** 50 journals and other
serials. **Services:** Library not open to public.

★1662★
BRODART, INC. - REFERENCE LIBRARY (Info Sci)
1609 Memorial Ave.   Phone: (717) 326-2461
Williamsport, PA 17705   Richard A. Russell, Libn.
Founded: 1958. **Staff:** Prof 1; Other 1. **Subjects:** Library science, technical
processing and services in libraries. **Holdings:** 550 books and bound periodical
volumes; 5 VF drawers of pamphlet material; films and filmstrips.
Subscriptions: 15 journals and other serials. **Services:** Interlibrary loans;
copying; library open to qualified adults.

BROEKER (Bernard D.) LAW LIBRARY
See: Bethlehem Steel Corporation - Bernard D. Broeker Law Library

★1663★
BROME COUNTY HISTORICAL SOCIETY - ARCHIVES (Hist)
P.O. Box 690   Phone: (514) 243-6782
Knowlton, PQ, Canada J0E 1V0   Marion L. Phelps, Cur. & Archv.
Founded: 1897. **Staff:** Prof 2. **Subjects:** Eastern Townships history; World
War I. **Special Collections:** McCorkill-Allsopp Journals and Papers; Pioneer
Papers; Hon. Christopher Dunkin File; Hon. Sydney Fisher File. **Holdings:** 2012
volumes; 12 drawers of subject, personages and genealogical files;
directories, documents, local newspapers. **Services:** Copying; archives open
to public for reference use only, by appointment only from September 1 to
June 1. **Special Catalogs:** Pioneer Papers catalog; card index for Eastern
Township books; finding aids for documents and papers.

BRONCK MUSEUM LIBRARY
See: Greene County Historical Society - Vedder Memorial Library

★1664★
BRONSON METHODIST HOSPITAL - HEALTH SCIENCES LIBRARY (Med)
252 Lovell St., E.   Phone: (616) 383-6318
Kalamazoo, MI 49007   Jeanne L. Hartenstein, Dir., Lib.Serv.
Founded: 1947. **Staff:** Prof 3; Other 1. **Subjects:** Medicine, nursing and
allied health sciences. **Holdings:** 9500 volumes; 12 VF drawers of information
files. **Subscriptions:** 345 journals and other serials. **Services:** Interlibrary
loans; copying; SDI; library open to public with restrictions. **Computerized
Information Services:** NLM. **Networks/Consortia:** Member of Kalamazoo Et
Al (KETAL); Michigan Area Serial Holdings Consortium (MASH). **Staff:** Clare
Hike, Asst.Libn.; Patricia Lang, Libn.

★1665★
BRONSON (Silas) LIBRARY - BUSINESS, INDUSTRY, AND TECHNOLOGY
   DEPARTMENT (Bus-Fin; Sci-Tech)
267 Grand St.   Phone: (203) 574-8233
Waterbury, CT 06702   Blanche T. Clark, Dept.Hd.
Founded: 1917. **Staff:** Prof 3. **Subjects:** Business, industry, technology.
Subscriptions: 285 journals and other serials. **Services:** Interlibrary loans;
copying; library open to public. **Computerized Information Services:**
DIALOG; computerized cataloging and circulation. **Remarks:** This is a U.S. and
Connecticut State Depository Library. **Staff:** Michael De Leo; Ellen Gambini .

★1666★
BRONX COUNTY BAR ASSOCIATION - LAW LIBRARY (Law)†
851 Grand Concourse   Phone: (212) 293-5600
Bronx, NY 10451
Founded: 1902. **Subjects:** Law. **Holdings:** 10,000 volumes. **Services:**
Library open only to members of the Bar.

★1667★
BRONX COUNTY HISTORICAL SOCIETY - LIBRARY (Hist)
3266 Bainbridge Ave.   Phone: (212) 881-8900
Bronx, NY 10467   Laura Tosi, Lib.Assoc.
Founded: 1955. **Staff:** Prof 3; Other 5. **Subjects:** Bronx and New York City
history. **Special Collections:** Complete run of the Bronx Home News, 1907-
1948 (hard copy and microfilm); County Archives; MacCracken Papers; R. Hoe
and Company records. **Holdings:** 1200 books; 50 bound periodical volumes;
current Bronx newspapers; photographs, maps, manuscripts, slides, microfilm.
Subscriptions: 20 journals and other serials; 12 newspapers. **Services:**
Copying; library open to public by appointment. **Publications:** List of
publications - available on request. **Special Indexes:** Index to Bronx County
Historical Journal (annual, distributed to members); index and obituary index to
Bronx Home News (in progress); two W.P.A. indexes to archives.

BRONX CRIMINAL-FAMILY COURT - LIBRARY
See: New York State Office of Court Administration

★1668★

BRONX-LEBANON HOSPITAL CENTER - CONCOURSE DIVISION MEDICAL LIBRARY (Med)
1650 Grand Concourse
Bronx, NY 10457
Phone: (212) 588-7000
Gerardo Gomez, Libn.
Founded: 1910. **Staff:** 2. **Subjects:** Medicine and related fields. **Holdings:** 1200 books; 3918 bound periodical volumes. **Subscriptions:** 130 journals and other serials. **Services:** Interlibrary loans; copying; library not open to public. **Networks/Consortia:** Member of Medical Library Center of New York (MLCNY). **Remarks:** Contains the holdings of its former Fulton Division Medical Library.

★1669★

BRONX-LEBANON HOSPITAL CENTER - FULTON DIVISION MEDICAL LIBRARY
1276 Fulton Ave., 169th St.
Bronx, NY 10456
Defunct. Holdings absorbed by Bronx-Lebanon Hospital Center - Concourse Division Medical Library.

BRONX MUNICIPAL HOSPITAL CENTER
See: Yeshiva University - Albert Einstein College of Medicine - Dept. of Psychiatry - J. Thompson Psychiatry Library

★1670★

BROOK LANE PSYCHIATRIC CENTER - MEDICAL LIBRARY (Med)
Box 1945
Hagerstown, MD 21740
Phone: (301) 733-0330
Staff: 1. **Subjects:** Psychiatry, child psychiatry, social work, psychiatric nursing. **Holdings:** 700 books; 5 other items. **Subscriptions:** 48 journals and other serials. **Services:** Interlibrary loans; library open to public with restrictions.

★1671★

BROOKDALE HOSPITAL MEDICAL CENTER - MARIE SMITH SCHWARTZ MEDICAL LIBRARY (Med)
Linden Blvd. & Rockaway Pkwy.
Brooklyn, NY 11212
Phone: (212) 240-5312
Sophie Winston, Chf.Med.Libn.
Staff: Prof 1; Other 3. **Subjects:** Medicine, health sciences, nursing. **Holdings:** 3000 books; 12,000 bound periodical volumes; 50 audiotapes; 40 slide programs; 80 videotapes. **Subscriptions:** 340 journals and other serials. **Services:** Interlibrary loans; library not open to public. **Computerized Information Services:** MEDLINE. **Networks/Consortia:** Member of Medical Library Center of New York (MLCNY).

BROOKE ARMY MEDICAL CENTER
See: U.S. Army Hospitals

BROOKE (Dr. H.H.W.) MEMORIAL LIBRARY
See: Burnaby General Hospital - Dr. H.H.W. Brooke Memorial Library

BROOKENS LIBRARY
See: Sangamon State University - Oral History Office

BROOKFIELD ZOO
See: Chicago Zoological Park

★1672★

BROOKGREEN GARDENS - LIBRARY (Sci-Tech)
Phone: (803) 237-4218
Murrells Inlet, SC 29576
G.L. Tarbox, Jr., Dir.
Staff: Prof 2. **Subjects:** Plant taxonomy, horticulture, sculpture, zoology, South Carolina history. **Holdings:** 1833 books; 100 bound periodical volumes; 1200 newspaper clippings; 10,000 slides; 1600 photographs. **Subscriptions:** 72 journals and other serials. **Services:** Library not open to public. **Publications:** Brookgreen Bulletin, quarterly. **Remarks:** Maintained by the Society for Southeastern Flora and Fauna. **Staff:** R.R. Salmon, Archv.

★1673★

BROOKHAVEN MEMORIAL HOSPITAL MEDICAL CENTER - MEDICAL LIBRARY (Med)
101 Hospital Rd.
Patchogue, NY 11772
Phone: (516) 654-7774
Mrs. Freddie Borock, Med.Libn.
Staff: Prof 1; Other 1. **Subjects:** Medicine, nursing and allied health fields. **Holdings:** 2000 books. **Subscriptions:** 202 journals and other serials. **Services:** Interlibrary loans (fee); copying; SDI; library open to public by appointment. **Computerized Information Services:** MEDLARS. **Networks/Consortia:** Member of Medical & Scientific Libraries of Long Island (MEDLI); MEDSHARE.

★1674★

BROOKHAVEN NATIONAL LABORATORY - ENERGY SYSTEMS LIBRARY (Energy)
Bldg. 475
Upton, NY 11973
Phone: (516) 282-7560
Patricia Aud-Isaacs, Libn.
Staff: Prof 1; Other 1. **Subjects:** Energy - policy, economics, assessments; environmental assessments; regional studies; developing countries; energy models. **Holdings:** 2800 books; 12,000 reports; 900 microfiche. **Subscriptions:** 202 journals and other serials. **Services:** Library open to public by appointment. **Computerized Information Services:** Online systems. **Publications:** ESL Notes, bimonthly - for internal distribution only. **Remarks:** The Brookhaven National Laboratory operates under contract to the U.S. Dept. of Energy.

★1675★

BROOKHAVEN NATIONAL LABORATORY - NATIONAL NUCLEAR DATA CENTER (Energy)
Bldg. 197 D
Upton, NY 11973
Phone: (516) 282-2901
Sol Pearlstein, Dir.
Staff: Prof 22; Other 8. **Subjects:** Neutron data, charged particle data, nuclear structure data, reactor physics data. **Special Collections:** Computerized libraries of evaluated nuclear data. **Holdings:** Figures not available. **Subscriptions:** 50 journals and other serials. **Services:** Interlibrary loans; copying; library open to public by appointment. **Computerized Information Services:** Internal database; computerized cataloging. **Publications:** Newsletter, quarterly; reports. **Special Indexes:** Index to bibliography, irregular. **Remarks:** The Brookhaven National Laboratory operates under contract to the U.S. Dept. of Energy.

★1676★

BROOKHAVEN NATIONAL LABORATORY - NUCLEAR SAFEGUARDS LIBRARY (Sci-Tech)
Bldg. 197C
Upton, NY 11973
Phone: (516) 282-2909
Donna M. Albertus, Libn.
Staff: Prof 1; Other 2. **Subjects:** Nuclear safeguards and nonproliferation. **Holdings:** 1800 books; 6400 reports. **Subscriptions:** 30 journals and other serials. **Services:** Interlibrary loans; copying; SDI; library open to public by appointment. **Computerized Information Services:** Lockheed, BRS, DOE/RECON; computerized cataloging (books only). **Networks/Consortia:** Member of Long Island Library Resources Council (LILRC). **Publications:** Library acquisitions newsletter, weekly - to selected recipients. **Special Indexes:** Keyword index for the field of nuclear safeguards (book). **Remarks:** The Brookhaven National Laboratory operates under contract to the U.S. Dept. of Energy.

★1677★

BROOKHAVEN NATIONAL LABORATORY - NUCLEAR WASTE MANAGEMENT LIBRARY (Sci-Tech)
Bldg. 830
Upton, NY 11973
Phone: (516) 282-7159
Sandra G. Lane, Sr.Libn.
Founded: 1980. **Staff:** Prof 1; Other 1. **Subjects:** Nuclear waste management, metals, corrosion, polymers and plastics, chelates, chemistry. **Special Collections:** Nuclear waste management. **Holdings:** 2600 books; 7000 bound reports; 300 unbound reports; 400 microfiche; 100 patents. **Subscriptions:** 72 journals and other serials. **Services:** Interlibrary loans; copying; library open to public by appointment. **Computerized Information Services:** DIALOG, DOE/RECON; internal database; computerized cataloging and acquisitions. **Publications:** Nuclear Waste Management Library Acquisitions Memo, 2/week - for internal distribution only. **Remarks:** The Brookhaven National Laboratory operates under contract to the U.S. Dept. of Energy.

★1678★

BROOKHAVEN NATIONAL LABORATORY - TECHNICAL INFORMATION DIVISION (Energy)
Phone: (516) 282-3489
Upton, NY 11973
Ken Ryan, Mgr., Tech.Info.Div.
Founded: 1947. **Staff:** Prof 12; Other 9. **Subjects:** Physics, chemistry, mathematics, biology, medicine, environment, energy, instrumentation, nuclear science and engineering. **Special Collections:** U.S. Department of Energy contractor reports; Environmental R&D administrative reports. **Holdings:** 35,000 books; 65,000 bound periodical volumes; 200,000 reports; 350,000 reports on microfiche. **Subscriptions:** 900 journals and other serials. **Services:** Interlibrary loans; library open to public by permission. **Computerized Information Services:** DIALOG, SDC, BRS, NLM, DOE/RECON; computerized serials. **Networks/Consortia:** Member of Long Island Library Resources Council. **Publications:** Monthly Acquisition List. **Remarks:** Brookhaven National Laboratory operates under contract to the U.S. Department of Energy. **Staff:** Marilyn Galli, Res.Lib.Adm.; Rosemary Cohen,

Hd., Tech.Serv.Br.; Judy Liu, Hd., Ref.Sect.; Doris Alkes, Hd., Acq.Sect.; Madeline Windsor, Hd., Rpts.Sect.; Carol Beckner, Hd., Access Serv.Sect.; Broni Orlowski, Hd., BNL Rpts.Sect.

★1679★
BROOKINGS INSTITUTION - LIBRARY (Soc Sci)
1775 Massachusetts Ave., N.W.   Phone: (202) 797-6240
Washington, DC 20036   Laura Walker, Libn.
Founded: 1927. **Staff:** Prof 5; Other 6. **Subjects:** Economics, political science, governmental studies, international relations. **Holdings:** 60,000 volumes; 60 VF drawers of pamphlets and government documents. **Subscriptions:** 550 journals and other serials. **Services:** Interlibrary loans; library not open to public. **Computerized Information Services:** DIALOG, SDC, New York Times Information Service. **Publications:** Books Added to Library and Selected Titles of Articles in Periodicals, biweekly - mimeographed lists distributed to Brookings' staff only. **Remarks:** Maintains the library of the Resources for the Future, Inc. **Staff:** Susan McGrath, Ref.Libn.; Marian Carroll, Cat.; Minnie Sue Ripy, Cat.; Nancy Barry, Acq./Per.Libn.

★1680★
BROOKLINE HOSPITAL - MEDICAL LIBRARY (Med)
165 Chestnut St.   Phone: (617) 734-1330
Brookline, MA 02146   Carole Foxman, Med.Libn.
Founded: 1959. **Staff:** Prof 1. **Subjects:** Medicine, biosciences. **Holdings:** 325 books; 500 bound periodical volumes; 15 indices and service publications; 2 file boxes of pamphlets; tapes. **Subscriptions:** 40 journals and other serials. **Services:** Interlibrary loans; copying; library open to community medical and paramedical personnel. **Publications:** Acquisitions and journal lists, semiannual - for internal distribution only.

★1681★
BROOKLYN BAR ASSOCIATION FOUNDATION, INC. - LIBRARY (Law)†
123 Remsen St.
Brooklyn, NY 11201
Staff: Prof 1. **Subjects:** Law. **Holdings:** 15,000 volumes. **Services:** Library not open to public.

★1682★
BROOKLYN BOTANIC GARDEN - LIBRARY (Sci-Tech)
1000 Washington Ave.   Phone: (212) 622-4433
Brooklyn, NY 11225   Brenda Weisman, Dir., Info.Serv.
Founded: 1911. **Staff:** Prof 2; Other 1. **Subjects:** Horticulture, botany. **Holdings:** 55,000 volumes. **Subscriptions:** 400 journals and other serials. **Services:** Library open to public for reference use only. **Staff:** Marie Giasi, Libn.

★1683★
BROOKLYN CHILDREN'S MUSEUM - CHILDREN'S RESOURCE LIBRARY (Educ)
145 Brooklyn Ave.   Phone: (212) 735-4400
Brooklyn, NY 11213   Susan J. Pober, Libn.
Founded: 1899. **Staff:** Prof 1. **Subjects:** Children's books - natural and cultural history, science and technology, folktales. **Holdings:** 1000 books. **Services:** Library open to children only, ages 6-14. **Publications:** B.C.M. Gazette (written by children), bimonthly - free upon request.

★1684★
BROOKLYN CHILDREN'S MUSEUM - STAFF RESEARCH LIBRARY (Hist)
145 Brooklyn Ave.   Phone: (212) 735-4400
Brooklyn, NY 11213   Cindy Schofield-Bodt, Staff Libn.
Founded: 1899. **Staff:** Prof 1. **Subjects:** Anthropology, history, arts and crafts, sciences, natural history. **Special Collections:** The Brooklyn Children's Museum Archives, 1899-1975. **Holdings:** 5000 books; 260 bound periodical volumes; pamphlets (uncataloged); maps; atlases; photographs. **Services:** Library open to public by appointment.

★1685★
BROOKLYN COLLEGE OF THE CITY UNIVERSITY OF NEW YORK - MUSIC LIBRARY (Mus)
417 Gershwin Hall   Phone: (212) 780-5289
Brooklyn, NY 11210   Prof. Dee Baily, Music Libn.
Founded: 1954. **Staff:** Prof 1; Other 3. **Subjects:** Music. **Special Collections:** Musical Festschriften, unpublished musicological translations; American music; Brooklyn College music theses; theoretical treatises. **Holdings:** 18,500 volumes; 4700 bound periodical volumes; 36,500 scores (cataloged); 17,500 phonograph records (cataloged); 12 VF drawers of clippings, pamphlets, libretti and program notes; 1000 reels of microfilm; octavo scores. **Subscriptions:** 140 journals and other serials. **Services:** Interlibrary loans; library open to public. **Computerized Information**

Services: DIALOG, BRS; computerized cataloging and serials. **Networks/Consortia:** Member of METRO. **Special Indexes:** AMS-MLA Translation Center Depository; computerized Union List of City University music periodicals; alphabetical listing of all chants in Liber Usualis (35 pages) - for sale.

★1686★
BROOKLYN DAILY LIBRARY (Publ)
338 3rd Ave.   Phone: (212) 858-3300
Brooklyn, NY 11215   Lionel Klass, Ed. & Libn.
Founded: 1950. **Staff:** Prof 1. **Subjects:** Newspaper reference topics. **Holdings:** Photographs; engravings; pictures of notables. **Services:** Library not open to public. **Remarks:** Merged with the Jewish Press.

★1687★
BROOKLYN HOSPITAL - MEDICAL LIBRARY (Med)†
121 DeKalb Ave.   Phone: (212) 270-4367
Brooklyn, NY 11201   Saul Kuchinsky, Libn.
Founded: 1935. **Staff:** Prof 1. **Subjects:** Medicine and medical specialities. **Holdings:** 1500 books; 6000 bound periodical volumes; 250 AV cassettes. **Subscriptions:** 120 journals and other serials. **Services:** Interlibrary loans; copying; library not open to public.

★1688★
BROOKLYN LAW SCHOOL - LAW LIBRARY (Law)
250 Joralemon St.   Phone: (212) 780-7974
Brooklyn, NY 11201   Charlotte L. Levy, Libn.
Founded: 1902. **Staff:** Prof 7; Other 15. **Subjects:** Law. **Holdings:** 160,000 volumes; 42,000 microforms. **Subscriptions:** 3546 journals. **Services:** Interlibrary loans; library open to Brooklyn Law School students and graduates. **Computerized Information Services:** LEXIS, WESTLAW; computerized cataloging. **Publications:** Brooklyn School Library Handbook, 1982. **Staff:** Linda Holmes, Asst.Libn.; James Gordon, Ref.Libn.; Lucienne Yoshinaga, Hd., Tech.Serv.; Mary Morrison, Cat.

★1689★
BROOKLYN MUSEUM - ART REFERENCE LIBRARY (Art)
188 Eastern Pkwy.   Phone: (212) 638-5000
Brooklyn, NY 11238   Mildred G. Iriberry, Asst.Libn. & Cat.
Founded: 1900. **Staff:** Prof 2; Other 2. **Subjects:** American art, primitive art, decorative arts, prints and drawings, Oriental art, Middle Eastern art, costume. **Special Collections:** American designer sketches (1900-1950). **Holdings:** 85,000 books; 20,000 bound periodical volumes; exhibition catalogs (cataloged); 100 VF drawers of ephemeral materials. **Subscriptions:** 400 journals and other serials. **Services:** Interlibrary loans; copying (both limited); library open to public for reference use by appointment only. **Special Indexes:** Chronological and subject indexes of Brooklyn Museum exhibitions on cards.

★1690★
BROOKLYN MUSEUM - WILBOUR LIBRARY OF EGYPTOLOGY (Art)
188 Eastern Pkwy.   Phone: (212) 638-5000
Brooklyn, NY 11238   Diane Guzman, Libn.
Founded: 1934. **Staff:** Prof 2; Other 1. **Subjects:** Ancient Egyptian art, archaeology, philology, travel in Egypt from antiquity to modern times. **Special Collections:** Egyptological collections of Charles Edwin Wilbour, Carl Richard Lepsius and Georg Steindorff. **Holdings:** 18,000 books; 11,000 bound periodical volumes; 4000 pamphlets (cataloged). **Subscriptions:** 200 journals and other serials. **Services:** Copying; library open to public by appointment. **Publications:** Egyptology Titles published at Heidelberg University, lists acquisitions of the institution.

★1691★
BROOKLYN PUBLIC LIBRARY - ART AND MUSIC DIVISION (Art; Mus)
Grand Army Plaza   Phone: (212) 780-7784
Brooklyn, NY 11238   Sue Sharma, Div.Chf.
Founded: 1941. **Staff:** Prof 5; Other 3. **Subjects:** Art history, architecture, design, photography, music, theater and dance, music scores, recreation and sport. **Special Collections:** Costume (1400 books and 375 bound periodical volumes); chess; art slides (1927). **Holdings:** 130,847 books; 2500 bound periodical volumes; 211 framed reproductions; 87,855 mounted pictures; 6868 sheets of music; 15 VF drawers of pamphlets; 5 VF drawers of artists' exhibition catalogs; framed prints; orchestra parts; microcards. **Subscriptions:** 420 journals and other serials. **Services:** Interlibrary loans; copying; library open to public. **Special Catalogs:** Catalog of orchestra parts (499 works). **Staff:** Richard Keller, Asst.Div.Chf.

★1692★
BROOKLYN PUBLIC LIBRARY - AUDIO VISUAL DIVISION (Aud-Vis)†
Grand Army Plaza
Brooklyn, NY 11238
Phone: (212) 780-7793
Kenneth W. Axthelm, Div.Chf.
Staff: Prof 3; Other 5. **Holdings:** 200 books; 2300 16mm sound films; 150 8mm sound film cartridges; 1690 filmstrips; 14,000 phonodiscs; 185 8mm films; 225 tape cassettes. **Subscriptions:** 45 journals and other serials. **Services:** Films may be borrowed by New York City residents only. **Publications:** Film Catalog. **Staff:** Catherine Grey, Asst.Chf.

★1693★
BROOKLYN PUBLIC LIBRARY - BUSINESS LIBRARY (Bus-Fin)
280 Cadman Plaza W.
Brooklyn, NY 11201
Phone: (212) 780-7800
Sylvia Mechanic, Bus.Libn.
Staff: Prof 9; Other 12. **Subjects:** Accounting, advertising, business management, business procedure, finance, insurance, public relations, real estate, taxation. **Special Collections:** Trade and professional directories; corporation annual and 10K reports; telephone directories (U.S. and foreign); financial and investment services. **Holdings:** 105,000 books; 33,000 microcards; 192,000 microfiche; 12,275 reels of microfilm; 32,000 microprints; 3000 directories; 36 VF drawers of geographic information; 20 VF drawers of business and economic information. **Subscriptions:** 5780 journals and other serials; 18 newspapers. **Services:** Interlibrary loans; self-service copying. **Computerized Information Services:** DIALOG, New York Times Information Service. **Networks/Consortia:** Member of METRO; New York State Interlibrary Loan Network (NYSILL). **Publications:** Service to Business and Industry, monthly (September-June) - free mailing. **Staff:** Dorothy Vogel, Asst.Bus.Libn.

★1694★
BROOKLYN PUBLIC LIBRARY - HISTORY, TRAVEL, RELIGION AND BIOGRAPHY DIVISION (Hist)
Grand Army Plaza
Brooklyn, NY 11238
Phone: (212) 780-7794
Henri Veit, Div.Chf.
Founded: 1941. **Staff:** Prof 6; Other 3. **Subjects:** History, travel, biography, religion. **Special Collections:** Local (Brooklyn) history; Brooklyn Eagle Morgue (210 VF cases); Brooklyn pictures (28 VF drawers); current Brooklyn materials (56 VF drawers); Civil War Collection-Map Collection (65,000 maps). **Holdings:** 240,000 books; 8000 bound periodical volumes; 11 VF cases of pamphlets; 10,000 negatives and prints in Brooklyn picture file. **Subscriptions:** 463 journals and other serials; 70 newspapers. **Services:** Interlibrary loans (except Brooklyn Collection materials); copying (except most Brooklyn Collection materials). **Staff:** Sue Habel, Asst.Div.Chf.

★1695★
BROOKLYN PUBLIC LIBRARY - LANGUAGE AND LITERATURE DIVISION (Hum)
Grand Army Plaza
Brooklyn, NY 11238
Phone: (212) 780-7733
Monte Olenick, Div.Chf.
Founded: 1941. **Staff:** Prof 6; Other 4. **Subjects:** Fiction, literary criticism, foreign languages, poetry, drama, essays, language learning, linguistics, books and libraries, computer science. **Special Collections:** Walt Whitman Collection (various editions plus biography and criticism; 465 items); Thomas Walsh letters and manuscripts; Benjamin De Casseres letters (274); H.L. Mencken letters (138); Puerto Rican Collection (1350 items in Spanish); large print books (2350 titles). **Holdings:** 391,406 books; 21,420 bound periodical volumes; 17,092 reels of microfilm; 100,100 microcards; 2750 microfiche. **Subscriptions:** 1105 journals and other serials; 60 newspapers. **Services:** Interlibrary loans; copying. **Special Indexes:** Index to Black Literature and Criticism. **Staff:** Vernon Jordan, Asst.Div.Chf.; Gaetano Verdini, Foreign Lang.Spec.; John Alfred Avant, Fiction Libn.

★1696★
BROOKLYN PUBLIC LIBRARY - SCIENCE AND INDUSTRY DIVISION (Sci-Tech)
Grand Army Plaza
Brooklyn, NY 11238
Phone: (212) 780-7745
Walter Wolff, Div.Chf.
Staff: Prof 5; Other 3. **Subjects:** Anthropology, automobiles, biology, birds, chemistry, cookery, engineering, geology, mathematics, product technology, radio, standards, television. **Special Collections:** Fire Protection Collection. **Holdings:** 160,000 books; 4700 bound periodical volumes; 40 VF drawers of pamphlets; specifications for chemical patents from July 1, 1952 through 1972. **Subscriptions:** 1000 journals and other serials. **Services:** Interlibrary loans; copying. **Publications:** Service to Business and Industry (published jointly with the Business Library), 10/year - free on request to local libraries, on exchange to others. **Staff:** Martin Leibowitz, Asst.Chf.

★1697★
BROOKLYN PUBLIC LIBRARY - SOCIAL SCIENCE DIVISION (Soc Sci)
Grand Army Plaza
Brooklyn, NY 11238
Phone: (212) 780-7746
Mary Gunning, Div.Chf.
Founded: 1941. **Staff:** Prof 6; Other 5. **Subjects:** Education, philosophy, international affairs, sociology, labor, social welfare, psychology, politics and government, folklore. **Special Collections:** Afro-American history; college histories; comparative folklore (in English); Prohibition; U.S. Government documents (partial depository); United Nations documents and official records. **Holdings:** 165,000 books; 8500 bound periodical volumes; 21 vertical files of pamphlets; 1500 New York City Civil Service examinations - current promotional only. **Subscriptions:** 1100 journals and other serials. **Services:** Interlibrary loans; copying. **Special Catalogs:** Information file; police file; annotated case study file (card); family life file. **Staff:** Leona Karten, Asst.Chf.; Rosemary Mesh, Doc.Libn.

BROOKS AIR FORCE BASE (TX)
See: U.S. Air Force - Human Resources Laboratory

★1698★
BROOKS INSTITUTE OF PHOTOGRAPHY - LIBRARY (Art)
2020 Alameda Padre Serra
Santa Barbara, CA 93103
Phone: (805) 969-2291
James B. Maher, Libn.
Staff: Prof 1; Other 2. **Subjects:** Photography - science, art, technology. **Holdings:** 4990 books; 1000 bound periodical volumes; 2500 pamphlets (cataloged). **Subscriptions:** 115 journals and other serials. **Services:** Library open to public for reference use only. **Remarks:** This library contains holdings of the former Montecito Branch Library. **Staff:** Gail Miller, Circ.Hd.

★1699★
BROOKS MEMORIAL ART GALLERY - LIBRARY (Art)†
Overton Pk.
Memphis, TN 38112
Phone: (901) 726-5266
Letitia B. Proctor, Libn.
Staff: Prof 2. **Subjects:** Art history, artists, decorative arts, printmaking, lithography. **Holdings:** 9000 books; 4000 bound periodical volumes; bulletins (cataloged); museum catalog, reproduction and artist files. **Subscriptions:** 32 journals and other serials. **Services:** Interlibrary loans; library open to public.

★1700★
BROOKS MINERALS, INC. - LIBRARY (Sci-Tech)
8700 W. 14th Ave.
Lakewood, CO 80215
Phone: (303) 232-5955
Lois J. Brooks, Libn.
Staff: Prof 1. **Subjects:** Geology, mining engineering. **Holdings:** 600 books; 100 bound periodical volumes; 100 technical reports; 50 reports on microfiche; 300 topographic maps. **Subscriptions:** 33 journals and other serials. **Services:** Library not open to public.

BROOKS (Walter) LIBRARY
See: New York Institute for the Education of the Blind - Walter Brooks Library

★1701★
BROOKSIDE HOSPITAL - MEDICAL STAFF LIBRARY (Med)
2000 Vale Rd.
San Pablo, CA 94806
Phone: (415) 235-7000
Barbara Dorham, Libn.
Staff: Prof 1. **Subjects:** Medicine. **Holdings:** 500 books. **Subscriptions:** 67 journals and other serials. **Services:** Library open to public for reference use only.

★1702★
BROOME COUNTY HISTORICAL SOCIETY - RESEARCH CENTER - JOSIAH T. NEWCOMB LIBRARY (Hist)
30 Front St.
Binghamton, NY 13905
Phone: (607) 772-0660
Marjory B. Hinman, Libn.
Founded: 1919. **Staff:** 1. **Subjects:** History - Broome County, New York State; genealogy; Northeastern Pennsylvania. **Special Collections:** William Bingham papers (100 pieces); Whitney Family papers (1800 pieces); patent medicine collection; Robert Harpur papers; circus archive; Broome County photographic archive; trade catalogs collection of Broome County firms; The Lacey Architecture Archives (1200 photographs, blueprints, correspondences); Daniel S. Dickinson papers; 1830s to 1860s (Lieutenant Governor and Senator; 150 pieces); J. Stuart Wells Collection (mayor; 217 pieces); Ben F. Sisson Collection (84 pieces); Locy Halsted Collection (245 pieces); William L. Ford Collection (1500 pieces); Uriah Gregory Collection (865 pieces); Dr. A.E. Stillson Collection (461 pieces); David Hotchkiss Family Collection (100 pieces); Richard Juliand land grant papers (125 pieces); Robert Harpur land account books, 1788-1818; Mersereau account book, 1765-1803; almanacs, 1799-1907 (100); 19th century American humor (100 volumes). **Holdings:** 2500 books; 125 bound periodical volumes; 5000

documents (cataloged); 18 VF drawers; personal letters; furnishings. **Services:** Copying; library open to public. **Remarks:** The Broome County Historical Society is a constituent member of Roberson Center for the Arts and Sciences and is housed there.

★1703★
BROTHERS THREE OF MORIARTY - LIBRARY (Rec)
1917 Fort Union Dr.   Phone: (505) 982-2947
Santa Fe, NM 87501   John Bennett Shaw, Owner
Subjects: Sherlock Holmes. **Holdings:** 4500 books; 100 bound periodical volumes; 3000 other cataloged items; 12,000 clippings; 200 games, puzzles and toys; 250 posters and prints. **Services:** Library open to public by appointment. **Remarks:** A private library (said to be the largest such collection) relating to all aspects of Sherlock Holmes.

★1704★
BROUGHTON HOSPITAL - MEDICAL LIBRARY (Med)†
1000 S. Sterling St.   Phone: (704) 433-2303
Morganton, NC 28655   Mary E. Bush, Libn.
Staff: Prof 1. **Subjects:** Psychiatry, psychiatric social work, psychology, child psychiatry, geriatric psychiatry, medicine. **Holdings:** 3100 books; 2000 bound periodical volumes; clippings; archives; publications. **Subscriptions:** 27 journals and other serials. **Services:** Interlibrary loans; copying (limited); library open to public. **Computerized Information Services:** MEDLINE, BRS. **Networks/Consortia:** Member of Northwest Area Health Center Consortium; Unifour Consortium.

BROUGHTON (L.A.) LIBRARY
See: Alberta School for the Deaf

BROUN (Heywood) LIBRARY
See: Newspaper Guild - Heywood Broun Library

★1705★
BROWARD COUNTY HISTORICAL COMMISSION - LIBRARY & ARCHIVES (Hist)*
100-B S. New River Dr., E.   Phone: (305) 765-5872
Fort Lauderdale, FL 33301   Carolyn Kayne, Coord.
Staff: Prof 1; Other 1. **Subjects:** History - local, state and regional. **Special Collections:** L. Clayton Nance Rare Book Collection; pioneer collection. **Holdings:** 600 books; 400 maps; 30 feet of archival material; 85 reels of microfilm. **Subscriptions:** 25 journals and other serials. **Services:** Library open to public. **Publications:** Broward Legacy.

★1706★
BROWARD COUNTY LAW LIBRARY (Law)
444 County Courthouse   Phone: (305) 765-4096
Fort Lauderdale, FL 33301   Jeanne Underhill, Dir.
Staff: Prof 2; Other 3. **Subjects:** Law. **Holdings:** 43,000 volumes. **Services:** Library open to public. **Staff:** Dorothy Brening, Asst.Libn.

★1707★
BROWARD COUNTY PUBLIC SCHOOLS - LEARNING RESOURCES - PROFESSIONAL LIBRARY (Educ)
6650 Griffin Rd.   Phone: (305) 765-6153
Davie, FL 33314   Helen S. Mattison, Educ.Spec., Media
Staff: Prof 2; Other 1. **Subjects:** Education. **Holdings:** 6343 books; 189,328 ERIC microfiche (cataloged); 1012 reels of microfilm; 12 VF drawers of clippings. **Subscriptions:** 155 journals and other serials. **Services:** Interlibrary loans; copying; library open to Broward County residents. **Staff:** Frances Hatfield, Dir.

★1708★
BROWN & BAIN, P.A. - LIBRARY (Law)
222 N. Central   Phone: (602) 257-8777
Phoenix, AZ 85004   Alison Ewing
Staff: Prof 1; Other 2. **Subjects:** Law. **Special Collections:** Antitrust law; American Indian law. **Holdings:** 18,000 books. **Subscriptions:** 350 journals and other serials; 10 newspapers. **Services:** Interlibrary loans; copying; SDI; library open to public by appointment. **Computerized Information Services:** DIALOG, Mead Data Central, Disclosure, Inc., New York Times Information Service. **Networks/Consortia:** Member of Phoenix Area Law Librarians.

★1709★
BROWN BROTHERS HARRIMAN & CO. - RESEARCH LIBRARY (Bus-Fin)
59 Wall St.   Phone: (212) 483-5517
New York, NY 10005   Agnes V. Kelly, Libn.
Staff: Prof 1; Other 4. **Subjects:** Banking, economic and business conditions, finance, investments, corporation records. **Holdings:** 1000 books; 125 bound

periodical volumes; 4000 microfiche files. **Subscriptions:** 400 journals and other serials. **Services:** Interlibrary loans to members of Special Libraries Association.

★1710★
BROWN BROTHERS - PHOTOGRAPH COLLECTION (Pict)
                                                Phone: (717) 689-9688
Sterling, PA 18463   Harry B. Collins, Jr., Pres.
Subjects: Stock photograph collection - news, history, geography. **Holdings:** 8 million photographs; old illustrations; movie stills; color transparencies. **Services:** Photographs available for reproduction on fee basis.

★1711★
BROWN & CALDWELL - LIBRARY (Sci-Tech)
1501 N. Broadway
Box 8045   Phone: (415) 937-9010
Walnut Creek, CA 94596   Bruce Hubbard, Libn.
Staff: Prof 2; Other 1. **Subjects:** Engineering - environmental, mechanical, structural; biological sciences; water resources. **Holdings:** 5000 books; 400 bound periodical volumes; 3000 vendors catalogs (cataloged). **Subscriptions:** 210 journals and other serials. **Services:** Interlibrary loans; library open to public with restrictions. **Computerized Information Services:** DIALOG. **Networks/Consortia:** Member of CLASS. **Publications:** Library Acquisitions. **Staff:** Nerisha Hihn, Libn.

BROWN (Charles Ewing) LIBRARY
See: Gulf Coast Bible College - Charles Ewing Brown Library

★1712★
BROWN COUNTY HISTORICAL SOCIETY - MUSEUM LIBRARY (Hist)
27 N. Broadway
Box 116   Phone: (507) 354-2016
New Ulm, MN 56073   Paul Klammer, Musm.Dir.
Founded: 1930. **Staff:** 2. **Subjects:** Local and regional history. **Special Collections:** Autographed portraits and letters (3000 figures in art, literature, and science, 1890-1925). **Holdings:** 1500 books; Family Record Files, 2500 families; 7 journals. **Services:** Copying; library open with restrictions for limited research and by special arrangement only. **Publications:** Newsnotes, quarterly - for internal distribution only. **Staff:** Darla Schnurrer, Musm.Asst.

★1713★
BROWN COUNTY MENTAL HEALTH CENTER - H.H. HUMPHREY MEMORIAL STAFF LIBRARY (Med)
2900 St. Anthony Dr.   Phone: (414) 468-1136
Green Bay, WI 54301   Nancy Hillen, Lib.Mgr.
Staff: Prof 2. **Subjects:** Psychiatry, psychology, social work, nursing, growth and development. **Holdings:** 1300 books; 100 bound periodical volumes; 100 AV items. **Subscriptions:** 45 journals and other serials. **Services:** Interlibrary loans; copying; library open to public by request.

BROWN (George) COLLEGE OF APPLIED ARTS & TECHNOLOGY
See: George Brown College of Applied Arts & Technology

BROWN (George Warren) SCHOOL OF SOCIAL WORK
See: Washington University - George Warren Brown School of Social Work

BROWN (Herbert C.) ARCHIVES
See: Purdue University - Chemistry Library

BROWN (John Carter) LIBRARY
See: Brown University - John Carter Brown Library

BROWN (John Young) MEMORIAL LIBRARY
See: St. John's Mercy Medical Center - John Young Brown Memorial Library

BROWN (Mary Ellen) MEDICAL CENTER LIBRARY
See: Presbyterian-University of Pennsylvania Medical Center - Mary Ellen Brown Medical Center Library

BROWN (Moses and Obadiah) LIBRARIES
See: Society of Friends - New England Yearly Meeting of Friends - Archives

BROWN (Ray E.) MANAGEMENT COLLECTION
See: American College of Hospital Administrators - Ray E. Brown Management Collection

★1714★
BROWN & ROOT, INC. - TECHNICAL LIBRARY (Sci-Tech)
Box 3   Phone: (713) 676-8693
Houston, TX 77001   Kathy Hubbard, Lib.Supv.
Founded: 1960. **Staff:** Prof 4; Other 4. **Subjects:** Engineering, construction, environmental science, technology. **Holdings:** 21,000 books; 6200 bound periodical volumes; 48 VF drawers of reports, dissertations and documents. **Subscriptions:** 260 journals and other serials. **Services:** Interlibrary loans; copying; library open to public by appointment. **Computerized Information Services:** DIALOG, SDC. **Publications:** Bridge the Gap. **Remarks:** Figures include the holdings of two branch libraries.

★1715★
BROWN UNIVERSITY - ART DEPARTMENT SLIDE ROOM (Art)
Box 1861, List Art Bldg.
64 College St.   Phone: (401) 863-3218
Providence, RI 02912   Norine Duncan Cashman, Cur.
Staff: Prof 2. **Subjects:** Architecture - modern, medieval, Renaissance and Baroque; painting and sculpture - modern, Renaissance and Baroque; Roman and Greek art and architecture. **Holdings:** 145,000 slides; 28,500 photographs; 6000 microfiche. **Services:** Slide room not open to public. **Staff:** Sheila Embury, Assoc.Cur.; Andrea Manzi, Asst.Cur.

★1716★
BROWN UNIVERSITY - JOHN CARTER BROWN LIBRARY (Hist)
Box 1894   Phone: (401) 863-2725
Providence, RI 02912
Founded: 1904. **Staff:** Prof 9; Other 3. **Subjects:** Discovery and exploration of the Americas; political and intellectual history of Europe and the Americas; maritime history; history of science; history of printing. **Special Collections:** American Indian linguistics (books and manuscripts); history of cartography (2000 books); American Revolution (15,000 items); Arnold-Green papers (132 linear feet); Bartlett papers (15 linear feet); Brown papers (681 linear feet). **Holdings:** 54,400 volumes; 3000 bound periodical volumes; 1200 maps; 350 bound volumes of codices; 36 linear feet of manuscripts. **Subscriptions:** 35 journals and other serials. **Services:** Library open to public with identification. **Computerized Information Services:** RLIN; computerized cataloging. **Networks/Consortia:** Member of RLG. **Publications:** Annual Report; exhibition catalogs, 2/year. **Special Catalogs:** Chronological files; imprint file, provenance file, engravers file, dedicatee file (all card). **Staff:** Everett C. Willkie, Jr., Bibliog.; Susan Danforth, Cur. of Maps & Prints; Earl Taylor, Chf., Cat.; Laurence C. Hardy, Adm.Supv.; Richard N. Hurley, Photographer.

★1717★
BROWN UNIVERSITY - POPULATION STUDIES AND TRAINING CENTER - DEMOGRAPHY LIBRARY (Soc Sci)
Sociology Dept., Box 1916   Phone: (401) 863-2668
Providence, RI 02912   Sidney Goldstein, Dir.
Founded: 1965. **Staff:** Prof 1; Other 1. **Subjects:** Population, human ecology, urbanization. **Holdings:** 2700 books; 1200 publications, 3500 reprints (cataloged); World Fertility Survey depository; recoded 1/1000 1960 U.S. Census tapes; Survey of Economic Opportunity tape; 1973 U.S. Census tapes; 1970 U.S. Census tapes; National Longitudinal Survey (Parnes); various KAP and Demographic Survey tapes; census tapes for selected developing countries; 300 foreign census reports; 1970 Canadian Census tapes; NORC general survey tapes, 1972-1978. **Subscriptions:** 61 journals and other serials. **Services:** Library not open to public. **Networks/Consortia:** Member of Association for Population/Family Planning Libraries and Information Centers International (APLIC). **Publications:** Accessions List - for internal distribution only. **Staff:** Joyce B. Coleman, Libn.; Carol L. Knopf, Libn.

★1718★
BROWN UNIVERSITY - SCIENCES LIBRARY (Sci-Tech)
Brown Univ. Library, Box I   Phone: (401) 863-2405
Providence, RI 02912   Ann K. Randall, Asst.Univ.Libn.
Founded: 1971. **Staff:** Prof 7; Other 15. **Subjects:** Health sciences, life sciences, physical sciences, engineering. **Special Collections:** Mathematics. **Holdings:** 300,000 books and bound periodical volumes. **Subscriptions:** 5164 journals and other serials. **Services:** Interlibrary loans (fee); copying; library open to public for bona fide scholarly use only. **Computerized Information Services:** DIALOG, BRS, SDC, MEDLARS; computerized circulation. **Networks/Consortia:** Member of Consortium of Rhode Island Academic and Research Libraries (CRIARL); OCLC through NELINET; New England Regional Medical Library Service; RLG. **Special Catalogs:** Serials Holdings List (microfiche). **Staff:** Ronald Fark, Hd., Circ.; Florence Doksansky, Hd., Ref.; Janet Crager, Biomed.Ref.Libn.; Patricia Galkowski, Phys.Sci.Ref.Libn.; Caroline Helie, Phys.Sci.Ref.Libn.; Betty Heller, Ser.Libn.; Frank Kellerman, Biology/Psych.Ref.Libn.

★1719★
BROWN UNIVERSITY - SPECIAL COLLECTIONS (Hist)
John Hay Library
20 Prospect St.   Phone: (401) 863-2146
Providence, RI 02912   Samuel A. Streit, Asst.Univ.Libn./Spec.Coll
Founded: 1939. **Staff:** Prof 8; Other 12. **Special Collections:** American poetry and plays (500,000 items); military history (5000); Lincoln and John Hay (17,500); American pamphlets (30,000); incunabula (700); Rhode Island history (13,500); Legend of Wandering Jew (1500); Thoreau (450); Whaling (1100); history of science; university archives. **Holdings:** 280,000 volumes; 110,000 historical and literary manuscripts; 40,000 broadsides (chiefly American verse and Lincoln); 40,000 prints, slides, drawings, photographs; 300,000 pieces of American sheet music. **Subscriptions:** 450 journals and other serials. **Services:** Copying; library open to public. **Computerized Information Services:** Computerized cataloging, acquisitions and serials. **Publications:** Books at Brown, annual. **Special Catalogs:** Dictionary Catalog of the Harris Collection of American Poetry and Plays, 1972, First Supplement, 1977; American Poetry 1609-1900 (microfilm). **Staff:** Martha L. Mitchell, Univ.Archv.; Mary T. Russo, Spec.Coll.Libn.; John H. Stanley, Spec.Coll.Libn.; Rosemary L. Cullen, Spec.Coll.Libn.; Jennifer B. Lee, Spec.Coll.Libn.; Mark N. Brown, Spec.Coll.Libn.; Catherine Denning, Cur.

BROWN (Dr. W. Gordon) MEMORIAL LIBRARY
See: Central Baptist Seminary - Dr. W. Gordon Brown Memorial Library

BROWN (W.R.) MEMORIAL LIBRARY
See: Arabian Horse Owners Foundation - W.R. Brown Memorial Library

★1720★
BROWN AND WILLIAMSON TOBACCO CORPORATION - RESEARCH LIBRARY (Sci-Tech)
1600 W. Hill St.
Box 35090   Phone: (502) 774-7683
Louisville, KY 40232   Carol S. Lincoln, Res.Libn.
Founded: 1958. **Staff:** Prof 1; Other 1. **Subjects:** Chemistry, tobacco, agriculture, chemical engineering, physics, statistics. **Holdings:** 3100 books; 3130 bound periodical volumes; 30,000 patents; 7000 company reports; 15 VF drawers of pamphlets and miscellaneous items. **Subscriptions:** 188 journals and other serials. **Services:** Interlibrary loans; copying; library not open to public. **Computerized Information Services:** Reports System - text searching; SDC, NLM. **Publications:** Monthly Accessions List - for internal distribution only.

★1721★
BROWN, WOOD, IVEY, MITCHELL & PETTY - LIBRARY (Law)
One World Trade Center   Phone: (212) 839-5444
New York, NY 10048   Connie L. Kluever, Libn.
Staff: Prof 1; Other 1. **Subjects:** Law. **Holdings:** 15,000 books. **Subscriptions:** 40 journals and other serials. **Services:** Library not open to public.

BROWNELL (Lois) RESEARCH LIBRARY
See: School of the Ozarks - Ralph Foster Museum - Lois Brownell Research Library

★1722★
BROWNING ARMS COMPANY - LIBRARY (Rec)
Route 1
Morgan, UT 84050
Subjects: Firearms, camping, fishing. **Holdings:** 400 books; 500 bound periodical volumes. **Subscriptions:** 12 journals and other serials. **Services:** Library not open to public.

BROWNING (Mc Pherson) MEMORIAL LIBRARY
See: Rehabilitation Institute, Inc. - Mc Pherson Browning Memorial Library

BROWNING MEMORIAL LIBRARY
See: Episcopal Theological Seminary in Kentucky

BRS LIBRARY
See: Bertrand Russell Society, Inc.

★1723★
BRUNDAGE, STORY & ROSE, INVESTMENT COUNSEL - LIBRARY (Bus-Fin)
1 Broadway   Phone: (212) 269-3050
New York, NY 10004   Julie L. Halston, Hd.Libn.
Staff: 2. **Subjects:** Investments, business, economics. **Special Collections:** Moody's Manuals, 1915 to present; Poor's Manual of Railroads; Wall Street

Journal, 1942 to present (microfilm); corporate annual reports. **Holdings:** 1120 books; 300 bound periodical volumes; 5100 company files, including annual and quarterly reports, proxies, prospectuses and 10K reports (both hard copy and microfiche). **Subscriptions:** 195 journals and other serials; 22 newspapers. **Services:** Interlibrary loans; library not open to public. **Staff:** Eileen Carney, Asst.Libn.

★1724★
BRUNSWICK CORPORATION - DEFENSE DIVISION - TECHNICAL LIBRARY (Bus-Fin; Sci-Tech)†
3333 Harbor Blvd.   Phone: (714) 546-8030
Costa Mesa, CA 92626   Clay Zlomke, Dir. of Engr.
Founded: 1962. **Staff:** Prof 1; Other 1. **Subjects:** Business and technical management, aerospace engineering. **Holdings:** 800 books; 7000 technical reports. **Subscriptions:** 100 journals and other serials. **Services:** Library not open to public.

★1725★
BRUNSWICK CORPORATION - MANAGEMENT LIBRARY
One Brunswick Plaza
Skokie, IL 60077
Defunct

★1726★
BRUSH WELLMAN, INC. - TECHNICAL LIBRARY (Sci-Tech)
17876 St. Clair Ave.   Phone: (216) 486-4200
Cleveland, OH 44110   Nancie J. Skonezny, Libn.
Staff: Prof 1; Other 1. **Subjects:** Beryllium metallurgy, metallurgy. **Holdings:** 1000 books; technical reports (uncataloged). **Subscriptions:** 110 journals and other serials. **Services:** Interlibrary loans; library open to public by appointment for on-site research. **Computerized Information Services:** DIALOG, Copper Development Association.

BRUTE LIBRARY
See: Old Cathedral Parish Church

★1727★
BRYAN, CAVE, MC PHEETERS & MC ROBERTS - LIBRARY (Law)
500 N. Broadway   Phone: (314) 231-8600
St. Louis, MO 63102   Rose J. Garrett, Libn.
Staff: Prof 3; Other 1. **Subjects:** American law. **Holdings:** 20,000 books. **Subscriptions:** 200 journals and other serials; 5 newspapers. **Services:** Interlibrary loans (limited); library open to clients. **Computerized Information Services:** LEXIS, New York Times Information Service. **Publications:** Annual report. **Staff:** Pete Sloan-Peterson, Asst.Libn.

★1728★
BRYAN (G. Werber) PSYCHIATRIC HOSPITAL - PROFESSIONAL LIBRARY (Med)
220 Faison Dr.   Phone: (803) 758-4839
Columbia, SC 29203   Virginia S. McEachern, Libn.
Founded: 1978. **Staff:** Prof 1. **Subjects:** Psychiatry, social work, psychology, recreation therapy. **Holdings:** 485 books. **Subscriptions:** 50 journals and other serials. **Services:** Interlibrary loans; copying; library open to Department of Mental Health employees. **Networks/Consortia:** Member of Columbia Medical Librarians Association.

BRYANS (Herbert L.) MEMORIAL LIBRARY
See: University Hospital and Clinic - Herbert L. Bryans Memorial Library

★1729★
BRYANT COLLEGE OF BUSINESS ADMINISTRATION - EDITH M. HODGSON MEMORIAL LIBRARY (Bus-Fin)
          Phone: (401) 231-1200
Smithfield, RI 02917   Dr. John P. Hannon, Dir.
Founded: 1955. **Staff:** Prof 4; Other 6. **Subjects:** Accounting, marketing, management, finance, business education, economics, law enforcement. **Holdings:** 95,000 books; 3700 bound periodical volumes; 6210 reels of microfilm. **Subscriptions:** 1042 journals and other serials; 18 newspapers. **Services:** Interlibrary loans; copying; library open to public. **Computerized Information Services:** Computerized cataloging. **Networks/Consortia:** Member of OCLC through NELINET; Consortium of Rhode Island Academic and Research Libraries (CRIARL); Rhode Island Interrelated Library Network. **Staff:** Connie Cameron, Asst.Libn.; Patrick Kelly, Asst.Libn.; Mary Maroney, Asst.Libn./Tech.Serv.

★1730★
BRYANT LIBRARY - LOCAL HISTORY COLLECTION (Hist)
Paper Mill Rd.   Phone: (516) 621-2240
Roslyn, NY 11576   Anthony M. Cucchiara, Cur.
Staff: Prof 1; Other 2. **Subjects:** Local history, literature. **Special Collections:** Christopher Morley Collection; William Cullen Bryant Collection; Long Island Collection; Roslyn Collection; Mackay Collection; business account books (early 19th century); Architecture Preservation Collection. **Holdings:** 8000 books; 300 bound periodical volumes; 250 local maps (cataloged); 338 Morley manuscripts and correspondence; 10,000 manuscripts, photographs and archives; 35 oral history tapes. **Subscriptions:** 46 journals and other serials. **Services:** Copying; library open to public.

★1731★
BRYANT AND STRATTON BUSINESS INSTITUTE - LIBRARY (Bus-Fin)
1028 Main St.   Phone: (716) 884-9120
Buffalo, NY 14202   Shirley R. Rowland, Media Supv.
Founded: 1854. **Staff:** Prof 1; Other 1. **Subjects:** Word processing, medical and dental assisting, accounting, advertising, business reference, economics, interior design, business correspondence, business education and careers, business psychology, retailing, computers and automation. **Holdings:** 2000 books; 250 corporation reports; 650 pamphlets; shorthand and machine transcription tapes. **Subscriptions:** 120 journals and other serials; 12 newspapers. **Services:** Library not open to public.

★1732★
BRYN MAWR COLLEGE - GEOLOGY LIBRARY (Sci-Tech)
          Phone: (215) 645-5118
Bryn Mawr, PA 19010   Anne Pringle, Hd., Sci. & Psych.Libs.
Founded: 1890. **Staff:** Prof 1; Other 1. **Subjects:** General geology, mineralogy, petrology, structural geology, geochemistry, stratigraphic geology, paleontology. **Special Collections:** U.S. Geological Survey publications and maps; Pennsylvania geologic and topographic publications; Geological Survey of Canada publications; guidebooks of geological societies. **Holdings:** 5475 books; 5800 bound periodical volumes; 12,650 surveys and reports (cataloged); 400 microfiche. **Subscriptions:** 120 journals and other serials. **Services:** Interlibrary loans; copying; library open to public with introduction of faculty member. **Computerized Information Services:** DIALOG, BRS; computerized cataloging. **Networks/Consortia:** Member of OCLC through PALINET & Union Library Catalogue of Pennsylvania.

★1733★
BRYN MAWR HOSPITAL - MEDICAL LIBRARY (Med)
          Phone: (215) 896-3160
Bryn Mawr, PA 19010   L.D. Gundry, Chf.Med.Libn.
Founded: 1893. **Staff:** Prof 2; Other 2. **Subjects:** Medicine, surgery and allied sciences. **Holdings:** 2500 books; 3800 bound periodical volumes. **Subscriptions:** 100 journals and other serials. **Services:** Interlibrary loans; copying; library open to public for reference use only. **Staff:** Alexander Kulchar, Med.Libn.; Helen Lonabaugh, Asst.Med.Libn.; Doris Mohn, Cat.

★1734★
BRYN MAWR HOSPITAL - MEDICAL LIBRARY - NURSING DIVISION (Med)
Lindsay Ave.   Phone: (215) 896-3084
Bryn Mawr, PA 19010   L.D. Gundry, Chf.Med.Libn.
Founded: 1953. **Staff:** Prof 3; Other 1. **Subjects:** Nursing, medicine. **Special Collections:** Nursing (historical). **Holdings:** 3500 books; 1100 bound periodical volumes. **Subscriptions:** 70 journals and other serials. **Services:** Interlibrary loans; copying; library open to public. **Staff:** Alexander Kulchar, Med.Libn.; Helen Lonabaugh, Asst.Med.Libn.; Mary Keating, Asst.Med.Libn.

★1735★
BUCHANAN COUNTY LAW LIBRARY (Law)
Buchanan County Courthouse   Phone: (816) 271-1462
St. Joseph, MO 64501
Staff: 1. **Subjects:** Law. **Holdings:** 50,000 volumes. **Services:** Copying; library open to public for reference use only. **Remarks:** Maintained by St. Joseph Bar Association.

BUCHANAN (James) FOUNDATION FOR THE PRESERVATION OF WHEATLAND
See: James Buchanan Foundation for the Preservation of Wheatland

★1736★
BUCK (Pearl S.) BIRTHPLACE FOUNDATION - LIBRARY (Hum)
Box 126   Phone: (304) 653-4430
Hillsboro, WV 24946   David C. Hyer, Exec.Dir.
Staff: 5. **Subjects:** Works by and about Pearl S. Buck in English and foreign languages. **Special Collections:** Original manuscripts of Pearl S. Buck (323

cataloged). **Holdings:** 500 books; tapes of seminars and various speeches involving Pearl S. Buck. **Services:** Library open to public. **Publications:** Periodical information letters to members of the foundation. **Remarks:** Manuscripts remain stored at West Virginia Wesleyan College, Buckhannon, WV, until suitable storage can be made available at Hillsboro. Manuscripts accessible to general public under specific requirements for care and usage.

BUCKEYE CELLULOSE CORPORATION
See: Procter & Gamble Company

★1737★
BUCKNELL UNIVERSITY - ARCHIVES (Hist)
Phone: (717) 524-1493
Lewisburg, PA 17837   William B. Weist, Univ.Archv.
Staff: Prof 1; Other 1. **Subjects:** Bucknell University history. **Special Collections:** David Jayne Hill Collection, U.S. Diplomatic Corps; university records, publications, papers. **Holdings:** 2500 books; 150 bound periodical volumes; 4000 other cataloged items. **Services:** Interlibrary loans (limited); copying; library open to public for reference use only.

★1738★
BUCKNELL UNIVERSITY - ELLEN CLARKE BERTRAND LIBRARY (Hum)
Phone: (717) 524-1661
Lewisburg, PA 17837   George M. Jenks, Coll.Dev.Libn.
Founded: 1846. **Staff:** Prof 1. **Subjects:** Irish authors. **Special Collections:** Letters and manuscripts of Oliver S. Gogarty (5 linear feet); D.H. Lawrence (5 items); William Bulter Yeats (letters); George Bernard Shaw (5 boxes of letters and pamphlets). **Holdings:** 5000 books and bound periodical volumes; 45 linear feet of manuscripts. **Services:** Interlibrary loans; copying; library open to public for reference use only. **Computerized Information Services:** Computerized cataloging. **Networks/Consortia:** Member of Associated College Libraries of Central Pennsylvania; Susquehanna Library Cooperative; OCLC through PALINET & Union Library Catalogue of Pennsylvania.

★1739★
BUCKS COUNTY COURIER TIMES - LIBRARY (Publ)
8400 Rte. 13   Phone: (215) 752-6877
Levittown, PA 19057   Susan Y. Ditterline, Libn./Supv.
Staff: Prof 1; Other 2. **Subjects:** Newspaper reference topics. **Holdings:** Newspaper clippings, photographs, directories, pamphlets, reference books. **Services:** Interlibrary loans; library open to public with restrictions.

★1740★
BUCKS COUNTY HISTORICAL SOCIETY - SPRUANCE LIBRARY (Hist)†
Pine & Ashland Sts.   Phone: (215) 345-0210
Doylestown, PA 18901   Terry A. McNealy, Lib.Dir.
Founded: 1880. **Staff:** Prof 2; Other 2. **Subjects:** Bucks County history and genealogy; history of crafts and technology. **Special Collections:** Manuscript collections concerned largely with Bucks County and its people; Durham Furnace account books; turnpike records; handwritten school books. **Holdings:** 18,000 volumes; 1000 cubic feet of Bucks County Archives. **Subscriptions:** 30 journals and other serials. **Services:** Copying; library open to public. **Publications:** Bucks County Historical Society Journal, semiannual.

★1741★
BUCKS COUNTY LAW LIBRARY (Law)
Court House   Phone: (215) 348-2911
Doylestown, PA 18901   Katharine P. Lehnig, Law Libn.
Staff: Prof 2; Other 1. **Subjects:** Law. **Holdings:** 22,500 volumes. **Subscriptions:** 124 journals and other serials. **Services:** Interlibrary loans; copying; library open for reference use to Bucks County residents. **Publications:** Newsletter, monthly. **Staff:** Terri Saye, Asst.Libn.

★1742★
BUCKS COUNTY PLANNING COMMISSION STAFF LIBRARY (Plan)
22-28 S. Main St.   Phone: (215) 348-2911
Doylestown, PA 18901   Jeffrey A. Vey, Info.Spec.
Founded: 1951. **Staff:** 2. **Subjects:** Land use planning, water resources management, agricultural preservation, waste water facility planning, demography, transportation planning. **Special Collections:** Bucks County Municipal Documents (300). **Holdings:** 6000 books; 30 bound periodical volumes; 200 pamphlets; 50 microfiche; 100 maps. **Subscriptions:** 70 journals and other serials; 7 newspapers. **Services:** Copying; library open to public for reference use only. **Staff:** John P. Nawyn, Libn.

★1743★
BUDD COMPANY TECHNICAL LIBRARY (Sci-Tech)
375 Commerce Dr.   Phone: (215) 643-2950
Fort Washington, PA 19034   Herbert A. Johnle, Mgr.
Founded: 1962. **Staff:** Prof 1. **Subjects:** Automotive and railroad engineering, metals, polymer chemistry, plastics, welding. **Special Collections:** Budd Company History (8000 photographs); Budd Rail Cars (photographs, 16 VF drawers). **Holdings:** 5300 books; 300 bound periodical volumes; 35 VF drawers of technical documents. **Subscriptions:** 180 journals and other serials. **Services:** Interlibrary loans; library open to public with permission of librarian only. **Computerized Information Services:** DIALOG.

BUDDEN (W.A.) MEMORIAL LIBRARY
See: Western States Chiropractic College - W.A. Budden Memorial Library

★1744★
BUENA VISTA COLLEGE - L.E. & E.L. BALLOU LIBRARY - SPECIAL COLLECTIONS (Educ)
Phone: (712) 749-2141
Storm Lake, IA 50588   Dr. Barbara R. Palling, Hd.Libn.
Founded: 1891. **Special Collections:** Iowa authors' books; curriculum collection; state, local and college history; textbooks; juvenile books. **Services:** Interlibrary loans; copying; library open to public. **Computerized Information Services:** DIALOG; computerized cataloging. **Networks/Consortia:** Member of Colleges of Mid-America, Inc.; Bibliographical Center for Research, Rocky Mountain Region, Inc. (BCR).

BUENGER MEMORIAL LIBRARY
See: Concordia College

★1745★
BUFFALO BILL HISTORICAL CENTER - HAROLD MC CRACKEN RESEARCH LIBRARY (Hist)
Box 1000   Phone: (307) 587-4771
Cody, WY 82414   Michael T. Kelly, Libn./Archv.
Founded: 1927. **Staff:** Prof 1; Other 6. **Subjects:** Western history and art, Plains Indians, firearms, museum administration. **Special Collections:** Buffalo Bill Archives; Valley Ranch manuscript collection; Charles Belden Photo Collection; Mercaldo Photo Archives of Western subjects; photographs of noted Indians, military leaders and Indian campaigns; Winchester Repeating Arms Company archives. **Holdings:** 5000 volumes; 30 volumes of press clippings; motion picture films; 714 reels and 7000 books in the Western Americana microfilm collection; 4 VF drawers of Western artists files. **Subscriptions:** 40 journals and other serials. **Services:** Copying; library open to qualified researchers and museum patrons.

★1746★
BUFFALO BILL MEMORIAL MUSEUM - INFORMATION CENTER (Hist)
Rte. 5, Box 950   Phone: (303) 526-0747
Golden, CO 80401   Stanley W. Zamonski, Cur.
Founded: 1921. **Subjects:** William F. Cody, Old American West. **Holdings:** 300 books; 220 pamphlets; 450 periodicals; 800 documents; 1500 photographs. **Services:** Copying; center open to public on request.

★1747★
BUFFALO COURIER-EXPRESS - LIBRARY (Publ)
795 Main St.   Phone: (716) 855-6583
Buffalo, NY 14240   Cynthia Hayes, Libn.
Staff: 3. **Subjects:** Newspaper reference topics. **Special Collections:** Early Buffalo newspapers on microfilm. **Holdings:** 390 books; 700 reports and government documents; 3 VF drawers of maps. **Services:** Interlibrary loans; copying; library open to public.

★1748★
BUFFALO & ERIE COUNTY HISTORICAL SOCIETY - LIBRARY (Hist)†
25 Nottingham Ct.   Phone: (716) 873-9644
Buffalo, NY 14216   Robert L. Damm, Dir.
Founded: 1862. **Staff:** Prof 11; Other 25. **Subjects:** City of Buffalo, Erie County, Western New York, Niagara Frontier, New York State, United States history (especially military history). **Special Collections:** Manuscript collections of Millard Fillmore; manuscript collections of Peter B. Porter; War of 1812 materials; Grover Cleveland papers (on microfilm); Niagara Falls; Erie Canal; Wilbur Porterfield photographic collection. **Holdings:** 60,000 bound volumes; 50,000 periodicals and ephemera; manuscripts collections of over 500,000 separate items (under supervision of curator of manuscripts); iconographic collections of over 130,000 separate items (under supervision of curator of iconography); large clipping file (indexed); large scrapbook collection (partly indexed); 1030 reels of 35mm microfilm; 300 tapes.

Subscriptions: 100 journals and other serials; 60 newspapers. **Services:** Interlibrary loans; copying; limited staff research for appropriate inquiries; library open to public for reference use only. **Publications:** Niagara Frontier, quarterly; Adventures in Western New York History, irregular; monthly newsletters; Erie County History 1870-1970. **Special Indexes:** All society publications and newspapers received are indexed. **Staff:** Dr. Herman Sass, Ref.Libn.; Raymond Hughes, Mus.Cur.; Clyde Helfter, Cur. of Iconography; Charles Brooks, Educ.Cur.; Kristin Keough, Act.Chf./Interp.

★1749★
BUFFALO & ERIE COUNTY PUBLIC LIBRARY - BUSINESS AND LABOR DEPARTMENT (Bus-Fin)
Lafayette Sq.   Phone: (716) 856-7525
Buffalo, NY 14203   Stanley P. Zukowski, Hd.
Staff: Prof 5; Other 3. **Subjects:** Economics, labor, finance, accounting, statistics, real estate, advertising, insurance, transportation, job information. **Holdings:** 62,000 books; 9800 bound periodical volumes; state industrial, trade and foreign directories; 20 VF cabinets; newspapers and periodicals on microfilm; annual reports of companies on the New York and American Stock Exchanges. **Subscriptions:** 890 journals and other serials. **Services:** Interlibrary loans; copying.

★1750★
BUFFALO & ERIE COUNTY PUBLIC LIBRARY - EDUCATION, SOCIOLOGY, PHILOSOPHY & RELIGION DEPARTMENT (Educ; Rel-Theol)
Lafayette Sq.   Phone: (716) 856-7525
Buffalo, NY 14203   Ann P. Miller, Hd.
Staff: Prof 4; Other 1. **Subjects:** Education, sociology, social welfare, philosophy, psychology, religion and history of religions. **Holdings:** 104,000 books; 11,500 bound periodical volumes; 8 VF drawers; 3500 college catalogs on microfiche. **Subscriptions:** 425 journals and other serials. **Services:** Interlibrary loans; copying.

★1751★
BUFFALO & ERIE COUNTY PUBLIC LIBRARY - FILM DEPARTMENT (Aud-Vis)
Lafayette Sq.   Phone: (716) 856-7525
Buffalo, NY 14203   Robert M. Gurn, Hd.
Staff: Prof 1; Other 5. **Holdings:** 1975 films. **Publications:** Film catalog.

★1752★
BUFFALO & ERIE COUNTY PUBLIC LIBRARY - HISTORY, TRAVEL AND GOVERNMENT DEPARTMENT (Hist)
Lafayette Sq.   Phone: (716) 856-7525
Buffalo, NY 14203   Ruth Willet, Dept.Hd.
Staff: Prof 9; Other 5. **Subjects:** History, travel, government, sports, archaeology, geography, numismatics. **Special Collections:** Local history (94 VF drawers); county, state and town histories; genealogy and heraldry. **Holdings:** 352,000 books; 11,900 bound periodical volumes; 39,500 maps. **Subscriptions:** 800 journals and other serials; 16 newspapers. **Services:** Interlibrary loans; copying.

★1753★
BUFFALO & ERIE COUNTY PUBLIC LIBRARY - LANGUAGE, LITERATURE AND ARTS DEPARTMENT (Hum)
Lafayette Sq.   Phone: (716) 856-7525
Buffalo, NY 14203   Ann P. Miller, Hd.
Staff: Prof 5; Other 1. **Subjects:** Fine arts and architecture, language, linguistics, journalism, literature, literary texts, history and criticism. **Holdings:** 208,000 books; 7700 bound periodical volumes; local theater programs. **Subscriptions:** 160 journals and other serials. **Services:** Interlibrary loans; copying.

★1754★
BUFFALO & ERIE COUNTY PUBLIC LIBRARY - MUSIC DEPARTMENT (Mus)
Lafayette Sq.   Phone: (716) 856-7525
Buffalo, NY 14203   Norma Jean Lamb, Hd.
Staff: Prof 3; Other 2. **Subjects:** Music and dance. **Special Collections:** 19th century American music - sheet music, bound volumes, songsters, tunebooks and broadsides. **Holdings:** 70,500 books and scores; 1800 bound periodical volumes; 78,600 song sheets; orchestral scores and parts (2600 titles); manuscripts of 8 contemporary composers; 65,500 phonograph records and tapes. **Subscriptions:** 250 journals and other serials. **Services:** Interlibrary loans; copying. **Special Indexes:** Index to song sheets and folios (titles on cards).

★1755★
BUFFALO & ERIE COUNTY PUBLIC LIBRARY - RARE BOOK ROOM (Rare Book)
Lafayette Sq.   Phone: (716) 856-7525
Buffalo, NY 14203   William H. Loos, Cur.
Founded: 1944. **Staff:** Prof 1; Other 1. **Subjects:** American history and literature, English literature, private press books, American almanacs, early Bibles, bibliography, costume and colorplate books, early medicine and science, music, minstrels, Shakers, antislavery movement, Western New York imprints and history. **Special Collections:** James Fenimore Cooper; Henry James; Dard Hunter; Julius J. Lankes; Elbert Hubbard and the Roycroft Press; Mark Twain; editions and translations of Huckleberry Finn; history of printing (43 incunabula); books illustrated with original photographs (200 titles). **Holdings:** 30,000 books; 4000 literary and historic manuscripts and letters, including manuscript of Huckleberry Finn; 220 Niagara Falls prints; 3800 posters, mostly World War I. **Services:** Copying (limited); room open to public. **Publications:** Checklists of Short Title Catalog, Wing, Evans, and Shaker holdings available.

★1756★
BUFFALO & ERIE COUNTY PUBLIC LIBRARY - SCIENCE AND TECHNOLOGY DEPARTMENT (Sci-Tech)
Lafayette Sq.   Phone: (716) 856-7525
Buffalo, NY 14203   Stanley P. Zukowski, Hd.
Staff: Prof 6; Other 2. **Subjects:** Engineering, mathematics, life sciences, earth sciences, agriculture, astronomy, military science, naval science. **Holdings:** 200,000 books; 46,500 bound periodical volumes; 20,500 volumes of U.S. Patent Office specifications and drawings; 95 boxes of U.S. Joint Publication Research Service reports in microform. **Subscriptions:** 1850 journals and other serials. **Services:** Interlibrary loans; copying.

★1757★
BUFFALO EVENING NEWS - LIBRARY (Publ)†
One News Plaza   Phone: (716) 849-4444
Buffalo, NY 14240   Sally G. Schlaerth, Hd.Libn.
Founded: 1920. **Staff:** Prof 6; Other 1. **Subjects:** Newspaper reference topics. **Special Collections:** Published reports of Buffalo Historical Society; Western New York history and biography. **Holdings:** 2000 volumes; 330 drawers and cases of pictures, clippings, maps, microfilms. **Services:** Library will sell news pictures; library not open to public. **Staff:** Robert Schoemann, Info.Spec.; Ann Joyce, Info.Spec.; Harvey Elsaesser, Info.Spec.; Joan Januszkiewicz, Info.Spec.

★1758★
BUFFALO GENERAL HOSPITAL, INC. - A.H. AARON MEDICAL LIBRARY (Med)
100 High St.   Phone: (716) 845-2878
Buffalo, NY 14203   Wentsing Liu, Dir.
Founded: 1920. **Staff:** Prof 1; Other 1. **Subjects:** Medicine, surgery, dentistry, pharmacology. **Special Collections:** Maisel Collection (gastroenterology); Norcross Collection (rheumatology); orthopedics. **Holdings:** 1800 books; 5000 bound periodical volumes; Audio-Digest tapes on internal medicine and surgery; 340 AV items. **Subscriptions:** 200 journals and other serials. **Services:** Interlibrary loans; copying; library open to public for reference use only. **Computerized Information Services:** BRS; computerized cataloging. **Networks/Consortia:** Member of Western New York Library Resources Council; Western New York Health Sciences Librarians. **Publications:** Aaron Announcement, quarterly.

BUFFALO MUSEUM OF SCIENCE
See: Buffalo Society of Natural Sciences

★1759★
BUFFALO PSYCHIATRIC CENTER - BPC LIBRARY (Med)
400 Forest Ave.   Phone: (716) 885-2261
Buffalo, NY 14213   Margaret Litzenberger, Asst.Libn.
Staff: Prof 1; Other 2. **Subjects:** Psychiatry, psychology, psychiatric nursing. **Holdings:** 6000 books; 686 bound periodical volumes; 5000 reports, pamphlets, clippings. **Subscriptions:** 101 journals and other serials. **Services:** Interlibrary loans; copying; library open to public with permission from librarian.

★1760★
BUFFALO SOCIETY OF NATURAL SCIENCES - RESEARCH LIBRARY (Sci-Tech)
Buffalo Musm. of Science
Humboldt Pkwy.   Phone: (716) 896-5200
Buffalo, NY 14211   Marcia Morrison, Libn.
Founded: 1861. **Staff:** Prof 1; Other 2. **Subjects:** Anthropology, astronomy,

geology, botany, zoology. **Special Collections:** Milestones of Science (200 items); Elizabeth W. Hamlin Oriental Library of Art and Archaeology (900 books); History of Writing Collection (200 items). **Holdings:** 10,000 books; 26,000 bound periodical volumes; 2 VF drawers of manuscripts; 1000 maps; 200 prints and drawings; 1415 microforms. **Subscriptions:** 620 journals and other serials. **Services:** Interlibrary loans; copying (limited); library open to public. **Networks/Consortia:** Member of Western New York Library Resources Council. **Special Catalogs:** Milestones of Science Catalog.

BUHL LIBRARY
See: University of Pittsburgh - School of Social Work

★1761★
BUILDING PRODUCTS OF CANADA LTD. - LIBRARY
10500 Cote de Liesse Rd., Suite 200
Lachine, PQ, Canada H8T 3E3
Defunct

★1762★
BUILT ENVIRONMENT COORDINATORS LIMITED - BEC INFORMATION SYSTEM (BIS) (Info Sci)
1947 Avenue Rd.   Phone: (416) 783-4277
Toronto, ON, Canada M5M 4A2   Jill Roughley, Dir.
Staff: Prof 2; Other 1. **Subjects:** Facility programming data. **Special Collections:** Generic activity data (3000 items). **Holdings:** 5000 books; 2500 bound periodical volumes; 14 cubic feet of vertical files; 500 slides; 1500 technical files; 200 technical reports; 200 floppy disks. **Subscriptions:** 33 journals and other serials. **Services:** Interlibrary loans; library not open to public. **Computerized Information Services:** Online systems; computerized cataloging. **Remarks:** This library provides backup data necessary to generate state-of-the-art predesign planning criteria for projects within the built environment. **Staff:** Elaine Borsuk, Lib.Techn.

BULEY (H.C.) LIBRARY
See: Southern Connecticut State College - H.C. Buley Library

★1763★
BULL, HOUSSER AND TUPPER - LIBRARY (Law)
3000 Royal Centre
1055 W. Georgia
P.O. Box 11130   Phone: (604) 687-6575
Vancouver, BC, Canada V6E 3R3   Susan Daly, Libn.
Staff: Prof 1; Other 1. **Subjects:** Law. **Holdings:** 14,000 books. **Services:** Library not open to public.

BULLER MEMORIAL LIBRARY
See: Canada - Agriculture Canada - Research Station, Winnipeg - Library

★1764★
BULOVA (Joseph) SCHOOL - LIBRARY (Sci-Tech)
40-24 62nd St.   Phone: (212) 424-2929
Woodside, Queens, NY 11377   James M. Devaney, Dir.
Founded: 1945. **Subjects:** Clock and watchmaking, machine-shop practice, jewelry repair, lapidary. **Holdings:** Figures not available. **Subscriptions:** 38 journals and other serials. **Services:** Interlibrary loans; library open to persons working in the jewelry field.

BULTEMA MEMORIAL LIBRARY
See: Grace Bible College

★1765★
BUNKER-RAMO CORPORATION - MAIN LIBRARY (Sci-Tech)†
Mail Code MS 3
31717 La Tienda Dr.   Phone: (213) 889-2211
Westlake, CA 91359   Mrs. Jan Krcmar, Chf.Libn.
Founded: 1958. **Staff:** Prof 1. **Subjects:** Electronics, human factors, undersea warfare. **Holdings:** 25,000 books; 20,000 bound periodical volumes; 14 VF drawers of pamphlets and reprints; 50,000 microfiche. **Subscriptions:** 150 journals and other serials. **Services:** Interlibrary loans; copying; library open to U.S. citizens by appointment. **Publications:** Information Center News, quarterly - for internal distribution only. **Special Catalogs:** Special documents and materials file maintained by Uniterm system.

BUNNELL COMMUNITY HOSPITAL
See: Community Hospital of Bunnell

★1766★
BURBANK COMMUNITY HOSPITAL - MEDICAL LIBRARY (Med)†
466 E. Olive Ave.   Phone: (213) 846-3135
Burbank, CA 91501   Narciso M. Garganta, Med.Libn.
Founded: 1973. **Staff:** Prof 1; Other 2. **Subjects:** Basic sciences, medicine, pharmacy, nursing, administration, allied health sciences. **Holdings:** 4500 books; 150 bound periodical volumes; Audio-Digest tapes; vertical files. **Subscriptions:** 235 journals and other serials. **Services:** Interlibrary loans; copying; library open to public for reference use only. **Computerized Information Services:** Internal database. **Publications:** Medical Library Hotline, quarterly - to medical staff and employees.

★1767★
BURBANK HOSPITAL - SCHOOL OF NURSING - GRACE GUMMO LIBRARY
Fitchburg, MA 01420
Defunct

★1768★
BURBANK PUBLIC LIBRARY - WARNER RESEARCH COLLECTION (Art)
110 N. Glenoaks Blvd.   Phone: (213) 847-9743
Burbank, CA 91501   Mary Ann Grasso, Lib.Coord.
Staff: Prof 1; Other 2. **Subjects:** Architecture, police and military, travel, transportation, history, costume. **Holdings:** 22,000 books; 5000 bound periodical volumes; 1 million clipping files; 500 research compilations; 14 VF drawers of license plates. **Subscriptions:** 78 journals and other serials. **Services:** Copying; library open with payment of fee and by appointment only. **Networks/Consortia:** Member of Metropolitan Cooperative Library System (MCLS). **Remarks:** The collection is designed to aid in the creative preparation of motion picture, television, and theatrical productions.

BURCHFIELD CENTER
See: SUNY - College at Buffalo

BUREAU OF AMERICAN ETHNOLOGY LIBRARY COLLECTION
See: Smithsonian Institution Libraries - National Museum of Natural History - Anthropology Branch Library

BUREAU OF APPLIED SOCIAL RESEARCH ARCHIVES
See: Columbia University - Herbert H. Lehman Library

★1769★
BUREAU COUNTY HISTORICAL SOCIETY - MUSEUM & LIBRARY (Hist)
109 Park Ave. W.
Princeton, IL 61356   Mrs. Howard Hilliard, Cur.
Founded: 1911. **Staff:** 2. **Subjects:** Histories and publications of Bureau County, Civil War histories, local genealogies, local newspapers. **Holdings:** 1500 books; 100 bound periodical volumes; 400 other cataloged items; 20 VF drawers of manuscripts, clippings. **Services:** Library open to public for reference use only. **Publications:** New Brochure. **Remarks:** Reprints of 1867 and 1885 histories of Bureau County, Illinois are available.

BUREAU OF FOODS LIBRARY
See: U.S. Food & Drug Administration

★1770★
BUREAU OF GOVERNMENTAL RESEARCH - LIBRARY (Soc Sci)
1308 Richards Bldg.   Phone: (504) 525-4152
New Orleans, LA 70112   John Brewer, Lib. Contact
Founded: 1932. **Staff:** Prof 1. **Subjects:** Public administration, city finances, personnel administration, police departments, fire departments, public works, recreation, intergovernmental relations. **Holdings:** 450 books; 450 bound periodical volumes; 7500 pamphlets (cataloged); 8 VF drawers of clippings; maps. **Subscriptions:** 200 journals and other serials. **Services:** Library open to BGR members and students. **Publications:** Reports on city finance, semiannual; research reports.

BUREAU D'INFORMATIQUE DANS LE DOMAINE DE LA SANTE
See: Health Computer Information Bureau

★1771★
BUREAU OF JEWISH EDUCATION - COMMUNITY LIBRARY (Rel-Theol)
2640 N. Forest Rd.   Phone: (716) 689-8844
Getzville, NY 14068   Abraham F. Yanover, Exec.Dir.
Founded: 1928. **Staff:** Prof 1. **Subjects:** Religion, philosophy, Bible, Jewish history, Hebraica, Jewish music, educational materials. **Holdings:** 9800 books; 2000 pamphlets; AV materials. **Subscriptions:** 75 journals and other serials. **Services:** Interlibrary loans; copying; library open to public. **Publications:** AV Catalog; Holocaust bibliography. **Staff:** Lenore Kulberg, Libn.

★1772★
BUREAU OF JEWISH EDUCATION - JEWISH COMMUNITY LIBRARY (Area-Ethnic)
601 14th Ave.   Phone: (415) 751-6983
San Francisco, CA 94118   Nanette Stahl, Hd.Libn.
Founded: 1950. **Staff:** Prof 2; Other 2. **Subjects:** Judaica, Jewish education, Bible, Jewish history, Israel, Jewish music. **Holdings:** 20,000 books; 400 phonograph records and tapes; vertical files. **Subscriptions:** 68 journals and other serials; 10 newspapers. **Services:** Copying; library open to public. **Publications:** Bibliographies on special holdings. **Staff:** Joyce Niles, Children's Libn.

BUREAU OF LABOR STATISTICS
See: U.S. Dept. of Labor

★1773★
BUREAU OF MUNICIPAL RESEARCH - LIBRARY (Plan)
73 Richmond St. W., Suite 404   Phone: (416) 363-9265
Toronto, ON, Canada M5H 2A1   Alice E. Bull, Libn.
Staff: Prof 4; Other 2. **Subjects:** Municipal planning, public administration. **Holdings:** 2000 books. **Subscriptions:** 46 journals and other serials. **Services:** Library open to public. **Publications:** Civic Affairs, 6-8/year. **Also Known As:** Toronto Bureau of Municipal Research.

★1774★
BUREAU OF NATIONAL AFFAIRS, INC. - LIBRARY AND INFORMATION CENTER (Soc Sci)
1231 25th St., N.W.   Phone: (202) 452-4466
Washington, DC 20037   Mildred Mason, Dir.
Staff: Prof 6; Other 4. **Subjects:** Law, labor-management relations, economics, government regulation, business, environment, energy, industrial safety and health. **Holdings:** 20,000 volumes. **Subscriptions:** 150 journals and other serials; 30 newspapers. **Services:** Interlibrary loans; library open to public by special arrangement only. **Computerized Information Services:** DIALOG, SDC, BRS, Dow Jones News Retrieval.

BUREAU OF RADIOLOGICAL HEALTH
See: U.S. Food & Drug Administration

★1775★
BUREAU OF SOCIAL SCIENCE RESEARCH - LIBRARY (Soc Sci)
1990 M St., N.W.   Phone: (202) 223-4300
Washington, DC 20036   Mary K. Hartz, User Serv.Libn.
Staff: 2. **Subjects:** Sociology, social policy, criminology and criminal justice, polls, social science methodology. **Holdings:** 8000 books; 700 bound periodical volumes. **Subscriptions:** 300 journals and other serials. **Services:** Interlibrary loans; copying; library open to qualified persons by appointment only. **Computerized Information Services:** DIALOG, SDC, BRS. **Networks/Consortia:** Member of Metropolitan Washington Library Council. **Publications:** Acquisitions list, quarterly. **Staff:** Lucy W. Duff, Coll.Mgt.Libn.

BURG (Louise) HOSPITAL - LIBRARY
See: Chicago College of Osteopathic Medicine - Alumni Memorial Library

BURGESS-CARPENTER LIBRARY
See: Columbia University

★1776★
BURGESS INDUSTRIES - ENGINEERING LIBRARY (Sci-Tech)†
8101 Carpenter Fwy.   Phone: (214) 631-1410
Dallas, TX 75247   Ernest L. Black, Mgr.
Founded: 1930. **Staff:** Prof 1; Other 1. **Subjects:** Acoustics, silencers, mechanical separators, fluid mechanics, thermodynamics, noise pollution, air pollution. **Special Collections:** Acoustical Society journals from first volume to present. **Holdings:** 200 books; 100 bound periodical volumes; 800 reports (cataloged). **Services:** Library not open to public.

BURGESS (Mary Ellen) DRAMA LIBRARY
See: Saskatchewan Teachers' Federation - Stewart Resources Centre

★1777★
BURKE & BURKE - LAW LIBRARY (Law)
529 Fifth Ave.   Phone: (212) 661-6600
New York, NY 10017   Peter Bartucca, Libn.
Staff: Prof 1; Other 1. **Subjects:** Law - general corporate, securities, mutual funds, banking, litigation, trust and estates, taxation, oil and gas. **Holdings:** 13,000 books and bound periodical volumes. **Subscriptions:** 30 journals and other serials. **Services:** Interlibrary loans; copying; library open to other firms. **Computerized Information Services:** LEXIS. **Networks/Consortia:** Member

of American Association of Law Libraries; Law Library Association of Greater New York.

BURKE (Carleton F.) MEMORIAL LIBRARY
See: California Thoroughbred Breeders Association - Carleton F. Burke Memorial Library

BURLEW MEDICAL LIBRARY
See: St. Joseph Hospital

★1778★
BURLINGTON COUNTY HISTORICAL SOCIETY - DELIA BIDDLE PUGH LIBRARY (Hist)
457 High St.   Phone: (609) 386-4773
Burlington, NJ 08016
Founded: 1915. **Subjects:** History of Burlington County and New Jersey; antiques; colonial arts and crafts; genealogy. **Special Collections:** James Fenimore Cooper works and critiques; imprints from presses of Stephen Ustick and Isaac Collins. **Holdings:** 1500 books; 300 bound periodical volumes; deeds; photographs; slides; clippings; maps; prints; postcards. **Services:** Copying; library open to public on a limited schedule.

★1779★
BURLINGTON COUNTY LYCEUM OF HISTORY AND NATURAL SCIENCE - MOUNT HOLLY LIBRARY (Hist)
307 High St.   Phone: (609) 267-7111
Mt. Holly, NJ 08060
Staff: Prof 2; Other 5. **Subjects:** Local history. **Special Collections:** Bridgetown Library Collection (c. 1765); Nathan Dunn Collection (c. 1844); Henry Shinn Collection (c. 1960); Levis Collection (19th century); Judge William Slaughter Collection of the American Indian. **Holdings:** 445 books; 1500 pamphlets, pictures, genealogical records, manuscripts, photographs. **Subscriptions:** 85 journals and other serials; 6 newspapers. **Services:** Copying; library open to public. **Remarks:** Holdings listed are for the historical collection only.

★1780★
BURLINGTON COUNTY MEMORIAL HOSPITAL - HEALTH SCIENCES LIBRARY (Med)
175 Madison Ave.   Phone: (609) 267-0700
Mt. Holly, NJ 08060   Betsy O'Connor, Libn.
Staff: Prof 1. **Subjects:** Health sciences. **Holdings:** 1100 books; 5000 bound periodical volumes; 80 other items; articles published by staff; 3 filing drawers of AV cassettes. **Subscriptions:** 300 journals and other serials. **Services:** Interlibrary loans; copying; library open to public with permission. **Computerized Information Services:** MEDLINE. **Networks/Consortia:** Member of Pinelands Consortium for Health Information. **Publications:** New Books, bimonthly; Administration Readings, bimonthly - both for internal distribution only.

★1781★
BURLINGTON COUNTY TIMES - LIBRARY (Publ)
Route 130   Phone: (609) 871-8000
Willingboro, NJ 08046   Helen Rosser, Libn.
Staff: Prof 1; Other 1. **Subjects:** Newspaper reference topics. **Holdings:** 160 books; newspapers on microfilm from 1955 to present. **Subscriptions:** 16 journals and other serials. **Services:** Library open to public with restrictions.

★1782★
BURLINGTON INDUSTRIES, INC. - LIBRARY INFORMATION SERVICES (Sci-Tech)
Box 20288
Greensboro, NC 27420   Darlene L. Ball, Mgr.
Founded: 1963. **Staff:** Prof 2; Other 2. **Subjects:** Textiles, chemistry, management. **Holdings:** 15,000 books; 12,000 bound periodical volumes. **Subscriptions:** 350 journals and other serials; 15 newspapers. **Services:** Library not open to public. **Computerized Information Services:** DIALOG, SDC, New York Times Information Service, Finsbury Data Services, Ltd., QUESTEL; computerized cataloging.

BURLINGTON LIBRARY
See: Arthur D. Little, Inc.

BURLINGTON TEXTILES LIBRARY
See: North Carolina State University

BURN CENTER
See: University of Michigan

★1783★
BURNABY GENERAL HOSPITAL - DR. H.H.W. BROOKE MEMORIAL LIBRARY
(Med)
3935 Kincaid St.   Phone: (604) 434-4211
Burnaby, BC, Canada V5G 2X6   Mr. Hoong Lim, Libn.
Staff: Prof 1. **Subjects:** Medicine, nursing, health care administration.
Holdings: 800 books; 400 bound periodical volumes; 2000 pamphlets and
clippings. **Subscriptions:** 75 journals and other serials. **Services:** Interlibrary
loans; copying; SDI; library open to public if cleared by administration.
Publications: Library Update, monthly - for internal distribution only.

★1784★
**BURNABY AND NEW WESTMINSTER SCHOOL BOARDS - REGIONAL FILM
LIBRARY SERVICES** (Aud-Vis)
Schou Educational Centre
4041 Canada Way   Phone: (604) 437-4511
Burnaby, BC, Canada V5G 1G6   R. Donald Lyon, Coord.
Founded: 1965. **Staff:** Prof 1; Other 2. **Subjects:** Elementary and secondary
school curriculum. **Holdings:** 1650 16mm films. **Services:** Interlibrary loans;
open to School Districts 40 and 41 and their municipal agencies.

★1785★
BURNABY SCHOOL BOARD - MEDIA LOANS (Aud-Vis)
Schou Educational Centre
4041 Canada Way   Phone: (604) 437-4511
Burnaby, BC, Canada V5G 1G6   R. Donald Lyon, Coord.
Staff: Prof 2; Other 7. **Subjects:** Education - instructional material for public
schools. **Holdings:** 12,000 AV items. **Services:** Copying; AV production,
inservice; library not open to public. **Publications:** Inside Schou, monthly -
distributed to Burnaby teachers. **Special Catalogs:** Book catalog of loan
materials. **Formerly:** Its District Resource Centre.

★1786★
BURNABY SCHOOL BOARD - TEACHERS' PROFESSIONAL LIBRARY (Educ)
Schou Educational Centre
4041 Canada Way
Burnaby, BC, Canada V5G 1G6   Phone: (604) 437-4511
Subjects: Teacher education, curriculum, philosophy, psychology, child study.
Holdings: 400 books. **Subscriptions:** 100 journals and other serials.
Services: Library not open to public. **Also Known As:** Jean Bailey Memorial
Library.

BURNAM (John Miller) CLASSICAL LIBRARY
See: University of Cincinnati - John Miller Burnam Classical Library

★1787★
BURNDY LIBRARY (Sci-Tech)
Electra Sq.   Phone: (203) 838-4444
Norwalk, CT 06856   Dr. Bern Dibner, Dir.
Founded: 1936. **Staff:** Prof 2; Other 2. **Subjects:** History of science to
1900. **Special Collections:** Electricity and magnetism; Galileo; Newton;
Einstein; Darwin; Pasteur; Volta. **Holdings:** 30,000 books; 100 letters and
manuscripts; 2000 portraits of scientists; 100 medals; 300 instruments.
Subscriptions: 25 journals and other serials. **Services:** Interlibrary loans;
copying; library open to scholars. **Publications:** Monographs in the history of
science. **Staff:** Dr. Philip Weimerskirch, Asst.Dir.; D. Nelhybel, Libn.

★1788★
**BURNET, DUCKWORTH & PALMER, BARRISTERS & SOLICITORS -
LIBRARY** (Law)
425 1st St., S.W., 32nd Fl.   Phone: (403) 260-0179
Calgary, AB, Canada T2P 3L8   Kathy Kurceba, Libn.
Staff: Prof 1; Other 1. **Subjects:** Law - Canada, Great Britain, United States.
Holdings: 8000 volumes. **Subscriptions:** 190 journals and other serials.
Services: Interlibrary loans; library not open to public. **Computerized
Information Services:** QL Systems.

BURNETT (Cordas C.) LIBRARY
See: Assemblies of God Graduate School - Cordas C. Burnett Library

★1789★
BURNETT (Leo) COMPANY, INC. - INFORMATION CENTER (Bus-Fin)
Prudential Plaza, 4th Fl.   Phone: (312) 565-5959
Chicago, IL 60601   Elizabeth Redmond, Libn.
Founded: 1938. **Staff:** Prof 4; Other 1. **Subjects:** Advertising, clients'
industries. **Services:** Library not open to public.

★1790★
BURNETT (Leo) COMPANY, INC. - RESEARCH LIBRARY (Bus-Fin)†
26555 Evergreen Rd.   Phone: (313) 355-1900
Southfield, MI 48076
Subjects: Advertising. **Holdings:** Figures not available.

BURNETT (Mary Couts) LIBRARY
See: Texas Christian University - Mary Couts Burnett Library

BURNHAM (Guy H.) MAP-AERIAL PHOTOGRAPH LIBRARY
See: Clark University - Graduate School of Geography - Guy H. Burnham
Map-Aerial Photograph Library

★1791★
BURNHAM HOSPITAL - LIBRARY (Med)
407 S. Fourth St.   Phone: (217) 337-2591
Champaign, IL 61820   Teresa M. Manthey, Libn.
Staff: Prof 1; Other 1. **Subjects:** Clinical medicine, nursing, health care
administration. **Holdings:** 600 books. **Subscriptions:** 201 journals and other
serials. **Services:** Interlibrary loans; copying; SDI; library open to public for
reference use only by telephone appointment. **Computerized Information
Services:** MEDLINE, DIALOG. **Networks/Consortia:** Member of Midwest
Health Science Library Network (MHSLN); Champaign-Urbana Consortium;
Lincoln Trail Library System.

BURNHAM LIBRARY
See: Art Institute of Chicago - Ryerson and Burnham Libraries

BURNHAM TAVERN MUSEUM
See: National Society, Daughters of the American Revolution - Hannah
Weston Chapter

★1792★
BURNS (Dean C.) HEALTH SCIENCES LIBRARY (Med)
                                                          Phone: (616) 348-4500
Petoskey, MI 49770   Kay Kelly, Med.Libn.
Staff: Prof 1; Other 2. **Subjects:** Health sciences. **Holdings:** 800 books;
4500 bound periodical volumes; slides, audio- and videotapes. **Subscriptions:**
250 journals and other serials. **Services:** Interlibrary loans; copying; library
open to public with restrictions. **Computerized Information Services:**
MEDLINE. **Networks/Consortia:** Member of Kentucky-Ohio-Michigan
Regional Medical Library Program; Michigan Area Serials Holdings Consortium
(MASH). **Remarks:** Maintained by Northern Michigan Hospitals, Inc. and Burns
Clinic Medical Center, P.C.

BURNS (Edward L.) HEALTH SCIENCES LIBRARY
See: Mercy Hospital - Edward L. Burns Health Sciences Library

★1793★
BURNS FRY LIMITED - RESEARCH LIBRARY (Bus-Fin)
1 First Canadian Place
P.O. Box 150   Phone: (416) 365-4444
Toronto, ON, Canada M5X 1H3   Ann Rait, Libn.
Founded: 1960. **Staff:** Prof 1; Other 1. **Subjects:** Stock market-investment,
Canadian and American companies. **Holdings:** 2100 books; 65 bound
periodical volumes; Canadian and American company files. **Subscriptions:** 20
journals and other serials; 15 newspapers. **Services:** Interlibrary loans; library
not open to public.

BURNS (Jacob) LAW LIBRARY
See: George Washington University - National Law Center - Jacob Burns
Law Library

BURNS (Landon) MEMORIAL LIBRARY
See: Carroll County Farm Museum - Landon Burns Memorial Library

★1794★
BURNS AND MC DONNELL ENGINEERING COMPANY - TECHNICAL LIBRARY
(Sci-Tech)
4600 E. 63rd St.
Box 173   Phone: (816) 333-4375
Kansas City, MO 64141   Adalene Stagner, Libn.
Founded: 1959. **Staff:** 4. **Subjects:** Civil, sanitary, electrical, mechanical and
electronic engineering; appraisals; public utilities; airports. **Holdings:** 4500
books; 1000 bound periodical volumes; 3650 government documents and
papers; 460 standards; 30 VF drawers of technical files; 7000
manufacturers' catalogs; 4 VF drawers of archives; 1 drawer of microfilm and
microfiche. **Subscriptions:** 215 journals and other serials; 10 newspapers.
Services: Library open to public for limited use. **Staff:** Valeeta Lucas,

Cat.Libn.; Frances Stanley, Asst.Libn.; Steve Goeckeler, Asst.Libn.

★1795★

BURNS AND ROE, INC. - JAMES MACLEAN TECHNICAL LIBRARY (Energy)†
185 Crossways Park Dr.　　　　　　Phone: (516) 677-2300
Woodbury, NY 11797　　　　　Emerenciana S. Santos, Tech.Libn.
Staff: Prof 1. **Subjects:** Engineering - nuclear, structural; energy technology.
Holdings: Codes and standards of engineering societies and organizations.
Services: Library not open to public.

★1796★

BURNS AND ROE, INC. - TECHNICAL LIBRARY (Sci-Tech)
800 Kinderkamack Rd.　　　　　　Phone: (201) 265-2000
Oradell, NJ 07649　　　　　　　Mrs. Ujwal Ranadive, Tech.Libn.
Staff: Prof 1; Other 1. **Subjects:** Engineering - nuclear, electrical, mechanical, civil and structural. **Holdings:** 2000 books; 12 VF drawers of industry standards; federal and military standards and specifications, federal construction regulations and vendor catalogs on microfilm (VSMF); preliminary and final safety analysis reports for 40 Nuclear Power Plants; 200 boxes of technical reports. **Subscriptions:** 175 journals and other serials. **Services:** Interlibrary loans; copying; library not open to public. **Staff:** Pat Bernstein, Tech.Lib.Asst.

★1797★

BURPEE ART MUSEUM/ROCKFORD ART ASSOCIATION - KATHERINE PEARMAN MEMORIAL LIBRARY (Art)
737 N. Main St.　　　　　　Phone: (815) 965-3131
Rockford, IL 61103　　　　　　Martin Dewitt, Dir./Cur.
Founded: 1960. **Staff:** 1. **Subjects:** Art, photography, crafts, graphics, conservation and restoration. **Holdings:** 500 books; 1000 bound periodical volumes; History of Art slides. **Subscriptions:** 12 journals and other serials. **Services:** Library open to public.

★1798★

BURR (Aaron) ASSOCIATION - LIBRARY (Hist)
R.D. 1, Rte. 33, Box 429　　　　　　Phone: (609) 448-2218
Hightstown, NJ 08520　　　　Dr. Samuel Engle Burr, Jr., Act.Libn.
Founded: 1950. **Staff:** Prof 1. **Subjects:** Biographies of Colonel Aaron Burr and other members of the Burr family; American history of the period of Burr's life. **Holdings:** 100 books. **Services:** Library may be used by special permission only.

★1799★

BURR-BROWN RESEARCH CORPORATION - LIBRARY (Sci-Tech)
Box 11400　　　　　　Phone: (602) 746-7305
Tucson, AZ 85734　　　　　　David B. Buus, Libn.
Founded: 1979. **Staff:** Prof 1; Other 1. **Subjects:** Semiconductors, microelectronics, hybrid fabrication, management. **Holdings:** 1500 books; 500 bound periodical volumes; 300 technical reports; 500 slides and cassettes; 850 federal specifications and standards; 1500 archival items. **Subscriptions:** 115 journals and other serials. **Services:** Interlibrary loans; copying; SDI; library not open to public. **Computerized Information Services:** DIALOG.

BURRITT (Elihu) LIBRARY
See: Central Connecticut State College - Elihu Burritt Library

★1800★

BURROUGHS CORPORATION - COMPUTER SYSTEMS GROUP - TECHNICAL INFORMATION RESOURCES CENTER (Sci-Tech)
460 Sierra Madre Villa　　　　　　Phone: (213) 351-6551
Pasadena, CA 91109　　　　　　Jean Robbins, Mgr.
Founded: 1956. **Staff:** Prof 1. **Subjects:** Digital computers, mathematics, electronics. **Holdings:** 6000 books; 3000 bound periodical volumes; 1500 technical reports. **Subscriptions:** 300 journals and other serials. **Services:** Interlibrary loans; copying; library open to public by appointment. **Computerized Information Services:** DIALOG; computerized acquisitions, circulation and Alert Bulletin & Service. **Networks/Consortia:** Member of Southern California Answering Network (SCAN); Southern California Interlibrary Loan Network (SCILL). **Publications:** DATALERT, monthly - for internal distribution only.

★1801★

BURROUGHS CORPORATION - CORPORATE INFORMATION RESEARCH CENTER (Sci-Tech; Bus-Fin)
Burroughs Place, Rm. 4C51　　　　　　Phone: (313) 972-7350
Detroit, MI 48232　　　　　　David R. Curry, Dir.
Founded: 1943. **Staff:** Prof 6; Other 3. **Subjects:** Computers, data processing, management, marketing, software. **Holdings:** 5000 books; 15 VF drawers and 8 shelves of internal reports and manuals; 20 VF drawers of pamphlets, clippings, annual reports and reprints; 25 shelves of directories and loose-leaf services. **Subscriptions:** 500 journals and other serials. **Services:** Interlibrary loans; copying; library open to public with restrictions. **Computerized Information Services:** DIALOG, SDC, Nexis; internal database. **Staff:** Carol C. Wildgen, Mgr., Info./Res.; Virginia Jeffers, Supv., Info. Liaison.

★1802★

BURROUGHS CORPORATION - ELECTRONIC COMPONENTS DIVISION - ENGINEERING LIBRARY (Sci-Tech)†
Box 1226
Plainfield, NJ 07061　　　　　　Phone: (201) 757-5000
Founded: 1963. **Staff:** 1. **Subjects:** Applied physics, computers, data processing, electronic components and engineering, electro-optical devices, behavioral sciences, industrial photography, product management. **Holdings:** 3500 books and bound periodical volumes. **Subscriptions:** 99 journals and other serials. **Services:** Library not open to public.

★1803★

BURROUGHS CORPORATION - LAW LIBRARY (Law)
Burroughs Pl.　　　　　　Phone: (313) 972-7895
Detroit, MI 48232　　　　　　Bernice C. Frank, Law Libn.
Staff: Prof 1; Other 1. **Subjects:** Labor, contracts, patents, trademarks, copyrights. **Holdings:** 11,000 volumes.

★1804★

BURROUGHS CORPORATION - LIBRARY (Sci-Tech)
25725 Jeronimo Rd.　　　　　　Phone: (714) 768-2685
Mission Viejo, CA 92691　　　　　M. Patricia Feeney, Tech.Libn.Sr.
Founded: 1974. **Staff:** Prof 1; Other 1. **Subjects:** Computers, digital engineering design, software engineering, programming, data communications, management. **Holdings:** 1800 books; 2000 technical reports. **Subscriptions:** 100 journals and other serials. **Services:** Interlibrary loans; copying; SDI (limited); library not open to public. **Computerized Information Services:** DIALOG, SDC, BRS; computerized circulation. **Networks/Consortia:** Member of Libraries of Orange County Network (LOCNET). **Publications:** Newsletter, quarterly. **Special Indexes:** KWOC Index of Technical Reports.

★1805★

BURROUGHS CORPORATION - RANCHO BERNARDO TECHNICAL INFORMATION CENTER (Sci-Tech)
10850 Via Frontera
Box 28810
San Diego, CA 92128　　　　　　Phone: (714) 451-4438
　　　　　　Marianna M. Seeley, Tech.Libn.
Founded: 1977. **Staff:** Prof 1. **Subjects:** Physics, semiconductors, electronics. **Holdings:** 600 books; 600 bound periodical volumes; 1500 proceedings and specifications; 250 technical reports. **Subscriptions:** 54 journals and other serials. **Services:** Interlibrary loans; copying; library open to public with approval of librarian. **Computerized Information Services:** DIALOG; computerized cataloging and acquisitions.

★1806★

BURROUGHS CORPORATION - SANTA BARBARA PLANT - LIBRARY
6300 Hollister Ave.
Goleta, CA 93017
Defunct

★1807★

BURROUGHS CORPORATION - TECHNICAL INFORMATION CENTER (Sci-Tech)
41100 Plymouth Rd.　　　　　　Phone: (313) 453-1400
Plymouth, MI 48170　　　　Dolores I. Schuller, Asst.Tech.Libn.
Founded: 1973. **Staff:** 1. **Subjects:** Engineering, computer technology. **Holdings:** 1500 books. **Subscriptions:** 95 journals and other serials; 5 newspapers. **Services:** Interlibrary loans; library open to public on request.

★1808★

BURROUGHS WELLCOME COMPANY - LIBRARY (Sci-Tech)
3030 Cornwallis Rd.　　　　　　Phone: (919) 541-9090
Research Triangle Park, NC 27709　　Ildiko Trombitas, Hd., Tech.Info.Dept.
Founded: 1929. **Staff:** Prof 13; Other 11. **Subjects:** Organic chemistry, medicine, biochemistry, pharmacology, microbiology, toxicology, business. **Holdings:** 19,736 books; 23,229 bound periodical volumes; 2 cabinets of product literature files; 3 bookcases of archives. **Subscriptions:** 1800 journals and other serials; 20 newspapers. **Services:** Interlibrary loans; copying; SDI; retrospective searches; library open to public by appointment. **Computerized Information Services:** NLM, DIALOG, SDC, BRS, Chemical Abstracts Service; internally developed computerized product information

system; serials control. **Networks/Consortia:** Member of OCLC through SOLINET. **Staff:** Barbara B. Abernathy, Hd., Lib.Serv.; Rolly L. Simpson, Hd., Prod.Sect.; Coyla McCullough, Hd., Res.Lit.Sect.; Robert B. Kilgore, Info.Spec.; Margaret Day, Info.Spec.; David Price, Info.Spec.; C. Gerken, Info.Spec.; H. Green, Info.Sci.; R. Larson, Info.Spec.; J. Mackars, Info.Spec.; M. Parker, Info.Spec.; M. Pratt, Info.Spec.

★1809★
BURROUGHS WELLCOME COMPANY - PLANT LIBRARY (Sci-Tech)
Box 1887   Phone: (919) 758-3436
Greenville, NC 27834   Laura Ann Bollinger, Plant Libn.
Founded: 1977. **Staff:** Prof 1; Other 1. **Subjects:** Pharmaceutical sciences and technology, chemistry, engineering, medicine. **Special Collections:** Pharmaceutical Technology (425 items). **Holdings:** 5332 books; 1507 bound periodical volumes; 5 VF drawers. **Subscriptions:** 200 journals and other serials. **Services:** Interlibrary loans; copying; SDI; library open to public with restrictions. **Computerized Information Services:** DIALOG, SDC, BRS, NLM. **Remarks:** The Plant Library is a satellite of the main library of the Burroughs Wellcome Company facility in Research Triangle Park, North Carolina.

BURROW (Edward F.) MEMORIAL LIBRARY
See: Grand View Hospital - Edward F. Burrow Memorial Library

★1810★
BURSON-MARSTELLER - INFORMATION SERVICE (Bus-Fin)
866 Third Ave.   Phone: (212) 752-6500
New York, NY 10022   Gayle Haring, Mgr., Info.Serv.
Founded: 1955. **Staff:** Prof 2; Other 2. **Subjects:** Advertising, public relations, marketing research. **Holdings:** 750 books. **Subscriptions:** 304 journals and other serials. **Services:** Interlibrary loans; library open to clients and librarians. **Computerized Information Services:** DIALOG, New York Times Information Service, NEXIS. **Staff:** Barbara MacCallum, Info.Spec.

BURTON HISTORICAL COLLECTION
See: Detroit Public Library

BUSH CENTER
See: St. John's Abbey and University - Hill Monastic Manuscript Library

★1811★
BUSHMAN (Ted) LAW OFFICES - LIBRARY (Law)
Bushman Bldg., Box 1261   Phone: (805) 773-4200
Santa Maria, CA 93456   Ted Bushman, Libn.
Founded: 1954. **Staff:** Prof 1. **Subjects:** Law, business, aviation. **Holdings:** 3000 books; 100 bound periodical volumes; 1000 audio cassettes; 5000 slides. **Subscriptions:** 50 journals and other serials; 5 newspapers. **Services:** Library not open to public.

★1812★
BUSHNELL CONGREGATIONAL CHURCH - LIBRARY (Rel-Theol)†
15000 Southfield Rd.   Phone: (313) 272-3550
Detroit, MI 48223   Mrs. George Unterburger, Lib.Cons.
Subjects: Bible and theology. **Holdings:** 1800 books; 19 bound periodical volumes; 310 filmstrips; 70 phonograph records; 50 slides. **Subscriptions:** 16 journals and other serials. **Services:** Library open to qualified persons by appointment.

★1813★
BUSINESS COMMUNICATIONS CO., INC. - LIBRARY (Sci-Tech; Energy)†
Box 2070C   Phone: (203) 325-2208
Stamford, CT 06906   Roger Memmott, Dir. of Oper.
Founded: 1971. **Staff:** Prof 12; Other 10. **Subjects:** Energy, transportation, plastics, chemicals, communications, foods, beverages. **Holdings:** 200 books; 10 VF drawers of clippings; 12 unbound manuscripts; research studies. **Subscriptions:** 8 journals and other serials. **Services:** Library not open to public. **Publications:** List of publications - available on request.

★1814★
BUSINESS INTERNATIONAL - RESEARCH LIBRARY (Bus-Fin)
One Dag Hammarskjold Plaza
Second Ave. & 47th St.   Phone: (212) 750-6383
New York, NY 10017   Audrey L. Bott, Dir. of Lib.Serv.
Founded: 1957. **Staff:** 7. **Subjects:** International aspects of economics, finance, marketing, management. **Special Collections:** Multinational corporations (books and files). **Holdings:** 500 books; 15,000 clippings of background data for countries on all subjects; 1000 files on U.S. and foreign corporations; several hundred clippings for marketing and product data. **Subscriptions:** 700 journals and other serials; 9 newspapers. **Services:** Interlibrary loans; copying (fee); library open to clients, subscribers and

graduate students by appointment only and to other business librarians. **Computerized Information Services:** BIDATA (economic and industry forecasts for 72 countries; internal database). **Special Indexes:** BI Master Key Index (computerized index to publications). **Staff:** Sergei Goregliad, Asst.Libn.

BUSINESS/PROFESSIONAL ADVERTISING ASSOCIATION (B/PAA)
See: Mc Graw-Hill Publications Company - Marketing Information Center

★1815★
BUSINESS AND PROFESSIONAL WOMEN'S FOUNDATION - MARGUERITE RAWALT RESOURCE CENTER (Soc Sci)
2012 Massachusetts Ave., N.W.   Phone: (202) 293-1200
Washington, DC 20036   Cheryl A. Sloan, Libn.
Founded: 1956. **Staff:** Prof 1; Other 1. **Subjects:** Women, with special emphasis on economic issues of importance to working women: jobs, careers, occupational segregation, comparable worth, sexual harassment, displaced homemakers and women's legal status. **Holdings:** 5000 books; 650 dissertations on microfilm (cataloged); 12,000 VF items; archival material. **Subscriptions:** 113 journals and other serials. **Services:** Interlibrary loans; copying; library open to public. **Computerized Information Services:** DIALOG. **Publications:** Selected Acquisitions, bimonthly; Information Digests, irregular.

BUSINESS WEEK MAGAZINE LIBRARY
See: Mc Graw-Hill, Inc.

BUSWELL (J. Oliver, Jr.) LIBRARY
See: Covenant Theological Seminary - J. Oliver Buswell, Jr. Library

★1816★
BUTEN MUSEUM OF WEDGWOOD - LIBRARY (Art)
246 N. Bowman Ave.   Phone: (215) 664-6601
Merion, PA 19066   David Buten, Dir.
Staff: Prof 3; Other 3. **Subjects:** Wedgwood and English ceramics, antique collecting, fine arts. **Special Collections:** Manuscripts and other material from the American sales branch of the Wedgwood Company; typescripts of Wedgwood - Bentley correspondence (18th century). **Holdings:** 1250 books; 10 VF drawers of newspaper clippings, magazine articles and other research materials. **Services:** Copying; library open to public by appointment.

★1817★
BUTLER, BINION, RICE, COOK, & KNAPP - LAW LIBRARY (Law)
1100 Esperson Bldg.   Phone: (713) 237-3140
Houston, TX 77002   Nell Booker, Libn.
Staff: Prof 1; Other 2. **Subjects:** Law - oil and gas, securities, tax, labor, patent. **Special Collections:** Early Laws of Texas (complete set); Corporate/International Law (1000 volumes). **Holdings:** 30,000 books. **Subscriptions:** 178 journals and other serials. **Services:** Interlibrary loans; library open to law librarians and to local law firm members. **Computerized Information Services:** LEXIS. **Publications:** Acquisition list, monthly - for internal distribution only.

BUTLER CENTER LIBRARY
See: Mansfield State College

★1818★
BUTLER COUNTY HISTORICAL SOCIETY - OLIVE CLIFFORD STONE LIBRARY (Hist)
381 E. Central
Box 696   Phone: (316) 321-9333
El Dorado, KS 67042   Anna Louise Borger, Libn.
Staff: Prof 1. **Subjects:** Local history, genealogy. **Holdings:** 2100 books. **Services:** Library open to public for reference use only.

★1819★
BUTLER COUNTY LAW LIBRARY (Law)
Court House   Phone: (412) 285-4731
Butler, PA 16001   Dolores Bradrick, Law Libn.
Staff: Prof 1. **Subjects:** Law. **Holdings:** 17,500 volumes; 130 volumes of Federal Regulation Codes; Federal Register (daily); 145 Advance Sheets; 35 binders of CCH Tax Service. **Subscriptions:** 12 journals and other serials. **Services:** Interlibrary loans; copying; library open to public.

★1820★
BUTLER COUNTY LAW LIBRARY ASSOCIATION (Law)
Court House Annex   Phone: (513) 867-5714
Hamilton, OH 45011   Anita K. Shew, Law Libn.
Staff: Prof 1; Other 2. **Subjects:** Law. **Holdings:** 32,000 volumes.

Subscriptions: 80 journals. Services: Library open to public with referral. Computerized Information Services: WESTLAW. Networks/Consortia: Member of OHIONET.

★1821★
BUTLER COUNTY MEMORIAL HOSPITAL - RUTH ARMSTRONG MEMORIAL MEDICAL LIBRARY (Med)
911 E. Brady St.   Phone: (412) 284-4240
Butler, PA 16001   Rita V. Liebler, Med.Libn.
Staff: Prof 1. Subjects: Medicine and health care administration. Holdings: 700 books; 200 bound periodical volumes. Subscriptions: 61 journals and other serials. Services: Interlibrary loans; copying; library open to public for reference use only, when librarian is present. Networks/Consortia: Member of Mideastern Regional Medical Library Service (MERMLS).

BUTLER (Edward H.) LIBRARY
See: SUNY - College at Buffalo - Edward H. Butler Library

BUTLER (Eva) LIBRARY
See: Indian and Colonial Research Center, Inc. - Eva Butler Library

BUTLER (Francis J.) HEALTH SCIENCE LIBRARY
See: Dakota Hospital - Francis J. Butler Health Science Library

★1822★
BUTLER HOSPITAL - ISAAC RAY MEDICAL LIBRARY (Med)
345 Blackstone Blvd.   Phone: (401) 456-3869
Providence, RI 02906   Erika Schmidt, Libn.
Founded: 1952. Staff: 1. Subjects: Psychiatry, psychology. Special Collections: Isaac Ray Collection (books from the early days of psychiatry). Holdings: 4330 books; 2192 bound periodical volumes; 1321 pamphlets. Subscriptions: 100 journals and other serials. Services: Interlibrary loans; copying; library not open to public. Publications: Isaac Ray Medical Library Bulletin, Volumes 1-3 (1953-55).

★1823★
BUTLER INSTITUTE OF AMERICAN ART - LIBRARY
524 Wick Ave.
Youngstown, OH 44502
Founded: 1919. Subjects: American art, graphic art. Holdings: 1200 books; 300 slides; files and catalogs on American artists. Remarks: Presently inactive.

BUTLER (John A.) LEARNING CENTER
See: Dunwoody Industrial Institute - John A. Butler Learning Center

BUTLER LIBRARY CIRCULATION DEPARTMENT
See: Columbia University

★1824★
BUTLER UNIVERSITY - IRWIN LIBRARY - HUGH THOMAS MILLER RARE BOOK ROOM (Area-Ethnic)
46th & Sunset   Phone: (317) 283-9227
Indianapolis, IN 46208   Gisela Hersch, Rare Bks.Libn.
Founded: 1931. Special Collections: William F. Charters South Sea Islands Collection (18th-20th centuries; 2000 volumes); Wesenberg Collection of 20th Century Poetry (first editions and manuscripts); Kate Greenaway Collection; early American botanic medicine and pharmacy; Kin Hubbard-Gaar Williams Collection of original cartoons, sketchbooks, books and memorabilia; Jeannette Siron Pelton Botanical Print Collection and zoological prints; 19th century American sheet music; Renfrew research collection on Madame de Stael. Services: Copying (limited); mail and telephone inquiries; library open to public for reference use only. Computerized Information Services: Computerized cataloging. Networks/Consortia: Member of OCLC. Special Catalogs: Card file for early imprints and printers.

★1825★
BUTLER UNIVERSITY - JORDAN COLLEGE OF FINE ARTS MUSIC LIBRARY (Mus)
46th & Sunset   Phone: (317) 283-9243
Indianapolis, IN 46208   Phyllis Schoonover, Music Libn.
Founded: 1951. Staff: Prof 2. Subjects: Art, music, music literature, dance,

radio and television, theater arts. Special Collections: Orchestral music section. Holdings: 6852 books; 1134 bound periodical volumes; 13,000 music scores (cataloged); 8515 recordings; 196 cassettes; 81 reel-to-reel tapes. Subscriptions: 81 journals and other serials. Services: Interlibrary loans; copying; library open to public for reference use only. Staff: Sheridan Stormes, Assoc. Music Libn.

BUTLER UNIVERSITY - KOSSUTH FOUNDATION
See: Kossuth Foundation

★1826★
BUTLER UNIVERSITY - SCIENCE LIBRARY (Sci-Tech)
46th & Sunset   Phone: (317) 283-9401
Indianapolis, IN 46208   Barbara Howes, Sci.Libn.
Founded: 1973. Staff: 2. Subjects: Botany, chemistry, environmental sciences, mathematics, pharmacy, physics, zoology. Holdings: 21,400 books; 18,400 bound periodical volumes; 36 VF drawers; 750 AV items. Subscriptions: 500 journals and other serials. Services: Interlibrary loans; copying; library open to public. Staff: Jean Cauger, Asst.Sci.Libn.

★1827★
BUTTE COUNTY LAW LIBRARY (Law)
Courthouse, One Court St.   Phone: (916) 534-4611
Oroville, CA 95965   Evlyn L. Turner, Law Libn.
Founded: 1907. Staff: 1. Subjects: Law. Holdings: 15,772 volumes. Subscriptions: 58 journals and other serials. Services: Library open to public.

BUTTENWIESER LIBRARY
See: 92nd Street Young Men's and Young Women's Hebrew Association

BUTTERICK FASHION MARKETING COMPANY
See: American Can Company

★1828★
BUTTERWORTH HOSPITAL - MEDICAL LIBRARY (Med)
100 Michigan, N.E.   Phone: (616) 774-1655
Grand Rapids, MI 49503   Eileen M. Dechow, Med.Libn.
Founded: 1948. Staff: Prof 1; Other 1. Subjects: Medicine, surgery. Holdings: 2000 books; 4000 bound periodical volumes; pamphlets; 650 AV cassettes. Subscriptions: 170 journals and other serials. Services: Interlibrary loans; copying; SDI; library open to public. Computerized Information Services: MEDLINE. Networks/Consortia: Member of Kentucky-Ohio-Michigan Regional Medical Library Network (KOMRML).

★1829★
BUTTERWORTH HOSPITAL - SCHOOL OF NURSING LIBRARY (Med)
335 Bostwick Ave., N.E.   Phone: (616) 774-1779
Grand Rapids, MI 49503   Betty Sherwood, Libn.
Founded: 1957. Staff: Prof 2; Other 3. Subjects: Nursing and nursing education, nursing specialties, anatomy and physiology, medical references, psychology, pharmacology, biography. Special Collections: National League for Nursing (NLN) publications (45 pamphlet boxes); Patient Information Section (104 items and 1 pamphlet subscription). Holdings: 4247 books; 633 bound periodical volumes; 5 VF drawers; 1295 AV software items. Subscriptions: 133 journals and other serials. Services: Interlibrary loans; copying; library open to public for reference use only by request. Staff: Marie Deyman, Asst.Libn.

BYRD MEMORIAL LIBRARY
See: Anderson College - School of Theology

BYRNE (John) MEMORIAL LIBRARY
See: Des Plaines Historical Society - John Byrne Memorial Library

C

C.B.I.C.
See: Canadian Book Information Centre

★1830★
C-E CREST ENGINEERING INC. - TECHNICAL LIBRARY (Sci-Tech)
4343 S. 118th E. Ave.   Phone: (918) 628-0800
Tulsa, OK 74145   Barbara Doty, Tech.Libn.
Staff: Prof 1. **Subjects:** Offshore drilling platforms, oil and gas production, fluid flow, chemical processing, oil and gas law. **Holdings:** 600 books; 50 bound periodical volumes; 2000 technical reports; 200 industry standards; 150 bound conference papers. **Subscriptions:** 66 journals and other serials. **Services:** Interlibrary loans; library open to public with restrictions. **Computerized Information Services:** SDC.

★1831★
C-I-L INC. - CENTRAL LIBRARY (Sci-Tech)
P.O. Box 200   Phone: (416) 226-6110
Willowdale, ON, Canada M2N 6H2   M.R. Weaver, Libn.
Founded: 1928. **Staff:** Prof 1; Other 2. **Subjects:** Chemistry, management, pollution control, explosives, plastics, engineering. **Holdings:** 10,000 books; 1000 bound periodical volumes; 3000 pamphlets; 1000 annual reports. **Subscriptions:** 300 journals and other serials; 5 newspapers. **Services:** Interlibrary loans; copying; library open to public by appointment. **Computerized Information Services:** SDC, DIALOG; computerized circulation.

★1832★
C-I-L INC. - CHEMICALS RESEARCH LABORATORY LIBRARY (Sci-Tech)
2101 Hadwen Rd.
Sheridan Park   Phone: (416) 823-7160
Mississauga, ON, Canada L5K 2L3   Joan L. Leishman, Libn.
Founded: 1945. **Staff:** Prof 1. **Subjects:** Chemistry, physics, chemical engineering, mathematics. **Holdings:** 3000 books; 4000 bound periodical volumes; 4 VF drawers of U.S. government reports; 5 VF drawers of patents; 700 internal reports. **Subscriptions:** 100 journals and other serials. **Services:** Interlibrary loans; copying; library open to public by appointment. **Computerized Information Services:** SDC, DIALOG, CAN/OLE; computerized cataloging. **Networks/Consortia:** Member of Sheridan Park Library and Information Science Committee.

★1833★
C-I-L PAINTS INC. - PAINT RESEARCH LABORATORY LIBRARY (Sci-Tech)
1330 Castlefield Ave.   Phone: (416) 787-2411
Toronto, ON, Canada M6B 4B3   M. Elaine Fitzpatrick, Libn.
Founded: 1955. **Staff:** Prof 1; Other 1. **Subjects:** Paint; chemistry - polymer, organic, analytical; chemical engineering. **Holdings:** 2500 books; 1500 bound periodical volumes; 12 VF drawers of pamphlets and reprints (cataloged); 44 VF drawers of company reports; 6 VF drawers of patents. **Subscriptions:** 100 journals and other serials. **Services:** Interlibrary loans; copying (limited); library open to public by special arrangement. **Computerized Information Services:** INFOMART, SDC. **Publications:** Acquisitions bulletin, monthly - for internal distribution only.

★1834★
C-I-L INC. - PATENT LIBRARY (Law)
P.O. Box 200   Phone: (416) 226-6110
Willowdale, ON, Canada M2N 6H2   Yolande D' Souza, Libn.
Staff: 2. **Subjects:** Patents. **Special Collections:** Chemical patents. **Holdings:** 1567 volumes. **Subscriptions:** 25 journals and other serials. **Services:** Library not open to public.

★1835★
C.I. POWER SERVICES - INFORMATION CENTRE (Energy)
2020 University St., Suite 1800   Phone: (514) 285-1414
Montreal, PQ, Canada H3A 2A5   Judith Joba, Info.Spec.
Founded: 1980. **Staff:** Prof 1. **Subjects:** Thermal power generation, energy, electrical and mechanical engineering. **Holdings:** 400 books; 8 VF drawers; 300 trade catalogs. **Subscriptions:** 50 journals and other serials. **Services:** Interlibrary loans; copying; SDI. **Computerized Information Services:** DIALOG, CAN/OLE.

★1836★
C.I.T. FINANCIAL CORPORATION - LAW LIBRARY (Law)
650 Madison Ave.   Phone: (212) 572-6500
New York, NY 10022   Doris McFalls, Libn.
Subjects: Law. **Holdings:** 9000 volumes.

★1837★
C.I.T. FINANCIAL CORPORATION - REFERENCE LIBRARY (Bus-Fin)
650 Madison Ave.   Phone: (212) 572-6412
New York, NY 10022   Marguerite Zambotti, Ref.Libn.
Founded: 1944. **Staff:** Prof 1; Other 1. **Subjects:** Banking, insurance, leasing, credit, industry files, country files. **Holdings:** 3000 books; 55 bound periodical volumes; 20 VF drawers of pamphlets. **Subscriptions:** 200 journals and other serials; 10 newspapers. **Services:** Interlibrary loans; copying; library not open to public. **Computerized Information Services:** Computerized cataloging. **Remarks:** C.I.T. Financial Corporation is a subsidiary of RCA Corporation.

★1838★
C.L.S.C. METRO - FAMILY LIFE EDUCATION SERVICES - PEEL CENTRE LIBRARY (Soc Sci)†
3647 Peel St.   Phone: (514) 844-8435
Montreal, PQ, Canada H3A 1X1
Staff: Prof 1. **Subjects:** Child development, family life education, mental health, leadership training, marital and premarital counselling. **Holdings:** 700 books; 400 pamphlets and reprints. **Subscriptions:** 25 journals and other serials. **Services:** Copying; library open to public with payment of membership fee. **Also Known As:** Centre Local de Service Communaute.

C & O HISTORICAL SOCIETY, INC.
See: Chesapeake & Ohio Historical Society, Inc.

CAB
See: U.S. Civil Aeronautics Board

★1839★
CABELL HUNTINGTON HOSPITAL - HEALTH SCIENCE LIBRARY (Med)
1340 Hal Greer Blvd.   Phone: (304) 696-2605
Huntington, WV 25701   Deborah L. Woodburn, Health Sci.Libn.
Staff: Prof 1. **Subjects:** Medicine, surgery, neonatal care, kidney dialysis and related health fields. **Holdings:** 720 books; 1250 bound periodical volumes. **Subscriptions:** 92 journals and other serials. **Services:** Interlibrary loans; copying; library not open to public. **Networks/Consortia:** Member of Huntington Health Science Library Consortium.

CABELL (James Branch) LIBRARY
See: Virginia Commonwealth University - James Branch Cabell Library

★1840★
CABLE TELEVISION INFORMATION CENTER (Aud-Vis)
1800 N. Kent St., Suite 1007   Phone: (703) 528-6846
Arlington, VA 22209   Harold E. Horn, Pres.
Founded: 1972. **Subjects:** Cable television. **Holdings:** Reports and papers available for purchase. **Services:** Center open to local government officials. **Publications:** CTIC CableReports, monthly newsletter; list of publications and reports - both free upon request. **Remarks:** The center is a nonprofit, nonpartisan membership organization designed to help local government officials make informed decisions about cable television by providing background information, valuable contacts and suggestions.

★1841★
CABOT CORPORATION - READING RESEARCH & DEVELOPMENT LIBRARY (Sci-Tech)
Box 1462   Phone: (215) 921-5262
Reading, PA 19603   Pamela L. Hehr, Libn.
Staff: Prof 1. **Subjects:** Metallurgy, beryllium, ceramics, composites. **Holdings:** 4000 volumes; 6000 patents, reports, documents. **Subscriptions:** 185 journals and other serials. **Services:** Interlibrary loans; copying.

★1842★
CABOT CORPORATION - RESEARCH & DEVELOPMENT LIBRARY (Sci-Tech)
Box 5001   Phone: (806) 669-2596
Pampa, TX 79065   Delores Martin, Libn./Off.Mgr.
Subjects: Thermodynamics, fluid flow, combustion, flame theory. **Holdings:** 650 books. **Subscriptions:** 22 journals and other serials. **Services:** Copying; library not open to public.

★1843★
CABOT CORPORATION - TECHNICAL INFORMATION CENTER (Sci-Tech)
1020 W. Park Ave.   Phone: (317) 456-6140
Kokomo, IN 46901   Betty S. Hollis, Tech.Libn.
Founded: 1952. **Staff:** Prof 3; Other 2. **Subjects:** Metallurgy, inorganic chemistry, marketing, finance, business. **Holdings:** 8000 books and bound periodical volumes; 12,000 technical reports; 10,000 technical reports on microfilm; slides; tapes. **Subscriptions:** 250 journals and other serials. **Services:** Interlibrary loans; copying; library open to public by special arrangement. **Computerized Information Services:** DIALOG, SDC; computerized cataloging. **Networks/Consortia:** Member of OCLC through INCOLSA. **Staff:** Amy J. Russell, Asst.Libn.; Mary S. Bonhomme, Mgr., Info./Commun.

★1844★
CABOT CORPORATION - TECHNICAL INFORMATION CENTER (Sci-Tech)
Concord Rd.   Phone: (617) 663-3455
Billerica, MA 01821   Barbara M. Davis, Mgr.
Founded: 1961. **Staff:** Prof 2; Other 3. **Subjects:** Chemistry, chemical engineering, polymers and plastics, paints, carbon black and white pigments, physics, metallurgy, inks, petroleum, rubber. **Holdings:** 6700 books; 7000 bound periodical volumes; 12 VF drawers of patents; 33 VF drawers of reprints and pamphlets; 15 VF drawers of trade literature; 150 VF drawers of company reports and correspondence; technical abstracts (40,000 cards). **Subscriptions:** 195 journals and other serials. **Services:** Interlibrary loans; library open to public by request. **Computerized Information Services:** DIALOG. **Staff:** Angea S. Reid, Libn.

CABOT (Godfrey Lowell) SCIENCE LIBRARY
See: Harvard University - Godfrey Lowell Cabot Science Library

CABOTS OLD INDIAN PUEBLO MUSEUM LIBRARY
See: Landmark Conservators

CABRILLO MARINE MUSEUM
See: Los Angeles - Department of Recreation and Parks

CABRILLO NATL. MONUMENT
See: U.S. Natl. Park Service

★1845★
CABRINI COLLEGE - HOLY SPIRIT LIBRARY - SPECIAL COLLECTIONS (Educ)
Eagle & King of Prussia Rds.   Phone: (215) 687-2100
Radnor, PA 19087   Claire Skerrett, Lib.Dir.
Founded: 1958. **Special Collections:** Special education (600 books; 425 bound periodical volumes; 200 reels of microfilm); 20th century Italian literature (496 books); Franklin Delano Roosevelt Collection (300 volumes). **Services:** Interlibrary loans; copying; library open to area residents and TCLC members. **Computerized Information Services:** BRS; computerized cataloging. **Networks/Consortia:** Member of Tri-state College Library Cooperative (TCLC); OCLC through PALINET & Union Library Catalogue of Pennsylvania.

★1846★
CABRINI MEDICAL CENTER - DR. MASSIMO BAZZINI MEMORIAL LIBRARY (Med)
227 E. 19th St.   Phone: (212) 725-6631
New York, NY 10003   Jeanne Becker, Med.Libn.
Founded: 1930. **Staff:** Prof 2; Other 5. **Subjects:** Medicine, surgery, nursing. **Holdings:** 3385 books; 4576 bound periodical volumes; 217 AV software programs. **Subscriptions:** 280 journals and other serials. **Services:** Interlibrary loans; library open to public by appointment. **Computerized Information Services:** NLM, BRS; computerized cataloging. **Networks/Consortia:** Member of Medical Library Center of New York (MLCNY); Manhattan-Bronx Health Sciences Library Group. **Staff:** Esther Silfen, Asst.Libn.

CADILLAC MOTOR CAR DIVISION
See: General Motors Corporation

★1847★
CAE ELECTRONICS, LTD. - ENGINEERING REFERENCE LIBRARY (Sci-Tech)†
P.O. Box 1800   Phone: (514) 341-6780
St. Laurent, PQ, Canada H4L 4X4   Sylvia Holloway
Founded: 1955. **Staff:** 1. **Subjects:** Component engineering, electrical engineering, computer systems, aeronautics, space technology, communications. **Holdings:** 2000 books; 4000 vendor catalogs; 6000 military specifications and federal standards. **Subscriptions:** 60 journals and other serials; 5 newspapers. **Services:** Interlibrary loans; library not open to

public. **Remarks:** Library located at 8585 Cote de Liesse Rd., Montreal, PQ, H4T 1G6.

CAFFERY (Jefferson) LOUISIANA ROOM
See: University of Southwestern Louisiana - Jefferson Caffery Louisiana Room

★1848★
CAHILL GORDON & REINDEL - LAW LIBRARY (Law)
80 Pine St.   Phone: (212) 825-0100
New York, NY 10005   Margaret J. Davenport, Libn.
Founded: 1920. **Staff:** Prof 3; Other 11. **Subjects:** Law - antitrust, corporation, securities, tax. **Holdings:** 6500 texts; 2600 bound periodical volumes; 20,000 other bound volumes; 40 VF drawers; 500 reels of microfilm. **Subscriptions:** 150 journals and other serials. **Services:** Interlibrary loans; copying; library may be visited by permission only. **Computerized Information Services:** DIALOG, SDC, LEXIS, New York Times Information Service, Dow Jones News Retrieval. **Staff:** Chan-Shen Lung, Asst.Libn.; Margo Edwards, Asst.Libn.

★1849★
CAI - TECHNICAL LIBRARY (Sci-Tech)
550 W. Northwest Hwy.   Phone: (312) 381-2400
Barrington, IL 60010   Steven Kormanak, Tech.Libn.
Staff: Prof 1; Other 1. **Subjects:** Mathematics, optics, electronics, photography. **Holdings:** 650 volumes; 4 VF drawers of patents; 8 VF drawers of pamphlets. **Subscriptions:** 110 journals and other serials. **Services:** Library not open to public. **Remarks:** Now a division of Recon/Optical, Inc. **Also Known As:** Chicago Aerial Industries.

★1850★
CAIN (J.B.) ARCHIVES OF MISSISSIPPI METHODISM AND MILLSAPS COLLEGE (Rel-Theol)
Millsaps College Library   Phone: (601) 354-5201
Jackson, MS 39210   James F. Parks, Hd.Libn.
Founded: 1934. **Staff:** 1. **Subjects:** Mississippi Methodist history, Millsaps College. **Special Collections:** New Orleans Christian Advocate, 1850-1946 (indexed); Nashville Advocate, 1890-1944; Mississippi Conference Journals, 1830 to present; North Mississippi Conference Journals, 1870 to present; papers of: Bishop Charles B. Galloway, William Winans, Lambuth family; history of Mississippi Conference; history of United Methodist women in the Mississippi Conference; histories of individual conferences; biographies of religious leaders; college administrative papers. **Holdings:** 1500 books; 500 bound periodical volumes. **Services:** Archives open to public by appointment. **Formed by the Merger of:** United Methodist Historical Society - Mississippi Conference - Archives and Millsaps College - Archives.

CAISSE DE DEPOT ET PLACEMENT DU QUEBEC
See: Quebec Province - Caisse de Depot et Placement du Quebec

★1851★
CALAIS FREE LIBRARY (Hum)
                                        Phone: (207) 454-3223
Calais, ME 04619   Helen R. Oliver, Libn.
Founded: 1892. **Staff:** Prof 3; Other 1. **Special Collections:** James Sheppard Pike Papers; Vroom Papers (35 newspaper articles); Hayden Diaries (60 notebooks); Ned Lamb Scrapbook (148 pages). **Holdings:** 14,498 volumes. **Subscriptions:** 31 journals and other serials. **Services:** Interlibrary loans; library open to public with restrictions. **Staff:** E. Marilyn Diffin, Asst.Libn.; Karen Pierce, Circ.

★1852★
CALAVERAS COUNTY LAW LIBRARY (Law)
Government Center   Phone: (209) 754-4252
San Andreas, CA 95249   Jeffrey Tuttle, Chm.
Subjects: Law, government code. **Holdings:** 6000 books. **Services:** Library open to public. **Staff:** B. Rutledge, Law Libn.

★1853★
CALAVERAS COUNTY MUSEUM AND ARCHIVES (Hist)
Government Center
30 N. Main St.   Phone: (209) 754-4203
San Andreas, CA 95249   Judith Cunningham, Dir./Cur.
Founded: 1977. **Staff:** 2. **Subjects:** Local and state history, mother lode region, mining, Indians. **Special Collections:** Calaveras County Archives (407 linear feet of inquests, probates, great registers, court records, assessments, tax records, mining claims in original form and on microfilm). **Holdings:** 350 books; 50 bound periodical volumes; diaries, manuscripts, documents, clippings; 120 oral history tapes; local maps. **Services:** Copying; library open

to public. **Publications:** Trips to the Mines. **Special Catalogs:** County Archives, newspapers, photographs. **Remarks:** Affiliated with the Calaveras Heritage Council.

★1854★
CALBIOCHEM-BEHRING CORPORATION - LIBRARY (Sci-Tech)
10933 N. Torrey Pines Rd.   Phone: (714) 453-7331
La Jolla, CA 92037   Aznive Sabonjian, Libn.
Founded: 1971. **Staff:** Prof 1. **Subjects:** Biochemistry, immunology, chemistry, biology. **Holdings:** 500 books; 1000 bound periodical volumes. **Subscriptions:** 100 journals and other serials; 5 newspapers. **Services:** Library open to public by appointment.

CALCULATOR INFORMATION CENTER
See: Ohio State University

CALDER (Louis) MEMORIAL LIBRARY
See: University of Miami - School of Medicine - Louis Calder Memorial Library

★1855★
CALGARY BOARD OF EDUCATION - PROFESSIONAL LIBRARY (Educ)
3610 9th St. S.E.   Phone: (403) 294-8581
Calgary, AB, Canada T2G 3C5   M. Jane Webb, Hd.Libn.
Founded: 1973. **Staff:** Prof 2; Other 2. **Subjects:** Education, library science. **Holdings:** 10,000 books; ERIC microfiche from 1969. **Subscriptions:** 700 journals and other serials. **Services:** Interlibrary loans; copying; library open to public for reference use only. **Computerized Information Services:** DIALOG. **Staff:** Carole Metcalfe, Libn.

★1856★
CALGARY CENTENNIAL PLANETARIUM & AERO-SPACE MUSEUM - LIBRARY & ARCHIVES (Sci-Tech; Trans)
Box 2100   Phone: (403) 264-2030
Calgary, AB, Canada T2P 2M5   S. Wieser, Dir.
Founded: 1967. **Subjects:** Astronomy, aircraft, railroads. **Holdings:** 610 books; 36 aircraft manuals and log books; 256 films and film clips. **Subscriptions:** 19 journals and other serials. **Services:** Library open to public for reference use only.

★1857★
CALGARY CITY ELECTRIC SYSTEM - RESOURCE CENTRE (Sci-Tech)
2808 Spiller Rd., S.E.
P.O. Box 2100   Phone: (403) 268-1100
Calgary, AB, Canada T2P 2M5   Ann K. Savage, Supv.
Staff: Prof 3. **Subjects:** Electrical engineering, transmission, distribution, customer relations, safety and training. **Holdings:** 500 books; 20 slides and films; 400 other cataloged items. **Subscriptions:** 200 journals and other serials; 8 newspapers. **Services:** Interlibrary loans; copying; SDI; library open to public. **Computerized Information Services:** DIALOG, CAN/OLE; internal database; computerized cataloging, acquisitions and serials. **Publications:** Library News, monthly - for internal distribution only. **Special Catalogs:** Book holdings (microfiche). **Staff:** Lanette Morden, Lib.Techn.; Shannon-Dean Ellison, Lib.Techn., Rec.

★1858★
CALGARY ECO-CENTRE SOCIETY - ENVIRONMENTAL INFORMATION CENTRE
204-223 12th Ave., S.W.
Calgary, AB, Canada T2R 0G9
Defunct

★1859★
CALGARY GENERAL HOSPITAL - LIBRARY SERVICES (Med)
841 Centre Ave., E.   Phone: (403) 268-9234
Calgary, AB, Canada T2E 0A1   Elizabeth Kirchner, Chf.Med.Libn.
Founded: 1940. **Staff:** Prof 2; Other 6. **Subjects:** Medicine, dentistry, hospital administration, nursing, paramedical fields, allied health sciences. **Holdings:** 10,000 books and bound periodical volumes; 400 tapes (cataloged). **Subscriptions:** 400 journals and other serials. **Services:** Interlibrary loans; copying; searches; LATCH; library open to public with permission from the Chief Medical Librarian.

★1860★
CALGARY HERALD - LIBRARY (Publ)
215 16th St., S.E.   Phone: (403) 269-6361
Calgary, AB, Canada T2G 3P2   Karen Liddiard, Chf.Libn.
Founded: 1929. **Staff:** Prof 1; Other 5. **Subjects:** Newspaper reference topics. **Holdings:** 700 books; 1000 pamphlets; 1440 microfilms of Calgary

Herald; clippings and pictures. **Services:** Copying; library open to serious researchers. **Computerized Information Services:** QL Systems.

CALGARY INSTITUTE OF RELIGION
See: Church of Jesus Christ of Latter-Day Saints

★1861★
CALGARY PLANNING DEPARTMENT - INFORMATION SERVICES (Plan)
Box 2100   Phone: (403) 268-5449
Calgary, AB, Canada T2P 2M5
Founded: 1965. **Staff:** Prof 3; Other 12. **Subjects:** City planning, housing and community renewal; land use and controls; transportation; environment; parks and recreation; citizen participation; urban affairs; records management. **Special Collections:** City of Calgary publications (500 documents). **Holdings:** 6000 books; clipping file. **Subscriptions:** 280 journals and other serials; 20 newspapers. **Services:** Interlibrary loans; copying; library open to public with prior arrangement. **Computerized Information Services:** Internal database; computerized cataloging and circulation. **Publications:** List of Publications, annual; What's New, weekly; Annual Report; Planning Library Bulletin, bimonthly; In the News, daily - all distributed on request. **Special Indexes:** KWOC index of holdings (COM). **Staff:** Linda D. Read, Supv.Plan.Lib.; Jodi R. Cohen, Supv.Rec.Ctr.; David M. Graham, Supv.Info.Ctr.

★1862★
CALGARY SOCIAL SERVICE DEPARTMENT - LIBRARY (Soc Sci)
Box 2100   Phone: (403) 268-5111
Calgary, AB, Canada T2P 2M5   Tahani Sarophim
Staff: 1. **Subjects:** Casework and counseling, social planning, day care and preschool education, child behavior and development, family therapy, neighborhood services. **Holdings:** 500 books; 145 bound periodical volumes. **Subscriptions:** 63 journals and other serials. **Services:** Copying; library open to public for reference use only. **Computerized Information Services:** Computerized cataloging and serials.

★1863★
CALGARY SUN - LIBRARY (Publ)
830 10th Ave., S.W.   Phone: (403) 263-7730
Calgary, AB, Canada T2R 0B1   Marilyn Wood, Libn.
Founded: 1955. **Staff:** Prof 1; Other 1. **Subjects:** Newspaper reference topics. **Holdings:** Newspaper clippings (20 years of Albertan and Calgary Herald); microfilm (Albertan, 1898-1982); photographs and pamphlets. **Services:** Copying.

★1864★
CALGARY ZOOLOGICAL SOCIETY - LIBRARY (Sci-Tech)
Box 3036, Sta. B.   Phone: (403) 265-9310
Calgary, AB, Canada T2M 4R8   Cheryl Chartrand, Animal Rec.Ck./Libn.
Staff: Prof 2. **Subjects:** Animal care, birds, mammals, reptiles. **Holdings:** 630 books; 4 drawers of manuscripts on wildlife management and specific species; 1 box of Canadian Wildlife Service reports. **Subscriptions:** 40 journals and other serials. **Services:** Copying; library open to public for reference use only. **Publications:** Dinny's Digest, quarterly. **Staff:** Kathy Lehnhardt, Interp.Off.

CALGON CORPORATION
See: Merck & Company, Inc.

CALHOUN (A.W.) MEDICAL LIBRARY
See: Emory University - School of Medicine - A.W. Calhoun Medical Library

★1865★
CALHOUN COUNTY HISTORICAL MUSEUM - LIBRARY (Hist)
680 Eighth St.
Rockwell City, IA 50579   Judy Webb, Libn.
Subjects: Local history, genealogy. **Special Collections:** Rare book collection. **Holdings:** 3000 books; 400 genealogy records; 80 scrapbooks; clippings; county records. **Services:** Library open to public under supervision.

★1866★
CALHOUN COUNTY METROPOLITAN PLANNING COMMISSION - PLANNING LIBRARY†
County Bldg., 315 W. Green St.
Marshall, MI 49068
Founded: 1968. **Subjects:** Planning, zoning, economic development, transportation, housing, parks, recreation, historic preservations. **Holdings:** 1450 books; 85 VF drawers containing small periodicals, newsletters, American Society of Planning Officials advisory service; American Institute of Planners Federal Register. **Publications:** Planning reports; Perspectives on Planning (newsletter). **Remarks:** Presently inactive.

★1867★

CALHOUN COUNTY MUSEUM - ARCHIVES AND LIBRARY (Hist)
303 Butler St.   Phone: (803) 874-3964
St. Matthews, SC 29135   Virginia D. Carroll, Libn.
Founded: 1952. **Staff:** Prof 1. **Subjects:** Genealogy, local history, archaeology, geology. **Special Collections:** Lawrence Keitt Papers; Geiger Collection; Olin M. Dantzler Papers (microfilm); Rev. Paul Turquand sermons (microfilm); 1850 Census of Orangeburgh District; cemetery, Bible and will records of the area. **Holdings:** 430 books; 320 bound periodical volumes; 200 plats and grants; 100 private papers; 50 oral histories (1952-1975). **Subscriptions:** 12 journals and other serials. **Services:** Interlibrary loans; copying; library open to public.

★1868★

CALIFORNIA ACADEMY OF SCIENCES - J.W. MAILLIARD, JR. LIBRARY (Env-Cons)
Golden Gate Park   Phone: (415) 221-5100
San Francisco, CA 94118   Ray Brian, Libn.
Founded: 1853. **Staff:** Prof 3; Other 3. **Subjects:** Botany, entomology, invertebrate zoology, geology, herpetology, ichthyology, mammalogy, ornithology, marine biology, paleontology, conservation/ecology. **Special Collections:** Diatom literature; Baja California; academy archives. **Holdings:** 85,000 volumes (75% of serial nature). **Subscriptions:** 2049 journals and other serials. **Services:** Interlibrary loans; copying (limited); library open to members of academy and qualified scholars (closed stacks). **Staff:** Mary L. Stilwell, Cat.; James E. Jackson, Asst.Libn.; Richard Pallowick, Asst.Libn.

★1869★

CALIFORNIA AIR RESOURCES BOARD - LIBRARY (Env-Cons)
1131 S St.
Box 2815
Sacramento, CA 95812   Phone: (916) 323-8377
     Mark T. Edwards, Libn.
Founded: 1976. **Staff:** Prof 2; Other 1. **Subjects:** Air - pollution, quality; environment. **Special Collections:** Air Pollution Technical Information Center reports (90,000 titles on microfiche); NTIS reports (air pollution; 20,000 on microfiche). **Holdings:** 5000 books. **Subscriptions:** 75 journals and other serials. **Services:** Interlibrary loans; library open to public. **Computerized Information Services:** DIALOG.

CALIFORNIA ARCHITECTURE/ENGINEERING LIBRARY
See: California State Office of the State Architect

★1870★

CALIFORNIA COLLEGE OF ARTS AND CRAFTS - MEYER LIBRARY (Art)
Broadway at College   Phone: (415) 653-8118
Oakland, CA 94618   Robert L. Harper, Hd.Libn.
Founded: 1907. **Staff:** Prof 2; Other 2. **Subjects:** Fine arts, art education, crafts. **Special Collections:** Jo Sinel Collection (Industrial Design) - clippings, prints, textiles. **Holdings:** 25,000 books; 2010 bound periodical volumes; 411 graduate projects (cataloged). **Subscriptions:** 364 journals and other serials. **Services:** Interlibrary loans; copying; library open to public with payment of deposit. **Networks/Consortia:** Member of Union of Independent Colleges of Art. **Staff:** Vanroy Burdick, Asst.Libn.; Arlene Talbot, Ser. & Circ.Supv.

★1871★

CALIFORNIA COLLEGE OF PODIATRIC MEDICINE - SCHMIDT MEDICAL LIBRARY (Med)†
Rincon Annex, Box 7855   Phone: (415) 563-3444
San Francisco, CA 94120   Leonard P. Shapiro, Dir.
Founded: 1914. **Staff:** Prof 1; Other 2. **Subjects:** Podiatry, orthopedics, sport medicine, basic and clinical sciences. **Special Collections:** Podiatry and lower extremity collection (500 volumes); orthopedics collection (1500 volumes); sports medicine collection (150 volumes). **Holdings:** 7800 books; 8527 bound periodical volumes; 200 AV items; 7 VF drawers of reprints; 3 VF drawers of city state file. **Subscriptions:** 500 journals and other serials. **Services:** Interlibrary loans; copying; SDI; library open to public with restrictions. **Computerized Information Services:** MEDLINE. **Networks/Consortia:** Member of San Francisco Biomedical Library Network; Pacific Southwest Regional Medical Library Service (PSRMLS). **Publications:** Acquisitions listing, quarterly; periodical listing, annual; handbook, biennial. **Remarks:** Located at 1210 Scott St., San Francisco, CA 94115. **Staff:** Robert D. Kearney, Asst.Dir.

★1872★

CALIFORNIA FEDERAL SAVINGS AND LOAN ASSOCIATION - MANAGEMENT LIBRARY (Bus-Fin)
5670 Wilshire Blvd.   Phone: (213) 932-4655
Los Angeles, CA 90036   Pamela J. Taranto, Libn.
Staff: Prof 1. **Subjects:** Savings and loan associations, banking, finance, housing, real estate, social issues. **Holdings:** 1500 books; 4 VF drawers of annual reports. **Subscriptions:** 200 journals and other serials; 8 newspapers. **Services:** Interlibrary loans; copying; SDI. **Computerized Information Services:** New York Times Information Service, SDC, DIALOG.

CALIFORNIA HISTORICAL RESEARCH COLLECTION
See: Tulare County Free Library

★1873★

CALIFORNIA HISTORICAL SOCIETY - HISTORY CENTER LIBRARY (Hist)
6300 Wilshire Blvd.   Phone: (213) 651-5655
Los Angeles, CA 90048   Jim Crowell, Cur.
Founded: 1978. **Staff:** Prof 2. **Subjects:** Local and state history. **Special Collections:** C.C. Pierce Collection; Southern California Photographic History (including mission, Indian, natural wonder and Los Angeles photographs); exhibits; Los Angeles County Business Incorporation Papers, 1850-1920 (130 cubic feet); Dominquez papers (6 cubic feet). **Holdings:** 2517 books; 100 bound periodical volumes; photographs; documents; maps; 25 lithographs. **Services:** Copying; library open to public. **Publications:** California History, quarterly; Courier (newsletter). **Special Indexes:** Index to California History. **Staff:** Bill Wurtz, Asst.Cur.

★1874★

CALIFORNIA HISTORICAL SOCIETY - SCHUBERT HALL LIBRARY (Hist)
2099 Pacific Ave.   Phone: (415) 567-1848
San Francisco, CA 94109   Bruce L. Johnson, Lib.Dir.
Founded: 1922. **Staff:** Prof 9; Other 1. **Subjects:** California history, genealogy, business history, theater, women in California, printing and publishing on the Pacific Coast. **Special Collections:** Genealogical collection (12,000 volumes); Edward C. Kemble Collections on Western Printing and Publishing (3500 volumes); Historic American Building Survey; Archive of Northern California American Civil Liberties Union (40 linear feet). **Holdings:** 40,000 volumes; 1800 bound periodical volumes; 3800 manuscript collections; 200,000 photographs; 4500 maps; 312 boxes, 17 VF drawers of ephemera. **Subscriptions:** 18 journals and other serials. **Services:** Copying; library open to public for a fee. **Staff:** Joy Berry, Ref.Libn.; Jocelyn Moss, Ref.Libn.; Judy Sheldon, Ref.Libn.; Douglas Haller, Cur. of Photographs; Carlen Luke, Photographs Asst.; Gerald D. Wright, Genealogist; Waverly Lowell, Cur. of Mss.

★1875★

CALIFORNIA HOSPITAL MEDICAL CENTER - MEDICAL STAFF LIBRARY (Med)
1414 South Hope St.   Phone: (213) 748-2411
Los Angeles, CA 90015   Anne G. Dillibe, Dir.
Founded: 1977. **Staff:** Prof 1; Other 1. **Subjects:** Clinical medicine, clinical oncology, cancer research, nursing, hospital administration. **Special Collections:** Albert Soiland Memorial Library (clinical oncology; 600 journal volumes); Southern California Cancer Center Research Department Collection (300 volumes). **Holdings:** 1500 books; 3500 bound periodical volumes; 500 audio cassettes. **Subscriptions:** 200 journals and other serials. **Services:** Copying; library open to public for reference use only. **Computerized Information Services:** Online systems.

CALIFORNIA INSTITUTE OF THE ARTS - ARNOLD SCHOENBERG INSTITUTE
See: Arnold Schoenberg Institute

★1876★

CALIFORNIA INSTITUTE OF THE ARTS - LIBRARY (Art)
24700 McBean Pkwy.   Phone: (805) 255-1050
Valencia, CA 91355   James Elrod, Lib.Dir.
Staff: Prof 6; Other 6. **Subjects:** Art, dance, design, film, music, theatre, general studies. **Special Collections:** Slide Collection of Women Artists; rare book collection on the development of film. **Holdings:** 53,505 books; 6547 bound periodical volumes; 713 films; 55,862 slides; 6687 reels of microfilm; 7022 exhibition catalogs; 10,857 recordings; 10,540 scores. **Subscriptions:** 535 journals and other serials; 19 newspapers. **Services:** Interlibrary loans; copying; library open to public for reference use only. **Computerized Information Services:** DIALOG, BRS, New York Times Information Service, RLIN; computerized cataloging and acquisitions. **Networks/Consortia:** Member of Total Interlibrary Exchange (TIE); OCLC. **Staff:** ; Fred Gardner, Hd., Pub.Serv.; Margie Hanft, Film Libn.Joan Anderson, Cat./Music Libn.; Evy White, Art/Slide Libn.

★1877★

CALIFORNIA INSTITUTE OF INTEGRAL STUDIES - LIBRARY (Hum; Area-Ethnic)
3494 21st St.   Phone: (415) 648-1489
San Francisco, CA 94110   Vern Haddick, Lib.Dir.
Founded: 1968. **Staff:** Prof 2; Other 3. **Subjects:** Philosophy, psychology and

counseling, religion, Hindu and Buddhist literature, Yoga and Zen discipline, Asian languages. **Special Collections:** Works of Sri Aurobindo, Gandhi, Sivananda, Vivekananda, Ramana Maharshi, Haridas Chandhuri. **Holdings:** 22,000 books; 65 masters dissertations; 40 doctoral dissertations; 500 philosophy and psychology tapes. **Subscriptions:** 100 journals and other serials. **Services:** Interlibrary loans; library serves the institute community. **Networks/Consortia:** Member of Bay Area Reference Center.

★1878★
CALIFORNIA INSTITUTE OF PUBLIC AFFAIRS - LIBRARY (Publ; Env-Cons)
226 W. Foothill Blvd.
Box 10   Phone: (714) 624-5212
Claremont, CA 91711   T.C. Trzyna, Pres.
Founded: 1969. **Staff:** Prof 1; Other 1. **Subjects:** California - current affairs, description and environmental issues; environmental, energy and natural resource policy, law and organizations (California and worldwide). **Holdings:** 1200 volumes; 125 file boxes of reports and clippings. **Subscriptions:** 200 journals and other serials. **Services:** Library open to public for reference use only by permission. **Publications:** List of publications - available on request. **Remarks:** The institute operates as an affiliate of the Claremont Colleges.

★1879★
CALIFORNIA INSTITUTE OF TECHNOLOGY - AERONAUTICS LIBRARY (Sci-Tech)
1201 E. California Blvd.   Phone: (213) 356-4521
Pasadena, CA 91125   Virginia N. Anderson, Libn.
Founded: 1940. **Staff:** Prof 1; Other 1. **Subjects:** Aeronautics, fluid and solid mechanics, acoustics, jet propulsion, hydrodynamics. **Special Collections:** National Advisory Committee for Aeronautics (NACA) and NASA reports; Advisory Group for Aerospace Research and Development (AGARD) reports; Aeronautical Research Council - CP reports. **Holdings:** 7350 books; 5488 bound periodical volumes; 225,350 microfiche; 210,300 reports. **Subscriptions:** 201 journals and other serials. **Services:** Interlibrary loans; copying; library open to public for reference use only. **Publications:** Additions to the Library, biweekly.

★1880★
CALIFORNIA INSTITUTE OF TECHNOLOGY - ASTROPHYSICS LIBRARY (Sci-Tech)
1201 E. California Blvd.   Phone: (213) 356-4008
Pasadena, CA 91125   Helen Z. Knudsen, Libn.
Founded: 1947. **Staff:** Prof 1; Other 1. **Subjects:** Astronomy, astrophysics. **Special Collections:** Palomar Sky Survey prints (1870 prints). **Holdings:** 6100 books; 6000 bound periodical volumes; 90 theses and dissertations; 350 unbound reports; 800 microforms; 2200 observatory publications (pamphlets); 1866 slides; 37 films; 450 microfiche; 43 sets of infrared prints. **Subscriptions:** 152 journals and other serials. **Services:** SDI; library not open to public; mail and telephone reference available. **Computerized Information Services:** ASTRODATA (internal database). **Remarks:** Figures given include holdings for branch libraries at Palomar Mountain Observatory, Owens Valley Radio Observatory and Big Bear Solar Observatory.

★1881★
CALIFORNIA INSTITUTE OF TECHNOLOGY - EARTHQUAKE ENGINEERING RESEARCH LIBRARY (Sci-Tech)
201 Thomas Lab.   Phone: (213) 356-4227
Pasadena, CA 91125   Kenneth D. Graham, Libn.
Founded: 1968. **Staff:** Prof 1; Other 3. **Subjects:** Earthquake engineering, vibration theory, structural mechanics, finite element analysis, seismology, disaster mitigation. **Holdings:** 10,000 books; 1400 bound periodical volumes; 7000 technical reports; 24,000 photographs, slides and maps; 550 seismographic records. **Subscriptions:** 120 journals and other serials. **Services:** Interlibrary loans; copying; literature searches; library open to public for reference use only. **Computerized Information Services:** Internal database. **Publications:** Publications list, monthly; serials list; reports list.

★1882★
CALIFORNIA INSTITUTE OF TECHNOLOGY - ENERGY RESEARCH LIBRARY (Energy)
1201 California Blvd.   Phone: (213) 356-4521
Pasadena, CA 91125   Virginia N. Anderson, Libn.
Founded: 1977. **Staff:** Prof 1; Other 1. **Subjects:** Energy. **Special Collections:** Windpower collection and bibliography (reports, clippings, books, microfiche). **Holdings:** 360 books; 61 bound periodical volumes; 4460 reports and 15,650 DOE microfiche. **Subscriptions:** 44 journals and other serials. **Services:** Interlibrary loans; copying; library open to public for reference use only.

★1883★
CALIFORNIA INSTITUTE OF TECHNOLOGY - ENVIRONMENTAL ENGINEERING LIBRARY (Env-Cons)
136 W.M. Keck Laboratory (138-78)   Phone: (213) 356-4381
Pasadena, CA 91125   Rayma Harrison, Assoc.Libn.
Founded: 1968. **Staff:** Prof 1; Other 1. **Subjects:** Environmental engineering and health, hydraulics, air pollution, water chemistry, water and wastewater treatment. **Holdings:** 3062 books; 819 bound periodical volumes; 19,400 technical and government reports; 87 volumes of dissertations. **Subscriptions:** 128 journals and other serials. **Services:** Library open to public with lending restrictions.

★1884★
CALIFORNIA INSTITUTE OF TECHNOLOGY - GEOLOGY LIBRARY (Sci-Tech)
201 North Mudd Bldg.   Phone: (213) 356-6699
Pasadena, CA 91125   Daphne Plane, Geology Libn.
Staff: Prof 2. **Subjects:** Geology, geophysics, geochemistry, planetary science. **Holdings:** 11,362 books; 16,677 bound periodical volumes; maps. **Subscriptions:** 798 journals and other serials. **Services:** Interlibrary loans; library open to public for reference use only. **Computerized Information Services:** DIALOG, SDC. **Staff:** Hoda Abdelghani, Ck.

★1885★
CALIFORNIA INSTITUTE OF TECHNOLOGY - INDUSTRIAL RELATIONS CENTER - MANAGEMENT LIBRARY (Soc Sci)
383 S. Hill (1-90)   Phone: (213) 356-4048
Pasadena, CA 91125   Mary MacKintosh, Libn.
Staff: Prof 1; Other 1. **Subjects:** Management, human resources, affirmative action and Equal Employment Opportunity. **Holdings:** 5700 books; 1000 bound periodical volumes; 106 VF drawers of business-related materials. **Subscriptions:** 131 journals and other serials. **Services:** Interlibrary loans; copying; library open to public. **Computerized Information Services:** DIALOG, New York Times Information Service; computerized cataloging.

★1886★
CALIFORNIA INSTITUTE OF TECHNOLOGY - JET PROPULSION LABORATORY - LIBRARY (Sci-Tech)
4800 Oak Grove Dr.   Phone: (213) 354-4200
Pasadena, CA 91103   D. Adel Wilder, Mgr., Lib.
Founded: 1948. **Staff:** Prof 12; Other 17. **Subjects:** Astronautics, space sciences, astronomy, engineering, communications, energy. **Special Collections:** Organic remote sensing collection. **Holdings:** 93,350 books; 38,000 bound periodical volumes; 70,000 technical reports; 926,500 microforms. **Subscriptions:** 2300 journals and other serials. **Services:** Interlibrary loans; copying; SDI; library open to public by appointment. **Computerized Information Services:** DIALOG, SDC, NASA/RECON, DOE/RECON; computerized cataloging and serials. **Networks/Consortia:** Member of National Aeronautics and Space Administration Library Network (NALNET). **Publications:** Library Additions, biweekly - for internal distribution only. **Staff:** Judith M. Castagno, Supv., Info.Serv.; Edward S. Jollie, Jr., Supv., Tech.Serv.

★1887★
CALIFORNIA INSTITUTE OF TECHNOLOGY - MILLIKAN LIBRARY (Sci-Tech)
1201 E. California Blvd.   Phone: (213) 356-6405
Pasadena, CA 91125   Roderick J. Casper, Act.Dir. of Libs.
Staff: Prof 11; Other 33. **Subjects:** Biology, chemistry, engineering, mathematics, physics, humanities, social sciences. **Special Collections:** History of science. **Holdings:** 182,360 books; 113,360 bound periodical volumes; 125,850 microforms; 1636 linear feet of documents; 500,000 institute archives. **Subscriptions:** 4220 journals and other serials; 15 newspapers. **Services:** Interlibrary loans; copying; library open to public for reference use only. **Computerized Information Services:** DIALOG, SDC, BRS, DTIC, MEDLINE, DOE/RECON; computerized cataloging and interlibrary loans. **Networks/Consortia:** Member of RLG; OCLC; Computerized Information Services. **Publications:** Serials and Journals in the CIT Libraries, annual - for sale. **Staff:** Edward R. Moser, Serials Libn.; Donald W. McNamee, Chf.Cat.; Dana L. Roth, Hd.Sci.Libn.;; Janet Casebier, Hd., Hum.Soc.Sci.Lib.; Bonnie Ludt, Hd., Acq.Dept.; Dr. Judith Goodstein, Inst.Archv.; Duane Helgeson, Hd., Physical Sci.; Nancy McLaughlin, Hd., Circ.Dept.

★1888★
CALIFORNIA INSTITUTE OF TECHNOLOGY - MUNGER AFRICANA LIBRARY (Area-Ethnic)
115 Baxter Hall   Phone: (213) 795-6811
Pasadena, CA 91125   Dr. Edwin S. Munger, Dir.
Founded: 1971. **Staff:** Prof 1; Other 2. **Subjects:** Africa - history, politics; sub-Sahara and South Africa. **Special Collections:** South African political ephemera (2000 items); African history (650 rare books and documents); antique maps. **Holdings:** 25,000 books; 900 journal titles cataloged; 34 VF

drawers of clippings. **Subscriptions:** 62 journals and other serials. **Services:** Copying; library open to public with restrictions. **Publications:** Munger Africana Library Notes, 5/year - by subscription.

★1889★
CALIFORNIA JOCKEY CLUB AT BAY MEADOWS - WILLIAM P. KYNE MEMORIAL LIBRARY (Rec)
Box 5050   Phone: (415) 574-7223
San Mateo, CA 94402   Gretchen G. Kramer, Libn.
Founded: 1973. **Staff:** Prof 1; Other 1. **Subjects:** Thoroughbred horses - racing, breeding, training, diseases, history; personalities in racing. **Special Collections:** Complete Racing Records Horses Foaled, 1960-1970 (microfiche); The Racing Calendar, 1727-1958. **Holdings:** 1681 books; 157 bound periodical volumes; photographs; national and international racing programs. **Services:** Copying; library open to public for reference use only.

★1890★
CALIFORNIA LUTHERAN COLLEGE - LIBRARY - SPECIAL COLLECTIONS (Rel-Theol)
                                                      Phone: (805) 492-2411
Thousand Oaks, CA 91360   Kenneth E. Pflueger, Dir., Lib.Serv.
Founded: 1961. **Special Collections:** Scandinavian Lutheranism and history (400 items); government documents (65,000). **Services:** Interlibrary loans; copying; library open to community - fee for borrowing. **Computerized Information Services:** DIALOG, BRS; computerized cataloging and ILL. **Networks/Consortia:** Member of OCLC; Total Information Exchange (TIE); CLASS. **Staff:** Ms. Joey Nelson, Doc.Libn.; Helen Parisky, Assoc.Libn. & Cat.; Mr. Armour Nelson, Spec.Coll. & Rare Books.

★1891★
CALIFORNIA MARITIME ACADEMY LIBRARY (Sci-Tech)†
Box 1392   Phone: (707) 644-5601
Vallejo, CA 94590   Paul W. O'Bannon, Sr.Libn.
Founded: 1959. **Staff:** Prof 2; Other 1. **Subjects:** Marine engineering and technology, navigation, ship operations, marine transportation, cargo handling. **Holdings:** 18,000 books; 12,000 technical reports on microfiche; 1000 bound periodical volumes; 1800 microforms of periodical back issues. **Subscriptions:** 385 journals and other serials; 5 newspapers. **Services:** Interlibrary loans; copying; library open to public. **Staff:** Nathan Plotkin, Libn.

★1892★
CALIFORNIA MEDICAL ASSOCIATION - LIBRARY (Med)
731 Market St.   Phone: (415) 777-2000
San Francisco, CA 94103   Clare J. Potter, Res.Libn.
Founded: 1959. **Staff:** Prof 1; Other 1. **Subjects:** Socio-medical economics, health insurance, public assistance. **Holdings:** 3600 books and pamphlets (cataloged). **Subscriptions:** 155 journals and other serials. **Services:** Interlibrary loans; copying; library open to members and health community only. **Publications:** Selected List of Acquisitions, quarterly. **Special Indexes:** Index to CMA minutes and resolutions (book).

★1893★
CALIFORNIA MISSIONARY BAPTIST INSTITUTE - LIBRARY (Rel-Theol)†
9246 Rosser
Box 848   Phone: (213) 925-4082
Bellflower, CA 90706   Edith Green, Libn.
Founded: 1957. **Staff:** Prof 1; Other 1. **Subjects:** Religion, church history. **Holdings:** 5000 books, bound periodical volumes, microfiche periodicals, association minutes. **Subscriptions:** 25 journals and other serials. **Services:** Interlibrary loans; copying; library open to public by appointment.

CALIFORNIA PETROLEUM INDUSTRY COLLECTION
See: Long Beach Public Library

★1894★
CALIFORNIA POLYTECHNIC STATE UNIVERSITY - ROBERT E. KENNEDY LIBRARY (Sci-Tech)
                                                      Phone: (805) 546-2344
San Luis Obispo, CA 93407   Dr. David B. Walch, Dir.
Founded: 1940. **Staff:** Prof 27; Other 49. **Subjects:** Engineering and technology, agriculture, architecture, home economics, business, science, social sciences, humanities. **Special Collections:** Fine Printing Collection (1750 items); Julia Morgan Papers (10,250 items); McCarthy Thoroughbred Horse Collection (125 items); Oyez Collection (150 items); Diablo Canyon Nuclear Plant Depository (5865 items). **Holdings:** 500,000 books; 65,000 bound periodical volumes; 60,000 other cataloged items; 38,000 theses; 420,000 government documents; 1.1 million microforms; 500 linear feet of university archives. **Subscriptions:** 6300 journals and other serials; 85 newspapers. **Services:** Interlibrary loans; copying; library open to public for

reference use only. **Computerized Information Services:** DIALOG, MEDLINE; computerized cataloging and circulation. **Networks/Consortia:** Member of OCLC; Total Interlibrary Exchange (TIE); CLASS. **Publications:** Annual Report; Information Guides; bibliography series. **Special Catalogs:** Periodical and Serials Holdings. **Staff:** Charles R. Beymer, Asst.Dir.

CALIFORNIA PRIMATE RESEARCH CENTER
See: University of California, Davis

★1895★
CALIFORNIA PROVINCE OF THE SOCIETY OF JESUS - JESUIT CENTER LIBRARY (Rel-Theol)
300 College Ave.
Box 128   Phone: (408) 354-9240
Los Gatos, CA 95031   Rev. Edward T. Burke, S.J., Libn.
Staff: Prof 1; Other 1. **Subjects:** Catholic theology, ecclesiastical history, Jesuitica. **Special Collections:** Jesuitica. **Holdings:** 40,000 books. **Services:** Interlibrary loans (limited); library open to public by appointment. **Remarks:** Maintained also by Sacred Heart Jesuit Center.

★1896★
CALIFORNIA RAILWAY MUSEUM - LIBRARY (Trans)
Star Rte. 283, Box 150   Phone: (415) 534-0071
Suisun City, CA 94585   Vernon J. Sappers, Cur.
Founded: 1946. **Staff:** Prof 1; Other 2. **Subjects:** Railroad - technology, history, fiction, maps. **Special Collections:** Vernon J. Sappers Collection (complete sets of Electric Railway Journal, Electric Traction; negative collection of 60,000 railroad subjects; bound sets of railroad employees timetables from major railroads of California); F.M. Smith Memorial Collection (corporate records of street railways serving Oakland, California from 1863-1946). **Holdings:** 5000 books; 100 bound periodical volumes; pamphlets; technical railroad newspaper clippings; maps; annual reports; timetables. **Services:** Library open to public with recommendation from outside sources. **Remarks:** Maintained by Bay Area Electric Railroad Association. **Staff:** Lisa Gorrell, Chf.Libn.; David Mitchell, Asst.Libn.; Robert S. Ford, Asst.Libn.

★1897★
CALIFORNIA REDWOOD ASSOCIATION - LIBRARY (Sci-Tech)
One Lombard St.   Phone: (415) 392-7880
San Francisco, CA 94111   L. Keith Lanning, Exec.V.P.
Subjects: Redwood and its uses. **Holdings:** 600 volumes; 5000 pamphlets on technical information concerning lumber and building.

★1898★
CALIFORNIA SCHOOL FOR THE BLIND - LIBRARY MEDIA CENTER (Aud-Vis)
500 Walnut Ave.   Phone: (415) 794-3800
Fremont, CA 94536   Vernalee Nullmeyer, Lib.Techn.
Founded: 1925. **Staff:** 1. **Subjects:** Books and media on elementary and high school levels for use by blind, multi-handicapped children. **Holdings:** 4500 books (Braille and print); 1350 talking books; 2200 records and tapes; 2000 models, realia, flash cards, games, maps, charts, kits; 51 boxes of pamphlets. **Subscriptions:** 73 journals and other serials. **Services:** Interlibrary loans; copying; library open to public by appointment.

CALIFORNIA SCHOOL FOR THE DEAF LIBRARY
See: California State Department of Education - School for the Deaf Library

★1899★
CALIFORNIA SCHOOL OF PROFESSIONAL PSYCHOLOGY - BERKELEY LIBRARY (Med)
1900 Addison   Phone: (415) 548-5415
Berkeley, CA 94704   Karen Hildebrand, Libn.
Staff: Prof 1; Other 2. **Subjects:** Psychology, psychoanalysis. **Special Collections:** Psychology of minority groups; psychological assessment. **Holdings:** 14,000 books; 4000 bound periodical volumes; 275 tapes; 400 dissertations. **Subscriptions:** 260 journals and other serials. **Services:** Interlibrary loans; copying; library open to public for reference use only. **Computerized Information Services:** DIALOG.

★1900★
CALIFORNIA SCHOOL OF PROFESSIONAL PSYCHOLOGY - FRESNO LIBRARY (Med)
1350 M St.   Phone: (209) 486-8424
Fresno, CA 93721   Inge Kauffman, Dir.
Founded: 1973. **Staff:** Prof 1; Other 3. **Subjects:** Psychology. **Special Collections:** Test collection (110 printed documents; 630 microfiche). **Holdings:** 7500 books; 800 bound periodical volumes; 28 VF drawers of documents and reprints; 1334 microforms; 250 audio cassettes.

Subscriptions: 180 journals and other serials. Services: Interlibrary loans; copying; library open to public for reference use only and to mental health professionals without restrictions. Computerized Information Services: BRS, DIALOG. Networks/Consortia: Member of Area Wide Library Network (AWLNET); 49/99 Cooperative Library System; Central Association of Libraries (CAL). Publications: Recent Acquisitions, quarterly; Serials Holdings, annual.

★1901★
CALIFORNIA SCHOOL OF PROFESSIONAL PSYCHOLOGY - LOS ANGELES LIBRARY (Med)
2235 Beverly Blvd.　Phone: (213) 665-4201
Los Angeles, CA 90057　Tobeylynn Birch, Hd.Libn.
Staff: Prof 2; Other 2. Subjects: Psychotherapy, women's issues, community and organizational consultation, program evaluation, child and family services. Holdings: 12,000 books; 300 bound periodical volumes; 610 government publications (especially National Institutes of Mental Health); 50 cassettes. Subscriptions: 180 journals and other serials. Services: Interlibrary loans; copying; library open to public by prior arrangement with librarian. Computerized Information Services: BRS, DIALOG (available to school members and staff only). Networks/Consortia: Member of CLASS. Staff: Emily Bergman, Asst.Libn.

★1902★
CALIFORNIA SCHOOL OF PROFESSIONAL PSYCHOLOGY - SAN DIEGO LIBRARY (Med)
3974 Sorrento Valley Blvd.　Phone: (714) 453-6880
San Diego, CA 92121　Richard Sanborn, Libn.
Staff: Prof 1; Other 2. Subjects: Psychology, sociology. Holdings: 11,000 books; 550 bound periodical volumes; 1100 cassette tapes. Subscriptions: 250 journals and other serials. Services: Interlibrary loans (limited); library open to local professionals and students for reference use only. Computerized Information Services: BRS.

★1903★
CALIFORNIA - STATE ARCHIVES (Hist)
Archives Bldg., Rm. 130
1020 O St.　Phone: (916) 445-4293
Sacramento, CA 95814　John F. Burns, Chf. of Archv.
Founded: 1850. Staff: Prof 7; Other 9. Subjects: Historical records of the California state government. Holdings: 50,000 cubic feet of documents, photographs, microforms, maps and related archival material. Services: Copying; library open to public.

★1904★
CALIFORNIA STATE AUTOMOBILE ASSOCIATION - LIBRARY (Trans)†
150 Van Ness Ave., B2-3F　Phone: (415) 565-2300
San Francisco, CA 94101　Pauline Jones Tighe, Libn.
Staff: Prof 1; Other 1. Subjects: Automobiles, traffic safety, driver education, automobile safety, traffic engineering, pedestrians, bicycles, motor vehicle accident statistics, highways and freeways. Holdings: Books, unbound reports, newspaper clippings, government documents. Subscriptions: 275 journals and other serials. Services: Library open to public by request.

★1905★
CALIFORNIA STATE BANKING DEPARTMENT - LIBRARY (Bus-Fin)
235 Montgomery St., Suite 750　Phone: (415) 557-4040
San Francisco, CA 94104　Paula Heiman, Libn.
Staff: Prof 1; Other 1. Subjects: Banking, law, economics. Special Collections: California Superintendent of Banks Annual Reports (1880 to present). Holdings: 3000 books; 100 bound periodical volumes; 100 bank stock offering circulars; 100 annual reports of state-chartered banks. Subscriptions: 279 journals and other serials; 6 newspapers. Services: Interlibrary loans; SDI; library open to public with restrictions. Computerized Information Services: DIALOG. Networks/Consortia: Member of CLASS.

★1906★
CALIFORNIA STATE BOARD OF EQUALIZATION - LAW LIBRARY (Law)
1020 North St., Rm. 289　Phone: (916) 445-7356
Sacramento, CA 95808　Barrie Griffith, Sr.Libn.
Staff: Prof 1. Subjects: Tax law - federal, state, local. Holdings: 7500 volumes. Services: Library open to public by appointment.

★1907★
CALIFORNIA STATE - COLORADO RIVER BOARD OF CALIFORNIA - LIBRARY (Env-Cons)
107 S. Broadway, Rm. 8103　Phone: (213) 620-4480
Los Angeles, CA 90012　Loretta E. Austin, Tech.Lib.Asst.
Founded: 1947. Staff: 1. Subjects: Hydrology, water resources,

conservation, Colorado River, engineering, agriculture, California water rights, salinity. Holdings: 9500 books; 300 pamphlets; 500 documents and reports; 60 VF drawers of maps and drafts. Subscriptions: 40 journals and other serials. Services: Interlibrary loans; library open to public by referral only. Publications: Annual Report to California State Library.

★1908★
CALIFORNIA STATE - COURT OF APPEAL, 2ND APPELLATE DISTRICT - LAW LIBRARY (Law)
3580 Wilshire Blvd., Rm. 448　Phone: (213) 736-2661
Los Angeles, CA 90010　Cheryl Stanwood, Law Libn.
Founded: 1967. Staff: Prof 2; Other 1. Subjects: Law. Holdings: 75,000 books. Subscriptions: 100 journals and other serials. Services: Library not open to public. Computerized Information Services: Online systems. Staff: Ruperta Reyes, Asst.Libn.

★1909★
CALIFORNIA STATE - COURT OF APPEAL, 4TH APPELLATE DISTRICT, DIVISION TWO - LAW LIBRARY (Law)
303 W. Third St.　Phone: (914) 383-4441
San Bernardino, CA 92401　Clint Rees, Libn.
Founded: 1966. Staff: 1. Subjects: Law. Holdings: 20,000 books; 380 bound periodical volumes. Services: Library not open to public.

★1910★
CALIFORNIA STATE - COURT OF APPEAL, 5TH APPELLATE DISTRICT - LAW LIBRARY (Law)
5002 State Bldg.　Phone: (209) 445-5686
Fresno, CA 93721　Cathy Pierce, Libn.
Staff: 1. Subjects: Law. Holdings: Figures not available. Services: Library open to attorneys during court sessions only.

★1911★
CALIFORNIA STATE DEPARTMENT OF ALCOHOL AND DRUG PROGRAMS - INFORMATION CLEARINGHOUSE (Soc Sci)
111 Capitol Mall　Phone: (916) 323-1873
Sacramento, CA 95814　Thomas D. Peck, Educ.Cons.
Staff: Prof 1; Other 1. Subjects: Alcohol and drug abuse, prevention. Holdings: 500 books; 1000 bound periodical volumes; 3500 reprints, clippings and reports; 200 films; 90 titles on microfilm. Subscriptions: 25 journals and other serials. Services: Interlibrary loans; copying (fee); clearinghouse open to public for reference use only. Computerized Information Services: Computerized cataloging. Publications: Film Catalogue.

★1912★
CALIFORNIA STATE DEPARTMENT OF DEVELOPMENTAL SERVICES - RESIDENTS LIBRARY (Med)
Agnews Residential Facility　Phone: (408) 262-2100
San Jose, CA 95134
Founded: 1948. Staff: Prof 1. Subjects: Mental retardation, developmental disabilities, neurology, psychology, psychiatric nursing, rehabilitation therapies. Holdings: 7000 books; 1020 bound periodical volumes; 125 tape recordings; 2 VF drawers. Subscriptions: 125 journals and other serials. Services: Interlibrary loans; copying; library open to state employees, students, parents and community. Networks/Consortia: Member of Medical Library Consortium of Santa Clara Valley; CIN. Publications: Acquisitions bibliography update; orientation booklet, annual.

CALIFORNIA STATE DEPARTMENT OF DEVELOPMENTAL SERVICES - STOCKTON STATE HOSPITAL
See: Stockton State Hospital

★1913★
CALIFORNIA STATE DEPARTMENT OF EDUCATION - SCHOOL FOR THE DEAF LIBRARY (Educ)
39350 Gallaudet Dr.　Phone: (415) 794-3666
Fremont, CA 94538　Elsa C. Kleinman, Libn.
Founded: 1860. Staff: Prof 1. Subjects: High interest, low vocabulary books suitable for K-12 deaf students. Special Collections: Education of the deaf (500 books). Holdings: 12,000 books; 119 bound periodical volumes. Services: Library open to public for reference use only.

★1914★
CALIFORNIA STATE DEPARTMENT OF HEALTH SERVICES - VECTOR BIOLOGY AND CONTROL SECTION - LIBRARY (Med)
2151 Berkeley Way　Phone: (415) 843-7900
Berkeley, CA 94704　Edna Hernandez, Libn.
Founded: 1947. Staff: Prof 1; Other 1. Subjects: Zoonoses, medical

entomology, vertebrate ecology, waste management, biostatistics, health education. **Holdings:** 2500 books and bound periodical volumes; 65,000 reports and reprints (cataloged); 3000 maps; 1600 slides and photographs; 20 reels of microfilm; 20 motion pictures and filmstrips. **Subscriptions:** 86 journals and other serials; 14 newspapers. **Services:** Interlibrary loans; library open to public. **Remarks:** Small technical libraries are located in field offices in Los Angeles, Fresno, Sacramento, San Bernardino, Santa Rosa, San Diego and Redding, California.

★1915★
CALIFORNIA STATE DEPARTMENT OF INDUSTRIAL RELATIONS - DIVISION OF LABOR STATISTICS AND RESEARCH LIBRARY (Soc Sci)
Box 603   Phone: (415) 557-2184
San Francisco, CA 94101   Ruth Mark, Res.Anl.
Founded: 1945. **Staff:** Prof 1; Other 1. **Subjects:** Labor statistics, employment, occupational injuries and illnesses, collective bargaining, industrial relations research. **Special Collections:** California Bureau of Labor Statistics (1883-1928). **Holdings:** 1044 shelf feet of books and pamphlets; 25 VF drawers of clippings and administrative memos. **Subscriptions:** 300 journals and other serials; 35 labor newspapers. **Services:** Library open to public for reference use only on request. **Publications:** Recent Publications of the Division of Labor Statistics Research, annual - by request. **Remarks:** Library located at 525 Golden Gate Ave., San Francisco, CA 94102.

★1916★
CALIFORNIA STATE DEPARTMENT OF JUSTICE - ATTORNEY GENERAL'S OFFICE - LAW LIBRARY (Law)
3580 Wilshire Blvd., Rm. 701   Phone: (213) 736-2196
Los Angeles, CA 90010   Janet T. Whitney, Supv.Libn.
Staff: Prof 2; Other 3. **Subjects:** Law. **Holdings:** 35,000 volumes. **Services:** Library not open to public. **Computerized Information Services:** WESTLAW. **Staff:** C. David Carlburg, Asst.Libn.

★1917★
CALIFORNIA STATE DEPARTMENT OF JUSTICE - ATTORNEY GENERAL'S OFFICE - LAW LIBRARY (Law)
110 West A St., Suite 600   Phone: (714) 237-7642
San Diego, CA 92101   Fay Henexson, Libn.
Founded: 1972. **Staff:** Prof 1; Other 1. **Subjects:** Law - California, United States. **Special Collections:** Opinions of the California Attorneys General, 1919 to present. **Holdings:** 15,500 books; 520 bound periodical volumes; 70 linear feet of California government documents; 20 linear feet of microfiche. **Subscriptions:** 52 journals and other serials; 4 newspapers. **Services:** Interlibrary loans; library open to public with restrictions; unique material available by appointment. **Computerized Information Services:** WESTLAW. **Special Indexes:** Index to opinions of the California Attorney General.

★1918★
CALIFORNIA STATE DEPARTMENT OF JUSTICE - ATTORNEY GENERAL'S OFFICE LIBRARY (Law)
6248 State Bldg.
San Francisco, CA 94102   Phone: (415) 557-2177
                                                   Malcolm Reynolds, Sr.Libn.
Staff: Prof 1; Other 3. **Subjects:** Law, government. **Special Collections:** Water and tidelands litigation; criminal appeals; California legislative hearings and reports. **Holdings:** 68,000 books; 2100 bound periodical volumes; 5000 documents (cataloged). **Subscriptions:** 258 journals and other serials; 11 newspapers. **Services:** Interlibrary loans; copying; library not open to public. **Computerized Information Services:** WESTLAW. **Special Indexes:** Index of Attorney General's opinions, letters of advice, and office memoranda.

CALIFORNIA STATE DEPARTMENT OF MENTAL HEALTH - METROPOLITAN STATE HOSPITAL
See: Metropolitan State Hospital

CALIFORNIA STATE DEPARTMENT OF PARKS AND RECREATION - CALIFORNIA STATE RAILROAD MUSEUM
See: California State Railroad Museum

★1919★
CALIFORNIA STATE DEPARTMENT OF TRANSPORTATION - DISTRICT 4 LIBRARY (Trans)
150 Oak St.
Box 7310
San Francisco, CA 94120   Phone: (415) 557-0567
                                                   Alice Y. Whitten, Lib.Tech.Asst.
Founded: 1972. **Staff:** 1. **Subjects:** Transportation planning, highway engineering. **Special Collections:** Highway Research Board pamphlets; California Division of Highway Statutes, 1929 to present; budget reports, 1925 to present; specifications, 1925 to present; California Highway and

Public Works documents, 1925-1966. **Holdings:** 5000 books; 180 bound periodical volumes; 2 shelves of clippings. **Subscriptions:** 30 journals and other serials. **Services:** Interlibrary loans; copying; library open to public for reference use only.

★1920★
CALIFORNIA STATE DEPARTMENT OF TRANSPORTATION - DISTRICT 7 LIBRARY (Trans; Plan)
120 N. Spring St.   Phone: (213) 620-5500
Los Angeles, CA 90012   Alyce L. Davis, Sr.Libn.
Founded: 1966. **Staff:** Prof 1; Other 1. **Subjects:** Engineering, transportation planning, supervision and management, environmental planning, freeway operations, drainage. **Special Collections:** Historical materials related to highways in Los Angeles, Orange and Ventura counties; project reports; oral interview techniques; study notes for engineering aids; surveys; chief of party training. **Holdings:** 21,000 books; 1000 bound periodical volumes; 1000 route planning reports; 500 California materials and research reports; 42 telephone directories; 100 earthquake materials; 400 construction project reports. **Subscriptions:** 52 journals and other serials; 63 newspapers. **Services:** Interlibrary loans; copying (limited); library open to public by referral. **Computerized Information Services:** Computer services. **Publications:** Intercom 7; monthly selected list of annotated recent books added to the library; informational catalogs about library's services. **Special Indexes:** Periodical indexes of library holdings.

★1921★
CALIFORNIA STATE DEPARTMENT OF TRANSPORTATION - DISTRICT 11 LIBRARY (Trans)
2829 Juan St.   Phone: (714) 237-6644
San Diego, CA 92110   Peggy A. Barton, Libn.
Staff: 1. **Subjects:** Multimodal transportation, planning, engineering. **Special Collections:** Highway/Transportation Research Board of National Academy of Science material; California Highways, 1925-1967. **Holdings:** 3000 volumes. **Subscriptions:** 75 journals and other serials; 25 newspapers. **Services:** Interlibrary loans; library open to public for reference use only. **Networks/Consortia:** Member of San Diego Greater Metropolitan Area Library and Information Agency Council. **Publications:** Bibliography of publications received, monthly.

★1922★
CALIFORNIA STATE DEPARTMENT OF TRANSPORTATION - LABORATORY LIBRARY (Sci-Tech; Trans)
5900 Folsom Blvd.   Phone: (916) 739-2152
Sacramento, CA 95819   Eva K. Caro, Sr.Libn.
Founded: 1965. **Staff:** Prof 1; Other 1. **Subjects:** Materials specifications, highway equipment testing, pollution measurement, soil mechanics, highway safety structures, geotechnical engineering. **Special Collections:** Road specifications of all U.S. states; complete American Society for Testing and Materials standards; F.H. Hveem papers. **Holdings:** 18,050 books, reports and bound periodical volumes; 4 VF drawers of pamphlets; 200 microfiche; 2000 other cataloged items. **Subscriptions:** 151 journals and other serials. **Services:** Interlibrary loans; copying; SDI; library open to public for reference use only. **Computerized Information Services:** Online systems; computerized cataloging and serials. **Publications:** List of publications - available upon request. **Also Known As:** TRANSLab Library.

★1923★
CALIFORNIA STATE DEPARTMENT OF TRANSPORTATION - LAW LIBRARY (Law)
1120 N St., Rm. 1315   Phone: (916) 445-2291
Sacramento, CA 95807   Lorna J. Flesher, Supv.Libn.
Staff: Prof 1; Other 1. **Subjects:** Torts, contracts, environmental law, multimodal transportation, real property. **Holdings:** Figures not available. **Services:** Copying; library not open to public.

★1924★
CALIFORNIA STATE DEPARTMENT OF TRANSPORTATION - TRANSPORTATION LIBRARY (Trans)
1120 N St.   Phone: (916) 445-3230
Sacramento, CA 95807   Edith Darknell, Supv.Libn.
Staff: Prof 3; Other 3. **Subjects:** Transportation, planning, highways, public transportation. **Holdings:** 50,000 volumes. **Subscriptions:** 250 journals and other serials. **Services:** Interlibrary loans; library open to public with restrictions. **Computerized Information Services:** DIALOG. **Remarks:** Library contains the collection of its Division of Structures - Technical Reference Section. **Staff:** Meredith Johanson, Libn.; Laurel Clark, Libn.

★1925★
CALIFORNIA STATE DEPARTMENT OF WATER RESOURCES - LAW LIBRARY (Env-Cons; Law)
1416 Ninth St., Rm. 1118-13   Phone: (916) 445-2839
Sacramento, CA 95814   Frances Pearson, Libn.
Staff: Prof 1; Other 1. **Subjects:** Water law - U.S. and California; water resources development. **Holdings:** 16,750 books and bound periodical volumes; 550 government documents. **Subscriptions:** 38 journals and other serials. **Services:** Interlibrary loans; copying; library open to public for reference use only.

★1926★
CALIFORNIA STATE DIVISION OF MINES AND GEOLOGY - LIBRARY (Sci-Tech)
Ferry Bldg.   Phone: (415) 557-0308
San Francisco, CA 94111   Angela Brunton, Libn.
Founded: 1880. **Staff:** Prof 1; Other 1. **Subjects:** Geology, mineralogy, mining engineering, petroleum. **Special Collections:** Gold rush and early California mining. **Holdings:** 25,000 volumes; 16,000 maps. **Subscriptions:** 225 journals and other serials. **Services:** Interlibrary loans; library open to public for reference use only.

★1927★
CALIFORNIA STATE HEALTH AND WELFARE AGENCY DATA CENTER - TECHNICAL LIBRARY UNIT (Sci-Tech)†
112 J St.   Phone: (916) 323-7739
Sacramento, CA 95814   Geraldine I. Fontes, Staff Serv.Anl.
Founded: 1978. **Staff:** 1. **Subjects:** Data processing. **Holdings:** 1500 books; 100 bound periodical volumes. **Services:** Library not open to public. **Computerized Information Services:** Online systems; computerized cataloging.

★1928★
CALIFORNIA STATE HEALTH AND WELFARE AGENCY - INTERDEPARTMENTAL LIBRARY
714 P St., Rm. 1800
Sacramento, CA 95814
Defunct

★1929★
CALIFORNIA STATE LIBRARY (Info Sci)
Library & Courts Bldg.
914 Capitol Mall
Box 2037   Phone: (916) 445-2585
Sacramento, CA 95809   Gary E. Strong, State Libn.
Founded: 1850. **Staff:** Prof 64; Other 125. **Subjects:** General research collection in support of state government; Californiana; law; genealogy; agriculture; Indians of North America; business; education; geology; mining; population; public administration; statistics; water resources. **Special Collections:** Regional library of books for the blind and physically handicapped; talking book phonograph records and cassettes; Braille books. **Holdings:** 3.1 million documents, books and bound periodical volumes; 1.1 million microforms; 62,657 maps and charts; 128 16mm films; 103 video recordings; 153,500 audio recordings. **Subscriptions:** 3635 journals, serials and newspapers. **Services:** Interlibrary loans; copying; administrative-legislative reference service for California state government; consultant service for public libraries; library open to public. **Computerized Information Services:** DIALOG, SDC, New York Times Information Service; computerized cataloging. **Publications:** Publications list available. **Remarks:** Includes the holdings of the State Law Library. **Staff:** Nancy W. Percy, Asst. State Libn.; Wes Doak, Chf. of Lib.Dev.; Collin Clark, Info.Mgr.; Sheila F. Thornton, Chf., State Lib.Serv.; Marion Bourke, Supv., Bks. For Blind; Gary Kurutz, Supv., Spec.Coll.; Jay Cunningham, Supv., Tech.Serv.; Charlotte Harriss, Supv., Pub.Serv.; Muriel Hoppes, Law Libn.

★1930★
CALIFORNIA STATE LIBRARY - SUTRO LIBRARY (Hist)
2495 Golden Gate Ave.   Phone: (415) 557-0374
San Francisco, CA 94118   Eleanor Capelle, Sr.Libn.
Founded: 1917. **Staff:** Prof 2; Other 5. **Subjects:** English history, history of science and technology, Americana, bibliography, voyages and travels, American local history and genealogy, Mexican history, Hebraica, natural history. **Special Collections:** Papers of Sir Joseph Banks, 1760-1820. **Holdings:** 100,000 volumes; 20,000 manuscripts. **Subscriptions:** 25 journals and other serials. **Services:** Interlibrary loans; copying; library open to public. **Computerized Information Services:** Computerized cataloging. **Publications:** Anatomy of a Library (brochure on the collection); New Arrivals in American Local History and Genealogy, quarterly - free upon request. **Remarks:** Library specializes in works published prior to 1900. **Staff:** Frank J.

Glover, Ref.Libn.

★1931★
CALIFORNIA STATE MEDICAL FACILITY - STAFF LIBRARY (Med)
1600 California Dr.   Phone: (707) 448-6841
Vacaville, CA 95696   Roberta Carson, Med.Rec.Libn.
Founded: 1950. **Subjects:** Psychiatry, medicine, surgery, penology, criminology, psychology, social work, nursing, hospital administration. **Holdings:** 6000 books; 130 bound periodical volumes; research materials relating to criminology and case work; reports from other state and national agencies; releases from federal, state and local agencies interested in inmate care and welfare and community adjustment. **Subscriptions:** 149 journals and other serials. **Services:** Interlibrary loans; bibliographies; research; library open to public for reference use only with consent of the superintendent.

★1932★
CALIFORNIA STATE OFFICE OF LEGISLATIVE COUNSEL - LIBRARY (Law)
3021 State Capitol   Phone: (916) 445-2609
Sacramento, CA 95814   Virginia Castro, Lib.Tech.Asst.
Founded: 1949. **Staff:** Prof 1; Other 2. **Subjects:** Law. **Special Collections:** Publications of the Legislature of California. **Holdings:** 22,000 books; 350 bound periodical volumes; 6000 other cataloged items; 6 boxes of ultrafiche of the National Reporter System, 1st series. **Subscriptions:** 153 journals and other serials. **Services:** Library not open to public. **Computerized Information Services:** LEXIS; internal database.

★1933★
CALIFORNIA STATE OFFICE OF THE STATE ARCHITECT - ARCHITECTURE/ENGINEERING LIBRARY (Plan)
1500 5th St.   Phone: (916) 445-8661
Sacramento, CA 95814   Rose A. Granados, Tech.Libn.
Staff: Prof 1. **Subjects:** Construction industry standards, architecture, electrical and mechanical engineering, building products, interior design. **Special Collections:** Architectural samples (6000). **Holdings:** 400 books; 30 bound periodical volumes; 5470 catalogs; 16 VF drawers of pamphlets; 16 volumes of State Fire Marshall listings; titles 1-25 of the California Administrative Code; microfilm. **Subscriptions:** 76 journals and other serials; 5 newspapers. **Services:** Interlibrary loans; copying; library open to other state agencies.

CALIFORNIA STATE PARKS SYSTEM - LA PURISIMA MISSION
See: La Purisima Mission

★1934★
CALIFORNIA STATE POLYTECHNIC UNIVERSITY, POMONA - LIBRARY - SPECIAL COLLECTIONS (Hum; Rec)
3801 W. Temple Ave.   Phone: (714) 598-4671
Pomona, CA 91768   Mary Lee DeVilbiss, Spec.Coll.Libn.
Founded: 1934. **Special Collections:** Arabian Horse Collection (1500 items); first editions of contemporary American and British authors (650 volumes); W.K. Kellogg Ranch papers. **Services:** Interlibrary loans; copying; library open to public with restrictions. **Computerized Information Services:** DIALOG, BRS, ISI; computerized cataloging. **Networks/Consortia:** Member of Inland Empire Academic Libraries Cooperative; California State University Mutual Use Program; CLASS. **Publications:** Arabian Horse bibliographies.

★1935★
CALIFORNIA STATE POSTSECONDARY EDUCATION COMMISSION - LIBRARY (Educ)
1020 Twelfth St.   Phone: (916) 322-8031
Sacramento, CA 95814   Elizabeth Testa, Sr.Libn.
Staff: Prof 1; Other 2. **Subjects:** Higher education. **Holdings:** 1000 books; 12,000 government documents; 6000 reports; 100,000 microfiche; 50 microfilms. **Subscriptions:** 270 journals and other serials. **Services:** Interlibrary loans; copying; library open for consultation to members of the state legislature and to state agencies. Public may write or call library for information. **Computerized Information Services:** Internal database on California higher education. **Publications:** New acquisitions list, irregular; list of other publications - available upon request.

★1936★
CALIFORNIA STATE RAILROAD MUSEUM - LIBRARY (Hist)
111 I St.   Phone: (916) 323-8073
Sacramento, CA 95814   Stephen E. Drew, Cur.
Founded: 1981. **Staff:** Prof 4. **Subjects:** History of railroads in California, Nevada and the West. **Special Collections:** Corporate records of Central Pacific, Southern Pacific and Western Pacific railroads and their subsidiary companies; Lima Locomotive Works construction drawings; Pullman Company glass negatives; C.P. Huntington papers (on microfilm); papers and collections

of the Pacific Coast Chapter of the Railway and Locomotive Historical Society; California State Railway Museum documents pertaining to its development and the restoration of locomotives and rolling stock on exhibit (total of 6000 cubic feet). **Holdings:** 1500 books; 200 periodical titles; 50,000 photographs, timetables, maps, drawings, railroad ephemera. **Subscriptions:** 43 journals and other serials. **Services:** Copying; library open to public for reference use only. **Special Indexes:** Index to selected railroad periodicals (card). **Remarks:** Maintained by the California State Department of Parks and Recreation. **Staff:** Walter P. Gray, III, Archv.; Ellen Schwartz, Libn.; Shirley M. Burman, Photographer.

★1937★
CALIFORNIA STATE REGIONAL WATER QUALITY CONTROL BOARD, SAN FRANCISCO BAY REGION - LIBRARY (Env-Cons)
1111 Jackson St., Rm. 6040   Phone: (415) 464-1255
Oakland, CA 94618   Lawrence P. Kolb, Hd.
Subjects: Water quality studies for San Francisco Bay Area. **Holdings:** 3600 studies and reports. **Services:** Copying; library open to public for reference use only.

★1938★
CALIFORNIA STATE REHABILITATION CENTER - RESIDENT LIBRARY (Soc Sci)
Box 841   Phone: (714) 737-2683
Norco, CA 91760   Gerald O. Nelson, Libn.
Founded: 1962. **Staff:** Prof 1; Other 6. **Subjects:** Social and behavioral sciences, black studies, law. **Holdings:** 13,460 books. **Subscriptions:** 19 journals and other serials; 24 newspapers. **Services:** Library not open to public. **Networks/Consortia:** Member of San Bernardino, Inyo, Riverside Counties United Library Services (SIRCULS).

★1939★
CALIFORNIA STATE RESOURCES AGENCY - LIBRARY (Env-Cons)
117 Resources Bldg.
1416 Ninth St.   Phone: (916) 445-7752
Sacramento, CA 95814   Madeleine A. Darcy, Sr.Libn.
Founded: 1927. **Staff:** Prof 1; Other 5. **Subjects:** Freshwater fisheries, game and game birds, forestry, park management, soil conservation, boats and boating, recreation, water pollution, engineering. **Holdings:** 20,000 books and bound periodical volumes; 6 VF drawers of reports. **Subscriptions:** 900 journals and other serials. **Services:** Interlibrary loans; copying; library open to public for reference use only. **Networks/Consortia:** Member of Western Forest Information Network (WESTFORNET). **Publications:** List of accessions, quarterly - distributed internally and to requesting libraries. **Remarks:** Library serves Departments of Fish and Game, Forestry, Parks & Recreation, Conservation, Water Resources and Water Resources Control Board.

★1940★
CALIFORNIA STATE SUPREME COURT LIBRARY (Law)
4241 State Bldg. Annex
455 Golden Gate Ave.   Phone: (415) 557-1922
San Francisco, CA 94102   John A. Sigel
Founded: 1868. **Staff:** Prof 1; Other 1. **Subjects:** Law. **Holdings:** 75,000 volumes. **Services:** Library not open to public.

★1941★
CALIFORNIA STATE UNIVERSITY, CHICO - MERIAM LIBRARY - SPECIAL COLLECTIONS (Educ)
First & Hazel Sts.   Phone: (916) 895-6212
Chico, CA 95929   William A. Jones, Spec.Coll.Libn.
Founded: 1887. **Special Collections:** Northeastern California Collection; regional information and records. **Holdings:** 324,444 government documents; 58,932 maps. **Services:** Interlibrary loans; copying; library open to public with courtesy card. **Computerized Information Services:** DIALOG, New York Times Information Service; computerized cataloging, serials and circulation. **Networks/Consortia:** Member of North State Cooperative Library System.

★1942★
CALIFORNIA STATE UNIVERSITY AND COLLEGES - MOSS LANDING MARINE LABORATORIES - LIBRARY (Sci-Tech)
Box 223   Phone: (408) 633-3304
Moss Landing, CA 95039   Sheila Baldridge, Libn.
Founded: 1966. **Staff:** Prof 1; Other 1. **Subjects:** Oceanography, marine biology and geology, trace metals research. **Special Collections:** Monterey Bay Collection. **Holdings:** 6000 books; 1574 bound periodical volumes; 950 nautical charts; 469 topographical maps; 1200 technical reports; 200 theses. **Subscriptions:** 96 journals and other serials. **Services:** Interlibrary loans (fee); copying; library open to public with restrictions. **Computerized**

Information Services: DIALOG. **Networks/Consortia:** Member of CIN.

★1943★
CALIFORNIA STATE UNIVERSITY, FRESNO - DEPARTMENT OF SPECIAL COLLECTIONS (Hum)
Fresno, CA 93740   Phone: (209) 487-2595
          Ronald J. Mahoney, Hd.
Staff: Prof 1; Other 1. **Subjects:** Fairs, history, viticulture, William Saroyan, Credit Foncier of Sinaloa Company. **Special Collections:** Donald G. Larson Collection of International Exhibitions and Fairs (5000 items); Harry Pidgeon Collection (645 negatives and prints); Viticulture and Enology Collection (5500 items); William Saroyan Collection (550 items); Roy J. Woodward Memorial Library of Californiana (11,000 items); Credit Foncier of Sinola Company Collection (587 photographs; 14,000 other items). **Holdings:** 17,000 books; 5000 bound periodical volumes; 1800 negatives. **Services:** Copying; library open to public for reference use only. **Computerized Information Services:** Online systems; computerized cataloging. **Networks/Consortia:** Member of Areawide Library Network (AWLNET); CLASS; RLG; OCLC. **Special Indexes:** San Joaquin Valley Index (card); Photographs of Panama-Pacific International Exposition Index (card); Enology Collection Index (card).

★1944★
CALIFORNIA STATE UNIVERSITY, FULLERTON - COLLECTION FOR THE HISTORY OF CARTOGRAPHY (Geog-Map; Hist)
The Library, Rm. L444-B
800 N. State College Blvd.
Box 4150   Phone: (714) 773-3444
Fullerton, CA 92634   Linda E. Herman, Spec.Coll.Libn.
Staff: Prof 1; Other 1. **Subjects:** Maps, history of cartography. **Holdings:** 3089 books; 722 pamphlets and periodicals; 1429 pre-1901 maps. **Subscriptions:** 35 journals and other serials. **Services:** Library open to public. **Publications:** Map exhibition catalog, annual - distributed to map libraries. **Staff:** Roy V. Boswell, Cur.

★1945★
CALIFORNIA STATE UNIVERSITY, FULLERTON - LIBRARY - FREEDOM CENTER (Soc Sci)
Box 4150   Phone: (714) 773-3186
Fullerton, CA 92634   Lynn M. Coppel, Coord.
Founded: 1965. **Staff:** Prof 1. **Subjects:** Political extremism, especially right-wing; contemporary culture; alternative life styles. **Holdings:** 10,000 pamphlets; 200 tapes; 4000 unbound periodical titles; 1000 folders of ephemeral material. **Subscriptions:** 300 journals and other serials; 10 newspapers. **Services:** Interlibrary loans; copying; library open to public for reference use only. **Computerized Information Services:** Computerized cataloging and serials.

CALIFORNIA STATE UNIVERSITY, LOS ANGELES - ARNOLD SCHOENBERG INSTITUTE
See: Arnold Schoenberg Institute

★1946★
CALIFORNIA STATE UNIVERSITY, LOS ANGELES - SCIENCE AND TECHNOLOGY REFERENCE ROOM (Sci-Tech)
John F. Kennedy Memorial Library
5151 State University Dr.   Phone: (213) 224-2232
Los Angeles, CA 90032   Cornelia O. Balogh, Act.Hd.
Founded: 1948. **Staff:** Prof 3; Other 6. **Subjects:** Science and technology. **Holdings:** 168,000 books; 51,201 bound periodical volumes; 9300 pamphlets; 8050 technical reports; 4108 microforms. **Subscriptions:** 2760 journals and other serials. **Services:** Interlibrary loans; copying; room open to public for reference use only. **Computerized Information Services:** DIALOG, BRS; computerized cataloging and circulation. **Networks/Consortia:** Member of CLASS; OCLC. **Staff:** Margaret Champlin, Sci. & Tech.Libn.; Sue Huddleson, Sci. & Tech.Libn.

★1947★
CALIFORNIA STATE UNIVERSITY, NORTHRIDGE - INSTRUCTIONAL MATERIALS LABORATORY (Educ)
South Library
18111 Nordhoff St.   Phone: (213) 885-2501
Northridge, CA 91330   Karin Duran, Dir.
Staff: Prof 1; Other 3. **Subjects:** Curriculum materials for all subjects K-12. **Special Collections:** Bilingual-bicultural curriculum materials (850 items). **Holdings:** 26,971 books; 14,326 nonbook materials; 2538 curriculum guides; 3500 filmstrips and sound filmstrips; 2500 phonograph records and cassettes; 1850 transparencies, slides, kits, games. **Services:** Copying; library open to public with fee for borrowing. **Publications:** Bibliography of

Bilingual-Bicultural Education Materials available at the Instructional Materials Laboratory; Special Education Materials available at the Instructional Materials Laboratory. **Special Catalogs:** Song file catalog (card). **Remarks:** The IML provides curriculum previewing areas and a workroom for the construction of instructional aids.

★1948★
CALIFORNIA STATE UNIVERSITY, NORTHRIDGE - LIBRARY - HEALTH SCIENCE COLLECTION (Med)
18111 Nordhoff St.   Phone: (213) 885-3012
Northridge, CA 91330   Snowdy Dodson, Sci.Ref.Libn.
Founded: 1965. **Staff:** Prof 2; Other 1. **Subjects:** Health education, nutrition, occupational health, sanitation, child and maternity care, medical statistics, preventive medicine, public health administration, physiology. **Holdings:** 29,000 books; 10,679 bound periodical volumes. **Subscriptions:** 516 journals and other serials. **Services:** Copying; library open to public. **Computerized Information Services:** NLM; computerized cataloging and circulation.

★1949★
CALIFORNIA STATE UNIVERSITY, NORTHRIDGE - WOMEN'S CENTER (Soc Sci)
18111 Nordhoff   Phone: (213) 885-2780
Northridge, CA 91330   Deborah Kae Walker, Dir.
Staff: 10. **Subjects:** Feminism, women in history, psychology, parenting, child development, sociology, employment and career development for women. **Holdings:** 1000 books; 700 bound periodical volumes; 500 reports and clippings. **Services:** Center open to public.

★1950★
CALIFORNIA STATE UNIVERSITY, SACRAMENTO - LIBRARY - MEDIA SERVICES CENTER (Aud-Vis)
6000 J St.   Phone: (916) 454-6466
Sacramento, CA 95819   Sheila J. Marsh, Media Libn.
Founded: 1947. **Staff:** Prof 1; Other 3. **Special Collections:** Slide collection (70,000 slides). **Holdings:** 902,000 microforms; 602 video cassettes; 340 filmstrips; 238 slide-tape programs; 1477 audio cassettes; 1663 language audio cassettes. **Services:** AV items available for reference use only; microforms available for interlibrary loan. **Publications:** Subject media bibliographies. **Special Catalogs:** Computer printouts of slide collection by artist, medium, country.

★1951★
CALIFORNIA STATE UNIVERSITY, SACRAMENTO - LIBRARY - SCIENCE & TECHNOLOGY REFERENCE DEPARTMENT (Sci-Tech)
2000 Jed Smith Dr.   Phone: (916) 454-6373
Sacramento, CA 95819   Barbara A. Charlton, Assoc.Libn.
Founded: 1953. **Staff:** Prof 4; Other 2. **Subjects:** Biology and environment, engineering, geology, chemistry, physics, mathematics, computer science, nursing, speech pathology, home economics. **Special Collections:** Powder Diffraction File (X-ray); Sadtler Standard Spectra (8 series). **Holdings:** 141,242 books; 49,452 bound periodical volumes; 18,500 microforms and AV materials; 11,000 topographic maps of California and neighboring states; 7280 pamphlets; 7945 clippings. **Subscriptions:** 1839 journals and other serials. **Services:** Interlibrary loans; copying; library open to public for reference use only. **Computerized Information Services:** BRS; computerized cataloging, serials and circulation. **Networks/Consortia:** Member of Mountain Valley Library System. **Publications:** Subject bibliographies. **Staff:** Joseph Kramer, Sr.Asst.Ref.Libn.; Eileen Heaser, Sr.Asst.Ref.Libn.; Donine Hedrick, Asst.Libn.

CALIFORNIA TEST BUREAU/MC GRAW-HILL
See: CTB/Mc Graw-Hill

★1952★
CALIFORNIA THOROUGHBRED BREEDERS ASSOCIATION - CARLETON F. BURKE MEMORIAL LIBRARY (Rec)
201 Colorado Pl.
Box 750
Arcadia, CA 91006   Phone: (213) 445-7800
                                      E. Brownie Working, Libn.
Staff: Prof 1. **Subjects:** Horses, thoroughbred breeding and racing, veterinary medicine. **Special Collections:** Edward E. Lasker Collection of Foreign Racing Records (2000 volumes); C.C. Mosely Collection on American Breeding. **Holdings:** 6500 books; 5500 bound periodical volumes; 600 microfiche. **Subscriptions:** 67 journals and other serials. **Services:** Copying; library open to public for reference use only. **Computerized Information Services:** Bloodstock Research & Statistical Service. **Special Indexes:** Index by dams to sales catalogs (card).

★1953★
CALIFORNIA WESTERN LAW SCHOOL - LIBRARY (Law)
350 Cedar St.   Phone: (714) 239-0391
San Diego, CA 92101   Chin Kim, Lib.Dir.
Staff: Prof 4; Other 5. **Subjects:** International and comparative law. **Holdings:** 81,923 books; 4220 bound periodical volumes; 26,146 books in microform. **Subscriptions:** 1300 journals and other serials; 10 newspapers. **Services:** Interlibrary loans (fee); copying; library open to public for reference use only. **Computerized Information Services:** WESTLAW; computerized cataloging. **Networks/Consortia:** Member of OCLC; San Diego Greater Metropolitan Area Library & Information Agency Council (METRO). **Staff:** Karla M. Randich, Dir., Pub.Serv.; Deborah C. Mattrey, Dir., Tech.Serv.

CALL-CHRONICLE NEWSPAPERS, INC.
See: Allentown Call-Chronicle

★1954★
CALLAWAY EDUCATIONAL ASSOCIATION - COLEMAN LIBRARY (Hum)
Lincoln St.   Phone: (404) 882-0948
LaGrange, GA 30240   Mary Lou Dabbs, Hd.Libn.
Founded: 1955. **Staff:** Prof 2; Other 10. **Subjects:** Children's literature, literary research, home and family. **Special Collections:** Georgia Collection (275 monographs); rare book collection (99 monographs). **Holdings:** 65,000 volumes; 3700 reels of microfilm; 1100 microfiche; 7100 phonograph records; 3125 filmstrips; 15 VF drawers. **Subscriptions:** 330 journals and other serials; 7 newspapers. **Services:** Copying; library open to members of the Callaway Educational Association. **Special Indexes:** Literary Reference File (card); Index to Georgia Magazines (card); The Herald (Troup County) Index (card).

CALLERY CHEMICAL COMPANY
See: Mine Safety Appliances Company - MSA Research Corporation

CALLIER CENTER FOR COMMUNICATIONS DISORDERS
See: University of Texas, Dallas

CALLIHAN (Gertrude) MEMORIAL LIBRARY
See: First United Methodist Church - Gertrude Callihan Memorial Library

CALLIOPEAN SOCIETY LIBRARY
See: Bridgeport Public Library - Historical Collections

★1955★
CALSPAN CORPORATION - TECHNICAL INFORMATION CENTER (Sci-Tech)
4455 Genesee St.   Phone: (716) 632-7500
Buffalo, NY 14225   Betty Miller, Supv.
Founded: 1946. **Staff:** Prof 1; Other 6. **Subjects:** Aerodynamics, aeronautics, electronics, transportation, computer sciences, meteorology, environmental sciences, aerospace sciences, applied sciences, applied physics. **Special Collections:** Complete output in microfiche of NTIS and American Institute of Aeronautics and Astronautics reports; National Advisory Committee for Aeronautics (NACA) Collection, 1915-1958. **Holdings:** 14,000 books; 564 reels of film and 14,000 microfiche backfiles of periodicals; 180,000 hard copy reports; 400,000 reports on microfiche. **Subscriptions:** 425 journals and other serials. **Services:** Interlibrary loans; copying; library open to public with restrictions. **Computerized Information Services:** DIALOG, SDC, NASA/RECON, ISI, MEDLINE, DTIC. **Networks/Consortia:** Member of Western New York Library Resources Council (WNYLRC).

★1956★
CALTEX PETROLEUM CORPORATION - BUSINESS LIBRARY (Bus-Fin; Energy)
Box 61500   Phone: (214) 830-1000
Dallas, TX 75261   Muriel H. Hummel, Libn.
Founded: 1953. **Staff:** Prof 1; Other 1. **Subjects:** Economics, intergovernmental affairs, statistics. **Holdings:** 1000 books; 500 pamphlet boxes. **Subscriptions:** 250 journals and other serials. **Services:** Interlibrary loans; library open by appointment to outside users from the petroleum industry or economic-related organizations on an in-house reference basis. **Computerized Information Services:** Online systems. **Formerly:** Its Planning and Economics Department Library, located in New York, NY.

CALUMET REGIONAL ARCHIVES
See: Indiana University Northwest

CALUMET ROOM
See: Hammond Historical Society

★1957★
CALVARY BAPTIST CHURCH - LIBRARY (Rel-Theol)
3921 Baltimore   Phone: (816) 531-1208
Kansas City, MO 64111   Carroll O'Neal, Dir.
Staff: Prof 2; Other 2. **Subjects:** Religion, history of the Southern Baptist church, children's religious literature, Bible, missions in foreign countries. **Holdings:** 2000 books. **Subscriptions:** 15 journals and other serials. **Services:** Interlibrary loans; library open to public for reference use only.

★1958★
CALVARY BAPTIST THEOLOGICAL SEMINARY - LIBRARY (Rel-Theol)
Valley Forge Rd. & Sumneytown Pike   Phone: (215) 368-7538
Lansdale, PA 19446   James F. Stitzinger, Libn.
Founded: 1975. **Staff:** Prof 1; Other 5. **Subjects:** Theology, Biblical studies. **Holdings:** 45,000 books; 4600 bound periodical volumes; 250 tapes. **Subscriptions:** 250 journals and other serials. **Services:** Copying; library open to public with restrictions. **Networks/Consortia:** Member of Southeastern Pennsylvania Theological Libraries Association (SEPTLA). **Staff:** Jean Kerr, Cat.

★1959★
CALVARY HOSPITAL - MEDICAL LIBRARY (Med)
1740-1770 Eastchester Rd.   Phone: (212) 430-4600
Bronx, NY 10461   Mary M. Carroll, Med.Libn.
Founded: 1963. **Staff:** Prof 1. **Subjects:** Medicine, cancer. **Holdings:** 500 books; 1400 bound periodical volumes; medical journal articles; 100 microfiche, slides, tapes. **Subscriptions:** 60 journals and other serials. **Services:** Interlibrary loans; copying; library not open to public. **Networks/Consortia:** Member of New York & New Jersey Regional Medical Library Program; Manhattan-Bronx Health Sciences Library Group.

CALVERT (Eleanor) MEMORIAL LIBRARY
See: Kitchener-Waterloo Art Gallery - Eleanor Calvert Memorial Library

★1960★
CALVERT MARINE MUSEUM - LIBRARY (Sci-Tech; Hist)
Box 97   Phone: (301) 326-3719
Solomons, MD 20688   Ralph Eshelman, Dir.
Founded: 1975. **Staff:** Prof 1. **Subjects:** Maritime history, Miocene and vertebrate paleontology, geology, marine biology. **Special Collections:** Budenhagen Collection (comprehensive Atlantic Coastal Plain geology and paleontology); M.M. Davis Collection (shipbuilding); Watermen of Patuxent River Region Collection (oral history tapes, photographs, slides). **Holdings:** 1443 books; 117 bound periodical volumes; 203 unbound periodicals; 860 local newspaper clippings; 2400 slides; 2500 photographs; 12.5 linear feet of business archives. **Subscriptions:** 34 journals and other serials. **Services:** Copying; library open to public for reference use only. **Staff:** Alice Viverette, Libn.

★1961★
CALVIN COLLEGE AND SEMINARY - LIBRARY (Rel-Theol)
3207 Burton St., S.E.   Phone: (616) 949-4000
Grand Rapids, MI 49506   Marvin E. Monsma, Dir.
Staff: Prof 6; Other 21. **Subjects:** Religion, philosophy, English literature, French literature and language, Dutch language and literature, history. **Special Collections:** Calvin and Calvinism; Colonial Origins of the Christian Reformed Church. **Holdings:** 285,000 books; 62,000 bound periodical volumes; 125,000 government documents; 20,000 microforms. **Subscriptions:** 2160 journals and other serials; 20 newspapers. **Services:** Interlibrary loans; copying; library open to public. **Computerized Information Services:** Computerized cataloging. **Networks/Consortia:** Member of OCLC through Michigan Library Consortium. **Special Indexes:** Card index to major publications (serials) of the Christian Reformed Church. **Staff:** Conrad J. Bult, Asst.Dir., Ref.; Peter De Klerk, Hd., Theological Div.; Stephen Lambers, Govt.Doc./Info.Serv.; Barbara Sluiter, Hd., Cat.; Herbert Brinks, Cur., Heritage Hall; Connie Van Sledright, Hd., Circ.; Marinus Goote, Theological Asst.; Jo Duyst, Acq.

CAM-I
See: Computer Aided Manufacturing-International, Inc.

★1962★
CAMARILLO STATE HOSPITAL - PROFESSIONAL LIBRARY (Med)
    Phone: (805) 484-3661
Camarillo, CA 93010   Melvin C. Oathout, Libn.
Founded: 1940. **Staff:** Prof 1. **Subjects:** Psychiatric and psychological treatment, medicine, social service, nursing, radiology, psychotherapy, adjunctive therapies, mental health. **Holdings:** 12,000 books; 1500 bound periodical volumes; 2600 unbound volumes of periodicals; 18 linear shelf feet

of pamphlets. **Subscriptions:** 175 journals and other serials. **Services:** Interlibrary loans; copying; library open to public for reference use only. **Networks/Consortia:** Member of California State Hospital Libraries Group; Pacific Southwest Regional Medical Library System (PSRMLS). **Publications:** Monthly and annual reports (restricted circulation); acquisition lists.

★1963★
CAMBRIA COUNTY FREE LAW LIBRARY (Law)
Courthouse   Phone: (814) 427-5440
Ebensburg, PA 15931   Judy Patterson, Libn.
Founded: 1906. **Staff:** Prof 1. **Subjects:** Law. **Holdings:** 35,000 volumes. **Services:** Library open to public.

★1964★
CAMBRIA COUNTY HISTORICAL SOCIETY - MUSEUM & LIBRARY (Hist)
521 W. High St.   Phone: (814) 472-6674
Ebensburg, PA 15931   Sara Leishman, Cur.
Founded: 1925. **Staff:** 1. **Subjects:** Genealogy; history of Cambria County; general history. **Holdings:** 2000 volumes. **Services:** Library open to public for reference use only.

★1965★
CAMBRIAN COLLEGE OF APPLIED ARTS AND TECHNOLOGY - LIBRARY (Sci-Tech)†
1400 Barrydowne Rd., Station A   Phone: (705) 566-8101
Sudbury, ON, Canada P3A 3V8   Bernard Bregaint, Mgr., Lib.Serv.
Founded: 1967. **Staff:** Prof 3; Other 10. **Subjects:** Mathematics, chemistry, physics, geology, metallurgy, mining, business, electronics, engineering, art, music. **Special Collections:** Metallurgy. **Holdings:** 40,000 books; 4 VF drawers of Cambriana Archives; 10 VF drawers of Statistics Canada material; 15 VF drawers of pamphlets and clippings; 10,000 microfiche; 1400 recordings. **Subscriptions:** 850 journals and other serials; 13 newspapers. **Services:** Interlibrary loans; copying; library open to public. **Computerized Information Services:** DIALOG. **Networks/Consortia:** Member of Bibliocentre. **Publications:** New Acquisitions List, monthly. **Staff:** Monique Chasse, Pub.Serv.Libn.

★1966★
CAMBRIDGE HISTORICAL COMMISSION - LIBRARY (Hist)
City Hall Annex
57 Inman St.   Phone: (617) 498-9040
Cambridge, MA 02139   Charles M. Sullivan, Exec.Dir.
Staff: Prof 3; Other 1. **Subjects:** Architectural history and development of Cambridge. **Holdings:** 300 books; 13,000 building inventory records (1963-1977); maps of Cambridge (1633-1930); 19,000 35mm negatives; 3500 negatives from city records (1919-1958); 3500 early views of Cambridge. **Services:** Copying; library open to public. **Publications:** Survey of Architectural History in Cambridge, 5 volumes. **Special Indexes:** Holdings organized by geographic location; card index of all Cambridge architects and builders. **Staff:** Robert H. Nylander, Arch.Hist.; Susan E. Maycock, Survey Dir.

★1967★
CAMBRIDGE HOSPITAL - MEDICAL LIBRARY (Med)†
1493 Cambridge St.   Phone: (617) 498-1439
Cambridge, MA 02139   Mrs. James H. Stanton, Med.Libn.
Staff: Prof 1. **Subjects:** Medicine, surgery, health sciences, nursing. **Holdings:** 550 books; 4500 bound periodical volumes. **Subscriptions:** 63 journals and other serials. **Services:** Library not open to public.

★1968★
CAMBRIDGE MENTAL HEALTH & DEVELOPMENTAL CENTER - STAFF & RESIDENT RESOURCE CENTER (Med)†
Rte. 35   Phone: (614) 439-1371
Cambridge, OH 43725   Nancy Bolin, Dir., Resource Serv.
Staff: Prof 2; Other 3. **Subjects:** Mental health, psychology, psychiatry, mental retardation. **Holdings:** 500 books; AV materials. **Subscriptions:** 100 journals and other serials. **Services:** Interlibrary loans; copying; library open to public with restrictions. **Networks/Consortia:** Member of Southeastern Ohio Library Organization (SOLO). **Publications:** Acquisitions list, bimonthly. **Special Catalogs:** AV Catalog. **Staff:** Mary Williams, Libn.

CAMBRIDGE MILITARY LIBRARY
See: Canada - National Defence

★1969★
CAMBRIDGE SCHOOL DEPARTMENT - TEACHERS' RESOURCE CENTER (Educ)
459 Broadway   Phone: (617) 492-8000
Cambridge, MA 02138   Sheila Morshead, Libn./Media Spec.
Founded: 1969. **Staff:** Prof 1; Other 1. **Subjects:** Education. **Holdings:**

9800 books; 15,000 other media materials; 1000 pamphlets (cataloged). **Subscriptions:** 110 journals and other serials. **Services:** Media production; library open to public for reference use only.

★1970★
CAMBRIDGE STATE HOSPITAL - LIBRARY (Med)
Cambridge, MN 55008

Phone: (612) 689-2121
Jean Peterson, Libn.

Staff: Prof 1. **Subjects:** Medicine, behavior modification. **Holdings:** 900 books. **Subscriptions:** 76 journals and other serials. **Services:** Interlibrary loans; copying; library open to public. **Networks/Consortia:** Member of Minnesota Department of Public Welfare Library Consortium. **Publications:** Newsletter - monthly.

CAMDEN-CARROLL LIBRARY
See: Morehead State University

★1971★
CAMDEN COUNTY BAR ASSOCIATION - LAW LIBRARY (Law)
Camden County Courthouse, Rm. 500
Camden, NJ 08101

Phone: (609) 757-6703
Diane Hollingshead, Libn.

Staff: Prof 1. **Subjects:** Law. **Holdings:** 20,000 books; 100 bound periodical volumes; U.S. and state statutes. **Services:** Library open to public for reference use only.

★1972★
CAMDEN COUNTY HISTORICAL SOCIETY - LIBRARY (Hist)
Park Blvd. & Euclid Ave.
Camden, NJ 08103

Phone: (609) 964-3333
Miriam Favorite, Libn.

Staff: Prof 1. **Subjects:** History of Camden, Camden County, New Jersey; decorative arts; Walt Whitman; genealogy. **Special Collections:** Manuscripts, building contracts, maps, deeds. **Holdings:** 18,000 books; 20 VF drawers of general material; 160 reels of microfilmed newspapers. **Subscriptions:** 15 journals and other serials. **Services:** Copying; library open to public. **Publications:** Bulletin, annual; newsletter, quarterly.

★1973★
CAMDEN DISTRICT HERITAGE FOUNDATION - HISTORIC CAMDEN (Hist)
Box 710
Camden, SC 29020

Phone: (803) 432-0764
Stephen Smith, Dir.

Staff: Prof 3. **Subjects:** Local history. **Holdings:** 100 volumes; 20 archeological reports; manuscript material pertaining to Camden from settlement in 1739 through 1865. **Subscriptions:** 10 journals and other serials. **Services:** Copying; library open to public. **Staff:** Shirley P. Ransom, Asst.Dir.

CAMERON (Angus L.) MEDICAL LIBRARY
See: Trinity Medical Center - Angus L. Cameron Medical Library

★1974★
CAMERON COUNTY HISTORICAL SOCIETY - LITTLE MUSEUM (Hist)
R.R. 2, Box 54
Emporium, PA 15834

Phone: (814) 483-3636
Mrs. Merle L. Bowser, Pres.

Staff: 2. **Subjects:** History of Cameron County; history of logging and early industry; genealogical material. **Special Collections:** Pictures, papers and books of Gen. Joseph T. McNarney, USAF; artifacts, papers, and photographs of Tom Mix, silent film star. **Holdings:** Cameron County documents; maps; 3 VF drawers of newspaper clippings and documents; microfilms of all tombstone inscriptions in 38 cemeteries and some church records. **Services:** Information prepared.

★1975★
CAMERON IRON WORKS, INC. - LIBRARY (Sci-Tech)†
1124 Silber Rd.
Houston, TX 77251

Phone: (713) 939-3789
Norma A. Gries, Libn.

Founded: 1967. **Staff:** Prof 1; Other 1. **Subjects:** Metallurgy, forging, oil tool technology. **Holdings:** 2000 books; 800 bound periodical volumes; 4 file drawers of microfiche. **Subscriptions:** 200 journals and other serials; 5 newspapers. **Services:** Interlibrary loans; copying (fee); library not open to public. **Computerized Information Services:** DIALOG. **Publications:** Library Bulletin - for internal distribution only.

★1976★
CAMP DRESSER & MC KEE, INC. - CDM ENVIRONMENTAL LIBRARY (Env-Cons; Energy)
11455 W. 48th Ave.
Wheat Ridge, CO 80033

Phone: (303) 422-0469
Sheila B. Weissberg, Libn.

Staff: Prof 1. **Subjects:** Environmental sciences, air and water pollution, ecology, environmental law, energy, mining. **Holdings:** 2000 books; 3000 government and technical documents. **Subscriptions:** 50 journals and other serials. **Services:** Interlibrary loans; copying; library open to public by appointment. **Computerized Information Services:** DIALOG, SDC.

★1977★
CAMP DRESSER & MC KEE, INC. - HERMAN G. DRESSER LIBRARY (Env-Cons)
One Center Plaza
Boston, MA 02108

Phone: (617) 742-5151
Virginia L. Carroll, Libn.

Founded: 1958. **Staff:** Prof 2; Other 1. **Subjects:** Environmental engineering, wastewater treatment, water treatment, solid waste management, industrial waste, resource recovery. **Holdings:** 13,000 books; 500 bound periodical volumes; 2500 reports (cataloged); 2800 report data (computations); 990 pamphlets; 325 reprints (articles written by employees); 250 microfiche. **Subscriptions:** 309 journals and other serials. **Services:** Interlibrary loans; copying; library open to public with restrictions. **Computerized Information Services:** DIALOG, SDC, BRS; computerized cataloging. **Networks/Consortia:** Member of New England On-Line Users Group; NELINET. **Publications:** Acquisitions list, monthly - for internal distribution only. **Special Indexes:** Report Index; computation index - both on rolodexes. **Staff:** Kathleen Houston, Asst.Libn.

CAMP H.M. SMITH LIBRARY
See: U.S. Marine Corps

★1978★
CAMP HILL HOSPITAL - DRUG INFORMATION CENTRE (Med)
1763 Robie St.
Halifax, NS, Canada B3H 3G2

Phone: (902) 423-1371
C. Brian Tuttle, Supv.

Staff: Prof 1; Other 1. **Subjects:** Therapeutics, pharmacology, toxicology, institutional and professional pharmacy practice. **Holdings:** 1512 files. **Subscriptions:** 18 journals and other serials. **Services:** Library open to public. **Computerized Information Services:** MEDLINE. **Publications:** The Distillate, quarterly.

★1979★
CAMP HILL HOSPITAL - HEALTH SCIENCES LIBRARY (Med)
1763 Robie St.
Halifax, NS, Canada B3H 3G2

Phone: (902) 423-1371
Verona Hall, Lib.Asst.

Staff: 1. **Subjects:** Medicine, surgery, psychiatry, nursing, gerontology, psychology, pharmacology. **Holdings:** 1050 books; 100 bound periodical volumes; tapes. **Subscriptions:** 250 journals and other serials. **Services:** Interlibrary loans; copying; library open to public.

CAMP PENDLETON
See: U.S. Marine Corps

CAMPBELL (Charles Mac Fie) MEMORIAL LIBRARY
See: Massachusetts Mental Health Center - Charles Mac Fie Campbell Memorial Library

CAMPBELL DISTRICT LIBRARY
See: Scarborough Public Library - Film Services

★1980★
CAMPBELL-EWALD COMPANY - REFERENCE CENTER (Bus-Fin)
30400 Van Dyke
Warren, MI 48093

Phone: (313) 574-3400
Susan B. Stepek, V.P. & Mgr.

Founded: 1925. **Staff:** Prof 6; Other 4. **Subjects:** Advertising, marketing, automotive industry, general business and reference. **Special Collections:** Automobilia; descriptive State file, art library; clips of advertisements. **Holdings:** 3200 books; 3100 bound periodical volumes; 2600 subject folders; 1200 reports, documents, bulletins, maps, client and company archives, government documents, services. **Subscriptions:** 500 journals and other serials (regular); 1800 journals and other serials (sample). **Services:** Library open to public by appointment. **Computerized Information Services:** DIALOG, New York Times Information Service, Dow Jones News Retrieval. **Publications:** Washington Scene, monthly; Social Change Briefs, bimonthly; Monthly Headline Services. **Staff:** Amber McCoy, Sr.Ref.Libn.

★1981★
CAMPBELL, GODFREY & LEWTAS - LIBRARY (Law)
Toronto Dominion Centre
Box 36
Toronto, ON, Canada M5K 1C5

Phone: (416) 362-2401
Clare-Marie Lyons, Libn.

Staff: Prof 2; Other 1. **Subjects:** Law, taxation. **Holdings:** 7000 books; 184 bound periodical volumes; 450 government documents; 3 VF drawers of annual reports. **Subscriptions:** 200 journals and other serials. **Services:** Interlibrary loans; copying; library open to public with restrictions.

Computerized Information Services: QL Systems, WESTLAW. **Publications:** Weekly newsletter. **Special Indexes:** Index of Canadian tax treaties (card); index of current bills in the Ontario and federal legislatures (card).

★1982★
CAMPBELL INSTITUTE FOR RESEARCH AND TECHNOLOGY - RESEARCH DEVELOPMENT LIBRARY (Sci-Tech; Food-Bev)
Campbell Pl.   Phone: (609) 964-4000
Camden, NJ 08101   CarolAnn Vincent, Res.Libn.
Founded: 1941. **Staff:** Prof 1; Other 1. **Subjects:** Food technology, biochemistry, microbiology, nutrition, home economics. **Holdings:** 5000 books; 2200 bound periodical volumes; 1500 pamphlets; 2500 patents. **Subscriptions:** 130 journals and other serials. **Services:** Interlibrary loans; copying; library not open to public. **Computerized Information Services:** Online systems. **Publications:** Library Bulletin, monthly.

CAMPBELL (John Bulow) LIBRARY
See: Columbia Theological Seminary - John Bulow Campbell Library

CAMPBELL LIBRARY
See: St. Joseph's University - Academy of Food Marketing

★1983★
CAMPBELL-MITHUN, INC. - LIBRARY (Bus-Fin)
Northstar Ctr.   Phone: (612) 347-1509
Minneapolis, MN 55402   Virginia Ferestad, Hd.Libn.
Founded: 1953. **Staff:** Prof 2; Other 3. **Subjects:** Advertising, marketing, Upper Midwest statistics. **Holdings:** 500 books; 400 volumes of client records; 500 files of pamphlets and clippings; 300 competitive advertising files; 1200 picture files. **Subscriptions:** 700 journals and other serials. **Services:** Interlibrary loans; copying; permission to use library may be requested. **Computerized Information Services:** New York Times Information Service, Mead Data Central. **Networks/Consortia:** Member of INSIDERS. **Staff:** Carol Delak, Assoc.Libn.

★1984★
CAMPBELL-MITHUN, INC. - RESEARCH INFORMATION CENTER (Bus-Fin)
111 E. Wacker Dr.   Phone: (312) 565-3800
Chicago, IL 60601   Steve Heffernan, Libn.
Founded: 1962. **Staff:** Prof 3. **Subjects:** Advertising, marketing, business, finance, food industry. **Holdings:** 1500 books; 500 government documents (cataloged); 174 VF drawers of clippings, pamphlets, pictures, annual reports. **Subscriptions:** 1000 journals and other serials; 10 newspapers. **Services:** Interlibrary loans; copying; library open to public by request. **Computerized Information Services:** DIALOG, SDC, New York Times Information Service, Mead Data Central, Dow Jones News Retrieval. **Networks/Consortia:** Member of Chicago Library System; Metropolitan Chicago Library Assembly. **Publications:** Fast Facts, monthly; The Future Book, monthly; Research Information Center Newsletter, monthly; Trends, quarterly - for distribution to Chicago office staff. **Special Indexes:** Information File Index (card); Corporation File Index (card).

CAMPBELL (R.B.) LIBRARY
See: Florida State Dept. of Natural Resources - Bureau of Geology Library

★1985★
CAMPBELL TAGGART, INC. - RESEARCH DIVISION - LIBRARY (Food-Bev)†
3401 Haggar Way   Phone: (214) 358-9211
Dallas, TX 75222   Sue Hammond, Libn.
Subjects: Food plant sanitation, chemistry, microbiology, nutrition, food technology and processing, cereal chemistry, machinery, marketing. **Special Collections:** U.S. Government data and regulations. **Holdings:** Figures not available. **Subscriptions:** 92 journals and other serials. **Services:** Interlibrary loans; library not open to public.

★1986★
CAMPBELL UNIVERSITY - SCHOOL OF LAW - LAW LIBRARY (Law)
Box 458   Phone: (919) 893-4111
Buies Creek, NC 27506   Karen C. Sorvari, Dir. of Res.
Staff: Prof 2; Other 5. **Subjects:** Law. **Holdings:** 60,500 books and bound periodical volumes; 3000 other cataloged items; 28,200 volumes on microform, including Supreme Court records and briefs, English ruling cases, English reports, and agency reports; AV materials. **Subscriptions:** 500 journals and other serials; 6 newspapers. **Services:** Copying; library open to public. **Computerized Information Services:** Online systems. **Staff:** Stanley F. Hammer, Asst.Libn.; Doris M. Hinson, Cat.Libn.; Barbara Ames, Ser.Asst.

CAMPBELL (William J.) LIBRARY OF THE UNITED STATES COURTS
See: William J. Campbell Library of the United States Courts

★1987★
CAMPION COLLEGE - LIBRARY (Hum)
University of Regina   Phone: (306) 586-4242
Regina, SK, Canada S4S 0A2   Myfanwy Truscott, Libn.
Staff: Prof 1; Other 2. **Subjects:** Religious studies, theology, philosophy, English literature, Canadian and medieval history, psychology. **Special Collections:** Jesuitica (1000 volumes). **Holdings:** 55,500 books; 4900 bound periodical volumes; 194 phonograph records; 10,000 microfiche; 148 maps. **Subscriptions:** 175 journals and other serials. 15 newspapers. **Subscriptions:** 200 journals and other serials. **Services:** Interlibrary loans (through University of Regina); copying; library open to public.

CAMPUS MARTIUS MUSEUM
See: Ohio Historical Society

★1988★
CAMROSE LUTHERAN COLLEGE - LIBRARY (Hum; Rel-Theol)
4503 50th St.   Phone: (403) 672-3381
Camrose, AB, Canada T4V 2R3   Asgeir Ingibergsson, Hd.Libn.
Staff: Prof 1; Other 5. **Subjects:** Religion, philosophy, history, music, social sciences, literature, sciences. **Holdings:** 30,000 books and bound periodical volumes; 1750 phonograph records; 1200 musical scores; 2000 microfiche; 53 volumes of debates of the Senate and House of Commons; 10 doctoral dissertations; 65 Princeton files of government documents. **Subscriptions:** 320 journals and other serials; 9 newspapers. **Services:** Interlibrary loans; copying; library open to public with restrictions. **Publications:** List of periodicals; monthly list of new acquisitions. **Staff:** Lila Majeski, Acq.; Margaret V. Nelson, Music; Nancy L. Money, Circ. & Ser.

★1989★
CAMSELL (Charles) GENERAL HOSPITAL - PETER WILCOCK LIBRARY (Med)
12815 115th Ave.   Phone: (403) 452-8770
Edmonton, AB, Canada T5M 3A4   Donna Dryden, Med.Libn.
Staff: Prof 1; Other 2. **Subjects:** Medicine, nursing, paramedical sciences, hospital administration. **Holdings:** 2000 books; 2300 bound periodical volumes; 1000 cassettes; 2 VF drawers of pamphlets and reports. **Subscriptions:** 250 journals and other serials; 9 newspapers. **Services:** Interlibrary loans; copying; library open to public for reference use only on request. **Computerized Information Services:** MEDLARS; computerized cataloging.

CANADA - AFFAIRES DES ANCIENS COMBATTANTS
See: Canada - Veterans Affairs Canada

CANADA - AFFAIRES EXTERIEURES CANADA
See: Canada - External Affairs Canada

CANADA - AFFAIRES INDIENNES ET DU NORD CANADA
See: Canada - Indian & Northern Affairs Canada

CANADA - AGENCE CANADIENNE DE DEVELOPPEMENT INTERNATIONAL
See: Canada - Canadian International Development Agency

★1990★
CANADA - AGRICULTURE CANADA - ANIMAL DISEASES RESEARCH INSTITUTE LIBRARY (Agri; Med)
Sta. H., P.O. Box 11300   Phone: (613) 998-9320
Ottawa, ON, Canada K2H 8P9   P. Atherton, Libn.
Staff: Prof 1; Other 1. **Subjects:** Veterinary medicine, virology, immunology, bacteriology. **Holdings:** 10,000 volumes. **Subscriptions:** 300 journals and other serials. **Services:** Interlibrary loans; copying; SDI; library open to public for reference use only.

★1991★
CANADA - AGRICULTURE CANADA - ANIMAL RESEARCH CENTRE LIBRARY (Sci-Tech)
Genetics Bldg.   Phone: (613) 994-9719
Ottawa, ON, Canada K1A 0C6   S. Yanosik
Staff: Prof 1. **Subjects:** Animal science and nutrition, genetics, physiology, biochemistry. **Holdings:** 3000 books; 4200 bound periodical volumes. **Subscriptions:** 200 journals and other serials. **Services:** Interlibrary loans; SDI; library open to public for reference use only.

★1992★
CANADA - AGRICULTURE CANADA - CANADIAN GRAIN COMMISSION - LIBRARY (Agri)
303 Main St., Rm. 1001   Phone: (204) 949-3360
Winnipeg, MB, Canada R3C 3G7   Lee Teal, Libn.
Founded: 1913. **Staff:** Prof 1; Other 1. **Subjects:** Cereal chemistry, cereals, grain industry and trade, baking, brewing. **Holdings:** 3000 books; 6000 bound periodical volumes; 1000 pamphlets; 800 slides. **Subscriptions:** 300 journals and other serials; 11 newspapers. **Services:** Interlibrary loans; copying; SDI; library open to public for reference use only. **Computerized Information Services:** DIALOG, CAN/OLE.

★1993★
CANADA - AGRICULTURE CANADA - ENTOMOLOGY RESEARCH LIBRARY (Sci-Tech)
K.W. Neatby Bldg., Rm. 4061
Central Experimental Farm   Phone: (613) 996-1665
Ottawa, ON, Canada K1A 0C6   Ruth Sharrett, Entomology Res.Libn.
Founded: 1919. **Staff:** Prof 2; Other 1. **Subjects:** Entomology, natural history, biology, evolution, nematology, paleontology. **Holdings:** 9000 books; 12,000 bound periodical volumes; 40,000 reprints; 5000 government documents. **Subscriptions:** 480 journals and other serials. **Services:** Interlibrary loans; copying; SDI; library open to public for reference use only.

★1994★
CANADA - AGRICULTURE CANADA - EXPERIMENTAL FARM LIBRARY (Agri)†
C.P. 400   Phone: (418) 856-3141
La Pocatiere, PQ, Canada G0R 1Z0   J. Deschenes
Staff: 1. **Subjects:** Plant pathology, mycology, biochemistry, plant physiology, general agriculture, plant breeding, botany, entomology, bacteriology. **Holdings:** 950 books; 1215 bound periodical volumes; 250 maps; 1200 aerial photographs; 150 boxes of reports; 425 boxes of reprints and bulletins. **Subscriptions:** 52 journals and other serials. **Services:** Interlibrary loans; library open to agronomists and research workers.

★1995★
CANADA - AGRICULTURE CANADA - LIBRARIES DIVISION (Agri)
Sir John Carling Bldg., Rm. 245   Phone: (613) 995-5219
Ottawa, ON, Canada K1A 0C5   M.L. Morton, Dir., Lib.Div.
Founded: 1910. **Staff:** Prof 39; Other 50. **Subjects:** Agriculture and related sciences, economics, veterinary medicine, chemistry, biochemistry, nutrition, management science. **Special Collections:** Chapais Collection (personal library of first Minister of Agriculture, Hon. Jean-Charles Chapais, and his son, Jean-Charles); Food and Agriculture Organization publications. **Holdings:** 1 million volumes; 10,000 microforms; 5000 translations. **Subscriptions:** 21,000 journals and other serials. **Services:** Interlibrary loans; copying; library open to public for reference use only. **Computerized Information Services:** CAN/SDI, CAN/OLE, DIALOG, SDC, QL Systems, MEDLINE, INFORMATECH; computerized cataloging and circulation. **Networks/Consortia:** Member of UTLAS, Inc. **Publications:** Selected List of Acquisitions, bimonthly - available on request; Current Periodicals, biennial; Union List of Serials in Canada Department of Agriculture Libraries; Publications of the Canada Department of Agriculture, 1867-1974; Agricultural Periodicals Published in Canada, 1836-1960; Chapais Collection. **Special Catalogs:** Catalogue of the Buller Memorial Library (located in Research Station, Winnipeg library); catalog of FAO publications; Union Catalog of Branch Library Holdings. **Remarks:** Maintains 25 branch libraries. **Staff:** M.J. MacIntosh, Asst.Dir., Hdq.; C. Bregaint, Asst.Dir., Field; O. Chumak, Chf., Tech.Serv.; J. Curren, Chf., Acq.Serv.; J. Wu, Sys.Libn.; R. Hodgins, Chf., Pub.Serv.

★1996★
CANADA - AGRICULTURE CANADA - LONDON RESEARCH CENTRE LIBRARY(Sci-Tech)
University Sub Post Office   Phone: (519) 679-4452
London, ON, Canada N6A 5B7   J. Giesbrecht, Area Coord.
Founded: 1951. **Staff:** Prof 1; Other 1. **Subjects:** Chemistry, entomology, plant pathology, fumigation, plant physiology, microbiology. **Holdings:** 4000 books; 7000 bound periodical volumes. **Subscriptions:** 200 journals and other serials. **Services:** Interlibrary loans; copying; SDI; library open to qualified persons. **Publications:** List of accessions, quarterly. **Staff:** Dorothy Drew, Libn.

★1997★
CANADA - AGRICULTURE CANADA - NEATBY LIBRARY (Sci-Tech)
K.W. Neatby Bldg., Rm. 3032
Central Experimental Farm   Phone: (613) 995-5011
Ottawa, ON, Canada K1A 0C6   Marcel Charette, Ck. in Charge
Founded: 1960. **Staff:** 3. **Subjects:** Biochemistry, biology, mineralogy, soils,

pesticides, soil and water pollution, bacteriology, microbiology, agrometeorology. **Holdings:** 5500 books; 5800 bound periodical volumes; 1000 microcards of Beilstein's Handbuch der Organischen Chemie. **Subscriptions:** 300 journals and other serials. **Services:** Interlibrary loans; copying; SDI; library open to public for reference use only. **Publications:** List of Acquisitions, bimonthly. **Staff:** M. Graham, ILL.

★1998★
CANADA - AGRICULTURE CANADA - PLANT RESEARCH LIBRARY (Agri)†
Biosystematics Research Inst., Bldg. 49   Phone: (613) 996-1665
Ottawa, ON, Canada K1A 0C6   Eva Gavora, Libn.
Founded: 1908. **Staff:** Prof 1; Other 1. **Subjects:** Botany, taxonomy, mycology. **Special Collections:** Linnean Collection, including early botany publications by Carl Linnaeus and revised editions by other botanists, mainly 1748-1825. **Holdings:** 9000 books; 11,000 bound periodical volumes; 14,000 microfiche (early taxonomic works and eleven European herbaria). **Subscriptions:** 700 journals and other serials. **Services:** Interlibrary loans; copying; library open to public. **Publications:** List of serial holdings, irregular; accessions list, quarterly.

★1999★
CANADA - AGRICULTURE CANADA - REGIONAL DEVELOPMENT & INTERNATIONAL AFFAIRS LIBRARY (Agri; Bus-Fin)
101-2050 Cornwall St.   Phone: (306) 359-5545
Regina, SK, Canada S4P 2K5   H.C. Vanstone, Lib. Techn.
Subjects: Agricultural economics. **Holdings:** 500 books; 200 bound periodical volumes; 3000 bulletins and reports. **Subscriptions:** 35 journals and other serials; 6 newspapers. **Services:** Interlibrary loans; library open to public by permission.

★2000★
CANADA - AGRICULTURE CANADA - RESEARCH STATION, BEAVERLODGE - LIBRARY (Agri)
Box 29   Phone: (403) 354-2212
Beaverlodge, AB, Canada T0H 0C0   Dr. L.P.S. Spangelo, Dir.
Subjects: Cereal breeding, plant management, forage crops, horticultural crops, pasture management, soil fertility, soil management, agrometeorology, apiculture. **Holdings:** 5000 volumes. **Subscriptions:** 60 journals and other serials. **Services:** Library not open to public. **Remarks:** All inquiries concerning this collection should be directed to the Area Coordinator, at the Regional Headquarters Library, Agriculture Canada, Lethbridge Research Station, Lethbridge, Alberta, T1G 4B1.

★2001★
CANADA - AGRICULTURE CANADA - RESEARCH STATION, CHARLOTTETOWN - LIBRARY (Agri)
P.O. Box 1210   Phone: (902) 892-5461
Charlottetown, PE, Canada C1A 7M8   Barrie Stanfield, Libn.
Founded: 1961. **Staff:** Prof 1. **Subjects:** Plant physiology and pathology; entomology; pest control; weed control; forage and cereal crops; animal science (cattle); soil science; vegetable crops. **Holdings:** 2000 books; 2000 bound periodical volumes; 200 boxes of government publications; 7 VF drawers of clippings and pamphlets. **Subscriptions:** 250 journals and other serials. **Services:** Interlibrary loans; copying; library open to public but material circulates to qualified users only.

★2002★
CANADA - AGRICULTURE CANADA - RESEARCH STATION, FREDERICTON - LIBRARY (Agri)
Box 20280   Phone: (506) 452-3260
Fredericton, NB, Canada E3B 4Z7   Donald B. Gammon, Area Coord. Atlantic
Founded: 1952. **Staff:** Prof 2; Other 1. **Subjects:** Agriculture, botany, zoology, soil science. **Holdings:** 2000 books; 2700 bound periodical volumes; 18,000 pamphlets and reprints. **Subscriptions:** 250 journals and other serials. **Services:** Interlibrary loans; copying; library open to public by permission. **Networks/Consortia:** Member of Agriculture Canada Network of Library Services. **Staff:** Norma Taniguchi, Libn.

★2003★
CANADA - AGRICULTURE CANADA - RESEARCH STATION, HARROW - LIBRARY (Agri)
     Phone: (519) 738-2251
Harrow, ON, Canada N0R 1G0   Eric A. Champagne, Libn.
Staff: Prof 1. **Subjects:** Agriculture and related topics. **Holdings:** 2000 books; 1800 bound periodical volumes; 300 government publications; 4 VF drawers. **Subscriptions:** 200 journals and other serials. **Services:** Interlibrary loans; SDI; library open to public for reference use only.

★2004★
CANADA - AGRICULTURE CANADA - RESEARCH STATION, KAMLOOPS - LIBRARY (Agri)
3015 Ord Rd.   Phone: (604) 376-5565
Kamloops, BC, Canada V2B 7V8   J.D. McElgunn, Dir.
Staff: 1. **Subjects:** Forage crops, range management, soils and fertilizers, cattle nutrition. **Holdings:** 1800 books; 2000 bound periodical volumes; research papers, reports, reprints, manuscripts and dissertations. **Subscriptions:** 186 journals and other serials. **Services:** Library open to public with restrictions. All inquiries concerning this collection should be addressed to the Main Library in Ottawa.

★2005★
CANADA - AGRICULTURE CANADA - RESEARCH STATION, KENTVILLE - LIBRARY (Agri)
                                               Phone: (902) 678-2171
Kentville, NS, Canada B4N 1J5   Jerry Miner, Libn.
Founded: 1953. **Staff:** Prof 1; Other 1. **Subjects:** Entomology, plant pathology, chemistry, fruit processing, field crops, small fruits, poultry, statistics, physiology of plant life. **Holdings:** 2000 books; 10,000 bound periodical volumes; 4000 reports; 412 boxes of government publications. **Subscriptions:** 300 journals and other serials. **Services:** Interlibrary loans; copying; library open to public.

★2006★
CANADA - AGRICULTURE CANADA - RESEARCH STATION, LACOMBE - LIBRARY (Agri)
                                               Phone: (403) 782-3316
Lacombe, AB, Canada T0C 1S0   D.E. Waldern, Dir.
Founded: 1907. **Staff:** 1. **Subjects:** Agriculture and related topics. **Holdings:** 1000 books; 1500 bound periodical volumes. **Subscriptions:** 80 journals and other serials; 10 newspapers. **Services:** Library not open to public. **Remarks:** All inquiries concerning this collection should be addressed to the main library in Ottawa.

★2007★
CANADA - AGRICULTURE CANADA - RESEARCH STATION, LETHBRIDGE - LIBRARY (Agri)
                                               Phone: (403) 327-4561
Lethbridge, AB, Canada T1J 4B1   John P. Miska, Area Coord.
Founded: 1950. **Staff:** Prof 2; Other 2. **Subjects:** Agriculture, biology, biochemistry, veterinary science, horticulture, environmental science. **Holdings:** 14,000 books; 8000 bound periodical volumes; 18,000 unbound periodicals; 170,000 unbound reports and bulletins; 2000 reprints; 200 reels of microfilm. **Subscriptions:** 1065 journals and other serials; 20 newspapers. **Services:** Interlibrary loans; copying; library open to public. **Computerized Information Services:** CAN/SDI; FAMULUS (internal database). **Publications:** Bibliographic Series, irregular - available for exchange; Library User's Manual, 1979; Library Accessions List, bimonthly; list of additional publications - available upon request. **Special Catalogs:** Periodicals Received (book). **Staff:** Cheryl M. Ronning Mains, Libn.

★2008★
CANADA - AGRICULTURE CANADA - RESEARCH STATION, MORDEN - LIBRARY (Agri)
P.O. Box 3001   Phone: (204) 822-4471
Morden, MB, Canada R0G 1J0   Mrs. D. Martinook, Sec.
Subjects: Biology, genetics, agronomy, plant pathology, plant physiology, horticulture. **Holdings:** 320 books; 500 bound periodical volumes; 50 shelf feet of annual reports, bulletins of agriculture research institutions. **Subscriptions:** 45 journals and other serials. **Services:** Library open to public by appointment. **Remarks:** All inquiries concerning this collection should be addressed to the Main Library in Ottawa.

★2009★
CANADA - AGRICULTURE CANADA - RESEARCH STATION, OTTAWA - LIBRARY (Agri)
                                               Phone: (613) 995-9428
Ottawa, ON, Canada K1A 0C6   S. Yanosik
Founded: 1925. **Staff:** 2. **Subjects:** Agriculture, cereal crops, horticulture, genetic engineering, cytogenetics, apiculture. **Holdings:** 3000 books; 2000 bound periodical volumes. **Subscriptions:** 170 journals and other serials. **Services:** Interlibrary loans; copying; SDI; library open to public for reference use only.

★2010★
CANADA - AGRICULTURE CANADA - RESEARCH STATION, REGINA - LIBRARY (Agri)
5000 Wascana Pkwy.
Box 440   Phone: (306) 585-0255
Regina, SK, Canada S4P 3A2   H.C. Vanstone, Lib.Techn.
Staff: 1. **Subjects:** Weed control, herbicides, biological control. **Special Collections:** Reports on weed control in Western Canada since 1928. **Holdings:** 800 books; 2100 bound periodical volumes; government publications. **Subscriptions:** 60 journals and other serials. **Services:** Interlibrary loans; copying; SDI; library open to public with permission of director.

★2011★
CANADA - AGRICULTURE CANADA - RESEARCH STATION, STE-FOY - LIBRARY (Agri)
2560 Hochelaga Blvd.   Phone: (418) 694-4017
Ste. Foy, PQ, Canada G1V 2J3   Paul R. Venne, Area Coord., Quebec
Founded: 1970. **Staff:** Prof 1; Other 1. **Subjects:** Plant physiology and pathology; cereal and forage breeding; economics. **Holdings:** 3500 books; 5000 bound periodical volumes; 250 maps. **Subscriptions:** 100 journals and other serials. **Services:** Interlibrary loans; copying; library open to public for reference use only. **Computerized Information Services:** Computerized cataloging. **Networks/Consortia:** Member of Agriculture Canada Network of Library Services; UTLAS, Inc. **Publications:** Accession List, irregular - for internal distribution only; list of French language agricultural journals and papers published in Canada, irregular - for internal distribution and to agricultural community leaders. **Special Catalogs:** Union catalog of research officers' textbooks; union catalog of holdings of other departmental libraries in Quebec.

★2012★
CANADA - AGRICULTURE CANADA - RESEARCH STATION, ST-JEAN - LIBRARY (Agri)
P.O. Box 457   Phone: (514) 346-4494
St. Jean-Sur-Richelieu, PQ, Canada J3B 6Z8   Ian Wallace, Libn.
Founded: 1952. **Staff:** Prof 1; Other 1. **Subjects:** Entomology, botany, agriculture, soil science, horticulture. **Holdings:** 2877 books; 2334 bound periodical volumes; 198 bound abstract volumes. **Subscriptions:** 350 journals and other serials. **Services:** Interlibrary loans; copying; SDI; translation; library open to qualified researchers only. **Computerized Information Services:** Computerized cataloging, serials and circulation.

★2013★
CANADA - AGRICULTURE CANADA - RESEARCH STATION, ST. JOHN'S WEST - LIBRARY (Agri)
Brookfield Rd.
P.O. Box 7098   Phone: (709) 772-4619
St. John's, NF, Canada A1E 3Y3   H.M. Stevenson, Off.Mgr.
Subjects: Horticulture, plant pathology, entomology, agronomy, poultry, meteorology. **Holdings:** 250 books; 100 bound periodical volumes; 325 Canadian Department of Agriculture publications; 75 boxes of pamphlets and Agriculture Canada reports; meteorological reports for 20 years. **Subscriptions:** 48 journals and other serials. **Services:** Interlibrary loans; library open to public for research only. **Remarks:** All inquiries concerning this collection should be addressed to the Main Library in Ottawa.

★2014★
CANADA - AGRICULTURE CANADA - RESEARCH STATION, SASKATOON - LIBRARY (Agri)
107 Science Cresc.   Phone: (306) 343-8214
Saskatoon, SK, Canada S7N 0X2   Marlene Glen, Libn.
Founded: 1957. **Staff:** Prof 1; Other 1. **Subjects:** Agriculture, entomology, crop science, plant breeding, plant pathology, oil seeds, pedology. **Holdings:** Reprint files. **Subscriptions:** 350 journals and other serials. **Services:** Interlibrary loans; copying; SDI; library open to public with restrictions. **Computerized Information Services:** Computerized indexing of special collections. **Publications:** Bibliographies excerpted from machine-searchable databases, published irregularly; acquisitions list, quarterly.

★2015★
CANADA - AGRICULTURE CANADA - RESEARCH STATION, SUMMERLAND - LIBRARY (Agri)
                                               Phone: (604) 494-7711
Summerland, BC, Canada V0H 1Z0   Vivienne B. Madsen, Libn.
Founded: 1951. **Staff:** Prof 1. **Subjects:** Horticulture, entomology, plant pathology, food processing, pomology, irrigation, plant nutrition. **Holdings:** 2000 books; 8000 bound periodical volumes; 5000 unbound periodicals; 20,500 pamphlets. **Subscriptions:** 160 journals and other serials. **Services:**

Interlibrary loans; copying; library open to public for reference use only.

★2016★
CANADA - AGRICULTURE CANADA - RESEARCH STATION, SWIFT CURRENT - LIBRARY (Agri)
Box 1030
Phone: (306) 773-4621
Swift Current, SK, Canada S9H 3X2
Karen E. Wilton, Libn.
Founded: 1921. **Staff:** Prof 1. **Subjects:** Cereal breeding, soil science, forage and range management, animal nutrition, irrigation, agrometeorology, agricultural engineering. **Holdings:** 1500 books; 2400 bound periodical volumes; 200 annual reports; 380 pamphlet boxes. **Subscriptions:** 270 journals and other serials; 5 newspapers. **Services:** Interlibrary loans; copying; SDI; library open to public with restrictions. **Special Indexes:** Swift Current Research Station Scientific Publications Index (computer printout).

★2017★
CANADA - AGRICULTURE CANADA - RESEARCH STATION, VANCOUVER - LIBRARY (Agri)
6660 N.W. Marine Dr.
Phone: (604) 224-4355
Vancouver, BC, Canada V6T 1X2
C.M. Cutler, Area Coord.
Founded: 1960. **Staff:** Prof 2; Other 1. **Subjects:** Plant pathology; virus chemistry and physiology; entomology; pedology and soil survey. **Special Collections:** Entomological Society of British Columbia Collection (130 books). **Holdings:** 1000 books. **Subscriptions:** 150 journals and other serials. **Services:** Interlibrary loans; copying; SDI; library open to public with restrictions.

★2018★
CANADA - AGRICULTURE CANADA - RESEARCH STATION, VINELAND STATION - LIBRARY (Agri)
Phone: (416) 562-4113
Vineland Station, ON, Canada L0R 2E0
M.-J. Boisvenue, Libn.
Staff: Prof 1. **Subjects:** Horticulture, fruits and vegetables, nematology, virology, pesticides. **Holdings:** 1000 books; 4000 bound periodical volumes; 345 unbound abstracts; 650 Agriculture Canada and Ontario Ministry of Agriculture publications; 161 unbound annual reports. **Subscriptions:** 49 journals and other serials. **Services:** Interlibrary loans; copying; library open to public by appointment.

★2019★
CANADA - AGRICULTURE CANADA - RESEARCH STATION, WINNIPEG - LIBRARY (Agri)†
195 Dafoe Rd.
Phone: (204) 269-2100
Winnipeg, MB, Canada R3T 2M9
M. Malyk, Libn.
Founded: 1957. **Staff:** Prof 2; Other 1. **Subjects:** Botany, plant pathology, cereal breeding, entomology, plant physiology, statistics. **Special Collections:** Buller Memorial Library (botanical collection). **Holdings:** 5000 books; 2600 bound periodical volumes; 30,000 reprints; 250 boxes of government bulletins; 1000 boxes of unbound journals. **Subscriptions:** 300 journals and other serials; 6 newspapers. **Services:** Interlibrary loans; SDI; library open to those with legitimate interest. **Special Catalogs:** Buller Memorial Library Catalog (book).

★2020★
CANADA - AGRICULTURE CANADA - SAANICHTON RESEARCH & PLANT QUARANTINE STATION - LIBRARY (Agri)†
8801 E. Saanich Rd.
Phone: (604) 656-1173
Sidney, BC, Canada V8L 1H3
Peggy Watson, Libn.
Founded: 1944. **Staff:** Prof 1. **Subjects:** Plant physiology, pathology, quarantine and physiology; entomology; ornamentals and greenhouse crops. **Holdings:** 1270 books; 2192 bound and unbound periodical volumes; 35,792 bulletins, documents, pamphlets. **Subscriptions:** 53 journals and other serials. **Services:** Interlibrary loans; copying; library open to public for reference use only. **Computerized Information Services:** CAN/SDI.

★2021★
CANADA - AIR POLLUTION TECHNICAL INFORMATION SECTION (Env-Cons)
12th Fl., Place Vincent Massey
351 St. Joseph Blvd.
Phone: (819) 994-0284
Hull, PQ, Canada J8Y 3Z5
Cheryl Trudeau, Mgr.
Founded: 1973. **Staff:** Prof 1; Other 1. **Subjects:** Air pollution - combustion, fuel, mineral and metal; chemical processes; acid rain; international policy. **Special Collections:** Air Pollution Technical Information Center (APTIC; microfiche). **Holdings:** 8000 books; 100,000 microforms; 4 VF drawers of unbound reports and manuscripts. **Subscriptions:** 120 journals and other serials. **Services:** Interlibrary loans; copying; SDI; library open to federal and provincial agencies on request with limited borrowing. **Computerized Information Services:** Online systems. **Publications:** List of publications -

available upon request. **Remarks:** Operated by Canada - Environment Canada - Air Pollution Control Directorate (APCD).

CANADA - ARCHIVES PUBLIQUES DU CANADA
See: Canada - Public Archives of Canada

★2022★
CANADA - ATMOSPHERIC ENVIRONMENT SERVICE - ATLANTIC REGIONAL LIBRARY (Sci-Tech)†
5th Fl., 1496 Bedford Hwy.
Phone: (902) 835-9529
Bedford, NS, Canada B4A 1E5
A.D. Gates
Founded: 1974. **Staff:** 1. **Subjects:** Meteorology, climatology. **Holdings:** 450 books; 1000 bound periodical volumes; 1000 microfiche of climatological data; 200 shelf feet of unbound reports, periodicals, summaries. **Subscriptions:** 30 journals and other serials. **Services:** Interlibrary loans; copying; library open to public by appointment.

★2023★
CANADA - ATMOSPHERIC ENVIRONMENT SERVICE - CENTRAL REGION LIBRARY (Sci-Tech)†
266 Graham Ave.
9th Fl., Post Office Bldg.
Phone: (204) 949-4389
Winnipeg, MB, Canada R3C 3V4
R.R. Tortorelli, Sci.Serv.Techn.
Subjects: Meteorology, climatology. **Holdings:** 250 books; 500 bound periodical volumes; 2000 scientific papers; 100 bound volumes of Canadian weather data; 1000 technical circulars. **Subscriptions:** 20 journals and other serials. **Services:** Library open to public for reference use only.

★2024★
CANADA - ATMOSPHERIC ENVIRONMENT SERVICE - LIBRARY (Sci-Tech)
4905 Dufferin St.
Phone: (416) 667-4500
Downsview, ON, Canada M3H 5T4
Mary M. Skinner, Chf.Lib.Serv.Div.
Founded: 1871. **Staff:** Prof 4; Other 5. **Subjects:** Meteorology, climatology, atmospheric sciences. **Special Collections:** Meteorological records for Canadian stations, 1873 to present; meteorological records for Toronto, 1839 to present; depository collection of World Meteorological Organization published documents. **Holdings:** 4400 books; 8300 bound periodical volumes; 1800 bound Canadian weather records; 9200 research and technical reports; 16 VF drawers of pamphlets; 14 VF drawers of reprints; 12 drawers of NTIS microfiche. **Subscriptions:** 550 journals and other serials; 7 newspapers. **Services:** Interlibrary loans; copying; library open for reference and limited borrowing. **Computerized Information Services:** DIALOG, CAN/OLE, QL Systems; computerized cataloging, acquisitions, serials and circulation. **Networks/Consortia:** Member of Environment Libraries Automated System (ELIAS). **Publications:** Selected List of Accessions, irregular - sent to all members of AES and to others on request. **Staff:** L. Stripnieks, Ref.Libn.; J.M. Glover, Hd.Lib.Oper.

★2025★
CANADA - ATMOSPHERIC ENVIRONMENT SERVICE - PACIFIC REGION - LIBRARY (Sci-Tech)
700-1200 W. 73rd Ave.
Phone: (604) 732-4830
Vancouver, BC, Canada V6P 6H9
D.A. Faulkner, Meteorologist
Staff: 1. **Subjects:** Meteorology, climatology. **Holdings:** 500 books; 100 bound periodical volumes. **Subscriptions:** 20 journals and other serials. **Services:** Library open to public with restrictions.

★2026★
CANADA - ATMOSPHERIC ENVIRONMENT SERVICE - QUEBEC REGION - BIBLIOTHEQUE REGIONALE (Sci-Tech)†
100 Blvd. Alexis-Nihon, 3rd Fl.
Phone: (514) 333-3020
St. Laurent, PQ, Canada H4M 2N6
Jacques Miron, Off.-in-Charge
Founded: 1950. **Staff:** 2. **Subjects:** Meteorology, weather forecasting, climatology. **Holdings:** 200 books; 50 bound periodical volumes; 1 drawer of microfiche. **Subscriptions:** 35 journals and other serials. **Services:** Library not open to public.

★2027★
CANADA - ATMOSPHERIC ENVIRONMENT SERVICE - WESTERN REGION HEADQUARTERS LIBRARY (Sci-Tech)
Argyll Centre
6325 103rd St.
Phone: (403) 437-1250
Edmonton, AB, Canada T6H 5H6
Larry Winstone, Meteorologist
Founded: 1960. **Staff:** 1. **Subjects:** Atmospheric sciences, including physics; climatology. **Holdings:** 450 books; 400 bound periodical volumes; 1500 unbound reports; 300 unbound periodicals; 2500 pamphlets. **Subscriptions:** 25 journals and other serials. **Services:** Library not open to public. **Networks/Consortia:** Member of Environment Canada Library Network.

CANADA - ATOMIC ENERGY OF CANADA, LTD.
See: Atomic Energy of Canada, Ltd.

CANADA - BANK OF CANADA
See: Bank of Canada

CANADA - BIBLIOTHEQUE NATIONALE DU CANADA
See: National Library of Canada

CANADA - BIBLIOTHEQUE DU PARLEMENT
See: Canada - Library of Parliament

★2028★
CANADA - CANADA CENTRE FOR REMOTE SENSING - TECHNICAL INFORMATION SERVICE (Sci-Tech)
240 Bank St., 5th Fl. Phone: (613) 995-5645
Ottawa, ON, Canada K2P 1X4 Brian McGurrin, Hd.
Staff: Prof 7; Other 3. **Subjects:** Remote sensing, scanning and imaging systems, pattern recognition, atmospheric optics, earth sciences. **Holdings:** 1000 books; 35,000 documents. **Subscriptions:** 100 journals and other serials. **Services:** Interlibrary loans; SDI; library open to public. **Computerized Information Services:** SDC, CAN/OLE; RESORS (internal database); computerized cataloging. **Networks/Consortia:** Member of UTLAS Inc. **Publications:** RESORS Keyword Dictionaries, irregular - to online users. **Staff:** Lidia Taylor, Ref.Libn.; Jacques Guerette, RESORS Mgr.

★2029★
CANADA - CANADA POST CORPORATION - LIBRARY (Bus-Fin)
Sir Alexander Campbell Bldg.
Riverside Dr. Phone: (613) 998-4463
Ottawa, ON, Canada K1A 0B1 Jean Weerasinghe, Corp.Libn.
Founded: 1948. **Staff:** Prof 1; Other 4. **Subjects:** Management, labour relations, public administration, postal operations, postal history, engineering. **Special Collections:** Union Postale Universelle publications. **Holdings:** 5000 books; 200 films. **Subscriptions:** 300 journals and other serials; 7 newspapers. **Services:** Interlibrary loans; copying; library open to public for reference use only. **Computerized Information Services:** DIALOG, QL Systems, Info Globe, SDC, DOBIS; computerized cataloging. **Publications:** Accessions report, quarterly. **Formerly:** Canada - Post Office Department - Library.

★2030★
CANADA - CANADIAN ADVISORY COUNCIL ON THE STATUS OF WOMEN - DOCUMENTATION CENTRE (Soc Sci)
Sta. B, Box 1541 Phone: (613) 995-8284
Ottawa, ON, Canada K1P 5R5 Nicole Proulx, Libn.
Founded: 1974. **Staff:** 1. **Subjects:** Women. **Special Collections:** Newsletters of Canadian women's groups; briefs and reports on status of women issues. **Holdings:** 500 books; 1000 reports and briefs; 15 drawers of clippings, manuscripts and dissertations. **Subscriptions:** 100 journals and other serials; 5 newspapers. **Services:** Interlibrary loans; centre open to public by invitation. **Publications:** Bibliographies, irregular.

CANADA - CANADIAN FORCES COLLEGE
See: Canada - National Defence - Canadian Forces College

CANADA - CANADIAN FORCES MEDICAL SERVICES SCHOOL
See: Canada - National Defence - Canadian Forces Medical Services School

★2031★
CANADA - CANADIAN FORESTRY SERVICE - GREAT LAKES FOREST RESEARCH CENTRE - LIBRARY (Sci-Tech)
P.O. Box 490 Phone: (705) 949-9461
Sault Ste. Marie, ON, Canada P6A 5M7 Sandra Burt, Libn.
Staff: Prof 1; Other 1. **Subjects:** Forestry, entomology, biochemistry, physiology, genetics, bioclimatology. **Holdings:** 6000 volumes. **Subscriptions:** 450 journals and other serials. **Services:** Interlibrary loans; copying; SDI; translation; library open to public with restrictions. **Computerized Information Services:** DIALOG, CAN/OLE. **Publications:** Accessions list, monthly - available upon request.

★2032★
CANADA - CANADIAN FORESTRY SERVICE - LAURENTIAN FOREST RESEARCH CENTRE - LIBRARY (Sci-Tech)
C.P. 3800, 1080 Route Du Vallon Phone: (418) 694-3989
Ste. Foy, PQ, Canada G1V 4C7 Monique Dupuis, Libn.
Founded: 1952. **Staff:** Prof 1; Other 1. **Subjects:** Forestry, entomology, plant pathology, silviculture, pedology, recreation, ecology. **Holdings:** 4000

books; 3000 bound periodical volumes; 12,000 serials (cataloged); 9 VF drawers of archives (researchers' scientific works). **Subscriptions:** 150 journals and other serials. **Services:** Interlibrary loans; copying; library open to public for reference use only. **Computerized Information Services:** Online systems; computerized cataloging and circulation. **Networks/Consortia:** Member of Environment Libraries Automated System (ELIAS). **Publications:** List of scientific publications, irregular. **Also Known As:** Centre de Recherches Forestieres des Laurentides.

★2033★
CANADA - CANADIAN FORESTRY SERVICE - MARITIMES FOREST RESEARCH CENTRE - LIBRARY (Sci-Tech)
P.O. Box 4000 Phone: (506) 452-3541
Fredericton, NB, Canada E3B 5P7 Barry Barner, Libn.
Founded: 1920. **Staff:** Prof 1; Other 1. **Subjects:** Forestry, forest ecology, silviculture, forest pathology, forest entomology, forest economics. **Holdings:** 4000 books; 5000 periodical volumes; 2000 boxes of pamphlets and technical reports (cataloged); microforms. **Subscriptions:** 300 journals. **Services:** Interlibrary loans; library open to public. **Computerized Information Services:** DIALOG, CAN/OLE, BRS.

★2034★
CANADA - CANADIAN FORESTRY SERVICE - NEWFOUNDLAND FOREST RESEARCH CENTRE - LIBRARY (Sci-Tech; Env-Cons)
P.O. Box 6028 Phone: (709) 772-4672
St. John's, NF, Canada A1C 5X8 Catherine E. Philpott, Libn.
Founded: 1950. **Staff:** 1. **Subjects:** Forestry, entomology, environmental research. **Holdings:** 1900 books; 320 bound periodical volumes. **Subscriptions:** 125 journals and other serials; 5 newspapers. **Services:** Interlibrary loans; copying; SDI; library open to public. **Networks/Consortia:** Member of Environment Canada Library Network.

★2035★
CANADA - CANADIAN FORESTRY SERVICE - NORTHERN FOREST RESEARCH CENTRE - LIBRARY (Sci-Tech; Env-Cons)
5320 122nd St. Phone: (403) 435-7323
Edmonton, AB, Canada T6H 3S5 D. Robinson, Libn.
Founded: 1952. **Staff:** Prof 1; Other 1. **Subjects:** Forestry, entomology, mycology, soil science, hydrology, environmental pollution. **Holdings:** 3000 books; 5000 bound periodical volumes; 20,000 reports and government publications; 3000 reprints and pamphlets; 248 microforms. **Subscriptions:** 300 journals and other serials. **Services:** Interlibrary loans; copying; library open to public for reference; loans made to qualified researchers.

★2036★
CANADA - CANADIAN FORESTRY SERVICE - PACIFIC FOREST RESEARCH CENTRE - LIBRARY (Sci-Tech; Env-Cons)
506 W. Burnside Rd. Phone: (604) 388-3811
Victoria, BC, Canada V8Z 1M5 Alice Solyma, Libn.
Founded: 1940. **Staff:** Prof 1; Other 1. **Subjects:** Forest science, land and environmental research, economics, entomology, fire research, hydrology, mensuration, meteorology, mycology, plant pathology. **Holdings:** 9750 books and bound periodical volumes; 42,000 reports and government documents. **Subscriptions:** 325 journals and other serials. **Services:** Interlibrary loans; copying; library open to public. **Computerized Information Services:** DIALOG, SDC, CAN/OLE. **Publications:** Monthly Accessions List.

CANADA - CANADIAN GOVERNMENT OFFICE OF TOURISM
See: Canada - Industry, Trade & Commerce

CANADA - CANADIAN GRAIN COMMISSION
See: Canada - Agriculture Canada - Canadian Grain Commission

★2037★
CANADA - CANADIAN INTERNATIONAL DEVELOPMENT AGENCY - DEVELOPMENT INFORMATION CENTRE (Soc Sci)†
Place du Centre
200 Promenade du Portage Phone: (819) 997-6212
Hull, PQ, Canada K1A 0G4 Monique Legere, Dir.
Founded: 1965. **Staff:** Prof 5; Other 5. **Subjects:** International development, project management. **Holdings:** 3000 books. **Subscriptions:** 1200 journals and other serials. **Services:** Interlibrary loans; copying; library open to public with restrictions. **Publications:** Focus, monthly accession list of monographs; Documents, monthly list of confidential material - available to agency officers only; Table of Contents, select list of periodicals dealing with sectoral or policy matters - for internal distribution only. **Also Known As:** Agence Canadienne de Developpement International. **Staff:** Nicole Smith, Coord.Doc./Info.; Lydia Oak, Coord.Ref./Coll.Dev.; Halina Lukasiewich, Coord.Biblog.Control; Colette Martineau, Hd., Acq.

CANADA - CANADIAN MILITARY ENGINEERS MUSEUM
See: Canadian Military Engineers Museum

CANADA - CANADIAN NATIONAL RAILWAYS
See: Canadian National Railways

★2038★
CANADA - CANADIAN RADIO-TELEVISION AND TELECOMMUNICATIONS COMMISSION - LIBRARY (Soc Sci)†
Phone: (613) 997-0313
Ottawa, ON, Canada K1A 0N2 Ms. M.A. Anschutz, Libn.
Founded: 1968. **Staff:** Prof 1; Other 4. **Subjects:** Broadcasting, mass media, telecommunications, communications. **Holdings:** 3000 books; pamphlets. **Subscriptions:** 350 journals and other serials. **Services:** Interlibrary loans; copying; library open to public. **Computerized Information Services:** DIALOG, SDC. **Publications:** Accessions List, monthly. **Remarks:** the library is located at Promenade du Portage, Hull, PQ. **Also Known As:** Conseil de la radiodiffusion et des telecommunications canadiennes.

★2039★
CANADA - CANADIAN TRANSPORT COMMISSION - LIBRARY (Trans)
Phone: (819) 997-7160
Ottawa, ON, Canada K1A 0N9 Marty H. Lovelock, Libn.
Staff: Prof 1; Other 3. **Subjects:** Transport policy, transportation economics, law. **Holdings:** 25,000 books and bound periodical volumes. **Subscriptions:** 250 journals and other serials. **Services:** Interlibrary loans; copying; library open to public with restrictions. **Publications:** Accession List, bimonthly. **Also Known As:** Commission Canadienne des Transports. **Staff:** Agathe Maccoll, ILL.

★2040★
CANADA - CANADIAN WILDLIFE SERVICE - ATLANTIC REGION LIBRARY (Env-Cons)
Box 1590 Phone: (506) 536-3025
Sackville, NB, Canada E0A 3C0 F. Helen Anderson, Libn.
Founded: 1970. **Staff:** 1. **Subjects:** Birds, mammals, conservation, habitat protection and management, pollution, national parks. **Holdings:** 1000 books; 40 bound periodical volumes; 60 boxes of manuscript reports; 70 boxes of reprints and reports; 300 national parks publications; 2800 microforms. **Subscriptions:** 60 journals and other serials. **Services:** Interlibrary loans; copying; library open to public with restrictions.

★2041★
CANADA - CANADIAN WILDLIFE SERVICE - ONTARIO REGION LIBRARY (Env-Cons)
1725 Woodward Dr., 5th Fl. Phone: (613) 998-4693
Ottawa, ON, Canada K1A 0E7 Katherine L. Mahoney, Libn.
Staff: Prof 1; Other 1. **Subjects:** Ornithology, mammalogy, wildlife management, environmental impact (wildlife). **Holdings:** 3500 books; 125 bound periodical volumes; 2000 pamphlets (cataloged); 950 reports. **Subscriptions:** 115 journals and other serials. **Services:** Interlibrary loans; copying; library open to qualified users for reference use only. **Publications:** Accession list, bimonthly - for internal distribution only.

★2042★
CANADA - CANADIAN WILDLIFE SERVICE - PRAIRIE MIGRATORY BIRD RESEARCH CENTRE - LIBRARY (Env-Cons)
115 Perimeter Rd. Phone: (306) 665-4087
Saskatoon, SK, Canada S7N 0X4 Cecilia J. Cote, Lib.Techn.
Staff: 1. **Subjects:** Birds, conservation, natural resources. **Holdings:** Manuscripts, satellite photographs, maps, microfilm. **Services:** Interlibrary loans; copying; library open to public with restrictions. **Computerized Information Services:** Computerized cataloging. **Remarks:** This library is part of the Western and Northern Region of the Canadian Wildlife Service, with headquarters in Edmonton, AB.

★2043★
CANADA - CANADIAN WILDLIFE SERVICE - WESTERN AND NORTHERN REGION LIBRARY (Env-Cons)
9942 108th St., Suite 1000 Phone: (403) 425-5891
Edmonton, AB, Canada T5K 2J5 Peter A. Jordan, Regional Libn.
Staff: Prof 1; Other 1. **Subjects:** Ornithology, botany, mammalogy, wildlife conservation, ecology, natural resources, limnology, land use, photogrammetry. **Special Collections:** Collection of aerial photographs. **Holdings:** 1300 books; 1600 bound periodical volumes; 4500 manuscripts; 50 VF drawers; 2800 reels of microfilm; 4500 government documents. **Subscriptions:** 270 journals and other serials. **Services:** Interlibrary loans; library open to public with restrictions. **Computerized Information Services:** DIALOG, QL Systems, CAN/OLE; Environmental Libraries Automated System

(ELIAS; internal database); computerized cataloging and serials. **Publications:** Accessions list, monthly. **Remarks:** Contains the holdings of the Environmental Protection Service - Edmonton Library.

CANADA - CENTRE DE DEVELOPPEMENT DES TRANSPORTS
See: Canada - Transport Canada - Transportation Development Centre

★2044★
CANADA CENTRE FOR INLAND WATERS - LIBRARY (Sci-Tech)
867 Lakeshore Rd.
Box 5050 Phone: (416) 637-4282
Burlington, ON, Canada L7R 4A6 Eve Dowie, Hd., Lib.Serv.
Founded: 1968. **Staff:** Prof 2; Other 3. **Subjects:** Limnology, water research, water pollution, hydraulics, sanitary engineering. **Holdings:** 20,000 books; 20,000 unbound periodicals; 150 dissertations; 15 drawers of microforms. **Subscriptions:** 1500 journals and other serials. **Services:** Interlibrary loans; copying; library open by appointment to persons engaged in water research. **Computerized Information Services:** SDC, CAN/OLE, QL Systems, DIALOG, MEDLINE.

CANADA CENTRE FOR MINERAL AND ENERGY TECHNOLOGY
See: Canada - Energy, Mines & Resources Canada - CANMET

CANADA CENTRE FOR REMOTE SENSING
See: Canada - Canada Centre for Remote Sensing

CANADA - COLLECTION NATIONALE DE CARTES & PLANS
See: Canada - Public Archives of Canada - National Map Collection

CANADA - COLLEGE MILITAIRE ROYAL DE ST-JEAN
See: College Militaire Royal de St-Jean

CANADA - COMMISSION CANADIENNE DES GRAINS
See: Canada - Agriculture Canada - Canadian Grain Commission

CANADA - COMMISSION CANADIENNE DES TRANSPORTS
See: Canada - Canadian Transport Commission

CANADA - COMMISSION DE LA FONCTION PUBLIQUE
See: Canada - Public Service Commission

CANADA - COMMISSION DE REFORME DU DROIT
See: Canada - Law Reform Commission of Canada

CANADA - COMMISSION DE REVISION DE L'IMPOT
See: Canada - Tax Review Board

CANADA - COMMISSION DU SYSTEME METRIQUE
See: Canada - Metric Commission

CANADA - CONSEIL CANADIEN DES RELATIONS DU TRAVAIL
See: Canada - Labour Relations Board

CANADA - CONSEIL ECONOMIQUE DU CANADA
See: Canada - Economic Council of Canada

CANADA - CONSEIL NATIONAL DE RECHERCHES
See: Canada - National Research Council

CANADA - CONSEIL DE LA RADIODIFFUSION ET DES TELECOMMUNICATIONS CANADIENNES
See: Canada - Canadian Radio-Television and Telecommunications Commission

★2045★
CANADA - CONSUMER AND CORPORATE AFFAIRS CANADA - DEPARTMENTAL LIBRARY (Bus-Fin)
Phone: (819) 997-1632
Ottawa, ON, Canada K1A 0C9 Corinne MacLaurin, Chf.Libn.
Founded: 1968. **Staff:** Prof 4; Other 10. **Subjects:** Consumer protection, restrictive trade practices, corporate and commercial law, intellectual property. **Special Collections:** Restrictive trade practices. **Holdings:** 25,000 books; 12,000 bound periodical volumes; 30,000 government documents; 6000 corporate annual reports. **Subscriptions:** 1500 journals and other serials; 50 newspapers. **Services:** Interlibrary loans; copying; library open to public with referral from another library. **Computerized Information Services:** DIALOG, SDC, QL Systems, Info Globe; computerized serials. **Publications:** Bulletin, monthly. **Also Known As:** Consommation et Corporations Canada.

CANADA - CONSUMER AND CORPORATE AFFAIRS CANADA - METRIC COMMISSION CANADA (M.C.C) - SIM RESEARCH UNIT
See: Canada - Metric Commission

★2046★
CANADA - CONSUMER AND CORPORATE AFFAIRS CANADA - PATENT OFFICE LIBRARY (Law)†
Place du Portage
Ottawa, ON, Canada K1A 0E1
Phone: (613) 997-2525
William Berdnikoff, Hd.
Founded: 1873. **Staff:** 27. **Subjects:** Patents of the world, patent acts and rules, copyrights. **Holdings:** 60,000 books; 5 million copies of patents of various countries; 15,000 gazettes and journals. **Subscriptions:** 150 journals and other serials. **Services:** Interlibrary loans; copying; library open to public. **Publications:** Canadian Patent Office Record. **Also Known As:** Consommation et Corporations Canada. **Staff:** Jules Lalonde, Pub. Search Rm.; Mary Morris, ILL & Ref.Libn.

CANADA - COUR SUPREME DU CANADA
See: Canada - Supreme Court of Canada

★2047★
CANADA - DEFENCE AND CIVIL INSTITUTE OF ENVIRONMENTAL MEDICINE - SCIENTIFIC INFORMATION CENTRE (Med; Sci-Tech)
1133 Sheppard Ave., W.
P.O. Box 2000
Downsview, ON, Canada M3M 3B9
Phone: (416) 635-2000
Anthony Cheung, Chf.Libn.
Founded: 1952. **Staff:** Prof 1; Other 2. **Subjects:** Aviation medicine, environmental physiology, biochemistry, biophysics, biostatistics, human engineering, electronics, aircraft accident investigation, computer systems. **Special Collections:** Canadian Aviation Medicine (16,000 reports). **Holdings:** 8000 books; 8000 bound periodical volumes; 20,000 reports; 200 microforms. **Subscriptions:** 250 journals and other serials. **Services:** Interlibrary loans; copying; Centre open to public with restrictions. **Computerized Information Services:** CAN/OLE, MEDLINE, DIALOG; computerized circulation. **Publications:** Bibliography of all reports published by Defence Research Establishment Toronto and Defence Research Medical Laboratories, 1951-1971; Recent Acquisitions, irregular - for internal distribution only.

★2048★
CANADA - DEFENCE RESEARCH ESTABLISHMENT ATLANTIC - LIBRARY (Sci-Tech)
P.O. Box 1012
Dartmouth, NS, Canada B2Y 3Z7
Phone: (902) 426-3100
Donna I. Collins, Hd.Info.Serv. Group
Founded: 1946. **Staff:** Prof 1; Other 2. **Subjects:** Underwater acoustics, electrical and mechanical engineering, computer science, analytical chemistry, naval architecture. **Holdings:** 4400 books; 2800 bound periodical volumes; 24,000 research reports. **Subscriptions:** 257 journals and other serials; 5 newspapers. **Services:** Interlibrary loans; library open to public with restrictions. **Computerized Information Services:** CAN/OLE, DIALOG. **Networks/Consortia:** Member of Nova Scotia On-Line Consortium. **Remarks:** The Defence Research Establishments are now administered by the Research and Development Branch of the Department of National Defence.

★2049★
CANADA - DEFENCE RESEARCH ESTABLISHMENT OTTAWA - LIBRARY (Sci-Tech)†
Ottawa, ON, Canada K1A 0Z4
Phone: (613) 596-9386
Tina Matiisen, Hd., Info.Serv.
Founded: 1950. **Staff:** Prof 1; Other 3. **Subjects:** Chemistry, physics, engineering, electronics, computer sciences. **Holdings:** 10,000 books; 12,000 bound periodical volumes; 75,000 technical reports; 1000 patents; 300 microforms. **Subscriptions:** 375 journals and other serials. **Services:** Interlibrary loans; copying; library not open to public. **Computerized Information Services:** CAN/OLE, CAN/SDI, DSIS. **Publications:** Accession lists.

★2050★
CANADA - DEFENCE RESEARCH ESTABLISHMENT PACIFIC - LIBRARY (Sci-Tech)†
Forces Mail Office
Victoria, BC, Canada V0S 1B0
Phone: (604) 388-1665
J.A. Wilson, Libn.
Founded: 1948. **Staff:** Prof 1; Other 1. **Subjects:** Physics, mathematics, computer programming, oceanography, metallurgy, chemical analysis, corrosion prevention, electrical engineering. **Holdings:** 6500 books; 1420 bound periodical volumes; 17,225 manuscript reports, pamphlets, reprints; 1200 microfiche. **Subscriptions:** 170 journals and other serials. **Services:** Interlibrary loans; library not open to public. **Computerized Information Services:** CAN/OLE, DIALOG.

★2051★
CANADA - DEFENCE RESEARCH ESTABLISHMENT SUFFIELD - INFORMATION SERVICES (Sci-Tech)
Ralston, AB, Canada T0J 2N0
Phone: (403) 544-3701
John G. Currie, Hd., Info.Serv.
Founded: 1981. **Staff:** Prof 2; Other 1. **Subjects:** Chemistry, biology, electronics, military science, medicine. **Holdings:** 25,000 books and bound periodical volumes; 50,000 technical and defence documents; 1200 Suffield publications; archives. **Subscriptions:** 325 journals and other serials. **Services:** Interlibrary loans; copying; SDI; library open to public with restrictions. **Computerized Information Services:** CAN/OLE, DIALOG; computerized serials. **Publications:** Serials list, annual. **Staff:** Clare Murray, Libn.

★2052★
CANADA - DEFENCE RESEARCH ESTABLISHMENT VALCARTIER - LIBRARY (Sci-Tech)
P.O. Box 8800
Courcelette, PQ, Canada G0A 1R0
Phone: (418) 844-4271
Real Menard, Chf.Libn.
Founded: 1945. **Staff:** Prof 1; Other 6. **Subjects:** Physics, chemistry, general sciences, mechanical engineering, military science. **Holdings:** 14,000 books; 3000 bound periodical volumes; 20,000 reports, patents, documents; 10,000 microforms. **Subscriptions:** 400 journals and other serials. **Services:** Interlibrary loans; copying; SDI; library not open to public. **Computerized Information Services:** Mechanized retrieval. **Publications:** Users Manual - for internal distribution only. **Special Catalogs:** Mechanized catalog for documents.

CANADA - DEFENSE NATIONALE
See: Canada - National Defence

CANADA - DEPARTEMENT DES ASSURANCES
See: Canada - Department of Insurance

CANADA - DEPARTMENT OF AGRICULTURE
See: Canada - Agriculture Canada

★2053★
CANADA - DEPARTMENT OF COMMUNICATIONS - COMMUNICATIONS RESEARCH CENTRE LIBRARY (Sci-Tech)
Sta. H., P.O. Box 11490
Ottawa, ON, Canada K2H 8S2
Phone: (613) 596-9250
Callista Kelly, Libn.
Founded: 1950. **Staff:** Prof 1; Other 3. **Subjects:** Telecommunications; aerospace, electrical and electronic engineering; computer science; physics; astronomy. **Holdings:** 10,000 books; 1106 bound periodical volumes; 231 technical reports. **Subscriptions:** 550 journals and other serials. **Services:** Interlibrary loans; copying; library not open to public. **Computerized Information Services:** CAN/OLE, SDC, DIALOG. **Also Known As:** Canada - Ministere des Communications - Bibliotheque du centre de recherches sur les communications.

★2054★
CANADA - DEPARTMENT OF COMMUNICATIONS - INFORMATION SERVICES (Sci-Tech)
300 Slater St., Rm. 1420
Ottawa, ON, Canada K1A 0C8
Phone: (613) 995-8883
Michel Granger, Chf.Libn.
Staff: Prof 3; Other 8. **Subjects:** Telecommunications; computer and satellite communications; cable television; privacy of information; social and environmental issues; Videotex, office of the future; arts and culture; broadcasting. **Special Collections:** International Telecommunications Union (ITU); Comite Consultatif International Telegraphique et Telephoniques (CCITT). **Holdings:** 13,000 books; 2200 technical reports; 5500 microfiche; 300 microfilms. **Subscriptions:** 900 journals and other serials; 20 newspapers. **Services:** Interlibrary loans; copying; library open to public for reference use only. **Computerized Information Services:** CAN/SDI, CAN/OLE, INFOMART; computerized serials. **Publications:** Union list of periodicals, biennial; acquisitions and conferences lists, bimonthly. **Also Known As:** Canada - Ministere des Communications. **Staff:** Monique Perrier, Hd., Ref.Serv.; Mrs. Z. Vandoros, Hd., Tech.Serv.

★2055★
CANADA - DEPARTMENT OF FINANCE - FINANCE/TREASURY BOARD LIBRARY (Bus-Fin)
Place Bell Canada, 17 Fl.
160 Elgin St.
Ottawa, ON, Canada K1A 0G5
Phone: (613) 996-5491
Mr. T. Reid, Chf.Libn.
Founded: 1947. **Staff:** Prof 8; Other 12. **Subjects:** Finance, economics, management, personnel management, public accounts, public administration. **Holdings:** 50,000 books and bound periodical volumes; Provincial and

Municipal Documents, 1973 to present, on microfiche. **Subscriptions:** 800 journals and other serials; 40 newspapers. **Services:** Interlibrary loans; copying; library open to public with restrictions; priority given to departmental clients. **Computerized Information Services:** DIALOG, SDC, Info Globe, QL Systems, New York Times Information Service, DOBIS; computerized cataloging. **Publications:** Library Guide; Accessions List; Daily Press Review. **Also Known As:** Canada - Ministere des Finances. **Staff:** R. Clement, ILL; Linda Ervin, Hd., Client Serv.; Eileen Bays-Coutts, Hd., Tech.Serv.; Frank White, Hd., Acq.Sect.

★2056★
CANADA - DEPARTMENT OF INSURANCE - LIBRARY (Bus-Fin)
140 O'Connor St., 16th Fl.
East Tower   Phone: (613) 996-5162
Ottawa, ON, Canada K1A 0H2   Luanne Larose, Lib.Techn.
Staff: Prof 1. **Subjects:** Insurance, finance. **Holdings:** 10,300 books. **Subscriptions:** 107 journals and other serials; 10 newspapers. **Services:** Interlibrary loans; library open to public with restrictions. **Also Known As:** Canada - Departement des Assurances.

★2057★
CANADA - DEPARTMENT OF JUSTICE - LIBRARY (Law)
Justice Bldg.
Kent & Wellington Sts.   Phone: (613) 995-0144
Ottawa, ON, Canada K1A 0H8   Susan Geggie, Dir., Lib.Serv.
Staff: Prof 5; Other 11. **Subjects:** Law. **Holdings:** 300,000 volumes. **Subscriptions:** 900 journals and other serials; 13 newspapers. **Services:** Interlibrary loans; copying; library not open to public. **Computerized Information Services:** QL Systems, WESTLAW, DIALOG, SDC; computerized cataloging. **Networks/Consortia:** Member of UTLAS, Inc. **Publications:** Library bulletin, monthly. **Also Known As:** Canada - Ministere de la Justice. **Staff:** Mireille McCullough, Hd., Ref. & Rd.Serv.; Edite Abols, Law Cat.; Cecilia Lo, Hd., Tech.Serv.

CANADA - DEPARTMENT OF NATIONAL HEALTH AND WELFARE
See: Canada - Health and Welfare Canada

CANADA - DEPARTMENT OF NATIONAL REVENUE
See: Canada - Revenue Canada

★2058★
CANADA - ECONOMIC COUNCIL OF CANADA - LIBRARY (Bus-Fin)
Sta. B, P.O. Box 527   Phone: (613) 993-1914
Ottawa, ON, Canada K1P 5V6   Irene Lackner, Libn.
Founded: 1964. **Staff:** Prof 3; Other 2. **Subjects:** Economics, sociology, finance, statistics. **Holdings:** 10,050 books; 10,306 government documents (cataloged); 2500 microfiche; 650 microfilms; 50 maps. **Subscriptions:** 1000 journals and other serials; 18 newspapers. **Services:** Interlibrary loans; copying; library open to students and researchers. **Computerized Information Services:** CANSIM, Info Globe; computerized serials. **Publications:** Accessions list, monthly; Library Guide; list of periodicals, irregular. **Remarks:** Library is located at 333 River Rd., Vanier, ON. **Also Known As:** Conseil Economique du Canada. **Staff:** Diane Melski, Cat.; Tybe Marcus, Ref./ILL.

★2059★
CANADA - EMPLOYMENT & IMMIGRATION CANADA - LIBRARY (Soc Sci)
                                       Phone: (819) 994-2603
Ottawa, ON, Canada K1A 0J9   P.E. Sunder-Raj, Chf.Libn.
Founded: 1966. **Staff:** Prof 7; Other 9. **Subjects:** Adult education, immigration, labour economics, management, income maintenance, social sciences. **Holdings:** 50,000 books and bound periodical volumes; 250 reels of microfilm; microforms. **Subscriptions:** 2000 journals and other serials. **Services:** Interlibrary loans; copying; library open to public. **Computerized Information Services:** INFOMART, QL Systems, DIALOG; computerized cataloging. **Networks/Consortia:** Member of UTLAS Inc. **Publications:** Accession List, monthly. **Remarks:** Library is located at Place du Portage, Phase IV, 150 Promenade du Portage, Hull, PQ. **Also Known As:** Emploi et Immigration Canada. **Staff:** Ms. B. Camfield, Hd., Lib.Info.Serv.; Mrs. M. Nowosielski, Hd., Tech.Serv.

★2060★
CANADA - EMPLOYMENT & IMMIGRATION CANADA - PUBLIC AFFAIRS - MANITOBA REGIONAL OFFICE LIBRARY (Soc Sci)
330 Graham Ave., Rm. 710   Phone: (204) 949-2868
Winnipeg, MB, Canada R3C 4B9   Win Kennedy, Regional Mgr.
Staff: 1. **Subjects:** Public affairs. **Holdings:** Figures not available. **Services:** Library for use of departmental employees only. **Also Known As:** Emploi et Immigration Canada.

★2061★
CANADA - EMPLOYMENT & IMMIGRATION CANADA - QUEBEC REGIONAL LIBRARY (Soc Sci)
550 Sherbrooke St., W., Rm. 424   Phone: (514) 283-4695
Montreal, PQ, Canada H3A 1B9   Claudine Lussier, Dir.
Staff: Prof 2; Other 3. **Subjects:** Manpower, immigration, adult education, counselling, employment, unemployment, economics. **Holdings:** 40,000 books and government documents; 60 bound periodical volumes; 1500 pamphlets. **Subscriptions:** 400 journals and other serials. **Services:** Interlibrary loans; copying; library open to public for reference use only. **Computerized Information Services:** SDC. **Publications:** Nouvelles Acquisitions, quarterly - free upon request. **Also Known As:** Emploi et Immigration Canada.

★2062★
CANADA - ENERGY, MINES & RESOURCES CANADA - CANMET - LIBRARY (Energy)
555 Booth St.   Phone: (613) 995-4132
Ottawa, ON, Canada K1A 0G1   Gloria M. Peckham, Chf.Libn.
Founded: 1913. **Staff:** Prof 4; Other 8. **Subjects:** Mining, mineral processing, metallurgy, energy technology. **Holdings:** 150,000 books and bound periodical volumes; 60 cabinets of unbound reports, patents, pamphlets, documents, standards and specifications, microforms. **Subscriptions:** 2000 journals and other serials. **Services:** Interlibrary loans; copying; translation; library open to public with restrictions. **Computerized Information Services:** DIALOG, SDC, CAN/OLE, CAN/SDI; Mining Information File (internal database); computerized cataloging. **Networks/Consortia:** Member of UTLAS Inc. **Publications:** Accession List, monthly - distributed on request. **Remarks:** CANMET is an acronym for Canada Centre for Mineral and Energy Technology. **Staff:** Mrs. K. Nagy, Hd., Rd.Serv.; Mr. J. Ho, Hd., Cat.Div.

★2063★
CANADA - ENERGY, MINES & RESOURCES CANADA - EARTH PHYSICS BRANCH LIBRARY (Energy)†
1 Observatory Crescent   Phone: (613) 995-5558
Ottawa, ON, Canada K1A 0Y3   W.M. Tsang, Chf.Libn.
Founded: 1905. **Staff:** Prof 1; Other 2. **Subjects:** Geophysics, seismology, gravity, geothermics, rock physics, geomagnetism, geodynamics, paleomagnetism, permafrost, earth tides. **Holdings:** 4000 books; 21,000 bound periodical volumes; 15,000 pamphlets, reports, reprints. **Subscriptions:** 1100 journals and other serials. **Services:** Interlibrary loans; library open to qualified users. **Publications:** Accession list, quarterly; serials list, irregular. **Staff:** J. C. Levesque, Asst.Libn.; Louise Dore, Techn.

★2064★
CANADA - ENERGY, MINES & RESOURCES CANADA - GEOGRAPHICAL SERVICES DIRECTORATE - MAP RESOURCE CENTRE
580 Booth St.
Ottawa, ON, Canada K1A 0E9
Founded: 1947. **Subjects:** Topography, geography, history. **Holdings:** 2000 books; topographical maps, atlases. **Remarks:** Presently inactive.

CANADA - ENERGY, MINES & RESOURCES CANADA - GEOLOGICAL SURVEY OF CANADA
See: Canada - Geological Survey of Canada

CANADA - ENERGY, MINES & MINERAL RESOURCES CANADA - INSTITUTE OF OCEAN SCIENCES
See: Insitute of Ocean Sciences

★2065★
CANADA - ENERGY, MINES & RESOURCES CANADA - RESOURCE ECONOMICS LIBRARY (Energy)
580 Booth St.   Phone: (613) 995-9466
Ottawa, ON, Canada K1A 0E4   F.B. Scollie, Chf.Libn.
Founded: 1958. **Staff:** Prof 3; Other 5. **Subjects:** Mineral and energy economics, policy, taxation, legislation and statistics, energy conservation. **Special Collections:** Energyfiche, 1973 to present; Statistics Canada microfiche collection, 1867-1980; Mineral Resources Branch and Mineral Policy Sector publications; provincial geological reports; Energy Sector publications. **Holdings:** 65,000 books and bound periodical volumes; 3000 reports; 156 shelf feet of microforms. **Subscriptions:** 1000 journals and other serials. **Services:** Interlibrary loans; copying; SDI; library open to public with approval of head librarian. **Computerized Information Services:** DIALOG, SDC, CAN/OLE, QL Systems, Info Globe; computerized cataloging. **Networks/Consortia:** Member of UTLAS Inc. **Publications:** Accession list, monthly - limited distribution. **Staff:** P. Gibson, Asst.Hd., Pub.Serv.; F. Mayrand, Asst.Hd., Tech.Serv.

★2066★
CANADA - ENERGY, MINES & RESOURCES CANADA - SURVEYS &
MAPPING BRANCH - LIBRARY (Geog-Map)
615 Booth St.   Phone: (613) 995-4071
Ottawa, ON, Canada K1A 0E9   Valerie E. Hoare, Chf.Libn.
Founded: 1962. **Staff:** Prof 1; Other 3. **Subjects:** Geodesy,
photogrammetry, cartography, toponymy, Canadian geography and history.
Holdings: 35,000 books; 12,000 bound periodical volumes. **Subscriptions:**
350 journals and other serials. **Services:** Interlibrary loans; copying; library
open to public with permission of librarian. **Networks/Consortia:** Member of
UTLAS Inc.

★2067★
CANADA - ENERGY, MINES & RESOURCES CANADA - SURVEYS &
MAPPING BRANCH - NATIONAL AIR PHOTO LIBRARY (Pict)
615 Booth St.   Phone: (613) 995-4650
Ottawa, ON, Canada K1A 0E9   Dianne Rombough, Hd.
Founded: 1925. **Staff:** Prof 15. **Subjects:** Mapping aerial photographs;
remote sensing photography. **Special Collections:** Photography for Canada,
1925 to present. **Holdings:** 4 million photographs; 11,900 index maps.
Services: Reproduction of aerial photography; library open to public. **Special**
Catalogs: Air photography index maps, catalogs and brochures.

CANADA - ENVIRONMENT CANADA - AIR POLLUTION CONTROL
DIRECTORATE (APCD)
See: Canada - Air Pollution Technical Information Section

CANADA - ENVIRONMENT CANADA - ATMOSPHERIC ENVIRONMENT
SERVICE
See: Canada - Atmospheric Environment Service

CANADA - ENVIRONMENT CANADA - CANADIAN FORESTRY SERVICE
See: Canada - Canadian Forestry Service

CANADA - ENVIRONMENT CANADA - CANADIAN WILDLIFE SERVICE
See: Canada - Canadian Wildlife Service

CANADA - ENVIRONMENT CANADA - ENVIRONMENTAL PROTECTION
SERVICE
See: Canada - Environmental Protection Service

CANADA - ENVIRONMENT CANADA - FISHERIES & MARINE SERVICE
See: Canada - Fisheries & Oceans

★2068★
CANADA - ENVIRONMENT CANADA - LIBRARY SERVICES BRANCH (Env-
Cons)
                                              Phone: (613) 997-1767
Ottawa, ON, Canada K1A 1C7   Mrs. A.M. Bystram, Dir., Lib.Serv.Br.
Founded: 1973. **Staff:** Prof 14; Other 17. **Subjects:** Forestry, land use
planning, national parks and historic sites, pollution prevention and control,
water resources, environmental planning and management, wildlife. **Holdings:**
88,500 books; 47,000 bound periodical volumes; 690 reels of microfilm;
10,000 microfiche reports from U.S. Environmental Protection Agency;
Environment Canada publications (depository). **Subscriptions:** 3282 journals
and other serials; 25 newspapers. **Services:** Interlibrary loans; copying; SDI;
translation of scientific and technical material; library open to public for
reference use only. **Computerized Information Services:** DIALOG, BRS,
MEDLINE, INFORMATECH, Info Globe, DOBIS, CAN/OLE, QL Systems, SDC,
RESORS; computerized cataloging, acquisitions and circulation. **Networks/**
Consortia: Headquarters of Environment Canada Library Network.
Publications: Ariel (Environment Canada Libraries newsletter), monthly;
Environment Canada Libraries Bibliography Series, irregular; Acquisitions List,
monthly; Library Services (brochure); Environment Canada Library Translation
Series. **Also Known As:** Ministere de l'environnement. **Staff:** Mrs. R.
Thompson, Assoc.Dir.; Mrs. M. Czanyo, Assoc.Dir.; Henne Kahwa, Hd.,
Rd.Serv.

CANADA - ENVIRONMENTAL PROTECTION SERVICE - EDMONTON
LIBRARY
See: Canada - Canadian Wildlife Service - Western and Northern Region
Library

★2069★
CANADA - ENVIRONMENTAL PROTECTION SERVICE - LIBRARY (Env-Cons)
25 St. Clair Ave., E.   Phone: (416) 966-5840
Toronto, ON, Canada M4T 1M2   Barbara Porrett, Libn.
Founded: 1975. **Staff:** Prof 1. **Subjects:** Air and water pollution - control and
prevention; waste management. **Special Collections:** Publications of the

Department of the Environment. **Holdings:** 6000 books; 1500 microfiche;
unpublished consultants' reports. **Subscriptions:** 90 journals and other serials.
Services: Interlibrary loans; library open to public by appointment.
Computerized Information Services: CAN/OLE; computerized cataloging.
Networks/Consortia: Member of Environment Libraries Automated System
(ELIAS). **Publications:** Monthly acquisitions list.

★2070★
CANADA - ENVIRONMENTAL PROTECTION SERVICE - PACIFIC REGION
LIBRARY (Env-Cons)
3rd Fl., Kapilano 100
Park Royal South   Phone: (604) 666-6711
West Vancouver, BC, Canada V7M 2N2   Kim MacDonald, Lib.Ck.
Founded: 1972. **Staff:** Prof 1; Other 1. **Subjects:** Pollution - air, water, land.
Holdings: 6750 monographs; 1900 pamphlets; 400 microforms; 20 VF
drawers of subject files; Canadian and U.S. government environmental
reports. **Subscriptions:** 102 journals and other serials. **Services:** Interlibrary
loans; copying; library open to public for reference use; loans to government
employees. **Networks/Consortia:** Member of Environment Canada Library
Network. **Publications:** EPS Reports, irregular.

CANADA - EXPANSION ECONOMIQUE REGIONALE
See: Canada - Regional Economic Expansion

★2071★
CANADA - EXTERNAL AFFAIRS CANADA - LIBRARY (Soc Sci)†
Lester B. Pearson Bldg.
Sussex Dr.   Phone: (613) 996-8691
Ottawa, ON, Canada K1A 0G2   Ruth Margaret Thompson, Dir.
Founded: 1931. **Staff:** Prof 9; Other 21. **Subjects:** Political science,
economics, history, geography, environment, sociology, literature. **Special**
Collections: International documents; international law. **Holdings:** 55,000
books; 2416 bound periodical volumes; 590,918 documents; 168,801
microforms. **Subscriptions:** 2939 journals and other serials; 60 newspapers.
Services: Interlibrary loans; copying; library open to public with restrictions.
Computerized Information Services: Computerized cataloging. **Networks/**
Consortia: Member of UTLAS Inc. **Publications:** Acquisitions List,
semimonthly. **Also Known As:** Affaires exterieures, Canada.

★2072★
CANADA - FARM CREDIT CORPORATION CANADA - LIBRARY (Agri)
Sta. D, Box 2314   Phone: (613) 996-6606
Ottawa, ON, Canada K1P 6J9   Violette Saunders, Info.Off.
Founded: 1976. **Staff:** 2. **Subjects:** Agriculture - economics, research,
management. **Holdings:** 1000 books; 200 series, unbound reports,
documents, annual reports and pamphlets; 25 shelves of archives.
Subscriptions: 82 journals and other serials; 16 newspapers. **Services:**
Library not open to public. **Publications:** FCC Annual Report; Financing Your
Farm Business; Farm Syndicates Loans; Federal Farm Credit Statistics books;
Farm Credit in the Financial System; Farm Credit 50 Years (history) - all free
upon request.

★2073★
CANADA - FISHERIES & OCEANS - BIOLOGICAL STATION LIBRARY (Sci-
Tech)
                                              Phone: (506) 529-8854
St. Andrews, NB, Canada E0G 2X0   Ms. C.R. Garnett, Libn.
Staff: 2. **Subjects:** Fisheries, aquatic biology, chemistry. **Holdings:** 6000
books; 8500 bound periodical volumes; 420 boxes of pamphlets.
Subscriptions: 715 journals and other serials. **Services:** Interlibrary loans;
copying; library open to qualified researchers. **Publications:** Circulars and
technical reports, irregular. **Also Known As:** Canada - Peches et Oceans.

★2074★
CANADA - FISHERIES & OCEANS - FISHERIES MANAGEMENT REGIONAL
LIBRARY (Sci-Tech; Env-Cons)†
1090 W. Pender St.   Phone: (604) 666-3851
Vancouver, BC, Canada V6E 2N9   Paulette Westlake, Lib.Techn.
Founded: 1962. **Staff:** 2. **Subjects:** Fisheries, biology, economics,
environment, engineering, northern development. **Holdings:** 5000 books; 250
bound periodical volumes; 65 shelves of reports and government documents;
22,000 pamphlets and photocopies; 450 translations; 125 microfiche.
Subscriptions: 500 journals and other serials. **Services:** Interlibrary loans;
library open to public for reference use only. **Publications:** Accession List.
Also Known As: Canada - Peches et Oceans.

★2075★
CANADA - FISHERIES & OCEANS - FRESHWATER INSTITUTE LIBRARY
(Sci-Tech)
501 University Crescent   Phone: (204) 269-7379
Winnipeg, MB, Canada R3T 2N6   K. Eric Marshall, Libn.
Founded: 1966. **Staff:** Prof 1; Other 3. **Subjects:** Fisheries, limnology.
Special Collections: Fritsch Collection of illustrations of freshwater algae
(microfiche); Arctic Petroleum Operators Association reports (microfiche).
Holdings: 16,000 books; 60,000 bound periodical volumes; 12,000
pamphlets; 200 pamphlet boxes of reports; 7000 microfiche; 300 reels of
microfilm; 15,000 cards of abstracts and indexes. **Subscriptions:** 1100
journals and other serials. **Services:** Interlibrary loans; copying; SDI; library
open to public. **Computerized Information Services:** DIALOG, SDC, QL
Systems, CAN/OLE, Institute for Scientific Information (ISI). **Publications:**
New Publications in the Library, monthly - for internal distribution only. **Also
Known As:** Canada - Peches et Oceans.

CANADA - FISHERIES & OCEANS - INSTITUTE OF OCEAN SCIENCES
See: Institute of Ocean Sciences

★2076★
CANADA - FISHERIES & OCEANS - LIBRARY (Sci-Tech)
240 Sparks St., 8th Fl. W.   Phone: (613) 995-9991
Ottawa, ON, Canada K1A 0E6   C.S. Boyle, Dir., Lib.Serv.
Staff: Prof 3; Other 2. **Subjects:** Fisheries, marine sciences. **Holdings:** 6000
books; 1000 bound periodical volumes. **Subscriptions:** 600 journals and
other serials; 10 newspapers. **Services:** Interlibrary loans; copying; SDI;
library open to public with restrictions on borrowing. **Publications:**
Acquisitions, bimonthly. **Special Indexes:** KWOC index of reports (loose-leaf).
Staff: C. Moise, Ref.; S.A. Farooqui, Cat.; D. Lasalle, ILL.

★2077★
CANADA - FISHERIES & OCEANS - NEWFOUNDLAND REGIONAL LIBRARY
(Sci-Tech; Env-Cons)
P.O. Box 5667   Phone: (709) 737-2022
St. John's, NF, Canada A1C 5X1   Audrey Conroy, Libn.
Founded: 1940. **Staff:** 4. **Subjects:** Marine biology, freshwater resource
development, fisheries, pollution. **Holdings:** 7000 books; 1500 linear feet of
serials. **Subscriptions:** 775 journals and other serials. **Services:** Interlibrary
loans; copying; SDI; computer searches for staff; library open to public.
Computerized Information Services: Online systems. **Also Known As:**
Canada - Peches et Oceans.

★2078★
CANADA - FISHERIES & OCEANS - PACIFIC BIOLOGICAL STATION -
LIBRARY (Sci-Tech)
                                                    Phone: (604) 758-5202
Nanaimo, BC, Canada V9R 5K6   G. Miller, Libn.
Staff: Prof 1; Other 2. **Subjects:** Fish biology, fish culture, marine ecology,
biological oceanography. **Holdings:** 3600 books. **Subscriptions:** 2400
journals and other serials. **Services:** Interlibrary loans; copying; SDI; library
open to public with restrictions. **Computerized Information Services:**
DIALOG, QL Systems, CAN/OLE; computerized cataloging. **Also Known As:**
Canada - Peches et Oceans.

★2079★
CANADA - FISHERIES & OCEANS - R&D DIRECTORATE - ARCTIC
BIOLOGICAL STATION LIBRARY (Sci-Tech; Env-Cons)
555 St. Pierre Blvd.   Phone: (514) 457-3660
Ste. Anne-De-Bellevue, PQ, Canada H9X 3R4   June Currie, Libn.
Founded: 1956. **Staff:** Prof 1. **Subjects:** Biological oceanography; marine
zoology; fishes and fisheries of Arctic and subarctic; ecology. **Special
Collections:** Primary and secondary literature on marine mammals. **Holdings:**
6000 books and bound periodical volumes; publications of Fisheries Research
Board of Canada. **Subscriptions:** 200 journals and other serials. **Services:**
Interlibrary loans; copying; library open to public for reference use only.
Computerized Information Services: CAN/OLE, QL Systems, DIALOG.
Publications: Monthly Current Awareness - for internal distribution only. **Also
Known As:** Canada - Peches et Oceans.

★2080★
CANADA - FISHERIES & OCEANS - SCOTIA-FUNDY REGIONAL LIBRARY
(Sci-Tech; Env-Cons)
P.O. Box 550   Phone: (902) 426-3972
Halifax, NS, Canada B3J 2S7   Anna Oxley, Regional Libn.
Founded: 1968. **Staff:** Prof 1; Other 3. **Subjects:** Fisheries, environmental
control, food technology. **Special Collections:** Atlantic Salmon. **Holdings:**
13,000 books; 2800 bound periodical volumes; 40,000 technical reports;
20,000 microfiche; 500 reels of microfilm. **Subscriptions:** 3150 journals

and other serials; 50 newspapers. **Services:** Interlibrary loans; copying; SDI;
library open to public with restrictions. **Computerized Information Services:**
Online systems. **Publications:** Atlantic Salmon Bibliography, annual. **Special
Indexes:** KWOC index to technical reports collection (COM microfiche).
Remarks: Contains the holdings of its R&D Directorate - Halifax Laboratory
Library. **Also Known As:** Canada - Peches et Oceans.

★2081★
CANADA - FISHERIES & OCEANS - SEA LAMPREY CONTROL CENTRE -
LIBRARY (Sci-Tech)
Huron St., Ship Canal P.O.   Phone: (705) 949-1102
Sault Ste. Marie, ON, Canada P6A 1P0   B.G.H. Johnson, Biologist
Founded: 1965. **Staff:** Prof 1. **Subjects:** Lamprey biology, fish and fishing,
vertebrate zoology, general biology, fisheries management and research.
Holdings: 300 books; 300 unbound periodicals; 1500 separates; 250
Fisheries Research Board manuscript reports; 650 Sea Lamprey Control
Centre annual reports; 400 unbound reports. **Subscriptions:** 30 journals and
other serials. **Services:** Copying; library open to public by appointment only,
for reference use. **Also Known As:** Canada - Peches et Oceans.

CANADA - GALERIE NATIONALE DU CANADA
See: Canada - National Gallery of Canada

CANADA - GENDARMERIE ROYALE DU CANADA
**See: Royal Canadian Mounted Police - Law Enforcement Reference
Centre**

★2082★
**CANADA - GEOLOGICAL SURVEY OF CANADA - INSTITUTE OF
SEDIMENTARY & PETROLEUM GEOLOGY - LIBRARY** (Sci-Tech)
3303 33rd St., N.W.   Phone: (403) 284-0301
Calgary, AB, Canada T2L 2A7   Marian Jones, Libn.
Founded: 1966. **Staff:** Prof 2; Other 2. **Subjects:** Geology. **Holdings:**
80,000 books; 1550 translations; 12 cabinets of maps. **Subscriptions:** 650
journals and other serials; 6 newspapers. **Services:** Copying; library open to
public by appointment. **Computerized Information Services:** CAN/OLE,
DIALOG, SDC. **Publications:** Monthly Accessions List. **Staff:** Dana Franck,
Asst.Libn.

★2083★
CANADA - GEOLOGICAL SURVEY OF CANADA - LIBRARY (Sci-Tech)
100 W. Pender St., 5th Fl.   Phone: (604) 666-3812
Vancouver, BC, Canada V6B 1R8   Mary Akehurst, Libn.
Founded: 1973. **Staff:** Prof 1; Other 1. **Subjects:** Earth sciences with
emphasis on the Western Cordillera and marine work on the Pacific Coast.
Special Collections: Reports and maps of the Geological Survey of Canada,
Dept. of Energy, Mines & Resources, Environment Canada and Fisheries and
Oceans; publications from U.S.G.S., U.S. Bureau of Mines and B.C. Ministry of
Energy, Mines & Petroleum Resources. **Holdings:** 103,000 volumes; 8000
maps; 25 VF drawers of unbound reports; 600 theses; microforms.
Subscriptions: 950 journals and other serials; 700 government serials.
Services: Copying on premises (limited); library open to public with
restrictions.

★2084★
CANADA - GEOLOGICAL SURVEY OF CANADA - LIBRARY (Sci-Tech)
601 Booth St., Rm. 350   Phone: (613) 995-4151
Ottawa, ON, Canada K1A 0E8   Miss A.E. Bourgeois, Hd., Lib.Serv.
Founded: 1844. **Staff:** Prof 9; Other 10. **Subjects:** Geology, paleontology,
geochemistry, geophysics, physical geography. **Holdings:** 400,000 books and
bound periodical volumes; 250,000 maps; 700 "open files" (unpublished
documents announced to users). **Subscriptions:** 4000 journals and other
serials. **Services:** Interlibrary loans; copying; SDI to Canadian users; library
open to public with restrictions. **Computerized Information Services:**
DIALOG, SDC, CAN/OLE, GEOSCAN. **Networks/Consortia:** Member of
UTLAS, Inc. **Publications:** Accession List, monthly; List of Translations,
annual. **Staff:** Mrs. L.A. Frieday, Hd., Automated Oper.; Mrs. E. Frebold, Hd.,
Info.Serv.; Miss T. Naraynsingh, Map Libn.; Mr. S. Alexander, Hd., Tech.Serv.

★2085★
CANADA - HEALTH AND WELFARE CANADA - DEPARTMENTAL LIBRARY
SERVICES (Med; Soc Sci)†
Brooke Claxton Bldg., Rm. 374
Tunney's Pasture   Phone: (613) 992-5743
Ottawa, ON, Canada K1A 0K9   Daphne Dolan, Chf.
Founded: 1944. **Staff:** Prof 13; Other 18. **Subjects:** Health sciences, public
health, social and economic welfare, economics, health care systems,
management, sociology, education, psychology. **Holdings:** 100,000 volumes.
Subscriptions: 4500 journals and other serials. **Services:** Interlibrary loans;

copying; SDI; library open to public for reference use only. **Computerized Information Services:** DIALOG, SDC, CAN/OLE, QL Systems, MEDLINE, New York Times Information Service, Union Book Catalogue. **Publications:** Accessions List, monthly. **Staff:** N. Wildgoose, Hd., Pub.Serv.; Mrs. F. Blacquiere, Sys.Libn.; Miss M. Marchand, Hd., Coll.Dev.; Mrs. J. Filipkowski, Hd., Tech.Serv.; Mrs. A. Cooke, Sr.Ref./SDI Libn.

★2086★
CANADA - HEALTH AND WELFARE CANADA - HEALTH PROTECTION BRANCH - REGIONAL LIBRARY (Sci-Tech; Med)
1001 W. Pender St., 6th Fl.   Phone: (604) 666-3147
Vancouver, BC, Canada V6E 2M7   Elizabeth Hardacre, Lib.Techn.
Founded: 1964. **Staff:** 1. **Subjects:** Food inspection and analysis; microbiology; pesticides; pharmaceuticals; illicit drug analysis. **Holdings:** 1500 books; 1000 bound periodical volumes. **Subscriptions:** 100 journals and other serials. **Services:** Interlibrary loans; copying; library not open to public.

★2087★
CANADA - HEALTH AND WELFARE CANADA - HEALTH PROTECTION BRANCH - REGIONAL LIBRARY (Sci-Tech; Med)
1001 Ouest Boul. St. Laurent, Ch. 321   Phone: (514) 283-5472
Longueuil, PQ, Canada J4K 1C7   Eleanora Ferenczy, Techn.
Founded: 1971. **Staff:** 1. **Subjects:** Food and drugs, organic chemistry, nutrition, pesticides, pharmacology, cosmetics. **Holdings:** 1500 books; 600 bound periodical volumes; 3500 pamphlets and other items. **Subscriptions:** 150 journals and other serials. **Services:** Interlibrary loans; copying; library open to public by appointment. **Computerized Information Services:** Computerized cataloging and serials.

★2088★
CANADA - HEALTH AND WELFARE CANADA - HEALTH PROTECTION BRANCH - TORONTO REGIONAL LIBRARY (Sci-Tech; Med)
2301 Midland Ave.   Phone: (416) 291-4231
Scarborough, ON, Canada M1P 4R7   S. Brockhurst, Lib.Techn.
Staff: 1. **Subjects:** Food analysis, food and drug legislation, microbiology, chemistry, pharmacology, toxicology, cosmetics, pesticides, narcotics. **Holdings:** 2500 books; 212 bound periodical volumes. **Subscriptions:** 97 journals and other serials. **Services:** Library open to public for reference use only.

★2089★
CANADA - HEALTH AND WELFARE CANADA - LIBRARY SERVICES (Sci-Tech; Med)
Sir F.G. Banting Research Centre, 3rd Fl., E.
Ross Ave., Tunney's Pasture   Phone: (613) 593-7603
Ottawa, ON, Canada K1A 0L2   Bonita Stableford, Chf., Lib.Serv.
Founded: 1969. **Staff:** Prof 7; Other 7. **Subjects:** Pharmacology, pharmaceutical chemistry, food science, nutrition research, microbiology, toxicology, medical sciences, environmental health, radiation protection, drug abuse. **Holdings:** 12,250 books and bound periodical volumes; 500 microforms. **Subscriptions:** 900 journals. **Services:** Interlibrary loans; copying; library open to public for reference use only. **Computerized Information Services:** Online systems. **Remarks:** The Ottawa libraries are organized at a directorate level and are located in the Laboratory Centre for Disease Control Building (593-4710), the Environmental Health Directorate Building (996-2635) and the Sir Frederick G. Banting Research Centre (593-6527), all on Tunney's Pasture. **Staff:** Ms. Merle McConnell, Banting Res. Centre; Ms. Terry Chernis, Env. Health; Susan Higgins, LCDC.

★2090★
CANADA - IMMIGRATION APPEAL BOARD - LIBRARY (Law)
116 Lisgar St.   Phone: (613) 995-6486
Ottawa, ON, Canada K1A 0K1   Philippa Wall, Hd.
Staff: 2. **Subjects:** Law, immigration. **Holdings:** 3176 books. **Services:** Interlibrary loans; library open to public for reference use only. **Staff:** Denise Groulx, Supv.

★2091★
CANADA - INDIAN & NORTHERN AFFAIRS CANADA - DEPARTMENTAL LIBRARY (Area-Ethnic; Hist)
     Phone: (819) 997-0799
Ottawa, ON, Canada K1A 0H4   Kamra Ramma, Hd.Libn.
Founded: 1966. **Staff:** Prof 9; Other 7. **Subjects:** Canada - native people, history, native crafts, arts, literature; Canadian North; Indians and Eskimos. **Special Collections:** Arctic collection. **Holdings:** 75,000 books; 20,000 bound periodical volumes; 3500 special government documents (cataloged); 3000 pamphlets; 3000 reels of microfilm. **Subscriptions:** 1200 journals and other serials; 20 newspapers. **Services:** Interlibrary loans; copying; library open to public with permission from chief librarian. **Computerized**

Information Services: DIALOG, BRS, QL Systems; computerized cataloging and circulation. **Networks/Consortia:** Member of UTLAS, Inc. **Publications:** Accessions List, monthly; Directory of Departmental Information Centres, irregular. **Remarks:** Library located at Terrasses de la Chandiere, Hull, PQ. **Also Known As:** Affaires indiennes et du Nord Canada. **Staff:** Ann Braden, Hd., Client Serv.

★2092★
CANADA - INDIAN & NORTHERN AFFAIRS CANADA - INUVIK SCIENTIFIC RESOURCE CENTRE - LIBRARY (Area-Ethnic)
P.O. Box 1430   Phone: (403) 979-3838
Inuvik, NT, Canada X0E 0T0   D.A. Sherstone, Scientist-in-Charge
Founded: 1963. **Staff:** Prof 1; Other 1. **Subjects:** General scientific subjects, Western Arctic region, Northern region. **Holdings:** 2000 books; 58 films; microfilm; maps. **Subscriptions:** 70 journals and other serials; 12 newspapers. **Services:** Interlibrary loans; copying; library open to public. **Also Known As:** Affaires indiennes et du Nord Canada.

★2093★
CANADA - INDUSTRY, TRADE & COMMERCE - CANADIAN GOVERNMENT OFFICE OF TOURISM (Bus-Fin)
Tourism Reference & Data Centre
235 Queen St.   Phone: (613) 995-2754
Ottawa, ON, Canada K1A 0H6   Rae Bradford, Mgr.
Founded: 1938. **Staff:** Prof 4; Other 2. **Subjects:** Tourism and travel; recreation and leisure; tourism marketing, planning and development. **Special Collections:** Canadian tourism research and statistics; international tourism statistics. **Holdings:** 5000 research and statistical reports in database; 100 pamphlet boxes. **Subscriptions:** 200 journals and other serials; 8 newspapers. **Services:** Interlibrary loans; copying; SDI; library open to public with restrictions on borrowing. **Computerized Information Services:** Online systems; computerized cataloging. **Publications:** Acquisition list, bimonthly. **Special Catalogs:** Bibliography of Tourism Research (book, English and French editions). **Staff:** Mrs. Frewen, Ref. Data Anl.; Mr. Rheal Viau, Database Anl.; Joyce Lockwood, Info.Anl.

CANADA - INDUSTRY, TRADE AND COMMERCE - CANADIAN INDUSTRIAL INNOVATION CENTRE/WATERLOO
See: Canadian Industrial Innovation Centre/Waterloo

★2094★
CANADA - INDUSTRY, TRADE & COMMERCE - LIBRARY (Bus-Fin; Sci-Tech)†
235 Queen St.   Phone: (613) 992-4947
Ottawa, ON, Canada K1A 0H6   Stephan Rush, Chf.Libn.
Staff: Prof 7; Other 12. **Subjects:** Economics, technology, science, manufactures, trades, administration. **Special Collections:** Documents of international organizations (20,000 items). **Holdings:** 100,000 volumes; 4000 pamphlets; 900 reels of microfilm. **Subscriptions:** 2000 journals and other serials; 25 newspapers. **Services:** Interlibrary loans; copying; SDI; library open to graduate students, faculty members and businessmen. **Computerized Information Services:** Computerized serials. **Publications:** Recent Additions, monthly - available on request. **Staff:** Miss E.J.V. Martin, Hd., Info.Serv.; Mr. J.L. Simon, Hd., Info.Proc.; Mr. G.J. Doherty, Hd., Intl.Doc.; Mrs. S.M. McLean, Hd., Purchasing.

CANADA - INSTITUT DE GENIE DES MATERIAUX
See: Canada - National Research Council - CISTI - Industrial Materials Research Institute Library

CANADA INSTITUTE FOR SCIENTIFIC AND TECHNICAL INFORMATION
See: Canada - National Research Council - CISTI

CANADA - INTERNATIONAL DEVELOPMENT RESEARCH CENTRE
See: International Development Research Centre

CANADA - INTERNATIONAL JOINT COMMISSION
See: International Joint Commission

★2095★
CANADA - LABOUR CANADA - LIBRARY - OCCUPATIONAL SAFETY AND HEALTH BRANCH - TECHNICAL RESOURCE CENTRE (Soc Sci)
     Phone: (819) 997-3100
Ottawa, ON, Canada K1A 0J3   John S.N. Chan, Br.Libn.
Founded: 1967. **Staff:** Prof 1; Other 1. **Subjects:** Occupational safety, health and medicine; industrial hygiene; safety engineering; Canadian OSH legislation. **Special Collections:** Standards from Canadian Standards Association and American National Standards Institute. **Holdings:** Figures not available. **Subscriptions:** 60 journals and other serials. **Services:** Library not open to

public. **Publications:** Occupational Safety and Health - A Bibliography (updated periodically). **Staff:** Dorothy Corneil, Asst. to Libn.

★2096★
CANADA - LABOUR CANADA - LIBRARY SERVICES (Soc Sci)
Ottawa, ON, Canada K1A 0J2   Phone: (819) 997-3540
    V.S. MacKelvie, Dir., Lib.Serv.
Founded: 1900. **Staff:** Prof 7; Other 9. **Subjects:** Industrial relations, labour economics, labour legislation, women in the work force, economic conditions, fair employment practices, technological change. **Special Collections:** Canadian labour history; labour union newspapers and proceedings; international labour publications. **Holdings:** 100,000 books; 10,000 bound periodical volumes; 1600 reels of microfilm (American and Canadian labour union newspapers). **Subscriptions:** 1300 journals and other serials. **Services:** Interlibrary loans; copying; library open to public. **Computerized Information Services:** SDC, Info Globe; internal database; computerized cataloging and indexing. **Publications:** Library Bulletin, weekly - for internal distribution only; Table of Contents - for internal distribution only; Guide to Library Services; Canadian Labour Papers on Microfilm; American Labour Papers on Microfilm; Canadian Labour Papers Currently Received; American Labour Papers Currently Received; General Periodicals Currently Received. **Special Indexes:** Periodicals index, 1970-1981. **Staff:** Vicki Milnes, Hd., Tech.Serv.; Suzanne Tourigny, Ref.Libn.; Fred Longley, Asst.Dir./Hd., Ref.; Ed Popoff, Ref./ Indexing/Microfilms.

★2097★
CANADA - LABOUR RELATIONS BOARD - LIBRARY (Law; Soc Sci)
Pearson Bldg., Tower D, 4th Fl.   Phone: (613) 995-0895
Ottawa, ON, Canada K1A 0X8   Denis Brazeau, Asst.Libn.
Founded: 1973. **Staff:** Prof 2; Other 2. **Subjects:** Labour law, collective bargaining, labour relations. **Holdings:** 3000 books. **Subscriptions:** 265 journals and other serials; 7 newspapers. **Services:** Interlibrary loans; copying; library open to public for reference use only. **Publications:** Library bulletin, monthly.

★2098★
CANADA - LAW REFORM COMMISSION OF CANADA - LIBRARY (Law)
130 Albert St., Rm. 809   Phone: (613) 995-8648
Ottawa, ON, Canada K1A 0L6   Judith Rubin, Libn.
Founded: 1972. **Staff:** Prof 1; Other 3. **Subjects:** Law - criminal, protection of life (medical, legal and ethical), administrative; revision of criminal code; police problems. **Special Collections:** Reports, study papers, research papers from other Law Reform Commissions. **Holdings:** 3650 books; 5532 bound periodical volumes; 560 other cataloged items. **Subscriptions:** 306 journals and other serials; 5 newspapers. **Services:** Interlibrary loans; copying; library open to public for research purposes. **Also Known As:** Commission de Reforme du Droit. **Staff:** Donna Hellman, Lib.Techn.; Francine Gauthier, Lib.Techn.

★2099★
CANADA - LIBRARY OF PARLIAMENT (Hist; Law)
Parliament Bldgs.   Phone: (613) 995-7113
Ottawa, ON, Canada K1A 0A9   Erik J. Spicer, Parliamentary Libn.
Founded: 1867. **Staff:** Prof 96; Other 131. **Subjects:** Parliamentary history and procedure; government and politics; foreign affairs; economics and finance; law; history; social welfare; Canadiana. **Special Collections:** U.K. parliamentary papers (3200 linear feet); U.S. Congressional and administrative publications (4140 linear feet); U.N. depository items (French and English; 1314 linear feet); Australia, New Zealand and South Africa federal parliamentary publications (846 linear feet); Canadian political pamphlets. **Holdings:** 570,000 books and bound periodical volumes; 21,200 reels of microfilmed newspapers; 126,639 microfiche of Canadian provincial and U.S. federal documents; 3336 files of clippings; 4761 unpublished research reports; 20,000 Canadian pamphlets. **Subscriptions:** 2490 journals and other serials; 663 newspapers. **Services:** Interlibrary loans; copying; library open to public for reference use only. **Computerized Information Services:** SDC, Infomart, CAN/OLE, New York Times Information Service, DIALOG, QL Systems, ANSSIR, Info Globe, SABINE, DOBIS; NIL (internal database); computerized cataloging. **Publications:** Selected Additions List, monthly; Selected Periodical Articles List, semimonthly; Your Library (revised as required); Periodicals and Newspapers in the Collection of the Library of Parliament; Annual Report of the Parliamentary Librarian - Current Issue Reviews, updated monthly; background papers; Quorum, daily during session; subject bibliographies - all distributed to senators, Members of Parliament and interested libraries. **Special Indexes:** Chronology of Legislation (loose-leaf), including index to bills by subject and sponsor (card), sessional with daily updates during session; indexes to Proceedings of Canadian Senate Committees, sessional (published by Supply and Services); clipping file subject headings; index to ministers' speeches. **Remarks:** Maintains 3 branch libraries

and 2 reading rooms in the parliamentary precincts. **Staff:** Richard Pare, Assoc.Libn.; Lloyd Heaslip, Dir., Info. & Ref.Br.; Hugh Finsten, Dir., Res.Br.; Bernard Dumouchel, Dir., Tech.Serv.Br.; J.J. Cardinal, Dir., Adm. & Personnel.

★2100★
CANADA LIFE ASSURANCE COMPANY - LIBRARY (Bus-Fin)
330 University Ave.   Phone: (416) 597-1456
Toronto, ON, Canada M5G 1R8   Gloria F.L. Johns, Libn.
Founded: 1931. **Staff:** 2. **Subjects:** Insurance and related fields. **Holdings:** 10,500 volumes; 32 VF drawers. **Subscriptions:** 145 journals and other serials. **Services:** Library open to representatives of other insurance companies and to members of the Special Libraries Association.

★2101★
CANADA - METRIC COMMISSION CANADA (M.C.C.) - SIM RESEARCH UNIT (Sci-Tech)
255 Argyle St.   Phone: (613) 996-8584
Ottawa, ON, Canada K1A 0C9   L. Gravel, Res.Off.
Founded: 1973. **Staff:** 3. **Subjects:** Systeme International, metric conversion and related data on standards, legislation, organizations, economics, statistics, technology. **Special Collections:** Documentation on metric conversion. **Holdings:** 600 books and pamphlets; 30,000 reports, periodicals and clippings on microfiche; parliamentary publications. **Services:** Library not open to public. **Computerized Information Services:** Mechanized services. **Remarks:** The Metric Commission - SIM Research Unit is affiliated with the Consumer and Corporate Affairs Canada - Departmental Library. **Also Known As:** Commission du systeme metrique.

CANADA - MINISTERE DES AFFAIRES DES ANCIENS COMBATTANTS
See: Canada - Veterans Affairs Canada

CANADA - MINISTERE DES AFFAIRES EXTERIEURES
See: Canada - External Affairs Canada

CANADA - MINISTERE DES AFFAIRES INDIENNES ET DU NORD CANADIEN
See: Canada - Indian & Northern Affairs Canada

CANADA - MINISTERE DE L'AGRICULTURE
See: Canada - Agriculture Canada

CANADA - MINISTERE DES COMMUNICATIONS
See: Canada - Department of Communications

CANADA - MINISTERE DE LA CONSOMMATION ET DES CORPORATIONS
See: Canada - Consumer and Corporate Affairs Canada

CANADA - MINISTERE DE LA DEFENSE NATIONALE
See: Canada - National Defence

CANADA - MINISTERE DE L'ENERGIE, DES MINES ET DES RESSOURCES
See: Canada - Energy, Mines & Resources Canada

CANADA - MINISTERE DE L'ENVIRONNEMENT
See: Canada - Environment Canada

CANADA - MINISTERE DE L'EXPANSION ECONOMIQUE REGIONALE
See: Canada - Regional Economic Expansion

CANADA - MINISTERE DES FINANCES
See: Canada - Department of Finance

CANADA - MINISTERE DE L'INDUSTRIE ET DU COMMERCE
See: Canada - Industry, Trade & Commerce

CANADA - MINISTERE DE LA JUSTICE
See: Canada - Department of Justice

CANADA - MINISTERE DU REVENU NATIONAL
See: Canada - Revenue Canada

CANADA - MINISTERE DE LA SANTE NATIONALE ET DU BIEN-ETRE SOCIAL
See: Canada - Health and Welfare Canada

CANADA - MINISTERE DU SECRETARIAT D'ETAT
See: Canada - Secretary of State

CANADA - MINISTERE DU SOLLICITEUR GENERAL
See: Canada - Solicitor General Canada

CANADA - MINISTERE DU TRAVAIL
See: Canada - Labour Canada

CANADA - MINISTERE DES TRAVAUX PUBLICS
See: Canada - Public Works Canada

★2102★
CANADA - MINISTRY OF STATE FOR SCIENCE AND TECHNOLOGY - LIBRARY (Sci-Tech)
270 Albert St.   Phone: (613) 992-7851
Ottawa, ON, Canada K1A 1A1   Carol P. Barton, Libn.
Founded: 1971. **Staff:** Prof 2; Other 1. **Subjects:** Science policy, futures, technological innovation, research and development. **Holdings:** 6000 books; 4200 reports (cataloged). **Subscriptions:** 350 journals and other serials; 12 newspapers. **Services:** Interlibrary loans; copying; SDI; library open to public for reference use only. **Computerized Information Services:** CAN/OLE, Infomart, QL Systems, Info Globe; online catalog searches available; computerized circulation. **Publications:** Accessions list, monthly - for internal distribution only. **Staff:** Carol O'Rourke, Lib.Asst.

CANADA - MINISTRY OF STATE FOR URBAN AFFAIRS - INFORMATION RESOURCE CENTER
See: Canada - Mortgage and Housing Corporation

CANADA - MINISTRY OF TRANSPORT
See: Canada - Transport Canada

★2103★
CANADA - MORTGAGE AND HOUSING CORPORATION - CANADIAN HOUSING INFORMATION CENTRE (Soc Sci; Plan)
Ground Fl., Annex, Montreal Rd.   Phone: (613) 746-4611
Ottawa, ON, Canada K1A 0P7   Leslie Jones, Mgr.
Founded: 1946. **Staff:** Prof 3; Other 4. **Subjects:** Housing, urban planning, community service, energy conservation, residential rehabilitation. **Special Collections:** Municipal information and maps (6000 items). **Holdings:** 40,000 books; 10,000 bound periodical volumes; 1000 vertical files; 3000 microfiche; 2000 maps; 2000 external research reports. **Subscriptions:** 800 journals and other serials; 6 newspapers. **Services:** Interlibrary loans; copying; library open to public for reference use only. **Computerized Information Services:** SDC, Info Globe, CAN/OLE, QL Systems; computerized cataloging. **Networks/Consortia:** Member of A Network of Social Security Information Resources (ANSSIR). **Publications:** Acquisitions list, monthly; research reports and projects, quarterly; Serials List, annual. **Remarks:** Includes the holdings of Canada - Ministry of State for Urban Affairs - Information Resource Centre. **Also Known As:** Societe Canadienne d'Hypotheques et de Logement. **Staff:** Marg Ahearn, Chf., Ref.Serv.

CANADA - MUSEE CANADIEN DE LA GUERRE
See: Canada - National Museums of Canada - Canadian War Museum

CANADA - MUSEES NATIONAUX DU CANADA
See: Canada - National Museums of Canada

CANADA - NATIONAL AIR PHOTO LIBRARY
See: Canada - Energy, Mines & Resources Canada - Surveys & Mapping Branch

★2104★
CANADA - NATIONAL DEFENCE - CAMBRIDGE MILITARY LIBRARY (Mil)†
Royal Artillery Pk.
1565 Queen St.   Phone: (902) 426-5142
Halifax, NS, Canada B3J 2H9
Staff: 1. **Subjects:** Military history, biography, art and science; strategy; 19th century travel; naval history. **Holdings:** 15,000 books; 500 bound periodical volumes. **Subscriptions:** 32 journals and other serials. **Services:** Interlibrary loans; library not open to public. **Remarks:** Library evolved from an officers' reading room established in 1817. **Also Known As:** Canada - Defense Nationale.

★2105★
CANADA - NATIONAL DEFENCE - CANADIAN FORCES COLLEGE - KEITH HODSON MEMORIAL LIBRARY (Mil)†
215 Yonge Blvd.   Phone: (416) 484-5742
Toronto, ON, Canada M5M 3H9   Mary Ash, Chf.Libn.
Staff: Prof 2; Other 3. **Subjects:** Military art and science, international relations, social sciences, history, management. **Holdings:** 35,000 books; 1000 bound periodical volumes; 500 reports; 5000 clippings; 1000 pamphlets; 2500 government documents; 1000 reels of microforms. **Subscriptions:** 200 journals and other serials; 15 newspapers. **Services:**

Copying; library open to public with restrictions. **Computerized Information Services:** SDC. **Also Known As:** Canada - Defense Nationale. **Staff:** Janice LeBlanc, Asst.Libn.

★2106★
CANADA - NATIONAL DEFENCE - CANADIAN FORCES COLLEGE - STAFF SCHOOL LIBRARY (Mil)
1107 Avenue Rd.   Phone: (416) 484-5645
Toronto, ON, Canada M5N 2E4   Coby Oates, Techn.-in-Charge
Subjects: Military art and science, international relations, management. **Holdings:** 13,000 books; 150 bound periodical volumes; 300 government documents and pamphlets. **Subscriptions:** 150 journals and other serials; 5 newspapers. **Services:** Interlibrary loans; copying; library not open to public except by special permission. **Computerized Information Services:** Infomart. **Also Known As:** Canada - Defense Nationale.

★2107★
CANADA - NATIONAL DEFENCE - CANADIAN FORCES MEDICAL SERVICES SCHOOL - LIBRARY (Med)
Canadian Forces Base   Phone: (705) 424-1200
Borden, ON, Canada L0M 1C0   Mrs. Marion Thomson, Libn.
Founded: 1946. **Staff:** 2. **Subjects:** Nursing, preventive medicine, hospital administration, military science. **Holdings:** 16,000 volumes. **Subscriptions:** 80 journals and other serials. **Services:** Interlibrary loans; library not open to public. **Also Known As:** Canada - Defense Nationale.

CANADA - NATIONAL DEFENCE - CANADIAN LAND FORCES COMMAND AND STAFF COLLEGE
See: Canada - National Defence - Fort Frontenac Library

CANADA - NATIONAL DEFENCE - CANADIAN MILITARY ENGINEERS MUSEUM
See: Canadian Military Engineers Museum

CANADA - NATIONAL DEFENCE - COLLEGE MILITAIRE ROYAL DE ST-JEAN
See: College Militaire Royal de St-Jean

CANADA - NATIONAL DEFENCE - DEFENCE AND CIVIL INSTITUTE OF ENVIRONMENTAL MEDICINE
See: Canada - Defence and Civil Institute of Environmental Medicine

CANADA - NATIONAL DEFENCE - DEFENCE RESEARCH ESTABLISHMENT
See: Canada - Defence Research Establishment

★2108★
CANADA - NATIONAL DEFENCE - DIRECTORATE OF HISTORY LIBRARY (Mil; Hist)
National Defence Headquarters   Phone: (613) 992-7849
Ottawa, ON, Canada K1A 0K2   Dr. W.A.B. Douglas, Dir.
Founded: 1919. **Staff:** Prof 2; Other 2. **Subjects:** History of Canadian Armed Forces, military history of Canada. **Special Collections:** Canadian and British military regulations and administrative orders. **Holdings:** 3500 books; 2500 bound periodical volumes; 1000 orders and regulations; 4000 feet of manuscript records of the Canadian Armed Forces. **Services:** Interlibrary loans; copying; library open to public by appointment. **Publications:** Official histories of the Canadian Armed Forces. **Also Known As:** Canada - Defense Nationale. **Staff:** Mr. O.A. Cooke, Sr. Archival Off.; Dr. S.J. Harris, Cat.

★2109★
CANADA - NATIONAL DEFENCE - FORT FRONTENAC LIBRARY (Mil)
Fort Frontenac   Phone: (613) 545-5829
Kingston, ON, Canada K7K 2X8   Mr. S.K. Kamra, Chf.Libn.
Founded: 1947. **Staff:** Prof 3; Other 5. **Subjects:** Military art and science; international relations; political and economic sciences; sociology. **Special Collections:** Military Strategy and World Politics. **Holdings:** 70,000 books; 2300 bound periodical volumes; 24 VF drawers. **Subscriptions:** 320 journals and other serials; 20 newspapers. **Services:** Interlibrary loans; library not open to public. **Remarks:** Fort Frontenac Library serves the National Defence College of Canada and Canadian Land Forces Command and Staff College. **Also Known As:** Canada - Defense Nationale. **Staff:** Mrs. J. Malach, Hd., Tech.Proc.

★2110★
CANADA - NATIONAL DEFENCE - MAPPING AND CHARTING ESTABLISHMENT TECHNICAL LIBRARY (Sci-Tech)
615 Booth St.   Phone: (613) 995-4411
Ottawa, ON, Canada K1A 0K2   Sergeant A. Therien, Libn.
Founded: 1974. **Staff:** Prof 1; Other 1. **Subjects:** Astronomy, cartography, photogrammetry, geology. **Holdings:** 3300 books; 25 bound periodical

volumes. **Subscriptions:** 16 journals and other serials; 5 newspapers. **Services:** Interlibrary loans; library not open to public.

CANADA - NATIONAL DEFENCE - NATIONAL DEFENCE COLLEGE OF CANADA
See: Canada - National Defence - Fort Frontenac Library

★2111★
CANADA - NATIONAL DEFENCE - NATIONAL DEFENCE MEDICAL CENTRE - MEDICAL LIBRARY (Med)
Alta Vista Dr. Phone: (613) 733-6600
Ottawa, ON, Canada K1A 0K6 Philip B. Allan, Med.Libn.
Staff: Prof 1; Other 1. **Subjects:** Medicine, nursing. **Special Collections:** Military medical history (500 volumes). **Holdings:** 4500 books; 11,500 bound periodical volumes; 1000 video and audio cassettes. **Subscriptions:** 301 journals and other serials. **Services:** Interlibrary loans; copying; library open to public with restrictions.

★2112★
CANADA - NATIONAL DEFENCE - NDHQ CHIEF CONSTRUCTION AND PROPERTIES LIBRARY (Sci-Tech)
101 Colonel By Drive
8th North Tower Phone: (613) 992-5710
Ottawa, ON, Canada K1A 0K2 Mr. C. Wakeford, Hd.
Staff: 2. **Subjects:** Architecture and building; engineering - civil, electrical, mechanical; fire prevention. **Holdings:** 3400 books; 10 bound periodical volumes; 3500 reports; property records. **Services:** Copying; current awareness; user orientation; library not open to public. **Publications:** Acquisitions list; guides to library collections.

★2113★
CANADA - NATIONAL DEFENCE - NDHQ COMPUTER CENTRE LIBRARY (Sci-Tech)
Canadian Bldg., 14th Fl.
219 Laurier Ave., W. Phone: (613) 996-6296
Ottawa, ON, Canada K1A 0K2 Hazel D. Rolland, Hd.
Staff: 2. **Subjects:** Computers, computer programming, electronics, data processing. **Special Collections:** IBM manuals (4890). **Holdings:** 5500 books; 1000 technical reports. **Subscriptions:** 43 journals and other serials. **Services:** Interlibrary loans; library not open to public.

★2114★
CANADA - NATIONAL DEFENCE - NDHQ LAND TECHNICAL LIBRARY (Mil)
305 Rideau St.
Bourque Memorial Bldg., Rm. 741 Phone: (613) 992-9862
Ottawa, ON, Canada K1A 0K2 D.J. Moyle, Hd.
Staff: 2. **Subjects:** Military vehicles, clothing, equipment and general stores; artillery and weapons; communications and electronics. **Holdings:** 5000 books; 15,000 technical reports. **Subscriptions:** 350 journals and other serials. **Services:** Interlibrary loans; copying; library not open to public. **Special Indexes:** Index to report literature (card).

★2115★
CANADA - NATIONAL DEFENCE - NDHQ LIBRARY (Mil)
101 Colonel By Drive, 2NT Phone: (613) 996-0831
Ottawa, ON, Canada K1A 0K2 Mr. R. Van Den Berg, Dept.Libn.
Founded: 1903. **Staff:** Prof 8; Other 27. **Subjects:** Military art and science, disarmament and peace keeping, naval science, aeronautics, political science, management, computer science. **Special Collections:** Charles H. Stewart Collection of Military Canadiana. **Holdings:** 105,000 books; 8000 bound periodical volumes; 1500 linear feet of government documents. **Subscriptions:** 2018 journals and other serials. **Services:** Interlibrary loans; copying; library open to members of other federal government libraries. **Computerized Information Services:** Computerized cataloging. **Networks/Consortia:** Member of UTLAS. **Also Known As:** Canada - Defense Nationale. **Staff:** J. LeBlanc, Hd., Rd.Serv.Sect.; L. Marsh, Hd., Branch Lib.

★2116★
CANADA - NATIONAL DEFENCE - NDHQ MARITIME TECHNICAL LIBRARY (Mil)
101 Colonel By Drive, 7ST Phone: (613) 996-2324
Ottawa, ON, Canada K1A 0K2 S. O'Neil, Hd.
Staff: 2. **Subjects:** Naval architecture, ship maintenance, undersea engineering and detection. **Holdings:** 4000 books; 5000 technical reports. **Subscriptions:** 17 journals and other serials. **Services:** Interlibrary loans; copying; library not open to public.

★2117★
CANADA - NATIONAL DEFENCE - NDHQ TECHNICAL LIBRARY (Mil; Sci-Tech)
Bldg. 155W, CFB Ottawa (N) Phone: (613) 993-2105
Ottawa, ON, Canada K1A 0K2 L. McKim, Libn.
Founded: 1952. **Staff:** 3. **Subjects:** Logistics support (military), aeronautical engineering, electronics, ground support and test equipment, mechanical and electrical engineering, management. **Special Collections:** Canadian Forces Technical Orders; federal supply catalogs; Canadian Forces publications; Canadian Forces Catalog of Materiel; USAF Technical Orders (140,000 items total). **Holdings:** 7500 books. **Subscriptions:** 325 journals and other serials. **Services:** Interlibrary loans; copying; library open to those who establish a need-to-know, with restrictions on classified material. **Also Known As:** Canada - Defense Nationale.

★2118★
CANADA - NATIONAL DEFENCE - NORTHERN REGION REFERENCE LIBRARY (Mil; Area-Ethnic)
Northern Region Headquarters
Evans Block, P.O. Box 6666 Phone: (403) 873-4011
Yellowknife, NT, Canada X1A 2R3 Sgt. A.A. Hiscock, Lib.Off.
Founded: 1970. **Staff:** Prof 1; Other 1. **Subjects:** Exploration, expeditions, Northern travel, native peoples, sociology, Northern reference, military history, geography. **Holdings:** 2500 volumes; 350 magazines; 800 reports. **Subscriptions:** 33 journals and other serials; 20 newspapers. **Services:** Interlibrary loans; copying; library open to public on request. **Remarks:** Library is a backup for Northern Region Operation Information Service. **Also Known As:** Canada - Defense Nationale. **Staff:** Betty Bryant, Libn.

★2119★
CANADA - NATIONAL DEFENCE - OFFICE OF THE JUDGE ADVOCATE GENERAL - LIBRARY (Law)
National Defence Headquarters Phone: (613) 996-3380
Ottawa, ON, Canada K1A 0K2 W.J. Kenney, Law Ck.
Founded: 1950. **Staff:** 2. **Subjects:** Law - general, military, international. **Special Collections:** Regulations and Orders - Canadian Army, Air Force and Navy and Canadian Forces since integration. **Holdings:** 7000 volumes; House of Commons Debates since 1939; Statutes of Canada since confederation in 1867; Federal Statutory Orders and Regulations since 1955. **Subscriptions:** 40 journals and other serials. **Services:** Library open to public for reference use only. **Publications:** Canada Court Martial Appeal Reports, Volumes I, II, III and Part I of Volume IV with current service updates. **Also Known As:** Canada - Defense Nationale.

CANADA - NATIONAL DEFENCE - RESEARCH AND DEVELOPMENT BRANCH - DEFENCE RESEARCH ESTABLISHMENT
See: Canada - Defence Research Establishment

CANADA - NATIONAL DEFENCE - ROYAL CANADIAN MILITARY INSTITUTE
See: Royal Canadian Military Institute

CANADA - NATIONAL DEFENCE - ROYAL MILITARY COLLEGE OF CANADA
See: Royal Military College of Canada

CANADA - NATIONAL DEFENCE - ROYAL MILITARY COLLEGE, ST-JEAN
See: College Militaire Royal de St-Jean

CANADA - NATIONAL DEFENCE - ROYAL ROADS MILITARY COLLEGE
See: Royal Roads Military College

★2120★
CANADA - NATIONAL ENERGY BOARD - LIBRARY (Energy)
473 Albert St., Rm. 962 Phone: (613) 996-0375
Ottawa, ON, Canada K1A 0E5 Ms. N.R. Park, Mgr.
Founded: 1959. **Staff:** Prof 3; Other 4. **Subjects:** Energy - technology, economics, policy and regulation; petroleum and natural gas pipeline technology; electric utilities. **Special Collections:** NEB Hearing Documents (10,000). **Holdings:** 7000 books. **Subscriptions:** 400 journals and other serials; 15 newspapers. **Services:** Interlibrary loans; copying; library open to public. **Computerized Information Services:** CAN/OLE, Infomart, Info Globe, DIALOG, QL Systems.

★2121★
CANADA - NATIONAL FILM BOARD OF CANADA - ATLANTIC REGION OFFICE - REFERENCE LIBRARY (Aud-Vis)
1572 Barrington St. Phone: (902) 426-6157
Halifax, NS, Canada B3J 1Z6 Harold Rennie, Info.Off.
Staff: Prof 1. **Subjects:** Film, maritime culture, Canadian literature. **Holdings:** 356 volumes; 50 internal reports and catalogs; 12 government reports.

Subscriptions: 38 journals and other serials. Services: Library open to public.

★2122★
CANADA - NATIONAL FILM BOARD OF CANADA - EDMONTON DISTRICT OFFICE - FILM LIBRARY (Aud-Vis)
Centennial Bldg.
10031 103rd Ave.   Phone: (403) 420-3010
Edmonton, AB, Canada T5J 0G9
Founded: 1940. Staff: Prof 4; Other 3. Subjects: Canada - the land, history, industry, native people; creative arts; literature; health and medicine; science; social science; sports and recreation. Special Collections: Films in French and English. Holdings: 5584 16mm films. Services: Library open to public; films may be borrowed free. Staff: Jean Claude Mahe, Distribution Rep.; Ursula Ulrich, Libn.; Juliette Paquette, Libn.; Graydon McCrea, Distribution Rep.

★2123★
CANADA - NATIONAL FILM BOARD OF CANADA - FILM PREVIEW LIBRARY (Aud-Vis)
3155 Cote de Liesse Rd.   Phone: (514) 333-3180
Montreal, PQ, Canada H4N 2N4   Antoinette LaPointe, Film Libn.
Staff: Prof 1; Other 2. Subjects: History, industry, health and medicine, social sciences, sports and recreation, social geography, animation. Special Collections: Archival films (9200); festival films (815 35mm films; 1758 16mm films); Canadian Broadcasting Corporation (CBC) films (300); Radio-Canada films (300); sponsored films (1000); films by Independent Canadian Filmmakers (150). Holdings: 14,217 16mm films; 5252 35mm films. Services: Library not open to public.

★2124★
CANADA - NATIONAL FILM BOARD OF CANADA - PHOTOTHEQUE (Pict)
Tunney's Pasture   Phone: (613) 593-5826
Ottawa, ON, Canada K1A 0M9   Lise Krueger, Photo Libn.
Founded: 1974. Staff: 4. Subjects: Social, economic and cultural life of Canada. Holdings: 200,000 black and white photographs; 25,000 color transparencies. Services: Library open to public. Publications: Photos Canada (7 volumes covering 1939-1980 have been published) - available for purchase.

★2125★
CANADA - NATIONAL FILM BOARD OF CANADA - REFERENCE LIBRARY (Soc Sci)
Sta. A, P.O. Box 6100   Phone: (514) 333-3141
Montreal, PQ, Canada H3C 3H5   Rose-Aimee Todd, Chf.Libn.
Staff: Prof 2; Other 4. Subjects: Film and filmmaking, photography, television, Canadian history, communication. Holdings: 17,500 books; 400 bound periodical volumes; 3000 pamphlets; 42 VF drawers; 10 drawers of maps; 370 reels of microfilm. Subscriptions: 800 journals and other serials; 25 newspapers. Services: Interlibrary loans; copying; library open to public by appointment. Computerized Information Services: DIALOG, QL Systems. Remarks: Library is located at 3155 Cote de Liesse Rd., Montreal, PQ H4N 2N4. Staff: Patricia Butler, Assoc.Libn.

CANADA - NATIONAL FILM, TELEVISION & SOUND ARCHIVES
See: Canada - Public Archives of Canada - Natl. Film, Television & Sound Archives

★2126★
CANADA - NATIONAL GALLERY OF CANADA - LIBRARY (Art)
75 Albert St., 4th Fl.   Phone: (613) 995-6245
Ottawa, ON, Canada K1A 0M8   J.E.B. Hunter, Chf.Libn.
Founded: 1918. Staff: Prof 7; Other 5. Subjects: Post-medieval Western art, Canadian art, photography. Special Collections: Canadiana Collection (Canadian art; 10,400 titles); Canadian art documentation (22,000 dossiers); restoration and conservation (1000 titles); prints and drawings (5000 titles). Holdings: 72,000 books and bound periodical volumes; 2 VF drawers of archives and manuscripts; 250 VF drawers of clippings and pamphlets; 1220 microfiche (dossiers of 200 Canadian artists); 102,250 other microforms; study collections of photographs and slides. Subscriptions: 1000 journals and other serials; 8 newspapers. Services: Interlibrary loans; copying; library open to public with restrictions. Computerized Information Services: Online systems; computerized cataloging and documentation. Networks/Consortia: Member of National Inventory, National Museums of Canada; UTLAS, Inc. Publications: Canadiana in the Library of the National Gallery of Canada, 1967 with supplements; Artists in Canada: A Union List, 1982 (files on microfiche); list of artists' files available on microfiche; Canadian art microdocuments: artists' files on microfiche - all available for purchase. Special Catalogs: Catalogue of the Library of the National Gallery of Canada, 1973 (book); supplement, 1981. Staff: Miss Maija Vilcins, Ref.Serv.; Isobel Van Lierde, Ser.Libn.; Susan Hasbury, Documentation; R. Engfield, Dp.Libn.

CANADA - NATIONAL LIBRARY OF CANADA
See: National Library of Canada

CANADA - NATIONAL MAP COLLECTION
See: Canada - Public Archives of Canada

★2127★
CANADA - NATIONAL MUSEUMS OF CANADA - CANADIAN CONSERVATION INSTITUTE LIBRARY (Art)
                                    Phone: (613) 998-3721
Ottawa, ON, Canada K1A 0M8   Mrs. M. Anderson, Libn.
Founded: 1973. Staff: Prof 1; Other 1. Subjects: Conservation and restoration of art objects; chemistry; fine arts; archeology; ethnology; photography. Holdings: 13,500 books; 100 bound periodical volumes; 3000 pamphlets and reprints. Subscriptions: 100 journals and other serials. Services: Interlibrary loans; copying; library open to serious scholars for reference use only. Also Known As: Institut Canadien de Conservation.

★2128★
CANADA - NATIONAL MUSEUMS OF CANADA - CANADIAN WAR MUSEUM - LIBRARY (Mil)
330 Sussex Dr.   Phone: (613) 996-4708
Ottawa, ON, Canada K1A 0M8   Mr. L. Kosche, Libn.
Founded: 1969. Staff: Prof 1. Subjects: Canadian military history, weapons, insignia, uniforms, military decorations. Special Collections: World War II newspaper clippings (80 VF drawers); Canadian Militia and Canadian Army Orders, 1899-1910 and 1914 to present; War Office list in changes of war materiel, 1883-1965 (incomplete). Holdings: 10,000 volumes, including bound periodical volumes and Canadian armed forces manuals. Subscriptions: 90 journals and other serials. Services: Interlibrary loans; library open to public for reference use only. Publications: Accessions list, bimonthly. Also Known As: Musee Canadien de la Guerre.

★2129★
CANADA - NATIONAL MUSEUMS OF CANADA - LIBRARY SERVICES (Sci-Tech)
                                    Phone: (613) 998-3923
Ottawa, ON, Canada K1A 0M8   Valerie Monkhouse, Mgr., Lib.Serv.
Founded: 1842. Staff: Prof 9; Other 17. Subjects: Natural sciences - botany, zoology and vertebrate paleontology; anthropology and archeology; folk culture; museology; military history; history of aviation and space; communications; ground transportation; Canadian science and technology. Special Collections: R.M. Anderson Collection (2000 items on mammalogy and ornithology); Canadian Arctic Expedition, 1913-1918; National Collection of Nature Photographs (500,000). Holdings: 80,000 books; 60,000 bound periodical volumes; 12 drawers of newspaper clippings; pamphlets; microtexts. Subscriptions: 2500 journals and other serials. Services: Interlibrary loans; copying; library open to public for reference use only. Computerized Information Services: DIALOG, SDC, CAN/OLE; computerized cataloging. Networks/Consortia: Member of UTLAS, Inc. Publications: Accessions list. Remarks: Figures include the staff and holdings of branch libraries and the former Photographic Division Library.

CANADA - NATIONAL MUSEUMS OF CANADA - NATIONAL GALLERY OF CANADA
See: Canada - National Gallery of Canada

★2130★
CANADA - NATIONAL MUSEUMS OF CANADA - NATIONAL MUSEUM OF SCIENCE AND TECHNOLOGY - LIBRARY (Sci-Tech)
                                    Phone: (613) 998-9520
Ottawa, ON, Canada K1A 0M8   Minda Bojin, Libn.
Staff: Prof 1; Other 1. Subjects: Aviation and space, communications, ground transportation, history of Canadian science and technology. Holdings: 12,000 books; 2200 bound periodical volumes. Subscriptions: 200 journals and other serials. Services: Interlibrary loans; SDI; library open to public for reference use only. Computerized Information Services: DIALOG, SDC, CAN/OLE; computerized cataloging. Networks/Consortia: Member of UTLAS.

★2131★
CANADA - NATIONAL MUSEUMS OF CANADA - PHOTOGRAPHIC DIVISION LIBRARY
Ottawa, ON, Canada K1A 0M8
Defunct. Holdings absorbed by Canada - National Museums of Canada - Library Services.

★2132★
CANADA - NATIONAL RESEARCH COUNCIL - ATLANTIC RESEARCH LABORATORY - LIBRARY (Sci-Tech)
1411 Oxford St.
Halifax, NS, Canada B3H 3Z1
Phone: (902) 426-8250
Annabelle Taylor, Libn.
Founded: 1951. Staff: Prof 1; Other 1. Subjects: Chemistry, marine botany, biochemistry and microbiology, phytochemistry, mass spectrometry, metallurgy, coal. Holdings: 5500 books; 13,500 bound periodical volumes. Subscriptions: 330 journals and other serials. Services: Interlibrary loans; copying; library open to public. Computerized Information Services: Online systems.

★2133★
CANADA - NATIONAL RESEARCH COUNCIL - CANADA INSTITUTE FOR SCIENTIFIC AND TECHNICAL INFORMATION (CISTI) (Sci-Tech)
Montreal Rd.
Ottawa, ON, Canada K1A 0S2
Phone: (613) 993-1600
Elmer V. Smith, Dir.
Staff: Prof 85; Other 120. Subjects: Science and technology, medicine. Holdings: 1.25 million volumes; 1.55 million microfiche. Subscriptions: 25,000 journals and other serials. Services: Interlibrary loans; copying; literature searches; library open to public. Computerized Information Services: CAN/SDI, CAN/OLE, CAN/SND, DOBIS, DIALOG, SDC, BRS, MEDLARS, Institute for Scientific Information; computerized cataloging. Publications: Scientific and Technical Societies of Canada; Directory of Federally Supported Research in Universities; Canadian Locations of Journals Indexed for MEDLINE. Special Catalogs: Union List of Scientific Serials in Canadian Libraries. Remarks: CISTI operates 11 branch libraries within the National Research Council. Also Known As: Institut Canadien de l'Information Scientifique et Technique. Staff: Inez Heseltine, Asst.Dir.; Norma Burns, Exec.Asst.; George Ember, Asst. to Dir.; Marianne Hurley, Hd. of Branches.

★2134★
CANADA - NATIONAL RESEARCH COUNCIL - CISTI - ADMINISTRATION BUILDING LIBRARY (Bus-Fin)
Montreal Rd.
Ottawa, ON, Canada K1A 0R6
Phone: (613) 993-1517
Dene McColm, Hd.
Staff: Prof 1; Other 1. Subjects: Administration, policy planning, management. Holdings: Figures not available.

★2135★
CANADA - NATIONAL RESEARCH COUNCIL - CISTI - AERONAUTICAL & MECHANICAL ENGINEERING BRANCH (Sci-Tech)
Montreal Rd., Bldg M-2
Ottawa, ON, Canada K1A 0R6
Phone: (613) 993-2431
Louise Fletcher, Libn.
Founded: 1941. Staff: Prof 3; Other 10. Subjects: Aeronautics; engineering - mechanical, structural; railway and marine transportation; tribology; fuels and lubricants; hydraulics. Special Collections: Unclassified NASA publications (depository). Holdings: 40,000 books; 10,000 bound periodical volumes; 450,000 technical reports; NASA microfiche (1962 to present); Supersonic Aircraft Engine (SAE) reprints (1962 to present); American Institute of Aeronautics and Astronautics reprints (1963 to present). Subscriptions: 2000 journals and other serials. Services: Interlibrary loans; copying; literature searches; library open to public. Publications: Recent acquisitions. Remarks: CISTI is the acronym for the Canada Institute for Scientific and Technical Information. Staff: Dawn Corbett, Hd., Tech.Proc.; Joan Leonardo, Hd., Info.Serv.

★2136★
CANADA - NATIONAL RESEARCH COUNCIL - CISTI - BUILDING RESEARCH BRANCH (Sci-Tech)
Montreal Rd.
Ottawa, ON, Canada K1A 0R6
Phone: (613) 993-2466
Joyce Waudby-Smith, Libn.
Founded: 1948. Staff: Prof 3; Other 5. Subjects: Construction, soil mechanics, acoustics, building services, fire research, building codes, building structures, materials, snow and ice research. Holdings: 10,000 books; 3000 bound periodical volumes; 90,000 reports. Subscriptions: 1500 journals and other serials. Services: Interlibrary loans; copying; library open to public. Publications: Canadian Building Abstracts, semiannual. Remarks: CISTI is the acronym for the Canada Institute for Scientific and Technical Information.

★2137★
CANADA - NATIONAL RESEARCH COUNCIL - CISTI - CHEMISTRY BRANCH (Sci-Tech)
Montreal Rd. Laboratories
Ottawa, ON, Canada K1A 0R9
Phone: (613) 993-2266
Nancy Ross, Libn.
Staff: Prof 1; Other 2. Subjects: Analytical chemistry, chemical engineering, colloid/clathrate chemistry, metallic corrosion/oxidation, high polymer chemistry, high pressure, kinetics/catalysis, sold state chemistry, textile chemistry. Special Collections: Complete Chemical Abstracts since 1907.

Holdings: Figures not available. Services: Interlibrary loans; copying; library open to public. Remarks: CISTI is the acronym for the Canada Institute for Scientific and Technical Information.

★2138★
CANADA - NATIONAL RESEARCH COUNCIL - CISTI - DOMINION ASTROPHYSICAL OBSERVATORY - LIBRARY (Sci-Tech)
5071 W. Saanich Rd.
R.R. 5
Victoria, BC, Canada V8X 3X3
Phone: (604) 388-0298
Eric S. LeBlanc, Libn.
Founded: 1918. Staff: 1. Subjects: Astronomy, mathematics, physics. Special Collections: Photographs, astronomical plates and machine-readable computer tapes. Holdings: 3000 books; 5000 bound periodical volumes and observatory publications. Subscriptions: 90 journals and other serials. Services: Interlibrary loans; library open to public. Computerized Information Services: CAN/OLE, DIALOG, QL Systems, SDC, DOBIS; computerized cataloging and serials. Networks/Consortia: Member of UTLAS, Inc. Publications: Publications of the Dominion Astrophysical Observatory - distributed to scientific institutions. Remarks: CISTI is the acronym for the Canada Institute for Scientific and Technical Information.

★2139★
CANADA - NATIONAL RESEARCH COUNCIL - CISTI - DOMINION RADIO ASTROPHYSICAL OBSERVATORY - LIBRARY (Sci-Tech)
Box 248
Penticton, BC, Canada V2A 6K3
Phone: (604) 497-5321
W. Gully, Libn.
Staff: 1. Subjects: Astronomy, physics, mathematics, electronics, astrophysics, geophysics, engineering sciences, seismology. Holdings: 2800 volumes; 8 VF drawers of reprints and research reports. Subscriptions: 75 journals and other serials. Services: Interlibrary loans; library open to public by permission. Remarks: CISTI is the acronym for the Canada Institute for Scientific and Technical Information.

★2140★
CANADA - NATIONAL RESEARCH COUNCIL - CISTI - ELECTRICAL ENGINEERING BRANCH (Sci-Tech)
Montreal Rd.
Ottawa, ON, Canada K1A 0R6
Phone: (613) 993-2006
Jane Dyment, Libn.
Staff: Prof 1; Other 1. Subjects: Electrical engineering, electronics, computer technology, biomedical engineering. Holdings: Figures not available. Services: Interlibrary loans; copying; library open to public. Remarks: CISTI is the acronym for the Canada Institute for Scientific and Technical Information.

★2141★
CANADA - NATIONAL RESEARCH COUNCIL - CISTI - ENERGY BRANCH (Energy)
Bldg. M-55, Montreal Rd.
Ottawa, ON, Canada K1A 0S2
Phone: (613) 993-3861
Raymond Jacyna, Libn.
Founded: 1979. Staff: Prof 3; Other 1. Subjects: Renewable energy, including solar, wind, biomass, geothermal, wave; energy policy in Canada. Services: Interlibrary loans; copying; library open to public. Remarks: The Energy Branch distributes publications of International Energy Agency and Biomass Technical Information Service. CISTI is the acronym for the Canada Institute for Scientific and Technical Information. Staff: Dorothy Evans, Asst.Libn.; Mary Balaisis, Energy Enquiry Ctr.

★2142★
CANADA - NATIONAL RESEARCH COUNCIL - CISTI - INDUSTRIAL MATERIALS RESEARCH INSTITUTE LIBRARY (Sci-Tech)
750 Rue Bel-Air
Montreal, PQ, Canada H4C 2K3
Phone: (514) 935-8513
Louise Venne, Libn.
Staff: Prof 1; Other 2. Subjects: Industrial materials, engineering, chemistry, metallurgy, plastics, corrosion, tribology. Holdings: 4000 volumes. Subscriptions: 350 journals and other serials. Services: Interlibrary loans; copying; library not open to public. Computerized Information Services: DIALOG, CAN/OLE; computerized cataloging and serials. Remarks: A branch of the Canada Institute for Scientific and Technical Information (CISTI). Also Known As: Institut de Genie des Materiaux (IGM).

★2143★
CANADA - NATIONAL RESEARCH COUNCIL - CISTI - PHYSICS BRANCH (Sci-Tech)
Division of Physics, Bldg. M-36
Ottawa, ON, Canada K1A 0S1
Phone: (613) 993-2483
Mary Van Buskirk, Libn.
Founded: 1962. Staff: Prof 1; Other 1. Subjects: Heat and thermometry; laser and plasma physics; optics; time and frequency; acoustics; x-ray and nuclear radiation; high energy physics; solid state; mechanical, optical and electrical standards. Special Collections: Photogrammetry. Holdings: Figures not available. Services: Interlibrary loans; copying; library open to public for

reference use only. **Remarks:** CISTI is the acronym for the Canada Institute for Scientific and Technical Information.

★2144★
CANADA - NATIONAL RESEARCH COUNCIL - CISTI - SUSSEX BRANCH LIBRARY (Sci-Tech)
100 Sussex Dr.   Phone: (613) 992-9151
Ottawa, ON, Canada K1A 0R6   Margaret Schade, Libn.
Staff: Prof 1; Other 4. **Subjects:** Biology, chemistry, physics, astronomy, astrophysics. **Holdings:** 40,000 volumes. **Subscriptions:** 1250 journals and other serials. **Services:** Interlibrary loans; copying; library open to public for reference use only. **Remarks:** CISTI is the acronym for the Canada Institute for Scientific and Technical Information.

★2145★
CANADA - NATIONAL RESEARCH COUNCIL - CISTI - UPLANDS BRANCH (Sci-Tech)
Montreal Rd.   Phone: (613) 998-3327
Ottawa, ON, Canada K1A 0R6   Alma Gorman, Hd.
Staff: Prof 1; Other 1. **Subjects:** Aeronautics, electronics, mathematics, computer science. **Special Collections:** Aerospace documents (NACA/NASA). **Holdings:** Figures not available. **Services:** Interlibrary loans; copying; SDI; library open to public with legitimate need for materials. **Remarks:** CISTI is the acronym for the Canada Institute for Scientific and Technical Information.

★2146★
CANADA - NATIONAL RESEARCH COUNCIL - PRAIRIE REGIONAL LABORATORY LIBRARY (Sci-Tech)
                                                              Phone: (306) 665-5256
Saskatoon, SK, Canada S7N 0W9   Flora Chen, Libn.
Founded: 1948. **Staff:** Prof 1; Other 1. **Subjects:** Production and utilization of legume seeds; fermentation technology; plant cell research; insect pheromones; microbial degradation of organic compounds; nitrogen fixation; bacteriology; plant leaf waxes; carbohydrates; proteins; wood extractives; biologically active compounds from plant sources and microorganisms. **Holdings:** 6623 books; 5761 bound periodical volumes; 4429 pamphlets, patents and documents; 78 translations; 25 drawers of microcards; 130 reels of microfilm; 30 titles on microfiche; 2827 indexed reprints. **Subscriptions:** 162 journals and other serials. **Services:** Interlibrary loans; library open to PRL staff, faculty and graduate students of University of Saskatchewan only. **Computerized Information Services:** CAN/SDI, CAN/OLE, DIALOG; FAMULUS (internal database). **Publications:** Library newsletter, irregular.

★2147★
CANADA - OFFICE OF THE COMMISSIONER OF OFFICIAL LANGUAGES - LIBRARY (Soc Sci)
66 Slater St., 20th Fl.   Phone: (613) 995-7717
Ottawa, ON, Canada K1A 0T8   Beryl Hunter
Staff: Prof 1; Other 1. **Subjects:** Bilingualism, official languages, ombudsman. **Holdings:** Figures not available. **Services:** Interlibrary loans; copying; library open to public.

CANADA - OFFICE OF THE DOMINION FIRE COMMISSIONER
See: **Canada - Public Works Canada - Office of the Dominion Fire Commissioner**

CANADA - OFFICE OF THE JUDGE ADVOCATE GENERAL
See: **Canada - National Defence - Office of the Judge Advocate General**

CANADA - OFFICE NATIONAL DE L'ENERGIE
See: **Canada - National Energy Board**

CANADA - OFFICE NATIONAL DU FILM
See: **Canada - National Film Board of Canada**

CANADA - OFFICE OF TOURISM
See: **Canada - Industry, Trade & Commerce - Canadian Government Office of Tourism**

CANADA - PARKS CANADA - BATTLEFORD NATIONAL HISTORIC PARK
See: **Battleford National Historic Park**

CANADA - PARKS CANADA - FORT MALDEN NATIONAL HISTORIC PARK
See: **Fort Malden National Historic Park**

CANADA - PARKS CANADA - FORTRESS OF LOUISBOURG NATIONAL HISTORIC PARK
See: **Fortress of Louisbourg National Historic Park**

★2148★
CANADA - PARKS CANADA, ONTARIO REGION - LIBRARY (Hist)
132 Second St., E.   Phone: (613) 933-9712
Cornwall, ON, Canada K6H 5V4   Michel R. Jesmer, Lib.Techn.
Staff: Prof 1; Other 1. **Subjects:** Natural history, Canadian history, industrial arts, archeology. **Special Collections:** National historic sites reports and manuscripts. **Holdings:** 11,000 books; 150 bound periodical volumes. **Subscriptions:** 350 journals and other serials. **Services:** Interlibrary loans; copying; library open to public with restrictions. **Networks/Consortia:** Member of Environment Libraries Automated System (ELIAS).

CANADA - PARKS CANADA - POINT PELEE NATIONAL PARK
See: **Point Pelee National Park**

★2149★
CANADA - PARKS CANADA, WESTERN REGION - LIBRARY (Env-Cons)
Parks Canada Library, Rm. 520
Sta. M, P.O. Box 2989   Phone: (403) 231-4455
Calgary, AB, Canada T2P 3H8   R.P. Morgan, Libn.
Founded: 1973. **Staff:** Prof 1. **Subjects:** Park planning and interpretation, environment, ecology, Western Canadian history. **Holdings:** 6000 books; 4200 internal reports; 30 microfiche; 45 films. **Subscriptions:** 100 journals and other serials. **Services:** Interlibrary loans; copying (limited); library open to public for reference use only. **Publications:** Library Information Bulletin, quarterly - for internal distribution only.

CANADA - PARLIAMENT OF CANADA - LIBRARY
See: **Canada - Library of Parliament**

CANADA - PATENT OFFICE LIBRARY
See: **Canada - Consumer and Corporate Affairs Canada**

CANADA - PECHES ET OCEANS
See: **Canada - Fisheries & Oceans**

CANADA POST CORPORATION
See: **Canada - Canada Post Corporation**

CANADA - POST OFFICE DEPARTMENT
See: **Canada - Canada Post Corporation**

★2150★
CANADA - PRAIRIE FARM REHABILITATION ADMINISTRATION - LIBRARY (Agri)
Motherwell Bldg.   Phone: (306) 359-5100
Regina, SK, Canada S4P 0R5   Charlene Kosack, Hd., Lib.Sect.
Founded: 1966. **Staff:** Prof 1; Other 2. **Subjects:** Water engineering, resource management and conservation, public administration, hydrology. **Holdings:** 9000 books; 300 bound periodical volumes; 1000 pamphlets; 2 shelves of archives. **Subscriptions:** 300 journals and other serials; 10 newspapers. **Services:** Interlibrary loans; copying; library open to public. **Computerized Information Services:** CAN/OLE, QL Systems, DIALOG; computerized cataloging. **Publications:** Library Newsletter, bimonthly. **Formerly:** Canada - Regional Economic Expansion - Prairie Farm Rehabilitation Administration.

★2151★
CANADA - PRIVY COUNCIL OFFICE - LIBRARY (Soc Sci)†
Blackburn Bldg.   Phone: (613) 992-7608
Ottawa, ON, Canada K1A 0A3
Staff: Prof 2; Other 25. **Subjects:** Political science, history, government. **Holdings:** 12,000 volumes. **Services:** Library not open to public.

★2152★
CANADA - PUBLIC ARCHIVES OF CANADA - FEDERAL ARCHIVES DIVISION (Hist)
395 Wellington St.   Phone: (613) 996-8507
Ottawa, ON, Canada K1A 0N3   E. Frost, Dir.
Founded: 1973. **Staff:** Prof 20; Other 38. **Subjects:** Activities of the Government of Canada, 1750-1960. **Holdings:** 80,000 linear feet of records; 9000 reels of microfilm. **Services:** Interlibrary loans; copying; library open to public with restrictions on some material. **Publications:** Inventories, updated as required. **Staff:** J.W. O'Brien, Chf., State & Mil.Rec.; T. Cook, Chf., Natural Res.Rec.; A. Martineau, Chf., Pub.Serv.; Ms. M. Matson, Chf., Commun.Rec.; M. Hopkins, Chf., Manpower Rec.; J.P. Lukowycz, Chf., Ref. & Info.Proc.

★2153★
CANADA - PUBLIC ARCHIVES OF CANADA - LIBRARY (Hist)
395 Wellington St.   Phone: (613) 992-2669
Ottawa, ON, Canada K1A 0N3   Normand St. Pierre, Chf.Libn.
Founded: 1872. **Staff:** Prof 6; Other 18. **Subjects:** Canadian history, archival science. **Special Collections:** R.J. Cyriax Collection (the Arctic search for Sir John Franklin); J.B. Milborne Collection (Masonic history); A. Merrilees Collection (railways); Pamphlet Collection (1492-1950; 22,000 volumes). **Holdings:** 120,000 books and bound periodical volumes; 1000 broadsides. **Subscriptions:** 2500 journals and other serials. **Services:** Copying; library open to public. **Publications:** Annual Report. **Special Catalogs:** Catalogue of Pamphlets in the Public Archives of Canada (two volumes); author/title and chronological list of pamphlets (12 volumes).

★2154★
CANADA - PUBLIC ARCHIVES OF CANADA - MANUSCRIPT DIVISION (Hist)
395 Wellington St.   Phone: (613) 995-8094
Ottawa, ON, Canada K1A 0N3   R.S. Gordon, Dir.
Founded: 1872. **Staff:** Prof 45; Other 27. **Subjects:** Canadian and related North American and European history. **Holdings:** 50,000 linear feet of manuscripts; 25,000 reels of microfilm. **Services:** Interlibrary loans (microfilms only); copying; search rooms open to public with restrictions on certain material. **Publications:** General Inventory, updated as required. **Special Catalogs:** Union List of Manuscripts. **Staff:** V. Chabot, Hd., French Archv.; G. Hyam, Hd., British Archv.; P. Kennedy, Preconfederation Archv.; C. Carroll, Hd., Pub.Aff.Archv.; I. McClymont, Prime Min.Archv.; J. Cumming, Hd., Soc./Cultural Archv.; P. Yurkiw, Hd., Tech.Serv.; W. Neutel, Hd., Ref.Rm.Serv.; M. Campeau, Hd., Curatorial Serv.; C. MacKinnon, Hd., Econ./Sci.Archv.; E. Laine, Natl. Ethnic Archv.; R.S. Gordon, Union List Mss.; J.-M. Le Blanc, Hd., Res./Inquiry Serv.

★2155★
CANADA - PUBLIC ARCHIVES OF CANADA - NATIONAL ETHNIC ARCHIVES (Area-Ethnic)
395 Wellington St.   Phone: (613) 996-7453
Ottawa, ON, Canada K1A 0N3   E. Laine, Chf.
Staff: Prof 6; Other 4. **Subjects:** Ethno-cultural groups in Canada, especially Finnish, Ukrainian, Jewish and Polish. **Holdings:** 1200 linear feet of manuscript collections. **Services:** Interlibrary loans (microfilms only); copying; archives open to public. **Special Catalogs:** Finding aids.

★2156★
CANADA - PUBLIC ARCHIVES OF CANADA - NATL. FILM, TELEVISION & SOUND ARCHIVES - DOCUMENTATION & PUB. SERV. (Aud-Vis)
395 Wellington St.   Phone: (613) 995-1311
Ottawa, ON, Canada K1A 0N3   S. Kula, Dir.
Founded: 1975. **Staff:** Prof 2; Other 1. **Subjects:** Film, television, recorded sound. **Holdings:** 8000 books; 500 bound periodical volumes; 144 drawers of clippings and documents; 48 drawers of microfiche. **Subscriptions:** 450 journals and other serials. **Services:** Interlibrary loans (limited); copying; library open to public for research. **Publications:** Books Received, quarterly; bibliography; FIAF Members Publication, annual. **Special Indexes:** Film Title Index (card); Film Personality Index (card). **Remarks:** Archives are located at 344 Wellington St., Ottawa, ON, K1A 0N3. **Staff:** Pamela Bruce, Libn.; Barbara Kaye, Cat.; Sylvie Robitaille, Info.Off.

★2157★
CANADA - PUBLIC ARCHIVES OF CANADA - NATIONAL MAP COLLECTION (Geog-Map)
395 Wellington St.   Phone: (613) 992-0468
Ottawa, ON, Canada K1A 0N3   Betty Kidd, Dir.
Founded: 1907. **Staff:** Prof 15; Other 10. **Subjects:** Historical cartography of Canada, current mapping of Canada, foreign current mapping, architectural plans. **Special Collections:** "Atlantic Neptune"; rare archival atlases. **Holdings:** 900,000 maps, charts, plans, atlases, globes, architectural and engineering plans, related cartobibliographical files. **Services:** Interlibrary loans (limited to foreign current material only); copying; library open to public. **Publications:** List of Publications of the National Map Collection - available on request. **Staff:** Mr. E. Dahl, Chf., Early Cart.Sect.; G. Langelier, Chf., Serv.Sect.; M. McCauley; Ms. V. Cartmell; Ms. D. Ahlgren, Chf., Govt.Rec.Sect.; H. Stibbe, Chf., Doc. Control; Ms. N. Kazymyra-Dzioba; Ms. H. Stevens; T. Nagy, Ref.Coord.; L. Cardinal, Chf., Modern Cart.Div; G. Caron; Ms. R. Werbin; L. Seboek; Ms. V. Parker .

★2158★
CANADA - PUBLIC SERVICE COMMISSION - LIBRARY SERVICES DIVISION (Soc Sci)
Esplanade-Laurier Bldg., Rm. 930, Tower 2
300 Laurier Ave.   Phone: (613) 996-6365
Ottawa, ON, Canada K1A 0M7   A. Campbell, Libn.
Founded: 1977. **Staff:** Prof 9; Other 21. **Subjects:** Public administration, personnel management, finance, linguistics. **Special Collections:** History of the Public Service. **Holdings:** 29,000 books; 400 bound periodical volumes; 350 films. **Subscriptions:** 500 journals and other serials. **Services:** Interlibrary loans; copying; library open to public for reference use only. **Computerized Information Services:** DIALOG, Informatech France-Quebec, DOBIS; computerized cataloging. **Publications:** Acquisitions list, monthly - for internal distribution only. **Also Known As:** Commission de la Fonction Publique - Division des Services de Bibliotheques. **Staff:** J. De Beaumont, Hd., Tech.Serv.; T. Jaansov-Boudreau, Hd., User Serv.

★2159★
CANADA - PUBLIC SERVICE STAFF RELATIONS BOARD - LIBRARY (Soc Sci)
Sta. B, P.O. Box 1525   Phone: (613) 992-3584
Ottawa, ON, Canada K1P 5V2   Charlene Elgee, Hd. & Ref.Libn.
Founded: 1967. **Staff:** Prof 2; Other 4. **Subjects:** Industrial and labor relations in the public sector; arbitration; collective bargaining; public administration; wages and working conditions. **Holdings:** 6000 books; 9000 bound periodical volumes. **Subscriptions:** 760 journals and other serials; 10 newspapers. **Services:** Interlibrary loans; copying; library open to public. **Publications:** Acquisitions List, monthly. **Staff:** Jocelyne Boutin, Hd., Tech.Serv.

★2160★
CANADA - PUBLIC WORKS CANADA - INFORMATION, RESEARCH & LIBRARY SERVICES (Sci-Tech; Energy)
Sir Charles Tupper Bldg.   Phone: (613) 998-8350
Ottawa, ON, Canada K1A 0M2   Mr. R. Gagnon, Chf.Libn.
Founded: 1955. **Staff:** Prof 5; Other 3. **Subjects:** Engineering - civil, mechanical, electrical; architecture and design; realty and property management; urban planning and design; energy conservation. **Special Collections:** Publications produced by or for the Department of Public Works (1000 titles). **Holdings:** 32,000 books; 2000 bound periodical volumes; 4000 federal government documents (cataloged); 100 linear feet of statistics; 100 linear feet of standards; 4000 microfiche. **Subscriptions:** 700 journals and other serials; 5 newspapers. **Services:** Interlibrary loans; copying; SDI; library open to public with restrictions on some material. **Computerized Information Services:** SDC, DIALOG, QL Systems, CAN/OLE, Info Globe, DOBIS. **Publications:** Bibliographies. **Special Catalogs:** Bilingual public card catalog. **Also Known As:** Travaux Publics Canada. **Staff:** Marilyn Dyck, Ref.Libn.; Patricia Madaire, Hd., Pub.Serv.

★2161★
CANADA - PUBLIC WORKS CANADA - OFFICE OF THE DOMINION FIRE COMMISSIONER - RESOURCE CENTRE (Sci-Tech)
Riverside Drive   Phone: (613) 998-4773
Ottawa, ON, Canada K1A 0M2   Mrs. M.L. Levesque, Fire Res.Off.
Staff: Prof 1. **Subjects:** Fire protection and prevention; fire loss statistics. **Special Collections:** Fire losses in Canada, 1922-1980; report of fire losses in Government of Canada properties, 1950-1980. **Holdings:** 3000 books; 500 bound periodical volumes; 31,500 pamphlets. **Subscriptions:** 93 journals and other serials. **Services:** Copying; library is open to local users only. **Publications:** Fire Losses in Canada, annual report - free to libraries on request. **Also Known As:** Travaux Publics Canada.

★2162★
CANADA - PUBLIC WORKS CANADA - ONTARIO REGIONAL LIBRARY (Sci-Tech)
4900 Yonge St.   Phone: (416) 224-4235
Willowdale, ON, Canada M2N 6A6   Rocco Cornacchia, Reg.Libn.
Founded: 1974. **Staff:** Prof 2; Other 4. **Subjects:** Engineering - civil, marine; design and construction; property management; municipal planning. **Holdings:** 48,000 technical drawings and support documents (cataloged); 10,000 books and reports; 5500 sets of aperture cards of microfilmed drawings. **Subscriptions:** 230 journals and other serials. **Services:** Interlibrary loans; library open to public for reference use only. **Also Known As:** Travaux Publics Canada. **Staff:** Edward M. Avey, Tech.Serv.Libn.

★2163★
CANADA - REGIONAL ECONOMIC EXPANSION - GOVERNMENT DOCUMENTATION CENTRE (Soc Sci)
800 Square Victoria
C.P. 247   Phone: (514) 283-7266
Montreal, PQ, Canada H4Z 1E8   Carole Laplante, Libn.
Founded: 1975. **Staff:** Prof 2. **Subjects:** Statistics, economics, regional development, computer science, finances, marketing. **Special Collections:** Complete collection of Statistics Canada and industrial studies. **Holdings:** 7500 volumes; government and annual reports. **Subscriptions:** 275 journals and other serials; 29 newspapers. **Services:** Interlibrary loans; copying; library open to public. **Publications:** Acquisitions Bulletin, monthly. **Also Known As:**

Canada - Expansion Economique Regionale. **Staff:** Claire Lavoie, ILL.

★2164★
CANADA - REGIONAL ECONOMIC EXPANSION - LIBRARY (Soc Sci)
235 Queen St., 3rd Fl. W.   Phone: (613) 997-6074
Ottawa, ON, Canada K1A 0M4   Diane Bays, Chf.Libn.
Founded: 1969. **Staff:** Prof 3; Other 4. **Subjects:** Regional development, land use, economics, business and industry. **Holdings:** 15,000 books. **Subscriptions:** 500 journals and other serials; 24 newspapers. **Services:** Interlibrary loans; copying; SDI; library open to public. **Computerized Information Services:** DIALOG, SDC, QL Systems; computerized serials routing systems. **Publications:** Acquisitions list, semimonthly - distributed on request. **Special Catalogs:** Computer-produced book catalog for holdings to 1978. **Remarks:** Library shares office space with Canada - Industry, Trade & Commerce - Library. **Also Known As:** Canada - Expansion Economique Regionale. **Staff:** Rosanne Pareanen, Hd., Ref.Serv.

CANADA - REGIONAL ECONOMIC EXPANSION - PRAIRIE FARM REHABILITATION ADMINISTRATION
See: Canada - Prairie Farm Rehabilitation Administration

CANADA - RESOURCE ECONOMICS LIBRARY
See: Canada - Energy, Mines & Resources Canada

★2165★
CANADA - REVENUE CANADA - CUSTOMS & EXCISE - COLLEGE LIBRARY (Educ; Bus-Fin)
                                              Phone: (514) 451-5357
Rigaud, PQ, Canada J0P 1P0   Marie Brunet, Lib.Ck.
Staff: Prof 1; Other 1. **Subjects:** Customs and excise, training and development, education. **Holdings:** 1500 volumes. **Subscriptions:** 100 journals and other serials; 8 newspapers. **Services:** Interlibrary loans; copying; library not open to public.

★2166★
CANADA - REVENUE CANADA - CUSTOMS & EXCISE - LEGAL SERVICES LIBRARY (Law)
3rd Fl. Connaught Bldg.
MacKenzie Ave.   Phone: (613) 996-9208
Ottawa, ON, Canada K1A 0L5   Diana Millar, Law Ck.
Staff: 1. **Subjects:** Law, statutes. **Holdings:** 1000 volumes; government documents. **Subscriptions:** 20 journals and other serials. **Services:** Library not open to public.

★2167★
CANADA - REVENUE CANADA - CUSTOMS & EXCISE LIBRARY (Bus-Fin)
Connaught Bldg., 2nd Fl.   Phone: (613) 995-0007
Ottawa, ON, Canada K1A 0L5   Dianne L. Parsonage, Dept.Libn.
Founded: 1952. **Staff:** 6. **Subjects:** Public finance, public administration, commerce and trade, industrial economics, history. **Special Collections:** Customs and excise administration. **Holdings:** 20,000 books; 3000 other cataloged items. **Subscriptions:** 300 journals and other serials; 22 newspapers. **Services:** Interlibrary loans; copying; library open to public with prior permission. **Publications:** Library Accessions List, quarterly - for internal distribution only. **Staff:** Suneeta Chander, Hd., Cat.Sect.

★2168★
CANADA - REVENUE CANADA - CUSTOMS & EXCISE - SCIENTIFIC AND TECHNICAL INFORMATION CENTRE (Sci-Tech)
79 Bentley Ave.   Phone: (613) 998-8510
Ottawa, ON, Canada K1A 0L5   Althea Sproule, Info.Serv.Techn.
Founded: 1974. **Staff:** Prof 1; Other 1. **Subjects:** Analytical and applied chemistry, chemical technology. **Special Collections:** Chemical Manufacturers Literature Files (950 folders); International and National Trade Classifications, Tariffs, Customs Co-operation Council Committees Notes (80 volumes). **Holdings:** 1950 books; 2300 bound periodical volumes; 45 internal technical and research reports; 315 reels of microfilmed Chemical Abstracts. **Subscriptions:** 120 journals and other serials. **Services:** Interlibrary loans; copying; SDI; library open to public with prior approval. **Computerized Information Services:** DIALOG, SDC, INFORMATECH, QL Systems, CAN/OLE; internal database. **Special Indexes:** Index to Manufacturers Literature files (card). **Remarks:** This information centre is part of the Laboratory & Scientific Services Division of Revenue Canada.

★2169★
CANADA - REVENUE CANADA - TAXATION LIBRARY (Bus-Fin)
Head Office, 875 Heron Rd.   Phone: (613) 996-9896
Ottawa, ON, Canada K1A 0L8   Lorraine Wilkinson, Chf., Lib.Serv.
Founded: 1953. **Staff:** Prof 3; Other 9. **Subjects:** Taxation, law, accounting,

electronic data processing, management, personnel management. **Holdings:** 5875 books; 5311 bound periodical volumes. **Subscriptions:** 660 journals and other serials; 7 newspapers. **Services:** Interlibrary loans; library open to public by appointment. **Computerized Information Services:** BRS, computerized cataloging. **Publications:** List of new acquisitions, monthly; list of serials currently received, annual; library guide - all distributed on request. **Staff:** Mary Butterill, Hd., Tech.Serv.; Margery Bull, Ref.Libn.

CANADA - ROYAL CANADIAN MOUNTED POLICE
See: Royal Canadian Mounted Police

★2170★
CANADA SAFETY COUNCIL (CSC) - LIBRARY (Med)
1765 St. Laurent Blvd.   Phone: (613) 521-6881
Ottawa, ON, Canada K1G 3V4   Charles James, Libn.
Founded: 1968. **Staff:** Prof 1. **Subjects:** Safety - public, occupational, traffic, motorcycle. **Special Collections:** Occupational Safety Data Sheets - Technical Information. **Holdings:** 4500 books; 1500 safety pamphlets; 2500 safety posters; 800 AV items. **Subscriptions:** 120 journals and other serials; 15 newspapers. **Services:** Interlibrary loans; copying; library open to specialists only.

CANADA - ST. LAWRENCE SEAWAY AUTHORITY
See: Canada - Transport Canada - St. Lawrence Seaway Authority

CANADA - SANTE ET BIEN-ETRE SOCIAL CANADA
See: Canada - Health and Welfare Canada

★2171★
CANADA - SCIENCE COUNCIL OF CANADA - LIBRARY (Sci-Tech)†
100 Metcalfe St.   Phone: (613) 996-3818
Ottawa, ON, Canada K1P 5M1   Ms. Frances Bonney, Libn.
Founded: 1967. **Staff:** Prof 1; Other 3. **Subjects:** Science, technology and public policy. **Holdings:** 1800 volumes. **Subscriptions:** 250 journals and other serials. **Services:** Library open to public. **Computerized Information Services:** DIALOG, SDC, INFORMATECH, Info Globe. **Publications:** Annotated list of articles concerning issues in science and technology, weekly - to interested individuals. **Remarks:** This is a current awareness collection receiving continual review.

CANADA - SECRETARIAT D'ETAT
See: Canada - Secretary of State

★2172★
CANADA - SECRETARY OF STATE - LIBRARY (Soc Sci)
15 Eddy St., 2nd Fl.   Phone: (819) 997-5467
Hull, PQ, Canada K1A 0M5   Claire Renaud-Frigon, Chf.Libn.
Founded: 1966. **Staff:** Prof 4; Other 5. **Subjects:** Social sciences, higher education, bilingualism, ethnic groups, native citizens, arts and culture. **Holdings:** 16,000 books; 750 bound periodical volumes; 3000 published and unpublished items of the department; 550 microforms; 25 feet of vertical files. **Subscriptions:** 850 journals and other serials. **Services:** Interlibrary loans; copying; library open to public with restrictions on circulation. **Publications:** Accessions List, monthly; Periodical List, annual. **Also Known As:** Canada - Secretariat d'Etat.

★2173★
CANADA - SECRETARY OF STATE - TRANSLATION BUREAU - DOCUMENTATION DIRECTORATE (Info Sci)
                                              Phone: (819) 997-3857
Ottawa, ON, Canada K1A 0M5   Suzanne Richer, Dir.
Staff: Prof 16; Other 32. **Subjects:** Science and technology, social science, translation, terminology. **Special Collections:** Bilingual (English-French) and multilingual dictionaries. **Holdings:** 70,000 books; 1000 bound periodical volumes; complete collection of International Science Organization and AFNOR standards. **Subscriptions:** 1975 journals and other serials; 26 newspapers. **Services:** Interlibrary loans; directorate open to public with restrictions. **Computerized Information Services:** DIALOG, SDC, Info Globe, Telesystemes, CAN/OLE, QL Systems, Institute for Scientific Information (ISI), International Development Research Centre, INFORMATECH; Government of Canada Terminology Data Bank (internal database); computerized cataloging. **Networks/Consortia:** Member of Library Delivery Service (LDS); UTLAS, Inc. **Publications:** List of publications - available upon request. **Special Catalogs:** Union catalogue of source codes (COM). **Also Known As:** Canada - Secretariat d'Etat. **Staff:** Mr. Rejean Heroux, Chf., Tech.Serv.; Jocelyne Beck, Chf., Ref.; J. Tomlinson, Chf., Lib. Network; Paula De Grace, Plan.Off.

★2174★
CANADA - SECRETARY OF STATE - TRANSLATION BUREAU - LIBRARY
(Info Sci)
Tour de la Cite, 15th Fl.
C.P. 970   Phone: (514) 283-7519
Montreal, PQ, Canada H2W 2R1   Cecile Mondou, Hd.Libn.
Staff: Prof 2; Other 2. **Subjects:** Translation, computer science, economics, management, technology, agriculture, medicine. **Special Collections:** Dictionaries, lexicons, vocabularies. **Holdings:** 14,000 books; 500 standards; 400 annual reports; 1500 documents and pamphlets. **Subscriptions:** 94 journals and other serials. **Services:** Interlibrary loans; copying; library open to public with prior telephone contact. **Computerized Information Services:** Computerized cataloging. **Networks/Consortia:** Member of UTLAS Inc. **Also Known As:** Canada - Secretariat d'Etat. **Staff:** Marie Lacoste, Lib.Techn.

CANADA - SERVICE CANADIEN DE LA FAUNE
See: Canada - Canadian Wildlife Service

CANADA - SERVICE CANADIEN DES FORETS
See: Canada - Canadian Forestry Service

CANADA - SERVICE DE L'ENVIRONNEMENT ATMOSPHERIQUE
See: Canada - Atmospheric Environment Service

CANADA - SERVICE DES PECHES ET DES SCIENCES DE LA MER
See: Canada - Fisheries & Oceans

CANADA - SERVICE DE LA PROTECTION DE L'ENVIRONNEMENT
See: Canada - Environmental Protection Service

CANADA - SOCIETE CANADIENNE D'HYPOTHEQUES ET DE LOGEMENT
See: Canada - Mortgage and Housing Corporation

★2175★
CANADA - SOLICITOR GENERAL CANADA - MINISTRY LIBRARY & REFERENCE CENTRE (Soc Sci)
340 Laurier Ave. W.   Phone: (613) 995-0144
Ottawa, ON, Canada K1A 0P8   Heather Moore, Chf.
Founded: 1969. **Staff:** Prof 5; Other 4. **Subjects:** Criminology, corrections, law, law enforcement. **Holdings:** 17,000 books; 5000 bound periodical volumes; National Criminal Justice Reference Service on 14,000 microfiche; Crime & Juvenile Delinquency Collection on 5000 microfiche. **Subscriptions:** 300 journals and other serials. **Services:** Interlibrary loans; library open to public if referred by another library. **Computerized Information Services:** DIALOG, QL Systems; computerized cataloging. **Networks/Consortia:** Member of UTLAS, Inc. **Publications:** Acquisitions list, irregular; Newsletter/Bulletin - free upon request. **Formerly:** Its Criminology Documentation Centre (CRIMDOC Centre). **Staff:** Mr. Heschel Hanley, Hd., Tech.Serv.; Mr. Tony Dittenhoffer, Ref.Coord.

★2176★
CANADA - STATISTICS CANADA - ADVISORY SERVICES - EDMONTON REFERENCE CENTRE (Soc Sci)
215 Hy's Centre
11010 101st St.   Phone: (403) 420-3027
Edmonton, AB, Canada T5H 4C5   L. Wiebe, Info.Off.
Founded: 1973. **Staff:** Prof 2; Other 2. **Subjects:** Canadian economic and social activity statistics. **Holdings:** Statistics Canada publications (about 1200 titles published annually); selected other federal and provincial government publications; census microforms and maps. **Services:** Copying; library open to public for reference use only and to purchase publications. **Computerized Information Services:** CANSIM. **Remarks:** In Alberta, toll-free access to the Edmonton office is available by calling 1-800-222-6400.

★2177★
CANADA - STATISTICS CANADA - ADVISORY SERVICES - HALIFAX REFERENCE CENTRE (Soc Sci)
1256 Barrington St., 3rd Fl.   Phone: (902) 426-5331
Halifax, NS, Canada B3J 1Y6
Staff: Prof 1; Other 4. **Subjects:** Canadian economic and social activity statistics. **Holdings:** Statistics Canada publications (about 1200 titles published annually); selected other federal and provincial government publications; census microforms and maps. **Services:** Copying; library open to public for reference use only and to purchase publications. **Computerized Information Services:** CANSIM. **Special Catalogs:** Statistics Canada Catalogue - free upon request. **Remarks:** In the Maritimes, toll-free access to the Halifax office is available by calling 1-800-565-7192.

★2178★
CANADA - STATISTICS CANADA - ADVISORY SERVICES - MONTREAL REFERENCE CENTRE (Soc Sci)†
Alexis Nihon Plaza, 7th Fl.
1500 Atwater Ave.   Phone: (514) 283-5725
Montreal, PQ, Canada H3Z 1Y2   Nicole Benoit
Founded: 1964. **Staff:** 9. **Subjects:** Canadian economic and social activity statistics. **Holdings:** Statistics Canada publications (about 1200 titles published annually); selected other federal and provincial government publications; census microforms and maps. **Services:** Copying; centre open to public for reference use only and to purchase publications. **Computerized Information Services:** CANSIM. **Staff:** Denis Boudreau, Regional Adv.

★2179★
CANADA - STATISTICS CANADA - ADVISORY SERVICES - REGINA REFERENCE CENTRE (Soc Sci)
530 Midtown Centre   Phone: (306) 359-5405
Regina, SK, Canada S4P 2B6   D. Lawrance, Regional Adv.
Staff: 3. **Subjects:** Canadian economic and social activity statistics. **Holdings:** Statistics Canada publications (about 1200 titles published annually); selected other federal and provincial government publications; census microforms and maps. **Services:** Copying; centre open to public for reference use only and to purchase publications. **Computerized Information Services:** CANSIM. **Remarks:** In Saskatchewan, toll-free access to the Regina office is available by calling 1-800-667-3524.

★2180★
CANADA - STATISTICS CANADA - ADVISORY SERVICES - ST. JOHN'S REFERENCE CENTRE (Soc Sci)†
Viking Bldg., 3rd Fl., Crosbie Rd.
Box 8556   Phone: (709) 772-4646
St. John's, NF, Canada A1B 3P2
Staff: 2. **Subjects:** Canadian economic and social activity statistics. **Holdings:** Statistics Canada publications (about 1200 titles published annually); selected other federal and provincial government publications; census microforms and maps. **Services:** Copying; centre open to public for reference use only and to purchase publications. **Computerized Information Services:** CANSIM.

★2181★
CANADA - STATISTICS CANADA - ADVISORY SERVICES - TORONTO REFERENCE CENTRE (Soc Sci)
25 St..Clair Ave., E., 10th Fl.   Phone: (416) 966-6586
Toronto, ON, Canada M4T 1M4
Staff: 12. **Subjects:** Canadian economic and social activity statistics. **Holdings:** Statistics Canada publications (about 1200 titles published annually); selected other federal and provincial government publications; census microforms and maps. **Services:** Copying; centre open to public for reference use only and to purchase publications. **Computerized Information Services:** CANSIM. **Remarks:** In Ontario, toll-free access to the Toronto office is available by calling 1-800-268-1151. **Staff:** V. Crompton, Co-Hd. of Inquiries; Sandra McIntyre, Co-Hd. of Inquiries.

★2182★
CANADA - STATISTICS CANADA - ADVISORY SERVICES - VANCOUVER REFERENCE CENTRE (Soc Sci)
1145 Robson St.   Phone: (604) 666-3695
Vancouver, BC, Canada V6E 3W8   C.G. Lenoski, Asst. Regional Dir.
Founded: 1967. **Staff:** 8. **Subjects:** Canadian social and economic activity statistics. **Holdings:** Statistics Canada publications (about 1200 titles published annually); selected other federal and provincial government publications; census microforms and maps. **Services:** Copying; centre open to public for reference use only. **Computerized Information Services:** CANSIM. **Remarks:** "A reference library with special emphasis on assisting users with data."

★2183★
CANADA - STATISTICS CANADA - ADVISORY SERVICES - WINNIPEG REFERENCE CENTRE (Soc Sci)
600 General Post Office
266 Graham Ave.   Phone: (204) 949-4020
Winnipeg, MB, Canada R3C 0K4   Mr. W.S. Pawluk, Asst. Regional Dir.
Staff: 3. **Subjects:** Canadian economic and social activity statistics. **Holdings:** Statistics Canada publications (about 1200 titles published annually); selected other federal and provincial government publications; census microforms and maps. **Services:** Copying; centre open to public for reference use only and to purchase publications. **Computerized Information Services:** CANSIM.

★2184★
CANADA - STATISTICS CANADA - LIBRARY (Soc Sci)
R.H. Coats Bldg., Tunney's Pasture　　Phone: (613) 992-2365
Ottawa, ON, Canada K1A 0T6　　Georgia Ellis, Chf.Libn.
Founded: 1918. **Staff:** Prof 11; Other 17. **Subjects:** Economic theory, demography, mathematics, statistics, labour, sociology. **Special Collections:** Official foreign statistics; historical collection of Statistics Canada publications. **Holdings:** 150,000 volumes; staff papers, microfilm, VF drawers. **Subscriptions:** 1800 journals and other serials. **Services:** Interlibrary loans; copying; library open to public. **Computerized Information Services:** DIALOG, SDC, QL Systems, New York Times Information Service, CANSIM. **Publications:** Accession List, bimonthly; Current Contents of Periodicals, monthly; List of Supplementary Documents. **Special Catalogs:** Master title file for all publications issued by Statistics Canada since its inception in 1918; card file of staff papers.

★2185★
CANADA - SUPPLY & SERVICE CANADA - CANADIAN GOVERNMENT EXPOSITIONS CENTRE - TECHNICAL LIBRARY
440 Coventry Rd.
Ottawa, ON, Canada K1A 0T1
Defunct

★2186★
CANADA - SUPREME COURT OF CANADA - LIBRARY (Law)
Supreme Court Bldg., Wellington St.　　Phone: (613) 995-6354
Ottawa, ON, Canada K1A 0J1
Founded: 1875. **Staff:** Prof 5; Other 10. **Subjects:** Law - civil, common. **Holdings:** 160,000 volumes. **Subscriptions:** 250 journals and other serials. **Services:** Interlibrary loans; copying; library open to qualified researchers. **Computerized Information Services:** QL Systems. **Staff:** Mary Jane T. Sinclair, Asst.Libn.; Johane Thibodeau, Asst.Libn.; Rosemary Murray-Lachapelle, Asst.Libn.

★2187★
CANADA SYSTEMS GROUP - REFERENCE LIBRARY (Sci-Tech)
2599 Speakman Dr.　　Phone: (416) 822-5200
Mississauga, ON, Canada L5K 1B1　　Janet Bycio, Libn.
Founded: 1971. **Staff:** 3. **Subjects:** Computer science. **Holdings:** 350 books and bound periodical volumes; 3000 computer manuals. **Subscriptions:** 107 journals and other serials. **Services:** Interlibrary loans; copying; library not open to public. **Computerized Information Services:** Online systems. **Networks/Consortia:** Member of Sheridan Park Library and Information Science Committee.

★2188★
CANADA - TAX REVIEW BOARD - TAX LIBRARY (Law)
381 Kent St.　　Phone: (613) 996-4762
Ottawa, ON, Canada K2P 0M1　　Mrs. N.C. Mecher, Act.Spec. Projects Off.
Founded: 1962. **Staff:** 1. **Subjects:** Income tax law, tax regulation, accounting. **Holdings:** 1560 books; 205 other catalogued items. **Subscriptions:** 9 journals and other serials. **Services:** Library open to public with restrictions. **Publications:** Annual Report of the Tax Review Board. **Remarks:** The Tax Review Board is a Court of Record and its library is maintained to assist board members in determining the merits of cases. **Also Known As:** Commission de Revision de l'Impot.

★2189★
CANADA - TELESAT CANADA - COMPANY LIBRARY (Sci-Tech)
333 River Rd.　　Phone: (613) 746-5920
Ottawa, ON, Canada K1L 8B9　　Eileen Foster, Lib.Mgr.
Founded: 1970. **Staff:** Prof 1; Other 1. **Subjects:** Satellite communications, microwaves, telemetry, computers, solar cells. **Holdings:** 3000 books; 6000 documents. **Subscriptions:** 350 journals and other serials. **Services:** Interlibrary loans; copying; library not open to public. **Publications:** Accession list, monthly.

★2190★
CANADA - TRANSPORT CANADA - CANADIAN AIR TRANSPORTATION ADMINISTRATION - WESTERN REGIONAL LIBRARY (Trans)
Federal Bldg.
9820 107th St., Rm. 10-76
Edmonton, AB, Canada T5K 1G3　　Phone: (403) 420-3801
　　P.J. Nelson, Regional Libn.
Founded: 1974. **Staff:** Prof 1; Other 3. **Subjects:** Air transportation; airports and construction; telecommunications; engineering; civil aeronautics; social and economic conditions of Alberta, Northwest Territories and Yukon; management; personnel. **Holdings:** 10,000 monographs and government documents; 8 VF drawers of clippings and pamphlets. **Subscriptions:** 200 journals and other serials; 30 newspapers. **Services:** Interlibrary loans;

copying; SDI; library open to public. **Networks/Consortia:** Member of Transport Canada Libraries and Information Centres. **Special Catalogs:** CODOC; union catalog of branch library holdings.

★2191★
CANADA - TRANSPORT CANADA - CANADIAN COAST GUARD COLLEGE - LIBRARY (Trans)
P.O. Box 4500　　Phone: (902) 539-2115
Sydney, NS, Canada B1P 6L1　　David N. MacSween, Libn.
Founded: 1965. **Staff:** Prof 2; Other 1. **Subjects:** Marine and mechanical engineering; navigation; technology. **Special Collections:** Magnetic compass; magnetism of ships (30 books). **Holdings:** 16,500 books; 3000 bound periodical volumes; 300 films. **Subscriptions:** 300 journals and other serials. **Services:** Interlibrary loans; library open to public. **Computerized Information Services:** CAN/OLE; computerized cataloging and acquisitions. **Networks/Consortia:** Member of UTLAS Inc. **Publications:** Library Bulletin, monthly - for internal distribution only. **Also Known As:** College de la Garde Cotiere Canadienne. **Staff:** Louise McKenna, Asst.Libn.

★2192★
CANADA - TRANSPORT CANADA - CANADIAN COAST GUARD, MARITIMES REGION - MARINE LIBRARY (Sci-Tech)
602-46 Portland St.
P.O. Box 1013　　Phone: (902) 426-5182
Dartmouth, NS, Canada B2Y 3Z7　　Mrs. Gaylan Ritchie, Regional Marine Libn.
Founded: 1973. **Staff:** Prof 1; Other 1. **Subjects:** Marine safety and engineering; maritime law; oil pollution and its prevention; naval architecture; oceanography; seamanship and navigation. **Holdings:** 3000 books; 19 folios of charts; VF drawers of reports, clippings, marine equipment brochures and catalogs. **Subscriptions:** 50 journals and other serials; 4 newspapers. **Services:** Interlibrary loans; copying; library open to public, identification required for borrowing. **Computerized Information Services:** CAN/OLE. **Special Catalogs:** Subject catalog to periodical articles concerned with marine safety (card).

CANADA - TRANSPORT CANADA - CENTRE DE DOCUMENTATION
See: Canada - Transport Canada - Library & Information Centre

★2193★
CANADA - TRANSPORT CANADA - LIBRARY & INFORMATION CENTRE (Trans)
Place de Ville, Tower C　　Phone: (613) 992-4529
Ottawa, ON, Canada K1A 0N5　　Serge G. Campion, Chf.Libn.
Founded: 1925. **Staff:** Prof 6; Other 24. **Subjects:** Transportation - air, marine, surface; management; data processing; civil and electrical engineering. **Special Collections:** List of Lights and Fog Signals (Canada), 1902 to present; List of Shipping (Canada), 1901 to present. **Holdings:** 11,000 books and bound periodical volumes; 95,000 government documents and technical reports; 4000 reels of microfilm; 410,000 microfiche. **Subscriptions:** 1800 journals and other serials; 21 newspapers. **Services:** Interlibrary loans; copying; SDI; library open to public. **Computerized Information Services:** DIALOG, SDC, CAN/OLE, BRS, QL Systems, Infomart, SABINE, DOBIS; Canadian Transportation Documentation System (CTDS; internal database); computerized cataloging. **Publications:** Accession List, bimonthly - distributed on request; Publications Catalogue, semiannual. **Also Known As:** Transport Canada - Centre de Documentation. **Staff:** B. Witt, Hd., Mktg. & Pub.Serv.; J. Cadieux, Hd., Tech.Serv.; H. Heyck, SDI Libn.; J. Gupta, Hd., Acq.; G. MacEwen, Field Serv.

CANADA - TRANSPORT CANADA - MARITIMES REGION - MARINE LIBRARY
See: Canada - Transport Canada - Canadian Coast Guard, Maritimes Region

★2194★
CANADA - TRANSPORT CANADA - ST. LAWRENCE SEAWAY AUTHORITY - INFORMATION OFFICE (Trans)
Place de Ville, 320 Queen St.　　Phone: (613) 992-3949
Ottawa, ON, Canada K1R 5A3　　G. Hemsley, Info.Off.
Founded: 1954. **Subjects:** St. Lawrence Seaway. **Holdings:** Studies, reports, general information material. **Services:** Collection open to public for reference use only on request.

★2195★
CANADA - TRANSPORT CANADA - TRAINING INSTITUTE - TECHNICAL INFORMATION CENTRE (Sci-Tech)
1950 Montreal Rd.
Bag Service 5400
Cornwall, ON, Canada K6H 6L2　　Phone: (613) 938-4344
　　Dianne Harding, Inst.Libn.
Staff: Prof 2; Other 2. **Subjects:** Electronics, management, electronic data

processing, aeronautics, naval arts and sciences, educational technology. **Holdings:** 4500 volumes; 3500 document titles; 48 feet of vertical files. **Subscriptions:** 300 journals and other serials; 26 newspapers. **Services:** Interlibrary loans; copying; library open to public. **Computerized Information Services:** CAN/OLE; DIALOG; Canadian Transportation Documentation System (CTDS; internal database). **Publications:** Library Accessions List, bimonthly - free upon request. **Staff:** Robert Amese, Asst.Libn.

★2196★
CANADA - TRANSPORT CANADA - TRANSPORTATION DEVELOPMENT CENTRE - LIBRARY (Trans)
1000 Sherbrooke St., W.
P.O. Box 549   Phone: (514) 283-4084
Montreal, PQ, Canada H3A 2R3   Judith Nogrady, Hd.
Founded: 1971. **Staff:** Prof 2; Other 3. **Subjects:** Transportation. **Special Collections:** Statistics Canada material (complete file, 1971 to present; 108 linear feet); NTIS microfiche (4000 items). **Holdings:** 8500 books; 1600 periodical volumes; 1200 technical reports; 450 pamphlets; 20 translations. **Subscriptions:** 460 journals and other serials; 5 newspapers. **Services:** Interlibrary loans; copying; library open to public for reference use by appointment. **Computerized Information Services:** DIALOG, SDC, CAN/OLE; computerized cataloging. **Networks/Consortia:** Member of UTLAS Inc. **Publications:** Recent Library Acquisitions, monthly; Serials Currently Received, annual. **Also Known As:** Centre de developpement des transports - Bibliotheque. **Staff:** A. George Ekins, Asst.Libn.

CANADA - TRAVAIL CANADA
See: Canada - Labour Canada

CANADA - TRAVAUX PUBLICS CANADA
See: Canada - Public Works Canada

CANADA - VETERANS AFFAIRS CANADA - DEER LODGE HOSPITAL
See: Deer Lodge Hospital

★2197★
CANADA - VETERANS AFFAIRS CANADA - LIBRARY (Mil; Soc Sci)
284 Wellington St.   Phone: (613) 593-4155
Ottawa, ON, Canada K1A 0P4   J. Cousineau, Lib.Mgr.
Founded: 1944. **Staff:** 2. **Subjects:** Canadian military history, management and personnel, social welfare, psychology. **Holdings:** 5200 books; 30 bound periodical volumes. **Subscriptions:** 200 journals and other serials; 7 newspapers. **Services:** Interlibrary loans; copying; library open to public for reference use only. **Publications:** Accession list, quarterly. **Also Known As:** Affaires des Anciens Combattants Canada.

★2198★
CANADA WIRE AND CABLE, LTD. - TECHNICAL LIBRARY (Sci-Tech)
22 Commercial Rd.   Phone: (416) 421-0440
Toronto, ON, Canada M4G 1Z4   Dianne Crompton, Lib.Techn.
Founded: 1965. **Staff:** Prof 1; Other 1. **Subjects:** Electrical engineering, mathematics, chemistry, management, marketing, mechanical engineering, industrial engineering. **Holdings:** 694 books and bound periodical volumes; 2000 patents; 1900 standards and specifications; 2 VF drawers of technical information; 1 VF drawer of archives. **Subscriptions:** 200 journals and other serials. **Services:** Interlibrary loans; copying; library open to public with restrictions.

★2199★
CANADAIR, LTD. - COMPANY LIBRARY (Sci-Tech)
P.O. Box 6087   Phone: (514) 744-1511
Montreal, PQ, Canada H3C 3G9   Margaret Levesque
Founded: 1946. **Staff:** 5. **Subjects:** Aeronautics, electronics, space research, transportation, management. **Holdings:** 7000 books; 2500 bound periodical volumes; 70,000 reports and pamphlets; 20,000 specifications. **Subscriptions:** 250 journals and other serials. **Services:** Interlibrary loans; library not open to public. **Computerized Information Services:** DIALOG. **Publications:** Library Accession List - for internal distribution only.

CANADAY (Ward M.) CENTER
See: University of Toledo - Ward M. Canaday Center

CANADIAN ADVISORY COUNCIL ON THE STATUS OF WOMEN
See: Canada - Canadian Advisory Council on the Status of Women

CANADIAN AIR TRANSPORTATION ADMINISTRATION
See: Canada - Transport Canada

★2200★
CANADIAN AMATEUR MUSICIANS-MUSICIENS AMATEURS DU CANADA (CAMMAC) - MUSIC LIBRARY (Mus)
4450 Sherbrooke St., W.
Montreal, PQ, Canada H3Z 1E6   Phone: (514) 935-2272
                                         Geoffrey Cooper, Chm., Lib.Comm.
Subjects: Choral, orchestral and chamber music. **Holdings:** 6000 titles. **Services:** Mail order service available in the United States and Canada; library open to public on a limited schedule. **Publications:** Catalog - free to members; Journal, 3-4/year - to members. **Remarks:** Library is a collection of performance music for amateurs and professionals, individuals and groups. **Staff:** Jan Simons, Gen.Dir.

CANADIAN ARCHITECTURAL ARCHIVES
See: University of Calgary - Environment-Science-Technology Library

★2201★
CANADIAN ASSOCIATION - LATIN AMERICA AND CARIBBEAN - INFORMATION CENTRE (Area-Ethnic)
42 Charles St., E.   Phone: (416) 964-6068
Toronto, ON, Canada M4Y 1T4   Maria A. Escriu, Chf.Libn.
Staff: Prof 1; Other 2. **Subjects:** Economics, finance, politics and current events throughout the Americas. **Special Collections:** Studies, reports, annual reports and statistics from Latin American governments, government institutions and business associations; English, Spanish and Portuguese periodicals from Canadian, U.S., British and Latin American sources. **Holdings:** Figures not available. **Subscriptions:** 300 journals and other serials. **Services:** Library not open to public. **Publications:** CALA Reports, monthly - by subscription; CALA Informa, quarterly (in Spanish); CALA Informa, quarterly (in Portuguese); CALA Update, quarterly (in English) - distributed to the Caribbean business community; Glossary of Institutions Concerned with Latin America, 2nd edition, 1978 - available for sale.

CANADIAN ASSOCIATION FOR THE MENTALLY RETARDED - NATIONAL INSTITUTE ON MENTAL RETARDATION
See: National Institute on Mental Retardation

★2202★
CANADIAN AUTOMOBILE ASSOCIATION - LIBRARY (Trans)
1775 Courtwood Crescent   Phone: (613) 226-7631
Ottawa, ON, Canada K2C 3J2   Linda Batoff, Libn.
Staff: Prof 1. **Subjects:** Urban transportation, traffic engineering, travel, energy conservation, traffic accidents and safety. **Holdings:** 1800 books; 2000 slides; 200 periodicals. **Subscriptions:** 245 journals and other serials; 5 newspapers. **Services:** Library not open to public.

CANADIAN BAPTIST ARCHIVES
See: Baptist Convention of Ontario and Quebec

★2203★
CANADIAN BIBLE COLLEGE/CANADIAN THEOLOGICAL SEMINARY - ARCHIBALD FOUNDATION LIBRARY (Rel-Theol)
4400 Fourth Ave.
Regina, SK, Canada S4T 0H8   Phone: (306) 545-1515
                                         Marguerite Porter, Dir., Lib.Serv.
Founded: 1941. **Staff:** Prof 1; Other 5. **Subjects:** Bible, missiology, theology, church growth and history, pastoral theology, Christian education. **Holdings:** 45,064 books; 1200 bound periodical volumes; 2800 audiovisual items; 3000 microfiche; 12 drawers of pamphlets. **Subscriptions:** 386 journals and other serials. **Services:** Interlibrary loans; copying; library open to public on request. **Computerized Information Services:** Computerized cataloging.

CANADIAN BOOK EXCHANGE CENTRE
See: National Library of Canada

★2204★
CANADIAN BOOK INFORMATION CENTRE (Publ)
70 the Esplanade, 3rd Fl.   Phone: (416) 362-6555
Toronto, ON, Canada M5E 1A6   Serge Lavoie, Project Mgr.
Staff: 8. **Subjects:** Canadian publications. **Holdings:** 3500 books. **Services:** Centre open to researchers and media reviewers. **Publications:** Checklist of Titles, annual; Bibliography of Bibliographies, annual; Canadian Media List, annual. **Special Catalogs:** Multiculturalism in Canada; Special Education. **Remarks:** Canadian Book Information Centre represents 130 Canadian-owned publishers and assists them with the marketing of their publications. C.B.I.C. directs its attention to promoting and increasing the level of awareness of Canadian materials. Branch offices are located in Vancouver, BC and Halifax, NS. **Also Known As:** C.B.I.C.

★2205★
CANADIAN BOOK PUBLISHERS' COUNCIL - LIBRARY (Publ)
45 Charles St., E., 7th Fl.   Phone: (416) 964-7231
Toronto, ON, Canada M4Y 1S2
Staff: 8. **Subjects:** Canadian publishing, education statistics, publishing trade. **Holdings:** 1000 books and bound periodical volumes. **Subscriptions:** 30 journals and other serials. **Services:** Copying; library open to public for reference use only. **Publications:** Communique, bimonthly - free upon request.

★2206★
CANADIAN BROADCASTING CORPORATION - ENGINEERING HEADQUARTERS LIBRARY (Sci-Tech)
7925 Cote St. Luc Rd.   Phone: (514) 488-2551
Montreal, PQ, Canada H4W 1R5   Mrs. E. Mercer, Act.Libn.
Founded: 1954. **Staff:** 1. **Subjects:** Radio and television, engineering, communications, photography. **Holdings:** 1000 volumes. **Subscriptions:** 130 journals and other serials. **Services:** Interlibrary loans; library open to public by request.

★2207★
CANADIAN BROADCASTING CORPORATION - HEAD OFFICE LIBRARY (Info Sci)
1500 Bronson Ave.
P.O. Box 8478   Phone: (613) 731-3111
Ottawa, ON, Canada K1G 3J5   N. Deschamps, Ref.Libn.
Founded: 1954. **Staff:** Prof 1; Other 1. **Subjects:** Communications, radio, television, advertising, social sciences. **Holdings:** 7000 books; 20 VF drawers of clippings and pamphlets. **Subscriptions:** 300 journals and other serials; 10 newspapers. **Services:** Interlibrary loans; copying; SDI; library open to public, borrowing by librarian's permission only. **Computerized Information Services:** Computerized cataloging and serials. **Publications:** Library News, irregular.

★2208★
CANADIAN BROADCASTING CORPORATION - LIBRARY (Info Sci)
C.P. 6000   Phone: (514) 285-3854
Montreal, PQ, Canada H3C 3A8   Michelle Bachand, Hd.Libn.
Founded: 1944. **Staff:** Prof 5; Other 9. **Subjects:** Broadcasting, Canadiana, communication, performing arts, current events. **Holdings:** 36,000 books; 24 VF drawers of clippings, pamphlets; 40 VF drawers of pictures; 307 reels of microfilmed journals; 1238 reels of microfilmed newspapers. **Subscriptions:** 637 journals and other serials; 16 newspapers. **Services:** Interlibrary loans; copying; library open to public by appointment. **Computerized Information Services:** Info Globe, SDC, New York Times Information Service, QUESTEL, SABINE; computerized serials. **Publications:** New acquisitions list - for internal distribution only. **Also Known As:** Societe Radio-Canada - Bibliotheque.

★2209★
CANADIAN BROADCASTING CORPORATION - MUSIC LIBRARY (Mus)
Sta. A., Box 500   Phone: (416) 925-3311
Toronto, ON, Canada M5W 1E6   John P. Lawrence, Coord., Music Lib.
Subjects: Music. **Special Collections:** CBC commissioned works; TV and radio scores and parts; Canadiana; popular sheet music, 1900-1955. **Holdings:** 910 books; 49 bound periodical volumes; 10 VF drawers of clippings under 4000 music headings; 8 VF drawers of publishers' catalogs; 115 VF drawers of CBC archival arrangements. **Subscriptions:** 33 journals and other serials. **Services:** Interlibrary loans; copying; library open to public for bona fide research. **Remarks:** Library is located at 90 Sumach Street, Toronto, ON. **Staff:** Pat Kellogg, Prog.Archv./Mus.Lib.Serv.

★2210★
CANADIAN BROADCASTING CORPORATION - MUSIC & RECORD LIBRARY (Mus)
541 Portage Ave.
P.O. Box 160   Phone: (204) 775-8351
Winnipeg, MB, Canada R3C 2H1   Don R. McLaren, Sr.Libn.
Founded: 1948. **Staff:** Prof 3. **Subjects:** Music, music industry. **Holdings:** 100,000 items of sheet music; 24,000 recordings. **Subscriptions:** 8 journals and other serials. **Services:** Interlibrary loans; library not open to public. **Staff:** Norma Lavich, Music Libn.; Mary Worobec, Record Libn.

★2211★
CANADIAN BROADCASTING CORPORATION - MUSIC & RECORD LIBRARY (Mus)
5600 Sackville St.
Box 3000   Phone: (902) 422-8311
Halifax, NS, Canada B3J 3E9   David S. Leadbeater, Sr.Rec.Libn.
Founded: 1936. **Staff:** Prof 1; Other 3. **Subjects:** Music. **Holdings:** 200 books; 40,000 phonograph records; 7000 items of sheet music and scores. **Subscriptions:** 12 journals and other serials. **Services:** Library open to public for serious reference use only.

★2212★
CANADIAN BROADCASTING CORPORATION - MUSIC SERVICES LIBRARY (Mus)
1400 Dorchester Blvd., E.
P.O. Box 6000   Phone: (514) 285-3900
Montreal, PQ, Canada H3C 3A8   Claude Gagnon, Hd., Music Serv.
Founded: 1936. **Subjects:** Music, music rights. **Special Collections:** 78rpm phonograph records (40,000). **Holdings:** 2000 books; 300,000 phonograph records; 175,000 titles of sheet music. **Subscriptions:** 35 journals and other serials. **Services:** Library not open to public. **Computerized Information Services:** Internal database; computerized circulation. **Staff:** Robert Ternisien, Supv., Music Copyrights; Conrad Sabourin, Delegate; Diane Leonard, Supv., Cat.Serv.; Fernand Bourdeau, Supv., Adm.Serv.; Louise Champeau, Supv., Music/Rec.Lib.

★2213★
CANADIAN BROADCASTING CORPORATION - PROGRAM ARCHIVES (Sound) (Aud-Vis)
Sta. A, Box 500   Phone: (416) 925-3311
Toronto, ON, Canada M5W 1E6   John P. Lawrence, Coord., Prog.Archv.
Founded: 1960. **Staff:** Prof 2; Other 9. **Subjects:** Radio network programming; audio of TCV programming (limited); Canadian politics, current events, cultural events, oral history. **Holdings:** 1050 books; 40 bound periodical volumes; 61,800 discs; 79,651 tapes. **Services:** Dubbing service; archives open to serious scholars and post-graduate students. **Staff:** Dido Mendl, Selection & Res.Off.

★2214★
CANADIAN BROADCASTING CORPORATION - RECORD LIBRARY (Mus)
Sta. A, Box 500   Phone: (416) 925-3311
Toronto, ON, Canada M5W 1E6   John P. Lawrence, Coord.
Staff: Prof 1; Other 8. **Subjects:** Music - literature, history. **Special Collections:** Canadiana. **Holdings:** 500 books; 600 bound periodical volumes; 250,000 phonograph records. **Subscriptions:** 92 journals and other serials. **Services:** Library not open to public. **Remarks:** The library is located at 100 Carlton St., Toronto, ON. **Staff:** Rose Geofroy, Sr. Record Libn.

★2215★
CANADIAN BROADCASTING CORPORATION - REFERENCE LIBRARY (Info Sci)
415 Yonge St.
Sta. A, Box 500
Toronto, ON, Canada M5W 1E6   Phone: (416) 925-3311
    Elizabeth Jenner, Hd.Libn.
Staff: Prof 5; Other 7. **Subjects:** Radio and television broadcasting, Canadiana, current affairs, drama. **Holdings:** 12,000 books; 8000 files of newspaper clippings. **Subscriptions:** 150 journals and other serials; 20 newspapers. **Services:** Interlibrary loans; copying; library open to public for research on CBC or broadcasting in Canada. **Computerized Information Services:** New York Times Information Service, QL Systems, DIALOG, Info Globe; computerized serials. **Publications:** Bibliotalk, irregular - for internal distribution only. **Staff:** Leone Earls, Libn.; Ann Irwin, Libn.; Lynda Barnett, Design Libn.; Ellen Levine, Libn.

★2216★
CANADIAN BROADCASTING CORPORATION - TV CURRENT AFFAIRS LIBRARY (Info Sci)
Sta. A, Box 500   Phone: (416) 925-3311
Toronto, ON, Canada M5W 1E6   Diana Redegeld, Lib.Techn.
Founded: 1975. **Staff:** Prof 1. **Subjects:** Canada - politics, current affairs, history. **Holdings:** 500 books; 1500 clipping files on all Canadian topics; 1000 cassettes. **Subscriptions:** 85 journals and other serials; 30 newspapers. **Services:** Library not open to public.

★2217★
CANADIAN CANNERS, LTD. - RESEARCH CENTRE - LIBRARY (Food-Bev)
1101 Walker's Line   Phone: (416) 335-9700
Burlington, ON, Canada L7N 2G4   Gisela Smithson, Tech.Libn.
Staff: Prof 1. **Subjects:** Food science, waste water technology, pesticides. **Special Collections:** History of canning industry in Canada (archives; 15 boxes); International CODEX files (food industry). **Holdings:** 800 books; 600 bound periodical volumes. **Subscriptions:** 46 journals and other serials. **Services:** Interlibrary loans; copying.

★2218★
CANADIAN CENTRE FOR ECUMENISM - LIBRARY (Rel-Theol)
2065 W. Sherbrooke   Phone: (514) 937-9176
Montreal, PQ, Canada H3H 1G6   Reginald Goulet, S.J., Dir.
Founded: 1963. **Staff:** Prof 3; Other 7. **Subjects:** Bible, ecumenism, interdenominational relations, theology. **Holdings:** 3600 volumes; 16 VF drawers of documentation; 700 pamphlets; AV materials; archives. **Subscriptions:** 140 journals and other serials; 10 newspapers. **Services:** Copying; library open to public with restrictions. **Publications:** Ecumenism/ Oecumenisme, quarterly. **Also Known As:** Centre Canadien d'Oecumenisme. **Staff:** Sr. Gabrielle Villemaire, S.S.A., Archv.; Marguerite-Marie d'Avignon, Bibliotechnician.

CANADIAN COAST GUARD COLLEGE
See: Canada - Transport Canada

CANADIAN CONSERVATION INSTITUTE LIBRARY
See: Canada - National Museums of Canada

★2219★
CANADIAN CONSULATE GENERAL - INFORMATION CENTER (Area-Ethnic)
310 S. Michigan Ave.   Phone: (312) 427-1031
Chicago, IL 60604   Carol A. Summers, Info.Mgr.
Subjects: Canada - literature, business, history, arts, social sciences. **Holdings:** 3500 books; 700 Canadian films; pamphlets and clippings. **Subscriptions:** 100 journals and other serials; 15 newspapers. **Services:** Interlibrary loans; library open to public with restrictions. **Networks/ Consortia:** Member of Chicago Library System.

★2220★
CANADIAN CONSULATE GENERAL - LIBRARY (Soc Sci)
1251 Ave. of the Americas   Phone: (212) 586-2400
New York, NY 10020   Sheila Purse, Hd.Libn.
Founded: 1945. **Staff:** Prof 2; Other 2. **Subjects:** Canadian government and politics, business, industry, trade, history, geography, literature, art, education, law, Canada-U.S. relations. **Special Collections:** Parliamentary Papers (beginning 1875); Canadian Government Publications (selective depository); Statistics Canada (full depository); Canada Treaty Series. **Holdings:** 4000 books; 6000 government documents; 30 drawers of news clippings and pamphlet files; 2 drawers of biography files; 10 drawers of corporation annual reports. **Subscriptions:** 360 journals and other serials; 20 newspapers. **Services:** Interlibrary loans; copying; library open to public by appointment only. **Computerized Information Services:** DIALOG, SDC, New York Times Information Service, Info Globe, Dow Jones New Retrieval, QL Systems. **Staff:** Carol Beyer, Asst.Libn.

★2221★
CANADIAN COUNCIL OF CHRISTIANS AND JEWS - JOHN D. HAYES LIBRARY OF HUMAN RELATIONS
49 Front St., E.
Toronto, ON, Canada M5E 1B3
Subjects: Group relationships, religion, Judaism, Catholicism, Protestantism, race relations, minority groups, police-community relations, labour-management relations. **Holdings:** 5000 books and bound periodical volumes; 11,000 pamphlets; films; records; tapes; maps; pictures. **Remarks:** Temporarily inactive.

★2222★
CANADIAN COUNCIL ON SOCIAL DEVELOPMENT - LIBRARY (Soc Sci)†
Sta. C, Box 3505   Phone: (613) 728-1865
Ottawa, ON, Canada K1Y 4G1   Ms. Pat Redhead, Libn.
Founded: 1921. **Staff:** Prof 1; Other 1. **Subjects:** Social welfare, social policy, housing, aging, poverty. **Special Collections:** Historical Canada Social Welfare Collection. **Holdings:** 12,000 books; 400 periodical titles; 7 drawers of subject files. **Subscriptions:** 335 journals and other serials; 7 newspapers. **Services:** Interlibrary loans; copying; library open to public. **Publications:** Accession list, irregular. **Remarks:** Library located at 55 Parkdale Ave., Ottawa, ON. **Also Known As:** Conseil Canadien de Developpement Social.

★2223★
CANADIAN COUNTY HISTORICAL MUSEUM - LIBRARY (Trans)
Wade & Grand Sts.   Phone: (405) 232-5121
El Reno, OK 73036   Mrs. Frank C. Ball, Cur.
Founded: 1970. **Staff:** 3. **Subjects:** Chicago, Rock Island & Pacific Railway; American railroads; history of Oklahoma and Canadian County; medicine; school textbooks. **Holdings:** 500 books; 200 other cataloged items; 3 VF drawers of pamphlets; 4 VF drawers of clippings; 3 VF drawers of documents; 30 cassette tapes; 3 VF drawers of old photographs. **Services:** Library open to public for reference use only. **Publications:** Bulletin, irregular. **Remarks:**

Maintained by Canadian County Historical Society. **Staff:** Leonard Schiffman, Co-Cur.

★2224★
CANADIAN CREDIT INSTITUTE - CREDIT RESEARCH AND LENDING LIBRARY (Bus-Fin)
931 Yonge St.   Phone: (416) 962-9911
Toronto, ON, Canada M4W 2H6   A.L. Peterman, Registrar
Founded: 1968. **Staff:** Prof 1; Other 1. **Subjects:** Credit management, commercial law, accounting, economics, administration, marketing. **Holdings:** 3500 volumes. **Subscriptions:** 44 journals and other serials. **Services:** Library open to members only.

★2225★
CANADIAN DENTAL ASSOCIATION - SYDNEY WOOD BRADLEY MEMORIAL LIBRARY (Med)
1815 Alta Vista Dr.   Phone: (613) 523-1770
Ottawa, ON, Canada K1G 3Y6   Margo M. Beres, Libn.
Founded: 1950. **Staff:** Prof 1. **Subjects:** Dentistry. **Holdings:** 5000 books; 100 bound periodical volumes. **Subscriptions:** 100 journals and newsletters. **Services:** Interlibrary loans.

CANADIAN DERMATOLOGICAL ASSOCIATION ARCHIVES
See: Mc Gill University - Osler Library

★2226★
CANADIAN EDUCATION ASSOCIATION - LIBRARY (Educ)
252 Bloor St., W., Suite 8-200   Phone: (416) 924-7721
Toronto, ON, Canada M5S 1V5   Diane Sibbett, Libn.
Founded: 1957. **Staff:** Prof 2. **Subjects:** Elementary and secondary education in Canada. **Holdings:** 3000 books; 30 VF drawers of clippings and pamphlets. **Subscriptions:** 250 journals and other serials. **Services:** Interlibrary loans; library open to public. **Also Known As:** Association canadienne d'education.

★2227★
CANADIAN EMBASSY - LIBRARY (Area-Ethnic)
1771 N St., N.W.   Phone: (202) 785-1400
Washington, DC 20036   Ms. Merle G. Fabian, Libn.
Founded: 1947. **Staff:** Prof 3; Other 2. **Subjects:** Canadiana, economics, biography, government, international affairs, Canadian-U.S. relations. **Special Collections:** Newspaper clippings and press releases (700 topics); Canadian government document depository (3500 documents). **Holdings:** 5000 books; 60 VF drawers of material on Canadian subjects. **Subscriptions:** 250 journals and other serials; 20 newspapers. **Services:** Interlibrary loans; copying (limited); library open to public. **Computerized Information Services:** Dow Jones News Retrieval, DIALOG, New York Times Information Service, Info Globe, QL Systems. **Publications:** Accession List, bimonthly. **Staff:** Angela Kilkenny, Asst.Libn.; Barbara Chinn, Ref.Libn.

CANADIAN ENERGY RESEARCH INSTITUTE - I.N. MC KINNON MEMORIAL LIBRARY
See: Mc Kinnon (I.N.) Memorial Library

★2228★
CANADIAN ETHNIC STUDIES ASSOCIATION - RESEARCH CENTRE (Area-Ethnic)
University of Calgary
2500 University Dr., N.W.   Phone: (403) 284-7257
Calgary, AB, Canada T2N 1N4   Dr. James S. Frideres, Dir.
Staff: Prof 10. **Subjects:** Ethnicity in sociology, anthropology and history. **Holdings:** Figures not available. **Services:** Centre not open to public. **Publications:** Canadian Ethnic Studies Journal, 3/year.

★2229★
CANADIAN EXPORT ASSOCIATION - LIBRARY (Bus-Fin)
99 Bank St., Suite 250   Phone: (613) 238-8888
Ottawa, ON, Canada K1P 6B9   J.D. Moore, Sec.
Founded: 1943. **Staff:** 2. **Subjects:** Trade statistics, regional geographic and economic groups, international organizations, international transport, export and international business, foreign investment. **Holdings:** 2000 books. **Services:** Interlibrary loans; copying; library open to public.

★2230★
CANADIAN FILM INSTITUTE - NATIONAL SCIENCE FILM LIBRARY (Sci-Tech; Aud-Vis)†
75 Albert St., Suite B20   Phone: (613) 232-2495
Ottawa, ON, Canada K1P 5E7   Peter Dyson-Bonter, Dir., N.S.F.L.
Founded: 1961. **Staff:** 2. **Subjects:** Health and medicine, earth sciences,

physical and engineering sciences, behavioral and biological sciences, geography and history, arts, performing arts and film. **Holdings:** 7400 titles of 16mm films. **Services:** Films available for loan in Canada only, with advance reservation; library open to public. **Publications:** Film catalogs on scientific disciplines. **Special Catalogs:** Price list of catalogs available upon request.

CANADIAN FORCES COLLEGE
See: Canada - National Defence

CANADIAN FORCES MEDICAL SERVICES SCHOOL
See: Canada - National Defence

CANADIAN FORESTRY SERVICE
See: Canada - Canadian Forestry Service

★2231★
CANADIAN FOUNDATION FOR ECONOMIC EDUCATION - RESOURCE CENTRE (Educ)
252 Bloor St. W., Suite 560   Phone: (416) 968-2236
Toronto, ON, Canada M5S 1V5   Judith Jackson, Resource Ctr.Dir.
Founded: 1977. **Staff:** Prof 1. **Subjects:** Economics, economic education. **Holdings:** 2000 books; 5 VF drawers of clippings. **Subscriptions:** 165 journals and other serials. **Services:** Interlibrary loans; copying; library open to public by appointment. **Special Indexes:** Index of journal articles received in resource centre (card).

★2232★
CANADIAN GAY ARCHIVES - LIBRARY (Soc Sci)
Sta. A, Box 639   Phone: (416) 863-6320
Toronto, ON, Canada M5W 1G2
Founded: 1973. **Staff:** Prof 6; Other 4. **Subjects:** Homosexuality, gay liberation movement, lesbianism. **Holdings:** 2000 books and bound periodical volumes; 25,000 clippings; 5000 journal articles; 300 hours of audiotapes; 16 hours of videotapes; 8000 periodicals (1400 titles). **Subscriptions:** 95 journals and other serials. **Services:** Copying; library open to public. **Publications:** Gay Archivist (newsletter), irregular; publications series (bibliographies, biographical sketches). **Special Indexes:** Index to published material (card); index to The Body Politic; index to clippings. **Staff:** Alan V. Miller, Collective Member; James A. Fraser, Collective Member.

★2233★
CANADIAN GENERAL ELECTRIC COMPANY, LTD. - CORPORATE INFORMATION CENTRE (Law; Bus-Fin)
Commerce Court Postal Station
P.O. Box 417   Phone: (416) 862-5598
Toronto, ON, Canada M5L 1J2   Anne Pashley, Mgr.
Founded: 1974. **Staff:** Prof 1; Other 1. **Subjects:** Law, business, economics. **Special Collections:** Company archives; Conference Board in Canada and C.D. Howe Institute publications. **Holdings:** 7500 volumes. **Subscriptions:** 75 journals and other serials; 6 newspapers. **Services:** Centre not open to public.

★2234★
CANADIAN GENERAL ELECTRIC COMPANY, LTD. - ENGINEERING LIBRARY (Sci-Tech)
107 Park St., N.   Phone: (705) 748-7745
Peterborough, ON, Canada K9J 7B5   Leida Madisso, Act.Libn.
Staff: Prof 1. **Subjects:** Science and technology, engineering. **Special Collections:** American Institute of Electrical Engineers (AIEE) and Institute of Electrical and Electronics Engineers (IEEE) transactions; Conference Internationale des Grands Reseaux Electriques/International Conference on Large High Tension Electric Systems (CIGRE) reports. **Subscriptions:** 203 journals and other serials. **Services:** Library not open to public. **Publications:** Library newsletter.

CANADIAN GERIATRICS RESEARCH SOCIETY - J.W. CRANE MEMORIAL LIBRARY
See: Crane (J.W.) Memorial Library

CANADIAN GOVERNMENT OFFICE OF TOURISM
See: Canada - Industry, Trade & Commerce

CANADIAN GRAIN COMMISSION
See: Canada - Agriculture Canada

★2235★
CANADIAN HEARING SOCIETY - LIBRARY (Med)
60 Bedford Rd.
Toronto, ON, Canada M5R 2K2   Phone: (416) 964-9595
                                          Dorothy Scott, Libn.
Subjects: Hearing impairment; education of the deaf; social work and

rehabilitation in the field of hearing loss. **Holdings:** 600 books; 3 VF drawers of reports and reprints. **Subscriptions:** 22 journals and other serials. **Services:** Copying; library open to public with restrictions.

★2236★
CANADIAN HOSPITAL ASSOCIATION - BLACKADER LIBRARY (Med)
410 Laurier W., Suite 800   Phone: (613) 238-8005
Ottawa, ON, Canada K1R 7T6
Founded: 1945. **Staff:** Prof 2; Other 1. **Subjects:** Health care administration. **Holdings:** 3000 books; 3400 reports; 1200 boxes of articles, pamphlets and ephemera; 200 titles of AV and learning materials. **Subscriptions:** 200 journals and other serials. **Services:** Interlibrary loans; copying; library open to personnel of hospitals and related institutions. **Publications:** Canadian Hospital Directory, annual - available for purchase; Dimensions in Health Service, monthly - by subscription; Directory of Long Term Centres in Canada - available for purchase; Hospital Trustee, bimonthly - by subscription; The Health Administrator's Library. **Also Known As:** Association des Hopitaux du Canada. **Staff:** Louise Gibson, Co-Dir., Lib.Serv.; Diane Thomson, Co-Dir., Lib.Serv.

CANADIAN HOUSING INFORMATION CENTRE
See: Canada - Mortgage and Housing Corporation

★2237★
CANADIAN IMPERIAL BANK OF COMMERCE - INFORMATION CENTRE (Bus-Fin)
Head Office - Commerce Court   Phone: (416) 862-3053
Toronto, ON, Canada M5L 1A2   Jane Cooney, Mgr.
Founded: 1971. **Staff:** Prof 5; Other 7. **Subjects:** Banking, economics, finance, Canadian economy and industry. **Special Collections:** Complete file of Statistics Canada publications; annual reports of Canadian chartered banks back to 1867. **Holdings:** 25,000 books; 700 bound periodical volumes; 1200 current subject files (clippings and pamphlets); 850 reels of microfilmed newspapers and periodicals; Canadian federal and provincial government documents on financial and commercial affairs on microfiche. **Subscriptions:** 2000 journals and other serials; 42 newspapers. **Services:** Interlibrary loans (fee); copying; library open to public with restrictions. **Computerized Information Services:** DIALOG, SDC, QL Systems, Info Globe, New York Times Information Service, BRS, Textline; computerized serials. **Publications:** New Books, monthly - for internal distribution only. **Special Indexes:** Index to internal staff publications (card). **Staff:** Helen Katz, Asst.Mgr., Info.Serv.; Mary-Lois Williams, Cat.; Philomena Pun, Ref.Libn.; Sue Merry, Asst.Mgr., Tech.Serv.

CANADIAN INDIAN RIGHTS COLLECTION
See: National Library of Canada

★2238★
CANADIAN INDUSTRIAL INNOVATION CENTRE/WATERLOO - RESOURCE CENTRE (Sci-Tech; Bus-Fin)
156 Columbia St., W.   Phone: (519) 885-5870
Waterloo, ON, Canada N2L 3L3
Staff: 1. **Subjects:** Technological innovation, invention, entrepreneurship, beginning businesses, patents, licensing. **Holdings:** 600 books and bound periodical volumes. **Services:** Copying; centre open to members and client companies. **Computerized Information Services:** Spires (University of Waterloo internal database); computerized cataloging. **Remarks:** Centre operated under the joint auspices of the University of Waterloo and Canada - Industry, Trade and Commerce.

CANADIAN INSTITUTE OF ADULT EDUCATION
See: Institut Canadien d'Education des Adultes

★2239★
CANADIAN INSTITUTE OF GUIDED GROUND TRANSPORT - INFORMATION CENTRE (Trans)
Queen's University   Phone: (613) 547-5777
Kingston, ON, Canada K7L 3N6   Jane Law, Info.Off.
Staff: Prof 1; Other 1. **Subjects:** Railroads and other modes of transportation. **Special Collections:** Hazardous materials transport; track/train dynamics; railway costs; energy. **Holdings:** 6000 monographs; microfiche. **Subscriptions:** 72 journals and other serials. **Services:** Interlibrary loans; copying; library open to public. **Computerized Information Services:** Online systems; internal database; computerized cataloging. **Networks/Consortia:** Member of Transport Canada Documents System. **Special Indexes:** Pre-catalog Information List, weekly - for internal distribution only.

★2240★
CANADIAN INSTITUTE OF HYPNOTISM - LIBRARY (Med)
Medical Towers Bldg., Suite 51
3465 Cote des Neiges Rd.
Montreal, PQ, Canada H3H 1T7   Phone: (514) 937-4488
                                             Jeanne Rigaud, Coord.
Subjects: Hypnosis - medical, dental, historical. **Holdings:** 1100 books; 45
bound periodical volumes. **Subscriptions:** 9 journals and other serials.
Services: Library open to public with restrictions.

★2241★
CANADIAN INSTITUTE OF INTERNATIONAL AFFAIRS - LIBRARY (Soc Sci)
15 King's College Circle   Phone: (416) 979-1851
Toronto, ON, Canada M5S 2V9   Jane R. Barrett, Libn.
Founded: 1945. **Staff:** Prof 1; Other 3. **Subjects:** International relations,
politics, Canadian foreign relations. **Special Collections:** United Nations
documents (depository). **Holdings:** 20,000 books; 3000 bound periodical
volumes; 9000 pamphlets (cataloged); 120 drawers of clippings.
Subscriptions: 250 journals and other serials; 15 newspapers. **Services:**
Interlibrary loans; copying; library open to public. **Publications:** Bibliography of
works on Canadian foreign relations, 1976-1980. **Staff:** Martha Foote,
Asst.Libn.; Nancy Clare, Cat.

CANADIAN INTERNATIONAL DEVELOPMENT AGENCY
See: Canada - Canadian International Development Agency

★2242★
CANADIAN JEWELLERS INSTITUTE - LIBRARY (Sci-Tech)
100 Front St., W.   Phone: (416) 368-8372
Toronto, ON, Canada M5J 1E3   Dolores T. Nelson, Registrar/Libn.
Staff: 1. **Subjects:** Precious metals, gemstones, watches, management,
salesmanship. **Holdings:** 400 books; 385 bound periodical volumes; trade
publications; government reports. **Subscriptions:** 16 journals and other
serials. **Services:** Interlibrary loans (to members only); library open to public
by special arrangement. **Publications:** Canadian Jewellers Institute News
Bulletin, quarterly - to members.

★2243★
CANADIAN JEWISH CONGRESS - NATIONAL ARCHIVES (Area-Ethnic)
1590 Ave. Docteur Penfield   Phone: (514) 931-7531
Montreal, PQ, Canada H3G 1C5   Judith Nefsky, Archv.
Founded: 1919. **Staff:** Prof 2; Other 2. **Subjects:** Jewish Canadiana.
Holdings: Records of the Canadian Jewish Congress; large collection of
personal and institutional archives relating to Canadian Jewish community.
Services: Copying; archives open to public by appointment. **Publications:**
Canadian Jewish Archives, irregular. **Formerly:** Its Library & Archives.

★2244★
CANADIAN LABOUR CONGRESS - LIBRARY (Soc Sci)
2841 Riverside Dr.   Phone: (613) 521-3400
Ottawa, ON, Canada K1V 8X7   Dawn Dobson, Libn.
Founded: 1962. **Staff:** Prof 1. **Subjects:** Industrial relations, economics,
political economy, international affairs, legislation, trade union history.
Holdings: 3500 books; 300 bound periodical volumes; archives; reports;
proceedings; government documents. **Subscriptions:** 90 journals and other
serials. **Services:** Interlibrary loans; library open to public for reference use
only.

★2245★
**CANADIAN LAW INFORMATION COUNCIL - RESOURCE CENTRE FOR
    COMPUTERS AND LAW** (Law; Info Sci)
Place de Ville, Suite 2010
112 Kent St.   Phone: (613) 236-9766
Ottawa, ON, Canada K1P 5P2   Lorna K. Rees-Potter, Dir. of Res.
Founded: 1980. **Staff:** Prof 1; Other 1. **Subjects:** Automated legal
information retrieval. **Special Collections:** Computers and law in Canada (200
items). **Holdings:** 25 books; 800 articles. **Subscriptions:** 40 journals and
other serials. **Services:** Copying; Centre open to public at the discretion of
director. **Computerized Information Services:** SDC, QL Systems.
Publications: Applications of Computer Technology to Law (1969-1978): A
Selected Bibliography; Automated Legal Research: A Manual for QL Users; A
Comparison of Automated and Manual Legal Research: A Computer Study.
Staff: M. Anne Foster, Dir. of Comp. & Law.

CANADIAN LIBRARY OF FAMILY MEDICINE
See: College of Family Physicians of Canada

★2246★
CANADIAN LIQUID AIR, LTD. - E & C LIBRARY (Sci-Tech)
1155 Sherbrooke St., W.   Phone: (514) 842-5431
Montreal, PQ, Canada H3A 1H8   Doris Hammond, Libn.
Founded: 1946. **Staff:** 1. **Subjects:** Chemical engineering, welding,
metallurgy, cryogenics, industrial gases. **Holdings:** 1700 books; 200 bound
periodical volumes; 10 cases of patents; 1 drawer of archives. **Subscriptions:**
130 journals and other serials; 6 newspapers. **Services:** Interlibrary loans;
copying; library not open to public. **Also Known As:** Air Liquide Canada Ltee.

★2247★
CANADIAN MARCONI COMPANY - LIBRARY (Sci-Tech)
2442 Trenton Ave.   Phone: (514) 341-7630
Montreal, PQ, Canada H3P 1Y9   Mrs. M. Benjamin, Libn.
Subjects: Electronics. **Holdings:** 5000 volumes. **Services:** Interlibrary loans;
library not open to public.

★2248★
CANADIAN MEDICAL ASSOCIATION - LIBRARY (Med)
1867 Alta Vista Dr.
P.O. Box 8650   Phone: (613) 731-9331
Ottawa, ON, Canada K1G 0G8   Kathleen Beaudoin, Libn.
Founded: 1955. **Staff:** Prof 2. **Subjects:** Medicine. **Holdings:** 900 books;
1250 bound periodical volumes; 900 other items. **Subscriptions:** 400
journals and other serials. **Services:** Interlibrary loans; copying; library open to
physicians and other libraries. **Special Indexes:** Index of Canadian Medical
Association Journal, semiannual; Canadian Journal of Surgery, annual.

★2249★
**CANADIAN MEMORIAL CHIROPRACTIC COLLEGE - C.C. CLEMMER
    LIBRARY** (Med)
1900 Bayview Ave.   Phone: (416) 482-2340
Toronto, ON, Canada M4G 3E6   J. Claire Callaghan, Dir.
Founded: 1945. **Staff:** Prof 3; Other 3. **Subjects:** Chiropractic, basic
sciences, sports medicine, nutrition, radiology, neurology. **Special
Collections:** History of chiropractic collection (200 books). **Holdings:** 8000
books; 1500 bound periodical volumes; 1500 reprints; 5000 slides; 150
slide-tape presentations; 25 transparencies; 44 cassettes; 9 realia.
Subscriptions: 350 journals and other serials. **Services:** Interlibrary loans;
copying; library open to public for reference use only. **Computerized
Information Services:** MEDLARS, DIALOG. **Networks/Consortia:** Member of
Toronto Medical Libraries Group; Chiropractic Library Consortium (CLIBCON).
Staff: Margaret Butkovic, AV Lib.Techn.; Leanne Johnson, Tech.Serv.Libn.

★2250★
CANADIAN MENTAL HEALTH ASSOCIATION - LIBRARY (Med)
2160 Yonge St., 3rd Fl.   Phone: (416) 484-7750
Toronto, ON, Canada M4S 2Z3
Subjects: Mental health and mental illness - all aspects. **Special Collections:**
Archives of the Canadian Mental Health Association. **Holdings:** 200 books;
pamphlets, articles, briefs. **Subscriptions:** 120 journals and other serials.
Services: Copying; library open to public by appointment, for reference use.
Also Known As: Association Canadienne pour la Sante Mentale.

★2251★
**CANADIAN MENTAL HEALTH ASSOCIATION - MANITOBA DIVISION
    LIBRARY**
330 Edmonton St.
Winnipeg, MB, Canada R3B 2L2
Defunct

★2252★
CANADIAN MILITARY ENGINEERS MUSEUM - LIBRARY (Mil)
M.P.O. 612   Phone: (604) 858-3311
C.F.B. Chilliwack, BC, Canada V0X 2E0
Founded: 1956. **Subjects:** Military engineering, military history, Corps of
Engineers history. **Holdings:** 2000 books; 1000 bound periodical volumes;
1000 pamphlets; 10 boxes of documents; 150 maps; 12 drawers of
photographs. **Services:** Library open to public for bona fide museum research
only.

★2253★
**CANADIAN MUSIC CENTRE - BRITISH COLUMBIA REGIONAL BRANCH
    LIBRARY** (Mus)
3-2007 W. 4th Ave.   Phone: (604) 734-4622
Vancouver, BC, Canada V6J 1N3   Colin Miles, Regional Dir.
Founded: 1977. **Staff:** Prof 1; Other 1. **Subjects:** Music by Canadian
composers. **Holdings:** 6000 published and unpublished scores; 200 files on
Canadian composers; 1700 recordings and cassettes; 250 information files

on Canadian music. **Subscriptions:** 20 journals and other serials. **Services:** Interlibrary loans; copying; library open to public. **Computerized Information Services:** Computerized cataloging. **Publications:** Centregramme (newsletter), 8/year. **Also Known As:** Centre de Musique Canadienne.

★2254★
CANADIAN MUSIC CENTRE - LIBRARY (Mus)
1263 Bay St.   Phone: (416) 961-6601
Toronto, ON, Canada M5R 2C1   H.A. Mutsaers, Libn.
Founded: 1959. **Staff:** Prof 3. **Subjects:** Music by Canadian composers. **Holdings:** 7000 published and unpublished scores; 500 discs and 2000 tapes of Canadian music; 175 extensive files on Canadian composers' biographies, program notes and publicity. **Subscriptions:** 20 journals and other serials. **Services:** Copying (of unpublished works with copyright holder's permission only); direct loans of scores to musicians and others throughout the world; library open to public. **Computerized Information Services:** Internal database. **Publications:** "Musicanada" (1967-1970); information lists, composer monographs, 3/year; Canadian Orchestral, Chamber, Choral, Vocal and Keyboard Music. **Remarks:** "The Canadian Music Centre exists to promote, disseminate and make readily available the music of Canadian composers, both in Canada and abroad." **Also Known As:** Centre de Musique Canadienne. **Staff:** John A. Miller, Exec.Dir.

★2255★
CANADIAN MUSIC CENTRE - LIBRARY (Mus)
1259 Rue Berri, Suite 300   Phone: (514) 849-9175
Montreal, PQ, Canada H2L 4C7   Mireille Gagne, Regional Dir.
Founded: 1973. **Staff:** Prof 4; Other 1. **Subjects:** Music, Canadian composers, musical societies. **Special Collections:** Music scores by Quebec and Canadian composers. **Holdings:** 6500 scores; 1700 audio cassettes and tapes; 500 discs. **Services:** Interlibrary loans; copying; library open to public. **Also Known As:** Centre de Musique Canadienne. **Staff:** Isabelle Bernier, Libn.

★2256★
CANADIAN MUSIC CENTRE - PRAIRIE REGION LIBRARY (Mus)
911 Library Tower
2500 University Dr., N.W.   Phone: (403) 284-7403
Calgary, AB, Canada T2N 1N4   Mr. Clare Richman, Regional Dir.
Founded: 1980. **Staff:** 2. **Subjects:** Canadian music. **Holdings:** 7000 published and unpublished scores; discs and tapes of Canadian music; biographies and program notes on Canadian composers. **Subscriptions:** 20 journals and other serials. **Services:** Interlibrary loans; copying; library open to public. **Publications:** Prairie Sounds, bimonthly newsletter; list of other publications - available on request.

★2257★
CANADIAN NATIONAL INSTITUTE FOR THE BLIND - NATIONAL LIBRARY SERVICES (Aud-Vis)
1929 Bayview Ave.   Phone: (416) 486-2579
Toronto, ON, Canada M4G 3E8   Francoise Hebert, Exec.Dir.
Founded: 1906. **Staff:** Prof 5; Other 75. **Subjects:** General and scholarly topics. **Special Collections:** Reference collection on blindness; titles produced in braille or audio format. **Holdings:** 5000 titles in braille; 5000 titles on audiotapes. **Subscriptions:** 66 journals and other serials. **Services:** Interlibrary loans; copying; special format materials available to handicapped persons only. **Computerized Information Services:** Computerized cataloging and braille production. **Publications:** Talking books available for sale to libraries; braille books and magazines - loaned through national distribution. **Special Catalogs:** Catalogs of the braille and talking books collections. **Also Known As:** CNIB. **Staff:** Helen Perry, Assoc.Dir./Tape Coord.; Lois Brown, Braille Coord.; Marilyn Schulz, Mgr., Acq. & Cat.; Margaret Matheson, Music Libn.

★2258★
CANADIAN NATIONAL INSTITUTE FOR THE BLIND - QUEBEC DIVISION LIBRARY (Aud-Vis)†
1181 Guy St.   Phone: (514) 931-7221
Montreal, PQ, Canada H3H 2K6   Jeannine Tardif, Lib.Supv.
Founded: 1965. **Staff:** 5. **Subjects:** General topics in the French language. **Holdings:** Braille books, sound reading material. **Services:** Textbooks read on tape (on special request from students); cassette reproducing; library open to registered blind persons only. **Remarks:** Library exchanges French sound reading material with others in Canada and the U.S. **Also Known As:** Institut National Canadien pour les Aveugles.

★2259★
CANADIAN NATIONAL RAIL - GREAT LAKES REGION LIBRARY (Trans; Sci-Tech)
20 York St.   Phone: (416) 860-2418
Toronto, ON, Canada M5J 1E7   Shirley K. Smith, Libn.
Founded: 1964. **Staff:** Prof 1. **Subjects:** Railroading, transportation, engineering, electronics, telecommunications. **Special Collections:** Canadian Railways. **Holdings:** 15,150 books; 972 bound periodical volumes; 264 CN speeches; 700 CN reports; 5480 unbound periodicals; 732 annual reports; 30 drawers of Statistics Canada material; 52 microfiche; 5 VF drawers; 92 federal and provincial annual reports; 42 reels of microfilmed catalog of all CN libraries holdings. **Subscriptions:** 532 journals and other serials; 8 newspapers. **Services:** Interlibrary loans; library open to public by special arrangement. **Computerized Information Services:** Computerized serials. **Publications:** Accession List, bimonthly - distributed to CN personnel only. **Formerly:** Canadian National Railways - Canadian National Telecommunications - Great Lakes Region Library. **Also Known As:** CN Rail.

★2260★
CANADIAN NATIONAL RAILWAYS - DECHIEF LIBRARY (Trans)
935 Lagauchetiere St., W.
B.P. 8100   Phone: (514) 877-4407
Montreal, PQ, Canada H3C 3N4   Kathleen Elliott, Sys.Libn.
Founded: 1923. **Staff:** Prof 4; Other 10. **Subjects:** Railroad engineering, operation, economics, history; commuter trains; rapid transit; management; industrial relations. **Holdings:** 32,000 books; 8600 bound periodical volumes; 46,500 pamphlets (cataloged); 1700 technical reports; 6500 microforms. **Subscriptions:** 900 journals and other serials. **Services:** Interlibrary loans; copying; SDI; library open to public for reference use only. **Computerized Information Services:** DIALOG, SDC, CAN/OLE, Info Globe, SABINE, QL Systems; computerized acquisitions and serials. **Publications:** A selected bibliography on Canadian railways; Current Awareness Bulletin, biweekly. **Staff:** Celia Donnelly, Info.Serv.Libn.

★2261★
CANADIAN NATIONAL RAILWAYS - PHOTOGRAPHIC LIBRARY (Pict)
P.O. Box 8100   Phone: (514) 877-4834
Montreal, PQ, Canada H3C 3N4   R. Susan Gallagher, Sys. Photo Libn.
Founded: 1930. **Staff:** Prof 1; Other 2. **Subjects:** Railways, telecommunications, marine service, hotels, Canadian travel scenics. **Special Collections:** Historical Railways (includes pictures dating back to the late 1800s). **Holdings:** 1000 photo albums of pictures; 250,000 black and white negatives; 80,000 color negatives and transparencies; 33,000 color slides. **Services:** Interlibrary loans; photographic reproduction; library open to public with restrictions.

★2262★
CANADIAN NATIONAL RAILWAYS - PUBLIC AFFAIRS DEPARTMENT LIBRARY (Trans)
935 Lagauchetiere St., W.
Sta. A, P.O. Box 8100
Montreal, PQ, Canada H3C 3N4   Phone: (514) 877-5584
                                     Dorothy Webb, Sys.Res.Off.
Staff: Prof 1; Other 2. **Subjects:** Railways and other transportation, telecommunications. **Holdings:** 65 VF drawers of clippings; government documents, translations. **Subscriptions:** 200 journals and other serials; 10 newspapers. **Services:** Copying; library open to public.

CANADIAN NEWSPAPERS, LTD.
See: Victoria Times-Colonist

★2263★
CANADIAN NUCLEAR ASSOCIATION - CNA LIBRARY (Energy)
111 Elizabeth St., 11th Fl.   Phone: (416) 977-6152
Toronto, ON, Canada M5G 1P7
Founded: 1974. **Staff:** 1. **Subjects:** Nuclear industry, nuclear energy, Canadian Deuterium Uranium (CANDU). **Special Collections:** CNA publications - Nuclear Canada and Annual International Conference Proceedings, both from 1961 to present. **Holdings:** 1000 books; 3 VF drawers of Atomic Energy of Canada Reports; 2 VF drawers of Royal Commission on Electric Power Planning Submissions. **Subscriptions:** 30 journals and other serials. **Services:** Copying; library open to public; borrowing restricted to CNA members. **Publications:** Nuclear Notes - to members; list of other publications - free upon request. **Remarks:** Primarily an information service to CNA staff and members, but public information is provided.

★2264★
CANADIAN NUMISMATIC ASSOCIATION - LIBRARY (Rec)†
P.O. Box 112   Phone: (705) 458-9242
Cookstown, ON, Canada L0L 1L0   Carol Gregory, Libn.
Founded: 1950. **Staff:** Prof 1. **Subjects:** Numismatics. **Special Collections:** Canadian Antiquarian and Numismatic Journal, 1872-1933. **Holdings:** 3500 books. **Subscriptions:** 58 journals and other serials. **Services:** Copying; library not open to public.

★2265★
CANADIAN NURSES ASSOCIATION - HELEN K. MUSSALLEM LIBRARY
   (Med)
50 The Driveway   Phone: (613) 237-2133
Ottawa, ON, Canada K2P 1E2   Linda Solomon Shiff, Chf.Libn.
Staff: Prof 3; Other 5. **Subjects:** Nursing. **Special Collections:** Repository Collection of Canadian Nursing Studies; provincial nursing legislation; biographies of Canadian nurses; Archives of Canadian Nursing; nursing education program information. **Holdings:** 14,000 books and documents; photographs. **Subscriptions:** 572 journals and other serials. **Services:** Interlibrary loans; copying; bibliographic services; library open to public. **Publications:** List of publications - available on request. **Special Indexes:** Index of Canadian Nursing Research.

★2266★
CANADIAN OLYMPIC ASSOCIATION - LIBRARY/INFORMATION SERVICES
   (Rec)
Olympic House, Cite du Havre   Phone: (514) 861-3371
Montreal, PQ, Canada H3C 3R4   Sylvia Doucette, Lib.Asst.
Staff: Prof 2. **Subjects:** Olympics, amateur sports. **Holdings:** 500 books; 100 boxes of reports, clippings and reprints; films and still photographs. **Subscriptions:** 225 journals and other serials. **Services:** Interlibrary loans; copying; library open to public with restrictions.

★2267★
CANADIAN OPERA COMPANY - ARCHIVES (Mus)
417 Queen's Quay West   Phone: (416) 363-6671
Toronto, ON, Canada M5V 1A2   Joan L. Baillie, Archv./Rec.Mgr.
Staff: Prof 1. **Subjects:** History of opera in Toronto and Canada. **Special Collections:** Records of Herman Geiger-Torel (12 feet, 26 document cases, 11 cartons and 1 display case); records of Vida Hampton Peene (12 document cases). **Holdings:** 39 volumes; 19 bound volumes of minutes; 12 bound volumes of program notes; 94 libretti; 10 file drawers of financial material; 85 document cases of publicity material; 81 feet of fund-raising material; 10 cartons of programs, schedules, set and costume designs; 8000 photographs and slides; 124 audio- and videotapes; 71 discs; 4 films; posters, 1959 to present. **Subscriptions:** 10 journals and other serials. **Services:** Copying; library open to public by appointment. **Publications:** Overtures, quarterly - by subscription; Opera Souvenir Book, annual - to patrons, researchers and libraries; Guild News, semiannual - to Canadian Opera Guild Members. **Special Indexes:** Indexes to corporate, administrative and artistic records, 1950 to present; Canadian Opera Company's seasons, repertoire, tours and artists; boards of directors, officers, committees, 1950 to present; items and photographs (all on cards).

CANADIAN PACIFIC AIRLINES, LTD.
See: CP Air

★2268★
CANADIAN PACIFIC, LTD. - CORPORATE LIBRARY/INFORMATION CENTRE
   (Trans)
Windsor Station
Sta. A, P.O. Box 6042   Phone: (514) 395-6617
Montreal, PQ, Canada H3C 3E4   A.A. DiIorio, Corp.Libn.
Founded: 1972. **Staff:** Prof 3; Other 3. **Subjects:** Transportation, business. **Holdings:** 7500 volumes. **Subscriptions:** 750 journals and other serials. **Services:** Interlibrary loans; copying; library open to public by appointment only. **Computerized Information Services:** DIALOG, SDC, Info Globe, CAN/OLE; computerized serials. **Publications:** Recent Additions, monthly. **Staff:** C. Olsen, Res.Libn.; H. Berardinucci, Supv., Cat. & Acq.

★2269★
CANADIAN PARAPLEGIC ASSOCIATION - LIBRARY (Med)
520 Sutherland Dr.   Phone: (416) 422-5640
Toronto, ON, Canada M4G 3V9   Peter Bernauer, Natl.Libn.
Founded: 1977. **Staff:** Prof 1; Other 2. **Subjects:** Spinal cord injury and rehabilitation; handicapped concerns, including equipment information and building modifications. **Holdings:** 800 books and bound periodical volumes; 900 reprints. **Subscriptions:** 60 journals and other serials. **Services:** Library open to staff and professionals in health and rehabilitation fields.

Publications: Up-date, irregular; New Materials.

CANADIAN PLAINS RESEARCH CENTER INFORMATION SYSTEM
See: University of Regina

★2270★
CANADIAN PRESS - LIBRARY (Publ)
36 King St., E.   Phone: (416) 364-0321
Toronto, ON, Canada M5C 2L9   Elizabeth Shewan, Libn.
Founded: 1932. **Subjects:** Canadian news events and biography; World War II; records of sports, crimes and disasters. **Holdings:** 250 books; 48 VF drawers.

★2271★
CANADIAN PSYCHOANALYTIC SOCIETY - LIBRARY (Med)†
7000 Cote des Neiges Rd.   Phone: (514) 738-6105
Montreal, PQ, Canada H3S 2C1   Nadia Gargour, Adm.Sec.
Founded: 1967. **Staff:** 2. **Subjects:** Psychoanalysis. **Holdings:** 4000 books. **Subscriptions:** 22 journals and other serials. **Services:** Library not open to public. **Also Known As:** Societe Canadienne de Psychanalyse.

CANADIAN RADIO-TELEVISION AND TELECOMMUNICATIONS COMMISSION
See: Canada - Canadian Radio-Television and Telecommunications Commission

★2272★
CANADIAN RAILROAD HISTORICAL ASSOCIATION - LIBRARY (Trans)†
Canadian Railway Museum
Sta. B, P.O. Box 22   Phone: (514) 632-2410
Montreal, PQ, Canada H3B 3J5   Dr. R.V.V. Nicholls, Archv./Libn.
Staff: Prof 1; Other 1. **Subjects:** Canadian railway and tramway history, technology and operation. **Special Collections:** Sir William Van Horne Collection (100 volumes). **Holdings:** 2500 books; 200 bound periodical volumes; 150 feet of archival material; 40,000 mechanical drawings. **Subscriptions:** 30 journals and other serials. **Services:** Library open to public by appointment.

★2273★
CANADIAN REAL ESTATE ASSOCIATION - LIBRARY
99 Duncan Mill Rd.
Don Mills, ON, Canada M3B 1Z2
Subjects: Real estate - advertising and marketing, land use, urbanization, appraising, investment and management, government programs, finance, taxation, statistics. **Holdings:** 2000 books; 230 bound periodical volumes; 15 VF drawers of pamphlets and newsletters. **Special Indexes:** Index to Canadian Real Estate Journal. **Remarks:** Presently inactive.

★2274★
CANADIAN RED CROSS SOCIETY - LIBRARY (Soc Sci)
95 Wellesley St., E.   Phone: (416) 923-6692
Toronto, ON, Canada M4Y 1H6   Mrs. S. Kenwell, Libn.
Founded: 1961. **Staff:** 1. **Subjects:** Canadian and International Red Cross. **Special Collections:** International humanitarian law (60 volumes). **Holdings:** 700 books; 450 bound periodical volumes; 100 boxes of archival material; 490 boxes of pamphlets, clippings, press releases; 50 reels of microfilmed C.R.C.S. minutes. **Subscriptions:** 454 journals and other serials. **Services:** Interlibrary loans; copying; library open to public.

★2275★
CANADIAN REHABILITATION COUNCIL FOR THE DISABLED - CRCD RESOURCE CENTRE (Soc Sci)
One Yonge St., Suite 2110   Phone: (416) 862-0340
Toronto, ON, Canada M5E 1E5   Maureen Vasey, Dir., Info.Serv.
Founded: 1962. **Staff:** Prof 6; Other 7. **Subjects:** Physical disabilities, rehabilitation. **Holdings:** 2500 books; 100 bound periodical volumes. **Subscriptions:** 100 journals and other serials. **Services:** Copying; library open to public. **Networks/Consortia:** Member of Rehabilitation Information Round Table (RIR). **Publications:** Rehabilitation Digest, quarterly - by subscription; film list; Access, quarterly newsletter - free upon request; list of additional publications - available upon request.

★2276★
CANADIAN REHABILITATION COUNCIL FOR THE DISABLED - NATIONAL INFORMATION RESOURCE CENTRE (Soc Sci)
One Yonge St., Suite 2110   Phone: (416) 862-0340
Toronto, ON, Canada M5E 1E5   Ms. Gartley Wagner, Libn.
Staff: Prof 1. **Subjects:** Physical disabilities; rehabilitation; disabled - aids and devices, housing, transportation, employment. **Holdings:** 2500 books; 100

reports, briefs, proposals; 18 films; 6 VF drawers. **Subscriptions:** 30 journals and other serials; 190 newspapers. **Services:** Copying; library open to public for reference use only. **Computerized Information Services:** Computerized cataloging. **Networks/Consortia:** Member of Rehabilitation Information Round Table. **Publications:** List of publications - available on request.

CANADIAN RESEARCH INSTITUTE
See: Criterion Instruments, Ltd. - Canadian Research Institute Division

★2277★
CANADIAN RESTAURANT & FOODSERVICES ASSOCIATION - RESOURCE CENTRE (Food-Bev)
80 Bloor St., W., Suite 904   Phone: (416) 923-8416
Toronto, ON, Canada M5S 2V1   Joyce Reynolds, Info.Spec.
Founded: 1972. **Staff:** Prof 1. **Subjects:** Food service, lodging, tourism, quantity cookery, statistics, legislation. **Special Collections:** Menu collection (600, mainly Canadian). **Holdings:** 1000 books; 15 VF drawers. **Subscriptions:** 78 journals and other serials. **Services:** Copying; SDI for members; library open to public on request, with service fee for nonmembers. **Publications:** Info Stats, monthly - to members. **Special Indexes:** Index of feature articles appearing in two major Canadian trade journals (card and book).

★2278★
CANADIAN STANDARDS ASSOCIATION - INFORMATION CENTRE (Sci-Tech)
178 Rexdale Blvd.   Phone: (416) 744-4058
Rexdale, ON, Canada M9W 1R3   Cameron D. Macdonald, Supv.
Founded: 1970. **Staff:** Prof 1; Other 3. **Subjects:** Engineering, product safety, quality control, certification of products, electrical engineering, consumerism. **Special Collections:** Engineering standards (60,000). **Holdings:** 2000 books; 1800 technical information files (cataloged). **Subscriptions:** 352 journals and other serials. **Services:** Interlibrary loans; library open to public with restrictions. **Computerized Information Services:** DIALOG, SDC. **Publications:** CSA Information Update, 8 times/year - by subscription. **Special Indexes:** Index of standards referenced in Canadian federal and provincial legislation (card). **Also Known As:** Association Canadienne de Normalisation.

★2279★
CANADIAN TAX FOUNDATION - LIBRARY (Soc Sci; Bus-Fin)
130 Adelaide St., W.   Phone: (416) 863-9784
Toronto, ON, Canada M5H 3P5   Marjorie Robinson, Libn.
Founded: 1946. **Staff:** Prof 1; Other 1. **Subjects:** Canadian and international taxation; public finance; government expenditures in Canada (including provincial); local government. **Special Collections:** Taxation services (loose-leaf); federal and provincial budgets and public accounts. **Holdings:** 13,000 books; 2500 bound periodical volumes; 3500 pamphlets (cataloged); 12 drawers of Royal Commission briefs; 16 drawers of Statistics Canada material. **Subscriptions:** 250 journals and other serials. **Services:** Interlibrary loans; copying; library open to public for reference use only. **Also Known As:** Association Canadienne d'Etudes Fiscales. **Staff:** Ronald K. MacLeod, Asst.Libn.

★2280★
CANADIAN TEACHERS' FEDERATION - GEORGE G. CROSKERY MEMORIAL LIBRARY (Educ)
110 Argyle Ave.   Phone: (613) 232-1505
Ottawa, ON, Canada K2P 1B4   Geraldine Channon, Dir., Res. & Info.Serv.
Founded: 1953. **Staff:** Prof 2; Other 2. **Subjects:** Education, research, economics and finance, teachers, teacher welfare, curriculum, labour relations, sociology, psychology. **Holdings:** 7000 books; 24 VF drawers and 200 boxes of documents and clippings; 220 reels of microfilmed back periodicals; 5000 microfiche. **Subscriptions:** 250 journals and other serials; 10 newspapers. **Services:** Interlibrary loans; copying; library open to public. **Publications:** Bibliographies, 5/year. **Also Known As:** Federation Canadienne des Enseignants. **Staff:** Marita Moll, Prog.Asst.; Ghyslaine Faubert, Lib.Techn.

★2281★
CANADIAN TELEPHONE EMPLOYEES' ASSOCIATION - LIBRARY (Soc Sci)
Place du Canada, Rm. 1465   Phone: (514) 861-9963
Montreal, PQ, Canada H3B 2N2   Miss E.A. Fenton, Gen.Sec.
Founded: 1945. **Staff:** Prof 1. **Subjects:** Labor relations, trade unions. **Holdings:** 200 books; CTEA publications. **Subscriptions:** 10 journals and other serials. **Services:** Library open to public.

CANADIAN THEOLOGICAL SEMINARY
See: Canadian Bible College/Canadian Theological Seminary

★2282★
CANADIAN THOROUGHBRED HORSE SOCIETY - LIBRARY (Rec)
Box 172   Phone: (416) 675-3602
Rexdale, ON, Canada M9W 5L1   D.M. Amos, Mgr.
Staff: Prof 1. **Subjects:** Thoroughbred horses. **Holdings:** Broodmare record books, daily racing form chart books, name charts on microfiche; pedigrees. **Subscriptions:** 12 journals and other serials. **Services:** Library open to public. **Publications:** C.T.H.S. Newsletter, bimonthly.

★2283★
CANADIAN TOBACCO MANUFACTURERS COUNCIL - LIBRARY (Med)
1808 Sherbrooke St., W.   Phone: (514) 937-7428
Montreal, PQ, Canada H3H 1E5   Myrna Cain, Council Libn.
Founded: 1973. **Staff:** Prof 1. **Subjects:** Smoking and health, tobacco, environment, pollution, biology, agriculture. **Holdings:** 520 books; 46 bound periodical volumes; 180 binders of clippings; 8 VF drawers of motion pictures and tapes; 80 boxes of reports; 20 boxes of pamphlets. **Subscriptions:** 130 journals and other serials; 20 newspapers. **Services:** Interlibrary loans; copying; library open to public by appointment only. **Formerly:** Its Smoking & Health Library.

CANADIAN TRANSPORT COMMISSION
See: Canada - Canadian Transport Commission

★2284★
CANADIAN TROTTING ASSOCIATION - STANDARDBRED CANADA LIBRARY (Rec)
233 Evans Ave.   Phone: (416) 252-3565
Toronto, ON, Canada M8Z 1J6   Margaret Neal, Coord. & Info.Spec.
Staff: Prof 1; Other 2. **Subjects:** Harness racing, standardbred horse breeding. **Special Collections:** Worldwide stud books; photographs; turf journals, current and historical. **Holdings:** 495 books and bound periodical volumes; 200 other cataloged items; 26 VF drawers of unbound periodicals; 1 drawer of microfiche; 4 VF drawers of photographs; 4 VF drawers of clippings; 1 filing drawer of historical race programs; oral history cassettes; films; videotapes. **Subscriptions:** 22 journals and other serials. **Services:** Library open to public. **Publications:** Trot Magazine - for sale.

★2285★
CANADIAN UNION COLLEGE - LIBRARY (Rel-Theol)
Box 430   Phone: (403) 782-6461
College Heights, AB, Canada T0C 0Z0   Keith H. Clouten, Libn.
Staff: Prof 2; Other 3. **Subjects:** Religion, social sciences, science. **Special Collections:** Seventh-Day Adventist history and publications. **Holdings:** 29,000 books; 5000 bound periodical volumes; films, tapes, records, curriculum materials; 300 maps. **Subscriptions:** 350 journals and other serials; 9 newspapers. **Services:** Interlibrary loans; library open to public.

CANADIAN UTILITIES LIMITED - CANADIAN WESTERN NATURAL GAS COMPANY LIMITED
See: Canadian Western Gas Company Limited

★2286★
CANADIAN UTILITIES LIMITED - LIBRARY (Energy)
10040 104th St.   Phone: (403) 420-7039
Edmonton, AB, Canada T5J 2V6   Donna I. Humphries, Libn.
Staff: Prof 2. **Subjects:** Public utilities, gas and electricity, engineering, management. **Holdings:** 4000 books; 500 annual reports; 200 standards; 3 VF drawers of pamphlets, clippings and technical papers. **Subscriptions:** 250 journals and other serials. **Services:** Interlibrary loans; copying; library open to public with restrictions. **Publications:** Library HiLites, semimonthly. **Special Indexes:** KWIC Index.

CANADIAN WAR MUSEUM
See: Canada - National Museums of Canada

★2287★
CANADIAN WESTERN NATURAL GAS COMPANY LIMITED - LIBRARY (Energy)
140 6th Ave., S.W.   Phone: (403) 245-7403
Calgary, AB, Canada T2P 0P6   Shelley J. Weatherhead, Libn.
Staff: Prof 1. **Subjects:** Public utilities, gas. **Holdings:** 2500 books; 3 VF drawers of pamphlets, files and technical papers; 7 VF drawers of annual reports. **Subscriptions:** 120 journals and other serials. **Services:** Interlibrary loans; library open to public with restrictions. **Remarks:** This library is a branch of the Canadian Utilities Limited main library in Edmonton.

★2288★
CANADIAN WILDLIFE FEDERATION - REFERENCE LIBRARY & INFORMATION CENTRE (Env-Cons)
1673 Carling Ave.   Phone: (613) 725-2191
Ottawa, ON, Canada K2A 1C4   Luba Mycio, Pub.Aff.
Founded: 1961. **Staff:** 2. **Subjects:** Wildlife, outdoor recreation, conservation, environment, natural history, energy. **Special Collections:** Canadian Wildlife Federation Archives. **Holdings:** 4000 books; 2500 bound periodical volumes; 215 items in subject file. **Subscriptions:** 42 journals and other serials. **Services:** Interlibrary loans (fee); copying; library open to public for reference use only. **Publications:** List of publications - available on request. **Special Catalogs:** Occasional bibliographies for internal use.

CANADIAN WILDLIFE SERVICE
See: Canada - Canadian Wildlife Service

★2289★
CANADIAN WOOD COUNCIL - LIBRARY (Sci-Tech)
85 Albert St., Suite 800   Phone: (613) 235-7221
Ottawa, ON, Canada K1P 6A4   D.H. Wilson, Dir. of Educ.
Staff: Prof 1; Other 2. **Subjects:** Wood products (technical literature). **Holdings:** 4000 publications; 6 slide cassette programs. **Services:** Library open to public with prior permission. **Publications:** Canadian Wood Construction; Fire Protective Design (both books for sale). **Staff:** Mrs. S. Doherty, Libn.

CANADIANA COLLECTION OF CHILDREN'S BOOKS
See: Toronto Public Library

CANADIANA GALLERY LIBRARY
See: Royal Ontario Museum

CANADORE COLLEGE LIBRARY
See: North Bay College Education Centre - Library

CANAL MUSEUM
See: Pennsylvania Canal Society

★2290★
CANAL MUSEUM - RESEARCH LIBRARY AND DOCUMENTATION CENTER (Trans)
Canal Museum Administration Bldg.
315 E. Water St.   Phone: (315) 471-0593
Syracuse, NY 13202   Todd S. Weseloh, Libn./Archv.
Founded: 1964. **Staff:** Prof 1; Other 2. **Subjects:** Canals - U.S. and foreign, history, economics, engineering, construction and operations; Syracuse local history. **Special Collections:** W.H. Campbell Collection (750 sketches with text of historic subjects in Central New York); N.Y.D.O.T. Collection (enlargement of New York canals, 1834-1918); Rossman Panama Canal Collection; St. Laurence Seaway Collection (construction of the seaway, 1942-1958). **Holdings:** 6500 books and bound periodical volumes; 8000 photographs; 7000 glass plate negatives; 4500 film negatives; 8000 slides; 500 linear feet of manuscript material; 4000 maps and plans; 700 prints; 1600 government documents. **Subscriptions:** 58 journals and other serials. **Services:** Copying; library open to public. **Publications:** Canal Packet, bimonthly - for museum associates.

★2291★
CANATOM INC. - LIBRARY (Sci-Tech; Energy)
Tour de la Bourse, C.P. 420   Phone: (514) 879-4810
Montreal, PQ, Canada H4Z 1K3   Marie-Anna Myers, Chf., Lib.Dept.
Founded: 1973. **Staff:** Prof 1; Other 4. **Subjects:** Nuclear energy; engineering - nuclear, civil, electrical, mechanical; construction. **Holdings:** 7000 books; 440 microfilm cartridges; 3800 pamphlets and reprints; 3500 specifications and standards; 5800 technical reports; 5000 manufacturers' catalogs. **Subscriptions:** 530 journals and other serials. **Services:** Interlibrary loans; copying; library open to public with restrictions. **Computerized Information Services:** CAN/OLE, DIALOG, SDC; computerized serials and circulation. **Publications:** Bulletin, monthly - for internal distribution only. **Remarks:** Library is located at 740 Notre-Dame St., W., Montreal, PQ, H3C 3X6.

★2292★
CANCER CARE, INC. - NATIONAL CANCER FOUNDATION LIBRARY
1 Park Ave.
New York, NY 10016
Defunct

★2293★
CANCER CONTROL AGENCY OF BRITISH COLUMBIA - LIBRARY (Med)†
2656 Heather St.   Phone: (604) 873-6212
Vancouver, BC, Canada V5Z 3J3   David Noble, Libn.
Staff: Prof 1; Other 2. **Subjects:** Radiotherapy, medical oncology, cancer nursing and immunology. **Holdings:** 2113 books; 2028 bound periodical volumes; 80 annual reports. **Subscriptions:** 213 journals and other serials. **Services:** Interlibrary loans; library open to cancer patients and families. **Computerized Information Services:** Online systems. **Publications:** Accession lists. **Also Known As:** British Columbia Cancer Institute.

★2294★
CANCER FEDERATION - LIBRARY (Med)
3530 9th St.   Phone: (714) 684-0508
Riverside, CA 92501   John Steinbacher, Dir.
Staff: 3. **Subjects:** Medicine, cancer, immunology. **Holdings:** Figures not available. **Services:** Library open to public. **Publications:** The Challenge, quarterly - by subscription.

CANCER INFORMATION CLEARINGHOUSE
See: U.S. Natl. Institutes of Health - National Cancer Institute

CANCER INSTITUTE OF ONTARIO
See: Ontario Cancer Institute

★2295★
CANDLER GENERAL HOSPITAL - MEDICAL LIBRARY (Med)
5353 Reynolds St.   Phone: (912) 356-6011
Savannah, GA 31412   Mary V. Fielder, Libn.
Founded: 1972. **Staff:** Prof 1. **Subjects:** Medicine, nursing, hospital administration, rehabilitation. **Holdings:** 800 books; 820 bound periodical volumes; 2 VF drawers of subject files. **Subscriptions:** 118 journals and other serials. **Services:** Interlibrary loans; copying; library not open to public.

★2296★
CANFIELD MEMORIAL LIBRARY - RUSSELL VERMONTIANA COLLECTION (Hist)
                                      Phone: (802) 375-6153
Arlington, VT 05250   Mary Henning, Libn.
Founded: 1956. **Staff:** 4. **Subjects:** History of Vermont, including counties adjoining Vermont in New York, Massachusetts and New Hampshire. **Special Collections:** Account books and journals. **Holdings:** 5000 books; 300 bound periodical volumes; maps; 4500 pamphlets, bulletins, notices; reports - especially regarding towns; 400 manuscript account books, journals, diaries; 5500 manuscript letters, deeds, court records. **Subscriptions:** 5 journals and other serials. **Services:** Library open to public by appointment. **Special Catalogs:** Bound copies of vital statistics of towns in the area; lists of gravestones and many cemeteries. **Staff:** David Thomas, Cur.; Mary Lou Thomas, Cur.

CANMET (Canada Centre for Mineral and Energy Technology)
See: Canada - Energy, Mines & Resources Canada - CANMET

CANNON AIR FORCE BASE (NM)
See: U.S. Air Force Base - Cannon Base Library

CANNON (Earnestine) MEMORIAL LIBRARY
See: Huntsville Memorial Hospital - School of Vocational Nursing - Earnestine Cannon Memorial Library

CANNON (Harry L.) MARINE STUDIES LABORATORY
See: University of Delaware, Newark - College of Marine Studies - Marine Studies Complex Library

★2297★
CANOCEAN RESOURCES LTD. - ENGINEERING LIBRARY (Sci-Tech; Energy)
610 Derwent Way
New Westminster, BC, Canada V3M 5P8   Ronald V. Simmer, Libn.
Staff: Prof 1. **Subjects:** Engineering - petroleum, marine, arctic; diving technology. **Special Collections:** Canadian Arctic environmental conditions; marine engineering in ice conditions. **Holdings:** 1418 books and bound periodical volumes; 300 conference proceedings; 150 internal reports; 350 industrial standards; 600 vendor catalogs. **Subscriptions:** 59 journals and other serials. **Services:** Interlibrary loans; copying; library open to public with restrictions. **Computerized Information Services:** Online systems. **Publications:** Bibliographies. **Formerly:** Lockheed Petroleum Services Ltd.

★2298★
CANTIGNY WAR MEMORIAL MUSEUM OF THE FIRST DIVISION - ARCHIVES ROOM (Mil)
1S151 Winfield Rd.   Phone: (312) 668-5161
Wheaton, IL 60187   Arthur Veysey, Gen.Mgr.
Subjects: Military history. **Special Collections:** Official First Division records of World War I and II. **Holdings:** 1894 books; photographs and documents. **Services:** Open to public.

★2299★
CANTON HISTORICAL SOCIETY - LIBRARY (Hist)
11 Front St.   Phone: (203) 693-2793
Collinsville, CT 06022   Jane L. Goedecke, Libn.
Founded: 1976. **Staff:** Prof 1; Other 1. **Subjects:** Local and state history, Victoriana, Collins Manufacturing Company. **Special Collections:** Collins Company (manufacturers of edge tools) of Collinsville, Connecticut, 1826-1966 (books, manuscripts, brochures, ledgers, patterns). **Holdings:** 154 books and bound periodical volumes; 73 years of annual reports; 30 deeds; 10 scrapbooks; 35 manuscripts; 2 cartons of clippings; 50 unbound magazines of historical interest. **Services:** Library open to public for reference use only. **Publications:** Newsletter, distributed to members. **Special Catalogs:** Catalog of holdings by subject and author (card). **Remarks:** Holdings are approximate. **Staff:** Robert Selb, Museum Cur.

★2300★
CANTON HISTORICAL SOCIETY - LIBRARY
1400 Washington St.
Canton, MA 02021
Subjects: Indian relics, household implements, farm implements, military material, woolen textiles. **Special Collections:** Official town records, 1636 to present; records and maps of towns of Stoughton and Sharon. **Holdings:** 558 books; 11 patents; 600 clippings; 380 pamphlets and documents; 300 programs and manuscripts; 5000 artifacts and photographs (cataloged). **Remarks:** Presently inactive.

★2301★
CAPE ANN HISTORICAL ASSOCIATION - LIBRARY (Hist)
27 Pleasant St.   Phone: (617) 283-0455
Gloucester, MA 01930   Deborah L. Goodwin, Cur.
Subjects: Gloucester - fishing industry, history and genealogy. **Special Collections:** Gordon Thomas Collection (photographs of fishing schooners at the Gloucester waterfront, 1870-1930; 4000 items). **Holdings:** 3000 books; 75 volumes of manuscripts and day books; 3 drawers of clippings; 3 drawers of Cape Ann Artists Archive. **Services:** Library open to public for reference use only. **Special Indexes:** Indexes to photographic and manuscript holdings (card).

★2302★
CAPE BRETON MINERS' MUSEUM - LIBRARY (Sci-Tech; Hist)†
Quarry Point   Phone: (902) 849-4522
Glace Bay, NS, Canada B1A 5T8   Thomas Miller, Cat.
Founded: 1967. **Staff:** 2. **Subjects:** Mining, geology, history, engineering, transportation. **Special Collections:** Institute of Mining Engineers, 1889-1938 (94 volumes); Mines of Nova Scotia reports, 1880 to present; Geological Survey of Canada, 1876-1903 (24 volumes). **Holdings:** 834 books; 187 newspapers; 150 magnetic tapes; 55 documents. **Services:** Interlibrary loans; library open to public with restrictions.

★2303★
CAPE COD MUSEUM OF NATURAL HISTORY - LIBRARY AND INFORMATION CENTER (Sci-Tech)
Main St.   Phone: (617) 896-3867
Brewster, MA 02631   Eileen R. Bush, Libn.
Staff: Prof 1; Other 8. **Subjects:** Natural history, zoology, botany, geology, ornithology. **Special Collections:** Slides of flowers, birds and marine life (500); teachers' collection; archeology collection. **Holdings:** 4000 books; 75 records of sounds of nature; VF drawers of pamphlets and clippings relating to all aspects of natural history. **Subscriptions:** 60 journals and other serials. **Services:** Library open to public with restrictions. **Publications:** Cape Naturalist, quarterly - distributed free to members, sold separately or by subscription.

CAPE COD NATL. SEASHORE
See: U.S. Natl. Park Service

CAPE COUNTY MEMORIAL MEDICAL LIBRARY, INC.
See: St. Francis Medical Center - Cape County Memorial Medical Library, Inc.

CAPE FEAR VALLEY HOSPITAL
See: Cumberland County Hospital System, Inc.

CAPE HATTERAS NATL. SEASHORE
See: U.S. Natl. Park Service

CAPE LOOKOUT NATL. SEASHORE
See: U.S. Natl. Park Service

★2304★
CAPE MAY COUNTY HISTORICAL & GENEALOGICAL SOCIETY - LIBRARY (Hist)
Rte. 9   Phone: (609) 465-3535
Cape May Court House, NJ 08210   Somers Corson, Act.Cur.
Founded: 1927. **Staff:** Prof 4; Other 6. **Subjects:** Local history and genealogy. **Special Collections:** H. Clifford Campion, Jr. Memorial Collection; Edward M. Post and Lewis T. Stevens Memorial Collection; Edmunds Collection. **Holdings:** 500 books; 20 bound periodical volumes; manuscripts; clippings; 31 volumes of New Jersey archives; bound newspapers. **Services:** Copying; library open to nonmembers for a fee. **Publications:** Cape May County, New Jersey Magazine of History & Genealogy, annual; quarterly newsletter. **Special Indexes:** Newspaper Indexes. **Staff:** Dawn M. Greek, Asst.Cur.; Hannah K. Swain, Libn.

CAPE PUBLICATIONS INC. - TODAY NEWSPAPER
See: Today Newspaper

CAPEN MEMORIAL LIBRARY
See: Second Presbyterian Church

CAPITAL BIBLE SEMINARY
See: Washington Bible College/Capital Bible Seminary

★2305★
CAPITAL DISTRICT LIBRARY COUNCIL FOR REFERENCE AND RESEARCH RESOURCES - BIBLIOGRAPHIC CENTER (Info Sci)
91 Fiddlers Lane   Phone: (518) 785-0798
Latham, NY 12110   Charles D. Custer, Exec.Dir.
Founded: 1968. **Staff:** Prof 3; Other 3. **Subjects:** Library networks and consortia, interlibrary cooperation, cooperative acquisitions, data files, library automation and administration. **Special Collections:** CDLC Union Catalog (1 million titles) and the data cards and holdings of the CDLC Union List of Serials (27,000 titles). **Holdings:** 1500 books and bound periodical volumes; 7 VF drawers of reports, directories and subject-related materials. **Subscriptions:** 80 journals and other serials. **Services:** Interlibrary loans; copying; SDI; bibliographic service to CDLC member libraries; library open by appointment to area and referred researchers. **Computerized Information Services:** Online systems; computerized cataloging, interlibrary loan and union list. **Networks/Consortia:** Member of SUNY/OCLC Library Network; New York State Interlibrary Loan Network (NYSILL access point for area libraries). **Publications:** RECAP, quarterly newsletter of CDLC; reports and directories - distributed to institutional and personal members; limited distribution to similar groups. **Special Catalogs:** Union List of Serials and Supplements; Directory of Collection Strengths; Union List of Newspapers; Computer Data Base Directory. **Remarks:** This library is the bibliographic center for the 19 academic libraries, 3 public library systems (65 public libraries) and 22 special libraries which are members of the Council as of May, 1981. **Staff:** Catherine L. Collins, Cat.Libn.; Carol D. Wait, Ser.Libn.

★2306★
CAPITAL DISTRICT PSYCHIATRIC CENTER - LIBRARY (Med)
75 New Scotland Ave.   Phone: (518) 445-6608
Albany, NY 12208   Bill McKewen, Libn.
Founded: 1978. **Staff:** Prof 1; Other 3. **Subjects:** Psychiatry, psychology. **Holdings:** 5000 books; 3600 bound periodical volumes. **Subscriptions:** 172 journals and other serials. **Services:** Interlibrary loans; copying; SDI; library open to allied health personnel. **Computerized Information Services:** BRS, NLM; computerized cataloging. **Networks/Consortia:** Member of Capital District Library Council; New York and New Jersey Regional Medical Library Program; OCLC. **Remarks:** Operated by the Albany Medical College under contract with the Capital District Psychiatric Center.

★2307★
CAPITAL RESEARCH COMPANY - RESEARCH LIBRARY (Bus-Fin)
333 S. Hope St., 51st Fl.   Phone: (213) 486-9261
Los Angeles, CA 90071   S. Kathleen Reilly, Libn.
Staff: Prof 1; Other 4. **Subjects:** Investment, management, corporation records, business and economic conditions, finance. **Holdings:** 1500 books; 500 bound periodical volumes; 6000 company files; 50 industry files.

Subscriptions: 450 journals and other serials; 25 newspapers. **Services:** Interlibrary loans; copying; library open to SLA members and other librarians. **Publications:** Monthly acquisitions list - for internal distribution only. **Special Indexes:** Index of corporate annual reports (card); index of internal reports; subject/industry/geographic index of subscriptions.

★2308★
CAPITAL SYSTEMS GROUP, INC. - LIBRARY (Trans; Info Sci)
11301 Rockville Pike   Phone: (301) 881-9400
Kensington, MD 20895   William A. Creager, Pres.
Founded: 1969. **Staff:** Prof 55; Other 45. **Subjects:** Aviation safety, information technology, petroleum transportation, quality of health care, innovation in scientific communication. **Special Collections:** Complete records of all general aviation accidents in the United States since January, 1969. **Holdings:** Complete file of 15,000 past and present pipeline tariffs for crude petroleum and petroleum products; complete file of textile manufacturers' registration numbers assigned by the Federal Trade Commission. **Subscriptions:** 100 journals and other serials. **Services:** Interlibrary loans; copying; data dissemination; library not open to public. **Computerized Information Services:** SDC, DIALOG, BRS, NLM; internal databases; computerized cataloging and serials. **Publications:** General Aviation Accident Report, weekly; Pipe Line Rates on Crude Petroleum Oil, monthly; Pipe Line Rates on Petroleum Products, monthly; Directory of Online Information Resources; Health Quality and Standards Report, monthly; RN & WPL Directory.

★2309★
CAPITAL SYSTEMS GROUP, INC. - NATIONAL HEALTH STANDARDS AND QUALITY INFORMATION CLEARINGHOUSE (Med)
11301 Rockville Pike   Phone: (301) 881-9400
Kensington, MD 20895   Marion Torchia, Dir.
Staff: Prof 4; Other 2. **Subjects:** Health care - quality assurance, utilization control; MEDICARE standards; survey and certification of health facilities. **Holdings:** 8000 reports, monographs and journal articles. **Subscriptions:** 50 journals and other serials; 40 newspapers. **Services:** Copying; SDI; clearinghouse not open to public. **Computerized Information Services:** Online systems; internal database. **Publications:** NHSQIC Information Bulletin, monthly newsletter; NHSQIC topical bibliography series. **Remarks:** Clearinghouse is operated under a contract from U.S. Dept. of Health and Human Services - Health Care Financing Administration.

★2310★
CAPITAL TIMES NEWSPAPER - LIBRARY (Publ)†
1901 Fish Hatchery Rd.
Box 8060
Madison, WI 53708   Phone: (608) 252-6412
                                    Ann Lund, Libn.
Staff: Prof 1; Other 1. **Subjects:** Subjects of current interest, local and state. **Holdings:** 200 books; 400 drawers of clippings; 10 drawers of photographs; Capital Times, 1917 to present, on microfilm. **Services:** Interlibrary loans by special arrangement; copying by special arrangement; library open to public with restrictions.

★2311★
CAPITAL UNIVERSITY - CHEMISTRY LIBRARY (Sci-Tech)
2199 E. Main St.   Phone: (614) 236-6500
Columbus, OH 43209   Albert F. Maag, Univ.Libn.
Founded: 1959. **Staff:** Prof 1; Other 1. **Subjects:** Chemistry. **Holdings:** 1785 books; 2400 bound periodical volumes. **Subscriptions:** 22 journals and other serials. **Services:** Copying; library open to public for reference use only. **Networks/Consortia:** Member of OHIONET.

CAPITAL UNIVERSITY - FEDERATION FOR UNIFIED SCIENCE EDUCATION
See: Federation for Unified Science Education

★2312★
CAPITAL UNIVERSITY - LAW SCHOOL LIBRARY (Law)
665 S. High St.   Phone: (614) 445-8634
Columbus, OH 43215   Leverett L. Preble, III, Hd. Law Libn./Prof.
Staff: Prof 6; Other 6. **Subjects:** Law, legal research. **Holdings:** 50,000 books; 12,000 bound periodical volumes; 78,000 other cataloged items; microforms. **Subscriptions:** 590 journals and other serials; 6 newspapers. **Services:** Interlibrary loans; copying; library open to public for reference use only. **Computerized Information Services:** LEXIS; computerized cataloging. **Networks/Consortia:** Member of OCLC. **Publications:** Readers' Guide, annual - for students only. **Staff:** William Newman, Ph.D., Asst. Law Libn.; Eileen Gruver, Asst. Law Libn.; Julee Pittman, Hd.Cat.; Val Bolen, Ph.D., Ref.Libn.; Nancy Miller, Ref.Libn.

★2313★
CAPITOL INSTITUTION OF TECHNOLOGY - CAPITOL TECH LIBRARY (Sci-Tech)
10335 Kensington Pkwy.   Phone: (301) 933-2599
Kensington, MD 20895   Patricia H. Wissinger, Libn.
Founded: 1932. **Staff:** Prof 1; Other 1. **Subjects:** Electronics engineering, computer science, mathematics. **Holdings:** 9000 books; 111 bound periodical volumes; 8 VF drawers. **Subscriptions:** 106 journals and other serials. **Services:** Interlibrary loans; copying; library not open to public. **Computerized Information Services:** Computerized acquisitions. **Networks/Consortia:** Member of Maryland Interlibrary Loan Organization (MILO); Interlibrary Users Association.

★2314★
CAPLIN & DRYSDALE - LIBRARY (Law)
1101 17th St., N.W., Suite 1100   Phone: (202) 862-5073
Washington, DC 20036   Karen M. Meyer, Law Libn.
Founded: 1964. **Staff:** Prof 2. **Subjects:** Law. **Holdings:** 12,000 books; 3000 bound periodical volumes. **Services:** Interlibrary loans; library not open to public. **Staff:** Ann Cromwell, Leg.Libn.

CAPS
See: ERIC Clearinghouse on Counseling and Personnel Services

★2315★
CARBON COUNTY LAW LIBRARY (Law)
Court House   Phone: (717) 325-3111
Jim Thorpe, PA 18229   Benjamin A. Lesniak, Libn.
Staff: 1. **Subjects:** Law. **Holdings:** 13,587 volumes. **Subscriptions:** 33 journals and other serials. **Services:** Copying; library open to public.

CARDEZA FOUNDATION
See: Jefferson (Thomas) University

CARDINAL BERAN LIBRARY
See: St. Mary's Seminary

★2316★
CARDINAL CUSHING GENERAL HOSPITAL - STAFF LIBRARY (Med)
235 N. Pearl St.   Phone: (617) 588-4000
Brockton, MA 02401   Nancy Sezak, Med.Libn.
Staff: 2. **Subjects:** Medicine. **Holdings:** 574 books; 941 bound periodical volumes; 340 unbound journals; 227 audiotape cassettes; 2 drawers of pamphlets and reprints. **Subscriptions:** 108 journals and other serials. **Services:** Interlibrary loans; copying (limited); library open to public with permission. **Networks/Consortia:** Member of Southeastern Massachusetts Health Sciences Libraries.

CARDINAL SPELLMAN LIBRARY
See: Friars of the Atonement

★2317★
CARDINAL SPELLMAN PHILATELIC MUSEUM, INC. - LIBRARY (Rec)
235 Wellesley St.   Phone: (617) 894-6735
Weston, MA 02193   Ruth Koved, Libn.
Founded: 1960. **Staff:** Prof 1; Other 2. **Subjects:** Philately; postal service. **Holdings:** 6300 books; 2100 bound periodical volumes; 1900 pamphlets (cataloged); 2500 volumes of auction catalogs (cataloged); 4430 unbound periodical volumes (cataloged); 2 VF drawers of pamphlets, clippings and documents. **Subscriptions:** 83 journals and other serials. **Services:** Interlibrary loans; copying; library open to public with permission of museum director.

CAREY (William) LIBRARY
See: New Orleans Baptist Theological Seminary - John T. Christian Library

★2318★
CARGILL, INC. - INFORMATION CENTER (Agri; Bus-Fin)
Box 9300   Phone: (612) 475-6498
Minneapolis, MN 55440   Julia Peterson, Mgr.
Staff: Prof 3; Other 3. **Subjects:** Grain storage and handling; commodity trading; agribusiness; finance; marketing; biochemistry; hybrid corn breeding and genetics; animal feeding and nutrition; vegetable oils - processing, chemistry; agricultural and food products; market research. **Holdings:** 10,000 books; 500 bound periodical volumes; 250 other items (cataloged); 7500 internal research reports; 2000 general information files; 300 vertical boxes (16,000 documents); 6 drawers of microforms. **Subscriptions:** 700 journals and other serials; 20 newspapers. **Services:** Interlibrary loans; copying; library open to graduate students or researchers by appointment only. **Computerized**

Information Services: DIALOG, SDC, New York Times Information Service, Dow Jones News Retrieval, NLM, Control Data Corporation, Mead Data Central, BRS; internal database; computerized cataloging and serials. **Networks/Consortia:** Member of OCLC; MINITEX. **Publications:** Monthly summary reports on research work to management; special bibliographies to company personnel; Recent Acquisitions List, bimonthly; Database Directory; Information Resources for Merchants. **Special Indexes:** Termatrex index - 10,000 items. **Staff:** Maggie Hansen, Res.Libn.; Sidnie Ross, Res.Libn.

★2319★
CARIBBEAN CENTER FOR ADVANCED STUDIES - LIBRARY (Soc Sci)
Minillas Sta., Box 41246   Phone: (809) 725-2458
Santurce, PR 00940   Betsaida Velez, Hd.Libn.
Founded: 1961. **Staff:** Prof 3; Other 5. **Subjects:** Psychology, Caribbean studies, social sciences. **Holdings:** 7000 books; 125 bound periodical volumes. **Subscriptions:** 87 journals and other serials; 4 newspapers. **Services:** Interlibrary loans; copying; library open to public for reference use only.

★2320★
CARIBBEAN REGIONAL LIBRARY (Area-Ethnic)
UPR Sta., Box 21927   Phone: (809) 764-0000
San Juan, PR 00931   Carmen M. Costa-Ramos, Dir.
Founded: 1946. **Staff:** Prof 1; Other 5. **Subjects:** The Caribbean - economics, agriculture, statistics, trade, tourism, education, political science, demography. **Special Collections:** Rare books on the Caribbean. **Holdings:** 117,000 volumes; 12 VF drawers of studies; 20 VF drawers of minutes of the Caribbean Organization and Caribbean Commission Meetings; pamphlets and official documents. **Subscriptions:** 220 journals and other serials; 12 newspapers. **Services:** Interlibrary loans; copying; bibliographies; library open to public for reference use only. **Publications:** Current Caribbean Bibliography, irregular - available on exchange or sale basis. **Remarks:** The library is located at the University of Puerto Rico, General Library, Rio Piedras.

CARIBBEAN RESEARCH CENTRE
See: Universite de Montreal - Centre de Recherches Caraibes

CARIBBEAN RESEARCH INSTITUTE
See: College of the Virgin Islands

★2321★
CARLE FOUNDATION HOSPITAL - LIBRARY (Med)
611 W. Park St.   Phone: (217) 337-3011
Urbana, IL 61801   Uden Rutter, Mgr., Lib.Serv.
Staff: Prof 1; Other 3. **Subjects:** Medicine and medical specialties. **Holdings:** 1020 books; 3590 bound periodical volumes. **Subscriptions:** 329 journals and other serials. **Services:** Interlibrary loans; copying; library open to public with restrictions. **Computerized Information Services:** MEDLINE. **Networks/Consortia:** Member of Champaign-Urbana Consortia; Regional Medical Library - Region 3; ILLINET. **Publications:** Selected Papers of the Carle Clinic and Carle Foundation, semiannual; CARLE NEWS, biweekly.

★2322★
CARLETON COLLEGE - SCIENCE LIBRARY (Sci-Tech)
                                            Phone: (507) 663-4415
Northfield, MN 55057   Elizabeth K. Tomlinson, Assoc.Sci.Libn.
Staff: Prof 1; Other 1. **Subjects:** Geology, physics, biology, chemistry. **Holdings:** 8000 books; 12,000 bound periodical volumes; microforms. **Subscriptions:** 237 journals and other serials. **Services:** Interlibrary loans; copying; SDI; library open to public with restrictions. **Computerized Information Services:** SDC; computerized cataloging. **Networks/Consortia:** Member of MINITEX. **Publications:** Acquisitions Bulletin, monthly.

CARLETON COUNTY LAW LIBRARY
See: County of Carleton Law Association

★2323★
CARLETON MEMORIAL HOSPITAL - HEALTH SCIENCES LIBRARY (Med)
Box 400   Phone: (506) 328-3391
Woodstock, NB, Canada E0J 2B0   Joanne E. Rosevear, Dir.
Founded: 1977. **Staff:** Prof 1; Other 1. **Subjects:** Medicine and allied health sciences. **Special Collections:** Archives. **Holdings:** 3500 books; 65 bound periodical volumes; 90 cassettes. **Subscriptions:** 65 journals and other serials; 5 newspapers. **Services:** Interlibrary loans; copying; library open to public with restrictions. **Staff:** Marilyn Sherman, Lib.Techn.

★2324★
CARLETON UNIVERSITY - MACODRUM LIBRARY - MAP LIBRARY (Geog-Map)
D299 Loeb Bldg., Colonel By Drive   Phone: (613) 231-4392
Ottawa, ON, Canada K1S 5B6   Barbara E. Farrell, Map Libn.
Founded: 1966. **Staff:** Prof 1; Other 2. **Subjects:** Geography, maps and atlases. **Special Collections:** Zaborski Collection of Maps of USSR and Eastern Europe (8000). **Holdings:** 600 books; 100,000 sheet maps; 800 atlases; 300 wall maps; 15 shelves of pamphlets; 25 reels of microfilmed atlases and maps; 27 microfiche of map catalogues and gazetteers; 2000 slides. **Subscriptions:** 30 journals and other serials. **Services:** Interlibrary loans; copying; library open to public. **Publications:** Acquisition lists; search aids, both irregular - both for internal distribution only.

★2325★
CARLETON UNIVERSITY - NORMAN PATERSON SCHOOL OF INTERNATIONAL AFFAIRS - RESOURCE CENTRE (Soc Sci)
Colonel By Drive   Phone: (613) 231-7182
Ottawa, ON, Canada K1B 5B6   Rede Widstrand, Coord.
Staff: Prof 1; Other 2. **Subjects:** International affairs, conflict analysis, international development and integration, foreign policy, strategy and security. **Special Collections:** Unpublished papers from conferences and research organizations (3000 papers). **Holdings:** 900 books; 1500 pamphlets (cataloged). **Subscriptions:** 380 journals and other serials; 10 newspapers. **Services:** SDI; centre open to public for reference use only. **Publications:** Bibliography series, irregular - available for purchase.

CARLSBAD CAVERNS NATL. PARK
See: U.S. Natl. Park Service

★2326★
CARLSBAD CITY LIBRARY - SPECIAL COLLECTIONS DEPARTMENT (Hist)
1250 Elm Ave.   Phone: (619) 438-5614
Carlsbad, CA 92008   Clifford E. Lange, Lib.Dir.
Subjects: Southwest history; China - history, description and travel. **Special Collections:** Southwest History (1300 volumes); Large Print Collection (2158 volumes); Spanish Collection (855 volumes); Patterns Collection (2156 items); Genealogy (7261 volumes); Toy Lending Library (250 items). **Holdings:** 139,435 books; 52,083 periodicals and newspapers in microform. **Services:** Interlibrary loans; copying; department open to public. **Computerized Information Services:** Computerized cataloging and circulation. **Special Catalogs:** Pattern Catalog (book); college catalogs (microfiche).

CARLSEN MEMORIAL LIBRARY
See: St. Olaf Lutheran Church

★2327★
CARLSMITH, CARLSMITH, WICHMAN & CASE - LIBRARY (Law)†
121 Waianuenue Ave.
Box 686   Phone: (808) 935-6644
Hilo, HI 96720   Raymond K. Hasegawa, Att.
Staff: Prof 1; Other 1. **Subjects:** Law. **Holdings:** 11,300 books; 100 bound periodical volumes; 10 VF drawers of legislative material; 1 VF drawer of pamphlets; 3 shelves of pamphlets. **Subscriptions:** 225 journals and other serials. **Services:** Library not open to public. **Special Indexes:** Index of current unbound Hawaii Supreme Court decisions (card). **Staff:** Hannah Nardini, Libn.

★2328★
CARLSON COMPANIES - LIBRARY (Bus-Fin)
12755 State Hwy. 55   Phone: (612) 540-5236
Minneapolis, MN 55441   Stella M. Rosow, Libn.
Founded: 1962. **Staff:** Prof 1; Other 1. **Subjects:** Business and finance, advertising, law, hotels and restaurants, catalog showrooms. **Holdings:** 1682 books; 100 pamphlets (cataloged); 16 VF drawers of company promotions and advertising materials. **Subscriptions:** 494 journals and other serials; 11 newspapers. **Services:** Interlibrary loans; copying; library not open to public.

CARLSON LIBRARY
See: University of Rochester

CARLSON MEMORIAL HEALTH SCIENCES LIBRARY
See: Park City Hospital

★2329★
CARLSON PROPERTIES, INC. - SECURITY LIFE LAW LIBRARY
1820 Security Life Bldg.
Denver, CO 80202
Defunct

CARLSON (Rena M.) LIBRARY
See: Clarion State College - Rena M. Carlson Library

CARLSON (William S.) LIBRARY
See: University of Toledo - Ward M. Canaday Center

★2330★
CARLTON, FIELDS, WARD, EMMANUEL, SMITH & CUTLER, P.A. - LIBRARY (Law)
610 N. Florida Ave., 20th Fl.
Exchange Bldg.   Phone: (813) 223-5366
Tampa, FL 33602   Donald G. Ziegenfuss, Law Libn.
Staff: Prof 1; Other 3. **Subjects:** Law. **Holdings:** 20,000 books and bound periodical volumes; memoranda and briefs (cataloged). **Subscriptions:** 120 journals and other serials; 10 newspapers. **Services:** Interlibrary loans; library open to lawyers. **Remarks:** Firm has branch libraries in Orlando, Pensacola and Tallahasee, FL.

★2331★
CARMEL UNITED PRESBYTERIAN CHURCH - MEMORIAL LIBRARY (Rel-Theol)
100 Edge Hill Rd.   Phone: (215) 887-1074
Glenside, PA 19038   Mrs. James T. Eaton, Libn.
Founded: 1943. **Subjects:** Religion, history, art, fiction. **Holdings:** 12,000 books. **Services:** Interlibrary loans (limited); library open to those regularly attending meetings in building.

★2332★
CARMELITANA COLLECTION (Rel-Theol)
1600 Webster St., N.E.   Phone: (202) 526-1221
Washington, DC 20017   Calvin Alderson, O.C., Dir.
Founded: 1948. **Staff:** Prof 1. **Subjects:** Carmelite order - history, Teresa of Avila, biography. **Special Collections:** Baptist of Mantua. **Holdings:** 7700 books; 995 bound periodical volumes; 100 reels of microfilmed medieval texts. **Subscriptions:** 33 journals and other serials. **Services:** Interlibrary loans; copying; library open to researchers from universities. **Special Catalogs:** Printed catalog (1958). **Remarks:** Maintained by the Carmelite Order of the Roman Catholic Church.

★2333★
CARMELITE MONASTERY - LIBRARY AND ARCHIVES (Rel-Theol)
1318 Dulaney Valley Rd.   Phone: (301) 823-7415
Baltimore, MD 21204   Sr. Constance Fitz Gerald, O.C.D., Archv.
Founded: 1790. **Staff:** 2. **Subjects:** Discalced Carmelite history and spirituality; Scripture; Catholic spirituality and theology; Roman Catholic missals and breviaries; biographies of the saints. **Special Collections:** Works of St. Teresa of Avila and St. John of the Cross in various languages; archives of the first community of Roman Catholic nuns in the Thirteen Colonies (founded in 1790) and other material relating to the history of the Catholic Church in the United States; Durham collection (extensive papers related to lawsuit). **Holdings:** 1000 volumes. **Services:** Library generally not open to public; access to archives limited and only by request.

★2334★
CARMELITE MONASTERY - LIBRARY OF THE IMMACULATE HEART OF MARY (Rel-Theol)
Beckley Hill   Phone: (802) 476-8362
Barre, VT 05641   Sr. Jeanne M. Gonyon, Libn.
Founded: 1950. **Staff:** Prof 1; Other 3. **Subjects:** Scripture, modern theology, philosophy, psychology, Carmelite spirituality, ecclesiology, social sciences, literature, biography of saints. **Special Collections:** Works of St. John of the Cross, St. Teresa of Jesus. **Holdings:** 5000 books; 400 bound periodical volumes; 4 VF drawers of reports of General Chapters, special meetings and unpublished material related to post Vatican II renewal. **Subscriptions:** 40 journals and other serials; 10 newspapers. **Services:** Interlibrary loans; library open to public with restrictions.

★2335★
CARNATION COMPANY - LIBRARY (Food-Bev; Bus-Fin)†
5045 Wilshire Blvd.   Phone: (213) 932-6558
Los Angeles, CA 90036   Vicki C. Giella, Info.Ctr.Coord.
Subjects: Food, marketing, business. **Holdings:** 100 books; 6 VF drawers of clippings; reports and documents. **Subscriptions:** 52 journals and other serials. **Services:** Copying; library not open to public. **Computerized Information Services:** DIALOG.

★2336★
CARNATION RESEARCH LABORATORIES - LIBRARY (Food-Bev)
8015 Van Nuys Blvd.   Phone: (213) 787-7820
Van Nuys, CA 91412   Kathryn A. Stewart, Libn.
Founded: 1940. **Staff:** Prof 1; Other 2. **Subjects:** Food science, nutrition, chemistry, biological science, veterinary science. **Special Collections:** Food ingredient suppliers file. **Holdings:** 3700 books; 4306 bound periodical volumes; 15,880 pamphlets, government reports; 4800 U.S. patents; 600 foreign patents. **Subscriptions:** 200 journals and other serials. **Services:** Interlibrary loans; library open to public on request. **Computerized Information Services:** DIALOG, SDC, BRS, NLM; internal technical reports on internal database. **Networks/Consortia:** Member of Metropolitan Cooperative Library System; Pacific Southwest Regional Medical Library Service (PSRMLS). **Publications:** Research Ripples, irregular - for internal distribution only; Current Awareness, weekly - for internal distribution only; Guide to the Library, annual; serial holdings, annual; Acquisitions List, quarterly.

★2337★
CARNEGIE ENDOWMENT FOR INTERNATIONAL PEACE - LIBRARY - NEW YORK (Soc Sci)
30 Rockefeller Plaza, 54th Fl.   Phone: (212) 572-8208
New York, NY 10020   Vivian D. Hewitt, Libn.
Founded: 1953. **Staff:** Prof 1; Other 2. **Subjects:** International affairs, international organization, pre-crisis fact finding, foreign relations of the U.S. with other countries. **Special Collections:** United Nations documents; Carnegie Endowment publications. **Holdings:** 5000 books; 15 VF drawers of uncataloged pamphlets. **Subscriptions:** 250 journals and other serials; 15 newspapers. **Services:** Interlibrary loans; copying; library not open to public. **Networks/Consortia:** Member of Consortium of Foundation Libraries; METRO.

★2338★
CARNEGIE FOUNDATION FOR THE ADVANCEMENT OF TEACHING - LIBRARY (Educ)
11 Dupont Circle, Suite 130   Phone: (202) 797-3650
Washington, DC 20036   Aletta Scuka, Libn.
Staff: Prof 1; Other 1. **Subjects:** Higher and secondary education; employment. **Holdings:** 3000 books; 200 boxes of vertical files; 80 volumes of the foundation's annual reports. **Subscriptions:** 111 journals and other serials. **Services:** Copying; library open to public by appointment.

★2339★
CARNEGIE INSTITUTION OF WASHINGTON - DEPARTMENT OF EMBRYOLOGY - LIBRARY (Sci-Tech)
115 W. University Pkwy.   Phone: (301) 467-1414
Baltimore, MD 21210
Staff: Prof 1. **Subjects:** Embryology, biochemistry. **Holdings:** 1275 books; 1800 bound periodical volumes; 775 periodicals. **Subscriptions:** 55 journals and other serials. **Services:** Copying (limited); library open to public.

★2340★
CARNEGIE INSTITUTION OF WASHINGTON - DEPARTMENT OF PLANT BIOLOGY - LIBRARY (Sci-Tech)
290 Panama   Phone: (415) 325-1521
Stanford, CA 94305   Dr. Jeanette S. Brown, Dir.
Founded: 1930. **Subjects:** Botany, plant physiology, biophysics, plant ecology, photosynthesis. **Special Collections:** Institute publications (200); reprint collections for photosynthesis and plant taxonomy. **Holdings:** 2000 books; 1130 bound periodical volumes; 64 volumes in Jens Clausen Memorial Library; 73 bound yearbooks. **Subscriptions:** 50 journals and other serials. **Services:** Copying; library open to public by appointment. **Computerized Information Services:** Plantbio bibliographic file (internal database). **Publications:** Year Book, annual - to scientists in biology and related fields.

★2341★
CARNEGIE INSTITUTION OF WASHINGTON - GEOPHYSICAL LABORATORY LIBRARY (Sci-Tech)
2801 Upton St., N.W.   Phone: (202) 966-0334
Washington, DC 20008   Dolores M. Petry, Libn.
Founded: 1908. **Staff:** 1. **Subjects:** Geochemistry, petrology, mineralogy, crystallography, geology, geophysics. **Special Collections:** Geophysical Laboratory reprints. **Holdings:** 3500 volumes. **Subscriptions:** 125 journals and other serials. **Services:** Interlibrary loans; copying; library not open to public.

★2342★
CARNEGIE INSTITUTION OF WASHINGTON - LIBRARY (Sci-Tech)
1530 P St., N.W.   Phone: (202) 387-6411
Washington, DC 20005   Pat Parratt, Libn.
Founded: 1903. **Staff:** Prof 2. **Subjects:** Astronomy, geophysics, botany, embryology, genetics, archaeology. **Special Collections:** All publications of the Carnegie Institution of Washington. **Holdings:** 1000 books; 195 bound periodical volumes; 333 reels of microfilm; SCIENCE (January, 1902 to present), NATURE (November, 1901 to present). **Services:** Interlibrary loans; open to public with restrictions. **Remarks:** This library serves primarily as a depository for publications of the Carnegie Institution of Washington.

★2343★
CARNEGIE INSTITUTION OF WASHINGTON - MOUNT WILSON & LAS CAMPANAS OBSERVATORIES - LIBRARY (Sci-Tech)
813 Santa Barbara St.   Phone: (213) 577-1122
Pasadena, CA 91101   Joan Gantz, Libn.
Founded: 1905. **Staff:** Prof 1. **Subjects:** Astronomy, astrophysics, physics. **Special Collections:** History of science; Newtoniana. **Holdings:** 26,000 volumes; 100 bound periodical volumes; observatory publications. **Services:** Copying; library open to public for reference use only by appointment.

★2344★
CARNEGIE INSTITUTION OF WASHINGTON - TERRESTRIAL MAGNETISM DEPARTMENT LIBRARY (Sci-Tech)
5241 Broad Branch Rd., N.W.   Phone: (202) 966-0863
Washington, DC 20015   Dorothy B. Dillin, Libn.
Subjects: Astrophysics, planetary physics, geophysics, seismology, geochemistry, nuclear and atomic physics, terrestrial magnetism. **Holdings:** 49,400 books, bound periodical volumes, pamphlets. **Services:** Interlibrary loans; library open to scientific institutions and government bureaus only. **Publications:** Annual reports; reprints.

★2345★
CARNEGIE LIBRARY - HENDERSON ROOM (Hist)
607 Broad St.   Phone: (404) 291-7568
Rome, GA 30161   Beatrice Millican, Spec.Coll.Libn.
Founded: 1911. **Staff:** Prof 5; Other 12. **Subjects:** Cherokee Indians, Georgia and local history, genealogy, Southern history. **Special Collections:** J.F. Brooks Cherokeeana Collection (401 books); Ellen Louise Axson Wilson Collection; John L. Harris Papers (3 VF drawers); George M. Battey, III Papers (5 VF drawers). **Holdings:** 6909 books; 552 bound periodical volumes; 30 VF drawers; 161 maps; 6183 microforms; 300 unbound magazines. **Subscriptions:** 71 journals and other serials. **Services:** Interlibrary loans; copying; library open to public with restrictions. **Remarks:** Carnegie Library is an affiliate of the Tri-County Regional Library. **Staff:** Emily H. Bradley, Asst.Libn.

★2346★
CARNEGIE LIBRARY OF PITTSBURGH - BUSINESS DIVISION (Bus-Fin)
Frick Bldg. Mezzanine
437 Grant St.   Phone: (412) 281-5945
Pittsburgh, PA 15219   Miriam S. Lerch, Div.Hd.
Founded: 1924. **Staff:** Prof 7; Other 2. **Subjects:** Investments, accounting, real estate, small business, insurance, banking, management, advertising. **Special Collections:** Foreign and state industrial and trade directories. **Holdings:** 8250 books and bound periodical volumes; 550 state and county industrial directories; 950 telephone directories; 100 boxes and 56 VF drawers of pamphlets; 5 services; 1000 reels of microfilm. **Subscriptions:** 80 journals and other serials; 6 newspapers. **Services:** Interlibrary loans; copying; library open to public. **Computerized Information Services:** DIALOG, SDC, Dow Jones News Retrieval, New York Times Information Service, WESTLAW; computerized cataloging. **Networks/Consortia:** Member of OCLC; Pittsburgh Regional Library Center. **Staff:** Carol A. Berthold, Asst.Div.Hd.; Selma Mellinger, Libn.; Eileen Grosh, Libn.

★2347★
CARNEGIE LIBRARY OF PITTSBURGH - CENTRAL CHILDREN'S ROOM HISTORICAL COLLECTION (Hum)
4400 Forbes Ave.   Phone: (412) 622-3122
Pittsburgh, PA 15213   Amy Kellman, Hd., Ch.Dept.
Staff: Prof 4; Other 4. **Subjects:** Folklore; 19th and 20th century children's literature. **Special Collections:** Alice Wirth Wirsing Collection. **Holdings:** 1910 books; 90 bound periodical volumes. **Services:** Copying; library open to public with restrictions. **Computerized Information Services:** Computerized cataloging. **Networks/Consortia:** Member of OCLC; Pittsburgh Regional Library Center. **Staff:** Mary Richardson, Libn.; Lea Blumenfeld, Libn.; Andrea Jones, Libn.

★2348★
CARNEGIE LIBRARY OF PITTSBURGH - MUSIC AND ART DEPARTMENT (Mus; Art)
4400 Forbes Ave.   Phone: (412) 622-3105
Pittsburgh, PA 15213   Ida Reed, Dept.Hd.
Founded: 1938. **Staff:** Prof 7; Other 10. **Subjects:** Music (including scores and parts); architecture; history of costume; painting; sculpture. **Special Collections:** Bernd Architectural Collection; Fashion Group Costume Collection; Boyd Memorial Collection (music and musicology); Merz Music Library (notable collection of 19th century American and German music journals). **Holdings:** 75,000 books; 60,000 volumes of music (cataloged); 30 VF drawers of clippings and pamphlets; 300,000 mounted pictures; 90,000 slides; 30,000 phonograph records. **Subscriptions:** 142 journals and other serials. **Services:** Interlibrary loans; copying; library open to public. **Computerized Information Services:** Computerized cataloging. **Networks/Consortia:** Member of OCLC; Pittsburgh Regional Library Center. **Staff:** Margaret C. Dusch, Asst.Dept.Hd.; Kirby Oilworth, Libn.; Deborah Greene, Libn.; A. Catherine Tack, Libn.; Ann Safley, Libn.; Katherine Kepes, Libn.

★2349★
CARNEGIE LIBRARY OF PITTSBURGH - PENNSYLVANIA DIVISION (Hist)
4400 Forbes Ave.   Phone: (412) 622-3154
Pittsburgh, PA 15213   Maria Zini, Hd.
Founded: 1928. **Staff:** Prof 3; Other 2. **Subjects:** Pennsylvania history, biography, economics and sociology, with emphasis on Pittsburgh and western Pennsylvania; genealogy; heraldry. **Special Collections:** Carnegie Collection (books and pamphlets written by and about Andrew Carnegie); Isaac Craig manuscripts; Pittsburgh Photographic Library. **Holdings:** 16,000 volumes; 100 VF drawers of clippings and pamphlets; 40,000 photographs; 8500 reels of microfilm. **Subscriptions:** 46 journals and other serials. **Services:** Copying. **Computerized Information Services:** Computerized cataloging. **Networks/Consortia:** Member of OCLC; Pittsburgh Regional Library Center. **Staff:** Lucille A. Tomko, Asst.Div.Hd.; Ann M. Loyd, Ref.Libn.

★2350★
CARNEGIE LIBRARY OF PITTSBURGH - SCIENCE AND TECHNOLOGY DEPARTMENT (Sci-Tech)
4400 Forbes Ave.   Phone: (412) 622-3138
Pittsburgh, PA 15213   Catherine Brosky, Hd.
Founded: 1895. **Staff:** Prof 9; Other 6. **Subjects:** Chemistry, physics, engineering, technology, geology, metallurgy, botany, biology, zoology. **Special Collections:** Complete sets of U.S. and British patent specifications and drawings; U.S. topographic maps, geologic maps, folios of the geologic atlas of the U.S.; soil surveys and maps; American National Standards (ANSI); British Standards (BSI); U. S. military and federal specifications; Brutcher translations; ISI translations; AEC translations; AEC reports; ERDA reports. **Holdings:** 361,814 books; 420,000 bound periodical volumes; 860,000 reels of microfilm and microfiche; 22,000 historical trade catalogs; complete sets of U.S. and British patents; complete sets of U.S. topographic maps. **Subscriptions:** 2300 journals and other serials. **Services:** Interlibrary loans; copying; library open to public. **Computerized Information Services:** DIALOG, SDC; computerized cataloging. **Networks/Consortia:** Member of OCLC; Pittsburgh Regional Library Center. **Publications:** Focus on Sci-Tech, irregular; Science and Technology, a Purchase Guide for Public Libraries, annual. **Staff:** Elizabeth Kinney, Libn.; Margery Peffer, Asst.Hd.; Martha Lyle, Libn.; Robert Matlack, Libn.; David Murdock, Libn.; Joan Anderson, Libn.; Sandra Janicki, Libn.; Dorothy Melamed, Libn.

★2351★
CARNEGIE-MELLON UNIVERSITY - AUDIO VISUAL SERVICES (Aud-Vis)
Hunt Library, Frew St.   Phone: (412) 578-2430
Pittsburgh, PA 15213   Stan Yoder, Hd.
Staff: Prof 3; Other 3. **Subjects:** Architecture, painting, psychology, history. **Special Collections:** Fine arts slide library (85,037 items); educational film library (300 titles). **Services:** Copying; equipment rental; presentation and production services; library open to public for reference use only. **Networks/Consortia:** Member of Pittsburgh Regional Library Center; Pittsburgh Council on Higher Education. **Special Catalogs:** Slide catalog (card); film-tape catalog (book). **Staff:** Maria Wilkinson, Slide Cur.; Joe Enck, Presentation Coord.

★2352★
CARNEGIE-MELLON UNIVERSITY - ENGINEERING & SCIENCE LIBRARY (Sci-Tech)
Schenley Park   Phone: (412) 578-2428
Pittsburgh, PA 15213   Mark H. Kibbey, Hd., Engr. & Sci.Lib.
Founded: 1971. **Staff:** Prof 3; Other 5. **Subjects:** Mathematics, physics, civil engineering, mechanical engineering, computer science, electrical engineering, biomedical engineering, chemical engineering, metallurgy and materials science, artificial intelligence, robotics, energy and environmental science.

Holdings: 271,740 books; 90,377 bound periodical volumes; CMU theses; Envirofiche and Energyfiche, 1971 to present. **Subscriptions:** 2503 journals and other serials. **Services:** Interlibrary loans; copying; library open to public with limited circulation. **Computerized Information Services:** DIALOG, New York Times Information Service, BRS, SDC. **Networks/Consortia:** Member of Pittsburgh Council on Higher Education; Pittsburgh Regional Library Center; OCLC. **Staff:** Timothy Wherry, Sci.Info.Spec.; Earl Mounts, Comp.Sci.Libn.; Cynthia Whittaker, Sci.Info.Spec.

★2353★
CARNEGIE-MELLON UNIVERSITY - HUNT INSTITUTE FOR BOTANICAL DOCUMENTATION (Sci-Tech)
Schenley Park
Pittsburgh, PA 15213
Phone: (412) 578-2434
Robert W. Kiger, Dir.
Founded: 1961. **Staff:** Prof 13; Other 10. **Subjects:** Botanical history, plant taxonomy, including 15th-17th century herbals, extensive collection of 18th and 19th century colorplate works, floras, monographic works and other works on natural history, early gardening and horticulture, plant exploration and introduction. **Special Collections:** Botanical art and illustration (25,000 paintings, drawings and prints); botanical portraiture (22,000); botanical biographies (15,000); bibliography of botanical biographies (185,000 citations); Strandell Collection of Linnaeana (7500 titles and 3600 processed clippings); library of Michel Adanson (128 books, 260 holographic letters). **Holdings:** 22,000 books. **Subscriptions:** 88 journals and other serials. **Services:** Interlibrary loans; copying; library open to public for reference use only. **Computerized Information Services:** Bibliographia Huntiana, an internal database maintaining bibliographic information on 35,000 books and 50,000 journal articles published in the field of botany between 1730 and 1840; Catalog of the Strandell Collection of Linnaeana; Catalog of Art Collection. **Networks/Consortia:** Member of OCLC through Pittsburgh Regional Library Center; Pittsburgh Council on Higher Education. **Publications:** Exhibition catalogs, Huntia, Hunt Monograph Series, Hunt Facsimile Series, Bibliographia Periodicum Huntianum. **Special Catalogs:** Catalog of Botanical Books in the Collection of Rachel McMasters Miller Hunt, 1477-1800; Catalog of Portrait Collection; Guide to Archives. **Staff:** Bernadette G. Callery, Libn.; Elizabeth Mosimann, Asst.Libn.; John V. Brindle, Cur. of Art Emeritus; James J. White, Cur. of Art; Donald E. Wendel, Asst.Cur. of Art; Gavin D.R. Bridson, Bibliog.; Jean Gunner, Bookbinder & Consrv.; Michael T. Stieber, Archv.; Anita L. Karg, Asst.Archv.; Mary Jo Lilly, Asst.Bibliog.; T.D. Jacobsen, Asst.Dir; Elizabeth Smith, Asst.Ed.

★2354★
CARNEGIE-MELLON UNIVERSITY - HUNT LIBRARY - SPECIAL COLLECTIONS (Sci-Tech; Hum)
Schenley Park
Pittsburgh, PA 15213
Phone: (412) 578-2447
Peggy Porter, Hd.
Founded: 1920. **Special Collections:** Fine and rare book collection: private press books noted for binding and illustration, incunabula, books by famous printers and first editions of English and American authors; architectural drawings; government documents (121,282). **Services:** Interlibrary loans; copying; microfiche duplication; library open to public. **Computerized Information Services:** DIALOG, New York Times Information Service, BRS, SDC; computerized cataloging and acquisitions. **Networks/Consortia:** Member of OCLC; Pittsburgh Regional Library Center; Pittsburgh Council on Higher Education. **Staff:** Mary Schall, Spec.Coll.Libn.

★2355★
CARNEGIE-MELLON UNIVERSITY - MELLON INSTITUTE LIBRARY (Env-Cons)
4400 Fifth Ave.
Pittsburgh, PA 15213
Phone: (412) 578-3172
Mary J. Volk, Libn.
Staff: Prof 2; Other 2. **Subjects:** Chemistry, biological sciences, environmental sciences. **Holdings:** 17,600 books; 46,757 bound periodical volumes. **Subscriptions:** 328 journals and other serials. **Services:** Interlibrary loans; copying; library open to public with limited circulation. **Computerized Information Services:** DIALOG, New York Times Information Service, BRS, SDC. **Networks/Consortia:** Member of Pittsburgh Regional Library Center; OCLC; Pittsburgh Council on Higher Education. **Staff:** Cynthia Whittaker, Sci.Info.Spec.

★2356★
CARNEGIE MUSEUM OF NATURAL HISTORY - LIBRARY (Sci-Tech)
4400 Forbes Ave.
Pittsburgh, PA 15213
Phone: (412) 622-3264
Anna R. Tauber, Libn.
Founded: 1898. **Staff:** Prof 1; Other 7. **Subjects:** Zoology, geology, paleontology, botany, anthropology, archeology. **Holdings:** 100,000 volumes. **Subscriptions:** 2157 journals and other serials. **Services:** Interlibrary loans; library open to staff members of colleges and other research workers.

★2357★
CARNEY HOSPITAL - MEDICAL LIBRARY (Med)
2100 Dorchester Ave.
Dorchester, MA 02124
Phone: (617) 296-4000
Frances E. O'Brien, Med.Libn.
Staff: Prof 1; Other 2. **Subjects:** Medicine. **Holdings:** 1200 books; 4500 bound periodical volumes; tapes. **Subscriptions:** 147 journals and other serials. **Services:** Interlibrary loans; copying; SDI; library not open to public. **Networks/Consortia:** Member of Boston Biomedical Library Consortium; Massachusetts Health Sciences Library Network.

★2358★
CAROLINA ART ASSOCIATION - LIBRARY & SOUTH CAROLINA ART ARCHIVES (Art)
Gibbes Art Gallery
135 Meeting St.
Charleston, SC 29401
Phone: (803) 722-2706
Martha Severens, Cur. of Coll.
Subjects: Art, architecture. **Special Collections:** Files on South Carolina artists; photographic collections showing development of Charleston. **Holdings:** 1500 books; 1200 bound periodical volumes. **Services:** Copying; books are available to members and teachers; all qualified researchers have access to archives by appointment.

★2359★
CAROLINA LIBRARY SERVICES, INC. (Info Sci)
106 Henderson St.
Chapel Hill, NC 27514
Phone: (919) 929-4870
Eva C. Metzger, Dir.
Staff: Prof 3; Other 8. **Subjects:** Information science. **Holdings:** 500 books. **Services:** Interlibrary loans; copying; SDI; document delivery; information services for a fee; library open to public. **Computerized Information Services:** DIALOG, SDC, DialOrder. **Staff:** Whit Price, Supv., Doc. Delivery.

★2360★
CAROLINA POPULATION CENTER - LIBRARY (Soc Sci)
University Sq., 123 W. Franklin St.
Chapel Hill, NC 27514
Phone: (919) 933-3081
Patricia E. Shipman, Hd.Libn.
Founded: 1967. **Staff:** Prof 4; Other 4. **Subjects:** Population dynamics, policy and education, abortion, family planning, fertility. **Special Collections:** India census on microfiche, 1890-1960; Census of Iran, 1966 (172 volumes); collected papers of the Population Associations of America (1968 to present); Area Files (7000); Reprint Files (8000); Bibliography File (700); Abortion File (800). **Holdings:** 8500 books; 1500 bound periodical volumes; 30,000 analytics (cataloged); 500 documents on microfiche. **Subscriptions:** 650 journals and other serials. **Services:** Interlibrary loans; copying; library open to public. **Computerized Information Services:** DIALOG, SDC, MEDLINE, POPLINE; computerized cataloging. **Publications:** International Directory of Population Information and Library Resources, Part 2: 1975 Address List; Population/Family Planning Thesaurus, 2nd edition, 1978, supplement, 1981. **Special Catalogs:** Microfiche catalog to entire collection. **Staff:** Cheryl Ward, Asst.Hd.Libn.; Lynn Richardson, Search Anl.; James Lewis, Ref.Libn.

★2361★
CAROLINA POWER & LIGHT COMPANY - TECHNICAL LIBRARY (Energy)
411 Fayetteville St.
Box 1551
Raleigh, NC 27602
Phone: (919) 836-6790
Anne P. Carmichael, Corp.Libn.
Founded: 1970. **Staff:** Prof 1; Other 1. **Subjects:** Engineering - electrical, mechanical, nuclear, civil, environmental; codes and standards; energy economics. **Special Collections:** Electric Power Research Institute (EPRI) reports; nuclear facility PSARs, FSARs; NRC regulatory documents. **Holdings:** 9000 volumes. **Subscriptions:** 125 journals and other serials. **Services:** Interlibrary loans; copying; SDI; library open to public by prior arrangement. **Computerized Information Services:** DIALOG.

★2362★
CARPENTER (Guy) & COMPANY, INC. - LIBRARY AND INFORMATION SERVICES (Bus-Fin)
110 William St.
New York, NY 10038
Phone: (212) 791-8665
John Cocke, Libn.
Founded: 1980. **Staff:** Prof 2; Other 1. **Subjects:** Property and casualty insurance, business. **Special Collections:** Reinsurance collection. **Holdings:** 500 books. **Subscriptions:** 73 journals and other serials. **Services:** Interlibrary loans; copying; library open to Special Libraries Association members by appointment. **Computerized Information Services:** DIALOG. **Staff:** Nancy Williamson, Asst.Libn.

★2363★

CARPENTER TECHNOLOGY CORPORATION - RESEARCH AND DEVELOPMENT CENTER LIBRARY (Sci-Tech)
Box 662   Phone: (215) 371-2583
Reading, PA 19603   Wendy M. Holt, Assoc.Libn.
Founded: 1950. **Staff:** Prof 1; Other 1. **Subjects:** Ferrous metallurgy, metal working, chemistry, electronics. **Holdings:** 4100 books; 10,000 bound periodical volumes; 8500 reports and pamphlets (hard copy); 10,000 microfiche (reports and pamphlets). **Subscriptions:** 200 journals and other serials. **Services:** Interlibrary loans; library open to public with permission. **Computerized Information Services:** DIALOG, SDC. **Networks/Consortia:** Member of Berks County Library Association. **Publications:** Acquisition List, quarterly; Patent Abstract Bulletin, weekly.

★2364★

CARR (Emily) COLLEGE OF ART - LIBRARY (Art)
1399 Johnston St.
Granville Island
Vancouver, BC, Canada V6H 3R9   Phone: (604) 687-2345
                                          Ken Chamberlain, Hd.Libn.
Staff: Prof 1; Other 4. **Subjects:** 20th century visual arts. **Holdings:** 7700 books; 350 bound periodical volumes; 35 linear feet of art exhibition catalogs. **Subscriptions:** 150 journals and other serials. **Services:** Interlibrary loans; copying; library open to public for reference use only. **Publications:** What's New in the Library, monthly - for internal distribution and to selected libraries.

CARR HEALTH SCIENCES LIBRARY
See: Somerville Hospital

★2365★

CARRAWAY METHODIST MEDICAL CENTER - MEDICAL LIBRARY (Med)
1600 N. 26th St.   Phone: (205) 254-6265
Birmingham, AL 35234   Mrs. Bobby H. Powell, Med.Libn.
Founded: 1942. **Staff:** Prof 1; Other 2. **Subjects:** Medicine, surgery, nursing, sciences. **Holdings:** 1347 books; 5795 bound periodical volumes. **Subscriptions:** 171 journals and other serials. **Services:** Interlibrary loans (limited); copying; library not open to public. **Networks/Consortia:** Member of Jefferson County Hospital Librarians' Association.

CARRIER CORPORATION - ELLIOTT COMPANY
See: United Technologies Corporation - Elliott Company

★2366★

CARRIER CORPORATION - LOGAN LEWIS LIBRARY (Sci-Tech)
Research Division, Carrier Pkwy.
Box 4808   Phone: (315) 432-6306
Syracuse, NY 13221   J. Huitfeldt, Mgr., Info.Res.
Founded: 1942. **Staff:** Prof 2. **Subjects:** Air conditioning, heating, refrigeration, ventilation, acoustics, electrical engineering, mechanical engineering, chemistry and chemical engineering, air and water pollution. **Special Collections:** Archives of Willis Carrier, Carrier Corporation history and history of air conditioning. **Holdings:** 6000 books; 2900 bound periodical volumes. **Subscriptions:** 350 journals and other serials. **Services:** Interlibrary loans; copying; library open to public with permission. **Computerized Information Services:** DIALOG, SDC; internal database. **Networks/Consortia:** Member of Central New York Library Resources Council. **Publications:** Bi-monthly Bulletin; Periodicals Received, annual - both distributed to area libraries upon request. **Remarks:** Carrier Corporation is an affiliate of United Technologies. **Staff:** L. Williams, Libn.

★2367★

CARRIER FOUNDATION - NOLAN D.C. LEWIS LIBRARY (Med)
Box 147   Phone: (201) 874-4000
Belle Mead, NJ 08502   Sharon Geiger, Dir.
Staff: Prof 2; Other 1. **Subjects:** Psychiatry, nursing, family therapy, psychology, allied mental health sciences, medicine. **Special Collections:** Nolan D.C. Lewis Collection of psychiatry and personal memorabilia. **Holdings:** 3500 books; 1500 bound periodical volumes. **Subscriptions:** 178 journals and other serials; 6 newspapers. **Services:** Interlibrary loans; copying; SDI; library open to public by appointment. **Networks/Consortia:** Member of Central Jersey Health Science Libraries Association; Health Sciences Library Association of New Jersey. **Staff:** Mary Chaikin, Asst.Libn.

★2368★

CARRINGTON, COLEMAN, SLOMAN & BLUMENTHAL - LIBRARY (Law)
2500 South Tower
Plaza of the Americas
Dallas, TX 75201   Phone: (214) 741-2121
                                          Sue H. Johnson, Libn.
Staff: 1. **Subjects:** Law. **Holdings:** 15,500 volumes. **Subscriptions:** 30 journals and other serials. **Services:** Library not open to public.

★2369★

CARROLL COLLEGE - LIBRARY (Rel-Theol; Hum)
                                          Phone: (406) 442-1295
Helena, MT 59601   Lois A. Fitzpatrick, Dir.
Founded: 1928. **Staff:** Prof 4; Other 25. **Subjects:** Drama, literary criticism, social work, philosophy, theology, biomedicine, Dante, ecology. **Holdings:** 94,000 books; 16 VF drawers of archival material relating to the Catholic Church in Montana; 675 microfiche on slavery in America; 500 magnetic tapes; 1500 microforms; 1500 phonograph records. **Subscriptions:** 470 journals and other serials; 16 newspapers. **Services:** Interlibrary loans; copying; library open to public for reference use only. **Computerized Information Services:** DIALOG; computerized cataloging, serials and circulation. **Networks/Consortia:** Member of Montana Information Network Exchange (MINE); Northwest Association of Private Colleges and Universities (NAPCU); OCLC. **Staff:** Sr. M. Padraig McRaith, O.P., Libn. Emeritus; Kathleen Fernandes, Tech.Proc.Libn.; Janet Wingenroth, Ref.Libn.; Gary Allan, Doc.Libn.

★2370★

CARROLL COUNTY BAR ASSOCIATION - LIBRARY (Law)
Court House   Phone: (301) 848-4500
Westminster, MD 21157   Florence Green, Libn.
Subjects: Law. **Holdings:** 10,000 volumes.

★2371★

CARROLL COUNTY FARM MUSEUM - LANDON BURNS MEMORIAL LIBRARY (Agri)
500 S. Center St.   Phone: (301) 848-7775
Westminster, MD 21157   Cindy Hofferberth, Dir. of Musm.
Subjects: Agriculture. **Holdings:** 500 books.

★2372★

CARROLL (John) UNIVERSITY - SEISMOLOGICAL LIBRARY (Sci-Tech)
                                          Phone: (216) 491-4361
Cleveland, OH 44118   Ann Mell, Libn.
Founded: 1905. **Staff:** Prof 2. **Subjects:** Seismological data, geophysics. **Special Collections:** Seismological bulletins from approximately 300 observatories throughout the world, going back to the dates of inception. **Holdings:** 200 books; 1000 bound periodical volumes; 10,000 seismological bulletins. **Services:** Interlibrary loans; copying; library open to public.

★2373★

CARSON COUNTY SQUARE HOUSE MUSEUM - INFORMATION CENTER (Hist)
Box 276   Phone: (806) 537-3118
Panhandle, TX 79068   Marvin T. Shickels, Dir.
Founded: 1967. **Staff:** 3. **Subjects:** Carson County history, pioneer health and medicine. **Special Collections:** Pioneer school textbooks (70 items); music, 1910-1940. **Holdings:** 100 books; 10,400 artifacts (cataloged); 10 interstate museum reports; 150 pamphlets; 40 maps. **Subscriptions:** 25 journals and other serials; 6 newspapers. **Services:** Copying; library open to public with restrictions. **Publications:** A Time to Purpose; Land of Coronado storybook; Voices of the Square House Museum; Square House Museum Cookbook - for sale. **Staff:** Beth Nobles, Cur. of Educ.

★2374★

CARSON (Kit) MEMORIAL FOUNDATION - HISTORICAL RESEARCH LIBRARY AND ARCHIVES (Hist)
E. Kit Carson Ave.
Box B   Phone: (505) 758-4741
Taos, NM 87571   Jack K. Boyer, Dir.
Founded: 1952. **Staff:** 1. **Subjects:** Early fur trade, Western Americana, Spanish-Colonial history, archeology and related subjects. **Special Collections:** Collection of literature on Kit Carson (250 items). **Holdings:** 3880 books; 5591 bound periodical volumes; 701 pamphlets (cataloged); 2 VF drawers of pamphlets (uncataloged); 8541 photographs and negatives; 919 maps; deeds; documents; letters; papers; manuscripts. **Subscriptions:** 23 journals and other serials. **Services:** Copying; library open to public for reference use only.

CARSON (Lucy) MEMORIAL LIBRARY
See: Western Montana College - Lucy Carson Memorial Library

CARSON (Rachel) COUNCIL, INC.
See: Rachel Carson Council, Inc.

CARSON (Russell M.L.) MEMORIAL LIBRARY
See: Glens Falls-Queensbury Historical Assoc. Inc. - Chapman Historical Museum - Russell M.L. Carson Mem. Library

★2375★
CARSON-TAHOE HOSPITAL - LAHONTAN BASIN MEDICAL LIBRARY (Med)
1201 N. Mountain St.
Box 2168   Phone: (702) 882-1361
Carson City, NV 89710   Mr. H. Pepper Sturm, Libn.
Staff: Prof 1; Other 1. **Subjects:** Clinical medicine, health care. **Holdings:**
500 books; 40 bound periodical volumes; unbound periodicals; 202 folders of
medical files. **Subscriptions:** 110 journals and other serials. **Services:**
Interlibrary loans; copying; library open to public with restrictions.
Computerized Information Services: MEDLINE; computerized cataloging.

★2376★
CARSTAB CORPORATION - RESEARCH LIBRARY (Sci-Tech)
West St.   Phone: (513) 554-1554
Cincinnati, OH 45215   Christine J. Gadker, Res.Libn.
Staff: Prof 1. **Subjects:** Organometallic chemistry; organic chemistry;
specialized information on additives for lubricants, plastics, foods. **Holdings:**
2800 books and bound periodical volumes; VF drawers of reprints, patents,
intercompany reports. **Subscriptions:** 80 journals and other serials. **Services:**
Interlibrary loans; library open to public with restrictions.

CARSWELL AIR FORCE BASE (TX)
See: U.S. Air Force Base - Carswell Base Library; U.S. Air Force Hospital -
    Medical Library (TX-Carswell AFB)

★2377★
CARTER (Amon) MUSEUM OF WESTERN ART - LIBRARY (Art)
3501 Camp Bowie Blvd.
Box 2365   Phone: (817) 738-1933
Fort Worth, TX 76113   Nancy G. Wynne, Libn.
Founded: 1961. **Staff:** Prof 2; Other 1. **Subjects:** Western Americana, North
American art, Canadiana. **Special Collections:** American newspapers before
1900 (6000 reels of microfilm). **Holdings:** 17,500 books; 1923 bound
periodical volumes. **Subscriptions:** 145 journals and other serials. **Services:**
Interlibrary loans; copying; library open to public by appointment. **Staff:** Milan
Hughston, Asst.Libn.

★2378★
CARTER & BURGESS, INC. ENGINEERS & PLANNERS - LIBRARY (Sci-Tech)
1100 Macon   Phone: (817) 335-2611
Fort Worth, TX 76102   Julia W. Sweet, Libn.
Staff: Prof 1; Other 5. **Subjects:** Engineering - hydraulic, environmental,
airport, highway and planning. **Special Collections:** FAA engineering
specifications (150); Fort Worth engineering specifications; federal
specifications and guidelines. **Holdings:** 1500 books; 1300 manufacturers'
specifications; ASTM set. **Subscriptions:** 180 journals and other serials; 10
newspapers. **Services:** Copying. **Special Catalogs:** Catalog for technical
reference material (card); CSI Manufacturer's Products Specifiers Catalogs.

★2379★
CARTER COUNTY MUSEUM - LIBRARY
Ekalaka, MT 59324
Subjects: Paleontology. **Holdings:** 250 books; 200 pamphlets (cataloged).
Remarks: Presently inactive.

CARTER (Gray) LIBRARY
See: Greenwich Hospital Association - Gray Carter Library

★2380★
CARTER (Larue D.) MEMORIAL HOSPITAL - MEDICAL LIBRARY (Med)
1315 W. 10th St.   Phone: (317) 634-8401
Indianapolis, IN 46202   Philip I. Enz, Adm.Libn.
Founded: 1953. **Staff:** Prof 2; Other 1. **Subjects:** Psychiatry, psychology,
social work, psychiatric nursing, rehabilitation therapies, mental health.
Special Collections: History of Mental Health. **Holdings:** 14,100 books and
bound periodical volumes; 100 audiotapes; 3 drawers of staff publications.
Subscriptions: 219 journals and other serials. **Services:** Interlibrary loans;
copying; library open to public for reference use only. **Networks/Consortia:**
Member of Regional Medical Library - Region 3. **Publications:** Mnemonic,
bimonthly (new books, bibliographies, abstracts) - free upon request. **Staff:**
Judith K. Smith, Libn.

★2381★
CARTER, LEDYARD AND MILBURN - LIBRARY (Law)†
2 Wall St.   Phone: (212) 732-3200
New York, NY 10005   Julius M. Pomerantz, Libn.
Staff: Prof 1; Other 2. **Subjects:** Law, philosophy of law. **Holdings:** 15,500
volumes. **Subscriptions:** 25 journals and other serials.

CARTER (Dr. Linden J.) LIBRARY
See: Berkshire Christian College - Dr. Linden J. Carter Library

★2382★
CARTER-WALLACE, INC. - LIBRARY (Med)
                                                    Phone: (609) 655-6297
Cranbury, NJ 08512   Arthur Hilscher, Dir.
Founded: 1948. **Staff:** Prof 3; Other 6. **Subjects:** Pharmacology,
experimental medicine, organic chemistry, medicine, toiletries, diagnostics.
Special Collections: Substituted Alkanediols (26,000 documents). **Holdings:**
3500 books; 1800 bound periodical volumes; 47,000 reports, pamphlets and
documents. **Subscriptions:** 350 journals and other serials. **Services:**
Interlibrary loans; copying; library open to special librarians. **Computerized
Information Services:** DIALOG; mechanized retrieval. **Networks/Consortia:**
Member of MEDCORE. **Publications:** Current Product Abstracts, monthly.
Staff: Jerry Zbehlik, Doc.Mgr.; Dolores Ureneck, Lib.Mgr.

★2383★
**CARTER (William) COLLEGE & EVANGELICAL THEOLOGICAL SEMINARY -
    WAGNER-KEVETTER LIBRARY (Rel-Theol)**
2306 E. Ash St.   Phone: (919) 735-0831
Goldsboro, NC 27530   Dr. Doris Byrd Thomas, Libn.
Founded: 1952. **Staff:** Prof 1; Other 2. **Subjects:** Religion, liberal arts,
philosophy, psychology, political science, sociology. **Special Collections:**
History of Germany prior to Hitler's regime. **Holdings:** 23,000 books.

CARTER'S INK COMPANY
See: Dennison Manufacturing Company

★2384★
CARVER BIBLE COLLEGE - LIBRARY (Rel-Theol)
437 Nelson St., S.W.
Atlanta, GA 30302   Ruth A. Wedel, Libn.
Staff: Prof 1; Other 2. **Subjects:** Biblical expositions, doctrinal theology,
missions, church history, Christian education, world religions, prophecy and
eschatology. **Holdings:** 13,000 books. **Subscriptions:** 69 journals and other
serials. **Services:** Library not open to public.

★2385★
CARVER COUNTY HISTORICAL SOCIETY, INC. - LIBRARY (Hist)
119 S. Cherry St.   Phone: (612) 442-4234
Waconia, MN 55387   Francis Klein, Pres.
Founded: 1940. **Staff:** Prof 1. **Subjects:** Carver County history. **Special
Collections:** Early 1860 library of Swedes and Germans in the locality.
Holdings: 5000 books; 8000 photographs. **Services:** Copying; museum open
to public; library open to public for reference use only.

CARVER (George Washington) NATIONAL MONUMENT
See: U.S. Natl. Park Service - George Washington Carver National
    Monument

CARVER PARK RESERVE - LOWRY NATURE CENTER
See: Hennepin County Park Reserve District - Lowry Nature Center

CARY ARBORETUM - LIBRARY
See: New York Botanical Garden

★2386★
CARY MEDICAL CENTER - HEALTH SCIENCE LIBRARY (Med)†
Van Buren Rd.
MRA Box 37   Phone: (207) 498-3131
Caribou, ME 04736   Donna E. Cote-Thibodeau, Libn.
Staff: 1. **Subjects:** Medicine. **Holdings:** 600 books and bound periodical
volumes. **Subscriptions:** 85 journals and other serials. **Services:** Interlibrary
loans; copying.

CARY (Melbert B., Jr.) GRAPHIC ARTS COLLECTION
See: Rochester Institute of Technology - Melbert B. Cary, Jr. Graphic Arts
    Collection

★2387★
CASA GRANDE VALLEY HISTORICAL SOCIETY - MUSEUM LIBRARY (Hist)
110 W. Florence Blvd.   Phone: (602) 836-2223
Casa Grande, AZ 85222   Kay Benedict, Cur.
Founded: 1964. **Staff:** 2. **Subjects:** Local history. **Holdings:** 500 volumes;
manuscripts and artifacts. **Services:** Library open to public. **Publications:**
Regular newsletter of the society; monographs on local historical subjects.
Special Indexes: Index of the local newspaper.

CASALS (Pablo) INTERNATIONAL CELLO LIBRARY
See: Arizona State University - Music Library

CASE
See: Council for Advancement and Support of Education

CASE MEMORIAL LIBRARY
See: Hartford Seminary Foundation

★2388★
CASE WESTERN RESERVE UNIVERSITY - ANDREW R. JENNINGS COMPUTING CENTER - DOCUMENTATION LIBRARY (Info Sci)
                                            Phone: (216) 368-2982
Cleveland, OH 44106   Gayle M. Lambert, Tech.Libn.
Founded: 1979. **Staff:** Prof 1; Other 1. **Subjects:** Computers - science, engineering, programming, applications; data communications; networks. **Holdings:** 502 books and bound periodical volumes. **Subscriptions:** 37 journals and other serials. **Services:** Library open to public with restrictions. **Computerized Information Services:** Computerized cataloging. **Special Indexes:** Index to major journal articles.

★2389★
CASE WESTERN RESERVE UNIVERSITY - APPLIED SOCIAL SCIENCES LIBRARY (Soc Sci)
School of Applied Social Sciences
2035 Abington Rd.
Cleveland, OH 44106   Phone: (216) 368-2302
                            Vlatka Ivanisevic, Libn.
Founded: 1927. **Staff:** Prof 1; Other 1. **Subjects:** Social work, social welfare, poverty, women's studies, black studies, alcoholism, corrections, aging, child welfare, minority group relations, community organization, psychiatry and mental health. **Special Collections:** Black studies and books by black authors. **Holdings:** 14,000 books; 1200 bound periodical volumes; 7000 pamphlets and monographs (cataloged). **Subscriptions:** 200 journals and other serials. **Services:** Interlibrary loans; copying; library open to public for reference use only. **Computerized Information Services:** Online systems. **Networks/Consortia:** Member of Cleveland Area Metropolitan Library System (CAMLS). **Publications:** Acquisitions list. **Special Catalogs:** Card catalog for all pamphlet material and minority's collection.

CASE WESTERN RESERVE UNIVERSITY - CLEVELAND HEALTH SCIENCES LIBRARY
See: Cleveland Health Sciences Library

CASE WESTERN RESERVE UNIVERSITY - DEPT. OF PATHOLOGY
See: University Hospitals of Cleveland

★2390★
CASE WESTERN RESERVE UNIVERSITY - LAW SCHOOL LIBRARY (Law)
11075 East Blvd.
Cleveland, OH 44106   Phone: (216) 368-2792
                            Simon L. Goren, Law Libn.
Founded: 1892. **Staff:** Prof 6; Other 9. **Subjects:** Law, international law, medical jurisprudence. **Special Collections:** American statute collection; foreign and international law. **Holdings:** 191,840 books; 47,482 microcards; 126 reels of microfilm; 57,379 microfiche; 501 VF items; 1700 unbound reports, pamphlets, documents. **Subscriptions:** 3610 journals and other serials; 12 newspapers. **Services:** Interlibrary loans; copying; library open to public with permission of law librarian. **Computerized Information Services:** LEXIS; computerized cataloging. **Networks/Consortia:** Member of OCLC. **Publications:** Table of Contents of selected legal periodicals, weekly; acquisitions list, monthly. **Special Catalogs:** Guide to Periodicals and Annuals in the Law Library, 1979. **Staff:** Vili Zadnikar, Assoc.Libn., Tech.Serv.; Loree E. Potash, Assoc.Libn., Pub.Serv.; Marsha Teitelbaum, Circ.; Helen C. Braznytez, Lib.Asst., Acq.; Sonia Solomonoff, Cat.; Kathleen Donnelly, Asst.Ref., AV/Govt.Doc.

★2391★
CASE WESTERN RESERVE UNIVERSITY - MATTHEW A. BAXTER SCHOOL OF LIBRARY & INFORMATION SCIENCE (Info Sci)
Newton D. Baker Bldg.
10950 Euclid Ave.
Cleveland, OH 44106   Phone: (216) 368-3524
                            Bettina R. MacAyeal, Libn.
Staff: Prof 1; Other 1. **Subjects:** Library science, information science. **Special Collections:** Juvenile Historical Collection (750 volumes); historical collection of library science materials (550 volumes); Eastman Collection of Printing and Bookmaking (400 volumes). **Holdings:** 15,000 volumes; 2000 microforms. **Subscriptions:** 356 journals and other serials. **Services:** Interlibrary loans; copying; SDI (by request); library open to public. **Networks/Consortia:** Member of OHIONET; Cleveland Area Metropolitan Library System (CAMLS). **Publications:** Acquisition list. **Staff:** Gretchen S.

Larson, Asst.Libn.

★2392★
CASE WESTERN RESERVE UNIVERSITY - SEARS LIBRARY (Sci-Tech; Env-Cons)†
10900 Euclid Ave.
Cleveland, OH 44106   Phone: (216) 368-4244
                            David Goding, Hd.Libn.
Staff: Prof 7; Other 16. **Subjects:** Astronomy, engineering, chemistry, earth sciences, mathematics, physics, economics, management. **Special Collections:** Environmental sciences. **Holdings:** 210,300 books and bound periodical volumes; 59,800 government documents; 34,000 technical reports; 975 reels of microfilm; 119,000 other microtexts; 67,000 geological maps. **Subscriptions:** 4000 journals and other serials; 11 newspapers. **Services:** Interlibrary loans; copying; library open to public with identification. **Computerized Information Services:** DIALOG, SDC, BRS, DOE/RECON; computerized serials. **Networks/Consortia:** Member of OCLC; NEOMAL; Cleveland Area Metropolitan Library System. **Special Catalogs:** Technical reports (card).

★2393★
CASE WESTERN RESERVE UNIVERSITY - UNIVERSITY ARCHIVES (Hist)
2040 Adelbert Rd.
Cleveland, OH 44106   Ruth Helmuth, Archv.
Staff: Prof 4; Other 1. **Subjects:** University related materials. **Holdings:** 4705 linear feet of publications, office files, personal papers, photographs, blueprints and other nontextual materials. **Services:** Copying; library open to public with restrictions. **Staff:** Laura Gorretta, Asst.Archv.; Jeffrey Rollison, Asst.Archv.; Victoria Sheffler, Asst.Archv.

★2394★
CASEMATE MUSEUM - LIBRARY (Hist)
Box 341
Ft. Monroe, VA 23651   Phone: (804) 727-3935
                            R. Cody Phillips, Musm.Cur.
Founded: 1951. **Staff:** Prof 5. **Subjects:** Civil War, military history, peninsula Virginia, Jefferson Davis, Fort Monroe and U.S. Army Coast Artillery. **Holdings:** 1200 volumes; 445 reels of microfilm; 27 boxes of manuscripts. **Subscriptions:** 14 journals and other serials. **Services:** Copying; library open to public for reference use only by appointment. **Publications:** Tales of Old Fort Monroe; Casemate Papers; Museum Guidebook.

CASEY, LANE & MITTENDORF
See: Lane & Mittendorf

CASEY MEMORIAL LIBRARY
See: U.S. Army Post - Fort Hood - MSA Division

CASTLE AIR FORCE BASE (CA)
See: U.S. Air Force Base - Castle Base - Baker Library

★2395★
CASTLE & COOKE, INC. - LAW & GOVERNMENT DEPARTMENT INFORMATION CENTER (Law)
50 California St., 18th Fl.
San Francisco, CA 94111   Phone: (415) 986-3000
                            Betty Hardin, Law Libn.
Founded: 1977. **Staff:** Prof 1. **Subjects:** Law, government, business. **Holdings:** 5115 volumes; uncataloged material. **Subscriptions:** 225 journals and other serials; 12 newspapers. **Services:** Library not open to public. **Special Indexes:** Index to files, legal memoranda and library holdings (computer).

★2396★
CASTLETON HISTORICAL SOCIETY - MUSEUM LIBRARY (Hist)†
Main St.
Castleton, VT 05735   Phone: (802) 468-2226
                            Mrs. Finley Shepard, Cur.
Founded: 1961. **Subjects:** Local history. **Special Collections:** Historical Vermont. **Holdings:** 50 books; photographs; newspapers; documents.

★2397★
CASTLETON STATE COLLEGE - CALVIN COOLIDGE LIBRARY - LEARNING RESOURCES CENTER (Educ)
                                            Phone: (802) 468-5611
Castleton, VT 05735   Joseph P. Santosuosso, Lib.Dir.
Founded: 1834. **Staff:** Prof 2; Other 6. **Subjects:** Education, nursing, criminal justice, U.S. and Vermont documents. **Special Collections:** Vermontiana (2600 items); U.S. Government Document Depository. **Holdings:** 69,000 books; 1200 bound periodical volumes; 28,771 U.S. documents (cataloged); 77,745 microforms; 318 phonograph records and audiotapes; 170 audio cassettes; 41 videotapes; 25 16mm films; 20 drawers of pamphlet files. **Subscriptions:** 765 journals and other serials; 7 newspapers.

Services: Interlibrary loans; copying; library open to public. **Computerized Information Services:** DIALOG. **Networks/Consortia:** Member of Vermont Union Catalog.

CATALINA MARINE SCIENCE CENTER
See: University of Southern California

★2398★
CATALYST - INFORMATION CENTER (Soc Sci)
14 E. 60th St.   Phone: (212) 759-9700
New York, NY 10022   Gurley Turner, Dir. of Info.Serv.
Staff: 3. **Subjects:** Women and work, career information. **Special Collections:** Family and career (two career families). **Holdings:** 5000 books; 5000 vertical files of government documents, studies and unpublished dissertations. **Subscriptions:** 125 journals and other serials. **Services:** Interlibrary loans; copying; center open to public. **Computerized Information Services:** BRS. **Networks/Consortia:** Member of Women's Information Services Network. **Publications:** List of bibliographies - available upon request.

★2399★
CATALYTIC, INC. - LIBRARY (Sci-Tech)
Centre Square West
1500 Market St.   Phone: (215) 864-8567
Philadelphia, PA 19102   Mary J. Kober, Dir.
Staff: Prof 1. **Subjects:** Engineering, chemical engineering. **Holdings:** 900 books; 703 bound periodical volumes; 200 vendors' catalogs; 10 VF drawers of vendors' bulletins; 35 VF drawers of standards, specifications, government publications. **Subscriptions:** 52 journals and other serials. **Services:** Interlibrary loans; copying; library not open to public.

★2400★
CATAWBA COUNTY HISTORICAL MUSEUM - LIBRARY (Hist)
U.S. Hwy. 321   Phone: (704) 465-0383
Newton, NC 28658   Sidney Halma, Dir.
Staff: Prof 1; Other 1. **Subjects:** Local history, genealogy. **Special Collections:** Mrs. D.M. Eaton Collection of correspondence and decorative arts reference books. **Holdings:** Figures not available. **Services:** Library open to public. **Publications:** Past Times, quarterly.

★2401★
CATERPILLAR TRACTOR COMPANY - BUSINESS LIBRARY (Bus-Fin)
100 N.E. Adams St.   Phone: (309) 675-4622
Peoria, IL 61629   Amy Wolf, Lib.Supv.
Founded: 1949. **Staff:** Prof 2; Other 6. **Subjects:** Economics, management, statistics, marketing, foreign trade. **Holdings:** 11,722 books; 130 bound periodical volumes; 39 VF drawers of pamphlets and government publications; annual reports. **Subscriptions:** 741 journals and other serials; 7 newspapers. **Services:** Interlibrary loans; copying; SDI; library open to public by prior arrangement. **Computerized Information Services:** DIALOG; computerized cataloging and ILL. **Networks/Consortia:** Member of Illinois Valley Library System. **Publications:** Business Update, bimonthly; Serials Holding List, annual - both for internal distribution only. **Staff:** Nancy B. McCully, Libn.

CATERPILLAR TRACTOR COMPANY - SOLAR TURBINES INCORPORATED
See: Solar Turbines Incorporated

★2402★
CATERPILLAR TRACTOR COMPANY - TECHNICAL INFORMATION CENTER (Sci-Tech)
Technical Center   Phone: (309) 578-6118
Peoria, IL 61629   Carol E. Mulvaney, Tech.Libn.
Founded: 1940. **Staff:** Prof 4; Other 4. **Subjects:** Mechanical engineering, metallurgy, enginology, soil mechanics. **Holdings:** 14,500 books and bound periodical volumes; 127 VF drawers of technical society papers and government reports; 8 VF drawers of bibliographies; 10 VF drawers of translations; 29 VF drawers of university publications; 297 VF drawers of internal reports. **Subscriptions:** 500 journals and other serials. **Services:** Interlibrary loans; library open to public on request. **Computerized Information Services:** DIALOG, SDC; computerized cataloging. **Networks/Consortia:** Member of Illinois Valley Library System; OCLC. **Publications:** TIC Update, semimonthly - for internal distribution only. **Staff:** Marilyn Ziebold, Asst.Libn.; John Serguison, Reports Indexer; Leon Decker, Cat.

★2403★
CATERPILLAR TRACTOR COMPANY - TRAINING LIBRARY
Bldg. W
East Peoria, IL 61630
Defunct

★2404★
CATHEDRAL OF ST. JOHN THE DIVINE - CATHEDRAL LIBRARY (Rel-Theol)
Cathedral Heights   Phone: (212) 678-6910
New York, NY 10025   Madeleine L'Engle Franklin, Writer in Residence
Staff: 1. **Subjects:** Religion, philosophy, theology, psychology, mythology and theological fantasy, church history, biography, ecclesiastical architecture. **Special Collections:** Bibles (200 volumes). **Holdings:** 15,000 books; 3000 unbound periodicals. **Subscriptions:** 15 journals and other serials. **Services:** Interlibrary loans; library open to public.

CATHER (Willa) HISTORICAL CENTER
See: Nebraska State Historical Society - Willa Cather Historical Center

CATHERWOOD (Martin P.) LIBRARY OF INDUSTRIAL AND LABOR RELATIONS
See: Cornell University - Martin P. Catherwood Library of Industrial and Labor Relations

CATHOLIC ARCHIVES OF TEXAS
See: Texas Catholic Historical Society

CATHOLIC ASSOCIATION FOR INTERNATIONAL PEACE - ARCHIVES
See: Marquette University - Department of Special Collections and University Archives

★2405★
CATHOLIC CENTER AT NEW YORK UNIVERSITY - CATHOLIC CENTER LIBRARY (Rel-Theol)
58 Washington Sq., S.   Phone: (212) 674-7236
New York, NY 10012
Founded: 1952. **Staff:** Prof 3. **Subjects:** Religion, theology, ethics, scripture, philosophy, Apologetics. **Special Collections:** John Henry Cardinal Newman (130 books). **Holdings:** 6000 books. **Services:** Interlibrary loans; library open to public.

★2406★
CATHOLIC CENTRAL UNION OF AMERICA - CENTRAL BUREAU LIBRARY (Soc Sci)
3835 Westminster Pl.   Phone: (314) 371-1653
St. Louis, MO 63108   Harvey J. Johnson, Dir.
Founded: 1908. **Staff:** 1. **Subjects:** Cooperatives, social action, biography. **Holdings:** 42,200 books; 5000 bound periodical volumes; 2000 pamphlets; 1200 reels of microfilm. **Subscriptions:** 41 journals and other serials. **Services:** Interlibrary loans; copying; library open to public by appointment.

CATHOLIC CONFERENCE DOCUMENTARY SERVICE
See: Diocese of Allentown - Pro-Life Library

CATHOLIC EDUCATION CENTRE LIBRARY
See: Metropolitan (Toronto) Separate School Board

CATHOLIC FOREIGN MISSIONARY SOCIETY OF AMERICA
See: Maryknoll Seminary

★2407★
CATHOLIC HEALTH ASSOCIATION OF THE UNITED STATES - INFORMATION RESOURCE CENTER (Med)
4455 Woodson Rd.   Phone: (314) 427-2500
St. Louis, MO 63134   Mark Unger, Dir., Info.Rsrcs.Ctr.
Staff: Prof 1; Other 2. **Subjects:** Health care administration, public health, nursing, paramedical areas, professional education, Catholic religion, business, safety. **Holdings:** Book and periodical holdings not available; 29 VF drawers of miscellaneous materials. **Subscriptions:** 228 journals and other serials. **Services:** Interlibrary loans; library open to public on request.

★2408★
CATHOLIC LIBRARY ASSOCIATION - NATIONAL HEADQUARTERS - LIBRARY (Rel-Theol; Publ)
461 W. Lancaster Ave.   Phone: (215) 649-5250
Haverford, PA 19041   Matthew R. Wilt, Exec.Dir.
Staff: Prof 6; Other 5. **Subjects:** Publishing. **Holdings:** Figures not available. **Services:** Library not open to public.

★2409★
CATHOLIC MEDICAL CENTER OF BROOKLYN & QUEENS, INC. - CENTRAL MEDICAL LIBRARY (Med)
88-25 153rd St.   Phone: (212) 290-3300
Jamaica, NY 11432   Sr. Regina Clare Woods, O.P., Coord./Med.Libs.
Founded: 1969. **Staff:** Prof 2; Other 2. **Subjects:** Medicine, surgery,

orthopedics, pathology, oncology, pediatrics. **Holdings:** 4500 books; 3000 bound periodical volumes; 8 VF drawers; 1150 Audio-Digest tapes; 35 sets of MEDCOM slides; microforms; 53 video cassettes. **Subscriptions:** 253 journals and other serials. **Services:** Interlibrary loans; copying; library open to public with identification. **Networks/Consortia:** Member of Medical Library Center of New York (MLCNY); Brooklyn-Queens-Staten Island Health Sciences Group (BQSI). **Special Catalogs:** Periodical Union List. **Remarks:** CMC includes Mary Immaculate, Jamaica; St. John's, Queens; St. Mary's, Brooklyn; The Hospital of Holy Family, Brooklyn. **Staff:** Sharon Barten, Asst.Libn.

★2410★
CATHOLIC MEDICAL CENTER OF BROOKLYN & QUEENS, INC. - ST. MARY'S HOSPITAL - MEDICAL ADMINISTRATIVE LIBRARY (Med)
170 Buffalo Ave.   Phone: (212) 774-3600
Brooklyn, NY 11213   Madeline A. Brown, Med.Libn.
Staff: 1. **Subjects:** Medicine and allied fields, nursing, sickle cell program, administration, drug addiction. **Special Collections:** Sickle Cell Anemia; health as related to blacks. **Holdings:** 1000 books; 100 administration items; Audio-Digest tapes; video cassettes. **Subscriptions:** 100 journals and other serials. **Services:** Interlibrary loans (to Catholic Medical Center hospitals only); copying; library open to paramedical personnel and Licensed Practical Nurses and others with proper identification. **Computerized Information Services:** MEDLINE. **Publications:** CMC Newsletter, quarterly. **Special Catalogs:** Book Catalog; audiovisual catalog.

★2411★
CATHOLIC MEDICAL CENTER - HEALTH SCIENCE LIBRARY (Med)
100 McGregor St.   Phone: (603) 668-3545
Manchester, NH 03102   Marcia K. Allen, Libn.
Staff: Prof 1; Other 3. **Subjects:** Medicine, nursing, allied health sciences. **Holdings:** 5162 books; 480 bound periodical volumes. **Subscriptions:** 135 journals and other serials. **Services:** Interlibrary loans; copying; library open to students, affiliated agencies, medical staff and hospital personnel. **Computerized Information Services:** MEDLINE. **Networks/Consortia:** Member of New England Regional Medical Library Service (NERMLS); Hospital Library Development Services.

CATHOLIC SCHOOL COMMISSION OF MONTREAL
See: Commission des Ecoles Catholiques de Montreal

★2412★
CATHOLIC SEMINARY FOUNDATION OF INDIANAPOLIS - LIBRARY (Rel-Theol)
4545 Northwestern Ave.   Phone: (317) 925-9095
Indianapolis, IN 46208   Rev. Ivan W. Hughes, O.S.B., Dir., Lib.Serv.
Founded: 1968. **Staff:** Prof 3. **Subjects:** Religion and theology, sociology, history, literature, biography. **Holdings:** 45,000 books; 657 bound periodical volumes; 800 phonograph records; 215 tapes. **Subscriptions:** 136 journals and other serials. **Services:** Interlibrary loans; copying (from Xerox only); library open to public with restrictions. **Networks/Consortia:** Member of Central Indiana Area Library Services Authority; Indianapolis Consortium for Urban Education. **Staff:** Rev. E. John Dorr, Libn.; Mary Jo Dorr, Asst.Libn.

★2413★
CATHOLIC SOCIAL SERVICES - LIBRARY (Soc Sci)
206 E. Michigan St.   Phone: (414) 271-2881
Milwaukee, WI 53202   Anne Kozlowski, Coord.
Staff: Prof 1. **Subjects:** Social work, psychotherapy, religion and psychiatry, psychology, medicine, education. **Special Collections:** National Catholic Charities Conference Reports since 1910; social welfare books since 1918. **Holdings:** 1250 books; 10 bound periodical volumes; 500 clippings, reports, pamphlets and brochures; 65 cassette tapes concerning social work and therapy. **Subscriptions:** 20 journals and other serials. **Services:** Library open to staff of local social agencies. **Remarks:** This library is primarily for the use of agency personnel, students assigned to the agency for field work and board members.

★2414★
CATHOLIC THEOLOGICAL UNION - LIBRARY (Rel-Theol)†
5401 S. Cornell Ave.   Phone: (312) 324-8000
Chicago, IL 60615   Rev. Kenneth O'Malley, C.P., Lib.Dir.
Founded: 1968. **Staff:** Prof 3; Other 2. **Subjects:** Catholic theology, scripture, canon law, missiology, patristics, homiletics. **Special Collections:** Franciscan Order - history, documents, spirituality. **Holdings:** 59,000 books; 25,000 bound periodical volumes; 560 AV materials (cataloged). **Subscriptions:** 450 journals and other serials; 5 newspapers. **Services:** Interlibrary loans; copying; library open to public for reference use only.

★2415★
CATHOLIC UNIVERSE BULLETIN - LIBRARY (Rel-Theol)
Chancery Bldg., 1027 Superior Ave.   Phone: (216) 696-6525
Cleveland, OH 44114   Edgar V. Barmann, Ed.
Subjects: Religious and lay leaders; welfare and educational institutions; churches; schools. **Holdings:** 98 bound periodical volumes; 60,500 photographs; 350,000 clippings. **Subscriptions:** 40 newspapers. **Services:** Copying; library open to public by appointment.

★2416★
CATHOLIC UNIVERSITY OF AMERICA - CHEMISTRY LIBRARY (Sci-Tech)
301 Maloney Bldg.   Phone: (202) 635-5389
Washington, DC 20064   N.L. Powell, Coord., Campus Libs.
Staff: 1. **Subjects:** Chemistry and related fields. **Holdings:** 10,243 books; 11,091 bound periodical volumes. **Subscriptions:** 149 journals and other serials. **Services:** Interlibrary loans; copying; library open to public. **Networks/Consortia:** Member of Consortium of Universities of the Washington Metropolitan Area; OCLC through CAPCON.

★2417★
CATHOLIC UNIVERSITY OF AMERICA - CLEMENTINE LIBRARY (Rel-Theol)
Mullen Library, Rm. 400-401   Phone: (202) 635-5091
Washington, DC 20064   Carolyn T. Lee, Cur.
Staff: Prof 1. **Subjects:** Pre-1800 theology; Jansenism; law; classical, European and Eastern languages and literature; Rome and the states of the church; missions; hagiography. **Holdings:** 9600 books. **Services:** Copying (limited); library open to public with restrictions. **Networks/Consortia:** Member of Consortium of Universities of the Washington Metropolitan Area; OCLC through CAPCON.

★2418★
CATHOLIC UNIVERSITY OF AMERICA - DEPARTMENT OF ARCHIVES AND MANUSCRIPTS (Hist)
Mullen Library, Rm. 4   Phone: (202) 635-5065
Washington, DC 20064   Dr. Anthony Zito, Univ.Archv.
Founded: 1948. **Staff:** Prof 1; Other 1. **Subjects:** 19th and 20th century American labor history; American Catholic Church history. **Special Collections:** Terence V. Powderly Papers; John Mitchell Papers; Lawrence F. Flick Papers; John Brophy Papers; John W. Hayes Papers; "Mother" Mary Harris Jones Papers; Philip Murray Papers; Aloisius Cardinal Muench Papers; Peter Guilday Papers; John A. Ryan Papers; National Catholic Welfare Conference Papers. **Holdings:** 3.5 million manuscript items. **Services:** Microfilming; copying; department open to scholars. **Networks/Consortia:** Member of Consortium of Universities of the Washington Metropolitan Area; OCLC through CAPCON. **Special Catalogs:** Finding aids for some papers. **Special Indexes:** Index to photographs of Archbishop Martin J. Connors papers.

★2419★
CATHOLIC UNIVERSITY OF AMERICA - ENGINEERING/ARCHITECTURE/ MATHEMATICS LIBRARY (Sci-Tech)
200 Pangborn Bldg.   Phone: (202) 635-5167
Washington, DC 20064   Robert Kimberlin, Act.Hd.
Staff: Prof 1; Other 2. **Subjects:** Engineering - aerospace, atmospheric, chemical, civil, mechanical, nuclear science, and electrical; architecture and planning; mathematics. **Holdings:** 28,368 books; 12,582 bound periodical volumes. **Subscriptions:** 535 journals and other serials. **Services:** Interlibrary loans; copying; library open to public. **Computerized Information Services:** MEDLINE, SDC. **Networks/Consortia:** Member of Consortium of Universities of the Washington Metropolitan Area; OCLC through CAPCON. **Remarks:** This library serves as the central office for all science libraries of the university.

★2420★
CATHOLIC UNIVERSITY OF AMERICA - HUMANITIES LIBRARY
Mullen Library, Rm. 114
Washington, DC 20064
Defunct. Merged with Theology/Philosophy/Canon Law/Religious Education Library to form Religious Studies/Philosophy/Humanities Division.

★2421★
CATHOLIC UNIVERSITY OF AMERICA - LIBRARY SCIENCE LIBRARY (Info Sci)
Marist Bldg.
620 Michigan Ave., N.E.   Phone: (202) 635-5092
Washington, DC 20064   Vivian Templin, Act.Hd.
Staff: Prof 1; Other 1. **Subjects:** Library science, history of books,

information retrieval, automation, book selection, cataloging. **Holdings:** 25,000 books; 25,000 bound periodical volumes; 1000 reels of microfilm (cataloged); 1500 VF materials; 2000 theses and research papers; annual reports; library school catalogs; handbooks. **Subscriptions:** 215 journals and other serials. **Services:** Interlibrary loans; copying; library open to public for reference use only. **Networks/Consortia:** Member of Consortium of Universities of the Washington Metropolitan Area; OCLC through CAPCON.

★2422★
CATHOLIC UNIVERSITY OF AMERICA - MUSIC LIBRARY (Mus)
Ward Music Bldg.   Phone: (202) 635-5424
Washington, DC 20064   Elizabeth M. Libbey, Music Libn.
Founded: 1952. **Staff:** Prof 1; Other 1. **Subjects:** Musicology, music education, performance. **Holdings:** 10,058 books; 1700 bound periodical volumes; 12,341 pieces of music (cataloged); 8360 recordings (cataloged); 572 tapes (cataloged); 4000 teaching aids. **Subscriptions:** 120 journals and other serials. **Services:** Interlibrary loans; library open to public with restrictions. **Networks/Consortia:** Member of Consortium of Universities of the Washington Metropolitan Area; OCLC through CAPCON. **Publications:** Major Holdings, every 5 years; periodical titles list, annual. **Special Catalogs:** Catalogs to recordings and tapes (card).

CATHOLIC UNIVERSITY OF AMERICA - NATIONAL REHABILITATION INFORMATION CENTER
See: National Rehabilitation Information Center

★2423★
CATHOLIC UNIVERSITY OF AMERICA - NURSING/BIOLOGY LIBRARY (Med)
                                    Phone: (202) 635-5411
Washington, DC 20064   N.L. Powell, Libn.
Staff: Prof 1; Other 2. **Subjects:** Nursing, medicine, social and physical sciences, biological and botanical sciences. **Holdings:** 38,230 books; 15,691 bound periodical volumes; 2505 reels of microfilm and 2727 theses (cataloged). **Subscriptions:** 382 journals and other serials. **Services:** Interlibrary loans; copying; library open to public for reference use only. **Computerized Information Services:** MEDLINE, SDC. **Networks/Consortia:** Member of Consortium of Universities of the Washington Metropolitan Area; OCLC through CAPCON.

★2424★
CATHOLIC UNIVERSITY OF AMERICA - OLIVEIRA LIMA LIBRARY (Area-Ethnic)
                                    Phone: (202) 635-5059
Washington, DC 20064   Manoel Cardozo, Cur.
Founded: 1916. **Staff:** Prof 2. **Subjects:** Brazil and Portugal - history, literature, church history, economic history, medical history; Portugal's colonial expansion and diplomatic history; Brazilian travel; European biography; Brazilian and African ethnography; native languages of Brazil, Africa, Argentina, Chile, Paraguay and Spain; Portuguese Africa; substantial materials on Spain, Spanish America, Great Britain, France, Germany, Italy, Japan, China. **Special Collections:** Lima Family papers; Tracts on the Portuguese Inquisition; collection of pamphlets on 19th century Portuguese liberalism; Dutch pamphlets on 17th century Brazil; Portuguese Restoration, 1640-1668; Society of Jesus; 19th century Brazilian newspapers; Portuguese newspapers of early liberal period. **Holdings:** 52,380 books; 1600 bound periodical volumes; 121,529 pages of manuscripts. **Subscriptions:** 73 journals and other serials; 7 newspapers. **Services:** Copying; library open to public with restrictions. **Networks/Consortia:** Member of Consortium of Universities of the Washington Metropolitan Area; OCLC through CAPCON. **Publications:** A Conspectus of the Oliveira Lima Library and its holdings (printed in both English and Portuguese versions); The Friends of the Oliveira Lima Library Newsletter; The Oliveira Lima Library, pamphlet - for internal distribution only; Oliveira Lima and the Catholic University of America. **Special Catalogs:** Bibliographical and Historical Description of the Rarest Books in the Oliveira Lima Collection at the Catholic University of America, 1 volume, 1927; A Guide to the Manuscripts in the Lima Library, The Catholic University of America, Washington, DC, 34 pages, 1971. **Staff:** Ralph J. Annicharico, Asst. to Cur.

★2425★
CATHOLIC UNIVERSITY OF AMERICA - PHYSICS LIBRARY (Sci-Tech)
208 Keane Bldg.   Phone: (202) 635-5320
Washington, DC 20064   N.L. Powell, Coord., Campus Libs.
Staff: 1. **Subjects:** Physics. **Holdings:** 7000 books; 3000 bound periodical volumes. **Subscriptions:** 179 journals and other serials. **Services:** Interlibrary loans; copying; library open to public. **Networks/Consortia:** Member of Consortium of Universities of the Washington Metropolitan Area; OCLC through CAPCON.

★2426★
CATHOLIC UNIVERSITY OF AMERICA - RELIGIOUS STUDIES/ PHILOSOPHY/HUMANITIES DIVISION LIBRARY (Rel-Theol; Hum)
Mullen Library, Rm. 300   Phone: (202) 635-5088
Washington, DC 20064   Bruce Miller, Coord.
Staff: Prof 3. **Subjects:** Theology, philosophy, canon law, religion, biblical studies, Christian literature, church history, art, ancient and medieval history, Greek and Latin, English, comparative literature, modern languages, speech and drama. **Special Collections:** Catholic Americana (10,000 volumes). **Holdings:** 230,000 books; 50,000 bound periodical volumes. **Subscriptions:** 1133 journals and other serials. **Services:** Interlibrary loans; library open to public. **Networks/Consortia:** Member of Consortium of Universities of the Washington Metropolitan Area; OCLC through CAPCON. **Formed by the Merger of:** Its Humanities Library with the Theology/Philosophy/Canon Law/ Religious Education Library.

★2427★
CATHOLIC UNIVERSITY OF AMERICA - SCHOOL OF LAW - ROBERT J. WHITE LAW LIBRARY (Law)
Michigan Ave.   Phone: (202) 635-5000
Washington, DC 20064   Prof. John R. Valeri, Dir.
Staff: Prof 4; Other 10. **Subjects:** Law. **Special Collections:** Religion and the law (500 volumes). **Holdings:** 123,000 volumes. **Subscriptions:** 1141 journals and other serials; 6 newspapers. **Services:** Interlibrary loans; copying; library open to public. **Staff:** Patrick Petit, Assoc. Law Libn.; Marie Sexton, Asst. Law Libn./Pub.Serv.

★2428★
CATHOLIC UNIVERSITY OF AMERICA - SEMITICS - INSTITUTE OF CHRISTIAN ORIENTAL RESEARCH (ICOR) LIBRARY (Hum)
Mullen Library, Rm. 18   Phone: (202) 635-5091
Washington, DC 20064   Carolyn T. Lee, Cur.
Staff: Prof 1; Other 1. **Subjects:** Coptic, Syriac, Arabic, Biblical Hebrew, Cuneiform languages; Christian Orient; theology; philosophy; Americana. **Special Collections:** Collection of the Institute of Christian Oriental Research, begun from the personal library of the founder, Monsignor H. Hyvernat (circa 25,000); Clementine Foster Stearns Collection on the Knights of Malta (400 titles); catechisms (1300 volumes). **Holdings:** 33,000 volumes; 145 volumes of photographs of Coptic manuscripts in Paris and Naples; 112 volumes of photographs of Coptic manuscripts in Pierpont Morgan Library; 52 VF drawers of offprints and department members' papers; 56 boxes of correspondence of Monsignor Hyvernat; 89 volumes of bound miscellanea (Christian Orient studies); 20 VF drawers of Catholic pamphlets; 2000 books and pamphlets on American Catholic local history. **Subscriptions:** 145 journals and other serials. **Services:** Copying (limited); library open to public with restrictions. **Networks/Consortia:** Member of Consortium of Universities of the Washington Metropolitan Area; OCLC through CAPCON.

CATHOLIC UNIVERSITY OF AMERICA - THEOLOGY/PHILOSOPHY/CANON LAW/RELIGIOUS EDUCATION LIBRARY
See: Catholic University of America - Religious Studies/Philosophy/ Humanities Division Library

★2429★
CATHOLIC UNIVERSITY OF PUERTO RICO - MONSIGNOR JUAN FREMIOT TORRES OLIVER LAW LIBRARY (Law)
                                    Phone: (809) 844-4150
Ponce, PR 00732   Noelia Padua-Flores, Dir.
Founded: 1960. **Staff:** Prof 4; Other 8. **Subjects:** Civil law, criminal law, constitutional law, torts. **Special Collections:** U.S. and United Nations documents. **Holdings:** 94,237 books; 10,468 bound periodical volumes; 1900 pamphlets (cataloged). **Subscriptions:** 1907 journals and other serials; 11 newspapers. **Services:** Interlibrary loans; copying; library open to public. **Publications:** Sumario de Revistas; Bolletin Trimestral. **Staff:** Gregorio Mejill, Cat.Dept.Dir.; Carmen Gonzalez, Acq.Dept.Dir.; Teresita Guillermard, Ref. & Circ.Dept.Dir.

CATLIN (George B.) MEMORIAL LIBRARY
See: Detroit News - George B. Catlin Memorial Library

★2430★
CATTARAUGUS COUNTY MEMORIAL AND HISTORICAL MUSEUM - LIBRARY (Hist)
Court St.   Phone: (716) 938-9111
Little Valley, NY 14755   Lorna Spencer, Cur.
Staff: 2. **Subjects:** Local history. **Holdings:** 300 books; 60 bound periodical volumes; 10 maps; 27 reels of microfilm; cemetery lists. **Services:** Copying; library open to public on a limited schedule. **Special Indexes:** Index to Cattaraugus County census, 1810-1860 (book).

CATTELL (Richard B.) MEMORIAL LIBRARY
See: Lahey Clinic Medical Center

★2431★
CAUDILL ROWLETT SCOTT - LIBRARY (Art; Plan)
1111 W. Loop S.
Box 22427   Phone: (713) 621-9600
Houston, TX 77027   Nancy S. Acker, Libn.
Founded: 1968. **Staff:** Prof 1. **Subjects:** Architecture, planning, engineering, landscape design, interior and graphic design, management. **Holdings:** 2100 books; 300 bound periodical volumes; 335 CRS reports (cataloged); 44 VF drawers research files. **Subscriptions:** 71 journals and other serials. **Services:** Interlibrary loans; copying; SDI; library open to public by appointment. **Computerized Information Services:** SDC, DIALOG, New York Times Information Service.

★2432★
CAUSE - LIBRARY (Info Sci)
737 29th St.   Phone: (303) 449-4430
Boulder, CO 80303   Charles R. Thomas, Exec.Dir.
Staff: Prof 3; Other 1. **Subjects:** Administrative information systems in higher education. **Holdings:** Figures not available. **Services:** Copying; library open to members only. **Publications:** List of publications - available upon request. **Special Indexes:** Exchange Index, a keyword listing of systems and documents available through the library; separate keyword listing of papers presented at the national conferences.

CAVAGNA LIBRARY
See: University of Illinois - Map and Geography Library

CAVEN LIBRARY
See: University of Toronto - Knox College

CAWP
See: Center for the American Woman & Politics

CAYCE (Edgar) FOUNDATION
See: Association for Research and Enlightenment - Edgar Cayce Foundation

★2433★
CAYLOR-NICKEL CLINIC AND HOSPITAL - MEDICAL LIBRARY (Med)
311 S. Scott St.   Phone: (219) 824-3500
Bluffton, IN 46714   Patricia Niblick, Med.Libn.
Founded: 1915. **Staff:** Prof 2. **Subjects:** Surgery, internal medicine, pathology, radiology, pediatrics, obstetrics, gynecology, urology, nursing, pharmacology, endocrinology. **Special Collections:** Complete set of the Collected Papers in Medicine and Surgery from the Mayo Clinic and the Mayo Foundation. **Holdings:** 9782 books; 5126 bound periodical volumes; 1 VF drawer of staff reprints (cataloged); 902 tapes (cataloged); 10 films (cataloged). **Subscriptions:** 417 journals and other serials. **Services:** Interlibrary loans; copying; library open to public with restrictions. **Computerized Information Services:** Computerized cataloging and serials. **Networks/Consortia:** Member of Northeast Indiana Health Sciences Libraries; Regional Medical Library - Region 3; TRI-ALSA. **Publications:** New Acquisitions list.

★2434★
CAYUGA COUNTY HISTORICAL RESEARCH CENTER - LIBRARY (Hist)
County Office Bldg.   Phone: (315) 253-1300
Auburn, NY 13021   Mrs. Leo Pinckney, Asst. County Hist.
Staff: 2. **Subjects:** Local history, genealogy. **Holdings:** 300 books; 500 bound periodical volumes; 50 boxes and 27 VF drawers of reports, manuscripts, letters, broadsides and clippings; 700 microfilms of newpapers; 1500 microfilms of records; photographs. **Subscriptions:** 16 journals and other serials. **Services:** Copying; library open to public for reference use only. **Publications:** Cayuga Gazette, annual. **Staff:** Malcolm Goodelle, Archv.

★2435★
CAYUGA MUSEUM OF HISTORY AND ART - LIBRARY & ARCHIVES (Hist)
203 Genesee St.   Phone: (315) 253-8051
Auburn, NY 13021   Prof. Walter K. Long, Dir.
Founded: 1936. **Staff:** Prof 1. **Subjects:** Central New York Indian history, local history. **Holdings:** 3000 books; 1000 bound periodical volumes. **Subscriptions:** 6 journals and other serials. **Services:** Interlibrary loans; library open to public during museum hours.

CBC
See: Canadian Broadcasting Corporation

★2436★
CBS INC. - CBS LAW LIBRARY (Law)
51 W. 52nd St.   Phone: (212) 975-4260
New York, NY 10019   Seth G. Alspaugh, Law Libn.
Staff: Prof 1. **Subjects:** Law. **Holdings:** 4500 books; 12 bound periodical volumes. **Subscriptions:** 30 journals and other serials; 10 newspapers. **Services:** Interlibrary loans; library open to public for reference use only on request.

★2437★
CBS INC. - CBS NEWS REFERENCE LIBRARY (Info Sci)
524 W. 57th St.   Phone: (212) 975-2877
New York, NY 10019   Laura B. Kapnick, Dir.
Founded: 1940. **Staff:** Prof 7; Other 8. **Subjects:** Radio, television, biography, government, politics. **Special Collections:** CBS News program transcripts (86 VF drawers). **Holdings:** 25,000 books; 420 bound periodical volumes; 420 VF drawers of clippings; 3700 reels of microfilm; 20,000 microfiche. **Subscriptions:** 250 journals and other serials; 10 newspapers. **Services:** Interlibrary loans; copying; library open to public by appointment with librarians approval. **Computerized Information Services:** New York Times Information Service. **Staff:** Carole D. Parnes, Mgr., Indus.Info.; Carolyn Wilder, Mgr., Lib.Serv.; Sara Wolozin, Mgr., Morgue Serv.

★2438★
CBS INC. - CBS TECHNOLOGY CENTER (Sci-Tech)
227 High Ridge Rd.   Phone: (203) 327-2000
Stamford, CT 06905   Rita Reade, Chf.Libn.
Founded: 1959. **Staff:** Prof 1. **Subjects:** Electronics, television, recording systems, acoustics. **Holdings:** 3000 books; 1000 bound periodical volumes. **Subscriptions:** 200 journals and other serials. **Services:** Library open for reference to members of local library groups. **Computerized Information Services:** DIALOG, SDC.

★2439★
CBS RECORDS - ARCHIVES (Mus)
49 E. 52nd St.   Phone: (212) 975-4949
New York, NY 10019   Martine Vinces, Archv.
Founded: 1964. **Staff:** Prof 1; Other 1. **Holdings:** 70,000 phonograph records (cataloged); Columbia catalogs, 1894 to present; 350,000 recording matrix cards; company memoranda; photograph archive. **Services:** Library open to professionals in the recording field by appointment only.

CCPM HISTORICAL COLLECTION/MUSEUM LIBRARY
See: Crosby County Pioneer Memorial

★2440★
CEDAR CREST COLLEGE - WOMEN'S CENTER (Soc Sci)
                                             Phone: (215) 437-4471
Allentown, PA 18104   Ginny Pityo Mihalik, Dir.
Staff: 2. **Subjects:** Women - career opportunities, money and credit, consciousness, personal growth; the women's movement. **Holdings:** 150 books; college guides, occupational reference materials. **Services:** Center open to public for reference use only.

★2441★
CEDAR FALLS HISTORICAL SOCIETY - ROWND HISTORICAL LIBRARY (Hist)
Cedar Falls Historical Museum
303 Clay St.   Phone: (319) 266-5149
Cedar Falls, IA 50613   Rosemary Beach, Dir.
Founded: 1968. **Staff:** Prof 4. **Subjects:** Local, state and U.S. history; natural ice industry; 19th century agriculture. **Special Collections:** Books by Cedar Falls authors (100 volumes); Cedar Falls Record, 1897-1950 (165 volumes); Diamonds Bulletin, 1932-1953 (25 volumes). **Holdings:** 400 books; 250 bound periodical volumes; 75 Roger Leavitt notebooks; 60 oral history tapes; 65 scrapbooks; 324 issues of The Palimpsest magazine, 1950 to present; 3 file cabinets of information files; 1 file cabinet of photographs. **Subscriptions:** 6 journals and other serials. **Services:** Library open to public for reference use only. **Publications:** Cedar Falls Historical Society Newsletter, monthly - to members.

★2442★
CEDAR RAPIDS MUSEUM OF ART - HERBERT S. STAMATS ART LIBRARY (Art)
324 3rd St., S.E.
Cedar Rapids, IA 52401   Phone: (319) 366-7503
Founded: 1967. **Staff:** 1. **Subjects:** Art history, architecture, archeology,

studio art, crafts, gardening. **Special Collections:** Grant Wood Archives. **Holdings:** 1000 books; 50 bound periodical volumes; museum catalogs; 2 VF drawers of clippings. **Subscriptions:** 60 journals and other serials. **Services:** Interlibrary loans with restrictions; library open to public for reference use only. **Formerly:** Cedar Rapids Art Center.

★2443★
CEDAR RAPIDS PUBLIC LIBRARY - BUSINESS CENTER
428 Third Ave., S.E.
Cedar Rapids, IA 52401
Defunct

★2444★
CEDAR SPRINGS FOUNDATION - LIBRARY (Hum)
42421 Auberry Rd.   Phone: (209) 855-2438
Auberry, CA 93602   William H. Young, Libn.
Staff: Prof 1. **Subjects:** Education, psychology, humanities, religion, philosophy. **Special Collections:** Agnosticism, free thought, humanism, peace, thanatology. **Holdings:** 4000 books; 50 cassette tapes; 30 boxes of reprints; 150 VF folders of clippings. **Subscriptions:** 105 journals and other serials. **Services:** Interlibrary loans; copying; library open to public by appointment. **Publications:** Newsletter, quarterly; occasional papers and bibliographies.

★2445★
CEDAR VALE REGIONAL HOSPITAL - LIBRARY (Med)†
Cedar St.
Box 398   Phone: (316) 758-2266
Cedar Vale, KS 67024   Mrs. Dera C. Brunstad, Libn.
Founded: 1972. **Staff:** 1. **Subjects:** Medicine and allied subjects. **Holdings:** 3000 books; teaching tapes and slides. **Subscriptions:** 32 journals and other serials. **Services:** Library open to public for reference use only. **Computerized Information Services:** Computerized cataloging and acquisitions. **Remarks:** The library is the private property of Dr. Rosellen E. Cohnberg and her husband, John F. Meyers, Administrator.

★2446★
CEDARCREST REGIONAL HOSPITAL - MEDICAL LIBRARY (Med)
525 Russell Rd.   Phone: (203) 666-4613
Newington, CT 06111   Helen Langin, Act.Libn.
Staff: 1. **Subjects:** Psychiatry, psychology, psychiatric nursing, medicine, mental health, pharmacology. **Holdings:** 1467 books; 768 bound periodical volumes; 165 cassettes; 166 pamphlets and reports. **Subscriptions:** 104 journals and other serials. **Services:** Interlibrary loans; copying; library open to CAHSL members and state facilities. **Networks/Consortia:** Member of State Library Services to Agencies and Institutions Network; Connecticut Association of Health Science Libraries (CAHSL).

★2447★
CEDARS OF LEBANON MEDICAL CENTER - MEDICAL LIBRARY (Med)
1400 N.W. 12th Ave.   Phone: (305) 325-5737
Miami, FL 33136   Irene Bohlmann, Hd.
Staff: Prof 1; Other 1. **Subjects:** Medicine, surgery, nursing, hospital administration. **Holdings:** 2500 books; 6500 bound periodical volumes; 50 AV cassettes; 150 audio cassettes; 10 video discs. **Subscriptions:** 132 journals and other serials. **Services:** Interlibrary loans; copying; SDI; library open to public by appointment. **Computerized Information Services:** MEDLINE. **Networks/Consortia:** Member of Miami Health Sciences Library Consortium. **Publications:** Under the Covers, bimonthly - to staff; Annual Report - to committee and administration. **Special Catalogs:** Catalog of serials (card and print).

★2448★
CEDARS-SINAI MEDICAL CENTER - HEALTH SCIENCES INFORMATION CENTER (Med)
8700 Beverly Blvd.
Box 48956   Phone: (213) 855-3751
Los Angeles, CA 90048   Ellen Wilson Green, Dir. of Libs.
Founded: 1953. **Staff:** Prof 4; Other 5. **Subjects:** Clinical medicine. **Holdings:** 10,000 books; 4 VF drawers of pamphlets; microfilm. **Subscriptions:** 561 journals and other serials. **Services:** Interlibrary loans; copying; library open to public for reference use only. **Computerized Information Services:** MEDLINE, SDC, BRS. **Staff:** Phyllis Soben, Med.Libn.; William Jacobs, Med.Libn.; Ellen Aaronson, Med.Libn.

★2449★
CEGEP ST-JEAN SUR RICHELIEU - BIBLIOTHEQUE (Hist; Hum)
30 Blvd. Du Seminaire
C.P. 1018
St. Jean, PQ, Canada J3B 5J4   Phone: (514) 347-5301
                                      Michel Robert, Chf.Libn.
Founded: 1968. **Staff:** Prof 2; Other 6. **Subjects:** History of Quebec, Quebec

literature. **Holdings:** 58,200 books; 6766 bound periodical volumes; 16,351 slides; 6040 cassettes, tapes and phonograph records; 401 films; 103 reels of microfilm. **Subscriptions:** 190 journals and other serials; 5 newspapers. **Services:** Interlibrary loans; copying; library open to public. **Publications:** Listes des nouveautes, monthly. **Staff:** Robert Dufort, Ref.Libn.

CEGEP DE ST-LAURENT - COLLEGE DE MUSIQUE SAINTE-CROIX
See: College de Musique Sainte-Croix

★2450★
CEGEP DE TROIS-RIVIERES - BIBLIOTHEQUE (Hum)
3500 De Courval   Phone: (819) 376-1721
Trois-Rivieres, PQ, Canada G9A 5E6   Denis Simard, Dir.
Founded: 1968. **Staff:** Prof 5; Other 13. **Subjects:** Literature, humanities, philosophy, pure and applied sciences, history, geography, linguistics. **Special Collections:** Materiautheque (architecture); Arteke (applied arts). **Holdings:** 95,000 books; 15,000 bound periodical volumes; AV material. **Subscriptions:** 454 journals and other serials. **Services:** Interlibrary loans; copying; library open to public. **Computerized Information Services:** DIALOG, Informatech France-Quebec. **Networks/Consortia:** Member of ASTED; Services Documentaires de la Region-04, Quebec (SDR-04). **Publications:** Bienvenue a la Bibliotheque. **Special Catalogs:** Liste des periodiques de la Region-04; Films de la Cinematheque. **Staff:** Le Duy Quy, Cat. & Clas.; Monique Roberge, Audiovideotheque; Raymond Levesque, Ref.; Solange Coulombe, Acq.; Danielle Baillargeon, Ref.; Solange Thibault, Per.

★2451★
CEGEP DU VIEUX MONTREAL - LIBRARY (Art)†
255 Ontario St. E.
Station N, P.O. Box 1444   Phone: (514) 279-1759
Montreal, PQ, Canada H2X 3M8
Staff: Prof 4; Other 3. **Subjects:** History of arts, advertising art, ceramics, interior decoration, industrial design, photography, architecture, graphic arts. **Holdings:** 8000 books; 6800 bound periodical volumes. **Subscriptions:** 280 journals and other serials. **Services:** Copying; library open to public.

★2452★
CELANESE CANADA, INC. - LIBRARY (Bus-Fin; Sci-Tech)
Sta. A., P.O. Box 6170   Phone: (514) 871-5789
Montreal, PQ, Canada H3C 3K8   Miss L. Trevaskis, Libn.
Founded: 1960. **Staff:** 2. **Subjects:** Business management, chemicals, economics, textiles, data processing. **Holdings:** 3000 books and bound periodical volumes; 12 drawers of annual reports of other companies; 25 drawers and shelves of government publications; 4 drawers of clippings; pamphlets and documents. **Subscriptions:** 200 journals and other serials; 10 newspapers. **Services:** Interlibrary loans; copying; library open to public with permission. **Remarks:** Library is located at 800 Dorchester Blvd., W., Montreal, PQ, H3B 1X9.

★2453★
CELANESE CORPORATION - CELANESE CHEMICAL COMPANY, INC. - TECHNICAL CENTER - LIBRARY (Sci-Tech)
Box 9077   Phone: (512) 241-2343
Corpus Christi, TX 78408   Betty Goodridge, Info.Ctr.Coord.
Founded: 1947. **Staff:** Prof 2; Other 4. **Subjects:** Organic aliphatic chemistry and derived technologies; physical chemistry of combustion; production of petroleum chemicals via direct oxidation. **Holdings:** 17,000 books; 9000 bound periodical volumes; 225,000 patents (U.S. and foreign); internal and government technical reports. **Subscriptions:** 300 journals and other serials. **Services:** Interlibrary loans. **Publications:** Patent Abstract Bulletin, weekly (abstracts of patents); report of recent acquisitions, monthly. **Computerized Information Services:** Online systems. **Remarks:** Includes the holdings of its Research and Development Laboratory - Clarkwood Library.

★2454★
CELANESE CORPORATION - CELANESE FIBERS COMPANY - TECHNICAL LIBRARY
Cherry Rd. Sta.
Rock Hill, SC 29730
Subjects: Textiles, chemistry, engineering, biochemistry, business. **Holdings:** 3000 books; 200 bound periodical volumes. **Remarks:** Presently inactive.

★2455★
CELANESE CORPORATION - CELANESE PLASTICS & SPECIALTIES COMPANY - INFORMATION CENTER (Bus-Fin)
26 Main St.   Phone: (201) 635-2600
Chatham, NJ 07928
Founded: 1952. **Staff:** Prof 1; Other 1. **Subjects:** Marketing material on plastics, business. **Holdings:** 1000 books; 600 market reports; 30 reels of

microfilm; 60 microfiche; 36 file drawers. **Subscriptions:** 120 journals and other serials; 5 newspapers. **Services:** Interlibrary loans; library open to students. **Computerized Information Services:** Online systems. **Publications:** Information Center Bulletin.

★2456★
CELANESE CORPORATION - SUMMIT RESEARCH LABORATORIES - TECHNICAL INFORMATION CENTER (Sci-Tech)
Box 1000   Phone: (201) 522-7500
Summit, NJ 07901   Dr. Gregory V. Nelson, Mgr., Info.Serv.
Staff: Prof 2; Other 1. **Subjects:** Polymers; plastics; fibers; chemicals; coatings; chemistry - organic, physical, analytical, inorganic. **Holdings:** 20,000 books; 20,000 bound and microform periodical volumes; 35,000 internal reports in hard copy and microform; 1.5 million patents in microform. **Subscriptions:** 400 journals and other serials; 6 newspapers. **Services:** Interlibrary loans; center open to public for reference use only by permission. **Computerized Information Services:** DIALOG, SDC; internal database. **Remarks:** Includes the holdings of the Plastics Research and Development Center. **Staff:** Mary Ann Bury, Supv., Info.Ctr.; Dr. Bernice I. Feuer, Info.Spec.

★2457★
CELANESE PLASTICS & SPECIALTIES COMPANY - TECHNICAL CENTER - RESEARCH LIBRARY (Sci-Tech)
9800 Bluegrass Pkwy.   Phone: (502) 585-8053
Jeffersontown, KY 40299   Robert A. McGrew, Libn.
Founded: 1947. **Staff:** Prof 1. **Subjects:** Polymer chemistry, organic chemistry, general physics, mathematics, paper technology, basic textile technology. **Holdings:** 1000 books; 3500 bound periodical volumes; 100,000 chemical patents, by class; U.S. chemical patents from 1968 on microfilm. **Subscriptions:** 130 journals and other serials. **Services:** Interlibrary loans; library not open to public. **Computerized Information Services:** DIALOG, SDC.

CENEX
See: Farmers Union Central Exchange, Inc.

★2458★
CENTENNIAL COLLEGE OF APPLIED ARTS & TECHNOLOGY - ASHTONBEE CAMPUS RESOURCE CENTRE (Sci-Tech)
Sta. A, P.O. Box 631   Phone: (416) 752-4444
Scarborough, ON, Canada M1K 5E9   Wendy Scott, Campus Libn.
Founded: 1972. **Staff:** Prof 1; Other 5. **Subjects:** Automotive technology; aircraft/avionics. **Holdings:** 13,680 volumes. **Subscriptions:** 182 journals and other serials. **Services:** Interlibrary loans; copying; library open to public. **Computerized Information Services:** DOBIS; computerized circulation. **Publications:** Student guide; faculty guide; fact sheet, annual. **Special Catalogs:** Videotape catalog; film catalog. **Remarks:** Library is located at 75 Ashtonbee Rd., Scarborough, ON, M1L 3Z6. **Staff:** Bette-Ann Fraser, Sr.Lib.Techn.

★2459★
CENTENNIAL COLLEGE OF APPLIED ARTS & TECHNOLOGY - EAST YORK CAMPUS RESOURCE CENTRE (Bus-Fin; Educ)
Sta. A, P.O. Box 631   Phone: (416) 469-5981
Scarborough, ON, Canada M1K 5E9   Ron Wood, Campus Libn.
Founded: 1979. **Staff:** Prof 1; Other 2. **Subjects:** Business. **Holdings:** 11,211 volumes. **Subscriptions:** 190 journals and other serials. **Services:** Interlibrary loans; copying; library open to public. **Computerized Information Services:** DOBIS; computerized circulation. **Publications:** Student guide; Faculty Guide, annual. **Remarks:** Library is located at 951 Carlaw Ave., East York, ON, M4K 3M2, and contains the holdings of the former Ontario Teacher Education College, Toronto.

★2460★
CENTENNIAL COLLEGE OF APPLIED ARTS & TECHNOLOGY - PROGRESS CAMPUS RESOURCE CENTRE (Bus-Fin; Sci-Tech)
Sta. A, P.O. Box 631   Phone: (416) 439-7180
Scarborough, ON, Canada M1K 5E9   Judy Downs, Campus Libn.
Founded: 1977. **Staff:** Prof 2; Other 7. **Subjects:** Business, engineering, law. **Holdings:** 25,307 volumes. **Subscriptions:** 211 journals and other serials. **Services:** Interlibrary loans; copying; library open to public. **Computerized Information Services:** DOBIS; computerized circulation. **Publications:** Student guide; faculty guide; fact sheet, annual. **Remarks:** Library is located at 41 Progress Ct., Scarborough, ON, M1L 3Z6. **Staff:** Susan Whitzman, Asst. Campus Libn.

★2461★
CENTENNIAL COLLEGE OF APPLIED ARTS & TECHNOLOGY - WARDEN WOODS CAMPUS RESOURCE CENTRE (Soc Sci)
Sta. A, P.O. Box 631   Phone: (416) 694-3241
Scarborough, ON, Canada M1K 5E9   Annetta Turner, Campus Libn.
Founded: 1966. **Staff:** Prof 2; Other 7. **Subjects:** Nursing; social sciences and humanities; women's studies; early childhood education; social services. **Holdings:** 35,736 volumes. **Subscriptions:** 332 journals and other serials; 6 newspapers. **Services:** Interlibrary loans; copying; library open to public. **Computerized Information Services:** DOBIS; computerized circulation. **Publications:** Student guide; faculty guide; fact sheet, annual. **Special Catalogs:** Videotape, nursing kits and film catalogs. **Remarks:** The library is located at 651 Warden Ave., Scarborough, ON, M1L 3Z6, and includes the libraries of the former Toronto East General Campus and the Scarborough Regional Campus. **Staff:** Holly Prue, Asst. Campus Libn.

CENTENNIAL MUSEUM LIBRARY
See: Royal Canadian Mounted Police

★2462★
CENTER FOR ACTION ON ENDANGERED SPECIES, INC. - LIBRARY (Env-Cons)
175 W. Main St.   Phone: (617) 772-0445
Ayer, MA 01432   Phoebe Wray, Exec.Dir.
Founded: 1973. **Staff:** 5. **Subjects:** Endangered species, marine mammals. **Special Collections:** Whales and whaling (750 reports, 200 volumes). **Holdings:** 1500 books; 4500 reports; 800 slides. **Subscriptions:** 75 journals and other serials. **Services:** Copying; library open to public for reference use only. **Special Catalogs:** Bibliographies on the bowhead whale, killer whale, animal rights.

★2463★
CENTER FOR ADVANCED STUDY IN THE BEHAVIORAL SCIENCES - LIBRARY (Soc Sci)
202 Junipero Serra Blvd.   Phone: (415) 321-2052
Stanford, CA 94305   Margaret Amara, Libn.
Founded: 1954. **Staff:** Prof 2. **Subjects:** Anthropology, history, philosophy, political science, psychology, sociology. **Special Collections:** Ralph W. Tyler Collection (585 publications representing works conceived, initiated or completed by Fellows during their stay at the center). **Holdings:** 4500 books. **Subscriptions:** 275 journals and other serials; 18 newspapers. **Services:** Library not open to public. **Computerized Information Services:** DIALOG, RLIN. **Special Catalogs:** Catalog of the Ralph W. Tyler Collection.

CENTER FOR AFRICAN ORAL DATA
See: Indiana University - Archives of Traditional Music

CENTER FOR AIR ENVIRONMENT STUDIES
See: Pennsylvania State University

CENTER FOR ALCOHOL STUDIES
See: University of North Carolina, Chapel Hill

★2464★
CENTER FOR THE AMERICAN WOMAN & POLITICS - LIBRARY (Soc Sci)
Eagleton Institute, Rutgers University
Wood Lawn, Neilson Campus   Phone: (201) 932-9384
New Brunswick, NJ 08901   Kathy Stanwick, Asst.Dir.
Founded: 1971. **Staff:** 9. **Subjects:** Women and American politics and government. **Holdings:** 500 books; 2000 papers, pamphlets, clippings. **Subscriptions:** 50 journals and other serials. **Services:** Copying; library open to public on request. **Publications:** List of publications - available on request. **Remarks:** CAWP is a research and education center committed to increasing knowledge about American women's participation in government and politics. **Staff:** Ruth B. Mandel, Dir.

★2465★
CENTER FOR THE ANALYSIS OF HEALTH PRACTICES - LIBRARY (Med)
Harvard School of Public Health
677 Huntington Ave.   Phone: (617) 732-1060
Boston, MA 02115   Sara Arnold, Libn.
Founded: 1974. **Staff:** Prof 1; Other 1. **Subjects:** Primary health care, decision analysis, operations research, health economics, public policy regarding health care. **Holdings:** 3156 books and bound periodical volumes. **Subscriptions:** 16 journals and other serials. **Services:** Copying; library not open to public. **Publications:** Newsletter, quarterly - distributed to deans and chairmen of departments of medicine and surgery at medical schools in the U.S. and to the Schools of Public Health as well as pertinent government agencies. **Remarks:** The collection is small and basically a research center

acquiring up-to-date material.

★2466★
CENTER FOR APPLIED RESEARCH IN THE APOSTOLATE - ARCHIVES AND RESEARCH LIBRARY (Rel-Theol)
3700 Oakview Terrace, N.E.
Washington, DC 20017   Phone: (202) 832-2300
Dolores Liptak, R.S.M., Spec.Libn./Archv.
Founded: 1965. **Staff:** Prof 1; Other 1. **Subjects:** Church personnel and management, religious life, parish development, pastoral research and planning, overseas ministry, health ministry. **Special Collections:** Chapter documents from 100 religious communities for men and women; American congregations history and materials; Seminary Directories, 1965 to present; diocesan surveys; Religious Life; American church. **Holdings:** 2000 monographs; 200 titles of CARA publications, 1965 to present; 300 cubic feet of working papers. **Subscriptions:** 25 journals and other serials; 5 newspapers. **Services:** Library open to public on request. **Publications:** CARA Report; Seminary Forum; Forum for Religions. **Formerly:** Its CARA Research Library.

CENTER FOR ARTS INFORMATION
See: Clearinghouse for Arts Information

CENTER FOR ASTROPHYSICS LIBRARY
See: Harvard University - Observatory Library

CENTER FOR BIOETHICS
See: Georgetown University - Kennedy Institute of Ethics

CENTER FOR BIOPOLITICAL RESEARCH
See: Northern Illinois University

CENTER FOR CLIMACTERIC STUDIES
See: University of Florida

★2467★
CENTER FOR COMMUNITY ECONOMIC DEVELOPMENT - LIBRARY
1320 19th St., N.W.
Washington, DC 20036
Defunct

★2468★
CENTER FOR COMPUTER/LAW - LIBRARY (Law)
Box 54308 T.A.
Los Angeles, CA 90054   Phone: (312) 623-3321
Michael D. Scott, Exec.Dir.
Founded: 1977. **Staff:** Prof 1; Other 1. **Subjects:** Law - computer, communication, information; automation. **Holdings:** 1200 books; 60 bound periodical volumes; 1250 pamphlets, reprints; 500 microfiche. **Subscriptions:** 50 journals and other serials; 8 newspapers. **Services:** Copying; library open to paid members only. **Computerized Information Services:** Computerized cataloging and serials. **Publications:** Computer/Law Journal, quarterly - by subscription; In the Center, occasional newsletter - to members. **Remarks:** Library is located at 3500 Figueroa, Suite 211, Los Angeles, CA 90014.

★2469★
CENTER OF CONCERN - INFORMATION CENTER (Soc Sci)
3700 13th St., N.E.
Washington, DC 20017   Phone: (202) 635-2757
Maria Riley, Ed.
Subjects: International social justice issues, international development, women, labor, social theology. **Holdings:** Figures not available. **Publications:** Center Focus, bimonthly newsletter - free upon request. **Remarks:** The Center of Concern is an independent, interdisciplinary team engaged in social analysis, religious reflection and public education around questions of social justice with particular stress on the international dimension.

CENTER FOR CONNECTICUT STUDIES
See: Eastern Connecticut State College

★2470★
CENTER FOR CREATIVE LEADERSHIP - LIBRARY (Soc Sci)
5000 Laurinda Dr.
Greensboro, NC 27402   Phone: (919) 288-7210
Frank H. Freeman, Dir.
Founded: 1969. **Staff:** Prof 2; Other 1. **Subjects:** Leadership, management, organizational behavior, creativity, social psychology, industrial psychology. **Special Collections:** Psychological assessment (500 documents); performance appraisal (250 documents). **Holdings:** 4000 books; 400 bound periodical volumes; 600 dissertations and reports (cataloged); 500 technical reports; 4500 reprints and unpublished papers. **Subscriptions:** 165 journals and other serials; 5 newspapers. **Services:** Interlibrary loans; copying; SDI;

library open to center participants or visiting scholars. **Computerized Information Services:** Online systems; FROLIC (internal database); computerized serials. **Publications:** Acquisitions list, monthly - for internal distribution only; topical bibliographies, irregular - by request. **Special Catalogs:** Leadership/Management (card).

★2471★
CENTER FOR CREATIVE STUDIES/COLLEGE OF ART & DESIGN - LIBRARY (Art)
245 E. Kirby
Detroit, MI 48202   Phone: (313) 872-3118
Jean Peyrat, Libn.
Founded: 1966. **Staff:** Prof 2. **Subjects:** Art. **Special Collections:** Art History (30,000 slides). **Holdings:** 13,000 books; 319 bound periodical volumes; 80,000 flat pictures. **Subscriptions:** 71 journals and other serials. **Services:** Library open to public for reference use only.

CENTER FOR DEFENSE INFORMATION
See: Fund for Peace

CENTER FOR DEMOGRAPHIC STUDIES
See: Duke University

CENTER FOR EARLY ADOLESCENCE
See: University of North Carolina, Chapel Hill

★2472★
CENTER FOR EARLY EDUCATION - LAURA M. ELLIS MEMORIAL LIBRARY (Educ)
563 N. Alfred St.
Los Angeles, CA 90048   Phone: (213) 655-4878
Barbara M. Whitney, Libn.
Founded: 1968. **Staff:** Prof 1; Other 1. **Subjects:** Psychology; education - elementary, preschool, teacher, special; psychoanalysis; sociology; human development; parenting. **Holdings:** 14,800 books; 500 other cataloged items. **Subscriptions:** 110 journals and other serials. **Services:** Interlibrary loans; copying; library open to public on request.

CENTER FOR EASTERN CHRISTIAN STUDIES
See: John XXIII Ecumenical Center, Inc.

CENTER FOR ECONOMIC RESEARCH
See: Long Island University - C.W. Post Center

★2473★
CENTER FOR ENERGY AND ENVIRONMENT - RESEARCH COLLECTION (Sci-Tech)
College Sta.
Mayaguez, PR 00708   Phone: (809) 832-1408
Norma I. Sojo Ramos, Asst.Libn.
Founded: 1960. **Staff:** Prof 1; Other 1. **Subjects:** Energy - solar, biomass, wind; ocean thermal energy conversion; energy conversion and conservation; marine sciences. **Holdings:** 4673 books; 2038 bound periodical volumes; 33,363 documents; 73,499 microcards; 105,104 microfiche; 401 films; 1 video cassette. **Subscriptions:** 32 journals and other serials. **Services:** Interlibrary loans; copying; SDI; library open to public. **Publications:** CEER Collection Bulletin of Information, monthly - free upon request.

CENTER FOR ENERGY POLICY AND RESEARCH
See: New York Institute of Technology

★2474★
CENTER FOR ENVIRONMENTAL INFORMATION - HARTWELL LIBRARY (Env-Cons)
33 S. Washington St.
Rochester, NY 14608   Phone: (716) 546-3796
Jean Thompson, Asst.Dir.
Staff: 2. **Subjects:** Environment. **Holdings:** 785 books; 250 bound periodical volumes; 5 VF drawers of newspaper clippings; 8 VF drawers plus 30 boxes of unbound periodicals and reports. **Subscriptions:** 68 journals and other serials; 10 newspapers. **Services:** Copying; library open to public for reference use only. **Publications:** The Link, monthly; newsletter. **Special Indexes:** Directory of Environmental Groups & Agencies.

★2475★
CENTER FOR FARM AND FOOD RESEARCH, INC. - LIBRARY (Agri)
Box 88
Falls Village, CT 06031   Phone: (203) 824-5945
Lucille Sadwith, Dir.
Founded: 1975. **Staff:** 1. **Subjects:** Food, agriculture, agricultural economics, energy, technology, multinational corporations. **Special Collections:** USDA and Food and Drug Administration publications and clippings. **Holdings:** 200 books; 10,000 clippings. **Subscriptions:** 30 journals and other serials; 15 newspapers. **Services:** Library open to public.

Publications: List of publications - available upon request. **Remarks:** The center is a nonprofit organization committed to the study and analysis of local, national and international food issues.

CENTER FOR GENEALOGICAL RESEARCH
See: Houston Public Library - Clayton Library

★2476★
CENTER FOR GOVERNMENTAL RESEARCH, INC. - LIBRARY (Soc Sci; Plan)
37 S. Washington St.   Phone: (716) 325-6360
Rochester, NY 14608   Christine Ryan, Info.Serv.Coord.
Founded: 1915. **Staff:** Prof 1; Other 1. **Subjects:** Government finance, urban studies, local government, planning, community services. **Special Collections:** Social indicators; Local Government Documents (500); Revenue Sharing (200). **Holdings:** 9000 books; 1000 other cataloged items; 500 reports by center from 1915; 10 VF drawers of center archives. **Subscriptions:** 150 journals and other serials. **Services:** Interlibrary loans; copying; library open to public for reference use only. **Networks/Consortia:** Member of Rochester Regional Research Library Council (RRRLC). **Publications:** Recent Acquisitions, monthly - distributed to center staff and other area libraries and interested individuals and groups.

CENTER FOR GREAT PLAINS STUDIES
See: University of Nebraska, Lincoln

CENTER FOR HELLENIC STUDIES
See: Harvard University

★2477★
CENTER FOR THE HISTORY OF AMERICAN NEEDLEWORK - LIBRARY (Rec)
Old Economy Village
14th & Church Sts.
Ambridge, PA 15003   Phone: (412) 266-6440
                                      Michele Palmer, Dir.
Staff: Prof 1. **Subjects:** Needlework, embroidery, quilting, spinning, textile fabrics, costume. **Holdings:** 3000 books; 300 patterns; 2100 slides; 500 items of needlework ephemera - postcards, trade cards, advertising, suppliers' catalogs. **Subscriptions:** 124 journals and other serials. **Services:** Copying; library open to public by appointment. **Publications:** Bibliographies and reference books on textile subjects; newsletter.

CENTER FOR HISTORY OF PHYSICS
See: American Institute of Physics

CENTER FOR HUMAN RESOURCE RESEARCH
See: Ohio State University

★2478★
CENTER FOR HUMANE OPTIONS IN CHILDBIRTH EXPERIENCES (CHOICE) - LIBRARY (Med)
739 S. James Rd.   Phone: (614) 237-0586
Columbus, OH 43227   Abby Kinne, Founder
Founded: 1977. **Staff:** Prof 4; Other 8. **Subjects:** Home birth, Lamaze method, natural childbirth, breast feeding, birth alternatives, nutrition, midwifery. **Holdings:** 200 books; films; pamphlets, statistical reports. **Services:** Copying; library open to public.

CENTER FOR INFORMATION AND NUMERICAL DATA ANALYSIS AND SYNTHESIS
See: Purdue University - CINDAS

CENTER FOR INTEGRATIVE STUDIES
See: SUNY at Buffalo

CENTER FOR INTERNATIONAL POLICY
See: Fund for Peace

★2479★
CENTER FOR INVESTIGATIVE REPORTING - LIBRARY (Publ)
1419 Broadway, Rm. 600   Phone: (415) 835-8525
Oakland, CA 94612   Dan Noyes, Mng.Ed.
Founded: 1977. **Staff:** 1. **Subjects:** Regulatory agencies, agriculture, environmental issues, nuclear power, pesticide use, immigration, military issues. **Special Collections:** Investigative methodology collection. **Holdings:** 550 books. **Services:** Library open to public on approval. **Publications:** Investigative Reports, 1978, 1979; Raising Hell - distributed to libraries and journalism schools; Circle of Poison, 1981 - distributed to libraries and bookstores and by mail order; Investigative Reports 1980-81; Nuclear California, 1982.

CENTER FOR JUDAIC STUDIES
See: Rocky Mountain Jewish Historical Society - Ira M. Beck Memorial Library

CENTER FOR KOREAN STUDIES
See: University of Hawaii

CENTER FOR LAKE ERIE AREA RESEARCH
See: Ohio State University

★2480★
CENTER FOR LAW AND EDUCATION - LIBRARY (Law; Educ)
6 Appian Way   Phone: (617) 495-4666
Cambridge, MA 02138   Ralph G. Oppenheim, Dir.
Founded: 1969. **Staff:** Prof 4. **Subjects:** Educational law and equality; student rights. **Holdings:** 4200 books; 3000 bound periodical volumes; 50 VF drawers of documents relating to legal problems in education. **Subscriptions:** 58 journals and other serials. **Services:** Library not open to public. **Publications:** Library Bulletin, 5/year. **Formerly:** Its Victoria Gregorian Library.

CENTER OF LEISURE STUDIES
See: University of Oregon

★2481★
CENTER FOR LIBERTARIAN STUDIES (Soc Sci)
200 Park Ave., S., Suite 911
New York, NY 10003   Phone: (212) 533-6600
                                      C.A. Drake
Subjects: Libertarianism. **Holdings:** 2000 books; 3000 unbound periodicals. **Services:** Library open to public for reference use only and with advance call. **Publications:** Journal of Libertarian Studies, quarterly - to mailing list.

CENTER FOR MARITIME STUDIES
See: Webb Institute of Naval Architecture - Livingston Library

★2482★
CENTER FOR MEDICAL CONSUMERS AND HEALTH INFORMATION - LIBRARY (Med)
237 Thompson St.   Phone: (212) 674-7105
New York, NY 10012   Arthur Levin, Dir.
Founded: 1976. **Staff:** 3. **Subjects:** Medicine, health, nutrition. **Holdings:** 1000 books; 10 bound periodical volumes. **Subscriptions:** 55 journals and other serials. **Services:** Copying; library open to public. **Publications:** Health Facts, monthly consumer newsletter.

CENTER FOR MEDIEVAL AND EARLY RENAISSANCE STUDIES
See: SUNY at Binghamton

CENTER FOR METEORITE STUDIES
See: Arizona State University

CENTER FOR METROPOLITAN PLANNING AND RESEARCH
See: Johns Hopkins University

CENTER FOR MIDDLE EASTERN STUDIES
See: Harvard University

★2483★
CENTER FOR MIGRATION STUDIES - CMS DOCUMENTATION CENTER (Soc Sci; Area-Ethnic)
209 Flagg Pl.   Phone: (212) 351-8800
Staten Island, NY 10304   Nancy F. Avrin, Libn./Archv.
Staff: Prof 2; Other 2. **Subjects:** Immigration, emigration, ethnicity, ethnic groups in the U.S., international migration, Italian Americans. **Special Collections:** Archival collections pertaining primarily to the Italian-American experience; ethnic press (microfilm). **Holdings:** 15,000 books and bound periodical volumes; 2000 reports; manuscripts. **Subscriptions:** 375 journals and other serials; 40 newspapers. **Services:** Interlibrary loans; copying (both limited); library open to public. **Staff:** Diana Zimmerman, Asst.Libn.

★2484★
CENTER FOR MODERN PSYCHOANALYTIC STUDIES - LIBRARY (Med)
16 W. 10th St.   Phone: (212) 260-7050
New York, NY 10011   C.Z. Meadow, Dir.
Staff: Prof 2; Other 2. **Subjects:** Psychoanalysis. **Special Collections:** Bound psychoanalytic research projects of center's graduates and other institute graduates' research. **Holdings:** 5000 books; 100 bound periodical volumes; 2000 reprints (cataloged); 120 lecture tapes. **Subscriptions:** 16 journals and other serials. **Services:** Copying; library open for research by appointment.

★2485★
CENTER FOR NATIONAL SECURITY STUDIES - CNSS LIBRARY (Soc Sci)
122 Maryland Ave., N.E.   Phone: (202) 544-5380
Washington, DC 20002
Staff: Prof 1. **Subjects:** Intelligence agencies, secrecy, terrorism, espionage, executive privilege, access to government information under the Freedom of Information Act. **Special Collections:** Intelligence-related materials; Congressional hearings and prints; documents from federal agencies obtained under the Freedom of Information Act. **Holdings:** 2000 books. **Subscriptions:** 80 journals and other serials. **Services:** Interlibrary loans; copying; library open to public by appointment.

CENTER FOR NAVAL ANALYSES
See: U.S. Navy

★2486★
CENTER FOR NEW SCHOOLS - RESOURCE CENTER (Educ)†
59 E. Van Buren St., Suite 1900   Phone: (312) 939-7025
Chicago, IL 60605   Robert O. Slater, Res.Ctr.Coord.
Staff: Prof 1. **Subjects:** Education, urban school problems. **Special Collections:** Community-based learning. **Holdings:** 1000 books; 1050 other cataloged items; 4 VF drawers of conference reports, journal articles, papers. **Subscriptions:** 30 journals and other serials. **Services:** Interlibrary loans; copying; library not open to public. **Computerized Information Services:** Online systems.

★2487★
CENTER FOR NONPROFIT ORGANIZATIONS, INC. - LIBRARY (Bus-Fin)
203 W. 25th St., 3rd Fl.   Phone: (212) 989-9026
New York, NY 10001   Howard E. Fischer, Dir.
Founded: 1978. **Staff:** Prof 1; Other 1. **Subjects:** Nonprofit organization law and management; fund raising; community development. **Special Collections:** 1000 fund raising resources. **Holdings:** 100 books; 300 bound periodical volumes; 500 clippings; 2000 fund raising program samples; studies of nonprofit organizations. **Subscriptions:** 50 journals and other serials; 20 newspapers. **Services:** Library open to public for a fee. **Publications:** Starting, Funding, Managing a Nonprofit Organization; Fund Raising Resource Directory; 101 Tips on Fund Raising; Nonprofit Organizations: Laws & Regulations Affecting Establishment & Operation. **Remarks:** The center also conducts research and provides consultation to businesses seeking to initiate or improve community relations and social responsibility programs. **Staff:** Robert Hess, Info.Off.

★2488★
CENTER FOR NORTHERN STUDIES - LIBRARY (Env-Cons)
Town Hill   Phone: (802) 888-4331
Wolcott, VT 05680   William E. Osgood, Libn.
Staff: Prof 1. **Subjects:** Arctic ecology, Quaternary studies, Inuit anthropology, resource management, environmental law, cold regions engineering. **Special Collections:** History of Arctic exploration. **Holdings:** 1100 books; 40 newsletter files; 60 reels of microfilm; 370 reprints of scientific papers; 500 maps. **Subscriptions:** 64 journals and other serials. **Services:** Interlibrary loans; copying; library open to public with restrictions. **Networks/Consortia:** Member of OCLC. **Remarks:** Library serves as a depository for the Cold Regions Research & Engineering Laboratory in Hanover, NH.

CENTER FOR PACIFIC NORTHWEST STUDIES
See: Western Washington University

CENTER FOR PEACE STUDIES
See: University of Akron

CENTER FOR PERFORMANCE ASSESSMENT
See: Northwest Regional Educational Laboratory

CENTER FOR POLICY ALTERNATIVES
See: Massachusetts Institute of Technology

CENTER FOR POPULATION & FAMILY HEALTH
See: Columbia University

CENTER FOR POPULATION RESEARCH
See: Georgetown University

CENTER FOR POPULATION STUDIES
See: Harvard University

CENTER FOR PRE-COLUMBIAN STUDIES
See: Harvard University - Dumbarton Oaks Center for Pre-Columbian Studies

CENTER FOR PUBLIC ECONOMICS LIBRARY
See: San Diego State University

CENTER FOR QUANTITATIVE SCIENCES
See: King Research, Inc.

★2489★
CENTER FOR REFORMATION RESEARCH - LIBRARY (Hist)
6477 San Bonita Ave.   Phone: (314) 727-6655
St. Louis, MO 63105   Dr. William Maltby, Exec.Dir.
Founded: 1957. **Staff:** Prof 1; Other 3. **Subjects:** History - Reformation, Renaissance, early modern, late medieval. **Special Collections:** Manuscripts on microfilm; political archives of Philipp of Hesse; Simmler Collection (Zurich Reformation); Baum Collection (Strassburg Reformation). **Holdings:** 2500 books; 1650 reels of microfilm; 1500 microcards. **Subscriptions:** 10 journals and other serials. **Services:** Interlibrary loans; copying; library open to public. **Publications:** Sixteenth Century Bibliography. **Special Indexes:** Finding Lists in Sixteenth Century Bibliography (a series).

★2490★
CENTER FOR RELIGION, ETHICS & SOCIAL POLICY - ANNE CARRY DURLAND MEMORIAL ALTERNATIVES LIBRARY (Soc Sci)
Cornell University
122 Anabel Taylor Hall   Phone: (607) 256-6486
Ithaca, NY 14853   Louise T. Fry, Libn.
Staff: Prof 1; Other 9. **Subjects:** Life styles, energy, ecology, justice, health, nutrition, gardening, agriculture, religion, politics, ethics. **Special Collections:** Peace and disarmament (100 items); American Indians (100 items). **Holdings:** 3500 books; 260 tapes and cassettes; unbound periodicals. **Subscriptions:** 142 journals and other serials. **Services:** Interlibrary loans; copying; library open to public with restrictions. **Remarks:** Maintained by Cornell University.

★2491★
CENTER FOR RESEARCH LIBRARIES (Info Sci)
5721 S. Cottage Grove Ave.   Phone: (312) 955-4545
Chicago, IL 60637   Donald B. Simpson, Dir.
Founded: 1949. **Staff:** Prof 16; Other 45. **Subjects:** Foreign doctoral dissertations; U.S. and foreign newspapers; foreign scientific and technical journals; archives on microfilm; state documents; infrequently used research materials. **Special Collections:** Russian Academy of Science publications (1958 to present). **Holdings:** Over three million volumes; 40,000 children's books; backfiles of college catalogs for 2000 schools; 80,000 primary and secondary textbooks; 600,000 foreign doctoral dissertations. **Subscriptions:** 14,400 journals and other serials; 325 newspapers. **Services:** Interlibrary loans; copying; library open to personnel of member institutions. **Networks/Consortia:** Resource center for libraries in Center for Research Libraries Consortia; member of OCLC. **Publications:** Focus newsletter; Handbook; printed catalogs (microfiche). **Staff:** Ray Boylan, Asst.Dir.; Alan Barney, Hd., Adm.Serv.Dept.; Cecelia Shores, Hd.Acq.Libn.; Karla D. Petersen, Hd., Cat.Dept.; Emma Davis, Circ.Libn.; Esther Smith, Coll.Dev.Libn.

CENTER FOR RURAL STUDIES
See: Earthwork

CENTER OF SCIENCE & INDUSTRY
See: Franklin County Historical Society

CENTER FOR SCIENCE AND INTERNATIONAL AFFAIRS LIBRARY
See: Harvard University

CENTER FOR SOCIAL ORGANIZATION OF SCHOOLS
See: Johns Hopkins University - Research & Development Center

★2492★
CENTER ON SOCIAL WELFARE POLICY AND LAW - LIBRARY (Law)
95 Madison Ave., Rm. 701   Phone: (212) 679-3709
New York, NY 10016   Henry A. Freedman, Dir.
Founded: 1967. **Subjects:** Law, public assistance programs, poverty, legal services. **Holdings:** 3000 books; federal public assistance materials; public assistance manuals for states and jurisdictions; 80 VF drawers of pamphlets, law reports, statutes, unpublished litigation papers. **Services:** Copying; library open to public by appointment only. **Publications:** Library Bulletin, weekly - for sale; other publications, irregular - request information. **Remarks:** Primarily for the use of its staff attorneys, the library is a grantee of the National Legal

Services Corporation.

★2493★
CENTER FOR SOUTHERN FOLKLORE - ARCHIVES (Hum; Mus)
1216 Peabody Ave.
Box 40105
Memphis, TN 38104
Phone: (901) 726-4205
Diane Yacoubian, Archv.
Founded: 1972. **Staff:** Prof 8; Other 6. **Subjects:** Folklife of the Deep South, folk music and religion, folktales, crafts, folk art and architecture, occupational lore, blues music, ethnic heritage, Memphis and Mississippi River history. **Special Collections:** The Reverend L.O. Taylor Collection (documentation of Memphis black community from the late 1920s to 1977). **Holdings:** 500 books; 500 unbound periodical volumes; 500 newsletters; phonograph records; 30,000 slides; 200,000 feet of film; 20,000 photographs; 2000 hours of audiotapes. **Subscriptions:** 100 journals and other serials. **Services:** Archives open to public by appointment. **Publications:** Southern Folklore Reports book series; Images of the South: Visits with Eudora Welty and Walker Evans (first in the series); American Folklore Films and Videotapes: An Index, volume 1; American Folklore Films and Videotapes: A Catalog, Volume 2. **Remarks:** This is "a nonprofit multimedia research center producing films, records, illustrated books, slide and tape programs, concert series and folklife festivals." **Staff:** Judy Peiser, Dir.; Bill Ferris, Pres.; Sharon Hesse, Off.Mgr.; Kini Kedigh, Ed.Prod.; Brett Robbs, Adm.Dir.; Rachelle Saltzman, Folklorist; George McDaniel, Dir. of Res.

CENTER OF SOUTHWEST STUDIES
See: Fort Lewis College

CENTER FOR SPACE RESEARCH
See: Massachusetts Institute of Technology

CENTER FOR STUDIES IN VOCATIONAL EDUCATION
See: Florida State University

CENTER FOR THE STUDY OF COMPARATIVE FOLKLORE AND MYTHOLOGY
See: University of California, Los Angeles - Wayland D. Hand Library of Folklore and Mythology

★2494★
CENTER FOR THE STUDY OF ETHICS IN THE PROFESSIONS - LIBRARY (Soc Sci)
Illinois Institute of Technology
IIT Center
Chicago, IL 60616
Phone: (312) 567-3017
David T. Thackery, Libn.
Founded: 1976. **Staff:** Prof 1; Other 2. **Subjects:** Professions - ethics, social responsibility, education, self-regulation, public regulation, sociology, public policy. **Special Collections:** Codes of ethics collection (600 items); referral bank of more than 250 programs and organizations concerned with professional ethics and related issues. **Holdings:** 1500 books; 5 videotapes; 3000 conference papers, court decisions, journal reprints. **Subscriptions:** 75 journals and other serials. **Services:** Copying; library open to public. **Publications:** Occasional papers series, irregular; Perspectives on the Professions, quarterly newsletter - both free upon request. **Special Catalogs:** Compilation of Statements Relating to Standards of Professional Responsibility and Freedom (booklet).

CENTER FOR THE STUDY OF ETHNIC PUBLICATIONS
See: Kent State University

★2495★
CENTER FOR THE STUDY OF HUMAN RIGHTS - LIBRARY (Soc Sci)
Columbia University
704 International Affairs Bldg.
New York, NY 10027
Phone: (212) 280-2479
Jane Callaghy, Adm.Asst.
Founded: 1978. **Staff:** 3. **Subjects:** Human rights in national societies - comparative and international perspectives, women and rights; health care and social welfare services. **Holdings:** 100 books; 50 bound periodical volumes; 1000 articles, reports and papers; 2 VF drawers of materials; 100 course curricula. **Subscriptions:** 30 journals and other serials. **Services:** Library open to public. **Publications:** Newsletter, 3/year; occasional papers and seminar reports; Human Rights Bibliography. **Special Indexes:** Teaching Human Rights.

★2496★
CENTER FOR STUDY OF MULTIPLE BIRTH - RESOURCE LIBRARY (Med)
333 E. Superior St., Suite 463-5
Chicago, IL 60611
Donald Keith, Exec.Dir.
Staff: Prof 1. **Subjects:** Conjoined twins, multiple births, raising children from multiple births. **Holdings:** Figures not available. **Subscriptions:** 10 journals and other serials. **Services:** Library open to public with restrictions.

★2497★
CENTER FOR THE STUDY OF THE PRESIDENCY - LIBRARY (Soc Sci)
208 E. 75th St.
New York, NY 10021
Phone: (212) 240-1200
Mr. Lee Tablewski, Libn.
Founded: 1965. **Staff:** Prof 2; Other 2. **Subjects:** American Presidency; U.S. Congress. **Holdings:** 3000 books; 1000 bound periodical volumes; 200 reels of microfilm. **Subscriptions:** 15 journals and other serials. **Services:** Copying; library open to public. **Publications:** Presidential Studies Quarterly; Proceedings, annual. **Staff:** Lenore Langerman, Asst.Libn.

★2498★
CENTER FOR THE STUDY OF YOUTH DEVELOPMENT, BOYS TOWN - LIBRARY SERVICES DIVISION
Father Flanagan's Boys' Home
Boys Town, NE 68010
Defunct

CENTER FOR TRANSPORTATION RESEARCH
See: University of Texas, Austin

★2499★
CENTER FOR ULCER RESEARCH AND EDUCATION FOUNDATION (CURE) - LIBRARY (Med)
VA Wadsworth Hospital Center
Bldg. 115, Rm. 203
Los Angeles, CA 90073
Phone: (213) 825-8095
Leona Green, Exec.Sec.
Subjects: Gastrointestinal diseases, peptic ulcers. **Holdings:** Figures not available for books; 500 bound periodical volumes; original manuscripts and research reports. **Services:** Copying; library open to public only with special permission. **Publications:** CURE News, 3/year.

CENTER FOR URBAN POLICY RESEARCH LIBRARY
See: Rutgers University, The State University of New Jersey

CENTER FOR WETLAND RESOURCES
See: Louisiana State University - Coastal Information Repository

★2500★
CENTER FOR WOMEN POLICY STUDIES - FAMILY VIOLENCE PROJECT LIBRARY (Soc Sci)
2000 P St., N.W., Suite 508
Washington, DC 20036
Phone: (202) 872-1770
Elinor Tucker, Supv.
Founded: 1979. **Staff:** Prof 1. **Subjects:** Family violence, spouse abuse, child sexual abuse, battered women. **Holdings:** Figures not available. **Services:** Copying; library open to public. **Publications:** Response, bimonthly newsletter.

★2501★
CENTER FOR WOMEN'S STUDIES AND SERVICES - CWSS LIBRARY (Soc Sci)
908 E St.
San Diego, CA 92101
Phone: (714) 233-8984
Lisa Cobbs, Libn.
Founded: 1972. **Staff:** Prof 1; Other 1. **Subjects:** Women's movement, women's fiction, biographies, nonsexist children's literature, radical movements. **Special Collections:** Women's liberation newspapers, 1969 to present. **Holdings:** 200 books. **Subscriptions:** 10 journals and other serials; 19 newspapers. **Services:** Interlibrary loans; copying; library open to public; returnable deposit for each book circulated. **Publications:** CWSS Feminist Bulletin, monthly - mail and hand distribution; Rainbow Snake, a woman's poetry anthology - for sale; The Longest Revolution, bimonthly newspaper. **Staff:** Joyce Lane, Asst.Dir.

CENTERS FOR DISEASE CONTROL
See: U.S. Centers for Disease Control

★2502★
CENTINELA HOSPITAL MEDICAL CENTER - EDWIN W. DEAN MEMORIAL LIBRARY (Med)
555 E. Hardy St.
Box 720
Inglewood, CA 90307
Phone: (213) 673-4660
Jeanne Spala, Med.Libn.
Staff: Prof 1; Other 2. **Subjects:** Sports medicine, orthopedics, clinical medicine, nursing. **Holdings:** 1000 books; 4200 bound periodical volumes. **Subscriptions:** 176 journals and other serials. **Services:** Interlibrary loans; copying; SDI; library open to public by appointment. **Computerized Information Services:** MEDLINE, DIALOG, SDC, BRS.

★2503★
CENTRAL AGENCY FOR JEWISH EDUCATION - EDUCATIONAL RESOURCE CENTER/LIBRARY (Area-Ethnic)
4200 Biscayne Blvd.   Phone: (305) 576-3030
Miami, FL 33137   Shirley Wolfe, Dir.
Founded: 1948. **Staff:** Prof 2; Other 2. **Subjects:** Israel, education, Hebrew language, Holocaust, Yiddish language, Judaica, Jewish ethnics. **Holdings:** 20,000 volumes; 50 file boxes of pamphlets; 1500 filmstrips; 1500 phonograph record albums; 200 tapes. **Subscriptions:** 70 journals and other serials; 8 newspapers. **Services:** Interlibrary loans; library open to public. **Computerized Information Services:** Computerized cataloging. **Networks/Consortia:** Member of OCLC through SOLINET. **Publications:** Audiovisual Catalog, annual - distributed to schools. **Staff:** Lillian Ross, Community Serv.Dir.

★2504★
CENTRAL ARIZONA MUSEUM - LIBRARY & ARCHIVES (Hist)
1242 N. Central Ave.   Phone: (602) 255-4470
Phoenix, AZ 85004   Janet Michaelieu, Libn.
Staff: Prof 1; Other 3. **Subjects:** Arizona and western history; antiques and preservation. **Holdings:** 1424 books and bound periodical volumes; 30 boxes of historic photographs; 82 boxes of manuscript and archival collections; 4 films and videotape programs; 5 boxes of oral history tapes. **Subscriptions:** 25 journals and other serials. **Services:** Interlibrary loans; copying; photographic reproduction; library open to public.

★2505★
CENTRAL BAPTIST CHURCH - MEDIA CENTER (Rel-Theol)
420 N. Roy   Phone: (612) 646-2751
St. Paul, MN 55104   Karen Johnson, Libn.
Founded: 1947. **Staff:** 5. **Subjects:** Bible, Christian life, Christian education, devotions, missions, biography. **Holdings:** 3400 books; slides, filmstrips; phonograph records, maps; pamphlets and denominational papers. **Subscriptions:** 6 journals and other serials. **Services:** Center open to public with restrictions.

CENTRAL BAPTIST HOSPITAL LIBRARY
See: Baptist Medical Center System

★2506★
CENTRAL BAPTIST SEMINARY - DR. W. GORDON BROWN MEMORIAL LIBRARY (Rel-Theol)
95 Jonesville Crescent   Phone: (416) 752-1976
Toronto, ON, Canada M4A 1H3   Ruth L. Kraulis, Libn.
Founded: 1949. **Staff:** Prof 1; Other 1. **Subjects:** Theology, Christian education, church history, Canadian Baptists. **Holdings:** 18,000 volumes; 1400 microfiche; slides. **Subscriptions:** 180 journals and other serials. **Services:** Interlibrary loans; copying; SDI (for faculty); library open to public for reference use only. **Staff:** Ann Johnson, Asst.Libn.

★2507★
CENTRAL BAPTIST THEOLOGICAL SEMINARY - LIBRARY (Rel-Theol)
Seminary Heights   Phone: (913) 371-1544
Kansas City, KS 66102   Dr. Henry R. Moeller, Libn.
Staff: Prof 1; Other 6. **Subjects:** Theology, particularly Protestant; Baptist doctrine and history. **Special Collections:** Fred E. Young Qumran Collection; Anabaptist Foundation Collection. **Holdings:** 58,670 books; 9866 bound periodical volumes; 6 VF drawers of pamphlets. **Subscriptions:** 299 journals and other serials. **Services:** Interlibrary loans; copying; library open to public with restrictions on borrowing. **Staff:** Miss Arel T. Lewis, Asst.Libn./ILL Libn.

★2508★
CENTRAL BIBLE COLLEGE - LIBRARY (Rel-Theol)
3000 N. Grant   Phone: (417) 833-2551
Springfield, MO 65802   Gerard J. Flokstra, Jr., Libn.
Staff: Prof 4; Other 23. **Subjects:** Bible and theology; missions; church history; religious education; psychology and philosophy; American history; music; sociology. **Special Collections:** Assemblies of God Collection; Holy Spirit Collection; Deaf and Deafness Collection; Curriculum Collection. **Holdings:** 88,433 books; 1714 bound periodical volumes; 74 VF drawers of clippings and pamphlets; 8 VF drawers of illustrated children's stories; 6001 cassette tapes (cataloged); 12,666 microfiche; 432 phonograph records. **Subscriptions:** 542 journals and other serials. **Services:** Interlibrary loans; copying; library open to public with fee charged to borrow materials. **Staff:** Mark Gentry, Ref.Libn.; Becky Brown, Tech.Serv.Libn.; Alice Murphy, Spec.Coll.Libn.

★2509★
CENTRAL CAROLINA TECHNICAL COLLEGE - LEARNING RESOURCE CENTER (Sci-Tech)
1105 Kelly Dr.   Phone: (919) 775-5401
Sanford, NC 27330   Jim Foster, Dir., LRC
Founded: 1965. **Staff:** Prof 4; Other 3. **Subjects:** Electronics; auto and motorcycle mechanics; tool and die making; veterinary medicine; nursing; law enforcement; business administration; radio-television broadcasting; secretarial science; paralegal technology; recreation technology; cosmetology; instrumentation. **Special Collections:** Veterinary medical technology (1043 books, 18 periodicals); law library collection (1138 volumes); nursing and medical library (500 volumes). **Holdings:** 22,884 books; 9 VF drawers of pamphlets and clippings; 3865 records, tapes, films, slides; 4495 microforms. **Subscriptions:** 268 journals and other serials; 15 newspapers. **Services:** Interlibrary loans; copying; center open to public. **Staff:** Gwen L. Glover, Libn.; Marian Bridges, ILL Libn.; Linda Halstead, Evening Libn.

★2510★
CENTRAL CHRISTIAN CHURCH - LIBRARY (Rel-Theol)
205 E. Short St.
Box 1354   Phone: (606) 233-1551
Lexington, KY 40590   Walter A. Hehl, Hd.
Founded: 1951. **Staff:** Prof 6; Other 4. **Subjects:** Religion, philosophy, biography. **Holdings:** 5100 books. **Services:** Library open to public. **Staff:** Miss Francis Cook, Libn.

★2511★
CENTRAL CHRISTIAN COLLEGE OF THE BIBLE - LIBRARY (Rel-Theol)
1093 Urbandale Rd.   Phone: (816) 263-3900
Moberly, MO 65270   Gareth L. Reese, Libn.
Staff: Prof 1; Other 2. **Subjects:** Theology. **Special Collections:** Walter S. Coble mission files. **Holdings:** 20,400 books; 1000 bound periodical volumes. **Subscriptions:** 134 journals and other serials. **Services:** Interlibrary loans; copying; library open to public.

★2512★
CENTRAL CONNECTICUT STATE COLLEGE - ELIHU BURRITT LIBRARY (Educ)
Wells St.   Phone: (203) 827-7530
New Britain, CT 06050   Robert E. Massmann, Dir.
Founded: 1859. **Staff:** Prof 18; Other 8. **Subjects:** Education and liberal arts. **Special Collections:** Elihu Burritt Collection (400 items); Mark Twain Collection (500 items); Thomas Hardy Collection (600 items); Bruce Rogers Collection (180 items); Dutch language children's books (275 items); Frederic W. Goudy Collection (200 items); Walter Hart Blumenthal Collection (700 items). **Holdings:** 261,726 books; 58,073 bound periodical volumes; 78,554 microforms (cataloged); 800 masters' theses; 5340 reels of microfilm; 4000 items Central Connecticut State College Archives. **Subscriptions:** 1685 journals and other serials; 25 newspapers. **Services:** Interlibrary loans; copying; library open to public. **Computerized Information Services:** Computerized cataloging. **Networks/Consortia:** Member of OCLC through NELINET. **Staff:** Mr. Francis J. Gagliardi, Assoc.Dir.; Marie Kascus, Ser.Libn.; Joan Garrett-Packer, Ref.Libn.; Dona Ostrander, Curric.Libn.; Martha Croft, Doc.Libn.; Elenore Zavez, Circ.Libn.; Priscilla Fox, Reserve Rd.Rm.Libn.; Robert Billings, Bibliog.; Jacqueline Isa, Acq.Libn.; Priya Rai, Chf., Tech.Proc.

★2513★
CENTRAL DU PAGE HOSPITAL - MEDICAL LIBRARY (Med)
0 North 025 Winfield Rd.   Phone: (312) 682-1600
Winfield, IL 60190   Dorothy B. Rowe, Libn.
Staff: Prof 2. **Subjects:** Medicine, nursing, allied health sciences. **Holdings:** 2000 books; bound periodical volumes; 8 VF drawers. **Subscriptions:** 200 journals and other serials. **Services:** Interlibrary loans; copying; SDI; library open to public for reference use only. **Networks/Consortia:** Member of Fox Valley Health Science Library Consortium; Midwest Health Science Library Network; Dupage Library System; ILLINET. **Staff:** Gloria Sullivan, Asst.Libn.

CENTRAL GREAT PLAINS RESEARCH STATION
See: U.S.D.A. - Agricultural Research Service

★2514★
CENTRAL INSTITUTE FOR THE DEAF - EDUCATIONAL RESEARCH LIBRARY (Med)
818 S. Euclid   Phone: (314) 652-3200
St. Louis, MO 63110   Mary M. Sicking, Libn.
Founded: 1929. **Staff:** Prof 1. **Subjects:** Audiology, early childhood education, behavioral sciences, speech pathology, physiology, otolaryngology, education of the deaf, electroacoustics, aural rehabilitation, neurophysiology. **Special Collections:** Max A. Goldstein Collection (evolution of nonelectric

hearing aids and early editions of books dealing with speech and hearing); Research Department Publications (periodicals). **Holdings:** 9339 books; 648 bound periodical volumes; 766 Research Publications (cataloged); 121 dissertations; 109 drawers of clippings; 10 reels of microfilm. **Subscriptions:** 68 journals and other serials. **Services:** Copying; library open to public with special permission. **Remarks:** The library is located in the Hearing Clinics & Research Bldg., 909 S. Taylor, St. Louis, MO 63110. The Max A. Goldstein Collection is housed at Washington University - School of Medicine Library.

★2515★
CENTRAL ISLIP PSYCHIATRIC CENTER - HEALTH SCIENCE LIBRARY (Med)†
Carlton Ave., Station H   Phone: (516) 234-6262
Central Islip, NY 11722   Mary Avlon, Libn.
Founded: 1973. **Staff:** Prof 1; Other 1. **Subjects:** Psychiatry, nursing, psychology, rehabilitation, retardation, developmental disabilities, geriatrics. **Special Collections:** John G. Walker Psychology Collection (180); old medicine and surgery textbooks (70). **Holdings:** 9011 books; 1257 bound periodical volumes; 20 VF drawers; 28 AV materials. **Subscriptions:** 188 journals and other serials. **Services:** Interlibrary loans; copying; library open to public for reference use only but LILRC patrons have borrowing privileges. **Computerized Information Services:** Internal database. **Networks/Consortia:** Member of Long Island Library Resources Council (LILRC); Suffolk Cooperative Library System. **Publications:** Accessions, monthly - for internal distribution only; Annual Report and Monthly Report (statistics).

★2516★
CENTRAL LOUISIANA STATE HOSPITAL - MEDICAL AND PROFESSIONAL LIBRARY (Med)
Box 31   Phone: (318) 445-2421
Pineville, LA 71360   Benton Carol McGee, Med.Libn.
Founded: 1958. **Staff:** Prof 1; Other 2. **Subjects:** Psychiatry, psychology, social work, occupational therapy, psychiatric nursing, psychiatric hospital administration. **Holdings:** 4000 books; 3500 bound periodical volumes; 12 VF drawers of pamphlets and reports. **Subscriptions:** 182 journals and other serials. **Services:** Interlibrary loans; copying; library open to public. **Publications:** Current Contents of Journals Received, weekly; Bibliographies - for hospital staff.

★2517★
CENTRAL MAINE MEDICAL CENTER - GERRISH-TRUE HEALTH SCIENCE LIBRARY (Med)
300 Main St.   Phone: (207) 795-2376
Lewiston, ME 04240   Diane Carroll, Lib.Dir.
Staff: Prof 6; Other 3. **Subjects:** Biomedicine, health care administration. **Holdings:** 1700 books; 3300 bound periodical volumes. **Subscriptions:** 402 journals and other serials; 8 newspapers. **Services:** Interlibrary loans; copying; SDI; library open to public. **Computerized Information Services:** Online systems. **Networks/Consortia:** Member of Health Science Library and Information Cooperative of Maine; New England Regional Medical Library Service. **Publications:** The Circuit-Rider, monthly - distributed to health professionals and libraries in central Maine. **Staff:** Linda Plunket, Project Coord.; Ann Mc Kay, Staff Libn./Tech.Serv.; Debra Warner, Staff Libn./Ref.Serv.; Raynna Bowlby Genetti, Principal Investigator; Maryanne Greven, Project Libn.

★2518★
CENTRAL MAINE POWER COMPANY - LIBRARY SERVICES (Energy)
Edison Dr.   Phone: (207) 623-3521
Augusta, ME 04336   Catharine Webber, Supv.
Founded: 1978. **Staff:** Prof 1; Other 2. **Subjects:** Engineering, electric utilities, energy, business, management. **Holdings:** 2000 books. **Subscriptions:** 100 journals and other serials; 5 newspapers. **Services:** Interlibrary loans; copying; library not open to public. **Computerized Information Services:** DIALOG, DOE/RECON.

★2519★
CENTRAL MICHIGAN UNIVERSITY - CLARKE HISTORICAL LIBRARY (Hist)
          Phone: (517) 774-3352
Mt. Pleasant, MI 48858   John Cumming, Dir.
Founded: 1955. **Staff:** Prof 3; Other 4. **Subjects:** Michigan, early travel in the Midwest, General George A. Custer, children's literature, manuscripts, maps. **Special Collections:** Lucile Clarke Memorial Children's Library; Reed Draper Angling Collection. **Holdings:** 47,000 books; 415 atlases; 3000 maps; 275,000 manuscripts; 2500 bound volumes of manuscripts; 1200 broadsides; 25,000 photographs; 6300 reels of microfilm. **Services:** Copying; use of collection for research may be requested. **Publications:** Annual report; occasional books. **Staff:** William Miles, Bibliog.; Stanley Max, Cat.

★2520★
CENTRAL MINNESOTA HISTORICAL CENTER - LIBRARY (Hist)
St. Cloud State University   Phone: (612) 255-3254
St. Cloud, MN 56301   Dr. Calvin W. Gower, Dir.
Founded: 1967. **Staff:** 2. **Subjects:** Church history, business, Minnesota politics and government, oral history. **Special Collections:** Rural Church Oral History Project. **Holdings:** 230 linear feet of local history materials. **Services:** Copying; library open to public. **Remarks:** The center is maintained by St. Cloud State University. **Formerly:** Minnesota Historical Society - Central Minnesota Historical Center.

★2521★
CENTRAL MISSOURI STATE UNIVERSITY - WARD EDWARDS LIBRARY - SPECIAL COLLECTIONS (Hist)
          Phone: (816) 429-4141
Warrensburg, MO 64093   Rosalie Schell, Dir., Rd.Serv.
Founded: 1937. **Special Collections:** Civil War; Izaak Walton's Compleat Angler; Missouri Speleology; government documents (218,692). **Services:** Interlibrary loans; copying; library open to public for reference use only. **Computerized Information Services:** DIALOG; computerized serials and circulation. **Networks/Consortia:** Member of OCLC; Kansas City Metropolitan Library Network; Missouri Library Network Corporation. **Special Catalogs:** National Defense Service Mapping Agency Depository Catalog.

★2522★
CENTRAL NAUGATUCK VALLEY REGIONAL PLANNING AGENCY - LIBRARY (Plan)
20 E. Main St.   Phone: (203) 757-0535
Waterbury, CT 06702   Duncan M. Graham, Exec.Dir.
Founded: 1960. **Subjects:** Planning, housing, demography, zoning, transportation, open space, government, education, economics. **Special Collections:** Census of Population and Housing, covering the decades from 1950 to 1980. **Holdings:** Figures not available. **Subscriptions:** 50 journals and other serials; 7 newspapers. **Services:** Library open to public by appointment.

★2523★
CENTRAL NEW YORK ACADEMY OF MEDICINE - LIBRARY (Med)
210 Clinton St.   Phone: (315) 735-2204
New Hartford, NY 13413   Mildred D. Timmerman, Libn.
Founded: 1925. **Staff:** 2. **Subjects:** Medicine, dentistry. **Holdings:** 5000 books; 4200 bound periodical volumes; 800 unbound journals. **Subscriptions:** 10 journals and other serials. **Services:** Interlibrary loans; copying; library open to public for reference use only. **Staff:** Olive A. Dorris, Asst.Libn.

★2524★
CENTRAL NEW YORK REGIONAL PLANNING & DEVELOPMENT BOARD - LIBRARY & INFORMATION CENTER (Plan)
700 E. Water St., Midtown Plaza   Phone: (315) 422-8276
Syracuse, NY 13210   Paul Jasek, Res.Asst.
Founded: 1966. **Staff:** Prof 1. **Subjects:** Land use planning, environmental and hazardous waste management, transportation, human resources, law enforcement, public utilities, grants assistance. **Special Collections:** U.S. Bureau of Census Products (500 items on U.S. census material); U.S. Census maps (150). **Holdings:** 3000 books; 900 bound periodical volumes; 200 maps and 800 pamphlets (cataloged); 1000 natural resources maps; 500 transportation maps; 150 local, state and federal regulations; 6 selected planning-regional council newsletters. **Subscriptions:** 200 journals and other serials; 8 newspapers. **Services:** Copying; SDI; library open to public for reference use only on request. **Networks/Consortia:** Member of Council of Planning Librarians. **Publications:** Library Acquisitions, monthly - for internal distribution only; Users Guide to the CNY RPDB Library, 1979 - local libraries. **Special Catalogs:** Catalog of Reports published by CNY Regional Planning Board; CARDS, periodical holdings (book).

CENTRAL OHIO RIVER VALLEY - HEALTH PLANNING & RESOURCES DEVELOPMENT ASSOCIATION - CORVA LIBRARY
See: Corva Library

★2525★
CENTRAL OHIO TRANSIT AUTHORITY - LIBRARY (Trans)
1600 McKinley Ave.   Phone: (614) 228-3831
Columbus, OH 43222   John T. Kniesner, Libn.
Founded: 1976. **Staff:** Prof 1. **Subjects:** Transportation. **Holdings:** Reports, pamphlets, documents. **Subscriptions:** 16 journals and other serials. **Services:** Library open to public. **Publications:** Bibliographies of new materials, quarterly.

★2526★
CENTRAL OPERA SERVICE - INFORMATION CENTER AND LIBRARY (Mus)
c/o Metropolitan Opera
Lincoln Center   Phone: (212) 957-9871
New York, NY 10023   Maria F. Rich, Exec.Dir.
Staff: 2. **Subjects:** Opera. **Special Collections:** Performance histories of
25,000 operas. **Holdings:** 500 books; 10 VF drawers of programs and
reviews. **Subscriptions:** 66 journals and other serials. **Services:** Library open
to members with restrictions. **Publications:** List of special directories -
available upon request. **Special Catalogs:** Annual survey of opera
performances in United States. **Staff:** Jeanne Kemp, Asst.Dir.

CENTRAL PENNSYLVANIA SYNOD ARCHIVES
See: Lutheran Theological Seminary - A.R. Wentz Library

★2527★
CENTRAL PRESBYTERIAN CHURCH - LIBRARY (Rel-Theol)†
1100 W. Capitol   Phone: (601) 353-2757
Jackson, MS 39203
Staff: Prof 1; Other 5. **Subjects:** Religion, Presbyterian Church. **Holdings:**
4000 books. **Services:** Copying; library open to public.

★2528★
CENTRAL PRESBYTERIAN CHURCH - LIBRARY (Rel-Theol)
3788 Richmond Ave.   Phone: (713) 621-2424
Houston, TX 77027   J.J. Britton, Libn.
Staff: 1. **Subjects:** Religion, education. **Holdings:** 4000 books.
Subscriptions: 12 journals and other serials. **Services:** Interlibrary loans;
library open to public on request.

★2529★
CENTRAL SOYA COMPANY, INC. - FOOD RESEARCH LIBRARY (Food-Bev)
Box 1400   Phone: (219) 489-1511
Fort Wayne, IN 46801-1400   Margaret Campbell, Libn.
Founded: 1940. **Staff:** Prof 1. **Subjects:** Soybeans, nutrition, proteins,
chemistry, food science. **Holdings:** 2750 books; 4025 bound periodical
volumes; 3 VF drawers of pamphlets; 80 reels of microfilm. **Subscriptions:**
53 journals and other serials. **Services:** Interlibrary loans; copying; library
open to public with restrictions.

★2530★
CENTRAL STATE HOSPITAL - HEALTH SCIENCES LIBRARY (Med)
Box 4030   Phone: (804) 861-7517
Petersburg, VA 23803   Mr. P.D. Upadhyaya, Med.Libn.
Staff: Prof 1; Other 4. **Subjects:** Psychiatry, psychiatric nursing, social work,
clinical psychology, mental retardation. **Holdings:** 10,700 books; 132 bound
periodical volumes. **Subscriptions:** 125 journals and other serials. **Services:**
Interlibrary loans; copying; library open to public by appointment.
Publications: Documentation List, monthly - free.

★2531★
CENTRAL STATE HOSPITAL - MEDICAL LIBRARY (Med)
                                                 Phone: (912) 453-4153
Milledgeville, GA 31062   Aurelia S. Spence, Lib.Dir.
Founded: 1961. **Staff:** Prof 1; Other 1. **Subjects:** Medicine, surgery and
related fields. **Holdings:** 2100 books and bound periodical volumes.
Subscriptions: 65 journals and other serials. **Services:** Interlibrary loans;
library open to students with authorization. **Networks/Consortia:** Member of
Health Science Libraries of Central Georgia; Department of Human Resources
Librarians.

★2532★
CENTRAL STATE HOSPITAL - MEDICAL LIBRARY (Med)
3000 W. Washington St.   Phone: (317) 639-3927
Indianapolis, IN 46222   Aurelia S. Baker, Libn.
Founded: 1954. **Staff:** Prof 1; Other 1. **Subjects:** Nursing, business and
management, psychiatry, psychology, geriatrics, mental health, mental
retardation, social work. **Holdings:** 7400 books; 3000 bound periodical
volumes; 300 archival items; 116 video cassettes; 450 audiotapes; 22 VF
drawers. **Subscriptions:** 141 journals and other serials. **Services:** Interlibrary
loans; copying; SDI; library open to public for reference use only. **Networks/
Consortia:** Member of Central Indiana Health Sciences Consortium; Central
Indiana Area Library Services Authority (CIALSA). **Publications:** Tables of
Contents; acquisitions lists - to staff.

★2533★
CENTRAL STATE HOSPITAL - MENTAL HEALTH LIBRARY (Med)
                                                 Phone: (912) 453-4371
Milledgeville, GA 31062   Kathy Ridley, Libn.
Staff: Prof 2. **Subjects:** Psychiatry, nursing, psychology, social work, religion,
anatomy, pharmacology. **Holdings:** 6000 books; 300 bound periodical
volumes. **Subscriptions:** 76 journals and other serials. **Services:** Interlibrary
loans; copying; library open to public with restrictions. **Networks/Consortia:**
Member of Department of Human Resources Library Group; Georgia Library
Information Network (GLIN); Health Science Libraries of Central Georgia
(HSLCG). **Staff:** Aurelia S. Spence, Dir.

★2534★
CENTRAL STATE HOSPITAL - PROFESSIONAL LIBRARY (Med)
Box 151   Phone: (405) 321-4880
Norman, OK 73069   Jane Marie Hamilton, Med.Libn.
Staff: Prof 1. **Subjects:** Psychiatry, psychology, medicine, nursing. **Special
Collections:** Child psychiatry; historical medical book collection, 1800s to
1915 (85 books). **Holdings:** 7800 books; 140 bound periodical volumes; 4
VF drawers of clippings and dissertations; 3 shelves of government
documents; 3 VF drawers of newsletters and nursing statements; 115 tapes;
20 films; 2 video cassettes; 200 filmstrips. **Subscriptions:** 106 journals and
other serials. **Services:** Interlibrary loans; copying; library open to public.
Networks/Consortia: Member of Oklahoma Regional Medical Libraries.
Publications: Bookends, irregular - to hospital staff.

★2535★
**CENTRAL STATE UNIVERSITY - LIBRARY - SPECIAL COLLECTIONS (Info
Sci)**
100 N. University Dr.   Phone: (405) 341-2980
Edmond, OK 73034   Dr. John L. Lolley, Dir. of Lib.Serv.
Founded: 1890. **Special Collections:** Microforms Research Center (79,156
reels of microfilm, 337,149 microfiche); Oklahoma Collection. **Services:**
Interlibrary loans; copying; library open to public with restrictions in some
subject fields. **Computerized Information Services:** BRS, DIALOG;
computerized cataloging, acquisitions and serials. **Networks/Consortia:**
Member of OCLC through AMIGOS Bibliographic Council, Inc.

★2536★
CENTRAL STATES INSTITUTE OF ADDICTIONS - LIBRARY (Med)
120 W. Huron St.   Phone: (312) 266-6100
Chicago, IL 60610   Mrs. Vi Springenberg, Libn.
Founded: 1963. **Staff:** 2. **Subjects:** Alcohol and alcoholism, addictions, drug
abuse education, alcohol and driving. **Holdings:** 3000 books; 500 government
publications; 600 pamphlets; newspaper clippings; 150 films on alcohol and
drug abuse. **Subscriptions:** 76 journals and other serials. **Services:**
Interlibrary loans; library open to public, borrowing restricted to members.

★2537★
CENTRAL SUFFOLK HOSPITAL - MEDICAL LIBRARY (Med)
1300 Roanoke Ave.   Phone: (516) 369-6088
Riverhead, NY 11901   Anne Kirsch, Med.Libn.
Founded: 1973. **Staff:** Prof 1. **Subjects:** Medicine, nursing, surgery, allied
health and hospital fields. **Holdings:** 650 books; 275 bound periodical
volumes; 125 cassettes; 4 VF drawers of pamphlets. **Subscriptions:** 89
journals and other serials. **Services:** Interlibrary loans; copying; library open by
referral and for research. **Networks/Consortia:** Member of Medical Libraries
of Long Island (MEDLI).

★2538★
**CENTRAL SYNAGOGUE OF NASSAU COUNTY - HELEN BLAU MEMORIAL
LIBRARY (Rel-Theol)**
430 DeMott Ave.   Phone: (516) 766-4300
Rockville Centre, NY 11570   Barbara Gresack, Libn.
Founded: 1959. **Staff:** Prof 1. **Subjects:** Religion, comparative religion,
sociology, history, biography. **Holdings:** 4000 books; 200 bound periodical
volumes; 200 filmstrips; maps; phonograph records. **Services:** Interlibrary
loans; reference service; library open to public.

CENTRAL TRANSPORTATION PLANNING STAFF
See: (Massachusetts) Central Transportation Planning Staff

★2539★
CENTRAL VERMONT HOSPITAL - MEDICAL LIBRARY (Med)
Box 547   Phone: (802) 229-9121
Barre, VT 05641   Betty-Jean Eastman, Med.Libn.
Staff: 1. **Subjects:** Medicine, surgery, nursing, and allied health sciences.
Holdings: 300 books. **Subscriptions:** 40 journals and other serials. **Services:**
Interlibrary loans; library open to persons in health science field.

★2540★
CENTRAL VERMONT PUBLIC SERVICE CORPORATION - TECHNICAL INFORMATION CENTER (Bus-Fin; Energy)
77 Grove St.   Phone: (802) 773-2711
Rutland, VT 05701   Linda G. Cameron, Libn.
Founded: 1952. **Staff:** Prof 1. **Subjects:** Energy, management, engineering, law, accounting, environment, personnel management, finance, public utility regulation, business, statistics. **Holdings:** 2400 books; 120 bound periodical volumes; 40 VF drawers of pamphlets. **Subscriptions:** 120 journals and other serials. **Services:** Interlibrary loans; center open to public with restrictions. **Computerized Information Services:** DIALOG; Information Management System (internal database); computerized serials, circulation and routing.

★2541★
CENTRAL WASHINGTON HOSPITAL - HEMINGER HEALTH SCIENCES LIBRARY (Med)
1211 Rosewood
Box 1887   Phone: (509) 662-1511
Wenatchee, WA 98801   Jane Belt, Med.Libn.
Staff: Prof 1. **Subjects:** Nursing, medicine including paramedicine, hospital administration. **Holdings:** 3000 books; 432 bound periodical volumes; 1000 tapes. **Subscriptions:** 125 journals and other serials. **Services:** Interlibrary loans; copying; library open to public with restrictions. **Computerized Information Services:** MEDLINE. **Networks/Consortia:** Member of Heminger (Ross A.) Health Sciences Library Consortia. **Publications:** Resources Newsletter, bimonthly.

★2542★
CENTRAL WASHINGTON UNIVERSITY - LIBRARY - CURRICULUM LABORATORY (Educ)
     Phone: (509) 963-1641
Ellensburg, WA 98926   Ann Donovan, Curric.Libn.
Founded: 1968. **Staff:** Prof 1; Other 1. **Subjects:** School texts and guides, children's literature. **Special Collections:** Early 20th century textbooks (80); picture books (200). **Holdings:** 25,000 volumes.

★2543★
CENTRAL WASHINGTON UNIVERSITY - LIBRARY DOCUMENTS DEPARTMENT (Info Sci)
     Phone: (509) 963-1541
Ellensburg, WA 98926   Ruth Dahlgren Hartman, Govt.Doc.Libn.
Founded: 1964. **Staff:** Prof 2; Other 3. **Subjects:** Documents - U.S., state, foreign, United Nations, international. **Holdings:** 300,000 items; microforms; maps. **Services:** Library open to public. **Staff:** Peter Stark, Asst.Doc.Libn.

★2544★
CENTRAL WASHINGTON UNIVERSITY - MAP LIBRARY (Geog-Map)
     Phone: (509) 963-1541
Ellensburg, WA 98926   Peter Stark, Map Libn.
Founded: 1950. **Staff:** Prof 1. **Subjects:** Washington State, geology. **Holdings:** 67 atlases; 67,193 maps (cataloged); 42 raised relief maps; 3 globes. **Services:** Interlibrary loans; copying; library open to public for reference use only. **Publications:** Map Acquisitions, semiannual. **Special Catalogs:** U.S. Geological Survey and Washington Geological Survey publications on Washington State.

★2545★
CENTRAL WASHINGTON UNIVERSITY - MEDIA LIBRARY SERVICES (Aud-Vis)
Instructional Media Center   Phone: (509) 963-2861
Ellensburg, WA 98926   Charles Vlcek, Dir.
Staff: Prof 1; Other 4. **Subjects:** Education, children's literature, psychology, sociology, anthropology, geography-geology. **Special Collections:** Archives (1064 16mm films). **Holdings:** 120 books; 3881 16mm films; 3526 other AV items; 54 8mm films. **Services:** Interlibrary loans; library open to public schools and public agencies in Northwest states. **Networks/Consortia:** Member of University Film Consortium. **Publications:** CWU Films for Teaching. **Special Indexes:** Filmographies in specialized subject areas.

★2546★
CENTRAL WASHINGTON UNIVERSITY - MUSIC LIBRARY (Mus)
     Phone: (509) 963-1841
Ellensburg, WA 98926   Paul Emmons, Music Libn.
Staff: Prof 1. **Subjects:** Music, music education. **Special Collections:** Paul Creston Collection. **Holdings:** 5400 books; 850 bound periodical volumes; 9300 phonograph records; 5700 magnetic tapes; 56 sets of collected works; 4200 scores; 20 volumes of microfilm. **Subscriptions:** 60 journals and other serials. **Services:** Interlibrary loans; copying; library open to public; recordings for reference use only; printed materials chargeable by arrangement.

Publications: New acquisitions list, quarterly. **Special Indexes:** Indexes of Broadway musicals, jazz artists and rock groups (card).

★2547★
CENTRALE DE L'ENSEIGNEMENT DU QUEBEC - CENTRE DE DOCUMENTATION (Educ)
2336 Chemin Ste-Foy   Phone: (418) 658-5711
Quebec, PQ, Canada G1V 4E5   Guy Duchesne
Staff: Prof 1; Other 6. **Subjects:** Education, social sciences. **Holdings:** 13,000 books, unbound reports, documents, papers; 250 reels of microfilm; 7400 current documents of CEQ. **Subscriptions:** 300 journals and other serials. **Services:** Interlibrary loans; copying; library open to public with restrictions. **Special Catalogs:** Uniterm catalog for papers; dictionary catalog for documents of CEQ; subject catalog for periodical articles.

★2548★
CENTRE D'ANIMATION, DE DEVELOPPEMENT ET DE RECHERCHE EN EDUCATION - BIBLIOTHEQUE (Educ)
1940 Blvd. Henri-Bourassa Est   Phone: (514) 381-8891
Montreal, PQ, Canada H2B 1S2   Jean-Luc Roy, Libn.
Founded: 1963. **Staff:** 5. **Subjects:** Sociology, education, psychology, school organization, teaching methods, institutional evaluation. **Holdings:** 10,000 books and bound periodical volumes. **Subscriptions:** 240 journals and other serials. **Services:** Library open to college teachers. **Publications:** Documents Recus, 4/year.

CENTRE CANADIEN D'OECUMENISME
See: Canadian Centre for Ecumenism

★2549★
CENTRE FOR CHRISTIAN STUDIES - LIBRARY (Rel-Theol; Educ)†
77 Charles St., W.   Phone: (416) 923-1168
Toronto, ON, Canada M5S 1K5   Mrs. Elfa M. Davidson, Libn.
Founded: 1954. **Staff:** Prof 1. **Subjects:** Religious education. **Holdings:** 6500 volumes; 15 VF drawers of pamphlets and pictures. **Subscriptions:** 60 journals and other serials. **Services:** Interlibrary loans; library not open to public.

★2550★
CENTRE COMMUNITY HOSPITAL - HEALTH SCIENCES LIBRARY (Med)
Orchard Rd.   Phone: (814) 234-6191
State College, PA 16801   Gloria Durbin Venett, Libn.
Founded: 1981. **Staff:** Prof 1. **Subjects:** Medicine, nursing, health care. **Holdings:** 836 books; 47 bound periodical volumes; 327 cassettes; 4 films; 104 multimedia kits; 20 slides. **Subscriptions:** 63 journals and other serials. **Services:** Interlibrary loans; copying; library not open to public. **Networks/Consortia:** Member of Central Pennsylvania Health Sciences Library Association (CPHSLA).

★2551★
CENTRE COUNTY LAW LIBRARY (Law)
Centre County Courthouse, Rm. 305   Phone: (814) 355-2861
Bellefonte, PA 16823   Lawrence C. Bickford, Court Adm.
Subjects: Law. **Holdings:** 500 books; 20,000 bound periodical volumes. **Subscriptions:** 150 journals and other serials. **Services:** Interlibrary loans; copying; library open to public.

CENTRE DE DEVELOPPEMENT DES TRANSPORTS
See: Canada - Transport Canada - Transportation Development Centre

CENTRE D'ETUDES ACADIENNES
See: Universite de Moncton

CENTRE D'ETUDES ET DE DOCUMENTATION EUROPEENNES
See: Universite de Montreal

★2552★
CENTRE D'ETUDES DU TOURISME - TECHNICAL INFORMATION CENTRE (Bus-Fin)†
1420 Saint Denis   Phone: (514) 282-9613
Montreal, PQ, Canada H2X 3J8   Mureille Bourque, Documentaliste
Founded: 1970. **Staff:** Prof 1; Other 3. **Subjects:** Tourism, leisure, outdoor recreation, travel research. **Special Collections:** Publications of World Tourism Organisation and Centre des Hautes Etudes Touristiques d'Aix-Marseille. **Holdings:** 2000 books; 500 microfiche; 18,000 documents, dissertations and unbound reports. **Subscriptions:** 350 journals and other serials. **Services:** Interlibrary loans; copying; library open to public. **Publications:** Notes du C.E.T., monthly. **Remarks:** Centre is an independent organization partially funded by the Quebec government.

CENTRE FOR EUROPEAN STUDIES
See: Universite de Montreal - Centre d'Etudes et de Documentation Europeennes

★2553★
LE CENTRE D'HERITAGE FRANCO-AMERICAIN - LIBRARY (Hist)*
133 Lisbon St.   Phone: (207) 783-8143
Lewiston, ME 04240   JoAnne D. Lapointe, Cur.
Staff: Prof 1; Other 1. **Subjects:** French genealogy and history. **Holdings:** 13,000 books; photographs; research papers; microfilm. **Services:** Library not open to public.

★2554★
CENTRE HOSPITALIER CHRIST-ROI - BIBLIOTHEQUE MEDICALE (Med)†
300, Boul. Wilfrid-Hamel   Phone: (418) 687-1711
Quebec, PQ, Canada G1M 2R9   Gratien Gelinas, Bibliothecaire
Founded: 1968. **Staff:** Prof 1; Other 1. **Subjects:** Medicine, nursing, pharmacy and related fields. **Holdings:** 2000 books; 5000 clippings; 75 magnetic tapes; AV items. **Subscriptions:** 150 journals and other serials. **Services:** Interlibrary loans; copying; SDI; library open to public for reference use only, on request.

★2555★
CENTRE HOSPITALIER COOKE - BIBLIOTHEQUE MEDICALE ET ADMINISTRATIVE (Med)†
3450 Rue Ste-Marguerite   Phone: (819) 375-7713
Trois-Rivieres, PQ, Canada G8Z 1X3   Helene H. Bouchard, Bibliotechnicienne
Staff: Prof 1. **Subjects:** Medicine and allied health sciences, administration. **Holdings:** 2480 volumes. **Subscriptions:** 135 journals and other serials. **Services:** Interlibrary loans; copying; library not open to public.

★2556★
CENTRE HOSPITALIER COTE-DES-NEIGES - CENTRE DE DOCUMENTATION (Med)
4565 Chemin de la Reine-Marie   Phone: (514) 344-3905
Montreal, PQ, Canada H3W 1W5   Jocelyne Blain-Juneau, Chf.Libn.
Founded: 1947. **Staff:** Prof 1. **Subjects:** Geriatrics, chronic care and related specialties, neurolinguistics, brain disorders. **Holdings:** 1500 books. **Subscriptions:** 100 journals and other serials. **Services:** Interlibrary loans; library open to public for reference use only. **Remarks:** New orientation (1978) from Veterans Hospital to Hospital for Geriatrics and Chronic Care.

★2557★
CENTRE HOSPITALIER DE L'HOTEL-DIEU DE GASPE - MEDICAL LIBRARY (Med)
     Phone: (418) 368-3301
Havre de Gaspe, PQ, Canada G0C 1S0   Mathilda Adams, Responsable
Founded: 1961. **Staff:** 1. **Subjects:** Medicine, surgery, pharmacy, radiology, cardiology, nursing, obstetrics. **Holdings:** 5073 books; 140 bound periodical volumes; 142 VF drawers. **Subscriptions:** 167 journals and other serials. **Services:** Interlibrary loans; copying; library open to public.

★2558★
CENTRE HOSPITALIER HOTEL-DIEU DE SHERBROOKE - BIBLIOTHEQUE (Med)
580 S. Bowen St.   Phone: (819) 569-2551
Sherbrooke, PQ, Canada J1G 2E8   Louise Cadieux, Chf.Libn.
Founded: 1954. **Staff:** Prof 1. **Subjects:** Medicine and medical specialties. **Holdings:** 1300 books; 2110 bound periodical volumes; 841 cassettes; 264 volumes of unbound periodicals. **Subscriptions:** 147 journals and other serials. **Services:** Interlibrary loans; copying; library open to medical personnel and students.

★2559★
CENTRE HOSPITALIER JACQUES-VIGER - CENTRE DE DOCUMENTATION (Med)
1051 St. Hubert St.   Phone: (514) 842-7181
Montreal, PQ, Canada H2L 3Y5   Conrad Tessier, Lib.Techn.
Founded: 1960. **Staff:** 1. **Subjects:** Geriatrics, gerontology, medicine, long term care. **Holdings:** 500 books; 300 bound periodical volumes; 200 brochures; 80 VF drawers of off prints. **Subscriptions:** 90 journals and other serials. **Services:** Interlibrary loans; copying; library open to public for reference use only. **Formerly:** Its Bibliotheque Medicale.

★2560★
CENTRE HOSPITALIER REGIONAL DE LANAUDIERE - BIBLIOTHEQUE MEDICALE (Med)
1000 Ste-Anne Blvd.   Phone: (514) 759-8222
Joliette, PQ, Canada J6E 6J2   Francine Garneau, Bibliothecaire
Staff: Prof 1; Other 1. **Subjects:** Medicine, psychiatry, addictions,

psychology, social work, nursing, hospital administration. **Holdings:** 13,000 books and bound periodical volumes; 393 other cataloged items; 400 cassettes. **Subscriptions:** 425 journals and other serials. **Services:** Interlibrary loans; copying; library open to public for reference use only.

★2561★
CENTRE HOSPITALIER ROBERT-GIFFARD - BIBLIOTHEQUE PROFESSIONNELLE (Med)
2601, de la Canardiere   Phone: (418) 663-5300
Beauport, PQ, Canada G1J 2G3   Yolande Plamondon, Techn.
Staff: Prof 1. **Subjects:** Psychiatry, neurology, general medicine, psychology, social sciences, nursing. **Holdings:** 9750 books; 5000 bound periodical volumes; 35 magnetic tapes; 17 cassettes. **Subscriptions:** 110 journals and other serials. **Services:** Interlibrary loans; copying; library open to public for reference use only. **Computerized Information Services:** MEDLINE.

★2562★
CENTRE HOSPITALIER STE. JEANNE D'ARC - BIBLIOTHEQUE MEDICALE (Med)
3570 Rue St. Urbain   Phone: (514) 842-6141
Montreal, PQ, Canada H2X 2N8   Louise Lemay, Chf.Libn.
Founded: 1957. **Staff:** Prof 2. **Subjects:** Medicine, psychology, psychiatry. **Holdings:** 2200 books; 1500 bound periodical volumes; 1300 cassettes. **Subscriptions:** 177 journals and other serials. **Services:** Interlibrary loans; copying; library open to public. **Staff:** Lise Forcier, Chf., Tech.Serv.

★2563★
CENTRE HOSPITALIER ST-JOSEPH - BIBLIOTHEQUE MEDICALE ET ADMINISTRATIVE (Med)
731 Rue Ste-Julie   Phone: (819) 379-8112
Trois-Rivieres, PQ, Canada G9A 1Y1   Solange De-Rouyn, Chf.
Founded: 1961. **Staff:** Prof 1. **Subjects:** Medicine, administration. **Holdings:** 3684 books; 4995 bound periodical volumes. **Subscriptions:** 254 journals and other serials. **Services:** Interlibrary loans (fee); copying; library open to public for reference use only.

CENTRE HOSPITALIER THORACIQUE DE MONTREAL
See: Montreal Chest Hospital Centre

★2564★
CENTRE HOSPITALIER DE L'UNIVERSITE LAVAL - BIBLIOTHEQUE DES SCIENCES DE LA SANTE (Med)
2705 Boul. Laurier   Phone: (418) 656-8188
Quebec, PQ, Canada G1X 3L9   Beatrice Dionne, Chf.
Staff: 2. **Subjects:** Medicine and allied health sciences. **Holdings:** 5000 books; 1300 bound periodical volumes. **Subscriptions:** 400 journals and other serials. **Services:** Interlibrary loans; copying; library open to public with fee for services. **Special Catalogs:** Catalog of health sciences periodicals of the Quebec region.

★2565★
CENTRE HOSPITALIER DE VERDUN - BIBLIOTHEQUE MEDICALE (Med)
4000 Blvd. Lasalle   Phone: (514) 761-3551
Verdun, PQ, Canada H4G 2A3   Mrs. Andree N. Mandeville, Libn.
Subjects: Medicine. **Holdings:** Figures not available.

CENTRE FOR HUMAN SETTLEMENTS
See: United Nations; University of British Columbia

★2566★
CENTRE INTERCULTUREL MONCHANIN - BIBLIOTHEQUE (Soc Sci)
4917 St-Urbain   Phone: (514) 288-7229
Montreal, PQ, Canada H2T 2W1   Real Bathalon, Libn.
Founded: 1963. **Staff:** Prof 1; Other 2. **Subjects:** Cultures and religions of the world. **Special Collections:** Complete works of Raimundo Panikkar. **Holdings:** 3600 books; records, slides, cassettes and tapes; 350 files on ethno-cultural organizations. **Subscriptions:** 106 journals and other serials. **Services:** Interlibrary loans; library open to public for reference use only. **Publications:** Bulletin, semiannual; Inter Culture, quarterly - both by subscription.

CENTRE INTERNATIONAL DE CRIMINOLOGIE COMPAREE
See: Universite de Montreal

CENTRE LOCAL DE SERVICE COMMUNAUTE
See: C.L.S.C. Metro

CENTRE DE MUSIQUE CANADIENNE
See: Canadian Music Centre

CENTRE FOR NEWFOUNDLAND STUDIES
See: Memorial University of Newfoundland - University Library

★2567★
CENTRE DE READAPTATION CONSTANCE-LETHBRIDGE - MEDICAL LIBRARY (Med)
7005 Boul. de Maisonneuve W.   Phone: (514) 487-1770
Montreal, PQ, Canada H4B 1T3   Jane Petrov, Libn.
Staff: Prof 1. **Subjects:** Rehabilitation medicine, physical and occupational therapy, vocational rehabilitation, psychology, speech. **Holdings:** 2500 books; 1000 bound periodical volumes. **Subscriptions:** 80 journals and other serials. **Services:** Interlibrary loans; copying; library open to public. **Networks/Consortia:** Member of McGill Medical and Health Libraries Association. **Formerly:** Centre de Readaptation Lethbridge.

★2568★
CENTRE DE RECHERCHE INDUSTRIELLE DU QUEBEC - DIRECTION DE L'INFO. TECHNOLOGIQUE ET DU TRANSFERT DE TECH. (Sci-Tech)
333 Rue Franquet   Phone: (418) 659-1550
Ste. Foy, PQ, Canada G1V 4C7   Francois Labrousse
Founded: 1970. **Subjects:** Industrial research - systems, materials, mechanics. **Holdings:** 3500 books. **Subscriptions:** 400 journals and other serials. **Services:** SDI; not open to public. **Computerized Information Services:** Banque de l'Information Industrielle Pont a Mousson. **Also Known As:** DITT.

CENTRE DE RECHERCHES CARAIBES
See: Universite de Montreal

CENTRE DE RECHERCHES FORESTIERES DES LAURENTIDES
See: Canada - Canadian Forestry Service - Laurentian Forest Research Centre

★2569★
CENTRE DE RECHERCHES EN RELATIONS HUMAINES - BIBLIOTHEQUE (Soc Sci)
2715 Cote St. Catherine Rd.   Phone: (514) 738-8076
Montreal, PQ, Canada H3T 1B6   Noel Mailloux, Dir./Prof. Emeritus
Founded: 1950. **Staff:** 1. **Subjects:** Psychology, social sciences, criminology. **Holdings:** 22,000 books; 10,000 bound periodical volumes. **Subscriptions:** 250 journals and other serials. **Services:** Library open to active qualified researchers only for reference use.

CENTRE FOR REMOTE SENSING
See: Canada - Canada Centre for Remote Sensing

★2570★
CENTRE DE RESSOURCES EDUCATIVES FRANCAISES - LIBRARY/TECHNICAL INFORMATION CENTER (Educ)
200, Ave. de la Cathedrale   Phone: (204) 237-6671
Saint-Boniface, MB, Canada R2H 0H7   Arsene Huberdeau, Dir.
Founded: 1978. **Staff:** Prof 3; Other 5. **Subjects:** Education, Manitoba, local production. **Special Collections:** Curriculum-support material, K-12, in the French language; illustrations; short plays (325). **Holdings:** 23,000 books; 400 Learning Centres; 1900 16mm films; 1300 35mm filmstrips; 850 media kits; 600 cassettes; 1300 records; 340 transparencies; 260 filmloops; 50 maps. **Subscriptions:** 40 journals and other serials. **Services:** Interlibrary loans; copying; lending service to all schools in Manitoba; library open to teachers. **Publications:** Le Bulletin, monthly. **Special Indexes:** Films catalog; AV catalog; short plays catalog. **Staff:** Doris Lemoine, Libn.; Gemma Lariviere, Libn.

★2571★
CENTRE DE SERVICES SOCIAUX DU MONTREAL METROPOLITAIN (CSSMM) - BIBLIOTHEQUE (Soc Sci)
1001 Est Boul. de Maisonneuve, 8th Fl.   Phone: (514) 527-7261
Montreal, PQ, Canada H2L 4R5   Micheline Gaudette, Bibliotechnicienne
Founded: 1955. **Staff:** Prof 1. **Subjects:** Social service, child welfare, juvenile delinquency, family therapy, aged, handicapped, psychotherapy. **Holdings:** 12,000 books; unbound periodicals (300 titles); 12 VF drawers of dossiers thematiques. **Subscriptions:** 50 journals and other serials. **Services:** Interlibrary loans; copying; library open to public for reference use only.

CENTRE DE SERVICES SOCIAUX VILLE MARIE
See: Ville Marie Social Service Centre

CENTRE ON TRANSNATIONAL CORPORATIONS
See: United Nations

CENTRO DE ESTUDIOS PUERTORRIQUENOS
See: CUNY - Centro de Estudios Puertorriquenos

★2572★
CENTURY ASSOCIATION - LIBRARY (Art)
7 W. 43rd St.   Phone: (212) 944-0090
New York, NY 10036   Andrew Zaremba, Libn.
Founded: 1847. **Subjects:** Art and architecture. **Special Collections:** Centuriana. **Holdings:** 25,000 volumes. **Services:** Library not open to public.

★2573★
CER CORPORATION - LIBRARY (Sci-Tech; Energy)
Desert Professional Plaza II
2225 E. Flamingo Rd.   Phone: (702) 735-7136
Las Vegas, NV 89109   Wendy M. Starkweather, Libn.
Founded: 1980. **Staff:** Prof 1; Other 1. **Subjects:** Natural gas and unconventional gas recovery; petroleum engineering and geology; geothermal and nuclear energy. **Special Collections:** Tight gas sands (1000 reports and reprints). **Holdings:** 700 books; 250 bound periodical volumes; 1500 technical reports; 150 project notebooks; 400 maps and charts; 2000 well logs; 5000 microfiche. **Subscriptions:** 101 journals and other serials. **Services:** Interlibrary loans; copying (limited); library open to public with restrictions.

★2574★
CESSNA AIRCRAFT COMPANY - WALLACE DIVISION - ENGINEERING LIBRARY (Sci-Tech)
Box 7704   Phone: (316) 946-6575
Wichita, KS 67277   Betty Parks, Libn.
Staff: Prof 1. **Subjects:** Aerodynamics. **Holdings:** 3500 volumes.

★2575★
CETUS CORPORATION - RESEARCH LIBRARY (Sci-Tech)
600 Bancroft Way   Phone: (415) 549-3300
Berkeley, CA 94710   Judy Labovitz, Mgr.
Founded: 1978. **Staff:** Prof 4; Other 5. **Subjects:** Microbiology, biotechnology. **Holdings:** 1900 books; 2000 bound periodical volumes. **Subscriptions:** 350 journals and other serials. **Services:** Interlibrary loans; copying; SDI; library not open to public. **Computerized Information Services:** Online systems; computerized cataloging. **Networks/Consortia:** Member of CLASS. **Staff:** Pamela Handman, Info.Spec.; George McGregor, Info.Spec.

CEUAT BIBLIOTHEQUE
See: Universite du Quebec

CHACO CANYON NATL. MONUMENT
See: U.S. Natl. Park Service

CHACO CENTER - LIBRARY
See: U.S. Natl. Park Service

★2576★
CHADBOURNE, PARKE, WHITESIDE, & WOLFF - LIBRARY (Law)
30 Rockefeller Plaza, 24th Fl.   Phone: (212) 344-8900
New York, NY 10112   Jeannine R. Esswein, Libn.
Staff: Prof 4; Other 3. **Subjects:** Law. **Special Collections:** Aviation law. **Holdings:** 25,000 books; 750 bound periodical volumes; 100 VF drawers of Civil Aeronautics Board orders and dockets. **Subscriptions:** 100 journals and other serials; 6 newspapers. **Services:** Interlibrary loans; copying; library open to members of American Association of Law Libraries and Special Libraries Association. **Computerized Information Services:** LEXIS, New York Times Information Service. **Staff:** Anna Smallen, Asst.Libn.; Allison J. Beier, Asst.Libn.; Charlotte Harrington, Asst.Libn.

★2577★
CHADWELL & KAYSER LTD. - LAW LIBRARY (Law)
233 S. Wacker Dr.
8500 Sears Tower   Phone: (312) 876-2209
Chicago, IL 60606-6592   Betty Roizman, Libn.
Staff: 1. **Subjects:** Law - antitrust, food and drug. **Holdings:** 16,525 books; 260 bound periodical volumes; 24 VF drawers of Justice Department files; pamphlets. **Subscriptions:** 99 journals and other serials. **Services:** Interlibrary loans; copying; library not open to public. **Formerly:** Chadwell, Kayser, Ruggles, Mc Gee & Hastings.

CHAIN STORE AGE - READER SERVICE RESEARCH
See: Lebhar-Friedman, Inc.

★2578★
CHAIT SALOMON - LIBRARY (Law)
1 Place Ville Marie, Suite 1901   Phone: (514) 879-1353
Montreal, PQ, Canada H3B 2C3   Shake Hagopian, Libn.
Founded: 1928. **Staff:** Prof 1; Other 1. **Subjects:** Law. **Holdings:** 500 books; 4500 bound periodical volumes. **Subscriptions:** 80 journals and other serials. **Services:** Interlibrary loans; copying; SDI; library open to public with restrictions. **Computerized Information Services:** Manac Systems (internal database). **Formerly:** Chait, Salomon, Gelber, Reis, Bronstein, Litvack, Echenberg & Lipper.

★2579★
CHALMERS (Dr. Everett) HOSPITAL - DR. GARFIELD MOFFATT HEALTH SCIENCES LIBRARY (Med)
Box 9000   Phone: (506) 452-5431
Fredericton, NB, Canada E3B 5N5   Cietta M. Babineau, Libn.
Staff: 2. **Subjects:** Medicine and related subjects. **Holdings:** 750 books; 350 bound periodical volumes. **Subscriptions:** 160 journals and other serials. **Services:** Interlibrary loans; copying; library open to public by prior arrangement. **Networks/Consortia:** Member of Nova Scotia On-line Consortium.

★2580★
CHAMBER OF COMMERCE OF HAWAII - INFORMATION OFFICE (Bus-Fin)
Dillingham Bldg., 735 Bishop St.   Phone: (808) 531-4111
Honolulu, HI 96813   Miss Tatsuko Honjo, Dir., Info.Off.Serv.
Founded: 1948. **Staff:** 1. **Subjects:** Statistics; commercial, trade and business information. **Special Collections:** Lists of Chamber of Commerce members providing special services. **Holdings:** 6000 pamphlets and reports; 8 VF drawers of newspaper clippings; directories; buyers' guides. **Subscriptions:** 10 journals and other serials. **Services:** Interlibrary loans; copying; office open to public. **Publications:** Trade Tips, monthly; Hawaii Facts and Figures, annual; Living and Working in Hawaii, irregular; Directory of Manufacturers, State of Hawaii, biennial; Directory of Shopping Centers - irregular.

★2581★
CHAMBER OF COMMERCE OF THE UNITED STATES OF AMERICA - LIBRARY (Bus-Fin)
1615 H St., N.W.   Phone: (202) 463-5448
Washington, DC 20062   Rose Racine, Libn.
Founded: 1917. **Staff:** Prof 1; Other 1. **Subjects:** Business, economics. **Special Collections:** Nation's Business Magazine (1912 to present on microfilm). **Holdings:** 10,000 books; 30 VF drawers. **Subscriptions:** 200 journals and other serials. **Services:** Library primarily for use by staff.

★2582★
CHAMBER OF MINES OF EASTERN BRITISH COLUMBIA - BUREAU OF INFORMATION (Sci-Tech)
215 Hall St.   Phone: (604) 352-5242
Nelson, BC, Canada V1L 5X4   George Murray, Mgr.
Founded: 1920. **Subjects:** British Columbian and Canadian mining - statistics, history, safety, regulations; geology; prospecting. **Special Collections:** British Columbia Minister of Mines reports from 1896; Geological Survey of Canada material from 1876 to 1972 (650 items). **Holdings:** 2000 books; 1500 bound periodical volumes; 600 other cataloged items; 12 volumes of press reports and archives; 200 pamphlets; 1200 maps. **Subscriptions:** 30 journals and other serials; 5 newspapers. **Services:** Copying; library open to public on request.

CHAMBERLAIN LABORATORIES
See: Norton Company

CHAMBLEE FACILITY LIBRARY
See: U.S. Centers for Disease Control

CHAMIZAL NATL. MEMORIAL
See: U.S. Natl. Park Service

★2583★
CHAMPAIGN COUNTY HISTORICAL ARCHIVES (Hist)
c/o Urbana Free Library
201 S. Race St.   Phone: (217) 367-4025
Urbana, IL 61801   Barbara Roberts, Dir.
Founded: 1956. **Staff:** Prof 3. **Subjects:** Champaign County history, genealogy. **Holdings:** 2500 books; 415 bound periodical volumes; 1400 reels of microfilm; 250 VF drawers of pictures, family information, clippings, manuscripts, documents, probate records; 100 oral history tapes. **Subscriptions:** 32 journals and other serials. **Services:** Interlibrary loans (limited); copying; archives open to public for reference use only; private researchers available. **Networks/Consortia:** Member of Lincoln Trail Libraries System. **Publications:** Champaign County Historical Archives Historical Publications Series: 1858 Alexander Bowman Map of Urbana; Combined 1893, 1913 and 1929 Atlases of Champaign County; Early History and Pioneers of Champaign County, 1891; 1863 Alexander Bowman Map of Champaign County; Ivesdale: A Photographic Essay. **Special Indexes:** Name indexes to Champaign County marriage license applications, cemetery inscriptions, funeral records, monument company records, probates. **Staff:** Jean Gordon, Archv.Asst.; Dorothy Benner, Archv.Asst.

★2584★
CHAMPAIGN COUNTY HISTORICAL MUSEUM - LIBRARY (Hist)†
709 W. University Ave.   Phone: (217) 356-1010
Champaign, IL 61820   Michael Cahall, Dir.
Staff: 2. **Subjects:** Local history. **Holdings:** 300 books; 75 bound periodical volumes; 100 photographs; 12 tapes. **Services:** Library open to public by appointment.

★2585★
CHAMPAIGN COUNTY LAW LIBRARY (Law)
County Court House   Phone: (513) 652-2222
Urbana, OH 43078   Judy K. Burnett, Libn.
Staff: 1. **Subjects:** Law. **Holdings:** 10,500 volumes. **Services:** Library open to public with restrictions.

★2586★
CHAMPAIGN NEWS-GAZETTE - LIBRARY (Publ)
48 Main St.   Phone: (217) 351-5228
Champaign, IL 61820   Deborah J. Voigt, Hd.Libn.
Staff: Prof 1; Other 1. **Subjects:** Newspaper reference topics. **Holdings:** 300 books; 200,000 newspaper clippings; 400 reels of microfilmed newspapers; 200 maps. **Services:** Library open to public.

★2587★
CHAMPION INTERNATIONAL - CHAMPION PAPERS TECHNICAL LIBRARY (Sci-Tech)
Knightsbridge Dr.   Phone: (513) 868-4578
Hamilton, OH 45020   Paul F. Bryant, Tech.Libn.
Founded: 1975. **Staff:** Prof 1; Other 1. **Subjects:** Pulp and paper, chemistry, chemical engineering, environment. **Special Collections:** Patents (any subject relative to company). **Holdings:** 3000 books; 300 bound periodical volumes; files on special subjects within the paper industry; IPC publications (research reports and bibliographies). **Subscriptions:** 100 journals and other serials. **Services:** Interlibrary loans; library open to public by appointment. **Computerized Information Services:** DIALOG, SDC; computerized serials.

★2588★
CHAMPION INTERNATIONAL - CORPORATE INFORMATION CENTER (Bus-Fin)
1 Champion Plaza   Phone: (203) 358-7390
Stamford, CT 06921   Phyllis Prince, Mgr.
Staff: Prof 3; Other 1. **Subjects:** Paper, building materials, forestry, business. **Special Collections:** Archival material. **Holdings:** 500 books; 150 bound periodical volumes; 100 research reports; 850 annual reports; microfiche. **Subscriptions:** 200 journals and other serials; 6 newspapers. **Services:** Interlibrary loans; copying; library open to public with restrictions. **Computerized Information Services:** DIALOG, SDC, BRS, New York Times Information Service. **Staff:** Lorain M. Kelley, Libn.; Christine Michigami, Libn.

★2589★
CHAMPION INTERNATIONAL - PACKAGING DIVISION - TECHNICAL CENTER LIBRARY (Sci-Tech)
2250 Wabash Ave.   Phone: (612) 641-4125
St. Paul, MN 55114   Jeanette Kustelski, Libn.
Staff: 1. **Subjects:** Paper technology, chemistry, packaging, plastics and polymers. **Special Collections:** Institute of Paper Chemistry (abstracts from 1930 to present). **Holdings:** 550 books; 129 bound periodical volumes; 705 project reports and bibliographies of the Institute of Paper Chemistry; 100 miscellaneous published reports. **Subscriptions:** 72 journals and other serials. **Services:** Library not open to public. **Networks/Consortia:** Member of METRONET. **Formerly:** Its Hoerner Waldorf Packaging Division - Technical Center Library.

★2590★

CHAMPLAIN VALLEY - PHYSICIANS HOSPITAL MEDICAL CENTER - MEDICAL LIBRARY (Med)
100 Beekman St.
Plattsburgh, NY 12901
Phone: (518) 561-2000
Judith El Reedy, Med.Libn.
Founded: 1972. **Staff:** Prof 1. **Subjects:** Medicine, nursing, health care. **Holdings:** 450 books. **Subscriptions:** 130 journals and other serials; 7 newspapers. **Services:** Interlibrary loans; copying; library open to public by appointment for reference use. **Computerized Information Services:** MEDLINE; computerized serials. **Networks/Consortia:** Member of North Country Reference and Research Resources Council (NCRRRC); Hospital Library Development Services; Northern New York Health Information Cooperative; OCLC.

CHAN (Stephen) LIBRARY OF FINE ARTS
See: New York University - Stephen Chan Library of Fine Arts

CHANCELLOR PATERSON LIBRARY
See: Lakehead University

★2591★

CHANDLER EVANS, INC. - COMPANY LIBRARY (Sci-Tech)†
One Charter Oak Blvd.
West Hartford, CT 06101
Phone: (203) 236-0651
Christina Jablonowski, Libn.
Staff: Prof 1. **Subjects:** Fluid mechanics, control engineering, missile technology, electrical engineering. **Holdings:** 2200 books; 10,000 reports. **Subscriptions:** 72 technical and management magazines. **Services:** Interlibrary loans; copying; library not open to public. **Publications:** Information Bulletin, quarterly - for internal distribution only.

CHANNEL ISLANDS ARCHIVE
See: Santa Barbara Museum of Natural History

CHANUTE AIR FORCE BASE (IL)
See: U.S. Air Force Base - Chanute Base Library; U.S. Air Force Hospital - Medical Library (IL-Rantoul)

★2592★

CHAPARRAL GENEALOGICAL SOCIETY - LIBRARY (Hist)
310 N. Live Oak
Box 606
Tomball, TX 77375
Phone: (713) 372-3738
Kathleen Glass, Libn.
Founded: 1973. **Staff:** 15. **Subjects:** Genealogy, local history. **Holdings:** 1000 books; 200 bound periodical volumes; 100 reels of microfilmed census records. **Subscriptions:** 71 journals and other serials. **Services:** Copying; library open to public. **Publications:** The Roadrunner, quarterly. **Special Indexes:** Indexes to early county censuses; Index to Waller County, Texas Cemeteries; marriage records from the following sixteen Texas counties: Austin, Brazos, Burleson, Fayette, Ft. Bend, Galveston, Grimes, Harris, Jefferson, Lee, Madison, Milam, Trinity, Washington, Waller and Montgomery.

CHAPELLE (Howard I.) MEMORIAL LIBRARY
See: Chesapeake Bay Maritime Museum - Howard I. Chapelle Memorial Library

CHAPIN LIBRARY
See: Williams College

★2593★

CHAPMAN (Bruce) COMPANY - LIBRARY (Info Sci)
Phone: (802) 843-2321
Grafton, VT 05146
William Chapman, Libn.
Founded: 1936. **Subjects:** Materials for radio and television documentary programs. **Holdings:** 3000 volumes; 100 VF drawers.

★2594★

CHAPMAN AND CUTLER - LAW LIBRARY (Law)
111 W. Monroe St.
Chicago, IL 60603
Phone: (312) 845-3749
Denis S. Kowalewski, Libn.
Staff: Prof 3; Other 2. **Subjects:** Law. **Holdings:** 30,000 volumes; loose-leaf services (cataloged). **Services:** Interlibrary loans; copying; library not open to public. **Computerized Information Services:** LEXIS. **Staff:** David Fanta, Asst.Libn.

CHAPMAN HISTORICAL MUSEUM
See: Glens Falls-Queensbury Historical Association, Inc.

★2595★

CHARETTE, FORTIN, HAWEY & COMPANY/TOUCHE, ROSS & COMPANY - LIBRARY (Bus-Fin)
One Place Ville Marie
Royal Bank Bldg.
Montreal, PQ, Canada H3B 2A3
Phone: (514) 861-8531
Nancy Bouchard, Libn.
Founded: 1961. **Staff:** Prof 1; Other 1. **Subjects:** Accounting, auditing, business management, data processing, management consulting services, organization, personnel management. **Holdings:** 4000 books. **Subscriptions:** 130 journals and other serials; 7 newspapers. **Services:** Interlibrary loans; copying; library open to public. **Special Catalogs:** Classification of business literature.

★2596★

CHARITY HOSPITAL - SCHOOL OF NURSING - LIBRARY (Med)
450 S. Claiborne Ave.
New Orleans, LA 70112
Phone: (504) 568-6431
Bruce T. Abbott, Coord., Lib.
Staff: Prof 2; Other 3. **Subjects:** Nursing. **Holdings:** 7500 books; 400 bound periodical volumes. **Subscriptions:** 100 journals and other serials. **Services:** Interlibrary loans; copying; library open to public. **Staff:** Kathleen Savoy, Libn.

★2597★

CHARLES RIVER ASSOCIATES, INC. - LIBRARY (Energy; Trans)
Box 708
Boston, MA 02117
Phone: (617) 266-0500
Nancy Jandl, Tech.Info.Mgr.
Staff: Prof 2; Other 1. **Subjects:** Economics, transportation, energy, metallurgy, environment, industrial organization. **Holdings:** 20,000 volumes. **Subscriptions:** 600 journals and other serials; 10 newspapers. **Services:** Interlibrary loans; library not open to public. **Computerized Information Services:** DIALOG, SDC, DOE/RECON; computerized cataloging. **Networks/Consortia:** Member of OCLC through NELINET.

★2598★

CHARLES RIVER BROADCASTING COMPANY - WCRB LIBRARY (Mus)
750 South St.
Waltham, MA 02154
Phone: (617) 893-7080
George C. Brown, Music Dir.
Staff: Prof 1. **Subjects:** Classical music recordings; live performance tapes of Boston Symphony Orchestra, Boston Pops and New York Philharmonic; music from Marlboro, Koussevitzky series. **Holdings:** 35,000 phonograph records. **Services:** Library not open to public. **Staff:** Louise Boyce, Libn.

CHARLESTON AIR FORCE BASE (SC)
See: U.S. Air Force Base - Charleston Base Library

★2599★

CHARLESTON AREA MEDICAL CENTER - GENERAL DIVISION - MEDICAL LIBRARY (Med)
MacCorkle Ave.
Box 1393
Charleston, WV 25325
Phone: (304) 347-1308
Mary A. Davis, Libn.
Staff: 1. **Subjects:** Medicine. **Special Collections:** Historical medical texts, primarily of the 1800s. **Holdings:** 175 books. **Subscriptions:** 25 journals and other serials. **Services:** Interlibrary loans; copying (limited); library open to public for reference use only. **Remarks:** This small core library is a branch of the West Virginia University Medical Center - Charleston Division - Learning Resources Center.

★2600★

CHARLESTON EVENING POST/NEWS AND COURIER - LIBRARY (Publ)
134 Columbus St.
Box 758
Charleston, SC 29402
Phone: (803) 577-7111
Mary S. Crockett, Chf.Libn.
Founded: 1946. **Staff:** Prof 3; Other 1. **Special Collections:** News and Courier on microfilm from 1803; Evening Post from 1894; Charleston City Year Books from 1880. **Holdings:** 1500 books; 350 bound periodical volumes; 169 VF drawers of newspaper clippings and microclips; 4 shelves of pamphlets (Lektriever); 10 file drawers of photograph files. **Subscriptions:** 50 newspapers. **Services:** Library open to public with restrictions. **Remarks:** Published by Evening Post Publishing Company. **Staff:** Robbie Goode, Libn.; Astrid Henriksen, Libn.

★2601★

CHARLESTON GAZETTE-MAIL - LIBRARY (Publ)
1001 Virginia St., E.
Charleston, WV 25330
Phone: (304) 348-4888
Ron Miller, Hd.Libn.
Founded: 1960. **Staff:** Prof 4. **Subjects:** West Virginia. **Holdings:** 36 bound periodical volumes; Charleston Gazette, 1888 to present and the Charleston Daily Mail, 1914 to present, both on microfilm (1416 reels; 40,000 microjackets). **Services:** Copying; library not open to public. **Staff:** Linda

Colvin, Asst.; Dreama Jil Bailey, Asst.; Kathy Bohnert, Asst.

★2602★
CHARLESTON LIBRARY SOCIETY (Hist)
164 King St.   Phone: (803) 723-9912
Charleston, SC 29401   Catherine E. Sadler, Libn.
Founded: 1748. **Staff:** Prof 4; Other 4. **Subjects:** History and literature.
Special Collections: South Caroliniana; Charleston newspapers from 1732;
18th century books and periodicals; books on architecture and furniture,
Jewish history, botany, South Carolina history. **Holdings:** 95,000 books and
bound periodical volumes; 1600 reels of microfilm. **Subscriptions:** 120
journals and other serials; 10 newspapers. **Services:** Interlibrary loans; library
open to public on membership basis. **Staff:** Theresa E. Wilson, Asst.Libn.;
Patricia G. Bennett, Asst.Libn.; Janice L. Grimes, Sec./Asst.Libn.

★2603★
CHARLESTON MUSEUM - LIBRARY (Hist; Art)
121 Rutledge Ave.   Phone: (803) 722-2996
Charleston, SC 29401   K. Sharon Bennett, Libn.
Founded: 1773. **Staff:** Prof 1; Other 2. **Subjects:** Natural history of South
Carolina, history of South Carolina, decorative arts, anthropology. **Special
Collections:** Print collection of South Carolina artists (200); Gov. Wm. Aiken
House Collection (5000 volumes); Manigault House Collection (300 volumes);
Heyward-Washington House Collection (400 volumes). **Holdings:** 10,000
books; 10,000 bound periodical volumes; 40 early maps of South Carolina; 30
documents; 200 pamphlets; 10 boxes of manuscripts. **Subscriptions:** 77
journals and other serials. **Services:** Interlibrary loans; copying; library open to
public by appointment only.

CHARLESTON NEWS AND COURIER
See: Charleston Evening Post/News and Courier

★2604★
CHARLOTTE LAW BUILDING ASSN. - CHARLOTTE LAW LIBRARY (Law)
730 E. Trade St.   Phone: (704) 334-4912
Charlotte, NC 28202   Elizabeth F. Ledford, Libn.
Founded: 1926. **Staff:** Prof 1. **Subjects:** Law. **Holdings:** 19,926 volumes.
Subscriptions: 47 journals and other serials. **Services:** Copying; library not
open to public.

★2605★
**CHARLOTTE AND MECKLENBURG COUNTY PUBLIC LIBRARY - CAROLINA
   ROOM** (Hist)
310 N. Tryon St.   Phone: (704) 374-2980
Charlotte, NC 28202   Mary Louise Phillips, Local Hist.Libn.
Staff: Prof 2; Other 1. **Subjects:** Local history, genealogy. **Special
Collections:** Harry Golden Collection (129 boxes of local author's
manuscripts, working papers and tapes). **Holdings:** 11,620 books; 364 bound
periodical volumes; 120 VF drawers of clippings and genealogical materials;
4800 reels of microfilmed Federal Population Schedules; 2125 reels of
microfilmed local newspapers; 360 reels of microfilmed county records.
Services: Copying; library open to public. **Networks/Consortia:** Member of
OCLC through SOLINET; Metrolina Library Association. **Staff:** Rosemary J.
Lands, Libn.

★2606★
**CHARLOTTE AND MECKLENBURG COUNTY PUBLIC LIBRARY - TEXTILE
   COLLECTION** (Sci-Tech)
310 N. Tryon St.   Phone: (704) 374-2725
Charlotte, NC 28202   Mae S. Tucker, Asst.Dir., Lib.Serv.
Staff: Prof 5; Other 2. **Subjects:** Textiles. **Holdings:** 4000 books; 6 16mm
films; 5 filmstrips; 3 slide sets; pamphlets and documents. **Subscriptions:**
100 journals and other serials. **Services:** Interlibrary loans; copying; library
open to public. **Networks/Consortia:** Member of OCLC through SOLINET.
Special Catalogs: Textiles: A Bibliography.

★2607★
**CHARLOTTE-MECKLENBURG SCHOOLS - CURRICULUM RESEARCH
   CENTER** (Educ)
428 W. Boulevard   Phone: (704) 376-0122
Charlotte, NC 28203   Bettye D. McCain, Hd., Media Spec.
Founded: 1957. **Staff:** Prof 2; Other 1. **Subjects:** Education. **Special
Collections:** Curriculum Development Library (on microfiche). **Holdings:**
12,700 books; unbound journals; 8 drawers of current publishers catalogs;
backfiles of 94 journals on microfilm; 4 VF drawers of pamphlets; 500
curriculum guides; ERIC collection. **Subscriptions:** 237 journals and other
serials. **Services:** Interlibrary loans; copying; center open to public but
circulation restricted to Charlotte-Mecklenburg Schools personnel.
Publications: Bibliographies. **Staff:** Beth M. Rountree, Media Spec.

★2608★
**CHARLOTTE MEMORIAL HOSPITAL AND MEDICAL CENTER - MEDICAL
   LIBRARY OF MECKLENBURG COUNTY/LRC OF CHARLOTTE AHEC** (Med)
Box 32681   Phone: (704) 373-3129
Charlotte, NC 28232   Donna Keklock, Chf.Libn.
Founded: 1977. **Staff:** Prof 2; Other 3. **Subjects:** Clinical medicine and allied
health fields. **Holdings:** 9000 books; 30,000 bound periodical volumes; 3 VF
drawers of pamphlets; 1200 video cassettes. **Subscriptions:** 330 journals
and other serials. **Services:** Interlibrary loans (fee); library not open to public.
Computerized Information Services: MEDLARS. **Networks/Consortia:**
Member of Charlotte Consortium; North Carolina Area Health Education
Centers Program (AHEC). **Publications:** Annual Report - to members of the
society. **Staff:** Ellen J. Medlin, Assoc.Libn.

★2609★
CHARLOTTE OBSERVER AND THE CHARLOTTE NEWS - LIBRARY (Publ)
600 S. Tryon St.
Box 32188   Phone: (704) 369-6889
Charlotte, NC 28232   Sara Gesler, Hd.Libn.
Founded: 1956. **Staff:** Prof 1; Other 6. **Subjects:** Newspaper reference
topics. **Holdings:** 800 VF drawers of clippings; 375 VF drawers of pictures;
25 VF drawers of microfilm. **Services:** Library is accessible through the
newspaper's promotion department. **Remarks:** Published by Knight Publishing
Company, Inc.

★2610★
CHARLTON PARK VILLAGE AND MUSEUM - LIBRARY (Hist)
2545 S. Charlton Park Rd.   Phone: (616) 945-3775
Hastings, MI 49058   Frank E. Walsh, Dir.
Subjects: Local history, crafts, agriculture. **Holdings:** Figures not available.
Services: Library open to public by appointment.

CHASE COLLECTION
See: Bradley University - Virginius H. Chase Special Collections Center

CHASE (Emory A.) MEMORIAL LIBRARY
See: New York State Supreme Court - 3rd Judicial District - Emory A.
   Chase Memorial Library

★2611★
CHASE MANHATTAN BANK, N.A. - INFORMATION CENTER (Bus-Fin)
One Chase Manhattan Plaza, 9th Fl.   Phone: (212) 552-0014
New York, NY 10081   Catherine R. Reilly, 2nd V.P., Mgr.
Staff: Prof 7; Other 14. **Subjects:** Banking, finance, industry, domestic and
foreign corporations, economics, data processing. **Holdings:** 18,000 books;
250 bound periodical volumes; 245 VF drawers; 60 periodical titles on
microfilm; Wall Street Journal since 1969 on microfilm; New York Times
since 1922 on microfilm. **Subscriptions:** 1500 journals and other serials; 15
newspapers. **Services:** Interlibrary loans; copying; research service for a fee;
library not open to public. **Computerized Information Services:** New York
Times Information Service, DIALOG, SDC, BRS, TEXTLINE, Dow Jones News
Retrieval, LEXIS, Spectrum; computerized cataloging, serials and routing.
Networks/Consortia: Member of OCLC. **Publications:** biz-dex, a monthly
abstracting service - available at a fee. **Remarks:** Contains the holdings of
Chase Manhattan Bank's former Systems Library. **Staff:** Ruby Fangemann,
Tech.Serv.; Lisa Whyte, Res.

★2612★
CHASE MANHATTAN BANK, N.A. - SYSTEMS LIBRARY
One New York Plaza
New York, NY 10004
Defunct. Holdings absorbed by Chase Manhattan Bank, N.A. - Information
Center.

CHASE (Salmon P.) COLLEGE OF LAW
See: Northern Kentucky University - Salmon P. Chase College of Law

★2613★
CHASE TRADE INFORMATION CORPORATION - LIBRARY
One World Trade Ctr.
New York, NY 10048
Subjects: Business conditions - Europe, Latin America, Middle East, North
Africa, Asia, China. **Holdings:** 2000 books; 40 VF drawers. **Remarks:**
Presently inactive.

CHASE (Virginius H.) SPECIAL COLLECTIONS CENTER
See: Bradley University - Virginius H. Chase Special Collections Center

CHASE (William Merritt) ARCHIVES
See: Parrish Art Museum - Library

★2614★
CHATTANOOGA-HAMILTON COUNTY BICENTENNIAL LIBRARY - LOCAL HISTORY AND GENEALOGICAL COLLECTIONS (Hist)
1001 Broad St.   Phone: (615) 757-5317
Chattanooga, TN 37402   Clara Swann, Hd.
Staff: Prof 1; Other 4. **Subjects:** Genealogy, local and state history, Tennessee writers. **Holdings:** 24,646 books; 257 manuscript collections; 100 VF drawers of clippings and photographs; 5500 reels of microfilmed county records and local newspapers; 4500 microfiche. **Subscriptions:** 145 journals and other serials; 5 newspapers. **Services:** Copying; library open to public for reference use only; requests for research by nonresidents may be subject to a fee. **Computerized Information Services:** Computerized cataloging. **Networks/Consortia:** Member of OCLC through SOLINET. **Publications:** Collections brochure, irregular. **Special Indexes:** Family surname index for materials in the department (card); local newspaper obituary indexes, 1897-1956, 1970 to present.

★2615★
CHATTANOOGA-HAMILTON COUNTY REGIONAL PLANNING COMMISSION - LIBRARY (Plan)
100 E. 11th St.
City Hall Annex, Rm. 200   Phone: (615) 757-5216
Chattanooga, TN 37402
Subjects: Conditions, growth and change in urban and regional areas. **Holdings:** 1050 books; 8 VF drawers of clippings; 480 loose-leaf notebooks; 46 drawers of maps; U.S. Census of 1970 for Tennessee. **Subscriptions:** 23 journals and other serials. **Services:** Library open to public for reference use only.

★2616★
CHATTANOOGA TIMES - LIBRARY (Publ)
117 E. 10th St.
Box 951   Phone: (615) 756-1234
Chattanooga, TN 37402   Lisa McCain, Libn.
Staff: Prof 1; Other 1. **Subjects:** Newspaper reference topics. **Holdings:** 500 books; 48,000 subject and biographical clipping files; 23 VF drawers of pictures; microfilm of newspaper from 1879; 300 pamphlets. **Subscriptions:** 15 newspapers. **Services:** Copying; library open to public for reference use only.

★2617★
CHATTEM DRUG AND CHEMICAL COMPANY - RESEARCH LIBRARY (Med)
1715 W. 38th St.   Phone: (615) 821-4571
Chattanooga, TN 37409   Tilda Wall, Libn.
Founded: 1915. **Staff:** 2. **Subjects:** Chemistry, engineering, medicine, pharmaceuticals. **Special Collections:** Antique herbals and antique almanacs. **Holdings:** 2100 books; 2200 bound periodical volumes; 200 pamphlets; 670 patents. **Subscriptions:** 92 journals and other serials; 34 newspapers. **Services:** Copying; library open to public for reference use only on request.

CHATTON (Milton J.) MEDICAL LIBRARY
See: Santa Clara Valley Medical Center - Milton J. Chatton Medical Library

★2618★
CHAUTAUQUA COUNTY HISTORICAL SOCIETY - LIBRARY (Hist)
Village Park   Phone: (716) 326-2977
Westfield, NY 14787   Maxine Smith, Hostess/Libn.
Founded: 1883. **Staff:** 1. **Subjects:** History of Chautauqua County. **Special Collections:** Tourgee papers; Civil War Muster Rolls of Chautauqua County; Foote Papers; Cushing Papers; Genealogy of Chautauqua County. **Holdings:** 2000 books. **Services:** Library open to public for reference use only. **Networks/Consortia:** Member of Chautauqua County Historical Agencies Consortium. **Publications:** History of Chautauqua County, 1938-1978 - available for sale. **Special Catalogs:** Local history collection (card); Foote papers (card). **Special Indexes:** Tourgee papers (book).

★2619★
CHAUTAUQUA COUNTY LAW LIBRARY (Law)
                                            Phone: (716) 753-4247
Mayville, NY 14757   Peggy Cross, Hd.Libn.
Staff: Prof 1. **Subjects:** Law. **Holdings:** 5000 volumes.

★2620★
CHAVES COUNTY DISTRICT COURT - LIBRARY (Law)
Box 1776   Phone: (505) 622-2212
Roswell, NM 88201
Staff: Prof 1. **Subjects:** Law. **Holdings:** 10,000 volumes. **Services:** Library open to public for reference use only. **Remarks:** Information concerning the library may be obtained by contacting the District Court office.

★2621★
CHELMSFORD HISTORICAL SOCIETY - BARRETT-BYAM HOMESTEAD LIBRARY (Hist)
40 Byam Rd.   Phone: (617) 256-2311
Chelmsford, MA 01824   Mrs. Donald Fogg, Curator
Founded: 1930. **Subjects:** Chelmsford and Massachusetts history, Civil War and Revolution, early agriculture. **Special Collections:** Historic music and school books. **Holdings:** Reports, pamphlets and deeds (Chelmsford history). **Subscriptions:** 10 journals and other serials. **Services:** Open to public with limited hours from mid-April to mid-December.

★2622★
CHEM-NUCLEAR SYSTEMS, INC. - INFORMATION CENTER (Sci-Tech)
240 Stoneridge Dr., Suite 100   Phone: (803) 256-0450
Columbia, SC 29210   Robin L. Deal, Info.Spec.
Founded: 1981. **Staff:** Prof 1. **Subjects:** Radioactive waste management, nuclear engineering, government regulations, radiation protection. **Holdings:** 150 books; 1000 technical reports (hard copy); 300 reports on microfiche; 10 VF drawers of subject files. **Subscriptions:** 18 journals and other serials. **Services:** Interlibrary loans; copying; library not open to public. **Computerized Information Services:** DIALOG. **Publications:** New Acquisitions, bimonthly - for internal distribution only.

★2623★
CHEM SYSTEMS INC. - INFORMATION CENTER (Sci-Tech)
303 S. Broadway   Phone: (914) 631-2828
Tarrytown, NY 10591   Maryann M. Grandy, Mgr., Info.Serv.
Founded: 1964. **Staff:** Prof 3; Other 1. **Subjects:** Chemical engineering, energy, organic chemicals. **Holdings:** 1100 books; 700 other cataloged items; 100 VF drawers of technical data; pamphlets; U.S. and foreign patents. **Subscriptions:** 80 journals and other serials. **Services:** Copying; library not open to public. **Staff:** Karen Stein, Res.Libn.; Milton Wenger, Info.Spec.

CHEMED CORPORATION - DEARBORN CHEMICAL (U.S.) LIBRARY
See: Grace (W.R.) and Company - Dearborn Chemical (U.S.) Library

★2624★
CHEMICAL ABSTRACTS SERVICE - LIBRARY (Sci-Tech; Info Sci)
Box 3012   Phone: (614) 421-3600
Columbus, OH 43210   Robert S. Tannehill, Jr., Lib.Mgr.
Founded: 1954. **Staff:** Prof 13; Other 42. **Subjects:** Chemistry, chemical engineering, chemical information sciences. **Special Collections:** Collection of primary chemical sciences literature (serials, proceedings of meetings and edited collections). **Holdings:** 20,000 books. **Subscriptions:** 12,000 journals and other serials. **Services:** Document Delivery Service; library open to public with restrictions. **Computerized Information Services:** DIALOG, SDC, BRS, NLM; computerized cataloging. **Networks/Consortia:** Member of OHIONET. **Publications:** Catalog of CAS publications and services - available on request. **Remarks:** This collection of primary chemical sciences literature is the most comprehensive in the world. Chemical Abstracts Service is a division of the American Chemical Society.

★2625★
CHEMICAL BANK - RESEARCH LIBRARY (Bus-Fin)
20 Pine St., Rm. 1915   Phone: (212) 770-3127
New York, NY 10015   Helen Traina, Chf.Libn.
Founded: 1966. **Staff:** Prof 4; Other 6. **Subjects:** Banking, economics, finance, international economics, management. **Holdings:** 9000 books; 800 periodical titles; 84,400 microforms; 150 VF drawers of pamphlets, speeches and miscellaneous material. **Subscriptions:** 1500 journals and other serials; 15 newspapers. **Services:** Interlibrary loans; copying (limited); library open to public for reference use only. **Computerized Information Services:** DIALOG, Source Telecomputing Corporation, TEXTLINE, New York Times Information Service; computerized serials. **Publications:** Recent Acquisitions, monthly - distribution by request on a letterhead. **Staff:** Peggy Pennell, Libn.; Ruth Bieble, Libn.; Maureen O'Donnell, Asst.Libn.

CHEMICAL INTERNATIONAL INFORMATION CENTER
See: Chemists' Club Library

★2626★
CHEMICAL MANUFACTURERS ASSOCIATION - LIBRARY (Sci-Tech)
2501 M St., N.W.   Phone: (202) 328-4229
Washington, DC 20037
Staff: Prof 1. **Subjects:** Chemical industry. **Holdings:** 1000 books; 60 VF drawers. **Subscriptions:** 50 journals and other serials. **Services:** Interlibrary loans; copying; library open to public.

CHEMICAL PROPULSION INFORMATION AGENCY
See: Johns Hopkins University - Applied Physics Laboratory

CHEMICAL THERMODYNAMICS DATA CENTER
See: U.S. Natl. Bureau of Standards

CHEMIN DE FER NATIONAUX DU CANADA
See: Canadian National Railways

★2627★
CHEMINEER, INC. - LIBRARY (Sci-Tech)
Box 1123   Phone: (513) 898-1111
Dayton, OH 45401   Dr. David S. Dickey, Technical Dir.
Subjects: Fluid agitation, mixing, mixing materials, impellers, mixing machinery, vessel design, CPI equipment design, chemical and mechanical engineering. **Holdings:** Books; journals; patents and data. **Services:** Copying; library open to qualified persons with permission only.

★2628★
CHEMISTS' CLUB LIBRARY - CHEMICAL INTERNATIONAL INFORMATION CENTER (Sci-Tech)
52 E. 41st St.   Phone: (212) 679-6383
New York, NY 10017   Elsie Lim, Libn.
Founded: 1898. **Staff:** Prof 3; Other 5. **Subjects:** Chemistry, pure and applied; chemical engineering; pharmacology; toxicology. **Special Collections:** Biographies and portraits of chemists. **Holdings:** 65,000 books and bound periodical volumes; microfilm. **Subscriptions:** 350 journals and other serials. **Services:** Copying; photostating orders accepted and quick reference questions answered by phone; library open to public. **Computerized Information Services:** MEDLINE, DIALOG, SDC, Derwent Publications Ltd. **Staff:** Dr. Sidney S. Tuwiner, Chm., Lib.Comm.

★2629★
CHEMPLEX COMPANY - LIBRARY (Sci-Tech)
3100 Golf Rd.   Phone: (312) 437-7800
Rolling Meadows, IL 60008   Frieda R. Oetting, Libn.
Founded: 1967. **Staff:** Prof 1; Other 1. **Subjects:** Polymer chemistry, polymer physics, general business, chemical engineering, statistics, mathematics. **Holdings:** 1600 books; 1545 bound periodical volumes; 460 technical abstracts (card); 650 annual reports and house organs; 390 pamphlets. **Subscriptions:** 230 journals and other serials. **Services:** Interlibrary loans; library open to public for reference use only by request. **Computerized Information Services:** DIALOG, SDC. **Publications:** Library Bulletin, monthly; Marketing Bibliography, monthly - for internal distribution only.

★2630★
CHEMUNG COUNTY HISTORICAL SOCIETY, INC. - MRS. ARTHUR W. BOOTH LIBRARY (Hist)
415 E. Water St.   Phone: (607) 734-4167
Elmira, NY 14901   Lyman D. Gridley, Pres.
Founded: 1923. **Staff:** 10. **Subjects:** New York State and local history, local authors, genealogies. **Special Collections:** Chemung County historical journals, 1955 to present; Chemung County historical records, maps and atlases; Genesee County historical records; Elmira city directories from 1857; all minutes of Elmira City Council and County Board of Supervisors. **Holdings:** 3000 volumes; letters; 10,000 manuscripts; historical pamphlets; 250 scrapbooks. **Services:** Copying; library open to public five days a week; open to groups and students for research by appointment. **Publications:** Chemung County Historical Journal. **Staff:** Martha K. Squires, Libn., Res.Ck.

★2631★
CHENANGO MEMORIAL HOSPITAL - MEDICAL LIBRARY (Med)
179 N. Broad St.   Phone: (607) 335-4159
Norwich, NY 13815   Ann L. Slocum, Med.Libn.
Founded: 1953. **Staff:** Prof 1. **Subjects:** Medicine, nursing and related fields. **Holdings:** 1000 books; 670 bound periodical volumes. **Subscriptions:** 186 journals and other serials. **Services:** Interlibrary loans; copying; library open to public by appointment. **Networks/Consortia:** Member of Health Resources Council of Central New York.

CHENEY (Anne Bunce) LIBRARY
See: University of Hartford - Anne Bunce Cheney Library

CHENEY COWLES MEMORIAL MUSEUM
See: Eastern Washington State Historical Society

CHERKASKY (Karl) SOCIAL MEDICINE LIBRARY
See: Montefiore Medical Center - Karl Cherkasky Social Medicine Library

★2632★
CHEROKEE COUNTY HISTORICAL SOCIETY - RESEARCH CENTER (Hist)
Box 247   Phone: (712) 436-2624
Cleghorn, IA 51014   Anne Wilberding, Pres.
Subjects: Local history, genealogy. **Special Collections:** Original pioneer materials and World War II data for Cherokee County. **Holdings:** Figures not available. **Services:** Copying; library open to public by appointment. **Publications:** Newsletter, monthly.

CHEROKEE GARDEN CLUB LIBRARY
See: Atlanta Historical Society - Archives

CHEROKEE NATIONAL ARCHIVES
See: Cherokee National Historical Society, Inc.

★2633★
CHEROKEE NATIONAL HISTORICAL SOCIETY, INC. - CHEROKEE NATIONAL ARCHIVES (Hist; Area-Ethnic)
Box 515
TSA-LA-GI   Phone: (918) 456-6007
Tahlequah, OK 74464   Duane King, Exec.Dir.
Founded: 1963. **Staff:** 1. **Subjects:** Cherokee history. **Special Collections:** W.W. Keeler (Principal Chief of Cherokees) papers; Cherokee National Executive Committee minutes 1948 (origin) to 1970 (disbandment); Cherokee Nation papers, 1969-1975; manuscript collections. **Holdings:** 3000 books; 500 bound periodical volumes; 100 reels of microfilm; 5 VF drawers of pamphlets; 7 VF drawers of papers and committee minutes. **Subscriptions:** 20 journals and other serials. **Services:** Interlibrary loans; copying; archives open to public on request.

★2634★
CHEROKEE REGIONAL LIBRARY - GEORGIA HISTORY & GENEALOGICAL ROOM (Hist; Area-Ethnic)
305 S. Duke St.
Box 707   Phone: (404) 638-2992
LaFayette, GA 30728   Diana Ray Tope, Dir.
Staff: Prof 2. **Subjects:** Local history, Cherokee Indians. **Holdings:** 625 books; 48 bound periodical volumes; 11 maps; 154 reels of microfilm with county census data; 242 reels of microfilm. **Services:** Interlibrary loans; copying; library open to public. **Special Catalogs:** Bibliographies of county histories; early Walker County History. **Special Indexes:** Deed Index I of Walker County; Index to Walker County History. **Staff:** Mary Robertson, Asst.Dir.

CHEROKEE STRIP LIVING MUSEUM
See: U.S. Natl. Park Service

★2635★
CHERRY HOSPITAL - LEARNING RESOURCE CENTER (Med)
                    Phone: (919) 731-3447
Goldsboro, NC 27530   Maxim Tabory, Libn./Dir. of LRC
Staff: Prof 1; Other 1. **Subjects:** Psychiatry, medicine, nursing, psychology, social work, allied health sciences. **Holdings:** 2000 books; 800 bound periodical volumes; 986 AV materials. **Subscriptions:** 112 journals and other serials. **Services:** Interlibrary loans; library open to state employees and health care workers. **Publications:** List of new acquisitions, quarterly - for internal distribution only; AV catalog - to selected state institutions. **Special Catalogs:** AV catalog (book).

CHESAPEAKE BAY CENTER FOR ENVIRONMENTAL STUDIES
See: Smithsonian Institution Libraries

★2636★
CHESAPEAKE BAY MARITIME MUSEUM - HOWARD I. CHAPELLE MEMORIAL LIBRARY (Hist)
Box 636   Phone: (301) 745-2916
St. Michaels, MD 21663   Mary Ruth Robertson, Libn.
Staff: Prof 2. **Subjects:** Chesapeake Bay history and marine life; boat construction, maintenance and handling; waterfowl; voyages and travel; naval and sailing craft history; ship models; steamboat history. **Holdings:** 2000

volumes. **Subscriptions:** 9 journals and other serials. **Services:** Library open to public with restrictions.

★2637★
CHESAPEAKE & OHIO HISTORICAL SOCIETY, INC. - C & O ARCHIVAL COLLECTION (Hist; Trans)
Christopher Newport College
50 Shoe Lane
Newport News VA 23606   Thomas W. Dixon, Jr., Pres.
Founded: 1970. **Staff:** 1. **Subjects:** C & O Railway history - steam/diesel locomotives, finance, operations. **Special Collections:** C & O Railway operations in the Steam Age and early Diesel era (4000 negatives). **Holdings:** 20 books; 25 bound periodical volumes; 1000 pamphlets; manuscripts and research notes. **Services:** Copying; archival facility open to researchers by advance appointment. **Publications:** Chesapeake & Ohio Historical Newsletter, monthly - by subscription; Chesapeake & Ohio Freight cars. **Special Indexes:** Card index to photographs by subject and location. **Remarks:** Appointments may be made by contacting the Assistant Archivist, Robert V. Gifford (804-898-5214), or by mail at 207 Brigade Drive, Yorktown, VA 23692. Corporate headquarters' address is Box 417, Alderson, WV 24910. **Staff:** Randolph Kean, Archv.; Robert V. Gifford, Asst.Archv.

★2638★
CHESAPEAKE AND OHIO RAILROAD COMPANY - TRAFFIC RESEARCH DEPARTMENT - LIBRARY (Bus-Fin; Trans)
One Charles Ctr., 16th Fl.   Phone: (301) 237-3742
Baltimore, MD 21201   R.M. Ruddle, Mgr., Traffic Res.
Founded: 1966. **Staff:** 1. **Subjects:** Industry, economics, statistics, transportation. **Special Collections:** Standard and Poor Corporate Records. **Holdings:** 3000 books and bound periodical volumes; 1000 pamphlets and reports; 1000 annual reports (corporate); 200 maps. **Subscriptions:** 120 journals and other serials; 10 newspapers. **Services:** Copying; library not open to public.

★2639★
CHESEBROUGH-POND'S, INC. - RESEARCH LIBRARY (Sci-Tech)
Trumbull Industrial Pk.   Phone: (203) 377-7100
Trumbull, CT 06611   Carol Gannon, Libn.
Founded: 1959. **Staff:** Prof 1; Other 1. **Subjects:** Chemistry, cosmetic science, food science, pharmacology. **Holdings:** 3800 books; 1860 bound periodical volumes; 20 lateral file drawers of patents, reprints, pamphlets; 40 cartridges of microfilm; 3 boxes of microfiche. **Subscriptions:** 130 journals and other serials. **Services:** Interlibrary loans; copying; library open to public by appointment. **Computerized Information Services:** DIALOG, TOXLINE, MEDLINE, SDC.

★2640★
CHESHIRE HOSPITAL - MEDICAL LIBRARY (Med)
580 Court St.   Phone: (603) 352-4111
Keene, NH 03431   Phyllis Askey, Med.Libn.
Founded: 1963. **Staff:** Prof 1; Other 1. **Subjects:** Medicine, nursing, related health areas. **Holdings:** 1000 books; 1600 bound periodical volumes; 165 indices (cataloged); 7 VF drawers of pamphlets. **Subscriptions:** 185 journals and other serials. **Services:** Interlibrary loans; copying; library open to public. **Networks/Consortia:** Member of New England Regional Medical Library Association; Vermont-New Hampshire-New York Hospital Libraries.

CHESS PRESS SYNDICATE
See: Kxe6s Verein Chess Society

★2641★
CHESTER COUNTY HISTORICAL SOCIETY - LIBRARY (Hist)
225 N. High St.   Phone: (215) 692-4800
West Chester, PA 19380   Rosemary B. Philips, Libn.
Founded: 1893. **Staff:** Prof 3. **Subjects:** Local history and politics, genealogy, decorative arts, church history. **Special Collections:** Albert Cook Myers' William Penn material (196 volumes and several boxes of Myers' personal papers); postal history (1000 items); almanacs (500 items); large collection of Chester County newspapers; county archives. **Holdings:** Book and periodical holdings not available; 140 VF drawers of newspaper clippings; 250 reels of microfilm. **Subscriptions:** 159 journals and other serials; 11 newspapers. **Services:** Copying; library open to nonmembers for a fee. **Special Indexes:** Name index to Chester County tax lists, 1699-1758, 1775-1783 (card); list of Chester County men on Revolutionary War rolls (card). **Staff:** Rita M. Moore, Asst.Libn.; Jack McCarthy, County Archv.

★2642★
CHESTER COUNTY LAW AND MISCELLANEOUS LIBRARY ASSOCIATION (Law)
Court House   Phone: (215) 431-6166
West Chester, PA 19380   Christine Harvan, Libn.
Founded: 1862. **Staff:** Prof 1; Other 2. **Subjects:** Law. **Holdings:** 21,000 books; 120 bound periodical volumes; 1 VF drawer of pamphlet material; 3 VF drawers of Chester County Township and Borough Ordinances. **Subscriptions:** 30 journals and other serials. **Services:** Interlibrary loans; copying; library open to public for reference use only. **Computerized Information Services:** WESTLAW. **Special Indexes:** Index to Chester County Township and Borough Ordinances. **Also Known As:** Chester County Law Library.

★2643★
CHESTERWOOD - LIBRARY (Art)
Box 248   Phone: (413) 298-3579
Stockbridge, MA 01262   Susan Frisch Lehrer, Cur.
Founded: 1969. **Staff:** Prof 2. **Subjects:** Sculpture, art, architecture, landscape architecture, decorative arts, historic preservation, history, travel, museum administration. **Special Collections:** Daniel Chester French collection of photographs, papers, blueprints, drawings and memorabilia (5000 items). **Holdings:** 5000 books; 25 bound periodical volumes; photographs (cataloged); 5 linear feet of papers of Mary French, William Penn Cresson and Margaret French Cresson; 13 oral history tapes of friends and relatives of Daniel Chester French and Chesterwood. **Services:** Library is open to scholars. **Remarks:** Maintained by the National Trust for Historic Preservation. **Staff:** Paul W. Ivory, Dir. of Chesterwood.

★2644★
CHESTNUT HILL HOSPITAL - SCHOOL OF NURSING LIBRARY (Med)
8835 Germantown Ave.
Philadelphia, PA 19118   Maude H. Meyerend, Libn.
Staff: Prof 2. **Subjects:** Nursing. **Holdings:** 2500 books; 155 bound periodical volumes; 112 filmstrips. **Subscriptions:** 47 journals and other serials. **Services:** Interlibrary loans; copying; library open to allied health personnel only.

★2645★
CHEVRON GEOSCIENCES COMPANY - LIBRARY (Sci-Tech)
Box 36487   Phone: (713) 781-3030
Houston, TX 77036   Francine Rorabaugh, Libn.
Founded: 1966. **Staff:** Prof 1; Other 1. **Subjects:** Geophysics, geology, mathematics. **Holdings:** 900 books and bound periodical volumes. **Subscriptions:** 43 journals and other serials. **Services:** Interlibrary loans; library not open to public.

★2646★
CHEVRON OIL FIELD RESEARCH COMPANY - TECHNICAL INFORMATION SERVICES (Energy)
Box 446   Phone: (213) 694-7500
La Habra, CA 90631   Ann S. Coppin, Supv.
Founded: 1947. **Staff:** Prof 3; Other 11. **Subjects:** Geology, petroleum engineering, oceanography, paleontology, physics, chemistry, mathematics. **Holdings:** 20,000 books; 18,500 bound periodical volumes; 6000 geologic maps (cataloged); 1700 reels of microfilm; 11,000 microfiche; 400 patents. **Subscriptions:** 1141 journals and other serials. **Services:** Interlibrary loans; copying; SDI; translations; center open to public by appointment or referral. **Computerized Information Services:** DIALOG, SDC; computerized cataloging, serials. **Networks/Consortia:** Member of Libraries of Orange County (LOCNET); RLG. **Publications:** Accessions List, weekly; book catalog, monthly cumulations - both for internal distribution only. **Special Catalogs:** Book catalog; corporate report bibliography and index. **Staff:** E. Susan Palmer, Tech.Info.Spec.; Elizabeth H. Ashton, Res.Libn.

★2647★
CHEVRON RESEARCH COMPANY - TECHNICAL INFORMATION CENTER (Energy)
576 Standard Ave.   Phone: (415) 237-4411
Richmond, CA 94802   J.M. Hubert, Mgr., Tech.Info.Ctr.
Founded: 1920. **Staff:** Prof 12; Other 16. **Subjects:** Chemistry, petroleum refining, petrochemicals, engineering, fuels and lubricants. **Holdings:** 12,500 books; 8500 bound periodical volumes; preprints of meeting papers (Society of Automotive Engineers, American Society of Mechanical Engineers); 2 million U.S. and foreign patents; 60,000 pamphlets; 20 file drawers of trade literature; 700 VF drawers of company reports and correspondence; 2 million pages of documents on microfilm. **Subscriptions:** 1400 journals and other serials. **Services:** Interlibrary loans; copying; translations; SDI profiles; library open to public by special request. **Computerized Information Services:** DIALOG, SDC, RLIN, BRS, New York Times Information Service, Chemical

Abstracts Service (CAS); computerized acquisitions, cataloging, serials and files system. **Networks/Consortia:** Member of RLG; CLASS. **Publications:** Technical Information Center Library Bulletin, semimonthly; Publications - Chevron Research Company, annual. **Staff:** H.D. Gholston, Supv.Tech.Lib.; M.S. Wawrzonek, Info.Anl.; A.A. Antony, Info.Anl.; J.J. Desoer, Res.Libn.; S.C. George, Info.Anl.; L.F. Herron, Res.Transl.; J.T. Kerns, Info.Anl.; C.L. Riley, Info.Anl.; H.G. Thompson, Central Files Spec.; W.W. West, Info.Anl.; L.W. White, Info.Anl.

★2648★
CHEVRON RESOURCES COMPANY - LIBRARY (Energy)
1746 Cole Blvd.   Phone: (303) 273-2700
Golden, CO 80401
Founded: 1973. **Staff:** Prof 1; Other 1. **Subjects:** Minerals exploration, earth science. **Holdings:** 3500 books; 200 bound periodical volumes; 180 tapes. **Subscriptions:** 200 journals and other serials; 10 newspapers. **Services:** Interlibrary loans; library open to public by appointment. **Computerized Information Services:** SDC; computerized cataloging and acquisitions. **Remarks:** Additional company resources collections are located in San Antonio, TX; Creede, CO; Reno, NV; Vernal, UT.

★2649★
CHEVRON STANDARD, LTD. - LIBRARY (Energy)
500 5th Ave., S.W.   Phone: (403) 234-5577
Calgary, AB, Canada T2P 0L7   Terri Pieschel, Supv. Lib.
Founded: 1952. **Staff:** Prof 1; Other 2. **Subjects:** Geology, geophysics, paleontology, palynology, petroleum engineering. **Holdings:** 7000 books and bound periodical volumes; 2000 research reports. **Subscriptions:** 450 journals and other serials. **Services:** Interlibrary loans; copying; library not open to public. **Computerized Information Services:** DIALOG, SDC; computerized cataloging and serials. **Publications:** Library News, monthly - for internal distribution only.

★2650★
CHEVRON USA INC. - CENTRAL REGION - TECHNICAL LIBRARY (Sci-Tech; Energy)
700 S. Colorado Blvd., Rm. 845   Phone: (303) 691-7347
Denver, CO 80222   Elaine Naranjo, Libn.
Staff: Prof 1. **Subjects:** Geology, geophysics, petroleum engineering. **Holdings:** 3000 books; 200 bound periodical volumes; 500 government publications. **Subscriptions:** 150 journals and other serials; 10 newspapers. **Services:** Interlibrary loans; copying; library open to public with restrictions.

CHEVRON USA INC. - EASTERN REGION LIBRARY
See: Standard Oil of California

★2651★
CHEVY CHASE BAPTIST CHURCH - SEBRING MEMORIAL LIBRARY (Rel-Theol)
5671 Western Ave., N.W.
Washington, DC 20015   May Kardell, Libn.
Staff: Prof 1. **Subjects:** Religion, biography, missions, children's literature. **Holdings:** 2800 books; 2 VF drawers of pictures; 1 VF drawer of archives; AV material. **Subscriptions:** 10 journals and other serials. **Services:** Interlibrary loans (limited); library open to public for reference use only; church members may borrow.

CHEYENNE FAMILY PRACTICE RESIDENCY PROGRAM
See: Family Practice Residency Program at Cheyenne

★2652★
CHEYENNE MOUNTAIN ZOOLOGICAL PARK - LIBRARY (Sci-Tech)
Box 158   Phone: (303) 633-0917
Colorado Springs, CO 80901   Bill Aragon, Cur.
Staff: Prof 2. **Subjects:** Zoology, biology, botany. **Holdings:** 500 books; zoo publications. **Subscriptions:** 16 journals and other serials. **Services:** Library not open to public.

CHI (John W.) MEMORIAL MEDICAL LIBRARY
See: Ingham Medical Center - John W. Chi Memorial Medical Library

★2653★
CHICAGO ACADEMY OF SCIENCES - MATTHEW LAUGHLIN MEMORIAL LIBRARY (Sci-Tech)
2001 N. Clark St.   Phone: (312) 549-0606
Chicago, IL 60614   Louise Lunak, Libn.
Founded: 1857. **Staff:** Prof 1; Other 2. **Subjects:** Ornithology, geology, biological science, physical sciences. **Holdings:** 30,000 volumes. **Services:** Library open to public with director's permission.

CHICAGO AERIAL INDUSTRIES
See: CAI

★2654★
CHICAGO BAR ASSOCIATION - LIBRARY (Law)
29 S. LaSalle St.   Phone: (312) 782-7348
Chicago, IL 60603   Stephen F. Czike, Exec.Libn.
Founded: 1874. **Staff:** Prof 3; Other 10. **Subjects:** Law and related subjects. **Holdings:** 160,000 volumes. **Services:** Not generally open to public; requests to use material will be considered on an individual basis.

★2655★
CHICAGO BOARD OF EDUCATION - LIBRARY (Educ)
228 N. LaSalle St., Rm. 846   Phone: (312) 641-4105
Chicago, IL 60601   Mary Ann Ross, Libn.
Founded: 1935. **Staff:** Prof 2; Other 1. **Subjects:** Education. **Holdings:** 14,000 books; archives; 6000 microforms; 244 tapes; 32 VF drawers. **Subscriptions:** 165 journals and other serials. **Services:** Interlibrary loans; library open to public for reference use only. **Networks/Consortia:** Member of Metropolitan Chicago Library Assembly. **Publications:** Relate, quarterly - to school personnel and others on request. **Staff:** Florence Williams, Asst.Libn.

★2656★
CHICAGO BOARD OF TRADE - LIBRARY (Bus-Fin)
141 W. Jackson Blvd.   Phone: (312) 435-3552
Chicago, IL 60604   Laura J. Miracle, Libn.
Founded: 1969. **Staff:** Prof 1; Other 1. **Subjects:** Commodity exchanges, futures trading, agriculture, agricultural economics, economics, finance. **Special Collections:** Statistical annuals of the Board of Trade from 1858, prices of commodities from 1858. **Holdings:** 3500 books; 550 bound periodical volumes; regulations, annual reports and statistics from commodity exchanges; 15 VF drawers of pamphlets, government reports, clippings, unbound reports, microfilm, state agricultural reports. **Subscriptions:** 400 journals and other serials; 9 newspapers. **Services:** Interlibrary loans; library open to public on a limited schedule. **Computerized Information Services:** Computerized cataloging. **Networks/Consortia:** Member of OCLC; ILLINET. **Publications:** Acquisitions list, quarterly; bibliographies, annual.

★2657★
CHICAGO BRIDGE & IRON COMPANY - TECHNICAL LIBRARY (Sci-Tech)
800 Jorie Blvd.   Phone: (312) 654-7279
Oak Brook, IL 60521   Suzanne D. Beatty, Tech.Libn.
Founded: 1963. **Staff:** Prof 1; Other 1. **Subjects:** Engineering - mechanical, civil, marine metals, structural; containers; seismology; soil mechanics. **Holdings:** 5000 books; 100 bound periodical volumes; 300 company reports; 4000 federal government documents; 300 association and state building codes. **Subscriptions:** 300 journals and other serials. **Services:** Interlibrary loans; copying; library not open to public.

★2658★
CHICAGO COLLEGE OF OSTEOPATHIC MEDICINE - ALUMNI MEMORIAL LIBRARY (Med)
5200 S. Ellis Ave.   Phone: (312) 947-4380
Chicago, IL 60615   Sandra A. Worley, Dir. of Lib.Serv.
Founded: 1913. **Staff:** Prof 4; Other 15. **Subjects:** Medicine and related subjects, osteopathy. **Special Collections:** Rare books on osteopathy. **Holdings:** 14,621 books; 22,831 bound periodical volumes; 6125 audiotape recordings; 1125 videotapes; 32,550 slides. **Subscriptions:** 1185 journals and other serials; 6 newspapers. **Services:** Interlibrary loans; library open to public for reference use. **Computerized Information Services:** MEDLINE, SDC, BRS, DIALOG; computerized serials. **Networks/Consortia:** Member of OCLC through ILLINET; Metropolitan Chicago Library Assembly; Regional Medical Library - Region 3. **Publications:** Library newsletter, quarterly - internal and mailing list distribution. **Special Indexes:** Subject index to serials. **Remarks:** There are two branch libraries: Olympia Fields Hospital Library, located at 203rd and Crawford, Olympia Fields, IL, 60461; and Louise Burg Hospital Library, located at 255 W. Cermak, Chicago, IL, 60616. **Staff:** Caryn Carr Lynn, Hd., Tech.Serv.; Vicki D. Bloom, Med.Libn.; Kathleen Despres, Med.Libn.

★2659★
CHICAGO COLLEGE OF OSTEOPATHIC MEDICINE - OLYMPIA FIELDS HOSPITAL LIBRARY (Med)
203rd and Crawford   Phone: (312) 747-4000
Olympia Fields, IL 60461   Lois F. Hayes, Libn.
Founded: 1978. **Staff:** Prof 1. **Subjects:** Medicine. **Holdings:** 1150 books; 900 bound periodical volumes; 200 videotapes. **Subscriptions:** 175 journals and other serials. **Services:** Interlibrary loans; copying; SDI; library open to public by appointment. **Computerized Information Services:** MEDLARS, BRS.

Networks/Consortia: Member of Chicago and South Consortium; Surburban Library System (SLS). **Publications:** Newsletter.

CHICAGO COMPREHENSIVE HEALTH COUNCIL
See: Comprehensive Health Council of Metropolitan Chicago

★2660★
CHICAGO DEPARTMENT OF HUMAN SERVICES - LIBRARY (Soc Sci)
640 N. LaSalle St.   Phone: (312) 744-6653
Chicago, IL 60610   Janice Bradshaw, Supv.
Staff: Prof 1; Other 3. **Subjects:** Human services. **Holdings:** 1300 books and bound periodical volumes; technical manuals. **Subscriptions:** 200 journals and other serials. **Services:** Interlibrary loans; copying; library open to public for reference use only.

★2661★
CHICAGO HISTORICAL SOCIETY - RESEARCH COLLECTIONS (Hist)
Clark St. at North Ave.   Phone: (312) 642-4600
Chicago, IL 60614
Founded: 1856. **Staff:** 16. **Subjects:** History - Chicago, Illinois, Civil War, Lincoln. **Special Collections:** Chicago directories; trade catalogs; advertising cards (6000); theater programs (12,000); sheet music (5400); personal papers and records of Chicago individuals and organizations from the city's early days to the present; negatives and prints from Chicago newspaper morgues, 1900-1965 (250,000); Meserve Americana (27 volumes, mostly of Civil War period; 8000 portraits); American city prints (historic); J. Norman Jensen Collection of Lake and River Disasters, 1679-1947 (8500 cards). **Holdings:** 110,000 books and pamphlets; 12,000 bound periodical volumes; 7500 volumes of newspapers; 16,000 broadsides and posters; 10,000 maps; 630 atlases; 37 VF drawers of clippings; 2500 volumes of CHS archives; 35,000 miscellaneous printed pieces; 9500 reels of microfilm; 8500 linear feet of manuscripts; 250,000 architectural drawings; 53,000 prints; 700,000 photographs; 12,000 reels of newsfilm. **Subscriptions:** 280 journals and other serials. **Services:** Copying; collections open to public for reference use only. **Staff:** Grant Dean, Assoc.Cur., Printed Coll.; Janice Soczka, Cur., Printed Coll.; Archie Motley, Cur. of Mss.; Larry Viskochil, Cur., Graphic Coll.; Ann Van Zanten, Cur., Arch.Coll.; Robert L. Brubaker, Cur., Spec.Coll.; Jane Stevens, Asst.Cur., Graphic Coll.; Linda J. Evans, Assoc.Cur., Mss.; Maureen O'Brien Will, Asst.Cur., Graphic Coll.

★2662★
CHICAGO INSTITUTE FOR PSYCHOANALYSIS - MC LEAN LIBRARY (Med)
180 N. Michigan Ave.   Phone: (312) 726-6300
Chicago, IL 60601   Glenn E. Miller, Libn.
Founded: 1932. **Staff:** Prof 1; Other 3. **Subjects:** Psychoanalysis, psychosomatic medicine, psychiatry, related social and behavioral sciences. **Special Collections:** Maxwell Gitelson Film Library (150 titles). **Holdings:** 10,000 books; 2000 bound periodical volumes; 3 VF drawers of archives of psychoanalytic society meetings; 8 VF drawers of archives of staff writings; 30 VF drawers of reprints and pamphlets; 600 reels of microfilm. **Subscriptions:** 200 journals and other serials. **Services:** Interlibrary loans; copying; library open to public with a fee for services. **Publications:** Chicago Psychoanalytic Literature Index, 1920-1970, published 1971 (3 volumes); with computer-compiled quarterly subject index, annually cumulated and bound for 1971 to present - by subscription; Gitelson Film Library Catalog. **Also Known As:** Institute for Psychoanalysis.

CHICAGO JAZZ ARCHIVE
See: University of Chicago - Music Collection

CHICAGO KENT LAW SCHOOL
See: Illinois Institute of Technology - Chicago Kent Law School

CHICAGO MEDICAL SCHOOL/UNIVERSITY OF HEALTH SCIENCES
See: University of Health Sciences/Chicago Medical School

CHICAGO METROPOLITAN SANITARY DISTRICT
See: Metropolitan Sanitary District of Greater Chicago

★2663★
CHICAGO MOUNTAINEERING CLUB - JOHN SPECK MEMORIAL LIBRARY (Rec)
739 Forest Ave.   Phone: (312) 469-3443
Glen Ellyn, IL 60137   George Pokorny, Libn.
Founded: 1950. **Staff:** 1. **Subjects:** Mountaineering expeditions, mountaineering techniques and safety, mountain areas of the world, climbing guidebooks, natural history and geology, skiing, mountaineering fiction, conservation, glaciology, mountain flora. **Holdings:** 2000 books; 500 bound periodical volumes; 200 pamphlets (cataloged); 200 maps. **Subscriptions:** 11

journals and other serials. **Services:** Interlibrary loans; copying; library available to other clubs for research purposes. **Special Catalogs:** Library catalog published for members and other clubs.

★2664★
CHICAGO MUNICIPAL REFERENCE LIBRARY (Soc Sci)
City Hall, Rm. 1004   Phone: (312) 744-4992
Chicago, IL 60602   Joyce Malden, Libn.
Staff: Prof 13; Other 15. **Subjects:** Municipal affairs (including city planning, criminology, public finance, housing, public administration, public personnel). **Special Collections:** City of Chicago documents. **Holdings:** 45,000 titles; 84 VF drawers of newspaper clippings; 48 VF drawers of pamphlets; maps; microfilms. **Subscriptions:** 1300 journals and other serials; 36 newspapers. **Services:** Interlibrary loans; copying; library open to public for reference use only. **Computerized Information Services:** SDC, DIALOG, New York Times Information Service; computerized cataloging. **Networks/Consortia:** Member of OCLC; ILLINET. **Publications:** Recent Additions, Municipal Reference Library, monthly; Checklist of Publications of the City of Chicago, quarterly; Facts about Chicago, annual; Recent Additions - Police Branch, bimonthly - all free upon request; Government of the City of Chicago, and Historical Information about Chicago - both for sale.

★2665★
CHICAGO PUBLIC LIBRARY CENTRAL LIBRARY - BUSINESS/SCIENCE/TECHNOLOGY DIVISION (Bus-Fin; Sci-Tech)
425 N. Michigan Ave.   Phone: (312) 269-2814
Chicago, IL 60611   Emelie Shroder, Division Chief
Founded: 1977. **Staff:** Prof 24; Other 18. **Subjects:** Business, technology, corporate and investment information, management, personnel management, patents, physical sciences, biological sciences, medicine, health, computer science, careers, environmental information, agriculture, gardening, cookbooks. **Special Collections:** U.S. and British Patents complete (38,202 volumes and 4135 reels of U.S. patents); gazettes complete; multilingual technical dictionaries (180 volumes); domestic and foreign automobile manuals; radio, TV, electrical schematics; industrial and product directories; career information; standards and specifications on microfilm including International Organization for Standardization (ISO). **Holdings:** 178,000 books; 34,821 bound periodical volumes; 321,724 microfiche 10K reports and prospectuses Leasco Disclosure Svc.; 8 VF drawers of federal specifications and standards; 6 VF drawers of American National Standards Institute standards; 50 VF drawers of pamphlets and corporate annual reports. **Subscriptions:** 2000 journals and other serials; 8 newspapers. **Services:** Interlibrary loans; copying; library open to public. **Computerized Information Services:** DIALOG, SDC, BRS, Dow Jones News Retrieval, New York Times Information Service; computerized cataloging. **Networks/Consortia:** Member of OCLC through ILLINET. **Publications:** Bibliography on special subjects, monthly. **Remarks:** The Science and Technology Information Center's telephone number is (312) 269-2865. **Staff:** John Moore, Engr.Sect.Hd.; Gerald Szesko, Tech.Sect.Hd.; David Rouse, Bus.Info.Ctr.Hd.; Lynda Sanford, Sci./Tech.Info.Hd.; Robert Bibbee, Per.Hd.; Carol Wilkens, Comp.Ref.Ctr.Hd.

★2666★
CHICAGO PUBLIC LIBRARY CENTRAL LIBRARY - GENERAL INFORMATION SERVICES DIVISION-BIBLIOGRAPHIC & ILL CENTER (Info Sci)
425 N. Michigan Ave.   Phone: (312) 269-2958
Chicago, IL 60611   Kathleen C. O'Meara, Hd.
Founded: 1977. **Staff:** Prof 10; Other 10. **Subjects:** Bibliographies - national, trade, selective, bibliography. **Holdings:** 11,875 books; 2 drawers publishers' catalogs. **Subscriptions:** 15 journals and other serials. **Services:** Interlibrary loans; copying; library open to public. **Computerized Information Services:** Computerized cataloging. **Networks/Consortia:** Member of OCLC through ILLINET. **Special Indexes:** Library order file; civil service examination "helps" subject index (both on cards). **Staff:** Marilyn Boria, Div.Chf., Gen.Info.

★2667★
CHICAGO PUBLIC LIBRARY CENTRAL LIBRARY - GENERAL INFORMATION SERVICES DIVISION - INFORMATION CENTER (Info Sci)
425 N. Michigan Ave.   Phone: (312) 269-2800
Chicago, IL 60611   Bronwyn Parhad, Hd.
Founded: 1971. **Staff:** Prof 12; Other 7. **Subjects:** Ready reference material in all subjects. **Holdings:** 1025 volumes; 96 card catalog drawers of biographical/obituary information; 51 card catalog drawers of Chicago curio information; 60 card catalog drawers of general information on Illinois, the United States and the world. **Services:** DIAL-LAW, a collection of tape-recorded messages giving general information about Illinois law and the legal system; DIAL-PET, giving general information about pet health and care; center open to public. **Networks/Consortia:** Member of OCLC through

ILLINET. **Staff:** Marilyn Boria, Div.Chf.

★2668★
CHICAGO PUBLIC LIBRARY CENTRAL LIBRARY - GENERAL INFORMATION SERVICES DIV. - NEWSPAPERS & GEN. PERIODICALS CTR. (Publ)
425 N. Michigan Ave.   Phone: (312) 269-2913
Chicago, IL 60611   Joy Gleason, Hd.
Staff: Prof 2; Other 6. **Subjects:** Newspapers, periodicals, reference tools. **Special Collections:** New York Times (indexed); London Times (indexed); Readex Microprint "Early American Newspapers"; Microphoto Underground Newspaper Collection; Foreign Language Press Survey. **Holdings:** 7332 books; 33,778 bound periodical volumes; 33,054 reels of positive microfilm, newspaper indexes, almanacs. **Subscriptions:** 90 journals and other serials; 269 newspapers. **Services:** Interlibrary loans; copying; library open to public. **Computerized Information Services:** Computerized cataloging. **Networks/Consortia:** Member of OCLC through ILLINET. **Staff:** Marilyn Boria, Div.Chf.

★2669★
CHICAGO PUBLIC LIBRARY CENTRAL LIBRARY - GOVERNMENT PUBLICATIONS DEPARTMENT (Info Sci)
425 N. Michigan Ave.   Phone: (312) 269-3002
Chicago, IL 60611   Elizabeth Willson, Dept.Hd.
Founded: 1979. **Staff:** Prof 5; Other 8. **Subjects:** United States, state and local documents. **Special Collections:** Declassified Documents Reference System; Congressional Information Service microfiche library; American Statistics Index microfiche library; Greenwood Press hearings on microfiche (1869-1946); Greenwood Press committee prints on microfiche. **Holdings:** 580,000 documents; 366,000 microforms; 53,000 maps. **Services:** Interlibrary loans; copying; library open to public. **Computerized Information Services:** SDC, DIALOG; Illinois State Legislature Legislative Information System; computerized cataloging and acquisitions. **Networks/Consortia:** Member of OCLC through ILLINET. **Publications:** Guide to the collection and selected finding tools.

★2670★
CHICAGO PUBLIC LIBRARY CENTRAL LIBRARY - NATIVE AMERICAN INFORMATION & REFERRAL CENTER (Area-Ethnic)
Social Sciences & History Division
425 N. Michigan Ave.   Phone: (312) 269-3229
Chicago, IL 60611   Lawrence A. D'Urso, Project Hd.
Founded: 1980. **Staff:** Prof 2. **Subjects:** History and contemporary concerns of North American Indians. **Special Collections:** Duke Indian Oral History Collection (310 microfiche). **Holdings:** 4000 books; 29 bound periodical volumes; 600 pamphlets. **Subscriptions:** 39 journals and other serials; 5 newspapers. **Services:** Interlibrary loans; copying (fee); SDI; library open to public. **Computerized Information Services:** DIALOG, New York Times Information Service; Native American Directory (internal database). **Networks/Consortia:** Member of Metropolitan Chicago Library Assembly; ILLINET; OCLC. **Staff:** Georgiana Oandasan, Project Asst.

★2671★
CHICAGO PUBLIC LIBRARY CENTRAL LIBRARY - PROFESSIONAL LIBRARY (Info Sci)
425 N. Michigan Ave.   Phone: (312) 269-2965
Chicago, IL 60611   Mildred Vannorsdall, Prof.Lib.Libn.
Founded: 1976. **Staff:** Prof 1. **Subjects:** Library science, Chicago Public Library and Chicago Library System. **Holdings:** 1978 books; 405 bound periodical volumes; 109 audio cassettes; 86 microforms; 127 current library school catalogs; 39 ARL Systems & Procedures Exchange Center Kits; 7 VF drawers of unbound reports, clippings, pamphlets and brochures. **Subscriptions:** 29 journals and other serials. **Services:** Interlibrary loans; library open to public. **Computerized Information Services:** Online systems; computerized cataloging and acquisitions. **Networks/Consortia:** Member of OCLC through ILLINET.

★2672★
CHICAGO PUBLIC LIBRARY CENTRAL LIBRARY - SOCIAL SCIENCES & HISTORY DIVISION (Soc Sci; Hist)
425 N. Michigan Ave.   Phone: (312) 269-2830
Chicago, IL 60611   Robert Baumruk, Div.Chf.
Founded: 1975. **Staff:** Prof 13; Other 6. **Subjects:** Sociology, history, education, religion, psychology, philosophy, political science, library science, sports, anthropology, law. **Special Collections:** ERIC microfiche (complete set); Newsbank-Urban Affairs Library; Library of American Civilization (12,500 microfiche); Migne's Patrologia Cursus Completus (221 volumes on microfiche). **Holdings:** 254,780 books; 27,398 bound periodical volumes; 343,410 microforms; 5627 pamphlets; 4600 college catalogs on microfiche; 2611 maps. **Subscriptions:** 1744 journals and other serials. **Services:** Interlibrary loans; copying; library open to public. **Computerized Information**

Services: Online systems; computerized cataloging, acquisitions, serials and circulation. **Networks/Consortia:** Member of OCLC through ILLINET. **Special Indexes:** Chicago History Index (card). **Staff:** Walter Grantham, Asst.Div.Chf.; Gerald Obrochta, Hd., Soc.Sci.Sect.; Jennifer Nesbit, Hd., Educ.Sect.; Ralph Schneider, Hd., Hist.Sect.; Marion Ferkull, Hd., Philosophy/Relg.Sect.

★2673★
CHICAGO PUBLIC LIBRARY CULTURAL CENTER - AUDIOVISUAL CENTER (Aud-Vis)
78 E. Washington St.   Phone: (312) 269-2910
Chicago, IL 60602   Barbara L. Flynn, Hd., AV Center
Staff: Prof 5; Other 10. **Subjects:** Motion pictures - art, history, reviews; radio - history, criticism; television - history, criticism, reviews. **Holdings:** 5093 books; 329 bound periodical volumes; 331 pamphlets; 3601 16mm sound films; 1408 8mm silent films; 26,108 slides; clippings from local newspapers of motion picture reviews, 1964 to present; 2118 audio cassettes; 734 video cassettes; 5754 spoken word recordings. **Subscriptions:** 60 journals and other serials. **Services:** Interlibrary loans; copying. **Computerized Information Services:** Computerized cataloging. **Networks/Consortia:** Member of OCLC through ILLINET. **Publications:** List of new 16mm films, bimonthly. **Special Catalogs:** 16mm film catalog in book form, 1981, updated with bimonthly list; 8mm film list; slide list; video cassette list.

★2674★
CHICAGO PUBLIC LIBRARY CULTURAL CENTER - FINE ARTS DIVISION - ART SECTION (Art)
78 E. Washington St.   Phone: (312) 269-2858
Chicago, IL 60602   Rosalinda Hack, Div.Chf.
Staff: Prof 8; Other 6. **Subjects:** Fine and applied art, architecture, decorative arts, crafts, dance, theater arts, photography, costume. **Special Collections:** Picture Collection, mounted and unmounted (secondary sources, over 1 million items); Folk Dance collection (50 loose-leaf volumes); Chicago Stagebills, 1937 to present. **Holdings:** 52,047 books; 5584 bound periodical volumes; 2 VF drawers of Chicago Artists file; 82 reels of Sears Roebuck catalogs on microfilm; 45 dance videotapes; 11 VF drawers of pamphlets; 661 volumes of monographs on microfilm; 5218 volumes of periodicals on microfilm. **Subscriptions:** 330 journals and other serials. **Services:** Interlibrary loans; copying; slide maker available for public use; library open to public. **Computerized Information Services:** Computerized cataloging. **Networks/Consortia:** Member of OCLC through ILLINET. **Publications:** Occasional annotated reading lists and/or bibliographies. **Special Indexes:** Paintings, Chicago architecture, artists, antiques, dance, Chicago theater, general art (all on cards). **Staff:** Yvonne Brown, Hd., Art Sect.; Virginia R. Smith, Hd.Asst./Pict.Libn.; Judith Rosenbaum-Cooper, Asst. Hd., Art Sect.

★2675★
CHICAGO PUBLIC LIBRARY CULTURAL CENTER - FINE ARTS DIVISION - MUSIC SECTION (Mus)
78 E. Washington St.   Phone: (312) 269-2886
Chicago, IL 60602   Rosalinda Hack, Div.Chf.
Founded: 1915. **Staff:** Prof 6; Other 8. **Subjects:** History and theory of music, biographies of musicians and composers, music education, opera, musical comedy, sacred music, popular music, discography, music business, musical instruments, vocal and instrumental pedagogy, music therapy, folk music, composition and orchestration, arranging. **Special Collections:** Chicago music programs (1873 to present); "Old Pops" collection of U.S. popular songs in original sheet music covers (10,314 pieces dating from 1830 to 1980s). **Holdings:** 17,000 books; 4000 bound periodical volumes; 17,000 bound volumes of music and 16,500 pieces of sheet music (cataloged); 11 VF drawers of pamphlets and clippings; 3 shelves of U.S. and foreign music school catalogs; 4225 microfiche of music; 1600 reels of microfilm of periodicals; 53,000 disc and cassette music recordings. **Subscriptions:** 333 journals and other serials. **Services:** Interlibrary loans; copying; Listening Center; Practice Rooms (3); library open to public. **Computerized Information Services:** Computerized cataloging. **Networks/Consortia:** Member of OCLC through ILLINET. **Publications:** Occasional annotated reading lists and/or bibliographies. **Special Indexes:** Indexes to songs, record titles, piano, violin and organ pieces in collections (card). **Staff:** Richard Schwegel, Act.Hd., Music Sect.; Felicia Carparelli, Rec.Libn.; Harry Purvis, First Asst.; Elizabeth L. Keenan, Rec.Libn.

★2676★
CHICAGO PUBLIC LIBRARY CULTURAL CENTER - LITERATURE AND LANGUAGE DIVISION (Hum)
78 E. Washington St.   Phone: (312) 269-2880
Chicago, IL 60602   David T. Bosca, Div.Chf.
Staff: Prof 10; Other 15. **Subjects:** Literature - American, English, foreign; language study; linguistics; foreign languages. **Special Collections:** Wright's

American Fiction (the novels, on microfilm); Library of English Literature (microfilm); Le Fin de Siecle literary magazines (microfilm); Spanish drama of the Golden Age (3500 plays on microfilm). **Holdings:** 350,000 books; 2000 bound periodical volumes; 100,000 books in microform. **Subscriptions:** 500 journals and other serials. **Services:** Interlibrary loans; copying; library open to public. **Computerized Information Services:** Computerized cataloging, acquisitions, serials and circulation. **Networks/Consortia:** Member of OCLC through ILLINET. **Special Catalogs:** Foreign language card catalog; Spanish Information Center - community and general information data files. **Staff:** Rosemary Dawood, Asst.Chf.; Edwin Suderow, Hd., Lit.Sect.; William McIlwain, Hd., Foreign Lang.Sect.; Yvonne Vargas, Hd., Spanish Info.Ctr.

★2677★
CHICAGO PUBLIC LIBRARY CULTURAL CENTER - SPECIAL COLLECTIONS DIVISION (Rare Book)
78 E. Washington St.   Phone: (312) 269-2926
Chicago, IL 60602   Susan Prendergast Schoelwer, Cur.
Founded: 1975. **Staff:** Prof 4. **Subjects:** Civil War and American history (1820-1880); Chicago history; Chicago authors and imprints; book arts; library archives; freedom of the press. **Special Collections:** Grand Army of the Republic Memorial Collection (1100 items); World's Columbian Exposition (470 items; 1200 manuscripts); Thomas Masaryk Collection (121 items); Deuel Collection (267 items); Lutz Collection (5400 items); Bruce Catton Collection (412 items); Goodman Theater Archives (75 cubic feet); Chicago Theater Arts (11 linear feet; 40 scrapbooks); Edward Weiss and Robert Nunn Autograph Collections (541 manuscript pieces); Chicago Public Library Archives; Lebold Miniature Book Collection (170 volumes). **Holdings:** 27,552 books; 1500 bound periodical volumes; miscellaneous manuscript collections. **Subscriptions:** 48 journals and other serials. **Services:** Copying; library open to public with identification. **Networks/Consortia:** Member of OCLC through ILLINET. **Publications:** Treasures of the Chicago Public Library - available for sale. **Staff:** Marta G. O'Neill, Asst.Cur.; Constance G. Gordon, Rare Book Cat.; Robert G. Marshall, Archival Spec.

★2678★
CHICAGO PUBLIC LIBRARY CULTURAL CENTER - THOMAS HUGHES CHILDREN'S LIBRARY (Hum)
78 E. Washington St.   Phone: (312) 269-2835
Chicago, IL 60602   Lillian R. New, Hd.
Founded: 1910. **Staff:** Prof 5; Other 4. **Subjects:** Children's books; preschool through 8th grade; books about children's books for adults; children's books in foreign languages; children's paperbacks. **Special Collections:** Historical collection of early children's books; out of print materials and illustrated classics, folk and fairy tales. **Holdings:** 63,000 books; 228 bound periodical volumes; 5992 recordings for children; 4746 paperbacks; 2144 pamphlets; 1231 filmstrips; 1757 cassettes and other nonbook materials. **Subscriptions:** 85 journals and other serials. **Services:** Interlibrary loans; copying; regularly scheduled story hours; class visits to the public library; librarians' visits to elementary schools; library open to public. **Computerized Information Services:** Computerized cataloging and acquisitions. **Networks/Consortia:** Member of OCLC through ILLINET. **Publications:** Calendar of Events; Summer Fun Programs; Brochure of Department - all free upon request; subject and graded reading lists. **Staff:** Mildred Williams, Hd.Asst.; Marsha Huddleston, Libn.; Irma Jean Patterson, Lib.Assoc.; Marian Sturm, Libn.

★2679★
CHICAGO PUBLIC LIBRARY CULTURAL CENTER - VIVIAN G. HARSH COLLECTION OF AFRO-AMERICAN HISTORY & LIT. (Area-Ethnic)
9525 S. Halsted St.   Phone: (312) 881-6910
Chicago, IL 60628   Hattie Power, Dir.
Founded: 1932. **Staff:** Prof 2; Other 8. **Subjects:** Afro-Americans - religion, sociology, art, music, history, international Black affairs. **Special Collections:** Illinois Writers Project; Heritage Press Archives; Carl Sang Collection of Afro-American History, 1684 to present; Charlemae Hill Rollins Collection of Children's Literature; Era Bell Thompson Collection on International Black Affairs; David P. Ross Collection of Reprints in Afro-Americana/Africana. **Holdings:** 27,225 books; 5000 bound periodical volumes; 4000 linear feet of manuscripts; 2500 phonograph records; 1500 cassette tapes; 8157 reels of microfilm. **Subscriptions:** 65 journals and other serials; 13 newspapers. **Services:** Interlibrary loans; copying; library open to public. **Computerized Information Services:** Computerized cataloging. **Networks/Consortia:** Member of OCLC through ILLINET. **Publications:** New Acquisitions in the Vivian G. Harsh Collection of Afro-American History and Literature. **Staff:** Sharon Scott, Asst.Cur.

★2680★
CHICAGO-READ MENTAL HEALTH CENTER - PROFESSIONAL LIBRARY (Med)
4200 N. Oak Park Ave.   Phone: (312) 794-3746
Chicago, IL 60634   Ruth Greenberg, Libn.
Staff: Prof 1; Other 1. **Subjects:** Psychiatry, psychology, medicine, mental retardation, mental health, crisis intervention. **Holdings:** 6000 books; 6000 bound periodical volumes; 2000 unbound items; 150 bibliographies. **Subscriptions:** 134 journals and other serials. **Services:** Interlibrary loans; copying (limited); library open to staff members only. **Networks/Consortia:** Member of Midwest Health Science Library Network (MHSLN); DMHDD Library Services Network; Chicago Library System.

★2681★
CHICAGO REGIONAL TRANSPORTATION AUTHORITY - INFORMATION SERVICES - LIBRARY (Trans)
300 N. State St.   Phone: (312) 836-4091
Chicago, IL 60610   Connie Tinner, Supv., Info.Serv.
Staff: Prof 3; Other 2. **Subjects:** Transportation. **Holdings:** 1850 books; RTA records. **Subscriptions:** 120 journals and other serials; 100 newspapers. **Services:** Interlibrary loans; copying; library open to public for reference use only. **Computerized Information Services:** Computerized cataloging and circulation. **Staff:** Catherina Hannah, Rec.Anl.

★2682★
CHICAGO SINAI CONGREGATION - EMIL G. HIRSCH LIBRARY (Rel-Theol)
5350 S. Shore Dr.   Phone: (312) 288-1600
Chicago, IL 60615   Howard A. Berman, Rabbi
Founded: 1950. **Staff:** Prof 1. **Subjects:** Judaica, Reform Judaism. **Special Collections:** Archives of Chicago Sinai Congregation 1861 to present. **Holdings:** 4500 books; 50 bound periodical volumes; 50 other items (cataloged). **Subscriptions:** 23 journals and other serials. **Services:** Library open to public. **Staff:** Ernest Rubinstein, Libn.

★2683★
CHICAGO STATE UNIVERSITY - DOUGLAS LIBRARY - SPECIAL COLLECTIONS (Educ)†
E. 95th St. & King Dr.   Phone: (312) 995-2254
Chicago, IL 60628   Dr. W. Patrick Leonard, Dean
Founded: 1868. **Special Collections:** Materials Center consisting of children's books (46,436 items); Division of Learning Resources (18,115 nonprint items); documents (92,520). **Services:** Interlibrary loans; library open to public for reference use only. **Computerized Information Services:** DIALOG, BRS; computerized cataloging. **Networks/Consortia:** Member of OCLC through ILLINET; Metropolitan Chicago Library Assembly; CRL; Regional Medical Library - Region 3. **Staff:** Dr. Serene Onesto, Coord., Lrng.Rsrcs.; Carol Bentley, Hd., Mtls.Ctr.

★2684★
CHICAGO SUN-TIMES - EDITORIAL LIBRARY (Publ)†
401 N. Wabash Ave.   Phone: (312) 321-2594
Chicago, IL 60611   Ernest Perez, Chf.Libn.
Founded: 1876. **Staff:** Prof 6; Other 18. **Subjects:** Current events, local government, political science, photography and graphic arts, newspaper reference topics. **Special Collections:** Newspaper clippings and microfilm dating back to 1876. **Holdings:** 3300 books; 200 bound periodical volumes; 600,000 files of clippings; 315,000 files of photographs; 260,000 negatives; 20 VF drawers of pamphlets. **Subscriptions:** 41 journals and other serials; 11 newspapers. **Services:** Library not open to public. **Computerized Information Services:** New York Times Information Service, DIALOG, SDC, Dow Jones News Retrieval, CompuServe, Inc.; Sun-Times News Index (internal database). **Networks/Consortia:** Member of Metropolitan Chicago Library Assembly; Chicago Library System. **Publications:** Monthly book list; Library Memo. **Staff:** Terri M. Golembiewski, Chf.Ref.Libn.; Michael Perlman, Ref.Libn.; Diana Boriss, Ref.Libn.; Virginia Davis, Ref.Libn.; Judith Halper, Ref.Libn.

★2685★
CHICAGO THEOLOGICAL SEMINARY - HAMMOND LIBRARY (Rel-Theol)
5757 S. University Ave.   Phone: (312) 752-5757
Chicago, IL 60637   Rev. Neil W. Gerdes, Libn.
Staff: Prof 3; Other 6. **Subjects:** Theology, Bible, social ethics, personality and religion, Congregational Church history, sociology and religion. **Special Collections:** Lowenbach collection of Congregational and Puritan history (8000 volumes); Anton Boisen Collection (papers and books on psychiatry, psychology and religion; 8000 volumes). **Holdings:** 96,000 books and bound periodical volumes; 12,000 volumes of church records from Midwest Congregational churches and societies; 740 microforms; 620 AV items. **Subscriptions:** 220 journals and other serials. **Services:** Interlibrary loans;

copying; library open to public with approval of librarian. **Computerized Information Services:** Online systems; computerized cataloging. **Networks/Consortia:** Member of ILLINET; Chicago Cluster of Theological Schools (CCTS). **Special Catalogs:** Chicago Union Card Catalog of Chicago Cluster Schools, the University of Chicago divinity collection and Newberry Library (microfiche). **Staff:** Joan Blocher, Asst.Libn.; Martha Butler, Tech.Asst.

★2686★
CHICAGO TRANSIT AUTHORITY - HAROLD S. ANTHON MEMORIAL LIBRARY (Trans)
Merchandise Mart Plaza
Box 3555   Phone: (312) 664-7200
Chicago, IL 60654   Joseph Benson, Dir., Info.Serv.
Founded: 1967. **Staff:** Prof 3; Other 1. **Subjects:** Urban transportation, transportation planning and engineering, business administration. **Holdings:** 15,000 books. **Subscriptions:** 550 journals and other serials. **Services:** Interlibrary loans; copying; Current Awareness Service; library open to public for reference use only on request. **Computerized Information Services:** DIALOG; computerized cataloging. **Networks/Consortia:** Member of OCLC through ILLINET; Metropolitan Chicago Library Assembly; Chicago Library System. **Publications:** Acquisitions list. **Staff:** Lillian D. Culbertson, Supv., Lib.Serv.; Violette Y. Brooks, Ref.Libn.

★2687★
CHICAGO TRIBUNE - INFORMATION CENTER (Publ)
435 N. Michigan Ave.   Phone: (312) 222-3871
Chicago, IL 60611   Barbara T. Newcombe, Mgr.
Founded: 1910. **Staff:** Prof 5; Other 14. **Subjects:** Newspaper reference topics, Chicago, Illinois, Midwest. **Holdings:** 8000 books; 15.5 million newspaper clippings; 9 million photographs; 3 million envelopes of negatives; Chicago Tribune on microfilm (1847-1883; 1900 to present); Chicago American & Today on microfilm (1950-74). **Subscriptions:** 90 journals and other serials; 8 newspapers. **Services:** Copies of Tribune photographs for sale; copying; center not open to public. **Computerized Information Services:** DIALOG, Dow Jones News Retrieval, New York Times Information Service. **Staff:** Mary Huschen, Asst.Mgr.; Katherine Ackerman, Libn.; Judy Redel, Libn.; Carol Bebb, Libn.

★2688★
CHICAGO TRIBUNE PRESS SERVICE - WASHINGTON BUREAU - LIBRARY (Publ)
1707 H St., N.W., 9th Fl.   Phone: (202) 785-9430
Washington, DC 20006   Carolyn J. Hardnett, Chf.Libn.
Staff: Prof 1; Other 1. **Subjects:** Politics, foreign affairs, economics, defense, history. **Holdings:** 3000 books; 2000 government documents; presidential documents. **Subscriptions:** 30 journals and other serials; 7 newspapers. **Services:** Interlibrary loans; copying; library open to public with restrictions.

★2689★
CHICAGO TRIBUNE - RESEARCH LIBRARY (Bus-Fin)
435 N. Michigan, 11th Fl.   Phone: (312) 222-3188
Chicago, IL 60610   Bernadette Szczech, Res.Libn.
Founded: 1964. **Staff:** Prof 1; Other 1. **Subjects:** Advertising, Chicago SCSA, marketing research, newspapers. **Holdings:** 500 books; 2 Lektrievers for vertical file information (150 feet). **Subscriptions:** 84 journals and other serials. **Services:** Interlibrary loans; library open to public by appointment. **Computerized Information Services:** New York Times Information Service. **Networks/Consortia:** Member of Chicago Library System. **Publications:** Digest of Chicago Market, annual - available for sale; New Store Openings, quarterly - by subscription.

★2690★
CHICAGO ZOOLOGICAL PARK - BROOKFIELD ZOO - LIBRARY (Sci-Tech)
8400 W. 31st St.   Phone: (312) 485-0263
Brookfield, IL 60513   Mary Rabb, Libn.
Staff: 2. **Subjects:** Zoology, animal behavior. **Holdings:** 4350 books; 1100 bound periodical volumes; slides and photographs (cataloged). **Subscriptions:** 175 journals and other serials. **Services:** Interlibrary loans; library open to public with restrictions. **Publications:** Zoo Guide; Brookfield Bison; Brookfield Bandarlog.

CHICKASAW COUNCIL HOUSE LIBRARY
See: Oklahoma Historical Society

CHICKASAW NATL. RECREATION AREA
See: U.S. Natl. Park Service

★2691★
CHICOPEE, INC. - RESEARCH DIVISION - LIBRARY (Sci-Tech)
2 Ford Ave.
Box 8   Phone: (201) 524-7872
Milltown, NJ 08850   Judith A. Hassert, Res.Libn.
Founded: 1947. **Staff:** Prof 1. **Subjects:** Textiles, chemistry, engineering. **Holdings:** 2000 books. **Subscriptions:** 96 journals and other serials. **Services:** Interlibrary loans; copying; library not open to public. **Computerized Information Services:** SDC, DIALOG, QUESTEL, Control Data Corporation. **Publications:** Library User's Guide - for internal distribution only. **Remarks:** Chicopee, Inc. is a division of Johnson and Johnson.

★2692★
CHILD CUSTODY EVALUATION SERVICES, INC. - RESOURCE CENTER (Soc Sci)
Box 202   Phone: (215) 576-0177
Glenside, PA 19038   Dr. Ken Lewis, Dir.
Staff: Prof 2; Other 1. **Subjects:** Child custody, single-parent families, divorce, child-snatching, mental health and law. **Special Collections:** Father's rights movements; men's and women's movements. **Holdings:** 800 books; 50 bound periodical volumes; 15 dissertation abstracts; 25 special reports; 12 grant narratives; 25 television and radio news documentaries; 50 monographs. **Subscriptions:** 75 journals and other serials; 25 newspapers. **Services:** Copying; library open to public by appointment. **Publications:** CCES Workshop Series. **Staff:** Rosemary Ryan, Mgr.

★2693★
CHILD WELFARE LEAGUE OF AMERICA, INC. - INFORMATIONAL RESOURCE SERVICES - DOROTHY L. BERNHARD LIBRARY (Soc Sci)
67 Irving Pl.   Phone: (212) 254-7410
New York, NY 10003   Marilyn Katz, Libn.
Founded: 1920. **Staff:** Prof 3; Other 1. **Subjects:** Child welfare, social work, social welfare, child development. **Special Collections:** Archives of the Child Welfare League of America and Florence Crittenton Association. **Holdings:** 3500 books; 30 VF drawers of USHHS Publications (comprehensive child welfare collection); 600 research reports limited to scope of the collection; 70 VF drawers. **Subscriptions:** 90 journals and other serials. **Services:** Interlibrary loans; copying; library not open to public. **Publications:** Subject bibliographies. **Special Catalogs:** AV catalog. **Remarks:** The services of the library are free only to agencies or individuals who have paid membership dues to the league.

★2694★
CHILDREN'S BOOK COUNCIL - LIBRARY (Educ)
67 Irving Pl.   Phone: (212) 254-2666
New York, NY 10003
Founded: 1960. **Subjects:** Children's books (both children's books and books about children's books). **Special Collections:** Permanent collection of selected prizewinning children's books. **Holdings:** 7000 books. **Subscriptions:** 30 journals and other serials. **Services:** Library open to public for reference use only.

★2695★
CHILDREN'S HOSPITAL OF BUFFALO - MEDICAL LIBRARY (Med)
219 Bryant St.   Phone: (716) 878-7304
Buffalo, NY 14222   Lucy Wargo, Med.Libn.
Founded: 1940. **Staff:** Prof 1; Other 1. **Subjects:** Pediatrics, general medicine. **Holdings:** 1715 books; 7458 bound periodical volumes. **Subscriptions:** 250 journals and other serials. **Services:** Interlibrary loans; copying; library open to public. **Computerized Information Services:** Online systems.

CHILDREN'S HOSPITAL OF THE EAST BAY
See: Children's Hospital Medical Center of Northern California

★2696★
CHILDREN'S HOSPITAL OF EASTERN ONTARIO - MEDICAL LIBRARY (Med)
401 Smyth Rd.   Phone: (613) 737-2206
Ottawa, ON, Canada K1H 8L1   Margaret P.J. Taylor, Dir., Lib.Serv.
Staff: Prof 3; Other 4. **Subjects:** Pediatrics, nursing, allied health sciences, general medicine, hospital management. **Special Collections:** Management Resource Centre (250 books and documents); child abuse file (500 pamphlets and reprints). **Holdings:** 5000 books; 2300 bound periodical volumes; 6 VF drawers of pamphlets and reprints; 500 AV items. **Subscriptions:** 445 journals and other serials. **Services:** Interlibrary loans; copying; SDI; library open to public. **Computerized Information Services:** MEDLARS, DIALOG. **Networks/Consortia:** Member of Ottawa-Hull Health Libraries Group; O.H.A. Region 9 Hospital Libraries Group. **Publications:** CHEO Library Acquisitions List, irregular; Pediatric Patient Education Directory; Management Resource

Centre Bibliography.

★2697★
CHILDREN'S HOSPITAL - FORBES MEDICAL LIBRARY (Med)
1056 E. 19th Ave.   Phone: (303) 861-6400
Denver, CO 80218   Melanie R. Birnbach, Med.Libn.
Staff: Prof 1; Other 2. **Subjects:** Medicine, nursing with emphasis on pediatrics. **Holdings:** 2000 books; 5000 bound periodical volumes; tapes, slides. **Subscriptions:** 200 journals and other serials. **Services:** Interlibrary loans; copying; library not open to public. **Computerized Information Services:** DIALOG, MEDLARS. **Networks/Consortia:** Member of Denver Area Health Sciences Library Consortium.

★2698★
CHILDREN'S HOSPITAL OF THE KING'S DAUGHTERS - MEDICAL LIBRARY (Med)
800 W. Olney Rd.   Phone: (804) 628-3180
Norfolk, VA 23507   Dolores M. Roberts, Dir. of Med.Rec.
Founded: 1979. **Staff:** Prof 1; Other 1. **Subjects:** Pediatrics. **Special Collections:** Maria Alexander Memorial Collection (endocrinology and metabolism; 23 books). **Holdings:** 397 books; 362 bound periodical volumes; 275 audio cassettes; 18 video cassettes; 5 slide collections on pediatric specialties. **Subscriptions:** 33 journals and other serials. **Services:** Interlibrary loans; copying; library not open to public. **Networks/Consortia:** Member of Tidewater Health Sciences Libraries (THSL).

★2699★
CHILDREN'S HOSPITAL OF LOS ANGELES - MEDICAL LIBRARY (Med)†
4650 Sunset Blvd.   Phone: (213) 663-3341
Los Angeles, CA 90027
Staff: Prof 1; Other 1. **Subjects:** Pediatrics. **Special Collections:** History of pediatrics. **Holdings:** 2500 books; 4000 bound periodical volumes. **Subscriptions:** 250 journals and other serials. **Services:** Interlibrary loans; copying; library open to health professionals. **Computerized Information Services:** MEDLINE.

★2700★
CHILDREN'S HOSPITAL MEDICAL CENTER OF NORTHERN CALIFORNIA - MEDICAL LIBRARY (Med)
51st & Grove Sts.   Phone: (415) 428-3000
Oakland, CA 94609   Barbara Davenport, Med.Libn.
Founded: 1938. **Staff:** 1. **Subjects:** Pediatrics, neonatology, pediatric hematology, growth and development, child psychology. **Holdings:** 1578 books; 3606 bound periodical volumes; 1793 unbound journals; 393 Audio-Digest tapes; 1351 titles; 103 videotapes. **Subscriptions:** 161 journals and other serials. **Services:** Interlibrary loans; copying; library not open to public. **Publications:** Bibliographies. **Also Known As:** Children's Hospital of the East Bay.

★2701★
CHILDREN'S HOSPITAL, INC. - MEDICAL LIBRARY (Med)†
3825 Greenspring Ave.   Phone: (301) 462-6800
Baltimore, MD 21211   Janet E.N. Bush, Med.Rec.Adm.
Staff: 2. **Subjects:** Orthopedics, plastic surgery, pediatrics, medicine. **Holdings:** 745 books; 260 bound periodical volumes. **Services:** Interlibrary loans; copying; library open to staff and allied health professionals.

★2702★
CHILDREN'S HOSPITAL, INC. - MEDICAL-NURSING LIBRARY (Med)
345 N. Smith Ave.   Phone: (612) 227-6521
St. Paul, MN 55102   Nancy W. Battaglia, Dir.
Founded: 1960. **Staff:** Prof 1. **Subjects:** Pediatrics, pediatric endocrinology, pediatric nursing, growth and development. **Holdings:** 1000 books; 600 bound periodical volumes; 2 VF drawers of reprints, photoduplicated articles on pediatric subjects; pediatric Audio-Digest - 100 cassette tapes, 100 35mm teaching slides on congenital malformations. **Subscriptions:** 100 journals and other serials. **Services:** Interlibrary loans; library open to qualified students and researchers for reference. **Computerized Information Services:** Computerized serials. **Networks/Consortia:** Member of Twin Cities Biomedical Consortium; Regional Medical Library - Region 3.

★2703★
CHILDREN'S HOSPITAL OF MICHIGAN - MEDICAL LIBRARY (Med)
3901 Beaubien   Phone: (313) 494-5322
Detroit, MI 48201   Michele S. Klein, Dir., Lib.Serv.
Staff: Prof 1; Other 3. **Subjects:** Pediatrics, growth and development, genetics, pediatric clinical research. **Holdings:** 2075 books; 3115 bound periodical volumes; 40 audiotapes. **Subscriptions:** 305 journals and other serials. **Services:** Interlibrary loans; copying; LATCH; library not open to

public. **Computerized Information Services:** DIALOG, MEDLINE; computerized cataloging. **Networks/Consortia:** Member of OCLC.

★2704★
CHILDREN'S HOSPITAL/NATIONAL MEDICAL CENTER - HOSPITAL LIBRARY (Med)
111 Michigan Ave., N.W.   Phone: (202) 745-3195
Washington, DC 20010   Deborah D. Gilbert, Chf.Hosp.Libn.
Staff: Prof 3; Other 2. **Subjects:** Pediatrics: child development, nursing, dentistry, psychiatry, ophthalmology. **Holdings:** 2953 books; 8254 bound periodical volumes; 300 AV items. **Subscriptions:** 550 journals and other serials. **Services:** Interlibrary loans; copying; LATCH; library open to public by appointment. **Computerized Information Services:** NLM, BRS, DIALOG; computerized cataloging. **Staff:** Shirley Knobloch, Asst.Libn.; Carolyn Willard, Family Libn.

★2705★
CHILDREN'S HOSPITAL OF PHILADELPHIA - MEDICAL LIBRARY (Med)
34th & Civic Center Blvd.   Phone: (215) 596-9673
Philadelphia, PA 19104   Mrs. Swaran Lata Chopra, Adm.Supv./Dir.
Founded: 1956. **Staff:** Prof 1; Other 3. **Subjects:** Pediatrics, medicine, nursing. **Holdings:** 3988 books; 7500 bound periodical volumes; 6 VF drawers of clippings and pamphlets. **Subscriptions:** 200 journals and other serials. **Services:** Interlibrary loans; copying; library open to public for reference use only.

★2706★
CHILDREN'S HOSPITAL OF PITTSBURGH - BLAXTER MEMORIAL LIBRARY (Med)
125 De Soto St.   Phone: (412) 647-5288
Pittsburgh, PA 15213   Nancy Dunn, Libn.
Staff: Prof 2; Other 1. **Subjects:** Pediatric medicine. **Holdings:** 900 books; 2900 bound periodical volumes. **Subscriptions:** 170 journals and other serials. **Services:** Interlibrary loans; copying; library open to public with restrictions. **Computerized Information Services:** NLM.

★2707★
CHILDREN'S HOSPITAL RESEARCH FOUNDATION - RESEARCH LIBRARY (Med)
Elland & Bethesda Sts.   Phone: (513) 559-4300
Cincinnati, OH 45229   Margaret L. Moutseous, Lib.Dir.
Founded: 1931. **Staff:** Prof 1; Other 1. **Subjects:** Pediatrics, medicine. **Holdings:** 7000 books; 15,000 bound periodical volumes. **Subscriptions:** 260 journals and other serials. **Services:** Interlibrary loans; copying; library open to physicians and other local research personnel for reference use only. **Computerized Information Services:** MEDLINE, DIALOG, BRS. **Networks/Consortia:** Member of Kentucky-Ohio-Michigan Regional Medical Libraries (KOMRML); Cincinnati Area Health Sciences Library Association; Cincinnati MEDLINE Consortium. **Publications:** Studies from the Children's Hospital Research Foundation.

★2708★
CHILDREN'S HOSPITAL OF SAN FRANCISCO - EMGE MEDICAL LIBRARY (Med)
Box 3805   Phone: (415) 387-8700
San Francisco, CA 94119   Angie Durso, Dir.
Founded: 1959. **Staff:** Prof 1; Other 1. **Subjects:** Medicine and related sciences. **Holdings:** 3500 books; 7000 bound periodical volumes; 13 videotape reels; 8 filmstrips and slide teaching units; 571 audiotapes. **Subscriptions:** 400 journals and other serials. **Services:** Interlibrary loans; copying; bibliographic services; library not open to public. **Computerized Information Services:** MEDLINE. **Networks/Consortia:** Member of San Francisco Biomedical Library Network. **Remarks:** Library located at 3700 California St., San Francisco, CA 94118.

★2709★
CHILDREN'S MEDICAL CENTER - LIBRARY (Med)
One Children's Plaza   Phone: (513) 226-8307
Dayton, OH 45404   Jane R. Bottoms, Libn.
Founded: 1967. **Staff:** Prof 1; Other 1. **Subjects:** Pediatrics and related fields. **Holdings:** 2000 books; 5000 bound periodical volumes. **Subscriptions:** 240 journals and other serials. **Services:** Interlibrary loans; copying; bibliographic and reference service available to professional staff of the center; library not open to public.

★2710★

CHILDREN'S MEMORIAL HOSPITAL - JOSEPH BRENNEMANN LIBRARY (Med)
2300 Children's Plaza   Phone: (312) 880-4505
Chicago, IL 60614   Leslie Goodale, Dir.
Founded: 1935. **Staff:** Prof 2; Other 4. **Subjects:** Pediatrics, surgery, genetics, child psychiatry. **Holdings:** 8500 books; 24,000 bound periodical volumes; 1470 AV items (cataloged). **Subscriptions:** 420 journals and other serials. **Services:** Interlibrary loans; copying; SDI; library not open to public. **Computerized Information Services:** NLM; computerized cataloging. **Networks/Consortia:** Member of Regional Medical Library - Region 3; Chicago Metropolitan Consortium; OCLC. **Publications:** Acquisitions/Newsletter, bimonthly - to hospital departments, employees and outside libraries on request. **Staff:** M. Rosemary Clark, Asst.Libn.

★2711★

CHILDREN'S MERCY HOSPITAL - MEDICAL LIBRARY (Med)
24th at Gillham Rd.   Phone: (816) 234-3001
Kansas City, MO 64108   Judy Vermillion, Med.Libn.
Founded: 1913. **Staff:** Prof 1; Other 1. **Subjects:** Pediatrics. **Special Collections:** William L. Bradford, M.D., Library of the History of Pediatrics (300 volumes). **Holdings:** 750 books; 3500 bound periodical volumes. **Subscriptions:** 180 journals and other serials. **Services:** Interlibrary loans; copying (limited to libraries); library open to public with restrictions. **Networks/Consortia:** Member of Kansas City Library Network Inc. **Publications:** CMH Book News, irregular - distributed to hospitals and libraries in the Greater Kansas City area. **Special Catalogs:** Children's Mercy Hospital Serial Holdings.

★2712★

CHILDREN'S MUSEUM OF INDIANAPOLIS - RAUH MEMORIAL LIBRARY (Hist)
3000 N. Meridian St.   Phone: (317) 924-5431
Indianapolis, IN 46208   George Hing, Libn.
Founded: 1975. **Staff:** Prof 1. **Subjects:** American history, American Indians, antiques, Indiana history, dolls, antique toys. **Special Collections:** Children's books (300). **Holdings:** 4000 books; 250 bound periodical volumes; 500 pamphlets; 500 vertical file materials. **Subscriptions:** 55 journals and other serials. **Services:** Interlibrary loans; copying; library open to public with restrictions. **Computerized Information Services:** Computerized cataloging. **Networks/Consortia:** Member of OCLC through INCOLSA.

★2713★

CHILDREN'S MUSEUM - RESOURCE CENTER (Educ)
Museum Wharf
300 Congress St.   Phone: (617) 426-6501
Boston, MA 02210   Caryl-Ann Feldman, Mgr., Rsrcs.Serv.
Staff: Prof 1; Other 6. **Subjects:** Education, native Americans, East Asian study, arts and crafts, museum studies, games, social studies, multicultures, early childhood, special needs, Americana, natural and physical sciences. **Special Collections:** Kits and games developed by Museum staff (700); cultural materials relating to native Americans (10,000). **Holdings:** 20,000 books and multimedia kits; slide collection; 150 bound periodical volumes; 1000 teaching aids (cataloged); 500 rental kits of materials (cataloged); 43 pamphlet boxes of publishers catalogs (cataloged); 25 pamphlet boxes of newsletters and museum brochures; 8 VF drawers of pamphlets and articles (cataloged). **Subscriptions:** 100 journals and other serials. **Services:** Interlibrary loans; copying; library open to public with restrictions. **Publications:** List of publications - available on request. **Special Catalogs:** Library resources; bibliographies; activity sheets.

★2714★

CHILDREN'S ORTHOPEDIC HOSPITAL & MEDICAL CENTER - HOSPITAL LIBRARY (Med)
4800 Sand Point Way N.E.   Phone: (206) 634-5081
Seattle, WA 98105   Tamara A. Turner, Dir.
Founded: 1946. **Staff:** Prof 1; Other 1. **Subjects:** Pediatrics, neonatology, adolescent medicine, orthopedics. **Special Collections:** Flashman Orthopedic Collection; Coe Surgical Collection; Resident's teaching files. **Holdings:** 2000 books; 3300 bound periodical volumes. **Subscriptions:** 400 journals and other serials. **Services:** Interlibrary loans; copying; SDI (manual); library open to public for reference use only. **Computerized Information Services:** MEDLINE; computerized serials. **Networks/Consortia:** Member of Seattle Area Hospital Libraries Consortium. **Publications:** Library Bulletin, quarterly.

CHILDREN'S PSYCHIATRIC RESEARCH INSTITUTE
See: University of Western Ontario - CPRI Library

★2715★

CHILDREN'S SPECIALIZED HOSPITAL - MEDICAL LIBRARY (Med)
150 New Providence Rd.   Phone: (201) 233-3720
Mountainside, NJ 07090   Emily L. Snitow, Libn.
Staff: Prof 1. **Subjects:** Pediatrics, rehabilitation, nursing. **Holdings:** 3000 books; 8 VF drawers; 320 audio cassettes; 105 filmstrip kits; 450 slides. **Subscriptions:** 90 journals and other serials. **Services:** Interlibrary loans; copying; library open to public on a limited basis. **Networks/Consortia:** Member of Cosmopolitan Biomedical Library Consortium.

CHILDREN'S THEATRE ARCHIVE
See: Arizona State University - Special Collections

★2716★

CHILDREN'S THEATRE COMPANY AND SCHOOL - LIBRARY (Theater)
2400 Third Ave. S.   Phone: (612) 874-0500
Minneapolis, MN 55404   Ingrid A. Liss, Theatre Sch.Asst.
Subjects: Acting technique, history of drama, technical theater, dance, children's literature. **Holdings:** Figures not available. **Services:** Library not open to public.

★2717★

CHILTON COMPANY - MARKETING & ADVERTISING INFORMATION CENTER (Bus-Fin; Publ)
One Chilton Way   Phone: (215) 687-8200
Radnor, PA 19089   Judith Skillings, Mgr., Info Ctr.
Founded: 1957. **Staff:** Prof 1; Other 3. **Subjects:** Advertising, marketing, publishing. **Special Collections:** Readership and Consumer Surveys; Chilton Archives. **Holdings:** 1000 books; 40 VF drawers of pamphlets, articles and government statistical reports (filed by subject); 240 microfilm reels of Chilton publications. **Subscriptions:** 110 journals and other serials. **Services:** Interlibrary loans; copying; library open to public with restrictions. **Computerized Information Services:** DIALOG, SDC, Dow Jones News Retrieval, New York Times Information Service. **Publications:** MAIC News, bimonthly - for internal distribution only; M.A.P. Releases, irregular. **Remarks:** Chilton Company is one of the American Broadcasting Companies. **Staff:** Carol Keegan, Asst.Libn.; Christine Sweely, Asst.Libn.

★2718★

CHILTON MEMORIAL HOSPITAL - MEDICAL LIBRARY (Med)
97 West Parkway   Phone: (201) 835-3700
Pompton Plains, NJ 07444   Janice Sweeton, Med.Libn.
Staff: Prof 1. **Subjects:** Medicine and allied sciences. **Holdings:** 800 books; 1500 bound periodical volumes. **Subscriptions:** 100 journals and other serials. **Services:** Interlibrary loans; copying; current awareness information service; preparation of bibliographies; library not open to public. **Networks/Consortia:** Member of Bergen/Passaic Health Sciences Library Consortium.

★2719★

CHINATOWN BUILDING AND EDUCATION FOUNDATION - CHINESE CULTURAL AND COMMUNITY CENTER (Area-Ethnic)
125 N. Tenth St.   Phone: (215) 923-6767
Philadelphia, PA 19107
Subjects: Chinese language publications. **Holdings:** Figures not available. **Services:** Library open to public.

★2720★

CHINESE CULTURAL CENTER - INFORMATION & COMMUNICATION DIVISION - LIBRARY (Area-Ethnic)
159 Lexington Ave.   Phone: (212) 725-4950
New York, NY 10016   Ming Tien Tsai, Libn.
Staff: Prof 1; Other 1. **Subjects:** Political, economic, cultural and social developments of the Republic of China; Chinese history, language, literature, art, philosophy, religion and related subjects; Chinese and international communism; foreign relations. **Holdings:** 14,000 books; 100 bound periodical volumes. **Subscriptions:** 100 journals and other serials; 30 newspapers (published in Taiwan and Hong Kong). **Services:** Copying; library open to public with restrictions. **Computerized Information Services:** Computerized acquisitions.

CHINESE CULTURAL AND COMMUNITY CENTER
See: Chinatown Building and Education Foundation

★2721★

CHINESE NATIONALIST LEAGUE OF CANADA - LIBRARY (Soc Sci; Area-Ethnic)†
529 Gore Ave.   Phone: (604) 681-6022
Vancouver, BC, Canada V6A 2Z6   James K. Cheng, Chf.Libn.
Founded: 1961. **Staff:** Prof 4; Other 6. **Subjects:** Chinese history, politics

and society; China Town and Canadian-Chinese history. **Special Collections:** History of the Chinese Nationalist League of Canada. **Holdings:** 31,000 books; 1000 bound periodical volumes. **Subscriptions:** 145 journals and other serials; 12 newspapers. **Services:** Interlibrary loans; copying; library open to public. **Staff:** Patrick Kwan, Supv., Pub.Serv.; Charlie Chan, Supv., Tech.Serv.

★2722★
CHIPPEWA VALLEY MUSEUM, INC. - LIBRARY (Hist)
9 Carson Park Dr.
Box 1204
Eau Claire, WI 54701   Phone: (715) 834-7871
    Alberta Rommelmeyer, Archv.
Founded: 1964. **Staff:** 6. **Subjects:** Local, area and state history. **Special Collections:** Oral history tapes (100). **Holdings:** 1100 books; 500 bound periodical volumes; 10 VF drawers of clippings; 12,000 photographs of early scenes and citizens; manuscripts; obituary file (2500 names); biographical file (500 names); document file (700 items). **Subscriptions:** 15 journals and other serials. **Services:** Copying; library open to public for reference use only. **Publications:** Guide to Archives and Manuscripts in Chippewa Valley Museum - cooperative project with Eau Claire Public Library and University of Wisconsin, Eau Claire.

★2723★
CHISHOLM TRAIL MUSEUM - ARCHIVES AND LIBRARY (Hist)
502 N. Washington Ave.   Phone: (316) 326-2174
Wellington, KS 67152   Anita Busch, Libn.
Staff: Prof 1. **Subjects:** Pioneer history - Kansas, Wellington and Sumner counties. **Special Collections:** Kansas Collection (100 volumes); antique and rare books; sheet music (100 items). **Holdings:** 500 books; 200 other cataloged items; 700 archival items. **Services:** Copying; library open to public for reference use only.

CHITTENDEN PIANOFORTE LIBRARY
See: Vassar College - George Sherman Dickinson Music Library

★2724★
CHOATE, HALL AND STEWART - LAW LIBRARY (Law)
60 State St.   Phone: (617) 227-5020
Boston, MA 02109   Joy Plunket, Libn.
Staff: Prof 1; Other 2. **Subjects:** Law. **Holdings:** 15,000 volumes. **Subscriptions:** 150 journals and other serials; 10 newspapers. **Services:** Interlibrary loans; copying; library not open to public. **Computerized Information Services:** LEXIS. **Networks/Consortia:** Member of Association of Boston Law Libraries.

CHOICE
See: Center for Humane Options in Childbirth Experiences

CHOMSKY (Elsie & William) EDUCATIONAL RESOURCE CENTER
See: Gratz College - Elsie & William Chomsky Educational Resource Center

★2725★
CHRIST CENTERED MINISTRIES - COLLEGE OF THE ROCKIES - LIBRARY (Rel-Theol)†
750 Clarkson
Denver, CO 80218   Phone: (303) 832-1547
Founded: 1961. **Staff:** 4. **Subjects:** Theology, liberal arts, psychology, liturgy. **Holdings:** 6000 books; 233 manuscripts, pamphlets and phonographs. **Subscriptions:** 15 journals and other serials.

CHRIST CHURCH, PHILADELPHIA - BRAY LIBRARY
See: Library Company of Philadelphia

★2726★
CHRIST HOSPITAL - HOSPITAL LIBRARY (Med)
4440 West 95th St.   Phone: (312) 425-8000
Oak Lawn, IL 60453   Gerald Dujsik, Lib.Mgr.
Staff: Prof 2; Other 2. **Subjects:** Medicine. **Holdings:** 3200 books; 2200 bound periodical volumes; 37 video cassettes; 475 audio cassettes. **Subscriptions:** 255 journals and other serials. **Services:** Interlibrary loans; library open to public for reference use only, by special permission. **Computerized Information Services:** NLM. **Networks/Consortia:** Member of Chicago and South Consortium; Suburban Library System. **Staff:** Mary Hanlon, Libn.

★2727★
CHRIST HOSPITAL INSTITUTE OF MEDICAL RESEARCH - LIBRARY (Med)
2141 Auburn Ave.   Phone: (513) 369-2540
Cincinnati, OH 45219   Lisa L. McCormick, Res.Libn.
Founded: 1932. **Staff:** Prof 1; Other 1. **Subjects:** Internal medicine, virology, oncology, microbiology, surgery. **Holdings:** 5000 books; 12,000 bound periodical volumes. **Subscriptions:** 253 journals and other serials. **Services:** Interlibrary loans; copying; SDI; library open to public with permission of librarian. **Computerized Information Services:** NLM, BRS; computerized cataloging. **Networks/Consortia:** Member of Cincinnati Area Health Sciences Library Association; Cincinnati MEDLINE Consortium.

★2728★
CHRIST THE KING SEMINARY - LIBRARY (Rel-Theol)
711 Knox Rd.   Phone: (716) 652-8959
East Aurora, NY 14052   Rev. Bonaventure F. Hayes, O.F.M., Lib.Dir.
Staff: Prof 3; Other 1. **Subjects:** Religion, theology. **Special Collections:** Msgr. James Bray Collection (500 volumes); early French Canadian and Niagara Frontier history. **Holdings:** 80,000 books and periodical volumes; 1500 pamphlets; 150 reels of taped lectures; 200 reels of microfilm; 300 tape cassettes. **Subscriptions:** 423 journals and other serials; 3 newspapers. **Services:** Interlibrary loans; copying; library open to public for reference use only. **Computerized Information Services:** Computerized cataloging. **Networks/Consortia:** Member of Western New York Library Resources Council (WNYLRC); OCLC. **Staff:** Sr. Consuela Scott, Asst.Libn./ILL; Mary Lee C. Xanco, Cat.Libn.

★2729★
CHRIST SEMINARY - SEMINEX LIBRARY (Rel-Theol)
539 N. Grand Blvd.   Phone: (314) 534-9410
St. Louis, MO 63103   Lucille Hager, Dir.
Founded: 1974. **Staff:** Prof 2; Other 2. **Subjects:** Biblical studies, Lutheran theology, church history, Judaica. **Holdings:** 34,000 books. **Subscriptions:** 345 journals and other serials. **Services:** Interlibrary loans; copying; library open to public. **Computerized Information Services:** Online systems; computerized cataloging. **Networks/Consortia:** Member of MIDLNET; St. Louis Regional Library Network. **Staff:** Mary Bischoff, Coord.Tech.Serv.; Elizabeth Danker, Circ./ILL; Anna Constable, Asst.Cat.

★2730★
CHRIST UNITED METHODIST CHURCH - LIBRARY (Rel-Theol)†
44 Highland Rd.   Phone: (412) 835-6621
Bethel Park, PA 15102
Staff: Prof 1. **Subjects:** Religion. **Holdings:** 3600 books; 300 filmstrips; 40 phonograph records; 50 phonotapes; 80 slides. **Services:** Library not open to public.

★2731★
CHRISTIAN BOARD OF PUBLICATION - MARION STEVENSON LIBRARY (Rel-Theol)†
2640 Pine St.   Phone: (314) 371-6900
St. Louis, MO 63166
Founded: 1943. **Staff:** Prof 1. **Subjects:** Religious education, Bible reference books, Christian churches (Disciples of Christ), religion, theology. **Special Collections:** Biographical file of Christian Churches (Disciples of Christ) - ministers, organizations, and institutions; Christian Church periodicals (1826-1967) and Christian-Evangelist and Christian (1874-1971) on microfilm. **Holdings:** Figures not available. **Services:** Interlibrary loans; copying; library open to area ministers and SLA members.

CHRISTIAN BROTHERS RARE WINE BOOKS LIBRARY
See: Wine Museum of San Francisco

★2732★
CHRISTIAN CHURCH (Disciples of Christ), INC. - DIVISION OF HIGHER EDUCATION - LIBRARY (Educ)
119 N. Jefferson Ave.   Phone: (314) 371-2050
St. Louis, MO 63103   Leslie P. Schroeder, Libn.
Founded: 1914. **Staff:** 1. **Subjects:** Higher education, theological education, histories of private/church-related colleges. **Special Collections:** Materials on the 32 higher education institutions historically established by the Christian Church (Disciples of Christ). **Holdings:** 2000 books; 575 college catalogs; 2000 higher education reports. **Subscriptions:** 20 journals and other serials. **Services:** Interlibrary loans; library open to public for reference use only.

★2733★
CHRISTIAN CHURCH (Disciples of Christ), INC. - LIBRARY (Rel-Theol)†
222 S. Downey Ave.
Box 1986   Phone: (317) 353-1491
Indianapolis, IN 46206   Doris Autrey Kennedy, Libn.
Founded: 1910. **Staff:** Prof 1; Other 1. **Subjects:** Religion, history of the Christian Church (Disciples of Christ), missions. **Holdings:** 6500 books; 500 bound periodical volumes; 1000 pamphlets (cataloged); 100 reports; 6 drawers of clippings. **Subscriptions:** 25 journals and other serials. **Services:** Interlibrary loans; copying; library open to public for reference use only. **Networks/Consortia:** Member of Central Indiana Area Library Services Authority. **Publications:** Books Added to Library, monthly - for internal distribution only. **Special Indexes:** Hymn Index (card).

★2734★
CHRISTIAN FARMERS FEDERATION OF ONTARIO - JUBILEE FOUNDATION FOR AGRICULTURAL RESEARCH - LIBRARY (Agri; Energy)
Box 698   Phone: (519) 338-2921
Harriston, ON, Canada N0G 1Z0   Elbert van Donkersgoed, Res. & Policy Dir.
Staff: Prof 1; Other 5. **Subjects:** Agriculture, stewardship, resource development, public participation, rural development, energy. **Holdings:** 1000 books; 25 filing drawers of agricultural policy development; 4 filing drawers of materials on agriculture and energy. **Subscriptions:** 168 journals and other serials. **Services:** Library open to public with restrictions. **Publications:** The Christian Farmer, quarterly. **Formerly:** Its Foundation for Christian Alternatives in Agriculture.

CHRISTIAN (John T.) LIBRARY
See: New Orleans Baptist Theological Seminary - John T. Christian Library

★2735★
CHRISTIAN RECORD BRAILLE FOUNDATION - CHRISTIAN RECORD FREE LENDING LIBRARY (Aud-Vis)
4444 S. 52nd St.   Phone: (402) 488-0981
Lincoln, NE 68506   Wendell Carpenter, Coord., Rd.Serv.
Staff: Prof 1; Other 15. **Subjects:** Adventure, character-building children's stories, devotions, diet and foods, health, music, nature, religion, travel. **Holdings:** 800 braille book titles; 2 Spanish braille titles; 80 disk titles; 12 Spanish disk titles; 713 cassette titles; 32 Spanish cassette titles; 12 full-vision titles; 65 large print titles; music album titles - 50 disk, 28 cassette. **Services:** Library open to blind and visually handicapped or those with physical handicaps which prevent them from following normal reading practices; materials sent free on 30-day loan basis with renewal privileges.

★2736★
CHRISTIAN SCIENCE MONITOR - RESEARCH LIBRARY (Publ)
One Norway St.   Phone: (617) 262-2300
Boston, MA 02115   Geoffrey Fingland, Libn.
Founded: 1908. **Staff:** Prof 5; Other 7. **Subjects:** Topics relating to national and international news; history; literature. **Holdings:** 10,000 books; 100 editorial research reports; three million clippings. **Subscriptions:** 50 journals and other serials. **Services:** Interlibrary loans (local only); copying; library not open to public. **Computerized Information Services:** NEXIS.

★2737★
CHRISTIAN THEOLOGICAL SEMINARY - LIBRARY (Rel-Theol)
1000 W. 42nd St.   Phone: (317) 924-1331
Indianapolis, IN 46208   Mr. Leslie R. Galbraith, Libn.
Founded: 1941. **Staff:** Prof 3; Other 5. **Subjects:** Religion, theology. **Special Collections:** Disciples of Christ historical materials. **Holdings:** 98,000 books; 7000 bound periodical volumes; 40 VF drawers of pamphlets. **Subscriptions:** 500 journals and other serials; 5 newspapers. **Services:** Interlibrary loans; copying; library open to public. **Computerized Information Services:** Computerized cataloging. **Networks/Consortia:** Member of Central Indiana Area Library Services; Indianapolis Consortium for Urban Education; INCOLSA. **Publications:** Encounter, quarterly - by subscription. **Staff:** Thelma F. Hodges, Assoc.Libn., Tech.Serv; William O. Harris, Asst.Libn., Rd.Serv.

CHRISTIE EDUCATION LIBRARY
See: Brandon University

★2738★
CHRISTMAS SEAL AND CHARITY STAMP SOCIETY - LIBRARY (Rec)†
5825 Dorchester Ave.
Chicago, IL 60637   Dr. H. Denny Donnell, Jr., Hist./Libn.
Founded: 1931. **Subjects:** Christmas seals of the world, especially the United States; charity seals of the world. **Special Collections:** Complete file of SEAL NEWS (and predecessor titles) representing official publications of the society from 1931 to present (1 VF drawer). **Holdings:** 3 VF drawers of pamphlets,

clippings, hobby newsletters describing seals and issuing societies; new issues of many nations and funds, errors, rarities, values, collections and exhibits of such. **Services:** Interlibrary loans; copying; questions answered by mail. **Publications:** Newsletter - to members and subscribers or exchanges.

CHRONICLE-HERALD NEWS
See: Augusta Chronicle-Herald News

★2739★
CHRONICLE OF HIGHER EDUCATION - LIBRARY (Educ)
1333 New Hampshire Ave., N.W.   Phone: (202) 828-3525
Washington, DC 20036   Edith Uunila, Sr.Ed.
Staff: 2. **Subjects:** Higher education. **Holdings:** 2500 books; 1500 booklets (cataloged); newspaper and magazine clippings. **Subscriptions:** 100 journals and other serials; 50 newspapers. **Services:** Interlibrary loans; copying; library open to public by appointment.

★2740★
CHRYSLER CORPORATION - ENGINEERING DIVISION - ENGINEERING LIBRARY (Sci-Tech)
Box 1118   Phone: (313) 956-4881
Detroit, MI 48073   Phyllis J. Sears, Supv.
Founded: 1933. **Staff:** Prof 1. **Subjects:** Automotive engineering, mechanical engineering, electrical engineering, chemistry, physics, mathematics. **Special Collections:** Service manuals. **Holdings:** 5000 books; 12,000 bound periodical volumes. **Subscriptions:** 300 journals and other serials. **Services:** Interlibrary loans; library open to public on request. **Computerized Information Services:** DIALOG, SDC.

CHRYSLER DEFENSE, INC.
See: General Dynamics Corporation - Land Systems Division

★2741★
CHRYSLER MUSEUM - JEAN OUTLAND CHRYSLER LIBRARY (Art)
Olney Rd. & Mowbray Arch   Phone: (804) 622-1211
Norfolk, VA 23510   Amy Navratil Ciccone, Libn.
Staff: Prof 2; Other 3. **Subjects:** Art history, glass, decorative arts. **Holdings:** 75,000 books; 50 VF drawers; 20,000 auction catalogs and 6000 exhibition catalogs on microfiche. **Subscriptions:** 55 journals and other serials. **Services:** Interlibrary loans; copying; library open to public by appointment. **Networks/Consortia:** Member of OCLC.

★2742★
CH2M HILL CORP. - LIBRARY (Energy; Env-Cons)
555 Capitol Mall, Suite 1290   Phone: (916) 441-3955
Sacramento, CA 95814   Joy Steveson, Libn.
Founded: 1973. **Staff:** Prof 1. **Subjects:** Water resources, energy, sanitation engineering, environmental planning. **Holdings:** 1000 books; 50 unbound periodicals; 1500 technical reports, proposals, contract documents, vendor catalogs. **Subscriptions:** 50 journals and other serials; 15 newspapers. **Services:** Interlibrary loans; library not open to public.

★2743★
CH2M HILL, INC. - CORVALLIS REGIONAL OFFICE LIBRARY (Sci-Tech)
Box 428   Phone: (503) 752-4271
Corvallis, OR 97330   Rebecca Pixler, Rec.Mgt.Coord.
Staff: Prof 1; Other 3. **Subjects:** Engineering, environmental science, geology, business administration. **Holdings:** 4000 books; 271 bound periodical volumes; 5000 manufacturers' catalogs; 20 boxes of archival material. **Subscriptions:** 271 journals and other serials. **Services:** Interlibrary loans; copying; library open to public with restrictions. **Special Catalogs:** Catalog to manufacturers' catalogs (card and book); catalog to internally generated materials (card). **Staff:** V. Fowler, Tech.Libn.

★2744★
CH2M HILL, INC. - INFORMATION CENTER (Sci-Tech)
1525 Court St.
Box 2088   Phone: (916) 243-5831
Redding, CA 96001   Virginia Merryman, Libn.
Founded: 1968. **Staff:** Prof 1; Other 1. **Subjects:** Engineering - sanitary, structural, agricultural; California weather; water resources. **Special Collections:** North American Weather Charts (1942 to present); California rainfall records (1956 to present). **Holdings:** 7500 books; 5000 U.S. Geological Survey topographical maps; 300 geological reports and maps; 300 California Department of Water Resources bulletins; 2000 project reports. **Subscriptions:** 342 journals and other serials. **Services:** Interlibrary loans;

copying; library open to public with restrictions.

★2745★
CH2M HILL, INC. - LIBRARY (Sci-Tech)
Box 22508   Phone: (303) 771-0900
Denver, CO 80222   LaRue Fontenot, Libn.
Staff: Prof 1; Other 1. **Subjects:** Water and wastewater, civil and mechanical engineering, climatology, mining. **Holdings:** 5500 books and bound periodical volumes; 2000 technical reports; 1100 trade catalogs; 300 Environmental Protection Agency documents; 300 U.S. Geological Survey topographical maps; 1000 archival items. **Subscriptions:** 150 journals and other serials; 10 newspapers. **Services:** Interlibrary loans; copying; library open to other CH2M Hill libraries. **Computerized Information Services:** Computerized acquisitions, serials and circulation.

★2746★
CH2M HILL, INC. - LIBRARY (Sci-Tech)
2020 S.W. 4th Ave., 2nd Fl.   Phone: (503) 224-9190
Portland, OR 97201   Polly Westover, Libn.
Founded: 1970. **Staff:** 2. **Subjects:** Engineering - wastes, water, structural, geotechnical; planning; economics. **Holdings:** 10,000 books; 6000 company reports; 4000 slides. **Subscriptions:** 200 journals and other serials; 37 newspapers. **Services:** Interlibrary loans; copying; library open to public.

★2747★
CH2M HILL SOUTHEAST, INC. - INFORMATION CENTER (Env-Cons)
7201 N.W. 11th Place   Phone: (904) 377-2442
Gainesville, FL 32602   Mary Gene Blanchard, Mgr., Rec.
Founded: 1968. **Staff:** Prof 1; Other 2. **Subjects:** Water supply; wastewater treatment and disposal; domestic and industrial waste treatment; solid and hazardous wastes disposal; environmental sciences; construction management. **Holdings:** 6200 books; 243 bound periodical volumes; 2600 engineering reports; 2500 specifications; 500 reels of microfilm; 5200 microfiche; AV equipment; maps. **Subscriptions:** 160 journals and other serials. **Services:** Interlibrary loans; copying; will answer brief questions and make referrals; library not open to public. **Publications:** Acquisition list, annual; newsletter, periodically. **Special Catalogs:** Catalog of bound company reports (card); catalog of bound specifications (card); catalog of original project drawings (card); catalog of manufacturers' catalogs (computerized).

★2748★
CH2M HILL - TECHNICAL INFORMATION CENTER (Sci-Tech)
1500 114th Ave., S.E.   Phone: (206) 453-5000
Bellevue, WA 98004   Kay M. Pflug-Felder, Rec.Mgt.Supv.
Staff: Prof 2; Other 1. **Subjects:** Engineering. **Holdings:** 4530 books. **Subscriptions:** 445 journals and other serials; 5 newspapers. **Services:** Library not open to public. **Computerized Information Services:** SDC. **Networks/Consortia:** Member of Washington Library Network (WLN). **Staff:** Gwen H. Bjorkman, Libn.

★2749★
CHURCH ARMY IN CANADA - COWAN MEMORIAL LIBRARY (Rel-Theol)
397 Brunswick Ave.   Phone: (416) 924-9279
Toronto, ON, Canada M5R 2Z2   Sr. Dianne McConachie, Libn.
Staff: Prof 1. **Subjects:** Old and New Testament, Christology, Christian doctrine, church history, homiletics and sermons. **Holdings:** 10,000 books; 100 tapes; 2 drawers of photographs; slides. **Services:** Interlibrary loans; copying; library not open to public. **Publications:** The Crusader, biennial - distributed throughout Canada.

★2750★
CHURCH OF THE BELOVED DISCIPLE - HOMOPHILE RESEARCH LIBRARY (Soc Sci)
348 W. 14th St.   Phone: (212) 242-6616
New York, NY 10014   Thor Wood, Libn.
Founded: 1953. **Subjects:** Homosexuality. **Special Collections:** Periodicals pertaining to the homophile/gay activist movement (i.e., the social movement devoted to improving the status of the homosexual); Archives of the Mattachine Society of New York. **Holdings:** 3500 books; 15 bound periodical volumes; 2 VF drawers of clippings and pamphlets; 14 VF drawers of archives and papers; 49 VF drawers of unbound periodicals; 1 drawer of audiotapes. **Subscriptions:** 20 journals and other serials. **Services:** Interlibrary loans; copying; library open to public. **Remarks:** Includes the holdings of the former Mattachine Society Inc. of New York, both Library and Archives.

★2751★
CHURCH OF THE BRETHREN GENERAL BOARD - BRETHREN HISTORICAL LIBRARY AND ARCHIVES (Rel-Theol)
1451 Dundee Ave.   Phone: (312) 742-5100
Elgin, IL 60120   James R. Lynch, Archv.
Founded: 1936. **Staff:** Prof 2; Other 3. **Subjects:** Church of the Brethren history; German Baptist Brethren history. **Holdings:** 7000 volumes; 2000 cubic feet of archival material and manuscript collection; 10 VF drawers of photographs; 1200 audiotapes; 400 reels of microfilm. **Services:** Interlibrary loans; copying; library open to public by appointment. **Computerized Information Services:** Computerized cataloging. **Networks/Consortia:** Member of ILLINET. **Publications:** Guide to the Brethren in Europe; Guide to Research in Brethren History; Guide for Local Church Historians - all three guides are pamphlets and are free upon request.

CHURCH OF CHRIST DISCIPLES ARCHIVES
See: **University of Toronto - Victoria University - Library**

CHURCH DIVINITY SCHOOL OF THE PACIFIC
See: **Graduate Theological Union**

★2752★
CHURCH OF ENGLAND INSTITUTE - LIBRARY (Rel-Theol)†
116 Princess St.   Phone: (506) 693-2295
Saint John, NB, Canada E2L 1K4   Mrs. F.H. Burton, Mgr.
Staff: 2. **Subjects:** Fiction. **Holdings:** 2000 books. **Services:** Library open to members.

CHURCH OF THE HOLY FAITH
See: **Episcopal Church of the Holy Faith**

★2753★
CHURCH OF THE INCARNATION - MARMION LIBRARY (Rel-Theol)
3966 McKinney Ave.   Phone: (214) 521-5101
Dallas, TX 75204-2099   Willa H. Johnson, Libn.
Founded: 1955. **Staff:** Prof 2. **Subjects:** Religion, history, biography, fiction. **Holdings:** 7000 books; 250 audiotapes. **Services:** Library not open to public. **Staff:** Frances Lawler, Mgr.

★2754★
CHURCH OF JESUS CHRIST OF LATTER-DAY SAINTS - ALBUQUERQUE BRANCH GENEALOGICAL LIBRARY (Hist)
Box 3568   Phone: (505) 255-1227
Albuquerque, NM 87110   David W. Seegmiller, Libn.
Staff: Prof 2; Other 13. **Subjects:** Genealogy, social history, heraldry, geography. **Special Collections:** New Mexico Genealogical Society card index to New Mexico cemetery, mortuary, probate and marriage records. **Holdings:** 750 books; 400 reels of microfilmed U.S. Census Records; 155 reels of microfilmed Boyd's Marriage Index; 200 reels of microfilmed U.S. records; microfilm of many New Mexico church records. **Services:** Copying; access to the microfilm collection of the main library in Salt Lake City; translation; library open to public.

★2755★
CHURCH OF JESUS CHRIST OF LATTER-DAY SAINTS - BOSTON BRANCH GENEALOGICAL LIBRARY (Hist)
Box 204   Phone: (617) 235-9892
Weston, MA 02193   Geoffrey P. Goldberg, Libn.
Founded: 1971. **Staff:** Prof 2; Other 6. **Subjects:** Genealogy, family histories. **Holdings:** 500 books; 50 bound periodical volumes; 10 manuscripts (cataloged); 68 million names on microfiche; microfilm. **Services:** Access to the microfilm collection of the main library in Salt Lake City; library open to public. **Remarks:** The library is located at Brown St. and South Ave., Weston, MA 02193.

★2756★
CHURCH OF JESUS CHRIST OF LATTER-DAY SAINTS - CALGARY INSTITUTE OF RELIGION - LIBRARY (Rel-Theol)†
3120 32nd Ave. N.W.   Phone: (403) 282-5426
Calgary, AB, Canada T2N 1N7   Merlin Olsen, Dir.
Founded: 1968. **Staff:** 1. **Subjects:** Religion, career information. **Holdings:** 680 books and bound periodical volumes. **Services:** Library open to public.

★2757★
CHURCH OF JESUS CHRIST OF LATTER-DAY SAINTS - CLEVELAND, OHIO STAKE BRANCH GENEALOGICAL LIBRARY (Hist)
25000 Westwood Rd.   Phone: (216) 777-1518
Westlake, OH 44145   Mary Phelps, Libn.
Subjects: Genealogy. **Holdings:** 88 reels of microfilm of U.S., British and

Canada collections; 112 reels of microfilm of non-English speaking countries (continental European, Afro-Asian, Latin American, Iberian Peninsula and Scandinavian Collections); 52 reels of microfilm of family names - all microfilm reels represent card catalog of collections. **Services:** Access to the microfilm collection of the main library in Salt Lake City; library open to public.

★2758★
CHURCH OF JESUS CHRIST OF LATTER-DAY SAINTS - DETROIT BRANCH GENEALOGICAL LIBRARY (Hist)†
425 N. Woodward   Phone: (313) 647-5671
Bloomfield Hills, MI 48103
Founded: 1970. **Staff:** Prof 19; Other 27. **Subjects:** Genealogy. **Holdings:** 150 books; 148 bound periodical volumes. **Services:** Interlibrary loans; copying; access to the microfilm collection of the main library in Salt Lake City; library open to public. **Special Indexes:** Index to Wayne County, MI, Probate Records; index to indefinite loan film collection.

★2759★
CHURCH OF JESUS CHRIST OF LATTER-DAY SAINTS - EL PASO BRANCH GENEALOGICAL LIBRARY (Hist)
3651 Douglas Ave.   Phone: (915) 565-9711
El Paso, TX 79903   H. Leroy Taylor, Libn.
Staff: Prof 2; Other 6. **Subjects:** Genealogy. **Holdings:** 175 books; 56 bound periodical volumes. **Services:** Copying; access to the microfilm collection of the main library in Salt Lake City; library open to public. **Staff:** Lovell K. Lovett, Asst.Libn.; Grace Wade, Asst.Libn.

★2760★
CHURCH OF JESUS CHRIST OF LATTER-DAY SAINTS - ELKO BRANCH GENEALOGICAL LIBRARY (Hist)
Box 651   Phone: (702) 738-4565
Elko, NV 89801   Bruce Hendrix, Libn.
Staff: 5. **Subjects:** Genealogy. **Holdings:** 200 books. **Services:** Library open to public.

★2761★
CHURCH OF JESUS CHRIST OF LATTER-DAY SAINTS - EUGENE, OREGON BRANCH GENEALOGICAL LIBRARY (Hist)
3550 W. 18th Ave.   Phone: (503) 343-3741
Eugene, OR 97402   Shirlee A. Bird, Libn.
Staff: Prof 1; Other 45. **Subjects:** Genealogy. **Special Collections:** County censuses for the state of Oregon. **Holdings:** 1100 books; 400 bound periodical volumes; 5 VF drawers (cataloged); 3 VF drawers of family histories; 600 reels of microfilm; 200 maps. **Subscriptions:** 75 journals and other serials. **Services:** Copying; access to the microfilm collection of the main library in Salt Lake City; library open to public.

★2762★
CHURCH OF JESUS CHRIST OF LATTER-DAY SAINTS - EUREKA, CALIFORNIA STAKE BRANCH GENEALOGICAL LIBRARY (Hist)
2734 Dolbeer St.   Phone: (707) 443-7411
Eureka, CA 95501   Grace M. Jones, Libn.
Founded: 1972. **Staff:** 18. **Subjects:** Genealogy. **Holdings:** 200 books; 150 bound periodical volumes; 20 volumes of indexed obituaries; 17 directories. **Services:** Access to the microfilm collection of the main library in Salt Lake City; library open to public.

★2763★
CHURCH OF JESUS CHRIST OF LATTER-DAY SAINTS - GENEALOGICAL LIBRARY (Hist)
50 E. North Temple St.   Phone: (801) 531-2331
Salt Lake City, UT 84150   David M. Mayfield, Dir.
Founded: 1894. **Staff:** Prof 105; Other 100. **Subjects:** Genealogy, family history, church and civil records, local history. **Special Collections:** Family Group Records Collection (8 million family reconstitution forms from the U.S. and foreign countries); oral genealogy tapes. **Holdings:** 150,000 books and bound periodical volumes; 1.2 million 100-foot reels of microfilm. **Subscriptions:** 1500 journals and other serials. **Services:** Copying; orientation tours; research classes; library open to public. **Computerized Information Services:** Computerized cataloging, acquisitions and circulation to branch libraries. **Publications:** Genealogical Research Papers, irregular. **Special Catalogs:** Genealogical Library Catalog (COM). **Special Indexes:** International Genealogical Index (includes 68 million names - COM). **Remarks:** Branch libraries having access to most film are added to the system on a continuing basis. **Staff:** Raymond Wright, Mgr., Pub.Serv.; Charles Clement, Mgr., Tech.Serv.; Glade Nelson, Mgr., Ext.Pub.Serv.; Jerry McMullin, Coord., Br.Libs.

★2764★
CHURCH OF JESUS CHRIST OF LATTER-DAY SAINTS - HELENA BRANCH GENEALOGICAL LIBRARY (Hist)
1610 E. Sixth Ave.
Box 811   Phone: (406) 443-1558
Helena, MT 59601   Esther M. Stratton, Br.Libn.
Founded: 1962. **Staff:** 12. **Subjects:** Genealogy. **Special Collections:** 1890 and 1900 Montana census. **Holdings:** 75 books; 98 reels of microfilm of maps and the card catalog of the Salt Lake City collection. **Services:** Interlibrary loans; copying; access to the microfilm collection of the main library in Salt Lake City; library open to public.

★2765★
CHURCH OF JESUS CHRIST OF LATTER-DAY SAINTS - HISTORICAL DEPARTMENT - CHURCH LIBRARY-ARCHIVES (Hist; Rel-Theol)
50 E. North Temple St.   Phone: (801) 531-2745
Salt Lake City, UT 84150   Donald T. Schmidt, Dir., Lib.Archv.
Staff: Prof 24; Other 35. **Subjects:** Mormonism. **Special Collections:** Publications, manuscripts and records of and pertaining to the Mormon Church. **Holdings:** 160,000 books, pamphlets and bound periodical volumes; 290,000 minute books and other handwritten volumes; 130,000 reels of microfilm; 60,000 microfiche; 11,500 transcriptions and tapes; 350 videotapes; 8000 manuscript histories; one million manuscript items. **Subscriptions:** 210 journals and other serials; 12 newspapers. **Services:** Copying; library open to public. **Special Catalogs:** Manuscript Card Catalog, Registers, Inventories and indexes of holdings of Library-Archives. **Staff:** Ronald Watt, Mgr., Tech.Serv.; Glenn N. Rowe, Mgr., Pub.Serv.

★2766★
CHURCH OF JESUS CHRIST OF LATTER-DAY SAINTS - JACKSONVILLE, FLORIDA BRANCH GENEALOGICAL LIBRARY (Hist)
4087 Hendricks Ave.   Phone: (904) 398-3487
Jacksonville, FL 32207   Elizabeth Shipp, Br. Genealogy Libn.
Staff: Prof 1; Other 7. **Subjects:** Genealogy, local history. **Special Collections:** Early Jacksonville newspaper clippings; local pedigree file. **Holdings:** 671 volumes; 1203 reels of microfilm; 25 drawers of newspaper vital statistics. **Services:** Copying; library open to public with restrictions.

★2767★
CHURCH OF JESUS CHRIST OF LATTER-DAY SAINTS - LAIE, HAWAII STAKE BRANCH GENEALOGICAL LIBRARY (Hist)
c/o BYU, Box 49   Phone: (808) 293-3880
Laie, HI 96762   Cassandra K. Johnson, Libn.
Founded: 1965. **Subjects:** Genealogy. **Special Collections:** Hawaiian and Polynesian genealogies. **Holdings:** 100 books; 1900 Hawaii Census; church records. **Services:** Access to the microfilm collection of the main library in Salt Lake City; library open to public.

★2768★
CHURCH OF JESUS CHRIST OF LATTER-DAY SAINTS - LANSING BRANCH GENEALOGICAL LIBRARY (Hist)
431 E. Saginaw
Box 801   Phone: (517) 332-2932
East Lansing, MI 48823   Azalia Benjamin, Branch Libn.
Founded: 1970. **Staff:** 30. **Subjects:** Genealogy. **Holdings:** 289 reels of microfilm of an index to the Salt Lake City Collection; 76 reels of microfilm of Gazetteers; 1048 reels of microfilm of family group sheets; index file to the computer holdings of the Genealogical Department of the Salt Lake City Library. **Services:** Copying; access to microfilm collection of the main library in Salt Lake City; library open to public. **Staff:** Maurine Wittwer, Patron Supv.

★2769★
CHURCH OF JESUS CHRIST OF LATTER-DAY SAINTS - LAS VEGAS BRANCH GENEALOGICAL LIBRARY (Hist)
509 S. Ninth St.   Phone: (701) 382-9695
Las Vegas, NV 89101   Earl C. Brunner, Jr., Hd.Libn.
Founded: 1966. **Staff:** 75. **Subjects:** Genealogy. **Holdings:** 5000 books; 1000 bound periodical volumes; 3500 reels of microfilm; 7000 microfiche. **Subscriptions:** 15 journals and other serials. **Services:** Copying; library open to public for reference use only. **Special Indexes:** Index to 1870 U.S. Census of Nevada. **Staff:** Joyce Musser, Asst.Hd.Libn.

★2770★
CHURCH OF JESUS CHRIST OF LATTER-DAY SAINTS - LONGVIEW BRANCH GENEALOGICAL LIBRARY (Hist)†
1700 Blueridge Pkwy.   Phone: (214) 759-7911
Longview, TX 75605
Founded: 1968. **Staff:** 10. **Subjects:** Genealogy. **Holdings:** 500 books. **Services:** Copying; access to the microfilm collection of the main library in

Salt Lake City; library open to public.

★2771★
CHURCH OF JESUS CHRIST OF LATTER-DAY SAINTS - LOVELL, WYOMING BRANCH GENEALOGICAL LIBRARY (Hist)
50 W. Main St.
Lovell, WY 82431
Phone: (307) 548-2963
Barbara C. Bassett, Libn.
Founded: 1965. **Staff:** 21. **Subjects:** Genealogy, history, biography. **Holdings:** 325 books; 200 bound periodical volumes; 20 unbound cemetery records; 1 set of unbound mortuary records; 10 folders of unbound obituary clippings; genealogy microforms. **Services:** Copying; library open to public.

★2772★
CHURCH OF JESUS CHRIST OF LATTER-DAY SAINTS - MESA BRANCH GENEALOGICAL LIBRARY (Hist)
464 E. First Ave.
Mesa, AZ 85204
Phone: (602) 964-1200
Joseph H. Lindblom, Pres.
Founded: 1930. **Subjects:** Genealogy. **Holdings:** 12,000 books; 200 bound periodical volumes; 15 volumes of clippings of the Hartford Times; 25,000 reels of microfilm; family histories; 10,000 indexed pedigree charts; obituaries from the Desert and Tribune News, 1851-1963. **Subscriptions:** 76 journals and other serials. **Services:** Copying; library open to public for reference use only.

★2773★
CHURCH OF JESUS CHRIST OF LATTER-DAY SAINTS - MORRISTOWN, NEW JERSEY BRANCH GENEALOGICAL LIBRARY (Hist)
283 James St.
Morristown, NJ 07960
Phone: (201) 539-5362
Ronald L. Wadsack, Hd.Libn.
Founded: 1968. **Staff:** 10. **Subjects:** Genealogy. **Holdings:** 150 books; 250 reels of microfilm; International Genealogical Index (microfiche). **Services:** Access to the microfilm collection of the main library in Salt Lake City; library open to public.

★2774★
CHURCH OF JESUS CHRIST OF LATTER-DAY SAINTS - MT. WHITNEY BRANCH GENEALOGICAL LIBRARY
Box 1090
Inyokern, CA 93527
Defunct

★2775★
CHURCH OF JESUS CHRIST OF LATTER-DAY SAINTS - SAFFORD-THATCHER STAKES - GENEALOGICAL LIBRARY (Hist)
Box 1218
Safford, AZ 85546
Phone: (602) 428-3194
Ervin Cluff, Libn.
Staff: 34. **Subjects:** Genealogy. **Special Collections:** Indian Tribes (pamphlets); World Conference, 1969 (18 volumes); Genealogical Society Series (12 volumes); World Conference, 1981 (13 volumes). **Holdings:** 2214 books; 1087 bound periodical volumes. **Subscriptions:** 21 journals and other serials. **Services:** Interlibrary loans; copying; library open to public.

★2776★
CHURCH OF JESUS CHRIST OF LATTER-DAY SAINTS - ST. GEORGE BRANCH GENEALOGICAL LIBRARY (Hist)
Box 417
St. George, UT 84770
Dr. David L. Morris, Libn.
Staff: Prof 3; Other 34. **Subjects:** Genealogy and history. **Special Collections:** Microfilmed church records for Southern Utah, Southern Nevada and Northern Arizona. **Holdings:** 3000 books and bound periodical volumes; 3000 reels of microfilm (cataloged). **Services:** Copying; library open to public. **Special Indexes:** Obituary Index for Mountain West.

★2777★
CHURCH OF JESUS CHRIST OF LATTER-DAY SAINTS - SOUTHERN CALIFORNIA AREA GENEALOGICAL LIBRARY (Hist)
10741 Santa Monica Blvd.
Los Angeles, CA 90025
Phone: (213) 474-9990
Fred E. Klingman, Pres.
Founded: 1964. **Staff:** Prof 3; Other 85. **Subjects:** Genealogy, local and county history. **Special Collections:** U.S. Censuses, 1790-1900; Index to Somerset House vital records, 1837-1902; Soundex 1880 and 1900 census; Hamburg Passenger List; Index to Pension Records, National Archives; Index to Passenger Lists, National Archives. **Holdings:** 10,500 books; 1500 bound periodical volumes; 35,000 reels of microfilm; 62 VF drawers of U.S. gazetteer files. **Subscriptions:** 60 journals and other serials. **Services:** Copying; member of the borrowing program of the Genealogical Society, Salt Lake City, UT; genealogical consultant services; library open to public. **Special Indexes:** Gazetteer card file of small or nonexistent towns; subject and locality index of periodicals.

★2778★
CHURCH OF JESUS CHRIST OF LATTER-DAY SAINTS - TACOMA BRANCH GENEALOGY LIBRARY (Hist)†
1102 S. Pearl
Tacoma, WA 98465
Phone: (206) 564-1103
Clifton M. Foreman, Libn.
Founded: 1976. **Staff:** 55. **Subjects:** Genealogy and local history. **Special Collections:** Family pedigree charts (800); family genealogies (180). **Holdings:** 600 volumes; 2000 reels of microfilm; 25 VF drawers of western Washington obituaries; 3 VF drawers of genealogy; hanging file of surnames; census records; films. **Services:** Interlibrary loans (fee); copying; access to the microfilm collection of the main library in Salt Lake City; library open to public.

★2779★
CHURCH OF JESUS CHRIST OF LATTER-DAY SAINTS - TAMPA BRANCH GENEALOGICAL LIBRARY (Hist)†
4106 E. Fletcher Ave.
Tampa, FL 33617
Phone: (813) 971-2869
Barbara M. Dalby, Libn.
Founded: 1968. **Staff:** 10. **Subjects:** Local history, genealogy. **Special Collections:** Mortuary and cemetery records of Hillsborough County, FL. **Holdings:** 1500 books; 200 bound periodical volumes; 2000 reels of microfilm (cataloged); 1000 unbound periodicals; 2500 clippings, maps and manuscripts. **Services:** Copying; access to the microfilm collection of the main library in Salt Lake City; library open to public.

★2780★
CHURCH OF JESUS CHRIST OF LATTER-DAY SAINTS - TRI-CITIES BRANCH GENEALOGICAL LIBRARY (Hist)
1720 Thayer
Richland, WA 99352
Phone: (509) 943-0921
Jay Jameson, Hd.
Founded: 1967. **Staff:** 30. **Subjects:** Genealogy. **Holdings:** 500 books; 200 bound periodical volumes; 3000 reels of microfilm. **Services:** Access to the microfilm collection of the main library in Salt Lake City; library open to public. **Remarks:** An alternate phone number is (509) 943-9733.

★2781★
CHURCH OF JESUS CHRIST OF LATTER-DAY SAINTS - UPPER SNAKE RIVER BRANCH GENEALOGICAL LIBRARY (Hist)†
Ricks College Library
Rexburg, ID 83440
Phone: (208) 356-2351
Neal S. Southwick, Libn.
Founded: 1965. **Staff:** Prof 2; Other 11. **Subjects:** History, biography, genealogy. **Holdings:** 1000 books; 100 bound periodical volumes; 5000 microfilms (cataloged). **Subscriptions:** 20 journals and other serials. **Services:** Interlibrary loans; copying; library open to public. **Computerized Information Services:** Computerized circulation. **Publications:** Bulletin showing use of library books and microfilm. **Staff:** Joyce Hathaway, Asst.Libn.

CHURCH OF JESUS CHRIST OF LATTER-DAY SAINTS - UTAH VALLEY BRANCH GENEALOGICAL LIBRARY
See: Brigham Young University - Utah Valley Branch Genealogical Library

★2782★
CHURCH OF JESUS CHRIST OF LATTER-DAY SAINTS - VENTURA BRANCH GENEALOGICAL LIBRARY (Hist)
3501 Loma Vista Rd.
Box 3517
Ventura, CA 93003
Phone: (805) 643-5607
Josephine P. McClure, Libn.
Staff: 21. **Subjects:** Genealogy. **Holdings:** 200 books; 400 reels of microfilm. **Subscriptions:** 10 journals and other serials. **Services:** Copying; access to microfilm collection of the main library in Salt Lake City; library open to public.

★2783★
CHURCH OF JESUS CHRIST OF LATTER-DAY SAINTS - WEST PALM BEACH FLORIDA STAKE BRANCH GENEALOGICAL LIBRARY (Hist)
1530 W. Camino Real
Box 2350
Boca Raton, FL 33432
Phone: (305) 395-6644
Phyllis M. Heiss, Supv.Libn.
Staff: Prof 1; Other 20. **Subjects:** Genealogy. **Holdings:** 500 books. **Services:** Copying; access to microfilm in Salt Lake City; library open to public.

★2784★
CHURCH OF THE NAZARENE - EDITORIAL LIBRARY (Rel-Theol)
6401 The Paseo
Kansas City, MO 64131
Phone: (816) 333-7000
Patricia F. Christie, Libn.
Staff: 1. **Subjects:** Bible, religious education, missions. **Holdings:** 8000 books; 200 bound periodical volumes; 20 VF drawers of pamphlets; 1 VF drawer of music scores; 100 cassette tapes. **Subscriptions:** 100 journals

and other serials. **Services:** Library not open to public.

CHURCHILL LIBRARY
See: Massachusetts College of Pharmacy & Allied Health Sciences

CHURCHILL (Winston) MEMORIAL AND LIBRARY
See: Westminster College - Winston Churchill Memorial and Library

★2785★
CIBA-GEIGY (Canada) LTD. - PHARMACEUTICAL LIBRARY (Med)
6860 Century Ave.
Mississauga, ON, Canada L5N 2W5   Heather Dansereau, Med.Libn.
Staff: Prof 1; Other 1. **Subjects:** Medicine, pharmacy, pharmacology, business. **Special Collections:** CIBA-GEIGY products, CIBA and GEIGY publications. **Holdings:** 3000 books and bound periodical volumes; 60,000 reels of microfilm. **Subscriptions:** 140 journals and other serials. **Services:** Interlibrary loans; copying; library open to public by appointment.

★2786★
CIBA-GEIGY CORPORATION - CORPORATE LIBRARY (Sci-Tech)
Saw Mill River Rd.   Phone: (914) 478-3131
Ardsley, NY 10502   Paul M. McIlvaine, Libn.
Founded: 1956. **Staff:** Prof 2; Other 2. **Subjects:** Organic chemistry, plastics and polymers, business administration and management. **Holdings:** 6000 books; 10,000 bound periodical volumes; 1500 reports; 3000 reels of microfilm; 1100 microfiche. **Subscriptions:** 825 journals and other serials. **Services:** Interlibrary loans; copying; library not open to public. **Computerized Information Services:** DIALOG, SDC, NLM, Dow Jones News Retrieval; computerized serials. **Publications:** Infoscope, bimonthly - for internal distribution only. **Staff:** Judith E. Shaw, Assoc.Libn.

★2787★
CIBA-GEIGY CORPORATION - PHARMACEUTICALS DIVISION - SCIENTIFIC INFORMATION CENTER (Med)
556 Morris Ave.   Phone: (201) 277-5544
Summit, NJ 07901   Dr. Karl Doebel, Dir.
Founded: 1937. **Staff:** Prof 15; Other 13. **Subjects:** Medicine, chemistry, pharmacology, pharmacy. **Holdings:** 7800 books; 24,400 bound periodical volumes; 120,000 product literature items; 2260 microfilm of journal holdings. **Subscriptions:** 600 journals and other serials. **Services:** Library not open to public. **Publications:** CIBA-GEIGY Summaries, weekly; New Drugs in Use or Research, monthly. **Special Indexes:** Author and archival number index to product literature on cards; partial subject index on computer printout. **Staff:** Adelaide Hammargren, Supv. of Lib.Serv.; Margaret Mulligan, Asst.Supv., Lib.Serv.

★2788★
CIBA-GEIGY CORPORATION - TECHNICAL INFORMATION SERVICE (Sci-Tech)
410 Swing Rd.   Phone: (919) 292-7100
Greensboro, NC 27409   Leonard Parker, Mgr., Tech.Info.Serv.
Staff: Prof 3. **Subjects:** Agriculture, organic chemistry, dyes, business, biochemistry. **Holdings:** 7800 books; 13,000 bound periodical volumes; 2250 reels of microfilm. **Subscriptions:** 753 journals and other serials. **Services:** Interlibrary loans; copying; SDI; library not open to public. **Computerized Information Services:** Online systems; computerized serials. **Publications:** Greensboro Library New Titles, bimonthly; DATAPUB, bimonthly - both for internal distribution only. **Staff:** E. Lynne Jacques, Libn.; Hilary Erskine, Tech.Info.Spec.

★2789★
CIBBARELLI & ASSOCIATES INC. - INFORMATION SERVICES (Info Sci)
Box 5337   Phone: (714) 842-6121
Huntington Beach, CA 92646
Staff: Prof 7. **Subjects:** Information science. **Services:** Information management consulting specializing in systems analysis and design, indexing and retrieval methodologies, software selection for automated retrieval systems, systems implementation, building special libraries, archives and records management, and personnel selection and training for information management. **Staff:** Kenneth H. Plate, Sr. Partner; Edward J. Kazlauskas, Sr. Partner.

★2790★
CIGAR ASSOCIATION OF AMERICA - LIBRARY
1120 19th St., N.W., Suite 410
Washington, DC 20036
Defunct

CIMARRON HEIGHTS LIBRARY
See: Eastern Orthodox Catholic Church in America

★2791★
CINCINNATI ART MUSEUM - LIBRARY (Art)
Eden Pk.   Phone: (513) 721-5204
Cincinnati, OH 45202   Patricia P. Rutledge, Libn.
Founded: 1881. **Staff:** Prof 2; Other 2. **Subjects:** Art. **Special Collections:** Cincinnati art; Cincinnati and vicinity artists. **Holdings:** 44,280 books and bound periodical volumes; 800 feet of U.S. and foreign museum, gallery and exhibition catalogs (cataloged); 250,000 pamphlets, clippings; 16,500 mounted pictures. **Subscriptions:** 350 journals and other serials. **Services:** Interlibrary loans; copying; library open to public. **Networks/Consortia:** Member of Greater Cincinnati Library Consortium (GCLC). **Special Catalogs:** File of exhibitions and artists shown at the museum since 1886 (card). **Staff:** Carole Schwartz, Asst.Libn., Archv.

CINCINNATI CENTER FOR DEVELOPMENTAL DISORDERS
See: University Affiliated Cincinnati Center for Developmental Disorders

CINCINNATI CHILDREN'S HOSPITAL - UNIVERSITY AFFILIATED CINCINNATI CENTER FOR DEVELOPMENTAL DISORDERS
See: University Affiliated Cincinnati Center for Developmental Disorders

★2792★
CINCINNATI CITY PLANNING COMMISSION - MUNICIPAL REFERENCE LIBRARY (Plan; Soc Sci)
Rm. 224, City Hall   Phone: (513) 352-3309
Cincinnati, OH 45202   Lawrence P. Annett, Libn.
Founded: 1928. **Staff:** Prof 3; Other 2. **Subjects:** Public administration, municipal government, city planning, urban development, personnel administration, housing, finance. **Special Collections:** Cincinnati government documents. **Holdings:** 7000 books; 42,000 other cataloged items; 40 VF drawers of clippings and pamphlets. **Subscriptions:** 350 journals and other serials. **Services:** Interlibrary loans (limited); library open to government agencies and libraries, civic organizations, and consultants working with the city. **Publications:** Municipal Library Bookshelf, monthly - distributed to city officials and administrators, libraries and local organizations. **Staff:** Iris M. Brawn, Asst.Libn.; Mary Schulte, Asst.Libn.

★2793★
CINCINNATI CITY PLANNING COMMISSION - PLANNING AND MANAGEMENT SUPPORT SYSTEM LIBRARY (Plan)
City Hall, Rm. 141
801 Plum St.   Phone: (513) 352-3441
Cincinnati, OH 45202   Larry Annett, Libn.
Staff: Prof 7; Other 1. **Subjects:** Cincinnati urban affairs and statistics. **Special Collections:** Cincinnati projects and programs (2000 vertical files). **Holdings:** 2000 local government documents; 11,500 slides; 800 data files. **Services:** Copying; library open to public for reference use only. **Computerized Information Services:** Internal database; computerized management reports. **Publications:** Information Update newsletter, monthly - selected recipients. **Staff:** Dick Moran, Hd. of Data Serv.

★2794★
CINCINNATI ELECTRONICS CORPORATION - TECHNICAL LIBRARY (Sci-Tech)
2630 Glendale-Milford Rd.   Phone: (513) 563-6000
Cincinnati, OH 45241   Lois D. Hammond, Chf.Tech.Libn.
Founded: 1955. **Staff:** Prof 2; Other 1. **Subjects:** Communications, electronics, infrared, optics, mathematics, physics. **Holdings:** 7500 books; 2213 bound periodical volumes; 31,000 documents (cataloged). **Subscriptions:** 175 journals and other serials. **Services:** Copying; library open to public for reference use only on request. **Publications:** Library Bulletin - irregular. **Staff:** Ms. Shelby J. Kehrer, Asst.Libn.

CINCINNATI AND HAMILTON COUNTY PUBLIC LIBRARY
See: Public Library of Cincinnati and Hamilton County

★2795★
CINCINNATI HISTORICAL SOCIETY - LIBRARY (Hist)
Eden Park   Phone: (513) 241-4622
Cincinnati, OH 45202   Laura L. Chace, Libn.
Founded: 1831. **Staff:** Prof 8; Other 9. **Subjects:** Northwest Territory, Miami Purchase, Hamilton County and Cincinnati metropolitan area, genealogy. **Special Collections:** James Albert Green Collection of William Henry Harrison; Peter G. Thomson Collection of Ohioana; Cornelius J. Hauck Collections (arboreta); rare books. **Holdings:** 70,000 books and bound periodical volumes; 4700 linear feet of manuscripts; 300,000 photographs; 12,000

slides; 4000 paintings and prints; 2500 maps; 4800 reels of microfilm; 1300 broadsides; 322 linear feet of clippings. **Subscriptions:** 200 journals and other serials. **Services:** Copying; library open to public for reference use only. **Networks/Consortia:** Member of Greater Cincinnati Library Consortium. **Publications:** Bulletin, quarterly. **Special Indexes:** Southwest Ohio vital statistics (card); local history index for Southwest Ohio (card). **Staff:** Gale E. Peterson, Dir.; Mrs. Elmer Forman, Ref.Libn.; Alden N. Monroe, Mss.Supv.; Steven Plattner, Photo Cur.

★2796★
CINCINNATI LAW LIBRARY ASSOCIATION (Law)
601 Courthouse   Phone: (513) 632-8372
Cincinnati, OH 45202   Carol E. Meyer, Hd.Libn.
Founded: 1847. **Staff:** Prof 2; Other 4. **Subjects:** Law. **Special Collections:** Supreme Court Briefs and Records; Ohio Law History; State Session Laws. **Holdings:** 165,000 books; Congressional Index Service; SEC No-Action Letters; Federal Register, 1971 to present; IRS Private Letter Rulings. **Subscriptions:** 425 journals and other serials. **Networks/Consortia:** Member of Greater Cincinnati Library Consortium (GCLC). **Publications:** Model Bibliography for County Law Libraries, 1979, in loose-leaf form; update 1979. **Staff:** Keith Blough, Asst. Law Libn.

★2797★
CINCINNATI MILACRON, INC. - CORPORATE INFORMATION CENTER (Sci-Tech)
4701 Marburg Ave.   Phone: (513) 841-8879
Cincinnati, OH 45209   Rory L. Chase, Corp.Libn.
Founded: 1968. **Staff:** Prof 2; Other 3. **Subjects:** Machine tools, metalworking, polymer chemistry, industrial controls, robotics, automated manufacturing. **Holdings:** 8000 books; 10,000 bound periodical volumes; 2500 other cataloged items; 65 cubic feet of company archival material. **Subscriptions:** 225 journals and other serials. **Services:** Interlibrary loans; copying; SDI; center open to public for reference use only on request. **Computerized Information Services:** DIALOG, BRS, SDC, New York Times Information Service, Dow Jones News Retrieval, MILDOCS (internal database); computerized union list of serials and cataloging. **Networks/Consortia:** Member of Greater Cincinnati Library Consortium (CGLC). **Publications:** NEWS, biweekly; Online Review, quarterly - both for internal distribution only. **Staff:** James W. Clasper, Asst.Corp.Libn.

★2798★
CINCINNATI MUSEUM OF NATURAL HISTORY - LIBRARY (Sci-Tech)
1720 Gilbert Ave.   Phone: (513) 621-3889
Cincinnati, OH 45202   DeVere Burt, Musm.Dir.
Subjects: Natural history. **Holdings:** 5000 books; 1000 bound periodical volumes. **Subscriptions:** 97 journals and other serials. **Services:** Interlibrary loans; copying; library open to museum members and specialists by appointment only.

★2799★
CINCINNATI POST - LIBRARY (Publ)
800 Broadway   Phone: (513) 352-2785
Cincinnati, OH 45202   Elmer L. Geers, Libn.
Founded: 1930. **Staff:** Prof 2. **Holdings:** 750 books; 280 VF drawers of pictures; 56 VF drawers of clippings; microfilm of materials from 1882 to present. **Services:** Library not open to public. **Staff:** Eric Davis, Asst.Libn.

★2800★
CINCINNATI PUBLIC SCHOOLS - PROFESSIONAL LIBRARY (Educ)†
230 E. Ninth St.   Phone: (513) 369-4734
Cincinnati, OH 45202   Paul J. Lee, Libn.
Staff: Prof 1; Other 1. **Subjects:** Education. **Special Collections:** Review collection of supplementary books approved by teacher committees for use in classrooms in support of curriculum. **Holdings:** 8261 books; 10 dissertations pertaining to education; 20 archives volumes on history of Cincinnati schools and Ohio; 618 reels of microfilm; 24,493 microfiche. **Subscriptions:** 182 journals and other serials. **Services:** Interlibrary loans; library open to public by special permission. **Special Catalogs:** Supplementary Books Bulletin, annual bound volume of titles approved for school purchase.

CINDAS
See: Purdue University

★2801★
CINEMATHEQUE QUEBECOISE - ARCHIVES & FILM MUSEUM (Aud-Vis)
335 Blvd. de Maisonneuve E.   Phone: (514) 842-9763
Montreal, PQ, Canada H2X 1K1   Robert Daudelin, Exec.Dir.
Founded: 1963. **Staff:** 20. **Subjects:** Canadian cinema, animation, film history. **Special Collections:** Documents and equipment illustrating the history

of cinema since 1870 (250 apparatus). **Holdings:** 11,000 films; 100,000 stills; 7000 posters; animation documents. **Services:** Facility open to public with restrictions. **Publications:** Copie Zero, bimonthly - by subscription; brochures on Canadian and foreign cinema and filmmakers - price list available. **Staff:** Gisele Cote, Acq.; Louise Beaudet, Hd. of Animation.

★2802★
CINEMATHEQUE QUEBECOISE - CENTRE DE DOCUMENTATION CINEMATOGRAPHIQUE (Aud-Vis)
335 Blvd. de Maisonneuve E.   Phone: (514) 842-9763
Montreal, PQ, Canada H2X 1K1   Rene Beauclair, Hd.Libn.
Staff: Prof 1; Other 5. **Subjects:** Canadian and international cinema, television, photography, mass media. **Special Collections:** Original scripts from Canadian movies. **Holdings:** 30,000 books; 125,000 bound periodical volumes; 300,000 clippings and pamphlets on actors and directors; 600 reels of microfilm; 30,000 vertical files on films and film personalities. **Subscriptions:** 200 journals and other serials; 20 newspapers. **Services:** Copying; library open to public with restrictions. **Publications:** Addition to "Copie Zero", 4/year; dossiers thematiques from press clippings. **Special Indexes:** List of screenplays available at the centre (card); indexes of films, personalities, subjects (card).

CINEMATHEQUE DE LA VILLE DE MONTREAL
See: Bibliotheque de la Ville de Montreal - Cinematheque

★2803★
CINTICHEM, INC. - LIBRARY (Med)
Box 816   Phone: (914) 351-2131
Tuxedo, NY 10987   Shirley Sollinger, Tech.Libn.
Founded: 1958. **Staff:** 1. **Subjects:** Radiopharmaceuticals, radioisotopes, nuclear medicine, biochemistry. **Holdings:** Figures not available for books, bound periodical volumes and microfilms; 40 VF drawers of reports. **Subscriptions:** 117 journals and other serials. **Services:** Interlibrary loans; copying; SDI; library not open to public. **Computerized Information Services:** DIALOG, SDC, MEDLINE. **Remarks:** Division of Medi-Physics, Inc.

★2804★
CIP INC. NATURE CENTRE - LIBRARY (Env-Cons)†
R.R. 2   Phone: (819) 242-6066
Calumet, PQ, Canada J0V 1B0   John Morrison, Ck.
Subjects: Ecology of native tree species, farm woodlot, forest and tree nursery management. **Holdings:** 182 books and bound periodical volumes; 2112 pamphlets and booklets; 700 slides.

★2805★
CIP RESEARCH, LTD. - LIBRARY (Sci-Tech)
                                         Phone: (613) 632-4121
Hawkesbury, ON, Canada K6A 2H4   Ms. M.J. Frey, Libn.
Founded: 1926. **Staff:** Prof 1; Other 1. **Subjects:** Chemistry, paper and allied trades, pulp and paper research, woodlands and forestry, textiles. **Holdings:** 5000 books; 6500 bound periodical volumes; 12,000 patents; 6000 pamphlets. **Subscriptions:** 150 journals and other serials. **Services:** Interlibrary loans; copying; library not open to public. **Computerized Information Services:** DIALOG, SDC, CAN/OLE.

★2806★
CIRCLEVILLE PRESBYTERIAN CHURCH - BOOK NOOK (Rel-Theol)
Rte. 302 & Goshen Tpke.   Phone: (914) 361-9552
Circleville, NY 10919
Staff: 1. **Subjects:** Theology, church history and music, children's literature, Christian living. **Holdings:** 1500 books; filmstrips; reel to reel tapes; cassette tapes; phonograph records. **Services:** Library open to public when church is open.

★2807★
CIRCUS HISTORICAL SOCIETY - LIBRARY (Hist)
2515 Dorset Rd.
Columbus, OH 43221   Fred D. Pfening, Jr.
Founded: 1954. **Subjects:** Circusiana. **Services:** Library not open to public; mail reference service not available.

★2808★
CIRCUS WORLD MUSEUM - LIBRARY (Hist)
415 Lynn St.   Phone: (608) 356-8341
Baraboo, WI 53913   Robert L. Parkinson, Chf.Libn. & Hist.
Founded: 1970. **Staff:** Prof 2. **Subjects:** Circus, Wild West. **Holdings:** 1000 books; 300 bound periodical volumes; 20,000 photographic prints, 19,000 photo negatives; 5000 pieces of circus band music; 6400 lithographs; 300 pieces of original circus lithograph art; 1900 circus programs, 400 route

books; business records, statistical and biographical files. **Services:** Interlibrary loans; copying (limited); library open to public. **Networks/Consortia:** Member of Madison Area Library Council (MALC). **Publications:** Circus World Museum Library - A Guide to its Holdings and Services; List of Loanable Circus Books; Circus Movies for Loan by Mail. **Special Indexes:** Index to 380,000 references to people in the circus field. **Remarks:** Maintained by State Historical Society of Wisconsin. **Staff:** Greg T. Parkinson, Asst.Libn. & Hist.

CIS
See: Congressional Information Service, Inc.

CISTI
See: Canada - National Research Council

★2809★
CITADEL GENERAL ASSURANCE COMPANY - INFORMATION CENTRE (Bus-Fin)
1075 Bay St.   Phone: (416) 928-8539
Toronto, ON, Canada M5S 2W5   Christine Macdonald, Mgr., Plan. & Res.
Founded: 1972. **Staff:** Prof 1; Other 1. **Subjects:** Insurance, business, finance. **Holdings:** 3000 books; 300 archival items; 5000 periodical volumes; 1000 pamphlets and government publications; 13 VF drawers of reprints, annual reports, clippings. **Subscriptions:** 230 journals and other serials; 7 newspapers. **Services:** Interlibrary loans; copying; library open to public by appointment. **Computerized Information Services:** DIALOG, SDC, Info Globe, QL Systems, TEXTLINE, New York Times Information Service. **Publications:** Library Annual Report; Selected List of New Acquisitions, monthly - both for internal distribution only. **Special Catalogs:** Library periodical holdings on MTST tapes.

★2810★
CITADEL - THE MILITARY COLLEGE OF SOUTH CAROLINA - ARCHIVES/ MUSEUM (Hist; Mil)
The Citadel   Phone: (803) 792-6846
Charleston, SC 29409   LCDR Mal J. Collet, Dir.
Staff: Prof 3. **Subjects:** History - military, state and local, Congressional, diplomatic. **Special Collections:** General Mark W. Clark Collection; General William C. Westmoreland; Congressman L. Mendel Rivers; Lt. General George M. Seignious III; VADM Fredrich Ruge, FGN; Bruce Catton; General Hugh P. Harris; The Citadel (1842 to present). **Holdings:** 1200 linear feet of manuscript material. **Services:** Interlibrary loans; copying; library open to public with prior permission. **Staff:** Jane Yates, Archv.; Dorothy S. Turner, Assoc.Cur. of Musm.

★2811★
CITADEL - THE MILITARY COLLEGE OF SOUTH CAROLINA - DANIEL LIBRARY (Mil)
    Phone: (803) 723-0711
Charleston, SC 29409   James M. Hillard, Dir. of Libs.
Founded: 1842. **Staff:** Prof 5; Other 12. **Subjects:** General academic with special emphasis on the military arts and South Carolina. **Holdings:** 178,000 books; 7300 bound periodical volumes; 36,000 government documents (cataloged); 400,000 microfiche. **Subscriptions:** 1417 journals and other serials; 14 newspapers. **Services:** Interlibrary loans; copying; library open to public for reference use only. **Computerized Information Services:** Computerized cataloging. **Networks/Consortia:** Member of OCLC through SOLINET; Low Country Consortium of Higher Education. **Staff:** Herbert T. Nath, Ref.Libn.; Arthur N. Corontzes, Assoc.Dir.; J. Edmund Maynerd, Circ.Libn.; Sherman E. Tyah, Docs. & Ser.

★2812★
CITE RESOURCE CENTER (Educ)
211 E. 7th St.
Southwest Tower   Phone: (512) 476-6861
Austin, TX 78701   Jan B. Anderson, Mgr.
Founded: 1971. **Staff:** Prof 3; Other 1. **Subjects:** Education. **Special Collections:** Curriculum guides; state programs/practices file; ERIC microfiche. **Holdings:** 4000 books and documents (cataloged); 3000 VF materials; 190,000 titles on microfiche. **Subscriptions:** 112 journals and other serials. **Services:** Copying; service open to public on subscription or fee basis. **Computerized Information Services:** DIALOG, BRS. **Publications:** Resource Bibliographies (selected topics). **Staff:** Deborah Daniels, Info.Cons.; Eva Westmoreland, Info.Cons.

★2813★
CITIBANK, N.A. - CITICORP LAW LIBRARY (Law; Bus-Fin)
399 Park Ave., 37th Fl.   Phone: (212) 559-2503
New York, NY 10043   Evelyn Sokol, Law Libn.
Staff: Prof 1; Other 1. **Subjects:** Law, banking. **Holdings:** 5500 books; 45 bound periodical volumes; legal memoranda; microfilm. **Subscriptions:** 24 journals and other serials. **Services:** Interlibrary loans; library not open to public.

★2814★
CITIBANK, N.A. - FINANCIAL LIBRARY (Bus-Fin)
399 Park Ave.   Phone: (212) 559-4559
New York, NY 10043   Conchita J. Pineda, Mgr.
Founded: 1907. **Staff:** Prof 5; Other 8. **Subjects:** Banking, business, economics, finance, management. **Holdings:** 22,550 books; 45,000 bound periodical volumes. **Subscriptions:** 3447 journals and other serials. **Services:** Interlibrary loans; library not open to public. **Computerized Information Services:** DIALOG, Dow Jones News Retrieval. **Publications:** Recent Additions List, bimonthly - for internal distribution only.

★2815★
CITIBANK, N.A. - INVESTMENT LIBRARY (Bus-Fin)
One Citicorp Ctr.
153 E. 53rd St.   Phone: (212) 559-9620
New York, NY 10043   Caroline Marks, Hd.Libn.
Staff: Prof 2; Other 6. **Subjects:** Corporate finance. **Special Collections:** Reports on obsolete companies. **Holdings:** 5000 books and bound periodical volumes; 950 VF drawers of corporate material; 10K reports on New York Stock Exchange and American Stock Exchange, 1969 to present. **Subscriptions:** 90 journals and other serials. **Services:** Interlibrary loans; copying; library open to corporate clients. **Computerized Information Services:** NEXIS.

★2816★
CITICORP/TRANSACTION TECHNOLOGY INC. - TECHNICAL INFORMATION RESEARCH CENTER (Sci-Tech; Bus-Fin)
3100 Ocean Park Blvd., Zone No. 26   Phone: (213) 450-9111
Santa Monica, CA 90405   Zorana Ercegovac, Info.Mgr.
Staff: Prof 2; Other 1. **Subjects:** Computer science and mathematics, banking, electronic funds transfer. **Special Collections:** Electronic Funds Transfer (EFT). **Holdings:** 4000 books; 1200 bound periodical volumes; 70 boxes of pamphlets; inhouse documents; microfiche. **Subscriptions:** 290 journals and other serials; 20 newspapers. **Services:** Interlibrary loans; copying; SDI; library not open to public. **Computerized Information Services:** DIALOG, SDC, BRS, Mead Data Central; computerized cataloging, serials and reference. **Networks/Consortia:** Member of OCLC. **Publications:** TTI Update, monthly. **Special Indexes:** EFT bibliographies. **Staff:** Melissa Jarvis, Lib.Asst.

★2817★
CITIES SERVICE COMPANY - CHEMICALS AND MINERALS MARKET RESEARCH LIBRARY (Sci-Tech)*
201 Bldg.
Box 300
Tulsa, OK 74102   Phone: (918) 561-4892
Founded: 1976. **Staff:** Prof 1. **Subjects:** Statistics, metals, minerals, chemicals, marketing, management. **Holdings:** 1500 books and bound periodical volumes; 16 VF drawers of annual reports; 12 VF drawers of clippings and pamphlets; 13 VF drawers of company reports. **Subscriptions:** 90 journals and other serials; 6 newspapers; 158 bulletins and newsletters. **Services:** Interlibrary loans; copying; library not open to public. **Computerized Information Services:** DIALOG, Copper Development Association; computerized serials, circulation and annual reports. **Publications:** Quarterly Acquisition List; Periodical Update, monthly - both for internal distribution only.

★2818★
CITIES SERVICE COMPANY - ERG - RESEARCH LIBRARY (Energy)
4500 S. 129 E. Ave.
Box 3908   Phone: (918) 561-5271
Tulsa, OK 74102   Linda L. Hill, Mgr.
Founded: 1954. **Staff:** Prof 3; Other 5. **Subjects:** Earth sciences, petroleum technology, paleontology, chemistry, engineering, mathematics, physics. **Holdings:** 9000 books; 1500 maps; 8500 company research reports, theses and government documents. **Subscriptions:** 595 journals and other serials. **Services:** Interlibrary loans; copying; library not open to public. **Computerized Information Services:** DIALOG, SDC; internal database. **Networks/Consortia:** Member of OCLC through AMIGOS Bibliographic Council, Inc. **Publications:** What's New in the Library, biweekly - for internal distribution only. **Staff:** Fred Stair, Libn.; Paige Graening, Libn.

★2819★
CITIES SERVICE COMPANY - LEGAL DIVISION LIBRARY (Law)
110 W. Seventh St.
Box 300   Phone: (918) 586-2272
Tulsa, OK 74102   Alberta Baker, Libn.
Founded: 1917. **Staff:** Prof 1; Other 1. **Subjects:** Oil and gas production, marketing law, taxation, labor law. **Holdings:** 15,000 volumes; 60 company reports; 69 shelves of miscellaneous reports, pamphlets, journals and bulletins; 7 VF drawers of opinions and briefs; 49 cassettes of magnetic tape. **Subscriptions:** 60 journals and other serials. **Services:** Interlibrary loans (limited); library not open to public. **Computerized Information Services:** LEXIS.

★2820★
CITIES SERVICE COMPANY - LIBRARY (Sci-Tech)*
Highway 68   Phone: (615) 496-7919
Copperhill, TN 37317   George DeWitt
Staff: 1. **Subjects:** Chemicals, metals, minerals, mining, pollution abatement. **Holdings:** 2000 books; 150 bound periodical volumes; 3500 magazines (cataloged). **Subscriptions:** 50 journals and other serials. **Services:** Interlibrary loans; copying; library open to public on a limited basis.

★2821★
CITIES SERVICE COMPANY - PLASTICS TECHNICAL CENTER - LIBRARY
3409 Prien Lake Rd.
Lake Charles, LA 70605
Founded: 1979. **Subjects:** Plastics research and development. **Holdings:** 1015 books; 2054 bound periodical volumes; 825 patents; 365 company reports. **Computerized Information Services:** SDC, DIALOG. **Remarks:** Presently inactive.

★2822★
CITIZENS ASSOCIATION FOR SOUND ENERGY (CASE) - LIBRARY (Energy)
Box 4123   Phone: (214) 946-9446
Dallas, TX 75208   Juanita Ellis, Pres.
Subjects: Energy, nuclear energy and waste. **Special Collections:** U.S. Nuclear Regulatory Commission information. **Holdings:** Figures not available. **Services:** Copying (limited); library open to public with restrictions. **Publications:** Newsletter, irregular.

★2823★
CITIZENS' ENERGY PROJECT, INC. - LIBRARY (Energy)
1110 Sixth St., N.W., Suite 300   Phone: (202) 387-8998
Washington, DC 20001   Ken Bossong, Coord.
Staff: Prof 5. **Subjects:** Solar and nuclear energy, environmental protection, appropriate technology. **Holdings:** 1000 books. **Subscriptions:** 100 journals and other serials; 10 newspapers. **Services:** Library open to public with restrictions. **Publications:** Soft Solar Notes, bimonthly.

★2824★
CITIZENS' ENERGY PROJECT, INC. - PASSIVE SOLAR FOUNDATION - LIBRARY (Energy)
1110 Sixth St., N.W., Suite 300   Phone: (202) 387-8998
Washington, DC 20001   Ken Bossong, Coord.
Staff: 2. **Subjects:** Passive solar design. **Holdings:** 150 books; newsletters and magazines. **Subscriptions:** 40 journals and other serials. **Services:** Library open to public with restrictions. **Publications:** Homeowners' Guide to Passive Solar (12-page report); National Passive Solar Directory; Passive Solar Retrofit Handbook.

★2825★
CITIZENS FORUM ON SELF-GOVERNMENT/NATIONAL MUNICIPAL LEAGUE, INC. - MURRAY SEASONGOOD LIBRARY (Soc Sci)
47 E. 68th St.   Phone: (212) 535-5700
New York, NY 10021   Joan A. Casey, Dir., Lib./Pubns.
Staff: Prof 1; Other 1. **Subjects:** Political science, public administration, state and local government, metropolitan areas. **Special Collections:** Municipal charters; state constitutional convention studies; reapportionment studies. **Holdings:** 10,000 volumes; 48 VF drawers. **Subscriptions:** 100 journals and other serials. **Services:** Interlibrary loans; library open to public for reference use only. **Publications:** Acquisitions listed in National Civic Review, monthly - to all league members.

★2826★
CITIZENS' GOVERNMENTAL RESEARCH BUREAU, INC. (Soc Sci)
125 E. Wells St., Rm. 616   Phone: (414) 276-8240
Milwaukee, WI 53202   Norman N. Gill, Exec.Dir.
Founded: 1913. **Subjects:** Local government, urban concerns of state government, municipal administration, local school districts. **Special**

Collections: Data about local governments and school districts in 4-county Milwaukee metropolitan area. **Holdings:** 3000 books; 100 bound periodical volumes; clippings files (cataloged); unbound reports, manuscripts, clippings, archives, documents. **Subscriptions:** 50 journals and other serials; 22 newspapers. **Services:** Interlibrary loans (limited); copying (limited); library open to public with permission. **Publications:** Bulletin, published 10 to 15 times/year - to mailing list of public officials and other opinion leaders.

★2827★
CITIZENS HOUSING AND PLANNING COUNCIL OF NEW YORK - LIBRARY (Plan)
20 W. 40th St.   Phone: (212) 391-9030
New York, NY 10018   Marian Sameth, Assoc.Dir.
Staff: 1. **Subjects:** Housing and planning. **Holdings:** 2000 books; 26 VF drawers of unbound material. **Subscriptions:** 13 journals and other serials. **Services:** Interlibrary loans; copying; library open to public for reference use only.

CITIZENS INFORMATION CENTER
See: Anthropology Research Center (ARC)

★2828★
CITIZENS LAW LIBRARY (Law)*
202 Courthouse Sq.   Phone: (412) 834-2191
Greensburg, PA 15601   Peter P. Cherellia, Libn.
Staff: 2. **Subjects:** Law. **Holdings:** 20,000 volumes. **Subscriptions:** 17 journals and other serials. **Services:** Copying; library open to public for reference use only. **Staff:** Gerald M. McClain, Libn.

★2829★
CITIZENS' RESEARCH FOUNDATION - LIBRARY (Soc Sci)
University of Southern California
Research Annex, 3716 S. Hope St.   Phone: (213) 743-5440
Los Angeles, CA 90007   Herbert E. Alexander, Dir.
Subjects: Political finance, fund-raising methods, campaign expenditures, group and individual financial participation in the electoral process. **Holdings:** 2000 volumes; files of research data. **Services:** Copying (limited); library open to public for reference use only.

CITIZENS SAVINGS ATHLETIC FOUNDATION
See: First Interstate Bank Athletic Foundation

★2830★
CITIZENS UNION OF THE CITY OF NEW YORK - LIBRARY (Soc Sci)
198 Broadway   Phone: (212) 227-0342
New York, NY 10038   Vance Benguiat, Exec.Dir.
Subjects: New York City politics and government since the turn of the century. **Holdings:** Figures not available for books and documents. **Services:** Library open to public by appointment; contact the executive director of the Citizen's Union.

CITRUS RESEARCH & DEVELOPMENT TECHNICAL LIBRARY
See: Coca-Cola Company - Foods Division

★2831★
CITY COLLEGE OF SAN FRANCISCO - HOTEL AND RESTAURANT DEPARTMENT - ALICE STATLER LIBRARY (Bus-Fin; Food-Bev)
50 Phelan Ave.   Phone: (415) 239-3460
San Francisco, CA 94112   Mary B. Smyth, Lib.Mgr.
Founded: 1964. **Staff:** Prof 1. **Subjects:** Public hospitality industries (including hotels, motels, restaurants, catering services, cafeterias, school lunches); cookery and nutrition; tourism; wines and other beverages. **Special Collections:** American Hotel Institute materials (nearly complete set, including texts, student manuals and instructors guides); menu collection from all over the world (2000 items); complete bound files of the seven leading magazines in the field, dating back to 1897. **Holdings:** 8300 books; 900 bound periodical volumes; 7000 pamphlets (cataloged); 16 16mm training films. **Subscriptions:** 85 journals and other serials. **Services:** Interlibrary loans; copying; library open to public for reference use only. **Computerized Information Services:** Computerized cataloging. **Publications:** Yearly acquisition lists; special subject lists - distributed on request. **Remarks:** "Our library has the most complete coverage of the public hospitality field in the West."

★2832★
CITY OF COMMERCE PUBLIC LIBRARY (Bus-Fin)
5655 Jillson St.   Phone: (213) 722-6660
Commerce, CA 90040   Lois E. McClish, Dir.
Founded: 1961. **Staff:** Prof 5; Other 20. **Subjects:** Business management,

coatings technology, investment, law, paint varnish. **Holdings:** 85,000 books; industrial directories. **Subscriptions:** 400 journals and other serials. **Services:** Interlibrary loans; copying; library open to public; registration fee charged to those who do not live in Commerce. **Networks/Consortia:** Member of Metropolitan Cooperative Library System (MCLS). **Publications:** Paint Bibliography. **Staff:** Catherine Penprase, Adult Serv.Supv.; Ruth Hergonson, Ch.Serv.Supv.; Corinne Bradbury, Tech.Serv.Supv.

★2833★
CITY OF HOPE NATIONAL MEDICAL CENTER - PINESS MEDICAL AND SCIENTIFIC LIBRARY (Med)
Duarte, CA 91010
Phone: (213) 359-8111
John L. Carrigan, Dir.
Staff: Prof 2; Other 3. **Subjects:** Neuroscience, immunology, biomedicine, medical genetics, biochemistry, biology, pediatrics, cancer pathology. **Holdings:** 4300 books; 20,000 bound periodical volumes. **Subscriptions:** 700 journals and other serials. **Services:** Interlibrary loans; copying; SDI; library open to public. **Computerized Information Services:** DIALOG, NLM, SDC, Lithium Library, RLIN, Chemical Information Services. **Networks/Consortia:** Member of OCLC. **Staff:** Joan Krinsky, Libn.

CITY HOSPITAL CENTER AT ELMHURST
See: Mount Sinai Hospital Services

★2834★
CITY OF INDUSTRY - RALPH W. MILLER GOLF LIBRARY (Hist)
One Industry Hills Pkwy.
Box 3287
City of Industry, CA 91744
Phone: (213) 965-0861
Jean Bryant, Lib.Dir.
Staff: Prof 1; Other 5. **Subjects:** Golf, Scottish history. **Special Collections:** Golf memorabilia and other museum items (500). **Holdings:** 4500 books; 500 bound periodical volumes; 7000 photographs, art and museum pieces; 2500 bound articles on golf, 1890 to present; newspaper clippings, 1900 to present, some on microfiche; 1 VF drawer of archival materials. **Subscriptions:** 40 journals and other serials. **Services:** Copying; library open to public for reference use only. **Special Indexes:** Subject index for newspaper clippings; subject and author index for magazine articles.

★2835★
CITY OF TORONTO ARCHIVES (Hist)
City Hall
100 Queen St., W.
Toronto, ON, Canada M5H 2N2
Phone: (416) 367-7483
R. Scott James, Dir. of Rec./City Archv.
Founded: 1960. **Staff:** Prof 15; Other 17. **Subjects:** Corporation of the city of Toronto. **Holdings:** 1100 books; 45,000 cubic feet of government records, papers of elected officials, papers of individuals and organizations related to the city of Toronto. **Subscriptions:** 6 journals and other serials. **Services:** Copying; archives open to public with restrictions. **Computerized Information Services:** Access to online systems. **Publications:** Market Gallery exhibition catalogs; guide to fine art collection; guide to record group collections. **Staff:** Victor L. Russell, Archv.Supv.

CITY UNIVERSITY OF NEW YORK
See: CUNY

CITYLINE INFORMATION SERVICE
See: Oakland Public Library

★2836★
CIVIC GARDEN CENTRE - LIBRARY (Sci-Tech)
777 Lawrence Ave., E.
Don Mills, ON, Canada M3C 1P2
Phone: (416) 445-1552
Pamela MacKenzie, Libn.
Founded: 1964. **Staff:** Prof 1; Other 2. **Subjects:** Horticulture, flower arranging, garden design, herbs, botany, natural history, Canadiana. **Special Collections:** Historical Canadian books on horticulture. **Holdings:** 5000 books; 9 VF drawers. **Subscriptions:** 43 journals and other serials. **Services:** Interlibrary loans; copying; library open to public for reference use only. **Publications:** Trellis, bimonthly - to members.

CIVIL AERONAUTICS BOARD
See: U.S. Civil Aeronautics Board

★2837★
CIVIL AIR PATROL - NATIONAL HEADQUARTERS AEROSPACE EDUCATION REFERENCE LIBRARY
National Headquarters
Maxwell AFB, AL 36112
Subjects: Aviation history, aerospace education, space exploration. **Remarks:** Presently inactive.

CIVIL ENGINEER CORPS
See: U.S. Navy - Naval School

CK PERMANENT PRESS - PARMAR ELDALIEVA LIBRARY
See: Parmar Eldalieva Library

★2838★
CLACKAMAS COUNTY, OREGON - ALDEN E. MILLER LAW LIBRARY (Law)
Clackamas County Courthouse, Rm. 302
Oregon City, OR 97045
Phone: (503) 655-8248
Ailsa Mackenzie Werner, Law Libn.
Staff: Prof 1. **Subjects:** Law. **Holdings:** 1000 books; 11,000 bound periodical volumes. **Subscriptions:** 700 journals and other serials. **Services:** Interlibrary loans; copying; library open to public for reference use only.

★2839★
CLAIROL, INC. - RESEARCH LIBRARY (Sci-Tech)
2 Blachley Rd.
Stamford, CT 06922
Phone: (203) 357-5001
Theodora J. Reardon, Libn.
Staff: Prof 2. **Subjects:** Chemistry and technology of cosmetics, hair dyes and dyeing, personal care, appliances. **Holdings:** 3500 books; 6000 bound periodical volumes; 30 titles on microfilm. **Subscriptions:** 230 journals and other serials. **Services:** Library open to public with restrictions. **Computerized Information Services:** DIALOG, SDC, NLM, NIH-EPA Chemical Information System. **Staff:** Gail C. Smith, Asst.Libn.

CLAPP (Mary Norton) LIBRARY
See: Occidental College - Mary Norton Clapp Library

CLAPP (William F.) LABORATORIES, INC.
See: Battelle New England Research Laboratory - William F. Clapp Laboratories, Inc.

CLAREMONT COLLEGES - CALIFORNIA INSTITUTE OF PUBLIC AFFAIRS
See: California Institute of Public Affairs

★2840★
CLAREMONT COLLEGES - ELLA STRONG DENISON LIBRARY (Hum)
Scripps College
Claremont, CA 91711
Phone: (714) 621-8000
Judy Harvey Sahak, Libn.
Founded: 1931. **Staff:** Prof 2; Other 2. **Subjects:** Humanities and fine arts. **Special Collections:** Perkins and Kirby (history of the book and book arts); Macpherson (women); Metcalf (Gertrude Stein); Pacific Coast Browning Foundation (Browning); Hanna (Southwest); Miller-Howard (Latin America); Ament (Melville); Louise Seymour Jones (3000 bookplates); original and revised versions of Richard W. Armour (62 titles including 43 manuscripts). **Holdings:** 89,770 books. **Services:** Interlibrary loans; copying; library open to public with restrictions. **Computerized Information Services:** Computerized cataloging, acquisitions, serials and circulation. **Networks/Consortia:** Member of OCLC. **Remarks:** This is one of the participating libraries of the Libraries of The Claremont Colleges. **Staff:** Susan Allen, Ref.Libn.

CLAREMONT COLLEGES - FRANCIS BACON FOUNDATION
See: Francis Bacon Foundation

CLAREMONT COLLEGES - FRANK P. BRACKETT OBSERVATORY LIBRARY
See: Claremont Colleges - Library

★2841★
CLAREMONT COLLEGES - LIBRARY (Hum; Soc Sci)
800 Dartmouth
Claremont, CA 91711
Phone: (714) 621-8000
Patrick Barkey, Dir.
Founded: 1952. **Staff:** Prof 22; Other 36. **Subjects:** Humanities, social sciences, natural science, science and technology. **Special Collections:** California and Western Americana (7189 volumes); Water Resources Development of Southern California (1309 volumes); Oxford and its Colleges (4457 volumes); Mrs. Humphry Ward (1800 items); Florentine Renaissance (3252 volumes); Hymnology (3452 volumes); Northern Europe and Scandinavia (3600 volumes); Oriental languages and literature (50,000 volumes). **Holdings:** 1 million books and bound periodical volumes; 23,300 reels of microfilm; 725,000 units of other forms of microtext. **Subscriptions:** 6575 journals and other serials. **Services:** Copying; library open to public with restrictions. **Computerized Information Services:** Computerized cataloging, acquisitions, serials, circulation and fund control. **Networks/Consortia:** Member of OCLC. **Remarks:** The Claremont Colleges are composed of Pomona College, Claremont Graduate School, Scripps College, Claremont Men's College, Harvey Mudd College, Pitzer College. The Claremont Colleges Libraries include the holdings of the library of the Frank P. Brackett Observatory. **Staff:** George M. Bailey, Assoc.Dir. of Libs.; Judy Harvey Sahak, Asst.Dir.; Robert F. Teare, Asst.Dir., Tech.Serv.; David Kuhner, Asst.Dir., Sci.

★2842★
CLAREMONT COLLEGES - NORMAN F. SPRAGUE MEMORIAL LIBRARY (Sci-Tech)
Harvey Mudd College
Claremont, CA 91711
Phone: (714) 621-8000
David Kuhner, Libn.
Founded: 1972. **Staff:** Prof 2; Other 2. **Subjects:** Science, history of science, engineering. **Special Collections:** The "De Re Metallica" Library of President and Mrs. Herbert Hoover (1010 volumes; 21 manuscripts; 441 letters); Carruthers' History of Aviation Collection (4000 volumes). **Holdings:** 60,000 books and bound periodical volumes; 105 reels of microfilm; 27,000 technical reports; 7000 microfiche; 35 film loops; 1050 pamphlets. **Subscriptions:** 663 journals and other serials. **Services:** Interlibrary loans; copying; library open to public with restrictions. **Computerized Information Services:** Computerized cataloging, acquisitions, serials and circulation. **Networks/Consortia:** Member of OCLC; Southern California Interlibrary Loan Network (SCILL). **Special Catalogs:** Bibliotheca De Re Metallica, 1980. **Remarks:** This is one of the participating libraries of the Libraries of The Claremont Colleges. **Staff:** Beverly McCracken, Ref.Libn.

CLAREMONT COLLEGES - POMONA SCIENCE LIBRARIES
See: Claremont Colleges - Seeley G. Mudd Science Library

★2843★
CLAREMONT COLLEGES - SEELEY G. MUDD SCIENCE LIBRARY (Sci-Tech)
Pomona College
Claremont, CA 91711
Phone: (714) 621-8000
David Kuhner, Libn.
Subjects: Botany, chemistry, geology, mathematics, physics-astronomy, and zoology. **Holdings:** 80,000 volumes; 500 reels of microfilm; 3000 microfiche. **Subscriptions:** 686 journals and other serials. **Services:** Interlibrary loans; copying; library open to public with restrictions. **Computerized Information Services:** Computerized cataloging, acquisitions, serials and circulation. **Networks/Consortia:** Member of OCLC. **Remarks:** These libraries are part of the Libraries of The Claremont Colleges. **Formerly:** The Pomona Science Libraries. **Staff:** Brian Ebersole, Ref.Libn.

★2844★
CLAREMONT GRADUATE SCHOOL - EDUCATIONAL RESOURCE & INFORMATION CENTER (Educ)
131 E. Tenth St.
Claremont, CA 91711
Phone: (714) 621-8000
Julie L. Robinson, Mng.Libn.
Founded: 1935. **Staff:** Prof 1; Other 1. **Subjects:** Education. **Holdings:** 5487 books; 6013 pamphlets; 496 critiques; 535 tests. **Subscriptions:** 60 journals and other serials. **Services:** Interlibrary loans; center open to public with restrictions (annual fee, otherwise no borrowing privileges).

★2845★
CLAREMONT GRADUATE SCHOOL - GEORGE G. STONE CENTER FOR CHILDREN'S BOOKS (Hum)
131 E. Tenth St.
Claremont, CA 91711
Phone: (714) 621-8000
Julie L. Robinson, Mng.Libn.
Founded: 1965. **Staff:** Prof 1; Other 1. **Subjects:** Children's literature; materials about children's literature; old children's books. **Holdings:** 14,000 books; 48 bound periodical volumes. **Subscriptions:** 26 journals and other serials. **Services:** Interlibrary loans; center open to public with restrictions (annual fee, otherwise no borrowing privileges). **Networks/Consortia:** Member of Southern California Answering Network (SCAN). **Publications:** Unicorn Booklist, semiannual; Children's Books for Holiday Giving, annual; Recognition of Merit, annual booklet; distributed to members, classes and from the library.

CLAREMONT MEN'S COLLEGE
See: Claremont Colleges - Library

CLAREMONT UNIVERSITY CENTER - BLAISDELL INSTITUTE FOR ADVANCED STUDY IN WORLD CULTURES AND RELIGIONS
See: Blaisdell Institute for Advanced Study in World Cultures and Religions

★2846★
CLARINDA MENTAL HEALTH INSTITUTION - RESIDENTS AND STAFF LIBRARY (Med)
Box 338
Clarinda, IA 51632
Phone: (712) 585-2161
Dorothy Horton, Libn.
Founded: 1941. **Staff:** Prof 1. **Subjects:** Psychiatry, psychology, psychiatric nursing, social services education, pastoral counseling, maintenance and dietary services. **Holdings:** 12,623 books; 481 bound periodical volumes; 3 VF drawers; 420 cassette tapes; 272 phonograph records. **Subscriptions:** 64 journals and other serials; 45 newspapers. **Services:** Interlibrary loans; library open to students and mental health professionals. **Remarks:** Maintained by Iowa State Mental Health Institute.

★2847★
CLARION COUNTY HISTORICAL SOCIETY - LIBRARY/MUSEUM (Hist)
18 Grant St.
Clarion, PA 16214
Phone: (814) 226-4450
Elisabeth S. Fulmer, Libn.
Founded: 1958. **Subjects:** Genealogy, Pennsylvania history. **Holdings:** 900 books; 50 bound newspapers; 2 files of pictures, pamphlets, documents, cemetery records. **Services:** Copying; library open to public with restrictions.

★2848★
CLARION STATE COLLEGE - RENA M. CARLSON LIBRARY (Educ)
Phone: (814) 226-2343
Clarion, PA 16214
Gerard B. McCabe, Dir. of Libs.
Founded: 1867. **Staff:** Prof 15; Other 17. **Subjects:** Business administration, education, teacher education, library science, special education. **Special Collections:** British Commonwealth History Collection. **Holdings:** 291,898 books; 35,727 bound periodical volumes; 786,019 microforms; 715 motion pictures; 5539 audio recordings; 3873 filmstrips; 4084 slides and overhead transparencies; 1702 maps and charts; 1669 mixed media items. **Subscriptions:** 1409 journals and newspapers. **Services:** Interlibrary loans; copying; library open to public. **Networks/Consortia:** Member of OCLC through Pittsburgh Regional Library Center; Northwest Interlibrary Cooperative of Pennsylvania. **Remarks:** Above figures include the holdings of the library at Venango Campus, Oil City, PA. **Staff:** Melayn Dorfler, Ser.Libn.; Mary E. Williams, Venango Campus Libn.; C. Richard Snow, Venango Campus Libn; Kenneth Emerick, Cat.; John Mager, Cat.; J. Kenneth Wyse, Cat.; Janice Horn, Hd.Cat.; Connie Gamaluddin, Ref.Libn.; Nancy McKee, Hd.Ref.Libn.; Roger Horn, Circ.Libn.; Elaine Moore, Lrng.Rsrcs.; James McDaniel, Instr.Mtls.Cat.; Debra Decker, Instr.Mtls.Ctr.

★2849★
CLARK COLLEGE - SOUTHERN CENTER FOR STUDIES IN PUBLIC POLICY - RESEARCH LIBRARY (Soc Sci)
240 Chestnut St., S.W.
Atlanta, GA 30314
Phone: (404) 752-6422
Mrs. Ollye G. Davis, Res.Libn.
Founded: 1968. **Staff:** Prof 2; Other 2. **Subjects:** Economic development, public policy, transportation, employment and labor, blacks and civil rights, poverty. **Special Collections:** Robert Brown Collection; Andrew Brimmer Papers (15 papers). **Holdings:** 5000 books; 325 bound periodical volumes; 6 VF drawers of clippings; 10 tapes each of the National Longitudinal Survey, the Panel Study of Income Dynamics, and the 1980 Census Report. **Subscriptions:** 185 journals and other serials; 6 newspapers. **Services:** Interlibrary loans; copying; library open to public for reference use only. **Computerized Information Services:** DIALOG; computerized cataloging. **Networks/Consortia:** Member of Atlanta Online Users Group. **Publications:** So You Are Doing Research, biennial. **Special Indexes:** Index of journal articles dealing with public policy issues. **Remarks:** Contains the holdings of the former Black Economic Research Center - Reference Library. **Staff:** Howard Pitts, Lib.Asst.

★2850★
CLARK COUNTY DISTRICT HEALTH DEPARTMENT - LIBRARY (Med)
625 Shadow Ln.
Las Vegas, NV 89127
Phone: (702) 385-1291
Janet Dolan, Health Info.Spec.
Founded: 1962. **Staff:** Prof 3. **Subjects:** Environmental health, emergency medical service, public health nursing, air pollution control, epidemiology. **Holdings:** 500 books; health pamphlets (cataloged); newsclippings; 3 VF drawers of health reprints; filmstrips; 16mm films. **Services:** Interlibrary loans; copying (limited); film loans; library open to public for reference use only.

★2851★
CLARK COUNTY HISTORICAL SOCIETY - LIBRARY (Hist)
Memorial Hall, 300 W. Main St.
Springfield, OH 45504
Phone: (513) 324-0657
Founded: 1897. **Subjects:** Clark County and Ohio history. **Special Collections:** Springfield city directories from 1852; newspapers from 1829. **Holdings:** 1000 books; 7500 archival items. **Subscriptions:** 10 journals and other serials. **Services:** Interlibrary loans; copying; library open to public. **Publications:** Monograph, annual; newsletter, monthly. **Special Catalogs:** Books, cemetery inscriptions, archival material, early businesses (card).

★2852★
CLARK COUNTY HISTORICAL SOCIETY - PIONEER MUSEUM - LIBRARY (Hist)
430 W. Fourth
Ashland, KS 67831
Phone: (316) 635-2227
Florence E. Hurd, Cur.
Founded: 1968. **Staff:** 1. **Subjects:** County and state history. **Special**

Collections: Early cattle era pictorial records; Kansas State Historical Society volumes, 1891 to present (214). **Holdings:** 10 VF drawers of manuscripts; Clark County newspapers, 1884 to present. **Services:** Library not open to public. **Publications:** Early Clark County, Kansas, 6 volumes; Kings and Queens of the Range, photographs of Clark County taken 1894-1904.

★2853★
CLARK COUNTY LAW LIBRARY
215 S. Third
Las Vegas, NV 89101
Founded: 1923. **Subjects:** Law. **Holdings:** 45,000 volumes, including all available Nevada case, statutory and legislative material, U.S. Supreme Court and federal cases, federal codes, cases and statutes of all 50 states, legal encyclopedias, periodicals, texts and treatises, loose-leaf services, form books, and city and county codes. **Special Indexes:** Legal Digests and Citators; Index to Legal Periodicals; Advance Nevada Digest. **Remarks:** Presently inactive.

★2854★
CLARK COUNTY LAW LIBRARY (Law)
Court House, Rm. 302
Box 5000   Phone: (206) 699-2268
Vancouver, WA 98668   Barbara Rowland, Libn.
Staff: 1. **Subjects:** Law. **Holdings:** 10,000 volumes. **Services:** Library open to public with restrictions. **Remarks:** Maintained by Clark County Bar Association.

★2855★
CLARK COUNTY MEMORIAL HOSPITAL - MEDICAL LIBRARY (Med)
1220 Missouri Ave.   Phone: (812) 283-2358
Jeffersonville, IN 47130   Becky Lacefield, Med.Libn.
Founded: 1971. **Staff:** Prof 1. **Subjects:** Medicine, nursing. **Holdings:** 400 books; 200 bound periodical volumes; 2 VF drawers of pamphlet material; 140 video cassettes; 1 video cassette series; 2 audio cassette series. **Subscriptions:** 80 journals and other serials. **Services:** Interlibrary loans; copying; library not open to public. **Networks/Consortia:** Member of Kentucky Health Sciences Library Consortium.

★2856★
CLARK COUNTY REGIONAL PLANNING COUNCIL - LIBRARY (Plan)†
1408 Franklin
Box 5000
Vancouver, WA 98668   Phone: (206) 699-2361
Founded: 1968. **Staff:** 1. **Subjects:** Planning, land use, urban studies, population, demography, pollution, recreation and parks, sewage disposal, water quality, transportation and zoning. **Subscriptions:** 24 journals and other serials. **Services:** Library open to public with restrictions.

CLARK (David G.) MEMORIAL PHYSICS LIBRARY
See: University of New Hampshire - David G. Clark Memorial Physics Library

★2857★
CLARK DIETZ ENGINEERS - LIBRARY (Sci-Tech)
211 N. Race St.   Phone: (217) 384-1400
Urbana, IL 61801   Felicia Bagby, Libn.
Staff: Prof 1; Other 1. **Subjects:** Environmental, structural and highway engineering; industrial wastes. **Holdings:** 3000 books; 1750 volumes of government publications; 1850 company specifications and reports. **Subscriptions:** 100 journals and other serials. **Services:** Copying; library not open to public. **Computerized Information Services:** DIALOG. **Networks/Consortia:** Member of ILLINET. **Remarks:** Library also houses the company archives.

CLARK (Edith M.) HISTORY ROOM
See: Rowan Public Library - Edith M. Clark History Room

CLARK FIELD ARCHIVES
See: University of New Mexico - Department of Anthropology

CLARK (Harold Terry) LIBRARY
See: Cleveland Museum of Natural History - Harold Terry Clark Library

CLARK (J. Reuben) LAW SCHOOL LIBRARY
See: Brigham Young University - J. Reuben Clark Law School Library

★2858★
CLARK, KLEIN AND BEAUMONT - LAW LIBRARY (Law)
1600 First Federal Bldg.
1001 Woodward Ave.   Phone: (313) 962-6492
Detroit, MI 48226
Staff: Prof 1. **Subjects:** Law - tax, antitrust and securities, corporate, real estate, labor, trial, interstate commerce, wills and trusts. **Holdings:** 10,761 books. **Subscriptions:** 15 journals and other serials. **Services:** Interlibrary loans; library open to public with restrictions.

CLARK (Dr. Leslie J.) MEMORIAL LIBRARY
See: Hemet Valley Hospital District - Dr. Leslie J. Clark Memorial Library

CLARK (Lydia Jane) LIBRARY
See: Pennsylvania Hospital - Department for Sick and Injured - Medical Library

CLARK SCIENCE LIBRARY
See: Smith College

★2859★
CLARK (Sterling and Francine) ART INSTITUTE - LIBRARY (Art)
South St.
Box 8   Phone: (413) 458-8109
Williamstown, MA 01267   Michael Rinehart, Libn.
Founded: 1962. **Staff:** Prof 4; Other 6. **Subjects:** European and American art. **Special Collections:** Juynboll collection (700,000 reproductions of works of art); Mary Ann Beinecke decorative art collection; Duveen Library and archive. **Holdings:** 75,000 volumes; 24,000 auction sales catalogs; 72,000 slides. **Subscriptions:** 474 journals and other serials. **Services:** Interlibrary loans; copying; library open to public. **Computerized Information Services:** Computerized cataloging. **Networks/Consortia:** Member of RLG. **Publications:** Occasional exhibition catalogs. **Special Indexes:** Index of auction sales catalogs (card). **Staff:** Susan Roeper, Cat.; Marshall Lapidus, Asst.Libn.; Dustin Wees, Slide Libn.

CLARK (Theda) REGIONAL MEDICAL CENTER
See: Theda Clark Regional Medical Center

★2860★
CLARK UNIVERSITY - GRADUATE SCHOOL OF GEOGRAPHY - GUY H. BURNHAM MAP-AERIAL PHOTOGRAPH LIBRARY (Geog-Map)
950 Main St.   Phone: (617) 793-7322
Worcester, MA 01610
Founded: 1920. **Staff:** Prof 1; Other 2. **Subjects:** General map library. **Special Collections:** Depository for Defense Mapping Agency and U.S. Geological Survey series; Libbey Lantern Slide Collection (slides of expeditions around the world); J.K. Wright Reading Room (geographic materials for Clark community). **Holdings:** 2000 books; 132,000 maps (cataloged); 200 documents (bound); 10,000 items of unbound material. **Subscriptions:** 25 journals and other serials. **Services:** Interlibrary loans; library open to public with restrictions. **Networks/Consortia:** Member of Worcester Consortium for Higher Education (WCHE). **Publications:** Clark Geophile, bimonthly.

CLARK (William Andrews) MEMORIAL LIBRARY
See: University of California, Los Angeles - William Andrews Clark Memorial Library

★2861★
CLARK (William H.) ASSOCIATES, INC. - RESEARCH LIBRARY (Bus-Fin)†
330 Madison Ave.   Phone: (212) 661-8760
New York, NY 10017   Judith Stein, Dir. of Res.
Founded: 1956. **Staff:** Prof 4. **Subjects:** Finance, real estate, manufacturing, consulting, engineering, medicine, pharmaceuticals, law, publishing, marketing, transportation, government, business. **Holdings:** 600 books; 21 volumes of studies on compensation; 26 drawers of unbound reports on corporations; 25,000 information files on business executives. **Subscriptions:** 35 journals and other serials; 6 newspapers. **Services:** Library open to public with permission. **Special Catalogs:** Industry Trends; Executive Compensation Trends. **Remarks:** Branch offices in Chicago and Los Angeles have microfilm indexes to this library.

CLARK (William J.) LIBRARY
See: Virginia Union University - William J. Clark Library

CLARKE HISTORICAL LIBRARY
See: Central Michigan University

★2862★
CLARKE INSTITUTE OF PSYCHIATRY - FARRAR LIBRARY (Med)†
250 College St.   Phone: (416) 979-2221
Toronto, ON, Canada M5T 1R8   Dawn Stewardson, Libn./Archv.
Subjects: Psychiatry, psychology, psychiatric nursing, neuroendocrinology, neurochemistry, occupational therapy, social work. **Holdings:** 6500 books; 6500 bound periodical volumes; 10 VF drawers of reprints; 12 VF drawers of staff publications; 2 VF drawers of government documents. **Subscriptions:** 350 journals and other serials. **Services:** Interlibrary loans; copying; library not open to public.

CLARKSON (Bishop) MEMORIAL HOSPITAL
See: Bishop Clarkson Memorial Hospital

★2863★
CLARKSON COLLEGE OF TECHNOLOGY - EDUCATIONAL RESOURCES CENTER (Sci-Tech)
                                             Phone: (315) 268-2292
Potsdam, NY 13676   Martin P. Wilson, Assoc.Dir.
Founded: 1980. **Staff:** Prof 7; Other 9. **Subjects:** Engineering - chemical, civil and environmental, mechanical and industrial, electrical and computer; chemistry; physics; biology; mathematics; management; humanities; social sciences. **Special Collections:** NASA Publication Program. **Holdings:** 83,137 books; 40,985 bound periodical volumes; 41,105 technical reports (hard copy); 2550 college catalogs (microfiche); 152 telephone books; 61,855 U.S. Government documents; 675 dissertations; 1814 master's theses; 39 maps; 4869 pamphlets; 1101 phonograph records; 6884 reels of microfilm; 145,088 microfiche. **Subscriptions:** 1937 journals and other serials; 13 newspapers. **Services:** Interlibrary loans; copying; SDI; library open to public with identification. **Computerized Information Services:** DIALOG, BRS, SDC, DOE/RECON; computerized cataloging, serials and circulation. **Networks/Consortia:** Member of OCLC; Associated Colleges of the St. Lawrence Valley, Inc.; North Country Reference & Research Resources Council (NCRRRC). **Publications:** Library Notes, irregular; Accession List, monthly - all distributed to college community and members of consortium. **Staff:** Rosanna H. Rosse, Hd., Rd.Serv.; J. Natalia Stahl, Ser. & Acq.Libn.; Gayle C. Berry, ILL Libn.; Byron V. Whitney, Hd., Tech.Serv.; Janet Van Weringh, Info.Ret.Libn.

★2864★
CLARKSON GORDON - BUSINESS LIBRARY (Bus-Fin)
630 Dorchester Blvd., West   Phone: (514) 875-6060
Montreal, PQ, Canada H3B 1T9   Margaret Cameron, Libn.
Founded: 1971. **Staff:** Prof 1. **Subjects:** Accounting, tax, management consulting. **Holdings:** 3000 books; 90 bound periodical volumes; 600 annual reports; 100 specialized marketing reports. **Subscriptions:** 120 journals and other serials; 10 newspapers. **Services:** Interlibrary loans; copying; library open to public by appointment. **Special Catalogs:** Internal publications catalog.

★2865★
CLARKSON, GORDON/WOODS, GORDON - LIBRARY (Bus-Fin)
Box 251, Toronto Dominion Centre   Phone: (416) 864-1234
Toronto, ON, Canada M5K 1J7   Karen Melville, Libn.
Founded: 1959. **Staff:** Prof 2; Other 2. **Subjects:** Accounting, tax legislation, management consulting, economics, marketing, data processing. **Special Collections:** Canadian companies financial reports and prospectuses (30 VF drawers). **Holdings:** 12,000 volumes; 12 VF drawers of U.S. and foreign financial reports; 1 VF drawer of maps. **Subscriptions:** 440 journals and other serials. **Services:** Interlibrary loans; copying; library not open to public. **Computerized Information Services:** DIALOG, SDC, Info Globe, New York Times Information Service, QL Systems; computerized serials. **Publications:** Acquisitions list, monthly; serials list, annual - for internal distribution only. **Special Indexes:** Subject guide to serials holdings. **Remarks:** This is a joint library serving the two firms. **Staff:** Lesia Korobaylo, Asst.Libn.

★2866★
CLARKSVILLE LEAF-CHRONICLE COMPANY - LIBRARY (Publ)
200 Commerce St.   Phone: (615) 552-1808
Clarksville, TN 37040   Lesley S. Potts, Libn.
Founded: 1968. **Staff:** Prof 1. **Subjects:** Newspaper reference topics. **Holdings:** 700 books; newspaper clippings; microfilm; 1 drawer of maps. **Subscriptions:** 15 newspapers. **Services:** Copying; library not open to public. **Special Catalogs:** Catalog to newspaper clippings on file and on microfilm (card).

CLARKWOOD LIBRARY
See: Celanese Corporation - Celanese Chemical Company, Inc. - Technical Center - Library

CLASS OF 1904 SCIENCE LIBRARY AND PHYSICS READING ROOM
See: Oberlin College

★2867★
CLASSIC AMX CLUB, INTERNATIONAL - AMX LIBRARY (Rec)
7963 Depew St.
Arvada, CO 80003   Larry G. Mitchell, Cur.
Founded: 1974. **Staff:** 1. **Subjects:** Sales and promotional material relating to American Motors' AMX automobile. **Holdings:** Sales and promotional books, folders, flyers and related items; 4 VF drawers; 200 loose-leaf binders; 273 assorted collectors items. **Services:** Copying; SDI; library open to public with restrictions. **Publications:** AMX-tra, bimonthly - to members. **Formerly:** Located in Loves Park, IL.

★2868★
CLAY COUNTY ARCHIVES (Hist)*
Box 99
Liberty, MO 64068   Ron Fuenfhausen, Cur.
Founded: 1979. **Staff:** 30. **Subjects:** Genealogy, local history, Civil War. **Special Collections:** Clay County probate records, 1821-1970; marriage records; Alexander Doniphan Chapter, Daughters of the American Revolution Collection; Liberty-Blue Mills Chapter, Children of the Confederacy; Nadene Hodges books on Missouri heritage. **Holdings:** 200 books; 5 reels of microfilm; local newspaper clippings; family photographs; diaries and letters. **Services:** Copying; archives open to public (fee). **Special Indexes:** Microfilm index of probate records.

★2869★
CLAY COUNTY HISTORICAL SOCIETY - ARCHIVES (Hist)
22 N. 8th St.
Box 501   Phone: (218) 233-4604
Moorhead, MN 56560   Kate Andrews, Adm.
Founded: 1932. **Staff:** Prof 2; Other 1. **Subjects:** Minnesota; Clay County and its cities and villages. **Special Collections:** Town, church and county histories (3 file drawers); autobiographical and biographical records of early Clay County pioneers (4 file drawers); glass negatives taken by pioneer photographers O.E. Flaten and S.P. Wange (1500). **Holdings:** 815 books and bound periodical volumes; 5 VF drawers of documents, pamphlets and clippings. **Subscriptions:** 10 journals and other serials. **Services:** Copying; library open to public for reference use only. **Networks/Consortia:** Member of Northern Lights Library Network. **Publications:** Monthly newsletter.

CLAYTON LIBRARY
See: Houston Public Library

CLAYTON (W.L.) RESEARCH CENTER
See: Anderson Clayton Foods - W.L. Clayton Research Center

★2870★
CLEARFIELD LAW LIBRARY (Law)†
Court House   Phone: (814) 765-9511
Clearfield, PA 16830   Carl Soderlund, Libn.
Subjects: Law. **Holdings:** 11,000 volumes.

★2871★
CLEARINGHOUSE FOR ARTS INFORMATION - CENTER FOR ARTS INFORMATION (Bus-Fin)
625 Broadway   Phone: (212) 677-7548
New York, NY 10012   Jana Jevnikar, Info.Coord.
Founded: 1976. **Staff:** Prof 3; Other 1. **Subjects:** Arts management, fund raising. **Holdings:** 5000 books; 500 files of arts service organizations; 250 subject files of arts management. **Subscriptions:** 300 journals and other serials. **Services:** Copying; library open to public by appointment. **Publications:** List of publications - available upon request.

★2872★
CLEARINGHOUSE ON CHILD ABUSE AND NEGLECT INFORMATION (Soc Sci)
Box 1182   Phone: (703) 558-8222
Washington, DC 20013   Joseph G. Wechsler, Dir.
Founded: 1975. **Staff:** Prof 5; Other 5. **Subjects:** Child abuse and neglect, child protective services. **Special Collections:** Indian tribal laws. **Holdings:** 5350 books, articles, reports and documents; state statutes; 101 research projects; 3362 programs; 466 AV items. **Subscriptions:** 30 journals and other serials. **Services:** Library open to public. **Computerized Information Services:** Online systems. **Publications:** Listing of the National Center on Child Abuse and Neglect publications - available upon request. **Remarks:** The Clearinghouse is maintained by the U.S. Department of Health & Human Services - National Center on Child Abuse and Neglect (NCCAN). **Staff:** Ruthann Bates, Proj.Dir.; Richard Roth, Proj.Mgr.; Fred Parris, Mgr., Info.Serv.

★2873★
CLEARINGHOUSE ON THE HANDICAPPED (Soc Sci)
U.S. Dept. of Education
Switzer Bldg., Rm. 3119 Phone: (202) 245-0080
Washington, DC 20202 Helga Roth, Chf., Clearinghouse
Staff: Prof 4; Other 2. **Subjects:** Handicapped - federal funding, legislation, programs. **Services:** Provides direct information services related to federal policies and programs for the physically and mentally handicapped; Clearinghouse open to public. **Computerized Information Services:** BRS. **Publications:** Newsletter, bimonthly; Directory of National Information Sources on Handicapping Conditions and Related Services. List of other publications - available upon request; no charge for publications.

CLEARINGHOUSE ON HEALTH INDEXES
See: National Center for Health Statistics

CLEARINGHOUSE FOR HOSPITAL MANAGEMENT ENGINEERING
See: American Hospital Association

CLEARINGHOUSE FOR OCCUPATIONAL SAFETY AND HEALTH INFORMATION
See: U.S. Natl. Institute for Occupational Safety & Health

★2874★
CLEARINGHOUSE FOR SOCIOLOGICAL LITERATURE (Soc Sci)
Dept. of Sociology
Northern Illinois Univ. Phone: (815) 753-0303
Dekalb, IL 60115 Hugo O. Engelmann, Ed.
Founded: 1965. **Staff:** 1. **Subjects:** Sociology, social psychology and related social scientific fields. **Holdings:** 100 articles and books on microfilm. **Services:** Copying; clearinghouse open to public. **Publications:** All deposits are abstracted in the Sociological Abstracts. **Remarks:** Appropriate manuscripts will be accepted from anyone. Manuscripts on deposit are available on request in full sized printout to any user upon payment of a user's fee.

★2875★
CLEARY, GOTTLIEB, STEEN & HAMILTON - LIBRARY (Law)
One State St. Plaza Phone: (212) 344-0600
New York, NY 10004 Karol M. Sokol, Libn.
Founded: 1946. **Staff:** Prof 2; Other 4. **Subjects:** Law. **Holdings:** 20,000 volumes. **Services:** Library not open to public.

CLEAVES (Nathan and Henry B.) LAW LIBRARY
See: Cumberland Bar Association - Nathan and Henry B. Cleaves Law Library

CLEMENS, SAMUEL LANGHORNE
See: Mark Twain

CLEMENTE (Roberto) LIBRARY
See: University of Connecticut - Puerto Rican Center - Roberto Clemente Library

CLEMENTINE LIBRARY
See: Catholic University of America

CLEMENTS HISTORY MEMORIAL LIBRARY
See: Franklin County Historical Society - Center of Science & Industry

CLEMENTS (William L.) LIBRARY
See: University of Michigan - William L. Clements Library

CLEMMER (C.C.) LIBRARY
See: Canadian Memorial Chiropractic College - C.C. Clemmer Library

★2876★
CLEMSON UNIVERSITY - EMERY A. GUNNIN ARCHITECTURAL LIBRARY (Art)
Lee Hall Phone: (803) 656-3081
Clemson, SC 29631 Dillman B. Sorrells, Arch.Lib.Spec.
Staff: 5. **Subjects:** Art, architecture, building science, city and regional planning. **Special Collections:** Slide collection (51,949). **Holdings:** 22,343 books; 4133 bound periodical volumes; 1721 city and regional planning documents. **Subscriptions:** 250 journals and other serials. **Services:** Interlibrary loans; copying; library open to public. **Computerized Information Services:** DIALOG. **Networks/Consortia:** Member of OCLC through SOLINET. **Publications:** Monthly acquisitions list. **Special Catalogs:** Selected bibliography of art and architecture materials. **Staff:** Phyllis Pivorun, Slide Cur.

★2877★
CLEMSON UNIVERSITY - ROBERT MULDROW COOPER LIBRARY (Sci-Tech; Agri)
Phone: (803) 656-3026
Clemson, SC 29631 Joseph Boykin, Dir.
Founded: 1893. **Staff:** Prof 20; Other 56. **Subjects:** Agriculture, engineering, chemistry, physics, mathematics, textiles, architecture. **Special Collections:** J. Strom Thurmond Papers; John C. Calhoun Papers; James F. Byrnes Papers; Edgar A. Brown Papers; Benjamin R. Tillman Papers. **Holdings:** 560,906 books; 298,555 bound periodical volumes; 20,172 reels of microfilm; 460,551 microfiche; 31,508 microcards; 27,515 maps. **Subscriptions:** 14,161 journals and other serials. **Services:** Copying; library open to public. **Computerized Information Services:** DIALOG. **Networks/Consortia:** Member of OCLC through SOLINET. **Publications:** Annual list of current periodicals and continuations received (alphabetical and classified); indexes, abstract journals and selected statistical sources found in the library. **Staff:** R.W. Meyer, Assoc.Dir.; Peggy Cover, Ref.Serv.; Michael Kohl, Spec.Coll.Libn.; Maureen Harris, Pub.Docs.

CLENDENING LIBRARY
See: University of Kansas Medical Center - College of Health Sciences and Hospital

★2878★
CLERMONT COUNTY LAW LIBRARY ASSOCIATION (Law)
Main St. Phone: (513) 732-7109
Batavia, OH 45103 Joyce B. Tedrick, Hd.Libn.
Founded: 1933. **Staff:** Prof 1; Other 2. **Subjects:** Taxation; bankruptcy; law - Ohio and federal; labor and employment; medicine. **Holdings:** Figures not available for ultrafiche. **Services:** Copying; library open to public for reference use only - staff not available for assistance. **Computerized Information Services:** WESTLAW.

CLEVELAND BOARD OF EDUCATION - MAX S. HAYES VOCATIONAL SCHOOL
See: Hayes (Max S.) Vocational School

★2879★
CLEVELAND CHIROPRACTIC COLLEGE - LIBRARY (Med)
6401 Rockhill Rd. Phone: (816) 333-8230
Kansas City, MO 64131 Marcia M. Thomas, Lib.Dir.
Staff: Prof 1; Other 3. **Subjects:** Health sciences, roentgenology, chiropractic, orthopedics, diagnosis, acupuncture. **Special Collections:** Chiropractic practice, history and philosophy (300 volumes). **Holdings:** 6500 books; 350 bound periodical volumes; 4100 radiographic films; 5000 radiographic slides; 5000 slides and tapes; 1 drawer of journals on microfiche. **Subscriptions:** 183 journals and other serials. **Services:** Interlibrary loans; copying; library open to public for reference use only. **Computerized Information Services:** DIALOG. **Networks/Consortia:** Member of Kansas City Library Network, Inc.; Chiropractic Library Consortium. **Publications:** New Books, 3/year - for internal distribution only.

★2880★
CLEVELAND CLINIC EDUCATION FOUNDATION - MEDICAL LIBRARY/ AUDIOVISUAL CENTER (Med)†
9500 Euclid Ave. Phone: (216) 444-5698
Cleveland, OH 44106 Elizabeth Joy, Hd.Med.Libn.
Founded: 1921. **Staff:** Prof 3; Other 5. **Subjects:** Medical sciences. **Holdings:** 3000 books; 17,600 bound periodical volumes; 440 AV items (cataloged). **Subscriptions:** 520 journals and other serials. **Services:** Interlibrary loans; copying; SDI; library not open to public. **Computerized Information Services:** MEDLINE. **Networks/Consortia:** Member of Kentucky-Ohio-Michigan Regional Medical Library Network (KOMRML). **Staff:** Lillian Mark, Med.Libn.; Kate Kretschmann, AV Libn.

★2881★
CLEVELAND COLLEGE OF JEWISH STUDIES - AARON GARBER LIBRARY (Area-Ethnic)
26500 Shaker Blvd. Phone: (216) 464-4050
Beachwood, OH 44122 Zipora Leiby, Chf.Libn.
Staff: Prof 3. **Subjects:** Judaica. **Special Collections:** Holocaust materials, Hebrew literature. **Holdings:** 20,000 volumes. **Subscriptions:** 125 journals and other serials. **Services:** Interlibrary loans; copying; library open to residents of Metropolitan Cleveland. **Staff:** Tikvah Krieger, Asst.Libn.; Betty Barson, Asst.Libn.

★2882★
CLEVELAND COUNCIL ON WORLD AFFAIRS - LIBRARY (Soc Sci)
601 Rockwell Ave.   Phone: (216) 781-3730
Cleveland, OH 44114
Founded: 1924. **Subjects:** Foreign affairs. **Special Collections:** U.S. Department of State's policy statements and background notes on individual countries. **Holdings:** Figures not available. **Services:** Library open to public. **Remarks:** "The library is used principally by the staff of the Council in the conduct of programs in secondary schools and in preparing speeches on world affairs."

★2883★
CLEVELAND - DEPARTMENT OF LAW LIBRARY (Law)
211 City Hall
601 Lakeside Ave.   Phone: (216) 664-2656
Cleveland, OH 44114   Jan Ryan Novak, Dept.Hd.
Founded: 1942. **Staff:** Prof 2; Other 2. **Subjects:** Federal and Ohio law, municipal corporation law, municipal codes and ordinances. **Holdings:** 20,000 books and bound periodical volumes. **Subscriptions:** 25 journals and other serials. **Services:** Library open to public. **Remarks:** Library is administered by the Public Administration Library, a department of the Cleveland Public Library.

★2884★
CLEVELAND ELECTRIC ILLUMINATING COMPANY - LAW LIBRARY (Law)
Public Square
Box 5000   Phone: (216) 622-9800
Cleveland, OH 44101   Judith A. Coll, Law Libn.
Staff: Prof 1. **Subjects:** Law, engineering, tax. **Holdings:** 4100 books. **Subscriptions:** 7 journals and other serials. **Services:** Library not open to public.

★2885★
CLEVELAND ELECTRIC ILLUMINATING COMPANY - LIBRARY (Energy)
Public Square, Rm. 504
Box 5000   Phone: (216) 622-9800
Cleveland, OH 44101   Paula Wilhelm, Assoc.Libn.
Founded: 1947. **Staff:** Prof 2. **Subjects:** Electric power engineering, energy, public utilities, management, business administration, finance. **Special Collections:** Electric Power Research Institute Reports. **Holdings:** 3000 books; 625 bound periodical volumes; 20,000 items in pamphlet file; 10,000 items in business services files; 650 microfiche; 102 audio cassettes. **Subscriptions:** 648 journals and other serials. **Services:** Interlibrary loans; copying; library open to public by appointment. **Computerized Information Services:** DIALOG. **Publications:** Library Bulletin, monthly; Acquisition List, monthly. **Special Indexes:** Pamphlet file index; Electric Power Research Institute (EPRI) Reports index (all on cards). **Staff:** Jean Ocampo, Assoc.Libn.

CLEVELAND FOUNDATION CENTER
See: Foundation Center - Cleveland

★2886★
CLEVELAND HEALTH SCIENCES LIBRARY (Med)
2119 Abington Rd.   Phone: (216) 368-3426
Cleveland, OH 44106   Robert G. Cheshier, Dir.
Founded: 1965. **Staff:** Prof 26; Other 20. **Subjects:** Medicine, dentistry, nursing, biology, nutrition. **Holdings:** 117,204 books; 191,377 bound periodical volumes; 2215 AV/television holdings; 100 microforms. **Subscriptions:** 1970 journals and other serials. **Services:** Interlibrary loans; copying; SDI; library open to public for reference use only. **Computerized Information Services:** MEDLINE. **Networks/Consortia:** Member of OCLC; Kentucky-Ohio-Michigan Regional Medical Library Network (KOMRML). **Publications:** Bulletin of Cleveland Medical Library Association, semiannual - to members. **Remarks:** The holdings of this library are divided among the Allen Memorial Library, Health Center Library and Howard Dittrick Museum of Historical Medicine. Maintained by Case Western Reserve University and Cleveland Medical Library Association.

★2887★
CLEVELAND HEALTH SCIENCES LIBRARY - ALLEN MEMORIAL LIBRARY (Med)
11000 Euclid Ave.   Phone: (216) 368-3640
Cleveland, OH 44106   Lydia Holian, Assoc.Dir.
Staff: Prof 17. **Subjects:** Medicine. **Holdings:** 67,727 books; 97,919 bound periodical volumes. **Services:** Interlibrary loans; copying; SDI; library open to public for reference use only. **Computerized Information Services:** MEDLINE, DIALOG, SDC. **Networks/Consortia:** Member of OCLC; Kentucky-Ohio-Michigan Regional Medical Library Network (KOMRML). **Staff:** Frederica Bolce, Ref.Libn.; Suzanne Marcy, Ref.Libn.; Susan Hill, ILL Libn.; Virginia Mattson, Circuit Libn.; Sylvia Feuer, Extramural Coord.; Jeanine Harkonen,

Circuit Libn.; Lillian Levine, ILL Libn.; Holly Sheldon, Circuit Libn.; Keith Stincic, Circuit Libn.; Dagny Roseboro, Circuit Libn.; Jean Stanley, Circuit Libn.; Joseph Hagloch, Circuit Libn.

★2888★
CLEVELAND HEALTH SCIENCES LIBRARY - HEALTH CENTER LIBRARY (Med)
2119 Abington Rd.   Phone: (216) 368-3426
Cleveland, OH 44106   Marjorie Saunders, Assoc.Dir.
Staff: Prof 9. **Subjects:** Medicine, nursing, dentistry, nutrition, biology. **Holdings:** 93,458 serials; 49,477 monographs. **Services:** Interlibrary loans; copying; SDI; library open to public for reference use only. **Computerized Information Services:** MEDLINE. **Networks/Consortia:** Member of OCLC; Kentucky-Ohio-Michigan Regional Medical Library Network (KOMRML). **Staff:** Mrs. Olyn Ruxin, Hd.Cat.Libn.; Jerianne Gross, Coll.Dev.-Ser.; Virginia Garvin, Coll.Dev. - Monographs; Kathleen Casteel, Hd.Ref.Libn./AV; Margaret Henning, Ed.; Karen Burt, Circ.Libn.; Miriam Gordon, Ref.; Toni Broygal, Acq.

★2889★
CLEVELAND HEALTH SCIENCES LIBRARY - HOWARD DITTRICK MUSEUM OF HISTORICAL MEDICINE (Med)
11000 Euclid Ave.   Phone: (216) 368-3648
Cleveland, OH 44106   Dr. Patsy A. Gerstner, Chf.Cur.
Staff: Prof 3. **Subjects:** History of medicine. **Special Collections:** Nicolaus Pol Collection of Incunabula (40); Sigmund Freud Collection (200); Harold N. Cole Collection of Venereals (235); Charles Darwin Collection of Books and Manuscripts (330 titles; 136 manuscripts); Marshall Collection of Herbals (350); historical biology (2000). **Holdings:** 20,000 books; 30,000 artifacts. **Computerized Information Services:** Computerized cataloging and serials. **Networks/Consortia:** Member of OCLC. **Staff:** James Edmonson, Assoc.Cur.; Glen Jenkins, Rare Bk.Libn./Archv.

★2890★
CLEVELAND HEARING AND SPEECH CENTER - LUCILE DAUBY GRIES MEMORIAL LIBRARY (Med)
11206 Euclid Ave.   Phone: (216) 231-8787
Cleveland, OH 44106   Mildred P. Grant, Libn.
Staff: Prof 1; Other 1. **Subjects:** Audiology, speech, language, deafness, rehabilitation, psychology. **Special Collections:** Technical journals dating from 1889 to present; AV file. **Holdings:** 1200 books; 490 bound periodical volumes; 90 dissertations; 4 VF drawers of reprints, abstracts, former comprehensive examinations. **Subscriptions:** 29 journals and other serials. **Services:** Library open to public for reference use only. **Publications:** Newsletter, monthly - for internal distribution only.

★2891★
CLEVELAND INSTITUTE OF ART - JESSICA R. GUND MEMORIAL LIBRARY (Art)
11141 East Blvd.   Phone: (216) 421-4322
Cleveland, OH 44106   Karen D. Tschudy, Lib.Dir.
Founded: 1882. **Staff:** Prof 4; Other 2. **Subjects:** Fine arts, industrial design, history of architecture, graphic arts, art history, humanities. **Holdings:** 35,086 books and bound periodical volumes; 9955 microforms; 48,262 AV items; file of 91,000 pictures; archives (35 volumes; boxed materials). **Subscriptions:** 225 journals and other serials. **Services:** Interlibrary loans; copying; library open to public. **Computerized Information Services:** Computerized cataloging. **Networks/Consortia:** Member of Union of Independent Colleges of Art; OCLC; Cleveland Area Metropolitan Library System (CAMLS). **Staff:** Christine Rom, Spec.Coll.Libn.; Hyosoo Lee, Tech.Serv.Libn.; M. Michelle Fowler, Slide Libn.

★2892★
CLEVELAND INSTITUTE OF MUSIC - LIBRARY (Mus)
11021 East Blvd.   Phone: (216) 791-5165
Cleveland, OH 44106   Karen K. Griffith, Dir., Lib.
Founded: 1922. **Staff:** Prof 3; Other 10. **Subjects:** Music - performance materials, scores, analytical works, bibliographies, biographies. **Holdings:** 44,400 books and scores; 1550 bound periodical volumes; 9000 phonograph records (cataloged); 2100 tapes (cataloged); 850 microcards (cataloged). **Subscriptions:** 157 journals and other serials. **Services:** Interlibrary loans; library open to public for reference use only. **Staff:** Sandra Cobb, Music Cat.; Pamela Schlenk, Record Libn.

★2893★
CLEVELAND LAW LIBRARY (Law)
404 County Court House   Phone: (216) 861-5070
Cleveland, OH 44113   Arthur W. Fiske, Libn.
Subjects: Law. **Holdings:** 136,362 volumes.

CLEVELAND MEDICAL LIBRARY ASSOCIATION
See: Cleveland Health Sciences Library

★2894★
CLEVELAND METROPARKS ZOOLOGICAL PARK - LIBRARY (Sci-Tech)
Brookside Pk.   Phone: (216) 661-6500
Cleveland, OH 44109   Charles R. Voracek, Pub.Info.Off.
Founded: 1882. **Subjects:** Zoo management, veterinary medicine, zoology, mammalogy, ornithology, herpetology. **Holdings:** 600 books; 20 bound periodical volumes. **Subscriptions:** 100 journals and other serials. **Services:** Library not open to public. **Publications:** Zoo News, 4/yr.

★2895★
CLEVELAND METROPOLITAN GENERAL HOSPITAL - HAROLD H. BRITTINGHAM MEMORIAL LIBRARY (Med)
3395 Scranton Rd.   Phone: (216) 459-5623
Cleveland, OH 44109   Christine Dziedzina, Chf.Libn.
Founded: 1937. **Staff:** Prof 2; Other 5. **Subjects:** Medicine, nursing. **Special Collections:** Stecher collection of arthritis and rheumatism journals. **Holdings:** 9273 books; 18,939 bound periodical volumes; 4 VF drawers of pamphlets. **Subscriptions:** 486 journals and other serials. **Services:** Interlibrary loans; copying (limited to hospital personnel); library open to public by special permission. **Computerized Information Services:** MEDLINE. **Networks/Consortia:** Member of Cleveland MEDLINE Consortium 2; Kentucky-Ohio-Michigan Regional Medical Library Network (KOMRML). **Remarks:** Includes the holdings of the Highland View Hospital - Medical Library. **Staff:** Janet P. Harouny, Asst.Libn.

★2896★
CLEVELAND MUSEUM OF ART - LIBRARY (Art)
11150 East Blvd.   Phone: (216) 421-7340
Cleveland, OH 44106   Jack Perry Brown, Libn.
Founded: 1916. **Staff:** Prof 9; Other 14. **Subjects:** Art, architecture, decorative arts, oriental art. **Special Collections:** Sothebys, Christies, and Parke-Bernet sales catalogs; Gernsheim photographs; Berenson Archive; D.I.A.L. **Holdings:** 111,000 books and bound periodical volumes; 260,000 slides; 250,000 photograph reference collection; 100 VF artist clippings. **Subscriptions:** 1400 journals and other serials. **Services:** Copying; library open to museum members, faculty, graduates and visiting scholars. **Computerized Information Services:** Computerized cataloging. **Networks/Consortia:** Member of Art Research Libraries of Ohio (ARLO); RLIN. **Publications:** ARLO Union list of serials and periodicals, 1974. **Special Catalogs:** Sales catalog (card). **Staff:** Judith G. Frost, Assoc.Libn.; Georgina Gy Toth, Assoc.Ref.Libn.; Sara J. Pearman, Slide Lib.; Su-Lee Huang, Assoc.Libn., Tech.Serv.

★2897★
CLEVELAND MUSEUM OF NATURAL HISTORY - HAROLD TERRY CLARK LIBRARY (Sci-Tech)
Wade Oval, University Circle   Phone: (216) 231-4600
Cleveland, OH 44106   Mary Baum, Libn.
Founded: 1921. **Staff:** Prof 2. **Subjects:** Natural history, ornithology, geology, astronomy, anthropology, zoology, entomology, botany, ichthyology, archaeology. **Special Collections:** Rare books (over 400 items). **Holdings:** 6000 books; 25,000 bound periodical volumes; 18 VF drawers of pamphlets. **Subscriptions:** 500 journals and other serials. **Services:** Interlibrary loans; copying; library open to public for reference use only.

★2898★
CLEVELAND MUSIC SCHOOL SETTLEMENT - KULAS LIBRARY
11125 Magnolia Dr.
Cleveland, OH 44106
Founded: 1911. **Subjects:** Music. **Holdings:** 4000 books and music scores; 2000 phonograph records. **Remarks:** Presently inactive.

★2899★
CLEVELAND PRESS - LIBRARY (Publ)†
901 Lakeside Ave.   Phone: (216) 623-6740
Cleveland, OH 44114   Thomas Barensfeld, Libn.
Staff: Prof 1; Other 6. **Subjects:** Newspaper reference topics. **Holdings:** 3000 books; one million clippings; one million pictures. **Subscriptions:** 10 journals and other serials; 20 newspapers. **Services:** Library open to graduate students only. **Computerized Information Services:** Mechanized services.

★2900★
CLEVELAND PSYCHIATRIC INSTITUTE - KARNOSH LIBRARY (Med)†
1708 Aiken Ave.   Phone: (216) 661-6200
Cleveland, OH 44109   Anna L. Harris, Libn.
Staff: 1. **Subjects:** Psychology, psychiatry, psychoanalysis, medicine,

sociology, clinical neurology. **Holdings:** 5653 books; 1819 bound periodical volumes; 5 VF drawers of pamphlets; 227 cassette tapes; 16 reels of tape; 64 slides. **Subscriptions:** 70 journals and other serials. **Services:** Interlibrary loans; copying; library open to public for reference use only on request. **Staff:** Dr. Edward Bakos, Med.Dir.; Dr. L. Rohira, Chm., Med.Lib.Comm.

★2901★
CLEVELAND PSYCHOANALYTIC SOCIETY - LIBRARY (Med)
11328 Euclid Ave., No. 205   Phone: (216) 229-2111
Cleveland, OH 44106   Murray A. Goldstone, M.D., Chm., Lib.Comm.
Founded: 1962. **Staff:** Prof 1. **Subjects:** Psychoanalysis, child therapy. **Special Collections:** Concordance to the Psychological Works of Sigmund Freud; Complete Psychological Works of Sigmund Freud (Standard Edition); Chicago Psychological Literature Index. **Holdings:** 980 books; 250 bound periodical volumes; 170 tape recordings of scientific psychoanalytic meetings; 8 shelves of unbound periodicals; 10 boxes of reprints; 25 boxes of unpublished papers. **Subscriptions:** 10 journals and other serials. **Services:** Copying; library open to persons with psychoanalytic background and training. **Staff:** Norrine E. Wild, Libn.

★2902★
CLEVELAND PUBLIC LIBRARY - BUSINESS, ECONOMICS & LABOR DEPARTMENT (Bus-Fin)
325 Superior Ave.   Phone: (216) 623-2927
Cleveland, OH 44114-1271   Marcella Matejka, Dept.Hd.
Founded: 1929. **Staff:** Prof 7; Other 11. **Subjects:** Investments and finance, marketing and advertising, insurance, accounting, real estate, communications, labor, taxation, salesmanship, banking, transportation. **Special Collections:** Trade directories (3000); Garfield Perry Philatelic Collection (2500 volumes). **Holdings:** 97,400 volumes; 38,857 bound periodical volumes; 25 VF drawers of economic and business subject files; 5000 companies' corporation files and annual reports, plus annual reports on microfiche for all companies on the New York and American Stock Exchanges; 100 loose-leaf services on investments, taxation, labor and employment. **Subscriptions:** 4000 journals and other serials. **Services:** Interlibrary loans; copying. **Computerized Information Services:** DIALOG, SDC, BRS, Dow Jones News Retrieval, New York Times Information Service, Institute for Scientific Information (ISI); internal database; computerized cataloging, serials and circulation. **Networks/Consortia:** Member of OHIONET; OCLC; Cleveland Area Metropolitan Library System (CAMLS). **Special Indexes:** Corporation File Index (card).

★2903★
CLEVELAND PUBLIC LIBRARY - CHILDREN'S LITERATURE DEPARTMENT (Hum)
325 Superior Ave.   Phone: (216) 623-2834
Cleveland, OH 44114-1271   Ruth M. Hadlow, Dept.Hd.
Founded: 1898. **Staff:** Prof 1; Other 2. **Subjects:** Children's materials. **Special Collections:** Treasure Room collection of Early Children's Books (1453 volumes); Lewis Carroll Collection (books by and about the author, 150 volumes). **Holdings:** 66,500 volumes; 535 bound periodical volumes; 45 RPM sound recordings. **Subscriptions:** 56 journals and other serials. **Services:** Interlibrary loans; copying. **Computerized Information Services:** DIALOG, SDC, BRS, Dow Jones News Retrieval, New York Times Information Service, Institute for Scientific Information (ISI); internal database; computerized cataloging, serials and circulation. **Networks/Consortia:** Member of OHIONET; OCLC; Cleveland Area Metropolitan Library System (CAMLS). **Publications:** Children's Books for Holiday Giving and Year 'Round Enjoyment, annual - available on request; Adventures in Reading (four lists by age groupings), every 3 years. **Special Indexes:** Author and illustrator index; fiction index; subject index: preschool through grade two.

★2904★
CLEVELAND PUBLIC LIBRARY - DOCUMENTS COLLECTION (Info Sci)
325 Superior Ave.   Phone: (216) 623-2870
Cleveland, OH 44114-1271   Elizabeth Fannon, Dept.Hd.
Staff: Prof 2; Other 2. **Subjects:** United States Government publications. **Special Collections:** Patent depository, 1790 to present (microfilm); U.S. Congressional committee prints, 1830s to present (6 drawers of microfiche); U.S. Bureau of Mines publications, 1910 to present (3 drawers of microfiche); U.S. NASA depository, 1968 to present (21 drawers of microfiche); U.S. NTIS subscription to Selected Research in Microfiche (SRIM) emphasizing environmental subjects, 1975 to present (30 drawers of microfiche); U.S. Department of Energy subscription (220 drawers of microfiche, 20 drawers of microcards). **Holdings:** Figures not available for hard copy holdings; 21 drawers of microfilm holdings of Government Printing Office depository; 48 drawers of microfiche. **Services:** Interlibrary loans; copying; library open to public. **Computerized Information Services:** DIALOG, SDC, BRS, Dow Jones News Retrieval, New York Times Information Service, Institute for Scientific

Information (ISI); internal database; computerized cataloging, serials and circulation. **Networks/Consortia:** Member of OHIONET; OCLC; Cleveland Area Metropolitan Library System (CAMLS).

★2905★
CLEVELAND PUBLIC LIBRARY - FINE ARTS DEPARTMENT (Art; Mus)
325 Superior Ave.   Phone: (216) 623-2848
Cleveland, OH 44114-1271   Joan Hoagland, Dept.Hd.
Founded: 1869. **Staff:** Prof 3; Other 2. **Subjects:** Art, architecture, sculpture, painting, music. **Holdings:** 144,900 books and bound periodical volumes; 200,000 pictures; 19,500 pieces of sheet music; 13,000 phonograph records. **Subscriptions:** 294 journals and other serials. **Services:** Interlibrary loans; copying. **Computerized Information Services:** DIALOG, BRS, SDC, Dow Jones News Retrieval, New York Times Information Service, Institute for Scientific Information (ISI); internal database; computerized cataloging, serials and circulation. **Networks/Consortia:** Member of OHIONET; OCLC; Cleveland Area Metropolitan Library System (CAMLS). **Publications:** Booklists, irregular.

★2906★
CLEVELAND PUBLIC LIBRARY - FOREIGN LITERATURE DEPARTMENT (Hum)
325 Superior Ave.   Phone: (216) 623-2895
Cleveland, OH 44114-1271   Natalia B. Bezugloff, Dept.Hd.
Founded: 1925. **Staff:** Prof 4; Other 2. **Subjects:** Collections in 36 modern languages which include classics and standard works with emphasis on belles-lettres, literary history and biography; books on learning languages; encyclopedias; dictionaries. **Special Collections:** Folk Arts Collections - artifacts, costumes, books and pamphlets on ethnic folk arts and customs. **Holdings:** 187,809 volumes; 4774 bound periodical volumes; 1906 phonograph records; 1102 cassettes (cataloged). **Subscriptions:** 147 journals and other serials. **Services:** Interlibrary loans; copying; file of teachers and translators in foreign languages. **Computerized Information Services:** DIALOG, SDC, BRS, Dow Jones News Retrieval, New York Times Information Service, Institute for Scientific Information (ISI); internal database; computerized cataloging, serials and circulation. **Networks/ Consortia:** Member of OHIONET; OCLC; Cleveland Area Metropolitan Library System (CAMLS). **Publications:** Booklists, phonodisc and cassette lists and descriptive brochures, irregular. **Special Catalogs:** Catalogs by languages and indexes to poetry, short stories, literary criticism, subject guide to fiction.

★2907★
CLEVELAND PUBLIC LIBRARY - GENERAL REFERENCE DEPARTMENT (Info Sci)
325 Superior Ave.   Phone: (216) 623-2856
Cleveland, OH 44114-1271   Joan L. Sorger, Dept.Hd.
Founded: 1875. **Staff:** Prof 5; Other 12. **Subjects:** Bibliography, cartography and maps, encyclopedias, newspapers, general reference. **Special Collections:** Obituary file of newspaper death notices. **Holdings:** 45,000 volumes; 23,400 bound periodical volumes; 40 VF drawers; 99,780 sheet maps; 36,206 microfiche cards of periodicals; 35,500 microfilm reels of periodicals and newspapers. **Subscriptions:** 500 journals and other serials; 153 newspapers. **Computerized Information Services:** DIALOG, SDC, BRS, Dow Jones News Retrieval, New York Times Information Service, Institute for Scientific Information (ISI); internal database; computerized cataloging, serials and circulation. **Networks/Consortia:** Member of OHIONET; OCLC; Cleveland Area Metropolitan Library System (CAMLS). **Publications:** Index to Cleveland Newspapers, monthly.

★2908★
CLEVELAND PUBLIC LIBRARY - HISTORY AND GEOGRAPHY DEPARTMENT (Hist; Geog-Map)
325 Superior Ave.   Phone: (216) 623-2864
Cleveland, OH 44114-1271   Donald Tipka, Dept.Hd.
Founded: 1869. **Staff:** Prof 3; Other 3. **Subjects:** History - ancient, medieval, modern; archaeology; local history; genealogy; heraldry; geography; black history; exploration and travel; numismatics. **Special Collections:** Latin American research sources; British learned society serials; 17th century political pamphlets; 19th century travel narratives; English parish register collection. **Holdings:** 230,400 volumes; 13,303 bound periodical volumes; 18,000 Cleveland pictures; 15,000 brochures and maps (current travel data); 2000 Mazarinades (17th century French political pamphlets); 2000 British 17th and 18th century political pamphlets; local history clipping file; Coat-of-Arms file. **Subscriptions:** 346 journals and other serials. **Services:** Interlibrary loans; copying. **Computerized Information Services:** DIALOG, SDC, BRS, Dow Jones News Retrieval, New York Times Information Service, Institute for Scientific Information (ISI); internal database; computerized cataloging, serials and circulation. **Networks/Consortia:** Member of OHIONET; OCLC; Cleveland Area Metropolitan Library System (CAMLS).

Publications: Book lists and descriptive brochures, irregular.

★2909★
CLEVELAND PUBLIC LIBRARY - JOHN G. WHITE COLLECTION OF FOLKLORE, ORIENTALIA, & CHESS (Rec; Rare Book)
325 Superior Ave.   Phone: (216) 623-2818
Cleveland, OH 44114-1271   Alice N. Loranth, Hd.
Founded: 1899. **Staff:** Prof 2; Other 2. **Special Collections:** Orientalia (52,100 volumes); folklore (39,500 volumes); chess and checkers (27,800 volumes); East India Company manuscript collection of official documents, correspondence, 1741-1859 (250 volumes); languages and linguistics (15,000 volumes); India and Southeast Asia (12,000 volumes); Near Eastern archeology (7000 volumes); early travel and voyages to the Orient and Africa (6500 volumes); Egyptology (5000 volumes); Chinese, Japanese and Tibetan religion and philosophy (5100 volumes); Arabic and Persian literature (4000 volumes); Omar Khayyam (1050 editions in 48 languages); Arabian Nights (600 volumes in 57 languages); Sanskrit literature (2810 volumes); Judaica (1600 volumes); manuscript catalogs (700 volumes); Madagascar (500 volumes); proverbs (2800 volumes); gypsies (600 volumes); chapbooks (1730 volumes); Robert Hays Gries Tobacco Collection (1360 volumes); occult sciences and witchcraft (2000 volumes); Medieval romance literature (3000 volumes); Celtic and Icelandic language and saga literature (1100 volumes); Tegner (225 19th century editions); Rabelais (163 16th-18th century editions); Catiglione (102 volumes); Vida (106 volumes); Derrydale Press (117 volumes); Cleveland Author Collection (2001 volumes); Cleveland Imprint Collection (441 volumes); 18th-19th century prostitution collection (233 volumes); early children's books (1453 volumes); Margaret Klipple Memorial Archives of African Folktales; Newbell Niles Puckett Memorial Archives of: Ohio Superstitions and Popular Beliefs, Black Names in America, Religious Beliefs of the Southern Negro and Canadian Lumberjack Songs. **Holdings:** 153,878 volumes, including rare books; 17,560 bound periodical volumes; 1500 bound manuscripts; 315 boxes and 40 VF drawers of clippings and pictorial material on chess; 147 tapes; 1768 reels of microfilm. **Subscriptions:** 743 journals and other serials. **Services:** Interlibrary loans; copying; exhibits; lectures; library open to public with valid identification. **Computerized Information Services:** DIALOG, SDC, BRS, Dow Jones News Retrieval, New York Times Information Service, Institute for Scientific Information (ISI); internal database; computerized cataloging, serials and circulation. **Networks/Consortia:** Member of OHIONET; OCLC; Cleveland Area Metropolitan Library Systems (CAMLS). **Publications:** John G. White Department of Folklore, Orientalia and Chess, irregular - available on request. **Special Catalogs:** Black Names in America: Origins and Usage; Catalog of the Chess Collection (including checkers) of the Cleveland Public Library (2 volumes); Catalog of Folklore, Folklife and Folk Songs of the Cleveland Public Library (3 volumes); Popular Beliefs and Superstitions: Compendium of American Folklore: From the Ohio Collection of Newbell Niles Puckett (3 volumes). **Special Indexes:** Index to chess biography, tournaments and historic chess columns; French, Spanish and Italian folksong and ballad index.

★2910★
CLEVELAND PUBLIC LIBRARY - LITERATURE DEPARTMENT (Hum; Theater)
325 Superior Ave.   Phone: (216) 623-2881
Cleveland, OH 44114-1271   Lucille R. Troph, Dept.Hd.
Founded: 1869. **Staff:** Prof 4; Other 2. **Subjects:** Fiction; drama and theater; film; radio, television scripts; poetry; essays; humor and satire; oratory and public speaking; craft of writing; literary criticism and biography; classical Greek and Latin; linguistics; journalism; book trade; printing; publishing; library and information science. **Special Collections:** Shakespeare and early English play collection; American drama including Barrett W. Clark collection of old paperbacks; William F. McDermott Memorial Theatre Collection; Weidenthal collection of theatrical memorabilia; Wertheimer theatre programs; W. Ward Marsh cinema archives. **Holdings:** 273,000 volumes; 6490 bound periodical volumes; 22,000 theater programs and playbills; 160,500 stills, photographs and pictures; 5130 titles of microprint editions of plays and miscellaneous items; 4650 phonograph records and cassette tapes. **Subscriptions:** 570 journals and other serials. **Services:** Interlibrary loans; copying. **Computerized Information Services:** DIALOG, SDC, BRS, Dow Jones News Retrieval, New York Times Information Service, Institute for Scientific Information (ISI); internal database; computerized cataloging, serials and circulation. **Networks/Consortia:** Member of OHIONET; OCLC; Cleveland Area Metropolitan Library System (CAMLS). **Publications:** Book lists and descriptive brochures, irregular. **Special Indexes:** Card indexes to clippings, theater programs, pictures, poems, plays, essays and parts of books having subject interest.

★2911★
CLEVELAND PUBLIC LIBRARY - POPULAR LIBRARY DEPARTMENT (Rec)
325 Superior Ave.   Phone: (216) 623-2842
Cleveland, OH 44114-1271   John Philip Ferguson, Dept.Hd.
Founded: 1869. **Staff:** Prof 2; Other 5. **Subjects:** Popular fiction and nonfiction; popular magazines. **Holdings:** 30,000 volumes. **Services:** Interlibrary loans; Books-by-Mail. **Computerized Information Services:** DIALOG, SDC, BRS, Dow Jones News Retrieval, New York Times Information Service, Institute for Scientific Information (ISI); internal database; computerized cataloging, serials and circulation. **Networks/Consortia:** Member of OHIONET; OCLC; Cleveland Area Metropolitan Library System (CAMLS).

★2912★
CLEVELAND PUBLIC LIBRARY - PUBLIC ADMINISTRATION LIBRARY (Soc Sci)
601 Lakeside Ave.   Phone: (216) 623-2919
Cleveland, OH 44114-1271   Jan Ryan Novak, Dept.Hd.
Founded: 1912. **Staff:** Prof 2; Other 2. **Subjects:** Municipal law, finance and engineering, public administration, city planning, police and fire protection. **Special Collections:** City of Cleveland Collection (5000 volumes). **Holdings:** 16,900 volumes; 7000 bound periodical volumes; 32 VF drawers of clippings, unbound reports and pamphlets; 46 VF drawers of documents. **Subscriptions:** 580 journals and other serials; 6 newspapers. **Services:** Interlibrary loans; copying. **Computerized Information Services:** DIALOG, SDC, BRS, Dow Jones News Retrieval, New York Times Information Service, Institute for Scientific Information (ISI); internal database; computerized cataloging, serials and circulation. **Networks/Consortia:** Member of OHIONET; OCLC; Cleveland Area Metropolitan Library System (CAMLS). **Publications:** Recent Acquisitions, bimonthly; Public Administration Library Digest, irregular - both available upon request. **Remarks:** Administers the Law Collection of the City Law Department.

★2913★
CLEVELAND PUBLIC LIBRARY - SCIENCE AND TECHNOLOGY DEPARTMENT (Sci-Tech)
325 Superior Ave.   Phone: (216) 623-2932
Cleveland, OH 44114-1271   Jean Z. Piety, Hd.
Founded: 1912. **Staff:** Prof 5; Other 10. **Subjects:** Engineering, science, metallurgy, aeronautics, mechanics, geology, environment, agriculture, history of science and technology, natural history, handicrafts, photography. **Special Collections:** Standards and specifications; dog stud books; Great Lakes Basin; cookbooks. **Holdings:** 140,130 books and bound periodical volumes. **Subscriptions:** 3552 journals and other serials. **Services:** Interlibrary loans; copying; Facts for a Fee. **Computerized Information Services:** DIALOG, SDC, BRS, Dow Jones News Retrieval, New York Times Information Service, Institute for Scientific Information (ISI); internal database; computerized cataloging, serials and circulation. **Networks/Consortia:** Member of OHIONET; OCLC; Cleveland Area Metropolitan Library System (CAMLS). **Special Indexes:** Card indexes to automobiles, Great Lakes, handicrafts, models, boats, history, standards and specifications.

★2914★
CLEVELAND PUBLIC LIBRARY - SOCIAL SCIENCES DEPARTMENT (Soc Sci)
325 Superior Ave.   Phone: (216) 623-2860
Cleveland, OH 44114-1271   Thelma J. Morris, Dept.Hd.
Founded: 1913. **Staff:** Prof 5; Other 5. **Subjects:** Government; education; general and child psychology; United Nations; Great Britain Command Papers; political and social sciences; religion; folklore; philosophy; law; logic; ethics; social welfare; crime; juvenile delinquency; psychic research; sports; dance; recreation; public administration. **Holdings:** 234,200 volumes; 48,000 bound periodical volumes. **Subscriptions:** 2040 journals and other serials. **Services:** Interlibrary loans; copying. **Computerized Information Services:** DIALOG, SDC, BRS, Dow Jones News Retrieval, New York Times Information Service, Institute for Scientific Information (ISI); internal database; computerized cataloging, serials and circulation. **Networks/Consortia:** Member of OHIONET; OCLC; Cleveland Area Metropolitan Library System (CAMLS).

★2915★
CLEVELAND STATE UNIVERSITY - JOSEPH W. BARTUNEK III LAW LIBRARY (Law)
Euclid Ave. At E. 18th St.   Phone: (216) 687-2250
Cleviand, OH 44115   W. Nicholas Pope, Asst.Prof./Law Libn.
Founded: 1897. **Staff:** Prof 5; Other 10. **Subjects:** Law. **Special Collections:** U.S. Government documents selective depository; Ohio and U.S. Supreme Court Records and Briefs (on microfilm). **Holdings:** 206,000 volumes. **Subscriptions:** 1938 journals and other serials. **Services:** Interlibrary loans; copying; library open to public for reference use only. **Computerized Information Services:** LEXIS; computerized cataloging and

acquisitions. **Networks/Consortia:** Member of OCLC. **Staff:** Judith Kaul, Media Libn.; Catherine A. Whipple, Cat.Libn.; Catherine H. Gillette, Asst.Dir., Pub.Serv.; Marie Rehmar, Asst.Dir., Tech.Serv.

★2916★
CLIFTON SPRINGS HOSPITAL AND CLINIC - MEDICAL LIBRARY (Med)†
2 Coulter Rd.   Phone: (315) 462-9561
Clifton Springs, NY 14432   Mary L. Button, Med.Rec.Libn.
Subjects: Medicine and medical specialities, history of medicine. **Special Collections:** Library of Dr. Foster, founder of the hospital. **Holdings:** 1827 books; 10,100 bound periodical volumes. **Subscriptions:** 31 journals and other serials. **Services:** Library open to public when approved by a physician on hospital staff.

CLIMAX MOLYBDENUM COMPANY
See: AMAX, Inc.

CLINE-TUNNELL LIBRARY
See: Western Conservative Baptist Seminary

★2917★
CLINICAL PHARMACOLOGY RESEARCH INSTITUTE - LIBRARY
2123 Addison St.
Berkeley, CA 94704
Founded: 1959. **Subjects:** Clinical pharmacology, medicine, statistics, pharmacology, biochemistry. **Holdings:** 3000 books and bound periodical volumes; 2000 pamphlets; 200 reprints; 3 VF drawers of drug information. **Remarks:** Presently inactive.

★2918★
CLINICAL RESEARCH INSTITUTE OF MONTREAL - MEDICAL LIBRARY (Med)
110 Pine Ave., W.   Phone: (514) 842-1481
Montreal, PQ, Canada H2W 1R7   Lorraine Bielmann, Hd.Libn.
Founded: 1967. **Staff:** Prof 2; Other 5. **Subjects:** Medicine and related fields. **Holdings:** 600 books; 50 bound periodical volumes; 135,000 reprints. **Subscriptions:** 100 journals and other serials. **Services:** Interlibrary loans; copying; translations; library not open to public. **Computerized Information Services:** MEDLINE. **Remarks:** The institute is affiliated with the Universite de Montreal. **Also Known As:** Institut de Diagnostic et de Recherches Cliniques de Montreal. **Staff:** Jocelyne Viel, Asst.Libn.; Dr. Jean Davignon, Cons.

★2919★
CLINTON HISTORICAL SOCIETY - LIBRARY (Hist)*
Andrews Memorial Town Hall
Box 174   Phone: (203) 669-2164
Clinton, CT 06413   Dr. Jesse H. Buell, Libn.
Founded: 1938. **Staff:** 1. **Subjects:** Local history and genealogy. **Holdings:** 300 books. **Services:** Library open to public by request.

★2920★
CLINTON RIVER WATERSHED COUNCIL - LIBRARY (Env-Cons)
8215 Hall Rd.   Phone: (313) 739-1122
Utica, MI 48087   Peggy B. Johnson, Exec.Sec.
Founded: 1973. **Staff:** 2. **Subjects:** Water - quality, management, recreation, associated land uses. **Special Collections:** Reports on the Clinton River. **Holdings:** 500 books; special reports (cataloged); engineering reports; dissertations, data collections. **Subscriptions:** 25 journals and other serials. **Services:** Copying; library open to public. **Publications:** Newsletter, quarterly; annual report - sent to mailing list; reports on special topics.

CLIO PRESS
See: American Bibliographical Center

★2921★
CLIVEDEN - LIBRARY (Hist)
6401 Germantown Ave.   Phone: (215) 848-1777
Philadelphia, PA 19144   Hope Hendrickson, Libn.
Staff: 5. **Special Collections:** Books and papers belonging to the Chew Family. **Holdings:** 200,000 manuscript pages of documents. **Services:** Library open to public with restrictions; telephone for appointment with administrator. **Remarks:** Maintained by National Trust for Historic Preservation.

CLOISTERS LIBRARY
See: Metropolitan Museum of Art

★2922★
CLOROX COMPANY - TECHNICAL CENTER LIBRARY (Sci-Tech)
7200 Johnson Dr.
Box 493   Phone: (415) 847-6343
Pleasanton, CA 94566   Mary Anne Hoopes, Libn.
Staff: Prof 1; Other 2. **Subjects:** Chemistry, chemical specialties, food, microbiology, toxicology. **Holdings:** 3500 books; 1800 bound periodical volumes; 1800 reports. **Subscriptions:** 402 journals and other serials. **Services:** Interlibrary loans; copying; SDI; library not open to public. **Computerized Information Services:** DIALOG, SDC, BRS, NLM, New York Times Information Service; computerized laboratory notebooks. **Networks/Consortia:** Member of CLASS. **Publications:** What's New In House, quarterly - research and corporate distribution.

★2923★
CLOUD COUNTY HISTORICAL MUSEUM - LIBRARY (Hist)
7th & Broadway   Phone: (913) 243-2866
Concordia, KS 66901   Thelma Schroth, Cur.
Founded: 1959. **Staff:** Prof 3; Other 2. **Subjects:** Local history. **Special Collections:** Microfilm of Concordia Blade Empire, 1870-1981; Royal Family books and scrapbooks (113 volumes). **Holdings:** 800 books; 40 bound periodical volumes; 10 cubic feet of historical files; atlases; newspapers. **Subscriptions:** 13 journals and other serials. **Services:** Library open to public for reference use only. **Staff:** Mildred Barber, Hist.; Clarence Paulsen, Hist.

CLOUGHLY (O.J.) ALUMNI LIBRARY
See: St. Louis College of Pharmacy - O.J. Cloughly Alumni Library

★2924★
CLUB MANAGERS ASSOCIATION OF AMERICA - INFORMATION, RESEARCH & STATISTICS DEPARTMENT (Food-Bev)
7615 Winterberry Place
Box 34482   Phone: (301) 229-3600
Washington, DC 20817   Carol A. Moody, Dir./Info., Res., Pubn.
Founded: 1927. **Staff:** 15. **Subjects:** Club management operations, private club administration, employment in club industry. **Holdings:** 250 books; 50 bound periodical volumes. **Subscriptions:** 25 journals and other serials. **Services:** Library not open to public. **Publications:** Professional Development Catalog of programs, services and publications available for sale.

CLUNY COLLECTIONS
See: Harvard University - Graduate School of Design - Frances Loeb Library

CMS DOCUMENTATION CENTER
See: Center for Migration Studies

CN
See: Canadian National Railways

CN RAIL
See: Canadian National Rail

★2925★
CNA LIBRARY (Bus-Fin)
CNA Plaza, Van Buren and Wabash   Phone: (312) 822-7630
Chicago, IL 60685   Sandra Masson, Mgr., Lib.
Founded: 1958. **Staff:** Prof 1; Other 3. **Subjects:** Insurance and business. **Holdings:** 13,000 books; 100 bound periodical volumes; 500 actuarial texbooks; 110 shelves of clipping files; microfiche clipping services. **Subscriptions:** 475 journals and other serials; 5 newspapers. **Services:** Interlibrary loans; library open to public by appointment. **Computerized Information Services:** Computerized serials. **Networks/Consortia:** Member of Chicago Library System; Metropolitan Chicago Library Assembly.

CNA LIBRARY
See: Canadian Nuclear Association

CNIB
See: Canadian National Institute for the Blind

COACH HOUSE PRESS ARCHIVES
See: University of Calgary - Special Collections Division

COACHING ASSOCIATION OF CANADA - SPORT INFORMATION RESOURCE CENTRE
See: Sport Information Resource Centre

COADY INTERNATIONAL INSTITUTE
See: St. Francis Xavier University

★2926★
COAL EMPLOYMENT PROJECT (CEP) - ARCHIVES (Soc Sci)
Box 3403   Phone: (615) 482-3428
Oak Ridge, TN 37830   Joyce Dukes, Asst.Dir.
Subjects: Women coalminers. **Holdings:** 100 clippings, 1978 to present; 15 videotapes; 3 audiotapes; 20 photographs. **Services:** Interlibrary loans; copying; library open to public with restrictions. **Publications:** Coalmining Women's Support Team News, monthly. **Staff:** Connie L. White, Community Educ.Coord.

★2927★
COASTAL ECOSYSTEMS MANAGEMENT, INC. - LIBRARY (Sci-Tech)†
3600 Hulen St.   Phone: (817) 731-3727
Fort Worth, TX 76107   Elizabeth L. Parker, Libn.
Founded: 1970. **Staff:** Prof 1. **Subjects:** Marine ecology, geology. **Holdings:** 700 books; 2000 bound periodical volumes; 3000 reprints and reports (cataloged). **Subscriptions:** 20 journals and other serials. **Services:** Library not open to public.

COASTAL ENGINEERING RESEARCH CENTER
See: U.S. Army - Corps of Engineers

COASTAL INFORMATION REPOSITORY
See: Louisiana State University

COBURN (O.W.) LAW LIBRARY
See: Oral Roberts University - O.W. Coburn Law Library

★2928★
COCA-COLA COMPANY - ARCHIVES & BUSINESS INFORMATION SERVICES
NAT-19, Drawer 1734
Atlanta, GA 30301
Defunct

★2929★
COCA-COLA COMPANY - FOODS DIVISION - CITRUS RESEARCH & DEVELOPMENT TECHNICAL LIBRARY (Food-Bev)
Orange St.
Box 550   Phone: (305) 886-1568
Plymouth, FL 32768   Mary Ivey-Clark, Libn.
Staff: 2. **Subjects:** Chemistry, food technology. **Holdings:** 800 books; 2 VF drawers of patents. **Subscriptions:** 26 journals and other serials. **Services:** Library open to public with restrictions.

★2930★
COCA-COLA COMPANY - LAW LIBRARY (Law; Bus-Fin)
Box 1734   Phone: (404) 898-2096
Atlanta, GA 30301   H. Christine Johnson, Law Libn.
Staff: Prof 2; Other 1. **Subjects:** Antitrust and trade regulations; food and drug laws; corporation law, Securities and Exchange Commission; labor and employee benefits; patents, trademarks and copyright; international law. **Special Collections:** Roy D. Stubbs Collection (40 volumes). **Holdings:** 11,000 books; 775 bound periodical volumes; Federal Register, 1970 to present (microfiche); Code of Federal Regulations, 1977 to present (microfiche); FTC Decisions (microfiche). **Subscriptions:** 110 journals and other serials; 10 newspapers. **Services:** Interlibrary loans; copying; SDI; library open to public with restrictions. **Computerized Information Services:** LEXIS; computerized cataloging. **Staff:** Philip Glenn Cooper, Asst. Law Libn.

★2931★
COCA-COLA COMPANY - MARKETING INFORMATION CENTER (Bus-Fin; Food-Bev)
310 North Ave.   Phone: (404) 898-3314
Atlanta, GA 30301   Judy A. Cassell, Libn.
Founded: 1968. **Staff:** Prof 1; Other 1. **Subjects:** Soft drinks and beverages; marketing; advertising. **Holdings:** 800 books; 5000 documents and reports; 6 VF drawers of microfilm and microfiche. **Subscriptions:** 176 journals and other serials. **Services:** Interlibrary loans; copying; center open to public by appointment. **Computerized Information Services:** DIALOG, New York Times Information Service; MIC document file (internal database). **Networks/Consortia:** Member of Georgia Library Information Network (GLIN); OCLC through SOLINET. **Publications:** Business Information Digest, monthly - for internal distribution only. **Special Indexes:** Document file subject index.

★2932★
COCA-COLA COMPANY - TECHNICAL INFORMATION SERVICES (Food-Bev)
Box 1734 Phone: (404) 898-2008
Atlanta, GA 30301 Bernard Prudhomme, Mgr.
Founded: 1967. **Staff:** Prof 3; Other 2. **Subjects:** Beverages, soft drinks, fruit juices, coffee, tea, wine, food technology, nutrition, chemistry, engineering. **Holdings:** 12,000 books; 3000 bound periodical volumes; 10,000 reprints and patents; 1700 internal reports. **Subscriptions:** 400 journals and other serials. **Services:** Interlibrary loans; copying; library open to public by request for reference use. **Computerized Information Services:** DIALOG, SDC; computerized cataloging. **Networks/Consortia:** Member of Georgia Library Information Network (GLIN); OCLC through SOLINET. **Publications:** Information Bulletin, quarterly - for internal distribution only. **Special Catalogs:** KWIC index for information bulletin; online indexing of internal reports and literature searches. **Staff:** Mary Jane Montesinos, Sr.Info.Sci.; I. Margareta Martin, Info.Sci.

★2933★
COCHISE COUNTY LAW LIBRARY (Law)
Drawer P Phone: (602) 432-5703
Bisbee, AZ 85603 Herlinda Tafoya, Libn.
Founded: 1932. **Staff:** 1. **Subjects:** Law. **Holdings:** 20,000 volumes. **Subscriptions:** 15 journals and other serials; 5 newspapers. **Services:** Library open to public for reference use only.

COCKERELL COLLECTION
See: Dalhousie University

★2934★
COCONINO COUNTY LAW LIBRARY (Law)
County Court House Phone: (602) 774-5011
Flagstaff, AZ 86001 Rebecca H. Ruiz, Law Libn.
Staff: 1. **Subjects:** Law. **Holdings:** 14,000 volumes. **Subscriptions:** 134 journals and other serials. **Services:** Copying; library open to public.

COE (William Robertson) LIBRARY
See: University of Wyoming

★2935★
COEN COMPANY, INC. - TECHNICAL LIBRARY (Sci-Tech)†
1510 Rollins Rd. Phone: (415) 697-0440
Burlingame, CA 94010 Clark Hutchason, Supv.
Staff: Prof 1. **Subjects:** Engineering, combustion, energy. **Holdings:** 400 books; 500 bound periodical volumes; 100 codes and standards. **Subscriptions:** 12 journals and other serials. **Services:** Library not open to public.

★2936★
COGSWELL COLLEGE - LIBRARY (Sci-Tech)
600 Stockton St. Phone: (415) 433-5550
San Francisco, CA 94108 Herbert E. Childs, Jr., Libn.
Founded: 1971. **Staff:** Prof 2. **Subjects:** Electronics, structural and mechanical engineering technology, industrial and fire safety, architecture. **Holdings:** 10,000 books. **Subscriptions:** 350 journals and other serials; 6 newspapers. **Services:** Interlibrary loans; copying; library open to public for reference use only. **Networks/Consortia:** Member of San Francisco Consortium; Bay Area Reference Center (BARC). **Publications:** What's New in the Cogswell Library, monthly. **Also Known As:** Cogswell Polytechnical College. **Staff:** Judith Carson-Croes, Asst.Libn.

COGSWELL MUSIC LIBRARY
See: Indiana University of Pennsylvania

COHEN (L. Lewis) MEMORIAL MEDICAL LIBRARY
See: Weiss (Louis A.) Memorial Hospital - L. Lewis Cohen Memorial Medical Library

COHEN (Morris Raphael) LIBRARY
See: CUNY - City College Library - Special Collections

COHEN (Ralph) MEMORIAL LIBRARY
See: Wise (Isaac M.) Temple - Ralph Cohen Memorial Library

★2937★
COHEN, SHAPIRO, POLISHER, SHIEKMAN AND COHEN - LIBRARY (Law)
12 S. 12th St. Phone: (215) 922-1300
Philadelphia, PA 19107 Betty Metz, Libn.
Staff: Prof 1; Other 2. **Subjects:** Law. **Holdings:** 11,000 books; 235 bound periodical volumes. **Subscriptions:** 100 journals and other serials; 16 newspapers. **Services:** Interlibrary loans; library not open to public. **Computerized Information Services:** LEXIS.

★2938★
COHEN AND URETZ - LAW LIBRARY (Law)
1775 K St., N.W. Phone: (202) 293-4740
Washington, DC 20006 Allen C. Story, Libn.
Staff: Prof 2; Other 2. **Subjects:** Federal taxation, real estate law. **Holdings:** Legislative histories of tax bills from 1909 to present (microfiche); all case material relating to federal taxes. **Subscriptions:** 100 journals and other serials. **Services:** Interlibrary loans; copying (limited); library open to visitors with permission of librarian. **Computerized Information Services:** LEXIS. **Staff:** Madonna Lyons, Asst.Libn.

COHN (Charles) MEMORIAL LIBRARY
See: North Shore Synagogue - Charles Cohn Memorial Library

★2939★
COLBY COLLEGE - MILLER LIBRARY - SPECIAL COLLECTIONS (Hum; Hist)
Phone: (207) 873-1131
Waterville, ME 04901 J. Fraser Cocks, III, Cur., Spec.Coll.
Founded: 1938. **Staff:** Prof 1; Other 1. **Subjects:** American regional literature, Irish literary renaissance. **Special Collections:** Colby College Archives; Edwin Arlington Robinson Collection (1500 printed and manuscript items); James A. Healy Collection of Irish Literature (5000 volumes); Thomas Hardy Collection (300 printed and manuscript items). **Holdings:** 30,000 books; 100 bound periodical volumes; 44,400 letters and manuscripts; 728 reels of microfilm. **Subscriptions:** 8 journals and other serials. **Services:** Copying; library open to public. **Special Catalogs:** Guide to James Augustine Healy Collection. **Staff:** P.A. Lenk, Spec.Coll.Asst.

COLBY (William E.) MEMORIAL LIBRARY
See: Sierra Club - William E. Colby Memorial Library

COLD REGIONS RESEARCH & ENGINEERING LABORATORY
See: Center for Northern Studies; U.S. Army

★2940★
COLD SPRING HARBOR LABORATORY - MAIN LIBRARY (Sci-Tech)
Box 100 Phone: (516) 692-6660
Cold Spring Harbor, NY 11724 Susan Gensel, Dir., Libs. & Marketing
Founded: 1906. **Staff:** Prof 2; Other 3. **Subjects:** Biological sciences, genetics, cancer research, cell science, neurobiology, virology. **Special Collections:** Carnegie Collection (genetics, eugenics and biochemistry historical collection; 3628 volumes). **Holdings:** 6400 books; 14,000 bound periodical volumes; 24 VF drawers of archives, letters, clippings; 4 boxes of pamphlets. **Subscriptions:** 359 journals and other serials. **Services:** Interlibrary loans; copying; library open to public by appointment with librarian only. **Computerized Information Services:** DIALOG. **Networks/Consortia:** Member of Long Island Library Resources Council (LILRC). **Remarks:** Original eugenics work of historical interest and much of the definitive work in genetics done at this site. **Staff:** Audrey Powers, Libn.; Laura Hyman, Asst.Libn.

COLE (Clinton L.) MARINE LIBRARY
See: University of Maine, Orono - Raymond H. Fogler Library - Special Collections Department

★2941★
COLE COUNTY HISTORICAL SOCIETY - MUSEUM AND LIBRARY (Hist)
109 Madison Phone: (314) 635-1850
Jefferson City, MO 65101 Lynn Rebbeor-Shay, Cur.
Staff: Prof 1; Other 1. **Subjects:** Cole County and local history, Missouri history, genealogy. **Holdings:** 600 books; 50 bound periodical volumes; 25 scrapbooks (cataloged); 200 books in the DAR Library; 100 documents and manuscripts; 28 VF drawers; 15 inaugural ball gowns of former Governors' wives. **Services:** Library open to public; admission fee charged.

COLE MEMORIAL LIBRARY OF THE PHYSICS AND ASTRONOMY DEPARTMENT
See: Ohio State University

★2942★
COLEBROOK HISTORICAL SOCIETY - LIBRARY AND ARCHIVES (Hist)
Phone: (203) 379-9773
Colebrook, CT 06021 George R. Rinhart, Cur.
Staff: 1. **Subjects:** Local history. **Holdings:** Books, town and church records, pictures and maps. **Services:** Collections open to public.

COLECCION TLOQUE NAHUAQUE
See: University of California, Santa Barbara - Library - Chicano Studies Collection

COLEMAN LIBRARY
See: Callaway Educational Association

COLEMAN LIBRARY
See: University of Toronto - Department of Geology

★2943★
COLER MEMORIAL HOSPITAL - MEDICAL LIBRARY (Med)
Roosevelt Island   Phone: (212) 688-9400
New York, NY 10044   Gina Buika, Ph.D., Dir., Med.Lib.
Founded: 1964. **Staff:** Prof 1; Other 1. **Subjects:** Medicine, chronic disease, geriatrics, rehabilitation, nursing and allied health sciences. **Special Collections:** Geriatrics. **Holdings:** Figures not available. **Subscriptions:** 160 journals. **Services:** Interlibrary loans; copying; library open to public with librarian's permission. **Networks/Consortia:** Member of Medical Library Center of New York (MLCNY). **Remarks:** Hospital is an affiliate of New York Medical College. **Formerly:** Bird S. Coler Hospital.

★2944★
COLES COUNTY HISTORICAL SOCIETY - GREENWOOD SCHOOL MUSEUM - LIBRARY (Hist)
800 Hayes Ave.   Phone: (217) 581-3310
Charleston, IL 61920   Dr. E. Duane Elbert, Musm.Cur.
Staff: Prof 1. **Subjects:** Local history. **Holdings:** 200 books; oral history tapes; clippings; documents. **Services:** Library open to public.

★2945★
COLGATE PALMOLIVE COMPANY - TECHNICAL INFORMATION CENTER (Sci-Tech)
909 River Rd.   Phone: (201) 463-1212
Piscataway, NJ 08854   Monica Grover, Sect.Hd.
Founded: 1936. **Staff:** Prof 3; Other 4. **Subjects:** Soaps and detergents, fats and oils, dentifrices, cosmetics, perfumes and essential oils, environmental pollution, foods, chemistry. **Holdings:** 18,000 books; 10,000 bound periodical volumes; 16,000 volumes of periodicals on 4000 reels of microfilm; 250 VF drawers of internal reports; 10 VF drawers of archives. **Subscriptions:** 400 journals and other serials; 3 newspapers. **Services:** Interlibrary loans; copying; SDI; library open to public with restrictions. **Computerized Information Services:** DIALOG, SDC, Derwent Publications Ltd., BRS, NLM, New York Times Information Service. **Publications:** Notes & Abstracts Bulletin, monthly. **Special Indexes:** Mechanized indexes to internal documents and compounds. **Staff:** Tina Velantzas, Info.Sci.; Mark Judman, Info.Sci.

★2946★
COLGATE ROCHESTER/BEXLEY HALL/CROZER THEOLOGICAL SEMINARIES - AMBROSE SWASEY LIBRARY (Rel-Theol)
1100 S. Goodman St.   Phone: (716) 271-1320
Rochester, NY 14620   Peter N. VandenBerge, Dir. of Lib.Serv.
Staff: Prof 2; Other 5. **Subjects:** World religions, Christian history, theology, worship and liturgy, marriage and family, Bible. **Holdings:** 200,000 books and bound periodical volumes; 1117 microforms; 665 audio recordings; 460 theses. **Subscriptions:** 975 journals and other serials. **Services:** Interlibrary loans; copying; library open to public with limited reference service. **Networks/Consortia:** Member of Rochester Regional Research Library Council (RRRLC). **Publications:** Book Lists, monthly; Guide to Ambrose Swasey Library. **Remarks:** Includes the holdings of Colburn Library, formerly at Bexley Hall, Gambier, OH, and portions of Bucknell Library, formerly located at Crozer Theological Seminary, Chester, PA. **Staff:** Robert Genovese, Cat.Libn.

COLGATE (Samuel) BAPTIST HISTORICAL LIBRARY
See: American Baptist Historical Society - Samuel Colgate Baptist Historical Library

★2947★
COLGATE UNIVERSITY - ARCHIVES (Hist)
                                         Phone: (315) 824-1000
Hamilton, NY 13346   Bruce M. Brown, Univ.Archv.
Founded: 1947. **Staff:** Prof 1. **Subjects:** Origin and development of Colgate University; its administrators, faculty, students and alumni. **Special Collections:** Edward H. Stone Memorial Collection (10,000 photographic negatives of people and places related to Hamilton, New York and Colgate University, for period 1900-1958). **Holdings:** 200 books; 25 filing cabinets and 300 boxes of archives. **Services:** Copying; archives open to public with

restrictions.

COLLECTION FOR THE HISTORY OF CARTOGRAPHY
See: California State University, Fullerton

★2948★
COLLECTOR CIRCLE - LIBRARY (Rec)
1313 S. Killian Dr.   Phone: (305) 845-6075
Lake Park, FL 33403   Roz Belford, Publ.
Staff: Prof 1; Other 1. **Subjects:** Thimbles - history, manufacture, usage, patents. **Special Collections:** Thimbles by Holmes; thimble related articles, 1867 to present (10 VF drawers of clippings). **Holdings:** 510 books and bound periodical volumes. **Subscriptions:** 35 journals and other serials; 40 newspapers.

★2949★
COLLECTORS CLUB OF CHICAGO - LIBRARY (Rec)†
1029 N. Dearborn St.   Phone: (312) 642-7981
Chicago, IL 60610   Lester E. Winick, Lib.Comm.
Staff: 1. **Subjects:** Philately. **Holdings:** 4000 books; 2000 bound periodical volumes. **Subscriptions:** 100 journals and other serials. **Services:** Interlibrary loans; library open to public. **Publications:** Books on postal history.

★2950★
COLLECTORS CLUB - LIBRARY (Rec)
22 E. 35th St.   Phone: (212) 683-0559
New York, NY 10016   Werner Elias, Libn.
Founded: 1896. **Subjects:** Philately, postal history. **Holdings:** 125,000 items. **Subscriptions:** 200 journals and other serials. **Services:** Interlibrary loans (fee); library open to public by appointment.

★2951★
COLLEGE DE L'ABITIBI-TEMISCAMINGUE - BIBLIOTHEQUE - SPECIAL COLLECTIONS (Area-Ethnic)
425 College Blvd.
Box 8000
Rouyn, PQ, Canada J9X 5M5
                                         Phone: (819) 762-0931
                                         Serge Allard, Dir.
Founded: 1953. **Special Collections:** Northwest Quebec (Abiti-Temiscamingue; 6608 books and 4 newspaper titles). **Services:** Interlibrary loans; copying; library open to public with restrictions. **Computerized Information Services:** DIALOG. **Networks/Consortia:** Member of BADADUQ. **Formerly:** College du Nord-Ouest.

COLLEGE OF THE AMERICAS - MUSEUM OF THE AMERICAS
See: Museum of the Americas

COLLEGE OF ART & DESIGN
See: Center for Creative Studies/College of Art & Design

COLLEGE BAND DIRECTORS NATIONAL ASSOCIATION ARCHIVES
See: University of Maryland, College Park - Libraries - Music Library

COLLEGE AT BROCKPORT
See: SUNY

COLLEGE AT BUFFALO
See: SUNY

★2952★
COLLEGE OF CAPE BRETON - BEATON INSTITUTE ARCHIVES (Hist)
Box 5300   Phone: (902) 564-6343
Sydney, NS, Canada B1P 6L2   Dr. R.J. Morgan, Dir.
Founded: 1957. **Staff:** Prof 1; Other 5. **Subjects:** Cape Breton Island - history, labour history, Gaelic literature, folklore, political history; traditional Scottish music of Cape Breton Island; genealogy. **Special Collections:** John Parker Nautical Collection (8.7 meters); Gaelic and Scottish collection (3000 volumes); political papers. **Holdings:** 5000 books; 200 bound periodical volumes; 200 unbound reports; 8000 photographs; 800 maps; 115 meters of manuscripts; 5 VF drawers of clippings; 600 reels of microfilm; 50 large scrapbooks; 3000 tapes; 600 slides; 50 videotapes. **Subscriptions:** 10 journals and other serials. **Services:** Copying; library open to public.

★2953★
COLLEGE CENTER OF THE FINGER LAKES - LIBRARY (Bus-Fin)
22 W. Third St.   Phone: (607) 962-3134
Corning, NY 14830   Julia Lonnberg, Libn.
Founded: 1965. **Staff:** 1. **Subjects:** Business, education, engineering. **Holdings:** 10,000 books. **Subscriptions:** 90 journals and other serials and newspapers. **Services:** Interlibrary loans; copying; library open to public for

reference use only. **Networks/Consortia:** Member of South Central Research Libraries Council (SCRLC).

COLLEGE AT CORTLAND
See: SUNY

★2954★
COLLEGE DOMINICAIN DE PHILOSOPHIE ET DE THEOLOGIE - BIBLIOTHEQUE (Rel-Theol)
96 Empress Ave.   Phone: (613) 233-5696
Ottawa, ON, Canada K1R 7G2   Jean-Jacques Robillard, Chf.Libn./Info.Dir.
Staff: Prof 3. **Subjects:** Theology, Near Eastern studies, Biblical studies, philosophy, medieval studies. **Holdings:** 81,150 books; 14,025 bound periodical volumes. **Subscriptions:** 423 journals and other serials; 10 newspapers. **Services:** Interlibrary loans; copying; library open to public. **Also Known As:** Dominican College of Philosophy and Theology. **Staff:** Angelo Ouellet, Asst.Libn.; Benoit Berthelot, Asst.Libn.

COLLEGE D'ENSEIGNEMENT GENERAL ET PROFESSIONNEL...
See: CEGEP...

COLLEGE OF ENVIRONMENTAL SCIENCE AND FORESTRY
See: SUNY

★2955★
COLLEGE OF FAMILY PHYSICIANS OF CANADA - CANADIAN LIBRARY OF FAMILY MEDICINE (Med)
Sciences Library
Natural Sciences Centre
University of Western Ontario   Phone: (519) 679-2537
London, ON, Canada N6A 5B7   Dorothy Fitzgerald, Libn.
Founded: 1972. **Staff:** Prof 1; Other 2. **Subjects:** Family medicine, general practice. **Services:** Copying; literature searches; library consultation; services available to health agencies and personnel interested in family medicine. **Computerized Information Services:** MEDLINE. **Publications:** Capsules from Family Medicine Literature, monthly, in Canadian Family Physician; Core Library List for Family Medical Centers or Small Hospital Libraries, every two years in Canadian Family Physician. **Special Catalogs:** Family Medicine Literature Index (FAMLI), quarterly with annual cumulations. **Remarks:** The Canadian Library of Family Medicine bases its services at the Sciences Library of the University of Western Ontario.

★2956★
COLLEGE OF FISHERIES, NAVIGATION, MARINE ENGINEERING AND ELECTRONICS - LIBRARY (Sci-Tech)
Parade St.
P.O. Box 4920   Phone: (709) 726-5272
St. John's, NF, Canada A1C 5R3   Mabel Farmer, Libn.
Founded: 1963. **Staff:** Prof 1; Other 2. **Subjects:** Fisheries and related fields; navigation; nautical science; marine engineering; electronics; food technology. **Holdings:** 13,000 books; 500 bound periodical volumes; 3000 government documents; 12 VF drawers of pamphlets, clippings and reprints (cataloged). **Subscriptions:** 250 journals and other serials; 14 newspapers. **Services:** Interlibrary loans; copying; library open to public with restrictions. **Publications:** Acquisitions list. **Special Catalogs:** Audio Visual Catalog.

COLLEGE AT FREDONIA
See: SUNY

COLLEGE DE LA GARDE COTIERE CANADIENNE
See: Canada - Transport Canada - Canadian Coast Guard College

COLLEGE AT GENESEO
See: SUNY

★2957★
COLLEGE FOR HUMAN SERVICES - LIBRARY (Soc Sci)
345 Hudson St.   Phone: (212) 989-2002
New York, NY 10014   Loretta Capers, Libn.
Staff: Prof 1; Other 1. **Subjects:** Human services, social sciences, humanities. **Holdings:** 18,200 books; 250 New Careers publications; 24 VF drawers articles and pamphlets. **Subscriptions:** 225 journals and other serials; 6 newspapers. **Services:** Interlibrary loans; library not open to public.

★2958★
COLLEGE OF IDAHO - REGIONAL STUDIES CENTER - LIBRARY (Env-Cons)
Boone Science Hall, Rm. 257   Phone: (208) 459-5214
Caldwell, ID 83605   Donna Parsons, Dir.
Staff: Prof 1; Other 1. **Subjects:** Snake River Basin and Idaho, folk-lore,

water quality, groundwater irrigation, natural resources, land use planning, environmental education. **Holdings:** 1500 books; 1000 35mm slides; 30 videotapes. **Services:** Interlibrary loans; library open to public.

COLLEGE OF INSURANCE - ASSOCIATION OF AVERAGE ADJUSTERS OF THE UNITED STATES
See: Association of Average Adjusters of the United States

★2959★
COLLEGE OF INSURANCE - INSURANCE SOCIETY OF NEW YORK - LIBRARY (Bus-Fin)
123 William St.   Phone: (212) 962-4111
New York, NY 10038   Donald Carson, Chf.Libn.
Founded: 1901. **Staff:** Prof 6; Other 1. **Subjects:** Insurance - casualty, fire, health, inland marine, life, marine, suretyship, unemployment, workmen's compensation, and all allied fields; fire and accident prevention; earthquakes; actuarial science. **Special Collections:** William Winter Marine Library (marine insurance); Heber B. Churchill earthquake collection. **Holdings:** 69,407 books; 12,502 bound periodical volumes; 52,247 pamphlets, clippings and speeches. **Subscriptions:** 418 journals and other serials; 6 newspapers. **Services:** Interlibrary loans; copying; reference service for members of society; library open to public for reference and research. **Publications:** Basic Insurance Books - send request to Insurance Information Institute, 110 William Street, New York, NY 10038. **Remarks:** Association of Average Adjusters of the U.S. is also located at this address. **Staff:** Beverly Rosignolo, Assoc.Libn.; Gladys Hodapp, Asst.Libn.; Paul Caricone, Cat.; Michael McKegney, Cat.

★2960★
COLLEGE OF INSURANCE - WESTERN DIVISION - LIBRARY (Bus-Fin)
3142 Wilshire Blvd.   Phone: (213) 738-9973
Los Angeles, CA 90010   Kathryn Lee, Libn.
Founded: 1979. **Staff:** Prof 1. **Subjects:** Insurance. **Holdings:** 1400 books. **Subscriptions:** 62 journals and other serials. **Services:** Interlibrary loans; library open to public with restrictions.

COLLEGE OF MEDICINE AND DENTISTRY OF NEW JERSEY
See: University of Medicine and Dentistry of New Jersey

★2961★
COLLEGE MILITAIRE ROYAL DE ST-JEAN - LIBRARY (Mil)
                                                      Phone: (514) 346-2131
St. Jean, PQ, Canada J0J 1R0   Armand Lamirande, Chf.Libn.
Founded: 1952. **Staff:** Prof 4; Other 6. **Subjects:** French Canadian literature, military science, Canadiana, Canadian history, sciences. **Holdings:** 102,951 books; 36,963 bound periodical volumes; 7345 pamphlets and government publications; French Canadian newspapers on microfilm; 170 tapes; 2451 reels of microfilm; 1915 slides; 1613 microfiche. **Subscriptions:** 870 journals and other serials. **Services:** Interlibrary loans; copying; library open to teachers, staff and families, and officer cadets. **Publications:** Accession Lists, monthly. **Remarks:** Maintained by Canada - National Defence. **Staff:** P. Tremblay, Ref.Libn.; L. Racicot, Asst. & Cat.; G. Cheung, Acq.Libn.

★2962★
COLLEGE DE MUSIQUE SAINTE-CROIX - BIBLIOTHEQUE (Mus)
637 Sainte-Croix Blvd.   Phone: (514) 747-6521
St. Laurent, PQ, Canada H4L 3X7   Lucienne Nadeau, Dir.
Founded: 1968. **Staff:** Prof 2; Other 2. **Subjects:** Music. **Special Collections:** Gregorian Chant number 800 with paleographic signs (Solesmes). **Holdings:** 4800 books; 170 bound periodical volumes; 4560 scores; Gregorian Chant microfilm; theses; documents on Canadian composers; tapes. **Subscriptions:** 46 journals and other serials. **Services:** Copying; library open to public by appointment. **Remarks:** College de Musique Sainte-Croix is part of the CEGEP de Saint-Laurent Music Department. **Staff:** Bertha Vermandere, Ref.Libn.

COLLEGE DU NORD-OUEST
See: College de l'Abitibi-Temiscaminque

COLLEGE AT ONEONTA
See: SUNY

COLLEGE AT OSWEGO
See: SUNY

★2963★
COLLEGE OF PHYSICIANS OF PHILADELPHIA - LIBRARY AND MEDICAL DOCUMENTATION SERVICE (Med)†
19 S. 22nd St.   Phone: (215) 561-6050
Philadelphia, PA 19103   Anthony Aguirre, Lib.Dir.
Founded: 1787. **Staff:** Prof 24; Other 33. **Subjects:** Medicine and medical

specialties; history of medicine. **Special Collections:** Incunabula, 16th, 17th, and 18th century works (423). **Holdings:** 293,885 accessioned items; 323,074 reports, theses, and dissertations; 1000 manuscripts and typescripts; 10,000 portraits, engravings and pictures; 10,000 autographs. **Subscriptions:** 2500 journals and other serials. **Services:** Interlibrary loans; copying; SDI; bibliographic searches; consultative library service. The Medical Documentation Service, established in 1953, provides current awareness, translation, indexing, abstracting, editing, data extraction and summary services as well as bibliographic searches - all on a fee basis; library open to public for reading and photocopy, other privileges restricted to registered borrowers. **Computerized Information Services:** MEDLINE. **Networks/Consortia:** Member of OCLC; headquarters of Mideastern Regional Medical Library Service (MERMLS). **Publications:** Annual Report, (both library and Regional Program); Booklist, 6/year. **Special Indexes:** Card file of portraits. **Staff:** June A. Poses, Asst. to Libn.; June M. Fulton, Dir., R.M.L.; Christine Ruggere, Cur./Hist.Coll.; Nina F. Galpern, MEDLINE; Cynthia Rourke, Regional Ext.Libn.; Dr. Ronald Kotrc, Dir., Med.Hist.Div.; Alberta D. Berton, Dir., Med.Doc.Serv.

★2964★
COLLEGE OF PHYSICIANS AND SURGEONS OF BRITISH COLUMBIA - MEDICAL LIBRARY SERVICE (Med)
Keith Library
1807 W. 10th Ave.   Phone: (604) 736-5551
Vancouver, BC, Canada V6J 2A9   C. William Fraser, Dir.
Founded: 1960. **Staff:** Prof 4; Other 6. **Subjects:** Medicine, medical history, medical biography. **Special Collections:** Vancouver Medical Association Historical Collection; British Columbia Archives of Medicine. **Holdings:** 8000 books; 40,000 bound periodical volumes; 1500 pamphlets; 8 VF drawers of archives; 3 shelves of reports; 1500 audiotapes. **Subscriptions:** 600 journals and other serials. **Services:** Interlibrary loans; copying; library open to qualified users. **Computerized Information Services:** MEDLINE. **Publications:** Books for Hospital Libraries, annual - distributed to British Columbia hospitals. **Also Known As:** British Columbia Medical Library Service. **Staff:** Adrienne Clark, Asst.Libn.

★2965★
COLLEGE PLACEMENT COUNCIL, INC. - RESOURCE INFORMATION CENTER (Educ)
Box 2263   Phone: (215) 868-1421
Bethlehem, PA 18001   Linda M. Pengilly, Info.Asst.
Staff: Prof 1. **Subjects:** Career planning and development, recruiting and placement, education statistics. **Holdings:** 500 books; 15 shelves of files. **Subscriptions:** 49 journals and other serials. **Services:** Library open to public.

COLLEGE AT PLATTSBURGH
See: SUNY

COLLEGE AT POTSDAM
See: SUNY

★2966★
COLLEGE OF PREACHERS - LIBRARY (Rel-Theol)
3510 Woodley Rd., N.W.
Washington, DC 20016   Mildred Coleman, Libn.
Subjects: Religion. **Holdings:** 8000 volumes. **Subscriptions:** 42 journals and other serials. **Services:** Library open to public by appointment.

★2967★
COLLEGE RETIREMENT EQUITIES FUND - CREF RESEARCH LIBRARY (Bus-Fin)
730 Third Ave.   Phone: (212) 916-4009
New York, NY 10017   Linda Bashover, Libn.
Founded: 1973. **Staff:** Prof 1; Other 2. **Subjects:** Investments, finance. **Holdings:** 520 books; 24 drawers of microfiche; 250 VF drawers of corporation records; 4 drawers of microfilm. **Subscriptions:** 260 journals and other serials; 24 newspapers. **Services:** Interlibrary loans; library open to SLA members.

COLLEGE OF THE ROCKIES
See: Christ Centered Ministries

★2968★
COLLEGE DE STE-ANNE-DE-LA-POCATIERE - BIBLIOTHEQUE (Hist; Hum)
100 Ave. Painchaud   Phone: (418) 856-3082
La Pocatiere, PQ, Canada G0R 1Z0   Marcel Mignault, Hd.
Founded: 1829. **Staff:** Prof 1; Other 2. **Subjects:** History of Canada, French-Canadian and French literature, regional history. **Holdings:** 80,000 books; 25,000 bound periodical volumes; 2000 pamphlets. **Subscriptions:** 150

journals and other serials. **Services:** Interlibrary loans; library open to public for reference use only.

★2969★
COLLEGE DE STE-ANNE-DE-LA-POCATIERE - SOCIETE HISTORIQUE-DE-LA-COTE-DU-SUD - BIBLIOTHEQUE (Hist)
C.P. 937   Phone: (418) 856-1525
La Pocatiere, PQ, Canada G0R 1Z0   Guy Theberge, Sec.
Founded: 1948. **Staff:** Prof 1. **Subjects:** Regional history, church history, genealogy, history of Canada. **Holdings:** 1200 books; 500 bound periodical volumes; 200 pamphlets. **Services:** Interlibrary loans; copying; library open to public for reference use only, on request. **Publications:** Cahiers d'Histoire.

★2970★
COLLEGE OF ST. CATHERINE - LIBRARY - RUTH SAWYER COLLECTION (Hum)
2004 Randolph Ave.   Phone: (612) 690-6553
St. Paul, MN 55105   Sr. Mary William Brady, Archv.
Staff: Prof 2. **Subjects:** Ruth Sawyer, children's literature, history and art of storytelling, folklore. **Special Collections:** Original manuscripts and drawings from several of Ruth Sawyer's books; honorary medals - Newbery, Wilder, Regina; artifacts of storybook characters. **Holdings:** 2039 books; 223 letters (cataloged). **Services:** Copying; library open to public with restrictions. **Computerized Information Services:** DIALOG; computerized cataloging. **Networks/Consortia:** Member of MINITEX; OCLC; Cooperating Libraries in Consortium (CLIC). **Publications:** The Ruth Sawyer Bibliography - in house only. **Remarks:** A nearly complete collection of Ruth Sawyer's writings, copies of works translated into foreign languages, correspondence and other personal memorabilia.

★2971★
COLLEGE OF ST. CATHERINE - LIBRARY - WOMAN'S COLLECTION (Soc Sci)
2004 Randolph Ave.   Phone: (612) 690-6648
St. Paul, MN 55105   Margaret Conant, Hd., Rd.Serv. & ILL
Staff: Prof 2. **Subjects:** Sociological and economic studies on women published in the early 20th century; psychological liberation of women; history, education, status of women in all phases of public and private life. **Special Collections:** Herstory: microfilm collection of 300 women's journals, newspapers and newsletters, 1956-1971 (23 reels); U.S. Dept. of Labor, Women's Bureau Bulletin, 1918-1954 (microfiche). **Holdings:** 3850 books; 20 bound periodical volumes; 8 VF drawers of pamphlets and clippings. **Services:** Interlibrary loans; copying; library open to public for reference use only. **Computerized Information Services:** DIALOG; computerized cataloging. **Networks/Consortia:** Member of MINITEX; OCLC; Cooperating Libraries in Consortium (CLIC).

★2972★
COLLEGE OF ST. CATHERINE - PERFORMING ARTS LIBRARY (Mus)
2004 Randolph Ave.   Phone: (612) 690-6696
St. Paul, MN 55105   Donald Bemis Jones, Libn.
Founded: 1970. **Staff:** Prof 2; Other 1. **Subjects:** Music, theater and drama, speech communication. **Holdings:** 10,000 books and scores; 6500 phonodiscs (cataloged). **Subscriptions:** 30 journals and other serials. **Services:** Interlibrary loans; library open to public with restrictions. **Computerized Information Services:** Computerized cataloging. **Networks/Consortia:** Member of OCLC; Cooperating Libraries in Consortium (CLIC). **Staff:** Anne Godine, Asst.Libn.

★2973★
COLLEGE OF ST. THOMAS - SPECIAL COLLECTIONS (Area-Ethnic)
O'Shaughnessy Library   Phone: (612) 647-5318
St. Paul, MN 55105   John B. Davenport, Spec.Coll.Libn.
Staff: Prof 2; Other 1. **Subjects:** Irish, Scottish and Welsh language, history, literature and folklore. **Special Collections:** Celtic Collection (4600 titles). **Holdings:** 5700 titles. **Services:** Copying; collection open to public 4 hours a week and upon written request. **Networks/Consortia:** Member of Cooperating Libraries in Consortium (CLIC); OCLC; MINITEX. **Staff:** James D. Kellen, Cat.; C. Ann Miller, Spec.Coll.Asst.

★2974★
COLLEGE OF THE SAN FRANCISCO ART INSTITUTE - ANNE BREMER MEMORIAL LIBRARY (Art)
800 Chestnut St.   Phone: (415) 771-7020
San Francisco, CA 94133   Sharon Chickanzeff, Lib.Dir.
Founded: 1871. **Staff:** Prof 2; Other 3. **Subjects:** Fine arts, photography, filmmaking, humanities and social sciences. **Special Collections:** Artists' book collection (300 volumes). **Holdings:** 20,000 books; 1200 bound periodical volumes; 30,000 slides; prints; 6 VF drawers; 300 volumes of archives; 100 manuscripts of information and school history; 25 cartons of documents,

clippings; 40 16mm films; 400 audiotapes. **Subscriptions:** 250 journals and other serials. **Services:** Copying; library open to public for reference use only. **Staff:** Charles Stephanian, Dir., Media Serv.

★2975★
COLLEGE OF TRADES AND TECHNOLOGY - LIBRARY (Sci-Tech; Med)
P.O. Box 1693   Phone: (709) 753-9360
St. John's, NF, Canada A1C 5P7   Patricia Rahal, Libn.
Founded: 1963. **Staff:** Prof 1; Other 5. **Subjects:** Business, engineering technology, electronics technology. **Holdings:** 25,000 books; 400 bound periodical volumes; 300 volumes of serials in microform. **Subscriptions:** 525 journals and other serials; 14 newspapers. **Services:** Interlibrary loans; copying; library open to public. **Computerized Information Services:** Computerized serials. **Publications:** Books added to the library, monthly - for internal distribution only.

★2976★
COLLEGE OF TRADES AND TECHNOLOGY - MEDICAL LIBRARY (Med)
Topsail Campus
P.O. Box 1693   Phone: (709) 368-2001
St. John's, NF, Canada A1C 5P7   Patricia Rahal, Libn.
Founded: 1975. **Staff:** 2. **Subjects:** Medical laboratory and x-ray technology, pharmacology, nursing, food management, forest technology, petroleum technology. **Holdings:** 7000 books; 600 bound periodical volumes; 100 films and models; 300 volumes of periodicals on microfiche. **Subscriptions:** 160 journals and other serials. **Services:** Interlibrary loans; copying; library open to public with restrictions. **Computerized Information Services:** Computerized serials. **Staff:** Mrs. D. Parrott, Lib.Techn.

★2977★
COLLEGE UNIVERSITAIRE DE ST. BONIFACE - BIBLIOTHEQUE UNIVERSITAIRE (Hum)
200 Ave. De La Cathedrale   Phone: (204) 233-0210
Saint-Boniface, MB, Canada R2H 0H7   Marcel Boulet, Hd.Libn.
Founded: 1818. **Staff:** Prof 3; Other 4. **Subjects:** French and French-Canadian literature, education, Canadian history, religion, philosophy, social sciences. **Holdings:** 60,000 volumes; 1500 reels of microfilm; 10,000 microfiche; 4253 audiovisual materials. **Subscriptions:** 325 journals and other serials; 9 newspapers. **Services:** Interlibrary loans; copying; library open to public. **Remarks:** The majority of holdings are French language. **Staff:** Marcel Lemieux, Asst.Libn.; Madeleine Samuda, Ref.

★2978★
COLLEGE OF THE VIRGIN ISLANDS - CARIBBEAN RESEARCH INSTITUTE - LIBRARY (Env-Cons; Energy; Soc Sci)
CRI Library   Phone: (809) 774-1252
St. Thomas, VI 00801   Anna Mae Brown-Comment, Adm.Asst.
Staff: Prof 1; Other 1. **Subjects:** Water resources, economics, social sciences, ecology, marine sciences, education, energy. **Special Collections:** Maps of the Caribbean, with emphasis on the Virgin Islands (50); Caribbean Shipwreck and other archeological documents (3 VF drawers); Alternate Energy Technologies (150 slides); Working Paper Series (Numbers 1 and 2); Microstate Studies Journal (Numbers 1 and 2). **Holdings:** 700 books; 500 documents on energy; 400 items of Caribbeana. **Subscriptions:** 53 journals and other serials. **Services:** Copying; library open to public with restrictions. **Publications:** Covicrier, quarterly newsletter; Caribbean Research Institute Biennial Report - both free upon request.

★2979★
COLLEGE OF THE VIRGIN ISLANDS - FOUNDATION CENTER REGIONAL COLLECTION (Soc Sci)
Paiewonsky Library   Phone: (809) 774-9200
St. Thomas, VI 00801   F. Keith Bingham
Founded: 1979. **Staff:** Prof 1. **Subjects:** Foundations, grants, fund-raising. **Holdings:** 65 books; 90 microfiche; 50 aperture cards; 180 annual reports and information brochures; 1 vertical file drawer. **Services:** Interlibrary loans; library open to public.

★2980★
COLLEGE OF WILLIAM AND MARY - EARL GREGG SWEM LIBRARY (Hist)†
                                       Phone: (804) 253-4404
Williamsburg, VA 23185   Clifford Currie, Libn.
Founded: 1693. **Staff:** Prof 16; Other 43. **Subjects:** Virginia history, U.S. history to 1830, dogs and hunting, history of American printing, college archives. **Special Collections:** Virginia Historical Manuscripts, 17th-20th centuries (900,000 items); Tucker-Coleman Papers, 1675-1956 (1500 volumes; 30,000 items); Peter Chapin Collection on dogs and hunting (3100 items); seed catalogs (800). **Holdings:** 703,541 books and bound periodical volumes; 1 million manuscripts; 290,769 documents (U.S. and Virginia);

435,250 microforms. **Subscriptions:** 4674 journals and other serials. **Services:** Interlibrary loans; copying; library open to public with borrower's card. **Computerized Information Services:** Computerized cataloging. **Networks/Consortia:** Member of OCLC through SOLINET; Association of Southeast Research Libraries. **Publications:** Library Contributions (numbered series), irregular. **Special Catalogs:** A Guide to Historical Materials in the Swem Library (book). **Staff:** Kay J. Domine, Coll.Archv.; Margaret C. Cook, Cur., Mss./Rare Bks.

COLLEGE OF WILLIAM & MARY - GRADUATE SCHOOL OF MARINE SCIENCE LIBRARY
See: Virginia Institute of Marine Science Library

COLLEGE OF WILLIAM AND MARY - INSTITUTE OF EARLY AMERICAN HISTORY AND CULTURE
See: Institute of Early American History and Culture

★2981★
COLLEGE OF WILLIAM AND MARY - MARSHALL-WYTHE LAW LIBRARY (Law)
                                       Phone: (804) 253-4680
Williamsburg, VA 23185   Edmund P. Edmonds, Act. Law Libn.
Staff: Prof 3; Other 9. **Subjects:** Law. **Special Collections:** Environmental law; taxation; Roman law; Thomas Jefferson Law Library. **Holdings:** 120,075 volumes; 46,919 volumes in microform; 167 AV items. **Subscriptions:** 3792 journals and other serials; 10 newspapers. **Services:** Interlibrary loans; copying; library open to public. **Computerized Information Services:** LEXIS; computerized cataloging. **Networks/Consortia:** Member of OCLC through SOLINET. **Staff:** Susan Dow, Ref./Doc.Libn.; Sue Welch, Hd., Tech.Serv.

★2982★
COLLEGE OF WILLIAM AND MARY - VIRGINIA ASSOCIATED RESEARCH CAMPUS LIBRARY (Sci-Tech)
12070 Jefferson Ave.   Phone: (804) 877-9231
Newport News, VA 23606
Staff: Prof 1; Other 1. **Subjects:** Physics, chemistry, biomedical sciences, environment. **Special Collections:** Energy. **Holdings:** 11,117 books; 10,308 bound periodical volumes; 3000 documents; 2000 microfiche. **Subscriptions:** 195 journals and other serials; 5 newspapers. **Services:** Interlibrary loans; copying; library open to public. **Computerized Information Services:** Computerized cataloging. **Networks/Consortia:** Member of Virginia Tidewater Consortium for Continuing Higher Education. **Publications:** Using the VARC Library, annual; Acquisitions List, monthly; Annotated Energy Bibliography, 1981 (book).

★2983★
COLLEGIATE REFORMED DUTCH CHURCH - LIBRARY (Hist)
45 John St.   Phone: (212) 233-1960
New York, NY 10038   Robert F. Williams, Chf.
Staff: 2. **Subjects:** Genealogical data from 1633. **Special Collections:** Minutes of board meetings from 1633. **Holdings:** 45 books; archives; documents. **Subscriptions:** 8 journals and other serials; 5 newspapers. **Services:** Copying; library open to public. **Publications:** Year Book.

★2984★
COLLIER STATE PARK LOGGING MUSEUM - LIBRARY (Hist)
Box 428   Phone: (503) 884-5145
Klamath Falls, OR 97601   Alfred D. Collier, Cur.
Founded: 1946. **Staff:** Prof 1. **Subjects:** Logging, forestry, fishery, Klamath Indians. **Special Collections:** Life of Jim McCrank, 96-year old lumberjack; Life of Jack Kimball Cruiser; logging equipment (650 pieces); Indian stone artifacts. **Holdings:** 50 books; logging magazines and newspapers; 3000 logging photographs; equipment catalogs; 20 tapes of autobiographies of loggers; Klamath Indian-English Dictionary dated 1870. **Subscriptions:** 6 journals and other serials. **Services:** Library not open to public. **Computerized Information Services:** Computerized cataloging. **Special Indexes:** Geological study of Collier State Park; Indexes of 600 exhibits. **Remarks:** Library is part of Oregon State Parks Department.

★2985★
COLLIN MEMORIAL HOSPITAL - MEDICAL LIBRARY (Med)†
1800 N. Graves St.
Box 370   Phone: (214) 542-2641
McKinney, TX 75069   Joan L. Thomas, Libn.
Founded: 1958. **Subjects:** Medicine. **Holdings:** 150 books and bound periodical volumes. **Services:** Library not open to public.

★2986★
COLLINS CANADA - TIC LIBRARY (Sci-Tech)
150 Bartley Dr.   Phone: (416) 757-1101
Toronto, ON, Canada M4A 1C7   Joan Ann Hall, Libn.
Founded: 1960. **Staff:** Prof 1. **Subjects:** Electronics and communications. **Holdings:** Figures not available for books, bound periodical volumes, pamphlets, reports, government documents. **Services:** Interlibrary loans; library open to public. **Remarks:** This is a subsidiary of Rockwell International of Canada, Ltd.

COLLINS COLLECTION OF THE DANCE
See: Birmingham Public and Jefferson County Free Library

COLLINS (Donald) MEMORIAL LIBRARY
See: American Society of Abdominal Surgeons - Donald Collins Memorial Library

COLLINS LIBRARY
See: Baker University - Archives and Historical Library

★2987★
COLOMBIERE COLLEGE - LIBRARY (Rel-Theol)
Box 139   Phone: (313) 625-5611
Clarkston, MI 48016   Rev. Stephen A. Meder, S.J., Libn.
Founded: 1959. **Staff:** 1. **Subjects:** Bible study, spiritual and ascetical works, spiritual exercises, Society of Jesus history and documents, theology, Greek and Latin classics. **Holdings:** 32,000 books; 4000 bound periodical volumes; 1 file drawer of spiritual exercises; 1 file drawer of U.S. Catholic Conference publications. **Subscriptions:** 70 journals and other serials. **Remarks:** Above information refers to the combined collections of the Dinan and Tertians Libraries.

★2988★
COLONIAL PENN GROUP, INC. - INFORMATION RESEARCH CENTER (Bus-Fin)
5 Penn Center Plaza   Phone: (215) 988-3796
Philadelphia, PA 19181   M. Diane Dugan, Sr.Info.Spec.
Founded: 1975. **Staff:** Prof 2; Other 2. **Subjects:** Insurance, senior citizen market, marketing, advertising, statistics. **Holdings:** 1500 books; 10 VF drawers of government document files; 80 VF drawers of general, company and project files. **Subscriptions:** 300 journals and other serials; 8 newspapers. **Services:** Interlibrary loans; copying; SDI; library not open to public. **Computerized Information Services:** DIALOG, SDC, New York Times Information Service. **Publications:** Annotated acquisitions list, monthly; Consumer Price Index Report, monthly. **Special Catalogs:** U.S. Government Agency Publications (card). **Special Indexes:** Index to annotated acquisitions list; index to research reports.

★2989★
COLONIAL WILLIAMSBURG - AUDIO-VISUAL LIBRARY (Aud-Vis)
                                         Phone: (804) 229-1000
Williamsburg, VA 23185   Patricia G. Maccubbin, Chf.Libn.
Founded: 1946. **Staff:** Prof 1; Other 2. **Subjects:** The Historic Area - its buildings, furnishings, gardens, flower arrangements, costumes and craft shops; historical collection - the history of the area as depicted by various artists. **Holdings:** Photographs, negatives, slides, photostats, clippings, films, sound tapes, discs and color transparencies. **Services:** Copying; library open to public. **Staff:** Julia Conlee, AV Libn.; Suzanne Brown, Asst.Libn.

COLONIAL WILLIAMSBURG FOUNDATION - INSTITUTE OF EARLY AMERICAN HISTORY AND CULTURE
See: Institute of Early American History and Culture

★2990★
COLONIAL WILLIAMSBURG - RESEARCH LIBRARY & ARCHIVES (Hist)
Box C   Phone: (804) 229-1000
Williamsburg, VA 23185   Louise A. Merriam, Res.Libn.
Staff: Prof 5; Other 2. **Subjects:** American and English History of the 18th century; history of Williamsburg; Virginia history; social life and customs of the colonial period; decorative arts; folk art; 18th century music. **Special Collections:** A.L. Kocher Collection of architectural books; Hopkins Collection of Landscape Architecture books; 18th century music and agriculture books; Tomlinson Collection of 18th and 19th century children's books; manuscript collections - Robert Anderson papers, Blathwayt papers, John Norton and Sons papers. **Holdings:** 32,500 books; 2000 reels of microfilm; 10,400 manuscripts; 5000 pictures; 1000 maps. **Subscriptions:** 200 journals and other serials. **Services:** Interlibrary loans; copying; library open to public by appointment. **Staff:** Susan Stromei, Asst.Libn.; Mary B. Haskell, Cat.; John E. Ingram, Archv.; Gail S. Terry, Asst.Archv.

COLORADO CHAUTAUQUA ASSOCIATION COLLECTION
See: Boulder Historical Society - Documentary Collections Department

★2991★
COLORADO COLLEGE - CHARLES LEAMING TUTT LIBRARY (Hum)
                                         Phone: (303) 473-2233
Colorado Springs, CO 80903   Prof. George V. Fagan, Hd.Libn.
Founded: 1874. **Staff:** Prof 6; Other 12. **Subjects:** Literature, especially 19th and 20th century; history, especially American West and Southwest; geology; anthropology. **Special Collections:** Colorado Collection; more than 500 manuscripts of British and American literary figures, statesmen and military leaders. **Holdings:** 304,250 books; 49,008 bound periodical volumes; 149,989 government documents; 3965 reels of microfilm; 36,120 microforms; 183 VF drawers of maps. **Subscriptions:** 1042 journals and other serials; 36 newspapers. **Services:** Interlibrary loans; copying; library open to public with restrictions. **Computerized Information Services:** DIALOG. **Networks/Consortia:** Member of Bibliographical Center for Research, Rocky Mountain Region, Inc. (BCR); OCLC.

★2992★
COLORADO COLLEGE - CHARLES LEAMING TUTT LIBRARY - SPECIAL COLLECTIONS (Hist)
Cascade & San Rafael   Phone: (303) 473-2233
Colorado Springs, CO 80903   Barbara L. Neilon, Cur., Spec.Coll.
Staff: Prof 1; Other 1. **Subjects:** History - Colorado, Colorado College, 19th and 20th century American West, printing. **Special Collections:** Colorado College Collection (1800 volumes); Colorado College (16,000 volumes); rare books (2100); special editions (6600); Justice Chess Collection (300 volumes); Alice Bemis Taylor Collection of historical manuscripts (300 items); Archer Butler Hulbert papers (13 feet); Charles C. Mierow papers (12 feet); Helen Hunt Jackson papers (7 feet); Donald Jackson Collection of Fine Printing (60 items); Spencer Penrose papers (53 feet); Thomas Nelson Haskell papers (8 feet); Theodore Roosevelt letters (57 items); Edward Royal Warren papers (12 feet); Philip Washburn papers (6 feet); Charles Collings Collection of historical manuscripts (57 items); oral history interviews (41 items). **Holdings:** 26,500 books; 275 bound periodical volumes; 350 linear feet of manuscripts; 122 oral history tapes; 10,000 photographs; 60 feet of college archives; 70 feet of ephemera; 81 historical tapes. **Services:** Copying; library open to public with restrictions. **Computerized Information Services:** Computerized cataloging and acquisitions. **Networks/Consortia:** Member of Bibliographical Center for Research, Rocky Mountain Region, Inc. (BCR); OCLC. **Publications:** Guides to manuscript collections. **Special Indexes:** Index to tape collection. **Staff:** Judith R. Finley, Dir., Oral Hist. Project.

COLORADO GEOLOGICAL SURVEY LIBRARY
See: Colorado State Department of Natural Resources

★2993★
COLORADO HISTORICAL SOCIETY - STEPHEN H. HART LIBRARY (Hist)
Colorado Heritage Ctr.
1300 Broadway   Phone: (303) 866-2305
Denver, CO 80203   Katherine Kane, Hd., Pub.Serv. & Access
Founded: 1879. **Staff:** Prof 3; Other 5. **Subjects:** Colorado - history, business history, mining, railroads, cattle, water resources. **Special Collections:** William Henry Jackson collection of glass negatives, west of the Mississippi (10,000). **Holdings:** 63,000 volumes; 100,000 glass plate negatives; 1 million manuscripts; 1000 tapes and phonograph records; 14,500 reels of television newsfilm; 27,700 reels of microfilm; 200,000 photographs; 200,000 clippings; 20,000 serials; 4000 newspapers; 2500 maps and atlases. **Subscriptions:** 275 journals and other serials; 135 newspapers. **Services:** Copying; library open to public. **Publications:** Guides to Manuscript Collections, Calendars - occasional. **Staff:** Catherine T. Engel, Ref.Libn.; Alice L. Sharp, Cat.

★2994★
COLORADO MINING ASSOCIATION - LIBRARY (Sci-Tech)
1515 Cleveland Place, Suite 410   Phone: (303) 534-1181
Denver, CO 80202
Staff: 1. **Subjects:** Mining operations and management, metals, government. **Special Collections:** Mining Year Books, 1969-1981. **Holdings:** Figures not available. **Services:** Library not open to public. **Publications:** Mining Year Book, annual - by subscription, for sale; Colorado Miner, quarterly - by subscription.

COLORADO PUBLIC SERVICE COMPANY
See: Public Service Company of Colorado

★2995★
COLORADO RAILROAD HISTORICAL FOUNDATION - LIBRARY (Hist)
17155 W. 44th Ave.
Box 10 Phone: (303) 279-4591
Golden, CO 80402 Robert W. Richardson, Exec.Dir.
Founded: 1958. **Staff:** Prof 1; Other 2. **Subjects:** Railroad history of
Colorado. **Special Collections:** Files, office and operating records of Rio
Grande Southern (narrow gauge) and Denver & Rio Grande System; Colorado
and Southern Railway. **Holdings:** 1900 books; 78 bound periodical volumes;
documents; photographs; recordings; 16,000 negatives; 3000 slides.
Subscriptions: 45 journals and other serials; 11 newspapers. **Services:**
Copying; collection may be consulted by appointment only. **Publications:** Iron
Horse News, 6/year.

COLORADO RIVER BOARD OF CALIFORNIA
See: California State - Colorado River Board of California

★2996★
COLORADO SCHOOL FOR THE DEAF AND THE BLIND - MEDIA CENTER
(Educ; Aud-Vis)
Kiowa at Institute Phone: (303) 636-5186
Colorado Springs, CO 80903 Janet L. Fleharty, Media Spec.
Founded: 1874. **Staff:** Prof 1; Other 1. **Subjects:** Books of interest to deaf
and blind children; professional books on deafness and blindness for staff and
parents. **Holdings:** 15,000 books; 200 bound periodical volumes.
Subscriptions: 122 journals and other serials. **Services:** Library open to
public. **Publications:** Colorado Index, quarterly - for staff, parents and
interested parties. **Staff:** Susan Cocherl, Lib.Asst.

★2997★
COLORADO SCHOOL OF MINES - ARTHUR LAKES LIBRARY (Sci-Tech;
Energy)
Phone: (303) 273-3665
Golden, CO 80401 Hartley K. Phinney, Jr., Dir.
Founded: 1874. **Staff:** Prof 8; Other 12. **Subjects:** Geology, mining
engineering, geophysics, petroleum engineering, metallurgy, chemical and
petroleum refining engineering, mineral economics, chemistry, physics,
mathematics. **Special Collections:** Original Mine Reports (2000 items);
Colorado Mining History (1500 items); Boettcher Collection on Energy,
Environment, Public Policy (7500 items). **Holdings:** 205,000 books and
bound periodical volumes; 100,000 maps (geologic, topographic, Defense
Mapping Agency Topographic Service); U.S. Geological Survey map depository;
house organs, trade publications; 26,000 microforms. **Subscriptions:** 2150
journals and other serials; 14 newspapers. **Services:** Interlibrary loans;
copying; library open to public for reference and research. **Computerized
Information Services:** DIALOG, SDC; computerized cataloging and circulation.
Networks/Consortia: Member of Bibliographic Center for Research, Rocky
Mountain Region, Inc. (BCR); Colorado Alliance of Research Libraries (CARL).
Publications: New Books List, biweekly. **Special Catalogs:** Serials Holdings
List (book). **Staff:** Marilyn Stark, Ref.Libn.; Mary Beth Vanderpoorten,
Acq.Libn.; Christine Ericson, Cat.Libn.; Margaret Smart, Doc.Libn.; Lee Carper,
Circ.Hd.; Mary Larsgaard, Map Libn.; Ann Lerew, Ref.Libn.; Diane Brown,
Boettcher Libn.

★2998★
**COLORADO SPRINGS FINE ARTS CENTER - REFERENCE LIBRARY AND
TAYLOR MUSEUM LIBRARY** (Art)
30 W. Dale St. Phone: (303) 634-5581
Colorado Springs, CO 80903 Roderick Dew, Libn.
Staff: Prof 1; Other 1. **Subjects:** Art history, drawing, painting, sculpture,
crafts, architecture, photography, graphic arts and printing, anthropology of
the Southwest, museums and private collections. **Special Collections:** Santos
Indians of the Southwest; Latin American folk and Colonial art. **Holdings:**
18,000 books; 950 bound periodical volumes; 12 shelves of biographical
files; 20 shelves of museum publications. **Subscriptions:** 88 journals and
other serials. **Services:** Art reference service; library open to public with
limited circulation.

★2999★
COLORADO SPRINGS GAZETTE TELEGRAPH - LIBRARY (Publ)
30 S. Prospect
Box 1779 Phone: (303) 632-5511
Colorado Springs, CO 80903 Carol A. Barber, Libn.
Staff: Prof 1; Other 1. **Subjects:** Newspaper reference topics. **Holdings:** 200
books and bound periodical volumes; 60 file drawers of newspaper clippings;
27 file drawers of photographs. **Services:** Copying; library open to public with
restrictions.

★3000★
**COLORADO SPRINGS PUBLIC SCHOOLS - DISTRICT NO. 11 - TEACHERS'
PROFESSIONAL LIBRARY** (Educ)
1036 N. Franklin St. Phone: (303) 635-6275
Colorado Springs, CO 80903 Sandy Patton, Media Supv.
Founded: 1959. **Staff:** Prof 2; Other 1. **Subjects:** Education. **Holdings:**
7161 books; 3568 nonprint items. **Subscriptions:** 97 journals and other
serials. **Services:** Library open to public with restrictions.

★3001★
**COLORADO STATE DEPARTMENT OF EDUCATION - INSTRUCTIONAL
MATERIALS CENTER FOR THE VISUALLY HANDICAPPED** (Aud-Vis)
1362 Lincoln St. Phone: (303) 839-2181
Denver, CO 80203 W. Buck Schrotberger, Sr.Cons.
Founded: 1971. **Staff:** Prof 2; Other 2. **Special Collections:** Large print,
braille and taped textbooks used by visually handicapped students in Colorado
schools, kindergarten through 12th grade. **Services:** Resources and materials
service for the visually handicapped; library not open to public. **Publications:**
Handbook of Resources and Materials for the Visually Handicapped in
Colorado. **Staff:** Barbara Z. Carr, Cons.

**COLORADO STATE DEPARTMENT OF LOCAL AFFAIRS - DIVISION OF
LOCAL GOVERNMENT**
See: Colorado State Division of Local Government

★3002★
**COLORADO STATE DEPARTMENT OF NATURAL RESOURCES - COLORADO
GEOLOGICAL SURVEY LIBRARY** (Sci-Tech)
1313 Sherman, Rm. 715 Phone: (303) 866-2611
Denver, CO 80203 Louise M. Slade, Staff Asst.
Founded: 1969. **Staff:** 1. **Subjects:** Geology, geophysics. **Special
Collections:** Colorado geology (500 volumes). **Holdings:** 2500 books; 500
bound periodical volumes; 1000 government documents; 1000 technical
reports; 1000 maps; depository for U.S. Geological Survey and the U.S.
Department of Energy. **Subscriptions:** 15 journals and other serials.
Services: Library open to public with restrictions. **Publications:** List of
publications - available upon request.

★3003★
COLORADO STATE DEPARTMENT OF SOCIAL SERVICE - LIBRARY (Soc Sci)
1575 Sherman St. Phone: (303) 866-2253
Denver, CO 80203 Margaret Umhoefer, Libn.
Founded: 1945. **Staff:** Prof 1. **Subjects:** Public and social welfare; child
welfare; adoption; foster care; aged; child development; handicapped and
defective; crime and juvenile delinquency; group work and community
organizations. **Holdings:** 10,000 volumes; 3 VF drawers of pamphlets; 18
16mm films; 20 filmstrips. **Subscriptions:** 40 journals and other serials.
Services: Library open to public.

★3004★
**COLORADO STATE DISTRICT COURT, 2ND JUDICIAL DISTRICT - LAW
LIBRARY** (Law)
389 City & County Bldg. Phone: (303) 575-2233
Denver, CO 80202 Jane E. Thompson, Law Libn.
Staff: Prof 1. **Subjects:** Law. **Holdings:** 15,000 books; 150 bound periodical
volumes. **Services:** Copying; library open to public. **Special Indexes:** Indexing
and abstracting of legal memoranda (card, book).

★3005★
**COLORADO STATE DISTRICT COURT, 6TH JUDICIAL DISTRICT - LAW
LIBRARY** (Law)
Box 3340 Phone: (303) 247-1301
Durango, CO 81301 Al H. Haas, Chf. Judge
Staff: Prof 1. **Subjects:** Law. **Holdings:** 10,000 volumes. **Services:** Copying;
library open to attorneys only.

★3006★
**COLORADO STATE DIVISION OF EMPLOYMENT & TRAINING - LABOR
MARKET INFORMATION LIBRARY** (Soc Sci)
251 E. 12th Ave. Phone: (303) 839-5833
Denver, CO 80203 Marvin H. Wojahn, Economist
Staff: Prof 1; Other 1. **Subjects:** Labor market information. **Special
Collections:** Colorado Manpower Review Series (1964 to present). **Holdings:**
200 books; 2000 unbound reports; 2000 unbound periodicals; all official
Colorado labor force estimates. **Subscriptions:** 50 journals and other serials.
Services: Library open to public for reference use only.

★3007★
COLORADO STATE DIVISION OF HIGHWAYS - TECHNICAL LIBRARY (Trans)
4340 E. Louisiana Ave., Rm. L201   Phone: (303) 757-9220
Denver, CO 80222   Joylyn A. Privette, Adm. Clerk
Founded: 1949. **Staff: Prof** 1. **Subjects:** Highway engineering, road planning and design, road and street research, road construction and maintenance, soils and materials, traffic safety and engineering, highway law, bridges and tunneling. **Holdings:** 730 books; 80 bound periodical volumes; 562 paperbound reports (cataloged); 400 pamphlets; magazine and newspaper clippings; 44 unbound periodicals. **Services:** Interlibrary loans; copying; library open to public.

★3008★
COLORADO STATE DIVISION OF LOCAL GOVERNMENT - LIBRARY (Plan)
1313 Sherman St., Rm. 520   Phone: (303) 866-2351
Denver, CO 80203   Philip Schmuck, Plan.Dir.
Subjects: Planning - state, regional, local. **Special Collections:** Environmental Impact Statements. **Holdings:** Figures not available. **Services:** Library open to public. **Remarks:** Maintained by Colorado State Department of Local Affairs. Contains the holdings of the former Colorado State Planning Library.

★3009★
COLORADO STATE DIVISION OF STATE ARCHIVES AND PUBLIC RECORDS (Hist)
Dept. of Administration
1313 Sherman St., Rm. 1B20   Phone: (303) 866-2055
Denver, CO 80203   George E. Warren, State Archv.
Founded: 1943. **Staff:** 13. **Subjects:** Noncurrent official public records and printed publications of the Territory and State of Colorado. **Holdings:** 56,000 cubic feet of public records. **Services:** Copying; certification; open to all who wish to consult records for legitimate purposes. **Publications:** Guide to the Resources of the Colorado State Archives (loose-leaf), updated periodically.

★3010★
COLORADO (State) DIVISION OF WILDLIFE - LIBRARY (Env-Cons)
6060 Broadway
Denver, CO 80216   Rita C. Green, Libn.
Staff: 1. **Subjects:** Wildlife, conservation, ecology, mammals and birds. **Holdings:** 1000 books; 500 bound periodical volumes; 325 films. **Subscriptions:** 15 journals and other serials. **Services:** Copying; library open to students or personnel in field. **Publications:** Game Research Reports, quarterly.

★3011★
COLORADO (State) DIVISION OF WILDLIFE - RESEARCH CENTER LIBRARY (Env-Cons)
317 W. Prospect   Phone: (303) 484-2836
Fort Collins, CO 80526   Marian Hershcopf, Libn.
Staff: Prof 1. **Subjects:** Wildlife biology, wildlife management, parks and recreation. **Holdings:** 500 books; 1000 bound periodical volumes; 1000 pamphlets and federal aid reports. **Subscriptions:** 10 journals and other serials. **Services:** Interlibrary loans; library open to public with some restrictions. **Publications:** Colorado Division of Wildlife Special Report; Technical Publication; Research Reviews Series - all three published irregularly and distributed to libraries and other state and federal agencies.

★3012★
COLORADO STATE HOME AND TRAINING SCHOOL - STAFF LIBRARY (Med)
10285 Ridge Rd.   Phone: (303) 424-7791
Wheat Ridge, CO 80033   Clara A. Glover, Supv.
Founded: 1968. **Staff: Prof** 1; **Other** 1. **Subjects:** Mental retardation, pediatrics, developmental disabilities. **Holdings:** 2000 books; 400 pamphlets; 10 periodicals on microfilm; 100 unbound periodicals. **Subscriptions:** 15 journals and other serials. **Services:** Library not open to public.

★3013★
COLORADO STATE HOSPITAL - PROFESSIONAL LIBRARY (Med)
1600 W. 24th St.   Phone: (303) 543-1170
Pueblo, CO 81003   Helen Wack, Libn.
Founded: 1925. **Staff: Prof** 1. **Subjects:** Psychiatry, mental health, psychology, surgery, internal medicine, social work. **Holdings:** 5329 books. **Subscriptions:** 109 journals and other serials. **Services:** Interlibrary loans; copying; library open to public with restrictions. **Networks/Consortia:** Member of Arkansas Valley Regional Library Service System; Midcontinental Regional Medical Library Program.

★3014★
COLORADO STATE LIBRARY
1362 Lincoln
Denver, CO 80203
Founded: 1876. **Holdings:** 90,000 government documents; state publications. **Computerized Information Services:** Computerized cataloging. **Networks/Consortia:** Member of Bibliographical Center for Research, Rocky Mountain Region, Inc. (BCR). **Remarks:** Presently inactive.

COLORADO STATE PLANNING LIBRARY
See: Colorado State Division of Local Government - Library

★3015★
COLORADO STATE SUPREME COURT LIBRARY (Law)
B 112 State Judicial Bldg.
2 E. 14th Ave.   Phone: (303) 861-1111
Denver, CO 80203   Frances D. Campbell, Libn.
Staff: Prof 3; **Other** 1. **Subjects:** Law. **Special Collections:** Water law collection (60 volumes). **Holdings:** 86,500 books; 4500 bound periodical volumes; 750 reels of microfilm; microfiche. **Subscriptions:** 275 journals and other serials. **Services:** Copying; library open to public. **Computerized Information Services:** Computerized cataloging. **Networks/Consortia:** Member of OCLC; Bibliographic Center for Research, Rocky Mountain Region, Inc. (BCR). **Staff:** Martha Campbell, Libn.; Linda Gruenthal, Libn.

★3016★
COLORADO STATE UNIVERSITY - ENGINEERING SCIENCES BRANCH LIBRARY (Sci-Tech; Energy)
        Phone: (303) 491-8694
Fort Collins, CO 80523   Barbara L. Burke, Asst.Engr.Sci.Libn.
Founded: 1961. **Staff: Prof** 1; **Other** 2. **Subjects:** Water resources, hydraulics, hydrology, fluid mechanics, lasers and quantum electronics, energy. **Special Collections:** Delft Hydraulics Laboratory Documentation Data; Asian Institute of Technology theses; E.W. Lane special collection on hydrology. **Holdings:** 4000 books; 1000 bound periodical volumes; 15,000 documents; 5 VF drawers of reprints; 10,000 unbound reports. **Subscriptions:** 300 journals and other serials. **Services:** Interlibrary loans; copying; library open to public by appointment. **Computerized Information Services:** DIALOG, SDC, DOE/RECON; internal database; computerized cataloging. **Networks/Consortia:** Member of RLG. **Special Indexes:** Energy from the Wind, annotated bibliography, annual updates planned; WASAR (Water and Soil in Arid Regions), An Index to Selected Materials in Colorado State University Libraries.

★3017★
COLORADO STATE UNIVERSITY - GERMANS FROM RUSSIA PROJECT LIBRARY (Area-Ethnic)
History Department   Phone: (303) 491-6854
Fort Collins, CO 80523   John Newman, Project Archv.
Staff: 1. **Subjects:** Germans from Russia. **Holdings:** 850 books; 40 bound periodical volumes; 100 manuscripts. **Services:** Interlibrary loans; copying; library open to public with prior arrangement. **Special Catalogs:** Germans from Russia in Colorado by Sidney Heitman, 1978.

★3018★
COLORADO STATE UNIVERSITY - WILLIAM E. MORGAN LIBRARY (Sci-Tech)
        Phone: (303) 491-5911
Fort Collins, CO 80523   LeMoyne W. Anderson, Dir. of Lib.
Founded: 1870. **Staff: Prof** 46; **Other** 90. **Subjects:** Hydraulic engineering, irrigation, water resources, soil mechanics, radiology and radiation biology, agronomy, horticulture, microbiology, mycology, parasitology, veterinary medicine, genetics, forestry. **Special Collections:** Western Imaginative Literature; Imaginary Wars. **Holdings:** 1.3 million books and bound periodical volumes; 697,728 microcards; 32,452 maps; 8076 audio reproductions. **Subscriptions:** 16,500 journals and other serials; 170 newspapers. **Services:** Interlibrary loans; copying; SDI; library open to public. **Computerized Information Services:** DIALOG, SDC, National Library of Medicine; computerized circulation. **Networks/Consortia:** Member of Bibliographical Center for Research, Rocky Mountain Region, Inc. (BCR); RLG; Center for Research Libraries. **Publications:** Library Series, irregular. **Special Catalogs:** Serials Book Catalog; CSU Dissertations and theses. **Remarks:** The William E. Morgan Library is the general library for the university. While it contains material to support a university curriculum and research program, the items listed under subjects are the areas in which the library is unusually strong. **Staff:** Richard Beeler, Bus./Econ.Libn.; Ronald DeWaal, Hum.Libn.; Curtis Gifford, Forestry/Agri.Sci.Libn.; Antoinette Lueck, Physical Sci.Libn.; Marjorie Rhoades, Engr.Sci.Libn.; Terry Hubbard, Soc.Sci.Libn.; Suzanne Johnson, Biomed.Sci.Libn.

★3019★
COLORADO STATE WATER CONSERVATION BOARD - LIBRARY
1313 Sherman St.
Denver, CO 80203
Founded: 1937. **Subjects:** Water, land, water laws; other natural resources. **Holdings:** 2400 books; 1200 bound periodical volumes; 250 reports (cataloged). **Remarks:** Presently inactive.

★3020★
COLT INDUSTRIES - CRUCIBLE RESEARCH CENTER - LIBRARY (Sci-Tech)
Box 88   Phone: (412) 923-2955
Pittsburgh, PA 15230   Patricia J. Aducci, Tech.Libn.
Subjects: Specialty steels and alloys; titanium and titanium alloys; particle metallurgy; powder-metal and alloys; product and process research, development and engineering. **Special Collections:** Iron and steel industry and related subject bibliographies. **Holdings:** 3500 books; 2500 periodical volumes; in-house technical reports (cataloged); 30 VF cabinets of technical documents; government reports; patents; mineral statistics; American Iron and Steel Institute (AISI) literature; company archives; in-house and NTIS reports on microfiche. **Subscriptions:** 190 journals and other serials. **Services:** Interlibrary loans. **Computerized Information Services:** DIALOG, SDC.

★3021★
COLT INDUSTRIES - FM ENGINE DIVISION LIBRARY (Sci-Tech)
701 Lawton St.   Phone: (608) 364-4411
Beloit, WI 53511   Wesley A. Brill, Act.Adm.
Founded: 1960. **Subjects:** Water and waste technology; metallurgy; diesel engines. **Holdings:** 1200 books; 400 bound periodical volumes; 1500 unbound professional reports and papers. **Subscriptions:** 30 journals and other serials. **Services:** Copying; library not open to public.

★3022★
COLTON HALL MUSEUM - LIBRARY (Hist)*
                                Phone: (408) 372-8121
Monterey, CA 93940   Dorothy Chesbro Ronald, Cur.
Staff: Prof 1. **Subjects:** California and local history. **Holdings:** 800 books; clipping files; early textbooks. **Subscriptions:** 11 journals and other serials. **Services:** Copying; library open to public with restrictions on some materials. **Remarks:** The Colton Hall Museum is owned and operated by the city of Monterey. Bilingual materials are available pertaining to the 1849 California Constitutional Convention.

COLTON (Harold S.) MEMORIAL LIBRARY
See: Museum of Northern Arizona - Harold S. Colton Memorial Library

★3023★
COLUMBIA BIBLE COLLEGE - LEARNING RESOURCES CENTER (Rel-Theol)
7435 Monticello Rd.
Box 3122
Columbia, SC 29230   Phone: (803) 754-4100
                                Laura Braswell, Dir.
Founded: 1923. **Staff:** Prof 2; Other 8. **Subjects:** Bible, theology, missions. **Special Collections:** Visual aids for religious education and Christian service; missionary curios. **Holdings:** 60,430 books and bound periodical volumes; 7780 AV items, 1435 cassette tapes and 890 phonograph records (cataloged); 40 VF drawers of pamphlets; 6 VF drawers of pictures. **Subscriptions:** 583 journals and other serials; 4 newspapers. **Services:** Interlibrary loans; copying; center open to public. **Computerized Information Services:** Computerized cataloging, acquisitions and serials. **Networks/Consortia:** Member of OCLC through SOLINET. **Special Indexes:** Index to mission boards, mission fields and sermons (card). **Staff:** Susan Webster, Circ.Supv.

★3024★
COLUMBIA CHRISTIAN COLLEGE - LIBRARY - SPECIAL COLLECTIONS (Hist)
200 N.E. 91st Ave.   Phone: (503) 255-7060
Portland, OR 97220   Dr. Richard Lee, Libn.
Staff: Prof 1. **Special Collections:** The Restoration (2000 volumes). **Services:** Interlibrary loans; copying; library open to public.

COLUMBIA COLLEGE LIBRARY
See: Columbia University

★3025★
COLUMBIA COUNTY HISTORICAL SOCIETY - HOUSE OF HISTORY LIBRARY (Hist)
                                Phone: (518) 758-9265
Kinderhook, NY 12106   Ruth Piwonka, Exec.Dir.
Founded: 1936. **Staff:** 2. **Subjects:** Columbia County, Hudson Valley regional and local history, biography, genealogy. **Special Collections:** Columbia County manuscript collections (2000 items); local history/old photographs; New York decorative arts in conjunction with museum offices. **Holdings:** 1718 books; 1448 pamphlets; clippings and maps. **Services:** Copying; library open to public June through August and by appointment the rest of the year. **Special Catalogs:** Calendars of manuscript collections.

★3026★
COLUMBIA COUNTY HISTORICAL SOCIETY - LIBRARY (Hist)
Box 197   Phone: (717) 683-6011
Orangeville, PA 17859   Edna Lynn, Exec.Dir.
Founded: 1914. **Staff:** Prof 2; Other 5. **Subjects:** Columbia County history; area history and genealogy. **Special Collections:** Late 19th century personal and small business accounts and correspondence of the county. **Holdings:** 850 books; 50 bound periodical volumes; 200 bound manuscripts and 20 linear feet of unbound manuscripts (cataloged); 48 scrapbooks (cataloged); 12 linear feet of pamphlet files cataloged by subject and area; 3 linear feet of Works Progress Administration files (mid-1930s historical and genealogical compilations); 36 reels of film and 50 unbound/bound volumes of county and area newspapers; 1100 photographs and maps (cataloged). **Services:** Copying; library open to public. **Publications:** The Columbian, 2/year; historical leaflets, 4/year. **Special Indexes:** List of area newspapers available in published booklet. **Staff:** Dr. Roy J. Haring, Lib.Exec.

★3027★
COLUMBIA COUNTY HISTORICAL SOCIETY - MUSEUM (Hist)
Old Courthouse   Phone: (503) 397-2805
St. Helens, OR 97051   Mildred Lain, Hist.
Founded: 1969. **Staff:** 1. **Subjects:** History of Columbia County, genealogy. **Holdings:** 250 books; 90 bound periodical volumes; deeds and contracts (cataloged); maps, local pictures, magazines, newspapers, scrapbooks. **Services:** Copying; library open to public for reference use only.

★3028★
COLUMBIA GAS SYSTEM SERVICE CORPORATION - LAW LIBRARY (Law)
20 Montchanin Rd.   Phone: (302) 429-5320
Wilmington, DE 19807   Kathryn C. Bossler, Law Libn.
Staff: 1. **Subjects:** Utility and corporate law, general law. **Holdings:** 4663 books; 72 periodical titles; 10 VF drawers. **Services:** Interlibrary loans; library not open to public.

★3029★
COLUMBIA GAS SYSTEM SERVICE CORPORATION - RESEARCH LIBRARY (Sci-Tech; Energy)
1600 Dublin Rd.   Phone: (614) 486-3681
Columbus, OH 43215   Camille Duer Greenwald, Res.Libn.
Staff: Prof 1. **Subjects:** Natural gas, petroleum, mechanical engineering, geology, pollution, management. **Holdings:** 4500 books; 25 bound periodical volumes; 8000 microfiche research reports; 30 serial titles on microfilm. **Subscriptions:** 232 journals and other serials. **Services:** Interlibrary loans; copying; SDI; library open to public by appointment. **Computerized Information Services:** SDC, DOE/RECON; computerized serials. **Networks/Consortia:** Member of CALICO. **Publications:** Union List of Technical Standards, annual - available by request; monthly acquisitions list.

★3030★
COLUMBIA GAS TRANSMISSION CORPORATION - LAW LIBRARY (Law; Energy)
Box 1273   Phone: (304) 346-0951
Charleston, WV 25325   Nina K. Angle, Law Libn.
Staff: Prof 1; Other 1. **Subjects:** Law, oil, gas, property, contracts, statutes. **Holdings:** 10,000 volumes, 346 VF drawers of law files. **Subscriptions:** 150 journals and other serials; 12 newspapers. **Services:** Library open to public with restrictions.

★3031★
COLUMBIA GULF TRANSMISSION COMPANY - ENGINEERING LIBRARY (Sci-Tech)
Box 683   Phone: (713) 621-1200
Houston, TX 77001   Jayne Young Benoit, Engr.Libn.
Founded: 1959. **Staff:** Prof 1. **Subjects:** Engineering - natural gas and petroleum; all other phases of engineering; business and management; information sciences. **Holdings:** 3700 books; 300 bound periodical volumes; 500 manufacturers' catalogs (cataloged); 4 VF drawers of maps; 4 VF drawers of clippings; 4 VF drawers of pictures; 15,052 microforms; 400 system (Columbia Gas) and company (Columbia Gulf) publications; government documents; standards. **Subscriptions:** 201 journals and other serials. **Services:** Interlibrary loans; copying; library open to public. **Computerized Information Services:** SDC; internal database; computerized cataloging and

acquisitions. **Publications:** Library Bulletin, bimonthly - for internal distribution only. **Remarks:** Library is located at 3805 W. Alabama, Rm. 334, Houston, TX 77027.

COLUMBIA HEALTH CENTER LIBRARY
See: Forbes Health System

★3032★
COLUMBIA HISTORICAL SOCIETY - LIBRARY (Hist)
1307 New Hampshire Ave., N.W.   Phone: (202) 785-2068
Washington, DC 20036   Perry G. Fisher, Exec.Dir./Libn.
Founded: 1894. **Staff:** 3. **Subjects:** Washington DC history. **Special Collections:** John Clagett Proctor Collection; Machen Collection (500 rare historical prints of the City of Washington). **Holdings:** 10,000 books and bound periodical volumes; 3000 manuscript items and diverse printed materials; 60 VF drawers of newspaper clippings; 40,000 picture items; scrapbooks relating to the history of the District of Columbia and its immediate environs. **Services:** Interlibrary loans; copying; library open to public. **Publications:** Records of the Columbia Historical Society, biennial hard-bound volume - first published in 1897; collection of articles. **Staff:** Elizabeth Jane Miller, Cur.

★3033★
COLUMBIA HOSPITAL - MEDICAL LIBRARY (Med)
2025 E. Newport Ave.   Phone: (414) 961-3858
Milwaukee, WI 53211   Ruth Holst, Med.Libn.
Founded: 1942. **Staff:** Prof 2; Other 3. **Subjects:** Medicine, nursing, hospital administration. **Special Collections:** Clinical medicine and nursing (150,000 reprints). **Holdings:** 1500 books; 6000 bound periodical volumes; 450 audio cassettes. **Subscriptions:** 270 journals and other serials. **Services:** Interlibrary loans; copying; SDI; library open to public by request. **Computerized Information Services:** NLM, DIALOG. **Networks/Consortia:** Member of Southeastern Wisconsin Health Science Library Consortium (SEWHSL); Library Council of Metropolitan Milwaukee (LCOMM); Regional Medical Library - Region 3. **Staff:** Susan Anderson, Assoc.Libn.

★3034★
COLUMBIA HOSPITAL - SCHOOL OF NURSING LIBRARY (Med)
2121 E. Newport Ave.   Phone: (414) 961-3533
Milwaukee, WI 53211   Shirley S. Chan, Libn.
Staff: Prof 1. **Subjects:** Nurses and nursing, nursing education, pharmacology, anatomy, physiology, psychology, sociology, nutrition. **Special Collections:** Historical Collection. **Holdings:** 3324 books; 446 bound periodical volumes; pamphlets on 124 subjects; 323 audio cassettes; 28 audiotapes; 175 phonograph records; 9 films; 328 filmstrips; 80 slide sets; 20 transparencies; 8 videotapes; 16 anatomical models; 8 games; 1 skeleton. **Subscriptions:** 88 journals and other serials. **Services:** Interlibrary loans; copying; SDI; library open to public for reference use only. **Networks/Consortia:** Member of Southeastern Wisconsin Health Science Libraries Consortium (SEWHSL); Library Council of Metropolitan Milwaukee, Inc. (LCOMM). **Publications:** AV Software list; Current Awareness on nursing journals - both for internal distribution only.

★3035★
COLUMBIA HOSPITAL FOR WOMEN - MEDICAL LIBRARY (Med)
2425 L St., N.W.   Phone: (202) 293-6560
Washington, DC 20037   Elizabeth M. Haggart, Libn.
Staff: Prof 1. **Subjects:** Gynecology, obstetrics. **Holdings:** 1200 books; 10 bound periodical volumes. **Subscriptions:** 85 journals and other serials. **Services:** Interlibrary loans; copying (limited); library not open to public. **Computerized Information Services:** MEDLINE.

★3036★
COLUMBIA MUSEUMS OF ART & SCIENCE - LIBRARY (Art)
1112 Bull St.   Phone: (803) 799-2810
Columbia, SC 29201   Cassandra S. Gissendanner, Hd.
Founded: 1950. **Staff:** 1; Other 4. **Subjects:** American art; European art - Renaissance through 20th century; biography of artists. **Holdings:** 5200 volumes; 6 VF drawers of pamphlets. **Subscriptions:** 49 journals and other serials. **Services:** Copying; library open to public for reference use only.

COLUMBIA NATIONAL FISHERIES RESEARCH LABORATORY LIBRARY
See: U.S. Fish & Wildlife Service

★3037★
COLUMBIA RIVER MARITIME MUSEUM - LIBRARY (Hist)
1792 Marine Dr.   Phone: (503) 325-2323
Astoria, OR 97103   Larry D. Gilmore, Cur.
Staff: Prof 1. **Subjects:** Ship construction, navigation, naval warfare,

exploration, U.S. Coast Guard, fishing, lighthouses, regional history. **Holdings:** 4000 books; 2000 photographs; 8 boxes of maps, charts and plans; 20 boxes of log books; journals and documents; 150 volumes of ship registers. **Subscriptions:** 12 journals and other serials. **Services:** Copying; library open to public for reference use only. **Publications:** Quarterdeck Review, quarterly newsletter - for museum members.

★3038★
COLUMBIA THEOLOGICAL SEMINARY - JOHN BULOW CAMPBELL LIBRARY (Rel-Theol)
701 Columbia Dr.   Phone: (404) 378-8821
Decatur, GA 30031   Dr. James A. Overbeck, Lib.Dir.
Founded: 1828. **Staff:** Prof 3; Other 1. **Subjects:** Biblical studies, church history, systematic theology, practical church work. **Holdings:** 82,000 books; 11,500 bound periodical volumes. **Subscriptions:** 240 journals and other serials. **Services:** Interlibrary loans; library open to public on a limited basis.

★3039★
COLUMBIA UNION COLLEGE - THEOFIELD G. WEIS LIBRARY (Rel-Theol)
7600 Flower Ave.   Phone: (301) 891-4217
Takoma Park, MD 20912   Margaret J. von Hake, Libn.
Founded: 1904. **Staff:** Prof 4; Other 1. **Subjects:** Religion, education, health sciences, history, natural sciences, psychology. **Special Collections:** Seventh-Day Adventist Collection - manuscripts, book rarities, mementos, theses and dissertations; Curriculum Library Collection (children's books, textbooks, curriculum guides and resource units). **Holdings:** 106,000 volumes; 32 VF drawers of reports, manuscripts and clippings; 38 trays of slides on geography and world travel. **Subscriptions:** 404 journals and other serials. **Services:** Interlibrary loans; copying; library open to public with references. **Publications:** Booklist, monthly - to faculty, students, selected libraries; Newsletter, bimonthly - to faculty, students. **Special Indexes:** Author, title, subject index to selected Seventh-Day Adventist serial publications (271,000 cards). **Staff:** Debbie Szasz, Acq.Techn.; Zella J. Holbert, Curric.Libn.; Leona P. Stone, Circ.Libn.; Lee M. Wisel, Cat.Libn.

★3040★
COLUMBIA UNIVERSITY - AMBROSE MONELL ENGINEERING LIBRARY (Sci-Tech)
422 Mudd   Phone: (212) 280-2976
New York, NY 10027
Founded: 1883. **Staff:** Prof 2; Other 5. **Subjects:** Aeronautics; engineering - chemical, civil, electrical, industrial, mechanical and nuclear; mining; metallurgy; applied mathematics; computer science. **Special Collections:** Archival material of New York Tunnel Authority; Regional Technical Report Center. **Holdings:** 200,000 volumes; 750,000 technical reports of DOE, NASA and NTIS. **Subscriptions:** 1375 journals and other serials. **Services:** Interlibrary loans; library open to public with restrictions. **Computerized Information Services:** DIALOG, SDC, BRS; computerized cataloging and acquisitions. **Networks/Consortia:** Member of RLG; CRL; METRO.

★3041★
COLUMBIA UNIVERSITY - AVERY ARCHITECTURAL AND FINE ARTS LIBRARY (Art; Plan)
Broadway & 116th St.   Phone: (212) 280-3501
New York, NY 10027   Angela Giral, Libn.
Founded: 1890. **Staff:** Prof 7; Other 7. **Subjects:** Architecture; painting, sculpture, decorative arts, city planning, archeology. **Special Collections:** Collection of original architectural drawings - Upjohn, A.J. Davis, Renwick, F.L. Wright, Lienau, Sullivan, Greene and Greene. **Holdings:** 200,000 volumes; 30,000 original architectural drawings; 1000 manuscripts, letters and clippings. **Subscriptions:** 1190 journals and other serials. **Services:** Copying; library open to public with restrictions. **Computerized Information Services:** Computerized cataloging and acquisitions. **Networks/Consortia:** Member of RLG; CRL; METRO. **Publications:** Avery Catalog; Avery Index, with supplements. **Staff:** Herbert Mitchell; William O'Malley; Janet Parks, Drawings Cur.; Christina Huemer, Fine Arts; Katharine Chibnik, Urban Plan.; Katharine Martinez, Hd., Access & Sup.Serv.

★3042★
COLUMBIA UNIVERSITY - BIOLOGICAL SCIENCES LIBRARY (Sci-Tech)
914 Schermerhorn Hall   Phone: (212) 280-4715
New York, NY 10027   Georgeanne M. O'Riordan, Libn.
Founded: 1912. **Staff:** Prof 2; Other 4. **Subjects:** Experimental zoology, neurosciences, genetics, molecular biology, cytology, histology, animal and plant physiology, biochemistry, cell biology. **Holdings:** 40,000 books and bound periodical volumes. **Subscriptions:** 315 journals and other serials. **Services:** Interlibrary loans; copying. **Computerized Information Services:** BRS. **Networks/Consortia:** Member of CRL; RLG; METRO. **Publications:** New Acquisitions List, monthly.

★3043★

COLUMBIA UNIVERSITY - BURGESS-CARPENTER LIBRARY (Hum; Soc Sci)
406 Butler Library
New York, NY 10027
Phone: (212) 280-4710
Frederick Byrne, Libn.
Staff: Prof 1; Other 10. **Subjects:** Social sciences, history, language and literature, classics in Greek and Latin. **Holdings:** 108,000 volumes; 25,000 Columbia master's essays; 3500 dissertations. **Services:** Interlibrary loans; copying. **Computerized Information Services:** Computerized circulation. **Networks/Consortia:** Member of RLG; CRL; METRO. **Special Indexes:** Card indexes to Columbia master's essays.

★3044★

COLUMBIA UNIVERSITY - BUTLER LIBRARY CIRCULATION DEPARTMENT (Hist; Hum)
303 Butler Library
New York, NY 10027
Phone: (212) 280-2235
Robert Pepin, Hd.
Staff: 50. **Subjects:** Literature, humanities, history. **Holdings:** 1.4 million volumes. **Services:** Interlibrary loans; copying; library open to public with restrictions. **Computerized Information Services:** Online systems; computerized circulation. **Networks/Consortia:** Member of RLG; CRL; METRO.

★3045★

COLUMBIA UNIVERSITY CANCER CENTER - INSTITUTE OF CANCER RESEARCH (Med)
701 W. 168th St.
New York, NY 10032
Phone: (212) 694-6948
Betty Rose Moore, Lib.Serv.Coord.
Founded: 1952. **Staff:** Prof 1. **Subjects:** Cancer. **Remarks:** Services are provided by the university's Health Sciences Library.

★3046★

COLUMBIA UNIVERSITY - CENTER FOR POPULATION & FAMILY HEALTH - LIBRARY/INFORMATION PROGRAM (Soc Sci)
60 Haven Ave.
New York, NY 10032
Phone: (212) 694-6985
Susan K. Pasquariella, Hd.Libn.
Founded: 1968. **Staff:** Prof 3; Other 3. **Subjects:** Family planning, evaluative methodology, operations research, demography. **Special Collections:** International family planning program evaluation. **Holdings:** 3000 books; 15,000 published and unpublished reports, manuscripts, reprints and other documents. **Subscriptions:** 231 journals and other serials. **Services:** Interlibrary loans; copying; SDI; prepare bibliographies; library open to public with restrictions. **Computerized Information Services:** Contributor to POPLINE database; computerized bibliographic searches. **Networks/Consortia:** Member of RLG; CRL; METRO; Association for Population/Family Planning Libraries and Information Centers - International (APLIC-Internatl.); United Nations Population Information Network (POPIN). **Publications:** POPLINE Thesaurus; Library Acquisitions List, monthly; POP/FAM Alert, bimonthly. **Remarks:** Center for Population & Family Health is a part of International Institute for the Study of Human Reproduction. **Staff:** Judith Wilkinson, Asst.Libn.; Claire Mayers, Ref.Libn.

COLUMBIA UNIVERSITY - CENTER FOR THE STUDY OF HUMAN RIGHTS
See: Center for the Study of Human Rights

★3047★

COLUMBIA UNIVERSITY - CHEMISTRY LIBRARY (Sci-Tech)
454 Chandler Hall
New York, NY 10027
Phone: (212) 280-4709
Elida B. Stein, Libn.
Founded: 1900. **Staff:** Prof 1; Other 1. **Subjects:** Chemistry, biochemistry. **Holdings:** 11,000 books; 23,000 bound periodical volumes. **Subscriptions:** 425 journals and other serials. **Services:** Interlibrary loans; copying. **Computerized Information Services:** Online systems. **Networks/Consortia:** Member of METRO; RLG; CRL.

★3048★

COLUMBIA UNIVERSITY - COLUMBIA COLLEGE LIBRARY (Soc Sci; Hum)
225 Butler Library
New York, NY 10027
Phone: (212) 280-3534
Frederick Byrne, Libn.
Founded: 1907. **Staff:** Prof 2; Other 12. **Subjects:** Humanities, social sciences, American history and literature, economics, English literature, philosophy. **Holdings:** 50,000 volumes. **Services:** Interlibrary loans; copying. **Networks/Consortia:** Member of RLG; CRL; METRO.

★3049★

COLUMBIA UNIVERSITY - COLUMBIANA (Hist)
210 Low Memorial Library
New York, NY 10027
Phone: (212) 280-3786
Paul R. Palmer, Cur.
Founded: 1883. **Staff:** Prof 1; Other 2. **Subjects:** Columbia University - history, biography. **Special Collections:** Columbia University archives; King's College Room (contains original library of King's College from Colonial America; portraits; furniture and other memorabilia). **Holdings:** 22,000 books; 6000 bound periodical volumes; 12,000 pamphlets; 18,000 photographs. **Services:** Copying. **Networks/Consortia:** Member of RLG; CRL; METRO.

★3050★

COLUMBIA UNIVERSITY - DEPARTMENT OF ART HISTORY & ARCHAEOLOGY - PHOTOGRAPH COLLECTION (Art)
420 Schermerhorn Hall
New York, NY 10027
Phone: (212) 280-5203
Prof. Jane Rosenthal, Rep.
Founded: 1952. **Staff:** Prof 3; Other 5. **Subjects:** Art - Primitive and Pre-Columbian, Near Eastern, Far Eastern, Greek, Roman, early Christian, Medieval, Renaissance, Baroque, 19th and 20th century. **Special Collections:** Berenson I-Tatti Archive (50,000 photographs); Dial Iconographic Index (12,580); Haseloff Archive (20,000); Bartsch Collection (10,640); Gaignieres Collection (3420); Arthur Kingsley Porter Collection (4000); Ware Collection; Courtauld Collection; Marburger Index on microfiche; Windsor Castle drawings; Chatsworth Collection; all James Austin offerings; special Alinari offerings; Bibles Moralisees in Vienna and Toledo; Arndt Einzelaufnamen (5100 photographs); Rudolph Wittkower Collection (5 VF drawers); Millard Meiss Collection (15 VF drawers); James Q. Reber Collection (1500 photographs). **Holdings:** 155,000 photographs exclusive of special collections; 15,000 gallery announcements (partially cataloged). **Services:** Copying; collection open to scholars with proper identification only and articles must not leave room. **Networks/Consortia:** Member of RLG; CRL; METRO. **Special Indexes:** Card index to Gaignieres Collection and Berenson Archive. **Staff:** Kathryn Kramer, Cur.; Polly Nooter, Asst.Cur.; Peggy Quisenberry, Asst.Cur.

★3051★

COLUMBIA UNIVERSITY - EAST ASIAN LIBRARY (Area-Ethnic)
300 Kent
New York, NY 10027
Phone: (212) 280-4318
James Reardon-Anderson, Libn.
Staff: Prof 12; Other 11. **Subjects:** China, Japan, Korea - humanities and social sciences. **Holdings:** Chinese - 201,400 books and 10,700 bound periodical volumes; Japanese - 121,400 books and 40,000 bound periodical volumes; Korean - 17,600 books and 7300 bound periodical volumes; Western languages - 20,100 books and 16,100 bound periodical volumes; 8800 microfilms; 4950 microfiche. **Subscriptions:** 1750 journals and other serials. **Services:** Interlibrary loans; copying. **Networks/Consortia:** Member of RLG; CRL; METRO.

COLUMBIA UNIVERSITY - ERIC CLEARINGHOUSE ON URBAN EDUCATION
See: ERIC Clearinghouse on Urban Education

COLUMBIA UNIVERSITY - FINE ARTS LIBRARY
See: Columbia University - Avery Architectural and Fine Arts Library

★3052★

COLUMBIA UNIVERSITY - GEOLOGY LIBRARY (Sci-Tech)
601 Schermerhorn
New York, NY 10027
Phone: (212) 280-4522
Susan Klimley, Libn.
Founded: 1912. **Staff:** Prof 1; Other 1. **Subjects:** Geology, mineralogy, stratigraphy, geophysics, geochemistry, remote sensing, petrology, sedimentology, economic geology. **Holdings:** 78,000 volumes. **Subscriptions:** 1400 journals and other serials. **Services:** Interlibrary loans; copying; SDI; library open to public with restrictions. **Computerized Information Services:** Online systems. **Networks/Consortia:** Member of RLG; CRL; METRO.

★3053★

COLUMBIA UNIVERSITY - HEALTH SCIENCES LIBRARY (Med)
701 W. 168th St.
New York, NY 10032
Phone: (212) 694-3688
Rachael K. Goldstein, Libn.
Founded: 1928. **Staff:** Prof 14; Other 28. **Subjects:** Anatomy, biochemistry, clinical medicine, dentistry, medicine (history and practice), microbiology, neurology, nursing, oncology, pathology, pharmacology, physiology, public health, surgery (general, orthopedic and plastic), thanatology. **Special Collections:** Jerome P. Webster Library of Plastic Surgery; George Sumner Huntington Collection (anatomy); John Green Curtis Collection (physiology); Sigmund Freud Library; Florence Nightingale Collection; Orton Collection (learning disorders); Lena Hyman Collection in the History of Anesthesia. **Holdings:** 375,000 volumes; 3000 AV titles. **Subscriptions:** 3100 journals and other serials. **Services:** Interlibrary loans; copying; SDI; library not open to public; some services on fee basis. **Computerized Information Services:** DIALOG, NLM, BRS, SDC, New York Times Information Service; computerized cataloging, acquisitions and serials. **Networks/Consortia:** Member of RLG; Medical Library Center of New York (MLCNY); METRO; CRL. **Staff:** Ellen

Nagle, Hd., Ref.Sect.; Vera Ortynsky, Hd., Cat.Sect.; Harriet Grossman, AV Libn.; Daniel Richards, Asst.Libn./Rsrcs. & Ref.

★3054★
COLUMBIA UNIVERSITY - HERBERT H. LEHMAN LIBRARY (Soc Sci; Geog-Map)
Intl. Affairs Bldg.
420 W. 118th St.   Phone: (212) 280-4170
New York, NY 10027   Betty L. Jenkins, Libn.
Founded: 1965. **Staff:** Prof 6; Other 8. **Subjects:** Political science, international affairs, sociology, anthropology, geography. **Special Collections:** Documents Service Center (51,237 standard printed materials; 354,305 microforms); PL 480 materials (50,000 volumes); Soviet Nationalities Collection (13,446 volumes); foreign newspapers (110); 19th and early 20th century Slavonic newspapers (823 titles). **Holdings:** 180,181 books and bound periodical volumes; 185,000 maps; 94,887 microforms; 13 shelves of American Enterprise Institute for Public Policy Research Rand Corporation Reports; 6 microfiche of Human Relations Area Files (HRAF) microfiles; 102 VF drawers of Bureau of Applied Social Research Archives; 10 VF drawers and 18 shelves of Radio Free Europe/Radio Liberty Library. **Subscriptions:** 1600 journals and other serials; 110 newspapers. **Services:** Interlibrary loans; copying; library open to public with restrictions. **Computerized Information Services:** DIALOG, BRS, New York Times Information Service; computerized cataloging and acquisitions. **Networks/Consortia:** Member of RLG; METRO; New York State Interlibrary Loan Network (NYSILL). **Special Catalogs:** Union List of Serials for the Social Science Division (book form). **Remarks:** Library has Reading Center for the Visually Disabled. Equipment includes 520 Visualtek Voyager enlarging machines; an IBM large print typewriter; and a "talking" calculator. **Staff:** J. Bryan May, Hd., Doc.Serv.Ctr.; Laura Binkowski, Ref.Libn.; Diane Goon, Ref.Libn.; Eileen Agard Glickstein, Hd., Access Serv.

COLUMBIA UNIVERSITY - HISPANIC INSTITUTE
See: Hispanic Institute

★3055★
COLUMBIA UNIVERSITY - LAMONT-DOHERTY GEOLOGICAL OBSERVATORY - GEOSCIENCE LIBRARY (Sci-Tech)
                                                   Phone: (914) 359-2900
Palisades, NY 10964   Susan Klimley, Libn.
Founded: 1960. **Staff:** Prof 1; Other 2. **Subjects:** Geophysics, geochemistry, oceanography, marine biology, seismology, meteorology. **Holdings:** 20,000 volumes. **Subscriptions:** 525 journals and other serials. **Services:** Interlibrary loans; copying. **Networks/Consortia:** Member of RLG; CRL; METRO.

★3056★
COLUMBIA UNIVERSITY - LAW LIBRARY (Law)
Law School
435 W. 116th St.   Phone: (212) 280-3737
New York, NY 10027   James L. Hoover, Law Libn.
Founded: 1910. **Staff:** Prof 12; Other 22. **Subjects:** Law - Anglo-American, foreign, international; Roman; criminology; trials; legal biography. **Special Collections:** League of Nations and United Nations documents; part of Law Library of James Kent; bar association reports. **Holdings:** 700,000 volumes. **Subscriptions:** 6000 journals and other serials. **Services:** Interlibrary loans; copying; telefacsimile transmission; library open to public with advance permission from librarian. **Computerized Information Services:** LEXIS, WESTLAW, DIALOG, New York Times Information Service, CCH ELSS; computerized cataloging. **Networks/Consortia:** Member of RLG. **Publications:** Selected Recent Acquisitions, monthly. **Staff:** Janet Tracy, Asst. Law Libn.; Harry Bitner, Legal Biblog.; Robert Buckwalter, Hd., Acq.; Samuel Cohen, Legal Res.Libn.; Barbara R. Kessler, Ref.Libn.; Diane Lee, Cat.; Bess Michaels, Hd., Access Serv.; Frantisek Mokry, Cat.; Philip Oxley, Ref.Libn.; John Zenelis, Hd., Law Cat.

★3057★
COLUMBIA UNIVERSITY - LIBRARY SERVICE LIBRARY (Info Sci)
606 Butler Library   Phone: (212) 280-3543
New York, NY 10027   Olha della Cava, Libn.
Founded: 1926. **Staff:** Prof 1; Other 3. **Subjects:** All aspects of librarianship and information science, library history, administration, bibliography, documentation, library schools and training, publishing, history of books and printing. **Special Collections:** Graphic Arts Collection (13,250 volumes). **Holdings:** 98,000 volumes. **Subscriptions:** 3200 journals and other serials. **Services:** Interlibrary loans; copying. **Networks/Consortia:** Member of RLG; CRL; METRO. **Publications:** Selected Acquisitions List - limited circulation.

★3058★
COLUMBIA UNIVERSITY - MATHEMATICS/SCIENCE LIBRARY (Sci-Tech)
303 Mathematics   Phone: (212) 280-4712
New York, NY 10027   Suzanne Fedunok, Libn.
Staff: Prof 1; Other 2. **Subjects:** Mathematics, history of science, mathematical statistics, general science. **Holdings:** 100,000 volumes. **Subscriptions:** 550 journals and other serials. **Services:** Interlibrary loans; copying; library not open to public. **Computerized Information Services:** RLIN. **Networks/Consortia:** Member of RLG; CRL; METRO.

★3059★
COLUMBIA UNIVERSITY - MUSIC LIBRARY (Mus)
701 Dodge   Phone: (212) 280-4711
New York, NY 10027   Thomas T. Watkins, Libn.
Founded: 1931. **Staff:** Prof 1; Other 4. **Subjects:** Music - analysis, interpretation, appreciation, bibliography, history, criticism, theory; musical instruments; musical notation; musicians; church music; ethnomusicology; composition. **Holdings:** 53,199 scores and literature; 15,996 phonograph records and tapes; 2488 manuscripts; 952 reels of microfilm; 3957 microcards. **Subscriptions:** 300 journals and other serials. **Services:** Interlibrary loans; copying; library open to public for unique materials only. **Networks/Consortia:** Member of RLG; CRL; METRO.

★3060★
COLUMBIA UNIVERSITY - ORAL HISTORY COLLECTION (Hist)
Butler Library
Box 20   Phone: (212) 280-2273
New York, NY 10027   Ronald J. Grele, Dir.
Founded: 1948. **Staff:** Prof 3; Other 4. **Subjects:** National affairs, international relations, culture and the arts, social welfare, business and labor, law, medicine, education, journalism, religion. **Special Collections:** The New Deal (50,000 pp.); Eisenhower Administration (36,000 pp.); Social Security, origins through Medicare (10,650 pp.); popular arts (7800 pp.); history of Carnegie Corporation (9928 pp.); aviation history (5400 pp.); radio pioneers (4765 pp.); Vietnam Veterans (3720 pp.); Columbia Crisis of 1968 (2450 pp.); psychoanalytic movement (2000 pp.); Nobel Laureates (1500 pp.); Women's History and Population Issues (2500 pp.); Occupation of Japan (1500 pp.); rare books (770 pp.); New York's Art World (1200 pp.); League of Nations (866 pp.); Hungarian Project (835 pp.); Poets on their Poetry (700 pp.). **Holdings:** 4800 volumes of edited transcript (cataloged); 2500 reels and cassettes of tapes, largely since 1963; microforms of one third of the Collection; supporting papers accompany some memoirs; data on other oral history holdings and centers worldwide. **Services:** Research Service available; copying (limited); collection open to public with restrictions. The office offers information kits on oral history for libraries. **Computerized Information Services:** Computerized cataloging. **Publications:** Oral History, annual report, 1949 to present; The Oral History Collection of Columbia University, 4th edition, 1979. **Staff:** Jeri Nunn, Adm.Asst.; Elizabeth B. Mason, Assoc.Dir.

★3061★
COLUMBIA UNIVERSITY - PATERNO LIBRARY (Area-Ethnic)
Casa Italiana, 1161 Amsterdam Ave.   Phone: (212) 280-2307
New York, NY 10027   Robert Connolly, Lib.Asst.
Founded: 1927. **Staff:** 1. **Subjects:** Italian literature and culture. **Holdings:** 20,000 volumes. **Subscriptions:** 50 journals and other serials; 10 newspapers. **Services:** Interlibrary loans; copying; library open to public with restrictions. **Networks/Consortia:** Member of RLG; CRL; METRO.

★3062★
COLUMBIA UNIVERSITY - PHILOSOPHY LIBRARY (Hum)
228 Butler Library   Phone: (212) 280-2259
New York, NY 10027   Frederick Byrne, Libn.
Staff: 2. **Subjects:** Philosophy. **Holdings:** 11,000 volumes; 300 dissertations. **Services:** Interlibrary loans; copying. **Networks/Consortia:** Member of RLG; CRL; METRO.

★3063★
COLUMBIA UNIVERSITY - PHYSICS LIBRARY (Sci-Tech)
810 Pupin Laboratories   Phone: (212) 280-3943
New York, NY 10027   Suzanne Fedunok, Libn.
Founded: 1898. **Staff:** Prof 1; Other 1. **Subjects:** Physics and astronomy. **Holdings:** 25,000 volumes. **Subscriptions:** 400 journals and other serials. **Services:** Interlibrary loans; copying. **Computerized Information Services:** DIALOG, SDC, BRS, RLIN; computerized cataloging and acquisitions. **Networks/Consortia:** Member of RLG; CRL; METRO.

★3064★
COLUMBIA UNIVERSITY - PSYCHOLOGY LIBRARY (Soc Sci)
409 Schermerhorn Hall   Phone: (212) 280-4714
New York, NY 10027   Georgeanne M. O'Riordan, Libn.
Founded: 1912. **Staff:** Prof 1; Other 9. **Subjects:** Psychology - abnormal, comparative, experimental, social, statistical, cognitive, physiological. **Special Collections:** Translations in the field of vision. **Holdings:** 25,000 volumes; 1850 microforms (cataloged). **Subscriptions:** 300 journals and other serials. **Services:** Interlibrary loans; copying; SDI; library open to public with restrictions. **Computerized Information Services:** Online systems. **Networks/Consortia:** Member of RLG; CRL; METRO. **Publications:** New Acquisitions List, monthly - distributed to faculty.

★3065★
COLUMBIA UNIVERSITY - RARE BOOK AND MANUSCRIPT LIBRARY (Rare Book)
801 Butler Library   Phone: (212) 280-2231
New York, NY 10027   Kenneth A. Lohf, Libn.
Founded: 1930. **Staff:** Prof 8; Other 7. **Subjects:** General rare book collections selected from the University Libraries - early printed books, rare editions, special copies; early manuscripts; the department also administers 2000 collections of correspondence and papers. **Special Collections:** Plimpton Library (history of textbooks from the manuscript period, calligraphy, mathematics, English and Latin grammars); David Eugene Smith Mathematical Library; Dale Library of Weights and Measures; Spinoza Collection; Seligman Library (history of economics); Epstean Collection (photography); Kilroe Collection (Tammaniana); Joan of Arc; Mary Queen of Scots; Bakhmeteff Archive of Russian and East European History and Culture; Columbiana; Gonzalez Lodge Collection; Book Arts Collection; Herbert H. Lehman Papers; David Abrahamson Collection; Park Benjamin Collection. **Holdings:** 500,000 books; 12 million manuscripts and papers. **Services:** Copying; library open to qualified researchers. **Computerized Information Services:** RLIN; computerized cataloging. **Networks/Consortia:** Member of RLG; CRL; METRO. **Publications:** Columbia Library Columns, 3/year - by subscription.

★3066★
COLUMBIA UNIVERSITY - SULZBERGER JOURNALISM LIBRARY (Info Sci)
304 Journalism Bldg.
Broadway & 116th St.   Phone: (212) 280-3860
New York, NY 10027   Wade A. Doares, Journalism Libn.
Founded: 1912. **Staff:** Prof 1; Other 4. **Subjects:** Journalism, current events. **Holdings:** 13,500 books and bound periodical volumes; 731 VF drawers of clippings. **Subscriptions:** 75 journals and other serials; 40 newspapers. **Services:** Interlibrary loans; copying; library open to faculty and students. **Computerized Information Services:** BRS; Lektrievers. **Networks/Consortia:** Member of RLG; METRO.

COLUMBIA UNIVERSITY - TEACHERS COLLEGE
See: Teachers College

★3067★
COLUMBIA UNIVERSITY - THOMAS J. WATSON LIBRARY OF BUSINESS AND ECONOMICS (Bus-Fin)
130 Uris Hall   Phone: (212) 280-4000
New York, NY 10027   Paula T. Kaufman, Bus.Libn.
Founded: 1920. **Staff:** Prof 4; Other 20. **Subjects:** Financial management, money and capital markets, marketing, international business, business and economic history, operations research, management science, economics, banking, labor and industrial relations, advertising, agriculture, transportation. **Special Collections:** Marvyn Scudder Financial Collection. **Holdings:** 329,000 volumes; 2681 reels of microfilm; 166,337 microforms of corporation 10K and annual reports; working papers of U.S. business schools; 10 VF drawers of pamphlets; 10 VF drawers of U.S. unions material. **Subscriptions:** 3000 journals and other serials and newspapers. **Services:** Interlibrary loans; copying; library open to public with restrictions. **Computerized Information Services:** DIALOG, BRS, SDC, New York Times Information Service; computerized acquisitions. **Networks/Consortia:** Member of RLG; CRL; METRO. **Publications:** Publications of the faculty and staff. **Special Catalogs:** Annual reports in microform (card); bound annual reports (book). **Special Indexes:** Index to New York Stock Exchange listing applications, 1959 to present (card). **Staff:** Lilita Gusts, Ref.Libn.; Jane E. Winland, Ref.Libn.; Jill Jennings, Ref.Libn.

★3068★
COLUMBIA UNIVERSITY - WHITNEY M. YOUNG, JR. MEMORIAL LIBRARY OF SOCIAL WORK (Soc Sci)
309 International Affairs Bldg.   Phone: (212) 280-5159
New York, NY 10027   Celestine C. Tutt, Libn.
Founded: 1898. **Staff:** Prof 2; Other 3. **Subjects:** Social work; community

organization; social policy development and administration; health and mental health, including mental retardation; social services - family and children, homemaker, day care, legal; aging; corrections and court services - probation, parole, diversionary treatment; alcoholism and drug addiction; industrial social welfare and manpower programs; urban education; intergroup relations; social and physical rehabilitation. **Special Collections:** The Mary Richmond Archives; The Homer Folks Archives; The Whitney M. Young, Jr. Papers; The Dorothy Hutchinson Collection on the Child; The Brookdale Collection on Gerontology. **Holdings:** 103,851 books, bound periodical volumes and pamphlets; student projects, dissertations, and agency reports. **Subscriptions:** 646 journals and other serials. **Services:** Interlibrary loans; copying. **Networks/Consortia:** Member of RLG; CRL; METRO.

★3069★
COLUMBIAN NEWSPAPER - LIBRARY (Publ)
329 North Rd.   Phone: (604) 521-2622
Coquitlam, BC, Canada V3L 4Z7   Una Broughton, Libn.
Founded: 1970. **Staff:** Prof 1. **Subjects:** Provincial and local government; local history. **Holdings:** 200 books; 10 bound periodical volumes; 52 VF drawers of news clippings; 446 reels of microfilm (complete collection of the newspaper). **Subscriptions:** 25 journals and other serials; 10 newspapers. **Services:** Interlibrary loans; copying; library not open to public.

★3070★
COLUMBIANA COUNTY LAW LIBRARY (Law)†
Court House   Phone: (216) 424-9511
Lisbon, OH 44432
Staff: 1. **Subjects:** Law. **Holdings:** 12,836 volumes. **Services:** Library open to public.

★3071★
COLUMBUS COLLEGE OF ART AND DESIGN - PACKARD LIBRARY (Art)
47 N. Washington Ave.   Phone: (614) 224-9101
Columbus, OH 43215   Chilin Yu, Hd.Libn.
Staff: Prof 3; Other 3. **Subjects:** Fine arts, architecture, literature, design. **Holdings:** 20,000 books; 2000 bound periodical volumes; 33,000 slides; 26,000 pictures and prints. **Subscriptions:** 142 journals and other serials; 7 newspapers. **Services:** Interlibrary loans; copying; library open to public for reference use only.

★3072★
COLUMBUS-CUNEO-CABRINI MEDICAL CENTER - COLUMBUS HOSPITAL MEDICAL LIBRARY (Med)
2520 N. Lakeview Ave.   Phone: (312) 883-7341
Chicago, IL 60614   James L. Finnerty, Ph.D., Chf.Med.Libn.
Staff: Prof 2; Other 1. **Subjects:** Clinical medicine, medical research, basic sciences in medicine. **Holdings:** 3600 books; 2200 bound periodical volumes; 250 videotapes. **Subscriptions:** 280 journals and other serials; 5 newspapers. **Services:** Interlibrary loans; copying; SDI; library not open to public. **Computerized Information Services:** BRS. **Networks/Consortia:** Member of Midwest Health Science Library Network (MHSLN); Metropolitan Consortium; Chicago Library System; ILLINET. **Publications:** Serial Holdings List; Subject Guide to Serials; Subject Guide to Videotapes (all annual). **Staff:** James Elledge, Asst.Med.Libn.

★3073★
COLUMBUS DEVELOPMENTAL CENTER - GOVE SCHOOL LIBRARY (Med)
1601 W. Broad St.   Phone: (614) 272-0509
Columbus, OH 43223   Charles Leisenheimer, Libn./Media Spec.
Staff: Prof 1. **Subjects:** Special education, mental retardation. **Holdings:** 4500 books; 1000 AV materials; 10 boxes of reports, curriculum guides, bibliographies; 100 games, pictures and manipulative materials. **Subscriptions:** 12 journals and other serials. **Services:** Interlibrary loans; copying; library open to public.

★3074★
COLUMBUS DISPATCH - EDITORIAL LIBRARY (Publ)
34 S. Third St.   Phone: (614) 461-5039
Columbus, OH 43216   James Hunter, Libn.
Staff: Prof 1; Other 3. **Subjects:** Newspaper reference topics. **Holdings:** 500 books; 30 bound periodical volumes; newspaper clippings; photographs. **Subscriptions:** 20 journals and other serials; 6 newspapers. **Services:** Library not open to public. **Networks/Consortia:** Member of Columbus Area Library & Information Council of Central Ohio (CALICO).

★3075★
COLUMBUS DOMINICAN EDUCATION CENTER
Nelson & Johnston Rds.
Columbus, OH 43219
Defunct. Holdings absorbed by Ohio Dominican College - Library.

★3076★
COLUMBUS HOSPITAL - HEALTH SCIENCES LIBRARY (Med)
Box 5013   Phone: (406) 727-3333
Great Falls, MT 59403   Sr. Margaret LaPorte, Dir.
Staff: Prof 1; Other 2. **Subjects:** Medicine, nursing, science. **Holdings:** 7500 books; 6000 bound periodical volumes; 6 VF drawers of pamphlets; 6 catalog drawers of drug description slips. **Subscriptions:** 350 journals and other serials. **Services:** Interlibrary loans; copying; library open to health care professionals and medical students. **Computerized Information Services:** MEDLINE. **Publications:** Cross-Currents, bimonthly publication of hospital.

COLUMBUS HOSPITAL MEDICAL LIBRARY
See: Columbus-Cuneo-Cabrini Medical Center

★3077★
COLUMBUS LAW LIBRARY ASSOCIATION (Law)†
Franklin County Hall of Justice
369 S. High St., 10th Fl.   Phone: (614) 221-4181
Columbus, OH 43215   Deborah J. Cannaday, Law Libn.
Staff: Prof 1; Other 3. **Subjects:** Law. **Holdings:** 80,000 volumes. **Services:** Copying; SDI; library open to public. **Computerized Information Services:** Computerized cataloging.

★3078★
COLUMBUS LEDGER-ENQUIRER - LIBRARY (Publ)
17 W. 12th St.   Phone: (404) 324-5526
Columbus, GA 31902   Patricia F. Hardy, Libn.
Founded: 1948. **Staff:** Prof 1; Other 2. **Subjects:** Newspaper reference topics. **Holdings:** Clippings; pamphlets; microfilm of newspapers since 1832 and microcards of old clippings.

COLUMBUS MEMORIAL LIBRARY
See: Organization of American States

★3079★
COLUMBUS MUSEUM OF ARTS AND SCIENCES - RESEARCH LIBRARY (Art)
1251 Wynnton Rd.   Phone: (404) 323-3617
Columbus, GA 31906   William E. Scheele, Dir.
Staff: Prof 2. **Subjects:** Art, crafts, archeology. **Holdings:** 1567 books; 34 bound periodical volumes; 800 items including biographical data of artists and craftsmen, museum newsletters and bulletins, and exhibition catalogs. **Subscriptions:** 15 journals and other serials. **Services:** Library open to public for research. **Staff:** Edge R. Reid, Volunteer Libn.

★3080★
COLUMBUS PUBLIC SCHOOLS - TEACHERS' PROFESSIONAL LIBRARY (Educ)
889 E. 17th Ave.   Phone: (614) 225-2815
Columbus, OH 43211   Hugh A. Durbin, Dir.
Staff: 1. **Subjects:** Education. **Holdings:** Figures not available. **Subscriptions:** 59 journals and other serials. **Services:** Copying; library not open to public. **Computerized Information Services:** Computerized cataloging. **Networks/Consortia:** Member of OHIONET; OCLC.

★3081★
COLUMBUS TECHNICAL INSTITUTE - EDUCATIONAL RESOURCES CENTER (Sci-Tech)
550 E. Spring St.
Box 1609   Phone: (614) 227-2400
Columbus, OH 43216   Linda Landis, Dir., ERC
Founded: 1968. **Staff:** Prof 7; Other 12. **Subjects:** Health, engineering, business, public service technologies. **Holdings:** 20,513 books; 30,142 media items (cataloged); 636 pamphlets; 1919 reels of microfilm. **Subscriptions:** 392 journals and other serials; 8 newspapers. **Services:** Copying; center open to public with courtesy card. **Computerized Information Services:** New York Times Information Service, DIALOG, SDC, BRS; computerized cataloging. **Networks/Consortia:** Member of OCLC; OHIONET; CALICO. **Publications:** Handbook; The Informer; Film Catalog, irregular. **Staff:** JoAnn Luzader, Libn., Pub.Serv.; Beverly Wilson, Libn., Tech.Serv.; Rosemary McMahon, Cat.Libn.; Ralph Bieber, Instr.Mtls.Spec.; John Manning, Media Serv.Coord.; Susan Pyle, Ref.Libn.

★3082★
COM/ENERGY SERVICES CO. - LIBRARY (Energy)
675 Massachusetts Ave.   Phone: (617) 864-3100
Cambridge, MA 02139   Esther A. Reppucci, Supv., Lib./Rec.Ctr.
Founded: 1958. **Staff:** Prof 1; Other 5. **Subjects:** Energy, electricity, gas, management, business. **Holdings:** 1000 books. **Subscriptions:** 125 journals and other serials. **Services:** Interlibrary loans; copying; library open to public by appointment. **Also Known As:** Commonwealth Energy System.

★3083★
COMBS COLLEGE OF MUSIC - LIBRARY (Mus)
100 Pelham Rd.   Phone: (215) 951-2259
Philadelphia, PA 19119   Kerry Birnbaum, Libn.
Staff: Prof 1; Other 1. **Subjects:** Music, music therapy. **Holdings:** 5000 books; 1050 microfiche; 10,000 music scores; 1750 phonograph records. **Subscriptions:** 72 journals and other serials. **Services:** Copying; library open to public. **Publications:** Newsletter, monthly - for internal distribution only.

★3084★
COMBUSTION ENGINEERING, INC. - C-E REFRACTORIES - RESEARCH & DEVELOPMENT LIBRARY
Box 828
Valley Forge, PA 19482
Defunct

★3085★
COMBUSTION ENGINEERING, INC. - METALLURGICAL AND MATERIALS LIBRARY (Sci-Tech)
911 W. Main St.   Phone: (615) 752-7132
Chattanooga, TN 37402   Nell T. Holder, Libn.
Founded: 1966. **Staff:** Prof 1. **Subjects:** Metallurgy, materials chemistry, computer science, physics, electronics, mechanical engineering. **Special Collections:** Combustion Engineering Technical Reports. **Holdings:** 15,000 books; 1200 bound periodical volumes; 3000 translations (cataloged); 200,000 microfiche of government documents. **Subscriptions:** 350 journals and other serials. **Services:** Interlibrary loans; literature searches; library open to public by appointment. **Computerized Information Services:** DIALOG, BRS.

★3086★
COMBUSTION ENGINEERING, INC. - POWER SYSTEMS GROUP LIBRARY SERVICES (Energy)
Dept. 6435-405   Phone: (203) 688-1911
Windsor, CT 06095   Zena C. Grot-Zakrzewski, Mgr.
Founded: 1956. **Staff:** Prof 6; Other 7. **Subjects:** Energy systems, fossil fuels technology and engineering, nuclear technology and engineering, environmental science and technology, management, marketing, business and finance, government regulations, physics, metallurgy, chemistry, computer science, engineering, mathematics. **Special Collections:** Government R&D reports; U.S. Nuclear Regulatory Commission Power Reactors Docket Material; standards (association, military, federal). **Holdings:** 20,000 books; 15,000 bound periodical volumes; 2000 conference proceedings (cataloged); 2000 reprints; 250,000 government documents on microfiche and 35,000 bound; 3000 technical manuals. **Subscriptions:** 650 journals and other serials. **Services:** Interlibrary loans; literature searching; translations; SDI; library not open to public. **Computerized Information Services:** DIALOG, BRS, NEXIS, New York Times Information Service, SDC, DOE/RECON. **Publications:** Technical Information Bulletin; Business Information Bulletin Daily; U.S. Nuclear Regulatory Commission Docket Material Acquisitions; U.S. DOE R&D Reports Accessions Listing, from the Federal Register. **Staff:** Joan Estoppey, Sr.Libn.; Catherine Fischer, Libn.; Rose Lane-Lopez, Libn.; Kathleen Monighetti, Asst.Libn.; Barbara Dembek, Libn.

★3087★
COMERICA INCORPORATED - RESEARCH LIBRARY (Bus-Fin)
211 W. Fort   Phone: (313) 222-9377
Detroit, MI 48231   Carol Pollack, Asst. V.P./Mgr.
Founded: 1974. **Staff:** Prof 2; Other 5. **Subjects:** Banking, economics, business, accounting, international business. **Holdings:** 15,000 books; 2000 unbound periodical volumes; 180 VF drawers of corporate and bank annual reports; 70 VF drawers of pamphlets and clippings. **Subscriptions:** 900 journals and other serials; 35 newspapers. **Services:** Interlibrary loans; library open to public by request. **Computerized Information Services:** New York Times Information Service, Dow Jones News Retrieval, DIALOG, TEXTLINE; computerized acquisitions, serials and circulation. **Publications:** Library Notes; Recent Additions to the Comerica Incorporated Research Library; Current Information in Banking, both monthly. **Formerly:** Detroitbank Corporation.

★3088★
COMICS MAGAZINE ASSOCIATION OF AMERICA, INC. - LIBRARY (Art)
60 E. 42nd St., Suite 1807   Phone: (212) 682-8144
New York, NY 10017   J. Dudley Waldner, Exec.Sec.
Subjects: Comics magazines. **Holdings:** 100 books; 2000 periodicals; 2 VF drawers. **Subscriptions:** 19 journals and other serials. **Services:** Library open to public by appointment.

★3089★
COMINCO LTD. - CENTRAL TECHNICAL LIBRARY (Sci-Tech)
    Phone: (604) 364-4409
Trail, BC, Canada V1R 4L8   Robert G. Lewis, Lib.Supv.
Founded: 1925. **Staff:** Prof 1; Other 2. **Subjects:** Chemistry, extractive metallurgy, mining and milling, engineering. **Holdings:** 6000 books; 12,000 bound periodical volumes; 2000 pamphlets (cataloged); 15,000 technical patents; 2000 U.S. Bureau of Mines reports and circulars; Chemical Abstracts from beginning in 1906; U.S. Patent Office Gazette since 1897; Canadian Patent Office Record since 1907. **Subscriptions:** 250 journals and other serials; 6 newspapers. **Services:** Interlibrary loans; copying; computerized literature searches; library open to public by personal arrangement with library supervisor.

★3090★
COMINCO LTD. - INFORMATION SERVICES (Bus-Fin)
200 Granville Sq., 24th Fl.   Phone: (604) 682-0611
Vancouver, BC, Canada V6C 2R2   Grace E. Rogozinska, Info.Anl.
Staff: Prof 1; Other 1. **Subjects:** Business, finance, statistics, geology. **Holdings:** 2000 books; 1200 reports and other items. **Subscriptions:** 210 journals and other serials; 20 newspapers. **Services:** Interlibrary loans; copying; library open to public by arrangement with librarian. **Computerized Information Services:** Info Globe, QL Systems, DIALOG, SDC, CAN/OLE. **Networks/Consortia:** Member of Central Vancouver Librarians Group. **Publications:** Acquisitions list, monthly - available upon request.

★3091★
COMINCO LTD. - PRODUCT RESEARCH CENTRE LIBRARY (Sci-Tech)
Sheridan Park   Phone: (416) 822-2022
Mississauga, ON, Canada L5K 1B4   Pat Doyle, Tech.Libn.
Founded: 1964. **Staff:** Prof 1. **Subjects:** Lead, zinc, corrosion, metallurgy. **Holdings:** 1700 books and bound periodical volumes; 10,000 pamphlets. **Subscriptions:** 146 journals and other serials. **Services:** Interlibrary loans; copying; answers brief inquiries from outside companies and makes referrals; library open to public by appointment. **Computerized Information Services:** DIALOG, CAN/OLE; Radioshack (internal database).

★3092★
COMINCO LTD. - SULLIVAN MINE LIBRARY (Sci-Tech)
P.O. Box 2000
Kimberley, BC, Canada V1A 2G3   Edna Gold, Libn.
Founded: 1946. **Staff:** 1. **Subjects:** Mining. **Holdings:** 480 books; 730 bound periodical volumes; 60 boxes of Bureau of Mines reports; 160 G.S.C. reports; British Columbia Minister of Mines reports, 1894 to present. **Subscriptions:** 56 journals and other serials. **Services:** Interlibrary loans; library open to public with restrictions.

★3093★
COMMERCE CLEARING HOUSE, INC. - BUSINESS LIBRARY (Bus-Fin)†
Quail Hill   Phone: (415) 472-3100
San Rafael, CA 94903   Patti Lusrano, Libn.
Founded: 1970. **Staff:** Prof 3. **Subjects:** Taxes - federal, state, inheritance; labor and arbitration; Social Security-Medicare; securities and finance; trade business; carriers-liquor-insurance; legislation. **Holdings:** 412 books; 335 bound periodical volumes; 405 other cataloged items; 63 Editorials on File; Canadian and Australian volumes regarding subjects listed. **Services:** Library open to public with restrictions.

COMMERCE PRODUCTIVITY CENTER
See: U.S. Dept. of Commerce

COMMERCE PUBLIC LIBRARY (Commerce, CA)
See: City of Commerce Public Library

★3094★
COMMERCE UNION BANK - LIBRARY (Bus-Fin)
One Commerce Pl.   Phone: (615) 749-3227
Nashville, TN 37219   John H. Thurman, Libn.
Founded: 1976. **Staff:** Prof 1. **Subjects:** Banking, economics, marketing. **Holdings:** 500 books; 4 VF drawers of archives; 4 VF drawers of annual reports; 4 VF drawers of newspaper clippings; 50 reels of microfilm.

Subscriptions: 160 journals and other serials. **Services:** Interlibrary loans; copying; library open to public with restrictions. **Computerized Information Services:** DIALOG, New York Times Information Service. **Formerly:** Tennessee Valley Bancorp.

COMMERCIAL APPEAL
See: Memphis Commercial Appeal

★3095★
COMMERCIAL UNION INSURANCE COMPANIES - RISK CONTROL TECHNICAL RESOURCE CENTER (Bus-Fin)
One Beacon St.   Phone: (617) 786-2155
Boston, MA 02108   Margaret Preston, Tech.Res.Assoc.
Founded: 1979. **Staff:** Prof 2. **Subjects:** Insurance, safety, risk control. **Holdings:** 1500 books; 250 AV items; 5 VF drawers. **Subscriptions:** 120 journals and other serials. **Services:** Interlibrary loans; copying; library open to public by appointment. **Computerized Information Services:** DIALOG, SDC, MEDLARS, Questel; computerized cataloging. **Staff:** Marcia A. Olson, Tech.Rsrcs.Libn.

COMMISSION CANADIENNE DES GRAINS
See: Canada - Agriculture Canada - Canadian Grain Commission

COMMISSION CANADIENNE DES TRANSPORTS
See: Canada - Canadian Transport Commission

COMMISSION ON CIVIL RIGHTS
See: U.S. Commission on Civil Rights

★3096★
COMMISSION DES ECOLES CATHOLIQUES DE MONTREAL - BIBLIOTHEQUE CENTRALE
3737 Sherbrooke E.
Montreal, PQ, Canada H1X 3B3
Founded: 1931. **Subjects:** Education, psychology, literature, philosophy, fine arts. **Special Collections:** Text books used in the schools of Montreal (1500 volumes). **Holdings:** 50,000 books and bound periodical volumes; 2800 microfilms. **Subscriptions:** 600 journals and other serials. **Special Indexes:** Index of articles on education (French). **Remarks:** Presently inactive. **Also Known As:** Catholic School Commission of Montreal.

COMMISSION D'ENERGIE ELECTRIQUE DU NOUVEAU BRUNSWICK
See: New Brunswick Electric Power Commission

COMMISSION OF THE EUROPEAN COMMUNITIES
See: European Community Information Service

COMMISSION DE LA FONCTION PUBLIQUE
See: Canada - Public Service Commission

COMMISSION DE REFORME DU DROIT
See: Canada - Law Reform Commission of Canada

COMMISSION DU SYSTEME METRIQUE
See: Canada - Metric Commission

COMMISSION DE TRANSPORT DE LA COMMUNAUTE URBAINE DE MONTREAL
See: Montreal Urban Community Transit Commission

COMMISSION ON WORSHIP LIBRARY
See: Lutheran Church - Missouri Synod

★3097★
COMMITTEE ON DIAGNOSTIC READING TESTS, INC. - LIBRARY (Educ)
    Phone: (704) 693-5223
Mountain Home, NC 28758   Dr. Frances Oralind Triggs, Chm.
Subjects: Psychology, reading development, statistics and measurement. **Holdings:** 10,000 books. **Subscriptions:** 100 journals and other serials. **Publications:** List of publications - available on request.

COMMITTEE OF SMALL PRESS EDITORS AND PUBLISHERS ARCHIVE
See: Temple University - Central Library System - Contemporary Culture Collection

COMMITTEE FOR THE VISUAL ARTS
See: Artists Space

★3098★

COMMODITY FUTURES TRADING COMMISSION - LAW LIBRARY (Bus-Fin; Law)†
2033 K St., N.W., Rm. 540   Phone: (202) 254-5901
Washington, DC 20581   Evangeline N. Jackson, Adm.Libn.
Staff: Prof 2; Other 3. **Subjects:** Commodity futures trading, economics, bankruptcy, law. **Special Collections:** Legislative Histories - Commodity Exchange Act, 1936; Futures Trading Act, 1978; CFTC Act, 1974. **Holdings:** 11,000 books; 1000 bound periodical volumes; microforms. **Services:** Interlibrary loans; library open to public, with borrowing only through ILL. **Computerized Information Services:** Online systems. **Publications:** New Acquisitions List, monthly. **Staff:** Suzanne Dawkins, Cat./Asst.Libn.

COMMONS (John R.) INDUSTRIAL RELATIONS REFERENCE CENTER
See: University of Wisconsin, Madison - Gerald G. Somers Graduate Reference Room

★3099★

COMMONWEAL - RESEARCH INSTITUTE LIBRARY (Med)
Box 316   Phone: (415) 868-0970
Bolinas, CA 94924   Jon Torkelson, Res.Libn.
Staff: Prof 1. **Subjects:** Health - environmental, occupational; environmental toxicology; nutrition; clinical ecology. **Holdings:** 1200 books; 16 VF drawers of articles, clippings and pamphlets on 500 topics; 300 government publications. **Subscriptions:** 153 journals and other serials. **Services:** Library open to public for reference use only.

★3100★

COMMONWEALTH EDISON COMPANY - LIBRARY (Energy)
Box 767   Phone: (312) 294-3064
Chicago, IL 60690   Barbara R. Kelly, Libn.
Founded: 1902. **Staff:** Prof 2; Other 3. **Subjects:** Public utilities, nuclear and electrical engineering, management. **Holdings:** 17,574 books and bound periodical volumes; 22 VF drawers of public utility reports; 59 VF drawers of pamphlets; 50 maps; microfiche. **Subscriptions:** 365 journals and other serials. **Services:** Interlibrary loans; library open to public for reference use only. **Publications:** Library Bulletin, monthly. **Staff:** Grace M. Pertell, Asst.Libn.

COMMONWEALTH ENERGY SYSTEM
See: COM/Energy Services Co.

COMMONWEALTH OF MASSACHUSETTS...
See: Massachusetts State...

★3101★

COMMONWEALTH MICROFILM LIBRARY (Publ)
760 Gordon Baker Rd.   Phone: (416) 497-8140
Willowdale, ON, Canada M2H 3B4   K.W. (Bill) Hayden, Dir.
Founded: 1971. **Staff:** Prof 2; Other 6. **Subjects:** Canadian newspapers and historical journals. **Special Collections:** North American Indian Collection; Negro Collection; Slavonic Collection; Index of Canadian Newspapers. **Holdings:** Books, periodicals and newspapers on microfilm; newspaper clipping file on microfiche. **Subscriptions:** 45 journals and other serials. **Services:** Copying; library not open to public.

★3102★

COMMUNICATIONS SATELLITE CORPORATION - CENTRAL LIBRARY (Sci-Tech)†
950 L'Enfant Plaza, S.W.   Phone: (202) 863-6834
Washington, DC 20024   Rita A. Carter, Libn.
Founded: 1968. **Staff:** Prof 2; Other 1. **Subjects:** Telecommunications, satellite technology, business, electrical engineering. **Holdings:** 10,000 books. **Subscriptions:** 600 journals and other serials. **Services:** Interlibrary loans; copying; library not open to public. **Computerized Information Services:** DIALOG, New York Times Information Service. **Networks/Consortia:** Member of OCLC. **Also Known As:** COMSAT. **Staff:** Mark A. Rohlf, Asst.Libn.

COMMUNICATIONS SATELLITE CORPORATION (COMSAT) - ENVIRONMENTAL RESEARCH & TECHNOLOGY, INC.
See: Environmental Research & Technology, Inc.

★3103★

COMMUNICATIONS SATELLITE CORPORATION - COMSAT LABORATORIES TECHNICAL INFORMATION CENTER (Sci-Tech)
22300 Comsat Dr.   Phone: (301) 428-4512
Clarksburg, MD 20734   Wayne Smith, Mgr., Tech.Info.Ctr.
Founded: 1967. **Staff:** Prof 2; Other 3. **Subjects:** Satellite communication, electronics engineering, computer science. **Special Collections:** Microfilm collection of design engineering and military specifications. **Holdings:** 14,000 books; 40,000 technical reports. **Subscriptions:** 380 journals and other serials. **Services:** Interlibrary loans; copying; library open to public with advance request. **Computerized Information Services:** DIALOG, SDC, NASA/RECON, DTIC, BRS, DOBIS; internal database; computerized acquisitions, serials and circulation. **Networks/Consortia:** Member of Interlibrary Users Association; OCLC. **Publications:** Information News, monthly; New Book List; journal holdings list. **Also Known As:** COMSAT. **Staff:** Merilee Worsey, Asst.Libn.

★3104★

COMMUNICATIONS WORKERS OF AMERICA - CWA INFORMATION LIBRARY (Bus-Fin)
1925 K St., N.W.   Phone: (202) 785-6799
Washington, DC 20006   Frances Snider, Libn.
Founded: 1975. **Staff:** Prof 1. **Subjects:** Trade unions, telecommunications industry, economics. **Holdings:** 2000 books; 10 VF drawers. **Subscriptions:** 204 journals and other serials. **Services:** Interlibrary loans; library open to public on request.

★3105★

COMMUNITY COLLEGE OF BALTIMORE - LIBRARIES/LEARNING RESOURCES CENTERS (Hist; Med)
Bard Library
2901 Liberty Heights Ave.   Phone: (301) 396-0432
Baltimore, MD 21213   Ellen I. Watson, Act.Dir.
Founded: 1947. **Staff:** Prof 9; Other 8. **Subjects:** Black history, health science, Baltimore and Maryland history, technology. **Holdings:** 101,200 books; 2250 bound periodical volumes; 100,000 pamphlets (uncataloged); 15,000 reels of microfilm; 20,000 items of nonprint media. **Subscriptions:** 800 journals and other serials; 15 newspapers. **Services:** Interlibrary loans; copying; library open to public for reference use only. **Computerized Information Services:** Mechanized circulation and shelflist files. **Remarks:** Includes the holdings of its Harbor Library/Learning Resources Center located at Lombard at Market Place, Baltimore, MD 21202. Its phone number is 396-1860. **Staff:** Dennis Mackowski, Asst.Dir., Media Serv.; Sue Wartzok, Tech.Serv.Libn.; Lynda B. Tabron, Per.Libn.; Dan Hancock, Pub.Serv.Libn.; Bruce Caroll, Circ.Libn.; Anne Cohen, Acq./Pub.Serv.Libn.; Stephanie Lea, Media & Pub.Serv.libn.

★3106★

COMMUNITY COLLEGE OF PHILADELPHIA - EDUCATION RESOURCES CENTER (Educ)
34 S. 11th St.   Phone: (215) 569-3680
Philadelphia, PA 19107   Sidney August, Dir.
Staff: Prof 12; Other 30. **Subjects:** Community colleges. **Holdings:** 70,000 books; 350 bound periodical volumes. **Subscriptions:** 500 journals and other serials; 5 newspapers. **Services:** Interlibrary loans; copying; center not open to public. **Computerized Information Services:** Computerized cataloging and circulation. **Networks/Consortia:** Member of OCLC through PALINET & Union Library Catalogue of Pennsylvania. **Publications:** ERC Handbook; ERC Faculty Newsletter. **Staff:** Donald Jones, Dept.Hd.; Aimee Weis, ILL.

★3107★

COMMUNITY ENVIRONMENTAL COUNCIL, INC. - ECOLOGY CENTER - LENDING LIBRARY (Energy)
924 Anacapa St., Suite B-4   Phone: (805) 962-2210
Santa Barbara, CA 93101   Lutie Fitzgerald, Ctr.Coord.
Founded: 1971. **Staff:** Prof 4; Other 10. **Subjects:** Energy - solar, resources, conservation; water and waste management; urban planning; gardening. **Special Collections:** Teachers' resources on energy and cancer treatment. **Holdings:** 4000 books; 5000 pamphlets. **Subscriptions:** 20 journals and other serials. **Services:** Copying; library open to public with restrictions. **Publications:** Publications list - for sale.

★3108★

COMMUNITY-GENERAL HOSPITAL OF GREATER SYRACUSE - STAFF LIBRARY (Med)
Broad Rd.   Phone: (315) 492-5500
Syracuse, NY 13215   Jessica Boysen, Staff Libn.
Staff: Prof 1; Other 1. **Subjects:** General medicine, nursing. **Holdings:** 2700 books; 2000 bound periodical volumes; 4 VF drawers of pamphlets and clippings. **Subscriptions:** 286 journals and other serials. **Services:** Interlibrary loans; copying; library open to area medical and nursing students, and to the general public by appointment. **Computerized Information Services:** NLM. **Networks/Consortia:** Member of Health Resources Council of Central New York. **Publications:** What's New in the Library, bimonthly.

★3109★
COMMUNITY HOSPITAL ASSOCIATION - MEDICAL LIBRARY (Med)*
183 West St.   Phone: (616) 963-5521
Battle Creek, MI 49016   Marilyn Cantrell, Dir., Med.Rec.
Staff: 2. **Subjects:** Biomedicine. **Holdings:** 650 books; 553 bound periodical volumes. **Subscriptions:** 43 journals and other serials. **Services:** Interlibrary loans; copying; library open to health technology students.

★3110★
COMMUNITY HOSPITAL OF BUNNELL - MEDICAL LIBRARY (Med)
Box 98   Phone: (904) 437-2211
Bunnell, FL 32010   Laine Bridges, Libn.
Staff: 1. **Subjects:** Medicine and allied sciences. **Holdings:** 51 books. **Services:** Library not open to public.

★3111★
COMMUNITY HOSPITAL AT GLEN COVE - MEDICAL LIBRARY (Med)
St. Andrews Ln.   Phone: (516) 676-5000
Glen Cove, NY 11542   Kathryn M. Gegan, Libn.
Staff: Prof 1. **Subjects:** Medicine. **Holdings:** 1000 books; 800 bound periodical volumes; reprints of publications by professional staff; 2 drawers of pamphlets; 5 drawers of tapes. **Subscriptions:** 99 journals and other serials. **Services:** Interlibrary loans; copying; library open to public with permission. **Networks/Consortia:** Member of Medical Libraries of Long Island (MEDLI).

★3112★
COMMUNITY HOSPITAL OF INDIANAPOLIS, INC. - LIBRARY (Med)†
1500 N. Ritter Ave.   Phone: (317) 353-5591
Indianapolis, IN 46219   Jean Bonner, Dir.
Staff: Prof 2; Other 2. **Subjects:** Medicine, nursing and allied health sciences. **Holdings:** 1200 books; 2000 bound periodical volumes; 4 VF drawers. **Subscriptions:** 225 journals and other serials. **Services:** Interlibrary loans; copying; library open to public with restrictions. **Networks/Consortia:** Member of Central Indiana Area Library Services Authority; Central Indiana Health Sciences Libraries Consortium (CIHSLC). **Staff:** Sr. Marianne Mader, Staff Libn.

★3113★
COMMUNITY HOSPITAL - MEDICAL LIBRARY (Med)
3325 Chanate Rd.   Phone: (707) 544-3340
Santa Rosa, CA 95404   Joan Chilton, Med.Libn.
Founded: 1962. **Staff:** Prof 1. **Subjects:** Medicine, psychiatry. **Holdings:** 1500 books; 3000 bound periodical volumes; Audio-Digest tapes, video cassettes. **Subscriptions:** 140 journals and other serials. **Services:** Interlibrary loans; copying; library open to medical, paramedical professionals and nursing students.

★3114★
COMMUNITY HOSPITAL OF THE MONTEREY PENINSULA - MEDICAL STAFF LIBRARY (Med)
Box HH   Phone: (408) 624-5311
Monterey, CA 93940   Ruthanne Lowe, Med. Staff Libn.
Staff: Prof 1. **Subjects:** Medicine and related fields. **Holdings:** 1600 books; 1700 bound periodical volumes; 650 audiotapes. **Subscriptions:** 130 journals and other serials. **Services:** Library not open to public. **Computerized Information Services:** MEDLINE. **Publications:** Monthly newsletter.

★3115★
COMMUNITY HOSPITAL OF SPRINGFIELD & CLARK COUNTY - HEALTH SCIENCES LIBRARY (Med)
2615 E. High St.   Phone: (513) 325-0531
Springfield, OH 45501   Jane Violet, Libn.
Staff: Prof 2; Other 1. **Subjects:** Medicine, nursing. **Holdings:** 1800 books; 950 bound periodical volumes; 400 audiovisual programs. **Subscriptions:** 120 journals and other serials. **Services:** Interlibrary loans; copying; library not open to public.

★3116★
COMMUNITY LEGAL SERVICES, INC. - LAW LIBRARY (Law)
Sylvania House
Juniper & Locust Sts.
Philadelphia, PA 19107   Phone: (215) 893-5368
                                            Diane Tierney, Libn.
Staff: Prof 1. **Subjects:** Law. **Holdings:** 12,000 books; 200 bound periodical volumes; 4 VF drawers. **Subscriptions:** 34 journals and other serials. **Services:** Interlibrary loans; copying; SDI; library not open to public. **Computerized Information Services:** LEXIS.

★3117★
COMMUNITY MEMORIAL GENERAL HOSPITAL - MEDICAL LIBRARY (Med)
5101 Willow Springs Rd.   Phone: (312) 352-1200
La Grange, IL 60525   Patricia J. Grundke, Libn.
Founded: 1955. **Staff:** Prof 1. **Subjects:** Medicine. **Holdings:** 550 books; 1500 bound periodical volumes. **Subscriptions:** 97 journals and other serials. **Services:** Interlibrary loans; library open to public with restrictions. **Computerized Information Services:** MEDLINE. **Networks/Consortia:** Member of Regional Medical Library - Region 3; Rush Affiliates Information Network (RAIN); Chicago and South Consortium; ILLINET; Suburban Library System.

★3118★
COMMUNITY MEMORIAL HOSPITAL OF MENOMONEE FALLS - MC KAY MEMORIAL LIBRARY (Med)
W180 N8085 Town Hall Rd.
Box 408   Phone: (414) 251-1000
Menomonee Falls, WI 53051   Sunja Shaikh, Libn.
Staff: Prof 1. **Subjects:** Medicine. **Holdings:** 236 books; 200 bound periodical volumes; 1859 slides; 50 video cassettes; 40 audio cassettes. **Subscriptions:** 157 journals and other serials. **Services:** Interlibrary loans; copying; SDI; library open to public for reference use only. **Networks/Consortia:** Member of Southeastern Wisconsin Health Sciences Library Consortium.

★3119★
COMMUNITY RELATIONS-SOCIAL DEVELOPMENT COMMISSION - RESEARCH LIBRARY (Soc Sci)
161 W. Wisconsin Ave., Rm. 7146   Phone: (414) 272-5600
Milwaukee, WI 53203   Pat Waddell, Res.Spec.
Founded: 1964. **Staff:** Prof 1; Other 1. **Subjects:** Poverty/social welfare, aging, employment and training, health, criminal justice, education. **Holdings:** 2500 books; 100 bound periodical volumes; 20 VF drawers; census and statistics collection; agency archives. **Subscriptions:** 40 journals and other serials; 6 newspapers. **Services:** Interlibrary loans; copying; library open to public with special arrangement. **Networks/Consortia:** Member of Library Council of Metropolitan Milwaukee, Inc. (LCOMM). **Publications:** Memorandum of new library materials, irregular - for internal distribution only.

★3120★
COMMUNITY SERVICE, INC. - LIBRARY (Soc Sci)
114 E. Whiteman St.   Phone: (513) 767-2161
Yellow Springs, OH 45387   Jane Folmer, Dir.
Staff: 2. **Subjects:** Communities - small, utopian and intentional; rural sociology; folk societies; communes; economics; education. **Special Collections:** Twentieth century intentional communities. **Holdings:** 1000 books and bound periodical volumes; 24 VF drawers of community development material, including commune newsletters from the 1950s and miscellaneous literature from communes and intentional communities. **Subscriptions:** 20 journals and other serials. **Services:** Library open to public for reference use only. **Publications:** Community Service Newsletter, bimonthly - to members.

★3121★
COMMUNITY SYSTEMS FOUNDATION - NUTRITION PLANNING INFORMATION SERVICE (Food-Bev)
1130 Hill St.   Phone: (313) 761-1357
Ann Arbor, MI 48103   Martha C. Gregg, Libn.
Founded: 1976. **Staff:** Prof 3; Other 2. **Subjects:** Community malnutrition, food policy, feeding programs, nutrition education, public health. **Special Collections:** Nutrition program evaluation (140 documents); nutrition planning (1870 documents abstracted in journal). **Holdings:** 150 books; 3000 documents; 1000 historical documents. **Publications:** Nutrition Planning: An International Journal of Abstracts about Food and Nutrition Policy, Planning and Programs, quarterly. **Special Indexes:** Geographic, Source, Subject Indexes, cumulated yearly. **Staff:** Naomi Gottlieb, Bus.Mgr.; Fe Susan Go, Doc.Libn.

★3122★
COMO ZOO - LIBRARY (Sci-Tech)
Midway Pkwy. & Kaufman Dr.   Phone: (612) 488-4041
St. Paul, MN 55103   Lala Byng, Libn.
Founded: 1955. **Staff:** Prof 1. **Subjects:** Animal studies, zoo-related studies. **Holdings:** 300 books. **Subscriptions:** 10 journals and other serials. **Services:** Library open to public for reference use only. **Special Indexes:** Animal inventory.

★3123★

COMPAGNIE DE JESUS - BIBLIOTHEQUE DE THEOLOGIE (Rel-Theol)
5605 Decelles Ave.   Phone: (514) 737-1465
Montreal, PQ, Canada H3T 1W4   Claude-Roger Nadeau, S.J., Dir.
Founded: 1882. **Staff:** Prof 1; Other 5. **Subjects:** Theology, scripture,
patristics, church history, canon law, history of religions, philosophy. **Special
Collections:** Canadiana; 16th, 17th and 18th century theological books; rare
books from the Ancien College des Jesuites de Quebec, established in 1635.
Holdings: 175,000 volumes. **Subscriptions:** 400 journals and other serials.
Services: Interlibrary loans; copying; library open to public with restrictions.

★3124★

COMPAGNIE DE JESUS - JESUITS LIBRARY (Rel-Theol)
C.P. 130   Phone: (514) 438-3593
St. Jerome, PQ, Canada J7Z 5T8   Joseph Cossette, S.J., Lib.Dir.
Founded: 1852. **Staff:** Prof 1; Other 1. **Subjects:** Spirituality, history.
Special Collections: Archives of the Society of Jesus (752 linear feet,
including 122 microfilms); history of Canada. **Holdings:** 72,137 books and
bound periodical volumes; numerous unbound items. **Subscriptions:** 147
journals and other serials; 11 newspapers. **Services:** Copying; library open to
graduates of the seminary. **Publications:** Cahiers d'Histoire des Jesuites, 3/
year.

COMPARATIVE ANIMAL RESEARCH LABORATORY LIBRARY
See: Oak Ridge Associated Universities

★3125★

**COMPLEXE SCIENTIFIQUE DU QUEBEC - SERVICE DE DOCUMENTATION ET
DE BIBLIOTHEQUE** (Sci-Tech)
2700 Einstein C-1-1   Phone: (418) 643-9730
Ste. Foy, PQ, Canada G1P 3W8   M. Levesque, Hd.Libn.
Founded: 1971. **Staff:** Prof 1; Other 7. **Subjects:** Marine biology, forestry,
agriculture, minerals. **Holdings:** 10,000 books; 900 bound periodical volumes.
Subscriptions: 350 journals and other serials; 10 newspapers. **Services:**
Interlibrary loans; copying; SDI; retrospective searches; library open to public.
Computerized Information Services: FIND/SVP; computerized cataloging.
Publications: Documentation, bimonthly - distributed to employees of
supporting services; Ref-Peches; Acquisitions Recentes.

★3126★

**COMPOSERS AND CHOREOGRAPHERS THEATRE, INC. - MASTER TAPE
LIBRARY** (Mus)
225 Lafayette St., No. 906   Phone: (212) 925-3721
New York, NY 10012   John Watts, Pres.
Founded: 1965. **Staff:** Prof 2; Other 1. **Subjects:** Contemporary American
music; modern dance; music and dance education; music and dance criticism.
Holdings: 2750 audio- and videotapes (cataloged) - 1000 hours from
concerts, radio broadcasts and lectures. **Subscriptions:** 35 journals and other
serials. **Services:** Interlibrary loans; copying; tape dubbing; library open to
public by membership or application. **Publications:** CCT Review, 4/year
distributed to members and professionals.

★3127★

**COMPREHENSIVE HEALTH COUNCIL OF METROPOLITAN CHICAGO -
ALCOHOLISM CENTER - LIBRARY** (Med; Soc Sci)
108 N. State St.   Phone: (312) 663-0610
Chicago, IL 60601   Karen L. Sincere, Adm.
Founded: 1977. **Staff:** Prof 2. **Subjects:** Alcohol, Fetal Alcohol Syndrome,
health promotion, disease prevention, polydrug, adolescent health. **Holdings:**
200 books; 28 films; 86 pamphlets; reprints; educational materials.
Subscriptions: 21 journals and other serials. **Services:** Copying; library open
to public. **Formerly:** Chicago Comprehensive Health Council - Alcoholism
Center.

★3128★

COMPREHENSIVE HEALTH PLANNING OF NORTHWEST ILLINOIS - LIBRARY
(Med)
206 W. State St., Suite 1008   Phone: (815) 968-0720
Rockford, IL 61101   Ray W. Peterson, Sr. Health Planner
Subjects: Health care, health services, population and demographics, health
statistics, health planning, hospitals. **Holdings:** 2242 books; unbound
periodicals; data files. **Subscriptions:** 36 journals and other serials. **Services:**
Interlibrary loans (fee); copying; library open to public. **Publications:** List of
publications - available on request.

★3129★

COMPTON ADVERTISING INC. - RESEARCH LIBRARY (Bus-Fin)
625 Madison Ave.   Phone: (212) 350-1570
New York, NY 10022   Shirley Damon, Hd.Libn.
Staff: Prof 2; Other 2. **Subjects:** Advertising, marketing. **Holdings:** 1220
books; 100 VF drawers. **Subscriptions:** 150 journals and other serials.
Services: Interlibrary loans; copying; library not open to public. **Computerized
Information Services:** DIALOG. **Staff:** Joyce Melito, Ref.Libn.

★3130★

**COMPUTER AIDED MANUFACTURING-INTERNATIONAL, INC. (CAM-I) -
LIBRARY** (Sci-Tech)
611 Ryan Plaza Dr., Suite 1107   Phone: (817) 860-1654
Arlington, TX 76011   Joanne E. Cruz, Lib.Coord.
Staff: 1. **Subjects:** Computer-aided manufacturing and design; numerical
control; automatically programmed tools (APT); process planning; geometric
modeling; factory management. **Special Collections:** APT documentation and
prototype software; CAM-I's Automated Process Planning (CAPP) system and
other process planning materials. **Holdings:** 1200 documents and
publications; 55 original magnetic tapes; 1 filing drawer of microfiche and
microfilm. **Services:** Copying (fee); library open to public with restrictions.
Special Catalogs: Catalog of Publications and Prototype Software - available
for sale. **Remarks:** CAM-I is a nonprofit membership corporation, engaged in
the research and development of computer-aided manufacturing technology.
CAM-I's member organizations, located throughout North America, Europe,
Japan and Australia, provide funds and manpower to support such research
and receive the benefits of new developments immediately upon completion.
After evaluation, the prototype developments are released to the public and
may then be obtained from CAM-I's library.

★3131★

COMPUTER HORIZONS, INC. - LIBRARY (Info Sci)
1050 Kings Hwy., N.
Cherry Hill, NJ 08034   Phone: (609) 779-0911
Staff: Prof 3; Other 1. **Subjects:** Bibliometrics, science and technology
indicators, science, social sciences. **Special Collections:** Bibliometrics
collection (75 books; approximately 750 papers); U.S. patents and patent
citations since 1971 (600,000). **Holdings:** 1000 books; 3000 papers in
subject areas (cataloged); 250 reels of magnetic computer tapes.
Subscriptions: 20 journals and other serials. **Services:** Library open to public
by appointment. **Computerized Information Services:** Internal database.
Special Indexes: Extensive scientific publication and citation data.

COMPUTER MODELLING GROUP - I.N. MC KINNON MEMORIAL LIBRARY
See: McKinnon (I.N.) Memorial Library

★3132★

COMPUTER PROCESSING INSTITUTE - INFORMATION CENTER (Info Sci)
111 Ash St.
East Hartford, CT 06108   Phone: (203) 528-9211
                                              Noreen M. Quinn, Dir., Info.Serv.
Staff: Prof 3; Other 2. **Subjects:** Data processing, business. **Holdings:** 1000
books; 1000 IBM manuals. **Subscriptions:** 60 journals and other serials; 10
newspapers. **Services:** Interlibrary loans; copying; SDI. **Networks/Consortia:**
Member of Capitol Region Library Council.

★3133★

**COMPUTER SCIENCES CORPORATION - SYSTEMS SCIENCES DIVISION -
TECHNICAL INFORMATION CENTER** (Sci-Tech; Info Sci)
8728 Colesville Rd.   Phone: (301) 589-1545
Silver Spring, MD 20910   Tenna Smelkinson, Mgr.
Staff: Prof 2; Other 3. **Subjects:** Computer science, aerospace, management,
mathematics. **Holdings:** 2500 books; reports on microfiche; programming
manuals. **Subscriptions:** 200 journals and other serials. **Services:** Interlibrary
loans; library not open to public. **Computerized Information Services:**
Computerized cataloging. **Networks/Consortia:** Member of Interlibrary
User's Association. **Publications:** COMDEX (book catalog of corporation
documents and reports), semiannual; New Acquisitions List, monthly. **Special
Catalogs:** Catalog of trade books and outside technical reports (card); catalog
of corporation reports, microfiche of reports and proposals (book).

★3134★

COMPUTER SCIENCES CORPORATION - TECHNICAL LIBRARY (Sci-Tech;
Info Sci)
650 N. Sepulveda Blvd.   Phone: (213) 615-0311
El Segundo, CA 90245   Jeannette H. Nelson, Mgr.
Founded: 1962. **Staff:** Prof 2; Other 2. **Subjects:** Data processing,
communications, information retrieval, programming, systems analysis,
business, management, operations research. **Holdings:** 3500 books; 1000
bound periodical volumes; 16,000 manuals, reports, and pamphlets; 2500

IBM manuals; 1000 microfiche. **Subscriptions:** 250 journals and other serials. **Services:** Interlibrary loans; copying; library open to public with restrictions. **Special Catalogs:** Book catalog to CSC technical reports and program documentation. **Special Indexes:** KWIC index to books, all serials and document holdings. **Staff:** Susan A. Tavetian, Sr.Libn.

★3135★
COMPUTER SCIENCES CORPORATION - TECHNICAL LIBRARY (Sci-Tech; Info Sci)
6565 Arlington Blvd.   Phone: (703) 237-2000
Falls Church, VA 22046   Ramona Briggs, Mgr.Tech.Lib.
Founded: 1963. **Staff:** Prof 4; Other 2. **Subjects:** Computers, communications, electronic engineering, operations research. **Holdings:** 12,000 books; 200 bound periodical volumes; 50,000 documents and reports; 10,000 microfiche; 300 reels of microfilm. **Subscriptions:** 350 journals and other serials; 10 newspapers. **Services:** Interlibrary loans; copying; library not open to public. **Computerized Information Services:** SDC; internal database. **Networks/Consortia:** Member of Interlibrary Users Association; Metropolitan Washington Library Council. **Special Indexes:** COMDEX (Computerized Documents Index) index to company reports; form is computer print-out, reduced and reproduced. **Staff:** Dorothy Barrett, Asst.Libn.

COMSAT
See: Communications Satellite Corporation

★3136★
CONAC - LIBRARY (Educ)
Binational Ctr. for Education
2717 Ontario Rd., N.W., Suite 200   Phone: (202) 223-1174
Washington, DC 20009   Cecelia Bustamante-Barron, Libn.
Founded: 1972. **Staff:** Prof 1; Other 3. **Subjects:** Higher education, Chicano literature, curriculum development, functional literacy, teacher and parent training. **Special Collections:** Fomento Literario - Chicano Literature (324 items). **Holdings:** 6000 books; 60 reports. **Services:** Copying; library open to public with restrictions. **Publications:** CONAC Boletin, monthly - to mailing list. **Also Known As:** El Congreso Nacional de Asuntos Colegiales.

CONANT LIBRARY
See: Nichols College

★3137★
CONCEPTION ABBEY AND SEMINARY - LIBRARY (Rel-Theol)
Phone: (816) 944-2211
Conception, MO 64433   Rev. Aidan McSorley, Hd.Libn.
Founded: 1873. **Staff:** Prof 2; Other 2. **Subjects:** Roman Catholic Church, philosophy, patrology, monasticism. **Special Collections:** Sixteenth to nineteenth century theological books (2600 volumes). **Holdings:** 77,577 books; 16,924 bound periodical volumes; 12 VF drawers of pamphlets; 9060 art and travel slides; 2661 music recordings; 53 incunabula; 663 tape recordings; 200 filmstrips; 130 reels of microfilm; 1200 art prints. **Subscriptions:** 308 journals and other serials. **Services:** Interlibrary loans; copying; library open to public with restrictions. **Networks/Consortia:** Member of Northwest Missouri Library Network. **Staff:** Bro. Leo Prichard, Asst.Libn.

★3138★
CONCORD ANTIQUARIAN SOCIETY - LIBRARY OF RALPH WALDO EMERSON (Hist)
Lexington Rd. & Cambridge Tpke.
Concord, MA 01742   Jim Fini, Dir.
Holdings: Figures not available. **Services:** Library not open to public. **Remarks:** A replica of Ralph Waldo Emerson's study, containing his library and original furnishings, on loan from the Emerson family.

★3139★
CONCORDIA COLLEGE - BUENGER MEMORIAL LIBRARY (Educ)
275 N. Syndicate   Phone: (612) 641-8240
St. Paul, MN 55104   Glenn W. Offermann, Hd.Libn.
Founded: 1893. **Staff:** Prof 4; Other 2. **Subjects:** Elementary education, religious education, church music. **Holdings:** 100,000 books; 12,000 periodical volumes (mostly in microform); 5000 nonbook items (cataloged); 250 motion pictures, filmloops; 2800 audio recordings; 1700 filmstrips; 3500 slides. **Subscriptions:** 450 journals and other serials; 6 newspapers. **Services:** Interlibrary loans; copying; library open to public with restrictions. **Networks/Consortia:** Member of Cooperating Libraries in Consortium (CLIC). **Staff:** Margaret Horn, Cat./Ref.Libn.; Martha Burkart, Curric.Coord.; Jeff Burkart, AV Dir.

★3140★
CONCORDIA COLLEGE - KLINCK MEMORIAL LIBRARY (Educ; Rel-Theol)
7400 Augusta St.   Phone: (312) 771-8300
River Forest, IL 60305   Henry R. Latzke, Dir., Lib.Serv.
Founded: 1864. **Staff:** Prof 5; Other 3. **Subjects:** Education, religion, psychology, church music. **Special Collections:** ERIC documents on microfiche (complete); hymnal collection. **Holdings:** 117,452 books; 10,842 bound periodical volumes; 10,000 curriculum laboratory materials; 1577 reels of microfilm; 252,872 microfiche; 1980 U.S. Census computer tapes. **Subscriptions:** 573 journals; 7 newspapers. **Services:** Interlibrary loans; copying; library open to public. **Computerized Information Services:** Computerized cataloging. **Networks/Consortia:** Member of OCLC; ILLINET; Surburban Library System (SLS). **Staff:** Cornell J. Kusmik, Acq.Libn.; Phyllis Masak, Cat. & Ref.Libn.; Audrey Roberts, Per. & Curric.Libn.; Richard Richter, Dir., Television.

CONCORDIA COLLEGE - LUTHERAN CHURCH - MISSOURI SYNOD - MICHIGAN DISTRICT ARCHIVES
See: Lutheran Church - Missouri Synod - Michigan District Archives

★3141★
CONCORDIA HISTORICAL INSTITUTE - DEPARTMENT OF ARCHIVES AND HISTORY (Rel-Theol)
801 DeMun Ave.   Phone: (314) 721-5934
St. Louis, MO 63105   August R. Suelflow, Dir.
Founded: 1927. **Staff:** Prof 2; Other 17. **Subjects:** Lutheranism in America; Archives of The Lutheran Church - Missouri Synod; Archives of the National Evangelical Lutheran Church; Archives of the Synod of Evangelical Lutheran Churches; Lutheran congregational histories; Evangelical Lutheran Synodical Conference Archives. **Special Collections:** Lutheran Foreign Mission resources; Lutheran Hour Broadcast discs; files and manuscripts of Lutheran leaders; Lutheran theological literature. **Holdings:** 58,000 books; 7800 bound periodical volumes; 2.5 million archival, document and manuscript materials; 156,000 feet of microfilm; 4700 phonograph records, discs, and tapes; 340 sets of slides and filmstrips; 5000 photographs, pictures, and museum items. **Subscriptions:** 130 journals and other serials; 35 newspapers. **Services:** Interlibrary loans (fee); copying; assistance in reference, research, bibliography, book identification, translation; library open to public. **Networks/Consortia:** Member of St. Louis Regional Library Network. **Publications:** Concordia Historical Insitute Quarterly; Historical Footnotes; Regional Archivist. **Special Indexes:** Index to Microfilm Holdings, 2 volumes. **Remarks:** Includes some of the holdings of the Lutheran Church - Missouri Synod - Lutheran Ministry to the Deaf, and other resources on specialized ministries.

★3142★
CONCORDIA SEMINARY - LIBRARY (Rel-Theol)
801 DeMun Ave.   Phone: (314) 721-5934
St. Louis, MO 63105   W. Larry Bielenberg, Dir., Lib.Serv.
Founded: 1839. **Staff:** Prof 3; Other 7. **Subjects:** Biblical studies, theology, patristics, Reformation and church history, hymnology and liturgics, sacred music. **Special Collections:** Lutherana (16th and 17th century Lutheran reformers and dogmaticians). **Holdings:** 133,377 books; 21,635 bound periodical volumes; 2566 reels of microfilm; 1484 phonodiscs; 756 filmstrips; 17,423 microfiche; 2914 cassettes; 943 microcards; 2782 slides. **Subscriptions:** 1082 journals and other serials; 9 newspapers. **Services:** Interlibrary loans; copying; library open to public for reference use only. **Networks/Consortia:** Member of St. Louis Regional Library Network. **Staff:** Joann Mirly, Asst.Dir.; Mark Wangerin, Coord., Pub.Serv.; Rev. William Engfehr, Dir., Educ. Media.

★3143★
CONCORDIA TEACHERS COLLEGE - LINK LIBRARY (Educ)
800 N. Columbia Ave.   Phone: (402) 643-3651
Seward, NE 68434   Vivian A. Peterson, Dir., Lib.Serv.
Founded: 1894. **Staff:** Prof 4; Other 6. **Subjects:** Education and religion. **Special Collections:** Koschmann Memorial Collection of Children's Literature. **Holdings:** 130,000 books and bound periodical volumes; 10,000 microforms; 9000 nonprint materials. **Subscriptions:** 650 journals and other serials. **Services:** Interlibrary loans; copying; library open to public. **Computerized Information Services:** Computerized cataloging. **Networks/Consortia:** Member of OCLC through NEBASE. **Staff:** Rebecca Bernthal, Pub.Serv.Libn.; Glenn Ohlmann, Tech.Serv.Libn.; Werner Klammer, Coord., AV Serv.

★3144★
CONCORDIA THEOLOGICAL SEMINARY - LIBRARY (Rel-Theol)
6600 N. Clinton   Phone: (219) 482-9611
Fort Wayne, IN 46825   Jeffrey Heard, Act.Dir., Lib.Serv.
Founded: 1846. **Staff:** Prof 3; Other 6. **Subjects:** Lutheran theology, church history, Lutherana, counseling, Spanish theological works. **Special Collections:**

Hermann Sasse Collection of European Theology; 16th and 17th century Lutheran Orthodoxy. **Holdings:** 107,862 books; 8000 bound periodical volumes; 1884 microforms; 2988 AV programs; 1495 other items. **Subscriptions:** 650 journals and other serials; 12 newspapers. **Services:** Interlibrary loans; copying; library open to public. **Computerized Information Services:** DIALOG, BRS; computerized cataloging, acquisitions and serials. **Networks/Consortia:** Member of OCLC through INCOLSA; TRI-ALSA. **Staff:** Norman Schell, Dir., Media Serv.; Janet Karius, Tech.Serv.Libn.

★3145★
CONCORDIA UNIVERSITY - SIR GEORGE WILLIAMS CAMPUS - GUIDANCE INFORMATION CENTRE (Educ)
1455 de Maisonneuve Blvd., W.   Phone: (514) 879-4443
Montreal, PQ, Canada H3G 1M8   Marlis Hubbard, Libn.
Founded: 1966. **Staff:** Prof 2; Other 3. **Subjects:** Educational planning, careers and career planning, financial aid, student life, study skills, personal development, job-hunting skills. **Holdings:** 950 books; 200 pamphlet boxes on careers; 3 VF drawers and 33 pamphlet boxes on financial aid; employer file of recruiting literature from 500 companies. **Subscriptions:** 80 journals and other serials. **Services:** Copying; centre open to public. **Publications:** Acquisitions List; Blueprint for a Guidance Information Centre; list of publications for sale - available upon request. **Special Catalogs:** Indexes to occupational and vocational collections. **Remarks:** Guidance Information Centre is maintained by Concordia Guidance Services. **Staff:** Susan Hawke, Libn.

★3146★
CONCORDIA UNIVERSITY - SIR GEORGE WILLIAMS CAMPUS - SCIENCE & ENGINEERING LIBRARY (Sci-Tech)
1455 De Maisonneuve Blvd., W.   Phone: (514) 879-4184
Montreal, PQ, Canada H3G 1M8   Z. Jirkovsky, Hd., Sci. & Engr.Lib.
Founded: 1966. **Staff:** Prof 5; Other 11. **Subjects:** Science, engineering, computer science. **Holdings:** Figures not available. **Services:** Interlibrary loans; copying; SDI; library open to public with restrictions. **Computerized Information Services:** DIALOG, SDC, CAN/OLE; computerized cataloging, serials and circulation. **Networks/Consortia:** Member of RIBLIN. **Special Catalogs:** Serials Holdings List.

★3147★
CONCORDIA UNIVERSITY - LOYOLA CAMPUS - DRUMMOND SCIENCE LIBRARY (Sci-Tech)
7141 Sherbrooke St., W.   Phone: (514) 482-0320
Montreal, PQ, Canada H4B 1R6   Tatiana Slivitzky, Supv.
Founded: 1962. **Staff:** Prof 1; Other 4. **Subjects:** Science, engineering, biophysical education. **Holdings:** Figures not available. **Services:** Library not open to public. **Computerized Information Services:** DIALOG, SDC, CAN/OLE; computerized cataloging and circulation. **Networks/Consortia:** Member of RIBLIN.

★3148★
CONCORDIA UNIVERSITY - LOYOLA CAMPUS - GEORGES P. VANIER LIBRARY (Soc Sci; Hum)
7141 Sherbrooke St., W.   Phone: (514) 482-0320
Montreal, PQ, Canada H4B 1R6   Irene Sendek, Hd., Loyola Libs.
Staff: Prof 6; Other 32. **Subjects:** Social sciences, humanities, communication arts, health, commerce, library studies. **Special Collections:** Africa Collection; D'Arcy McGee Collection of Irish Material; Masonic Collection (400 items); Rudnyc'ki Archives; Hilaire Belloc Collection. **Holdings:** Figures not available. **Services:** Interlibrary loans; copying; library open to public with restrictions on borrowing. **Computerized Information Services:** DIALOG, SDC, CAN/OLE; computerized cataloging and circulation. **Networks/Consortia:** Member of RIBLIN. **Staff:** Mrs. L. Boucher, Ref.Libn.; Mr. H. Perron, Ref.Libn.; Mr. M. Orbach, Ref.Libn.; J. Appleby, Ref.Libn.; Miss H. Gamiero, Ref.Libn.

CONCRETE TECHNOLOGY INFORMATION ANALYSIS CENTER
See: U.S. Army - Engineer Waterways Experiment Station

★3149★
CONDE NAST PUBLICATIONS, INC. - LIBRARY (Publ)
350 Madison Ave., 11th Fl.   Phone: (212) 880-8244
New York, NY 10017   Dianne Weber Spoto, Sr.Libn.
Founded: 1935. **Staff:** Prof 3. **Subjects:** Fashion, houses, gardens, home furnishings, interior design, health, personalities. **Special Collections:** Magazine photographs; complete bound volumes of House & Garden, Vogue, Vanity Fair, Glamour, Mademoiselle, Brides, Self, Gentlemen's Quarterly. **Holdings:** 5100 volumes. **Subscriptions:** 100 journals and other serials; 5 newspapers. **Services:** Copying; library open to public by appointment. **Special Indexes:** Index to Vogue, 1892 to present; index to Vanity Fair,

1913-1936. **Staff:** Theo Tarter; Cynthia Cathcart .

★3150★
CONDELL MEMORIAL HOSPITAL - FOHRMAN LIBRARY (Med)†
900 S. Garfield Ave.   Phone: (312) 362-2900
Libertyville, IL 60048   Emily Bergmann, Libn.
Founded: 1963. **Staff:** 2. **Subjects:** Medicine and surgery. **Holdings:** 1000 books and bound periodical volumes; 200 pamphlets; 500 audio cassettes. **Subscriptions:** 100 journals and other serials. **Services:** Interlibrary loans. **Networks/Consortia:** Member of Lake County Consortium; Regional Medical Library - Region 3; North Suburban Library System.

★3151★
CONDIESEL MOBILE EQUIPMENT - ENGINEERING LIBRARY (Sci-Tech)
1700 E. Putnam Ave.   Phone: (203) 637-6140
Old Greenwich, CT 06870   Denise M. Mellott, Tech.Libn.
Staff: Prof 1. **Subjects:** Military and commercial specifications; engineering. **Holdings:** 64 VF drawers of government and commercial specifications and standards. **Services:** Interlibrary loans (limited); copying; library open to public on a limited basis.

CONE LIBRARY
See: Marycrest College

★3152★
CONE MILLS CORPORATION - LIBRARY (Sci-Tech; Bus-Fin)
1106 Maple St.   Phone: (919) 379-6215
Greensboro, NC 27405   Arletta M. Kluttz, Libn.
Founded: 1944. **Staff:** Prof 1. **Subjects:** Textile technology, marketing, industrial relations, management, chemistry. **Holdings:** 3888 books; 1880 bound periodical volumes; 5890 patents. **Subscriptions:** 100 journals and other serials; 6 newspapers. **Services:** Interlibrary loans; copying; library open to public with company approval.

★3153★
CONE (Moses H.) MEMORIAL HOSPITAL - MEDICAL LIBRARY (Med)
1200 N. Elm St.   Phone: (919) 379-4484
Greensboro, NC 27420   Leslie G. Mackler, Dir., Med.Lib.
Founded: 1953. **Staff:** 4. **Subjects:** Medicine and medical specialities. **Holdings:** 2000 books; 1500 bound periodical volumes; 1200 AV items. **Subscriptions:** 130 journals and other serials. **Services:** Interlibrary loans; copying; library open to health care professionals in the Greensboro Area Health Education Center and health care students from local colleges for reference use only. **Computerized Information Services:** MEDLINE.

★3154★
CONEMAUGH VALLEY MEMORIAL HOSPITAL - HEALTH SCIENCES LIBRARY (Med)
1086 Franklin St.   Phone: (814) 536-6671
Johnstown, PA 15905   Fred L. Wilson, Jr., Med. Staff Libn.
Staff: Prof 2. **Subjects:** Medicine, nursing, allied health sciences. **Holdings:** 3000 books; 5000 bound periodical volumes; 450 Audio-Digest tapes; 80 videotapes. **Subscriptions:** 228 journals and other serials. **Services:** Interlibrary loans; copying; library not open to public. **Computerized Information Services:** NLM. **Networks/Consortia:** Member of Laurel Highlands Health Sciences Library Consortium. **Staff:** Gloria M. Cowie, Libn.

★3155★
CONESTOGA COLLEGE OF APPLIED ARTS & TECHNOLOGY, GUELPH CENTRE - HEALTH SCIENCES DIV. LEARNING RESOURCE CENTRE (Med)
70 Westmount Rd.   Phone: (519) 824-2950
Guelph, ON, Canada N1H 5H7   Joy Weiss, Libn.
Founded: 1967. **Staff:** 2. **Subjects:** Nursing, medicine, surgery, education. **Holdings:** 4100 books; 183 bound periodical volumes; 1500 items of AV software; 5 VF drawers of clippings, pamphlets, reports. **Subscriptions:** 58 journals and other serials. **Services:** Interlibrary loans; copying; library open to public with restrictions. **Networks/Consortia:** Member of Bibliocentre; Wellington County Health Library Network. **Special Catalogs:** Union card catalog and serials list for Wellington County Health Library Network. **Staff:** Louise Malison, AV Techn.

★3156★
CONEY ISLAND HOSPITAL - HAROLD FINK MEMORIAL LIBRARY (Med)
Ocean & Shore Pkwys.   Phone: (212) 743-4100
Brooklyn, NY 11235   Ronnie Joan Mark, Dir.
Founded: 1951. **Staff:** Prof 1; Other 5. **Subjects:** Medicine, nursing, pharmacy. **Holdings:** 4300 books; 8000 bound periodical volumes; 100 video cassettes; 50 slides with audio cassettes; 150 slides with pamphlets. **Subscriptions:** 215 journals and other serials. **Services:** Interlibrary loans;

copying; library open to librarians.

★3157★
CONFEDERATE MEMORIAL LITERARY SOCIETY - MUSEUM OF THE CONFEDERACY - ELEANOR S. BROCKENBROUGH LIBRARY (Hist)
1201 E. Clay St.
Phone: (804) 649-1861
Richmond, VA 23219
Cathleen A. Carlson, Cur. of Mss.
Founded: 1890. Staff: Prof 6. Subjects: Confederate military history; Confederate civil history; history of the South; military history. Special Collections: Confederate manuscripts and imprints; Jefferson Davis letters; Robert E. Lee letters. Holdings: Figures not available. Services: Copying; library primarily serves scholars. Publications: Newsletter, quarterly - to members. Staff: Edward D. C. Campbell, Jr., Dir.; Betsy McKemie, Cur. of House; Patricia Lockridge, Cur. of Educ.; David Hahn, Cur. of Coll.; Mercedes Tromley, Adm.Asst.

CONFEDERATE RESEARCH CENTER AND GUN MUSEUM
See: Hill Junior College

★3158★
CONFEDERATION DES CAISSES POPULAIRES ET D'ECONOMIE DESJARDINS DU QUEBEC - SERVICE DE DOCUMENTATION (Bus-Fin)
100 Ave. Des Commandeurs
Phone: (418) 835-2468
Levis, PQ, Canada G6V 7N5
Louise Tremblay
Founded: 1971. Staff: Prof 2; Other 5. Subjects: Cooperation, finance, economy, education. Holdings: 3000 books. Subscriptions: 30,000 journals and other serials. Services: Centre open to public.

★3159★
CONFEDERATION CENTRE ART GALLERY AND MUSEUM - ART REFERENCE LIBRARY (Art)
P.O. Box 848
Phone: (902) 892-2464
Charlottetown, PE, Canada C1A 7L9
David Webber, Dir.
Founded: 1964. Subjects: Art, architecture, sculpture. Holdings: 3500 books; numerous unbound periodicals. Subscriptions: 10 journals and other serials. Services: Library open to public.

★3160★
CONFEDERATION COLLEGE OF APPLIED ARTS & TECHNOLOGY - RESOURCE CENTRE (Sci-Tech; Bus-Fin)
Box 398
Phone: (807) 475-6241
Thunder Bay, ON, Canada P7C 4W1
J.R. Rapino, Dir.
Founded: 1967. Staff: Prof 1; Other 13. Subjects: Applied arts, business, technology. Holdings: 30,000 books; 5000 AV items (cataloged). Subscriptions: 500 journals and other serials; 50 newspapers. Services: Interlibrary loans; centre open to public. Computerized Information Services: Internal database; computerized circulation. Staff: G.W. Maki, Hd.Libn.

★3161★
CONFEDERATION LIFE INSURANCE COMPANY - LIBRARY (Bus-Fin)
321 Bloor St., E.
Phone: (416) 967-8326
Toronto, ON, Canada M4W 1H1
Lynne M. Cousins, Libn.
Founded: 1871. Staff: Prof 1; Other 2. Subjects: Actuarial science, group insurance, investments, law, management, marketing, personnel administration. Holdings: 10,000 books; 130 bound periodical volumes; 10 VF drawers of Life Insurance Marketing and Research Association (LIMRA) and Life Office Management Association (LOMA) reports; 17 VF drawers of U.S. and Canadian legislation; 5 VF drawers of association material; 1 VF drawer of maps; 2000 pamphlets. Subscriptions: 300 journals and other serials. Services: Interlibrary loans; copying; library open to librarians in insurance field.

★3162★
CONFERENCE BOARD OF CANADA - LIBRARY & INFORMATION CENTER (Bus-Fin)
25 McArthur Rd., Suite 100
Phone: (613) 746-1261
Ottawa, ON, Canada K1L 6R3
George Khoury, Dir., Info.Serv.
Founded: 1916. Staff: Prof 4; Other 2. Subjects: Management practice, statistics, economics, compensation. Special Collections: Complete holdings of the Conference Board (Canadian, American and European). Holdings: 2500 books; Canadian and U.S. government publications; pamphlets. Subscriptions: 200 journals and other serials; 12 newspapers. Services: Interlibrary loans; copying; library open to public with restrictions. Publications: Library acquisitions, monthly - for internal distribution only. Special Indexes: Cumulative index, annual (book). Staff: Theresa Bruneau, Libn.; Barbara Jardine, Lib.Techn.

★3163★
CONFERENCE BOARD, INC. - INFORMATION SERVICE (Bus-Fin)
845 3rd Ave.
Phone: (212) 759-0900
New York, NY 10022
Tamsen M. Hernandez, Dir.
Founded: 1916. Staff: Prof 10; Other 10. Subjects: Statistics, finance, management, personnel, marketing, economics. Holdings: 25,000 books and pamphlets; 300 bound periodical volumes; 150 VF drawers of pamphlets (uncataloged); 900 reels of microfilm. Subscriptions: 1700 journals and other serials. Services: Interlibrary loans (to members); copying; open only to Conference Board members, and faculty. Computerized Information Services: DIALOG, I.P. Sharpe Associates, Ltd.; internal database. Special Indexes: Cumulative Index to Conference Board Publications. Staff: Carol Estoppey, Supv., Tech.Serv.; Ellen Ackerman, Supv., Ref.Serv.; Judy Silverman, Sr.Info.Spec., Econ.; Mary Moore, Sr.Info.Spec., Mgt.; Riva Pearl, Info.Spec.; Arthur Di Meglio, Info.Spec.; Cecilia Dewey, Info.Spec.; Hilma Ebanks, Info.Spec.; Leslie Tobias, Info.Spec.

★3164★
CONFERENCE ON ECONOMIC PROGRESS - LIBRARY (Bus-Fin)
2610 Upton St., N.W.
Phone: (202) 363-6222
Washington, DC 20008
Leon H. Keyserling, Pres./Dir. of Staff
Subjects: U.S. economic problems and policies. Holdings: 3000 books; 500 bound periodical volumes. Publications: Coming Crisis in Housing, 1972; Wages, Prices and Profits, 1971; Toward Full Employment within Three Years, 1976; Full Employment without Inflation, 1975; The Scarcity School of Economics, 1973; Liberal & Conservative National Economic Policies & Their Consequences, 1919-1979, 1979; Money, Credit and Interest Rates and their Gross Mismanagement by the Federal Reserve System, 1980; list of other publications - available on request.

★3165★
CONFERENCE DES RECTEURS ET DES PRINCIPAUX DES UNIVERSITES DU QUEBEC - CENTRE DE DOCUMENTATION (Educ)
2 Complexe Desjardins, Suite 1817
C.P. 124
Phone: (514) 288-8524
Montreal, PQ, Canada H3B 1B3
Marie Brie-Berard, Documentaliste
Founded: 1967. Staff: Prof 1. Subjects: Education, communication, industrial relations, library science, economics. Holdings: 4500 books; 55 bound periodical volumes. Services: Interlibrary loans; library open to public. Also Known As: Conference of Rectors and Principals of Quebec Universities.

★3166★
CONGOLEUM CORPORATION - RESILIENT FLOORING DIVISION - TECHNICAL RESEARCH LIBRARY (Sci-Tech)†
Box 3127
Phone: (609) 587-1000
Trenton, NJ 08619
Doris Maul Fair, Libn.
Founded: 1920. Staff: Prof 1. Subjects: Plastics, chemistry, paper, floor coverings, coatings. Holdings: 2500 books; 350 bound periodical volumes; 15 VF drawers of technical bulletins, pamphlets, clippings, patents. Subscriptions: 60 journals and other serials. Services: Interlibrary loans; copying; library not open to public.

★3167★
CONGREGATION ADATH ISRAEL - LIBRARY (Rel-Theol)
Longwood Ave. & The Riverway
Phone: (617) 566-3960
Boston, MA 02215
Elaine B. Wilton, Libn.
Staff: Prof 1; Other 1. Subjects: Judaica. Holdings: 8500 books. Subscriptions: 30 journals and other serials. Services: Library open to congregation and religious school.

★3168★
CONGREGATION ADATH JESHURUN - GOTTLIEB MEMORIAL LIBRARY (Rel-Theol)
York & Ashbourne Rds.
Phone: (215) 635-1337
Elkins Park, PA 19117
Carole G. Ozeroff, Libn.
Staff: Prof 1; Other 2. Subjects: Judaica, religion, Bible. Holdings: 3000 books; 6 VF drawers of clippings; 60 phonograph records. Subscriptions: 8 journals and other serials. Services: Interlibrary loans; copying; library open to public with restrictions.

★3169★
CONGREGATION AGUDAS ACHIM - BERNARD RUBENSTEIN LIBRARY (Rel-Theol)†
1201 Donaldson Ave.
Phone: (512) 736-4216
San Antonio, TX 78228
Marie Bartman, Libn.
Staff: 3. Subjects: Judaica. Holdings: 3000 books and bound periodical volumes; magazines of Jewish content (cataloged); 20 phonograph records. Services: Copying; library open to public for reference use only.

★3170★
CONGREGATION OF THE ALEXIAN BROTHERS - PROVINCIAL ARCHIVES
  (Rel-Theol)
600 Alexian Way
Elk Grove Village, IL 60007   Bro. Roy Godwin, C.F.A., Prov.Archv.
Founded: 1971. Staff: Prof 1; Other 1. Subjects: History of the Alexian
Brothers; Roman Catholic Church history. Special Collections: Materials
relating to the congregation's hospitals and nursing homes and church history
from areas served by the Alexians (702 linear feet). Services: Archives open
to public with restrictions.

★3171★
CONGREGATION BETH ACHIM - JOSEPH KATKOWSKY LIBRARY (Rel-
  Theol)†
21100 Twelve Mile Rd., W.   Phone: (313) 352-8670
Southfield, MI 48076   Dr. Israel Wiener, Lib.Chm./Libn.
Founded: 1964. Staff: Prof 2. Subjects: Judaica, Bible/Old Testament,
cantorial liturgy, Jewish history. Special Collections: Classic Cantorial Liturgy;
Isaacs Collection (children's books). Holdings: 10,000 books; 80 records of
liturgical music (Hebrew and Yiddish); 75 pamphlets. Subscriptions: 25
journals and other serials; 5 newspapers. Services: Interlibrary loans; library
open to public. Staff: Judith Lawson, Asst.Libn.

★3172★
CONGREGATION BETH AM - DOROTHY G. FELDMAN LIBRARY (Rel-Theol)
3557 Washington Blvd.   Phone: (216) 321-1000
Cleveland Heights, OH 44118   Mrs. Louis L. Powers, Libn.
Founded: 1935. Staff: Prof 1. Subjects: Judaica. Holdings: 6500 volumes;
records. Subscriptions: 22 journals and other serials. Services: Interlibrary
loans; library open to public.

★3173★
CONGREGATION BETH AM - LIBRARY (Rel-Theol)†
26790 Arastradero Rd.   Phone: (415) 493-4661
Los Altos Hills, CA 94022   Ken Fehl, Chm., Lib.Comm.
Founded: 1961. Staff: 3. Subjects: Judaica. Holdings: 2500 books.
Subscriptions: 20 journals and other serials. Services: Library open to public
subject to approval. Staff: Elise Zentner, Libn.; Jan Lieberman, Libn.

★3174★
CONGREGATION BETH JACOB - GOODWIN FAMILY LIBRARY (Rel-Theol)†
109 E. Maple Ave.   Phone: (609) 662-4509
Merchantville, NJ 08109   Marilyn Kirshbaum, Libn.
Founded: 1956. Staff: 1. Subjects: Judaica. Holdings: 5500 volumes.
Subscriptions: 15 journals and other serials. Services: Library open to public.

★3175★
CONGREGATION BETH SHALOM - RABBI MORDECAI S. HALPERN
  MEMORIAL LIBRARY (Rel-Theol)
14601 W. Lincoln Rd.   Phone: (313) 547-7970
Oak Park, MI 48237   Eleanor Smith, Libn.
Founded: 1966. Staff: Prof 1. Subjects: Judaica. Holdings: 8000 books;
200 phonograph records; 200 Hebrew language story books. Subscriptions:
13 journals and other serials. Services: Library open to public.

★3176★
CONGREGATION BRITH SHALOM - MORRIS P. RADOV JEWISH CENTER
  LIBRARY (Rel-Theol)
3207 State St.   Phone: (814) 454-2431
Erie, PA 16508
Founded: 1950. Staff: Prof 5. Subjects: Talmud, Bible, Judaica, Midrash,
Rabbinics, Mysticism, Kabbalah, Chasidism. Holdings: 2500 books. Services:
Interlibrary loans; copying; library open to public. Computerized Information
Services: Online system.

★3177★
CONGREGATION EMANU-EL B'NE JESHURUN - RABBI DUDLEY WEINBERG
  LIBRARY (Rel-Theol)
2419 E. Kenwood Blvd.   Phone: (414) 964-4100
Milwaukee, WI 53211   Shirley Rumack, Libn.
Founded: 1930. Staff: Prof 1. Subjects: Judaica, Talmud, and general
reference. Special Collections: Jewish children's books (1500). Holdings:
6750 books and other items. Subscriptions: 20 journals and other serials.
Services: Interlibrary loans; library open to public by recommendation and
identification.

★3178★
CONGREGATION EMANU-EL - IVAN M. STELTENHEIM LIBRARY (Rel-Theol)†
6th Ave. & 65th St.   Phone: (212) 744-1400
New York, NY 10021   Marianne Winkler, Libn.
Founded: 1906. Staff: 1. Subjects: Judaica, American Jewish literature.
Holdings: 20,000 books. Subscriptions: 15 journals and other serials.
Services: Library open to public for reference use only.

CONGREGATION OF THE HOLY NAME
See: Dominican Sisters

★3179★
CONGREGATION KENESETH ISRAEL - LIBRARY (Rel-Theol)
2227 Chew St.   Phone: (215) 435-9074
Allentown, PA 18104   Ruth Y. Radin, Lib. Chairperson
Subjects: Religion, Bible, history, literature, biography, reference. Special
Collections: Judaica (adult and juvenile). Holdings: 4109 books; recordings; 2
VF drawers of pamphlets. Subscriptions: 10 journals and other serials.
Services: Interlibrary loans; library open to public.

★3180★
CONGREGATION KINS OF WEST ROGERS PARK - JORDAN E. FEUER
  LIBRARY (Rel-Theol)
2800 W. North Shore   Phone: (312) 761-4000
Chicago, IL 60645   Mrs. Milton Greenstein, Libn.
Staff: Prof 1; Other 5. Subjects: Religion and Hebraica. Special Collections:
Phonograph records dealing with Judaica (175 albums). Holdings: 3383
books; 200 pamphlets; 60 filmstrips. Subscriptions: 10 journals and other
serials.

★3181★
CONGREGATION MISHKAN ISRAEL - ADULT LIBRARY (Rel-Theol)
785 Ridge Rd.   Phone: (203) 288-3877
Hamden, CT 06517   Jay M. Brown, Chm., House Comm.
Staff: 1. Subjects: Judaica. Special Collections: Congregation archives.
Holdings: 1500 books. Services: Interlibrary loans; library open to public by
arrangement.

★3182★
CONGREGATION MISHKAN TEFILA - HARRY AND ANNA FEINBERG
  LIBRARY (Rel-Theol)
300 Hammond Pond Pkwy.   Phone: (617) 332-7770
Chestnut Hill, MA 02167   Carol Lurie, Libn.
Founded: 1920. Staff: Prof 1; Other 2. Subjects: Judaica. Holdings: 4000
books. Subscriptions: 20 journals and other serials. Services: Library open to
public by permission. Formerly: Temple Mishkan Tefila.

★3183★
CONGREGATION OF THE PASSION - HOLY CROSS PROVINCE -
  PROVINCIAL LIBRARY (Rel-Theol)
1924 Newburg Rd.   Phone: (502) 451-2330
Louisville, KY 40205   Fr. Germain Legere, C.P., Libn.
Founded: 1965. Staff: Prof 1; Other 1. Subjects: Philosophy, theology.
Special Collections: History of Passionist Congregation (800 volumes).
Holdings: 16,000 books; 2300 bound periodical volumes. Subscriptions: 20
journals and other serials; 5 newspapers.

★3184★
CONGREGATION RODEPH SHALOM - LIBRARY (Rel-Theol)
1338 Mount Vernon St.   Phone: (215) 627-6747
Philadelphia, PA 19123   Mildred Kurland, Libn.
Founded: 1802. Staff: Prof 1; Other 1. Subjects: Judaica; Jewish history
and religion, especially American. Special Collections: Roberta Lee Magaziner
Music Memorial (Jewish music, 340 books and sheet music). Holdings:
10,251 books; 8 VF drawers of clippings and pamphlets. Subscriptions: 24
journals and other serials. Services: Interlibrary loans; library open to public
for reference use only. Remarks: Branch library located at 8201 High School
Rd., Elkins Park, PA

★3185★
CONGREGATION RODFEI ZEDEK - J.S. HOFFMAN MEMORIAL LIBRARY
  (Rel-Theol)†
5200 Hyde Park Blvd.   Phone: (312) 752-4489
Chicago, IL 60615   Henrietta Schultz, Libn.
Founded: 1950. Staff: Prof 1; Other 1. Subjects: Judaica, Americana,
Lincolniana. Holdings: 8000 books; phonograph records (cataloged).
Subscriptions: 30 journals and other serials. Services: Library open to public.

★3186★
CONGREGATION SHAAREY ZEDEK - LEARNING RESOURCE CENTER (Rel-Theol)†
27375 Bell Rd. Phone: (313) 357-5544
Southfield, MI 48034 Albert E. Karbal, Dir.
Staff: Prof 1; Other 1. **Subjects:** Hebraica and Judaica. **Special Collections:** Yiddish (3500 volumes); Cantor Sonenklar Music Collection (75 items); Irwin T. Holtzman Israeli Literature (50 items). **Holdings:** 26,000 volumes; 20 VF drawers of pamphlets, clippings and pictures; 4 drawers of filmstrips; 2 drawers of cassettes; 200 phonograph records. **Subscriptions:** 35 journals and other serials. **Services:** Production of educational materials; library open to public. **Publications:** LRC Media Education, irregular. **Remarks:** Provides both remedial and individualized instruction as well as independent study for the students of the congregation's religious school.

★3187★
CONGREGATION SHALOM - SHERMAN PASTOR MEMORIAL LIBRARY (Rel-Theol)
7630 N. Santa Monica Blvd. Phone: (414) 352-9288
Milwaukee, WI 53217 Ellen Mandelman, Libn.
Founded: 1970. **Staff:** Prof 1; Other 4. **Subjects:** Bible, Jewish history, Israel, Jewish biography, and holidays. **Holdings:** 3500 books; 200 magazines and pamphlets (cataloged). **Services:** Library open to public with restrictions. **Special Catalogs:** Books for the Jewish Child (reading list).

★3188★
CONGREGATION SHEARITH ISRAEL - SOPHIE AND IVAN SALOMON LIBRARY COLLECTION (Rel-Theol)
8 W. 70th St. Phone: (212) 873-0300
New York, NY 10023 Anita Notrica, Libn.
Founded: 1956. **Staff:** Prof 1; Other 1. **Subjects:** Judaica, Hebraica. **Special Collections:** American Jewish Archive. **Holdings:** 5500 books. **Subscriptions:** 15 journals and other serials. **Services:** Library open to public for reference use only with permission.

★3189★
CONGREGATION SOLEL - LIBRARY (Rel-Theol)†
1301 Clavey Rd.
Box 838 Phone: (312) 433-3555
Highland Park, IL 60035 M.W. Hanig, Lib.Chm.
Founded: 1960. **Subjects:** Jewish religion and philosophy, Bible, Talmud, sociology, history, fiction; anti-semitism, Israel, Holocaust. **Special Collections:** Art books; Hagaddot; Holocaust photographs and maps of towns destroyed. **Holdings:** Figures not available. **Subscriptions:** 20 journals and other serials. **Services:** Library open to public, use of library encouraged.

CONGREGATIONAL LIBRARY
See: American Congregational Association

CONGRESS WATCH
See: Public Citizen

★3190★
CONGRESSIONAL BUDGET OFFICE - LIBRARY (Bus-Fin)
House Office Bldg., Annex 2
2nd & D Sts., S.W. Phone: (202) 225-4525
Washington, DC 20515 Jane T. Sessa, Libn.
Staff: Prof 2; Other 1. **Subjects:** Economics, federal budget, congressional budget process, economic policy. **Holdings:** 10,000 books; 800 bound periodical volumes; 1000 economics working papers; Serial Set on microfiche, 86th Congress to present. **Services:** Interlibrary loans; copying; library open to public. **Computerized Information Services:** DIALOG, BRS, New York Times Information Service; computerized circulation. **Networks/Consortia:** Member of OCLC through FEDLINK; Metropolitan Washington Library Council. **Publications:** Serials received by the Congressional Budget Office Library, irregular.

★3191★
CONGRESSIONAL CLEARINGHOUSE ON THE FUTURE (Sci-Tech; Educ; Energy)
H2-555 House Annex 2 Phone: (202) 225-3153
Washington, DC 20515 Elaine Wicker, Ed.
Subjects: Agriculture, appropriate technology, education, energy. **Holdings:** Figures not available. **Services:** Interlibrary loans; clearinghouse open to public. **Publications:** What's Next (newsletter), monthly.

★3192★
CONGRESSIONAL INFORMATION SERVICE, INC. (Publ)
4520 East-West Hwy., Suite 800 Phone: (301) 654-1550
Bethesda MD 20814 Paul P. Massa, Pres.
Founded: 1970. **Staff:** 225. **Subjects:** U.S. Congress and statistics. **Holdings:** Congressional publications, 1789 to present; U.S. government statistical publications; selected statistical publications from U.S. sources other than the federal government; statistical publications from major international intergovernmental organizations. **Services:** Library not open to public. **Computerized Information Services:** DIALOG, SDC. **Publications:** CIS/Index, monthly with annual cumulation; American Statistics Index, annual with monthly supplements; Statistical Reference Index, monthly with annual cumulation; Index to International Statistics, monthly with annual cumulation; CIS Legislative History Service; ASI Microfiche Library; CIS Microfiche Library; SRI Microfiche Library; IIS Microfiche Library. **Remarks:** CIS created the first standard indexes to Congressional publications and to U.S. government statistics. It collects, analyzes, abstracts and microfilms the publications indexed.

CONGRESSIONAL INFORMATION SERVICE, INC. - GREENWOOD PRESS
See: Greenwood Press

CONGRESSIONAL RESEARCH SERVICE
See: Library of Congress

★3193★
CONNAUGHT LABORATORIES, LTD. - BALMER NEILLY LIBRARY (Med)
1755 Steeles Ave., W. Phone: (416) 667-2921
Willowdale, ON, Canada M2R 3T4 Elaine Selke, Libn.
Founded: 1921. **Staff:** Prof 1; Other 3. **Subjects:** Immunology, virology, bacteriology, veterinary medicine, chemistry. **Holdings:** 19,455 volumes; 610 pamphlets. **Subscriptions:** 350 journals and other serials. **Services:** Interlibrary loans; copying; library open to public by appointment. **Computerized Information Services:** SDC. **Publications:** Acquisitions List, quarterly - for internal distribution only.

★3194★
CONNECTICUT AERONAUTICAL HISTORICAL ASSOCIATION - BRADLEY AIR MUSEUM REFERENCE LIBRARY
Bradley International Airport
Windsor Locks, CT 06096
Founded: 1965. **Subjects:** Aviation. **Holdings:** Figures not available. **Remarks:** Presently inactive.

★3195★
CONNECTICUT AGRICULTURAL EXPERIMENT STATION - OSBORNE LIBRARY (Agri)
123 Huntington St.
Box 1106 Phone: (203) 789-7265
New Haven, CT 06504 Paul Gough, Libn.
Founded: 1875. **Staff:** 2. **Subjects:** Botany, chemistry, entomology. **Holdings:** 23,050 books and bound periodical volumes. **Subscriptions:** 401 journals and other serials. **Services:** Interlibrary loans; copying; library open to qualified researchers. **Staff:** Victoria Jacobine, Asst.Libn.

★3196★
CONNECTICUT AUDUBON CENTER - LIBRARY (Env-Cons)
2325 Burr St. Phone: (203) 259-6305
Fairfield, CT 06430 Leslie N. Corey, Jr., Exec.Dir.
Founded: 1898. **Subjects:** Ornithology, botany, herpetology, mammalogy, natural history. **Holdings:** 5000 books; 2500 ornithology journals. **Subscriptions:** 25 journals and other serials. **Services:** Library open to public for reference use only. **Publications:** CAS Bulletin, bimonthly; CAS Reports, 3/year. **Remarks:** Maintained by Connecticut Audubon Society.

★3197★
CONNECTICUT COLLEGE - GREER MUSIC LIBRARY (Mus)
Phone: (203) 447-1911
New London, CT 06320 Philip Youngholm, Music Libn.
Founded: 1969. **Staff:** Prof 1; Other 1. **Subjects:** Music. **Special Collections:** American tunebooks of the 19th century (100); Richard C. Shelley Jazz and Blues Recordings Collection (2770 phonograph records); John H. Hilliar Collection of Opera Recordings (1500 phonograph records). **Holdings:** 5000 books; 650 bound periodical volumes; 1150 sound recordings; 8400 scores; 250 magnetic tapes. **Subscriptions:** 50 journals and other serials. **Services:** Interlibrary loans; copying; library open to public for reference use on request; phonograph records and tapes do not circulate. **Networks/Consortia:** Member of OCLC through NELINET.

★3198★
CONNECTICUT COLLEGE - LIBRARY - SPECIAL COLLECTIONS (Hum)
Mohegan Ave.　　　　　　　　　　　Phone: (203) 442-1630
New London, CT 06320　　　　　　Brian D. Rogers, Coll.Libn.
Subjects: Literature, history, art history, fine printing. **Special Collections:**
Coudert Collection of Oriental Art (500 volumes); Downs Collection of fish and
angling (1400 volumes); Helen O. Gildersleeve Collection of 19th and early
20th century children's literature (1500 volumes); Simmon's Collection of
John Masefield; Palmer Collection of Americana, history and theater (1750
volumes); Wyman Ballad Collection (350 volumes); first editions of Faulkner,
Frost, O'Neill, Stein and Yeats; manuscripts and papers of Prudence Crandall,
Alice Hamilton, Richard Mansfield, Belle Moskowitz, Eugene O'Neill, Frances
Perkins and Lydia Sigourney; New London County History (200 volumes).
Holdings: 11,000 books; 770 bound periodical volumes; 830 Little
Magazines. **Services:** Copying; library open to public. **Computerized
Information Services:** Online systems; computerized cataloging. **Networks/
Consortia:** Member of OCLC through NELINET; CTUW Project; Southeast
Connecticut Library Association. **Publications:** Library Acquisitions, bimonthly;
Library Bulletin, irregular. **Special Catalogs:** Palmer Collection Catalog (card).
Staff: W. James MacDonald, Ref.Libn.; Mary T. Odyniec, Assoc.Ref.Libn.;
Thelma Gilkes, Cat.Libn.

★3199★
**CONNECTICUT ELECTRIC RAILWAY ASSOCIATION, INC. - LIBRARY
　　DEPARTMENT** (Trans)
Box 360　　　　　　　　　　　　　　Phone: (203) 623-7417
East Windsor, CT 06088　　　　　　W.E. Wood, Libn.
Founded: 1940. **Staff:** 1. **Subjects:** Transportation, electric railways, trolley
data. **Holdings:** 1600 books; 370 bound periodical volumes; I.C.C. reports;
pictures; magazines; maps; time-tables; builders' plans. **Services:** Collection is
not centralized; open to public by special request.

★3200★
CONNECTICUT GENERAL LIFE INSURANCE COMPANY - LIBRARY (Bus-Fin)
　　　　　　　　　　　　　　　　　Phone: (203) 726-4327
Hartford, CT 06152　　　　　　　　Brenda H. Claflin, Corp.Libn.
Founded: 1919. **Staff:** Prof 2; Other 5. **Subjects:** Life insurance, health
insurance, pensions, law, business management, economics. **Special
Collections:** Company history. **Holdings:** 42,230 books and bound periodical
volumes; 3000 annual reports (cataloged); 10 VF drawers of pamphlets,
documents and clippings. **Subscriptions:** 1000 journals and other serials; 10
newspapers. **Services:** Interlibrary loans; library open to public by
appointment. **Computerized Information Services:** DIALOG, SDC, New York
Times Information Service; computerized serials. **Publications:** Library
Listings, bimonthly. **Remarks:** The library is located at 900 Cottage Grove
Rd., Bloomfield, CT 06002. **Staff:** Irene Goldman, Asst.Libn.

**CONNECTICUT HISTORICAL COMMISSION - PRUDENCE CRANDALL
　　MEMORIAL MUSEUM**
See: Crandall (Prudence) Memorial Museum

★3201★
CONNECTICUT HISTORICAL SOCIETY - LIBRARY (Hist)
1 Elizabeth St.　　　　　　　　　　Phone: (203) 236-5621
Hartford, CT 06105　　　　　　　　Elizabeth Abbe, Libn.
Founded: 1825. **Staff:** Prof 3. **Subjects:** New England and Connecticut
history and genealogy, colonial sources. **Special Collections:** Connecticut
imprints, city directories, maps and atlases, photographs and prints, almanacs,
children's books, sermons, broadsides, trade catalogs, historical and
genealogical manuscripts, account books and diaries. **Holdings:** 65,000
books; 400 bound periodical volumes; 1 million manuscripts; 2500 volumes of
18th and early 19th century newspapers. **Subscriptions:** 62 journals and
other serials. **Services:** Copying; library open to public. **Publications:** Bulletin,
quarterly; annual reports; monographs and occasional publications. **Special
Indexes:** Connecticut imprints by date; chronological index of manuscripts;
index to Connecticut Courant, 1764-1820. **Staff:** Ruth Blair, Mss.Cat.; Diana
McCain, Book Cat.

★3202★
**CONNECTICUT MUTUAL LIFE INSURANCE COMPANY - BUSINESS
　　INFORMATION SERVICES** (Bus-Fin)
140 Garden St.　　　　　　　　　　Phone: (203) 727-6500
Hartford, CT 06115　　　　　　　　Ellen Cartledge, Libn.
Founded: 1957. **Staff:** Prof 2; Other 2. **Subjects:** Life insurance and
business. **Special Collections:** Company archives; company publications.
Holdings: 6000 books and bound periodical volumes; 20 VF drawers of
pamphlets and current material; 24 VF drawers of archival material.
Subscriptions: 111 journals and 180 other serials. **Services:** Interlibrary
loans; library open to public for reference use only, on request. **Computerized**

Information Services: DIALOG, BRS, New York Times Information Service,
Dow Jones News Retrieval; computerized serials. **Publications:** Business
Information Services Bulletin, irregular; Business Information Services
Periodical Review, weekly - both for internal distribution only.

★3203★
CONNECTICUT NEWSPAPERS INC. - ADVOCATE LIBRARY (Publ)
75 Tresser Blvd.
Stamford, CT 06901　　　　　　　　Anne McRae, Libn.
Staff: Prof 1; Other 1. **Subjects:** Newspaper reference topics. **Special
Collections:** Antique newspapers and posters. **Holdings:** Clippings; local and
state documents; microfilm; photographs. **Services:** Library open to public
with permission. **Special Catalogs:** Catalogs of clipping file and photograph
file.

★3204★
CONNECTICUT POLICE ACADEMY - RESOURCE CENTER (Soc Sci)
285 Preston Ave.　　　　　　　　　Phone: (203) 238-6531
Meriden, CT 06450　　　　　　　　Theresa A. Wyser, Libn.
Founded: 1972. **Staff:** Prof 1. **Subjects:** Police science and administration,
criminal investigation, Connecticut law and penal codes, criminology,
constitutional law, motor vehicle law and safety. **Special Collections:** Law
reference library (756 volumes). **Holdings:** 1710 books; 1 VF drawer of
clippings, reports and articles; 1500 government documents and pamphlets;
473 AV programs. **Subscriptions:** 60 journals and other serials. **Services:**
Interlibrary loans; copying; library open to public with restrictions. **Networks/
Consortia:** Member of National Criminal Justice Reference Service.
Publications: Bibliographies; Audio Visual Catalog, 1980, with annual
supplements. **Special Indexes:** Index to AV materials (book).

★3205★
CONNECTICUT RIVER WATERSHED COUNCIL - LIBRARY (Env-Cons)
125 Combs Rd.　　　　　　　　　　Phone: (413) 584-0057
Easthampton, MA 01027　　　　　　Terry Blunt, Exec.Dir.
Staff: Prof 2; Other 2. **Subjects:** Water resources, water law, Connecticut
River studies. **Holdings:** 1000 books. **Subscriptions:** 7 journals and other
serials. **Services:** Copying; library open to public for reference use only.

★3206★
**CONNECTICUT STATE BOARD OF EDUCATION - J.M. WRIGHT TECHNICAL
　　SCHOOL - LIBRARY** (Sci-Tech)
Box 1416　　　　　　　　　　　　　Phone: (203) 324-7363
Stamford, CT 06904　　　　　　　　Iris W. Hill, Lib./Media Spec.
Founded: 1959. **Staff:** 1. **Subjects:** Automobile engineering, auto body
repair, welding, cosmetology, building trades, drafting, dental hygiene,
electricity, electronics, food economics and nutrition, machine tool and die,
industrial chemistry, practical nursing. **Special Collections:** Professional books
relative to teaching, especially vocational and art subjects. **Holdings:** 7290
books; 269 pamphlets (cataloged); 400 pamphlets; 252 files of magazines; 8
VF drawers of monographs, excerpts and catalogs. **Subscriptions:** 64 journals
and other serials. **Services:** Interlibrary loans; library open to public if material
cannot be obtained elsewhere.

★3207★
**CONNECTICUT STATE DEPARTMENT OF EDUCATION - LEARNING
　　RESOURCES AND TECHNOLOGY UNIT** (Educ)
Rm. 375, State Office Bldg.
165 Capitol Ave.　　　　　　　　　Phone: (413) 566-5582
Hartford, CT 06106　　　　　　　　Dorothy W. Headspeth, Educ.Asst.Libn.
Founded: 1981. **Staff:** Prof 1. **Subjects:** Education in Connecticut. **Special
Collections:** Connecticut State Department of Education Publications.
Holdings: 20 VF drawers of unbound reports; 514 volumes of pamphlets and
documents; 20 Princeton files of curriculum guides. **Subscriptions:** 20
journals and other serials. **Services:** library open to public for reference use
only. **Publications:** LRT Newsletter, 4/year. **Formerly:** Its Charles D. Hine
Library.

★3208★
**CONNECTICUT STATE DEPARTMENT OF HEALTH SERVICES - STANLEY H.
　　OSBORN MEDICAL LIBRARY** (Med)
79 Elm St., Rm. 315　　　　　　　　Phone: (203) 566-2198
Hartford, CT 06115　　　　　　　　Margery A. Cohen, Libn.
Staff: Prof 1; Other 1. **Subjects:** Public health, medicine. **Special
Collections:** Connecticut statutes and legislation, 1700s to present.
Holdings: 2610 books; 400 bound periodical volumes; 5126 pamphlets; 450
Children's Bureau publications; 2000 Public Health Service publications.
Subscriptions: 200 journals and other serials. **Services:** Interlibrary loans;
copying; library open to public for reference use only.

★3209★
CONNECTICUT STATE LIBRARY (Hist; Law)
231 Capitol Ave.   Phone: (203) 566-4777
Hartford, CT 06115   Clarence R. Walters, State Libn.
Founded: 1854. **Staff:** Prof 46; Other 141. **Subjects:** Library science, local history and genealogy, state and federal law, politics and government, legislative reference. **Special Collections:** Barbour Index of Connecticut Vital Records to 1850; Connecticut newspapers, town documents and probate records; pictorial archives; genealogical files (pre-1850); early automobile catalogs; almanacs. **Holdings:** 650,000 books; 30,000 bound periodical volumes; 2 million manuscripts (cataloged); 200 feet of photographs; newspaper clipping files, 1927 to present; 6000 reels of microfilm; 6000 maps; 1 million U.S. documents; 50,000 state documents; regional federal documents depository. **Subscriptions:** 1640 journals and other serials; 100 newspapers. **Services:** Interlibrary loans; copying; library open to public. **Computerized Information Services:** Online systems; computerized cataloging. **Networks/Consortia:** Member of OCLC through NELINET; New England Library Board. **Publications:** The Provisioner; Guide to Archives in the Connecticut State Library, 3rd edition, 1981; Connecticut State Library Monthly New Booklist; Checklist of Publications of Connecticut State Agencies; Historical and Genealogical Materials in the Connecticut State Library, 1981; Agency Newsletter, quarterly. **Special Indexes:** Index to Connecticut Legislative Journals, 1911 to present. **Staff:** Mark Jones, Archv.; Kenneth F. Rieke, Chf., Rec.Ctr.; Samuel E. Molod, Dp. State Libn.; David A. Peck, Personnel; Dominic A. Persempere, Pub.Rec.Adm.; Arlene F. Bielefield, Div.Hd.; Maureen D. Well, Law Libn.; Theodore O. Wohlsen, Archv./Hist./ Genealogy; Lynne N. Newell, Chf., Tech.Proc.; Patricia Owens, Div.Hd.; Leon Shatkin, Hd., ILL Ctr.; Mary Anna Tien, Middletown Dir.; Barbara Van Der Lyke, Willimantic Dir.; Dale Jeske, Hd.Libn. for Blind; Leslie Burger, Plan.Supv.; Barry Woods, Genealogy/Doc.

★3210★
CONNECTICUT STATE LIBRARY - FILM SERVICE (Aud-Vis)
Middletown Library Service Ctr.
786 S. Main St.   Phone: (203) 344-2645
Middletown, CT 06457   Mary Anna Tien, Dir.
Staff: Prof 1; Other 4. **Special Collections:** Home economics films. **Holdings:** Figures not available. **Subscriptions:** 12 journals and other serials. **Services:** Interlibrary loans; library not open to public. **Computerized Information Services:** Computerized film circulation.

★3211★
CONNECTICUT STATE LIBRARY - HARTFORD LAW BRANCH (Law)†
95 Washington St.   Phone: (203) 566-3900
Hartford, CT 06106   Evangeline Luddy, Libn.
Founded: 1854. **Staff:** Prof 1. **Subjects:** Law. **Holdings:** 35,000 books and bound periodical volumes. **Subscriptions:** 55 journals and other serials. **Services:** Interlibrary loans; copying; library open to public.

★3212★
CONNECTICUT STATE LIBRARY - LAW LIBRARY AT BRIDGEPORT (Law)
1061 Main St., 7th Fl.
New Court House   Phone: (203) 579-6237
Bridgeport, CT 06604   Robert Nathan Plotnick, Libn.
Founded: 1886. **Staff:** Prof 2; Other 2. **Subjects:** Law - admiralty, bailments, debtor-creditor, evidence, pleadings, negligence, zoning, wills and estates. **Special Collections:** Connecticut Collection from Colonial days to the present. **Holdings:** 100,000 books; 5000 bound periodical volumes; 5000 reports. **Subscriptions:** 150 law journals. **Services:** Interlibrary loans; copying; library open to public for reference use only. **Remarks:** Branches of the State Law Library System are located in Stamford, Danbury, Hartford, New Haven, Waterbury, Middletown, Rockville, Litchfield, Putnam, Willimantic, Norwich and New London. **Staff:** Louise Baldyga, Asst.Libn.

★3213★
CONNECTICUT STATE LIBRARY - LAW LIBRARY AT LITCHFIELD (Law)
Court House, West St.   Phone: (203) 567-0598
Litchfield, CT 06759   Evelina E. Lemelin, Libn.
Founded: 1976. **Staff:** 1. **Subjects:** Law. **Holdings:** 8000 volumes. **Subscriptions:** 56 journals. **Services:** Copying; library open to public.

★3214★
CONNECTICUT STATE LIBRARY - LAW LIBRARY AT NEW HAVEN (Law)
County Courthouse
235 Church St.   Phone: (203) 789-7889
New Haven, CT 06510   Martha J. Sullivan, Lib.Adm.
Founded: 1848. **Staff:** Prof 2. **Subjects:** Law. **Holdings:** 50,000 volumes. **Subscriptions:** 60 journals and other serials. **Services:** Interlibrary loans; copying; library open to public. **Remarks:** Contains the holdings of the former

New Haven County Law Library. **Staff:** Ann Lenz .

★3215★
CONNECTICUT STATE LIBRARY - LAW LIBRARY AT PUTNAM (Law)
155 Church St.   Phone: (203) 928-3716
Putnam, CT 06260   Donna R. Izbicki, Libn.
Staff: Prof 1. **Subjects:** Law. **Holdings:** 12,000 books. **Subscriptions:** 150 journals and other serials. **Services:** Interlibrary loans; library not open to public.

★3216★
CONNECTICUT STATE LIBRARY - LAW LIBRARY AT ROCKVILLE (Law)
Box 510   Phone: (203) 875-6294
Rockville, CT 06066   Virginia Scanlon, Libn.
Staff: 1. **Subjects:** Law. **Holdings:** 12,500 books. **Services:** Library open to public.

★3217★
CONNECTICUT STATE LIBRARY - LAW LIBRARY AT STAMFORD (Law)
Court House, 123 Hoyt St.   Phone: (203) 359-1114
Stamford, CT 06905   Jonathan C. Stock, Libn.
Staff: Prof 1; Other 1. **Subjects:** Law. **Holdings:** 18,000 books. **Services:** Interlibrary loans; copying; library open to public. **Publications:** Connecticut State Library-Law Library/Stamford, quarterly newsletter - to attorneys and corporations.

★3218★
CONNECTICUT STATE LIBRARY - LAW LIBRARY AT WATERBURY (Law)†
Court House, 300 Grand St.   Phone: (203) 754-2644
Waterbury, CT 06702   Lucy L. Cyr, Libn.
Subjects: Law. **Holdings:** 18,000 volumes. **Remarks:** Contains the holdings of the Waterbury Bar Library.

★3219★
CONNECTICUT STATE LIBRARY - LIBRARY FOR THE BLIND AND PHYSICALLY HANDICAPPED (Aud-Vis)
90 Washington St.   Phone: (203) 566-3028
Hartford, CT 06106   Dale Jeske, Dir.
Founded: 1968. **Staff:** Prof 1; Other 13. **Holdings:** Braille and talking books. **Services:** Library open to visually impaired or physically handicapped residents of Connecticut. **Remarks:** Service may be conducted by mail or telephone. Books and playback equipment are sent postage free.

★3220★
CONNECTICUT STATE OFFICE OF POLICY AND MANAGEMENT - LIBRARY
80 Washington St.
Hartford, CT 06115
Founded: 1978. **Subjects:** Energy, state budget, planning. **Special Collections:** Connecticut Regional Planning Agencies reports; energy reports. **Holdings:** 300 books; 11,000 documents; 40 pamphlets. **Remarks:** Contains the holdings of the Connecticut State Energy Library. Presently inactive.

★3221★
CONNECTICUT VALLEY HISTORICAL MUSEUM - RESEARCH LIBRARY (Hist; Bus-Fin)
194 State St.   Phone: (413) 732-3080
Springfield, MA 01103   Gregory Farmer, Dir.
Staff: Prof 2; Other 2. **Subjects:** Connecticut Valley business history, 17th-century to 1956 (manuscript business records of companies now defunct). **Special Collections:** John Pynchon Account Books, 1651-1713; diaries, letters and personal papers of Connecticut Valley residents, 1650-1950. **Services:** Library open to public by request. **Publications:** List of publications - available on request.

★3222★
CONNECTICUT VALLEY HOSPITAL - HALLOCK MEDICAL LIBRARY (Med)
Box 351   Phone: (203) 344-2304
Middletown, CT 06457   Mildred Asbell, Med.Libn.
Founded: 1946. **Staff:** Prof 1. **Subjects:** Psychiatry, neurology, medicine. **Holdings:** 4500 books; 2500 bound periodical volumes. **Subscriptions:** 77 journals and other serials. **Services:** Interlibrary loans; library open to medical and psychology students and physicians.

★3223★
CONNER PRAIRIE PIONEER SETTLEMENT - RESEARCH DEPARTMENT LIBRARY (Hist)
30 Conner Lane   Phone: (317) 773-3633
Noblesville, IN 46060   John Lauritz Larson, Hist.
Staff: Prof 2. **Subjects:** History of central Indiana to 1850 - culture,

architecture, ideas and institutions. **Holdings:** 2000 books; maps; newspapers; journals; account books; microfilm and other copies of local government documents. **Services:** Library open to public on approval.

CONOCO COAL DEVELOPMENT COMPANY
See: Conoco Inc. - Coal Research Division

★3224★
CONOCO INC. - COAL RESEARCH DIVISION - TECHNICAL LIBRARY (Energy)
4000 Brownsville Rd.　　　　　　　　Phone: (412) 831-6688
Library, PA 15129　　　　　　　　Kristin E. Henson, Tech.Libn.
Founded: 1947. **Staff:** Prof 1. **Subjects:** Coal and fuel - chemistry and technology. **Holdings:** 10,000 books; 2500 bound periodical volumes; 26 VF drawers; 54 boxes of reprints; 38 boxes of microfilm; selected government microfiche and reports. **Subscriptions:** 250 journals and other serials. **Services:** Interlibrary loans; copying; library open to public with restrictions. **Computerized Information Services:** DIALOG, SDC, DOE/RECON, NTIS. **Formerly:** Conoco Coal Development Company.

★3225★
CONOCO, INC. - INTERNATIONAL PRODUCTION - CENTRAL FILES/ LIBRARY (Energy)
Conoco Tower, Suite 1821
Greenway Plaza E.　　　　　　　　Phone: (713) 965-2499
Houston, TX 77046　　　　　　　　Frances A. Nowak, Supv.
Founded: 1958. **Staff:** Prof 1; Other 3. **Subjects:** Geology, petroleum, geophysics, business. **Special Collections:** Arab International and World Petroleum Congress - bibliographies and indexes; Oil & Gas Journal, 1968 to present. **Holdings:** 5000 volumes; 42 VF drawers; conference papers; proceedings; technical manuals; atlases. **Subscriptions:** 70 journals and other serials. **Services:** Interlibrary loans; copying; library open to public with restrictions. **Computerized Information Services:** DIALOG, SDC. **Remarks:** Serves as central files for its International Production Department and houses well files of its International Production and International Exploration Departments. **Formerly:** Its International Exploration and Production Library.

★3226★
CONOCO, INC. - LEGAL INFORMATION CENTER (Law)
5 Greenway Plaza E., Suite 1614
Box 2197　　　　　　　　　　　Phone: (713) 965-2592
Houston, TX 77001　　　　　　Robert S. Grundy, Law Libn./Att.
Staff: Prof 2; Other 2. **Subjects:** U.S. law - cases and statutes; oil and gas law; international law. **Special Collections:** Backfile of Federal Register and Code of Federal Regulations (complete set on microfiche). **Holdings:** 25,000 books; 500 bound periodical volumes; legal department memos and briefs; company annual reports. **Subscriptions:** 125 journals and other serials; 12 newspapers. **Services:** Interlibrary loans; copying; SDI; library open with librarian's permission. **Computerized Information Services:** Mead Data Central, SDC, DIALOG, Dow Jones New Retrieval; internal data base; computerized cataloging, acquisitions and serials. **Publications:** Acquisitions list/newsletter - for internal distribution only.

★3227★
CONOCO, INC. - MINERALS LIBRARY (Energy)
555 17th St.　　　　　　　　　　Phone: (303) 575-6025
Denver, CO 80202　　　　　　　　Sharon Brown, Libn.
Staff: Prof 1. **Subjects:** Geology, mining engineering, physical science, business, environment. **Special Collections:** Annual reports of mining industry companies (350). **Holdings:** 6000 books; 250 microfiche and 700 maps (cataloged); unbound periodicals. **Subscriptions:** 100 journals and other serials; 5 newspapers. **Services:** Copying; library not open to public. **Computerized Information Services:** DIALOG, SDC. **Publications:** Minerals Library Bulletin, monthly - to field offices. **Special Catalogs:** Catalog of books and maps.

★3228★
CONOCO, INC. - RESEARCH AND DEVELOPMENT DEPARTMENT - TECHNICAL INFORMATION SERVICES (Energy)
　　　　　　　　　　　　　　　Phone: (405) 767-4719
Ponca City, OK 74601　　　Dr. Harold H. Eby, Dir., Corp.Serv.Sect.
Founded: 1952. **Staff:** Prof 4; Other 4. **Subjects:** Petroleum, chemicals, mining. **Holdings:** 10,000 books; 18,000 bound periodical volumes; 2500 pamphlets (cataloged); 250,000 patents; 3000 reports in VF; microfilm: API Abstracts, Petroleum Abstracts (University of Tulsa), Chemical Abstracts, U.S. Patents (1952 to present), U.S. Patent Gazette (1930 to present); magnetic tape: IFI's U.S. Chemical Patents (1950 to present); API Abstracts, 13,000 Proprietary Research Reports. **Subscriptions:** 550 journals and other serials. **Services:** Interlibrary loans; copying; literature searches; contracted SDI; contracted translations; library open to public by request. **Computerized**

Information Services: SDC, DIALOG, NLM, DOE/RECON. **Publications:** Library Bulletin, biweekly. **Staff:** John F. Foell, Sr.Info.Spec.; Dr. John T. Minor, Sr.Info.Spec.; Mrs. Pat S. Hoskins, Hd.Libn.

CONOLE (Frances R.) ARCHIVE OF SOUND RECORDINGS
See: SUNY at Binghamton - Special Collections

★3229★
CONRAD GREBEL COLLEGE - LIBRARY/ARCHIVES (Hist; Rel-Theol)
　　　　　　　　　　　　　　　Phone: (519) 885-0220
Waterloo, ON, Canada N2L 3G6　　　Samuel Steiner, Libn. & Archv.
Founded: 1964. **Staff:** Prof 1; Other 2. **Subjects:** Anabaptist/Mennonite history, peace studies. **Special Collections:** Mennonite Archives of Ontario (300 feet, 6600 feet on microfilm). **Holdings:** 15,000 books; 1000 bound periodical volumes; 800 microforms; 10 feet of clipping files; 300 oral history cassettes. **Subscriptions:** 150 journals and other serials; 10 newspapers. **Services:** Interlibrary loans; copying; library open to public; archives open to public by appointment.

CONRAD (Joseph) LIBRARY
See: Seamen's Church Institute of New York - Joseph Conrad Library

CONRAD TECHNICAL LIBRARY
See: U.S. Army Signal Center & Fort Gordon

CONSEIL CANADIEN DE DEVELOPPEMENT SOCIAL
See: Canadian Council on Social Development

CONSEIL CANADIEN DES RELATIONS DU TRAVAIL
See: Canada - Labour Relations Board

CONSEIL ECONOMIQUE DU CANADA
See: Canada - Economic Council of Canada

CONSEIL NATIONAL DE RECHERCHES DU CANADA
See: Canada - National Research Council

CONSEIL DE LA RADIODIFFUSION ET DES TELECOMMUNICATIONS CANADIENNES
See: Canada - Canadian Radio-Television and Telecommunications Commission

CONSERVATION ANALYTICAL LABORATORY
See: Smithsonian Institution Libraries

★3230★
CONSERVATION COUNCIL OF ONTARIO - LIBRARY (Env-Cons; Energy)
45 Charles St. E., 6th Fl.　　　　　　Phone: (416) 961-6830
Toronto, ON, Canada M4Y 1S2　　　Arthur M. Timms, Exec.Dir.
Staff: 4. **Subjects:** Water quality, parks, land use planning, energy. **Holdings:** 1000 books. **Subscriptions:** 10 journals and other serials; 10 newspapers. **Services:** Library open to public.

★3231★
CONSERVATION DISTRICTS FOUNDATION - DAVIS CONSERVATION LIBRARY (Env-Cons)
408 E. Main St.
Box 776　　　　　　　　　　　Phone: (713) 332-3404
League City, TX 77573　　　　　　Mary M. Wooley, Libn.
Founded: 1962. **Staff:** Prof 1. **Subjects:** Conservation, natural resources, soil, water, agriculture, forests, cities and towns (planning), conservation of wild life, water resources development, ecology. **Special Collections:** History of soil and water conservation districts movement in America. **Holdings:** 2500 books; 55 bound periodical volumes; 300 pamphlets; 50 VF drawers of the History of the National Association of Conservation Districts and related history of conservation. **Subscriptions:** 24 journals and other serials. **Services:** Interlibrary loans; copying; library open to public through request placed at one's local Conservation District.

★3232★
CONSERVATION FOUNDATION - LIBRARY (Env-Cons)
1717 Massachusetts Ave., N.W.　　　Phone: (202) 797-4300
Washington, DC 20036　　　　　　Barbara K. Rodes, Libn.
Founded: 1949. **Staff:** 1. **Subjects:** Natural resource conservation, water resources, pollution, land use planning, energy pricing and regulation. **Holdings:** 3000 books; clippings file. **Subscriptions:** 120 journals and other serials. **Services:** Interlibrary loans; library open to public by appointment. **Computerized Information Services:** DIALOG. **Publications:** Acquisitions List, monthly.

★3233★
CONSERVATION AND RENEWABLE ENERGY INQUIRY AND REFERRAL SERVICE (Energy)†
Franklin Research Center
20th & Cherry Sts.   Phone: (800) 523-2929
Philadelphia, PA 19103   Ken Bordner, Dir.
Founded: 1976. **Staff:** Prof 10; Other 100. **Subjects:** Solar heating and cooling, solar water heating. **Holdings:** 1000 books and pamphlets; 3000 reports; 5700 articles; 2000 clippings; 100 microforms; 1200 slides. **Subscriptions:** 90 journals and other serials. **Services:** Library not open to public. **Computerized Information Services:** DOE/RECON; INQUIRE (internal database). **Publications:** Solar heating and cooling pamphlets, fact sheets, bibliographies - on request. **Remarks:** The Conservation and Renewable Energy Inquiry and Referral Service operates under contract to the U.S. Dept. of Energy. In Pennsylvania, the tollfree number is 800-462-4983; in Hawaii and Alaska, the tollfree number is 800-523-4700; in the remaining states, it is 800-523-2929. **Formerly:** Franklin Research Center - National Solar Heating & Cooling Information Center. **Staff:** Gloria Fultz, Lib.Mgr.; Marcia Ballen, Data Bank Mgr.; Diana Fortvaler.

★3234★
CONSERVATIVE BAPTIST THEOLOGICAL SEMINARY - CAREY S. THOMAS LIBRARY (Rel-Theol)
Univ.Pk.Sta.
Box 10,000   Phone: (303) 781-8691
Denver, CO 80210   Sarah Lyons, Libn.
Founded: 1950. **Staff:** Prof 2; Other 8. **Subjects:** Bible, theology, missions, church history, Christian education, homiletics, philosophy, pastoral theology. **Holdings:** 70,500 volumes; filmstrips, microfilms and slides; cassette and reel tapes; pamphlets. **Subscriptions:** 475 journals and other serials. **Services:** Interlibrary loans; copying; library open to public. **Computerized Information Services:** Computerized cataloging. **Networks/Consortia:** Member of OCLC. **Staff:** Jeannette France, Asst.Libn.

★3235★
CONSERVATOIRE D'ART DRAMATIQUE DE QUEBEC - BIBLIOTHEQUE (Theater)†
30 St-Denis   Phone: (418) 643-2139
Quebec, PQ, Canada G1R 4B6   Georgette Laki, Bibliothecaire
Staff: Prof 1; Other 1. **Subjects:** All aspects of the theater, dramatic criticism. **Holdings:** 4566 books; 4000 slides in 80 series; 2000 unbound periodicals. **Subscriptions:** 20 journals and other serials. **Services:** Interlibrary loans; library open to public for consultation; restricted borrowing. **Special Indexes:** Index to number of characters in each play (card). **Remarks:** All holdings are in French.

★3236★
CONSERVATOIRE DE MUSIQUE DE MONTREAL - CENTRE DE DOCUMENTATION (Mus)
100 rue Notre-Dame est   Phone: (514) 873-4031
Montreal, PQ, Canada H2Y 1C1   Nicole Boisclair, Directrice
Staff: Prof 1; Other 4. **Subjects:** Music. **Special Collections:** Emil Cooper; Jean Deslauriers; Arthur Garami. **Holdings:** 7000 books; 47,000 scores; 8000 sound recordings; 240 magnetic tapes. **Subscriptions:** 50 journals and other serials. **Services:** Interlibrary loans; library open to public with restrictions. **Also Known As:** Montreal Conservatory of Music - Documentation Centre.

CONSERVATORIO DE MUSICA DE PUERTO RICO
See: Festival Casals, Inc.

★3237★
CONSOLIDATED-BATHURST INC. - RESEARCH CENTRE LIBRARY (Sci-Tech)
                Phone: (819) 538-3341
Grand Mere, PQ, Canada G9T 5L2   Gilberte Angel, Libn.
Staff: 1. **Subjects:** Pulp and paper, chemistry, physics. **Holdings:** 900 books; 2000 bound periodical volumes. **Subscriptions:** 30 journals and other serials. **Services:** Library not open to public.

★3238★
CONSOLIDATED EDISON COMPANY OF NEW YORK, INC. - LIBRARY (Energy)
4 Irving Pl., Rm. 1650-S   Phone: (212) 460-4228
New York, NY 10003   Steven Jaffe, Libn.
Founded: 1906. **Staff:** Prof 2; Other 3. **Subjects:** Electricity; gas; public utility economics; atomic power. **Holdings:** 35,000 books; 10,000 bound periodical volumes; 40 cabinets of pamphlets on labor, political science; microforms. **Subscriptions:** 380 journals and other serials. **Services:** Interlibrary loans; copying; library open to public by appointment.

Computerized Information Services: DIALOG, SDC, DOE/RECON, New York Times Information Service, Control Data Corporation, Electric Power Research Institute (EPRI), BRS. **Publications:** Con Edison Library Bulletin, monthly. **Staff:** Peter James Dietrich, Assoc.Libn.

CONSOLIDATED HOSPITALS OF IDAHO FALLS
See: Idaho Falls Consolidated Hospitals

★3239★
CONSOLIDATED NATURAL GAS SERVICE CO., INC. - RESEARCH DEPARTMENT LIBRARY (Sci-Tech; Energy)
11001 Cedar Ave.   Phone: (216) 421-6310
Cleveland, OH 44106   Carol A. Brown, Supv., Info.Serv.
Staff: Prof 1; Other 1. **Subjects:** Natural gas, liquefied natural gas, public utilities, management. **Holdings:** 4000 books; 350 periodical volumes on microfilm; 3000 other cataloged items; 45 vertical files; 20,000 government documents on microfiche. **Services:** Interlibrary loans; copying; SDI; library open to public by appointment with librarian. **Computerized Information Services:** DOE/RECON, DIALOG, SDC, Control Data Corporation. **Publications:** Library Acquisition List, bimonthly. **Special Catalogs:** Subject bibliographies.

★3240★
CONSOLIDATED PAPERS, INC. - RESEARCH AND DEVELOPMENT LIBRARY (Sci-Tech)
Box 50   Phone: (715) 422-3768
Wisconsin Rapids, WI 54494   Helen W. Sanborn, Supv., Info.Serv.
Founded: 1966. **Staff:** Prof 1; Other 2. **Subjects:** Pulp paper technology; graphic arts; management. **Holdings:** 10,000 books; 700 bound periodical volumes; 3000 reprints; 12 drawers of patents. **Subscriptions:** 1800 journals and other serials; 12 newspapers. **Services:** Library open to public with restrictions. **Computerized Information Services:** Computerized acquisitions and circulation.

★3241★
CONSOLIDATION COAL COMPANY - EXPLORATION LIBRARY (Sci-Tech; Energy)
Consol Plaza
1800 Washington Rd.   Phone: (412) 831-4513
Pittsburgh, PA 15241   Eva Marie Tomassetti, Land Ck.
Founded: 1973. **Staff:** 1. **Subjects:** Geology, geography, mining engineering, hydrology. **Special Collections:** Submittals (1000). **Holdings:** 5600 books; 30 bound periodical volumes; 2000 volumes of exploration reports; 34 VF drawers of exploration-mine maps; 1000 volumes of Drill Hole Data (50,000 drill holes). **Subscriptions:** 20 journals and other serials. **Services:** Interlibrary loans; library open to public by appointment. **Special Indexes:** File indexes arranged by subject and geographic area (book form); computer index for submittals and project reports.

CONSOMMATION ET CORPORATIONS CANADA
See: Canada - Consumer and Corporate Affairs Canada

CONSTANTINE (Mother M.) MEMORIAL LIBRARY
See: Mount Carmel Medical Center - Mother M. Constantine Memorial Library

★3242★
CONSTITUTION ISLAND ASSOCIATION, INC. - WARNER HOUSE LIBRARY (Hist)
Box 41   Phone: (914) 446-8676
West Point, NY 10996
Subjects: Warner family library, including books written by Susan and Anna Warner. **Holdings:** 2000 books; 300 periodicals; 8 VF drawers of Warner correspondence, family records, manuscripts, drawings and photographs. **Services:** Library open to public with restrictions. **Publications:** Annual report; bibliography of Warner books, 1976; biography of Susan and Anna Warner, 1978.

★3243★
CONSTRUCTION CONSULTANTS, INC. - LIBRARY (Sci-Tech)
900 Pallister   Phone: (313) 874-2770
Detroit, MI 48202   Joan M. Boram, Libn.
Founded: 1974. **Staff:** Prof 1; Other 1. **Subjects:** Waterproofing, roofing, concrete. **Special Collections:** Legal documents related to roofing failures. **Holdings:** 500 books. **Subscriptions:** 24 journals and other serials. **Services:** Interlibrary loans; copying; library open to public with restrictions.

★3244★
CONSULATE GENERAL OF DENMARK - DANISH INFORMATION OFFICE
(Area-Ethnic)
280 Park Ave.   Phone: (212) 697-5107
New York, NY 10017   Else Rothe, Libn.
Founded: 1945. **Subjects:** Denmark and Danish subjects. **Special Collections:** Danish authors in Danish. **Holdings:** 2000 books. **Services:** Office open to public for reference use only.

★3245★
CONSULATE GENERAL OF INDIA - INFORMATION SERVICE OF INDIA LIBRARY (Area-Ethnic)†
3 E. 64th St.   Phone: (212) 879-7800
New York, NY 10021   Mrs. Pushpa Gupta, Libn.
Founded: 1958. **Staff:** Prof 1; Other 1. **Subjects:** India - all fields of information. **Special Collections:** Collected works of Mahatma Gandhi (55 volumes). **Holdings:** 6636 books; ministry's annual report; clippings of Indian newspapers. **Subscriptions:** 40 journals and other serials; 15 newspapers. **Services:** Library open to public.

CONSULATE GENERAL OF IRELAND
See: Ireland Consulate General

★3246★
CONSULATE GENERAL OF ISRAEL - LT. DAVID TAMIR LIBRARY AND READING ROOM (Area-Ethnic)
800 Second Ave.   Phone: (212) 697-5500
New York, NY 10017   Ralene Levy, Info.Off.
Founded: 1948. **Staff:** 1. **Subjects:** Israel, Middle East. **Holdings:** Figures not available. **Services:** Library not open to public. **Special Catalogs:** Israel Speakers Bureau Catalog; Films of Israel Catalog. **Remarks:** Publishes and distributes free of charge literature on all aspects of Israel's life and development. Maintains a speakers' bureau. Provides display material including photographs. Has available a radio series, tapes, films and publications.

★3247★
CONSULATE GENERAL OF JAPAN - JAPAN INFORMATION CENTER - LIBRARY (Area-Ethnic)†
One Citicorp Center
153 E. 53rd St., 44th Fl.   Phone: (212) 986-1600
New York, NY 10022   Masakatsio Wajima, Libn.
Founded: 1959. **Staff:** 1. **Subjects:** Japan. **Special Collections:** Classic and modern Japanese literature. **Holdings:** 8000 books; 35 bound periodical volumes; 1450 other cataloged items; 43 VF drawers. **Subscriptions:** 100 journals and other serials; 15 newspapers. **Services:** Library open to public. **Publications:** Japan Report, monthly.

★3248★
CONSULATE-GENERAL OF JAPAN - JAPANESE CONSULATE LIBRARY (Area-Ethnic)†
10020 100th St., Suite 2600
Edmonton, AB, Canada T5J 0N4   Phone: (403) 422-3752
Staff: 1. **Subjects:** Japanese history, culture and economics. **Holdings:** 500 books; 500 bound periodical volumes; 500 government reports; 100 films; 500 slides; 300 maps, annual reports and pamphlets. **Subscriptions:** 120 journals and other serials; 7 newspapers. **Services:** Copying; library open to public. **Staff:** Valerie Bowyer, Pub.Serv. & Info.

★3249★
CONSULATE GENERAL OF THE NETHERLANDS - PRESS AND CULTURAL SECTION
One Rockefeller Plaza
New York, NY 10020
Subjects: Dutch history, economy, political system, geography and cultural life. **Holdings:** 3000 volumes; pamphlets; photographs; films; slides; travelling exhibits. **Remarks:** Presently inactive.

CONSUMER AND CORPORATE AFFAIRS CANADA
See: Canada - Consumer and Corporate Affairs Canada

★3250★
CONSUMER EDUCATION RESOURCE NETWORK (CERN) (Bus-Fin; Educ)
1555 Wilson Blvd., Suite 600   Phone: (703) 522-4616
Rosslyn, VA 22209   Celia Szarejko, Mgr., Info.Sys. & Lib.
Founded: 1978. **Staff:** Prof 6; Other 3. **Subjects:** Consumer - education, protection, movement, rights and responsibilities; complaint handling; consumers-in-the-marketplace. **Holdings:** 3000 books; 3000 pamphlets; information on 4500 organizations in the consumer field. **Subscriptions:** 60 journals and other serials. **Services:** Copying; library open to public by

appointment. **Computerized Information Services:** DIALOG, BRS, Source Telecomputing Corporation; CERN Bibliographic and Directory of Consumer Organizations (internal databases). **Publications:** ConCERNs, newsletter, 11/year - to mailing list; Consumer Education Resource Inventory, 3 updates/year - for sale; Bibliographies on Selected Consumer Issues, monthly. **Remarks:** The Consumer Education Resource Network is operated by InterAmerica Research Associates, Inc. under contract to the U.S. Dept. of Education. **Staff:** Janet O. Cochran, Mgr., Info.Serv.

CONSUMER INFORMATION CENTER
See: U.S. General Services Administration

★3251★
CONSUMER PRODUCT SAFETY COMMISSION - LIBRARY (Soc Sci; Bus-Fin)
5401 Westbard Ave.   Phone: (301) 492-6544
Washington, DC 20207   Elizabeth D. Goldberg, Adm.Libn.
Founded: 1973. **Staff:** Prof 1; Other 4. **Subjects:** Consumer product safety and standards, law, product testing, management and administration, science and technology. **Special Collections:** Standards Collection; Office of Production Management Regulatory Development Files; CPSC Management Records and Archives (11 cubic feet). **Holdings:** 15,000 books; 12,000 indexed documents and 125,000 news clippings on product safety; 350 journals on microfilm, 1970 to present. **Subscriptions:** 500 journals and other serials; 40 newspapers. **Services:** Interlibrary loans; copying; library open to public. **Computerized Information Services:** New York Times Information Service, DIALOG, SDC, MEDLINE; internal database; computerized cataloging. **Networks/Consortia:** Member of OCLC through FEDLINK; Metropolitan Washington Library Council.

CONSUMER PRODUCT SAFETY COMMISSION - NATIONAL INJURY INFORMATION CLEARINGHOUSE
See: National Injury Information Clearinghouse

★3252★
CONSUMERS' GAS COMPANY - LIBRARY SERVICES (Energy)
P.O. Box 650   Phone: (416) 492-5490
Scarborough, ON, Canada M1K 5E3   Donna M. Ivey, Supv., Lib.Serv.
Founded: 1961. **Staff:** Prof 2; Other 3. **Subjects:** Natural gas distribution, public utility regulation, industrial fuel applications, management. **Special Collections:** History of early gas industry in Toronto. **Holdings:** 5000 books; 5800 reports. **Subscriptions:** 440 journals and other serials. **Services:** Interlibrary loans; copying; library open to public by permission. **Computerized Information Services:** DIALOG, SDC, Info Globe. **Publications:** Newsletter, semimonthly - for internal distribution only.

★3253★
CONSUMERS GLASS COMPANY LIMITED - LIBRARY (Sci-Tech)
703 Evans Ave., Suite 301   Phone: (416) 232-3275
Etobicoke, ON, Canada M9C 5A6   Barbara Presho, Libn.
Subjects: Plastics, packaging. **Holdings:** 100 books. **Subscriptions:** 50 journals and other serials. **Services:** Interlibrary loans; copying; SDI; library not open to public. **Networks/Consortia:** Member of Sheridan Park Association.

★3254★
CONSUMERS POWER COMPANY - LAW LIBRARY (Law)
212 W. Michigan Ave.   Phone: (517) 788-1088
Jackson, MI 49201   Beulah I. Standish, Libn.
Staff: Prof 1. **Subjects:** Federal and Michigan Statutes and administrative law materials, energy, environment, labor, public utilities. **Special Collections:** Company history. **Holdings:** 12,200 books; 250 reports, newsletters, pamphlets. **Subscriptions:** 25 journals and other serials. **Services:** Interlibrary loans; library open to public with restrictions. **Publications:** Letter regarding new material, irregular.

★3255★
CONSUMERS POWER COMPANY - PARNALL TECHNICAL LIBRARY (Energy)
1945 Parnall Rd.   Phone: (517) 788-0541
Jackson, MI 49201   Kay E. Stevens, Libn.
Staff: Prof 1; Other 1. **Subjects:** Energy - electric, gas, nuclear; environment; business. **Holdings:** 4500 books and bound periodical volumes; 15,000 reports, pamphlets and standards. **Subscriptions:** 225 journals and other serials. **Services:** Interlibrary loans; library open to public with restrictions. **Computerized Information Services:** DIALOG, DOE/RECON; computerized cataloging. **Networks/Consortia:** Member of Capitol Area Library Network (CALNET). **Publications:** Library Lines - News and Views of Parnall Technical Library - bimonthly. **Staff:** Jean A. Walczak, Asst.Libn.

★3256★
CONSUMERS' RESEARCH, INC. - LIBRARY (Bus-Fin)
Box 168
Washington, NJ 07882   F.J. Schlink, Tech.Dir.
Subjects: Automobiles and accessories; home electric appliances; economics of consumption; food and health; textiles and clothing; photographic equipment; housing (materials and equipment); cleaning products. **Special Collections:** Special technical information relating to consumer goods, specifications for them, and methods for testing them. **Holdings:** 15,000 subject files; pamphlet collection. **Services:** Library open to public with restrictions.

★3257★
CONSUMERS UNION FOUNDATION - CENTER FOR THE STUDY OF THE CONSUMER MOVEMENT - LIBRARY
256 Washington St.
Mount Vernon, NY 10550
Defunct. Holdings absorbed by the Consumers Union of United States, Inc. - Library.

★3258★
CONSUMERS UNION OF UNITED STATES, INC. - LIBRARY (Bus-Fin)
256 Washington St.   Phone: (914) 664-6400
Mount Vernon, NY 10550   Lynn P. Freedman, Mgr.
Founded: 1936. **Staff:** Prof 5; Other 3. **Subjects:** Consumer goods, standards and specifications, consumer economics, history of the consumer movement, health and medicine. **Holdings:** 5000 books; 1500 volumes of periodicals on microfilm; 20,000 issues of unbound journals; 15,000 pamphlets; 215 VF drawers of laboratory test project data, company documents and correspondence; archives. **Subscriptions:** 500 journals and other serials. **Services:** Interlibrary loans; library open to researchers and librarians. **Computerized Information Services:** DIALOG, SDC, NLM, New York Times Information Service. **Publications:** Consumers Union News Digest, semimonthly - available for sale; List of Publications Received, monthly - for internal distribution only. **Special Indexes:** Consumer Reports Index; Consumer Union News Digest Index. **Remarks:** Contains the holdings of the former Consumers Union Foundation - Center for the Study of the Consumer Movement - Library. **Staff:** Ellen Carney, Res.Libn.; Wendy Goldman, Res.Libn.; Elizabeth Hamilton, Res.Libn.; Leslie Rosen, Res.Libn.

★3259★
CONTACT, INC. - AAAA CONTACT CENTER (Educ)
Box 81826   Phone: (402) 464-0602
Lincoln, NE 68501-1826   Rhonda Kadavy, Dir.
Staff: 4. **Subjects:** Illiteracy, adult basic education, literacy. **Holdings:** Figures not available. **Services:** Center open to public for reference use only. **Publications:** The Written Word, monthly newsletter; Reducing Functional Illiteracy: A National Guide to Facilities and Services, annual. **Also Known As:** American Association of Advertising Agencies - Literacy Clearinghouse.

★3260★
CONTEL INFORMATION SYSTEMS - LIBRARY (Info Sci)
130 Steamboat Rd.   Phone: (516) 829-5900
Great Neck, NY 11024   Harriet Z. Fadem, Libn.Mgr.
Staff: Prof 2; Other 1. **Subjects:** Telecommunications, computer applications, data processing. **Holdings:** 200 books; reports; archival material. **Subscriptions:** 97 journals and other serials; 12 newspapers. **Services:** Interlibrary loans; copying; library not open to public. **Computerized Information Services:** DIALOG. **Publications:** Acquisitions Lists; Seminar Information - both for internal distribution only. **Staff:** Danuta Obojski, Libn.

CONTEMPORARY AUTHORS ARCHIVES
See: Gale Research Company - Library

★3261★
CONTEMPORARY CRAFTS ASSOCIATION - LIBRARY (Art)†
3934 S.W. Corbett Ave.   Phone: (503) 223-2654
Portland, OR 97201   LaVerne Kuchler, Act.Libn.
Founded: 1971. **Staff:** Prof 2. **Subjects:** Ceramics and pottery, weaving and textiles, Pacific Northwest craftsmen, contemporary designers, metalwork and jewelry, contemporary glass, sculpture. **Holdings:** 250 books; 74 bound and 125 unbound periodical volumes; 235 exhibition catalogs. **Publications:** Contemporary Crafts Association News, quarterly - mailed to members.

CONTEMPORARY MUSIC PROJECT LENDING SERVICE
See: University of Maryland, College Park - Libraries - Music Library

CONTINENTAL BAKING COMPANY
See: ITT Continental Baking Company

★3262★
CONTINENTAL CARBON COMPANY - TECHNICAL LIBRARY (Sci-Tech)
10500 Richmond Ave.
Box 42817   Phone: (713) 975-5802
Houston, TX 77042   Linda M. Malisheski, Libn./Sec.
Founded: 1947. **Staff:** Prof 1. **Subjects:** Carbon black, rubber, chemistry, physics, engineering, chemical technology, industrial chemistry, combustion and flame technology. **Holdings:** 1100 books; 5500 patents; 500 technical and research reports; 2000 progress reports; 80 large binders of technical data and clippings; 4 legal drawers of technical papers from special technical meetings. **Subscriptions:** 12 serials. **Services:** Library not open to public.

★3263★
CONTINENTAL CHEMISTE CORPORATION - LIBRARY (Sci-Tech)
2256 W. Ogden Ave.   Phone: (312) 226-2134
Chicago, IL 60612   Kenneth J. Kass, Pres.
Founded: 1945. **Staff:** Prof 1; Other 1. **Subjects:** Pesticides, entomology, metallurgy, toxicology, chemicals, business administration, aviation, astronomy. **Holdings:** 1000 books; 500 bound periodical volumes; 500 unbound volumes; 1000 articles; 100 reels of microfilm. **Subscriptions:** 25 journals and other serials. **Services:** Library not open to public. **Staff:** Fred Targ, V.P.

★3264★
CONTINENTAL GROUP, INC. - INFORMATION RESOURCE CENTER (Bus-Fin)
1 Harbor Plaza   Phone: (203) 964-6593
Stamford, CT 06904   Candace Stuart, Mgr.
Staff: Prof 1. **Subjects:** Business, economics, packaging, forest industries, insurance, energy. **Holdings:** 1000 books; 5 drawers of microfilm; 3 drawers of microfiche. **Subscriptions:** 180 journals and other serials. **Services:** Interlibrary loans; SDI; library open to public by appointment. **Computerized Information Services:** DIALOG, New York Times Information Service, Mead Data Central, SDC; computerized cataloging. **Networks/Consortia:** Member of Southwestern Connecticut Library Council (SWLC).

★3265★
CONTINENTAL ILLINOIS NATIONAL BANK AND TRUST COMPANY OF CHICAGO - INFORMATION SERVICES DIVISION (Bus-Fin)
231 S. La Salle St.   Phone: (312) 828-8580
Chicago, IL 60693   Susan J. Montgomery, Mgr.
Founded: 1925. **Staff:** Prof 8; Other 13. **Subjects:** Banking, industry, finance, management. **Holdings:** 24,800 books. **Subscriptions:** 1500 journals and other serials. **Services:** Interlibrary loans; library open to bank personnel. **Computerized Information Services:** New York Times Information Service, DIALOG, SDC, Dow Jones News Retrieval, LEXIS, NEXIS, Data Resources, Inc.; computerized cataloging and acquisitions. **Networks/Consortia:** Member of Chicago Library System; RLG. **Staff:** Janet S. Reed, Asst.Mgr.; James C. Moulton, Sr.Info.Anl.; Jane G. Fouser, Sr.Info.Anl.; Susan J. Glodkowski, Info.Anl.; Rita R. Dermody, Law Libn.; Peggy L. Popa, Tech.Serv.Supv.; Mary G. Kreinbring, Tech.Serv.Libn.

★3266★
CONTINENTAL PAGE ENGINEERS, INC. - INFORMATION CENTER (Sci-Tech)
801 Follin Ln.   Phone: (703) 938-4000
Vienna, VA 22180   Eileen C. Durham, Libn.
Founded: 1955. **Staff:** Prof 1. **Subjects:** Communication systems, system installation. **Special Collections:** 10,000 maps. **Holdings:** 4000 books; 1000 bound periodical volumes; 10,000 maps (cataloged); military standards; specifications; government reports and documents. **Subscriptions:** 102 journals and other serials. **Services:** Interlibrary loans; copying; library open to public. **Remarks:** Company is a subsidiary of Continental Telephone Company. **Formerly:** Page Communications Engineers, Inc.

★3267★
CONTINENTAL TELEPHONE LABORATORIES - WALTER L. ROBERTS TECHNICAL LIBRARY (Sci-Tech)
270 Scientific Dr., Suite 10
Technology Park/Atlanta
Norcross, GA 30092   Phone: (404) 448-2206
                                                Virginia Lawrence, Libn.
Staff: Prof 3. **Subjects:** Telephony, telecommunications, electrical engineering, mathematics, electronics, polymer chemistry, materials science, research management. **Special Collections:** Bell System technical journals (volumes 1-60). **Holdings:** 6500 books; 180 bound periodical volumes; 3000 technical papers; 1200 wire and cable industry product specifications; 750 films and slides. **Subscriptions:** 66 journals and other serials. **Services:** Interlibrary loans; copying; library not open to public. **Publications:** Literature

Survey and Acquisitions, monthly - for internal distribution only. **Staff:** Shirley Schumhl; Jerry Bradley .

★3268★
CONTRA COSTA COUNTY - CENTRAL LIBRARY - LOCAL HISTORY COLLECTION (Hist)
1750 Oak Park Blvd.   Phone: (415) 944-3434
Pleasant Hill, CA 94523   Ruth Russell, Hd., Ctrl.Lib.
Founded: 1961. **Subjects:** Local history. **Holdings:** 3200 books; 32 feet of VF drawers. **Services:** Interlibrary loans; copying; library open to public. **Staff:** Thomas Gates, Hist.Spec.

★3269★
CONTRA COSTA COUNTY LAW LIBRARY (Law)
Court House   Phone: (415) 372-2783
Martinez, CA 94553   Jean Steffensen, Law Libn.
Subjects: Law. **Holdings:** 50,000 volumes. **Services:** Copying; library open to public. **Remarks:** Branch law library (17,000 volumes) is located at 100 37th St., Richmond, CA 94805.

★3270★
CONTRA COSTA COUNTY SUPERINTENDENT OF SCHOOLS - ACCESS INFORMATION CENTER & PROFESSIONAL LIBRARY (Educ)
2371 Stanwell Dr.   Phone: (415) 671-4318
Concord, CA 94520   Marilyn Matosian, Sr.Res., Lib./Res.Serv.
Staff: Prof 1; Other 4. **Subjects:** Teaching methodology, administration, educational research, special education. **Special Collections:** ERIC abstracts and document collection; collection of research documents. **Holdings:** 15,000 books; 300,000 microfiche (cataloged); 2000 textbooks in sample textbook collection; 6000 documents; 3000 learning activity packages; 1000 curriculum guides; 1500 books in juvenile review book collection. **Subscriptions:** 300 journals and other serials. **Services:** Copying; tie-in by computer with the ERIC indexes; center is open to outside users in area only. **Publications:** Dateline, a newsletter published 2/week for district administrators.

★3271★
CONTRA COSTA TIMES - LIBRARY (Publ)
2640 Shadelands Dr.
Box 5088
Walnut Creek, CA 94596   Phone: (415) 935-2525
     Ellen D. Wood, Libn.
Staff: Prof 1; Other 2. **Subjects:** Newspaper reference topics. **Holdings:** 150 books; 120 VF drawers of clippings; 30 VF drawers of photographs; 4 VF drawers of microfilmed Contra Costa Times, 1913 to present; 4 drawers of microfilm of the Concord Transcript, 1905-1982. **Subscriptions:** 20 journals and other serials; 15 newspapers. **Services:** Copying; SDI; library open to public by appointment. **Networks/Consortia:** Member of Bay Area Library and Information System (BALIS). **Formerly:** Walnut Creek - Contra Costa Times - Library.

★3272★
CONTROL DATA CORPORATION - GOVERNMENT SYSTEMS LIBRARY (Sci-Tech)
1800 N. Beauregard St.   Phone: (703) 998-4606
Alexandria, VA 22311   Barbara B. Harris, Libn.
Staff: Prof 1. **Subjects:** Engineering, management, computer science. **Holdings:** 2400 books; 500 microforms; 500 reports. **Subscriptions:** 45 journals and other serials. **Services:** Interlibrary loans; copying; library open to public by appointment. **Networks/Consortia:** Member of Interlibrary Users Association. **Publications:** Newsletter - for internal distribution only.

★3273★
CONTROL DATA CORPORATION - LIBRARY (Info Sci)
215 Moffett Park Dr.   Phone: (408) 744-5798
Sunnyvale, CA 94086   Jaxon K. Matthews, Libn.
Founded: 1967. **Staff:** Prof 1. **Subjects:** Computer science and programming, communications, business. **Holdings:** 1427 books; 150 bound periodical volumes; 205 government reports on computers; 332 microfiche of government reports. **Subscriptions:** 92 journals and other serials. **Services:** Interlibrary loans; copying; library not open to public. **Computerized Information Services:** Mechanized services; computerized cataloging. **Networks/Consortia:** Member of CIN.

★3274★
CONTROL DATA CORPORATION - LIBRARY/INFORMATION CENTER (Sci-Tech)
2800 E. Old Shakopee Rd.
Box 1249, Bldg. HQM 250
Minneapolis, MN 55440   Phone: (612) 853-4229
     Gloria T. Andrew, Mgr.
Founded: 1958. **Staff:** Prof 4; Other 1. **Subjects:** Computer science,

electronic technology, microelectronics, management science, marketing. **Special Collections:** IBM, Honeywell, Digital Equipment and UNIVAC reference manuals (10,000). **Holdings:** 4000 books; 1000 bound periodical volumes. **Subscriptions:** 400 journals and other serials. **Services:** Interlibrary loans; library open to public by permission. **Computerized Information Services:** SDC, New York Times Information Service, DIALOG, CYBERNET; computerized cataloging and circulation. **Publications:** Library Bulletin, monthly. **Staff:** Doris A. Dingley, Libn.; Kathleen Edwards, Libn.; Kimberly Hicks, Lib.Asst.

★3275★
CONTROL DATA CORPORATION - TECHNOLOGY & INFORMATION SERVICES LIBRARY (Bus-Fin; Sci-Tech)
245 E. 6th St.
Box 0 -- HQV001
Minneapolis, MN 55440   Phone: (612) 853-6133
     James R. Donaldson, Mgr.
Founded: 1981. **Staff:** Prof 6. **Subjects:** Market research, small business, technology transfer. **Holdings:** 1200 books. **Subscriptions:** 285 journals and other serials; 15 newspapers. **Services:** Interlibrary loans; copying; SDI; library not open to public. **Computerized Information Services:** DIALOG, SDC, BRS, Control Data Corporation, Cybernet; internal database. **Staff:** Crystal A. Clift, Info.Cons.; William B. DeWitt, Info.Cons.; Stella A. Pagonis, Info.Cons.; Joanne P. Rongitsch, Info.Cons.

CONTROLLED FUSION ATOMIC DATA CENTER
See: Oak Ridge National Laboratory

★3276★
CONVALESCENT HOSPITAL FOR CHILDREN - LIBRARY (Med)
2075 Scottsville Rd.   Phone: (716) 436-4442
Rochester, NY 14623   Christine S. Bonati, Libn.
Founded: 1967. **Staff:** Prof 1. **Subjects:** Child psychiatry, clinical psychology, community and child mental health, psychiatric social work. **Holdings:** 1400 books; 300 bound periodical volumes. **Subscriptions:** 70 journals and other serials. **Services:** Interlibrary loans; copying; library open to public. **Networks/Consortia:** Member of Rochester Regional Research Library Council.

★3277★
CONVERSE CONSULTANTS - CORPORATE LIBRARY (Sci-Tech)†
126 W. Del Mar Blvd.   Phone: (213) 795-0461
Pasadena, CA 91105   Andrea B. Berman, Corp.Libn.
Founded: 1980. **Staff:** Prof 1. **Subjects:** Engineering - geotechnical, earthquake, mathematics; soils; foundations; groundwater hydrology. **Holdings:** 1000 books; 200 government reports in microform; 100 company reports; 1 file drawer of clippings. **Subscriptions:** 52 journals and other serials. **Services:** Interlibrary loans; copying (both with branch offices only); library not open to public. **Computerized Information Services:** SDC. **Formerly:** Converse Ward Davis Dixon.

★3278★
CONVERSE CONSULTANTS - LIBRARY (Sci-Tech)
91 Roseland Ave.
Box 91
Caldwell, NJ 07006   Phone: (201) 226-9191
     Roslyn M. Terry, Libn.
Staff: 1. **Subjects:** Geology, soil mechanics and related subjects. **Holdings:** 3000 volumes. **Subscriptions:** 25 journals and other serials. **Services:** Library open to public by appointment. **Formerly:** Converse Ward Davis Dixon.

CONVERSE (J.G.) MEMORIAL LIBRARY
See: Winter Haven Hospital - J.G. Converse Memorial Library

CONVERSE MEMORIAL LIBRARY
See: Harvard University - Chemistry Library

CONVERSE WARD DAVIS DIXON
See: Converse Consultants

★3279★
CONWAY (E.A.) MEMORIAL HOSPITAL - MEDICAL LIBRARY (Med)
Box 1881   Phone: (318) 387-8460
Monroe, LA 71201   Linda Darnell, Libn.
Founded: 1941. **Subjects:** Medicine and allied subjects. **Holdings:** 612 volumes. **Subscriptions:** 69 journals and other serials. **Services:** Interlibrary loans; copying; library not open to public.

★3280★
CONWED CORPORATION - BUSINESS INFORMATION CENTER (Bus-Fin)
444 Cedar St.
Box 43237   Phone: (612) 221-1271
St. Paul, MN 55164   Charlotte Feist, Mgr.
Staff: Prof 1. **Subjects:** Business, plastics, construction. **Holdings:** 800 books; 12 pamphlets and reports; product literature. **Subscriptions:** 200 journals and other serials. **Services:** Interlibrary loans; copying; center not open to public. **Computerized Information Services:** DIALOG.

CONWELLANA-TEMPLANA COLLECTION
See: Temple University - Central Library System

★3281★
COOK COUNTY HISTORICAL SOCIETY - GRAND MARAIS LIBRARY (Hist)
                                 Phone: (218) 387-1678
Grand Marais, MN 55604   Mary Alice Harvey, Libn.
Staff: Prof 2. **Subjects:** Pioneer life stories; community histories; history of organizations, schools, churches, industries. **Special Collections:** Thomsonites (400 mounted in special show cases). **Holdings:** Files of information on lumbering, fishing, organizations, school, churches, pioneers and industries; 40 transcriptions; newspapers and census on microfilm. **Services:** Interlibrary loans; copying; library open to public. **Special Indexes:** Annual and biennial reports.

★3282★
COOK COUNTY HOSPITAL - HEALTH SCIENCE LIBRARY (Med)†
1900 W. Polk St.   Phone: (312) 633-7979
Chicago, IL 60612   Estela Escudero, Libn.
Staff: Prof 4; Other 7. **Subjects:** Nursing and allied health sciences. **Special Collections:** Original letters of Florence Nightingale. **Holdings:** 3000 books; AV collection. **Subscriptions:** 200 journals and other serials; 6 newspapers. **Services:** Interlibrary loans; library open to public for reference use only. **Computerized Information Services:** MEDLARS. **Remarks:** Operated by the Cook County Board.

★3283★
COOK COUNTY HOSPITAL - TICE MEMORIAL LIBRARY (Med)†
720 S. Wolcott St.   Phone: (312) 633-6724
Chicago, IL 60612   Grace Auer, Hd.Med.Libn.
Founded: 1953. **Staff:** Prof 4; Other 7. **Subjects:** Medicine and surgery. **Special Collections:** Frederick Tice Collection of rare books in medicine. **Holdings:** 3000 books; 6500 bound periodical volumes; AV collection. **Subscriptions:** 300 journals and other serials. **Services:** Interlibrary loans; copying; library open to public for reference use only. **Computerized Information Services:** MEDLARS. **Networks/Consortia:** Member of Illinois Health Libraries Consortium. **Remarks:** Operated by the Cook County Board.

★3284★
COOK COUNTY LAW LIBRARY (Law)
2900 Richard J. Daley Ctr.   Phone: (312) 443-5423
Chicago, IL 60602   William J. Powers, Jr., Exec. Law Libn.
Founded: 1966. **Staff:** Prof 22. **Subjects:** Law - Anglo-American, foreign and international; government documents. **Holdings:** 208,589 books; 13,105 bound periodical volumes. **Subscriptions:** 1000 journals and other serials; 20 newspapers; CIS Legislative History Service (in microform). **Services:** Interlibrary loans; SDI; library open to public with restrictions. **Computerized Information Services:** New York Times Information Service, WESTLAW; Illinois Legislative Information System (internal database); computerized cataloging. **Publications:** Acquisitions List, bimonthly; Newsletter, 6/year. **Special Catalogs:** Union Card Catalog. **Staff:** Lee Burstin, Chf.Acq.Libn.; Frederic C. Pearson, Circ.Libn.; Alfred Kulys, Cat.Libn.; Antonio Naranjo, Foreign Law Libn.

★3285★
COOK COUNTY LAW LIBRARY - CRIMINAL COURT BRANCH (Law)
2650 S. California Ave., Rm. 4D00   Phone: (312) 890-7396
Chicago, IL 60608   Bennie E. Martin, Chf.Libn.
Staff: Prof 1; Other 1. **Subjects:** Criminal law. **Holdings:** 4000 books. **Subscriptions:** 8 journals and other serials. **Services:** Interlibrary loans; copying; library open to public.

★3286★
COOK COUNTY STATE'S ATTORNEY'S OFFICE LIBRARY (Law)
500 Richard J. Daley Center   Phone: (312) 443-8723
Chicago, IL 60602   Valerie K. Kruk, Libn.
Staff: Prof 1; Other 6. **Subjects:** Law. **Holdings:** 30,000 books; 6000 bound periodical volumes. **Subscriptions:** 110 journals and other serials. **Services:** Library not open to public.

COOK (Oscar G.) MEMORIAL LIBRARY
See: Oxford United Methodist Church - Oscar G. Cook Memorial Library

COOK (Sigga) MEMORIAL LIBRARY
See: Saskatoon Cancer Clinic - Library & Sigga Cook Memorial Library

COOKE (J.C.) LIBRARY
See: Northwest Bible College - J.C. Cooke Library

★3287★
COOLEY, GODWARD, CASTRO, HUDDLESON & TATUM - LIBRARY (Law)†
1 Maritime Plaza, 20th Fl.   Phone: (415) 981-5252
San Francisco, CA 94111   Mary J. Hays, Libn.
Staff: Prof 1; Other 2. **Subjects:** Law. **Holdings:** 12,000 books. **Services:** Interlibrary loans; library open to attorneys and clients only. **Computerized Information Services:** LEXIS.

★3288★
COOLEY (Thomas M.) LAW SCHOOL - LIBRARY (Law)†
217 S. Capitol Ave.
Box 13038   Phone: (517) 371-5140
Lansing, MI 48901   Peter M. Kempel, Dir., Res.Serv.
Founded: 1973. **Staff:** Prof 4; Other 10. **Subjects:** Law. **Holdings:** 20,829 books; 46,829 bound periodical volumes; 53,187 volumes on microfiche. **Subscriptions:** 1715 journals and other serials; 15 newspapers. **Services:** Interlibrary loans; copying; library open to public. **Networks/Consortia:** Member of Capitol Area Library Network (CALNET). **Publications:** Library User's Guide. **Staff:** Maria Nevai, Tech.Serv.Libn.; Barbara Bonge, Rd.Serv.Libn.; Robert K. Wolfe, Rd.Serv.Libn.

COOLIDGE (Calvin) LIBRARY
See: Castleton State College - Calvin Coolidge Library

COOMBE (Lee) MEMORIAL LIBRARY
See: Memorial Sloan-Kettering Cancer Center - Lee Coombe Memorial Library

COOPER-HEWITT MUSEUM OF DESIGN - DORIS & HENRY DREYFUSS MEMORIAL STUDY CENTER
See: Smithsonian Institution Libraries - Cooper-Hewitt Museum of Design - Doris & Henry Dreyfuss Memorial Study Ctr.

★3289★
COOPER MEDICAL CENTER - REUBEN L. SHARP HEALTH SCIENCE LIBRARY (Med)
One Cooper Plaza   Phone: (609) 963-7230
Camden, NJ 08103   Patricia Solin, Dir.
Founded: 1971. **Staff:** Prof 2; Other 2. **Subjects:** Medicine, nursing, paraprofessional health sciences, patient education. **Special Collections:** History of medicine in Camden County; Cooper Medical Center history of medicine (200 volumes). **Holdings:** 1500 books; 5100 periodicals - bound and on microfiche; 120 journal titles, 1976 to present; filmstrips; slide shows; video and audio cassettes. **Subscriptions:** 350 journals and other serials. **Services:** Interlibrary loans; copying; LATCH; library open to public for reference use only. **Computerized Information Services:** MEDLARS. **Networks/Consortia:** Member of Southwest New Jersey Consortium for Health Information Services. **Publications:** New Acquisitions, monthly. **Staff:** Kathleen Schwartz, Ref.Libn.

COOPER (Robert Muldrow) LIBRARY
See: Clemson University - Robert Muldrow Cooper Library

★3290★
COOPER SCHOOL OF ART - LIBRARY (Art)
1951 W. 26th St.   Phone: (216) 241-1486
Cleveland, OH 44113   Barbara Hammerlund, Hd.Libn.
Founded: 1936. **Staff:** 4. **Subjects:** Art history, graphic design, contemporary illustration, biographies of artists, photography, commercial and interior design. **Special Collections:** Art history slide collection (5000 slides). **Holdings:** 1500 books. **Subscriptions:** 40 journals and other serials; 7 newspapers. **Services:** Library not open to public.

COOPER (Thomas) LIBRARY
See: University of South Carolina - Thomas Cooper Library

★3291★
COOPER UNION FOR THE ADVANCEMENT OF SCIENCE AND ART - LIBRARY (Art; Sci-Tech)
41 Cooper Sq.   Phone: (212) 254-6300
New York, NY 10003   Elizabeth A. Vajda, Coord. for Lib.Serv.
Founded: 1859. **Staff:** Prof 4; Other 4. **Subjects:** Architecture, art, engineering. **Special Collections:** Cooper-Hewitt Collection - papers of Peter Cooper and Abram S. Hewitt and partial school archives (2000 pieces and 5 linear feet). **Holdings:** 74,500 books; 12,950 bound periodical volumes; 42,300 slides. **Subscriptions:** 309 journals and other serials. **Services:** Interlibrary loans; copying; library not open to public. **Computerized Information Services:** Computerized cataloging and circulation. **Networks/Consortia:** Member of Research Library Consortium of South Manhattan. **Staff:** Herbert Bott, Asst. to the Coord.; Virginia Weimer, Asst.Libn., Art & Arch.; Irene Perry, Asst.Libn., Engr./ILL; Carol Abatelli, Asst.Libn., Slides.

★3292★
CO-OPERATIVE COLLEGE OF CANADA - LIBRARY SERVICES (Bus-Fin)
141 105th St., W.   Phone: (306) 373-0474
Saskatoon, SK, Canada S7N 1N3   Leona Olson, Lib.Supv.
Founded: 1966. **Staff:** 1. **Subjects:** Cooperatives, management, employee training, adult education. **Holdings:** 3500 books; 35 films; 52 videotapes; 33 VF drawers. **Subscriptions:** 55 journals and other serials; 10 newspapers. **Services:** Interlibrary loans; copying; library open to public with restrictions. **Publications:** Library Services Bulletin, monthly - for internal distribution only.

COOPERATIVE INFORMATION CENTER FOR HOSPITAL MANAGEMENT STUDIES
See: University of Michigan

★3293★
COOPERS & LYBRAND - AUDIT LIBRARY (Bus-Fin)
222 Riverside Plaza   Phone: (312) 648-1133
Chicago, IL 60606   Isa Lang, Audit Libn.
Staff: Prof 1. **Subjects:** Business, finance. **Holdings:** 1000 books; 50 bound periodical volumes; 30 audio- and videotapes. **Subscriptions:** 85 journals and other serials. **Services:** Interlibrary loans; copying; library open to public with restrictions.

★3294★
COOPERS & LYBRAND - LIBRARY (Bus-Fin)†
1000 W. 6th St.   Phone: (213) 481-1000
Los Angeles, CA 90017   June B. Williams, Libn.
Staff: Prof 2. **Subjects:** Accounting, taxes. **Holdings:** 4000 books; 4000 annual reports. **Subscriptions:** 250 journals and other serials; 15 newspapers. **Services:** Interlibrary loans; copying; will answer brief inquiries; library open to clients and librarians by appointment. **Staff:** Jeffrey Lambert, Asst.Libn.

★3295★
COOPERS & LYBRAND - LIBRARY (Bus-Fin)
333 Market St.   Phone: (415) 957-3172
San Francisco, CA 94105   Karen E. Ivy, Libn.
Founded: 1974. **Staff:** Prof 1; Other 1. **Subjects:** Accounting, auditing, taxation, management consulting. **Holdings:** 2400 books; 90 bound periodical volumes; 1 VF drawer of pamphlets; 1500 annual reports. **Subscriptions:** 160 journals and other serials. **Services:** Interlibrary loans; library open by appointment to researchers in the field. **Computerized Information Services:** Computerized circulation. **Publications:** New Books List, monthly.

★3296★
COOPERS & LYBRAND - LIBRARY AND INFORMATION CENTER (Bus-Fin)
One Post Office Sq.   Phone: (617) 423-4200
Boston, MA 02109   Kathleen Healy, Libn.
Founded: 1945. **Staff:** Prof 1; Other 1. **Subjects:** Accounting, taxation. **Holdings:** 4500 books; 600 bound periodical volumes; 200 services. **Subscriptions:** 250 journals and other serials; 15 newspapers. **Services:** Copying (limited); library open to clients and reciprocating libraries.

★3297★
COOPERS & LYBRAND - NATIONAL LIBRARY (Bus-Fin)†
1251 Ave. of the Americas   Phone: (212) 536-2000
New York, NY 10020   Dorothy Kasman, Chf.Libn.
Staff: Prof 4; Other 5. **Subjects:** Accounting, taxation. **Holdings:** 10,000 books. **Subscriptions:** 500 journals and other serials. **Services:** Interlibrary loans; copying (limited); library not open to public. **Computerized Information Services:** New York Times Information Service, INFORM, Dow Jones News Retrieval, SDC, National Automated Accounting Research System, LEXIS, Mead Data Central.

COOPERSMITH (Jacob) LIBRARY OF HANDELIANA
See: University of Maryland, College Park - Libraries - Music Library

★3298★
COORS (Adolph) COMPANY - TECHNICAL LIBRARY (Food-Bev)
Mail 105   Phone: (303) 279-6565
Golden, CO 80401   Mary Bond, Libn.
Staff: Prof 1. **Subjects:** Brewing, microbiology, chemistry, law, engineering. **Holdings:** 3000 books; 6000 internal reports; patents, clippings and pamphlets. **Subscriptions:** 160 journals and other serials; 10 newspapers. **Services:** Copying; library open to public with restrictions. **Publications:** Library Bulletin, monthly.

★3299★
COPLEY PRESS, INC. - THE JAMES S. COPLEY LIBRARY (Hist)
Box 1530   Phone: (714) 454-0411
La Jolla, CA 92038   Richard Reilly, Cur.
Founded: 1966. **Staff:** Prof 5. **Subjects:** American Revolutionary War, history of the West, John Charles Freemont, Mark Twain, American newspaper history, art. **Special Collections:** Autographs of the signers of the Declaration of Independence; American Revolutionary War documents and letters. **Holdings:** 8000 books; 750 letters, documents and manuscripts. **Services:** Interlibrary loans (limited); copying; library open only to researchers by appointment. **Remarks:** The library is located at 1134 Kline St., La Jolla, CA 92037. **Staff:** Suzanne M. Carnes, Libn.; Carol Herron, Asst. to the Cur.; Harold Kopelke, Cons.; Tina Hendricks, Lib.Asst.

COPPER DATA CENTER
See: Battelle-Columbus Laboratories; Copper Development Association, Inc.

★3300★
COPPER DEVELOPMENT ASSOCIATION, INC. - COPPER DATA CENTER (Sci-Tech)
405 Lexington Ave.   Phone: (212) 953-7300
New York, NY 10017   Mary W. Covington, Supv., Tech.Info.
Founded: 1965. **Subjects:** Copper technology from refining of metal through end-use performance of copper and copper alloys; iron and steel with copper as an alloying element; copper chemicals, materials and processes used in insulated wire and cable; competitive materials. **Services:** Retrieval services are available to the technical community at large. **Computerized Information Services:** Computer retrieval using online remote terminals. **Publications:** Extracts of Copper Technology, Thesaurus of Terms on Copper Technology - distribution to members. **Remarks:** The center covers the world literature on copper technology and is operated by CDA under a contract with the Columbus Laboratories of Battelle Memorial Institute, Columbus, Ohio.

COPYRIGHT PUBLIC INFORMATION OFFICE
See: Library of Congress

★3301★
CORCORAN MUSEUM AND SCHOOL OF ART - LIBRARY (Art)
17th St. & New York Ave., N.W.   Phone: (202) 638-3211
Washington, DC 20006   Ann Maginnis, Lib.Dir.
Founded: 1982. **Staff:** Prof 2. **Subjects:** Art history, with emphasis on American art; art techniques, photography. **Holdings:** 5000 books; 600 bound periodical volumes. **Subscriptions:** 112 journals and other serials. **Services:** Interlibrary loans; copying; library open to public. **Computerized Information Services:** Computerized cataloging. **Networks/Consortia:** Member of OCLC through CCLC. **Publications:** Acquisitions list, monthly. **Formed by the Merger of:** Corcoran School of Art Library and the Corcoran Museum - Curatorial Library.

★3302★
CORDIS CORPORATION - LIBRARY (Med)
Box 525700   Phone: (305) 551-2380
Miami, FL 33152   Cindy Salkeld, Corp.Libn.
Founded: 1980. **Staff:** Prof 1; Other 2. **Subjects:** Pacemakers, catheters, neurology. **Holdings:** 1000 books; 300 bound periodical volumes. **Subscriptions:** 153 journals and other serials. **Services:** Interlibrary loans; copying; SDI; library open to public by appointment. **Computerized Information Services:** BRS, DIALOG, SDC. **Networks/Consortia:** Member of Miami Health Sciences Library Consortium; South Florida Online Searchers.

★3303★
CORE LABORATORIES, INC. - LIBRARY (Sci-Tech)
7501 Stemmons
Box 47547   Phone: (214) 631-8270
Dallas, TX 75247   Christine B. Dobson, Libn.
Staff: Prof 1. **Subjects:** Petroleum engineering, geology, chemistry,

mathematics. **Holdings:** 1500 books; 300 bound periodical volumes; 100 technical reports. **Subscriptions:** 50 journals and other serials. **Services:** Interlibrary loans; copying; library not open to public. **Computerized Information Services:** DIALOG, SDC, DOE/BETC (Bartlesville Energy Technology Center). **Publications:** Library Log, bimonthly - for internal distribution only.

CORGAN (D. Leonard) LIBRARY
See: King's College - D. Leonard Corgan Library

CORN INDUSTRIES RESEARCH FOUNDATION
See: Corn Refiners Association, Inc.

★3304★
CORN REFINERS ASSOCIATION, INC. - CORN INDUSTRIES RESEARCH FOUNDATION - LIBRARY (Food-Bev)
1001 Connecticut Ave., N.W.   Phone: (202) 331-1634
Washington, DC 20036
Founded: 1932. **Subjects:** Food science. **Holdings:** Figures not available. **Services:** Library not open to public.

CORN RESEARCH CENTER
See: De Kalb Agresearch Inc.

★3305★
CORNELL COLLEGE - CHEMISTRY LIBRARY (Sci-Tech)
West Science Hall   Phone: (319) 895-8811
Mount Vernon, IA 52314   Stuart A. Stiffler, Dir., Lib.Serv.
Staff: Prof 4; Other 3. **Subjects:** Chemistry. **Holdings:** 4068 volumes. **Services:** Interlibrary loans; library open to public. **Computerized Information Services:** DIALOG, SDC, BRS. **Networks/Consortia:** Member of Iowa Library Information Teletype Exchange (ILITE); OCLC.

CORNELL LIBRARY OF SCIENCE AND ENGINEERING
See: Swarthmore College

CORNELL MEDICAL CENTER
See: New York Hospital-Cornell Medical Center

CORNELL MILL MUSEUM
See: Missisquoi Historical Society

CORNELL MODERN INDONESIA PROJECT
See: Cornell University - Southeast Asia Program

★3306★
CORNELL UNIVERSITY - AFRICANA STUDIES AND RESEARCH CENTER LIBRARY (Area-Ethnic)
310 Triphammer Rd.   Phone: (607) 256-3822
Ithaca, NY 14853   Marvin Williams, Adm.Supv.
Founded: 1972. **Staff:** 5. **Subjects:** African, Afro-American, Caribbean peoples - history, culture, life styles; current materials on their economic, social and political development. **Holdings:** 7223 books; 313 bound periodical volumes; 23 theses (cataloged); 225 reels of microfilm; 30 unbound reports; 2 boxes of clippings. **Subscriptions:** 105 journals and other serials; 35 newspapers. **Services:** Interlibrary loans; copying; library open to public with restrictions. **Networks/Consortia:** Member of RLG; OCLC through FAUL; CONSER.

★3307★
CORNELL UNIVERSITY - ALBERT R. MANN LIBRARY (Agri; Soc Sci; Food-Bev)
          Phone: (607) 256-2285
Ithaca, NY 14853   Jan Olsen, Libn.
Founded: 1952. **Staff:** Prof 18; Other 32. **Subjects:** Agriculture, biological sciences, human ecology, nutrition. **Special Collections:** Everett Franklin Phillips Beekeeping Collection (5000 volumes); James E. Rice Poultry Library (5500 volumes). **Holdings:** 516,000 books and bound periodical volumes; 3100 maps; 306,000 microforms. **Subscriptions:** 9600 journals and other serials. **Services:** Interlibrary loans; copying; library open to public. **Computerized Information Services:** DIALOG, BRS; computerized cataloging and acquisitions. **Networks/Consortia:** Member of RLG; OCLC through FAUL. **Remarks:** The library serves the New York State College of Agriculture & Life Sciences, the New York State College of Human Ecology, the Division of Biological Sciences, and the Division of Nutritional Sciences. **Staff:** Henry Murphy, Coll.Dev./Acq.Libn.; Meeri Kaaret, Cat.Libn.; Virginia Carsello, Reserve Libn.; Jean Barrile, Circ.Supv.

★3308★
CORNELL UNIVERSITY - ARECIBO OBSERVATORY - LIBRARY (Sci-Tech)
Box 995   Phone: (809) 878-2612
Arecibo, PR 00613   Carmen G. Segarra, Libn.
Founded: 1963. **Staff:** Prof 2. **Subjects:** Astronomy, mathematics, radio and radar astronomy, upper atmosphere, computer science. **Holdings:** 4000 books; 800 bound periodical volumes; 800 Center for Radiophysics and Space Research reports; 29 Arecibo Observatory reports; 133 National Astronomy and Ionosphere Center reports; reprints, maps, charts, slides. **Subscriptions:** 80 journals and other serials. **Services:** Interlibrary loans; copying; library open to public with permission. **Computerized Information Services:** Computerized cataloging, acquisitions, serials and circulation. **Staff:** Garred Giles, Scientific Serv.

★3309★
CORNELL UNIVERSITY - AUDIO-VISUAL RESOURCE CENTER (Aud-Vis)
8 Research Park   Phone: (607) 256-2091
Ithaca, NY 14850   Carol Doolittle, AV Coord.
Founded: 1948. **Staff:** Prof 2; Other 2. **Subjects:** Agriculture, food and nutrition, child development, home management. **Special Collections:** Films: horses (30 titles); nutrition and food (50 titles); safety (40 titles); child development (80 titles); child abuse (40 titles); horticulture (80 titles); home management (100 titles); ecology (90 titles); apiculture (10 titles). **Holdings:** 500 16mm films; 180 35mm slide sets; 200 videotapes; 30 audiotapes. **Services:** Interlibrary loans (fee); library open to public. **Networks/Consortia:** Member of Consortium of University Film Centers; Educational Film Library Association. **Publications:** Film rental and sale catalog - free upon request.

★3310★
CORNELL UNIVERSITY - BAILEY HORTORIUM LIBRARY (Sci-Tech)
Mann Library, Rm. 467   Phone: (607) 256-2132
Ithaca, NY 14853   D.M. Bates, Dir.
Subjects: Taxonomic botany and horticulture. **Special Collections:** World-wide collection of seed and plant lists and catalogs from both botanical gardens and commercial sources; card file of sources for plant materials. **Holdings:** 12,000 volumes; 20,000 reprints on taxonomic botany and related subjects; 8000 photographs of type specimens and other important specimens in European herbaria. **Subscriptions:** 214 journals and other serials. **Services:** Interlibrary loans; library open to public. **Remarks:** This library serves the New York State College of Agriculture & Life Sciences at Cornell University.

CORNELL UNIVERSITY - BOYCE THOMPSON INSTITUTE
See: Thompson (Boyce) Institute

CORNELL UNIVERSITY - CENTER FOR RELIGION, ETHICS & SOCIAL POLICY
See: Center for Religion, Ethics & Social Policy

★3311★
CORNELL UNIVERSITY - DEPARTMENT OF MANUSCRIPTS AND UNIVERSITY ARCHIVES (Hist)
101 Olin Research Library   Phone: (607) 256-3530
Ithaca, NY 14853   Kathleen Jacklin, Archv.
Founded: 1942. **Staff:** Prof 4; Other 10. **Subjects:** Cornell University history; economic and social regional history; city and regional planning; 19th and 20th century politics; social and civil service reform; land policy; agriculture; railroads; forest products; diplomatic history; medicine; law; manufacturing. **Holdings:** 22,500 cubic feet of archives, manuscripts and ephemera; 2100 reels of microfilm; 4100 tape recordings; 50,000 photographs. **Subscriptions:** 90 journals and other serials; 22 newspapers. **Services:** Interlibrary loans; copying; collection open to public. **Staff:** H. Thomas Hickerson, Chm.; Gould Colman, Univ.Archv.; Elaine Engst, Asst.Archv.

★3312★
CORNELL UNIVERSITY - ENGINEERING LIBRARY (Sci-Tech)
Carpenter Hall   Phone: (607) 256-4318
Ithaca, NY 14853   Susan Markowitz, Engr.Libn.
Founded: 1937. **Staff:** Prof 3; Other 6. **Subjects:** Engineering - aerospace, chemical, civil, electrical, industrial, mechanical, nuclear; theoretical and applied mechanics; space science and technology; water resources development; computer science; operations research; energy; materials science; earth science. **Special Collections:** NTIS Reports; American Society of Mechanical Engineers Technical Papers; Research and Development Reports; Society of Automotive Engineers Papers. **Holdings:** 280,000 volumes; 134 reels of microfilm; 625,000 microtext items. **Subscriptions:** 2280 journals and other serials. **Services:** Interlibrary loans; copying. **Computerized Information Services:** DIALOG, SDC, BRS. **Networks/**

Consortia: Member of RLG; OCLC through FAUL. **Publications:** Monthly book list - distributed to all engineering faculty and any others requesting it. **Staff:** John Saylor, Bibliog./Ref.Libn.; Jane Hall, Circ. Reserve Supv.; Gloria Kulhawy, Tech.Serv.Libn.

★3313★
CORNELL UNIVERSITY - ENTOMOLOGY LIBRARY (Sci-Tech)
Comstock Hall   Phone: (607) 256-3265
Ithaca, NY 14853   David L. Thomas, Entomology Libn.
Founded: 1914. **Staff:** Prof 1; Other 1. **Subjects:** General and applied entomology; medical entomology; parasitology. **Special Collections:** Collected reprints of important entomological writers; collected reprints for each order of insects. **Holdings:** 27,000 volumes. **Subscriptions:** 500 journals and other serials. **Services:** Interlibrary loans; copying. **Networks/Consortia:** Member of RLG; OCLC through FAUL. **Special Indexes:** Author index to reprint collections (card).

★3314★
CORNELL UNIVERSITY - FINE ARTS LIBRARY (Art; Plan)
Sibley Dome   Phone: (607) 256-3710
Ithaca, NY 14853   Judith E. Holliday, Libn.
Founded: 1871. **Staff:** Prof 2; Other 4. **Subjects:** Art, history of art, architecture, city and regional planning. **Holdings:** 110,000 books and bound periodical volumes. **Subscriptions:** 1900 journals and other serials. **Services:** Interlibrary loans; copying. **Networks/Consortia:** Member of RLG; OCLC through FAUL. **Staff:** Pat Sullivan, Asst.Libn.

★3315★
CORNELL UNIVERSITY - FLOWER VETERINARY LIBRARY (Med)
Schurman Hall   Phone: (607) 256-2083
Ithaca, NY 14853   Susanne K. Whitaker, Libn.
Founded: 1897. **Staff:** Prof 2; Other 5. **Subjects:** Veterinary medicine and supporting biomedical subjects. **Holdings:** 69,300 volumes. **Subscriptions:** 1030 journals and other serials. **Services:** Interlibrary loans; copying; library open to public for reference use only. **Computerized Information Services:** MEDLINE, DIALOG, BRS. **Networks/Consortia:** Member of RLG; OCLC through FAUL; CONSER. **Remarks:** This library serves the New York State College of Veterinary Medicine at Cornell University.

★3316★
CORNELL UNIVERSITY - GRADUATE SCHOOL OF BUSINESS AND PUBLIC ADMINISTRATION - LIBRARY (Bus-Fin)
Malott Hall   Phone: (607) 256-3389
Ithaca, NY 14853   Betsy Ann Olive, Libn.
Staff: Prof 3; Other 5. **Subjects:** Business and public administration, finance, investment, accounting, marketing, hospital administration, managerial economics, operations management and information systems, personnel, quantitative analysis. **Special Collections:** Corporation reports (275,000 microtext editions); pamphlet collection on U.S. corporations. **Holdings:** 130,000 volumes. **Subscriptions:** 3000 journals and other serials. **Services:** Interlibrary loans; copying. **Networks/Consortia:** Member of RLG; OCLC through FAUL. **Publications:** Occasional bibliographies - distribution usually restricted to other schools of management.

★3317★
CORNELL UNIVERSITY - HISTORY OF SCIENCE COLLECTIONS (Hist; Sci-Tech)
215 Olin Research Library   Phone: (607) 256-4033
Ithaca, NY 14853   David W. Corson, Hist. of Sci.Libn.
Founded: 1961. **Staff:** Prof 1; Other 3. **Subjects:** History of the biological and physical sciences, medicine and technology. **Special Collections:** Adelmann Collection (history of embryology and anatomy; 5400 volumes); Baldassare Boncompagni archives (history of mathematics and physical sciences; 3400 items); Benoist LaForte archives (late 18th century chemistry; 3000 manuscript items); Hollister Collection (history of civil engineering; 300 volumes); Lavoisier Collection (18th and early 19th century chemistry; 2000 volumes, 525 manuscript items); medical dissertations (16th-19th centuries, mainly German; 6500 items); Boyle Collection (writings of Robert Boyle; 150 volumes); rare books. **Holdings:** 32,000 books. **Services:** Copying (limited); collections open to public for reference use only. **Special Catalogs:** Catalog of manuscripts; catalogs by provenance, publisher, printer and imprint date (all card).

CORNELL UNIVERSITY - HUMAN DEVELOPMENT AND FAMILY STUDIES DEPARTMENT
See: National Center on Child Abuse and Neglect - Region II Child Abuse and Neglect Resource Center

★3318★
CORNELL UNIVERSITY - ICELANDIC COLLECTION (Area-Ethnic)
Olin Research Library   Phone: (607) 256-6462
Ithaca, NY 14853   Vilhjalmur Bjarnar, Cur.
Founded: 1905. **Staff:** Prof 1. **Subjects:** Icelandic and Old Norse literature and language; Icelandic and early Scandinavian history; Iceland. **Holdings:** 33,000 volumes; 270 reels of microfilm; 600 maps. **Subscriptions:** 80 journals and other serials. **Services:** Interlibrary loans (limited); copying; collection open to public with restrictions on circulation. **Networks/Consortia:** Member of RLG; OCLC through FAUL. **Publications:** Islandica, irregular - by subscription and exchange, available for sale from Cornell University Press. **Special Catalogs:** Catalog of Runic Literature.

★3319★
CORNELL UNIVERSITY - JOHN M. ECHOLS COLLECTION ON SOUTHEAST ASIA (Area-Ethnic)
Olin Library   Phone: (607) 256-4189
Ithaca, NY 14853   Giok Po Oey, Cur.
Staff: Prof 5; Other 3. **Subjects:** Southeast Asia. **Holdings:** 153,000 books; 14,000 serials; 843 newspapers; 4000 titles on microfilm; 1400 maps. **Subscriptions:** 3500 journals and other serials; 86 newspapers. **Services:** Interlibrary loans; copying; collection open to public for reference use only. **Computerized Information Services:** Online systems; computerized cataloging, acquisitions and serials. **Networks/Consortia:** Member of Southeast Asia Microform Project; National Program for Acquisitions and Cataloging. **Publications:** Accessions list, monthly - by subscription. **Special Catalogs:** Southeast Asia Catalog, 7 volume book catalog, published 1976; list of special catalogs - available upon request. **Staff:** Marguerite C. Crawford, Res.Spec.; R.M. Suprapto, Indonesian Cat.; Tjeng Sioe The, Indonesian Cat.; Sari Devi Suprapto, Thai Cat.; John Hickey, Vietnamese Cat.

★3320★
CORNELL UNIVERSITY - LABORATORY OF ORNITHOLOGY - LIBRARY (Sci-Tech)
159 Sapsucker Woods Rd.   Phone: (607) 256-5056
Ithaca, NY 14850   Helen Lapham, Supv.
Staff: 1. **Subjects:** Ornithology. **Special Collections:** Books illustrated by Louis A. Fuertes (100). **Holdings:** 3500 books; 600 bound periodical volumes; 10,000 ornithological reprints. **Subscriptions:** 275 journals and other serials. **Services:** Copying; library open to public with restrictions.

★3321★
CORNELL UNIVERSITY - LABORATORY OF ORNITHOLOGY - LIBRARY OF NATURAL SOUNDS (Env-Cons)
159 Sapsucker Woods Rd.   Phone: (607) 256-5056
Ithaca, NY 14850   Dr. James L. Gulledge, Dir.
Founded: 1948. **Staff:** Prof 1; Other 1. **Subjects:** Vocalizations - bird, amphibian, mammal; environmental sounds. **Holdings:** 40,000 sound recordings. **Services:** Copying; library not open to public. **Publications:** Bioacoustics, bulletin temporarily discontinued - back issues available.

★3322★
CORNELL UNIVERSITY - LAW LIBRARY (Law)
Myron Taylor Hall   Phone: (607) 256-7236
Ithaca, NY 14853   Jane L. Hammond, Law Libn.
Founded: 1887. **Staff:** Prof 7; Other 13. **Subjects:** Law. **Holdings:** 360,000 volumes. **Services:** Interlibrary loans; copying; library open to public with restrictions. **Computerized Information Services:** LEXIS; computerized cataloging. **Networks/Consortia:** Member of New York State Interlibrary Loan Network (NYSILL); South Central Research Libraries Council (SCRLC); RLG.

★3323★
CORNELL UNIVERSITY - MAPS, MICROTEXT, NEWSPAPERS DEPARTMENT (Geog-Map)
Olin Research Library   Phone: (607) 256-5258
Ithaca, NY 14853   Marie Gast, Libn.
Staff: Prof 3; Other 3. **Holdings:** 146,500 sheet maps; 1.2 million microforms. **Subscriptions:** 399 newspapers. **Services:** Copying; restricted circulation. **Staff:** Barbara Berthelsen, Map Libn.; Joan Smith, Sr.Asst.Libn.

★3324★
CORNELL UNIVERSITY - MARTIN P. CATHERWOOD LIBRARY OF INDUSTRIAL AND LABOR RELATIONS (Soc Sci)
Ives Hall   Phone: (607) 256-2277
Ithaca, NY 14853   Shirley F. Harper, Libn.
Founded: 1945. **Staff:** Prof 11; Other 15. **Subjects:** Labor-management relations; labor law and legislation; labor organization; industrial and labor conditions; labor economics; manpower; social security; personnel

administration and supervision; human relations in industry; industrial psychology; industrial safety; international labor conditions and problems; industrial education; organization behavior. **Special Collections:** Labor union journals, labor union proceedings and labor union constitutions; Labor Management Documentation Center (manuscripts and current documents). **Holdings:** 140,000 volumes; 172,000 pamphlets and documents ; 6500 linear feet of manuscripts. **Subscriptions:** 4100 journals and other serials. **Services:** Interlibrary loans; copying; primarily for, but not limited entirely to, residents and organizations in New York State; fee-based reference service called ILR: ACCESS. **Computerized Information Services:** DIALOG, SDC, BRS, New York Times Information Service, Dow Jones News Retrieval, Source Telecomputing Corporation, Citibank Economic Database, Conference Board, Inc. **Networks/Consortia:** Member of RLG; OCLC through FAUL. **Publications:** Acquisitions List, monthly; Recent Publications, quarterly - issued as part of the Industrial and Labor Relations Review; finding guides have been prepared for some manuscript collections. **Remarks:** This library serves the New York State School of Industrial and Labor Relations at Cornell University. **Staff:** Phillip Dankert, Coll.Dev.; Chung N. Kim, Cat.Libn.; Gordon T. Law, Ref.Libn.; M. Constance Buckley, Doc.Ctr.; Richard Strassberg, Asst.Libn., LMD Ctr.; Harold E. Way, Ref.Libn.; Carolyn Zimmerman, Hd., Circ. & Reserve; Carla M. Weiss, Cat.; Karen A. Wilson, Cat.

★3325★
CORNELL UNIVERSITY - MATHEMATICS LIBRARY (Sci-Tech)
White Hall   Phone: (607) 256-5076
Ithaca, NY 14853   Steven W. Rockey, Supv.
Founded: 1953. **Staff:** 2. **Subjects:** Pure mathematics, applied mathematics, mathematical statistics, mathematical logic, history of mathematics. **Holdings:** 27,000 books and bound periodical volumes. **Subscriptions:** 325 journals and other serials. **Services:** Interlibrary loans; copying; library open to public for reference use only. **Networks/Consortia:** Member of RLG; OCLC through FAUL. **Publications:** List of new acquisitions, monthly.

★3326★
CORNELL UNIVERSITY - MEDICAL COLLEGE - SAMUEL J. WOOD LIBRARY (Med)
1300 York Ave.   Phone: (212) 472-5300
New York, NY 10021   Erich Meyerhoff, Libn.
Founded: 1899. **Staff:** Prof 11; Other 18. **Subjects:** Medicine and nursing. **Holdings:** 41,756 books; 78,574 bound periodical volumes; 1909 microfiche; 192 audio recordings; 21 video cassettes; 15 reels of microfilm. **Subscriptions:** 1769 journals and other serials. **Services:** Interlibrary loans; copying; library open to public by appointment. **Computerized Information Services:** PHILSOM, BRS, DIALOG, NLM; computerized cataloging and serials. **Networks/Consortia:** Member of Medical Library Center of New York; OCLC. **Publications:** News of Books and Journals, monthly. **Staff:** Emi Akiyama, Assoc.Libn.; Doris Lowe, Ref.; Linda Methlie-Spitzer, Circ.; Josefina Lim, Hd., Tech.Serv.; Jean Reibman, Hd., Cat.; Sylvia Sentner, ILL; Ellen Poison, Ref.; Andrea Sherman, Media; Sylvia Diaz, Ref.

★3327★
CORNELL UNIVERSITY - MUSIC LIBRARY (Mus)
225 Lincoln Hall   Phone: (607) 256-4011
Ithaca, NY 14853   Lenore Coral, Music Libn.
Founded: 1958. **Staff:** Prof 2; Other 5. **Subjects:** Musicology, music, opera, chamber music, contemporary music. **Special Collections:** Vocal music published in U.S. - 18th-20th century (12,150 items); early 16th century music (500 reels of microfilm); chamber music (4700 items); Denkmaler, collected sets, Monuments of Music (7325 items); Archive of Field Recordings (251 items). **Holdings:** 71,832 books and bound periodical volumes; 29,090 phonograph records (cataloged). **Subscriptions:** 711 journals and other serials. **Services:** Interlibrary loans; library open to public. **Computerized Information Services:** Computerized cataloging, acquisitions and bibliographic searching. **Networks/Consortia:** Member of RLG; OCLC through FAUL; CONSER. **Special Catalogs:** Materials relating to Alessandro Scarlatti's operas (book catalog); Archive of Field Recordings (book catalog). **Special Indexes:** Index to sheet music; index to performers on LP phonograph records.

★3328★
CORNELL UNIVERSITY - NEW YORK STATE AGRICULTURAL EXPERIMENT STATION - LIBRARY (Agri; Food-Bev)
W. North St.   Phone: (315) 787-2214
Geneva, NY 14456   Gail L. Hyde, Libn.
Founded: 1882. **Staff:** Prof 1; Other 1. **Subjects:** Agriculture, fruit and vegetable breeding, food science, wines, seed investigation, entomology, plant pathology. **Special Collections:** Large collection of books and journals on grapes and wine. **Holdings:** 48,000 books and bound periodical volumes. **Subscriptions:** 1000 journals and other serials. **Services:** Interlibrary loans;

copying; library open to public for reference use only. **Computerized Information Services:** DIALOG. **Publications:** New in the Library, monthly - for internal distribution only.

★3329★
CORNELL UNIVERSITY - PHYSICAL SCIENCES LIBRARY (Sci-Tech)
Clark Hall   Phone: (607) 256-5288
Ithaca, NY 14853   Ellen Thomas, Libn.
Founded: 1965. **Staff:** Prof 2; Other 5. **Subjects:** Astronomy; chemistry - analytical, inorganic, organic; physics - applied, experimental, theoretical; biochemistry; biophysics; crystallography; electron microscopy; optics; quantum theory. **Special Collections:** X-ray powder diffraction cards of American Society for Testing and Materials; spectral indexes of Sadtler Research, and Texas A & M University Thermodynamics Research Center. **Holdings:** 72,094 books and bound periodical volumes. **Subscriptions:** 931 journals and other serials. **Services:** Interlibrary loans; copying. **Networks/Consortia:** Member of RLG; OCLC through FAUL. **Publications:** List of new acquisitions, monthly.

★3330★
CORNELL UNIVERSITY - PROGRAM ON PARTICIPATION AND LABOR-MANAGED SYSTEMS - DOCUMENTATION CENTER (Bus-Fin)
490 Uris Hall   Phone: (607) 256-4070
Ithaca, NY 14853
Founded: 1978. **Staff:** Prof 1. **Subjects:** Workers self-management, participation and control; production cooperatives; self-help. **Holdings:** 250 books; 900 manuscripts; 50 dissertations; 3700 bibliographic citations with abstracts. **Services:** Copying; reference search services (fee); library open to public with restrictions. **Publications:** PPLMS Annual Report.

★3331★
CORNELL UNIVERSITY - RARE BOOKS DEPARTMENT (Rare Book)
Olin Research Library   Phone: (607) 256-4211
Ithaca, NY 14853   Donald Eddy, Libn.
Staff: Prof 2; Other 3. **Subjects:** Antislavery, Daniel and Philip Berrigan, Charles X of France, Dante, Robert Dodsley, Ford Madox Ford, Franco-Americana, French Revolution, Samuel Johnson, James Joyce, Marquis de Lafayette, Wyndham Lewis, A.J. Liebling, Comte de Maurepas, George Jean Nathan, Petrarch, Alexander Pope, George Bernard Shaw, Jonathan Swift, E.B. White, Witchcraft, William Wordsworth. **Holdings:** 121,000 books; 1.5 million manuscripts. **Services:** Copying; library open to public. **Publications:** Catalogs. **Staff:** Charles B. McNamara, Assoc.Libn.

CORNELL UNIVERSITY - REGION II CHILD ABUSE AND NEGLECT RESOURCE CENTER
See: National Center on Child Abuse and Neglect - Region II Child Abuse and Neglect Resource Center

★3332★
CORNELL UNIVERSITY - RESOURCE INFORMATION LABORATORY (Geog-Map)
Box 22, Roberts Hall   Phone: (607) 256-6520
Ithaca, NY 14853   Eugenia M. Barnaba, Mgr., Tech.Serv.
Founded: 1972. **Staff:** Prof 2; Other 3. **Subjects:** New York State - air photos, maps, satellite images. **Holdings:** 3000 books and bound periodical volumes; 100,000 air photos; 8000 units of maps; 2000 volumes of statistical data of land use. **Subscriptions:** 20 journals and other serials. **Services:** Library open to public. **Special Catalogs:** Available air photos for New York State; Land Use Inventory of New York State. **Remarks:** This library serves the New York State College of Agriculture & Life Sciences at Cornell University. **Staff:** Arlyn Ingram, Techn.; Steve Smith, Techn.

★3333★
CORNELL UNIVERSITY - SCHOOL OF HOTEL ADMINISTRATION LIBRARY (Bus-Fin; Food-Bev)
Statler Hall   Phone: (607) 256-3673
Ithaca, NY 14853   Margaret J. Oaksford, Libn.
Founded: 1950. **Staff:** Prof 2; Other 3. **Subjects:** Hotel, motel and restaurant administration; personnel administration, accounting, food and food chemistry, food facilities engineering, sanitation, advertising, sales promotion, public relations, marketing, environmental law, real estate, tourist industry, resort development. **Special Collections:** Menu Collection; rare cookbooks. **Holdings:** 20,000 volumes. **Subscriptions:** 397 journals and other serials. **Services:** Interlibrary loans; copying; library open to public with restrictions. **Computerized Information Services:** DIALOG, BRS. **Networks/Consortia:** Member of RLG; OCLC through FAUL; South Central Research Library Council (SCRLC). **Publications:** A Bibliography: Hotel and Restaurant Administration and Related Subjects, annual.

★3334★
CORNELL UNIVERSITY - SHOALS MARINE LABORATORY - LIBRARY (Sci-Tech)
G14 Stimson Hall   Phone: (607) 256-3717
Ithaca, NY 14853   Linda Mahon, Adm.Sec.
Staff: 1. **Subjects:** Marine biology and geology, oceanography, meteorography, physical science. **Holdings:** 1000 books; pamphlets, articles, theses. **Services:** Library not open to public.

★3335★
CORNELL UNIVERSITY - SOUTHEAST ASIA PROGRAM - CORNELL MODERN INDONESIA PROJECT (Area-Ethnic)
102 West Ave.   Phone: (607) 256-4359
Ithaca, NY 14850   Audrey Kahin
Staff: 3. **Subjects:** Indonesia, Southeast Asia, East Asia. **Special Collections:** Publications of Cornell Modern Indonesia Project (60 volumes); publications of Southeast Asia Program (100 volumes). **Holdings:** 300 books; 200 bound periodical volumes; 5 volumes of Indonesia Press Survey, 1955-1963; 6 volumes of Indonesia Current Affairs; 5 volumes of Report on Indonesia; 500 volumes of Far Eastern Economic Review. **Services:** Library open to public with permission. **Publications:** Indonesia, semiannual - by subscription; irregular publications.

★3336★
CORNELL UNIVERSITY - WASON COLLECTION (Area-Ethnic)
Olin Library   Phone: (607) 256-4357
Ithaca, NY 14853   James H. Cole, Cur.
Staff: Prof 3; Other 8. **Subjects:** China, Japan, Korea and Southeast Asia. **Holdings:** 467,663 volumes; 600 manuscripts; 26,824 reels of microfilm; 15,075 microfiche. **Subscriptions:** 3500 journals and other serials; 72 newspapers. **Services:** Interlibrary loans; copying; library open to public with restrictions. **Computerized Information Services:** Computerized serials and acquisitions (Western Language). **Networks/Consortia:** Member of RLG; OCLC through FAUL. **Special Catalogs:** Catalog of the Wason Collection on China and the Chinese, 7 volumes, 1980. **Staff:** Paul P.W. Cheng, East Asian Libn.; Jen-Yuan Wang, East Asian Cat.

CORNETTE LIBRARY
See: West Texas State University

★3337★
CORNING GLASS WORKS/CORNING MEDICAL & SCIENTIFIC - DAVID R. STEINBERG MEMORIAL LIBRARY & INFO. CENTER (Med; Bus-Fin)
63 North St.   Phone: (617) 359-7711
Medfield, MA 02052   Joyce Newton, Info.Spec.
Founded: 1978. **Founded:** Prof 1. **Subjects:** Clinical medicine, market research, engineering, business. **Special Collections:** Market research collection pertaining to the medical instruments and diagnostics markets (800 items); competitive file. **Holdings:** 350 books; 150 bound periodical volumes; 50 patents; 50 internal research reports. **Subscriptions:** 90 journals and other serials. **Services:** Interlibrary loans; copying; SDI; library open to public with restrictions. **Computerized Information Services:** DIALOG. **Publications:** Library Notes, monthly; circulation list, weekly; acquisitions list, monthly.

★3338★
CORNING GLASS WORKS - TECHNICAL INFORMATION CENTER (Sci-Tech)
Sullivan Pk.   Phone: (607) 974-3258
Corning, NY 14831   Raymond R. Barber, Libn.
Founded: 1936. **Staff:** Prof 2; Other 3. **Subjects:** Glass technology, ceramics, physics, chemistry, electronics, business. **Holdings:** 10,000 books; 15,000 bound periodical volumes; 10,000 internal company technical reports; 2500 translations. **Subscriptions:** 500 journals and other serials. **Services:** Copying; library not open to public. **Publications:** TIC Bulletin; BIC Newsletter, both monthly - for internal distribution only.

★3339★
CORNING MUSEUM OF GLASS - LIBRARY (Art; Sci-Tech)
Corning Glass Ctr.   Phone: (607) 937-5371
Corning, NY 14831   Dr. John H. Martin, Dir.
Founded: 1951. **Staff:** Prof 2; Other 2. **Subjects:** Art, history and archaeology of glass; glass manufacture and technology prior to 1900; glass painting and staining; history of science and technology; decorative arts; museology; conservation. **Special Collections:** Rare books, incunabula and early manuscripts dealing with art and history of glass; 1200 manufacturers' trade catalogs on microfiche. **Holdings:** 22,000 books; 6000 bound periodical volumes; 600 documents (cataloged); 80,000 2x2 colored transparent slides; 25 VF drawers of ephemeral material; 700 fine art prints and photographs; 45 boxes of company records of defunct glass firms; 1

drawer of patents; 240 reels of microfilm of journals; 150 films (converted to videotape). **Subscriptions:** 500 journals and other serials. **Services:** Interlibrary loans; copying; library open to public for reference use only. **Computerized Information Services:** OBCAT (internal database); computerized cataloging. **Networks/Consortia:** Member of OCLC; South Central Research Libraries Council (SCRLC). **Publications:** Journal of Glass Studies, annual; New Glass Review, annual - both by subscription; exhibition catalogs, occasional - direct order; Acquisitions List, monthly - for internal distribution only. **Special Indexes:** Check List of Recently Published Articles and Books on Glass, annual, published in Journal of Glass Studies. **Staff:** Norma P.H. Jenkins, Libn.; Virginia Wright, Asst.Libn.

CORNING (Warren H.) LIBRARY
See: Holden Arboretum - Warren H. Corning Library

★3340★
CORNISH INSTITUTE - LIBRARY (Art)
710 E. Roy St.   Phone: (206) 323-1400
Seattle, WA 98102   Ronald G. McComb, Hd.Libn.
Founded: 1974. **Staff:** Prof 1; Other 3. **Subjects:** Fine arts, design, music, dance, theatre. **Holdings:** 7000 books; 6000 slides. **Subscriptions:** 90 journals and other serials. **Services:** Interlibrary loans; library open to public with restrictions.

★3341★
CORPORATE-TECH PLANNING - RESEARCH LIBRARY (Sci-Tech; Energy)
275 Wyman St.   Phone: (617) 890-2600
Waltham, MA 02154   Susan M. Montigny, Res.Libn.
Founded: 1978. **Staff:** Prof 1. **Subjects:** Automotive engineering, computer science, telecommunications, electronics, environment, energy. **Special Collections:** Motor Vehicle Manufacturers Association (MVMA) specifications, 1975 to present. **Holdings:** 200 books; 2 VF drawers of annual reports and product literature; 480 technical reports; 25 microfiche. **Subscriptions:** 64 journals and other serials. **Services:** Interlibrary loans; copying; library open to public with restrictions. **Publications:** CTP Monthly Acquisitions - for internal distribution only. **Special Catalogs:** Automotive engineering media reference file (book).

★3342★
CORPORATION PROFESSIONNELLE DES MEDECINS DU QUEBEC - INFORMATHEQUE (Med)
1440 Ste. Catherine St., W., Rm. 914   Phone: (514) 878-4441
Montreal, PQ, Canada H3G 1S5   Marthe Dumont Salvail, Hd.Libn.
Staff: Prof 2. **Subjects:** Social medicine, legal medicine, health insurance, medical education, medical ethics, hospital administration, social security, state medicine. **Special Collections:** Medical laws. **Holdings:** 5500 books; 1400 bound periodical volumes; 800 federal, provincial and U.S. government publications. **Subscriptions:** 130 journals and other serials; 10 newspapers. **Services:** Interlibrary loans; copying; library open to public with restrictions. **Also Known As:** Professional Corporation of Physicians of Quebec.

CORPUS CHRISTI ART FOUNDATION
See: Art Museum of South Texas

★3343★
CORPUS CHRISTI CALLER-TIMES - LIBRARY (Publ)
Box 9136   Phone: (512) 884-2011
Corpus Christi, TX 78408   Margaret J. Neu, Hd.Libn.
Founded: 1954. **Staff:** Prof 1; Other 3. **Subjects:** Newspaper reference topics. **Holdings:** Books, microfilm, clippings, photographs, maps. **Services:** Library open with limited public access. **Remarks:** Library is located at 820 Lower N. Broadway, Corpus Christi, TX 78401.

★3344★
CORPUS CHRISTI MUSEUM - STAFF LIBRARY (Soc Sci)
1900 N. Chaparral   Phone: (512) 883-2862
Corpus Christi, TX 78401   Aalbert Heine, Musm.Dir.
Founded: 1967. **Staff:** Prof 1. **Subjects:** Natural history, museology, malacology, anthropology, ornithology, botany. **Special Collections:** Juveniles Series Collection; Netting Periodicals Collection; Museological Collection; Law Collection (19th century). **Holdings:** 9000 volumes; 28 VF drawers; 20 map case drawers; 180 sound recordings. **Subscriptions:** 77 journals and other serials. **Services:** Interlibrary loans; library open to public with restrictions. **Staff:** Diane DeLa Portilla, Libn.

★3345★
CORRECTIONAL SERVICE OF MINNESOTA - LIBRARY (Soc Sci)
1427 Washington Ave., S.   Phone: (612) 340-5432
Minneapolis, MN 55454   Richard C. Ericson, Exec.Dir.
Founded: 1957. **Staff:** 17. **Subjects:** Crime and crime prevention, delinquency, law enforcement, courts, corrections, victim services. **Holdings:** 200 16mm films (K-12 and college education films; public education films); cassette tapes; books; games; posters. **Services:** Sale or rental of materials; research and community planning in criminal justice field; operation of 5 Crime Victim Center Offices; services to wives and families of inmates. **Special Catalogs:** Catalog of educational materials.

★3346★
CORRY AREA HISTORICAL SOCIETY - LIBRARY (Hist)*
Box 107
Corry, PA 16407   Mrs. Keppel Tiffany
Staff: 2. **Subjects:** Climax locomotives, local history. **Holdings:** 100 volumes; 200 old newspapers; city directories. **Services:** Library open to public by appointment.

CORSELIUS (F.M.) LIBRARY
See: All Saints Episcopal Hospital - F.M. Corselius Library

★3347★
CORTEZ PUBLIC LIBRARY - SOUTHWEST COLLECTION (Hist)
802 E. Montezuma   Phone: (303) 565-8117
Cortez, CO 81321   Maryellen Brubaker, Lib.Dir.
Subjects: Local history. **Holdings:** Figures not available for tapes. **Services:** Interlibrary loans; copying; library open to public with fee for borrowing. **Computerized Information Services:** Computerized cataloging.

CORTICELLI (Belding) RESEARCH CENTER
See: Belding Hemingway Company - Belding Corticelli Research Center

★3348★
CORTLAND COUNTY HISTORICAL SOCIETY - LIBRARY (Hist)
25 Homer Ave.   Phone: (607) 756-6071
Cortland, NY 13045   Shirley G. Heppell, Libn.
Staff: Prof 1; Other 2. **Subjects:** Cortland County history and genealogy. **Holdings:** 2056 books; 91 bound periodical volumes; 187 reels of microfilm; 619 cubic feet of manuscripts; 55 linear feet of cemetery records and vital records; 225 titles (journals and other serials); 148 maps; 3000 photographs; 24 oral history tapes. **Services:** Copying; library open to public. **Special Indexes:** 1810 population finding list; 1820-1880 federal census of Cortland County; 1855-1875 New York census of Cortland County; 1900 federal census index of Cortland County.

★3349★
CORVA LIBRARY (Med)
35 E. 7th St., Suite 608   Phone: (513) 621-2434
Cincinnati, OH 45252   Susanne Gilliam, Libn.
Founded: 1978. **Staff:** Prof 1; Other 1. **Subjects:** Health planning, emergency medical services, ambulatory care, home health care. **Holdings:** 1500 volumes; microfiche. **Subscriptions:** 40 journals and other serials; 5 newspapers. **Services:** Interlibrary loans; copying; library open to public. **Networks/Consortia:** Member of Cincinnati Area Health Sciences Library Association. **Remarks:** Maintained by the Health Planning & Resources Development Association of the Central Ohio River Valley.

CORWIN (Joseph H.) MEMORIAL LIBRARY
See: Temple Israel of Hollywood - Joseph H. Corwin Memorial Library

COTSIDAS-TONNA LIBRARY
See: Hellenic College and Holy Cross Greek Orthodox School of Theology

★3350★
COTTAGE HOSPITAL - DAVID L. REEVES MEDICAL LIBRARY (Med)
320 W. Pueblo St.   Phone: (805) 966-7393
Santa Barbara, CA 93105   Evelyn Fay, Lib.Supv.
Founded: 1942. **Staff:** Prof 2; Other 2. **Subjects:** Medicine, surgery and related sciences. **Holdings:** 3000 books; 6000 bound periodical volumes; 1000 other items (cataloged). **Subscriptions:** 200 journals and other serials. **Services:** Interlibrary loans; copying; library open to medical patrons, and for reference to public.

★3351★
COTTAGE HOSPITAL OF GROSSE POINTE - MEDICAL LIBRARY (Med)
159 Kercheval Ave.   Phone: (313) 884-8600
Grosse Pointe Farms, MI 48236   Carol Attar, Lib.Dir.
Staff: Prof 1; Other 2. **Subjects:** Medicine, nursing, and allied sciences. **Holdings:** 1272 books; 319 bound periodical volumes; 4 VF drawers of clippings and pamphlets; 4 video cassettes; 66 audiovisual slide-tape programs; 60 audio cassettes. **Subscriptions:** 145 journals and other serials. **Services:** Interlibrary loans; copying; library open to public with restrictions. **Computerized Information Services:** MEDLINE, BRS.

★3352★
COTTONWOOD COUNTY HISTORICAL SOCIETY - LIBRARY (Hist)
812 4th Ave.   Phone: (507) 831-1134
Windom, MN 56101   Lucille Stahl, Pres.
Founded: 1901. **Staff:** 2. **Subjects:** County history. **Holdings:** Clippings and pamphlets; 2 filing cases of obituaries and history. **Services:** Copying; library open to public. **Publications:** History of Cottonwood County, 1870-1970 - for sale.

COUCH (John N.) LIBRARY
See: University of North Carolina, Chapel Hill - John N. Couch Library

COUCHMAN MEMORIAL LIBRARY
See: Schools of Theology in Dubuque - Libraries

★3353★
COUDERT BROTHERS - LIBRARY (Law)
200 Park Ave.   Phone: (212) 880-4796
New York, NY 10166   Jane C. Rubens, Libn.
Staff: Prof 3; Other 5. **Subjects:** Law. **Holdings:** 21,000 books. **Subscriptions:** 55 journals and other serials; 12 newspapers. **Services:** Interlibrary loans (local); copying; library open to clients and members of Special Libraries Association. **Staff:** Judith Popik, Asst.Libn.; Virginia Creesy, Cat.Libn.

COULEE DAM NATL. RECREATION AREA
See: U.S. Natl. Park Service

★3354★
COUNCIL FOR ADVANCEMENT AND SUPPORT OF EDUCATION - REFERENCE CENTER (Soc Sci)
Eleven Dupont Circle, N.W., Suite 400   Phone: (202) 328-5900
Washington, DC 20036   Cynthia Snyder, Dir.
Founded: 1974. **Staff:** Prof 1. **Subjects:** Alumni administration; educational fund raising; government relations; institutional relations/information services; periodicals and publications; executive management. **Holdings:** 600 books; reports, studies, speeches, surveys; college and university publications and literature; 100 titles on microfiche. **Subscriptions:** 23 journals and other serials. **Services:** Copying; library open to public for reference use only. **Also Known As:** CASE.

COUNCIL FOR EXCEPTIONAL CHILDREN
See: ERIC Clearinghouse on Handicapped & Gifted Children

★3355★
COUNCIL FOR FINANCIAL AID TO EDUCATION - LIBRARY (Educ; Bus-Fin)
680 Fifth Ave.   Phone: (212) 541-4050
New York, NY 10019
Founded: 1953. **Staff:** Prof 1. **Subjects:** Financing of higher education, corporate support of higher education. **Holdings:** 1500 volumes. **Subscriptions:** 36 journals and other serials. **Services:** Library open to public by appointment for reference use only.

★3356★
COUNCIL ON FOREIGN RELATIONS - LIBRARY (Soc Sci)
58 E. 68th St.   Phone: (212) 734-0400
New York, NY 10021   Janet Rigney, Libn.
Founded: 1929. **Staff:** Prof 4; Other 3. **Subjects:** International relations, international organizations, economics, political science. **Special Collections:** Documentation on the United Nations and the various European Communities. **Holdings:** 45,255 volumes; 105,000 United Nations documents and those of the Specialized Agencies; 340 VF drawers of clipping files. **Subscriptions:** 200 journals and other serials. **Services:** Interlibrary loans; copying; library open to public if approved by the librarian. **Staff:** Virginia Etheridge, Cat.; Janis Kreslins, Ref.Asst.; Barbara Miller, Doc.Asst.

COUNCIL OF FOREST INDUSTRIES OF BRITISH COLUMBIA
See: British Columbia - Council of Forest Industries of British Columbia

★3357★
COUNCIL OF JEWISH FEDERATIONS - LIBRARY (Area-Ethnic)†
575 Lexington Ave.
New York, NY 10022
Phone: (212) 751-1311
Zalman Alpert, Libn.
Staff: Prof 1; Other 1. **Subjects:** Jewish social welfare, community organization. **Holdings:** 300 books; 237 VF drawers of pamphlets, reports, speeches, studies, local agency material, correspondence and minutes. **Subscriptions:** 135 journals and other serials; 55 newspapers. **Services:** Interlibrary loans; library not open to public. **Publications:** Major Council Publications, A Selected Bibliography, biennial.

★3358★
COUNCIL ON NATIONAL LITERATURES - INFORMATION CENTER (Hum)
Box 81
Whitestone, NY 11357
Phone: (212) 767-8380
Anne Paolucci, Pres./Exec.Dir.
Staff: 2. **Subjects:** Integration of Western and non-Western literatures; overviews of national literatures. **Holdings:** Figures not available. **Services:** Library not open to public. **Publications:** List of publications - available on request.

COUNCIL OF PLANNING LIBRARIANS
See: Merriam Center Library

★3359★
COUNCIL OF STATE GOVERNMENTS - STATES INFORMATION CENTER (Soc Sci)
Iron Works Pike
Box 11910
Lexington, KY 40578
Phone: (606) 252-2291
Nanette D. Eichell, Info.Rsrcs.Coord.
Staff: Prof 1; Other 4. **Subjects:** State government organization and administration; legislative processes and procedures; intergovernmental relations. **Holdings:** 17,000 documents; checklists of state libraries from 50 states; state's bluebooks and budgets. **Subscriptions:** 206 journals and other serials; 8 newspapers. **Services:** Interlibrary loans; center open to public with restrictions on circulation. **Computerized Information Services:** DIALOG; internal database: licensing information; computerized cataloging. **Networks/Consortia:** Member of OCLC through SOLINET. **Publications:** State Government Research Checklist, bimonthly.

COUNCIL ON WORLD AFFAIRS
See: Cleveland Council on World Affairs

★3360★
COUNTRY DOCTOR MUSEUM - LIBRARY (Med; Hist)★
Vance St.
Box 34
Bailey, NC 27807
Phone: (919) 235-4165
Joyce R. Cooper, Exec.Sec.
Staff: 1. **Subjects:** Medicine, pharmacy. **Holdings:** 738 volumes. **Services:** Library not open to public.

★3361★
COUNTRY MUSIC FOUNDATION - LIBRARY AND MEDIA CENTER (Mus)
4 Music Square E.
Nashville, TN 37203
Phone: (615) 256-7008
Danny R. Hatcher, Dp.Dir. for Lib.Serv.
Staff: Prof 9; Other 5. **Subjects:** Country and popular music; music publishing and recording; recorded sound technology; music copyright. **Special Collections:** Acuff Collection (films, books, photographs, clippings, tapes and manuscripts pertaining to the career of Roy Acuff); National Academy of Recording Arts & Sciences (700 records, tapes and printed material related to NARAS-Award nominees). **Holdings:** 7500 books; 1500 bound periodical volumes; 85,000 recorded discs; 4550 audio- and videotapes; 1000 16mm films; 4000 pieces of sheet music; 1200 vertical file folders; 10,000 photographs. **Subscriptions:** 300 journals and other serials; 10 newspapers. **Services:** Copying; library open to public by appointment. **Publications:** Journal of Country Music, 3/year - by subscription. **Staff:** Terry Gordon, Hd., Tech.Serv.; Ronnie Pugh, Ref.Libn.; Bob Pinson, Principal Res.; Bob Oermann, Print Cat.; Kayce Cawthon, Lib.Sec.; Alan Stoker, Audio/Video Engr.; Becky Bell, Ser.Libn.; John Rumble, Oral Hist.

★3362★
COUNTRYSIDE HOME - STAFF LIBRARY (Med)
Hwy. W.
Jefferson, WI 53549
Phone: (414) 674-3170
Catherine M. Rueth, Sec./Libn.
Founded: 1971. **Staff:** 1. **Subjects:** Medicine, nursing and related subjects. **Holdings:** 1011 books. **Subscriptions:** 50 journals and other serials. **Services:** Interlibrary loans; copying; library not open to public. **Publications:**

Annual reports; library newspaper, monthly.

COUNTWAY (Francis A.) LIBRARY
See: Harvard University - Schools of Medicine, Dental Med. & Health, Boston Med. Lib. - Francis A. Countway Lib.

★3363★
COUNTY OF CARLETON LAW ASSOCIATION - LAW LIBRARY (Law)
Court House, 2 Daly Ave.
Ottawa, ON, Canada K1N 6E2
Phone: (613) 233-7386
Wanda T. Walsh, Libn.
Founded: 1888. **Staff:** 2. **Subjects:** Law. **Holdings:** 11,500 volumes. **Subscriptions:** 365 journals and other serials. **Services:** Interlibrary loans; copying; library not open to public. **Formerly:** Carleton County Law Library. **Staff:** Suzanne Lucier, Asst.Libn.

★3364★
COUNTY OF YORK LAW ASSOCIATION - COURT HOUSE LIBRARY (Law)
361 University Ave.
Toronto, ON, Canada M5G 1T3
Phone: (416) 965-7488
Anna M. MacIver, Libn./Adm.
Staff: Prof 2; Other 1. **Subjects:** Law. **Holdings:** 18,500 volumes. **Subscriptions:** 10 journals and other serials. **Services:** Copying; library not open to public. **Formerly:** York County Law Association.

COUR SUPREME DU CANADA
See: Canada - Supreme Court of Canada

★3365★
COURAGE CENTER LIBRARY (Med)
3915 Golden Valley Rd.
Golden Valley, MN 55422
Phone: (612) 588-0811
Mary Lindgren, Libn.
Founded: 1965. **Staff:** Prof 1. **Subjects:** Rehabilitation, handicapping conditions. **Special Collections:** Rehabilitation engineering (1000 documents). **Holdings:** 1000 books; pamphlets. **Subscriptions:** 50 journals and other serials. **Services:** Interlibrary loans; copying; library open to public. **Computerized Information Services:** BRS. **Networks/Consortia:** Member of Midwest Health Science Library Network (MHSLN); METRONET.

COURANT INSTITUTE OF MATHEMATICAL SCIENCES
See: New York University

★3366★
COURIER-JOURNAL AND LOUISVILLE TIMES - LIBRARY (Publ)
525 W. Broadway
Louisville, KY 40202
Phone: (502) 582-4184
Doris J. Batliner, Chf.Libn.
Founded: 1920. **Staff:** Prof 4; Other 12. **Subjects:** General reference and state and local information; Indiana information; law; current events. **Special Collections:** Newspaper clippings (5 million, classed); photograph collection (250,000); tapes on management. **Holdings:** 7000 books; Courier-Journal on microfilm, November 1868 to present; Louisville Times on microfilm, May 1884 to present; 15,000 pamphlets (cataloged); 350,000 clippings on microfilm, accessed by computer. **Subscriptions:** 50 journals and other serials; 15 newspapers. **Services:** Interlibrary loans; copying; SDI; library open to public (fee basis). **Computerized Information Services:** DIALOG, SDC, New York Times Information Service, INFO-KY. **Networks/Consortia:** Member of OCLC. **Publications:** Acquisitions Bulletin. **Staff:** Berenice Franklin, Mgr./Lib. Photo Serv.; Sharon Bidwell, Mgr./Lib.Ref.Serv.; Sonny Tharp, Asst.Libn.

★3367★
COURIER - LIBRARY (Publ)
701 W. Sandusky St.
Findlay, OH 45840
Phone: (419) 422-5151
Betty B. Edie, Libn.
Founded: 1886. **Staff:** 1. **Holdings:** Microfilm files of The Courier newspaper, 1846 to present. **Services:** Copying; library open to public. **Special Indexes:** Daily listing of news stories (card). **Remarks:** Published by the Findlay Publishing Company.

COURVILLE-ABBOTT MEMORIAL LIBRARY
See: White Memorial Medical Center

COUTTS (H.T.) LIBRARY
See: University of Alberta - H.T. Coutts Library

★3368★
COVENANT THEOLOGICAL SEMINARY - J. OLIVER BUSWELL, JR. LIBRARY (Rel-Theol)
12330 Conway Rd., Creve Coeur
St. Louis, MO 63141
Phone: (314) 434-4044
Dr. Joseph H. Hall, Libn.
Founded: 1955. **Staff:** Prof 2; Other 2. **Subjects:** Bible, theology, church

history, practical theology. **Special Collections:** Blackburn Library; Presbyteriana. **Holdings:** 42,000 books; 700 bound periodical volumes; 10 VF drawers of archives and pamphlets; theses and recordings. **Subscriptions:** 325 journals and other serials. **Services:** Interlibrary loans; copying; library open to qualified persons on request. **Computerized Information Services:** Computerized cataloging. **Staff:** George F. Johnston, Asst.Libn.

★3369★
COVINGTON AND BURLING - LIBRARY (Law)
1201 Pennsylvania Ave., N.W.   Phone: (202) 662-6152
Washington, DC 20004   Ellen P. Mahar, Libn.
Staff: Prof 5; Other 8. **Subjects:** Law - taxation, antitrust, labor, administrative, corporation, aviation. **Special Collections:** Legislative histories of selected federal laws. **Holdings:** 40,000 books; 1800 bound periodical volumes; 40 VF drawers and 100 boxes of pamphlets. **Subscriptions:** 200 journals and other serials. **Services:** Interlibrary loans; copying; library open to public by special permission only. **Computerized Information Services:** DIALOG, BRS, SDC, Dow Jones News Retrieval, Mead Data Central; computerized cataloging. **Networks/Consortia:** Member of OCLC through CAPCON. **Publications:** Annual Report of the Librarian; Library Bulletin, bimonthly - for internal distribution only. **Staff:** Ms. M. Dzurinko, Asst.Libn.; Ms. C. White, Asst.Libn.; Ms. D. Anderson, Ref.Libn.; Ms. J. LaPrade, Ref.Libn.

COWAN MEMORIAL LIBRARY
See: Church Army in Canada

★3370★
COWETA COUNTY GENEALOGICAL SOCIETY - LIBRARY (Hist)
Box 1014
Newnan, GA 30264   Norma Gunby, Owner
Founded: 1981. **Subjects:** Genealogy, local history. **Special Collections:** Local histories; census. **Holdings:** Books, magazines, microfilm, newspapers and other genealogical material. **Services:** Library open to public by appointment. **Publications:** Coweta County Genealogical Magazine, quarterly.

COWLES FOUNDATION FOR RESEARCH IN ECONOMICS
See: Yale University

COWLES PUBLISHING COMPANY - SPOKANE SPOKESMAN-REVIEW AND SPOKANE CHRONICLE
See: Spokane Spokesman-Review and Spokane Chronicle

COWLEY COUNTY GENEALOGICAL SOCIETY
See: U.S. Natl. Park Service - Cherokee Strip Living Museum - Docking Research Center Archives Library

★3371★
COX (Lester E.) MEDICAL CENTER - DOCTORS' LIBRARY (Med)
1423 N. Jefferson St.   Phone: (417) 836-3238
Springfield, MO 65802   Theresa Wimsatt, Asst.Dir., Med.Rec.
Staff: Prof 2; Other 1. **Subjects:** Medicine. **Holdings:** 260 books. **Subscriptions:** 40 journals and other serials. **Services:** Interlibrary loans; copying; library open to medical personnel and students affliated with the hospital. **Computerized Information Services:** MEDLINE, OCTANET. **Networks/Consortia:** Member of Midcontinental Regional Medical Library Program. **Staff:** Cynthia Walker, Rec.Techn.

★3372★
COYOTE POINT MUSEUM - RESOURCE CENTER (Env-Cons)
Coyote Point Dr.   Phone: (415) 342-7755
San Mateo, CA 94401   Lori Mann, Educ.Dir.
Staff: 2. **Subjects:** Natural science, biology, environmental science. **Holdings:** 700 books; 175 unbound reports; 2 drawers of clippings; documents. **Services:** Library open to docents with the museum. **Publications:** Coyote Point Museum Newsletter, bimonthly - to members and the public. **Staff:** Celia Cuomo, Educ.Asst.

★3373★
CP AIR - ENGINEERING LIBRARY (Sci-Tech)
One Grant McConachie Way
Vancouver International Airport
Vancouver, BC, Canada V7B 1V1   Phone: (604) 270-5211
Founded: 1942. **Staff:** 2. **Subjects:** Aviation, engineering, government regulations. **Holdings:** 7000 books; 300 unbound periodicals; 40,000 engineering drawings; 2300 microfiche of maintenance manuals, overhaul manuals, service bulletins and stock catalogs; business and government documents. **Subscriptions:** 15 journals and other serials. **Services:** Interlibrary loans; copying; library open to public with prior approval.

★3374★
CPC INTERNATIONAL - BEST FOODS RESEARCH CENTER - INFORMATION CENTER (Food-Bev)
1120 Commerce Ave.
Box 1534   Phone: (201) 688-9000
Union, NJ 07083   Anne Troop, Mgr., Info.Serv.
Founded: 1970. **Staff:** Prof 2; Other 2. **Subjects:** Nutrition, food technology, cookery, food microbiology, food analysis. **Holdings:** 5000 books; company reports on microfiche; 14 drawers of patents. **Subscriptions:** 300 journals and other serials. **Services:** Interlibrary loans; center open to public with permission of director. **Computerized Information Services:** DIALOG, SDC, MEDLINE; internal databases. **Publications:** Monthly list of acquisitions; annual periodicals holdings list. **Staff:** Diane Malakoff, Info.Spec.

★3375★
CPC INTERNATIONAL - MOFFETT TECHNICAL LIBRARY (Food-Bev)
Box 345   Phone: (312) 458-2000
Argo, IL 60501   Joy Louise Caruso, Mgr., Info.Serv.
Founded: 1939. **Staff:** Prof 3; Other 2. **Subjects:** Chemistry, chemical engineering, food chemistry. **Special Collections:** Carbohydrate chemistry (125 volumes and 12 periodicals). **Holdings:** 7200 books; 4700 bound periodical volumes; 15 shelves of pamphlets; 20 VF drawers of reprints; 600 cassettes of microfilmed periodicals. **Subscriptions:** 300 journals and other serials. **Services:** Library open to public by request. **Computerized Information Services:** DIALOG, SDC; internal database; computerized cataloging and circulation. **Networks/Consortia:** Member of Suburban Library System. **Publications:** Current Awareness Bulletin - for internal distribution only. **Staff:** Diane M. Whitt, Tech.Lit. Searcher; Elizabeth F. Shepard, Rec.Ctr.Supv.

CRABBE (John Grant) LIBRARY
See: Eastern Kentucky University - John Grant Crabbe Library

★3376★
CRAFT CENTER MUSEUM - CRAFT CENTER LIBRARY (Art)★
78 Danbury Rd.
Box 488
Wilton, CT 06897   Miss E. Gilbaine, Libn.
Founded: 1925. **Staff:** 2. **Subjects:** Architecture, sculpture, metalwork, general artwork. **Holdings:** 6000 books; 100 VF drawers. **Subscriptions:** 300 journals, serials and newspapers. **Services:** Interlibrary loans; copying; library open to public by appointment. **Remarks:** Part of the Craft Center School in Long Island City, NY; library evolved from a collection of ornamental ironwork books gathered in 1875.

★3377★
CRAFT AND FOLK ART MUSEUM - LIBRARY/MEDIA RESOURCE CENTER (Art)
5814 Wilshire Blvd.   Phone: (213) 937-5544
Los Angeles, CA 90036   Joan M. Benedetti, Media Libn.
Staff: Prof 1; Other 3. **Subjects:** Folk art - international, traditional and contemporary; contemporary crafts. **Special Collections:** Slide Registry of Contemporary Craftspeople; L.A. Community Research Project (slides, audiotapes and reports on living folk artists in Los Angeles). **Holdings:** 1200 books; 6 VF drawers of clippings; brochures and ephemera; 3 VF drawers of archival materials; 4 VF drawers of biographical materials; information and referral files. **Subscriptions:** 80 journals and other serials. **Services:** Library open to public for reference use only.

★3378★
CRAFTS GUILD OF MANITOBA - LIBRARY (Art)
183 Kennedy St.   Phone: (204) 943-1190
Winnipeg, MB, Canada R3C 1S6   Betty Andrich, Chm.
Founded: 1928. **Staff:** 6. **Subjects:** Crafts - weaving, pottery, embroidery, knitting, crochet, macrame. **Holdings:** 1200 volumes; 600 slides. **Services:** Library not open to public.

CRAGMONT MEDICAL LIBRARY
See: Madison State Hospital

★3379★
CRAIG DEVELOPMENTAL CENTER - MARGARET A. KENNGOTT MEMORIAL LIBRARY OF THE HEALTH SCIENCES (Med)
          Phone: (716) 658-2221
Sonyea, NY 14556   Audrey Algier, Dir., Staff Dev.
Staff: 1. **Subjects:** Medicine, nursing, developmental disabilities therapy, neurology, psychiatry. **Holdings:** 1200 books; 168 bound periodical volumes; 125 medical index volumes and catalogs; 20 newsletter titles. **Subscriptions:** 30 journals and other serials. **Services:** Library open to staff for reference

use only. **Remarks:** Maintained by New York State Office of Mental Retardation/Developmental Disabilities.

★3380★
CRAIN COMMUNICATIONS, INC. - INFORMATION CENTER (Publ; Bus-Fin)
740 N. Rush St.   Phone: (312) 649-5476
Chicago, IL 60611   Carol A. David, Libn.
Founded: 1930. **Staff:** Prof 2; Other 3. **Subjects:** Advertising, marketing. **Holdings:** 1900 books; 260 bound periodical volumes; clipping file. **Subscriptions:** 400 journals and other serials. **Services:** Library not open to public. **Special Indexes:** Index to Advertising Age, Business Insurance, Crain's Chicago Business and other periodicals (card and microfiche). **Remarks:** Second office located at 220 E. 42nd St., New York, NY 10017; phone: (212) 210-0100. **Staff:** Alice Troyer, Asst.Libn.

★3381★
CRANBROOK ACADEMY OF ART - LIBRARY (Art)
500 Lone Pine Rd.
Box 801   Phone: (313) 645-3355
Bloomfield Hills, MI 48013   Diane Vogt O'Connor, Hd.Libn.
Founded: 1932. **Staff:** Prof 3; Other 6. **Subjects:** History of art, photography, painting, ceramics, architecture, fiber/textiles, sculpture, metalsmithing, printmaking, design, philosophy. **Special Collections:** Cranbrook Press publications; Fine Binding Collection; exhibit catalog collection; lectures by visiting artists (500 cassette tapes). **Holdings:** 25,000 books; 18 VF drawers of clippings on artists and art; 5 VF drawers of clippings on CAA alumni and staff; 14 VF drawers of exhibit catalogs on artists; 25,000 slides. **Subscriptions:** 65 journals and other serials; 5 newspapers. **Services:** Interlibrary loans; copying; library open to public for reference use only. **Networks/Consortia:** Member of Michigan Library Consortium; Southeastern Michigan League of Libraries. **Publications:** Bibliographies; Pathfinders - both for internal distribution only. **Staff:** Carol Doll, Cat.

★3382★
CRANBROOK INSTITUTE OF SCIENCE - LIBRARY (Sci-Tech)
500 Lone Pine Rd.
Box 801   Phone: (313) 645-3255
Bloomfield Hills, MI 48013   Christine Bartz, Hd.Libn.
Founded: 1935. **Staff:** Prof 1; Other 1. **Subjects:** Anthropology, ethnology, natural sciences, physics, astronomy. **Holdings:** 16,000 books; 25 VF drawers of pamphlets (cataloged); 2000 maps; slides and phonograph records; depository for U.S. Government Documents in subject fields. **Subscriptions:** 210 journals and other serials. **Services:** Interlibrary loans; copying; library open to public. **Publications:** Annual Report - free to libraries on request; Newsletter, 10/year - free to members, libraries and on exchange; bulletins, irregular. **Staff:** Eleanore Kellogg, Asst.Libn.

★3383★
CRANDALL (Prudence) MEMORIAL MUSEUM - LIBRARY (Hist; Educ)
Box 12   Phone: (203) 566-3005
Canterbury, CT 06331   Margaret W. Nareff, Cur.Assoc.
Staff: Prof 1. **Subjects:** Black history, schools for blacks, life of Prudence Crandall, history of Canterbury. **Holdings:** 1000 books. **Services:** Copying; library open to public by appointment for reference use only. **Remarks:** Maintained by Connecticut Historical Commission.

CRANE (Charles) MEMORIAL LIBRARY
See: University of British Columbia - Charles Crane Memorial Library

★3384★
CRANE COMPANY - HYDRO-AIRE DIVISION - TECHNICAL LIBRARY (Sci-Tech)
3000 Winona Ave.   Phone: (213) 842-6121
Burbank, CA 91510   Douglas Longyear, Engr.Dir.
Founded: 1955. **Staff:** 1. **Subjects:** Aeronautics, engineering. **Special Collections:** Federal Aviation Administration reports; American Society Testing Materials; Air Force reports; NASA documents; American Society for Nondestructive Testing. **Holdings:** 1750 books and bound periodical volumes; 5000 cataloged reports; 45 VF drawers of government specifications and handbooks; 16 VF drawers of miscellaneous reports and documents. **Services:** Interlibrary loans; library not open to public. **Staff:** Joanne Mandeville, Libn.; George Frie, Engr.Adm.

★3385★
CRANE (J.W.) MEMORIAL LIBRARY (Med)
351 Christie St.   Phone: (416) 537-6000
Toronto, ON, Canada M6G 3C3   Elaine DuWors, Libn.
Founded: 1962. **Staff:** 2. **Subjects:** Aged, aging, geriatrics, gerontology. **Special Collections:** Crane Historical Collection (history of medicine, general

literature). **Holdings:** 3500 books, pamphlets and reprints; 130 bound periodical volumes; 1 VF drawer; 200 audio cassettes. **Subscriptions:** 115 journals and other serials. **Services:** Interlibrary loans; copying; library open to public. **Networks/Consortia:** Member of Toronto Medical Libraries Group. **Publications:** New Acquisitions, annual. **Special Indexes:** Index to periodical literature in geriatrics and gerontology (card). **Remarks:** Maintained by the Canadian Geriatrics Research Society.

CRANE MUSIC LIBRARY
See: SUNY - College at Potsdam

★3386★
CRANE PACKING COMPANY - TECHNICAL LIBRARY (Sci-Tech)
6400 Oakton St.   Phone: (312) 967-3790
Morton Grove, IL 60053   Margaret W. Ashworth, Libn.
Founded: 1967. **Staff:** Prof 1. **Subjects:** Metallurgy, chemistry, engineering, management, patents. **Holdings:** 3000 books; 4000 technical abstract research projects (9x12 cards); 3500 chemistry abstract research projects (5x8 cards). **Subscriptions:** 300 journals and other serials. **Services:** Interlibrary loans; copying; library open to public with restrictions.

★3387★
CRANFORD HISTORICAL SOCIETY - MUSEUM LIBRARY (Hist)
124 N. Union Ave.   Phone: (201) 276-0082
Cranford, NJ 07016   Loretta A. Widdows, Cur.
Founded: 1927. **Staff:** Prof 2. **Subjects:** History of Cranford, New Jersey. **Holdings:** Books, pictures, clippings and articles. **Services:** Library open to public for reference use only. **Publications:** 300 Years at Crane's Ford. **Staff:** Evelyn Turner, Asst.Cur.

★3388★
CRANFORD UNITED METHODIST CHURCH - LIBRARY (Rel-Theol)†
201 E. Lincoln Ave.   Phone: (201) 276-0936
Cranford, NJ 07016   Laura Engel, Libn.
Founded: 1960. **Staff:** Prof 1; Other 1. **Subjects:** Religion, history, philosophy, psychology, children's books. **Holdings:** 3000 books; 300 unbound reports and pamphlets; picture file. **Subscriptions:** 8 journals and other serials. **Services:** Library not open to public.

CRAPPER (Sir Thomas) MEMORIAL ARCHIVES
See: International Brotherhood of Old Bastards, Inc. - Sir Thomas Crapper Memorial Archives

CRATER LAKE NATL. PARK
See: U.S. Natl. Park Service

★3389★
CRAVATH, SWAINE, & MOORE - LAW LIBRARY (Law)
1 Chase Manhattan Plaza   Phone: (212) 422-3000
New York, NY 10005   Jean Strohofer, Libn.
Founded: 1819. **Staff:** Prof 8; Other 12. **Subjects:** Law. **Special Collections:** Corporate precedent files (100 VF drawers); tender offer library (60 VF drawers); government documents (100 VF drawers). **Holdings:** 40,000 books; 600 VF drawers. **Services:** Interlibrary loans; copying; library not open to public. **Computerized Information Services:** DIALOG, Dun & Bradstreet, Inc., Data Resources, Inc., Legi-Slate, SDC, LEXIS, New York Times Information Service, Dow Jones News Retrieval, Control Data Corporation (CDC), RLIN; computerized circulation. **Networks/Consortia:** Member of Law Library Association of Greater New York. **Special Indexes:** Proxy and Prospectus Index. **Staff:** Arlene Stern, Assoc.Libn.; Penny Frank, Info.Spec.; Marilyn Adamo, Corp.Info.Spec.; John Manchesi, Corp.Info.Spec.; Paulette Toth, Info.Spec.

★3390★
CRAVEN FOUNDATION - AUTOMOTIVE REFERENCE LIBRARY (Sci-Tech)
760 Lawrence Ave. W.   Phone: (416) 789-3432
Toronto, ON, Canada M6A 1B8   Frank Francis, Gen.Mgr.
Staff: 1. **Subjects:** Automotive reference. **Holdings:** 6000 volumes. **Subscriptions:** 145 journals and other serials. **Services:** Copying; library open to public by appointment. **Remarks:** This library is sponsored by Rothmans of Pall Mall Canada, Ltd.

CRAWFORD COLLECTION ON THE MODERN DRAMA
See: Yale University

★3391★
CRAWFORD COUNTY BAR ASSOCIATION - LAW LIBRARY (Law)
Court House, Rm. 212   Phone: (814) 336-1151
Meadville, PA 16335   William K. Reid, Libn.
Staff: 1. **Subjects:** Law. **Holdings:** 16,375 books; 145 bound periodical volumes; 2000 volumes on ultrafiche. **Services:** Library open to public with restrictions.

★3392★
CRAWFORD COUNTY HISTORICAL SOCIETY - LIBRARY AND ARCHIVES (Hist)
848 N. Main St.   Phone: (814) 724-6080
Meadville, PA 16335   Robert Ilisevich, Libn.
Founded: 1880. **Staff:** 1. **Subjects:** Local history and genealogy. **Special Collections:** Federal census for county, 1800-1900; county tax records, 1800-1897; local newspapers, 1805 to present. **Holdings:** 2600 books; 500 bound periodical volumes; 600 reels of microfilm; 22 cabinets of pamphlets, clippings, documents, letters, manuscripts, census records, newspapers, maps, ledgers and day books, audio- and videotapes. **Subscriptions:** 15 journals and other serials. **Services:** Copying; library open to public. **Publications:** Newsletter, semiannual - to members. **Special Indexes:** Crawford County cemetery, birth, death and newspaper indexes; manuscript collection indexes.

★3393★
CRAWFORD (F. Marion) MEMORIAL SOCIETY - BIBLIOTHECA CRAWFORDIANA (Hist)
Saracinesca House
3610 Meadowbrook Ave.   Phone: (615) 292-9695
Nashville, TN 37205   John C. Moran, Dir.
Founded: 1975. **Staff:** Prof 1. **Subjects:** Works by and about F.M. Crawford, fantastic literature, modern Romanticism, post-1850 literature. **Special Collections:** Francis Marion Crawford, 1854-1909 (225 items). **Holdings:** 1000 books; 5 letters and autographed items; 250 microfilmed and photocopied letters; 1 thesis and 100 miscellaneous items. **Subscriptions:** 7 journals and other serials. **Services:** Copying; library open to public by appointment. **Publications:** The Romantist, annual - limited to 300 numbered copies; The Worthies Library (series of small books). **Remarks:** The society is interested in acquiring anything by and about Crawford which its library does not already have.

★3394★
CRAWFORD AND RUSSELL, INC. - TECHNICAL LIBRARY (Sci-Tech)
17 Amelia Pl.   Phone: (203) 327-1450
Stamford, CT 06904   Bonnie Russ, Tech.Libn.
Founded: 1977. **Subjects:** Chemical engineering, chemical process technology. **Holdings:** 1200 books; 500 bound periodical volumes; 12 VF drawers of physical properties files. **Subscriptions:** 47 journals and other serials. **Services:** Interlibrary loans; copying; SDI; library open to public by appointment. **Computerized Information Services:** DIALOG. **Networks/Consortia:** Member of Southwestern Connecticut Library Council.

★3395★
CRAWFORD W. LONG MEMORIAL HOSPITAL - LIBRARY (Med)
35 Linden Ave., N.E.   Phone: (404) 892-4411
Atlanta, GA 30365   Mrs. Girija Vijay, Dir., Med.Lib.
Founded: 1942. **Staff:** Prof 2; Other 3. **Subjects:** Medicine, nursing, allied health sciences. **Holdings:** 3884 books; 5920 bound periodical volumes; 587 VF folders; 724 audio cassettes; 1115 slides; 12 phonograph records; 39 charts and pictures; 7 teaching aids. **Subscriptions:** 419 journals and other serials. **Services:** Interlibrary loans (fee); copying; library not open to public. **Computerized Information Services:** NLM. **Networks/Consortia:** Member of Atlanta Health Science Libraries Consortium; Georgia Library Information Network (GLIN). **Also Known As:** Crawford W. Long Memorial Hospital of Emory University. **Staff:** Jane Roach, Asst.Libn.

CRAWFORD (Woodruff L.) BRANCH LIBRARY OF THE HEALTH SCIENCES
See: University of Illinois - College of Medicine at Rockford - Library of the Health Sciences

★3396★
CRC PRESS, INC. - LIBRARY (Sci-Tech)
2000 Corporate Blvd., N.W.   Phone: (305) 994-0555
Boca Raton, FL 33431   Janelle Sparks, Ed.
Staff: Prof 3; Other 1. **Subjects:** Chemistry, ecology, medicine, engineering, food technology. **Holdings:** 1000 books and bound periodical volumes. **Subscriptions:** 25 journals and other serials. **Services:** Library not open to public. **Staff:** Sandy Pearlman, Mng.Ed.

★3397★
CREARE, INC. - LIBRARY (Sci-Tech)
Box 71   Phone: (603) 643-3800
Hanover, NH 03755   Margaret Ackerson, Hd., Tech.Info.Serv.
Founded: 1961. **Staff:** 2. **Subjects:** Fluid mechanics and machinery, heat transfer, multiphase flow, gas turbines, computers. **Special Collections:** Loss-of-coolant accident file (16 VF drawers). **Holdings:** 1000 books; 18,000 other cataloged items; 500 patents; 1400 company reports and proposals. **Subscriptions:** 100 journals and other serials. **Services:** Library not open to public. **Computerized Information Services:** DIALOG. **Publications:** Acquisitions list, monthly - for internal distribution only.

★3398★
CREATION-SCIENCE RESEARCH CENTER - INFORMATION CENTER (Rel-Theol)†
5466 Complex St.   Phone: (619) 569-8673
San Diego, CA 92123
Founded: 1971. **Staff:** Prof 3; Other 2. **Subjects:** Creation-science and history. **Holdings:** 1800 books; clippings (cataloged). **Services:** Library not open to public.

CREDIT RESEARCH AND LENDING LIBRARY
See: Canadian Credit Institute

★3399★
CREDIT UNION NATIONAL ASSOCIATION - INFORMATION RESOURCE CENTER (Bus-Fin)
5710 W. Mineral Point Rd.
Box 431   Phone: (608) 231-4170
Madison, WI 53701   Judith Sayrs, Ref.Libn.
Founded: 1958. **Staff:** Prof 2; Other 2. **Subjects:** Credit unions, economics, business, finance. **Special Collections:** Edward A. Filene papers; Roy F. Bergengren papers; history of the credit union movement. **Holdings:** 2000 books; 6000 historical items (cataloged); 4000 credit union documents (cataloged); 10,000 historical documents; microfilm (minutes of Credit Union National Association, World Council of Credit Unions, CUNA Supply Corporation; annual reports of state, provincial and national credit union leagues). **Subscriptions:** 400 journals and newsletters. **Services:** Interlibrary loans; copying; library open to public by appointment. **Special Catalogs:** Cross-indexed catalog of historical credit union documents. **Staff:** Jerry Burns, Hist.Libn.

★3400★
CREEDMOOR PSYCHIATRIC CENTER - HEALTH SCIENCES LIBRARY (Med)
80-45 Winchester Blvd.   Phone: (212) 464-7500
Queens Village, NY 11427   Susan Taubman, Lrng.Rsrcs.Coord.
Staff: Prof 2; Other 1. **Subjects:** Psychiatry, psychology, medicine, sociology, hospital administration. **Holdings:** 12,000 books; 1600 bound periodical volumes; 2209 other cataloged items; 3198 pamphlets. **Subscriptions:** 180 journals and other serials. **Services:** Interlibrary loans; library open to public by appointment. **Computerized Information Services:** Online systems. **Networks/Consortia:** Member of Brooklyn-Queens-Staten Island Health Science Librarians; New York and New Jersey Regional Medical Library Program; Medical and Scientific Libraries of Long Island. **Special Indexes:** List of new acquisitions by subject (pamphlet); list of current subscription journals. **Remarks:** Maintained by the New York State Office of Mental Health. **Staff:** Pushpa Bhati, Sr.Libn.

★3401★
CREEK INDIAN MEMORIAL ASSOCIATION - CREEK COUNCIL HOUSE MUSEUM - LIBRARY (Hist)†
Town Square
106 W. 6th St.   Phone: (918) 756-2324
Okmulgee, OK 74447   Bruce M. Shackelford, Cur./Dir.
Founded: 1930. **Staff:** Prof 1. **Subjects:** Oklahoma history, Creek Indian history and culture. **Holdings:** 200 books; 60 bound periodical volumes; 2 VF drawers of clippings and biography notes; 150 documents and records of the Creek Nation. **Subscriptions:** 7 journals and other serials. **Services:** Library open to public with permission of director.

★3402★
CREIGHTON UNIVERSITY - ALUMNI MEMORIAL LIBRARY (Hum)
2500 California St.   Phone: (402) 280-2705
Omaha, NE 68178   Ray B. Means, Lib.Dir.
Founded: 1878. **Staff:** Prof 7; Other 9. **Subjects:** Religion, philosophy. **Special Collections:** Japanese history and culture. **Holdings:** 240,000 books; 36,000 bound periodical volumes; 38,400 books on microfiche; 50,000 U.S. government documents; 97,800 microforms; 1600 cassettes. **Subscriptions:** 1400 journals and other serials; 33 newspapers. **Services:**

Interlibrary loans; copying; library open to public. **Computerized Information Services:** DIALOG; computerized cataloging and serials. **Networks/Consortia:** Member of OCLC through NEBASE; Nebraska Library Commission.

★3403★
CREIGHTON UNIVERSITY - HEALTH SCIENCES LIBRARY (Med)
California at 24th St.   Phone: (402) 280-2908
Omaha, NE 68178   Marjorie Wannarka, Dir.
Founded: 1910. **Staff:** Prof 6; Other 18. **Subjects:** Medicine, pharmacy, dentistry, nursing and allied health sciences. **Special Collections:** Von Schulte Rare Book Collection; Levine Collection (history of scurvy). **Holdings:** 30,145 books; 46,930 bound periodical volumes; 553 audio cassettes; 1498 slide-tape programs; 1763 video cassettes; 176 filmstrips; 126 super 8 films; 102 teaching packages; 14,164 microforms. **Subscriptions:** 1378 journals and other serials; 6 newspapers. **Services:** Interlibrary loans; copying; library open to public. **Computerized Information Services:** MEDLINE, BRS, OCTANET, Canadian Micrographic Society; Creighton Online Multiple Medical Educational Services (COMMES; internal database); computerized cataloging and serials. **Networks/Consortia:** Member of OCLC through NEBASE; Midcontinental Regional Medical Library Program (MCMRLP). **Publications:** New Accessions List, monthly - faculty distribution. **Special Indexes:** Learning Resources Center Audiovisual Catalog; Creighton University Health Science Serials. **Staff:** Geraldine Dell, Circ.Libn.; Earl M. Boulton, Ref.Libn.; Nannette Bedrosky, Cat.Libn.; Sandra Arnesen, Dir., LRC.

★3404★
CREIGHTON UNIVERSITY - LAW SCHOOL - KLUTZNICK LIBRARY (Law)
2500 California St.   Phone: (402) 280-2875
Omaha, NE 68178   Robert Q. Kelly, Dir.
Staff: Prof 4; Other 5. **Subjects:** Law - international, Anglo-American, comparative, foreign. **Special Collections:** Early history of English law; Anglo-American Legal History, 1600-1900 (900 volumes). **Holdings:** 104,561 books; 22,176 bound periodical volumes; 5073 documents; 1431 rolls of 35mm film; 27,900 microfiche; 86 audio cassettes; 89 videotape cassettes. **Subscriptions:** 1935 journals and other serials; 14 newspapers. **Services:** Interlibrary loans; copying; library open to public with restrictions. **Networks/Consortia:** Member of OCLC through NEBASE; Nebraska Library Commission. **Publications:** Creighton Law Review; acquisitions list, monthly. **Staff:** Elizabeth C. Kelly, Assoc.Dir.; Paul F. Hill, Ref.Libn.; Brian D. Striman, Cat.Libn.

★3405★
CRERAR (John) LIBRARY (Sci-Tech; Med)
35 W. 33rd St.   Phone: (312) 225-2526
Chicago, IL 60616   William S. Budington, Exec.Dir./Libn.
Staff: Prof 12; Other 35. **Subjects:** Sciences - physical, biological, medical, engineering and other fields. **Holdings:** 700,000 volumes; microfilm; microcards; microfiche. **Subscriptions:** 7000 journals and other serials. **Services:** Interlibrary loans; copying; contract bibliographic services - retrospective searches; current awareness reporting; abstracting; library open to public. **Computerized Information Services:** Online systems; computerized cataloging. **Networks/Consortia:** Member of Midwest Health Science Library Network (MHSLN); OCLC through ILLINET. **Publications:** Leukemia Abstracts, monthly - free to qualified researchers in leukemia and blood research; Translations Register-Index, monthly - fee. **Staff:** Ammiel Prochovnick, Asst.Libn.; J. Walter Shelton, Assoc.Libn.

CRERAR (John) LIBRARY - NATIONAL TRANSLATIONS CENTER
See: National Translations Center

★3406★
CRESAP, MC CORMICK, AND PAGET, INC. - LIBRARY (Bus-Fin)
245 Park Ave., 30th Fl.   Phone: (212) 953-7157
New York, NY 10167   Helen Garvey, Libn.
Founded: 1946. **Staff:** Prof 1; Other 1. **Subjects:** Management, business organization, marketing, retailing, health, education, government. **Holdings:** 1600 books; 70 VF drawers of pamphlets and clippings; 16 VF drawers of annual reports. **Subscriptions:** 110 journals and other serials. **Services:** Interlibrary loans; library not open to public.

★3407★
CRESCENT AVENUE PRESBYTERIAN CHURCH - LIBRARY (Rel-Theol)†
716 Watchung Ave.
Plainfield, NJ 07060   Mary McDougall
Staff: 3. **Subjects:** Religion, American history. **Holdings:** 3000 books. **Services:** Library open to public. **Remarks:** Library may be reached by telephone at (201) 756-2469.

★3408★
CRESCENT HEIGHTS BAPTIST CHURCH - LIBRARY (Rel-Theol)†
1902 N. Mockingbird Ln.   Phone: (915) 677-3749
Abilene, TX 79603   Mrs. Bill Jonas, Dir. of Lib.Serv.
Founded: 1959. **Staff:** Prof 4; Other 6. **Subjects:** Christian life, church, Baptists, religious education, missions, devotional literature, family. **Holdings:** 2194 books; 110 bound periodical volumes; 5 VF drawers of resource material; slides; filmstrips; cassette tapes; phonograph records. **Subscriptions:** 22 journals and other serials. **Services:** Interlibrary loans; library open to public.

CRESS
See: ERIC Clearinghouse on Rural Education and Small Schools

CRI LIBRARY
See: College of the Virgin Islands - Caribbean Research Institute

CRIME CONTROL PLANNING BOARD
See: Minnesota State Department of Energy Planning and Development - Criminal Justice Program

★3409★
CRIME & JUSTICE FOUNDATION - MASCARELLO LIBRARY OF CRIMINAL JUSTICE (Law)
19 Temple Pl.   Phone: (617) 426-9800
Boston, MA 02111   Cynthia Brophy, Project Dir.
Founded: 1977. **Subjects:** Criminal justice, correction, probation, parole, courts, police. **Special Collections:** Early Prison Societies in Boston, 1820s to present; annotated laws of Massachusetts. **Holdings:** 2500 volumes; 9 films. **Subscriptions:** 22 journals and other serials. **Services:** Interlibrary loans; library open to public for reference use only. **Publications:** Comparative Analysis of Adult Correctional Standards; Comparative Analysis of Standards for Juvenile Probation and After Care Services; Comparative Analysis of Standards for Administration of Correctional Agencies.

★3410★
CRISWELL CENTER FOR BIBLICAL STUDIES - LIBRARY (Rel-Theol)†
525 N. Ervay, 10th Fl.   Phone: (214) 742-3111
Dallas, TX 75201   John A. Burns, Libn.
Founded: 1979. **Staff:** Prof 1; Other 10. **Subjects:** Theology, Baptists, Anabaptists, Bible commentaries, church history, history, literature. **Special Collections:** Baptist history; Dr. W.A. Criswell manuscripts; Dr. George W. Truett memorabilia; First Baptist Church, Dallas, Texas scrapbooks. **Holdings:** 65,000 books; 10,000 bound periodical volumes; 525 cassette tapes; 4000 microforms. **Subscriptions:** 400 journals and other serials. **Services:** Interlibrary loans; copying; library open to public with restrictions.

★3411★
CRITERION INSTRUMENTS LTD. - CANADIAN RESEARCH INSTITUTE DIVISION - LIBRARY
30 Progress Ave.
Scarborough, ON, Canada M1P 4W8
Founded: 1938. **Subjects:** Electronics, electricity, physics, instrumentation. **Holdings:** 60 books and bound periodical volumes; 2000 historical and current catalogs of scientific instruments. **Remarks:** Presently inactive. **Formerly:** Located in Don Mills, ON.

★3412★
CROATIAN-SLOVENIAN-SERBIAN GENEALOGICAL SOCIETY - LIBRARY (Area-Ethnic)
2527 San Carlos Ave.   Phone: (415) 592-1190
San Carlos, CA 94070   Adam S. Eterovich, Dir.
Staff: 4. **Subjects:** Genealogy, heraldry, census, U.S. history prior to 1900. **Special Collections:** 120,000 index cards on individuals in the U.S. prior to 1910. **Holdings:** 500 books; 20 bound periodical volumes; 20 drawers of index cards; 30 manuscripts. **Subscriptions:** 10 journals and other serials; 5 newspapers. **Services:** Library open to public by appointment. **Publications:** Bulletins, monographs.

★3413★
CROCKER ART MUSEUM - RESEARCH LIBRARY (Art)
216 O St.   Phone: (916) 446-4677
Sacramento, CA 95814   Richard Vincent West, Musm.Dir.
Staff: Prof 3; Other 3. **Subjects:** Painting, sculpture, graphic arts, ceramics, glass, photography, art reference, textiles. **Special Collections:** Works about James McNeill Whistler; Numa Trivas collection of books on European art; original E.B. Crocker Library. **Holdings:** 3500 books; 5000 exhibition and museum catalogs (most since 1970). **Subscriptions:** 25 journals and other serials. **Services:** Interlibrary loans; library open to public with permission of

staff. **Staff:** Roger D. Clisby, Cur.; Joanna Ownby, Asst.Cur.; K.D. Kurutz, Cur., Educ.

CROCKER BUSINESS LIBRARY
See: University of Southern California

★3414★
CROCKER NATIONAL BANK - LIBRARY (Bus-Fin)
Box 38000   Phone: (415) 477-3581
San Francisco, CA 94138   Inga Govaars, Libn.
Founded: 1944. **Staff:** Prof 2; Other 2. **Subjects:** Business, finance, economics. **Services:** Interlibrary loans; library open to public by referral. **Computerized Information Services:** New York Times Information Service, DIALOG, Dow Jones News Retrieval. **Publications:** Monthly Acquisition List. **Remarks:** Library is located at 1 Montgomery St., West Tower, San Francisco, CA 94104. **Staff:** Kathleen E. Gardiser, Libn.

★3415★
CROMPTON & KNOWLES CORPORATION - DYES AND CHEMICALS DIVISION - GIBRALTAR RESEARCH LIBRARY (Sci-Tech)
Box 341   Phone: (215) 582-8765
Reading, PA 19603   Betty Hanf, Sr.Info.Chem.
Staff: Prof 1. **Subjects:** Dyes, organic chemistry, textiles. **Holdings:** 1300 books; 1200 bound periodical volumes; 16 VF drawers of patents; 4 VF drawers of trade literature. **Subscriptions:** 36 journals and other serials. **Services:** Interlibrary loans; copying (both limited); library open to public by appointment. **Computerized Information Services:** DIALOG, SDC. **Networks/Consortia:** Member of Berks County Library Association; Mideastern Regional Medical Library Service (MERMLS); Three-Valley On-line Users Group. **Special Catalogs:** Dye patents (card); dye structures (card). **Formerly:** Its Central Information Service, located in Charlotte, NC.

CROMWELL (William Nelson) LIBRARY
See: American Bar Foundation - William Nelson Cromwell Library

CRONK (Betty) MEMORIAL LIBRARY
See: Rochester Business Institute - Betty Cronk Memorial Library

CROP SCIENCE SOCIETY OF AMERICA
See: American Society of Agronomy

★3416★
CROSBY COUNTY PIONEER MEMORIAL - CCPM HISTORICAL COLLECTION/MUSEUM LIBRARY (Hist)
101 Main St.
Box 386   Phone: (806) 675-2331
Crosbyton, TX 79322   Verna Anne Wheeler, Exec.Dir.
Staff: Prof 1. **Subjects:** West Texas history. **Holdings:** 3000 volumes; 5 vertical files; The Crosbyton Review on microfilm (1909 to present). **Subscriptions:** 17 journals and other serials. **Services:** Copying; library open to public for reference use only. **Publications:** Newsletter, quarterly. **Special Indexes:** Index to the Crosbyton Review.

★3417★
CROSBY, HEAFEY, ROACH & MAY - LAW LIBRARY (Law)
1939 Harrison St.   Phone: (415) 834-4820
Oakland, CA 94612   Patrick O'Leary, Libn.
Founded: 1969. **Staff:** Prof 2; Other 2. **Subjects:** Civil litigation, taxation, labor law, medical jurisprudence. **Holdings:** 11,000 books; 100 bound periodical volumes; 300 legal briefs; 480 legal audiotapes. **Subscriptions:** 172 journals and other serials; 9 newspapers. **Services:** Interlibrary loans; copying; library not open to public. **Computerized Information Services:** DIALOG, SDC, LEXIS. **Staff:** Nora Skrukrud, Asst.Libn.

CROSBY LIBRARY
See: Gonzaga University

★3418★
CROSIER HOUSE OF STUDIES - LIBRARY (Rel-Theol)
2620 E. Wallen Rd.   Phone: (219) 489-3521
Fort Wayne, IN 46825   Rev. Ervin J. Rausch, O.S.C., Hd.Libn.
Founded: 1948. **Staff:** Prof 1. **Subjects:** Scripture, theology, philosophy, canon law, church history, sociology. **Holdings:** 22,449 books; 1660 bound periodical volumes. **Subscriptions:** 50 journals and other serials; 5 newspapers. **Services:** Interlibrary loans; library open to public.

★3419★
CROSIER SEMINARY - LIBRARY (Rel-Theol)
                                                   Phone: (612) 532-3103
Onamia, MN 56359   Richard McGrath, Dir.
Staff: Prof 1; Other 2. **Subjects:** Roman Catholic theology. **Holdings:** 20,000 books and bound periodical volumes. **Subscriptions:** 112 journals and other serials; 12 newspapers. **Services:** Interlibrary loans; copying; library open to public with restrictions.

CROSKERY (George G.) MEMORIAL LIBRARY
See: Canadian Teachers' Federation - George G. Croskery Memorial Library

★3420★
CROSS CANCER INSTITUTE - LIBRARY (Med)
11560 University Ave.   Phone: (403) 432-8593
Edmonton, AB, Canada T6G 1Z2   Katherine Sharma, Libn.
Founded: 1968. **Staff:** Prof 1. **Subjects:** Neoplastic diseases. **Holdings:** 3500 books; 860 bound periodical volumes; 40 tapes; 2 drawers of pamphlets; government documents. **Subscriptions:** 161 journals and other serials. **Services:** Interlibrary loans; copying; library open to medical personnel only.

CROUCH MUSIC LIBRARY
See: Baylor University

★3421★
CROUSE-IRVING MEMORIAL HOSPITAL - LIBRARY (Med)
736 Irving Ave.   Phone: (315) 424-6380
Syracuse, NY 13210   Frances Shelander, Libn.
Founded: 1913. **Staff:** Prof 4; Other 2. **Subjects:** Nursing and medicine. **Holdings:** 5000 books; 260 bound periodical volumes; 3 VF drawers of pamphlets and ephemeral material; 500 AV items. **Subscriptions:** 110 journals and other serials. **Services:** Interlibrary loans; copying; library open to public with permission of librarians. **Computerized Information Services:** MEDLARS; computerized cataloging (through Upstate Medical Library) and acquisitions. **Networks/Consortia:** Member of Health Resources Council of Central New York. **Staff:** Dorothea Shultes, Libn.; Connie D'Accurzio, Libn.; Gretchen Roberts, Media Coord.

★3422★
CROW WING COUNTY HISTORICAL SOCIETY - MUSEUM LIBRARY (Hist)
320 Laurel St.
Box 722
Brainerd, MN 56401   Catherine M. Ebert, Dir.
Staff: Prof 1. **Subjects:** Old textbooks; old books on religion, literature, railroading, history, arts, social sciences; Bibles. **Special Collections:** Works Progress Administration (WPA) biographies of local residents. **Holdings:** City and county records; historical scrapbooks and photograph albums; oral history collection; county jail records, 1894-1910; Brainerd city directories, 1901-1963. **Services:** Library open to public for reference use only. **Special Indexes:** Index to WPA Biographies.

★3423★
CROWELL & MORING - LIBRARY (Bus-Fin; Law)
1100 Connecticut Ave., N.W.   Phone: (202) 452-5857
Washington, DC 20036   Janet P. Klingaman, Libn.
Staff: Prof 3; Other 5. **Subjects:** Government contracts; transportation; tax; law - corporate, environmental, energy. **Special Collections:** Legislative histories (90 titles). **Holdings:** 19,980 books; 1372 bound periodical volumes; 6000 microfiche; 100 video cassettes; 1000 volumes of Congressional hearings and reports. **Subscriptions:** 125 journals and other serials; 8 newspapers. **Services:** Interlibrary loans; SDI; library open by appointment only. **Computerized Information Services:** LEXIS, New York Times Information Service. **Special Indexes:** Legal Memoranda File (card). **Staff:** Julie Fields, Asst.Libn., Rd.Serv.; Fern Sikkema, Asst.Libn., Leg.Serv.

★3424★
CROWN LIFE INSURANCE COMPANY - LAW LIBRARY (Law)
120 Bloor St., E.   Phone: (416) 928-4563
Toronto, ON, Canada M4W 1B8   Mari White, Law Libn.
Founded: 1973. **Staff:** Prof 1. **Subjects:** Law - life insurance, labour, corporation, securities, taxation. **Holdings:** 3400 books; 366 bound periodical volumes; 2200 reports, pamphlets and other items; 31 loose-leaf services. **Subscriptions:** 24 journals and other serials. **Services:** Interlibrary loans (with restrictions); copying; library not open to public. **Computerized Information Services:** Computerized acquisitions. **Networks/Consortia:** Member of Canadian Association of Law Libraries.

★3425★
CROWN LIFE INSURANCE COMPANY - LIBRARY (Bus-Fin)†
120 Bloor St., E.   Phone: (416) 928-4650
Toronto, ON, Canada M4W 1B8   H. Elizabeth Angus, Libn.
Founded: 1900. **Staff:** Prof 1; Other 1. **Subjects:** Business, life insurance, personnel management, actuarial science. **Holdings:** 15,000 books. **Subscriptions:** 250 journals and other serials. **Services:** Interlibrary loans; copying.

★3426★
CROWN ZELLERBACH CORPORATION - CENTRAL RESEARCH LIBRARY (Sci-Tech)†
349 N.W. Seventh Ave.   Phone: (206) 834-4444
Camas, WA 98607
Founded: 1938. **Staff:** Prof 3; Other 1. **Subjects:** Paper technology, chemistry, forestry, wood products, textiles, plastics, engineering. **Holdings:** 5000 books and bound periodical volumes. **Subscriptions:** 500 journals and other serials; 10 newspapers. **Services:** Interlibrary loans; copying; library open to public by appointment. **Staff:** Jan Hopkins, Cat.Libn.; Dorothea Crawford, Acq.Libn.; Nancy Huddleston, Per.Libn.

★3427★
CROWN ZELLERBACH CORPORATION - CORPORATE INFORMATION CENTER (Bus-Fin)
One Bush St.   Phone: (415) 823-5403
San Francisco, CA 94104   Gloria Capel, Adm.
Founded: 1953. **Staff:** 4. **Subjects:** Marketing research, marketing, forest products and paper industry, economics, statistics (business). **Special Collections:** Trade journals of the forest products and paper industry. **Holdings:** 5900 books; 3500 pamphlets (cataloged); 12 VF drawers of trade association material; 2 drawers of microforms. **Subscriptions:** 350 journals and other serials. **Services:** Interlibrary loans; library not open to public. **Computerized Information Services:** DIALOG, SDC, ORI, Inc., RLIN; computerized periodical circulation. **Networks/Consortia:** Member of CLASS. **Staff:** Ann Hardham, Ref.Libn.

★3428★
CROZER CHESTER MEDICAL CENTER - MEDICAL LIBRARY (Med)
15th St. & Upland Ave.   Phone: (215) 447-2600
Chester, PA 19013   Elizabeth R. Warner, Med.Libn.
Founded: 1966. **Staff:** Prof 1; Other 1. **Subjects:** Medicine, nursing, allied health sciences. **Holdings:** 600 books; 4500 bound periodical volumes. **Subscriptions:** 350 journals and other serials. **Services:** Interlibrary loans; copying; library open to public by appointment. **Computerized Information Services:** BRS, NLM. **Networks/Consortia:** Member of Consortium for Health Information and Library Services (CHI); Mideastern Regional Medical Library Service (MERMLS). **Publications:** Newsletter, quarterly - for internal distribution only.

CROZER THEOLOGICAL SEMINARY
See: Colgate Rochester/Bexley Hall/Crozer Theological Seminaries

CRUCIBLE RESEARCH CENTER
See: Colt Industries

★3429★
CRUM AND FORSTER CORPORATION - CORPORATE LIBRARY (Bus-Fin)
U.S. Insurance Group
305 Madison Ave.
Box 2387
Morristown, NJ 07960   Phone: (201) 455-0707
     Rosemary W. Leckie, Corp.Libn.
Founded: 1971. **Staff:** Prof 1; Other 2. **Subjects:** Insurance - property and casualty; personnel; investment; management; training; data processing. **Special Collections:** Company historical materials (6 cartons). **Holdings:** 1700 books; 200 bound periodical volumes; 5 VF drawers of clippings. **Subscriptions:** 350 journals and other serials; 10 newspapers. **Services:** Interlibrary loans; copying; SDI; library not open to public. **Computerized Information Services:** DIALOG. **Publications:** From the Bookshelf, quarterly; The Bookshelf Companion, irregular; Film Directory, irregular - all for internal distribution only.

CRUMB (Frederick W.) MEMORIAL LIBRARY
See: SUNY - College at Potsdam - Frederick W. Crumb Memorial Library

CRYOGENIC TECHNOLOGY, INC.
See: Helix Technology Corporation

CSC
See: Canada Safety Council

★3430★
CTB/MC GRAW-HILL - LIBRARY (Educ)
Del Monte Research Park   Phone: (408) 649-7919
Monterey, CA 93940   Phyllis H. O'Donovan, Libn.
Staff: 6. **Subjects:** Education, educational psychology, statistics, psychology, sociology. **Holdings:** 7500 books; 100 bound periodical volumes; 800 research reports. **Subscriptions:** 200 journals and other serials; 10 newspapers. **Services:** Interlibrary loans; copying; library open to graduate students with restrictions on some materials. **Special Catalogs:** Annual periodical holdings listing. **Also Known As:** California Test Bureau.

CUBBERLEY EDUCATION LIBRARY
See: Stanford University

★3431★
CUBIC CORPORATION - LIBRARY (Sci-Tech)
Box 80787   Phone: (714) 277-6780
San Diego, CA 92138   Maxine Moser, Mgr.
Staff: Prof 2; Other 1. **Subjects:** Electronics, aeronautics, management, mathematics, physics, communications, radar, computer science. **Holdings:** 2100 books; 900 bound periodical volumes; 22,000 microfiche reports; 4200 paper reports; 1000 maps. **Subscriptions:** 350 journals and other serials; 5 newspapers. **Services:** Interlibrary loans; copying; library open to public by appointment. **Computerized Information Services:** DIALOG, BRS, RLIN, DROLS, SDC; online bibliographic search services for employees. **Publications:** Acquisitions List, monthly. **Staff:** Liz Pope, Online Coord.; Wanda Marchbanks, Lib.Techn.

CUDAHY MEMORIAL LIBRARY
See: Loyola University of Chicago

CUE
See: ERIC Clearinghouse on Urban Education

CULBERTSON (William S.) LIBRARY
See: National Presbyterian Church - William S. Culbertson Library

★3432★
CULINARY INSTITUTE OF AMERICA - KATHARINE ANGELL LIBRARY (Food-Bev)
North Rd.   Phone: (914) 452-9600
Hyde Park, NY 12538   Eileen De Vries, Libn.
Founded: 1972. **Staff:** Prof 2; Other 2. **Subjects:** Cookery, food service, restaurant management. **Special Collections:** Louis P. DeGouy notebooks (261). **Holdings:** 20,000 volumes; 3400 menus; 6000 pamphlets. **Subscriptions:** 250 journals and other serials. **Services:** Interlibrary loans; copying; library open to public by appointment. **Staff:** Gertrude D. Trani, Asst.Libn.

CULLMAN (Howard S.) LIBRARY
See: Tobacco Merchants Association of the U.S. - Howard S. Cullman Library

CULLOM-DAVIS LIBRARY
See: Bradley University - Virginius H. Chase Special Collections Center

★3433★
CULTURAL SURVIVAL, INC. - LIBRARY (Area-Ethnic)
11 Divinity Ave.   Phone: (617) 495-2562
Cambridge, MA 02138   Jason W. Clay, Dir. of Res.
Staff: 3. **Subjects:** Indigenous populations, ethnic minorities, human rights, development, social impact, culture change. **Holdings:** 1000 books; 5000 clippings; 250 unpublished social impact assessments; 300 reports and documents. **Subscriptions:** 80 journals and other serials; 20 newspapers. **Services:** Copying (fee); library open to public. **Publications:** Newsletter, quarterly; occasional papers, monthly; special reports, 4/year.

★3434★
CULVER PICTURES, INC. - LIBRARY (Pict)
660 First Ave.   Phone: (212) 684-5054
New York, NY 10016   Roberts Jackson, Dir.
Founded: 1926. **Staff:** Prof 7. **Holdings:** 5000 books; 1000 bound periodical volumes; over 9 million photographs, prints and engravings. **Services:** Illustrated material available to publishers and advertisers for reproduction on a fee basis; library not open to public.

★3435★

CUMBERLAND BAR ASSOCIATION - NATHAN AND HENRY B. CLEAVES LAW LIBRARY (Law)

County Court House, 142 Federal St. Phone: (207) 773-9712
Portland, ME 04111 Ann Pierce, Libn.
Founded: 1811. **Staff:** Prof 1; Other 1. **Subjects:** Law. **Special Collections:** Briefs and records of the Supreme Judicial Court of Maine. **Holdings:** 26,871 volumes. **Subscriptions:** 126 journals and other serials. **Services:** Copying; library open to public as guests of members of Cumberland Bar Association.

★3436★

CUMBERLAND COUNTY HISTORICAL SOCIETY & HAMILTON LIBRARY (Hist)

21 N. Pitt St.
Box 626 Phone: (717) 249-7610
Carlisle, PA 17013 Ann Kramer Hoffer, Pres.
Founded: 1874. **Staff:** Prof 1; Other 3. **Subjects:** Cumberland County history, Pennsylvania history. **Special Collections:** Local newspapers from 1785 to present (microfilm, microfiche and bound volumes); Carlisle Indian Industrial School memorabilia (1879-1918); papers of Robert Whitehill, Judge James Hamilton, George Stevenson and Samuel Postlethwaite; business records of Cumberland County firms. **Holdings:** 5000 books; 63 linear feet of Cumberland County documents including tax lists from 1750-1886; 18 linear feet of manuscripts; 30 VF drawers; 270 maps; 820 reels of microfilm; 125 microcards. **Subscriptions:** 22 journals and other serials. **Services:** Copying; library open to public for reference use only. **Staff:** Mrs. James Hertzler, Chm., Lib.Comm.; Roger Steck, Exec.Sec.; Cordelia M. Neitz, Libn.

★3437★

CUMBERLAND COUNTY HISTORICAL SOCIETY - PIRATE HOUSE LIBRARY (Hist)

Box 16 Phone: (609) 455-8580
Greenwich, NJ 08323 Carl L. West, Hd.Libn.
Founded: 1908. **Subjects:** History and genealogy of New Jersey and Cumberland County. **Special Collections:** Photographs of Cumberland County (1000); deeds, 1674-1850 (500); survey maps (800); Washington Whig Newspapers (bound, 1815-1837); Bridgeton Chronicle (bound, 1853-1858, 1863-1865, 1880-1883); New Jersey Patriot (bound, 1869-1891). **Holdings:** 1500 books; 4 VF drawers of family genealogical data; 5 VF drawers of historical data; 2 VF drawers of maps and charts; 1 map case; deeds. **Services:** Copying; library open to public on a limited schedule. **Special Indexes:** Index of South Jersey families (card); index to deeds and maps (card). **Staff:** Mildred Harris, Libn.; June Queripel, Libn.

★3438★

CUMBERLAND COUNTY HOSPITAL SYSTEM, INC. - CAPE FEAR VALLEY HOSPITAL - MEDICAL LIBRARY (Med)

Box 2000 Phone: (919) 323-6708
Fayetteville, NC 28302 Barbara Beattie, Dir., Med.Lib.
Staff: Prof 1; Other 1. **Subjects:** Medicine, surgery, rehabilitation. **Holdings:** 1000 books. **Subscriptions:** 72 journals and other serials. **Services:** Interlibrary loans; copying; library not open to public. **Networks/Consortia:** Member of Cape Fear Health Sciences Information Consortium.

★3439★

CUMBERLAND COUNTY LAW LIBRARY (Law)

County Court House
W. Broad & Fayette Sts. Phone: (609) 451-8000
Bridgeton, NJ 08302 John R. Reinard, Law Libn.
Founded: 1909. **Staff:** Prof 1; Other 1. **Subjects:** Law. **Holdings:** 5000 books. **Services:** Library open to public with restrictions.

★3440★

CUMBERLAND COUNTY LAW LIBRARY (Law)

Court House, S. Hanover St. Phone: (717) 249-1133
Carlisle, PA 17013 Mary S. Rykoskey, Libn.
Staff: 1. **Subjects:** Law. **Holdings:** 18,018 volumes. **Services:** Library open to public with restrictions.

★3441★

CUMBERLAND COUNTY PLANNING BOARD - TECHNICAL REFERENCE LIBRARY (Plan)

800 E. Commerce St. Phone: (609) 451-8000
Bridgeton, NJ 08302 Carl B. Holm, Prin. Planner
Staff: 1. **Subjects:** Planning theory and history, land and land utilization, statistics, traffic and transportation, utilities and housing, agriculture and agricultural retention, parks and recreation, government finance and administration, community facilities, history and preservation. **Holdings:** 700 books and bound periodical volumes; 350 pamphlets; 30 file boxes of newsletters and reports; 200 maps. **Subscriptions:** 10 journals and other serials. **Services:** Interlibrary loans; copying; library open to public. **Publications:** Cumberland Planner - issued periodically to all county officials. **Remarks:** Library is an affiliate of New Jersey State Data Center.

★3442★

CUMBERLAND COUNTY PUBLIC LIBRARY - NORTH CAROLINA FOREIGN LANGUAGE CENTER (Hum)

328 Gillespie St. Phone: (919) 483-5022
Fayetteville, NC 28301 Patrick M. Valentine, Coord./Libn.
Founded: 1976. **Staff:** Prof 1; Other 2. **Subjects:** Languages - European, Asian; English as a second language. **Holdings:** 20,000 books; 2000 cassette tapes and phonograph records. **Subscriptions:** 40 journals and other serials. **Services:** Interlibrary loans; library open to public. **Publications:** Newsletter, monthly - free upon request.

CUMBERLAND GAP NATL. HISTORICAL PARK
See: U.S. Natl. Park Service

★3443★

CUMBERLAND MUSEUM AND SCIENCE CENTER - LIBRARY (Hist)

800 Ridley Ave. Phone: (615) 242-1858
Nashville, TN 37203 Mary S. Thieme, Cur.
Founded: 1945. **Subjects:** Natural history, ornithology. **Holdings:** 3000 books. **Subscriptions:** 40 journals and other serials. **Services:** Library open to researchers with permission.

CUMBERLAND SCHOOL OF LAW
See: Samford University

★3444★

CUMMER GALLERY OF ART - LIBRARY (Art)

829 Riverside Ave. Phone: (904) 356-6857
Jacksonville, FL 32204 Laura R. Joost, Chm., Lib.Comm.
Founded: 1961. **Staff:** Prof 1; Other 4. **Subjects:** Western and Eastern visual arts. **Special Collections:** European porcelains, especially Meissen, including many rare sales catalogs, clippings and photographs (600 volumes). **Holdings:** 3000 books; 1200 bound periodical volumes; 10,000 art slides. **Subscriptions:** 24 journals and other serials. **Services:** Copying; library open to public upon application on a limited schedule. **Publications:** Museum notices and catalogs.

CUMMINGS (Dorothy) MEMORIAL LIBRARY
See: American Indian Bible Institute - Dorothy Cummings Memorial Library

★3445★

CUMMINS ENGINE CO., INC. - LIBRARIES (Sci-Tech)

M/C 50120, Box 3005 Phone: (812) 379-6959
Columbus, IN 47201 W.E. Poor, Lib.Serv.Mgr.
Staff: Prof 2; Other 4. **Subjects:** Diesel engineering, business. **Holdings:** 10,000 books; 1000 bound periodical volumes; 10,000 research reports; 5000 society technical papers; 1000 patents; 5000 reels of microfilm. **Subscriptions:** 400 journals and other serials; 12 newspapers. **Services:** Interlibrary loans; library not open to public. **Computerized Information Services:** DIALOG, SDC; computerized acquisitions, serials, and circulation. **Staff:** M.H. Meredith, Bus.Libn.

CUMMINS (J.W.) MEMORIAL LIBRARY
See: Farmland Industries, Inc. - J.W. Cummins Memorial Library

CUNNINGHAM MEMORIAL LIBRARY
See: Indiana State University

★3446★

CUNNINGHAM AND WALSH, INC. - INFORMATION CENTER (Bus-Fin)

260 Madison Ave. Phone: (212) 683-4900
New York, NY 10016 Ruth Fromkes, Hd., Info.Ctr.
Founded: 1940. **Staff:** Prof 1; Other 1. **Subjects:** Advertising, marketing. **Holdings:** 1600 books; 60 bound periodical volumes; 189 reference items (cataloged); 96 VF drawers of clippings, reports and pamphlets; picture/scrap collection. **Subscriptions:** 147 journals and other serials. **Services:** Interlibrary loans; library not open to public. **Computerized Information Services:** New York Times Information Service.

CUNY - BERNARD M. BARUCH COLLEGE
See: Baruch (Bernard M.) College of the City University of New York

CUNY - BROOKLYN COLLEGE
See: Brooklyn College of the City University of New York

★3447★
CUNY - CENTRO DE ESTUDIOS PUERTORRIQUENOS (Area-Ethnic)
445 W. 59th St.   Phone: (212) 489-5262
New York, NY 10019   Nelida Perez, Libn.
Staff: Prof 3; Other 1. **Subjects:** Puerto Rico - history, culture, literature; Puerto Ricans in the U.S., particularly New York City. **Holdings:** 5000 books; 150 bound periodical volumes; 600 theses; 4 VF drawers of government documents; 10 VF drawers of reports and pamphlets; 20 drawers of microfilm material, including 19th and 20th century Puerto Rican papers, rare pamphlets, literary journals and historical documents. **Subscriptions:** 100 journals and other serials. **Services:** Copying; center open to public. **Computerized Information Services:** Computerized cataloging. **Networks/Consortia:** Member of OCLC; METRO. **Publications:** List of publications - available on request. **Staff:** Amilcar Tirado, Libn.; Angel Aponte, Cat.

★3448★
CUNY - CITY COLLEGE LIBRARY - ARCHITECTURE LIBRARY (Art; Plan)
3300 Broadway, Rm. 206   Phone: (212) 690-5329
New York, NY 10031   Sylvia H. Wright, Libn.-in-Charge
Founded: 1967. **Staff:** Prof 2; Other 1. **Subjects:** Architecture, urban planning, landscape architecture, structural technology. **Holdings:** 14,000 books; 2300 bound periodical volumes; 11,000 pamphlets, pictures, newspaper and periodical clippings. **Subscriptions:** 149 journals and other serials. **Services:** Interlibrary loans; copying; library open to public for reference use only. **Computerized Information Services:** Computerized cataloging. **Special Catalogs:** Union List of New York City Locations for Periodicals in the Avery Index (30 page pamphlet).

★3449★
CUNY - CITY COLLEGE LIBRARY - COLLEGE ARCHIVES (Educ)
North Academic Center
Convent Ave. & W. 137th St.   Phone: (212) 690-5367
New York, NY 10031   Barbara J. Dunlap, Archv.
Founded: 1960. **Staff:** Prof 1; Other 1. **Subjects:** Publications of and about City College, including official records and papers; selected publications of alumni and faculty; biographical material on alumni; private papers and other memorabilia of some alumni and faculty; student life - clubs, publications and activities. **Special Collections:** Papers of Cleveland Abbe, Charles Baskerville, R.R. Bowker, Alfred G. Compton, Abraham Goldforb, Townsend Harris, Ira Marion, Lewis F. Mott, Henry Neumann, Edward M. Shepard and Everett Wheeler; some official publications of the City University and Board of Higher Education. **Holdings:** 1700 linear feet of official and alumni related records (includes bound, boxed, oversize and VF materials); 140 reels of microfilm; 110 phonograph records; 13,000 photographs; 1300 blueprints. **Services:** Archives open to public. **Special Indexes:** Guides to some portions of the collection; indexes to certain publications; register of Townsend Harris Papers - all available for on-site use.

CUNY - CITY COLLEGE LIBRARY - MORRIS RAPHAEL COHEN LIBRARY
See: CUNY - City College Library - Special Collections

★3450★
CUNY - CITY COLLEGE LIBRARY - MUSIC LIBRARY (Mus)
Shepard Hall, Rm. 318A
Convent Ave. & W. 138th St.   Phone: (212) 690-4174
New York, NY 10031   Melva Peterson, Chf., Music Lib.
Founded: 1948. **Staff:** Prof 2; Other 1. **Subjects:** Music. **Holdings:** 7680 books; 13,450 scores; 10,800 phonograph records; 550 titles in microform. **Subscriptions:** 175 journals and other serials. **Services:** Interlibrary loans; copying; division open to public for reference use only. **Staff:** Ruth Henderson, Libn.

CUNY - CITY COLLEGE LIBRARY - PHONOGRAPHIC LIBRARY OF CONTEMPORARY POETS
See: CUNY - City College Library - Special Collections

★3451★
CUNY - CITY COLLEGE LIBRARY - SCIENCE/ENGINEERING DIVISION (Sci-Tech)†
Science Bldg., Rm. 29
New York, NY 10031   Phone: (212) 690-8243
                                 Marlin Demlinger, Lib.Chf.
Founded: 1936. **Staff:** Prof 4; Other 3. **Subjects:** Biology; chemistry; earth sciences; mathematics; oceanography; physics; nursing; medicine; computer sciences; technology; engineering - chemical, civil, electrical and mechanical. **Holdings:** 99,685 books; 64,446 bound periodical volumes; 1100 pamphlets and catalogs; 2873 reels of journals on microfilm. **Subscriptions:** 1475

journals and other serials. **Services:** Interlibrary loans; copying; library open to public for reference use only. **Computerized Information Services:** BRS. **Staff:** Anabel Meister; Stephen Janofsky, Med.Libn.; Frances Chambers.

★3452★
CUNY - CITY COLLEGE LIBRARY - SPECIAL COLLECTIONS (Rare Book)
North Academic Center
Convent Ave. & W. 137th St.   Phone: (212) 690-5367
New York, NY 10031   Barbara Jane Dunlap, Chf., Archv. & Spec.Coll.
Founded: 1960. **Staff:** Prof 1; Other 1. **Subjects:** English literature, drama. **Special Collections:** City College Phonographic Library of Contemporary Poets (books and recordings of poets active 1932-1942); English Civil War pamphlets; W.B. Yeats (books only); library of Morris Raphael Cohen; Russell Sage Collection (labor and social welfare; 100,000 pamphlets, annual reports, conference proceedings and serials, to circa 1965). **Services:** Copying; collections available to outside users.

★3453★
CUNY - GRADUATE SCHOOL AND UNIVERSITY CENTER - LIBRARY (Soc Sci)
33 W. 42nd St.   Phone: (212) 790-4541
New York, NY 10036   Jane R. Moore, Chf.Libn.
Founded: 1964. **Staff:** Prof 12; Other 9. **Subjects:** Humanities, social sciences, mathematics. **Special Collections:** U.S. Presidential Papers; Human Relations Area Files (paper set); CUNY doctoral dissertations. **Holdings:** 170,000 books and bound periodical volumes; 12,500 reels of microfilm; 253,000 microfiche; 107,000 art slides; 1400 music scores. **Subscriptions:** 1400 journals and other serials. **Services:** Interlibrary loans; copying; library open to faculty and students of other educational institutions. **Computerized Information Services:** Computerized acquisitions, serials and ILL. **Networks/Consortia:** Member of OCLC; METRO. **Publications:** Acquisition Policy of the Graduate School and University Center Library; List of Periodicals in the Library of the Graduate School and University Center (1975); Bibliography of Dissertation Bibliographies (1975); Reference Resources in German Literature (1975); reference guide leaflets - Interlibrary Loan Procedures, How to Use the ERIC System, How to Use IBZ; Library Handbook, annual. **Staff:** Claire D. Bowie, Chf., Rd.Serv.; Helga Feder, Hum.Ref.Libn.; Carol Fitzgerald, Soc.Sci.Ref.Libn.; Constance Beavon, Art Libn.; Lois Hacker, Chf.Tech.Serv.Libn.; Susan Levkovitz, Chf.Cat.Libn.; Priscilla M. Pereira, Educ.Ref.Libn.; Minna C. Saxe, Chf.Ser.Libn.; William Shank, Music Libn.; George Simor, Chf. Book Acq.Libn.; Rosl Smith, Cat.Libn.

CUNY - HUNTER COLLEGE
See: Hunter College of the City University of New York

CUNY - JOHN JAY COLLEGE OF CRIMINAL JUSTICE
See: John Jay College of Criminal Justice of the City University of New York

CUNY - MOUNT SINAI SCHOOL OF MEDICINE
See: Mount Sinai School of Medicine of the City University of New York

★3454★
CUNY - NEW YORK CITY TECHNICAL COLLEGE LIBRARY/LEARNING RESOURCE CENTER (Sci-Tech)
300 Jay St.   Phone: (212) 643-5240
Brooklyn, NY 11201   Catherine T. Brody, Chf.Libn.
Founded: 1947. **Staff:** Prof 13; Other 11. **Subjects:** Paramedical fields; graphic arts; hotel and restaurant management; Afro-American studies; engineering technology. **Special Collections:** Voorhees Branch Collection (17,944 volumes); Jay Street Branch Collection (6699 volumes). **Holdings:** 127,043 books; 4654 bound periodical volumes; 117 VF drawers of pamphlet material; 3 VF drawers of menus; 15 VF drawers of pictures; 7 VF drawers of career material; 4 VF drawers of company history; 4693 reels of microfilm; 1740 phonograph records; 785 8mm film loops; 194 cassette tapes. **Subscriptions:** 514 journals and other serials; 14 newspapers. **Services:** Interlibrary loans; copying; library open to public for reference use only. **Computerized Information Services:** Computerized cataloging. **Networks/Consortia:** Member of METRO; Academic Libraries of Brooklyn; OCLC. **Publications:** Library Notes, irregular - distributed to faculty and to others on request. **Staff:** Paul T. Sherman, Adm.Serv.Libn.; Richard Luxner, Voorhees Br.Libn.; Jacqueline Jefferson, Jay St.Br.Libn.

CUNY - QUEENS COLLEGE
See: Queens College of the City University of New York

CUNY - RESEARCH CENTER FOR MUSICAL ICONOGRAPHY
See: Repertoire International d'Iconographie Musicale

CURE
See: Center for Ulcer Research and Education Foundation

★3455★
CURRIE, COOPERS & LYBRAND, LTD. - INFORMATION CENTRE (Bus-Fin)
630 Dorchester Blvd., W.   Phone: (514) 866-3721
Montreal, PQ, Canada H3B 1W5   Johan Mady, Libn.
Staff: 1. **Subjects:** Management - systems, finance, planning, human resources, production and operations, health. **Holdings:** 600 books; 9 VF drawers of technical files (cataloged). **Subscriptions:** 47 journals and other serials. **Services:** Interlibrary loans; copying; library not open to public. **Computerized Information Services:** Infomart, DIALOG, CANSIM, New York Times Information Service.

★3456★
CURRIE, COOPERS & LYBRAND, LTD. - LIBRARY/INFORMATION CENTRE
   (Bus-Fin)
145 King St., W.   Phone: (416) 366-1921
Toronto, ON, Canada M5H 1J8   Stephen K. Abram, Libn.
Founded: 1966. **Staff:** Prof 1; Other 2. **Subjects:** Accounting, business, auditing, management consulting. **Holdings:** 6000 books; 50 bound periodical volumes; 3000 confidential client reports; 10 drawers of technical files; 11 drawers of industrial files. **Subscriptions:** 225 journals and other serials; 7 newspapers. **Services:** Interlibrary loans; copying; SDI; library open to public by appointment. **Computerized Information Services:** DIALOG, SDC, Mead Data Central, Info Globe, New York Times Information Service. **Remarks:** Includes holdings of Coopers & Lybrand.

★3457★
CURRY COLLEGE - LOUIS R. LEVIN MEMORIAL LIBRARY - SPECIAL
   COLLECTIONS (Educ)
1071 Blue Hill Ave.   Phone: (617) 333-0500
Milton, MA 02186   Dr. Marshall Keys, Dir.
Staff: Prof 3; Other 4. **Special Collections:** Speech; learning disabilities; U.S. government documents (38,943). **Services:** Interlibrary loans; copying; library open to public. **Computerized Information Services:** Computerized cataloging. **Networks/Consortia:** Member of OCLC through NELINET. **Publications:** Bibliographic Instruction, Orientation - for internal distribution only. **Staff:** Elaine Nolan, Hd., Ser. & Cat.; Mary Ryan, Rd.Serv.Libn.; Gay Hughes, Doc.Supv.

CURTIS (Helene) INDUSTRIES, INC.
See: Helene Curtis Industries, Inc.

★3458★
CURTIS INSTITUTE OF MUSIC - LIBRARY (Mus)
Rittenhouse Sq.
1726 Locust St.   Phone: (215) 893-5265
Philadelphia, PA 19103   Elizabeth Walker, Libn.
Founded: 1925. **Staff:** Prof 3. **Subjects:** Music - orchestral, chamber, solo instrumental, vocal. **Special Collections:** Jarvis Memorial Collection of 19th century piano, violin and chamber music (1700 items); Leopold Stokowski Collection of Orchestral Music (1500 items). **Holdings:** 8000 books; 42,700 scores; 5100 phonograph records; 1700 tapes. **Subscriptions:** 30 journals and other serials. **Services:** Interlibrary loans; library open to public by appointment. **Staff:** Anne Sebastian, Asst.Libn.; Dr. Edwin Heilakka, Orchestra Libn.

★3459★
CURTIS, MALLET-PREVOST, COLT AND MOSLE - LIBRARY (Law)
101 Park Ave.   Phone: (212) 248-8111
New York, NY 10178   Janet P. Tidwell, Libn.
Founded: 1897. **Staff:** Prof 3; Other 4. **Subjects:** Anglo-American law. **Special Collections:** Legislation of Central and Latin America. **Holdings:** 60,000 books; 2000 bound periodical volumes; 20 VF drawers of pamphlet material; 800 reels of microfilm; microfiche. **Subscriptions:** 500 journals and other serials; 10 newspapers. **Services:** Interlibrary loans. **Computerized Information Services:** LEXIS; computerized circulation. **Special Indexes:** Index to Laws of Latin American Countries (book). **Staff:** Gary Jaskula, Assoc.Libn.

CURTIS (Mary Beth) HEALTH SCIENCE LIBRARY
See: Elmbrook Memorial Hospital - Mary Beth Curtis Health Science
   Library

★3460★
CURTIS PUBLISHING COMPANY - ARCHIVES (Publ)
1100 Waterway Blvd.   Phone: (317) 634-1100
Indianapolis, IN 46202   Carol Brown McShane, Libn./Archv.
Staff: Prof 1; Other 1. **Subjects:** Advertising, marketing, general fiction. **Special Collections:** Correspondence of Cyrus H.K. Curtis, 1900-1930 (15 VF drawers); complete files of Saturday Evening Post, Jack and Jill, Country Gentleman. **Holdings:** 4500 volumes; 4 VF drawers of manuscripts; clippings and pamphlets. **Subscriptions:** 100 journals and other serials. **Services:** Copying; library not open to public. **Special Indexes:** Author, title and subject card index of the Saturday Evening Post, 1900 to present; Saturday Evening Post cartoonists, 1971 to present, and artists, 1920 to present.

★3461★
CURTISS (Glenn H.) MUSEUM OF LOCAL HISTORY - MINOR SWARTHOUT
   MEMORIAL LIBRARY (Rec)
Lake & Main St.   Phone: (607) 569-2160
Hammondsport, NY 14840   Merrill Stickler, Dir./Cur.
Founded: 1975. **Staff:** Prof 1. **Subjects:** Aviation. **Holdings:** 400 books; 4000 aviation periodicals; 600 early Curtiss aviation photographs. **Services:** Library open to public by appointment.

★3462★
CURTISS-WRIGHT CORPORATION - INFORMATION SERVICES LIBRARY
   (Sci-Tech; Energy)†
1 Passaic St.   Phone: (201) 777-2900
Wood-Ridge, NJ 07075
Founded: 1930. **Staff:** Prof 1. **Subjects:** Aeronautics, engineering, fossil energy, metallurgy. **Holdings:** 6000 books; 150 bound periodical volumes; 20,000 technical reports. **Subscriptions:** 125 journals and other serials. **Services:** Interlibrary loans; copying; library not open to public. **Staff:** Harold Moak, Dir./Engr.Plan.

CUSHING (Cardinal) GENERAL HOSPITAL
See: Cardinal Cushing General Hospital

★3463★
CUSHING HOSPITAL - PROFESSIONAL LIBRARY (Med)
Dudley Rd.
Box 190   Phone: (617) 872-4301
Framingham, MA 01701   Susan M. Wald, Libn.
Founded: 1959. **Staff:** Prof 1. **Subjects:** Geriatrics, aging, psychology. **Holdings:** 3000 books; 1172 bound periodical volumes. **Subscriptions:** 36 journals and other serials. **Services:** Interlibrary loans; library not open to public.

CUSHING HOUSE MUSEUM
See: Historical Society of Old Newbury

★3464★
CUSHMAN (Charlotte) CLUB - THEATRE RESEARCH LIBRARY (Theater)
239 S. Camac St.   Phone: (215) 735-4676
Philadelphia, PA 19107   Jean Rapp, Lib.Chm.
Founded: 1907. **Staff:** Prof 1. **Subjects:** History of the stage, histories of city theaters, plays, theatrical biographies, picture books, books on theater, programs and playbills, pictures and picture books on stage and cinema. **Holdings:** 2900 books; 25 bound volumes of Theatre Arts; 112 scrapbooks; 2000 clippings and letters; 5000 programs; 100 items of theatrical memorabilia. **Services:** Library open to public for reference use only.

CUSTER BATTLEFIELD NATL. MONUMENT
See: U.S. Natl. Park Service

★3465★
CUSTER COUNTY HISTORICAL SOCIETY - LIBRARY (Hist)
225 S. 10th Ave.   Phone: (308) 872-2203
Broken Bow, NE 68822   David K. Wilson, Cur.
Staff: Prof 3; Other 3. **Subjects:** History - state, local, national and world; genealogy; American Indian history; archeology. **Special Collections:** Census of the 81 county cemeteries in Nebraska. **Holdings:** 2000 books; collection of Indian artifacts 110 volumes of bound newspapers; 700 photographs; 250 maps; 221 reels of microfilm; 12 VF drawers of obituaries and biographical materials. **Subscriptions:** 7 newspapers. **Services:** Interlibrary loans; copying; library open to public. **Publications:** Centennial Inquirer, irregular - for members and county residents. **Special Indexes:** Index to Butcher Photograph Collection, city and county histories, obituaries from 1874 to present. **Staff:** Phillip Gardner; Harry Richardson .

CUSTER (General George Armstrong) COLLECTION
See: Monroe County Library System - General George Armstrong Custer Collection

CUTLER ARMY HOSPITAL
See: U.S. Army Hospitals

CUTLER-HAMMER LIBRARY
See: Eaton Corporation

CUTTER LABORATORIES, INC. - BAYVET
See: BAYVET

★3466★
CUTTER LABORATORIES - LIBRARY (Med)
4th & Parker Sts.
Box 1986   Phone: (415) 420-5188
Berkeley, CA 94710   Hwei Wen Ng, Libn.
Founded: 1940. **Staff:** Prof 2; Other 1. **Subjects:** Biomedicine, pharmaceutical sciences, nutrition. **Holdings:** 19,000 volumes. **Subscriptions:** 800 journals and other serials. **Services:** Interlibrary loans; copying; library not open to public. **Computerized Information Services:** MEDLINE, DIALOG. **Publications:** Acquisitions list, monthly, and list of journals received, annual - for internal distribution only.

★3467★
CUYAHOGA COUNTY REGIONAL PLANNING COMMISSION - LIBRARY (Plan)
415 The Arcade   Phone: (216) 861-6805
Cleveland, OH 44114   Robert Parry, Dp.Dir.
Founded: 1947. **Staff:** Prof 12. **Subjects:** Planning - regional, urban; population; transportation; housing; employment. **Holdings:** 400 books; 50 bound periodical volumes; VF drawers of documents and pamphlets; 3 cases of archives; 550 reports (cataloged). **Subscriptions:** 25 journals and other serials; 5 newspapers. **Services:** Interlibrary loans; copying; library open to public for reference use only. **Publications:** Community and regional reports; County Data Newsletter. **Staff:** Phyllis Gordon, Libn.

★3468★
CYRUS J. LAWRENCE, INC. - LIBRARY (Bus-Fin)
115 Broadway   Phone: (212) 962-2200
New York, NY 10006   Joan Grant, Libn.
Founded: 1965. **Staff:** Prof 1; Other 1. **Subjects:** Business, finance, investments, government. **Special Collections:** Company reports. **Holdings:** 300 books; 150 bound periodical volumes; 28 VF drawers on business; 156 VF drawers of corporate records; 20 VF drawers of research notes; 6500 microfiche of Security Exchange Commission filings. **Subscriptions:** 350 journals and other serials; 25 newspapers. **Services:** Interlibrary loans; copying; library open to SLA members by appointment.

D

DACRON RESEARCH LABORATORY
See: Du Pont De Nemours (E.I.) & Company, Inc.

DADE COUNTY AUXILIARY LAW LIBRARY
See: Florida State Supreme Court - 11th Judicial Circuit

★3469★
DADE COUNTY LAW LIBRARY (Law)
321A County Court House   Phone: (305) 579-5422
Miami, FL 33130   Robert B. Wallace, Libn.
Staff: Prof 4; Other 4. **Subjects:** Law. **Special Collections:** All Florida Statutes and Session laws (1846 to present); instructional law cassettes. **Holdings:** 83,000 volumes; microforms. **Subscriptions:** 600 journals and other serials. **Services:** Copying; library open to public at librarian's discretion. **Computerized Information Services:** WESTLAW, DIALOG. **Staff:** Larry Cortek, Asst.Libn., Tech.Serv.; Eric Welsh, Ref.Libn.; Barbara Hunt, Asst.Libn., Adm.

DAFOE (Elizabeth) LIBRARY
See: University of Manitoba

DAG HAMMARSKJOLD COLLEGE ARCHIVES
See: Georgetown University - Special Collection Division

DAHLGREN MEMORIAL LIBRARY
See: Georgetown University - Medical Center

DAILY EVENING ITEM - NEWSPAPER MORGUE
See: Hastings & Sons Publishers

DAILY PANTAGRAPH
See: Bloomington-Normal Daily Pantagraph

DAIR (Carl) ARCHIVE
See: Massey College - Robertson Davies Library

★3470★
DAIRY RESEARCH, INC. - TECHNICAL INFORMATION SERVICE (Food-Bev)
6300 N. River Rd.   Phone: (312) 696-1870
Rosemont, IL 60018   William W. Menz, Vice-Pres., Res.
Staff: Prof 1; Other 2. **Subjects:** Dairy products, food, nutrition, chemistry. **Holdings:** 450 books and bound periodical volumes; reports, pamphlets, patents and dissertations. **Subscriptions:** 80 journals and other serials; 15 newspapers. **Services:** Copying; service is available to public. **Publications:** Dairy Research Digest, monthly - distributed to qualified readers free of charge upon special request.

★3471★
DAIRY SOCIETY INTERNATIONAL - LIBRARY (Agri)
3008 McKinley St., N.W.   Phone: (202) 363-3359
Washington, DC 20015   George W. Weigold, Mng.Dir.
Founded: 1946. **Subjects:** Milk, dairy products, dairy technology. **Special Collections:** Country files on status of dairy industry. **Holdings:** 1000 volumes; 16 VF drawers. **Subscriptions:** 70 journals and other serials. **Services:** Library not open to public.

★3472★
DAIRYLAND POWER COOPERATIVE - LIBRARY (Sci-Tech)
2615 E. Ave. South   Phone: (608) 788-4000
La Crosse, WI 54601   Dolly Matthes, Rec.Coord.
Staff: Prof 1; Other 1. **Subjects:** Rural electrification, electric cooperatives, public utilities. **Holdings:** Figures not available. **Subscriptions:** 60 journals and other serials.

★3473★
DAKOTA COUNTY HISTORICAL SOCIETY - LIBRARY AND MUSEUM (Hist)
130 3rd Ave. N.   Phone: (612) 451-6260
South St. Paul, MN 55075   Frances Miller, Dir./Cur.
Founded: 1940. **Staff:** 7. **Subjects:** Minnesota, Dakota County, local, and United States history. **Holdings:** 210 volumes; county newspapers and census on microfilm. **Services:** Copying; library open to public for reference use only.

★3474★
DAKOTA HOSPITAL - FRANCIS J. BUTLER HEALTH SCIENCE LIBRARY (Med)
1720 S. University Dr.   Phone: (701) 280-4187
Fargo, ND 58103   Ardis Haaland, Med.Libn.
Staff: Prof 1. **Subjects:** Internal medicine, obstetrics and gynecology, physical medicine and rehabilitation, nursing, surgery, pediatrics. **Holdings:** 925 books; 2400 bound periodical volumes; 600 titles of AV materials. **Subscriptions:** 225 journals and other serials. **Services:** Interlibrary loans; copying; library open to students from affiliated institutions. **Networks/ Consortia:** Member of Valley Medical Network.

★3475★
DAKOTA STATE COLLEGE - KARL E. MUNDT LIBRARY (Educ)
      Phone: (605) 256-3551
Madison, SD 57042   Joseph T. Paulukonis, Dir.
Founded: 1881. **Staff:** Prof 3; Other 2. **Subjects:** Education; South Dakota. **Special Collections:** Karl E. Mundt Archives (2500 linear feet). **Holdings:** 71,000 books; 11,900 bound periodical volumes; 200 reels of microfilm of Indian Affairs in Dakota, 1850-1890; complete kinescopes of the Army-McCarthy Hearings. **Subscriptions:** 510 journals and other serials; 16 newspapers. **Services:** Interlibrary loans; copying; library open to public. **Staff:** Marcel Selgestad, Asst.Libn., Acq./Cat.; Harlan Hallstrom, Asst.Libn., Pub.Serv.; Pearl Hefte, Archv.

★3476★
DALCHO HISTORICAL SOCIETY OF THE PROTESTANT EPISCOPAL CHURCH IN SOUTH CAROLINA - LIBRARY AND ARCHIVES (Rel-Theol)
Box 2127   Phone: (803) 722-4075
Charleston, SC 29403   George W. Williams, Pres.
Founded: 1945. **Subjects:** History of the Episcopal Church in South Carolina. **Services:** Collection open to public.

DALE (Edgar) EDUCATIONAL MEDIA & INSTRUCTIONAL MATERIAL LABORATORY
See: Ohio State University - Edgar Dale Educational Media & Instructional Material Laboratory

DALE LIBRARY OF WEIGHTS AND MEASURES
See: Columbia University - Rare Book and Manuscript Library

★3477★
DALHOUSIE UNIVERSITY - BACON COLLECTION (Hum)
University Library   Phone: (902) 424-3615
Halifax, NS, Canada B3H 4H8
Staff: Prof 1; Other 1. **Subjects:** Pre-1750 monographs by and about Sir Francis Bacon. **Holdings:** 300 volumes; 180 seventeenth century imprints. **Services:** Library open to public by appointment.

★3478★
DALHOUSIE UNIVERSITY - COCKERELL COLLECTION (Publ)
University Library   Phone: (902) 424-3615
Halifax, NS, Canada B3H 4H8
Founded: 1936. **Staff:** Prof 1; Other 1. **Subjects:** Representative bindings of the 15th to 18th centuries assembled by Douglas Cockerell, the famous English bookbinder. **Holdings:** 140 volumes. **Services:** Library open to public by appointment.

★3479★
DALHOUSIE UNIVERSITY - INSTITUTE OF PUBLIC AFFAIRS - LIBRARY (Soc Sci)
6086 University Ave.   Phone: (902) 424-2526
Halifax, NS, Canada B3H 3J5   Faustina Chen, Libn.
Founded: 1936. **Staff:** Prof 1; Other 1. **Subjects:** Management, commerce, regional development, labor, business, government, political science, industrial relations, economics. **Holdings:** 17,528 books; 2 drawers of clippings. **Subscriptions:** 300 serials. **Services:** Interlibrary loans; library open to public. **Staff:** Janice Kay .

★3480★
DALHOUSIE UNIVERSITY - KIPLING COLLECTION (Hum)
University Library   Phone: (902) 424-3615
Halifax, NS, Canada B3H 4H8
Founded: 1954. **Staff:** Prof 1; Other 1. **Subjects:** Kiplingiana. **Holdings:** 1606 books; 309 bound periodical volumes; 653 unbound periodicals; 144 manuscripts; 64 musical selections; 226 photostats and clippings. **Services:** Library open to public.

★3481★

DALHOUSIE UNIVERSITY - LAW LIBRARY (Law)
Weldon Law Bldg.
Halifax, NS, Canada B3H 4H9
Phone: (902) 424-2124
Christian L. Wiktor, Law Libn.
Founded: 1883. **Staff:** Prof 6; Other 15. **Subjects:** Law - Canadian, English, Commonwealth, American. **Special Collections:** Maritime law; international law. **Holdings:** 142,000 volumes. **Subscriptions:** 3350 journals and other serials. **Services:** Interlibrary loans; copying; library open to public with restrictions. **Special Indexes:** Index to Commonwealth Legal Periodicals; Marine Affairs Bibliography. **Staff:** Heather E. Creech, Ref.Libn.; Dorothy A. Long, Pub.Serv.Libn.; Linda S. Aiken, Acq.Libn.; Joan Simpson, Cat.; Leslie A. Foster, Res.Asst.

★3482★

DALHOUSIE UNIVERSITY - MACDONALD SCIENCE LIBRARY (Sci-Tech)
University Library
Halifax, NS, Canada B3H 4J3
Phone: (902) 424-2059
Sylvia J. Fullerton, Asst.Univ.Libn., Sci.
Staff: Prof 5; Other 11. **Subjects:** Biological sciences, psychology, computers, physical sciences. **Special Collections:** Map collection (54,500). **Holdings:** 116,750 books and bound periodical volumes; 25,600 documents. **Subscriptions:** 2222 journals and other serials. **Services:** Interlibrary loans; copying; SDI; library open to public. **Computerized Information Services:** CAN/OLE, SDC, DIALOG, QL Systems, Infodata Systems, Inc.; computerized circulation. **Networks/Consortia:** Member of Nova Scotia Online Consortium. **Publications:** Information Bulletin, irregular; subject bibliographies; guides to the library. **Special Indexes:** Government document keyword index (printout).

★3483★

DALHOUSIE UNIVERSITY - MARITIME SCHOOL OF SOCIAL WORK - LIBRARY (Soc Sci)
6420 Coburg Rd.
Halifax, NS, Canada B3H 3J5
Phone: (902) 424-3760
Mrs. Jean O. Hattie, Libn.
Founded: 1941. **Staff:** Prof 1; Other 1. **Subjects:** Social work, social welfare, sociology, psychology, counselling, corrections, community development. **Special Collections:** Native Peoples Collection (on Indians, Eskimos and metis). **Holdings:** 21,900 books and bound periodical volumes; 400 AV items; 12 VF drawers. **Subscriptions:** 202 journals and other serials. **Services:** Interlibrary loans; copying; library open to public. **Computerized Information Services:** Computerized serials.

★3484★

DALHOUSIE UNIVERSITY - OCEAN STUDIES PROGRAMME - LIBRARY (Sci-Tech)
1321 Edward St.
Halifax, NS, Canada B3H 4H9
Phone: (902) 424-6557
Judy Reade, Libn.
Staff: Prof 1; Other 1. **Subjects:** Fisheries in Nova Scotia and the Atlantic provinces, fishing industry, Bay of Fundy/Gulf of Maine, oil and gas operations, law of the sea. **Holdings:** 500 books; 2000 reports and reprints. **Subscriptions:** 34 journals and other serials. **Services:** Interlibrary loans; copying; library not open to public. **Computerized Information Services:** Computerized cataloging.

★3485★

DALHOUSIE UNIVERSITY - W.K. KELLOGG HEALTH SCIENCES LIBRARY (Med)
Sir Charles Tupper Medical Bldg.
Halifax, NS, Canada B3H 4H7
Phone: (902) 424-2458
Ann Nevill, Health Sci.Libn.
Founded: 1889. **Staff:** Prof 8; Other 28. **Subjects:** Medicine, dentistry, nursing, pharmacy, physiotherapy, physical education, human communication disorders. **Special Collections:** History of Medicine (emphasizing the Atlantic region). **Holdings:** 140,000 books and bound periodical volumes; 3500 audiotapes, videotapes and slide-tape programs. **Subscriptions:** 3000 journals and other serials. **Services:** Interlibrary loans; copying; Regional Loan and Information Service; library open to public. **Computerized Information Services:** MEDLINE, CAN/OLE, CAN/SDI, SDC, DIALOG; computerized serials. **Networks/Consortia:** Member of Nova Scotia Online Consortium. **Publications:** List of Recent Acquisitions, monthly. **Staff:** Linda Harvey, Hd., Pub.Serv.; Peter King, Hd., Ed.Serv.; Eugene Pelchat, Hd., Tech.Serv.; Tom Flemming, Hd., ILL.

★3486★

DALLAS BIBLE COLLEGE - GOULD MEMORIAL LIBRARY (Rel-Theol)
8733 LaPrada Dr.
Dallas, TX 75228
Phone: (214) 328-7171
John R. Stanley, Libn.
Founded: 1972. **Staff:** Prof 2; Other 5. **Subjects:** Theology, philosophy, history, psychology, sociology. **Holdings:** 32,000 books; 220 bound periodical volumes; 2700 AV items (cataloged). **Subscriptions:** 120 journals and other serials. **Services:** Interlibrary loans; library open to public with restrictions.

★3487★

DALLAS BUDGET & RESEARCH LIBRARY (Soc Sci)
City Hall
Dallas, TX 75201
Phone: (214) 670-4248
Kathryn W. Martin, Libn.
Staff: Prof 1. **Subjects:** Dallas - city government, budgeting, transportation. **Special Collections:** City government budgets; published articles by city employees; consultants' reports. **Holdings:** 2000 books; 4 VF drawers of newspaper clippings; 4 VF drawers of city subject files. **Subscriptions:** 150 journals and other serials; 5 newspapers. **Services:** Interlibrary loans; copying; library open to public for reference use only. **Computerized Information Services:** Computerized cataloging. **Special Indexes:** Indexes to consultants' reports and Budget & Research publications. **Formerly:** Dallas Management Services Library.

★3488★

DALLAS CHRISTIAN COLLEGE - LIBRARY (Rel-Theol)
2700 Christian Pkwy.
Dallas, TX 75234
Phone: (214) 241-3371
Richard Hathaway, Libn.
Founded: 1950. **Staff:** 2. **Subjects:** Theology. **Special Collections:** Restoration Library (history of Churches of Christ). **Holdings:** 30,000 books. **Subscriptions:** 125 journals and other serials. **Services:** Interlibrary loans; copying; library open to public with specific needs. **Computerized Information Services:** Computerized cataloging. **Networks/Consortia:** Member of OCLC through AMIGOS Bibliographic Council, Inc.

★3489★

DALLAS CIVIC GARDEN CENTER - HORTICULTURE LIBRARY (Sci-Tech)
Fair Park
First at Martin Luther King Blvd.
Dallas, TX 75226
Phone: (214) 428-7476
Susan Miller, Libn.
Founded: 1957. **Staff:** Prof 1; Other 7. **Subjects:** Gardening, botany, floriculture, greenhouse management, flower arranging, pest control. **Holdings:** 4233 books; 34 bound periodical volumes; herbarium collection. **Subscriptions:** 12 journals and other serials. **Services:** Copying; library open to public. **Publications:** The Garden Gate - newsletter.

★3490★

DALLAS COUNTY CIRCUIT COURT - LIBRARY (Law)
Dallas County Courthouse
Box 1158
Selma, AL 36701
Phone: (205) 872-3461
Subjects: Law. **Special Collections:** Rare law books. **Holdings:** 9786 books; 678 bound periodical volumes. **Services:** Interlibrary loans; library open to public for reference use only.

★3491★

DALLAS COUNTY LAW LIBRARY (Law)
Government Ctr. Bldg., 2nd Fl.
Dallas, TX 75202
Phone: (214) 749-8481
Zanna L. Moore, Act.Libn.
Founded: 1931. **Staff:** Prof 2. **Subjects:** Law. **Holdings:** 45,000 volumes; 2000 bound periodical volumes; 246 cassette tapes; state reports and Federal Register on microfiche. **Subscriptions:** 200 journals and other serials. **Services:** Copying; library open to public for reference use only. **Staff:** Valerie Rodawalt, Asst.Libn.

★3492★

DALLAS-FORT WORTH MEDICAL CENTER - DR. PHIL R. RUSSELL LIBRARY (Med)†
2709 Hospital Blvd.
Grand Prairie, TX 76010
Phone: (214) 641-5086
Founded: 1964. **Staff:** Prof 2. **Subjects:** Medicine. **Holdings:** 532 books; 380 bound periodical volumes; 75 audiotapes. **Subscriptions:** 33 journals and other serials. **Services:** Library open to public for reference use only. **Formerly:** Grand Prairie Community Hospital.

★3493★

DALLAS HISTORICAL SOCIETY - RESEARCH CENTER (Hist)
Hall of State, Fair Park
Box 26038
Dallas, TX 75226
Phone: (214) 421-5136
John W. Crain, Dir.
Founded: 1922. **Staff:** Prof 3; Other 1. **Subjects:** Dallas, Texas and Southwestern history. **Special Collections:** Sarah Horton Cockrell, Charles E. Arnold and Johnson Photograph Collections, Howard Library Collection; papers of Hatton W. Sumners, Thomas B. Love and Joseph W. Bailey. **Holdings:** 14,000 books and bound periodical volumes; 2 million archival items. **Subscriptions:** 35 journals and other serials. **Services:** Interlibrary loans (fee); copying; library open to public with restrictions. **Publications:** Dallas Rediscovered, DHS Report. **Staff:** Peggy Riddle, Dir., Res.; Casey Greene, Archv.

DALLAS INDEPENDENT SCHOOL DISTRICT - DALLAS SKILLS CENTER
See: Dallas Skills Center

DALLAS MANAGEMENT SERVICES LIBRARY
See: Dallas Budget & Research Library

★3494★
DALLAS MORNING NEWS - REFERENCE DEPARTMENT (Publ)
Communications Center   Phone: (214) 745-8302
Dallas, TX 75265   Judy Metcalf, Ref.Ed.
Founded: 1906. **Staff:** Prof 5; Other 11. **Subjects:** Newspaper reference topics. **Special Collections:** Texana and local Dallas history (600 books devoted to Texas history). **Holdings:** 5000 books; 150,000 pictures; 8 million clippings. **Subscriptions:** 115 newspapers and periodicals. **Services:** SDI; library open to other libraries. **Computerized Information Services:** DIALOG, SDC, New York Times Information Service, Dow Jones News Retrieval; computerized subject and name authority files. **Also Known As:** The Dallas News Reference Library. **Staff:** Judy Sall, Asst.Ref.Ed.; Bonnie Lovell, Text Libn.; Pamela Bonnell, Photo Libn.; Jerome Sims, Night Libn.

★3495★
DALLAS MUSEUM OF FINE ARTS - REFERENCE LIBRARY (Art)†
Fair Park
Box 26250   Phone: (214) 421-4187
Dallas, TX 75226   Donna E. Rhein, Dir.
Founded: 1936. **Staff:** Prof 1. **Subjects:** Art history, painting, sculpture, architecture, Pre-Columbian and primitive art. **Holdings:** 16,500 books; 500 bound periodical volumes; artist files; 20 VF drawers of museum publications. **Subscriptions:** 51 journals and other serials. **Services:** Interlibrary loans; copying; library open to public for reference use only.

★3496★
DALLAS POWER AND LIGHT COMPANY - RESEARCH LIBRARY (Energy; Bus-Fin)
1506 Commerce St., Rm. 1801   Phone: (214) 698-7000
Dallas, TX 75201   Mrs. I. Naraine, Libn.
Founded: 1940. **Staff:** 1. **Subjects:** Public utility regulation, statistics, business, economics, electrical engineering, accounting. **Holdings:** 700 books; 200 bound periodical volumes. **Subscriptions:** 80 journals and other serials. **Services:** Interlibrary loans (limited); copying (limited); library not open to public.

★3497★
DALLAS PUBLIC LIBRARY - BUSINESS AND TECHNOLOGY DIVISION (Bus-Fin)
1515 Young St.   Phone: (214) 749-4100
Dallas, TX 75201   Sarabeth Sullivan, Div.Hd.
Founded: 1955. **Staff:** Prof 11; Other 9. **Subjects:** Business economics, management, energy, foreign trade, construction, transportation, data processing, finance. **Special Collections:** Business History Collection; automobile shop manuals; corporate reports; business and industrial trade directories; standards and specifications. **Holdings:** 106,000 books; 36,000 bound periodical volumes; 13,000 microcards; 300,000 microfiche; 6500 reels of microfilm; 12 VF drawers of pamphlets. **Subscriptions:** 4000 journals and other serials; 20 newspapers. **Services:** Interlibrary loans; copying; telephone reference; library open to public. **Computerized Information Services:** DIALOG, SDC, New York Times Information Service, Dow Jones News Retrieval; computerized cataloging. **Publications:** Business information for Dallas, bimonthly. **Special Catalogs:** Book Catalog of Library's Business History Collection. **Staff:** Carolyn Davis, Asst. to Div.Hd.; Carla LaCroix, Libn.; Lloyd Loving, Libn.; Marian Waite, Libn.; Phyllis Hulse, Libn.; Ellen Derey, Libn.; Loring Palmlund, Libn.; Barbara Kowalski, Libn.; Jimmi Fischer, Libn.; Janelle Dodson, Libn.

★3498★
DALLAS PUBLIC LIBRARY - CUSTOM RESEARCH SERVICE/BIBLIOGRAPHIC CENTER (Info Sci)
1515 Young St.   Phone: (214) 749-4321
Dallas, TX 75201   Wayne Gray, Div.Hd.
Staff: Prof 4; Other 3. **Holdings:** 7900 books; 130 bound periodical volumes; 10,000 microfiche; 75 reels of microfilm. **Subscriptions:** 130 journals and other serials. **Services:** Interlibrary loans; copying; center open to public. **Computerized Information Services:** DIALOG, SDC, New York Times Information Service, Dow Jones News Retrieval; internal database; computerized cataloging and circulation. **Networks/Consortia:** Member of AMIGOS Bibliographic Council, Inc.; Texas State Library Communications Network; Northeast Texas Library System. **Special Indexes:** Central Research Library Periodicals List (loose-leaf book). **Staff:** Marsha Fleckenstein, First Asst.; Jane Mann, Bibliog.Spec.; Ben Rodriguez, Per. Controller.

★3499★
DALLAS PUBLIC LIBRARY - FILM SERVICE (Aud-Vis)
1515 Young St.   Phone: (214) 749-4474
Dallas, TX 75201   Julie Travis, Supv.Mgr.
Founded: 1942. **Staff:** Prof 3; Other 8. **Holdings:** 2500 films. **Subscriptions:** 25 journals and other serials. **Services:** Library open to public, and through Northeast Texas Library System, serves 58 libraries in 33 counties. **Computerized Information Services:** Computerized cataloging. **Special Catalogs:** Book catalog of films. **Staff:** Masha R. Porte, Film Spec.; Victor F. Kralisz, Adm.Mgr.

★3500★
DALLAS PUBLIC LIBRARY - FINE ARTS DIVISION (Art; Mus)
1515 Young St.   Phone: (214) 749-4236
Dallas, TX 75201   Jane Holahan, Div.Hd.
Founded: 1955. **Staff:** Prof 7; Other 9. **Subjects:** Theater, music, painting, sculpture, architecture, prints and printmaking, dance, photography, crafts. **Special Collections:** Margo Jones Theatre; W.E. Hill Theatre; John Rosenfield Collection; Marion Flagg Papers (music educator); Lawrence Kelly Collection of Opera Renderings; Dallas Little Theatre; local theater archives; Interstate Theatre Collection. **Holdings:** 66,257 books; 7725 pieces of sheet music; 35,100 recordings; 475 cassette tapes; 30 video cassettes; 64,000 mounted pictures; 494,000 vertical file items in theater, art and music. **Subscriptions:** 900 journals and other serials. **Services:** Interlibrary loans; copying; library open to public with restrictions. **Computerized Information Services:** Computerized cataloging and circulation. **Remarks:** An alternate telephone number is (214)749-4100. **Staff:** James Calhoun, Music Libn.; Robert Eason, Theater Libn.; William Haddaway, Art Libn.; Donna Mendro, Recordings Libn.; Jon Held, Video Libn.

★3501★
DALLAS PUBLIC LIBRARY - FINE BOOKS DIVISION (Rare Book)
1515 Young St.   Phone: (214) 749-4154
Dallas, TX 75201   Marvin H. Stone, Fine Bks.Libn.
Founded: 1956. **Staff:** Prof 3. **Subjects:** History of printing and the book. **Holdings:** 2500 books. **Services:** Paper preservation laboratory; library open to public.

★3502★
DALLAS PUBLIC LIBRARY - GENEALOGY COLLECTION (Hist)
1515 Young St.   Phone: (214) 749-4129
Dallas, TX 75201   Lloyd DeWitt Bockstruck, Div.Hd.
Staff: Prof 1; Other 8. **Subjects:** Genealogy, heraldry, onomatology, local history. **Holdings:** 17,130 books; 6719 bound periodical volumes; 9973 reels of microfilm; 2125 microcards; 6778 microfiche. **Subscriptions:** 560 journals and other serials. **Services:** Copying; collection open to public.

★3503★
DALLAS PUBLIC LIBRARY - GOVERNMENT PUBLICATIONS DIVISION (Soc Sci)
1515 Young St.   Phone: (214) 749-4176
Dallas, TX 75201   Frank Lee, Div.Hd.
Founded: 1978. **Staff:** Prof 5; Other 6. **Subjects:** Official publications - United States, Texas, international; patents; maps and atlases. **Holdings:** 10,000 books; 6000 bound periodical volumes; 650,000 U.S. government publications; 10,000 Texas state publications; 10,000 international government documents; 3000 reels of microfilm (U.S. patents, 1950 to present); 20,000 maps; 100,000 microfiche; Texas geological publications. **Subscriptions:** 400 journals and other serials. **Services:** Interlibrary loans; copying; library open to public. **Computerized Information Services:** DIALOG, SDC, New York Times Information Service, U.S. Patent Office; internal database; computerized cataloging and circulation. **Networks/Consortia:** Member of AMIGOS Bibliographic Council, Inc.; Northeast Texas Library System. **Staff:** John George, Sr.Doc.Libn.; Marie Hartman, First Asst./U.S.Doc.Libn.; Emily Matteucci, Map Libn.; Johanna Johnson, Patent Libn.

★3504★
DALLAS PUBLIC LIBRARY - HISTORY AND SOCIAL SCIENCES DIVISION (Hist; Soc Sci)
1515 Young St.   Phone: (214) 749-4123
Dallas, TX 75201   Thomas M. Bogie, Div.Hd.
Founded: 1973. **Staff:** Prof 6; Other 4. **Subjects:** History and travel, law, political science, education, psychology, sociology, social welfare, biography, military and naval sciences, public administration. **Special Collections:** College catalogs (600). **Holdings:** 136,340 books; 15,062 bound periodical volumes; 310,000 microfiche; 2454 reels of microfilm; 52 VF drawers of travel material and pamphlets. **Subscriptions:** 1050 journals and other serials. **Services:** Interlibrary loans; copying. **Remarks:** Includes the holdings of the U.S. Office of Education - Region VI - Research Information Center. **Staff:**

Nellie Kendall, Libn.; Paul Oswalt, Libn.; Michael K. Smith, Libn.; Carolyn Starks, Libn.; Heather Williams, First Asst.

★3505★
DALLAS PUBLIC LIBRARY - HUMANITIES DIVISION (Hum)
1515 Young St.　　　　　　　　Phone: (214) 749-4100
Dallas, TX 75201　　　　　　　　Frances Bell, Div.Hd.
Founded: 1979. **Staff:** Prof 8; Other 6. **Subjects:** Literary criticism, children's literature, language, fiction, drama, journalism, poetry, library science, essays, philosophy, religion. **Special Collections:** Children's literature (47,000 volumes). **Holdings:** 203,000 books; 12,700 bound periodical volumes. **Subscriptions:** 700 journals and other serials. **Services:** Interlibrary loans; copying. **Special Indexes:** Play index which provides author-title analytics for anthologies not included in standard indexes (card). **Staff:** Ronald Boyd, First Asst.; Muriel Brown, Children's Lit.Spec.; Rita Foudray, Libn.; Stephen Housewright, Libn.; Marie Musick, Asst.Ch.Lit.Spec.; Jeanne Schorr, Libn.; Robert Slaymaker, Prof.Asst.

★3506★
DALLAS PUBLIC LIBRARY - TEXAS/DALLAS HISTORY AND ARCHIVES DIVISION (Hist)
1515 Young St.　　　　　　　　Phone: (214) 749-4151
Dallas, TX 75201　　　　　　　　Katherine P. Jagoe, Div.Hd.
Founded: 1979. **Staff:** Prof 6; Other 5. **Subjects:** Dallas and Texas history, literature by Texas and Dallas authors. **Special Collections:** Margo Jones Collection (75 cubic feet); Mayor Wes Wise City Council Files (12 cubic feet); Juanita Craft Collection (42 cubic feet; 21 boxes); Dallas American Revolution Bicentennial Corporation (17 cubic feet); Interstate Theatre Collection (300 cubic feet); Texas Pacific Land Trust (261 volumes; 18 cubic feet; 21 boxes). **Holdings:** 35,020 books and bound periodical volumes; 27 cabinets of news clippings; 10,833 microforms; 230 oral history interviews; 108 cubic feet of local history archives; 150,000 historic photgraphs. **Subscriptions:** 251 journals and other serials; 30 newspapers. **Services:** Copying; photograph copying; library open to public with restrictions. **Computerized Information Services:** Internal database; computerized cataloging, serials and circulation. **Networks/Consortia:** Member of AMIGOS Bibliographic Council, Inc; Northeast Texas Library System. **Staff:** Gary Jennings, First Asst.; Lucile Boykin, Local Hist.Spec.; Marcelle Hull, Archival Libn.; Gerald Saxon, Oral Hist.Libn.

★3507★
DALLAS PUBLIC LIBRARY - URBAN INFORMATION CENTER (Plan)
1515 Young St.　　　　　　　　Phone: (214) 749-4170
Dallas, TX 75201　　　　　　　　Mary Tod, Mgr.
Staff: Prof 5; Other 2. **Subjects:** City service management and administration, public administration, grants, urban planning, transportation, citizen participation and awareness. **Special Collections:** Foundation Center Collection; City of Dallas documents. **Holdings:** 7058 books; 846 bound periodical volumes; 922 Rand reports; 10,000 microfiche; 4 video cassettes. **Subscriptions:** 136 journals and other serials. **Services:** Interlibrary loans; copying; center open to public. **Computerized Information Services:** DIALOG, New York Times Information Service. **Publications:** Urban Information Review; Open Dallas. **Special Catalogs:** APL/CAT (A Public Library Community Access Tool; cards on 3000 local community organizations). **Staff:** Connie Brouillette, Libn.; Lisa Faulkner, Grants Libn.; Karen Fagg, Lib.Assoc.; David Darnell, Libn.

★3508★
DALLAS SKILLS CENTER - LEARNING LAB (Educ)†
1403 Corinth
Dallas, TX 75215　　　　　　　Cynthia A. Teter, Lrng.Ctr.Instr.
Founded: 1973. **Staff:** Prof 1. **Subjects:** Math, job development skills, English, social studies, science, literature. **Holdings:** 800 books; 250 bound periodical volumes; 100 sound filmstrip sets; 175 cassette and worksheet lessons; 60 film loops. **Subscriptions:** 13 journals and other serials. **Services:** Library not open to public. **Remarks:** The Skills Center is maintained by the Dallas Independent School District.

DALLAS THEATER CENTER LIBRARY
See: Trinity University

★3509★
DALLAS THEOLOGICAL SEMINARY - MOSHER LIBRARY (Rel-Theol)
3909 Swiss Ave.　　　　　　　　Phone: (214) 824-3094
Dallas, TX 75204　　　　　　　　Dr. John A. Witmer, Dir.
Founded: 1924. **Staff:** Prof 5; Other 12. **Subjects:** Theology, Bible, Biblical languages, Christian literature, church history, world missions, Christian education, practical theology; devotional literature. **Special Collections:** Biblical Languages Research Library. **Holdings:** 100,000 books and bound

periodical volumes; 2500 tapes and cassettes; 10,000 microforms. **Subscriptions:** 800 journals and other serials. **Services:** Interlibrary loans; copying; library open to public with annual fee required for checking out books. **Publications:** Mosher Periodical Index, monthly - by subscription; Recent Accessions List, bimonthly - free; List of Theses and Dissertations, annual - free. **Staff:** John Beverage, Pub.Serv.Libn.; Stephen Harthan, Tech.Serv.Libn.; Marvin Hunn, Ref.Libn.; Timothy Hui, Ser.Libn.

★3510★
DALLAS TIMES-HERALD - LIBRARY (Publ)
1101 Pacific St.
Box 5445　　　　　　　　　　Phone: (214) 744-6240
Dallas, TX 75202　　　　　　　Elaine B. Walden, Libn.
Founded: 1973. **Staff:** Prof 3; Other 3. **Subjects:** Newspaper reference topics. **Holdings:** 882 books; newspaper on microfilm from 1886 to present. **Subscriptions:** 12 newspapers. **Services:** Copying; library not open to public. **Computerized Information Services:** New York Times Information Service.

DALMO VICTOR OPERATIONS
See: Textron, Inc. - Bell Aerospace Textron

★3511★
DALY (Leo A.) COMPANY - YEE DIVISION - LIBRARY (Sci-Tech)
1441 Kapiolani Blvd., Suite 810　　Phone: (808) 946-3161
Honolulu, HI 96814　　　　　　Ann L. Marsteller, Libn.
Staff: Prof 1. **Subjects:** Structural engineering, precast and prestressed concrete, architecture. **Holdings:** 2000 books; 33 bound periodical volumes; 46 VF drawers of clippings, archives, photographs and manufacturers' literature; slides; maps. **Subscriptions:** 75 journals and other serials; 6 newspapers. **Services:** Library not open to public; reference services for librarians and qualified researchers. **Computerized Information Services:** DIALOG. **Formerly:** Yee (Alfred A.) & Associates Inc.

★3512★
DAMES & MOORE - CHICAGO LIBRARY (Sci-Tech)
1550 Northwest Highway
Park Ridge, IL 60068　　　　　Phone: (312) 297-6120
　　　　　　　　　　　　　Patricia Krzysiak, Libn.
Founded: 1975. **Staff:** Prof 1. **Subjects:** Geotechnical, aquatic, soil and atmospheric engineering, environmental science. **Special Collections:** House reports on nuclear power plants, environmental reports, preliminary and final safety analysis reports (PSAR and FSAR); State File (selected state documents with emphasis on midwest states). **Holdings:** 2000 books and reports; 20 VF drawers of topographical maps. **Subscriptions:** 84 journals and other serials. **Services:** Interlibrary loans; copying; library open to public by appointment. **Computerized Information Services:** DIALOG, SDC. **Networks/Consortia:** Member of North Suburban Library System; ILLINET.

★3513★
DAMES & MOORE - ENGINEERING LIBRARY (Sci-Tech)†
1626 Cole Blvd.　　　　　　　Phone: (303) 232-6262
Golden, CO 80401　　　　　　Ellie Reiter, Libn.
Founded: 1975. **Staff:** Prof 1; Other 1. **Subjects:** Mining engineering, rock mechanics, geology, water resources (technical information), air quality, environment including Rocky Mountains. **Special Collections:** U.S. Geological Survey Geologic Atlas of the United States, 1894. **Holdings:** 3500 books; 20 VF drawers of unbound reports and clippings; 100 VF drawers of internal reports; 350 topographic and geological maps. **Subscriptions:** 105 journals and other serials. **Services:** Interlibrary loans; copying; library open to public by request. **Computerized Information Services:** DIALOG, SDC.

★3514★
DAMES & MOORE - LIBRARY (Sci-Tech)
1100 Glendon Ave., Suite 1000
Los Angeles, CA 90024　　　　Phone: (213) 879-9700
　　　　　　　　　　　　　Alice Ohst, Libn.
Founded: 1966. **Staff:** Prof 1; Other 1. **Subjects:** Soil mechanics and foundation engineering, oceanography, geology. **Holdings:** 7000 books; 500 pamphlets; 34 VF drawers of pamphlets (uncataloged); 10,000 maps. **Subscriptions:** 200 journals and other serials. **Services:** Interlibrary loans; copying; SDI; library not open to public. **Computerized Information Services:** DIALOG, SDC, NIH-EPA Chemical Information System.

★3515★
DAMES & MOORE - LIBRARY (Sci-Tech)
445 East Paces Ferry Rd., N.E., Suite 200
Atlanta, GA 30363　　　　　　Phone: (404) 262-2915
　　　　　　　　　　　　　Becky Kear, Libn.
Founded: 1974. **Staff:** Prof 1. **Subjects:** Civil engineering, nuclear power plants, meteorology, geology, water resources, biology, environment, pollution. **Holdings:** 3000 books; 150 environmental reports; 4 VF drawers of technical material; 1500 maps. **Subscriptions:** 53 journals and other serials.

Services: Interlibrary loans; library open to public with restrictions. **Computerized Information Services:** DIALOG. **Publications:** New Book List, monthly - for internal distribution only. **Special Catalogs:** Dames & Moore book catalog, quarterly on microfiche - distributed to D & M Libraries.

★3516★
DAMES & MOORE - LIBRARY (Sci-Tech)
7101 Wisconsin Ave., Suite 700
Bethesda, MD 20814
Founded: 1975. **Staff:** Prof 1. **Subjects:** Geology, civil engineering, meteorology, environmental science. **Holdings:** 1300 books; 500 geological survey bulletins and reports. **Subscriptions:** 100 journals and other serials. **Services:** Library not open to public.

★3517★
DAMES & MOORE - LIBRARY
6 Commerce Dr.
Cranford, NJ 07016
Founded: 1974. **Subjects:** Geology, soils and soil mechanics. **Holdings:** 2000 books. **Remarks:** Presently inactive.

★3518★
DAMES & MOORE - LIBRARY AND INFORMATION CENTER (Sci-Tech)
4321 Directors Row, Suite 200   Phone: (713) 688-4541
Houston, TX 77092
Founded: 1973. **Subjects:** Civil engineering, geology, seismology, meteorology, hydrology, oceanography, biology, demography. **Holdings:** 1248 books; 1163 pamphlets; 1939 maps; 693 microfiche. **Subscriptions:** 100 journals and other serials. **Services:** Interlibrary loans; copying; library open to public by request.

★3519★
DAMES & MOORE - SEATTLE OFFICE LIBRARY (Sci-Tech)
155 N.E. 100th St., Suite 500   Phone: (206) 523-0560
Seattle, WA 98125   Ruth L. Van Dyke, Libn.
Staff: Prof 1. **Subjects:** Aquatic biology, socioeconomics, geology, civil engineering, hydrology, meteorology. **Holdings:** 2500 books; 500 technical reports. **Subscriptions:** 75 journals and other serials. **Services:** Interlibrary loans; SDI; library open to public with restrictions and for reference use only. **Computerized Information Services:** DIALOG; internal database. **Networks/Consortia:** Member of Washington Library Network (WLN). **Publications:** Info, monthly - for internal distribution only.

★3520★
DAMIEN DUTTON SOCIETY FOR LEPROSY AID, INC. - LIBRARY (Med)
616 Bedford Ave.   Phone: (516) 221-5829
Bellmore, NY 11710   Howard E. Crouch, Pres.
Subjects: Leprosy and leprosy research. **Holdings:** 250 books; 500 bound periodical volumes.

★3521★
DAN RIVER, INC. - RESEARCH LIBRARY (Sci-Tech)
                                       Phone: (804) 799-7103
Danville, VA 24541   W.K. Adams, Asst. to Res.Dir.
Subjects: Textiles, organic chemistry. **Holdings:** 1000 books; 300 bound periodical volumes. **Subscriptions:** 50 journals and other serials. **Services:** Library open to public by appointment.

DANA BIOMEDICAL LIBRARY
See: Dartmouth College

DANA (Charles A.) LAW LIBRARY
See: Stetson University - College of Law - Charles A. Dana Law Library

DANA (Charles A.) MEDICAL LIBRARY
See: University of Vermont - Division of Health Sciences - Charles A. Dana Medical Library

★3522★
DANA COLLEGE - C.A. DANA-LIFE LIBRARY (Area-Ethnic; Hum)
College Dr.   Phone: (402) 426-4101
Blair, NE 68008   Ronald D. Johnson, Lib.Dir.
Founded: 1884. **Staff:** Prof 2; Other 4. **Subjects:** Danish literature and language; history, humanities. **Special Collections:** Lauritz Melchior Memorial (records, scores, tapes, scrapbooks, artifacts, paintings). **Holdings:** 113,331 books; microfilm; records; pamphlets. **Subscriptions:** 522 journals and other serials; 8 newspapers. **Services:** Interlibrary loans; copying; library not open to public. **Computerized Information Services:** Computerized cataloging. **Networks/Consortia:** Member of OCLC. **Remarks:** Library is said to be one

of the best collections of Danish literature in translation and in the original language in the U.S. **Staff:** Ruth Rasmussen, Libn.

★3523★
DANA CORPORATION - WEATHERHEAD DIVISION - LIBRARY AND TECHNICAL INFORMATION CENTER (Sci-Tech)†
767 Beta Dr.   Phone: (216) 449-6500
Cleveland, OH 44143   Dorothy Schaberl, Libn.
Founded: 1956. **Staff:** 1. **Subjects:** Engineering - chemical, metallurgical, automotive; aircraft; hydraulics. **Holdings:** 500 books; technical files; Society of Automotive Engineers (SAE) papers. **Subscriptions:** 28 journals and other serials. **Services:** Interlibrary loans; copying; library not open to public.

DANA (John Cotton) LIBRARY
See: Woodstock Historical Society, Inc. - John Cotton Dana Library

DANA RESEARCH CENTER
See: Northeastern University

DANA SCIENCE & ENGINEERING LIBRARY
See: University of Hartford

★3524★
DANBURY HOSPITAL - HEALTH SCIENCES LIBRARY (Med)†
24 Hospital Ave.   Phone: (203) 797-7279
Danbury, CT 06810   Maryanne Witters, Dir.
Staff: Prof 1; Other 3. **Subjects:** Medicine, nursing, hospitals, allied health sciences. **Holdings:** 3720 books; 5060 bound periodical volumes; 781 AV items; 2 VF drawers of reports; 40 cases of pamphlets; 12 VF drawers of clippings. **Subscriptions:** 432 journals and other serials. **Services:** Interlibrary loans; copying; SDI; library open to public for reference use only. **Computerized Information Services:** MEDLINE. **Networks/Consortia:** Member of Northwestern Connecticut Health Science Library Consortium.

★3525★
DANBURY SCOTT-FANTON MUSEUM AND HISTORICAL SOCIETY - LIBRARY (Hist)
45 Main St.   Phone: (203) 743-5200
Danbury, CT 06810   Julie B. Barrows, Dir.
Subjects: Town and state history, genealogy, hat industry and other local industries. **Holdings:** 800 books; 50 bound periodical volumes; manuscripts, diaries, deeds and maps; negatives and prints of local scenes from 1875. **Services:** Library open to public with restrictions.

★3526★
DANCE FILMS ASSOCIATION, INC. (Aud-Vis)
241 E. 34th St., Rm. 301   Phone: (212) 686-7019
New York, NY 10016   Susan Braun, Pres.
Founded: 1956. **Subjects:** Dance on film. **Holdings:** Slides and films on dance. **Services:** Film projection and production services; film rental library for members - members may also order most films not in the library; annual dance film and video festival in New York City. **Publications:** News bulletin, monthly - to members; catalogs of films and videotapes on dance and mime (1980 edition available). **Remarks:** Organization is nonprofit and tax-exempt.

★3527★
DANCER FITZGERALD SAMPLE, INC. - INFORMATION CENTER (Bus-Fin)†
405 Lexington Ave.   Phone: (212) 661-0800
New York, NY 10174   Carolyn Gutierrez, Libn.
Founded: 1945. **Staff:** Prof 1. **Subjects:** Advertising, marketing. **Holdings:** 750 books. **Subscriptions:** 160 journals and other serials. **Services:** Interlibrary loans; library open to SLA members and to the public by appointment.

★3528★
DANE COUNTY LAW LIBRARY (Law)
230 City-County Bldg.
210 Monona Ave.   Phone: (608) 266-4230
Madison, WI 53709   Lorraine Breszee, Libn.
Founded: 1957. **Staff:** 1. **Subjects:** Law. **Holdings:** 8000 volumes. **Services:** Copying; library not open to public.

★3529★
DANE COUNTY REGIONAL PLANNING COMMISSION - LIBRARY (Plan)
City-County Bldg., Rm. 114   Phone: (608) 266-4137
Madison, WI 53709   Pamela Czapla, Libn.
Founded: 1964. **Staff:** 1. **Subjects:** Transportation, land use and development, census and population, water resources. **Holdings:** 3900 government reports; 3000 maps. **Subscriptions:** 14 journals and other

serials; 110 newsletters. **Services:** Interlibrary loans; library open to public.

DANIEL (Allen Mercer) LAW LIBRARY
See: Howard University - School of Law - Allen Mercer Daniel Law Library

★3530★
DANIEL FREEMAN HOSPITAL - VICTOR J. WACHA MEDICAL LIBRARY (Med)
333 N. Prairie Ave.   Phone: (213) 674-7050
Inglewood, CA 90301   Gillian Olechno, Dir.
Staff: Prof 1; Other 2. **Subjects:** Medicine, nursing. **Holdings:** 672 books; 3445 bound periodical volumes; 998 cassette tapes; 18 audiovisual cassettes. **Subscriptions:** 225 journals and other serials. **Services:** Interlibrary loans; copying; SDI; library open to public with permission. **Computerized Information Services:** DIALOG, SDC, MEDLARS. **Publications:** Medical Library Bulletin, irregular - for internal distribution only.

DANIEL LIBRARY
See: Citadel - The Military College of South Carolina

★3531★
DANIEL, MANN, JOHNSON AND MENDENHALL - LIBRARY (Plan)
3250 Wilshire Blvd.   Phone: (213) 381-3663
Los Angeles, CA 90010   Marlene Barkley, Corp.Libn.
Staff: Prof 1; Other 2. **Subjects:** Area statistics and information, transportation, architecture, planning, recreation, environment, water resources, engineering - civil, structural and mechanical. **Holdings:** 7500 books; 135 bound periodical volumes; 340 Transportation Research Board reports; 800 maps; 135 microfiche; 10,000 35mm slides. **Subscriptions:** 250 journals and other serials. **Services:** Interlibrary loans; copying; library open to public for reference use only by appointment. **Computerized Information Services:** Computerized circulation. **Publications:** What's New in the DMJM Library, monthly.

★3532★
DANIEL WEBSTER COLLEGE - LIBRARY (Sci-Tech; Bus-Fin)
University Dr.   Phone: (603) 883-3556
Nashua, NH 03063   Patience K. Jackson, Lib.Dir.
Founded: 1966. **Staff:** Prof 2; Other 4. **Subjects:** Aeronautics, business administration, computers. **Special Collections:** Aeronautics, aviation history, computer systems. **Holdings:** 18,000 books. **Subscriptions:** 300 journals and other serials; 10 newspapers. **Services:** Interlibrary loans; copying; library open to public. **Networks/Consortia:** Member of New Hampshire College and University Council; Nashua Area Materials Exchange (NAME). **Staff:** Doris G. Webb, Ref./ILL.

★3533★
DANISH BAPTIST GENERAL CONFERENCE OF AMERICA - ARCHIVES (Rel-Theol)
American Baptist Historical Society
1106 S. Goodman St.
Rochester, NY 14620   Phone: (716) 473-1740
                                             William H. Brackney, Exec.Dir.
Founded: 1910. **Staff:** Prof 2; Other 3. **Subjects:** Denominational history and records. **Holdings:** Annual reports; local church records; manuscripts; newspapers; hymn books; tracts; devotional books; photographs. **Remarks:** Archives have been in the care of the American Baptist Historical Society since 1958 when the Danish General Conference consolidated with the American Baptist Churches U.S.A.

DANISH CONSULATE GENERAL
See: Consulate General of Denmark

DANNER (E.H.) LIBRARY OF TELEPHONY
See: General Telephone Company of the Southwest - E.H. Danner Library of Telephony

DANVERS ARCHIVAL CENTER
See: Peabody Institute Library

★3534★
DANVERS STATE HOSPITAL - MAC DONALD MEDICAL LIBRARY
Box 50
Hathorne, MA 01937
Defunct. Holdings absorbed by Hogan (Charles V.) Regional Center - Staff Library.

★3535★
DANVILLE STATE HOSPITAL - MEDICAL LIBRARY (Med)†
                                             Phone: (717) 275-7011
Danville, PA 17821
Staff: 1. **Subjects:** Psychiatry, psychiatric nursing, psychotherapy. **Holdings:** 700 books. **Subscriptions:** 110 journals and other serials. **Services:** Interlibrary loans; library open to public with permission of hospital superintendent.

DARCO EXPERIMENTAL LABORATORY LIBRARY
See: ICI Americas Inc.

★3536★
D'ARCY-MAC MANUS AND MASIUS - LIBRARY (Bus-Fin)†
One S. Memorial Dr.   Phone: (314) 342-8818
St. Louis, MO 63102   Jean Kammer, Libn.
Staff: Prof 1; Other 5. **Subjects:** Advertising. **Holdings:** 750 volumes; 375 VF drawers of pamphlets and clippings. **Subscriptions:** 750 journals and other serials. **Services:** Copying.

★3537★
D'ARCY-MAC MANUS AND MASIUS - LIBRARY
360 Madison Ave.
New York, NY 10017
Defunct

★3538★
D'ARCY-MAC MANUS AND MASIUS - LIBRARY INFORMATION SERVICES (Bus-Fin)
Long Lake at Woodward   Phone: (313) 646-1000
Bloomfield Hills, MI 48013   Lois W. Collet, Mgr.
Founded: 1952. **Staff:** Prof 3; Other 2. **Subjects:** Marketing, advertising, automotive history. **Holdings:** 3000 books; 400 bound periodical volumes; 170,000 VF items; corporation files; 50,000 pictures; 2500 government documents. **Subscriptions:** 1200 journals and other serials; 20 newspapers. **Services:** Interlibrary loans; copying; library open to public by appointment. **Computerized Information Services:** DIALOG, New York Times Information Service; computerized circulation. **Publications:** Hi, Look Us Over, monthly - for internal distribution only. **Staff:** Wallace Szumni, Ref.; Harriet Siden, Art Libn.

DARDEN (Colgate) GRADUATE SCHOOL OF BUSINESS ADMINISTRATION
See: University of Virginia - Colgate Darden Graduate School of Business Administration

★3539★
DARGAN-CARVER LIBRARY (Rel-Theol)
127 Ninth Ave., N.   Phone: (615) 251-2133
Nashville, TN 37234   Lynn E. May, Joint Lib.Dir.
Founded: 1951. **Staff:** Prof 4; Other 6. **Subjects:** Baptist history, Baptist biography, bibliography, hymnology. **Special Collections:** Southern Baptist archives; Baptist associational minutes; Baptist Sunday School Board archives. **Holdings:** 55,000 books; 8725 bound periodical volumes; 10,885 pamphlets (cataloged); 818 feet of Convention Archives; 10,336 reels of microfilm; Baptist reference file (65,847 3x5 cards). **Subscriptions:** 414 journals and other serials. **Services:** Interlibrary loans; copying; library open to public for reference use only. **Networks/Consortia:** Member of Baptist Information and Retrieval System (BIRS). **Publications:** Baptist History and Heritage. **Remarks:** Dargan-Carver Library is a joint project of the Southern Baptist Historical Commission and the Baptist Sunday School Board. **Staff:** Howard Gallimore, Supv.; Ramona Denton, Rsrcs.Libn.; Yolanda Canas, Cat.Libn.

DARLING (Ira C.) CENTER LIBRARY
See: University of Maine, Orono - Ira C. Darling Center Library

DARLING (Roger) MEMORIAL LIBRARY
See: Ashland Theological Seminary - Roger Darling Memorial Library

DARLING (Samuel Taylor) MEMORIAL LIBRARY
See: Gorgas Army Hospital - Samuel Taylor Darling Memorial Library

★3540★
DARLINGTON COUNTY HISTORICAL COMMISSION - DARLINGTON COUNTY ARCHIVES (Hist)*
Court House, Rm. 307
Darlington, SC 29532   Horace Fraser Rudisill, Hist.
Staff: 1. **Subjects:** Local history and genealogy. **Holdings:** Books, documents, pamphlets and journals. **Services:** Copying; library open to public. **Special Indexes:** Index to church and land record groups (card and notebook).

DARLINGTON MEMORIAL LIBRARY
See: University of Pittsburgh

DARLINGTON TECHNICAL COLLEGE
See: Florence-Darlington Technical College

DARNALL ARMY HOSPITAL
See: U.S. Army Hospitals

★3541★
DARTMOUTH COLLEGE - DANA BIOMEDICAL LIBRARY (Med)
Dartmouth-Hitchcock Medical Center   Phone: (603) 646-2858
Hanover, NH 03756   Shirley J. Grainger, Libn.
Founded: 1797. Staff: Prof 6; Other 10. Subjects: Medicine, life sciences, nursing, agriculture. Special Collections: Conner Collection of Rare Medical Classics; Raymond Pearl Longevity Collection; Henry A. Schroeder papers (11,281 items); Henry Kumm Index on Poliomyelitis and tropical medicine; Dartmouth Medical School Eye Institute Reprint File. Holdings: 135,000 books and bound periodical volumes; Dartmouth Medical School faculty reprints; 15,000 AV items; microforms; subject pamphlets; dissertations. Subscriptions: 2600 journals and other serials. Services: Interlibrary loans; copying; SDI; library open to public for reference use only. Computerized Information Services: MEDLINE, DIALOG, New York Times Information Service, SDC, BRS; computerized cataloging, acquisitions and serials. Networks/Consortia: Member of National Library of Medicine; OCLC through NELINET; RLG. Publications: Dana Nurse Interface, A Guide to Dana Biomedical Library; Community Health Collection (pamphlet/poster). Special Catalogs: Computerized serials list; automated AV catalog.

★3542★
DARTMOUTH COLLEGE - FELDBERG LIBRARY (Bus-Fin; Sci-Tech)
                                       Phone: (603) 646-2191
Hanover, NH 03755   Margaret M. Link, Libn.
Founded: 1972. Staff: Prof 3; Other 5. Subjects: Business administration and management; engineering - biomedical, electrical, environmental/natural resource systems analysis and policy design, mechanical; cold regions science and engineering; computer applications and information systems. Special Collections: Thayer Collection (books in mathematics, civil engineering and military engineering donated by General Thayer; 1565 volumes). Holdings: 74,853 books and bound periodical volumes; 6546 reels of microfilm; 311,205 microfiche. Subscriptions: 2574 journals and other serials; 21 newspapers. Services: Interlibrary loans; copying; library open to public. Computerized Information Services: DIALOG, SDC, BRS, DOE/RECON; computerized cataloging, acquisitions and serials. Networks/Consortia: Member of OCLC through NELINET; RLG.

★3543★
DARTMOUTH COLLEGE - KRESGE PHYSICAL SCIENCES LIBRARY (Sci-Tech)
                                       Phone: (603) 646-3564
Hanover, NH 03755   Monique C. Cleland, Libn.
Founded: 1974. Staff: Prof 3; Other 3. Subjects: Chemistry, earth sciences, physics, astronomy, climatology. Holdings: 80,000 volumes. Subscriptions: 1349 journals and other serials. Services: Interlibrary loans (fee); copying; library open to public. Computerized Information Services: DIALOG, BRS; computerized cataloging, acquisitions and serials. Networks/Consortia: Member of OCLC through NELINET; RLG.

★3544★
DARTMOUTH COLLEGE - MAP SECTION (Geog-Map)
Baker Library   Phone: (603) 646-2579
Hanover, NH 03755   John F. Berthelsen, Spec. Subject Asst.
Founded: 1946. Staff: 1. Subjects: Topography, geology, oceanography, local history, historical cartography, New England. Special Collections: New Hampshire; polar regions; Soviet Russia. Holdings: 107,000 maps; 3600 reference books and atlases; 23 globes; 560 relief models; 285 aerial photographs; 300 rolled wall maps. Subscriptions: 15 journals and other serials. Services: Interlibrary loans; copying; library open to public. Computerized Information Services: DIALOG, BRS; computerized cataloging, acquisitions and serials. Networks/Consortia: Member of OCLC through NELINET; RLG. Publications: A Guide to the Map Room; List of Known Maps of New Hampshire to 1800. Remarks: This library serves as a Map Depository for the Defense Mapping Agency, the U.S. Geological Survey, the Canadian Department of Energy, Mines and Resources and U.S. Government publications.

★3545★
DARTMOUTH COLLEGE - PADDOCK MUSIC LIBRARY (Mus)
                                       Phone: (603) 646-3234
Hanover, NH 03755   Patricia B. Fisken, Asst.Libn.
Founded: 1975. Staff: 2. Subjects: Music. Holdings: 3000 books; 350 bound periodical volumes; 12,300 musical scores; 11,300 phonograph records; 500 cassette tapes. Subscriptions: 34 journals and other serials. Services: Library open to public for reference use only. Computerized Information Services: DIALOG, BRS; computerized cataloging, acquisitions and serials. Networks/Consortia: Member of RLG; OCLC through NELINET. Special Indexes: Computer-produced index to recordings.

★3546★
DARTMOUTH COLLEGE - SANBORN HOUSE ENGLISH LIBRARY (Hum)
                                       Phone: (603) 646-2312
Hanover, NH 03755   Charlotte S. McCanna, Branch Lib.Adm.Asst.
Founded: 1929. Subjects: English and American literature. Special Collections: Shakespeare collection; spoken word phonograph record collection; works by English-American poets published since 1912 (1500 volumes). Holdings: 7016 books; 325 sound recordings; 260 cassettes. Subscriptions: 23 journals and other serials. Computerized Information Services: DIALOG, BRS; computerized cataloging, acquisitions and serials. Networks/Consortia: Member of OCLC through NELINET; RLG.

★3547★
DARTMOUTH COLLEGE - SHERMAN ART LIBRARY (Art)
Carpenter Hall   Phone: (603) 646-2305
Hanover, NH 03755   Jeffrey L. Horrell, Libn.
Staff: Prof 1; Other 3. Subjects: Art, architecture and photography. Holdings: 52,839 books and bound periodical volumes; 24 VF drawers of pamphlets. Subscriptions: 370 journals and other serials. Services: Interlibrary loans; library open to public with restrictions. Computerized Information Services: DIALOG, BRS; computerized cataloging, acquisitions and serials. Networks/Consortia: Member of OCLC through NELINET; RLG.

★3548★
DARTMOUTH COLLEGE - SPECIAL COLLECTIONS
Dartmouth College Library   Phone: (603) 646-2571
Hanover, NH 03755   Stanley W. Brown, Cur., Rare Books
Staff: Prof 3; Other 7. Subjects: American calligraphy; bookplates; broadsides; Dartmouth Archives and local history; Abenaki Indians; Don Quixote; American, English, French and German plays; George Ticknor; Great Awakening; Hanover genealogy; movie scripts; New England illustrated books, 1769-1869; New England railroads; New Hampshire history and imprints; Polar regions, including manuscripts and memoirs of explorers; private presses; sheet music; Spanish civilization and plays; theater (primarily American); White Mountains. Special Collections: Vilhjalmur Stefansson correspondence and papers; principal collection of works by and about authors and statesmen - Sherman Adams, Josiah Bartlett, Robert P. Bass, Rupert Brooke, Robert Burns, Witter Bynner, Erskine Caldwell, Salmon P. Chase, Rufus Choate, Winston Churchill (American novelist), Grenville Clark, Joseph Conrad, Stephen Crane, Silas Dinsmore, Richard Eberhart, Corey Ford, Robert Frost, John Galsworthy, Robert Bontine Cunninghame Graham, Ramon Guthrie, John P. Hale, James G. Huneker, Aldous Huxley, J.J. Lankes, T.E. Lawrence, E.V. Lucas, Benton, Percy, and Steele MacKaye, David McClure, Herman Melville, H.L. Mencken, Henry Miller, Eugene O'Neill, Kenneth Roberts, Count Rumford, Rudolph Ruzicka, Augustus Saint Gaudens, William Shakespeare, Wallace Stevens, Genevieve Taggard, Isaiah Thomas, Charles W. Tobey, Daniel Webster, Eleazar Wheelock, Weeks family of Lancaster, NH; Nathaniel Whitaker, Ben Ames Williams, Levi Woodbury, Charles A. Young. Services: Copying; collections open to public. Publications: Dartmouth College Library Bulletin, semiannual - on request to libraries; guides and microform publications relating to resources. Staff: Kenneth C. Cramer, College Archv.; Philip N. Cronenwett, Cur. of Mss.

DARTMOUTH-HITCHCOCK MEDICAL CENTER
See: Dartmouth College - Dana Biomedical Library

★3549★
DARTNELL CORPORATION - PUBLISHING-RESEARCH LIBRARY (Publ)
4660 N. Ravenswood Ave.   Phone: (312) 561-4000
Chicago, IL 60640   Juanita Roberts, Libn.
Founded: 1963. Staff: Prof 1. Subjects: Publishing, salesmanship, sales management. Holdings: 2400 volumes. Subscriptions: 240 journals and other serials; 11 newspapers. Services: Interlibrary loans; copying; library open to public on request.

DATA CENTER ON ATOMIC TRANSITION PROBABILITIES
See: U.S. Natl. Bureau of Standards

★3550★
DATA CENTER - INVESTIGATIVE RESOURCE CENTER (Soc Sci)
464 19th St.   Phone: (415) 835-4692
Oakland, CA 94612   Fred Goff, Pres.
Founded: 1977. **Staff:** Prof 2; Other 9. **Subjects:** Corporations, labor,
international trade, industry, military, intelligence, Latin America. **Special
Collections:** The New Right (2 boxes); plant closures (4 boxes); toxics in the
environment (3 boxes). **Holdings:** 5000 books; 28 VF drawers of files on
5000 corporations; 100 corporate profiles; 70,000 articles on Latin America;
600 boxes of alternative publications from the 1960s and 1970s.
Subscriptions: 435 journals and other serials; 15 newspapers. **Services:**
Copying; center open to public with restrictions. **Publications:** ISLA
(Information Services on Latin America), monthly; Data Center Press Profiles;
Data Center Corporate Profiles. **Staff:** Zoia Horn, Libn.

★3551★
DATA GENERAL CORPORATION - CORPORATE LIBRARY (Sci-Tech)
4400 Computer Dr., M.S. C-236   Phone: (617) 366-8911
Westborough, MA 01581   Roberta Ferguson, Sr.Res.Libn.
Founded: 1977. **Staff:** Prof 1; Other 2. **Subjects:** Computer science,
engineering, mathematics, business. **Holdings:** 1100 books. **Subscriptions:**
150 journals and other serials; 10 newspapers. **Services:** Interlibrary loans;
library not open to public. **Computerized Information Services:** DIALOG.
Networks/Consortia: Member of OCLC through NELINET. **Publications:**
Monthly Newsletter.

★3552★
DATA SYSTEMS ANALYSTS - TECHNICAL LIBRARY (Info Sci)
North Park Dr. & Airport Hwy.   Phone: (609) 665-6088
Pennsauken, NJ 08109   Elizabeth Colabrese, Libn.
Staff: Prof 1. **Subjects:** Data processing, data communications, computer
programming, computer networks. **Holdings:** 2550 books; 900 bound
periodical volumes; 30 VF drawers of computer manuals; 54 VF drawers of
reports. **Subscriptions:** 115 journals and other serials. **Services:** Interlibrary
loans; library not open to public.

★3553★
DATA USE AND ACCESS LABORATORIES (DUALABS) - LIBRARY (Soc Sci)
1515 Wilson Blvd., Suite 607   Phone: (703) 525-1480
Arlington, VA 22209   Deborah S. Pomerance, Libn.
Founded: 1972. **Staff:** Prof 1. **Subjects:** Census, demography, social science
data use, information science. **Special Collections:** Full range of 1960-1980
Census of Population and Housing Summary and Public Use Sample computer
tapes and related printed report series; special extracts and reaggregations of
census data (3000 tape files); National Crime Survey tapes; Current
Population Survey tapes; Emergency Housing Allowance Program tapes.
Holdings: Figures not available. **Subscriptions:** 40 journals; 40 newsletters.
Services: Interlibrary loans; copying; cost estimates for retrieval of federal,
publicly available data from tapes; library open to public. **Publications:** Review
of Public Data Use, bimonthly - available by subscription. **Also Known As:**
DUALabs.

★3554★
DATACROWN, INC. - LIBRARY SERVICES (Bus-Fin)
650 McNicoll Ave.   Phone: (416) 497-1012
Willowdale, ON, Canada M2H 2E1   Lucille Slack, Mgr., Lib.Serv.
Founded: 1977. **Staff:** Prof 1; Other 3. **Subjects:** Computer science,
management, business, marketing. **Special Collections:** Computer manuals.
Holdings: 400 books; 10,000 manuals. **Subscriptions:** 135 journals and
other serials; 5 newspapers. **Services:** Library open to public by appointment.
Computerized Information Services: Computerized indexes.

DATAGRAPHIX, INC.
See: General Dynamics Corporation

DAUGHTERS OF THE AMERICAN REVOLUTION
See: National Society, Daughters of the American Revolution

★3555★
DAUGHTERS OF THE REPUBLIC OF TEXAS - LIBRARY (Hist)
Box 2599   Phone: (512) 225-1071
San Antonio, TX 78299   Sharon R. Crutchfield, Dir.
Founded: 1950. **Staff:** Prof 5; Other 1. **Subjects:** Texas history, Texana.
Special Collections: William E. Howard Collection; Hill Collection; John W.
Smith Collection; Bustillo Collection; Bowie Family Letters; Spanish Kings and
Viceroys. **Holdings:** 12,000 books; 112 bound periodical volumes; 10,000

manuscripts and documents; 66 VF drawers of clippings; 8 VF drawers of
pictures and photographs; 150 maps. **Subscriptions:** 21 journals and other
serials. **Services:** Copying; library open to public for research only.
Publications: Library brochure. **Staff:** Martha Utterback, Asst.Dir.; Sandi
Hood, Cat.; Jeannette Phinney, Ref.; Bernice Strong, Ref.

★3556★
**DAUGHTERS OF UNION VETERANS OF THE CIVIL WAR - NATIONAL
HEADQUARTERS LIBRARY** (Hist)
503 S. Walnut St.
Springfield, IL 62704   Phone: (217) 544-0616
                                                Vivian Gertz, Natl.Treas.
Staff: Prof 1. **Subjects:** Civil War. **Holdings:** Figures not available; paintings,
glass windows, Civil War guns. **Services:** Library open to public on limited
schedule and by appointment.

★3557★
DAUPHIN COUNTY LAW LIBRARY (Law)
Dauphin County Court House   Phone: (717) 234-7001
Harrisburg, PA 17101   Brenda Mull, Libn.
Founded: 1865. **Staff:** 2. **Subjects:** Law. **Holdings:** 32,000 volumes.
Services: Library open to public for reference use only; only members of the
bar may borrow books.

**DAUPHIN ISLAND SEA LAB - MARINE ENVIRONMENTAL SCIENCES
CONSORTIUM**
See: Marine Environmental Sciences Consortium - Library

DAVA
See: U.S. Defense Audiovisual Agency

DAVEE (Chalmer) LIBRARY
See: University of Wisconsin, River Falls - Chalmer Davee Library

★3558★
DAVENPORT ART GALLERY - ART REFERENCE LIBRARY (Art)
1737 W. 12th St.   Phone: (319) 326-7804
Davenport, IA 52804   Gladys Hitchings, Cur.
Founded: 1925. **Staff:** Prof 4; Other 11. **Subjects:** Art. **Holdings:** 3660
books; 4798 pamphlets; slides. **Subscriptions:** 19 journals and other serials.
Services: Library open to public.

★3559★
DAVID LIBRARY OF THE AMERICAN REVOLUTION (Hist)
River Rd.
Rte. 32, Box 48   Phone: (215) 493-6776
Washington Crossing, PA 18977   Joseph J. Felcone, Libn.
Founded: 1959. **Staff:** Prof 2; Other 2. **Subjects:** American Revolution.
Special Collections: Sol Feinstone Collection of the American Revolution
(original letters and manuscripts). **Holdings:** 2500 books; 6000 reels of
microfilm. **Services:** Copying; library open to public. **Special Catalogs:**
Abstracts of New Jersey Manuscripts in Sol Feinstone Collection (book).
Special Indexes: Index to microfilm edition of Sol Feinstone Collection (book).
Staff: Linda H. Witman, Assoc.Libn.

★3560★
DAVID THOMPSON UNIVERSITY CENTRE - SPECIAL COLLECTIONS (Hist)
820 Tenth St.
Nelson, BC, Canada V1L 3C7   Phone: (604) 352-2241
                                                Ronald J. Welwood, Chm.
Founded: 1963. **Staff:** Prof 2; Other 7. **Subjects:** Kootenaiana. **Holdings:**
1075 volumes; 920 photographs. **Services:** Interlibrary loans; copying;
collections open to public. **Computerized Information Services:**
Computerized cataloging. **Networks/Consortia:** Member of British Columbia
Union Catalogue Project. **Publications:** Kootenaiana: a listing of books,
government publications, monographs, journals, pamphlets, etc. relating to the
Kootenay area, 1976.

DAVIDSON COUNTY PUBLIC LIBRARY
See: Public Library of Nashville and Davidson County

★3561★
**DAVIES (Ralph K.) MEDICAL CENTER - FRANKLIN HOSPITAL MEDICAL
LIBRARY** (Med)
Castro & Duboce St.   Phone: (415) 565-6352
San Francisco, CA 94114   Anne Shew, Med.Libn.
Staff: Prof 1. **Subjects:** Biomedical sciences. **Holdings:** 1160 books; 4000
bound periodical volumes; 208 audio cassette tapes; 135 videotapes.
Subscriptions: 178 journals and other serials. **Services:** Interlibrary loans;
copying; bibliographies on request; SDI; library open to public with special
permission. **Computerized Information Services:** MEDLARS, DIALOG, SDC,

BRS. **Networks/Consortia:** Member of Pacific Southwest Regional Medical Library Service (PSRMLS); San Francisco Biomedical Libraries Network. **Publications:** Acquisitions list, irregular; serials holdings - available on request.

DAVIES (Robertson) LIBRARY
See: **Massey College - Robertson Davies Library**

DAVIS (Chester) MEMORIAL LIBRARY
See: **National Association of Precancel Collectors, Inc. - Chester Davis Memorial Library**

★3562★
DAVIS & COMPANY - LAW LIBRARY (Law)
1400-1030 W. Georgia St.   Phone: (604) 687-9444
Vancouver, BC, Canada V6E 3C2   Joan Mulholland, Libn.
Staff: Prof 1; Other 3. **Subjects:** Law. **Holdings:** 8000 books; 150 bound periodical volumes. **Subscriptions:** 375 journals and other serials. **Services:** Interlibrary loans; copying; library open to local law firms.

DAVIS CONSERVATION LIBRARY
See: **Conservation Districts Foundation**

DAVIS (Emert L.) MEMORIAL LIBRARY
See: **U.S. Army - Patton Museum of Cavalry & Armor - Emert L. Davis Memorial Library**

★3563★
DAVIS, GRAHAM & STUBBS/COLORADO NATIONAL BUILDING - CNB LAW LIBRARY (Law)
2500 Colorado National Bldg.
950 17th St.   Phone: (303) 892-9400
Denver, CO 80202   Pamela K. Lewis, Law Libn.
Staff: Prof 3; Other 2. **Subjects:** Law. **Holdings:** 30,000 volumes. **Subscriptions:** 353 journals and other serials; 13 newspapers. **Services:** Interlibrary loans; copying; library not open to public. **Computerized Information Services:** New York Times Information Service; LEXIS; computerized cataloging. **Publications:** CNB Law Library Newsletter, quarterly. **Staff:** Linda Fields, Asst.Libn.

DAVIS (Harwell Goodwin) LIBRARY
See: **Samford University - Harwell Goodwin Davis Library**

★3564★
DAVIS (J.M.) GUN MUSEUM - RESEARCH LIBRARY (Hist)
333 N. Lynn Riggs Blvd.
Box 966   Phone: (918) 341-5707
Claremore, OK 74017   Sue E. Cook, Adm.
Founded: 1969. **Subjects:** Firearms, edged weapons, American Indian artifacts, steins, music instruments. **Holdings:** 800 books; 30 bound periodical volumes; old gun catalogs (cataloged); World War I posters; pins, buttons and badges. **Subscriptions:** 15 journals and other serials. **Services:** Library open to public for reference use only.

DAVIS LIBRARY
See: **Mote Marine Laboratory**

DAVIS (Michael M.) READING ROOM
See: **Association of University Programs in Health Administration - Resource Center for Health Services Adm. Education**

DAVIS (Sir Mortimer B.) JEWISH GENERAL HOSPITAL
See: **Sir Mortimer B. Davis Jewish General Hospital**

★3565★
DAVIS POLK & WARDWELL - LIBRARY (Law)
One Chase Manhattan Plaza   Phone: (212) 530-4267
New York, NY 10005   Nuchine Nobari, Chf.Libn.
Founded: 1881. **Staff:** Prof 5; Other 11. **Subjects:** Law - tax, antitrust, international and corporate. **Special Collections:** Opinions & Memoranda of Law; United States Supreme Court Briefs. **Holdings:** 60,000 volumes. **Subscriptions:** 550 journals and other serials; 25 newspapers. **Services:** Interlibrary loans; copying; library not open to public. **Computerized Information Services:** DIALOG, SDC, BRS, LEXIS, New York Times Information Service; computerized serials and circulation. **Networks/Consortia:** Member of OCLC; Law Library Association of Greater New York. **Publications:** DPW Library Bulletin. **Special Catalogs:** Memoranda of law. **Staff:** Daniel J. Hanson, Ref.Libn.; Jean Jarosek, Ref.Libn.; Susannah K. Scott, Corp.Libn.; Laura Sale, Tech.Serv.Libn.

DAVISON ART CENTER
See: **Wesleyan University - Art Library**

★3566★
DAWES ARBORETUM - LIBRARY (Agri)
7770 Jacksontown Rd., S.E.   Phone: (614) 323-2355
Newark, OH 43055   Alan D. Cook, Horticulturist
Founded: 1929. **Staff:** 2. **Subjects:** Horticulture, botany, ecology, nature, forestry. **Holdings:** 5000 books. **Subscriptions:** 28 journals and other serials. **Services:** Copying; library open to public for reference use only.

DAWES (Charles Gates) HOME
See: **Evanston Historical Society - Charles Gates Dawes Home**

★3567★
DAWE'S LABORATORIES, LTD. - TECHNICAL AND AGRICULTURAL LIBRARIES (Agri)
7100 N. Tripp Ave.   Phone: (312) 982-9540
Lincolnwood, IL 60646   Cameron Gillingham
Founded: 1929. **Staff:** Prof 1. **Subjects:** Animal nutrition, feed fortifiers, organic chemistry, biochemistry, microbiology. **Holdings:** 1500 books; 21,000 bound periodical volumes; 10 VF drawers of patents (cataloged). **Subscriptions:** 125 journals and other serials; 5 newspapers. **Services:** Interlibrary loans; copying; library open to small company libraries. **Publications:** Frontiers in Nutrition Supplement - free upon request.

★3568★
DAWGWOOD RESEARCH LIBRARY (Hist)†
Oak & Ymbacion Sts.   Phone: (512) 526-2451
Refugio, TX 78377   Hobart Huson, Owner
Founded: 1940. **Subjects:** Local and regional history, Pythagorana, Greek and Roman classics, pre-Christian religion. **Special Collections:** Historical manuscripts and documents; collection of special editions; travel literature (Europe and North America; 20 VF drawers). **Holdings:** 10,000 books; 150 bound periodical volumes; bound county newspapers, 1895 to present; 200 pamphlets (cataloged); 15,000 items of bibliographic reference material on Pythagoras; 25,000 Pythagorean reference slips; 150 maps (Greek and local); 16mm film on ancient Greece and Italy. **Subscriptions:** 10 journals and other serials. **Services:** Interlibrary loans (limited); correspondence with reference to Pythagoras and local history; library open for reference use on request. **Publications:** District Judges of Refugio County; Refugio, A History, 2 volumes; Pearls of Pythagorean Philosophy; Dr. Bernard's Journal, 1835-1836; Pythagoras and Christianity; Pythagoron; Eucharistia; Captain Dimmitt's Commandancy of Goliad 1835-1836 (published 1974) - all materials and price list - available upon request.

DAWSON (Dana) LIBRARY
See: **St. Paul School of Theology - Dana Dawson Library**

DAWSON (J.M.) CHURCH-STATE RESEARCH CENTER
See: **Baylor University - J.M. Dawson Church-State Research Center**

DAY (Timothy C.) TECHNICAL LIBRARY
See: **University of Cincinnati - OMI College of Applied Science - Timothy C. Day Technical Library**

★3569★
DAY & ZIMMERMANN, INC. - LIBRARY (Sci-Tech)
1818 Market St., 21st Fl.   Phone: (215) 299-8222
Philadelphia, PA 19103   Jenny Kuan, Libn.
Founded: 1945. **Staff:** Prof 1. **Subjects:** Engineering - mechanical, chemical, electrical. **Holdings:** 2200 books; 22 VF drawers of specifications, technical reports. **Subscriptions:** 90 journals and other serials. **Services:** Interlibrary loans; library open to public for reference use only.

★3570★
DAYTON ART INSTITUTE - LIBRARY (Art)
Forest & Riverview Aves.
Box 941   Phone: (513) 223-5277
Dayton, OH 45401   Helen L. Pinkney, Libn.
Staff: Prof 1; Other 2. **Subjects:** Art and architecture. **Special Collections:** Lott Memorial Architectural Library. **Holdings:** 22,869 books; 2569 bound periodical volumes; 24,023 slides; 317 VF drawers of museum catalogs and bulletins; 820 microfiche. **Subscriptions:** 120 journals and other serials; 5 newspapers. **Services:** Interlibrary loans; copying; library open to public for reference use only. **Staff:** Evelyn L. Higgins, Asst.Libn.; Renate W. Harlan, Asst.Libn.

★3571★

DAYTON CHILDREN'S PSYCHIATRIC HOSPITAL - LIBRARY
141 Firwood Dr.
Dayton, OH 45419
Founded: 1959. **Subjects:** Psychiatry, psychology, psychiatric social work. **Holdings:** 2500 books; 360 bound periodical volumes. **Remarks:** Presently inactive.

★3572★

DAYTON HUDSON CORPORATION LIBRARY (Bus-Fin)
777 Nicollet Mall   Phone: (612) 370-6769
Minneapolis, MN 55402   Barbara Schultz, Corp.Libn.
Staff: Prof 1; Other 1. **Subjects:** Retailing, business. **Holdings:** 500 books. **Subscriptions:** 200 journals and other serials. **Services:** Interlibrary loans; library open to public by special permission. **Computerized Information Services:** New York Times Information Service, DIALOG, NEXIS. **Networks/Consortia:** Member of Insiders. **Publications:** Retail Bulletin, monthly - for internal distribution only.

★3573★

DAYTON LAW LIBRARY (Law)†
505 Montgomery County Courts Bldg.
41 N. Perry St.   Phone: (513) 225-4505
Dayton, OH 45422   Betty Busch, Libn.
Founded: 1868. **Staff:** Prof 1; Other 3. **Subjects:** Law. **Special Collections:** Rare books (145). **Holdings:** 80,000 volumes; 892 binders; 270 Princeton files. **Subscriptions:** 209 journals and other serials. **Services:** Copying.

★3574★

DAYTON MENTAL HEALTH CENTER - STAFF LIBRARY (Med)
2611 Wayne Ave.   Phone: (513) 258-0440
Dayton, OH 45420   Leonard Skonecki, Libn.
Founded: 1950. **Staff:** Prof 1. **Subjects:** Psychiatry, psychology, medicine, social work. **Holdings:** 660 books. **Subscriptions:** 17 journals and other serials. **Services:** Interlibrary loans; copying; library not open to public. **Networks/Consortia:** Member of Miami Valley Association of Health Science Libraries.

★3575★

DAYTON AND MONTGOMERY COUNTY PUBLIC LIBRARY - INDUSTRY AND SCIENCE DIVISION (Bus-Fin; Sci-Tech)
215 E. Third St.   Phone: (513) 224-1651
Dayton, OH 45402   Martha A. Overwein, Hd.
Founded: 1962. **Staff:** Prof 5; Other 3. **Subjects:** Industry, business, commerce, statistics, finance, pure and applied sciences. **Special Collections:** Dayton newspapers on microfilm since 1808. **Holdings:** 53,000 books. **Subscriptions:** 400 journals and other serials; 35 newspapers. **Services:** Interlibrary loans; copying; library open to public. **Computerized Information Services:** Computerized cataloging. **Networks/Consortia:** Member of OCLC; OHIONET. **Publications:** BITS (Business, Industry, Technology), 10/year.

★3576★

DAYTON AND MONTGOMERY COUNTY PUBLIC LIBRARY - LITERATURE AND FINE ARTS DIVISION (Hum)
215 E. Third St.   Phone: (513) 224-1651
Dayton, OH 45402   Donald T. Paul, Hd.
Founded: 1962. **Staff:** Prof 6; Other 2. **Subjects:** Literature, art, music, sports, crafts. **Special Collections:** Foreign languages; miniature scores. **Holdings:** Figures not available for books; 15 VF drawers of sheet music. **Subscriptions:** 208 journals and other serials. **Services:** Interlibrary loans; copying; library open to public. **Networks/Consortia:** Member of OHIONET.

★3577★

DAYTON AND MONTGOMERY COUNTY PUBLIC LIBRARY - NON-PRINT MEDIA CENTER (Aud-Vis)
215 E. Third St.   Phone: (513) 224-1651
Dayton, OH 45402   Theodore J. Nunn, Jr., Hd.
Founded: 1973. **Staff:** Prof 2; Other 5. **Holdings:** 3200 16mm films; 1750 8mm films; 1400 filmstrips; 29,000 slides; 28,000 phonodiscs; 7600 audiocassettes; 26,200 photographs and pictures. **Services:** Library open to public. **Publications:** 16mm Film Catalog; 35mm color slide catalog; 35mm filmstrip catalog - all three with supplements.

★3578★

DAYTON AND MONTGOMERY COUNTY PUBLIC LIBRARY - SOCIAL SCIENCES DIVISION (Soc Sci; Hist)
215 E. Third St.   Phone: (513) 224-1651
Dayton, OH 45402   Laura J. Smith, Hd.
Staff: Prof 4; Other 3. **Subjects:** Dayton history, Montgomery County history, local genealogy. **Special Collections:** Valandingham materials; Dayton history collection; Paul Laurence Dunbar Collection; Dayton and Montgomery County Picture File (2000 - reproductions may be made from negatives). **Holdings:** Figures not available; unpublished letters and manuscripts on local history; special clipping files. **Subscriptions:** 300 journals and other serials. **Services:** Interlibrary loans; copying; preliminary genealogy work; library open to public. **Computerized Information Services:** Computerized cataloging. **Networks/Consortia:** Member of OHIONET. **Special Indexes:** Local genealogy index (150 card file drawers).

★3579★

DAYTON NEWSPAPERS INC. - REFERENCE LIBRARY (Publ)
37 S. Ludlow St.   Phone: (513) 225-2430
Dayton, OH 45402   Mr. Harish Trivedi, Ref. & Res.Dir.
Founded: 1979. **Staff:** Prof 1; Other 8. **Special Collections:** Dayton Journal Herald/Dayton Daily News on microfilm since 1837. **Holdings:** 3500 books; 3500 pamphlets (cataloged); newspaper clippings, microfiche and microfilm; pictures, photographs. **Subscriptions:** 25 journals and other serials. **Services:** Copying; library open to public by appointment.

DAZIAN LIBRARY OF THEATRICAL DESIGN
See: Museum of the City of New York - Theatre Collection

DE BELLIS (Frank V.) COLLECTION
See: San Francisco State University - Frank V. de Bellis Collection

★3580★

DE CORDOVA MUSEUM - LIBRARY (Art)†
Sandy Pond Rd.   Phone: (617) 259-8355
Lincoln, MA 01773   Bee Warren, Libn.
Founded: 1950. **Staff:** 1. **Subjects:** Fine arts and crafts. **Holdings:** 2500 books. **Subscriptions:** 17 journals and other serials. **Services:** Interlibrary loans; library serves museum associates. **Publications:** "ETC" Newsletter; catalogs of special exhibitions.

DE FOREST MEMORIAL ARCHIVES
See: Foothill College

★3581★

DE FOREST RESEARCH - LIBRARY (Info Sci)†
5451 Marathon St.   Phone: (213) 468-5000
Hollywood, CA 90038   Kellam de Forest, Dir.
Subjects: Research material for motion pictures and television. **Holdings:** 30,000 books; 2000 bound periodical volumes; 4000 files of photographs and clippings; 6500 motion picture and television scripts. **Subscriptions:** 10 journals and other serials. **Services:** Library not open to public. **Remarks:** This is a private research organization which provides legal and authenticating information for the movie and television industry.

DE GUIGNE TECHNICAL CENTER
See: Stauffer Chemical Company

DE HAEN (Paul) DRUG INFORMATION SYSTEMS
See: Micromedex, Inc. - Paul de Haen Drug Information Systems

★3582★

DE HAVILLAND AIRCRAFT OF CANADA, LTD. - ENGINEERING LIBRARY (Sci-Tech)
Garratt Blvd.
Downsview, ON, Canada M3K 1Y5   Phone: (416) 633-7310
                                          Mrs. C. Parsons, Libn.
Founded: 1955. **Staff:** Prof 1; Other 2. **Subjects:** Aeronautics. **Special Collections:** Canadian and international reports, papers, regulations and standards dealing with aeronautics. **Holdings:** 2000 books; 600 bound periodical volumes; 90,000 reports (cataloged); 3000 microfiche. **Subscriptions:** 112 journals and other serials; 6 newspapers. **Services:** Interlibrary loans; copying (limited); SDI (internal); library open to public with restrictions on borrowing.

★3583★

DE KALB AGRESEARCH INC. - CORN RESEARCH CENTER - LIBRARY (Agri)
Sycamore Rd.   Phone: (815) 758-3461
DeKalb, IL 60115   Dr. Charles F. Krull, V.P., Corn Res.
Founded: 1965. **Staff:** 1. **Subjects:** Agriculture and related topics. **Holdings:** Figures not available. **Services:** Library not open to public.

DE KALB COUNTY BOARD OF EDUCATION - FERNBANK SCIENCE CENTER
See: Fernbank Science Center

★3584★
DE KALB GENERAL HOSPITAL - MEDICAL LIBRARY (Med)
2701 N. Decatur Rd.   Phone: (404) 292-4444
Decatur, GA 30033   Marilyn Osborne Gibbs, Med.Libn.
Founded: 1974. **Staff:** Prof 1; Other 1. **Subjects:** Clinical medicine.
Holdings: 500 books; 2000 periodical volumes. **Subscriptions:** 135 journals
and other serials. **Services:** Interlibrary loans; copying; library not open to
public. **Computerized Information Services:** Online systems. **Networks/
Consortia:** Member of Atlanta Health Science Libraries Consortium; Georgia
Library Information Network (GLIN).

★3585★
DE LEUW, CATHER AND COMPANY - LIBRARY (Sci-Tech)
165 W. Wacker Dr.   Phone: (312) 346-0424
Chicago, IL 60601   Leslie Ewing, Libn.
Founded: 1971. **Staff:** Prof 2; Other 1. **Subjects:** Civil engineering;
transportation and urban planning; structural engineering. **Special Collections:**
Company reports (1700). **Holdings:** 6000 books; 4000 other cataloged
items. **Subscriptions:** 200 journals and other serials. **Services:** Interlibrary
loans; SDI; library open to public for reference use only by request.
Computerized Information Services: DIALOG. **Networks/Consortia:**
Member of Chicago Library System; Metropolitan Chicago Library Assembly.
Publications: Recent acquisitions, irregular.

★3586★
DE PAUL HOSPITAL - DR. HENRY BOONE MEMORIAL LIBRARY (Med)
Kingsley Ln. & Granby St.   Phone: (804) 489-5270
Norfolk, VA 23505   Ramona C. Parrish, Libn.
Staff: Prof 1. **Subjects:** Medicine. **Holdings:** 1439 books; 2663 bound
periodical volumes; 765 Audio-Digest tapes. **Subscriptions:** 130 journals and
other serials. **Services:** Interlibrary loans; library open to public for reference
use only with appointment.

★3587★
DE PAUL HOSPITAL - SCHOOL OF NURSING LIBRARY (Med)
150 Kingsley Ln.   Phone: (804) 489-5386
Norfolk, VA 23505   Elinor B. Arsic, Libn.
Staff: Prof 1; Other 1. **Subjects:** Medicine and religion. **Special Collections:**
Historical nursing books. **Holdings:** 4111 books; 397 bound periodical
volumes; 2893 AV items; 9 VF drawers of clippings and pamphlets.
Subscriptions: 69 journals and other serials. **Services:** Interlibrary loans;
library open to hospital personnel with restrictions.

★3588★
DE PAUL UNIVERSITY - LAW SCHOOL LIBRARY (Law)
25 E. Jackson Blvd.   Phone: (312) 321-7710
Chicago, IL 60604   Susan Beverly Kuklin, Dir.
Founded: 1915. **Staff:** Prof 7; Other 14. **Subjects:** Anglo-American law.
Special Collections: Municipal Codes for all Illinois municipalities with
populations over 10,000. **Holdings:** 130,000 books and bound periodical
volumes; 70,000 volumes on microform. **Subscriptions:** 2887 journals and
other serials and newspapers. **Services:** Interlibrary loans; library open to
public. **Computerized Information Services:** LEXIS; computerized cataloging
and circulation. **Staff:** Mary Lu Linnane, Hd., Tech.Serv.; Milta Hall, Hd.,
Pub.Serv.; Raminta Sinkus, Hd., Cat.Serv; Charlotte Palmer, Cat.Libn.; Carol
Caughran, Ref.Libn.; Joyce Olin, Govt.Docs./Ref.Libn.

★3589★
**DE PAUL UNIVERSITY, LINCOLN PARK CAMPUS LIBRARY - SPECIAL
   COLLECTIONS DEPARTMENT (Hum)**
2323 N. Seminary   Phone: (312) 321-7940
Chicago, IL 60614   Kathryn DeGraff, Spec.Coll.Libn.
Founded: 1975. **Staff:** Prof 1; Other 1. **Subjects:** French Revolution,
humanities. **Special Collections:** Napoleon Collection (4000 volumes); rare
books (2000 volumes); Dickens Collection (590 volumes); sports (900
volumes); book arts (170 volumes); Horace Collection (212 volumes).
Holdings: 7872 books; 598 bound periodical volumes; 70 manuscripts.
Services: Interlibrary loans; copying; library open to public. **Computerized
Information Services:** BRS; computerized cataloging, serials and circulation.
Networks/Consortia: Member of OCLC through ILLINET; Chicago Academic
Library Council (CALC); Metropolitan Chicago Library Assembly. **Special
Catalogs:** Napoleon Library Catalog, 1941; revised addenda 1978.

★3590★
**DE PAUW UNIVERSITY - ARCHIVES OF DE PAUW UNIVERSITY AND
   INDIANA UNITED METHODISM (Rel-Theol; Hist)**
Roy O. West Library   Phone: (317) 658-4501
Greencastle, IN 46135   David E. Horn, Archv.
Founded: 1951. **Staff:** Prof 1; Other 2. **Subjects:** DePauw University history;

United Methodist Church of Indiana. **Special Collections:** Histories of Indiana
United Methodist Churches and early Methodist Church records of Indiana;
records of DePauw from the university's founding in 1837. **Holdings:** 800
books; 350 bound periodical volumes; 250 volumes of Methodist Conference
minutes; 1800 church histories of Indiana Methodism; 1500 cubic feet of
manuscripts pertaining to the history of the university and the church; tape
recordings, microfilm and photographs. **Subscriptions:** 9 journals and other
serials. **Services:** Interlibrary loans (microfilm only); copying; genealogical
research service on a fee basis; archives open to public. **Publications:** Annual
Report - for internal distribution only.

★3591★
DE SALES HALL SCHOOL OF THEOLOGY - LIBRARY
5001 Eastern Ave.
Hyattsville, MD 20782
Defunct

★3592★
DE SALES PREPARATORY SEMINARY - LIBRARY
3501 S. Lake Dr.
Milwaukee, WI 53207
Defunct

★3593★
DE SOTO, INC. - INFORMATION CENTER (Sci-Tech)
1700 S. Mt. Prospect Rd.   Phone: (312) 391-9556
Des Plaines, IL 60018   Cathy Collins Kozelka, Mgr.
Founded: 1965. **Staff:** Prof 2; Other 3. **Subjects:** Chemical coatings,
polymer and analytical chemistry, management, business. **Holdings:** 9500
books; 7200 microforms; 2200 microfilm cartridges; 4 VF drawers of
military and federal specifications and standards; 130 AV materials.
Subscriptions: 275 journals; 7 newspapers. **Services:** Interlibrary loans;
copying; reference service; library open to public by appointment.
Computerized Information Services: DIALOG, SDC, NLM; computerized
cataloging. **Networks/Consortia:** Member of North Suburban Library System;
Center for Research Libraries (CRL); ILLINET. **Publications:** Patent Alert Line
(U.S.), weekly; Patent Alert Line (foreign), weekly - both for internal
distribution only.

DE SOTO NATL. MEMORIAL
See: U.S. Natl. Park Service

DE VALDES (Juan) LIBRARY
See: Evangelical Seminary of Puerto Rico - Juan de Valdes Library

DE VRY INSTITUTE OF TECHNOLOGY
See: Bell & Howell Education Group

DE YOUNG (M.H.) MEMORIAL MUSEUM
See: Fine Arts Museums of San Francisco

★3594★
**DEACONESS COMMUNITY LUTHERAN CHURCH OF AMERICA - LUTHERAN
   DEACONESS COMMUNITY LIBRARY (Rel-Theol)**
801 Merion Sq. Rd.   Phone: (215) 642-8838
Gladwyne, PA 19035   Sr. Dorothy Goff, Libn.
Founded: 1946. **Staff:** Prof 1. **Subjects:** Religion, theology, Christian
education, church history, Bible, psychology, education, social work, women's
work in the church. **Special Collections:** Historical and archival collection of
Deaconess Community, LCA (26 VF drawers; 95 documentary storage boxes;
2 memorabilia cabinets; 150 books and bound periodical volumes). **Holdings:**
9000 books and bound periodical volumes; 50 pamphlet cases of audiovisual
and curriculum material for Christian education; 6 VF drawers of miscellaneous
material. **Subscriptions:** 50 journals and other serials. **Services:** Library open
to public by appointment. **Publications:** The Deaconess, semiannual
publication of the Deaconess Community. **Remarks:** The Historical Collection
listed above is located in a separate room and is open by appointment for
research. **Staff:** Sr. Louise Burroughs, Archv.

DEACONESS HALL LIBRARY
See: Lutheran Deaconess Association

★3595★
DEACONESS HOSPITAL - DRUSCH PROFESSIONAL LIBRARY (Med)†
6150 Oakland Ave.   Phone: (314) 645-8510
St. Louis, MO 63139   Jane Whalen, Libn.
Founded: 1943. **Staff:** Prof 1; Other 1. **Subjects:** Nursing, medicine,
surgery, paramedical sciences. **Special Collections:** Book collection of
Greater St. Louis Society of Clinical Hypnosis; Dermatology Collection of

Norman Tobias. **Holdings:** 3382 books; 2400 bound periodical volumes; 12 VF drawers of ephemeral files; 10 VF drawers of reports (unbound); films; filmstrips; tapes; Audio-Digest tapes. **Subscriptions:** 150 journals and other serials. **Services:** Interlibrary loans; copying; library open to public with permission of librarian and hospital administration. **Networks/Consortia:** Member of Midcontinental Regional Medical Library Program. **Publications:** New Book List, quarterly; Annual Report. **Special Catalogs:** Card catalog of AV equipment, hard and soft ware, and hospital literature.

★3596★
DEACONESS HOSPITAL - HEALTH SCIENCE LIBRARY (Med)
600 Mary St.   Phone: (812) 426-3385
Evansville, IN 47747   Millie H. Grunow, Med.Libn.
Founded: 1969. **Staff:** Prof 1; Other 2. **Subjects:** Nursing education, clinical medicine and allied health sciences. **Holdings:** 5800 books; 3700 bound periodical volumes; 1440 items of AV material. **Subscriptions:** 200 journals and other serials; 5 newspapers. **Services:** Interlibrary loans; copying; library open to health personnel. **Computerized Information Services:** NLM. **Networks/Consortia:** Member of Evansville Area Health Science Library Consortium. **Remarks:** In 1969 several departmental libraries joined to form the present library and only materials which had been acquired or reclassified since 1960 are shelved in the new facility.

DEACONESS HOSPITAL - HEALTH SCIENCE LIBRARY (Milwaukee, WI)
See: Good Samaritan Medical Center - Deaconess Hospital Campus

★3597★
DEACONESS HOSPITAL - MEDICAL LIBRARY (Med)
1001 Humboldt Parkway   Phone: (716) 886-4400
Buffalo, NY 14208   Donna Browning, Med.Libn.
Staff: Prof 1; Other 1. **Subjects:** Medicine, surgery, and related sciences. **Holdings:** 500 books; 4000 bound periodical volumes. **Subscriptions:** 143 journals and other serials. **Services:** Interlibrary loans; copying; library not open to public.

★3598★
DEACONESS HOSPITAL - SCHOOL OF NURSING - RICHARD W. ANGERT MEMORIAL LIBRARY (Med)
415 Straight St.   Phone: (513) 559-2285
Cincinnati, OH 45219   Valerie J. Eliot, Libn.
Founded: 1967. **Staff:** Prof 1. **Subjects:** Nursing and allied health subjects. **Holdings:** 3355 books; 370 bound periodical volumes; 481 AV programs; 8 VF drawers of pamphlets, articles, pictures. **Subscriptions:** 51 journals and other serials. **Services:** Interlibrary loans; copying; library open to public with restrictions. **Networks/Consortia:** Member of Cincinnati Area Health Science Libraries Association.

★3599★
DEAF SMITH GENERAL HOSPITAL - LIBRARY (Med)
801 E. 3rd St.   Phone: (806) 364-2141
Hereford, TX 79045   Vicky L. Higgins, Dir., Med.Rec.
Staff: Prof 1; Other 2. **Subjects:** Medicine and allied health sciences. **Holdings:** 175 volumes. **Services:** Copying; library not open to public.

DEAN (Edwin W.) MEMORIAL LIBRARY
See: Centinela Hospital Medical Center - Edwin W. Dean Memorial Library

DEAN (Mallette) ARCHIVE
See: University of San Francisco - Special Collections Department/ Donohue Rare Book Room

DEAN MEMORIAL LIBRARY
See: American Museum of Natural History - Department of Ichthyology

DEAN MUSEUM ART REFERENCE LIBRARY
See: Edward-Dean Museum Art Reference Library

★3600★
DEAN WITTER REYNOLDS, INC. - LIBRARY (Bus-Fin)
130 Liberty St.   Phone: (212) 524-2745
New York, NY 10006   Barbara C. White, Chf.Libn.
Founded: 1970. **Staff:** Prof 2; Other 4. **Subjects:** Corporation records; economic conditions. **Holdings:** 1300 books. **Subscriptions:** 400 journals and other serials. **Services:** Interlibrary loans. **Computerized Information Services:** Dow Jones News Retrieval, New York Times Information Service, DIALOG, SDC, Source Telecomputing Corporation, NEXIS, Info Globe, Economic Information Systems, Inc., TEXTLINE, Computer Directions Advisors, Inc.; internal databases; computerized circulation. **Staff:** Merill Losick, Ref.Libn.

★3601★
DEAN WITTER REYNOLDS, INC. - RESEARCH DEPARTMENT LIBRARY (Bus-Fin)†
5 World Trade Center   Phone: (212) 524-2222
New York, NY 10048   Beth Morris, Res.Dept.Libn.
Founded: 1978. **Staff:** Prof 1; Other 1. **Subjects:** Finance, investments, economics, business. **Special Collections:** Corporation records (8000). **Holdings:** 250 books. **Subscriptions:** 305 journals and other serials. **Services:** Interlibrary loans; library not open to public. **Computerized Information Services:** DIALOG, SDC, New York Times Information Service, Dow Jones News Retrieval. **Special Indexes:** Index to research reports.

DEARBORN CHEMICAL (U.S.) LIBRARY
See: Grace (W.R.) and Company

DEARBORN (Frederick M.) MEDICAL LIBRARY
See: Metropolitan Hospital Center - Frederick M. Dearborn Medical Library

★3602★
DEARBORN HISTORICAL MUSEUM - RESEARCH DIVISION - ARCHIVES AND LIBRARY (Hist)
915 S. Brady St.   Phone: (313) 565-3000
Dearborn, MI 48124
Staff: Prof 2; Other 2. **Subjects:** Local history. **Holdings:** 2517 books; 353 bound periodical volumes; 15 VF drawers of manuscripts; 50 VF drawers of clippings, pamphlets, photographs and maps; 11 storage cabinets of diaries, documents and archival material; 400 reels of microfilm of local newspapers and records; 16,000 feet of tape of oral history. **Subscriptions:** 31 journals and other serials. **Services:** Copying; library open to public for reference use only. **Publications:** Museum Quarterly; Annual Report. **Special Catalogs:** Manuscript, history, newspaper and photo catalogs (card). **Remarks:** Library under direction of Dearborn Historical Commission. **Staff:** Virginia Sherk, Archv.Spec.; Donald V. Baut, Cur. of Res.

DEATH VALLEY NATL. MONUMENT
See: U.S. Natl. Park Service

DEATS (Hiram E.) MEMORIAL LIBRARY
See: Hunterdon County Historical Society - Hiram E. Deats Memorial Library

★3603★
DEBEVOISE & LIBERMAN - LAW LIBRARY (Law)
26 Broadway   Phone: (212) 248-6900
New York, NY 10004   Ben Schneberg, Law Libn.
Staff: Prof 1. **Subjects:** U.S. and N.Y. law, public utilities, U.S. Securities and Exchange Commission rules and regulations, corporations. **Holdings:** 8000 books; 94 bound periodical volumes. **Subscriptions:** 134 journals and other serials. **Services:** Interlibrary loans; copying; library not open to public. **Formerly:** Berlack, Israels and Liberman.

★3604★
DEBEVOISE & PLIMPTON - LAW LIBRARY (Law)†
875 Third Ave.   Phone: (212) 909-6275
New York, NY 10022   Denis R. O'Connor, Libn.
Staff: Prof 2; Other 5. **Subjects:** Law. **Holdings:** 30,000 books; 500 bound periodical volumes; 3000 pamphlets. **Subscriptions:** 20 journals and other serials. **Services:** Interlibrary loans; library open to clients; SLA members and others may visit by appointment. **Computerized Information Services:** LEXIS, New York Times Information Service. **Formerly:** Debevoise, Plimpton, Lyons and Gates.

★3605★
DEBORAH HEART AND LUNG CENTER - MEDICAL LIBRARY (Med)
One Trenton Rd.   Phone: (609) 893-6611
Browns Mills, NJ 08015   Carol A. Harris, Med.Libn.
Founded: 1971. **Staff:** Prof 1. **Subjects:** Cardiology, respiratory diseases, cardiothoracic surgery, medicine, pathology, nursing. **Holdings:** 3500 books; 2000 bound periodical volumes; AV materials. **Subscriptions:** 175 journals and other serials. **Services:** Interlibrary loans; copying; library not open to public. **Networks/Consortia:** Member of New York & New Jersey Regional Medical Library Program; Pinelands Consortium for Health Information.

★3606★
DEBS (Eugene V.) FOUNDATION - LIBRARY (Hist)
451 N. 8th St.   Phone: (812) 232-2163
Terre Haute, IN 47807   Curtis Culver, Exec.V.P.
Staff: 1. **Subjects:** Eugene V. Debs. **Holdings:** Brotherhood Locomotive

Magazine, bound files, 1878-1894; Brotherhood of Locomotive Firemen and Enginemen Convention Proceedings, 1873-1960; scrapbooks of Mrs. Eugene V. Debs; 75 letters of Eugene V. Debs; Appeal to Reason (Girard, KS), bound files, 1907-1914. **Services:** Library open to public.

★3607★
DECATUR DEPARTMENT OF COMMUNITY DEVELOPMENT - PLANNING LIBRARY (Plan)
One Civic Center Plaza
Decatur, IL 62523
Phone: (217) 424-2778
Robert Menzies, Plan.Coord.
Subjects: Land use planning, transportation, housing, economics, urban redevelopment, demographics, community facilities studies, natural resources and environment. **Holdings:** 75 books; 1500 other cataloged items; 25 pieces of census material; 100 Illinois Geological Survey reports; 10 dissertations; 100 unbound periodicals. **Services:** Library open to qualified researchers.

★3608★
DECATUR HERALD AND REVIEW - LIBRARY (Publ)†
601 E. William St.
Box 311
Decatur, IL 62523
Phone: (217) 429-5151
Faye Spencer, Libn.
Founded: 1890. **Staff:** 8. **Subjects:** Newspaper reference topics, local history. **Holdings:** 1500 books; 929,600 clippings; 90,000 photographs and maps; microfilm (Decatur newspapers, 1873 to present). **Subscriptions:** 100 newspapers. **Services:** Interlibrary loans; copying; library may be consulted for information unavailable elsewhere.

★3609★
DECATUR MEMORIAL HOSPITAL - HEALTH SCIENCE LIBRARY (Med)
2300 N. Edward St.
Decatur, IL 62526
Phone: (217) 877-8121
John W. Law, Libn.
Staff: Prof 1. **Subjects:** Nursing, general medicine. **Holdings:** 2065 books; 2454 bound periodical volumes; AV materials. **Subscriptions:** 125 journals and other serials. **Services:** Interlibrary loans; copying; library not open to public. **Networks/Consortia:** Member of Regional Medical Library - Region 3; Central Illinois Consortium of Health Science Libraries; ILLINET; Rolling Prairie Library System.

★3610★
DECHERT, PRICE AND RHOADS - LIBRARY (Law)
3400 Centre Sq. W.
1500 Market St.
Philadelphia, PA 19102
Phone: (215) 972-3453
Susan Jane Gibbons, Libn.
Staff: Prof 2; Other 3. **Subjects:** Law. **Holdings:** 19,000 books; 1300 bound periodical volumes; 14 VF drawers of Memoranda of Law; 13 VF drawers of annual reports, prospectuses and proxy statements. **Subscriptions:** 60 journals and other serials; 6 newspapers. **Services:** Interlibrary loans; copying (limited); library not open to public. **Computerized Information Services:** LEXIS, DIALOG. **Publications:** Developments in the European Countries, published monthly by the members of the firm in the Brussels office. **Special Indexes:** Card index to the Memoranda of Law, Business Forms file, prospectuses. **Staff:** Elizabeth A. McNerlin, Asst.Libn.

DECHIEF LIBRARY
See: Canadian National Railways

★3611★
DECISIONS AND DESIGNS, INC. - LIBRARY (Sci-Tech)
8400 Westpark Dr., Suite 600
Box 907
McLean, VA 22101
Phone: (703) 821-2828
Vicki Holcomb, Lib./Pubns.Mgr.
Staff: Prof 1; Other 1. **Subjects:** Decision theory, computer science, applied psychology, mathematics/statistics, systems analysis, project management. **Special Collections:** Journal reprints by foremost decision theorists (1000). **Holdings:** 500 books; 3000 technical reports, government documents; 300 reports on microfiche; 300 DDI technical reports. **Subscriptions:** 50 journals and other serials. **Services:** Interlibrary loans; copying; library open to public by appointment. **Computerized Information Services:** DIALOG, SDC. **Networks/Consortia:** Member of Interlibrary Users Association; Metropolitan Washington Library Council. **Special Indexes:** DDI technical reports index. **Staff:** William H. Shawcross, Mgr. of Serv.

DECKER LIBRARY
See: Maryland Institute, College of Art

★3612★
DEDHAM HISTORICAL SOCIETY - LIBRARY (Hist)
612 High St.
Dedham, MA 02026
Phone: (617) 326-1385
Muriel N. Peters, Libn.
Founded: 1859. **Staff:** 2. **Subjects:** Dedham history and genealogy. **Special Collections:** Fisher Ames Papers (1758-1808; 400 items); Nathaniel Ames Diary (1758-1821); Horace Mann lecture notes (1796-1859). **Holdings:** 8000 volumes; account books; documents, manuscripts. **Services:** Copying; library open to public for reference use only with limited hours.

DEEP CANYON DESERT RESEARCH CENTER
See: University of California, Riverside

DEER CREEK LIBRARY
See: Hewlett-Packard Company - HP Laboratories

★3613★
DEER ISLE-STONINGTON HISTORICAL SOCIETY - LIBRARY (Trans; Hist)
Phone: (207) 348-2886
Deer Isle, ME 04627
Genice Welcome, Exec.Sec.
Founded: 1959. **Subjects:** Marine vessels, steamboats and yachts, early children's books and school books. **Special Collections:** Area customhouse books (30); Richardson collection of steamboat photographs. **Holdings:** 200 books; early scrapbooks; information file of clippings of typed information on local subjects; diaries, photographs. **Services:** Library open to public with restrictions. **Publications:** Newsletter, annual.

★3614★
DEER LODGE HOSPITAL - MEDICAL REFERENCE LIBRARY (Med)
2109 Portage Ave.
Winnipeg, MB, Canada R3J 0L3
Phone: (204) 837-1301
J.L. Saunders, Libn.
Staff: 2. **Subjects:** Medicine, surgery, geriatrics. **Holdings:** 231 books; 1471 bound periodical volumes. **Subscriptions:** 79 journals and other serials. **Services:** Library open to medical staff. **Remarks:** Maintained by Canada - Veterans Affairs Canada.

★3615★
DEERE & COMPANY - LAW LIBRARY (Law)
John Deere Rd.
Moline, IL 61265
Phone: (309) 752-4165
Donna Eudaley, Adm.Sec.
Subjects: Law. **Holdings:** 5700 volumes. **Services:** Library not open to public.

★3616★
DEERE & COMPANY - LIBRARY (Agri; Sci-Tech)
John Deere Rd.
Moline, IL 61265
Phone: (309) 752-4442
Betty Hagberg, Mgr., Lib.Serv.
Founded: 1958. **Staff:** Prof 4; Other 7. **Subjects:** Agriculture, engineering, business, economics, management, materials science. **Special Collections:** Deere & Company history. **Holdings:** 25,000 books; 500 bound periodical volumes; state documents; publications of agricultural experiment stations and extension services; federal documents; 8 drawers of microfiche; 800 reels of microfilm; 100 audiotapes. **Subscriptions:** 2500 journals and other serials; 10 newspapers. **Services:** Interlibrary loans; copying; library open to public for reference use only on request. **Computerized Information Services:** New York Times Information Service, MEDLARS, DIALOG, NEXIS, SDC; computerized cataloging, acquisitions, circulation and serials. **Networks/Consortia:** Member of OCLC through ILLINET. **Publications:** Staying Ahead: Reading for Self-Development, irregular. **Special Indexes:** Computerized Furrow Index; online index to archival holdings. **Staff:** Les Stegh, Archv.; Diana Polk, Ref.Libn.; Eileen Holmer, Ref.Libn.

DEERE & COMPANY - PRODUCT ENGINEERING CENTER
See: John Deere Product Engineering Center

★3617★
DEERE & COMPANY - TECHNICAL CENTER LIBRARY (Sci-Tech)
3300 River Dr.
Moline, IL 61265
Phone: (309) 757-5363
Donna M. Morgan, Ref.Libn.
Staff: Prof 1. **Subjects:** Engineering, materials science, metallurgy, chemistry. **Holdings:** 5000 books; 200 bound periodical volumes; 1520 hard copy technical reports; 1790 reports on microfiche; 230 videotapes. **Subscriptions:** 175 journals and other serials. **Services:** Interlibrary loans; copying; library open to public with restrictions. **Computerized Information Services:** DIALOG, SDC, BRS; computerized acquisitions and circulation.

DEFENCE AND CIVIL INSTITUTE OF ENVIRONMENTAL MEDICINE
See: Canada - Defence and Civil Institute of Environmental Medicine

DEFENCE RESEARCH ESTABLISHMENT
See: Canada - Defence Research Establishment

DEFENSE COMMUNICATIONS ENGINEERING CENTER
See: U.S. Defense Communications Agency - Technical Library and Information Center

DEFENSE CONSTRUCTION SUPPLY CENTER
See: U.S. Defense Logistics Agency

DEFENSE GENERAL SUPPLY CENTER
See: U.S. Defense Logistics Agency

DEFENSE INDUSTRIAL PLANT EQUIPMENT CENTER
See: U.S. Dept. of Defense

DEFENSE INDUSTRIAL SUPPLY CENTER
See: U.S. Defense Logistics Agency

DEFENSE LOGISTICS SERVICES CENTER
See: U.S. Defense Logistics Agency

DEFENSE NATIONALE
See: Canada - National Defence

DEFENSE PERSONNEL SUPPORT CENTER
See: U.S. Defense Logistics Agency

DEFENSE PEST MANAGEMENT INFORMATION ANALYSIS CENTER
See: U.S. Army - Armed Forces Pest Management Board

★3618★
DEFENSE RESEARCH INSTITUTE, INC. - BRIEF BANK (Law)
733 N. Van Buren St.   Phone: (414) 272-5995
Milwaukee, WI 53202   Fred L. Bardenwerper, Asst.Res.Dir.
Founded: 1961. **Staff:** Prof 9; Other 15. **Subjects:** Briefs filed in appellate cases; civil litigation. **Special Collections:** Tort Liability Research Library; insurance law. **Holdings:** 5000 books; 6000 briefs (case files). **Subscriptions:** 100 journals and other serials. **Services:** Copying (limited); DRI Defense Services for members; bank not open to public. **Publications:** Brief Bank Indexes, annual cumulative supplements and quarterly inserts. **Special Indexes:** Brief Bank Indexes listed by legal subject.

DEGOLYER LIBRARY
See: Southern Methodist University - Fikes Hall of Special Collections and DeGolyer Library

★3619★
DEGOLYER AND MAC NAUGHTON - LIBRARY (Energy)
One Energy Sq.   Phone: (214) 368-6391
Dallas, TX 75206   Eleanor Maclay
Founded: 1939. **Staff:** Prof 1. **Subjects:** Petroleum and natural gas, economics, minerals, geology, engineering. **Holdings:** 16,000 books; 3800 bound periodical volumes; 21,000 pamphlets (cataloged); 4500 geologic maps; 85 pamphlet boxes of preprints. **Subscriptions:** 150 journals and other serials. **Services:** Interlibrary loans; copying; library open to public by appointment. **Networks/Consortia:** Member of Industrial Information Service.

DEHON (Leo) LIBRARY
See: Sacred Heart Monastery - Leo Dehon Library

★3620★
DEL MAR COLLEGE - MUSIC LIBRARY (Mus)
Music Dept.   Phone: (512) 881-6386
Corpus Christi, TX 78404   Ralph Thibodeau, Prof. of Music
Staff: Prof 1; Other 3. **Subjects:** Music; scores; classical music; performance music - choral, instrumental. **Holdings:** 5774 books, scores, bound periodical volumes; 3898 classical recordings; 5179 performance scores and parts. **Subscriptions:** 38 journals and other serials. **Services:** Interlibrary loans; library open to public with restrictions. **Computerized Information Services:** Computerized serials. **Special Catalogs:** Bach Gesamtausgabe (Breitkopf and Haertel; card).

★3621★
DEL NORTE COUNTY HISTORICAL SOCIETY - LIBRARY (Hist)
577 H St.   Phone: (707) 464-3922
Crescent City, CA 95531   Judy Knitter, Pres.
Subjects: History of Del Norte County and California; history of southern

Oregon. **Holdings:** 500 books; 2000 personal papers, diaries and other material; area photographs; Yurok and Tolowa Indian artifacts. **Services:** Library open to public on a limited schedule. **Publications:** Bulletin, 11/year; local history pamphlets.

★3622★
DEL NORTE COUNTY LAW LIBRARY (Law)
Courthouse   Phone: (707) 464-4139
Crescent City, CA 95531   Patricia Lamb, Law Libn.
Subjects: Law. **Holdings:** 5811 volumes. **Services:** Library open to public for reference use only.

DELAP (Loyd) LAW LIBRARY
See: Klamath County - Loyd Delap Law Library

★3623★
DELAVAN CORPORATION - ENGINEERING LIBRARY (Sci-Tech)
Box 100   Phone: (515) 274-1561
West Des Moines, IA 50265   Gwen Hartman, Libn.
Founded: 1955. **Staff:** 1. **Subjects:** Liquid atomization; spray nozzles; fuel injectors; fuel combustion; fluid flow and hydraulics; pumps; engineering design; properties of materials; ultrasonics and electronics. **Holdings:** 1000 books; 500 bound periodical volumes; 10,000 papers and articles (cataloged); manufacturers' catalogs; 1800 patents related to company products; 400 technical reports (for company use); microfilms, microfiche and motion pictures. **Subscriptions:** 100 journals and other serials. **Services:** Library principally for organization use. **Publications:** Library bulletin - for internal distribution only. **Special Catalogs:** Index card files based on author, title and key words. **Staff:** R.W. Tate, Dir. of Res.

★3624★
DELAWARE ACADEMY OF MEDICINE - LIBRARY (Med)
1925 Lovering Ave.   Phone: (302) 656-1629
Wilmington, DE 19806   Gail P. Gill, Libn.
Founded: 1930. **Staff:** Prof 1. **Subjects:** Medicine. **Special Collections:** 50 state medical journals (20-year holding). **Holdings:** 6000 books; 8500 journals. **Subscriptions:** 200 journals and other serials. **Services:** Interlibrary loans; copying; library open to public for reference use only. **Computerized Information Services:** MEDLARS; computerized cataloging. **Networks/ Consortia:** Member of Wilmington Area Biomedical Library Consortium; Delaware Library Consortium.

★3625★
DELAWARE ART MUSEUM - LIBRARY (Art)
2301 Kentmere Pkwy.   Phone: (302) 571-9590
Wilmington, DE 19806   Anne Marie Haslam, Libn.
Founded: 1912. **Staff:** Prof 1. **Subjects:** American art history; history of illustration; pre-Raphaelites. **Special Collections:** Bancroft Pre-Raphaelite Library (3000 volumes); Howard Pyle Library (3000 volumes); N.C. Wyeth Collection (150 volumes); John Sloan Memorial Library (2500 volumes); John Sloan, Everett Shinn, Jerome Myers and Frank Schoonover collections. **Holdings:** 25,000 books; 360 bound periodical volumes; 40 shelves of unbound periodicals; 260 reels of microfilmed illustrated periodicals (1890-1940); 38 VF drawers of exhibition catalogs; 20 VF drawers of pamphlets and clippings; 20 shelves of auction catalogs; 8 VF drawers of manuscripts. **Subscriptions:** 50 journals and other serials. **Services:** Interlibrary loans; copying; library open to public on a limited schedule or by appointment.

★3626★
DELAWARE COUNTY HISTORICAL SOCIETY - LIBRARY (Hist)
Box 1036, Widener University   Phone: (215) 874-6444
Chester, PA 19013   Edna S. Sweely, Cur.
Founded: 1895. **Staff:** 2. **Subjects:** Delaware County history and genealogy. **Special Collections:** Partial 1790-1900 Census of Delaware County; Baker Collection of local historic data (105 notebooks); atlas books of early land holdings; Pennsylvania, New Jersey and Delaware archives; out-of-print newspapers (1840-1935). **Holdings:** 5000 books; 140 bound periodical volumes; 4500 files of clippings and pictures (cataloged); maps. **Subscriptions:** 19 journals and other serials. **Services:** Interlibrary loans; copying; library open to public for reference use only. **Computerized Information Services:** Computerized cataloging. **Publications:** Delaware County Historical Society Bulletin, quarterly. **Remarks:** Holdings of the library are housed in the Wolfgram Memorial Library at Widener University.

★3627★
DELAWARE COUNTY LAW LIBRARY (Law)
Court House   Phone: (614) 363-4632
Delaware, OH 43015   Sherman Moist, Libn.
Founded: 1900. **Staff:** 1. **Subjects:** Law. **Holdings:** 12,000 volumes.

Services: Library open to members of the bar and students by special permission.

★3628★
DELAWARE COUNTY LAW LIBRARY (Law)
Courthouse
Media, PA 19063
Phone: (215) 891-2380
Charlotte H. Hewlings, Libn.
Staff: 1. **Subjects:** Law. **Holdings:** 26,000 volumes. **Services:** Copying; library open to public.

★3629★
DELAWARE COUNTY PLANNING COMMISSION - LIBRARY AND DATA SECTION (Plan)
Watkins Bldg.
350 N. Middletown Rd.
Lima, PA 19037
Phone: (215) 891-5656
Jane Taggart Quinn, Libn.
Founded: 1968. **Staff:** Prof 1. **Subjects:** Land use, population and demography, mapping of area, zoning and planning, economic statistics, environmental resources, data about minor civil division, housing. **Holdings:** 1500 books; 100 bound periodical volumes; 5000 binders of report material from government sources; 150 microfiche; 8 VF drawers. **Subscriptions:** 70 journals and other serials. **Services:** Interlibrary loans; copying; SDI; library open to public. **Publications:** Acquisition lists, bimonthly - for libraries in area. **Formerly:** Located in Media, PA.

★3630★
DELAWARE LAW SCHOOL OF WIDENER UNIVERSITY - LAW LIBRARY (Law)
Concord Pike, Box 7475
Wilmington, DE 19803
Phone: (302) 478-5280
Richard Humphreys, Libn.
Founded: 1971. **Staff:** Prof 6; Other 6. **Subjects:** Law. **Holdings:** 105,000 books; 45,000 volumes in microform. **Subscriptions:** 490 journals and other serials. **Services:** Interlibrary loans; copying; library open to public. **Computerized Information Services:** LEXIS; computerized cataloging, acquisitions, serials and ILL. **Networks/Consortia:** Member of Delaware Library Consortium. **Staff:** David Voisinet, Asst.Libn.; Eileen Cooper, Asst.Libn.; Jacquelin Paul, Asst.Libn.; Evelyn Brownlee, Asst.Libn.; Karin Thurman, Asst.Libn.; Mary Alice Peeling, Asst.Libn.

★3631★
DELAWARE MUSEUM OF NATURAL HISTORY - LIBRARY (Sci-Tech)
Kennett Pike, Rte. 52
Box 3937
Greenville, DE 19807
Phone: (302) 658-9111
Robert L. Dimit, Dir.
Staff: 1. **Subjects:** Malacology (mollusks), ornithology, mammalogy, natural history. **Special Collections:** Books by and about Linneaus (600 books; 200 reprints). **Holdings:** 5000 books; 1000 bound periodical volumes; 10,000 unbound reprints on mollusks; 4000 unbound reprints on birds. **Subscriptions:** 100 journals and other serials. **Services:** Interlibrary loans; copying; library open to public by prior arrangement. **Publications:** Indo-Pacific Mollusca, irregular; Nemouria, irregular; Living Volutes, 1970; Philippine Birds, 1971; South Pacific Birds, 1976; Exotic Conchology, 1976; Woodpeckers of the World, 1982. **Special Indexes:** Index Nudibranchia, 1971.

★3632★
DELAWARE RIVER BASIN COMMISSION - TECHNICAL LIBRARY (Env-Cons)
25 State Police Dr.
Box 7360
Trenton, NJ 08628
Phone: (609) 883-9500
Mary Frances Wightman, Tech.Libn.
Founded: 1962. **Staff:** Prof 1. **Subjects:** Delaware River, water resources, water pollution, aquatic biology, geology, hydrology. **Holdings:** 1500 books; 550 bound periodical volumes; 10,000 technical reports (cataloged); 1 map case; 500 slides. **Subscriptions:** 100 journals and other serials. **Services:** Interlibrary loans; copying; library open to public by appointment. **Computerized Information Services:** DIALOG.

DELAWARE STATE ARCHIVES
See: Delaware State Division of Historical & Cultural Affairs

★3633★
DELAWARE STATE DEPARTMENT OF COMMUNITY AFFAIRS - DIVISION OF LIBRARIES
43 S. Dupont Hwy.
Dover, DE 19901
Phone: (302) 736-4749
Sylvia Short, State Libn.
Founded: 1901. **Staff:** Prof 4; Other 14. **Subjects:** Adult nonfiction. **Special Collections:** Delaware state documents on microfiche. **Holdings:** 42,000 books; 60 periodical titles on microfilm; 1400 reels of microfilm; 5 VF drawers of pamphlets; 10,000 talking books and cassettes. **Subscriptions:** 125 journals and other serials; 5 newspapers. **Services:** Interlibrary loans; copying; library open to public. **Computerized Information Services:**

Computerized cataloging. **Networks/Consortia:** Member of OCLC through PALINET & Union Library Catalogue of Pennsylvania. **Publications:** Chicken Scratch and Star. **Special Catalogs:** Large Print Books in Delaware Public Libraries (book). **Staff:** Lee Steele, Ref.Libn.; Jane Buch, Tech.Serv.Supv.; Diane Greenwald, Network Serv.

★3634★
DELAWARE STATE DEPARTMENT OF PUBLIC INSTRUCTION - LIBRARY (Educ)
Townsend Bldg.
Box 1402
Dover, DE 19901
Phone: (302) 736-4692
Richard L. Krueger, Libn.
Founded: 1970. **Staff:** Prof 1; Other 1. **Subjects:** Education - administration and supervision; school finance; school plant planning; school law. **Special Collections:** Laws of Delaware; Delaware Code Annotated; Delaware history of education. **Holdings:** 6500 books; 206 bound periodical volumes; minutes of the State Board of Education; Department reports; information files. **Subscriptions:** 250 journals and other serials; 25 newspapers. **Services:** Interlibrary loans; copying; library open to public. **Computerized Information Services:** DIALOG. **Networks/Consortia:** Member of Delaware Dissemination Network. **Publications:** Compilation of School Laws of Delaware, updated periodically for school personnel. **Remarks:** Library's ERIC collection is the only complete microfiche set in Delaware.

★3635★
DELAWARE STATE DEPARTMENT OF TRANSPORTATION - LIBRARY (Trans)
Rte. 113, Administrative Bldg.
Dover, DE 19901
Phone: (302) 678-4157
Juliana Cheng, Libn.
Staff: 1. **Subjects:** Traffic studies, highway design, mass transportation. **Special Collections:** Transportation Research Board Reports. **Holdings:** 3000 books; 2000 reports. **Subscriptions:** 25 journals and other serials. **Services:** Interlibrary loans; library open to public with restrictions. **Publications:** Acquisitions list, irregular.

★3636★
DELAWARE STATE DEVELOPMENT OFFICE - TECHNICAL LIBRARY (Plan; Bus-Fin)
Townsend Bldg., 3rd Fl.
Dover, DE 19901
Phone: (302) 736-4271
Cora Bonniwell
Founded: 1981. **Staff:** 1. **Subjects:** Business development, planning, land use, statistics, economics. **Holdings:** 480 books and bound periodical volumes; studies; pamphlets. **Subscriptions:** 40 journals and other serials. **Services:** Library open to public with restrictions. **Publications:** Dimensions on Delaware, A Statistical Abstract. **Remarks:** The Office also houses the State Data Center. **Formerly:** Delaware State Office of Management, Budget & Planning.

★3637★
DELAWARE STATE DIVISION OF HISTORICAL & CULTURAL AFFAIRS - DELAWARE STATE ARCHIVES (Hist)
Hall of Records
Dover, DE 19901
Phone: (302) 736-5318
Roy H. Tryon, Chf./Archv. & Rec.Mgt.Bur.
Founded: 1911. **Staff:** Prof 3; Other 5. **Subjects:** Delaware history and government; county and city records. **Special Collections:** Tatnall Tombstone collection (2 volumes); Turner genealogical collection (21 cubic feet); transcribed church records (35 volumes). **Holdings:** 2000 books; 5000 maps and architectural drawings; 50,000 photographs and slides; 13,100 reels of microfilm. **Services:** Copying; archives open to public. **Networks/Consortia:** Member of Kent County Library Network. **Publications:** Delaware Documentation, quarterly checklist of state publications - national distribution. **Staff:** Joanne A. Mattern, Archv.Br.Supv.; C. Russell McCabe, Archv.

DELAWARE STATE - DIVISION OF LIBRARIES
See: Delaware State Department of Community Affairs

★3638★
DELAWARE STATE GEOLOGICAL SURVEY - LIBRARY (Sci-Tech)
101 Penny Hall
University of Delaware
Newark, DE 19711
Phone: (302) 738-2834
Robert R. Jordan, State Geologist
Subjects: Geology, mineral and water resources, seismology, well sampling, cartography. **Special Collections:** Core and sample library (25,000 items); repository for geophysical logs and seismic sections. **Holdings:** Figures not available. **Services:** Library open to public for reference and by arrangement only. **Staff:** Thomas E. Pickett, Assoc.Dir.

★3639★

DELAWARE STATE HOSPITAL - MEDICAL LIBRARY (Med)†
Rte. 13   Phone: (302) 421-6368
New Castle, DE 19720   Ruth A. Irwin, Libn.
Staff: Prof 1; Other 1. **Subjects:** Psychiatry, psychology, medicine, social science, nursing, pastoral care. **Holdings:** 4000 books; 1240 bound periodical volumes; 220 cassettes (cataloged); 8 VF drawers of pamphlets. **Subscriptions:** 153 journals and other serials. **Services:** Interlibrary loans; copying; library open to public for reference use only. **Networks/Consortia:** Member of Wilmington Area Biomedical Libraries Consortium; Mideastern Regional Medical Library Service (MERMLS).

★3640★

DELAWARE STATE LAW LIBRARY IN KENT COUNTY (Law)
Kent County Courthouse   Phone: (302) 736-5467
Dover, DE 19901   Carol N. Russell, Law Libn.
Staff: Prof 1; Other 1. **Subjects:** Law. **Holdings:** 39,000 volumes. **Services:** Copying; library open to public.

DELAWARE STATE OFFICE OF MANAGEMENT, BUDGET & PLANNING
See: Delaware State Development Office

★3641★

DELAWARE STATE TRAVEL SERVICE (Bus-Fin)
630 State College Rd.
Box 1401   Phone: (302) 678-4254
Dover, DE 19901   J.C. Geddes, Dir. of Tourism
Staff: Prof 3; Other 4. **Subjects:** State of Delaware - travel information, tourism, promotional and statistical material. **Holdings:** Figures not available; maps and brochures. **Services:** Service open to public. **Remarks:** The toll-free number is 800-441-8846.

★3642★

DELAWARE VALLEY COLLEGE OF SCIENCE AND AGRICULTURE - JOSEPH KRAUSKOPF MEMORIAL LIBRARY (Agri)
                                            Phone: (215) 345-1500
Doylestown, PA 18901   Constance R. Shook, Hd.Libn.
Founded: 1925. **Staff:** Prof 5; Other 7. **Subjects:** Agronomy, animal husbandry, dairy husbandry, food industry, horticulture, ornamental horticulture, poultry husbandry, biology, chemistry, business administration. **Special Collections:** Memorial Collection of Judaica. **Holdings:** 49,197 books; 9018 bound periodical volumes; 17,000 U.S. Department of Agriculture and State Agricultural Experiment Station bulletins (subject indexed); 1390 reels of microfilm; 1300 microfiche. **Subscriptions:** 600 journals and other serials; 6 newspapers. **Services:** Interlibrary loans; copying; library open to public for reference use only. **Networks/Consortia:** Member of Mideastern Regional Medical Library Service (MERMLS); Tri-State College Library Cooperative (TCLC). **Staff:** Cynthia Spell, Cat./Ref.Libn.; June Bitzer, Acq./Ref.Libn.; Nora O'Malley, AV Libn.; Bruce Hanson, Circ./Ref.Libn.

★3643★

DELAWARE VALLEY MEDICAL CENTER - JOHN A. WHYTE MEDICAL LIBRARY (Med)
Wilson Ave. & Pond St.   Phone: (215) 245-2335
Bristol, PA 19007   Marian C. Moran, Med.Libn.
Staff: Prof 1. **Subjects:** Medicine. **Holdings:** 800 books; 15 bound periodical volumes; 400 cassettes and videotapes. **Subscriptions:** 87 journals and other serials. **Services:** Interlibrary loans; copying; library not open to public. **Computerized Information Services:** NLM. **Networks/Consortia:** Member of Mideastern Regional Medical Library Service (MERMLS); Delaware Valley Information Consortium (DEVIC).

DELBAY PHARMACEUTICALS
See: Miles Laboratories, Inc.

DELCO ELECTRONICS DIVISION
See: General Motors Corporation

DELHOM-GAMBRELL REFERENCE LIBRARY
See: Mint Museum of Art - Library

★3644★

DELL PUBLISHING COMPANY, INC. - LIBRARY (Publ)†
One Dag Hammarskjold Plaza   Phone: (212) 605-3000
New York, NY 10017   Janie Fabian, Libn.
Founded: 1936. **Staff:** Prof 1; Other 2. **Subjects:** Publishing, authors, movie personalities. **Special Collections:** Dell publications (5000 volumes). **Holdings:** 2000 volumes; 174 VF drawers of movie personality photographs and biographies; 34 VF drawers of movie production stills; 8 VF drawers of TV material; hard cover books; paperback books; comic and activity books. **Subscriptions:** 319 journals and other serials. **Services:** Library open to SLA members by appointment. **Remarks:** Includes Reference Library, TV/Movie Reference and Stills Library, and Archives. **Staff:** Gem Spence, Per.

★3645★

DELLCREST CHILDREN'S CENTRE - LIBRARY (Soc Sci)
1645 Sheppard Ave. W.   Phone: (416) 633-0515
Downsview, ON, Canada M3M 2X4   Lois Elliott, Libn.
Staff: Prof 1; Other 1. **Subjects:** Children - psychotherapy, welfare and development; parenting and family therapy. **Holdings:** 1124 books and bound periodical volumes; 41 cassettes; 36 VF drawers of pamphlets. **Subscriptions:** 72 journals and other serials. **Services:** Library open to public with restrictions.

★3646★

DELOITTE HASKINS & SELLS - AUDIT/MAS & TAX LIBRARY (Bus-Fin)†
44 Montgomery St.   Phone: (415) 393-4300
San Francisco, CA 94104   Eunice J. Azzani, Libn.
Staff: 1. **Subjects:** Accounting, auditing, business, management advisory and tax services. **Holdings:** 1800 books. **Subscriptions:** 150 journals and other serials; 5 newspapers. **Services:** Interlibrary loans; library open to public with permission from librarian.

★3647★

DELOITTE HASKINS & SELLS - EXECUTIVE OFFICE LIBRARY (Bus-Fin)
1114 Ave. of the Americas   Phone: (212) 790-0639
New York, NY 10036   Rhea Tabakin, Exec.Off.Libn.
Founded: 1895. **Staff:** Prof 2; Other 4. **Subjects:** Accounting, auditing, business and finance, taxation, electronic data processing. **Holdings:** 5750 books; 250 bound periodical volumes; 7500 pamphlets. **Subscriptions:** 450 journals and other serials. **Services:** Interlibrary loans; library open to librarians, clients and researchers by appointment. **Computerized Information Services:** DIALOG, SDC, New York Times Information Service, Mead Data Central. **Remarks:** Corporate annual reports kept in Research Department. **Staff:** Elaine Miller, Asst.Libn.

★3648★

DELOITTE HASKINS & SELLS - LIBRARY (Bus-Fin)
1101 15th St., N.W., 9th Fl.   Phone: (202) 862-3548
Washington, DC 20005   Nancy Holland, Libn.
Founded: 1977. **Staff:** Prof 1. **Subjects:** Accounting, auditing, banking, data processing, management, taxation. **Holdings:** 1000 books; 20 bound periodical volumes; 300 pamphlets; 150 technical reports; 6 VF drawers of clippings, annual reports and pamphlets. **Subscriptions:** 85 journals and other serials; 5 newspapers. **Services:** Interlibrary loans; copying; SDI; library open to public with restrictions.

★3649★

DELOITTE HASKINS & SELLS - LIBRARY (Bus-Fin)
625 Fourth Ave. S., Suite 1000   Phone: (612) 333-2900
Minneapolis, MN 55402   Richard G. Reynen, Libn.
Staff: Prof 1. **Subjects:** Accounting, auditing, taxation. **Holdings:** 2500 books; 30 bound periodical volumes. **Subscriptions:** 95 journals and other serials; 5 newspapers. **Services:** Interlibrary loans; copying; library open to public with restrictions.

★3650★

DELOITTE HASKINS & SELLS - LIBRARY (Bus-Fin)
2500 Three Girard Plaza   Phone: (215) 569-3500
Philadelphia, PA 19102   Lenka Berlin, Libn.
Founded: 1970. **Staff:** Prof 1; Other 1. **Subjects:** Accounting and auditing, U.S. taxation, management and business. **Holdings:** 1800 books; 750 bound periodical volumes; 8 VF drawers of published annual reports; 12 VF drawers of pamphlets and clippings. **Subscriptions:** 325 journals and other serials. **Services:** Interlibrary loans; copying; library open to public by appointment.

DELOITTE HASKINS & SELLS TAX RESEARCH ROOM
See: University of Minnesota

DELTA BRANCH EXPERIMENT STATION LIBRARY
See: Mississippi State Agricultural & Forestry Experiment Station

★3651★

DELTA COUNTY HISTORICAL SOCIETY MUSEUM LIBRARY (Hist)
Ludington Park, Box 1776
Escanaba, MI 49829   William G. Daniels, Pres.
Founded: 1956. **Subjects:** History of Delta County, railroads, lumbering, families. **Holdings:** Local subjects files. **Services:** Library not open to public.

★3652★
DELTA ENGINEERING CORPORATION - LIBRARY (Sci-Tech)
7400 Harwin
Box 36255
Houston, TX 77036
Phone: (713) 783-9120
Jacquelyn D. Davis, Libn.
Founded: 1981. **Staff:** Prof 1. **Subjects:** Petroleum - engineering, production, refining, offshore production; construction. **Special Collections:** Job archives of Delta Projects Limited, Canada (1200 documents). **Holdings:** 110 books; 60 bound periodical volumes; 400 reels of microfilm; 2700 pieces of archival material; 10,000 drawings. **Subscriptions:** 37 journals and other serials. **Services:** Interlibrary loans; copying; library not open to public. **Publications:** DEC/Library Newsletter, irregular - for internal distribution only. **Special Indexes:** Index to job archives on microfilm (book).

DELTA OMICRON MUSIC COMPOSERS LIBRARY
See: Public Library of Cincinnati and Hamilton County - Art and Music Department

DELTA REGIONAL PRIMATE RESEARCH CENTER
See: Tulane University of Louisiana

★3653★
DELTA WATERFOWL RESEARCH STATION - LIBRARY (Sci-Tech)
R.R. 1
Portage La Prairie, MB, Canada R1N 3A1
Phone: (204) 857-9125
Shirley Rutledge, Libn.
Founded: 1951. **Staff:** 1. **Subjects:** Zoology, botany, ornithology, earth sciences, natural history. **Holdings:** 3200 books; 2500 bound periodical volumes; 300 pamphlet boxes; 50 magnetic tapes. **Subscriptions:** 70 journals and other serials. **Services:** Interlibrary loans; copying; library open to university and government agency personnel.

★3654★
DELTIOLOGISTS OF AMERICA - LIBRARY (Rec)
10 Felton Ave.
Ridley Park, PA 19078
Phone: (215) 353-1689
James L. Lowe, Dir.
Founded: 1960. **Staff:** 1. **Subjects:** Deltiology (publishing and collecting of picture postcards), 1870 to present. **Special Collections:** Picture postcard publications. **Holdings:** 250 books; 400 bound periodical volumes; 3000 clippings in 5 file drawers; 400,000 picture postcards in 300 file drawers. **Subscriptions:** 20 journals and other serials. **Services:** Interlibrary loans; copying; library not open to public. **Publications:** Deltiology, bimonthly, limited circulation; Bibliography of Postcard Literature; Standard Postcard Catalog; Lincoln Postcard Catalog; Pictures in the Past; Picture Postcards of the Golden Age; Detroit Publishing Company Collector's Guide.

★3655★
DEMOCRATIC NATIONAL COMMITTEE - RESEARCH LIBRARY (Soc Sci)
1625 Massachusetts Ave., N.W.
Washington, DC 20036
Phone: (202) 797-5900
John Francis Bierlein, Dir., Res.Dev.
Staff: Prof 1; Other 2. **Subjects:** Politics - party and national; news - national, legislative, international. **Special Collections:** Most of the Democratic National Convention proceedings since 1856. **Holdings:** 500 books. **Subscriptions:** 34 journals and other serials. **Services:** Copying (limited); library open to public.

DENALI NATL. PARK
See: U.S. Natl. Park Service

DENISON (Ella Strong) LIBRARY
See: Claremont Colleges - Ella Strong Denison Library

DENISON MEMORIAL LIBRARY
See: University of Colorado Health Sciences Center

DENKMANN MEMORIAL LIBRARY
See: Augustana College

DENNIS (Fred O.) LAW LIBRARY
See: Georgetown University - Fred O. Dennis Law Library

★3656★
DENNISON MANUFACTURING COMPANY - RESEARCH LIBRARY (Sci-Tech)
300 Howard St.
Framingham, MA 01701
Phone: (617) 879-0511
Eva M. Bonis, Mgr., Lib. & Info.Serv.
Founded: 1935. **Staff:** Prof 1; Other 1. **Subjects:** Chemistry, chemical engineering, physics, mechanical engineering, business, marketing. **Special Collections:** Patents on copiers and adhesives (14,000). **Holdings:** 3600 books; 4 VF drawers of reprints. **Subscriptions:** 109 journals and other serials. **Services:** Interlibrary loans; copying; library not open to public.

Computerized Information Services: DIALOG, SDC; computerized circulation. **Publications:** Library News, 3-4/month - for internal distribution only. **Remarks:** Contains the holdings of Carter's Ink Company - Technical Library. **Staff:** Maryellen White, Asst.Libn.

★3657★
DENNY'S INC. - COMPUTER SERVICES LIBRARY (Info Sci)†
14256 E. Firestone Blvd.
La Mirada, CA 90637
Phone: (714) 739-8100
Penny Shubnell, Tech.Libn.
Founded: 1972. **Staff:** Prof 1. **Subjects:** Computers. **Holdings:** 500 books. **Services:** Library not open to public. **Computerized Information Services:** Computerized cataloging.

★3658★
DENOYER-GEPPERT COMPANY - EDITORIAL LIBRARY (Publ)
5235 Ravenswood Ave.
Chicago, IL 60640
Dr. Daniel H. Franck, Libn.
Staff: Prof 1; Other 1. **Subjects:** Middle Eastern business, education. **Holdings:** 3200 books; sales catalogs of 700 companies; clipping file. **Subscriptions:** 170 journals and other serials. **Services:** Library open to public by appointment. **Networks/Consortia:** Member of OCLC through ILLINET. **Publications:** New Titles, bimonthly - for internal distribution only.

DENTAL RESEARCH DATA OFFICE
See: National Institute of Dental Research

★3659★
DENVER ART MUSEUM - FREDERIC H. DOUGLAS LIBRARY OF ANTHROPOLOGY AND ART (Art)
100 W. 14th Ave. Pkwy.
Denver, CO 80204
Phone: (303) 575-2256
Margaret Goodrich, Libn.
Founded: 1929. **Staff:** Prof 1. **Subjects:** American Indians, African and Oceanic art, anthropology, primitive art. **Special Collections:** American Indians. **Holdings:** 50,000 books and bound periodical volumes; 30 boxes of clippings and pamphlets. **Subscriptions:** 75 journals and other serials. **Services:** Copying; library open to public by appointment. **Computerized Information Services:** BRS; computerized cataloging and serials. **Networks/Consortia:** Member of Central Colorado Library System; OCLC.

DENVER BAPTIST BIBLE COLLEGE/DENVER BAPTIST BIBLE INSTITUTE
See: Denver Theological Seminary/Bible Institute

★3660★
DENVER BOTANIC GARDENS - HELEN FOWLER LIBRARY (Sci-Tech)
909 York St.
Denver, CO 80206
Phone: (303) 575-2548
Solange G. Gignac, Libn.
Staff: Prof 1. **Subjects:** Horticulture, botany. **Special Collections:** Watercolors of Colorado and Oregon wild flowers; Waring Collection (rare horticulture and botany books). **Holdings:** 12,000 books; 2000 pamphlets (cataloged); 300 brochures describing botanic gardens; 6000 pamphlets (uncataloged); 675 slides; 150 index seminum lists. **Subscriptions:** 300 journals and other serials. **Services:** Interlibrary loans; copying; library open to public but only members may borrow. **Networks/Consortia:** Member of Central Colorado Library System. **Publications:** Library Lines, bimonthly; accessions list, monthly. **Special Indexes:** Index to Green Thumb, quarterly.

DENVER GENERAL HOSPITAL LIBRARY
See: Denver Public Library

★3661★
DENVER MEDICAL LIBRARY (Med)
1601 E. 19th Ave.
Denver, CO 80218
Phone: (303) 839-6670
Mary De Mund, Lib.Dir.
Founded: 1871. **Staff:** Prof 2; Other 1. **Subjects:** Medicine, dentistry, history of medicine, socioeconomics, health adminisration. **Special Collections:** Hubert Work Collection (neuropsychiatry, 4200 volumes). **Holdings:** 7272 books; 27,200 bound periodical volumes. **Subscriptions:** 504 journals and other serials. **Services:** Interlibrary loans; copying; computer literature searching; library open to public with permission from society member. **Computerized Information Services:** NLM, Mile High Media Center, BRS. **Staff:** Martha Burroughs, Ref.Libn.

★3662★
DENVER MUSEUM OF NATURAL HISTORY - LIBRARY (Sci-Tech)
City Park
Denver, CO 80205
Phone: (303) 575-3610
Stephanie H. Stowe, Libn.
Founded: 1908. **Staff:** Prof 1. **Subjects:** Anthropology (Southwest United States), geology, paleontology, ornithology. **Holdings:** 20,000 volumes. **Subscriptions:** 200 journals and other serials. **Services:** Interlibrary loans;

copying; library open to public with restrictions. **Computerized Information Services:** Computerized cataloging. **Networks/Consortia:** Member of OCLC; Central Colorado Library System.

★3663★
DENVER POST - LIBRARY (Publ)
650 15th St.
Denver, CO 80202
Phone: (303) 820-1691
Marilyn Harrison, Asst.Libn.
Staff: Prof 1; Other 6. **Holdings:** 200 books and bound periodical volumes. **Services:** Copying; library not open to public. **Special Indexes:** Index of Denver Post articles since 1901 (1 million cards).

★3664★
DENVER PUBLIC LIBRARY - ARCHERY COLLECTION (Rec)
1357 Broadway
Denver, CO 80203
Phone: (303) 571-2036
Georgiana Tiff, Dept.Mgr.
Subjects: History and techniques of archery. **Holdings:** 230 books; 34 bound periodical volumes; uncataloged pamphlet collection. **Services:** Interlibrary loans; copying; library open to public for reference use only. **Remarks:** Collection is part of Arts and Recreation Department.

★3665★
DENVER PUBLIC LIBRARY - CONSERVATION LIBRARY (Env-Cons; Energy)
1357 Broadway
Denver, CO 80203
Phone: (303) 571-2000
Linda L. Cumming, Subject Dept.Mgr.
Staff: Prof 2; Other 1. **Subjects:** Conservation of natural resources, energy, environment, wilderness, pollution, wildlife, land use. **Special Collections:** American Bison Society; Howard Zahniser Memorial Wilderness Collection; Ira Gabrielson; Alberta Oil Sands Environmental Research Program; Alaska Coalition; Velma B. "Wild Horse Annie" Johnston; Wilderness Society; Rocky Mountain Center on Environment; Conservation Foundation; Rosalie Edge. **Holdings:** 10,000 books; 650 bound periodical volumes; 1200 linear feet of manuscripts; 243 linear feet of pamphlets; 130 oral history tapes; 200 reels of microfilm; 2000 microfiche; 10,000 photographs; 5000 documents; access to state and federal document depository. **Subscriptions:** 600 journals and other serials. **Services:** Interlibrary loans; copying; library open to public for reference use only with approval required for manuscript use. **Computerized Information Services:** DIALOG, SDC, BRS; computerized cataloging, acquisitions, serials and circulation. **Publications:** Forest Service Endangered Species Reports; Wild Horse and Wild Burro Report; Bureau of Land Management Technical Bulletins on Endangered Species; Energy/ Environment Information (newsletter), quarterly. **Special Indexes:** Index of all pamphlets, environmental impact statements, periodical articles and state documents not indexed commercially; index of manuscript collection; referral file.

★3666★
DENVER PUBLIC LIBRARY - DENVER GENERAL HOSPITAL LIBRARY (Med)
W. 8th & Cherokee Sts.
Denver, CO 80204
Phone: (303) 893-7422
Anita F. Westwood, Med. Subject Spec.
Founded: 1939. **Staff:** Prof 1; Other 1. **Subjects:** Clinical medicine, nursing, surgery, public health. **Holdings:** 2500 books; 10,500 bound periodical volumes. **Subscriptions:** 204 journals and other serials. **Services:** Interlibrary loans; copying; library open to public with restrictions. **Computerized Information Services:** Mile High Media Center, BRS, MEDLARS; computerized cataloging, acquisitions and ILL. **Networks/Consortia:** Member of Colorado Council of Medical Librarians; Midcontinental Regional Medical Library Program. **Publications:** Union List of Serials. **Special Catalogs:** Library Catalog (book).

★3667★
DENVER PUBLIC LIBRARY - FISH AND WILDLIFE REFERENCE SERVICE (Env-Cons)
3840 York St., Unit I
Denver, CO 80205
Phone: (303) 571-4656
Merveit Alkhoudairy, Proj.Mgr.
Founded: 1965. **Staff:** Prof 3; Other 2. **Subjects:** Wildlife management, fisheries management, endangered species. **Special Collections:** Selected Federal Aid in Fish and Wildlife Restoration Reports; selected Anadromous (sport) Fish Conservation Reports; Cooperative Fishery and Wildlife Research Units Reports; Endangered Species Act Reports/Recovery Plans. **Holdings:** 15,500 Federal Aid reports on microfiche (indexed); 65,000 segment reports. **Services:** Copying; SDI; library open to public. **Computerized Information Services:** DIALOG. **Publications:** Fish and Wildlife Reference Service Newsletter, quarterly - free upon request; Fish and Wildlife Thesaurus. **Special Indexes:** Indexes to computer-based system holdings for each state and territory of the U.S. (microfiche or hardcopy). **Remarks:** Primary function is to provide custom literature searches of computer files on fish and wildlife management research reports from state game and fish agencies. **Staff:** Wayne R. Coffey, Ref.Spec.; Jim Pinamont, Indexing Spec.

★3668★
DENVER PUBLIC LIBRARY - FOLK MUSIC COLLECTION, FRIENDS OF MUSIC (Mus)
1357 Broadway
Denver, CO 80203
Phone: (303) 571-2036
Georgiana Tiff, Dept.Mgr.
Subjects: Folk music with emphasis on ballads and Anglo-American tradition; ethnomusicology; contemporary folk music. **Holdings:** 1750 books and song collections; 47 bound periodical volumes. **Subscriptions:** 15 journals and other serials. **Services:** Interlibrary loans (limited); copying; collection open to public for reference use only. **Remarks:** Collection is part of the Arts and Recreation Department.

★3669★
DENVER PUBLIC LIBRARY - GENEALOGY DIVISION (Hist)
1357 Broadway
Denver, CO 80203
Phone: (303) 571-2077
Joanne Classen, Subject Spec.
Staff: Prof 2. **Subjects:** County, state and town histories; census schedules, 1790-1880; genealogy; military rosters; heraldry. **Special Collections:** Denver obituaries, 1900 to present (21 reels of microfilm, 9 volumes, 16 file drawers; 13 microfiche); notebook file of Colorado pioneers (2 VF drawers); genealogical manuscripts and clippings (20 VF drawers); genealogical charts (2 map cases). **Holdings:** 17,500 books; 2000 bound periodical volumes; 2550 reels of microfilmed census schedules; 2500 microcards; vital records; census indexes; 9 boxes of manuscripts; 2 VF drawers of non-Denver obituaries. **Subscriptions:** 150 journals and other serials. **Services:** Copying. **Special Indexes:** Index to obituaries published in 2 major Denver newspapers; Index to anniversary announcements published in 2 major Denver newspapers; family name file; coat of arms file - all on cards.

★3670★
DENVER PUBLIC LIBRARY - SPECIAL COLLECTIONS ROOM (Hist; Hum)
1357 Broadway
Denver, CO 80203
Phone: (303) 571-2010
Eleanor M. Gehres, Hd., Western Hist.Dept.
Special Collections: Eugene Field Collection (400 books; 900 manuscripts); Ross-Barrett Historical Aeronautics Collection (12,000 books; 900 bound periodical volumes; 4 VF drawers of pamphlets; 600 pictures; 16 manuscripts; 48 films); Douglas Collection of Fine Printing (1500 books). **Services:** Interlibrary loans (limited); copying (limited); room open to public with restrictions, and with a fee for nonresidents.

★3671★
DENVER PUBLIC LIBRARY - WESTERN HISTORY DEPARTMENT (Hist)
1357 Broadway
Denver, CO 80203
Phone: (303) 571-2009
Eleanor M. Gehres, Hd.
Staff: Prof 7; Other 5. **Subjects:** History of U.S. west of Mississippi River with special emphasis on Rocky Mountain region. **Special Collections:** Western states mining collection; Spanish land grants; western railroads; Nate Salsbury-Buffalo Bill Collection; Western newspapers on microfilm; Frontier Theater Collection (5000 items). **Holdings:** 60,000 books and pamphlets; 285,000 prints and photographs; 182 VF drawers of clippings; 4500 maps; 6000 reels of microfilm; 1000 feet of manuscripts. **Subscriptions:** 200 journals and other serials; 60 newspapers. **Services:** Interlibrary loans (limited); copying; photographic prints; department open to public, with a fee for nonresidents. **Publications:** Occasional books and catalogs; Oral History Workshop Guide; Nothing Is Long Ago: A Documentary History of Colorado 1776/1976. **Special Catalogs:** Colorado Photographers, 1858-1940; David Barry pictures published catalog; Otto Perry Railroad published catalog, volumes 1 and 2. **Special Indexes:** General Western Index (4 million entries).

★3672★
DENVER PUBLIC SCHOOL DISTRICT 1 - PROFESSIONAL LIBRARY (Educ)
3800 York St., Bldg.1, Unit B
Denver, CO 80205
Phone: (303) 837-1000
Phyllis Dodd, Supv.
Founded: 1923. **Staff:** Prof 3; Other 6. **Subjects:** Education - materials for teachers, pupils and curriculum. **Special Collections:** Multi-ethnic print and nonprint media; instruction in the use of the library/IMC (nonprint); materials to be used with gifted, talented, and creative students. **Holdings:** 61,832 books; 421 bound periodical volumes; 847 microfilms and microfiche; 4078 nonprint items. **Subscriptions:** 140 journals and other serials. **Services:** Interlibrary loans (limited); copying; library open to public with restrictions.

★3673★
DENVER REGIONAL COUNCIL OF GOVERNMENTS - DRCOG LIBRARY (Plan)
2480 W. 26th Ave., Suite 200B
Denver, CO 80211
Phone: (303) 455-1000
Dianna L. Waterworth, Libn.
Staff: Prof 1. **Subjects:** Regional planning, transportation, environmental planning, population and housing, aging and health, criminal justice. **Special Collections:** DRCOG publications (500 titles). **Holdings:** 5500 books; 2 VF drawers of pamphlets and clippings; 75 files and notebooks of computer

materials. **Subscriptions:** 82 journals and other serials; 8 newspapers. **Services:** Interlibrary loans; copying; library open to public with restrictions and on a limited schedule. **Publications:** DRCOG Notes and Notations, monthly - to interested groups and libraries.

DENVER REGIONAL TRANSPORTATION DISTRICT
See: Regional Transportation District (Metropolitan Denver Area)

DENVER RESEARCH INSTITUTE
See: University of Denver and Denver Research Institute

★3674★
DENVER THEOLOGICAL SEMINARY/BIBLE INSTITUTE - SAMUEL JAMES BRADFORD MEMORIAL LIBRARY (Rel-Theol)
1200 Miramonte St.
Broomfield, CO 80020   Anita R. Meyer, Act.Libn.
Founded: 1953. **Staff:** 3. **Subjects:** Religion and theology. **Holdings:** 20,000 books; 186 bound periodical volumes; 160 record albums; 200 language tapes; 6 drawers slides; 4 VF drawers of pamphlets; 7 VF drawers of maps, mission boards, bibliographies and transparencies. **Subscriptions:** 151 journals and other serials. **Services:** Interlibrary loans; copying; literature searches; library open to public. **Also Known As:** Denver Baptist Bible College/Denver Baptist Bible Institute.

★3675★
DENVER ZOOLOGICAL GARDEN - LIBRARY (Sci-Tech)
23rd & Steele   Phone: (303) 575-2432
Denver, CO 80205   Paul Linger, Asst.Dir.
Founded: 1970. **Subjects:** Animal husbandry, endangered species, natural history. **Holdings:** 300 books; 50 bound periodical volumes; 500 annual reports, guidebooks of other zoos and other items. **Subscriptions:** 50 journals and other serials.

★3676★
DES MOINES ART CENTER - LIBRARY (Art)
Greenwood Park   Phone: (515) 277-4405
Des Moines, IA 50312   Margaret Buckley, Libn.
Founded: 1948. **Staff:** Prof 1. **Subjects:** Painting, graphics, sculpture, architecture, art, textiles, drawing. **Holdings:** 8050 books; 402 bound periodical volumes; 15 VF drawers of pamphlets on individual artists; 15 VF drawers of museum catalogs and other related material; 3 VF drawers of subject files. **Subscriptions:** 24 journals and other serials. **Services:** Interlibrary loans; copying; library open to public for reference use only.

★3677★
DES PLAINES HISTORICAL SOCIETY - JOHN BYRNE MEMORIAL LIBRARY (Hist)
789 Pearson St.   Phone: (312) 391-5399
Des Plaines, IL 60016   James R. Williams, Musm.Dir.
Founded: 1967. **Staff:** 3. **Subjects:** Local history. **Holdings:** 500 books; 4 VF drawers of clippings; 4 boxes of documents; 2 VF drawers of photographs; microfilm, magnetic tapes. **Subscriptions:** 30 journals and other serials. **Services:** Copying; library open to public by appointment on weekdays only. **Publications:** Cobweb, monthly newsletter issued by society includes library information.

DESCHATELETS LIBRARY
See: Oblate Fathers - Bibliotheque Deschatelets

★3678★
DESERET NEWS - LIBRARY (Publ)
30 E. First S.   Phone: (801) 237-2155
Salt Lake City, UT 84111   Connie Christensen, Libn.
Staff: 5. **Subjects:** Newspaper reference topics. **Holdings:** Newspaper clippings, pictures, negatives, reference books and microfilm. **Services:** Copying; reprints of photographs; library not open to public.

★3679★
DESERT BOTANICAL GARDEN - RICHTER LIBRARY (Sci-Tech)
Papago Pk.
1201 N. Galvin Pkwy.   Phone: (602) 941-1217
Phoenix, AZ 85008   Betsy Lambie, Libn.
Founded: 1937. **Staff:** Prof 1; Other 2. **Subjects:** Cacti and other succulents; desert trees and shrubs. **Special Collections:** M.C. Richter Collection; botanical print collection (500). **Holdings:** 3550 volumes; 650 VF items. **Subscriptions:** 76 journals and other serials. **Services:** Interlibrary loans; copying; library open to public for reference use only on a limited schedule. **Networks/Consortia:** Member of Council on Botanical and Horticultural Libraries; Intermountain Union List of Serials (IMULS).

Publications: Saguaroland Bulletin, monthly - to members and others on exchange basis; Science Bulletin, irregular. **Special Indexes:** Desert Botanical Garden Index Seminum.

DESERT RESEARCH INSTITUTE
See: University of Nevada, Reno

★3680★
DESIGN PROFESSIONALS FINANCIAL CORPORATION - LIBRARY (Bus-Fin; Sci-Tech)
P.O. Drawer DPFC   Phone: (408) 649-5522
Monterey, CA 93942   Annette C. Gaskin, Libn.
Founded: 1975. **Staff:** Prof 1. **Subjects:** Insurance, psychology, architecture, business management, engineering, law. **Holdings:** 1000 books; 1400 clippings. **Subscriptions:** 84 journals and other serials. **Services:** Interlibrary loans; copying; library open to public with approval of librarian. **Formerly:** Located in San Francisco, CA.

★3681★
DESJARDINS DUCHARME DESJARDINS & BOURQUE - LAW LIBRARY (Law)
635 W. Dorchester Blvd., Suite 1200   Phone: (514) 878-9411
Montreal, PQ, Canada H3B 1R9   Jacques Cartier, Law Libn.
Staff: Prof 1; Other 1. **Subjects:** Law - corporate, tax, bankruptcy, labor, insurance; general liability. **Special Collections:** Canadian Jurisprudence (2000 volumes). **Holdings:** 7000 books; 1000 bound periodical volumes; 25,000 reports on microfiche. **Subscriptions:** 100 journals and other serials; 5 newspapers. **Services:** Copying; library not open to public.

★3682★
DETREX CHEMICAL INDUSTRIES, INC. - RESEARCH LABORATORIES - LIBRARY (Sci-Tech)†
Box 501   Phone: (313) 868-8402
Detroit, MI 48232   Sondra E. Schader, Libn.
Subjects: Chemistry and chemical engineering. **Holdings:** 2800 books and bound periodical volumes.

★3683★
DETROIT BAR ASSOCIATION FOUNDATION - LIBRARY (Law)
600 Woodward Ave.   Phone: (313) 961-3507
Detroit, MI 48226   Elizabeth T. Stajniak, Dir.
Founded: 1853. **Staff:** Prof 2; Other 6. **Subjects:** Law. **Holdings:** 100,000 books; 6500 bound periodical volumes; 60 newsletters (cataloged); 130,0000 microforms. **Subscriptions:** 190 journals and other serials; 6 newspapers. **Services:** Interlibrary loans (for members only); copying; library not open to public. **Computerized Information Services:** WESTLAW. **Staff:** Lillian Suchyta, Hd.Proc.Dept.

★3684★
DETROIT COLLEGE OF LAW - LIBRARY (Law)
130 E. Elizabeth St.   Phone: (313) 965-0150
Detroit, MI 48201   Mario A. Ceresa, Hd.Libn.
Staff: Prof 3; Other 4. **Subjects:** Law. **Holdings:** 63,419 books and bound periodical volumes; 70,256 volumes in microform. **Subscriptions:** 1689 journals and other serials. **Services:** Interlibrary loans; copying; library open to public with restrictions. **Computerized Information Services:** LEXIS. **Publications:** Acquisitions list, bimonthly. **Staff:** Lorraine K. Lorne, Assoc.Libn.; Sheryl H. Summers, Asst.Libn.

DETROIT DIESEL ALLISON DIVISION
See: General Motors Corporation

★3685★
DETROIT EDISON COMPANY - REFERENCE SERVICES (Energy)
2000 Second Ave.   Phone: (313) 237-9216
Detroit, MI 48226   Susan D. Clement, Supv., Ref.Serv.
Founded: 1915. **Staff:** Prof 3; Other 4. **Subjects:** Public utilities, electrical and mechanical engineering, business management. **Special Collections:** Electric Power Research Institute reports. **Holdings:** 6000 books; videotapes; industry standards on microfiche. **Subscriptions:** 300 journals and other serials. **Services:** Interlibrary loans; copying; library open to public by appointment. **Computerized Information Services:** New York Times Information Service, DIALOG, SDC, NEXIS; computerized cataloging, circulation and ILL. **Networks/Consortia:** Member of OCLC; Michigan Library Consortium. **Publications:** New Publications Newsletter, bimonthly. **Staff:** Vicki C. Hooft, Ref.Libn.; Martha McGee, Ref.Libn.

★3686★

DETROIT FREE PRESS - LIBRARY (Publ)
321 W. Lafayette   Phone: (313) 222-6897
Detroit, MI 48231   Michele Ann Kapecky, Chief Libn.
Founded: 1925. **Staff:** Prof 7; Other 5. **Subjects:** Newspaper reference topics. **Holdings:** 600 books; clippings on microfilm, 1971-1981; Free Press on microfilm, 1925 to present; 800,000 photographs. **Subscriptions:** 50 journals and other serials; 15 newspapers. **Services:** Library not open to public. **Computerized Information Services:** New York Times Information Service, QL Systems, full text online retrieval of newspaper stories. **Staff:** Bernadine Aubert, Asst.Chf.Libn.

★3687★

DETROIT GARDEN CENTER - LIBRARY (Sci-Tech)
1460 E. Jefferson Ave.   Phone: (313) 259-6363
Detroit, MI 48207   Jeanne C. Hillmer, Chm. of Lib.
Founded: 1932. **Staff:** Prof 1. **Subjects:** Horticulture and flora culture. **Holdings:** 4000 books. **Subscriptions:** 10 journals and other serials. **Services:** Library open to public for research. **Publications:** Detroit Garden Center Bulletin. **Remarks:** Moross House, the oldest known brick residence in Detroit, has been restored under the auspices of the Detroit Historical Commission. The Horticultural Library is on the second floor. **Staff:** Nona Duffey, Libn.

★3688★

DETROIT INSTITUTE OF ARTS - RESEARCH LIBRARY (Art)
5200 Woodward Ave.   Phone: (313) 833-7926
Detroit, MI 48202   Constance Wall, Libn.
Founded: 1905. **Staff:** Prof 2; Other 3. **Subjects:** Painting, sculpture, furniture, decorative arts, history of art, architecture. **Special Collections:** Paul McPharlin collection of puppetry and theater material; Grace Whitney Hoff collection of fine bindings; Albert Kahn Architecture Library. **Holdings:** 65,000 books; 6500 bound periodical volumes; 1500 bulletins; 40,000 2x2 slides; 27,000 3x4 slides; 166,000 pamphlets and museum and sale catalogs; 83,000 photographs. **Subscriptions:** 263 journals and other serials. **Services:** Interlibrary loans; copying; library open to public. **Computerized Information Services:** Computerized cataloging. **Networks/Consortia:** Member of Michigan Library Consortium. **Special Indexes:** D.I.A. Bulletin Index; American and Foreign Art Institution File; microfilm clipping file. **Staff:** Lynne Garza, Asst.Libn.

★3689★

DETROIT INSTITUTE OF TECHNOLOGY - JAMES C. GORDON MEMORIAL LIBRARY
2727 Second Ave.
Detroit, MI 48201
Defunct

★3690★

DETROIT JAZZ CENTER - JAZZ ARCHIVE (Mus)†
2626 Webb   Phone: (313) 867-4141
Detroit, MI 48206   John Sinclair, Dir.
Founded: 1979. **Staff:** Prof 1; Other 1. **Subjects:** Detroit and U.S. jazz artists. **Special Collections:** Current Detroit jazz artists (300 tapes); historical performances of Detroit jazz artists (100 tapes). **Holdings:** 200 books; 500 unbound jazz magazines; 1000 original photographs of Detroit jazz artists; 1000 posters, flyers, ephemera. **Subscriptions:** 10 journals and other serials. **Services:** Copying; library open to public by appointment. **Publications:** Jazz Space Detroit (book); Detroit Jazz Center Calendar, annual; World Stage Newsletter, monthly.

★3691★

DETROIT MACOMB HOSPITALS ASSOCIATION - HOSPITAL LIBRARY (Med)
690 Mullett   Phone: (313) 225-5185
Detroit, MI 48226   Lynn Sorensen Sutton, Corp.Dir. of Libs.
Staff: Prof 2; Other 1. **Subjects:** Medicine. **Holdings:** 2200 books; 1500 bound periodical volumes. **Subscriptions:** 250 journals and other serials. **Services:** Interlibrary loans; copying; SDI; library open to public by appointment. **Computerized Information Services:** Online systems. **Networks/Consortia:** Member of Metropolitan Detroit Medical Library Group (MDMLG); Detroit Cooperative Cataloging Center. **Publications:** Libraryline, bimonthly. **Staff:** Victoria A. Staniszewski, Asst.Libn.; Teresa Ocholik, Asst.Libn.

★3692★

DETROIT MACOMB HOSPITALS ASSOCIATION - SOUTH MACOMB HOSPITAL LIBRARY (Med)
11800 Twelve Mile Rd.   Phone: (313) 573-5117
Warren, MI 48093   Lynn Sorensen Sutton, Corp.Dir. of Libs.
Founded: 1974. **Staff:** Prof 2; Other 1. **Subjects:** Medicine, surgery,

obstetrics and gynecology, respiratory medicine. **Holdings:** 1300 books; 978 bound periodical volumes; 3 VF drawers. **Subscriptions:** 170 journals and other serials. **Services:** Interlibrary loans; copying; SDI; library open to public by appointment. **Computerized Information Services:** NLM, BRS, DIALOG; computerized cataloging. **Networks/Consortia:** Member of Metropolitan Detroit Medical Library Group; Detroit Cooperative Cataloging Center. **Publications:** Libraryline, bimonthly.

★3693★

DETROIT NEWS - GEORGE B. CATLIN MEMORIAL LIBRARY (Publ)
615 W. Lafayette St.   Phone: (313) 222-2110
Detroit, MI 48231   Betty W. Havlena, Chf.Libn.
Staff: Prof 3; Other 8. **Subjects:** Newspaper reference topics. **Holdings:** 20,000 books; 250 bound periodical volumes; 3 million clippings; 1 million photographs; 5000 pamphlets; microfilm. **Subscriptions:** 75 journals and other serials; 6 newspapers. **Services:** Interlibrary loans; library not open to public. **Staff:** Diane M. Dunn, Hd., Ref.Dept.

★3694★

DETROIT OSTEOPATHIC HOSPITAL - MEDICAL LIBRARY (Med)
12523 Third Ave.   Phone: (313) 869-1200
Highland Park, MI 48203   Gayle Williams, Dir. of Libs.
Founded: 1944. **Staff:** Prof 2; Other 1. **Subjects:** Medicine, orthopedics, surgery, ophthalmology, otolaryngology, nephrology, cardiology. **Special Collections:** Osteopathy classics. **Holdings:** 1600 books; 4160 bound periodical volumes; 200 audiotapes. **Subscriptions:** 175 journals and other serials. **Services:** Interlibrary loans; library open to public with restrictions. **Computerized Information Services:** MEDLINE, DIALOG. **Networks/Consortia:** Member of Kentucky-Ohio-Michigan Regional Medical Library Network (KOMRML); Metropolitan Detroit Medical Library Group (MDMLG). **Staff:** Lucie Beard, Libn.

★3695★

DETROIT PSYCHIATRIC INSTITUTE - LIBRARY (Med)
1151 Taylor   Phone: (313) 876-4170
Detroit, MI 48202   Rita H. Bigman, Libn.
Staff: Prof 1. **Subjects:** Psychiatry, psychoanalysis, social work, psychology, psychiatric nursing, general medicine. **Holdings:** 1445 books; 219 bound periodical volumes; 5 VF drawers of psychoanalysis articles; 3 VF drawers of government documents. **Subscriptions:** 66 journals and other serials. **Services:** Interlibrary loans; copying; SDI; library not open to public. **Computerized Information Services:** DIALOG.

★3696★

DETROIT PUBLIC LIBRARY - BURTON HISTORICAL COLLECTION (Hist)
5201 Woodward Ave.   Phone: (313) 833-1480
Detroit, MI 48202   Alice C. Dalligan, Chf.
Founded: 1914. **Staff:** Prof 8; Other 3. **Subjects:** History - Detroit, Michigan, Old Northwest, local (U.S. and Canada), Great Lakes; genealogy. **Special Collections:** Edgar DeWitt Jones - Lincoln Collection; Ernie Harwell Sports Collection (guides, periodicals, record books, yearbooks, rule books - 18,985 volumes). **Holdings:** 250,000 books and bound periodical volumes; 12,000 pamphlets and 4800 bound volumes of newspapers (cataloged); 4700 feet of manuscripts and personal papers; 9500 feet of archives; 20,000 reels of microfilm; 6000 microfiche; 1100 microcards; 50,000 pictures; 4000 maps; 5000 glass negatives; 6800 scrapbooks; 1000 color transparencies; 1000 lantern slides; 4050 maps; 325 broadsides. **Subscriptions:** 500 journals and other serials. **Services:** Copying; collection open to public. **Special Indexes:** Manuscripts reported in National Union List of Manuscripts. **Staff:** Joseph Oldenberg, Mss.Spec.; Benedict Markowski, Fld.Archv.; Margaret Ward, Fld.Archv.

★3697★

DETROIT PUBLIC LIBRARY - BUSINESS AND FINANCE DEPARTMENT (Bus-Fin)
5201 Woodward Ave.   Phone: (313) 833-1420
Detroit, MI 48202   Margaret Hammond, Chf.
Founded: 1924. **Staff:** Prof 5; Other 2. **Subjects:** Corporations, accounting, insurance, banking, advertising, real estate, business administration, investments, marketing. **Special Collections:** Corporation annual reports (paper and microfiche); trade directories. **Holdings:** 50,000 books; 8000 bound periodical volumes; 35 VF drawers; U.S. and foreign telephone directories. **Subscriptions:** 650 journals and other serials; 12 newspapers. **Services:** Interlibrary loans; copying; library open to public. **Computerized Information Services:** New York Times Information Service.

★3698★
DETROIT PUBLIC LIBRARY - FILM DEPARTMENT
5201 Woodward Ave.
Detroit, MI 48202
Founded: 1947. **Subjects:** Interpersonal relations, psychology, science, sports, lands and peoples, children's films, comedies (Laurel & Hardy, Charlie Chaplin, etc.), black studies, U.S. history, travel. **Holdings:** 2500 16mm sound films, 250 video cassettes. **Remarks:** Temporarily inactive.

★3699★
DETROIT PUBLIC LIBRARY - FINE ARTS DEPARTMENT (Art)
5201 Woodward Ave.   Phone: (313) 833-1467
Detroit, MI 48202   Shirley Solvick, Chf.
Founded: 1921. **Staff:** Prof 4; Other 1. **Subjects:** Art, architecture, handicrafts, design and drawing, cartooning, pottery and porcelain, prints, photography. **Special Collections:** Picture file - Collection of about 500,000 separate pictures covering all subjects. **Holdings:** 58,000 books; 9000 bound periodical volumes; 800 color prints (cataloged). **Subscriptions:** 290 journals and other serials. **Services:** Interlibrary loans; copying; department open to public with restrictions. **Special Indexes:** Subject index (card file analyzing books and periodicals); Picture heading list (card file of picture file subjects with references). **Staff:** Jean Comport, First Asst.; Ruth Barton, Libn.; Dora Deitch, Libn.

★3700★
DETROIT PUBLIC LIBRARY - FOREIGN LANGUAGE COLLECTION (Hum)
Downtown Library, 121 Gratiot   Phone: (313) 833-9800
Detroit, MI 48226   Carol Ferrero, Foreign Lang.Spec.
Staff: Prof 2. **Subjects:** Works in 47 foreign languages on all subjects. **Holdings:** 65,000 books; 2258 bound periodical volumes. **Subscriptions:** 70 journals and other serials; 53 newspapers. **Services:** Interlibrary loans; copying; deposit collections available to Michigan public libraries upon request. **Publications:** Periodic lists of new books in specific languages - internal distribution and to others upon request.

★3701★
DETROIT PUBLIC LIBRARY - GENERAL INFORMATION DEPARTMENT (Info Sci)
5201 Woodward Ave.   Phone: (313) 833-1400
Detroit, MI 48202   Margaretta Sandula, Chf.
Founded: 1948. **Staff:** Prof 7; Other 3. **Subjects:** Bibliography, biography, library science, sports, gardening, home economics, journalism. **Holdings:** 95,000 books; 31,000 bound periodical volumes; 16 vertical files of pamphlets and clippings; 14,000 reels of microfilm. **Subscriptions:** 700 journals and other serials; 9 newspapers. **Services:** Interlibrary loans; copying; library open to public.

★3702★
DETROIT PUBLIC LIBRARY - HISTORY AND TRAVEL DEPARTMENT (Hist; Geog-Map)
5201 Woodward Ave.   Phone: (313) 833-1445
Detroit, MI 48202   Anna DiPiazza, Chf.
Founded: 1949. **Staff:** Prof 4; Other 3. **Subjects:** History - political and social; archaeology, including Indians; geography; travel. **Special Collections:** Map Collection (150,095 sheet maps; 3314 atlases). **Holdings:** 145,484 books and bound periodical volumes; 88 VF drawers of travel pamphlets; 10 VF drawers of map publishers catalogs. **Subscriptions:** 336 journals and other serials. **Services:** Interlibrary loans; copying. **Computerized Information Services:** Computerized cataloging (maps). **Special Catalogs:** Map card catalog (area and subject arrangement).

★3703★
DETROIT PUBLIC LIBRARY - LABOR COLLECTION (Soc Sci)
5201 Woodward Ave.   Phone: (313) 833-1440
Detroit, MI 48202   Doris Detwiler, Chf.
Subjects: History of U.S. and foreign labor movement and individual unions; U.S. and foreign labor laws and legislation; collective bargaining and arbitration; labor relations; statistics on wages, hours of labor. **Special Collections:** Labor union contracts and agreements; labor union constitutions; files of labor laws; labor union convention proceedings. **Holdings:** 20,000 books; 1500 bound periodical volumes; 8000 cataloged pamphlets; 16 VF drawers of uncataloged pamphlets and clippings; 1000 reels of microfilm. **Subscriptions:** 100 journals and other serials; 130 newspapers. **Services:** Interlibrary loans; copying; library open to public. **Remarks:** Collection housed in Sociology and Economics Department.

★3704★
DETROIT PUBLIC LIBRARY - LANGUAGE AND LITERATURE DEPARTMENT (Hum)
5201 Woodward Ave.   Phone: (313) 833-1470
Detroit, MI 48202   Ann Rabjohns, Chf.
Founded: 1949. **Staff:** Prof 4; Other 1. **Subjects:** Literary history and criticism; drama; poetry; essays and belles lettres; public speaking; language and linguistics; folklore. **Special Collections:** Reference collection of foreign language dictionaries; reference and research collection of fiction; reference and research collection of children's literature. **Holdings:** 145,500 books; 7150 bound periodical volumes; 32 VF drawers of clippings and pamphlets. **Subscriptions:** 500 journals and other serials. **Services:** Interlibrary loans; copying. **Special Indexes:** Files include play index, poetry by subject and individial poems, biography and criticism of dramatists, poets, novelists and other writers of belles-lettres (card).

★3705★
DETROIT PUBLIC LIBRARY - MUNICIPAL REFERENCE LIBRARY (Soc Sci)
Rm. 1004, City County Bldg.
2 Woodward Ave.   Phone: (313) 224-3885
Detroit, MI 48226   Patricia Stobbe, Chf.
Founded: 1945. **Subjects:** Public administration, municipal government, transportation, city planning, public health, urban sociology, police, fire, housing, human resources. **Special Collections:** City of Detroit documents since 1945; Wayne County and municipal documents exchange with 19 similar libraries in the country; grantsmanship center including information on government and foundation funding sources and proposal writing. **Holdings:** 32,000 volumes; 100 legal drawers of pamphlets; 165,000 clippings. **Subscriptions:** 700 journals and other serials. **Services:** Interlibrary loans (limited); copying (limited); routing of periodicals; library open to public for reference use only. **Publications:** MRL Bulletin, quarterly - to city and county employees, and interested governmental agencies.

★3706★
DETROIT PUBLIC LIBRARY - MUSIC AND PERFORMING ARTS DEPARTMENT (Mus; Theater)
5201 Woodward Ave.   Phone: (313) 833-1460
Detroit, MI 48201   Agatha Pfeiffer Kalkanis, Chf.
Founded: 1921. **Staff:** Prof 5; Other 5. **Subjects:** Music, theater, moving pictures, radio and television, broadcasting, dance, bullfighting, circus, rodeo. **Special Collections:** E. Azalia Hackley Collection (Negroes in the performing arts); Michigan Collection (music by Michigan composers or with Michigan associations). **Holdings:** 30,000 books; 6000 bound periodical volumes; 56,000 music scores (cataloged); 30,000 recordings; 20,000 titles of popular sheet music; 124 VF drawers; 6 VF drawers of photographs; 1000 cassettes. **Subscriptions:** 300 journals and other serials. **Services:** Interlibrary loans; copying.

★3707★
DETROIT PUBLIC LIBRARY - NATIONAL AUTOMOTIVE HISTORY COLLECTION (Trans)
5201 Woodward   Phone: (313) 833-1456
Detroit, MI 48202   Gloria Francis, Chf.
Founded: 1953. **Staff:** Prof 1; Other 1. **Subjects:** Automobiles, almost all facets - historical, technological, financial, legal, biographies and history of advertising; men and companies associated with auto industry; carriage making and design; trucks; buses; motorcycles; bicycles. **Special Collections:** Papers of pioneer auto-makers; records of corporations; races; accessory companies; legal cases. **Holdings:** 14,250 books; 8300 bound periodical volumes; 300,000 photographs; 80,000 advertising catalogs (vehicles and accessories); 13 VF cabinets of pamphlets, clippings, sheet music, blueprints, phonograph records, race programs, other miscellany. **Subscriptions:** 182 journals and other serials. **Services:** Copying; collection open to public with staff supervision. **Special Catalogs:** Subject guide to the holdings of the Automotive History Collection of the Detroit Public Library.

★3708★
DETROIT PUBLIC LIBRARY - PHILOSOPHY, RELIGION AND EDUCATION DEPARTMENT (Hum; Educ)
5201 Woodward Ave.   Phone: (313) 833-1430
Detroit, MI 48202   Geraldine Frenette, Chf.
Founded: 1950. **Staff:** Prof 4; Other 6. **Subjects:** Philosophy, psychology, psychiatry, religion, education. **Holdings:** 92,000 books; 8800 bound periodical volumes; 2800 government documents and reports; 307 boxes of occupations pamphlets; 303 boxes of school catalogs; 75 VF drawers of clippings and pamphlets; 71 boxes of documents. **Subscriptions:** 260 journals and other serials; 6 newspapers. **Services:** Interlibrary loans; copying; library open to public. **Networks/Consortia:** Member of Michigan Occupational Information System. **Special Indexes:** Index to occupations collection (card);

index to vertical file (card).

★3709★
DETROIT PUBLIC LIBRARY - RARE BOOK DIVISION
5201 Woodward Ave.
Detroit, MI 48202
Founded: 1954. **Subjects:** Rare books in all subject areas; history of printing and writing; book arts (illustration, bindings); bibliography. **Special Collections:** Bibles, children's books (early); cookbooks; Samuel L. Clemens; Kate Greenaway; Robinson Crusoe; Walter Crane; important first editions (American and English); modern press books. **Holdings:** 27,700 books; 1100 bound periodical volumes; 1100 pamphlets (including catalogs); 9000 bookplates; 250 literary manuscripts and letters. **Remarks:** Temporarily inactive.

★3710★
DETROIT PUBLIC LIBRARY - SOCIOLOGY AND ECONOMICS DEPARTMENT (Soc Sci)
5201 Woodward Ave.　　　　Phone: (313) 833-1440
Detroit, MI 48202　　　　Doris Detwiler, Chf.
Staff: Prof 6; Other 3. **Subjects:** Sociology, social work, economics, labor, political science, international relations, public administration, law, public health, city planning. **Holdings:** 182,000 books; 14,000 bound periodical volumes; 900 bound newspapers; 75,000 paper items; 2000 reels of microfilm; 131 VF drawers of pamphlets, clippings and releases. **Subscriptions:** 750 journals and other serials; 60 newspapers. **Services:** Interlibrary loans; copying. **Remarks:** Houses the Labor Collection and regional U.S. Documents Depository.

★3711★
DETROIT PUBLIC LIBRARY - TECHNOLOGY AND SCIENCE DEPARTMENT (Sci-Tech)
5201 Woodward Ave.　　　　Phone: (313) 833-1450
Detroit, MI 48202　　　　George Unterburger, Chf.
Founded: 1917. **Staff:** Prof 7; Other 3. **Subjects:** Metals and metal technology; engineering - automotive, mechanical, civil, electronic, nuclear; biological sciences; space sciences. **Special Collections:** National Automotive History Collection. **Holdings:** 110,000 books; 87,000 bound periodical volumes; U.S. patent collection; 200,000 government reports; 50 VF drawers of pamphlets and trade catalogs; 70,000 microcards and microfiche. **Subscriptions:** 2000 journals and other serials. **Services:** Interlibrary loans; copying. **Computerized Information Services:** New York Times Information Service. **Staff:** Carol Wischmeyer, Lit.Spec.

★3712★
DETROIT PUBLIC SCHOOLS - PROFESSIONAL LIBRARY (Educ)
5057 Woodward Ave.　　　　Phone: (313) 494-1626
Detroit, MI 48202　　　　Charles V. Partridge, Libn.
Founded: 1966. **Staff:** Prof 1; Other 2. **Subjects:** Education. **Holdings:** 6000 books and bound periodical volumes; 3000 pamphlets (cataloged). **Subscriptions:** 200 journals and other serials. **Services:** Copying; library open to public for reference use only.

★3713★
DETROIT RECEIVING HOSPITAL & UNIVERSITY HEALTH CENTER - LIBRARY (Med)
4201 St. Antoine　　　　Phone: (313) 494-4475
Detroit, MI 48201　　　　Cherrie M. Mudloff, Libn.
Staff: Prof 1; Other 2. **Subjects:** Medicine. **Holdings:** Figures not available. **Subscriptions:** 267 journals and other serials. **Services:** Interlibrary loans; copying; library open to own personnel and Metropolitan Detroit Medical Library Group. **Computerized Information Services:** NLM. **Networks/Consortia:** Member of OCLC.

★3714★
DETROIT SYMPHONY ORCHESTRA - LIBRARY (Mus)
1 W. Jefferson　　　　Phone: (313) 567-9000
Detroit, MI 48226　　　　Albert P. Steger, Libn.
Staff: Prof 2. **Subjects:** Orchestral scores and parts. **Special Collections:** Original prints and manuscripts. **Holdings:** Figures not available. **Services:** Library not open to public. **Staff:** Charles Weaver, Asst.Libn.

★3715★
DETROIT UNIVERSITY CLUB - LIBRARY (Hist)
1411 E. Jefferson
Detroit, MI 48207　　　　Phone: (313) 567-9280
Subjects: Detroit and Michigan - history and fiction. **Holdings:** 5000 books. **Subscriptions:** 47 journals and other serials. **Services:** Library open to members only.

DETROITBANK CORPORATION
See: Comerica Incorporated

DEUTSCH (Dr. Joseph) MEMORIAL LIBRARY
See: Illinois Masonic Medical Center - School of Nursing - Dr. Joseph Deutsch Memorial Library

★3716★
DEUTSCH, KERRIGAN AND STILES - LAW LIBRARY (Law)
4700 One Shell Sq.　　　　Phone: (504) 581-5141
New Orleans, LA 70139　　　　Jean Sandel, Libn.
Staff: Prof 1. **Subjects:** Law - federal, state (Louisiana), admiralty, labor, tax and aviation; insurance; contracts. **Special Collections:** 19th century individual state reports (1624 volumes); collection of Great Britain legal materials (1382 volumes). **Holdings:** 30,000 volumes. **Subscriptions:** 59 journals and other serials; 6 newspapers. **Services:** Library not open to public.

DEUTZ DIESEL (Canada) LIMITED
See: KHD (Canada) Ltd.

DEVEREAUX LIBRARY
See: South Dakota School of Mines & Technology

★3717★
DEVEREUX FOUNDATION - PROFESSIONAL LIBRARY (Soc Sci)
Devon, PA 19333　　　　Annetta Zulick, Libn.
Staff: Prof 1. **Subjects:** Clinical psychology, special education, psychiatry, child care, vocational rehabilitation, psychoanalysis. **Special Collections:** Clinical training audiotape library (700). **Holdings:** 3000 books; 100 bound periodical volumes; 6 multimedia training programs; 200 selected reprints. **Subscriptions:** 100 journals and other serials. **Services:** Interlibrary loans; library open to professionals by appointment. **Special Catalogs:** Catalog of training tapes.

DEVONIAN LIBRARY
See: Western Canadian Universities - Marine Biological Society

★3718★
DEWEY, BALLANTINE, BUSHBY, PALMER & WOOD - LIBRARY (Law)
140 Broadway　　　　Phone: (212) 820-1300
New York, NY 10005　　　　Gitelle Seer, Libn.
Staff: Prof 7; Other 11. **Subjects:** Law - antitrust, securities, taxation, real property, trusts and estates, corporate. **Holdings:** 30,000 volumes. **Services:** Interlibrary loans; library open to members of SLA by appointment. **Computerized Information Services:** LEXIS, New York Times Information Service, DIALOG, SDC, Dow Jones News Retrieval, Control Data Corporation, Computer Directions Advisors, Inc. (CDA). **Staff:** Daniel Pelletier, Asst.Libn.; Shirley E. Diamond, Corp.Libn.; Jane Hoffman, Tax Libn.; Diane Hayward, Asst.Libn./Midtown Lib.

DEWEY LIBRARY
See: Massachusetts Institute of Technology

★3719★
DEWITT HISTORICAL SOCIETY OF TOMPKINS COUNTY - ARCHIVE/LIBRARY/MUSEUM (Hist)
116 N. Cayuga St.　　　　Phone: (607) 273-8284
Ithaca, NY 14850　　　　Craig Williams, Dir.
Founded: 1863. **Staff:** 7. **Subjects:** Genealogy, local history. **Special Collections:** Ithaca Imprints (500 volumes). **Holdings:** 3000 books; 200 bound periodical volumes; 500 boxes of manuscripts; 200 maps; 5000 photographs; 10,000 negatives (glass plate); 300 scrapbooks (indexed); 30 multi-media kits; genealogy letter files. **Services:** Copying; library open to public. **Publications:** DeWitt Historical Society Newsletter, quarterly - to members. **Staff:** Elizabeth Gibson, Cur. of Coll.; Amy Humber, Archv.; Susan Eleuterio-Comer, Cur. of Educ.; Carl Koski, Cur. of Exhibits; Francis Yaple, Cur.Asst.; Millie Russell, Cur.Asst.

★3720★
DEXTER CORPORATION - C.H. DEXTER DIVISION - TECHNICAL LIBRARY (Sci-Tech)
Two Elm St.　　　　Phone: (203) 623-9801
Windsor Locks, CT 06096　　　　Fred N. Masters, Jr., Mgr.Tech.Info.Rsrcs.
Founded: 1965. **Staff:** Prof 1; Other 1. **Subjects:** Papermaking, synthetic fiber papers. **Holdings:** Figures not available. **Subscriptions:** 200 journals and other serials. **Services:** Interlibrary loans; library open to public by request. **Computerized Information Services:** DIALOG, SDC. **Publications:** Library Bulletin, monthly; Technical Abstracts, monthly; Patent Announcements, monthly; Facts and Figures, weekly.

★3721★
DI CYAN AND BROWN - LIBRARY (Med)
1486 E. 33rd St.
Brooklyn, NY 11234   Phone: (212) 252-8844
Subjects: Pharmacology, neuropharmacology, therapeutics, biochemistry, drugs, psychopharmacology, cosmetics. **Holdings:** 2000 volumes. **Services:** Library not open to public.

DIABLO SYSTEMS, INC.
See: Xerox Corporation

★3722★
DIALOG INFORMATION SERVICES, INC. (Info Sci)
3460 Hillview Ave.   Phone: (415) 858-3785
Palo Alto, CA 94304   Dr. Roger K. Summit, Pres.
Subjects: Chemistry, science and technology, engineering, social sciences and humanities, business, economics, medicine, popular magazine literature, research in progress, law. **Holdings:** 55 million computer accessible citations and abstracts on subject fields listed above. **Services:** Computer-based retrospective and SDI support services to remote terminals; service available to public for a fee. Additional private file service provides use of DIALOG hardware and software for storing and accessing customer developed databases; training seminar in online searching of DIALOG databases; DIALORDER. **Publications:** Chronolog, monthly - distributed to users of service; Guide to DIALOG Searching; user's manual; DIALOG Databases documentation chapters. **Remarks:** Branch offices are maintained in Boston, Los Angeles, New York City, Washington, DC, Chicago, Houston, London, Germany, Tokyo, Toronto, Sydney. **Formerly:** Lockheed Missiles & Space Company, Inc. - Lockheed Information Systems. **Staff:** Robert Donati, Dir., Domestic Oper.; Betty Davis, Marketing Dir.; Charles Meadow, Mgr., Customer Serv.

DIAMOND (Harry) LABORATORIES
See: U.S. Army - Electronic R & D Command - Harry Diamond Laboratories

★3723★
DIAMOND SHAMROCK CORPORATION - CORPORATE LIBRARY (Bus-Fin; Sci-Tech)
Box 348   Phone: (216) 357-3475
Painesville, OH 44077   Marilyn Graubart, Mgr.Lib.Serv.
Founded: 1980. **Staff:** Prof 7; Other 5. **Subjects:** Chemistry, energy, business, finance, management, statistics, engineering. **Special Collections:** Internal engineering records on microfilm (500 reels). **Holdings:** 10,000 books; 4500 bound periodical volumes; 8800 reels of microfilm; 300,000 patents; 6700 reports; 3000 pamphlets; 550 dissertations. **Subscriptions:** 1002 journals and other serials. **Services:** Interlibrary loans; copying; library open to public by authorization by Diamond Shamrock personnel. **Computerized Information Services:** DIALOG, SDC, BRS, DOE/RECON, NLM, New York Times Information Service, Dow Jones News Retrieval; computerized circulation. **Publications:** Library Line, 6/year - for internal distribution only; Research Readings, monthly. **Staff:** Donna Hiznay, Supv.Ref.Serv.; Sharon DeLong, Eng.Info.Anl.; Lois Evans, Adm.Libn.; Renee Guttman, Tech.Serv.Supv.

★3724★
DIAMOND SHAMROCK CORPORATION - PROCESS CHEMICALS DIVISION - LIBRARY (Sci-Tech)
350 Mt. Kemble Ave.
Box 2386-R   Phone: (201) 267-1000
Morristown, NJ 07960   Marilyn Swetell, Libn.
Founded: 1934. **Staff:** Prof 2; Other 2. **Subjects:** Chemistry - organic, textile, paper, polymer, leather; fats and oils. **Holdings:** 11,000 volumes; 32 VF drawers of U.S. patents; U.S. Chemicals patents, 1959 to present on microfilm; 28 VF drawers of technical data sheets. **Subscriptions:** 310 journals and other serials. **Services:** Interlibrary loans; copying; library not open to public. **Publications:** Patent Research Review, biweekly - for internal distribution only. **Staff:** Amy Meskin, Asst.Libn.

DIBNER LIBRARY
See: Smithsonian Institution Libraries - Special Collections Branch

★3725★
DICK (A.B.) COMPANY - LIBRARY (Sci-Tech)
5700 W. Touhy Ave.   Phone: (312) 763-1900
Chicago, IL 60648   Jo Ann Miller, Assoc.Libn.
Founded: 1945. **Staff:** 1. **Subjects:** Chemistry, business, electronics, graphic arts. **Holdings:** 3300 books; 2300 bound periodical volumes; 15 VF drawers of patents; 30 VF drawers of manufacturers' catalogs; 16 VF drawers of pamphlets and clippings. **Subscriptions:** 240 journals and other serials. **Services:** Interlibrary loans; copying; Interlibrary loans not open to public. **Computerized Information Services:** DIALOG, SDC.

DICKERSON (O.D.) MEMORIAL LIBRARY
See: American Institute for Property & Liability Underwriters - Insurance Institute of America

DICKEY (Donald R.) LIBRARY OF VERTEBRATE ZOOLOGY
See: University of California, Los Angeles - Biomedical Library

DICKHAUT (John W.) LIBRARY
See: Methodist Theological School in Ohio - John W. Dickhaut Library

★3726★
DICKINSON COLLEGE - LIBRARY - SPECIAL COLLECTIONS (Hist)
College Library   Phone: (717) 245-1399
Carlisle, PA 17013   Martha Calvert Slotten, Cur.
Founded: 1784. **Staff:** 2. **Subjects:** College archives and historical manuscripts; rare books. **Special Collections:** Papers of Founders, James Buchanan, Roger Brooke Taney, Joseph Priestley, Carl Sandburg, John Drinkwater, Moncure Conway, Robert Bridges (American editor); Books from the Library of Isaac Norris (1671-1735); John F. Kennedy Collection (6600 items). **Holdings:** 20,000 volumes; 1000 feet of manuscripts and archives. **Services:** Copying; library open to public. **Networks/Consortia:** Member of OCLC. **Publications:** Guide to the Archives and Manuscripts Collection of Dickinson College, 1972; John and Mary's Journal. **Staff:** Marie Booth Ferre, Asst.Cur.

DICKINSON (George Sherman) MUSIC LIBRARY
See: Vassar College - George Sherman Dickinson Music Library

★3727★
DICKINSON SCHOOL OF LAW - SHEELY-LEE LAW LIBRARY (Law)
150 S. College St.   Phone: (717) 243-4611
Carlisle, PA 17013   James R. Fox, Law Libn.
Founded: 1834. **Staff:** Prof 5; Other 3. **Subjects:** Law. **Special Collections:** Intellectual property law; Jewish, Israeli and Italian law; law and medicine. **Holdings:** 135,000 volumes; 20 VF drawers of records and briefs of the U.S. Supreme Court (microforms); 365 shelves of records and briefs of Pennsylvania Supreme, Superior and Commonwealth Courts. **Subscriptions:** 1238 journals and other serials; 10 newspapers. **Services:** Interlibrary loans; copying; library open to public for reference use only. **Computerized Information Services:** LEXIS, WESTLAW; computerized cataloging. **Networks/Consortia:** Member of OCLC through PALINET & Union Library Catalogue of Pennsylvania. **Publications:** Selected acquisitions, irregular. **Staff:** Mary E. Lefkowski, Govt.Doc.Libn.; Dana Spitzform, Cat.; Debra Jones, Reader Serv.; Sharon Anderson, Ref.Libn.

★3728★
DICKINSON STATE COLLEGE - STOXEN LIBRARY (Educ)
     Phone: (701) 227-2135
Dickinson, ND 58601   Bernnett Reinke, Lib.Dir.
Founded: 1918. **Staff:** Prof 4; Other 1. **Subjects:** Education. **Special Collections:** Theodore Roosevelt Collection (200 volumes). **Holdings:** 65,000 volumes. **Subscriptions:** 510 journals and other serials; 10 newspapers. **Services:** Interlibrary loans; copying; library open to public with deposit required. **Computerized Information Services:** Computerized cataloging. **Networks/Consortia:** Member of MINITEX; OCLC; North Dakota Network for Knowledge; North Dakota Union List of Serials. **Staff:** James Martz, Acq.Libn.; Louise Pearson, Cat.; Eileen Kopron, Circ.; Lillian Sorenson, ILL.

★3729★
DICKINSON, WRIGHT, MOON, VAN DUSEN & FREEMAN - LIBRARY (Law)
800 First National Bldg.   Phone: (313) 223-3500
Detroit, MI 48226   Valerie Hanafee, Libn.
Founded: 1878. **Staff:** 3. **Subjects:** Law - general civil practice, corporation, taxation, banking, probate and insurance, labor, municipal finance. **Holdings:** 20,000 volumes. **Subscriptions:** 1500 journals and other serials. **Services:** Interlibrary loans; library not open to public. **Computerized Information Services:** LEXIS, WESTLAW, DIALOG; internal database. **Networks/Consortia:** Member of Detroit Associated Libraries Region of Cooperation. **Remarks:** Branch libraries are located at 525 N. Woodward Ave., Box 509, Bloomfield Hills, MI 48013; 121 E. Allegan St., Lansing, MI 48933; and 1901 L St., N.W., Suite 801, Washington, DC 20036. **Formerly:** Dickinson, Wright, McKean, Cudlip & Moon.

★3730★

DIEBOLD GROUP, INC. - LIBRARY (Bus-Fin)
475 Park Ave., S.   Phone: (212) 684-4700
New York, NY 10016   Judy Lee, Libn.
Founded: 1950. **Staff:** Prof 1; Other 1. **Subjects:** Data processing, computer and management information systems, communications, business, automation, telecommunications. **Holdings:** 3500 books; 3000 annual reports and pamphlets; 500 computer manufacturers' catalogs; 1500 clipping files. **Subscriptions:** 102 journals and other serials. **Services:** Interlibrary loans; library not open to public. **Computerized Information Services:** DIALOG.

DIETHELM (Oskar) HISTORICAL LIBRARY
See: New York Hospital-Cornell Medical Center - Oskar Diethelm Historical Library

★3731★

DIETRICH COLLECTION (Art; Area-Ethnic)
RFD 1, West Farms Rd.   Phone: (603) 632-7156
West Canaan, NH 03741   Dr. R. Krystyna Dietrich, Dir.
Founded: 1962. **Staff:** Prof 1. **Subjects:** Polish art; Polish translations of American literature; Polish reference. **Special Collections:** Original and graphic works by Alexander Orlowski (1777-1832); graphic works by Daniel Chodowiecki (1726-1801); graphic works by Jean Pierre Norblin de la Gourdaine (1745-1830). **Holdings:** 6000 volumes; 4500 other items. **Services:** Copying (for museums and libraries only); collection open to public by appointment. **Special Catalogs:** U.S. Literature in Poland, 1790-1960 (typed bibliography, 1500 pp.); works by and about Alexander Orlowski in the collection and elsewhere in America (1200 cards); works by and about Daniel Chodowiecki in the collection (1800 cards). **Remarks:** This is said to be the largest American collection of works by and about Orlowski and Chodowiecki, as well as the only collection of American literature in Polish, in the U.S.

DIFFUSION IN METALS DATA CENTER
See: U.S. Natl. Bureau of Standards - Metallurgy Division

★3732★

DIGITAL EQUIPMENT CORPORATION - HUDSON LSI LIBRARY (Sci-Tech)
HLO2-2/NO6
77 Reed Rd.   Phone: (617) 568-5258
Hudson, MA 01749   E. Ann Baker-Shear, Tech.Libn.
Staff: Prof 2; Other 2. **Subjects:** Semiconductor technology, computer architecture, employee development. **Special Collections:** Semiconductor technology (videotape series; technical reports). **Holdings:** 1800 books; 500 videotapes; 4000 unbound journals; 600 technical reports; 150 sets of microfiche and microfilm. **Subscriptions:** 245 journals and other serials; 7 newspapers. **Services:** Interlibrary loans (books only); copying; library open to public with restrictions. **Computerized Information Services:** DIALOG, NEXIS, Institute for Scientific Information (ISI); internal database; computerized cataloging, serials and reference. **Networks/Consortia:** Member of Digital Library Network. **Publications:** Listings of recent acquisitions, conferences and seminars, monthly; monthly column in local newsletter; bibliographies and special publications, irregular. **Special Catalogs:** AV catalog; training materials catalog. **Staff:** Howard M. Williams, Assoc.Libn.

★3733★

DIGITAL EQUIPMENT CORPORATION - MARLBORO LIBRARY (Info Sci)
200 Forest St., MR01-2/A94   Phone: (617) 467-5040
Marlboro, MA 01752   Michelle Johnson, Tech.Libn.
Staff: Prof 1; Other 1. **Subjects:** Computer engineering, marketing, management. **Holdings:** 2500 books; 100 technical reports. **Subscriptions:** 150 journals and other serials; 10 newspapers. **Services:** Interlibrary loans; library not open to public. **Computerized Information Services:** DIALOG, NEXIS, Institute for Scientific Information (ISI); computerized cataloging. **Networks/Consortia:** Member of Digital Library Network. **Publications:** Recent Acquisitions, monthly - for internal distribution only; Audio & Video Course list, irregular - for internal distribution only; Journal List, irregular - for internal distribution only.

★3734★

DIGITAL EQUIPMENT CORPORATION - MAYNARD LIBRARY (Sci-Tech; Bus-Fin)
146 Main St., MLO 4-3/A20   Phone: (617) 493-6231
Maynard, MA 01754   Janice Eifrig
Founded: 1974. **Staff:** Prof 6; Other 10. **Subjects:** Computer science, electronics, electrical engineering, management. **Holdings:** 14,000 books; 1000 bound periodical volumes; 600 AV items; 2000 volumes of company literature; 3000 volumes of technical reports. **Subscriptions:** 500 journals

and other serials; 20 newspapers. **Services:** Interlibrary loans; library open to public with restrictions. **Computerized Information Services:** DIALOG, BRS, NEXIS, Dow Jones News Retrieval; internal database; computerized cataloging. **Networks/Consortia:** Member of OCLC through NELINET; Digital Library Network. **Publications:** Library newsletter, monthly; periodicals list, annual - both for internal distribution only. **Staff:** Carol Henley, Supv., Tech.Serv.; Jeanne Thompson, Supv., Info.Serv.; Betsey Cane, Ref.; Richard Maxfield, Ref.; Helen MacFadyen, ILL; Lisa Schiffman, Cat.

★3735★

DIGITAL EQUIPMENT CORPORATION - SPIT BROOK LIBRARY (Info Sci)
110 Spit Brook Rd.   Phone: (603) 884-8036
Nashua, NH 03061   Charles Matthews, Tech.Libn.
Founded: 1980. **Staff:** Prof 2. **Subjects:** Software engineering, programming languages, technical documentation. **Holdings:** 750 books; 400 manuals; 300 reports; 120 AV items; 2 VF drawers. **Subscriptions:** 120 journals and other serials; 10 newspapers. **Services:** Interlibrary loans; SDI; library not open to public. **Computerized Information Services:** DIALOG; internal database; computerized cataloging. **Networks/Consortia:** Member of NELINET; Digital Library Network. **Publications:** Spit Brook Compiler, bimonthly - for internal distribution only. **Staff:** Dorothy Mamos, Assoc.Libn.

★3736★

DIGITAL EQUIPMENT CORPORATION - TEWKSBURY LIBRARY (Sci-Tech)
1925 Andover St., TWO/BIO   Phone: (617) 851-5071
Tewksbury, MA 01876   Janet Slinn, Tech.Libn.
Founded: 1979. **Staff:** Prof 2; Other 1. **Subjects:** Computers, distributed systems. **Holdings:** 1200 books; technical reports; pamphlets; AV materials. **Subscriptions:** 110 journals and other serials; 10 newspapers. **Services:** Interlibrary loans; library not open to public. **Computerized Information Services:** DIALOG; computerized cataloging. **Networks/Consortia:** Member of NELINET. **Staff:** Janet Potter, Assoc.Libn.

★3737★

DILLON, READ & COMPANY, INC. - LIBRARY (Bus-Fin)
46 William St.   Phone: (212) 285-5690
New York, NY 10005   Nancy J. Bowles, Libn.
Founded: 1966. **Staff:** Prof 2; Other 8. **Subjects:** Finance - corporate and municipal; securities regulations; public utilities. **Holdings:** 3000 books; 300 lateral shelves of corporate and municipal reports; 65 lateral shelves of subject files. **Subscriptions:** 575 journals and other serials. **Services:** Interlibrary loans (New York City only); copying; library open to librarians only. **Computerized Information Services:** DIALOG, SDC, Mead Data Central, New York Times Information Service, Control Data Corporation, Computer Directions Advisors, Inc. (CDA), Dow Jones News Retrieval. **Staff:** Gloria Dean McDonald, Asst.Libn.

DIMOND LIBRARY
See: University of New Hampshire

DINAN AND TERTIANS LIBRARIES
See: Colombiere College - Library

DINOSAUR NATL. MONUMENT
See: U.S. Natl. Park Service

★3738★

DINOSAUR NATURAL HISTORY MUSEUM - REFERENCE LIBRARY (Sci-Tech)
235 E. Main St.   Phone: (801) 789-3799
Vernal, UT 84078   Alden Hamblin, Dir.
Founded: 1948. **Staff:** Prof 3; Other 3. **Subjects:** Natural history, geology, paleontology, archaeology. **Holdings:** 4000 books. **Services:** Library open to public.

★3739★

DINSMORE & SHOHL - LIBRARY (Law)
2100 Fountain Sq. Plaza
511 Walnut St.   Phone: (513) 621-6747
Cincinnati, OH 45202   Sharon A. Jones, Libn.
Staff: Prof 1; Other 1. **Subjects:** Law. **Holdings:** 20,012 volumes. **Subscriptions:** 12 journals and other serials. **Services:** Library not open to public. **Computerized Information Services:** LEXIS.

★3740★

DIOCESAN SEMINARY OF THE IMMACULATE CONCEPTION - LIBRARY (Rel-Theol)
1903 E. Lake Dr.   Phone: (217) 529-2213
Springfield, IL 62707
Founded: 1961. **Staff:** 1. **Subjects:** Philosophy, theology, history, literature.

Holdings: 11,000 books. **Services:** Library not open to public.

★3741★
DIOCESE OF ALLENTOWN - PRO-LIFE LIBRARY (Soc Sci)
1135 Stefko Blvd.   Phone: (215) 691-0380
Bethlehem, PA 18018   Rev. Stephen T. Forish, Dir.
Staff: Prof 2; Other 1. **Subjects:** Bioethics, abortion, sexuality, death and
dying. **Special Collections:** United States Catholic Conference Documentary
Service; Origins Documentary Service. **Holdings:** 530 books and bound
periodical volumes; 500 audiotapes; 20 videotapes; 90 pamphlets and
booklets; 50 government statistics and reports; newspaper clippings.
Subscriptions: 11 journals and other serials. **Services:** Interlibrary loans;
copying; library open to public. **Publications:** Life Issues in America, monthly -
by subscription. **Staff:** Sr. M. Irene, O.S.F., Libn.

DIOCESE OF CALGARY
See: Anglican Church of Canada

DIOCESE OF INDIANAPOLIS, INDIANA - PROTESTANT EPISCOPAL CHURCH
See: Protestant Episcopal Church

★3742★
DIOCESE OF LAFAYETTE, LOUISIANA - ARCHIVES (Hist)*
Drawer 3387   Phone: (318) 361-5639
Lafayette, LA 70501   Rev. James F. Geraghty, Archv.
Founded: 1918. **Staff:** Prof 1; Other 2. **Subjects:** History of diocese
parishes and Southwest Louisiana. **Special Collections:** Bishop Maurice
Schexnayder papers, 1895-1981 (50 linear feet). **Holdings:** 500 books;
1500 linear feet of archives; 200 reels of microfilm of sacramental records,
1756-1978. **Subscriptions:** 15 journals and other serials. **Services:**
Interlibrary loans; copying; library open to public with restrictions. **Special
Indexes:** Correspondence of the Most Rev. Jules Jeanmard, 1st Bishop of
Lafayette, 1918-1956 (card).

DIOCESE OF MONTREAL
See: Anglican Church of Canada

DIOCESE OF NEW WESTMINSTER
See: Anglican Church of Canada - Ecclesiastical Province of British
Columbia and Diocese of New Westminster

★3743★
DIOCESE OF OGDENSBURG - ARCHIVES (Rel-Theol; Hist)
622 Washington St.
Box 369   Phone: (315) 393-2920
Ogdensburg, NY 13669   Rev. Lawrence E. Cotter, Archv.
Subjects: Church history. **Special Collections:** Journal of Father Picquet,
founder of Fort LaPresentation (later Ogdensburg). **Holdings:** Figures not
available for books; correspondence. **Services:** Copying; archives open to
public with restrictions.

DIOCESE OF PENNSYLVANIA
See: Protestant Episcopal Church

★3744★
DIOCESE OF PITTSBURGH - LEARNING MEDIA CENTER (Rel-Theol)
111 Blvd. of the Allies   Phone: (412) 456-3120
Pittsburgh, PA 15222   Carole Oluokta, Dir.
Staff: Prof 1; Other 2. **Subjects:** Religion, theology, liturgy, educational
methods. **Holdings:** Textbooks; resource materials; AV materials.
Subscriptions: 30 journals and other serials; 4 newspapers. **Services:** AV
material available on rental basis. **Special Catalogs:** AV catalog and
supplements.

★3745★
DIOCESE OF SPOKANE - DIOCESAN CHANCERY ARCHIVES (Rel-Theol)
1023 W. Riverside Ave.
Box 1453   Phone: (509) 456-7100
Spokane, WA 99210   Rev. Edward J. Kowrach, Archv.
Staff: Prof 1. **Subjects:** Northwest religious history, church records. **Special
Collections:** Eastern Washington Catholic Church records. **Holdings:** 15,000
volumes; 5000 reels of microfilm of records of Eastern Washington.
Subscriptions: 12 journals and other serials. **Services:** Interlibrary loans;
copying; library open to public with restrictions.

DIOCESE OF TORONTO
See: Anglican Church of Canada

★3746★
DIOCESE OF TUCSON - REGINA CLERI RESOURCE LIBRARY (Rel-Theol)
8800 E. 22nd St.   Phone: (602) 886-5201
Tucson, AZ 85710   Sr. Bibiane Roy, O.P., Coord.
Subjects: Theology, sacred scripture, spirituality, family life, church history
and renewal. **Holdings:** 15,000 books; 200 filmstrips; 25 films; Spanish
language materials (700 books; 20 AV items). **Subscriptions:** 73 journals and
other serials. **Services:** Library open to public on a limited schedule.

★3747★
DIRECT MAIL/MARKETING ASSOCIATION, INC. - INFORMATION CENTER
(Bus-Fin)
6 E. 43rd St., 12th Fl.   Phone: (212) 689-4977
New York, NY 10017   Karen Burns, Dir., Info. & Res.
Founded: 1946. **Staff:** Prof 1; Other 4. **Subjects:** Direct mail advertising and
marketing. **Holdings:** 325 books and bound periodical volumes; 2500 bound
portfolios of direct marketing campaigns; 700 color microfiche; 45 VF
drawers of direct mail samples and articles; cassettes; slides. **Subscriptions:**
65 journals and other serials. **Services:** Copying; library open to public by
appointment. **Publications:** Direct Marketing Monograph Series; Features of
the Month (newsletter); Direct Mail Marketing Manual; Monograph Series.

**DIRECTION DE L'INFORMATION TECHNOLOGIQUE ET DU TRANSFERT DE
TECHNOLOGIE**
See: Centre de Recherche Industrielle du Quebec

★3748★
**DIRKSEN (Everett McKinley) CONGRESSIONAL LEADERSHIP RESEARCH
CENTER - LIBRARY** (Hist)
Broadway & Fourth St.   Phone: (309) 347-7113
Pekin, IL 61554   Frank H. Mackaman, II, Exec.Dir.
Founded: 1975. **Staff:** Prof 3; Other 3. **Subjects:** Everett McKinley Dirksen;
U.S. Congressional leadership; U.S. Congress; Harold Himmel Velde. **Special
Collections:** Dirksen Papers, ca. 1900-1970 (1800 linear feet); Velde
Papers, ca. 1940-1956 (16 linear feet). **Holdings:** 2000 linear feet of
archives; 1500 items of memorabilia; 8000 photographs; 800 AV items.
Services: Copying; library open to public with donor-imposed restrictions.
Special Indexes: Guides to open manuscript collection.

DIS
See: University of Minnesota - Drug Information Services

★3749★
DISADA PRODUCTIONS LTD. - WALT DISNEY MEMORIAL LIBRARY
(Theater)
5788 Notre Dame de Grace Ave.   Phone: (514) 489-0527
Montreal, PQ, Canada H4A 1M4   Sherrill Barth, Libn.
Founded: 1967. **Staff:** 1. **Subjects:** Motion pictures. **Holdings:** 600 books;
4000 bound periodical volumes; 850 other cataloged items; 700 films and
tapes; 350 items of original artwork; 2000 posters, stills, pressbooks; 400
items of special film material. **Services:** Copying; screening facilities; library
open to public by appointment.

DISASTER RESEARCH CENTER
See: Ohio State University

DISCIPLES OF CHRIST
See: Christian Church (Disciples of Christ), Inc.

★3750★
DISCIPLES OF CHRIST HISTORICAL SOCIETY - LIBRARY (Hist)
1101 19th Ave., S.   Phone: (615) 327-1444
Nashville, TN 37212   David I. McWhirter, Dir. of Lib./Archv.
Founded: 1941. **Staff:** Prof 2. **Subjects:** Christian Church, Disciples of
Christ, Churches of Christ. **Holdings:** 24,000 books and bound periodical
volumes; 150 record groups of archives; 500 collections of personal papers;
manuscripts, microfilm, phonograph records. **Subscriptions:** 250 journals and
other serials. **Services:** Interlibrary loans; copying; library open to members.
Publications: Disciplina, quarterly - distributed to Society members. **Special
Catalogs:** Preliminary Guide to Black Materials in the Disciples of Christ
Historical Society (book). **Staff:** Stephen Berry, Lib.Asst.

★3751★
DISCOVERY HALL MUSEUM - RESEARCH LIBRARY (Hist)
120 S. St. Joseph St.   Phone: (219) 284-9714
South Bend, IN 46601   Marsha Mullin, Cur.
Staff: Prof 2. **Subjects:** Local and industrial history of South Bend, IN area.
Special Collections: Studebaker Archives (3000 linear feet); Oliver
Photographic Collection (10,000 negatives, ca. 1900-1950 from Oliver

Corporation, manufacturers of farm equipment). **Holdings:** 300 books; 60 reels of microfilm; 15 VF drawers of trade catalogs and advertising; 12 VF drawers of photographs. **Subscriptions:** 27 journals and other serials. **Services:** Interlibrary loans; copying; library open to public. **Publications:** Discovering, bimonthly - by membership and exchange. **Staff:** Geoffrey Huys, Res.Hist.

DISNEY (Walt E.) ENTERPRISES
See: WED Enterprises

DISNEY (Walt) MEMORIAL LIBRARY
See: Disada Productions Ltd. - Walt Disney Memorial Library

★3752★
DISNEY (Walt) PRODUCTIONS - ARCHIVES (Hist; Rec)
500 S. Buena Vista   Phone: (213) 840-5424
Burbank, CA 91521   David R. Smith, Archv.
Founded: 1970. **Staff:** Prof 2; Other 1. **Subjects:** Walt Disney, Disneyland, Walt Disney World. **Holdings:** 5000 square feet of archival material - correspondence, publications, music, photographs, character merchandise, film, production files, original artwork. **Services:** Copying; archives open to public by appointment. **Staff:** Paula M. Sigman, Asst.Archv.

★3753★
DISNEY (Walt) PRODUCTIONS - LIBRARY (Art)
500 S. Buena Vista   Phone: (213) 840-5326
Burbank, CA 91521   Mary Jo Terry, Libn.
Staff: Prof 3; Other 1. **Subjects:** Nature, art, history, social life and customs. **Special Collections:** Humor collection of jokes and cartoons. **Holdings:** 21,000 books; 150 VF drawers of photographs, clippings and pamphlets for background research in motion pictures. **Subscriptions:** 120 journals and other serials. **Services:** Interlibrary loans; copying; library open to serious students. **Special Indexes:** Index of illustrations and articles appearing in periodicals (card). **Staff:** Gale Musker, Res.; Laueen McCoy, Res.; Elizabeth Gnerre, Asst.Res.

★3754★
DISTILLED SPIRITS COUNCIL OF THE U.S., INC. - LIBRARY (Food-Bev)†
1300 Pennsylvania Bldg.
425 13th St., N.W.   Phone: (202) 628-3544
Washington, DC 20004   Elizabeth Sharer, Libn.
Staff: 2. **Subjects:** Distilled spirits industry, prohibition, alcoholism, liquor laws and taxation, highway safety. **Holdings:** 2000 volumes. **Subscriptions:** 200 journals and other serials. **Services:** Copying; library open to researchers with prior notice.

DISTRICT OF COLUMBIA BAR ASSOCIATION
See: Bar Association of the District of Columbia

★3755★
DISTRICT OF COLUMBIA - CORPORATION COUNSEL LAW LIBRARY (Law)
Rm. 302, District Bldg.
14th & E Sts., N.W.   Phone: (202) 727-6274
Washington, DC 20004   Deborah M. Murray, Law Libn.
Founded: 1932. **Staff:** Prof 1; Other 1. **Subjects:** Law. **Holdings:** 24,000 volumes. **Services:** Interlibrary loans; copying; library not open to public. **Computerized Information Services:** Mead Data Central. **Networks/ Consortia:** Member of Metropolitan Washington Library Council.

★3756★
DISTRICT OF COLUMBIA DEPARTMENT OF HOUSING AND COMMUNITY DEVELOPMENT LIBRARY (Plan)
1133 North Capitol St., Rm. 203   Phone: (202) 535-1004
Washington, DC 20002   Anne L. Meglis, Libn.
Founded: 1966. **Staff:** Prof 1; Other 1. **Subjects:** Urban renewal, housing, city planning, community development, historic preservation, urban affairs. **Special Collections:** Archives (600 items on the District of Columbia Redevelopment Land Agency); photograph collection of before-and-after photographs of urban renewal project areas and public housing projects from 1930 to present (6 VF drawers). **Holdings:** 2400 books; 75 boxes of pamphlets; newspaper clippings on all urban renewal project areas dating from 1954 (partially indexed). **Subscriptions:** 125 journals and other serials. **Services:** Interlibrary loans; copying; library open to public with restrictions. **Publications:** Bibliographic Tour of Washington, D.C., 1974 - individual copies free upon request.

★3757★
DISTRICT OF COLUMBIA GENERAL HOSPITAL - MEDICAL LIBRARY (Med)†
19th St. & Massachusetts Ave., S.E.   Phone: (202) 675-5348
Washington, DC 20003   Mrs. Dale Eliasson, Libn.
Staff: Prof 3; Other 1. **Subjects:** Medicine, nursing, allied health sciences. **Holdings:** 8188 books; 8992 bound periodical volumes. **Subscriptions:** 599 journals and other serials. **Services:** Interlibrary loans; copying; SDI for staff; library not open to public. **Computerized Information Services:** MEDLINE. **Networks/Consortia:** Member of District of Columbia Health Sciences Information Network (DOCHSIN). **Publications:** Acquisitions list, quarterly. **Special Catalogs:** Alphabetical and subject lists of journal holdings. **Staff:** Johanne Holmes, Ser. & Circ.Libn.

DISTRICT OF COLUMBIA - METROPOLITAN COUNCIL OF GOVERNMENTS
See: Metropolitan Washington Council of Governments

★3758★
DISTRICT OF COLUMBIA PUBLIC LIBRARY - ART DIVISION (Art)
Martin Luther King Memorial Library
901 G St., N.W.   Phone: (202) 727-1291
Washington, DC 20001   Lois Kent Stiles, Chf.
Founded: 1927. **Staff:** Prof 3. **Subjects:** Art history, painting, architecture, drawing, sculpture, artists, city planning, landscape architecture, arts and crafts, aesthetics, graphic arts, photography, stamps, coins, paper money. **Special Collections:** Material on 400 artists in the District of Columbia Metropolitan area. **Holdings:** 20,253 books; 800 bound periodical volumes; 197,457 mounted pictures; 48 VF drawers. **Subscriptions:** 90 journals and other serials. **Services:** Interlibrary loans. **Staff:** Mary Ternes, Rd.Adv.; Sarah E. McBryde, Rd.Adv.

★3759★
DISTRICT OF COLUMBIA PUBLIC LIBRARY - AUDIOVISUAL DIVISION (Aud-Vis)
Martin Luther King Memorial Library
901 G St., N.W.   Phone: (202) 727-1265
Washington, DC 20001   Diane Henry, Chf.
Staff: Prof 2; Other 4. **Subjects:** Black awareness; film as art; film history; human relations. **Holdings:** 201 books; 2467 film reels; 2179 spoken recordings; 321 videotapes; 457 cassettes. **Subscriptions:** 17 journals and other serials. **Publications:** Monthly and weekly film programs. **Special Catalogs:** Book Film Catalog. **Staff:** David Duff, Rd.Adv.

★3760★
DISTRICT OF COLUMBIA PUBLIC LIBRARY - BIOGRAPHY DIVISION (Hist)
Martin Luther King Memorial Library
901 G St., N.W.   Phone: (202) 727-1234
Washington, DC 20001   Helen Bergan, Chf.
Staff: Prof 2. **Subjects:** Biography, heraldry, genealogy. **Holdings:** 27,000 books; 90 VF drawers of pamphlets and clippings. **Services:** Interlibrary loans. **Staff:** Marian Holt, Rd.Adv.

★3761★
DISTRICT OF COLUMBIA PUBLIC LIBRARY - BLACK STUDIES DIVISION (Area-Ethnic)
Martin Luther King Memorial Library
901 G St., N.W.   Phone: (202) 727-1211
Washington, DC 20001   Alice B. Robinson, Chf.
Founded: 1971. **Staff:** Prof 3. **Subjects:** Slavery in the U.S. and Caribbean; history, science and technology, business, social conditions, literature, Afro-American culture, civil rights, biography. **Special Collections:** Beatrice Murphy Foundation (1700 books); Juvenile Reference Collection (637 books). **Holdings:** 12,725 books; 15 bound periodical volumes; 152 framed prints; 72 phonograph records; 98 reels of microfilm; 97 catalogs of Black colleges and universities; 18 VF drawers. **Subscriptions:** 83 journals and other serials; 48 newspapers. **Services:** Copying; holdings do not circulate. **Publications:** Booklists on special subject, irregular - free. **Special Indexes:** Index of Black literary magazines (card). **Staff:** Deborah Lockhart, Rd.Adv.; Joe Lewis, Rd.Adv.

★3762★
DISTRICT OF COLUMBIA PUBLIC LIBRARY - BUSINESS, ECONOMICS & VOCATIONS DIVISION (Bus-Fin)
Martin Luther King Memorial Library
901 G St., N.W.   Phone: (202) 727-1171
Washington, DC 20001   Wayne D. Kryszak, Chf.
Founded: 1907. **Staff:** Prof 4. **Subjects:** Statistics, economics, vocations, commerce, management, marketing, labor, transportation. **Special Collections:** Current telephone and business directories; U.S. Census 1790 to present; company annual reports; Small Business Center (SBC); Mini

Employment Information Center (MEIC). **Holdings:** 21,000 books; 840 bound periodical volumes; 400 business directories; 6000 pamphlets; 750 telephone directories; 2244 reels of microfilm; 88 microcards; 2450 microfiche. **Subscriptions:** 370 journals and other serials; 16 newspapers and financial services. **Publications:** Booklists of special subjects, irregular - free. **Special Indexes:** Title index to American Management Association and Conference Board publications (card). **Staff:** Jane Cates, Rd.Adv.; Sun Shin, Rd.Adv.; Elizabeth Hale, Rd.Adv.

★3763★
DISTRICT OF COLUMBIA PUBLIC LIBRARY - CHILDREN'S DIVISION (Hum)
Martin Luther King Memorial Library
901 G St., N.W.   Phone: (202) 727-1248
Washington, DC 20001   Barbara F. Geyger, Chf.
Staff: Prof 3. **Subjects:** Children's literature. **Special Collections:** Illustrators Collection, 18th century to present (11,000 volumes); historical children's books and periodicals (1500 books, 558 bound periodical volumes); source collection for children's literature (200 volumes). **Holdings:** 41,338 books; 600 bound periodical volumes; 221 phonograph records; 19 cassettes; 69 filmstrips. **Subscriptions:** 38 journals and other serials. **Services:** Division open to public. **Publications:** Graded and subject lists, irregular - free. **Staff:** Beulah Holbert, Rd.Adv.; Margaret Flynn, Rd.Adv.

★3764★
DISTRICT OF COLUMBIA PUBLIC LIBRARY - HISTORY AND GEOGRAPHY DIVISION (Hist; Geog-Map)
Martin Luther King Memorial Library
901 G St., N.W.   Phone: (202) 727-1161
Washington, DC 20001   Eleanor A. Bartlett, Chf.
Founded: 1949. **Staff:** Prof 3. **Subjects:** History, geography, travel. **Holdings:** 42,901 books; 44 VF drawers of pamphlets and clippings; 2620 reels of microfilm; 737 microcards; 2873 microfiche. **Subscriptions:** 143 journals and other serials. **Services:** Interlibrary loans; copying. **Staff:** Nineta Rozen, Rd.Adv.; Ethel L. Sumpter, Rd.Adv.

★3765★
DISTRICT OF COLUMBIA PUBLIC LIBRARY - LANGUAGE, LITERATURE & FOREIGN LANGUAGE DIVISION (Hum)
Martin Luther King Memorial Library
901 G St., N.W.   Phone: (202) 727-1281
Washington, DC 20001   Octave S. Stevenson, Chf.
Founded: 1949. **Staff:** Prof 3. **Subjects:** Poetry, drama, general and literary essays, literary history and criticism, philology, journalism, library science, foreign languages, language instruction. **Holdings:** 38,979 books; 76 bound periodical volumes; 1000 pamphlets; 1096 microforms; 658 phonograph records. **Subscriptions:** 117 journals and other serials. **Services:** Interlibrary loans. **Staff:** Barbara Gloriod, Rd.Adv.; Alexander Geyger, Rd.Adv.

★3766★
DISTRICT OF COLUMBIA PUBLIC LIBRARY - LIBRARY FOR THE BLIND AND PHYSICALLY HANDICAPPED (Aud-Vis)
Martin Luther King Memorial Library
901 G St., N.W.   Phone: (202) 272-2142
Washington, DC 20001   Grace Lyons, Chf.
Staff: Prof 2; Other 8. **Subjects:** Popular and general material in special formats; information on legislation and services for the disabled; volunteer production of graduate and post-secondary school and work-related materials in special formats; reference material on aging and the handicapped. **Special Collections:** Recorded books (96,115); large-print books (4195); Books in braille (4137). **Holdings:** 646 books; 2700 phonograph records. **Subscriptions:** 145 journals and other serials (50 print and braille, 95 recorded). **Services:** Interlibrary loans; certification required with talking book materials; production of taped materials for disabled. **Publications:** Newsletter, quarterly - large-print distributed to blind and disabled readers and to local and national organizations serving the disabled. **Staff:** Edith Lewis, Libn.

★3767★
DISTRICT OF COLUMBIA PUBLIC LIBRARY - MUSIC & RECREATION DIVISION (Mus; Rec)
Martin Luther King Memorial Library
901 G St., N.W.   Phone: (202) 727-1285
Washington, DC 20001   Mary Elliott, Chf.
Founded: 1934. **Staff:** Prof 3. **Subjects:** Music, recreation. **Special Collections:** Hans Kindler Collection of orchestral scores and parts. **Holdings:** 12,300 books; 1000 bound periodical volumes; 17,319 recordings; 6153 sheet music items; 24,480 scores; 303 cassette tapes; 121 reels of microfilm. **Subscriptions:** 132 journals and other serials. **Special Indexes:** Song index. **Staff:** Bonnie Jo Dopp, Rd.Adv.; Victor P. Dyni, Rd.Adv.

★3768★
DISTRICT OF COLUMBIA PUBLIC LIBRARY - PHILOSOPHY, PSYCHOLOGY AND RELIGION DIVISION (Hum)
Martin Luther King Memorial Library
901 G St., N.W.   Phone: (202) 727-1251
Washington, DC 20001   Vicky Rogers, Chf.
Founded: 1956. **Staff:** Prof 3. **Subjects:** Religion, psychology, philosophy. **Holdings:** 27,628 books; 771 bound periodical volumes; 50 reports; 200 clippings; 19 VF drawers of pamphlets; reels of microfilm; 2239 microcards. **Subscriptions:** 131 journals and other serials. **Services:** Interlibrary loans. **Special Indexes:** Indexes to prayers, sermons, gods and goddesses of classical mythology and Oriental mythology. **Staff:** Lois Bell, Rd.Adv.; Ellen Flaherty, Asst.Chf.

★3769★
DISTRICT OF COLUMBIA PUBLIC LIBRARY - POPULAR LIBRARY (Hum)
Martin Luther King Memorial Library
901 G St., N.W.   Phone: (202) 727-1295
Washington, DC 20001   Mildred R. Greene, Chf.
Staff: Prof 4. **Subjects:** Fiction and nonfiction. **Holdings:** 63,063 books; 605 bound periodical volumes; 4 drawers of pamphlets; 2960 reels of microfilm. **Subscriptions:** 61 journals and other serials. **Services:** Interlibrary loans. **Publications:** Booklists of fiction and other subjects, irregular - free. **Special Indexes:** Subject index of fiction; title index of fiction; author index of short stories (all on cards). **Staff:** Jacqueline J. Sein, Asst.Chf.; Eleanor Dore, Rd.Adv.; Gloria Thornton, Rd.Adv.

★3770★
DISTRICT OF COLUMBIA PUBLIC LIBRARY - SOCIOLOGY, GOVERNMENT & EDUCATION DIVISION (Soc Sci; Educ)
Martin Luther King Memorial Library
901 G St., N.W.   Phone: (202) 727-1261
Washington, DC 20001   Ann K. Ross, Chf.
Founded: 1927. **Staff:** Prof 3. **Subjects:** Social sciences, sociology, education, customs, folklore, military science, government, political science, costume. **Special Collections:** Adult Basic Education. **Holdings:** 49,884 books; 950 bound periodical volumes; 90 VF drawers of pamphlets; 2826 reels of microfilm; 6417 microfiche (college catalogs). **Subscriptions:** 196 journals and other serials. **Services:** Interlibrary loans; copying. **Publications:** How to Prepare for the High School Equivalency Exam - free to patrons. **Staff:** Eloise Fogo, Rd.Adv.; Monica O'Connell, Rd.Adv.

★3771★
DISTRICT OF COLUMBIA PUBLIC LIBRARY - TECHNOLOGY AND SCIENCE DIVISION (Sci-Tech)
Martin Luther King Memorial Library
901 G St., N.W.   Phone: (202) 727-1175
Washington, DC 20001   Barbara Lundquist, Chf.
Founded: 1907. **Staff:** Prof 4. **Subjects:** Mathematics, biology, domestic arts, earth sciences, chemistry, physics, engineering, agriculture, gardening, medicine, psychiatry, astronomy, consumer information. **Holdings:** 35,800 books; 2300 bound periodical volumes; 4868 microforms; 65 VF drawers. **Subscriptions:** 300 journals and other serials. **Staff:** Bonnie C. Minton, Asst.Chf.; Ruby Ramer, Rd.Adv.; Theresa Hung, Rd.Adv.

★3772★
DISTRICT OF COLUMBIA PUBLIC LIBRARY - WASHINGTONIANA DIVISION (Hist)
Martin Luther King Memorial Library
901 G St., N.W.   Phone: (202) 727-1213
Washington, DC 20001   Roxanne Deane, Chf.
Founded: 1907. **Staff:** Prof 3; Other 1. **Subjects:** District of Columbia - history, current affairs, government, biography, organizations. **Special Collections:** History of Washington, DC from its founding to the present; Washington Star Library (13 million clippings; 1 million photographs). **Holdings:** 13,863 books; 50 bound periodical volumes; over one million newspaper clippings and pamphlets; 5515 reels of microfilm; 20,000 mounted pictures; 2000 maps. **Subscriptions:** 86 journals and other serials. **Staff:** Kathryn Ray, Asst.Chf.; Charles Hicks, Rd.Adv.; G.R.F. Key, Rd.Adv.

★3773★
DISTRICT OF COLUMBIA PUBLIC SCHOOLS - DIVISION OF QUALITY ASSURANCE - RESEARCH INFORMATION CENTER (Educ)
415 12th St., N.W.   Phone: (202) 724-4249
Washington, DC 20004   Erika Robinson, Coord.
Founded: 1969. **Staff:** Prof 1; Other 1. **Subjects:** Education. **Services:** School system historical documents and budgets. **Holdings:** 1000 books and reports; Research in Education and Current Index to Journals in Education; 100 VF drawers of fugitive material; ERIC microfiche collection.

Subscriptions: 70 journals and other serials. Services: Interlibrary loans; copying; computer searches; center open to public for reference use only. Computerized Information Services: DIALOG. Formerly: Its Division of Research and Evaluation.

DISTRICT OF COLUMBIA - REDEVELOPMENT LAND AGENCY
See: District of Columbia Department of Housing and Community Development Library

DISTRICT OF COLUMBIA TEACHERS COLLEGE
See: University of District of Columbia

★3774★
DISTRICT ONE TECHNICAL INSTITUTE - LIBRARY - EDUCATIONAL RESOURCE CENTER (Educ)
620 W. Clairemont Ave.　　　　　　Phone: (715) 836-4756
Eau Claire, WI 54701　　　　Lorraine Kearney, Coord., Lib.Serv.
Founded: 1966. Staff: Prof 4; Other 10. Subjects: Electronics, fluid power, health occupations, quantity foods, data processing, police science, accounting, business education, law, automotive technology. Special Collections: Repository for the National Clearinghouse on Aging's Service Center for Aging Information (SCAN). Holdings: 36,000 books; 7000 other cataloged items; 4000 microfiche on aging. Subscriptions: 890 journals and other serials; 43 newspapers. Services: Interlibrary loans; copying; library open to public with restrictions. Computerized Information Services: DIALOG, Control Data Corporation. Networks/Consortia: Member of OCLC. Publications: Handbook, bibliographies - on request. Special Catalogs: AV listing. Staff: David Olson, Asst.Libn.; Sandy Hoch, Asst.Libn.; Jane White, Asst.Libn.; Kris Carr, Asst.Libn.

DITT
See: Centre de Recherche Industrielle du Quebec - Direction de l'Info. Technologique et du Transfert de Tech.

★3775★
DITTBERNER ASSOCIATES, INC. - LIBRARY (Bus-Fin)
4903 Auburn Ave.　　　　　　Phone: (301) 652-8350
Bethesda, MD 20814　　　　　　Ingrid C.D. Mayr, Libn.
Founded: 1965. Staff: Prof 1. Subjects: Computers, telephone switching equipment, business statistics (national and international). Holdings: 700 books; 13 VF drawers of industry files (cataloged); 60 VF drawers of telecommunication market and technology information. Subscriptions: 85 journals and other serials. Services: Library not open to public. Remarks: Library is used primarily in conjunction with consulting services performed by the corporation.

DITTRICK (Howard) MUSEUM OF HISTORICAL MEDICINE
See: Cleveland Health Sciences Library - Howard Dittrick Museum of Historical Medicine

★3776★
DIVERSEY WYANDOTTE INC. - RESEARCH CENTRE LIBRARY (Sci-Tech)
2645 Royal Windsor Dr.　　　　　　Phone: (416) 822-3511
Mississauga, ON, Canada L5J 1L1　　　　　　Mr. D. Mul
Founded: 1969. Staff: 1. Subjects: Chemistry - organic, physical, inorganic, analytical. Holdings: 400 books; 10 binders of government and customer specifications; patents. Subscriptions: 15 journals and other serials. Services: Library not open to public.

★3777★
DIVINE PROVIDENCE HOSPITAL - MEDICAL LIBRARY (Med)
1100 Grampian Blvd.　　　　　　Phone: (717) 326-8153
Williamsport, PA 17701　　　　Janet Anderson, Med.Rec.Adm.
Founded: 1951. Subjects: Medicine. Holdings: 781 books; 2458 bound periodical volumes. Subscriptions: 86 journals and other serials. Services: Interlibrary loans; copying; library open to public by appointment.

★3778★
DIVINE WORD INTERNATIONAL RELIGIOUS EDUCATION CENTRE - LIBRARY
Box 2400
London, ON, Canada N6A 4G3
Founded: 1966. Subjects: Scripture, theology, anthropology, religious education, social analysis. Holdings: 6000 books. Remarks: Presently inactive.

★3779★
DIVINE WORD SEMINARY - LIBRARY (Rel-Theol)
101 Park St.　　　　　　Phone: (609) 298-0549
Bordentown, NJ 08505　　　　　　John McCullough, Libn.
Staff: Prof 1; Other 1. Subjects: History, religion, social studies, literature. Holdings: 15,000 volumes; 900 reports and clippings; 100 tapes; 300 recordings. Subscriptions: 70 journals and other serials; 5 newspapers. Services: Interlibrary loans.

★3780★
DIVINE WORD SEMINARY OF ST. AUGUSTINE - LIBRARY†
201 Ruella St.
Bay St. Louis, MS 39520
Founded: 1923. Subjects: Negro history and literature, ethnology, philosophy, Catholic theology, social sciences, pure and applied sciences, literature, geography, history. Holdings: 26,000 books; 3500 bound periodical volumes. Remarks: Presently inactive.

DIX (Dorothea) HOSPITAL
See: Dorothea Dix Hospital

DIX (Dorothea) MUSEUM
See: Harrisburg State Hospital - Staff Library

★3781★
DIXMONT STATE HOSPITAL - PERSONNEL LIBRARY (Med)
　　　　　　　　　　　Phone: (412) 761-1780
Sewickley, PA 15143　　　　Ta-Liang Daisy Yao Tang, Libn.
Founded: 1965. Staff: Prof 1. Subjects: Psychiatric medicine and allied fields. Special Collections: Works on and by Sigmund Freud (41 volumes). Holdings: 1200 books; 11 bound periodical volumes; 130 pamphlets. Subscriptions: 25 journals and other serials. Services: Interlibrary loans; copying; library open to public with restrictions. Networks/Consortia: Member of Mideastern Regional Medical Library Service (MERMLS). Publications: Acquisition lists. Remarks: Maintained by Pennsylvania State Department of Public Welfare.

★3782★
DIXON DEVELOPMENTAL CENTER - PROFESSIONAL LIBRARY (Med)
2600 N. Brinton Ave.　　　　　　Phone: (815) 288-5561
Dixon, IL 61021　　　　　　Sarah Haff, Libn.
Founded: 1967. Staff: 1. Subjects: Mental retardation, psychology, psychiatry, medicine, special education, speech and hearing, sociology. Holdings: 3102 books; 584 bound periodical volumes; 1875 phonograph records (cataloged); 1500 VF items; 50 microfiche. Subscriptions: 40 journals and other serials. Services: Interlibrary loans; copying; library open to public with approval of librarian. Remarks: Maintained by Illinois State Department of Mental Health and Developmental Disabilities.

★3783★
DIXON GALLERY AND GARDENS - LIBRARY (Art)
4339 Park Ave.　　　　　　Phone: (901) 761-5250
Memphis, TN 38117　　　　　　Michael Milkovich, Dir.
Staff: 1. Subjects: Impressionist art, horticulture, 18th and 19th century British art, art history, porcelain. Holdings: 3000 volumes; 150 boxes of notebooks and periodicals. Subscriptions: 81 journals and other serials. Services: Interlibrary loans; copying; library open to public for reference use only. Staff: Reba Russell, Cur. of Educ.

★3784★
DMS, INC. - TECHNICAL LIBRARY (Sci-Tech)
100 Northfield St.　　　　　　Phone: (203) 661-7800
Greenwich, CT 06830　　　　　　Frank Dahm, Dir.
Founded: 1967. Staff: Prof 1; Other 2. Subjects: Aerospace, avionics, aircraft missiles, research and development of engines, ships and vehicles ordnance, environmental and civil programs, government defense contracts. Holdings: Figures not available. Subscriptions: 100 journals and other serials; 50 newspapers. Services: Interlibrary loans; copying; library not open to public. Staff: Rose Marie De Natale, Libn.

★3785★
DOALL COMPANY - LIBRARY (Sci-Tech)†
245 N. Laurel Ave.　　　　　　Phone: (312) 824-1122
Des Plaines, IL 60016
Subjects: Machine tool operation, cutting tools, gauging equipment, metallurgy, metrology. Holdings: Books; films; photographs; data and other nonprint material. Services: Library open to qualified users.

★3786★
DOANE-WESTERN, INC. - INFORMATION CENTER (Agri)
8900 Manchester Rd.
Phone: (314) 968-1000
St. Louis, MO 63144
Mary E. Aversa, Mgr.
Founded: 1947. **Staff:** Prof 1; Other 2. **Subjects:** Agriculture, economics, business management, law. **Holdings:** 2000 books; 1000 bound periodical volumes; 10,000 college, state and USDA publications (cataloged); 30 VF drawers of subject files; 8 VF drawers of state agricultural statistics; government documents; agricultural college publications. **Subscriptions:** 365 journals and other serials; 6 newspapers. **Services:** Interlibrary loans; copying; library open to public with restrictions. **Computerized Information Services:** DIALOG, SDC, BRS, Dow Jones News Retrieval, Source Telecomputing Corporation, I.P. Sharp Associates, Ltd.; internal database; computerized cataloging and serials. **Publications:** Weekly Acquisitions. **Special Indexes:** Ag Index, monthly cumulative subject index - available by subscription. **Formerly:** Doane Agricultural Service, Inc.

DOBLITZ (Ray) MEMORIAL LIBRARY
See: Ohev Shalom Synagogue - Ray Doblitz Memorial Library

DOCKING RESEARCH CENTER ARCHIVES LIBRARY
See: U.S. Natl. Park Service - Cherokee Strip Living Museum

★3787★
DOCTORS HOSPITAL - ALEXANDER RAXLER LIBRARY (Med)
45 Brunswick Ave.
Phone: (416) 963-5464
Toronto, ON, Canada M5S 2M1
Margy Chan, Libn.
Staff: Prof 1. **Subjects:** Clinical medicine, nursing, hospital administration. **Holdings:** 1500 books; 500 cassettes. **Subscriptions:** 157 journals and other serials. **Services:** Interlibrary loans; library not open to public. **Computerized Information Services:** MEDLARS. **Networks/Consortia:** Member of Toronto Medical Libraries Group. **Publications:** Acquisitions list, bimonthly - for internal distribution only.

★3788★
DOCTORS' HOSPITAL - MEDICAL LIBRARY (Med)
5000 University Dr.
Phone: (305) 666-2111
Miami, FL 33143
Lyn O'Brien, Med.Libn.
Staff: Prof 1. **Subjects:** Medicine. **Holdings:** 1050 books; 176 bound periodical volumes; video and audio cassettes. **Subscriptions:** 47 journals and other serials. **Services:** Interlibrary loans; copying; library open to public with approval of administration and librarian. **Networks/Consortia:** Member of Miami Health Sciences Library Consortium (MHSLC).

★3789★
DOCTORS HOSPITAL INC. OF STARK COUNTY - MEDICAL LIBRARY (Med)
400 Austin Ave., N.W.
Phone: (216) 837-7371
Massillon, OH 44646
Christine J. Williams, Dir.Lib.Serv.
Staff: Prof 1; Other 1. **Subjects:** Medicine, osteopathy. **Holdings:** 750 books; 1380 bound periodical volumes. **Subscriptions:** 124 journals and other serials. **Services:** Interlibrary loans; copying; SDI; library not open to public. **Computerized Information Services:** BRS. **Networks/Consortia:** Member of Canton-Massillon BRS Consortia.

★3790★
DOCTORS HOSPITAL - W.S. KONOLD MEMORIAL LIBRARY (Med)
1087 Dennison Ave.
Phone: (614) 421-4113
Columbus, OH 43201
Joseph Muzzo, Dir.
Founded: 1973. **Staff:** Prof 1; Other 3. **Subjects:** Medicine, nursing, allied health sciences. **Holdings:** 2000 books; 4000 bound periodical volumes; 300 AV items; 4 VF drawers of pamphlet material; 300 slide sets; 77 video cassette titles; 500 videotapes; 900 audiotapes. **Subscriptions:** 225 journals and other serials. **Services:** Interlibrary loans; copying; SDI; library open to public for reference use only. **Computerized Information Services:** MEDLINE. **Networks/Consortia:** Member of Kentucky-Ohio-Michigan Regional Medical Library Network (KOMRML); Central Ohio Hospital Library Consortium. **Publications:** Journal of the Columbus Clinical Group.

★3791★
DOCTORS' MEDICAL CENTER - PROFESSIONAL LIBRARY (Med)
1441 Florida Ave.
Box 4138
Phone: (209) 578-1211
Modesto, CA 95352
Margaret F. Luebke, Med.Libn.
Founded: 1966. **Staff:** Prof 1; Other 1. **Subjects:** Medicine, nursing. **Holdings:** 360 books; 150 bound periodical volumes. **Subscriptions:** 126 journals and other serials. **Services:** Interlibrary loans; copying; SDI; library open to public for reference use only. **Computerized Information Services:** MEDLINE. **Networks/Consortia:** Member of 49-99 Cooperative Library System.

★3792★
DOCUMENTATION ASSOCIATES (Soc Sci; Info Sci)
Box 84005
Phone: (213) 477-5081
Los Angeles, CA 90073
Skye Atman, Pres.
Founded: 1971. **Staff:** Prof 4. **Subjects:** Drug abuse, aging, suicide, environmental sciences, education, engineering, social sciences. **Holdings:** 1000 journal articles, pamphlets and reports on drug abuse; 3000 citations to literature on aging; 200 reports on technology assessment. **Services:** SDI; abstracting, indexing, library development, database construction, thesaurus development, consulting, literature searching; open to public with fee for services. **Staff:** Donna Chamberlain, V.P.

DODGE (Austin A.) PHARMACY LIBRARY
See: University of Mississippi - School of Pharmacy - Austin A. Dodge Pharmacy Library

★3793★
DODGE COUNTY HISTORICAL SOCIETY - LOUIS E. MAY MUSEUM (Hist)
1643 N. Nye
Phone: (402) 721-4515
Fremont, NE 68025
Loell R. Jorgensen, Musm.Dir.
Staff: 1. **Subjects:** Dodge County history, historic preservation, 19th century decorative arts. **Special Collections:** Historical photographs (1000). **Holdings:** 1220 books and bound periodical volumes; 1 VF drawer of maps; 12 file boxes of documents; 2 manuscripts. **Subscriptions:** 14 journals and other serials.

DODGE (Robert Gray) LIBRARY
See: Northeastern University - Robert Gray Dodge Library

★3794★
DOFASCO INC. - MAIN OFFICE LIBRARY (Sci-Tech)
1330 Burlington St. E.
P.O. Box 460
Phone: (416) 544-3761
Hamilton, ON, Canada L8N 3J5
Mrs. Mina Gucma, Libn.
Founded: 1961. **Staff:** Prof 2. **Subjects:** Metallurgy, steel industry, business, occupational medicine, engineering. **Special Collections:** British Iron and Steel Industry and Brutcher metallurgical translations; metallurgical patents (4 VF drawers). **Holdings:** 5000 books; 750 bound periodical volumes; 17 VF drawers of reports, clippings and pamphlets. **Subscriptions:** 1120 journals and other serials; 12 newspapers. **Services:** Interlibrary loans; copying; library open to public on application to librarian. **Staff:** Liz Godin, Asst.Libn.

★3795★
DOFASCO INC. - RESEARCH INFORMATION CENTRE (Sci-Tech; Energy)
1390 Burlington St., E.
Box 460
Phone: (416) 544-3761
Hamilton, ON, Canada L8N 3J5
Ann M. Duff, Res.Libn.
Staff: Prof 1; Other 1. **Subjects:** Iron and steel production, chemical engineering, coal, coke. **Holdings:** 5000 books; 375 bound periodical volumes; 700 reels of microfilm; 1000 patents; 1500 reports. **Subscriptions:** 255 journals and other serials. **Services:** Interlibrary loans; copying; SDI; library open to public by appointment. **Computerized Information Services:** DIALOG, SDC; computerized cataloging. **Networks/Consortia:** Member of Sheridan Park Association.

DOHENY (Edward Laurence) MEMORIAL LIBRARY
See: St. John's Seminary - Edward Laurence Doheny Memorial Library

★3796★
DOME PETROLEUM LIMITED - CORPORATE LIBRARY (Energy)
P.O. Box 200
Phone: (403) 260-2674
Calgary, AB, Canada T2P 2H8
H.W. McNaught, Corp.Libn.
Founded: 1979. **Staff:** Prof 4; Other 3. **Subjects:** Petroluem exploration and production, geology, engineering, arctic research, marine architecture. **Holdings:** 5000 books; 7000 government documents (catatloged). **Subscriptions:** 700 journals and other serials; 10 newspapers. **Services:** Interlibrary loans; SDI; library open to public by appointment. **Computerized Information Services:** DIALOG, SDC, New York Times Information Service, QL Systems, CANSIM, CAN/OLE, Info Globe, Dow Jones News Retrival; computerized cataloging and serials. **Remarks:** Contains the holdings of the former Hudson's Bay Oil & Gas Company, Ltd. - Corporate Library.

★3797★
DOMGLAS INC. - CORPORATE LIBRARY (Sci-Tech; Bus-Fin)
2070 Hadwen Rd.
Phone: (416) 823-3860
Mississauga, ON, Canada L5K 2C9
Mary MacKinnon
Founded: 1971. **Staff:** 1. **Subjects:** Glass technology, engineering, marketing, business. **Holdings:** 2000 books; 150 bound periodical volumes; 2000 patents; reports. **Subscriptions:** 200 journals and other serials.

Services: Interlibrary loans; copying; library open to public by appointment. **Computerized Information Services:** CAN/OLE, QL Systems, DIALOG. **Networks/Consortia:** Member of Sheridan Park Association.

DOMINGO TOLEDO ALAMO LAW LIBRARY
See: Interamerican University of Puerto Rico

★3798★
DOMINICAINS DE ST-ALBERT-LE-GRAND, MONTREAL - INSTITUT D'ETUDES MEDIEVALES - BIBLIOTHEQUE (Hist)
2715 Chemin de la Cote Ste-Catherine   Phone: (514) 739-9868
Montreal, PQ, Canada H3T 1B6   Yvon-D. Gelinas, O.P., Hd.Libn.
Founded: 1942. **Staff:** Prof 2; Other 3. **Subjects:** Medieval civilization - philosophy, theology, literature, history, including economic and political history; church history; classics; ancient philosophy and patristics (texts and studies); canon law; medieval art history; paleography. **Holdings:** 65,000 books; 15,000 bound periodical volumes; 300 reels of microfilm of manuscripts. **Subscriptions:** 400 journals and other serials. **Services:** Interlibrary loans; copying; library open for consultation only.

★3799★
DOMINICAN COLLEGE LIBRARY (Rel-Theol)
487 Michigan Ave., N.E.   Phone: (202) 529-5300
Washington, DC 20017-1584   Rev. J. Raymond Vandegrift, O.P., Libn.
Founded: 1905. **Staff:** Prof 2; Other 3. **Subjects:** Scholastic and modern theology; Thomistic and modern philosophy; scripture; patristics. **Special Collections:** Dominicana (Dominican Order - history and authors); Thomas Aquinas; Dominican Dissertations; rare books. **Holdings:** 44,088 books; 9738 bound periodical volumes. **Subscriptions:** 302 journals and other serials. **Services:** Interlibrary loans; copying; library open to public. **Computerized Information Services:** Computerized cataloging. **Networks/Consortia:** Member of Washington Theological Consortium; CAPCON; Cluster of Independent Theological Schools. **Special Catalogs:** Analytical Catalog of Dominican Authors. **Remarks:** Maintained by the Dominican House of Studies. **Staff:** E. Matthew Rzeczkowski, O.P., Asst.Libn.; Serilda Lango, Circ./ILL.

DOMINICAN COLLEGE OF PHILOSOPHY AND THEOLOGY
See: College Dominicain de Philosophie et de Theologie

DOMINICAN COLLEGE OF SAN RAFAEL - AMERICAN MUSIC RESEARCH CENTER
See: American Music Research Center

DOMINICAN CONVENT OF SAN RAFAEL - ARCHIVES
See: Dominican Sisters - Congregation of the Holy Name

★3800★
DOMINICAN EDUCATION CENTER - LIBRARY (Rel-Theol)
          Phone: (608) 748-4411
Sinsinawa, WI 53824   Sr. Coronata Harvey, Dir.
Staff: Prof 2; Other 2. **Subjects:** Theology, philosophy, scripture, fine arts. **Holdings:** 24,000 volumes; indexes. **Subscriptions:** 55 journals and other serials; 8 newspapers. **Services:** Interlibrary loans; copying; library open to public. **Remarks:** This is an extension of the Rosary College Library, River Forest, IL 60305. **Staff:** Sr. John Bosco Hyland, Cat.

DOMINICAN HOUSE OF STUDIES
See: Dominican College Library

★3801★
DOMINICAN SANTA CRUZ HOSPITAL - MEDICAL LIBRARY (Med)
1555 Soquel Dr.   Phone: (408) 476-0220
Santa Cruz, CA 95065   Mrs. Merle Ochs, Med.Libn.
Staff: Prof 1; Other 1. **Subjects:** Medicine, nursing and related subjects. **Holdings:** 835 books; 2040 bound periodical volumes. **Subscriptions:** 104 journals and other serials. **Services:** Interlibrary loans; copying; library open to public for reference use only. **Computerized Information Services:** MEDLINE.

DOMINICAN SCHOOL OF PHILOSOPHY AND THEOLOGY
See: Graduate Theological Union

★3802★
DOMINICAN SISTERS - CONGREGATION OF THE HOLY NAME - ARCHIVES (Rel-Theol; Hist)
1520 Grand Ave.   Phone: (415) 454-9221
San Rafael, CA 94901   Sr. Justin Barry, O.P., Archv.
Founded: 1930. **Staff:** 2. **Subjects:** History of the congregation. **Holdings:** 175 linear feet of archives including letters, ledgers, publications, photographs

and clippings. **Services:** Copying; library open to public by appointment. **Remarks:** Archives located at the Dominican Convent of San Rafael. **Staff:** Sr. Martin Barry, Asst.Archv.

DOMINION ASTROPHYSICAL OBSERVATORY
See: Canada - National Research Council - CISTI

★3803★
DOMINION ENGINEERING WORKS, LTD. - LIBRARY
795 1st Ave.
Lachine, PQ, Canada H8S 2S8
Founded: 1954. **Subjects:** Pulp and paper machinery; water power engineering; rubber, mining and plastics machinery. **Holdings:** 3000 volumes; 20 VF drawers of pamphlets and annual reports. **Remarks:** Presently inactive.

DOMINION RADIO ASTROPHYSICAL OBSERVATORY
See: Canada - National Research Council - CISTI

★3804★
DOMTAR, INC. - CENTRAL LIBRARY (Bus-Fin)†
P.O. Box 7210   Phone: (514) 282-5039
Montreal, PQ, Canada H3C 3M1   Elyse Therrien, Libn.
Founded: 1962. **Staff:** Prof 1; Other 1. **Subjects:** Management, business, pulp and paper. **Holdings:** 1200 books; 600 periodical volumes. **Subscriptions:** 150 journals and other serials. **Services:** Interlibrary loans; copying; library open to public by appointment. **Computerized Information Services:** DIALOG, SDC, Info Globe, Informatech. **Remarks:** Library is located at 395 de Maisonneuve Blvd., W., Montreal, PQ.

★3805★
DOMTAR, INC. - RESEARCH CENTRE LIBRARY (Sci-Tech)
C.P. 300   Phone: (514) 457-6810
Senneville, PQ, Canada H9X 3L7   Barbara G. Bolton, Libn.
Founded: 1963. **Staff:** Prof 1; Other 1. **Subjects:** Pulp and paper, chemical engineering, building products, environment. **Holdings:** 1600 books; 3200 bound periodical volumes; 500 pamphlets. **Subscriptions:** 200 journals and other serials. **Services:** Interlibrary loans; copying; library open to public for reference use only by request. **Computerized Information Services:** DIALOG, SDC, CAN/OLE. **Publications:** Periodicals list - distributed on request. **Special Indexes:** Index to internal reports.

★3806★
DON BOSCO TECHNICAL INSTITUTE - LEE LIBRARY (Sci-Tech)
1151 N. San Gabriel Blvd.   Phone: (213) 280-0451
Rosemead, CA 91770   Phyllis Swistock, Hd.Libn.
Founded: 1957. **Staff:** Prof 1. **Subjects:** Metallurgy, electronics, drafting, mathematics, religion, history, English, chemistry, physics, general science. **Holdings:** 15,000 volumes. **Subscriptions:** 110 journals and other serials. **Services:** Copying; library is AV center for institute.

★3807★
DONALDSON COMPANY, INC. - INFORMATION CENTER (Sci-Tech)
Box 1299   Phone: (612) 887-3019
Minneapolis, MN 55440   Arlene Louton, Libn.
Founded: 1969. **Staff:** Prof 1; Other 2. **Subjects:** Filtration, pollution engineering, particle technology, control systems, acoustics, hydraulics and pneumatics, aerodynamics and fluid mechanics, business. **Holdings:** 7000 books; 20,000 internal reports; 3000 external reports; 4000 vendors' catalogs on microcartridge; complete set of military standards on microcartridge. **Subscriptions:** 400 journals and other serials. **Services:** Interlibrary loans; copying; center open to public with permission of librarian. **Computerized Information Services:** DIALOG; internal database; computerized cataloging and circulation. **Publications:** New Publications List, monthly - for internal distribution only. **Remarks:** Information Center is located at 1400 W. 94th St., Minneapolis, MN 55431.

★3808★
DONALDSON, LUFKIN AND JENRETTE, INC. - CORPORATE INFORMATION CENTER (Bus-Fin)
140 Broadway, 34th Fl.   Phone: (212) 902-2375
New York, NY 10005   Leslie A. Wheaton, Asst. V.P./Mgr.
Founded: 1962. **Staff:** Prof 4; Other 12. **Subjects:** Business, finance, pensions, investment companies. **Special Collections:** Financial history of the American Revolution. **Holdings:** 6000 books; 300 bound periodical volumes; 50,000 microfiche; 500 reels of microfilm; 422 drawers of corporate files on 8360 companies. **Subscriptions:** 2000 journals and other serials; 15 newspapers. **Services:** Interlibrary loans; library not open to public. **Computerized Information Services:** DIALOG, New York Times Information Service, Dow Jones News Retrieval, Info Globe, Computer Directions

Advisors, Inc. (CDA), ADP Network Services, Inc., Control Data Corporation, NEXIS; computerized acquisitions and mechanized routing of serials. **Publications:** DLJ Index of Research Publications. **Staff:** Lola McComb, Ref.; Jeanne Byrnes, Ref.; Peter Piroq, Cat.

DONNELL LIBRARY CENTER
See: New York Public Library

DONNELLEY LIBRARY
See: Lake Forest College

★3809★
DONNELLY MIRRORS, INC. - LIBRARY (Bus-Fin; Sci-Tech)
414 East 40th St.   Phone: (616) 394-2268
Holland, MI 49423   Nancy Yetman, Tech.Libn.
Founded: 1972. **Staff:** Prof 1. **Subjects:** Business, management, glass, plastics, physics, vacuum technology, chemistry, transportation. **Holdings:** 2000 books; 2000 unbound periodicals; 8 drawers of patents (rear view mirrors for automobiles); 8 drawers of reports. **Subscriptions:** 125 journals and other serials. **Services:** Interlibrary loans; copying; open to public with permission. **Computerized Information Services:** DIALOG. **Networks/Consortia:** Member of Holland Zeeland Cooperative Library Association. **Special Catalogs:** Periodical holdings (book, in preparation). **Remarks:** "Donnelly Mirrors is one of the foremost U.S. authorities in automotive rear vision."

DONOHUE (Countess Bernadine Murphy) **ROOM FOR SPECIAL COLLECTIONS**
See: University of San Francisco - Special Collections Department/ Donohue Rare Book Room

★3810★
DONORS FORUM OF CHICAGO - LIBRARY (Soc Sci)
208 S. LaSalle St., Rm. 600   Phone: (312) 726-4882
Chicago, IL 60604   Susan M. Levy, Libn.
Staff: Prof 2. **Subjects:** Philanthropy, grants and funding, foundations and corporate giving, nonprofit organizations. **Special Collections:** Federal tax return cards (forms 990AR, 990PF) for private foundations in seven midwest states and major national foundations elsewhere; information on nonprofit organizations in the Chicago area; files on private foundations and corporate giving including annual reports. **Holdings:** 1000 books; 100,000 cards of foundation tax returns; 22 VF drawers. **Subscriptions:** 82 journals and other serials. **Services:** Copying; library open to public. **Publications:** Chicago Corporate Connection, biennial; Corporate Philanthropy: An Annotated Bibliography. **Special Catalogs:** Donors Forum Members Grants List, annual. **Staff:** Amy Dobratz, Asst.Libn.

DONORS FORUM OF FORSYTH COUNTY
See: Winston-Salem Foundation

★3811★
DONOVAN, LEISURE, NEWTON & IRVINE - LIBRARY (Law)
30 Rockefeller Plaza   Phone: (212) 489-4293
New York, NY 10112   Albert P. Borner, Libn.
Staff: Prof 1; Other 5. **Subjects:** Law. **Special Collections:** Antitrust briefs and pleadings. **Holdings:** 24,000 volumes; 20 VF drawers of pamphlets. **Services:** Interlibrary loans; library open to clients and SLA members.

DONOVICK LIBRARY
See: American Type Culture Collection

★3812★
DORCHESTER HISTORICAL SOCIETY - ROBINSON-LEHANE LIBRARY (Hist)
195 Boston St.   Phone: (617) 436-8367
Dorchester, MA 02125   Anthony Mitchell Sammarco, Vice Pres.
Subjects: Local history. **Special Collections:** Huebener Brick Collection; Badlam Collection of Revolutionary War papers; Baker Chocolate Company collection (2 Hollinger boxes). **Holdings:** 1500 books; 250 cataloged items; 1000 manuscripts; 100 newspapers and clippings. **Services:** Library open to public by appointment. **Publications:** Dorchester Courier, quarterly - to members. **Special Catalogs:** Catalogs to manuscript and photograph collections.

DORFMAN (Irving) **MEMORIAL MEDICAL LIBRARY**
See: Jewish Memorial Hospital - Irving Dorfman Memorial Medical Library

★3813★
DOROTHEA DIX HOSPITAL - F.T. FULLER STAFF LIBRARY (Med)
                                           Phone: (919) 733-5111
Raleigh, NC 27611   Spanola M. Eubanks, Dir., Lib.Serv.
Founded: 1957. **Staff:** Prof 1; Other 1. **Subjects:** Psychiatry, psychiatric nursing, social service, psychology. **Holdings:** 8500 books; 3200 bound periodical volumes; 350 reels of microfilm; 146 cassette tapes. **Subscriptions:** 113 journals and other serials. **Services:** Interlibrary loans; copying; library open to public for reference use only. **Remarks:** Library maintains Learning Lab equipped with AV equipment and materials.

★3814★
DORR-OLIVER INC. - CENTRAL TECHNOLOGY LIBRARY (Sci-Tech)
77 Havemeyer Lane   Phone: (203) 358-3770
Stamford, CT 06904   William D. Kallaway, Tech.Libn.
Founded: 1937. **Staff:** Prof 1; Other 1. **Subjects:** Engineering, chemistry, sanitation, pollution control, management, mining, metallurgy. **Special Collections:** Kirk-Othmer Encyclopedia of Chemical Technology; Purdue Waste Conference collection. **Holdings:** 3500 books; 2500 bound periodical volumes; internal reports; manuals; American Society for Testing and Materials standards. **Subscriptions:** 210 journals and other serials. **Services:** Interlibrary loans; copying; library open to public by appointment. **Publications:** Library Bulletin, irregular. **Special Catalogs:** Catalog to Ph.D. theses.

★3815★
DORSEY, & WHITNEY - LAW LIBRARY (Law)
2300 First National Bank Bldg.   Phone: (612) 340-2613
Minneapolis, MN 55402   Ann M. Carter, Libn.
Staff: Prof 3; Other 3. **Subjects:** Law. **Holdings:** 28,000 volumes; 45 cassette tapes; 1700 volumes on microfilm. **Subscriptions:** 375 journals and other serials; 10 newspapers. **Services:** SDI; library not open to public. **Computerized Information Services:** LEXIS, WESTLAW, DIALOG, New York Times Information Service. **Networks/Consortia:** Member of Downtowners. **Publications:** The Digest, for internal distribution only. **Formerly:** Dorsey, Windhorst, Hannaford, Whitney & Halladay. **Staff:** Jamie Niss Dunn, Asst.Libn.; Helga Eckhoff, Ser.Libn.

DOSSIN GREAT LAKES MUSEUM INFORMATION CENTER
See: Great Lakes Maritime Institute

DOUGLAS AIRCRAFT COMPANY
See: Mc Donnell Douglas Corporation

★3816★
DOUGLAS COUNTY HISTORICAL SOCIETY - FAIRLAWN MUSEUM LIBRARY (Hist)
906 E. 2nd St.   Phone: (715) 394-5712
Superior, WI 54880   Florence Walde, Chm., Lib.Comm.
Founded: 1902. **Staff:** Prof 2. **Subjects:** History of Douglas County, Superior, Wisconsin, Northwest Wisconsin, Northwest Minnesota and Lake Superior. **Holdings:** 200 books; 100 bound periodical volumes; photographs; whaleback material; 100 maps of the area. **Services:** Interlibrary loans (limited); copying (limited); copying of photographs; library open to public with restrictions.

★3817★
DOUGLAS COUNTY LAW LIBRARY (Law)
Hall of Justice
17th & Farnam   Phone: (402) 444-7174
Omaha, NE 68183   Carol Gendler, Libn.
Founded: 1905. **Staff:** Prof 1. **Subjects:** Law. **Holdings:** 25,000 volumes. **Services:** Copying; library open to public with restrictions. **Computerized Information Services:** WESTLAW. **Special Catalogs:** Book catalog.

★3818★
DOUGLAS COUNTY LAW LIBRARY (Law)†
1313 Belknap St.
Court House   Phone: (715) 394-0239
Superior, WI 54880   Carol Wittke, Libn.
Staff: 1. **Subjects:** Law. **Holdings:** 10,500 volumes. **Services:** Library open to public.

★3819★
DOUGLAS COUNTY MUSEUM - LAVOLA BAKKEN MEMORIAL LIBRARY (Hist)
Box 1550   Phone: (503) 440-4507
Roseburg, OR 97470   Ella Mae Young, Res.Hist.
Staff: Prof 1. **Subjects:** Douglas County history, Umpqua Indians, logging,

sawmills and grist mills, marine history, mining, development of area towns, railroads, agriculture. **Special Collections:** Herbarium collection of Douglas County. **Holdings:** 2000 books; 135 vertical files of letters, diaries, manuscripts, genealogies, census and cemetery records; 188 oral histories. **Services:** Copying; library open to public for reference use only. **Networks/ Consortia:** Member of Lane-Douglas Consortia.

DOUGLAS (Frederic H.) LIBRARY OF ANTHROPOLOGY AND ART
See: Denver Art Museum - Frederic H. Douglas Library of Anthropology and Art

★3820★
DOUGLAS HOSPITAL CENTRE - STAFF LIBRARY (Med)
6875 La Salle Blvd.
Montreal, PQ, Canada H4H 1R3   Elaine Mancina, Chf.Libn.
Staff: 1. **Subjects:** Psychiatry, psychopharmacology, psychology, child psychiatry, psychiatric nursing. **Holdings:** 3000 books; 2000 bound periodical volumes; bibliographies. **Subscriptions:** 210 journals and other serials. **Services:** Interlibrary loans; library open to public, but material does not circulate.

DOUGLAS (Jane H.) MEMORIAL LIBRARY
See: Amateur Astronomers Association

DOUGLAS LIBRARY
See: Chicago State University

DOUGLAS LIBRARY
See: Queen's University at Kingston - Special Collections

★3821★
DOUGLAS OIL COMPANY OF CALIFORNIA - RESEARCH AND TECHNOLOGY DEPARTMENT - LIBRARY
14700 Downey Ave.
Paramount, CA 90723
Defunct

★3822★
DOUGLASS BOULEVARD CHRISTIAN CHURCH - LIBRARY (Rel-Theol)†
2005 Douglass Blvd.   Phone: (502) 452-2620
Louisville, KY 40205   Mrs. Eugene R. Cruikshank
Founded: 1940. **Staff:** Prof 1. **Subjects:** Religion, Bible study, family and community, fiction. **Holdings:** 2500 volumes; family life and community action pamphlets. **Services:** Library not open to public.

DOUGLASS (Frederick) HOME AND VISITOR CENTER
See: U.S. Natl. Park Service - Frederick Douglass Home and Visitor Center

DOUGLASS-TRUTH BRANCH LIBRARY
See: Seattle Public Library

DOVER AIR FORCE BASE (DE)
See: U.S. Air Force Base - Dover Base Library

★3823★
DOVER PUBLICATIONS, INC. - PICTORIAL ARCHIVES LIBRARY (Pict)
180 Varick St.   Phone: (212) 255-3755
New York, NY 10014
Staff: Prof 1. **Subjects:** Pre-1900 portraits, natural history, photographs, 19th century trades and manufacturers. **Special Collections:** American portraits (20,000 portraits of Americans in all walks of life who lived prior to 1900); European portraits (30,000 portraits of Europeans in all walks of life who lived prior to 1900). **Holdings:** 400 books; 200 bound periodical volumes. **Services:** Library not open to public; mail applications will be considered on an individual basis.

★3824★
DOW CHEMICAL CANADA INC. - LIBRARY (Sci-Tech)
P.O. Box 1012   Phone: (519) 339-3663
Sarnia, ON, Canada N7T 7K7   Barbara R. Buchanan, Libn.
Staff: 3. **Subjects:** Chemistry, chemical engineering. **Holdings:** 4000 books; 5600 bound periodical volumes; microfiche report collection. **Subscriptions:** 400 journals and other serials. **Services:** Interlibrary loans; copying; library open to public by appointment. **Computerized Information Services:** SDC.

★3825★
DOW CHEMICAL COMPANY - LEGAL LIBRARY (Law)
2030 Dow Center   Phone: (517) 636-6648
Midland, MI 48640   Doris L. Steiner, Supv.
Staff: 3. **Subjects:** Law. **Holdings:** 11,000 books. **Subscriptions:** 58 journals and other serials. **Services:** Library open to company attorneys; others by permission. **Computerized Information Services:** Mead Data Central.

★3826★
DOW CHEMICAL COMPANY - MERRELL DOW PHARMACEUTICALS, INC. - RESEARCH CENTER LIBRARY (Med)
2110 E. Galbraith Rd.   Phone: (513) 948-9111
Cincinnati, OH 45215   Elaine Besterman, Mgr.Lib.Serv.
Founded: 1922. **Staff:** Prof 4; Other 2. **Subjects:** Chemistry, medicine, pharmacology, pharmacy. **Holdings:** 10,600 books; 17,450 bound periodical volumes; 2 VF drawers of pamphlets; 1902 microfilm cartridges of journals; 1534 microfiche. **Subscriptions:** 540 journals and other serials. **Services:** Interlibrary loans; copying; SDI; translations; library open to public by appointment. **Computerized Information Services:** DIALOG, SDC, NLM. **Networks/Consortia:** Member of Cincinnati Area Health Sciences Libraries Association. **Publications:** Monthly Report - for internal distribution only. **Staff:** Emily Rahe, Lit. Searcher; Francine Rosenthal, Lit. Searcher; Robert Schutz, Transl.

★3827★
DOW CHEMICAL COMPANY - RESEARCH CENTER LIBRARY (Med)
Box 68511   Phone: (317) 873-3000
Indianapolis, IN 46268   Maxine Tomlin, Libn.
Founded: 1947. **Staff:** Prof 1; Other 1. **Subjects:** Pharmacology, analytical and clinical chemistry, medicine, hematology, virology. **Holdings:** 6500 books; 15,000 bound periodical volumes; abstract services; chemical patent file on microfilm; 7 file drawers of annual reports of other companies; research notebooks on microfilm. **Subscriptions:** 1200 journals and other serials. **Services:** Interlibrary loans; SDI; library open to public with management approval. **Computerized Information Services:** Pharmaco-Medical Documentation Inc., MEDLARS. **Publications:** Additions list, monthly.

★3828★
DOW CHEMICAL COMPANY - TECHNICAL INFORMATION SERVICES - CENTRAL REPORT INDEX (Sci-Tech)
566 Bldg.   Phone: (517) 636-3754
Midland, MI 48640   Paula B. Moses, Mgr.
Founded: 1945. **Staff:** Prof 5; Other 11. **Holdings:** 200,000 proprietary technical research and development reports; 230,000 chemical registry items. **Services:** Copying; SDI; searches; department not open to public. **Computerized Information Services:** Online systems; computerized processing of all materials for storage and retrieval. **Special Indexes:** Indexes, guides and bulletins to the proprietary collection (hardcopy and microform). **Staff:** M.L. Dilling; S.P. Klesney; L.E. Nelson; S.A. Buck .

★3829★
DOW CHEMICAL COMPANY - TECHNICAL INFORMATION SERVICES - CHEMICAL LIBRARY (Sci-Tech)
566 Bldg.
Box 1704   Phone: (517) 636-1098
Midland, MI 48640   Paula B. Moses, Mgr.
Founded: 1920. **Staff:** Prof 10; Other 9. **Subjects:** Chemistry, plastics, agriculture, process engineering, chemical engineering, metallurgy, physics, biology, business. **Holdings:** 25,000 books; 1800 journal titles; 45,000 microfilm cartridges of 250 journal titles. **Subscriptions:** 800 journals and other serials. **Services:** Interlibrary loans; copying; technical literature searches; translation; library open to public. **Computerized Information Services:** Online systems; computerized serials and circulation. **Special Catalogs:** Union List of Serials for Dow Division Libraries' Holdings. **Staff:** M.M. Brumm; S.A. Buck; A.G. Buske; A.L. Clemons; K.A. Friewer; R.F. Helmreich; S.P. Klesney; F.K. Voci .

★3830★
DOW CHEMICAL U.S.A. - BUSINESS INFORMATION CENTER (Bus-Fin)
2020 Dow Center   Phone: (517) 636-3779
Midland, MI 48640   Phae H. Dorman, Mgr.
Founded: 1968. **Staff:** Prof 1; Other 2. **Subjects:** Business, economics, chemical business intelligence, plastics business intelligence, marketing research, international investment, management, finance. **Special Collections:** Chemical economics and marketing. **Holdings:** 5000 books; annual reports; 60 journals on microfilm. **Subscriptions:** 300 journals and other serials; 10 newspapers. **Services:** Interlibrary loans; library open to public with restrictions. **Computerized Information Services:** DIALOG, Dow

Jones News Retrieval, NEXIS. **Publications:** Acquisition Bulletin, monthly.

★3831★
DOW CHEMICAL U.S.A. - HOUSTON DOW CENTER LIBRARY (Sci-Tech)
400 West Belt South
Houston, TX 77042
Phone: (713) 978-2694
Alice Harris, Libn.
Founded: 1965. **Staff:** Prof 1; Other 1. **Subjects:** Engineering, minerals. **Special Collections:** Engineering Standards (current and obsolete). **Holdings:** 3000 books and bound periodical volumes; 3350 manufacturers' catalogs; 4500 standards. **Subscriptions:** 103 journals and other serials. **Services:** Interlibrary loans; library open to public for reference use only on request.

★3832★
DOW CHEMICAL U.S.A. - LOUISIANA DIVISION - LIBRARY (Sci-Tech)
Box 400
Plaquemine, LA 70764-0400
Phone: (504) 389-8859
James H. Modeen, Mgr.
Staff: Prof 1; Other 2. **Subjects:** Chemistry, physical sciences, plastics, chemical engineering, process chemistry. **Holdings:** 3800 books; 2700 bound periodical volumes; 4500 pamphlets; chemical abstracts; U.S. chemical patents; 120,000 company reports in microform; official gazette. **Subscriptions:** 146 journals and other serials. **Services:** Interlibrary loans; copying; library open to public with restrictions. **Computerized Information Services:** DIALOG, SDC; internal databases; computerized acquisitions, serials and circulation.

★3833★
DOW CHEMICAL U.S.A. - TEXAS DIVISION - LIBRARY (Sci-Tech)
Freeport, TX 77541
Phone: (409) 238-3512
Carl F. Wolfe, Res.Libn.
Founded: 1944. **Staff:** Prof 2; Other 3. **Subjects:** Chemistry, physical sciences, chemical engineering. **Holdings:** 10,000 books, 16,000 bound periodical volumes; 2000 pamphlets; 120,000 company reports; 600,000 index cards to company research. **Subscriptions:** 375 journals and other serials. **Services:** Interlibrary loans; copying; library open to public by appointment. **Computerized Information Services:** DIALOG, SDC, NLM; proprietary reports from internal databases; computerized cataloging, serials and holdings list. **Networks/Consortia:** Member of OCLC through AMIGOS Bibliographic Council, Inc. **Staff:** L. Levine, Sr.Tech.Info.Spec.

★3834★
DOW CHEMICAL U.S.A. - WESTERN DIVISION - LIBRARY (Sci-Tech)
Box 1398
Pittsburg, CA 94565
Phone: (415) 432-5199
Mary Ellen Christensen, Libn.
Staff: Prof 1; Other 2. **Subjects:** Chemistry, engineering, business administration. **Holdings:** 7000 books and bound periodical volumes; reports, documents, industrial literature (all cataloged). **Subscriptions:** 400 journals and other serials. **Services:** Library not open to public. **Computerized Information Services:** Computerized serials and circulation.

★3835★
DOW CHEMICAL U.S.A. - WESTERN DIVISION RESEARCH LABORATORIES - LIBRARY (Sci-Tech)
Box 9002
Walnut Creek, CA 94598
Phone: (415) 944-2064
Mary Lao, Libn.
Staff: Prof 2; Other 2. **Subjects:** Chemistry, physics, engineering, agricultural sciences, mining engineering. **Holdings:** 20,000 volumes; reports, patents, documents, and industrial literature. **Subscriptions:** 425 journals and other serials. **Services:** Library not open to public.

★3836★
DOW CORNING CORPORATION - BUSINESS INFORMATION CENTER (Bus-Fin)
2200 W. Salzburg Rd.
Midland, MI 48640
Phone: (517) 496-4941
Fred Lee, Libn.
Founded: 1965. **Staff:** Prof 1; Other 2. **Subjects:** Business, marketing, management, chemistry, economics, statistics. **Holdings:** 3500 books; 2000 pamphlets; 600 reports; 80 reels of microfilm; 150 maps. **Subscriptions:** 300 journals and other serials. **Services:** Interlibrary loans; copying; library open to public for reference use only on request. **Publications:** Selected New Titles; Reference Source Courses; Business Information Topics.

★3837★
DOW CORNING CORPORATION - TECHNICAL INFORMATION SERVICE LIBRARY (Sci-Tech)
Midland, MI 48640
Phone: (517) 496-4957
Lori T. Karnath, Libn.
Founded: 1948. **Staff:** Prof 1; Other 2. **Subjects:** Chemistry, organosilicon chemistry, polymer chemistry. **Holdings:** 2500 books; 2100 bound periodical volumes; 320 dissertations; 15 drawers of trade literature; 1500 cartridges

of periodicals on microfilm; 150 hardcopy and 8500 microfiche government contract reports. **Subscriptions:** 150 journals and other serials. **Services:** Interlibrary loans; copying; library open to researchers by special arrangement. **Computerized Information Services:** DIALOG, SDC, NLM; mechanized retrieval in field of organosilicon chemistry (TIS Information Systems). **Publications:** Bi-weekly Library Bulletin; List of Contract Reports.

★3838★
DOW JONES & CO. - LIBRARY (Bus-Fin)
22 Cortlandt
New York, NY 10007
Phone: (212) 285-5075
Lottie Lindberg, Libn.
Staff: Prof 1; Other 11. **Subjects:** Business, finance, investment. **Special Collections:** Clipping file of Wall Street Journal. **Holdings:** Figures not available. **Services:** Copying; library not open to public. **Computerized Information Services:** Dow Jones News Retrieval. **Special Indexes:** Wall Street Journal Index, monthly with annual cumulations; Barron's Index, annual.

★3839★
DOW, LOHNES & ALBERTSON - LAW LIBRARY (Law)
1225 Connecticut Ave., Suite 500
Washington, DC 20036
Phone: (202) 862-8021
Susanne D. Thevenet, Libn.
Staff: Prof 1; Other 2. **Subjects:** Law, communications. **Holdings:** 14,000 books; 500 bound periodical volumes; 60 legislative histories. **Subscriptions:** 25 journals and other serials; 4 newspapers. **Services:** Interlibrary loans; library open to public with prior permission. **Computerized Information Services:** LEXIS, New York Times Information Service.

DOWDEN, HUTCHINSON & ROSS, INC.
See: Hutchinson Ross Publishing Company

★3840★
DOWNEY COMMUNITY HOSPITAL - HEALTH SCIENCES LIBRARY (Med)
11500 Brookshire Ave.
Downey, CA 90241
Phone: (213) 869-3061
Marguerite Bladen, Med.Lib.Cons.
Staff: Prof 1. **Subjects:** Medicine, nursing. **Holdings:** 559 books. **Subscriptions:** 22 journals and other serials. **Services:** Interlibrary loans; copying; library not open to public. **Networks/Consortia:** Member of Southeast Hospital Librarians Group.

★3841★
DOWNEY HISTORICAL SOCIETY MUSEUM - LIBRARY (Hist)
12458 Rives Ave.
Box 554
Downey, CA 90241
Phone: (213) 869-7367
Barbara Callarman, Dir.
Staff: Prof 2; Other 1. **Subjects:** Local history and genealogy. **Special Collections:** Genealogical Records for Los Nietos Valley pioneers. **Holdings:** 500 books; complete records of Downey Cemetery with tombstone inscriptions; 8 VF drawers of records, clippings and photographs; 1850-1910 census on microfilm. **Subscriptions:** 10 journals and other serials. **Services:** Copying; library open to public. **Networks/Consortia:** Member of Southern California Consortium. **Publications:** Downey Historical Society Annual; A Brief History of John G. Downey.

DOWNSTATE MEDICAL CENTER
See: SUNY

★3842★
DOYLE DANE BERNBACH/WEST - RESEARCH LIBRARY (Bus-Fin)
5900 Wilshire Blvd.
Los Angeles, CA 90036
Phone: (213) 937-5100
Lois S. Steinmann, Mgr., Info.Serv.
Founded: 1980. **Staff:** Prof 1. **Subjects:** Advertising, marketing, business. **Holdings:** 500 books; 200 market reports; 1 VF drawer of pamphlets; 3 VF drawers of subject clipping files. **Subscriptions:** 82 journals and other serials. **Services:** Copying (limited); telephone reference for other librarians; library open to clients only.

★3843★
DRACKETT COMPANY - RESEARCH AND DEVELOPMENT LIBRARY (Bus-Fin; Sci-Tech)
5020 Spring Grove Ave.
Cincinnati, OH 45232
Phone: (513) 632-1449
Patti Beck, Res.Libn.
Founded: 1925. **Staff:** Prof 1; Other 1. **Subjects:** Science and technology; business and finance. **Holdings:** 4300 books; 66 bound periodical volumes; 8800 patents (cataloged); 100 technical reports; 310 cartridges of microfilm. **Subscriptions:** 190 journals and other serials; 6 newspapers. **Services:** Interlibrary loans; copying; library open to public with restrictions. **Computerized Information Services:** DIALOG, SDC. **Publications:** Inter-Company New Acquisitions Bulletin. **Remarks:** Drackett Company is a division of Bristol-Myers.

DRAKE (Joseph F.) MEMORIAL LEARNING RESOURCES CENTER
See: Alabama A & M University - Joseph F. Drake Memorial Learning
      Resources Center

DRAKE MEMORIAL LIBRARY
See: SUNY - College at Brockport

★3844★
DRAKE UNIVERSITY - COLLEGE OF PHARMACY - LIBRARY (Med)
28th & Forest Ave.   Phone: (515) 271-2172
Des Moines, IA 50311   Margaret Daly Granberg, Libn.
Founded: 1970. **Staff:** Prof 1; Other 2. **Subjects:** Biology and chemistry,
pharmacy and related subjects, medicine, veterinary medicine, dentistry.
Holdings: 3800 books and bound periodical volumes; 100 government
documents. **Subscriptions:** 122 journals and other serials. **Services:**
Interlibrary loans; library open to public.

★3845★
DRAKE UNIVERSITY - LAW LIBRARY (Law)
Carnegie Hall
27th & Carpenter   Phone: (515) 271-2141
Des Moines, IA 50311   Juan F. Aguilar, Dir.
Founded: 1875. **Staff:** Prof 4; Other 5. **Subjects:** Law. **Special Collections:**
Foreign law, including English law (400 volumes). **Holdings:** 101,898 books;
12,643 bound periodical volumes; 691 government documents (cataloged);
124 audio recordings; 10 video recordings; 95 titles of microforms.
Subscriptions: 2322 journals and other serials; 6 newspapers. **Services:**
Interlibrary loans; copying; library open to public with permission.
Computerized Information Services: LEXIS; computerized cataloging.
Networks/Consortia: Member of OCLC through Bibliographical Center for
Research, Rocky Mountain Region, Inc.; Mid-America Law School Library
Consortium. **Publications:** Current Acquistions List, semiannual. **Special
Catalogs:** Periodicals holdings list. **Staff:** Kaye Stoppel, Asst.Libn.; Susan
Catterall, Ref./Circ.Libn.; Shirley Fosher, Tech.Serv.Libn.

DRAKE WELL MUSEUM
See: Pennsylvania State Historical & Museum Commission

★3846★
**DRAPER (Charles Stark) LABORATORY, INC. - TECHNICAL INFORMATION
      CENTER (Sci-Tech)**
555 Technology Sq., Mail Sta. 74
Cambridge, MA 02139   Phone: (617) 258-3555
                                       M. Hope Coffman, Mgr.
Staff: Prof 5; Other 9. **Subjects:** Flight control, inertial guidance, aerospace
technology, computer science. **Special Collections:** Technical Report
Literature Collection in Aerospace Technology. **Holdings:** 12,000 books; 65
bound periodical volumes; 34,000 technical reports (cataloged); 7500
archival items; 600 theses. **Subscriptions:** 305 journals and other serials.
Services: Interlibrary loans; copying; center not open to public.
Computerized Information Services: DIALOG, BRS, DTIC, NASA/RECON;
internal database of archival materials; computerized cataloging and journal
routing. **Networks/Consortia:** Member of OCLC through NELINET.
Publications: TIC Bulletin, weekly - for internal distribution only. **Staff:** Cary
Graham Citron, Hd.Libn.; Laurie D. Rotman, Asst.Libn.; Gary D. Ambush, Chf.
of Doc. Control; Elizabeth D. Edwards, Cat.

DRAPER FUND
See: Population Crisis Committee/Draper Fund

DRAPER HALL LIBRARY
See: Metropolitan Hospital Center

DRAUGHON (Ralph B.) LIBRARY
See: Auburn University - Archives

★3847★
DRAVO CORPORATION - LIBRARY (Sci-Tech)
1 Oliver Plaza   Phone: (412) 566-5075
Pittsburgh, PA 15222   Alice Patience, Lib.Mgr.
Founded: 1949. **Staff:** Prof 2; Other 1. **Subjects:** Engineering, industrial
construction, business administration, mining. **Holdings:** 15,000 books; 960
bound periodical volumes; 40 vertical files of pamphlets and professional
association publications; U.S. patents on microfilm, 1966 to present.
Subscriptions: 1100 journals and other serials; 15 newspapers. **Services:**
Interlibrary loans; copying; library open to public with permission of library
manager. **Computerized Information Services:** DIALOG, Info Globe, Dow
Jones News Retrieval; computerized circulation of magazines. **Publications:**
International Information, annual; The Library Informer, semimonthly;
Periodicals List, quarterly. **Staff:** Nancy J. Leuzinger, Libn.

DRESSER (Herman G.) LIBRARY
See: Camp Dresser & McKee, Inc. - Herman G. Dresser Library

★3848★
DRESSER INDUSTRIES, INC. - MAGCOBAR RESEARCH LIBRARY (Energy)
10201 Westheimer, Bldg. 1A, Rm. 100
Houston, TX 77042   Phone: (713) 784-6611
                          Dr. Aliyah Von Nussbaumer, Res.Libn.
Staff: Prof 2; Other 1. **Subjects:** Chemistry, petroleum, geology, mining
engineering, management, safety engineering, statistics. **Holdings:** 6000
books and bound periodical volumes; 28,000 patents (cataloged); 1200
American Petroleum Institute pamphlets; 500 maps; 5000 papers of Society
of Petroleum Engineers. **Subscriptions:** 250 journals and other serials; 10
newspapers. **Services:** Interlibrary loans; copying; library open to public by
appointment only. **Staff:** Mary Kluttz Dimataris, Tech.Libn.

★3849★
DREW COUNTY HISTORICAL SOCIETY - MUSEUM AND ARCHIVES (Hist)
404 S. Main St.   Phone: (501) 367-7446
Monticello, AR 71655   Mrs. Clyde Rogers, Hostess
Staff: 4. **Subjects:** Local and Arkansas history. **Holdings:** Figures not available
for books; local Drew County records on microfilm; family histories; original
Goodspeeds; textile collection, quilts and looms; early printing press, Indian
artifacts. **Services:** Library open to public with restrictions.

★3850★
DREW UNIVERSITY - LIBRARY (Rel-Theol)
                                       Phone: (201) 377-3000
Madison, NJ 07940   Dr. Arthur E. Jones, Jr., Dir.
Founded: 1867. **Staff:** Prof 14; Other 17. **Subjects:** Theology, religion,
history, Methodistica, English and American literature, patristics, liberal arts,
Biblical archaeology, art, United Nations, European Common Market. **Special
Collections:** U.S. Depository Collection (100,000 items); Tyerman Collection
of Methodist Pamphlets; Tipple and Maser Collections of Wesleyana;
Methodist Manuscript Collection; David Creamer Hymnology Collection; Walter
Koehler Collection in Reformation History. **Holdings:** 410,000 books; 52,000
bound periodical volumes; 11,800 reels of microfilm; 14,300 microfiche;
1102 phonograph records; 120 VF drawers of manuscripts; 70,000
pamphlets. **Subscriptions:** 1540 journals and other serials; 14 newspapers.
Services: Interlibrary loans; copying; library open to public for reference use
only; annual fee for borrowers. **Computerized Information Services:**
DIALOG; computerized cataloging, acquisitions and ILL. **Networks/
Consortia:** Member of OCLC. **Special Catalogs:** Methodist Union Catalog
published since 1975 (book). **Staff:** Kenneth E. Rowe, Methodist Libn.;
Caroline M. Coughlin, Asst.Dir.; Jean A. Schoenthaler, Hd., Tech.Serv.

★3851★
DREXEL BURNHAM LAMBERT INC. - RESEARCH LIBRARY (Bus-Fin)
60 Broad St.   Phone: (212) 480-6475
New York, NY 10004   Laura G. Ripin, Lib.Dir.
Staff: Prof 1; Other 3. **Subjects:** Business, finance, accounting, corporations,
investing. **Special Collections:** Commercial and Financial Chronicle, 1903 to
present. **Holdings:** 3500 corporate files; 10Ks, 10Qs, prospectuses, proxy
statements, registration statements on microfiche. **Subscriptions:** 125
journals and other serials; 6 newspapers. **Services:** Interlibrary loans; library
not open to public. **Computerized Information Services:** DIALOG,
Interactive Data Corporation.

DREXEL LIBRARY
See: St. Joseph's University

★3852★
DREXEL UNIVERSITY LIBRARY - SPECIAL COLLECTIONS (Soc Sci)
32nd & Chestnut Sts.   Phone: (215) 895-2755
Philadelphia, PA 19104   Michael Halperin, Hd.
Founded: 1891. **Special Collections:** Drexeliana (material concerning the
university, the Drexel family, faculty and student publications); government
documents (106,188). **Services:** Interlibrary loans; copying; SDI; library open
to public for reference use only. **Computerized Information Services:**
DIALOG, SDC, BRS, Dow Jones News Retrieval, IN/FORM Data Services;
computerized cataloging and ILL. **Networks/Consortia:** Member of OCLC
through PALINET & Union Library Catalogue of Pennsylvania. **Staff:** Marjorie
Rothberg, Govt.Doc.Libn.; Ann Preston, Spec.Coll.Libn.

★3853★
DREXEL UNIVERSITY - SCIENCE AND TECHNOLOGY LIBRARY (Sci-Tech)†
32nd & Chestnut Sts.   Phone: (215) 895-2765
Philadelphia, PA 19104   William Page, Hd., Sci. & Tech.Lib.
Founded: 1959. **Staff:** Prof 2; Other 3. **Subjects:** Biology; biomedical
engineering; chemistry; nutrition; physics; mathematics; engineering -

aeronautical, civil, chemical, mechanical, electrical, metallurgical and environmental. **Special Collections:** American National Standards Institute Standards (complete set). **Holdings:** 87,849 books; 46,507 bound periodical volumes; 186,312 microfiche; 1479 reels of microfilm. **Subscriptions:** 1597 journals and other serials. **Services:** Interlibrary loans; copying; library open to public for reference use only. **Computerized Information Services:** DIALOG, SDC, BRS; computerized cataloging and ILL. **Networks/Consortia:** Member of OCLC through PALINET & Union Library Catalogue of Pennsylvania. **Staff:** Charlotte Duvally, Engr.Libn.; Deidre Harper, ILL.

★3854★
DREYFUS CORPORATION - INFORMATION CENTER (Bus-Fin)
767 Fifth Ave.   Phone: (212) 935-8405
New York, NY 10153   Cytheria Theodos, Dir.Info.Serv.
Staff: Prof 2; Other 6. **Subjects:** Corporation records, investment companies, business, finance, industries. **Holdings:** 2000 books; 10,000 microfiche of reports; 4000 files of corporation records; 100 drawers of subject files. **Subscriptions:** 400 journals and other serials; 20 newspapers. **Services:** Interlibrary loans; library not open to public. **Computerized Information Services:** DIALOG, New York Times Information Service, Dow Jones News Retrieval, SDC. **Staff:** Barbara D. Smith, Asst.Libn.

DREYFUSS (Doris & Henry) MEMORIAL STUDY CENTER
See: Smithsonian Institution Libraries - Cooper-Hewitt Museum of Design - Doris & Henry Dreyfuss Memorial Study Ctr.

DREYOUS (Felix J.) LIBRARY
See: New Orleans Museum of Art - Felix J. Dreyous Library

★3855★
DRINKER, BIDDLE & REATH - LAW LIBRARY (Law)
1100 Philadelphia National Bank Bldg.
Broad & Chestnut Sts.   Phone: (215) 988-2951
Philadelphia, PA 19107   Nancy H. Rosenberg, Hd., Law Lib.
Staff: Prof 1; Other 1. **Subjects:** Law. **Holdings:** 15,000 volumes. **Services:** Interlibrary loans; copying; library open to public for reference use only on request. **Computerized Information Services:** LEXIS.

DRINKER LIBRARY OF CHORAL MUSIC
See: Free Library of Philadelphia - Music Department - Drinker Library of Choral Music

DRIPPS (Robert Dunning) LIBRARY OF ANESTHESIA
See: Hospital of the University of Pennsylvania - Robert Dunning Dripps Library of Anesthesia

★3856★
DRISCOLL FOUNDATION CHILDREN'S HOSPITAL - MEDICAL LIBRARY (Med)†
3533 Alameda
Box 6530   Phone: (512) 854-5341
Corpus Christi, TX 78411   Becky Melton, Lib.Mgr.
Staff: 1. **Subjects:** General pediatrics, neonatology, pediatric surgery, pediatric cardiology. **Holdings:** 330 books; 4000 bound periodical volumes. **Subscriptions:** 80 journals and other serials. **Services:** Library open to professionals. **Networks/Consortia:** Member of Coastal Bend Health Sciences Library Consortium.

★3857★
DROPSIE COLLEGE - LIBRARY (Rel-Theol; Area-Ethnic)
Broad & York Sts.   Phone: (215) 229-1566
Philadelphia, PA 19132   Sarah N. Levy, Lib.Dir.
Founded: 1907. **Staff:** Prof 2; Other 3. **Subjects:** Biblical and post-Biblical learning, Semitic languages, Jewish studies, Assyriology, Egyptology, Rabbinic literature, Ancient Near East. **Special Collections:** Genizah fragments (500 items); Oriental manuscripts (256 volumes); correspondence relating to activities in America and its territories, 1800-1980. **Holdings:** 150,000 books; Abraham I. Katsh microfilm collection of Hebraica manuscripts and documents from the U.S.S.R., Poland and Hungary; microfilm of the Vatican Hebrew manuscript collection. **Subscriptions:** 300 journals and other serials. **Services:** Interlibrary loans; library open to public. **Staff:** Susan Sobel, Asst.Libn.

DRUG INFORMATION SERVICES
See: University of Minnesota

DRUID CITY HOSPITAL - MEDICAL LIBRARY
See: University of Alabama - College of Community Health Sciences - Health Sciences Library

DRUMMOND SCIENCE LIBRARY
See: Concordia University - Loyola Campus

DRUSCH PROFESSIONAL LIBRARY
See: Deaconess Hospital

DRUSKIN (Dr. Sidney) MEMORIAL LIBRARY
See: New York College of Podiatric Medicine - Dr. Sidney Druskin Memorial Library

DRYDEN BUSINESS LIBRARY
See: Prudential Insurance Company of America

DRYDEN FLIGHT RESEARCH CENTER
See: U.S. NASA - Dryden Flight Research Center

DTIC
See: U.S. Defense Technical Information Center

★3858★
DU PAGE COUNTY LAW LIBRARY (Law)
Courthouse
201 Reber St.   Phone: (312) 682-7337
Wheaton, IL 60187   Charlean Eggert, Hd. Law Libn.
Staff: Prof 1; Other 2. **Subjects:** Law, Illinois law. **Special Collections:** Illinois Revised Statutes, 1816 to present. **Holdings:** 23,790 books and bound periodical volumes. **Subscriptions:** 18 journals and other serials; 7 newspapers. **Services:** Copying; library open to public for reference use only. **Computerized Information Services:** WESTLAW.

★3859★
DU PAGE LIBRARY SYSTEM - SYSTEM CENTER (Info Sci)
127 S. First St.
Box 268   Phone: (312) 232-8457
Geneva, IL 60134   Alice E. McKinley, Dir.
Staff: Prof 7; Other 14. **Subjects:** Library science, management and history. **Holdings:** 50,000 books; 1700 pieces of framed art; 3000 audio cassettes; 1700 pieces of sheet music. **Subscriptions:** 200 journals and other serials. **Services:** Interlibrary loans; copying; library open to public. **Computerized Information Services:** Computerized circulation. **Networks/Consortia:** Member of DuPage Library System; ILLINET. **Publications:** Crossroads, monthly - to library staffs and public library trustees; Miscellany, biweekly - to library staffs. **Remarks:** DuPage Library System is a cooperative organization of 106 academic, public, school and special libraries. **Staff:** Carol Morrison, Network Coord.

★3860★
DU PONT (Alfred I.) INSTITUTE OF THE NEMOURS FOUNDATION LIBRARY (Med)
Box 269   Phone: (302) 651-5820
Wilmington, DE 19899   Mrs. Gene Schiefelbein, Libn.
Founded: 1940. **Staff:** Prof 1. **Subjects:** Orthopedics, biochemistry, microbiology, pediatrics, birth defects. **Holdings:** 4000 books; 16,000 bound periodical volumes. **Subscriptions:** 300 journals and other serials. **Services:** Interlibrary loans; library open to public for reference use only. **Networks/Consortia:** Member of Wilmington Area Biomedical Libraries Consortium; Mideastern Regional Medical Library Service; Delaware Library Consortium.

★3861★
DU PONT CANADA, INC. - CENTRAL LIBRARY (Bus-Fin)
Streetsville Postal Sta., Box 2300   Phone: (416) 821-5781
Mississauga, ON, Canada L5M 2J4   Martha Pettit, Libn.
Founded: 1954. **Staff:** Prof 1; Other 1. **Subjects:** Business, management, marketing, economics, statistics, chemicals and chemical industry, textile fibres industry, plastics industry, government. **Holdings:** 10,000 books; 20 VF drawers of annual reports; 16 VF drawers of information files; 32 VF drawers of Statistics Canada reports. **Subscriptions:** 251 journals and other serials; 8 newspapers. **Services:** Interlibrary loans; copying; library not open to public. **Computerized Information Services:** Info Globe, QL Systems, SDC, DIALOG; computerized cataloging and serials. **Publications:** New Books Listing, bimonthly - for internal distribution only.

★3862★
DU PONT CANADA, INC. - CUSTOMER TECHNICAL CENTRE LIBRARY (Sci-Tech)†
P.O. Box 3500   Phone: (613) 544-6000
Kingston, ON, Canada K7L 5A1   L.A. Collins
Founded: 1968. **Staff:** Prof 1; Other 1. **Subjects:** Textiles, rubber goods, plastics, industrial chemicals, economics, management. **Holdings:** 1050

books; 300 bound periodical volumes; 1000 pamphlets and booklets; 33 VF drawers of internal reports, manuals, special studies; 36 shelves of unbound periodicals; 2 VF drawers and 2 shelves of manufacturers' literature; 1 VF drawer of patents. **Subscriptions:** 128 journals and other serials. **Services:** Interlibrary loans; library not open to public. **Publications:** Monthly summary of developments on specific topics (based on literature received during month); List of Accessions, bimonthly; bibliographies, as required - all for internal distribution only. **Special Indexes:** Subject indexes of internal reports and manufacturers' literature (card); subject indexes of periodical articles in areas of particular interest (book).

★3863★

DU PONT CANADA, INC. - MAITLAND WORKS LIBRARY (Sci-Tech)†
P.O. Box 611
Maitland, ON, Canada K0E 1P0
Phone: (613) 348-3611
H.M. Perrott, Libn.
Founded: 1953. **Staff:** Prof 1. **Subjects:** Chemical engineering, chemical plant operation, organic chemistry, management, occupational health, synthetic fiber manufacture. **Holdings:** 2045 books; 1450 bound periodical volumes; 6929 reports, patents and other items. **Subscriptions:** 175 journals and other serials; 5 newspapers. **Services:** Interlibrary loans; copying; SDI; library open to public with clearance from management. **Computerized Information Services:** SDC; computerized serials and circulation. **Publications:** New Books and Reports, quarterly; Procedures Manual, irregular - limited distribution.

★3864★

DU PONT CANADA, INC. - PATENT DIVISION LIBRARY (Law)
Streetsville Postal Sta., Box 2200
Mississauga, ON, Canada L5M 2H3
Phone: (416) 821-5504
Joan E. Leedale, Libn.
Founded: 1954. **Staff:** Prof 2. **Subjects:** Law, patents. **Holdings:** 3000 books; 150,000 patents. **Subscriptions:** 40 journals and other serials. **Services:** Interlibrary loans; library not open to public. **Staff:** Lynn Assadourian

★3865★

DU PONT CANADA, INC. - RESEARCH CENTRE LIBRARY (Sci-Tech)
P.O. Box 5000
Kingston, ON, Canada K7L 5A5
Phone: (613) 544-6400
B.F. Swerbrick, Libn.
Founded: 1954. **Staff:** Prof 1; Other 1. **Subjects:** Chemistry, chemical engineering, mathematics, electronics, physics, computers, plastics, management, economics, textile fibers, occupational health and safety. **Holdings:** 8000 books; 4200 bound periodical volumes; 25 VF drawers of unbound materials; 145 VF drawers of internal reports. **Subscriptions:** 250 journals and other serials. **Services:** Interlibrary loans; library not open to public. **Computerized Information Services:** CAN/OLE, DIALOG.

★3866★

DU PONT DE NEMOURS (E.I.) & COMPANY, INC. - BENGER LABORATORY - LIBRARY (Sci-Tech)
Waynesboro, VA 22980
Phone: (703) 949-8141
Virginia G. Mize, Libn.
Founded: 1947. **Staff:** 1. **Subjects:** Polymer chemistry, fiber technology. **Holdings:** 5000 books; 3500 bound periodical volumes; 1700 pamphlets (cataloged). **Subscriptions:** 100 journals and other serials. **Services:** Interlibrary loans; copying; library open to public by appointment.

★3867★

DU PONT DE NEMOURS (E.I.) & COMPANY, INC. - CHEMICALS & PIGMENTS DEPT. - JACKSON LABORATORY LIBRARY (Sci-Tech)
Wilmington, DE 19898
Phone: (609) 299-5000
W.B. McCormack, R&D Libn.
Founded: 1925. **Staff:** Prof 4; Other 7. **Subjects:** Chemistry - organic, physical, petroleum, textile, analytical; dyes and dyeing; pigments; chemical engineering; fluorine. **Holdings:** 15,000 books; 18,000 periodical volumes; 100 VF drawers of pamphlets (cataloged); 35 VF drawers of pamphlets (uncataloged); 3600 reels of microfilm; 400 microcards. **Subscriptions:** 500 journals and other serials. **Services:** Interlibrary loans; copying; translations; library not open to public. **Computerized Information Services:** Online systems; computerized serials and circulation. **Publications:** It's New (additions list); translation lists - for internal distribution only. **Staff:** R.N. Dion, Supv.; Louise G. Del Signore, Libn.; R.M. Irelan, Tech.Spec.; G.C. Meyer, R&D Chemist.

★3868★

DU PONT DE NEMOURS (E.I.) & COMPANY, INC. - DACRON RESEARCH LABORATORY - TECHNICAL LIBRARY (Sci-Tech)
Box 800
Kinston, NC 28501
Phone: (919) 522-6406
Louis G. Boccetti, Libn.
Founded: 1954. **Staff:** Prof 1; Other 1. **Subjects:** Textile fibers, polymers

and polymerization, organic chemistry, textile industry, fabrics. **Holdings:** 3300 books; 1750 bound periodical volumes. **Subscriptions:** 160 journals and other serials. **Services:** Library not open to public.

★3869★

DU PONT DE NEMOURS (E.I.) & COMPANY, INC. - HASKELL LABORATORY FOR TOXICOLOGY & INDUSTRIAL MEDICINE - LIBRARY (Med)
Elkton Rd.
Box 50
Newark, DE 19711
Phone: (302) 366-5225
Nancy S. Selzer, Libn.
Founded: 1935. **Staff:** Prof 1; Other 2. **Subjects:** Industrial medicine and toxicology. **Holdings:** 5500 books; 15,500 bound periodical volumes. **Subscriptions:** 255 journals and other serials. **Services:** Interlibrary loans; copying; library open to qualified persons. **Computerized Information Services:** DIALOG, SDC, BRS, MEDLARS; computerized cataloging. **Networks/Consortia:** Member of Mideastern Regional Medical Library System (MERMLS); Wilmington Area Biomedical Libraries Consortium; Delaware Library Consortium.

★3870★

DU PONT DE NEMOURS (E.I.) & COMPANY, INC. - LAVOISIER LIBRARY (Sci-Tech)
Central Research & Development Dept.
Experimental Sta.
Wilmington, DE 19898
Phone: (302) 772-2086
Frances E. Parsons, Lib.Supv.
Founded: 1917. **Staff:** Prof 8; Other 18. **Subjects:** Chemistry, physics, engineering, biology. **Holdings:** 90,288 books and bound periodical volumes; 388 VF drawers of pamphlets; 4989 microfilm cartridges. **Subscriptions:** 959 journals and other serials. **Services:** Interlibrary loans; library not open to public. **Computerized Information Services:** DIALOG, SDC; computerized cataloging, serials, circulation and ILL. **Networks/Consortia:** Member of OCLC through PALINET & Union Library Catalogue of Pennsylvania. **Publications:** Additions to the Library, Calendar of Scientific Meetings, both monthly; Letter from Lavoisier, irregular - all for internal distribution only.

★3871★

DU PONT DE NEMOURS (E.I.) & COMPANY, INC. - LEGAL DEPARTMENT LIBRARY (Law)
6067 Du Pont Bldg.
Wilmington, DE 19898
Phone: (302) 774-3307
M. Jane DiCecco, Libn.
Staff: Prof 1; Other 1. **Subjects:** Law. **Holdings:** 16,000 books; 800 bound periodical volumes; 100 pamphlets (cataloged); 61 reels of microfilm. **Subscriptions:** 274 journals and other serials. **Services:** Private library open to public with permission. **Computerized Information Services:** LEXIS, New York Times Information Service; computerized cataloging. **Networks/Consortia:** Member of Delaware Library Consortium.

★3872★

DU PONT DE NEMOURS (E.I.) & COMPANY, INC. - MARSHALL LABORATORY LIBRARY (Sci-Tech)
3500 Grays Ferry Ave.
Box 3886
Philadelphia, PA 19146
Phone: (215) 339-6314
Virginia L. Maier, Libn.
Founded: 1951. **Staff:** Prof 1; Other 2. **Subjects:** Polymer chemistry, organic coatings, finishes, organic chemistry, chemical engineering. **Holdings:** 2700 books; 1000 bound periodical volumes; 2000 departmental technical reports (1000 on microfilm). **Subscriptions:** 220 journals and other serials. **Services:** Interlibrary loans; library not open to public. **Computerized Information Services:** DIALOG. **Publications:** Library Bulletin, monthly - for internal distribution only.

★3873★

DU PONT DE NEMOURS (E.I.) & COMPANY, INC. - PHOTO PRODUCTS DEPARTMENT - INFORMATION CENTER (Sci-Tech)
Parlin, NJ 08859
Phone: (201) 257-4600
Peggy J. Joplin, Supv.
Founded: 1940. **Staff:** Prof 1; Other 2. **Subjects:** Photography, graphic arts, chemistry, physics, polymers, plastics. **Holdings:** 2500 books; 5500 bound periodical volumes; 120 trade catalogs and directories; 70 VF drawers of company reports; 55 VF drawers of pamphlets, translations and photocopies; 10 VF drawers of trade literature; 154 reels of microfilm; 3500 microcards. **Subscriptions:** 175 journals and other serials. **Services:** Interlibrary loans; copying (for employees); library not open to public. **Computerized Information Services:** DIALOG. **Publications:** Additions to the Library, monthly - for internal distribution only.

★3874★
DU PONT DE NEMOURS (E.I.) & COMPANY, INC. - POLYMER PRODUCTS DEPARTMENT - TECHNICAL LIBRARY (Sci-Tech)
Sabine River Works
Box 1089   Phone: (713) 886-6418
Orange, TX 77630   Patsy Holland, Tech.Libn.
Staff: Prof 1; Other 1. **Subjects:** Chemistry, chemical engineering. **Holdings:** 5000 books; 1000 bound periodical volumes. **Subscriptions:** 150 journals and other serials. **Services:** Library open to public by appointment. **Computerized Information Services:** DIALOG; computerized circulation.

★3875★
DU PONT DE NEMOURS (E.I.) & COMPANY, INC. - POLYMER PRODUCTS LIBRARY (Sci-Tech; Energy)†
Hwy. 347
Box 3269   Phone: (713) 727-9606
Beaumont, TX 77704   Roberta L. Howard, Tech.Libn.
Staff: Prof 1. **Subjects:** Chemistry, plastics, polymer science, elastomers, energy, environmental control, computer science. **Holdings:** 960 books; 328 bound periodical volumes; 1600 U.S. and foreign patents; 4000 reports; 4 shelves of government documents; 400 reels of microfilm; 28 shelves of miscellaneous drawings, booklets and manuals. **Subscriptions:** 57 journals and other serials. **Services:** Interlibrary loans; copying; library not open to public.

DU PONT DE NEMOURS (E.I.) & COMPANY, INC. - SAVANNAH RIVER LABORATORY
See: Savannah River Laboratory

★3876★
DU PONT DE NEMOURS (E.I.) & COMPANY, INC. - STINE LABORATORY LIBRARY (Med)
Box 30   Phone: (302) 366-5354
Newark, DE 19711   Virginia Bredemeier, Libn.
Founded: 1947. **Staff:** Prof 1; Other 2. **Subjects:** Medicine, pharmacology, biochemistry, biology, microbiology. **Holdings:** 3000 books; 4800 bound periodical volumes; 2 VF drawers of pamphlets. **Subscriptions:** 304 journals and other serials. **Services:** Interlibrary loans; library not open to public. **Computerized Information Services:** DIALOG. **Networks/Consortia:** Member of Wilmington Area Biomedical Libraries. **Special Indexes:** Indexes to holdings (punched card).

★3877★
DU PONT DE NEMOURS (E.I.) & COMPANY, INC. - TECHNICAL LIBRARY SYSTEM - HEADQUARTERS (Sci-Tech)
3155 Du Pont Bldg.
Tenth & Market Sts.   Phone: (302) 774-7232
Wilmington, DE 19898   Helen S. Strolle, Mgr.
Founded: 1919. **Staff:** Prof 25; Other 28. **Subjects:** Chemistry, business and economics, fibers and films, paints and lacquers, plastics. **Special Collections:** Safety; statistics; Du Pont authors; annual reports of corporations; house organs. **Holdings:** 16,100 books; 3575 bound periodical volumes; 88 drawers and 215 shelves of pamphlet material. **Subscriptions:** 1700 journals and other serials. **Services:** Interlibrary loans; library open to public by appointment only. **Remarks:** The Du Pont Technical Library System consists of the main library in the Du Pont Building and four branches. The total staff figures given above include personnel in all the units. The Technical Library System is part of the Du Pont Company Information Systems Department.

★3878★
DU PONT DE NEMOURS (E.I.) & COMPANY, INC. - TECHNICAL LIBRARY SYSTEM - LOUVIERS BRANCH (Sci-Tech)
    Phone: (302) 366-3791
Wilmington, DE 19898   Marilyn L. Evans, Br.Supv.
Founded: 1952. **Staff:** Prof 4; Other 6. **Subjects:** Engineering - chemical, civil, electrical, management, mechanical. **Special Collections:** Safety material; standards and specifications. **Holdings:** 10,500 books; 3050 bound periodical volumes; 84 VF drawers and 18 lateral files of pamphlet material. **Subscriptions:** 843 journals and other serials. **Services:** Interlibrary loans; library open to public by appointment only. **Publications:** Library Notes, monthly - distributed to Engineering Department employees.

★3879★
DU PONT DE NEMOURS (E.I.) & COMPANY, INC. - TECHNICAL LIBRARY SYSTEM - PIONEERING RESEARCH LABORATORY BRANCH (Sci-Tech)
Experimental Sta., Bldg. 302   Phone: (302) 772-3451
Wilmington, DE 19898   Mrs. Bohuslawa Z-P. Bass, Br.Supv.
Founded: 1928. **Staff:** Prof 2; Other 2. **Subjects:** Polymer chemistry, organic and analytical chemistry, textile fibers, chemical engineering.

Holdings: 2700 books; 2800 bound periodical volumes; 20,000 Du Pont Company research reports; pamphlets (cataloged); 18 VF drawers of company reports on microfiche. **Subscriptions:** 150 journals and other serials; 5 newspapers. **Services:** Interlibrary loans; library open to public by appointment only. **Publications:** Report Book Bulletin and Newsletter, monthly - for internal distribution only.

★3880★
DU PONT DE NEMOURS (E.I.) & COMPANY, INC. - TECHNICAL LIBRARY SYSTEM - SPRUANCE RESEARCH LABORATORY BRANCH (Sci-Tech)
Box 27001
Spunbonded Products, Nomex Division   Phone: (804) 743-2616
Richmond, VA 23261   Luella G. Wills, Info.Anl.
Founded: 1943. **Staff:** Prof 1; Other 1. **Subjects:** Polymer science and technology, textile fibers, chemistry, paper, engineering, statistics. **Holdings:** 2600 books; 900 bound periodical volumes; 225 pamphlets (cataloged); research reports on microfiche. **Subscriptions:** 115 journals. **Services:** Interlibrary loans; copying; SDI; library open to public by appointment only. **Computerized Information Services:** SDC. **Publications:** Library Bulletin - for internal distribution only.

★3881★
DU PONT DE NEMOURS (E.I.) & COMPANY, INC. - TECHNICAL LIBRARY SYSTEM - TEXTILE RESEARCH LABORATORY BRANCH (Sci-Tech)
Chestnut Run   Phone: (302) 999-3473
Wilmington, DE 19898   Mrs. Bohuslawa Z-P. Bass, Br.Supv.
Founded: 1958. **Staff:** Prof 2; Other 1. **Subjects:** Textile fibers and fabrics. **Holdings:** 3800 books; 1300 bound periodical volumes; 43 lateral files of pamphlet material. **Subscriptions:** 350 journals and other serials. **Services:** Interlibrary loans; library open to public by appointment only. **Publications:** Library Notes, monthly - for internal distribution only.

★3882★
DU PONT DE NEMOURS (E.I.) & COMPANY, INC. - VICTORIA PLANT LIBRARY (Sci-Tech)
Box 2626   Phone: (512) 572-1111
Victoria, TX 77901   Debbie A. Ganem, Libn.
Founded: 1950. **Staff:** 1. **Subjects:** Chemistry, mathematics, engineering, management. **Holdings:** 3250 books and bound periodical volumes; 75 volumes of engineering standards and codes; 800 reels of microfilm; 300 chemical and equipment catalogs. **Subscriptions:** 150 journals and other serials. **Services:** Library not open to public.

★3883★
DU PONT (Henry Francis) WINTERTHUR MUSEUM - LIBRARY (Art; Hist)
    Phone: (302) 656-8591
Winterthur, DE 19735   Dr. Frank H. Sommer, III, Hd. of Lib.
Founded: 1951. **Staff:** Prof 7; Other 8. **Subjects:** Art - American, British, French and Italian (with emphasis on decorative arts); cultural history. **Special Collections:** Waldron P. Belknap Research Library of American Painting; E.D. Andrews Memorial Shaker Collection; Downs Manuscript & Microfilm Collection; Decorative Arts Photographic Collection; Slide Library; Maxine Waldron Collection; Estate Archives. **Holdings:** 53,000 books and bound periodical volumes; 57,600 manuscripts; 132,700 photographs; 90,000 slides; 3000 microforms; 1500 feet of archival material. **Subscriptions:** 300 journals and other serials; 10 newspapers. **Services:** Interlibrary loans; copying; library open to public. **Computerized Information Services:** Computerized cataloging and acquisitions. **Networks/Consortia:** Member of OCLC through PALINET and Union Library Catalogue of Pennsylvania. **Special Indexes:** Collection of Printed Books, Guide to Archives. **Staff:** Kathryn K. McKenney, Slide Libn.; Barbara Hearn, Archv.; Beatrice K. Taylor, Mss.Libn.; Eleanor M. Thompson, Libn., Print Bk.; Bert Denker, DAPC Libn.; Richard McKinstry, Asst.Libn., Print Bk.

DU PONT (Jean Austin) LIBRARY
See: University of Pennsylvania - New Bolton Center - Jean Austin Du Pont Library

DU PONT (Jessie Ball) MEMORIAL LIBRARY
See: Lee (Robert E.) Memorial Association, Inc. - Jessie Ball DuPont Memorial Library

DU PONT LIBRARY
See: University of the South

★3884★

DU SABLE MUSEUM OF AFRICAN AMERICAN HISTORY - LIBRARY (Area-Ethnic)

740 E. 56th Pl. Phone: (312) 947-0600
Chicago, IL 60637 Dr. Margaret Burroughs, Libn.
Founded: 1961. **Staff:** Prof 3. **Subjects:** Black history, sociology, politics, religion, fiction and biography, Africana. **Holdings:** 3000 volumes; 500 other items (cataloged); 100 oral history tapes; 50 manuscripts; 85 VF drawers of clippings. **Services:** Copying; library open to public for reference use only. **Publications:** Calendar, annual. **Staff:** Eugene Feldman, Dir. of Res. & Pubn.; Charles Burroughs, Asst.

DUANE LIBRARY
See: Fordham University - Special Collections

★3885★

DUANE, MORRIS & HECKSCHER - LAW LIBRARY (Law)

1500 One Franklin Plaza Phone: (215) 854-6248
Philadelphia, PA 19102 Teresa N. Clarkson, Libn.
Staff: Prof 1; Other 3. **Subjects:** Law. **Holdings:** 12,000 books; 4000 bound periodical volumes; 15 VF drawers of maps, reports and pamphlets. **Subscriptions:** 145 journals and other serials; 6 newspapers. **Services:** Interlibrary loans; copying; library open to public with restrictions. **Computerized Information Services:** Online systems.

DUANE PHYSICAL LABORATORIES
See: University of Colorado, Boulder - Mathematics & Physics Library

DUCHOW (Marvin) MUSIC LIBRARY
See: Mc Gill University - Marvin Duchow Music Library

★3886★

DUCKS UNLIMITED CANADA - LIBRARY (Env-Cons)

1190 Waverley St. Phone: (204) 477-1760
Winnipeg, MB, Canada R3T 2E2 Marlene Hilland, Adm.Sec.
Founded: 1938. **Staff:** Prof 1. **Subjects:** Conservation, waterfowl biology, water management, wildlife habitat development. **Special Collections:** Complete collection of "The Auk"; Proceedings of North American Wildlife Conference; Journal of Wildlife Management. **Holdings:** 500 books; 1000 bound periodical volumes. **Subscriptions:** 10 journals and other serials; 15 newspapers. **Services:** Interlibrary loans; copying; library open to public with restrictions.

DUDLEY OBSERVATORY
See: Union University

DUERKSEN (Walter) FINE ARTS CENTER
See: Wichita State University - Thurlow Lieurance Memorial Music Library

★3887★

DUFF AND PHELPS, INC. - RESEARCH LIBRARY (Bus-Fin)

55 E. Monroe St., Suite 4000 Phone: (312) 263-2610
Chicago, IL 60603 Sheila A. Collins, Libn.
Staff: Prof 1; Other 2. **Subjects:** Financial analysis, public utilities, industry analysis, economics. **Holdings:** 700 books; U.S. Securities and Exchange Commission (SEC) microfiche; annual reports for 2000 companies. **Subscriptions:** 356 journals and other serials. **Services:** Interlibrary loans; copying; library not open to public. **Computerized Information Services:** Online systems. **Publications:** Library News, monthly - for internal distribution only.

DUGWAY PROVING GROUND
See: U.S. Army

★3888★

DUKE POWER COMPANY - DAVID NABOW LIBRARY (Sci-Tech; Energy)

Charlotte, NC 28242 Phone: (704) 373-4095
  Peggy B. Lambert, Libn.
Founded: 1967. **Staff:** Prof 2; Other 2. **Subjects:** Environment; engineering - electrical, civil and mechanical; soils; water resources; design of dams; building; standards. **Special Collections:** Nuclear Regulatory Commission reports and standards; Electric Power Research Institute reports. **Holdings:** 3700 books; 1375 bound periodical volumes; 6000 standards. **Subscriptions:** 302 journals and other serials. **Services:** Interlibrary loans; copying; library open to public with restrictions. **Computerized Information Services:** DIALOG, SDC, DOE/RECON; internal database. **Publications:** Acquisitions List, monthly; Safety Analysis Reports and Periodicals List, both quarterly. **Staff:** Harriet A. Webster, Info.Sci.

★3889★

DUKE POWER COMPANY - PRODUCTION DEPARTMENTS - INFORMATION RESOURCE CENTER (IRC) (Sci-Tech; Energy)

Box 670 Phone: (704) 875-1686
Cornelius, NC 28031 Ella Butler Scarborough, Supv., IRC
Founded: 1975. **Staff:** Prof 2; Other 3. **Subjects:** Nuclear and fossil fuels, mathematics, physics, chemistry, mechanical engineering, electronics. **Special Collections:** Electric Power Research Institute (EPRI). **Holdings:** 4500 books; 1500 manuals (cataloged); 3600 slides; 150 films; 130 kits; 22 charts; 7 models; subject vertical files; standards. **Subscriptions:** 150 journals and other serials. **Services:** Interlibrary loans; copying; library open to community use at intervals. **Computerized Information Services:** DIALOG, DOE/RECON; 17,000 technical reports on internal database. **Special Indexes:** Printouts of library holdings, quarterly (microfiche). **Staff:** Mr. R.M. Koehler, Mgr., Tech.Trng.Ctr.

★3890★

DUKE UNIVERSITY - ARCHIVES (Hist)

341 Perkins Phone: (919) 684-5637
Durham, NC 27706 William E. King, Univ.Archv.
Staff: Prof 2. **Subjects:** University history and records; 19th century Methodism. **Special Collections:** Triangle Universities Computation Center; Hispanic American Historical Review. **Holdings:** 1100 books; 400 bound periodical volumes; 11,000 dissertations; 2750 cubic feet of records, manuscripts and photographs. **Subscriptions:** 26 journals and other serials. **Services:** Copying; archives open to public. **Staff:** G. Edwin Southern, Jr., Asst.Univ.Archv.

★3891★

DUKE UNIVERSITY - BIOLOGY-FORESTRY LIBRARY (Sci-Tech; Env-Cons)

  Phone: (919) 684-2381
Durham, NC 27706 Bertha Livingstone, Libn.
Founded: 1938. **Staff:** Prof 1; Other 2. **Subjects:** Botany, zoology, forestry and environmental studies. **Holdings:** 138,064 volumes. **Subscriptions:** 1000 journals and other serials. **Services:** Interlibrary loans; copying. **Computerized Information Services:** Online systems.

★3892★

DUKE UNIVERSITY - CENTER FOR DEMOGRAPHIC STUDIES - REFERENCE LIBRARY (Soc Sci)

2117 Campus Dr. Phone: (919) 684-6126
Durham, NC 27706 Michael McFee, Libn.
Founded: 1964. **Staff:** Prof 6. **Subjects:** Demography; human ecology; census, vital statistics and other data sources; methods of research and analysis; population dynamics; urban and regional studies; economics of population size and distribution; migration studies; gerontology. **Special Collections:** Joseph J. Spengler Collection (several thousand books, periodicals, serials, reprints and clippings - on population and related topics, from the library of Professor Emeritus Spengler); Urban and Migration Reprint - reference files, 200 entries each; National Center for Health Statistics Mortality Data; 1960 and 1970 Public Use Samples; reprint files on aging, migration, human ecology. **Holdings:** 5000 books (cataloged); 175 bound periodical volumes; 2000 census volumes (cataloged); 30 dissertations; 125 maps; 350 microfiche; documents; program documentation. **Subscriptions:** 60 journals and other serials. **Services:** Copying (fee basis); library open to outside users actively engaged in demographic research. **Publications:** Reprint series; Working Paper Series - both periodically distributed on request. **Special Catalogs:** ABC's - Annotated Bibliographic Compiling System. **Special Indexes:** Computerized bibliography on aging and population modeling. **Staff:** George C. Myers, Dir. of Ctr.; Kenneth G. Manton, Asst.Dir.

★3893★

DUKE UNIVERSITY - CHEMISTRY LIBRARY (Sci-Tech)

  Phone: (919) 684-3004
Durham, NC 27706 Kitty Porter, Libn.
Founded: 1927. **Staff:** Prof 1. **Subjects:** Chemistry and related subjects. **Special Collections:** Sadtler Standard Spectra collections (UV, IR-Grating, NMR, C-13, Raman); API and TRC Catalogs of Standard Spectra. **Holdings:** 39,230 volumes. **Subscriptions:** 628 journals and other serials. **Services:** Interlibrary loans; copying; SDI; library open to public. **Computerized Information Services:** DIALOG, BRS, NLM. **Publications:** Recent Acquisitions List, monthly.

★3894★

DUKE UNIVERSITY - DIVINITY SCHOOL LIBRARY (Rel-Theol)

  Phone: (919) 684-3691
Durham, NC 27706 Donn Michael Farris, Libn.
Staff: Prof 2; Other 3. **Subjects:** Jansenism, Jesuits, the Wesleys and Methodism, Judaic studies, Quakerism, religions and related subjects.

Holdings: 207,513 volumes. **Subscriptions:** 600 journals and other serials. **Staff:** Harriet Leonard, Ref.Libn.

★3895★
DUKE UNIVERSITY - MANUSCRIPT DEPARTMENT (Hum)
344 Perkins Library   Phone: (919) 684-3372
Durham, NC 27706   Mattie Underwood Russell, Cur. of Mss.
Staff: Prof 6; Other 1. **Subjects:** Southern history and literature; U.S. history; British history and literature; Latin American, Spanish and French history. **Holdings:** 7.25 million manuscripts; 50,000 manuscript volumes. **Services:** Copying. **Publications:** Guide to the Cataloged Collections in the Manuscript Department of the William R. Perkins Library, 1980 (1005 pages). **Special Catalogs:** Autograph, geographic and picture files (card). **Staff:** William R. Erwin, Jr., Asst.Cur., Cat.; Ellen G. Gartrell, Asst.Cur., Rd.Serv.; Robert L. Byrd, Mss.Libn.

★3896★
DUKE UNIVERSITY - MARINE LABORATORY - A.S. PEARSE MEMORIAL LIBRARY (Sci-Tech)
Beaufort, NC 28516   Phone: (919) 728-2111
     Jean S. Williams, Sr.Lib.Asst.
Founded: 1954. **Staff:** 2. **Subjects:** Marine sciences, oceanography. **Holdings:** 12,000 books and bound periodical volumes. **Subscriptions:** 150 journals and other serials. **Services:** Interlibrary loans (fee); copying; library open to public with restrictions. **Computerized Information Services:** Computerized cataloging, acquisitions, serials and circulation. **Networks/Consortia:** Member of OCLC. **Publications:** Serial Publications, 1979 - upon request.

★3897★
DUKE UNIVERSITY - MATH-PHYSICS LIBRARY (Sci-Tech)
233 Physics Bldg.   Phone: (919) 684-8118
Durham, NC 27706   Mary Ann W. Southern, Libn.
Staff: Prof 1; Other 2. **Subjects:** Mathematics, physics. **Special Collections:** University of Ulm Microwave Catalog. **Holdings:** 64,853 books and bound periodical volumes; 115,000 technical reports on microfiche. **Subscriptions:** 606 journals and other serials. **Services:** Interlibrary loans; copying; library open to public. **Computerized Information Services:** DIALOG, BRS; TSDB (internal database); computerized cataloging and acquisitions. **Networks/Consortia:** Member of OCLC through SOLINET.

★3898★
DUKE UNIVERSITY - MEDICAL CENTER LIBRARY (Med)
Durham, NC 27710   Phone: (919) 684-2092
     Warren Bird, Dir.
Staff: Prof 10; Other 21. **Subjects:** Medicine and related sciences. **Special Collections:** Josiah C. Trent Collection (history of medicine). **Holdings:** 183,500 books and bound periodical volumes. **Subscriptions:** 2974 journals and other serials. **Services:** Interlibrary loans; copying; SDI; library open to public with librarian's permission. **Computerized Information Services:** DIALOG, SDC, BRS, NLM; computerized acquisitions and serials. **Publications:** North Carolina Union List of Biomedical Serials (NORCUL); Library Telecommunications Directory, Canada & U.S.

★3899★
DUKE UNIVERSITY - MUSIC LIBRARY (Mus)
College Sta., Box 6695   Phone: (919) 684-6449
Durham, NC 27708   J. Samuel Hammond, Libn.
Staff: Prof 1; Other 2. **Subjects:** Music. **Holdings:** 52,000 books and periodicals; 500 reels of microfilm; music scores; music literature. **Subscriptions:** 180 journals and other serials. **Services:** Interlibrary loans; library open to public for reference use only. **Special Indexes:** Card index to manuscript inventories and descriptions.

★3900★
DUKE UNIVERSITY - SCHOOL OF ENGINEERING LIBRARY (Sci-Tech)
Durham, NC 27706   Phone: (919) 684-2371
     Eric J. Smith, Libn.
Founded: 1923. **Staff:** Prof 1; Other 2. **Subjects:** Engineering - mechanical, electrical, civil, biomedical; materials and computer science. **Holdings:** 66,322 volumes; 4500 NASA Research Reports. **Subscriptions:** 900 journals and other serials. **Services:** Interlibrary loans; copying; library open to public with restrictions. **Computerized Information Services:** DIALOG, SDC, MEDLINE; computerized cataloging, acquisitions, and serials. **Networks/Consortia:** Member of OCLC through SOLINET.

★3901★
DUKE UNIVERSITY - SCHOOL OF LAW LIBRARY (Law)
     Phone: (919) 684-2847
Durham, NC 27706   Richard Danner, Dir.
Staff: Prof 8; Other 12. **Subjects:** Law. **Holdings:** 302,959 volumes. **Subscriptions:** 4245 journals and other serials. **Services:** Interlibrary loans; copying; library open to public for reference use only. **Computerized Information Services:** LEXIS; computerized cataloging and acquisitions. **Networks/Consortia:** Member of OCLC through SOLINET. **Publications:** D.U.L.L. News, monthly. **Staff:** Janeen Denson, Circ.Libn.; Claire Germain, Hd.Ref.Libn.; Kathy Kott, Hd., Tech.Serv.; Kathryn Christie, Ref./Res.Libn.; Gretchen Wolf, Acq.Libn.; Hope Breeze, Asst.Cat.Libn.; Michael Chiorazzi, Ref.Libn.

★3902★
DUKES COUNTY HISTORICAL SOCIETY - LIBRARY (Hist)
Cooke & School Sts.
Box 827   Phone: (617) 627-4441
Edgartown, MA 02539   Thomas E. Norton, Dir.
Founded: 1922. **Staff:** 4. **Subjects:** History of Martha's Vineyard, genealogy, whaling history, shipping, maritime history, history of Island Indians, literature by Island authors. **Special Collections:** Whaling logbooks and account books. **Holdings:** 3000 volumes; 154 boxes of archive material; microfilm of customs office and of the whaling logbooks and account books. **Services:** Interlibrary loans; copying; library open to public. **Publications:** Dukes County Intelligencer, quarterly. **Staff:** Muriel Crossman, Ref.Libn.

★3903★
DULUTH BAR LIBRARY ASSOCIATION (Law)
515 St. Louis County Court House   Phone: (218) 723-3563
Duluth, MN 55802   Michele Milinovich, Libn.
Founded: 1889. **Staff:** Prof 1. **Subjects:** Law. **Holdings:** 35,000 books. **Services:** Copying; library circulates to members only.

★3904★
(Duluth) NEWS-TRIBUNE & HERALD - LIBRARY (Publ)
424 W. 1st St.   Phone: (218) 723-5309
Duluth, MN 55801   Lana Michelizzi, Libn.
Staff: Prof 1; Other 2. **Subjects:** Newspaper reference topics. **Holdings:** 550 books; 1300 bound periodical volumes; 825,000 newspaper clippings; 1000 reels of microfilm; 75,000 photographs. **Subscriptions:** 10 journals and other serials. **Services:** Library not open to public.

DUMBARTON OAKS...
See: Harvard University

★3905★
DUN AND BRADSTREET, INC. - BUSINESS LIBRARY (Bus-Fin)
99 Church St.   Phone: (212) 285-7304
New York, NY 10007   Carol Stankiewicz, Libn.
Founded: 1939. **Staff:** Prof 2; Other 3. **Subjects:** Economics, marketing, business statistics, credit, management, small business. **Holdings:** 15,000 volumes; 1 set microfiche D-U-N-S Account Identifier; 300 VF drawers of pamphlets and clippings. **Subscriptions:** 400 journals and other serials. **Services:** Interlibrary loans; copying; library open to public by appointment. **Computerized Information Services:** DIALOG, New York Times Information Service. **Publications:** Library Bulletin, New Acquisitions, Periodical list, irregular, free. **Special Catalogs:** Operating Ratios (card). **Staff:** Eileen Rourke, Ref.Libn.

★3906★
DUNHAM TAVERN MUSEUM - LIBRARY (Hist)
6709 Euclid Ave.   Phone: (216) 431-1060
Cleveland, OH 44103   Elizabeth Martel, Libn.
Staff: 1. **Subjects:** Collecting china, pottery, pewter, furniture, history of Cleveland and Ohio. **Special Collections:** Antiques (complete set of magazine, from 1922 to present). **Holdings:** 1000 books. **Services:** Library open to members only. **Remarks:** Maintained by the Society of Collectors, Inc.

★3907★
DUNHILL COMPANY - BUSINESS RESEARCH LIBRARY (Bus-Fin)
2430 W. Oakland Park Blvd.   Phone: (305) 484-8300
Fort Lauderdale, FL 33311   Ruth Balaban, Libn.
Staff: Prof 2. **Subjects:** Manufacturing, wholesalers, retailers, religious market, clubs and organizations, finance, associations and members, service organizations. **Holdings:** Trade directories. **Services:** Library not open to public. **Remarks:** This company is a subsidiary of Dunhill International List Company, Inc.

★3908★
DUNKIRK OBSERVER - LIBRARY (Publ)†
8 E. Second St.
Dunkirk, NY 14048   Phone: (716) 366-3000
Founded: 1882. **Staff:** 1. **Subjects:** Newspaper reference topics, Dunkirk and area events. **Holdings:** Newspapers on microfilm (1882 to present). **Services:** Library open to public by permission.

★3909★
DUNLAP AND ASSOCIATES, INC. - LIBRARY (Soc Sci)†
One Parkland Dr.   Phone: (203) 655-3971
Darien, CT 06820   Joan Edwards, Dir.
Founded: 1948. **Staff:** Prof 1. **Subjects:** Psychology, human factors, statistics, military science, drug abuse, accidents (including alcohol-related). **Holdings:** 2500 books; 100 bound periodical volumes; 80 VF drawers of reports, government documents and pamphlets. **Subscriptions:** 50 journals and other serials; 5 newspapers. **Services:** Interlibrary loans; copying; library open to public by appointment.

DUNLAP (David) OBSERVATORY
See: University of Toronto - David Dunlap Observatory

★3910★
DUNLOP RESEARCH CENTRE - LIBRARY (Sci-Tech)
Sheridan Park   Phone: (416) 822-4711
Mississauga, ON, Canada L5K 1Z8   Shirley A. Morrison, Libn.
Staff: Prof 1; Other 1. **Subjects:** Rubber chemistry and technology; plastics technology; polymer chemistry. **Holdings:** 1200 books; 300 bound periodical volumes; reports and patents. **Subscriptions:** 125 journals and other serials. **Services:** Interlibrary loans; copying; SDI; library open to public by appointment. **Computerized Information Services:** DIALOG, SDC, BRS, CAN/OLE, Info Globe.

★3911★
DUNS SCOTUS LIBRARY (Rel-Theol)
20000 W. Nine Mile Rd.   Phone: (313) 357-3070
Southfield, MI 48075   Bro. Gabriel Balassone, Libn.
Founded: 1930. **Staff:** 1. **Subjects:** Philosophy, theology, Franciscana, literature, liberal arts, sociology. **Special Collections:** Renaissance manuscripts (2); Incunabula (16); books printed in the 16th century (95); books printed in the 17th century (164); books printed in the 18th century (440); books printed in the 19th century; Franciscana (2530). **Holdings:** 36,000 books; 8000 bound periodical volumes. **Subscriptions:** 60 journals and other serials. **Services:** Interlibrary loans; copying; library open to public for reference use only. **Remarks:** Maintained by the Order of Friars Minor (Franciscans).

★3912★
DUNWOODY INDUSTRIAL INSTITUTE - JOHN A. BUTLER LEARNING CENTER (Sci-Tech)
818 Wayzata Blvd.   Phone: (612) 374-5800
Minneapolis, MN 55403   Lillian V. Carlson, Libn.
Staff: Prof 1; Other 2. **Subjects:** Printing, mechanical and architectural drafting, electronics, refrigeration, baking, electrical and mechanical engineering, welding, auto mechanics. **Holdings:** 10,184 books. **Subscriptions:** 56 journals and other serials. **Services:** Copying (fee); library not open to public.

DUPLICATE EXCHANGE CLEARINGHOUSE
See: Universal Serials & Book Exchange, Inc.

DUPRE LIBRARY
See: University of Southwestern Louisiana - Jefferson Caffery Louisiana Room

DUPUIS HALL LIBRARY
See: Queen's University at Kingston

★3913★
DUQUESNE UNIVERSITY - LAW LIBRARY (Law)†
600 Forbes Ave.   Phone: (412) 434-6293
Pittsburgh, PA 15282   Frank Yining Liu, Law Libn.
Founded: 1911. **Staff:** Prof 5. **Subjects:** Law. **Holdings:** 76,000 volumes; 2000 volumes in microform. **Subscriptions:** 847 journals and other serials. **Services:** Interlibrary loans; library use restricted to attorneys. **Computerized Information Services:** LEXIS. **Publications:** Duquesne Law Library Notes, quarterly; Short Subjects, monthly - both for internal distribution only. **Staff:** Doris M.E. Corsello, Cat.; Agnes F. Robinson, Asst. Law Libn.; Virginia C. Esckridge, Ref.Libn.

★3914★
DURACELL INC. - RESEARCH LIBRARY (Sci-Tech)
2333 N. Sheridan Way
Sheridan Park   Phone: (416) 823-4410
Mississauga, ON, Canada L5K 1A7   Valerie F. Potter, Libn.
Staff: 1. **Subjects:** Electrochemistry, powder metallurgy, batteries. **Holdings:** 2000 books; 400 bound periodical volumes; 3000 clippings. **Subscriptions:** 100 journals and other serials. **Services:** Interlibrary loans; copying; library not open to public. **Computerized Information Services:** BRS, DIALOG, CISTI, INFOLINE, SDC. **Networks/Consortia:** Member of Sheridan Park Association.

★3915★
DURACELL INC. - TECHNICAL INFORMATION CENTER (Sci-Tech)
Northwest Industrial Pk.   Phone: (617) 272-4100
Burlington, MA 01803   Mildred Keller, Mgr., Tech.Info.Serv.
Founded: 1969. **Staff:** Prof 2; Other 1. **Subjects:** Electrochemistry, physical chemistry, metallurgy, materials science, environmental science, computer science. **Holdings:** 4500 books; 2140 bound periodical volumes; 2750 reprints and pamphlets (cataloged); 7 VF drawers of battery patents; 3000 government contract reports; 4 VF drawers of literature searches; 750 microforms. **Subscriptions:** 197 journals and other serials. **Services:** Interlibrary loans; copying; library open to public for reference use only by request. **Computerized Information Services:** DIALOG, SDC; internal database. **Networks/Consortia:** Member of New England On-line Users Group. **Publications:** TIC Topics, bimonthly; Abstracts of Current Battery Patents, monthly - both for internal distribution only. **Staff:** Richard Dupont, Asst.Libn.

★3916★
DURANT FAMILY REGISTRY - LIBRARY (Rec)
2700 Timber Ln.
Green Bay, WI 54303   Phone: (414) 499-8797
                                     Jeff Gillis, Hd.
Staff: 1. **Subjects:** Automobiles - Durant, DeVaux, Star, Flint, Rugby, Canadian Frontenac. **Special Collections:** Sales literature, owners manuals, factory photographs, related information pertaining to cars produced by W.C. Durant from 1921-1932. **Holdings:** Figures not available. **Services:** Copying (fee); library open to public. **Publications:** The Registry, quarterly - to members in North America, Europe, Africa and Australia.

★3917★
DURHAM COLLEGE OF APPLIED ARTS AND TECHNOLOGY - MAIN LIBRARY & SIMCOE RESOURCE CENTRE (Sci-Tech)
Simcoe St., N.
Box 385
Oshawa, ON, Canada L1H 7L7   Phone: (416) 576-0210
                                     Susan Barclay, Coll.Libn.
Founded: 1967. **Staff:** Prof 1; Other 8. **Subjects:** Technology, business, applied arts, health sciences. **Holdings:** 20,000 books; 1750 bound periodical volumes; 1300 federal and provincial government documents; 5300 slides; 2000 pamphlets; 620 filmstrips; 339 records; 1580 tapes and cassettes. **Subscriptions:** 250 journals and other serials; 7 newspapers. **Services:** Interlibrary loans; copying; library open to local and regional library system users. **Computerized Information Services:** Computerized cataloging and acquisitions.

★3918★
DURHAM COUNTY HOSPITAL CORPORATION - WATTS SCHOOL OF NURSING - LIBRARY (Med)
3643 N. Roxboro Rd.   Phone: (919) 471-3411
Durham, NC 27704   Priscilla W. Hoover, Libn.
Founded: 1895. **Staff:** Prof 1; Other 1. **Subjects:** Nursing and nursing education, pediatrics, obstetrics and gynecology, sociology and psychology. **Holdings:** 6457 books; 218 bound periodical volumes; 3 VF drawers; 20 boxes of pamphlets. **Subscriptions:** 50 journals and other serials. **Services:** Interlibrary loans; copying; library open to hospital personnel and nursing students only.

★3919★
DURHAM HERALD-SUN NEWSPAPER - LIBRARY (Publ)
115 Market St.   Phone: (919) 682-8181
Durham, NC 27702   Barbara P. Semonche, Chf.Libn.
Staff: Prof 2; Other 5. **Subjects:** Newspaper reference topics. **Special Collections:** Durham Herald-Sun Newspaper Microfilm Collection (1900 to present). **Holdings:** 3000 books; 60,000 photographs; 40 VF drawers; Duke University Index to Herald-Sun Newspapers (1930-1977). **Subscriptions:** 34 journals and other serials; 23 newspapers. **Services:** Library not open to public. **Publications:** Library Bulletin, annual; Newspaper Libraries in North Carolina; Carolina Live Wire (newsletter), 3/year. **Special Indexes:** IND-EX, computerized local news index. **Staff:** Gloria Colvin, Assoc.Libn.; Kate

Mooneyham, Asst.Libn.

DURKEE FOODS DIVISION
See: SCM Corporation - Glidden Coatings & Resins Div./Durkee Foods
Division

DURLAND (Anne Carry) MEMORIAL ALTERNATIVES LIBRARY
See: Center for Religion, Ethics & Social Policy - Anne Carry Durland
Memorial Alternatives Library

★3920★
DURO-TEST CORPORATION - TECHNICAL LIBRARY (Sci-Tech; Med)†
2321 Kennedy Blvd.   Phone: (201) 867-7000
North Bergen, NJ 07047   Dorothy K. Jakubczak, Tech.Libn.
Staff: Prof 1. **Subjects:** Illuminating engineering, medical applications of light.
Holdings: 850 books; 100 bound periodical volumes; U.S. and British patents.
Subscriptions: 60 journals and other serials. **Services:** Interlibrary loans;
library not open to public. **Networks/Consortia:** Member of New Jersey
Library Network Services; New York & New Jersey Regional Medical Library
Program.

★3921★
**DUTCHESS COUNTY DEPARTMENT OF PLANNING - INFORMATION
CENTER** (Plan)
47 Cannon St.   Phone: (914) 485-9890
Poughkeepsie, NY 12601   Charles J. Murphy, Pub.Info.Off.
Founded: 1980. **Staff:** Prof 1. **Subjects:** Land use, transportation,
environmental planning, parks and recreation, housing and energy, refuse
disposal. **Special Collections:** Tri-State Regional Planning Commission
Reports; American Society of Planning Officials Reports; Urban Land Institute
reports. **Holdings:** 300 books; 31 county and municipal master plans; New
York State statistical yearbooks; 10,000 slides; 1000 pamphlets and
unpublished reports; U.S. and county census data. **Subscriptions:** 25 journals
and other serials; 5 newspapers. **Services:** Copying; library open to public for
reference use only. **Publications:** County data book; land use, housing and
school reports; census tract plans.

★3922★
DUTCHESS COUNTY GENEALOGICAL SOCIETY - LIBRARY (Hist)
LDS Church
Spackenkill Rd., Box 708
Poughkeepsie, NY 12602
Founded: 1975. **Subjects:** Genealogy, history, heraldry. **Holdings:** 75 books;
60 pamphlets; 1790 census on 3 reels of microfilm; 1810 census on 71 reels
of microfilm; census of 1820 and 1840-1880 (ten year intervals) on
microfilm. **Subscriptions:** 80 journals and other serials. **Services:** Library
open to public. **Remarks:** The Genealogical Society's collection is housed in
the library of the LDS Church.

★3923★
DUTCHESS COUNTY MENTAL HEALTH LIBRARY (Med; Soc Sci)
230 North Rd.   Phone: (914) 485-9700
Poughkeepsie, NY 12601   Barbara B. Pantridge, Libn.
Founded: 1969. **Staff:** Prof 1; Other 1. **Subjects:** Psychiatry, child
psychiatry, alcoholism, drug abuse, psychology, mental retardation, the family.
Holdings: 1477 books; 129 bound periodical volumes; 85 films; 29
audiotapes; 4 videotapes; 4 VF drawers of clippings, pamphlets, reprints; 10
filmstrips. **Subscriptions:** 73 journals and other serials. **Services:** Interlibrary
loans; copying; library open to public with restrictions. **Networks/Consortia:**
Member of Southeastern New York Library Resources Council; Health
Information Libraries of Westchester (HILOW). **Publications:** Accessions
Lists, 2/year; AV catalog, irregular; brochure. **Special Indexes:** Indexes on
child abuse, deinstitutionalization, suicide and other mental health subjects
(book). **Remarks:** Maintained by the Mental Health Association in Dutchess
County.

DUVAL (Addison M.) LIBRARY
See: Georgia State Department of Human Resources - Georgia Mental
Health Institute - Addison M. Duval Library

★3924★
DUVAL COUNTY LAW LIBRARY (Law)
220 Court House   Phone: (904) 633-4756
Jacksonville, FL 32202   Jack T. Sheng, Law Libn.
Founded: 1939. **Staff:** Prof 1; Other 3. **Subjects:** Law - Florida, English,
taxation, criminal. **Special Collections:** Old English law. **Holdings:** 31,500
books; 3000 bound periodical volumes; 950 other cataloged items; 20 maps;
125 tapes. **Subscriptions:** 152 journals and other serials; 5 newspapers.
Services: Copying; library open to county residents.

DUVEEN LIBRARY
See: Clark (Sterling and Francine) Art Institute - Library

★3925★
DWORMAN (Thomas J.) - LIBRARY (Trans)
20210 Archer   Phone: (313) 255-2132
Detroit, MI 48219   Thomas J. Dworman
Founded: 1946. **Staff:** Prof 1. **Subjects:** Detroit area electric railways, local
streetcars, interurbans and electrified portions of main line railways. **Holdings:**
3000 pictures; track and route maps; equipment rosters; pamphlets;
transfers. **Services:** Interlibrary loans; copying (limited); will answer questions
or supply data when possible; collection accessible to public by appointment.

DYE (F.W. and Bessie) MEMORIAL LIBRARY
See: Texas Woman's University, Dallas Center - F.W. and Bessie Dye
Memorial Library

DYER INSTITUTE OF INTERDISCIPLINARY STUDIES
See: U.S. Army Military History Institute

DYER OBSERVATORY
See: Vanderbilt University Library

DYESS AIR FORCE BASE (TX)
See: U.S. Air Force Base - Dyess Base Library

★3926★
DYKEMA, GOSSETT, SPENCER, GOODNOW & TRIGG - LAW LIBRARY (Law)
400 Renaissance Center, 35th Fl.   Phone: (313) 568-6715
Detroit, MI 48243   Suzanne S. Schriefer, Mgr., Lib.Serv.
Staff: Prof 1; Other 3. **Subjects:** Law - tax, corporate, labor. **Holdings:**
16,000 books; 2000 bound periodical volumes; 6 VF drawers. **Subscriptions:**
102 journals and other serials; 25 newspapers. **Services:** Interlibrary loans;
library not open to public. **Computerized Information Services:** LEXIS,
WESTLAW, DIALOG, SDC, New York Times Information Service, Dow Jones
New Retrieval, BRS.

★3927★
DYNAMICS RESEARCH CORPORATION - LIBRARY (Sci-Tech)
60 Concord St.   Phone: (617) 658-6100
Wilmington, MA 01887   Sheila Elfman, Lib.Spec.
Founded: 1962. **Staff:** Prof 1. **Subjects:** Inertial navigation systems,
computer programming, guidance and control. **Holdings:** 1000 books; 8000
documents, pamphlets and periodicals. **Subscriptions:** 20 journals and other
serials. **Services:** Library not open to public.

★3928★
DYNAPOL - LIBRARY (Sci-Tech; Food-Bev)
445 Cambridge Ave.   Phone: (415) 321-1032
Palo Alto, CA 94304   Sharon R. Hamrick, Libn.
Founded: 1972. **Staff:** Prof 1. **Subjects:** Food chemicals, food additives,
polymers, toxicology, organic chemistry, microbiology. **Holdings:** 2000 books;
World Health Organization reports; Food and Agriculture Organization reports.
Subscriptions: 125 journals and other serials. **Services:** Interlibrary loans;
copying; literature surveys; library open to public by appointment.
Computerized Information Services: DIALOG. **Networks/Consortia:**
Member of CIN; CLASS. **Special Indexes:** Index to the Dynapol collection of
WHO reports; Books on Toxicology - A Survey of 14 San Francisco Bay Area
Libraries.

★3929★
DYNATECH CORPORATION LIBRARY (Sci-Tech)†
99 Erie St.   Phone: (617) 868-8050
Cambridge, MA 02139   Jane I. Petschaft, Libn.
Founded: 1962. **Staff:** Prof 1. **Subjects:** Chemical engineering,
bioengineering, thermal engineering. **Holdings:** 2500 books; 1500 technical
reports (cataloged); 5 drawers of technical reports on microfiche.
Subscriptions: 95 journals and other serials. **Services:** Interlibrary loans;
library not open to public.

E

★3930★

E-SYSTEMS, INC. - DIVISION LIBRARY (Sci-Tech)
Box 1056
Greenville, TX 75401   Phone: (214) 454-4580
    Joleta Moore, Supv.
Founded: 1960. **Staff:** Prof 1; Other 2. **Subjects:** Electronics, mathematics, physics, research and development, airborne equipment. **Holdings:** 3100 books; 200 bound periodical volumes; 20,000 military specifications and standards; Armed Services Technical Information Agency (ASTIA) documents; 2600 technical manuals; 8000 reports. **Subscriptions:** 75 journals and other serials. **Services:** Interlibrary loans; library not open to public.

★3931★

E-SYSTEMS, INC. - ECI DIVISION - TECHNICAL INFORMATION CENTER (Sci-Tech)
1501 72nd St., N.
Box 12248
St. Petersburg, FL 33733   Susan Weiss, Tech.Info. Data Spec.
Founded: 1958. **Staff:** 1. **Subjects:** Electronics, communications, electrical engineering. **Holdings:** 5000 books; 1000 bound periodical volumes; 12,000 documents (cataloged). **Subscriptions:** 150 journals and other serials. **Services:** Interlibrary loans; copying; library not open to public. **Computerized Information Services:** DIALOG, SDC, DTIC, DOE/RECON, DMS INC.; computerized cataloging and circulation.

★3932★

E-SYSTEMS, INC. - GARLAND DIVISION - TECHNICAL LIBRARY (Sci-Tech)
Box 226118   Phone: (214) 272-0515
Dallas, TX 75266   Charlene Morris, Tech.Libn.
Founded: 1952. **Staff:** 1. **Subjects:** Astronautics, electronics, communications systems, data processing, display systems, optics. **Holdings:** 7200 books; 725 bound periodical volumes; 65,000 technical reports (cataloged); 100 microfiche. **Subscriptions:** 80 journals and other serials. **Services:** Interlibrary loans; copying; library not open to public.

★3933★

E-SYSTEMS, INC. - MELPAR DIVISION - TECHNICAL LIBRARY (Sci-Tech)
7700 Arlington Blvd.   Phone: (703) 560-5000
Falls Church, VA 22046   Mary A. Albertson, Libn.
Staff: Prof 1; Other 2. **Subjects:** Electronic communications. **Holdings:** 6000 books; 600 bound periodical volumes; 5000 company notebooks, proposals and reports; vendor catalogs; military standards and specifcations. **Subscriptions:** 94 journals and other serials. **Services:** Interlibrary loans; copying; SDI; library open to public by appointment. **Computerized Information Services:** DIALOG.

★3934★

EAGLE PUBLISHING COMPANY - EAGLE LIBRARY (Publ)
33 Eagle St.   Phone: (413) 447-7311
Pittsfield, MA 01201   Madeline F. Winter, Libn.
Founded: 1891. **Staff:** 2. **Subjects:** Newspaper reference topics. **Holdings:** 500,000 clippings; current and historical pictures. **Services:** Copying; library open to public. **Formerly:** Berkshire Eagle - Library.

EAGLETON INSTITUTE, RUTGERS UNIVERSITY
See: Center for the American Woman & Politics

★3935★

EAGLEVILLE HOSPITAL - HENRY S. LOUCHHEIM LIBRARY (Med)
Box 45   Phone: (215) 539-6000
Eagleville, PA 19408   Patricia C. Moretti, Dir., Spec.Serv.
Founded: 1971. **Staff:** Prof 3; Other 6. **Subjects:** Alcoholism, drug addiction, psychology, psychiatry. **Special Collections:** History and Philosophy of Community Living (350 items). **Holdings:** 3500 books; 32 drawers of archives and reprints; 750 audio cassettes (cataloged). **Subscriptions:** 252 journals and other serials. **Services:** Interlibrary loans; copying; library open to public for reference use only with approval of librarian. **Computerized Information Services:** DIALOG, BRS. **Networks/Consortia:** Member of Consortium for Health Information & Library Services. **Publications:** Openline (newsletter), weekly - for internal distribution only. **Special Indexes:** Indexes to proceedings, directories, reprints and card files. **Staff:** Harold Selix, Asst.Dir., Lib.Serv.; Jane Peltier, Acq.Libn.

★3936★

EARLHAM COLLEGE - JOSEPH MOORE MUSEUM - HADLEY LIBRARY (Sci-Tech)
Box 68
Richmond, IN 47374   Phone: (317) 962-6561
    John Iverson, Musm.Dir.
Subjects: Ornithology, mammals. **Holdings:** 1000 books; 200 bound periodical volumes. **Services:** Library open to public with restrictions.

★3937★

EARLHAM COLLEGE - QUAKER COLLECTION (Rel-Theol)
Lilly Library
Richmond, IN 47374   Phone: (317) 962-6561
    Philip Shore, Assoc.Libn.
Founded: 1909. **Staff:** Prof 1; Other 1. **Subjects:** Society of Friends (Quaker); Earlham College. **Special Collections:** Indian Affairs; Collections of Chas. F. Coffin, Elbert Russell, Marcus Mote, Clifford Crump, Esther Griffin White and Harlow Lindley; Earlham College Historical Collection. **Holdings:** 8000 books; 550 bound periodical volumes; 5000 pamphlets, manuscripts and photographs (cataloged); 60 volumes of printed and bound theses; 250 reels of audiotapes. **Subscriptions:** 70 journals and other serials. **Services:** Interlibrary loans; copying; library open to public. **Computerized Information Services:** Computerized cataloging. **Networks/Consortia:** Member of INCOLSA. **Special Catalogs:** Catalog of archive items (card). **Staff:** J. Arthur Funston, Archv.

★3938★

EARLY AMERICAN INDUSTRIES ASSOCIATION - LIBRARY (Hist)
Bucks County Historical Society
Pine St.   Phone: (215) 345-0210
Doylestown, PA 18901   Terry A. McNealy, Libn.
Staff: 1. **Subjects:** Early American tools and technology. **Special Collections:** Ephemera Collection; early tools. **Holdings:** 1500 books; 500 catalogs and broadsides. **Services:** Library open to public. **Publications:** Chronicle, quarterly.

EARTH AND MINERAL SCIENCES LIBRARY
See: Pennsylvania State University

EARTH RESOURCES OBSERVATION SYSTEMS DATA CENTER
See: U.S. Geological Survey - EROS Data Center

EARTH TECHNOLOGY CORPORATION
See: ERTEC Western, Inc.

★3939★

EARTHMIND - LIBRARY (Env-Cons; Energy)
4844 Hirsch Rd.
Mariposa, CA 95338   Michael A. Hackleman, Res.Dir.
Founded: 1972. **Staff:** 1. **Subjects:** Alternative energy sources and architecture, homesteading, organic gardening. **Holdings:** 1000 books; 2000 color slides. **Subscriptions:** 20 journals and other serials. **Services:** Library open to public by appointment. **Publications:** Wind & Windspinners; The Homebuilt Wind-Generated Electricity Handbook; Electric Vehicles; other energy publications.

EARTHQUAKE ENGINEERING RESEARCH CENTER LIBRARY
See: University of California, Berkeley

EARTHQUAKE ENGINEERING RESEARCH LIBRARY
See: California Institute of Technology

★3940★

EARTHWATCH - LIBRARY (Env-Cons)
10 Juniper Rd.
Box 127
Belmont, MA 02178   Phone: (617) 489-3030
    Brian Rosborough, Pres.
Founded: 1971. **Staff:** Prof 25; Other 10. **Subjects:** Archeology, restoration, conservation, marine science, endangered species. **Holdings:** Figures not available. **Subscriptions:** 30 journals and other serials. **Publications:** Earthwatch Research Expedition Magazine, 3/year. **Staff:** Ann Austin, Res.

★3941★

EARTHWORK - CENTER FOR RURAL STUDIES (Env-Cons)
Box 8445
Minneapolis, MN 55408   Mark Ritchie
Staff: Prof 1. **Subjects:** Food, agriculture, land, rural affairs. **Holdings:** Figures not available. **Publications:** Monthly indexed clipping service on food, land and agriculture. **Formerly:** Located in San Francisco, CA.

★3942★
EARTHWORM, INC. - RECYCLING INFORMATION SERVICES (Env-Cons)
186 Lincoln St.   Phone: (617) 426-7344
Boston, MA 02111
Founded: 1970. Staff: 4. Subjects: Recycling, hazardous wastes, cooperatives. Holdings: 100 volumes; publications from Environmental Protection Agency, food cooperatives, environmental and commercial organizations; Earthworm News. Subscriptions: 5 journals and other serials. Services: Slide shows; library open to public by appointment. Publications: Earthworm News, semiannual - to mailing list.

★3943★
EAST CAROLINA UNIVERSITY - HEALTH SCIENCES LIBRARY (Med)
                               Phone: (919) 757-6961
Greenville, NC 27834   JoAnn Bell, Dir.
Founded: 1969. Staff: Prof 14; Other 21. Subjects: Medicine and allied health sciences; social welfare. Holdings: 40,323 books; 83,163 bound periodical volumes; 3956 school catalogs, pamphlets and brochures. Subscriptions: 1977 journals and other serials. Services: Interlibrary loans; copying; library open to public. Computerized Information Services: DIALOG, BRS, NLM; computerized cataloging. Networks/Consortia: Member of OCLC through SOLINET. Publications: Updater, monthly; Library Handbook; Nonprint Media Catalog. Staff: Bernice McKibben, Assoc.Dir.

★3944★
EAST CAROLINA UNIVERSITY - MUSIC LIBRARY (Mus)
Music Library, School of Music
East Carolina University   Phone: (919) 757-6250
Greenville, NC 27834   Mary Lou Jensen, Music Libn.
Staff: Prof 2; Other 1. Subjects: Music. Special Collections: East Carolina University faculty recital tapes. Holdings: 3350 books; 1050 bound periodical volumes; 10,000 scores; 6870 phonograph records; 860 tapes. Subscriptions: 67 journals and other serials. Services: Interlibrary loans; copying; library open to public. Computerized Information Services: Computerized cataloging. Networks/Consortia: Member of SOLINET. Special Indexes: Song index (cards).

★3945★
EAST CENTRAL LEGAL SERVICES - LIBRARY (Law)
1616 Meridian St.   Phone: (317) 644-2816
Anderson, IN 46016   John E. Fidler, Libn.
Founded: 1977. Staff: 2. Subjects: Law - federal, Indiana, administrative, poverty, consumer. Holdings: 1516 books; 24 bound periodical volumes. Services: Interlibrary loans; library not open to public. Formerly: Legal Services Organization of Indiana, Inc. - Delaware County Office, located in Muncie, IN.

★3946★
EAST CENTRAL OKLAHOMA STATE UNIVERSITY - OKLAHOMA ENVIRONMENTAL INFORMATION/MEDIA CENTER (Env-Cons)
                               Phone: (405) 332-8000
Ada, OK 74820   John Walker, Dir.
Founded: 1971. Staff: Prof 1. Subjects: Air quality, water quality, appropriate technology, solid waste, energy, occupational safety and health, environmental education. Special Collections: Envirofiche (Environmental Information Center, New York, NY). Holdings: 9500 books; 550 bound periodical volumes; 52,000 titles Envirofiche; 3000 government documents. Subscriptions: 100 journals and other serials. Services: Interlibrary loans; copying; searches from a total text system; library open primarily to Oklahomans. Computerized Information Services: DIALOG, SDC, BRS; computerized cataloging and ILL. Networks/Consortia: Member of OCLC through AMIGOS Bibliographic Council, Inc. Publications: Resources, irregular. Staff: Cynthia M. Coulter, Libn.

★3947★
EAST CHICAGO HISTORICAL SOCIETY - LIBRARY (Hist)
East Chicago Public Library
2401 E. Columbus Dr.   Phone: (219) 397-2453
East Chicago, IN 46312   Rose LeVan, Pres.
Founded: 1966. Staff: 2. Subjects: Local history, industry and urban problems. Holdings: Figures not available for books; pamphlets; community center records; church histories; Indiana Theatre records; oral tape collection. Services: Copying; library open to public with restrictions. Staff: E.S. Johnston, Libn.

★3948★
EAST DALLAS CHRISTIAN CHURCH - HAGGARD MEMORIAL LIBRARY (Rel-Theol)†
629 N. Peak St.   Phone: (214) 542-8441
Dallas, TX 75246   Mrs. Alfred C. Grosse, Lib.Chm.
Founded: 1950. Staff: Prof 1; Other 6. Subjects: Religion, missions, education, recreation, literature, art, Americana, psychology, science. Special Collections: The Christian Church (Disciples of Christ) history, theology and work in the world. Holdings: 15,500 books; 300 filmstrips plus scripts and/or records; 5 cassette tapes. Services: Library open to community residents for planned activities.

★3949★
EAST HAMPTON FREE LIBRARY - LONG ISLAND COLLECTION (Hist)
159 Main St.   Phone: (516) 324-0222
East Hampton, NY 11937   Dorothy T. King, Libn.
Founded: 1930. Staff: Prof 1. Subjects: Long Island history, biography and genealogy; Long Island imprints; books by Long Island authors. Special Collections: Thomas Moran Biographical Art Collection; memorabilia and other material related to T. Moran (1837-1926), his wife, brothers and son; Herbert F. Seversmith Collection 1904-1967 (Long Island genealogy, 395 items); Jeannette Edwards Rattray Collection (shipwrecks of Long Island; East Hampton Genealogy). Holdings: 3500 books; 300 bound periodical volumes; 90 VF drawers of reports, manuscripts, clippings, pamphlets, documents and maps; microfilm of Long Island newspapers, Whaling Log Books, Suffolk County Federal Census, 1820-1880, 1900 (102 reels). Subscriptions: 11 journals and other serials. Services: Copying; collection open to public. Special Catalogs: Catalog to Long Island Collection (card); Thomas Moran Biographical Collection (card); Herbert F. Seversmith Collection (card); East Hampton Star Index (book). All special card catalogs are on microfilm (8 reels).

★3950★
EAST LIBERTY PRESBYTERIAN CHURCH - LIBRARY (Rel-Theol)†
116 S. Highland Mall   Phone: (412) 441-3800
Pittsburgh, PA 15206   Barbara I. Lewis, Libn.
Subjects: Religion and theology. Holdings: 1200 volumes. Services: Library open to public with restrictions.

★3951★
EAST ORANGE GENERAL HOSPITAL - HEALTH SERVICES LIBRARY (Med)
300 Central Ave.   Phone: (201) 672-8400
East Orange, NJ 07019   Joann Mehalick, Mgr. of Lib.Serv.
Founded: 1974. Staff: Prof 1. Subjects: Medicine, mental health, allied health fields. Holdings: 1200 books. Subscriptions: 60 journals and other serials. Services: Interlibrary loans; copying; SDI; current awareness; LATCH; library open to public for reference service on request. Networks/Consortia: Member of Cosmopolitan Biomedical Library Consortium.

EAST PATTEE LIBRARY
See: Pennsylvania State University - Life Sciences Library

EAST ROUTT LIBRARY DISTRICT - ROUTT COUNTY COLLECTION
See: Tread of Pioneers Museum

★3952★
EAST STROUDSBURG STATE COLLEGE - KENT LIBRARY (Educ)
                               Phone: (717) 424-3465
East Stroudsburg, PA 18301   Russell J. Emele, Dir. Of Lib.
Staff: Prof 10; Other 13. Subjects: Health and physical education, education, history, political science, sociology, biology. Holdings: 296,191 books; 63,461 bound periodical volumes; 43,043 government documents; early American imprints and early English books in microform; 10,501 microcards; 277,619 microprints; 442,427 microfiche; 24,443 reels of microfilm; ERIC microfiche (complete). Subscriptions: 1300 journals and other serials; 26 newspapers. Services: Interlibrary loans; copying; library open to public for reference use only. Computerized Information Services: Computerized cataloging, circulation and serials. Networks/Consortia: Member of OCLC through PALINET & Union Library Catalogue of Pennsylvania; Interlibrary Delivery Service of Pennsylvania (IDS). Staff: Patricia J. Jersey, Ref./ILL Libn.; Leslie Berger, Ref./ILL Libn.; A. Angelini, Hd.Cat.; M. Paul Beaty, Asst.Cat.; Alvin C. Berger, Act.Dir.; Judith M. Feller, Doc.Libn.; John B. Lalley, Hd., Acq.; Gwynne H. Reese, Per.Libn.; Ellis F. Riebel, Asst.Circ.Libn.; A. Susan Bromer, Curric.Mtls.Libn.

EAST SUBURBAN HEALTH CENTER
See: Forbes Health System

★3953★
EAST TENNESSEE BAPTIST HOSPITAL - HEALTH SCIENCES LIBRARY
(Med)
Box 1788   Phone: (615) 632-5618
Knoxville, TN 37920   Mary Evelyn Lynn, Libn.
Founded: 1949. **Staff:** 2. **Subjects:** Nursing, allied health fields, cardiology, gerontology. **Holdings:** 2948 books; 107 bound periodical volumes. **Subscriptions:** 75 journals and other serials. **Services:** Interlibrary loans; copying; library open to area professionals only. **Computerized Information Services:** MEDLINE; computerized cataloging. **Networks/Consortia:** Member of Knoxville Area Health Sciences Library Consortium. **Publications:** Acquisitions list, monthly - to hospital departments, physicians and area schools. **Special Catalogs:** AV catalog. **Staff:** Betsy Bean, Asst.Libn.

EAST TENNESSEE HISTORICAL CENTER
See: Knoxville-Knox County Public Library System - Mc Clung Historical Collection

★3954★
EAST TENNESSEE STATE UNIVERSITY - ARCHIVES OF APPALACHIA (Hist)
Sherrod Library   Phone: (615) 929-4338
Johnson City, TN 37614   Dr. Richard M. Kesner, Dir.
Staff: Prof 7; Other 7. **Subjects:** Appalachia - history, economic development, material culture, folklore; Tennessee - history, educational institutions. **Special Collections:** Congress for Appalachian Development Collection; Burton-Manning Folklore Collection; Broadside Television, Inc. Collection; WSJK-TV Collection; Clinchfield Railroad Collection; ET and WNC Collection; East Tennessee State University papers. **Holdings:** 1000 books; 1000 bound periodical volumes; vertical files; 4000 feet of archives and manuscripts; 400 hours of audiotapes; 600 hours of videotapes. **Services:** Copying; library open to public. **Computerized Information Services:** Computerized cataloging. **Publications:** Archives of Appalachia Newsletter, quarterly - free upon request or by subscription.

★3955★
EAST TENNESSEE STATE UNIVERSITY, QUILLEN-DISHNER COLLEGE OF MEDICINE - DEPT. OF LEARNING RSRCS. - MEDICAL LIBRARY (Med)
Box 23290A   Phone: (615) 928-6426
Johnson City, TN 37614   Janet S. Fisher, Asst. Dean
Founded: 1975. **Staff:** Prof 6; Other 11. **Subjects:** Medicine. **Special Collections:** Hardy Long Collection (history of medicine). **Holdings:** 19,638 books; 28,341 bound periodical volumes; 6866 AV items; government documents; microforms; vertical files. **Subscriptions:** 1465 journals and other serials. **Services:** Interlibrary loans; copying; SDI; library open to public with restrictions. **Computerized Information Services:** BRS, DIALOG, NLM; computerized cataloging and serials. **Networks/Consortia:** Member of OCLC; Tri-Cities Area Health Sciences Libraries Consortium; PHILSOM. **Publications:** Actus Medicus, monthly; Library Guide, annual - to mailing list. **Staff:** Martha Whaley, Cat.Libn.; Betsy Williams, Asst.Libn.; Patsy Stranberg, Hd., ILL/Circ.; Frieda Davison, Hd., Tech.Serv.; Jim Curtis, AV Libn.

★3956★
EAST TEXAS BAPTIST COLLEGE - MAMYE JARRETT LEARNING CENTER
(Educ)
1209 North Grove   Phone: (214) 938-2636
Marshall, TX 75670   E.M. Adams, Jr., Libn.
Founded: 1917. **Staff:** Prof 4; Other 3. **Subjects:** English language, literature, teacher education, history, business, biology, chemistry, mathematics, music, religion. **Special Collections:** Lentz Collection of manuscripts on Harrison County; Millard Cope Collection of Texana. **Holdings:** 95,000 books; 14,000 bound periodical volumes; 125 manuscripts on local history; 3200 recordings; 2500 microforms. **Subscriptions:** 617 journals and other serials; 13 newspapers. **Services:** Interlibrary loans; copying; center open to graduates, area teachers, ministers and East Texas history research students. **Networks/Consortia:** Member of East Texas Higher Education Information Exchange. **Staff:** Gene Futrell, Curric.Lab.Libn.; Carolyn Jackson, Cat.; Dorothy Meadows, ILL.

★3957★
EAST TEXAS GENEALOGICAL ASSOCIATION - LIBRARY (Hist)
Rte. 2, Box 39
Tenaha, TX 75974
Founded: 1967. **Subjects:** Genealogy, local history. **Holdings:** 750 books; 32 bound periodical volumes; 125 reels of microfilm; 740 sound recordings; 6 VF drawers. **Formerly:** Southwest Texas Genealogical Association, located in Del Rio, TX.

★3958★
EAST TEXAS LEGAL SERVICES - LIBRARY (Law)
527 Forsythe   Phone: (713) 835-4971
Beaumont, TX 77701   Lana Caswell Garcia, Law Libn./Res.Spec.
Staff: Prof 1; Other 7. **Subjects:** Law, poverty law. **Holdings:** 15,000 books; 33 bound periodical volumes; 2 VF drawers of poverty files; 125 briefs; 1 filing drawer of forms; 25 tapes. **Subscriptions:** 50 journals and other serials; 25 newspapers. **Services:** Library open to area bar associations and their representatives. **Publications:** ETLS Library Newsletter, monthly - to professional staff of program. **Remarks:** Branch libraries are located in Huntsville, Jasper, Longview, Nacogdoches, Paris, Texarkana and Tyler.

★3959★
EAST TEXAS STATE UNIVERSITY - JAMES GILLIAM GEE LIBRARY (Educ)
East Texas Sta.   Phone: (214) 886-5717
Commerce, TX 75428   Mary E. Cook, Dir. of Lib.Serv.
Founded: 1889. **Staff:** Prof 17; Other 23. **Subjects:** Teacher education, liberal arts and sciences, Texas history, business. **Special Collections:** Historical textbooks; early imprints; Texana, especially Texas county histories; collection of pamphlets on printing by Douglas McMurtrie. **Holdings:** 426,774 books; 104,643 bound periodical volumes; 256,283 U.S. government documents; 101,012 books on microforms; 171,546 items in ERIC Collection; 30,192 items in VF drawers. **Subscriptions:** 7670 journals and other serials; 64 newspapers. **Services:** Interlibrary loans; copying; printout of library shelf list according to Library of Congress classification available on request; library open to public. **Computerized Information Services:** DIALOG, SDC, BRS; computerized cataloging, acquisitions and circulation. **Networks/Consortia:** Member of OCLC through AMIGOS Bibliographic Council, Inc.; Association for Higher Education of the North Texas Area; Federation of North Texas Area Universities. **Publications:** Ex Libris, monthly - select mailing list. **Special Catalogs:** Shelf list maintained on magnetic tape. **Staff:** Donald R. Kerr, Assoc.Dir.; Diane Saucier, Hd., Ref.Dept.; Jan Kemp, ILL Libn.

EAST TEXAS STATE UNIVERSITY - JAMES GILLIAM GEE LIBRARY - PLACE NAME SURVEY OF THE UNITED STATES
See: American Name Society - Place Name Survey of the United States

★3960★
EAST TEXAS STATE UNIVERSITY - ORAL HISTORY PROGRAM (Hist)
James Gilliam Gee Library
East Texas Sta.
Commerce, TX 75428   Phone: (214) 886-5738
                                                    James Conrad, Coord.
Founded: 1968. **Staff:** Prof 1; Other 1. **Subjects:** History of East Texas - railroad, cotton, blacks, medicine; Senator A.M. Aikin, Jr. project; institutional history; Fletcher Warren project. **Special Collections:** Dallas Mayors Project. **Holdings:** 150 volumes; 425 cassette tapes of interviews. **Services:** Copying; library open to public with restrictions. **Computerized Information Services:** Computerized cataloging. **Special Catalogs:** Oral history catalog (in progress).

★3961★
EAST-WEST CENTER - EAPI/PI/RSI RESEARCH MATERIALS COLLECTION
(Soc Sci)
1777 East-West Rd.   Phone: (808) 944-7451
Honolulu, HI 96848   Alice D. Harris, Res.Info.Spec.
Founded: 1969. **Staff:** Prof 3; Other 2. **Subjects:** Demography, population problems and policy in Hawaii, Asian countries and Pacific area; family planning programs; environment; energy; agriculture; resource systems. **Special Collections:** Population of Mainland China and Thailand; census and government publications of Korea, Taiwan, Indonesia, Malaysia. **Holdings:** 10,000 books; 100 bound periodical volumes; 8000 reprints/papers; 43 films; 160 reels of microfilm; 6 tapes; maps. **Subscriptions:** 200 journals and other serials. **Services:** Interlibrary loans; copying; SDI; collection open to public. **Computerized Information Services:** DIALOG; computerized cataloging. **Networks/Consortia:** Member of OCLC; Association for Population/Family Planning Libraries and Information Centers-International (APLIC-Internatl.). **Publications:** Accession List, 5-6/year. **Formerly:** East-West Population Institute Resource Materials Collection. **Staff:** Phyllis Kagehiro, Jr.Lib.Spec.; Terese Leber, Jr.Lib.Spec.

★3962★
EAST-WEST CULTURE LEARNING INSTITUTE - RESOURCE MATERIALS COLLECTION (Soc Sci)
East-West Ctr.
1777 East-West Rd.
Honolulu, HI 96848   Phone: (808) 944-7345
                                                    Sumiye Konoshima, Res.Mtls.Spec.
Staff: Prof 2; Other 2. **Subjects:** Cross-cultural education and literature, cultural problems in treaty negotiation, methods for analyzing cultural

misunderstanding, transnational interaction, English as an international language. **Holdings:** 3000 books; tape recordings; videotapes; slides; photographs; reprints. **Subscriptions:** 150 journals and other serials. **Services:** Copying; library open to public with restrictions. **Publications:** Culture Learning Institute Report, quarterly; Language Planning Newsletter, quarterly.

★3963★
EAST-WEST GATEWAY COORDINATING COUNCIL - REFERENCE AREA (Plan)
112 N. 4th St., Suite 1200   Phone: (314) 421-4220
St. Louis, MO 63102   Henrietta Whiteside, Info.Serv.Coord.
Founded: 1966. **Staff:** Prof 1. **Subjects:** Transportation, regional comprehensive planning, environmental planning, solid waste, regional census data, housing. **Holdings:** 5000 books; 8 VF drawers of pamphlets; regional maps. **Subscriptions:** 200 journals and other serials. **Services:** Interlibrary loans; copying; library open to public by appointment. **Publications:** Annual reports of the council. **Special Indexes:** Index listing of agency-produced publications.

EAST-WEST POPULATION INSTITUTE RESOURCE MATERIALS COLLECTION
See: East-West Center

★3964★
EAST YORK BOARD OF EDUCATION - PROFESSIONAL LIBRARY (Educ)
840 Coxwell Ave.   Phone: (416) 465-4631
Toronto, ON, Canada M4C 2V3   Martha Pluscauskas, Coord.
Founded: 1973. **Staff:** Prof 1; Other 3. **Subjects:** Education. **Holdings:** 8000 books. **Subscriptions:** 252 journals and other serials. **Services:** Interlibrary loans; copying; library open to employees of the Board of Education, residents of East York and student teachers.

EAST YORK CAMPUS RESOURCE CENTRE
See: Centennial College of Applied Arts & Technology

★3965★
EASTCHESTER HISTORICAL SOCIETY - LIBRARY (Hist)
Box 37   Phone: (914) 793-1900
Eastchester NY 10709   Madeline Schaeffer, Libn.
Staff: Prof 1. **Subjects:** Juvenile literature, 1795-1905; local and general history. **Special Collections:** Juvenile textbooks, 1790-1900. **Holdings:** 8000 books; manuscripts, diaries. **Subscriptions:** 25 journals and other serials. **Services:** Copying; library open to public with restrictions.

★3966★
EASTER SEAL REHABILITATION CENTER OF SOUTHWESTERN CONNECTICUT - FRANCIS M. HARRISON MEMORIAL LIBRARY (Med)
26 Palmer's Hill Rd.   Phone: (203) 325-1544
Stamford, CT 06902   Ruth C. Adams, Libn.
Founded: 1961. **Staff:** 1. **Subjects:** Rehabilitation. **Holdings:** 500 books; 240 bound periodical volumes; 6 VF drawers of pamphlets, brochures; 3 shelves of reports, catalogs. **Subscriptions:** 18 journals and other serials. **Services:** Interlibrary loans; library open to public for reference and research by appointment.

★3967★
EASTERN BAPTIST THEOLOGICAL SEMINARY - LIBRARY (Rel-Theol)
Lancaster Ave. & City Line   Phone: (215) 896-5000
Philadelphia, PA 19151   Rev. R. David Koch, Assoc.Libn./Tech.Serv.
Founded: 1925. **Staff:** Prof 2; Other 2. **Subjects:** Theology and related subjects. **Special Collections:** Russel H. MacBride Collection of Philosophy, Religion and Classical Literature (4300 volumes). **Holdings:** 81,000 books; 9000 bound periodical volumes. **Subscriptions:** 420 journals and other serials. **Services:** Interlibrary loans; copying; library open to graduate students and ministers. **Computerized Information Services:** Computerized cataloging. **Networks/Consortia:** Member of OCLC through PALINET & Union Library Catalogue of Pennsylvania; Southeastern Pennsylvania Theological Libraries Association. **Staff:** Dr. William J. Hand, Assoc.Libn./Adm.

★3968★
EASTERN CONNECTICUT STATE COLLEGE - CENTER FOR CONNECTICUT STUDIES (Hist)
J. Eugene Smith Library   Phone: (203) 456-2231
Willimantic, CT 06226   Dr. David M. Roth, Dir.
Founded: 1970. **Staff:** Prof 1; Other 1. **Subjects:** Education, politics, religion, economic development, town history, folklore. **Holdings:** 2618 books; 62 bound periodical volumes; 300 folders (cataloged); 339 volumes of town annual reports; 96 folders of Connecticut dissertations and theses; 24

maps and prints. **Subscriptions:** 40 journals and other serials. **Services:** Interlibrary loans; copying; library open to public. **Publications:** Series in Connecticut History (list available on request). **Special Indexes:** Punched card index to all holdings.

EASTERN ENVIRONMENTAL RADIATION LAB
See: Environmental Protection Agency

★3969★
EASTERN KENTUCKY UNIVERSITY - JOHN GRANT CRABBE LIBRARY (Educ)
     Phone: (606) 622-3606
Richmond, KY 40475   Ernest E. Weyhrauch, Dean of Libs.
Founded: 1906. **Staff:** Prof 28; Other 60. **Subjects:** Humanities, nursing, education, law enforcement. **Special Collections:** ERIC; Learning Resources Center; government documents. **Holdings:** 681,045 books and bound periodical volumes; 682,208 microfiche; 30,905 microprint; 28,633 reels of microfilm. **Subscriptions:** 3535 journals and other serials; 111 newspapers. **Services:** Interlibrary loans; copying; library open to public with restrictions. **Computerized Information Services:** DIALOG, BRS; computerized cataloging. **Networks/Consortia:** Member of OCLC through SOLINET. **Publications:** Newsletters and subject bibliographies. **Staff:** Kenneth Barksdale, Acq.Libn.; June Martin, Circ.Libn.; Rebecca Turner, Ref.Libn.; Miko Pattie, Cat.; Marilee Gabbard, LRC Libn.; Sharon Marsh, Doc. Libn.; Genevieve J. Clay, Per.Libn.

★3970★
EASTERN KENTUCKY UNIVERSITY - JOHN GRANT CRABBE LIBRARY - JOHN WILSON TOWNSEND ROOM (Hist)
     Phone: (606) 622-7348
Richmond KY 40475   Sharon McConnell, Libn.
Staff: Prof 1; Other 1. **Subjects:** Kentucky and Kentuckians, genealogy. **Special Collections:** Kentucky collection of autographed first editions by Kentuckians or about Kentucky. **Holdings:** 15,000 books; 310 bound periodical volumes; 24 VF drawers of manuscripts; 18 VF drawers of clippings; 277 reels of microfilm; 2498 sheets of microprint; 6597 microfiche. **Subscriptions:** 26 journals and other serials. **Services:** Copying; room open to public for reference use only.

★3971★
EASTERN KENTUCKY UNIVERSITY - LAW ENFORCEMENT LIBRARY (Soc Sci)
Stratton Bldg.   Phone: (606) 622-5234
Richmond, KY 40475   Verna Casey, Libn.
Founded: 1975. **Staff:** Prof 1; Other 2. **Subjects:** Law enforcement, fire science, traffic safety, criminal law. **Holdings:** 11,638 books and bound periodical volumes; 201 theses; 9319 microfiche; 110 reels of microfilm. **Subscriptions:** 139 journals and other serials. **Services:** Interlibrary loans; copying; library open to public. **Computerized Information Services:** Computerized cataloging. **Networks/Consortia:** Member of OCLC through SOLINET.

★3972★
EASTERN KENTUCKY UNIVERSITY - MUSIC LIBRARY (Mus)
     Phone: (606) 622-4944
Richmond, KY 40475   Elizabeth K. Baker, Libn.
Founded: 1969. **Staff:** Prof 1; Other 11. **Subjects:** Music. **Holdings:** 11,253 books; 597 bound periodical volumes; 6771 recordings; 477 tapes; 601 reels of microfilm; 818 microfiche. **Subscriptions:** 65 journals and other serials. **Services:** Interlibrary loans. **Computerized Information Services:** Access to online systems. **Networks/Consortia:** Member of OCLC through SOLINET.

★3973★
EASTERN MAINE MEDICAL CENTER - HEALTH SCIENCES LIBRARY (Med)
489 State St.   Phone: (207) 947-3711
Bangor, ME 04401   Jean S. Doty, Libn.
Staff: Prof 5; Other 3. **Subjects:** Medicine, surgery, obstetrics/gynecology, pediatrics, orthopedics, neurology. **Special Collections:** Nursing School Collection; Alcohol Abuse Collection. **Holdings:** 3528 book titles; 6754 bound periodical volumes; 5 VF drawers of archive material. **Subscriptions:** 435 journals and other serials. **Services:** Interlibrary loans; copying; library open to public with fee charged for services. **Computerized Information Services:** MEDLARS, BRS, DIALOG. **Networks/Consortia:** Member of Health Science Library and Information Cooperative of Maine (HSLIC). **Staff:** Suellen Jagels, Asst.Libn.; Catherine L. Smith, Asst.Libn.; Margaret C. Speirs, Asst.Libn.; Margene Fennell, Asst.Libn.; Lucy Butler, Asst.Libn.

★3974★

EASTERN MENNONITE COLLEGE - MENNO SIMONS HISTORICAL LIBRARY AND ARCHIVES (Hist)

Harrisonburg, VA 22801

Phone: (703) 433-2771
Grace Showalter, Libn.

Founded: 1943. **Staff:** Prof 2. **Subjects:** Anabaptist and Mennonite history, German culture in Eastern United States, history of the Shenandoah Valley, genealogy. **Holdings:** 14,796 volumes; 237 reels of microfilm; 214 microfiche; 433 reels of magnetic tape; 287 linear feet of manuscript and archival material; 63 VF drawers and 42 linear feet of general files. **Subscriptions:** 180 journals and other serials; 12 newspapers. **Services:** Interlibrary loans (limited); copying (limited); library open to public for reference use only. **Computerized Information Services:** Computerized cataloging. **Networks/Consortia:** Member of OCLC through SOLINET. **Publications:** Historical Library Bulletin, irregular. **Staff:** Lois B. Bowman, Asst.

★3975★

EASTERN MICHIGAN UNIVERSITY - CENTER OF EDUCATIONAL RESOURCES - ARCHIVES/SPECIAL COLLECTIONS (Soc Sci)

Ypsilanti, MI 48197

Phone: (313) 487-3423
Margaret Eide, Act.Archv.

Staff: Prof 1; Other 1. **Subjects:** History of Eastern Michigan University and of education. **Holdings:** 1025 linear feet and 171 VF drawers of university publications, photographs, transcripts of oral history tapes, correspondence, papers and ephemera. **Networks/Consortia:** Member of Michigan Library Consortium through University Library.

★3976★

EASTERN MICHIGAN UNIVERSITY - CENTER OF EDUCATIONAL RESOURCES - GOVERNMENT DOCUMENTS COLLECTION (Soc Sci)

Ypsilanti, MI 48197

Phone: (313) 487-2280
Clare Beck, Govt.Doc.Libn.

Staff: Prof 1; Other 1. **Subjects:** U.S. government and population, economics, education, health, social conditions. **Special Collections:** U.S. government publications, selective depository. **Holdings:** 134,059 documents. **Networks/Consortia:** Member of Michigan Library Consortium through University Library.

★3977★

EASTERN MICHIGAN UNIVERSITY - CENTER OF EDUCATIONAL RESOURCES - INSTRUCTIONAL MATERIALS CENTER (Educ)

Ypsilanti, MI 48197

Phone: (313) 487-0490
Margaret Best, Libn.

Staff: Prof 1; Other 1. **Subjects:** Instructional materials for examination and use by students in education. **Holdings:** 11,052 items including pamphlets, posters, media kits, curriculum units and textbooks. **Networks/Consortia:** Member of Michigan Library Consortium through University Library.

★3978★

EASTERN MICHIGAN UNIVERSITY - CENTER OF EDUCATIONAL RESOURCES - MAP LIBRARY (Geog-Map)

Ypsilanti, MI 48197

Phone: (313) 487-3191
Joanne Hansen, Sci. & Tech.Libn.

Staff: Prof 1; Other 1. **Subjects:** Cartography. **Holdings:** 35,161 maps; atlases. **Networks/Consortia:** Member of Michigan Library Consortium through University Library.

★3979★

EASTERN MONTANA COLLEGE - LIBRARY - SPECIAL COLLECTIONS (Hist)

1500 N. 30th St.
Billings, MT 59101

Phone: (406) 657-2262
Ed Neroda, Dir., Lib.Serv.

Special Collections: Custer Collection (formerly held at Custer Battlefield National Monument; 100 volumes, 71 boxes); Dora C. White Memorial Collection (local correspondence and works, Billings and Yellowstone County; 3100 volumes, 700 pictures and photographs); federal and Montana documents (154,365). **Services:** Interlibrary loans; copying; library open to public. **Computerized Information Services:** BRS; computerized cataloging, acquisitions and serials. **Networks/Consortia:** Member of Pacific Northwest Bibliographic Center (PNBC); WLN.

★3980★

EASTERN NEBRASKA GENEALOGICAL SOCIETY - LIBRARY (Hist)

Box 541
Fremont, NE 68025

Phone: (402) 721-9553
Claire Mares, Ed.

Founded: 1971. **Subjects:** Local history, genealogy. **Holdings:** 100 books; genealogies and pedigree sheets. **Subscriptions:** 100 journals and other serials. **Services:** Library open to public for reference use only. **Publications:** Roots and Leaves, quarterly. **Special Catalogs:** 1885 census of Dodge County, Nebraska (card); obituary file of local area (card); all Dodge County cemeteries (microfilm). **Special Indexes:** History of Czechs in Nebraska; Special Index and Compilation on Czech Settlers in Nebraska, 1879; 1885 Census - Dodge, Saunders and Washington Counties (card); 1902 Dodge County Plat Atlas; 1885 Mortality Schedule for Burt, Colfax, Cuming, Dodge, Rural Douglas, Saunders and Washington Counties (book); marriage records from beginning of county to 1900 for Dodge, Cuming and Washington Counties; Indexes to 1870 Nebraska Census of Dodge and Washington Counties (card); Index to Nebraska cemeteries of Colfax, Saunders, and Washington Counties (microfilm and card).

★3981★

EASTERN NEW MEXICO UNIVERSITY - GOLDEN LIBRARY (Hum)

Portales, NM 88130

Phone: (505) 562-2624
Peggy M. Tozer, Lib.Dir.

Staff: Prof 9; Other 14. **Subjects:** Liberal arts and sciences, fine arts, education, business administration. **Special Collections:** Science fiction (5000 volumes, 43.5 cubic feet of archives); Roosevelt County, New Mexico history (75 cubic feet of papers, 6353 photographs, 3500 slides, 750 cassette tapes, 164 newspaper titles); University Archives (521 cubic feet); educational film library (4500 titles); instructional media (textbooks, study guides, psychological tests). **Holdings:** 194,164 books; 41,142 bound periodical volumes; 376,877 microforms; 154,229 government documents; 4500 educational films; 34,667 non-print items. **Subscriptions:** 1220 journals and other serials; 50 newspapers. **Services:** Interlibrary loans; library open to public. **Computerized Information Services:** Computerized cataloging. **Networks/Consortia:** Member of OCLC through AMIGOS Bibliographic Council, Inc. **Staff:** Cecil Clotfelter, Asst.Dir.Tech.Serv.; Mary Jo Walker, Spec.Coll.; Laura McGuire, Doc.Libn.; Edward Richter, Hd.Ref.Libn.; Mary Lee Moris, Cat.Libn.; Laurie Eagleson, Cat.Libn.; Wanda Graham, AV Dir.; Jackson Carter, Ser.Libn.; Gloria Townsend, ILL; Leo Tormes, Film Lib.Dir.

★3982★

EASTERN OREGON HOSPITAL AND TRAINING CENTER - PROFESSIONAL LIBRARY (Med)

Box A
Pendleton, OR 97801

Phone: (503) 276-1711

Founded: 1919. **Subjects:** Mental health and retardation. **Holdings:** 1700 volumes. **Subscriptions:** 10 journals and other serials. **Services:** Library open to public with permission from the superintendent of the hospital.

★3983★

EASTERN ORTHODOX CATHOLIC CHURCH IN AMERICA - CIMARRON HEIGHTS LIBRARY (Rel-Theol)

Rt. 1, Paradise Valley
Coyle, OK 73027

Phone: (405) 466-3960
Kay Adair, Libn.

Staff: 3. **Subjects:** Eastern Orthodox theology, patristics, Biblical theology, liturgics, Byzantine music, philosophy, psychology, homiletics, Roman Catholic theology, Anglican theology. **Special Collections:** Monumentae Musicae Byzantinae - 11th through 17th century Byzantine music manuscripts on microfilm (100). **Holdings:** 12,000 books; 5000 bound periodical volumes; 300 microfilms (cataloged); 3000 unbound periodicals; 1000 leaflets, pamphlets; 500 phonograph recordings. **Subscriptions:** 12 journals and other serials. **Services:** Interlibrary loans; library open to public with restrictions. **Formerly:** Its Three Hierarchs Seminary Library.

EASTERN PENNSYLVANIA MENNONITE HISTORICAL LIBRARY
See: Mennonite Historical Library of Eastern Pennsylvania

EASTERN PENNSYLVANIA PSYCHIATRIC INSTITUTE
See: Medical College of Pennsylvania

★3984★

EASTERN SHORE HOSPITAL CENTER - PROFESSIONAL LIBRARY (Med)

R.D. 1
Box 800
Cambridge, MD 21613

Phone: (301) 228-0800
Estella C. Clendaniel, Supv., Lib. & Files

Founded: 1953. **Staff:** 1. **Subjects:** Psychiatry, medicine, nursing. **Holdings:** 2647 books; 303 bound periodical volumes; 4 VF drawers of pamphlets. **Subscriptions:** 35 journals and other serials. **Services:** Interlibrary loans; copying; library open to public with restrictions. **Computerized Information Services:** MEDLARS. **Networks/Consortia:** Member of Maryland Association of Health Science Librarians. **Remarks:** Maintained by Maryland State Department of Health & Mental Hygiene.

EASTERN STATE HOSPITAL LIBRARY (Medical Lake, WA)
See: Washington State Library - Eastern State Hospital Library

★3985★

EASTERN STATE HOSPITAL - PROFESSIONAL LIBRARY (Med)
Drawer A
Williamsburg, VA 23185
Phone: (804) 253-5457
Barbara Dike, Lib.Asst.
Founded: 1942. **Staff:** 1. **Subjects:** Psychiatry, psychology, medicine, nursing. **Special Collections:** Library of John Minson Galt II, M.D. **Holdings:** 3824 books; 151 bound periodical volumes; 410 AV items. **Subscriptions:** 68 journals and other serials. **Services:** Interlibrary loans; copying; library open to public for reference use only.

★3986★

EASTERN STATE HOSPITAL - RESOURCE LIBRARY (Med)†
627 W. Fourth St.
Lexington, KY 40508
Phone: (606) 255-1431
Juanita H. Morrill, Libn.
Staff: 1. **Subjects:** Psychiatry, psychology, psychiatric nursing and social work, community and public health, medicine. **Holdings:** 2000 books; 200 bound periodical volumes. **Subscriptions:** 64 journals and other serials. **Services:** Interlibrary loans (fee); copying; library not open to public.

★3987★

EASTERN STATE SCHOOL AND HOSPITAL - STAFF LIBRARY (Med)
3740 Lincoln Hwy.
Trevose, PA 19047
Phone: (215) 671-3389
Elizabeth Sorg, Libn.
Founded: 1963. **Staff:** Prof 1; Other 1. **Subjects:** Child psychiatry, nursing, psychology, social services, special education, pediatrics. **Holdings:** 2770 books; 194 bound periodical volumes; 59 dissertations; 1740 ERIC microfiche; 87 pamphlets. **Subscriptions:** 100 journals and other serials. **Services:** Interlibrary loans; copying; library open to public for reference use only. **Networks/Consortia:** Member of Delaware Valley Information Consortium (DEVIC).

EASTERN TOWNSHIP HISTORICAL SOCIETY
See: Societe d'Histoire des Cantons de l'Est

★3988★

EASTERN VIRGINIA MEDICAL SCHOOL - MOORMAN MEMORIAL LIBRARY (Med)
700 Olney Rd.
Box 1980
Norfolk, VA 23501
Phone: (804) 446-5845
Anne Cramer, Dir.
Staff: Prof 5; Other 9. **Subjects:** Medicine, allied health sciences, behavioral sciences. **Holdings:** 11,564 books; 26,965 bound periodical volumes. **Subscriptions:** 1046 journals and other serials. **Services:** Interlibrary loans; copying; library open to public. **Computerized Information Services:** BRS, MEDLARS; computerized cataloging and ILL. **Networks/Consortia:** Member of SOLINET. **Publications:** INFORM (newsletter), monthly; BAVIT: Biomedical Audiovisuals in Tidewater. **Staff:** Richard J. Harris, Tech.Serv.Libn.; Kerrie Shaw, Ref.Libn.; Ethel Pollock, Ref.Libn.; Jane Pellegrino, Community Prog.Coord.

★3989★

EASTERN WASHINGTON STATE HISTORICAL SOCIETY - LIBRARY (Hist)
Cheney Cowles Memorial Museum
W. 2316 First Ave.
Spokane, WA 99204
Phone: (509) 456-3931
Douglas A. Olson, Libn.
Staff: Prof 1. **Subjects:** History of the Inland Empire with emphasis on the Spokane area; Pacific Northwest history; Indian history and ethnology; fur traders; explorers; geology; fine arts. **Special Collections:** Photographs, including early photography, tintypes and prints; manuscripts (1500 feet). **Holdings:** 5600 books; 185 bound periodical volumes; 40 VF drawers of pamphlets and newspaper clippings; 700 oral history tapes; 31 one-hour videotapes; 3 music tapes; 9 reels of microfilm; 12 drawers of maps; 25,000 photographs; 645 manuscripts and records; 70,000 Expo '74 and AV files. **Subscriptions:** 59 journals and other serials. **Services:** Interlibrary loans (limited); copying; library open to public. **Publications:** Libbys' Spokane: A Visual Retrospect, 1980. **Special Indexes:** Pacific Northwesterner Index, vols. 1-20 (1957-1966).

★3990★

EASTERN WASHINGTON UNIVERSITY - INSTRUCTIONAL MEDIA CENTER (Educ)
Cheney, WA 99004
Phone: (509) 359-2265
Jerome S. Donen, Dir.
Staff: Prof 6; Other 6. **Subjects:** Instructional media, teaching-learning resources. **Holdings:** Filmstrips; 8 and 16mm films; audio cassettes; videotapes; slides. **Services:** Center open to public.

★3991★

EASTERN WASHINGTON UNIVERSITY - MUSIC LIBRARY (Mus)†
Music Bldg.
Cheney, WA 99004
Phone: (509) 359-7843
Karen Olson, Hd.
Founded: 1950. **Staff:** Prof 1; Other 3. **Subjects:** Music. **Holdings:** 6000 phonograph records; 7000 scores (cataloged). **Services:** Library open to public.

EASTMAN ARBITRATION LIBRARY
See: American Arbitration Association

★3992★

EASTMAN DENTAL CENTER - BASIL G. BIBBY LIBRARY (Med)
625 Elmwood Ave.
Rochester, NY 14620
Phone: (716) 275-5010
June Glaser, Libn.
Staff: 2. **Subjects:** Dentistry. **Holdings:** 2650 books; 4200 bound periodical volumes. **Subscriptions:** 146 journals and other serials. **Services:** Interlibrary loans; library open to public by appointment. **Computerized Information Services:** MEDLARS. **Networks/Consortia:** Member of Rochester Regional Research Library Council (RRRLC); Rochester Area Libraries in Healthcare. **Publications:** EDC Library Gazette, quarterly.

EASTMAN (George) HOUSE
See: International Museum of Photography at George Eastman House

★3993★

EASTMAN KODAK COMPANY - BUSINESS INFORMATION CENTER (Bus-Fin)
343 State St.
Rochester, NY 14650
Phone: (716) 724-3041
M. Lois Gauch, Libn.
Founded: 1926. **Staff:** Prof 1; Other 3. **Subjects:** General business, photography. **Holdings:** 7000 books. **Subscriptions:** 300 journals and other serials; 6 newspapers. **Services:** Interlibrary loans; copying; center not open to public. **Computerized Information Services:** Online systems; computerized cataloging and circulation. **Networks/Consortia:** Member of Rochester Regional Research Library Council (RRRLC). **Publications:** What's New List, monthly - for internal distribution only.

★3994★

EASTMAN KODAK COMPANY - COLORADO DIVISION - ENGINEERING AND INFORMATION SERVICES LIBRARY (Sci-Tech)
Bldg. CS02A
Windsor, CO 80551
Phone: (303) 686-7611
Audrey Hoover, Libn.
Founded: 1970. **Staff:** 1. **Subjects:** Engineering, construction. **Holdings:** 750 books. **Subscriptions:** 40 journals and other serials. **Services:** Library not open to public.

★3995★

EASTMAN KODAK COMPANY - EASTMAN CHEMICALS DIVISION - RESEARCH LIBRARY (Sci-Tech)
Box 511
Kingsport, TN 37662
Phone: (615) 229-3870
Michael W. Ubaldini, Res.Libn.
Founded: 1944. **Staff:** Prof 2; Other 6. **Subjects:** Organic chemistry, polymer chemistry, physics, textiles. **Holdings:** 35,000 volumes; 150 VF drawers of patents; 10 VF drawers of pamphlets; 150 VF drawers of microfilm. **Subscriptions:** 750 journals and other serials. **Services:** Interlibrary loans; copying; library open to public for reference use with approval. **Computerized Information Services:** Computerized serials and circulation. **Publications:** New Acquisitions, bimonthly. **Staff:** M. Gail Preslar, Asst.Res.Libn.

★3996★

EASTMAN KODAK COMPANY - ENGINEERING LIBRARY (Sci-Tech)
Kodak Park Division, Bldg. 23
Rochester, NY 14650
Phone: (716) 722-2356
Raymond W. Curtin, Libn.
Founded: 1948. **Staff:** Prof 1; Other 3. **Subjects:** Engineering - chemical, civil, electrical, environmental, electronic, mechanical, structural. **Holdings:** 3500 books; 35 shelves of bound periodical volumes; 12,000 manufacturers' catalogs (cataloged); 15,000 microfiche of standards, law and codes; 2 visual search microfilm file services. **Subscriptions:** 463 journals and other serials. **Services:** Interlibrary loans; copying; library open to professionals by appointment. **Computerized Information Services:** DIALOG, SDC. **Networks/Consortia:** Member of Rochester Regional Research Library Council (RRRLC). **Publications:** Quarterly Report - for internal distribution only. **Special Catalogs:** Union Book Catalog (microfiche); Union Subscription list (computer printout) - with company libraries; Engineering Library Periodical Holdings.

★3997★

EASTMAN KODAK COMPANY - HEALTH, SAFETY AND HUMAN FACTORS LABORATORY - LIBRARY (Med)
Kodak Park Division, Bldg. 320
Rochester, NY 14650
Phone: (716) 458-1000
Rita B. Stack, Libn.
Founded: 1952. **Staff:** Prof 1; Other 4. **Subjects:** Toxicology, occupational medicine, environmental hygiene, biochemistry. **Holdings:** 8000 books and government publications; 5000 bound periodical volumes. **Subscriptions:** 365 journals and other serials. **Services:** Interlibrary loans; copying; library open to public by appointment. **Computerized Information Services:** DIALOG, SDC, NLM; computerized cataloging. **Networks/Consortia:** Member of Rochester Regional Research Library Council (RRRLC); Rochester Area Libraries in Healthcare.

★3998★

EASTMAN KODAK COMPANY - KODAK APPARATUS DIVISION - LIBRARY (Sci-Tech)
901 Elmgrove Rd.
Rochester, NY 14650
Phone: (716) 726-2127
Marie Jean Bonn, Supv.Libn.
Founded: 1944. **Staff:** Prof 2; Other 3. **Subjects:** Engineering, chemistry, physics, electronics, materials, mathematics, metallurgy, metallography, optics, photography, plastics, finishes, aerospace, industrial management, systems. **Special Collections:** Medical Library. **Holdings:** 19,000 books; 1500 bound periodical volumes; 3000 pamphlets; 1500 Company reports; 6000 government documents; 2500 standards; 2000 codes, microfilms, microfiche. **Subscriptions:** 750 journals and other serials; 5 newspapers. **Services:** Interlibrary loans; copying; library open to public by advance request to Industrial Relations Department. **Computerized Information Services:** DIALOG, SDC; computerized cataloging, acquisitions and serials. **Publications:** Technical Information Services Listing Booklet; Recent Additions Bulletin, monthly; periodical listings, semiannual. **Special Catalogs:** Book catalog (microfiche; updated monthly). **Staff:** Jeffrey C. Yu, Libn.

★3999★

EASTMAN KODAK COMPANY - MANAGEMENT SERVICES - LIBRARY (Sci-Tech)
Kodak Park, Bldg. 56
Rochester, NY 14650
Phone: (716) 722-1184
Deborah Mourey, Libn.
Staff: Prof 1; Other 3. **Subjects:** Industrial engineering, computer science, statistics, behavorial science. **Holdings:** 6000 books; 150 bound periodical volumes. **Subscriptions:** 210 journals and other serials; 10 newspapers. **Services:** Interlibrary loans; copying; SDI; library not open to public. **Computerized Information Services:** DIALOG, BRS, SDC, New York Times Information Service, Institute for Scientific Information (Compumath); computerized acquisitions, serials and circulation. **Networks/Consortia:** Member of Rochester Regional Research Library Council; Monroe County Library System. **Publications:** MSD Library Newsletter; Computer and Information Systems Newsletter, both monthly - both for internal distribution only.

★4000★

EASTMAN KODAK COMPANY - PHOTOGRAPHIC TECHNOLOGY DIVISION - LIBRARY (Sci-Tech)
Kodak Park Division
Rochester, NY 14650
Phone: (716) 722-2341
Ruth H. Donoghue, Supv., Info.Serv.
Founded: 1948. **Staff:** 2. **Subjects:** Chemistry, physics, mathematics, color photography, color science, color vision, psychology of vision. **Holdings:** 3000 books; 34,000 microforms. **Subscriptions:** 300 journals and other serials. **Services:** Interlibrary loans; copying; library not open to public. **Computerized Information Services:** Computerized cataloging and acquisitions. **Networks/Consortia:** Member of Rochester Regional Research Library Council (RRRLC).

★4001★

EASTMAN KODAK COMPANY - RESEARCH LIBRARY (Sci-Tech)
Kodak Park, Bldg. 83
Rochester, NY 14650
Phone: (716) 722-2723
Elizabeth W. Kraus, Info.Assoc./Lib.Mgr.
Founded: 1912. **Staff:** Prof 6; Other 12. **Subjects:** Photography, chemistry, physics. **Special Collections:** Old photographic books and journals. **Holdings:** 37,000 books; 85,000 bound periodical volumes; 6000 microfilmed articles; 9000 translations; 32,000 external research reports on microfiche. **Subscriptions:** 1200 journals and other serials. **Services:** Interlibrary loans; copying; library open to public by appointment. **Computerized Information Services:** DIALOG, SDC, BRS, NEXIS, New York Times Information Service; computerized cataloging, acquisitions and serials. **Networks/Consortia:** Member of Rochester Regional Research Library Council (RRRLC). **Publications:** Research Library Bulletin. **Special Catalogs:** Microfiche catalog for books. **Staff:** Clare Freund, Cat.; Marcia B. McDugle, Per.Libn.; Mary Connolly, Ref.Libn.; Barbara Brockman, Tech.Proc./Circ.; Ardelle Kocher, Ref.Libn.

★4002★

EASTMAN KODAK COMPANY - TENNESSEE EASTMAN COMPANY - BUSINESS LIBRARY (Bus-Fin)
Box 511
Kingsport, TN 37662
Phone: (615) 229-2071
Sandra H. Boyd, Lib.Asst.
Founded: 1947. **Staff:** 2. **Subjects:** Business, economics, statistics. **Holdings:** 2500 volumes. **Subscriptions:** 250 journals and other serials. **Services:** Library not open to public.

★4003★

EASTMAN KODAK COMPANY - TEXAS EASTMAN COMPANY - BUSINESS LIBRARY (Bus-Fin)
Box 7444
Longview, TX 75607
Phone: (214) 757-6611
Carol Kinsey, Bus.Libn.
Founded: 1973. **Staff:** Prof 1. **Subjects:** Business. **Holdings:** 1200 books. **Subscriptions:** 102 journals and other serials; 11 newspapers. **Services:** Interlibrary loans; copying; library open to public with restrictions.

★4004★

EASTMAN KODAK COMPANY - TEXAS EASTMAN COMPANY - RESEARCH & DEVELOPMENT LIBRARY (Sci-Tech)†
Box 7444
Longview, TX 75607
Phone: (214) 236-5000
Jack T. Buchanan, Res.Libn.
Staff: Prof 1. **Subjects:** Chemistry and chemical engineering. **Holdings:** 10,000 books. **Subscriptions:** 400 journals and other serials. **Services:** Interlibrary loans; library open to public with restrictions.

EASTMAN MEMORIAL FOUNDATION - LAUREN ROGERS LIBRARY AND MUSEUM OF ART
See: Lauren Rogers Library and Museum of Art

EASTMAN SCHOOL OF MUSIC
See: University of Rochester

★4005★

EASTMINSTER PRESBYTERIAN CHURCH - LIBRARY (Rel-Theol)
106 N. Riverside Dr.
Indialantic, FL 32903
Phone: (305) 723-8371
Gratia Richman, Libn.
Staff: 4. **Subjects:** Religion. **Holdings:** 3000 volumes. **Services:** Library open to public.

★4006★

EASTMORELAND GENERAL HOSPITAL - HEALTH SCIENCES LIBRARY (Med)
2900 S.E. Steele St.
Portland, OR 97202
Phone: (503) 234-0411
Ann H. Haines, Med.Libn.
Subjects: Osteopathic medicine, medicine, nursing. **Holdings:** 489 books; 119 bound periodical volumes; 510 cassette tapes; 17 slide-tape kits. **Subscriptions:** 68 journals and other serials. **Services:** Interlibrary loans; copying; SDI; library open to public with librarian's permission. **Computerized Information Services:** MEDLINE. **Networks/Consortia:** Member of Oregon Health Information Network (OHIN); Portland Area Health Sciences Librarians.

★4007★

EASTON HOSPITAL - MEDICAL LIBRARY (Med)
21st & Lehigh Sts.
Easton, PA 18042
Phone: (215) 250-4130
Mary James, Libn.
Staff: Prof 1. **Subjects:** Medicine and related fields. **Holdings:** 910 books; 3410 bound periodical volumes. **Subscriptions:** 167 journals and other serials. **Services:** Interlibrary loans. **Networks/Consortia:** Member of Cooperating Hospital Libraries of the Lehigh Valley Area.

★4008★

EATON CORPORATION - AIL DIVISION - RESEARCH LIBRARY (Sci-Tech)
Walt Whitman Rd.
Melville, NY 11747
Phone: (516) 595-4400
Laurel D. Meyerhoff, Libn.
Founded: 1945. **Staff:** Prof 1; Other 3. **Subjects:** Electronics, navigation, space science, antennas, aircraft landing systems. **Holdings:** 28,000 books; 8000 bound periodical volumes; company project reports. **Subscriptions:** 200 journals and other serials. **Services:** Interlibrary loans; copying; literature searching; library open to public with restrictions; security clearance is required. **Computerized Information Services:** DIALOG. **Networks/Consortia:** Member of Long Island Library Resources Council (LILRC). **Publications:** Library Bulletin, semimonthly.

★4009★

EATON CORPORATION - CORPORATE LIBRARY
100 Erieview Plaza
Cleveland, OH 44114
Defunct

★4010★
EATON CORPORATION - CUTLER-HAMMER LIBRARY (Sci-Tech)
4201 N. 27th St.
Box 463-464
Milwaukee, WI 53201
Phone: (414) 449-7679
Herbert J. Seuss, Libn.
Founded: 1960. **Staff:** Prof 2. **Subjects:** Electric control, control systems, electrical/electronic engineering, management. **Holdings:** 4473 books; 450 vendor catalogs; 25 journals on microfilm from 1955; 4791 subject classifications in vertical file; 450 internal reports. **Subscriptions:** 277 journals and other serials. **Services:** Interlibrary loans; copying; SDI; library open to public by appointment. **Computerized Information Services:** DIALOG, Dow Jones News Retrieval; New York Times Information Service; computerized cataloging. **Networks/Consortia:** Member of Library Council of Metropolitan Milwaukee. **Publications:** CIS News, monthly; Table of Contents, weekly - company-wide distribution. **Special Catalogs:** Vendor File on cards. **Remarks:** Maintains a Technical Information Center at 4265 N. 30th St., Milwaukee, WI. **Staff:** Ardyce Milton, Asst.Libn.

★4011★
EATON CORPORATION - ENGINEERING & RESEARCH CENTER LIBRARY (Sci-Tech)
Box 766
Southfield, MI 48037
Phone: (313) 354-6979
Mary E. Montgomery, Res.Libn.
Staff: Prof 1; Other 1. **Subjects:** Automotive and mechanical engineering, metallurgy. **Holdings:** 2000 books; 1500 bound periodical volumes; 75 VF drawers of internal reports, federal government reports, clippings, translations. **Subscriptions:** 402 journals and other serials. **Services:** Interlibrary loans (limited); copying; SDI; library open by referral. **Computerized Information Services:** DIALOG, SDC, New York Times Information Service, BRS. **Networks/Consortia:** Member of Wayne Oakland Region of Interlibrary Cooperation. **Publications:** 30 Minutes a Day, monthly listing of acquisitions - for internal distribution only. **Remarks:** Library is located at 26201 Northwestern Hwy., Southfield, MI 48076.

★4012★
EBASCO SERVICES, INC. - INFORMATION CENTER/LIBRARY (Sci-Tech)
2 World Trade Ctr., 92nd Fl.
New York, NY 10048
Phone: (212) 839-2021
Veronica C. Pidala, Lib./Rec.Adm.
Staff: Prof 1; Other 2. **Subjects:** Engineering - power, nuclear, utilities; environmental services; consulting services; finance. **Special Collections:** Water Supply Papers, 1966-1974 (by state). **Holdings:** 12,500 volumes. **Subscriptions:** 400 journals and other serials. **Services:** Interlibrary loans; library open to public by appointment only. **Computerized Information Services:** DIALOG, SDC, Dun & Bradstreet; computerized serials.

★4013★
EBERSTADT (F.) AND COMPANY - BUSINESS LIBRARY (Bus-Fin)
61 Broadway
New York, NY 10006
Phone: (212) 480-0807
Mrs. Pat Salandy, Libn.
Founded: 1972. **Staff:** Prof 1; Other 1. **Subjects:** Investment banking, investment research, chemicals, data processing. **Holdings:** 500 books; 71 cabinets of VF items. **Subscriptions:** 300 journals and other serials; 13 newspapers. **Services:** Interlibrary loans; copying; library not open to public. **Special Catalogs:** Corporate Catalog (card); periodical catalog (card).

ECCLES (Spencer S.) HEALTH SCIENCES LIBRARY
See: University of Utah - Spencer S. Eccles Health Sciences Library

ECCLESIASTICAL PROVINCE OF BRITISH COLUMBIA AND DIOCESE OF NEW WESTMINSTER
See: Anglican Church of Canada

ECHOLS (John M.) COLLECTION ON SOUTHEAST ASIA
See: Cornell University - John M. Echols Collection on Southeast Asia

ECKHART LIBRARY
See: University of Chicago

★4014★
ECOLE DES HAUTES ETUDES COMMERCIALES DE MONTREAL - BIBLIOTHEQUE (Bus-Fin)
5255 Decelles Ave.
Montreal, PQ, Canada H3T 1V6
Phone: (514) 343-4481
Rodolphe Lavergne, Chf.Libn.
Founded: 1916. **Staff:** Prof 11; Other 31. **Subjects:** Human management, finance, marketing, advertising, production management, accounting, auditing, business economics, quantitative methods, operation research, human organization, industrial relations. **Holdings:** 130,000 books; 90,000 bound periodical volumes; 3000 reels of microfilm. **Subscriptions:** 4300 journals and other serials. **Services:** Interlibrary loans; copying; library open to public with restrictions on borrowing. **Computerized Information Services:** DIALOG, SDC; computerized circulation. **Publications:** New Acquisitions, monthly. **Special Catalogs:** Catalogue of periodicals (computer). **Remarks:** An affiliate of the Universite de Montreal. **Staff:** Vasile Tega, Ref.Libn.; Louise Goulet, Chf. of Cat.Dept.; Gerald Boudreau, Chf. of Acq.Dept.

ECOLE NATIONALE D'ADMINISTRATION PUBLIQUE
See: Universite du Quebec

★4015★
ECOLE POLYTECHNIQUE - BIBLIOTHEQUE (Sci-Tech)
C.P. 6079, Succursale A
Montreal, PQ, Canada H3C 3A7
Phone: (514) 344-4847
Roger Bonin, Dir.
Founded: 1873. **Staff:** Prof 6; Other 24. **Subjects:** Engineering. **Holdings:** 98,014 books; 235,300 bound periodical volumes; 45,000 reports (cataloged); 28,000 pamphlets (uncataloged); 48,500 maps; 13,500 reels of microfilm. **Subscriptions:** 2310 journals and other serials. **Services:** Interlibrary loans; copying; SDI; library open to public with restrictions. **Computerized Information Services:** CAN/OLE, SDC, DIALOG, QUESTEL; computerized cataloging. **Publications:** Acquisitions List, monthly; Library Guide, annual; Periodical List. **Remarks:** An affiliate of the Universite de Montreal. **Staff:** Olivier Paradis, Proc.Libn.; Claire Pelletier, Acq.Libn.; Josee Schepper, Ref.Libn.

★4016★
ECOLOGY CENTER - LIBRARY (Env-Cons; Energy)†
2701 College Ave.
Berkeley, CA 94705
Phone: (415) 548-2221
Michael Austin, Coord.
Founded: 1969. **Staff:** 1. **Subjects:** Solid waste, energy, San Francisco Bay area environment, air pollution, water resources, land use planning. **Special Collections:** Solid Waste Management. **Holdings:** 4000 volumes including Environmental Impact Review (EIR) documents, monographs; 34 bound periodical volumes; 20 vertical files. **Subscriptions:** 34 journals and other serials. **Services:** Copying; library open to public for reference use only; members may borrow. **Publications:** Ecology Center Newsletter, monthly - available to members and by subscription. **Special Indexes:** Indexes of books and periodicals (card).

★4017★
ECOLOGY CENTER OF SOUTHERN CALIFORNIA (Env-Cons; Energy)
P.O. Box 35473
Los Angeles, CA 90035
Phone: (213) 559-9160
Nancy Pearlman, Exec.Dir.
Founded: 1972. **Staff:** Prof 1. **Subjects:** Environment, ecological education, pollution, land use, resources, wildlife, population, urban affairs, planning, energy, waste, open space. **Special Collections:** Environmental impact reports; city, county and federal plans and programs documents. **Holdings:** 50 books; 3000 unbound magazines; 50 booklets and pamphlets; 5000 informational sheets and newsletters; VF drawers; simulation games, posters, items; 275 cassettes of weekly radio show, "Environmental Directions." **Subscriptions:** 125 magazines and newsletters. **Services:** Reference materials open to public on request. **Publications:** The Compendium, bimonthly newsletter listing environmental activities in Los Angeles and Orange Counties; 1982 Directory of Environmental Organizations, 7th edition, a comprehensive list of international, national, state, county and city groups; reprints of weekly newspaper column "Special Environmental Report." **Remarks:** Project of Educational Communications, Inc. (nonprofit). Holdings are decentralized; materials available from committee coordinators and at selected libraries, galleries and educational centers in Southland.

★4018★
ECOLOGY & ENVIRONMENT, INC. - LIBRARY (Env-Cons)
195 Sugg Rd.
Box D
Buffalo, NY 14225
Phone: (716) 632-4491
Theresa L. Wolfe, Info.Spec.
Staff: 1. **Subjects:** Environment and ecology. **Holdings:** 5500 books. **Subscriptions:** 130 journals and other serials. **Services:** Library not open to public.

ECONOMIC COUNCIL OF CANADA
See: Canada - Economic Council of Canada

★4019★
ECONOMICS LABORATORY, INC. - CORPORATE INFORMATION CENTER (Sci-Tech)
Osborn Bldg.
St. Paul, MN 55102
Phone: (612) 451-5651
D.M. Sontag Bradt, Mgr.
Founded: 1947. **Staff:** Prof 3; Other 2. **Subjects:** Organic and surfactant chemistry, water pollution and treatment, dairy and food processing technology. **Holdings:** 18,000 books; 800 bound periodical volumes; 15 VF

drawers of patents; 4 VF drawers of government reports; 10 VF drawers of corporate and public information reports. **Subscriptions:** 667 journals and other serials. **Services:** Copying; center open to professionals in allied subject fields. **Computerized Information Services:** DIALOG, SDC, BRS, Pergamon International Information Corporation, CAS Online, Information Handling Services, CHEMSHARE; computerized cataloging and circulation. **Staff:** K.J. Hayes-Clabots, Libn.; D.A. Neuburger, Chem.Info.Spec.; N.A. Fenton, Asst.Libn.

★4020★
ECONOMICS RESEARCH ASSOCIATES - LIBRARY (Plan)†
10960 Wilshire Blvd. Phone: (213) 477-9585
Los Angeles, CA 90024 Barbara J. Thompson, Libn.
Founded: 1968. **Staff:** Prof 1; Other 1. **Subjects:** Real estate development, land use, housing, recreation, tourism, urban affairs. **Holdings:** 750 books; 50 bound periodical volumes; 2000 government publications (cataloged); 5000 internal reports; 75 VF drawers of geographic data; 20 VF drawers of newspaper clippings and brochures. **Subscriptions:** 504 journals and other serials. **Services:** Interlibrary loans (limited); copying.

★4021★
ECUMENICAL FORUM OF CANADA - LIBRARY (Rel-Theol)
11 Madison Ave. Phone: (416) 924-9351
Toronto, ON, Canada M5R 2S2
Founded: 1921. **Subjects:** Missions, ecumenics, development. **Holdings:** 10,000 books; 240 bound periodical volumes; 50 boxes of pamphlets on missions and ecumenics; 7 VF drawers of other pamphlets. **Subscriptions:** 130 journals and other serials. **Services:** Interlibrary loans; library open to qualified persons.

★4022★
ECUMENICAL LIBRARY (Rel-Theol)
475 Riverside Dr., Rm. 1372 Phone: (212) 870-3600
New York, NY 10115 Betty Ljungberg, Libn.
Founded: 1978. **Staff:** Prof 1. **Subjects:** Missions, theology, social issues, ecumenical relations. **Special Collections:** H. Paul Douglass Collection of Religious Research Reports (2000); Denominational Yearbooks (1000). **Holdings:** 10,000 books; 50 file drawers of pamphlets and clippings. **Subscriptions:** 125 journals and other serials. **Services:** Interlibrary loans; copying; library open to public by appointment. **Remarks:** Created in 1978 by the merger of the Research Library of the National Council of Churches with the United Mission Library of the United Methodist and United Presbyterian Churches. This library is administered by an ecumenical committee composed of representatives of the Interchurch Center, the National Council of Churches and agencies of the United Methodist and United Presbyterian churches.

★4023★
EDDY (E.B.) FOREST PRODUCTS, LTD. - LIBRARY (Sci-Tech)
P.O. Box 600
Hull, PQ, Canada J8X 3Y7 J.D. Hall, Mgr., R & D
Founded: 1946. **Staff:** 1. **Subjects:** Pulp and paper manufacture, physics, chemistry. **Holdings:** 800 volumes. **Subscriptions:** 100 journals and other serials. **Services:** Library not open to public.

EDEN ARCHIVES
See: Evangelical and Reformed Historical Society

★4024★
EDEN HISTORICAL SOCIETY - TOWN HISTORIAN'S OFFICE AND HISTORICAL SOCIETY LIBRARY (Hist)
8584 S. Main St. Phone: (716) 992-9141
Eden, NY 14057 Nathalie B. Leonard, Town Hist./Cur.
Staff: 1. **Subjects:** Local history and genealogy. **Holdings:** 300 books; 30 scrapbooks; 8 boxes of deeds, tax records, road warrants, tavern licenses, school district records; 10 photograph albums; 11 drawers of local history and genealogy files; 110 reels of microfilm. **Subscriptions:** 15 journals and other serials. **Services:** Copying; library open to public by appointment. **Special Indexes:** Indexes to town records, church records, scrapbooks, daybooks, histories of town, 1847-1851 vital records, original deeds, cemetery inscriptions, death notices, gazetteers (card). **Remarks:** The library is jointly maintained by the town of Eden and the Eden Historical Society.

★4025★
EDEN THEOLOGICAL SEMINARY - LIBRARY (Rel-Theol)
475 E. Lockwood Phone: (314) 961-3627
Webster Groves, MO 63119 Rev. Warren R. Mehl, Libn.
Founded: 1850. **Staff:** Prof 6; Other 9. **Subjects:** Religion, philosophy, theology. **Special Collections:** Reformed Church history and catechisms. **Holdings:** 59,561 books; 7531 bound periodical volumes. **Subscriptions:**

275 journals and other serials; 5 newspapers. **Services:** Interlibrary loans; copying; library open to public. **Networks/Consortia:** Member of OCLC. **Staff:** Marilyn Berra, Circ.Supv.; Betty Brookes, AV; Rose Brady, Circ.; Elaine Harvey, Acq.Libn.; Anne Moedritzer, Ref.Libn.; Maya Grauch, Acq.Asst.; Emilia Rogers, Acq.Asst.; Eunice Hayes, Acq.Asst.; Mahala Cox, Curric.Libn.; Jane Kropa, Cat.Libn.

★4026★
EDGEWATER BAPTIST CHURCH - LIBRARY (Rel-Theol)
5501 Chicago Ave. Phone: (612) 827-3803
Minneapolis, MN 55417 Gordon Krantz, Libn.
Subjects: Religion. **Holdings:** 800 books; tapes, records, flannelgraphs. **Services:** Library not open to public.

★4027★
EDGEWATER HOSPITAL - MEDICAL LIBRARY (Med)
5700 N. Ashland Ave. Phone: (312) 878-6000
Chicago, IL 60660 Laura Wimmer, Dir., Lib.Serv.
Staff: Prof 1. **Subjects:** Internal medicine, cardiology, surgery, orthopedics, obstetrics. **Holdings:** 800 books; 2500 bound periodical volumes; 250 Audio Digest tapes. **Subscriptions:** 90 journals and other serials. **Services:** Interlibrary loans; copying; library open to public. **Networks/Consortia:** Member of Metropolitan Consortium; Regional Medical Library - Region 3; ILLINET. **Publications:** Periodicals Holding List, annual.

★4028★
EDGEWOOD COLLEGE - MAUDE WEBSTER MIDDLETON NURSING LIBRARY (Med)
1010 Mound St. Phone: (608) 267-6313
Madison, WI 53715 Vicki Schluge, Instr.Rsrcs.Mgr.
Founded: 1926. **Staff:** Prof 1; Other 5. **Subjects:** Nursing, education, management, patient education. **Holdings:** 2100 books; 390 bound periodical volumes; 542 assorted AV items; pamphlets. **Subscriptions:** 65 journals and other serials. **Services:** Interlibrary loans; copying; library open to nursing staff and students. **Computerized Information Services:** MEDLINE; computerized cataloging. **Networks/Consortia:** Member of Southern Wisconsin Health Science Library Consortia; Consortia of Health Audiovisual Resources of Madison (CHARM). **Publications:** From the Stacks, monthly. **Formed by the Merger of:** Madison General Hospital - Nursing Education and Edgewood College.

EDIE (Lionel D.) AND COMPANY, INC.
See: Lionel D. Edie and Company, Inc.

EDINBORO STATE COLLEGE - ANTHROPOLOGY DEPARTMENT - FORT LE BOEUF MUSEUM
See: Pennsylvania State Historical & Museum Commission - Fort Le Boeuf Museum

★4029★
EDINBORO STATE COLLEGE - BARON-FORNESS LIBRARY (Educ)
  Phone: (814) 732-2780
Edinboro, PA 16444 Saul Weinstein, Dir.
Founded: 1867. **Staff:** Prof 16; Other 9. **Subjects:** Art, history, literature. **Special Collections:** Southeast Asia; Erie Indians; curriculum materials. **Holdings:** 290,300 books; 50,650 bound periodical volumes; 30,110 government documents (U.S., Pennsylvania and U.N.); 946,147 microforms. **Subscriptions:** 2080 journals and other serials; 25 newspapers. **Services:** Interlibrary loans; copying; SDI; library open to public with restrictions. **Computerized Information Services:** Computerized cataloging and circulation. **Networks/Consortia:** Member of OCLC through Pittsburgh Regional Library Center; Northwest Interlibrary Cooperative of Pennsylvania; Council of Pennsylvania State College & University Library Directors (COPSCAULD). **Staff:** John Fleming, Spec.Coll.Libn.; Susan Hennip, ILL.

★4030★
EDISON ELECTRIC INSTITUTE - LIBRARY (Energy)
1111 19th St., N.W. Phone: (202) 828-7520
Washington, DC 20036 Ethel Tiberg, Mgr.Lib.Serv.
Founded: 1917. **Staff:** Prof 3; Other 3. **Subjects:** Electric utilities, legislation, regulations, statistics, economics, environment. **Holdings:** 11,035 volumes; 1045 bound periodical volumes; 143 VF drawers; government documents; technical reports. **Subscriptions:** 605 journals and other serials. **Services:** Interlibrary loans; use of library for reference use may be requested. **Computerized Information Services:** SDC, New York Times Information Service, DOE/RECON, BRS; computerized routing. **Staff:** Susan Farkas, Gen.Ref.Libn.; Jo Yellis, Leg.Libn.

EDISON INSTITUTE
See: Henry Ford Museum and Greenfield Village

EDISON NATL. HISTORIC SITE
See: U.S. Natl. Park Service

★4031★
EDITOR & PUBLISHER - LIBRARY (Publ)
575 Lexington Ave.　　　　　　Phone: (212) 752-7050
New York, NY 10022　　　　　　　　Beth Scott, Libn.
Founded: 1884. **Staff:** Prof 1; Other 1. **Subjects:** Daily newspaper field. **Holdings:** 500 books; bound volumes of Editor & Publisher, 1900 to present; 200 reels of microfilms. **Subscriptions:** 90 journals and other serials; 10 newspapers. **Services:** Interlibrary loans; copying; library open to public by appointment. **Special Indexes:** Periodical index (card).

★4032★
EDMONTON ART GALLERY - REFERENCE LIBRARY (Art)
2 Sir Winston Churchill Sq.　　　Phone: (403) 429-6781
Edmonton, AB, Canada T5J 2C1　　　Brenda Banks, Libn.
Staff: Prof 1; Other 1. **Subjects:** Contemporary art and artists (including Canadian); art history; art education. **Special Collections:** Old exhibition catalogs, 1900-1950 (20). **Holdings:** 6650 books and bound periodical volumes; 8500 slides; 45 videotapes; 7 drawers of clippings of artist biographical information; 2 drawers of photographs of art; 40 annual reports; 40 press releases from other galleries; 272 microfiche. **Subscriptions:** 41 journals and other serials. **Services:** Interlibrary loans; copying; library open to public for reference use only.

★4033★
EDMONTON CITY ARCHIVES (Hist)
10105 112th Ave.　　　　　　Phone: (403) 479-2069
Edmonton, AB, Canada T5G 0H1　Helen LaRose, Supv., Archv.
Founded: 1973. **Staff:** 5. **Subjects:** Alberta and Edmonton history. **Holdings:** 3000 books; 120 City of Edmonton reports; 2500 pamphlets and maps; 10,000 photographs; city records; manuscripts; plans. **Subscriptions:** 11 journals and other serials. **Services:** Copying; archives open to public for reference use only. **Staff:** John McIsaac, Asst.Archv.

★4034★
EDMONTON CITY PLANNING DEPARTMENT - LIBRARY/RESOURCE CENTRE (Plan)
11th Fl., Phipps-McKinnon Bldg.
10020 101A Ave.　　　　　　Phone: (403) 428-2665
Edmonton, AB, Canada T5J 3G2　　　Coreen Douglas, Libn.
Staff: 1. **Subjects:** Planning, land use and resources, housing and urban renewal, land economics, social and economic planning, public administration and finance, transportation. **Holdings:** 5000 books; 33 volumes of aerial photographs; newspaper clippings for 1980-1982. **Subscriptions:** 125 journals and other serials; 10 newspapers. **Services:** Interlibrary loans; copying; library open to public for reference use only. **Special Indexes:** KWOC index to document collection.

★4035★
EDMONTON GENERAL HOSPITAL - HEALTH SCIENCES LIBRARY (Med)
11111 Jasper Ave.　　　　　　Phone: (403) 482-8301
Edmonton, AB, Canada T5K 0L4　　Jake Vande Brink, Hd.Libn.
Founded: 1970. **Staff:** Prof 1; Other 2. **Subjects:** Medicine, nursing, geriatrics. **Holdings:** 4031 books; 1441 bound periodical volumes; 300 audio cassettes. **Subscriptions:** 192 journals and other serials. **Services:** Interlibrary loans; copying; library open to health care professionals. **Computerized Information Services:** MEDLINE. **Publications:** Medical and Nursing Update, monthly.

★4036★
EDMONTON JOURNAL - LIBRARY (Publ)†
101st St. & 100th Ave.
Box 2421
Edmonton, AB, Canada T5J 2S6　　Phone: (403) 420-1919
　　　　　　　　　　　　　　　Patricia Garneau, Libn.
Founded: 1903. **Staff:** Prof 1; Other 8. **Subjects:** Current events. **Holdings:** 500 volumes; clippings and photographs; microfilm of the newspaper from 1903 to present. **Services:** Copying; library not open to public. **Computerized Information Services:** INFO-KY (internal database). **Special Indexes:** Index of newspaper clippings.

★4037★
EDMONTON POWER - LIBRARY (Sci-Tech; Energy)
10250 101st St., Suite 700　　　Phone: (403) 428-4302
Edmonton, AB, Canada T5J 3P4　　　Ronald Friesen, Libn.
Founded: 1972. **Staff:** Prof 1; Other 1. **Subjects:** Electrical and electronics engineering; power transmission and distribution; energy resources and conservation; electric lighting; accounting; management; city planning. **Holdings:** 2000 books; 400 bound periodical volumes; 850 reports and documents; 420 manufacturers' catalogs; 900 standards; 3 VF drawers of technical papers. **Subscriptions:** 225 journals and other serials. **Services:** Interlibrary loans; copying; SDI; library open to public by appointment. **Computerized Information Services:** SDC. **Special Indexes:** Manufacturers' catalogs indexed by subject and manufacturer. **Remarks:** Edmonton Power is a department of the city of Edmonton.

★4038★
EDMONTON PUBLIC SCHOOL BOARD - LEARNING RESOURCES PROFESSIONAL LIBRARY (Educ)
10010 107A Ave.　　　　　　Phone: (403) 429-5621
Edmonton, AB, Canada T5H 0Z8　　　Marilyn Elliott, Libn.
Founded: 1961. **Staff:** Prof 1; Other 2. **Subjects:** Education. **Special Collections:** Elementary and junior high school display collection (2268 books); curriculum guides (400). **Holdings:** 12,310 books; 184 bound periodical volumes; 208 dissertations; 13 drawers of pamphlets; 100 unbound reports; 1009 microfiche. **Subscriptions:** 347 journals and other serials. **Services:** Interlibrary loans; library not open to public. **Computerized Information Services:** SPIRES. **Publications:** New Editions, monthly listing of recent materials received.

EDMONTON SCHOOL FOR AUTISTIC CHILDREN
See: Alberta Society for Autistic Children - Library

★4039★
EDMONTON SEPARATE SCHOOL BOARD - PROFESSIONAL LIBRARY (Educ; Rel-Theol)
9807 106th St.　　　　　　　Phone: (403) 429-7631
Edmonton, AB, Canada T5K 1C2　　　C. Hornby, Res.Libn.
Staff: 2. **Subjects:** Education, Catholicism. **Holdings:** 5000 books. **Subscriptions:** 200 journals and other serials. **Services:** Library not open to public.

★4040★
EDMONTON SOCIAL SERVICES DEPARTMENT - LIBRARY (Soc Sci)
CN Tower, 6th Fl.
10004 104th Ave.　　　　　　Phone: (403) 428-5927
Edmonton, AB, Canada T5J 0K1
Staff: Prof 1; Other 1. **Subjects:** Social services, welfare services, social and urban planning, community organization, poverty, preventive social service. **Holdings:** 775 books and bound periodical volumes. **Subscriptions:** 30 journals and other serials; 20 newspapers. **Services:** Library not open to public.

★4041★
EDMONTON SUN - NEWSPAPER LIBRARY (Publ)
9405 50th St.　　　　　　　Phone: (403) 468-5111
Edmonton, AB, Canada T6B 2T4　　　John M. Sinclair, Libn.
Founded: 1978. **Staff:** Prof 1; Other 5. **Subjects:** Current affairs. **Special Collections:** Commonwealth Games, 1978 (2 drawers of clippings; brochures, pamphlets, books); Wayne Gretzky, Edmonton Oilers and Edmonton Eskimos clippings and photographs. **Holdings:** 60 books; 225,000 clippings; all editions of Edmonton Sun on microfilm. **Subscriptions:** 16 journals and other serials. **Services:** Copying; library not open to public. **Publications:** Edmonton Sun on microfilm, monthly.

★4042★
EDMUNDSON (Jennie) MEMORIAL HOSPITAL - LIBRARY (Med)
933 E. Pierce St.　　　　　　Phone: (712) 328-6130
Council Bluffs, IA 51501　　　Patricia A. Blanchard, Libn.
Founded: 1959. **Staff:** Prof 1; Other 1. **Subjects:** Nursing, medicine, paramedicine, hospital literature. **Holdings:** 8655 books; 2421 bound periodical volumes; 19 VF drawers of pamphlets and clippings; AV materials. **Subscriptions:** 169 journals and other serials. **Services:** Interlibrary loans; copying; library open to public for reference use only. **Computerized Information Services:** MEDLINE, BRS. **Networks/Consortia:** Member of Regional Medical Library - Region 3. **Publications:** Orientation Manual; Annual Report; Library Newsletter; AV catalog. **Remarks:** An alternate telephone number is (712) 328-6203.

★4043★
EDO CORPORATION - ENGINEERING LIBRARY (Sci-Tech)
14-04 111th St.   Phone: (212) 445-6000
College Point, NY 11356   Robin I. Praver, Libn.
Founded: 1939. Staff: Prof 1; Other 2. Subjects: Electronics, underwater acoustical equipment, sonar, hydrodynamics, hydrofoils, fluid mechanics. Holdings: 4800 books; 120 VF drawers of documents and over 6500 documents on microfiche (cataloged); 1350 filmstrips; 1288 film reels; 48 VF drawers of company reports; 400 Vugraphs. Subscriptions: 80 journals and other serials. Services: Interlibrary loans; library open to public with restrictions. Computerized Information Services: New England Research Application Center, DIALOG.

★4044★
EDUCATIONAL BROADCASTING CORPORATION - THIRTEEN RESEARCH
    LIBRARY (Info Sci)
356 W. 58th St.   Phone: (212) 560-3063
New York, NY 10019   Victoria A. Dawson, Mgr.
Founded: 1972. Staff: Prof 1; Other 2. Subjects: Current events. Special Collections: MacNeil/Lehrer Report printed index and microfiche; Thirteen viewer guides from 1972 to present. Holdings: 2318 books; 932 bound periodical volumes; 216 VF drawers of news clippings; 1935 reels of microfilmed newspapers. Subscriptions: 200 journals and other serials; 17 newspapers. Services: Interlibrary loans; copying; library not open to public. Computerized Information Services: New York Times Information Service. Staff: Harriett Obus, Ref.

EDUCATIONAL COMMUNICATIONS, INC. - ECOLOGY CENTER OF
    SOUTHERN CALIFORNIA
See: Ecology Center of Southern California

★4045★
EDUCATIONAL FILM LIBRARY ASSOCIATION - LIBRARY AND
    INFORMATION CENTER (Aud-Vis)
43 W. 61st St., 9th Fl.   Phone: (212) 246-4533
New York, NY 10023   Maryann Chach, Film Ref.Libn.
Staff: Prof 1; Other 1. Subjects: Educational and theatrical film, library and school media. Holdings: 2000 books; 144 linear feet of clippings; educational film card file (20,000 entries). Subscriptions: 150 journals and newsletters. Services: Copying; library open to public with restrictions. Publications: Sightlines, quarterly; EFLA Bulletin, quarterly. Special Indexes: 16mm Distribution Handbook; filmographies. Staff: Nadine Covert, Exec.Dir.

★4046★
EDUCATIONAL FOUNDATION FOR HUMAN SEXUALITY - HARRY A.
    SPRAGUE LIBRARY (Soc Sci)
Montclair State College
Valley Rd. & Normal Ave.   Phone: (201) 893-4000
Upper Montclair, NJ 07043   Blanche Haller, Dir., Lib.Serv.
Founded: 1967. Subjects: Human sexuality, sex education, research in human sexuality, marriage and the family, world population, black-white relations, aging and death. Holdings: 2500 books; 200 bound periodical volumes; 4000 reprints; 10 VF drawers of clippings; 17 films; 70 sound filmstrip sets; miscellaneous tapes, microfilm and slide sets.

★4047★
EDUCATIONAL RECORDS BUREAU - LIBRARY (Educ)
Bardwell Hall
37 Cameron St.   Phone: (617) 235-8920
Wellesley, MA 02181   R. Bruce McGill, Pres.
Subjects: Educational testing. Holdings: 500 books; 500 research reports; 1 million test scores. Services: Library open to qualified persons with permission only.

★4048★
EDUCATIONAL RESEARCH SERVICE - LIBRARY (Educ)
1800 N. Kent St.   Phone: (703) 243-2100
Arlington, VA 22209   Josephine Franklin, Coord., Info.Serv.
Founded: 1973. Staff: Prof 9; Other 1. Subjects: Educational administration, policy and practices; school management. Holdings: 3500 books; 11,000 reports, booklets and documents; 224 file drawers of journal articles, clippings and newsletters. Subscriptions: 140 journals and other serials. Services: Copying; library open to public with restrictions. Computerized Information Services: Online systems. Publications: ERS Bulletin, monthly (September-June) - by subscription; ERS Information Aids; ERS Reports; ERS Research Briefs; ERS Monographs; ERS School Research Forum - all available for sale. Staff: Jocelyn Petrov, Asst.Coord., Info.Serv.

EDUCATIONAL RESOURCES INFORMATION CENTER CLEARINGHOUSE
See: ERIC Clearinghouse

★4049★
EDUCATIONAL TESTING SERVICE - CARL CAMPBELL BRIGHAM LIBRARY
    (Soc Sci)
Rosedale Rd.   Phone: (609) 921-9000
Princeton, NJ 08541   Janet Williams, Libn.
Staff: Prof 2; Other 3. Subjects: Psychology, education, psychometrics. Special Collections: College catalogs. Holdings: 16,200 books; 10,000 bound periodical volumes; 6000 technical reports (cataloged). Subscriptions: 400 journals and other serials. Services: Interlibrary loans; copying; library open to public for reference use only. Computerized Information Services: DIALOG; computerized cataloging. Networks/Consortia: Member of RLG. Publications: Pamphlets on library and literature search services. Special Catalogs: Periodical holdings (punched cards). Special Indexes: KWOC Index to technical reports (punched cards). Staff: Adrienne Richter, Assoc.Libn.; Hinda Greenberg, Assoc.Libn.

EDUCATIONAL TESTING SERVICE - ERIC CLEARINGHOUSE ON TESTS,
    MEASUREMENT AND EVALUATION
See: ERIC Clearinghouse on Tests, Measurement and Evaluation

★4050★
EDUCATIONAL TESTING SERVICE - TEST COLLECTION (Educ)
Rosedale Rd.   Phone: (609) 734-5686
Princeton, NJ 08541   Marilyn Halpern, Hd., Test Coll.
Staff: Prof 1; Other 3. Subjects: Educational tests; measurement instruments; achievement and aptitude tests; interest and aptitude tests; sensory-motor tests; vocational tests. Special Collections: Tests (11,000), many with accompanying manuals. Holdings: 200 test publishers' catalogs; 550 tests on microfiche; 3000 reels of microfilm of tests. Services: Library open to public with restrictions. Publications: News on Tests, 10/year - by subscription; Tests in Microfiche, annual - by request. Special Indexes: Annotated bibliographies listing tests by type or subject (200).

★4051★
EDUCOM, INTERUNIVERSITY COMMUNICATIONS COUNCIL, INC. - LIBRARY
    (Educ)
Rosedale Rd.
Box 364   Phone: (609) 921-7575
Princeton, NJ 08540   Eleanor G. Sayles, Libn.
Staff: Prof 1; Other 1. Subjects: Computer applications in academic organizations. Holdings: Over 300 documents and research reports. Services: Library not open to public. Networks/Consortia: EDUCOM is a nonprofit consortium of over 360 colleges, universities, and educational service organizations with an interest and involvement in the use of computers and communications technology in higher education. It also promotes sharing of resources in these areas by annual conferences and seminars, and by consulting activities. Two activities of EDUCOM are EDUNET, a national computing network for higher education and research and EFPM, the EDUCOM Financial Planning Model - a computer-based interactive model-building system. Publications: EDUCOM, Bulletin of the Interuniversity Communications Council Inc., quarterly; list of other publications available on request. Special Indexes: Subject Index of the Bulletin, 1965-1975; Author/ Title Index annually.

★4052★
EDWARD-DEAN MUSEUM ART REFERENCE LIBRARY (Art)
9401 Oak Glen Rd.   Phone: (714) 845-2626
Cherry Valley, CA 92223   Jan Holmlund, Dir.
Founded: 1964. Staff: Prof 1; Other 1. Subjects: Furniture, decorative arts, sculpture, architecture, costume design, history. Holdings: 1200 books. Services: Library open to public by special permission. Remarks: Maintained by Riverside County Art & Culture Center, Edward-Dean Museum of Decorative Arts.

EDWARDS AIR FORCE BASE (CA)
See: U.S. Air Force Base - Edwards Base Library; U.S. Air Force - Flight
    Test Center

★4053★
EDWARDS (Jacob) LIBRARY (Sci-Tech)
236 Main St.   Phone: (617) 764-2544
Southbridge, MA 01550   Ronald B. Latham, Dir.
Staff: Prof 2; Other 12. Special Collections: Dirlam Collection on whaling and the Arctic; local history; McNitt Collection of Fine Printing. Holdings: 46,644 books; 291 bound periodical volumes. Subscriptions: 222 journals and other serials; 17 newspapers. Services: Interlibrary loans; copying; library open to

public. **Computerized Information Services:** Computerized cataloging and circulation. **Networks/Consortia:** Member of Central Massachusetts Regional Library System. **Staff:** Evelyn Petrelli, Asst.Libn.

EDWARDS (Ward) LIBRARY
See: Central Missouri State University - Ward Edwards Library

EEOC
See: U.S. Equal Employment Opportunity Commission

EFFIGY MOUNDS NATL. MONUMENT
See: U.S. Natl. Park Service

★4054★
EG&G, INC. - CORPORATE HEADQUARTERS - BUSINESS & FINANCIAL REFERENCE LIBRARY (Bus-Fin)
45 William St.   Phone: (617) 237-5100
Wellesley, MA 02181   Raymond J. Champoux
Founded: 1970. **Staff:** Prof 1; Other 1. **Subjects:** Business reference. **Holdings:** 50 books; 50 bound periodical volumes; 500 credit reports. **Subscriptions:** 95 journals and other serials; 5 newspapers. **Services:** Library open to public by specific request.

★4055★
EG&G, INC. - IDAHO NATIONAL ENGINEERING LABORATORY - INEL TECHNICAL LIBRARY (Sci-Tech; Energy)
Box 1625   Phone: (208) 526-1195
Idaho Falls, ID 83415   Brent N. Jacobsen, Lib.Supv.
Founded: 1952. **Staff:** Prof 4; Other 7. **Subjects:** Nuclear energy and technology, metallurgy and material science, chemistry and chemical engineering, alternative energy sources, physics, fluid mechanics and heat transfer, engineering, mathematics and computer science. **Special Collections:** U.S. Dept. of Energy Reports (550,000); power reactor docket information (150,000 items on microfiche). **Holdings:** 33,000 books; 11,600 bound periodical volumes; 650,000 research and development report titles. **Subscriptions:** 475 journals and other serials. **Services:** Interlibrary loans; copying; library open to public with restrictions. **Computerized Information Services:** DIALOG, SDC, BRS, DOE/RECON; computerized cataloging, acquisitions, serials and circulation. **Publications:** Library Service Notes, monthly - local distribution. **Special Catalogs:** Book Catalogs of the INEL Technical Library; Technical Journals at the INEL; The INEL Technical Library (brochure). **Remarks:** EG&G, Inc. operates under contract to the U.S. Department of Energy. **Staff:** George B. Stultz, Acq./Cat.; David P. Klepich, Hd., Tech.Serv.; Heather M. Redding, Ref.Libn.

★4056★
EG&G, INC. - MASON RESEARCH INSTITUTE - LIBRARY (Med)
57 Union St.   Phone: (617) 791-0931
Worcester, MA 01608   Evelyn M. Brann, Libn.
Founded: 1956. **Staff:** Prof 1. **Subjects:** Carcinogenesis (invitro and invivo), mutagenesis, toxicology, pathology, immunobiology, endocrinology, reproductive physiology, biochemistry, computer software, tissue culture, veterinary medicine. **Special Collections:** Bioassay data on 3000 steroids. **Holdings:** 1700 books; 2100 bound periodical volumes; 20,500 reprints; 10,650 unbound reports; 1500 staff personal publications; 5000 pamphlets and reprints (uncataloged). **Subscriptions:** 48 journals and other serials. **Services:** Interlibrary loans; copying; literature searching; abstracting; library open to public for reference use only. **Networks/Consortia:** Member of Central Massachusetts Health Related Libraries. **Publications:** Bibliographies of scientific work on the dog.

★4057★
EG&G, INC. - SANTA BARBARA DIVISION - LIBRARY (Energy)
130 Robin Hill Rd.
Box 98   Phone: (805) 967-0456
Goleta, CA 93117   Richard H. Clow, Libn.
Founded: 1960. **Staff:** Prof 1. **Subjects:** Nuclear science, electronics, energy. **Holdings:** 4500 books; 700 bound periodical volumes; 2500 technical reports; 25,000 reports on microfiche; 90 reels of microfilm. **Subscriptions:** 50 journals and other serials. **Services:** Interlibrary loans; copying; library not open to public. **Computerized Information Services:** DIALOG, SDC.

★4058★
EG&G, INC. - TECHNICAL LIBRARY (Energy)†
680 E. Sunset Rd.
Box 1912   Phone: (702) 734-8181
Las Vegas, NV 89101   Anna Lee Kaighn, Libn.
Founded: 1955. **Staff:** Prof 1; Other 1. **Subjects:** Electronic engineering, physics, nuclear energy, photography, electricity, management, environmental studies, computer languages. **Holdings:** 10,000 books; 1500 bound periodical volumes; 2000 reports (cataloged); 10 VF drawers of patents, clippings, pamphlets and reprints; 60 films. **Subscriptions:** 225 journals and other serials. **Services:** Interlibrary loans; library open for limited research only.

★4059★
EG&G, INC. - WASHINGTON ANALYTICAL SERVICES CENTER - INFORMATION CENTER (Sci-Tech)
2150 Fields Rd.   Phone: (301) 840-3243
Rockville, MD 20850   Vanessa R.L. Schroader, Mgr.
Staff: Prof 14; Other 3. **Subjects:** Electrical engineering, acoustics, physics, mathematics, oceanography, environmental sciences. **Holdings:** 1050 books; 155 bound periodical volumes; 4200 military specifications and standards; 380 technical reports on energy; 440 visual search microfilm files. **Subscriptions:** 135 journals and other serials; 24 newspapers. **Services:** Interlibrary loans; center not open to public. **Computerized Information Services:** Computerized cataloging. **Publications:** Engineering Information Bulletin. **Staff:** Dick Golemboski, Supv., Info. Center; Janet Tkaczyk, Supv., Data Banks; Maria Shih, Supv., Res./Ref.; Carol Suthard, Hd., Marketing Serv.

EGLIN AIR FORCE BASE (FL)
See: U.S. Air Force Base - Eglin Base Library

EHRENKRANTZ (Edward) LIBRARY
See: Temple Sharey Tefilo - Edward Ehrenkrantz Library

EHRMAN (Frederick L.) MEDICAL LIBRARY
See: New York University Medical Center - Frederick L. Ehrman Medical Library

EIELSON AIR FORCE BASE (AK)
See: U.S. Air Force Base - Eielson Base Library

EIMAC DIVISION - TECHNICAL LIBRARY
See: Varian Associates

★4060★
EIMCO PROCESS EQUIPMENT COMPANY - TECHNICAL LIBRARY (Env-Cons)
Box 300   Phone: (801) 526-2492
Salt Lake City, UT 84110
Founded: 1976. **Staff:** 1. **Subjects:** Water treatment, waste management, solid/liquid separation technology. **Special Collections:** Manufacturers' catalogs. **Holdings:** 1550 books; 500 bound periodical volumes; 500 documents; 40 VF drawers of technical files. **Subscriptions:** 105 journals and other serials. **Services:** Interlibrary loans; library open to public with restrictions. **Publications:** The Clarifier - for internal distribution only. **Formerly:** Eimco PMD Technology & Development.

EINSTEIN (Albert) COLLEGE OF MEDICINE
See: Yeshiva University - Albert Einstein College of Medicine

★4061★
EINSTEIN (Albert) MEDICAL CENTER - MT. SINAI-DAROFF DIVISION - MEDICAL LIBRARY (Med)
5th & Reed Sts.   Phone: (215) 465-1100
Philadelphia, PA 19147   Rena E. Hawes, Lib.Dir.
Founded: 1932. **Staff:** Prof 1. **Subjects:** Medicine. **Holdings:** 2075 books; 2856 bound periodical volumes. **Subscriptions:** 178 journals and other serials. **Services:** Interlibrary loans; copying.

★4062★
EINSTEIN (Albert) MEDICAL CENTER - NORTHERN DIVISION - LURIA MEDICAL LIBRARY (Med)
York & Tabor Roads   Phone: (215) 456-6345
Philadelphia, PA 19141   Marion H. Silverman, Dir.
Founded: 1951. **Staff:** Prof 3; Other 3. **Subjects:** Medicine. **Holdings:** 1500 books; 11,000 bound periodical volumes. **Subscriptions:** 227 journals and other serials. **Services:** Interlibrary loans; copying; library open to public for reference use only with identification. **Computerized Information Services:** MEDLARS. **Networks/Consortia:** Member of Mideastern Regional Medical Library Service (MERMLS).

★4063★

EINSTEIN (Albert) MEDICAL CENTER - SCHOOL OF NURSING LIBRARY
(Med)
11th & Tabor Rds.   Phone: (215) 329-0700
Philadelphia, PA 19141   Mary M. McCrory, Libn.
Founded: 1954. **Staff:** 2. **Subjects:** Professional nursing, public health,
nursing research, general education, natural and social sciences, medicine,
psychology, religion, hospital economy, biography. **Holdings:** 4300 volumes.
200 cassettes and filmstrips. **Subscriptions:** 80 journals and other serials.
Services: Interlibrary loans; copying; library open to public with restrictions.
Also Known As: A.E.M.C. Alumni Library.

EISENBERG MEDICAL STAFF LIBRARY
See: Sinai Hospital of Baltimore, Inc.

EISENHOWER (D.D.) ARMY MEDICAL CENTER
See: U.S. Army Hospitals - D.D. Eisenhower Army Medical Center

EISENHOWER (Dwight D.) LIBRARY
See: U.S. Presidential Libraries - Dwight D. Eisenhower Library

★4064★

EISENHOWER MEDICAL CENTER - WALTER M. LEUTHOLD MEDICAL
LIBRARY (Med)
39000 Bob Hope Dr.   Phone: (714) 340-3911
Rancho Mirage, CA 92270   Jean Atkinson, Chf.Med.Libn.
Founded: 1973. **Staff:** Prof 1; Other 2. **Subjects:** Medicine, health sciences.
Holdings: 4000 books; 4000 bound periodical volumes; 8 VF drawers of
reprints and reports. **Subscriptions:** 305 journals and other serials. **Services:**
Interlibrary loans; copying; library not open to public.

EISENHOWER (Milton S.) LIBRARY
See: Johns Hopkins University - Milton S. Eisenhower Library

EKSTROM LIBRARY
See: University of Louisville - University Archives and Records Center

EL CONGRESO NACIONAL DE ASUNTOS COLEGIALES
See: CONAC

★4065★

EL DORADO COUNTY LAW LIBRARY (Law)
495 Main St.   Phone: (916) 626-2416
Placerville, CA 95667   James Blackford, Lib.Adm.
Staff: 1. **Subjects:** Law - California and federal. **Holdings:** 8100 volumes
Services: Copying; library open to public.

★4066★

EL MONTE HISTORICAL SOCIETY - MUSEUM LIBRARY (Hist)
3100 Tyler Ave.   Phone: (213) 444-3813
El Monte, CA 91733   Lillian Wiggins, Dir.-Cur.
Founded: 1958. **Staff:** Prof 2; Other 12. **Subjects:** History - local and state.
Holdings: 3000 books; manuscripts, photographs, films, diaries.
Subscriptions: 15 journals and other serials; 5 newspapers. **Services:** Library
open to public for reference use only. **Publications:** The Landmark, quarterly.
Staff: Peggy Lowe, Sec.Asst.

★4067★

EL PASO COUNTY LAW LIBRARY (Law)
104 Judicial Bldg.
20 E. Vermijo   Phone: (303) 471-5419
Colorado Springs, CO 80903   Margaret B. Walker, Law Libn.
Staff: Prof 2. **Subjects:** Law - corporate, state, tax, inheritance, labor,
pension plan. **Holdings:** 15,600 volumes. **Services:** Copying; library open to
public. **Staff:** Barbara C. Rainwater, Law Libn.

★4068★

EL PASO COUNTY LAW LIBRARY (Law)
508 City-County Bldg.
500 San Antonio St.
El Paso, TX 79901   Phone: (915) 543-2917
                                         June D. Haggin, Libn.
Founded: 1950. **Staff:** Prof 1; Other 2. **Subjects:** Law. **Holdings:** 24,422
volumes. **Subscriptions:** 49 journals and other serials. **Services:** Interlibrary
loans; copying; library open to public for reference use only.

★4069★

EL PASO HERALD-POST - LIBRARY (Publ)
401 Mills St.   Phone: (915) 747-6950
El Paso, TX 79999   Trinidad B. Acosta, Libn.
Staff: 1. **Subjects:** Newspaper reference topics. **Holdings:** Figures not
available. **Subscriptions:** 12 newspapers. **Services:** Library open to public
with editor's consent.

★4070★

EL PASO NATURAL GAS COMPANY - TECHNICAL INFORMATION CENTER
(Energy)
Box 1492   Phone: (915) 541-3085
El Paso, TX 79978   Anne S. Wise, Coord.
Founded: 1974. **Staff:** Prof 1; Other 2. **Subjects:** Natural gas transmission,
gas industry and technology, alternate fuels, business and economics.
Holdings: 5000 books. **Subscriptions:** 400 journals and other serials.
Services: Interlibrary loans; copying; SDI; center open to public by
appointment. **Computerized Information Services:** DIALOG, SDC.
Publications: Monthly bulletin; serials list, biennial.

★4071★

EL PASO PRODUCTS COMPANY - RESEARCH AND DEVELOPMENT
LIBRARY (Sci-Tech)
Box 3986   Phone: (915) 333-8497
Odessa, TX 79760   R.A. Landis, Info. Chemist
Founded: 1957. **Staff:** Prof 1. **Subjects:** Chemistry, chemical engineering,
marketing research, computer science. **Holdings:** 7000 books; 4000 bound
periodical volumes; 1000 pamphlets; 24 VF drawers of reports; 8 VF drawers
of patents; 4 VF drawers of catalogs; 300 reels of patents on microfilm.
Subscriptions: 150 journals and other serials. **Services:** Interlibrary loans;
copying; SDI; library open to public with permission of head of Research and
Development Department. **Computerized Information Services:** DIALOG,
SDC.

★4072★

EL PASO PUBLIC LIBRARY - GENEALOGY SECTION (Hist; Soc Sci)
501 N. Oregon St.   Phone: (915) 541-4873
El Paso, TX 79901   Jeanne C. Reynolds, Genealogy Libn.
Staff: Prof 1; Other 3. **Subjects:** Genealogy. **Special Collections:** Daughters
of the American Revolution Lineage Books; official records of the Union and
Confederate Armies. **Holdings:** 3850 books; 640 bound periodical volumes; 5
VF drawers; 20 reels of microfilm. **Subscriptions:** 50 journals and other
serials. **Services:** Copying; library open to public. **Computerized Information
Services:** Computerized cataloging. **Networks/Consortia:** Member of OCLC
through AMIGOS Bibliographic Council, Inc.

★4073★

EL PASO PUBLIC LIBRARY - SOUTHWEST RESEARCH COLLECTION (Hist)
501 N. Oregon St.   Phone: (916) 543-3815
El Paso, TX 79901   Mary A. Sarber, Hd.
Staff: Prof 1; Other 2. **Subjects:** El Paso, Texas, New Mexico and Arizona,
Mexican Revolution. **Special Collections:** Aultman Collection (6000 negatives
and prints); Trost Architectural Collection (150 sets of plans, 600
photographs); Rusk-Edwards papers. **Holdings:** 14,000 books; 2500 bound
periodical volumes; 18,000 photographs, negatives and prints; 400
architectural plans; 200 linear feet of archives and manuscripts; 75 VF
drawers. **Subscriptions:** 50 journals and other serials. **Services:** Interlibrary
loans; copying; library open to public.

EL SEGUNDO LIBRARY
See: Hughes Aircraft Company

EL TORO AIR STATION LIBRARY
See: U.S. Marine Corps

ELBEL (Frederick) LIBRARY
See: Northern Indiana Historical Society - Frederick Elbel Library

ELBIN LIBRARY
See: West Liberty State College

★4074★

**ELDORADO NUCLEAR, LTD. - RESEARCH & DEVELOPMENT LIBRARY (Sci-
Tech; Energy)**
400-255 Albert St.   Phone: (613) 238-5222
Ottawa, ON, Canada K1P 6A9   Karen Julian, Chf.Libn.
Founded: 1962. **Staff:** 1. **Subjects:** Metallurgy, uranium, inorganic
chemistry, solvent extraction, zirconium, mining, nuclear energy, mineralogy,
cobalt. **Holdings:** 2200 books; 100 bound periodical volumes; 5080 reports;

120 microfiche; Nuclear Science Abstracts, 1943 to present (complete run). **Subscriptions:** 79 journals and other serials. **Services:** Interlibrary loans; copying; library not open to public. **Publications:** List of periodicals, annual; document accession list, quarterly; New Books, annual - for internal distribution only. **Special Catalogs:** Catalogue of Books (book form).

★4075★
ELECTRIC POWER RESEARCH INSTITUTE - TECHNICAL LIBRARY (Energy)
3412 Hillview Ave.　　　　　　　Phone: (415) 855-2355
Palo Alto, CA 94304　　　　　　Stephen B. Parker, Libn.
Staff: Prof 2; Other 2. **Subjects:** Energy, nuclear engineering, environmental studies, health physics, electric power sources and transmissions, economics. **Special Collections:** U.S. DOE unclassified scientific reports (microfiche); EPRI reports. **Holdings:** 6000 books; 10,000 microfiche; 700 pamphlets; U.S. utility annual reports. **Subscriptions:** 500 journals and other serials; 7 newspapers. **Services:** Interlibrary loans; copying; SDI; library open to public by appointment. **Computerized Information Services:** DIALOG, SDC, DOE/RECON, Ontyme - II; internal database. **Networks/Consortia:** Member of CLASS; CIN; RLIN.

ELECTROMAGNETIC COMPATIBILITY ANALYSIS CENTER
See: IIT Research Institute

ELECTROMAGNETIC SYSTEMS LABORATORIES
See: ESL, Inc./Subsidiary of TRW

★4076★
ELECTRO-MECHANICS COMPANY - LIBRARY
Box 1546
Austin, TX 78767
Defunct

ELECTRONIC PROPERTIES INFORMATION CENTER
See: Purdue University - CINDAS

ELECTRONICS MUSEUM
See: Foothill College

ELECTRONICS PARK LIBRARY
See: General Electric Company

★4077★
ELEUTHERIAN MILLS HISTORICAL LIBRARY (Bus-Fin; Hist)
Greenville
Box 3630　　　　　　　　　　　Phone: (302) 658-2400
Wilmington, DE 19807　　　　Dr. Richmond D. Williams, Lib.Dir.
Founded: 1961. **Staff:** Prof 8; Other 10. **Subjects:** Business, industrial and technological history, French Revolution, explosives, naval history, aeronautics. **Special Collections:** Papers of Du Pont Family (1760-1954) and Company (1802-1915); business and industrial records of over 500 companies in the Mid-Atlantic state area. **Holdings:** 154,000 books, bound periodical volumes, pamphlets and trade catalogs; 18 million manuscripts and archival materials; 9000 microforms; 280,000 photographs, prints, engineering drawings. **Subscriptions:** 220 journals and other serials. **Services:** Interlibrary loans; copying; library open to public. **Computerized Information Services:** Computerized cataloging. **Networks/Consortia:** Member of OCLC through PALINET & Union Library Catalogue of Pennsylvania. **Publications:** Occasional guides to collections and other bibliographical aids. **Special Indexes:** "Optical Incidence" Information Retrieval System for Manuscript Collections; Guide to Manuscripts (1970; 1978 supplement); Pictorial Collections brochure. **Remarks:** This library is part of the Eleutherian Mills-Hagley Foundation, Inc. **Staff:** Heddy A. Richter, Imprints Libn.; Nina Walls, Cat.; Betty P. Low, Res. & Ref.Libn.; Daniel T. Muir, Cur. Pictorial Coll.

★4078★
ELEVENTH BOMBARDMENT GROUP (H) ASSOCIATION - ARCHIVES (Hist)
1106 Maplewood Ave.　　　　　Phone: (603) 436-5835
Portsmouth, NH 03801　　　　　W.M. Cleveland, Hist.
Subjects: Eleventh bombardment group. **Holdings:** 20 books; 5 bound periodical volumes; 35 albums of photographs; 60 cubic feet of unbound combat records, reports, personal narratives, drawings and maps. **Services:** Copying; library open to public. **Publications:** Newsletter, quarterly; Plane Names; Grey Geese Calling; Grey Geese Flyer.

ELFTMAN MEMORIAL LIBRARY
See: Salvation Army School for Officers Training

★4079★
ELGIN MENTAL HEALTH CENTER - ANTON BOISEN PROFESSIONAL LIBRARY (Soc Sci; Med)
750 S. State St.　　　　　　　Phone: (312) 742-1040
Elgin, IL 60120　　　　　　　　Jennifer Ford, Libn.
Staff: Prof 1; Other 3. **Subjects:** Psychology, psychiatry, medicine, social work, nursing. **Holdings:** 4000 books; 649 bound periodical volumes; 400 cassettes. **Subscriptions:** 80 journals and other serials. **Services:** Interlibrary loans; copying; library open to public with restrictions on borrowing. **Networks/Consortia:** Member of Regional Medical Library - Region 3; Fox Valley Health Science Library Consortium; Illinois Department of Mental Health and Developmental Disabilites Library Services Network (DMHDD/LISN). **Publications:** Serials Holdings List, annual. **Remarks:** Maintained by the Illinois State Department of Mental Health & Developmental Disabilities.

★4080★
ELI LILLY AND COMPANY - BUSINESS LIBRARY (Bus-Fin)
307 E. McCarty St.　　　　　　Phone: (317) 261-3241
Indianapolis, IN 46285　　　　Helen E. Loftus, Dept.Hd.
Founded: 1950. **Staff:** Prof 2; Other 3. **Subjects:** Management, marketing, finance, advertising, engineering. **Holdings:** 10,000 books; 65 VF drawers of pamphlets and clippings; annual reports. **Subscriptions:** 900 journals and other serials. **Services:** Interlibrary loans; copying; library open to public with restrictions. **Computerized Information Services:** DIALOG, SDC, New York Times Information Service, Dow Jones News Retrieval; computerized cataloging and circulation. **Networks/Consortia:** Member of OCLC through INCOLSA. **Special Catalogs:** Business information abstract file (card).

★4081★
ELI LILLY AND COMPANY - GREENFIELD LABORATORIES - LIBRARY AGRICULTURAL SERVICE (Agri)
Box 708　　　　　　　　　　　Phone: (317) 462-8225
Greenfield, IN 46140　　　　Bernas Downing, Supv., Lit.Serv.
Founded: 1957. **Staff:** Prof 3; Other 2. **Subjects:** Plant science, animal nutrition, veterinary medicine, toxicology. **Holdings:** 4000 books; 6300 bound periodical volumes. **Subscriptions:** 650 journals and other serials. **Services:** Interlibrary loans; library open to public with restrictions. **Computerized Information Services:** DIALOG, SDC, BRS. **Networks/Consortia:** Member of INCOLSA.

★4082★
ELI LILLY AND COMPANY - LILLY ARCHIVES (Pict; Bus-Fin)
Lilly Center
307 E. McCarty St.　　　　　　Phone: (317) 261-2173
Indianapolis, IN 46285　　　　Anita Martin, Archv.
Founded: 1956. **Staff:** Prof 1; Other 1. **Subjects:** Lilly family, company administration, engineering, finance, industrial relations, marketing, production, research, foreign operations and subsidiary companies (all subjects relate to the operation of Eli Lilly and Company). **Special Collections:** Company publications (indexed). **Holdings:** 250 volumes; 40,000 pictures; 15,000 35mm slides; 300 reels of 16mm movies. **Services:** Copying; archives not open to public.

★4083★
ELI LILLY AND COMPANY - SCIENTIFIC LIBRARY (Sci-Tech)
307 E. McCarty St.　　　　　　Phone: (317) 261-4452
Indianapolis, IN 46285　　　　Adele Hoskin, Chf.Libn.
Founded: 1890. **Staff:** Prof 5; Other 9. **Subjects:** Chemistry, medicine, biological sciences, pharmacy, cosmetics. **Special Collections:** Drug product compendia and encyclopedias (foreign and domestic); worldwide Pharmacopoeias; history of pharmacy. **Holdings:** 35,000 volumes; 22,125 pamphlets; 200 annual reports of organizations; 350 government documents; 49,000 clippings; 56,500 pieces of promotional literature; 6000 pictures; 1.7 million drug product information cards; 50 audiotapes; extensive microfilm periodical holdings. **Subscriptions:** 1600 journals and other serials. **Services:** Interlibrary loans; copying; translation arrangements; literature searching; computerized SDI using ISI tapes in-house; library open to public with advance approval. **Computerized Information Services:** DIALOG, SDC, BRS, NLM; computerized cataloging and serials. **Networks/Consortia:** Member of INCOLSA; Regional Medical Library - Region 3. **Publications:** Scientific Library Bulletin, semiweekly - for internal distribution only. **Special Catalogs:** Lilly Serial Periodical Holdings (loose-leaf book); drug product information (card file); bound volumes of publications from research and scientific divisions of Eli Lilly and Company. **Remarks:** Maintains a branch library, Bldg. 88 Library, whose holdings are included here. **Staff:** Carol Andrejasich, Cat.; Lee Ann Bertram, Ref.Libn.; Jacqui Bridgeforth, Ref.Libn.

★4084★
ELIASON (Frank) CENTRE - HEALTH SCIENCES LIBRARY (Med)
2003 Arlington Ave.　　　Phone: (306) 373-2151
Saskatoon, SK, Canada S7J 2H6　　Kristine Wisser, Dir. of Med.Rec.
Founded: 1974. **Staff:** 1. **Subjects:** Gerontology, rehabilitation, anatomy, multiple sclerosis, cerebral palsy, Parkinson's disease, nursing. **Holdings:** 281 books; 36 boxes of unbound journals. **Subscriptions:** 18 journals and other serials. **Services:** Interlibrary loans; copying; library open to public with restrictions.

ELIOT (Charles) COLLECTION
See: Harvard University - Graduate School of Design - Frances Loeb Library

ELIZABETH FREE PUBLIC LIBRARY
See: Free Public Library of Elizabeth, NJ

★4085★
ELIZABETH GENERAL HOSPITAL & DISPENSARY - CHARLES H. SCHLICHTER, M.D. HEALTH SCIENCE LIBRARY (Med)
925 E. Jersey St.　　　Phone: (201) 289-8600
Elizabeth, NJ 07201　　　Catherine M. Boss, Dir.
Staff: Prof 2; Other 1. **Subjects:** Nursing, medicine, science. **Holdings:** 4736 books; 1778 bound periodical volumes; 1100 items of AV software. **Subscriptions:** 187 journals and other serials. **Services:** Interlibrary loans; copying; SDI; library open to public with restrictions. **Networks/Consortia:** Partners for Learning (PFL). **Publications:** SDI for nursing personnel - bimonthly. **Special Catalogs:** Catalog of audiovisuals (card and book). **Staff:** Donald Miller, Libn.

ELIZABETHAN CLUB COLLECTION
See: Yale University

★4086★
ELIZABETHTOWN COLLEGE - ZUG MEMORIAL LIBRARY - ARCHIVES (Hist)
　　　Phone: (717) 367-1151
Elizabethtown, PA 17022　　　Anna M. Carper, Dir.
Staff: Prof 4; Other 6. **Special Collections:** Archives of Elizabethtown College, Brethren Heritage Room (materials by and about members of the Church of the Brethren, 27 VF drawers and 244 boxes). **Services:** Interlibrary loans; copying; library open to public for reference use only. **Networks/Consortia:** Member of Associated College Libraries of Central Pennsylvania; OCLC through PALINET & the Union Library Catalogue of Pennsylvania. **Staff:** E. Margaret Gabel; Michael W. Andrews, Rd.Serv.Libn.

★4087★
ELKEM METALS COMPANY - TECHNOLOGY CENTER - HAYNES-BECKET MEMORIAL LIBRARY (Sci-Tech)
4625 Royal Ave.
Box 1344
Niagara Falls, NY 14302　　　Phone: (716) 286-7498
　　　Lorraine Hayes, Libn.
Staff: Prof 2. **Subjects:** Metallurgy, solid state physics, inorganic chemistry, chemical engineering. **Special Collections:** Structure reports; U.S. Bureau of Mines publications; historical files. **Holdings:** 15,500 books; 10,000 bound periodical volumes; 12,000 external technical reports, translations and photocopies; 9 drawers of division historical files; 100 drawers of U.S. and foreign patents. **Subscriptions:** 302 journals and other serials; 6 newspapers. **Services:** Interlibrary loans; copying; library open to public by appointment. **Computerized Information Services:** SDC; computerized cataloging. **Networks/Consortia:** Member of Western New York Library Resources Council (WNYLRC). **Staff:** Carol Thomson, Lib.Asst.

★4088★
ELKO MEDICAL CLINIC - LIBRARY (Med)
762 14th St.　　　Phone: (702) 738-3111
Elko, NV 89801　　　Dr. George T. Manilla
Founded: 1930. **Staff:** Prof 1; Other 1. **Subjects:** Medicine and allied health sciences. **Holdings:** 1025 books; 1950 bound periodical volumes; 50 unbound medical volumes (cataloged); 721 postgraduate tapes. **Subscriptions:** 108 journals and other serials. **Services:** Interlibrary loans; copying; library open to public.

ELKS LIBRARY
See: Barlow Hospital

ELLINGTON AGRICULTURAL CENTER
See: Tennessee State Department of Agriculture - Lou Wallace Library

ELLIOTT COMPANY
See: United Technologies Corporation

★4089★
ELLIS COUNTY HISTORICAL SOCIETY - ARCHIVES (Hist)
100 W. 7th St.　　　Phone: (913) 628-2624
Hays, KS 67601　　　Rev. Blaine Burkey, Archv./Hist.
Founded: 1971. **Staff:** Prof 1. **Subjects:** Local history, Volga-German migration. **Special Collections:** Records of the Munjor Town and Grazing Company (1/2 foot); miscellaneous papers of former U.S. Congresswoman Kathryn O'Loughlin McCarthy (1/2 foot); Volga-German Centennial photograph collection (2000). **Holdings:** 48 feet of archives. **Services:** Copying; library open to public by appointment. **Publications:** Homesteader, irregular - to membership.

ELLIS (Dean B.) LIBRARY
See: Arkansas State University - Dean B. Ellis Library

★4090★
ELLIS FISCHEL STATE CANCER CENTER - LIBRARY & INFORMATION CENTER (Med)
Business Loop 70 & Garth Ave.　　Phone: (314) 875-2100
Columbia, MO 65201　　　Charles A. O'Dell, Libn.
Founded: 1968. **Staff:** Prof 1. **Subjects:** Neoplastic diseases, clinical medicine. **Holdings:** 4000 books; 6208 bound periodical volumes; 5 VF drawers (cataloged); bound volumes of staff publications, 1940-1979; 368 reels of microfilm; 1 drawer of archives of hospital history. **Subscriptions:** 200 journals and other serials. **Services:** Copying; library open to public by staff request or through application. **Computerized Information Services:** MEDLINE. **Publications:** Checklist of articles on cancer, and acquisitions list, weekly - to staff and interested parties.

★4091★
ELLIS HOSPITAL - MAC MILLAN LIBRARY (Med)
1101 Nott St.　　　Phone: (518) 382-4381
Schenectady, NY 12308　　　Dorothy Dralle, Libn.
Founded: 1930. **Staff:** Prof 2; Other 2. **Subjects:** Medicine, nursing, hospital administration. **Holdings:** 2401 books; 4023 bound periodical volumes; 5 VF drawers of clippings; Audio-Digest tapes. **Subscriptions:** 150 journals and other serials. **Services:** Interlibrary loans; copying; library not open to public. **Computerized Information Services:** MEDLARS. **Networks/Consortia:** Member of Capital District Library Council for Reference and Research Resources; SAVE.

ELLIS (Laura M.) MEMORIAL LIBRARY
See: Center for Early Education - Laura M. Ellis Memorial Library

ELLIS (Richard) LIBRARY AND ARCHIVE
See: Temple University - Central Library System - Rare Book & Manuscript Collection

ELLISTON (George) POETRY COLLECTION
See: University of Cincinnati - George Elliston Poetry Collection

ELLWANGER & BARRY HORTICULTURAL LIBRARY
See: University of Rochester - Department of Rare Books and Special Collections

★4092★
ELMBROOK MEMORIAL HOSPITAL - MARY BETH CURTIS HEALTH SCIENCE LIBRARY (Med)
19333 W. North Ave.　　　Phone: (414) 782-2222
Brookfield, WI 53005　　　Harvada Oitzinger, Med.Libn.
Staff: Prof 1. **Subjects:** Medicine, nursing, hospital administration. **Holdings:** 1600 books; 35 boxes of pamphlets; 4 VF drawers; periodical microfilm (200 cassettes). **Subscriptions:** 130 journals and other serials. **Services:** Interlibrary loans; copying; library open to public for reference use only. **Networks/Consortia:** Member of Southeastern Wisconsin Health Sciences Library Consortium (SWHSLC). **Publications:** Acquisitions lists, monthly - for internal distribution only.

ELMENDORF AIR FORCE BASE (AK)
See: U.S. Air Force Hospital - Medical Library (AK-Elmendorf AFB)

★4093★
ELMHURST HISTORICAL MUSEUM - LIBRARY (Hist)
120 E. Park Ave.　　　Phone: (312) 833-1457
Elmhurst, IL 60126　　　Virginia Stewart, Act.Dir.
Staff: 2. **Subjects:** Local history - Elmhurst, DuPage County; genealogy;

museology. **Holdings:** 350 books; 142 reels of microfilm of local newspapers and Federal censuses of DuPage County; 1400 slides; 100 oral history tapes and cassettes; 175 linear feet of archives, manuscripts, maps and photographs. **Subscriptions:** 15 journals and other serials. **Services:** Copying; library open to public for reference use only. **Special Catalogs:** Guide to Research Collections of Elmhurst Historical Museum (loose-leaf); manuscript and iconographic catalog (card).

★4094★
ELMIRA PSYCHIATRIC CENTER - PROFESSIONAL LIBRARY (Med)
Caller 1527
Elmira, NY 14902
Phone: (607) 737-4769
Victoria G. Pifalo, Asst.Libn.
Founded: 1973. **Staff:** Prof 1; Other 1. **Subjects:** Psychiatry, psychology, sociology. **Holdings:** 2416 books; 798 AV items. **Subscriptions:** 58 journals and other serials. **Services:** Interlibrary loans; copying; library open to public. **Networks/Consortia:** Member of South Central Research Library Council (SCRLC). **Special Catalogs:** Sheaf catalog of AV holdings.

★4095★
ELMIRA STAR GAZETTE - LIBRARY (Publ)
201 Baldwin St.
Elmira, NY 14902
Phone: (607) 734-5151
Jean M. Strong, Libn.
Staff: 1. **Subjects:** Newspaper reference topics. **Special Collections:** Microfilm of paper from 1835 to present. **Holdings:** 50 books; 9 VF drawers of photographs; 130 VF drawers of clippings. **Services:** Library open to public with restrictions.

ELNA
See: Esperanto League for North America

ELON COLLEGE LIBRARY - AMERICAN THEATRE ORGAN SOCIETY
See: American Theatre Organ Society

★4096★
ELRICK AND LAVIDGE, INC. - LIBRARY (Bus-Fin)†
10 S. Riverside Plaza
Chicago, IL 60606
Phone: (312) 726-0666
G. Birch Ripley, Libn.
Founded: 1965. **Staff:** Prof 1. **Subjects:** Marketing research. **Special Collections:** Primary research reports (3000). **Holdings:** 100 books; 7 VF drawers of pamphlets; 2 drawers of maps; 300 directories; 25 telephone directories; census publications. **Subscriptions:** 65 journals and other serials. **Services:** Interlibrary loans; library not open to public. **Computerized Information Services:** DIALOG. **Special Catalogs:** Catalog to primary research reports (card).

ELVEHJEM MUSEUM OF ART
See: University of Wisconsin, Madison - Kohler Art Library

★4097★
ELWYN INSTITUTES - LIBRARY (Med)
Elwyn, PA 19063
Phone: (215) 358-6487
Joyce Lentz, Libn.
Founded: 1968. **Staff:** Prof 1. **Subjects:** Mental retardation, special education, vocational rehabilitation, psychology, medicine. **Holdings:** 3500 books and bound periodical volumes; 8 VF drawers of reprints, reports, bibliographies and brochures. **Subscriptions:** 50 journals and other serials. **Services:** Interlibrary loans; copying; library open to public for reference use only. **Networks/Consortia:** Member of Mideastern Regional Medical Library Service (MERMLS); Consortium for Health Information and Library Services (CHI).

★4098★
ELYRIA CHRONICLE-TELEGRAM - LIBRARY (Publ)
225 East Ave.
Elyria, OH 44036
Phone: (216) 329-7000
Jeanne D. Meredith, Libn.
Founded: 1955. **Staff:** 5. **Subjects:** Newspaper reference topics. **Holdings:** Figures not available for newspaper clippings, photographs, negatives. **Services:** Library open to public with restrictions.

★4099★
ELYRIA MEMORIAL HOSPITAL - LIBRARY (Med)†
630 E. River St.
Elyria, OH 44035
Phone: (216) 323-3221
Linda Masek, Hd.Libn.
Founded: 1975. **Staff:** Prof 1; Other 3. **Subjects:** Orthopedics, nursing, pediatrics. **Holdings:** 3783 books; 3102 bound periodical volumes; 20 VF drawers of pamphlets, reports, clippings, bibliographies and AV aids. **Subscriptions:** 260 journals and other serials. **Services:** Interlibrary loans; copying; library not open to public. **Computerized Information Services:** MEDLINE. **Networks/Consortia:** Member of Kentucky-Ohio-Michigan

Regional Medical Library Network (KOMRML).

★4100★
EMANUEL HOSPITAL - LIBRARY SERVICES (Med)†
2801 N. Gantenbein Ave.
Portland, OR 97227
Phone: (503) 280-3558
Katherine W. Rouzie, Dir., Lib.Serv.
Staff: Prof 2; Other 2. **Subjects:** Medicine, nursing, allied health sciences. **Special Collections:** Burn care; surgery; trauma care. **Holdings:** 1500 books; 4 VF drawers of ephemera; 50 video cassettes; 40 audio cassettes. **Subscriptions:** 250 journals and other serials. **Services:** Interlibrary loans; SDI; library open to public for reference use only. **Computerized Information Services:** MEDLARS. **Networks/Consortia:** Member of Oregon Health Information Network (OHIN). **Remarks:** Includes the holdings of the School of Nursing Library. **Staff:** Sharon A. Tashjian, AV Libn.

★4101★
EMANUEL MEDICAL CENTER - MEDICAL LIBRARY (Med)
Box 2120
Turlock, CA 95381-2120
Phone: (209) 634-9151
Donna Cardoza, Lib.Ck.
Staff: 1. **Subjects:** Medicine and allied health sciences. **Holdings:** 676 books; 210 bound periodical volumes. **Subscriptions:** 122 journals and other serials. **Services:** Interlibrary loans; copying; library open for professional use. **Networks/Consortia:** Member of Pacific Southwest Regional Medical Library Service (PSRMLS); 49-99 Cooperative Library System.

EMBASSY OF INDIA
See: India - Embassy of India

★4102★
EMBASSY OF ZIMBABWE - LIBRARY (Area-Ethnic)
2852 McGill Terrace, N.W.
Washington, DC 20008
Phone: (202) 332-7100
Staff: 1. **Subjects:** Rhodesia. **Holdings:** Figures not available for books, government publications and reports; current issues of the national newspapers and Rhodesian magazines. **Services:** Copying; library open to public. **Remarks:** The office issues two publications which are available upon request. These include Focus on Rhodesia and Zimbabwe Rhodesia Viewpoint.

★4103★
EMBROIDERERS' GUILD OF AMERICA, INC. - LIBRARY (Rec)
6 E. 45th St.
New York, NY 10017
Phone: (212) 986-0460
Grace R. Gutberlet, Lib.Chm.
Subjects: Embroidery. **Holdings:** 1000 books. **Services:** Library open to members only. **Publications:** Needle Arts, quarterly.

★4104★
EMBRY RIDDLE AERONAUTICAL UNIVERSITY - LEARNING RESOURCES CENTER (Trans)
Regional Airport
Daytona Beach, FL 32014
Phone: (904) 252-5561
M. Judy Luther, Dir., Lrng.Rsrcs.
Founded: 1965. **Staff:** Prof 11; Other 7. **Subjects:** Aviation, management, aeronautical engineering. **Special Collections:** Aviation history (10,000 volumes). **Holdings:** 30,000 books; 5000 bound periodical volumes; 20,000 documents; 18,500 reports on microfiche; 1000 AV items; 1156 journal titles. **Subscriptions:** 570 journals and other serials. **Services:** Interlibrary loans; copying; library open to public. **Computerized Information Services:** DIALOG; computerized cataloging. **Networks/Consortia:** Member of SOLINET. **Special Catalogs:** Periodicals Holdings List; Media Catalog. **Staff:** Kathleen Paro, Instr.Serv.Libn.; Charlotte Minor, Coll.Dev.Libn.; Elena Eckley, Media Serv.Libn.; Diana Ramsden, Ser.Libn.; Vicki Killion, Circ.Mgt.Libn.

★4105★
EMERGENCY CARE RESEARCH INSTITUTE - LIBRARY (Med)
5200 Butler Pike
Plymouth Meeting, PA 19462
Phone: (215) 825-6000
June P. Katucki, Hd.Libn.
Staff: Prof 1; Other 2. **Subjects:** Medical devices, bio-medical engineering, hospital safety. **Special Collections:** Health Devices Evaluation Services (medical and manufacturing literature). **Holdings:** 1000 books; 150 VF drawers of annual reports, technical reports and evaluation data. **Subscriptions:** 300 journals and other serials. **Services:** Interlibrary loans; library open to public by appointment. **Computerized Information Services:** DIALOG; Health Devices Thesaurus (in-house computer-generated database). **Networks/Consortia:** Member of Mideastern Regional Medical Library Service (MERMLS); Delaware Valley Information Consortium (DEVIC). **Publications:** Health Devices; Health Devices Alerts; Health Devices Sourcebook, annual - for sale.

★4106★

EMERSON COLLEGE - LIBRARY (Med; Theater)
150 Beacon St.   Phone: (617) 262-2010
Boston, MA 02116   Donna T. Ravn, Dir.
Founded: 1892. **Staff:** Prof 6; Other 7. **Subjects:** Speech communication, mass communications, speech pathology, theater arts. **Holdings:** 68,554 books; 881 bound periodical volumes; 413 phonotapes; 3173 phonograph records; 3782 microforms; 32 videotapes; 95 filmstrips; 3376 slides; 106 films; 57 models. **Subscriptions:** 540 journals and other serials; 14 newspapers. **Services:** Interlibrary loans; library open to public with college identification card or letter of introduction from other library. **Computerized Information Services:** DIALOG; computerized cataloging and ILL. **Networks/ Consortia:** Member of Fenway Library Consortium; OCLC through NELINET. **Staff:** Cynthia Alcorn, Hd., Coll.Dev.; Elizabeth Bezera, Hd., Pub.Serv.; Mary Curtin-Stevenson, Hd.Cat.; Maureen Tripp, Hd., Media Serv.

★4107★

EMERSON ELECTRIC COMPANY - SPACE AND ELECTRONICS DIVISION - ENGINEERING LIBRARY (Sci-Tech)
8100 W. Florissant Ave.
St. Louis, MO 63136   Marian S. Shaffer, Tech.Libn.
Staff: Prof 1; Other 1. **Subjects:** Engineering, physics, mathematics, computers, data processing, systems management. **Special Collections:** Military specifications and standards. **Holdings:** Figures not available.

EMERSON (Haven) PUBLIC HEALTH LIBRARY
See: New York City - Municipal Reference and Research Center - Haven Emerson Public Health Library

EMERSON (Ralph Waldo), LIBRARY OF
See: Concord Antiquarian Society - Library of Ralph Waldo Emerson

★4108★

EMERY INDUSTRIES, INC. - RESEARCH LIBRARY (Sci-Tech)
4900 Este Ave.   Phone: (513) 482-2157
Cincinnati, OH 45232   B.A. Bernard, Res.Libn.
Staff: Prof 1; Other 1. **Subjects:** Organic chemistry and allied sciences. **Holdings:** Figures not available. **Services:** Interlibrary loans; copying.

EMGE MEDICAL LIBRARY
See: Children's Hospital of San Francisco

★4109★

EMHART INDUSTRIES, INC. - HARTFORD DIVISION LIBRARY
123 Day Hill Rd.
Box 700
Windsor, CT 06095
Subjects: Glass technology, physics, metallurgy, machine design, refractories, ceramics. **Special Collections:** U.S. glass patents. **Holdings:** 4000 books; 2700 bound periodical volumes; 1000 other cataloged items; 10,000 miscellaneous reports, patents and data relating to glass manufacturing. **Remarks:** Presently inactive.

★4110★

EMMAUS BIBLE SCHOOL - LIBRARY (Rel-Theol)
156 N. Oak Park Ave.   Phone: (312) 383-7000
Oak Park, IL 60301   Ruth Marshall, Libn.
Staff: Prof 2. **Subjects:** Biblical studies. **Special Collections:** Plymouth Brethren Writings (books, pamphlets and periodicals). **Holdings:** 16,000 books and multimedia materials; 1500 bound periodical volumes. **Subscriptions:** 250 journals and other serials. **Services:** Interlibrary loans; copying; library open to public with restrictions. **Staff:** Betty Canell, Asst.Libn.

★4111★

EMMAUS LUTHERAN CHURCH - LIBRARY (Rel-Theol)
3120 Irving St.   Phone: (303) 477-5358
Denver, CO 80211   Herbert Harms, Libn.
Founded: 1959. **Staff:** Prof 1; Other 4. **Subjects:** Religion. **Holdings:** 3000 books and bound periodical volumes. **Subscriptions:** 10 journals and other serials. **Services:** Library open to public.

★4112★

EMORY AND HENRY COLLEGE - APPALACHIAN ORAL HISTORY COLLECTION (Hist)
Drawer S   Phone: (703) 944-3121
Emory, VA 24327   George Stevenson, Dir.
Staff: 1. **Subjects:** Southwest Virginia, East Tennessee, social and economic history, agricultural and mining history, personal memoirs. **Holdings:** 1200 hours of tapes; 500 transcripts. **Services:** Copying; collection open to public

for reference use only.

EMORY UNIVERSITY - CHEMISTRY LIBRARY
See: Emory University - James Samuel Guy Library

EMORY UNIVERSITY - CRAWFORD W. LONG MEMORIAL HOSPITAL
See: Crawford W. Long Memorial Hospital

★4113★

EMORY UNIVERSITY - DIVISION OF LIBRARY AND INFORMATION MANAGEMENT LIBRARY (Info Sci)
420 Candler Library Bldg.   Phone: (404) 329-6846
Atlanta, GA 30322   Martha Fisher Buckley, Libn.
Founded: 1930. **Staff:** Prof 2; Other 3. **Subjects:** Library and information science. **Special Collections:** Pettus Collection on the History of the Book; Caylor Collection (Newbery and Caldecott Awards); Holme Collection (early children's books). **Holdings:** 32,698 volumes; 437 reels of microfilm; 6156 microforms; 140 AV units; 50 microcomputer diskettes. **Subscriptions:** 732 journals and other serials. **Services:** Interlibrary loans; copying; library open to public. **Computerized Information Services:** Computerized cataloging. **Networks/Consortia:** Member of SOLINET. **Staff:** Victoria Norman, Asst.Libn.

★4114★

EMORY UNIVERSITY - DOCUMENTS DEPARTMENT (Info Sci)
Woodruff Library   Phone: (404) 329-6880
Atlanta, GA 30322   Elizabeth A. McBride, Doc.Libn.
Founded: 1956. **Staff:** Prof 1; Other 4. **Subjects:** U.S. government publications, U.N. publications, League of Nations publications, Organization of American States official records, selected publications of foreign governments. **Holdings:** 8000 linear feet of books and bound periodical volumes; 900 linear feet of microprint and microfilm; 60,000 microfiche; 8 VF drawers. **Services:** Interlibrary loans; copying; U.S. collection open to public. **Computerized Information Services:** DIALOG, SDC. **Networks/ Consortia:** Member of OCLC; Georgia Library Information Network (GLIN). **Publications:** List of publications - available upon request.

★4115★

EMORY UNIVERSITY - JAMES SAMUEL GUY LIBRARY (Sci-Tech)
440 Chemistry Bldg.   Phone: (404) 329-6618
Atlanta, GA 30322   Pamela E. Pickens, Chem.Libn.
Founded: 1951. **Staff:** Prof 1; Other 4. **Subjects:** Organic, physical and analytical chemistry. **Holdings:** 7000 books; 9000 bound periodical volumes; 1500 microfiche. **Subscriptions:** 205 journals and other serials. **Services:** Interlibrary loans; copying; SDI; library not open to public. **Computerized Information Services:** DIALOG, SDC, BRS. **Networks/Consortia:** Member of OCLC; Georgia Library Information Network (GLIN).

★4116★

EMORY UNIVERSITY - PITTS THEOLOGY LIBRARY (Rel-Theol)
Theology Bldg.   Phone: (404) 329-4166
Atlanta, GA 30322   Channing R. Jeschke, Libn.
Founded: 1914. **Staff:** Prof 7; Other 7. **Subjects:** Theology. **Special Collections:** Wesleyana Collection (2700 volumes); hymnology (8800 volumes); theology (30,000 volumes); Cardinal Henry Edward Manning Library (4300 books; 1500 manuscripts). **Holdings:** 373,177 books and bound periodical volumes; 6700 United Methodist Conference Reports; 2223 reels of microfilm; 15,074 microfiche. **Subscriptions:** 1284 journals and other serials. **Services:** Interlibrary loans; copying; library open to public. **Computerized Information Services:** Computerized cataloging. **Staff:** David Chen, Asst.Libn./Tech.Serv.; Sara Mobley, Asst.Libn./Pub.Serv.; Achilla I. Erdican, Cat.Libn.; Fred A. Grater, Cat.Libn.; Cynthia G. Runyon, Per.Libn.; Anita K. Delaries, Cur. of Archv. & Mss.

★4117★

EMORY UNIVERSITY - SCHOOL OF DENTISTRY - SHEPPARD W. FOSTER LIBRARY (Med)
1462 Clifton Rd., N.E.
Atlanta, GA 30322   Phone: (404) 329-6695
                       Lucy L. Duke, Libn.
Founded: 1917. **Staff:** Prof 2; Other 2. **Subjects:** Dentistry, medical sciences. **Special Collections:** History of dentistry in the South. **Holdings:** 19,756 books and bound periodical volumes. **Subscriptions:** 237 journals and other serials. **Services:** Interlibrary loans.

★4118★

EMORY UNIVERSITY - SCHOOL OF LAW LIBRARY (Law)
Gambrell Hall   Phone: (404) 329-6823
Atlanta, GA 30322   Adrien C. Hinze, Law Libn.
Founded: 1916. **Staff:** Prof 5; Other 12. **Subjects:** Law. **Holdings:** 181,487

volumes. **Subscriptions:** 3231 journals and other serials. **Services:** Interlibrary loans; copying; library open to members of Bench and Bar. **Computerized Information Services:** LEXIS. **Networks/Consortia:** Member of OCLC. **Staff:** Angelina Way, Ref.Libn.; Malvina Bechor, Cat.Libn.; Joice Elam, Doc.Libn.

★4119★
EMORY UNIVERSITY - SCHOOL OF MEDICINE - A.W. CALHOUN MEDICAL LIBRARY (Med)

Atlanta, GA 30322

Phone: (404) 329-5820
Miriam H. Libbey, Libn.

Founded: 1923. **Staff:** Prof 12; Other 25. **Subjects:** Medicine and related sciences. **Holdings:** 47,568 books; 86,231 bound periodical volumes; 2731 AV titles. **Subscriptions:** 2407 journals and other serials. **Services:** Interlibrary loans; copying; library open to health professionals in the metropolitan area. **Computerized Information Services:** BRS, MEDLINE, SDC, DIALOG. **Networks/Consortia:** Member of University Center in Georgia, Inc.; Atlanta Health Science Libraries Consortium. **Publications:** Book Ends. **Staff:** E. Louise Warren, Asst.Libn., Tech.Serv.; Carol A. Burns, Asst.Libn., Pub.Serv.; Lauren A. Benevich, Ref.Libn.; Elaine Keefer, Ref.Libn.; Nena K. Perry, Ref.Libn.; Linda Garr Markwell, Grady Br.Libn.; Archie Martin, AV Libn.; Robin Raquet, Ref.Libn.; Joan E. Spring, Cat.; J. Stevens Foote, Ser.Cat.

★4120★
EMORY UNIVERSITY - SCIENCE LIBRARY (Sci-Tech)
Woodruff Library
Atlanta, GA 30322

Phone: (404) 329-6885
Irene K. Mallison, Hd., Sci.Dept.

Founded: 1955. **Staff:** Prof 1; Other 1. **Subjects:** Biology, psychology, physics, geology, mathematics, sociology of medicine. **Holdings:** 53,300 books. **Subscriptions:** 1270 journals and other serials. **Services:** Interlibrary loans; copying; library not open to public. **Computerized Information Services:** DIALOG, SDC, BRS; computerized cataloging. **Networks/Consortia:** Member of OCLC; Georgia Library Information Network (GLIN). **Publications:** Guide to Library Resources in Chemistry, 1976; Guide to Library Resources and Services in Psychology, 1981; Guide to Library Resources and Services in the Biological Sciences, 1982; Guide to Energy Information, 1981; Library Resources for Authors of Scientific Papers, 1981; Library Resources for the Study of Communicative Disorders, 1982; Guide to Library Materials for the Study of Earth Resources, 1982.

★4121★
EMORY UNIVERSITY - SPECIAL COLLECTIONS DEPARTMENT (Hist)
Woodruff Library
Atlanta, GA 30322

Phone: (404) 329-6887
Linda M. Matthews, Hd.

Founded: 1926. **Staff:** Prof 3; Other 4. **Subjects:** Methodism, Confederate history, Southern history, Southern journalists, Southern women, British and Anglo-Irish literature, American and Asian Communism, Emory archives. **Special Collections:** Joel Chandler Harris Collection; Candler Family papers; Alexander H. Stephens; John Wesley papers; Wesleyan Collection; Julian LaRose Harris papers; Ralph McGill papers; Mildred Seydell papers; William Butler Yeats; Lady Augusta Gregory and Sir William Gregory; Theodore Draper; Philip Jaffe; Richard H. Rich; William B. Hartsfield. **Holdings:** 16,000 books; 300 bound periodical volumes; 800 maps (cataloged); 3000 linear feet of manuscripts; 4700 volumes of Emory University dissertations and theses; 265 reels of microfilm. **Services:** Copying; department open to qualified researchers. **Computerized Information Services:** Computerized cataloging. **Networks/Consortia:** Member of OCLC. **Publications:** The Robert W. Woodruff Library for Advanced Studies, Special Collections (brochure describing major holdings); Manuscript Sources for Women's History, a Descriptive List of Holdings in the Special Collections Department, revised 1978; A Guide to Manuscript Sources in the Special Collections Department for Atlanta, 1978; Lucy M. Stanton, Artist, 1975; Guide to the Charles Holmes Herty Papers, 1981; John Hill Hewitt, Sources and Bibliography, 1981. **Staff:** Virginia J.H. Cain, Proc.Archv.

★4122★
EMORY UNIVERSITY - YERKES REGIONAL PRIMATE CENTER - LIBRARY (Sci-Tech)

Atlanta, GA 30322

Phone: (404) 329-7764
Nellie Johns, Lib.Coord.

Founded: 1945. **Staff:** Prof 1. **Subjects:** Primatology. **Special Collections:** Rare books on primates; collected reprints on primates (3000). **Holdings:** 3000 books; 2000 bound periodical volumes; 1500 bound faculty publications, 1925 to present. **Subscriptions:** 60 journals and other serials. **Services:** Interlibrary loans; copying; library open to Atlanta Health Science Libraries Consortium members. **Networks/Consortia:** Member of Atlanta Health Science Libraries Consortium. **Publications:** Yerkes, fifty years of publications 1925-1974.

EMPIRE STATE COLLEGE
See: SUNY

EMPLOI ET IMMIGRATION CANADA
See: Canada - Employment & Immigration Canada

★4123★
EMPLOYEE BENEFIT RESEARCH INSTITUTE - LIBRARY (Soc Sci)
1920 M St., N.W., Suite 520
Washington, DC 20036

Margaret B. Riordan, Libn.

Staff: Prof 1. **Subjects:** Retirement income, health benefits. **Holdings:** 500 books; 3000 documents. **Subscriptions:** 22 journals and other serials. **Services:** Interlibrary loans; library not open to public. **Publications:** List of publications - available upon request.

EMPLOYMENT & IMMIGRATION CANADA
See: Canada - Employment & Immigration Canada

★4124★
EMPORIA STATE UNIVERSITY - WILLIAM ALLEN WHITE LIBRARY - SPECIAL COLLECTIONS (Hum)
1200 Commercial
Emporia, KS 66801

Phone: (316) 343-1200
Mary E. Bogan, Spec.Coll.Libn.

Staff: Prof 1; Other 2. **Special Collections:** William Allen White Collection (1216 items); Mary White Collection (64 items); Normaliana Collection (1051 volumes, 28,698 items); May Massee Collection (3819 items); Lois Lenski Collection (268 items); Children's Literature Collection (29,000 volumes); Rare Book Collection (1414 volumes); Dunning Antique Collection; W.A. White Children's Books; Award Collection (611 volumes); Archives (34 linear feet); Elizabeth Yates Collection (142 items); Ruth Garver Gagliardo Collection (1804 volumes); Historical Children's Literature Collection (436 volumes). **Services:** Interlibrary loans; copying; SDI; library open to public with borrowing privileges reserved for Kansas residents with library card. **Computerized Information Services:** Online systems; computerized cataloging and circulation. **Networks/Consortia:** Member of OCLC; Bibliographical Center for Research, Rocky Mountain Region, Inc. (BCR); Kansas Nebraska Interlibrary Loan Project. **Publications:** A Bibliography of William Allen White, 1969, 2 volumes; The May Massee Collection: Creative Publishing for Children, 1923-1963, A Checklist, Dr. George V. Hodowanec, Editor, 1979; The William Allen White Children's Book Award, Books on the Master Lists, 1952-1953 through 1982-1983 - all for sale. **Special Catalogs:** May Massee Collection (card); Normaliana (card); Ruth Garver Gagliardo (card).

EMR PHOTOELECTRIC-SCHLUMBERGER LTD.
See: Sangamo-Weston Group - EMR Photoelectric Division

★4125★
EMR TELEMETRY-SANGAMO WESTON - TECHNICAL INFORMATION CENTER
Box 3041
Sarasota, FL 33578
Defunct

ENCINO HISTORICAL SOCIETY, INC.
See: Los Encinos Docent Association

★4126★
ENCYCLOPAEDIA BRITANNICA, INC. - EDITORIAL LIBRARY (Publ)
425 N. Michigan Ave.
Chicago, IL 60611

Phone: (312) 321-7221
Terry Miller, Hd.Libn.

Founded: 1920. **Staff:** Prof 2; Other 2. **Subjects:** Reference, foreign statistics. **Holdings:** 25,000 books and bound periodical volumes; 3000 unbound geographical and statistical publications; 1920 reels of microfilm. **Subscriptions:** 491 journals and other serials; 6 newspapers. **Services:** Interlibrary loans; copying; library not open to public. **Staff:** Shantha Channabasappa, Assoc.Libn.

★4127★
ENDO LABORATORIES, INC. - LIBRARY (Med)
1000 Stewart Ave.
Garden City, NY 11530

Phone: (516) 832-2113
Virginia Steinberger, Mgr.

Founded: 1960. **Staff:** Prof 1; Other 2. **Subjects:** Medicine; pharmacology; chemistry - organic, medicinal, pharmaceutical; pharmaceutical sciences. **Holdings:** 1500 books; 3000 bound periodical volumes; reprints (confidential); 15,000 U.S. and 1000 foreign pharmaceutical patents; 12 journals on microfilm cassettes. **Subscriptions:** 325 journals and other serials; 15 newspapers. **Services:** Interlibrary loans; copying; SDI; library not open to public. **Computerized Information Services:** NLM, DIALOG, SDC.

Publications: Abstracts; SDI Bulletins - for internal distribution only.

★4128★

ENERGY IMPACT ASSOCIATES, INC. - LIBRARY (Env-Cons)
Box 1899   Phone: (412) 351-5800
Pittsburgh, PA 15230   Jacqueline A. Dasch, Libn.
Founded: 1971. **Staff:** Prof 1. **Subjects:** Environment, energy, ecology, pollution. **Special Collections:** Environmental reports, water quality data, state pollution regulations, Federal Register. **Holdings:** 6500 books and bound periodical volumes; 80 journals; company reports. **Subscriptions:** 71 journals and other serials. **Computerized Information Services:** DIALOG, SDC; computerized acquisitions. **Remarks:** The Library is located at 2400 Ardmore Blvd., Pittsburgh, PA 15221.

ENERGY AND MINERAL RESOURCES RESEARCH INSTITUTE
See: Iowa State University

ENERGY, MINES & RESOURCES CANADA
See: Canada - Energy, Mines & Resources Canada

ENERGY REFERENCE AND RESEARCH CENTER
See: National Energy Foundation

★4129★

ENERGY RESOURCES COMPANY - LIBRARY (Energy)
1 Alewife Pl.   Phone: (617) 661-3111
Cambridge, MA 02140
Founded: 1977. **Staff:** Prof 2. **Subjects:** Energy - fluidized bed combustion, geothermal; environment; solid waste; wastewater; toxicology. **Holdings:** 5500 books; 4000 microfiche. **Subscriptions:** 129 journals and other serials. **Services:** Interlibrary loans; copying; SDI; library not open to public. **Computerized Information Services:** DIALOG, NLM, DOE/RECON. **Staff:** Drusilla Raiford, Asst.Libn.

ENERGY RESOURCES CONSERVATION BOARD
See: Alberta - Energy Resources Conservation Board

★4130★

ENERGY, INC. - TECHNICAL LIBRARY (Energy)
Box 736   Phone: (208) 529-1000
Idaho Falls, ID 83402   Jacqueline Loop, Libn.
Founded: 1975. **Staff:** Prof 1; Other 1. **Subjects:** Nuclear engineering. **Holdings:** 1500 books; 6000 technical reports (hardcopy); 150,000 technical reports (microfiche). **Subscriptions:** 80 journals and other serials. **Services:** Interlibrary loans; copying; library open to public with restrictions. **Computerized Information Services:** DIALOG.

ENGEL (R.A.) TECHNICAL LIBRARY
See: Monsanto Company - Fisher Controls Company

ENGEL (William P.) LIBRARY
See: Temple Emanu-El - William P. Engel Library

★4131★

ENGELHARD CORPORATION - TECHNICAL INFORMATION CENTER (Sci-Tech)
Menlo Park   Phone: (201) 321-5271
Edison, NJ 08818   Roger L. Meyer, Mgr., Tech.Info.Serv.
Staff: Prof 5; Other 3. **Subjects:** All aspects of noble metals-platinum group metals; gold and silver; catalysis; air pollution control; Kaolin clays; ore dressing; paper making and converting. **Holdings:** 25,000 books; 5000 bound periodical volumes; 1000 other cataloged items; 20,000 special reports; 50,000 foreign patents; complete U.S. patents 1974 to present. **Subscriptions:** 450 journals and other serials. **Services:** Interlibrary loans; copying; library open to public with prior approval. **Computerized Information Services:** Online systems. **Publications:** Review of Current Technical Literature and Patent Bulletin, monthly. **Staff:** Maurica Fedors, Tech.Info.Spec.; Marguerite Bebbington, Tech.Info.Spec.; Maryann Sobin, Libn.

★4132★

ENGINEERING DYNAMICS, INC. - LIBRARY (Sci-Tech)
3925 S. Kalamath   Phone: (303) 761-4367
Englewood, CO 80110   Howard McGregor, Pres.
Founded: 1975. **Staff:** Prof 1. **Subjects:** Acoustics, vibration, information science. **Holdings:** 150 books; 50 cases of reports and reprints by subject; 25 telephone books. **Subscriptions:** 10 journals and other serials; 5 newspapers. **Services:** Interlibrary loans; copying; SDI; retrieval services available on fee basis; library open to public with restrictions. **Computerized**

Information Services: Online systems.

★4133★

ENGINEERING-SCIENCE, INC. - TECHNICAL LIBRARY
125 W. Huntington Dr.
Arcadia, CA 91006
Founded: 1979. **Subjects:** Wastewater engineering, water pollution control. **Holdings:** 500 books; 150 bound periodical volumes; 2000 in-house reports; 1000 Environmental Protection Agency reports on water pollution control. **Computerized Information Services:** DIALOG. **Remarks:** Presently inactive.

★4134★

ENGINEERING SOCIETIES LIBRARY (Sci-Tech)
United Engineering Ctr.
345 E. 47th St.   Phone: (212) 644-7611
New York, NY 10017   S.K. Cabeen, Dir.
Founded: 1913. **Staff:** Prof 13; Other 27. **Subjects:** Engineering - chemical, civil, electrical, mechanical, mining; history of engineering; fuels; metallurgy. **Holdings:** 115,000 books; 135,000 bound periodical volumes; 10,000 maps; 6500 searches. **Subscriptions:** 5500 journals and other serials. **Services:** Copying; literature searches available as paid service; library open to public. **Computerized Information Services:** Online systems. **Publications:** Bibliographies; Periodicals Currently Received - both irregular. **Staff:** Carmela Carbone, Dp.Dir.; Ari Cohen, Hd., Cat.Dept.; Dan Wood, Hd., Acq.Dept.

★4135★

ENGINEERING SOCIETY OF BALTIMORE, INC. - LIBRARY (Sci-Tech)
11 W. Mt. Vernon Pl.   Phone: (301) 539-6914
Baltimore, MD 21201
Subjects: Engineering. **Holdings:** Figures not available.

★4136★

ENGINEERS' CLUB OF DAYTON - LIBRARY (Sci-Tech)†
110 E. Monument Ave.   Phone: (513) 228-2148
Dayton, OH 45402   Susan Marks, Libn.
Founded: 1918. **Staff:** 1. **Subjects:** Engineering - electrical, civil, mechanical; mathematics; aviation and space technology; chemistry; physics. **Holdings:** 3500 books; 1950 bound periodical volumes; 150 pamphlets (cataloged); 300 pamphlets (uncataloged); 460 reels of microfilm. **Subscriptions:** 110 journals and other serials. **Services:** Interlibrary loans; copying; library open to public with restrictions. **Networks/Consortia:** Member of Dayton-Miami Valley Consortium.

★4137★

ENGINEERS AND SCIENTISTS OF CINCINNATI - LIBRARY
1349 E. McMillan St.
Cincinnati, OH 45206
Defunct

ENGLAND AIR FORCE BASE (LA)
See: U.S. Air Force Base - England Base Library

ENGLAND (Joseph W.) LIBRARY
See: Philadelphia College of Pharmacy and Science - Joseph W. England Library

★4138★

ENGLEWOOD HOSPITAL - MEDICAL LIBRARY (Med)
350 Engle St.   Phone: (201) 894-3070
Englewood, NJ 07631   Katherine L. Lindner, Dir.
Staff: Prof 2; Other 2. **Subjects:** Medicine and allied fields. **Special Collections:** Internal medicine and surgery AV materials. **Holdings:** 2000 books; 10,000 bound periodical volumes. **Subscriptions:** 200 journals and other serials. **Services:** Interlibrary loans; copying; library open to public by appointment. **Computerized Information Services:** MEDLINE. **Networks/Consortia:** Member of Bergen-Passaic Health Sciences Library Consortium. **Special Catalogs:** Catalog of audiovisual materials; listing of health education resources for patients and community members.

★4139★

ENGLEWOOD HOSPITAL - SCHOOL OF NURSING LIBRARY (Med)
350 Engle St.   Phone: (201) 894-3326
Englewood, NJ 07631   Patricia Young, Libn.
Staff: Prof 1; Other 1. **Subjects:** Nursing. **Holdings:** 5500 books; 310 bound periodical volumes; 8 VF drawers; 325 cassette and filmstrip titles; 50 film titles; 20 slides and cassettes. **Subscriptions:** 49 journals and other serials. **Services:** Library open to public by appointment.

ENGLISH LANGUAGE INSTITUTE
See: University of Michigan

★4140★
ENGLISH, MC CAUGHAN AND O'BRYAN - LAW LIBRARY (Law)
Box 14098   Phone: (305) 462-3301
Fort Lauderdale, FL 33302   Angela R. Stramiello, Libn.
Staff: Prof 1. **Subjects:** Law. **Holdings:** 6000 volumes.

★4141★
**ENGLISH-SPEAKING UNION OF THE U.S.A. - BOOKS ACROSS THE SEA
LIBRARY** (Area-Ethnic)
16 E. 69th St.   Phone: (212) 879-6800
New York, NY 10021   Catherine Nolan, Libn.
Founded: 1942. **Staff:** Prof 1; Other 1. **Subjects:** Britain and the other
Commonwealth countries. **Holdings:** 8600 books. **Subscriptions:** 14 journals
and other serials. **Services:** Interlibrary loans; lending services to schools,
libraries and colleges; library open to public for research and study.

★4142★
**ENGLISH-SPEAKING UNION OF THE U.S.A. - WASHINGTON D.C. BRANCH
LIBRARY** (Area-Ethnic)
2131 S St., N.W.   Phone: (202) 234-4602
Washington, DC 20008   Eleanor Johnson, Libn.
Staff: 1. **Subjects:** English history, biography, travel, historical novels,
aspects of Commonwealth life. **Special Collections:** Works of Churchill.
Holdings: 500 volumes. **Services:** Interlibrary loans; library open to public for
reference use only on request.

★4143★
ENI COMPANIES - INFORMATION CENTER (Bus-Fin)
110 110th Ave., N.E.   Phone: (206) 451-4000
Bellevue, WA 98009   Wendy Doty, Hd.
Founded: 1977. **Staff:** 2. **Subjects:** Petroleum, securities, finance, natural
gas, marketing, business. **Holdings:** 350 books; 20 maps; 10 VF drawers of
subject files; 200 cassette tapes; 1650 research files. **Subscriptions:** 182
journals and other serials. **Services:** Copying; library not open to public.

★4144★
ENOCH PRATT FREE LIBRARY - AUDIO-VISUAL DEPARTMENT (Aud-Vis)
400 Cathedral St.   Phone: (301) 396-4616
Baltimore, MD 21201   Helen W. Cyr, Hd.
Founded: 1949. **Staff:** Prof 4; Other 10. **Subjects:** History of film,
experimental film, music, art, social sciences, other arts and crafts, religion,
black history/culture, children's films. **Special Collections:** Maryland and
Baltimore history. **Holdings:** 5194 16mm films; 161 super and standard 8mm
films; 486 filmstrips; 36,805 slides; 926 videotapes; 120 videodiscs; 412
audiotape cassettes. **Subscriptions:** 14 journals and other serials. **Services:**
Interlibrary loans (within Maryland only); library open to public. **Staff:** John
Carey, Asst.Hd.; Carolyn Hauck, AV Spec.; Dorry Ipolito, Ref.Libn.

★4145★
**ENOCH PRATT FREE LIBRARY - BUSINESS, SCIENCE AND TECHNOLOGY
DEPARTMENT** (Bus-Fin; Sci-Tech)
400 Cathedral St.   Phone: (301) 396-5316
Baltimore, MD 21201   Margaret L. Jacobs, Dept.Hd.
Founded: 1916. **Staff:** Prof 12; Other 3. **Subjects:** Science, business,
economics, technology, census material, medicine, consumerism. **Special
Collections:** Directories (14 shelves); auto repair (40 VF drawers). **Holdings:**
122,769 books; 3750 bound periodical volumes; 128 VF drawers of
pamphlets; 2176 shelves of U.S. documents; 360 periodical titles on
microfiche; 34 VF drawers of U.S. documents on microfiche. **Subscriptions:**
1002 journals and other serials. **Services:** Interlibrary loans; copying; library
open to public. **Computerized Information Services:** New York Times
Information Service. **Networks/Consortia:** Member of Maryland Interlibrary
Loan Organization (MILO).

★4146★
**ENOCH PRATT FREE LIBRARY - FINE ARTS AND RECREATION
DEPARTMENT** (Art; Mus)
400 Cathedral St.   Phone: (301) 396-5491
Baltimore, MD 21201   Joan Stahl, Dept.Hd.
Staff: Prof 5; Other 3. **Subjects:** Art, music, architecture, sports and
recreation, antiques, dance, prints. **Special Collections:** Holme Collection (a
chronological record of illustrated books). **Holdings:** 41,000 books and bound
periodical volumes; 18,865 musical recordings; 64 VF drawers; 196 VF
drawers of pictures; 35,000 libretti; 11,800 pieces of sheet music.
Subscriptions: 172 journals and other serials. **Services:** Interlibrary loans;
copying; library open to public. **Computerized Information Services:** New

York Times Information Service. **Networks/Consortia:** Member of Maryland
Interlibrary Loan Organization (MILO). **Special Indexes:** Song index; analytical
index; popular sheet music index; dance index; games index (all on cards).
Staff: Margaret Ericson, Prof.Asst.; Rosalia Shriver, Prof.Asst.; Ruth
Sundermeyer, Prof.Asst.; Marta-Marie Graziani, Prof.Asst.

ENOCH PRATT FREE LIBRARY - GEORGE PEABODY DEPARTMENT
See: Johns Hopkins University - Milton S. Eisenhower Library - George
      Peabody Collection

★4147★
ENOCH PRATT FREE LIBRARY - JOB AND CAREER INFORMATION CENTER
(Soc Sci)
400 Cathedral St.
Baltimore, MD 21201   Patricia Dougherty, Libn./Counselor
Founded: 1981. **Subjects:** Vocational guidance, job/person matching,
trades. **Holdings:** Figures not available for books; 270 reference titles; 16 VF
drawers. **Subscriptions:** 22 journals and other serials. **Services:** Center open
to public. **Remarks:** The center is contained in Enoch Pratt Free Library -
Business, Science and Technology Department.

★4148★
ENOCH PRATT FREE LIBRARY - MARYLAND DEPARTMENT (Hist)
400 Cathedral St.   Phone: (301) 396-5468
Baltimore, MD 21201   Morgan H. Pritchett, Hd.
Founded: 1934. **Staff:** Prof 4; Other 5. **Subjects:** State of Maryland -
persons, places, subjects. **Holdings:** 40,000 volumes; 7000 uncataloged
documents; 2100 maps; 24,000 photographs; 1272 fine prints; 4000
postcards; vertical files of clippings, pamphlets. **Subscriptions:** 40 journals
and other serials. **Services:** Interlibrary loans; copying; library open to public.
Special Indexes: Biography file, query file, documents file (all card). **Staff:**
Eva Slezak, Spec.; Robert Stevens, Libn.; Patricia Andrews, Libn.

★4149★
**ENOCH PRATT FREE LIBRARY - SOCIAL SCIENCE AND HISTORY
DEPARTMENT** (Soc Sci; Hist)
400 Cathedral St.   Phone: (301) 396-5430
Baltimore, MD 21201   Marva Belt, Hd.
Staff: Prof 10; Other 3. **Subjects:** Sociology, biography, travel, anthropology,
political science, law, history, education. **Special Collections:** Foundation
Center Collection; college catalogs (4225). **Holdings:** 250,000 volumes; 161
VF drawers; 250 recordings; depository library for government documents.
Subscriptions: 625 journals and other serials. **Services:** Interlibrary loans;
copying; open to public. **Computerized Information Services:** New York
Times Information Service. **Networks/Consortia:** Member of Maryland
Interlibrary Loan Organization (MILO). **Staff:** Harriet Jenkins, Asst.Hd.

★4150★
ENQUIRER AND NEWS - EDITORIAL REFERENCE LIBRARY (Publ)
155 W. Van Buren St.   Phone: (616) 964-7161
Battle Creek, MI 49016   Wanda G. Halsey, Libn.
Staff: Prof 1; Other 3. **Subjects:** Local events, area history. **Special
Collections:** Battle Creek newspapers dating back to 1846 (on microfilm).
Holdings: 1100 books; 900 reels of microfilm; maps; newspaper clippings,
photographs. **Services:** Library open to public for reference use only with
permission.

★4151★
**ENSANIAN PHYSICOCHEMICAL INSTITUTE - INFORMATION CENTER FOR
GRAVITATION CHEMISTRY** (Sci-Tech)
Box 98   Phone: (814) 225-3296
Eldred, PA 16731   Elizabeth A. Ensanian, Chf.Libn.
Founded: 1968. **Staff:** Prof 3. **Subjects:** Gravitation, chemistry, physics,
biology, engineering. **Special Collections:** Reports of zero gravity drop tower
experiments. **Holdings:** 1300 books; 2000 bound periodical volumes; 850
reports (cataloged); 400 reprints on gravity phenomena; 350 microfiche.
Subscriptions: 43 journals and other serials; 5 newspapers. **Services:** Will
answer brief inquiries and make referrals; library open to public with
restrictions. **Publications:** Literature Survey, quarterly - for internal
distribution only; Annual Review of Gravitational Chemistry - for internal
distribution only; Journal of the Ensanian Physicochemical Institute (book
form). **Staff:** Armand O. Ensanian, Ref.Libn.; Bernard Caplan, Res.Spec.;
Tamara Ensanian, Res.Spec.

★4152★
ENSCO, INC. - TECHNICAL LIBRARY (Sci-Tech; Trans)
5400 Port Royal Rd.   Phone: (703) 321-4604
Springfield, VA 22151   Sue E. Littlepage, Res.Libn.
Staff: Prof 1; Other 1. **Subjects:** Railroad and highway safety technology,

mining safety, electronics, seismic detection, surface radar. **Special Collections:** Railroad technology (1200 volumes). **Holdings:** 3500 books and bound periodical volumes; 1200 railroad slides; 17 VF drawers of technical reports and reprints. **Subscriptions:** 115 journals and other serials. **Services:** Interlibrary loans; copying; library not open to public. **Computerized Information Services:** SDC, DTIC, DIALOG. **Special Catalogs:** Rail Technology Thesaurus.

ENTOMOLOGICAL SOCIETY OF BRITISH COLUMBIA COLLECTION
See: Canada - Agriculture Canada - Research Station, Vancouver - Library

★4153★
ENVIRODYNE ENGINEERS, INC. - LIBRARY (Env-Con)
12161 Lackland Rd.　　　　　　　Phone: (314) 434-6960
St. Louis, MO 63141　　　　　Kathryn L. Flowers, Libn./Info.Spec.
Staff: Prof 1; Other 1. **Subjects:** Water and air pollution, wastewater treatment, hazardous waste management, chemical analysis. **Holdings:** 1800 books; 900 government documents. **Subscriptions:** 87 journals and other serials. **Services:** Interlibrary loans; copying; library open to public by appointment. **Computerized Information Services:** DIALOG. **Networks/Consortia:** Member of St. Louis Regional Library Network.

★4154★
ENVIRONIC FOUNDATION INTERNATIONAL, INC. - LIBRARY AND FILES
(Plan)
Box 88　　　　　　　　　　Phone: (219) 233-3357
Notre Dame, IN 46556　　　　　　Patrick Horsbrugh, Chm.
Founded: 1970. **Staff:** 4. **Subjects:** Urban planning; geotecture (subterranean accommodation); thalatecture (construction in the shallows); hypostecture (high structures); limnotecture (design of lakes); nesotecture (design of islands); synecotecture (structures that accomodate vegetation in association with human requirements); synecopolis (design of cities using synecological principles); poietic encyclement (remaking all that is made - the ultimate technological achievement); person/plant proxemics (the values of close interrelationships between vegetation and human well-being). **Special Collections:** John Bunge Papers; Thames Barrage Project, 1927-1957; High Paddington (London) Papers, 1950-1954; New Barbican (London) Papers, 1954-1955. **Holdings:** 6000 books. **Subscriptions:** 64 journals and other serials. **Services:** Library open to public for reference use only on request.

ENVIRONMENT CANADA
See: Canada - Environment Canada

★4155★
ENVIRONMENT INFORMATION CENTER, INC. (Env-Cons; Energy)
48 W. 38th St.　　　　　　　Phone: (212) 944-8500
New York, NY 10018　　　　　James G. Kollegger, Pres. & Pub.
Founded: 1970. **Subjects:** Genetic engineering - impacts, constraints, legal issues, industrial applications, energy applications, food applications, crops, human, animals, research; environment - noise pollution, population control, renewable resources-terrestrial, renewable resources-water, wildlife, weather; energy - policy, coal, natural gas, petroleum, electricity, solar, nuclear. **Special Collections:** Microfiche collection. **Holdings:** 10,000 books. **Subscriptions:** 6000 journals and other serials. **Services:** Copying. **Computerized Information Services:** DIALOG, BRS, SDC; Telegenline, Enviroline, Energyline, Energynet (internal databases). **Publications:** List of publications - available on request. **Staff:** Monica Pronin, Dir., Ed.Prod.

★4156★
ENVIRONMENTAL ACTION COALITION - LIBRARY/RESOURCE CENTER
(Env-Cons)
417 Lafayette St.　　　　　　Phone: (212) 677-1601
New York, NY 10003　　　　　Diane Buxbaum, Off.Mgr.
Staff: Prof 3. **Subjects:** Natural resources, urban forestry, energy, pollution, solid and toxic waste, natural sciences, alternative lifestyles. **Holdings:** 3000 books; 500 bound periodical volumes; reports; 4 volumes of newspaper clippings; 30 films; AV items; VF drawers. **Subscriptions:** 13 journals and other serials. **Services:** Library open to public with borrowing privileges reserved for members. **Publications:** ECO News; ECO-facts; Cycle; Waste Paper (periodicals); It's Your Environment (book).

ENVIRONMENTAL CONSERVATION LIBRARY OF MINNESOTA
See: Minneapolis Public Library & Information Center

ENVIRONMENTAL DATA & INFORMATION SERVICE
See: U.S. Natl. Oceanic & Atmospheric Administration

★4157★
ENVIRONMENTAL EDUCATION GROUP - LIBRARY (Env-Cons)
5762 Firebird Ct.　　　　　　Phone: (213) 340-7309
Camarillo, CA 93010　　　　　Alan Arthur Tratner, Exec.Dir.
Founded: 1972. **Staff:** Prof 2. **Subjects:** Air pollution, water pollution, anti-pollution technologies, land use, environment, energy alternatives, geothermal information. **Special Collections:** Public Interest Reports; Energy Charts. **Holdings:** 300 books; back issues of environmental journals and magazines; 2000 slides on all subjects. **Subscriptions:** 35 journals and other serials. **Services:** Interlibrary loans; research services and consultation for environmental education; library open to public by written request. **Publications:** Pollution Watch; Public Interest Reports. **Special Indexes:** Environmental bibliographies, energy information. **Staff:** Karen Lee Darwin, Projects Ed.

★4158★
ENVIRONMENTAL IMPACT PLANNING CORPORATION - LIBRARY (Env-Cons)
319 Eleventh St.　　　　　　Phone: (415) 864-2311
San Francisco, CA 94103　　　　Cathleen Galloway Brown, Libn.
Founded: 1972. **Staff:** Prof 1. **Subjects:** Environment, natural resources, pollution, hydrology, geology, community planning. **Holdings:** 4000 reports and other items. **Subscriptions:** 72 journals and other serials. **Services:** Interlibrary loans; library open to public by appointment.

★4159★
ENVIRONMENTAL LAW INSTITUTE - LIBRARY (Law; Env-Cons)
1346 Connecticut Ave., N.W., Suite 620　Phone: (202) 452-9600
Washington, DC 20036　　　　　Iva Futrell, Libn.
Staff: Prof 1. **Subjects:** Environmental law, toxic substances, natural resources, energy, air and water pollution. **Special Collections:** Federal Environmental Impact Statements (9000). **Holdings:** 5000 books. **Subscriptions:** 318 journals and other serials. **Services:** Interlibrary loans; copying (fee); library open to public by appointment. **Computerized Information Services:** DIALOG, New York Times Information Service. **Special Indexes:** Subject index to environmental law articles in selected law journals (card).

ENVIRONMENTAL MUTAGEN INFORMATION CENTER
See: Oak Ridge National Laboratory - Information Division

★4160★
ENVIRONMENTAL PROTECTION AGENCY - ANDREW W. BREIDENBACH ENVIRONMENTAL RESEARCH CTR., CINCINNATI - TECH.LIB. (Env-Cons)
26 W. St. Clair Ave.　　　　　Phone: (513) 684-7701
Cincinnati, OH 45268　　　　　JoAnn Johnson, Chf., Lib.Serv.
Founded: 1971. **Staff:** Prof 6; Other 11. **Subjects:** Environmental pollution, solid waste, chemistry, medical science, biology, instrumentation. **Holdings:** 30,000 books; 10,000 bound periodical volumes; 50,000 technical reports. **Subscriptions:** 1300 journals and other serials; 7 newspapers. **Services:** Interlibrary loans; copying; SDI; library open to public for reference use only. **Computerized Information Services:** Computer database retrieval on 50 systems; computerized cataloging, serials and circulation. **Networks/Consortia:** Member of OCLC; Greater Cincinnati Library Consortium; Kentucky-Ohio-Michigan Regional Medical Libraries; Cincinnati Area Health Sciences Library Association (CAHSLA). **Publications:** Serials Holding List; Computerized Literature Searching and Data Bases. **Special Catalogs:** Document Control System. **Staff:** Dottie F. Brofft, Ref.Libn.; Harriet Rusin, Lit. Searcher; Mary L. Burbage, Cat.; Maxine M. Smith, Lit. Searcher; Jonda Byrd, ILL Libn.; Lilian Bosworth, Coll.Dev./Circ.; Larry Cline, Doc. Control.

★4161★
ENVIRONMENTAL PROTECTION AGENCY - CENTRAL REGIONAL LABORATORY - LIBRARY (Env-Cons)
839 Bestgate Rd.　　　　　　Phone: (301) 224-2740
Annapolis, MD 21401　　　　　Margaret Munro, Libn.
Founded: 1964. **Staff:** Prof 1. **Subjects:** Water quality management, marine environment, biological indicators, mathematical modeling, toxic substances. **Special Collections:** Scientific studies of Chesapeake Bay. **Holdings:** 600 books; 3000 reprints; 140 Annapolis Field Office publications; 2000 EPA R&D reports. **Subscriptions:** 68 journals and other serials. **Services:** Interlibrary loans; copying; library open to public for reference use only.

★4162★
ENVIRONMENTAL PROTECTION AGENCY - DIVISION OF METEOROLOGY - INFORMATION SERVICE CENTER (Env-Cons)
　　　　　　　　　　Phone: (919) 541-4536
Research Triangle Park, NC 27711　Evelyn M. Poole-Kober, Tech.Info.Ck.
Founded: 1971. **Subjects:** Air pollution, meteorology. **Holdings:** 1200 books;

13,000 hard copy documents and technical reports; microfiche. **Subscriptions:** 125 journals and other serials. **Services:** Interlibrary loans; library open to Environmental Protection Agency (EPA) personnel and others under contract to the agency.

★4163★

ENVIRONMENTAL PROTECTION AGENCY - EASTERN ENVIRONMENTAL RADIATION LAB - LIBRARY (Sci-Tech; Env-Cons)
Box 3009   Phone: (205) 272-3402
Montgomery, AL 36193   Charles M. Petko, Supv., Spec.Serv.
Founded: 1960. **Subjects:** Analytical chemistry of radionuclides, electronic products, microwave energy, nuclear power reactors and their environmental effects. **Holdings:** 1050 books; 4000 technical reports; 7000 technical reports on microfiche. **Subscriptions:** 120 journals and other serials. **Services:** Interlibrary loans; library not open to public.

★4164★

ENVIRONMENTAL PROTECTION AGENCY - ENVIRONMENTAL MONITORING SYSTEMS LABORATORY - LIBRARY
Box 15027
Las Vegas, NV 89114
Defunct. Holdings merged into University of Nevada's general collection.

★4165★

ENVIRONMENTAL PROTECTION AGENCY - ENVIRONMENTAL RESEARCH LABORATORY, ATHENS - LIBRARY (Env-Cons)
College Station Rd.   Phone: (404) 546-3324
Athens, GA 30613   Charlotte C. Folk, Libn.
Founded: 1967. **Staff:** Prof 1; Other 1. **Subjects:** Sanitary engineering, chemistry, biology, environmental systems, aquatic biology. **Holdings:** 5000 books; 7000 government documents; 100 journals on microfilm. **Subscriptions:** 170 journals and other serials. **Services:** Interlibrary loans; copying; library open to public. **Computerized Information Services:** Online systems; computerized cataloging and circulation.

★4166★

ENVIRONMENTAL PROTECTION AGENCY - ENVIRONMENTAL RESEARCH LABORATORY, CORVALLIS - LIBRARY (Env-Cons)
200 S.W. 35th St.   Phone: (503) 757-4731
Corvallis, OR 97330   Betty M. McCauley, Libn.
Founded: 1966. **Staff:** Prof 1; Other 1. **Subjects:** Effects of air, water and soil pollutants on the ecosystem; marine and freshwater ecosystems; toxic substances; fish toxicology; hazardous waste. **Special Collections:** Acid rain (4000 documents). **Holdings:** 2200 books; 6200 reports; 15,000 microforms. **Subscriptions:** 153 journals and other serials. **Services:** Interlibrary loans; copying; library open to public for reference use only. **Computerized Information Services:** Computerized cataloging, circulation. **Networks/Consortia:** Member of U.S. Environmental Protection Agency System; OCLC; FEDLINK.

★4167★

ENVIRONMENTAL PROTECTION AGENCY - ENVIRONMENTAL RESEARCH LABORATORY, GULF BREEZE - LIBRARY (Env-Cons)
Sabine Island, 6   Phone: (904) 932-5311
Gulf Breeze, FL 32561   Andree Lowry, Libn.
Founded: 1967. **Staff:** Prof 1; Other 1. **Subjects:** Pesticides, microbial ecology, marine ecology, fishery biology, carcinogens. **Holdings:** 2000 books; 4000 reprints; 14,000 publications on microfiche. **Subscriptions:** 200 journals and other serials. **Services:** Interlibrary loans; copying; library open to public for reference use only on a limited basis. **Computerized Information Services:** DIALOG, SDC, BRS, NLM; computerized cataloging and circulation. **Networks/Consortia:** Member of U.S. Environmental Protection Agency System; OCLC. **Publications:** List of publications - available on request.

★4168★

ENVIRONMENTAL PROTECTION AGENCY - ENVIRONMENTAL RESEARCH LABORATORY, NARRAGANSETT - LIBRARY (Env-Cons)†
South Ferry Rd.   Phone: (401) 789-1071
Narragansett, RI 02882   Rose Ann Gamache, Libn.
Founded: 1966. **Staff:** 1. **Subjects:** Biological oceanography, marine ecology, biomedical science, fisheries biology, chemistry. **Holdings:** 15,000 technical reports, collected reprints; microforms. **Subscriptions:** 45 journals and other serials. **Services:** Interlibrary loans; copying; library open to public with restrictions. **Computerized Information Services:** Online system; computerized cataloging and serials.

★4169★

ENVIRONMENTAL PROTECTION AGENCY - HEADQUARTERS LIBRARY (Env-Cons)
401 M St., S.W., Rm. 2404   Phone: (202) 755-0308
Washington, DC 20460   Sami Klein, Chf.
Founded: 1971. **Staff:** Prof 5; Other 4. **Subjects:** Water pollution and control, environment, pesticides, air pollution, solid waste, noise pollution, environmental health and law, toxic substances control. **Holdings:** 6000 books; 25,000 unbound reports and documents; 300 reels of microfilm; 200,000 microfiche; periodicals (unbound and on film). **Subscriptions:** 904 journals and other serials. **Services:** Interlibrary loans; translations (both limited); library open to public. **Computerized Information Services:** DIALOG, SDC, BRS, MEDLARS, JOURNALINK, New York Times Information Service; computerized cataloging and circulation. **Networks/Consortia:** Headquarters of U.S. Environmental Protection Agency System; member of OCLC; FEDLINK; COG. **Publications:** Journal Holdings Report, annual - distributed to other libraries; Users Guide to the EPA Library System - all distributed to EPA staff and its library system. **Special Catalogs:** Journal Holdings Report and the upcoming Book Holdings Report are maintained on computer tape and are published on COM microfiche. **Staff:** Claudia Norwood, Ref.Sect.; Alice Wills, Tech.Serv.; Bruce Ingalls, Ref.Sect.

★4170★

ENVIRONMENTAL PROTECTION AGENCY - LIBRARY SERVICES (Env-Cons)†
MD 35   Phone: (919) 541-2777
Research Triangle Park, NC 27711   Libby Smith, Libn.
Founded: 1970. **Staff:** Prof 4; Other 10. **Subjects:** Air pollution effects and control. **Special Collections:** APTIC (Air Pollution Technical Information Center) Collection; Environmental Protection Agency document distribution center. **Holdings:** 4000 books and bound periodical volumes; 12,000 technical reports; 200,000 microfiche. **Subscriptions:** 550 journals and other serials. **Services:** Interlibrary loans; copying; SDI (all services limited); library open to public. **Computerized Information Services:** DIALOG, SDC, MEDLINE; computerized cataloging, serials and circulation. **Publications:** Combined journal holdings list for the Environmental Protection Agency - Library Services and the National Institute of Environmental Health Sciences Library, both located at Research Triangle Park, NC. **Staff:** Harriet J. Myers, Lib.Techn.; John Knight, Comp.Prog.Techn.

★4171★

ENVIRONMENTAL PROTECTION AGENCY - MOTOR VEHICLE EMISSION LABORATORY - LIBRARY (Env-Cons)
2565 Plymouth Rd.   Phone: (313) 668-4311
Ann Arbor, MI 48105   Debra Talsma, Libn.
Staff: Prof 1. **Subjects:** Automotive engineering, air pollution from mobile sources, alternative fuels for motor vehicles. **Special Collections:** SAE papers (4000); automotive service/shop manuals (350); EPA final and technical reports (1000). **Holdings:** 360 books; 15,000 reports on microfiche; 300 legislative documents; patents. **Subscriptions:** 64 journals and other serials. **Services:** Interlibrary loans; copying; library not open to public. **Special Catalogs:** EPA Motor Vehicle Emmission Laboratory final and technical report listing.

★4172★

ENVIRONMENTAL PROTECTION AGENCY - NATIONAL ENFORCEMENT INVESTIGATIONS - LIBRARY (Env-Cons)
Denver Federal Ctr., Bldg. 53
Box 25227   Phone: (303) 234-5765
Denver, CO 80225   Mary Quinlivan, Libn.
Founded: 1972. **Staff:** Prof 1; Other 1. **Subjects:** Water quality, industrial and agricultural pollution abatement practices, air pollution, pesticides, hazardous wastes. **Holdings:** 1000 volumes; 150,000 microfiche; technical reports; R&D reports, conference documents, state of the art on municipal, industrial and agricultural pollution abatement practices. **Subscriptions:** 150 journals and other serials. **Services:** Interlibrary loans; copying; library open to public with restrictions. **Computerized Information Services:** DIALOG, SDC, DOE/RECON, NLM, New York Times Information Service, WESTLAW, NIH-EPA Chemical Information System; computerized cataloging and serials. **Staff:** Charlene Swibas, Tech.Info.Spec.

★4173★

ENVIRONMENTAL PROTECTION AGENCY - REGION I LIBRARY (Env-Cons)
JFK Bldg., Rm. 2100-B   Phone: (617) 223-5791
Boston, MA 02203   Ruth K. Seidman, Libn.
Founded: 1970. **Subjects:** Solid waste management, air pollution, pesticides, radiation, noise abatement, water quality. **Special Collections:** Documerica (picture index to 150,000 photographs). **Holdings:** 10,000 books, government documents and technical reports; 100,000 microfiche.

Subscriptions: 250 journals and other serials. **Services:** Interlibrary loans; Current Awareness services (limited); library open to public for reference use only; borrowing through ILL only. **Computerized Information Services:** BRS. **Networks/Consortia:** Member of Environmental Protection Agency System.

★4174★

ENVIRONMENTAL PROTECTION AGENCY - REGION II FIELD OFFICE - TECHNICAL LIBRARY (Env-Cons)

Edison, NJ 08837

Phone: (201) 321-6000
Dorothy Szefczyk, Lib.Techn.

Founded: 1967. **Staff:** 1. **Subjects:** Water pollution, water quality, environmental quality. **Holdings:** 2100 books; 15 bound periodical volumes; 10,000 federal and state reports; 50,000 microfiche. **Subscriptions:** 40 journals and other serials. **Services:** Interlibrary loans; copying; library open to public. **Networks/Consortia:** Member of OCLC. **Publications:** Selected Acquisitions - distributed within the region, to other EPA libraries.

★4175★

ENVIRONMENTAL PROTECTION AGENCY - REGION II LIBRARY (Env-Cons)

26 Federal Plaza, Rm. 1002
New York, NY 10007

Phone: (212) 264-2881
Christopher E. James, Lib.Techn.

Founded: 1965. **Staff:** 2. **Subjects:** Environmental quality, aquatic biology, energy resources. **Holdings:** 4200 books; 900 bound periodical volumes; 21,000 reports (cataloged); 170,000 microfiche. **Subscriptions:** 315 journals and other serials. **Services:** Interlibrary loans; library open to public for reference use only. **Computerized Information Services:** JOURNALINK; computerized cataloging. **Networks/Consortia:** Member of U.S. Environmental Protection Agency System; OCLC. **Publications:** Library Acquisitions; occasional bibliographies.

★4176★

ENVIRONMENTAL PROTECTION AGENCY - REGION III LIBRARY (Env-Cons)

Curtis Bldg., 6th & Walnut Sts.
Philadelphia, PA 19106

Phone: (215) 597-0580
Diane M. McCreary, Libn.

Founded: 1972. **Staff:** Prof 1; Other 1. **Subjects:** Environmental sciences and law, management, economics, toxicology. **Special Collections:** Wetland ecology. **Holdings:** 5600 books; 7000 technical reports; 75,000 microfiche. **Subscriptions:** 203 journals and other serials. **Services:** Interlibrary loans; copying; library open to public for reference use only. **Computerized Information Services:** DIALOG, MEDLARS, LEXIS; computerized circulation. **Publications:** User's guide; bimonthly acquisitions list; periodical holdings list; subject bibliographies.

★4177★

ENVIRONMENTAL PROTECTION AGENCY - REGION IV LIBRARY (Env-Cons)

345 Courtland St.
Atlanta, GA 30308

Phone: (404) 881-4216
Carolyn W. Mitchell, Hd.Libn.

Founded: 1973. **Staff:** Prof 1; Other 3. **Subjects:** Water, air and noise pollution, solid waste management, toxic substances, Southeastern U.S. ecology. **Special Collections:** Environmental impact statements. **Holdings:** 2000 books; 110,000 documents (cataloged); state environmental laws on microfiche. **Subscriptions:** 253 journals and other serials. **Services:** Interlibrary loans; copying; SDI; library open to public. **Computerized Information Services:** Online systems; computerized cataloging, acquisitions, serials and circulation; EPA reports, documents catalog, hardbound books - all online. **Networks/Consortia:** Member of U.S. Environmental Protection Agency System; OCLC through FEDLINK. **Publications:** Monthly Acquisitions - for internal distribution only. **Special Catalogs:** Document Control System.

★4178★

ENVIRONMENTAL PROTECTION AGENCY - REGION V LIBRARY (Env-Cons)

230 S. Dearborn St., Rm. 1420
Chicago, IL 60604

Phone: (312) 353-2022
Ms. Lou W. Tilley, Regional Libn.

Founded: 1972. **Staff:** Prof 2; Other 1. **Subjects:** Water quality and supply; air quality and air pollution; solid waste management; pesticides; radiation; noise; energy; hazardous wastes; toxic substances; environmental science; environmental law - emphasis on the Great Lakes and six states in the region: Illinois, Indiana, Michigan, Minnesota, Ohio and Wisconsin. **Special Collections:** Environmental Protection Agency and predecessor agency reports (complete set); Air Pollution Technical Information Center (APTIC) file. **Holdings:** 3550 books; 18,000 state and federal documents (cataloged); 10 VF drawers; 56 VF drawers of microforms; **Subscriptions:** 465 journals and other serials. **Services:** Interlibrary loans; copying; SDI (for staff only); library open to public for reference use only. **Computerized Information Services:** Internal databases; computerized cataloging, circulation and ILL. **Networks/Consortia:** Member of U.S. Environmental Protection Agency System; OCLC. **Publications:** Region V Library Selected Acquisitions, quarterly - in-house and available on request; Fact Sheet, irregular.

★4179★

ENVIRONMENTAL PROTECTION AGENCY - REGION VI LIBRARY (Env-Cons)

First International Bldg.
1201 Elm St.
Dallas, TX 75270

Phone: (214) 767-7341

Founded: 1971. **Subjects:** Law, river basins, environmental science, toxicology, water, air, solid waste, radiation. **Holdings:** 4100 books; 600 bound periodical volumes; 5725 cataloged documents; 323 drawers of microfiche; 425 reels of microfilm; 7650 maps. **Subscriptions:** 150 journals and other serials. **Services:** Interlibrary loans; copying; Current Awareness reports; library open to public with restrictions. **Computerized Information Services:** DIALOG, SDC, MEDLINE, JOURNALINK; computerized cataloging and circulation. **Networks/Consortia:** Member of OCLC through FEDLINK. **Publications:** What's New, monthly - to employees.

★4180★

ENVIRONMENTAL PROTECTION AGENCY - REGION VII LIBRARY (Env-Cons)

324 E. 11th St., 16th Fl.
Kansas City, MO 64106

Phone: (816) 374-3497
Connie McKenzie, Libn.

Founded: 1970. **Subjects:** Air and water pollution, solid waste, pesticides, environmental law, radiation, agricultural pollution, water hygiene, chemistry, biology, ecology, management, geology. **Holdings:** 1000 books; 3000 technical reports; 100,000 technical reports on microfiche. **Subscriptions:** 50 journals and other serials. **Services:** Interlibrary loans.

★4181★

ENVIRONMENTAL PROTECTION AGENCY - REGION VIII LIBRARY (Env-Cons)

1860 Lincoln St., Suite 103
Denver, CO 80295-0699

Phone: (303) 837-2560
Dolores D. Eddy, Regional Libn.

Founded: 1973. **Staff:** Prof 1; Other 1. **Subjects:** Water, air, solid waste management, pesticides, radiation, noise, toxic substances, energy. **Special Collections:** Microfiche collections of air pollution literature and of EPA technical reports. **Holdings:** 1200 books; 14,000 EPA and technical reports; 110,000 microfiche. **Subscriptions:** 353 journals and other serials. **Services:** Interlibrary loans; library open to public for reference use only. **Computerized Information Services:** Computerized cataloging. **Networks/Consortia:** Member of U.S. Environmental Protection Agency System. **Publications:** Library Acquisitions Update, monthly - available in the library.

★4182★

ENVIRONMENTAL PROTECTION AGENCY - REGION IX LIBRARY/ INFORMATION CENTER (Env-Cons)

215 Fremont St.
San Francisco, CA 94105

Phone: (415) 974-8076
Jean Circiello, Libn.

Founded: 1969. **Staff:** Prof 5; Other 2. **Subjects:** Environment including water and air pollution, solid waste management, noise and radiation, especially in California, Arizona, Nevada, Hawaii and the Pacific Islands. **Special Collections:** Environmental Impact Statements. **Holdings:** 4000 books; 2000 bound periodical volumes; 225,000 reports (cataloged); 150,000 reports on microfiche. **Subscriptions:** 300 journals and other serials. **Services:** Interlibrary loans; copying; library open to public for reference use only. **Computerized Information Services:** DIALOG; computerized cataloging, circulation and literature searches. **Networks/Consortia:** Member of U.S. Environmental Protection Agency System; OCLC; CLASS. **Publications:** List of Acquisitions, monthly; Fact Sheet, EPA Region IX Library.

★4183★

ENVIRONMENTAL PROTECTION AGENCY - REGION X LIBRARY (Env-Cons)

1200 Sixth Ave.
Seattle, WA 98101

Phone: (206) 442-1289
Julienne Sears, Regional Libn.

Founded: 1971. **Staff:** Prof 1; Other 2. **Subjects:** Environmental pollution. **Holdings:** Figures not available. **Subscriptions:** 125 journals and other serials. **Services:** Interlibrary loans; library open to public for reference use only. **Computerized Information Services:** Computerized cataloging and circulation.

★4184★

ENVIRONMENTAL PROTECTION AGENCY - ROBERT S. KERR ENVIRONMENTAL RESEARCH CENTER - LIBRARY (Env-Cons)†

Box 1198
Ada, OK 74820

Phone: (405) 332-8800
Ms. LoRene Fuller, Libn.

Founded: 1966. **Staff:** Prof 1; Other 1. **Subjects:** Water pollution, agricultural pollution, ground water quality and pollution, soil treatment and aquaculture technology, chemical pollution, chemistry, sanitary engineering, aquatic biology. **Special Collections:** Animal Waste Management Collection (over 5000 items on animal waste, treatment, disposal, utilization). **Holdings:** 2000 volumes; 2100 maps; 25,000 reports (hard copy and/or microfiche).

Subscriptions: 196 journals and other serials. Services: Interlibrary loans; copying; library open to public for reference use only. Computerized Information Services: Online systems; computerized cataloging, serials, maps and reports. Networks/Consortia: Member of OCLC. Publications: Publication List.

★4185★
ENVIRONMENTAL PROTECTION AGENCY - WENATCHEE PESTICIDES RESEARCH BRANCH - LIBRARY
Box 219
Wenatchee, WA 98801
Defunct

ENVIRONMENTAL PROTECTION SERVICE
See: Canada - Environmental Protection Service

★4186★
ENVIRONMENTAL RESEARCH INSTITUTE OF MICHIGAN - ERIM INFORMATION CENTER (Env-Cons; Sci-Tech)
Box 8618
Ann Arbor, MI 48107
Phone: (313) 994-1200
Corliss A. Hugg, Mgr.
Founded: 1977. Staff: Prof 1; Other 2. Subjects: Remote sensing; infrared and electro-optical technology and related topics. Holdings: 12,000 books; 1500 bound periodical volumes; 70,000 unbound reports; 500 maps; LANDSAT, radar and aerial photographs. Subscriptions: 350 journals and other serials. Services: Interlibrary loans; copying; library open to public by appointment. Computerized Information Services: DIALOG, DTIC, SPIRES. Publications: ERIM Bibliography, irregular - distributed on request; Information Center Acquisitions, monthly - for internal distribution only.

★4187★
ENVIRONMENTAL RESEARCH INSTITUTE OF MICHIGAN - INFRARED INFORMATION AND ANALYSIS CENTER (IRIA) (Sci-Tech)
Box 8618
Ann Arbor, MI 48107
Phone: (313) 994-1200
George J. Zissis, Dir.
Founded: 1956. Staff: Prof 4; Other 4. Subjects: Infrared and electro-optical technology and associated topics. Holdings: 1000 books; 37,000 technical reports. Subscriptions: 25 journals and other serials. Services: Center open to visitors with security clearance. Computerized Information Services: DIALOG, DTIC; computer printed bibliographies for subscribers. Publications: Proceedings of IRIA; annotated bibliographies; state-of-the-art reports; The Infrared Handbook. Remarks: Dept. of Defense information and analysis center providing bibliographic and other information services to authorized requesters includes the infrared and optical collection of the Ballistic Missile Radiation Analysis Center (BAMIRAC); formerly associated with the University of Michigan. Staff: Mildred F. Denecke, Mgr.

ENVIRONMENTAL RESEARCH LABORATORIES, EPA
See: Environmental Protection Agency - Environmental Research Laboratory ...

ENVIRONMENTAL RESEARCH LABORATORIES, NOAA
See: U.S. Natl. Oceanic & Atmospheric Administration

★4188★
ENVIRONMENTAL RESEARCH & TECHNOLOGY, INC. - ENVIRONMENTAL CONTRACTING CENTER LIBRARY (Env-Cons; Energy)
Box 2105
Fort Collins, CO 80522
Phone: (303) 493-8878
Sally Ramsey, Adm.
Founded: 1972. Staff: Prof 1. Subjects: Ecology, pollution, environmental science, energy, impact assessment, mining reclamation. Special Collections: Oil shale; environmental impact statements; federal and state regulations and guidelines for the Rocky Mountain region; oil spills. Holdings: 3500 books; 200 bound technical reports; 700 technical reports; 500 maps; reprints. Subscriptions: 200 journals and other serials; 10 newspapers. Services: Interlibrary loans; copying; SDI; library open to public for reference use only. Computerized Information Services: Online systems. Special Indexes: Reprint literature for benthos, fishes, ornithology, mammology, water quality, hydrology, air quality, vegetation. Remarks: Library is located at 1716 Heath Pkwy., Fort Collins, CO 80524. Formerly: Its Life Sciences Information Center.

★4189★
ENVIRONMENTAL RESEARCH & TECHNOLOGY, INC. - INFORMATION CENTER (Env-Cons)
696 Virginia Rd.
Concord, MA 01742
Phone: (617) 369-8910
Brenda Y. Allen, Libn.
Founded: 1972. Staff: Prof 2; Other 1. Subjects: Environmental sciences, meteorology, biology, chemistry, energy, mathematical modeling. Holdings:

4000 books; 10,000 scientific and technical reports; microfiche collection. Subscriptions: 400 journals and other serials; 10 newspapers. Services: Interlibrary loans; copying; SDI; library open to public by appointment. Computerized Information Services: DIALOG, SDC, Dun & Bradstreet, Inc.; computerized cataloging. Networks/Consortia: Member of OCLC. Publications: Accessions list, monthly - for internal distribution only; Environmental News Alert, biweekly - for internal distribution only. Remarks: Company is a subsidiary of Communications Satellite Corporation (COMSAT). Also Known As: ERT, Inc. Staff: Deanna C. Lynn, Asst.Libn.

★4190★
ENVIRONMENTAL RESEARCH & TECHNOLOGY, INC. - WESTERN REGIONAL OFFICE - LIBRARY (Env-Cons)
2625 Townsgate Rd., Suite 360
Westlake Village, CA 91361
Phone: (213) 889-5313
Marcia Henry, Libn.
Founded: 1977. Staff: Prof 1; Other 1. Subjects: Air pollution, environmental chemistry, environmental impact statements. Holdings: 150 books; 1000 technical reports, state documents, environmental impact statements; 1200 company reports; 500 Environmental Protection Agency reports; 1000 microfiche; 300 U.S. Geological Survey maps. Subscriptions: 60 journals and other serials. Services: Interlibrary loans; copying; SDI; library not open to public. Computerized Information Services: DIALOG, NLM. Networks/Consortia: Member of OCLC. Publications: Library newsletter, biweekly - for internal distribution only.

ENVIRONMENTAL TERATOLOGY INFORMATION CENTER
See: National Institute of Environmental Health Sciences

★4191★
ENVIROTECH CORPORATION - LIBRARY
3000 Sand Hill Rd.
Menlo Park, CA 94025
Defunct

EPA
See: Environmental Protection Agency

EPHRATA CLOISTER
See: Pennsylvania State Historical & Museum Commission

EPILEPSY FOUNDATION OF AMERICA
See: National Epilepsy Library and Resource Center

★4192★
EPISCOPAL CHURCH OF THE HOLY FAITH - PARISH LIBRARY (Rel-Theol)
311 E. Palace Ave.
Box 1848
Santa Fe, NM 87501
Phone: (505) 982-4447
Katherine Landers, Libn.
Founded: 1949. Staff: 14. Subjects: Comparative religion, arts and symbolism, Bible, altar, festivals, drama, music, church and related subjects. Holdings: 5063 books; unbound magazines. Subscriptions: 12 journals and other serials. Services: Interlibrary loans; copying; library open to public, circulation by mail. Publications: Lent and Advent Book Lists, annual; supplements to catalog, biennial; Newsletter, quarterly.

EPISCOPAL DIOCESE OF CONNECTICUT
See: Protestant Episcopal Church

EPISCOPAL DIOCESE OF EASTERN OREGON
See: Protestant Episcopal Church

EPISCOPAL DIOCESE OF MASSACHUSETTS
See: Protestant Episcopal Church

EPISCOPAL DIOCESE OF MISSOURI
See: Protestant Episcopal Church - Missouri Diocese

EPISCOPAL DIOCESE OF NEW YORK
See: Protestant Episcopal Church

EPISCOPAL DIOCESE OF SOUTH DAKOTA
See: Protestant Episcopal Church

EPISCOPAL DIOCESE OF SPRINGFIELD, ILLINOIS
See: Protestant Episcopal Church

★4193★

EPISCOPAL HOSPITAL - MEDICAL LIBRARY (Med)
Front St. & Lehigh Ave.
Philadelphia, PA 19125   Phone: (215) 427-7487
      Margaret Flanagan, Med.Libn.
Staff: Prof 1; Other 1. **Subjects:** Medicine and nursing. **Holdings:** 6000 books; 4112 bound periodical volumes; 6 VF drawers of pamphlets; 500 cassettes. **Subscriptions:** 180 journals and other serials. **Services:** Interlibrary loans; copying; library not open to public. **Publications:** Newsletter.

★4194★

EPISCOPAL THEOLOGICAL SEMINARY IN KENTUCKY - BROWNING MEMORIAL LIBRARY (Rel-Theol)
544 Sayre Ave.
Lexington, KY 40508   Phone: (606) 255-9591
      Dorie Ann Stapleton, Libn.
Staff: Prof 1. **Subjects:** Anglican theology, Catholic spirituality, Orthodox works, church history, liturgics, patrology. **Special Collections:** Barnes Collection - Orthodox Eastern Church. **Holdings:** 9500 books and bound periodical volumes. **Subscriptions:** 35 journals and other serials. **Services:** Interlibrary loans; library open to public with special borrower's card.

★4195★

EPISCOPAL THEOLOGICAL SEMINARY OF THE SOUTHWEST - LIBRARY (Rel-Theol)
Box 2247
Austin, TX 78768   Phone: (512) 472-4134
      Harold H. Booher, Libn.
Founded: 1953. **Staff:** Prof 2; Other 2. **Subjects:** Theology, English Church history, biblical criticism, church history (other than English), church and culture, pastoral care, ethics, philosophy, politics, sociology. **Special Collections:** Black Collection of fine editions of nineteenth century English and American literature; Winterbotham Collection (history, geography, language, literature, art and culture of Spanish America). **Holdings:** 78,922 books; 4778 bound periodical volumes. **Subscriptions:** 265 journals and other serials. **Services:** Interlibrary loans; copying; library open to public. **Staff:** Robert E. Cogswell, Cat.; Patricia M. Booher, Circ.Libn.

★4196★

EPPLEY INSTITUTE FOR RESEARCH IN CANCER & ALLIED DISEASES - LIBRARY (Med)
University of Nebraska Medical Ctr.
42nd & Dewey
Omaha, NE 68105   Phone: (402) 541-7669
Founded: 1962. **Subjects:** Chemical and general carcinogenesis, pathology, toxicology. **Holdings:** 1100 books; 2800 bound periodical volumes; 365 institute reprints. **Subscriptions:** 65 journals and other serials. **Services:** Interlibrary loans; copying; library not open to public. **Computerized Information Services:** Online systems.

EPSTEIN (Max) ARCHIVE
See: University of Chicago - Department of Art - Max Epstein Archive

EQUAL EMPLOYMENT OPPORTUNITY COMMISSION
See: U.S. Equal Employment Opportunity Commission

★4197★

EQUIFAX, INC. - CORPORATE LIBRARY (Bus-Fin)
Box 4081
Atlanta, GA 30302   Phone: (404) 885-8320
      Michael McDavid, Corp.Libn.
Founded: 1910. **Staff:** Prof 1; Other 2. **Subjects:** Management, marketing, economics, insurance, general business, employee development. **Special Collections:** American Management Association and Conference Board studies and reports (19 VF drawers); company archives. **Holdings:** 11,000 books; management and self-development tapes; telephone directories. **Subscriptions:** 300 journals and other serials; 10 newspapers. **Services:** Interlibrary loans; copying; library open to public by appointment. **Computerized Information Services:** DIALOG, Dow Jones News Retrieval, New York Times Information Service; computerized periodical routing. **Networks/Consortia:** Member of Georgia Library Information Network (GLIN); SOLINET. **Publications:** Library Update, bimonthly - distributed to management personnel; Reading for Management, annual - distributed to managers.

★4198★

EQUITABLE LIFE ASSURANCE SOCIETY OF THE U.S. - INFORMATION SERVICES DIVISION (Bus-Fin)
1285 Ave. of the Americas
New York, NY 10019   Phone: (201) 554-2491
      Jean Carrigan, Dir.
Founded: 1886. **Staff:** Prof 5; Other 5. **Subjects:** Actuarial science, life insurance, health insurance, social insurance, employee benefits, business

management, finance, economic conditions, computer science. **Special Collections:** Company archives. **Holdings:** 40,000 books and bound periodical volumes; 60 VF drawers of clippings, releases and pamphlets. **Subscriptions:** 370 journals and other serials. **Services:** Interlibrary loans; library may be consulted by permission. **Computerized Information Services:** DIALOG, BRS, New York Times Information Service. **Publications:** Library Bulletin, monthly. **Formerly:** Its General Library. **Staff:** Veronica Viger, Ref.Libn.; Kathryn Marsala, Ref.Libn.; Arline Schneider, Ref.Libn.; Carol Gee, Cat.

★4199★

EQUITABLE LIFE ASSURANCE SOCIETY OF THE U.S. - MEDICAL AND HEALTH INFORMATION CENTER (Med)
1285 Ave. of the Americas
New York, NY 10019   Phone: (212) 554-2935
      Susan Voge, Med.Libn.
Founded: 1954. **Staff:** Prof 1; Other 1. **Subjects:** Medicine, public health, occupational medicine, health economics, self health. **Holdings:** 2700 books; 470 bound periodical volumes; 50 VF drawers; 396 reels of microfilmed journals. **Subscriptions:** 330 journals and other serials. **Services:** Interlibrary loans; copying; library open to public by appointment. **Computerized Information Services:** DIALOG, BRS, MEDLINE; computerized cataloging. **Networks/Consortia:** Member of Manhattan-Bronx Health Sciences Library Group; OCLC; METRO; Union Catalog of Medical Periodicals (UCMP). **Publications:** Periodicals Holdings, annual - on request; What's New in the Medical Library, biannual - to routing list.

★4200★

EQUITABLE LIFE ASSURANCE SOCIETY OF THE U.S. - TECHNICAL INFORMATION CENTER (Sci-Tech; Info Sci)
1285 Ave. of the Americas, Rm. 3I
New York, NY 10019   Phone: (212) 554-4064
      Kathryn Marsala, Mgr., Tech.Info.Ctr.
Founded: 1965. **Staff:** Prof 1; Other 1. **Subjects:** Computers, systems analysis, training programming, operations research, telecommunications, office automation, data communications, electronic data processing, office of the future, word processing. **Special Collections:** Diebold management studies; privacy and security; database management; guide proceedings; share proceedings. **Holdings:** 1800 books; 94 bound periodical volumes; slides, microfiche, videotapes, audiotapes, cassettes, Deltack. **Subscriptions:** 101 journals and other serials. **Services:** Interlibrary loans; copying; library open to Special Libraries Association members and professionals. **Computerized Information Services:** DIALOG, SDC, BRS, New York Times Information Service; computerized cataloging and circulation. **Networks/Consortia:** Member of OCLC. **Publications:** Library Bulletin, monthly.

★4201★

ERC MANAGEMENT CORPORATION - JUNE AUSTIN PARRISH MEMORIAL LIBRARY (Bus-Fin)
5200 Metcalf
Box 2991
Overland Park, KS 66201   Phone: (913) 676-5681
      Jeanne Wood, Libn.
Founded: 1940. **Staff:** Prof 2. **Subjects:** Reinsurance - all lines; insurance; law. **Special Collections:** Collection of clippings on reinsurance, domestic and international. **Holdings:** 10,000 books; 100 bound periodical volumes; 111 VF drawers of pamphlets, bulletins and proceedings from insurance associations, bureaus and organizations. **Subscriptions:** 104 journals and other serials. **Services:** Interlibrary loans; copying; library open to public with restrictions. **Formerly:** ERC Corporation, located in Kansas City, MO.

★4202★

ERCO INDUSTRIES, LTD. - LIBRARY (Sci-Tech)
2 Gibbs Rd.
Islington, ON, Canada M9B 1R1   Phone: (416) 239-7111
      Douglas G. Suarez, Corp.Libn.
Founded: 1898. **Staff:** Prof 1; Other 1. **Subjects:** Phosphorus and phosphates, pulp and paper bleaching chemicals, electrochemistry, business. **Holdings:** 5000 books; 1800 bound periodical volumes; 50 VF drawers; 20 government documents; 500 microfiche. **Subscriptions:** 153 journals and other serials. **Services:** Interlibrary loans; copying; SDI; library open to public by appointment. **Computerized Information Services:** SDC, Info Globe; computerized cataloging. **Networks/Consortia:** Member of Sheridan Park Association. **Publications:** Acquisitions list, quarterly - distributed on request.

★4203★

ERIC CLEARINGHOUSE ON ADULT, CAREER AND VOCATIONAL EDUCATION - NATL. CTR. FOR RESEARCH IN VOCATIONAL EDUC. (Educ)
Ohio State University
1960 Kenny Rd.
Columbus, OH 43210   Phone: (614) 486-3655
      Juliet V. Miller, Dir.
Founded: 1966. **Staff:** Prof 2; Other 10. **Subjects:** Education - adult, career and vocational. **Holdings:** 51,000 books; 215,000 ERIC microfiche. **Subscriptions:** 100 journals and other serials. **Services:** Copying; SDI; library

open to public for reference use only. **Computerized Information Services:** DIALOG, BRS; computer search in subject areas. **Publications:** Publications list - available on request. **Special Catalogs:** Directories of databases and educational dissemination systems; bibliographies in scope area. **Remarks:** Toll-free phone number is (800) 848-4815. **Staff:** Sandra Kerka, Acq.Coord.; Judith O. Wagner, User Serv.Coord.; Susan Imel, Asst.Dir.

★4204★
ERIC CLEARINGHOUSE ON ADULT, CAREER & VOCATIONAL EDUC. - NATL. CTR. FOR RES. IN VOCATIONAL EDUC. - RES. LIB. (Educ)
Ohio State University
1960 Kenny Rd. Phone: (614) 486-3655
Columbus, OH 43212 Meg Trauner, Res.Libn.
Staff: Prof 2; Other 3. **Subjects:** Education - vocational, adult, career; educational evaluation; youth unemployment; special populations. **Holdings:** 50,000 books; 3700 bound periodical volumes; 210,000 microforms; 5000 dissertations; 1500 instruments. **Subscriptions:** 350 journals and other serials; 5 newspapers. **Services:** Interlibrary loans; copying; SDI; library not open to public. **Computerized Information Services:** Lockheed; Resource and Referral Service (RRS), Resources in Vocational Education (RIVE), Library Control System (LCS; internal databases). **Publications:** SDI, biweekly; Periodical List, annual. **Special Catalogs:** Data collection instrument file (card). **Staff:** Marjorie Freshwater, Cat.; Lawrence Sheeley, Acq.; Steven Chambers, Ref.

★4205★
ERIC CLEARINGHOUSE ON COUNSELING AND PERSONNEL SERVICES - LEARNING RESOURCES CENTER (Educ)
School of Education Bldg.
University of Michigan Phone: (313) 764-9492
Ann Arbor, MI 48109 Carol Mills, Coord., LRC
Founded: 1966. **Staff:** Prof 2; Other 2. **Subjects:** Guidance, counseling, student and educational psychology, helping services. **Special Collections:** Career Resource Center. **Holdings:** 500 books; 200,000 microfiche (cataloged). **Subscriptions:** 70 journals and other serials; assorted newsletters. **Services:** Center open to public. **Computerized Information Services:** Online searches. **Publications:** Searchlights, newsletter; monographs and special papers. **Also Known As:** ERIC/CAPS. **Staff:** Helen L. Mamarchev, Asst.Dir.

★4206★
ERIC CLEARINGHOUSE ON EDUCATIONAL MANAGEMENT (Educ)
College of Education
University of Oregon Phone: (503) 686-5043
Eugene, OR 97403 Dr. Philip K. Piele, Prof./Dir.
Staff: Prof 9; Other 6. **Subjects:** Educational management, facilities, planning and evaluation; school administration, organization, finance, building design and construction. **Holdings:** 500 books; 250,000 ERIC documents on microfiche; 10,000 ERIC documents on educational management on microfiche. **Subscriptions:** 75 journals and other serials. **Services:** Clearinghouse open to public with restrictions. **Computerized Information Services:** DIALOG. **Publications:** Bibliographies; reviews; monographs; books; newsletter, quarterly. **Staff:** Stuart C. Smith, Asst.Dir. & Ed.; Clarice Watson, Acq.Libn.

★4207★
ERIC CLEARINGHOUSE ON ELEMENTARY AND EARLY CHILDHOOD EDUCATION (Educ)
University of Illinois
1310 S. 6th St. Phone: (217) 333-1386
Champaign, IL 61820 Lilian G. Katz, Dir.
Founded: 1966. **Staff:** Prof 8; Other 3. **Subjects:** Early childhood, elementary education, day care, parent education, child development and education through age 12. **Holdings:** ERIC microfiche collection; VF drawers; small resource library of early childhood materials. **Subscriptions:** 150 journals and other serials. **Services:** Reference service; SDI; library open to public for reference use only. **Computerized Information Services:** ERIC; computerized cataloging. **Networks/Consortia:** Member of Lincoln Trail Library System Affiliate. **Publications:** Publication list - available on request; ERIC-EECE Newsletter; resource lists - free upon request. **Staff:** Mima Spencer, Assoc.Dir.; Dianne Rothenberg, Asst.Dir., Acq.; Karen Steiner, Ed.; Norma Howard, User.Serv.

★4208★
ERIC CLEARINGHOUSE ON HANDICAPPED & GIFTED CHILDREN - CEC INFORMATION SERVICES (Educ)
Council for Exceptional Children
1920 Association Dr. Phone: (703) 620-3660
Reston, VA 22091 Lynn Smarte, Asst.Dir./User Serv.
Founded: 1966. **Staff:** Prof 9; Other 5. **Subjects:** Exceptional child

education, handicapped, gifted, special education. **Holdings:** 48,000 bound documents and microfiche; ERIC collection and private collection on microfiche. **Subscriptions:** 250 journals and other serials. **Services:** Copying; center open to public for reference use only. **Computerized Information Services:** DIALOG, BRS. **Staff:** Donald Erickson, Dir.; June Jordan, Assoc.Dir.; Dorothy Beling, Asst.Dir., Database Oper.

★4209★
ERIC CLEARINGHOUSE ON HIGHER EDUCATION (Educ)
George Washington University
One Dupont Circle, Suite 630 Phone: (202) 296-2597
Washington, DC 20036 Dr. Jonathan D. Fife, Dir.
Founded: 1968. **Staff:** Prof 8. **Subjects:** Higher education. **Holdings:** 12,000 cataloged items, primarily reports; ERIC microfiche collection. **Subscriptions:** 52 journals and other serials. **Services:** Copying; clearinghouse open to public. **Computerized Information Services:** DIALOG; computer generated bibliographies (individualized). **Publications:** ERIC/Higher Education Research Report Series, 10/year; Research Currents, 5/year; Administrator's Update, 3/year; bibliographies; CRIB Sheets. **Staff:** Marilyn S. Shorr, Assoc.Dir.; Lynn Barnett, Asst.Dir.

★4210★
ERIC CLEARINGHOUSE ON INFORMATION RESOURCES (Info Sci; Educ)
Syracuse Univ., School of Education
150 Marshall St. Phone: (315) 423-3640
Syracuse, NY 13210 Dr. Donald Ely, Dir.
Founded: 1974. **Staff:** Prof 6; Other 5. **Subjects:** Library science, information science, educational media and technology, simulation games, radio and television, film, computer assisted instruction, programmed instruction. **Special Collections:** Complete ERIC Collection on microfiche (210,000 documents). **Holdings:** 3600 books; 6000 unbound reports. **Subscriptions:** 250 journals and newsletters. **Services:** Copying; reference; library open to public. **Computerized Information Services:** DIALOG, BRS. **Publications:** Newsletter; information analysis products and user services products in scope area. **Staff:** Marilyn Laubacher, User Serv.Coord.; B.J. Vaughn, Acq.Dir.; Barbara Minor, Pubn.Coord.

★4211★
ERIC CLEARINGHOUSE FOR JUNIOR COLLEGES (Educ)
University of California, Los Angeles
96 Powell Library Phone: (213) 825-3931
Los Angeles, CA 90024 Arthur M. Cohen, Dir.
Founded: 1966. **Staff:** Prof 4; Other 3. **Subjects:** Planning and operation of community/junior/two-year colleges - administration, students, staff, instruction, curriculum. **Holdings:** 7000 research reports (cataloged). **Subscriptions:** 11 journals and other serials. **Services:** Literature searches; SDI; library open to public for reference use only. **Computerized Information Services:** DIALOG, SDC, BRS; internal database. **Networks/Consortia:** Member of Educational Resources Information Center (ERIC). **Publications:** Topical Paper Series, irregular - by request; Junior College Resource Review series, irregular - by request; monographs, occasional; columns in Com/Junior College Research Quarterly, Community College Review, Com Services Catalyst, Community College Frontiers and New Directions for Community Colleges, Journal of Developmental and Remedial Education. **Special Indexes:** Index of the Junior Colleges' holdings (card). Dr. John Lombardi, Res.Educ.; Dr. Florence B. Brawer, Res.Educ.; Anita Colby, Doc.Coord.; Jim Palmer, User Serv.Spec.; Gayle Byock, Assoc.Dir.

★4212★
ERIC CLEARINGHOUSE ON LANGUAGES AND LINGUISTICS (Hum)
3520 Prospect St., N.W. Phone: (703) 528-4312
Washington, DC 20007 John L.D. Clark, Dir.
Founded: 1966. **Staff:** Prof 6; Other 2. **Subjects:** Foreign languages; theoretical and applied linguistics; second language instruction; first and second language acquisition; bilingualism; bilingual education; English as a second/foreign language. **Holdings:** ERIC microfiche (200,000 items); 65 state foreign language newsletters. **Subscriptions:** 50 journals and other serials. **Services:** Center open to public. **Computerized Information Services:** DIALOG. **Publications:** Language in Education: Theory and Practice Series; ERIC/CLL News Bulletin. **Staff:** Mary M. Niebuhr, Assoc.Dir.

★4213★
ERIC CLEARINGHOUSE ON READING AND COMMUNICATIONS SKILLS (Educ)
National Council of Teachers of English
1111 Kenyon Rd. Phone: (217) 328-3870
Urbana, IL 61801 Dr. Bernard O'Donnell, Dir.
Founded: 1967. **Staff:** Prof 12; Other 4. **Subjects:** Reading, teaching and learning English, educational journalism, speech communication, advertising

education, mass media. **Holdings:** 200,000 documents on microfiche. **Subscriptions:** 60 journals and other serials. **Services:** Copying; SDI; library open to public. **Computerized Information Services:** Computer search of ERIC database. **Publications:** Bibliographies; monthly journal articles; State-of-the-Art monographs; Theory and Research into Practice (TRIP) booklets; Recommended Curriculum Guides, annual; ERIC First Analysis. **Staff:** Karl Koenke, Assoc.Dir.; Jane McClellan, Asst.Dir.; William Work, Module Dir.; Dorcas Rohn, Doc.Coord.; Anne Auten, User Serv.Coord.

★4214★

ERIC CLEARINGHOUSE ON RURAL EDUCATION AND SMALL SCHOOLS (Educ)
New Mexico State University
Box 3AP
Las Cruces, NM 88003
Phone: (505) 646-2623
Dr. Everett D. Edington, Dir.
Founded: 1966. **Staff:** 12. **Subjects:** Education - rural, small schools, Mexican-American, American Indian, migrant, outdoor. **Holdings:** 220,000 ERIC microfiche. **Subscriptions:** 26 journals and other serials. **Services:** Interlibrary loans (fee); copying; clearinghouse open to public for reference use only. **Computerized Information Services:** DIALOG, SDC, BRS. **Publications:** Newsletter, semiannual; Information Analysis Products, annual - each distributed by mailing list and for sale. **Also Known As:** CRESS. **Staff:** Betty Rose Rios, Asst.Dir.; Manuela Quezada-Aragon, Info.Spec.; Elaine Benally, Info.Spec.; Amelita Hill, User Serv.

★4215★

ERIC CLEARINGHOUSE FOR SCIENCE, MATHEMATICS AND ENVIRONMENTAL EDUCATION (Educ; Sci-Tech)
Ohio State University
1200 Chambers Rd.
Columbus, OH 43212
Phone: (614) 422-6717
Robert W. Howe, Dir.
Founded: 1966. **Staff:** Prof 7. **Subjects:** Curriculum, teacher education, instruction, learning, research reporting and methodology. **Holdings:** 70,000 documents. **Subscriptions:** 75 journals and other serials. **Services:** Copying; SDI; abstracting and indexing; consulting; open to public. **Computerized Information Services:** DIALOG, SDC, BRS, ERIC; computer literature search; local tapes. **Publications:** Newsletter, bibliographies, research reviews, directories, instructional activities manuals (20-25 per year). **Special Indexes:** Indexes for science, mathematics and environmental education, biennial. **Staff:** Patricia Blosser, Assoc.Dir., User Serv.; Stanley Helgeson, Assoc.Dir., Sci.; Marilyn Suydam, Assoc.Dir., Math.; John Disinger, Assoc.Dir., Env.Educ.

★4216★

ERIC CLEARINGHOUSE FOR SOCIAL STUDIES/SOCIAL SCIENCE EDUCATION - RESOURCE & DEMONSTRATION CENTER (Educ; Soc Sci)
Social Science Education Consortium
855 Broadway
Boulder, CO 80302
Phone: (303) 492-8434
Regina McCormick, Staff Assoc.
Founded: 1970. **Staff:** 10. **Subjects:** Social studies, social sciences. **Holdings:** 18,000 social studies/social science materials for elementary and secondary teachers including games and simulations, multimedia kits, curriculum guides, textbooks, professional books, catalogs, resource file on institutions and organizations in social science; complete collection of ERIC microfiche. **Services:** Workshop program; consultation program; mail and phone request service; center open to public. **Computerized Information Services:** Computer search of ERIC database. **Networks/Consortia:** Operates in conjunction with the Social Science Education Consortium. **Publications:** List of publications - available on request. **Remarks:** The Resource and Demonstration Center houses the joint collection of ERIC Clearinghouse for Social Studies/Social Science Education and the Social Science Education Consortium.

★4217★

ERIC CLEARINGHOUSE ON TEACHER EDUCATION (Educ)
American Assn. of Colleges
For Teacher Education
One Dupont Circle, N.W., Suite 610
Washington, DC 20036
Phone: (202) 293-2450
Dean A. Schwanke, User Serv.Coord.
Staff: Prof 7; Other 5. **Subjects:** Teacher education; health, physical and recreation education. **Holdings:** 200,000 microfiche (cataloged). **Subscriptions:** 25 journals and other serials. **Services:** Copying; library open to public. **Computerized Information Services:** DIALOG; computer search of ERIC database. **Networks/Consortia:** Member of Educational Resources Information Center (ERIC).

★4218★

ERIC CLEARINGHOUSE ON TESTS, MEASUREMENT AND EVALUATION (Educ)
Educational Testing Service
Rosedale Rd.
Princeton, NJ 08541
Phone: (609) 734-5181
Dr. S. Donald Melville, Dir.
Founded: 1971. **Staff:** Prof 5; Other 3. **Subjects:** Tests, measurement and evaluation, human growth and development, learning theory. **Special Collections:** Microfiche for the entire ERIC system (195,000 documents); ERIC/TM reports, highlights, annotated bibliographies and updates; complete collection of Resources in Education (RIE) and Current Index to Journals in Education (CIJE). **Services:** Abstracting; workshops; indexing; library open to public. **Computerized Information Services:** DIALOG, SDC, BRS. **Publications:** Current publications list - free upon request. **Staff:** Barbara M. Wildemuth, Assoc.Dir.; Louisa Coburn, User Serv.Coord.

★4219★

ERIC CLEARINGHOUSE ON URBAN EDUCATION (Educ)
Box 40, Teachers College
Columbia University
New York, NY 10027
Phone: (212) 678-3437
Dr. Erwin Flaxman, Dir.
Founded: 1965. **Staff:** Prof 4; Other 7. **Subjects:** Education of urban and minority children and youths; psychology; sociology. **Holdings:** 1000 books; 15,500 reports, manuscripts and other documentation (cataloged); 200,000 titles in ERIC microfiche collection. **Subscriptions:** 60 journals and other serials. **Services:** Reference services by mail in the form of prepared bibliographies and other ERIC/CUE publications; library open to public by appointment. **Computerized Information Services:** DIALOG. **Publications:** IRCD Bulletin, 1965-1982 - for sale; Urban Diversity Series, irregular - free; Equal Opportunity Review Series, irregular - free; Doctoral Research Series, irregular - free. **Also Known As:** CUE. **Staff:** Michael Webb, Asst.Dir.; Darryl Alladice, Processer; Maryellen LoBosco, Ed./Pub.Rel.

★4220★

ERIC PROCESSING AND REFERENCE FACILITY (Educ; Info Sci)
4833 Rugby Ave., Suite 301
Bethesda, MD 20814
Phone: (301) 656-9723
Wesley T. Brandhorst, Dir.
Founded: 1966. **Staff:** Prof 11; Other 7. **Subjects:** Education, lexicography, document and information processing, abstracting, indexing, reference. **Special Collections:** Complete collection of ERIC Clearinghouse products; complete ERIC microfiche collection. **Holdings:** 500 books and bound periodical volumes. **Subscriptions:** 25 journals and other serials. **Services:** Information processing services; facility open to public with restrictions. **Computerized Information Services:** ERIC database in machine-readable form available. **Publications:** Resources in Education, monthly abstract journal; updates to the ERIC Processing Manual, Directory of Clearinghouses, the System Documentation; Directory of ERIC Microfiche Collections; Directory of ERIC Search Services; Bibliography of ERIC Information Analysis Products. **Special Indexes:** ERIC Thesaurus; Source Directory; Contract/Grant Number Index; Report/Project Number Index; Clearinghouse Number/ED Number Cross Reference Listing; Title Index - all for sale. **Remarks:** The facility is a centralized editing and information processing facility maintaining the ERIC database and serving all components of the ERIC network. It is operated for the National Institute of Education by ORI, Inc., Information Systems Division.

★4221★

ERIE COUNTY HISTORICAL SOCIETY (Hist)
Cashiers House, 417 State St.
Erie, PA 16501
Phone: (814) 454-1813
Robert F. Taft, Pres.
Staff: Prof 3. **Subjects:** History, genealogy, preservation. **Special Collections:** Pennsylvania Population Company records (3 VF drawers). **Holdings:** 5450 volumes; 20 boxes of papers. **Services:** Copying; library open to public with restrictions. **Publications:** Journal of Erie Studies (jointly with Mercyhurst College). **Staff:** J.R. Claridge, Exec.Dir.; Mrs. C.B. Andrews, Libn.; Doris Nicholson, Cur.

★4222★

ERIE COUNTY LAW LIBRARY (Law)
Court House, 1st Fl.
Sandusky, OH 44870
Phone: (419) 626-4823
Robin A. Muratori, Lib. Aide
Founded: 1890. **Subjects:** Law. **Holdings:** 12,000 volumes. **Services:** Library not open to public.

★4223★

ERIE COUNTY LAW LIBRARY (Law)
Court House
Erie, PA 16501
Phone: (814) 452-3333
Max C. Peaster, Libn.
Staff: Prof 1. **Subjects:** Law. **Holdings:** 32,610 books and bound periodical

volumes; 3121 microforms. **Subscriptions:** 66 journals and other serials. **Services:** Interlibrary loans; copying; library open to public for reference use only. **Networks/Consortia:** Member of NICOP.

★4224★
ERIE COUNTY MEDICAL CENTER - MEDICAL LIBRARY (Med)
462 Grider St.   Phone: (716) 898-3939
Buffalo, NY 14215   Anthony Ciko, Sr.Med.Libn.
Founded: 1921. **Staff:** Prof 2; Other 2. **Subjects:** Medicine, nursing, dentistry, biological sciences. **Holdings:** 2300 books; 10,000 bound periodical volumes; 900 AV programs; 12 VF drawers of reprints and pamphlets. **Subscriptions:** 320 journals and other serials. **Services:** Interlibrary loans; copying; library open to public for reference use only. **Networks/Consortia:** Member of New York and Northern New Jersey Regional Medical Library System; Western New York Library Resources Council (WNYLRC). **Staff:** Edward Leisner, Med.Libn.

★4225★
ERIKSON INSTITUTE - LIBRARY (Soc Sci)
1525 E. 53rd St., Rm. 1001   Phone: (312) 493-0200
Chicago, IL 60615   Maija B. May
Staff: 1. **Subjects:** Child development, psychology, anthropology. **Special Collections:** RoAnn Nesbit Harris Collection (100 volumes). **Holdings:** 1500 books; 6 VF drawers of pamphlets; films, filmstrips and tapes. **Subscriptions:** 28 journals and other serials.

ERIM INFORMATION CENTER
See: Environmental Research Institute of Michigan

★4226★
ERLANGER MEDICAL CENTER - MEDICAL LIBRARY (Med)
975 E. Third St.   Phone: (615) 778-7498
Chattanooga, TN 37403   Margarette D. Koplan, Chf.Libn.
Founded: 1963. **Staff:** Prof 1; Other 2. **Subjects:** Orthopedics, surgery, internal medicine, obstetrics, gynecology, pediatrics, family medicine. **Special Collections:** William Moore Bogart Memorial Collection (historic and cultural medicine); History of Medicine Collection; T.C.T. Children's Medical Center Pediatric Library (1500 books and bound periodical volumes; 37 subscriptions). **Holdings:** 8000 books; 25,000 bound periodical volumes; 4 VF drawers of archives and clippings; 4 VF drawers of pamphlets and pictures; 500 cassette tapes; 2 VF drawers of prepared bibliographies. **Subscriptions:** 352 journals and other serials. **Services:** Interlibrary loans; copying; library open to public for reference use only. **Computerized Information Services:** NLM. **Networks/Consortia:** Member of East Tennessee Online Users Group; Southeastern Regional Medical Library Program (SERMLP); Health Education Library Program (HELP); Tennessee Health Science Library Association. **Publications:** Bibliographies, accessions lists; new books lists, monthly. **Special Indexes:** Index of bibliographies (card).

★4227★
ERLANGER MEDICAL CENTER - SCHOOL OF NURSING - SARAH C. BARTON LIBRARY (Med)
975 E. Third St.   Phone: (615) 265-3254
Chattanooga, TN 37403   Margarette D. Koplan, Chf.Libn.
Staff: Prof 1; Other 2. **Subjects:** Nursing, medicine, psychology, education, general sciences. **Holdings:** 3000 books; 800 bound periodical volumes; 1550 pamphlets; 370 filmstrips; 100 videotapes; 500 slides; 250 cassette tapes; 250 phonograph records. **Subscriptions:** 87 journals and other serials. **Services:** Interlibrary loans; copying; SDI; library open to public for reference use only. **Networks/Consortia:** Member of Southeastern Regional Medical Library Program (SERMLP); Health Education Library Program (HELP); Tennessee Health Science Library Association. **Publications:** New Book lists, monthly - to faculty and hospital staff. **Remarks:** This library is a part of the Erlanger Medical Center. **Staff:** Ruth Kee, Nursing Educ.Libn.

★4228★
ERNST & WHINNEY - DATA SYSTEMS LIBRARY (Sci-Tech)
153 E. 53rd St.   Phone: (212) 888-9100
New York, NY 10022   Janet How, Dir., Lib.Serv.
Staff: Prof 1; Other 1. **Subjects:** Electronic data processing. **Special Collections:** IBM technical manuals; application manuals; vendor files; subject files. **Holdings:** 20 file drawers of materials. **Subscriptions:** 54 journals and other serials; 5 newspapers.

★4229★
ERNST & WHINNEY - GENERAL LIBRARY (Bus-Fin)
153 E. 53rd St.   Phone: (212) 752-8100
New York, NY 10022   Janet How, Dir., Lib.Serv.
Founded: 1967. **Staff:** Prof 2; Other 2. **Subjects:** Accounting, business, management. **Holdings:** 5000 books; 172 bound periodical volumes; 20 VF drawers. **Subscriptions:** 208 journals and other serials. **Services:** Interlibrary loans. **Computerized Information Services:** DIALOG, SDC, New York Times Information Service, Mead Data Central, Dow Jones News Retrieval, Informetrica Limited. **Publications:** Update; Essence. **Staff:** Bonnie Figgatt, Asst.Libn.

★4230★
ERNST & WHINNEY - INTERNATIONAL LIBRARY (Bus-Fin)
153 E. 53rd St.   Phone: (212) 888-9100
New York, NY 10022   Janet How, Dir., Lib.Serv.
Staff: Prof 1; Other 1. **Subjects:** International taxation, accounting, trade, business. **Holdings:** 1000 books; 8 VF drawers of pamphlets. **Subscriptions:** 160 journals and other serials.

★4231★
ERNST & WHINNEY - LIBRARY (Bus-Fin)
515 S. Flower St.   Phone: (213) 621-1666
Los Angeles, CA 90071   Sherry du Roy, Libn.
Staff: Prof 1. **Subjects:** Accounting, business, electronic data processing, health care. **Holdings:** Figures not available. **Subscriptions:** 204 journals and other serials. **Services:** Interlibrary loans; SDI; library not open to public. **Computerized Information Services:** DIALOG, SDC; PREPARE (internal database).

★4232★
ERNST & WHINNEY - LIBRARY (Bus-Fin)
100 Renaissance Center, Suite 200   Phone: (313) 354-4600
Detroit, MI 48243   Lynne Taft, Libn.
Subjects: Accounting. **Holdings:** Figures not available. **Subscriptions:** 100 journals and other serials. **Services:** Library not open to public.

★4233★
ERNST & WHINNEY - NATIONAL OFFICE LIBRARY (Bus-Fin)
2000 National City Ctr.   Phone: (216) 861-5000
Cleveland, OH 44114   Naomi Clifford, Natl.Off.Libn.
Founded: 1960. **Staff:** Prof 2; Other 1. **Subjects:** Business - accounting, auditing, management. **Special Collections:** American Institute of Certified Public Accountants and Financial Accounting Standards Board publications. **Holdings:** 5600 books and bound periodical volumes; 20 VF drawers; 6000 annual reports. **Subscriptions:** 400 journals and other serials; 15 newspapers. **Services:** Interlibrary loans; copying; library open to public by appointment. **Computerized Information Services:** DIALOG, New York Times Information Service, Mead Data Central; computerized cataloging. **Networks/Consortia:** Member of OHIONET. **Staff:** Lynn Sniderman, Asst.Libn.

★4234★
ERNST & WHINNEY - TAX LIBRARY (Bus-Fin)
153 E. 53rd St.   Phone: (212) 888-9100
New York, NY 10022   Robin Ahern, Tax Libn.
Staff: Prof 1. **Subjects:** U.S. taxation. **Holdings:** 2500 books; 375 bound periodical volumes; 7 VF drawers of Ernst & Whinney publications. **Subscriptions:** 251 journals and other serials. **Services:** Interlibrary loans; copying; library not open to public. **Computerized Information Services:** LEXIS, NEXIS.

EROS DATA CENTER
See: U.S. Geological Survey

ERT, INC.
See: Environmental Research & Technology, Inc.

★4235★
ERTEC WESTERN, INC. - LIBRARY (Sci-Tech)
3777 Long Beach Blvd.   Phone: (213) 595-6611
Long Beach, CA 90807   Fia Vitar, Libn.
Founded: 1978. **Staff:** Prof 1. **Subjects:** Engineering, geology, hydrology, seismology, nuclear waste plants and management systems. **Special Collections:** U.S. Air Force MX surveys and site investigations. **Holdings:** 40,000 books; 3000 bound periodical volumes; 2000 maps; 660 technical reports; 100 microfiche. **Subscriptions:** 60 journals and other serials; 10 newspapers. **Services:** Interlibrary loans; copying; SDI; library open to users with security clearance. **Computerized Information Services:** SDC; internal database; computerized circulation. **Publications:** Confidential reports for clients. **Also Known As:** Earth Technology Corporation.

★4236★
ESCAMBIA COUNTY HEALTH DEPARTMENT - LIBRARY (Med)†
Box 12604　Phone: (904) 438-8571
Pensacola, FL 32574-2604　Barbara McCullough, Health Educ.
Subjects: Health, public health. **Holdings:** Vertical files on health subjects.
Services: Copying; library open to public.

★4237★
ESCO CORP. - LIBRARY (Sci-Tech)†
2141 N.W. 25th Ave.　Phone: (503) 228-2141
Portland, OR 97210　Leroy Finch, Sr. Metallurgist
Founded: 1977. **Staff:** 1. **Subjects:** Metallurgical technology, public relations.
Holdings: 700 volumes.

★4238★
ESHERICK, HOMSEY, DODGE & DAVIS - LIBRARY (Energy)
2789 25th St.　Phone: (415) 285-9193
San Francisco, CA 94110　Fran Brunet, Libn.
Founded: 1970. **Staff:** Prof 1; Other 1. **Subjects:** Architecture, construction, energy conservation, solar energy. **Holdings:** 2600 books; 41,500 slides and photographs; 1000 product literature catalogs; 16 VF drawers of product literature; blueprints; archives. **Subscriptions:** 130 journals and other serials. **Services:** Interlibrary loans (limited); library not open to public.

ESKATON AMERICAN RIVER HOSPITAL
See: American River Hospital

★4239★
ESL, INC./SUBSIDIARY OF TRW - RESEARCH LIBRARY (Sci-Tech)
495 Java Dr.
Box 510　Phone: (408) 738-2888
Sunnyvale, CA 94086　Verna Van Velzer, Chf.Libn.
Founded: 1966. **Staff:** Prof 1; Other 1. **Subjects:** Electronics, astrophysics, computer science, physics, mathematics, military science. **Holdings:** 20,000 books and bound periodical volumes. **Subscriptions:** 250 journals and other serials. **Services:** Interlibrary loans; library not open to public. **Computerized Information Services:** DIALOG, SDC, Ontyme-II; computerized serials. **Networks/Consortia:** Member of Cooperative Information Network. **Remarks:** ESL, Inc. is a subsidiary of TRW, Inc. **Also Known As:** Electromagnetic Systems Laboratories.

★4240★
ESOTERIC PHILOSOPHY CENTER, INC. - LIBRARY (Rec)†
517 Lovett Blvd.　Phone: (713) 526-5998
Houston, TX 77006　Jannah Gibson, Libn.
Founded: 1970. **Staff:** 1. **Subjects:** Metaphysics, occult doctrine, sound, color, vibration, astrology, numerology, tarot, palmistry, yoga. **Holdings:** 2460 books. **Services:** Library open to members or with payment of yearly fee. **Publications:** The Centric, quarterly.

★4241★
ESPERANTIC STUDIES FOUNDATION - LIBRARY (Hum)
6451 Barnaby St., N.W.　Phone: (202) 362-3963
Washington, DC 20015　E. James Lieberman, Dir.
Founded: 1968. **Staff:** 1. **Subjects:** Esperanto, international communication. **Holdings:** 300 books; 30 file boxes of U.S., European and Asian unbound journals in Esperanto. **Services:** Library open to public by appointment. **Publications:** Esperanto and International Language Problems: A Research Bibliography, 4th edition, 1977.

★4242★
ESPERANTO LEAGUE FOR NORTH AMERICA - ESPERANTO INFORMATION SERVICE (Hum)
Box 1129　Phone: (415) 653-0998
El Cerrito, CA 94530　Donald J. Harlow, Dir.
Staff: Prof 1. **Subjects:** Book service listing over 1000 titles in Esperanto for sale in many subjects including language, history, interlinguistics, prose, drama, poetry, biography, politics, philosophy, science, geography, travel, music. **Services:** Universal Esperanto Association (Rotterdam), of which ELNA is an affiliate, provides copy service for out-of-print publications for a fee. **Publications:** Book catalog published by Esperanto Book Service with occasional appendices. **Also Known As:** ELNA.

★4243★
ESPEY MFG. & ELECTRONICS CORP. - COMPONENT SPECIFICATIONS LIBRARY (Sci-Tech)†
Ballston at Congress Ave.
Box 422　Phone: (518) 584-4100
Saratoga Springs, NY 12866　Cathi Jackson, Libn.
Subjects: Electronics, engineering, finishing materials. **Holdings:** 1000 volumes; government and military specifications. **Services:** Interlibrary loans; copying; library open to public with restrictions. **Computerized Information Services:** Computerized cataloging.

★4244★
ESSEX COUNTY HISTORICAL SOCIETY - LIBRARY (Hist)*
Court St.　Phone: (518) 873-6466
Elizabethtown, NY 12932　Dorothy A. Plum, Libn.
Founded: 1956. **Staff:** Prof 1; Other 5. **Subjects:** Adirondack history, folklore, literature; Indians of North America; Northern New York guidebooks; Essex County, New York. **Holdings:** 5399 books; 91 bound periodical volumes; 5000 pamphlets; 20 VF drawers of ephemeral material; 350 manuscripts; 123 reels of microfilm; 78 newspaper titles; 246 maps; 162 microforms and AV items. **Subscriptions:** 78 journals and other serials. **Services:** Copying (limited); library open to public by appointment. **Special Indexes:** Index to cemetery records; index to place names.

★4245★
ESSEX COUNTY HOSPITAL CENTER - HAMILTON MEMORIAL LIBRARY (Med)
Box 500　Phone: (201) 228-8002
Cedar Grove, NJ 07009　Elizabeth B. Guarducci, Med.Libn.
Founded: 1958. **Staff:** 4. **Subjects:** Psychiatry, psychology, mental health, psychotherapy, medicine, social work. **Holdings:** 2500 books. **Subscriptions:** 135 journals and other serials; 7 newspapers. **Services:** Interlibrary loans; copying; library open to public with restrictions. **Networks/Consortia:** Member of Cosmopolitan Biomedical Library Consortium. **Publications:** Acquisitions list, quarterly.

★4246★
ESSEX COUNTY LAW LIBRARY (Law)†
34 Federal St.　Phone: (617) 741-0200
Salem, MA 01970　J. Joseph Gilligan, Libn.
Staff: Prof 1; Other 1. **Subjects:** Law - Massachusetts and New England; federal cases and statutes. **Special Collections:** Maritime law and law of the seas cases. **Holdings:** 34,000 books; 10,000 bound periodical volumes; law archives; Massachusetts statutes. **Services:** Interlibrary loans; copying; library open to public. **Computerized Information Services:** Computerized acquisitions.

★4247★
ESSEX COUNTY LAW LIBRARY (Law)
512 County Courts Bldg.
50 W. Market St.　Phone: (201) 961-7293
Newark, NJ 07102　Jill Wright, Law Libn.
Founded: 1896. **Staff:** 2. **Subjects:** Law. **Holdings:** 20,000 volumes. **Services:** Library open to county judges and attorneys.

★4248★
ESSEX INSTITUTE - JAMES DUNCAN PHILLIPS LIBRARY (Hist)
132-134 Essex St.　Phone: (617) 744-3390
Salem, MA 01970　Bryant F. Tolles, Jr., Libn.
Founded: 1848. **Staff:** Prof 5; Other 1. **Subjects:** Essex County history, New England maritime history and culture, Americana, genealogy, China and the Chinese. **Special Collections:** Almanacs; juvenile literature; trade catalogs; history of China; American fine and decorative arts; Hawthorne; Whittier. **Holdings:** 400,000 books; bound periodical volumes; Early American broadsides; directories; newspapers (complete for Salem); business records and personal papers of merchants and families; log books, journals and diaries; manuscripts of American literary writers; maps; photographs. **Subscriptions:** 60 journals and other serials. **Services:** Copying; library open to public with payment of fee. **Staff:** Robinson Murray, III, Assoc.Libn.; Caroline Preston, Mss.Libn.

★4249★
ESSEX LAW ASSOCIATION - LIBRARY (Law)
County Court House
245 Windsor Ave.　Phone: (519) 252-8418
Windsor, ON, Canada N9A 1J2　Anne Matthewman, Libn.
Staff: 1. **Subjects:** Law. **Holdings:** 10,000 volumes. **Services:** Copying; library open to University law students for reference use only.

ESSEX PRESBYTERY OF UNITED CHURCH OF CANADA
See: United Church of Canada - Essex Presbytery

★4250★

ESSO EASTERN, INC. - LIBRARY (Bus-Fin)
Box 1415
Houston, TX 77001
Phone: (713) 978-5346
Carrie W. Eagon, Libn.
Founded: 1956. Staff: Prof 1; Other 1. Subjects: Petroleum, economics, finance, business, law, Asia, Oceania. Holdings: 4000 books; 2200 bound periodical volumes. Subscriptions: 300 journals and other serials; 5 newspapers. Services: Interlibrary loans; copying; library not open to public. Computerized Information Services: Computerized cataloging, acquisitions and serials. Special Indexes: Index to Selected Periodicals, cumulative.

★4251★

ESSO RESOURCES CANADA LIMITED - LIBRARY INFORMATION CENTRE
(Energy)
237 4th Ave., S.W.
Calgary, AB, Canada T2P 0H6
Phone: (403) 237-4500
Terri A. Harris, Act.Coord. of Libs.
Founded: 1957. Staff: Prof 11; Other 7. Subjects: Petroleum exploration, production and research, business, minerals. Special Collections: Engineering standards; Northern Environmental Information. Holdings: 10,000 books; 6000 bound periodical volumes; 7000 external reports; 10,000 internal reports. Subscriptions: 400 journals and other serials. Services: Interlibrary loans; copying; SDI (in library); editorial and computer processing services. Computerized Information Services: DIALOG, SDC, BRS, CAN/OLE, Info Globe, SPIRES, QL Systems; computerized cataloging, acquisitions and circulation. Publications: Current Awareness, biweekly. Special Indexes: Internal computer-produced indexes. Staff: Roxanne Roebroek, Act.Coord., Info.Spec.; Ken Reeson, Info.Spec.; Dan Pauli, Info.Spec.; V. Kohse, Libn., Res.; Tobe Odell, Libn., Lib.Serv.; J. Poffenroth, Lib.Asst., Engr.Lib.

★4252★

ESSO RESOURCES CANADA LIMITED - RESEARCH DEPARTMENT LIBRARY
(Sci-Tech)
339 50th Ave., S.E.
Calgary, AB, Canada T2G 2B3
Phone: (403) 259-0303
Vicki Kohse, Res.Dept.Libn.
Founded: 1956. Staff: Prof 1; Other 2. Subjects: Chemistry, chemical engineering, physics, petroleum engineering, paleontology, ice engineering, oceanography. Holdings: 3500 books; 500 bound periodical volumes; 3400 company reports; 1000 pamphlets and patents. Subscriptions: 300 journals and other serials; 5 newspapers. Services: Interlibrary loans; library open to public with restrictions. Computerized Information Services: CAN/OLE, DIALOG, SDC; computerized cataloging.

★4253★

ESTERLINE ANGUS INSTRUMENT CORPORATION - COMPANY LIBRARY
(Sci-Tech)
1201 Main St.
Indianapolis, IN 46224
Phone: (317) 244-7611
Kelli R. Norris, Co.Libn.
Founded: 1964. Staff: 1. Subjects: Electrical and mechanical instruments. Holdings: 757 books. Subscriptions: 20 journals and other serials. Services: Interlibrary loans; library open to public. Remarks: Esterline Angus is an Esterline Company.

ESTES (Margaret) LIBRARY
See: Le Tourneau College - Margaret Estes Library

ESTES (W.L., Jr.) MEMORIAL LIBRARY
See: St. Luke's Hospital of Bethlehem, Pennsylvania - W.L. Estes, Jr. Memorial Library

★4254★

ETHICON, INC. - SCIENTIFIC INFORMATION SERVICES (Sci-Tech; Med)
Rte. 22
Somerville, NJ 08076
Phone: (201) 524-3402
Dr. Charles G. Fritz, Dir.
Founded: 1956. Staff: Prof 5; Other 3. Subjects: Biological and physical sciences, sterilization, polymer chemistry, surgery. Holdings: 5000 books; 20,000 bound periodical volumes; 8 VF drawers of U.S. and foreign patents. Subscriptions: 320 journals and other serials. Services: Interlibrary loans; copying; SDI. Computerized Information Services: NLM, SDC, DIALOG, BRS; computerized acquisitions and circulation. Networks/Consortia: Member of MEDCORE. Publications: Current Literature, weekly; Scientific Information Reports, monthly; SCAN, biweekly - all for internal distribution only. Staff: Dr. Edgar Schipper, Lit.Sci.; Jane T. Minckler, Res.Libn.; Norma K. Stavetski, Assoc.Info.Sci.; Ms.Leslie Douglass, Asst.Libn.

★4255★

ETHYL CORPORATION - INFORMATION & LIBRARY SERVICES LIBRARY
(Sci-Tech)
Box 2246
Baton Rouge, LA 70821
Phone: (504) 359-2182
Lois M. Skinner, Chem./Libn.
Staff: Prof 3; Other 2. Subjects: Chemistry, chemical engineering, mathematics. Holdings: 14,000 books; 6000 bound periodical volumes. Subscriptions: 1300 journals and other serials. Services: Interlibrary loans (limited); library open to public by appointment. Computerized Information Services: DIALOG, SDC; computerized serials. Publications: New Books Bulletin. Formerly: Its Chemical Development Library. Staff: Elizabeth A. Weaver, Lit.Chem.; Louise O. Pearce, Asst.Libn.

★4256★

ETHYL CORPORATION - RESEARCH LABORATORIES - RESEARCH LIBRARY
(Energy)
1600 W. Eight Mile Rd.
Ferndale, MI 48220
Phone: (313) 399-9600
Gloria M. Smith, Libn.
Founded: 1950. Staff: Prof 1; Other 3. Subjects: Chemistry, fuel technology, physical sciences. Holdings: 10,000 books; 10,000 bound periodical volumes; 3600 internal reports; 748 VF drawers of research data, memoranda, reports and publications; 51 VF drawers of patents; trays of drawings; 29 VF drawers of photographs; 32 drawers of lantern slides; 1250 reels of microfilm. Subscriptions: 370 journals and other serials. Services: Interlibrary loans; copying; library not open to public. Publications: Technical Information Bulletin, monthly - for internal distribution only.

★4257★

ETOBICOKE BOARD OF EDUCATION - RESOURCE LIBRARY (Educ)
1 Civic Centre Court
Etobicoke, ON, Canada M9C 2B3
Phone: (416) 626-4360
Alice Churchman, Coord.
Founded: 1969. Staff: Prof 2; Other 3. Subjects: Education, psychology, social sciences, curriculum subjects. Holdings: 30,000 books; 40 VF drawers of clippings. Subscriptions: 452 journals and other serials. Services: Interlibrary loans; copying; library open to public. Computerized Information Services: DIALOG, SDC, Info Globe. Staff: Barbara Dewsnap, Cons.

★4258★

ETOBICOKE GENERAL HOSPITAL - MEDICAL LIBRARY (Med)
101 Humber College Blvd.
Rexdale, ON, Canada M9V 1R8
Phone: (416) 744-3334
Joyce Gitt, Lib.Techn.
Founded: 1973. Staff: Prof 1. Subjects: Medicine and allied health sciences. Holdings: 2272 books; 127 bound periodical volumes; 2 VF drawers of Where to Look files; 2 drawers of cassettes. Subscriptions: 125 journals and other serials. Services: Interlibrary loans; copying; library open to affiliated students.

★4259★

EUGENE HEARING AND SPEECH CENTER - LIBRARY (Med)
1202 Almaden
Box 2087
Eugene, OR 97402
Phone: (503) 485-8521
Ned Risbrough, Exec.Dir.
Subjects: Audiology, speech pathology, child development, special education. Holdings: 350 books. Subscriptions: 49 journals and other serials. Services: Library open to public with restrictions.

★4260★

EUGENE HOSPITAL AND CLINIC - DOCTORS' LIBRARY (Med)
1162 Willamette St.
Eugene, OR 97401
Phone: (503) 687-6000
Dr. Byron Musa, Chm., Lib.Comm.
Subjects: Medicine and allied sciences. Holdings: 100 books; 150 bound periodical volumes. Subscriptions: 10 journals and other serials. Services: Library open to staff only.

★4261★

EUGENE O'NEILL MEMORIAL THEATER CENTER, INC. - THEATER COLLECTION AND LIBRARY (Theater)†
325 Pequot Ave.
New London, CT 06320
Phone: (203) 443-0051
Sally Thomas Pavetti, Cur.
Founded: 1967. Staff: Prof 2. Subjects: Drama, dramatic literature, costume design, theater memorabilia. Special Collections: Johnson Briscoe Drama Collection; Virginia Dean Collection; Harold Friedlander Playbill Collection; Eugene O'Neill letters to Edward R. Keefe and to Charles O'Brien Kennedy; O'Neill Theater Center National Playwrights Conference Scripts, 1966-1978; other miscellaneous original letters; Pulitzer Prizes and Drama Circle Awards of Tennessee Williams and William Inge; original manuscript material from playwrights Frank Gagliano, Ron Cowen, Paul Foster and Israel Horovitz; Frederick Adler Collection of color movie window cards. Holdings: 1000 books; playbills; theater scrapbooks; photographic stills; manuscripts; letters; set and costume designs; television manuscripts; National Theater of the Deaf Scripts; clipping files; periodicals. Services: Copying; library open to public. Staff: Lois E. McDonald, Asst.Cur.

★4262★

EUGENE REGISTER-GUARD - NEWS LIBRARY (Publ)
975 High St.
Box 10188
Eugene, OR 97440   Phone: (503) 485-1234
    Marijoy Rubaloff, Libn.
Founded: 1950. **Staff:** Prof 1; Other 1. **Subjects:** Newspaper reference topics. **Holdings:** 1500 books; newspaper clippings. **Subscriptions:** 25 journals and other serials; 10 newspapers. **Services:** Library open to public with restrictions.

★4263★

EUROPEAN ART COLOR - PETER ADELBERG ARCHIVE (Pict)
120 W. 70th St.   Phone: (212) 877-9654
New York, NY 10023   Greta Adelberg, Pict.Libn.
Subjects: Art photographs - paintings, frescoes, mosaics, sculpture, illuminated manuscripts, stained glass windows, burnt enamel (cloisonne), textiles, architecture, views. **Holdings:** 6000 color slides and transparencies. **Services:** Slides and transparencies for sale or loan, reproduction fees charged. **Publications:** General Catalog, 1953-1971 - for sale.

★4264★

EUROPEAN COMMUNITY INFORMATION SERVICE - LIBRARY (Soc Sci)
2100 M St., N.W., Suite 707
Washington, DC 20037   Phone: (202) 862-9500
    Ella Krucoff, Chf., Ref. & Doc.
Founded: 1963. **Staff:** Prof 3; Other 2. **Subjects:** International relations and economics; trade affairs; European affairs; political science; international monetary affairs. **Special Collections:** Information on and official documents of the European Economic Community, the European Coal and Steel Community, and the European Atomic Energy Community. **Holdings:** 28,000 books; 2700 pamphlets (cataloged); VF materials on over 1300 subjects relating to the community and related affairs. **Subscriptions:** 9 newspapers. **Services:** Interlibrary loans (limited); copying; library open to public. **Publications:** European Community, bimonthly. **Staff:** Barbara Sloan, Info.Spec.; Melinda Bills, Info.Spec.

★4265★

EUROPEAN COMMUNITY INFORMATION SERVICE - LIBRARY (Soc Sci)
245 E. 47th St.   Phone: (212) 371-3804
New York, NY 10017   Elizabeth Grant, Info.Spec.
Staff: Prof 2; Other 1. **Subjects:** European economic policies, European political integration, Common Market law, multinationals. **Special Collections:** European Common Market. **Holdings:** 1500 books; 1000 bound periodical volumes; 30 file cabinets of dossiers on special topics. **Subscriptions:** 50 journals and other serials; 7 newspapers. **Services:** Copying; library open to public for reference use only on a limited schedule. **Publications:** European Community, monthly - available upon request. **Also Known As:** Commission of the European Communities.

EURY (Jessie C.) LIBRARY
See: Lincoln Christian College & Seminary - Jessie C. Eury Library

★4266★

EVALUATION, DISSEMINATION & ASSESSMENT CENTER - EDAC RESEARCH LIBRARY (Educ)
Lesley College
49 Washington Ave.
Cambridge, MA 02140   Phone: (617) 492-0505
    Molly Leong, Bilingual Res.Libn.
Founded: 1976. **Staff:** Prof 1; Other 2. **Subjects:** Bilingual education, testing, curricula, assessment, evaluation, English as a second language. **Special Collections:** Bilingual Teaching Materials (1300 volumes; filmstrips, cassettes, films). **Holdings:** 4000 books; 70 microfiche; 37 cassettes; 74 AV kits; 139 slides; 55 filmstrips; 250 titles of periodicals; 4 VF drawers of publishers' catalogs. **Subscriptions:** 62 journals and other serials; 8 newspapers. **Services:** Copying; library open to public for reference use only. **Computerized Information Services:** BRS.

EVALUATION DOCUMENTATION CENTER (EDC)
See: U.S. Dept. of Health and Human Services

EVANGELICAL COVENANT CHURCH OF AMERICA - ARCHIVES
See: North Park College and Theological Seminary - Mellander Library

★4267★

EVANGELICAL COVENANT CHURCH OF AMERICA - COVENANT ARCHIVES AND HISTORICAL LIBRARY (Hist; Rel-Theol)
5125 N. Spaulding Ave.
Chicago, IL 60625   Phone: (312) 583-2700
    Sigurd F. Westberg, Archv.
Founded: 1935. **Staff:** Prof 1; Other 3. **Subjects:** Denominational historical records of the Covenant and related denominations; historical records of local

Covenant Churches. **Special Collections:** Local church records; pictures of church pioneers; newspapers and church records (microfilm); denominational and regional conference headquarters correspondence and records (50 VF drawers). **Holdings:** 4500 books; 600 bound periodical volumes; 325 pamphlets (cataloged); 95 VF drawers of clippings, diaries, correspondence, music, departmental publications; 750 reels of microfilm; photographs. **Subscriptions:** 12 journals and other serials. **Services:** Copying; microfilm printing; library open to public by appointment. **Special Indexes:** Indexes to photographs, people, records, books, newspapers and periodicals (all on cards).

★4268★

EVANGELICAL COVENANT CHURCH - LIBRARY (Rel-Theol)†
1260 Jefferson
Muskegon, MI 49440   Phone: (616) 728-5385
    Carolyn M. Brooks, Libn.
Founded: 1957. **Staff:** Prof 1; Other 2. **Subjects:** Christian fiction and nonfiction. **Holdings:** 3100 books; 25 cassette tapes; 124 filmstrips. **Subscriptions:** 11 journals and other serials. **Services:** Library not open to public.

EVANGELICAL FRIENDS CHURCH, EASTERN REGION
See: Society of Friends - Ohio Yearly Meeting - Westgate Friends Library

EVANGELICAL LUTHERAN SYNODICAL CONFERENCE ARCHIVES
See: Concordia Historical Institute

★4269★

EVANGELICAL AND REFORMED HISTORICAL SOCIETY - EDEN ARCHIVES (Hist)
475 E. Lockwood Ave.
Webster Groves, MO 63119   Phone: (314) 961-3627
    Gary W. Kwiatek, Archv.
Staff: Prof 2; Other 1. **Subjects:** Evangelical Synod of North America; Evangelical & Reformed Church; United Church of Christ - all relating to German Protestant missions in the U.S. and elsewhere, principally midwestern U.S. **Special Collections:** Records of Evangelical Synod Church. **Holdings:** 4400 books and bound periodical volumes; 200 VF drawers of reports, manuscripts and archives; 35 volumes of photoduplicated German-American immigration-mission documents; 95 reels of microfilmed church records. **Services:** Interlibrary loans; copying; library open to public; genealogical service available for a fee. **Publications:** Newsletter, biennial; in cooperation with Evangelical & Reformed Historical Society, Lancaster Theological Seminary, Lancaster, PA, 17603 and Historical Council, United Church of Christ, 105 Madison Ave., New York, NY 10016. **Staff:** Prof. Lowell H. Zuck, Libn.

★4270★

EVANGELICAL AND REFORMED HISTORICAL SOCIETY - LANCASTER CENTRAL ARCHIVES AND LIBRARY (Hist; Rel-Theol)
Lancaster Theological Seminary
555 W. James St.
Lancaster, PA 17603   Phone: (717) 393-0654
    Florence M. Bricker, Archv.
Founded: 1863. **Staff:** Prof 3; Other 3. **Subjects:** Reformed Church in the United States; Evangelical and Reformed Church; United Church of Christ; Mercersburg theology. **Special Collections:** Reformed Church in the United States (transcribed church records of the 18th century, principally in southeastern Pennsylvania). **Holdings:** 6100 books; 700 bound periodical volumes; 90 manuscript boxes and 40 VF drawers of reports, manuscripts, archives; 160 reels of microfilmed church records. **Subscriptions:** 12 journals and other serials. **Services:** Copying; library open to public. **Remarks:** Includes the archives of the United Church of Christ. **Staff:** Elizabeth Sanders, Res.; Edna M. Hafer, Asst.Res.; Josephine Roye, Cat.; Herbert B. Anstaett, Exec.Sec.

★4271★

EVANGELICAL SCHOOL OF NURSING - WOJNIAK MEMORIAL LIBRARY (Med)
9345 S. Kilbourn
Oak Lawn, IL 60453   Phone: (312) 425-8000
    Gerald Dujsik, Lib.Mgr.
Founded: 1965. **Staff:** Prof 1; Other 2. **Subjects:** Nursing education. **Holdings:** 3000 books and bound periodical volumes; 8 VF drawers of pamphlets; videotapes, films, filmstrips and audiotapes. **Subscriptions:** 100 journals and other serials. **Services:** Interlibrary loans; copying; library open to public with permission. **Networks/Consortia:** Member of Chicago and South Consortium; Regional Medical Library - Region 3; Suburban Library System (SLS). **Publications:** Library Handbook; Acquisitions List.

★4272★
EVANGELICAL SCHOOL OF THEOLOGY - ROSTAD LIBRARY (Rel-Theol)
121 S. College St.   Phone: (717) 866-5775
Myerstown, PA 17067   Terry M. Heisey, Libn.
Staff: Prof 1; Other 1. **Subjects:** Theology, church history, pastoral psychology, Christian education. **Special Collections:** Publications relating to the Evangelical Congregational Church and the United Evangelical Church. **Holdings:** 41,000 books; 6500 bound periodical volumes. **Subscriptions:** 282 journals and other serials. **Services:** Interlibrary loans; copying; library open to public. **Networks/Consortia:** Member of Southeastern Pennsylvania Theological Libraries Association (SEPTLA).

★4273★
EVANGELICAL SEMINARY OF PUERTO RICO - JUAN DE VALDES LIBRARY
   (Rel-Theol)
Ave. Ponce de Leon 776   Phone: (809) 751-6483
Hato Rey, PR 00918   Hector Ruben Sanchez, Lib.Dir.
Founded: 1958. **Staff:** Prof 2; Other 1. **Subjects:** Theology, religious education, Bible, study of history of religions. **Special Collections:** Works of Spanish reformers of the 16th century. **Holdings:** 31,515 books and bound periodical volumes; 265 volumes in microform; 64 boxes of historical documents. **Subscriptions:** 250 journals and other serials; 7 newspapers. **Services:** Interlibrary loans; copying; library open to public for reference use only. **Also Known As:** Seminario Evangelico de Puerto Rico. **Staff:** Gloria M. Mercado .

EVANGELICAL THEOLOGICAL SEMINARY
See: Carter (William) College & Evangelical Theological Seminary

★4274★
EVANGELICAL UNITED BRETHREN CHURCH - HISTORICAL SOCIETY OF
   THE EASTERN CONFERENCE - ARCHIVES ROOM (Rel-Theol)
Gossard Memorial Library
Lebanon Valley College   Phone: (717) 867-4411
Annville, PA 17003   Rev. Herbert R. Blouch, Conf.Hist.
Founded: 1957. **Subjects:** Eastern Conference materials, general Evangelical United Brethren Church materials. **Holdings:** 578 books; 42 bound periodical volumes; 463 conference proceedings; 53 VF drawers unbound archival materials. **Services:** Archives Room open to public by appointment.

★4275★
EVANS, KITCHEL & JENCKES, P.C. - LIBRARY (Law)
363 N. First Ave.   Phone: (602) 262-8811
Phoenix, AZ 85003   Patricia A. Wood, Libn.
Staff: Prof 1; Other 1. **Subjects:** Law. **Special Collections:** Mining (200 volumes); labor (400 volumes). **Holdings:** 14,800 books; 200 bound periodical volumes. **Subscriptions:** 278 journals and other serials. **Services:** Interlibrary loans; copying; library not open to public. **Computerized Information Services:** LEXIS, Disclosure, Inc., New York Times Information Service.

EVANS MEMORIAL LIBRARY
See: Good Samaritan Medical Center - Lutheran Campus

EVANS (Sterling C.) LIBRARY
See: Texas A & M University

EVANSON (Lulu) RESOURCE LIBRARY
See: North Dakota Farmers Union - Lulu Evanson Resource Library

★4276★
EVANSTON HISTORICAL SOCIETY - CHARLES GATES DAWES HOME -
   LIBRARY (Hist)
225 Greenwood St.   Phone: (312) 475-3410
Evanston, IL 60201   Margaret Nicholsen, Libn.
Founded: 1898. **Staff:** 5. **Subjects:** History - Evanston, Illinois. **Special Collections:** Biographical materials on Charles G. Dawes (1865-1951). **Holdings:** 2500 books; 250 bound periodical volumes; 7000 photographs; clippings; local government documents and reports; Evanston newspapers dating from 1873. **Subscriptions:** 10 journals and other serials. **Services:** Copying; library open to public. **Staff:** Mikell C. Darling, Dir.

★4277★
EVANSTON HOSPITAL - WEBSTER MEDICAL LIBRARY (Med)
2650 Ridge Ave.   Phone: (312) 492-4585
Evanston, IL 60201   Rose Slowinski, Dir.
Founded: 1912. **Staff:** Prof 1; Other 2. **Subjects:** Medicine and related fields. **Holdings:** 2500 books; 7500 bound periodical volumes. **Subscriptions:** 180 journals and other serials. **Services:** Interlibrary loans;

copying; library open to public for reference use only. **Networks/Consortia:** Member of Metropolitan Consortium.

★4278★
EVANSVILLE MUSEUM OF ARTS AND SCIENCE - LIBRARY (Art)
411 S.E. Riverside Dr.   Phone: (812) 425-2406
Evansville, IN 47713   Mary McNamee Schnepper, Cur. of Coll.
Founded: 1927. **Staff:** 2. **Subjects:** Art, history, anthropology, science, technology, natural history, architecture, antiques. **Special Collections:** Henry B. Walker, Jr. Memorial Art Library; Evansville and Vanderburgh County, Indiana history archives (19 VF drawers); art archives (13 VF drawers of catalogs, show notices and manuscripts of biographical data). **Holdings:** 3500 books; 2000 unbound periodicals; letters, documents, maps. **Subscriptions:** 54 journals and other serials. **Services:** Copying; library open to public for reference use only.

★4279★
EVANSVILLE PSYCHIATRIC CHILDREN'S CENTER - STAFF LIBRARY (Med)
3330 E. Morgan Ave.   Phone: (812) 477-6436
Evansville, IN 47715   Juanita J. Massie, Med.Rec.Adm./Libn.
Founded: 1966. **Staff:** 1. **Subjects:** Psychotherapy, child development, recreation therapy, psychopathology, education, nursing. **Special Collections:** Children's psychiatric diseases (400 volumes). **Subscriptions:** 14 journals and other serials. **Services:** Interlibrary loans; copying; library open to professionals and students in related fields. **Networks/Consortia:** Member of Evansville Area Health Science Libraries Consortium.

EVENING POST PUBLISHING COMPANY - CHARLESTON EVENING POST/
   NEWS AND COURIER
See: Charleston Evening Post/News and Courier

EVERGLADES NATL. PARK
See: U.S. Natl. Park Service

★4280★
EVERSON MUSEUM OF ART - LIBRARY (Art)
401 Harrison St.   Phone: (315) 474-6064
Syracuse, NY 13202   Jeffrey J. York, Libn.
Staff: Prof 1. **Subjects:** Contemporary and traditional American artists, ceramics, Chinese art, film, photography, video, sculpture, architecture. **Holdings:** 6500 books, exhibition and museum catalogs; 6000 slides. **Subscriptions:** 35 journals and other serials. **Services:** Interlibrary loans; library open to members for reference use only.

EVERYWOMAN CENTER
See: Richland College

★4281★
EVERYWOMAN OPPORTUNITY CENTER, INC. - LIBRARY (Soc Sci)
237 Main St., Suite 725
Buffalo, NY 14203
Subjects: Career and vocational guidance. **Holdings:** 350 volumes. **Subscriptions:** 10 journals and other serials. **Services:** Library open to public. **Publications:** Newsletter, 3-4/year.

EWING MEMORIAL LIBRARY
See: First Presbyterian Church

★4282★
EXCERPTA MEDICA - DATABASE DIVISION (Med)
Box 3085   Phone: (609) 896-9450
Princeton, NJ 08540   Alex Adler, Pres.
Founded: 1968. **Subjects:** Clinical medicine, biological sciences, environmental health, drug information, pharmacy and pharmacology, hospital management. **Holdings:** Excerpta Medica publications since 1947; microfiche of 3000 biomedical periodicals since 1960 (held at Royal Netherlands Academy of Science in Amsterdam). **Subscriptions:** 3500 journals and other serials. **Services:** SDI; retrospective searches; translations; abstracting; bibliographies; Drugdoc; library not open to public; services provided on subscription. **Publications:** 43 regular abstract bulletins; 15 special bulletins; Proceedings in the International Congress Series; Drug Literature Index; Adverse Reactions Titles; MALIMET, Master List of Medical Indexing Terms (thesaurus); EMCLAS (classification system). **Remarks:** Main office and library located in Amsterdam, Netherlands. Magnetic tape, SDI and online retrieval services based on the Excerpta Medica database are provided in North America by DIALOG Information Services, Inc. **Staff:** Marianne M. Meyer, Promotion Mgr.

EXECUTIVE OFFICE OF THE PRESIDENT
See: U.S. Executive Office of the President

EXLEY (Frederick) ARCHIVE
See: University of Rochester - Department of Rare Books and Special Collections

★4283★

EX-MOON INC. - BUSINESS LIBRARY
Box 62
Brookline, MA 02146
Defunct

EXPANSION ECONOMIQUE REGIONALE
See: Canada - Regional Economic Expansion

★4284★

EXPERIENCE, INC. - INFORMATION CENTER (Agri)
1930 Dain Tower   Phone: (612) 333-5231
Minneapolis, MN 55402   Grieg Aspnes, Mgr., Info.Serv.
Founded: 1981. Staff: Prof 2. Subjects: Agriculture, agribusiness, rural development, food processing. Holdings: 200 books; 1500 internal project reports. Subscriptions: 104 journals and other serials. Services: Interlibrary loans; copying; library open to public with restrictions. Computerized Information Services: DIALOG, SDC; internal database; computerized cataloging. Special Indexes: Book catalog; internal reports index.

★4285★

EXPERIMENT IN INTERNATIONAL LIVING - SCHOOL FOR INTERNATIONAL TRAINING - DONALD B. WATT LIBRARY (Soc Sci)
Kipling Rd.   Phone: (802) 257-7751
Brattleboro, VT 05301   Shirley Capron, Pub.Serv.Libn.
Founded: 1968. Staff: Prof 2; Other 1. Subjects: Social sciences and area studies; languages and linguistics; educational research; psychology; French; Spanish. Special Collections: Linguistics. Holdings: 26,000 books; 850 microfiche on language, teaching, linguistics and education; pamphlets; reports; case studies; listing of organizations of international nature. Subscriptions: 300 journals and other serials; 18 newspapers. Services: Interlibrary loans; copying; library open to public for reference use only.

★4286★

EXPERIMENTAL AIRCRAFT ASSOCIATION - AVIATION FOUNDATION - LIBRARY
EAA Aviation Center
Oshkosh, WI 54901
Founded: 1972. Subjects: Aeronautical history, aircraft design, amateur construction. Special Collections: Aeronautical ephemera. Holdings: 200 books; 1500 bound periodical volumes; technical reports. Remarks: Presently inactive. Formerly: Located in Hales Corners, WI.

EXPERIMENTAL SURGERY LIBRARY
See: Mc Gill University

★4287★

EXPLORERS CLUB - JAMES B. FORD MEMORIAL LIBRARY (Geog-Map)
46 E. 70th St.   Phone: (212) 628-8383
New York, NY 10021
Founded: 1904. Staff: Prof 1; Other 3. Subjects: Exploration, chiefly 18th and 19th centuries; ethnology. Special Collections: Admiral Robert Peary Library; 18th century travel. Holdings: 20,000 books; 1000 bound periodical volumes. Subscriptions: 100 journals and other serials. Services: Copying; library open to professional researchers by appointment.

★4288★

EXPORT DEVELOPMENT CORPORATION - LIBRARY (Bus-Fin)
110 O'Connor St.
Box 655
Ottawa, ON, Canada K1P 5T9   Phone: (613) 237-2570
                                          Ann James, Libn.
Staff: Prof 1; Other 2. Subjects: Economics, international banking and finance, commerce. Holdings: 8000 volumes; 8000 annual reports. Subscriptions: 600 journals and other serials; 21 newspapers. Services: Interlibrary loans; copying; library open to public by appointment. Publications: Acquisitions list; list of periodicals received - both for internal distribution only.

★4289★

EXPORT-IMPORT BANK OF THE UNITED STATES - LIBRARY (Bus-Fin)
811 Vermont Ave., N.W.   Phone: (202) 566-8897
Washington, DC 20571   Theodora McGill, Libn.
Founded: 1945. Staff: Prof 2; Other 1. Subjects: Banking, economics, finance, commerce, trade statistics, exports and imports. Special Collections: Economist Intelligence Unit (EIU) collection of quarterly economic reviews. Holdings: 2000 books; 10,000 other cataloged items; 20 VF drawers of Congressional materials; 5 VF drawers of clippings; 2 VF drawers of press releases. Subscriptions: 900 journals and other serials; 20 newspapers. Services: SDI; library open to public. Computerized Information Services: Computerized serials. Publications: Bibliographies on financial statements or other subjects of interest; Acquisitions List, biweekly - internal distribution, available to libraries on request. Staff: John R. Posniak, Asst.Libn.

EXPRESS-NEWS CORPORATION - SAN ANTONIO EXPRESS AND NEWS
See: San Antonio Express and News

★4290★

EXTEL CORPORATION - TEHNICAL LIBRARY (Sci-Tech)
4000 Commercial Ave.   Phone: (312) 291-2766
Northbrook, IL 60062   Elizabeth Ziegler, Tech.Libn.
Staff: Prof 1. Subjects: Electrical engineering, telecommunications, computers. Holdings: 600 books; 15 VF drawers of U.S. and foreign standards. Subscriptions: 120 journals and other serials; 5 newspapers. Services: Interlibrary loans; copying; SDI; library open to public with restrictions.

EXTERNAL AFFAIRS CANADA
See: Canada - External Affairs Canada

EXTINCT SPECIES MEMORIAL FUND
See: Whale Center

EXXON COMMUNICATIONS SYSTEMS
See: Verbex Corporation - Exxon Communications Systems

★4291★

EXXON COMPANY, U.S.A. - EXPLORATION LIBRARY (Energy)
Box 4279, Rm. 3350   Phone: (713) 999-9257
Houston, TX 77001   Roza Ekimov, Libn.
Founded: 1971. Staff: Prof 1; Other 1. Subjects: Geology, geophysics, oceanography, paleontology. Special Collections: Alaska; Arctic. Holdings: 7260 volumes; 4300 other cataloged items. Subscriptions: 205 journals and other serials. Services: Interlibrary loans; library open to public for reference use only by appointment. Publications: Library Bulletin, biweekly.

★4292★

EXXON COMPANY, U.S.A. - EXXON RESEARCH & DEVELOPMENT LABORATORIES LIBRARY (Energy)
Box 2226   Phone: (504) 359-7681
Baton Rouge, LA 70821   Nima T. Cotton
Founded: 1944. Subjects: Chemical engineering, chemical refining, petroleum, petrochemicals. Holdings: 5000 volumes. Services: Library not open to public.

★4293★

EXXON COMPANY, U.S.A. - GENERAL SERVICES - LIBRARY
Box 2180
Houston, TX 77001
Defunct

★4294★

EXXON COMPANY, U.S.A. - LAW LIBRARY (Law)
Box 2180   Phone: (713) 656-2019
Houston, TX 77001   Mrs. Del Wherry, Libn.
Staff: Prof 2; Other 2. Subjects: Law. Holdings: 30,000 volumes. Services: Copying; library not open to public.

★4295★

EXXON COMPANY, U.S.A. - TECHNICAL SERVICES - ENGINEERING LIBRARY (Sci-Tech)
Box 3950   Phone: (713) 425-4487
Baytown, TX 77520   Bethany Picard, Libn.
Staff: Prof 1; Other 1. Subjects: Engineering - civil, mechanical, electrical, chemical; instrumentation; mathematics; computing; systems. Holdings: 10,000 books; 75 bound periodical volumes; 30,000 manufacturers' catalogs on microfilm. Subscriptions: 150 journals and other serials.

Services: Interlibrary loans; copying; library open to public by special arrangement. **Computerized Information Services:** SDC. **Publications:** Periodical holdings, annual; Acquisition List, quarterly.

★4296★

EXXON CORPORATION - COMMUNICATIONS AND COMPUTER SCIENCE DEPARTMENT- TECHNICAL LIBRARY (Sci-Tech)
180 Park Ave., Bldg. 103
Florham Park, NJ 07932
Phone: (201) 765-7533
P. Neubig, Ref.Sys.Supv.
Staff: Prof 1; Other 2. **Subjects:** Mathematics, computer science. **Holdings:** 2000 books. **Subscriptions:** 150 journals and other serials. **Services:** Library not open to public. **Computerized Information Services:** DIALOG, SDC.

★4297★

EXXON CORPORATION - LAW-TAX LIBRARY (Law)
1251 Ave. of the Americas, 45th Fl.
New York, NY 10020
Phone: (212) 398-3247
Mary K. Moynihan, Libn.
Staff: Prof 1; Other 1. **Subjects:** Corporate law, taxation. **Holdings:** 30,000 books; 250 bound periodical volumes. **Subscriptions:** 44 journals and other serials. **Services:** Library not open to public.

★4298★

EXXON CORPORATION - MEDICAL LIBRARY (Med)
1251 Ave. of the Americas
New York, NY 10020
Phone: (212) 398-2504
Constance M. Lima, Med.Libn.
Founded: 1945. **Staff:** Prof 1. **Subjects:** Clinical medicine, industrial medicine and hygiene, preventive medicine and public health. **Holdings:** 900 books; 300 bound periodical volumes; 1900 pamphlets. **Subscriptions:** 80 journals and other serials. **Services:** Interlibrary loans; use of library may be requested.

★4299★

EXXON CORPORATION - MEDICINE & ENVIRONMENTAL HEALTH DEPT. - RESEARCH & ENVIRONMENTAL HEALTH DIV.LIB. (Med)
Mettlers Rd.
Box 235
East Millstone, NJ 08873
Phone: (201) 474-2506
Patricia Hodge, Group Ldr., Lib/Off.Serv.
Founded: 1952. **Staff:** Prof 3; Other 2. **Subjects:** Toxicology, industrial hygiene, epidemiology, industrial medicine. **Holdings:** 1000 books; 1500 bound periodical volumes; government reports, clippings, pamphlets and reprints. **Subscriptions:** 303 journals and other serials. **Services:** Library open to the public with director's permission. **Computerized Information Services:** SDC, DIALOG, NLM; computerized serials. **Special Catalogs:** Abstracts of related literature (card and microfiche). **Also Known As:** Exxon Biomedical Sciences Inc. **Staff:** Rosemarie Parker, Sr.Info.Sci.; Janet Chapman, Info.Anl.

★4300★

EXXON RESEARCH AND ENGINEERING COMPANY - FLORHAM PARK INFORMATION CENTER (Sci-Tech; Energy)
Box 101
Florham Park, NJ 07932
Phone: (201) 765-6704
Martin Cosgrave, Sect.Hd.
Founded: 1961. **Staff:** Prof 12; Other 26. **Subjects:** Engineering - petroleum, chemical, mechanical, civil; materials science; environment; metallurgy; energy; related business subjects. **Holdings:** 9700 books; 8000 bound periodical volumes; 1544 reels of microfilm; 281 microfiche; company reports on microfilm and microfiche; mechanical catalogs; Esso Abstract Card Files on microfilm; engineering drawings. **Subscriptions:** 350 journals and other serials. **Services:** Library not open to public. **Computerized Information Services:** Online systems. **Staff:** J.P. Saldinger, Libn.; B.A. Short, Libn.

★4301★

EXXON RESEARCH AND ENGINEERING COMPANY - INFORMATION SERVICES (Sci-Tech; Energy)†
Box 121
Linden, NJ 07036
Phone: (201) 474-0100
Margaret H. Graham, Mgr.
Founded: 1919. **Staff:** Prof 35; Other 62. **Subjects:** Petroleum refining processes and products; petrochemical processes and products, engineering, chemistry, physics, metallurgy, science and technology. **Holdings:** 61,000 books and bound periodical volumes, including microforms; 66,000 proprietary reports; patent holdings. **Subscriptions:** 900 journals and other serials. **Services:** Copying; services not open to public. **Computerized Information Services:** Online systems; text processing; computerized cataloging, acquisitions and serials. **Publications:** Technical Information News - for internal distribution only. **Special Catalogs:** Current Journal Orders and Holdings. **Special Indexes:** Technical Reports Index, bimonthly; cumulation to annual microfiche and computer database.

★4302★

EXXON RESEARCH AND ENGINEERING COMPANY - LIBRARY (Energy)
Box 4178
Baytown, TX 77520
Phone: (713) 428-5100
Geraldine Gieger, Res.Libn.
Founded: 1938. **Staff:** Prof 1; Other 2. **Subjects:** Chemistry, chemical engineering, petrochemicals, physics, mathematics. **Holdings:** 25,000 books and bound periodical volumes. **Subscriptions:** 300 journals and other serials. **Services:** Interlibrary loans; copying (limited); library open to public by appointment. **Computerized Information Services:** DIALOG, SDC. **Publications:** Acquisitions List and list of journal holdings - for internal distribution only.

★4303★

EYE AND EAR HOSPITAL OF PITTSBURGH - BLAIR-LIPPINCOTT LIBRARY (Med)
230 Lothrop St.
Pittsburgh, PA 15213
Phone: (412) 647-2287
Bruce Johnston, Med.Libn.
Founded: 1922. **Staff:** Prof 1; Other 1. **Subjects:** Ophthalmology, otolaryngology, audiology. **Holdings:** 3000 books; 4000 bound periodical volumes. **Subscriptions:** 120 journals and other serials. **Services:** Interlibrary loans; copying; library open to public with special permission necessary for borrowing. **Computerized Information Services:** MEDLARS.

★4304★

EYE FOUNDATION HOSPITAL - JOHN E. MEYER EYE FOUNDATION LIBRARY (Med)
1720 8th Ave., S.
Birmingham, AL 35233
Phone: (205) 325-8505
Hugh Thomas, Med.Libn.
Founded: 1977. **Staff:** Prof 1. **Subjects:** Ophthalmology, otolaryngology, general medicine, plastic surgery, hospital administration. **Holdings:** 1000 books; 1100 bound periodical volumes; 500 slides and cassettes. **Subscriptions:** 81 journals and other serials. **Services:** Interlibrary loans; copying; library open to medical professionals.

F

F.B.I. ACADEMY
See: U.S. Dept. of Justice - Federal Bureau of Investigation

★4305★
FACTORY MUTUAL SYSTEM - FACTORY MUTUAL RESEARCH CORPORATION - LIBRARY (Sci-Tech)
1151 Boston-Providence Tpke.
Norwood, MA 02062
Phone: (617) 762-4300
Bruce P. Mattoon, V.P.
Staff: Prof 1; Other 6. Subjects: Engineering - emphasis on fire research and loss prevention. Holdings: 5000 books; 500 bound periodical volumes; 2000 technical reports. Subscriptions: 150 journals and other serials. Services: Interlibrary loans; library open to public by appointment. Computerized Information Services: DIALOG. Staff: Florice T. Madden, Libn.

FACULTE ST-JEAN
See: University of Alberta

★4306★
FAEGRE & BENSON - LAW LIBRARY (Law)
1300 Northwestern Bank Bldg.
Minneapolis, MN 55402
Phone: (612) 371-5300
Carolyn Scott, Libn.
Staff: Prof 2; Other 1. Subjects: Law. Holdings: 20,800 books; 1200 bound periodical volumes. Subscriptions: 75 journals and other serials; 5 newspapers. Services: Library open to other law librarians and firms with special permission. Computerized Information Services: LEXIS. Staff: Rhonda Greenwood, Libn.

FAIRBANK (John K.) CENTER FOR EAST ASIAN RESEARCH
See: Harvard University - John K. Fairbank Center for East Asian Research

★4307★
FAIRBANKS ENVIRONMENTAL CENTER - LIBRARY (Env-Cons)
218 Driveway
Fairbanks, AK 99701
Phone: (907) 452-5021
Brian Allen, Dir.
Founded: 1972. Staff: 1. Subjects: Alaska - land use, pipelines for oil and gas, wildlife, highways and transportation, environment. Holdings: 500 books; 1500 pamphlets; VF drawers on environmental concerns (5 on Alaskan, 1 on Fairbanks and 3 on national). Services: Copying; library open to public. Publications: The Northern Line, bimonthly - distributed to members or by subscription.

★4308★
FAIRBANKS MUSEUM AND PLANETARIUM - LIBRARY (Sci-Tech)†
Main and Prospect Sts.
St. Johnsbury, VT 05819
Phone: (802) 748-2378
Howard B. Reed, Assoc.Dir., Musm.Coll.
Founded: 1890. Staff: 1. Subjects: Natural history, physical science, history, energy technology. Holdings: 2200 books; 550 bound periodical volumes; 5 boxes of unbound reports; 5 boxes of historical archives. Subscriptions: 15 journals and other serials. Services: Interlibrary loans; copying; library open to public for reference use only.

FAIRCHILD AERIAL PHOTOGRAPH COLLECTION
See: Whittier College - Department of Geology

FAIRCHILD AIR FORCE BASE (WA)
See: U.S. Air Force Base - Fairchild Base Library; U.S. Air Force Hospital - Technical Library

★4309★
FAIRCHILD CAMERA AND INSTRUMENT CORPORATION - R & D LIBRARY (Sci-Tech)†
4001 Miranda Ave.
Palo Alto, CA 94303
Phone: (415) 493-7250
Founded: 1960. Staff: Prof 1; Other 1. Subjects: Semiconductors. Holdings: Figures not available. Services: Library not open to public.

★4310★
FAIRCHILD INDUSTRIES - FAIRCHILD REPUBLIC COMPANY - TECHNICAL INFORMATION CENTER (Sci-Tech)
Conklin St.
Farmingdale, NY 11735
Phone: (516) 531-3497
George A. Mauter, Supv.
Founded: 1942. Staff: Prof 1; Other 2. Subjects: Aeronautics, astronautics, aircraft, fluid dynamics, propulsion, materials, engineering sciences,
electronics, military science. Special Collections: NACA and NASA Reports; Aeronautical Research Council (U.K.) reports. Holdings: 20,000 books and bound periodical volumes; 135,000 technical reports (paper copy); 510,000 technical reports on microforms; 23,000 society papers. Subscriptions: 235 journals and other serials. Services: Interlibrary loans; copying; SDI; library open to public by appointment. Computerized Information Services: DIALOG, DTIC, Dow Jones News Retrieval, New York Times Information Service, Data Resources Inc. (DRI); computerized circulation. Networks/Consortia: Member of Long Island Library Resources Council. Publications: Acquisitions Bulletin, monthly; The Source, bimonthly. Special Indexes: KWIC Index. Formerly: Its Engineering Library.

★4311★
FAIRCHILD INDUSTRIES - TECHNICAL INFORMATION SERVICE - LIBRARY (Sci-Tech)
Sherman Fairchild Technology Ctr.
20301 Century Blvd.
Germantown, MD 20874
Phone: (301) 428-6415
Hazel M. More, Tech.Libn.
Staff: Prof 1. Subjects: Electronics, aerospace science, communication satellites. Special Collections: Collection of the National Advisory Committee for Aeronautics (NACA) Tech Memos on microfiche. Holdings: 2000 books; 2000 bound periodical volumes; 96 file drawers of microfiche. Subscriptions: 250 journals and other serials. Services: Interlibrary loans.

★4312★
FAIRCHILD TROPICAL GARDEN - MONTGOMERY LIBRARY (Sci-Tech)
10901 Old Cutler Rd.
Miami, FL 33156
Phone: (305) 667-1651
John Popenoe, Dir.
Founded: 1940. Subjects: Botany, horticulture. Special Collections: Manuscripts and correspondence of Dr. David Fairchild (4 filing cabinets). Holdings: 5000 volumes. Services: Library open to public by appointment.

★4313★
FAIRCHILD-WESTON SYSTEMS INC. - WESTON CONTROLS DIVISION - TECHNICAL LIBRARY (Sci-Tech)
Kennedy Dr.
Archbald, PA 18403
Phone: (717) 876-1500
Arlene F. Kohl, Tech.Libn.
Staff: Prof 1. Subjects: Science, technology, electronics, nuclear instrumentation, metallurgy. Holdings: 3000 books; potentiometer patents. Subscriptions: 55 journals and other serials; 5 newspapers. Services: Interlibrary loans; copying; library not open to public. Remarks: Company is a division of Schlumberger, Ltd.

★4314★
FAIRFAX COUNTY - COMPREHENSIVE PLANNING LIBRARY (Plan)
4100 Chain Bridge Rd.
Fairfax, VA 22030
James L. Linard, Res.Libn.
Staff: Prof 1. Subjects: Urban planning. Special Collections: Fairfax County Planning. Holdings: 500 books; 100 periodical volumes; 2000 reports/studies. Subscriptions: 50 journals and other serials. Services: Interlibrary loans; copying; library open to public with restrictions.

★4315★
FAIRFAX COUNTY LAW LIBRARY (Law)
4110 Chain Bridge Rd.
Fairfax, VA 22030
Phone: (703) 691-2170
Judith A. Meadows, Law Libn.
Staff: Prof 1; Other 2. Subjects: Law. Special Collections: Virginia law. Holdings: 17,000 books and bound periodical volumes. Services: Interlibrary loans; copying; library open to public. Computerized Information Services: WESTLAW.

★4316★
FAIRFAX COUNTY PUBLIC LIBRARY - BUSINESS & TECHNICAL SECTION (Bus-Fin; Sci-Tech)
3915 Chain Bridge Rd.
Fairfax, VA 22030
Phone: (703) 691-2121
Bergliot G. Sleight, Libn.
Founded: 1972. Staff: Prof 3; Other 1. Subjects: Management, economics, investments, electronics, engineering. Holdings: 15,000 books; 350 telephone directories; annual reports and proxy statements, 1978 to present, on microfiche; Dun & Bradstreet Account Identification file on microfiche. Subscriptions: 300 journals and other serials. Services: Interlibrary loans; copying; library open to public. Computerized Information Services: DIALOG; computerized cataloging and circulation.

★4317★
FAIRFAX COUNTY PUBLIC LIBRARY - VIRGINIA ROOM (Hist)
3915 Chain Bridge Rd.
Fairfax, VA 22030
Phone: (703) 691-2123
Suzanne S. Levy, Libn.
Founded: 1940. Staff: Prof 1; Other 2. Subjects: Virginia - history,

government, genealogy. **Special Collections:** Fairfax County History; Virginia Legislative Information; Fairfax County Photographic Archives; microfilm collection; map collection; Virginia and Fairfax city and county documents. **Holdings:** 19,200 books; 900 bound periodical volumes; 8 VF drawers of Historic Landmarks Files; 1090 reels of microfilm; 116 boxes of manuscripts and scrapbooks; 6500 photographs; 1931 microfiche; 461 microcards. **Subscriptions:** 248 journals and other serials; 20 newspapers. **Services:** Interlibrary loans; copying; library open to public. **Computerized Information Services:** Virginia State Division of Legislative Services; computerized cataloging and circulation. **Publications:** Fairfax County Public Library Guide to the Virginia General Assembly, annual - to legislative service users. **Special Indexes:** Fairfax County History Index; Fairfax County Cemetery Index; Local Newspaper Index; Local and State Periodical Index.

★4318★
FAIRFAX COUNTY PUBLIC SCHOOLS - PROFESSIONAL REFERENCE LIBRARY IN EDUCATION (Educ)
3500 Old Lee Hwy.   Phone: (703) 591-4514
Fairfax, VA 22030   Betty Chilton, Lib.Spec.
Staff: Prof 1; Other 1. **Subjects:** Education. **Holdings:** 13,500 books; ERIC microfiche collection. **Subscriptions:** 200 journals and other serials. **Services:** Library open to public for reference use only.

★4319★
FAIRFAX HOSPITAL - JACOB D. ZYLMAN MEMORIAL LIBRARY (Med)
3300 Gallows Rd.   Phone: (703) 698-3234
Falls Church, VA 22046   Alice J. Sheridan, Dir.
Staff: Prof 3; Other 4. **Subjects:** Medicine, nursing, hospital management. **Holdings:** 5000 books; 5000 bound periodical volumes; 1000 audiotapes. **Subscriptions:** 300 journals and other serials. **Services:** Interlibrary loans; copying; library open to public for reference use only. **Computerized Information Services:** MEDLARS, DIALOG, BRS.

★4320★
FAIRFIELD HILLS HOSPITAL - MEDICAL LIBRARY (Med)
Box W   Phone: (203) 426-2531
Newtown, CT 06470   Pauline A. Kruk, Libn.
Founded: 1933. **Staff:** 3. **Subjects:** Psychiatry, psychology, medicine, social service, dentistry, rehabilitation. **Holdings:** 3500 books; 2000 bound periodical volumes; 150 cataloged reference materials; 350 pamphlets and periodicals; AV materials. **Subscriptions:** 133 journals and other serials. **Services:** Interlibrary loans; library open to public for reference use only. **Networks/Consortia:** Member of Connecticut Association of Health Science Libraries (CAHSL); Southwestern Connecticut Library Council (SCLC).

★4321★
FAIRFIELD HISTORICAL SOCIETY - REFERENCE AND RESEARCH LIBRARY (Hist)
636 Old Post Rd.   Phone: (203) 259-1598
Fairfield, CT 06430   Irene K. Miller, Libn.
Founded: 1903. **Staff:** Prof 1; Other 4. **Subjects:** Local history, genealogy. **Holdings:** 8000 books; 750 bound periodical volumes; 200 linear feet of manuscript material including 18th to 20th century family, church, school and town records, personal diaries, scrapbooks, account books and records of merchants, craftsmen, professional men and organizations, and local ephemera; maps; photographs; 28 VF drawers of local history and genealogy. **Subscriptions:** 22 journals and other serials. **Services:** Copying; library open to public for reference use only. **Publications:** Fairfield in Connecticut, 1776-1976; Naval History of Fairfield County Men in the Revolution; Walking Through History - The Seaports of Black Rock and Southport; Newsletter, quarterly. **Special Indexes:** Indexes to selected manuscript collections.

FAIRLAWN MUSEUM LIBRARY
See: Douglas County Historical Society

★4322★
FAIRLEIGH DICKINSON UNIVERSITY - MESSLER LIBRARY - NEW JERSEY ROOM (Hist; Soc Sci)
Montross Ave.   Phone: (201) 933-5000
Rutherford, NJ 07070   Catharine M. Fogarty, NJ Rm.Libn.
Staff: Prof 1; Other 1. **Subjects:** New Jersey - state and local history, social and economic conditions, politics and government. **Holdings:** 5512 books; 604 bound periodical volumes; 3626 documents; 558 pamphlets; 732 maps; 36 feet of manuscripts; 346 reels of microfilm; 263 microcards; 177 cards of microfiche. **Subscriptions:** 373 journals and other serials. **Services:** Interlibrary loans; copying; open to public by request. **Computerized Information Services:** DIALOG; computerized cataloging. **Networks/Consortia:** Member of PALINET & Union Library Catalogue of Pennsylvania. **Publications:** Accessions lists; Documents of New Jersey Local Governments,

published in 1969. **Special Catalogs:** A Guide to Manuscripts on Microfilm, 1976 (pamphlet).

★4323★
FAIRLEIGH DICKINSON UNIVERSITY - SCHOOL OF DENTISTRY LIBRARY (Med)
110 Fuller Pl.   Phone: (201) 836-6300
Hackensack, NJ 07601   Kathy Marousek, Act. Dental Libn.
Founded: 1956. **Staff:** Prof 1; Other 4. **Subjects:** Dentistry and allied health sciences. **Special Collections:** Museum items (dental instruments and equipment; 600 items). **Holdings:** 12,320 books; 6596 bound periodical volumes; 352 audiotapes; 475 videotapes; 79 motion pictures; 28,107 slides; 1900 reels of microfilm. **Subscriptions:** 516 journals and other serials. **Services:** Interlibrary loans; copying; library open to medical and health professionals for specific needs. **Computerized Information Services:** BRS; computerized cataloging. **Networks/Consortia:** Member of Medical Library Network. **Publications:** Dental Library Notes, irregular - for internal distribution only.

★4324★
FAIRLEIGH DICKINSON UNIVERSITY - WEINER LIBRARY - REFERENCE/GOVERNMENT DOCUMENTS DEPARTMENT (Soc Sci)
1000 River Rd.   Phone: (201) 692-2290
Teaneck, NJ 07666   Michelle Fanelli, Hd.
Founded: 1963. **Staff:** Prof 2; Other 2. **Subjects:** Census, environment, energy, education, business, government. **Special Collections:** Depository for selected U.S. government documents. **Holdings:** 52,107 documents; microforms. **Services:** Interlibrary loans; copying; department open to public. **Computerized Information Services:** BRS; computerized cataloging. **Networks/Consortia:** Member of PALINET & Union Library Catalogue of Pennsylvania.

★4325★
FAIRMOUNT TEMPLE - SAM AND EMMA MILLER LIBRARY (Rel-Theol)
23737 Fairmount Blvd.   Phone: (216) 464-1330
Cleveland, OH 44122
Founded: 1927. **Staff:** Prof 1; Other 1. **Subjects:** Judaica. **Holdings:** 18,000 subject files. **Subscriptions:** 80 journals and other serials; 6 newspapers. **Services:** Interlibrary loans; library open to public.

★4326★
FAIRVIEW COLLEGE - LEARNING RESOURCES CENTRE (Agri)
Box 3000   Phone: (403) 835-2213
Fairview, AB, Canada T0H 1L0   Olive V. Lancaster, Chm., LRC
Founded: 1951. **Staff:** Prof 1; Other 4. **Subjects:** Agriculture, animal health, beekeeping, trades technology, turfgrass, business, local history. **Holdings:** 23,000 books; 113 bound periodical volumes; 2000 AV items; 150 pamphlets; 900 bulletins. **Subscriptions:** 10 newspapers. **Services:** Interlibrary loans; copying; library open to public. **Remarks:** Administered by the Board of Governors.

★4327★
FAIRVIEW COMMUNITY HOSPITALS - HEALTH SCIENCES LIBRARY (Med)
2312 S. Sixth St.   Phone: (612) 371-6545
Minneapolis, MN 55454   Linda McIntosh, Dir.
Founded: 1971. **Staff:** Prof 1; Other 4. **Subjects:** Medicine, orthopedics, nursing. **Holdings:** 3067 books; 4500 bound periodical volumes; 233 audiotapes (cataloged). **Subscriptions:** 300 journals and other serials. **Services:** Library not open to public. **Computerized Information Services:** BRS, MEDLINE. **Networks/Consortia:** Member of Twin Cities Biomedical Consortium.

FAIRVIEW COMMUNITY HOSPITALS - TEL-MED HEALTH INFORMATION SERVICE
See: Tel-Med Health Information Service

★4328★
FAIRVIEW DEACONESS HOSPITAL - MEDICAL LIBRARY (Med)
1400 E. 24th St.   Phone: (612) 721-9475
Minneapolis, MN 55404   Susan Clark, Libn.
Staff: Prof 1; Other 1. **Subjects:** Nursing, medicine, religion. **Holdings:** 2500 books; 160 bound periodical volumes; 10 filing cabinets of pamphlets and clippings; 180 AV items. **Subscriptions:** 145 journals and other serials. **Services:** Interlibrary loans; copying; SDI; library not open to public. **Computerized Information Services:** MEDLINE, SUNY-Biomedical Communication Network (BCN). **Networks/Consortia:** Member of Twin Cities Biomedical Consortium (TCBC); Regional Medical Library - Region 3. **Publications:** FDH Library Recent Acquisitions, quarterly. **Formerly:** Lutheran Deaconess Hospital.

★4329★
FAIRVIEW GENERAL HOSPITAL - HEALTH MEDIA CENTER (Med)
18101 Lorain Ave.   Phone: (216) 476-7118
Cleveland, OH 44111   Susan L. Favorite, Dir.
Staff: Prof 1; Other 4. **Subjects:** Internal medicine, obstetrics, gynecology, surgery, pediatrics, nursing. **Holdings:** 7516 books; 3120 bound periodical volumes. **Subscriptions:** 442 journals and other serials. **Services:** Interlibrary loans; copying; library not open to public. **Computerized Information Services:** MEDLINE. **Networks/Consortia:** Member of Cleveland MEDLINE Consortium. **Remarks:** Includes the holdings of the School of Nursing Library.

★4330★
FAIRVIEW SOUTHDALE HOSPITAL - MARY ANN KING HEALTH SCIENCES LIBRARY (Med)
6401 France Ave., S.   Phone: (612) 924-5005
Edina, MN 55435   Lisa C. Bjerken, Dir., Lib.Serv.
Founded: 1975. **Staff:** Prof 1. **Subjects:** Medicine, nursing, allied health sciences, hospital administration and management. **Holdings:** 1100 books; 300 bound periodical volumes; vertical files. **Subscriptions:** 160 journals and other serials. **Services:** Interlibrary loans; copying; SDI; library open to public with restrictions. **Computerized Information Services:** BRS, MEDLINE. **Networks/Consortia:** Member of Region Medical Library - Region 3; Twin Cities Biomedical Consortium (TCBC).

FAIRVIEW SOUTHDALE HOSPITAL - TEL-MED HEALTH INFORMATION SERVICE
See: Tel-Med Health Information Service

★4331★
FAIRVIEW STATE HOSPITAL - STAFF LIBRARY (Med; Soc Sci)
2501 Harbor Blvd.   Phone: (714) 957-5394
Costa Mesa, CA 92626   Barbara Rycroft, Sr.Libn.
Founded: 1960. **Staff:** Prof 1. **Subjects:** Mental retardation, developmental disabilities, psychology, special education, medicine, social work. **Holdings:** 2502 books; 2675 bound periodical volumes; 45 staff research reports; 5 VF drawers of pamphlets. **Subscriptions:** 117 journals and other serials. **Services:** Interlibrary loans; copying; library open to public for reference use only. **Networks/Consortia:** Member of Pacific Southwest Regional Medical Library Service (PSRMLS); Nursing Information Consortium of Orange County (NICOC).

★4332★
FAITH EVANGELICAL LUTHERAN SEMINARY - LIBRARY (Rel-Theol)
3504 N. Pearl
Box 7186
Tacoma, WA 98407   Phone: (206) 752-2020
      Rev. Osborne Y. Bruland, Libn.
Founded: 1969. **Staff:** Prof 1. **Subjects:** Theology, church history, missions. **Holdings:** 9366 books; 84 bound periodical volumes. **Subscriptions:** 21 journals and other serials. **Services:** Interlibrary loans; library open to public. **Remarks:** The seminary is sponsored and supported by Lutherans Alert National.

FAKE (Warren H.) LIBRARY
See: Hahnemann Medical College & Hospital - Warren H. Fake Library

★4333★
FALCONBRIDGE NICKEL MINES, LTD. - FALCONBRIDGE INFORMATION CENTRE (Sci-Tech)
Commerce Court West
P.O. Box 40
Toronto, ON, Canada M5L 1B4   Phone: (416) 863-7227
      Stewart Collett, Mgr.
Founded: 1964. **Staff:** Prof 2; Other 1. **Subjects:** Metallurgy, geology, mining engineering, mineralogy, mechanical engineering, finance. **Holdings:** 10,000 books; 650 bound periodical volumes; 45,000 inputs in original form and microfilm covering all subjects with KWIC index. **Subscriptions:** 172 journals and other serials; 14 newspapers. **Services:** Interlibrary loans; copying; library not open to public. **Computerized Information Services:** Internal database; computerized cataloging. **Publications:** KWIC indexes, annual with monthly supplements. **Staff:** Joan Cox, Asst.; Virginia Dodd, Asst.

★4334★
FALCONBRIDGE NICKEL MINES, LTD. - METALLURGICAL LABORATORIES INFORMATION SERVICES (Sci-Tech)
Box 900
Thornhill, ON, Canada L3T 4A8   Phone: (416) 889-6221
      Doris George, Libn.
Founded: 1957. **Staff:** 3. **Subjects:** Physical metallurgy, extractive metallurgy, analytical chemistry, mineralogy, geology. **Holdings:** 2500 books; 2200 bound periodical volumes; 20,000 separate articles. **Subscriptions:** 170 journals and other serials. **Services:** Interlibrary loans; copying; library

open to SLA members and individuals approved by management. **Computerized Information Services:** DIALOG, SDC, Falconbridge Laboratories Information Search System (FLISS-internal database). **Networks/Consortia:** Member of Sheridan Park Association. **Publications:** Library Review, monthly; Nickel News, quarterly. **Staff:** Miss B. Maxwell, Asst.Libn.; Mrs. S. Simpson, Ck.

FALCONER BIOLOGY LIBRARY
See: Stanford University

FALES LIBRARY
See: New York University

FALK LIBRARY OF THE HEALTH SCIENCES
See: University of Pittsburgh

★4335★
FALKIRK HOSPITAL - LIBRARY (Med)
Box 194   Phone: (914) 928-2256
Central Valley, NY 10917   Maria Gern
Founded: 1889. **Staff:** Prof 2; Other 1. **Subjects:** Psychiatry, psychology, medicine, alcoholism, drug addiction. **Special Collections:** Papers and monographs of Dr. Charles W. Pilgrim; Falkirk Hospital papers from 1889. **Holdings:** 2250 books; 350 bound periodical volumes. **Subscriptions:** 57 journals and other serials; 14 newspapers. **Services:** Interlibrary loans; copying; library not open to public. **Computerized Information Services:** Computerized cataloging, serials and circulation.

FALL (Bernard B.) COLLECTION
See: Howard University - Bernard B. Fall Collection

★4336★
FALL RIVER HISTORICAL SOCIETY - MUSEUM/LIBRARY (Hist)
451 Rock St.   Phone: (617) 679-1071
Fall River, MA 02720   Florence C. Brigham, Cur.
Staff: Prof 2. **Subjects:** Fall River Line, cotton textile industry; local history and genealogy. **Holdings:** Figures not available. **Services:** Museum open to public.

★4337★
FALL RIVER LAW LIBRARY (Law)
Superior Court House
441 N. Main St.   Phone: (617) 676-8971
Fall River, MA 02720   Mary L. Sullivan, Libn.
Staff: Prof 1. **Subjects:** Law. **Special Collections:** Massachusetts reports, papers and briefs; English reports. **Holdings:** 24,439 books and bound periodical volumes. **Subscriptions:** 51 journals and other serials. **Services:** Library open to public for reference use only. **Remarks:** The library is sponsored by the Fall River Bar Association. **Formerly:** Bristol County Bar Association - Fall River Law Library.

FALL RIVER MARINE MUSEUM
See: Marine Museum at Fall River, Inc.

★4338★
FALLSVIEW PSYCHIATRIC HOSPITAL - STAFF LIBRARY (Med)
330 Broadway E.   Phone: (216) 929-8301
Cuyahoga Falls, OH 44221   David Allen, Libn.
Staff: Prof 1. **Subjects:** Psychology, psychiatry, nursing, social work, gerontology, pastoral counseling. **Holdings:** 3000 books. **Subscriptions:** 30 journals and other serials. **Services:** Interlibrary loans; library open to public with restrictions. **Computerized Information Services:** Computerized cataloging. **Networks/Consortia:** Member of Northeastern Ohio Universities College of Medicine (NEOUCOM).

★4339★
FALMOUTH HISTORICAL SOCIETY - RESOURCES CENTER - HISTORY & GENEALOGY ARCHIVES (Hist)
Palmer Ave. at the Village Green
Box 174
Falmouth, MA 02541   Phone: (617) 548-4857
      Dudley W. Hallett, Pres.
Staff: 4. **Subjects:** Local history, genealogy. **Special Collections:** Old deeds and wills. **Holdings:** 500 books; 30 ships logs (from 1820); 100 boxes of archival materials. **Staff:** Capt. Charles A. Davis, Recorder.

FAMILY LIFE EDUCATION SERVICES
See: C.L.S.C. Metro

FAMILY PLANNING INFORMATION CENTER
See: Hawaii Planned Parenthood

FAMILY PLANNING LIBRARIES & INFORMATION CENTERS INTERNATIONAL
See: Association for Population/Family Planning Libraries & Information Centers International

★4340★
FAMILY PRACTICE RESIDENCY PROGRAM AT CHEYENNE - FAMILY PRACTICE LIBRARY AT CHEYENNE (Med)
821 E. 18th St.   Phone: (307) 777-7911
Cheyenne, WY 82001-4797   Carol Seebaum, Med.Libn.
Founded: 1980. **Staff:** Prof 1. **Subjects:** Clinical medicine. **Holdings:** 300 books; 1500 bound periodical volumes; 1500 current journals on microfilm. **Subscriptions:** 82 journals and other serials. **Services:** Interlibrary loans; copying; library open to medical professionals. **Computerized Information Services:** MEDLARS. **Networks/Consortia:** Member of Southeast Wyoming Health Sciences Library Consortium.

FAMILY RESOURCE & REFERRAL CENTER
See: National Council on Family Relations

★4341★
FAMILY SERVICE ASSOCIATION OF AMERICA - LIBRARY (Soc Sci)
44 E. 23rd St.   Phone: (212) 674-6100
New York, NY 10010   Joan Fenton, Libn.
Founded: 1939. **Staff:** Prof 1; Other 1. **Subjects:** Family life education, social casework, psychology, psychiatry, sociology, administration of local family service agencies. **Holdings:** 3000 books; 150 VF drawers of pamphlets, reports, speeches, studies, minutes, correspondence and local agency material. **Subscriptions:** 120 journals and other serials. **Services:** Interlibrary loans. **Publications:** Directory of FSAA Member Agencies, annual - for sale; bibliographies on selected subjects of FSAA publications - free upon request.

FAMILY VIOLENCE PROJECT LIBRARY
See: Center for Women Policy Studies

★4342★
FANNY ALLEN HOSPITAL - INFORMATION CENTER (Med)
101 College Pkwy.   Phone: (802) 655-1234
Winooski, VT 05404   Ann M. Bousquet, Med.Libn.
Founded: 1971. **Staff:** 1. **Subjects:** Medicine, nursing, hospital administration. **Holdings:** 550 books; patient education pamphlets; AV materials. **Subscriptions:** 85 journals and other serials. **Services:** Interlibrary loans; copying; LATCH; library open to public with restrictions. **Networks/Consortia:** Member of Vermont-New Hampshire-New York Hospital Libraries.

★4343★
FANSHAWE COLLEGE OF APPLIED ARTS AND TECHNOLOGY - LEARNING RESOURCE CENTRE - VICTORIA CAMPUS LIBRARY (Med)
Sta. C, P.O. Box 4005   Phone: (519) 433-6157
London, ON, Canada N5W 5H1   Jennifer Morrissey, Libn.
Founded: 1964. **Staff:** Prof 1; Other 3. **Subjects:** Nursing, medicine, medical laboratory technology, psychology, sociology, education. **Holdings:** 6624 books; 1336 bound periodical volumes; 447 AV items; 8 drawers of clippings and pamphlets. **Subscriptions:** 107 journals and other serials. **Services:** Library open to public for reference use only. **Remarks:** Library is located at 373 Hill St., London, ON, N6A 1E4.

★4344★
FANSHAWE COLLEGE OF APPLIED ARTS AND TECHNOLOGY - MAIN LIBRARY (Bus-Fin; Sci-Tech)
P.O. Box 4005   Phone: (519) 452-4350
London, ON, Canada N5W 5H1   Annette K. Frost, Mgr., Lib.Serv.
Founded: 1967. **Staff:** Prof 5; Other 13. **Subjects:** Business, mathematics, science, electrical technology, electronics, civil technology, health sciences and nursing, social sciences, fine arts, communication arts, design, psychology, library science, law, secretarial science. **Special Collections:** Statistics Canada material; annual reports of business corporations. **Holdings:** 41,491 books; 5069 bound periodical volumes; 4974 pamphlets; 686 films; 452 cassettes; 1049 videotapes; 506 kits; 4 transparencies; 52 filmstrips; flash cards; 35 film loops. **Subscriptions:** 665 journals and other serials; 13 newspapers. **Services:** Interlibrary loans; copying; library open to public for reference use only. **Computerized Information Services:** Computerized circulation. **Publications:** DIG, monthly during school year. **Staff:** Suzanne O'Neill, Pub.Serv.Libn.; Vicky Mok, Tech.Serv.Libn.

★4345★
FANTUS COMPANY - LIBRARY (Env-Cons; Bus-Fin)
3330 Prudential Plaza   Phone: (312) 346-1940
Chicago, IL 60601   Kathy J. Morris, Libn.
Staff: Prof 1. **Subjects:** Geography, government finance, employment and earnings, environment. **Holdings:** 100 books; 20 volumes of the Environmental Reporter; 160 volumes of EPA regulations; labor market letters and industrial directories. **Subscriptions:** 10 journals and other serials. **Services:** Copying; library not open to public.

★4346★
FAR EAST MERCHANTS ASSOCIATION - FEMAS TRADE LIBRARY
1597 Curtis St.
Berkeley, CA 94702
Defunct

★4347★
FAR EAST RESEARCH LIBRARY (Area-Ethnic)
5812 Knox Ave., S.   Phone: (612) 926-6887
Minneapolis, MN 55419   Dr. Jerome Cavanaugh, Dir.
Staff: Prof 1; Other 3. **Subjects:** China - language, literature, history; Japan; Indonesia; Southeast Asia. **Special Collections:** Chinese dialects (2500 items). **Holdings:** 38,000 books; 1500 bound periodical volumes. **Subscriptions:** 245 journals and other serials. **Services:** Interlibrary loans; copying; library open to public for validated research projects. **Publications:** An Index to Four Collections of Chinese Book Collectors' Biographies, 1977 - for sale. **Remarks:** Majority of library holdings are written in Chinese and Japanese.

★4348★
FAR WEST LABORATORY FOR EDUCATIONAL RESEARCH AND DEVELOPMENT - LIBRARY AND ARCHIVES (Educ)
1855 Folsom St.   Phone: (415) 565-3211
San Francisco, CA 94103   Lillian Chinn, Libn.
Founded: 1966. **Staff:** 1. **Subjects:** Education, research methods, teaching, educational psychology, curricula, tests and measurement, minority education and minorities, women's educational equity, child development, environmental education. **Special Collections:** Research and Development documents; Far West Laboratory Archives. **Holdings:** 15,000 books; 3000 laboratory reports (cataloged); 2100 laboratory archives; complete set of ERIC microfiche. **Subscriptions:** 100 journals and other serials. **Services:** Interlibrary loans; copying; library open to public for reference use only. **Networks/Consortia:** Member of Bay Area Education Libraries.

FARADAY LIBRARY
See: Northern Illinois University

FARB (Jean) MEDICAL LIBRARY
See: Mercy Hospital and Medical Center - Jean Farb Medical Library

★4349★
FARIBAULT STATE HOSPITAL - LIBRARY (Med)
                                     Phone: (507) 332-3274
Faribault, MN 55021   Mary K. Heltsley, Libn.
Staff: Prof 1. **Subjects:** Mental retardation. **Holdings:** 2200 books; 379 bound periodical volumes; 9 VF drawers of pamphlets; 210 pamphlet boxes of unbound periodicals. **Subscriptions:** 66 journals and other serials. **Services:** Interlibrary loans; library open to public. **Networks/Consortia:** Member of Minnesota Department of Public Welfare Library Consortium.

FARLOW REFERENCE LIBRARY
See: Harvard University

FARM CREDIT CORPORATION CANADA
See: Canada - Farm Credit Corporation Canada

★4350★
FARM JOURNAL, INC. - MARKETING RESEARCH LIBRARY (Agri)
230 W. Washington Sq.   Phone: (215) 574-1360
Philadelphia, PA 19105   Kandace Herzog, Libn.
Founded: 1945. **Staff:** Prof 1; Other 1. **Subjects:** Farm markets, U.S. agriculture, advertising and media, marketing. **Holdings:** 962 books; 400 bound periodical volumes; 148 VF drawers of clippings, U.S. government periodicals in farm field, Farm Journal statistical materials. **Subscriptions:** 209 journals and other serials. **Services:** Interlibrary loans; library open to public on a limited basis.

★4351★

FARM LABOR ORGANIZING COMMITTEE - LIBRARY (Soc Sci)
714 1/2 S. St. Clair St.   Phone: (419) 243-3456
Toledo, OH 43609   Ernesto Reza, Coord.
Staff: 1. **Subjects:** Farm labor organization, labor history, international labor movement. **Holdings:** 500 books; committee newspapers since 1968. **Subscriptions:** 25 journals and other serials. **Services:** Library open to public with restrictions. **Publications:** Nuestra Lucha.

★4352★

FARMERS INSURANCE GROUP - LIBRARY (Bus-Fin)†
4680 Wilshire Blvd.
Terminal Annex, Box 2478   Phone: (213) 932-3200
Los Angeles, CA 90010   Tish Wallace, Libn.
Founded: 1945. **Staff:** 1. **Subjects:** Insurance, business and business methods, finance, safety, driver education. **Holdings:** 5000 books; 45 VF drawers of statistics and reports. **Subscriptions:** 166 journals and other serials. **Services:** Library not open to public.

★4353★

FARMERS UNION CENTRAL EXCHANGE, INC. - INFORMATION CENTER
    (Agri)
Box 43089   Phone: (612) 451-5133
St. Paul, MN 55164   Margaret Ludvigsen, Mgr., Info.Serv.
Founded: 1967. **Staff:** Prof 1; Other 1. **Subjects:** Agriculture and cooperatives. **Holdings:** Figures not available. **Services:** Interlibrary loans; copying; library not open to public. **Also Known As:** CENEX. **Remarks:** The Information Center is located in Inver Grove Heights, MN 55075.

★4354★

FARMINGDALE PUBLIC SCHOOLS - PROFESSIONAL LIBRARY (Educ)
East Memorial at Mill Lane School
Mill Lane   Phone: (516) 752-6553
Farmingdale, NY 11735   Geoffrey L. Mattocks, Adm.Dir.
Founded: 1957. **Staff:** Prof 2; Other 2. **Subjects:** Education. **Holdings:** 2000 books; unbound periodicals and pamphlets. **Subscriptions:** 19 journals and other serials. **Services:** Library open to public on a limited basis. **Remarks:** Includes the holdings of Library Audio-Visual Services, East Memorial Mill Lane School.

★4355★

FARMLAND INDUSTRIES, INC. - FARMLAND AGRISERVICES, INC. MANUFACTURING PRODUCTS DIVISION (Agri)
960 N. Halstead   Phone: (316) 663-5711
Hutchinson, KS 67501   Peggy Anderson, Exec.Sec.
Staff: Prof 35. **Subjects:** Soy products, feed processing, energy, alcohol, microbiology, animal fat, grain storage, grain products. **Holdings:** Figures not available. **Subscriptions:** 20 journals and other serials; 10 newspapers.

★4356★

FARMLAND INDUSTRIES, INC. - J.W. CUMMINS MEMORIAL LIBRARY (Agri)
3315 N. Oak Trafficway
Box 7305   Phone: (816) 459-6606
Kansas City, MO 64116   Sarah Davidson, Info.Coord.
Founded: 1950. **Staff:** 1. **Subjects:** Cooperatives, agriculture, economics. **Special Collections:** Farmland News, December 1933 to present; American Cooperation (proceedings of annual summer institutes of American Institute of Cooperation), 1926 to present. **Holdings:** 2085 books and bound periodical volumes; Teammates and Inside Farmland (1950 to present), an employee publication; microfilm cassettes for all years of above publications. **Services:** Library open to public by appointment.

★4357★

FARNHAM (Frank C.) COMPANY, INC. - LIBRARY (Sci-Tech)
1930 Chestnut St., 8th Fl.   Phone: (215) 567-1500
Philadelphia, PA 19103   Katherine C. Jordan, Sci.Ed.
Staff: Prof 1; Other 1. **Subjects:** Medicine, chemistry, electronics, mining, history and art of translation. **Special Collections:** Bilingual and multilingual dictionaries (300). **Holdings:** 1100 books; 18,000 translations from patent and periodical literature; 2500 foreign ads, speeches, direct mail pieces. **Subscriptions:** 21 journals and other serials. **Services:** Library not open to public. **Publications:** Guidelines for Translation Buyers. **Special Indexes:** Word and phrase indexes for in-house use. **Remarks:** We specialize in foreign sales communication and English translation of patent and periodical literature.

★4358★

FARNSWORTH (William A.) - ART MUSEUM AND LIBRARY (Art; Hist)
                                                 Phone: (207) 596-6457
Rockland, ME 04841   Marius B. Peladeau, Dir.
Founded: 1948. **Staff:** Prof 1; Other 1. **Subjects:** Art - decorative, American, European, Oriental; local marine history. **Special Collections:** Winlock Collection of Egyptian Archeology (25 volumes); rare and illustrated books; Louise Nevelson Archives; N.C. Wyeth Collection; Maine artists archives (includes Robert Indiana, George Bellows, Waldo Peirce, Andrew Wyeth, Jonathan Fisher, Jamie Wyeth, William Barrett). **Holdings:** 3000 books; 100 early Maine imprints. **Subscriptions:** 15 journals and other serials. **Services:** Copying; library open to public by appointment. **Publications:** Annual Report; catalogs of special exhibitions.

FARRAR LIBRARY
See: Clarke Institute of Psychiatry

FARRELL LIBRARY
See: Kansas State University

★4359★

FARRIS, VAUGHAN, WILLS & MURPHY - LIBRARY (Law)
700 W. Georgia St.
Box 10026   Phone: (604) 684-9151
Vancouver, BC, Canada V7Y 1B3   Fiona Anderson, Libn.
Staff: Prof 1; Other 1. **Subjects:** Law - tax, corporate/commercial, municipal, labour. **Holdings:** 3500 volumes. **Subscriptions:** 103 journals and other serials. **Services:** Interlibrary loans (limited); library not open to public.

★4360★

FASHION INSTITUTE OF DESIGN & MERCHANDISING - LIBRARY (Art)
790 Market St.   Phone: (415) 433-6691
San Francisco, CA 94102   F. Samuel Douglas, Libn.
Founded: 1977. **Staff:** Prof 1; Other 1. **Subjects:** Fashion design and merchandising, interior design. **Special Collections:** Designers File (700 international designers). **Holdings:** 3200 books; 500 AV items; 400 annual reports and pamphlets; 700 newspaper clipping files. **Subscriptions:** 50 journals and other serials. **Services:** Copying; library open to public for reference use only. **Networks/Consortia:** Member of Bay Area Reference Center (BARC).

★4361★

FASHION INSTITUTE OF DESIGN & MERCHANDISING - RESOURCE AND RESEARCH CENTER (Art)
818 W. 7th St.   Phone: (213) 624-1200
Los Angeles, CA 90017   Kaycee Hale, Dir.
Staff: Prof 2; Other 8. **Subjects:** Fashion design and merchandising, interior design, business, art. **Special Collections:** Costume collection (1855 to present, 1100 garments); International Fashion Designers File (1650 files, biographies, pictures, press releases); rare books; textiles. **Holdings:** 8350 books; 387 bound periodical volumes; 350 corporate annual reports; 5700 slides and AV cassettes; 4350 newspaper clipping files; 300 pictures; 450 retail catalogs. **Subscriptions:** 185 journals and other serials; 15 newspapers. **Services:** Copying; library open to public with restrictions. **Networks/Consortia:** Member of Southern California Answering Network (SCAN). **Publications:** Acquisitions list - for internal distribution only; Resource & Research Center Newsletter, quarterly - for internal distribution only. **Staff:** Clemente Mascio, Libn.; Bescye Powell, Libn.

★4362★

FASHION INSTITUTE OF TECHNOLOGY - LIBRARY (Art)
227 W. 27th St.   Phone: (212) 760-7695
New York, NY 10001
Founded: 1953. **Staff:** Prof 16; Other 29. **Subjects:** Costume, fashion, interior design, management engineering technology, fashion buying and merchandising, textiles, advertising. **Special Collections:** Lady Duff-Gordon collection (sketches and photographs); Max Meyer Collection; Haft-Swansdown Collection (sketches); Fredrick Milton Collection (sketches); Berley Collection (sketches); Millinery Trade Review; Du Barry Fashion Studios Sketchbooks (55 volumes); Bergdorf Goodman Collection (sketches); Davidow Collection (sketches); Muriel King Collection (sketches). **Holdings:** 74,413 books; 3518 bound periodical volumes; 108 VF drawers of clippings and pamphlets on art and design; 105 VF drawers of clippings and pamphlets on business and technology; 33 titles on microfilm. **Subscriptions:** 562 journals and other serials; 35 newspapers. **Services:** Interlibrary loans; copying; library open to public for reference use only. **Networks/Consortia:** Member of METRO. **Publications:** Newsletter, quarterly - for internal distribution only. **Special Indexes:** Bibliographies in subject areas including management engineering, clothing and home sewing, fashion, costume accessories,

production, advertising, cosmetics, fashion buying, direct marketing, international trade, textile design, textile science. **Staff:** Marjorie Miller, Ref.Libn.; Sweetman R. Smith, Ref.Libn.; Judy Wood, Acq.Libn.; Eunice Walker, Cat.Libn.; Lionel White, Instr. Media Spec.; Beryl Rentof, Ref.Libn.; Lorraine Weberg, Evening Ref.Libn.; Stephen Rosenberger, Evening Ref.Libn.

★4363★
FASKEN & CALVIN, BARRISTERS AND SOLICITORS - LIBRARY (Law)
Toronto Dominion Centre, Box 30   Phone: (416) 366-8381
Toronto, ON, Canada M5K 1C1   Bettina Hakala, Libn.
Staff: 2. **Subjects:** Law - corporate, administrative, real estate, estate; taxation; litigation. **Holdings:** 7000 books; 75 bound periodical volumes; federal and provincial legislation. **Subscriptions:** 130 journals and other serials. **Services:** Interlibrary loans; library open to public with librarian's permission. **Publications:** What's New in the Library, monthly; How to Use Your Law Library - to new students; OSC Bulletins/Policy Statement handbook. **Special Indexes:** Index to current legislation (federal and provincial); index to legal memorandum.

★4364★
FATHER FLANAGAN'S BOYS' HOME - BOYS TOWN SEARCH SERVICE (Soc Sci)
Boys Town Center
14100 Crawford St.   Phone: (402) 498-1426
Boys Town, NE 68010   Donna L. Richardson, Search Serv.Mgr.
Founded: 1982. **Staff:** Prof 1; Other 1. **Subjects:** Children and youth. **Holdings:** 750 books. **Services:** Interlibrary loans (document delivery). **Computerized Information Services:** DIALOG, SDC, BRS, New York Times Information Service, Dow Jones News Retrieval. **Networks/Consortia:** Member of OCLC; Bibliographic Center for Research, Rocky Mountain Region, Inc. (BCR).

★4365★
FAUCETT (Jack) ASSOCIATES - LIBRARY (Bus-Fin; Energy)
5454 Wisconsin Ave., Suite 1100   Phone: (301) 657-8223
Chevy Chase, MD 20815   Robert J. Skarr, Libn.
Founded: 1963. **Staff:** Prof 1; Other 2. **Subjects:** Economics, energy, transportation, environment, capital investment. **Holdings:** 16,000 books, technical reports, statistical series in both hard copy and microform. **Subscriptions:** 150 journals and other serials. **Services:** Interlibrary loans; copying; SDI; library not open to public. **Computerized Information Services:** DIALOG. **Networks/Consortia:** Member of Metropolitan Washington Library Council. **Publications:** Library Bulletin - for internal distribution only; JFA Technical Reports List, annual. **Staff:** Ruth Geldon, Asst.Libn.

★4366★
FAULKNER HOSPITAL - INGERSOLL BOWDITCH LIBRARY (Med)
1153 Centre St.   Phone: (617) 522-5800
Jamaica Plain, MA 02130   Barbara P. Pastan, Lib.Dir.
Founded: 1940. **Staff:** Prof 2. **Subjects:** Medicine, surgery, nursing, administration. **Holdings:** 650 books; 5000 bound periodical volumes; hospital reports (cataloged); 350 audiotapes; 25 videotape cassettes; 25 slide/tape programs; microfiche. **Subscriptions:** 175 journals and other serials. **Services:** Interlibrary loans; copying; SDI; library open to health professionals. **Computerized Information Services:** NLM. **Networks/Consortia:** Member of New England Regional Medical Library Service (NERMLS); Boston Biomedical Library Consortium; Tufts/Maine Area Health Education Center.

FAY (Oliver J.) MEMORIAL LIBRARY
See: Iowa Methodist Medical Center

★4367★
FAYETTE COUNTY LAW LIBRARY (Law)
Fayette County Court House
Washington Court House, OH 43160
Founded: 1920. **Staff:** 1. **Subjects:** Case law. **Holdings:** 14,000 volumes. **Services:** Library open to public.

★4368★
FAYETTE COUNTY LAW LIBRARY (Law)
Court House
Uniontown, PA 15401   Elnora E. Mullooly, Libn.
Subjects: Law. **Holdings:** 20,000 volumes.

FAYETTE URBAN COUNTY PLANNING COMMISSION
See: Lexington-Fayette Urban County Planning Commission

★4369★
FAYETTEVILLE AREA HEALTH EDUCATION CENTER - LIBRARY (Med)
1601 Owen Dr.
Box 64699   Phone: (919) 323-1152
Fayetteville, NC 28306   Patricia J. Powell, Libn.
Staff: Prof 2; Other 2. **Subjects:** Medicine, nursing, allied health sciences. **Holdings:** 1500 books; 1050 bound periodical volumes; 400 AV items; 1 drawer of clippings; 1 drawer of pamphlets. **Subscriptions:** 192 journals and other serials. **Services:** Interlibrary loans; copying; SDI; library open to public with restrictions. **Computerized Information Services:** MEDLARS. **Networks/Consortia:** Member of Cape Fear Health Sciences Information Consortium; Area Health Education Centers of North Carolina; Mid-Atlantic Regional Medical Library. **Publications:** Calendar and acquisitions list, monthly - to health professionals. **Staff:** Barbara Wright, Ref.Libn.

★4370★
FAYETTEVILLE PUBLISHING COMPANY - NEWSPAPER LIBRARY (Publ)
Box 849   Phone: (919) 323-4848
Fayetteville, NC 28302   Daisy D. Maxwell, Libn.
Staff: Prof 1; Other 2. **Subjects:** Newspaper reference topics. **Holdings:** 1000 books; 10,000 pictures; 69 drawers of newspaper clippings; 547 reels of microfilm. **Subscriptions:** 25 journals and other serials; 57 newspapers. **Services:** Copying; library open to public.

FCC
See: U.S. Federal Communications Commission

FDA
See: U.S. Food & Drug Administration

FDIC
See: U.S. Federal Deposit Insurance Corporation

FEDERAL ARCHIVES AND RECORDS CENTER
See: U.S. Natl. Archives & Records Service

FEDERAL AVIATION ADMINISTRATION
See: U.S. Federal Aviation Administration

FEDERAL BAR FOUNDATION LIBRARY
See: Foundation of the Federal Bar Association

FEDERAL BUREAU OF INVESTIGATION
See: U.S. Dept. of Justice

★4371★
FEDERAL BUSINESS DEVELOPMENT BANK - LIBRARY (Bus-Fin)
360, rue St-Jacques W., Suite 320   Phone: (514) 283-7632
Montreal, PQ, Canada H2Y 1P5   Julia E. McIntosh, Hd.Libn.
Founded: 1977. **Staff:** Prof 2; Other 4. **Subjects:** Small business, development banking, management, banking and finance. **Holdings:** 3000 books. **Subscriptions:** 500 journals and other serials; 10 newspapers. **Services:** Interlibrary loans; copying; SDI; library open to public by appointment only. **Publications:** Library Bulletin, monthly - for internal distribution only. **Staff:** David G. Rowe, Cat.Libn.

FEDERAL COMMUNICATIONS BAR ASSOCIATION ARCHIVE
See: Broadcast Pioneers Library

FEDERAL COMMUNICATIONS COMMISSION
See: U.S. Federal Communications Commission

FEDERAL DEPOSIT INSURANCE CORPORATION
See: U.S. Federal Deposit Insurance Corporation

★4372★
FEDERAL ELECTION COMMISSION - NATIONAL CLEARINGHOUSE ON ELECTION ADMINISTRATION - DOCUMENT CENTER (Law; Soc Sci)
1325 K St., N.W.   Phone: (800) 424-9530
Washington, DC 20463   Gwenn Hofmann, Asst. to Dir.
Founded: 1976. **Staff:** Prof 3. **Subjects:** Elections administration, federal and state election laws and grants, census data, contract research projects. **Holdings:** 3000 volumes; state legislative research reports. **Subscriptions:** 20 journals and other serials. **Services:** Copying; library open to public.

FEDERAL HOME LOAN BANK BOARD
See: U.S. Federal Home Loan Bank Board

★4373★
FEDERAL HOME LOAN BANK OF SAN FRANCISCO - LIBRARY (Bus-Fin)
Box 7948   Phone: (415) 393-1215
San Francisco, CA 94120   Molly M. Skeen, Libn.
Staff: Prof 1; Other 2. **Subjects:** Housing, savings and loan industry, economics, finance. **Holdings:** 800 books. **Subscriptions:** 811 journals and other serials. **Services:** Interlibrary loans; library open to public with restrictions. **Computerized Information Services:** DIALOG, Dow Jones News Retrieval; computerized serials. **Networks/Consortia:** Member of Bay Area Reference Center (BARC); CLASS.

FEDERAL JUDICIAL CENTER
See: U.S. Federal Judicial Center

FEDERAL MARITIME COMMISSION
See: U.S. Federal Maritime Commission

FEDERAL PRISON SYSTEM
See: U.S. Dept. of Justice

FEDERAL RAILROAD ADMINISTRATION - TRANSPORTATION TEST CENTER
See: U.S. Dept. of Transportation - Transportation Test Center

FEDERAL REPUBLIC OF GERMANY - GERMAN INFORMATION CENTER
See: German Information Center

★4374★
FEDERAL RESERVE BANK OF ATLANTA - RESEARCH LIBRARY (Bus-Fin)
Box 1731   Phone: (404) 586-8829
Atlanta, GA 30301   Leigh Watson Healy, Libn.
Founded: 1938. **Staff:** Prof 2; Other 4. **Subjects:** Banking, finance, economics, statistics, agriculture, industry, foreign trade, domestic trade. **Special Collections:** Publications of the Federal Reserve Board and Federal Reserve Banks. **Holdings:** 30,000 volumes; 56 legal file drawers. **Subscriptions:** 1217 journals and other serials; 48 newspapers. **Services:** Interlibrary loans; copying; library open to public by appointment. **Computerized Information Services:** DIALOG, New York Times Information Service; computerized cataloging and ILL. **Networks/Consortia:** Member of OCLC through SOLINET; Georgia Library Information Network (GLIN). **Publications:** Newsletters, acquisitions lists - for internal distribution only. **Staff:** Cynthia Walsh-Kloss, Assoc.Libn.

★4375★
FEDERAL RESERVE BANK OF BOSTON - LAW LIBRARY (Law)
600 Atlantic Ave.
Boston, MA 02106
Subjects: Banking law, finance. **Services:** Library not open to public.

★4376★
FEDERAL RESERVE BANK OF BOSTON - RESEARCH LIBRARY (Bus-Fin)†
600 Atlantic Ave., T-28   Phone: (617) 973-3393
Boston, MA 02210   Mary C. Vlantikas, Libn.
Founded: 1921. **Staff:** Prof 2; Other 5. **Subjects:** Economics, money and banking, international economics, regional economics, public finance, business conditions. **Special Collections:** Federal Reserve System material. **Holdings:** 40,000 books; 650 bound periodical volumes; 6000 microforms. **Subscriptions:** 1500 journals and other serials; 6 newspapers. **Services:** Interlibrary loans; library open to member bank personnel, graduate students, research workers and government personnel. **Networks/Consortia:** Member of OCLC through NELINET. **Publications:** Book News, biweekly. **Staff:** Sandra Cram, Asst.Libn.; Joyce Hannan, Cat. & Clas.

★4377★
FEDERAL RESERVE BANK OF CHICAGO - LIBRARY (Bus-Fin)
164 W. Jackson
Box 834
Chicago, IL 60690   Phone: (312) 322-5824
                                            Dorothy Phillips, Adm.
Founded: 1920. **Staff:** Prof 5; Other 4. **Subjects:** Banking, finance, agriculture, business conditions, statistics, economics, taxation. **Holdings:** 15,000 books and annual reports; 3000 bound periodical volumes; 394 VF drawers of pamphlets and statistical releases. **Subscriptions:** 600 journals and other serials. **Services:** Interlibrary loans; library open to public for use of Federal Reserve publications. **Computerized Information Services:** SDC, DIALOG; computerized cataloging. **Networks/Consortia:** Member of ILLINET; Chicago Library System (CLS). **Staff:** Barbara Mayer, Sr.Res.Libn.; Elizabeth C. Ryan, Sr.Res.Libn.; Geraldine Purpur, Res.Libn.; Kathryn Moon, Res.Libn.

★4378★
FEDERAL RESERVE BANK OF CLEVELAND - PITTSBURGH BRANCH LIBRARY (Bus-Fin)
717 Grant St.
Pittsburgh, PA 15230   Phone: (412) 261-7915
                                            Dolores Craft, Act.Libn.
Founded: 1943. **Staff:** 1. **Subjects:** Banking and finance. **Holdings:** 500 volumes; 6 VF drawers of pamphlets, clippings, and releases; Federal Reserve bulletins, 1978-1982; films on the Federal Reserve System. **Subscriptions:** 50 journals and other serials; 6 newspapers. **Services:** Interlibrary loans; library open to public for reference use only.

★4379★
FEDERAL RESERVE BANK OF CLEVELAND - RESEARCH LIBRARY (Bus-Fin)
Box 6387   Phone: (216) 241-2800
Cleveland, OH 44101   Elizabeth Maynard, Libn.
Founded: 1918. **Staff:** Prof 2; Other 3. **Subjects:** Banking, finance, business, economics. **Holdings:** 20,000 books and bound periodical volumes; 175 VF drawers of pamphlets. **Subscriptions:** 500 journals and other serials; 25 newspapers. **Services:** Interlibrary loans; copying; library open to public with restrictions. **Computerized Information Services:** LEXIS, NEXIS; internal database. **Staff:** Linda Suzuki, Assoc.Libn.

★4380★
FEDERAL RESERVE BANK OF DALLAS - RESEARCH LIBRARY (Bus-Fin)
400 S. Akard St.   Phone: (214) 651-6392
Dallas, TX 75222   Victoria M. Roberts, Res.Libn.
Founded: 1943. **Staff:** Prof 1; Other 3. **Subjects:** Banking, finance, economics, industry, labor, statistics. **Special Collections:** Foreign central bank publications from 60 countries. **Holdings:** 8500 books. **Subscriptions:** 900 journals and other serials; 10 newspapers. **Services:** Interlibrary loans; copying; SDI; library open to public by appointment. **Computerized Information Services:** DIALOG; computerized cataloging. **Publications:** Recent Additions to the Research Library.

★4381★
FEDERAL RESERVE BANK OF KANSAS CITY - LAW LIBRARY (Law)
925 Grand Ave.   Phone: (816) 881-2557
Kansas City, MO 64198   Jann Faltermeier, Law Libn.
Subjects: Law. **Holdings:** Figures not available. **Services:** Library not open to public.

★4382★
FEDERAL RESERVE BANK OF KANSAS CITY - RESEARCH LIBRARY (Bus-Fin)
                                            Phone: (816) 881-2676
Kansas City, MO 64198   Ellen M. Johnson, Libn.
Staff: Prof 2; Other 3. **Subjects:** Economics, agriculture, statistics, banking. **Holdings:** 14,000 books and bound periodical volumes. **Subscriptions:** 757 journals and other serials. **Services:** Interlibrary loans; library open to public for reference use only.

★4383★
FEDERAL RESERVE BANK OF MINNEAPOLIS - LAW LIBRARY (Law)
250 Marquette Ave.   Phone: (612) 340-2412
Minneapolis, MN 55480   James M. Lyon, Dir.
Staff: Prof 4; Other 2. **Subjects:** Law. **Holdings:** 5000 volumes. **Services:** Library not open to public.

★4384★
FEDERAL RESERVE BANK OF MINNEAPOLIS - LIBRARY (Bus-Fin)
250 Marquette, S.   Phone: (612) 340-2292
Minneapolis, MN 55480   Joanne E. Farley, Mgr., Lib.Serv.
Staff: Prof 3; Other 2. **Subjects:** Economic theory, agriculture, business, banking. **Holdings:** 20,000 books; 2000 bound periodical volumes; 3500 pamphlets (cataloged); 87 VF drawers of government documents and releases. **Subscriptions:** 3000 journals and other serials; 19 newspapers. **Services:** Interlibrary loans; copying; library open to public for reference use only. **Computerized Information Services:** Computerized serials. **Publications:** Library Record, monthly - for internal distribution only. **Staff:** Amy Hargens, Assoc.Libn.; Janet Swan, Assoc.Libn.

★4385★
FEDERAL RESERVE BANK OF NEW YORK - COMPUTER SCIENCES LIBRARY (Info Sci)
33 Liberty St.   Phone: (212) 791-5766
New York, NY 10045   Joan A. LaBudde, Hd.Libn.
Staff: Prof 2; Other 2. **Subjects:** Data processing, telecommunications, system development. **Holdings:** 2000 books; 250 reels of microfilmed periodicals; 400 internal documents; 1500 vendor manuals; 4 VF drawers.

Subscriptions: 100 journals and other serials. Services: Interlibrary loans; copying; SDI; library not open to public. Computerized Information Services: DIALOG. Publications: Computer Sciences Library Notes, 8/year; Periodicals Available in the Computer Sciences Library, semiannual; News of the Day, daily - all for internal distribution only. Staff: Dale Rosenberg, Sr.Libn.

★4386★
FEDERAL RESERVE BANK OF NEW YORK - LAW LIBRARY DIVISION (Law)
33 Liberty St.   Phone: (212) 791-5012
New York, NY 10045   Rodney H. Congdon, Chf.Law Libn.
Founded: 1930. Staff: Prof 6; Other 4. Subjects: Banking law. Special Collections: Legislative histories regarding Federal Reserve System. Holdings: 22,000 books and bound periodical volumes; 265 VF drawers of legal precedent, legislative and litigation files; 1035 reels of microfilm. Subscriptions: 182 journals and other serials. Services: Interlibrary loans. Computerized Information Services: WESTLAW. Staff: Giuliano Chicco, Asst.Chf. Law Libn.; Roberta G. Friedman, Sr. Law Libn.; John H. Williams, Sr. Law Libn.; Lucy Curci, Law Libn.; Edith Feder, Law Libn.

★4387★
FEDERAL RESERVE BANK OF NEW YORK - RESEARCH LIBRARY (Bus-Fin)
33 Liberty St.
New York, NY 10045   Jean Deuss, Chf.Libn.
Founded: 1918. Staff: Prof 7; Other 7. Subjects: Economics, finance, business conditions, balance of international payments, international finance, monetary policy, central banking, foreign area economic and financial conditions. Holdings: 58,000 books and bound periodical volumes; 3600 reels of microfilm; 300 microfiche; 180 VF drawers of pamphlet material. Subscriptions: 2000 journals and other serials. Services: Library open to public only for information on Federal Reserve System and financial operations of the U.S. government. Computerized Information Services: DIALOG, New York Times Information Service; computerized periodical routing. Staff: Ruth Schaefer, Asst.Chf.Libn.; Joan Breitbart, Sr.Libn.; Emily Trueblood, Sr.Libn.; Jean Wooten, Sr.Libn.; Barbara Macey, Sr.Libn.

★4388★
FEDERAL RESERVE BANK OF PHILADELPHIA - LIBRARY (Bus-Fin)
Box 66   Phone: (215) 574-6540
Philadelphia, PA 19105   Aileen C. Boer, Libn.
Founded: 1922. Staff: Prof 4; Other 3. Subjects: Money, banking, prices, finance. Holdings: 15,000 volumes; 5000 pamphlets (cataloged); 147 legal file drawers of releases. Subscriptions: 283 journals and other serials. Services: Interlibrary loans; SDI; library open to public for reference use only. Computerized Information Services: New York Times Information Service, SDC, DIALOG, Dow Jones News Retrieval. Networks/Consortia: Member of PALINET and Union Library Catalogue of Pennsylvania. Publications: Index to Monthly Reviews of Federal Reserve Banks, 1950-1976, biennial - available on request; FED in Print, semiannual cumulative index to monthly reviews of Federal Reserve banks and board - available on request. Staff: Barbara Turnbull, Assoc.Libn.; Deborah Naulty, Ref.Libn.; Caren Brodsky, Ref.Libn.

★4389★
FEDERAL RESERVE BANK OF RICHMOND - RESEARCH LIBRARY (Bus-Fin)
Box 27622   Phone: (804) 643-1250
Richmond, VA 23261   Ruth M.E. Cannon, Libn.
Founded: 1920. Staff: Prof 3; Other 5. Subjects: Banking, money, statistics, finance, agriculture, economics, business and industry. Holdings: 18,000 books; 1500 bound periodical volumes; 144 VF drawers of pamphlets, statistical releases, clippings and reference material. Subscriptions: 950 journals and other serials; 18 newspapers. Services: Interlibrary loans; library open to public by appointment. Computerized Information Services: DIALOG; computerized cataloging. Networks/Consortia: Member of OCLC through FEDLINK. Publications: Library Bulletin. Staff: Connie B. Thompson, Assoc.Libn.; Susan Miles, Ref.Libn.

★4390★
FEDERAL RESERVE BANK OF ST. LOUIS - RESEARCH LIBRARY (Bus-Fin)
Box 442   Phone: (314) 444-8552
St. Louis, MO 63166   Carol J. Thaxton, Hd.Libn.
Founded: 1922. Staff: Prof 2; Other 3. Subjects: Federal Reserve, money, banking, finance, economics, agriculture. Holdings: 15,000 books; 2170 bound periodical volumes; 136 VF drawers of pamphlets (cataloged). Subscriptions: 800 journals and other serials; 15 newspapers. Services: Interlibrary loans; library open to public with restrictions. Computerized Information Services: Computerized cataloging. Networks/Consortia: Member of OCLC; MIDNET. Staff: Anita Boyd, Libn. A.

★4391★
FEDERAL RESERVE BANK OF SAN FRANCISCO - RESEARCH LIBRARY (Bus-Fin)
101 Market St.
Box 7702   Phone: (415) 544-2358
San Francisco, CA 94120   Miriam Ciochon, Lib.Mgr.
Staff: Prof 5; Other 4. Subjects: Central banking, banking and finance, economics, business. Subscriptions: 1600 journals and other serials. Services: Interlibrary loans; copying; library open to public for reference use only. Computerized Information Services: DIALOG, New York Times Information Service, RLIN, BRS; computerized serials. Publications: Accessions List, weekly - for internal distribution only.

★4392★
FEDERAL RESERVE SYSTEM - BOARD OF GOVERNORS - LAW LIBRARY (Law; Bus-Fin)
20th & Constitution Ave., N.W.   Phone: (202) 452-3284
Washington, DC 20551   Judith M. Weiss, Law Libn.
Founded: 1975. Staff: Prof 2; Other 1. Subjects: Banking law, general federal law, state codes. Special Collections: Legislative histories on banking, monetary policy and economic affairs (300 titles). Holdings: 13,500 books; 200 bound periodical volumes; 150 reels of microfilm; 3000 microfiche. Subscriptions: 150 journals and other serials. Services: Interlibrary loans; copying; SDI; library open to public by appointment. Computerized Information Services: DIALOG, SDC, New York Times Information Service, LEXIS. Publications: Legislative newsletter, weekly - for internal distribution only. Staff: Jan D. Reagan, Leg.Libn.

★4393★
FEDERAL RESERVE SYSTEM - BOARD OF GOVERNORS - RESEARCH LIBRARY (Bus-Fin)
20th & Constitution Ave., N.W.   Phone: (202) 452-3332
Washington, DC 20551   Ann Roane Clary, Chf.Libn.
Founded: 1914. Staff: Prof 6; Other 5. Subjects: Banking, money, finance, economic conditions (U.S. and foreign), economic theory, monetary, credit and fiscal policy. Special Collections: Federal Reserve System; Foreign Central Banking. Holdings: 85,500 books; 8000 bound periodical volumes. Subscriptions: 2500 journals and other serials; 20 newspapers. Services: Interlibrary loans (limited to special libraries in Washington); library open to public with restrictions or by special permission. Computerized Information Services: DIALOG, New York Times Information Service (for staff only); computerized cataloging. Networks/Consortia: Member of OCLC through FEDLINK. Publications: Research Library-Recent Acquisitions, monthly - free upon request. Staff: Julia G. Back, Rd.Serv.Libn.; Jean Rhodes, Govt.Doc.Libn.; Ioana Ratesh, Cat.; Susan Vincent, Ref.Libn.; Bernice Coles, Per.Libn.

FEDERAL TRADE COMMISSION
See: U.S. Federal Trade Commission

★4394★
FEDERATED CONSERVATIONISTS OF WESTCHESTER COUNTY - FCWC OFFICE RESOURCE LIBRARY (Env-Cons)
Natural Science Bldg., Rm. 1002
SUNY   Phone: (914) 253-8046
Purchase, NY 10577   Carolyn Cunningham, Exec.Dir.
Staff: 1. Subjects: Wetland legislation, water supply and quality, air pollution. Holdings: Figures not available; government reports; environmental impact statements; legal cases; 15 file drawers of resource materials. Subscriptions: 12 journals and other serials. Services: Library open to public for reference use only. Publications: Westchester Environment, bimonthly.

★4395★
FEDERATION DES ADMINISTRATEURS DES SERVICES DE SANTE ET DES SERVICES SOCIAUX DU QUEBEC - BIBLIOTHEQUE (Bus-Fin)†
4237 rue Bordeaux   Phone: (514) 526-0875
Montreal, PQ, Canada H2H 1Z4   Claude Magnon, Dir.
Subjects: Hospital management, administration. Holdings: 2000 volumes. Subscriptions: 80 journals and other serials. Services: Library not open to public.

FEDERATION CANADIENNE DES ENSEIGNANTS
See: Canadian Teachers' Federation

★4396★
FEDERATION EMPLOYMENT & GUIDANCE SERVICE - RICHARD J. BERNHARD MEMORIAL LIBRARY (Soc Sci)
510 6th Ave.   Phone: (212) 741-7151
New York, NY 10011   Otto Kanocz, Chf.Libn.
Staff: Prof 1. Subjects: Occupational and vocational guidance, vocational

rehabilitation, education, labor market information. **Special Collections:** College catalogs; scholarship information. **Holdings:** 4000 books; 35,000 clippings and pamphlets (classified by subject); 500 microforms. **Subscriptions:** 170 journals and other serials; 5 newspapers. **Services:** Interlibrary loans; copying (limited); library open to public during business hours. **Computerized Information Services:** New York City University Data Bank.

★4397★
FEDERATION DES MEDECINS OMNIPRACTICIENS DU QUEBEC - DOCUMENTATION CENTRE (Med)
1440 Ouest Ste-Catherine, Suite 1100   Phone: (514) 878-1911
Montreal, PQ, Canada H3G 1R8   Ghislaine Lincourt, Adm.
Founded: 1966. **Staff:** Prof 2. **Subjects:** Medicine - social aspects, unions, law, teaching. **Holdings:** 4000 books; 600 bound periodical volumes; government publications; reports. **Subscriptions:** 192 journals and other serials; 8 newspapers. **Services:** Interlibrary loans; copying; library not open to public. **Publications:** Liste d'acquisition; Bulletin signaletique. **Staff:** Madeleine Savard, Lib.Techn.

★4398★
FEDERATION FOR UNIFIED SCIENCE EDUCATION - FUSE CENTER LIBRARY (Educ)
231 Battelle Hall of Science
Capital University   Phone: (614) 236-6816
Columbus, OH 43209   Dr. Victor M. Showalter, Dir.
Founded: 1972. **Subjects:** Unified science education, philosophy of science, science teaching materials and media. **Holdings:** 800 books; 250 program descriptions; 20 VF drawers. **Services:** Copying; library open to public for reference use only.

FEEHAN MEMORIAL LIBRARY
See: St. Mary of the Lake Seminary

★4399★
FEHL (Fred) PHOTOGRAPHER - INFORMATION CENTER (Pict)
415 W. 115th St.   Phone: (212) 662-2253
New York, NY 10025
Staff: Prof 2. **Subjects:** Performance photographs of Broadway and Off-Broadway productions; ballet and dance in America since 1940; New York City opera, all productions; orchestra conductors and musicians; color slides of U.S. National Parks, historic monuments, art treasures and scenic pictures of Europe. **Services:** Photographs are available for publications on a fee basis.

FEINBERG (Benjamin F.) LIBRARY
See: SUNY - College at Plattsburgh - Special Collections

FEINBERG (Harry and Anna) LIBRARY
See: Congregation Mishkan Tefila - Harry and Anna Feinberg Library

FEINSTONE (Sol) LIBRARY
See: Bishop's Mill Historical Institute - Sol Feinstone Library

FEINSTONE (Sol) LIBRARY FOR THE SURVIVAL OF FREEDOM
See: American Security Council Education Foundation - Sol Feinstone Library

FELDBERG LIBRARY
See: Dartmouth College

FELDHEYM (Norman F.) LIBRARY
See: St. Bernardine Hospital - Norman F. Feldheym Library

FELDMAN (Dorothy G.) LIBRARY
See: Congregation Beth Am - Dorothy G. Feldman Library

★4400★
FELETI PACIFIC LIBRARY (Area-Ethnic)
Box 1329   Phone: (684) 633-1181
Pago Pago, AS 96799   Papa Fiaui, Lib.Asst.
Staff: Prof 1; Other 18. **Subjects:** South Pacific islands, American Samoa. **Special Collections:** Robert Louis Stevenson Collection (50 volumes); South Pacific Commission (10 VF drawers). **Holdings:** 5500 books; 95 bound periodical volumes; 25 VF drawers of publications of the government of American Samoa; 10 VF drawers of materials on General Pacific; 12 VF drawers of South Pacific Commission publications. **Subscriptions:** 56 journals and other serials; 5 newspapers. **Services:** Interlibrary loans; copying; library open to public for reference use only. **Remarks:** Library is administered by the American Library Association - Office of Library Services. **Staff:** Emma F.C.

Pen, Lib.Prog.Dir.

FELICIAN SISTERS - ST. MARY HOSPITAL
See: St. Mary Hospital - Medical Library

★4401★
FELLOWSHIP COMMISSION - LIBRARY
117 S. 17th St.
Philadelphia, PA 19103
Defunct

★4402★
FELLOWSHIP OF RECONCILIATION - LIBRARY (Soc Sci)
Box 171   Phone: (914) 358-4601
Nyack, NY 10960
Subjects: Peace movements, disarmament, human rights. **Special Collections:** Manuscripts by A.J. Muste. **Holdings:** 1800 books; 42 bound periodical volumes. **Subscriptions:** 208 journals and other serials. **Services:** SDI; library open to public with restrictions. **Special Indexes:** Index of pamphlets from Institute for World Order (card).

★4403★
FELLOWSHIP OF RELIGIOUS HUMANISTS - BRANCH LIBRARY (Rel-Theol)
1044 Samar Rd.   Phone: (305) 783-8359
Cocoa Beach, FL 32931   Rev. Edwin H. Wilson, Hist.
Founded: 1970. **Staff:** Prof 1. **Subjects:** Religious and naturalistic humanism, positivism, church and state separation. **Special Collections:** Works of Julian Huxley, George Santayana; collections of Humanist and Free Thought publications. **Holdings:** 1305 books; 26 bound periodical volumes; 50 VF drawers. **Services:** Answers inquiries; library open to students of humanism by mail or special appointment.

★4404★
FELLOWSHIP OF RELIGIOUS HUMANISTS - LIBRARY (Rel-Theol)
Box 278
Yellow Springs, OH 45387   Edwin H. Wilson, Hist.
Staff: Prof 1; Other 1. **Subjects:** Humanism, American Humanist Association, separation of Church and State, positivism, International Humanist and Ethical Union. **Special Collections:** Copies of material on Alfred Loisy, Catholic modernist. **Holdings:** Complete archives of Humanist movement dating from 1932, including files of the American Humanist Association from 1941-1963; tape recordings of broadcasts over New York City radio stations; reprints of James H. Leuba articles. **Subscriptions:** 22 journals and other serials. **Services:** Library open to public by appointment.

FELS RESEARCH INSTITUTE - JENNIE MAY FELS MEMORIAL LIBRARY
See: Wright State University - Health Sciences Library

FELTON (Charlotte Ashley) MEMORIAL LIBRARY
See: Stanford University - Department of Special Collections

★4405★
FENCO ENGINEERS, INC. - LIBRARY (Env-Cons)
33 Yonge St.   Phone: (416) 365-9955
Toronto ON, Canada M5E 1E7   Agnes M. Croxford, Chf.Libn.
Staff: Prof 2; Other 2. **Subjects:** Engineering, hydrology, nuclear science, pollution control, waste management, urban and regional planning. **Holdings:** 16,000 books; 650 bound periodical volumes; 1500 maps; 250 vertical files. **Subscriptions:** 250 journals and other serials; 10 newspapers. **Services:** Interlibrary loans; copying; library open to public with restrictions. **Computerized Information Services:** SDC, DIALOG, CAN/OLE, QL Systems; ADLIB (internal database); computerized cataloging and serials. **Publications:** Library Bulletin, bimonthly - for internal distribution only. **Remarks:** Library is formed by the merger of the libraries of several organizations including Maclaren Engineers Planners & Scientists Inc. and Fenco Engineers, Inc., but the companies have remained separate. **Staff:** Kaili Sermat-Harding, Asst.Libn.

★4406★
FENTON HISTORICAL SOCIETY - LIBRARY (Hist)
67 Washington St.   Phone: (716) 661-2296
Jamestown, NY 14701
Founded: 1964. **Staff:** Prof 1; Other 1. **Subjects:** Genealogy, local history, Civil War. **Special Collections:** Early local photographs. **Holdings:** 4000 books; local daybooks, account books, town and school district records; 4 drawers of clippings and pamphlets; 11 shelves and 5 drawers of manuscripts. **Subscriptions:** 20 journals and other serials. **Services:** Interlibrary loans; copying; library open to public. **Publications:** Jamestown & Chautauqua County Trolleys; Chautauqua Lake Steamboats; History of Post Offices of

Jamestown, N.Y. **Special Indexes:** Newspaper deaths and marriages (card); Index to Biographical Cyclopedia of Chautauqua County, by B.F. Dilley (book); Index to Early History of Ellicott, by Hazeltine (book); A Complete Index to More Than 10,000 Personal Names Mentioned in Andrew W. Young's History of Chautauqua County, New York (book). **Staff:** Ellen Fessenden, Adm.Coord.; Candace Larson, Adm.Coord.

FER ET TITANE DU QUEBEC, INC.
See: Q.I.T. - Fer et Titane Inc.

★4407★
FERGUS FALLS STATE HOSPITAL - LIBRARY (Med)
Corner of Fir & Union
Box 157
Fergus Falls, MN 56537

Phone: (218) 739-7327
Elizabeth Swenson, Libn.

Founded: 1900. **Staff:** Prof 1. **Subjects:** Medicine, nursing, psychiatry, special education, drug abuse. **Holdings:** 6500 books; 800 other professional items (cataloged); 2000 articles. **Subscriptions:** 55 journals and other serials; 60 newspapers. **Services:** Interlibrary loans; copying; library open to public. **Networks/Consortia:** Member of Minnesota Department of Public Welfare Library Consortium. **Remarks:** Library is a combination of patients' library and professional library.

★4408★
FERGUSON BAPTIST CHURCH - LIBRARY (Rel-Theol)
602 Gover Ln.
Ferguson, KY 42533

Phone: (606) 679-1690
Dorothy Holloway, Dir.

Staff: Prof 3. **Subjects:** Religion, biography, history, missions. **Special Collections:** Devotionals. **Holdings:** 4000 books; 3 VF drawers; 1 missionary tape. **Services:** Library is open to church families. **Staff:** Stelma Haynes, Lib.Asst.; Dorothy Hughes, Lib.Asst.

FERGUSON (Charles) MEDICAL LIBRARY
See: Bayley Seton Hospital - Charles Ferguson Medical Library

★4409★
FERGUSON LIBRARY - BUSINESS-TECHNOLOGY DEPARTMENT (Bus-Fin; Sci-Tech)
96 Broad St.
Stamford, CT 06901

Phone: (203) 964-1000
Doris Goodlett, Hd., Adult Serv.

Staff: Prof 12; Other 10. **Subjects:** Business, technology. **Holdings:** 15,000 books; 96 VF drawers. **Subscriptions:** 300 journals and other serials; 10 newspapers. **Services:** Interlibrary loans; copying; library open to public. **Computerized Information Services:** Computerized cataloging and circulation. **Networks/Consortia:** Member of OCLC through NELINET. **Publications:** Booklists. **Staff:** Louisa Campbell, Bus.Spec.

FERMI (Enrico) CULTURAL CENTER
See: New York Public Library - Belmont Regional Library

★4410★
FERMI NATIONAL ACCELERATOR LABORATORY - LIBRARY (Sci-Tech)
Box 500
Batavia, IL 60510

Phone: (312) 840-3401
Roger S. Thompson, Libn.

Founded: 1967. **Staff:** Prof 1; Other 2. **Subjects:** High energy physics, particle accelerators, particle physics. **Holdings:** 4000 books; 3500 bound periodical volumes; 4000 reprints and reports; 1000 microfiche. **Subscriptions:** 175 journals and other serials. **Services:** Interlibrary loans; library open to public for reference use only. **Computerized Information Services:** SPIRES. **Networks/Consortia:** Member of DuPage Library System. **Staff:** May West, Asst.Libn.

★4411★
FERNBANK SCIENCE CENTER - LIBRARY (Sci-Tech)
156 Heaton Park Dr., N.E.
Atlanta, GA 30307

Phone: (404) 378-4311
Mary Larsen, Libn.

Staff: Prof 1; Other 1. **Subjects:** Astronomy, biology, geology, meteorology, horticulture, forestry. **Holdings:** 15,000 books; 4300 bound periodical volumes; 10,000 slides; microfilm; 5 VF drawers of pamphlets and maps. **Subscriptions:** 355 journals and other serials; 7 newspapers. **Services:** Interlibrary loans; copying; library open to public for reference use only. **Computerized Information Services:** DIALOG; computerized journal. **Networks/Consortia:** Member of OCLC through SOLINET; Atlanta Health Science Libraries Consortium. **Remarks:** Maintained by the DeKalb County Board of Education.

★4412★
FERRIS STATE COLLEGE - LIBRARY (Med)†
901 S. State St.
Big Rapids, MI 49307

Phone: (616) 796-0461
Mary M. Bower, Dir.

Founded: 1884. **Staff:** Prof 12; Other 32. **Subjects:** Pharmacy, health sciences, optometry. **Special Collections:** Woodbridge N. Ferris letters and materials relative to founding of the college (12,000 items). **Holdings:** 190,000 books; 15,000 bound periodical volumes; 63,665 pamphlets and documents (cataloged); 147,684 titles in microform; 22,368 records, tapes and slides. **Subscriptions:** 16,500 journals and other serials; 15 newspapers. **Services:** Interlibrary loans; copying; library open to public. **Computerized Information Services:** DIALOG, BRS. **Networks/Consortia:** Member of OCLC through Michigan Library Consortium (MLC). **Staff:** R. Lawrence Martin, Archv.

★4413★
FERRIS STATE COLLEGE - SCHOOL OF PHARMACY - PHARMACY READING ROOM (Med)
901 S. State St.
Big Rapids, MI 49307

Phone: (616) 796-2641
Mary M. Bower, Dir.

Founded: 1972. **Staff:** Prof 1; Other 3. **Subjects:** Pharmacy, pharmaceutical sciences. **Special Collections:** Catalog of faculty publications. **Holdings:** 1500 books; pamphlets and reprints; 150 tapes, slides, filmstrips; Iowa Drug Information Service, 1966 to present on microfiche; DRUGDEX. **Subscriptions:** 160 journals and other serials. **Services:** Interlibrary loans; copying; library open to public for reference use only by request. **Special Catalogs:** Periodical Holdings; Non-Print materials - both mimeographed lists. **Formerly:** Its Periodical Reading Room.

★4414★
FERRO CORPORATION - FERRO CHEMICAL DIVISION - FERRO CHEMICAL LIBRARY (Sci-Tech)
7040 Krick Rd.
Bedford, OH 44146

Phone: (216) 641-8580
Mary Jane Campbell, Libn.

Founded: 1957. **Staff:** 2. **Subjects:** Chemistry - polymer, paint, organic, analytical; polymer and paint technology. **Holdings:** 3500 books; 1000 bound periodical volumes; 4 VF drawers of patents and patent applications; 12 VF drawers of manufacturers' literature; 4 VF drawers of photocopies, reports, clippings and specifications. **Subscriptions:** 135 journals and other serials. **Services:** Interlibrary loans; library not open to public. **Computerized Information Services:** DIALOG, MEDLINE, Dow Jones News Retrieval, DTSS Inc., SDC. **Publications:** Lists of abstracts and acquisitions, semimonthly - for internal distribution only.

★4415★
FERRO CORPORATION - LIBRARY (Sci-Tech)
7500 E. Pleasant Valley Rd.
Independence, OH 44131

Phone: (216) 641-8580
Kathleen Fuller, Hd.Libn.

Founded: 1943. **Staff:** Prof 2; Other 1. **Subjects:** Ceramics, glazes, coatings, porcelain enamels. **Holdings:** 4900 books; 850 bound periodical volumes; 2800 microfiche of government documents; 24 VF drawers of research and laboratory notebooks; 18 VF drawers of pamphlets. **Subscriptions:** 273 journals and other serials. **Services:** Interlibrary loans; library not open to public. **Computerized Information Services:** DIALOG, SDC; computerized circulation. **Publications:** Current Awareness Bulletin - for internal distribution only. **Staff:** Robert Clement, Lit.Chem.

FERRY-MORSE ARCHIVE
See: University of California, Davis - University Libraries

★4416★
FERTILIZER INSTITUTE (Agri)
1015 18th St., N.W.
Washington, DC 20036

Phone: (202) 466-2700
Donald N. Collins, V.P., Commun.

Subjects: Agriculture (especially fertilizers and soils). **Remarks:** Although the library holdings have been dispersed, the institute still serves as a source for fertilizer and soil fertility information.

★4417★
FESTIVAL CASALS, INC. - PUERTO RICO INDUSTRIAL DEVELOPMENT COMPANY - CONSERVATORIO DE MUSICA - LIBRARY (Mus)
Minillas Sta., Box 41227
Santurce, PR 00940

Phone: (809) 751-0160
Ines Mora Gordon, Libn.

Founded: 1962. **Staff:** Prof 1; Other 3. **Subjects:** Music. **Special Collections:** Complete works of Brahms, Bach; Romero, Ramos and Monsita Ferrer. **Holdings:** 3422 books; 11,023 musical scores and parts; 900 orchestral music scores and parts; 400 pieces of choral music; 40 pieces of band music; 10 binders of microfiche; 70 albums of clippings; 500 librettos, college and publishers' catalogs; 2926 phonograph records. **Subscriptions:**

48 journals and other serials. **Services:** Library open to public for reference use only. **Remarks:** Library is located at Ave. Roosevelt, Esquina Lamar, Hato Rey, PR 00918. **Also Known As:** Conservatorio de Musica de Puerto Rico - Biblioteca.

FEUER (Jordan E.) LIBRARY
See: Congregation Kins of West Rogers Park - Jordan E. Feuer Library

FIBER GLASS RESEARCH CENTER
See: PPG Industries, Inc.

★4418★
FIBER MATERIALS, INC. - TECHNICAL LIBRARY (Sci-Tech)
Biddeford Industrial Park   Phone: (207) 282-5911
Biddeford, ME 04005   Susan A. Walker, Tech.Libn.
Staff: Prof 1. **Subjects:** Materials science, composites, ablation, carbon. **Holdings:** 1000 books; 8 bound periodical volumes; 2250 technical reports. **Subscriptions:** 124 journals and other serials. **Services:** Interlibrary loans; copying; SDI; library not open to public.

FIBERS & PLASTICS COMPANY
See: Allied Corporation

★4419★
FIDELITY & DEPOSIT COMPANY OF MARYLAND - LAW LIBRARY (Law)
302 Fidelity Bldg.
Box 1227   Phone: (301) 539-0800
Baltimore, MD 21203   Mary Teresa Jerscheid, Law Libn.
Founded: 1922. **Staff:** Prof 1. **Subjects:** Law. **Holdings:** 22,000 volumes. **Services:** Interlibrary loans; library open to building tenants.

★4420★
FIDELITY MANAGEMENT & RESEARCH COMPANY - LIBRARY (Bus-Fin)
82 Devonshire St.   Phone: (617) 726-0293
Boston, MA 02109   Catharine Schoellkopf, Hd.Libn.
Staff: Prof 4; Other 5. **Subjects:** Investment and securities, stock market behavior, economic and business conditions. **Special Collections:** Municipal collection (finance). **Holdings:** 3000 books; 10 VF drawers of mutual fund literature; Securities and Exchange Commission document file. **Subscriptions:** 750 journals and other serials; 10 newspapers. **Services:** Interlibrary loans; copying; SDI; library not open to public. **Computerized Information Services:** DIALOG, SDC, Dow Jones News Retrieval. **Networks/Consortia:** Member of New England On-Line Users Group. **Publications:** Acquisition list, monthly. **Staff:** Cynthia Wolfe, Assoc.Libn.; Virginia Adams, Info.Spec.

★4421★
FIDELITY MUTUAL LIFE INSURANCE COMPANY - LIBRARY ARCHIVES (Bus-Fin)†
Fidelity Mutual Life Bldg., S. Penn Sq.
Box 7318   Phone: (215) 977-8093
Philadelphia, PA 19101   Renee Walker, Libn.
Founded: 1878. **Staff:** 1. **Subjects:** Business, life insurance. **Holdings:** 15,000 books; 44 bound periodical volumes. **Subscriptions:** 44 journals and other serials. **Services:** Interlibrary loans; copying; library open to public with restrictions.

★4422★
FIDUCIARY TRUST COMPANY OF NEW YORK - RESEARCH LIBRARY (Bus-Fin)
2 World Trade Ctr., 94th Fl.   Phone: (212) 466-4100
New York, NY 10048   Marilyn Armeit, Libn.
Founded: 1933. **Staff:** Prof 1; Other 2. **Subjects:** Corporate records, banks and finance, investment, international trade, economics. **Special Collections:** Moody's manuals, 1945 to present. **Holdings:** 2500 books; 200 bound periodical volumes; 30 VF drawers of Extra annuals; 19 VF drawers of corporate records; 16 VF drawers of industry information; corporation files on 4500 companies; 10K, 10Q, 8K and prospectuses of 226 companies on microfiche. **Subscriptions:** 175 journals and other serials; 11 newspapers. **Services:** Interlibrary loans; copying; library open to public by phone request only. **Publications:** Research Library Bulletin. **Special Indexes:** Index to company economic and financial review.

★4423★
FIELD (Eugene) HOUSE AND TOY MUSEUM - LIBRARY (Hum)
634 S. Broadway   Phone: (314) 421-4689
St. Louis, MO 63102   John Scholz, Dir.
Subjects: Eugene Field. **Special Collections:** Editions of the works of Eugene Field (225 volumes). **Holdings:** 17 manuscripts of Eugene Field; 3 feet of clippings; 2 VF drawers of photographs; 6 VF drawers of correspondence and memorabilia. **Services:** Library open to public with restrictions.

★4424★
FIELD MUSEUM OF NATURAL HISTORY - LIBRARY (Sci-Tech)
Roosevelt Rd. & Lake Shore Dr.   Phone: (312) 922-9410
Chicago, IL 60605   W. Peyton Fawcett, Hd.Libn.
Founded: 1893. **Staff:** Prof 5; Other 4. **Subjects:** Anthropology, botany, geology, zoology. **Special Collections:** Ayer Ornithology Library; Laufer Collection of Far Eastern Studies; Schmidt Herpetology Library. **Holdings:** 200,000 books and bound periodical volumes. **Subscriptions:** 4000 journals and other serials. **Services:** Interlibrary loans; copying; library open to public. **Networks/Consortia:** Member of OCLC through ILLINET; Chicago Library System (CLS); Metropolitan Chicago Library Assembly. **Staff:** Eugenia Jang, Ser.Libn.; Alfreda Rogowski, Acq.Libn.; Chi-Wei Pan, Cat.; Michele Calhoun, Ref.Libn.

FIKES HALL OF SPECIAL COLLECTIONS AND DEGOLYER LIBRARY
See: Southern Methodist University

★4425★
FILLMORE (Millard) HOSPITAL - KIDENEY HEALTH SCIENCES LIBRARY (Med)
3 Gates Circle   Phone: (716) 887-4848
Buffalo, NY 14209   Aniela Lichtenstein, Hd.Libn.
Staff: Prof 1; Other 3. **Subjects:** Clinical medicine, nursing. **Holdings:** 4415 books; 4390 bound periodical volumes; 8 VF drawers of pamphlets and articles; 1007 audio cassettes. **Subscriptions:** 198 journals and other serials. **Services:** Interlibrary loans; copying; SDI; library open to public for reference use only. **Special Catalogs:** Subject catalog of articles in clinical medicine (card).

FILM CULTURE NON-PROFIT CORPORATION
See: Anthology Film Archives

★4426★
FILSON CLUB - LIBRARY (Hist)
118 W. Breckinridge St.   Phone: (502) 582-3727
Louisville, KY 40203   Dorothy C. Rush, Libn.
Founded: 1884. **Staff:** Prof 5; Other 6. **Subjects:** Kentucky and Virginia history, genealogy. **Holdings:** 40,000 books and bound periodical volumes; manuscripts (private papers); 20,000 pictures; clippings on Kentucky; 1500 maps of Kentucky and the U.S. **Subscriptions:** 85 journals and other serials. **Services:** Copying (limited); library open to public. **Publications:** Filson Club History Quarterly; occasional books. **Special Catalogs:** Chronological catalog to manuscripts (card).

★4427★
FINANCIAL ACCOUNTING STANDARDS BOARD (FASB) - LIBRARY (Bus-Fin)
High Ridge Pk.   Phone: (203) 329-8401
Stamford, CT 06905   Marianne Losch, Libn.
Staff: Prof 1; Other 2. **Subjects:** Accounting, finance. **Holdings:** 2500 books and bound periodical volumes; 2000 other cataloged items. **Subscriptions:** 200 journals and other serials. **Services:** Interlibrary loans; copying; library not open to public. **Computerized Information Services:** SDC, LEXIS. **Staff:** Judith T. Rosum, Asst.Libn.

★4428★
FINANCIAL EXECUTIVES RESEARCH FOUNDATION - LIBRARY (Bus-Fin)
10 Madison Ave.
Box 1938
Morristown, NJ 07960   Moreen Hopkins
Founded: 1944. **Staff:** Prof 1. **Subjects:** Financial management and controllership on executive level, accounting, banking and finance. **Subscriptions:** 70 journals and other serials. **Services:** Library not open to public. **Publications:** Foundation's Research Studies - for sale; Financial Executive, monthly - by subscription, details on request. **Formerly:** Located in New York, NY.

★4429★
FINANCIAL TIMES OF CANADA - LIBRARY (Publ; Bus-Fin)
920 Yonge St., Suite 500   Phone: (416) 922-1133
Toronto, ON, Canada M4W 3L5   Jane Wachna, Libn.
Founded: 1962. **Staff:** Prof 1; Other 2. **Subjects:** Canadian business, government and economics. **Holdings:** 2000 current clippings (48 drawers). **Subscriptions:** 80 journals and other serials; 20 newspapers. **Services:** Interlibrary loans; copying; library open to public by permission. **Computerized Information Services:** New York Times Information Service, CANSIM.

★4430★
FINCH ARBORETUM - LIBRARY
W. 3404 Woodland Blvd.
Spokane, WA 99204
Defunct

★4431★
FIND/SVP - LIBRARY (Bus-Fin; Info Sci)
500 Fifth Ave.   Phone: (212) 354-2424
New York, NY 10110   Kathleen S. Bingham, Exec.V.P.
Staff: Prof 45; Other 10. **Subjects:** Business, health care, food, advertising, chemistry, transportation, energy, metals. **Holdings:** 2500 books; 5000 subject files including pamphlets, statistics and government material; annual reports, 10Ks and proxies of 10,000 companies; 1600 U.S. and foreign telephone directories; 20,000 microfiche of 10K reports, Census, New York Times, Wall Street Journal; 100 periodical titles on microfiche. **Subscriptions:** 800 journals and other serials. **Services:** Interlibrary loans; copying; translations, market studies, telephone surveys, current awareness services; library not open to public. **Computerized Information Services:** DIALOG, SDC, BRS, Dow Jones News Retrieval, New York Times Information Service, National CSS, Inc., TEXTLINE, MEDLINE. **Publications:** Inside FIND, monthly newsletter - sent to clients; FINDEX, annual; Information Catalog, quarterly - for sale. **Remarks:** Maintained by Information Clearing House, Inc., this organization offers a complete package of information gathering, fact-finding and research services. **Staff:** Edith Rood, Dir., Info.Serv.; Deonna Taylor, Mgr., Lib.Serv.; Anne Potter Dennis, Dir., Info.Rsrcs.

FINDLAY PUBLISHING COMPANY
See: Courier

★4432★
FINE ARTS GALLERY OF SAN DIEGO - LIBRARY (Art)
Box 2107   Phone: (714) 232-7931
San Diego, CA 92112   Nancy J. Andrews, Libn.
Founded: 1926. **Staff:** Prof 1; Other 1. **Subjects:** Art - Renaissance, Spanish Baroque, Oriental. **Special Collections:** Contemporary artists (23 VF cabinets); exhibition catalogs (33,000); San Diego artists (6 VF drawers). **Holdings:** 9500 books; 350 bound periodical volumes; 16,500 slides; museum scrapbooks; 16,000 other cataloged items. **Subscriptions:** 36 journals and other serials. **Services:** Copying; library open to members. **Publications:** Exhibition catalogs, occasional. **Special Catalogs:** File of all biographical material contained in the library holdings of exhibition catalogs (card).

★4433★
FINE ARTS MUSEUMS OF SAN FRANCISCO - LIBRARY (Art)
M.H. De Young Memorial Museum
Golden Gate Pk.   Phone: (415) 558-2887
San Francisco, CA 94118   Jane Gray Nelson, Musm.Libn.
Founded: 1930. **Staff:** Prof 1. **Subjects:** Art - French, American, African, Oceania; art history. **Special Collections:** Achenbach Foundation for Graphic Arts Reference Library (3500 volumes); Bothin American Art Library Collection. **Holdings:** 25,000 books; 15,000 bound periodical volumes; auction sales catalogs; exhibition catalogs. **Subscriptions:** 100 journals and other serials. **Services:** Copying; library open to museum staff only. **Publications:** Catalogs of museum collections and exhibitions.

FINK (Harold) MEMORIAL LIBRARY
See: Coney Island Hospital - Harold Fink Memorial Library

FINKELSTEIN LIBRARY
See: St. Mary's Hospital

FINNEY (Dr. John M.T., Jr.) MEMORIAL MEDICAL LIBRARY
See: Union Memorial Hospital - Dr. John M.T. Finney, Jr. Memorial Medical Library

FINNEY MEMORIAL LIBRARY
See: St. Mary-Corwin Hospital

FINNEY (Theodore M.) MUSIC LIBRARY
See: University of Pittsburgh - Theodore M. Finney Music Library

★4434★
FINNISH-AMERICAN HISTORICAL ARCHIVES (Hist)
Suomi College   Phone: (906) 482-5300
Hancock, MI 49930   Robin L. Alanen, Archv.
Founded: 1932. **Staff:** Prof 1. **Subjects:** Finnish churches in North America, immigration, temperance, cooperatives, workers' organizations, Kaleva

Society. **Special Collections:** Archives of Suomi Synod (125 feet) and Suomi College (28 feet); manuscript music of Martti Nisonen (11 feet); Help Finland (19 feet); Temperance (98 feet); Oral History Collection; rare books; Finnish Library. **Holdings:** 5360 books; 760 bound periodical volumes; 2000 photographs; 152,000 manuscripts; 760 tapes. **Subscriptions:** 21 journals and other serials; 5 newspapers. **Services:** Copying; archives open to public by appointment.

★4435★
FINNISH AMERICAN HISTORICAL SOCIETY OF MICHIGAN (Area-Ethnic)
19885 Melrose
Southfield, MI 48075   Felix V. Jackonen, Pres.
Founded: 1945. **Subjects:** Finnish history, culture and religion; books in Finnish. **Holdings:** 200 books; archives; clippings; pamphlets. **Services:** Archives not open to public.

FIRE CENTER
See: University of Minnesota

FIRE RESEARCH INFORMATION SERVICES
See: U.S. Natl. Bureau of Standards

★4436★
FIREARMS RESEARCH AND IDENTIFICATION ASSOCIATION - LIBRARY (Rec)
18638 Alderbury Dr.   Phone: (213) 964-7885
Rowland Heights, CA 91748   John Armand Caudron, Pres.
Staff: Prof 3. **Subjects:** Firearms, weapons, aircraft, military history. **Holdings:** 84 books; 12 technical reports. **Services:** Library not open to public. **Publications:** Snyder Research Newsletter, monthly.

★4437★
FIREFIGHTERS' MUSEUM OF NOVA SCOTIA - LIBRARY & INFORMATION CENTER (Sci-Tech)
451 Main St.   Phone: (902) 742-5525
Yarmouth, NS, Canada B5A 1G9   Helen J. Goodwin, Cur.
Founded: 1977. **Staff:** 1. **Subjects:** Firefighting. **Holdings:** 200 books; 400 magazines. **Subscriptions:** 12 journals and other serials. **Services:** Library open to public for reference use only.

★4438★
FIREMAN'S FUND INSURANCE COMPANIES - LIBRARY (Bus-Fin)†
3333 California St.
Box 3395   Phone: (415) 929-2871
San Francisco, CA 94119   Oda Bali Hansen, Libn.
Staff: Prof 6; Other 4. **Subjects:** Insurance - property/casualty, life/health. **Holdings:** Figures not available. **Services:** Interlibrary loans; copying; library open to public. **Publications:** Recent Acquisitions, monthly. **Staff:** Eugenia Ironside, Asst.Libn.; Albert Muto, Asst.Libn.; Molly Skeen, Asst.Libn.; Kirsten Cutler, Jr.Libn.; Rebecca Farmer, Law Libn.

FIRESTONE (Idabelle) AUDIO LIBRARY
See: New England Conservatory of Music - Harriet M. Spaulding Library

FIRESTONE LIBRARY
See: Princeton University

★4439★
FIRESTONE TIRE AND RUBBER COMPANY - BUSINESS LIBRARY (Bus-Fin)
1200 Firestone Pkwy.   Phone: (216) 379-6650
Akron, OH 44317   Shirley Evans, Libn.
Staff: 1. **Subjects:** Tire industry and rubber manufacturing. **Holdings:** Figures not available. **Subscriptions:** 200 journals and other serials; 5 newspapers. **Services:** Library not open to public.

★4440★
FIRESTONE TIRE AND RUBBER COMPANY - CENTRAL RESEARCH LIBRARY (Sci-Tech)
1200 Firestone Pkwy.   Phone: (216) 379-7430
Akron, OH 44317   S. Koo, Sr.Res.Libn.
Founded: 1945. **Staff:** Prof 1; Other 1. **Subjects:** Rubber, plastics, textiles, chemical engineering, mechanical engineering, polymer chemistry. **Holdings:** 7500 books; 11,000 bound periodical volumes; 46 VF drawers of patents; 12 VF drawers of pamphlets; 2000 government documents; 3750 reels of microfilm; 3000 microfiche; 10,000 internal research reports. **Subscriptions:** 250 journals and other serials. **Services:** Interlibrary loans; copying; SDI; library open to public with restrictions. **Computerized Information Services:** DIALOG, SDC; computerized circulation. **Publications:** U.S. Patents Bulletin, weekly; Table of Contents Bulletin, biweekly; New

Booklist, semiannual; Translation Bulletin, irregular; German Patent Applications Bulletin, irregular; List of Released Research Reports, monthly.

★4441★

FIRESTONE TIRE AND RUBBER COMPANY - DEFENSE RESEARCH AND PRODUCTS DIVISION - LIBRARY (Sci-Tech)
1200 Firestone Pkwy.
Akron, OH 44317   Phone: (216) 379-7467
     Sandra Keller, Staff Asst.
Subjects: Ordnance, shaped charge manufacturing technology. **Holdings:** 400 books; 3000 technical reports; 400 microfiche. **Subscriptions:** 12 journals and other serials. **Services:** Library not open to public.

★4442★

FIRST ASSEMBLY OF GOD - CHURCH LIBRARY (Rel-Theol)
22nd & Franklin Sts.
North Little Rock, AR 72114   Phone: (501) 758-8553
     Joye Murry, Dir.
Founded: 1952. **Staff:** 3. **Subjects:** Religion, fiction. **Holdings:** 3000 books; 3 VF drawers of pamphlets; 90 filmstrips; 120 slides; 210 AV items. **Services:** Library open to public with recommendation from pastor or educational director.

FIRST BAPTIST ACADEMY
See: First Baptist Church of Dallas

★4443★

FIRST BAPTIST CHURCH OF DALLAS - FIRST BAPTIST ACADEMY - GEORGE W. TRUETT MEMORIAL LIBRARY (Rel-Theol)†
1707 San Jacinto
Dallas, TX 75201   Phone: (214) 742-5765
     Mildred L. Lively, Dir. of Lib.Serv.
Founded: 1936. **Staff:** Prof 2. **Subjects:** Religion, Christian education, theology. **Holdings:** 28,000 books; archives and dissertations; VF materials and AV media (cataloged). **Subscriptions:** 129 journals and other serials. **Services:** Interlibrary loans; copying; library open to public for reference use only. **Remarks:** Library also serves 12 grades in a Christian Day School. **Staff:** Mary Anne Schmidt, Libn.

★4444★

FIRST BAPTIST CHURCH - E.F. WALKER MEMORIAL LIBRARY (Rel-Theol)
218 N. Magnolia
Box 90
Luling, TX 78648   Phone: (512) 875-2227
     Mrs. Raymond Matthews, Libn.
Founded: 1957. **Staff:** 3. **Subjects:** Theology, missions, biography. **Holdings:** 1775 books; 1200 slides; 3 VF drawers; 125 filmstrips; 45 magnetic tapes; 45 phonograph records. **Services:** Library open to public. **Staff:** Mrs. Ben Fuller, Asst.; Mrs. William Smith, Asst.

★4445★

FIRST BAPTIST CHURCH - I.C. ANDERSON MEMORIAL LIBRARY & MEDIA CENTER (Rel-Theol)
Fifth & Webster Sts.
Box 1847
Waco, TX 76703   Phone: (817) 752-3000
     Esther Davis, Dir. of Lib.Serv.
Founded: 1952. **Staff:** Prof 1; Other 5. **Subjects:** Religion, philosophy, Christian life, Bible, literature, children's books, biography. **Special Collections:** First Baptist Church history (100 books, pamphlets, bulletins, pictures, yearbooks); rare books. **Holdings:** 16,000 books; 80 bound periodical volumes; 800 filmstrips; 200 cassette tapes. **Subscriptions:** 26 journals and other serials. **Services:** Library open to Waco residents with church affiliation. **Special Catalogs:** Media Directory (loose-leaf). **Staff:** Jane Campbell, Circ.Dir.

★4446★

FIRST BAPTIST CHURCH - JOHN L. WHORTON MEDIA CENTER (Rel-Theol)
209 E. South St.
Longview, TX 75601   Phone: (214) 758-0681
     Sandra Trippett, Dir.
Founded: 1942. **Staff:** Prof 2; Other 11. **Subjects:** Religion, Bible, inspirational material, Baptist church. **Holdings:** 13,000 books; 703 AV items (cataloged). **Services:** Library open to public with restrictions.

★4447★

FIRST BAPTIST CHURCH OF LAKEWOOD - CHURCH LIBRARY (Rel-Theol)
5336 Arbor Rd.
Long Beach, CA 90808   Phone: (213) 420-1471
     Judy L. Hughes, Libn.
Founded: 1955. **Staff:** Prof 1; Other 13. **Subjects:** Bible study, devotions, Christian living, missions, biography, children's literature. **Holdings:** 5500 books; 700 recordings; 1000 cassette tapes of the pastor's sermons; 100 cassette albums; 15 cassette-book sets; mission fields information. **Services:** Library open to public with restrictions. **Special Catalogs:** Cassette catalog of sermons, 1975-1980 (pamphlet).

★4448★

FIRST BAPTIST CHURCH - LIBRARY (Rel-Theol)
Box 162
Slocomb, AL 36375   Phone: (205) 886-2533
     Norma Foster, Libn.
Founded: 1963. **Staff:** Prof 1; Other 3. **Subjects:** Religion, philosophy, biography, history. **Holdings:** 3289 books; 143 filmstrips; 172 recordings; 2 vertical files; 189 slides; 20 cassette tapes. **Services:** Library open to public. **Publications:** Weekly column in church bulletin. **Special Catalogs:** Catalog of First Baptist Church History (local).

★4449★

FIRST BAPTIST CHURCH - LIBRARY (Rel-Theol)†
561 Main St.
Melrose, MA 02176   Phone: (617) 665-4470
     Ruth Richardson, Libn.
Staff: Prof 1. **Subjects:** Religion. **Holdings:** 1000 volumes. **Services:** library open to public with restrictions.

★4450★

FIRST BAPTIST CHURCH - LIBRARY (Rel-Theol)†
Exchange & Meridian
Spring Lake, MI 49456   Phone: (616) 842-1974
Staff: 4. **Subjects:** Religion, biography. **Holdings:** 2500 volumes. **Services:** Library not open to public.

★4451★

FIRST BAPTIST CHURCH - LIBRARY (Rel-Theol)
Ninth & Wacouta Sts.
St. Paul, MN 55101   Phone: (612) 222-0718
     Ann Fitch, Libn.
Staff: Prof 1; Other 3. **Subjects:** Religion, Christian education, biography, social concerns, psychology. **Holdings:** 3000 books. **Services:** Library not open to public.

★4452★

FIRST BAPTIST CHURCH - LIBRARY (Rel-Theol)
First at Church St.
Booneville, MS 38825   Phone: (601) 728-6272
     Stanley Barnett, Libn.
Staff: 1. **Subjects:** Religion. **Holdings:** 2376 books; 38 bound volumes of church bulletins; 103 filmstrips; 90 cassettes. **Services:** Library open to public with restrictions.

★4453★

FIRST BAPTIST CHURCH - LIBRARY (Rel-Theol)
300 St. Francis St.
Kennett, MO 63857   Phone: (314) 888-4689
     Pearl Young, Libn.
Founded: 1946. **Staff:** Prof 1; Other 1. **Subjects:** Religious commentary, biography. **Holdings:** 3500 books. **Services:** Library open to public with restrictions.

★4454★

FIRST BAPTIST CHURCH - LIBRARY (Rel-Theol)
2205 Iron St.
North Kansas City, MO 64116   Phone: (816) 842-1175
     Esther St. John, Hd.Libn.
Staff: 7. **Subjects:** Bible study, Christian education, Christian ethics, children's books, biography. **Holdings:** 2000 books; audiovisual materials. **Services:** Library open to public with restrictions.

★4455★

FIRST BAPTIST CHURCH - LIBRARY (Rel-Theol)
1000 W. Friendly
Box 5443
Greensboro, NC 27403   Phone: (919) 274-3286
     Charlotte M. Bell, Dir., Media Serv.
Founded: 1947. **Staff:** Prof 1; Other 36. **Subjects:** Religion, biography, art, children's literature, history, social sciences. **Holdings:** 13,000 books; 1300 cassette tapes; 33 8mm films; 600 filmstrips. **Subscriptions:** 43 journals and other serials. **Services:** Copying (limited); library open to public.

★4456★

FIRST BAPTIST CHURCH - LIBRARY (Rel-Theol)
1401 S. Covell
Sioux Falls, SD 57105   Phone: (605) 336-0966
     Chris Carstensen, Libn.
Staff: 2. **Subjects:** Religion, theology. **Holdings:** 2500 books. **Subscriptions:** 10 journals and other serials. **Services:** Library open to public.

★4457★

FIRST BAPTIST CHURCH - LIBRARY (Rel-Theol)†
1200 Beech St.
McAllen, TX 78501   Phone: (512) 686-7418
     Mrs. Hans Wells, Dir.
Founded: 1960. **Staff:** 6. **Subjects:** Religion, Bible, sociology, literature. **Holdings:** 4349 books; 207 filmstrips; 74 records. **Services:** Library open to

public with restrictions.

★4458★
FIRST BAPTIST CHURCH - LIBRARY (Rel-Theol)
515 McCullough Ave.
San Antonio, TX 78215
Phone: (512) 226-0363
Virginia Patterson, Libn.
Founded: 1939. Staff: Prof 1; Other 5. Subjects: Baptist history and doctrines, Bible, family religious life. Holdings: 16,000 books; 440 bound periodical volumes; 10 VF drawers of church archives; 1400 filmstrips; 950 tapes. Subscriptions: 35 journals and other serials. Services: Interlibrary loans; copying; library open to public for reference use only.

★4459★
FIRST BAPTIST CHURCH - MATTIE D. HALL LIBRARY (Rel-Theol)
Front St.
Box 125
Rosedale, MS 38769
Phone: (601) 759-6378
Staff: 7. Subjects: Theology, Christian living. Holdings: 3200 books. Services: Library open to public with restrictions.

★4460★
FIRST BAPTIST CHURCH - MEDIA CENTER (Rel-Theol)
425 W. University Ave.
Gainesville, FL 32601
Phone: (904) 376-2131
Dorothy S. Hammond, Dir. of Lib.Serv.
Founded: 1953. Staff: Prof 2; Other 6. Subjects: Religion, Christian living, missionary biography, fiction, children's books. Holdings: 8000 books; 490 filmstrips; 200 phonograph records; 4 VF drawers of pamphlets; 335 slides; flipcharts and maps; 150 cassettes. Subscriptions: 20 journals and other serials. Services: Interlibrary loans; use of AV material and equipment available to county Baptist churches; library open to public. Publications: Catalog of filmstrip holdings in pamphlet form, biennial. Staff: Mrs. Robert Hyatt.

★4461★
FIRST BAPTIST CHURCH - MEDIA CENTER (Rel-Theol)†
Box 1996
Roswell, NM 88201
Phone: (505) 623-2640
Jeannine Miller, Dir. of Media Ctr.
Founded: 1956. Staff: 6. Subjects: Religion, Christian life, psychology, children's literature. Holdings: 3610 books; 318 filmstrips; 157 phonograph records; 141 slides; 50 maps and realia. Services: Interlibrary loans; library open to organizations with restrictions.

★4462★
FIRST BAPTIST CHURCH - MEDIA CENTER (Rel-Theol)
122 Gaston St.
Brevard, NC 28712
Phone: (704) 883-8251
Carole Jackson, Chm., Media Ctr.Comm.
Staff: 4. Subjects: Religion, children's books, fiction. Holdings: 5000 books. Services: Library open to public. Staff: Edna Bryson, Libn.; Ann Runyan, Asst.Libn.; Mrs. Perry Brown, Asst.Libn.

★4463★
FIRST BAPTIST CHURCH - MEDIA LIBRARY (Rel-Theol)
Box 85
Abilene, TX 79604
Phone: (915) 673-5031
Ruth Dahlstrom, Lib.Dir.
Founded: 1948. Staff: Prof 4; Other 6. Subjects: Religion, biography, history, travel, fiction, fine arts, philosophy, family life, children's literature. Holdings: 18,000 books; 650 cassette recordings; 30 phonograph records; 400 filmstrips; 4 VF drawers; 185 slides. Subscriptions: 12 journals and other serials. Services: Library open to public with restrictions. Networks/Consortia: Member of Texas Church Library Association.

★4464★
FIRST BAPTIST CHURCH OF RICHMOND - LIBRARY (Rel-Theol)†
Monument & Boulevard
Richmond, VA 23220
Phone: (804) 355-8637
Staff: Prof 10; Other 5. Subjects: Bible and Bible study, theology, Christian life, prayer, devotional literature, biography. Holdings: 9000 books; 500 filmstrips and recordings; 2 VF drawers of clippings, articles, folders and pamphlets; 600 slides; 50 cassette tapes and phonograph records. Subscriptions: 35 journals and other serials. Services: Library open to public. Publications: Current Book List and Memorials, monthly.

★4465★
FIRST BAPTIST CHURCH - STINCEON IVEY MEMORIAL LIBRARY (Rel-Theol)†
Box 663
Fairmont, NC 28340
Phone: (919) 628-6844
Mrs. Jack Waters, Lib.Asst.
Staff: 5. Subjects: Religion. Holdings: 3898 books. Services: Library open to public.

★4466★
FIRST BOSTON CORPORATION - INFORMATION CENTER (Bus-Fin)
Park Avenue Plaza
New York, NY 10055
Phone: (212) 825-7781
Julia B. Shibla, Asst.V.P./Mgr.
Founded: 1963. Staff: Prof 5; Other 8. Subjects: Finance, corporations, business, industries, investment and securities. Special Collections: Corporation records, U.S. and foreign; Securities and Exchange Commission files (microfiche). Holdings: 2000 books; 500 bound periodical volumes; 300,000 microfiche; 1000 reels of microfilm. Subscriptions: 600 journals and other serials; 25 newspapers. Services: Interlibrary loans; copying; library open to Special Libraries Association members, with restriction to others. Computerized Information Services: Dow Jones News Retrieval, Mead Data Central, DIALOG, SDC, BRS, Info Globe, New York Times Information Service, Source Telecomputing Corporation, Control Data Corporation, COMPMARK Data Services, Spectrum Data Base, Dun & Bradstreet, Inc.; internal database; computerized cataloging, acquisitions and serials. Publications: New Acquisitions, bimonthly. Staff: Regina M. Galligan, Asst.Mgr./Ref.Libn.

★4467★
FIRST CATHOLIC SLOVAK UNION OF U.S.A. AND CANADA (Area-Ethnic)
3289 E. 55th St.
Cleveland, OH 44127
Phone: (216) 341-3355
Stephen F. Ungvarsky, Exec.Sec.
Subjects: Slovakia. Special Collections: Books by Slovak authors. Remarks: Publications for this organization are handled by Joseph C. Krajsa, Editor and Manager, JEDNOTA Printery, Box 150, Middletown, PA 17057. The phone number is (717) 944-0461.

★4468★
FIRST CHRISTIAN CHURCH - LIBRARY (Rel-Theol)†
Walnut & Tenth Sts.
Columbia, MO 65201
Phone: (314) 449-7265
Subjects: Bible, theology, philosophy, religious education, ecumenical church, missions, socioeconomic problems, Christian life and worship. Holdings: 4000 books; AV collection.

★4469★
FIRST CHRISTIAN CHURCH - LIBRARY (Rel-Theol)†
Tenth & Faraon Sts.
St. Joseph, MO 64501
Phone: (816) 233-2556
Founded: 1957. Staff: 3. Subjects: Religion, social problems. Holdings: 2300 books. Services: Interlibrary loans; library open to public with restrictions.

★4470★
FIRST CHRISTIAN CHURCH - LIBRARY (Hist)
On The Diamond
New Castle, PA 16101
Mrs. H.E. McEwen, Libn.
Founded: 1959. Staff: 5. Holdings: 2411 books; 9 boxes of historical materials. Subscriptions: 8 journals and other serials. Services: Interlibrary loans; library open to public.

★4471★
FIRST CHRISTIAN CHURCH - LIBRARY (Rel-Theol)†
2723 King St.
Alexandria, VA 22302
Phone: (703) 549-3911
Sue Solomon, Libn.
Founded: 1954. Staff: 1. Subjects: Theology, philosophy, biography, history. Special Collections: Robin June Gustafson Memorial Collection of Children's Books. Holdings: 2500 books; 50 sermons and pamphlets; 40 slides and filmstrips. Services: Interlibrary loans; library open to public with permission of librarian. Publications: Selected Current Acquisitions Lists, irregular.

★4472★
FIRST CHRISTIAN CHURCH - WINONA ROEHL LIBRARY (Rel-Theol)†
211 W. 5th Ave.
Knoxville, TN 37917
Phone: (615) 522-0545
Mrs. E.R. Snyder, Libn.
Founded: 1953. Staff: Prof 2. Subjects: Religion, teaching aids, biography, children's books. Special Collections: E. Stanley Jones; Jane Merchant. Holdings: 3400 books and bound periodical volumes; audiovisual items. Services: Library open to public.

★4473★
FIRST CHRISTIAN REFORMED CHURCH - LIBRARY (Rel-Theol)
15 S. Church St.
Zeeland, MI 49464
Betty G. Shoemaker, Church Libn.
Founded: 1928. Staff: 5. Subjects: Religion. Holdings: 3950 books; 60 bound periodical volumes. Subscriptions: 20 journals and other serials. Services: Library open to public.

★4474★
FIRST CHURCH IN ALBANY (Reformed) - LIBRARY (Rel-Theol)
N. Pearl & Clinton Sq.   Phone: (518) 463-4449
Albany, NY 12210   E. Helen Gardner, Libn.
Founded: 1958. **Staff:** Prof 1; Other 1. **Subjects:** Religion, Albany history. **Holdings:** 2000 volumes; 1700 church records. **Services:** Library open to public by application.

★4475★
FIRST CHURCH OF CHRIST CONGREGATIONAL - JOHN P. WEBSTER LIBRARY (Rel-Theol)
12 S. Main St.   Phone: (203) 233-9605
West Hartford, CT 06107   Rev. Lee K. Ellenwood, Lib.Dir.
Founded: 1978. **Staff:** Prof 1; Other 2. **Subjects:** Religion, psychology, social issues. **Holdings:** 7500 books. **Subscriptions:** 62 journals and other serials. **Services:** Interlibrary loans; library open to public.

★4476★
FIRST CHURCH OF CHRIST SCIENTIST - ARCHIVES AND LIBRARY (Rel-Theol)
Christian Science Ctr.   Phone: (617) 262-2300
Boston, MA 02115   Lee Z. Johnson, Archv.
Staff: Prof 14; Other 4. **Subjects:** Christian Science; Church of Christ, Scientist; Mary Baker Eddy. **Holdings:** 2500 books; 250 bound periodical volumes; manuscript material. **Services:** Interlibrary loans; copying; library accessible with restrictions. **Staff:** Stephen R. Howard, Assoc.Archv.

★4477★
FIRST CONGREGATIONAL CHURCH OF AUBURN - LIBRARY (Rel-Theol)†
128 Central St.   Phone: (617) 832-2845
Auburn, MA 01501   Mrs. Leroy H. LaPlante, Chm.
Founded: 1959. **Staff:** 6. **Subjects:** Bible commentary and history, religion, missions, education, current issues, family life, juvenile literature. **Holdings:** 3500 books; 8 VF drawers of unbound materials. **Services:** Library open to public with restrictions.

★4478★
FIRST CONGREGATIONAL CHURCH OF CHESHIRE - LIBRARY (Rel-Theol)†
Church Dr.   Phone: (203) 272-5323
Cheshire, CT 06410
Staff: 9. **Subjects:** Religion. **Holdings:** 3000 books. **Services:** Library not open to public.

★4479★
FIRST CONGREGATIONAL CHURCH - LIBRARY (Rel-Theol)†
1985 Louis Rd.   Phone: (415) 856-6662
Palo Alto, CA 94303
Staff: 1. **Subjects:** Religion, Christian doctrines. **Holdings:** 1000 books; sermons of G. Arthur Casaday (cataloged). **Services:** Library not open to public.

★4480★
FIRST CONGREGATIONAL CHURCH - LIBRARY (Rel-Theol)
2001 Niles Ave.   Phone: (616) 983-5519
St. Joseph, MI 49085   Arlene Emery, Libn.
Founded: 1957. **Staff:** 1. **Subjects:** Religion, social science, fine arts, ethics, family life. **Holdings:** 3680 books. **Services:** Library not open to public.

★4481★
FIRST CONGREGATIONAL CHURCH IN WELLESLEY HILLS - LIBRARY (Rel-Theol)
207 Washington St.   Phone: (617) 235-4424
Wellesley Hills, MA 02181   Dr. Lorraine E. Tolman, Lib.Coord.
Founded: 1955. **Staff:** 7. **Subjects:** Bible study, Christian education. **Special Collections:** Audiovisual Resource Center. **Holdings:** 3500 books. **Subscriptions:** 10 journals and other serials.

FIRST FEDERAL SAVINGS & LOAN ASSOCIATION OF BROWARD COUNTY
See: Glendale Federal Savings & Loan Association

★4482★
FIRST FEDERAL SAVINGS AND LOAN ASSOCIATION OF FORT WAYNE - LIBRARY (Bus-Fin)†
719 Court St.   Phone: (219) 423-2377
Fort Wayne, IN 46801   Robert P. Norton, V.P.
Founded: 1966. **Staff:** Prof 1; Other 2. **Subjects:** Savings and loan associations, financial institutions, economics, business, housing. **Holdings:** 2800 books; 125 bound periodical volumes. **Subscriptions:** 95 journals and other serials. **Services:** Library open to public by appointment. **Networks/**

Consortia: Member of OCLC through INCOLSA. **Publications:** First Federal Flash - for internal distribution only.

★4483★
FIRST HAWAIIAN BANK - RESEARCH DIVISION LIBRARY (Bus-Fin)
Box 3200   Phone: (808) 525-6229
Honolulu, HI 96847   Mary I. Kuramoto, Res.Libn.
Staff: Prof 2; Other 1. **Subjects:** Banking, economics, business in Hawaii. **Holdings:** 5030 books; 40 bound periodical volumes; 20 VF drawers of news clippings; 20 VF drawers of newsletters; telephone books for major U.S. cities on microfiche; 68 VF drawers of government documents. **Subscriptions:** 295 journals and other serials; 10 newspapers. **Services:** Interlibrary loans; copying; library open to public. **Special Catalogs:** Hawaii Business Magazine, Discover Hawaii, Honolulu (card). **Staff:** Helen L. Bevens, Asst.V.P., Supv./Libn.

★4484★
FIRST INTERSTATE BANK ATHLETIC FOUNDATION - LIBRARY (Rec)
2141 W. Adams Blvd.   Phone: (213) 614-2995
Los Angeles, CA 90018   W.R. Bill Schroeder, Mng.Dir.
Founded: 1936. **Staff:** Prof 2. **Subjects:** Sports - history and instruction. **Special Collections:** Olympic Games Official Reports (1896-1980); athletic and sports guides. **Holdings:** 10,000 books; 10,000 bound periodical volumes; bound newspaper sport pages; sports record files; historical documents; scrap books; souvenir programs; sports photographs. **Subscriptions:** 52 journals and other serials. **Services:** Copying (limited); library open to public for reference use only. **Publications:** Press-media announcements and special research. **Remarks:** Library holdings of sports record ephemera and other documentary materials are among the most comprehensive in existence.

★4485★
FIRST INTERSTATE BANK OF CALIFORNIA - LIBRARY (Bus-Fin)
Terminal Annex
Box 3666   Phone: (213) 614-4097
Los Angeles, CA 90051   Peggy Wilson, Chf.Libn.
Founded: 1955. **Staff:** Prof 2; Other 1. **Subjects:** Banking and finance, business and industry, accounting, management, economics, personnel. **Special Collections:** Federal Reserve Reports; American Bankers Association publications. **Holdings:** 12,000 volumes; 45 VF drawers of clippings, pamphlets, maps, special reports, newsletters. **Subscriptions:** 325 journals and other serials; 23 newspapers. **Services:** Interlibrary loans; copying; library open to area bank and business libraries. **Computerized Information Services:** DIALOG, New York Times Information Service.

★4486★
FIRST INTERSTATE BANK - LIBRARY (Bus-Fin)†
1300 S.W. 5th
Box 3131   Phone: (503) 225-4193
Portland, OR 97208   Sue Pettis, Libn.
Staff: Prof 1; Other 1. **Subjects:** Banking, business, personnel administration, management. **Holdings:** 1150 books; 2400 American Institute of Banking textbooks; theses; pamphlets. **Subscriptions:** 25 journals and other serials. **Services:** Interlibrary loans; library not open to public. **Publications:** Library Listing, biennial. **Formerly:** First National Bank of Oregon.

FIRST (Joseph M.) LIBRARY
See: Akiba Hebrew Academy

★4487★
FIRST LUTHERAN CHURCH - ADULT LIBRARY (Rel-Theol)
1000 3rd Ave., S.E.   Phone: (319) 365-1494
Cedar Rapids, IA 52403   Ortha Harstad
Founded: 1959. **Staff:** 14. **Subjects:** Religion, works of Luther, family, Bible. **Holdings:** 2500 books; 75 audio cassettes. **Services:** Library open to public.

★4488★
FIRST LUTHERAN CHURCH OF THE LUTHERAN CHURCH IN AMERICA - SCHENDEL MEMORIAL LIBRARY (Rel-Theol)
615 5th St.   Phone: (612) 388-9311
Red Wing, MN 55066   Mrs. Delma Rigelman, Libn.
Founded: 1951. **Subjects:** Bible, Christian life, prayer. **Special Collections:** Luther's complete works; 20th century theology (50 titles). **Holdings:** 4000 books; 2 VF drawers of clippings, pamphlets and maps. **Subscriptions:** 10 journals and other serials. **Services:** Library open to Lutheran congregations in the area. **Staff:** Viola Vogt, Cat.Libn.

★4489★
FIRST LUTHERAN CHURCH - PARISH LIBRARY (Rel-Theol)
415 Vine St.   Phone: (814) 536-7521
Johnstown, PA 15901   Elizabeth J. Will, Libn.
Founded: 1954. **Staff:** 2. **Subjects:** Religion, church history. **Holdings:** 4500 books; 2 VF drawers of pamphlets. **Subscriptions:** 12 journals and other serials. **Services:** Library open to public.

★4490★
FIRST MERIDIAN HEIGHTS PRESBYTERIAN CHURCH - HUDELSON LIBRARY
    (Rel-Theol)†
4701 N. Central Ave.   Phone: (317) 283-1305
Indianapolis, IN 46205   Linda K. Harris, Chm., Lib.Comm.
Staff: 9. **Subjects:** Religion. **Holdings:** 3000 books; 15 bound periodical volumes; 150 recordings. **Services:** Library open to public. **Computerized Information Services:** Computerized cataloging. **Networks/Consortia:** Member of INCOLSA.

FIRST METHODIST CHURCH
See also: First United Methodist Church

★4491★
FIRST METHODIST CHURCH - BLISS MEMORIAL LIBRARY (Rel-Theol)
Head of Texas St.   Phone: (318) 424-7771
Shreveport, LA 71101   Mrs. Dick Towery, Libn.
Founded: 1946. **Staff:** Prof 2; Other 6. **Subjects:** Religion, history, biography. **Special Collections:** Articles for Worship Centers; religious maps. **Holdings:** 10,000 books; 86 bound periodical volumes; Methodist Conference proceedings; 80 tapes. **Services:** Copying; library open to public. **Staff:** Mrs. John Hanks, Libn.

★4492★
FIRST NATIONAL BANK OF BOSTON - LIBRARY (Bus-Fin)
100 Federal St.   Phone: (617) 434-8440
Boston, MA 02110   Jane E. Gutowski-Connell, Libn.
Staff: Prof 2; Other 3. **Subjects:** Banking and business. **Special Collections:** Archives and bank history (8 VF drawers). **Holdings:** 14,700 books and bound periodical volumes; 76 VF drawers of business-financial and related subjects; 40 VF drawers of international material (country files). **Subscriptions:** 750 journals and other serials. **Services:** Interlibrary loans; copying (limited); library open to clients, students and other librarians with restrictions. **Computerized Information Services:** DIALOG, New York Times Information Service. **Publications:** Monthly Recent Acquisitions.

★4493★
FIRST NATIONAL BANK OF CHICAGO - INFORMATION TECHNOLOGY
    LIBRARY (Info Sci)
1 First National Plaza   Phone: (312) 732-4760
Chicago, IL 60670   Naomi Adler, Mgr./Info.Spec.
Staff: Prof 1; Other 1. **Subjects:** Bank data processing, computer security, electronic fund transfer, software engineering and reliability, information science. **Holdings:** 2395 books. **Services:** Interlibrary loans; library not open to public. **Computerized Information Services:** DIALOG, SDC.

★4494★
FIRST NATIONAL BANK OF CHICAGO - LIBRARY (Bus-Fin)†
One First National Plaza, Suite 0477   Phone: (312) 732-3590
Chicago, IL 60670   Martha Whaley, Libn.
Founded: 1931. **Staff:** Prof 4; Other 6. **Subjects:** Banking, economics, business, industries. **Holdings:** 5000 books; 1175 bound periodical volumes. **Services:** Interlibrary loans. **Networks/Consortia:** Member of Metropolitan Chicago Library Assembly. **Publications:** Library News, bimonthly - limited distribution.

★4495★
FIRST NATIONAL BANK OF FORT WORTH - LIBRARY (Bus-Fin)†
Box 2260   Phone: (817) 390-6161
Fort Worth, TX 76101   Bonner Garmon, Libn.
Staff: 1. **Subjects:** Banking, bonds, management, real estate. **Holdings:** 1500 books. **Subscriptions:** 75 journals and other serials. **Services:** Library open to bank employees only.

FIRST NATIONAL BANK OF OREGON
See: First Interstate Bank

★4496★
FIRST PENNSYLVANIA BANK, N.A. - MARKETING INFORMATION CENTER
    (Bus-Fin)†
Center Sq. Tower, 40th Fl.
1500 Market St.   Phone: (215) 786-5980
Philadelphia, PA 19101   Vernice W. Berry, Mgr.
Founded: 1973. **Staff:** Prof 1; Other 2. **Subjects:** Marketing, banking, management, industry. **Holdings:** 2000 books; 90 drawers of industry reports; periodic internal reports; 88 marketing research reports; 100 banking reports; computer programs. **Subscriptions:** 162 journals and other serials. **Services:** Interlibrary loans; copying; library open to public by appointment. **Publications:** Source Network, annual - to personnel.

★4497★
FIRST PRESBYTERIAN CHURCH OF CHARLESTON - LIBRARY (Rel-Theol)
16 Broad St.   Phone: (304) 343-8961
Charleston, WV 25301   Susan Perkins, Dir., Educ.Rsrcs.
Staff: 10. **Subjects:** Religion. **Holdings:** 8000 books; 200 records. **Services:** Library open to public with restrictions.

★4498★
FIRST PRESBYTERIAN CHURCH - CHRISTIAN EDUCATION DEPARTMENT -
    LIBRARY (Rel-Theol)†
320 Date St.   Phone: (619) 232-7513
San Diego, CA 92101   L.A. Schworer, Sec./Christian Educ.
Staff: 1. **Subjects:** Religion, Christian biography and autobiography. **Holdings:** 3459 books. **Subscriptions:** 51 journals and other serials. **Services:** Library open to public.

★4499★
FIRST PRESBYTERIAN CHURCH - EWING MEMORIAL LIBRARY (Rel-Theol)
5300 S. Main   Phone: (713) 526-2525
Houston, TX 77004   Elizabeth Orr, Libn.
Staff: Prof 1; Other 14. **Subjects:** Religion. **Holdings:** 8000 books. **Services:** Library not open to public.

★4500★
FIRST PRESBYTERIAN CHURCH OF FLINT - PEIRCE MEMORIAL LIBRARY
    (Rel-Theol)
746 S. Saginaw St.   Phone: (313) 234-8673
Flint, MI 48502   Barbara Spaulding Westcott, Lib.Chm.
Staff: 8. **Subjects:** Christianity, church history, ancient history, other religions. **Holdings:** 2000 books; magazines and papers. **Services:** Copying; library open to public.

★4501★
FIRST PRESBYTERIAN CHURCH OF GADSDEN - LIBRARY (Rel-Theol)
530 Chestnut St.
Box 676   Phone: (201) 547-5747
Gadsden, AL 35902   Mrs. Tom Smith, Libn.
Founded: 1959. **Staff:** 4. **Subjects:** Religion. **Holdings:** 3000 books. **Subscriptions:** 10 journals and other serials. **Services:** Library not open to public.

★4502★
FIRST PRESBYTERIAN CHURCH - JOHN C. GARDNER MEMORIAL LIBRARY
    (Rel-Theol)
219 E. Bijou   Phone: (303) 634-4301
Colorado Springs, CO 80903   Elouise Young, Libn.
Staff: 2. **Subjects:** Religion. **Holdings:** 3700 books. **Subscriptions:** 25 journals and other serials. **Services:** Library open to public with restrictions.

★4503★
FIRST PRESBYTERIAN CHURCH - LIBRARY (Rel-Theol)
869 N. Euclid Ave.   Phone: (714) 982-8811
Upland, CA 91786   Courtney Brunworth, Libn.
Founded: 1966. **Staff:** Prof 1. **Subjects:** Religion and theology, missions, children's and young adult books. **Holdings:** 1700 volumes. **Services:** Library open to public with restrictions.

★4504★
FIRST PRESBYTERIAN CHURCH - LIBRARY (Rel-Theol)
724 N. Woodland Blvd.   Phone: (904) 734-6212
De Land, FL 32720   Dorthea Beiler, Libn.
Founded: 1955. **Subjects:** Religion, Bible, Christian education, family living, Presbyterianism, devotional literature. **Holdings:** 3655 books. **Services:** Library open to public.

★4505★
FIRST PRESBYTERIAN CHURCH - LIBRARY (Rel-Theol)†
225 W. Maple Ave.   Phone: (312) 362-2174
Libertyville, IL 60048
Subjects: Bible, religion, biography, children's books. **Holdings:** 1800 books.
Services: Library open to residents of Libertyville.

★4506★
FIRST PRESBYTERIAN CHURCH - LIBRARY (Rel-Theol)
1432 Washtenaw Ave.   Phone: (313) 662-4466
Ann Arbor, MI 48104
Subjects: Church history, theology, Christian education, missions, family life.
Holdings: 3200 books. **Subscriptions:** 10 journals and other serials.
Services: Library not open to public.

★4507★
FIRST PRESBYTERIAN CHURCH - LIBRARY (Rel-Theol)†
321 W. South St.   Phone: (616) 344-0119
Kalamazoo, MI 49006   Lillian B. Auducon
Founded: 1956. **Staff:** Prof 5. **Subjects:** Religion and allied fields. **Holdings:**
2500 books. **Services:** Library not open to public.

★4508★
FIRST PRESBYTERIAN CHURCH - LIBRARY (Rel-Theol)
7th at Lincoln Ave.   Phone: (402) 462-5147
Hastings, NE 68901   Mrs. Harrold Shiffler, Libn.
Founded: 1950. **Staff:** Prof 1; Other 5. **Subjects:** Christian religion,
philosophy, sociology, art and music. **Holdings:** 6000 books. **Subscriptions:**
12 journals and other serials. **Services:** Library open to public. **Networks/
Consortia:** Member of Hastings Area Librarians.

★4509★
FIRST PRESBYTERIAN CHURCH - LIBRARY (Rel-Theol)†
823 S.E. Lane   Phone: (503) 673-5559
Roseburg, OR 97470   Nancy Nixon, Libn.
Founded: 1950. **Staff:** Prof 1. **Subjects:** Religion. **Holdings:** 1000 books.
Services: Library not open to public.

★4510★
FIRST PRESBYTERIAN CHURCH - LIBRARY (Rel-Theol)†
Main St.   Phone: (215) 933-8816
Phoenixville, PA 19460   Elizabeth Holden, Libn.
Staff: 5. **Subjects:** Religion. **Holdings:** 4050 books. **Services:** Library open
to public with restrictions.

★4511★
FIRST PRESBYTERIAN CHURCH - LIBRARY (Rel-Theol)
1340 Murchison Dr.   Phone: (915) 533-7551
El Paso, TX 79902
Founded: 1955. **Staff:** Prof 1; Other 2. **Subjects:** Theology. **Holdings:** 2800
books. **Services:** Library open to public.

★4512★
**FIRST PRESBYTERIAN CHURCH - THOMAS E. BOSWELL MEMORIAL
LIBRARY** (Rel-Theol)
1427 Chicago Ave.   Phone: (312) 864-1472
Evanston, IL 60201   Joan Borg, Libn.
Founded: 1962. **Staff:** Prof 1; Other 4. **Subjects:** Christian theology, Bible,
family life, children's literature, fine arts, biography. **Holdings:** 4000 books;
12 tapes (cataloged). **Subscriptions:** 16 journals and other serials. **Services:**
Library open to public. **Publications:** Book Shelf, monthly newsletter - for local
church.

★4513★
FIRST SOUTHERN BAPTIST CHURCH - LIBRARY (Rel-Theol)
445 E. Speedway   Phone: (602) 623-5858
Tucson, AZ 85705   Eleanor Potts, Dir.
Founded: 1957. **Staff:** Prof 1; Other 9. **Subjects:** Religion. **Holdings:** 5500
books; 27 transparencies; 295 filmstrips; 307 cassette tapes; 338
phonograph records. **Subscriptions:** 25 journals and other serials. **Services:**
Library open to members of this church. **Publications:** Messenger, weekly.

★4514★
FIRST UNITED METHODIST CHURCH OF ALHAMBRA - LIBRARY (Rel-
Theol)†
9 N. Almansor   Phone: (213) 289-4258
Alhambra, CA 91801   Dorothy Hooper, Chm., Lib.Comm.
Staff: Prof 1; Other 5. **Subjects:** Religion, psychology, devotions, children's
books, biography, social science. **Holdings:** 4000 books. **Services:** Library not

open to public.

★4515★
FIRST UNITED METHODIST CHURCH - ALLEN LIBRARY (Rel-Theol)†
212 S. Park St.   Phone: (616) 381-6340
Kalamazoo, MI 49006   Mildred S. Hedrick, Libn.
Founded: 1952. **Staff:** Prof 6; Other 6. **Subjects:** Religion, family-home,
Christian ethics, biography, history, devotional and children's literature, race
relations. **Holdings:** 6700 books; pictures; maps; pamphlets; 150 AV
materials; 221 filmstrips; 75 phonograph records; 14 tapes; 12 kits.
Services: Interlibrary loans; copying; library open to public with restrictions.

★4516★
**FIRST UNITED METHODIST CHURCH - GERTRUDE CALLIHAN MEMORIAL
LIBRARY** (Rel-Theol)†
129 W. Hutchinson
Box 2490   Phone: (512) 392-6001
San Marcos, TX 78666   Hilda Carlisle, Lib.Chm.
Staff: Prof 1; Other 3. **Subjects:** Religion. **Holdings:** 3000 books. **Services:**
Library open to public.

★4517★
**FIRST UNITED METHODIST CHURCH - JENNIE E. WEAVER MEMORIAL
LIBRARY** (Rel-Theol)†
7 Elm St.   Phone: (518) 725-9313
Gloversville, NY 12078
Staff: 3. **Subjects:** Religion. **Holdings:** 2476 volumes. **Services:** Library not
open to public.

★4518★
FIRST UNITED METHODIST CHURCH - LIBRARY (Rel-Theol)
424 Forest Ave.   Phone: (312) 469-3510
Glen Ellyn, IL 60137   Kathryn Collord, Libn.
Founded: 1959. **Staff:** 10. **Subjects:** Religion, religious education, devotional
materials. **Holdings:** 4500 books; AV materials. **Services:** Interlibrary loans;
library open to public by appointment.

★4519★
FIRST UNITED METHODIST CHURCH - LIBRARY (Rel-Theol)†
1115 S. Boulder   Phone: (918) 587-9481
Tulsa, OK 74119   Marie Tongue, Dir. of Lib.Serv.
Founded: 1930. **Staff:** Prof 3; Other 11. **Subjects:** Religion, Bible, theology,
Christian life, religious art, archeology, psychology, handicrafts. **Special
Collections:** Methodist history/biography (360 volumes); Methodist rare
books. **Holdings:** 11,000 books and bound periodical volumes; vertical files
on church related subjects; cassette tapes; phonograph records; large print
books. **Services:** Library open to church members and to public for reference
only.

★4520★
FIRST UNITED METHODIST CHURCH - MEMORIAL LIBRARY (Rel-Theol)
305 E. Anapamu St.   Phone: (805) 963-3579
Santa Barbara, CA 93101   Homer W. Freeman, Church Libn.
Staff: Prof 1. **Subjects:** Bible, devotions, inspiration, local church history.
Holdings: 2000 volumes; 2 VF drawers; 300 children's books. **Services:**
Interlibrary loans; copying; library open to public with restrictions.

★4521★
**FIRST UNITED PRESBYTERIAN CHURCH OF THE COVENANT - BRITTAIN
LIBRARY** (Rel-Theol)†
250 W. 7th St.   Phone: (814) 456-4243
Erie, PA 16501   Louise Loesel, Libn.
Founded: 1930. **Staff:** Prof 1; Other 4. **Subjects:** Religion, philosophy,
science, art, biography, children's books. **Holdings:** 7000 books. **Services:**
Library open to public with restrictions.

★4522★
FIRST UNITED PRESBYTERIAN CHURCH - LIBRARY (Rel-Theol)
215 Locust St., N.E.   Phone: (505) 247-9594
Albuquerque, NM 87102   Anita Odermann, Dir./Christian Educ.
Staff: Prof 3; Other 9. **Subjects:** Religion, Bible, philosophy, geography, the
arts, history, fiction, Southwest. **Holdings:** 3500 books. **Subscriptions:** 15
journals and other serials. **Services:** Interlibrary loans; library open to public.

FISCHEL (Ellis) STATE CANCER CENTER
See: Ellis Fischel State Cancer Center

★4523★

FISCHER & PORTER CO. - CORPORATE ENGINEERING LIBRARY (Sci-Tech)
125 E. County Line Rd.   Phone: (215) 674-6834
Warminster, PA 18974   Cheryl A. Cherry, Libn.
Staff: Prof 1. **Subjects:** Process control, engineering. **Holdings:** 2150 books;
500 reels of microfilm; 21 VF drawers of technical reports and standards.
Subscriptions: 190 journals and other serials. **Services:** Interlibrary loans;
SDI; library open to public by appointment. **Computerized Information
Services:** DIALOG. **Publications:** Engineering Library Bulletin - for internal
distribution only.

★4524★

**FISH DOCTOR CLINICAL CENTER, INC. - MERYMAN LIBRARY OF AQUATIC
    RESEARCH** (Sci-Tech)
10408 Bloomingdale Ave.   Phone: (813) 626-1805
Riverview, FL 33569   Dr. Charles Dale Meryman, Pres.
Staff: Prof 2; Other 1. **Subjects:** Fish, aquatic life, fisheries. **Holdings:** 3000
books; 42 bound periodical volumes; 475 photographs and slides; 2000
manuscripts; 500 clippings; 50 unbound reports. **Subscriptions:** 30 journals
and other serials; 5 newspapers. **Services:** Interlibrary loans; copying; library
open to public by appointment. **Computerized Information Services:** Internal
database; computerized cataloging. **Publications:** Contemporary
Pathobiology; F.D.C.C. Technical Papers. **Special Indexes:** Special Breakdown
on Fisheries and Aquatic Animal Health. **Staff:** Elisabeth Lynch, Supv.,
Lib.Serv.; Heidi Norton, Supv., Tech.Info.

FISH FARMING EXPERIMENTAL STATION
See: U.S. Fish & Wildlife Service

★4525★

FISH MEMORIAL HOSPITAL - MEDICAL LIBRARY (Med)
245 E. New York Ave.   Phone: (904) 734-2323
De Land, FL 32720   Paula Greenwood, Circuit Libn.
Founded: 1952. **Staff:** Prof 1; Other 2. **Subjects:** Medicine, nursing and
related subjects. **Holdings:** 100 books; 20 unbound periodicals.
Subscriptions: 20 journals and other serials. **Services:** Interlibrary loans;
library open to public for reference use only. **Computerized Information
Services:** MEDLINE. **Networks/Consortia:** Member of Shared Hospital
Services of Florida, Inc.

★4526★

FISH AND NEAVE - LIBRARY (Law)
875 Third Ave.   Phone: (212) 715-0600
New York, NY 10022   Janet M. Stark, Libn.
Staff: Prof 2; Other 2. **Subjects:** Law - patent, trademark, unfair competition.
Holdings: 10,000 books; 34 bound periodical volumes. **Subscriptions:** 65
journals and other serials. **Services:** Interlibrary loans; copying; library not
open to public. **Computerized Information Services:** LEXIS. **Staff:** Louise E.
Studer, Asst.Libn.

FISHBON (Harris M.) MEMORIAL LIBRARY
See: Mount Zion Hospital and Medical Center - Harris M. Fishbon
    Memorial Library

FISHER (B.L.) LIBRARY
See: Asbury Theological Seminary - B.L. Fisher Library

FISHER CONTROLS COMPANY
See: Monsanto Company

FISHER LIBRARY
See: University of Toronto - University Archives

FISHER (Thomas) RARE BOOK LIBRARY
See: University of Toronto - Thomas Fisher Rare Book Library

FISHKILL HISTORICAL SOCIETY, INC. - VAN WYCK HOMESTEAD MUSEUM
See: Van Wyck Homestead Museum

FISK (Pliny) LIBRARY OF ECONOMICS AND FINANCE
See: Princeton University - Pliny Fisk Library of Economics and Finance

★4527★

**FISK UNIVERSITY - MOLECULAR SPECTROSCOPY RESEARCH
    LABORATORY - LIBRARY** (Sci-Tech)
Box 8   Phone: (615) 329-8620
Nashville, TN 37203   E. Silberman, Prof./Dir.
Staff: 2. **Subjects:** Spectroscopy - infrared, raman, molecular. **Holdings:** 300
books. **Subscriptions:** 10 journals and other serials. **Services:** Library open to

public by appointment.

★4528★

FISK UNIVERSITY - SPECIAL COLLECTIONS DEPARTMENT (Hum)
17th at Jackson St.   Phone: (615) 329-8646
Nashville, TN 37203   Ann Allen Shockley, Assoc.Libn./Archv.
Founded: 1866. **Staff:** Prof 3. **Special Collections:** Negro Collection;
Fiskiana Collection (9 VF drawers); Yorkshire Collection; George Gershwin
Collection; Langston Hughes Phonograph Collection; Black Oral History
Collection (600 tapes); audiotape collection (183 tapes). **Holdings:** 48,000
books; 1565 bound periodical volumes; 3050 microfilms by and about blacks;
2000 phonograph records; 4 VF drawers of pictures; 2 VF drawers of
newspaper clippings; 4 VF drawers of biographical information by or about
blacks; 878 masters' theses (Fisk University); 75 archive and manuscript
collections. **Subscriptions:** 110 journals and other serials; 20 newspapers.
Services: Copying; library open to public with restrictions. **Special Catalogs:**
Dictionary catalog on the Negro Collection; catalog to Oral History Collection;
shelf lists for archives and manuscripts collections. **Staff:** Beth M. Howse,
Spec.Coll.Libn.

FITCH (Albert) MEMORIAL LIBRARY
See: Pennsylvania College of Optometry - Albert Fitch Memorial Library

★4529★

FITCHBURG HISTORICAL SOCIETY - LIBRARY (Hist)
50 Grove St.
Box 953
Fitchburg, MA 01420   Eleanora F. West, Cur. of Musm.
Founded: 1892. **Staff:** Prof 1; Other 1. **Subjects:** Fitchburg and vicinity.
Special Collections: Files of Fitchburg papers from 1838; Norcross Room,
collection of paintings and memorabilia; City Directories, 1835 to present;
area photographs. **Holdings:** 9000 books and bound periodical volumes;
photographs; manuscripts; artifacts; pamphlets. **Services:** Library open to
public with restrictions.

★4530★

FITCHBURG LAW LIBRARY (Law)
Court House, Elm St.   Phone: (617) 345-6726
Fitchburg, MA 01420   Ann E. O'Connor, Law Libn.
Founded: 1871. **Staff:** Prof 1. **Subjects:** Law. **Holdings:** 16,590 books; 200
bound periodical volumes. **Subscriptions:** 292 journals and other serials.
Services: Interlibrary loans; copying; library open to public.

★4531★

FITCHBURG STATE COLLEGE - LIBRARY (Educ)†
Pearl St.   Phone: (617) 345-2151
Fitchburg, MA 01420   William T. Casey, Lib.Dir.
Founded: 1895. **Staff:** Prof 7; Other 7. **Subjects:** Education, special
education, nursing, industrial arts, liberal arts. **Special Collections:** Finnish
Collection. **Holdings:** 155,000 books; 14,000 bound periodical volumes;
4000 pamphlets (cataloged); 175,000 ERIC microfiche; 3500 ultrafiche.
Subscriptions: 2082 journals and other serials; 10 newspapers. **Services:**
Interlibrary loans; library open to public for reference use only. **Staff:**
Jeremiah Greene, Cat.; Faith Antilla, Per.Libn.; Bruce McSheehey, Ref.Libn.;
Robert Foley, ILL; Eini Woods, Circ.Libn.; Lind Cowe, Circ.Asst.

FITZ HUGH LUDLOW MEMORIAL LIBRARY
See: Ludlow (Fitz Hugh) Memorial Library

★4532★

FITZGERALD, ABBOTT AND BEARDSLEY - LAW LIBRARY (Law)†
1330 Broadway
Oakland, CA 94612   Lawrence R. Shepp
Subjects: Law. **Holdings:** 15,000 volumes.

FITZSIMONS ARMY MEDICAL CENTER
See: U.S. Army Hospitals

★4533★

FLAG RESEARCH CENTER - LIBRARY (Rec)
3 Edgehill Rd.   Phone: (617) 729-9410
Winchester, MA 01890   Whitney Smith, Dir.
Founded: 1962. **Staff:** Prof 1. **Subjects:** Flags, heraldry, symbolism. **Special
Collections:** Old flag charts; U.S. flag histories; Argentine flag books.
Holdings: 6000 books; 90 bound periodical volumes; 100 cubic feet of
correspondence on flags, news clippings, pictures, and pamphlets; 200 charts;
1700 unbound periodicals; 20,000 cards of flag information; 1000 flags.
Subscriptions: 50 journals and other serials. **Services:** Copying; consultation;
translation provided to organizations; library open to those stating purpose of

research by prior application. **Publications:** The Flag Bulletin, bimonthly; chart of flags of the world; occasional pamphlets; books. **Special Catalogs:** Flag bibliography (partially published and on cards); list of vexillologists (flag historians) and flag manufacturers. **Remarks:** The Flag Research Center is in touch with numerous private flag book collectors around the world and is familiar with the holdings of public and university libraries; its library will answer questions relating to this subject.

FLAGLER (Henry Morrison) MUSEUM - HISTORICAL SOCIETY OF PALM BEACH COUNTY
See: Historical Society of Palm Beach County

★4534★
FLAGLER HOSPITAL - MEDICAL LIBRARY†
Marine St.
St. Augustine, FL 32084
Subjects: Medicine, surgery, nursing. **Holdings:** 350 books; 235 bound periodical volumes; 322 Audio-Digest tapes; pamphlets. **Networks/ Consortia:** Member of Halifax Hospital Medical Center. **Remarks:** Presently inactive.

FLATHEAD NATL. FOREST CENTER
See: U.S. Forest Service

FLEISCHMANN COLLEGE OF AGRICULTURE
See: University of Nevada, Reno - Life and Health Sciences Library

FLEISCHMANN (Max C.) MEDICAL LIBRARY
See: St. Mary's Hospital - Max C. Fleischmann Medical Library

FLEISHER (Edwin A.) COLLECTION OF ORCHESTRAL MUSIC
See: Free Library of Philadelphia - Edwin A. Fleisher Collection of Orchestral Music

FLEMING (Sir Sanford) COLLEGE OF APPLIED ARTS & TECHNOLOGY
See: Sir Sanford Fleming College of Applied Arts & Technology

★4535★
FLETCHER, MAYO, ASSOCIATES, INC. - LIBRARY (Agri; Bus-Fin)
Sta. E, Box B   Phone: (816) 233-8261
St. Joseph, MO 64505   Sue Becker, Libn.
Staff: Prof 1. **Subjects:** Advertising, marketing, agriculture. **Special Collections:** Agricultural Print Media Report. **Holdings:** 200 books; 500 unbound periodicals. **Subscriptions:** 340 journals and other serials; 10 newspapers. **Services:** Interlibrary loans; copying; library open to public by appointment. **Networks/Consortia:** Member of Northwest Missouri Library Network. **Special Catalogs:** IQ/III (agricultural production facts) - book.

FLETCHER SCHOOL OF LAW & DIPLOMACY
See: Tufts University

★4536★
FLEXIBLE CAREERS - LIBRARY (Soc Sci)*
37 S. Wabash
Chicago, IL 60603   Gertrude D. Schwerin, Libn.
Staff: Prof 1. **Subjects:** Women, careers. **Holdings:** 215 books; 225 VF drawers. **Services:** Library open to public for reference use only.

★4537★
FLICKINGER FOUNDATION FOR AMERICAN STUDIES, INC. - LIBRARY (Hist)
300 St. Dunstan's Rd.   Phone: (301) 323-6284
Baltimore, MD 21212   B. Floyd Flickinger, Pres.
Staff: Prof 1; Other 1. **Subjects:** Americana, American travel, American Revolution, Virginia, Maryland, American military. **Special Collections:** General Daniel Morgan manuscripts; Quaker records; American clergy and educators manuscripts; early American travel. **Holdings:** 10,000 books; 40 VF drawers; 50 boxes of pamphlets; 1000 historic prints and engravings. **Subscriptions:** 60 journals and other serials; 6 newspapers. **Services:** Library open to scholars by appointment. **Remarks:** Foundation is most concerned with the Potomac-Chesapeake-Alleghany region of the U.S.

★4538★
FLINT DEPARTMENT OF COMMUNITY DEVELOPMENT - LIBRARY (Plan)
1101 S. Saginaw St., Rm. 6   Phone: (313) 766-7355
Flint, MI 48502   Dianne Montgomery, Adm. Aide
Staff: 1. **Subjects:** Planning, zoning, housing, transportation, grants information. **Holdings:** 500 books. **Subscriptions:** 17 journals and other serials. **Services:** Library not open to public.

★4539★
FLINT HILLS AREA VOCATIONAL-TECHNICAL SCHOOL - LIBRARY (Sci-Tech)†
3301 W. 18th Ave.
Emporia, KS 66801   Phone: (316) 342-6404
                                           Jane M. Birchard, Libn.
Founded: 1966. **Staff:** Prof 1. **Subjects:** Automotive mechanics, electronics, building trades, food preparation and management, practical nursing, welding, dental assisting, machine tooling, distributive education, farm and ranch management, vocational agriculture, office occupations, graphic arts. **Holdings:** 4000 books; 25 bound periodical volumes. **Subscriptions:** 60 journals and other serials. **Services:** Interlibrary loans; copying; library open to public with restrictions.

★4540★
FLINT INSTITUTE OF ARTS - LIBRARY (Art)†
1120 E. Kearsley St.   Phone: (313) 234-1695
Flint, MI 48503   Diane Oliver, Act.Libn.
Subjects: Art - North American Indian, African, decorative, Oriental, contemporary; glass (paperweights); painting; sculpture. **Holdings:** 2000 books; catalogs of museums' collections; exhibition catalogs. **Subscriptions:** 19 journals and other serials. **Services:** Library open to members and to public with permission.

★4541★
FLINT JOURNAL - EDITORIAL LIBRARY (Publ)
200 E. First St.   Phone: (313) 767-0660
Flint, MI 48502   David W. Larzelere, Chf.Libn.
Founded: 1935. **Staff:** Prof 1; Other 3. **Subjects:** Journalism, local history, news events. **Holdings:** 2000 books; 1000 pamphlets; 1000 maps; 175,000 photographs; 3400 reels of microfilmed newspapers; 1 million newspaper clippings; 32,000 microfiche jackets of clippings. **Subscriptions:** 40 journals and other serials. **Services:** Copying; library not open to public.

★4542★
FLINT NEWMAN CENTER - LIBRARY AND CATHOLIC INFORMATION CENTER (Rel-Theol)
609 E. 5th Ave.   Phone: (313) 239-9391
Flint, MI 48503   Rev. James B. Bettendorf, Dir.
Founded: 1966. **Staff:** 3. **Subjects:** Theology, philosophy, ethics, scripture, church history, aesthetics, sociology. **Special Collections:** Orestes Brownson's works. **Holdings:** 2390 books. **Subscriptions:** 41 journals and other serials; 14 newspapers. **Services:** Library open to public.

★4543★
FLINT OSTEOPATHIC HOSPITAL - DR. E. HERZOG MEMORIAL MEDICAL LIBRARY (Med)
3921 Beecher Rd.
Flint, MI 48502   Phone: (313) 762-4587
                                           Doris M. Blauet, Libn.
Staff: Prof 1; Other 1. **Subjects:** Clinical medicine. **Holdings:** 1500 books; 3556 bound periodical volumes. **Subscriptions:** 260 journals and other serials. **Services:** Interlibrary loans; copying; SDI; library not open to public. **Computerized Information Services:** MEDLARS. **Networks/Consortia:** Member of Flint Area Health Science Library Network; Metropolitan Detroit Medical Library Group; Kentucky-Ohio-Michigan Regional Medical Library Program (KOMRML).

★4544★
FLINT PUBLIC LIBRARY - ART, MUSIC & DRAMA DEPARTMENT (Art; Mus)
1026 E. Kearsley St.
Flint, MI 48502   Phone: (313) 232-7111
                                           James Kangas, Hd.
Staff: Prof 4; Other 1. **Subjects:** Art, drama, music, antiques, theater, architecture, photography, radio, television, motion pictures, crafts, costume, city planning, gardening, dance, circus, interior decoration. **Holdings:** 41,410 books; 3522 bound periodical volumes; 91 VF drawers of pictures; 15 VF drawers of mounted reproductions for study; 65 VF drawers of pamphlets and clippings; 8 VF drawers of music, record, play, picture and crafts catalogs; 1906 posters; 2417 pieces of sheet music; 410 anthem titles (5 to 100 copies per title); 92 cassette tapes; 143 8-track tapes; 12,343 phonograph records; 242 librettos. **Subscriptions:** 169 journals and other serials. **Services:** Interlibrary loans; copying; library open to public with annual borrowing fee for nonresidents. **Computerized Information Services:** Computerized circulation. **Networks/Consortia:** Member of Michigan Library Consortium. **Special Indexes:** Plays, Tune-Dex, portraits, biographies, Roland Scott Joke File, film reviews, songs, Flint Symphony and May Festival (Ann Arbor) program notes (all on cards). **Staff:** Patricia A. Legg, First Asst.

★4545★
FLINT PUBLIC LIBRARY - AUTOMOTIVE HISTORY COLLECTION (Hist)
1026 E. Kearsley St.   Phone: (313) 232-7111
Flint, MI 48502   Joyce E. Peck, Dept.Hd.
Staff: Prof 1. **Subjects:** History of automotive industry. **Special Collections:** Buick and Chevrolet shop manuals. **Holdings:** 1100 books; 175 bound periodical volumes; 15 VF drawers of clippings, pamphlets and owners' manuals. **Subscriptions:** 10 journals and other serials. **Services:** Interlibrary loans; copying; library open to public with annual borrowing fee for nonresidents. **Special Indexes:** Book collection partially indexed by vehicle make and model (book).

★4546★
FLINT PUBLIC LIBRARY - BUSINESS AND INDUSTRY DEPARTMENT (Bus-Fin; Sci-Tech)
1026 E. Kearsley St.   Phone: (313) 232-7111
Flint, MI 48502   Joyce E. Peck, Dept.Hd.
Staff: Prof 5; Other 1. **Subjects:** Economics, labor, investments, management, real estate, insurance, physical sciences, technology. **Special Collections:** Telephone directories (466); trade directories (200). **Holdings:** 33,500 books; 5600 bound periodical volumes; 2000 corporation annual reports; 56 VF drawers of pamphlets and clippings. **Subscriptions:** 375 journals and other serials. **Services:** Interlibrary loans; copying; library open to public with annual borrowing fee for nonresidents. **Publications:** Business and Industry Bulletin, monthly - distributed to local businessmen and libraries.

★4547★
FLINT PUBLIC LIBRARY - CHILDREN'S DEPARTMENT (Hum)
1026 E. Kearsley St.   Phone: (313) 232-7111
Flint, MI 48502   Marcia Carlsten, Hd.
Staff: Prof 3; Other 2. **Subjects:** Fairy tales. **Special Collections:** History and criticism of children's literature; first editions. **Holdings:** 1700 books; 42 bound periodical volumes. **Services:** Library open to public for reference use only.

★4548★
FLINT PUBLIC LIBRARY - MICHIGAN ROOM (Hist)
1026 E. Kearsley St.   Phone: (313) 232-7111
Flint, MI 48502   Judith J. Field, Hd., Gen.Ref.
Founded: 1972. **Staff:** Prof 1. **Subjects:** Local history, Michigan history, genealogy. **Special Collections:** Genesee Biography File; Flint directories, 1860 to present; Flint newspapers, 1839 to present; oral history tapes (43). **Holdings:** 13,525 books; 67 VF drawers; 1100 microcards; 2500 microfiche; 823 reels of census material; 313 drawers of specialized indexes; Michigan document depository. **Subscriptions:** 250 journals. **Services:** Copying; mail inquiries will be answered; room open to public. **Special Indexes:** Name index to Genesee county obituaries in local newspapers, 1850-1876, 1898-1955, 1968 to present.

FLINTKOTE BUILDING PRODUCTS COMPANY
See: Genstar-Flintkote Building Products Company

★4549★
FLOATING POINT SYSTEMS, INC. - INFORMATION CENTER/LIBRARY (Sci-Tech)
3601 S.W. Murray Blvd.   Phone: (503) 641-3151
Beaverton, OR 97005   Richard Grahner, Hd.Libn.
Founded: 1977. **Staff:** Prof 2; Other 1. **Subjects:** Computer science, mathematics, electronics, business, physics. **Special Collections:** Military specifications and standards. **Holdings:** 7000 books; 150 bound periodical volumes; 500 annual reports; 200 telephone directories. **Subscriptions:** 250 journals and other serials; 15 newspapers. **Services:** Interlibrary loans; copying; library open to public. **Computerized Information Services:** DIALOG, RLIN, Information Handling Services; computerized cataloging. **Networks/Consortia:** Member of Washington County Cooperative Library Services; CLASS. **Formerly:** Its Technical Library. **Staff:** Dorcas Phelan, Media Tech.Asst.

★4550★
FLORENCE CITY SCHOOLS - CENTRAL RESOURCE CENTER (Educ)†
541 Riverview Dr.   Phone: (205) 766-3234
Florence, AL 35630   Lois E. Henderson, Lib.Supv.
Staff: Prof 1. **Subjects:** Curriculum, social studies, language arts, school administration, arts and crafts. **Special Collections:** Black history (300 16mm films; 500 multimedia kits). **Holdings:** 5000 books. **Subscriptions:** 35 journals and other serials; 5 newspapers. **Services:** Interlibrary loans; copying; library open to staff.

★4551★
FLORENCE-DARLINGTON TECHNICAL COLLEGE - LIBRARY (Sci-Tech)
Drawer 8000   Phone: (803) 662-8151
Florence, SC 29501   Jeronell White, Lib.Coord.
Staff: Prof 2; Other 3. **Subjects:** Health, business, data processing, secretarial science, civil engineering, fashion merchandising. **Special Collections:** Technology (7500 volumes). **Holdings:** 26,000 books; 657 bound periodical volumes; 1500 pamphlets; 3441 microforms. **Subscriptions:** 321 journals and other serials; 19 newspapers. **Services:** Interlibrary loans; copying; library open to public for reference use only. **Computerized Information Services:** Computerized cataloging. **Networks/Consortia:** Member of OCLC through SOLINET. **Staff:** Helen Alsbrooks, Asst.Libn.

★4552★
FLORENCE DEVELOPMENT DIVISION - PLANNING AND DEVELOPMENT LIBRARY (Plan)
City-County Complex, Drawer FF   Phone: (803) 665-3141
Florence, SC 29501   Elizabeth Shaw, Libn.
Staff: Prof 1. **Subjects:** City and rural planning, state and federal administration, housing, finance, taxation. **Special Collections:** City plans (150); city maps (50 on microfilm); multi-family studies (30). **Holdings:** 1500 books; 40 bound periodical volumes; 20 departmental reports. **Subscriptions:** 27 journals and other serials. **Services:** Library open to public with restrictions. **Computerized Information Services:** Computerized acquisitions. **Formerly:** Its Research and Planning Library.

FLORES (Arturo Taracena) LIBRARY
See: University of Texas, Austin - Benson Latin America Collection

★4553★
FLORES (Nieves M.) MEMORIAL LIBRARY (Area-Ethnic; Aud-Vis)
Box 652   Phone: (471) 472-6417
Agana, GU 96910   Magdalena S. Taitano, Territorial Libn.
Founded: 1949. **Staff:** Prof 5; Other 33. **Special Collections:** Guam history; Western Pacific; subregional library for blind and physically handicapped. **Holdings:** 184,886 books; 1784 bound periodical volumes; 61,771 U.S. documents; 1370 pamphlets; 1072 cassettes; 45 video cassettes; 2460 phonograph records; 361 tapes; 1624 films and filmstrips; 1779 local documents; 2682 microforms. **Subscriptions:** 520 journals and other serials; 20 newspapers. **Services:** Interlibrary loans; copying; library open to public. **Computerized Information Services:** Internal database; computerized acquisitions and registration. **Publications:** Union List of Serials, annual - distributed to contributors and by request; Union Catalog of Guam and Pacific Area Materials, 1979. **Special Indexes:** Index to the Guam Recorder; Index to the Guam Newsletter. **Remarks:** Maintains four branch libraries. **Staff:** Alvina M. Quan, Ser.Libn.; Beata C. Borja, Br.Lib.Supv.; Mildred C. Tai, Clerical Staff Supv.; Virginia A. Leon Guerrero, Children's Libn.

★4554★
FLORIDA A&M UNIVERSITY - ARCH/TECH LIBRARY (Sci-Tech)
B.B. Tech Center A-301
Box 164   Phone: (904) 599-3050
Tallahassee, FL 32307   Margaret F. Wilson, Assoc.Univ.Libn.
Staff: Prof 1; Other 1. **Subjects:** Electronics, civil engineering, data processing, architecture, graphic arts, computer technology. **Holdings:** 10,678 books; 2500 bound periodical volumes; 573 reels of microfilm; 100 filmstrips; 35 films; 112 microfiche; 250 slides. **Subscriptions:** 150 journals and other serials. **Services:** Interlibrary loans; copying; library open to public. **Computerized Information Services:** Computerized cataloging. **Networks/Consortia:** Member of OCLC.

★4555★
FLORIDA A&M UNIVERSITY - PHARMACY LIBRARY (Med)
Box 367   Phone: (904) 599-3304
Tallahassee, FL 32307   Pauline Hicks, Assoc.Univ.Libn.
Founded: 1957. **Staff:** Prof 1; Other 1. **Subjects:** Pharmacy, pharmaceutical chemistry, pharmacology, pharmacognosy, clinical pharmacy, toxicology. **Holdings:** 9800 books; 5000 bound periodical volumes; AV materials. **Subscriptions:** 468 journals and other serials. **Services:** Interlibrary loans (fee); copying; SDI; library open to public with restrictions. **Computerized Information Services:** MEDLINE, TOXLINE; computerized acquisitions and circulation. **Publications:** New Acquisitions List; How to Find it Out in Pharmacy Library.

★4556★

FLORIDA A&M UNIVERSITY - SCHOOL OF BUSINESS & INDUSTRY LIBRARY (Bus-Fin)
Box 309
Tallahassee, FL 32307
Phone: (904) 599-3457
Elizabeth N. Carr, Libn.
Staff: Prof 1. **Subjects:** Management, finance, accounting, marketing, economics, labor relations. **Special Collections:** Robert Trueblood Collection; SBA Collection (2 VF drawers). **Holdings:** 5200 books; 550 bound periodical volumes; 8 VF drawers of career materials; 8 VF drawers of annual reports; 8 VF drawers of information files. **Subscriptions:** 240 journals and other serials; 22 newspapers. **Services:** Interlibrary loans; copying; library open to public with restrictions. **Publications:** Acquisitions list - for internal distribution only.

★4557★

FLORIDA A&M UNIVERSITY - SCHOOL OF NURSING LIBRARY (Med)
Box 136
Tallahassee, FL 32307
Phone: (904) 599-3048
Marva L. Carter, Lib.Tech.Asst.Supv.
Staff: 2. **Subjects:** Nursing - pediatric, surgical, community health, obstetric, psychiatric. **Holdings:** 5000 books; 325 bound periodical volumes; 437 AV materials; VF drawers. **Subscriptions:** 31 journals and other serials. **Services:** Library open to students on campus. **Special Catalogs:** Media catalog, vertical file catalog (both on cards).

★4558★

FLORIDA AUDUBON SOCIETY - INFORMATION CENTER
1101 Audubon Way
Maitland, FL 32751
Subjects: Energy, environment, pollution, land use, endangered species, water resources, planning - Florida. **Special Collections:** Audubon Book Collection (housed at Maitland Public Library). **Holdings:** 1000 books; 1000 reports and documents; microfilmed source materials. **Remarks:** Presently inactive.

FLORIDA BAPTIST HISTORICAL COLLECTION
See: Stetson University - Florida Baptist Historical Collection

FLORIDA COASTAL ENGINEERING ARCHIVES
See: University of Florida - Coastal & Oceanographic Engineering Department - Coastal Engineering Archives

FLORIDA EDUCATIONAL INFORMATION SERVICE
See: Florida State University - Ctr. for Studies in Vocational Educ.

★4559★

FLORIDA FOLKLIFE PROGRAM - ARCHIVES (Hist)
Box 265
White Springs, FL 32096
Phone: (904) 397-2192
Charles Robert (Bob) McNeil, Archv.Asst.
Staff: Prof 1; Other 1. **Subjects:** Folklife - arts and crafts, storytelling, music, foodways, architecture; ethnic music; occupations. **Special Collections:** Florida Folk Festival recordings (400 audiotapes); Thelma Boltin papers (3 linear feet); folklore and folklife field recordings (200 audiotapes and cassettes); folk related slides and photographs (4000 pieces). **Holdings:** 500 books; 6 VF drawers of clippings, newsletters and pamphlets; 14 boxes of sound recordings. **Subscriptions:** 37 journals and other serials. **Services:** Copying; library open to public with restrictions. **Publications:** Florida Folklife News, bimonthly; Festival Programs, annual; Florida Folk Arts Directory, 1979. **Special Indexes:** Accession Register (notebook); indexes and work sheets for reel-to-reel tapes and cassettes.

★4560★

FLORIDA HISTORICAL SOCIETY - LIBRARY (Hist)
Univ. of South Florida Library
Tampa, FL 33620
Phone: (813) 974-2732
Paul Eugen Camp, Exec.Sec.
Founded: 1856. **Subjects:** Florida history. **Subscriptions:** 73 journals and other serials on exchange. **Services:** Copying; library open to public. **Publications:** Florida Historical Quarterly.

★4561★

FLORIDA HOSPITAL - MEDICAL LIBRARY (Med)
601 E. Rollins St.
Orlando, FL 32803
Phone: (305) 896-6611
Meredith Semones, Libn.
Founded: 1950. **Staff:** Prof 1; Other 3. **Subjects:** Medicine, surgery. **Special Collections:** Nursing (350 books; 104 bound periodical volumes). **Holdings:** 800 books; 3180 bound periodical volumes; 1 VF drawer; 25 titles on microfiche. **Subscriptions:** 144 journals and other serials. **Services:** Interlibrary loans; copying; library open to public by telephone request. **Computerized Information Services:** MEDLARS.

★4562★

FLORIDA INSTITUTE OF PHOSPHATE RESEARCH - LIBRARY AND INFORMATION CLEARINGHOUSE (Env-Cons)
Box 877
Bartow, FL 33830
Phone: (813) 533-0983
Patricia W. Boody, Info.Sci.
Founded: 1980. **Staff:** Prof 1; Other 1. **Subjects:** Reclamation, ecology, phosphate mining, radiation, fertilizers. **Holdings:** 1100 books; 200 bound periodical volumes; 300 technical reports on microfiche; 250 maps. **Subscriptions:** 76 journals and other serials. **Services:** Interlibrary loans; copying; SDI; library open to public. **Computerized Information Services:** DIALOG, SDC, QL Systems; computerized cataloging and serials. **Networks/Consortia:** Member of Florida Library Information Network; Tampa Bay Library Consortium. **Publications:** Library and Information Clearinghouse Newsletter, monthly - by subscription. **Remarks:** FIPR is a state supported research organization.

★4563★

FLORIDA INSTITUTE OF TECHNOLOGY - LIBRARY (Sci-Tech)
Box 1150
Melbourne, FL 32901
Phone: (305) 723-3701
Llewellyn L. Henson, Dir.
Staff: Prof 5; Other 15. **Subjects:** Engineering - electrical, mechanical, civil, ocean; sciences - biological, mathematical, management, psychological, medical, space; oceanography; physics; science education. **Special Collections:** General (Ret.) John Bruce Medaris Collection of personal papers and memorabilia; U.S. government document depository. **Holdings:** 125,000 books; 11,000 bound periodical volumes; 15 feet of institute archives and masters' theses; 20 feet of technical reports; 12 VF drawers of pamphlets and clippings. **Subscriptions:** 1250 journals and other serials. **Services:** Interlibrary loans; copying; library open to public. **Computerized Information Services:** DIALOG, SDC; computerized cataloging and acquisitions. **Networks/Consortia:** Member of OCLC through SOLINET. **Staff:** Barbara Markham, Assoc.Dir./Tech.Serv.; Judy Henson, Act.Hd., Ref.Serv.; Elizabeth Dugoff, MRI Libn.; Eleanor Harris, JBC Libn.

★4564★

FLORIDA INSTITUTE OF TECHNOLOGY - SCHOOL OF APPLIED TECHNOLOGY - LIBRARY (Sci-Tech; Env-Cons)
1707 N.E. Indian River Dr.
Jensen Beach, FL 33457
Phone: (305) 334-4200
Eleanor S. Harris, Br.Libn.
Staff: Prof 4; Other 2. **Subjects:** Oceanography, aquaculture, marine science, environmental technology, underwater technology, electronics, photography, computer technology. **Special Collections:** Fisheries & Aquaculture (300 books). **Holdings:** 21,000 books; 1254 bound periodical volumes; 3 VF drawers of technical reports; 475 EPA reports; 24 VF drawers of pamphlets, clippings; theses. **Subscriptions:** 212 journals and other serials; 6 newspapers. **Services:** Interlibrary loans (fee); copying; library open to public. **Staff:** Roberta Fitzpatrick, Asst.Libn.; Nicole Lebeau, Tech.Serv.; Olga Figueredo, Per.Libn.

★4565★

FLORIDA POWER CORPORATION - CORPORATE LIBRARY (Energy)
Box 14042
St. Petersburg, FL 33733
Phone: (813) 866-5458
Genevieve Joyner, Libn.
Founded: 1972. **Staff:** Prof 1; Other 2. **Subjects:** Electric utilities; electric power and power resources; environmental engineering; ecology; atomic power plants; electrical engineering; manpower; personnel management. **Special Collections:** Florida Power Corporation publications (500). **Holdings:** 7000 books; 2085 bound periodical volumes; 800 technical reports (cataloged). **Subscriptions:** 390 journals and other serials; 10 newspapers. **Services:** Interlibrary loans; copying; library open to public by appointment. **Computerized Information Services:** DIALOG. **Publications:** Library Bulletin, as needed. **Remarks:** Library is located at 3201 34th St., S., St. Petersburg, FL 33711.

★4566★

FLORIDA POWER & LIGHT COMPANY - CORPORATE LIBRARY (Bus-Fin; Energy)†
9250 W. Flagler St.
Box 529100
Miami, FL 33152
Phone: (305) 552-3210
Caryl Congleton, Libn.
Founded: 1975. **Staff:** Prof 1; Other 2. **Subjects:** Public utilities, nuclear science, mechanical and nuclear engineering, management and business, mathematics and statistics, safety engineering, energy, environment, materials technology. **Special Collections:** VSMF industry and military standards; product catalogs. **Holdings:** 5000 books; 200,000 microfiche; 3200 technical reports (uncataloged). **Subscriptions:** 600 periodicals; 15 newspapers. **Services:** Interlibrary loans; copying; library not open to public. **Computerized Information Services:** New York Times Information Service, SDC, Informatics. **Publications:** Books 'N Stacks, Fiche 'N Facts, quarterly -

to personnel.

★4567★
FLORIDA PUBLISHING CO. - EDITORIAL LIBRARY (Publ)
1 Riverside Ave.   Phone: (904) 359-4237
Jacksonville, FL 32202   Martin L. Crotts, Dir.
Founded: 1967. **Staff:** Prof 5; Other 2. **Subjects:** Newspaper reference
topics. **Holdings:** 2000 books; 2400 reports, pamphlets and studies; 2.7
million clippings; 610,000 photographs. **Subscriptions:** 14 journals and other
serials; 60 newspapers. **Services:** Interlibrary loans; copying (fee); library
open to public with director's approval for a fee. **Staff:** Pauline Sauer,
Hd.Lib.Asst.

FLORIDA REGIONAL LIBRARY FOR THE BLIND & PHYSICALLY
   HANDICAPPED
See: Florida State Division of Blind Services

★4568★
FLORIDA SCHOOL FOR THE DEAF AND BLIND - LIBRARY FOR THE DEAF
   (Educ)
Box 1209   Phone: (904) 824-1654
St. Augustine, FL 32084   Joan Embry, Hd.Libn.
Staff: Prof 3; Other 3. **Subjects:** Education of the deaf; fiction and nonfiction
(low level, high interest). **Special Collections:** Professional collection
(audiology, sign language, speech pathology). **Holdings:** 16,574 books; 500
bound periodical volumes; pamphlets, filmstrips, captioned films, film loops.
Subscriptions: 45 journals and other serials. **Services:** Interlibrary loans;
library open to public with restrictions. **Staff:** Marydel Alford, Media Spec.;
Bob Graham, Media Coord.

★4569★
FLORIDA SOLAR ENERGY CENTER - LIBRARY (Energy)
300 State Rd. 401   Phone: (305) 783-0300
Cape Canaveral, FL 32920   Iraida B. Rickling, Libn.
Founded: 1975. **Staff:** Prof 1; Other 3. **Subjects:** Solar and alternative
sources of energy, science, technology. **Holdings:** 5653 books; 535 bound
periodical volumes; 4039 technical documents (cataloged); 841 folders of
manufacturers' brochures and product bulletins; 4780 slides; 31,822
microfiche; 9 films. **Subscriptions:** 250 journals and other serials. **Services:**
Interlibrary loans; copying; library open to public with restrictions.
Computerized Information Services: DOE/RECON; computerized cataloging.
Networks/Consortia: Member of OCLC through SOLINET. **Publications:**
Acquisitions bulletin, monthly - for internal distribution only; Current
Awareness Bulletin. **Remarks:** The Florida Solar Energy Center is part of the
Florida State University System and is affiliated with the University of Central
Florida. An additional phone line called SUNCOM is 364-1120.

FLORIDA STATE ARCHIVES
See: Florida State Division of Archives, History & Records Management

★4570★
FLORIDA STATE BOARD OF REGENTS - RECORDS AND ARCHIVES (Educ)
107 W. Gaines St.   Phone: (904) 488-6826
Tallahassee, FL 32304   Carol Wade, Rec.Adm.
Founded: 1963. **Staff:** Prof 1; Other 2. **Subjects:** Higher education,
educational finance, planning, manpower. **Holdings:** 3000 books; 150 other
cataloged items; 1200 microforms; 26 shelves of college catalogs; 18 VF
drawers of pamphlets; 20 VF drawers of archives. **Subscriptions:** 200
journals and other serials; 12 newspapers. **Services:** Interlibrary loans; library
open to public by appointment. **Publications:** List of current library
acquisitions, monthly; List of publications available, revised annually - free
upon request. **Special Catalogs:** Archival records and records management
(card).

★4571★
FLORIDA STATE COURT OF APPEAL - 3RD DISTRICT - LAW LIBRARY (Law)
2001 S.W. 117th Ave.
Box 650307   Phone: (305) 552-2900
Miami, FL 33165   Rosemary E. Helsabeck, Libn.
Founded: 1960. **Staff:** Prof 1. **Subjects:** Law. **Holdings:** 36,000 volumes.
Subscriptions: 56 journals and other serials. **Services:** Library open to
attorneys and law students.

★4572★
FLORIDA STATE DEPT. OF AGRICULTURE AND CONSUMER SERVICES -
   DIVISION OF PLANT INDUSTRY - LIBRARY (Sci-Tech)
Box 1269   Phone: (904) 372-3505
Gainesville, FL 32602   June B. Jacobson, Libn.
Founded: 1915. **Staff:** Prof 1; Other 1. **Subjects:** Entomology, apiary, plant

pathology, plant inspection, nematology. **Special Collections:** Taxonomic
Entomology Collection; Division of Plant Industry Historical Archives and
Entomology Museum. **Holdings:** 10,972 volumes; 124 microfiche units.
Subscriptions: 452 journals and other serials. **Services:** Copying; library open
to public for reference use only. **Publications:** List of publications - available
on request.

★4573★
FLORIDA STATE DEPT. OF COMMERCE - RESEARCH LIBRARY (Bus-Fin)
Fletcher Bldg., Rm. 408   Phone: (904) 487-2971
Tallahassee, FL 32301   Marilyn Cramer, Libn.
Staff: Prof 1. **Subjects:** Florida - economic development, census, cities,
counties, travel, history, description; employment and unemployment;
environment; ecology; international trade; tourism; statistics. **Holdings:** 900
books; 4100 technical reports; 2000 subject folders in 100 VF drawers.
Subscriptions: 74 journals and other serials. **Services:** Copying; library open
to public for reference use only. **Networks/Consortia:** Member of North
Florida Library Association.

★4574★
FLORIDA STATE DEPT. OF ENVIRONMENTAL REGULATION - LIBRARY
   (Env-Cons)
2600 Blair Stone Rd.   Phone: (904) 488-0870
Tallahassee, FL 32301   Kathleen Everall, Dir.
Founded: 1973. **Staff:** Prof 1; Other 1. **Subjects:** Environmental sciences,
water pollution, coastal zone management, air pollution, solid and hazardous
wastes, noise pollution. **Special Collections:** National Oceanic and
Atmospheric Administration climatic data; HURD aerial photographs; U.S.
Environmental Protection Agency, U.S. Geological Survey and Florida Bureau
of Geology reports. **Holdings:** 17,000 books and technical reports; 19 VF
drawers of newsletters and special subject articles; 1500 maps.
Subscriptions: 150 journals and other serials. **Services:** Interlibrary loans;
copying; library open to public for reference use only. **Publications:** Monthly
acquisitions list.

★4575★
FLORIDA STATE DEPT. OF HEALTH & REHABILITATIVE SERVICES - HRS
   RESOURCE CENTER
1217 Pearl St.
Box 210
Jacksonville, FL 32231
Defunct. Holdings absorbed by Jacksonville Health Education Programs, Inc. -
Borland Health Sciences Library.

★4576★
FLORIDA STATE DEPT. OF HEALTH & REHABILITATIVE SERVICES -
   RESOURCE CENTER
1317 Winewood Blvd., Bldg. 2, Rm. 118
Tallahassee, FL 32301
Defunct

★4577★
FLORIDA STATE DEPT. OF LEGAL AFFAIRS - ATTORNEY GENERAL'S
   LIBRARY (Law)
Capitol Bldg.   Phone: (904) 488-6040
Tallahassee, FL 32301   Ann C. Kaklamanos, Libn.
Staff: Prof 1; Other 1. **Subjects:** Law and related subjects. **Holdings:** 35,000
volumes. **Services:** Interlibrary loans; copying; library open to public.
Computerized Information Services: LEXIS, WESTLAW.

★4578★
FLORIDA STATE DEPT. OF NATURAL RESOURCES - BUREAU OF GEOLOGY
   LIBRARY (Sci-Tech)
903 W. Tennessee St.   Phone: (904) 488-9380
Tallahassee, FL 32304   Mary Ann Cleveland, Libn.
Founded: 1908. **Staff:** Prof 1; Other 1. **Subjects:** Mineral commodities,
mining and reclamation, stratigraphy, micropaleontology, petroleum
engineering, water resources. **Special Collections:** Robert Burns Campbell
Collection of geology (1400 items of general works and geological works -
personal library of R.B. Campbell, geologist); rare books in geology (150
volumes); photographic archives (2500 slides and prints); H.S. Puri
micropaleontology collection. **Holdings:** 2300 books; 3000 bound journal
volumes; 10,000 bound federal and state documents; 190 pamphlets, 500
reports and journal article reprints; 200 reels of microfilm; 1500 aerial
photographs; 9000 maps. **Subscriptions:** 35 journals and other serials.
Services: Interlibrary loans; copying (fee); SDI; library open to public for
reference use only, circulation only to approved patrons. **Computerized
Information Services:** Online systems, through Florida State University,
Strozier Library. **Networks/Consortia:** Member of Florida Library Information

Network (FLIN). **Special Indexes:** Unpublished subject bibliographies; geology indexes.

★4579★

FLORIDA STATE DEPT. OF NATURAL RESOURCES - DIV. OF STATE LANDS - BUREAU OF STATE LAND MANAGEMENT - TITLE SECTION (Plan)
3900 Commonwealth Blvd.   Phone: (904) 488-8123
Tallahassee, FL 32303   F.R. Williams, Adm., Land Records
Founded: 1908. **Staff:** 3. **Subjects:** Land matters involving the title and description of the public domain. **Special Collections:** Spanish Archives (dealing with land matters). **Holdings:** 750 volumes; surveys, plats, maps, field notes, patents. **Services:** Copying; collection open to public. **Staff:** Kathy Miklus, Rec.Spec.; Irene Randolph, Field Note Spec.

★4580★

FLORIDA STATE DEPT. OF NATURAL RESOURCES - MARINE RESEARCH LABORATORY - LIBRARY (Sci-Tech)
100 Eighth Ave., S.E.   Phone: (813) 896-8626
St. Petersburg, FL 33701   Mary G. Krost, Libn.
Staff: Prof 1; Other 2. **Subjects:** Marine biology, ichthyology, invertebrata, algology, mariculture, ecology. **Holdings:** 1925 books; 2500 bound periodical volumes; 31,500 reprints (cataloged). **Subscriptions:** 500 journals and other serials. **Services:** Interlibrary loans; library open to public for reference use only. **Computerized Information Services:** DIALOG. **Publications:** Florida Marine Research Publications, irregular; Memoirs of the Hourglass Cruises, irregular.

★4581★

FLORIDA STATE DEPT. OF STATE TREASURER - DIVISION OF INSURANCE - LEGAL BUREAU LIBRARY (Law)
Rm. 413-B Larson Bldg.
200 E. Gaines St.   Phone: (904) 488-3243
Tallahassee, FL 32304   Sandra L. Brooks
Staff: 1. **Subjects:** Law, insurance law. **Holdings:** 2000 volumes. **Services:** Library open to public on a limited basis.

★4582★

FLORIDA STATE DEPT. OF TRANSPORTATION - CENTRAL REFERENCE LIBRARY (Trans)
Burns Bldg.
Tallahassee, FL 32301   Phone: (904) 488-8572
                                          Robert Morse, Libn.
Founded: 1969. **Staff:** Prof 1; Other 1. **Subjects:** Transportation - land, air, water; accounting; law; administration. **Special Collections:** Transportation research; road operations; materials and mass transit. **Holdings:** 300 books; 200 pamphlets; 500 research reports and documents (cataloged); 8 VF drawers; unbound periodicals in boxes. **Subscriptions:** 125 journals and other serials. **Services:** Interlibrary loans; copying; library open to public with restrictions.

★4583★

FLORIDA STATE DIVISION OF ARCHIVES, HISTORY & RECORDS MANAGEMENT - FLORIDA PHOTOGRAPHIC COLLECTION (Pict)
Florida State Archives
R.A. Gray Bldg., Rm. 107
Tallahassee, FL 32301   Phone: (904) 487-2073
                                          Joan L. Morris, Archv.Supv.
Founded: 1952. **Staff:** Prof 1; Other 2. **Subjects:** Florida - places and people. **Special Collections:** 4x5 negatives from the Jacksonville Journal, 1951-1959 and the Tallahassee Democrat, 1955-1969; negatives by Gordon Spottswood & Son, 1916-1967; negatives by Harvey Slade, 1947-1974; prints and negatives by William A. Fishbaugh, Alvan S. Harper, Stanley J. Morrow, Red Kerce, Forrest Granger and from the Seldomridge portrait studio; prints from Brugert Bros. Collection, the Richard B. Hoit Collection and the Charles T. Cottrell Collection; prints by Gleason W. Romer. **Holdings:** 277,262 items, including negatives, contact prints, original prints, prints, glass negatives. **Services:** Copying; library open to public; sale of photographs. **Special Catalogs:** Index of people who appear in photographs (card). **Formerly:** Florida State University - Florida Photographic Archives.

★4584★

FLORIDA STATE DIVISION OF ARCHIVES, HISTORY & RECORDS MANAGEMENT - FLORIDA STATE ARCHIVES (Hist)
R.A. Gray Bldg.
500 S. Bronough   Phone: (904) 487-2073
Tallahassee, FL 32301   Ed Tribble, State Archv.
Staff: Prof 9; Other 2. **Subjects:** Florida history. **Holdings:** 16,000 cubic feet of state historical records; 9000 reels of microfilmed local historical records; 400 linear feet of manuscripts, 1822 to present. **Services:** Copying. **Computerized Information Services:** SPINDEX (Natl. Archives) from internal database. **Publications:** Catalog of the Florida State Archives. **Staff:** Isabell

Kirkwood, Tech.Serv.Supv.; Richard Roberts, Ref.Supv.; Carla Kemp, Pub.Rec.Supv.

★4585★

FLORIDA STATE DIVISION OF BLIND SERVICES - FLORIDA REGIONAL LIB. FOR THE BLIND & PHYSICALLY HANDICAPPED (Aud-Vis)
Box 2299   Phone: (904) 252-4722
Daytona Beach, FL 32015   Donald John Weber, Dir.
Founded: 1950. **Staff:** Prof 5; Other 24. **Subjects:** Recreational reading material for the print handicapped, blindness, physical handicaps, rehabilitation. **Special Collections:** Braille and recorded books about Florida and the South. **Holdings:** 350,000 books recorded on disc, open-reel tape, and cassette; 10,000 books in braille. **Subscriptions:** 180 journals and other serials. **Services:** Interlibrary loans; copying; library open to public; serves all legally blind and physically handicapped residents of Florida. **Computerized Information Services:** DIALOG, BRS, SDC; computerized circulation. **Networks/Consortia:** Member of U.S. Library of Congress, National Library Service for the Blind & Physically Handicapped, Regional Libraries; Southern Conference of Libraries for the Blind and Physically Handicapped. **Publications:** Newsletter, quarterly - general distribution. **Remarks:** The Florida Regional Library for the Blind and Physically Handicapped is part of the Division of Blind Services of the Florida State Department of Education. It maintains seven subregional libraries in public libraries in Hollywood, Jacksonville, Miami, Orlando, West Palm Beach, Bradenton, and Tampa. It also houses the Multistate Center for the Blind under contract from the Library of Congress. Statewide toll-free telephone number is 1-800-342-5627. **Staff:** Billie Jean Ouellette, Assoc.Dir.; Dorothy Minor, Tech.Serv./Ref.Libn.; Marjorie A. Foley, Fld.Serv.; Diane Schultz, Volunteer Coord.

FLORIDA STATE - HISTORIC PENSACOLA PRESERVATION BOARD
See: Historic Pensacola Preservation Board

★4586★

FLORIDA STATE HOSPITAL - HEALTH SCIENCE LIBRARY (Med)
Chattahoochee, FL 32324   Phone: (904) 663-7205
                                          Ada C. Ethridge, Med.Libn.
Staff: 2. **Subjects:** Psychiatry, medicine, psychology, nursing, social service. **Holdings:** 2000 books; 75 bound periodical volumes. **Subscriptions:** 50 journals and other serials; 5 newspapers. **Services:** Copying; library not open to public.

★4587★

FLORIDA STATE HOSPITAL - PATIENT/STAFF LIBRARY (Soc Sci)
Chattahoochee, FL 32324   Phone: (904) 663-7453
                                          R. Michael Collard, Act.Dir.
Founded: 1945. **Staff:** Prof 4; Other 3. **Subjects:** General and mental health topics. **Special Collections:** Career planning; sexual education; poster collection; comic book collection. **Holdings:** 15,000 volumes; 800 films and filmstrips; realia (toys, games, models); 400 record albums; photographs. **Subscriptions:** 108 journals and other serials; 11 newspapers. **Services:** Interlibrary loans; library open to hospital staff, patients and other libraries in the area. **Networks/Consortia:** Member of Gadsden-Jackson Counties Librarians's Caucus. **Special Catalogs:** Audiovisual catalog (book). **Staff:** Alexis Dean, Civil Libn.; Lenore Hart, Forensic Libn.; Ann Bruce, Libn.

★4588★

FLORIDA STATE LEGISLATURE - DIVISION OF LEGISLATIVE LIBRARY SERVICES (Soc Sci; Law)
701, The Capitol   Phone: (904) 488-2812
Tallahassee, FL 32301   B. Gene Baker, Dir.
Founded: 1949. **Staff:** Prof 3; Other 3. **Subjects:** Law, public administration, finance, welfare and transportation, natural resources. **Special Collections:** Journals of House and Senate, 1901 to present; Laws of Florida, 1822 to present; Florida Statutes, 1847 to present. **Holdings:** 30,000 classified books, general reference works and state and federal documents; 168 VF drawers of committee reports and subject files; 540 reels of microfilm; 3300 microfiche of federal documents, state session laws and periodicals. **Subscriptions:** 350 journals and other serials; 12 newspapers. **Services:** Interlibrary loans; copying; library open to public on a limited basis. **Publications:** Summary of General Legislation, annual; User's Manual, irregular - free upon request. **Staff:** Janet Lanigan, Libn.; Marjorie Lee, Libn.

FLORIDA STATE LIBRARY
See: State Library of Florida

★4589★
FLORIDA STATE MEDICAL ENTOMOLOGY LABORATORY LIBRARY (Sci-Tech)
IFAS, University of Florida
Box 520
Vero Beach, FL 32960
Phone: (305) 562-5435
Carolee Zimmerman, Sec. II-Libn.
Staff: 1. **Subjects:** Biology, biochemistry, ecology, entomology, physiology. **Holdings:** 5300 volumes. **Subscriptions:** 131 journals and other serials. **Services:** Copying; library not open to public.

FLORIDA STATE MUSEUM LIBRARY
See: University of Florida

★4590★
FLORIDA STATE OFFICE OF THE COMPTROLLER - DEPARTMENT OF BANKING & FINANCE - LEGAL LIBRARY (Law)
The Capitol, Suite 1302
Tallahassee, FL 32301
Phone: (904) 488-9896
Linda Blackwell, Sec. IV/Hd.Libn.
Staff: Prof 1; Other 2. **Subjects:** Administrative law, securities, banking, finance, accounting and auditing. **Holdings:** 2250 books; 200 bound periodical volumes; 15 Continuing Legal Education items; 30 Florida Attorney General's Reports. **Services:** Interlibrary loans; library open to public for reference use only.

★4591★
FLORIDA STATE - SOUTH FLORIDA WATER MANAGEMENT DISTRICT - REFERENCE CENTER (Env-Cons)
Box V
West Palm Beach, FL 33402-4238
Phone: (305) 686-8800
Cynthia H. Plockelman, Ref.Libn.
Founded: 1951. **Staff:** 2. **Subjects:** Flood control, hydrology, conservation of natural resources, land and water economics, water rights and legislation, land use, recreation, Florida agriculture, Florida environmental history, environmental engineering, limnology, wetland and coastal ecology. **Holdings:** 90 shelves of pamphlets, documents, reports, and statistics. **Subscriptions:** 124 journals and other serials. **Services:** Interlibrary loans; library open to public for reference use only with restrictions.

★4592★
FLORIDA STATE - SOUTHWEST FLORIDA MANAGEMENT DISTRICT - LIBRARY (Energy)
2379 Broad St.
Brooksville, FL 33512-9712
Phone: (904) 796-7201
Charles Tornabene, Jr., Libn.
Staff: Prof 1; Other 1. **Subjects:** Water resources, urban planning, ecology, engineering. **Holdings:** 10,000 books. **Subscriptions:** 50 journals and other serials. **Services:** Copying; library open to public. **Publications:** Basin Literature Assessments, annual.

★4593★
FLORIDA STATE SUPREME COURT - 11TH JUDICIAL CIRCUIT - DADE COUNTY AUXILIARY LAW LIBRARY (Law)
420 Lincoln Rd., Suite 245
Miami Beach, FL 33139
Phone: (305) 538-0314
Johanna Porpiglia, Br.Libn.
Staff: Prof 1. **Subjects:** Law. **Holdings:** 16,000 books; 200 bound periodical volumes. **Subscriptions:** 121 journals and other serials. **Services:** Copying; library open to public with restrictions.

★4594★
FLORIDA STATE SUPREME COURT LIBRARY (Law)
Supreme Court Bldg.
Tallahassee, FL 32304
Phone: (904) 488-8919
Brian S. Polley, Libn.
Founded: 1845. **Staff:** Prof 3; Other 1. **Subjects:** Law. **Holdings:** 78,500 volumes. **Subscriptions:** 350 journals and other serials. **Services:** Open to public by permission of court. **Computerized Information Services:** WESTLAW, DIALOG, Auto-Cite. **Staff:** Joan D. Cannon, Asst.Libn.; Jo A. Dowling, Ref.Libn.

★4595★
FLORIDA STATE UNIVERSITY - CTR. FOR STUDIES IN VOCATIONAL EDUC. - FLORIDA EDUCATIONAL INFO. SERV. (Educ)
2003 Apalachee Pkwy.
Tallahassee, FL 32301
Phone: (904) 644-6454
Margaret Winkler, Coord.
Staff: Prof 5; Other 10. **Subjects:** Education - vocational, technical; education theory; instructional design and innovative programs. **Holdings:** 3000 volumes; archives; ERIC microfiche collection; 8 cabinets of publisher's listings of instructional materials. **Subscriptions:** 20 journals and other serials. **Services:** Interlibrary loans; copying; SDI; library open to public. **Computerized Information Services:** DIALOG, BRS; FREE Data Base (internal database). **Publications:** F.E.I.S. Information Series, irregular. **Special Indexes:** Subject index to publisher's listings of instructional materials; thesaurus of vocational subject headings. **Staff:** Lynn Badger, Mgr./Online Searching; Peggy Haskin, Libn.; Phyllis Broomfield, Libn.; Rebecca Augustyniak, Libn.

★4596★
FLORIDA STATE UNIVERSITY - COMMUNICATION RESEARCH CENTER - LIBRARY (Soc Sci)
College of Communication
401A Diffenbaugh Bldg.
Tallahassee, FL 32306
Phone: (904) 644-5034
Dr. Barry S. Sapolsky, Dir.
Founded: 1980. **Staff:** Prof 1; Other 2. **Subjects:** Communications, research methodology, social psychology. **Special Collections:** Unpublished communication papers (500). **Holdings:** 200 books; 1500 unbound periodicals; 200 indices. **Subscriptions:** 10 journals and other serials. **Services:** Library open to public. **Publications:** Communication Research Center Research Reports series; CRC Bulletin.

FLORIDA STATE UNIVERSITY - FLORIDA PHOTOGRAPHIC ARCHIVES
See: Florida State Division of Archives, History & Records Management

FLORIDA STATE UNIVERSITY - FLORIDA SOLAR ENERGY CENTER
See: Florida Solar Energy Center

★4597★
FLORIDA STATE UNIVERSITY - INSTRUCTIONAL SUPPORT CENTER - FILM LIBRARY (Aud-Vis)
Phone: (904) 644-2820
Tallahassee, FL 32306
Dr. John W. McLanahan, Dir.
Staff: Prof 2; Other 5. **Subjects:** Language arts, literature, humanities, social sciences, science, mathematics, art, music, history, social studies, guidance, character development. **Holdings:** 4500 16mm educational films and videotapes. **Services:** Rental and referral services; center open to public. **Networks/Consortia:** Member of Consortium of University Film Centers (CUFC). **Publications:** Florida State University Films, annual - distributed in Florida and throughout the United States - upon request.

★4598★
FLORIDA STATE UNIVERSITY - LAW LIBRARY (Law)
Phone: (904) 644-1004
Tallahassee, FL 32306
Edwin M. Schroeder, Dir.
Founded: 1966. **Staff:** Prof 6; Other 8. **Subjects:** Law. **Holdings:** 217,825 volumes; 4722 reels of microfilm; 377,641 microfiche; 518 audiotapes; 131 videotapes. **Subscriptions:** 4282 journals and other serials; 26 newspapers. **Services:** Interlibrary loans; copying; library open to public. **Computerized Information Services:** LEXIS; computerized cataloging. **Networks/Consortia:** Member of SOLINET. **Publications:** Current Acquisitions List, biweekly; Law Library Handbook, annual. **Special Catalogs:** COM Catalog of Law Library holdings. **Staff:** Gail G. Reinertsen, Asst.Dir.; Wallis D. Hoffsis, Acq.Libn.; Anne D. Bardolph, Cat.Libn.; Patricia K. Simonds, Ref.Libn.; Mark S. Evans, Circ.Libn.

★4599★
FLORIDA STATE UNIVERSITY - LIBRARY SCIENCE LIBRARY (Info Sci)
Robert Manning Strozier Library
Tallahassee, FL 32306
Phone: (904) 644-1803
Adeline W. Wilkes, Univ.Libn.
Founded: 1947. **Staff:** Prof 1; Other 5. **Subjects:** Library and information science. **Special Collections:** Picture and children's books; personal papers of Joseph Wheeler and Paul Howard. **Holdings:** 57,600 books and bound periodical volumes; 3517 AV items (cataloged); annual reports of libraries; F.S.U. masters' theses (library science). **Subscriptions:** 439 journals and other serials. **Services:** Interlibrary loans; copying; library open to public for reference use only.

★4600★
FLORIDA STATE UNIVERSITY - SPECIAL COLLECTIONS (Hum)
Robert Manning Strozier Library
Tallahassee, FL 32306
Phone: (904) 644-3271
Opal M. Free, Hd.
Staff: Prof 3; Other 3. **Subjects:** Florida, Florida State University, early Americana, Confederate imprints, book arts, herbals, poetry, Napoleon, history of area business. **Special Collections:** Florida Collection (11,894 items); Childhood in Poetry (24,232 items); Rare Books (11,505); Florida State University Archives (65,124 items); Napoleon Collection (11,300 items); Scottish Collection (1673 items); Blue Ridge Institute for Southern Community Service Executives (4000 items); McGregor Collection (337 items); Lois Lenski Collection (867 items); Night Before Christmas Collection (257 items); Christmas Greetings (259 items); Fuller Warren Papers (60,900); Richard Ervin Papers (22,239); Allen Morris Papers (16,084); William S. Rosasco Papers (5184); George R. Fairbanks Papers (2017). **Holdings:** 72,590 books and bound periodical volumes; 11,332 theses and

dissertations (cataloged); 985,541 manuscripts and papers; 130,488 maps; authors' manuscripts (310 items); 52,057 archival clippings, miscellaneous serials and pamphlets; 173,670 Florida clippings and pamphlets. **Subscriptions:** 267 journals and other serials. **Services:** Copying; collection open to public. **Special Catalogs:** The Lois Lenski Collection in the Florida State University Library, compiled by Nancy Bird, 1966 (book); The French Revolution and Napoleon Collection at Florida State University, compiled by Donald D. Horward, 1973 (book); Childhood in Poetry, compiled by John MacKay Shaw, 1968 (book), Supplement 1, 1972, Supplement 2, 1976 (2 volumes); The Parodies of Lewis Carroll and Their Originals: Catalog of an Exhibition with Notes by John MacKay Shaw, 1960 (book); St. Nicholas Poetry Index, 1873-1943, compiled by John MacKay Shaw, 1965 (book); What the Poets Have to Say About Childhood: An Exhibition of One Hundred Books...John MacKay Shaw, 1966 (book); The Poetry of Sacred Song; A Short-Title List Supplementing Childhood in Poetry - A Catalog, compiled by John MacKay Shaw, 1972 (book); A Sketch of the Fuller Warren Papers in the Special Collections Division of the Florida State University Library, 1974 (book); A Sketch of the Doak Campbell Papers in the Special Collections Division of the Florida State University Library, 1974 (book); A List of the Records of the Blue Ridge Institute for Southern Community Service Executives, 1927-1977, compiled by Shirley J. Fogle, on deposit in the Florida State University Library. **Staff:** Susan Hamburger, Asst.Libn.; Burton Altman, Assoc.Libn./Pepper Coll.

★4601★
FLORIDA STATE UNIVERSITY - WARREN D. ALLEN MUSIC LIBRARY (Mus)
Phone: (904) 644-5028
Tallahassee, FL 32306　　Dale L. Hudson, Music Libn.
Staff: Prof 1; Other 2. **Subjects:** Music. **Holdings:** 16,000 books; 2500 bound periodical volumes; 38,000 music scores and 21,500 music recordings (cataloged). **Subscriptions:** 100 journals and other serials. **Services:** Interlibrary loans; library open to public with permission of librarian. **Computerized Information Services:** Computerized circulation. **Special Indexes:** Song Index of recordings and song collections in library (card).

FLORISSANT FOSSIL BEDS NATIONAL MONUMENT
See: U.S. Natl. Park Service

FLOROVSKY (Fr. Georges) LIBRARY
See: St. Vladimir's Orthodox Theological Seminary - Fr. Georges Florovsky Library

FLOWER VETERINARY LIBRARY
See: Cornell University

★4602★
FLOYD MEDICAL CENTER - LIBRARY (Med)
Turner McCall Blvd.　　Phone: (404) 295-5500
Rome, GA 30161　　Mark W. Lashley, Med.Libn.
Founded: 1960. **Staff:** Prof 1. **Subjects:** Medicine, nursing, hospital administration. **Holdings:** 1115 books; 2295 bound periodical volumes. **Subscriptions:** 100 journals and other serials. **Services:** Interlibrary loans; copying; library open to public with restrictions.

FLUID POWER NATIONAL INFORMATION CENTER
See: National Fluid Power Association

★4603★
FLUIDYNE ENGINEERING CORPORATION - TECHNICAL LIBRARY (Sci-Tech; Energy)
5900 Olson Memorial Hwy.　　Phone: (612) 544-2721
Minneapolis, MN 55422　　Marlys J. Johnson, Tech.Libn.
Staff: Prof 1; Other 1. **Subjects:** Fluidized bed combustion, magnetohydrodynamics, aerospace, alternate sources of energy. **Holdings:** 1000 books; 50 bound periodical volumes; 35,000 documents. **Subscriptions:** 100 journals and other serials. **Services:** Interlibrary loans; copying; library open to public with restrictions. **Computerized Information Services:** DIALOG, DOE/RECON, NASA/RECON. **Networks/Consortia:** Member of Twin Cities Standards Cooperators.

★4604★
FLUKE (John) MANUFACTURING CO., INC. - LIBRARY (Sci-Tech)
6920 Seaway Blvd.
Everett, WA 98206　　Gladys Cloakey, Libn.
Founded: 1965. **Subjects:** Electronics. **Holdings:** 1500 books; manufacturers' catalogs; military specifications. **Subscriptions:** 105 journals and other serials. **Services:** Interlibrary loans; copying; library not open to public.

★4605★
FLUOR CORPORATION - FLUOR POWER SERVICES, INC. - LIBRARY (Sci-Tech)
200 W. Monroe　　Phone: (312) 368-3719
Chicago, IL 60606　　Eileen J. Seaberg, Hd.Libn.
Staff: Prof 2. **Subjects:** Engineering - civil, mechanical, electrical, nuclear, environmental. **Holdings:** 4500 books; 118 bound periodical volumes; engineering standards. **Subscriptions:** 120 journals and other serials. **Services:** Interlibrary loans; library open to local libraries. **Networks/Consortia:** Member of Council of Planning Librarians (CPL). **Staff:** Jolanta Mielniewski, Lib.Asst.

★4606★
FLUOR ENGINEERS, INC. - ENGINEERING LIBRARY (Bus-Fin; Sci-Tech)
3333 Michelson Dr.　　Phone: (714) 975-2000
Irvine, CA 92730　　Pam Sammons, Tech.Libn.
Founded: 1972. **Staff:** Prof 1; Other 3. **Subjects:** Engineering - structural, mechanical, piping, electrical, vessel, control systems; management. **Special Collections:** Standards (3000); contract data; codes. **Holdings:** 2000 books; 30 bound periodical volumes; 11,000 other cataloged items; 5000 catalogs; 3000 contract materials. **Subscriptions:** 85 journals and other serials. **Services:** Library not open to public. **Computerized Information Services:** SDC; computerized cataloging. **Publications:** Attention, newsletter, monthly. **Special Indexes:** Vendor catalog (computerized index).

★4607★
FLUOR ENGINEERS, INC. - FLUOR HOUSTON LIBRARY (Energy)
Box 35000　　Phone: (713) 662-3960
Houston, TX 77035　　Camille M. Powell, Tech.Libn.
Founded: 1967. **Staff:** Prof 1; Other 2. **Subjects:** Engineering - petroleum, chemical, design, environmental; occupational safety; construction. **Special Collections:** Coal and oil shale technologies. **Holdings:** 4000 books and bound periodical volumes; 5000 descriptive job books. **Subscriptions:** 61 journals and other serials. **Services:** Interlibrary loans; copying; SDI; library open to public by appointment. **Computerized Information Services:** DIALOG, SDC, DOE/RECON. **Publications:** Library Highlights.

★4608★
FLUOR OCEAN SERVICES, INC. - ENGINEERING LIBRARY (Sci-Tech)
6200 Hillcroft
Box 36878　　Phone: (713) 776-4369
Houston, TX 77036　　Juanna I. Gee, Libn.
Founded: 1972. **Staff:** Prof 1; Other 1. **Subjects:** Offshore construction, ocean engineering. **Special Collections:** Offshore Technology Conference Proceedings. **Holdings:** 1000 books; 200 society specifications and codes; 200 navigation charts. **Subscriptions:** 35 journals and other serials. **Services:** Interlibrary loans (fee); copying; library open to public by appointment. **Computerized Information Services:** DIALOG, SDC.

★4609★
FLUSHING HOSPITAL AND MEDICAL CENTER - MEDICAL LIBRARY (Med)
4500 Parsons Blvd.　　Phone: (212) 670-5653
Flushing, NY 11355-9980　　Maria Czechowicz, Dir.
Founded: 1940. **Staff:** Prof 1; Other 2. **Subjects:** Medicine and allied sciences. **Holdings:** 5500 books; 1900 bound periodical volumes; 5 VF drawers of pamphlets and clippings; Audio-Digest tapes. **Subscriptions:** 242 journals and other serials. **Services:** Interlibrary loans; copying; library open to public for reference use only.

FLYNT (Henry N.) LIBRARY
See: Historic Deerfield, Inc. - Henry N. Flynt Library

★4610★
FMC CORPORATION - AGRICULTURAL CHEMICAL GROUP - RESEARCH AND DEVELOPMENT DEPT. - TECHNICAL LIBRARY
100 Niagara St.
Middleport, NY 14105
Defunct. Holdings absorbed by FMC Corporation - Chemical Research & Development Center - Technical Information Service.

★4611★
FMC CORPORATION - CENTRAL ENGINEERING LABORATORIES - LIBRARY (Sci-Tech)
1185 Coleman Ave.
Box 580
Santa Clara, CA 95052　　Phone: (408) 289-2529
　　Keye L. Luke, Libn.
Founded: 1960. **Staff:** Prof 2; Other 1. **Subjects:** Agricultural and mining machinery, food processing equipment, industrial materials handling, construction equipment, materials testing, packaging machinery. **Holdings:**

4800 books; 2000 industrial standards; 9800 technical reports. **Subscriptions:** 447 journals and other serials. **Services:** Interlibrary loans; copying; SDI; library open to public for reference use only. **Computerized Information Services:** DIALOG, SDC, BRS. **Networks/Consortia:** Member of CIN; CLASS. **Publications:** Library Acquisitions Bulletin, monthly - to employees; Periodicals Received, annual. **Staff:** Cheryl L. Groen, Asst.Libn.

FMC CORPORATION - CHAIN DIVISION
See: PT Components, Inc. - Chain Division

★4612★
FMC CORPORATION - CHEMICAL RESEARCH & DEVELOPMENT CENTER - TECHNICAL INFORMATION SERVICES (Sci-Tech)
Box 8   Phone: (609) 452-2300
Princeton, NJ 08540   Paul Garwig, Mgr., Tech.Info.Serv.
Founded: 1956. **Staff:** Prof 9; Other 7. **Subjects:** Chemistry, chemical engineering, agricultural chemicals. **Holdings:** 20,000 books; 20,000 bound periodical volumes; reports; U.S. chemical patents since 1955 (microform). **Subscriptions:** 700 journals and other serials. **Services:** Interlibrary loans; copying; literature searching; library open to public on a limited basis. **Computerized Information Services:** Online systems; computerized circulation. **Remarks:** Contains holdings of the former FMC Corporation - Agricultural Chemical Group - Research and Development Dept. - Technical Library.

★4613★
FMC CORPORATION - CORPORATE LIBRARY (Bus-Fin)
200 E. Randolph   Phone: (312) 861-5705
Chicago, IL 60601   Marjorie L. Lock, Corp.Libn.
Founded: 1979. **Staff:** Prof 1; Other 1. **Subjects:** Business, management, finance. **Holdings:** 3000 books; 200 bound periodical volumes; 1000 SRI Technical reports; 500 A.D. Little reports; 1500 Conference Board publications. **Subscriptions:** 100 journals and other serials; 5 newspapers. **Services:** Interlibrary loans; copying; SDI; library open to other libraries. **Computerized Information Services:** DIALOG, Dow Jones News Retrieval, SDC, New York Times Information Service; computerized cataloging. **Networks/Consortia:** Member of Chicago Library System.

★4614★
FMC CORPORATION - MARINE COLLOIDS DIVISION - LIBRARY (Sci-Tech)
Box 308   Phone: (207) 594-4436
Rockland, ME 04841   Barbara Swift, Libn.
Staff: Prof 1. **Subjects:** Colloid science, chemistry, biochemistry, clinical chemistry, seaweeds. **Holdings:** 2500 books; 250 bound periodical volumes; 10,000 reprints. **Subscriptions:** 60 journals and other serials. **Services:** Interlibrary loans; library open to public with restrictions. **Computerized Information Services:** DIALOG. **Networks/Consortia:** Member of Health Science Library Information Cooperative. **Publications:** Newsletter, irregular - to library users.

★4615★
FMC CORPORATION - ORDNANCE DIVISION - OD TECHNICAL LIBRARY (Sci-Tech)
1105 Coleman Ave.
Box 1201   Phone: (408) 289-3490
San Jose, CA 95108   Sheila Smokey, Supv., Tech.Lib.
Staff: Prof 3; Other 1. **Subjects:** Armored military vehicles; ordnance; weapon systems; engineering - mechanical, electrical, human factors. **Holdings:** 2100 books; 35,000 specifications and technical reports (hard copy and microfiche); 3000 military technical manuals; 4000 in-house test reports. **Subscriptions:** 284 journals and other serials. **Services:** Interlibrary loans; copying; library open to public by appointment. **Computerized Information Services:** DIALOG, TECH-NET, SDC, DTIC, ON-TYME; internal database; computerized cataloging, acquisitions and circulation. **Networks/Consortia:** Member of CIN. **Publications:** Monthly acquisitions list. **Staff:** Kathy Koch, Asst.Libn., Cat.; Sumedha Shende, Asst.Libn., Ref.

FOGELMAN (Raymond) LIBRARY
See: New School for Social Research - Raymond Fogelman Library

FOGG ART MUSEUM
See: Harvard University - Fine Arts Library

FOGG (James Lemont) MEMORIAL LIBRARY
See: Art Center College of Design - James Lemont Fogg Memorial Library

FOGLER (Raymond H.) LIBRARY
See: University of Maine, Orono - Raymond H. Fogler Library

FOHRMAN LIBRARY
See: Condell Memorial Hospital

★4616★
FOI SERVICES, INC. - LIBRARY (Food-Bev)
12315 Wilkins Ave.   Phone: (301) 881-0410
Rockville, MD 20852   John E. Carey, Gen.Mgr.
Founded: 1975. **Staff:** Prof 6; Other 2. **Subjects:** Food and Drug Administration documents. **Holdings:** 35,000 documents. **Services:** Copying; library open to clients only. **Computerized Information Services:** Online systems. **Publications:** FDA Freedom of Information Log; Index of FDA Regulatory Letters; EPA Freedom of Information Log, all weekly - by subscription. **Also Known As:** Freedom of Information Services, Inc. **Staff:** Francine R. Klein, Off.Mgr.; Andrea Kronzek, Info.Spec.; Reba R. Heyman, Info.Spec.; Mary Hoffman, Info.Spec.

★4617★
FOLEY & LARDNER - LIBRARY (Law)
777 E. Wisconsin Ave.   Phone: (414) 271-2400
Milwaukee, WI 53202   Noreen Link, Libn.
Staff: Prof 1; Other 4. **Subjects:** Law - general, labor, banking, antitrust; taxation. **Holdings:** 18,500 books; 25 bound periodical volumes; 550 pamphlets (cataloged); 20 series in microform. **Subscriptions:** 300 journals and other serials. **Services:** Interlibrary loans; copying; library not open to public. **Computerized Information Services:** LEXIS. **Networks/Consortia:** Member of Library Council of Metropolitan Milwaukee, Inc. (LCOMM). **Publications:** Information Bulletin; Summary of Wisconsin Legislation - both for internal distribution only. **Staff:** Susan O'Toole, Asst.Libn.

★4618★
FOLGER SHAKESPEARE LIBRARY (Hum)
201 E. Capitol St.   Phone: (202) 544-4600
Washington, DC 20003   Dr. O.B. Hardison, Jr., Dir.
Founded: 1932. **Staff:** Prof 40; Other 28. **Subjects:** Shakespeare; history of English and Western civilization in the 16th and 17th centuries; history of the theater in England especially in the 16th to 18th centuries; Renaissance drama, history and literature. **Holdings:** 230,000 books and bound periodical volumes; 50,000 manuscripts; 1000 reels of microfilm. **Subscriptions:** 198 journals and other serials. **Services:** Copying; library open to public with restrictions. **Networks/Consortia:** Member of RLG. **Publications:** Folger Library Newsletter, 5/year; series of publications in paper and hard cover editions. **Special Catalogs:** Catalog of Folger Books and Catalog of Folger Manuscripts (published). **Remarks:** Largest collection of Shakespeariana in the world. **Staff:** Dr. Philip A. Knachel, Assoc.Dir.; Dr. John Andrews, Dir. of Res.; Dr. Robert Glick, Dir. of Dev.; Lilly Lievsay, Hd.Cat. & Cur.; Dr. Nati H. Krivatsy, Ref.Libn.; Elizabeth Niemyer, Acq.Libn.

FOLK-MUSIC COLLECTION, FRIENDS OF MUSIC
See: Denver Public Library

FOLKLORE AND LANGUAGE ARCHIVE
See: Memorial University of Newfoundland

FOLKS (Homer) ARCHIVES
See: Columbia University - Whitney M. Young, Jr. Memorial Library of Social Work

FOLSOM LIBRARY
See: Rensselaer Polytechnic Institute

FOND DU LAC COUNTY LAW LIBRARY
See: Wisconsin State

FONDREN LIBRARY
See: Rice University

FONDREN LIBRARY
See: Southern Methodist University - Mc Cord Theater Collection

★4619★
FONTENELLE FOREST NATURE CENTER - REFERENCE LIBRARY (Env-Cons; Hist)
1111 Bellevue Blvd., N.   Phone: (402) 731-3140
Bellevue, NE 68005   Robert W. Fluchel, Dir.
Founded: 1974. **Subjects:** Natural history and ecology, Missouri Valley history. **Special Collections:** Rare books on natural history. **Holdings:** 700 books; 32 bound periodical volumes; 1000 pamphlets; extensive clipping file of nature magazines. **Subscriptions:** 20 journals and other serials. **Services:** Library open to public for reference use only. **Remarks:** Maintained by the

Fontenelle Forest Association.

FOOD AND FEED GRAIN INSTITUTE
See: Kansas State University

★4620★

FOOD MARKETING INSTITUTE - INFORMATION SERVICE (Bus-Fin; Food-Bev)
1750 K St., N.W.   Phone: (202) 452-8444
Washington, DC 20006   Barbara L. McBride, Mgr., Info.Serv.
Founded: 1952. **Staff:** 6. **Subjects:** Food distribution. **Services:** Interlibrary loans; copying; service open to public by appointment. **Publications:** Reference Point, Food Industry Abstracts, monthly; Weekly Card Service; Cumulative Index; Scanning Installation Update, monthly - to members; for sale to nonmembers.

FOOD AND NUTRITION INFORMATION CENTER
See: U.S.D.A. - Human Nutrition Information Service

★4621★

FOOD PROTEIN RESEARCH AND DEVELOPMENT CENTER - LIBRARY (Food-Bev)
Texas A & M University, F.E. Box 183   Phone: (713) 845-2741
College Station, TX 77843   Dr. E.W. Lusas, Dir.
Subjects: Processing of soybeans, peanuts, cotton-seed, sunflower and sesame. **Subscriptions:** 32 journals and other serials. **Remarks:** Collection of reference texts and reprints is on file for internal use and is available to the public with restrictions.

FOOD RESEARCH INSTITUTE
See: Stanford University

★4622★

FOOTE CONE & BELDING - CREATIVE ARCHIVES (Bus-Fin)
101 Park Ave.   Phone: (212) 907-1577
New York, NY 10178   Barbara Hogenson, Dir.
Founded: 1982. **Staff:** Prof 1; Other 1. **Subjects:** Advertising. **Special Collections:** Historical collection of Foote Cone & Belding advertisements and commercials. **Holdings:** 80 books; 8000 slides; 3000 commercials. **Subscriptions:** 50 journals and other serials; 5 newspapers. **Services:** Archives open to public by appointment. **Computerized Information Services:** Computerized cataloging. **Formerly:** Its Library.

★4623★

FOOTE CONE & BELDING - INFORMATION CENTER (Bus-Fin)
401 N. Michigan Ave.   Phone: (312) 467-9200
Chicago, IL 60611   John Kok, Dir.
Founded: 1977. **Staff:** Prof 12; Other 4. **Subjects:** Advertising and marketing. **Holdings:** 1000 books and bound periodical volumes; 1500 subject files; 750 company files. **Subscriptions:** 640 journals and other serials; 10 newspapers. **Services:** Center open to public by appointment. **Computerized Information Services:** DIALOG, SDC, New York Times Information Service, Advertising and Marketing Intelligence Service (AMI), Dow Jones News Retrieval, Info Globe. **Networks/Consortia:** Member of Metropolitan Chicago Library Assembly; Chicago Library System. **Staff:** Janice Johnson, Hd.Libn.; Faye Brill, Mgr., Desk Res.; Nada Trifunovich, Desk Res.; Sharon Waycuilis, Desk Res.; Marsha Smisko, Desk Res.; Mary McCormick, Libn.; Mary Blankenheim, Libn.; Joanne Humphreville, Libn.; Mary Beth Markus, Libn.

★4624★

FOOTE MINERAL COMPANY - RESEARCH AND ENGINEERING DEPARTMENT LIBRARY (Sci-Tech)†
Rte. 100   Phone: (215) 363-6500
Exton, PA 19341   M.R. Abernathy, Libn.
Founded: 1948. **Staff:** Prof 1. **Subjects:** Chemistry, metallurgy, ceramics. **Holdings:** 3400 volumes; company reports and patents; microfilm. **Services:** Interlibrary loans; copying (by special request); library may be consulted by special authorization.

★4625★

FOOTHILL COLLEGE - ELECTRONICS MUSEUM - DE FOREST MEMORIAL ARCHIVES (Sci-Tech)
12345 El Monte Rd.   Phone: (415) 948-8590
Los Altos Hills, CA 94022   Len Lansdowne, Cur.
Founded: 1973. **Staff:** Prof 2; Other 3. **Subjects:** Early radio, electronics. **Special Collections:** Collections of Dr. Lee de Forest, Dr. Cledo Brunetti, Harold Elliott, Douglas Perham and Royden Thornberg. **Holdings:** 1342 books; 125 bound periodical volumes; 1400 museum artifacts (cataloged); 30 boxes of manuscripts; 6 boxes of patents; 9 VF drawers of documents and clippings; 10 boxes of scrapbooks; microfilm; pamphlets. **Subscriptions:** 10 journals and other serials. **Services:** Library open to qualified researchers. **Staff:** Walter Warren, Dir.

★4626★

FOOTHILLS HOSPITAL EDUCATIONAL SERVICES CENTER (Med)
1403 29th St. N.W.   Phone: (403) 270-1460
Calgary, AB, Canada T2N 2T9   Ruth MacRae, Coord.
Founded: 1965. **Staff:** 3. **Subjects:** Nursing. **Holdings:** 3500 books and bound periodical volumes; 1000 AV items. **Subscriptions:** 63 journals and other serials. **Services:** Interlibrary loans; library open to public with restrictions. **Formerly:** Its School of Nursing - Library.

★4627★

FOOTHILLS PIPE LINES (Yukon) LTD. - LIBRARY (Sci-Tech)
205 5th Ave., S.W., No. 1600   Phone: (403) 294-4606
Calgary, AB, Canada T2P 2V7   Oresta Esquibel, Hd.Libn.
Founded: 1976. **Staff:** 3. **Subjects:** Engineering, pipelines, northern environment, regulations. **Holdings:** 10,000 books and documents. **Subscriptions:** 300 journals and other serials; 10 newspapers. **Services:** Interlibrary loans; copying; SDI; library open to public. **Computerized Information Services:** SDC, CAN/OLE, Info Globe. **Publications:** Current awareness bulletin, quarterly.

★4628★

FORBES HEALTH SYSTEM - COLUMBIA HEALTH CENTER LIBRARY (Med)
Penn Ave. & West St.   Phone: (412) 247-2541
Pittsburgh, PA 15221   Susan V. Reber, Libn.
Founded: 1941. **Staff:** Prof 1; Other 1. **Subjects:** Nursing and medicine. **Holdings:** 2495 books; 1176 bound periodical volumes; 4 VF drawers of material. **Subscriptions:** 122 journals and other serials. **Services:** Interlibrary loans; copying; SDI; library open to hospital personnel. **Networks/Consortia:** Member of Pittsburgh-East Hospital Library Cooperative. **Publications:** Forbes Libraries Booktales, quarterly.

★4629★

FORBES HEALTH SYSTEM - CORPORATE OFFICE LIBRARY (Med; Bus-Fin)
500 Finley St.   Phone: (412) 665-3570
Pittsburgh, PA 15206   Susan V. Reber, Libn.
Founded: 1976. **Staff:** Prof 1; Other 1. **Subjects:** Business management, medicine, law. **Holdings:** 1278 books; 24 bound periodical volumes; 55 tapes; 3 VF drawers of pamphlets and clippings. **Services:** Interlibrary loans; copying; SDI; library open to public with restrictions. **Networks/Consortia:** Member of Pittsburgh-East Hospital Library Cooperative. **Publications:** Forbes Libraries Booktales, biennial.

★4630★

FORBES HEALTH SYSTEM - EAST SUBURBAN HEALTH CENTER - MEDICAL LIBRARY (Med)
2570 Haymaker Rd.   Phone: (412) 273-2422
Monroeville, PA 15146   Elisabeth Barclay, Med.Libn.
Founded: 1978. **Staff:** Prof 1. **Subjects:** Medicine, nursing, family practice, obstetrics, gynecology, pediatrics. **Holdings:** 1614 books; 462 bound periodical volumes; Audio-Digest tapes. **Subscriptions:** 94 journals and other serials. **Services:** Interlibrary loans; copying; SDI; library open to affiliated allied health programs. **Computerized Information Services:** MEDLARS. **Networks/Consortia:** Member of Pittsburgh-East Hospital Library Cooperative. **Publications:** Forbes Libraries Booktales, irregular.

★4631★

FORBES HEALTH SYSTEM - PITTSBURGH SKILLED NURSING CENTER LIBRARY (Med)
Frankstown Ave. & Washington Blvd.   Phone: (412) 665-3050
Pittsburgh, PA 15206   Susan V. Reber, Libn.
Staff: Prof 1; Other 1. **Subjects:** Medicine, nursing, geriatrics. **Holdings:** 773 books; 117 bound periodical volumes; reprints and clippings. **Subscriptions:** 72 journals and other serials. **Services:** Interlibrary loans; copying; library open to public with restrictions. **Networks/Consortia:** Member of Pittsburgh-East Hospital Library Cooperative. **Publications:** Forbes Libraries Booktales, biennial.

★4632★

FORBES LIBRARY (Hist)
20 West St.   Phone: (413) 584-8550
Northampton, MA 01060   Blaise Bisaillon, Dir.
Founded: 1895. **Staff:** Prof 5; Other 37. **Special Collections:** Calvin Coolidge Memorial Room Collection; Kingsley Room (Northampton history) Collection; genealogical collection; Connecticut Valley History; Japan and

Japanese books; Walter E. Corbin Collection of Photographic Prints and Slides. **Holdings:** 297,500 volumes; musical scores. **Services:** Interlibrary loans; copying; library open to public. **Special Indexes:** Index to local news in Daily Hampshire Gazette. **Staff:** Stanley Greenberg, Asst.Dir.

★4633★
FORBES, INC. - LIBRARY (Bus-Fin; Publ)
60 Fifth Ave.   Phone: (212) 620-2237
New York, NY 10011   Dolores Lataniotis, Libn.
Founded: 1960. **Staff:** Prof 5; Other 4. **Subjects:** Finance, investments, company history, business. **Holdings:** 2000 volumes; 311 VF drawers of company annual reports, brokerage reports, clippings and industry subject files; 30 drawers of newspapers on microfilm. **Subscriptions:** 300 journals and other serials; 12 newspapers. **Services:** Interlibrary loans; library open to public for approved research projects. **Special Indexes:** Index to Forbes Magazine, 1917 to present (card). **Staff:** Clarita Jones, Asst.Libn.

FORBES MEDICAL LIBRARY
See: Children's Hospital

★4634★
FORD AEROSPACE & COMMUNICATIONS CORP. - AERONUTRONIC DIVISION - TECHNICAL INFORMATION SERVICES (Sci-Tech)
Ford Rd.   Phone: (714) 720-5872
Newport Beach, CA 92663   L.H. Linder, Mgr., Tech.Info.Serv.
Founded: 1957. **Staff:** Prof 2; Other 1. **Subjects:** Mathematics, astronomy, physics, meteorology, metallurgy, chemistry, biology, engineering and management, aerospace research, electronics. **Holdings:** 19,400 books; 6680 bound periodical volumes; 402,000 technical reports. **Subscriptions:** 211 journals and other serials. **Services:** Interlibrary loans; copying; translation; current awareness searching; retrospective literature searching. **Computerized Information Services:** DIALOG, DTIC. **Publications:** Acquisitions List; Periodical Holdings; Handbook, irregular. **Staff:** I. Mann, Res.Libn.

★4635★
FORD AEROSPACE & COMMUNICATIONS CORP. - COMMUNICATIONS SYSTEMS LIBRARY
2101 Blair Mill Rd.
Willow Grove, PA 19090
Defunct

★4636★
FORD AEROSPACE & COMMUNICATIONS CORP. - WESTERN DEVELOPMENT LABORATORIES (WDL) - TECHNICAL LIBRARY (Sci-Tech)†
3939 Fabian Way   Phone: (415) 494-7400
Palo Alto, CA 94303   Cynthia Turgeon, Libn.
Founded: 1959. **Staff:** Prof 1. **Subjects:** Higher mathematics, electronics, space sciences, physics. **Special Collections:** Bell System Laboratories Monographs, 1926-1972. **Holdings:** 9000 books; 800 bound periodical volumes; 14,000 technical reports; 6 VF drawers of government documents; 3 VF drawers of meeting papers. **Subscriptions:** 151 journals and other serials. **Services:** Interlibrary loans; copying; library not open to public.

FORD ARCHIVES
See: Henry Ford Museum and Greenfield Village

★4637★
FORD, BACON & DAVIS, INC. - LIBRARY (Energy)†
2 Broadway   Phone: (212) 344-3200
New York, NY 10004   Joan Frick, Libn.
Founded: 1894. **Staff:** Prof 1. **Subjects:** Public utilities, valuation, power plants, water supply, petroleum, natural gas, geology, oil and gas pipelines. **Holdings:** 10,000 volumes. **Subscriptions:** 100 journals and other serials. **Services:** Interlibrary loans; library open to SLA members.

FORD FORESTRY CENTER
See: Michigan Technological University

★4638★
FORD FOUNDATION - INVESTMENT RESEARCH LIBRARY (Bus-Fin)
320 E. 43rd St., 9th Fl.   Phone: (212) 573-5221
New York, NY 10017   Mary Camper-Titsingh, Investment Res.Libn.
Founded: 1971. **Staff:** Prof 2; Other 1. **Subjects:** U.S. and international investments; money and banking; business conditions (U.S. and international); statistics; social responsibility. **Holdings:** 450 books; 2500 corporate files; 50 industry and subject files. **Subscriptions:** 200 journals and other serials. **Services:** Interlibrary loans; copying; library not open to public. **Computerized**

Information Services: DIALOG, SDC, New York Times Information Service. **Staff:** Nick Sayward, Asst.Libn.

★4639★
FORD FOUNDATION - LIBRARY (Soc Sci)
320 E. 43rd St.   Phone: (212) 573-5155
New York, NY 10017   Susan T. Newman, Libn.
Founded: 1953. **Staff:** Prof 3; Other 2. **Subjects:** Economic and technical assistance, urban affairs, education, philanthropy, social sciences, population. **Holdings:** 20,575 volumes; 1500 reels of microfilm. **Subscriptions:** 765 journals and other serials. **Services:** Interlibrary loans; copying; SDI; library open to public if material not available elsewhere. **Computerized Information Services:** DIALOG, New York Times Information Service. **Networks/Consortia:** Member of METRO; Consortium of Foundation Libraries. **Staff:** Martha Lazarevic, Tech.Serv.Libn.; Mary Harding, Ref.Libn.; Miss Jan Ferrell, Ser.Acq.Supv.; Carol Gjeruldsen, Book Acq.Supv.

FORD (Henry) HOSPITAL
See: Henry Ford Hospital

FORD (Henry) MUSEUM
See: Henry Ford Museum and Greenfield Village

FORD (James B.) MEMORIAL LIBRARY
See: Explorers Club - James B. Ford Memorial Library

★4640★
FORD MOTOR COMPANY - TECHNICAL INFORMATION SECTION (Sci-Tech)
20000 Rotunda Dr.   Phone: (313) 323-1059
Dearborn, MI 48121   Douna Seiler Estry, Supv., Tech.Info.Sect.
Founded: 1920. **Staff:** Prof 5; Other 5. **Subjects:** Engineering - automotive, electrical, metallurgical, mechanical; chemistry; mathematics; physics; electronics; engineering mechanics; statistics; energy; materials; pollution; environmental health; transportation. **Holdings:** 23,000 books; 40,000 bound periodical volumes; 85 journal titles on microfilm. **Subscriptions:** 1000 journals and other serials. **Services:** Interlibrary loans; use of library for reference may be requested. **Computerized Information Services:** New York Times Information Service, NLM, DIALOG, SDC; computerized cataloging and periodical routing; thesaurus. **Publications:** Technical Reports, monthly. **Special Indexes:** Index to automotive periodical and technical literature, to technical report literature on pollution and environmental health, automotive safety, transportation, energy, and material resources (card). **Remarks:** Library serves company personnel. **Formerly:** Its Technical Information Service & Engineering & Research Library.

FORDHAM UNIVERSITY - BIOLOGY LIBRARY
See: Fordham University - Mulcahy Science Library

FORDHAM UNIVERSITY - CHEMISTRY LIBRARY
See: Fordham University - Mulcahy Science Library

★4641★
FORDHAM UNIVERSITY - LIBRARY AT LINCOLN CENTER (Educ; Soc Sci)
W. 60th St. and Columbus Ave.   Phone: (212) 841-5130
New York, NY 10023   Clement J. Anzul, Libn.
Founded: 1969. **Staff:** Prof 6; Other 8. **Subjects:** Education, educational testing and measurement, educational psychology, guidance, mental health, business, liberal arts, social work and casework, community organization, government and social welfare, delinquency and crime. **Special Collections:** ERIC; SCAN documents depository. **Holdings:** 269,157 books and bound periodical volumes; Alcohol Abstracts. **Subscriptions:** 1219 journals and other serials. **Services:** Interlibrary loans; copying; library open to public for reference use only with letter of introduction required. **Computerized Information Services:** DIALOG, Dow Jones News Retrieval. **Staff:** Anne M. Finnan, Ref.Libn.; Corinne A. Freeman, Soc.Serv.Libn.; William Austin, Circ.Libn.; Barbara A. Sykes, Cat.Libn.; Zoe Salem, Bus.Ref.Libn.

FORDHAM UNIVERSITY - LOYOLA REFERENCE LIBRARY
See: Loyola Reference Library

★4642★
FORDHAM UNIVERSITY - MULCAHY SCIENCE LIBRARY (Sci-Tech)
Mulcahy Hall, Rm. 420   Phone: (212) 933-2233
Bronx, NY 10458   Edmund P. Maloney, Circ.Libn.
Founded: 1979. **Staff:** Prof 2; Other 1. **Subjects:** Chemistry and chemical industry, seismology, spectroscopy, electronics, atomic and nuclear physics, pure mathematics, mathematical statistics, bacteriology, cytology, embryology, genetics, insects, physiology. **Holdings:** 64,659 books and bound periodical volumes. **Subscriptions:** 492 journals and other serials. **Services:**

Interlibrary loans; copying; library open to public for reference use only with letter of introduction. **Formed by the Merger of:** Its Chemistry Library and Biology Library with its Physics/Mathematics Library.

FORDHAM UNIVERSITY - PHYSICS/MATHEMATICS LIBRARY
See: Fordham University - Mulcahy Science Library

★4643★
FORDHAM UNIVERSITY - SCHOOL OF LAW LIBRARY (Law)
Lincoln Sq., 140 W. 62nd St.   Phone: (212) 956-6601
New York, NY 10023   Dr. Ludwik A. Teclaff, Law Libn.
Staff: Prof 7; Other 10. **Subjects:** Law. **Holdings:** 265,000 books and bound periodical volumes. **Subscriptions:** 3200 journals and other serials. **Services:** Copying; library open to public for reference use only on request. **Computerized Information Services:** LEXIS; computerized cataloging. **Networks/Consortia:** Member of OCLC. **Staff:** Gersten Rappaport, Asst.Libn.

★4644★
FORDHAM UNIVERSITY - SPECIAL COLLECTIONS (Hum)
Duane Library   Phone: (212) 933-2233
Bronx, NY 10458   Mary Riley, Chf.Ref.Libn.
Staff: Prof 4. **Subjects:** Literature, history, Gaelic language and literature. **Special Collections:** Charles Allen Munn Collection of Revolutionary and Early Federal Americana (98 volumes); Joseph Givernaud Collection on the French Revolution (5200 volumes); Zema Memorial Collection on Monastic History of the Middle Ages (600 volumes); McGarry Collection on Criminology (450 volumes); McGuire-McLees Collection of Gaelic Language and Literature (700 volumes); William Cobbett Collection (80 monographs and 20 manuscript letters). **Services:** Copying; library open to public with restrictions. **Computerized Information Services:** DIALOG; computerized cataloging. **Networks/Consortia:** Member of METRO.

FORE RESOURCE CENTER
See: American Medical Record Association

★4645★
FOREIGN CLAIMS SETTLEMENT COMMISSION OF THE UNITED STATES - LIBRARY (Law)†
1111 20th St., N.W., Rm. 401   Phone: (202) 653-6166
Washington, DC 20579   Karl D. Klauck, Dp.Gen.Couns.
Staff: Prof 1. **Subjects:** Commission decisions, international law, federal regulations, U.S. code and statutes. **Services:** Library open to public by appointment.

★4646★
FOREIGN MISSIONS SOCIETY OF QUEBEC - LIBRARY (Rel-Theol)
180, place Juge-Desnoyers   Phone: (514) 667-4190
Pont-Viau, Ville Laval, PQ, Canada H7G 1A4   Florian Vachon, Lib.Dir.
Founded: 1924. **Staff:** Prof 1; Other 1. **Subjects:** Theology, missiology, Holy Scripture, social sciences, biography, languages. **Holdings:** 25,000 volumes. **Subscriptions:** 121 journals and other serials. **Services:** Interlibrary loans; library not open to public.

★4647★
FOREIGN POLICY RESEARCH INSTITUTE - LIBRARY (Soc Sci)
3508 Market St., Suite 350   Phone: (215) 382-2054
Philadelphia, PA 19104
Founded: 1955. **Staff:** Prof 1; Other 1. **Subjects:** American foreign policy, regional studies, international relations, strategic and military studies. **Special Collections:** Congressional hearings collection (400). **Holdings:** 3000 books; 100 bound periodical volumes; foreign broadcast information service reports, 1952-72 (microfilm), 1972 to present (unbound volumes); Foreign Policy Research Institute publications, 1955 to present; ORBIS archives, 1957 to present. **Subscriptions:** 250 journals and other serials. **Services:** Copying; library open to public for reference use only.

★4648★
FOREIGN SERVICES RESEARCH INSTITUTE - WHITEFORD MEMORIAL LIBRARY (Soc Sci)
Box 6317   Phone: (202) 362-1588
Washington, DC 20015-0317   Ellspath Lawrence, Libn.
Staff: 3. **Subjects:** Political science, international relations, humanities, education. **Special Collections:** Prix Teilhard/Londres award manuscripts; Primers for the Age of Inner Space series books. **Holdings:** 1800 books. **Subscriptions:** 31 journals and other serials. **Services:** Interlibrary loans; library not open to public. **Publications:** Primers for the Age of Inner Space, irregular - free to university libraries. **Remarks:** Publishes research papers via Forders Press.

FOREMAN (Dr. Robert C.) HEALTH SCIENCES LIBRARY
See: Scottsdale Memorial Hospital - Dr. Robert C. Foreman Health Sciences Library

★4649★
FOREMOST INSURANCE COMPANY - LIBRARY
5800 Foremost Dr., S.E.
Box 2450
Grand Rapids, MI 49501
Defunct

★4650★
FOREMOST-MC KESSON - R & D CENTER LIBRARY (Food-Bev)
Box 2277   Phone: (415) 828-1440
Dublin, CA 94566   Joan La Manna, Libn.
Staff: Prof 1; Other 1. **Subjects:** Food technology, dairy technology, biochemistry. **Holdings:** 2600 books; 3000 bound periodical volumes; 13 VF drawers of patents; 10 VF drawers of research reports; 40 VF drawers of clippings and pamphlets (uncataloged). **Subscriptions:** 200 journals and other serials. **Services:** Interlibrary loans; will answer brief inquiries from libraries; library open to public on a contract basis. **Computerized Information Services:** DIALOG, BRS, New York Times Information Service. **Remarks:** Includes the holdings of the Foremost Dairies Company Research Department Library.

FORENSIC SCIENCE SERVICES LIBRARY
See: Orange County Sheriff/Coroner

★4651★
FOREST ENGINEERING RESEARCH INSTITUTE OF CANADA - LIBRARY (Sci-Tech)
143 Place Frontenac   Phone: (514) 694-1140
Pointe Claire, PQ, Canada H9R 4Z7   Christel Mukhopadhyay, Libn.
Founded: 1976. **Staff:** Prof 1; Other 1. **Subjects:** Forest engineering, forestry, biomass energy, transport of wood, mechanical engineering. **Special Collections:** Logging machinery patents (30 linear feet). **Holdings:** 1819 books; 2658 uncataloged reports in series; 420 periodical volumes; 4 VF drawers of annual reports; 4 linear feet of pamphlets and reprints. **Subscriptions:** 218 journals. **Services:** Interlibrary loans; copying; SDI; library open to public with restrictions. **Computerized Information Services:** DIALOG, SDC, Info Globe, QL Systems. **Publications:** Serials list, annual; Library Communications, quarterly accessions list - both distributed internally, to member companies and to selected libraries.

★4652★
FOREST HISTORY SOCIETY, INC. - LIBRARY AND ARCHIVES (Env-Cons; Hist)
109 Coral St.   Phone: (408) 426-3770
Santa Cruz, CA 95060   Mary E. Johnson, Libn.
Founded: 1946. **Staff:** Prof 1; Other 2. **Subjects:** History of forest resources and conservation. **Special Collections:** Oral history interviews with leaders of forestry and forest products industries; historical picture collection (24 VF drawers); archival collections of American Forest Institute, American Forestry Association, National Forest Products Association, Society of American Foresters and papers of foresters. **Holdings:** 3120 books; 500 bound periodical volumes; 900 archives boxes of manuscripts; 195 VF drawers of pamphlets and documents; 59 VF drawers of photograph collections; 693 oral history tapes; 100 reels of microfilmed records. **Subscriptions:** 240 journals and other serials. **Services:** Interlibrary loans; copying; library open to public for reference use only. **Publications:** Journal of Forest History, quarterly - by subscription. **Special Indexes:** Guides to Forest and Conservation History of North America. **Remarks:** The Forest History Society refers the great bulk of all forest history source materials which it finds to repositories in the U.S. and Canada which are focal points for research in forest history.

★4653★
FOREST INSTITUTE OF PROFESSIONAL PSYCHOLOGY - LIBRARY (Med)
1717 Rand Rd.   Phone: (312) 635-4333
Des Plaines, IL 60090   Donna E. Bush, Dir., Lib.Serv.
Founded: 1979. **Staff:** Prof 2; Other 1. **Subjects:** Psychology, psychiatry, medicine, family therapy, drugs, alcoholism, aging. **Holdings:** 6000 books; 210 bound periodical volumes; 2000 unbound periodicals; 100 articles. **Subscriptions:** 175 journals and other serials. **Services:** Interlibrary loans; copying; library open to public with restrictions; special borrowing provision with Morton Grove Public Library. **Computerized Information Services:** DIALOG, SDC, BRS; internal database; computerized reference. **Networks/Consortia:** Member of North Suburban Library System. **Publications:** Newsletter, weekly bulletins - for internal distribution only.

★4654★
FOREST PRODUCTS ACCIDENT PREVENTION ASSOCIATION - LIBRARY
(Sci-Tech)
Box 270   Phone: (705) 472-4120
North Bay, ON, Canada P1B 8H2   James Nugent
Staff: 1. **Subjects:** Accident and fire prevention; industrial and occupational diseases; forests and forestry; management; total loss control. **Holdings:** 160 books; 122 16mm films; 42 videotapes. **Subscriptions:** 30 journals and other serials. **Services:** Interlibrary loans; copying; library open to public with restrictions on borrowing. **Publications:** Tallyboard, bimonthly - distributed to members. **Special Catalogs:** Film catalog; Educational Materials catalog.

FOREST PRODUCTS LABORATORY LIBRARY
See: U.S. Forest Service

★4655★
FOREST PRODUCTS RESEARCH SOCIETY - AIDS INFORMATION SERVICE
(Sci-Tech; Info Sci; Energy)
2801 Marshall Ct.   Phone: (608) 231-1361
Madison, WI 53705   Mary Gordon, AIDS Abstractor
Founded: 1974. **Staff:** Prof 1; Other 1. **Subjects:** Timber - resources and harvesting; wood - machining, mechanical properties, energy; plywood and particleboard. **Holdings:** Magnetic tape database of 16,500 citations with 1000 entries/year; copies of all English articles in the AIDS system are available either on microfiche or hardcover. **Subscriptions:** 100 journals and other serials. **Services:** Interlibrary loans; copying; center open to public. **Computerized Information Services:** SDC; internal database tapes can be leased. **Publications:** 1981 Energy Bibliography; bibliographies on wood energy, noise, control in wood processing, computerized processing systems; and wood construction topics; keyword thesaurus - available on request. **Special Indexes:** Author, subject, keyword and species index to database (microfiche). **Remarks:** The AIDS database is also called Forest or Forest Products when accessed online via SDC. Over 200 worldwide references are abstracted including periodicals and government, education and trade association publications.

★4656★
FORESTA INSTITUTE FOR OCEAN AND MOUNTAIN STUDIES - ENVIRONMENTAL STUDIES CENTER
6205 Franktown Rd.
Carson City, NV 89701
Founded: 1960. **Subjects:** Ichthyology, plant and animal ecology, Western American and Nevada environment and ecology. **Special Collections:** Antarctica (2500 books, reprints, maps); rare and endangered species (2000 books, reprints). **Holdings:** 7000 books; 100 bound periodical volumes; 3000 reprints and pamphlets (cataloged); 2000 color slides; 200 maps. **Remarks:** Presently inactive.

★4657★
FORINTEK CANADA CORPORATION - EASTERN LABORATORY - LIBRARY
(Sci-Tech)
800 Montreal Rd.   Phone: (613) 744-0963
Ottawa, ON, Canada K1G 3Z5   Marjorie Wickens, Libn.
Founded: 1913. **Staff:** Prof 1; Other 1. **Subjects:** Forest products, wood chemistry and engineering; wood as an energy source. **Holdings:** 9246 books and bound periodical volumes. **Subscriptions:** 400 journals and other serials. **Services:** Interlibrary loans; copying; library open to public with restrictions. **Computerized Information Services:** DIALOG, SDC, CAN/OLE. **Networks/Consortia:** Member of Council of Federal Libraries; Ottawa-Hull Area Library Delivery Service. **Publications:** Accession lists; List of Publications, annual.

★4658★
FORINTEK CANADA CORP. - WESTERN LABORATORY - LIBRARY (Sci-Tech)
6620 N.W. Marine Dr.   Phone: (604) 224-3221
Vancouver, BC, Canada V6T 1X2   Mrs. Marion E. Johnson, Hd., Info.Rsrcs.
Founded: 1927. **Staff:** Prof 1; Other 2. **Subjects:** Wood chemistry and identification; timber engineering; wood protection and preservation; sawmilling and wood seasoning; wood machining; glues and gluing; pulping technology. **Holdings:** 3700 books; 3200 bound periodical volumes; 500 microfiche; 42 reels of microfilm; 160 VF drawers of pamphlets, reprints, internal publications; 4 films. **Subscriptions:** 303 journals and other serials. **Services:** Interlibrary loans; copying (limited); library open to public with restrictions. **Computerized Information Services:** DIALOG, SDC; computerized cataloging, acquisitions and serials. **Publications:** Occasional bibliographies; technical reports.

★4659★
FORSYTH DENTAL CENTER - PERCY HOWE MEMORIAL LIBRARY (Med)
140 The Fenway   Phone: (617) 262-5200
Boston, MA 02115   Roberta Oppenheim, Libn.
Founded: 1914. **Staff:** Prof 1; Other 4. **Subjects:** Dentistry, dental hygiene, biochemistry, microbiology, anthropology, anatomy, immunology. **Special Collections:** History of the Forsyth Dental Center (photographs); archives - photographs and memorabilia, rare books and antique dental instruments. **Holdings:** 3900 books; 6500 bound periodical volumes; pamphlets; photographs; staff reprints. **Subscriptions:** 192 journals and other serials. **Services:** Interlibrary loans (fee); library open to public with restrictions. **Computerized Information Services:** DIALOG, NLM, BRS. **Publications:** Acquisitions list, quarterly; newsletter, bimonthly.

★4660★
FORSYTH MEMORIAL HOSPITAL - JOHN C. WHITAKER LIBRARY (Med)
3333 Silas Creek Pkwy.   Phone: (919) 773-3995
Winston-Salem, NC 27103   Sandra L. Lawson, Med.Libn.
Founded: 1964. **Staff:** Prof 1; Other 1. **Subjects:** Medicine and allied health sciences. **Holdings:** 2409 books; 4294 bound periodical volumes; 237 tapes (cataloged). **Subscriptions:** 129 journals and other serials. **Services:** Computer searching; current awareness; library open to public for reference use only. **Computerized Information Services:** MEDLINE.

★4661★
FORSYTH TECHNICAL INSTITUTE - LIBRARY (Sci-Tech; Bus-Fin)
2100 Silas Creek Pkwy.   Phone: (919) 723-0371
Winston-Salem, NC 27103   Audrey B. Zablocki, Dir.
Staff: Prof 2; Other 4. **Subjects:** Technology, health, law, business, psychology, art. **Holdings:** 27,850 books; 1317 bound periodical volumes. **Subscriptions:** 303 journals and other serials; 6 newspapers. **Services:** Interlibrary loans; copying; library open to public for reference use only. **Staff:** Tom Gordon, Rd.Serv.Libn.

★4662★
FORT BELKNAP ARCHIVES, INC. - LIBRARY (Hist)
Route 1, Box 27   Phone: (817) 549-1856
Newcastle, TX 76372   K.F. Neighbours, Archv.
Founded: 1961. **Staff:** Prof 2; Other 4. **Subjects:** History - local, Texas, Southwest, frontier; genealogy; Texana and Americana. **Holdings:** 3000 books; 500 bound periodical volumes; 500 manuscripts; 10,000 clippings; 500 documents; 10 reels of microfilm of U.S. Archives documents. **Subscriptions:** 15 journals and other serials; 10 newspapers. **Services:** Copying; library open to public for reference use only. **Publications:** Report, annual; Fort Belknap Archives, Inc.; A Tour Through Fort Belknap and its Archives; Fort Belknap Frontier Saga, 1790-1980. **Remarks:** Maintained by the Board of Directors of Fort Belknap Archives, Inc. Barbara A. Ledbetter, Asst.Archv.

FORT BURGWIN RESEARCH CENTER
See: Southern Methodist University

FORT CARSON ARMY HOSPITAL
See: U.S. Army Hospitals

★4663★
FORT COLLINS PUBLIC LIBRARY - ORAL HISTORY COLLECTION (Hist)
201 Peterson   Phone: (303) 493-4422
Fort Collins, CO 80524   Charlene Tresner, Local Hist.Coord.
Staff: 1. **Subjects:** Local history. **Holdings:** 368 tapes. **Subscriptions:** 5 journals and other serials; 10 newspapers. **Services:** Copying; library open to public.

★4664★
FORT CONCHO REFERENCE LIBRARY (Hist)
213 E. Ave. D   Phone: (915) 655-9121
San Angelo, TX 76903   Wayne Daniel, Libn./Archv.
Founded: 1971. **Staff:** Prof 1. **Subjects:** Local and regional civilian and military history. **Special Collections:** M.C. Ragsdale Photographic Collection (over 500 photographs of early Fort Concho and West Texas); Oscar Ruffini Collection (drawings and specifications by pioneer architect); Papers of Captain George Gibson Huntt, 4th Calvary. **Holdings:** 3000 books; 3000 photographs (cataloged); 300 maps; 104 reels of microfilm; 10,000 pieces of archival material; 400 file folders of research material. **Subscriptions:** 30 journals and other serials. **Services:** Interlibrary loans; copying; library open to public for reference use only. **Publications:** Fort Concho Report, quarterly newsletter; Medical History of Fort Concho; Fort Concho in 1877 - all for sale.

FORT DAVIS NATL. HISTORIC SITE
See: U.S. Natl. Park Service

FORT FRONTENAC LIBRARY
See: Canada - National Defence

★4665★
FORT HAMILTON-HUGHES MEMORIAL HOSPITAL CENTER - SOHN MEMORIAL HEALTH SERVICES LIBRARY (Med)
630 Eaton Ave.   Phone: (513) 867-2310
Hamilton, OH 45013   Lois Protzman, Libn.
Founded: 1959. **Staff:** Prof 1. **Subjects:** Medicine. **Holdings:** 1000 books; 467 bound periodical volumes. **Subscriptions:** 50 journals and other serials. **Services:** Interlibrary loans; copying; library not open to public.

★4666★
FORT HAYS STATE UNIVERSITY - STERNBERG MEMORIAL MUSEUM - LIBRARY (Sci-Tech)
                     Phone: (913) 628-4286
Hays, KS 67601   Dr. Richard J. Zakrzewski, Musm.Dir.
Founded: 1953. **Staff:** 1. **Subjects:** Paleontology, geology, archeology, history. **Holdings:** 300 books; 4646 unbound periodicals (cataloged); 19 boxes of pamphlets. **Services:** Library open to qualified researchers.

FORT LARAMIE NATL. HISTORIC SITE
See: U.S. Natl. Park Service

★4667★
FORT LARNED HISTORICAL SOCIETY, INC. - SANTA FE TRAIL CENTER LIBRARY (Hist)
Rte. 3   Phone: (316) 285-2054
Larned, KS 67550   Ruth Olson, Archv.
Staff: 1. **Subjects:** History - Civil War, counties along the Santa Fe Trail, Kansas. **Special Collections:** R.R. Smith Glass Magic Lantern Slide Collection (2300 slides); Grand Army of the Republic records, B.F. Larned Post (30 boxes). **Holdings:** 2000 books; 100 bound periodical volumes; 11 boxes of W.P.A. county histories; 2 boxes of maps relating to the Santa Fe Trail; 100 items of historic sheet music; Pawnee County Archives; photographic collection; Civil War official records. **Services:** Copying; library open to public with restrictions.

FORT LARNED NATL. HISTORIC SITE
See: U.S. Natl. Park Service

★4668★
FORT LAUDERDALE HISTORICAL SOCIETY - LIBRARY & ARCHIVES (Hist)
219 Southwest 2nd Ave.   Phone: (305) 463-4431
Fort Lauderdale, FL 33301   Daniel T. Hobby, Exec.Dir.
Staff: Prof 3; Other 5. **Subjects:** Local and state history, historic preservation, genealogy. **Holdings:** 2500 books; 450 bound periodical volumes; 50 feet of manuscripts; 210 oral history cassettes; 200,000 photographs and slides. **Subscriptions:** 25 journals and other serials. **Services:** Copying; library open to public by appointment. **Publications:** New River News; In-house Guide.

FORT LE BOEUF MUSEUM
See: Pennsylvania State Historical and Museum Commission

★4669★
FORT LEE PUBLIC LIBRARY - SILENT FILM PHOTO COLLECTION (Theater; Pict)
320 Main St.   Phone: (201) 592-3614
Fort Lee, NJ 07024   Rita Altomara, Project Coord.
Staff: Prof 1; Other 1. **Subjects:** Silent films; actors and actresses; Fort Lee film studios. **Special Collections:** Silent Film Photo Collection (1000 photographs); videotaped history of Fort Lee films. **Holdings:** 500 books; periodicals on microfilm; 10 interviews on tape; 32 silent films, most made in Fort Lee. **Services:** Interlibrary loans (books only); copying; library open to public. **Networks/Consortia:** Member of Bergen County Cooperative Library System.

★4670★
FORT LEWIS COLLEGE - CENTER OF SOUTHWEST STUDIES (Area-Ethnic)
Fort Lewis College Library   Phone: (303) 247-7456
Durango, CO 81301   Dr. Robert W. Delaney, Dir.
Subjects: U.S. history, American Indians, railroads, mining, energy, water. **Special Collections:** Spanish exploration and colonization; Indians; records of geological surveys; mining; military; newspapers; railroads. **Holdings:** 7000 books; 500 bound periodical volumes; maps and photographs. **Services:**

Interlibrary loans; copying; library open to public. **Networks/Consortia:** Member of Colorado Southwest Systems. **Publications:** Occasional papers. **Special Catalogs:** Opportunities for Research, 1979.

★4671★
FORT LEWIS MILITARY MUSEUM - MUSEUM RESEARCH LIBRARY (Hist; Mil)
Main St., Bldg. 4320   Phone: (206) 967-7206
Fort Lewis, WA 98433   Barbara A. Bower, Dir.
Founded: 1974. **Staff:** 3. **Subjects:** History - war, Northwest military, Washington State. **Special Collections:** Women's Army Auxiliary Corps (letters and scrapbooks); engineer records on Fort Lewis buildings and land (100 handwritten volumes). **Holdings:** 4000 books; 1000 bound periodical volumes; 2000 technical and field manuals; 12 diaries; 200 letters; 4 VF drawers of manuscripts concerning unit histories. **Services:** Copying; library open to public on weekdays only.

★4672★
FORT LIGONIER MEMORIAL FOUNDATION - HENRY BOUQUET ROOM (Hist)
S. Market St.   Phone: (412) 238-9701
Ligonier, PA 15658   J. Martin West, Dir./Cur.
Founded: 1974. **Staff:** 1. **Subjects:** Fort Ligonier; French and Indian War; historical archeology; Arthur St. Clair; Ligonier Valley, 1758-90; fortifications. **Holdings:** 400 books; 25 notebooks of archeological field records; 10 unpublished reports manuscripts; 650 pages of correspondence on historical archeology; 800 unbound periodicals and pamphlets. **Subscriptions:** 13 journals and other serials. **Services:** Copying; library open to public by appointment. **Remarks:** The Henry Bouquet Room is a research facility dedicated to historical archeology. Fort Ligonier is a restored English frontier fort and museum.

★4673★
FORT LOGAN MENTAL HEALTH CENTER - MEDICAL LIBRARY (Med)
3520 Oxford Ave., W.   Phone: (303) 761-0220
Denver, CO 80236   Bernice N. Stone, Supv.Libn.
Founded: 1963. **Staff:** Prof 1. **Subjects:** Social psychiatry including social work, therapeutic community work and day hospital care; psychiatry; psychology; behavioral sciences. **Holdings:** 6201 books; 3213 bound periodical volumes; 5 VF drawers of pamphlets and reports. **Subscriptions:** 83 journals and other serials. **Services:** Interlibrary loans; copying; library open to public for reference use only.

FORT MC HENRY NATL. MONUMENT
See: U.S. Natl. Park Service

★4674★
FORT MALDEN NATIONAL HISTORIC PARK - LIBRARY & ARCHIVES (Hist)
100 Laird Ave.
Box 38
Amherstburg, ON, Canada N9V 2Z2   Phone: (519) 736-5416
                      Sally Snyder, Libn.
Founded: 1941. **Staff:** Prof 2; Other 1. **Subjects:** Fort Malden, War of 1812, Rebellion of 1837, Essex County history (original material and secondary sources); British and American military before 1860; weapons; domestic life in Upper Canada. **Holdings:** 1500 books; 7 VF drawers of information files; 200 photographs of Essex County. **Subscriptions:** 10 journals and other serials. **Services:** Interlibrary loans; library open to public by appointment only. **Remarks:** Maintained by Parks Canada. **Staff:** Harry Bosveld, Park Supt.

★4675★
FORT MASSAC HISTORIC SITE - LIBRARY (Hist)
Box 708   Phone: (618) 524-9321
Metropolis, IL 62960   Paul E. Fellows, Site Supt.
Founded: 1973. **Staff:** 2. **Subjects:** U.S. military history (1750-1830); weapons of early America; guides to collections in U.S. archives; plant life of Illinois. **Special Collections:** Typed copies of original Fort Massac documents, 1794-1835, (22 volumes). **Holdings:** 60 books; 15 bound periodical volumes; 35 maps (North America, 1700-1900); 6 archaeological reports of Fort Massac; 21 reels of microfilm (Anthony Wayne Papers); 5 reels of microfilm (Issac Craig Papers, 1787-1809). **Services:** Library open to public for reference use only. **Publications:** Fort Massac - Yesterday & Today, bimonthly series - for area newspapers. **Special Catalogs:** Catalogue of Fort Massac Museum acquisitions - for internal distribution only. **Remarks:** Maintained by Illinois State Department of Conservation.

FORT MEADE ARMY EDUCATION CENTER, LANGUAGE LABORATORY
See: U.S. Army - Language Training Facility

FORT MEADE MUSEUM
See: U.S. Army

FORT MIAMI HERITAGE SOCIETY
See: Genealogical Association of Southwestern Michigan

FORT NECESSITY NATL. BATTLEFIELD
See: U.S. Natl. Park Service

★4676★
FORT ONTARIO - LIBRARY (Hist)†
Oswego, NY 13126
Phone: (315) 343-4711
Wallace Workmaster, Historic Site Mgr.
Founded: 1960. **Subjects:** European, American, state and local history; Oswego military fortifications. **Holdings:** 900 volumes; 150 photographs; 1 case of vertical files; 675 slides. **Services:** Library open to public upon application.

FORT PITT MUSEUM
See: Pennsylvania State Historical & Museum Commission

FORT POLK ARMY HOSPITAL
See: U.S. Army Hospitals

FORT PULASKI NATL. MONUMENT
See: U.S. Natl. Park Service

FORT ROBINSON MUSEUM
See: Nebraska State Historical Society

★4677★
FORT SANDERS REGIONAL MEDICAL CENTER - MEDICAL/NURSING LIBRARY (Med)
1915 White Ave.
Knoxville, TN 37916
Phone: (615) 971-1293
Nedra Cook, Libn.
Staff: Prof 2; Other 4. **Subjects:** Nursing and nursing education, medicine. **Special Collections:** National League of Nursing Publication Collection. **Holdings:** 5900 books; 600 bound periodical volumes; 16 VF drawers; 75 charts, posters, transparencies; 15 cassettes, slide or filmstrip kits. **Subscriptions:** 153 journals and other serials. **Services:** Interlibrary loans; copying; library open to public. **Networks/Consortia:** Member of Knoxville Area Health Science Library Consortium. **Staff:** Sandra Chesney, Lib.Asst.

FORT SNELLING BRANCH LIBRARY
See: Minnesota Historical Society

FORT SPOKANE VISITOR CENTER
See: U.S. Natl. Park Service - Coulee Dam Natl. Recreation Area

FORT SUMTER NATL. MONUMENT
See: U.S. Natl. Park Service

★4678★
FORT TICONDEROGA ASSOCIATION, INC. - LIBRARY (Hist)
Box 390
Ticonderoga, NY 12883
Phone: (518) 585-2821
Jane M. Lape, Cur.-Libn.
Founded: 1908. **Staff:** Prof 2. **Subjects:** Champlain Valley history; United States colonial history; fortifications; early United States military history. **Special Collections:** Colonial and Revolutionary history. **Holdings:** 3500 books; 1500 bound periodical volumes; 2500 manuscripts (mainly early history of Fort Ticonderoga and Champlain Valley). **Services:** Interlibrary loans (limited); copying (limited); library open to public only by special arrangement with librarian. **Publications:** Bulletin of the Fort Ticonderoga Museum.

FORT UNION NATL. MONUMENT
See: U.S. Natl. Park Service

★4679★
FORT VALLEY STATE COLLEGE - HENRY ALEXANDER HUNT MEMORIAL LEARNING RESOURCES CENTER (Agri; Educ)†
State College Dr.
Fort Valley, GA 31030
Phone: (912) 825-6342
Dorothy Haith, Libn.
Staff: Prof 7; Other 8. **Subjects:** Education, business and economics, agriculture, science, home economics. **Special Collections:** Fort Valley State College Ethnic Heritage Collection (5293 volumes); Experiment Station Collection (3831 items). **Holdings:** 133,275 books; 26,137 bound periodical volumes; 3684 phonograph records; 719 tapes; 161,986 microtext items. **Subscriptions:** 1612 journals and other serials; 50 newspapers. **Services:** Interlibrary loans; copying; library open to public for reference use only.

Computerized Information Services: GIDC; computerized cataloging. **Networks/Consortia:** Member of OCLC through SOLINET; Central Georgia Associated Libraries. **Publications:** What's New in the LRC, quarterly. **Special Catalogs:** Ethnic heritage; microprint; Experimental Station Collection (card catalogs). **Staff:** Doris Gosier, Coord.Pub.Serv.; Elizabeth Brinson, Assoc.Dir., LRC.

FORT VANCOUVER NATL. HISTORIC SITE
See: U.S. Natl. Park Service

★4680★
FORT WARD MUSEUM - DOROTHY C.S. STARR CIVIL WAR RESEARCH LIBRARY (Hist)
4301 W. Braddock Rd.
Alexandria, VA 22304
Phone: (703) 838-4848
Wanda S. Dowell, Cur.
Founded: 1972. **Staff:** 2. **Subjects:** Civil War. **Holdings:** 1000 books; 100 unbound publications on the Civil War. **Services:** Library open to public by prior arrangements. **Remarks:** Maintained by City of Alexandria.

★4681★
FORT WAYNE BIBLE COLLEGE - S.A. LEHMAN MEMORIAL LIBRARY (Rel-Theol)
919 W. Rudisill Blvd.
Fort Wayne, IN 46807
Phone: (219) 456-2111
Wava Bueschlen, Dir. of the Lib.
Founded: 1905. **Staff:** Prof 2; Other 3. **Subjects:** Theology, education. **Holdings:** 53,000 books; 1913 bound periodical volumes; 3342 teaching aids (cataloged). **Subscriptions:** 369 journals and other serials. **Services:** Interlibrary loans; copying; library open to public with restrictions. **Computerized Information Services:** Computerized cataloging. **Networks/Consortia:** Member of OCLC through INCOLSA. **Publications:** Library Handbook.

FORT WAYNE HISTORICAL SOCIETY
See: Allen County-Fort Wayne Historical Society

★4682★
FORT WAYNE JOURNAL-GAZETTE - NEWSPAPER LIBRARY (Publ)
600 W. Main St.
Fort Wayne, IN 46802
Phone: (219) 461-8377
Rosalina Stier, Libn.
Staff: Prof 1; Other 4. **Subjects:** Newspaper reference topics. **Holdings:** 200 books; 325,502 clippings; 46,851 photographs; 748 reels of microfilm. **Services:** Copying; library open to public on a fee basis.

★4683★
FORT WORTH ART MUSEUM - LIBRARY (Art)
1309 Montgomery St.
Fort Worth, TX 76107
Phone: (817) 738-9215
David Ryan, Dir.
Founded: 1971. **Staff:** Prof 1. **Subjects:** 20th century art in all countries and all media including painting, sculpture, graphics, architecture, design, photography, video and film. **Holdings:** 5000 books; 200 bound periodical volumes; 2000 museum catalogs; 8 VF drawers containing 2000 items; 5000 slides. **Subscriptions:** 50 journals and other serials. **Services:** Interlibrary loans; copying; library open to public for research only.

★4684★
FORT WORTH PUBLIC LIBRARY - ARTS DEPARTMENT (Art; Mus)
300 Taylor St.
Fort Worth, TX 76102
Phone: (817) 870-7739
Heather L. Goebel, Dept.Mgr.
Staff: Prof 3. **Subjects:** Drawing, painting, sculpture, music and dance, entertainment, theater, movies, bullfight and rodeo, handicrafts and hobbies, architecture and city planning, antiques and interior decorating, photography, games and sports. **Special Collections:** Sheet music and scores; picture file; Mrs. John F. Lyons Collection of autographed performing artists' photographs; Hal Coffman Collection (original cartoon art); Nancy Taylor Collection (bookplates); collection of rare books. **Holdings:** 85,000 books; 6700 bound periodical volumes; 22,000 pieces of sheet music, scores and tune cards; 83 framed reproductions of paintings; 44 drawers of mounted pictures, clipped pictures, articles, pamphlets, programs. **Subscriptions:** 135 journals and other serials. **Services:** Interlibrary loans; copying; library open to public. **Networks/Consortia:** Member of North Texas Library System. **Publications:** Bibliographies, irregular. **Special Indexes:** Sheet Music Index. **Formerly:** Its Humanities Department. **Staff:** Shakuntala Gokhale, Libn.

★4685★
FORT WORTH PUBLIC LIBRARY - BUSINESS AND TECHNOLOGY DEPARTMENT (Bus-Fin; Sci-Tech)
300 Taylor St.
Fort Worth, TX 76102
Phone: (817) 870-7727
John McCracken, Sect.Mgr.
Staff: 4. **Subjects:** Business, economics, investments, science, technology.

Holdings: 62,000 books; 28 VF drawers of pamphlets and clippings. **Subscriptions:** 350 journals and other serials. **Services:** Interlibrary loans; copying. **Publications:** Bibliographies and booklists, irregular. **Staff:** Don Toups, Libn.; Ellen Wartoe, Libn.; Vi Easley, Lib. Aide.

★4686★
FORT WORTH PUBLIC LIBRARY - BUSINESS AND TECHNOLOGY DEPARTMENT - EARTH SCIENCE LIBRARY (Energy)
300 Taylor St.   Phone: (817) 870-7727
Fort Worth, TX 76102   John McCracken, Sect.Mgr.
Founded: 1957. **Subjects:** Geology, petroleum, mineralogy, paleontology, geophysics, surveying, petrology, oil economics. **Holdings:** 4500 volumes; 15,500 U.S. and state documents on geology and petroleum; 5000 maps; 4 VF drawers of pamphlets. **Subscriptions:** 56 journals and other serials. **Services:** Interlibrary loans; copying.

★4687★
FORT WORTH PUBLIC LIBRARY - GENEALOGY AND LOCAL HISTORY DEPARTMENT (Hist)
300 Taylor St.   Phone: (817) 870-7740
Fort Worth, TX 76102   Patricia Chadwell, Unit Supv., Soc.Sci.Div.
Founded: 1956. **Staff:** Prof 1; Other 3. **Subjects:** Local history, genealogy. **Special Collections:** Mary Daggett Lake Collection (300 linear feet); Texas Writers Project, Research Data, Fort Worth and Tarrant County (21 linear feet); Texas family manuscripts and Bible records (12 linear feet). **Holdings:** 25,000 books; 8000 bound periodical volumes; 4050 reels of microfilm; 5000 microcards; 50 titles on microfiche; 50 lateral file drawers of pamphlets and clippings on local history; 135 linear feet of miscellaneous manuscript material; 1200 photographs. **Subscriptions:** 245 journals and other serials. **Services:** Copying; library open to public. **Networks/Consortia:** Member of North Texas Library System. **Special Indexes:** Index to local events in Fort Worth newspapers, 1966 to present (card); Tarrant County Index (analytical index to published and manuscript material).

★4688★
FORT WORTH STAR-TELEGRAM - LIBRARY (Publ)
400 W. 7th St.   Phone: (817) 390-7740
Fort Worth, TX 76102   Hettie Arleth, Chf.Libn.
Founded: 1909. **Staff:** Prof 1; Other 4. **Subjects:** Newspaper reference topics. **Holdings:** 720 books; clippings; photographs. **Services:** Copying; library open to public.

FORTIER MEMORIAL LIBRARY
See: Manistee County Historical Museum

★4689★
FORTRESS OF LOUISBOURG NATIONAL HISTORIC PARK - LIBRARY (Hist)
P.O. Box 160   Phone: (902) 733-2280
Louisbourg, NS, Canada B0A 1M0   Judith-Marie Romard, Archv./Lib.Techn.
Founded: 1964. **Staff:** 1. **Subjects:** 18th century European and Canadian history. **Special Collections:** Rare Book Collection (18th and early 19th century, including Diderot's "Encyclopedie"); 18th century picture file. **Holdings:** 7500 books; 2000 bound periodical volumes; 150 unpublished reports; 500,000 frames of manuscripts (copies and microfilm); 500 maps, drawings, plans, views. **Subscriptions:** 40 journals and other serials. **Services:** Interlibrary loans (no rare books); copying; library open to researchers only. **Remarks:** Maintained by Parks Canada.

★4690★
FORUM PUBLISHING CO. - LIBRARY (Publ)
Box 2020   Phone: (701) 235-7311
Fargo, ND 58102   Andrea H. Halgrimson, Hd.Libn.
Founded: 1922. **Staff:** Prof 2; Other 2. **Subjects:** Newspaper reference topics. **Holdings:** 100,000 biographical and subject files; newspapers on microfilm. **Services:** Library not open to public.

FOSCUE (Edwin) MAP LIBRARY
See: Southern Methodist University - Science/Engineering Library

FOSSOM (Earl) MEMORIAL LIBRARY
See: Society of Costa Rica Collectors (SOCORICO) - Earl Fossom Memorial Library

★4691★
FOSTER ADVERTISING COMPANY, LTD. - INFORMATION CENTRE (Bus-Fin)
40 St. Clair Ave., W.   Phone: (416) 924-8090
Toronto, ON, Canada M4V 1M6   A. Slamen, Libn.
Founded: 1954. **Staff:** Prof 1; Other 1. **Subjects:** Advertising, marketing, statistics, business, sales promotion. **Holdings:** 200 books; 75 Statistics

Canada reports; 32 VF drawers of clippings and research studies. **Subscriptions:** 100 journals and other serials; 5 newspapers. **Services:** Library open to public for reference use only.

★4692★
FOSTER ASSOCIATES, INC. - LIBRARY (Energy)
1101 17th St., N.W.   Phone: (202) 296-2380
Washington, DC 20036   Ann Blandamer, Libn.
Founded: 1956. **Staff:** Prof 1; Other 2. **Subjects:** Public utilities regulation, energy resources, communications, transportation. **Holdings:** 15,000 books; 35 VF drawers; 4 drawers of microfiche. **Subscriptions:** 106 journals and other serials. **Services:** Interlibrary loans; copying; library not open to public.

FOSTER HALL COLLECTION
See: University of Pittsburgh

★4693★
FOSTER, PEPPER & RIVIERA - LAW LIBRARY (Law)
1111 Third Ave. Bldg.   Phone: (206) 447-4400
Seattle, WA 98101   Jane Cargill, Libn.
Staff: Prof 1; Other 1. **Subjects:** Law - tax, securities, banking, business, real estate; litigation. **Holdings:** 8500 volumes. **Subscriptions:** 110 journals and other serials; 6 newspapers. **Services:** Interlibrary loans; library not open to public.

FOSTER (Ralph) MUSEUM
See: School of the Ozarks - Ralph Foster Museum

FOSTER (Sheppard W.) LIBRARY
See: Emory University - School of Dentistry - Sheppard W. Foster Library

★4694★
FOSTER WHEELER DEVELOPMENT CORPORATION - RESEARCH INFORMATION CENTER AND LIBRARY (Sci-Tech)
9 Peach Tree Hill Rd.   Phone: (201) 533-3663
Livingston, NJ 07039   Karlo J. Mirth, Mgr.
Founded: 1944. **Staff:** Prof 2; Other 2. **Subjects:** Solid mechanics; applied thermodynamics; metallurgy; engineering - mechanical, chemical, nuclear; air pollution control; steam generating equipment; process plants. **Holdings:** 8700 books and bound periodical volumes; 12,000 technical reports; 6000 reports and documents; 6400 microfiche. **Subscriptions:** 270 journals and other serials. **Services:** Interlibrary loans; library open to members of American Society for Information Science and Special Libraries Association. **Computerized Information Services:** Computerized circulation. **Publications:** Current Technical Papers, monthly. **Staff:** June Lewis, Acq.Libn.

FOULGER (Peter) LIBRARY
See: Nantucket Historical Association - Peter Foulger Library

★4695★
FOUNDATION FOR BLIND CHILDREN - LIBRARY (Educ)
1201 North 85th Pl.   Phone: (602) 947-3744
Scottsdale, AZ 85257   Bess D. Kaplan, Materials Coord.
Founded: 1959. **Staff:** 3. **Subjects:** Educational material for visually impaired students. **Special Collections:** Professional material pertaining to visual impairment and related handicaps (200 books; tapes and journals). **Holdings:** 26,000 large-type textbooks, braille books and supplemental reading material (9930 titles). **Subscriptions:** 12 journals and other serials. **Services:** Interlibrary loans; copying (from master braille and large-type titles only); library open to public.

★4696★
FOUNDATION FOR BLOOD RESEARCH - LIBRARY (Med)
Route 1
Box 428   Phone: (207) 883-4132
Scarborough, ME 04074   Maxine L. Brady, Libn.
Staff: Prof 1. **Subjects:** Immunology, genetics, pediatrics, rheumatology, prenatal diagnosis. **Holdings:** 550 books; 1030 bound periodical volumes. **Subscriptions:** 62 journals and other serials. **Services:** Interlibrary loans; copying; library open to medical professionals. **Computerized Information Services:** New England Research Application Center (NERAC). **Networks/Consortia:** Member of Health Science Library and Information Cooperative (HSLIC). **Publications:** Genetics Education, bimonthly during the academic year - by mail.

★4697★
FOUNDATION CENTER - CLEVELAND - KENT H. SMITH LIBRARY (Soc Sci)
739 National City Bank Bldg.   Phone: (216) 861-1933
Cleveland, OH 44114   Jeanne Bohlen, Dir.
Founded: 1977. **Staff:** 2. **Subjects:** Reports by and of foundations; foundation tax returns; government grants; corporate philanthropy; grantsmanship and proposal writing; general information in fields of health, education and welfare; biography. **Special Collections:** Tax returns (in microform) for foundations in Ohio, Illinois, Indiana, Kentucky, Michigan, Missouri, Pennsylvania and Wisconsin. **Holdings:** 500 books and bound periodical volumes; 500 pamphlets (cataloged); 400 current annual reports of foundations; clippings on philanthropic foundations; tax returns (in microform) for foundations in the above states. **Subscriptions:** 10 journals and other serials. **Services:** Interlibrary loans; instructional sessions in the use of specialized materials on grants; library open to public. **Computerized Information Services:** DIALOG. **Networks/Consortia:** Field office of Foundation Center of New York; member of Cleveland Area Metropolitan Library System (CAMLS). **Publications:** Library brochure; worksheets for grantseekers.

★4698★
FOUNDATION CENTER - NEW YORK - LIBRARY (Soc Sci)
888 7th Ave., 26th Fl.   Phone: (212) 975-1120
New York, NY 10106   Carol M. Kurzig, Dir.Pub.Serv.
Founded: 1956. **Staff:** Prof 5; Other 5. **Subjects:** Foundations, philanthropy. **Special Collections:** Computer Data Bases - Foundation Directory, Foundation Grants Index, National; Foundation annual reports and IRS information returns. **Holdings:** 2500 books; 3250 pamphlets; 500 American and foreign foundation annual reports and retrospective collection; 165 reels of microfilm of 1970 foundation tax returns; approximately 480,000 aperture cards of 1972-1981 foundation tax returns. **Subscriptions:** 155 journals and other serials. **Services:** Interlibrary loans; copying. Operates libraries in New York, Washington, DC, Cleveland and San Francisco and coordinates networks of over 100 regional cooperating collections in all 50 states, the Virgin Islands, Mexico, Canada and Puerto Rico. All libraries open to public without charge. Center-operated libraries offer free weekly orientations on funding research; special services for annual fee include tollfree telephone reference, custom computer search service, library research service. **Computerized Information Services:** DIALOG, SDC, New York Times Information Service, FAPRS. **Networks/Consortia:** Member of Consortium of Foundation Libraries. **Publications:** Foundation Directory; Foundation Grants Index; Foundation Center Source Book Profiles; Foundation Center National Data Book; Foundation Grants to Individuals; COMSEARCH Printouts; Foundation Fundamentals. **Remarks:** To locate your nearest Foundation Center regional or cooperating collection, call toll free (800) 424-9836. **Staff:** Stephen Seward, Dir. N.Y. Lib.; Donna V. Dunlop, Ref.Libn.; JoAlyce Newgaard, Ref.Libn.; Jane Malik, Ref.Libn.; Candace Kuhta, Ref.Libn.

FOUNDATION CENTER REGIONAL COLLECTION
See: Grand Rapids Public Library; College of the Virgin Islands

★4699★
FOUNDATION CENTER - SAN FRANCISCO OFFICE - LIBRARY (Soc Sci)
312 Sutter St., 3rd Fl.   Phone: (415) 397-0902
San Francisco, CA 94108   Caroline McGilvray, Dir.
Founded: 1977. **Staff:** Prof 1; Other 1. **Subjects:** Philanthropic foundations, fund raising, corporate contributions, nonprofit organizations. **Holdings:** 550 books; 4000 foundation annual reports; 75,000 aperture cards of foundation tax returns; 12 VF drawers of clippings; 500 pamphlets. **Subscriptions:** 25 journals and other serials. **Services:** Copying; library open to public. **Computerized Information Services:** DIALOG.

★4700★
FOUNDATION CENTER - WASHINGTON BRANCH LIBRARY (Soc Sci)
1001 Connecticut Ave., N.W., Suite 938   Phone: (202) 331-1400
Washington, DC 20036   Margot Brinkley, Dir.
Founded: 1964. **Staff:** Prof 2; Other 2. **Subjects:** Philanthropic foundations. **Special Collections:** Private foundation information returns; printed annual reports issued by private foundations; books and articles on private foundations, philanthropy and philanthropists, establishing and managing nonprofit organizations, fund raising, grants for individuals. **Holdings:** 1200 volumes. **Services:** Copying; library open to public. **Computerized Information Services:** DIALOG; internal database. **Staff:** Mary Resnik, Libn.

★4701★
FOUNDATION FOR CITIZEN EDUCATION - ANNA LORD STRAUSS LIBRARY (Hist; Soc Sci)
817 Broadway   Phone: (212) 677-5050
New York, NY 10003   Alice Vielehr, Libn.
Founded: 1972. **Staff:** Prof 1; Other 1. **Subjects:** Woman's suffrage,

government, politics, international relations. **Holdings:** 600 books. **Services:** Library open to public. **Remarks:** Associated with the League of Women Voters of the City of New York.

★4702★
FOUNDATION FOR ECONOMIC EDUCATION - LIBRARY (Soc Sci)
30 S. Broadway   Phone: (914) 591-7230
Irvington-On-Hudson, NY 10533   Brian Summers, Libn.
Founded: 1946. **Subjects:** Economics, political theory. **Holdings:** 5000 books; 3000 pamphlets. **Subscriptions:** 130 journals and other serials. **Services:** Library open to public by appointment. **Publications:** The Freeman, monthly - free upon request.

★4703★
FOUNDATION OF THE FEDERAL BAR ASSOCIATION - FEDERAL BAR FOUNDATION LIBRARY (Law)
1815 H St., N.W.   Phone: (202) 638-1956
Washington, DC 20006   Richard M. Flynn, Libn.
Staff: Prof 1; Other 7. **Subjects:** Law - federal, administrative, tax, trade regulation, government procurement, condominium. **Holdings:** 30,000 volumes. **Subscriptions:** 343 journals and other serials. **Services:** Copying; library open to persons authorized by National Lawyer Club members and to members of the Federal Bar Association. **Computerized Information Services:** WESTLAW.

★4704★
FOUNDATION HISTORICAL ASSOCIATION - SEWARD HOUSE (Hist)
33 South St.   Phone: (315) 252-1283
Auburn, NY 13021   Betty Mae Lewis, Cur.
Founded: 1955. **Subjects:** Civil War, Alaska, local history. **Holdings:** 10,000 volumes. **Services:** Library open to public for reference use only.

★4705★
FOUNDATION FOR PUBLIC AFFAIRS - RESOURCE CENTER (Soc Sci)
1220 16th St., N.W.   Phone: (202) 872-1750
Washington, DC 20036   Jane Sennett Long, Dir.
Founded: 1976. **Staff:** Prof 4; Other 2. **Subjects:** Public interest groups; corporate public affairs programs; business issues. **Special Collections:** Files on 2000 public interest groups. **Holdings:** 500 books; 50 VF drawers of clippings, program materials, newsletters. **Subscriptions:** 200 journals and other serials. **Services:** Copying; library open to public by appointment. **Computerized Information Services:** Online systems. **Publications:** Public Interest Profiles, biennial; Policy Networks, monthly newsletter; miscellaneous bibliographies. **Staff:** John F. Mancini, Dir. of Res.; Leslie Swift-Rosenzweig, Res.Assoc.; Linda Johnson, Res.Asst.; Beth Bolton-Armani, Adm.Asst.

FOUNDATION OF RECORD EDUCATION (FORE)
See: American Medical Record Association

FOUNDATION FOR REFORMATION RESEARCH
See: Center for Reformation Research

★4706★
FOUNDATION FOR RESEARCH ON THE NATURE OF MAN - INSTITUTE FOR PARAPSYCHOLOGY - RESEARCH LIBRARY (Soc Sci)
College Station
Box 6847   Phone: (919) 688-8241
Durham, NC 27708   G. Rani Rao, Libn.
Founded: 1942. **Staff:** Prof 1; Other 2. **Subjects:** Parapsychology, including extrasensory perception (clairvoyance, telepathy, precognition) and psychokinesis; psychology. **Special Collections:** The J.B. and Louisa Rhine Collection; original records of published experiments. **Holdings:** 2500 books; 400 bound periodical volumes; 500 manuscripts (cataloged); 2 files of published and unpublished manuscripts. **Subscriptions:** 57 journals and other serials. **Services:** Interlibrary loans; copying; library open to serious students. **Publications:** Recommended Books Available on Parapsychology.

★4707★
FOUNDATION FOR STUDENT COMMUNICATION - LIBRARY AND RESOURCE CENTER
305 Aaron Burr Hall
Princeton University
Princeton, NJ 08540
Founded: 1969. **Subjects:** Business-government relations, economic policy and history, corporate publications. **Special Collections:** Corporate histories (80). **Holdings:** 500 books; 50 boxes of magazines; 5 boxes of government pamphlets; 10 boxes of economic foundation material. **Remarks:** Presently inactive.

★4708★

FOUNDATION FOR THE STUDY OF CYCLES INC. - LIBRARY (Sci-Tech)
124 S. Highland Ave.   Phone: (412) 441-1666
Pittsburgh, PA 15206   Gertrude F. Shirk, Ed.
Founded: 1941. **Staff:** Prof 4. **Subjects:** Rhythmic and periodic phenomena. **Holdings:** 2750 volumes and papers. **Subscriptions:** 15 journals and other serials. **Services:** Copying; library open to public. **Publications:** Cycles Magazine, 9/year. **Staff:** John T. Burns, Exec.Dir.

★4709★

FOUNDATION FOR THE STUDY OF PRESIDENTIAL AND CONGRESSIONAL TERMS - LIBRARY (Soc Sci)
1019 19th St., N.W., Suite 1010   Phone: (202) 466-2311
Washington, DC 20036   Alice O'Connor, Dir.
Staff: 4. **Subjects:** Congress, Presidency, politics, American political history. **Holdings:** 253 books and bound periodical volumes; 3 volumes of clippings; 6 symposia tape recordings; 1 volume of research reports; 3 VF drawers. **Subscriptions:** 14 journals and other serials. **Services:** Library open to public by appointment. **Remarks:** The foundation is a nonprofit research group looking into the questions of term limitation.

FOUNDERS MEMORIAL LIBRARY
See: Northern Illinois University - Southeast Asia Collection

FOUNDRY SCHOOL MUSEUM
See: Putnam County Historical Society

FOUR COUNTY LAW LIBRARY
See: Rolloff (C.A.) Four County Law Library

★4710★

FOUR-PHASE SYSTEMS - CORPORATE LIBRARY (Bus-Fin)
10700 N. De Anza Blvd.   Phone: (408) 255-0900
Cupertino, CA 95014   Linda McKell, Lib.Mgr.
Staff: Prof 2; Other 1. **Subjects:** Computers, business, engineering, mathematics. **Holdings:** 3000 books; 800 conference proceedings. **Subscriptions:** 250 journals and other serials. **Services:** Interlibrary loans; SDI; library open to public with restrictions. **Computerized Information Services:** Online systems; computerized cataloging and acquisitions. **Networks/Consortia:** Member of RLG; CLASS; CIN. **Publications:** Library Bulletin, monthly.

FOURNIER NEWSPAPERS
See: Valley Newspapers

FOWLER (Helen) LIBRARY
See: Denver Botanic Gardens - Helen Fowler Library

FOWLER (Richard S.) MEMORIAL LIBRARY
See: Hall of Flame - Richard S. Fowler Memorial Library

FOX CHASE CANCER CENTER
See: Institute for Cancer Research

FOX FOREST LIBRARY
See: New Hampshire State Division of Forests and Lands

FOX (Judge Raymond) MEMORIAL LIBRARY
See: Kalamazoo County Law Library - Judge Raymond Fox Memorial Library

★4711★

FOX RESEARCH AND LIBRARY SERVICE (Sci-Tech)
309 Yale Ave.   Phone: (215) 543-2801
Swarthmore, PA 19081   Jane G. Fox, Libn.
Staff: Prof 2; Other 1. **Subjects:** Latex compounding, rubber compounding, adhesives, paper, textiles, coatings, impregnating, laminating. **Special Collections:** Toxicity and chemical control; technology utilization; water pollution; solar energy; coal liquification. **Holdings:** 200 volumes; 15 VF drawers; 12 storage files. **Subscriptions:** 27 journals and other serials. **Services:** Copying; library open to public. **Publications:** Monthly Research Newsletter - by subscription; occasional bibliographies; semi-annual reports to clients. **Staff:** Karl M. Fox, Info.Cons.

★4712★

FOXBORO COMPANY - RD & E LIBRARY (Sci-Tech)
38 Neponset Ave.   Phone: (617) 543-8750
Foxboro, MA 02035   Helen E. Stevens, Tech.Libn.
Founded: 1963. **Staff:** Prof 1; Other 1. **Subjects:** Engineering, chemistry,

physics, mathematics, management, marketing, instrumentation, electronics, automation. **Holdings:** 6500 books; 15,000 other cataloged items. **Subscriptions:** 93 journals and other serials. **Services:** Interlibrary loans; copying; will answer brief inquiries and make referrals; library not open to public. **Computerized Information Services:** DIALOG.

FPIC
See: Hawaii Planned Parenthood - Family Planning Information Center

★4713★

FRAMINGHAM UNION HOSPITAL - CESARE GEORGE TEDESCHI LIBRARY (Med)
115 Lincoln St.   Phone: (617) 879-7111
Framingham, MA 01701   Sandra Clevesy, Dir.Lib.Serv.
Founded: 1960. **Staff:** Prof 1; Other 4. **Subjects:** Medicine, nursing, nursing education, health care delivery. **Special Collections:** Framingham Union Hospital Archives (1500 photographs; 9 linear feet of documents). **Holdings:** 5400 books; 5500 bound periodical volumes; 9 VF drawers of pamphlets. **Subscriptions:** 371 journals and other serials. **Services:** Interlibrary loans; copying; SDI; library open to public; LATCH; clinical librarian available. **Computerized Information Services:** NLM; computerized cataloging. **Networks/Consortia:** Member of OCLC; Consortium for Information Resources (CIR). **Publications:** Books Added, monthly - to staff, consortium members, and others on request; Framingham Medical Reflections.

FRANCES-HENRY LIBRARY
See: Hebrew Union College - Jewish Institute of Religion

★4714★

FRANCIS BACON FOUNDATION - LIBRARY (Hum)
655 N. Dartmouth Ave.   Phone: (714) 624-6305
Claremont, CA 91711   Elizabeth S. Wrigley, Dir.-Libn.
Founded: 1938. **Staff:** Prof 3; Other 2. **Subjects:** Francis Bacon; 16th-18th century English and American literature and history; Dante; anti-Shakespeareana. **Special Collections:** Lee-Bernard Collection of 18th century American political theory; 16th and 17th century Emblem literature; Arensberg Archives (manuscripts and letters relating to 20th century art, Dada period - 650 items); cryptography; Rosicrucians. **Holdings:** 10,500 books; 25 bound periodical volumes; 85 Princeton files of pamphlets; 25 maps; 2 VF drawers of clippings; 4 VF drawers of photographs and photostats; 35 manuscripts; 75 reels of microfilm. **Subscriptions:** 35 journals and other serials. **Services:** Interlibrary loans (limited); copying; library open to public for reference use only. **Networks/Consortia:** Member of Cooperating Libraries in Consortium; Cooperating Librarians in Claremont. **Publications:** Catalogs: STC numbers (1475-1640) in the Bacon Library - free to libraries only; Wing numbers (1641-1700) in the Bacon Library - free to libraries only; Supplement to STC and Wing holdings in the Library - for sale. **Special Catalogs:** Lee-Bernard Collection (long-title) - available for purchase; Cryptography (book); Shakespeare (book); Bacon (book); Rosicrucian and Occult (book); Emblems (book); Brown Collection of Elizabethan and Jacobean Literature (book). **Remarks:** Foundation is affiliated with the Claremont Colleges. **Staff:** Naomi S. Gorse, Tech.Serv.Libn.; Thelma S. Davies, Spec.Serv.Libn.

FRANCISCAN FATHERS OF CALIFORNIA - SANTA BARBARA MISSION ARCHIVE-LIBRARY
See: Santa Barbara Mission Archive-Library

★4715★

FRANCISCAN FATHERS OF CINCINNATI, OHIO - ST. LEONARD COLLEGE - LIBRARY
8100 Clyo Rd.
Dayton, OH 45459
Defunct

★4716★

FRANCISCAN FRIARS - ASSUMPTION FRIARY LIBRARY (Rel-Theol)
Franciscan Center
143 E. Pulaski St.   Phone: (414) 822-3291
Pulaski, WI 54162   Joseph Krymkowski, O.F.M., Libn.
Founded: 1943. **Staff:** Prof 1. **Subjects:** Religion, general interest. **Special Collections:** Polish Collection (7000 volumes of religious and literary works); Franciscana (500 volumes). **Holdings:** 16,000 books; 70 file boxes of pamphlets. **Services:** Interlibrary loans; library open to public by appointment.

★4717★

FRANCISCAN FRIARS OF THE ATONEMENT - ATONEMENT SEMINARY LIBRARY (Rel-Theol)
145 Taylor St., N.E.   Phone: (202) 529-1114
Washington, DC 20017   Bro. Edward Rankey, S.A., Libn.
Founded: 1961. **Staff:** Prof 2. **Subjects:** Ecumenism - theological and

historical development; 19th century church history in Great Britain. **Special Collections:** Anglican Reformation History. **Holdings:** 42,200 books; 5000 bound periodical volumes; 300 reels of periodicals on microfilm. **Subscriptions:** 190 journals and other serials. **Services:** Library open to public by appointment. **Staff:** Bernard Fortier, Cat.

FRANCISCAN INSTITUTE LIBRARY
See: St. Bonaventure University

★4718★
FRANCISCAN MONASTERY LIBRARY (Rel-Theol)†
1400 Quincy St., N.E. Phone: (202) 526-6800
Washington, DC 20017 Bartholomew Bengisser, Dir.
Staff: 1. **Subjects:** Theology and religion, Franciscan studies, Holy Land. **Special Collections:** Montgomery Carmichael (300 volumes); Franciscana (3000 volumes); Near East, Palestine and the Holy Land and religion (3500 volumes). **Holdings:** 28,000 books; 4000 bound periodical volumes; 1000 other bound volumes; 50 maps. **Subscriptions:** 50 journals and other serials. **Services:** Permission to use library may be requested.

FRANCISCAN ORDER - OLD SPANISH MISSIONS HISTORICAL RESEARCH LIBRARY
See: Our Lady of the Lake University - Old Spanish Missions Historical Research Library

FRANCISCAN SCHOOL OF THEOLOGY
See: Graduate Theological Union

FRANCO-AMERICAN HERITAGE CENTER
See: Le Centre d'Heritage Franco-Americain

★4719★
FRANK, BERNSTEIN, CONAWAY & GOLDMAN - LIBRARY (Law)
2 Hopkins Plaza, Suite 1300 Phone: (301) 625-3503
Baltimore, MD 21201 Nina Ogden, Libn.
Staff: Prof 1; Other 2. **Subjects:** Law. **Holdings:** 14,000 books; 300 bound periodical volumes; 50 tapes (cataloged); microfiche. **Subscriptions:** 55 journals and other serials. **Services:** Interlibrary loans; copying; SDI; library open to public with prior permission. **Computerized Information Services:** LEXIS.

FRANK (Samuel) MEDICAL LIBRARY
See: Sinai Hospital of Detroit - Samuel Frank Medical Library

FRANKFORD ARSENAL ARCHIVE (Philadelphia, PA)
See: U.S. Army - Armament Research & Development Command - Scientific and Technical Information Division

★4720★
FRANKFORD HOSPITAL - HOSPITAL LIBRARIES (Med)
Frankford Ave. & Wakeling St. Phone: (215) 831-2182
Philadelphia, PA 19124 Dianne E. Rose, Med.Libn.
Founded: 1950. **Staff:** Prof 1; Other 3. **Subjects:** Medicine, surgery, nursing, obstetrics, administration. **Special Collections:** Christine Putney Hostelley Ophthalmologic Collection (53 volumes). **Holdings:** 3100 books and bound periodical volumes. **Subscriptions:** 138 journals and other serials. **Services:** Interlibrary loans; copying; library open to public with restrictions. **Networks/Consortia:** Member of Mideastern Regional Medical Library Service (MERMLS); Delaware Valley Information Consortium (DEVIC). **Remarks:** Holdings and services listed include those for the Torresdale Division Library at Red Lion and Knight's Rd., Philadelphia, PA 19114.

★4721★
FRANKFORD HOSPITAL - SCHOOL OF NURSING - STUDENT LIBRARY (Med)
4918 Penn St. Phone: (215) 831-2372
Philadelphia, PA 19124 Dianne Rose, Med.Libn.
Staff: Prof 1; Other 1. **Subjects:** Nursing, sciences, medicine. **Holdings:** 2000 books and bound periodical volumes; records and filmstrips. **Subscriptions:** 55 journals and other serials. **Services:** Interlibrary loans; copying; library open to public with restrictions. **Networks/Consortia:** Member of Delaware Valley Information Consortium.

FRANKLIN (Benjamin) COLLECTION
See: Yale University - Benjamin Franklin Collection

★4722★
FRANKLIN COLLEGE - SPECIAL COLLECTIONS (Hist)
Franklin College Library Phone: (317) 736-8441
Franklin, IN 46131 Mary Alice Medlicott, Cur.
Staff: Prof 1; Other 1. **Subjects:** Indiana Baptist Church, Indiana history and literature. **Special Collections:** David Demaree Banta Collection of Indiana history and literature (10,000 volumes); Indiana Baptist Collection (300 volumes). **Holdings:** 11,000 books; 200 bound periodical volumes; 250 boxes of manuscripts; maps. **Services:** Interlibrary loans; copying; library open to public. **Computerized Information Services:** Computerized cataloging. **Networks/Consortia:** Member of OCLC through INCOLSA; Central Indiana Area Library Services Authority (CIALSA). **Staff:** Robert Y. Coward, Hd.Libn.

★4723★
FRANKLIN COUNTY HISTORICAL SOCIETY - CENTER OF SCIENCE & INDUSTRY - CLEMENTS HISTORY MEMORIAL LIBRARY (Hist; Sci-Tech)
280 E. Broad St. Phone: (614) 228-5613
Columbus, OH 43215 Daniel F. Prugh, Dir., Hist./Pub.Rel.
Founded: 1948. **Staff:** 2. **Subjects:** Science, health science, space science, history and genealogy of Franklin County. **Special Collections:** Oral F. Heffner Theatrical Collection; Myron and Dorothy Seifert Valentine Collection (circa 1900-1920). **Holdings:** 3500 volumes; clippings and photographs of city, county and state. **Subscriptions:** 25 journals and other serials. **Services:** Interlibrary loans; copying; library open to members and researchers by appointment. **Publications:** COSI Sights and Sounds, Newsletter - distribution to members and interested people upon request. **Staff:** William C. Schmitt, Dir. of Educ.

★4724★
FRANKLIN COUNTY HISTORICAL SOCIETY - STANLEY LIBRARY (Hist)
Ferrum College Phone: (703) 365-2121
Ferrum, VA 24088 J.B. Mitchell, Hd.Libn.
Subjects: Local history and genealogy. **Holdings:** 100 books; 1500 pamphlets; 15 tape recordings; 1000 photographs; 250 maps; genealogical files, clippings, newspapers. **Subscriptions:** 12 journals and other serials. **Services:** Copying; library open to public with permission.

★4725★
FRANKLIN COUNTY LAW LIBRARY (Law)
Court House Phone: (717) 263-4809
Chambersburg, PA 17201 Paula S. Rabinowitz, Libn.
Staff: 1. **Subjects:** Law. **Holdings:** 17,800 volumes. **Subscriptions:** 50 journals and other serials. **Services:** Library open to public when librarian is present.

FRANKLIN COUNTY TRIAL COURT - LAW LIBRARIES
See: Massachusetts State Trial Court - Franklin County Law Library

★4726★
FRANKLIN FURNACE ARCHIVES, INC. - LIBRARY (Art)
112 Franklin St. Phone: (212) 925-4671
New York, NY 10013 Matthew Hogan, Archv.
Founded: 1976. **Staff:** Prof 1; Other 6. **Subjects:** Artists' books and other ephemeral published artworks. **Holdings:** 11,000 books; 24 VF drawers of reference materials on artists' books; periodicals; postcards; records; cassette tapes; posters; pamphlets. **Subscriptions:** 1000 journals and other serials. **Services:** Library open to public by appointment. **Publications:** Franklin Furnace, quarterly; The Flue (newsletter). **Special Indexes:** Franklin Furnace Artists' Book Bibliography (card). **Remarks:** Franklin Furnace Archives, Inc. is a nonprofit organization dedicated to the preservation of printed edition books by artists.

★4727★
FRANKLIN GENERAL HOSPITAL - MEDICAL LIBRARY (Med)
900 Franklin Ave. Phone: (516) 825-8800
Valley Stream, NY 11580 Kathryn A. Boccieri, Libn.
Founded: 1964. **Staff:** Prof 1. **Subjects:** Medicine. **Holdings:** 1000 books; 2000 bound periodical volumes; Audio-Digest tapes; slides. **Subscriptions:** 50 journals and other serials. **Services:** Interlibrary loans; copying; library open to medical students. **Networks/Consortia:** Member of Medical and Scientific Libraries of Long Island (MEDLI).

★4728★
FRANKLIN (H.H.) CLUB - LIBRARY (Rec)
Cazenovia College
Cazenovia, NY 13035 Lee Schopmeier, Libn.
Founded: 1951. **Staff:** 1. **Subjects:** Franklin automobiles - preservation, technical data, related topics. **Holdings:** Figures not available. **Services:**

Copying; library not open to public.

FRANKLIN HOSPITAL MEDICAL LIBRARY
See: Davies (Ralph K.) Medical Center

★4729★
FRANKLIN HOSPITAL - MEDICAL STAFF LIBRARY (Med)
1 Spruce St.   Phone: (814) 437-7000
Franklin, PA 16323   Mr. L.P. Gilliland, Libn.
Staff: Prof 1. **Subjects:** Medicine, nursing. **Holdings:** 400 books; 600 bound periodical volumes. **Subscriptions:** 65 journals and other serials. **Services:** Interlibrary loans; copying; library open to public by appointment. **Networks/Consortia:** Member of Erie Area Health Information Library Cooperative; Mideastern Regional Medical Library Service (MERMLS); Northwest Interlibrary Cooperative of Pennsylvania.

★4730★
FRANKLIN INSTITUTE OF BOSTON - LIBRARY (Sci-Tech)
41 Berkeley St.   Phone: (617) 423-4632
Boston, MA 02116   Bonnie L. Wilson, Libn.
Staff: 1. **Subjects:** Architecture; chemistry; engineering - civil, electrical, mechanical; photography; physics. **Special Collections:** Ravich Collection in photographic science. **Holdings:** 8500 volumes. **Subscriptions:** 119 journals and other serials. **Services:** Interlibrary loans; copying; library open to public by appointment.

★4731★
FRANKLIN INSTITUTE - FRANKLIN RESEARCH CENTER - INFORMATION MANAGEMENT DEPARTMENT (Sci-Tech)
20th & Race Sts.   Phone: (215) 448-1227
Philadelphia, PA 19103   J. Lifsey, V.P.
Founded: 1961. **Staff:** Prof 120; Other 30. **Subjects:** Air pollution, water pollution and management, pesticides, food additives, occupational hazards, carcinogenesis, gerontology, toxicology, cancer research, solar energy, nuclear safety, ozone technology, consumer product safety, national highway traffic safety. **Services:** Manual and automated literature searching and screening; abstracting; reviewing; acquisitioning international publications; technical data compilation; translation; technology utilization surveys; evaluation studies; designing and operating manual information storage and retrieval systems; operation of on-site facilities; monographs; bibliographies; directories; customized hierarchical indexes; state-of-the-art reports; training programs; conferences and symposia. **Computerized Information Services:** Machine conversion and computer storage; designing and operating automated information storage and retrieval systems. **Publications:** Ozone Chemistry and Technology; books and monographs through the Franklin Institute Press. **Remarks:** This is a separate cost center of The Franklin Institute with an operating branch office in Silver Spring, MD. Its activity is sponsored by government agencies and private industries on a contractual basis. It is audited by DOD and has facilities for confidential and secret work. Library services are based on collections of the Franklin Institute Library and affiliated libraries in Philadelphia, Europe, and the Far East. **Staff:** L.H. Freiser, Chf.Libn.; B.E. Epstein, V.P.

★4732★
FRANKLIN INSTITUTE - LIBRARY (Sci-Tech)
20th & Benjamin Franklin Pkwy.   Phone: (215) 448-1321
Philadelphia, PA 19103   Leonard H. Freiser, Libn.
Founded: 1824. **Staff:** Prof 10; Other 15. **Subjects:** Astronomy, physics, geophysics, mathematics, history of science, solar energy, carcinogenesis, biomedicine, pollution, environment, toxicology, chemistry, oncology, pharmacology, engineering, industrial hygiene, aging, energy, metallurgy, underwater man, motor technology. **Special Collections:** Ware Reference Collection on Sugar; Wright Brothers Aeronautical Engineering Collection; Lenthall Collection on Naval Vessels; Underwater Man Library Section. **Holdings:** 60,000 books; 240,000 bound periodical volumes. **Subscriptions:** 4000 journals and other serials. **Services:** Interlibrary loans; copying; current awareness screening; retrospective bibliographic searching of the world's published scientific and technical literature (automated and manual); cataloging, abstracting and indexing of documents for both computerized information systems and abstract journals; develops thesauri; operates scientific and technical libraries at other locations; library open to public for U.S. patent use only. **Computerized Information Services:** Computerized serials. **Networks/Consortia:** Member of PALINET & Union Library Catalogue of Pennsylvania. **Special Catalogs:** Horological Bibliography (book); Sugar Bibliography; Serial Titles in the Academy of Natural Sciences and Franklin Institute Libraries, 1981. **Staff:** Barbara Dean, Sec.; Lenore Hardy, Lib.Oper.Supv.; Linda Henson, Indexing & Abstracting; Warren Marshall, Reprographics; Hana Rozsypal, Acq.; Pearl Stark, Screening; Charles Wilt, Industrial Serv.

★4733★
FRANKLIN AND MARSHALL COLLEGE - BIOLOGY LIBRARY (Sci-Tech)
                                       Phone: (717) 291-4118
Lancaster, PA 17604
Subjects: Biology. **Holdings:** Figures not available for books. **Subscriptions:** 86 journals and other serials. **Services:** Copying; library open to public for reference use only.

★4734★
FRANKLIN AND MARSHALL COLLEGE - CHEMISTRY DEPARTMENT - WILLIAM SHAND, JR. MEMORIAL LIBRARY (Sci-Tech)
                                       Phone: (717) 291-4123
Lancaster, PA 17604
Subjects: Chemistry. **Holdings:** 2050 volumes; 11,000 microcards. **Subscriptions:** 35 journals and other serials. **Services:** Library open to public with permission.

★4735★
FRANKLIN & MARSHALL COLLEGE - DEPARTMENT OF GEOLOGY - LIBRARY (Sci-Tech)
                                       Phone: (717) 291-4133
Lancaster, PA 17604   Ed Beutner, Chm.
Subjects: Geology. **Holdings:** Figures not available for books. **Subscriptions:** 20 journals and other serials.

★4736★
FRANKLIN AND MARSHALL COLLEGE - DEPARTMENT OF PHYSICS - LIBRARY (Sci-Tech)
                                       Phone: (717) 291-4136
Lancaster, PA 17604
Subjects: Physics and related subjects. **Holdings:** 2700 books. **Subscriptions:** 30 journals and other serials. **Services:** Library open to College community.

★4737★
FRANKLIN AND MARSHALL COLLEGE - PSYCHOLOGY LIBRARY (Soc Sci)
                                       Phone: (717) 291-4202
Lancaster, PA 17604
Subjects: Psychology. **Holdings:** 500 books. **Subscriptions:** 138 journals and other serials. **Services:** Copying; library open to public for reference use only.

★4738★
FRANKLIN AND MARSHALL COLLEGE - SHADEK-FACKENTHAL LIBRARY - SPECIAL COLLECTIONS (Hum)
                                       Phone: (717) 291-4216
Lancaster, PA 17604   ·   Kathleen J. Moretto, Dir.
Founded: 1787. **Staff:** Prof 8; Other 11. **Special Collections:** Alexander Corbett Collection of Theatre Memorabilia (600 photographs and letters); German American Imprint Collection (4000 volumes); W.W. Griest Collection of Lincoln Pictures (300 photographs, engravings, etchings); Napoleon Collection (1700 volumes); Franklin J. Schaffner Film Library (shooting scripts and memorabilia). **Holdings:** 161,875 volumes; 5406 linear feet of U.S. Government documents; 101,957 microforms. **Services:** Interlibrary loans; copying; library open to public for reference use only. **Networks/Consortia:** Member of OCLC through PALINET & Union Library Catalogue of Pennsylvania; Associated College Libraries of Central Pennsylvania (ACLCP); Central Pennsylvania Consortium (CPC). **Formerly:** Its Fackenthal Library. **Staff:** Martin Gordon, Per.Libn.; Renate Sachse, Cat.Libn.; Robert A. Siever, Asst.Dir.Tech.Serv.; Ann. F. Bevilacqua, Doc.Libn.; David W. Lewis, Asst.Dir.Pub.Serv.; C. Paul Vincent, Hum.Ref.Libn.; Mary Eleanor Brennan, Ref.Libn.

★4739★
FRANKLIN MEMORIAL HOSPITAL - TURNER MEMORIAL LIBRARY (Med)†
RFD No. 2
Wilton Rd.   Phone: (207) 778-6031
Farmington, ME 04938   Marilyn G. Courtney, Med.Libn.
Staff: 1. **Subjects:** Medicine. **Holdings:** 100 books. **Subscriptions:** 37 journals and other serials. **Services:** Interlibrary loans; copying.

★4740★
FRANKLIN MINT - INFORMATION RESEARCH SERVICES (Hist)
                                       Phone: (215) 459-6374
Franklin Center, PA 19091   Nancy Davis, Dir.
Staff: Prof 18; Other 7. **Subjects:** American history, art, description and travel, numismatics, natural history, philatelics. **Holdings:** 16,500 volumes; 50 VF drawers of pictures. **Subscriptions:** 120 journals and other serials; 8 newspapers. **Services:** Interlibrary loans; copying; open to public with permission of librarian. **Computerized Information Services:** DIALOG, New

York Times Information Service, Dow Jones News Retrieval; internal database. **Publications:** New Book List, monthly - for internal distribution only. **Staff:** Ruth S. Burns, Mgr., Lib.Serv.

★4741★
FRANKLIN PIERCE LAW CENTER - LIBRARY (Law)
2 White St. Phone: (603) 228-1541
Concord, NH 03301 Thomas M. Steele, Law Libn.
Staff: Prof 3; Other 4. **Subjects:** Law. **Special Collections:** Energy Law Institute Collection (1000 volumes). **Holdings:** 80,000 books; 10,000 bound periodical volumes. **Subscriptions:** 1500 journals and other serials; 5 newspapers. **Services:** Interlibrary loans; copying; SDI; library open to public for reference use only. **Computerized Information Services:** LEXIS. **Publications:** Bibliography series; Legal Research series, both irregular. **Staff:** Judith Gire Norcross, Asst.Libn.

FRANKLIN RESEARCH CENTER - NATIONAL SOLAR HEATING & COOLING INFORMATION CENTER
See: Conservation and Renewable Energy Inquiry and Referral Service

FRANKLIN RESEARCH CENTER - SCIENCE INFORMATION SERVICES
See: Franklin Institute

FRANKLIN RESEARCH CENTER - U.S. INTERAGENCY ADVANCED POWER GROUP
See: U.S. Interagency Advanced Power Group

★4742★
FRANKLIN UNIVERSITY - LIBRARY (Bus-Fin)
201 S. Grant Ave. Phone: (614) 224-6237
Columbus, OH 43215 Mr. Allyn Ehrhardt, Libn.
Founded: 1966. **Staff:** Prof 6; Other 2. **Subjects:** Economics, business, social sciences. **Holdings:** 52,000 books; 5100 bound periodical volumes; 488 tapes; 10K reports; NYSE, AMEX, OHIO; 12 drawers of annual reports; 12 drawers of pamphlets; 10,800 reels of microfilm; 31,193 microfiche. **Subscriptions:** 1200 journals and other serials; 9 newspapers. **Services:** Interlibrary loans; copying; Telefax; library open to public. **Computerized Information Services:** DIALOG, SDC, BRS, New York Times Information Service, Information Handling Services, Finsbury Data Services, Ltd. **Networks/Consortia:** Member of CALICO; OHIONET; OCLC. **Staff:** Fred Helser, Assoc.Libn.; Mr. Beauford McCall, Ser.Libn.

FRANKS (Virginia L.) MEMORIAL LIBRARY
See: University of Wisconsin, Madison - School of Social Work - Virginia L. Franks Memorial Library

FRANZHEIM ARCHITECTURE LIBRARY
See: University of Houston

★4743★
FRASER AND BEATTY - LIBRARY (Law)
First Canadian Place
P.O. Box 100
Toronto, ON, Canada M5X 1B2 Phone: (416) 863-4527
 Joan Hudson, Libn.
Staff: Prof 1; Other 1. **Subjects:** Law. **Holdings:** 7000 volumes; government documents, law reports and statutes. **Subscriptions:** 45 journals and other serials; 6 newspapers. **Services:** Library not open to public. **Computerized Information Services:** WESTLAW, Info Globe, QL Systems. **Special Indexes:** Legal Memoranda of Law Collection (by subject, author and statutes).

★4744★
FRASER INC. - CENTRAL TECHNICAL DEPARTMENT LIBRARY (Sci-Tech)
 Phone: (506) 735-5551
Edmundston, NB, Canada E3V 1S9 Lloyd G. Hinton, Mgr., Process Dev.
Founded: 1940. **Subjects:** Pulp and paper. **Holdings:** 1494 books; 1497 bound periodical volumes. **Subscriptions:** 60 journals and other serials. **Services:** Copying; library not open to public.

★4745★
FRASER-HICKSON INSTITUTE, MONTREAL - FREE LIBRARY - SPECIAL COLLECTIONS (Hist)
4855 Kensington Ave. Phone: (514) 489-5301
Montreal, PQ, Canada H3X 3S6 Margery W. Trenholme, Chf.Libn.
Founded: 1885. **Special Collections:** Canadiana; 19th century newspapers. **Holdings:** Figures not available. **Services:** Copying; library open to public.

★4746★
FRASER HYNDMAN, BARRISTERS & SOLICITORS - LAW LIBRARY (Law)
32nd Fl., Four Bentall Centre
1055 Dunsmuir St.
P.O. Box 49360 Phone: (604) 687-3216
Vancouver, BC, Canada V7X 1P2 Gillian Crabtree, Law Libn.
Staff: Prof 1; Other 1. **Subjects:** Law. **Holdings:** 1800 books. **Services:** Library not open to public.

FRASER (Simon) UNIVERSITY
See: Simon Fraser University

FRAUNCES TAVERN MUSEUM - SONS OF THE REVOLUTION IN THE STATE OF NEW YORK
See: Sons of the Revolution in the State of New York - Library

FRAZIER MEMORIAL LIBRARY
See: National Wildlife Federation

FREDERICK CANCER RESEARCH FACILITY
See: U.S. Natl. Institutes of Health - National Cancer Institute

★4747★
FREDERICK COUNTY LAW LIBRARY (Law)
Court House Phone: (301) 663-8300
Frederick, MD 21701 Janet D. Rippeon, Law Libn.
Subjects: Law. **Holdings:** 25,000 volumes. **Services:** Library not open to public.

★4748★
FREDERICK COUNTY PLANNING COMMISSION - LIBRARY (Plan)†
Winchester Hall, E. Church St. Phone: (301) 694-1153
Frederick, MD 21701 Theresa K. Alexander, Sec.
Founded: 1970. **Staff:** Prof 1. **Subjects:** Planning and zoning in urban, rural and regional areas. **Holdings:** 275 books; 32 bound periodical titles; 1400 plans, studies and reports; 5 VF drawers of Frederick County information; 4 VF drawers of general information; maps and slides; tape recordings of planning and zoning and board of appeals meetings and hearings. **Subscriptions:** 42 journals and other serials. **Services:** Library open to public for reference use only.

★4749★
FREDERICK MEMORIAL HOSPITAL - WALTER F. PRIOR MEDICAL LIBRARY (Med)
Park Place & W. 7th St. Phone: (301) 694-3459
Frederick, MD 21701 Chadwick Gibbs, Med.Libn.
Staff: Prof 1. **Subjects:** Medicine and related topics. **Holdings:** 1500 books and bound periodical volumes. **Subscriptions:** 75 journals and other serials. **Services:** Interlibrary loans; copying; library open to authorized persons and students for reference use on request.

FREDERICKSBURG & SPOTSYLVANIA NATL. MILITARY PARK
See: U.S. Natl. Park Service

★4750★
FREE LIBRARY OF PHILADELPHIA - ART DEPARTMENT (Art)
Logan Sq. Phone: (215) 686-5403
Philadelphia, PA 19103 Marianne Promos, Hd.
Staff: Prof 5; Other 2. **Subjects:** Art techniques and history, architecture, painting, sculpture, costume, drawing, decorative arts, ceramics, cartoons, creative crafts, commercial art, photography, graphic arts, antiques, numismatics, interior decorating. **Special Collections:** 18th and 19th century architectural pattern books; American Institute of Architects, original measured drawings of colonial Philadelphia buildings; John Frederick Lewis Collection of books on fine prints and printmaking (2645 volumes); Lawrence B. Saint formulas and cartoons for stained glasswork. **Holdings:** 151,000 volumes; 33,839 pamphlets and clippings; 735 periodical titles; card index of artists (15,700 names); card index of exhibition catalogs of Pennsylvania Academy of the Fine Arts (10,000 names). **Subscriptions:** 175 journals and other serials. **Services:** Interlibrary loans; copying.

★4751★
FREE LIBRARY OF PHILADELPHIA - BUSINESS, SCIENCE AND INDUSTRY DEPARTMENT (Bus-Fin; Sci-Tech)
Logan Sq. Phone: (215) 686-5394
Philadelphia, PA 19103 Alex S. Weinbaum, Hd.
Founded: 1953. **Staff:** Prof 6; Other 5. **Subjects:** Business, economics, investment and banking, insurance, pure and applied sciences, automotive literature, technology, philately. **Special Collections:** Automobile Reference

Collection; Klein-Deats Philatelic Literature Collection. **Holdings:** Figures not available for book and periodical holdings; 165 VF drawers of pamphlets; 39,000 microcards; 10,000 microfiche; 16,000 reels of microfilm. **Subscriptions:** 1150 journals and other serials. **Services:** Interlibrary loans (limited); copying; will answer questions by mail, particularly in special collections areas.

★4752★
FREE LIBRARY OF PHILADELPHIA - EDUCATION, PHILOSOPHY, RELIGION DEPARTMENT (Educ; Hum)
Logan Sq.   Phone: (215) 686-5392
Philadelphia, PA 19103   Esther J. Maurer, Hd.
Founded: 1954. **Staff:** Prof 5; Other 3. **Subjects:** Education, philosophy, psychology, religion, library science. **Special Collections:** College and school catalogs (2300 items); Judaica (primarily history and religion). **Holdings:** Figures not available for books and periodical holdings; 49 VF drawers of clippings and pamphlets; 2538 reels of microfilm; 4464 microfiche sheets. **Subscriptions:** 670 journals and other serials; annual reports for 46 libraries. **Services:** Interlibrary loans; copying.

★4753★
FREE LIBRARY OF PHILADELPHIA - EDWIN A. FLEISHER COLLECTION OF ORCHESTRAL MUSIC (Mus)
Logan Sq.   Phone: (215) 686-5313
Philadelphia, PA 19103   Sam Dennison, Cur.
Founded: 1929. **Staff:** Prof 3; Other 3. **Subjects:** Conductors' scores, orchestral parts, program information. **Holdings:** 13,140 sets of performance materials (scores and parts); 1350 reference scores; 450 audiotape recordings (primarily the Recording Guarantee Project of the American International Music Fund); 155 phonograph records; 177 reels of microfilm; composer, publisher and agent files. **Services:** Interlibrary loans; collection available to public for reference use only; materials are lent to organizations for performance, although copyrighted works must be cleared in advance. **Publications:** Edwin A. Fleisher Collection of Orchestral Music in the Free Library of Philadelphia, A Cumulative Catalog, 1929-1977. **Special Catalogs:** Master catalog of Fleisher Collection holdings (card); union card catalog of orchestral music, scores and theater arrangements; special subject indices and complete title index available by consulting collection.

★4754★
FREE LIBRARY OF PHILADELPHIA - FILMS DEPARTMENT (Aud-Vis)
Logan Sq.   Phone: (215) 686-5367
Philadelphia, PA 19103   Steven J. Mayover, Lib. Film Oper.Supv.
Founded: 1958. **Staff:** Prof 2; Other 5. **Subjects:** Films emphasize subjects such as intercultural relations, social problems, science and travel; collection includes outstanding documentaries and short subjects and full-length features. **Holdings:** 2555 16mm sound films; 12 VF drawers of pamphlets. **Services:** Interlibrary loans (limited to Delaware County, PA); department open to public. **Publications:** Annotated Catalog of 16mm Films. **Staff:** Margaret K. Turanski, Asst.Hd.

★4755★
FREE LIBRARY OF PHILADELPHIA - GOVERNMENT PUBLICATIONS DEPARTMENT (Info Sci)
Logan Sq.   Phone: (215) 686-5330
Philadelphia, PA 19103   William A. Felker, Hd.
Founded: 1900. **Staff:** Prof 6; Other 5. **Subjects:** Publications of municipal, state, federal and official international agencies. **Holdings:** 72,763 bound volumes; 961,881 unbound documents; 390,489 microprint cards; 6217 reels of microfilm; 284,752 microfiche. **Subscriptions:** 3000 journals and other serials. **Services:** Interlibrary loans; telephone and mail service; department open to public, material generally not for circulation.

★4756★
FREE LIBRARY OF PHILADELPHIA - LIBRARY FOR THE BLIND AND PHYSICALLY HANDICAPPED (Aud-Vis)
919 Walnut St.   Phone: (215) 925-3213
Philadelphia, PA 19107   Michael P. Coyle, Hd.
Staff: Prof 4; Other 21. **Holdings:** 9000 braille books; 16,000 talking book titles; 16,500 cassette tapes; 5000 large print books. **Networks/Consortia:** Member of National Library Service for the Blind & Physically Handicapped, Library of Congress.

★4757★
FREE LIBRARY OF PHILADELPHIA - LITERATURE DEPARTMENT (Hum)
Logan Sq.   Phone: (215) 686-5402
Philadelphia, PA 19103   Maryann Baker, Hd.
Staff: Prof 5; Other 3. **Subjects:** Literature, criticism, foreign language literature, theater, language, folklore, journalism. **Special Collections:**

Theater Collection; Granger collection of poetry anthologies. **Holdings:** 130,000 books; 35,000 bound periodical volumes; 11 VF drawers of pamphlets; 7700 reels of microfilm; 3500 audio recordings of speech, drama, poetry and language instruction. **Subscriptions:** 275 journals and other serials. **Services:** Interlibrary loans; copying.

★4758★
FREE LIBRARY OF PHILADELPHIA - MERCANTILE LIBRARY (Bus-Fin)
1021 Chestnut St.   Phone: (215) 627-1231
Philadelphia, PA 19107   James B. Woy, Hd.
Founded: 1953. **Staff:** Prof 4; Other 5. **Subjects:** Business, investments, real estate. **Special Collections:** Telephone and trade directories. **Holdings:** 45,000 books; 19 VF drawers of pamphlets and maps; all current annual reports of New York and American Stock Exchange companies on negative microfiche. **Subscriptions:** 450 journals and other serials; 100 investment and other loose-leaf services. **Services:** Interlibrary loans. **Computerized Information Services:** DIALOG.

★4759★
FREE LIBRARY OF PHILADELPHIA - MICROFORMS AND NEWSPAPERS DEPARTMENT (Info Sci)
Logan Sq.   Phone: (215) 686-5431
Philadelphia, PA 19103   Bernard F. Pasqualini, Hd.
Founded: 1979. **Staff:** Prof 2; Other 7. **Subjects:** Philadelphia area newspapers from colonial times to present; major current national and foreign newspapers. **Holdings:** Over 16,000 reels of positive microfilm of newspapers; partial indexing for the Philadelphia Press, the Public Ledger/Evening Ledger; indexes to major newspapers; over 65,000 reels of positive microfilm of periodicals; several hundred thousand microfiche. **Services:** Photocopies from newspapers and positive prints from microforms.

★4760★
FREE LIBRARY OF PHILADELPHIA - MUSIC DEPARTMENT (Mus)
Logan Sq.   Phone: (215) 686-5316
Philadelphia, PA 19103   Frederick J. Kent, Hd.
Founded: 1927. **Staff:** Prof 5; Other 4. **Subjects:** Music and dance. **Special Collections:** Edward I. Keffer Collection of Early American musical imprints; Harvey Husten Jazz Library (recordings); sheet music (piano and vocal); library of the Musical Fund Society of Philadelphia; chamber music; historical collection of records (RCA Victor Masterworks before LP). **Holdings:** 70,000 volumes; 4000 bound periodical volumes; 45,000 phonograph records; 150,000 pieces of sheet music; librettos; pamphlets; clippings. **Subscriptions:** 180 current serial titles. **Services:** Interlibrary loans; copying.

★4761★
FREE LIBRARY OF PHILADELPHIA - MUSIC DEPARTMENT - DRINKER LIBRARY OF CHORAL MUSIC (Mus)
Logan Sq.   Phone: (215) 686-5364
Philadelphia, PA 19103   Frederick J. Kent, Hd.
Staff: Prof 1; Other 2. **Subjects:** Choral music (men's voices, women's voices, mixed voices); liturgical music for chorus - chorales, music and texts. **Special Collections:** Bach cantatas; Brahms solo songs; English translations of the texts of the vocal works of Bach, Brahms, Schumann, Schutz and Schubert (edited, arranged and translated by Henry S. Drinker); Library of American Choral Foundation (primarily 20th century works). **Holdings:** 348,000 unbound choral parts; 25,000 unbound instrumental parts for accompaniment to choral parts; 3000 unbound texts of vocal works; 10,000 solo songs. **Services:** Circulation restricted to subscribers. **Publications:** Catalog of the Drinker Library of Choral Music; Bach 389 Chorales. **Staff:** Robert C. Williams

★4762★
FREE LIBRARY OF PHILADELPHIA - PRINT AND PICTURE COLLECTION (Pict)
Logan Sq.   Phone: (215) 686-5405
Philadelphia, PA 19103   Robert F. Looney, Cur.
Founded: 1953. **Staff:** Prof 1; Other 3. **Subjects:** Loan collection of pictures on all subjects; reference collection of fine prints. **Special Collections:** John Frederick Lewis Portrait Collection (220,000 items); Philadelphiana Collection (10,000 items); Americana (1194 items); John Gibb Smith Collection of Philadelphia streetcars (906 items); WPA Collection of Prints (1415 items); Napoleonic Prints (3379 items); Rosenthal and Bendiner collections of American drawings of the 19th and 20th centuries (1000 items); American photographs of the 19th and 20th centuries (1200 items). **Holdings:** 1500 original graphics, 1491 to present; loan collection pictures; 800,000 items of photographs and art reproductions; postcards, greeting cards and travel posters. **Services:** Copying; exhibitions and displays.

★4763★

FREE LIBRARY OF PHILADELPHIA - RARE BOOK DEPARTMENT (Rare Book)
Logan Sq.
Philadelphia, PA 19103   Phone: (215) 686-5416
Howell J. Heaney, Rare Book Libn.
Founded: 1949. **Staff:** Prof 4; Other 1. **Subjects:** Cuneiform tablets; illuminated manuscripts (European and Oriental); Bibles; common law; British and American legal autographs and prints; Horace; incunabula; Americana (discovery and exploration); early American children's books (including American Sunday-School Union collection); Oliver Goldsmith; Charles Dickens; Edgar Allan Poe; Pennsylvania German Fraktur and imprints; Irish and American pamphlets (18th and 19th centuries); Wing and short title catalogue books; calligraphy; English and American library and auction catalogs; 19th century English and American literature; British engravers; giftbooks; letters of the preseidents of the United States; angling prints; Philadelphia prints; Arthur Rackham; Kate Greenaway; Beatrix Potter; A.B. Frost; Howard Pyle; Joseph Conrad; Rudyard Kipling; Robert Louis Stevenson; James Branch Cabell; Bret Harte; Mark Twain; Agnes Repplier; William Cowper; Palmer Cox; A. Edward Newton; Robert Lawson. **Holdings:** 39,235 books; 6725 pamphlets; 2800 cuneiform tablets; 168 horn books; 21,733 prints and broadsides; 1100 Pennsylvania German Fraktur; 1350 Oriental miniatures; 2200 illuminated European miniatures and leaves; 17,083 manuscripts, letters and documents. **Services:** Microfilming (positive only supplied), photographs; department open to public to view exhibitions; use of materials restricted to qualified research workers.

★4764★

FREE LIBRARY OF PHILADELPHIA - SOCIAL SCIENCE & HISTORY DEPARTMENT (Soc Sci; Hist)
Logan Sq.
Philadelphia, PA 19103   William Handley, Hd.
Founded: 1953. **Staff:** Prof 6; Other 4. **Subjects:** History, biography, social sciences, books and printing, law, travels and geography, archeology, anthropology, bibliography, sports and games. **Special Collections:** American Indians (Wilberforce Eames); chess (Charles Willing); Confederate imprints (Simon Gratz); Regional Foundation Collection. **Holdings:** 167,500 volumes; 47,500 pamphlets; 19 VF drawers of clippings; 370 boxes of microcards; 4000 annual reports. **Subscriptions:** 715 journals and other serials. **Services:** Interlibrary loans.

★4765★

FREE LIBRARY OF PHILADELPHIA - SOCIAL SCIENCE & HISTORY DEPARTMENT - MAP COLLECTION (Geog-Map)
Logan Sq.
Philadelphia, PA 19103   Phone: (215) 686-5397
J.B. Post, Map Libn.
Staff: Prof 1; Other 1. **Subjects:** General map collection with emphasis on local area. **Special Collections:** Kelso collection of Jansson-Visscher maps of America (20 sheets); fire insurance and ward atlases of Philadelphia (500 volumes); Pennsylvania county atlases. **Holdings:** 15,000 atlases, gazetteers, cartobibliographies; 130,000 maps; 200 aerial photographs.

★4766★

FREE LIBRARY OF PHILADELPHIA - THEATRE COLLECTION (Theater)
Logan Sq.
Philadelphia, PA 19103   Phone: (215) 686-5427
Geraldine Duclow, Libn.-In-Charge
Founded: 1951. **Staff:** Prof 1; Other 2. **Subjects:** Theater, film, television, radio, circus, minstrels. **Special Collections:** 19th century playbills; Lubin Film Company archives; Philadelphia playbills from 1803. **Holdings:** Over a million items including programs, playbills, scrapbooks, 3500 books, 100 titles of periodicals, posters, biographical newspaper clippings, reviews of movies and plays, pictures of productions and film stills, microfilm. **Services:** Copying. **Special Indexes:** Philadelphia Theatre Index (card index of productions since 1855).

★4767★

FREE METHODIST CHURCH OF NORTH AMERICA -MARSTON MEMORIAL HISTORICAL LIBRARY (Rel-Theol)
901 College Ave.
Winona Lake, IN 46590   Phone: (219) 267-7656
Evelyn Mottweiler, Libn.
Staff: Prof 1; Other 1. **Subjects:** Free Methodist and Methodist history, Wesleyana, Holiness literature. **Holdings:** 5000 books; 500 bound periodical volumes; manuscripts, journals, letters, photographs, pamphlets, microfilms, cassette tapes. **Subscriptions:** 10 journals and other serials. **Services:** Interlibrary loans; copying; library open to public. **Publications:** The Free Methodist Church: A Bibliography - by order. **Staff:** Arlene Clyde, Asst.Libn.

★4768★

FREE PUBLIC LIBRARY OF ELIZABETH, NJ - ART AND MUSIC DEPARTMENT (Art; Mus)
11 S. Broad St.
Elizabeth, NJ 07202   Phone: (201) 354-6060
Roman A. Sawycky, Supv.Libn.
Staff: Prof 4; Other 5. **Subjects:** Painting, sculpture, art and music education, history of art and music, art and music biography, music appreciation. **Special Collections:** Japanese prints from Primitive Period through Revival (250 items). **Holdings:** 25,000 books; 1000 pamphlets (cataloged); music scores; 13,000 phonograph records; 400 35mm filmstrips; 350 16mm motion picture films; 200,000 mounted pictures; 800 study art prints. **Subscriptions:** 58 journals and other serials. **Services:** Interlibrary loans; copying; Spanish, Slavonic languages capability; audiovisual programs assistance; library open to public. **Special Catalogs:** Separate printed catalogs for the Filmstrip Collection and Motion Pictures (annotated). **Staff:** Doris Fichtelberg, Supv.Libn., Music; Daisy Tamayo, Prin.Libn., Art.

FREE UNIVERSITY NETWORK
See: Learning Resources Network

FREE WILL BAPTIST HISTORICAL COLLECTION
See: Mount Olive College

★4769★

FREEBORN COUNTY HISTORICAL SOCIETY - NELSON LIBRARY (Hist)
North Bridge St.
Box 105
Albert Lea, MN 56007   Phone: (507) 373-8003
Georges Denzene, Libn.
Founded: 1980. **Staff:** Prof 2; Other 2. **Subjects:** Local history and genealogy, Minnesota history. **Holdings:** 1500 books; 1000 bound periodical volumes; 100 boxes of manuscripts; 1500 slides and photographs; 35 reels of microfilm; 20 VF drawers. **Services:** Copying; library open to public for reference use only. **Staff:** Roger D. Lonning, Supv.

FREEDOM EDUCATION CENTER
See: Northwood Institute of Texas

★4770★

FREEDOM HOUSE - INFORMATION CENTER (Soc Sci)
20 W. 40th St.
New York, NY 10018   Phone: (212) 730-7744
Leonard R. Sussman, Exec.Dir.
Subjects: Foreign affairs, problems of higher education, international communication, American heritage. **Services:** Freedom House/Books U.S.A. (120 volumes) available as gifts to Africa, Asia and Latin America; Comparative Survey of Freedom. **Publications:** Freedom at Issue, bimonthly; Freedom in the World: Political Rights and Civil Liberties, a yearbook.

FREEDOM FROM HUNGER FOUNDATION
See: Meals for Millions/Freedom from Hunger Foundation

FREEDOM OF INFORMATION CENTER - UNIVERSITY OF MISSOURI
See: Investigative Reporters and Editors, Inc. - Paul Williams Memorial Resource Center

FREEDOM OF INFORMATION SERVICES, INC.
See: FOI Services, Inc.

★4771★

FREEDOMS FOUNDATION AT VALLEY FORGE - LIBRARY (Hist)
Valley Forge, PA 19481   Phone: (215) 933-8825
Harold Badger, Libn.
Staff: 1. **Subjects:** U.S. history - social, political, economic and foreign policy; 20th century totalitarianism; modern economic and political systems; current events and public policy issues. **Special Collections:** U.S. Radical Movements collection. **Holdings:** 30,000 books; 6000 bound periodical volumes; 1000 linear feet of unbound serials; pamphlets; posters; fugitive literature. **Subscriptions:** 125 journals and other serials. **Services:** Copying; library open to public. **Networks/Consortia:** Member of Collector's Network. **Remarks:** Library was established in 1965 to support the Freedoms Foundation educational programs.

FREEL (Eugene L.) LIBRARY
See: North Adams State College - Eugene L. Freel Library

★4772★

FREELANCE PHOTOGRAPHERS GUILD, INC. (Pict)
251 Park Ave., S.
New York, NY 10010   Phone: (212) 777-4210
Gary R. Heller, Natl. Sales Mgr.
Founded: 1937. **Staff:** Prof 10; Other 20. **Subjects:** Photography - scenery,

industry, sports, human interest, science. **Special Collections:** Photoworld black and white archives from middle 1800s to mid-1970s (5 million prints); Alpha Photo Associates color transparencies (3 million). **Services:** Library open to public, reproduction fee charged. **Publications:** Newsletter of new submissions to the files, bimonthly; color file guide available. **Staff:** Janis Lobel, Mgr., Color Res.Dept.; Mary Jane Cannizzaro, Mgr., Black & White Dept.

FREEMAN (Daniel) HOSPITAL
See: Daniel Freeman Hospital

FREEMAN (George E.) LIBRARY
See: State Technical Institute at Memphis - George E. Freeman Library

FREEMAN (Larry) DECORATIVE ARTS LIBRARY
See: American Life Foundation and Study Institute

FREEMAN (Thomas Oscar) MEMORIAL LIBRARY
See: Lake Forest College - Thomas Oscar Freeman Memorial Library

FREER GALLERY OF ART
See: Smithsonian Institution

FREITAS (J.A.) LIBRARY
See: U.P.E.C. Cultural Center - J.A. Freitas Library

★4773★
FRENCH AMERICAN CULTURAL SERVICES AND EDUCATIONAL AID (FACSEA) (Area-Ethnic)
972 Fifth Ave.   Phone: (212) 737-9700
New York, NY 10021   Anne Marie Morotte, Exec.Dir.
Founded: 1955. **Subjects:** French history and culture. **Holdings:** 6500 films; 800 scientific and medical films; television newsreels; French language radio cassettes; French language courses. **Publications:** Catalogs available for each department.

★4774★
FRENCH AMERICAN METALS CORPORATION - LIBRARY
9580 W. 14th Ave.
Lakewood, CO 80215
Defunct

★4775★
FRENCH-CANADIAN GENEALOGICAL SOCIETY OF CONNECTICUT, INC. - LIBRARY (Hist)
Box 262   Phone: (203) 529-9040
Rocky Hill, CT 06067   Henri E. Carrier, Pres.
Founded: 1981. **Staff:** Prof 1; Other 7. **Subjects:** French-Canadian genealogy and history. **Holdings:** 200 books. **Services:** Library open to public with restrictions.

FRENCH (Harley E.) MEDICAL LIBRARY
See: University of North Dakota - School of Medicine - Harley E. French Medical Library

★4776★
FRENCH INSTITUTE/ALLIANCE FRANCAISE - LIBRARY (Area-Ethnic)
22 E. 60th St.   Phone: (212) 355-6100
New York, NY 10022   Fred J. Gitner, Libn.
Founded: 1911. **Staff:** Prof 2; Other 2. **Subjects:** French literature, art, history and civilization; Paris. **Holdings:** 37,000 books; 750 bound periodical volumes; readers for students; 800 phonograph records (cataloged). **Subscriptions:** 75 journals and other serials. **Services:** Copying; books may be borrowed by mail (if member, with fee); library open to public for reference use only. **Publications:** List of new acquisitions, quarterly - free upon request. **Staff:** Aline Locascio, Asst.Libn.

★4777★
FRENCH LIBRARY IN BOSTON, INC. (Area-Ethnic)
53 Marlborough St.   Phone: (617) 266-4351
Boston, MA 02116   Mylo Housen, Exec.Dir.
Founded: 1945. **Staff:** Prof 7. **Subjects:** Classical and contemporary French literature including criticism; French history, politics, social life; language and art; cinema; education; architecture. **Special Collections:** Local depository for French-Canadian literature. **Holdings:** 40,000 books; major depository for French film classics including Renoir, Truffaut, Rene Clair. **Subscriptions:** 18 journals and other serials. **Services:** Interlibrary loans; activities for members; library open to public for reference use only. **Publications:** Le Bibliophile, bimonthly newsletter, published September through July. **Special Catalogs:** Printed catalog (1982) of 60 feature and documentary films available for

rental by institutions. **Remarks:** This library serves the New England area primarily. Salles Carne (Mariel Carne) is said to be the only archive of a French filmmaker in the U.S. **Staff:** Jane Stahl, Libn.; Marga McCormick, Libn.

★4778★
FRENCH (R.T.) COMPANY - TECHNICAL LIBRARY (Food-Bev)
Box 23450
Rochester, NY 14692   Phone: (716) 482-8000
                                           Enna L. Breton, Adm.
Staff: Prof 1. **Subjects:** Food technology, chemistry, animal nutrition and care, biology. **Holdings:** 800 books; 580 bound periodical volumes; 1500 pamphlets (cataloged); 900 patents; 3 VF drawers of reprints of articles. **Subscriptions:** 25 journals and other serials. **Services:** Copying (limited); library open to public by appointment. **Publications:** List of Periodicals Currently Received, annual.

FRESHWATER INSTITUTE LIBRARY
See: Canada - Fisheries & Oceans

★4779★
FRESNO CITY AND COUNTY HISTORICAL SOCIETY - ARCHIVES (Hist)†
7160 W. Kearney Blvd.
Fresno, CA 93706   Phone: (209) 441-0862
                                           Sharon Hiigel, Archv.
Founded: 1919. **Staff:** Prof 1; Other 3. **Subjects:** Fresno County history, city and county records. **Special Collections:** A.W. Peters glass negative plates (833 showing the history of Fresno County); Paul Hutchinson glass negative plates (250 showing the history of Fowler); subject and portrait photograph collection (1000 items). **Holdings:** 3000 books; 50 bound periodical volumes; 400 pamphlets (cataloged); 40 manuscripts; Ben Walker file (250,000 newspaper clippings); 100 bound city and county records; 30,000 unbound city and county records. **Subscriptions:** 30 journals and other serials; 10 newspapers. **Services:** Copying; archives open to public by appointment. **Publications:** Fresno Past & Present, quarterly. **Special Catalogs:** A Guide to the Fresno County Historical Society Archives.

★4780★
FRESNO COMMUNITY HOSPITAL - MEDICAL LIBRARY (Med)
Box 1232
Fresno, CA 93715   Phone: (209) 442-6000
                                           Ann Keeney, Med.Libn.
Staff: Prof 1; Other 2. **Subjects:** Biological sciences. **Holdings:** 3000 books; 2500 bound periodical volumes; 8 VF drawers of pamphlets and clippings. **Subscriptions:** 640 journals and other serials. **Services:** Interlibrary loans; copying; library not open to public. **Computerized Information Services:** SDC, BRS, MEDLINE, DIALOG.

★4781★
FRESNO COUNTY DEPARTMENT OF EDUCATION - IMC-LIBRARY (Educ)†
2314 Mariposa St.   Phone: (209) 488-3272
Fresno, CA 93721   Stephen E. Goodson, Dir.
Founded: 1945. **Staff:** Prof 2; Other 19. **Subjects:** Education, children's literature. **Special Collections:** Curriculum guides for California schools (5400 volumes). **Holdings:** 120,000 books; 500 bound periodical volumes; 5 VF drawers of pamphlets; 2 drawers of microfiche; 900 bilingual books, kits and games; 291 affective education books and kits; 15,000 16mm films; 11,000 other nonprint materials; 3000 publisher's review copies. **Subscriptions:** 100 journals and other serials. **Services:** Interlibrary loans; copying; library open only to educators whose schools have a service contract with the IMC-Library; public may use curriculum guides and publishers' samples. **Networks/Consortia:** Member of Area Wide Library Network (AWLNET). **Publications:** IMC Book Talk, 2-3/year - distributed to county schools; New Book Reviews, annual - distributed to county schools and on request; bibliographies - available on request. **Special Catalogs:** Catalog of 16mm films; catalog of building level materials. **Remarks:** Library is a textbook display center for California textbook adoption. **Staff:** Tom Westre, Libn.

★4782★
FRESNO COUNTY LAW LIBRARY (Law)
Fresno County Courthouse, Rm. 600
1100 Van Ness Ave.   Phone: (209) 237-2227
Fresno, CA 93721   Dorothy G. Morris, Libn.
Founded: 1891. **Staff:** Prof 2; Other 1. **Subjects:** Law, including medicolegal material. **Holdings:** 51,687 volumes. **Subscriptions:** 337 journals and other serials. **Services:** Library open to public for reference use only.

★4783★
FRESNO DIOCESAN LIBRARY (Rel-Theol)
Box 1668
Fresno, CA 93717   Phone: (209) 237-5125
                                           Fr. Walter Minhoto, Libn.
Founded: 1933. **Staff:** 2. **Subjects:** Roman Catholicism, Californiana.

Special Collections: Material concerning Central California. **Holdings:** 20,000 books; 500 bound periodical volumes; 75 VF drawers of unbound material, microfilm, pictures and maps concerning Central California Catholic churches. **Subscriptions:** 59 journals and other serials. **Services:** Library not open to public. **Remarks:** Library is located at 1550 N. Fresno St., Fresno, CA 93707.

★4784★
FRESNO GENEALOGICAL SOCIETY - LIBRARY (Hist)
Box 1429
Fresno, CA 93716   Ruby Newell Jeter, Libn.
Founded: 1965. **Staff:** 5. **Subjects:** Genealogy. **Holdings:** 400 books; 50 unbound periodicals; 250 bound periodical volumes; 8 reels of microfilm. **Subscriptions:** 71 journals and other serials. **Services:** Library open to public with restrictions. **Publications:** Ash Tree Echo, quarterly, with index.

FREUND LAW LIBRARY
See: Washington University - School of Law - Freund Law Library

★4785★
FRIARS OF THE ATONEMENT - CARDINAL SPELLMAN LIBRARY (Rel-Theol)
Graymoor   Phone: (914) 424-3671
Garrison, NY 10524   Rev. Alexander Kelliher, S.A., Mgr.
Founded: 1952. **Staff:** Prof 2; Other 1. **Subjects:** Ecumenical theology, church history, ecclesiology. **Special Collections:** Archives of the Franciscan Friars of the Atonement (documents and books about the history of the Graymoor Friars). **Holdings:** 85,000 books; 140 bound periodical volumes; 450 reels of microfilm of Library of Church Unity periodicals. **Subscriptions:** 160 journals and other serials; 30 newspapers. **Services:** Interlibrary loans; copying; library open to public. **Publications:** Ecumenical Trends; AT-ONE-MENT. **Formerly:** Graymoor Ecumenical Institute. **Staff:** Sally Kearnan, Libn.

★4786★
FRICK ART REFERENCE LIBRARY (Art)
10 E. 71st St.   Phone: (212) 288-8700
New York, NY 10021   Helen Sanger, Libn.
Founded: 1920. **Staff:** Prof 7; Other 25. **Subjects:** Art. **Special Collections:** Books and photographs of American and European paintings, drawings and sculpture; illuminated manuscripts and enamels from the early Christian era to 1860. **Holdings:** 150,400 books and bound periodical volumes; 53,300 sales catalogs; 416,900 study photographs. **Subscriptions:** 200 journals and other serials. **Services:** Copying; print orders can be filled from collection of 60,000 negatives with the permission of the owner of the original work of art; library open to serious graduate students of history of art. **Publications:** The Story of the Frick Art Reference Library: The Early Years (1979) - for sale. **Staff:** Marie C. Keith, Asst.Libn.

FRICK CHEMICAL LABORATORY
See: Princeton University - Chemistry & Biochemistry Library

FRICK (Henry Clay) FINE ARTS LIBRARY
See: University of Pittsburgh - Henry Clay Frick Fine Arts Library

★4787★
FRIED FRANK HARRIS SHRIVER JACOBSON - LIBRARY & INFORMATION CENTER (Law)†
1 New York Plaza   Phone: (212) 820-8000
New York, NY 10004   Stewart F. Deutsch, Exec.Libn.
Staff: 12. **Subjects:** Law - securities, Anglo-American, real estate, corporate, tax. **Holdings:** 25,000 books; 10,000 bound periodical volumes; 1000 prospectuses (cataloged); 200 microforms; 50 VF drawers of pamphlets. **Subscriptions:** 175 journals and other serials. **Services:** Interlibrary loans; copying; library not open to public. **Computerized Information Services:** Online systems. **Special Catalogs:** Catalog of company prospectuses and office legal memoranda. **Staff:** Warren Gordon, Asst.Exec.Libn.; Beth Abend, Gen.Libn.; Karen McShane, Tax Libn.

★4788★
FRIED FRANK HARRIS SHRIVER & KAMPELMAN - LIBRARY (Law)
600 New Hampshire Ave., N.W.   Phone: (202) 342-3681
Washington, DC 20037   Terezia Rubai, Dir.
Staff: Prof 3; Other 3. **Subjects:** Law, international trade, business. **Holdings:** 17,000 volumes. **Subscriptions:** 104 journals and other serials. **Services:** Interlibrary loans; copying; library open to public by appointment. **Computerized Information Services:** DIALOG, SDC, LEXIS, New York Times Information Service. **Publications:** Library newsletter, monthly.

FRIEDENWALD (Jonas S.) LIBRARY
See: Johns Hopkins University - Wilmer Ophthalmological Institute - Jonas S. Friedenwald Library

★4789★
FRIEDMAN & KOVEN - LAW LIBRARY (Law)
208 S. LaSalle St.   Phone: (312) 346-8500
Chicago, IL 60604   Cynthia Lowe Rynning, Hd. Law Libn.
Staff: Prof 1; Other 2. **Subjects:** Law - antitrust, securities, taxation, labor. **Holdings:** 13,000 books. **Subscriptions:** 100 journals and other serials; 10 newspapers. **Services:** Interlibrary loans; library not open to public. **Computerized Information Services:** DIALOG, LEXIS, New York Times Information Service, AUTO-CITE, Disclosure, Inc. **Publications:** Library Bulletin, 2/month - for internal distribution only. **Special Catalogs:** Form Catalog for litigation and business forms.

★4790★
FRIENDS COMMITTEE ON NATIONAL LEGISLATION - LEGISLATIVE LIBRARY (Soc Sci)
245 2nd St., N.E.   Phone: (202) 547-6000
Washington, DC 20002
Founded: 1943. **Staff:** 1. **Subjects:** Disarmament, basic human needs, world institutions, domestic and international agriculture, American Indians. **Holdings:** 300 boxes of reports, Congressional documents. **Subscriptions:** 50 journals and other serials. **Services:** Copying; library open to public by appointment. **Remarks:** Archival materials housed in Swarthmore College - Friends Historical Library - Peace Collection.

FRIENDS FREE LIBRARY
See: Germantown Friends Meeting

FRIENDS HISTORICAL LIBRARY
See: Swarthmore College

★4791★
FRIENDS HOSPITAL - NORMAN D. WEINER PROFESSIONAL LIBRARY (Med)
Roosevelt Blvd. & Adams Ave.   Phone: (215) 831-4763
Philadelphia, PA 19124   Donna M. Zoccola, Libn.
Founded: 1974. **Staff:** Prof 1; Other 2. **Subjects:** Psychoanalysis, psychiatry, psychology, behavioral sciences, human life cycle. **Special Collections:** Archival collection of history of Friends Hospital and other hospitals. **Holdings:** 2650 books; 2500 bound periodical volumes; VF drawers; 275 audiotapes. **Subscriptions:** 105 journals and other serials. **Services:** Interlibrary loans; library open to public by appointment. **Computerized Information Services:** DIALOG, NLM, Lithium Information Center, BRS. **Networks/Consortia:** Member of Mideastern Regional Medical Library System.

FRIENDS HOUSE LIBRARY
See: Society of Friends

FRIENDS MEETING OF WASHINGTON
See: Society of Friends

★4792★
FRIENDS OF THE THIRD WORLD INC. - WHOLE WORLD BOOKS (Soc Sci)
611 W. Wayne St.   Phone: (219) 422-6821
Fort Wayne, IN 46802   Marian R. Waltz, Resource Coord.
Staff: Prof 1; Other 2. **Subjects:** Hunger, population, international politics and economics, U.S. minorities, food and nutrition, international and national poverty issues, American lifestyles and the environment. **Special Collections:** Alternative periodicals and newsletters; research files on Third World Handicraft production (600). **Holdings:** 800 books; 2000 pamphlets and periodicals; 24 VF drawers. **Subscriptions:** 30 journals and other serials. **Services:** Copying; library open to public for reference use only; requests for information or referral are answered by mail. **Publications:** Library catalog, annual.

★4793★
FRIENDS UNIVERSITY - EDMUND STANLEY LIBRARY (Rel-Theol)
2100 University Ave.   Phone: (316) 261-5800
Wichita, KS 67213   Hans Bynagle, Dir., Lrng.Res.
Founded: 1898. **Staff:** Prof 5; Other 4. **Subjects:** Religion, humanities, social sciences, natural sciences. **Special Collections:** Quaker heritage and work among the Indians; Noble Cain Collection of Music and Memorabilia; Friends University; family life. **Holdings:** 75,000 books; 14,000 bound periodical volumes; 4500 microforms and AV items; 25 VF drawers of Kansas Yearly Meeting of Friends Archives. **Subscriptions:** 516 journals and other serials; 10 newspapers. **Services:** Interlibrary loans; copying; library open to public with restrictions. **Computerized Information Services:** Computerized cataloging. **Networks/Consortia:** Member of OCLC; Kansas Library Network. **Staff:** Helen Wood, Cur., Quaker Coll.

★4794★
FRIENDS OF THE WESTERN PHILATELIC LIBRARY (Rec)
Box 2219　　　　　　　　　　　Phone: (408) 245-9171
Sunnyvale, CA 94087　　　　　　Richard E. Clever, Pres.
Staff: 1. **Subjects:** Stamp collecting. **Holdings:** 2000 books; 3000 bound periodical volumes; 10 cabinets of pamphlets and files. **Subscriptions:** 150 journals and other serials. **Services:** Interlibrary loans; copying; library open to public. **Computerized Information Services:** Computerized circulation. **Publications:** Monthly newsletter. **Remarks:** The library is housed in the Sunnyvale Public Library, 665 W. Olive, Sunnyvale, CA 94087.

FRISSELL (Hollis Burke) LIBRARY-ARCHIVES
See: Tuskegee Institute - Hollis Burke Frissell Library-Archives

★4795★
FRITO-LAY, INC. - LIBRARY (Food-Bev)†
6400 Harry Hines
Box 35034　　　　　　　　　　Phone: (214) 351-7298
Dallas, TX 75235　　　　　　　Rosemary Barrett, Libn.
Staff: 2. **Subjects:** Snack foods, business management, grocery/marketing. **Holdings:** 350 books; 40 bound periodical volumes. **Subscriptions:** 353 journals and other serials. **Services:** Interlibrary loans; copying; library open to public for reference use only. **Staff:** Helen R. Harden, Dept.Supv.

★4796★
FRITO-LAY, INC. - TECHNICAL INFORMATION CENTER (Sci-Tech; Food-Bev)
7929 Brookriver Dr.　　　　　Phone: (214) 689-1708
Dallas, TX 75247　　　　　　　Suzanne M. Ogden, Tech.Libn.
Founded: 1980. **Staff:** Prof 1. **Subjects:** Engineering, computer science, food science, pollution control. **Special Collections:** Vendor catalogs of required products (1200). **Holdings:** 320 books; 4 file drawers of technical reports; 4 file drawers of journal articles (cataloged by subject); 150 phone directories and maps of plant sites; 48 volumes of ASTM Standards; 4 file drawers of ANSI Standards. **Subscriptions:** 152 journals and other serials. **Services:** Interlibrary loans; copying; SDI; library open to other librarians. **Computerized Information Services:** DIALOG; computerized cataloging. **Networks/Consortia:** Member of Metroplex Council of Health Science Librarians; Brookhollow Area Librarians Association. **Publications:** TIC Acquisitions Newsletter, monthly; descriptive brochure of services; TIC Policy Manual (both updated as needed). **Special Catalogs:** Catalog of vendor catalogs; catalog of technical reports and catalog of standards (both hardcopy).

FRITZ (Chester) LIBRARY
See: University of North Dakota

★4797★
FRITZSCHE, DODGE AND OLCOTT, INC. - RESEARCH LIBRARY (Sci-Tech)
76 Ninth Ave.　　　　　　　　Phone: (212) 929-4100
New York, NY 10011　　　　　Dr. Roman T. Koenig, Info.Dir.
Founded: 1930. **Staff:** Prof 2. **Subjects:** Essential oils, aromatic chemicals, perfume and flavor raw materials. **Holdings:** 5000 volumes and bound periodical volumes. **Subscriptions:** 200 journals and other serials. **Services:** Interlibrary loans; copying (limited); library not open to public. **Computerized Information Services:** DIALOG, SDC. **Publications:** Fritzsche, D & O Library Bulletin, monthly - free upon request. **Staff:** Rita Intal, Asst.Libn.

FRITZSCHE (Paul) LIBRARY
See: Johnson & Wales College - Paul Fritzsche Library

FROMKIN (Morris) MEMORIAL COLLECTION
See: University of Wisconsin, Milwaukee

★4798★
FRONTIER GATEWAY MUSEUM - LIBRARY (Hist)
Belle Prairie Frontage Rd., Box 1181
Glendive, MT 59330　　　　　Louise Cross, Cur.
Subjects: Homesteading in Montana; Indians of eastern Montana; prehistoric fossils; ranching, rural education, early businesses. **Special Collections:** Senator George McCone collection (40 items); M.E. Sutton Memorial Indian display (156 items); fossil collection. **Holdings:** 300 books; 279 unbound research items (cataloged); 45 maps; 3 VF drawers of pictures; 7 VF drawers of clippings. **Services:** Interlibrary loans (limited); library open to public.

FROSST LABORATORIES
See: Merck Frosst Laboratories

FROST ENTOMOLOGICAL MUSEUM
See: Pennsylvania State University

FROST LIBRARY
See: New York University - Elmer Holmes Bobst Library

FROST (Robert) COLLECTION
See: Plymouth State College - Herbert H. Lamson Library - Robert Frost Collection

★4799★
FROSTBURG STATE COLLEGE - LIBRARY (Educ)
　　　　　　　　　　　　　　Phone: (301) 689-4396
Frostburg, MD 21532　　　　John Zimmerman, Lib.Dir.
Staff: Prof 13; Other 18. **Subjects:** Business, teacher education, liberal arts. **Special Collections:** Depository for selected U.S. Government documents, Appalachian Regional Commission and U.S. Defense Mapping Agency, Topographic Center. **Holdings:** 151,553 books; 24,008 bound periodical volumes; 90,941 government documents; 50,784 AV materials; 86,832 microforms. **Subscriptions:** 1284 journals; 25 newspapers. **Services:** Interlibrary loans; copying; library open to public. **Computerized Information Services:** Computerized cataloging. **Networks/Consortia:** Member of OCLC. **Publications:** Monographs, irregular.

★4800★
FRUEHAUF CORPORATION - RESEARCH AND DEVELOPMENT DIVISION - LIBRARY (Sci-Tech; Trans)
10825 Harper　　　　　　　　Phone: (313) 267-1504
Detroit, MI 48213　　　　　　Rita Van Assche Bueter, Libn.
Staff: Prof 1. **Subjects:** Trailers, mechanical engineering, metallurgy, containers, freight transportation, welding. **Holdings:** 350 books; 1000 manufacturers' catalogs; 500 technical reports; 500 in-house projects and reports. **Subscriptions:** 50 journals and other serials. **Services:** Interlibrary loans; copying; library not open to public. **Computerized Information Services:** DIALOG. **Publications:** R & D Library Newsletter, monthly - for internal distribution only. **Special Indexes:** Manufacturers' catalogs and products cross index (card).

★4801★
FRUITLANDS MUSEUMS - LIBRARY (Hist)
Prospect Hill Rd.
R.R. 2, Box 87　　　　　　　　Phone: (617) 456-3924
Harvard, MA 01451　　　　　　Richard S. Reed, Musm.Dir.
Staff: 2. **Subjects:** American Indians, American paintings, Transcendentalist history, Shaker history. **Special Collections:** Shaker journals (25). **Holdings:** 5000 books; 3000 bound periodical volumes; 1000 manuscipts; 200 unbound reports. **Subscriptions:** 25 journals and other serials. **Services:** Library open to public with restrictions.

FRY CONSULTANTS INCORPORATED - MANAGEMENT CENTRE
See: Mac Farlane & Company, Inc.

FRY (J.A.B.) RESEARCH LIBRARY
See: United Methodist Church - Northern California-Nevada Conference - J.A.B. Fry Research Library

★4802★
FRYE (Charles and Emma) ART MUSEUM - LIBRARY (Art)
Box 3005　　　　　　　　　　Phone: (206) 622-9250
Seattle, WA 98114　　　　　　Mrs. W.S. Greathouse, Pres.
Subjects: European and American art of late 19th-century. **Holdings:** Figures not available. **Subscriptions:** 8 journals and other serials. **Services:** Library not open to public.

★4803★
FRYE-SILLS, INC. - LIBRARY (Bus-Fin)
5500 S. Syracuse Circle　　　Phone: (303) 773-3900
Englewood, CO 80111　　　　Libbie Gottschalk, Libn.
Founded: 1978. **Staff:** Prof 1. **Subjects:** Advertising and marketing; graphic arts. **Special Collections:** Frye-Sills Archives. **Holdings:** 250 books; 3 VF drawers; 15 scrapbooks. **Services:** Library not open to public. **Remarks:** Subsidiary of Young and Rubicam, Inc.

FTC
See: U.S. Federal Trade Commission - Library

FUDGER HEALTH SCIENCES LIBRARY
See: Toronto General Hospital

FUEL SYSTEMS INFORMATION CENTER
See: Westinghouse Hanford Company

★4804★
FUGRO GULF, INC. - LIBRARY (Sci-Tech)
10101 Harwin, Suite 200   Phone: (713) 777-2641
Houston, TX 77036   Gloria Bellis, Libn.
Founded: 1977. **Staff:** Prof 1. **Subjects:** Soil mechanics; engineering - geotechnical, ocean, highway; geology. **Holdings:** 1010 books and bound periodical volumes; 120 technical reports; 550 reports on microfiche; 325 maps. **Subscriptions:** 52 journals and other serials. **Services:** Interlibrary loans; copying. **Computerized Information Services:** SDC.

★4805★
FULBRIGHT & JAWORSKI - LIBRARY (Law)
Bank of the Southwest Bldg.   Phone: (713) 651-5151
Houston, TX 77002   Jane D. Holland, Libn.
Founded: 1919. **Staff:** Prof 2; Other 8. **Subjects:** Law. **Holdings:** 47,000 volumes. **Subscriptions:** 1500 journals and other serials; 8 newspapers. **Services:** Interlibrary loans; copying; library open to other attorneys by invitation. **Computerized Information Services:** LEXIS. **Staff:** Violanda Fabugais, Asst.Libn.

FULD (Helene) LEARNING RESOURCE CENTER
See: St. Joseph's Hospital - Helene Fuld Learning Resource Center

FULD (Helene) LIBRARY
See: New England Baptist Hospital - Helene Fuld Library

FULD (Helene) MEDICAL CENTER
See: Helene Fuld Medical Center

FULLER (F.T.) STAFF LIBRARY
See: Dorothea Dix Hospital - F.T. Fuller Staff Library

FULLER (George F.) LIBRARY
See: Worcester Foundation for Experimental Biology - George F. Fuller Library

★4806★
FULLER & HENRY - LIBRARY (Law)
12th Fl., Edison Plaza
300 Madison Ave.   Phone: (419) 255-8220
Toledo, OH 43604   Melvia A. Scott, Libn.
Staff: Prof 1; Other 1. **Subjects:** Law. **Holdings:** 20,000 volumes; loose-leaf services; periodicals; government reports. **Services:** Library not open to public. **Computerized Information Services:** LEXIS. **Publications:** Internal newsletter. **Formerly:** Fuller, Henry, Hodge & Snyder.

FULLER MEMORIAL LIBRARY
See: Brockton Art Museum

FULLER (Ralph) MEDICAL LIBRARY
See: St. Mary's Hospital & Health Center - Ralph Fuller Medical Library

★4807★
FULLER THEOLOGICAL SEMINARY - MC ALISTER LIBRARY (Rel-Theol)
135 N. Oakland Ave.   Phone: (213) 449-1745
Pasadena, CA 91101   Christine C. Jewett, Libn.
Founded: 1948. **Staff:** Prof 8; Other 7. **Subjects:** Biblical studies, theology, religion, missiology, philosophy, psychology. **Holdings:** 140,000 books and bound periodical volumes. **Subscriptions:** 725 journals and other serials. **Services:** Interlibrary loans; copying; library open to public but borrowing restricted to students, faculty and alumni. **Networks/Consortia:** Member of Western Association of Theological Schools; American Theological Library Association; OCLC. **Staff:** Karen Cranston, Ref.; Lura Stockett, Circ.Libn.; E. Yeung, Tech.Serv.; Olivia Ruth, Hd., Comp.Serv.; Hildegard Nelson, Per.Libn.

★4808★
FULTON COUNTY HISTORICAL AND GENEALOGICAL SOCIETY - RESEARCH ROOM (Hist)†
Parlin-Ingersoll Library
205 W. Chestnut   Phone: (309) 647-0328
Canton, IL 61520   Beverly Stewart, Hd.Libn.
Staff: Prof 8. **Subjects:** Genealogy, history. **Special Collections:** Historical scrapbooks. **Holdings:** 600 books; diaries, scrapbooks. **Subscriptions:** 12 journals and other serials. **Services:** Interlibrary loans; copying; library open to public.

★4809★
FULTON COUNTY HISTORICAL SOCIETY - LIBRARY (Hist)
7th & Pontiac   Phone: (219) 223-4436
Rochester, IN 46975   Shirley Willard, Dir.
Founded: 1963. **Staff:** 10. **Subjects:** Local history and genealogy, Elmo Lincoln (first movie Tarzan), Potawatomi Indians. **Special Collections:** Trail of Death removal of Potawatomi Indians from Indiana to Kansas in 1838. **Holdings:** 500 books; 7 file cabinets of clippings; 1 file cabinet of documents; 4 films; 5 rooms of archives. **Subscriptions:** 29 journals and other serials. **Services:** Copying; library open to public for reference use only. **Publications:** Fulton County Historical Society Quarterly - for members; Fulton County Folks (volumes 1 and 2); **Special Catalogs:** Card file of objects, books, donors; catalog of accession sheets.

★4810★
FULTON COUNTY HISTORICAL SOCIETY - LIBRARY (Hist)
Box 115
McConnellsburg, PA 17233
Founded: 1976. **Subjects:** Local history and genealogy. **Special Collections:** Cemetery file; Fulton Republican newspaper, 1865-1900; Fulton Democrat newspaper on microfilm, 1900-1970; old school photographs; local family histories; county histories; church records. **Holdings:** 200 books; U.S. Census on microfilm for Bedford and Fulton Counties, 1790-1900; 100 volumes of Pennsylvania archives; Bedford County wills and deeds on microfilm, 1771-1850. **Services:** Library open to public with restrictions.

★4811★
FULTON COUNTY LAW LIBRARY (Law)†
709 Courthouse
136 Pryor St., S.W.   Phone: (404) 572-2330
Atlanta, GA 30303   Margaret D. Martin, Law Libn.
Founded: 1913. **Staff:** Prof 1; Other 1. **Subjects:** Law - local, county, state, federal. **Holdings:** 15,000 volumes. **Services:** Copying; library open to public.

★4812★
FULTON COUNTY LAW LIBRARY ASSOCIATION - LAW LIBRARY (Law)†
Court House   Phone: (419) 335-8863
Wauseon, OH 43567   Marilyn Horner, Libn.
Staff: 2. **Subjects:** Law. **Holdings:** 10,000 volumes; 50 audio cassettes. **Services:** Copying; library open to public with restrictions. **Special Catalogs:** Book catalog.

FULTON-HAYDEN MEMORIAL LIBRARY
See: Amerind Foundation, Inc.

★4813★
FULTON STATE HOSPITAL - MEDICAL LIBRARY (Med)†
E. Fifth St.   Phone: (314) 642-3311
Fulton, MO 65251   Berneice Deloney, Libn.
Staff: 1. **Subjects:** Medicine, psychiatry. **Holdings:** 900 books; 250 bound periodical volumes. **Subscriptions:** 40 journals and other serials. **Services:** Library open to public.

★4814★
FUND FOR MODERN COURTS - LIBRARY (Law)
36 W. 44th St., Rm. 711   Phone: (212) 575-1577
New York, NY 10036   Dr. M.L. Henry, Jr., Exec.Dir.
Staff: 6. **Subjects:** Judicial selection, court unification and administration, criminal justice, citizen participation. **Special Collections:** Court Monitoring; Citizen's Court Projects Manual; Family & Criminal Court Handbook. **Holdings:** 1000 volumes; 8 VF drawers of clippings and newsletters. **Services:** Interlibrary loans; library open to public with restrictions. **Special Indexes:** Clipping index.

★4815★
FUND FOR PEACE - CENTER FOR DEFENSE INFORMATION - LIBRARY (Mil)
303 Capital Gallery West
600 Maryland Ave., S.W.   Phone: (202) 484-9490
Washington, DC 20024   Richard Fieldhouse, Res.Libn.
Founded: 1972. **Staff:** Prof 1; Other 2. **Subjects:** Defense information, Defense Department budgets, foreign affairs, military posture, nuclear weapons, arms control. **Special Collections:** Stockholm International Peace Research Institute (SIPRI) yearbooks (12 linear feet); arms control and armaments (11 volumes); defense-related Congressional Budget Office reports (2 linear feet); defense-related General Accounting Office reports. **Holdings:** 800 books; 1200 bound periodical volumes; 2500 Congressional hearing reports; 9 linear feet of intelligence reports; 8 linear feet of Defense Department posture statements and reports; 36 file boxes on special topics; 12 VF drawers of defense information; 50 audio- and videotapes; 400

pamphlets, reports and manuscripts. **Subscriptions:** 140 journals and other serials; 6 newspapers. **Services:** Copying; library open to public for reference use only. **Publications:** Defense Monitor, 10/year.

★4816★
FUND FOR PEACE - CENTER FOR INTERNATIONAL POLICY - INFORMATION CENTER (Soc Sci)
120 Maryland Ave., N.E.   Phone: (202) 544-4666
Washington, DC 20002   Virginia Adams, Adm.Dir.
Founded: 1975. **Staff:** 7. **Subjects:** United States human rights policy and foreign assistance; U.S.-Indochina relations. **Holdings:** Figures not available. **Subscriptions:** 20 journals and other serials; 20 newspapers.

FUNDAMENTAL CONSTANTS DATA CENTER
See: U.S. Natl. Bureau of Standards

★4817★
FUNDING INFORMATION LIBRARY (Soc Sci)
1120 Milam Bldg.
406 W. Market St.
San Antonio, TX 78205   Phone: (512) 227-4333
    Candes Chumney, Supv.
Founded: 1974. **Staff:** Prof 3. **Subjects:** Foundations, grants, proposal writing, federal and corporate funding, nonprofit organizations. **Holdings:** 1000 books and bound periodical volumes; 12 thesauri; 13,000 microfiche; 8 VF drawers of clippings and reports. **Subscriptions:** 15 journals and other serials; 10 newspapers. **Services:** Copying; library open to public. **Computerized Information Services:** DIALOG. **Networks/Consortia:** Member of Foundation Center of New York; San Antonio Online Users Group. **Publications:** FIL Handbook. **Special Catalogs:** Local foundation notebooks; file of corporate and business gifts to nonprofit organizations (card). **Special Indexes:** San Antonio Foundations Grants Index, 1979-1980. **Remarks:** FIL is now a separate nonprofit and tax-exempt corporation. **Formerly:** Minnie Stevens Piper Foundation - Funding Information Library.

★4818★
FURMAN UNIVERSITY LIBRARY - SPECIAL COLLECTIONS (Hist)
    Phone: (803) 294-2194
Greenville, SC 29613   Dr. J. Glen Clayton, Spec.Coll.Libn.
Founded: 1826. **Staff:** Prof 1; Other 1. **Subjects:** South Carolina Baptist history. **Special Collections:** South Carolina Collection (2750 books); Furman University Collection (150 books and 325 theses and projects); Furman archives; Rare Books (275); Baptist Historical Collection (1400 books, 150,000 pages on microfilm, 12,000 manuscripts). **Services:** Interlibrary loans; collections open to public for reference use only. **Publications:** Journal of South Carolina Baptist Historical Society, annual - to members and by subscription.

FURNESS (Horace Howard) MEMORIAL LIBRARY
See: University of Pennsylvania - Horace Howard Furness Memorial Library

★4819★
FURNITURE LIBRARY ASSOCIATION (Art)
1009 N. Main St.   Phone: (919) 883-4011
High Point, NC 27262   Jo Ellen Godfrey, Libn.
Subjects: Early architecture; design - interior, furniture, fabric. **Special Collections:** Original complete volumes of Chippendale, Hepplewhite, Sheraton and other 18th century designers (unique to this library). **Holdings:** 4500 books and bound periodical volumes including over 100 years of Furniture World; other trade journals. **Services:** Copying; library open to public.

FUSE CENTER LIBRARY
See: Federation for Unified Science Education

FUSZ MEMORIAL LIBRARY
See: St. Louis University - College of Philosophy and Letters

★4820★
FUTURE AVIATION PROFESSIONALS OF AMERICA (FAPA) - INFORMATION CENTER (Educ)
3000B S. Highland Dr.   Phone: (702) 737-0897
Las Vegas, NV 89109   W. Louis Smith, Pres.
Founded: 1975. **Staff:** 15. **Subjects:** Professional pilot careers. **Holdings:** 52 books and periodicals. **Subscriptions:** 22 journals and other serials. **Services:** Personal career counseling to members; statistics provided to airline industry; employment information for professional air crews and computer job assistance for air crew applicants; computerized selection of pilot applicants supplied to airlines, commuter lines, corporate and FBO employers. **Publications:** Information packet; monthly newsletter for pilots; monthly newsletter for flight attendants; pilot employment guide; flight attendant employment guide.

★4821★
FUTURE HOMEMAKERS OF AMERICA - NATIONAL HEADQUARTERS & LEADERSHIP CENTER - RESOURCE CENTER (Educ)
1910 Association Drive   Phone: (703) 476-4900
Reston, VA 22091   Polli Howard, Dir. of Commun.
Founded: 1973. **Staff:** Prof 5. **Subjects:** Home economics education, vocational education, child/adolescent care, nutrition. **Holdings:** Figures not available. **Subscriptions:** 36 journals and other serials. **Services:** Library not open to public.

★4822★
FUTURES GROUP, INC. - LIBRARY (Soc Sci)
76 Eastern Blvd.   Phone: (203) 633-3501
Glastonbury, CT 06033   Katherine H. Willson, Mgr., Info.Serv.
Founded: 1971. **Staff:** Prof 2; Other 2. **Subjects:** Futures research, technology assessment, energy, business, economics, materials. **Holdings:** 9000 books; 950 bound periodical volumes; 3500 other cataloged items; 3500 clippings and unbound reports. **Subscriptions:** 150 journals and other serials. **Services:** Interlibrary loans; copying; SDI; library not open to public. **Computerized Information Services:** Online systems.

G

★4823★

G & W NATURAL RESOURCES GROUP - ZERBE RESEARCH CENTER - TECHNICAL LIBRARY (Sci-Tech)
1 Highland Ave.   Phone: (215) 866-9235
Bethlehem, PA 18017   W.S. Castor, Jr., Mgr.
Founded: 1913. **Subjects:** Pigments, metallurgy (chiefly titanium and zinc), chemistry, physics, optics, paint, paper, plastics, rubber. **Holdings:** 4000 books; 2500 bound periodical volumes; 20,000 U.S. and foreign patents. **Subscriptions:** 80 journals and other serials. **Services:** Interlibrary loans; copying; library not open to public. **Computerized Information Services:** SDC.

GAAR (Julia Meek) WAYNE COUNTY HISTORICAL MUSEUM
See: Wayne County Historical Museum

★4824★

GAF CORPORATION - LEGAL DEPARTMENT LIBRARY (Bus-Fin; Law)†
140 W. 51st St.   Phone: (212) 621-5000
New York, NY 10020
Subjects: Business, law. **Holdings:** 2000 volumes.

★4825★

GAF CORPORATION - PROCESS DEVELOPMENT DEPARTMENT - RESEARCH LIBRARY
40 Charles St.
Binghamton, NY 13902
Defunct

★4826★

GAF CORPORATION - TECHNICAL INFORMATION SERVICES (Sci-Tech)
1361 Alps Rd.   Phone: (201) 628-3321
Wayne, NJ 07470   Ira Naznitsky, Mgr.
Founded: 1942. **Staff:** Prof 3; Other 2. **Subjects:** Chemistry, engineering, plastics, pulp and paper, petroleum, polymers, surfactants, brighteners, chemical intermediates, textile assistants, organic chemistry. **Holdings:** 6800 books; 8000 bound periodical volumes; 400 unbound journal volumes; 250,000 U.S. patents; 3000 foreign patents; 950 reels of microfilm; 63 VF drawers of pamphlets (cataloged). **Subscriptions:** 212 journals and other serials. **Services:** Interlibrary loans; copying; use of library for reference may be requested. **Computerized Information Services:** SDC, NLM, BRS, DOE, DIALOG, Chemical Abstracts Service. **Publications:** Internal Reports; Searches; Translations. **Staff:** Helen Carini, Supv.Libn.; Ceil Garcia, Info.Spec.

GAGE (Homer) LIBRARY
See: Memorial Hospital - Homer Gage Library

★4827★

GAGE & TUCKER - LIBRARY (Law)
2345 Grand Ave.   Phone: (816) 474-6460
Kansas City, MO 64108   Mary Traylor Troup, Libn.
Staff: Prof 1; Other 1. **Subjects:** Law. **Holdings:** 3000 books; 300 bound periodical volumes. **Services:** Interlibrary loans; copying; library open to public with restrictions. **Computerized Information Services:** LEXIS.

★4828★

GAINESVILLE SUN - LIBRARY (Publ)
Drawer A   Phone: (904) 378-1411
Gainesville, FL 32602   Robert Ivey, Libn.
Staff: Prof 1; Other 1. **Subjects:** Newspaper reference topics. **Holdings:** 600 books; 12,000 photographs; 320 reels of microfilmed newspapers; 150 maps; 200 VF drawers of tearsheets. **Services:** Copying; library not open to public.

★4829★

GALE RESEARCH COMPANY - LIBRARY (Publ)
Penobscot Bldg.   Phone: (313) 961-2242
Detroit, MI 48226   Annie M. Brewer, Sr.Ed.
Founded: 1954. **Staff:** Prof 1; Other 1. **Subjects:** Associations and professional societies, collected biography, military history (especially code names), acronyms and initialisms, tradenames, library science and history, special libraries, research programs, newsletters, lexicology, onomatology, music, art, occult. **Special Collections:** Contemporary Authors Archives; Association Archives (200,000 items on 15,000 organizations); Print Collection (2500 prints); biographical dictionaries (3000). **Holdings:** 65,100

volumes. **Subscriptions:** 1300 journals and other serials; 20 newspapers. **Services:** Copying; library open to public for reference use only by permission. **Computerized Information Services:** DIALOG, SDC.

★4830★

GALESBURG COTTAGE HOSPITAL - HEALTH SERVICES LIBRARY (Med)
695 N. Kellogg St.   Phone: (309) 343-8131
Galesburg, IL 61401   Barbara Olson Bullis, Libn.
Founded: 1950. **Staff:** Prof 1. **Subjects:** Medicine, nursing, allied health sciences, hospital administration. **Holdings:** 1200 books. **Subscriptions:** 130 journals and other serials. **Services:** Interlibrary loans; copying; library open to public. **Networks/Consortia:** Member of Regional Medical Library - Region 3; Heart of Illinois Library Consortium; Rush Affiliates Information Network (RAIN). **Publications:** Recent acquisitions list, quarterly - distributed to medical staff and hospital employees.

★4831★

GALESBURG MENTAL HEALTH CENTER - HIMWICH LIBRARY OF THE NEUROSCIENCES (Med)
1801 N. Seminary   Phone: (309) 344-2141
Galesburg, IL 61401   Margo McClelland, Med.Libn.
Founded: 1953. **Staff:** Prof 1; Other 1. **Subjects:** Psychiatry, mental retardation, neurology, biochemistry, neurochemistry, psychology, social service, nursing, medicine, activities therapy. **Holdings:** 5800 books; 4500 bound periodical volumes; 2000 reprints; 10 dissertations; 590 publications from Galesburg State Research Hospital Laboratory. **Subscriptions:** 80 journals and other serials. **Services:** Interlibrary loans; copying; current awareness; library open to public. **Networks/Consortia:** Member of Heart of Illinois Library Consortium; Illinois Department of Mental Health and Developmental Disabilitites Library Services Network (DMHDD/LISN). **Publications:** New Acquisitions List, quarterly. **Remarks:** Maintained by Illinois State Department of Mental Health and Developmental Disabilities.

GALLAGHER (Marian Gould) LAW LIBRARY
See: University of Washington - Marian Gould Gallagher Law Library

★4832★

GALLAUDET COLLEGE LIBRARY - SPECIAL COLLECTIONS (Educ)
Seventh & Florida Aves., N.E.   Phone: (202) 651-5566
Washington, DC 20002   Fern Edwards, College Libn.
Founded: 1854. **Staff:** Prof 12; Other 18. **Subjects:** Deafness and the deaf; remedial speech and hearing. **Holdings:** 12,000 books and AV items; 500 other cataloged items (Baker Collection); 100 VF drawers; college archives; 3000 theses and dissertations on microfilm; ERIC microfiche; films. **Services:** Interlibrary loans; copying; collection open to public for reference use only. **Computerized Information Services:** DIALOG, BRS; Linguistic Research Laboratory sign language collection and deafness collection, available through SIRE; computerized cataloging. **Networks/Consortia:** Member of Consortium of Universities of the Washington Metropolitan Area (CUMWA). **Special Catalogs:** COM catalog of deafness collection. **Staff:** Theresa Chang, Hd., Tech.Serv.; Jeanne Conway, Hd., Pub.Serv.; Thomas Harrington, Media Libn.

★4833★

GALLAUDET COLLEGE - NATIONAL INFORMATION CENTER ON DEAFNESS (Educ)
T-6 Gallaudet College   Phone: (202) 651-5109
Washington, DC 20002   Jane Mortenson, Dir.
Founded: 1980. **Staff:** Prof 4; Other 6. **Subjects:** Deafness. **Holdings:** 75 books; 3 VF drawers of subject files; 4 VF drawers of deafness agency/organization files. **Subscriptions:** 10 journals and other serials. **Services:** Center open to public with restrictions. **Staff:** Arlynn Snukals, Sr.Info.Anl; Craig Speicher, Sr.Info.Anl.; Kay Fitzgerald, Promotional Coord.

★4834★

GALLERY/STRATFORD - JOHN MARTIN LIBRARY (Art)
54 Romeo St.   Phone: (519) 271-5271
Stratford, ON, Canada N5A 4S9   Bruce White, Coord., Educ. & Ext.
Founded: 1968. **Subjects:** Fine arts. **Holdings:** 900 books; 3000 exhibition catalogs (Canadian, U.S., European). **Services:** Library open to gallery members, educators, students and researchers by appointment.

★4835★

GALLO (E. & J.) WINERY - LIBRARY (Food-Bev)
Box 1130   Phone: (209) 521-3230
Modesto, CA 95353   Jill Elliott, Libn.
Founded: 1969. **Staff:** Prof 1. **Subjects:** Wine technology; chemical and biological research; statistics; packaging. **Holdings:** 9000 books; 750 bound periodical volumes; 3800 VF items (cataloged); 400 catalogs; 8 VF drawers

of trade literature. **Subscriptions:** 450 journals and other serials. **Services:** Library not open to public. **Publications:** New Material Received, weekly; Current Abstracts, monthly - both for internal distribution only. **Special Catalogs:** Wine technology bibliography, prepared from Current Abstracts.

GALLOUPE (Charles William) LIBRARY
See: Beverly Historical Society - Library and Archives

★4836★
GALLOWAY (Ewing) PHOTO AGENCY
342 Madison Ave.
New York, NY 10017
Defunct

★4837★
GALLUP INDIAN MEDICAL CENTER - MEDICAL LIBRARY (Med; Area-Ethnic)
East Nizhoni Blvd.
Box 1337   Phone: (505) 722-1119
Gallup, NM 87301   Patricia V. Bradley, Med.Libn.
Founded: 1961. **Staff:** Prof 1. **Subjects:** Medicine, surgery, dentistry. **Special Collections:** Navajo Indians. **Holdings:** 2000 books. **Subscriptions:** 240 journals and other serials. **Services:** Interlibrary loans; library open to public with restrictions. **Formerly:** U.S. Public Health Service Hospital.

GAMBLE (David B.) HOUSE
See: Greene and Greene Library

GAMING RESEARCH CENTER
See: University of Nevada, Las Vegas

★4838★
GANNETT (Guy) PUBLISHING COMPANY - PRESS HERALD-EVENING EXPRESS LIBRARY (Publ)†
390 Congress St.   Phone: (207) 775-5811
Portland, ME 04104   Mary N. Sparrow, Chf.Libn.
Founded: 1912. **Staff:** Prof 1; Other 5. **Subjects:** Newspaper reference topics. **Special Collections:** City directories, 1856 to present; state registers, 1872 to present. **Holdings:** 1000 books; 250,000 newspaper clipping files; 100,000 photographs; 12 VF drawers of pamphlets and microfilmed newspapers from 1924 to present. **Services:** Copying; library open to public with restrictions and for reference only.

GANNETT NEWSPAPERS
See: Binghamton Press and Sun Bulletin; Bridgewater Courier-News; Oakland Tribune; (Shreveport) Times

GANNON MUSEUM OF WAGONS
See: Yakima Valley Museum and Historical Association

GANONG LIBRARY
See: New Brunswick Museum - Library and Archives Department

GANSER (Helen A.) LIBRARY
See: Millersville State College - Helen A. Ganser Library

GANT (John R.) LIBRARY
See: Wisconsin School for the Deaf - John R. Gant Library

GAO
See: U.S. General Accounting Office

★4839★
GARBELL RESEARCH FOUNDATION - LIBRARY (Sci-Tech)†
1714 Lake St.   Phone: (415) 752-0871
San Francisco, CA 94121
Subjects: Aerodynamics, aeronautical engineering, meteorology, space flight, theoretical physics. **Holdings:** 5000 volumes.

GARBER (Aaron) LIBRARY
See: Cleveland College of Jewish Studies

GARBER RESEARCH CENTER LIBRARY
See: Harbison-Walker Refractories Company

GARBRECHT (Donald L.) LAW LIBRARY
See: University of Maine School of Law - Donald L. Garbrecht Law Library

GARCEAU LIBRARY
See: St. Vincent's Hospital

★4840★
GARD, INC. - LIBRARY (Sci-Tech)
7449 N. Natchez Ave.   Phone: (312) 647-9000
Niles, IL 60648   Ida Carter, Tech.Libn.
Founded: 1965. **Staff:** Prof 1; Other 1. **Subjects:** Engineering, energy applications, manufacturing technology, materials engineering, mechanics research, instrumentation and controls, nondestructive testing. **Holdings:** 4800 books and bound periodical volumes; 12 drawers of military and federal standards and specifications; 700 technical reports. **Subscriptions:** 328 journals and other serials. **Services:** Interlibrary loans; library open to public with prior approval. **Computerized Information Services:** DIALOG, DOE/RECON, DTIC, TECHNOTEC. **Networks/Consortia:** Member of Metropolitan Chicago Library Assembly; North Suburban Library System; ILLINET. **Publications:** New Arrivals, monthly - for internal distribution only. **Remarks:** GARD is a subsidiary of GATX Corporation.

★4841★
GARDEN CENTER OF GREATER CLEVELAND - ELEANOR SQUIRE LIBRARY (Sci-Tech)
East Blvd.   Phone: (216) 721-1600
Cleveland, OH 44106   Richard T. Isaacson, Libn.
Founded: 1930. **Staff:** Prof 1. **Subjects:** Gardening, horticulture, landscape architecture. **Special Collections:** Warren H. Corning Collection of Horticultural Classics. **Holdings:** 11,000 books; 150 bound periodical volumes; 500 seed and nursery catalogs; clippings, pamphlets, illustrations, photographs, slides and botanical prints. **Subscriptions:** 183 journals and other serials. **Services:** Interlibrary loans; copying; personal consultations on gardening problems and on program planning; library open to public. **Special Indexes:** Index of colored botanical illustrations (card); Flowering Plant Index.

★4842★
GARDEN CENTER OF ROCHESTER - LIBRARY (Sci-Tech)
5 Castle Park   Phone: (716) 473-5130
Rochester, NY 14620   Mrs. Robert Baschnagel, Libn.
Founded: 1945. **Staff:** 7. **Subjects:** Horticulture, landscaping, plant identification, garden history, nature study, flower arrangement. **Holdings:** 3000 books; 1000 bound periodical volumes; 12 VF drawers of clippings and bound periodical volumes. **Subscriptions:** 34 journals and other serials. **Services:** Interlibrary loans; library open to members only on limited schedule. **Publications:** The Garden Center Bulletin, 10/year - to members.

★4843★
GARDEN GROVE HISTORICAL SOCIETY - E.G. WARE LIBRARY (Hist)
12174 Euclid Ave.   Phone: (714) 530-8871
Garden Grove, CA 92640   Terry B. Thomas, Pres.
Founded: 1971. **Staff:** 4. **Subjects:** Local history. **Special Collections:** Garden Grove photographs (750); fire department records from founding of volunteers to formal incorporation of city of Garden Grove. **Holdings:** Figures not available. **Services:** Library open to public by appointment.

GARDEN LIBRARY OF THE CENTER FOR STUDIES IN LANDSCAPE ARCHITECTURE
See: Harvard University - Dumbarton Oaks Garden Library of the Center for Studies in Landscape Architecture

★4844★
GARDNER ADVERTISING COMPANY - INFORMATION CENTER (Bus-Fin)
10 Broadway   Phone: (314) 444-2357
St. Louis, MO 63102   Delores Borders, Info.Ctr.Mgr.
Founded: 1902. **Staff:** 3. **Subjects:** Marketing, advertising, media, creative writing. **Holdings:** 1500 books; 900 periodicals. **Subscriptions:** 15 journals and other serials. **Services:** Interlibrary loans; library not open to public.

GARDNER (Carol Mc Donald) RARE BOOK ROOM
See: St. Louis Public Library - Carol Mc Donald Gardner Rare Book Room

GARDNER (Charles B.) LIBRARY
See: Wheaton Historical Association - Library & Research Office

★4845★
GARDNER (Isabella Stewart) MUSEUM, INC. - STAFF LIBRARY (Art)
2 Palace Rd.   Phone: (617) 566-1401
Boston, MA 02115   Susan Sinclair, Archv.
Staff: Prof 1. **Subjects:** Art - history, criticism, technique, conservation; artists; art museums; galleries; exhibition catalogs. **Special Collections:** Correspondence and papers of Isabella Stewart Gardner (6000 items; these

are also on microfilm at the Archives of American Art); Library of Isabella Stewart Gardner (1000 volumes including rare books, fine bindings, literary and historical manuscripts, French horae, 17th and 18th century illustrated works, novels, memoirs, American first editions of 19th and early 20th century; collected letters). **Holdings:** 2000 books; 200 bound periodical volumes; 75 other items; archives memorabilia, clippings, photographs. **Subscriptions:** 20 journals and other serials. **Services:** Library open to public by appointment. **Publications:** Isabella Stewart Gardner Museum; Fenway Court (annual report); Guide to the Collection; Drawings Catalog; Paintings Catalog; Isabella Stewart Gardner and Fenway Court; Sculpture Catalog. **Remarks:** The staff library contains only material "related to the art collection of the museum."

GARDNER (John C.) MEMORIAL LIBRARY
See: First Presbyterian Church - John C. Gardner Memorial Library

GARDNER LIBRARY
See: National Center on Child Abuse and Neglect - Region I Child Abuse and Neglect Resource Center

GARDNER (Yvelin) ALCOHOLISM LIBRARY
See: National Council on Alcoholism, Inc. - Yvelin Gardner Alcoholism Library

★4846★
GARIBALDI AND MEUCCI MEMORIAL MUSEUM - LIBRARY OF THE ITALIAN RISORGIMENTO (Hist)
John Jay Homestead, Box AH
Katonah, NY 10536
Phone: (914) 232-3667
Lino S. Lipinsky de Orlov, Dir.
Founded: 1956. **Subjects:** History of Italian Unification Wars. **Special Collections:** Garibaldi mementoes. **Holdings:** 1250 volumes. **Services:** Library open to public. **Remarks:** The library is located at 420 Tompkins Ave., Rosebank, NY 10305.

★4847★
GARLAND COUNTY HISTORICAL SOCIETY - ARCHIVES (Hist)
Rugg & Olive Sts.
Hot Springs, AR 71901
Phone: (501) 623-5875
Inez E. Cline, City/County Hist.
Founded: 1978. **Staff:** 1. **Subjects:** Local history, genealogy. **Special Collections:** 1880 county census. **Holdings:** 100 books; 58 unbound periodical volumes; 15 file cabinets of clippings; 15 scrapbooks; 5 shelves of old newspapers; 5 ledgers and account books. **Subscriptions:** 58 journals and other serials. **Services:** Library open to public by appointment. **Publications:** The Record, annual. **Special Indexes:** Index to 1880 census of Garland County.

GARRETT (Bruce A.) MEMORIAL LIBRARY & MEDIA CENTER
See: Baptist Memorial Hospital System - Bruce A. Garrett Memorial Library & Media Center

★4848★
GARRETT CORPORATION - AIRESEARCH MANUFACTURING COMPANY - TECHNICAL LIBRARY (Sci-Tech)
Dept. 93-45
2525 W. 190th St.
Torrance, CA 90509
Phone: (213) 512-3667
Joanna M. Sutton, Hd.Libn.
Staff: Prof 2; Other 2. **Subjects:** Engineering - aeronautical, material, mechanical; heat transfer; energy; turbomachinery. **Special Collections:** NACA Technical Reports. **Holdings:** 14,000 books and bound periodical volumes; 130,000 technical reports. **Subscriptions:** 350 journals and other serials. **Services:** Interlibrary loans; copying; library not open to public. **Computerized Information Services:** DIALOG, NASA/RECON, SDC. **Special Indexes:** Index of Garrett-Airesearch Reports. **Staff:** Oakley J. Stephens, Asst.Libn.

★4849★
GARRETT CORPORATION - GARRETT TURBINE ENGINE COMPANY - ENGINEERING LIBRARY (Sci-Tech)
111 S. 34th St.
Box 5217
Phoenix, AZ 85010
Phone: (602) 267-2062
Dr. Nelson W. Hope, Tech.Res.Libn.
Staff: Prof 2; Other 1. **Subjects:** Engineering, automotive engineering, aeronautics, chemistry, mathematics, management, metallurgy, solar energy. **Holdings:** 12,500 books; 2200 bound periodical volumes; 10,000 hard copy government reports; 300,000 government reports on microfiche. **Subscriptions:** 300 journals and other serials. **Services:** Interlibrary loans; SDI; library open to public by arrangement. **Computerized Information Services:** DIALOG. **Publications:** What's New in the Engineering Library, quarterly. **Staff:** Denise Birnbaum, Tech.Libn.

GARRETT (Eileen J.) LIBRARY
See: Parapsychology Foundation - Eileen J. Garrett Library

★4850★
GARRETT-EVANGELICAL/SEABURY-WESTERN THEOLOGICAL SEMINARIES LIBRARY (Rel-Theol)†
2021 Sheridan Rd.
Evanston, IL 60201
Phone: (312) 866-3900
Founded: 1857. **Staff:** Prof 5; Other 9. **Subjects:** General theology, Wesleyana, British and American Methodism, Anglicana, Semitic languages and literature. **Special Collections:** Deering-Jackson Methodistica (500 titles). **Holdings:** 231,000 volumes. **Subscriptions:** 1823 journals and other serials. **Services:** Interlibrary loans; copying; library open to public for reference use only on payment of borrowing fee. **Computerized Information Services:** Computerized cataloging, acquisitions and serials. **Publications:** Garrett-Evangelical Bibliographic Lectures, annual - available for purchase.

GARRETT (John Work) LIBRARY
See: Johns Hopkins University - John Work Garrett Library

★4851★
GARRETT MANUFACTURING, LTD. - ENGINEERING LIBRARY (Sci-Tech)
255 Attwell Dr.
Rexdale, ON, Canada M9W 5B8
Phone: (416) 675-1411
Louis J. Hale, Standards Engr.
Founded: 1967. **Staff:** 4. **Subjects:** Electronics, circuit design, properties of materials, metal fabrication, mechanical engineering. **Holdings:** 800 books; 2000 technical papers (cataloged). **Subscriptions:** 80 journals and other serials. **Services:** Interlibrary loans; library not open to public.

GARVIN LIBRARY
See: Shaker Heights City School District

★4852★
GARY POST-TRIBUNE - LIBRARY (Publ)
1065 Broadway
Gary, IN 46402
Phone: (219) 886-5078
Louise K. Tucker, Hd.Libn.
Staff: Prof 1; Other 2. **Subjects:** Newspaper reference topics. **Holdings:** 300 books; 55 VF drawers of biographical clippings; 67 VF drawers of subject clipping files; 16 VF drawers of local and national photographs; microfilm from 1906 to present. **Services:** Library open to public with restrictions.

GASPIRALI (Ismail) LIBRARY
See: American Association of Crimean Turks, Inc. - Ismail Gaspirali Library

★4853★
GASTON SNOW & ELY BARTLETT (Law)
One Federal St.
Boston, MA 02110
Phone: (617) 426-4600
Catherine F. Breen, Libn.
Staff: Prof 2; Other 2. **Subjects:** Law, business. **Holdings:** 17,000 books; 1000 bound periodical volumes. **Subscriptions:** 80 journals and other serials; 8 newspapers. **Services:** Interlibrary loans; copying; library open to public with restrictions. **Computerized Information Services:** LEXIS, New York Times Information Service. **Networks/Consortia:** Member of Association of Boston Law Librarians. **Publications:** GS & EB newsletter. **Staff:** Jan O'Rourke, Libn.

★4854★
GATES CORPORATION - TECHNICAL INFORMATION CENTER (Sci-Tech)
900 S. Broadway
Box 5887
Denver, CO 80217
Phone: (303) 744-4150
Kathryn L. Mikol, Res.Libn.
Founded: 1945. **Staff:** Prof 1; Other 1. **Subjects:** Rubber, chemistry, physics, management, plastics, textiles. **Holdings:** 2000 books; 140 bound periodical volumes; 40 VF drawers of research reports; 5 VF drawers of catalogs and bulletins. **Subscriptions:** 150 journals and other serials; 10 newspapers. **Services:** Interlibrary loans; copying; library open to public by appointment. **Computerized Information Services:** DIALOG, BRS, SDC.

★4855★
GATEWAY VOCATIONAL TECHNICAL & ADULT EDUCATION DISTRICT - LEARNING RESOURCES CENTER (Educ)
3520 30th Ave.
Kenosha, WI 53141
Phone: (414) 656-6924
Gerald F. Perona, District Libn.
Founded: 1964. **Staff:** Prof 3; Other 7. **Subjects:** Office education, law enforcement, nursing and allied health sciences, horticulture, aeronautics, electronics. **Special Collections:** Fire technology (300 items); career education (1000 items); vocational education (1500 items); hearing impaired (2000 items). **Holdings:** 42,608 books; 4560 periodical volumes including microfilm; 356 bound theses; 4624 pamphlets; 400 16mm films; 295 video cassettes; 3900 other AV materials. **Subscriptions:** 456 journals and other

serials. **Services:** Interlibrary loans; copying; library open to public. **Computerized Information Services:** DIALOG; computerized cataloging. **Networks/Consortia:** Member of Tri County Library Council; Regional Medical Library - Region 3. **Publications:** LRC Student Handbook. **Special Catalogs:** COM Catalog; Gateway Film and Videotape Catalog. **Remarks:** This library has campus locations at Kenosha, Racine and Elkhorn. **Staff:** Kathy Orth, Racine & Elkhorn Libn.; Araxie Kalvonjian, Tech.Proc./Acq.Libn.

★4856★
GATEWAYS HOSPITAL AND COMMUNITY MENTAL HEALTH CENTER - PROFESSIONAL LIBRARY (Med; Soc Sci)
1891 Effie St.   Phone: (213) 666-0171
Los Angeles, CA 90026   Celia Palant, Libn.
Founded: 1965. **Staff:** Prof 1. **Subjects:** Psychiatry, community mental health, penology. **Special Collections:** Karpf Collection - social psychology (100 titles); hyperkinesis (500 titles). **Holdings:** 1000 books; 100 unbound periodical volumes; 500 pamphlets and government documents; 50 tape cassettes. **Subscriptions:** 25 journals and other serials. **Services:** Interlibrary loans; copying; library open to public with permission.

GATX CORPORATION - GARD INC.
See: GARD, Inc.

GAUVIN (Marshall) LIBRARY OF FREE THOUGHT AND RATIONALIST LITERATURE
See: University of Manitoba - Archives and Special Collections

★4857★
GAY TASK FORCE - INFORMATION CENTER (Soc Sci)
Box 2383   Phone: (215) 471-3322
Philadelphia, PA 19103   Barbara Gittings, Coord.
Founded: 1970. **Subjects:** Homosexuality, lesbianism/feminism, gay rights. **Holdings:** 2000 books, pamphlets, periodical titles. **Publications:** Gay Bibliography, frequently revised - for sale; complete list of publications available upon request. **Remarks:** This Information Center is affiliated with the American Library Association, Social Responsibilities Round Table.

★4858★
GAYLORD HOSPITAL - MEDICAL LIBRARY (Med)
Box 400   Phone: (203) 269-3344
Wallingford, CT 06492   Ruth Ford, Med.Libn.
Founded: 1962. **Staff:** Prof 1. **Subjects:** Rehabilitation, psychology, social service, psychiatry, medicine, nursing. **Holdings:** 1250 books. **Subscriptions:** 35 journals and other serials. **Services:** Interlibrary loans; copying; library open to public with restrictions.

GAYLORD MUSIC LIBRARY
See: Washington University

★4859★
GCA CORPORATION - TECHNOLOGY DIVISION - LIBRARY (Env-Cons)
213 Burlington Rd.   Phone: (617) 275-5444
Bedford, MA 01730   Josephine Silvestro, Libn.
Founded: 1960. **Staff:** Prof 2; Other 1. **Subjects:** Pollution - air, water, solid waste; meteorology; analytical chemistry; planning - land use, transportation; energy. **Special Collections:** Archive collection of GCA reports and papers appearing in the open literature. **Holdings:** 7000 books; 3500 bound periodical volumes; 7500 unbound reports; 6000 microfiche. **Subscriptions:** 250 journals and other serials. **Services:** Interlibrary loans; copying; library open to public through arrangement with library. **Computerized Information Services:** DIALOG. **Staff:** Linda A. Callahan, Asst.Libn.

★4860★
GCG ENGINEERING PARTNERSHIP - LIBRARY (Trans)†
17420 Stony Plain Rd.   Phone: (403) 483-8094
Edmonton, AB, Canada T5S 1K6   Heather Grimble, Lib.Techn.
Subjects: Transportation, highways, mass transit. **Holdings:** 4000 books. **Subscriptions:** 75 journals and other serials. **Services:** Library open to public by permission.

GE
See: General Electric Company

★4861★
GEAUGA COUNTY HISTORICAL SOCIETY - LIBRARY (Hist)
14653 E. Park St.   Phone: (216) 834-1492
Burton, OH 44021   Marlene F. Collins, Off.Mgr.
Staff: 1. **Subjects:** Local history. **Special Collections:** Early land grants and township records; diaries; genealogy. **Special Collections:** Personal papers of

Hitchcock and Hickox families. **Holdings:** 1000 books; letters of President Garfield. **Services:** Library open to public with restrictions.

★4862★
GEAUGA COUNTY LAW LIBRARY (Law)
Court House   Phone: (216) 285-2222
Chardon, OH 44024   Violet R. Amnasan, Libn.
Founded: 1968. **Staff:** 1. **Subjects:** Law. **Holdings:** 12,500 volumes; Court of Appeals Rulings for the 11th District, 1969-1982. **Services:** Copying; library open to persons authorized by ORC. 3375.55.

★4863★
GEBBIE PRESS, INC. - HOUSE MAGAZINE LIBRARY (Publ)
                                          Phone: (914) 255-7560
New Paltz, NY 12561   A. Gebbie, Pres.
Holdings: House organs of more than 3000 companies.

GEE (James Gilliam) LIBRARY
See: American Name Society

GEE (James Gilliam) LIBRARY
See: East Texas State University - James Gilliam Gee Library

★4864★
GEE & JENSON ENGINEERS, ARCHITECTS, PLANNERS, INC. - LIBRARY (Plan)
2090 Palm Beach Lakes Blvd.
Drawer 4600   Phone: (305) 683-3301
West Palm Beach, FL 33402   Helen M. Foster, Lib.Mgr.
Founded: 1953. **Staff:** Prof 2; Other 3. **Subjects:** Florida water resources and land development; wastewater plants; Florida ports, paving and drainage. **Special Collections:** Development of Disneyworld; Development of Canaveral Port; Florida weather data, 1950 to present. **Holdings:** 6200 books; 86 bound periodical volumes; 2000 drawings; Corps of Engineers design memorandum; American Society of Civil Engineers Transactions (1936 to present); Florida Soil Conservation Service Surveys (complete from 1930); 3 VF drawers of Florida city and county rules and regulations; 2 VF drawers of Florida maps; 2 drawers of microforms; drawings and specifications; reports of Gee & Jenson from 1953 to present; file hearings and plans of the Cross Florida Barge Canal. **Subscriptions:** 304 journals and other serials; 23 newspapers. **Services:** Interlibrary loans (limited); copying; library open to public with permission from the Board of Directors. **Computerized Information Services:** Internal database; computerized circulation. **Publications:** New book and periodical listings, monthly; employee orientation manuals. **Special Indexes:** Gee & Jenson drawings, reports and specifications (card). **Staff:** Jackie Zabrosky, Ref.Libn.

★4865★
GEERS GROSS ADV. INC. - LIBRARY (Bus-Fin)
845 Third Ave.   Phone: (212) 350-9234
New York, NY 10022   Janet Jacquette, Libn.
Founded: 1956. **Staff:** Prof 1; Other 1. **Subjects:** Advertising, marketing, nutrition. **Holdings:** 400 books. **Subscriptions:** 100 journals and other serials; 8 newspapers. **Services:** Interlibrary loans; library open to public with restrictions.

GEHRKENS (Karl W.) MUSIC EDUCATION LIBRARY
See: Oberlin College - Conservatory of Music - Mary M. Vial Music Library

GEIGY CORPORATION
See: CIBA-GEIGY Corporation

GEISEL (Helen Palmer) LIBRARY
See: La Jolla Museum of Contemporary Art - Helen Palmer Geisel Library

GEISEL LIBRARY
See: St. Anselm's College

★4866★
GEISINGER MEDICAL CENTER - MEDICAL LIBRARY (Med)
N. Academy Ave.   Phone: (717) 275-6463
Danville, PA 17822   Britain G. Roth, Mgr., Lib.Serv.
Founded: 1927. **Staff:** Prof 2; Other 4. **Subjects:** Medicine and paramedical fields. **Holdings:** 25,000 volumes; 1500 audio cassettes; 150 slide sets; 200 videotapes. **Subscriptions:** 780 journals and other serials. **Services:** Interlibrary loans; copying; SDI; library open to public. **Computerized Information Services:** MEDLINE. **Networks/Consortia:** Member of Susquehanna Library Cooperative; Central Pennsylvania Health Sciences Library Association (CPHSLA); OCLC. **Publications:** Library Bulletin, quarterly.

Staff: Selma Etler, Ref.Libn.

★4867★
GEISINGER MEDICAL CENTER - SCHOOL OF NURSING LIBRARY (Med)
Danville, PA 17822
Phone: (717) 271-6288
Claire A. Huntington, Libn.
Founded: 1938. Staff: Prof 1. Subjects: Nursing and related subjects. Holdings: 5470 books; 186 bound periodical volumes; 4 VF drawers of pamphlet material. Subscriptions: 88 journals and other serials; 5 newspapers. Services: Interlibrary loans; copying; library open to public for reference use only. Computerized Information Services: Computerized cataloging. Networks/Consortia: Member of OCLC.

★4868★
GELBERG & ABRAMS - LAW LIBRARY (Law)
711 Third Ave.
New York, NY 10017
Phone: (212) 599-3200
Jennifer L. Elden, Libn.
Founded: 1979. Staff: Prof 1; Other 1. Subjects: Law - tax, securities, real estate, bankruptcy; litigation; ERISA (Employment Retirement Income Security Act). Holdings: 6000 books; 100 bound periodical volumes. Subscriptions: 150 journals and other serials; 10 newspapers. Services: Interlibrary loans; copying; SDI; library open to public with restrictions. Computerized Information Services: LEXIS, New York Times Information Service; computerized serials. Publications: Library Bulletin, monthly - to attorneys.

★4869★
GEM VILLAGE MUSEUM - GREEN MEMORIAL LIBRARY (Hum)
39671 Highway 160
Bayfield, CO 81122
Phone: (303) 884-2811
Elizabeth X. Gilbert, Sec.-Tres.
Founded: 1948. Staff: 1. Subjects: Occult, ESP research, Edgar Cayce, human auras, local archeology and geology. Holdings: 319 books; 2 cartons of unpublished research papers. Services: Library open to public by appointment only.

★4870★
GEMOLOGICAL INSTITUTE OF AMERICA - RESEARCH LIBRARY (Sci-Tech)
1660 Stewart St.
Santa Monica, CA 90404
Phone: (213) 829-2991
Dona Mary Dirlam, Info./Res.
Founded: 1931. Staff: Prof 1. Subjects: Gemology; mineralogy; jewelry - retailing, design, history. Holdings: 3000 volumes. Subscriptions: 100 journals and other serials. Services: Copying; library open to public with restrictions. Computerized Information Services: SDC. Publications: Gems and Gemology, quarterly - by subscription.

GENDARMERIE ROYALE DU CANADA
See: Royal Canadian Mounted Police - Law Enforcement Reference Centre

★4871★
GENEALOGICAL ASSOCIATION OF SOUTHWESTERN MICHIGAN - MAUD PRESTON PALENSKE MEMORIAL LIBRARY (Hist)
Box 573
St. Joseph, MI 49085
Marjorie Pearson, Res.Chm.
Founded: 1971. Staff: 1. Subjects: Genealogy. Holdings: 4 VF drawers; card file of burials in Berrien County, MI (75,000 names). Subscriptions: 30 journals and other serials. Services: Library open to public; search of card file by request only, for a small fee. Publications: The Pastfinder, quarterly (bulletin); Cemetery Records of Bainbridge, Baroda, Bertrand and New Buffalo Townships, Berrien County, MI, early 1800s to 1972. Also Known As: Fort Miami Heritage Society's Committee on Genealogy. Staff: Edith Zuppann, Pub.Chm.

★4872★
GENEALOGICAL CENTER - LIBRARY FOR THE BLIND & PHYSICALLY HANDICAPPED, INC. (Hist)
Box 88534
Atlanta, GA 30356-8534
Phone: (404) 393-9777
Diane Dieterle, Dir.
Founded: 1975. Subjects: Genealogy. Special Collections: Genealogical materials in braille, large print and cassettes. Holdings: 3000 books; 8000 genealogical magazines; 200 cassettes; 6 videotapes of genealogy lessons in sign language. Subscriptions: 25 journals and other serials. Services: Copying; library open to public for a fee. Computerized Information Services: Computerized cataloging. Networks/Consortia: Member of Georgia Library Information Network (GLIN). Publications: The Guild Newsletter, detailing genealogical instruction. Special Catalogs: 25,000 surname catalog; 5000 card locality catalog.

★4873★
GENEALOGICAL FORUM OF PORTLAND OREGON, INC. - LIBRARY (Hist)
1410 S.W. Morrison St.
Portland, OR 97205
Phone: (503) 227-2398
Emily Reding, Libn.
Subjects: Genealogy, history. Holdings: 5000 books; 1000 vertical files; unbound periodicals. Subscriptions: 130 journals and other serials. Services: Library open to public. Publications: Quarterly Bulletin. Staff: Mary Lou Stroup, Libn.

★4874★
GENEALOGICAL PERIODICALS LIBRARY (Hist)
709 E. Main St.
Middletown, MD 21769
Phone: (301) 371-6293
George Ely Russell, Genealogist
Staff: Prof 1. Subjects: Genealogy (English language). Holdings: 800 bound periodical volumes. Subscriptions: 50 journals and other serials. Services: Consultation service to editors, librarians, bibliographers. Publications: Genealogical Periodical Annual Index, 1966-1969, US ISSN 0072-0593.

GENEALOGICAL SOCIETY OF THE CHURCH OF JESUS CHRIST OF LATTER-DAY SAINTS
See: Church of Jesus Christ of Latter-Day Saints. Genealogical branch libraries are listed under the above heading and their specific names - e.g. Church of Jesus Christ of Latter-Day Saints - Tampa Branch Genealogical Lib.

★4875★
GENEALOGICAL SOCIETY OF NEW JERSEY - MANUSCRIPT COLLECTIONS (Hist)
Rutgers University Library
College Ave.
New Brunswick, NJ 08903
Phone: (201) 932-7510
Ruth J. Simmons, Sr.Archv./Coord.Spec.Coll
Founded: 1921. Staff: Prof 8; Other 4. Subjects: Genealogical records and information pertaining to New Jersey families. Special Collections: Bible records, gravestone records, family notes, John P. Dornan Collection. Services: Copying; collections open to public. Networks/Consortia: Member of RLG through Rutgers University Library. Publications: Genealogical Magazine of N.J., quarterly - to members. Special Indexes: Bible records; New Jersey family files; gravestone records; John P. Dornan Collection (all on cards). Remarks: Collections maintained in Rutgers University Library - Special Collections Department. Staff: Ronald L. Becker; Clark L. Beck, Jr.; Anne Brugh; Marjorie Li; Maxine Lurie; William Miller; Janet Kiemer; Jolan Szendey .

★4876★
GENEALOGICAL SOCIETY OF PENNSYLVANIA - LIBRARY (Hist)
1300 Locust St.
Philadelphia, PA 19107
Phone: (215) 545-0391
Founded: 1892. Subjects: Records of early churches, wills and cemeteries; family genealogies. Holdings: 4000 books; 4000 reels of microfilm. Services: Library open to public. Publications: Pennsylvania Genealogical Magazine, semiannual.

★4877★
GENERAL AMERICAN INVESTORS CO., INC. - LIBRARY (Bus-Fin)
330 Madison Ave.
New York, NY 10017
Phone: (212) 949-1763
Jennifer Jones, Libn.
Founded: 1929. Staff: Prof 2. Subjects: Investments, finance, economics. Special Collections: Corporation material, including annual reports. Holdings: 1000 books; 250 VF drawers of economic data. Subscriptions: 200 journals and other serials. Services: Library not open to public. Staff: Marie T. Grimes, Asst.Libn.

GEOTHERMAL RESOURCE AREAS DATABASE
See: Lawrence Berkeley Laboratory

★4878★
GENERAL ATOMIC COMPANY - LIBRARY (Sci-Tech; Energy)
Box 81608
San Diego, CA 92138
Phone: (714) 455-3322
Richard J. Tommey, Libn.
Founded: 1956. Staff: Prof 1; Other 2. Subjects: Energy technology, nuclear fusion, high temperature gas-cooled reactors, training reactor for isotope production, electronic instrumentation, fluidized bed combustion. Special Collections: U.S. Atomic Energy Commission R&D Reports. Holdings: 32,000 books; 15,000 bound periodical volumes; 75,000 government research and development reports. Subscriptions: 902 journals and other serials. Services: Interlibrary loans; copying; library open to public by appointment. Computerized Information Services: DIALOG, BRS, DTIC, DOE/RECON. Networks/Consortia: Member of San Diego Greater Metropolitan Area Library and Information Agency Council (METRO). Publications: Selected Acquisitions, weekly - for internal distribution only.

★4879★
GENERAL CABLE COMPANY - RESEARCH CENTER LIBRARY (Sci-Tech)
160 Fieldcrest Ave.   Phone: (201) 225-4780
Edison, NJ 08818   Benjamin L. De Witt, Mgr., Tech.Info.Serv.
Staff: Prof 1; Other 1. **Subjects:** Telecommunications, fiber optics, electronics, polymers and plastics, materials science. **Special Collections:** Patents of fiber optics **Holdings:** 1000 books; 50 bound periodical volumes; 200 other cataloged items. **Subscriptions:** 162 journals and other serials. **Services:** Interlibrary loans; copying; library not open to public. **Computerized Information Services:** DIALOG, NLM, BRS, DOE/RECON, Pergamon-InfoLine. **Publications:** Fiber Optics Patent Bulletin, monthly.

GENERAL COMMISSION ON CHAPLAINS AND ARMED FORCES PERSONNEL
See: National Conference on Ministry to the Armed Forces

★4880★
GENERAL DATACOMM INDUSTRIES, INC. - CORPORATE LIBRARY (Info Sci)
One Kennedy Ave.   Phone: (203) 797-0711
Danbury, CT 06810   Catherine Greene, Libn.
Staff: Prof 1. **Subjects:** Telecommunications, computers. **Holdings:** 300 books; 13 volumes of Datapro reports; 2 volumes of Federal Communications Commission rules and regulations; 12 volumes of Bell technical references; regulations and specifications. **Subscriptions:** 60 journals and other serials; 5 newspapers. **Services:** Interlibrary loans; copying; library not open to public. **Computerized Information Services:** Internal database; computerized cataloging and acquisitions. **Networks/Consortia:** Member of Southwestern Connecticut Library Council (SCLC).

GENERAL DOUGLAS MAC ARTHUR MEMORIAL - LIBRARY AND ARCHIVES
See: Mac Arthur (General Douglas) Memorial - Library and Archives

★4881★
GENERAL DRAFTING COMPANY, INC. - MAP LIBRARY (Geog-Map)
Canfield Rd.   Phone: (201) 538-7600
Convent Station, NJ 07961   Allan Freeman, Libn.
Founded: 1952. **Staff:** Prof 1. **Subjects:** Travel, geography, cartography, maps, atlases. **Special Collections:** Exxon Road Maps (U.S. and foreign). **Holdings:** 1500 books; 100,000 maps (U.S. and foreign). **Subscriptions:** 102 journals and other serials. **Services:** Interlibrary loans; library open to public by special request only.

★4882★
GENERAL DYNAMICS CORPORATION - CONVAIR DIVISION - RESEARCH LIBRARY (Sci-Tech)
Box 80986   Phone: (714) 277-8900
San Diego, CA 92138   Urban J. Sweeney, Chf.Libn.
Founded: 1956. **Subjects:** Aerospace, aircraft, electronics, missiles, spacecraft, computer technology. **Special Collections:** NASA reports; DOD report collections. **Holdings:** 40,000 books; 15,000 bound periodical volumes; one million microfiche reports. **Subscriptions:** 500 journals and other serials; 20 newspapers. **Services:** Interlibrary loans; copying; SDI; library not open to public. **Computerized Information Services:** STAIRS (internal database); computerized cataloging; computer literature searches (internal use only). **Staff:** Robert E. Arndal, Info.Spec.; Colleen Alexander, Computer Searches.

★4883★
GENERAL DYNAMICS CORPORATION - DATAGRAPHIX, INC. - ENGINEERING LIBRARY (Sci-Tech)
Box 82449   Phone: (714) 291-9960
San Diego, CA 92138
Founded: 1963. **Staff:** 1. **Subjects:** Computer output microfilm, optics, photographic science and engineering, electronics, electronic data processing. **Holdings:** 3000 books and bound periodical volumes. **Subscriptions:** 141 journals and other serials. **Services:** Interlibrary loans; copying; library open to public by application. **Publications:** Acquisitions lists, information service descriptor lists, irregular - for internal distribution only.

★4884★
GENERAL DYNAMICS CORPORATION - ELECTRIC BOAT DIVISION - DIVISION LIBRARY (Sci-Tech)
Eastern Point Rd.   Phone: (203) 446-3481
Groton, CT 06340   Charles E. Giles, Chf.Libn.
Founded: 1955. **Staff:** Prof 2; Other 1. **Subjects:** Electrical and marine engineering, underwater sciences, naval architecture, oceanography, submarine construction, metal and metal joining, underwater acoustics. **Holdings:** 30,000 books and bound periodical volumes; 30,000 technical reports. **Subscriptions:** 1100 journals and other serials. **Services:** Interlibrary

loans; copying; library not open to public.

★4885★
GENERAL DYNAMICS CORPORATION - FORT WORTH DIVISION - TECHNICAL LIBRARY (Sci-Tech)
Grant's Lane, MZ2246
Box 748   Phone: (817) 732-4811
Fort Worth, TX 76101   P. Roger de Tonnancour, Chf.Libn.
Founded: 1949. **Staff:** Prof 2; Other 4. **Subjects:** Aerospace technology, mathematics, nuclear physics, materials technology. **Special Collections:** Technical documents (500,000 microforms). **Holdings:** 45,000 books; 10,000 bound periodical volumes; 150,000 technical reports. **Subscriptions:** 800 journals and other serials; 6 newspapers. **Services:** Interlibrary loans; copying; SDI; translation; library open to public by appointment. **Computerized Information Services:** Online systems. **Publications:** Guides, accessions lists, special reports. **Staff:** Pier R. Aultto, Tech.Info.Spec.

★4886★
GENERAL DYNAMICS CORPORATION - LAND SYSTEMS DIVISION - TECHNICAL LIBRARY (Sci-Tech)
Box 1901   Phone: (313) 497-0495
Warren, MI 48090   Margaret vonRosen, Libn.
Founded: 1954. **Staff:** Prof 2. **Subjects:** Combat and special purpose vehicles, ordnance systems, fire control, optics, reliability, electro-hydraulics, human factors engineering. **Holdings:** 1985 books; 30,000 scientific and technical documents; 56 drawers of military and federal specifications and standards. **Subscriptions:** 81 journals and other serials. **Services:** Interlibrary loans; library not open to public. **Remarks:** Includes the holdings of the Chrysler Missile Division. Library is located at 25999 Lawrence Ave., Center Line, MI 48105. **Formerly:** Chrysler Defense, Inc. - Engineering Division - Technical Library. **Staff:** Shirley Maguire, Asst.Libn.

★4887★
GENERAL DYNAMICS CORPORATION - POMONA DIVISION - DIVISION LIBRARY MZ 4-20 (Sci-Tech)
Box 2507   Phone: (714) 620-7511
Pomona, CA 91769   N.S. Fredrick, Chf.Libn.
Founded: 1952. **Staff:** Prof 4; Other 4. **Subjects:** Tactical missiles, electronics. **Holdings:** 14,000 books; 1875 bound periodical volumes; 80,000 technical documents (cataloged). **Subscriptions:** 500 journals and other serials. **Services:** Interlibrary loans; library not open to public. **Computerized Information Services:** DIALOG, DTIC, SDC; STAIRS (internal database); computerized cataloging and reference system. **Staff:** S. Linnell, Engr.Libn.; C.M. Busch, Engr.Libn.; J.G. Boyajian, Engr.Libn.

★4888★
GENERAL DYNAMICS CORPORATION - PUBLIC AFFAIRS LIBRARY (Sci-Tech)
Pierre Laclede Ctr.   Phone: (314) 889-8200
St. Louis, MO 63105   Barbara Elliott, Chf.Libn.
Staff: Prof 3. **Subjects:** Aerospace, shipping, electronics, resources and building materials, communications. **Services:** Copying; library not open to public. **Computerized Information Services:** New York Times Information Service. **Staff:** Kathi Harrison, Lib.Asst.; Elliott Blevins, Asst.Libn.

★4889★
GENERAL DYNAMICS CORPORATION - QUINCY SHIPBUILDING DIVISION LIBRARY (Sci-Tech)†
97 E. Howard St.   Phone: (617) 471-4200
Quincy, MA 02169   G. Richard Myers, Libn.
Founded: 1967. **Staff:** Prof 1; Other 1. **Subjects:** Shipbuilding, naval architecture, marine engineering. **Holdings:** 3255 books; 1530 bound periodical volumes; 4000 reports (cataloged); 1545 reports of Society of Naval Architects & Marine Engineers. **Subscriptions:** 75 journals and other serials; 3 newspapers. **Services:** Library open to qualified users by appointment. **Computerized Information Services:** Computerized cataloging. **Publications:** Supplements to U.S. Coast Guard Rules & Regulations, monthly - for internal distribution only.

★4890★
GENERAL ELECTRIC COMPANY - ADVANCED REACTOR SYSTEMS DEPT. - LIBRARY (Sci-Tech)
310 DeGuigne Drive
Box 5020   Phone: (408) 738-7177
Sunnyvale, CA 94086   Dorothy Hutson, Mgr., Tech.Serv.
Founded: 1968. **Staff:** Prof 2; Other 1. **Subjects:** Liquid metal fast breeder reactors; nuclear energy. **Holdings:** 2500 books; 40,000 technical reports; 30,000 reports on microfiche. **Subscriptions:** 203 journals and other serials. **Services:** Interlibrary loans; copying; SDI; library not open to public.

Computerized Information Services: DIALOG, DOE/RECON; computerized cataloging and serials. Networks/Consortia: Member of CLASS; OCLC. Special Catalogs: Computer produced book and report catalogs. Staff: Doris Robinson, Rpt.Spec.

★4891★
GENERAL ELECTRIC COMPANY - AIRCRAFT ENGINE GROUP - DR. C.W. SMITH TECHNICAL INFORMATION CENTER (Sci-Tech)
1000 Western Ave.   Phone: (617) 594-5363
Lynn, MA 01910   Sandra S. Moltz, Supv.
Founded: 1953. Staff: Prof 2; Other 2. Subjects: Aeronautics, aircraft gas turbine engines, thermodynamics, aeronautical engineering, materials science, engine noise control. Special Collections: C.W. Smith Collection of Gas-turbine Literature. Holdings: 10,000 books; 3500 bound periodical volumes; 110,000 technical reports; 14,500 microforms. Subscriptions: 300 journals and other serials. Services: Interlibrary loans; center not open to public. Computerized Information Services: DIALOG; internal databases. Publications: Acquisitions list, biweekly; List of Journal Holdings, annual. Special Catalogs: Termatrex Thesaurus for information retrieval (book and punched cards). Staff: Helen G. Brown, Info.Anl.

★4892★
GENERAL ELECTRIC COMPANY - AIRCRAFT ENGINE GROUP - LAW LIBRARY (Law)
Mail Drop F17   Phone: (513) 243-2298
Cincinnati, OH 45215   Peggy Edwards
Founded: 1950. Subjects: Government contracts, labor law, patents, antitrust laws, product liability. Holdings: 6498 volumes; patents. Services: Library not open to public.

★4893★
GENERAL ELECTRIC COMPANY - AIRCRAFT ENGINE GROUP - TECHNICAL INFORMATION CENTER (Sci-Tech)
Bldg. 700, N-32   Phone: (513) 243-4333
Cincinnati, OH 45215   L.W. Kozerski, Mgr.
Founded: 1950. Staff: Prof 3; Other 2. Subjects: Aerospace materials, aeronautical engineering, physical sciences, mathematics, computer science. Special Collections: Aircraft Engine Group Technical Information Series Reports and Technical Memoranda (50,000). Holdings: 20,000 books; 14,000 bound periodical volumes; 4500 pamphlets; 180,000 technical reports; 13,000 technical society papers; 5000 U.S. and foreign patents; 785,000 reports on microfiche. Subscriptions: 160 journals and other serials. Services: Literature research; center not open to public. Computerized Information Services: DIALOG, SDC; ARTIC (internal database); computerized circulation. Publications: Technical Information Preview Series (TIPS), semimonthly; bibliographies, biblioabstracts and special reports as required. Staff: P.L. Sewell, Hd.Libn.; W.C. Rowe, Tech.Info.Prog.Engr.

★4894★
GENERAL ELECTRIC COMPANY - AIRCRAFT EQUIPMENT DIV. - AEROSPACE ELECTRONIC SYSTEMS DEPT. - INFO.RSRCS. CENTER (Sci-Tech)
901 Broad St.   Phone: (315) 793-5716
Utica, NY 13503   Catherine Walsh, Supv.
Founded: 1955. Staff: Prof 2; Other 3. Subjects: Aerospace electronic, radar, optics, communication, management, reliability. Special Collections: Institute of Electrical and Electronics Engineering (IEEE) proceedings and transactions. Holdings: 6000 books; 300 bound periodical volumes; 100 cassettes; 9000 technical reports. Subscriptions: 193 journals and other serials. Services: Interlibrary loans; copying; library open to public by appointment. Computerized Information Services: DIALOG; General Electric Company Libraries (internal database); computerized information retrieval, cataloging, serials and circulation. Networks/Consortia: Member of Central New York Library Resources Council. Publications: Library News Quarterly. Staff: Lori Scoones, Asst.Libn.

★4895★
GENERAL ELECTRIC COMPANY - AIRCRAFT EQUIPMENT DIV. - ARMAMENT & ELECTRICAL SYSTEMS DEPT. ENGINEERING LIBRARY (Sci-Tech)
Lakeside Ave.   Phone: (802) 657-6598
Burlington, VT 05402   Raymond M. Palmer, Tech.Libn.
Founded: 1949. Staff: Prof 1; Other 1. Subjects: Armament and weapon systems, electronics, mathematics, integrated circuits, ammunition, ground support equipment, feed systems, fuses. Holdings: 5000 books; 20,000 technical reports; military, commercial and federal specifications and standards. Subscriptions: 300 journals and other serials. Services: Interlibrary loans; copying; microfilm/microfiche reproduction; library not

open to public.

★4896★
GENERAL ELECTRIC COMPANY - APOLLO SYSTEMS - TECHNICAL AND SERVICES SUPPORT LIBRARY (Sci-Tech)
1830 Nasa Blvd.
Box 58408   Phone: (713) 332-4511
Houston, TX 77058   C.E. Colburn, Libn.
Founded: 1963. Staff: 1. Subjects: Aerospace, reliability, Apollo program, management. Holdings: Figures not available. Services: Library not open to public.

★4897★
GENERAL ELECTRIC COMPANY - CARBOLOY SYSTEMS DEPARTMENT - CSD LIBRARY (Sci-Tech)
Box 237, G.P.O.   Phone: (313) 536-9100
Detroit, MI 48232   Frances M. Briggs, Libn.
Founded: 1939. Staff: Prof 1. Subjects: Metals, powder metals, cemented carbides, refractory materials, metal cutting (machining). Holdings: 4355 books; 1053 bound periodical volumes; 7000 patents; 4000 company and government reports (cataloged); 2000 slides, films, microfiche and cassettes on language; 1000 slides, 1000 microfiche of government and company reports and books; 6 shelves of military, federal and other standards. Subscriptions: 275 journals and other serials; 5 newspapers. Services: Interlibrary loans; copying; library open to public with special permission.

★4898★
GENERAL ELECTRIC COMPANY - COMPUTER MANAGEMENT OPERATION LIBRARY (Sci-Tech)
Bldg. 30ES
1285 Boston Ave.   Phone: (203) 382-3921
Bridgeport, CT 06602   Wendy Berger, Info.Spec.
Staff: Prof 1; Other 2. Subjects: Computers, microprocessors, software. Holdings: Figures not available. Subscriptions: 225 journals and other serials. Services: Interlibrary loans; SDI. Computerized Information Services: Online systems. Networks/Consortia: Member of Southwest Connecticut Library Council.

★4899★
GENERAL ELECTRIC COMPANY - CORPORATE RESEARCH & DEVELOPMENT - WHITNEY INFORMATION SERVICES (Sci-Tech; Energy)
Box 8   Phone: (518) 385-8791
Schenectady, NY 12301   Maryde Fahey King, Mgr.
Founded: 1900. Staff: Prof 7; Other 5. Subjects: Energy, physics, chemistry, electronics, metallurgy, ceramics, mathematics. Holdings: 15,000 books; 25,000 bound periodical volumes; 5000 microforms including 500 bibliographies, 1200 pamphlets, 800 dissertations. Subscriptions: 500 journals and other serials. Services: Interlibrary loans; SDI; library open to public by appointment. Computerized Information Services: DIALOG, SDC, BRS, New York Times Information Service, TOXLINE, Mead Data Central, Source Telecomputing Corporation; computerized cataloging. Networks/Consortia: Member of Capital District Library Council. Publications: Bibliogram, semimonthly - for internal distribution only. Staff: Ella R. Kunes, Libn.-Cat.; Judith A. Lent, Libn.-Ref. & ILL; Carolyn Warden, Libn.-Search & Ret.; Edith M. Raviola, Libn.; Beth H. Mazin, Ref. & Cat.; Joann Deitlen, Ser.Libn.; David Bates, Ref. & Copyright Libn.

★4900★
GENERAL ELECTRIC COMPANY - DIRECT CURRENT MOTOR AND GENERATOR DEPARTMENT - LIBRARY
3001 E. Lake Rd.
Erie, PA 16531
Founded: 1956. Subjects: Electricity, chemistry, business, mathematics, electro-mechanics. Holdings: 4500 books; 350 bound periodical volumes; 1000 patents (uniterm indexed); 4500 data folders (uniterm indexed); 300 reels of microfilm. Computerized Information Services: Computerized circulation. Remarks: Presently inactive.

★4901★
GENERAL ELECTRIC COMPANY - ELECTRONICS PARK LIBRARY (Sci-Tech)†
Electronics Park, Bldg. 3, Rm. 154   Phone: (315) 456-2023
Syracuse, NY 13221   C.S. Webb, Mgr., Info.Serv.
Founded: 1948. Staff: Prof 2; Other 3. Subjects: Communications, electronics, radio, television, microwave engineering, physics, chemistry, mathematics, business, computers. Special Collections: Technical reports on microfiche (25,000). Holdings: 6000 books; 1750 bound periodical volumes. Subscriptions: 260 journals and other serials. Services: Interlibrary loans; copying; SDI; library open to public by appointment. Computerized

Information Services: DIALOG, SDC, New York Times Information Service; computer-produced card catalog. **Networks/Consortia:** Member of Central New York Library Resources Council. **Publications:** Current Awareness Bulletins (40 topics), semimonthly - for internal distribution only. **Remarks:** This library serves all General Electric departments in Syracuse. **Staff:** Gerry Radway, Libn.

★4902★
GENERAL ELECTRIC COMPANY - INFORMATION RESOURCES (Sci-Tech)
French Rd., MD300　　　　　　　　Phone: (315) 793-7875
Utica, NY 13503　　　　　　　　　Catherine Walsh, Supv.
Founded: 1982. **Staff:** 2. **Subjects:** Aerospace electronics, radar, optics, management, computers, reliability. **Holdings:** 200 books. **Subscriptions:** 52 journals and other serials. **Services:** Interlibrary loans; copying; library not open to public. **Computerized Information Services:** DIALOG; internal database; computerized cataloging, serials and circulation. **Publications:** Library News, quarterly. **Staff:** Lori Scoones, Asst.Libn.

★4903★
GENERAL ELECTRIC COMPANY - LAMP GLASS & COMPONENTS LIBRARY (Sci-Tech)†
24400 Highland Rd.　　　　　　　Phone: (216) 266-3653
Richmond Heights, OH 44143　　　Jeanne Parker
Staff: 1. **Subjects:** Glass research and manufacturing, ceramics. **Holdings:** 1500 books; 500 bound periodical volumes; patents; in-house and government reports. **Subscriptions:** 15 journals and other serials.

★4904★
GENERAL ELECTRIC COMPANY - LIGHTING RESEARCH AND TECHNICAL SERVICES OPERATIONS - LIBRARY (Sci-Tech)
Nela Park　　　　　　　　　　　Phone: (216) 266-3216
Cleveland, OH 44112　　　　　　　Sue Haase, Info.Spec.
Founded: 1914. **Staff:** Prof 1. **Subjects:** Lighting technology, ceramics, refractory metals, physical and inorganic chemistry, plasma physics, optics. **Holdings:** 10,000 books; 7500 bound periodical volumes; 700 feet of various internal reports, manuscripts, patents, clippings, pamphlets, dissertations, and documents. **Subscriptions:** 250 journals and other serials. **Services:** Interlibrary loans (limited); copying (limited); SDI; library open to public by previous arrangement. **Computerized Information Services:** DIALOG; internal database. **Publications:** Various internal publications.

★4905★
GENERAL ELECTRIC COMPANY - MAIN LIBRARY (Sci-Tech; Bus-Fin)
One River Rd.　　　　　　　　　Phone: (518) 385-3652
Schenectady, NY 12345　　　　　　Julia Hewitt, Mgr.
Founded: 1899. **Staff:** Prof 3; Other 1. **Subjects:** Engineering - mechanical and electrical; metals and materials; business and management. **Special Collections:** General Electric Company history and publications; standards. **Holdings:** 16,000 books; 17,000 bound periodical volumes; 48,000 pamphlets, translations, NASA reports and other documents. **Subscriptions:** 600 journals and other serials. **Services:** Translations; literature searching; library open to public by appointment. **Computerized Information Services:** DIALOG, SDC, NEXIS. **Networks/Consortia:** Member of OCLC. **Publications:** Library Acquisitions Bulletin. **Staff:** Marian Smith, Online Serv.; Diane C. Glock, Cat.

★4906★
GENERAL ELECTRIC COMPANY - METER BUSINESS DEPARTMENT - LIBRARY & DATA BUREAU (Sci-Tech)
130 Main St.　　　　　　　　　Phone: (603) 692-2100
Somersworth, NH 03878　　　　　　Dave Weatherby
Founded: 1954. **Staff:** Prof 1; Other 1. **Subjects:** Electrical and mechanical engineering. **Special Collections:** Technical reports by Meter Department authors pertaining to watt-hour meters, instrument transformers, and current potential transformers. **Holdings:** 650 books; 225 patents; 67 reels of microfilm. **Subscriptions:** 73 journals and other serials. **Services:** Interlibrary loans; copying. **Publications:** Technical Topics, weekly - for internal distribution only. **Special Catalogs:** File of technical reports - by author and key words (card).

★4907★
GENERAL ELECTRIC COMPANY - NUCLEAR ENERGY GROUP - LIBRARY (Energy)
175 Curtner Ave.　　　　　　　Phone: (408) 925-3522
San Jose, CA 95125　　　　　Mrs. Scotty A. McEwen, Tech.Libn.
Founded: 1955. **Staff:** Prof 1; Other 5. **Subjects:** Nuclear power. **Holdings:** 8000 books; 60,000 documents; 300,000 microfiche. **Subscriptions:** 502 journals and other serials. **Services:** Interlibrary loans; copying; library open to public by special permission. **Computerized Information Services:** DIALOG,

DOE/RECON. **Publications:** Monthly accession list - for internal distribution only.

★4908★
GENERAL ELECTRIC COMPANY - ORDNANCE SYSTEMS - ENGINEERING LIBRARY (Sci-Tech)
100 Plastics Ave., Rm. 2168　　　Phone: (413) 494-4207
Pittsfield, MA 01201　　　　　　Ann B. Rauch, Tech.Libn.
Founded: 1958. **Staff:** Prof 1; Other 1. **Subjects:** Inertial guidance; electronic and mechanical engineering; space navigation; underwater engineering; environmental technology; computers and cybernetics; mathematics; stabilization; transmissions; weapon control, directors and mounts. **Holdings:** 7723 books; 1800 bound periodical volumes; 10 file cabinets of documents. **Subscriptions:** 200 journals and other serials. **Services:** Interlibrary loans; copying (limited); library not open to public.

★4909★
GENERAL ELECTRIC COMPANY - REFRACTORY METAL PRODUCTS DEPARTMENT - LIBRARY (Sci-Tech)†
21800 Tungsten Rd.　　　　　　Phone: (216) 266-3736
Cleveland, OH 44117　　　　　　Patricia A. Loucka, Libn.
Founded: 1955. **Staff:** Prof 1. **Subjects:** Metallurgy, refractory metals, analytical chemistry, powder metallurgy, spectroscopy, microscopy, marketing information. **Special Collections:** Tungsten and molybdenum. **Holdings:** 5500 books; 1500 bound periodical volumes; 4 VF drawers of patents; 63 VF drawers of reports and dissertations; 6 VF drawers of reprints; 2 VF drawers of translations; 1 VF drawer of specifications. **Subscriptions:** 200 journals and other serials. **Services:** Interlibrary loans; library not open to public. **Publications:** From the Library, monthly - for internal distribution only. **Special Catalogs:** Periodical Holdings List (book).

★4910★
GENERAL ELECTRIC COMPANY - RSD BRANCH LIBRARY
3198 Chestnut St.
Philadelphia, PA 19104
Defunct

★4911★
GENERAL ELECTRIC COMPANY - SILICONE PRODUCTS DIVISION - LIBRARY (Sci-Tech)
　　　　　　　　　　　　　Phone: (518) 237-3330
Waterford, NY 12188　　　　　　Marianne K. Pouliott, Libn.
Subjects: Silicone chemistry; organic chemistry; business, marketing and management of the silicone industry. **Holdings:** Figures not available. **Computerized Information Services:** DIALOG, SDC; computerized cataloging. **Networks/Consortia:** Member of Capital District Library Council (CDLC); G.E. Libraries.

★4912★
GENERAL ELECTRIC COMPANY - SPACE/SYSTEMS DIVISION LIBRARIES (Sci-Tech; Energy)
Box 8555　　　　　　　　　　Phone: (215) 962-4700
Philadelphia, PA 19101　　　　　　Larry Chasen, Mgr.
Founded: 1945. **Staff:** Prof 5. **Subjects:** Aerospace technology, energy, chemistry, ocean systems, physics, sensor physics, computer technology. **Special Collections:** World War II Captured German War Documents on V-2. **Holdings:** 75,000 books and 750 bound periodical volumes; 800,000 documents; complete NASA collection on microfiche. **Subscriptions:** 255 journals and other serials. **Services:** Interlibrary loans; direct input/output to cataloging daily so the collection of 250,000 publications is current for retrieval purposes; library open to public by appointment and only for open literature. **Computerized Information Services:** DIALOG; U.S. DOE, NASA, DTIC; GE Corporate R and D Center Databases (internal); computerized cataloging, circulation. **Publications:** Technical Abstracts Bulletin, 2/month; Company Newspaper. **Remarks:** This library is described as having the first online information retrieval system in an industrial library in the world. **Staff:** Isabella Hopkins, Spec., Tech.Info.; Shirley J. Rockefeller, Tech.Libn.; Denise A. Rich, Info.Sys.Libn.; Eugenia V. Sowicz, Supv. Book & Journal Lib.

★4913★
GENERAL ELECTRIC COMPANY - TECHNICAL INFORMATION EXCHANGE (Sci-Tech)
Bldg. 5, Rm. 321
One River Rd.　　　　　　　　Phone: (518) 385-3615
Schenectady, NY 12345　　　　　　P.A. Oliver, Mgr.
Staff: Prof 3; Other 11. **Subjects:** Turbines, motors, switchgear, jet engines, space vehicles, management, data processing, electronic equipment, materials. **Holdings:** 185,000 internal technical reports. **Services:** Exchange not open to public.

★4914★
GENERAL ELECTRIC COMPANY - TRANSPORTATION TECHNOLOGY CENTER - TECHNICAL INFORMATION CENTER (Sci-Tech)
Bldg. 14, Rm. 123A
2901 E. Lake Rd.
Erie, PA 16531   Phone: (814) 455-5466
    Robert H. Berry, Tech.Info.Spec.
Founded: 1940. **Staff:** Prof 1. **Subjects:** Railroad business and technology; rapid transit systems; mechanical, electrical and control engineering. **Holdings:** Figures not available. **Subscriptions:** 300 journals and other serials. **Services:** Interlibrary loans; copying; library open to public with restrictions. **Computerized Information Services:** DIALOG; computerized cataloging.

★4915★
GENERAL ELECTRIC COMPANY - WILLIAM STANLEY LIBRARY
100 Woodlawn Ave.
Pittsfield, MA 01201
Defunct

★4916★
GENERAL ELECTRODYNAMICS CORPORATION - LIBRARY (Sci-Tech)†
4430 Forest Ln.   Phone: (214) 276-1161
Garland, TX 75040
Staff: 2. **Subjects:** Chemistry, physics, electronics and optics. **Holdings:** 500 books and bound periodical volumes; 400 government research reports; 2 VF drawers of patents. **Subscriptions:** 20 journals and other serials. **Services:** Interlibrary loans; library open to public for reference use only.

★4917★
GENERAL FOODS CORPORATION - INFORMATION SERVICES DEPARTMENT - INFORMATION CENTER (Info Sci)
250 North St., S1-4   Phone: (914) 335-3805
White Plains, NY 10625   Theresa Maylone, Lib.Serv.Spec.
Founded: 1980. **Staff:** Prof 1; Other 1. **Subjects:** Data and information processing, computers, business information systems, management. **Holdings:** 500 books; 400 data processing manuals; 150 systems documentation items; 1000 noncurrent periodicals on microfiche; 500 program lists and other reference materials on microfiche. **Subscriptions:** 100 journals and other serials; 8 newspapers. **Services:** Center open to public for reference use only by appointment. **Computerized Information Services:** DIALOG, SDC; Library Information Catalog System (LICS; internal databases); computerized acquisitions, serials and circulation.

★4918★
GENERAL FOODS CORPORATION - MARKETING INFORMATION CENTER (Bus-Fin)
250 North St.   Phone: (914) 683-3911
White Plains, NY 10625   Lois Seulowitz, Mgr.
Founded: 1973. **Staff:** Prof 3; Other 3. **Subjects:** Marketing, advertising, business, public relations. **Holdings:** Figures not available. **Services:** Interlibrary loans; copying (limited); library not open to public. **Computerized Information Services:** DIALOG, SDC, New York Times Information Service, Dow Jones News Retrieval, BRS, Source Telecomputing Corporation. **Publications:** Currents, Cross-Currents, New Products Report and other newsletters. **Staff:** Grace Filipak, Sr.Info.Spec./Ref.; Patricia Miller, Info.Spec./Tech.Serv.

★4919★
GENERAL FOODS CORPORATION - MAXWELL HOUSE - TECHNICAL INFORMATION CENTER (Sci-Tech)
1125 Hudson St.   Phone: (201) 420-3309
Hoboken, NJ 07030   Anne Marie Civinskas, Adm.
Staff: Prof 1; Other 1. **Subjects:** Food technology, chemical engineering, coffee processing. **Holdings:** 2000 books; 6 VF drawers of internal reports; 90 binders of patents; 6 VF drawers of clippings; catalogs. **Subscriptions:** 90 journals and other serials. **Services:** Interlibrary loans; copying; library not open to public. **Computerized Information Services:** SDC; GENIUS (internal database).

★4920★
GENERAL FOODS CORPORATION - TECHNICAL CENTER - TARRYTOWN TECHNICAL INFORMATION CENTER (Sci-Tech; Food-Bev)
    Phone: (914) 683-6827
White Plains, NY 10625   Elinor Cohen, Adm., Tech.Info.Serv.
Founded: 1939. **Staff:** Prof 6; Other 4. **Subjects:** Food technology, biochemistry, chemistry, nutrition, taste-testing. **Holdings:** 10,000 books; 60 VF drawers of pamphlets; 9000 reels of periodicals on microfilm. **Subscriptions:** 400 journals and other serials. **Services:** Interlibrary loans; library open to members of Special Libraries Association. **Computerized Information Services:** Online systems; computerized cataloging. **Networks/**

Consortia: Member of SUNY/OCLC Library Network. **Publications:** TRENDS, biweekly - for internal distribution only. **Special Indexes:** GF Union List of Reference Books (booklet); GF Union List of Periodicals (booklet). **Remarks:** Library located at 555 S. Broadway, Tarrytown, NY.

★4921★
GENERAL FOODS, LTD. - INFORMATION CENTRE (Bus-Fin)
Terminal A, P.O. Box 4019   Phone: (416) 481-4211
Toronto, ON, Canada M5W 1J6   Carol Symon, Supv., Info.Ctr.
Founded: 1957. **Staff:** 1. **Subjects:** Marketing, management, advertising. **Holdings:** 2000 books; pamphlets; 54 VF drawers of market research reports; 12 shelves of Neilsen reports; 10 shelves of government documents. **Subscriptions:** 65 journals and other serials. **Services:** Interlibrary loans; copying; library not open to public. **Computerized Information Services:** DIALOG.

★4922★
GENERAL HOSPITAL - HEALTH SCIENCES LIBRARY (Med)
941 Queen St. E.   Phone: (705) 254-5181
Sault Ste. Marie, ON, Canada P6A 2B8   Kathy You, Libn.
Founded: 1978. **Staff:** Prof 1. **Subjects:** Medicine, nursing, hospital administration. **Holdings:** 600 books; journals kept for 10 years (unbound). **Subscriptions:** 64 journals and other serials. **Services:** Interlibrary loans; copying; library open to all hospital staff and nursing students for reference.

★4923★
GENERAL INSTRUMENT CORPORATION, GOVERNMENT SYSTEMS DIVISION - ENGINEERING LIBRARY (Sci-Tech)
600 West John St.   Phone: (516) 733-3000
Hicksville, NY 11802   Hilda N. Shevack, Logistics/Data Mgr.
Staff: Prof 2; Other 1. **Subjects:** Electronics and engineering, electronic warfare, physics and mathematics, management. **Holdings:** 3000 books; 500 bound periodical volumes; 10,000 other cataloged items; 2000 engineering notebooks; 1000 microforms; military specifications; technical publications. **Subscriptions:** 200 journals and other serials; 10 newspapers. **Services:** Interlibrary loans; copying; library open to public with restrictions. **Staff:** Irene Meier, Engr.Libn.

GENERAL LIBRARY OF THE PERFORMING ARTS
See: New York Public Library

★4924★
GENERAL MILLS, INC. - GENERAL OFFICE LIBRARY/INFORMATION CENTER (Bus-Fin; Food-Bev)
9200 Wayzata Blvd.   Phone: (612) 540-3536
Minneapolis, MN 55426   Duane R. Day, Mgr.Lib.Serv.
Founded: 1947. **Staff:** Prof 3; Other 2. **Subjects:** Marketing, food, economics, advertising, personnel management, marketing research. **Holdings:** 4000 volumes. **Subscriptions:** 45 journals and other serials. **Services:** Interlibrary loans; copying; library not open to public. **Computerized Information Services:** DIALOG, NEXIS, New York Times Information Service; internal abstract database; computerized serials. **Publications:** Newsletter-Bulletin, monthly. **Staff:** Elaine Madigan, Libn.

★4925★
GENERAL MILLS, INC. - JAMES FORD BELL TECHNICAL CENTER - TECHNICAL INFORMATION SERVICES (Sci-Tech; Food-Bev)
9000 Plymouth Ave., N.   Phone: (612) 540-3464
Minneapolis, MN 55427   Dr. Curtis H.. Hallstrom, Mgr., Tech.Info.Serv.
Founded: 1961. **Staff:** Prof 7; Other 5. **Subjects:** Food and chemical research. **Holdings:** 6500 books; 3500 bound periodical volumes; 2500 unbound periodical volumes; 53 VF drawers of patents; 44 VF drawers of documents and pamphlets; 6 VF drawers of annual reports; 1230 reels of microfilmed periodicals; 750 reels of patents; 2 VF drawers of translations. **Subscriptions:** 900 journals and other serials. **Services:** Interlibrary loans; literature surveys; coordinate SDI service; library open to public with advance request and approval by management. **Computerized Information Services:** DIALOG, Info Globe, Questel, Pergamon-InfoLine, Dow Jones News Retrieval, Source Telecomputing Corporation, New England Research Application Center, SDC, BRS, New York Times Information Service, Control Data Corporation, Mead Data Central, NLM; internal database; computerized serials, cataloging and acquisitions. **Networks/Consortia:** Member of OCLC; MINITEX. **Publications:** Library Bulletin, semimonthly - to employees; World Patent Alert, monthly - to employees. **Staff:** Jacqueline Angus, Supv., Lib.Sec.; Harvey G. Johnson, Info.Sci.; Dr. H. Eugene Miller, Info. Res./Sec.Ldr.; Nancy W. Cervone, Info.Sci.; Dr. William D. Davidson, Sr.Res.Info.Sci.; Rick Samuelson, Info.Sci.

★4926★

GENERAL MILLS, INC. - LAW LIBRARY (Law)
Box 1113
Minneapolis, MN 55440
Phone: (612) 540-2047
Rhonda E. Greenwood, Law Libn.
Staff: 1. **Subjects:** Law - patent, trademark and copyright. **Holdings:** 10,000 books and bound periodical volumes; microfilm of Official Gazette of the U.S. Patent and Trademark Office since 1955. **Subscriptions:** 30 journals and other serials. **Services:** Interlibrary loans; library open only to law librarians. **Computerized Information Services:** DIALOG, WESTLAW.

★4927★

GENERAL MILLS, INC. - MARKETING RESEARCH INFORMATION CENTER (Bus-Fin)
Box 1113
Minneapolis, MN 55440
Phone: (612) 540-2070
Judith A. Galt, Mktg.Res.Info.Spec.
Founded: 1976. **Staff:** Prof 1; Other 1. **Subjects:** Marketing and advertising research; food and food industry. **Holdings:** 700 books; 20 bound periodical volumes; 9200 internal reports (in hard copy and microfiche); Roper Reports (1975 to present); Gallup Food Preparation studies (1977 to present); Marketing Science Institute studies (1975 to present); 12 VF drawers of clippings; 7 VF drawers of promotional materials from market research supply houses. **Subscriptions:** 80 journals and other serials. **Services:** Copying; library not open to public. **Computerized Information Services:** DIALOG, New York Times Information Service; internal database. **Publications:** MRIC Newsletter, monthly; Marketing Research Information Services Booklet, semiannual - both for internal distribution only. **Special Indexes:** Index to in-house research reports (computer).

★4928★

GENERAL MOTORS CORPORATION - AC SPARK PLUG DIVISION - ENGINEERING LIBRARY (Sci-Tech)
1300 N. Dort Hwy.
Flint, MI 48556
Phone: (313) 766-2655
Eileen L. Lane, Libn.
Staff: Prof 1. **Subjects:** Ceramics, engineering, automotive technology. **Special Collections:** Ceramics - books and bound journals of the American Ceramic Society Bulletin dating back to 1922. **Holdings:** 1500 books; 80 bound periodical volumes; 5 VF drawers of engineering reports; 300 theses. **Subscriptions:** 200 journals and other serials. **Services:** Interlibrary loans; copying; library not open to public. **Computerized Information Services:** DIALOG. **Publications:** Newsletter, 4/year - distributed to management.

★4929★

GENERAL MOTORS CORPORATION - CADILLAC MOTOR CAR DIVISION - ENGINEERING DIVISION LIBRARY (Sci-Tech)
2860 Clark
Detroit, MI 48232
Phone: (313) 554-7689
Subjects: Automotive engineering, Cadillac history. **Holdings:** Figures not available.

★4930★

GENERAL MOTORS CORPORATION - CURRENT PRODUCT ENGINEERING - INFORMATION MANAGEMENT (Sci-Tech)
WO-INFO MGMT,
General Motors Technical Ctr.
Warren, MI 48090
Phone: (313) 575-1112
John L. Thompson, Libn.
Founded: 1959. **Staff:** Prof 1; Other 5. **Subjects:** Automotive engineering and design, engineering, science and technology, business and management. **Holdings:** 5700 books; 1430 bound periodical volumes; 500 unrestricted internal reports; 106 VF drawers of corporate reports, pamphlets, government documents, SAE papers, translations. **Subscriptions:** 476 journals and other serials. **Services:** Interlibrary loans; copying; library open to public by appointment. **Computerized Information Services:** DIALOG, SDC; computerized cataloging, acquisitions, serials and circulation. **Special Indexes:** Index to automotive road test data. **Formerly:** Its Technical Information Center.

★4931★

GENERAL MOTORS CORPORATION - DELCO ELECTRONICS DIVISION - TECHNICAL LIBRARY (Sci-Tech)
6767 Hollister Ave.
Goleta, CA 93017
Phone: (805) 961-5080
Kenneth C. Crombie, Tech.Libn.
Staff: Prof 1. **Subjects:** Physics, astronautics, aeronautics, mathematics, astronomy, electronics, electrical engineering, oceanography, geophysics. **Holdings:** 3100 books; 8900 bound periodical volumes. **Subscriptions:** 200 journals and other serials; 10 newspapers. **Services:** Interlibrary loans; library not open to public. **Special Indexes:** Uniterm retrieval system for reports.

★4932★

GENERAL MOTORS CORPORATION - DELCO ELECTRONICS DIVISION - TECHNICAL LIBRARY (Sci-Tech)
Box 797
Kokomo, IN 46902
Phone: (317) 459-7262
R.E. Sparks, Tech.Libn.
Founded: 1961. **Staff:** Prof 1; Other 1. **Subjects:** Electronics, semiconductors, acoustics, mechanics, physics, metallurgy, chemistry, mathematics, communications, research management. **Holdings:** 2500 books; 550 bound periodical volumes; 8500 technical reports. **Subscriptions:** 425 journals and other serials. **Services:** Interlibrary loans; copying; library not open to public - use for reference may be requested. **Computerized Information Services:** DIALOG; computerized cataloging. **Networks/Consortia:** Member of OCLC through INCOLSA. **Publications:** Library Broadcast.

★4933★

GENERAL MOTORS CORPORATION - DESIGN STAFF LIBRARY (Art)
General Motors Technical Ctr.
12 Mile & Mound Rds.
Warren, MI 48090
Phone: (313) 575-1957
Mrs. Biljana Delevich, Design Libn.
Founded: 1945. **Staff:** Prof 1. **Subjects:** Industrial and automotive design, art. **Special Collections:** General Motors, other American and foreign automobile brochures and advertisements (76 VF drawers). **Holdings:** 3750 books; 439 bound periodical volumes; 20 VF drawers. **Subscriptions:** 162 journals and other serials. **Services:** Interlibrary loans; copying; library not open to public. **Special Indexes:** Road Test Index, updated monthly - computer printout.

★4934★

GENERAL MOTORS CORPORATION - DETROIT DIESEL ALLISON DIVISION - LIBRARY (Sci-Tech)
Plant No. 8
Box 894
Indianapolis, IN 46206
Phone: (317) 243-5651
W.H. Richardson, Libn.
Founded: 1941. **Staff:** Prof 1; Other 1. **Subjects:** Gas turbine engines, transmissions, diesel engines, metallurgy, fluid mechanics, heat transfer, combustion. **Holdings:** 10,000 books; 2000 bound periodical volumes; 50,000 technical reports. **Subscriptions:** 250 journals and other serials. **Services:** Interlibrary loans; copying; library open to public with restrictions. **Networks/Consortia:** Member of OCLC through INCOLSA.

★4935★

GENERAL MOTORS CORPORATION - ECONOMICS STAFF LIBRARY (Bus-Fin)
767 Fifth Ave., 26th Fl.
New York, NY 10153
Phone: (212) 486-5092
Lourdes P. Lim, Libn.
Founded: 1980. **Staff:** Prof 1; Other 1. **Subjects:** Automotive industry (non-technical material), economics, foreign trade. **Special Collections:** United Nations; International Monetary Fund; Organization for Economic Cooperation and Development (OECD); General Agreement on Tariffs and Trade (GATT). **Holdings:** 4000 volumes; 55 VF drawers of clippings and foreign publications. **Subscriptions:** 116 journals and other serials. **Services:** Interlibrary loans; library not open to public. **Publications:** List of recent acquisitions, 6/year - for internal distribution only. **Special Indexes:** Automotive industry studies (card).

★4936★

GENERAL MOTORS CORPORATION - ELECTRO-MOTIVE DIVISION - ENGINEERING LIBRARY (Sci-Tech)
9301 55th St.
La Grange, IL 60525
Phone: (312) 387-6706
Eleanor Spolarich, Libn.
Founded: 1935. **Staff:** Prof 1. **Subjects:** Diesel engines, gas turbines, locomotives, industrial and marine engines, power plants. **Holdings:** 4000 books; 23 bound periodical titles; 3000 reports. **Subscriptions:** 70 journals and other serials. **Services:** Library not open to public.

★4937★

GENERAL MOTORS CORPORATION - INFORMATION SYSTEMS & COMMUNICATIONS ACTIVITY - TECHNICAL INFORMATION CENTER (Sci-Tech)
2912 GMISCA Bldg.
7000 Chicago Rd.
Warren, MI 48090
Phone: (313) 492-3574
Patricia Cupoli, Libn.
Staff: Prof 1. **Subjects:** Data processing and communications, office automation. **Holdings:** 1000 books; 500 microfiche; technical reports and proceedings. **Subscriptions:** 40 journals and other serials; 5 newspapers. **Services:** Interlibrary loans; copying; SDI; library open to public by appointment. **Computerized Information Services:** DIALOG, SDC, New York Times Information Service; STAIRS (internal database); computerized

cataloging. **Publications:** Bibliographies.

★4938★
GENERAL MOTORS CORPORATION - LEGAL STAFF LIBRARY (Law)
14-224 General Motors Bldg.
3044 W. Grand Blvd.   Phone: (313) 556-4010
Detroit, MI 48202   Sheila M. Sweeny, Legal Staff Libn.
Staff: Prof 2; Other 4. **Subjects:** Anglo-American, foreign and international law. **Special Collections:** Selected legislative histories. **Holdings:** 60,000 volumes; U.S. Hearings and Reports. **Subscriptions:** 300 journals and other serials; 15 newspapers. **Services:** Interlibrary loans; library open to public with restrictions.

★4939★
GENERAL MOTORS CORPORATION - MANUFACTURING, ENGINEERING & DEVELOPMENT - MANUFACTURING DEVELOPMENT LIBRARY (Sci-Tech)
GM Technical Center   Phone: (313) 575-0652
Warren, MI 48090-9040   Jean Schlage, Libn.
Staff: Prof 1. **Subjects:** Materials science, robotics, automation, manufacturing. **Holdings:** Figures not available for books; 413 internal technical reports; 1.5 VF drawers of clippings **Subscriptions:** 231 journals and other serials. **Services:** Interlibrary loans; copying; SDI; library not open to public. **Computerized Information Services:** DIALOG; internal database. **Publications:** GMMD Technical Reports list, annual.

★4940★
GENERAL MOTORS CORPORATION - PUBLIC RELATIONS STAFF LIBRARY (Bus-Fin)
General Motors Bldg., Rm. 11-235
3044 W. Grand Blvd.   Phone: (313) 556-2051
Detroit, MI 48202   Nettie H. Seabrooks, Mgr.
Founded: 1946. **Staff:** Prof 4; Other 2. **Subjects:** Automotive industry (non-technical material), business, economics, public relations, labor relations, personnel administration. **Special Collections:** Publications by and about General Motors Corporation and its divisions. **Holdings:** 7500 books; 350 bound periodical volumes; 10,000 pamphlets. **Subscriptions:** 300 journals and other serials; 10 newspapers. **Services:** Interlibrary loans; copying; library open to outside organizations. **Computerized Information Services:** DIALOG, New York Times Information Service, Dow Jones News Retrieval. **Staff:** Suzanne M. Petre, Libn.; Carol A. Lehman, Libn.; Catherine F. Cochran, Libn.

★4941★
GENERAL MOTORS CORPORATION - RESEARCH LABORATORIES LIBRARY (Sci-Tech)
General Motors Technical Center
12 Mile & Mound Rd.   Phone: (313) 575-2736
Warren, MI 48090   Robert W. Gibson, Jr., Dept.Hd.
Founded: 1917. **Staff:** Prof 11; Other 12. **Subjects:** Automotive engineering, physical sciences, mechanical engineering, chemistry, biomedicine, societal analysis. **Special Collections:** Automotive catalogs; shop manuals. **Holdings:** 52,000 books; 54,000 bound periodical volumes; 1500 other items (cataloged); 1800 translations; 90,000 indexed items. **Subscriptions:** 1300 journals and other serials. **Services:** Interlibrary loans; library open to public with prior permission. **Computerized Information Services:** DIALOG, SDC, MEDLARS, Research Reports Series on KWOC (from internal database); computerized circulation. **Networks/Consortia:** Member of MIDLNET; OCLC. **Publications:** New Acquisitions (GMR only). **Staff:** Neil K. VanAllen, Staff Libn.; Mary C. Babian, Staff Libn.; Helene Brown, Biomed.Br.Libn.; Delores E. Maximena, Trans.Libn.; Ernest L. Horne, Cat.; Richard E. Stoey, Libn.; Margaret E. Shepard, Libn.; Neville L. Grow, Sr.Libn.; Donald E. Sunday, Libn.; Barbara K. Kunkel, Sr.Libn.

GLAD (Edward A.) MEMORIAL LIBRARY
See: Red Cross of Constantine - United Grand Imperial Council - Edward A. Glad Memorial Library

★4942★
GENERAL MOTORS CORPORATION - TAX SECTION LIBRARY (Law)
12-135 General Motors Bldg.   Phone: (313) 556-1567
Detroit, MI 48202   Geraldyne J. Musser, Asst.Libn.
Founded: 1966. **Staff:** 1. **Subjects:** Foreign and domestic tax law, employee benefits. **Special Collections:** Canadian income tax law (250 volumes). **Holdings:** 3200 books; 240 bound periodical volumes; 1500 loose-leaf services and 750 pamphlets (cataloged); 3000 United States and Canada bills of importance; 400 reels of microfilm. **Subscriptions:** 259 journals and other serials. **Services:** Interlibrary loans; limited copying; library not open to public. **Computerized Information Services:** LEXIS. **Publications:** Acquisition and selected reading list, bimonthly - for General Motors Central Office only.

GENERAL MOTORS INSTITUTE
See: GMI Engineering & Management Institute

GENERAL RADIO COMPANY
See: GenRad, Inc.

★4943★
GENERAL RAILWAY SIGNAL CO. - TECHNICAL LIBRARY (Sci-Tech)
801 West Ave.
Box 600   Phone: (716) 436-2020
Rochester, NY 14692   Kathy Zuidema, Libn.
Founded: 1967. **Staff:** Prof 1; Other 1. **Subjects:** Electrical and systems engineering, electronics, railroads, rapid transit. **Special Collections:** Railroads/Railroading - historical collection of early journals, proceedings, product catalogs. **Holdings:** 1600 books; 1000 bound periodical volumes; technical reports, archives, vendor catalogs. **Subscriptions:** 170 journals and other serials. **Services:** Interlibrary loans; copying; SDI; library open to public by appointment. **Computerized Information Services:** DIALOG, SDC; online literature searching. **Networks/Consortia:** Member of Rochester Regional Research Library Council (RRRLC). **Publications:** SDI Journal Publication, weekly; newsletter, irregular.

★4944★
GENERAL REFRACTORIES COMPANY - U.S. REFRACTORIES DIVISION - RESEARCH CENTER LIBRARY (Sci-Tech)
Box 1673   Phone: (301) 355-3400
Baltimore, MD 21203   A.G. Parsons, Libn.
Staff: 1. **Subjects:** Refractories, ceramics, mineralogy, chemical engineering, metallurgical engineering, petrography, chemistry, spectroscopy. **Holdings:** 300 books; 400 bound periodical volumes; 130 U.S. Bureau of Mines reports; 4 boxes of technical papers; 11 boxes of technical reports from U.S. and technical societies. **Subscriptions:** 30 journals and other serials. **Services:** Library open to public for reference use on request. **Remarks:** Library is located at 7th & Maude Ave., Baltimore, MD 21225. **Staff:** Jeffrey A. Tripp, Mgr.; David W. Robertson, Asst. to the Mgr.

★4945★
GENERAL RESEARCH CORPORATION - LIBRARY (Sci-Tech)
Box 6770   Phone: (805) 964-7724
Santa Barbara, CA 93111   Kathryn Tammen, Supv., Acq.
Founded: 1961. **Staff:** 2. **Subjects:** Aerospace technology, radar and systems analysis, data processing, computer science, transportation, mathematics. **Holdings:** 7000 books and bound periodical volumes. **Subscriptions:** 135 journals and other serials; 8 newspapers. **Services:** Library not open to public. **Staff:** Cindy Machado, Acq.Spec.

★4946★
GENERAL RESEARCH CORPORATION - LIBRARY (Sci-Tech)
7655 Old Springhouse Rd.   Phone: (703) 893-5900
McLean, VA 22102   Robert M. Greathouse, Dir.
Founded: 1948. **Staff:** Prof 1; Other 1. **Subjects:** Research and development, biomedical sciences, military history, economics, mathematics, statistics, operations research. **Special Collections:** World War II history; operations research history. **Holdings:** 27,500 books; 700 bound periodical volumes. **Subscriptions:** 450 journals and other serials; 10 newspapers. **Services:** Interlibrary loans; copying; library not open to public. **Computerized Information Services:** DIALOG. **Special Catalogs:** Index to operations research literature (card). **Remarks:** Includes the holdings of the Lambda Corporation Library.

★4947★
GENERAL SOCIETY OF MECHANICS AND TRADESMEN OF THE CITY OF NEW YORK - LIBRARY (Hum)
20 W. 44th St.   Phone: (212) 921-1767
New York, NY 10036   Margery Peters, Libn.
Staff: Prof 1; Other 3. **Subjects:** History, biography, fiction. **Special Collections:** Gilbert and Sullivan. **Holdings:** 140,000 books and bound periodical volumes. **Subscriptions:** 35 journals and other serials. **Services:** Library open to public with restrictions; annual subscription fee for borrowing books. **Networks/Consortia:** Member of METRO.

GENERAL STEEL WARES ARCHIVE
See: Mc Master University - Archives and Research Collections Division

★4948★
GENERAL TELEPHONE OF CALIFORNIA - FILM LIBRARY (Aud-Vis)
12211 Washington Blvd.   Phone: (213) 390-9064
Los Angeles, CA 90066   Pegi Matsuda, Community Rel.Rep.
Founded: 1956. **Staff:** Prof 1; Other 3. **Subjects:** Telephone usage

techniques, social studies, sports and travel, nature, health and safety, communication and transportation, career education, arts and music, science. **Holdings:** 1200 16mm films. **Services:** Films are available to schools and organizations only within General Telephone Company of California's service area. **Publications:** Motion Picture Catalog.

★4949★
GENERAL TELEPHONE COMPANY OF THE SOUTHWEST - E.H. DANNER LIBRARY OF TELEPHONY (Bus-Fin; Sci-Tech)
2701 S. Johnson St.
Box 1001
San Angelo, TX 76904
Phone: (915) 944-5149
Aline H. Taylor, Libn.
Founded: 1966. **Staff:** 3. **Subjects:** Management, business, engineering, finance, public utilities, economics. **Holdings:** 6500 books; 400 video cassette tapes; 50 16mm films; 16 drawers of newsletters, bulletins, reports, clippings, pamphlets. **Subscriptions:** 200 journals and other serials. **Services:** Interlibrary loans; copying; library open to public with permission of librarian. **Publications:** Catalog - for internal distribution only.

GENERAL TELEPHONE AND ELECTRONICS CORPORATION
See: GTE

★4950★
GENERAL THEOLOGICAL LIBRARY (Rel-Theol)
14 Beacon St.
Boston, MA 02108
Phone: (617) 227-4557
Ruth Pragnell, Libn.
Founded: 1860. **Staff:** Prof 1. **Subjects:** Theology, philosophy, sociology, psychology, New Testament-Old Testament studies, religions, archeology, literature. **Holdings:** 35,000 books; 550 bound periodical volumes. **Subscriptions:** 58 journals and other serials. **Services:** Interlibrary loans; mail service to U.S.; library open to public with restrictions. **Publications:** Bulletin of the General Theological Library, quarterly. **Remarks:** Multi-denominational Board includes Jewish, Roman Catholic, Orthodox, Anglican, Protestant clergy and lay persons. **Staff:** James Heney, Asst.Libn.

★4951★
GENERAL THEOLOGICAL SEMINARY OF THE PROTESTANT EPISCOPAL CHURCH IN THE U.S.A. - ST. MARK'S LIBRARY (Rel-Theol)
175 Ninth Ave.
New York, NY 10011
Phone: (212) 243-5150
David Green, Libn.
Founded: 1817. **Staff:** Prof 2; Other 4. **Subjects:** Biblical studies, theology, patristics, church history, ecumenical movement, PECUSA materials (printed and manuscript), liturgics, English theology. **Special Collections:** Latin Bible (800 editions); Early English Theology Collection (6600 titles printed before 1701 on the Church of England). **Holdings:** 198,000 books; manuscripts, clippings, microforms. **Subscriptions:** 1100 journals and other serials. **Services:** Interlibrary loans; copying; library open to public for reference use only. **Networks/Consortia:** Member of OCLC. **Publications:** Annual Report; Library Manual. **Staff:** Jonathan Beasley, Cat.

★4952★
GENERAL TIRE AND RUBBER COMPANY - RESEARCH DIVISION INFORMATION CENTER (Sci-Tech)
2990 Gilchrist Rd.
Akron, OH 44305
Phone: (216) 798-3496
B.D. Farah, Hd., Info.Ctr.
Founded: 1946. **Staff:** Prof 3; Other 2. **Subjects:** Rubber and plastics; chemistry - inorganic, organic, analytical; safety; research management. **Holdings:** Figures not available. **Subscriptions:** 400 journals and other serials. **Services:** Interlibrary loans; literature and online searches; copying; SDI; library open to public. **Staff:** W.A. Williams, Info.Spec.; D.A. Kramer, Info.Spec.

★4953★
GENESEE COUNTY CIRCUIT COURT - LAW LIBRARY (Law)
401 County Court House
Flint, MI 48502
Phone: (313) 766-8896
Janet E. Patsy, Law Libn.
Staff: 1. **Subjects:** Law. **Special Collections:** Michigan Supreme Court records and briefs, 1977 to present. **Holdings:** 13,000 volumes. **Subscriptions:** 49 journals and other serials. **Services:** Copying; library open to public.

★4954★
GENESEE COUNTY - DEPARTMENT OF HISTORY - RESEARCH LIBRARY (Hist)
131 W. Main St.
Batavia, NY 14020
Phone: (716) 343-2550
Susan L. Conklin, Hist.
Staff: Prof 3. **Subjects:** History - local, area (original Genesee County), state; western New York land grants and genealogy records; famous people of the area. **Special Collections:** Captain Charles Rand, General Emory Upton,

General Ely Parker, William Morgan; Genesee County early railroads; industries, architecture of area; Staples Genealogy of Town of Elba; Cooley's genealogy file; Saulsbury Notes; tax rolls, 1838-1905. **Holdings:** 1663 books; 400 bound periodical volumes; 32 bound atlases; daily newspapers (1823-1974); 28 reels of microfilm; 288 slides; 29 cassette tapes; 4 rolls 1200 ft. tapes; VF drawers of people, places, things, organizations, churches, schools, local history - town and county; newsletters from historical societies; genealogy queries and answers; 50 reels of microfilm of Federal Census of Genesee County, 1810-1880; 11 bound volumes of Genesse County Federal Census Records, 1820-1870. **Services:** Copying; department open to public for reference use only. **Special Indexes:** Indexes of microfilm collection, photographs, map file, 1820-1870 federal census records.

★4955★
GENESEE HOSPITAL - SAMUEL J. STABINS, M.D., HEALTH SCIENCES LIBRARY (Med)
224 Alexander St.
Rochester, NY 14607
Phone: (716) 263-6305
Sally M. Gerling, Chf.Libn.
Staff: Prof 1; Other 3. **Subjects:** Medicine, nursing and allied sciences. **Holdings:** 4000 books; 4700 bound periodical volumes; slide/tape programs; videotapes; audiotapes. **Subscriptions:** 200 journals and other serials. **Services:** Interlibrary loans; SDI; online bibliographic searching; library open to health professionals only. **Computerized Information Services:** MEDLINE. **Networks/Consortia:** Member of Rochester Regional Research Library Council. **Publications:** Newsletter, monthly.

★4956★
GENESEE-LAPEER-SHIAWASSEE REGION V PLANNING & DEVELOPMENT COMMISSION - LIBRARY (Plan)
1602 W. Third Ave.
Flint, MI 48504
Phone: (313) 234-0340
Verna L. McColley, Lib.Techn.
Staff: 1. **Subjects:** Water quality, transportation, housing, land use. **Holdings:** 3600 volumes; 2 VF drawers of newspaper clippings; 2 VF drawers of agency newsletters. **Subscriptions:** 15 journals and other serials; 11 newspapers. **Services:** Copying; library open to public with restrictions. **Publications:** New Publications in the GLS Library, newsletter, 3/month - by request.

GENESIS INSTITUTE
See: Bible Science Association

★4957★
GENEVA HISTORICAL SOCIETY AND MUSEUM - JAMES D. LUCKETT MEMORIAL ARCHIVES (Hist)
543 S. Main St.
Geneva, NY 14456
Phone: (315) 789-5151
Eleanore R. Clise, Chf.Archv.
Founded: 1960. **Staff:** 3. **Subjects:** Local history, architecture, genealogy. **Special Collections:** James G. Vail collection of photographic plates of Geneva scenes and genre, 1862-1880 (900 subjects). **Holdings:** 5000 books; 15,000 photographs; 185 boxes and 15 VF drawers of clippings, manuscripts, pamphlets, documents and diaries; 39 reels of 19th century Geneva newspapers, 27 reels of Federal Census for Ontario County, NY (1820-1925), 7 reels of early Geneva church records, all on microfilm; 64 cassette tapes of local oral history; antiques and costumes. **Services:** Copying; genealogical research; library open to public for reference use only. **Publications:** Newsletter, monthly. **Also Known As:** Prouty-Chew Museum and Library.

GENEVA MEDICAL COLLEGE LIBRARY
See: SUNY - Upstate Medical Center Library

★4958★
GENRAD, INC. - LIBRARY (Sci-Tech)
300 Baker Ave.
Concord, MA 01742
Phone: (617) 369-4400
Subjects: Engineering - electronic, software. **Special Collections:** General Radio experimenters. **Holdings:** 1000 books; 50 bound periodical volumes. **Subscriptions:** 35 journals and other serials. **Services:** Interlibrary loans; copying; library not open to public. **Also Known As:** General Radio Company.

★4959★
GENSTAR CEMENT, LTD. - TECHNICAL LIBRARY (Sci-Tech)
Sta. D, P.O. Box 3961
Edmonton, AB, Canada T5L 4P8
Phone: (403) 452-8290
Miss V.W. Cameron, Sec.
Founded: 1958. **Staff:** 1. **Subjects:** Cement, concrete. **Holdings:** 106 pamphlets and reports; 47 films on concrete applications. **Services:** Interlibrary loans; copying; film loans; library open to public.

★4960★
GENSTAR CORP. - LIBRARY (Bus-Fin)
4 Embarcadero Center, Suite 3700
San Francisco, CA 94111   Jana Selph, Libn.
Founded: 1960. **Subjects:** Business and finance, management, housing, construction. **Special Collections:** Annual reports of 1200 companies. **Holdings:** 500 books. **Subscriptions:** 100 journals and other serials; 7 newspapers. **Services:** Library not open to public. **Computerized Information Services:** DIALOG, SDC.

★4961★
GENSTAR-FLINTKOTE BUILDING PRODUCTS COMPANY - CORPORATE R&D LIBRARY (Sci-Tech)
3241 W. Story Rd.   Phone: (214) 659-9800
Irving, TX 75062   Charles A. Pagen, Ph.D., Dir. of Res.
Subjects: Asphalt, rubber, resins, cellulose, petroleum, gypsum, plastics, building material. **Holdings:** 4500 books; 1000 bound periodical volumes; 30 VF drawers of pamphlets. **Subscriptions:** 60 journals and other serials. **Remarks:** Presently inactive. **Formed by the Merger of:** Flintkote Building Products Company and Genstar-Flintkote.

★4962★
GEOGRAPHICAL SOCIETY OF PHILADELPHIA - LIBRARY (Geog-Map)
21 S. 12th St., Rm. 909   Phone: (215) 563-0127
Philadelphia, PA 19107
Founded: 1891. **Staff:** 1. **Subjects:** Travel and exploration. **Holdings:** 2000 books. **Services:** Library open to public for reference use only.

★4963★
GEOLOGICAL INFORMATION LIBRARY OF DALLAS (GILD) (Energy)
One Energy Sq., Suite 100
4925 Greenville Ave.   Phone: (214) 363-1078
Dallas, TX 75206   G. Frederick Shepherd, Dir.
Founded: 1969. **Subjects:** Geology, geophysics, engineering, mathematics, geochemistry, solid minerals, hydrocarbons, energy resources. **Special Collections:** Maps; scout tickets; production data; completion cards; well histories. **Holdings:** 50,000 basic texts, journals and publications of international, national and local scientific societies, associations and trade organizations. **Services:** Research services are available at an hourly rate; borrowing privileges reserved for members; library open to public with restrictions. **Computerized Information Services:** Computerized retrieval of production statistics via internal database. **Publications:** Dallas Geological & Geophysical Societies Newsletter, monthly; annotated bibliographies of the region - for sale. **Remarks:** Affiliated with the University of Texas at Dallas. **Staff:** Lois Dillard, Ref.Libn.

★4964★
GEOLOGICAL SURVEY OF ALABAMA - LIBRARY (Energy)†
Drawer O   Phone: (205) 349-2852
University, AL 35486   Dorothy L. Brady, Libn.
Founded: 1910. **Staff:** Prof 1; Other 1. **Subjects:** Hydrology, oil and gas, geology, paleontology, geophysics, energy resources research, economic geology. **Holdings:** 65,000 books; 7900 bound periodical volumes; 22 films (cataloged); 6 VF drawers of manuscripts; 91 theses. **Subscriptions:** 184 journals and other serials. **Services:** Library open to public for reference use on request. **Also Known As:** Alabama State Geological Survey.

GEOLOGICAL SURVEY OF CANADA
See: Canada - Geological Survey of Canada

★4965★
GEOLOGICAL SURVEY OF WYOMING - PUBLIC RECORDS SECTION (Env-Cons; Energy)
Box 3008, University Sta.   Phone: (307) 742-2054
Laramie, WY 82071   Gary B. Glass, Dir./State Geologist
Subjects: Mineral resources, environment, oil and gas, geology. **Holdings:** 100 books; 1000 unbound reports and periodicals; 20,000 oil and gas records; 2000 mineral files; 3000 maps and miscellaneous items. **Subscriptions:** 14 journals and other serials. **Services:** Copying; library open to public with restrictions. **Special Indexes:** Oil and Gas (card); USGS open-file reports (card). **Also Known As:** Wyoming Geological Survey.

★4966★
GEOMET TECHNOLOGIES INC. - INFORMATION CENTER (Med)
1801 Research Blvd., 6th Fl.   Phone: (301) 424-9133
Rockville, MD 20850
Subjects: Toxicology, environmental health, industrial and occupational medicine. **Holdings:** 500 books; 650 bound periodical volumes; 15,000 reprints; 3000 translations. **Subscriptions:** 50 journals and other serials; 10 newspapers. **Services:** Interlibrary loans; copying; SDI; library open to public by appointment. **Computerized Information Services:** DIALOG, SDC, NLM.

★4967★
GEOPHOTO SERVICES, LTD. - LIBRARY
906 12th Ave., S.W.
Calgary, AB, Canada T2R 1K7
Subjects: Geology, geochemistry, photogrammetry, surveying. **Holdings:** 250 shelf feet. **Remarks:** Presently inactive.

GEOPHYSICAL FLUID DYNAMICS LABORATORY
See: U.S. Natl. Oceanic & Atmospheric Administration

GEORGE AIR FORCE BASE (CA)
See: U.S. Air Force Base - George Base Library

★4968★
GEORGE BROWN COLLEGE OF APPLIED ARTS & TECHNOLOGY - ARCHIVES (Soc Sci)
Sta. B, Box 1015   Phone: (416) 967-1212
Toronto, ON, Canada M5T 2T9   John L. Hardy, Archv.
Founded: 1975. **Staff:** Prof 1. **Subjects:** College history, labour relations, fashion industry. **Special Collections:** Dr. Louis Fine Papers - Labour Relations Consultant's File; records of the Men's Clothing Manufacturer's Association of Ontario (2 metres); history project collection of the Association of Colleges of Applied Arts and Technology of Ontario (8 metres); records of the Nightingale School of Nursing (7 metres); records of the Committee of Registrars and Admissions Officers of the Colleges of Applied Arts and Technology of Ontario (38 cm.); records of the Committee of Librarians of the Colleges of Applied Arts and Technology of Ontario (1.3 metres). **Holdings:** 300 metres of records and manuscripts. **Services:** Library open to public with restrictions.

★4969★
GEORGE BROWN COLLEGE OF APPLIED ARTS & TECHNOLOGY - LIBRARY (Sci-Tech; Med)
Sta. B, Box 1015   Phone: (416) 967-1212
Toronto, ON, Canada M5T 2T9   Rita L. Edwards, Dir./Lib. & AV Serv.
Founded: 1968. **Staff:** Prof 21. **Subjects:** Engineering and architectural technology; nursing; business and commerce; food technology; fashion technology; child care; addiction counselling. **Holdings:** 93,000 books; 1600 bound periodical volumes; 900 films; 180 metres of archives. **Subscriptions:** 652 journals and other serials; 6 newspapers. **Services:** Library open to public for reference use only, on request. **Publications:** Acquisition list, monthly; film catalog. **Remarks:** The library's holdings are dispersed among the college's four campuses. **Staff:** Robert Anthony, Group Ldr.; Mrs. E. Crawshaw, Group Ldr.; Judy Lister, Group Ldr.; Miss D. Chant, Group Ldr.; Miss I. Ferdinand, Libn.; Mr. J. Hardy, Archivist; Miss M. Pulleyblank, Libn.; Mrs. E. Schumann, Libn.

★4970★
GEORGE (Henry) SCHOOL OF LOS ANGELES - RESEARCH LIBRARY (Soc Sci)
10242 Mahogany Trail
Box 655   Phone: (213) 352-4141
Tujunga, CA 91042   Mrs. G.E. Pollard, Libn.
Founded: 1949. **Staff:** 3. **Subjects:** Henry George; land-value taxation; single tax history; political economy theory; tax practices; property tax analysis. **Holdings:** 2000 books. **Subscriptions:** 9 journals and other serials. **Services:** Copying; library open to public by appointment.

★4971★
GEORGE (Henry) SCHOOL OF SOCIAL SCIENCE - RESEARCH LIBRARY (Soc Sci)
3410 19th St.   Phone: (415) 362-7944
San Francisco, CA 94110   Robert Scrofani, Exec. V.P.
Founded: 1949. **Staff:** 1. **Subjects:** Land economics, economics, single tax. **Holdings:** 450 volumes; 3 VF drawers of news clippings; 300 pamphlets. **Subscriptions:** 10 journals and other serials. **Services:** Copying; library open to public for reference use only on request.

GEORGE MASON UNIVERSITY - AMERICAN SYMPHONY ORCHESTRA LEAGUE ARCHIVES
See: American Symphony Orchestra League

★4972★
GEORGE MASON UNIVERSITY - SCHOOL OF LAW - LIBRARY (Law)
3401 N. Fairfax Dr.   Phone: (703) 841-2652
Arlington, VA 22201   Stephen L. Burnett, Dir.
Founded: 1971. **Staff:** Prof 3; Other 5. **Subjects:** Law. **Special Collections:**

U.S. App. D.C. records and briefs (2500 volumes); Murdock International Law Collection (1500 volumes). **Holdings:** 135,000 books; 10,000 bound periodical volumes; 31,000 volumes in microform. **Subscriptions:** 570 journals and other serials; 11 newspapers. **Services:** Interlibrary loans; copying; library open to public. **Computerized Information Services:** LEXIS; Dataphase (internal database); computerized cataloging. **Networks/Consortia:** Member of EDUCOM; CAPCON. **Staff:** Linda Smith, Asst.Libn./Acq.; Michael J. Petit, Asst.Libn./Tech.Serv.

GEORGE WASHINGTON UNIVERSITY - ERIC CLEARINGHOUSE ON HIGHER EDUCATION
See: ERIC Clearinghouse on Higher Education

★4973★
GEORGE WASHINGTON UNIVERSITY - INSTITUTE FOR SINO-SOVIET STUDIES LIBRARY (Area-Ethnic)†
2130 H St., N.W.   Phone: (202) 676-7105
Washington, DC 20052   Alice E. Kopp, Libn.
Staff: Prof 1. **Subjects:** Russia, China, Japan, Korea - political science, history, economics, geography, philosophy; Eastern Europe, World Communist Movement. **Special Collections:** Translations of foreign press, foreign broadcast information service - China, USSR, Eastern Europe, Western Europe, Middle East, North Africa, Sub-Sahara Africa, Asia and Pacific. **Holdings:** 10,000 books; 210 bound periodical volumes; 18 atlases (cataloged); 20 VF drawers of reports, manuscripts, reprints and clippings. **Subscriptions:** 200 journals and other serials; 7 newspapers. **Services:** Copying; library open to public with permission of Director. **Networks/Consortia:** Member of CAPCON; Consortium of Universities of the Washington Metropolitan Area. **Publications:** ISSS Library Press Clips - for internal distribution only.

★4974★
GEORGE WASHINGTON UNIVERSITY - MEDICAL CENTER - PAUL HIMMELFARB HEALTH SCIENCES LIBRARY (Med)
2300 Eye St., N.W.   Phone: (202) 676-3528
Washington, DC 20037   Shelley A. Bader, Dir.
Staff: Prof 8; Other 15. **Subjects:** Medicine and allied health sciences. **Holdings:** 17,500 books; 63,000 bound periodical volumes; 850 titles of AV items. **Subscriptions:** 1281 journals and other serials. **Services:** Interlibrary loans; copying; SDI; library open to public with restrictions. **Computerized Information Services:** DIALOG, BRS, NLM, computerized cataloging, serials and circulation. **Networks/Consortia:** Member of Mid-Atlantic Regional Medical Library Program (MARMLP); District of Columbia Health Sciences Information Network (DOCHSIN). **Publications:** Information Interface, 10/year to Medical Center faculty, staff and students upon request. **Staff:** Suzanne Grefsheim, Assoc.Dir./Chf.Tech Serv.; Jim Gobeille, Access/Facilities Serv.; Cathy Harbert, Hd., Ref./ILL; Christine Matthews, Hd., On-line Serv.; Pamela Meredith, Ser.

★4975★
GEORGE WASHINGTON UNIVERSITY - NATIONAL LAW CENTER - JACOB BURNS LAW LIBRARY (Law)
716 20th St., N.W.   Phone: (202) 676-6646
Washington, DC 20052   Anita K. Head, Libn.
Founded: 1865. **Staff:** Prof 8; Other 14. **Subjects:** Law - Anglo-American, international, comparative. **Special Collections:** U.N. publications; records and briefs of U.S. Court of Customs and patent appeals; U.S. Supreme Court records and briefs (1959 to present); selective U.S. Government Documents depository. **Holdings:** 220,000 books; 335,000 microforms. **Subscriptions:** 3400 journals and other serials; 19 newspapers. **Services:** Interlibrary loans; copying (both limited); library open to public with special permission of librarian; government documents open to public. **Computerized Information Services:** LEXIS. **Networks/Consortia:** Member of OCLC through CAPCON; EDUCOM. **Publications:** Monthly Accession List; Guide to Law Library. **Staff:** Robert G. Bidwell, Assoc.Libn; Brian R. Dixon, Assoc.Libn.

★4976★
GEORGESON & COMPANY - LIBRARY (Bus-Fin)
Wall St. Plaza   Phone: (212) 440-9949
New York, NY 10005   Aileen V. Burnes, Libn.
Founded: 1939. **Staff:** Prof 2; Other 3. **Subjects:** Proxy solicitation, stockholder relations. **Special Collections:** Corporate records (annual reports, proxies) for all companies listed on the New York and American Stock Exchanges. **Holdings:** 135 books; 450 VF drawers. **Subscriptions:** 45 journals and other serials; 5 newspapers. **Services:** Interlibrary loans; library open to SLA members by appointment. **Special Indexes:** Index to proxies. **Staff:** Eileen Lewis-Lurin, Asst.Libn.

★4977★
GEORGETOWN UNIVERSITY - BLOMMER SCIENCE LIBRARY (Sci-Tech)
Reiss Science Bldg., 3rd Fl.
Box 37445   Phone: (202) 625-4733
Washington, DC 20013   Peg O'Rourke
Founded: 1962. **Staff:** Prof 1; Other 2. **Subjects:** Chemistry, physics, biology, mathematics, computer science, general science. **Holdings:** 57,922 books and bound periodical volumes; 160 motion picture loop cassettes. **Subscriptions:** 750 journals and other serials. **Services:** Interlibrary loans; copying; library open to public. **Computerized Information Services:** DIALOG, BRS; computerized cataloging. **Networks/Consortia:** Member of Consortium of Universities of the Washington Metropolitan Area; CAPCON; OCLC.

★4978★
GEORGETOWN UNIVERSITY - CENTER FOR POPULATION RESEARCH - LIBRARY (Soc Sci)
3520 Prospect St., N.W.   Phone: (202) 625-4333
Washington, DC 20057   Joan Helde, Libn.
Founded: 1962. **Staff:** 1. **Subjects:** Demography, U.S. census material, U.S. vital statistics. **Holdings:** 2000 books; 110 bound periodical volumes; 8 VF drawers of demographic reprints; census publications; 35 masters' theses. **Subscriptions:** 60 journals and other serials. **Services:** Interlibrary loans; copying; library open to scholars.

★4979★
GEORGETOWN UNIVERSITY - EAST CAMPUS DATA LIBRARY
35th & N Sts., N.W.
249A Nevils Bldg.
Washington, DC 20057
Defunct

★4980★
GEORGETOWN UNIVERSITY - FRED O. DENNIS LAW LIBRARY (Law)†
600 New Jersey Ave., N.W.   Phone: (202) 624-8260
Washington, DC 20001   Robert L. Oakly, Law Libn.
Founded: 1870. **Staff:** Prof 14; Other 21. **Subjects:** Law, international law. **Special Collections:** Environmental Resources, Federal Legislative Histories, United Nations documents. **Holdings:** 203,819 books and bound periodical volumes; 98,243 microforms. **Subscriptions:** 3300 journals and other serials. **Services:** Interlibrary loans; copying; library open to alumni (free) and attorneys (for a fee). **Computerized Information Services:** LEXIS; computerized cataloging. **Networks/Consortia:** Member of Consortium of Universities of the Washington Metropolitan Area; Metropolitan Washington Library Council. **Publications:** Library Guide; Title Page (acquisitions list and periodical tables of contents); Verso (Library Science Acquisitions List); bibliographies and reference aides - irregular. **Staff:** Elizabeth S. Jackson, Assoc.Libn.; Barbara Pawloski, Doc.Libn.; Tessa Perry, Order Libn.; Gretchen Feltes, Circ.Libn.; Sharon Cunningham, Media & Online Serv.; Lynn Wishart, Asst.Libn., Res.Serv.; Rick Ericson, Acq.Libn.; Richard Greenfield, Intl. Law Libn.; Bill Maxon, Ref.Libn.; Linda Davis, Asst.Cat.; Linda Wirth, Cat.Libn.; Linda Siler-Regan, Asst.Libn.Biblog.Control; Vivian L. Campbell, Asst.Libn., Coll.Dev.

★4981★
GEORGETOWN UNIVERSITY - KENNEDY INSTITUTE OF ETHICS - CENTER FOR BIOETHICS LIBRARY (Soc Sci)
3520 Prospect St., N.W.   Phone: (202) 625-2383
Washington, DC 20057   Doris Goldstein, Dir., Lib. & Info.Serv.
Founded: 1971. **Staff:** Prof 5; Other 4. **Subjects:** Ethics, bioethics, medical ethics, human experimentation, death and dying, physician-patient relationship, genetic intervention. **Holdings:** 8200 books; 28,000 articles (cataloged); 1 file of organizations in the field. **Subscriptions:** 180 journals and other serials. **Services:** Interlibrary loans (photocopies only); copying; library open to public. **Computerized Information Services:** MEDLARS, BIOETHICSLINE. **Networks/Consortia:** Member of OCLC; CAPCON. **Publications:** Bibliography of Bioethics, edited by Dr. LeRoy Walters, Volume I, 1975 - annual; New Titles in Bioethics, edited by Betsy Walkup, Volume I, 1975 - monthly current awareness service - by subscription; Bioethics: A Guide to Information Sources, 1982, compiled by Doris Goldstein. **Staff:** Judith Misticabelli, Sr.Libn.; Joy Kahn, Sr.Bibliog.

★4982★
GEORGETOWN UNIVERSITY - MEDICAL CENTER - DAHLGREN MEMORIAL LIBRARY (Med)
3900 Reservoir Rd.
Washington, DC 20007   Phone: (202) 625-7673
    Naomi C. Broering, Libn.
Founded: 1912. **Staff:** Prof 13; Other 26. **Subjects:** Medicine, dentistry, nursing hospital administration. **Special Collections:** History of Medicine (700

rare books); Carrel Collection (archival; 200 books and manuscripts). **Holdings:** 41,100 books; 59,600 bound periodical volumes; 1400 AV programs; 1000 historical items. **Subscriptions:** 1508 journals and other serials. **Services:** Interlibrary loans (fee); copying; SDI; library open to public for reference use only. **Computerized Information Services:** MEDLINE, DIALOG, SDC, BRS; PHILSOM (internal database); computerized cataloging, acquisitions, serials, circulation and bibliographic ILL. **Networks/Consortia:** Member of District of Columbia Health Sciences Information Network (DOCHSIN); CAPCON; Consortium of Academic Health Sciences Libraries of D.C.; Mid-Atlantic Regional Medical Library, Region IV. **Publications:** LOGIN (newsletter), 9/year; Faculty Publications Bulletin; Library Guide, annual. **Special Catalogs:** Dental Bibliography; AV Catalog. **Staff:** Clementine Pellegrino, Spec.Coll.Libn.; Margaret Kaiser, AV Serv.Libn.; Karen Shaines, Ref.Libn.; Helen Bagdoyan, Asst.Libn./Pub.Serv.; Linda Blackburn, Ref.Libn.; Karen Stesis, Acq.Libn.; Bonnie Cannard, Asst.Libn./Tech.Serv.; Patricia Patel, Resource Serv.Libn.; Wilma Ewens, Hd.Cat.; Susan Anderson, Ref.Libn.; MaryAnn Blake, Clinical Libn.

GEORGETOWN UNIVERSITY - MEDICAL SCHOOL - NATIONAL BIOMEDICAL RESEARCH FOUNDATION
See: National Biomedical Research Foundation

★4983★
GEORGETOWN UNIVERSITY - SPECIAL COLLECTION DIVISION - LAUINGER MEMORIAL LIBRARY (Hist)
37th and O Sts., N.W.   Phone: (202) 635-3230
Washington, DC 20057   George M. Barringer, Spec.Coll.Libn.
Staff: Prof 4; Other 2. **Subjects:** U.S. - political science, Catholic history, diplomacy and foreign affairs; English and American literature. **Special Collections:** Archives of Maryland Province, Society of Jesus; Archives of Woodstock College; Archives of the American Political Science Association; Archives of Dag Hammarskjold College. **Holdings:** 45,000 books; 1250 bound periodical volumes; 5000 linear feet of manuscripts in 600 separate collections; 2000 linear feet of University archives; 125,000 photographs (including 55,000 on motion picture history in the Quigley Photographic Archive); 2500 maps and graphics. **Services:** Copying; library open to public. **Computerized Information Services:** Computerized cataloging. **Networks/Consortia:** Member of OCLC; Consortium of Universities of the Washington Metropolitan Area. **Publications:** Exhibit catalogs and ephemera, irregular - distributed on item-by-item basis. **Special Catalogs:** Finding aids for manuscript collections, University Archives. **Staff:** Jon K. Reynolds, Univ.Archv.; L. Carl Chamberlain, Rare Books Cat.; Nicholas B. Scheetz, Mss.Libn.

GEORGETOWN UNIVERSITY - WOODSTOCK THEOLOGICAL CENTER
See: Woodstock Theological Center

GEORGIA AGRICULTURAL EXPERIMENT STATION LIBRARY
See: University of Georgia

★4984★
GEORGIA BAPTIST HISTORICAL SOCIETY - LIBRARY (Hist)
Stetson Memorial Library   Phone: (912) 744-2700
Macon, GA 31207   Mary E. Overby, Spec.Coll.Asst.
Staff: 1. **Subjects:** Mercer University history, local history. **Special Collections:** Georgia Baptist Convention minutes, 1822 to date; Georgia Baptist Associations; Southern Baptist Convention annuals. **Holdings:** Figures not available. **Remarks:** Library holdings located at Mercer University.

★4985★
GEORGIA BAPTIST MEDICAL CENTER - MEDICAL LIBRARY (Med)
300 Boulevard, N.E.   Phone: (404) 653-4603
Atlanta, GA 30312   Fay E. Boyer, Med.Libn.
Staff: Prof 1; Other 2. **Subjects:** Medicine and allied sciences. **Holdings:** 1500 books; 5000 bound periodical volumes; 7 volumes of audio cassettes. **Subscriptions:** 199 journals and other serials; 15 newspapers. **Services:** Interlibrary loans; copying; research; library open to medical and paramedical personnel. **Computerized Information Services:** MEDLINE. **Networks/Consortia:** Member of Atlanta Health Sciences Libraries Consortium. **Special Catalogs:** Reprint file; bibliography file; periodical holdings catalog (book).

GEORGIA COASTAL PLAIN EXPERIMENT STATION LIBRARY
See: University of Georgia

★4986★
GEORGIA COLLEGE - INA DILLARD RUSSELL LIBRARY (Hum)
231 W. Hancock   Phone: (912) 453-4047
Milledgeville, GA 31061   Janice C. Fennell, Lib.Dir.
Founded: 1889. **Staff:** Prof 7; Other 10. **Subjects:** Education, liberal arts,

science, business, social sciences, medicine. **Special Collections:** Flannery O'Connor; Georgia Authors; Georgia Collections; horology collection. **Holdings:** 125,354 books; 16,538 bound periodical volumes; 32,140 government documents; 298,460 microtexts (cataloged); 15,445 reels of microfilm (cataloged); 11,701 other nonprint materials (cataloged). **Subscriptions:** 1495 journals and other serials; 32 newspapers. **Services:** Interlibrary loans; copying; SDI; library open to public. **Computerized Information Services:** Computerized cataloging. **Networks/Consortia:** Member of OCLC through SOLINET; East Georgia Library Triangle; Central Georgia Associated Libraries; Health Science Libraries of Central Georgia. **Publications:** The Flannery O'Connor Bulletin. **Special Indexes:** Flannery O'Connor Manuscript Collection Index; Southern Recorder (Union Recorder) Index. **Staff:** Katherine Davis, Coord., Media Serv.; Anne L. Harman, Coord., Tech.Serv.; Jeremy Sayles, Info.Libn.

★4987★
GEORGIA COLLEGE - LEARNING RESOURCES CENTER (Educ)
                                        Phone: (912) 453-4714
Milledgeville, GA 31061
Founded: 1972. **Staff:** Prof 2; Other 2. **Subjects:** K-12 education, textbooks. **Special Collections:** All textbooks on the Georgia State Department of Education approved textbook list. **Holdings:** 6269 books; 7969 nonprint materials (cataloged); government documents, microtext, microfilm. **Services:** Interlibrary loans; library open to public with restrictions. **Computerized Information Services:** Computerized cataloging. **Networks/Consortia:** Member of OCLC through SOLINET; East Georgia Library Triangle; Central Georgia Associated Libraries. **Staff:** Katherine Davis, Coord., Media Serv.

★4988★
GEORGIA CONSERVANCY, INC. - LIBRARY (Env-Cons)
3110 Maple Dr., Suite 407   Phone: (404) 262-1967
Atlanta, GA 30305
Subjects: Conservation, ecology and pollution with special emphasis on the state of Georgia. **Holdings:** 425 books; 300 other items (cataloged). **Subscriptions:** 22 journals and other serials. **Services:** Copying; library open to public.

★4989★
GEORGIA HISTORICAL SOCIETY - LIBRARY (Hist)
W.B. Hodgson Hall
501 Whitaker St.   Phone: (912) 944-2128
Savannah, GA 31499   Anthony R. Dees, Dir.
Founded: 1839. **Staff:** Prof 3; Other 1. **Subjects:** Savannah history, Georgia history, genealogy. **Holdings:** 30,000 books; 1385 feet of manuscripts (private papers); Savannah newspapers, 1763 to present, on microfilm; maps of Savannah, Georgia and U.S.; collection of photographs and prints of Savannah and Georgia; Federal censuses of Georgia, 1820 to 1860, on microfilm; 216 feet of noncurrent Chatham County records (naturalization and various courts); 966 feet of noncurrent City of Savannah records. **Subscriptions:** 82 journals and other serials. **Services:** Copying; library open to public. **Publications:** Georgia Historical Quarterly; Collections of the Georgia Historical Society, irregular; G.H.S. Foot-Notes, quarterly. **Staff:** Barbara S. Bennett, Asst.Dir.; Anne P. Smith, Cat.; Karen Osvald, Archv.Asst.

★4990★
GEORGIA INSTITUTE OF TECHNOLOGY - PRICE GILBERT MEMORIAL LIBRARY (Sci-Tech)
Campus Dr.   Phone: (404) 894-4510
Atlanta, GA 30332   Dr. Edward Graham Roberts, Dir.
Founded: 1900. **Staff:** Prof 43; Other 82. **Subjects:** Engineering - aerospace, ceramic, chemical, civil, electrical, industrial, systems, mechanical, nuclear, textile; architecture; biology; chemistry; science and mechanics; geophysical science; industrial management; information and computer sciences; mathematics; physics; psychology. **Special Collections:** Maps (123,000); patents (4.2 million); technical reports (1.5 million); government documents (540,000). **Holdings:** 1.1 million volumes; 19,000 pictures; 30,000 pamphlets; 1700 films. **Subscriptions:** 13,800 journals and other serials. **Services:** Interlibrary loans; copying; fee-based computer literature searches; library open to public with fee charged to noncampus users. **Computerized Information Services:** Online systems; computerized cataloging, circulation and serials. **Networks/Consortia:** Member of OCLC through SOLINET. **Publications:** Serials Holdings List and Catalogs on microfiche. **Staff:** Dr. Arthur Kittle, Assoc.Dir.; Ruth Hale, Hd., Bibliog.Serv.Div.; James B. Dodd, Hd., User Serv.Div.; Helen Walzer, Hd., Coll. Organization; Mildred Emmon, Hd., Coll.Dev.Div.

★4991★

GEORGIA INSTITUTE OF TECHNOLOGY - PRICE GILBERT MEMORIAL LIBRARY - ARCHITECTURE LIBRARY (Art)

Atlanta, GA 30332

Phone: (404) 894-4877

Kathryn S. Brackney, Arch.Libn.

Staff: Prof 1; Other 5. **Subjects:** Architecture, architectural history; industrial, interior and urban design; building construction. **Special Collections:** Art Nouveau, a select group of drawings by architect Neel Reid. **Holdings:** 15,000 volumes; 47,570 slides; 3663 pamphlets. **Subscriptions:** 100 journals and other serials. **Services:** Interlibrary loans; copying; library open to public with fee for noncampus users. **Computerized Information Services:** DIALOG, BRS, SDC; computerized circulation.

★4992★

GEORGIA KRAFT COMPANY - TECHNICAL DEVELOPMENT CENTER LIBRARY (Sci-Tech)†

Box 1551

Rome, GA 30161

Phone: (404) 291-6920

Founded: 1966. **Staff:** 1. **Subjects:** Pulp and paper manufacture, pollution control, chemistry. **Holdings:** 950 books and bound periodical volumes; 4 VF drawers of technical papers and reports. **Subscriptions:** 60 journals and other serials. **Services:** Copying; library open to public by special request. **Staff:** Carol Osborn, Sec./Libn.

GEORGIA LAND OFFICE

See: Georgia State Surveyor General Department

GEORGIA MENTAL HEALTH INSTITUTE

See: Georgia State Department of Human Resources

★4993★

GEORGIA MUNICIPAL ASSOCIATION - LIBRARY (Soc Sci)

34 Peachtree St., N.W.

Atlanta, GA 30303

Phone: (404) 688-0472

W.E. George, Exec.Dir.

Founded: 1934. **Staff:** Prof 13; Other 7. **Subjects:** Municipal government including charters, codes, ordinances, taxation, planning and zoning, traffic, courts, economics, fiscal reports. **Holdings:** 300 books; 430 bound periodical volumes; 600 magazines and reports; 8 VF drawers. **Subscriptions:** 53 journals and other serials. **Services:** Interlibrary loans; library open to qualified persons.

★4994★

GEORGIA-PACIFIC CORPORATION - HISTORICAL MUSEUM (Sci-Tech)

900 S.W. 5th Ave.

Portland, OR 97204

Phone: (503) 222-5561

Richard M. Thompson, Info.Spec./Musm.Mgr.

Founded: 1973. **Staff:** 2. **Subjects:** Forestry, forest railroad technology, forest history. **Holdings:** 350 volumes; films, slides and videotapes. **Services:** Interlibrary loans (fee); copying; film lending.

★4995★

GEORGIA POWER COMPANY - LIBRARY SERVICES (Energy)

333 Piedmont Ave.

Box 4545

Atlanta, GA 30302

Phone: (404) 526-6857

Beth Ansley, Lib.Serv.Supv.

Founded: 1957. **Staff:** Prof 3; Other 1. **Subjects:** Energy technology, law, management, public relations, computer science, social sciences. **Special Collections:** Engineering publications; government documents; public utility annual reports; company history; E.P.R.I. **Holdings:** 15,000 books; 2000 bound periodical volumes; 1000 microfiche. **Subscriptions:** 500 journals and other serials. **Services:** Interlibrary loans; document retrieval; library not open to public. **Computerized Information Services:** DIALOG, SDC, New York Times Information Service, Legi-Slate, DOE/RECON, Dow Jones News Retrieval; internal database; computerized cataloging. **Staff:** Scott Muir, Libn.; Katherine J. Schreiner, Libn.

★4996★

GEORGIA REGIONAL HOSPITAL AT AUGUSTA - HOSPITAL LIBRARY (Med)

3405 Old Savannah Rd.

Box 327

Gracewood, GA 30812

Phone: (404) 790-2399

Barbara Avrett, Libn.

Founded: 1970. **Staff:** 1. **Subjects:** Psychiatry, nursing, psychology, social work, chaplaincy, recreation. **Holdings:** 2748 books; 834 cassettes and 28 games (cataloged); 3 VF drawers; 103 phonograph records; 55 maps; 63 slides; 2 filmstrips. **Subscriptions:** 101 journals and other serials. **Services:** Interlibrary loans; library open to public for reference use only. **Networks/Consortia:** Member of Southeastern Regional Medical Library Program (SERMLP); Augusta Area Committee for Health Services Resources. **Special Catalogs:** Cassette catalog.

★4997★

GEORGIA SOUTHERN COLLEGE - ARCHIVES/SPECIAL COLLECTIONS (Hist)

College Library

Landrum Box 8074

Statesboro, GA 30460

Phone: (912) 681-5645

Andrew Penson, Asst.Ref.Libn.

Staff: Prof 16; Other 21. **Subjects:** History. **Special Collections:** College Archives; Spencer H. and Spencer W. Cone papers (200 letters and documents); Conrad Aiken collection; Margaret Mitchell's letters to Leodel Coleman. **Holdings:** 1650 books; 215,826 documents; 457,547 microforms. **Services:** Interlibrary loans; copying; archives and special collections open to public for reference use only. **Computerized Information Services:** Computerized cataloging, acquisitions and serials. **Networks/Consortia:** Member of OCLC through SOLINET; East Georgia Library Triangle; Central Georgia Associated Libraries. **Staff:** Wendell Barbour, Assoc.Dir./Rd.Serv.

★4998★

GEORGIA STATE DEPARTMENT OF ARCHIVES AND HISTORY - CENTRAL RESEARCH LIBRARY (Hist)†

330 Capitol Ave., S.E.

Atlanta, GA 30334

Phone: (404) 656-2350

Ruth L. Corry, Hd., Ctrl.Res.

Founded: 1918. **Staff:** Prof 13; Other 2. **Subjects:** Georgia, southeastern U.S., genealogy. **Special Collections:** Georgia state records (45,000 cubic feet); county records (7500 cubic feet and 22,000 reels of microfilm); private papers (2500 cubic feet). **Holdings:** 14,000 volumes; 2000 reels of microfilm of newspapers; 6000 maps; 20,000 prints and photographs. **Subscriptions:** 323 journals and other serials; 91 newspapers. **Services:** Copying; library open to public. **Publications:** List of publications of the Georgia State Department of Archives and History - free upon request. **Special Catalogs:** Civil War Pension Index (microfilm); Family Surname File; descriptive inventories for individual official record groups and of manuscript collections. **Staff:** Sally Moseley, Hd., Microfilm Lib.

★4999★

GEORGIA STATE DEPARTMENT OF EDUCATION - DIVISION OF PUBLIC LIBRARY SERVICES (Educ)

156 Trinity Ave., S.W.

Atlanta, GA 30303

Phone: (404) 656-2461

Joe B. Forsee, Dir.

Staff: Prof 17; Other 32. **Subjects:** Education, Georgia. **Special Collections:** Public Library Film Collection, Juvenile and Young Adult. **Holdings:** 310,562 books; 839 bound periodical volumes; 299,438 microfiche; 10,000 reels of microfilm; 30 VF drawers of pamphlets; 2400 films. **Subscriptions:** 874 journals and other serials. **Services:** Interlibrary loans; copying; library open to public for reference use only. **Computerized Information Services:** Computerized cataloging. **Networks/Consortia:** Member of Georgia Library Information Network (GLIN); OCLC through SOLINET. **Publications:** Selected List of Books for Teachers, irregular; Georgia Public Library Statistics, annual - both available on request. **Staff:** Lucia Patrick, Cons., Rd.Serv.; Martha Covey, Hd., Ref.; Richard B. Hall, Cons., Bldg./Films; Jim DeJarnatt, Cons., Lib. for Blind; Linda Raye Osborn, Cons., Ch.Serv.; Robyn Hollar, Hd., Circ.; Katherine Swint, Hd., Tech.Serv.

★5000★

GEORGIA STATE DEPARTMENT OF EDUCATION - LIBRARY FOR THE BLIND & PHYSICALLY HANDICAPPED (Aud-Vis)

1050 Murphy Ave., S.W.

Atlanta, GA 30310

Phone: (404) 656-2465

Jim DeJarnatt, Dir.

Staff: Prof 3; Other 12. **Special Collections:** History of Georgia, books written by Georgians, blindiana. **Holdings:** 110,000 talking books; books in braille and large print; tapes and cassettes. **Services:** Interlibrary loans; copying; tape duplication. **Networks/Consortia:** Member of U.S. Library of Congress - Division for the Blind and Physically Handicapped Regional Libraries. **Remarks:** Coordinates talking book centers in Albany, Athens, Augusta, Bainbridge, Brunswick, Columbus, Dublin, Gainesville, LaFayette, Macon, Savannah, Rome, and Valdosta. **Staff:** Iona Foreman, Textbook Cons.; Emily Yeh, Vol.Coord.

★5001★

GEORGIA STATE DEPARTMENT OF HUMAN RESOURCES - GEORGIA MENTAL HEALTH INSTITUTE - ADDISON M. DUVAL LIBRARY (Med)

1256 Briarcliff Rd., N.E.

Atlanta, GA 30306

Phone: (404) 894-5663

Brenda Scott, Dir. of Libs.

Founded: 1966. **Staff:** Prof 2; Other 1. **Subjects:** Psychiatry, nursing, social work, chaplaincy, activities therapy, psychology. **Special Collections:** Department of Human Genetics Collection (600 books, 35 subscriptions); Department of Biological Psychiatry Collection (100 books, 11 subscriptions). **Holdings:** 15,000 books; 3400 bound periodical volumes. **Subscriptions:** 150 journals and other serials; 2 newspapers. **Services:** Interlibrary loans; clinical librarian service; copying; SDI; library open to public with a deposit.

Networks/Consortia: Member of Atlanta Health Sciences Libraries Consortium. Publications: Acquisition List, bimonthly. Remarks: The Grady Jackson Memorial Library, a patient library containing 1000 volumes is also located at the above address. Staff: Stephen M. Koplan, Libn.; Z.C. Martin, ILL.

★5002★

GEORGIA STATE DEPARTMENT OF HUMAN RESOURCES - LIBRARY (Med)
534-H, 47 Trinity Ave., S.W.   Phone: (404) 656-4969
Atlanta, GA 30334-1202   Miriam Boland, Lib.Dir.
Founded: 1940. Staff: Prof 1; Other 1. Subjects: Public health, sociology. Special Collections: U.S. Public Health Service Reports. Holdings: 19,000 books; 5000 bound periodical volumes. Subscriptions: 100 journals and other serials. Services: Interlibrary loans; copying; library open to public for reference use only. Networks/Consortia: Member of Atlanta Health Science Libraries Consortium.

★5003★

GEORGIA STATE DEPARTMENT OF NATURAL RESOURCES - COASTAL RESOURCES DIVISION - ANDERSON LIBRARY (Env-Cons)
1200 Glynn Ave.   Phone: (912) 264-7330
Brunswick, GA 31523   Eleanor Y. Waters, Libn.
Staff: Prof 1; Other 1. Subjects: Shellfish, sport fishing, fish, estuarine ecology. Holdings: 1000 books; 600 bound periodical volumes; 6000 reprints. Services: Interlibrary loans; copying; SDI; library open to public for reference use only. Publications: Contributions column for Coastlines Georgia; Coast Cards. Remarks: Library contains the holdings of library of William W. Anderson, Senior Scientist for the U.S. government and the state of Georgia.

★5004★

GEORGIA STATE DEPARTMENT OF OFFENDER REHABILITATION - REFERENCE/RESOURCE CENTER (Law)
205 Butler St., S.E.   Phone: (404) 894-5383
Atlanta, GA 30334   Karen Dornseif, Libn.
Founded: 1974. Staff: Prof 1; Other 1. Subjects: Corrections, criminal justice, grants, counseling, rehabilitation, management. Special Collections: Project reports (200); female offenders (150 items). Holdings: 1500 books; 125 periodicals. Subscriptions: 80 journals and newsletters. Services: Interlibrary loans; copying; library open to public for reference use only. Computerized Information Services: Computerized cataloging and acquisitions. Networks/Consortia: Member of Georgia Library Information Network. Publications: Reference/Resource Center News, bimonthly - to department staff and to others upon request; bibliographies.

★5005★

GEORGIA STATE DEPARTMENT OF TRANSPORTATION - RESEARCH LIBRARY (Trans)
15 Kennedy Dr.   Phone: (404) 363-7567
Atlanta, GA 30050   Alfredia A. Scott, Libn.
Founded: 1974. Staff: Prof 1; Other 1. Subjects: Transportation, statistics. Special Collections: Transportation Research Board publications. Holdings: 5000 volumes; 50 bound periodical volumes; 6021 State DOT research reports; 7235 US DOT documents; 8 drawers of clippings; materials and testing standards and specifications. Subscriptions: 66 journals and other serials. Services: Interlibrary loans; copying; library open to public for reference use only on request.

★5006★

GEORGIA STATE FORESTRY COMMISSION - LIBRARY (Sci-Tech)†
Box 819   Phone: (912) 744-3231
Macon, GA 31202   Al Smith, Hd.
Founded: 1956. Staff: 1. Subjects: Forestry, entomology. Holdings: 2240 books; 100 bound periodical volumes; 21 shelves of pamphlets; 5 VF drawers of reference files. Services: Interlibrary loans; copying; library not open to public.

★5007★

GEORGIA STATE LIBRARY (Info Sci)†
301 Judicial Bldg.
40 Capitol Sq., S.W.   Phone: (404) 656-3468
Atlanta, GA 30334   Carroll T. Parker, State Libn.
Founded: 1831. Staff: Prof 3; Other 4. Subjects: Law, government, economics, politics. Special Collections: Georgia Collection (20,000 volumes). Holdings: 100,000 books; 7250 bound periodical volumes; federal and Georgia documents. Subscriptions: 329 journals and other serials. Services: Interlibrary loans (limited); copying; library open to public. Publications: Checklist of Official Publications of the State of Georgia, quarterly - by exchange. Special Indexes: Index of legislative bills (card).

Staff: John E. Poe, Ref./Rd.Serv.Libn.; Martha Mashburn, Doc./Tech.Serv.Libn.

★5008★

GEORGIA STATE OFFICE OF PLANNING AND BUDGET - STATE DATA CENTER (Soc Sci; Plan)
270 Washington St., S.W., Rm. 608   Phone: (404) 656-2191
Atlanta, GA 30334   Thomas M. Wagner, Prog.Mgr.
Founded: 1970. Staff: Prof 2. Subjects: Population, education, economics, health, crime. Special Collections: Georgia County Population Estimates and Projections. Holdings: 1500 books; 300 U.S. government publications; 100,000 pages of computer printouts; 175 reels of computer tapes; 300 primary data files; 2500 maps. Subscriptions: 15 journals and other serials. Services: Copying; library open to public but some files are confidential. Computerized Information Services: Computerized acquisitions; online access to census data for Georgia. Publications: Georgia County Population Estimates and Projections, annual. Remarks: Inventory includes all census data relevant to the state of Georgia.

★5009★

GEORGIA STATE SUPREME COURT LIBRARY (Law)
Judicial Bldg., 5th Fl.
40 Capitol Sq., S.W.   Phone: (404) 656-4212
Atlanta, GA 30334   Curtis M. French, Libn.
Staff: Prof 1. Subjects: Law. Holdings: 10,000 volumes. Subscriptions: 10 journals and other serials. Services: Library open to attorneys of record.

★5010★

GEORGIA STATE SURVEYOR GENERAL DEPARTMENT - LIBRARY (Hist; Geog-Map)
330 Capitol Ave.
Archives & Records Bldg.   Phone: (404) 656-2367
Atlanta, GA 30334   Mr. Marion R. Hemperley, Dp. Surveyor Gen.
Staff: Prof 3. Subjects: Georgia - history and geography. Special Collections: John H. Goff Collection of Georgia history. Holdings: 2000 manuscript volumes containing 1.5 million grants and plats of survey for Georgia; 10,000 maps; 200 papers, theses and dissertations. Services: Copying; library open to public. Publications: Occasional publications from original holdings. Remarks: The Surveyor General Department is the Land Office for Georgia. Staff: Margaret Johnsen, Sr.Archv.; Ingrid Shields, Archv.

★5011★

GEORGIA STATE UNIVERSITY - SMALL BUSINESS DEVELOPMENT CENTER (Bus-Fin)
Box 874, University Plaza   Phone: (404) 658-3550
Atlanta, GA 30303   Peggy Triplett
Founded: 1979. Staff: 1. Subjects: Small business. Holdings: Figures not available; business directories; government publications and journals. Services: Counseling; library open to public with restrictions. Remarks: Library is located at 40-42 Pryor St., Atlanta, GA.

★5012★

GEORGIA STATE UNIVERSITY - SOUTHERN LABOR ARCHIVES (Soc Sci; Hist)
                                                Phone: (404) 658-2476
Atlanta, GA 30303   Leslie S. Hough, Archv.
Founded: 1969. Staff: Prof 4; Other 9. Subjects: Southern labor history, Georgia State University history, 20th-century popular music. Special Collections: Records of the United Textile Workers of America, the United Furniture Workers of America and numerous collections from regional and local union offices; the Johnny Mercer papers; personal papers of trade union activists; university records. Holdings: 150 books; 12 bound periodical volumes; 3500 cubic feet of manuscripts. Subscriptions: 110 journals and other serials; 110 newspapers. Services: Interlibrary loans; copying; library open to public with restrictions on selected collections. Publications: Southern Labor Archives Report. Staff: Robert Dinwiddie, Asst.Archv.; Karen Bouffard, Archv.Asst.

★5013★

GEOSCIENCE, LTD. - LIBRARY (Sci-Tech)
410 S. Cedros Ave.   Phone: (714) 755-9396
Solana Beach, CA 92075   D. Gossett, Libn.
Founded: 1961. Staff: Prof 1. Subjects: Mathematics, physics, medicine. Holdings: 700 volumes. Services: Library not open to public.

★5014★

GEOSOURCE INC. - SMITH METER DIVISION - ENGINEERING TECHNICAL LIBRARY (Sci-Tech)
1602 Wagner Ave.
Box 10428   Phone: (814) 899-0661
Erie, PA 16514   Sharon D. Carter, Engr.Coord.
Founded: 1980. **Staff:** Prof 1. **Subjects:** Flow technology, mechanical and electrical engineering, drafting. **Holdings:** 1000 books; 50 technical studies; 100 patents; 500 standards. **Subscriptions:** 16 journals and other serials. **Services:** Library not open to public.

★5015★

GEO-TECH ARCHIVES LTD. - PALEONTOLOGICAL RESEARCH LABORATORY - LIBRARY
3616 Garden Club Ln.
Charlotte, NC 28210
Defunct

★5016★

GEOTHERMAL RESOURCES COUNCIL - LIBRARY (Energy)
Box 1350   Phone: (916) 758-2360
Davis, CA 95617   David N. Anderson, Exec.Dir.
Staff: 3. **Subjects:** Geothermal resources. **Holdings:** Figures not available. **Services:** Copying; library open to public. **Publications:** List of publications - available on request. **Staff:** Beverly A. Hall, Asst.Dir.

★5017★

GEOTHERMAL WORLD CORPORATION - INFORMATION CENTER (Energy)
5762 Firebird Ct.   Phone: (805) 482-6288
Camarillo, CA 93010   Alan A. Tratner, Dir.
Founded: 1978. **Staff:** Prof 3. **Subjects:** Geothermal energy - research and development. **Special Collections:** Geothermal World Directory, 1972-1982. **Holdings:** 500 volumes; Geothermal Energy Monthly Journal, 1973-1982, volumes 1-10 (microfiche); maps; slides. **Subscriptions:** 10 journals and other serials. **Services:** Copying; requests for information accepted by mail. **Special Indexes:** Geothermal Energy, cumulative index; Geothermal World Directory index.

★5018★

GEOTRONICS LABORATORIES, INC. - LIBRARY (Sci-Tech)
115 West Greenbriar Lane   Phone: (214) 946-7573
Dallas, TX 75208
Subjects: Engineering, research and development. **Holdings:** Figures not available.

GERAGHTY & MILLER, INC. - WATER INFORMATION CENTER, INC.
See: Water Information Center, Inc.

★5019★

GERBER PRODUCTS COMPANY - CORPORATE LIBRARY (Food-Bev)
445 State St.   Phone: (616) 928-2631
Fremont, MI 49412   Sherrie Anderson, Libn.
Founded: 1946. **Staff:** Prof 1; Other 3. **Subjects:** Food processing, infant nutrition, business administration, marketing, chemistry, microbiology, agriculture. **Special Collections:** Company archives. **Holdings:** 6500 books; 2800 bound periodical volumes; 125 AV programs; 2000 patents on microfiche; 10,000 photoprints and pamphlets in hardcopy or on microfiche. **Subscriptions:** 1000 journals and other serials; 20 newspapers. **Services:** Interlibrary loans; copying; library open to public with permission. **Computerized Information Services:** DIALOG; Gerber Retrieval System (internal database); computerized cataloging and circulation. **Publications:** Library Newsletter, monthly - for internal distribution only. **Special Catalogs:** Serial holdings list (card and book).

GERHARDT LIBRARY OF MUSICAL INFORMATION
See: Towson State University

GERHARDT MARIMBA AND XYLOPHONE COLLECTION
See: Towson State University

GERMAN CULTURAL CENTER
See: Goethe Institut Chicago; Goethe Institute Atlanta

GERMAN CULTURAL CENTRE
See: Goethe Institute Montreal

GERMAN CULTURAL INSTITUTE - GOETHE HOUSE NEW YORK
See: Goethe House New York

★5020★

GERMAN INFORMATION CENTER - FEDERAL REPUBLIC OF GERMANY (Area-Ethnic)
410 Park Ave.   Phone: (212) 888-9840
New York, NY 10022
Subjects: General information on the Federal Republic of Germany. **Holdings:** Figures not available. **Services:** Center open to public with restrictions.

★5021★

GERMAN SOCIETY OF PENNSYLVANIA - JOSEPH HORNER MEMORIAL LIBRARY (Area-Ethnic)
611 Spring Garden St.   Phone: (215) 627-4365
Philadelphia, PA 19123   Christine E. Richardson, Libn.
Founded: 1817. **Staff:** Prof 1; Other 1. **Subjects:** All subjects with special emphasis on history, biography, literature (85% in German language); juvenile literature in German. **Special Collections:** Americana-Germanica (12,000 volumes). **Holdings:** 75,000 books including 12,000 items of archival collection. **Subscriptions:** 15 journals. **Services:** Interlibrary loans (fee); copying; library open to members; reference use only to all others. **Publications:** Newsletters to members of German Society. **Staff:** Gisela Hill Cannan, Libn.

★5022★

GERMAN SOCIETY OF WINNIPEG - LIBRARY (Area-Ethnic)
121 Charles St.   Phone: (204) 589-7724
Winnipeg, MB, Canada R2W 4A6
Founded: 1958. **Subjects:** General topics in the German language. **Holdings:** 1200 books. **Services:** Library open to public on special request to president.

GERMANS FROM RUSSIA PROJECT LIBRARY
See: Colorado State University

★5023★

GERMANTOWN FRIENDS MEETING - FRIENDS FREE LIBRARY (Rel-Theol)
5418 Germantown Ave.   Phone: (215) 438-6023
Philadelphia, PA 19144   Sara G. Woy, Hd.Libn.
Founded: 1848. **Staff:** Prof 3; Other 3. **Special Collections:** Quaker Collection; Germantown history; Irvin Poley Theater History of Philadelphia - 1904-1965 (250 scrapbooks). **Holdings:** 54,811 books. **Subscriptions:** 170 journals and other serials; 7 newspapers. **Services:** Interlibrary loans; copying; library open to public.

★5024★

GERMANTOWN HISTORICAL SOCIETY - LIBRARY (Hist)
5214 Germantown Ave.   Phone: (215) 844-0514
Philadelphia, PA 19144   Marilyn R. Drinker, Libn.
Founded: 1908. **Staff:** Prof 1. **Subjects:** History of Germantown, Mt. Airy, Chestnut Hill and East Falls sections of Philadelphia. **Special Collections:** Books and Bibles printed in Germantown. **Holdings:** 3200 books; scrapbooks; photographs; post-cards; newspapers published in Germantown since 1830; deeds and briefs of title; local genealogies. **Subscriptions:** 12 journals and other serials. **Services:** Copying; research for a fee; library open to public. **Publications:** Germantown Crier, quarterly.

★5025★

GERMANTOWN HOSPITAL AND MEDICAL CENTER - LIBRARY (Med)
One Penn Blvd.   Phone: (215) 438-9700
Philadelphia, PA 19144   Kathleen A. Leigh, Libn.
Founded: 1982. **Staff:** Prof 1. **Subjects:** Medicine, nursing. **Holdings:** 2200 books; 900 bound journals. **Subscriptions:** 150 journals and other serials. **Services:** Interlibrary loans; copying; library open to medical personnel, nursing staff, allied health staff, students and all hospital personnel. **Networks/Consortia:** Member of Mid-Eastern Regional Medical Library Service (MERMLS). **Formed by the Merger of:** Its Medical Staff Library and the Nursing School Library.

★5026★

GERMANTOWN HOSPITAL AND MEDICAL CENTER - NURSING SCHOOL LIBRARY
One Penn Blvd.
Philadelphia, PA 19144
Defunct. Merged into Germantown Hospital and Medical Center - Library.

GERONTOLOGY LEARNING RESOURCES CENTER
See: Institute of Gerontology

GERONTOLOGY RESEARCH CENTER
See: National Institute on Aging

GERRISH-TRUE HEALTH SCIENCE LIBRARY
See: Central Maine Medical Center

GERSTENZANG SCIENCE LIBRARY
See: Brandeis University

GERUNTINO (A.J.) LIBRARY
See: Southwestern University - A.J. Geruntino Library

★5027★
GESSLER CLINIC - MEDICAL LIBRARY
635 First St., North
Winter Haven, FL 33880
Founded: 1971. **Subjects:** Medicine. **Holdings:** 300 books; 700 bound periodical volumes. **Remarks:** Presently inactive.

GEST (John Marshall) MEMORIAL LIBRARY
See: Jenkins (Theodore F.) Memorial Law Library Company

GEST ORIENTAL LIBRARY AND EAST ASIAN COLLECTIONS
See: Princeton University

★5028★
GESTAS INC. - DOCUMENTATION CENTER (Bus-Fin)
410 St. Nicolas St.   Phone: (514) 288-5611
Montreal, PQ, Canada H2Y 2P5   Monique Dumont, Libn.
Founded: 1975. **Staff:** Prof 1; Other 1. **Subjects:** Insurance, law, management. **Holdings:** 5000 books; 300 bound periodical volumes; 600 insurance judgments; 200 financial statements. **Subscriptions:** 200 journals and other serials; 10 newspapers. **Services:** Interlibrary loans; copying; library not open to public. **Publications:** Appraisal of Periodicals, bimonthly - for internal distribution only. **Special Indexes:** Index of Insurance Judgements (card). **Remarks:** Company is a member of Sodarcan, Ltd. **Staff:** Michele Laurin, Tech.Libn.

★5029★
GETHSEMANI ABBEY - LIBRARY (Rel-Theol)†
                    Phone: (502) 549-3117
Trappist, KY 40073   Fr. Hilarion Schmock, O.C.S.O., Libn.
Founded: 1848. **Staff:** 2. **Subjects:** Scripture, Christian and monastic writers, Benedictine/Cistercian monasticism, religious life, non-Christian religions, theology, liturgy, prayer, mysticism. **Special Collections:** Thomas Merton Collection; printed editions of the Rule of St. Benedict, 1500 to present (300). **Holdings:** 30,000 books; 1000 bound periodical volumes; 30 manuscripts and 60 incunabula on microfilm. **Subscriptions:** 70 journals and other serials; 10 newspapers. **Services:** Interlibrary loans; copying; library open to public for specific research. **Remarks:** Rare books on Cisterian history and St. Bernard, manuscripts and incunabula on permanent loan to Institute of Cistercian Studies at Western Michigan University. **Staff:** Fr. Bede Kok, O.C.S.O., Libn.

★5030★
GETTY (J. Paul) MUSEUM - RESEARCH LIBRARY (Art)
17985 Pacific Coast Hwy.   Phone: (213) 459-2306
Malibu, CA 90265   Anne-Mieke Halbrook, Hd.Libn.
Staff: Prof 4; Other 3. **Subjects:** Art - Greek and Roman, 18th-century French decorative; European painting 13th-19th centuries. **Holdings:** 40,000 volumes including sale and auction catalogs; 400 reels of microfilm; 6 VF drawers of microfiche; 8 VF drawers of pamphlets and clippings. **Subscriptions:** 80 journals and other serials. **Services:** Interlibrary loans (selective); copying; library open to public by appointment. **Computerized Information Services:** Computerized cataloging. **Networks/Consortia:** Member of RLG. **Staff:** Bethany Mendenhall, Assoc.Libn.

★5031★
GETTY OIL COMPANY, INC. - LIBRARY (Energy)
3810 Wilshire Blvd.   Phone: (213) 381-7151
Los Angeles, CA 90005   Mary Krupp, Adm., Corp.Lib.
Founded: 1954. **Staff:** Prof 1; Other 2. **Subjects:** Geology, petroleum, business. **Holdings:** 18,650 books and bound periodical volumes; 112 pamphlet boxes; 15 VF drawers and 2 map cases of maps. **Subscriptions:** 200 journals and other serials; 19 newspapers. **Services:** Interlibrary loans; library open to public with restrictions. **Computerized Information Services:** DIALOG, SDC. **Publications:** Titles and Topics, monthly - for internal distribution only.

★5032★
GETTY OIL COMPANY, INC. - RESEARCH CENTER LIBRARY (Energy)
10201 Westpark Dr.
Box 770070   Phone: (713) 972-1749
Houston, TX 77215-0070   Elaine P. Adams, Supv., Lib.Serv.
Founded: 1960. **Staff:** Prof 3; Other 4. **Subjects:** Petroleum engineering, chemistry, geology, environmental science, technology. **Holdings:** 12,000 books; 400 bound periodical volumes; AV materials; maps; company documents. **Subscriptions:** 260 journals and other serials. **Services:** Interlibrary loans; copying; library open to public by appointment. **Computerized Information Services:** DIALOG, SDC. **Networks/Consortia:** Member of Regional Information and Communication Exchange (RICE). **Publications:** Announcements of acquisitions and services, monthly. **Staff:** Debra J. Clay, Tech.Lit.Libn.; Katherine B. Ellwood, Doc.Libn.

★5033★
GETTY REFINING AND MARKETING COMPANY - LAW LIBRARY (Law)
Box 1650   Phone: (918) 560-6136
Tulsa, OK 74102   Margaret A. Brookfield, Law Libn.
Staff: Prof 1. **Subjects:** Law. **Holdings:** 15,000 books. **Services:** Library not open to public. **Computerized Information Services:** LEXIS.

★5034★
GETTY REFINING AND MARKETING COMPANY - TECHNICAL LIBRARY (Energy)†
                    Phone: (302) 834-6247
Delaware City, DE 19706   J.G. Mitchell, Libn.
Founded: 1957. **Subjects:** Petroleum processing and related subjects. **Holdings:** 2500 books; 2100 bound periodical volumes. **Subscriptions:** 50 journals and other serials. **Services:** Interlibrary loans; copying; library not open to public.

★5035★
GETTYSBURG COLLEGE - DEPARTMENT OF CHEMISTRY - LIBRARY (Sci-Tech)
Breidenbaugh Hall
Gettysburg, PA 17325   Lillian S. Jackson, Chem. Faculty
Subjects: Chemistry. **Holdings:** 2000 books. **Subscriptions:** 23 journals and other serials.

★5036★
GETTYSBURG COLLEGE - MUSSELMAN LIBRARY - SPECIAL COLLECTIONS (Hist; Soc Sci)
                    Phone: (717) 334-3131
Gettysburg, PA 17325   James H. Richards, Jr., Libn.
Staff: Prof 7; Other 14. **Special Collections:** Civil War (4400 volumes); American Indian Collection (700 volumes); H.L. Mencken (250 volumes and clippings). **Holdings:** 266,000 volumes. **Subscriptions:** 1198 journals and other serials. **Services:** Interlibrary loans; copying; library open to public with restrictions. **Computerized Information Services:** Computerized cataloging, acquisitions and serials. **Networks/Consortia:** Member of CentralPennsylvania Consortium (CPC); Associated College Libraries of Central Pennsylvania (ACLCP). **Publications:** Breviaria, irregular. **Staff:** Anna Jane Moyer, ILL Libn.; Mary G. Burel, Acq.Libn.; David T. Hedrick, AV Libn.; Dwight Huseman, Ser., Doc., Sys.Libn.; Nancy Scott, Archv.

GETTYSBURG NATL. MILITARY PARK
See: U.S. Natl. Park Service

GEY (George and Margaret) LIBRARY
See: Jones (W. Alton) Cell Science Center - George and Margaret Gey Library

★5037★
GHOST RANCH CONFERENCE CENTER - GHOST RANCH LIBRARY (Rel-Theol)
                    Phone: (505) 685-4333
Abiquiu, NM 87510   Lidie Miller, Libn.
Staff: Prof 1. **Subjects:** Theology, Bible study, Christian education, Southwest, ecology, archeology, paleontology, fine arts. **Holdings:** 12,000 books; 2 VF drawers of pamphlets. **Subscriptions:** 35 journals and other serials. **Services:** Library open to ranch guests. **Remarks:** The Conference Center operates under the auspices of the United Presbyterian Church in the U.S.A. - Program Agency.

GIANNINI FOUNDATION OF AGRICULTURAL ECONOMICS
See: University of California, Berkeley

GIBBES ART GALLERY - CAROLINA ART ASSOCIATION
See: Carolina Art Association

★5038★
GIBBS AND COX, INC. - TECHNICAL INFORMATION CENTER (Sci-Tech)
119 W. 31st St.   Phone: (212) 613-1300
New York, NY 10001   J.W. Hoffman, Jr., Mgr.
Founded: 1930. **Staff:** Prof 3; Other 3. **Subjects:** Naval architecture, marine engineering. **Holdings:** 6000 books; 1000 bound periodical volumes; 3000 vendor catalogs; 10,000 reports. **Subscriptions:** 100 journals and other serials. **Services:** Library not open to public. **Computerized Information Services:** Complete microfilm service; company documents on internal database with search capabilities.

★5039★
GIBBS & HILL, INC. - LIBRARY (Sci-Tech)
393 Seventh Ave.   Phone: (212) 760-5062
New York, NY 10001   Ralph F. DeAngelis, Chf.Libn.
Staff: Prof 2; Other 1. **Subjects:** Nuclear engineering; nuclear safety; fossil power plants; alternative energy technology; environmental science and technology; engineering - electrical, civil, mechanical. **Special Collections:** Nuclear Safety Library (500 volumes); standards and specifications (3000). **Holdings:** 3000 books; 100 bound periodical volumes; 1500 company reports; 3500 technical reports (hard copy); 1500 vendor catalogs; 35,000 reports on microfiche; 300 cassettes of vendor information and standards. **Subscriptions:** 333 journals and other serials. **Services:** Interlibrary loans; copying; library not open to public. **Computerized Information Services:** DIALOG. **Publications:** Current Awareness Microfiche Bulletin, monthly; Library Bulletin, monthly - to management and professionals. **Staff:** Kathy Evans, Asst.Libn.

GIBRALTAR RESEARCH LIBRARY
See: Crompton & Knowles Corporation - Dyes and Chemicals Division

★5040★
GIBSON, DUNN & CRUTCHER - LAW LIBRARY (Law)
515 S. Flower St.   Phone: (213) 488-7216
Los Angeles, CA 90071   Irwin G. Manley, Adm., Info.Serv.
Staff: Prof 4; Other 8. **Subjects:** Law. **Holdings:** 33,000 books; 1600 bound periodical volumes; 210 law memoranda (cataloged); 600 pamphlets; 600 tape cassettes; 10,000 microfiche. **Subscriptions:** 170 journals and other serials; 8 newspapers. **Services:** Library not open to public. **Computerized Information Services:** LEXIS, WESTLAW, New York Times Information Service, DIALOG, SDC; internal database. **Special Catalogs:** Catalog to collection of bound Memoranda of Law, 1928 to present (online). **Special Indexes:** Index to tape cassettes (visible file). **Staff:** Pamela Robinson, Libn.; Susan I-Man Liu, Cat.; Donald Spring, Ref.

GIBSON LIBRARY
See: Kentucky Mountain Bible Institute

GIBSON MEDICAL LIBRARY
See: St. Mary's of the Lake Hospital

GIBSON (R.E.) LIBRARY
See: Johns Hopkins University - Applied Physics Laboratory - R.E. Gibson Library

★5041★
GIFFELS ASSOCIATES, INC. - LIBRARY (Sci-Tech)
Box 5025   Phone: (313) 355-4600
Southfield, MI 48037   William H. Dukes, Libn.
Staff: 1. **Subjects:** Engineering, architecture. **Holdings:** 1100 books. **Subscriptions:** 80 journals and other serials. **Services:** Interlibrary loans; copying; library open to public with restrictions. **Remarks:** Library is located at 25200 Telegraph Rd., Southfield, MI 48034.

GIFFORD (John H.) MEMORIAL LIBRARY & INFORMATION CTR.
See: American Chemical Society, Inc. - Rubber Division - John H. Gifford Memorial Library & Information Ctr.

★5042★
GIFFORD MEMORIAL HOSPITAL - HEALTH INFORMATION CENTER (Med)†
44 S. Main St.   Phone: (802) 728-3366
Randolph, VT 05060   Patience L. Crowley, Dir.
Staff: 1. **Subjects:** Medicine, nursing. **Holdings:** 325 books; 1 VF drawer of pamphlets; 150 government publications; 50 tapes and filmstrips. **Subscriptions:** 45 journals and other serials. **Services:** Interlibrary loans; copying; library open to public with restrictions.

GILA CLIFF DWELLINGS NATL. MONUMENT
See: U.S. Natl. Park Service

★5043★
GILA COUNTY LAW LIBRARY (Law)
1400 E. Ash   Phone: (602) 425-3231
Globe, AZ 85501
Staff: 1. **Subjects:** Law. **Holdings:** 16,000 books; 8000 bound periodical volumes. **Services:** Copying; library open to public. **Staff:** Dave Crossett, Libn.; Barbara Rice, Asst.Libn.

★5044★
GILBERT ASSOCIATES, INC. - CORPORATE LIBRARY (Env-Cons)
Box 1498   Phone: (215) 775-2600
Reading, PA 19603   Deborah Bosler, Supv.
Founded: 1979. **Staff:** Prof 3; Other 5. **Subjects:** Engineering and management for power industry; energy research; environmental engineering. **Special Collections:** Coal conversion (6000 reports). **Holdings:** 66,000 books; 15,000 government reports (cataloged); 500 16mm VSMF cartridges of vendor catalogs and standards; 9000 microfiche; 8 VF drawers and 60 volumes of engineering standards. **Subscriptions:** 430 journals and other serials. **Services:** SDI; library open to public by appointment. **Computerized Information Services:** DIALOG, DOE/RECON; Spindex (internal database); computerized cataloging. **Networks/Consortia:** Member of Berks County Library Consortium. **Publications:** Library Bulletin (list of new materials received in company), monthly. **Staff:** Bryan Leithiser, Info.Spec.; Frances Calvaresi, Libn.

GILBERT (Price) MEMORIAL LIBRARY
See: Georgia Institute of Technology - Price Gilbert Memorial Library

GILBREATH (Margaret Clark) MEMORIAL LIBRARY
See: Baptist Medical Center System - Margaret Clark Gilbreath Memorial Library

GILBRETH (Frank & Lilian) MEMORIAL LIBRARY
See: American Institute of Industrial Engineers, Inc. - Frank & Lilian Gilbreth Memorial Library

★5045★
GILCREASE (Thomas) INSTITUTE OF AMERICAN HISTORY AND ART - LIBRARY (Hist)
1400 N. 25th West Ave.   Phone: (918) 531-5311
Tulsa, OK 74127   Sarah Hirsch, Libn.
Founded: 1955. **Staff:** Prof 1. **Subjects:** History - Colonial, Western, Spanish Southwest, Indian. **Special Collections:** Hispanic documents, 1500-1800; John Ross papers (Chief of Cherokees, 1814-1870); Peter P. Pitchlynn papers (Chief of Choctaws); Grant Foreman Collection. **Holdings:** 35,000 books; 35,000 government documents; 25 VF drawers of historic photographs and manuscripts; broadsides; maps; photostats. **Subscriptions:** 20 journals and other serials. **Services:** Copying (limited); library open to public by appointment. **Special Catalogs:** Guide to Manuscripts; Gilcrease-Hargrett Catalog; Hispanic Documents Catalog (out of print).

GILFILLAN ENGINEERING LIBRARY
See: ITT Corporation

★5046★
GILFORD INSTRUMENT LABORATORIES, INC. - TECHNICAL LIBRARY (Sci-Tech)
132 Artino St.   Phone: (216) 774-1041
Oberlin, OH 44074   Marjorie Mulder, Libn.
Founded: 1971. **Staff:** Prof 1. **Subjects:** Biochemistry, electronics, optics. **Holdings:** 1750 books; 94 bound periodical volumes; 10 VF drawers of Gilford archival material. **Subscriptions:** 155 journals and other serials. **Services:** Interlibrary loans; copying; library open to researchers in a related field. **Computerized Information Services:** DIALOG. **Networks/Consortia:** Member of Cleveland Medical Library Association.

★5047★
GILLETTE CHILDREN'S HOSPITAL - PROFESSIONAL LIBRARY (Med)
200 E. University   Phone: (612) 291-2848
St. Paul, MN 55101   K. McCarty
Staff: Prof 1. **Subjects:** Orthopedics, pediatrics. **Holdings:** 2584 books; 54 bound periodical volumes. **Subscriptions:** 48 journals and other serials. **Services:** Copying; library open to health professionals.

★5048★
GILLETTE COMPANY - PERSONAL CARE DIVISION - INFORMATION CENTER
(Sci-Tech)
Box 2131   Phone: (617) 463-2800
Boston, MA 02106   M. McDonough, Asst.Libn.
Staff: Prof 1; Other 1. **Subjects:** Chemistry, hair, skin, cosmetics. **Holdings:** 2400 books; 875 bound periodical volumes; microfilm of complete runs of 7 journals; 32 VF drawers of company reports. **Subscriptions:** 150 journals and other serials. **Services:** Interlibrary loans; copying; library not open to public. **Publications:** List of Journal Holdings, biennial - for internal distribution only.

★5049★
GILLETTE MEDICAL EVALUATION LABORATORIES - INFORMATION CENTER (Sci-Tech)
1413 Research Blvd.   Phone: (301) 424-2000
Rockville, MD 20850   Patrick J. Dexter, Info.Serv.Supv.
Founded: 1974. **Staff:** Prof 2; Other 2. **Subjects:** Toxicology; cosmetics; dermatology; chemistry - organic, textile, surface; biology. **Special Collections:** Reprints dealing with cosmetics and dermatology (9000). **Holdings:** 4900 books; 2900 bound periodical volumes; 700 government documents; 12,000 reprints; 30 notebooks of OTC meeting minutes. **Subscriptions:** 450 journals and other serials; 5 newspapers. **Services:** Interlibrary loans; SDI; library open to public by appointment. **Computerized Information Services:** DIALOG, SDC, New York Times Information Service, Chemical Abstract Services. **Networks/Consortia:** Member of Interlibrary Users Association. **Special Indexes:** Index to Gillette Company Research Reports. **Remarks:** Center contains the holdings of the Gillette Research Institute - Technical Library.

★5050★
GILLETTE RESEARCH INSTITUTE - TECHNICAL LIBRARY
1413 Research Blvd.
Rockville, MD 20850
Defunct. Holdings absorbed by Gillette Medical Evaluation Laboratories - Information Center.

★5051★
GILMAN MUSEUM - LIBRARY (Sci-Tech)
At the Cave   Phone: (215) 838-8767
Hellertown, PA 18055   Naomi P. Gilman, Info.Dir.
Founded: 1955. **Staff:** 4. **Subjects:** Rocks and minerals, fossils, lapidary work, mining and prospecting. **Holdings:** 500 volumes. **Services:** Library open to public for reference use only.

GILMORE (D.S.) RESEARCH LABORATORIES
See: Upjohn Company - D.S. Gilmore Research Laboratories

GILSON (Etienne) ARCHIVE
See: University of Toronto - St. Michael's College - John M. Kelly Library

GIMBEL (Adam L.) DESIGN LIBRARY
See: Parsons School of Design - Adam L. Gimbel Design Library

GIMBEL (Col. Richard) AERONAUTICS HISTORY LIBRARY
See: U.S. Air Force Academy - Library

★5052★
GINN AND COMPANY - EDITORIAL LIBRARY (Publ)
3771 Victoria Park Ave.   Phone: (416) 497-4600
Scarborough, ON, Canada M1W 2P9   Ann Doyle, Libn.
Founded: 1980. **Staff:** Prof 1. **Subjects:** Textbooks, Ginn Canada publications, education. **Holdings:** 6000 books. **Subscriptions:** 80 journals and other serials. **Services:** Interlibrary loans; copying; library open to public by appointment.

GINN AND COMPANY LIBRARY
See: Xerox Corporation

GINN (Edwin) LIBRARY
See: Tufts University - Fletcher School of Law & Diplomacy - Edwin Ginn Library

★5053★
GIRARD BANK - INFORMATION CENTER (Bus-Fin)
Girard Plaza   Phone: (215) 585-3313
Philadelphia, PA 19101   Lee Ann Dean, Mgr.
Founded: 1972. **Staff:** Prof 2. **Subjects:** Banking, finance, economics. **Holdings:** 2500 books; 200 bound periodical volumes; 20 file drawers of 10Ks and 10Qs on microfiche; 5 file drawers of journals on microfiche; 15 VF drawers of pamphlets, documents, reports. **Subscriptions:** 200 journals and other serials; 6 newspapers. **Services:** Interlibrary loans; SDI; library open to public by appointment. **Computerized Information Services:** Dow Jones News Retrieval, DIALOG, IN/FORM Data Services, SDC, Data Resources, Inc. **Staff:** Theresa L. McMonagle, Info.Spec.

★5054★
GIRL SCOUTS OF RACINE COUNTY, INC. - LIBRARY (Rec)†
816 6th St.   Phone: (414) 633-2409
Racine, WI 53403   Betsy Marron, Prog.Serv.Dir.
Founded: 1960. **Staff:** 2. **Subjects:** Youth programs (games and crafts), camping and outdoors, human relations, music and songs. **Holdings:** 500 books; 55 serial books (cataloged). **Subscriptions:** 15 journals and other serials. **Services:** Interlibrary loans; library open to public with permission of program director. **Publications:** The Lingo, monthly newsletter covering all aspects of council operations. **Staff:** Leigh Tomlinson, Res.Ctr.Coord.

★5055★
GIRL SCOUTS OF THE USA - JULIETTE GORDON LOW GIRL SCOUT NATIONAL CENTER (Hist; Rec)
142 Bull St.   Phone: (912) 233-4501
Savannah, GA 31401   Susan T. Mason, Prog.Spec.
Staff: Prof 1. **Subjects:** Juliette Gordon Low, early Girl Scout history. **Holdings:** 100 books; 2 boxes of manuscripts; 2 lateral file drawers of archival material; 1000 historical photographs; 1000 stereoviews. **Services:** Copying; limited research by staff; library open to public by appointment.

★5056★
GIRL SCOUTS OF THE USA - LIBRARY/ARCHIVES (Rec)
830 Third Ave. & 51st St.   Phone: (212) 940-7500
New York, NY 10022   Juana Alers-Quinones, Libn./Archv.
Staff: Prof 1. **Subjects:** Education, training, camp and camping, arts and crafts. **Special Collections:** Girl Scout publications (4000 titles). **Holdings:** 7000 books; 88 bound periodical volumes; records; 5000 photos; 200 uniforms; memorabilia; 35 shelves of publications. **Subscriptions:** 400 journals and other serials; 10 newspapers. **Services:** Copying (limited); SDI (limited); library open to public by special arrangement. **Publications:** Acquisitions Notices, monthly - for internal distribution only. **Special Catalogs:** Memorabilia catalog (card); inventory list of archives records (loose-leaf).

GITELSON (Maxwell) FILM LIBRARY
See: Chicago Institute for Psychoanalysis

★5057★
GIUFFRE MEDICAL CENTER - LIBRARY (Med)
8th & Girard Ave.   Phone: (215) 787-2228
Philadelphia, PA 19122   Allathea Ames, Libn.
Staff: Prof 1. **Subjects:** Medicine, surgery, nursing, alcoholism, drug abuse. **Holdings:** 1700 books; 300 bound periodical volumes; 11 VF drawers; 20 films; 50 AV items. **Subscriptions:** 150 journals and other serials. **Services:** Interlibrary loans; copying; library open to public by appointment. **Networks/Consortia:** Member of Delaware Valley Information Consortium; Mideastern Regional Medical Library Service (MERMLS).

★5058★
GIVAUDAN CORPORATION - LIBRARY (Sci-Tech)
125 Delawanna Ave.   Phone: (201) 365-8563
Clifton, NJ 07014   Roberta F. Nugent, Chf.Libn.
Staff: Prof 1; Other 1. **Subjects:** Fragrances, aroma chemicals, flavors. **Holdings:** 10,000 books and bound periodical volumes; 17 VF drawers of U.S. and foreign patents; Chemical Abstracts on microfilm; 36 VF drawers of reprints and pamphlets. **Subscriptions:** 129 journals and other serials. **Services:** Interlibrary loans; copying; library not open to public. **Remarks:** This library is part of the Research Department of Givaudan Corporation. **Staff:** Elaine Lembeck, Asst.Libn.

GLACIER NATL. PARK
See: U.S. Natl. Park Service

★5059★
GLADMAN (Everett A.) MEMORIAL HOSPITAL - MEDICAL LIBRARY (Med)
2633 East 27th St.   Phone: (415) 536-8111
Oakland, CA 94601   Elizabeth Edelstein, Libn.
Staff: Prof 1. **Subjects:** Psychiatry, psychology, medicine. **Holdings:** 500 books. **Subscriptions:** 60 journals and other serials. **Services:** Library not open to public.

GLASS (E. Gordon, M.D.) MEMORIAL LIBRARY
See: Muhlenberg Hospital - E. Gordon Glass, M.D., Memorial Library

GLASS MEMORIAL LIBRARY
See: Johnson Bible College

GLASS RESEARCH CENTER
See: PPG Industries, Inc.

★5060★
GLASSBORO STATE COLLEGE - SAVITZ LIBRARY - LLOYD V. MANWILLER CURRICULUM LABORATORY (Educ)
Rte. 322   Phone: (609) 445-5335
Glassboro, NJ 08028   Kathleen Kennedy, Educ.Libn.
Founded: 1956. **Staff:** Prof 1; Other 4. **Subjects:** Teaching aids, reference works. **Holdings:** 7331 volumes; 13,922 pamphlets; 2711 curriculum guides; 946 tests; 1426 AV items. **Services:** Copying; library open to public; circulation limited to loans of AV items to college community.

★5061★
GLASSBORO STATE COLLEGE - SAVITZ LIBRARY - STEWART ROOM (Hist)
                                                  Phone: (609) 445-6303
Glassboro, NJ 08028   Clara Kirner, Spec.Coll.Libn.
Staff: Prof 1; Other 1. **Subjects:** New Jersey history (rare books, deeds, surveys, marriage licenses, acts of assembly); early religious history; genealogy; Indians of North America; Revolutionary War; War of 1812; Grinnell Arctic expedition. **Special Collections:** Family papers - Howell, Inskeep, Haines, Lippincott; Frank H. Stewart Collection (8000 volumes); Charles A. Wolverton Papers (10 boxes); Summit Conference Papers (4 boxes); Satterthwaite Genealogical Collection (24 VF drawers). **Holdings:** 14,000 books; 416 bound periodical volumes; 5000 manuscripts (cataloged); 13 VF drawers of college archives; 3700 volumes of masters theses. **Subscriptions:** 23 journals and other serials. **Services:** Copying (limited); center open to public for reference use only. **Publications:** Guide to the Special Collections - distributed by request.

★5062★
GLATFELTER (P.H.) COMPANY - RESEARCH LIBRARY (Sci-Tech)
                                                  Phone: (717) 225-4711
Spring Grove, PA 17362   Jean Bailey, Libn.
Staff: 1. **Subjects:** Pulp and paper, organic and inorganic chemistry, management, statistics, environment. **Holdings:** 1890 books; 207 bound periodical volumes; 5 VF drawers of patents; 12 VF drawers of information retrieval materials. **Subscriptions:** 100 journals and other serials. **Services:** Interlibrary loans; library open to public for reference use only.

★5063★
GLAXO CANADA, LTD. - LIBRARY (Med)
1025 The Queensway   Phone: (416) 252-2281
Toronto, ON, Canada M8Z 5S6   Dr. V. Chivers Wilson, Dir., Res./Dev.
Staff: Prof 2; Other 2. **Subjects:** Medicine, pharmacy, pharmacology, chemistry, microbiology. **Holdings:** 500 books. **Subscriptions:** 155 journals and other serials. **Services:** Interlibrary loans; copying; library not open to public. **Computerized Information Services:** Internal database; computerized cataloging, serials and circulation. **Special Indexes:** Card index. **Staff:** Dr. M. Nadasdi, Med.Dir.

GLEASON (Madeline) POETRY ARCHIVE
See: University of San Francisco - Special Collections Department/Donohue Rare Book Room

GLEDHILL LIBRARY
See: Santa Barbara Historical Society

GLEESON (Richard A.) LIBRARY
See: University of San Francisco - Special Collections Department/Donohue Rare Book Room

★5064★
GLEN HELEN ASSOCIATION - LIBRARY (Env-Cons)
Glen Helen Bldg.
405 Corry St.
Yellow Springs, OH 45387   Phone: (513) 767-7375
                                            Mrs. George Asakawa, Libn.
Founded: 1973. **Staff:** 1. **Subjects:** Environmental protection, resource management, natural area preservation, forestry, outdoor recreation and education, wildlife. **Holdings:** 602 books; 234 volumes of U.S. Environmental Protection Agency reports; 14 VF drawers of pamphlets; 7 VF drawers of maps; 5 reels of film; 16 tapes; 44 volumes of NASA Technical Support Package; 10 volumes of U.S. Department of Interior Third Nationwide

Outdoor Recreation Plan; 1 set color reproductions of John James Audubon's The Birds of America with text; 6 carousel trays of slides; 6 games. **Subscriptions:** 70 journals and other serials. **Services:** Library open to public. **Remarks:** There is also a small reference library at the Trailside Museum for staff and junior naturalists. The library is associated with Anitoch University.

★5065★
GLENBOW-ALBERTA INSTITUTE - LIBRARY & ARCHIVES (Hist)
130 9th Ave., S.E.   Phone: (403) 264-8300
Calgary, AB, Canada T2G 0P3   Leonard J. Gottselig, Chf.Libn.
Founded: 1955. **Staff:** Prof 8; Other 9. **Subjects:** Western Canada, Canadian Arctic, Indians of North America, fur trade, missionaries, local history, Canadian art. **Special Collections:** Dewdney papers; J.J. Bowlen papers; George Coote papers; Sir F.W.G. Haultain papers. **Holdings:** 35,000 books; 800 bound periodical volumes; 300,000 pages of manuscripts; 1000 reels of microfilm; 48 VF drawers of newspaper clippings; 30 VF drawers of trade catalogs; 1500 Western Canadian political pamphlets and leaflets; 100 motion picture films; 250,000 photographs; 1200 tape recordings. **Subscriptions:** 300 journals and other serials; 15 newspapers. **Services:** Interlibrary loans (limited); copying; library open to public for reference use only. **Special Catalogs:** Catalog of Glenbow Historical Library (book); list of Glenbow-Alberta Institute publications - available on request. **Staff:** Lindsay Moir, Asst.Libn.; Miss M. Knox, Bookbinder & Consrv.; William C. McKee, Chf.Archv.; Georgeen Klassen, Asst.Chf.Archv.; Lynette Walton, Archv.; D. Cass, Archv.; Jennifer Hamblin, Archv.; Don Bourdon, Archv.

★5066★
GLENDALE ADVENTIST MEDICAL CENTER - LIBRARY (Med)
1509 Wilson Terrace   Phone: (213) 244-8000
Glendale, CA 91206   Eugenie Prime, Lib.Dir.
Staff: Prof 10; Other 7. **Subjects:** Medicine, nursing, paramedicine, health education. **Holdings:** 6165 books; 8966 bound periodical volumes; 875 AV items. **Subscriptions:** 475 journals and other serials. **Services:** Interlibrary loans; SDI; copying; current awareness service; literature searches; library open to public for reference use only. **Computerized Information Services:** MEDLINE, SDC, BRS, DIALOG. **Publications:** Cumulative Index to Nursing and Allied Health Literature. **Staff:** Carolyn Fishel, Asst.Lib.Dir.; DeLauna Lockwood, Editor CINAHL.

★5067★
GLENDALE CITY - PLANNING DIVISION - TECHNICAL LIBRARY (Plan)
633 E. Broadway   Phone: (213) 956-2144
Glendale, CA 91205   Gerald J. Jamriska, Dir. of Plan.
Staff: 1. **Subjects:** Planning, urban development, zoning law, organization, legal codes and requirements, public administration, population and housing data, land use data. **Special Collections:** Historic Preservation; Glendale data (Planning Division publications, hill development proposals, tract developments, zoning information and related material). **Holdings:** 510 books; 126 bound periodical volumes; 147 unbound items. **Services:** Interlibrary loans (limited loans of division publications to public); library open to public with approval of the Planning Director. **Publications:** List of publications - available on request.

★5068★
GLENDALE FEDERAL SAVINGS & LOAN ASSOCIATION - CORPORATE LIBRARY (Bus-Fin)†
301 E. Las Olas Blvd.
Box 14370
Fort Lauderdale, FL 33302   Phone: (305) 763-1121
                                             Ava Goldman, Corp.Libn.
Founded: 1979. **Staff:** Prof 1. **Subjects:** Finance - savings and loans. **Special Collections:** Savings & Loan News, 1955 to present. **Holdings:** 100 books. **Subscriptions:** 65 journals and other serials; 13 newspapers. **Services:** Interlibrary loans; copying; SDI; library open to public with restrictions. **Publications:** Library News - quarterly. **Formerly:** First Federal Savings & Loan Association of Broward County.

★5069★
GLENDALE PUBLIC LIBRARY - BRAND LIBRARY (Art; Mus)†
1601 W. Mountain St.   Phone: (213) 956-2051
Glendale, CA 91201   Jane Hagan, Lib.Serv.Supv.
Founded: 1955. **Staff:** Prof 2; Other 6. **Subjects:** Art history, music of all countries, architecture, crafts, photography, art for artists, sculpture. **Special Collections:** Dieterle Collection (mounted art prints); Rempel Collection (watercolors, woodcuts, engravings); Ross Collection of 78 rpm recordings; Edwards Collection of Scrapbooks (1849-1930 art illustrations). **Holdings:** 33,123 books; 3000 bound periodical volumes; 10,000 pieces of sheet music; 23,050 phonograph records and 1700 cassettes (cataloged); 197 piano rolls (1895-1924); 1578 art reproductions and prints; 10,000 drawings and clippings; 1600 78 rpm recordings (inactive). **Subscriptions:**

102 journals and other serials. **Services:** Research for motion pictures and television studios; framed prints for loan; library open to public. **Networks/Consortia:** Member of Metropolitan Cooperative Library System (MCLS). **Publications:** Events of the Month. **Special Indexes:** Song Index (card). **Remarks:** Brand Library is the art and music department of the Glendale Public Library. It contains gallery and recital hall. **Staff:** Ellen Dworkin, Sr.Libn.

★5070★
GLENDALE UNIVERSITY - COLLEGE OF LAW LIBRARY (Law)
220 N. Glendale Ave.   Phone: (213) 247-0770
Glendale, CA 91206   Judy Greitzer, Lib.Adm.
Staff: Prof 2; Other 12. **Subjects:** Law - tax, accounting. **Special Collections:** English law; early English and American law books. **Holdings:** 85,000 volumes. **Subscriptions:** 376 journals and other serials. **Services:** Copying; library not open to public. **Staff:** Herman Lancaster, Dir., Res.

★5071★
GLENGARRY GENEALOGICAL SOCIETY - HIGHLAND HERITAGE RESEARCH LIBRARY (Hist)
11 Oak St.
P.O. Box 460   Phone: (613) 347-3719
Lancaster, ON, Canada K0C 1N0   Alex W. Fraser, Pres.
Founded: 1974. **Staff:** 2. **Subjects:** Genealogy, church records. **Special Collections:** Roots Glengarry (church records and index). **Holdings:** 380 volumes; 49 reels of microfilm of St. Raphael's and St. Andrew's church records, Glengarry News; 4 manuscripts on gravestones of Glengarry; 5 binders of clippings of birth, death and marriage records; 18 binders of local church records; 70 binders of family genealogies. **Subscriptions:** 18 journals and other serials. **Services:** Family tree research; library open to public by appointment. **Publications:** Highland Heritage, quarterly; Family Genealogies, semiannual - both for sale. **Special Indexes:** 50,000 names from local church, cemetery and newspaper records (card). **Staff:** Rhoda Ross, V.P.

GLENMARY HOME MISSIONERS
See: Home Missioners of America

★5072★
GLENS FALLS-QUEENSBURY HISTORICAL ASSN., INC. - CHAPMAN HISTORICAL MUSM. - RUSSELL M.L. CARSON MEMORIAL LIB. (Hist)
348 Glen St.   Phone: (518) 793-2826
Glens Falls, NY 12801   Joseph A. Cutshall King, Dir.
Founded: 1967. **Subjects:** Local history, Adirondacks. **Holdings:** 700 books; 20,000 photographs; 15 VF drawers of business records of the Glens Falls Insurance Company (1849-1968) and 30 VF drawers of the YMCA (1887-1969); clippings, archives. **Services:** Copying; library open to public by appointment.

★5073★
GLENVIEW AREA HISTORICAL SOCIETY - LIBRARY (Hist)
1121 Waukegan Rd.   Phone: (312) 724-2235
Glenview, IL 60025   Richard L. Hibbard, Supv.
Founded: 1967. **Staff:** Prof 1; Other 8. **Subjects:** Local history. **Holdings:** Figures not available. **Services:** Copying; library open to public by appointment with supervisor. **Publications:** Glenview 1899-1974.

★5074★
GLENWOOD STATE HOSPITAL-SCHOOL - STAFF LIBRARY (Med)
711 S. Vine   Phone: (712) 527-4811
Glenwood, IA 51534   Claire Osterholm, Assoc.Libn.
Staff: Prof 1. **Subjects:** Mental retardation, psychiatry, psychology, medicine, special education. **Holdings:** 3540 books; 500 bound periodical volumes. **Subscriptions:** 155 journals and other serials. **Services:** Interlibrary loans; copying; library open to families of employees.

GLIDDEN COATINGS & RESINS DIV./DURKEE FOODS DIVISION
See: SCM Corporation

GLOBAL COMMUNITY CENTRE
See: Kitchener-Waterloo Overseas Aid Inc.

★5075★
GLOBAL EDUCATION ASSOCIATES - CURRICULUM RESOURCE LIBRARY (Educ)
552 Park Ave.   Phone: (201) 675-1409
East Orange, NJ 07017   Anna Flynn, Libn.
Founded: 1973. **Subjects:** Global education, world order, alternative futures, conflict management, values, world religions. **Special Collections:** Curricula resource lists, United Nations documents. **Holdings:** 3000 books and bound periodical volumes; clippings, pamphlets, manuscripts. **Subscriptions:** 85

journals and other serials. **Services:** Library open to public for reference use only. **Publications:** Associates newsletter; The Whole Earth papers; Toward a Human World Order. **Special Catalogs:** Curricula resource lists related to global education.

★5076★
GLOBAL ENGINEERING DOCUMENTS - LIBRARY (Sci-Tech)
2625 Hickory St.   Phone: (714) 540-9870
Santa Ana, CA 92707   Jerome H. Lieblich, Pres.
Founded: 1968. **Staff:** Prof 8; Other 22. **Holdings:** 500,000 specifications, standards and manuals (cataloged). **Subscriptions:** 1000 journals and other serials. **Services:** Copying; technical manual preparation; spares provisioning. **Publications:** Drawing Requirements Manual; Qualified Products List and Sources, biannual; Instructions for Technical Manual Preparation; Plating Manual; Printed Circuit Manual. **Remarks:** Library makes available specifications and standards from 3000 government, industry, military and trade societies. This company is a division of Information Handling Services which is owned by Indian Head Company.

GLOBE AND MAIL, LTD.
See: Toronto Globe and Mail, Ltd.

★5077★
GLOBE PHOTOS, INC. - LIBRARY (Pict)
275 7th Ave., 21st Fl.   Phone: (212) 689-1340
New York, NY 10001
Subjects: Current events, personalities, features. **Holdings:** 10 million original color transparencies and black/white photos. **Remarks:** Library contains subjects of interest to advertising agencies and publishers of magazines, books, encyclopedias.

★5078★
GLOUCESTER COUNTY HISTORICAL SOCIETY - LIBRARY (Hist)
17 Hunter St.   Phone: (609) 845-4771
Woodbury, NJ 08096   Edith Hoelle, Libn.
Staff: 5. **Subjects:** Genealogy, New Jersey history, U.S. history. **Special Collections:** Richard Somers Collection (100 original documents pertaining to Richard Somers and the U.S. Navy in early 1800s); Howell Collection (3800 items concerning the Howell family from 1739 to 1890). **Holdings:** 4000 books; 425 reels of microfilmed documents; 114 bound volumes of newspapers (cataloged); 70,000 county manuscripts, 1686-1870; 44 VF drawers of files of genealogy and history, photographs, typescripts, clippings. **Services:** Copying; library open to public with restrictions.

GLOVER MEMORIAL MEDICAL AND NURSING LIBRARY
See: Altoona Hospital

★5079★
GMI ENGINEERING & MANAGEMENT INSTITUTE - LIBRARY (Sci-Tech)
Chevrolet & Third Aves.   Phone: (313) 762-7814
Flint, MI 48502   Emily R. Mobley, Dir.
Founded: 1927. **Staff:** Prof 4; Other 5. **Subjects:** Engineering, business. **Special Collections:** Undergraduate theses. **Holdings:** 45,000 books; 10,000 bound periodical volumes; 25,600 other cataloged items. **Subscriptions:** 750 journals and other serials; 25 newspapers. **Services:** Interlibrary loans; copying; library open to public with permission. **Computerized Information Services:** DIALOG. **Formerly:** General Motors Institute - Library. **Staff:** Cheryl Pfeifer, Ref.; Dorcas Watkins, Acq.; Betty Holifield, Cat.

★5080★
GNOSTIC CONCEPTS, INC. - TECHNICAL LIBRARY (Sci-Tech)
2710 Sand Hill Rd.   Phone: (415) 854-4672
Menlo Park, CA 94025   A. Jeannine Caudill, Mgr., Lib.Serv.
Founded: 1976. **Staff:** Prof 1; Other 3. **Subjects:** Electronics, computers, communications. **Holdings:** 2000 books; 80 VF drawers of annual reports and 10K reports of electronics companies. **Subscriptions:** 325 journals and other serials; 25 newspapers. **Services:** Interlibrary loans; copying; library not open to public. **Computerized Information Services:** DIALOG, Dun & Bradstreet. **Networks/Consortia:** Member of CLASS; RLG.

GODDARD (Edward P., M.D.) MEMORIAL LIBRARY
See: Medical Center Hospital of Oroville - Edward P. Goddard, M.D., Memorial Library

GODDARD INSTITUTE FOR SPACE STUDIES
See: U.S. NASA

GODDARD LIBRARY
See: Gordon-Conwell Theological Seminary

GODDARD SPACE FLIGHT CENTER
See: U.S. NASA

★5081★
GODFREY MEMORIAL LIBRARY (Hist)
134 Newfield St.   Phone: (203) 346-4375
Middletown, CT 06457   Doris Post, Dir.
Founded: 1947. **Staff:** 4. **Subjects:** Genealogy, local history, biography.
Holdings: 16,000 books; 7 million items in genealogical reference file.
Subscriptions: 12 journals and other serials. **Services:** Interlibrary loans
(limited); copying; genealogical research; library open to public. **Publications:**
American Genealogical-Biographical Index, quarterly - by subscription (1982 -
6 volumes); microfiche in the fields of genealogy and local history.

★5082★
GOETHE HOUSE NEW YORK - LIBRARY (Area-Ethnic)
1014 Fifth Ave.   Phone: (212) 744-8310
New York, NY 10028   Freya Jeschke, Libn.
Founded: 1957. **Staff:** Prof 1; Other 1. **Subjects:** Germany - literature, the
arts, history, politics; social sciences. **Special Collections:** Collected works in
German and English of Goethe and other famous German writers. **Holdings:**
16,000 books; 20 reports on Germany and German affairs; 1000 records
(cataloged). **Subscriptions:** 120 journals and other serials; 14 newspapers.
Services: Interlibrary loans; library open to public. **Remarks:** Branch of
German Cultural Institute/Goethe Institute Munich.

★5083★
GOETHE INSTITUT CHICAGO - GERMAN CULTURAL CENTER - LIBRARY
   (Area-Ethnic)
401 N. Michigan Ave.   Phone: (312) 329-0915
Chicago, IL 60611   Christiane Schmidt, Libn.
Staff: Prof 1. **Subjects:** Contemporary German literature, German cinema,
German social issues. **Holdings:** 6000 books; 577 cassettes; 240 slides; 60
videotapes; 360 phonograph records. **Subscriptions:** 30 journals and other
serials; 10 newspapers. **Services:** Interlibrary loans; copying; library open to
public. **Publications:** Cultural Events, monthly; New Acquisitions, semiannual;
Midwest Announcements, monthly. **Special Catalogs:** Catalog of AV materials
for use in the German classroom.

★5084★
GOETHE INSTITUTE ATLANTA - GERMAN CULTURAL CENTER - LIBRARY
   (Area-Ethnic)
400 Colony Sq.   Phone: (404) 892-2226
Atlanta, GA 30361   Margit Rostock, Libn.
Founded: 1977. **Staff:** Prof 2. **Subjects:** Germany - contemporary literature,
social science, geography, history. **Holdings:** 9500 books; 150 bound
periodical volumes; 3000 tapes; 500 slide series; 4 VF drawers of movie
review clippings. **Subscriptions:** 50 journals and other serials; 5 newspapers.
Services: Interlibrary loans; copying; library open to public. **Special Indexes:**
Tape catalog (book); slide catalog (book). **Remarks:** This institute is the
German cultural center for the southeastern United States. It is a branch of
the Goethe Institute Munich. **Staff:** Sharon Hoogerwerf, Libn.

★5085★
GOETHE INSTITUTE BOSTON - LIBRARY (Area-Ethnic)
170 Beacon St.   Phone: (617) 262-6050
Boston, MA 02116   Dorothee Burney, Hd.Libn.
Founded: 1966. **Staff:** Prof 1. **Subjects:** Germany - literature, language,
geography, customs, fine arts, history and politics, sociology, philosophy,
theology and psychology. **Holdings:** 8500 books. **Subscriptions:** 63 journals;
17 newspapers. **Services:** Interlibrary loans; copying; library open to public.
Networks/Consortia: Member of Goethe Institute Munich. **Publications:**
Calendar of events. **Remarks:** This is the German cultural center for New
England. The holdings are in German with about 20% English translation.

★5086★
GOETHE INSTITUTE - LIBRARY (Area-Ethnic)
530 Bush St.   Phone: (415) 391-0370
San Francisco, CA 94108   Helmi Schluter, Libn.
Founded: 1970. **Staff:** Prof 1. **Subjects:** Germany - contemporary literature,
classics, history, political science, art, economics, education. **Holdings:** 8000
books; 30 bound periodical volumes; slides, tapes and phonograph records.
Subscriptions: 68 journals and other serials; 6 newspapers. **Services:**
Interlibrary loans; library open to public. **Publications:** Recent acquisitions.
Special Catalogs: Tape Catalog; record catalog; slide catalog (all card).
Remarks: 90% of books are in German; 10% are translations from German to

English.

★5087★
GOETHE INSTITUTE MONTREAL - GERMAN CULTURAL CENTRE - LIBRARY
   (Area-Ethnic; Hum)
Place Bonaventure
P.O. Box 428   Phone: (514) 866-1081
Montreal, PQ, Canada H5A 1B8   Elisabeth Morf, Libn.
Staff: Prof 1. **Subjects:** German literature and history. **Special Collections:**
German language textbooks; English and French translations of German
authors. **Holdings:** 11,000 books; 400 phonograph records; 600 magnetic
tapes; 150 slide series. **Subscriptions:** 20 journals and other serials; 7
newspapers. **Services:** Interlibrary loans; copying; library open to public.

★5088★
GOETHE INSTITUTE OTTAWA - LIBRARY (Area-Ethnic)
300 Slater St.   Phone: (613) 235-5124
Ottawa, ON, Canada K1P 6A6
Founded: 1969. **Staff:** 2. **Subjects:** German literature, literary history and
criticism, history and arts, Germany. **Holdings:** 3500 books. **Subscriptions:**
21 journals and other serials. **Services:** Library open to public. **Remarks:** This
institute is a branch of the Goethe Institute Munich.

★5089★
GOETHE INSTITUTE TORONTO - LIBRARY (Area-Ethnic; Hum)
1067 Yonge St.   Phone: (416) 924-3327
Toronto, ON, Canada M4W 2L2   Ulla Habekost, Libn.
Founded: 1962. **Staff:** Prof 1. **Subjects:** Modern German literature, German
literary history, language and linguistics, visual and performing arts in
Germany, children's literature. **Holdings:** 7500 books; 478 phonograph
records; 575 tapes; 332 slides; 118 German language films. **Subscriptions:**
61 journals and other serials; 7 newspapers. **Services:** Library open to public.

★5090★
GOLD INFORMATION CENTER (Sci-Tech)
Olympic Tower, 645 Fifth Ave.   Phone: (212) 688-0474
New York, NY 10022   Ms. Leslie Mirin Domino, Mgr.
Founded: 1977. **Subjects:** Gold. **Holdings:** 250 books; VF drawers;
periodicals; AV materials. **Services:** Telephone and mail reference service for
organizations and individuals with a professional interest in gold; library not
open to public. **Publications:** Occasional bibliographies. **Remarks:** The Gold
Information Center collects and makes available information concerning gold,
its properties and usage in all fields of human activities. **Staff:** Jean L. McHale,
Gold Info.Coord.

★5091★
GOLD PARACHUTE LIBRARY, ARCHIVES & TECHNICAL INFORMATION
   CENTER (Rec)
741 W. Haloid Ave.
Ridgecrest, CA 93555   Dave Gold, Dir. & Archv.
Staff: 1. **Subjects:** Parachute - development, history, manufacture,
parachuting, philately. **Special Collections:** Foreign and domestic parachute
collection. **Holdings:** Figures not available for books, scrapbooks and
photographs. **Services:** Library open to public by appointment. **Publications:**
Let's Talk Parachutes, quarterly - to members.

GOLDBERG (David) MEMORIAL MEDICAL LIBRARY
See: Pascack Valley Hospital - David Goldberg Memorial Medical Library

GOLDBERG (Max & Ann) LIBRARY
See: Temple Beth El - Max & Ann Goldberg Library

GOLDEN BEAR DIVISION - QC/R & D Library
See: WITCO Chemical Corporation

★5092★
GOLDEN GATE BAPTIST THEOLOGICAL SEMINARY - LIBRARY (Rel-Theol)
Strawberry Point   Phone: (415) 388-8080
Mill Valley, CA 94941   Cecil R. White, Libn.
Founded: 1944. **Staff:** Prof 3; Other 8. **Subjects:** Bible texts and
commentaries; church history; philosophy; Christian ethics; Bible archeology;
comparative religion; preaching; patristics; missions; systematic theology;
religious education. **Special Collections:** Old and rare hymnals (115).
Holdings: 102,523 books; 8500 bound periodical volumes; 22 VF drawers of
pamphlets; 2805 microforms. **Subscriptions:** 615 journals and other serials.
Services: Interlibrary loans; library open to public. **Networks/Consortia:**
Member of Graduate Theological Union - Library; Marin Consortium for Higher
Education. **Staff:** J. Craig Kubic, Act.Rd.Serv.Libn.; Elizabeth Ashley, Dir. of
Tech.Serv.

GOLDEN GATE NATIONAL RECREATION AREA - NATIONAL MARITIME MUSEUM
See: National Maritime Museum

★5093★
GOLDEN GATE UNIVERSITY - LIBRARIES (Bus-Fin)
536 Mission St.   Phone: (415) 442-7242
San Francisco, CA 94105   Harold E. Korf, Dir.
Founded: 1851. Staff: Prof 5; Other 7. Subjects: Business, public administration. Holdings: 150,000 volumes. Services: Interlibrary loans; copying; libraries not open to public except by fee. Computerized Information Services: DIALOG, BRS, RLIN, SDC, New York Times Information Service; The Golden Retriever (internal database). Networks/Consortia: Member of RLG. Staff: Catriona Wendroff, Ref.

★5094★
GOLDEN GATE UNIVERSITY - SCHOOL OF LAW LIBRARY (Law)
536 Mission St.   Phone: (415) 442-7260
San Francisco, CA 94105   Nancy Carol Carter, Dir.
Founded: 1901. Staff: Prof 4; Other 6. Subjects: Law. Special Collections: Taxation, land use, legal periodicals. Holdings: 170,000 volumes. Subscriptions: 2000 journals and other serials; 5 newspapers. Services: Interlibrary loans; copying; library open to public. Computerized Information Services: LEXIS, RLIN; computerized cataloging. Networks/Consortia: Member of RLG; CLASS. Staff: Scott B. Pagel, Pub.Serv.Libn.; William E. Benemann, Tech.Serv.Libn.; Susan Huff, Spec.Res.Libn.

GOLDEN LIBRARY
See: Eastern New Mexico University

★5095★
GOLDEN VALLEY HEALTH CENTER - MEDICAL LIBRARY (Med)
4101 Golden Valley Rd.   Phone: (612) 588-2771
Golden Valley, MN 55422   Carol Nordby, Lib.Ck.
Founded: 1973. Staff: Prof 1. Subjects: Medicine, nursing, psychiatry. Holdings: 700 books; 65 bound periodical volumes; 200 cassette tapes (cataloged). Subscriptions: 85 journals and other serials. Services: Interlibrary loans; copying; SDI; library not open to public. Networks/Consortia: Member of Twin Cities Biomedical Consortium (TCBC); Regional Medical Library - Region 3.

★5096★
GOLDEN VALLEY LUTHERAN COLLEGE - LIBRARY (Rel-Theol)†
6125 Olson Hwy.   Phone: (612) 542-1210
Minneapolis, MN 55422   Richard Serena, Libn.
Founded: 1919. Staff: Prof 5; Other 2. Subjects: Religion, social sciences, literature, pure science, music, physical education. Holdings: 28,500 books; 950 bound periodical volumes. Subscriptions: 255 journals and other serials; 5 newspapers. Services: Interlibrary loans; copying; library open to public. Publications: Acquisitions list, monthly - to faculty. Staff: Lola Steidl, Cat.; Una Lamb, Asst. to Libn.; Orlette Tatley, Asst. to Libn.

★5097★
GOLDER (H.Q.) & ASSOCIATES - LIBRARY (Sci-Tech)
3151 Wharton Way   Phone: (416) 625-0094
Mississauga, ON, Canada L4X 2B6   Mary Anne Smyth, Lib.Techn.
Staff: 1. Subjects: Geology, geophysics, engineering geology. Holdings: 2000 books; maps. Subscriptions: 60 journals and other serials. Services: Library not open to public. Computerized Information Services: DIALOG.

★5098★
GOLDEY BEACOM COLLEGE - J. WILBUR HIRONS LIBRARY (Bus-Fin)
4701 Limestone Rd.   Phone: (302) 998-8814
Wilmington, DE 19808   R.M. Beach, Dir.
Founded: 1965. Staff: Prof 2; Other 2. Subjects: Business, management, accounting, business administration, marketing, computer science, secretarial studies. Holdings: 11,500 books; 2700 bound periodical volumes; transparencies; maps; 1110 AV units; 600 reels of microfilm; 4289 microfiche; 245 corporation annual reports. Subscriptions: 326 journals and other serials. Services: Interlibrary loans; copying; library open to public for reference use only. Staff: G. Coe, Ref.Libn.; M. Baird, Tech.Serv.

★5099★
GOLDMAN, SACHS AND COMPANY - LIBRARY (Bus-Fin)
55 Broad St.   Phone: (212) 676-7400
New York, NY 10004   Elizabeth O'Mahoney, V.P.
Founded: 1933. Staff: Prof 3; Other 18. Subjects: Corporation records, banking, finance, commercial paper. Special Collections: U.S. and foreign corporation records (30,000). Holdings: 9000 books; 400 bound periodical volumes; disclosure service - annual reports, 10Ks, 10Qs, 8Ks, proxies and municipal bonds (500,000 microfiche); 200 reels of microfilm. Subscriptions: 400 journals and other serials; 15 newspapers. Services: Interlibrary loans; copying; library not open to public. Computerized Information Services: DIALOG, New York Times Information Service, Dow Jones News Retrieval. Staff: Katherine Cray, Asst.Mgr.; Patricia Magee, Ref.Asst.

GOLDSMITH CIVIC GARDEN CENTER LIBRARY
See: Memphis Botanic Garden Foundation, Inc.

GOLDSTEIN (Morris) LIBRARY
See: Magnes (Judah L.) Memorial Museum - Morris Goldstein Library

GOLDTHWAIT POLAR LIBRARY
See: Ohio State University - Institute of Polar Studies

★5100★
GOLDWATER MEMORIAL HOSPITAL - HEALTH SCIENCES LIBRARY (Med)†
New York Univ. Medical Center Affiliate   Phone: (212) 750-6749
Franklin D. Roosevelt Island, NY 10044   Martin M. Leibovici, Libn.
Founded: 1939. Staff: Prof 1; Other 2. Subjects: General medicine, rehabilitation medicine, geriatrics, chronic disease. Holdings: 8000 volumes; 2 VF drawers. Subscriptions: 188 journals and other serials. Services: Interlibrary loans; copying; library open to scholars by appointment. Computerized Information Services: MEDLINE; computerized cataloging. Networks/Consortia: Member of Medical Library Center of New York (MLCNY). Publications: Acquisitions lists.

GOLDWATER (Robert) LIBRARY
See: Metropolitan Museum of Art - Robert Goldwater Library

★5101★
GOLF COURSE SUPERINTENDENTS ASSOCIATION OF AMERICA - GCSAA LIBRARY (Rec)
1617 St. Andrews Dr.   Phone: (913) 841-2240
Lawrence, KS 66044   Barbara Gentry, Educ.Sec.
Staff: 1. Subjects: Landscaping, turfgrass and golf course management. Holdings: 133 books; slides and films. Services: Library open to public with restrictions.

GOLF HOUSE LIBRARY
See: United States Golf Association

★5102★
GONZAGA UNIVERSITY - CROSBY LIBRARY (Hum)
502 E. Boone Ave.   Phone: (509) 328-4220
Spokane, WA 99258   Robert L. Burr, Dir.
Founded: 1887. Staff: Prof 7; Other 10. Special Collections: Gerard Manley Hopkins Collection (4900 items); Crosby Memorabilia; Biology-Chemistry Library in Hughes Hall. Holdings: 230,649 books; 61,355 bound periodical volumes; 62,000 microforms. Subscriptions: 1419 journals and other serials. Services: Interlibrary loans; copying; library open to public with restrictions. Computerized Information Services: DIALOG, SDC; computerized cataloging and acquisitions. Networks/Consortia: Member of Washington Library Network (WLN). Publications: Crosby News & Notes. Special Catalogs: Hopkins Collected at Gonzaga by Ruth Seelhammer, 1970 (book). Remarks: Crosby Library also houses the Society of Jesus (Oregon Province) Archives. Staff: Carol F. Burroughs, Hd., Pub.Serv.; Mary M. Carr, Hd., Tech.Serv.

GONZAGA UNIVERSITY - CROSBY LIBRARY - OREGON PROVINCE ARCHIVES
See: Society of Jesus - Oregon Province Archives

★5103★
GONZAGA UNIVERSITY SCHOOL OF LAW - LIBRARY (Law)
600 E. Sharp Ave.
Box 3528   Phone: (509) 328-4220
Spokane, WA 99220   Dennis J. Stone, Law Libn.
Founded: 1912. Staff: Prof 6; Other 13. Subjects: Law. Holdings: 180,000 volumes; 60,000 volumes in microform. Subscriptions: 2300 journals and other serials. Subscriptions: Interlibrary loans; library open to public for reference use only. Computerized Information Services: WESTLAW; computerized cataloging and acquisitions. Networks/Consortia: Member of Washington Library Network (WLN). Staff: Elizabeth Thweatt, Doc./Acq.Libn.; Larry Deemer, Pub.Serv.Libn.; Lorraine E. Rodich, Asst.Libn.; Bernice Owen, Cat.Libn.; John H. Davis, Ref.Libn.

★5104★

GOOD SAMARITAN HOSPITAL - HEALTH SCIENCE LIBRARY (Med)
Box 2989   Phone: (602) 257-4353
Phoenix, AZ 85062   Betty J. Kjellberg, Libn.
Staff: Prof 1; Other 4. **Subjects:** Medicine, nursing, hospital administration. **Holdings:** 3500 books; 6000 bound periodical volumes; 8 drawers of pamphlets. **Subscriptions:** 280 journals and other serials. **Services:** Interlibrary loans; copying; SDI; library not open to public. **Computerized Information Services:** NLM, BRS.

★5105★

GOOD SAMARITAN HOSPITAL - HEALTH-SCIENCE LIBRARY (Med)
605 N. 12th St.   Phone: (618) 242-4600
Mt. Vernon, IL 62864   Debbie Greene, Libn.
Staff: Prof 1; Other 1. **Subjects:** Hospital administration, medicine, nursing. **Holdings:** 900 books; 500 periodical volumes. **Subscriptions:** 200 journals and other serials. **Services:** Interlibrary loans; copying; SDI; library open to medical staff and hospital employees. **Networks/Consortia:** Member of Areawide Hospital Library Consortium of Southwestern Illinois; Cumberland Trail Library System; Regional Medical Library - Region 3.

★5106★

GOOD SAMARITAN HOSPITAL - KROHN MEMORIAL LIBRARY (Med)
4th & Walnut Sts.   Phone: (717) 272-7611
Lebanon, PA 17042   Susan Foltz, Libn.
Founded: 1955. **Staff:** Prof 1. **Subjects:** Medicine, surgery, toxicology. **Holdings:** 500 books. **Subscriptions:** 51 journals and other serials. **Services:** Interlibrary loans; copying; library not open to public.

★5107★

GOOD SAMARITAN HOSPITAL - LIBRARY (Med)
407 14th Ave., S.E.   Phone: (206) 848-6661
Puyallup, WA 98371   Linda Ziemke, Dir.
Subjects: Medicine. **Holdings:** 200 books. **Subscriptions:** 12 journals and other serials. **Services:** Interlibrary loans; library not open to public. **Networks/Consortia:** Member of Pierce County Medical Library Consortium.

★5108★

GOOD SAMARITAN HOSPITAL AND MEDICAL CENTER - LIBRARY (Med)
1015 N.W. 22nd Ave.   Phone: (503) 229-7336
Portland, OR 97210   Melvina Stell, Hd.Libn.
Staff: Prof 2; Other 2. **Subjects:** Medicine, nursing. **Special Collections:** Ophthalmology Collection (250 items). **Holdings:** 3000 books; 3500 bound periodical volumes; 4 VF drawers of pamphlets; 505 AV cassettes, filmstrips, slide sets. **Subscriptions:** 320 journals and other serials. **Services:** Interlibrary loans; library open to public for reference use only. **Computerized Information Services:** MEDLINE. **Networks/Consortia:** Member of Oregon Health Information Network (OHIN). **Publications:** Library Notes, bimonthly - for internal distribution only.

★5109★

GOOD SAMARITAN HOSPITAL - MEDICAL LIBRARY (Med)
1000 Montauk Hwy.   Phone: (516) 669-6670
West Islip, NY 11795   Helen Matlin, Libn.
Staff: Prof 1. **Subjects:** Medicine, surgery, obstetrics, pediatrics. **Holdings:** 150 books; 4000 bound periodical volumes. **Subscriptions:** 60 journals and other serials. **Services:** Interlibrary loans; copying; library open to public with restrictions. **Networks/Consortia:** Member of Medical and Scientific Libraries of Long Island (MEDLI).

★5110★

GOOD SAMARITAN HOSPITAL - MEDICAL LIBRARY (Med)
3217 Clifton Ave.   Phone: (513) 872-2433
Cincinnati, OH 45220   Rosalie V. Zajac, Med.Libn.
Founded: 1915. **Staff:** Prof 1; Other 4. **Subjects:** Clinical medicine, clinical surgery. **Holdings:** 2730 books; 7606 bound periodical volumes; 179 AV programs (cataloged); 2 VF drawers of pamphlets; 900 audio cassettes. **Subscriptions:** 275 journals and other serials. **Services:** Interlibrary loans; copying; SDI; library open to public by special arrangement with the librarian. **Computerized Information Services:** MEDLINE, MEDLARS, BRS, SDC; computerized cataloging. **Networks/Consortia:** Member of Cincinnati Area Health Sciences Library Association; Kentucky-Ohio-Michigan Regional Medical Libraries (KOMRML); Cincinnati Area Medline Consortium. **Publications:** Medical Library Newsletter, quarterly - to staff. **Special Catalogs:** Book catalog.

★5111★

GOOD SAMARITAN HOSPITAL OF ORANGE COUNTY, INC. - MEDICAL LIBRARY (Med)†
1025 S. Anaheim Blvd.   Phone: (714) 533-6220
Anaheim, CA 92805   Evelyn Simpson, Med.Libn.
Founded: 1972. **Staff:** Prof 1. **Subjects:** Surgery, podiatry, nursing. **Holdings:** 1200 books; cassettes (cataloged); 1 VF drawer of reprints and pamphlets. **Subscriptions:** 120 journals and other serials. **Services:** Interlibrary loans; library open to public for reference use only. **Networks/Consortia:** Member of Nursing Information Consortium of Orange County.

★5112★

GOOD SAMARITAN HOSPITAL - RICHARD S. BEINECKE MEDICAL LIBRARY (Med)
Box 3166   Phone: (305) 655-5511
West Palm Beach, FL 33402   Elizabeth H. Day, Med.Libn.
Founded: 1968. **Staff:** Prof 2. **Subjects:** Medicine, surgery, nursing, hospital literature. **Holdings:** 3210 books; 6905 bound periodical volumes; 150 rare books; 300 videotape cassettes; 1010 audiotape cassettes. **Subscriptions:** 230 journals and other serials. **Services:** Interlibrary loans; copying; library open to public with restrictions. **Computerized Information Services:** MEDLARS. **Networks/Consortia:** Member of Southeastern Regional Medical Library Program (SERMLP); Palm Beach County Health Science Libraries Consortium; Miami Health Sciences Library Consortium. **Staff:** Linda J. O'Callaghan, Med.Libn./Anl.

★5113★

GOOD SAMARITAN HOSPITAL - SHANK MEMORIAL LIBRARY (Med)
2222 Philadelphia Dr.   Phone: (513) 278-2612
Dayton, OH 45406   Elizabeth A. Robinson, Libn.
Staff: Prof 2; Other 1. **Subjects:** Medicine. **Holdings:** 8000 books; 14,000 bound periodical volumes; 1026 Audio-Digest tapes; 8 VF drawers of pamphlets. **Subscriptions:** 480 journals and other serials. **Services:** Interlibrary loans; copying; library open to public with restrictions. **Computerized Information Services:** MEDLINE, BRS. **Networks/Consortia:** Member of Miami Valley Association of Health Sciences Libraries; Dayton Area MEDLINE Consortium. **Special Indexes:** Dayton Area Health Sciences AV Union List (card). **Staff:** Marcia Dorfman, Asst.Libn.

★5114★

GOOD SAMARITAN MEDICAL CENTER - DEACONESS HOSPITAL CAMPUS - HEALTH SCIENCE LIBRARY (Med)†
620 N. 19th St.   Phone: (414) 933-9600
Milwaukee, WI 53233   Julia Woodward Schleif, Libn.
Staff: 1. **Subjects:** Medicine and nursing. **Holdings:** 3600 books and bound periodical volumes; 27 VF drawers of clippings and pamphlets; 325 slides; 400 tapes. **Subscriptions:** 136 journals and other serials. **Services:** Interlibrary loans; copying. **Networks/Consortia:** Member of Southeastern Wisconsin Health Science Library Consortium (SWHSL).

★5115★

GOOD SAMARITAN MEDICAL CENTER - LUTHERAN CAMPUS - EVANS MEMORIAL LIBRARY (Med)
2200 W. Kilbourn Ave.
Milwaukee, WI 53233   Ann Towell, Med.Libn.
Founded: 1940. **Subjects:** Medicine, nursing, hospital administration. **Holdings:** 900 volumes; 4 VF drawers of professional pamphlets. **Subscriptions:** 250 periodical titles. **Services:** Interlibrary loans available to medical staff and hospital personnel; copying; library open to public with restrictions. **Computerized Information Services:** MEDLARS. **Networks/Consortia:** Member of Southeastern Wisconsin Health Science Libraries Consortium (SWHSL). **Publications:** Acquisitions list, irregular.

★5116★

GOOD SAMARITAN SOCIETY - LIBRARY (Med)
Good Samaritan Auxiliary Hospital
9649 71st Ave.   Phone: (403) 439-6381
Edmonton, AB, Canada T6E 5J2   Geraldine Ridge, Libn.
Founded: 1975. **Staff:** Prof 1. **Subjects:** Geriatrics, long-term care, rehabilitation, pastoral care. **Holdings:** 1000 books; 5 16mm films; 23 filmstrips/cassette sets; 50 cassette tapes; 600 slides. **Subscriptions:** 36 journals and other serials. **Services:** Copying; library open to public for reference use only.

GOODFELLOW AIR FORCE BASE (TX)
See: U.S. Air Force Base - Goodfellow Base Library

★5117★
GOODHUE COUNTY HISTORICAL SOCIETY - LIBRARY (Hist)
1166 Oak St.   Phone: (612) 388-6024
Red Wing, MN 55066   Orville K. Olson, Cur. of Musm.
Staff: 6. **Subjects:** Goodhue County, local and state history. **Special Collections:** Rare books which belonged to early settlers. **Holdings:** 500 books; 3000 clippings and manuscripts; 8000 photographs. **Services:** Library open to public for reference use on a limited schedule. **Publications:** Goodhue County Historical News, 3/year.

GOODLETT (Caroline Meriwether) LIBRARY
See: **United Daughters of the Confederacy - Caroline Meriwether Goodlett Library**

★5118★
GOODMAN AND CARR - LIBRARY (Law)
2800 York Centre
145 King St., W.   Phone: (416) 868-1234
Toronto, ON, Canada M5H 3K1   Carol L. Malcolm, Libn.
Staff: Prof 1; Other 2. **Subjects:** Corporate and commercial law, taxation, real estate, estate planning, leasing, litigation. **Holdings:** 7150 books; 350 bound periodical volumes. **Subscriptions:** 102 journals and other serials. **Services:** Interlibrary loans; library not open to public.

★5119★
GOODMAN AND GOODMAN - LIBRARY (Law)
20 Queen St., W., Suite 3000
Box 30   Phone: (416) 979-2211
Toronto, ON, Canada M5H 1V5   Michele L. Miles, Libn.
Staff: Prof 1; Other 1. **Subjects:** Law - commercial, corporate and securities, bankruptcy, entertainment, planning and administrative; litigation; real estate; estates and trusts; taxation. **Holdings:** 5000 volumes. **Subscriptions:** 61 journals and other serials. **Services:** Interlibrary loans; library open to public by appointment.

GOODMAN LIBRARY
See: **Napa County Historical Society**

GOODMAN (Louis E.) MEMORIAL LIBRARY
See: **U.S. District Court - Northern California District - Louis E. Goodman Memorial Library**

GOODMAN THEATER ARCHIVES
See: **Chicago Public Library Cultural Center - Special Collections Division**

★5120★
GOODRICH (B.F.) COMPANY - AKRON INFORMATION CENTER (Bus-Fin; Sci-Tech)
500 S. Main St.   Phone: (216) 374-4368
Akron, OH 44318   Virginia Gallicchio, Mgr.
Founded: 1971. **Staff:** Prof 3; Other 1. **Subjects:** Rubber, polymers, tires, business, management. **Holdings:** 2500 books; 30 VF drawers of pamphlets. **Subscriptions:** 220 journals and other serials. **Services:** Interlibrary loans; SDI; library open to public with advance clearance. **Computerized Information Services:** New York Times Information Service, DIALOG, SDC, TOXLINE, MEDLINE, INFOLINE, Dow Jones News Retrieval; B.F. Goodrich Technical Information Retrieval (internal database). **Networks/Consortia:** Member of OHIONET. **Publications:** Alerting bulletins, irregular - for internal distribution only. **Special Catalogs:** Tire pamphlet file; Journal Holdings. **Staff:** Peter Bowler, Sr.Info.Spec., Bus.; Sherrill Snedeker, Sr.Info.Spec., Tech.

★5121★
GOODRICH (B.F.) COMPANY - GOODRICH CHEMICAL DIVISION TECHNICAL CENTER - INFORMATION CENTER (Sci-Tech)
Box 122   Phone: (216) 933-6181
Avon Lake, OH 44012   Carol Ann Lioce, Mgr., Info.Ctr.
Founded: 1959. **Staff:** Prof 3; Other 2. **Subjects:** Polymerization technology, plastics applications, rubber applications, specialty polymers. **Holdings:** 7000 books and bound periodical volumes; 75,000 company technical reports on microfilm; U.S. and foreign patents with translations, 1964 to present. **Subscriptions:** 250 journals and other serials. **Services:** Library open to public with restrictions. **Computerized Information Services:** DIALOG, SDC; internal databases; computerized cataloging. **Staff:** R.B. Davidson, Sr.Info.Spec.; J.W. Frimel, Info.Anl.

★5122★
GOODRICH (B.F.) COMPANY - RESEARCH AND DEVELOPMENT CENTER - BRECKSVILLE INFORMATION CENTER (Sci-Tech)
9921 Brecksville Rd.   Phone: (216) 447-5299
Brecksville, OH 44141   Carol A. Lioce, Mgr., Info.Ctr.
Founded: 1914. **Staff:** Prof 3; Other 2. **Subjects:** Rubber, plastics, polymer chemistry. **Holdings:** 10,000 books; 20,000 bound periodical volumes; 150,000 patents; 12,000 pamphlets and reports; 50,000 internal reports; 800 tape cassettes. **Subscriptions:** 328 journals and other serials. **Services:** Interlibrary loans; SDI; center open to public with restrictions. **Computerized Information Services:** DIALOG, SDC; internal database; computerized cataloging. **Publications:** Information Center Bulletin, monthly; current awareness bulletins, biweekly - both for internal distribution only. **Special Catalogs:** Book Catalog; Journal Holdings; KWIC and KWOC indexes. **Staff:** Ruth A. Spindler, Sr.Info.Spec.; Lillian A. Devault, Info.Spec.

GOODRICH MEMORIAL LAW LIBRARY
See: **Ossining Historical Society Museum**

GOODWIN FAMILY LIBRARY
See: **Congregation Beth Jacob**

★5123★
GOODWIN, PROCTER & HOAR - LAW LIBRARY (Law)
28 State St., 22nd Fl.   Phone: (617) 523-5700
Boston, MA 02109   Mary Jo Poburko, Hd.Libn.
Staff: Prof 1; Other 2. **Subjects:** Law - taxation, labor, securities, litigation, real estate, probate. **Holdings:** 17,000 books; 500 bound periodical volumes. **Subscriptions:** 200 journals and other serials. **Services:** Interlibrary loans; copying; SDI; library not open to public. **Computerized Information Services:** LEXIS.

★5124★
GOODYEAR AEROSPACE CORPORATION - LIBRARY (Sci-Tech)
1210 Massillon Rd.   Phone: (216) 796-2557
Akron, OH 44315   Louise Lariccia, Libn.
Staff: Prof 2; Other 3. **Subjects:** Aeronautics, electronics, mathematics, physics, computer science, material science. **Special Collections:** Lighter-than-air craft. **Holdings:** 7782 books; 1569 bound periodical volumes; 183,000 technical reports; archives; 131,747 microforms. **Subscriptions:** 667 journals and other serials. **Services:** Interlibrary loans; copying (limited); library open to public with restrictions. **Computerized Information Services:** DIALOG, NASA/RECON, DTIC, SDC; Goodyear Engineering Reports (GERS - internal database); computerized serials. **Networks/Consortia:** Member of OCLC. **Publications:** Library Bulletin, bimonthly - for internal distribution only. **Special Indexes:** Airship Index; Lighter-than-Air Archives Index.

GOODYEAR ATOMIC CORPORATION
See: **Goodyear Tire and Rubber Company**

★5125★
GOODYEAR TIRE AND RUBBER COMPANY - BUSINESS INFORMATION CENTER (Bus-Fin)†
142 Goodyear Blvd.   Phone: (216) 794-2790
Akron, OH 44316   Dori Rogers, Bus.Info.Spec.
Founded: 1978. **Staff:** Prof 2; Other 1. **Subjects:** Management, administration, marketing, economics, international relations, foreign statistics. **Special Collections:** Company publications. **Holdings:** 2000 books; 150 16mm films. **Subscriptions:** 217 journals and other serials; 8 newspapers. **Services:** Interlibrary loans; library not open to public. **Computerized Information Services:** DIALOG, BRS, MEDLINE, New York Times Information Service, Dow Jones News Retrieval, SDC; computerized cataloging. **Staff:** Judy Hale, Mgr., Info.Serv.

★5126★
GOODYEAR TIRE AND RUBBER COMPANY - GOODYEAR ATOMIC CORPORATION - TECHNICAL LIBRARY (Sci-Tech)
Box 628   Phone: (614) 289-2331
Piketon, OH 45661   Robert P. Holland, Supv.
Founded: 1952. **Staff:** Prof 2; Other 3. **Subjects:** Atomic and nuclear science, chemistry, physics, chemical engineering, mechanical engineering, electrical engineering, industrial safety, metallurgical science, mathematics. **Holdings:** 21,000 books; 6000 bound periodical volumes; 38,000 technical reports; 80,000 technical reports on microforms. **Subscriptions:** 518 journals and other serials; 8 newspapers. **Services:** Interlibrary loans; copying; library not open to public. **Computerized Information Services:** Computer com-share facilities. **Special Catalogs:** Union List. **Staff:** Marvin L. Rice, Tech.Libn.; Phyl A. Hopkins, Engr.Libn.

★5127★
GOODYEAR TIRE AND RUBBER COMPANY - TECHNICAL INFORMATION CENTER (Sci-Tech)
142 Goodyear Blvd.
Akron, OH 44316
Phone: (216) 796-6540
Judy E. Hale, Mgr., Info.Serv.
Founded: 1942. **Staff:** Prof 8; Other 4. **Subjects:** Rubber, plastics, environment, organic chemistry, fibers, radiation. **Special Collections:** Government Rubber Reserve Reports. **Holdings:** 6000 books; 4465 bound periodical volumes. **Subscriptions:** 554 journals and other serials. **Services:** Copying (limited); library open to public with restrictions. **Computerized Information Services:** DIALOG, Derwent, SDC, NLM, BRS; computerized serials. **Staff:** Genevieve Heineking, Sect.Hd.; Dori Rogers, Staff Lit.Chem.; Betty Cole, Lit.Chem.; Robin Waynesboro, Lit.Chem.; Eileen Ambelang, Lit.Chem.; Gina Conti, Lit.Chem.; Cynthia Smith, Lit.Chem.; Randall Walker, Lit.Chem.

GORDON (Bruce) MEMORIAL LIBRARY
See: Beth Emet, The Free Synagogue - Bruce Gordon Memorial Library

★5128★
GORDON COLLEGE - WINN LIBRARY (Hum)
255 Grapevine Rd.
Wenham, MA 01984
Phone: (617) 927-2300
John Beauregard, Dir.
Staff: Prof 3; Other 5. **Subjects:** Liberal arts, humanities, North American ethnology, Shakespeare, linguistics. **Special Collections:** Edward Payson Vining Collection. **Holdings:** 122,000 books; 29,600 other cataloged items. **Subscriptions:** 637 journals and other serials. **Services:** Interlibrary loans; copying; library open to public with restrictions. **Computerized Information Services:** DIALOG. **Networks/Consortia:** Member of Essex County Cooperating Libraries; Northeast Consortium of Colleges and Universities in Massachusetts. **Staff:** Mary A. Shakelton, Ref./Circ.Libn.

★5129★
GORDON-CONWELL THEOLOGICAL SEMINARY - GODDARD LIBRARY (Rel-Theol)
130 Essex St.
South Hamilton, MA 01982
Phone: (617) 468-7111
Robert Dvorak, Dir.
Founded: 1945. **Staff:** Prof 3; Other 5. **Subjects:** Theology, Biblical studies, church history, church ministry, Christian education, world missions, evangelism, Christianity and society. **Special Collections:** Mercer Collection of Assyrio-Babylonian materials; Roger Babson Collection of rare Bibles (especially early English Bibles). **Holdings:** 105,000 books and bound periodical volumes; 2250 cassettes; 893 reels of microfilm; 952 microfiche; 152 sermon tapes; 4733 microcards; 279 phonodiscs. **Subscriptions:** 952 journals and other serials; 7 newspapers. **Services:** Interlibrary loans; copying; library open to public. **Computerized Information Services:** Online systems; computerized cataloging. **Networks/Consortia:** Member of Boston Theological Institute; OCLC through NELINET. **Staff:** Kenneth Umenhofer, Assoc.Libn.; Norman E. Anderson, Assoc.Libn.

GORDON (Donald B.) MEMORIAL LIBRARY
See: Morikami Museum of Japanese Culture - Donald B. Gordon Memorial Library

GORDON (George C.) LIBRARY
See: Worcester Polytechnic Institute - George C. Gordon Library

GORDON (J. Roy) RESEARCH LABORATORY
See: INCO Metals Company - J. Roy Gordon Research Laboratory

★5130★
GORE PLACE SOCIETY, INC. - LIBRARY (Hum)
52 Gore St.
Waltham, MA 02154
Phone: (617) 894-2798
Charles Hammond, Dir.
Staff: Prof 1. **Subjects:** 18th-century English literature; law; history; philosophy; landscape and horticulture; works of Christopher Gore. **Holdings:** 2000 books; 100 manuscripts. **Services:** Library open to public.

★5131★
GORGAS ARMY HOSPITAL - SAMUEL TAYLOR DARLING MEMORIAL LIBRARY (Med)
USA MEDDAC Panama
APO Miami, FL 34004
Barbara Poole, Chf. MEDDAC Libn.
Founded: 1918. **Staff:** Prof 2; Other 1. **Subjects:** Medicine and related fields. **Holdings:** 3000 books; 20,000 journals; 1000 videotapes; 300 items of AV software. **Subscriptions:** 500 journals and other serials. **Services:** Interlibrary loans; copying; library open to the medical community. **Remarks:** Hospital maintained by the U.S. Army MEDDAC (Panama); located in Ancon, Panama. **Staff:** Patricia Mead, Asst.Med.Libn.

★5132★
GORGAS MEMORIAL LABORATORY OF TROPICAL AND PREVENTIVE MEDICINE, INC. - BIO-MEDICAL RESEARCH LIBRARY (Med)
Box 935
APO Miami, FL 34002
Prof. Manuel Victor De Las Casas, Dir. & Med.Libn.
Founded: 1928. **Staff:** Prof 1; Other 3. **Subjects:** Arboviruses, malaria, leishmaniasis, trypanosomiasis, vertebrate zoology, parasitology, bacteriology, entomology, ecology, yellow fever. **Special Collections:** Tropical Medicine; Gorgas Memorial Laboratory Publications (900 reprints). **Holdings:** 4000 books; 9000 bound periodical volumes; 95 boxes of reprints and other material; 17 VF drawers of pamphlets. **Subscriptions:** 503 journals and other serials. **Services:** Interlibrary loans; copying; library open for the use of physicians, medical students, scientists, nurses and laboratory technicians. **Publications:** Annual Report; Bibliography of Publications of the Gorgas Memorial Laboratory; Evaluacion Ambiental y Efectos del Proyecto Hidroelectrico Fortuna; El Laboratorio Conmemorativo Gorgas: Su Historia y Su Labor - all free upon request. **Remarks:** Phone number is 27-4111. Main library is located at Justo Arosemena Ave., No. 35-30, Republic of Panama.

★5133★
GORGAS MEMORIAL LABORATORY OF TROPICAL AND PREVENTIVE MEDICINE, INC. - VIROLOGY UNIT LIBRARY (Med)
Box 935
APO Miami, FL 34002
Prof. Manuel Victor De Las Casas, Dir. & Med.Libn.
Founded: 1975. **Staff:** Prof 1; Other 2. **Subjects:** Virology, ecology, animal care, cytology and tissue culture, epidemiology, statistics, parasitology, pathology, entomology, veterinary medicine, microbiology. **Holdings:** 1500 books; 1161 bound periodical volumes; 20 VF drawers of reprints; 10 VF drawers of maps. **Subscriptions:** 22 journals and other serials. **Services:** Interlibrary loans; copying; library open for reference to Gorgas Hospital staff and area physicians and scientists. **Computerized Information Services:** Online systems. **Publications:** Annual Report; Bibliography of the Publications of the Gorgas Memorial Laboratory; El Laboratorio Conmemorativo Gorgas, Su Historia y Su Labor; Evaluacion Ambiental y Efectos del Proyecto Hidroelectrico Fortuna - all free upon request. **Special Catalogs:** Arbovirus Catalog. **Remarks:** This library is an extension of the Gorgas Memorial Laboratory Library. It is located at Gorgas Rd., Bldg. 265, Ancon, Republic of Panama. The phone numbers are 62-0864 and 27-4111.

GORNO MEMORIAL MUSIC LIBRARY
See: University of Cincinnati - College Conservatory of Music

GORTON (Thomas) MUSIC LIBRARY
See: University of Kansas - Thomas Gorton Music Library

GOSHEN COLLEGE - MENNONITE HISTORICAL LIBRARY
See: Mennonite Historical Library

★5134★
GOSHEN HISTORICAL SOCIETY - LIBRARY (Hist)
Old Middle Rd.
Goshen, CT 06756
Phone: (203) 491-2665
Mrs. John Tuttle, Cur.
Staff: 5. **Subjects:** Local history, genealogy. **Holdings:** Figures not available. **Services:** Copying; library open to public with restrictions. **Computerized Information Services:** Computerized acquisitions.

GOSS HISTORY OF ENGINEERING LIBRARY
See: Purdue University - Engineering Library

GOSSARD MEMORIAL LIBRARY
See: Evangelical United Brethren Church

GOTTESMAN (D. Samuel) LIBRARY
See: Yeshiva University - Albert Einstein College of Medicine - D. Samuel Gottesman Library

GOTTESMAN (Mendel) LIBRARY OF HEBRAICA AND JUDAICA
See: Yeshiva University - Mendel Gottesman Library of Hebraica and Judaica

GOTTLIEB MEMORIAL LIBRARY
See: Congregation Adath Jeshurun

GOTTSCHO PACKAGING INFORMATION CENTER
See: Rutgers University, The State University of New Jersey

★5135★
GOULD INC. - GOULD INFORMATION CENTER (Sci-Tech)
40 Gould Center   Phone: (312) 640-4423
Rolling Meadows, IL 60008   Mala Laurin, Dir., Info.Rsrcs.
Staff: Prof 4; Other 4. **Subjects:** Electronics, energy, batteries, business. **Holdings:** 4000 books. **Subscriptions:** 600 journals and other serials. **Services:** Interlibrary loans; copying; library open to public by appointment. **Computerized Information Services:** DIALOG, SDC, New York Times Information Service, NEXIS; computerized cataloging, serials, circulation, SDI and mailing lists. **Networks/Consortia:** Member of North Suburban Library System; OCLC. **Staff:** Mark Casey, Supv., Lib.Serv.; Terry Murphy, Info.Spec.; Barbara Nelson, Sr.Lib.Tech.Asst.; Mel Budzol, Info.Spec.

GOULD, INC. - GOULD INFORMATION CENTER (Cleveland, OH)
See: Imperial Clevite Inc. - IC Information Center

GOULD MEMORIAL LIBRARY
See: Dallas Bible College

★5136★
GOULD, INC. - NAVCOM SYSTEMS DIVISION - TECHNICAL LIBRARY (Sci-Tech)†
Hoffman Electronic Pk.
4323 N. Arden Dr.   Phone: (213) 442-0123
El Monte, CA 91731   Nora Hubert, Libn.
Founded: 1953. **Staff:** 1. **Subjects:** Electronics, engineering, navigation, industrial psychology, astronomy, business management, chemistry, physics, aeronautics. **Holdings:** 5000 volumes; 6000 other items. **Subscriptions:** 142 journals and other serials. **Services:** Interlibrary loans; copying; library not open to public. **Publications:** Acquisitions list, monthly - for internal distribution only.

★5137★
GOULD, INC. - OCEAN SYSTEMS INFORMATION CENTER (Sci-Tech)
Plant 2
18901 Euclid Ave.   Phone: (216) 486-8300
Cleveland, OH 44117   Robert J. Rittenhouse, Tech.Info.Spec. & Mgr.
Staff: Prof 1; Other 1. **Subjects:** Military electronics, acoustics, underwater ocean technology, reliability, military science, computer hardware and software, materials (including composites). **Special Collections:** Military specifications, standards, handbooks, industrial specifications, catalogs, U.S. government documents. **Holdings:** 2000 books; 20,000 documents. **Subscriptions:** 450 journals and other serials; 10 newspapers. **Services:** Interlibrary loans; copying; library not open to public. **Computerized Information Services:** DIALOG, Tech-net, SDC. **Networks/Consortia:** Member of OCLC. **Publications:** Ocean System Information Center Newsletter.

★5138★
GOULD, INC. - S.E.L. COMPUTER SYSTEMS DIVISION - TECHNICAL INFORMATION CENTER (Sci-Tech)
6901 W. Sunrise Blvd.   Phone: (305) 587-2900
Fort Lauderdale, FL 33313   L. Susan Hayes, Info.Spec.
Staff: Prof 1; Other 1. **Subjects:** Computers, electrical engineering. **Holdings:** 1500 volumes; 700 microforms. **Subscriptions:** 100 journals and other serials. **Services:** Interlibrary loans; copying; SDI; library open to public by appointment. **Computerized Information Services:** DIALOG, SDC, BRS; internal database. **Publications:** Newsletter, monthly.

GOVE SCHOOL LIBRARY
See: Columbus Developmental Center

★5139★
GOVERNMENT RESEARCH CORPORATION - LIBRARY (Soc Sci)
1730 M St., N.W.   Phone: (202) 857-1400
Washington, DC 20036   Jennifer De Toro, Dir., Lib.Serv.
Founded: 1969. **Staff:** 7. **Subjects:** Federal government operations. **Holdings:** 1500 books; 50 VF drawers of clippings; 32 VF drawers of biographies; congressional hearings and other government documents. **Subscriptions:** 300 journals and newsletters; 8 newspapers. **Services:** Interlibrary loans; copying; reference and bibliographic services for clients and National Journal subscribers; library not open to public. **Publications:** National Journal. **Staff:** Linda K. Fowlie, Ref.Libn.

GOVERNMENTAL SERVICES INSTITUTE
See: Louisiana State University

★5140★
GOVERNOR BACON HEALTH CENTER - MEDICAL LIBRARY (Med)
     Phone: (302) 834-9201
Delaware City, DE 19706   Ivonne K. Go, Libn.
Founded: 1948. **Staff:** Prof 1. **Subjects:** Psychiatry, social service, psychology. **Holdings:** 850 books and bound periodical volumes. **Subscriptions:** 18 journals and other serials. **Services:** Interlibrary loans; copying; library not open to public. **Networks/Consortia:** Member of Medical Library Resource Improvement Consortium (MEDICKS); LINCK.

★5141★
GOWANDA PSYCHIATRIC CENTER - HEALTH SCIENCES LIBRARY (Med)
Rte. 62   Phone: (716) 532-3311
Helmuth, NY 14079   Mark Wudyka, Libn.
Founded: 1961. **Staff:** Prof 1; Other 1. **Subjects:** Psychiatry, psychology, nursing. **Holdings:** 4215 volumes. **Subscriptions:** 66 journals and other serials. **Services:** Interlibrary loans; copying; library open to public by appointment. **Networks/Consortia:** Member of Western New York Library Resources Council (WNYLRC).

★5142★
GPU NUCLEAR - HEADQUARTERS LIBRARY (Energy; Bus-Fin)
100 Interpace Pkwy.   Phone: (201) 263-4900
Parsippany, NJ 07054   Jan Thompson, Libn.
Staff: Prof 1; Other 2. **Subjects:** Electrical and mechanical engineering, management, nuclear power, electrical utility business. **Special Collections:** Electric Power Research Institute Reports (2500); Nuclear Regulatory Commission Reports (2700). **Holdings:** 2000 books; 40 bound periodical volumes; 8500 technical reports; VSMF industry standards. **Subscriptions:** 570 journals and other serials; 6 newspapers. **Services:** Interlibrary loans; copying SDI; library not open to public. **Computerized Information Services:** Online systems; CARIRS (internal database); computerized acquisitions, serials and circulation. **Publications:** Library Bulletin, monthly - for internal distriubtion.

★5143★
GPU NUCLEAR - LIBRARY (Energy; Bus-Fin)
Rte. 183 & Van Reed Rd.   Phone: (215) 371-1001
Reading, PA 19601   Jan Thompson, Libn.
Staff: Prof 1; Other 1. **Subjects:** Electric utility business, electrical and mechanical engineering. **Holdings:** 500 books; 15 bound periodical volumes; 500 government documents. **Subscriptions:** 98 journals and other serials. **Computerized Information Services:** Online systems.

★5144★
GPU NUCLEAR - OYSTER CREEK TECHNICAL LIBRARY (Sci-Tech)
Oyster Creek Nuclear Generating Sta.
Box 338
Forked River, NJ 08731   Carlyn Ewald, Tech.Libn.
Founded: 1981. **Staff:** 1. **Subjects:** Nuclear power and engineering. **Special Collections:** Engineering and nuclear industry standards (microfiche and paper copies). **Holdings:** 500 books; 800 technical reports. **Subscriptions:** 55 journals and other serials. **Services:** Interlibrary loans; copying; library not open to public. **Computerized Information Services:** DIALOG; CARIRS (internal database). **Networks/Consortia:** Member of GPU Nuclear Libraries Network.

★5145★
GPU NUCLEAR - TECHNICAL LIBRARY (Energy; Bus-Fin)
100 Interpace Pkwy.   Phone: (201) 299-2159
Parsippany, NJ 07054   Toby E. Necht, Tech.Libn.
Staff: Prof 1. **Subjects:** Nuclear power, mechanical and electrical engineering, utility industry. **Special Collections:** Nuclear Regulatory Commission Reports (500). **Holdings:** 250 books; 3000 engineering standards; 500 technical reports. **Subscriptions:** 15 journals and other serials. **Services:** Interlibrary loans; copying; library not open to public. **Computerized Information Services:** DIALOG, SDC; CARIRS (internal database); computerized acquisitions, serials and circulation.

★5146★
GPU NUCLEAR - TMI TECHNICAL LIBRARY (Sci-Tech)
Three Mile Island Nuclear Generating Sta.
Box 480   Phone: (717) 948-8105
Middletown, PA 17057   Joan H. Slavin, Tech.Libn.
Staff: Prof 1; Other 1. **Subjects:** Nuclear and electric power. **Holdings:** 750 books; 500 standards; 1000 technical reports. **Services:** Interlibrary loans; library not open to public. **Computerized Information Services:** Computerized cataloging, serials. **Networks/Consortia:** Member of GPU Nuclear Libraries Network.

★5147★

GRACE BIBLE COLLEGE - BULTEMA MEMORIAL LIBRARY (Rel-Theol)
1011 Aldon St., S.W.
Box 910
Grand Rapids, MI 49509
Phone: (616) 538-2332
Guni Olson, Hd.Libn.
Staff: Prof 2; Other 2. **Subjects:** Theology, Biblical studies, missions, Christian education, practical theology, general education. **Special Collections:** Dispensational Theology (71 books and pamphlets). **Holdings:** 27,482 books; 920 bound periodical volumes; 200 records (cataloged); 27 microforms. **Subscriptions:** 103 journals and other serials. **Services:** Interlibrary loans; copying; library open to public for reference use only. **Staff:** R.E. Reich, Cat. & Acq.Libn.

★5148★

GRACE COLLEGE OF THE BIBLE - LIBRARY (Rel-Theol)
1515 S. Tenth St.
Omaha, NE 68108
Phone: (402) 342-3377
Norma McWilliams, Hd.Libn.
Founded: 1943. **Staff:** Prof 1; Other 2. **Subjects:** Bible and theology, history, literature. **Holdings:** 50,400 books; 3900 bound periodical volumes; 900 phonograph records; 130 elementary education filmstrips and kits; clippings; maps; pamphlets; tapes and cassettes. **Subscriptions:** 130 journals and other serials. **Services:** Interlibrary loans; copying; library open to public from metropolitan area.

★5149★

GRACE GENERAL HOSPITAL - CHESLEY A. PIPPY, JR. MEDICAL LIBRARY (Med)
LeMarchant Rd.
St. John's, NF, Canada A1E 1P9
Phone: (709) 778-6796
Elizabeth Duggan, Med.Libn.
Staff: 1. **Subjects:** Medicine. **Holdings:** 950 books; 1200 bound periodical volumes. **Subscriptions:** 110 journals and other serials. **Services:** Interlibrary loans; copying; library not open to public. **Publications:** Newsletter and recent acquisitions, quarterly. **Remarks:** Maintained by Salvation Army.

★5150★

GRACE GENERAL HOSPITAL - SCHOOL OF NURSING LIBRARY (Med)†
LeMarchant Rd.
St. John's, NF, Canada A1E 1P9
Phone: (709) 778-6645
Catherine Ryan, Libn.
Founded: 1964. **Staff:** 1. **Subjects:** Nursing. **Holdings:** 2200 books; 130 bound periodical volumes; 20 boxes of pamphlets. **Services:** Interlibrary loans; library open to public for reference use only.

GRACE HOSPITAL
See: Harper-Grace Hospitals

★5151★

GRACE LUTHERAN CHURCH - LIBRARY (Rel-Theol)
18360 Minnetonka Blvd.
Wayzata, MN 55391
Phone: (612) 473-2362
Betty LeDell, Libn.
Founded: 1958. **Staff:** Prof 1; Other 4. **Subjects:** Religion, social problems. **Holdings:** 3200 books; 3 VF drawers of pictures, clippings and pamphlets; 5 drawers of cassette tapes. **Subscriptions:** 12 journals and other serials. **Services:** Library open to public.

★5152★

GRACE MATERNITY HOSPITAL - MEDICAL LIBRARY (Med)
5821 University Ave.
Halifax, NS, Canada B3H 1W3
Phone: (902) 422-6501
Donna M. Gallivan, Dir., Med.Rec.Dept.
Subjects: Obstetrics and gynecology, pediatrics, surgery, medicine. **Holdings:** 400 books. **Subscriptions:** 15 journals and other serials. **Services:** Library open to public with restrictions.

★5153★

GRACE THEOLOGICAL SEMINARY - LIBRARY (Rel-Theol)†
Wooster Rd.
Winona Lake, IN 46590
Phone: (219) 267-8191
Robert Ibach, Dir.
Founded: 1939. **Staff:** Prof 3. **Subjects:** Bible, archeology, history, missions, Christian education, philosophy. **Special Collections:** Billy Sunday Papers (28 cubic feet); Grace Brethren denominational archives. **Holdings:** 40,000 books; 3200 bound periodical volumes. **Subscriptions:** 300 journals and other serials. **Services:** Interlibrary loans; copying; library open to public. **Computerized Information Services:** Computerized cataloging. **Networks/Consortia:** Member of INCOLSA. **Staff:** William Darr, Asst.Dir.; Floyd Votaw, Hd. of Tech.Serv.

★5154★

GRACE (W.R.) AND COMPANY - AGRICULTURAL CHEMICALS GROUP - PLANNING SERVICES LIBRARY (Agri)
100 N. Main Bldg.
Box 277
Memphis, TN 38101
Phone: (901) 522-2385
Carolyn Wilhite, Libn.
Founded: 1956. **Staff:** Prof 1; Other 1. **Subjects:** Agriculture, chemistry, chemical engineering, animal nutrition. **Holdings:** 7000 books; 1500 bound periodical volumes; 3 VF drawers of patents; 200 VF drawers of agricultural related materials; Biological Abstracts on microfilm, 1927-1982; Chemical Abstracts, 1917-1982; 400 cataloged microforms. **Subscriptions:** 725 journals and other serials; 25 newspapers. **Services:** Interlibrary loans; copying; library open to public by appointment. **Computerized Information Services:** DIALOG, SDC; computerized cataloging.

★5155★

GRACE (W.R.) AND COMPANY - CRYOVAC DIVISION - TECHNICAL LIBRARY (Sci-Tech)
Box 464
Duncan, SC 29334
Phone: (803) 439-4121
Margaret M. Ezell, Tech.Libn.
Founded: 1960. **Staff:** Prof 1; Other 2. **Subjects:** Plastic film, packaging, food packaging, polymer chemistry. **Holdings:** 6500 books; 220 bound periodical volumes; 70 VF drawers of technical reports and other materials; 640 microforms. **Subscriptions:** 200 journals and other serials; 5 newspapers. **Services:** Interlibrary loans; copying; automated ISRS; library open to public with advance notice.

★5156★

GRACE (W.R.) AND COMPANY - CHEMED CORPORATION - DEARBORN CHEMICAL (U.S.) LIBRARY (Env-Cons)
300 Genesee St.
Lake Zurich, IL 60047
Phone: (312) 483-8241
Martha M. Mitchell, Libn.
Founded: 1940. **Staff:** Prof 1; Other 1. **Subjects:** Water treatment, corrosion, inorganic chemistry, organic chemistry (polymers), environmental engineering, pollution control, water bacteriology, spectroscopy. **Holdings:** 3000 books; 2100 bound periodical volumes; 850 research notebooks; 6000 U.S. and foreign patents; 5300 research reports; 5000 pamphlets and clippings. **Subscriptions:** 140 journals and other serials. **Services:** Interlibrary loans; copying; library open to public by appointment. **Computerized Information Services:** DIALOG, SDC. **Networks/Consortia:** Member of North Suburban Library System (NSLS). **Publications:** Literature Index and Recent Book Acquisitions - for internal distribution only. **Formerly:** Chemed Corporation - Dearborn Chemical (U.S.) Library.

★5157★

GRACE (W.R.) AND COMPANY - INDUSTRIAL CHEMICALS GROUP - LIBRARY (Sci-Tech)
62 Whittemore Ave.
Cambridge, MA 02140
Phone: (617) 876-1400
Marjorie Metcalf, Libn.
Staff: Prof 1; Other 1. **Subjects:** Chemistry - organic, colloidal, inorganic, analytical, polymer; rheology; rubber. **Holdings:** 3000 books; 1000 bound periodical volumes. **Subscriptions:** 350 journals and other serials. **Services:** Interlibrary loans; copying; library open to public by appointment. **Computerized Information Services:** DIALOG.

★5158★

GRACE (W.R.) AND COMPANY - NATURAL RESOURCES GROUP - INFORMATION CENTER (Sci-Tech)
3400 First International Bldg.
Dallas, TX 75270
Phone: (214) 658-1030
Jane Johnston, Mgr.
Founded: 1975. **Staff:** Prof 3; Other 2. **Subjects:** Petroleum, mining and paper industries. **Special Collections:** Energy industry annual reports file (2000 reports). **Holdings:** 3000 books; 4000 microforms; 50 boxes of pamphlets. **Subscriptions:** 280 journals and other serials; 25 newspapers. **Services:** Interlibrary loans; copying; library open to other special librarians. **Computerized Information Services:** DIALOG, New York Times Information Service, SDC, Dow Jones News Retrieval, Dun & Bradstreet, Inc.; computerized cataloging and serials. **Publications:** Periodicals list, bimonthly; publications list, bimonthly - both for internal distribution only. **Staff:** Ernestine Chipman, Libn.; Dorothy Stevenson, Sr.Rec.Techn.; Mary T. Sullivan, Asst.Mgr.

★5159★

GRACE (W.R.) AND COMPANY - RESEARCH DIVISION LIBRARY (Sci-Tech)
7379 Route 32
Columbia, MD 21044
Phone: (301) 531-4269
Jeanette S. Hamilton, Supv., Info.Ctr.
Founded: 1953. **Staff:** Prof 2. **Subjects:** Biochemistry, chemical engineering, chemistry - inorganic, nuclear, organic. **Holdings:** 20,000 books; 3000 internal reports; microfiche. **Subscriptions:** 225 journals and other serials; 10

newspapers. **Services:** Interlibrary loans; copying (limited); library open to public. **Computerized Information Services:** DIALOG, SDC, BRS, DOE/RECON, MEDLARS, Dow Jones News Retrieval. **Publications:** Acquisitions list. **Staff:** Caroline A. Sasser, Supv. of Lib.

★5160★
GRACELAND COLLEGE - FREDERICK MADISON SMITH LIBRARY (Hum)
Lamoni, IA 50140
Phone: (515) 784-3311
Volante H. Russell, Dir.
Founded: 1895. **Staff:** Prof 2; Other 7. **Subjects:** Religion, literature, psychology, history, philosophy, education, art, economics, music, social and behavioral sciences. **Special Collections:** Mormonism; 20th century American literature. **Holdings:** 91,000 books; 10,000 bound periodical volumes; 1426 microforms (cataloged); 6000 pamphlets; 65,000 government documents. **Subscriptions:** 500 journals and other serials; 15 newspapers. **Services:** Interlibrary loans; copying; library open to public. **Computerized Information Services:** Computerized cataloging. **Networks/Consortia:** Member of Kansas City Regional Council for Higher Education (KRCHE); Iowa Library Information Teletype Exchange (ILITE); Bibliographical Center for Research, Rocky Mountain Region, Inc. (BCR). **Special Catalogs:** Mormonism (card). **Staff:** Jill Seymour, Asst.Libn.

★5161★
GRACEWOOD STATE SCHOOL AND HOSPITAL - LIBRARY (Med)
Gracewood, GA 30812
Phone: (404) 790-2183
Alice K. Garren, Libn.
Founded: 1964. **Staff:** 1. **Subjects:** Mental retardation, pediatrics, psychology, medicine, dentistry, nursing. **Special Collections:** Pediatric tape collection (800 reels and cassettes); Mental Retardation and Reinforcement Therapy (4 films). **Holdings:** 3100 books; 600 bound periodical volumes; 1800 cassette tapes; 2185 reprints; 700 pamphlets; 3 films (cataloged). **Subscriptions:** 99 journals and other serials. **Services:** Interlibrary loans; copying; library open to public with restrictions. **Networks/Consortia:** Member of Georgia Health Sciences Libraries; Georgia Department of Human Resources Library Consortium. **Special Catalogs:** Reprint index, tapes catalog.

★5162★
GRADUATE HOSPITAL - LIBRARY (Med)†
One Graduate Plaza
Philadelphia, PA 19146
Phone: (215) 893-2401
Diane M. Farny, Libn.
Founded: 1977. **Staff:** Prof 1. **Subjects:** Medicine, nursing, patient health education. **Special Collections:** M. Harris Samitz Dermatology Collection. **Holdings:** 3000 books; 3000 bound periodical volumes. **Subscriptions:** 202 journals and other serials. **Services:** Interlibrary loans (fee); library open to public with permission. **Networks/Consortia:** Member of Mideastern Regional Medical Library Service (MERMLS); Delaware Valley Information Consortium.

★5163★
GRADUATE THEOLOGICAL UNION - LIBRARY (Rel-Theol)
2400 Ridge Rd.
Berkeley, CA 94709
Phone: (415) 841-8222
John. D. Baker-Batsel, Dir.
Founded: 1969. **Staff:** Prof 10; Other 17. **Subjects:** Bible, denominations, theology including practical theology, church history, religion, new American religious movements. **Holdings:** 353,284 books; 40,000 bound periodical volumes; 5000 pamphlets (cataloged); 965 cubic feet of archival material; 117,000 tapes and microforms (cataloged); 1800 phonograph records (cataloged). **Subscriptions:** 1895 journals and other serials. **Services:** Interlibrary loans; copying; library open to public with restrictions. **Computerized Information Services:** BRS; computerized cataloging and acquisitions. **Networks/Consortia:** This is a library consortium, uniting the holdings of the libraries of nine seminaries: American Baptist Seminary of the West; Church Divinity School of the Pacific; Franciscan School of Theology; Pacific Lutheran Theological Seminary; Jesuit School of Theology at Berkeley; Dominican School of Philosophy and Theology; San Francisco Theological Seminary; Pacific School of Religion; and Starr King School for the Ministry; also a member of Marin Library Network. **Publications:** Catalog of the Graduate Theological Union Library, 15 volumes; Check-It-Out (newsletter) - irregular. **Remarks:** The Graduate Theological Union Library works cooperatively with the library of the Canon Law Collection of the University of California Law School. **Staff:** Libby Flynn, Asst.Dir.

★5164★
GRAFTON HISTORICAL MUSEUM (Hist)
Main St.
Grafton, VT 05146
Phone: (802) 843-2388
Helen M. Pettengill, Musm.Dir.
Founded: 1962. **Subjects:** Grafton history, genealogy. **Special Collections:** 500 photographs of old time Grafton; historical artifacts. **Services:** Library open to public for reference use only on a limited schedule. **Publications:**

Grafton History, 1754-1976; Innkeeping 100 Years Ago, Barrett Store, 1815-1830; Grafton Cornet Band; Life of a Vermont Farmer from Diaries; Nine Historical Grafton Walks.

GRAHAM (Billy) CENTER LIBRARY
See: Wheaton College - Billy Graham Center Library

★5165★
GRAHAM (Billy) EVANGELISTIC ASSOCIATION - LIBRARY (Rel-Theol)
1300 Harmon Place
Minneapolis, MN 55403
Phone: (612) 338-0500
Rev. Roger C. Palms, Ed.
Staff: 1. **Subjects:** Religion, biography, history. **Special Collections:** Billy Graham articles; magazine and newspaper clippings concerning Billy Graham. **Holdings:** 6000 books; 50 bound periodical volumes; 1000 other items (cataloged); 25 reels of microfilm. **Subscriptions:** 200 journals and other serials. **Services:** Library open to public for reference use only on request. **Staff:** David G. Stiff, Libn.

GRAHAM (Billy) ROOM
See: Southern Baptist Theological Seminary - Billy Graham Room

GRAHAM (F.P.) RESOURCE CENTER
See: National Sharecroppers Fund/Rural Advancement Fund - F.P. Graham Resource Center

GRAHAM (Dr. H. Carson) MEMORIAL LIBRARY
See: Lions Gate Hospital - Dr. H. Carson Graham Memorial Library

★5166★
GRAHAM HOSPITAL ASSOCIATION - MEDICAL STAFF LIBRARY (Med)
210 W. Walnut St.
Canton, IL 61520
Phone: (309) 647-5240
Mrs. Moneta Bedwell, Libn.
Staff: Prof 1. **Subjects:** Surgery, internal medicine. **Holdings:** 500 books; 40 bound periodical volumes; Audio-Digest tapes. **Subscriptions:** 25 journals and other serials. **Services:** Interlibrary loans; copying; library not open to public. **Networks/Consortia:** Member of Heart of Illinois Consortium; Illinois Valley Library System.

★5167★
GRAHAM HOSPITAL ASSOCIATION - SCHOOL OF NURSING LIBRARY (Med)
210 W. Walnut St.
Canton, IL 61520
Phone: (309) 647-5240
Mrs. Moneta Bedwell, Libn.
Founded: 1930. **Staff:** Prof 1. **Subjects:** Nursing and medicine, chemistry, social sciences, psychology, nutrition. **Special Collections:** Historical textbooks; dolls costumed as historical nursing persons. **Holdings:** 3000 books; 112 bound periodical volumes; 3 VF drawers of pamphlets and clippings; 60 filmstrips; 15 filmloops; 300 slides. **Subscriptions:** 60 journals and other serials. **Services:** Interlibrary loans; copying; library open to public for reference use only. **Networks/Consortia:** Member of Heart of Illinois Consortium; Illinois Valley Library System.

GRAHAM LIBRARY
See: Jones and Laughlin Steel Corporation

★5168★
GRAIN PROCESSING CORPORATION - TECHNICAL INFORMATION CENTER, R&D (Sci-Tech)
1600 Oregon St.
Box 349
Muscatine, IA 52761
Phone: (319) 264-4389
Maurene Failor, Libn.
Staff: 2. **Subjects:** Paper technology, animal nutrition, antibiotics, protein, vitamins. **Holdings:** 1500 books; 1300 bound periodical volumes; 35 VF drawers of technical reports, patents, reprints. **Subscriptions:** 150 journals and other serials. **Services:** Interlibrary loans; copying; library open to public by request. **Computerized Information Services:** Computerized retrieval system. **Publications:** Bulletin, monthly - for internal distribution only. **Staff:** Dr. Donald L. Kiser, Supv.

GRAND CANYON RESEARCH LIBRARY
See: U.S. Natl. Park Service

★5169★
GRAND ENCAMPMENT MUSEUM, INC. - LIBRARY (Hist)
Encampment, WY 82325
Phone: (307) 327-5310
Vera Oldman, Pres., Musm.Corp.
Founded: 1967. **Staff:** 1. **Subjects:** Area history. **Special Collections:** Library of W.T. Peryam, a pioneer settler. **Holdings:** 100 books; 100 pamphlets (cataloged); 5 reels of microfilm of old area newspapers; pioneer oral history tapes; 1000 historical pictures; 100 historical manuscripts; file of

Saratoga Lyre, 1888; file of Grand Encampment Herald, 1898-1912; maps. **Services:** Library open to public with restrictions on a limited schedule. **Publications:** Museum Newsletter, annual.

GRAND FORKS ENERGY TECHNOLOGY CENTER LIBRARY
See: U.S. Dept. of Energy

★5170★
GRAND LODGE OF ANCIENT FREE AND ACCEPTED MASONS OF MARYLAND - LIBRARY (Rec)
225 N. Charles St.   Phone: (301) 752-1198
Baltimore, MD 21201
Staff: 2. **Subjects:** Freemasonry. **Holdings:** Figures not available. **Services:** Library open to public by request.

★5171★
GRAND LODGE OF FREE AND ACCEPTED MASONS OF CALIFORNIA - LIBRARY AND MUSEUM (Rec)
1111 California St.   Phone: (415) 776-7000
San Francisco, CA 94108   Robert A. Klinger, Grand Libn.
Founded: 1958. **Staff:** Prof 1; Other 9. **Subjects:** Freemasonry, freemasonry in California, philosophy, religion, history. **Special Collections:** Papers of Charles Albert Adams, founder of Public Schools Week; 200 volumes of archives, clippings, photographs, and documents of Masonic historical significance. **Holdings:** 10,000 books, 250 bound periodical volumes; 150 boxes of Masonic pamphlets, reports and proceedings of worldwide Masonic bodies. **Services:** Loans open to Freemasons only. Other scholars may use by special request.

★5172★
GRAND LODGE OF FREE AND ACCEPTED MASONS OF PENNSYLVANIA - LIBRARY (Rec)
Masonic Temple, 1 N. Broad St.   Phone: (215) 988-1933
Philadelphia, PA 19107   Frank W. Bobb, Libn. & Cur.
Staff: Prof 4. **Subjects:** Freemasonry. **Holdings:** 75,000 volumes. **Services:** Library open to public.

★5173★
GRAND LODGE OF IOWA, A.F. AND A.M. - IOWA MASONIC LIBRARY (Rec)
813 First Ave., S.E.
Box 279
Cedar Rapids, IA 52406   Phone: (319) 365-1438
     Tom Eggleston, Grand Sec.
Founded: 1845. **Staff:** Prof 2. **Subjects:** Freemasonry, literature, history, Iowa, biography, religion. **Special Collections:** Robert Burns; Abraham Lincoln; A.E. Waite. **Holdings:** 105,000 books; 7000 bound periodical volumes; pamphlets, clippings, autographs, certificates, documents and microfilms. **Subscriptions:** 250 journals and other serials. **Services:** Interlibrary loans; copying; research assistance for those who request it; library open to public. **Special Indexes:** Index Rerum (card). **Staff:** William Durow, Asst.Libn.

★5174★
GRAND LODGE OF MANITOBA, A.F. AND A.M. - MASONIC LIBRARY (Rec)†
Masonic Memorial Temple
420 Corydon Ave.   Phone: (204) 284-2423
Winnipeg, MB, Canada R3L 0N8   W.F.L. Hyde, Grand Libn.
Founded: 1896. **Staff:** 1. **Subjects:** Freemasonry and early history of Western Canada. **Holdings:** 2870 books; 58 bound periodical volumes; 86 tape recordings. **Services:** Interlibrary loans; copying; library open to public.

★5175★
GRAND LODGE OF MASSACHUSETTS, A.F. AND A.M. - LIBRARY (Rec)
Masonic Temple, 186 Tremont St.   Phone: (617) 426-6040
Boston, MA 02111   Roberta A. Hankamer, Libn.
Staff: Prof 1; Other 1. **Subjects:** Freemasonry and related subjects. **Holdings:** 60,000 volumes; 60 drawers of clippings and pamphlet material. **Subscriptions:** 100 journals and other serials. **Services:** Interlibrary loans; copying; library open to public for research only. **Publications:** Short list of books on Freemasonry.

★5176★
GRAND LODGE OF NEW YORK, F. AND A.M. - LIBRARY AND MUSEUM (Rec)
71 W. 23rd St.   Phone: (212) 741-4500
New York, NY 10010   Allan Boudreau, Dir. & Cur.
Founded: 1781. **Staff:** Prof 3; Other 3. **Subjects:** Freemasonry, New York history. **Special Collections:** Haywood Memorial (1000 items on religion); Abraham Felt Memorial (New York City history); local history; New York State county histories. **Holdings:** 60,000 books; 5000 bound periodical volumes;

100 VF drawers; 3000 manuscripts; photographs, slides, recordings, microfilms. **Subscriptions:** 120 journals and other serials. **Services:** Interlibrary loans; copying; library open to public for scholarly purpose - in-house use only. **Computerized Information Services:** Internal database. **Publications:** Empire State Mason (magazine); American Lodge of Research Transactions; Masonic Philatelist (magazine). **Special Indexes:** Lodges in New York State; Freemasons in the American Revolution. **Staff:** Allan Zweibach, Tech.Serv.; Aydin Y. Turkmen, Ref.Lib.

GRAND MARAIS LIBRARY
See: Cook County Historical Society

GRAND PORTAGE NATL. MONUMENT
See: U.S. Natl. Park Service

GRAND PRAIRIE COMMUNITY HOSPITAL
See: Dallas-Fort Worth Medical Center

★5177★
GRAND RAPIDS ART MUSEUM - MC BRIDE LIBRARY (Art)
155 N. Division   Phone: (616) 459-4676
Grand Rapids, MI 49503   Luci King, Lib.Chm.
Subjects: Art and art history. **Special Collections:** Publicity scrapbooks from 1911-1979. **Holdings:** 3527 volumes; brochures, catalogs, periodicals. **Subscriptions:** 27 journals and other serials. **Services:** Copying; library open to public for reference use only.

★5178★
GRAND RAPIDS LAW LIBRARY (Law)
200 Monroe, N.W., Suite 400   Phone: (616) 454-9493
Grand Rapids, MI 49503   Marjorie C. Wilcox, Exec.Dir.
Founded: 1887. **Staff:** 4. **Subjects:** Law. **Holdings:** 30,000 volumes; 2700 microfiche (1st Reporter Series); 200 Internal Revenue Service Letter Rulings. **Services:** Interlibrary loans; library not open to public. **Computerized Information Services:** WESTLAW. **Publications:** Newsletter, monthly.

★5179★
GRAND RAPIDS PRESS - REFERENCE LIBRARY (Publ)
Press Plaza, Vandenberg Ctr.   Phone: (616) 459-1474
Grand Rapids, MI 49502   Diane L. Wheeler, Libn.
Founded: 1963. **Subjects:** Newspaper reference topics. **Staff:** Prof 1; Other 5. **Holdings:** 250,000 files of clippings, pictures and veloxes. **Services:** Library open to public for reference use only.

★5180★
GRAND RAPIDS PUBLIC LIBRARY - FOUNDATION CENTER REGIONAL COLLECTION (Soc Sci)
60 Library Plaza, N.E.   Phone: (616) 456-4411
Grand Rapids, MI 49503   James Langmo, Ref.Libn.
Founded: 1973. **Subjects:** Private foundations. **Holdings:** IRS forms 990PF and 990AR for Michigan foundations on film; all publications of the Foundation Center, New York; Foundation Grants Index: Subjects, on film; complete set of Comsearch printouts (grant records by subject). **Services:** Collection open to public for reference use only. **Publications:** Bibliography.

★5181★
GRAND RAPIDS PUBLIC LIBRARY - FURNITURE DESIGN COLLECTION (Art)
60 Library Plaza, N.E.   Phone: (616) 456-4410
Grand Rapids, MI 49503   Lucija Skuja, Art Libn.
Subjects: Furniture history and design - all periods and styles. **Holdings:** 1500 books; 980 bound periodical volumes. **Subscriptions:** 8 journals and other serials. **Services:** Interlibrary loans; copying; collection open to public for reference use only upon request. **Publications:** Grand Rapids Public Library List of Books on Furniture, 1927, supplement 1954. **Remarks:** The collection of furniture books (housed in a separate room) is under the supervision of the Art Department. Since the city has been commonly recognized as the "Furniture Capital of America," the library has always taken a great interest in books on furniture. The figures given above are for the reference collection; the circulation department also has an outstanding collection on the subject.

★5182★
GRAND RAPIDS PUBLIC LIBRARY - MICHIGAN ROOM (Hist)
60 Library Plaza, N.E.   Phone: (616) 456-4424
Grand Rapids, MI 49503   Gordon Olson, Hd.
Staff: Prof 1; Other 1. **Subjects:** Michigan and Old Northwest history, genealogy, heraldry. **Holdings:** 14,000 books. **Subscriptions:** 100 journals and other serials. **Services:** Copying; library open to public for reference use only.

★5183★
GRAND SEMINAIRE DE MONTREAL - BIBLIOTHEQUE (Rel-Theol)
2065 Sherbrooke, W.
Montreal, PQ, Canada H3H 1G6
Phone: (514) 932-9918
Rev. Jacques Viger, S.S., Hd.Libn.
Staff: Prof 1; Other 1. **Subjects:** Religion (especially Bible), Church law and history, religious biographies, philosophy. **Special Collections:** Migne's Patrologies (378 volumes, in Greek and Latin). **Holdings:** 85,000 books; 16,000 bound periodical volumes. **Subscriptions:** 100 journals and other serials. **Services:** Interlibrary loans; copying; library open to public for reference use only. **Special Indexes:** Fichier Liturgique, Mont-Cesar Abbey (card). **Staff:** Laurette Allard .

★5184★
GRAND SEMINAIRE DES SAINTS APOTRES - BIBLIOTHEQUE (Rel-Theol)
130 Cathedrale
C.P. 430
Sherbrooke, PQ, Canada J1H 5K1
Phone: (819) 562-4552
Raynald Provencher, Sec.
Staff: 3. **Subjects:** Theology, religion, pastoral literature. **Special Collections:** J.P. Migne (412 volumes). **Holdings:** 28,000 books; archives; manuscripts. **Subscriptions:** 162 journals and other serials. **Services:** Interlibrary loans; copying; library open to public.

GRAND TETON NATL. PARK
See: U.S. Natl. Park Service

★5185★
GRAND VIEW COLLEGE - ARCHIVES (Area-Ethnic)†
1351 Grandview
Des Moines, IA 50316
Phone: (515) 263-2800
Thorvald Hansen, Archv.
Founded: 1896. **Staff:** Prof 1. **Subjects:** Danish-American church life, 1871-1962; Danish-American culture; Danish literature, 18th to 20th century. **Holdings:** 2500 volumes. **Services:** Interlibrary loans; copying; archives open to public. **Computerized Information Services:** Computerized cataloging. **Staff:** Barbara L. Burn, Libn.

★5186★
GRAND VIEW HOSPITAL - EDWARD F. BURROW MEMORIAL LIBRARY (Med)
700 Lawn Ave.
Sellersville, PA 18960
Phone: (215) 257-3611
Linda M. Beach, Med.Libn.
Staff: Prof 1. **Subjects:** Medicine, nursing, administration. **Holdings:** 500 volumes; 1100 bound periodical volumes; 2 VF drawers of pamphlets; 30 AV tapes; 1 VF drawer of bibliographies. **Subscriptions:** 40 journals and other serials. **Services:** Interlibrary loans; copying; library open to persons with referrals from medical and professional staff members. **Networks/Consortia:** Member of Delaware Valley Information Consortium (DEVIC). **Formerly:** Its Medical Resource Library.

★5187★
GRANDE PRAIRIE GENERAL HOSPITAL - LIBRARY (Med)†
10409 98th St.
Grande Prairie, AB, Canada T8V 2E8
S. Black, Libn.
Staff: Prof 1. **Subjects:** Medicine. **Holdings:** 200 books; 220 bound periodical volumes. **Subscriptions:** 21 journals and other serials. **Services:** Library not open to public.

★5188★
GRANDVIEW HOSPITAL - MEDICAL LIBRARY (Med)
405 Grand Ave.
Dayton, OH 45405
Phone: (513) 226-3379
Loma Pallman, Dir.
Staff: Prof 3; Other 1. **Subjects:** Medicine, nursing, hospital administration, allied health sciences. **Holdings:** 5200 books; 6500 bound periodical volumes. **Subscriptions:** 237 journals and other serials. **Services:** Interlibrary loans; copying; library not open to public. **Computerized Information Services:** MEDLINE, BRS. **Staff:** Candy Winteregg, Asst.Dir.

★5189★
GRANGE-FARM FILM FOUNDATION - LIBRARY (Agri; Aud-Vis)
1616 H St., N.W.
Washington, DC 20006
Phone: (202) 628-3507
Judy T. Massabny, Exec.Dir.
Founded: 1946. **Staff:** 3. **Subjects:** Agriculture. **Holdings:** 16mm films (90 titles). **Services:** Interlibrary loans. **Publications:** Annual list of available titles.

★5190★
GRANGER COLLECTION (Pict)
1841 Broadway
New York, NY 10023
Phone: (212) 586-0971
William Glover, Dir.
Founded: 1964. **Staff:** Prof 2; Other 3. **Subjects:** People, places, things and events of the past in pictures. **Holdings:** 2000 books; 1000 bound periodical volumes; 5 million prints, photographs, printed ephemera, color transparencies, woodcuts, engravings, movie stills and other graphics. **Subscriptions:** 40 journals and other serials. **Services:** Copying; illustrations available to publishers and other professional users of illustrations on a fee basis; open to professional users of illustrations. **Staff:** Erika Glover, Assoc.Dir.

★5191★
GRANT (Alexander) & COMPANY - CHICAGO OFFICE LIBRARY (Bus-Fin)
600 Prudential Plaza
Chicago, IL 60601
Phone: (312) 856-0200
Mary T.R. Mowery, Libn.
Staff: Prof 2. **Subjects:** Accounting and auditing, domestic and international tax. **Holdings:** Figures not available. **Subscriptions:** 88 journals and other serials; 10 newspapers. **Services:** Interlibrary loans; copying; SDI; library not open to public. **Computerized Information Services:** Online systems. **Staff:** Duane Wenzel, Asst.Libn.

★5192★
GRANT (Alexander) & COMPANY - NATIONAL OFFICE LIBRARY (Bus-Fin)
Prudential Plaza 3900
Chicago, IL 60601
Phone: (312) 856-0001
Nancy Wilkinson, Libn.
Staff: Prof 1. **Subjects:** Accounting, auditing, Securities and Exchange Commission regulations. **Holdings:** 1560 books; 3 bound periodical volumes. **Subscriptions:** 53 journals and other serials. **Services:** Interlibrary loans; library not open to public. **Computerized Information Services:** DIALOG, SDC, New York Times Information Service, National Automated Accounting Research System (NAARS).

★5193★
GRANT COUNTY HISTORICAL SOCIETY - LIBRARY (Hist)
Elbow Lake, MN 56531
Phone: (218) 685-4864
George M. Shervey, Pres.
Subjects: Local and state history; archeology. **Holdings:** 1000 books; microfilm of all Grant County, MN newspapers; biographies; 100 tape recordings of local people and events.

GRANT (David) MEDICAL CENTER
See: U.S. Air Force Hospital - David Grant Medical Center

★5194★
GRANT HOSPITAL OF CHICAGO - LIBRARY (Med)
550 W. Webster Ave.
Chicago, IL 60614
Phone: (312) 883-2230
Dalia S. Kleinmuntz, Lib.Dir.
Staff: Prof 1; Other 2. **Subjects:** Medicine, nursing, hospital administration. **Holdings:** 1600 books; 2500 bound periodical volumes. **Subscriptions:** 170 journals and other serials. **Services:** Interlibrary loans; copying; SDI; library open to public by special permission. **Computerized Information Services:** MEDLINE, BRS. **Networks/Consortia:** Member of Metropolitan Consortium; Regional Medical Library - Region 3; Rush Affiliates Information Network (RAIN); Chicago Library System. **Publications:** Newsletter, quarterly; serial list, annual; Annual Report.

★5195★
GRANT HOSPITAL - MEDICAL LIBRARY (Med)
309 E. State St.
Columbus, OH 43215
Phone: (614) 461-3467
Nancy Cohen, Med.Libn.
Founded: 1961. **Staff:** Prof 1; Other 1. **Subjects:** Medicine, nursing, and allied health sciences. **Holdings:** 5000 books; 5550 bound periodical volumes; audiotapes (cataloged); 3 VF drawers. **Subscriptions:** 215 journals and other serials. **Services:** Interlibrary loans; copying; bibliographic searches; library not open to public.

GRANT LAW LIBRARY
See: Scott County Bar Association

★5196★
GRAPHIC ARTS TECHNICAL FOUNDATION - E.H. WADEWITZ MEMORIAL LIBRARY (Sci-Tech)
4615 Forbes Ave.
Pittsburgh, PA 15213
Phone: (412) 621-6941
Janice L. Lloyd, Libn.
Founded: 1944. **Staff:** Prof 1; Other 1. **Subjects:** Printing processes, especially lithography; paper; ink; metal decorating; packaging; chemistry; physics; environmental control; safety and health; photography. **Holdings:** 2500 books; 2800 bound periodical volumes; 16 VF drawers of pamphlets and trade catalogs; 3 drawers of patents; 90,000 cataloged abstracts. **Subscriptions:** 240 journals and other serials; 5 newspapers. **Services:** Interlibrary loans; copying; literature searches; library open to public for reference use only. **Publications:** Graphic Arts Abstracts, monthly - to membership, some schools and associations. **Special Indexes:** Indexes to

Graphic Arts Abstracts 1972-1980, annual.

★5197★
GRAPHIC COMMUNICATIONS WORLD/TECHNICAL INFORMATION, INC. - LIBRARY (Publ; Sci-Tech)
Box 9500
Tallahassee, FL 32303
Phone: (904) 385-1131
A.E. Gardner, Libn.
Staff: Prof 4; Other 5. **Subjects:** Automated typesetting and photocomposition, printing industry technology, micrographics. **Subscriptions:** 150 journals and other serials. **Services:** Library open to subscribers. **Formerly:** Located in Tequesta, FL.

★5198★
GRATZ COLLEGE - ELSIE AND WILLIAM CHOMSKY EDUCATIONAL RESOURCE CENTER (CERC) (Educ; Area-Ethnic)
10th St. & Tabor Rd.
Philadelphia, PA 19141
Phone: (215) 329-3363
Eileen L. Samuelson, Coord.
Staff: Prof 1; Other 2. **Subjects:** Jewish history, holidays and customs; Hebrew language and literature; Bible; ethics; prayer. **Holdings:** 500 books; 12 VF drawers of instructional materials. **Services:** Copying; SDI; library open to public. **Publications:** CERC Newsletter, 2-3/year - to all Jewish religious school teachers in the Philadelphia area. **Special Indexes:** Subject, age and method index.

★5199★
GRATZ COLLEGE - LIBRARY (Educ)
10th St. & Tabor Rd.
Philadelphia, PA 19141
Phone: (215) 329-3363
Michael Grunberger, Libn.
Founded: 1895. **Staff:** 4. **Subjects:** Hebraica, Judaica, education. **Holdings:** 35,000 books; 1000 bound periodical volumes; 1000 pamphlets. **Subscriptions:** 100 journals and other serials. **Services:** Interlibrary loans; copying; bibliographic and reference services; library open to public. **Staff:** Eliezer Wise, Asst.Libn.; Eileen Samuelson, Asst.Libn.

GRAVES (Henry S.) MEMORIAL LIBRARY
See: Yale University - Forestry Library

GRAVES (L.M.) MEMORIAL LIBRARY
See: Harding Graduate School of Religion - L.M. Graves Memorial Library

GRAVES (Lulu G.) MEMORIAL LIBRARY
See: American Dietetic Association - Lulu G. Graves Memorial Library

GRAVES (Robert) ARCHIVES
See: University of Victoria - Mc Pherson Library - Special Collections

★5200★
GRAVURE RESEARCH INSTITUTE - LIBRARY (Sci-Tech)
22 Manhasset Ave.
Port Washington, NY 11050
Phone: (516) 883-6670
Harvey F. George, Res.Dir.
Subjects: Graphic arts technology; gravure processes and equipment; environmental control. **Holdings:** Figures not available. **Services:** Facility not open to public.

GRAY (Bowman) SCHOOL OF MEDICINE
See: Wake Forest University - Bowman Gray School of Medicine

★5201★
GRAY, CARY, AMES & FRYE - LAW LIBRARY (Law)
525 B St., Suite 2100
San Diego, CA 92101
Phone: (714) 236-1661
June F. Mac Leod, Law Libn.
Staff: Prof 1; Other 5. **Subjects:** Law. **Special Collections:** Annual reports; firm history. **Holdings:** 17,000 volumes. **Subscriptions:** 230 journals and other serials; 9 newspapers. **Services:** Copying (limited); library open to public by appointment. **Computerized Information Services:** LEXIS, NEXIS, New York Times Information Service, Disclosure, Inc.; computerized circulation. **Publications:** Monthly newsletter - for internal distribution only. **Special Catalogs:** Legal research memos (computer printout).

GRAY (Garland) RESEARCH CENTER & LIBRARY
See: Historic Lexington Foundation - Garland Gray Research Center & Library

GRAY HERBARIUM
See: Harvard University - Arnold Arboretum & Gray Herbarium

★5202★
GRAY PANTHERS - NATIONAL OFFICE LIBRARY (Soc Sci)
3635 Chestnut St.
Philadelphia, PA 19104
Jean G. Hopper, Libn.
Staff: Prof 1. **Subjects:** Aging - housing, health care, retirement and alternative work patterns, education, consciousness-raising; intergenerational programs - housing, education. **Holdings:** 150 boxes of clippings, government publications, and pamphlets. **Subscriptions:** 100 journals and other serials. **Services:** Copying; library open to public for reference use only.

★5203★
GRAY, PLANT, MOOTY, MOOTY, AND BENNETT - LAW LIBRARY (Law)†
300 Roanoke Bldg.
Minneapolis, MN 55402
Phone: (612) 343-2800
Annette Jenson, Libn.
Staff: 1. **Subjects:** Law, taxes. **Holdings:** 10,000 books; 300 bound periodical volumes; 35 loose-leaf services (cataloged); in-house brief and memoranda file. **Services:** Interlibrary loans; library not open to public. **Computerized Information Services:** LEXIS.

GRAYMOOR ECUMENICAL INSTITUTE
See: Friars of the Atonement

★5204★
GRAYS HARBOR COUNTY LAW LIBRARY (Law)†
Courthouse, 2nd Fl.
Montesano, WA 98563
Phone: (206) 249-4211
E. Urquhart, Libn.
Staff: Prof 1; Other 1. **Subjects:** Law. **Holdings:** 12,000 volumes. **Services:** Library open to public for reference use only.

★5205★
GREAT FALLS CLINIC - MEDICAL LIBRARY (Med)
1220 Central Ave.
Great Falls, MT 59401
Phone: (406) 454-2171
Bethel Bolstad, Libn.
Founded: 1928. **Staff:** 1. **Subjects:** Medicine and related fields. **Holdings:** 3212 volumes. **Subscriptions:** 87 journals and other serials. **Services:** Interlibrary loans; copying; library open to public with restrictions.

★5206★
GREAT FALLS GENEALOGY SOCIETY - LIBRARY (Hist)
Paris Gibson Sq.
1400 First Ave., N.
Great Falls, MT 59401
Phone: (406) 727-8255
Thelma L. Marshall, Libn.
Founded: 1975. **Staff:** 25. **Subjects:** Genealogy, local history. **Special Collections:** Census (210 reels of microfilm). **Holdings:** 2500 books; 500 unbound society publications; 200 telephone books. **Subscriptions:** 60 genealogy society exchanges. **Services:** Copying; seminars and training courses in genealogy conducted; library open to public for reference use only. **Publications:** Treasure State Lines, quarterly - by membership and exchange. **Special Indexes:** Surname index; Great Falls Tribune obituaries, 1976 to present; Cascade County Cemetery Records.

★5207★
GREAT LAKES BASIN COMMISSION - GREAT LAKES BASIN LIBRARY
3475 Plymouth Rd.
Box 999
Ann Arbor, MI 48106
Defunct. Merged with International Joint Commission - Great Lakes Regional Office Library.

★5208★
GREAT LAKES CHEMICAL CORPORATION - LIBRARY (Sci-Tech)
1975 Green Rd.
Ann Arbor, MI 48105
Phone: (313) 994-8000
Barbara V. Chandik, Info.Spec.
Staff: Prof 1. **Subjects:** Chemistry, polymer science, fire and flammability. **Holdings:** 1200 books; 1575 bound periodical volumes; 350 government reports. **Subscriptions:** 35 journals and other serials. **Services:** Library open to public with restrictions. **Computerized Information Services:** DIALOG. **Formerly:** Velsicol Chemical Corporation - Technical Information Center.

★5209★
GREAT LAKES COLLEGES ASSOCIATION - PHILADELPHIA URBAN SEMESTER - LIBRARY (Soc Sci)
1227-29 Walnut St.
Philadelphia, PA 19107
Phone: (215) 574-9490
Lisa M. Dyckman, Prog.Asst./Libn.
Founded: 1968. **Staff:** Prof 1. **Subjects:** Urban studies, experiential education, Philadelphia studies. **Holdings:** 2000 books. **Subscriptions:** 27 journals and other serials. **Services:** Interlibrary loans; copying; library open to public with restrictions. **Networks/Consortia:** Member of Great Lakes Colleges Association.

GREAT LAKES ENVIRONMENTAL RESEARCH LABORATORY LIBRARY
See: U.S. Natl. Oceanic & Atmospheric Administration

GREAT LAKES FISHERY LABORATORY
See: U.S. Fish & Wildlife Service - John Van Oosten Great Lakes Fishery Research Library

GREAT LAKES FOREST RESEARCH CENTRE
See: Canada - Canadian Forestry Service

★5210★
GREAT LAKES HISTORICAL SOCIETY - CLARENCE METCALF RESEARCH LIBRARY (Hist)†
480 Main St.   Phone: (216) 967-3467
Vermilion, OH 44089   Dr. Robert M. Hosler
Founded: 1953. **Staff:** 8. **Subjects:** Great Lakes - history, ship building, shipwrecks, shipping records, battle of Lake Erie in 1812, lighthouses, lifesaving service, ship log books. **Special Collections:** Great Lakes Historical Society Photo Collection; St. Clair Collection; Beeeson's, Greens, Red Book, Merchant Vessels of the U.S., and Lloyd's Registers Marine Directories. **Holdings:** 2500 books; 10,000 photographs; records of shipping firms; log books. **Services:** Library open to members only. **Publications:** Inland Seas, quarterly journal - mailed to society members; Chadburn Society newsletter.

GREAT LAKES LABORATORIES - LIMNOLOGY LIBRARY
See: SUNY - College at Buffalo

★5211★
GREAT LAKES MARITIME INSTITUTE - DOSSIN GREAT LAKES MUSEUM INFORMATION CENTER (Hist)
Belle Isle   Phone: (313) 824-3157
Detroit, MI 48207   John F. Polacsek, Cur.
Founded: 1960. **Staff:** Prof 2. **Subjects:** Great Lakes history, ship history, records, and plans. **Holdings:** 15,000 items including logs, corporate records, clippings, advertising, lithographs, and paintings of Great Lakes maritime subjects; 200 feet of shelving and 50 file drawers, 800 prints and negatives. **Services:** Inquiries answered if accompanied by self-addressed stamped envelope; center open to public by appointment. **Publications:** Telescope Magazine (Great Lakes history and current events), bimonthly - by subscription.

★5212★
GREAT LAKES RESEARCH CORPORATION - RESEARCH LIBRARY (Sci-Tech)
Box 1031   Phone: (615) 543-3111
Elizabethton, TN 37643   Joan Warden, Libn.
Founded: 1962. **Staff:** Prof 1. **Subjects:** Carbon and graphite technology. **Holdings:** 5250 books; 7000 bound periodical volumes; 4500 government publications; 42 VF drawers of reports, reprints, pamphlets. **Subscriptions:** 300 journals and other serials. **Services:** Interlibrary loans; copying; library not open to public.

GREAT PLAINS RESEARCH LIBRARY AND ARCHIVES
See: Museum of the Great Plains

★5213★
GREAT PLAINS ZOO - REFERENCE LIBRARY (Sci-Tech)
Sioux Falls Park & Recreation Dept.
600 E. 7th   Phone: (605) 339-7059
Sioux Falls, SD 57102   Keith Halverson, Zoo Dir.
Founded: 1966. **Subjects:** Natural history. **Special Collections:** The Royal Natural History; Zoo Yearbooks. **Holdings:** 125 books. **Services:** Library open to public for reference use only. **Remarks:** Maintained by Sioux Falls Park & Recreation Department.

GREAT SMOKY MOUNTAINS NATL. PARK
See: U.S. Natl. Park Service

★5214★
GREAT-WEST LIFE ASSURANCE COMPANY - LIBRARY (Bus-Fin)
60 Osborne St., N.   Phone: (204) 946-9225
Winnipeg, MB, Canada R3C 3A5   Mary F. Keelan, Sr.Libn.
Founded: 1928. **Staff:** 3. **Subjects:** Life and health insurance, insurance law, economics, business management, accounting, taxation. **Holdings:** 12,000 volumes; 40 files of clippings, pamphlets and reports. **Subscriptions:** 128 journals and other serials. **Services:** Interlibrary loans; copying; library open to public with restrictions.

★5215★
GREAT WESTERN SUGAR COMPANY - AGRICULTURAL RESEARCH CENTER - RESEARCH LIBRARY (Food-Bev; Agri)
11939 Sugarmill Rd.   Phone: (303) 776-1802
Longmont, CO 80501   James F. Gonyou, Dir.
Founded: 1910. **Subjects:** Plant breeding, plant physiology, agronomy, nematology, weed control, organic chemistry. **Holdings:** 650 books and bound serials; 5100 slides; 900 photographs. **Subscriptions:** 50 journals and other serials. **Services:** Interlibrary loans; copying; library open to public with prior approval of librarian or ARC Director.

★5216★
GREATER BALTIMORE MEDICAL CENTER - DR. JOHN E. SAVAGE MEDICAL STAFF LIBRARY (Med)
6701 N. Charles St.   Phone: (301) 828-2530
Baltimore, MD 21204   Michael Houck, Libn.
Founded: 1958. **Staff:** Prof 1; Other 1. **Subjects:** Medicine. **Holdings:** 900 books; 3000 bound periodical volumes; audiovisuals. **Subscriptions:** 165 journals and other serials. **Services:** Interlibrary loans; copying; library not open to public. **Computerized Information Services:** MEDLINE. **Networks/Consortia:** Member of Baltimore Consortia for Resource Sharing.

★5217★
GREATER DALLAS PLANNING COUNCIL - LIBRARY AND INFORMATION CENTER
Fidelity Union Tower, 16th Fl.
Dallas, TX 75201
Defunct

★5218★
GREATER EGYPT REGIONAL PLANNING AND DEVELOPMENT COMMISSION - LIBRARY-RESEARCH CENTER (Plan)†
Box 3160   Phone: (618) 549-3306
Carbondale, IL 62901   Kay Clary, Res.Anl.
Founded: 1961. **Staff:** 1. **Subjects:** Regional planning, social-economic development, criminal justice planning, water resources, zoning, housing. **Special Collections:** Local government and regional planning (64 VF drawers of material); Commission's publications collection (600 reports and special studies); federal government publications. **Holdings:** 6514 books and bound periodical volumes; 322 other cataloged items; 1500 maps (county, municipality, regional); 377 microfiche documents; 193 sets of slides, filmstrips, videotapes; 30 reels of 16mm films. **Subscriptions:** 152 journals and other serials; 11 newspapers. **Services:** Interlibrary loans; copying; library open to public for reference use only.

★5219★
GREATER LOS ANGELES ZOO ASSOCIATION - LIBRARY (Sci-Tech)
5333 Zoo Dr.   Phone: (213) 661-2184
Los Angeles, CA 90027   Ruth Anne Barton, Chm., Lib.Commn.
Founded: 1964. **Staff:** Prof 1; Other 5. **Subjects:** Mammals, birds, reptiles, amphibians, conservation, ecology. **Holdings:** 1300 books; 25 bound periodical volumes; 2 cabinets of unbound magazines and journals. **Subscriptions:** 15 journals and other serials. **Services:** Library open by special arrangement. **Formerly:** Its Andrew Norman Education Center. **Staff:** Kathryn Fine, Cat.

★5220★
GREATER MADISON CHAMBER OF COMMERCE - MATERIALS REFERENCE LIBRARY (Soc Sci)
Box 71   Phone: (608) 256-8348
Madison, WI 53701   Robert Brennan, Pres.
Subjects: Wisconsin legislature bills; information on Madison and Dane County. **Special Collections:** Telephone and city directories of selected major U.S. cities; census tract data; city and county demographic data; small business operation information. **Services:** Copying; library open to public. **Publications:** Greater Madison, monthly; Statistical Bulletin, semimonthly; Issues in Review (legislative information), monthly. **Remarks:** This library had been destroyed by fire in May of 1978 and is being reestablished at present.

★5221★
GREATER NEW YORK SAFETY COUNCIL, INC. - ACCIDENT PREVENTION REFERENCE LIBRARY†
989 Avenue of the Americas
New York, NY 10018
Founded: 1936. **Subjects:** Accident prevention; safety - home, school, public, recreation, industrial, traffic, transportation. **Holdings:** 750 books; 1800 pamphlets; 35 VF drawers; 123 films. **Remarks:** Presently inactive.

★5222★
GREATER SOUTHEAST COMMUNITY HOSPITAL - LURA HEALTH SCIENCES LIBRARY (Med)
1310 Southern Ave., S.E.
Washington, DC 20032
Phone: (202) 574-6793
Brenda Lewis, Chf.Libn.
Staff: Prof 2. **Subjects:** Medicine, nursing, general management. **Special Collections:** Patient Education Center (pamphlets and booklets on various diseases, 100 titles). **Holdings:** 2000 books; periodicals. **Subscriptions:** 175 journals and other serials. **Services:** Interlibrary loans; copying; library open to public for reference use only. **Computerized Information Services:** MEDLINE. **Networks/Consortia:** Member of Maryland and D.C. Consortium of Resource Sharing (MADCORS). **Staff:** Shirley Taylor, Co-Libn.

GREATER SYRACUSE COMMUNITY-GENERAL HOSPITAL
See: Community-General Hospital of Greater Syracuse

★5223★
GREATER VANCOUVER REGIONAL DISTRICT - LIBRARY (Plan)
2294 W. 10th Ave.
Vancouver, BC, Canada V6K 2H9
Phone: (604) 731-1155
Frances Christopherson, Libn.
Founded: 1970. **Staff:** Prof 1; Other 1. **Subjects:** Regional government. **Holdings:** 6000 books; 80 feet of unbound periodicals; annual reports; 60 feet of statistics; 12 VF drawers of pamphlets; 4 shelves of legislative material; 2 VF drawers of newspaper clippings; 18 VF drawers of publications of the district and its predecessor. **Subscriptions:** 274 journals and other serials; 24 newspapers. **Services:** Interlibrary loans; copying; library open to public with restrictions on loans. **Publications:** Accessions list, monthly. **Special Catalogs:** List of GVRD publications, revised semiannually. **Remarks:** Library is located at 2034 W. 12th Ave., Vancouver, BC V6J 2G2.

GREBEL (Conrad) COLLEGE
See: Conrad Grebel College

★5224★
GREELEY AND HANSEN - LIBRARY (Env-Cons)
222 S. Riverside Plaza
Chicago, IL 60606
Phone: (312) 648-1155
Elizabeth L. Ell, Libn.
Founded: 1914. **Staff:** Prof 1; Other 1. **Subjects:** Wastewater and water treatment, solid waste disposal, sewerage, flood control, hydraulics. **Holdings:** 6000 books; 300 bound periodical volumes; 10,000 in-house reports, drawings; 30,000 microforms; 1400 municipal annual reports. **Subscriptions:** 354 journals and other serials. **Services:** Interlibrary loans; copying; SDI; library open to public with restrictions. **Computerized Information Services:** DIALOG, SDC; computerized cataloging. **Networks/Consortia:** Member of OCLC through ILLINET; Metropolitan Chicago Library Assembly.

★5225★
GREELEY MUNICIPAL MUSEUM - LIBRARY (Hist)
Civic Ctr. Complex, 919 7th St.
Greeley, CO 80631
Phone: (303) 353-6123
Peggy A. Ford, Musm.Coord.
Founded: 1968. **Staff:** 3. **Subjects:** Greeley and Weld County history, biographies of early pioneers, Colorado history. **Special Collections:** Record books of the Union Colony (founding colony of Greeley). **Holdings:** 1000 books; 100 bound periodical volumes; Nunn newspaper for 29 years on microfilm; 28 scrapbooks of clippings, carded and cataloged; 5 VF drawers of manuscripts, clippings, maps, photographs. **Services:** Copying; library open to public with restrictions.

★5226★
GREELEY PUBLIC LIBRARY - SPECIAL COLLECTIONS (Hist; Area-Ethnic)
City Complex Bldg.
Greeley, CO 80631
Phone: (303) 353-6123
Esther Fromm, Archv./Dir., GPL
Staff: Prof 1; Other 3. **Subjects:** Germans from Russia - history, genealogy, personal reminiscences. **Holdings:** 1300 books; tapes; maps; newpapers on microfilm. **Services:** Interlibrary loans; copying; library open to public with identification card. **Formerly:** American Historical Society of Germans from Russia - Greeley Public Library. **Staff:** Shirley Soenksen, Ref.Libn.

GREELY (General A.W.) POLAR LIBRARY
See: National Geographic Society - Library

★5227★
GREEN BAY PRESS-GAZETTE - LIBRARY (Publ)
435 E. Walnut St.
Green Bay, WI 54305
Phone: (414) 435-4411
Diane L. Laes, Libn.
Founded: 1957. **Staff:** Prof 2. **Subjects:** Biography, newspaper reference topics. **Holdings:** 500 books; 50 other cataloged items; 8000 subject files; 15,000 biography files; 650 reels of microfilm; 18,000 negative files.

Subscriptions: 20 newspapers. **Services:** Copying; library open to public. **Remarks:** Maintained by Green Bay Newspaper Company. **Staff:** Jean Eggert, Photo.Libn.

GREEN (Cecil H.) LIBRARY
See: Stanford University

★5228★
GREEN CLINIC - LIBRARY (Med)†
709 S. Vienna St.
Box 310
Ruston, LA 71270
Phone: (318) 255-3690
Louise M. Allen, Libn.
Founded: 1955. **Staff:** Prof 1. **Subjects:** Internal medicine, surgery, pediatrics, obstetrics and gynecology, ophthalmology, otolaryngology, radiology, dentistry, adolescent medicine, urology, family practice. **Holdings:** 1160 books; 2378 bound periodical volumes; 962 bound single issues of hardbacked medical journals and yearbooks (cataloged); 50 volumes of unbound medical journals; 92 volumes of revisions for various specialties in binders; 1175 tapes; 4 VF drawers of unbound material. **Subscriptions:** 110 journals and other serials; 9 newspapers. **Services:** Copying; library open to public only when librarian is present; materials do not circulate.

GREEN (David W.) MEDICAL LIBRARY
See: Salem County Memorial Hospital - David W. Green Medical Library

GREEN (Francis Harvey) LIBRARY
See: West Chester State College - Francis Harvey Green Library

★5229★
GREEN GIANT/PILLSBURY COMPANY - LIBRARY
1100 N. 4th St.
Le Sueur, MN 56058
Defunct. Holdings absorbed by Pillsbury Company - Technical Information Center.

GREEN MEMORIAL LIBRARY
See: Gem Village Museum

★5230★
GREEN THUMB LIBRARY (Soc Sci)†
1401 Wilson Blvd., Suite 100
Arlington, VA 22209
Phone: (703) 276-0750
Fred Twombley, Sr.Adm.Asst.
Founded: 1975. **Subjects:** Employment, aging, rural development, management. **Holdings:** Congressional reports; 20 Senate hearings on aging; 1 film. **Services:** Library open to public with restrictions. **Formerly:** Located in Washington, DC.

★5231★
GREENBERG AND GLUSKER - LIBRARY (Law)
1900 Avenue of the Stars
Los Angeles, CA 90067
Lisa Winslow, Law Libn.
Staff: Prof 1; Other 1. **Subjects:** Law. **Holdings:** 15,000 books. **Subscriptions:** 200 journals and other serials. **Services:** Interlibrary loans; copying; library open to public with librarian's permission. **Computerized Information Services:** LEXIS.

GREENBLATT (Robert B.) LIBRARY
See: University of Florida - Center for Climacteric Studies - Robert B. Greenblatt Library

★5232★
GREENBRIER HISTORICAL SOCIETY - ARCHIVES (Hist)
North House, Church St.
Lewisburg, WV 24901
Phone: (304) 645-3503
Frances A. Swope, Archv.
Founded: 1963. **Subjects:** History of Greenbrier Valley area. **Special Collections:** Mrs. Alex McVeigh Miller Collection (dime novels from 1890s). **Holdings:** 438 titles; 40 periodicals; 6 VF drawers of manuscripts, clippings and pamphlets; 1 VF drawer of pictures. for sale to others; Harrison-Handley Map of Greenbrier County, 1887; Map of Lewisburg, 1880; Bicentennial Map of Greenbrier County, 1978 - all three for sale.

★5233★
GREENE COUNTY DISTRICT LIBRARY - GREENE COUNTY ROOM (Hist)
76 E. Market St.
Box 520
Xenia, OH 45385
Phone: (513) 376-2995
Julie M. Overton, Coord., Local Hist.
Staff: Prof 1; Other 14. **Subjects:** Local history and genealogy. **Special Collections:** William Galloway papers (4 feet); Fred C. Kelly papers (1 foot). **Holdings:** 1200 books; 107 bound periodical volumes; 607 reels of

microfilm; 60 cassette tapes of local history interviews. **Services:** Copying; room open to public. **Computerized Information Services:** Computerized cataloging. **Networks/Consortia:** Member of OCLC. **Publications:** Library Lights, weekly newspaper column.

★5234★
GREENE COUNTY HISTORICAL SOCIETY - LIBRARY AND MUSEUM (Hist)
R.F.D. 2   Phone: (412) 627-9513
Waynesburg, PA 15370   Kathryn Gooden, Libn.
Staff: Prof 1; Other 1. **Subjects:** Greene County and Western Pennsylvania history and genealogy; Union and Confederate armies. **Special Collections:** Greene County Cemetery Records; Shaker Material; War of the Rebellion; Greene County obituaries. **Holdings:** Figures not available. **Services:** Copying; library and museum open to public for reference use only (fee for nonmembers).

★5235★
GREENE COUNTY HISTORICAL SOCIETY - VEDDER MEMORIAL LIBRARY
(Hist)
R.D. 1, Box 10A   Phone: (518) 731-6822
Coxsackie, NY 12051   Raymond Beecher, Libn.
Founded: 1964. **Staff:** Prof 1; Other 1. **Subjects:** Greene County, The Catskills, mid-Hudson River Valley region. **Holdings:** Full figures not available; 1102 manuscript volumes; 29 VF drawers and 93 boxes of manuscripts; 8 boxes of postcards; county newspapers, 1792 to present; pictorial file. **Services:** Library open to public by appointment; closed winters. **Also Known As:** Bronck Museum Library.

★5236★
GREENE COUNTY LAW LIBRARY (Law)
Court House   Phone: (513) 376-5115
Xenia, OH 45385   Jill LeSourd, Libn.
Subjects: Law. **Holdings:** 27,000 volumes.

★5237★
GREENE COUNTY LAW LIBRARY (Law)†
Court House   Phone: (412) 852-1171
Waynesburg, PA 15370   Wanda B. Smith, Libn.
Founded: 1924. **Staff:** Prof 1. **Subjects:** Law. **Holdings:** 10,000 volumes. **Services:** Library open to public for reference use only.

GREENE COUNTY PUBLIC LIBRARY
See: Springfield-Greene County Public Libraries

★5238★
GREENE AND GREENE LIBRARY (Art)
David B. Gamble House
4 Westmoreland Pl.   Phone: (213) 793-3334
Pasadena, CA 91103   Mary Alice Waugh, Lib.Comm.Chm.
Founded: 1966. **Staff:** 8. **Subjects:** Architecture, Greene and Greene, craftsman period, Tiffany glass, arts and crafts. **Special Collections:** Drawings, blueprints, tissues, sketches and personal items of the Greene brothers. **Holdings:** 450 books; 125 bound periodical volumes; pamphlets and photographs (cataloged); 4 pamphlet file cabinets; 20 map case drawers of plans and drawings; 230 file boxes. **Services:** Copying; library open to students by appointment. **Remarks:** Library is maintained by the City of Pasadena and the University of Southern California School of Architecture.

★5239★
GREENE, MANN, ROWE, STANTON, MASTRY & BURTON - LIBRARY (Law)
1030 First Federal Bldg.   Phone: (813) 896-7171
St. Petersburg, FL 33701   Cindy Schartner, Libn.
Founded: 1935. **Staff:** 1. **Subjects:** Law. **Holdings:** 11,822 books; 200 bound periodical volumes; 700 research memoranda files. **Subscriptions:** 142 journals and other serials. **Services:** Library not open to public. **Computerized Information Services:** LEXIS.

GREENE MEMORIAL MUSEUM
See: University of Wisconsin, Milwaukee

GREENE (Stephen) MEMORIAL LIBRARY
See: Association of American Publishers - Publishing Education Information Service - Stephen Greene Memorial Library

GREENFIELD (Albert M.) LIBRARY
See: Philadelphia College of Art - Albert M. Greenfield Library

★5240★
GREENFIELD COMMUNITY COLLEGE   FOUNDATION - ARCHIBALD MAC LEISH COLLECTION (Hum)
One College Dr.   Phone: (413) 774-3131
Greenfield, MA 01301   Margaret E.C. Howland, Cur.
Founded: 1974. **Staff:** Prof 2. **Subjects:** Archibald MacLeish. **Special Collections:** Interviews with Archibald MacLeish, 1976-1981 (41 cassettes). **Holdings:** 178 books; 125 bound periodical volumes; 174 letters; 52 manuscripts; 264 nonprint items; 35 pamphlets; 104 posters; 24 photographs. **Services:** Copying; collection open to public by appointment. **Special Catalogs:** Bibliography of works by and about Archibald MacLeish (card). **Staff:** Carol G. Letson, Libn.

★5241★
GREENFIELD COMMUNITY COLLEGE - PIONEER VALLEY RESOURCE CENTER (Hist)
One College Dr.   Phone: (403) 774-3131
Greenfield, MA 01301   Carol G. Letson, Pioneer Valley Stud.Libn.
Founded: 1981. **Staff:** Prof 2. **Subjects:** Pioneer Valley of Western Massachusetts. **Special Collections:** Elmina Bennet Lee Collection, 1846-1885 (family history); Howes Photographic Collection, 1882-1907 (29 reels of microfilm, 200 prints); oral history (29 cassettes). **Holdings:** 807 books; 67 nonprint items. **Services:** Interlibrary loans; copying; center open to public.

GREENFIELD (Frederick William) YOUNG PEOPLE'S LIBRARY
See: 92nd Street Young Men's and Young Women's Hebrew Association - Buttenwieser Library

GREENFIELD LABORATORIES
See: Eli Lilly and Company

GREENFIELD VILLAGE
See: Henry Ford Museum and Greenfield Village

GREENLEY (Thomas D.) LIBRARY
See: SUNY - Agricultural and Technical College at Farmingdale - Thomas D. Greenley Library

GREENPOINT HOSPITAL AFFILIATION
See: Jewish Hospital and Medical Center of Brooklyn

★5242★
GREENSBORO DAILY NEWS AND RECORD - LIBRARY (Publ)
Box 20848   Phone: (919) 373-7044
Greensboro, NC 27420   R.L. Beall, Lib.Dir.
Staff: Prof 1; Other 2. **Subjects:** Newspaper reference topics. **Holdings:** Reference books; clippings; photographic negatives; microfilm. **Services:** Files not open to public.

★5243★
GREENSBORO HISTORICAL MUSEUM (Hist)
130 Summit Ave.   Phone: (919) 373-2043
Greensboro, NC 27408   William J. Moore, Dir. of Mus.
Staff: 9. **Subjects:** Local history. **Holdings:** 500 books; 13 VF drawers of archival material. **Services:** Open to outside users for reference use only upon application. **Publications:** Journal (newsletter).

★5244★
GREENSBORO HISTORICAL MUSEUM - ARCHIVES (Hist)
130 Summit Ave.   Phone: (919) 373-2043
Greensboro, NC 27408   Karen Carroll, Archv.
Founded: 1924. **Staff:** Prof 1. **Subjects:** O. Henry, Dolley Madison, decorative arts. **Holdings:** 500 linear feet of books; 100 linear feet of manuscripts; 4500 photographs; 100 state and local maps. **Services:** Copying; library open to public by appointment. **Publications:** Journal, bimonthly newsletter.

★5245★
GREENSBORO MASONIC MUSEUM LIBRARY (Rec)
426 W. Market St.
Box 466
Greensboro, NC 27402   Robert A. Pinnix, Cur.
Founded: 1932. **Staff:** 1. **Subjects:** Masonic history, papers and pamphlets; ancient Egyptian history. **Special Collections:** Masonic papers published by the Grand Lodge of A.F. & A.M. of North Carolina (1931 to present). **Holdings:** 500 volumes. **Services:** Library not open to public.

★5246★

GREENSBORO PLANNING & COMMUNITY DEVELOPMENT DEPARTMENT - LIBRARY (Plan)
Drawer W-2
Greensboro, NC 27402   Phone: (919) 373-2144
                              Arthur Davis, III, Data & Anl.Spec.
Staff: Prof 2. **Subjects:** Municipal planning and development. **Holdings:** 225 books; 100 bound periodical volumes. **Subscriptions:** 100 journals and other serials; 5 newspapers. **Services:** Copying; library open to public with restrictions. **Staff:** Rondal Alexander, Data Anl. Planner.

★5247★

GREENSBORO PUBLIC LIBRARY - BUSINESS LIBRARY (Bus-Fin)
201 N. Greene St.
Greensboro, NC 27402   Phone: (919) 373-2471
                              Ms. Lebby B. Lamb, Bus.Libn.
Founded: 1952. **Staff:** Prof 1. **Subjects:** Management, investment, automation, salesmanship, marketing, economics, real estate, taxes, accounting. **Holdings:** 12,000 books; 300 pamphlets; 1 VF drawer of government documents. **Subscriptions:** 400 journals and other serials. **Services:** Interlibrary loans; copying; library open to public. **Computerized Information Services:** Computerized cataloging, acquisitions and circulation. **Publications:** Bibliographies, irregular.

★5248★

GREENSFELDER, HEMKER, WIESE, GALE & CHAPPELOW - LIBRARY (Law)
1800 Equitable Bldg.
10 S. Broadway
St. Louis, MO 63102   Phone: (314) 241-9090
                              Helen R. Gibson, Libn.
Staff: Prof 1; Other 1. **Subjects:** Law - Missouri, Illinois, federal, corporate, tax, construction. **Holdings:** 5000 books; 100 bound periodical volumes. **Subscriptions:** 103 journals and other serials. **Services:** Interlibrary loans; copying; library open to public by recommendation of firm member. **Computerized Information Services:** LEXIS.

★5249★

GREENVALE EDITORIAL SERVICES, INC. - LIBRARY (Bus-Fin)
2 Haven Ave.
Port Washington, NY 11050   Phone: (516) 944-8066
                              Joan Casson Sauer, Libn.
Staff: Prof 1; Other 1. **Subjects:** Federal income and estate taxation, corporations, real estate, pensions, life insurance. **Holdings:** Figures not available. **Services:** Library not open to public. **Remarks:** Greenvale is a subsidiary of Prentice-Hall.

★5250★

GREENVILLE COUNTY PLANNING COMMISSION - PLANNING TECHNICAL LIBRARY (Plan)
Courthouse Annex, Box 1947
Greenville, SC 29602   Phone: (803) 298-8671
                              Robin Hughes Gordon, Econ. Planner
Founded: 1964. **Staff:** 1. **Subjects:** Urban planning, land use, housing, zoning, Greenville, South Carolina. **Holdings:** 6450 volumes; maps, aerial photographs, census data. **Subscriptions:** 30 journals and other serials. **Services:** Interlibrary loans; copying; library open to public for reference use only. **Publications:** Listing printout, quarterly.

★5251★

GREENVILLE GENERAL HOSPITAL - MEDICAL LIBRARY (Med)†
701 Grove Rd.
Greenville, SC 29605   Phone: (803) 242-8628
                              Susan Chappell, Med.Libn.
Staff: Prof 2; Other 1. **Subjects:** Medicine, nursing, allied health sciences, hospital administration. **Holdings:** 1300 books; 7500 bound periodical volumes; AV materials. **Subscriptions:** 225 serials. **Services:** Interlibrary loans; copying; library open to public during regular hours but only hospital personnel may check out materials. **Computerized Information Services:** NLM. **Remarks:** Greenville General Hospital also maintains branch libraries at Greenville Memorial Hospital, Roger C. Peace Institute of Rehabilitative Medicine and Marshall I. Pickens Psychiatric Hospital. **Staff:** Karen Wieckowski, Asst.Libn.

★5252★

GREENVILLE LAW LIBRARY (Law)
Court House
Greenville, OH 45331   Phone: (513) 548-1430
                              Helen V. Pierce, Libn.
Staff: 1. **Subjects:** Law. **Holdings:** 1100 books. **Services:** Copying; library open to public for reference use only.

★5253★

GREENVILLE MENTAL HEALTH CENTER - LIBRARY (Med)
715 Grove Rd.
Greenville, SC 29605   Phone: (803) 235-0184
                              Laura F. Pitzer, Libn.
Founded: 1969. **Staff:** Prof 1. **Subjects:** Mental health, psychiatry, psychology, counseling and therapy, social work. **Special Collections:** Pastoral Care Section - Psychiatry and Religion (75 volumes); Crisis Intervention. **Holdings:** 2600 books; 317 bound periodical volumes; 200 pamphlets and unbound periodicals (cataloged); 4 VF drawers of pamphlet material. **Subscriptions:** 73 journals and other serials. **Services:** Interlibrary loans; copying; library open to public for research only with prior arrangement with librarian. **Networks/Consortia:** Member of Southeastern Regional Medical Library Program (SERMLP).

★5254★

GREENVILLE TECHNICAL COLLEGE - LEARNING RESOURCES CENTER (Sci-Tech)
Box 5539
Greenville, SC 29606   Phone: (803) 242-3170
                              Martin R. Pautz, Dean, Lrng.Rsrcs.
Founded: 1962. **Staff:** Prof 4. **Subjects:** Technical, scientific and business education. **Holdings:** 35,000 books; 1200 bound periodical volumes; 2500 government documents; 186 state documents; 721 pamphlets; 5176 ERIC microforms. **Subscriptions:** 500 journals and other serials; 13 newspapers. **Services:** Interlibrary loans; library open to public with restrictions.

★5255★

GREENWICH HOSPITAL ASSOCIATION - GRAY CARTER LIBRARY (Med)
                              Phone: (203) 869-7000
Greenwich, CT 06830   Carmel Fedors, Lib.Mgr.
Staff: Prof 1; Other 1. **Subjects:** Medicine and related fields, nursing, hospital administration. **Holdings:** 1617 books; 1949 bound periodical volumes. **Subscriptions:** 190 journals and other serials. **Services:** Interlibrary loans; library open to public by appointment with approval. **Computerized Information Services:** MEDLARS, MEDLINE, BRS. **Networks/Consortia:** Member of Southwestern Library Council.

★5256★

GREENWICH LIBRARY - ORAL HISTORY PROJECT (Hist)
101 W. Putnam Ave.
Greenwich, CT 06830   Phone: (203) 622-7900
                              Katherine M. McLennan, Local Hist.Ref.Libn.
Founded: 1973. **Staff:** 30. **Subjects:** Local history. **Special Collections:** Transcriptions of oral history interviews (366); published edited transcriptions (82). **Holdings:** 629 oral history cassettes; 355 microfiche of transcriptions. **Services:** Interlibrary loans (limited to bound edited titles); copying; collection open to public with restrictions. **Special Indexes:** Composite index of all transcriptions.

★5257★

GREENWOOD PRESS - LIBRARY (Publ)
88 Post Rd., W.
Box 5007
Westport, CT 06881   Phone: (203) 226-3571
                              Mary Kalb, Info.Dir.
Subjects: Urban affairs. **Special Collections:** Urban Documents Microfiche Collection (21,000 local government documents from the United States and Canada). **Services:** Library not open to public. **Computerized Information Services:** Computerized Index to Current Urban Documents and an internal database of the more than 12,000 titles in print from Greenwood Press. **Publications:** Index to Current Urban Documents, quarterly with annual cumulation. **Remarks:** Greenwood Press is a division of Congressional Information Service, Inc. **Staff:** Mary Rose Denaro; Laura Kaminsky .

GREENWOOD SCHOOL MUSEUM
See: Coles County Historical Society

GREER MUSIC LIBRARY
See: Connecticut College

GRESSETTE LEARNING RESOURCE CENTER
See: Orangeburg-Calhoun Technical College

★5258★

GREY ADVERTISING, INC. - RESEARCH LIBRARY (Bus-Fin)†
777 3rd Ave.
New York, NY 10017   Phone: (212) 546-2000
                              Genette P. Lieb, Libn.
Founded: 1948. **Staff:** Prof 2; Other 1. **Subjects:** Advertising, marketing, retailing. **Holdings:** 500 books; 1000 bound periodical volumes; 300 directories; 300 VF drawers of reports and documents. **Subscriptions:** 250 journals and other serials; 10 newspapers. **Services:** Interlibrary loans to SLA members; library not open to public. **Computerized Information Services:** New York Times Information Service, DIALOG. **Staff:** Janet K. Barnett, Asst.Libn.

★5259★

GREYHOUND CORPORATION - LAW DEPARTMENT LIBRARY (Law)†
Greyhound Tower
111 W. Clarendon Ave.
Phoenix, AZ 85077
Phone: (602) 248-4000
Ms. E. Feltz, Law Dept.Adm.
Subjects: Law. **Holdings:** 3000 volumes. **Services:** Library not open to public.

★5260★

GREYHOUND CORPORATION - PATENT LAW DEPARTMENT LIBRARY (Law; Food-Bev)
Armour Research Center
15101 N. Scottsdale Rd.
Scottsdale, AZ 85260
Phone: (602) 998-6365
Frank T. Barber, Chf., Patent Counsel
Staff: Prof 2. **Subjects:** Meat products; dairy, poultry and edible oils; food processing and apparatus; grocery products; soaps and detergents; cosmetics. **Holdings:** 40,000 U.S. patents; 12,000 foreign patents, patent law, trademark and technical and scientific volumes. **Subscriptions:** 10 journals and other serials. **Services:** Library not open to public. **Computerized Information Services:** DIALOG, BRS, SDC, Pergamon International Information Corporation (PIIC). **Publications:** Patent Newsletter, monthly - for internal distribution only. **Special Indexes:** Uniterm Index to Chemical Patents; Derwent World Patents Index; U.S. Patent Indexes. **Staff:** Shirley C. Blazer, Patent Coord.

★5261★

GREYSTONE PARK PSYCHIATRIC HOSPITAL - HEALTH SCIENCE LIBRARY (Med)
Box A
Greystone Park, NJ 07950
Phone: (201) 538-1800
Brian C. Hamilton, Libn.
Founded: 1930. **Staff:** Prof 1; Other 1. **Subjects:** Psychiatry, psychiatric nursing, psychology, medicine. **Holdings:** 2245 books; 51 bound periodical volumes; 82 pamphlets; 34 other cataloged items; 123 microfiche. **Subscriptions:** 85 journals and other serials. **Services:** Interlibrary loans (fee); library open to public with permission. **Computerized Information Services:** NLM.

GRIES (Lucile Dauby) MEMORIAL LIBRARY
See: Cleveland Hearing and Speech Center - Lucile Dauby Gries Memorial Library

GRIES (Robert Hays) TOBACCO COLLECTION
See: Cleveland Public Library - John G. White Collection of Folklore, Orientalia, & Chess

GRIFFIN (Patrick Henry) SURGICAL LIBRARY
See: St. Louis University - Medical Center Library

GRIFFISS AIR FORCE BASE (NY)
See: U.S. Air Force Hospital - Medical Library (NY-Rome); U.S. Air Force - Rome Air Development Center

★5262★

GRIFFITH OBSERVATORY - LIBRARY (Sci-Tech)
2800 E. Observatory Rd.
Los Angeles, CA 90027
Phone: (213) 664-1181
Dr. E.C. Krupp, Dir.
Founded: 1934. **Subjects:** Astronomy, astrophysics, earth sciences, physical sciences. **Holdings:** 3300 books; 200 bound periodical volumes. **Subscriptions:** 20 journals and other serials. **Services:** Copying (limited); library not open to public. **Publications:** Griffith Observer, monthly - by subscription. **Remarks:** Maintained by City of Los Angeles.

GRINBERG (Sherman) FILM LIBRARIES, INC.
See: Sherman Grinberg Film Libraries, Inc.

GRISSOM AIR FORCE BASE (IN)
See: U.S. Air Force Base - Grissom Base Library

★5263★

GROLIER CLUB OF NEW YORK - LIBRARY (Rare Book; Hum)
47 E. 60th St.
New York, NY 10022
Phone: (212) 838-6690
Robert Nikirk, Libn.
Founded: 1884. **Staff:** Prof 2. **Subjects:** Bibliography, history of printing, book-collecting, bookselling, arts of the book. **Special Collections:** Early printing, historical and fine book bindings; private library catalogs; auction and bookseller catalogs. **Holdings:** 65,000 volumes; 1000 prints (largely portraits); bookplates. **Subscriptions:** 30 journals and other serials. **Services:** Library open to qualified scholars and collectors.

★5264★

GROLIER INCORPORATED - LIBRARY (Publ)
Sherman Tpk.
Danbury, CT 06816
Phone: (203) 792-1200
Chun Chuan Chang, Chf.Libn.
Staff: Prof 1; Other 1. **Subjects:** General reference. **Holdings:** 14,000 books. **Subscriptions:** 160 journals and other serials. **Services:** Library not open to public.

GROSS (Jenny) MEMORIAL LIBRARY
See: Adath Jeshurun Congregation - Jenny Gross Memorial Library

GROSSMAN (Jacob and Rose) LIBRARY
See: Hebrew College - Jacob and Rose Grossman Library

★5265★

GROUP HEALTH ASSOCIATION OF AMERICA, INC. - GERTRUDE STURGES MEMORIAL LIBRARY (Med; Soc Sci)
624 9th St., N.W.
Washington, DC 20001
Phone: (202) 737-4311
Nina M. Lane, Lib.Dir.
Founded: 1972. **Staff:** Prof 2; Other 1. **Subjects:** Health maintenance organizations, health insurance and administration, medical economics. **Holdings:** 2100 books. **Subscriptions:** 80 journals and other serials. **Services:** Interlibrary loans; copying; SDI; library open to public by appointment. **Computerized Information Services:** SDC, MEDLINE. **Networks/Consortia:** Member of District of Columbia Health Sciences Information Network (DOCHSIN). **Staff:** Anna T. Stocker, Lib.Res.Asst.

★5266★

GROUP HEALTH COOPERATIVE OF PUGET SOUND - MEDICAL LIBRARY (Med)
200 15th Ave., E.
Seattle, WA 98112
Phone: (206) 326-6093
Katherine Warren, Dir.
Founded: 1969. **Staff:** Prof 2; Other 3. **Subjects:** Clinical medicine, group medical plans, hospital administration, nursing. **Special Collections:** Audio-Digest tapes in major medical fields, 1972 to present; core collections for family practice in satellite clinics (14). **Holdings:** 4000 books; 2500 bound periodical volumes; 4 VF drawers of pamphlets; 4000 audiotape cassettes. **Subscriptions:** 410 journals and other serials. **Services:** Interlibrary loans; copying; library open occasionally to public by permission. **Computerized Information Services:** NLM, BRS. **Networks/Consortia:** Member of Seattle Area Hospital Library Consortium. **Remarks:** Branch Library at Eastside Hospital located at 2700 152nd N.E., Redmond, WA, 98052. **Staff:** Sherry Dodson, Libn.

★5267★

GROUT MUSEUM OF HISTORY AND SCIENCE - GENEALOGY, ARCHIVES AND REFERENCE LIBRARY (Hist; Sci-Tech)
503 South St.
Waterloo, IA 50701
Phone: (319) 234-6357
Mary B. Miller, Archv.
Founded: 1956. **Staff:** Prof 1; Other 1. **Subjects:** Genealogy, area histories. **Special Collections:** Rare books of area history, Indians, Civil War; books by Iowa authors; Iowa school book collection. **Holdings:** 1800 books; 250 bound periodical volumes; 3000 clippings; 1500 archival items; 950 photographs. **Services:** Copying; library open to public for reference use only.

GROVE (V.G.) RESEARCH LIBRARY OF MATHEMATICS-STATISTICS
See: Michigan State University - V.G. Grove Research Library of Mathematics-Statistics

GROW (Malcolm) MEDICAL CENTER
See: U.S. Air Force Hospital - Malcolm Grow Medical Center

★5268★

GRUMMAN AEROSPACE CORPORATION - TECHNICAL INFORMATION CENTER (Sci-Tech)
Plant 35
Bethpage, NY 11714
Phone: (516) 575-3912
Royal Scheiman, Chf.Libn.
Founded: 1955. **Staff:** Prof 5; Other 9. **Subjects:** Aerospace technology, electrical engineering, physics, mathematics, management. **Holdings:** 19,000 books; 11,500 bound periodical volumes; 32,000 other cataloged items; 100,000 technical reports; 650,000 microfiche, 750 reels of microfilm. **Subscriptions:** 500 journals and other serials; 5 newspapers. **Services:** Interlibrary loans; copying; SDI; library not open to public. **Computerized Information Services:** Online systems; computerized serials and circulation. **Special Catalogs:** Computer-printed periodical list. **Staff:** John Burden, Per.Libn.; Robert Jenkins, Cat.; Teresa Wilkins, Ref.Libn.; Joan Clemens, Retrieval Libn.

GRUND (Henry J.) LIBRARY
See: Library of Henry J. Grund

GRUNER (Heinz) LIBRARY
See: American Society of Photogrammetry

★5269★
GRUY (H.J.) & ASSOCIATES, INC. - LIBRARY (Energy)
150 W. Carpenter Fwy.   Phone: (214) 659-3200
Irving, TX 75062   Nancy Cooper, Dir., Lib./Info.Serv.
Staff: Prof 2. **Subjects:** Petroleum engineering, geology, energy, economics.
Holdings: 7000 books. **Subscriptions:** 200 journals and other serials.
Computerized Information Services: SDC, DIALOG; computerized serials
and map cataloging. **Staff:** Leo Papa, Libn.

GS & T CORPORATE ENGINEERING LIBRARY
See: Gulf Oil Corporation

★5270★
GTE AUTOMATIC ELECTRIC - LIBRARY (Sci-Tech)
400 N. Wolf Rd., A-6
Box 2317   Phone: (312) 681-7118
Northlake, IL 60164   Jane Yu Lee, Libn.
Founded: 1962. **Staff:** Prof 1; Other 1. **Subjects:** Mathematics, electronics,
telephony, electricity, radio, computers. **Holdings:** 5000 books; 700 bound
periodical volumes; other unbound periodicals, government reports,
pamphlets, standards and translations. **Subscriptions:** 265 journals and other
serials. **Services:** Interlibrary loans; copying (internal only); library not open to
public. **Computerized Information Services:** DIALOG. **Publications:** Library
Bulletin.

★5271★
GTE - COMMUNICATION SYSTEMS DIVISION - MAIN LIBRARY (Sci-Tech)
77 A St.   Phone: (617) 449-2000
Needham Heights, MA 02194   Michael D. Snow, Supv., Lib.Serv.
Founded: 1952. **Staff:** Prof 3; Other 2. **Subjects:** Electronics, electronic
devices, communications, antennas, detection systems, countermeasures,
command and control systems, computer and data processing systems,
physics, mathematics. **Holdings:** 12,000 books; 3500 bound periodical
volumes; 12,000 technical reports. **Subscriptions:** 350 journals and other
serials. **Services:** Interlibrary loans; library open to public by appointment.
Computerized Information Services: DIALOG; internal database. **Networks/
Consortia:** Member of Wellesley-Lexington Area Consortium of Libraries
(WELEXACOL). **Also Known As:** General Telephone and Electronics
Corporation. **Staff:** Jean King, Acq.Libn.; Ruth Ann Donaldson, Doc.Libn.

★5272★
GTE LABORATORIES - LIBRARY (Sci-Tech)
40 Sylvan Rd.   Phone: (617) 890-8460
Waltham, MA 02254   David R. Jelley, Hd.Libn.
Founded: 1971. **Staff:** Prof 4; Other 5. **Subjects:** Communication,
semiconductors and solid state, telecommunications, materials analysis, life
sciences. **Holdings:** 35,000 volumes. **Subscriptions:** 650 journals and other
serials; 7 newspapers. **Services:** Interlibrary loans; copying; SDI; library open
to public upon request. **Computerized Information Services:** DIALOG, SDC,
BRS; computerized cataloging, acquisitions, serials and circulation. **Special
Catalogs:** Catalog of journals; book catalog.

★5273★
GTE LENKURT, INC. - TECHNICAL LIBRARY, M679 (Sci-Tech)†
1105 County Rd., MS-M679
San Carlos, CA 94070   Patrick R. Marshment, Tech.Libn.
Founded: 1952. **Staff:** Prof 1; Other 2. **Subjects:** Telecommunications, radio
communication, microwaves, optical communication. **Special Collections:**
Patent collection (indexed by subject); major telecommunications &
electronics serials; foreign telecommunications serials. **Holdings:** 12,000
books; 1300 bound periodical volumes; 19 VF drawers of patents; 26 VF
drawers of unbound reports; 6 VF drawers of pamphlets. **Subscriptions:** 316
journals and other serials; 13 newspapers. **Services:** Interlibrary loans;
copying; library open with permission of librarian. **Computerized Information
Services:** DIALOG. **Networks/Consortia:** Member of CIN; CLASS.
Publications: Lenkurt Library Newsletter, monthly - for internal distribution
only. **Special Catalogs:** Subject catalog to patents (card); catalog to
standards & specifications (card). **Staff:** Mary Vandever, Asst.Tech.Libn.

★5274★
**GTE PRODUCTS CORPORATION - SYLVANIA SYSTEMS GROUP -
WESTERN DIVISION - LIBRARY (Sci-Tech)**
Box 188   Phone: (415) 966-3082
Mountain View, CA 94042   Julie del Fierro, Lib.Serv.Supv.
Founded: 1952. **Staff:** Prof 2; Other 3. **Subjects:** Communications, physics,
electronics, mathematics. **Special Collections:** Military specifications and
standards; vendors' catalogs. **Holdings:** 10,000 books; 25,000 technical
reports (cataloged). **Subscriptions:** 400 journals and other serials. **Services:**
Interlibrary loans; copying; library not open to public. **Computerized
Information Services:** DIALOG, SDC. **Networks/Consortia:** Member of
CLASS; CIN.

★5275★
GTE SYLVANIA - ENGINEERING LIBRARY (Sci-Tech)
100 Endicott St.   Phone: (617) 777-1900
Danvers, MA 01923   Mildred A. McKenna, Libn.
Staff: Prof 1. **Subjects:** Engineering, lighting. **Holdings:** 8000 volumes; 1976
journals on microfilm. **Subscriptions:** 175 journals and other serials.
Services: Interlibrary loans; copying; SDI; library not open to public.

★5276★
GUADALUPE MEDICAL CENTER - MEDICAL STAFF LIBRARY (Med)
2430 W. Pierce St.   Phone: (505) 887-6633
Carlsbad, NM 88220   Dorothy Eswein, Med.Rec.Dir./Libn.
Staff: Prof 1; Other 1. **Subjects:** Medicine and allied health sciences.
Holdings: 562 books; 212 bound periodical volumes; 5 VF drawers of
Pediatric Notes; 51 VF drawers of medical journals. **Subscriptions:** 17
journals and other serials. **Services:** Interlibrary loans (fee); copying; library
not open to public. **Special Indexes:** Attrition book and card indexes by title
and author.

★5277★
GUAM MEMORIAL HOSPITAL AUTHORITY - MEDICAL LIBRARY (Med)
Box AX   Phone: (717) 646-5801
Agana, GU 96910   Juliana C. Salumbides, Med.Libn.
Staff: Prof 1. **Subjects:** Medicine, nursing, hospital administration. **Special
Collections:** Health and Medicine in Guam and Micronesia (2 VF drawers).
Holdings: 1400 books; 551 bound periodical volumes; Audio-Digest tapes -
896 reel-to-reel, 3359 cassette; 2 VF drawers of pamphlets. **Subscriptions:**
68 journals and other serials. **Services:** Interlibrary loans; copying; library
open to public for reference use only. **Networks/Consortia:** Member of
Pacific Southwest Regional Medical Library Service (PSRMLS). **Special
Indexes:** Health & Medicine in Guam & Micronesia (list and cards).

★5278★
GUAM TERRITORIAL LAW LIBRARY (Law)
141 San Ramon Rd.   Phone: (671) 477-7623
Agana, GU 96910   Colette H. Gomoto, Law Libn.
Staff: Prof 1. **Subjects:** Law. **Holdings:** 15,000 books; 100 bound periodical
volumes. **Subscriptions:** 80 journals and other serials. **Services:** Copying;
SDI; library open to public.

★5279★
GUEDEL MEMORIAL ANESTHESIA CENTER - LIBRARY (Med)
2395 Sacramento St.
Box 7999
San Francisco, CA 94120   Harold R. Gibson, Libn.
Staff: Prof 1. **Subjects:** Anesthesiology. **Holdings:** 762 books; 385 bound
periodical volumes; 623 cassette tapes; exhibits, artifacts. **Subscriptions:** 25
journals and other serials. **Services:** Interlibrary loans; copying; library open to
anesthesiologists and members.

★5280★
GUERNSEY COUNTY LAW LIBRARY (Law)
Court House
Cambridge, OH 43725   Phone: (614) 439-3916
                    Frank C. Leyshon, Libn.
Staff: Prof 1; Other 1. **Subjects:** Law. **Holdings:** 8000 books; 500 bound
periodical volumes. **Services:** Copying; library open to public with restrictions.

★5281★
GUGGENHEIM (Solomon R.) MUSEUM - LIBRARY (Art)†
1071 5th Ave.   Phone: (212) 860-1338
New York, NY 10028   Sonja Bay, Libn.
Founded: 1953. **Staff:** 1. **Subjects:** Painting and sculpture of the 20th
century. **Holdings:** 30,000 books; 1260 bound periodical volumes; 50,000
file folders of pamphlets; 2500 slides; 300 tapes. **Subscriptions:** 50 journals
and other serials. **Services:** Interlibrary loans; copying; library open to public
by appointment. **Staff:** Mrs. Marion Wolf, Assoc.Libn.

GUIDANCE AND CONTROL INFORMATION ANALYSIS CENTER
See: IIT Research Institute

★5282★
GUILD OF BOOK WORKERS - LIBRARY (Publ)
Boston Athenaeum
10 1/2 Beacon St.   Phone: (617) 227-0270
Boston, MA 02108   Stanley Ellis Cushing, Lib.Chm.
Staff: Prof 1; Other 1. **Subjects:** Bookbinding, history of the book, calligraphy, printing, paper making. **Holdings:** 500 books. **Services:** Library not open to public.

★5283★
GUILD OF CARILLONNEURS IN NORTH AMERICA - ARCHIVES (Mus)
900 Burton Memorial Tower
University of Michigan   Phone: (313) 764-2539
Ann Arbor, MI 48109   William De Turk, Archv.
Founded: 1936. **Staff:** Prof 1. **Subjects:** Carillons, chimes, campanology. **Holdings:** 8 VF drawers of archives, tapes, records, books. **Services:** Archives not open to public but information can be obtained by contacting archivist. **Publications:** Newsletter, semiannual; Bulletin, annual.

GUILD OF ST. LUKE BIOETHICS COLLECTION
See: Boston College - School of Nursing Library

GUILFORD CENTER LIBRARY
See: Western Electric Company, Inc.

★5284★
GUILFORD COLLEGE - LIBRARY - SPECIAL COLLECTIONS (Educ)
5800 W. Friendly Ave.   Phone: (919) 292-5511
Greensboro, NC 27410   Dr. Herbert Poole, Dir.
Founded: 1837. **Special Collections:** Friends Historical Collection (original records and minutes of the Society of Friends in North Carolina); science fiction; American Revolution; North Caroliniana. **Holdings:** 145,000 books; 14,500 bound periodical volumes; 11,500 microforms; 12,000 AV materials; 9000 pamphlets. **Subscriptions:** 897 journals and other serials; 20 newspapers. **Services:** Interlibrary loans; copying; media production; library open to public with restrictions. **Networks/Consortia:** Member of Greensboro Regional Consortium. **Publications:** Occasional papers; The Southern Friend: Journal of the North Carolina Friends Historical Society. **Staff:** Damon D. Hickey, Assoc.Lib.Dir./Cur.; Carole Treadway, Quaker Bibliog.

★5285★
GUILFORD KEEPING SOCIETY, INC. - LIBRARY (Hist)
171 Boston St.
Box 363   Phone: (203) 453-3176
Guilford, CT 06437   Joel Helander, Lib.Comm.Chm.
Founded: 1947. **Subjects:** Local history. **Holdings:** 100 books; 1000 photographs; town documents, maps, letters, deeds. **Remarks:** Library is housed in the Guilford Public Library.

★5286★
GUILFORD TECHNICAL INSTITUTE - LEARNING RESOURCE CENTER (Educ)
Box 309   Phone: (919) 292-1101
Jamestown, NC 27282   Mertys W. Bell, Dean, LRC
Founded: 1963. **Staff:** Prof 10; Other 7. **Subjects:** Technology, vocational education, commercial art, nursing, dental technology, business, engineering, aviation, criminal justice, architecture, child care, electronics, fire science. **Holdings:** 42,684 books; 989 bound periodical volumes; 16 VF drawers of clippings and pamphlets; 8 VF drawers of archives; 7765 films, filmstrips, tapes, recordings, slides and transparencies; 2867 microforms. **Subscriptions:** 473 journals and other serials; 20 newspapers. **Services:** Interlibrary loans; copying; media production; library open to public. **Networks/Consortia:** Member of Central Piedmont Consortium of Community Colleges and Technical Institutes. **Publications:** LRC Handbook, annual; List of AV Materials; Periodicals List, annual - all distributed to faculty and students; Faculty Guide to LRC. **Staff:** Thomasine C. Gant, Coord., Instr.Serv.; A. Beverley Gass, Coord., Lib.Serv.; Lytton T. Barker, Tech.Serv.Libn.; John B. Mann, Coord., AV Serv.; Mary Breeze, Team Ldr., Career Ctr.

GUILFORD TOWNSHIP HISTORICAL COLLECTION
See: Plainfield Public Library

★5287★
GUITAR FOUNDATION OF AMERICA - ARCHIVE (Mus)
Wisconsin Conservatory of Music
1584 N. Prospect Ave.
Milwaukee, WI 53202   George Lindquist, Assoc.Archv.
Staff: 2. **Subjects:** Guitar music. **Holdings:** 36 volumes; 2500 scores; 7 dissertations on the guitar; 1 VF drawer of information on guitarists and the guitar; 2 VF drawers of modern guitar music. **Services:** Copying; library open to public. **Computerized Information Services:** Computerized cataloging. **Remarks:** Mail orders are handled at above address; acquisition and cataloging are done by Dr. Thomas Heck of Ohio State University Music Library, 1813 N. High St., Columbus, OH, 43210; (614) 422-2310.

★5288★
GULF CANADA LIMITED - CENTRAL LIBRARY (Sci-Tech; Bus-Fin; Energy)
800 Bay St.
Sta. A, P.O. Box 460   Phone: (416) 924-4141
Toronto, ON, Canada M5W 1E5   Wendy A. Davis, Sr.Libn.
Staff: Prof 3; Other 2. **Subjects:** Energy, petroleum industry, business economics, marketing, personnel development, industrial hygiene and safety, public relations, environmental studies. **Holdings:** 7500 books; 75 bound periodical volumes; archives; 3000 annual reports and pamphlets (cataloged); 600 reels of microfilm; 4000 microfiche. **Subscriptions:** 780 journals and other serials; 35 newspapers. **Services:** Interlibrary loans; copying; library open to public for reference use only, by appointment. **Computerized Information Services:** Online systems; computerized cataloging and acquisitions (serials). **Publications:** Central Library Newsletter - for internal distribution only. **Special Catalogs:** Catalog of archive material; catalog of internally produced publications. **Staff:** Patricia Hrycyna, Per.Libn.; Roni Epstein, Bus.Info.Libn.; Jean Tepper, Lib.Asst.

★5289★
GULF CANADA LIMITED - LIBRARY (Energy)
P.O. Box 130   Phone: (403) 233-3804
Calgary, AB, Canada T2P 2H7   Ms. S. Crozier-Parkinson, Sr.Libn.
Staff: Prof 2; Other 2. **Subjects:** Petroleum industry, petroleum engineering, geology, exploration, production, marketing. **Holdings:** 15,000 volumes; 4800 reports; 6000 maps. **Subscriptions:** 375 journals and other serials. **Services:** Interlibrary loans; copying; library open to public with approval from management. **Computerized Information Services:** SDC, Info Globe. **Publications:** Acquisition list, monthly.

★5290★
GULF CANADA LIMITED - RESEARCH & DEVELOPMENT DEPARTMENT - LIBRARY (Sci-Tech)
2489 N. Sheridan Way
Sheridan Park   Phone: (416) 822-6770
Mississauga, ON, Canada L5K 1A8   Ann Neilson, Libn.
Staff: Prof 2; Other 1. **Subjects:** Petroleum and energy technology, analytical chemistry. **Holdings:** 5200 books; 1793 bound periodical volumes; 2600 reels of microfilm; 24,000 microfiche; 24 VF drawers. **Subscriptions:** 323 journals and other serials. **Services:** Interlibrary loans; copying; SDI; library open to public by arrangement. **Computerized Information Services:** Online systems. **Networks/Consortia:** Member of Sheridan Park Association. **Publications:** Acquisitions list, monthly - for internal distribution only. **Special Indexes:** Miscellaneous KWIC indexes (computer printout). **Staff:** R.E. Metcalfe, Info. Chemist.

★5291★
GULF COAST BIBLE COLLEGE - CHARLES EWING BROWN LIBRARY (Rel-Theol)
Box 7889   Phone: (713) 862-3800
Houston, TX 77270   Ronald W. Kriesel, Hd.Libn.
Founded: 1953. **Staff:** Prof 2; Other 4. **Subjects:** Bible, theology, Christian education, music, professional ministries, pre-nursing. **Holdings:** 37,048 books; 1025 bound periodical volumes; 1500 pamphlets; 15,679 microforms; 13,066 microbooks; 492 audio cassettes; 389 filmstrips. **Subscriptions:** 243 journals and other serials; 5 newspapers. **Services:** Copying (limited); library open to public with restrictions. **Remarks:** Library is located at 911 W. 11th St., Houston, TX 77008. **Staff:** Ruth Kirks, Asst.Libn.

★5292★
GULF COAST RESEARCH LABORATORY - GORDON GUNTER LIBRARY (Sci-Tech)
Phone: (601) 875-2244
Ocean Springs, MS 39564   Malcolm S. Ware, Sr.Libn.
Founded: 1947. **Staff:** Prof 1; Other 2. **Subjects:** Marine sciences, including biology, microbiology, physiology, parasitology, geology, chemistry, botany, ecology, oceanography, zoology, toxicology; fisheries research and

management. **Special Collections:** Piatt Collection/Embryology (3775 papers); Gunter Collection/Marine Biology (2700 papers); Bennett Collection/Marine Invertebrates (2000 papers). **Holdings:** 15,000 books; 3000 bound periodical volumes; 14 journal titles on microfilm; 45 journal titles on microcard; 30,000 reprints (accessioned or cataloged). **Subscriptions:** 310 journals and other serials. **Services:** Interlibrary loans; copying (limited); library open to public for reference use only. **Networks/Consortia:** Member of Gulf Coast Biomedical Library Consortium; International Association of Marine Science Libraries and Information Centers; Coastal Mississippi Library Cooperative. **Publications:** Gulf Research Reports, irregular - exchange basis; Marine Briefs, quarterly - mailing list basis.

★5293★
GULF COAST WASTE DISPOSAL AUTHORITY - RESEARCH AND DEVELOPMENT LIBRARY
910 Bay Area Blvd.
Houston, TX 77058
Defunct

★5294★
GULF COMPANIES - LAW LIBRARY (Law)
Box 4553　　　　　　　　　　　　Phone: (713) 754-3172
Houston, TX 77210　　　　　Frederick A. Riemann, Law Libn.
Founded: 1933. **Staff:** Prof 2; Other 2. **Subjects:** Law, foreign law. **Holdings:** 30,000 books; 1000 bound periodical volumes; 200 cassette tapes. **Subscriptions:** 500 journals and other serials; 10 newspapers. **Services:** Interlibrary loans (fee); library open to public by appointment. **Computerized Information Services:** LEXIS; computerized cataloging. **Publications:** Acquisitions List, monthly - for internal distribution only. **Staff:** S. Gail Sisson, Asst.Libn.

GULF MINERAL RESOURCES COMPANY
See: Gulf Oil Corporation

★5295★
GULF OIL CHEMICALS COMPANY - CHEMICAL INFORMATION CENTER (Bus-Fin)
Box 3766
Houston, TX 77001
Joel A. Beale, Libn.
Staff: Prof 1; Other 2. **Subjects:** Business, chemicals, marketing. **Holdings:** 4000 books; 300 periodical volumes on microfiche; company annual reports. **Subscriptions:** 250 journals and other serials; 12 newspapers. **Services:** Interlibrary loans; SDI; library open to public by appointment. **Computerized Information Services:** Online systems; computerized circulation. **Publications:** What's New, monthly. **Formerly:** Its Business Information Center.

★5296★
GULF OIL CHEMICALS COMPANY - POLYMER RESEARCH LIBRARY (Sci-Tech)
Box 79070　　　　　　　　　　　Phone: (713) 754-7421
Houston, TX 77079　　　　　　R.C. Sartorius, Info.Anl.
Founded: 1976. **Staff:** Prof 1; Other 1. **Subjects:** Chemistry. **Holdings:** 6000 books; 500 bound periodical volumes; 1000 unbound periodicals; 1600 microforms; archive boxes, files. **Subscriptions:** 103 journals and other serials. **Services:** Interlibrary loans; copying; SDI; library not open to public. **Computerized Information Services:** Online systems. **Formerly:** Its Houston Research Library. **Staff:** J.N. Carrol, Asst.

★5297★
GULF OIL CORPORATION - BUSINESS RESEARCH LIBRARY (Bus-Fin; Energy)
Box 1166　　　　　　　　　　　Phone: (412) 263-6040
Pittsburgh, PA 15230　　　　Phyllis McCanna, Lib.Supv.
Founded: 1978. **Staff:** Prof 2; Other 6. **Subjects:** Petroleum, economics, energy, management, business, finance. **Special Collections:** Microfiche collection of 10K reports of corporations on the New York and American Stock Exchanges; all SEC filings on major petroleum companies; SRI Business Intelligence Program Chemical Economics Handbook. **Holdings:** 3000 books and bound periodical volumes; 35 VF drawers of annual company reports; New York Times on microfiche (1969 to present); selected periodicals on microfilm (1973 to present). **Subscriptions:** 580 journals and other serials; 20 newspapers. **Services:** Interlibrary loans; library open to public by appointment. **Computerized Information Services:** DIALOG, SDC, Dow Jones News Retrieval, New York Times Information Service. **Networks/Consortia:** Member of Pittsburgh Regional Library Center. **Publications:** At a Glance in Energy & Business; Monthly Acquisitions list; Checklist of Services and Periodicals; Quarterly Newsletter. **Staff:** Rita Evans .

★5298★
GULF OIL CORPORATION - GS & T CORPORATE ENGINEERING LIBRARY (Sci-Tech)
Box 1357　　　　　　　　　　　Phone: (713) 754-3624
Houston, TX 77001　　　　　　Margaret A. Sirman, Libn.
Founded: 1977. **Staff:** Prof 1. **Subjects:** Engineering. **Holdings:** 300 books; 200 bound periodical volumes; 500 codes and standards. **Subscriptions:** 51 journals and other serials. **Services:** Interlibrary loans; copying; library open to public with permission. **Computerized Information Services:** Online systems; computerized cataloging, acquisitions, serials and circulation. **Special Indexes:** Kardex Periodicals File; listing of codes and standards, company files; computerized listing of files. **Remarks:** Library is located at 2 Houston Center, Room 761, Houston, TX 77010.

★5299★
GULF OIL CORPORATION - GULF MINERAL RESOURCES COMPANY - LIBRARY AND INFORMATION CENTER (Sci-Tech)
1720 S. Bellaire St.　　　　　Phone: (303) 759-6821
Denver, CO 80222　　　　　　Marriott W. Smart, Libn.
Founded: 1979. **Staff:** Prof 1. **Subjects:** Geology, minerals, mining, coal. **Special Collections:** Federal and state Geological Survey publications; U.S. Department of Energy Open File reports (7 drawers of microfiche); in-house technical reports (2 drawers). **Holdings:** 7000 books and bound periodical volumes; 8 drawers of technical reports on microfiche; 24 VF drawers of geological maps. **Subscriptions:** 70 journals and other serials; 5 newspapers. **Services:** Interlibrary loans; library not open to public. **Computerized Information Services:** SDC, DIALOG; GGIS (internal database); computerized cataloging. **Publications:** Acquisitions list, semimonthly; periodicals list, annual. **Formerly:** Its Exploration Library.

★5300★
GULF OIL CORPORATION - LIBRARY AND INFORMATION CENTER (Energy; Bus-Fin)
Box 2100　　　　　　　　　　　Phone: (713) 226-1632
Houston, TX 77252　　　　　　Stanley E. Brewer, Hd.Libn.
Founded: 1974. **Staff:** Prof 2; Other 3. **Subjects:** Petroleum industry, general business, business statistics, economics, planning, management, marketing, exploration and production, geology, biography. **Special Collections:** Annual Reports (250 companies in petroleum and related industries). **Holdings:** 7000 books; 50 bound periodical volumes; N.Y. Times, 1969 to present on microfiche; NTIS microfiche in energy-related areas; 500 U.S. government documents. **Subscriptions:** 350 journals and other serials; 10 newspapers. **Services:** Interlibrary loans; library open to public by appointment. **Computerized Information Services:** DIALOG, SDC, Dow Jones News Retrieval, New York Times Information Service; computerized cataloging and acquisitions. **Publications:** Acquisitions List, monthly - for internal distribution only. **Formerly:** Gulf Refining & Marketing Company. **Staff:** Charlotte A. Wagner, Asst.Libn.; Pamela J. Batiste, Info.Spec.

★5301★
GULF PUBLISHING CO., INC. - EDITORIAL LIBRARY (Publ)
Debuys Rd.
Box 4567
Biloxi, MS 39531　　　　　　　Phone: (601) 896-2314
Marilyn Pustay, Libn.
Staff: 2. **Subjects:** Newspaper reference topics. **Holdings:** 120 VF drawers of Biloxi Sun and Herald clippings; 300 reports of state and local agencies; microfilm of the Herald and the Sun, 1880 to present. **Subscriptions:** 16 journals and other serials. **Services:** Copying; library open to public with restrictions.

GULF REFINING & MARKETING COMPANY
See: Gulf Oil Corporation - Library and Information Center

★5302★
GULF RESEARCH AND DEVELOPMENT COMPANY - TECHNICAL INFORMATION SERVICES (Energy)
Drawer 2038　　　　　　　　　Phone: (412) 665-6000
Pittsburgh, PA 15230　　　　Tina B. Ross, Dir., Tech.Info.Serv.
Founded: 1935. **Staff:** Prof 6; Other 19. **Subjects:** Petroleum, chemistry, engineering, earth sciences, energy and the environment. **Holdings:** 60,000 books; 15,000 bound periodical volumes; 3000 cartridges of microfilm; 27,000 microfiche. **Subscriptions:** 1000 journals and other serials; 15 newspapers. **Services:** Interlibrary loans; copying; SDI; library open to public for reference use only on request. **Computerized Information Services:** SDC, DIALOG, BRS, DOE/RECON, NLM, NIH/EPA Chemical Information System, Petroleum Data Service. **Publications:** Technical Information Accessions, monthly - for internal distribution only. **Special Catalogs:** Periodical Holdings (book form) - for internal distribution only. **Staff:** G. Louise McCleary, Lib. Unit Hd.; Autumn E. Colby, Res.Info.Spec.; Nickolas C. Kotow,

Info.Spec.

★5303★
GULF RESOURCES AND CHEMICAL CORPORATION - LITHIUM CORPORATION OF AMERICA, INC. - RESEARCH LIBRARY (Sci-Tech)
Box 795   Phone: (704) 692-2282
Bessemer City, NC 28016   JoAnn Trull, Libn.
Founded: 1958. **Staff:** Prof 1. **Subjects:** Lithium, chemistry, chemical engineering, metallurgy. **Holdings:** 1500 books; 800 bound periodical volumes; 600 government reports; 7 VF drawers of patents; 75 drawers of technical abstracts on cards; 250 reels of microfilm. **Subscriptions:** 63 journals and other serials. **Services:** Interlibrary loans; Chemical Abstracts on Microfilm Recordak Retrieval; library not open to public. **Publications:** Annotated bibliography, monthly - for internal distribution only.

★5304★
GULF SOUTH RESEARCH INSTITUTE - LIBRARY (Sci-Tech)
Box 26518   Phone: (504) 283-4223
New Orleans, LA 70186   Jim Hobbs, Tech.Libn.
Founded: 1965. **Staff:** Prof 1. **Subjects:** Polymer chemistry, membrane science, analytical chemistry, desalination. **Holdings:** 500 books; 14 bound periodical volumes; 400 technical reports. **Subscriptions:** 50 journals and other serials. **Services:** Interlibrary loans; copying; SDI; library open to public with restrictions. **Computerized Information Services:** DIALOG, MEDLINE.

★5305★
GULF STATES UTILITIES COMPANY - CORPORATE LIBRARY (Energy; Bus-Fin)
Box 2951   Phone: (713) 838-6631
Beaumont, TX 77704   Karen S. McConnell, Corp.Libn.
Founded: 1956. **Staff:** Prof 2; Other 6. **Subjects:** Public utility industry and regulations; electrical engineering; nuclear power, engineering and licensing; management, government, business, accounting. **Holdings:** 6000 books and bound periodical volumes; 160 films; U.S. Federal Register and Code of Federal Regulations, 1936 to present on microfiche. **Subscriptions:** 700 journals and other serials. **Services:** Interlibrary loans; copying; library open to public with restrictions. **Computerized Information Services:** DIALOG, SDC, BRS, DOE/RECON, NIH/EPA Chemical Information System, Tech-Net; computerized cataloging and acquisitions. **Networks/Consortia:** Member of OCLC through AMIGOS Bibliographic Council, Inc. **Remarks:** Center is located at 350 Pine St., Beaumont, TX 77701. **Staff:** Katherine Pfeiffer, Licensing Libn.

★5306★
GULF STATES UTILITIES COMPANY - FINANCE LIBRARY (Bus-Fin)
285 Liberty Ave.   Phone: (713) 838-6631
Beaumont, TX 77701   Hal G. Tierney, Supv. of Adm.
Staff: 2. **Subjects:** Banking and finance. **Holdings:** 220 books; 64 bound periodical volumes; speeches and reports. **Services:** Copying; library open to public for reference use only.

★5307★
GULF STATES UTILITIES COMPANY - LAW LIBRARY (Law)
285 Liberty
Box 2951   Phone: (713) 838-6631
Beaumont, TX 77704   Tonya Vineyard, Legal Asst.
Subjects: Texas statutes, public utility law, labor relations, federal regulations. **Holdings:** 2175 books; bound periodical volumes. **Subscriptions:** 11 journals and other serials. **Services:** Library open to other attorneys for reference use.

★5308★
GULF STATES UTILITIES COMPANY - NUCLEAR LIBRARY (Sci-Tech; Energy)
Box 2951   Phone: (713) 838-3843
Beaumont, TX 77704   Katherine N. Pfeiffer, Licensing Anl./Libn.
Founded: 1979. **Staff:** Prof 1; Other 1. **Subjects:** Nuclear regulation. **Special Collections:** Nuclear power plants licensing regulations. **Holdings:** 800 titles of Nuclear Regulatory Commission publications; 350 federal reports; 300 utility safety analysis documents; 150 River Bend Nuclear Station materials; 400 corporation and regulatory documents. **Subscriptions:** 32 journals and other serials. **Services:** Interlibrary loans; copying; library open to public with permission of librarian. **Computerized Information Services:** NOTEPAD. **Networks/Consortia:** Member of OCLC.

★5309★
GULF & WESTERN MANUFACTURING COMPANY - MARKETING LIBRARY (Bus-Fin)
26261 Evergreen Rd.
Box 999   Phone: (313) 355-8517
Southfield, MI 48037   Carole Hango-Hanlon, Marketing Libn.
Founded: 1980. **Staff:** Prof 1. **Subjects:** Business, marketing. **Holdings:** 50

books; corporate annual and 10K reports; government documents; VF materials. **Subscriptions:** 350 journals and other serials; 6 newspapers. **Services:** Interlibrary loans; copying; SDI; library open to public by appointment. **Computerized Information Services:** DIALOG, SDC, New York Times Information Service, Dow Jones News Retrieval.

GUND (Jessica R.) MEMORIAL LIBRARY
See: Cleveland Institute of Art - Jessica R. Gund Memorial Library

GUNDRY (L.P.) HEALTH SCIENCES LIBRARY
See: St. Agnes Hospital - L.P. Gundry Health Sciences Library

GUNNIN (Emery A.) ARCHITECTURAL LIBRARY
See: Clemson University - Emery A. Gunnin Architectural Library

GUNST (Morgan A. and Aline D.) MEMORIAL LIBRARY OF THE BOOK ARTS
See: Stanford University - Department of Special Collections

★5310★
GUNSTON HALL PLANTATION - HOUSE MUSEUM - LIBRARY (Hist; Rare Book)†
                                                Phone: (703) 550-9220
Lorton, VA 22079   Bennie Brown, Jr., Libn.
Founded: 1974. **Staff:** Prof 1. **Subjects:** George Mason and Mason family, John Mercer, early Virginia, northern Virginia, law and government, art and architecture. **Special Collections:** Mason-Mercer Rare Book Collection (2000 volumes representing library holdings of 18th century gentleman); Pamela C. Copeland Collection (500 volumes on Virginiana and genealogy); Robert Carter of Nomini Hall Collection (170 volumes). **Holdings:** 6000 books; 500 bound periodical volumes; 35 papers and letters of George Mason; photostats of 5000 Mason Family papers; 200 maps; 100 reels of microfilm. **Subscriptions:** 20 journals and other serials; 5 newspapers. **Services:** Copying; library open to public by appointment. **Publications:** Library search list, periodically - for internal distribution only.

GUNTER AIR FORCE STATION (AL)
See: U.S. Air Force Base - Gunter Base Library

GUNTER (Gordon) LIBRARY
See: Gulf Coast Research Laboratory - Gordon Gunter Library

GUNTER (Jean) SOCIAL WELFARE LIBRARY
See: Mississippi State Department of Public Welfare - Jean Gunter Social Welfare Library

★5311★
GUSTAVUS ADOLPHUS COLLEGE - LUND MUSIC LIBRARY (Mus)
                                                Phone: (507) 931-7365
St. Peter, MN 56082   Mary Behrends, Music Lib.Asst.
Founded: 1971. **Staff:** 1. **Subjects:** Music. **Special Collections:** Mettetal Record Collection (8000 records). **Holdings:** 4500 books; 3200 scores. **Services:** Interlibrary loans; library open to public with restrictions. **Computerized Information Services:** Computerized cataloging. **Networks/Consortia:** Member of OCLC; MINITEX. **Special Indexes:** Index of Swedish music in the library (notebook).

GUTHEIL (Emil A.) MEMORIAL LIBRARY
See: Postgraduate Center for Mental Health - Emil A. Gutheil Memorial Library

GUTHRIE THEATER ARCHIVES
See: University of Minnesota - Manuscripts Division

★5312★
GUTHRIE THEATER FOUNDATION - GUTHRIE THEATER STAFF REFERENCE LIBRARY (Theater)
725 Vineland Pl.   Phone: (612) 377-2824
Minneapolis, MN 55403   Melissa J. Brechon, Libn./Res.
Staff: Prof 1. **Subjects:** Decorative arts, costume, plays, history of theater and costume, architecture. **Special Collections:** Ladies Home Companion, The Designer, Delineator, 1908-1950. **Holdings:** 2500 books; 200 bound periodical volumes; 150 photographs; 200 plays; 4 VF drawers of slides; 4 VF drawers of photographs of past productions; 100 audio- and videotapes. **Subscriptions:** 14 journals and other serials. **Services:** Interlibrary loans; copying; library open to public with restrictions. **Networks/Consortia:** Member of METRONET.

GUTMAN LIBRARY
See: Harvard University - Graduate School of Education

GUTTMAN (Paul H.) LIBRARY
See: Sacramento-El Dorado Medical Society

GUTTORMSSON LIBRARY OF ICELANDIC CANADIAN POETRY
See: University of Manitoba - Archives and Special Collections

GUY (James Samuel) LIBRARY
See: Emory University - James Samuel Guy Library

H

★5313★
H.M.S. BOUNTY SOCIETY, INTERNATIONAL - RESEARCH LIBRARY AND DEPOSITORY (Hist)
174 Trinidad Dr.   Phone: (415) 435-9749
Tiburon, CA 94920   A. Munro Christian, Dir.
Founded: 1971. **Staff:** Prof 1; Other 5. **Subjects:** HMS Bounty history, genealogy, Christian heraldry, Pitcairn/Norfolk Island history. **Special Collections:** Christian family pedigree from 13th to 20th Century; HMS Bounty historical documents. **Holdings:** 1000 books; 5 bound periodical volumes; 150 manuscripts. **Subscriptions:** 9 journals and other serials. **Services:** Copying; library open to public for research use only.

HAAS (John A.W.) LIBRARY
See: Muhlenberg College - John A.W. Haas Library

HAAS (Ruth A.) LIBRARY
See: Western Connecticut State College - Ruth A. Haas Library

HABITAT
See: United Nations - Centre for Human Settlements

★5314★
HABITAT INSTITUTE - NATURAL HISTORY LIBRARY (Env-Cons)
10 Juniper Rd.
Box 136   Phone: (617) 489-3850
Belmont, MA 02178   Jean L. Rosenberg, Prog.Dir.
Founded: 1970. **Staff:** Prof 1. **Subjects:** Natural history, environmental education. **Holdings:** 3000 books; 500 bound periodical volumes. **Subscriptions:** 125 journals and other serials. **Services:** Interlibrary loans; library open to public with restrictions. **Publications:** Habitat Newsletter, quarterly - for members. **Formerly:** Its Environmental Studies Library.

★5315★
HACKENSACK MEDICAL CENTER - MEDICAL LIBRARY (Med)
Hospital Pl.   Phone: (201) 441-2326
Hackensack, NJ 07601   Duressa Pujat, Libn.
Founded: 1951. **Staff:** Prof 2; Other 2. **Subjects:** Medicine, surgery, nursing, hospital administration. **Special Collections:** Hospital archives. **Holdings:** 5200 books; 15,000 bound periodical volumes; vertical files; pamphlets; 500 tapes. **Subscriptions:** 272 journals and other serials. **Services:** Interlibrary loans; copying; library open to public. **Computerized Information Services:** NLM, SDC. **Networks/Consortia:** Member of Bergen/Passaic Health Sciences Library Consortium. **Publications:** Accessions List, quarterly - for internal distribution only. **Staff:** Cynthia Schutzer, Assoc.Libn.

★5316★
HACKETT (G.D.) PHOTO AGENCY AND ARCHIVES (Pict)
130 W. 57th St.   Phone: (212) 265-6842
New York, NY 10019   Gabriel D. Hackett, Owner, Ed.
Subjects: History - World Wars I and II, Russian Revolution; music; counter culture and social problems; Americana; fine arts - Europe, Far East; religions; American Indians. **Special Collections:** Bartok; Gershwin; Beethoven; Russian music; Magritte; Picasso. **Holdings:** 200,000 negatives; photographs.

★5317★
HACKETTSTOWN HISTORICAL SOCIETY - MUSEUM (Hist)
106 Church St.   Phone: (201) 852-8797
Hackettstown, NJ 07840   Milton K. Thorp, Cur.
Staff: 2. **Subjects:** Local history and genealogy. **Holdings:** 535 books; 262 newspapers dating from 1874; 301 documents; 72 genealogies; 30 volumes of Warren County Cemetery Records; 32 oral histories; 2 volumes of historical buildings in Hackettstown; 3 histories of Hackettstown by local historians. **Services:** Museum open to public.

★5318★
HACKLEY HOSPITAL - EDUCATION LIBRARY (Med)
1700 Clinton St.   Phone: (616) 728-4897
Muskegon, MI 49443   Betty Rogers, Libn.
Founded: 1982. **Staff:** Prof 1. **Subjects:** Nursing, health sciences. **Holdings:** 2800 books; 191 bound periodical volumes; 286 AV items. **Subscriptions:** 103 journals and other serials. **Services:** Interlibrary loans; copying; library open to public with restrictions. **Networks/Consortia:** Member of Michigan Area Serial Holdings (MASH); Kentucky-Ohio-Michigan Regional Medical Library Program (KOMRML). **Formerly:** Its Medical Library.

HADLEY (Ernest E.) MEMORIAL LIBRARY
See: Washington Psychoanalytic Society - Ernest E. Hadley Memorial Library

HADLEY LIBRARY
See: Earlham College - Joseph Moore Museum

HAGAN LIBRARY
See: Louisville Baptist Hospitals, Inc.

HAGGARD MEMORIAL LIBRARY
See: East Dallas Christian Church

★5319★
THE HAGGIN MUSEUM - ALMEDA MAY CASTLE PETZINGER LIBRARY (Hist; Art)
1201 N. Pershing Ave.   Phone: (209) 462-4116
Stockton, CA 95203   Raymond W. Hillman, Hist.Cur.
Founded: 1948. **Staff:** Prof 1; Other 1. **Subjects:** California history, local biography, agricultural technology of San Joaquin Valley, Caterpillar tractors, local business and industry. **Special Collections:** Ralph Yardley drawings of early Stockton history; Bert Whitman's editorial cartoons; V. Covert Martin Photo Collection; Holt Manufacturing Company archives; Stephens Bros. Boat Works archives. **Holdings:** 5300 books; 280 bound periodical volumes; 60,000 manuscripts, maps, business records, diaries, documents and photographs. **Subscriptions:** 14 journals and other serials. **Services:** Copying; library open to public for reference use only by appointment. **Formerly:** Pioneer Museum and Haggin Galleries.

HAGLEY FOUNDATION
See: Eleutherian Mills Historical Library

HAHLO (Helen) LIBRARY
See: Waterbury State Technical College - Helen Hahlo Library

★5320★
HAHNEMANN MEDICAL COLLEGE & HOSPITAL - WARREN H. FAKE LIBRARY (Med)†
245 N. 15th St.   Phone: (215) 448-7184
Philadelphia, PA 19102   Eleanora M. Kenworthy, Dir.
Founded: 1850. **Staff:** Prof 6; Other 16. **Subjects:** Medicine, allied health professions, nursing, mental health. **Special Collections:** Paracelsus (189 items); homeopathy (200 volumes); history of medicine (620 volumes). **Holdings:** 30,773 books; 35,375 bound periodical volumes; 231 theses; 1000 government and miscellaneous reports; 6 VF drawers; 493 reels of microfilm; 8005 microfiche and microcards; 2677 audiotapes and cassettes; 105 videotapes; 3107 slides; 54 films and filmstrips. **Subscriptions:** 1003 journals and other serials. **Services:** Interlibrary loans; copying; library open to medical and scientific personnel for reference only. **Computerized Information Services:** MEDLINE, DIALOG, SDC, BRS; computerized cataloging. **Networks/Consortia:** Member of Mideastern Regional Medical Library System (MERMLS); Tri-State College Library Cooperative (TCLC); OCLC; Interlibrary Delivery Service of Pennsylvania (IDS). **Staff:** Judith Baker, Assoc.Dir.; Margaret Hoffman, Tech.Serv.Libn.; Fran Sina, Ref./Circ.Supv.; Richard Aldred, Cat./Acq.Supv.; Sonia Lavilla, ILL; Gwen MacMurray, Per.Supv.

★5321★
HAIGHT, GARDNER, POOR AND HAVENS - LIBRARY (Law)
One State St. Plaza   Phone: (212) 344-6800
New York, NY 10004   Hortense Zeller, Libn.
Staff: Prof 1. **Subjects:** Law - admiralty and aviation; legal aspects of medicine. **Holdings:** 13,000 books; 400 bound periodical volumes; 7 VF drawers of maps and charts; 15 VF drawers of pamphlets; 5 VF drawers of legal forms. **Subscriptions:** 30 journals and other serials; 14 newspapers. **Services:** Interlibrary loans; library open to public by appointment.

HAILEYBURY SCHOOL OF MINES
See: Northern College

★5322★
HAKLUYT MINOR - LIBRARY (Rec; Trans)
9206 N.E. 180th St.   Phone: (206) 485-2124
Bothell, WA 98011   Richard G. McCloskey, Dir.
Staff: 2. **Subjects:** One and two-man transocean cruising. **Special Collections:** Books published on this subject from 1857-1957. **Holdings:** 1300 books; 400 bound periodical volumes; 4 VF drawers of files on each transocean passage. **Subscriptions:** 12 journals and other serials. **Services:** Copying; library open to public. **Publications:** Bibliography; Journal, monthly.

★5323★

HALCON SD GROUP, INC. - TECHNICAL INFORMATION CENTER (Sci-Tech)
2 Park Ave. Phone: (212) 689-1222
New York, NY 10016 R. Rosen, Hd.Libn.
Founded: 1952. **Staff:** Prof 3. **Subjects:** Chemical industry, petrochemicals. **Holdings:** 6500 books; 1500 bound periodical volumes; 21,000 patents; 300 VF drawers of technical data; 1000 microforms. **Subscriptions:** 200 journals and other serials. **Services:** Copying; library not open to public. **Computerized Information Services:** DIALOG, SDC; STAIRS (internal database). **Staff:** E. Stout, Lib.Asst.

★5324★

HALE AND DORR - LIBRARY (Law)
60 State St. Phone: (617) 742-9100
Boston, MA 02109 Mary Catherine H. Crowley, Libn.
Founded: 1960. **Staff:** Prof 2; Other 2. **Subjects:** Law. **Holdings:** 15,000 volumes. **Subscriptions:** 200 journals and other serials. **Services:** Interlibrary loans; copying; SDI; library not open to public. **Computerized Information Services:** DIALOG, SDC, New York Times Information Service, LEXIS. **Networks/Consortia:** Member of Association of Boston Law Libraries. **Publications:** Acquisitions list, monthly - for internal distribution only.

HALE HOSPITAL
See: Haverhill Municipal (Hale) Hospital

HALEAKALA NATL. PARK
See: U.S. Natl. Park Service

HALEY (Rosalind Kress) LIBRARY
See: Northwood Institute of Texas - Rosalind Kress Haley Library

★5325★

HALIFAX BOARD OF TRADE - LIBRARY (Bus-Fin)
Suite 400, 5251 Duke St. Phone: (902) 422-6447
Halifax, NS, Canada B3J 1P3 G.H. Lummis, Exec.V.P.
Subjects: Trade. **Special Collections:** City directories, trade directories. **Holdings:** Figures not available. **Services:** Library open to public. **Staff:** Myrtle Corkum, Mgr., Member Serv.

★5326★

HALIFAX HISTORICAL SOCIETY, INC. - LIBRARY (Hist)
Box 2682 Phone: (904) 255-6976
Daytona Beach, FL 32015 Susan Lofaro, Pres.
Staff: Prof 2; Other 2. **Subjects:** Florida history, automobiles, history, educational institutions. **Special Collections:** Aerospace history. **Holdings:** 550 books; 170 bound periodical volumes; 30 VF drawers of photographs, scrapbooks, postcards, maps, clippings, slides. **Services:** Copying; library open to public for reference use only by appointment. **Publications:** Halifax Historical Herald, quarterly - to members or for sale. **Remarks:** Library is located at 128 Orange Ave., Daytona Beach, FL 32014. **Staff:** Elizabeth Baker, Cons.

★5327★

HALIFAX HOSPITAL MEDICAL CENTER - MEDICAL LIBRARY (Med)
Clyde Morris Blvd. Phone: (904) 258-1544
Daytona Beach, FL 32014 Ken Mead, Dir., Med.Lib.
Founded: 1963. **Staff:** Prof 1; Other 1. **Subjects:** Medicine, nursing, hospital administration. **Holdings:** 3300 books; 4400 bound periodical volumes; 21 subscriptions for cassette tapes; 1 subscription Network for Continuing Medical Education Video Cassette films. **Subscriptions:** 200 journals and other serials. **Services:** Interlibrary loans; copying; research and bibliographies; library open to students and local attorneys and to others by special permission. **Networks/Consortia:** Halifax Medical Library is MEDLINE Center and head of a consortium of six hospital libraries located in Ormond Beach, Deland and New Smyrna. **Publications:** Newsletter, monthly - for internal distribution only. **Special Indexes:** Special article-bibliography file; hospital directory.

★5328★

HALIFAX INFIRMARY - HEALTH SERVICES LIBRARY (Med)
1335 Queen St. Phone: (902) 428-3058
Halifax, NS, Canada B3J 2H6 Dr. Anitra Laycock, Libn.
Founded: 1963. **Staff:** Prof 1; Other 1. **Subjects:** Medicine, nursing and allied health services, administration. **Holdings:** 1500 books; 5000 slides, archives and videotapes. **Subscriptions:** 350 journals and other serials. **Services:** Interlibrary loans; copying; SDI; library open to public with restrictions. **Computerized Information Services:** Online systems; computerized serials. **Special Indexes:** KWIC index of audiovisual holdings.

★5329★

HALIFAX REGIONAL VOCATIONAL SCHOOL - LIBRARY (Sci-Tech; Bus-Fin)
1825 Bell Rd. Phone: (902) 422-8301
Halifax, NS, Canada B3H 2Z4 Joann Morris, Libn.
Staff: Prof 1; Other 1. **Subjects:** Vocational trades, business administration, data processing, secretarial science. **Holdings:** 24,800 books; 2000 pocketbooks; 50 films; 150 transparencies, filmstrips, record kits. **Subscriptions:** 140 journals and other serials. **Services:** Interlibrary loans; copying; library open to public with restrictions. **Networks/Consortia:** Member of Nova Scotia Provincial Library and Union Catalogue (NOVANET).

★5330★

HALL-BROOKE HOSPITAL - PROFESSIONAL LIBRARY (Med)
47 Long Lots Rd. Phone: (203) 227-1251
Westport, CT 06881 Janet Pankiewicz, Libn.
Founded: 1960. **Staff:** Prof 1. **Subjects:** Psychiatry, psychology, mental health, psychiatric nursing, family therapy. **Holdings:** 1300 books; 500 bound periodical volumes; Hall-Brooke Roundtable Tapes, 1968-1973. **Subscriptions:** 120 journals and other serials. **Publications:** Selected List of Tables of Contents of Psychiatric Periodicals, monthly - distributed to mental health professionals. **Services:** Interlibrary loans; copying; library open to public only when librarian is available. **Networks/Consortia:** Member of Southwestern Health Science Library Consortium; Connecticut Association of Health Sciences Libraries (CAHSL); Southwestern Connecticut Library Council.

★5331★

HALL COUNTY MUSEUM BOARD - STUHR MUSEUM - LIBRARY AND ARCHIVES (Hist)
3133 W. Highway 34 Phone: (308) 384-1380
Grand Island, NE 68801 Dr. Robert Manley, Sr.Hist.
Founded: 1961. **Subjects:** Local and state history. **Holdings:** 3000 books; 50 boxes of unbound periodicals; 40 shelves of documents, diaries, letters, manuscripts, business ledgers and photographs. **Subscriptions:** 12 journals and other serials. **Services:** Copying; library open to public. **Publications:** Stuhr Museum of the Prairie Pioneer Newsletter, monthly - distributed to members.

HALL (Edward T.) LIBRARY
See: University of Arizona Environmental Psychology Program - Library

★5332★

HALL OF FLAME - RICHARD S. FOWLER MEMORIAL LIBRARY (Sci-Tech)
6101 E. Van Buren Phone: (602) 275-3473
Phoenix, AZ 85008 George F. Getz, Jr., Pres.
Founded: 1968. **Staff:** 2. **Subjects:** Disasters, fires, fire departments and salvage corps, fire prevention and fire services. **Special Collections:** Catalogs of fire apparatus manufacturers; histories of major fires; photographs of fires; service manuals and others relating to fire departments and the fire service. **Holdings:** 4000 books; 300 bound periodical volumes; company reports; newspaper clippings, photographs of fires. **Services:** Library open to public for reference use only. **Remarks:** The phone number above is designed to read ASK FIRE. This library is operated by the National Historical Fire Foundation.

HALL (George Talbot) LIBRARY
See: Bloomfield College - George Talbot Hall Library

HALL (James) LIBRARY
See: Vandalia Historical Society

★5333★

HALL OF JUSTICE LIBRARY (Law)†
850 Bryant St., Rm. 305 Phone: (415) 553-1763
San Francisco, CA 94103 Robert R. Schmidt, Libn.
Staff: Prof 1. **Subjects:** Law. **Holdings:** 6000 volumes; 1000 bound and unbound serials; 500 microforms. **Services:** Interlibrary loans; copying (fee); library open to public by special permission. **Computerized Information Services:** LEXIS. **Remarks:** Library serves the San Francisco District Attorney and the San Francisco Public Defender offices.

HALL (Linda) LIBRARY
See: Linda Hall Library

HALL (Mattie D.) LIBRARY
See: First Baptist Church - Mattie D. Hall Library

HALL (Paul) LIBRARY AND MARITIME MUSEUM
See: Lundeberg Maryland Seamanship School - Paul Hall Library and Maritime Museum

HALL SCHOOL OF NURSING
See: Northeast Georgia Medical Center and Hall School of Nursing

HALL (Wilford) U.S.A.F. MEDICAL CENTER
See: U.S. Air Force Medical Center - Wilford Hall U.S.A.F. Medical Center

★5334★
HALL (William S.) PSYCHIATRIC INSTITUTE - PROFESSIONAL LIBRARY (Med)
Box 202   Phone: (803) 758-5370
Columbia, SC 29202   Mrs. Neeta N. Shah, Chf.Med.Libn.
Founded: 1964. Staff: Prof 1; Other 2. Subjects: Psychiatry, psychology, sociology, neurology, pastoral counseling, genetics, psychopharmacology, nursing, occupational therapy. Special Collections: Historical collection; Asylum reports from 1836; Transactions of the American Medico-Psychological Association from 1901; Annual reports of the South Carolina State Hospital from 1853. Holdings: 10,594 books; 6925 bound periodical volumes; 20 tapes; 550 cassettes; 12 VF drawers of pamphlets and reprints. Subscriptions: 320 journals and other serials. Services: Interlibrary loans; copying; library open to public for reference use only. Computerized Information Services: MEDLARS, DIALOG. Networks/Consortia: Member of Columbia Area Medical Librarians Association. Publications: Psychiatric Forum, 3/year - to selected institutions.

HALLAUER (George) MEMORIAL LIBRARY
See: Western Evangelical Seminary - George Hallauer Memorial Library

HALLETT (Dessie M.) LIBRARY
See: Mount Vernon Place United Methodist Church - Dessie M. Hallett Library

HALLIBURTON LAW LIBRARY
See: Mercer University - Law School

HALLIBURTON (Richard) MAP COLLECTION
See: Princeton University - Richard Halliburton Map Collection

★5335★
HALLMARK CARDS, INC. - CREATIVE RESEARCH LIBRARY (Art)
25th & McGee   Phone: (816) 274-5525
Kansas City, MO 64108   Jon M. Henderson, Mgr., Lib.Serv.
Founded: 1930. Staff: Prof 1; Other 2. Subjects: Fine art, lettering, advertising, graphic art, design, illustration, pictures. Special Collections: Old and rare books collection. Holdings: 10,000 books; 50 bound periodical volumes; 100,000 pictures and clippings in 32 VF drawers. Subscriptions: 125 journals and other serials; 5 newspapers. Services: Interlibrary loans; copying; library not open to public. Special Catalogs: Cross-index file for clippings.

HALLOCK MEDICAL LIBRARY
See: Connecticut Valley Hospital

HALPERN (Rabbi Mordecai S.) MEMORIAL LIBRARY
See: Congregation Beth Shalom - Rabbi Mordecai S. Halpern Memorial Library

HALPIN MEMORIAL LIBRARY
See: University of Wisconsin, Madison - Poultry Science Department

HAMADY HEALTH SCIENCES LIBRARY
See: Hurley Medical Center

HAMBER (Eric W.) LIBRARY
See: University of British Columbia - Eric W. Hamber Library

★5336★
HAMBURG CENTER FOR THE MENTALLY RETARDED - STAFF DEVELOPMENT LIBRARY (Med)
                                            Phone: (215) 562-7511
Hamburg, PA 19526   Marie D. Fortney, Libn.
Founded: 1960. Staff: 1. Subjects: Mental retardation, medicine, surgery, psychiatry, diagnosis, chest, heart, anatomy, cancer. Holdings: 306 books; 396 other cataloged items; 19 volumes of the Laws of Pennsylvania. Subscriptions: 15 journals and other serials. Services: Library not open to public. Remarks: Maintains a small Client Library.

HAMBURGER (Ferdinand, Jr.) ARCHIVES
See: Johns Hopkins University - Ferdinand Hamburger, Jr. Archives

★5337★
HAMILTON ACADEMY OF MEDICINE - LIBRARY (Med)
286 Victoria Ave., N.   Phone: (416) 528-1611
Hamilton, ON, Canada L8L 5G4   Bessie J. McKinlay, Libn.
Founded: 1931. Staff: Prof 1; Other 2. Subjects: Medicine. Holdings: 3500 books; 8000 bound periodical volumes. Subscriptions: 130 journals and other serials. Services: Interlibrary loans; copying; library not open to public.

★5338★
HAMILTON BOARD OF EDUCATION - EDUCATION CENTRE LIBRARY (Educ)
100 Main St., W.   Phone: (416) 527-5092
Hamilton, ON, Canada L8P 1H6   E. Birgit Langhammer, Libn.
Founded: 1967. Staff: Prof 3; Other 4. Subjects: Teaching methods, educational philosophy, educational psychology, history of education, special education, guidance, child psychology. Holdings: 20,000 books; 1400 phonograph records; 4000 slides; 300 filmstrips; 500 film loops; 800 kits; 20 VF drawers of clippings and pamphlets; 8 VF drawers of pictures; 1500 reels of microfilm; 132,000 microfiche. Subscriptions: 575 journals and other serials; 7 newspapers. Services: Interlibrary loans; copying; library open to public for reference use only. Publications: Subject Bibliographies, irregular - for internal distribution only; Periodical Content Listing, 8/year - for internal distribution only; Just Arrived, monthly; Update, news and reviews, irregular. Staff: Fotoula Pantazis, Asst.Libn.

★5339★
HAMILTON CITY HALL - LIBRARY (Plan)
71 Main St., W.   Phone: (416) 527-0241
Hamilton, ON, Canada L8N 3T4   S.G. Hollowell, Rec.Adm.
Founded: 1975. Staff: 2. Subjects: Municipal government, urban and regional planning. Holdings: 10,000 items. Subscriptions: 35 journals and other serials. Services: Library open to public for reference use only. Computerized Information Services: Online systems; computerized cataloging. Remarks: This is a depository of city and regional government publications.

HAMILTON COUNTY PUBLIC LIBRARY
See: Public Library of Cincinnati and Hamilton County

★5340★
HAMILTON LAW ASSOCIATION - LAW LIBRARY (Law)
50 Main St., E.   Phone: (416) 522-1563
Hamilton, ON, Canada L8N 1E9   W. Hearder-Moan, Libn.
Founded: 1879. Staff: Prof 1; Other 2. Subjects: Law. Holdings: 16,000 volumes. Services: Library open to public with permission.

HAMILTON LIBRARY
See: Cumberland County Historical Society & Hamilton Library

HAMILTON LIBRARY
See: University of Hawaii

HAMILTON MEMORIAL LIBRARY
See: Essex County Hospital Center

★5341★
HAMILTON PUBLIC LIBRARY - SPECIAL COLLECTIONS (Hist)
55 York Blvd.   Phone: (416) 529-8111
Hamilton, ON, Canada L8R 3K1   Judith McAnanama, Chf.Libn.
Founded: 1890. Staff: Prof 2; Other 4. Subjects: Canadiana. Special Collections: Local history and archives; Canadian Association in Support of the Native Peoples material (12 VF drawers, update on microfiche); government documents (full depository - federal/provincial/municipal). Services: Interlibrary loans; copying; library open to public. Computerized Information Services: DIALOG, SDC, QL Systems, CAN/OLE, DOBIS; computerized cataloging, serials and circulation. Networks/Consortia: Member of South Central Regional Library System; UTLAS Inc. Special Indexes: Extensive index to local history material (card); Canadian composers/artists index (card). Staff: Katharine Greenfield, Coord.

★5342★
HAMILTON SPECTATOR - REFERENCE LIBRARY (Publ)
44 Frid St.   Phone: (416) 526-3315
Hamilton, ON, Canada L8N 3G3   Jean M. Tebbutt, Chf.Libn.
Founded: 1935. Staff: Prof 1; Other 3. Subjects: History, general reference. Holdings: 3000 books; clippings on 30,000 subjects; microfilm of Spectator from 1847 to present. Subscriptions: 15 journals and other serials; 30 newspapers. Services: Library open to public for reference use only by request. Staff: Heather Hopgood, Asst.Libn.

HAMILTONIAN LIBRARY
See: National Hamiltonian Party

★5343★
HAMLINE UNIVERSITY SCHOOL OF LAW - LIBRARY (Law)
1536 Hewitt Ave.   Phone: (612) 641-2119
St. Paul, MN 55104   Nicholas Triffin, Libn.
Founded: 1973. Staff: Prof 5; Other 4. Subjects: Law. Holdings: 22,000
books; 11,000 bound periodical volumes; 62,000 case reports, statutes and
other items; microform holdings - Congressional Information Services, 1970-
1980; U.S. Supreme Court Record and Briefs, 1940 to present; Codes of
Federal Regulations; Federal Register. Subscriptions: 650 journals and other
serials; 7 newspapers. Services: Interlibrary loans; copying; library open to
public. Computerized Information Services: DIALOG, WESTLAW;
computerized cataloging. Networks/Consortia: Member of MINITEX. Staff:
Susan Kiefer, Asst.Libn., Pub.Serv.; Suzanne Thorpe, Asst.Libn., Cat.; Eleanor
Noll, Asst.Libn., Acq.; Marilyn Soullen, Asst.Libn., Govt.Doc.

HAMMARSKJOLD (Dag) LIBRARY
See: United Nations Headquarters - Dag Hammarskjold Library

★5344★
HAMMER, SILER, GEORGE ASSOCIATES - LIBRARY (Plan)
1111 Bonifant St.   Phone: (301) 565-5200
Silver Spring, MD 20910
Founded: 1954. Staff: Prof 1; Other 1. Subjects: Economic development,
environmental control, housing, land use, planning, transportation, historic
preservation, commercial revitalization. Special Collections: Census
Collection (Census of Population, Housing, Business, Manufacturing,
Agriculture, Census Tract from 1950 to present; 55 shelves); Geographic
Collection (2500 items; data on states arranged by area and subject).
Holdings: 7000 volumes; 2000 HSGA company reports; 8 shelves of state
employment statistics. Subscriptions: 33 journals and other serials.
Services: Interlibrary loans; copying; SDI; library open to public by
appointment. Networks/Consortia: Member of Regional and Urban
Information Network (RUIN). Special Catalogs: Geographic and subject
catalog for in-house company reports. Formerly: Located in Washington, DC.

★5345★
HAMMERMILL PAPER COMPANY - TECHNICAL LIBRARY (Sci-Tech)
East Lake Rd.
Box 10050
Erie, PA 16533   Phone: (814) 456-8811
Founded: 1966. Staff: 1. Subjects: Paper manufacture, pulp manufacture,
black liquor recovery, water pollution. Holdings: 1100 books; 6200 bound
periodical volumes; technical information exchange reports (cataloged); 6500
patents on paper manufacturing from 1926 to present; 1000 pamphlets and
articles in keyword file. Subscriptions: 50 journals and other serials.
Services: Interlibrary loans; copying; library open to business people in the
Erie area. Formerly: Its Central Research Technical Library.

★5346★
HAMMOND, INC. - EDITORIAL DIVISION LIBRARY (Geog-Map)
515 Valley St.   Phone: (201) 763-6000
Maplewood, NJ 07040   W.Z. Myers, Libn.
Founded: 1945. Staff: 1. Subjects: Geography, cartography, astronomy,
anthropology, history, archeology. Special Collections: U.S. and foreign
census publications. Holdings: 12,000 books; 60 VF drawers of pamphlets
and clippings; 17,000 maps; 350 atlases. Subscriptions: 250 journals and
other serials. Services: Library not open to public.

★5347★
HAMMOND HISTORICAL SOCIETY - CALUMET ROOM (Hist)
564 State St.   Phone: (219) 931-5100
Hammond, IN 46320   Kathryn Thegzi, Libn.
Staff: Prof 1. Subjects: History of Hammond and the Calumet Region.
Holdings: 600 books; 12 VF drawers of pamphlets and clippings (cataloged);
96 VF drawers of newspaper negatives; 30 personal scrapbooks. Services:
Interlibrary loans; copying; library open to public with restrictions. Remarks:
Maintained by Hammond Public Library.

HAMMOND (Horace) MEMORIAL LIBRARY
See: Birmingham Botanical Gardens - Horace Hammond Memorial Library

HAMMOND LIBRARY
See: Chicago Theological Seminary

★5348★
HAMOT MEDICAL CENTER - LIBRARY SERVICES (Med)
201 State St.   Phone: (814) 455-6711
Erie, PA 16512   Jean A. Maurer, Dir., Lib.Serv.
Founded: 1963. Staff: Prof 1; Other 3. Subjects: Medicine, surgery, nursing
and related sciences. Holdings: 2200 books; 4500 bound periodical volumes.
Subscriptions: 270 journals and other serials. Services: Interlibrary loans;
copying; library open to public with authorization from librarian. Computerized
Information Services: DIALOG, MEDLARS. Networks/Consortia: Member of
Erie Area Health Information Library Cooperative; Northwest Interlibrary
Cooperative of Pennsylvania.

★5349★
HAMPDEN COUNTY LAW LIBRARY (Law)
50 State St.
Box 559   Phone: (413) 781-8100
Springfield, MA 01101   Carol A. Baker, Act.Libn.
Founded: 1900. Staff: Prof 1; Other 2. Subjects: Law. Holdings: 43,000
books; 2000 bound periodical volumes. Subscriptions: 50 journals and other
serials. Services: Interlibrary loans; library open to public.

HAMPDEN DISTRICT MEDICAL SOCIETY - SPRINGFIELD ACADEMY OF
    MEDICINE
See: Springfield Academy of Medicine

HAMPDEN (Walter) MEMORIAL LIBRARY
See: Walter Hampden - Edwin Booth Theater Collection and Library

★5350★
HAMPSHIRE COUNTY LAW LIBRARY (Law)
Court House   Phone: (413) 586-2297
Northampton, MA 01060   Barbara Fell-Johnson, Libn.
Founded: 1908. Staff: Prof 1. Subjects: Law. Special Collections: New
England statutes; English cases. Holdings: 24,000 books and bound periodical
volumes. Subscriptions: 50 journals and other serials. Services: Interlibrary
loans; copying; library open to public for reference use only.

★5351★
HAMPTON GENERAL HOSPITAL - MEDICAL LIBRARY (Med)
3120 Victoria Blvd.   Phone: (804) 727-7102
Hampton, VA 23669   Minette Brooks, Med.Libn.
Founded: 1892. Staff: Prof 1. Subjects: Medical sciences, hospital
administration, nursing. Holdings: 599 books; 1100 bound periodical
volumes. Subscriptions: 68 journals and other serials. Services: Interlibrary
loans; copying; library open to public with restrictions.

HAMPTON HISTORICAL SOCIETY
See: Meeting House Green Memorial and Historical Association, Inc.

★5352★
HAMPTON INSTITUTE - COLLIS P. HUNTINGTON MEMORIAL LIBRARY -
    SPECIAL COLLECTIONS (Soc Sci)
                                          Phone: (804) 727-5371
Hampton, VA 23668   Jason C. Grant, III, Dir.
Founded: 1904. Special Collections: George Foster Peabody Collection of
Negro Literature and History; Hampton Institute Archives (2 million items);
U.S. Government documents (partial depository). Holdings: Figures not
available. Services: Interlibrary loans; copying; library open to public.
Networks/Consortia: Member of Virginia Tidewater Consortium for
Continuing Higher Education. Special Catalogs: Dictionary Catalog of the
George Foster Peabody Collection of Negro Literature and History, 1972.

★5353★
HAMPTON MARINERS MUSEUM - LIBRARY (Hist)
120 Turner St.   Phone: (919) 728-7317
Beaufort, NC 28516   Jean Potter
Staff: Prof 1. Subjects: Current and historical boat building and design,
natural history, navigation, voyages. Holdings: 750 books; building plans for
vessels. Subscriptions: 14 journals and other serials. Services: Copying;
library open to public.

★5354★
HANCOCK (Allan) FOUNDATION - HANCOCK LIBRARY OF BIOLOGY &
    OCEANOGRAPHY (Sci-Tech)
University of Southern California
University Pk.   Phone: (213) 743-6005
Los Angeles, CA 90089-0371   Kimberly Douglas, Dir.
Founded: 1944. Staff: Prof 3; Other 2. Subjects: Marine biology, geology,
zoology, botany, paleontology. Special Collections: Early scientific

expeditions; natural history. **Holdings:** 30,000 books; 65,000 bound periodical volumes; scientific reprints and pamphlets. **Subscriptions:** 2330 journals and other serials. **Services:** Interlibrary loans; library open to advanced workers in subject area. **Computerized Information Services:** DIALOG. **Staff:** Vicki L. Griffith, Libn.; Florence E. Lewis, Libn.

★5355★
HANCOCK COUNTY LAW LIBRARY, INC. (Law)*
60 State St.
Ellsworth, ME 04605   Margaret A. Cunningham, Libn.
Founded: 1907. **Staff:** 1. **Subjects:** Law. **Holdings:** 6000 books. **Services:** Public must register at office of Clerk of Courts to use library.

★5356★
HANCOCK COUNTY LAW LIBRARY ASSOCIATION (Law)
Hancock County Courthouse   Phone: (419) 424-7077
Findlay, OH 45840   Ruth A. Long, Asst. Law Libn.
Staff: 1. **Subjects:** Law. **Holdings:** 20,000 volumes. **Services:** Library for use of members, members of the courts, local attorneys, county officials and the public.

★5357★
HANCOCK, ESTABROOK, RYAN, SHOVE & HUST - LAW LIBRARY (Law)
One Mony Plaza   Phone: (315) 471-3151
Syracuse, NY 13202   Paula G. Niemi, Libn.
Staff: Prof 1. **Subjects:** State and federal law, labor relations, taxes, securities, estates and trusts, negligence, products liability, malpractice, municipalities, real property. **Special Collections:** Colonial Laws of New York (5 volumes). **Holdings:** 9000 books; 10 shelves of pamphlets. **Subscriptions:** 57 journals and other serials. **Services:** Interlibrary loans; library open to public with restrictions. **Publications:** Newsletter, quarterly - for internal distribution only.

HANCOCK (John) MUTUAL LIFE INSURANCE COMPANY
See: John Hancock Mutual Life Insurance Company

HAND (Wayland D.) LIBRARY OF FOLKLORE AND MYTHOLOGY
See: University of California, Los Angeles - Wayland D. Hand Library of Folklore and Mythology

HANDLEMAN INSTITUTE OF RECORDED SOUND ARCHIVES
See: University of Miami - School of Music - Albert Pick Music Library

★5358★
HANDWRITING ANALYSIS RESEARCH - LIBRARY (Soc Sci)
91 Washington St.   Phone: (413) 774-4667
Greenfield, MA 01301   Robert E. Backman, Cur.
Founded: 1949. **Staff:** Prof 1. **Subjects:** Graphology, handwriting, handwriting analysis, penmanship. **Special Collections:** Phyllis Grossberg Memorial Collection (7000 classified handwriting samples); Anna Aab Memorial Collection (551 penmanship books, booklets, copy slips); Gene Steccone Memorial Collection (311 books, pamphlets, articles). **Holdings:** 4511 books; 121 bound periodical volumes; 1214 research reports; 41,216 manuscripts, clippings, photocopies; 621 translated items; 6913 abstracts (all cataloged); archival records of 5 defunct handwriting analysis organizations (closed reserve). **Subscriptions:** 11 journals and other serials. **Services:** Interlibrary loans; copying; library open to public for reference use only by appointment. **Publications:** Schools, Teachers and Penmanship; reprints of historical items on graphology, handwriting, handwriting analysis and penmanship; Graphological Abstracts (book). **Special Indexes:** Bibliographic card file; abstracts card file; special subject and topic index (card).

★5359★
HANDY ASSOCIATES, INC. - RESEARCH LIBRARY (Bus-Fin)
245 Park Ave.   Phone: (212) 867-8444
New York, NY 10167   Ann Barry, Dir. of Res.
Founded: 1955. **Staff:** Prof 2; Other 1. **Subjects:** Business, economics, management, personnel administration, executive compensation and benefits. **Holdings:** 1500 books; 50 VF drawers of company annual reports, proxies and clippings. **Subscriptions:** 100 journals and other serials. **Services:** Interlibrary loans; library not open to public. **Staff:** Donna Siefert, Libn.

HANNA (Wilson C.) LIBRARY/RESEARCH LIBRARY
See: San Bernardino County Museum - Wilson C. Hanna Library/Research Library

HANSCOM AIR FORCE BASE (MA)
See: U.S. Air Force Base - Hanscom Base Library

★5360★
HANSELL, POST, BRANDON & DORSEY - LIBRARY (Law)
3300 First National Bank Tower   Phone: (404) 581-8000
Atlanta, GA 30383   Mildred Rosser, Libn.
Staff: Prof 1; Other 1. **Subjects:** Law. **Holdings:** 20,000 books.

★5361★
HANSEN (Clark Bradley) PRIVATE LIBRARY (Hum)†
3901 E. 49th St.   Phone: (612) 722-3630
Minneapolis, MN 55417   Clark B. Hansen, Dir.
Founded: 1968. **Staff:** Prof 1. **Subjects:** Minnesota history and travel, theology, philosophy, literature and literary criticism, natural history, science, book trades, art. **Holdings:** 12,000 volumes. **Services:** Library open to public by appointment for reference use. **Publications:** Inquire about publications and items available for sale.

★5362★
HANSON ENGINEERS, INC. - TECHNICAL LIBRARY (Sci-Tech)
1525 S. Sixth St.   Phone: (217) 788-2483
Springfield, IL 62703   Silvey W. Barge, Tech.Libn.
Staff: 1. **Subjects:** Civil engineering, Illinois geology, soil mechanics, geotechnical engineering, structural engineering. **Holdings:** 4769 volumes. **Subscriptions:** 80 journals and other serials. **Services:** Library not open to public. **Networks/Consortia:** Member of Rolling Prairie Library System.

★5363★
HANSON MATERIALS ENGINEERING (Western) LTD. - CORPORATE LIBRARY (Sci-Tech)
7450 18th St.   Phone: (403) 464-7916
Edmonton, AB, Canada T6P 1N8   Irene J. Caine, Libn.
Founded: 1966. **Staff:** Prof 1. **Subjects:** Metallurgy, metallography, welding technology, materials engineering, nondestructive testing, heat treating. **Special Collections:** Metallurgical and nondestructive testing specifications (550). **Holdings:** 800 books; 250 handbooks; 700 technical files; 5000 consulting engineering reports. **Subscriptions:** 45 journals and other serials; 10 newspapers. **Services:** Library not open to public. **Formerly:** Its Business Library.

★5364★
HAR ZION TEMPLE - IDA AND MATTHEW RUDOFKER LIBRARY (Rel-Theol)
Hagy's Ford & Hollow Rd.   Phone: (215) 667-5000
Penn Valley, PA 19072   Jessie Rubenstone, Libn.
Founded: 1924. **Staff:** Prof 2; Other 1. **Subjects:** Judaica. **Holdings:** 6000 books. **Subscriptions:** 30 journals and other serials. **Services:** Library open to members of congregation and to affiliated organizations. **Staff:** Cyndi Schoenbrun, Asst.Libn.

★5365★
HARBISON-WALKER REFRACTORIES COMPANY - GARBER RESEARCH CENTER LIBRARY (Sci-Tech)
Box 98037   Phone: (412) 469-3880
Pittsburgh, PA 15227   Harriet Gillespie, Res.Libn.
Founded: 1925. **Staff:** Prof 1; Other 1. **Subjects:** Refractories, ceramics, geology, metallurgy. **Holdings:** 2500 books; 3000 bound periodical volumes. **Subscriptions:** 320 journals and other serials. **Services:** Interlibrary loans; library open to public.

★5366★
HARBOR BRANCH FOUNDATION, INC. - LIBRARY (Sci-Tech)
R.R.1, Box 196   Phone: (305) 465-2400
Fort Pierce, FL 33450   Kristen L. Metzger, Libn.
Staff: Prof 2. **Subjects:** Marine sciences, marine engineering, marine ecology, biological oceanography, fisheries science. **Holdings:** 2800 books; 4300 bound periodical volumes; 720 reels of microfilm of periodicals. **Subscriptions:** 260 journals and other serials. **Services:** Interlibrary loans; copying; library open to public by appointment. **Computerized Information Services:** DIALOG, SDC. **Staff:** Carol F. Browder, Asst.Libn.

HARBOR LIBRARY/LEARNING RESOURCES CENTER
See: Community College of Baltimore

HARBORVIEW MEDICAL CENTER
See: University of Washington - Health Sciences Library - K.K. Sherwood Library

★5367★

HARBRIDGE HOUSE, INC. - LIBRARY (Bus-Fin)
12 Arlington St.   Phone: (617) 267-6410
Boston, MA 02116   Martha J. Berglund, Dir. of Lib.
Staff: Prof 2; Other 2. **Subjects:** Business and management, management training and development, public administration, transportation, finance, environmental studies. **Holdings:** 5000 books; 2000 in-house reports; 100 boxes of microfilm; 20 films; 4 VF drawers of pamphlets. **Subscriptions:** 85 journals and other serials; 6 newspapers. **Services:** Copying; library open to public by appointment. **Computerized Information Services:** Lockheed. **Special Catalogs:** Harbridge House studies and reports catalog (card). **Staff:** Bedia Ahmad, Asst.Libn.

★5368★

HARCOURT BRACE JOVANOVICH, INC. - EDITORIAL LIBRARY (Publ)
757 Third Ave.   Phone: (212) 888-3497
New York, NY 10017   Ron Coplen, Libn.
Founded: 1958. **Staff:** Prof 1; Other 4. **Subjects:** Reference, literature, education. **Special Collections:** Archives of Harcourt Brace Jovanovich (15,000). **Holdings:** 30,000 books. **Subscriptions:** 800 journals and other serials; 5 newspapers. **Services:** Interlibrary loans; copying; library open to public.

★5369★

HARCOURT BRACE JOVANOVICH, INC. - PICTURE RESEARCH LIBRARY (Pict)
757 Third Ave., 7th Fl.   Phone: (212) 888-3645
New York, NY 10017   Mudite Austrins, Pict.Libn.
Founded: 1958. **Staff:** 2. **Subjects:** American history, art. **Holdings:** 5000 books; 70,000 black and white photographs; 20,000 slides (31 VF drawers of black and white, 180 VF drawers of color). **Subscriptions:** 100 journals and other serials. **Services:** Library not open to public.

HARCOURT BRACE JOVANOVICH, INC. - SEA WORLD
See: Sea World, Inc.

HARDIE (Grace) CHILDREN'S BOOKS COLLECTION
See: Birmingham Public and Jefferson County Free Library - Youth Department

HARDING (Bernice) LIBRARY
See: San Diego Hall of Science - Bernice Harding Library

★5370★

HARDING GRADUATE SCHOOL OF RELIGION - L.M. GRAVES MEMORIAL LIBRARY (Rel-Theol)†
1000 Cherry Rd.   Phone: (901) 761-1354
Memphis, TN 38117   Annie May Alston Lewis, Libn.
Founded: 1958. **Staff:** Prof 2; Other 2. **Subjects:** Bible and religion, philosophy, church history, missions, counseling. **Special Collections:** Restoration history; religious education curriculum library. **Holdings:** 68,000 volumes. **Subscriptions:** 550 journals and other serials. **Services:** Interlibrary loans; copying; library open to public with restrictions. **Staff:** Don Meredith, Assoc.Libn.

★5371★

HARDWOOD PLYWOOD MANUFACTURERS ASSOCIATION - LIBRARY (Sci-Tech)
1825 Michael Faraday Dr.
Box 2789
Reston, VA 22090   Phone: (703) 435-2900
     Clark E. McDonald, Pres.
Founded: 1921. **Staff:** 12. **Subjects:** Hardwood plywood; hardwood veneer; testing - flamespread, formaldehyde, adhesive, structural; building codes. **Holdings:** 200 books; 25 bound periodical volumes. **Subscriptions:** 60 journals and other serials. **Services:** Interlibrary loans; copying; library open to public with restrictions. **Publications:** Members Bulletin, monthly; Furniture Bulletin; Import Report; Export Report; Literature Survey. **Staff:** Myrna Downey, Libn.

★5372★

HARDY ASSOCIATES (1978) LTD. - LIBRARY (Sci-Tech)
4810 93rd St.
Box 746
Edmonton, AB, Canada T5J 2L4   Phone: (403) 436-2152
     Alice R. Lechelt, Lib.Techn.
Staff: 2. **Subjects:** Engineering - geotechnical, materials, metallurgical; analytical chemistry; environment. **Holdings:** 5000 books; 200 bound periodical volumes; 1000 maps; 8 VF drawers. **Subscriptions:** 65 journals and other serials. **Services:** Interlibrary loans; copying; SDI; library open to public. **Computerized Information Services:** DIALOG, SDC, CAN/OLE, QL

Systems; computerized cataloging.

HARDY (Carrie) MEMORIAL LIBRARY
See: Open Bible College - Carrie Hardy Memorial Library

HARDYMON (Philip B.) LIBRARY
See: St. Anthony Hospital - Philip B. Hardymon Library

★5373★

HARKNESS (Edward S.) EYE INSTITUTE - JOHN M. WHEELER LIBRARY (Med)
635 W. 165th St.   Phone: (212) 694-2916
New York, NY 10032   Albertina F. Mount, Lib.Supv.
Founded: 1933. **Staff:** Prof 1; Other 1. **Subjects:** Ophthalmology. **Special Collections:** Early ophthalmic instruments; memorabilia. **Holdings:** 13,550 books; 1400 bound periodical volumes; 4250 reprints (cataloged); 360 audiotapes. **Subscriptions:** 90 journals and other serials. **Services:** Interlibrary loans (photocopies only); copying. **Computerized Information Services:** Access to Columbia University Health Sciences Library through internal database. **Staff:** Winston H. Smith, Asst.Libn.

★5374★

HARLEM HOSPITAL MEDICAL CENTER - HEALTH SCIENCES LIBRARY (Med)
506 Lenox Ave., KP 6108   Phone: (212) 694-8261
New York, NY 10037   Mr. Manny Chowdhury, Libn.
Staff: Prof 3; Other 5. **Subjects:** Medicine, dentistry, nursing, allied health sciences. **Holdings:** 22,011 books; 8612 bound periodical volumes; 1100 other cataloged items. **Subscriptions:** 451 journals and other serials; 5 newspapers. **Services:** Interlibrary loans; copying; library open to public for reference use only on request. **Computerized Information Services:** BRS; computerized cataloging, acquisitions and serials. **Networks/Consortia:** Member of Medical Library Center of New York. **Publications:** Newsletter, bimonthly; Acquisitions List, quarterly; annual reports; Library Guide; Serials Lists, annual; bibliographies.

★5375★

HARLEM VALLEY PSYCHIATRIC CENTER - INTERDISCIPLINARY LIBRARY (Med)
     Phone: (914) 832-6611
Wingdale, NY 12594   Virginia Lewandowski, Libn.
Founded: 1973. **Staff:** Prof 1; Other 1. **Subjects:** Psychology, psychiatry, medicine, nursing, social work. **Special Collections:** History of New York State Department of Mental Hygiene; collection of AV items in mental health. **Holdings:** 3500 books; 800 bound periodical volumes; audiovisual materials. **Subscriptions:** 60 journals and other serials. **Services:** Interlibrary loans; copying; library open to public. **Networks/Consortia:** Member of New York & Northern New Jersey Regional Medical Library; Southeastern New York Bibliographic Center. **Publications:** Library Services at Harlem Valley, annual - for internal distribution only.

★5376★

HARLEY-DAVIDSON MOTOR CO. - ENGINEERING LIBRARY
3700 W. Juneau Ave.
Box 653
Milwaukee, WI 53201
Founded: 1978. **Subjects:** Motorcycles, motor vehicles, engineering. **Holdings:** 385 volumes; SAE technical reports. **Remarks:** Presently inactive. **Formerly:** AMF/Harley Davidson Motor Co.

HARMAN LIBRARY
See: United Cooperatives of Ontario

★5377★

HARMARVILLE REHABILITATION CENTER - STAFF LIBRARY (Med)
Guys Run Rd.
Box 11460
Pittsburgh, PA 15238   Phone: (412) 781-5700
     Alice B. Kuller, Dir.
Staff: Prof 2. **Subjects:** Rehabilitation of the physically handicapped adult, spinal cord injuries, hemiplegia, paraplegia, architectural accessibility, sexual aspects of disability. **Holdings:** 1300 books; 700 bound periodical volumes; 150 nonprint items; 100 videotapes; 300 films; 8 audio cassette albums; 12 slide/sound programs. **Subscriptions:** 121 journals and other serials. **Services:** Interlibrary loans; copying; SDI; library open to public for reference use only. **Computerized Information Services:** BRS. **Networks/Consortia:** Member of Mideastern Regional Medical Library Service (MERMLS). **Staff:** Patricia Carle, Asst.Libn.

HARMONY FOUNDATION
See: Society for the Preservation and Encouragement of Barber Shop Quartet Singing in America

★5378★
HARPER-GRACE HOSPITALS - DRUG INFORMATION CENTER (Med)
3990 John R St.   Phone: (313) 494-8626
Detroit, MI 48201   Gerald W. Zieg, Dir.
Staff: Prof 2. **Subjects:** Drugs - dosage, availability, metabolism, side effects, toxicity, therapeutic compatibility, adverse reactions, pharmaceutical compatibility. **Special Collections:** DeHaen: Drugs in Use and Drugs in Research Abstracts; Iowa Microfiche Drug Information Service; DrugDex. **Holdings:** 325 books; 120 bound periodical volumes; International Pharmaceutical Abstracts; 6000 FDA clinical experience abstracts; 1600 individual drug entity files; 300 drug therapy audio cassettes. **Subscriptions:** 41 journals and other serials. **Services:** Interlibrary loans; copying; center open to public with restrictions. **Computerized Information Services:** MEDLINE. **Publications:** Harper-Grace Hospital Drug Therapy Newsletter. **Staff:** Dr. Susan Hatfield .

★5379★
HARPER-GRACE HOSPITALS - GRACE HOSPITAL DIVISION - OSCAR LE SEURE PROFESSIONAL LIBRARY (Med)
18700 Meyers Rd.   Phone: (313) 927-3277
Detroit, MI 48235   Frances M. Phillips, Chf.Libn.
Founded: 1914. **Staff:** Prof 2; Other 2. **Subjects:** Medicine and the medical specialties, nursing. **Holdings:** 2500 books; 7000 bound periodical volumes; 391 AV software items. **Subscriptions:** 300 journals and other serials. **Services:** Interlibrary loans; copying; AV production; library open to students in hospital for medical training. **Computerized Information Services:** MEDLINE. **Networks/Consortia:** Member of Pontiac-Allen Park-Detroit Consortium. **Remarks:** Grace Hospital joined Harper Hospital to form Harper-Grace Hospitals. **Staff:** Mary A. Dery, Asst.Libn.

★5380★
HARPER-GRACE HOSPITALS - HARPER HOSPITAL DIVISION - DEPARTMENT OF LIBRARIES (Med)
3990 John R St.   Phone: (313) 494-8264
Detroit, MI 48201   Barbara Coe Johnson, Dir. of Libs.
Founded: 1890. **Staff:** Prof 4; Other 8. **Subjects:** Medicine, nursing, hospital administration. **Special Collections:** Patients' library satellites and booktrain; hard and softbound books of recreational and lay medical orientation (2000 volumes); hospital and corporate archives; professional library. **Holdings:** 8500 book titles; 17,000 bound periodical volumes; 8 VF drawers of pamphlets; tapes; AV software and hardware. **Subscriptions:** 720 journals and other serials. **Services:** Interlibrary loans; copying; library open to community professionals on application to librarian; open to public by physician referral only; general library open to patients, their families and hospital staff only. **Computerized Information Services:** MEDLARS (in-house staff only), DIALOG, BRS. **Networks/Consortia:** Member of OCLC; Biomedical Communication Network (BCN); Metropolitan Detroit Medical Library Group (MDMLG); Detroit Cooperative Cataloging Consortium Center (DC3). **Remarks:** Harper Hospital joined Grace Hospital to form Harper-Grace Hospitals, Inc. of Detroit. **Staff:** Edna Lee Jolliff, Assoc.Libn.; Sandra I. Martin, Asst.Libn.; Kathleen M. Carmichael, Asst.Libn.

★5381★
HARPER & ROW, PUBLISHERS, INC. - SCHOOL DIVISION LIBRARY (Educ; Publ)
10 E. 53rd St., 16th Fl.   Phone: (212) 593-7379
New York, NY 10022   Beth Murphy, Mgr., Lib.
Staff: Prof 1; Other 2. **Subjects:** Education, publishing, English language. **Special Collections:** Row, Peterson textbooks; Harper & Row textbooks and trade books. **Holdings:** 8000 books; 2 VF drawers of publishers' catalogs; 3 VF drawers of language arts material. **Subscriptions:** 90 journals and other serials. **Services:** Interlibrary loans; library open to company staff only. **Computerized Information Services:** DIALOG, SDC. **Publications:** List of New Acquisitions - for internal distribution only.

HARPERS FERRY CENTER LIBRARY
See: U.S. Natl. Park Service

★5382★
HARRAH'S AUTOMOTIVE LIBRARY (Trans)
Box 10   Phone: (702) 786-3232
Reno, NV 89504   Jim Edwards, Oper.Mgr.
Founded: 1961. **Staff:** Prof 2; Other 1. **Subjects:** Antique and classic automobiles, special interest vehicles, motorcycles, boats, airplanes. **Holdings:** 800 books; 4500 bound periodical volumes; 2335 manufacturers'

parts, price manuals and wiring diagrams (cataloged); 12 VF drawers of vehicle accessory catalogs and manuals; 119 VF drawers of vehicle manufacturers' catalogs and manuals, 1896-1974. **Subscriptions:** 54 journals and other serials; 24 newspapers. **Services:** Copying; library not open to public. **Staff:** Ray Borges, Automotive Res.; Pete Grosso, Automotive Res.

HARRELL (George T.) LIBRARY
See: Pennsylvania State University - College of Medicine - George T. Harrell Library

HARRER (Joseph M.) LIBRARY
See: Midwest College of Engineering - Joseph M. Harrer Library

★5383★
HARRINGTON INSTITUTE OF INTERIOR DESIGN - DESIGN LIBRARY (Art)
410 S. Michigan, Rm. 541   Phone: (312) 939-4975
Chicago, IL 60605   Adeline Schuster, Libn.
Staff: Prof 1; Other 2. **Subjects:** Architecture, building construction, decorative arts, furniture history, environmental psychology. **Special Collections:** Current manufacturers' catalogs (furniture, lighting, hardware). **Holdings:** 3700 books; 300 bound periodical volumes; 500 pamphlets; 2000 sample paint colors; 300 sample ceramic tiles; 1000 sample plastic laminates. **Subscriptions:** 80 journals and other serials. **Services:** Interlibrary loans; copying; library open to public for reference use only. **Computerized Information Services:** Computerized cataloging. **Networks/Consortia:** Member of Chicago Library System; OCLC; ILLINET. **Publications:** Subject bibliography, irregular.

HARRINGTON LIBRARY OF THE HEALTH SCIENCES
See: Texas Tech University - Health Sciences Center

HARRINGTON MEETING HOUSE
See: Pemaquid Historical Association

HARRIS (Al) LIBRARY
See: Southwestern Oklahoma State University - Al Harris Library

★5384★
HARRIS CORPORATION - PRD ELECTRONICS DIVISION - INFORMATION CENTER (Sci-Tech)
6801 Jericho Tpke.   Phone: (516) 496-8700
Syosset, NY 11791   Eleanor Pienitz, Libn./Info.Spec.
Staff: Prof 1. **Subjects:** Electronics. **Holdings:** 1103 books; 377 bound periodical volumes. **Services:** Interlibrary loans; library not open to public. **Computerized Information Services:** DIALOG. **Networks/Consortia:** Member of Long Island Library Resources Council (LILRC).

★5385★
HARRIS COUNTY HERITAGE SOCIETY - LIBRARY (Hist; Art)†
1100 Bagby St.   Phone: (713) 223-8367
Houston, TX 77002   Mrs. T.J. Burnett, Jr., Chm.
Founded: 1954. **Staff:** 15. **Subjects:** 19th century decorative arts, history of Houston, Texas and Southwest, art and artists, architecture, restoration. **Special Collections:** Houston history. **Holdings:** 1200 books; 120 bound periodical volumes; newspaper articles (cataloged); 1 VF drawer of pamphlets; maps; slides of 19th century decorative arts, homes, tombstones and history. **Subscriptions:** 13 journals and other serials. **Services:** Copying; library open to public with restrictions. **Publications:** Compendium, annual. **Special Catalogs:** Docent subjects (card).

★5386★
HARRIS COUNTY LAW LIBRARY (Law)
101 Civil Courts Bldg.   Phone: (713) 221-5183
Houston, TX 77002   Eugene Chambers, Dir., Law Lib.
Founded: 1913. **Staff:** Prof 3; Other 4. **Subjects:** Law. **Special Collections:** American and foreign law reviews; U.S. and Canada statutes; official reports for all states; English reports; old legal periodicals. **Holdings:** 75,000 books; 35,000 bound periodical volumes; Texas Criminal Slip Opinions. **Subscriptions:** 1000 journals and other serials. **Services:** Copying; library serves only lawyers, litigants and judges. **Staff:** Clytie Sonnier, Asst. Law Libn.; Vienda Hill, Asst. Law Libn.; Doris Howard, Asst. Law Libn.

★5387★
HARRIS & GIFFORD - LIBRARY (Pict)
2037 N. Glebe Rd.   Phone: (202) 628-8700
Arlington, VA 22207   R.A. Gifford, Owner
Subjects: Supreme Court, President Ford, formal and candid portraits of notables. **Holdings:** 50,000 black/white original photographs and color transparencies.

★5388★
HARRIS HOSPITAL - MEDICAL LIBRARY (Med)
1300 W. Cannon St.
Fort Worth, TX 76104
Phone: (817) 334-6474
Vaida Durham, Libn.
Founded: 1949. Staff: 1. Subjects: Medicine and surgery. Holdings: 1800 books; 3500 bound periodical volumes; 2266 tapes and cassettes. Subscriptions: 143 journals and other serials. Services: Interlibrary loans; copying; library open to public for reference use only.

★5389★
HARRIS (Louis) & ASSOCIATES, INC. - INFORMATION SERVICES (Soc Sci)
630 Fifth Ave.
New York, NY 10111
Phone: (212) 975-1695
Sally Reed, Dir.
Staff: Prof 2. Subjects: Public opinion. Holdings: 500 books; 100 unbound periodicals; Harris Surveys; in-house reports; 2 VF drawers of clippings. Subscriptions: 104 journals and other serials. Services: Interlibrary loans; copying; service not open to public. Special Indexes: Index to the Harris Survey public opinion (book). Staff: Ann Gladwin, Libn.; Barbara Winokur, Libn.

HARRIS (Louis) DATA CENTER
See: University of North Carolina, Chapel Hill - Institute for Research in Social Science

HARRIS (Chancellor R.V.) MEMORIAL LIBRARY
See: Anglican Church of Canada - Church House Library

★5390★
HARRIS-STOWE STATE COLLEGE LIBRARY (Educ)
3026 Laclede Ave.
St. Louis, MO 63103
Phone: (314) 533-3366
Martin Knorr, Dir.
Founded: 1857. Staff: Prof 4; Other 6. Subjects: Education and related subjects. Special Collections: Elementary education; Education of Exceptional Children; Black Studies. Holdings: 80,000 books; 2400 reels of microfilmed periodicals. Subscriptions: 347 journals and other serials; 9 newspapers. Services: Interlibrary loans; copying; library not open to public. Networks/Consortia: Member of St. Louis Regional Library Network; Learning Resources Council of the Higher Education Center of St. Louis, MO. Staff: Julia Broad, Libn.; Marie Wakefield, Libn.; Tom Rick, Libn.

★5391★
HARRIS TRUST AND SAVINGS BANK - RESEARCH LIBRARY (Bus-Fin)
111 W. Monroe St.
Chicago, IL 60603
Phone: (312) 461-7625
Claudette S. Warner, Info.Serv.Off.
Staff: Prof 2; Other 2. Subjects: Banking, economics, finance. Holdings: 4500 books; Securities and Exchange Commission filings for New York and American Stock Exchanges. Subscriptions: 200 journals and other serials. Services: Interlibrary loans; library open to public with restrictions. Computerized Information Services: DIALOG, SDC, Dow Jones News Retrieval, New York Times Information Service; computerized cataloging and circulation. Networks/Consortia: Member of Metropolitan Chicago Library Assembly; Chicago Library System; ILLINET. Publications: New acquisitions list, biweekly - on exchange. Staff: Elizabeth Dreazen, Info.Spec.

★5392★
HARRISBURG HOSPITAL - LIBRARY/MEDIA SERVICES (Med)
S. Front St.
Harrisburg, PA 17101
Phone: (717) 782-5511
Cheryl A. Capitani, Dir., Lib./Media Serv.
Founded: 1936. Staff: Prof 3; Other 2. Subjects: Clinical medicine, nursing, hospital administration, consumer health education. Holdings: 3214 volumes; 3905 bound periodical volumes; 200 AV programs; 214 reels of microfilm. Subscriptions: 388 journals. Services: Interlibrary loans; copying; library open to public for reference use only with permission of director. Computerized Information Services: BRS, NLM; computerized cataloging. Networks/Consortia: Member of Central Pennsylvania Health Science Library Association; Mideastern Regional Medical Library Service (MERMLS); OCLC. Publications: Library Newsletter, bimonthly; Nursing Contents, monthly. Staff: Elizabeth E. Coldsmith, Asst.Libn.; Ray A. Wingert, Media Spec.; Barbara E. Thompson, Lib.Tech.Serv.

★5393★
HARRISBURG STATE HOSPITAL - STAFF LIBRARY (Med)
Cameron & Maclay Sts.
Pouch A
Harrisburg, PA 17105
Phone: (717) 787-9215
Glenn Wayne Miller, Staff Libn.
Founded: 1851. Staff: Prof 2. Subjects: Psychiatry, psychology, social work, medicine, nursing. Special Collections: Audio-Visual Collection. Holdings: 2500 books; 20 linear feet of hospital archives, 1845-1900; Dorothea Dix Museum (housed in Building 09). Subscriptions: 53 journals and other serials. Services: Interlibrary loans; copying; library open to public. Networks/

Consortia: Member of Central Pennsylvania Health Sciences Library Association. Special Catalogs: Current Books of the Staff Library (1973-1982); Accessions for all Hospital Departments (pamphlet). Staff: Mary Kaye Kent, Patient Libn.

★5394★
HARRISON (Benjamin) MEMORIAL HOME - LIBRARY (Hist)
1230 N. Delaware St.
Indianapolis, IN 46202
Phone: (317) 631-1898
Patricia Ronsheim, Cur.
Staff: 5. Subjects: Political history, government reports. Holdings: 1500 books; 500 pamphlets. Services: Library open to public for research on premises. Remarks: Maintained by the President Benjamin Harrison Foundation.

★5395★
HARRISON COMMUNITY HOSPITAL - LIBRARY (Med)
26755 Ballard Rd.
Mt. Clemens, MI 48043
Phone: (313) 465-5501
Bina Wagner, Libn.
Staff: Prof 1; Other 1. Subjects: Podiatry, orthopedics, pediatrics, cardiology, surgery, drug abuse and alcoholism. Holdings: 600 books; 60 bound periodical volumes. Subscriptions: 73 journals and other serials; 5 newspapers. Services: Interlibrary loans; copying; SDI; library not open to public. Networks/Consortia: Member of Macomb Area Libraries Health Information Consortium.

★5396★
HARRISON COUNTY HISTORICAL MUSEUM - LIBRARY (Hist)
Peter Whetstone Sq.
Marshall, TX 75670
Phone: (214) 938-2680
Inez H. Hughes, Dir.
Founded: 1965. Staff: 3. Subjects: Civil War, local and Texas history, genealogy, railroads, music. Special Collections: Judaism (200 books); historical and genealogical periodicals. Holdings: 500 books; 16 VF drawers of clippings; 120 scrapbooks; 100 maps. Services: Library open to public with restrictions.

HARRISON (Francis M.) MEMORIAL LIBRARY
See: Easter Seal Rehabilitation Center of Southwestern Connecticut - Francis M. Harrison Memorial Library

HARRISON (Harold E.) LIBRARY
See: Baltimore City Hospitals - Harold E. Harrison Library

HARRISON (Mel) MEMORIAL LIBRARY
See: Temple Judea - Mel Harrison Memorial Library

★5397★
HARRISON MEMORIAL HOSPITAL - HEALTH SCIENCES LIBRARY (Med)
2520 Cherry St.
Bremerton, WA 98310
Phone: (206) 377-3911
Selma Kannel, Med.Libn.
Founded: 1980. Staff: Prof 1. Subjects: Clinical sciences, nursing, hospital administration. Holdings: 450 books; 900 unbound periodical volumes. Subscriptions: 76 journals and other serials. Services: Interlibrary loans; copying; library not open to public. Computerized Information Services: MEDLARS.

★5398★
HARRISONBURG-ROCKINGHAM HISTORICAL SOCIETY AND MUSEUM - JOHN W. WAYLAND LIBRARY (Hist)†
301 S. Main St.
Box 1141
Harrisonburg, VA 22801
Phone: (703) 434-4762
Julia A. Drinkard, Info.Dir.
Subjects: History of Rockingham County and Harrisonburg. Special Collections: Writings and printed works of Joseph Funk and other family members who were music publishers in the county (150); Henkel Press publications and family correspondence (200 items). Holdings: 600 books; 3 VF drawers of genealogical materials; 6 VF drawers of local newspaper obituaries; 3 VF drawers of miscellany. Services: Copying; library open to public for reference use only. Publications: Rockingham Recorder, occasional.

HARSH (Vivian G.) COLLECTION OF AFRO-AMERICAN HISTORY AND LITERATURE
See: Chicago Public Library Cultural Center - Vivian G. Harsh Collection of Afro-American History & Lit.

HART (Stephen H.) LIBRARY
See: Colorado Historical Society - Stephen H. Hart Library

★5399★
HARTFORD - CITY PLAN LIBRARY (Plan)
550 Main St.   Phone: (203) 722-6630
Hartford, CT 06103   Patricia Williams, Planning Dir.
Subjects: Planning, development, redevelopment, housing, zoning, design. **Special Collections:** General plans of cities and towns in the U.S. **Holdings:** 1220 items, primarily reports and studies. **Subscriptions:** 24 journals and other serials.

★5400★
HARTFORD COURANT - NEWS LIBRARY (Publ)
285 Broad St.   Phone: (203) 249-6411
Hartford, CT 06115   Kathleen McKula, News Libn.
Staff: Prof 1; Other 4. **Subjects:** Newspaper reference topics. **Holdings:** Figures not available.

★5401★
HARTFORD FEMINIST LIBRARY (Soc Sci)
350 Farmington Ave.   Phone: (203) 232-7393
Hartford, CT 06105   Irene Scheibner, Contact
Staff: Prof 2; Other 5. **Subjects:** Women - fiction, literature, political issues, health. **Special Collections:** Nonsexist children's books. **Holdings:** 900 books. **Services:** Library open to public with fee.

★5402★
HARTFORD HOSPITAL - HEALTH SCIENCE LIBRARIES (Med)
80 Seymour St.   Phone: (203) 524-2971
Hartford, CT 06115   Gertrude Lamb, Ph.D., Dir.
Staff: Prof 8; Other 9. **Subjects:** Clinical medicine, nursing, education, administration, gerontology, allied health specialties. **Special Collections:** Foley Collection (early books on nursing). **Holdings:** 7700 books; 8268 bound periodical volumes; 30 VF drawers of pamphlets; 37 series of audio cassettes; 170 video cassettes; 155 slide sets and kits; 10 16mm films. **Subscriptions:** 587 journals and other serials. **Services:** Interlibrary loans; copying; SDI; library open to public for reference use only. **Computerized Information Services:** NLM, BRS. **Networks/Consortia:** Member of Capitol Area Health Consortium Libraries; Connecticut Association of Health Science Libraries. **Also Known As:** Robinson Library - Medical Library. **Staff:** Virginia Corcoran, Robinson Libn.; Steve Lytle, Archv.; Holly B. Clark, Clinical Libn./Pediatrics; Alice Briggs, Med.Libn.; Sherry Morgan, Ref.Libn.; Suzanne LaRue, Clinical Libn., Surgery; Valori Banfi, Clinical Libn./Med.

★5403★
HARTFORD INSURANCE GROUP - CORPORATE LIBRARY (Bus-Fin)
Hartford Plaza   Phone: (203) 547-5516
Hartford, CT 06115   Bonnie Jean Woodworth, Corp.Libn.
Founded: 1968. **Staff:** Prof 1; Other 2. **Subjects:** Finance. **Special Collections:** Moody's Industrials, 1919 to present. **Holdings:** 2000 books; 166 legal file drawers of corporate and financial information. **Subscriptions:** 250 journals and other serials. **Services:** Interlibrary loans; copying; library open to public by appointment. **Networks/Consortia:** Member of Capitol Region Library Council.

★5404★
HARTFORD INSURANCE GROUP - LOSS CONTROL DEPARTMENT LIBRARY (Sci-Tech)
Hartford Plaza   Phone: (203) 547-5000
Hartford, CT 06115   Gail M. Thompson, Libn.
Staff: Prof 1; Other 1. **Subjects:** Engineering, environmental science, safety engineering, chemistry. **Holdings:** 2000 books. **Subscriptions:** 130 journals and other serials. **Services:** Library not open to public. **Computerized Information Services:** MEDLARS.

HARTFORD LAW BRANCH
See: Connecticut State Library

★5405★
HARTFORD MEDICAL SOCIETY - WALTER STEINER MEMORIAL LIBRARY (Med)
230 Scarborough St.   Phone: (203) 236-5613
Hartford, CT 06035   William E. Hart, M.D., Libn.
Founded: 1873. **Staff:** Prof 1. **Subjects:** Medicine, history of medicine, anesthesiology. **Special Collections:** Gershom Bulkeley manuscripts; Hartford imprints; medical and dental tools and artifacts. **Holdings:** 33,850 volumes. **Subscriptions:** 138 journals and other serials. **Services:** Copying; library open to public for reference use only. **Special Catalogs:** A Catalogue of Selected Objects from The Historical Museum of Medicine and Dentistry.

★5406★
HARTFORD PUBLIC LIBRARY - ART, MUSIC AND RECREATION DEPARTMENT (Art; Mus)
500 Main St.   Phone: (203) 525-9121
Hartford, CT 06103   Vernon Martin, Hd.
Staff: Prof 4. **Subjects:** Art, music, recreation. **Holdings:** 327,997 pictures; 16,910 pamphlets; 563 films; 9393 phonograph records. **Subscriptions:** 44 journals and other serials. **Services:** Interlibrary loans; copying; library open to public. **Publications:** Film catalog; monthly film lists; book lists - distributed to patrons. **Special Indexes:** Song, piano, organ, violin indexes; film index. **Staff:** Jonathan Porter; Betty Raynor; Kathleen Brophy.

★5407★
HARTFORD PUBLIC LIBRARY - BUSINESS, SCIENCE & TECHNOLOGY DEPARTMENT (Bus-Fin; Sci-Tech)
500 Main St.   Phone: (203) 525-9121
Hartford, CT 06103   Charles S. Griffen, Hd.
Founded: 1929. **Staff:** Prof 5; Other 2. **Subjects:** Commerce, economics, statistics, applied science, science and technology, mathematics, natural sciences. **Special Collections:** Commercial Airplane Catalog files; corporate annual reports; radio and television service manuals. **Holdings:** 32,000 books and bound periodical volumes; 28 VF drawers of pamphlets; 170,000 government documents; 1180 reels of microfilm. **Subscriptions:** 410 journals and other serials. **Services:** Interlibrary loans; copying; library open to public. **Special Indexes:** Consumer product, automobile, and audio/hi-fi equipment evaluation indexes (card). **Staff:** Marlene Melcher; Ann Santos; Angela Chase, Govt.Doc.Libn.; James Gold .

★5408★
HARTFORD PUBLIC LIBRARY - REFERENCE AND GENERAL READING DEPARTMENT (Hist)
500 Main St.   Phone: (203) 525-9121
Hartford, CT 06103   Martha D. Nolan, Hd.
Founded: 1774. **Staff:** 11. **Subjects:** History; biography; travel; literature; social sciences; philosophy; psychology; religion; political science; performing arts - theater, motion pictures, radio and television. **Special Collections:** Hartford Collection (35,000 cataloged items); Foundation Center Regional Collection; Municipal Reference Collection. **Holdings:** 100,000 books; 20,500 pamphlets and reports; 30,000 maps; depository for U.S. and Connecticut government documents; Defense Mapping Agency depository; 1900 reels of microfilm; 1700 microfiche; 3000 pictures; 400 recordings. **Subscriptions:** 400 journals and other serials; 26 newspapers. **Services:** Interlibrary loans; copying; library open to public. **Computerized Information Services:** Online systems (through NELINET). **Networks/Consortia:** Member of Capitol Region Library Council. **Special Indexes:** Index to Hartford Courant, 1945 to present; Hartford Times, 1945 to 1976. **Staff:** Beverly Loughlin, Adm.Asst.; Evelyn Ball; Dorothy Brickett; Rosalie Fawcett; Carol Fitting; James Gold; Shirley Kiefer; Fernando Labault; Betty Mullendore; Evelyn Seltzer

★5409★
HARTFORD SEMINARY FOUNDATION - CASE MEMORIAL LIBRARY (Rel-Theol)†
77 Sherman St.   Phone: (203) 232-4451
Hartford, CT 06105   Nancy Lee Harney, Libn.
Founded: 1834. **Staff:** 1. **Subjects:** Theology, church history, missions, sociology, education. **Special Collections:** Duncan Black Macdonald Collection of Arabian Nights (1000 volumes); Beck Collection of Martin Luther (1000 volumes); Arabic manuscripts (1200). **Holdings:** 80,000 volumes; 5000 bound periodical volumes; 100,000 archival items; 20,000 microforms. **Subscriptions:** 1100 journals and other serials. **Services:** Interlibrary loans; copying; library open to public. **Staff:** Willem Bijlefeld, Supv., Lib.Comm.

★5410★
HARTFORD STATE TECHNICAL COLLEGE - GROM HAYES LIBRARY (Sci-Tech)
401 Flatbush Ave.   Phone: (203) 527-4111
Hartford, CT 06106   Larry W. Yother, Libn.
Founded: 1963. **Staff:** Prof 2. **Subjects:** Engineering- civil, mechanical, tool; computer and electronic technology. **Special Collections:** Architecture history. **Holdings:** 9000 books. **Subscriptions:** 78 journals and other serials. **Services:** Interlibrary loans; copying; library open to state residents. **Computerized Information Services:** Computerized cataloging, acquisitions, serials, circulation and inventory. **Publications:** Automation systems manual, semiannual. **Staff:** Grom M. Hayes, Libn. Emeritus.

HARTMAN LIBRARY
See: Ortho Pharmaceutical Corporation

HARTNESS LIBRARY
See: Vermont Technical College

HARTT SCHOOL OF MUSIC
See: University of Hartford

HARTWELL LIBRARY
See: Center for Environmental Information

HARVARD BLACK ROCK FOREST LIBRARY
See: Harvard University

HARVARD FOREST LIBRARY
See: Harvard University

★5411★
HARVARD LIBRARY IN NEW YORK (Hum)
27 W. 44th St.   Phone: (212) 840-6600
New York, NY 10036   Adrienne G. Fischier, Libn.
Founded: 1978. **Staff:** 2. **Special Collections:** Harvardiana. **Holdings:** 25,000 books; 600 bound periodical volumes; 500 catalogs, reports, pamphlets. **Subscriptions:** 120 journals and other serials; 10 newspapers. **Services:** Interlibrary loans (limited); library open to public by appointment.

HARVARD MEDICAL SCHOOL
See: Harvard University - School of Medicine

★5412★
HARVARD MUSICAL ASSOCIATION - LIBRARY (Mus)
57A Chestnut St.   Phone: (617) 523-2897
Boston, MA 02108   Natalie Palme, Libn.
Founded: 1837. **Staff:** Prof 1; Other 1. **Subjects:** Printed music, music books, music manuscripts. **Holdings:** 2130 books; 325 bound periodical volumes; 7512 other items of music (cataloged). **Services:** Interlibrary loans; library open to public.

HARVARD NEGOTIATION PROJECT LIBRARY
See: Harvard University

HARVARD UKRAINIAN RESEARCH INSTITUTE
See: Harvard University

★5413★
HARVARD UNIVERSITY - ARCHIVES (Hist)
Pusey Library   Phone: (617) 495-2461
Cambridge, MA 02138   Harley P. Holden, Cur.
Staff: Prof 6; Other 5. **Subjects:** Harvard University (archives, publications of, books about); Harvard graduates (biography and clippings about); Harvard professors (private papers). **Special Collections:** Harvard University theses and dissertations. **Holdings:** 81,706 volumes and pamphlets. **Services:** Copying; reference service on Harvard University and Harvard people; archives open to public. **Networks/Consortia:** Member of OCLC through NELINET; CRL. **Publications:** Descriptive Guide, by Clark Elliott, 1974; Visual Collections Manual, by Karen R. Lewis, 1982. **Staff:** Clark A. Elliott, Assoc.Cur.

★5414★
HARVARD UNIVERSITY - ARNOLD ARBORETUM & GRAY HERBARIUM - LIBRARY (Sci-Tech)
22 Divinity Ave.   Phone: (617) 495-2366
Cambridge, MA 02138   Barbara A. Callahan, Libn.
Founded: 1890. **Staff:** Prof 1; Other 3. **Subjects:** Botany and horticulture. **Special Collections:** Manuscript letters from botanists. **Holdings:** 150,000 books, bound periodical volumes, and pamphlets. **Subscriptions:** 913 journals and other serials. **Services:** Copying; library open to public for reference use only on a limited basis. **Networks/Consortia:** Member of OCLC through NELINET; CRL. **Publications:** Gray Herbarium Index - reproduction of 259,000 cards with names and literature citations of newly described or established vascular plants of the Western Hemisphere.

★5415★
HARVARD UNIVERSITY - BIOLOGICAL LABORATORIES LIBRARY (Sci-Tech)
16 Divinity Ave.   Phone: (617) 495-3944
Cambridge, MA 02138   Dorothy J. Solbrig, Libn.
Staff: Prof 1; Other 1. **Subjects:** Cell and developmental biology, biochemistry, plant and animal physiology, genetics. **Holdings:** 21,853 books and bound periodical volumes. **Subscriptions:** 260 journals and other serials. **Services:** Interlibrary loans; library open to public. **Computerized Information Services:** BRS; computerized cataloging. **Networks/Consortia:**

Member of OCLC through NELINET; CRL.

★5416★
HARVARD UNIVERSITY - CENTER FOR EUROPEAN STUDIES - LIBRARY (Area-Ethnic)†
5 Bryant St.   Phone: (617) 495-4150
Cambridge, MA 02138   Loren Goldner, Libn.
Founded: 1969. **Staff:** Prof 1. **Subjects:** Contemporary European domestic politics, history, sociology, economics and labor relations. **Special Collections:** German domestic politics and history; books, pamphlets, journals and newspapers for Laurence Wylie's Bibliography on France: the events of May-June 1968. **Holdings:** 4069 books; 1 VF drawer of information on European archives; 25 years of Le Monde newspaper; 300 papers on European politics; 20 dissertations; 5 boxes of seminar and conference papers. **Subscriptions:** 82 journals and other serials; 18 newspapers. **Services:** Interlibrary loans; copying; library open to public but borrowing is limited to students and faculty in the Greater Boston area. **Networks/Consortia:** Member of OCLC through NELINET; CRL. **Publications:** Monographs on Europe, casebooks; list of publications - available upon request. **Special Catalogs:** Union catalog of West European newspapers in the Boston area.

★5417★
HARVARD UNIVERSITY - CENTER FOR HELLENIC STUDIES - LIBRARY (Hum; Hist)
3100 Whitehaven St., N.W.   Phone: (202) 234-3738
Washington, DC 20008   Jeno Platthy, Ph.D., Libn.
Staff: Prof 1; Other 1. **Subjects:** Ancient Greek history and civilization, literature, religion. **Holdings:** 40,500 books, bound periodical volumes, and pamphlets. **Subscriptions:** 205 journals and other serials. **Services:** Interlibrary loans; library open to qualified scholars. **Networks/Consortia:** Member of OCLC through NELINET; CRL.

★5418★
HARVARD UNIVERSITY - CENTER FOR INTERNATIONAL AFFAIRS - LIBRARY (Soc Sci)
Coolidge Hall
1737 Cambridge St.   Phone: (617) 495-2173
Cambridge, MA 02138   Julie M. Blattner, Libn.
Staff: Prof 1. **Subjects:** International relations. **Holdings:** 11,250 books. **Subscriptions:** 35 journals and other serials. **Services:** Interlibrary loans; copying; library open to public with restrictions. **Networks/Consortia:** Member of OCLC through NELINET; CRL.

★5419★
HARVARD UNIVERSITY - CENTER FOR MIDDLE EASTERN STUDIES - LIBRARY (Area-Ethnic)
Coolidge Hall
1737 Cambridge St.   Phone: (617) 495-2173
Cambridge, MA 02138   Julie M. Blattner, Libn.
Founded: 1959. **Subjects:** History of Islam; ancient and modern Middle East - Turkey, Iran, Egypt, Syria, Jordan, Israel, Libya, North Africa, Caucasus, Central Asia. **Special Collections:** Army maps of Middle Eastern area. **Holdings:** 5005 books, bound periodical volumes and pamphlets.

★5420★
HARVARD UNIVERSITY - CENTER FOR POPULATION STUDIES LIBRARY (Soc Sci)
665 Huntington Ave.   Phone: (617) 732-1234
Boston, MA 02115   Wilma E. Winters, Libn.
Founded: 1965. **Staff:** Prof 1; Other 1. **Subjects:** Population studies and demography. **Holdings:** 20,000 volumes. **Subscriptions:** 235 journals and other serials. **Services:** Interlibrary loans; copying; library open to public with restrictions. **Networks/Consortia:** Member of Association for Population/Family Planning Libraries and Information Centers - International (APLIC-Internatl.).

★5421★
HARVARD UNIVERSITY - CENTER FOR SCIENCE AND INTERNATIONAL AFFAIRS LIBRARY (Soc Sci)
79 Boylston St.   Phone: (617) 495-1408
Cambridge, MA 02138   Lisbeth Bernstein, Libn.
Founded: 1973. **Staff:** Prof 1; Other 1. **Subjects:** Arms control, international affairs, energy policy. **Holdings:** 3420 books and bound periodical volumes. **Subscriptions:** 125 journals and other serials; 15 newspapers. **Services:** Interlibrary loans; copying; library not open to public. **Computerized Information Services:** Computerized cataloging. **Networks/Consortia:** Member of OCLC through NELINET. **Publications:** International Security, quarterly - by subscription.

★5422★

HARVARD UNIVERSITY - CHEMISTRY LIBRARY (Sci-Tech)
Converse Memorial Library   Phone: (617) 495-4079
Cambridge, MA 02138   Ludmila Birladeanu, Supv.
Staff: Prof 1; Other 1. **Subjects:** Chemistry. **Special Collections:** Foreign dissertations. **Holdings:** 49,469 books, bound periodical volumes and pamphlets. **Subscriptions:** 411 journals and other serials. **Services:** Interlibrary loans (fee); copying; library open to public with restrictions. **Networks/Consortia:** Member of OCLC through NELINET; CRL.

★5423★

HARVARD UNIVERSITY - DIVINITY SCHOOL - ANDOVER-HARVARD THEOLOGICAL LIBRARY (Rel-Theol)
45 Francis Ave.   Phone: (617) 495-5770
Cambridge, MA 02138   Maria Grossmann, Libn.
Founded: 1812. **Staff:** Prof 7; Other 8. **Subjects:** Theology, Bible, Protestantism and material related to this field. **Special Collections:** American Congregational, Unitarian and Universalist materials. **Holdings:** 362,775 volumes; 1800 filing boxes of manuscripts; 7502 microforms. **Subscriptions:** 2060 journals and other serials. **Services:** Interlibrary loans; copying; library open to public on special application. **Computerized Information Services:** Computerized cataloging and acquisitions. **Networks/Consortia:** Member of OCLC through NELINET; CRL; Boston Theological Institute. **Publications:** Guide. **Staff:** Theodore Pulcini, Pub.Serv.; Russell Pollard, Tech.Serv.; Alan Seaburg, Mss. and Archv.; Doris Freitag, Consrv.

★5424★

HARVARD UNIVERSITY - DUMBARTON OAKS CENTER FOR PRE-COLUMBIAN STUDIES - LIBRARY (Area-Ethnic)
1703 32nd St., N.W.   Phone: (202) 342-3265
Washington, DC 20007   Carlos Arostegui, Asst.Cur.
Founded: 1963. **Staff:** 1. **Subjects:** Pre-Columbian archeology and art history; Mesoamerican linguistics; Latin American ethnology. **Special Collections:** Maya Linguistics (105 volumes). **Holdings:** 12,000 volumes; 6 VF drawers of photographs and clippings; 32 reels of microfilm; 43 conference tapes; 8900 slides, 20 microfiche. **Subscriptions:** 65 journals and other serials. **Services:** Copying; library open to qualified scholars by appointment. **Publications:** List of publications - available upon request.

★5425★

HARVARD UNIVERSITY - DUMBARTON OAKS GARDEN LIBRARY OF THE CENTER FOR STUDIES IN LANDSCAPE ARCHITECTURE (Hist; Art)
1703 32nd St., N.W.   Phone: (202) 342-3280
Washington, DC 20007   Laura Byers, Libn.
Founded: 1963. **Staff:** Prof 1; Other 1. **Subjects:** History - gardens and garden design, landscape architecture, garden ornaments and horticulture. **Special Collections:** Rare books, drawings, prints and floral illustrations. **Holdings:** 12,000 books; 350 bound periodical volumes; photograph and slide collection; 4 VF drawers of pamphlet material, microfiche. **Subscriptions:** 12 journals and other serials. **Services:** Interlibrary loans; copying; library open to scholars and professionals with appointment. **Computerized Information Services:** Online systems; computerized cataloging and serials. **Networks/Consortia:** Member of Consortium of Universities of the Washington Metropolitan Area. **Publications:** Colloquium on the History of Landscape Architecture, annual - for sale.

★5426★

HARVARD UNIVERSITY - DUMBARTON OAKS RESEARCH LIBRARY AND COLLECTION (Hist)
1703 32nd St., N.W.   Phone: (202) 342-3240
Washington, DC 20007   Irene Vaslef, Libn.
Founded: 1940. **Staff:** Prof 3; Other 5. **Subjects:** Early Christian, Byzantine and medieval civilization - art, archeology, religion, history, source material. **Holdings:** 88,000 volumes; 84,000 photographs and slides; 550 microforms. **Subscriptions:** 877 journals and other serials. **Services:** Interlibrary loans; copying; library open to research scholars. **Computerized Information Services:** Computerized cataloging. **Networks/Consortia:** Member of OCLC through CAPCON; CRL.

HARVARD UNIVERSITY - EAST ASIAN RESEARCH CENTER
See: Harvard University - John K. Fairbank Center for East Asian Research

★5427★

HARVARD UNIVERSITY - ECONOMIC BOTANY LIBRARY (Sci-Tech)†
10 Oxford St.   Phone: (617) 495-2326
Cambridge, MA 02138   Wesley Wong
Founded: 1876. **Staff:** 1. **Subjects:** Ethnobotany, economic botany, medical botany, herbals, plant foods, agronomy. **Special Collections:** The Oakes Ames Collection of Linneana (150 volumes). **Holdings:** 27,539 volumes; 8 VF drawers of student theses and dissertations, pre-publication manuscripts, clippings. **Subscriptions:** 83 journals and other serials. **Services:** Interlibrary loans (fee); copying; library open to public for reference use only. **Networks/Consortia:** Member of OCLC through NELINET; CRL. **Publications:** Botanical Museum Leaflets, 10 issues/volume - international distribution. **Also Known As:** Oakes Ames Library of Economic Botany.

★5428★

HARVARD UNIVERSITY - EDA KUHN LOEB MUSIC LIBRARY (Mus)†
                                     Phone: (617) 495-2794
Cambridge, MA 02138   Michael Ochs, Libn.
Staff: Prof 4; Other 12. **Subjects:** Music. **Special Collections:** Isham Memorial Library of rare materials and microfilms of early music prints and manuscripts. **Holdings:** 88,798 books and scores; 25,000 recordings; 14,741 reels of microfilm. **Subscriptions:** 527 journals and other serials. **Services:** Interlibrary loans (fee); library use requires a letter of introduction; fee for extended use. **Staff:** Larry G. Mowers, Asst.Libn.; Robert J. Dennis, Recorded Sound Libn.; Florence Lynch, Cat.

★5429★

HARVARD UNIVERSITY - FARLOW REFERENCE LIBRARY (Sci-Tech)
20 Divinity Ave.   Phone: (617) 495-2369
Cambridge, MA 02138   Geraldine C. Kaye, Libn.
Subjects: Cryptogamic botany - algae, bryophytes, fungi, lichens. **Holdings:** 60,000 books and pamphlets; manuscript and portrait collections. **Subscriptions:** 105 journals and other serials. **Services:** Copying; library open to public. **Publications:** Occasional papers. **Special Catalogs:** Author/Title/Subject catalog (book), 6 volumes.

★5430★

HARVARD UNIVERSITY - FINE ARTS LIBRARY (Art)
Fogg Art Museum   Phone: (617) 495-3373
Cambridge, MA 02138   Wolfgang Freitag, Libn.
Staff: Prof 11; Other 16. **Subjects:** History of art. **Special Collections:** Exhibition catalogs; auction sale catalogs; Classical Art and Archeology; Islamic Architecture; Italian Renaissance painting; German Expressionism; Rubel Asiatic Research Collection of the arts of the Far East, India and Central Asia. **Holdings:** 197,000 volumes; 60 boxes of pamphlets and catalogs; 1.1 million slides and photographs; 25,650 microforms. **Subscriptions:** 1163 journals and other serials. **Services:** Copying; library open to members of the university. **Networks/Consortia:** Member of RLG; OCLC through NELINET; CRL. **Publications:** Harvard List of Books on Art. **Special Catalogs:** Book Catalog (15 volumes) published in 1971, 3 volume supplement, 1976. **Remarks:** Library maintains the Documentation Center for the Aga Khan Program in Islamic Architecture. **Staff:** James Hodgson, Acq.Libn.; Jane Knuttunen, Hd., Tech.Serv.; Helene Roberts, Cur. of Visual Coll.; Richard Simpson, Pub.Serv.Libn.; Mrs. Yen-Shew Lynn Chao, Cur. of Rubel Coll.; Dolores Fairbanks, Bibliog., Islamic Arch.

★5431★

HARVARD UNIVERSITY - GEOLOGICAL SCIENCES LIBRARY (Sci-Tech)
24 Oxford St.   Phone: (617) 495-2029
Cambridge, MA 02138   Julian Green, Libn.
Founded: 1960. **Staff:** Prof 1; Other 2. **Subjects:** Mineralogy, petrology, mining geology. **Holdings:** 50,221 books and bound periodical volumes; 15,000 geological maps. **Subscriptions:** 912 journals and other serials. **Services:** Interlibrary loans; copying. **Networks/Consortia:** Member of OCLC through NELINET; CRL.

★5432★

HARVARD UNIVERSITY - GODFREY LOWELL CABOT SCIENCE LIBRARY (Sci-Tech)
Science Ctr., One Oxford St.   Phone: (617) 495-5353
Cambridge, MA 02138   Alan E. Erickson, Sci.Spec.
Founded: 1973. **Staff:** Prof 4; Other 10. **Subjects:** All sciences listed in the undergraduate curriculum, pure mathematics and theoretical statistics research. **Holdings:** 125,353 books and bound periodical volumes. **Subscriptions:** 815 journals and other serials. **Services:** Interlibrary loans; bibliographic instruction. **Computerized Information Services:** DIALOG, BRS; computerized cataloging and acquisitions. **Networks/Consortia:** Member of OCLC through NELINET; CRL. **Staff:** William A. Bourque, Tech.Serv.Libn.; Mary Morrison, Ref.Libn.; Carrie Kent, Ref.Libn.; Alice Dalton, Hd., Circ.

★5433★

HARVARD UNIVERSITY - GORDON MC KAY LIBRARY - DIVISION OF APPLIED SCIENCES (Sci-Tech)†
Pierce Hall, 29 Oxford St.   Phone: (617) 495-2836
Cambridge, MA 02138   Julie Sandall Barlas, Libn.
Founded: 1919. **Staff:** Prof 2; Other 3. **Subjects:** Applied mathematics,

applied physics, computers, environment, mechanics, electronics. **Special Collections:** Blue Hill Collection (meteorology and oceanography; 5120 volumes). **Holdings:** 75,000 books; 34,000 bound periodical volumes; 75,369 technical reports on microcards; 130,876 technical reports on microfiche. **Subscriptions:** 878 journals and other serials. **Services:** Interlibrary loans (fee); copying; library open to public for reference use only. **Computerized Information Services:** Computerized cataloging and acquisitions. **Networks/Consortia:** Member of OCLC through NELINET; CRL.

★5434★

HARVARD UNIVERSITY - GRADUATE SCHOOL OF BUSINESS ADMINISTRATION - BAKER LIBRARY (Bus-Fin)
Soldiers Field Rd.   Phone: (617) 495-6395
Boston, MA 02163   Mary Chatfield, Libn.
Founded: 1908. **Staff:** Prof 12; Other 26. **Subjects:** Business and economics. **Special Collections:** Kress Library of Business and Economics (publications before 1850; 30,000 volumes); corporate reports on 19,340 companies; manuscripts and archives (80,000 volumes). **Holdings:** 540,000 books, bound periodical volumes and pamphlets; 322,258 microfiche; 7344 reels of microfilm. **Subscriptions:** 6473 journals and other serials. **Services:** Interlibrary loans; copying; library open to qualified persons for reference. **Computerized Information Services:** Online systems; computerized cataloging and serials. **Networks/Consortia:** Member of OCLC through NELINET. **Publications:** Business Forecasting for the 1980s - and Beyond; Business Intelligence and Strategic Planning; Baker Library Mini-Lists; Business Reference Sources; Core Collection: An Author and Subject Guide, annual; Current Periodical Publications in Baker Library, annual; Recent Additions to Baker Library, monthly; Working Papers in Baker Library: A Quarterly Checklist; List of Business Manuscripts in Baker Library. **Special Catalogs:** Book Catalog (32 volumes) published in 1971, first supplements 1974; Kress Catalog (3 volumes, plus 1967 supplement). **Staff:** Nancy Bowen, Ref.; Mary Barnard, Ref.; Enanu Dixon, Ref.; Ruth Reinstein Rogers, Kress Lib.; Florence Bartoshesky, Mss. and Archv.; Lorna M. Daniells, Bus.Bibliog.

★5435★

HARVARD UNIVERSITY - GRADUATE SCHOOL OF DESIGN - FRANCES LOEB LIBRARY (Art)†
Gund Hall   Phone: (617) 495-2574
Cambridge, MA 02138   Angela Giral, Libn.
Founded: 1902. **Staff:** Prof 6; Other 10. **Subjects:** Architecture, landscape architecture, city and regional planning. **Special Collections:** Charles Mulford Robinson Collection; Charles Eliot Collection; Warren Manning Collection (exposition); Cluny Collections; Le Corbusier Collection. **Holdings:** 208,750 books, bound periodical volumes and pamphlets; 10,000 maps; plans; 5000 architectural blueprints; 76,000 slides. **Subscriptions:** 903 journals and other serials. **Services:** Interlibrary loans; copying; library open to public for reference use only. **Computerized Information Services:** Computerized cataloging, acquisitions and reserves. **Networks/Consortia:** Member of OCLC through NELINET; CRL. **Staff:** Judith Auerbach, Acq.Libn.; Christopher Hail, Asst. And Ref.Libn.; Hinda Sklar, Hd., Tech.Serv.; Katherine Poole, Lrng.Rsrcs.Libn.

★5436★

HARVARD UNIVERSITY - GRADUATE SCHOOL OF EDUCATION - GUTMAN LIBRARY (Educ)†
Appian Way   Phone: (617) 495-4225
Cambridge, MA 02138   Inabeth Miller, Libn.
Founded: 1920. **Staff:** Prof 10; Other 15. **Subjects:** Education, tests and measurements, urban and minority education, curriculum, textbooks. **Holdings:** 134,825 volumes; 294,518 microfiche. **Subscriptions:** 1238 journals and other serials. **Services:** Interlibrary loans; copying; library open to public for reference use only. **Computerized Information Services:** DIALOG. **Networks/Consortia:** Member of OCLC through NELINET; CRL. **Publications:** Guide; Newsletter. **Staff:** Susan Baughman, Asst.Libn.; Virginia Stein, Hd., Circ.

★5437★

HARVARD UNIVERSITY - HARVARD BLACK ROCK FOREST LIBRARY (Sci-Tech)†
                                            Phone: (914) 534-4517
Cornwall, NY 12518   Jack J. Karnig, Forest Mgr.
Subjects: Forestry. **Holdings:** 9536 books and bound periodical volumes. **Subscriptions:** 36 journals and other serials. **Services:** Library not open to public. **Networks/Consortia:** Member of OCLC through NELINET; CRL.

★5438★

HARVARD UNIVERSITY - HARVARD FOREST LIBRARY (Sci-Tech)
Shaler Hall   Phone: (617) 724-3285
Petersham, MA 01366   Catherine M. Danahar, Libn.
Founded: 1908. **Subjects:** Forestry. **Holdings:** 10,307 volumes. **Subscriptions:** 140 journals and other serials. **Services:** Interlibrary loans; library not open to public. **Networks/Consortia:** Member of OCLC through NELINET; CRL.

★5439★

HARVARD UNIVERSITY - HARVARD NEGOTIATION PROJECT LIBRARY (Soc Sci)
Pound Hall 500
Harvard Law School   Phone: (617) 495-1684
Cambridge, MA 02138   Bruce M. Patton, Assoc.Dir./Lib.Hd.
Staff: 2. **Subjects:** Negotiation theory and technique; international negotiations. **Holdings:** 74 books. **Services:** Library open to public with permission. **Staff:** Jody Bailey, Libn.

★5440★

HARVARD UNIVERSITY - HARVARD UKRAINIAN RESEARCH INSTITUTE - REFERENCE LIBRARY (Area-Ethnic)
1583 Massachusetts Ave.   Phone: (617) 495-5224
Cambridge, MA 02138   Larisa Trolle, Libn.
Founded: 1973. **Staff:** Prof 1; Other 1. **Subjects:** Ukraine - history, culture, linguistics, literature, religion, social sciences, societies and institutions; ancillary historical disciplines (textology, historiography, filangrology). **Special Collections:** Specialized bibliographies of monographs and serials; works of major Ukrainian authors (including translations of scholarly and literary importance); classic textbooks in history, literature, linguistics, religion, theology and the social sciences; offprints of articles of Ukrainian scholars (all disciplines) and those relating to Ukraine; national bibliography. **Holdings:** 8571 books; periodicals; atlases; classic textbooks; offprints. **Subscriptions:** 84 journals and other serials. **Services:** Copying (limited); library open to public with restrictions. **Publications:** Harvard Ukrainian Studies, quarterly journal; Ukrainica in the Harvard University Library (1975 to present); Harvard Series in Ukrainian Studies volumes.

★5441★

HARVARD UNIVERSITY - HARVARD-YENCHING LIBRARY (Area-Ethnic)
2 Divinity Ave.   Phone: (617) 495-2756
Cambridge, MA 02138   Eugene Wu, Libn.
Staff: Prof 13; Other 13. **Subjects:** Humanities and social sciences relating to China, Japan, and Korea. **Special Collections:** Rare Chinese books and manuscripts; Chinese rubbings; Tibetan and Mongolian Tripitaka; Manchu publications; Nakhi manuscripts; Vietnamese publications. **Holdings:** 612,881 volumes; 12,189 reels of microfilm; 10,207 journals; 309 newspapers. **Subscriptions:** 2146 journals and other serials; 46 newspapers. **Services:** Interlibrary loans; copying; library open to those with identification and a fee for borrowing. **Networks/Consortia:** Member of CRL. **Publications:** Occasional Reference Notes; Harvard-Yenching Library Bibliographical Series. **Staff:** George E. Potter, Pub.Serv.Libn.; John Yung-Hsiang Lai, Assoc.Libn./Cat.; Chia-Yaung Hu, Hd., Chinese Sect.; Toshiyuki Aoki, Hd., Japanese Sect.; Sungha Kim, Hd., Korean Sect.; Sidney Tai, Supv., Rare Bks.Rm.; Raymond D. Lum, Hd., Western Sect.

★5442★

HARVARD UNIVERSITY - HISTORY OF SCIENCE LIBRARY (Sci-Tech)
Widener Library, Rm. 91
Cambridge, MA 02138
                                            Erwin N. Hiebert
Subjects: History of science. **Holdings:** 23,783 volumes. **Services:** Library not open to public. **Networks/Consortia:** Member of OCLC through NELINET; CRL.

★5443★

HARVARD UNIVERSITY - HOUGHTON LIBRARY (Rare Book)
                                            Phone: (617) 495-2440
Cambridge, MA 02138   Roger E. Stoddard, Assoc.Libn./Houghton Lib.
Subjects: Major collection of rare books and manuscripts in all fields, with some emphasis on literature, history, theater history and typography. **Special Collections:** Archives of United Church Board for World Ministries. **Holdings:** 440,000 volumes, printed books; manuscripts occupying 14,775 linear feet. **Services:** Copying; library open to public. **Networks/Consortia:** Member of OCLC through NELINET; CRL. **Staff:** Lawrence R. Dowler, Assoc.Libn./Harvard Coll.; F. Thomas Noonan, Cur., Reading Rm.; Rodney G. Dennis, Cur. of Mss.; Eleanor M. Garvey, Cur., Printing; Jeanne Newlin, Cur., Theater Coll.; James E. Walsh, Kpr., Printed Bks.

★5444★
HARVARD UNIVERSITY - INSTITUTE FOR INTERNATIONAL DEVELOPMENT - LIBRARY (Soc Sci)
Coolidge Hall
1737 Cambridge St. Phone: (617) 495-2173
Cambridge, MA 02138 Julie M. Blattner, Libn.
Founded: 1958. **Staff:** Prof 1. **Subjects:** Economic and rural development, underdeveloped countries. **Holdings:** 16,000 books and bound periodical volumes; clippings; special studies. **Subscriptions:** 62 journals and other serials. **Services:** Interlibrary loans; copying; library open to public with restrictions. **Networks/Consortia:** Member of OCLC through NELINET; CRL. **Publications:** Development Discussion Papers, 10-15/year - for sale.

★5445★
HARVARD UNIVERSITY - JOHN FITZGERALD KENNEDY SCHOOL OF GOVERNMENT - LIBRARY (Soc Sci)
79 John F. Kennedy St. Phone: (617) 495-1302
Cambridge, MA 02138 Malcolm C. Hamilton, Libn.
Founded: 1978. **Staff:** Prof 3; Other 8. **Subjects:** Policy analysis and policy making; public management. **Special Collections:** Science and International Affairs (4000 volumes). **Holdings:** 20,000 books and bound periodical volumes; 3500 working papers. **Subscriptions:** 2000 journals and other serials. **Services:** Interlibrary loans (fee); copying; library open to public for reference use only. **Computerized Information Services:** DIALOG, BRS; computerized cataloging. **Special Indexes:** Papers in the Policy Sciences, quarterly with annual cumulations (computer printout). **Staff:** David Reikowski, Hd. of Circ.; Ellen Isenstein, Ref.Libn.; Jennie Meyer Howard, Hd. of Tech.Serv.

★5446★
HARVARD UNIVERSITY - JOHN K. FAIRBANK CENTER FOR EAST ASIAN RESEARCH - LIBRARY (Area-Ethnic)
1737 Cambridge St. Phone: (617) 495-5753
Cambridge, MA 02138 Nancy Hearst, Libn.
Founded: 1963. **Staff:** Prof 1. **Subjects:** China since 1949; post-World War II Japan. **Holdings:** 6873 books and bound periodical volumes. **Subscriptions:** 125 journals and other serials. **Services:** Copying; library open to public with restrictions.

★5447★
HARVARD UNIVERSITY - LAW SCHOOL LIBRARY (Law)
Langdell Hall Phone: (617) 495-3170
Cambridge, MA 02138 Harry Martin, Libn.
Founded: 1817. **Staff:** Prof 28; Other 51. **Subjects:** Law in all its aspects. **Special Collections:** International law serials, treatises and documents dealing with all aspects of international law, international transactions and the work of international organizations; Treasure Room (collection of rare books and legal incunabula); records and briefs on appeal of the Supreme Court of the U.S., Massachusetts, and of the Federal Courts of Appeal. **Holdings:** 1.4 million volumes. **Subscriptions:** 8000 journals and other serials. **Services:** Interlibrary loans; copying; library open for legal research to those requiring these library resources. **Computerized Information Services:** LEXIS, RLIN; computerized cataloging and acquisitions. **Networks/Consortia:** Member of CRL; RLG. **Staff:** Sandra Coleman, Dp.Libn.; Richard Greenfield, Asst.Libn.Intl.LegalStud.; Lee W. Leighton, Asst.Libn., Cat.Serv.; Erika S. Chadbourn, Cur. of Mss.; Edith G. Henderson, Cur./Treasure Rm.

★5448★
HARVARD UNIVERSITY - LITTAUER LIBRARY (Soc Sci)†
Phone: (617) 495-2105
Cambridge, MA 02138 James Damaskos, Libn.
Founded: 1938. **Staff:** Prof 4; Other 9. **Subjects:** Economics, statistics, government (including official documents), manpower and industrial relations. **Holdings:** 424,423 volumes, including 120,000 state and city documents and 35,000 foreign documents. **Subscriptions:** 3200 journals and other serials; 435 newspapers. **Services:** Interlibrary loans (fee); copying; library open to qualified users. **Computerized Information Services:** Computerized cataloging and acquisitions. **Networks/Consortia:** Member of OCLC through NELINET; CRL. **Staff:** Maury D. Feld, Ref.Libn.; Claire L. Brown, Spec.; Catherine B. Carpenter, Chf.Cat.

★5449★
HARVARD UNIVERSITY - MAP COLLECTION (Geog-Map)
Pusey Library
Cambridge, MA 02138 Phone: (617) 495-2417
Frank E. Trout, Cur.
Founded: 1818. **Staff:** Prof 1; Other 2. **Subjects:** Atlases and maps (general and special). **Special Collections:** U.S. Defense Mapping Agency; Hydrographic/Topographic Center; U.S. National Oceanic and Atmospheric Administration; U.S. Geological Survey. **Holdings:** 10,000 volumes; 500,000 maps. **Services:** Library for U.S. Government depository use only.

★5450★
HARVARD UNIVERSITY - MATHEMATICAL LIBRARY (Sci-Tech)†
Science Center
1 Oxford St. Phone: (617) 495-2147
Cambridge, MA 02138 Philip A. Griffiths
Subjects: Mathematics. **Holdings:** 9132 books, bound periodical volumes and pamphlets; 1050 reports. **Subscriptions:** 76 journals and other serials. **Services:** Interlibrary loans; copying; library open to public for reference use only. **Networks/Consortia:** Member of OCLC through NELINET; CRL. **Also Known As:** George David Birkhoff Library.

★5451★
HARVARD UNIVERSITY - MUSEUM OF COMPARATIVE ZOOLOGY - LIBRARY (Sci-Tech)†
Oxford St. Phone: (617) 495-2475
Cambridge, MA 02138 Eva Jonas, Libn.
Founded: 1859. **Staff:** Prof 3; Other 8. **Subjects:** Zoology, paleontology, oceanography. **Special Collections:** Original drawings, manuscripts and archives. **Holdings:** 225,302 volumes. **Subscriptions:** 1888 journals and other serials. **Services:** Interlibrary loans; copying; library open to public for reference use only. **Networks/Consortia:** Member of OCLC through NELINET; CRL.

★5452★
HARVARD UNIVERSITY - NEW ENGLAND REGIONAL PRIMATE RESEARCH CENTER - LIBRARY (Sci-Tech)
One Pine Hill Dr. Phone: (617) 481-0400
Southborough, MA 01772 Sydney Fingold, Libn.
Founded: 1966. **Subjects:** Primatology, veterinary research, cardiophysiology, cytogenetics, reproductive physiology, pharmacology, immunology, nutrition, pathology. **Holdings:** 3000 books; 2500 bound periodical volumes. **Subscriptions:** 110 journals and other serials. **Services:** Interlibrary loans; library open to qualified scientific researchers. **Networks/Consortia:** Member of Central Massachusetts Consortium of Health Related Libraries.

★5453★
HARVARD UNIVERSITY - OAKES AMES ORCHID LIBRARY (Sci-Tech)
University Herbarium Phone: (617) 495-2360
Cambridge, MA 02138 Herman R. Sweet, Libn.
Subjects: Orchids. **Holdings:** 4806 volumes. **Subscriptions:** 19 journals and other serials. **Services:** Library not open to public. **Networks/Consortia:** Member of OCLC through NELINET; CRL.

★5454★
HARVARD UNIVERSITY - OBSERVATORY LIBRARY (Sci-Tech)
60 Garden St. Phone: (617) 495-5488
Cambridge, MA 02138 Estelle Karlin, Libn.
Founded: 1849. **Staff:** Prof 1; Other 1. **Subjects:** Astronomy and astrophysics. **Holdings:** 58,066 volumes; VF collection (25,000 items); 500,000 astronomical photographic plates. **Subscriptions:** 666 journals and other serials. **Services:** Interlibrary loans; copying; library open to public. **Networks/Consortia:** Member of OCLC through NELINET; CRL. **Also Known As:** John G. Wolbach Library; Center for Astrophysics Library.

★5455★
HARVARD UNIVERSITY - PHYSICS RESEARCH LIBRARY (Sci-Tech)
450 Jefferson Library Phone: (617) 495-2878
Cambridge, MA 02138 Nina McMaster, Libn.
Founded: 1931. **Staff:** Prof 1; Other 1. **Subjects:** Physics. **Holdings:** 17,900 volumes. **Subscriptions:** 137 journals and other serials. **Services:** Library open to public for reference use only. **Computerized Information Services:** Computerized cataloging. **Networks/Consortia:** Member of OCLC through NELINET; CRL.

★5456★
HARVARD UNIVERSITY - PSYCHOLOGY RESEARCH LIBRARY (Sci-Tech)
33 Kirkland St. Phone: (617) 495-3858
Cambridge, MA 02138 Annelise Katz, Libn.
Staff: Prof 1. **Subjects:** Experimental psychology, history of psychology, cognitive processes, physiological psychology, animal behavior, psychology of motivation and learning, psychological aspects of language and communication, biological and experimental aspects of developmental and abnormal psychology, psychophysics. **Holdings:** 9778 books and bound periodical volumes; 540 theses. **Subscriptions:** 149 journals and other serials. **Services:** Copying; library open for research and graduate work only. **Computerized Information Services:** Computerized cataloging.

Networks/Consortia: Member of OCLC through NELINET; CRL.

★5457★

HARVARD UNIVERSITY - RADCLIFFE COLLEGE - MORSE MUSIC LIBRARY (Mus)
59 Shepard St.   Phone: (617) 495-8730
Cambridge, MA 02138   Stephan B. Fuller, Music Libn.
Founded: 1927. **Staff:** Prof 1. **Subjects:** Music. **Holdings:** 3000 books; 500 bound periodical volumes; 6500 phonograph records; 6000 scores. **Subscriptions:** 17 journals and other serials. **Services:** Interlibrary loans; library open to students of Radcliffe College and Harvard University and registered guests. **Networks/Consortia:** Member of OCLC through NELINET; CRL.

★5458★

HARVARD UNIVERSITY - RADIO ASTRONOMY STATION - LIBRARY (Sci-Tech)
Fort Davis, TX 79734   Phone: (915) 426-3201
                              A. Maxwell, Project Dir.
Founded: 1956. **Staff:** 1. **Subjects:** Astronomy, mathematics, physics, electronics. **Holdings:** 1070 books, bound periodical volumes, pamphlets and reports (cataloged); 6500 reprints. **Subscriptions:** 20 journals and other serials. **Services:** Copying; library open to visiting scientists. **Networks/Consortia:** Member of OCLC through NELINET; CRL.

★5459★

HARVARD UNIVERSITY - ROBBINS LIBRARY (Hum)†
Emerson Hall   Phone: (617) 495-2193
Cambridge, MA 02138   Susan Neiman, Asst.Libn.
Staff: 2. **Subjects:** Philosophy. **Holdings:** 8625 books and bound periodical volumes. **Subscriptions:** 72 journals and other serials. **Services:** Library open to public. **Networks/Consortia:** Member of OCLC through NELINET; CRL.

★5460★

HARVARD UNIVERSITY - RUSSIAN RESEARCH CENTER - LIBRARY (Area-Ethnic)†
Coolidge Hall Library
1737 Cambridge St.   Phone: (617) 495-4030
Cambridge, MA 02138   Susan Jo Gardos, Libn.
Staff: Prof 1. **Subjects:** Soviet Union. **Holdings:** 12,800 volumes. **Subscriptions:** 211 journals and other serials. **Networks/Consortia:** Member of OCLC through NELINET; CRL.

★5461★

HARVARD UNIVERSITY - SCHOOL OF MEDICINE - LUCIEN HOWE LIBRARY OF OPHTHALMOLOGY (Med)
243 Charles St.   Phone: (617) 523-7900
Boston, MA 02114   Charles Snyder, Libn.
Founded: 1928. **Staff:** Prof 1; Other 1. **Subjects:** Ophthalmology and otolaryngology. **Holdings:** 14,000 books, bound periodical volumes and pamphlets; 300 stereophotographs of diseases of the eye. **Subscriptions:** 183 journals and other serials. **Services:** Interlibrary loans; library open to public for reference use only. **Networks/Consortia:** Member of RLG; OCLC through NELINET; CRL.

★5462★

HARVARD UNIVERSITY - SCHOOL OF MEDICINE - SCHERING FOUNDATION LIBRARY OF HEALTH CARE (Med)
643 Huntington Ave.   Phone: (617) 732-2101
Boston, MA 02115   Anne Alach, Libn.
Founded: 1970. **Staff:** Prof 1. **Subjects:** Community health care, preventive and social medicine. **Holdings:** 4000 volumes. **Subscriptions:** 38 journals and other serials. **Services:** Interlibrary loans; library open to Harvard community for reference use only. **Computerized Information Services:** DIALOG, SDC, BRS. **Networks/Consortia:** Member of New England On-Line Users Group. **Also Known As:** Harvard Medical School.

HARVARD UNIVERSITY - SCHOOL OF PUBLIC HEALTH - CENTER FOR ANALYSIS OF HEALTH PRACTICES
See: Center for Analysis of Health Practices

★5463★

HARVARD UNIVERSITY - SCHOOL OF PUBLIC HEALTH - HEALTH SERVICES LIBRARY (Med)
677 Huntington Ave.   Phone: (617) 732-1146
Boston, MA 02115   Peg Hewitt, Libn.
Founded: 1975. **Staff:** Prof 1; Other 1. **Subjects:** Health services policy, management, economics, maternal and child health. **Holdings:** 5000 books. **Subscriptions:** 77 journals and other serials. **Services:** Interlibrary loans;

copying; library open to public with restrictions. **Computerized Information Services:** NLM, BRS, DIALOG, SDC. **Networks/Consortia:** Member of New England On-line Users Group; North Atlantic Health Sciences Libraries.

★5464★

HARVARD UNIVERSITY - SCHOOLS OF MEDICINE, DENTAL MED. & PUBLIC HEALTH, BOSTON MED.LIB. - FRANCIS A. COUNTWAY LIB. (Med)
10 Shattuck St.   Phone: (617) 732-2136
Boston, MA 02115   C. Robin LeSueur, Libn.
Founded: 1964. **Staff:** Prof 20; Other 41. **Subjects:** Anatomy, biochemistry, dentistry, history of medicine, legal medicine, microbiology, parasitology, physiology, public health. **Special Collections:** History of medicine (810 incunabula); European books printed from 16th through 19th centuries; English books published from 1475 to 1800; American books from 1668-1870, especially New England imprints and Bostoniana; medical Hebraica and Judaica from the 14th centuries; manuscripts and archives, especially of New England origin; national archive of medical illustration; Warren Collection of early books in the history of medicine; world-famous collection of medical medals and collection of portraits. **Holdings:** 502,859 volumes. **Subscriptions:** 4976 journals and other serials. **Services:** Interlibrary loans; copying; library open to those with a vocational interest in the technical literatures of the health sciences. **Computerized Information Services:** MEDLINE, DIALOG, BRS, CATLINE. **Networks/Consortia:** Member of OCLC through NELINET; CRL. **Publications:** Library Guide. **Staff:** Charles C. Colby, III, Assoc.Libn./BML Serv; Susan E. Whitehead, Hd., Ref.Dept.; Miriam Allman, Acq.Libn.; Elaine E. Ciarkowski, Circ.Libn.; Richard J. Wolfe, Cur., Rare Bks. & Mss.; Mary E. Van Winkle, Asst.Cur., Rare Bks.; Jo S. Wang, Chf.Cat.

★5465★

HARVARD UNIVERSITY - SOCIAL RELATIONS/SOCIOLOGY LIBRARY (Soc Sci)
33 Kirkland St.   Phone: (617) 495-3838
Cambridge, MA 02138   Annelise Katz, Libn.
Staff: Prof 1. **Subjects:** Sociology, social psychology, personality, abnormal psychology. **Holdings:** 16,219 books and bound periodical volumes. **Subscriptions:** 108 journals and other serials. **Services:** Library open to public with restrictions. **Computerized Information Services:** Computerized cataloging. **Networks/Consortia:** Member of OCLC through NELINET; CRL.

★5466★

HARVARD UNIVERSITY - STATISTICS LIBRARY (Sci-Tech)†
Science Center
1 Oxford St.   Phone: (617) 495-5496
Cambridge, MA 02138   William Glynn, Lib.Asst.
Founded: 1959. **Subjects:** Statistical theory and applied statistics. **Holdings:** 2002 volumes; reprints and dissertations. **Subscriptions:** 20 journals and other serials. **Services:** Permission to use library may be requested. **Networks/Consortia:** Member of OCLC through NELINET; CRL.

★5467★

HARVARD UNIVERSITY - THEATRE COLLECTION (Theater)
Pusey Library   Phone: (617) 495-2445
Cambridge, MA 02138   Jeanne T. Newlin, Cur.
Founded: 1901. **Staff:** Prof 3; Other 1. **Subjects:** Performing arts - theater, dance, circus, minstrels, popular entertainment. **Special Collections:** Angus McBean Collection; H.W.L. Dana Collection; William Como Collection on Modern Dance; John and Rita Russell Viennese Collection; George Pierce Baker Collection; George Chaffee Ballet Collection; Robert Gould Shaw Collection; Edward B. Sheldon Collection; E.J. Wendell Collection. **Holdings:** 25,000 books; playbills and programs (3 million); photographs (over 500,000); engraved portraits and scenes (250,000); scenery and costume designs (15,000); manuscripts, documents, prompt books, posters, clippings. **Subscriptions:** 125 journals and other serials. **Services:** Copying (limited); Sheldon Exhibition Rooms open to all; library open to public with restrictions. **Networks/Consortia:** Member of OCLC through NELINET; CRL. **Publications:** Catalog of Dramatic Portraits in the Theatre Collection of the Harvard College Library, 4 volumes. **Staff:** Martha R. Mahard, Assoc.Cur.

★5468★

HARVARD UNIVERSITY - TICKNOR LIBRARY
Boylston Hall
Cambridge, MA 02138
Founded: 1959. **Subjects:** Languages and literature - Germanic, Romance, Slavic. **Holdings:** 7518 books. **Subscriptions:** 25 journals and other serials. **Remarks:** Library contains a reference collection primarily for the use of the Division of Modern Languages. Presently inactive.

★5469★
HARVARD UNIVERSITY - TOZZER LIBRARY (Soc Sci)
21 Divinity Ave.   Phone: (617) 495-2253
Cambridge, MA 02138   Nancy J. Schmidt, Libn.
Staff: Prof 4; Other 11. **Subjects:** Anthropology, ethnology, prehistoric
archeology. **Special Collections:** Central American and Mexican archeology
and linguistics. **Holdings:** 145,000 volumes. **Subscriptions:** 1500 journals
and other serials. **Services:** Interlibrary loans; copying; library open to public
for reference use only. **Networks/Consortia:** Member of OCLC through
NELINET; CRL. **Publications:** Quarterly Journal, Anthropological Literature.
Special Catalogs: Book Catalog (53 volumes) published 1963; 12 volume
supplement, 1970; 7 volume supplement, 1976; 7 volume supplement, 1979.
Formerly: Its Peabody Museum of Archaeology and Ethnology. **Staff:** Sharon
Morita, Cat.; Joanne Serreno, Cat.; John Weeks, Indexer.

★5470★
**HARVARD UNIVERSITY - W.E.B. DU BOIS INSTITUTE FOR AFRO-
  AMERICAN RESEARCH - LIBRARY**
Canaday Hall B
Cambridge, MA 02138
Defunct. Holdings absorbed by Harvard University - Afro-American Reading
Room.

★5471★
HARVARD UNIVERSITY - WOODBERRY POETRY ROOM (Hum)
Lamont Library   Phone: (617) 495-2454
Cambridge, MA 02138   Stratis Haviaras, Cur.
Founded: 1931. **Staff:** Prof 1; Other 1. **Subjects:** 20th century poetry and
poetics. **Holdings:** 10,543 books and bound periodical volumes; 3800
phonograph records; 1500 magnetic tapes; 150 cassette tapes.
Subscriptions: 250 journals and other serials. **Services:** Interlibrary loans;
copying; library open to poets and qualified scholars for reference use.
Computerized Information Services: Computerized acquisitions. **Networks/
Consortia:** Member of OCLC through NELINET; CRL. **Publications:** The
Poet's Voice (cassette recordings).

HARVARD-YENCHING LIBRARY
See: Harvard University

HARWOOD (E.C.) LIBRARY
See: American Institute for Economic Research - E.C. Harwood Library

★5472★
**HARWOOD FOUNDATION LIBRARY OF THE UNIVERSITY OF NEW MEXICO
  (Hum)**
25 Ledoux St.
Box 766   Phone: (505) 758-3063
Taos, NM 87571   David Caffey, Dir.
Founded: 1923. **Staff:** Prof 1; Other 6. **Subjects:** Art, Southwestern
Americana, books by and about D.H. Lawrence. **Holdings:** 25,000 books.
Subscriptions: 75 journals and other serials. **Services:** Interlibrary loans;
copying. **Remarks:** Serves as the only public library in Taos County, NM.

HASELOFF ARCHIVE
**See: Columbia University - Department of Art History & Archaeology -
  Photograph Collection**

★5473★
**HASHOMER HATZAIR-ZIONIST YOUTH MOVEMENT - LIBRARY (Area-
  Ethnic)**
150 Fifth Ave.   Phone: (212) 929-4955
New York, NY 10011   Natan Gottesman, Pres.
Founded: 1923. **Staff:** 1. **Subjects:** Jewish history, modern Israel and
Zionism, problems of youth, scouting, Jewish sociology, socialism, kibbutzim.
Special Collections: Yehuda Krantz Memorial Collection (500 volumes).
Holdings: 5000 books; 50 bound periodical volumes; 8 VF drawers and 6
cases of archival materials; unbound pamphlets and periodicals.
Subscriptions: 50 journals and other serials. **Services:** Interlibrary loans;
copying; library open to public with permission of staff. **Publications:** Youth &
Nation, quarterly; The Young Guard, bimonthly.

HASKELL LABORATORY FOR TOXICOLOGY & INDUSTRIAL MEDICINE
See: Du Pont de Nemours (E.I.) & Company, Inc.

★5474★
HASKINS LABORATORIES - LIBRARY (Med)
270 Crown St.   Phone: (203) 436-1774
New Haven, CT 06510   Nancy O'Brien, Libn.
Staff: 1. **Subjects:** Speech communication, linguistics, experimental

psychology, speech physiology, computers and programming. **Holdings:** 2500
books; 70 bound periodical volumes; 120 file boxes of irregular serials/
occasional papers from other research groups and organizations; 20 file boxes
of Haskins Laboratories publications, 1939 to present. **Subscriptions:** 165
journals and other serials. **Services:** Interlibrary loans; copying; library open to
public on written request. **Publications:** Haskins Laboratories Status Report
on Speech Research, quarterly - available to libraries serving research
colleagues.

★5475★
HASSARD, BONNINGTON, ROGERS & HUBER - LIBRARY (Law)
44 Montgomery St., Suite 3500   Phone: (415) 781-8787
San Francisco, CA 94104   Linda Conley, Libn.
Staff: Prof 1; Other 2. **Subjects:** Law, medical malpractice, taxation.
Holdings: 5000 books; 300 bound periodical volumes. **Subscriptions:** 100
journals and other serials. **Services:** Interlibrary loans; library not open to
public. **Computerized Information Services:** LEXIS.

HASTINGS CENTER
See: Institute of Society, Ethics & the Life Sciences

HASTINGS COLLEGE OF THE LAW
See: University of California, San Francisco

★5476★
HASTINGS REGIONAL CENTER - MEDICAL LIBRARY (Med)
                                                    Phone: (402) 463-2471
Hastings, NE 68901   Ruth Swingle, Libn.
Staff: Prof 1. **Subjects:** Psychiatry, psychiatric nursing, psychiatric social
work, medicine, patient education, mental health. **Holdings:** 5799 books; 500
bound periodical volumes; 9 boxes of pamphlets, reports, papers; 4 VF
drawers of pamphlets and reprints. **Subscriptions:** 33 journals and other
serials. **Services:** Interlibrary loans; copying; library open to public with
restrictions.

★5477★
**HASTINGS & SONS PUBLISHERS - DAILY EVENING ITEM - NEWSPAPER
  MORGUE (Publ)**
38 Exchange St.   Phone: (617) 593-7700
Lynn, MA 01903   NancyAnn Rogers, Res.Libn.
Staff: Prof 1. **Subjects:** Newspaper reference topics. **Special Collections:**
Historical photographs and clippings. **Holdings:** 68 VF drawers of clippings;
microfilmed newspapers, 1877 to present; newspaper photographs. **Services:**
Copying; library open to public with restrictions.

★5478★
HATBORO BAPTIST CHURCH - LIBRARY (Rel-Theol)
32 N. York Ave.   Phone: (215) 675-8400
Hatboro, PA 19040   Carolyn Zimmerman, Libn.
Founded: 1950. **Staff:** Prof 1. **Subjects:** Bible commentaries, Bible histories,
missions, church organization, church history, inspiration, Christian education
and ethics, theology and doctrine. **Holdings:** 4714 books.

★5479★
HATCH-BILLOPS COLLECTION, INC. (Area-Ethnic)
491 Broadway, 7th Fl.   Phone: (212) 966-3231
New York, NY 10012   Camille Billops, Exec.Dir.
Staff: Prof 1. **Subjects:** Afro-Americana, theater, visual arts. **Special
Collections:** Oral history interviews (800); art slides (10,000); Owen Dodson
plays and manuscripts; Theodore Ward plays. **Holdings:** 4000 books; 1000
black and white photographs; 300 posters; 300 playbills; 300 art catalogs.
Subscriptions: 12 journals and other serials. **Services:** Library open to public
by written appointment. **Special Catalogs:** Catalog of oral history holdings
with abstracts; Artists and Influence Series transcripts. **Staff:** James V. Hatch

HATCHER GRADUATE LIBRARY
See: University of Michigan

**HATHAWAY (Harry S.) LIBRARY OF NATURAL HISTORY AND
  CONSERVATION**
**See: Audubon Society of Rhode Island - Harry S. Hathaway Library of
  Natural History and Conservation**

HATHEWAY ENVIRONMENTAL EDUCATION INSTITUTE
See: Massachusetts Audubon Society

HAUGHTON (Peter D.) MEMORIAL LIBRARY
See: Trotting Horse Museum - Peter D. Haughton Memorial Library

HAUSMAN (William A.) MEDICAL LIBRARY
See: Sacred Heart Hospital - William A. Hausman Medical Library

★5480★
HAVERFORD COLLEGE - TREASURE ROOM AND QUAKER COLLECTION
(Rel-Theol; Hum)
Haverford College Library   Phone: (215) 649-9600
Haverford, PA 19041   Edwin B. Bronner, Cur.
Founded: 1833. **Staff:** Prof 3; Other 2. **Subjects:** History, drama, poetry, fiction, biography, and other subjects relating to Society of Friends throughout the world; rare books and manuscripts; mysticism. **Special Collections:** William H. Jenks Collection (1600 seventeenth-century Quaker tracts); Charles Roberts autograph collection (20,000 items); Haverfordiana; Rufus M. Jones collection on mysticism (1400 books and pamphlets); William Pyle Philips Collection (rare books and manuscripts, mostly of Renaissance period); Harris collection of ancient and Oriental manuscripts (60 items); Lockwood Collection of Italian Humanists; Dictionary of Quaker Biography (typescript containing 15,000 biographical sketches). **Holdings:** 25,000 books and bound periodical volumes; 248,300 Quaker manuscripts; 20,000 other manuscripts; pictures; maps, photographs and microfilm. **Subscriptions:** 300 journals and other serials. **Services:** Interlibrary loans (limited); copying; permission to use library may be requested. **Computerized Information Services:** DIALOG, BRS, SDC; computerized cataloging, acquisitions and serials. **Networks/Consortia:** Member of PALINET and Union Library Catalogue of Pennsylvania. **Special Catalogs:** Quaker research in progress (cards); Quaker necrology (cards); index to pamphlet collection (cards); Bleyden Survey: Index to all manuscript collections. **Remarks:** Has absorbed partial holdings of the Society of Friends - Philadelphia Yearly Meeting. **Staff:** Diana Alten, Mss.Cat.; Elisabeth P. Brown, Quaker Bibliog.

★5481★
HAVERFORD STATE HOSPITAL - MEDICAL LIBRARY (Med)†
3500 Darby Rd.   Phone: (215) 525-9620
Haverford, PA 19041   Joyce Matheson, Dir., Lib.Serv.
Founded: 1963. **Staff:** Prof 1. **Subjects:** Psychiatry, psychology, sociology, medicine. **Holdings:** 3500 books; 1500 bound periodical volumes; 200 cassette tapes (cataloged). **Subscriptions:** 101 journals and other serials. **Services:** Interlibrary loans; copying; library open to public with permission of hospital librarian. **Networks/Consortia:** Member of Consortium for Health Information & Library Services (CHI).

★5482★
HAVERFORD TOWNSHIP HISTORICAL SOCIETY - LIBRARY (Hist)
Box 825
Havertown, PA 19083   Margaret E. Johnston, Cur.
Subjects: History of Haverford Township, Delaware County and Pennsylvania. **Special Collections:** Collections on 1810 Nitre Hall Powder Mills and Philadelphia/West Chester Transit Line. **Holdings:** Figures not available; photographs. **Services:** Library open to public with restrictions. **Publications:** Newsletter, semiannual.

★5483★
HAVERHILL MUNICIPAL (Hale) HOSPITAL - MEDICAL LIBRARY (Med)
40 Buttonwoods Ave.   Phone: (617) 372-7141
Haverhill, MA 01830   Eleanor Howard, Med.Libn.
Staff: Prof 1. **Subjects:** Medicine, nursing, allied health. **Holdings:** 850 books; 1800 bound periodical volumes; 300 cassettes; 100 unbound journals; 4 VF drawers of pamphlets; 50 filmstrips with records; 5 2x2 slide series; 10 films. **Subscriptions:** 55 journals and other serials. **Services:** Interlibrary loans; copying; literature searches; library open to public with permission. **Networks/Consortia:** Member of Northeast Consortium for Health Information (NECHI); Haverhill Area Library Resources Consortium.

★5484★
HAVERHILL PUBLIC LIBRARY - SPECIAL COLLECTIONS DIVISION (Hist)
99 Main St.   Phone: (617) 373-1586
Haverhill, MA 01830   Howard W. Curtis, Cur.
Founded: 1874. **Staff:** Prof 2; Other 5. **Subjects:** Genealogy and local history, John Greenleaf Whittier, art, early children's books. **Special Collections:** John Greenleaf Whittier Collection (2500); Gale Art Collection (5300); Haverhill History Collection (4000); Pecker Local History and Genealogy Collection (7600). **Holdings:** 22,000 books; 700 bound periodical volumes; 800 pamphlets; 4000 manuscripts; 400 broadsides; 250 maps; 1000 reels of microfilm; city documents in manuscript; 10,000 Haverhill photographs; 375 volumes of bound Haverhill newspapers; 200 volumes of clippings; genealogical microfiche. **Subscriptions:** 18 journals and other

serials. **Services:** Interlibrary loans (microfilm only; fee); copying; library open to public. **Networks/Consortia:** Member of Haverhill Library Resources Consortium; Eastern Massachusetts Regional Library System. **Publications:** Annual Report, special publication; Architectural Heritage of Haverhill. **Special Catalogs:** Whittier Collection Holdings (book); Haverhill History (card). **Staff:** Gregory H. Laing, Genealogist.

HAVIGHURST (Walter) SPECIAL COLLECTIONS LIBRARY
See: Miami University - Walter Havighurst Special Collections Library

HAVILAND RECORDS ROOM
See: Society of Friends - New York Yearly Meeting - Records Committee

★5485★
HAWAII CHINESE HISTORY CENTER (Area-Ethnic)†
111 N. King St., No. 410   Phone: (808) 521-5948
Honolulu, HI 96817   Violet L. Lai, Hd.Libn.
Staff: 2. **Subjects:** Chinese - societies, language schools, churches; biographies of Chinese; early Chinese immigration; historic sites; Chinese-Americans in U.S., especially Hawaii. **Holdings:** 650 books; 1 VF drawer of newspaper clippings; 164 taped recordings of old Chinese residents; 1 VF drawer of information on Chinese societies; 1/2 VF drawer of old documents; 10 maps of South China; 100 photographs of old Chinese in Hawaii; 25 genealogies of local Chinese families. **Subscriptions:** 22 journals and other serials. **Services:** Library open to public for reference use only. **Publications:** Newsletter, quarterly - to members; list of other publications - available on request. **Staff:** Irma Tam Soong, Exec.Dir. Emeritus.

★5486★
HAWAII EMPLOYERS COUNCIL - LIBRARY (Soc Sci)†
2682 Waiwai Loop   Phone: (808) 836-1511
Honolulu, HI 96819
Founded: 1943. **Staff:** Prof 1; Other 2. **Subjects:** Labor relations, labor law, management, compensation and benefits, personnel administration, employment systems and development, industrial psychology, labor economics and living costs, employment and unemployment statistics. **Special Collections:** Local collective bargaining agreements; industrial films; company employee publications; employers' association publications; newspaper clippings concerning labor history and development in Hawaii. **Holdings:** 6000 books; 150 bound periodical volumes; 50 Council research publications; 600 current local collective bargaining agreements and related documents; 120 local collective bargaining agreements and related documents on microfilm, 1944-1966; 115 industrial films and tapes; federal and local government documents; local newspaper clippings. **Subscriptions:** 336 journals and other serials; 17 newspapers. **Services:** Interlibrary loans; copying; library open to council staff, member companies and students.

★5487★
HAWAII INSTITUTE OF GEOPHYSICS - LIBRARY (Sci-Tech)
University of Hawaii
2525 Correa Rd.   Phone: (808) 948-7040
Honolulu, HI 96822   Patricia E. Price, Libn.
Staff: Prof 1; Other 3. **Subjects:** Geology, geophysics, oceanography, meteorology. **Holdings:** 2000 books; 4700 bound periodical volumes; 22,000 unbound serial volumes; 8000 maps and charts; 20,000 reprints; 5000 reports. **Subscriptions:** 145 journals and other serials. **Services:** Interlibrary loans; copying; library open to public.

★5488★
HAWAII MEDICAL LIBRARY, INC. (Med)
1221 Punchbowl St.   Phone: (808) 536-9302
Honolulu, HI 96813   John A. Breinich, Dir.
Founded: 1913. **Staff:** Prof 4; Other 8. **Subjects:** Medicine, nursing, tropical diseases. **Holdings:** 15,000 books; 45,000 bound periodical volumes; 500 pamphlets; 500 audio cassette tapes. **Subscriptions:** 1400 journals and other serials. **Services:** Interlibrary loans; copying; library open to public. **Computerized Information Services:** MEDLINE; computerized cataloging. **Networks/Consortia:** Member of OCLC.

★5489★
HAWAII NEWSPAPER AGENCY - LIBRARY (Publ)
News Bldg., 605 Kapiolani Blvd.   Phone: (808) 525-7669
Honolulu, HI 96813   Beatrice S. Kaya, Chf.Libn.
Staff: Prof 2; Other 7. **Subjects:** Newspaper reference topics. **Special Collections:** Hawaiiana. **Holdings:** 2000 books and pamphlets; dissertations; reports; 2971 reels of microfilm. **Services:** Library not open to public. **Staff:** Margaret Iwamoto, Asst.Libn.

★5490★

HAWAII PLANNED PARENTHOOD - FAMILY PLANNING INFORMATION CENTER (FPIC) - LIBRARY (Soc Sci)
1136 Union Mall, Suite 702
Honolulu, HI 96813
Phone: (808) 531-1327
Sandi Grundmanis, FPIC Supv.
Founded: 1979. **Staff:** Prof 1. **Subjects:** Family planning, sex education, population, birth control, pregnancy. **Special Collections:** Birth control methods and their history; books and films on human sexuality and the mentally retarded; religious materials related to family planning and human sexuality. **Holdings:** 1000 books and bound periodical volumes; 3000 other cataloged items; 5000 newspaper clippings; health education kits; 100 multimedia items. **Subscriptions:** 32 journals and other serials. **Services:** Library open to public. **Networks/Consortia:** Member of Planned Parenthood Federation of America, Inc.

★5491★

HAWAII STATE CIRCUIT COURT - 2ND CIRCUIT - LAW LIBRARY (Law)
Box P
Wailuku, HI 96793
Phone: (808) 244-5227
Sandra Wada, Libn.
Founded: 1907. **Staff:** 1. **Subjects:** Real property, criminal law, juveniles, personal injury, local government, federal laws. **Holdings:** 13,200 volumes. **Subscriptions:** 35 journals and other serials. **Services:** Interlibrary loans; library open to public.

★5492★

HAWAII STATE CIRCUIT COURT - 3RD CIRCUIT - LAW LIBRARY (Law)
Federal Bldg., 75 Aupini St.
Box 1007
Hilo, HI 96720
Phone: (808) 961-7226
Staff: 1. **Subjects:** Law. **Holdings:** 17,000 books; **Services:** Interlibrary loans; copying; library open to public for reference use only.

★5493★

HAWAII STATE DEPARTMENT OF ACCOUNTING AND GENERAL SERVICES - PUBLIC ARCHIVES (Hist)
Iolani Palace Grounds
Honolulu, HI 96813
Phone: (808) 548-2357
Founded: 1906. **Staff:** Prof 8; Other 5. **Subjects:** Hawaiian history and government. **Special Collections:** Captain Cook Collection (on Cook and discovery of Hawaiian Islands). **Holdings:** 2000 books; 160 bound periodical volumes; 12,000 government documents; 300 cubic feet of manuscripts (private collections); 9000 cubic feet of official archives; 41,000 prints and negatives; 750 maps. **Subscriptions:** 6 newspapers. **Services:** Copying; archives open to public. **Staff:** Richard Thompson, Libn.

★5494★

HAWAII STATE DEPARTMENT OF EDUCATION - AUDIOVISUAL SERVICES (Educ; Aud-Vis)
641 18th Ave.
Honolulu, HI 96816
Phone: (808) 732-2824
Franklin S. Tamaribuchi, TAC Spec.
Founded: 1946. **Staff:** Prof 1; Other 7. **Subjects:** Language arts; social sciences; mathematics; science; music; health; art; education - physical, career, environmental, business; guidance; industrial arts; home economics. **Holdings:** 15,000 prints of 16mm sound motion picture films; 5600 titles of audiotape masters. **Subscriptions:** 8 journals and other serials. **Services:** Films from NASA, Department of Energy and NIMH may be used by others upon availability; library not open to public. **Computerized Information Services:** Computerized circulation. **Special Catalogs:** Audiotape Catalog;16mm Film Catalog and supplements; DOE/NASA film holdings. **Remarks:** Maintained by the Office of Instructional Services, Multimedia Services Branch, Technical Assistance Center Section.

HAWAII STATE DEPARTMENT OF EDUCATION - HAWAII STATE LIBRARY - FEDERAL DOCUMENTS SECTION
See: Hawaii State Library - Federal Documents Section

★5495★

HAWAII STATE DEPARTMENT OF HEALTH - HASTINGS H. WALKER MEDICAL LIBRARY (Med)
Leahi Hospital
3675 Kilauea Ave.
Honolulu, HI 96816
Phone: (808) 734-0221
Jean K. Yee, Lib.Asst.
Founded: 1944. **Staff:** Prof 1. **Subjects:** Clinical medicine, tuberculosis and respiratory diseases, tropical medicine, psychiatry, hospital administration, nursing, leprosy. **Holdings:** 6000 books; 1500 bound periodical volumes; 57 pamphlets. **Subscriptions:** 141 journals and other serials. **Services:** Interlibrary loans; library open to public for reference use only.

★5496★

HAWAII STATE DEPARTMENT OF PLANNING & ECONOMIC DEVELOPMENT - LIBRARY (Plan)
Box 2359
Honolulu, HI 96804
Phone: (808) 548-3059
Anthony M. Oliver, Libn.
Founded: 1967. **Staff:** Prof 2; Other 3. **Subjects:** Economics, statistics, planning, land use, energy, economic development, agriculture, international trade, science and technology, tourism, public administration. **Holdings:** 8000 titles (chiefly government reports); 1500 microfiche. **Subscriptions:** 200 journals and other serials; 6 newspapers. **Services:** Interlibrary loans; copying; library open to public. **Computerized Information Services:** DIALOG, SDC, New York Times Information Service; computerized cataloging.

★5497★

HAWAII STATE HOSPITAL - MEDICAL LIBRARY (Med)
45-710 Keaahala Rd.
Kaneohe, HI 96744
Phone: (808) 247-2191
Diana C. Stephens, Med.Libn.
Founded: 1950. **Staff:** Prof 1. **Subjects:** Behavioral sciences, psychiatry, psychology, neuropsychology, psychiatric nursing, mental health. **Holdings:** 5000 books; 1400 bound periodical volumes; 8 VF drawers of unbound materials; 200 magnetic tapes; 100 cassette tapes; current and historic collection of Hawaii State Department of Health publications. **Subscriptions:** 98 journals and other serials. **Services:** Interlibrary loans; library open to public by permission. **Computerized Information Services:** DIALOG, MEDLINE. **Publications:** HSH Medical Library Bulletin, bimonthly - for internal distribution only.

★5498★

HAWAII STATE - LEGISLATIVE REFERENCE BUREAU LIBRARY (Soc Sci)
State Capitol
Honolulu, HI 96813
Phone: (808) 548-7853
Hanako Kobayashi, Res.Libn.
Founded: 1943. **Staff:** Prof 3; Other 4. **Subjects:** Public administration, legislative procedure, public finance, state government. **Holdings:** 70,000 books and pamphlets. **Subscriptions:** 250 journals and other serials. **Services:** Interlibrary loans; library open to public.

★5499★

HAWAII STATE LIBRARY - BUSINESS, SCIENCE, TECHNOLOGY UNIT (Bus-Fin; Sci-Tech)
478 S. King St.
Honolulu, HI 96813
Joyce Kidani, Act.Hd.
Subjects: Economics, commmerce, transportation, natural sciences, technological sciences. **Holdings:** 42,696 books; 15,750 pamphlets. **Subscriptions:** 399 journals and other serials. **Services:** Interlibrary loans; library open to public. **Computerized Information Services:** DIALOG.

★5500★

HAWAII STATE LIBRARY - EDNA ALLYN ROOM (Area-Ethnic)
478 S. King St.
Honolulu, HI 96813
Phone: (808) 548-2341
Shirley S. Naito, Oahu Ch.Coord.
Staff: Prof 3; Other 2. **Subjects:** Children's books, Hawaiiana, foreign books for children. **Special Collections:** Historical collection of "out-of-print" and rare children's books; alphabet books; autographed Nene Award books. **Holdings:** 63,646 books; 4105 phonograph records; 1860 tapes. **Subscriptions:** 26 journals and other serials. **Services:** Interlibrary loans; copying; library open to public. **Staff:** Delia Fukuji, Libn.; Alice Bartelli, Libn.

★5501★

HAWAII STATE LIBRARY - FEDERAL DOCUMENTS SECTION (Info Sci)
478 S. King St.
Honolulu, HI 96813
Phone: (808) 548-2386
Norma T. Herkes, Hd.
Staff: Prof 1; Other 2. **Subjects:** U.S. Government documents. **Special Collections:** Popular collection for inventors. **Holdings:** 117,153 documents (paper); 337,241 documents in microform; international and state documents. **Services:** Interlibrary loans; copying; SDI (limited); library open to public. **Computerized Information Services:** DIALOG. **Remarks:** Maintained by the Hawaii State Department of Education.

★5502★

HAWAII STATE LIBRARY - FINE ARTS AND AUDIOVISUAL SECTION (Art)
478 S. King St.
Honolulu, HI 96813
Phone: (808) 548-2340
Eloise Van Niel, Hd.
Staff: Prof 4; Other 4. **Subjects:** Art, theater, music, motion pictures, dance, sports, recreation. **Holdings:** 33,930 books; 3016 film reels; 10,098 music scores; 20,170 phonograph records; 52,090 pictures. **Subscriptions:** 213 journals and other serials. **Services:** Interlibrary loans; library open to public. **Staff:** Mary Lu Kipilii, Libn./AV Spec.; Chitra Stuiver, Libn./Art Spec.

★5503★
HAWAII STATE LIBRARY - HAWAII AND PACIFIC SECTION I (Area-Ethnic; Hist)
478 S. King St.　　　　　　　　Phone: (808) 548-2346
Honolulu, HI 96813　　　　　　William R. Ranger, Act.Hd.
Founded: 1913. **Staff:** Prof 5; Other 5. **Subjects:** Hawaiiana, Pacifica. **Special Collections:** Hawaii and the Pacific Collection (48,544 volumes); State Documents Collection (30,560); Hawaii Historical Collection (42,800); Admiral Thomas Papers (130); Phillips Collection (1705 items). **Holdings:** 50,000 books; 256 bound periodical volumes; 55,400 pamphlets and newspaper clippings; 27,760 state documents on microfiche; 40 titles of periodicals on microfilm. **Subscriptions:** 188 journals and other serials; 24 newspapers. **Services:** Interlibrary loans; copying; library open to public. **Computerized Information Services:** DIALOG. **Publications:** Hawaii Documents; Basic Hawaiiana; What to Read About Hawaii; other bibliographies. **Special Indexes:** Index to Honolulu Star-Bulletin and Advertiser; Hawaii Documents, biennial; Basic Hawaiiana. **Staff:** Mrs. Oi-Yung Chow, Dir., State Lib.; Mrs. Proserfina Strona, Hd., Doc.Ctr.

★5504★
HAWAII STATE LIBRARY - LANGUAGE, LITERATURE AND HISTORY SECTION (Hum)
478 S. King St.　　　　　　　　Phone: (808) 548-4165
Honolulu, HI 96813　　　　　　Bessie Wenkam, Section Hd.
Staff: Prof 6; Other 4. **Subjects:** Language, literature, history, travel. **Special Collections:** Genealogy (1266 items); Foreign Language (9701 items). **Holdings:** 119,972 books; 11,107 pamphlets; 3456 maps; 131 titles on microfiche. **Subscriptions:** 318 journals and other serials. **Services:** Interlibrary loans; library open to public. **Computerized Information Services:** Computerized cataloging; online bibliographic searching. **Publications:** Various bibliographies.

★5505★
HAWAII STATE LIBRARY - SERIALS SECTION (Bus-Fin; Hum)
478 S. King St.　　　　　　　　Phone: (808) 548-2389
Honolulu, HI 96813　　　　　　Vincent Van Brocklin, Ser. Unit Hd.
Staff: Prof 6; Other 7. **Subjects:** Business, science, fine arts and literature, sports, language, social sciences, history. **Special Collections:** Staff collection of library periodicals (85 titles). **Holdings:** 132 titles; 12,991 reels of microfilm. **Subscriptions:** 1575 journals and other serials; 73 newspapers. **Services:** Interlibrary loans; copying; library open to public.

★5506★
HAWAII STATE LIBRARY - SOCIAL SCIENCE AND PHILOSOPHY SECTION (Soc Sci; Hum)
478 S. King St.　　　　　　　　Phone: (808) 548-2340
Honolulu, HI 96813　　　　　　Judith Middlebrook Prakash, Section Hd.
Founded: 1967. **Staff:** Prof 3; Other 1. **Subjects:** Social science, religion, philosophy, psychology, education, government, law, folklore. **Holdings:** 56,673 books; 5152 social science pamphlets; 13,402 college catalogs (microfiche and paperbound). **Subscriptions:** 409 journals and other serials. **Services:** Interlibrary loans; copying; library open to public. **Computerized Information Services:** DIALOG. **Staff:** Kay H. Ogata, Libn.; Colette F.H. Young, Libn.

★5507★
HAWAII STATE LIBRARY - STATE LIBRARY FOR THE BLIND AND PHYSICALLY HANDICAPPED (Aud-Vis)
402 Kapahulu Ave.　　　　　　Phone: (808) 732-7767
Honolulu, HI 96815　　　　　　Lydia S. Ranger, Hd.Libn.
Staff: Prof 3; Other 11. **Subjects:** General. **Holdings:** 3896 braille books; 23,019 talking books; 4098 open reel tapes; 3888 large-type books; 22,277 cassette tapes; 1642 phonograph records; 1804 inkprint books; 1438 pamphlets; 714 film loops; 211 filmstrips; 13 16mm films; 163 manipulatives; 490 multimedia kits; 6 video cassettes. **Subscriptions:** 174 journals in various media. **Services:** Interlibrary loans; duplicating; transcribing; circulation of talking books and other media; machine lending service; institutional library services; library open to all persons requiring materials in special media. **Publications:** News is Getting Around the Pacific, quarterly - available by request to registered patrons and agencies working with the handicapped. **Special Catalogs:** Spiral bound catalog of holdings. **Staff:** Sue Sugimura, Pub.Serv.Libn.; Fusako Miyashiro, Inst.Libn.

★5508★
HAWAII STATE LIBRARY - YOUNG ADULT SECTION (Educ)
478 S. King St.　　　　　　　　Phone: (808) 548-2337
Honolulu, HI 96813　　　　　　Sylvia C. Mitchell, Young Adult Libn.
Staff: Prof 1. **Subjects:** Young adult books, Hawaiiana, occupational information. **Holdings:** 22,447 books; 5339 pamphlets; 629 audio cassettes.

Subscriptions: 18 journals and other serials; 8 school newspapers. **Services:** Interlibrary loans; copying; library open to public.

★5509★
HAWAII STATE SUPREME COURT - LAW LIBRARY (Law)
Box 779　　　　　　　　　　　Phone: (808) 548-7432
Honolulu, HI 96808　　　　　　Momoe Tanaka, State Law Libn.
Founded: 1851. **Staff:** Prof 3; Other 5. **Subjects:** Law. **Holdings:** 75,000 volumes. **Subscriptions:** 290 journals and other serials. **Services:** Interlibrary loans; library open to public for reference use only. **Staff:** Ann S. Koto, Asst. Law Libn.; Irene Wong, Pub.Serv.Libn.

HAWAII VOLCANOES NATL. PARK
See: U.S. Natl. Park Service

★5510★
HAWAIIAN ELECTRIC CO., INC. - CORPORATE LIBRARY (Energy)
Box 2750　　　　　　　　　　Phone: (808) 548-7915
Honolulu, HI 96840　　　　　　Deborah Knowlton, Corp.Libn.
Founded: 1980. **Staff:** Prof 1. **Subjects:** Electric utility management, personnel training, law. **Holdings:** 350 books; 2 VF drawers of archives and artifacts. **Subscriptions:** 19 journals and other serials. **Services:** Library open by appointment only to university students. **Computerized Information Services:** DIALOG; internal database; computerized cataloging. **Publications:** Library Highlights - monthly. **Remarks:** Library is located at 900 Richards St., Honolulu, HI 96813.

★5511★
HAWAIIAN ELECTRIC CO., INC. - ENGINEERING LIBRARY (Sci-Tech; Energy)
820 Ward Ave.
Box 2750　　　　　　　　　　Phone: (808) 548-7915
Honolulu, HI 96840　　　　　　Deborah Knowlton, Corp.Libn.
Founded: 1965. **Staff:** Prof 1; Other 1. **Subjects:** Electrical engineering, mechanical engineering, energy, air and water pollution, civil engineering. **Holdings:** 2800 books; 740 trade catalogs (cataloged); 1900 pamphlets. **Subscriptions:** 120 journals and other serials. **Services:** Interlibrary loans (limited); library open to college and university students by appointment. **Computerized Information Services:** DIALOG, DOE/RECON; internal database; computerized cataloging. **Publications:** Library Highlights, monthly - distributed to engineering personnel. **Special Indexes:** Technical file index (book).

★5512★
HAWAIIAN HISTORICAL SOCIETY - MISSION-HISTORICAL LIBRARY (Hist)
560 Kawaiahao St.　　　　　　Phone: (808) 537-6271
Honolulu, HI 96813　　　　　　Barbara E. Dunn, Libn.
Founded: 1893. **Staff:** Prof 1. **Subjects:** Pacific and round the world voyages, history of Hawaiian Islands and Polynesia, local biography. **Special Collections:** Newspapers printed in Hawaiian Islands, 1836-1900; Hawaiian language imprints, 1822-1900 (600 volumes). **Holdings:** 10,000 volumes; 2808 pamphlets; 5 VF drawers of manuscripts; 10 VF drawers of clippings; 5 VF drawers of photographs; microfilmed early newspapers; 3 VF drawers of maps; 1 VF drawer of broadsides; 50 photograph albums and scrapbooks. **Subscriptions:** 28 journals and other serials. **Services:** Copying; library open to public, but it is primarily for researchers. **Publications:** Hawaiian Journal of History, annual - free to members of society, for sale to others.

★5513★
HAWAIIAN MISSION CHILDREN'S SOCIETY - MISSION-HISTORICAL LIBRARY (Hist)
553 S. King St.　　　　　　　　Phone: (808) 531-0481
Honolulu, HI 96813　　　　　　Mary Jane Knight, Libn.
Founded: 1920. **Staff:** Prof 2. **Subjects:** 19th century Hawaiian history, history of Protestant missionaries in Hawaii. **Special Collections:** Manuscripts of missionaries including letters, journals, reports; books in the Hawaiian language; early Hawaiian newspapers and magazines. **Holdings:** 12,000 books; 400 bound periodical volumes; 3 drawers of microfilm; 245 linear feet of manuscript material; 20 boxes of unclassified manuscripts; engravings, drawings, daguerrotypes, photographs. **Subscriptions:** 15 journals and other serials. **Services:** Copying (very limited); qualified researchers may use manuscript material; library open to public. **Special Catalogs:** Guide to Manuscript Collections (pamphlet); Guide to Journals of Missionaries in Hawaii: Hawaiian Mission Children's Society Holdings (book; in progress). **Staff:** Lela Goodell, Asst.Libn.

★5514★
HAWAIIAN SUGAR PLANTERS' ASSOCIATION EXPERIMENT STATION -
  LIBRARY (Agri; Sci-Tech)†
99-193 Aiea Heights Dr.
Box 1057
Aiea, HI 96701   Phone: (808) 487-5561
      Mary O. Matsuoka, Libn.
Staff: Prof 1; Other 2. **Subjects:** Sugar technology, plant breeding and physiology, entomology, chemistry, plant pathology, agriculture. **Special Collections:** Project files of experiment station (5000 folders). **Holdings:** 90,000 volumes. **Subscriptions:** 800 journals and other serials. **Services:** Interlibrary loans; library open to researchers with permission from director or librarian.

★5515★
HAWAIIAN TELEPHONE COMPANY - LIBRARY (Bus-Fin)†
1177 Bishop St.
Box 2200
Honolulu, HI 96841   Phone: (808) 546-2600
      Michelle A. Pommer, Libn.
Staff: Prof 1; Other 1. **Subjects:** Telecommunications, telephony, management, business. **Holdings:** 1750 books and bound periodical volumes. **Subscriptions:** 56 journals and other serials. **Services:** Interlibrary loans; copying; library open to public for reference use only when material is not available elsewhere. **Computerized Information Services:** DIALOG.

★5516★
HAWKER SIDDELEY CANADA INC. - ORENDA DIVISION - ENGINEERING
  LIBRARY
Box 6001, A.M.F.
Toronto, ON, Canada L5P 1B3
Founded: 1960. **Subjects:** Engines, space aircraft. **Holdings:** 7000 volumes. **Remarks:** Presently inactive.

★5517★
HAWKINS, DELAFIELD & WOOD - LIBRARY (Law)
67 Wall St.   Phone: (212) 952-4772
New York, NY 10005   Peggy Martin, Libn.
Founded: 1896. **Staff:** Prof 2; Other 4. **Subjects:** Law. **Special Collections:** Municipal bond law; constitutional law. **Holdings:** 18,000 volumes. **Services:** Interlibrary loans; copying; library not open to public. **Computerized Information Services:** LEXIS, New York Times Information Service; computerized circulation. **Special Indexes:** Bond memoranda of law index. **Staff:** Debra Glessner, Asst.Libn.

HAWLEY (Rose) MUSEUM AND HISTORICAL LIBRARY
See: Mason County Historical Society - Rose Hawley Museum and Historical Library

★5518★
HAY ASSOCIATES - RESEARCH LIBRARY (Bus-Fin)
229 S. 18th St., Rittenhouse Sq.   Phone: (215) 875-2300
Philadelphia, PA 19103   Lynn Dunwody, Res.Libn.
Staff: Prof 1; Other 1. **Subjects:** Management, compensation, personnel, pensions and benefits. **Holdings:** 3000 books; 2500 company files. **Subscriptions:** 150 journals and other serials. **Services:** Interlibrary loans; library not open to public. **Computerized Information Services:** DIALOG, SDC, Dow Jones News Retrieval, Dun & Bradstreet, Inc.

HAY (John) LIBRARY
See: Brown University - Special Collections

HAYDEN LIBRARY
See: Arizona Historical Foundation; Arizona State University

HAYDEN LIBRARY
See: Massachusetts Institute of Technology - Institute Archives and Special Collections

HAYDEN PLANETARIUM
See: American Museum of Natural History

HAYES (Grom) LIBRARY
See: Hartford State Technical College - Grom Hayes Library

HAYES (Helen) HOSPITAL
See: Helen Hayes Hospital

★5519★
HAYES/HILL INCORPORATED - LIBRARY (Bus-Fin)
20 N. Wacker Dr., Suite 3330   Phone: (312) 984-5250
Chicago, IL 60606   Sandra K. Rollheiser, Res.Mgr.
Founded: 1975. **Staff:** 6. **Subjects:** Business and industry, wage and salary administration. **Holdings:** 500 books; 1200 annual reports. **Subscriptions:** 102 journals and other serials. **Services:** Interlibrary loans; copying (limited); library open to other librarians. **Computerized Information Services:** DIALOG. **Networks/Consortia:** Member of Chicago Library System; Metropolitan Chicago Library Assembly.

HAYES (John D.) LIBRARY OF HUMAN RELATIONS
See: Canadian Council of Christians and Jews - John D. Hayes Library of Human Relations

★5520★
HAYES (Max S.) VOCATIONAL SCHOOL - LIBRARY (Sci-Tech)
4600 Detroit Ave.   Phone: (216) 631-1528
Cleveland, OH 44102   Robert Stephen, Libn.
Founded: 1958. **Staff:** Prof 1; Other 1. **Subjects:** Automotive trades, metalwork, machine shop work, vocational education, construction, textile fabrication. **Holdings:** 12,000 books and bound periodical volumes; complete U.S. and foreign car shop manuals, 1960 to present. **Subscriptions:** 106 journals and other serials. **Services:** Interlibrary loans; copying; library open to public by appointment. **Remarks:** Maintained by the Cleveland Board of Education.

HAYES REGIONAL ARBORETUM
See: Hayes (Stanley W.) Research Foundation

★5521★
HAYES (Rutherford B.) PRESIDENTIAL CENTER - LIBRARY (Hist)
Spiegel Grove   Phone: (419) 332-2081
Fremont, OH 43420   Leslie H. Fishel, Jr., Dir.
Founded: 1911. **Staff:** Prof 16; Other 10. **Subjects:** Rutherford B. Hayes library and papers; Hayes family papers and papers of many of the President's contemporaries; Civil War and Reconstruction in the South; black studies; American railroads; American travel; presidents of the U.S.; U.S. political and economic history; American biography; American letters; Ohio history; Sandusky River Valley history; Great Lakes marine collections. **Holdings:** 65,000 books and bound periodical volumes; one million manuscripts; 50,000 photographs; census manuscripts and newspapers on microfilm; tapes, pictures, films and slides. **Services:** Interlibrary loans; copying; library open to public. **Staff:** Thomas A. Smith, Mss.Cur.; Roberta L. Hudson, Libn.; Janice L. Haas, Ref.Libn.; Petrene P. Wilkins, Photograph Cur.

HAYES (Samuel P.) RESEARCH LIBRARY
See: Perkins School for the Blind - Samuel P. Hayes Research Library

★5522★
HAYES, SEAY, MATTERN & MATTERN - TECHNICAL LIBRARY (Sci-Tech)
1315 Franklin Rd., S.W.
Box 13446
Roanoke, VA 24034   Phone: (703) 343-6971
      Nancy H. Seamans, Libn.
Founded: 1958. **Staff:** Prof 1. **Subjects:** Architecture, engineering, planning, construction, highways. **Holdings:** 8500 books; folders of letters, clippings and brochures. **Subscriptions:** 188 journals and other serials. **Services:** Interlibrary loans; copying; library not open to public.

★5523★
HAYES (Stanley W.) RESEARCH FOUNDATION - LIBRARY (Env-Cons)†
Box 1404   Phone: (317) 962-3745
Richmond, IN 47374   D.R. Hendricks, Pres.
Subjects: Ecology, entomology, ornithology, geology, biology. **Holdings:** 1300 volumes. **Remarks:** Library located on grounds of Hayes Regional Arboretum.

★5524★
HAYHURST (F.H.) COMPANY, LTD. - MEDIA RESEARCH LIBRARY (Bus-Fin)
55 Eglinton Ave., East   Phone: (416) 487-4371
Toronto, ON, Canada M4P 1G9   J. Marcotte, Media Supv.
Founded: 1959. **Staff:** Prof 1. **Subjects:** Advertising, media, marketing. **Holdings:** 230 books; 2600 magazines and periodicals; 16 drawers of clippings; 12 drawers of Statistics Canada material. **Subscriptions:** 80 journals and other serials. **Services:** Interlibrary loans; library not open to public. **Publications:** Media Research Bulletin, monthly - to company personnel and agency clients.

HAYNES-BECKET MEMORIAL LIBRARY
See: Elkem Metals Company - Technology Center

HAYNES MEMORIAL LIBRARY
See: Living Desert Reserve

HAYNES YELLOWSTONE NATIONAL PARK LIBRARY
See: Montana State University - Roland R. Renne Library - Special Collections

HAYS (George H.) MEMORIAL LIBRARY
See: Mount Sinai Medical Center of Cleveland - George H. Hays Memorial Library

★5525★
HAYSTACK MOUNTAIN SCHOOL OF CRAFTS - LIBRARY (Art)
                                      Phone: (207) 348-6946
Deer Isle, ME 04627
Staff: Prof 1. **Subjects:** Crafts, ceramics, weaving, glassblowing, jewelry. **Holdings:** 300 books. **Subscriptions:** 19 journals and other serials. **Services:** Library open to public.

HAYT (Lillian R.) MEMORIAL LIBRARY
See: Hospital Educational and Research Fund - Lillian R. Hayt Memorial Library

HAZARDVILLE CATHOLIC LIBRARY
See: St. Bernard's Parish

★5526★
HAZELDEN FOUNDATION - STAFF LIBRARY (Soc Sci)
Box 11   Phone: (612) 257-4010
Center City, MN 55012   Joan A. Frederickson, Libn.
Staff: Prof 1; Other 2. **Subjects:** Alcoholism, drug abuse. **Holdings:** 4000 books; 100 bound periodical volumes; 150 cassette tapes; 145 Hazelden studies. **Subscriptions:** 100 journals and other serials. **Services:** Copying. **Networks/Consortia:** Member of Twin Cities Biomedical Consortium. **Formerly:** Its Staff & Research Libraries.

★5527★
HAZELTON RALTECH, INC. - LIBRARY (Sci-Tech)
3301 Kinsman Blvd.
Box 7545
Madison, WI 53707   Phone: (608) 241-4471
                                      Patricia Riese, Libn.
Staff: Prof 1. **Subjects:** Food science, chemistry, toxicology, drugs and cosmetics, laboratory animals. **Holdings:** 3000 books; 3000 bound periodical volumes. **Subscriptions:** 212 journals and other serials. **Services:** Interlibrary loans; copying; library open to public with restrictions. **Computerized Information Services:** DIALOG. **Networks/Consortia:** Member of Regional Medical Library - Region 3. **Formerly:** Raltech Scientific Services.

HEADLEY (Louis S.) MEMORIAL LIBRARY
See: Science Museum of Minnesota - Louis S. Headley Memorial Library

HEAFEY (Edwin A.) LAW LIBRARY
See: University of Santa Clara - Edwin A. Heafey Law Library

★5528★
HEALD COLLEGE OF ENGINEERING AND ARCHITECTURE - LIBRARY (Sci-Tech)†
1215 Van Ness Ave.   Phone: (415) 441-5562
San Francisco, CA 94109   Catherine Matteucig, Dir.
Staff: Prof 1; Other 2. **Subjects:** Mathematics, architecture, chemistry, engineering. **Holdings:** 6900 books; 6 cases of unbound periodicals; 1200 bound theses. **Subscriptions:** 37 journals and other serials. **Services:** Copying; library open to public with restrictions.

★5529★
HEALTH COMPUTER INFORMATION BUREAU (Med; Info Sci)
10504A 169th St.   Phone: (403) 489-4553
Edmonton, AB, Canada T5P 3X6   Steven A. Huesing, HCIB Secretariat
Staff: 1. **Subjects:** Computer applications in health. **Holdings:** Figures not available. **Services:** Library not open to public. **Publications:** Health Computer Applications in Canada (Volumes I-VI presently available), annual - by order. **Also Known As:** Bureau d'Informatique dans le Domaine de la Sante.

★5530★
HEALTH EDUCATION CENTER LIBRARY (Med)
200 Ross St.   Phone: (412) 392-3165
Pittsburgh, PA 15219   Susan J. Stapley, Libn.
Founded: 1976. **Staff:** Prof 1. **Subjects:** Health education and planning, prevention, self-care, health care delivery, disease, patient education. **Special Collections:** Consumer health education materials (10,000 items). **Holdings:** 500 books; 20,000 newsletters, reports, preprints. **Subscriptions:** 150 journals and newsletters. **Services:** Interlibrary loans; copying; library open to public. **Computerized Information Services:** Computerized cataloging. **Networks/Consortia:** Member of Pittsburgh Consortium for Health Education Information; Pittsburgh Regional Library Center. **Publications:** Update (newsletter), bimonthly; Recent Acquisitions, 4/year; list of publications - available upon request. **Special Catalogs:** Directory for Sources of Health Information Materials in Southwestern Pennsylvania.

HEALTH INSURANCE ASSOCIATION OF AMERICA
See: American Council of Life Insurance

★5531★
HEALTH POLICY ADVISORY CENTER (HEALTH/PAC) - LIBRARY (Med)
17 Murray St.   Phone: (212) 267-8890
New York, NY 10007   Kate Pfordresher, Assoc.Ed.
Staff: 2. **Subjects:** U.S. health care system, women's health, medical self-help. **Special Collections:** Health Policy Advisory Center Bulletin (1968 to present). **Holdings:** 1000 books; 50 bound periodical volumes. **Services:** Library open to public by appointment. **Publications:** Health Policy Advisory Center Bulletin, monthly - by subscription.

★5532★
HEALTH RESEARCH AND EDUCATIONAL TRUST OF NEW JERSEY - LEARNING CENTER (Med)
760 Alexander Rd. (CN-1)   Phone: (609) 452-9280
Princeton, NJ 08540   Michelle Pentland, Program Coord.
Staff: Prof 1. **Subjects:** Hospital and health care administration, consumer health education, hospital and in-service education, business and management. **Special Collections:** Diagnostic Related Group Reference Material. **Holdings:** 1500 books; 115 bound periodical volumes; 55 films; 15 videotapes; 96 audiotapes; 8 VF drawers of related material; 2 files of archival material. **Subscriptions:** 170 journals and other serials; 6 newspapers. **Services:** Interlibrary loans; copying; library open to public with restrictions. **Computerized Information Services:** BRS. **Networks/Consortia:** Member of MEDCORE. **Publications:** Selected Recent Acquisitions, monthly - for New Jersey hospital libraries; Library Bulletins, monthly - for New Jersey hospital libraries and selected personnel. **Special Indexes:** Acquisitions update (notebook).

HEALTH AND WELFARE CANADA
See: Canada - Health and Welfare Canada

★5533★
HEALTH AND WELFARE COUNCIL OF CENTRAL MARYLAND, INC. - STAFF REFERENCE LIBRARY (Soc Sci)
22 Light St.   Phone: (301) 752-4146
Baltimore, MD 21202   John G. Geist, Exec.Dir.
Founded: 1960. **Staff:** 1. **Subjects:** Regional planning; personnel practices and agency management; census; employment and manpower; child welfare and day care; rehabilitation and aging; health, welfare, education, court and correction services; social service delivery systems; information and referral services. **Holdings:** 500 books; 2750 other cataloged items; 42 looseleaf binders of Health and Welfare Council Studies and Reports; 10 pamphlet boxes of annual reports of Maryland State and Baltimore City departments; 120 loose-leaf binders of agency newsletters and U.S. Health, Education and Welfare statistics and research notes. **Subscriptions:** 31 journals and other serials; 5 newspapers. **Services:** Library not open to public; open to community agencies under special arrangement.

★5534★
HEALTH AND WELFARE PLANNING ASSOCIATION OF ALLEGHENY COUNTY - LIBRARY (Soc Sci)
200 Ross St.   Phone: (412) 261-6010
Pittsburgh, PA 15219   Mary Lou Charlton, Libn.
Founded: 1952. **Staff:** Prof 1. **Subjects:** Health and welfare planning and financing; social agency administration; family and child welfare; housing; rehabilitation; problems of aged; group work and recreation; health (including mental health); crime and correction. **Special Collections:** Annual reports of governmental and social agencies. **Holdings:** 1200 books; pamphlets. **Subscriptions:** 61 journals and other serials. **Services:** Interlibrary loans; library open to public on request for limited use.

★5535★
HEARD MUSEUM - LIBRARY (Art)
22 E. Monte Vista Rd. Phone: (602) 252-8840
Phoenix, AZ 85004 Mary E. Graham, Libn.
Founded: 1929. **Staff:** Prof 1; Other 12. **Subjects:** Ethnology, social anthropology, American Indian, archeology, primitive art, American Indian painting, Southwest travel and exploration. **Special Collections:** Spanish and Mexican colonial architecture, art and decorating. **Holdings:** 50,000 volumes; 9 films; 300 maps; 31 records; 1000 pamphlets. **Subscriptions:** 500 journals and other serials. **Services:** Interlibrary loans; copying; library open to public for reference use only. **Networks/Consortia:** Member of ARLIS; Intermountain Union List of Serials (IMULS). **Publications:** Heard Museum Newsletter, bimonthly - distributed to members; special publications by the staff, irregular - for sale. **Special Catalogs:** Intermountain Union List of Serials (IMULS).

HEARST CORPORATION - HOUSE BEAUTIFUL - STAFF LIBRARY
See: House Beautiful - Staff Library

★5536★
HEARST METROTONE NEWS - FILM LIBRARY (Info Sci)
235 E. 45th St. Phone: (212) 682-7690
New York, NY 10017 Ted Troll, Chf.Libn.
Staff: Prof 1. **Subjects:** Newsreel films; special documentary and film projects. **Special Collections:** Screen News Digest; educational films for schools. **Holdings:** Figures not available.

HEARST-METROTONE NEWSREEL LIBRARY
See: University of California, Los Angeles - UCLA Film Archives

★5537★
HEARST (Phoebe Apperson) HISTORICAL SOCIETY, INC. - MUSEUM CENTER (Hist)
850 Walton
Box 1842
St. Clair, MO 63077 Phone: (314) 629-3186
 Mabel Reed, Sec. in Charge
Founded: 1961. **Staff:** 1. **Subjects:** Archeology, history, radio programs. **Holdings:** Historical books, Congressional Records, clippings, tapes, slides, photographs, phonograph records, manuscripts. **Services:** Interlibrary loans; library open to public. **Publications:** Newsletter. **Staff:** Ralph Gregory, Pres.

★5538★
HEART OF AMERICA GENEALOGICAL SOCIETY & LIBRARY, INC. (Hist)
311 E. 12th St. Phone: (816) 221-2685
Kansas City, MO 64106 Maida Whitten, Pres.
Subjects: Genealogy. **Holdings:** 7000 books; 1500 bound periodical volumes. **Subscriptions:** 125 journals and other serials. **Services:** Copying; library open to public. **Publications:** The Kansas City Genealogist, quarterly - by subscription and exchange. **Special Indexes:** Family Record Sheets (60,000 names). **Remarks:** The genealogy collection is housed in the Kansas City Public Library.

HEARTMAN COLLECTION
See: Texas Southern University - Library

★5539★
HEBREW COLLEGE - JACOB AND ROSE GROSSMAN LIBRARY (Educ; Rel-Theol)
43 Hawes St. Phone: (617) 232-8710
Brookline, MA 02146 Maurice S. Tuchman, Libn.
Founded: 1922. **Staff:** Prof 4; Other 1. **Subjects:** Education, Jewish history, Hebrew literature, Bible, Israel, children's literature, Rabbinic literature. **Special Collections:** Responsa literature; Kabbalah and Hassidic literature; Jewish education; Large-print Judaica; Dr. Harry A. and Beatrice Savitz Jewish Medical History Collection; Russian Judaica. **Holdings:** 80,000 books; 1300 bound periodical volumes; 2 incunabula; 300 16th and 17th century rare books; 72 manuscripts; 600 phonograph records; 60 maps and charts; 600 reels of microfilm; 100 slides. **Subscriptions:** 210 journals and other serials; 11 newspapers. **Services:** Interlibrary loans; copying; library open to public. **Networks/Consortia:** Member of Fenway Library Consortium. **Special Catalogs:** Manuscript catalog (book form); Russian Judaica; Microform Judaica. **Staff:** Helen Sarna, Asst.Libn.; Shalva Siegel, Spec. Subjects Cat.; Judy Schiff, Ref.Libn.

★5540★
HEBREW EDUCATIONAL ALLIANCE - LIBRARY (Rel-Theol)
1555 Stuart St. Phone: (303) 629-0410
Denver, CO 80204 William David Ellis, Libn.
Founded: 1932. **Staff:** 1. **Subjects:** Judaica and Hebraica. **Holdings:** 2000 books. **Subscriptions:** 20 journals and other serials. **Services:** Library open to public.

★5541★
HEBREW INSTITUTE OF PITTSBURGH - SOL ROSENBLOOM LIBRARY (Rel-Theol; Educ)
6401 Forbes Ave. Phone: (412) 521-1100
Pittsburgh, PA 15217 Michaella Segall, Libn.
Founded: 1916. **Staff:** Prof 2. **Subjects:** Juvenile literature, Bible, Bible commentary, religion, language, education, Jewish community reference, history of Israel. **Special Collections:** Gertrude Nachman Memorial Collection of Juvenile Books. **Holdings:** Figures not available. **Subscriptions:** 45 journals and other serials; 5 newspapers. **Services:** Interlibrary loans; copying; library open to public.

★5542★
HEBREW THEOLOGICAL COLLEGE - SAUL SILBER MEMORIAL LIBRARY (Rel-Theol)
7135 N. Carpenter Rd. Phone: (312) 267-9800
Skokie, IL 60077 Leah Mishkin, Libn. & Cur.
Staff: Prof 4. **Subjects:** Judaica, philosophy, ethics, Hebraica, Rabbinics, Biblical literature, Jewish history, Zionism. **Special Collections:** J. Rapoport; R. Farber; Saul Silber; Max Shulman Zionist Library; Rev. Newman Hebrew Periodical Collection; Rabbi Simon H. Album Halakha Collection; Rabbi Leonard C. Mishkin Holocaust Collection. **Holdings:** 61,000 volumes; manuscripts and microfilm. **Subscriptions:** 170 journals and other serials. **Services:** Interlibrary loans; library open to public. **Staff:** Joseph Bachrach, Asst.Libn.; Don Rosenbaum, Libn.

★5543★
HEBREW UNION COLLEGE - JEWISH INSTITUTE OF RELIGION - AMERICAN JEWISH ARCHIVES (Hist)
3101 Clifton Ave. Phone: (513) 221-1875
Cincinnati, OH 45220 Fannie Zelcer, Archv.
Founded: 1947. **Staff:** Prof 4; Other 13. **Subjects:** Western Hemisphere Jewish history and culture. **Holdings:** 7 million manuscript pages. **Subscriptions:** 5000 journals and other serials. **Services:** Interlibrary loans; copying; services available to all scholars and researchers in the field of Western Hemisphere Jewish history. **Publications:** American Jewish Archives, semiannual. **Special Catalogs:** Manuscript catalog of the American Jewish Archives, 5 volumes; Guide to the Holdings of the American Jewish Archives, by James Clasper and M. Carolyn Delenbach (1979). **Staff:** Dr. Abraham J. Peck, Assoc.Dir.; Prof. Jacob R. Marcus, Dir.

★5544★
HEBREW UNION COLLEGE - JEWISH INSTITUTE OF RELIGION - AMERICAN JEWISH PERIODICAL CENTER (Rel-Theol)
3101 Clifton Ave. Phone: (513) 221-1875
Cincinnati, OH 45220 Jacob R. Marcus, Dir.
Founded: 1956. **Staff:** Prof 1; Other 2. **Subjects:** American Jewish periodicals and newspapers on microfilm. **Holdings:** 7600 reels of microfilm (cataloged). **Services:** Interlibrary loans; copying; center open to public. **Publications:** Catalog of American Jewish Newspapers and Periodicals on Microfilm (1957); First Supplement (1960). **Staff:** Herbert C. Zafren, Co-Dir.

★5545★
HEBREW UNION COLLEGE - JEWISH INSTITUTE OF RELIGION - FRANCES-HENRY LIBRARY (Rel-Theol)
3077 University Ave. Phone: (213) 749-3424
Los Angeles, CA 90007 Harvey P. Horowitz, Libn.
Founded: 1958. **Staff:** Prof 1; Other 3. **Subjects:** Bible, Talmud, Rabbinics, Jewish history, philosophy, art, Jewish communal service, Hebrew literature, religion, Zionism. **Special Collections:** Rare Hebraica; Joseph H. Rosenberg American Jewish Archives. **Holdings:** 70,000 books; 2500 bound periodical volumes; 4000 reels of microfilm; 70 dissertations. **Subscriptions:** 350 journals and other serials; 25 newspapers. **Services:** Interlibrary loans; copying; library open to public.

★5546★
HEBREW UNION COLLEGE - JEWISH INSTITUTE OF RELIGION - KLAU LIBRARY (Rel-Theol)
1 W. Fourth St. Phone: (212) 674-5300
New York, NY 10012 Philip E. Miller, Libn.
Founded: 1922. **Staff:** Prof 2; Other 4. **Subjects:** Jewish literature, history, sociology, music; Near Eastern languages including Hebrew and Aramaic; philosophy; archeology; religious education. **Holdings:** 112,000 books. **Subscriptions:** 300 journals and other serials; 30 newspapers. **Services:** Interlibrary loans; copying; library open to public for reference use only. **Networks/Consortia:** Member of New York Area Theological Library

Association. **Publications:** Studies in Bibliography & Booklore. **Staff:** Susan Tabor, Circ.; Catherine Markush, ILL; Debra K. Reed, Judaica Ref.

★5547★
HEBREW UNION COLLEGE - JEWISH INSTITUTE OF RELIGION - KLAU LIBRARY (Area-Ethnic)
3101 Clifton Ave.   Phone: (513) 221-1875
Cincinnati, OH 45220   Herbert C. Zafren, Lib.Dir.
Founded: 1875. **Staff:** Prof 9; Other 14. **Subjects:** Judaica, Hebraica, ancient Near East, Biblica, Rabbinics. **Special Collections:** Spinoza; Jewish music; rare books and manuscripts; Anti-Semitism; maps and broadsides; Jewish Americana; Josephus; Judeo-Persian; Yiddish theater. **Holdings:** 315,000 volumes; 6331 reels of microfilm; 14,046 microfiche; 3000 volumes of manuscripts. **Subscriptions:** 1952 journals and other serials. **Services:** Interlibrary loans; copying; library open to public. **Computerized Information Services:** Computerized cataloging. **Publications:** Studies in Bibliography and Booklore, irregular - available by subscription; Bibliographica Judaica, monograph series. **Staff:** David J. Gilner, Ref./Pub.Serv.Libn.; Ellen S. Kovacic, Cat.Libn.; James I. Neiger, Adm./Coll.Dev.Libn.; Bernard H. Rabenstein, Acq.Libn.; Jonathan H. Rodgers, Spec.Coll.Libn.; Arnona Rudavsky, Judaica Libn.; Gloria Wolfson, Off.Mgr.

HECHT (Sigmund) LIBRARY
See: Wilshire Boulevard Temple - Sigmund Hecht Library

HEDBERG (Carl A.) HEALTH SCIENCE LIBRARY
See: Augustana Hospital and Health Care Center - Carl A. Hedberg Health Science Library

HEGGEN (Thomas) MEMORIAL LIBRARY
See: University of Minnesota - Eric Sevareid Journalism Library

★5548★
HEIDRICK & STRUGGLES, INC. - LIBRARY RESEARCH CENTER (Bus-Fin)
125 S. Wacker Dr., Suite 2800   Phone: (312) 372-8811
Chicago, IL 60606   Margaret E. Bremner, Libn.
Staff: Prof 1; Other 1. **Subjects:** Corporate data. **Holdings:** 1000 books; 7000 annual reports and proxies; industry directories; 12 VF drawers of clippings. **Subscriptions:** 95 journals and other serials; 5 newspapers. **Services:** Interlibrary loans; copying; SDI; library open to public with restrictions. **Computerized Information Services:** DIALOG, New York Times Information Service, Dow Jones News Retrieval. **Networks/Consortia:** Member of Chicago Library System; Metropolitan Chicago Library Assembly.

HEIM MEMORIAL LIBRARY
See: Allentown State Hospital

★5549★
HEINZ (H.J.) COMPANY - LIBRARY (Food-Bev)
1062 Progress St.
Box 57
Pittsburgh, PA 15230   Phone: (412) 237-5948
     Nancy M. Wright, Libn.
Founded: 1903. **Staff:** Prof 2; Other 1. **Subjects:** Food processing and engineering, agriculture, statistics, packaging, chemistry, bacteriology, marketing, advertising, selling. **Special Collections:** Company archives. **Holdings:** 5000 books; 6000 bound periodical volumes; 16,000 pamphlets (cataloged); patents, clippings, house organs, road maps, microfilm. **Subscriptions:** 800 journals and other serials; 6 newspapers. **Services:** Interlibrary loans; copying (fee); library not open to public. **Computerized Information Services:** DIALOG; internal database. **Publications:** Weekly Abstract of Magazines - intracompany distribution; Recent Acquisitions. **Staff:** Joan R. Myers, Asst.Libn.

★5550★
HEISEY COLLECTORS OF AMERICA, INC. - HCA LIBRARY & ARCHIVES (Rec)
Sixth & Church Sts.
Box 27
Newark, OH 43055   Phone: (614) 345-2932
     Robert McClain, Pres.
Founded: 1971. **Staff:** 4. **Special Collections:** Heisey glassware made in Newark from 1896-1957. **Holdings:** Figures not available for Heisey catalogs and related material; microfiche. **Services:** Copying (limited); library open to public with restrictions. **Publications:** Heisey News - monthly newsletter distributed to members; Encyclopedia of Heisey Glassware, Etchings & Carvings; Heisey by Imperial, 2nd edition; Heisey Toothpick Holders; reprints of original catalogs.

★5551★
HELD-POAGE MEMORIAL HOME & RESEARCH LIBRARY (Hist)
603 W. Perkins St.   Phone: (707) 462-6969
Ukiah, CA 95482   Mrs. Lila J. Lee, Libn.
Staff: 2. **Subjects:** History - Mendocino County, California, U.S., Civil War; Pomo and other Indians. **Special Collections:** Writings of Edith Van Allen Murphey, Dr. John Whiz Hudson, Helen Carpenter. **Holdings:** 3150 books; photographs, maps, bound county records, clippings, genealogies. **Subscriptions:** 13 journals and other serials. **Services:** Interlibrary loans; copying; library open to public for reference use only, by appointment. **Remarks:** Maintained by Mendocino County Historical Society.

★5552★
HELEN HAYES HOSPITAL - LIBRARY (Med)
Route 9W   Phone: (914) 947-3000
West Haverstraw, NY 10993   Kathleen Kuczynski, Lib.Dir.
Staff: Prof 2; Other 2. **Subjects:** Orthopedics, rehabilitation medicine, neurology, physical therapy, occupational therapy, biomedical engineering, psychology, psychiatry, speech and hearing. **Holdings:** 5000 books; 5000 bound periodical volumes. **Subscriptions:** 200 journals and other serials. **Services:** Interlibrary loans; library open to health professionals. **Networks/Consortia:** Member of New York and New Jersey Regional Medical Library System; Southeastern New York Library Resources Council (SENYLRC); Health Information Libraries of Westchester; Ramapo Catskill Library System.

★5553★
HELEN KELLER NATIONAL CENTER - REFERENCE LIBRARY (Med)
111 Middle Neck Rd.   Phone: (516) 944-8900
Sands Point, NY 11050   Gertrude Queen, Libn.
Staff: Prof 1. **Subjects:** Deafness, blindness, Usher's Syndrome, rubella. **Holdings:** 700 books. **Subscriptions:** 14 journals and other serials. **Services:** Interlibrary loans; copying; library open to public. **Publications:** Nat-Cent News, quarterly - to deaf/blind people and those working with them.

★5554★
HELENE CURTIS INDUSTRIES, INC. - CORPORATE LIBRARY (Sci-Tech; Bus-Fin)
4401 W. North Ave.   Phone: (312) 292-2280
Chicago, IL 60639   Jacquelyn B. Becker, Corp.Libn.
Founded: 1952. **Staff:** Prof 1; Other 1. **Subjects:** Cosmetics, chemistry, textiles, dermatology, toxicology, marketing, management. **Holdings:** 2000 books; 500 bound periodical volumes; files for 500 companies (annual reports and 10Ks); 7 drawers of patents; 24 VF drawers of pamphlets; company archives. **Subscriptions:** 250 journals and other serials. **Services:** Interlibrary loans; copying; library open to public for reference use only with prior permission from librarian. **Computerized Information Services:** DIALOG, New York Times Information Service, Source Telecomputing Corporation, Dialcom, Inc., SDC, NLM. **Networks/Consortia:** Member of OCLC through ILLINET.

★5555★
HELENE FULD MEDICAL CENTER - HEALTH SCIENCES LIBRARY (Med)
750 Brunswick Ave.   Phone: (609) 394-6065
Trenton, NJ 08638   Kathy Goldberg, Dir.
Staff: Prof 1; Other 2. **Subjects:** Medicine, nursing, allied health sciences. **Holdings:** 3500 books; 2917 bound periodical volumes; 8 VF drawers of clippings and pictures. **Subscriptions:** 185 journals and other serials. **Services:** Interlibrary loans; copying; SDI; library open to public for reference use only. **Computerized Information Services:** MEDLARS. **Networks/Consortia:** Member of Health Sciences Library Association of New Jersey; Central Jersey Health Sciences Library Association.

★5556★
HELIX TECHNOLOGY CORPORATION - LIBRARY (Sci-Tech)
266 Second Ave.   Phone: (617) 890-9400
Waltham, MA 02254   Carole B. Shutzer, Libn.
Staff: Prof 1; Other 1. **Subjects:** Cryogenics, engineering. **Holdings:** 1000 books; 250 technical reports. **Subscriptions:** 150 journals and other serials. **Services:** Interlibrary loans; copying; library open to public with restrictions. **Computerized Information Services:** DIALOG, SDC, Information Handling Service. **Publications:** Acquisitions list, monthly - by request; Information Alert, monthly.

★5557★
HELLENIC COLLEGE AND HOLY CROSS GREEK ORTHODOX SCHOOL OF THEOLOGY - COTSIDAS-TONNA LIBRARY (Rel-Theol)
50 Goddard Ave.   Phone: (617) 731-3500
Brookline, MA 02146   Rev. George. C. Papademetriou, Dir. of Lib.
Founded: 1954. **Staff:** Prof 2; Other 2. **Subjects:** Classical and modern

Greek literature, Greek Orthodox theology, Byzantine history and culture, patristic literature, Orthodox liturgics, Byzantine music. **Holdings:** 80,000 volumes. **Subscriptions:** 250 journals and other serials; 20 newspapers. **Services:** Interlibrary loans; copying; library open to public for reference use only. **Computerized Information Services:** Computerized cataloging. **Networks/Consortia:** Member of Boston Theological Institute. **Staff:** Gladys I. Dratch, Assoc.Dir./Cat.; Helen Katre, Acq.Libn.; Sophia Tsangali, Greek Acq.

★5558★
HELLER, EHRMAN, WHITE & MC AULIFFE - LIBRARY (Law)
44 Montgomery St., 30th Fl.   Phone: (415) 772-6105
San Francisco, CA 94104   Loretta Mak, Libn.
Founded: 1921. **Staff:** Prof 1; Other 4. **Subjects:** Law. **Holdings:** 22,000 volumes. **Subscriptions:** Loose-leaf services; journals and other serials. **Services:** Interlibrary loans; copying; library not open to public.

HELM-CRAVENS LIBRARY
See: Western Kentucky University - Folklore, Folklife, & Oral History Archives

HELPERN (Milton) CENTER
See: International Reference Organization in Forensic Medicine and Sciences

HELPERN (Milton) LIBRARY OF LEGAL MEDICINE
See: New York City - Office of Chief Medical Examiner - Milton Helpern Library of Legal Medicine

★5559★
HEMET VALLEY HOSPITAL DISTRICT - DR. LESLIE J. CLARK MEMORIAL LIBRARY (Med)
1116 E. Latham Ave.   Phone: (714) 652-2811
Hemet, CA 92343   Dixie Cirocco, Dir.
Staff: Prof 1; Other 1. **Subjects:** Clinical medicine, nursing, psychiatry. **Holdings:** 736 books; 918 bound periodical volumes. **Subscriptions:** 106 journals and other serials. **Services:** Interlibrary loans; copying; library open to public by appointment. **Computerized Information Services:** MEDLINE. **Networks/Consortia:** Member of Inland Empire Medical Library Cooperative.

HEMINGER HEALTH SCIENCES LIBRARY
See: Central Washington Hospital

★5560★
HENDERSHOT BIBLIOGRAPHY & CONSULTANTS - LIBRARY (Educ)
4114 Ridgewood
Bay City, MI 48706   Dr. Carl H. Hendershot, Publ.
Founded: 1963. **Staff:** 2. **Subjects:** Self instructional materials. **Holdings:** 2500 books; research and historical materials on programmed instruction, self-study and learner-paced instruction. **Subscriptions:** 25 journals and other serials. **Services:** Library open to public with restrictions. **Publications:** Programmed Learning & Individually Paced Instruction - bibliography.

HENDERSON (Charles W.) MEMORIAL LIBRARY
See: U.S. Bureau of Mines - Charles W. Henderson Memorial Library

HENDERSON (Maurine) LIBRARY
See: Travis Avenue Baptist Church - Maurine Henderson Library

HENDERSON ROOM
See: Carnegie Library

HENDERSON TECHNICAL LIBRARY
See: Titanium Metals Corporation of America

★5561★
HENDRICK MEDICAL CENTER - MARY MEEK SCHOOL OF NURSING - LIBRARY (Med)
N. 19th & Hickory Sts.   Phone: (915) 677-3551
Abilene, TX 79601   Mrs. Frances Brookreson, Libn.
Founded: 1924. **Staff:** Prof 1. **Subjects:** Nursing, medicine, radiology. **Holdings:** 2160 books; 339 bound periodical volumes; 4 VF drawers of clippings; TV available through continuing education. **Subscriptions:** 50 journals and other serials. **Services:** SDI; library open to public for reference use only.

HENDRY (W. Candler) LIBRARY OF THE OCCULT
See: Tree of Life Press - Library and Archives

★5562★
HENKEL CORPORATION - HENNEPIN TECHNICAL CENTER LIBRARY (Sci-Tech)
2010 E. Hennepin Ave.   Phone: (612) 378-8758
Minneapolis, MN 55413   A. Rahman Khan, Mgr., Tech.Info.Serv.
Founded: 1937. **Staff:** Prof 7; Other 6. **Subjects:** Chemical research, chemical engineering. **Holdings:** 5500 books; 2600 bound periodical volumes; 2000 unbound periodicals; 167 VF drawers of company reports and correspondence; 1050 reels of microfilmed periodicals and documents; 600 reels of microfilmed patents. **Subscriptions:** 600 journals and other serials. **Services:** Interlibrary loans; literature surveys; SDI; library open to public with advance request and approval by management. **Computerized Information Services:** DIALOG, SDC, NLM, Control Data Corporation, General Electric; computerized cataloging. **Networks/Consortia:** Member of OCLC. **Special Indexes:** Termatrex index to internal reports. **Staff:** Dorthea Hicks, Info.Spec.; Margaret A. Drews, Libn.

★5563★
HENNEPIN COUNTY HISTORICAL SOCIETY - ARCHIVES (Hist)
2303 Third Ave., S.   Phone: (612) 870-1329
Minneapolis, MN 55404   Donna Lind, Exec.Dir.
Staff: 1. **Subjects:** Local history, lumber and milling industries, transportation. **Special Collections:** St. Anthony Falls Water Power Company (5 boxes of photographs and maps); Civil War (145 volumes); Abraham Lincoln (80 volumes). **Holdings:** 2000 books; 551 bound periodical volumes; 1200 photographs (cataloged); 31 VF drawers of clippings and ephemera; 30 boxes and 20 VF drawers of archives, maps and atlases; 19 volumes of Sanborn Insurance Maps. **Subscriptions:** 67 newsletters; 17 newspapers. **Services:** Copying; library open to public for reference use only. **Publications:** Hennepin County History, quarterly; Newsletter, irregular - both to members. **Special Indexes:** Index of photograph collection (card); index of archival holdings and maps (card); index of clipping and ephemera files (card); index of biographies (card).

★5564★
HENNEPIN COUNTY LAW LIBRARY (Law)
C2451 Government Ctr.   Phone: (612) 348-3022
Minneapolis, MN 55487   Anne W. Grande, Dir.
Founded: 1883. **Staff:** Prof 3; Other 6. **Subjects:** Law. **Holdings:** 65,000 books; 7000 bound periodical volumes. **Subscriptions:** 350 journals and other serials. **Services:** Interlibrary loans; copying; library open to public. **Computerized Information Services:** WESTLAW. **Publications:** Acquisitions List, bimonthly - local distribution. **Staff:** Margaret Hall, Asst.Libn.; Barbara Golden, Ref.Libn.

★5565★
HENNEPIN COUNTY LIBRARY SYSTEM - GOVERNMENT CENTER INFORMATION LIBRARY (Soc Sci)
C-2359 Government Center
300 S. Sixth St.   Phone: (612) 348-2024
Minneapolis, MN 55487   Carol LeDuc, Sr.Libn.
Staff: Prof 2; Other 2. **Subjects:** Local government, public administration, management, planning, human services, urban affairs. **Holdings:** 2100 books. **Subscriptions:** 400 journals and other serials; 13 newspapers. **Services:** Interlibrary loans; copying; library open to public for reference use only. **Computerized Information Services:** DIALOG, BRS, SDC, New York Times Information Service. **Networks/Consortia:** Member of Metropolitan Library Services Agency (MELSA); MINITEX. **Publications:** Information Bulletin, bimonthly - to county departments. **Staff:** Jan Price, Libn.

★5566★
HENNEPIN COUNTY MEDICAL CENTER - HEALTH SCIENCES LIBRARY (Med)
701 Park Ave.   Phone: (612) 347-2710
Minneapolis, MN 55415   Patricia A. Williams, Sr.Libn.
Staff: Prof 2; Other 5. **Subjects:** Clinical medicine, nursing, allied health fields. **Holdings:** 25,000 books and bound periodical volumes; 200 video cassettes; AV materials. **Subscriptions:** 505 journals and other serials. **Services:** Interlibrary loans; copying; SDI; Current Awareness Service; library open to public for reference use only. **Computerized Information Services:** MEDLINE, BRS. **Networks/Consortia:** Member of Twin Cities Biomedical Consortium (TCBC); Regional Medical Library - Region 3. **Publications:** Library Handbook; Library Newsletter; annual report; Serial Title List; Book Review, bimonthly - for internal distribution only. **Staff:** Judi Unruh, Libn.

★5567★
HENNEPIN COUNTY PARK RESERVE DISTRICT - LOWRY NATURE CENTER - LIBRARY (Sci-Tech)†
Carver Park Reserve
Rt. 1, Box 690   Phone: (612) 472-4911
Excelsior, MN 55331   Dale Rock, Naturalist
Founded: 1970. **Staff:** Prof 4. **Subjects:** Natural history, ornithology,

mammology, ichthyology, herpetology, botany and forestry, wildlife management, ecology, entomology. **Holdings:** 650 books; 4 VF drawers of natural history material, organizational material, maps, pamphlets. **Services:** Library open to public for reference use only.

HENNEPIN TECHNICAL CENTER LIBRARY
See: Henkel Corporation

★5568★
HENROTIN HOSPITAL - MEDICAL LIBRARY (Med)†
111 West Oak St.   Phone: (312) 440-7759
Chicago, IL 60610   Penny Thomas-Jackson, Med.Libn.
Founded: 1925. **Staff:** Prof 1. **Subjects:** Medical sciences. **Holdings:** 350 books; 325 bound periodical volumes. **Subscriptions:** 45 journals and other serials. **Services:** Library not open to public.

★5569★
HENRY COUNTY HISTORICAL SOCIETY - LIBRARY (Hist)
Henry County Historical Bldg.
606 S. 14th St.   Phone: (317) 529-4028
New Castle, IN 47362   Wilma Kern, Pres.
Staff: 4. **Subjects:** Henry County and Indiana history. **Holdings:** Manuscripts, letters, photographs, paintings, scrapbooks, county histories and atlases. **Services:** Library open to public. **Publications:** Newsletter, 2/year. **Remarks:** The library does genealogical research on a fee basis for people living outside the county. **Staff:** Evelyn S. Clift, Cur.

★5570★
HENRY COUNTY LAW LIBRARY (Law)
Court House
Napoleon, OH 43545
                                           James Donovan, Libn.
Subjects: Law. **Holdings:** 5000 volumes. **Services:** Library not open to public.

★5571★
HENRY FORD HOSPITAL - FRANK J. SLADEN LIBRARY (Med)
2799 W. Grand Blvd.   Phone: (313) 876-2550
Detroit, MI 48202   Nardina L. Namath, Dir., Lib./AV Serv.
Founded: 1915. **Staff:** Prof 5; Other 8. **Subjects:** Medicine, biochemistry, physics. **Special Collections:** History of Medicine (1100 volumes). **Holdings:** 20,000 books; 33,000 bound periodical volumes; 150 videotapes (cataloged). **Subscriptions:** 1200 journals and other serials. **Services:** Interlibrary loans; copying; library open to public by permission. **Computerized Information Services:** MEDLINE, TOXLINE, CATLINE, DIALOG, BRS; computerized cataloging and ILL. **Networks/Consortia:** Member of OCLC; Michigan Library Consortium (MLC).

★5572★
HENRY FORD MUSEUM AND GREENFIELD VILLAGE - ARCHIVES & RESEARCH LIBRARY (Hist)
Village Rd.   Phone: (313) 271-1620
Dearborn, MI 48121   Douglas A. Bakken, Dir.
Founded: 1929. **Staff:** Prof 4; Other 5. **Subjects:** History of American technology including agriculture, community and domestic life, entertainment and leisure, trades and manufactures, transportation and communication, Henry Ford, Ford Motor Company. **Special Collections:** Edison Institute Archives; Ford Motor Company Historical Records (includes Henry Ford Papers, Stout Metal Airplane Company, Ford Motor Company Production, public relations, sales and advertising, finance, subsidiary companies, international operations, engineering and purchasing records from 1903 to 1950, Ford Motor Company Photographic Archives from 1910 to 1950, Ford Oral History Program (400 interviews)); graphics collection including Detroit Publishing Company, Enterprise Chair Company, Autocar Company Photographic Archives, Lincoln Motor Company Photographic Archives, cased, card and mounted photograph collection, Decorative Art Print Collections and Detroit, Toledo & Ironton Railroad photographs; manuscripts of Thomas A. Edison, Boston & Sandwich Glass Company, D.S. Morgan Company and Stickley Furniture Collection; Johnson Collection (350 steam traction and portable engine trade catalogs); Sullivan Collection (Americana; 500 trade catalogs); Dreppard Study Collection (Americana, 1795-1940); Scher Automotive Literature Collection (1902-1970); music sheets; McGuffey Readers and Almanacs (20 million items total). **Holdings:** 20,000 monographs; 750 periodicals. **Services:** Copying (fee); library open to researchers by appointment. **Publications:** Guide to the Archives & Research Library, 1982; Guide to the Ford Archives Photograph Print Collection, 1981; Henry Ford, A Personal History, revised edition, 1980. **Special Indexes:** Finding guides to collections. **Also Known As:** Edison Institute. **Formed by the Merger of:** Henry Ford Museum and Greenfield Village - Ford Archives and its Robert H. Tannahill Research Library. **Staff:** David R. Crippen, Ref.Archv.;

Joan Gartland, Cur., Print; Cynthia Read, Asst.Cur., Graphics.

★5573★
HENRY FORD MUSEUM AND GREENFIELD VILLAGE - ROBERT H. TANNAHILL RESEARCH LIBRARY
Village Rd.
Dearborn, MI 48124
Defunct. Merged with Henry Ford Museum and Greenfield Village - Ford Archives to form Henry Ford Museum and Greenfield Museum - Archives & Research Library.

★5574★
HENRY (J.J.) CO., INC. - ENGINEERING LIBRARY (Mil; Sci-Tech)
West Park Dr.
Mt. Laurel Ind. Pk.   Phone: (609) 234-3880
Moorestown, NJ 08057   Lorraine Van Leir, Libn.
Staff: 5. **Subjects:** Marine engineering, naval architecture, Coast Guard. **Holdings:** 25,000 military specifications and standards; 8000 instruction materials; 6000 technical reports; 5000 Navy standard drawings; 4000 vendor catalogs; 2000 special reports and drawings on specific contracts; 1700 naval technical manuals; 360 Marine handbooks; 170 classified documents; 100 directories. **Subscriptions:** 154 journals and other serials; 5 newspapers. **Services:** Library not open to public. **Staff:** A. Brown, Jr., Hd., Engr.Serv.

★5575★
HEPBURN (A. Barton) HOSPITAL - MEDICAL LIBRARY (Med)†
214 King St.   Phone: (315) 393-3600
Ogdensburg, NY 13669   M. Bridget Doyle, Med.Libn.
Founded: 1960. **Staff:** Prof 1. **Subjects:** Medicine and related fields. **Holdings:** 700 books; 300 bound periodical volumes. **Subscriptions:** 32 journals and other serials. **Services:** Interlibrary loans; copying; library open to public with permission of librarian. **Computerized Information Services:** MEDLARS. **Networks/Consortia:** Member of North Country Reference and Research Resources Council; Northern New York Health Information Cooperative.

★5576★
HERALD PUBLISHING COMPANY - HERALD LIBRARY (Publ)
One Herald Square   Phone: (203) 225-4601
New Britain, CT 06050   Cheryl B. Archer, Libn.
Staff: Prof 1. **Subjects:** Newspaper reference topics. **Special Collections:** New Britain Herald history (1 VF drawer). **Holdings:** 200 books; bound newspapers, 1880 to present; 6 VF drawers of photographs and negatives; newspapers on microfilm, 1937-1947, 1954 to present; 5 VF drawers of clippings and pamphlets. **Services:** Library open to public. **Special Indexes:** Herald index, 1954 to present (card). **Formerly:** New Britain Herald.

HERBERT (George) COLLECTION
See: University of North Carolina, Greensboro - George Herbert Collection

★5577★
HERCULES, INC. - AEROSPACE DIVISION - MC GREGOR TECHNICAL INFORMATION CENTER (Sci-Tech)
Box 548   Phone: (817) 840-2811
McGregor, TX 76657   D.A. Browne, Pubn.Coord.
Founded: 1952. **Staff:** 2. **Subjects:** Solid rocketry, engineering, chemistry, mathematics, physics, management. **Holdings:** 3000 volumes; 20,000 technical reports in computerized data retrieval system. **Subscriptions:** 50 journals and other serials. **Services:** Interlibrary loans; copying; library not open to public. **Networks/Consortia:** Member of Hercules Aerospace Division Group Information System. **Publications:** Library Bulletins; Library Accession List.

★5578★
HERCULES, INC. - BACCHUS WORKS INFORMATION SERVICES (Sci-Tech)
Box 98   Phone: (801) 250-5911
Magna, UT 84044   Dorothy H. Alley, Ref.Libn.
Founded: 1959. **Staff:** Prof 2; Other 6. **Subjects:** Chemical propulsion, rocketry, explosives, space technology, graphite fiber, ammunition, composite materials. **Holdings:** 2100 books; 280 bound periodical volumes; 90,000 technical reports; 9000 STAR NASA reports on 14,000 microfiche sheets. **Subscriptions:** 252 journals and other serials. **Services:** Interlibrary loans; services open to public with proper security clearance and demonstrated need-to-know. **Computerized Information Services:** DIALOG. **Publications:** Weekly report accessions list - distribution to Hercules personnel. **Special Indexes:** Computerized index to report collection - 50,000 accessions. **Staff:** Loralynn Nay, Doc. Procurement Libn.

★5579★

HERCULES, INC. - HATTIESBURG PLANT LABORATORY - LIBRARY (Sci-Tech)†
Box 1937   Phone: (601) 545-3450
Hattiesburg, MS 39401   Georgia Kay Carter, Supv. Chemist
Staff: 1. **Subjects:** Chemistry, chemical engineering. **Holdings:** 3000 books; 3000 bound periodical volumes; 2000 reprints; 6000 Hercules Research Investigation files; 200 Naval Stores translations. **Subscriptions:** 25 journals and other serials. **Services:** Library not open to public. **Publications:** New listings, semiannual.

★5580★

HERCULES, INC. - LAW DEPARTMENT LIBRARY (Law)
910 Market St., 14th Fl.   Phone: (302) 575-7019
Wilmington, DE 19899   Brenda S. Burris, Law Libn.
Subjects: Law, business. **Holdings:** 5000 books. **Subscriptions:** 15 journals and other serials. **Services:** Library not open to public.

★5581★

HERCULES, INC. - LIBRARY (Bus-Fin)
Hercules Tower, Rm. 1401-T
910 Market St.   Phone: (302) 575-5401
Wilmington, DE 19899   Barbara Beaman, Supv.
Founded: 1918. **Staff:** Prof 3; Other 2. **Subjects:** Business, explosives, management, pine and paper chemicals, synthetics. **Holdings:** 10,675 volumes. **Subscriptions:** 625 journals and other serials. **Services:** Interlibrary loans; copying; library open to public on request. **Staff:** Vera C. Newell, Libn.

★5582★

HERCULES, INC. - PICCO RESINS DIVISION - LIBRARY (Sci-Tech)
120 State St.   Phone: (412) 233-8600
Clairton, PA 15025   Norman E. Daughenbaugh, Tech.Libn.
Staff: 1. **Subjects:** Chemistry. **Holdings:** 400 books; 700 bound periodical volumes. **Subscriptions:** 15 journals and other serials. **Services:** Library open to public with restrictions.

★5583★

HERCULES, INC. - RESEARCH CENTER - TECHNICAL INFORMATION DIVISION (Sci-Tech)
                                                            Phone: (302) 995-3484
Wilmington, DE 19899   Robert N. Manning, Mgr.
Founded: 1928. **Staff:** Prof 10; Other 13. **Subjects:** Chemistry, engineering, physics. **Holdings:** 13,000 books; 25,500 bound periodical volumes; 2000 pamphlets; research reports; patents; correspondence. **Subscriptions:** 600 journals and other serials. **Services:** Interlibrary loans; copying; library open to public on request. **Computerized Information Services:** DIALOG, SDC, BRS, NLM; computerized cataloging, serials and circulation. **Publications:** Journal Literature Bulletin, biweekly; online bulletin, biweekly; Marketing Information Bulletin, biweekly; New Additions to Library, monthly. **Staff:** Thomas L. Martinke, Lib.Supv.; Antoinette Sansone, Asst.Libn.; Lucille Golt, Abstractor/Indexer; Leslie Truono, Abstractor/Indexer; John T. Hays, Tech.Ed.; Ruth E. Curtiss, Online Search; Z.B. Blums, Transl.

HERITAGE PRESS ARCHIVES
See: Chicago Public Library Cultural Center - Vivian G. Harsh Collection of Afro-American History & Lit.

★5584★

HERKIMER COUNTY LAW LIBRARY (Law)
Court House, Main St.   Phone: (315) 867-1172
Herkimer, NY 13350   Jane C. Gilbert, Law Lib.Ck.
Staff: 1. **Subjects:** Law. **Holdings:** 9000 volumes. **Services:** Interlibrary loans; library open to public.

★5585★

HERKIMER-ONEIDA COUNTIES COMPREHENSIVE PLANNING PROGRAM - LIBRARY (Plan)†
800 Park Ave.   Phone: (315) 798-5721
Utica, NY 13501   Michael Gapin, Prog.Dir.
Founded: 1964. **Staff:** 1. **Subjects:** Urban and regional planning. **Holdings:** 1500 volumes. **Computerized Information Services:** New York State Data Center.

★5586★

HERMAN MILLER, INC. - RESOURCE CENTER (Bus-Fin)
                                                            Phone: (616) 772-3629
Zeeland, MI 49464   Linda M. Wagenveld, Mgr.
Founded: 1977. **Staff:** Prof 2; Other 2. **Subjects:** Business, management, marketing, interior design. **Special Collections:** Corporate Archives; Designer/Product Archives (16 VF drawers); Eames Film Collection (55 films). **Holdings:** 1500 books; 300 pieces of furniture. **Subscriptions:** 125 journals and other serials. **Services:** Interlibrary loans; SDI; library not open to public. **Computerized Information Services:** DIALOG, SDC, MEDLARS, Source Telecomputing Corporation. **Publications:** Guide to Statistical Resources; Economic Review, bimonthly - both for internal distribution only. **Staff:** Lynne Miller, Libn.

HERMAN (Woody) ARCHIVES
See: Berklee College of Music - Library

HERMANN (Grover M.) ENGINEERING LIBRARY
See: Manhattan College - Grover M. Hermann Engineering Library

★5587★

HERMANN HOSPITAL - SCHOOL OF VOCATIONAL NURSING LIBRARY (Med)†
1203 Ross Sterling   Phone: (713) 797-4080
Houston, TX 77030   Helen C. Harrell, Dir.
Founded: 1941. **Staff:** 1. **Subjects:** Nursing, medicine, related subjects. **Holdings:** 2083 books and bound periodical volumes. **Services:** Interlibrary loans (limited); library open to professional personnel in center.

★5588★

HERMES ELECTRONICS LTD. - LIBRARY (Sci-Tech)
Box 1005   Phone: (902) 466-7491
Dartmouth, NS, Canada B2Y 4A1   Vaila S. Mowat, Hd., Engr.Doc.
Staff: Prof 1; Other 1. **Subjects:** Electronics, mechanical engineering, oceanography, acoustical engineering. **Special Collections:** Dr. Hans Castelliz Collection of general interest engineering. **Holdings:** 4000 books; 38 VF drawers of company technical documents; 1050 product catalogs; 100 microfiche. **Subscriptions:** 15 journals and other serials. **Services:** Interlibrary loans; copying; library open to public with restrictions. **Computerized Information Services:** Infomart. **Special Indexes:** KWIC index for company technical documents.

HERNER AND COMPANY - ARTHRITIS INFORMATION CLEARINGHOUSE
See: Arthritis Information Clearinghouse

★5589★

HERNER AND COMPANY - LIBRARY (Info Sci)
1700 N. Moore St.   Phone: (703) 558-8200
Arlington, VA 22209   Nancy D. Wright, V.P. for Lib.Serv.
Founded: 1955. **Staff:** Prof 3; Other 1. **Subjects:** Information science, library science. **Holdings:** 1300 books; 226 company technical reports; 3000 reports in microform; 12,000 environmental impact statements on microfiche. **Subscriptions:** 87 journals and other serials. **Services:** Interlibrary loans; copying; SDI; library open to public by appointment. **Computerized Information Services:** DIALOG, BRS, SDC, MEDLINE. **Networks/Consortia:** Member of Interlibrary Users Association. **Remarks:** Herner and Company is a library and information science consulting and service firm. **Staff:** Michael Tomaski, Libn.

★5590★

HERRICK HOSPITAL AND HEALTH CENTER - PSYCHIATRIC LIBRARY (Med)
2001 Dwight Way   Phone: (415) 845-0130
Berkeley, CA 94704   Marlene Rozofsky, Libn.
Founded: 1957. **Staff:** Prof 2. **Subjects:** Psychiatry, psychology, neurology. **Holdings:** 7000 books and bound periodical volumes; 6 VF drawers of reports, reprints and pamphlets. **Subscriptions:** 99 journals and other serials. **Services:** Interlibrary loans; copying; library open to individuals in the area working in the mental health field.

HERRICK (Margaret) LIBRARY
See: Academy of Motion Picture Arts and Sciences - Margaret Herrick Library

HERRICK MEMORIAL LIBRARY
See: Alfred University

★5591★

HERRICK AND SMITH - LAW LIBRARY (Law)
100 Federal St.   Phone: (617) 357-9000
Boston, MA 02110   Faith M. Lane, Libn.
Staff: Prof 1; Other 1. **Subjects:** Law. **Holdings:** 13,000 volumes. **Computerized Information Services:** LEXIS.

HERRON SCHOOL OF ART OF INDIANA UNIVERSITY
See: Indiana University, Indianapolis - University Library/Herron School of
Art

★5592★

HERSHEY FOODS CORPORATION - COMMUNICATIONS CENTER (Food-Bev)
1025 Reese Ave.   Phone: (717) 534-5106
Hershey, PA 17033   William M. Woodruff, Mgr., Commun.Ctr.
Founded: 1968. **Staff:** Prof 2; Other 2. **Subjects:** Confectionery, chocolate,
food science, nutrition, chemistry, engineering. **Holdings:** 4000 books; 50
journal titles in microform; 15 VF drawers of unbound material, including
patents and reports. **Subscriptions:** 300 journals and other serials; 7
newspapers. **Services:** Interlibrary loans; copying; library open to public by
appointment. **Computerized Information Services:** DIALOG, BRS,
TEXTLINE, NIH/EPA Chemical Information System; internal database.
Networks/Consortia: Member of PALINET and Union Library Catalogue of
Pennsylvania; Central Pennsylvania SLA Users Group; Three Valley On-Line
Users Group. **Publications:** Communications Center Newsletter, monthly;
Weekly Facts. **Staff:** Barbara Hundertmark, Tech.Commun.Spec.

**HERSHEY (Milton S.) MEDICAL CENTER - PENNSYLVANIA STATE
UNIVERSITY - COLLEGE OF MEDICINE**
See: Pennsylvania State University - College of Medicine - George T.
Harrell Library

HERSKOVITS (Melville J.) LIBRARY OF AFRICAN STUDIES
See: Northwestern University - Melville J. Herskovits Library of African
Studies

★5593★

HERTY FOUNDATION - LIBRARY (Sci-Tech)
Brampton Rd.
Box 1963
Savannah, GA 31402   Phone: (912) 964-5541
                                         J. Robert Hart, Dir.
Staff: 1. **Subjects:** Pulp, paper, chemistry, chemical engineering, physics,
forest products. **Holdings:** 2500 volumes. **Subscriptions:** 15 journals and
other serials. **Services:** Library open to public by appointment.

HERTZBERG (Harry) CIRCUS COLLECTION
See: San Antonio Public Library - Harry Hertzberg Circus Collection

★5594★

HERTZLER RESEARCH FOUNDATION LIBRARY (Med)†
3rd & Chestnut St.   Phone: (316) 835-2241
Halstead, KS 67056
Founded: 1907. **Staff:** 1. **Subjects:** Pathology, endocrinology, hematology
and surgery. **Holdings:** 4000 books; 6662 bound periodical volumes.
Subscriptions: 160 journals and other serials. **Services:** Interlibrary loans;
library open to public.

HERZOG (Dr. E.) MEMORIAL MEDICAL LIBRARY
See: Flint Osteopathic Hospital - Dr. E. Herzog Memorial Medical Library

HETERICK MEMORIAL LIBRARY
See: Ohio Northern University

★5595★

HEWITT ASSOCIATES - LIBRARY (Bus-Fin)
100 Half Day   Phone: (312) 295-5000
Lincolnshire, IL 60015   Loralie Van Sluys, Libn.
Founded: 1948. **Staff:** Prof 5. **Subjects:** Compensation, employee benefits,
wage and salary administration, actuarial science, insurance, business,
finance, general management, personnel. **Holdings:** 6500 volumes; 5000
employee benefit plan booklets; 8000 proxy statements (annually).
Subscriptions: 500 journals and other serials; 12 newspapers. **Services:**
Interlibrary loans; library open to SLA members. **Publications:** What's New in
Recent Writings, monthly. **Staff:** Marj Simmet, Asst.

★5596★

HEWLETT-PACKARD COMPANY - ANDOVER DIVISION LIBRARY (SciTech)
1776 Minuteman Rd.   Phone: (617) 687-1501
Andover, MA 01810   Carol Miller, Libn.
Founded: 1977. **Staff:** Prof 1; Other 1. **Subjects:** Cardiology, electronic
design, ultrasound, computer programming, business. **Holdings:** 1000 books;
50 bound periodical volumes; 25 videotapes. **Subscriptions:** 183 journals and
other serials. **Services:** Interlibrary loans; copying; library open to public with
permission. **Computerized Information Services:** BRS, DIALOG;
computerized cataloging.

★5597★

HEWLETT-PACKARD COMPANY - AVONDALE DIVISION LIBRARY (Sci-Tech)
Route 41 & Starr Rd.   Phone: (215) 268-2281
Avondale, PA 19311   Shirley Boyd, Clerk
Staff: 1. **Subjects:** Gas and liquid chromatography. **Holdings:** 1500 books;
150 bound periodical volumes. **Subscriptions:** 144 journals and other serials.
Services: Interlibrary loans; copying (limited); library not open to public.

★5598★

**HEWLETT PACKARD COMPANY - BOISE SITE SCIENCE/TECHNICAL
LIBRARY** (Sci-Tech)
11413 Chinden Blvd.   Phone: (208) 376-6000
Boise, ID 83702   Gail Prescott, Libn.
Founded: 1979. **Staff:** Prof 1. **Subjects:** Computers, electronics,
engineering, physics. **Holdings:** 700 books. **Subscriptions:** 80 journals and
other serials; 5 newspapers. **Services:** Interlibrary loans; copying; SDI; library
not open to public. **Computerized Information Services:** DIALOG.
Networks/Consortia: Member of RLG; CLASS.

★5599★

**HEWLETT-PACKARD COMPANY - COLORADO SPRINGS DIVISION -
ENGINEERING RESOURCE CENTER** (Sci-Tech)
Box 2197   Phone: (303) 598-1900
Colorado Springs, CO 80901-2197   Jacquelyn Nichols, Libn.
Founded: 1970. **Staff:** Prof 1. **Subjects:** Electronics, computer sciences,
chemistry, management. **Holdings:** 1400 books; 231 bound periodical
volumes; 791 microforms. **Subscriptions:** 131 journals and other serials.
Services: Copying; library not open to public. **Computerized Information
Services:** RLIN. **Publications:** Technical Communications Letter. **Remarks:**
Center is located at 1900 Garden of the Gods Rd., Colorado Springs, CO
80907.

★5600★

HEWLETT-PACKARD COMPANY - CORPORATE LIBRARY (Sci-Tech)
1501 Page Mill Rd.   Phone: (415) 857-3091
Palo Alto, CA 94304   Mark H. Baer, Dir. of Libs.
Founded: 1952. **Staff:** Prof 8; Other 11. **Subjects:** Computers, electronics,
solid state physics, instrumentation, medical electronics, chemistry, business
and management, physics. **Holdings:** 25,000 books; 30,000 bound periodical
volumes; 1500 reports; 3500 literature searches; 6000 Hewlett-Packard
instrument manuals on microfiche; 500 videotape training films; New York
Stock Exchange, American Stock Exchange, and 10K reports on microfiche;
37 shelves of specifications and standards. **Subscriptions:** 950 journals and
other serials; 10 newspapers. **Services:** Interlibrary loans; copying; SDI;
literature searches; library open to public by appointment. **Computerized
Information Services:** New York Times Information Service, DIALOG, SDC,
BRS, RLIN, Source Telecomputing Corporation; internal database;
computerized cataloging and serials. **Networks/Consortia:** Member of CIN;
CLASS; RLG. **Publications:** Library Bulletin, monthly - for internal distribution
only. **Special Catalogs:** Online and printed Union List of Hewlett-Packard
libraries literature searches; computer-produced union list of Hewlett-Packard
libraries periodical holdings (book); Union catalog of Hewlett-Packard Library
Network (card). **Staff:** William C. Petru, Mgr., Lib.Oper.; Olga Kallos, Mgr.,
Tech.Proc.; Teresa Lau, Cat.Libn.; Michael Okajima, Mgr., Info.Serv.; Linda
Mullins, Sr.Info.Spec.

★5601★

**HEWLETT-PACKARD COMPANY - CORVALLIS DIVISION TECHNICAL
INFORMATION CENTER** (Sci-Tech)
1000 N.E. Circle Blvd.   Phone: (503) 757-2000
Corvallis, OR 97330   Shari Morwood, Dir.
Founded: 1980. **Staff:** Prof 1; Other 2. **Subjects:** Electrical engineering,
computers, calculators, business. **Special Collections:** Specifications;
standards; annual reports. **Holdings:** Figures not available. **Services:**
Interlibrary loans; copying; SDI; library not open to public. **Computerized
Information Services:** DIALOG, BRS, RLIN; computerized cataloging.

★5602★

HEWLETT-PACKARD COMPANY - CUPERTINO LIBRARY (Sci-Tech)†
11000 Wolfe Rd.   Phone: (408) 257-7000
Cupertino, CA 95014   Catherine Biggs, Libn.
Founded: 1969. **Staff:** Prof 1. **Subjects:** Computers, programming,
programming languages, electronics. **Holdings:** 3500 volumes.
Subscriptions: 175 journals and other serials. **Services:** Interlibrary loans;
copying; library open to public for reference use only on request. **Networks/
Consortia:** Member of CIN.

★5603★
HEWLETT-PACKARD COMPANY - FORT COLLINS FACILITY LIBRARY (Sci-Tech)
3404 E. Harmony Rd.   Phone: (303) 226-3800
Fort Collins, CO 80525   Jane Fiasconaro, Libn.
Founded: 1978. **Staff:** 2. **Subjects:** Computers, electronics. **Holdings:** 1500 books. **Subscriptions:** 200 journals and other serials; 8 newspapers. **Services:** Interlibrary loans; copying; library open to public by appointment. **Computerized Information Services:** OnTyme.

★5604★
HEWLETT-PACKARD COMPANY - HP LABORATORIES - DEER CREEK LIBRARY (Sci-Tech)
Box 10350   Phone: (415) 857-5205
Palo Alto, CA 94303-0867   Nancy E. Lem, Libn.
Founded: 1975. **Staff:** Prof 1; Other 2. **Subjects:** Computer science, electronics, physics, science technology. **Holdings:** 1700 books; 700 bound periodical volumes; 600 bibliographies. **Subscriptions:** 282 journals and other serials; 7 newspapers. **Services:** Interlibrary loans; copying; SDI; library open to public by appointment. **Computerized Information Services:** DIALOG, SDC, BRS, New York Times Information Service, Derwent; computerized cataloging. **Networks/Consortia:** Member of HP Library/Information Network. **Publications:** Library Bulletin, monthly - for internal distribution only; List of Periodicals, semiannual.

★5605★
HEWLETT-PACKARD COMPANY - LOVELAND FACILITY LIBRARY (Sci-Tech)
Box 301   Phone: (303) 667-5000
Loveland, CO 80537   Marsha Haugen, Libn.
Staff: Prof 1; Other 2. **Subjects:** Electronics, electrical engineering, computers, business. **Holdings:** 3000 books; 500 bound periodical volumes. **Subscriptions:** 204 journals and other serials. **Services:** Interlibrary loans; copying; library open to public with restrictions. **Computerized Information Services:** SDC, BRS, DIALOG; computerized cataloging. **Networks/Consortia:** Member of RLG; CLASS.

★5606★
HEWLETT-PACKARD COMPANY - MEDICAL PRODUCTS GROUP - LIBRARY (Med; Sci-Tech)
175 Wyman St.   Phone: (617) 890-6300
Waltham, MA 02154   Susan Saraidaridis, Libn.
Founded: 1957. **Staff:** Prof 1; Other 2. **Subjects:** Medicine, engineering, business. **Holdings:** 6000 books; 1200 bound periodical volumes. **Subscriptions:** 425 journals and other serials; 7 newspapers. **Services:** Interlibrary loans (limited); library not open to public. **Computerized Information Services:** DIALOG, Ontyme, BRS; internal database; computerized cataloging and journal routing. **Publications:** Library Lines, bimonthly - for internal distribution only. **Formerly:** Its Medical Electronics Division.

★5607★
HEWLETT-PACKARD COMPANY - SAN DIEGO DIVISION - TECHNICAL LIBRARY (Sci-Tech)
16399 W. Bernardo Drive   Phone: (714) 487-4100
San Diego, CA 92127   Cherlyn A. Williams, Lib.Spec.
Founded: 1979. **Staff:** 1. **Subjects:** Engineering - mechanical, electronic, chemical; computer science. **Holdings:** 650 books. **Subscriptions:** 120 journals and other serials. **Services:** Interlibrary loans; copying; library open to public with restrictions.

★5608★
HEWLETT-PACKARD COMPANY - SANTA CLARA DIVISION LIBRARY (Sci-Tech)
5301 Stevens Creek Blvd.   Phone: (408) 246-4300
Santa Clara, CA 95050   Diana Robba, Lib.Spec.
Staff: 1. **Subjects:** Technology, engineering, electrical engineering and industries, physics. **Holdings:** 1800 books; 100 bound periodical volumes. **Subscriptions:** 200 journals and other serials. **Services:** Interlibrary loans; copying; library not open to public.

HEYE FOUNDATION - MUSEUM OF THE AMERICAN INDIAN
See: Huntington Free Library - Museum of the American Indian

★5609★
HIALEAH HOSPITAL - HEALTH SCIENCE LIBRARY (Med)
651 East 25th St.   Phone: (305) 835-4635
Hialeah, FL 33013   Yvonne Barkman, Health Sci.Libn.
Founded: 1969. **Staff:** Prof 1. **Subjects:** Medicine, surgery, nursing,

paramedics. **Holdings:** 2000 books; 800 bound periodical volumes; 15 volumes of cassettes; 3 VF drawers of pamphlets and clippings; 75 AV materials. **Subscriptions:** 102 journals and other serials. **Services:** Interlibrary loans; copying; library open to public with restrictions. **Networks/Consortia:** Member of Miami Health Sciences Library Consortium.

HIBBS (Russell A.) LIBRARY
See: New York Orthopaedic Hospital - Russell A. Hibbs Library

HICKOX (Edward J. and Gena G.) LIBRARY
See: Naismith Memorial Basketball Hall of Fame - Edward J. and Gena G. Hickox Library

HICKS (Gerald) MEMORIAL LIBRARY
See: Lorain County Historical Society - Gerald Hicks Memorial Library

★5610★
HIDALGO COUNTY LAW LIBRARY (Law)
Courthouse, Box 215   Phone: (512) 383-2751
Edinburg, TX 78539   Aurora Rutledge, Libn.
Founded: 1954. **Staff:** Prof 1. **Subjects:** Law, Texas statutes. **Holdings:** Figures not available. **Services:** Copying; library open to out-of-town attorneys and Pan American students. **Remarks:** This library serves Hidalgo County attorneys.

HIEBERT LIBRARY
See: Mennonite Brethren Biblical Seminary

★5611★
HIGGINS ARMORY MUSEUM - MEMORIAL LIBRARY (Hist)
100 Barber Ave.   Phone: (617) 853-6015
Worcester, MA 01606   Walter J. Karcheski, Jr., Asst.Cur.
Founded: 1966. **Staff:** Prof 1; Other 1. **Subjects:** Arms and armor, archeology, stained glass, history, art, military history. **Holdings:** 2500 books and bound periodical volumes. **Services:** Library open to public for reference use only by appointment. **Publications:** Ventail Voice, quarterly. **Special Catalogs:** Catalog of Armour (cloth). **Formerly:** John Woodman Higgins Armory, Inc.

HIGGINS (F. Hal) LIBRARY OF AGRICULTURAL TECHNOLOGY
See: University of California, Davis - F. Hal Higgins Library of Agricultural Technology

HIGGINS LIBRARY OF AGRICULTURAL TECHNOLOGY
See: University of California, Davis - University Libraries

★5612★
HIGGS, FLETCHER & MACK - LAW LIBRARY (Law)†
707 Broadway, Suite 1800
Box 568   Phone: (619) 236-1551
San Diego, CA 92112   Lauren Reznack, Law Libn.
Staff: Prof 1; Other 1. **Subjects:** Law - aviation, bankruptcy, corporate, securities, tax. **Holdings:** 12,000 books and bound periodical volumes; 500 items in the legal research file. **Subscriptions:** 37 journals and other serials. **Services:** SDI; library not open to public. **Special Indexes:** Attorney specialty file (card); legal research file index (card); form file (card).

HIGH ALTITUDE OBSERVATORY LIBRARY
See: National Center for Atmospheric Research

★5613★
HIGH PRESSURE DATA CENTER (Sci-Tech)
Box 7246   Phone: (801) 224-0389
Provo, UT 84602   Dr. Leo Merrill, Dir.
Staff: Prof 1; Other 1. **Subjects:** Pressure, thermodynamics, equilibrium, material phases, calibration, crystallography. **Holdings:** Original scientific papers and critical evaluations of experimental data. **Services:** Copying; library open to public. **Publications:** Bibliography on High Pressure Research.

HIGH ROCK PARK CONSERVATION CENTER
See: Staten Island Institute of Arts and Sciences

★5614★
HIGH STREET CHRISTIAN CHURCH - H.A. VALENTINE MEMORIAL LIBRARY (Rel-Theol)
131 S. High St.   Phone: (216) 434-1039
Akron, OH 44308   Evelyn R. Ling, Libn.
Founded: 1965. **Staff:** 25. **Subjects:** Religion, Christian education. **Special Collections:** Church Archives. **Holdings:** 5200 books. **Services:** Library open

to public by special permission.

★5615★

HIGH VOLTAGE ENGINEERING CORPORATION - LIBRARY
S. Bedford St.
Burlington, MA 01803
Founded: 1946. **Subjects:** Particle accelerators, magnets, and related fields. **Holdings:** 2160 books and bound periodical volumes; 1100 technical reports; 900 reprints. **Remarks:** Includes the holdings of Ion Physics Corporation. Presently inactive.

★5616★

HIGHLAND COUNTY LAW LIBRARY (Law)
High & Main Sts., Court House
Hillsboro, OH 45133
Phone: (513) 393-4863
Michelle Vanzant, Law Libn.
Founded: 1936. **Staff:** Prof 1. **Subjects:** Law. **Holdings:** 6648 books; 90 bound periodical volumes; 2150 microforms. **Services:** Interlibrary loans; copying; library open to public for reference use only. **Computerized Information Services:** WESTLAW; computerized cataloging.

HIGHLAND HERITAGE RESEARCH LIBRARY
See: Glengarry Genealogical Society

★5617★

HIGHLAND HOSPITAL, INC. - MEDICAL LIBRARY (Med)
2412 50th St.
Lubbock, TX 79412
Phone: (806) 795-8251
Margaret Bussey, Med.Libn./Dir., Med.Rec.
Staff: 1. **Subjects:** Medicine and related health sciences. **Holdings:** 400 books; 200 bound periodical volumes; 312 audio cassettes. **Subscriptions:** 28 journals and other serials. **Services:** Interlibrary loans; copying; library not open to public.

★5618★

HIGHLAND HOSPITAL OF ROCHESTER - THE WILLIAMS HEALTH SCIENCES LIBRARY (Med)
South Ave. at Bellevue Dr.
Rochester, NY 14620
Phone: (716) 473-2200
Helen King Murphy, Dir.
Founded: 1956. **Staff:** Prof 1; Other 1. **Subjects:** Medicine and allied fields, family medicine, nursing. **Holdings:** 4604 books; bound periodical volumes; 19 VF drawers (including 7 drawers of archival materials); cassettes. **Subscriptions:** 190 journals and other serials. **Services:** Interlibrary loans; copying; library open to public for reference use only. **Computerized Information Services:** NLM.

★5619★

HIGHLAND PARK HERBARIUM - LIBRARY (Sci-Tech)†
375 Westfall Rd.
Rochester, NY 14620
Phone: (716) 244-4640
James W. Kelly, Cur.
Founded: 1888. **Staff:** Prof 1. **Subjects:** Plant taxonomy, dendrology, horticulture, plant pathology, landscaping, agriculture, forestry, toxicology, anthropology, history. **Special Collections:** 7 volume collection: Fruits of New York by E. P. Hedrick; Wild Flowers of New York, by the State University of New York; Trees of Great Britain and Ireland by H.J. Elwes; The Lilac by S.D. McKelvey. **Holdings:** 835 books; 110 bound periodical volumes; 2299 photographs of trees and panoramas of the parks of Monroe County; 552 slides of trees and shrubs of Monroe County; 500 card file of birds of Monroe County; 15,204 specimens in adjacent herbarium. **Subscriptions:** 19 journals and other serials. **Services:** Interlibrary loans; copying; library open to public for reference use only. **Publications:** Highland Park Lilac Tour; Highland Park Conifer Tour; Rhododendron Collections of Monroe County Department of Parks, 1978. **Remarks:** Maintained by Monroe County Department of Parks.

★5620★

HIGHLAND PARK HISTORICAL SOCIETY - LIBRARY (Hist)
326 Central Ave.
Box 56
Highland Park, IL 60035
Phone: (312) 432-7090
Henry X. Arenberg.
Staff: 1. **Subjects:** Local history. **Holdings:** 500 books; 1000 photographs; 2500 35mm slides. **Services:** Library open to public. **Publications:** Newsletter, bimonthly.

★5621★

HIGHLAND PARK PRESBYTERIAN CHURCH - MADELINE ROACH MEYERCORD LIBRARY (Rel-Theol)
3821 University Blvd.
Dallas, TX 75205
Phone: (214) 526-7457
Mrs. David P. Smith, Chm.
Founded: 1953. **Staff:** 30. **Subjects:** Religion, family relationships, children's literature. **Holdings:** 13,000 books. **Subscriptions:** 15 journals and other serials. **Services:** Library open to public with restrictions on time.

★5622★

HIGHLAND PARK UNITED METHODIST CHURCH - LIBRARY (Rel-Theol)
3300 Mockingbird Ln.
Dallas, TX 75205
Phone: (214) 521-3111
Adele Ervine, Libn.
Staff: Prof 1; Other 16. **Subjects:** Religion, children's literature, history, biography, art, technology, fiction. **Holdings:** 18,913 books; films and filmstrips (cataloged); slides, records, maps, tapes. **Services:** Library open to public.

★5623★

HIGHLAND UNITED PRESBYTERIAN CHURCH - LIBRARY (Rel-Theol)
708 Highland Ave.
New Castle, PA 16101
Phone: (412) 654-7391
Elizabeth Milholland, Libn.
Founded: 1967. **Staff:** 2. **Subjects:** Bible, Christian life. **Holdings:** 1872 books; church history and annual reports. **Subscriptions:** 18 journals and other serials. **Services:** Library open to public with restrictions. **Networks/Consortia:** Member of Tri-County Library Consortium.

HIGHLANDS BAPTIST HOSPITAL
See: Louisville Baptist Hospitals, Inc.

HIGHLY (Henry G.) LIBRARY
See: Los Angeles College of Chiropractic - Henry G. Highly Library

★5624★

HIGHTOWER (Sara) REGIONAL LIBRARY - BUSINESS LIBRARY (Bus-Fin)†
606 W. First St.
Box 277
Rome, GA 30161
Phone: (404) 291-9360
Jim L. Doyle, Bus.Libn.
Founded: 1967. **Staff:** Prof 1; Other 1. **Subjects:** Investment, management, consumer information, small business information, company information. **Holdings:** 1700 volumes; 12 VF drawers of clippings and pamphlets; 18 magazines on microfiche; 104 reels of microfilm. **Subscriptions:** 126 journals and other serials; 8 newspapers. **Services:** Interlibrary loans; copying; library open to public. **Publications:** Brochures on offerings of Business Library, irregular. **Special Catalogs:** Union List of Periodicals maintained by all the libraries in the area (card).

HIGHWAY RESEARCH INFORMATION SERVICE
See: National Academy of Sciences - National Research Council

HIGHWAY SAFETY RESEARCH CENTER
See: University of North Carolina, Chapel Hill

HIGHWAY SAFETY RESEARCH INSTITUTE
See: University of Michigan

★5625★

HIGHWAY USERS FEDERATION - LIBRARY
1776 Massachusetts Ave., N.W.
Washington, DC 20036
Founded: 1937. **Subjects:** Highway safety and planning, traffic engineering, urban affairs, transportation and related legal and economic research. **Holdings:** 16,000 books and bound periodical volumes; 50 VF drawers of unbound material. **Remarks:** Presently inactive.

HILANDAR ROOM
See: Ohio State University

HILDRETH (Harold M.) MEMORIAL LIBRARY
See: Institute for Studies of Destructive Behaviors and the Suicide Prevention Center - Harold M. Hildreth Mem.Lib.

★5626★

HILL AND BARLOW - LIBRARY (Law)
225 Franklin St.
Boston, MA 02110
Phone: (617) 423-6200
Carol S. Wellington, Libn.
Staff: Prof 1; Other 1. **Subjects:** Law. **Holdings:** 11,000 volumes. **Services:** Library not open to public. **Computerized Information Services:** LEXIS.

HILL (D.H.) LIBRARY
See: North Carolina State University - D.H. Hill Library

HILL (Edwin Bliss) ARCHIVE
See: Arizona State University - Special Collections

★5627★
HILL, FARRER & BURRILL - LAW LIBRARY (Law)†
445 S. Figueroa St.
Union Bank Bldg., 34th Fl.   Phone: (213) 620-0460
Los Angeles, CA 90071   Fleur C. Osmanson, Libn.
Staff: Prof 1; Other 1. **Subjects:** Law. **Holdings:** 12,000 books; 350 bound periodical volumes; 1300 legal memoranda. **Subscriptions:** 350 journals and other serials. **Services:** Library not open to public.

★5628★
HILL (James Jerome) REFERENCE LIBRARY (Bus-Fin; Trans)
Fourth St. at Market   Phone: (612) 227-9531
St. Paul, MN 55102   Virgil F. Massman, Exec.Dir.
Founded: 1921. **Staff:** Prof 11; Other 21. **Subjects:** Business, economics, transportation, railroad history. **Special Collections:** James Jerome Hill's collection of local history books covering Minnesota and the regions to the north and west; Seth Eastman watercolors of American Indians; Frank P. Donovan, Jr. Collection on Railroads in Literature (3200 volumes). **Holdings:** 197,000 volumes; Karl Bodmer prints; 10K and proxy reports for 12 states. **Subscriptions:** 1500 journals and other serials; 11 newspapers. **Services:** Interlibrary loans; copying; library open to public. **Computerized Information Services:** DIALOG, SDC, BRS; computerized cataloging. **Networks/Consortia:** Member of Cooperating Libraries in Consortium (CLIC); MINITEX; Metropolitan Library Services (MELSA); headquarters of Twin Cities Standards Cooperative (TCSC). **Special Catalogs:** The Hill Directory of Library and Informational Resources in the Twin City Area (book); Union Catalog of 7 private Twin City colleges and Hill Library; Twin Cities Standards Cooperative Catalog (card). **Special Indexes:** Standards Cross-Reference List.

★5629★
HILL JUNIOR COLLEGE - CONFEDERATE RESEARCH CENTER AND GUN MUSEUM (Hist; Mil)
                              Phone: (817) 582-2555
Hillsboro, TX 76645   AnnieLee Wright, Libn.
Founded: 1964. **Staff:** Prof 1; Other 2. **Subjects:** Civil War, military history, Texas history, guns and ammunition, artillery. **Special Collections:** Hood's Texas Brigade, Army of Northern Virginia; special library on guns, edged weapons, artillery and ammunition (150 volumes). **Holdings:** 2500 books; 500 bound periodical volumes; 200 booklets; 2 VF drawers of unpublished manuscripts, diaries and letters; 3 VF drawers of photographs, muster roll compilations, and miscellaneous Civil War items; 3 VF drawers of microfilm of Texas forts (1848-1861); service records for Hood's Texas Brigade; Texas newspapers (1846-1861). **Subscriptions:** 49 journals and other serials. **Services:** Interlibrary loans; copying; library open to public.

HILL MONASTIC MANUSCRIPT LIBRARY
See: St. John's Abbey and University

★5630★
HILLCREST MEDICAL CENTER - LIBRARY (Med)
1144 S. Troost   Phone: (918) 584-1351
Tulsa, OK 74120   Peggy Cook, Hosp.Libn.
Staff: Prof 1; Other 2. **Subjects:** Medicine, nursing. **Holdings:** 3500 books; 2150 bound periodical volumes; 600 AV items; 8 VF drawers of pamphlets; 1 VF drawer of bibliographies; 1 VF drawer of newsletters. **Subscriptions:** 162 journals and other serials. **Services:** Interlibrary loans; copying; library open to public for reference use only. **Publications:** List of Recent Acquisitions in hospital newsletter, bimonthly.

★5631★
HILLCREST REGIONAL CENTER FOR DEVELOPMENTAL DISABILITIES - MEDICAL LIBRARY
600 County Farm Rd.
Box M-155
Howell, MI 48843
Defunct

HILLERUD MEMORIAL LIBRARY
See: Northwest Bible College - J.C. Cooke Library

HILLES (Florence Bayard) LIBRARY
See: National Woman's Party - Florence Bayard Hilles Library

HILLMAN (James Frazer) HEALTH SCIENCES LIBRARY
See: Shadyside Hospital - James Frazer Hillman Health Sciences Library

HILLMAN LIBRARY
See: University of Pittsburgh

★5632★
HILLSBOROUGH COUNTY HISTORICAL COMMISSION - LIBRARY (Hist)
County Court House   Phone: (813) 272-5919
Tampa, FL 33602   Anthony P. Pizzo, Chm.
Founded: 1949. **Staff:** 1. **Subjects:** History of Florida and other southern states; genealogy. **Services:** Library open to the public. **Staff:** Mrs. G.B. Jones, Libn.

★5633★
HILLSBOROUGH COUNTY LAW LIBRARY (Law)
County Court House
Tampa, FL 33602   William M. Bailey, Libn.
Staff: Prof 1; Other 2. **Subjects:** Law. **Holdings:** 40,000 volumes. **Subscriptions:** 100 journals and other serials. **Services:** Copying; library open to public with restrictions. **Computerized Information Services:** WESTLAW.

HILLSIDE MEDICAL CENTER
See: Long Island Jewish-Hillside Medical Center

HILLYER ART LIBRARY
See: Smith College

★5634★
HILO HOSPITAL - FRED IRWIN MEDICAL LIBRARY (Med)
1190 Waianuenue Ave.   Phone: (808) 961-4331
Hilo, HI 96720   Hazel M. Takemoto
Founded: 1920. **Staff:** 1. **Subjects:** Medicine and related subjects. **Holdings:** 492 books; 1296 cassette tapes. **Subscriptions:** 45 journals and other serials. **Services:** Interlibrary loans; library open to medical staff and other health care professionals. **Networks/Consortia:** Member of Hawaii Medical Library; Pacific Southwest Regional Medical Library Service.

HILTON-DAVIS CHEMICAL COMPANY DIVISION
See: Sterling Drug, Inc.

HILTY (Mae) MEMORIAL LIBRARY
See: Texas Chiropractic College - Mae Hilty Memorial Library

HIMMELFARB (Paul) HEALTH SCIENCES LIBRARY
See: George Washington University - Medical Center - Paul Himmelfarb Health Sciences Library

HIMWICH LIBRARY OF THE NEUROSCIENCES
See: Galesburg Mental Health Center

★5635★
HINCKLEY FOUNDATION MUSEUM - LIBRARY (Hist)
410 E. Seneca St.   Phone: (607) 273-7053
Ithaca, NY 14850   Ellen Baker Wikotrom, Dir.
Staff: Prof 2. **Subjects:** Local history. **Special Collections:** Ithaca imprints; Hinckley family papers; Celia Smith papers. **Holdings:** 1000 books; 10 boxes of papers. **Services:** Library open to public for reference use only.

★5636★
HINDS GENERAL HOSPITAL - WILLIAM M. SUTTLE MEDICAL LIBRARY (Med)
1850 Chadwick Dr.   Phone: (601) 376-1148
Jackson, MS 39204   Dale Badger, Libn.
Staff: 1. **Subjects:** Medicine, hospital administration. **Holdings:** 525 books; 1400 bound periodical volumes. **Subscriptions:** 112 journals and other serials. **Services:** Interlibrary loans; copying; library open to public with approval from administration. **Networks/Consortia:** Member of Central Mississippi Council of Medical Libraries; Central Mississippi Library Council.

HINES (Edward, Jr.) MEDICAL CENTER
See: U.S. Veterans Administration (IL-Hines)

HINKLE (Walter C.) MEMORIAL LIBRARY
See: SUNY - Agricultural and Technical College at Alfred - Walter C. Hinkle Memorial Library

★5637★
HINSDALE SANITARIUM AND HOSPITAL - A.C. LARSON LIBRARY (Med)
120 N. Oak St.   Phone: (312) 887-2868
Hinsdale, IL 60521   Richard L. Cook, Hosp.Libn.
Founded: 1970. **Staff:** Prof 3. **Subjects:** Nursing, religion, medicine. **Special Collections:** Ellen G. White Collection (200 volumes). **Holdings:** 10,000 books; 1000 bound periodical volumes; 150 rare items (cataloged); 19 VF drawers of pamphlets; 5 films; 200 miscellaneous items. **Subscriptions:** 180

journals and other serials. **Services:** Interlibrary loans; copying; library open to public for reference use only. **Staff:** Bonnie Son, Asst.Libn.; Guinevere Cook, Asst.Libn.

HIRAM WALKER HISTORICAL MUSEUM
See: Walker (Hiram) Historical Museum

HIRONS (J. Wilbur) LIBRARY
See: Goldey Beacom College - J. Wilbur Hirons Library

HIRSCH (Emil G.) LIBRARY
See: Chicago Sinai Congregation - Emil G. Hirsch Library

HIRSCH LIBRARY
See: Museum of Fine Arts, Houston

HIRSHHORN MUSEUM AND SCULPTURE GARDEN
See: Smithsonian Institution

★5638★
HISPANIC INSTITUTE - LIBRARY (Hum)†
Casa Hispanica, Columbia University
612 W. 116th St.   Phone: (212) 280-4187
New York, NY 10027
Subjects: Literature. **Holdings:** 10,000 books. **Services:** Library open to public by permission.

★5639★
HISPANIC SOCIETY OF AMERICA - DEPARTMENT OF ICONOGRAPHY - GENERAL REFERENCE FILE (Pict)
Broadway & 155th St.   Phone: (212) 926-2234
New York, NY 10032   Lydia Dufour, Assoc.Cur., Iconography
Subjects: 150,000 photographs of Spanish and Portuguese art (fine and applied); views of cities and buildings in Spain and Portugal and their former possessions; costumes and customs of Spain and Portugal. **Services:** Photographs available for study.

★5640★
HISPANIC SOCIETY OF AMERICA - LIBRARY (Area-Ethnic)
Broadway & 155th St.   Phone: (212) 926-2234
New York, NY 10032   Jean R. Longland, Cur.
Founded: 1904. **Staff:** Prof 5; Other 6. **Subjects:** Art, history, literature and general culture of Spain, Portugal and colonial Hispanic America. **Special Collections:** Books printed before 1701; manuscripts. **Holdings:** 150,000 volumes; 200,000 manuscripts; 113 VF drawers of clippings; 50 manuscript maps; periodicals. **Services:** Copying (rare books only); library open to public. **Publications:** List of publications - available upon request. **Staff:** Juliette L. Sobon, Asst.Cur. of Lib.; Martha M. De Narvaez, Mss./Rare Bks.Cur.; John S. Robotham, Asst.; Irene S. Frye, Per.Libn.

★5641★
HISTORIC ANNAPOLIS, INC. - LIBRARY (Hist)
194 Prince George St.   Phone: (301) 267-7619
Annapolis, MD 21401   Mrs. John Symonds, Pres.
Founded: 1952. **Staff:** Prof 1; Other 1. **Subjects:** Preservation, urban planning, state and local history, genealogy, decorative arts. **Special Collections:** Annapolis Community Study 1650-1850. **Holdings:** 500 books; Annapolis and Anne Arundel County history records on 500,000 index cards; extensive 19th and 20th century photographic files; computer file of 17th and 18th century Anne Arundel County probate records; 30 volumes of clippings; architectural databank; maps. **Subscriptions:** 13 journals and other serials. **Services:** Interlibrary loans; copying; library open to serious scholars only. **Staff:** Mrs. Robert L. Baker, Jr., Dir. of Res.

★5642★
HISTORIC BETHLEHEM INC. - LIBRARY/ARCHIVES (Hist)
501 Main St.   Phone: (215) 868-6311
Bethlehem, PA 18018   Becky Hoskins, Cur.
Staff: Prof 1. **Subjects:** Bethlehem history, museum studies literature. **Special Collections:** Photograph collection of Bethlehem history. **Holdings:** 1500 books. **Subscriptions:** 12 journals and other serials. **Services:** Library open to public for reference use only by appointment.

HISTORIC CAMDEN
See: Camden District Heritage Foundation

★5643★
HISTORIC DEERFIELD, INC. - HENRY N. FLYNT LIBRARY - POCUMTUCK VALLEY MEMORIAL ASSOCIATION (Hist)
Memorial St.
Box 53   Phone: (413) 774-5581
Deerfield, MA 01342   David R. Proper, Libn.
Founded: 1870. **Staff:** Prof 2; Other 3. **Subjects:** History - Deerfield and Western Massachusetts; decorative arts. **Special Collections:** Works by local authors; manuscripts and account books of local persons; Western Massachusetts imprints. **Holdings:** 18,000 books; 175 bound periodical volumes; 250 boxes of family manuscripts, diaries and letters; 387 account books; 110 boxes of town, business and miscellaneous papers; 15 boxes of photographs; travel accounts; hymnals; 135 reels of microfilm. **Subscriptions:** 25 journals and other serials. **Services:** Copying; library open to public for reference use only. **Staff:** Mrs. Lloyd W. Perrin, Lib.Asst.

★5644★
HISTORIC LANDMARKS FOUNDATION OF INDIANA, INC. - INFORMATION CENTER (Art; Hist)
3402 Boulevard Pl.   Phone: (317) 926-2301
Indianapolis, IN 46208   Christine Connor, Dir. of Pubns./Pub.Info.
Founded: 1960. **Staff:** 1. **Subjects:** State architectural surveys, architecture, history, adaptive use, historic preservation, restoration techniques, neighborhood preservation, art, antiques. **Holdings:** 750 books; 14,000 color slides; 1200 black/white photographs; 230 unbound reports; 550 pamphlets; clippings; 4500 black/white negatives. **Subscriptions:** 62 journals and other serials. **Services:** Copying; library open to public with restrictions. **Computerized Information Services:** Computerized cataloging. **Publications:** Properties brochures; The Indiana Preservationist, bimonthly; Preservation Bulletin, occasional; publications of preservation, occasional. **Special Indexes:** Indiana architects; Indiana historic structures, listed by county (both on cards).

★5645★
HISTORIC LEXINGTON FOUNDATION - GARLAND GRAY RESEARCH CENTER & LIBRARY (Hist)
Stonewall Jackson House
8 E. Washington St.   Phone: (703) 463-2552
Lexington, VA 24450   Ms. Michael Anne Lynn, Dir.
Subjects: Thomas J. "Stonewall" Jackson, Civil War, historic preservation, museum practices, decorative arts. **Special Collections:** Jackson correspondence copies; T.M. Wade Collection. **Holdings:** 800 books. **Services:** Copying; library open to public by appointment. **Publications:** The Genealogies of the Jackson, Junkin and Morrison Families.

★5646★
HISTORIC MOBILE PRESERVATION SOCIETY - MITCHELL ARCHIVES (Hist)†
350 Oakleigh Pl.   Phone: (205) 432-1281
Mobile, AL 36604   Mrs. Carter Smith, Archv.
Founded: 1940. **Staff:** Prof 1. **Subjects:** Mobile history, Mardi Gras, Mobiliana. **Special Collections:** William E. Wilson Collection of Mobile scenes and people, 1895-1910 (2000 glass negatives); worldwide architectural books (500). **Holdings:** 500 books; 15 VF drawers of clippings; 4 VF drawers of documents; 4 VF drawers of photographs; 5 VF drawers of maps and prints. **Services:** Research on premises; fee for use of photographic prints commercially; send stamped envelope with out-of-town inquiries.

★5647★
HISTORIC NEW ORLEANS COLLECTION - LIBRARY (Hist)
533 Royal St.   Phone: (504) 523-4662
New Orleans, LA 70130   Kenneth T. Urquhart, Hd., Res.Lib.
Staff: Prof 4. **Subjects:** History - New Orleans, Louisiana, Southern States; New Orleans architecture. **Special Collections:** Vieux Carre Survey (New Orleans architecture - French Quarter, 150 binders). **Holdings:** 8000 books; 100 bound periodical volumes; 22 VF drawers of pamphlets. **Subscriptions:** 30 journals and other serials. **Services:** Copying; library open to public. **Remarks:** Collection is administered by The Kemper and Leila Williams Foundation. **Staff:** Florence M. Jumonville, Hd.Libn.; Pamela D. Arceneaux, Ref.Libn.; Judith L. McMillan, Asst.Libn.

★5648★
HISTORIC PENSACOLA PRESERVATION BOARD - LIBRARY (Hist)
205 E. Zaragoza St.   Phone: (904) 434-1042
Pensacola, FL 32501   Linda V. Ellsworth, Hist.
Subjects: Historic preservation, Florida and regional history, museum administration, architectural history, antiques. **Holdings:** 1000 books; 2 scrapbooks; 30 oral history tapes. **Subscriptions:** 20 journals and other serials. **Services:** Library open to public for reference use only. **Remarks:** Maintained by State of Florida.

HISTORIC RUGBY, INC. - THOMAS HUGHES LIBRARY
See: Hughes (Thomas) Library

★5649★

HISTORIC ST. AUGUSTINE PRESERVATION BOARD - HISPANIC RESEARCH LIBRARY (Hist)
Box 1987
St. Augustine, FL 32084

Phone: (904) 824-3355
Dr. Amy Turner Bushnell, Hist.

Founded: 1963. **Staff:** Prof 2; Other 1. **Subjects:** St. Augustine and Florida history; Hispanic and Southeastern ethnography and material culture; cultural resource management. **Special Collections:** 16th-18th century Spanish documents (transcripts and translations); St. Augustine preservation projects files; historical maps. **Holdings:** 2800 books; 55 bound periodical volumes; 4500 slides; 800 maps; 3500 negatives; 100 reels of microfilm; 45 VF drawers of research materials; 350 architectural drawings. **Subscriptions:** 10 journals and other serials. **Services:** Copying (limited); library open by introduction and appointment. **Staff:** Robert H. Steinbach, Sr.Musm.Cur.

★5650★

HISTORIC SCHAEFFERSTOWN, INC. - THOMAS R. BRENDLE MEMORIAL LIBRARY & MUSEUM (Hist)
N. Market St.
Schaefferstown, PA 17088

Mrs. Paul Skewis

Staff: 1. **Subjects:** Local history, Pennsylvania German folklore. **Special Collections:** Thomas R. Brendle Collection of Pennsylvania German Folklore. **Holdings:** 1000 books; Brendle Family manuscripts. **Services:** Library open to public on request.

★5651★

HISTORIC WALKER'S POINT, INC. - LIBRARY (Hist)†
734 S. 5th St.
Milwaukee, WI 53204

Phone: (414) 645-6681
Diane Kealty, Pres.

Founded: 1974. **Subjects:** Milwaukee history, preservation, architecture. **Holdings:** 250 books; clipping files and slides. **Subscriptions:** 25 journals and other serials. **Services:** Library open to public. **Publications:** Historic Walker's Point News, 9/year.

★5652★

HISTORICAL ASSOCIATION OF SOUTHERN FLORIDA - CHARLTON W. TEBEAU LIBRARY OF FLORIDA HISTORY (Hist)
3280 S. Miami Ave., Bldg. B
Miami, FL 33129

Phone: (305) 854-3289
Rebecca A. Smith, Libn./Archv.

Founded: 1940. **Staff:** Prof 1; Other 1. **Subjects:** Florida history, especially South Florida; Caribbean; Dade County history; Bahamas. **Special Collections:** Early telephone and business directories; family scrapbooks; photographs, including the works of Claude Matlack, Richard B.Hoit, Ralph Munroe, and Annette and Rudi Rada; manuscripts, including the papers of Carl Fisher, George Merrick, James Jaudon, Gilpin Family, Julia Tuttle and Reginald V. Waters. **Holdings:** 3000 books; 300 bound periodical volumes; 1200 maps; 146 reels of microfilm; 20 VF drawers of pamphlets and clippings; 73,000 photographs; 180 linear feet of archives and manuscripts; 100 oral history tapes, with transcripts. **Subscriptions:** 50 journals and other serials. **Services:** Copying; SDI; library open to public for research use only. **Publications:** Tequesta, annual; Update, quarterly.

★5653★

HISTORICAL COMMITTEE OF THE MENNONITE CHURCH - ARCHIVES OF THE MENNONITE CHURCH (Rel-Theol; Hist)
Goshen College
Goshen, IN 46526

Phone: (219) 533-3161
Leonard Gross, Archv.

Founded: 1911. **Staff:** Prof 2; Other 2. **Subjects:** Official records of the Mennonite Church, its boards, committees, agencies and institutions; peace collections; archives collection of the Mennonite Central Committee; private papers of 600 church leaders. **Special Collections:** J.F. Funk and H.S. Bender Collections of manuscripts and papers. **Holdings:** 10 million items. **Services:** Copying; archives open to public. **Publications:** Mennonite Historical Bulletin, quarterly - subscription. **Special Catalogs:** Inventory listings of major collections.

★5654★

HISTORICAL FOUNDATION OF THE PRESBYTERIAN AND REFORMED CHURCHES - LIBRARY AND ARCHIVES (Rel-Theol)
Box 847
Montreat, NC 28757

Phone: (704) 669-7061
Jerrold Lee Brooks, Dir.

Founded: 1927. **Staff:** Prof 8; Other 3. **Subjects:** Presbyterian and Reformed churches of the world. **Special Collections:** History of churches and women's work in the Presbyterian Church, U.S. (6000 volumes and manuscripts); records and minutes of Presbyterian and Reformed Churches of the world (7500 volumes). **Holdings:** 40,000 books; 25,000 bound periodical volumes; 75,000 other items (cataloged); 3500 linear feet of manuscripts; 3000 reels of microfilm. **Subscriptions:** 150 journals and other serials. **Services:** Interlibrary loans; copying; library open to public. **Publications:** Historical Foundation News, quarterly - to ministers and subscribers. **Special Catalogs:** Catalogs of Presbyterian and Reformed institutions (printed); Survey of Records and Minutes in the Historical Foundation (printed); The Historical Foundation and its Treasures (printed); Stuart Robinson (1814-1881) Working Bibliography, Early American Church Music from the Colonies to the Mid-Nineteenth Century, Eighteenth-Century American Publications (printed). **Special Indexes:** Individuals, local churches, photographs (card). **Staff:** Mary G. Lane, Sr.Libn.; Kay L. Stockdale, Libn.; John M. Walker, III, Tech.Serv.Libn.; Jane P. Britton, Archv.; Joel L. Alvis, Jr., Local Church Hist.

★5655★

HISTORICAL AND GENEALOGICAL SOCIETY OF INDIANA COUNTY - LIBRARY AND ARCHIVES (Hist)
Silas M. Clark House
S. Sixth & Wayne Ave.
Indiana, PA 15701

Phone: (412) 463-9600
Margaret Rees Derwart, Libn.

Founded: 1938. **Staff:** Prof 2; Other 1. **Subjects:** Local history and genealogy, Pennsylvania regimental histories, historic preservation. **Special Collections:** Extensive genealogical files; Frances Strong Helman Collection. **Holdings:** 4000 books; 150 volumes of newspapers on microfilm; manuscripts. **Services:** Interlibrary loans; copying; library open to public during specified hours. **Staff:** Wanda Rife, Co-Libn.

★5656★

HISTORICAL AND GENEALOGICAL SOCIETY OF SOMERSET COUNTY - COUNTY HISTORICAL LIBRARY AND RESEARCH CENTER (Hist)
Somerset Historical Ctr.
R.F.D. 2, Box 238
Somerset, PA 15501

Phone: (814) 445-6077
Mark D. Ware, Musm.Asst.

Founded: 1960. **Staff:** 1. **Subjects:** Somerset County history, genealogy. **Holdings:** 300 books; 5 drawers of source materials on local history and genealogy; films of documents and source material; 200 reels of microfilm. **Subscriptions:** 25 journals and other serials. **Services:** Copying; microfilm printing; library open to public. **Publications:** Laurel Messenger, quarterly.

★5657★

HISTORICAL PICTURES SERVICE, INC. (Pict; Hist)
601 W. Randolph St.
Chicago, IL 60606

Phone: (312) 346-0599
Jeane M. Williams, Archv.

Founded: 1900. **Staff:** Prof 4. **Subjects:** Documentary history - political, diplomatic, military, economic, technological, social and aesthetic. **Special Collections:** Harris and Ewing collection of news events photographs (1900-1955) and prominent persons photographs (1900-1973); Chicago history (5000 prints); religion (15,000 prints); labor history (2500 prints); Americana (35,000 prints); portraits (500,000 prints). **Holdings:** 3000 books; 3.5 million prints and photographs, largely predating 1900, illustrating cultural history throughout the world. **Services:** Copying; pictures available on a fee basis; collection open to public by appointment. **Staff:** Monika Franzen, Res.Assoc.; Durrett Wagner, Ed.Cons.

★5658★

HISTORICAL SOCIETY OF BERKS COUNTY - LIBRARY (Hist)†
940 Centre Ave.
Reading, PA 19601

Phone: (215) 375-4375
Aimee Devine Sanders, Lib.Cons.

Staff: Prof 2. **Subjects:** History of Reading and Berks County, with Pennsylvania background. **Special Collections:** Reading and Berks County imprints; slide collection of barn signs; original account books of early forges and furnaces of Berks County. **Holdings:** 15,000 volumes; church archives; microfilm; maps. **Subscriptions:** 31 journals and other serials. **Services:** Library open to public on a limited schedule. **Publications:** Historical Review of Berks County, quarterly. **Staff:** Barbara Gill, Libn.

★5659★

HISTORICAL SOCIETY OF THE COCALICO VALLEY - MUSEUM AND LIBRARY (Hist)
249 W. Main St.
Ephrata, PA 17522

Phone: (717) 733-1616
Clarence E. Spohn, Cur.

Subjects: Local history, genealogy. **Special Collections:** Milton H. Heinecke Collection of manuscript notebooks on local history (52); Col. George Sallade Howard Collection (first conductor of the U.S. Air Force Band; manuscripts, photographs). **Holdings:** 2588 books; 2241 manuscripts and typescripts; 1647 photographs; 107 tapes and reels of microfilm. **Services:** Copying; library open to public on a limited schedule. **Publications:** Journal of the Historical Society of the Cocalico Valley, annual.

★5660★

HISTORICAL SOCIETY OF DAUPHIN COUNTY - LIBRARY (Hist)
219 S. Front St.   Phone: (717) 233-3462
Harrisburg, PA 17104   Michael Barton, Ph.D., Pres.
Founded: 1869. **Staff:** 4. **Subjects:** Dauphin County history. **Special Collections:** Simon Cameron papers; Bucher papers; Rev. John Elder papers; Joseph Wallace papers; Kelker collection; DeWitt papers; Charles C. Rawn papers (3000 photographs; 100 paintings). **Holdings:** 1000 volumes. **Services:** Copying; library open to members; fee required for nonmembers. **Staff:** Mary H. Redus, Cur.; Joan L. Romig, Asst.Cur.; James F. Davis, Spec. Projects Dir.

★5661★

HISTORICAL SOCIETY OF DELAWARE - LIBRARY (Hist)
505 Market Street Mall   Phone: (302) 655-7161
Wilmington, DE 19801   Dr. Barbara E. Benson, Dir. of Lib.
Founded: 1864. **Staff:** Prof 3; Other 2. **Subjects:** Delaware - history, business, industry; politics and diplomacy; law; religion; genealogy. **Special Collections:** Delaware newspapers; rare books, pamphlets and Delaware imprints; photographs (150,000); maps (1000); business, organization and personal papers. **Holdings:** 50,000 books; 10,000 pamphlets; 53 cubic feet of ephemera; 12 VF drawers and 60 catalog drawers of reference and genealogical files. **Subscriptions:** 80 journals and other serials; 5 newspapers. **Services:** Interlibrary loans (limited); copying; photograph reproduction; library open to public. **Networks/Consortia:** Member of Council of Historical Libraries in Delaware. **Publications:** Delaware History, semiannual. **Special Catalogs:** Imprints, photograph, maps, newspapers (card); manuscript catalog (card and inventory); manuscript books catalog (printed); special subjects catalog (card). **Staff:** Constance Cooper, Mss.Libn.; Carolyn Stallings, Ref.Libn.

★5662★

HISTORICAL SOCIETY OF EARLY AMERICAN DECORATION, INC. - LIBRARY (Art)†
19 Dove St.   Phone: (518) 462-1676
Albany, NY 12210   Mrs. Charles Coffin, Libn.
Founded: 1958. **Subjects:** Decorated tinware, furniture, stencilled walls and floors, glass, clocks, antiques. **Holdings:** 142 books; 23 bound periodical volumes; 30 VF drawers of recordings of original patterns; 13 VF drawers of other recordings and miscellaneous material. **Services:** Library open to members of society and bona fide researchers. **Publications:** The Decorator, semiannual; The Ornamented Chair, 1959 (out of print); The Ornamented Tray, 1969 - both edited by Zilla Lea; An Illustrated Glossary of Decorated Antiques, by Maryjane Clark, 1970.

HISTORICAL SOCIETY OF THE EASTERN CONFERENCE
See: Evangelical United Brethren Church

★5663★

HISTORICAL SOCIETY OF HADDONFIELD - LIBRARY (Hist)†
343 King's Hwy. East   Phone: (609) 429-7375
Haddonfield, NJ 08033   Gertrude D. Hess, Libn.
Staff: Prof 1; Other 4. **Subjects:** Local and state history, genealogy. **Holdings:** 2500 volumes; 3 VF drawers of maps; 15 VF drawers of manuscripts; pamphlets collection; newspapers on microfilm; history recordings. **Services:** Library open to public on a limited schedule. **Publications:** Bulletin, 3/year - to members and other historical societies.

★5664★

HISTORICAL SOCIETY OF LONG BEACH - ARCHIVES (Hist; Pict)
Rancho Los Cerritos
4600 Virginia Rd.
Long Beach, CA 90807   Zona Gale Forbes, Archv.
Staff: 3. **Subjects:** Local history. **Special Collections:** Photograph collection (25,000 negatives and contact prints). **Holdings:** 2000 slides; 20 scrapbooks; 3 VF drawers of newspaper clippings; 3 VF drawers of pamphlets and ephemera. **Services:** Copying; library open to public. **Publications:** Photograph Journals, irregular; Newsletter, monthly.

★5665★

HISTORICAL SOCIETY OF NEWBURGH BAY AND THE HIGHLANDS - LIBRARY (Hist)
189 Montgomery St.   Phone: (914) 561-2585
Newburgh, NY 12550   Helen VerNooy Gearn, Chm. of Lib.Comm.
Staff: Local history. **Holdings:** 3000 books. **Services:** Library open to public with restrictions.

★5666★

HISTORICAL SOCIETY OF OKALOOSA & WALTON COUNTIES, INC. - MUSEUM LIBRARY (Hist)
115 Westview Ave.   Phone: (904) 678-2615
Valparaiso, FL 32580   Christian LaRoche, Musm.Dir.
Staff: Prof 1. **Subjects:** Local and Florida history, Civil War, antiques, folk crafts, genealogy. **Holdings:** 1300 volumes; 35 boxes of letters, clippings and brochures; 12 boxes of newspapers; 70 oral history tapes; 20 folders of maps. **Subscriptions:** 32 journals and other serials; 8 newspapers. **Services:** Library open to public.

★5667★

HISTORICAL SOCIETY OF OLD NEWBURY - LIBRARY (Hist)
Cushing House Museum
98 High St.   Phone: (603) 462-2681
Newburyport, MA 01950   Wilhelmina V. Lunt, Cur.
Founded: 1877. **Staff:** 3. **Subjects:** History of Old Newbury, genealogy. **Special Collections:** Mary Adams Rolfe Genealogical Collection (handwritten). **Holdings:** 1500 books; 50 bound periodical volumes; 10,000 manuscripts. **Services:** Society open to public with fee.

★5668★

HISTORICAL SOCIETY OF PALM BEACH COUNTY - LIBRARY, ARCHIVES AND MUSEUM (Hist)
Henry Morrison Flagler Museum
One Whitehall Way
Box 1147   Phone: (305) 655-1492
Palm Beach, FL 33480   Maxine Wisner Banash, Dir.
Founded: 1937. **Staff:** Prof 2; Other 2. **Subjects:** History of Palm Beach County, local authors, Florida history. **Special Collections:** Palm Beach Post-Times, 1916 to 1932, being microfilmed; Palm Beach Post Times, 1933 to 1953 (microfilm); Addison Mizner architectural drawings (500 drawings from 67 projects). **Holdings:** 3000 books; 160 bound periodical volumes; 2800 photographs (cataloged); early slides of Palm Beach County (cataloged); 11 VF drawers of pamphlets, documents, reports; 6 files of postcards of Florida; 16 reels of recorded tapes of Palm Beach history. **Subscriptions:** 8 journals and other serials; 6 newspapers. **Services:** Copying; library open to public by appointment. **Publications:** The Sunlit Road, newsletter - 5/year; Selected Reading List on Florida History, 1968 (in process of revision). **Staff:** Jon A. von Gunst-Andersen, Cur.

★5669★

HISTORICAL SOCIETY OF PENNSYLVANIA - LIBRARY (Hist)
1300 Locust St.   Phone: (215) 732-6200
Philadelphia, PA 19107   John H. Platt, Hd.Libn.
Founded: 1824. **Staff:** Prof 10; Other 2. **Subjects:** History - U.S., Colonial, Pennsylvania; genealogy. **Holdings:** 553,400 books; 14 million manuscripts; 2800 microcards; 7133 microfiche; 10,936 reels of microfilm; maps, prints, pictures, newspapers, documents. **Subscriptions:** 467 journals and other serials. **Services:** Interlibrary loans; copying; library open to public with fee. **Publications:** The Pennsylvania Magazine of History and Biography Quarterly; The Pennsylvania Correspondent. **Staff:** Peter J. Parker, Chf. of Mss.; James E. Mooney, Dir.

★5670★

HISTORICAL SOCIETY OF PORTER COUNTY - LIBRARY (Hist)
Porter County Museum Old Jail   Phone: (219) 464-8661
Valparaiso, IN 46383   Bertha Stalbaum, Dir./Cur.
Staff: 1. **Subjects:** History - Porter, Lake and LaPorte Counties; Indiana. **Special Collections:** The War of the Rebellion; Official Records of Union and Confederate Armies, series 1-4; applications for Grand Army of the Republic (G.A.R.) membership of Porter County Civil War veterans and naturalization records, 1854-1955. **Holdings:** Figures not available. **Services:** Library open to public with restrictions.

★5671★

HISTORICAL SOCIETY OF PRINCETON - LIBRARY (Hist)
158 Nassau St.   Phone: (609) 921-6817
Princeton, NJ 08540   Lisa Cziffra, Libn.
Founded: 1938. **Staff:** 5. **Subjects:** Princeton and New Jersey history and genealogy. **Holdings:** 4000 volumes; 500 manuscript collections; 10,000 glass plate negatives; photographs, maps, microfilm, post cards. **Subscriptions:** 18 journals and other serials. **Services:** Copying (limited); library open to public for reference use only during limited hours. **Publications:** Princeton History, irregular; News and Notes, newsletter, quarterly. **Special Indexes:** Index to Hageman's History of Princeton.

★5672★
HISTORICAL SOCIETY OF QUINCY AND ADAMS COUNTY - LIBRARY (Hist)†
425 S. 12th St.   Phone: (217) 222-1835
Quincy, IL 62301   Ned Broemmel, Pres.
Founded: 1896. **Staff:** 1. **Subjects:** History and biography of Quincy and Adams County. **Special Collections:** Papers of Gen. John D. Morgan; books by Quincy authors. **Holdings:** 1000 volumes; manuscripts. **Services:** Library open to public for reference use only, by written request.

★5673★
HISTORICAL SOCIETY OF ROCKLAND COUNTY - LIBRARY (Hist)
20 Zukor Rd.   Phone: (914) 634-9629
New City, NY 10956
Founded: 1959. **Subjects:** Local history. **Holdings:** 500 books.

★5674★
HISTORICAL SOCIETY OF SARATOGA SPRINGS - MUSEUM AND LIBRARY (Hist)
Casino, Congress Park
Box 216   Phone: (518) 584-6920
Saratoga Springs, NY 12866   Heidi A. Fuge, Dir.
Founded: 1911. **Staff:** 2. **Subjects:** Historical Saratoga Springs. **Special Collections:** Documents of Chancellor Walworth; papers and manuscripts of Frank Sullivan. **Holdings:** 500 books; 4 VF files of pamphlets, photographs, clippings, scrapbooks. **Services:** Copying (fee); library open to public by appointment. **Publications:** Newsletter, monthly - to members. **Special Indexes:** Walworth Collection (card). **Staff:** Carol A. Lumia, Asst.Dir.

★5675★
HISTORICAL SOCIETY OF THE TARRYTOWNS - HEADQUARTERS LIBRARY (Hist)
19 Grove St. & 1 Grove St.   Phone: (914) 631-8374
Tarrytown, NY 10591   Adelaide R. Smith, Cur.
Founded: 1889. **Staff:** Prof 1. **Subjects:** General history of the communities and the region; capture of Major John Andre at Tarrytown, September 23, 1780, and related events; Westchester County and New York State history; local genealogy. **Holdings:** 3000 books; 100 bound periodical volumes; 15 VF drawers of clippings, letters, documents, and pictures; 500 cataloged maps dating from 1785; Civil War manuscripts and records; local weekly newspapers on microfilm, 1875-1946; bound volumes of The Daily News, 1916-1937, 1943, 1953. **Services:** Library open to public during specified hours. **Remarks:** Maintains small junior library. **Staff:** Ruth Neuendorffer, Libn.

★5676★
HISTORICAL SOCIETY OF THE TOWN OF NORTH HEMPSTEAD - LIBRARY (Hist)
220 Plandome Rd.   Phone: (516) 627-0590
Manhasset, NY 11030   F.J. Pistone, Pres.
Staff: Prof 1. **Subjects:** Town of North Hempstead, Long Island, Nassau County, New York State. **Special Collections:** History of Town of North Hempstead by areas (manuscript form). **Holdings:** Figures not available; unbound reports, manuscripts, clippings, dissertations. **Services:** Interlibrary loans; copying; library open to public by appointment.

★5677★
HISTORICAL SOCIETY OF WESTERN PENNSYLVANIA - LIBRARY (Hist)
4338 Bigelow Blvd.   Phone: (412) 681-5533
Pittsburgh, PA 15213   Helen M. Wilson, Libn.
Founded: 1915. **Staff:** Prof 2. **Subjects:** History of Pittsburgh and Western Pennsylvania. **Special Collections:** Papers of John and William Thaw, William J. Holland, Jacob D. Mathiot, Isaac and Neville Craig, Denny O'Hara, Max Henrici; John Covode; Pittsburgh Common and Select Council records; business ledger collections (200 cubic feet). **Holdings:** 27,119 books; 890 bound periodical volumes; 225 reels of microfilm; 90 boxes of unbound newspapers; 28 VF drawers of pamphlets and clippings; 456 linear feet and 859 bound volumes of manuscripts. **Subscriptions:** 75 journals and other serials. **Services:** Copying; library open to public. **Publications:** Western Pennsylvania Historical Magazine, quarterly; Guide to the Old Stone Blast Furnaces in Western Pennsylvania; Point of Empire; Oildom's Photographic Historian. **Special Indexes:** Cumulative Index and Supplement to Western Pennsylvania Historical Magazine, volumes 1-53. **Staff:** Ruth S. Reid, Archv./Rare Bk.Cur.

★5678★
HISTORICAL SOCIETY OF YORK COUNTY - LIBRARY AND ARCHIVES (Hist)†
250 E. Market St.   Phone: (717) 848-1587
York, PA 17403   Landon C. Reisinger, Libn.
Founded: 1895. **Staff:** Prof 2; Other 1. **Subjects:** York County and city history, York County genealogy, fine and decorative arts. **Special Collections:** Lewis Miller Collection of Folk Art; Shettle Collection of Theatre and Circusiana. **Holdings:** 16,000 books; 1400 bound periodical volumes; 15,000 York County land records; 18,000 York County tax records, 1762-1900; 150 linear feet of York County manuscripts; 5000 photographs and negatives of York County; 1000 reels of microfilm of York County newspapers and manuscripts. **Subscriptions:** 36 journals and other serials. **Services:** Copying; library open to public. **Special Catalogs:** Inventories of manuscript collections (pamphlets).

HISTORY LIBRARY OF MISSIONS
See: Yale University - Divinity School Library

★5679★
HITCO - TECHNICAL LIBRARY (Sci-Tech)
1600 W. 135th St.   Phone: (213) 321-8080
Gardena, CA 90249   Anita Hicks, Tech.Libn.
Founded: 1940. **Staff:** Prof 1; Other 1. **Subjects:** Carbon fibers, composites, advanced materials and structures. **Holdings:** 4100 books and bound periodical volumes; 2800 technical reports; 10,250 patents. **Subscriptions:** 98 journals and other serials. **Services:** Interlibrary loans; limited public access upon approval. **Computerized Information Services:** DIALOG; computerized cataloging. **Remarks:** Hitco is a division of Armco, Inc.

HITE (Allen R.) ART INSTITUTE
See: University of Louisville - Allen R. Hite Art Institute

★5680★
HITTMAN ASSOCIATES, INC. - TECHNICAL INFORMATION DEPARTMENT - LIBRARY
9190 Red Branch Rd.
Columbia, MD 21045
Subjects: Environment, synthetic fuels, energy conservation, solar energy. **Holdings:** 2000 books; 10,000 technical reports. **Remarks:** Presently inactive.

★5681★
HJK&A ADVERTISING & PUBLIC RELATIONS - INFORMATION CENTER (Bus-Fin)
2233 Wisconsin Ave., N.W.   Phone: (202) 333-0700
Washington, DC 20007   Jennifer White, Info.Spec.
Staff: Prof 1; Other 1. **Subjects:** Advertising and marketing, industry. **Holdings:** 500 books; 2 VF drawers of pictures; 5000 slides; 5 VF drawers of clippings; 75 unbound periodicals. **Subscriptions:** 200 journals and other serials; 8 newspapers. **Services:** Interlibrary loans; copying; library not open to public. **Computerized Information Services:** DIALOG, New York Times Information Service. **Publications:** Acquisitions Newsletter, quarterly.

HJORTH (Norman S.) MEMORIAL LIBRARY
See: Trinity United Presbyterian Church - Norman S. Hjorth Memorial Library

★5682★
HOAG MEMORIAL HOSPITAL-PRESBYTERIAN - MEDICAL LIBRARY (Med)
301 Newport Blvd.
Box Y   Phone: (714) 760-2308
Newport Beach, CA 92663   Mrs. Ute Simons, Med.Libn.
Staff: Prof 2; Other 2. **Subjects:** Medicine, nursing, psychiatry. **Holdings:** 5000 books; 8000 bound periodical volumes; 1500 audio cassettes and other AV items. **Subscriptions:** 350 journals and other serials. **Services:** Interlibrary loans; copying; SDI; library open to public with restrictions. **Computerized Information Services:** MEDLINE and other databases. **Networks/Consortia:** Member of Nursing Information Consortium of Orange County (NICOC).

HOAGLAND MEDICAL LIBRARY
See: Long Island College Hospital

★5683★
HOARD HISTORICAL MUSEUM - LIBRARY (Hist)
407 Merchant Ave.   Phone: (414) 563-4521
Fort Atkinson, WI 53538   Hannah W. Swart, Cur.
Founded: 1933. **Staff:** Prof 2. **Subjects:** Black Hawk War, 1800-1840; local Indians and history; birds; quilts; furniture. **Special Collections:** Rare books on Black Hawk War, local history and regional birds; Winnebago Indian artifacts dating 7000 B.C. to 1840s; National Dairy Shrine Museum. **Holdings:** 5108 books; 4813 local pictures. **Subscriptions:** 17 journals and other serials. **Services:** Interlibrary loans; copying; library open to public. **Publications:** Bibliography (Jefferson County).

★5684★
HOBART BROTHERS TECHNICAL CENTER - JOHN H. BLANKENBUEHLER MEMORIAL LIBRARY (Sci-Tech)
Trade Square E.　　　　　　　Phone: (513) 339-6011
Troy, OH 45373　　　　　　　Martha A. Baker, Libn.
Staff: Prof 2. **Subjects:** Welding, metallurgy. **Special Collections:** Current files of the American Welding Society, American Society of Mechanical Engineers, military specifications, American Society for Testing and Materials and foreign standards and specifications related to welding procedures and processes. **Holdings:** 1500 books; 500 bound periodical volumes; 25 VF drawers of educational material and government publications; 1 drawer of microfiche; 50 volumes of government documents; 20 volumes of International Institute of Welding documents. **Subscriptions:** 75 journals and other serials. **Services:** Interlibrary loans; copying; library open to public with permission of director. **Staff:** Howard B. Cary, Dir.

★5685★
HOBART HISTORICAL SOCIETY, INC. - MARIAM J. PLEAK MEMORIAL LIBRARY AND ARCHIVE (Hist)
706 E. Fourth St.
Box 24
Hobart, IN 46342　　　　　Elin B. Christianson, Cur.
Staff: Prof 1. **Subjects:** Local history and genealogy. **Holdings:** 1200 books; 36 VF drawers of archival material; 50 reels of microfilm of Hobart newspapers. **Services:** Library open to public. **Special Indexes:** Index to families listed in 1850-1880 federal censuses for Hobart Township.

★5686★
HOBE SOUND BIBLE COLLEGE - LIBRARY (Rel-Theol)
Box 1065　　　　　　　　Phone: (305) 546-5534
Hobe Sound, FL 33455　　　　Estaline Allison, Dir.
Staff: Prof 2; Other 13. **Subjects:** Religion, elementary education, literature, music, math, science, business. **Holdings:** 20,700 books; 122 bound periodical volumes; 1254 AV programs; 406 microfiche; 1500 pamphlets. **Subscriptions:** 204 journals and other serials. **Services:** Interlibrary loans; copying; library open to public with restrictions. **Staff:** Barbara Burgess, Asst.Libn.

HOBLITZELLE THEATRE ARTS LIBRARY
See: University of Texas, Austin - Humanities Research Center

★5687★
HOCKEY HALL OF FAME - LIBRARY (Rec)
Exhibition Place　　　　　　Phone: (416) 595-1345
Toronto, ON, Canada M6K 3C3　　M.H. (Lefty) Reid, Dir. & Cur.
Subjects: Hockey. **Special Collections:** Turofsky Collection (21,000 negatives). **Holdings:** 1100 books; 300 bound periodical volumes; 40,000 photographs; uncataloged scrapbooks; 6000 35mm slides (current players); microfilm; scrapbooks. **Subscriptions:** 15 journals and other serials. **Services:** Copying; library open to public with restrictions. Some photographs available for purchase by mail.

★5688★
HOCKING TECHNICAL COLLEGE - LIBRARY (Sci-Tech)
Rt. 1　　　　　　　　　Phone: (614) 753-3591
Nelsonville, OH 45764　　　Margy L. Kramer, Libn.
Founded: 1969. **Staff:** Prof 1; Other 1. **Subjects:** Wildlife, parks and recreation, forestry, police science, corrections, nursing, hotel/motel administration, ceramic engineering. **Holdings:** 18,000 books; 450 bound periodical volumes; AV items (cataloged); 18 VF drawers of pamphlets. **Subscriptions:** 270 journals and other serials; 7 newspapers. **Services:** Interlibrary loans; copying; library open to public.

HODGKINS (Clara) MEMORIAL HEALTH SCIENCES LIBRARY
See: Mid-Maine Medical Center - Clara Hodgkins Memorial Health Sciences Library

HODGSON (Edith M.) MEMORIAL LIBRARY
See: Bryant College of Business Administration - Edith M. Hodgson Memorial Library

HODSON (Keith) MEMORIAL LIBRARY
See: Canada - National Defence - Canadian Forces College - Keith Hodson Memorial Library

★5689★
HOECHST-ROUSSEL PHARMACEUTICALS, INC. - LIBRARY (Med)†
Route 202-206, North　　　　Phone: (201) 231-2394
Somerville, NJ 08876　　　　Loretta F. Stangs, Mgr., Lib.Serv.
Staff: Prof 11; Other 5. **Subjects:** Chemistry, pharmacology, toxicology, medicine, pharmaceutical marketing, pesticides, psychopharmacology, industrial management. **Holdings:** 10,183 books; 8500 bound periodical volumes; 4000 reels of microfilm of journals and patents; 800 AV materials. **Subscriptions:** 875 journals and other serials. **Services:** Interlibrary loans; copying; SDI; translations; library open to public by request. **Computerized Information Services:** DIALOG, SDC, Derwent, MEDLINE; computerized cataloging, serials, circulation and product information. **Publications:** H-RPI Notes & Abstracts; H-RPI Current Literature: Furosemide; H-RPI Current Literature: IND Products; Medical Bulletin - all published monthly; Book Acquisitions List, quarterly. All publications are distributed on site and overseas. **Staff:** Ann Van Dine, Asst.Mgr., Lib.Serv.; June Strupczewski, Info.Sci.; Tanya Eichholz, Info.Sci.; Alina Lysiuk, Asst.Med.Libn.; Joanne Reed, Prod.Info.Coord.; Eileen Tortora, Ser.Libn.; Barbara Boyajian, Med.Libn.; Kitty Druck, Hd., Transl.Dept.

HOFFMAN (Charles A.) LIBRARY OF THE HISTORY OF MEDICAL SCIENCES
See: Marshall University - James E. Morrow Library - Special Collections

HOFFMAN (J.S.) MEMORIAL LIBRARY
See: Congregation Rodfei Zedek - J.S. Hoffman Memorial Library

★5690★
HOFFMANN-LA ROCHE, INC. - BUSINESS INFORMATION CENTER (Bus-Fin)
340 Kingsland St.　　　　　Phone: (201) 235-3901
Nutley, NJ 07110　　　　　Goldie Rosenberg, Mgr.
Founded: 1963. **Staff:** Prof 6; Other 4. **Subjects:** Business, marketing, pharmaceuticals, health care. **Holdings:** 6650 books; 35 bound periodical titles; 213 annual reports; 196 subject files. **Subscriptions:** 630 journals and other serials; 8 newspapers. **Services:** Interlibrary loans; library open to public with approval of library manager. **Computerized Information Services:** DIALOG, New York Times Information Service; computerized circulation. **Publications:** Periodical List, annual; RAP, weekly; Digests, monthly; Scan, daily. **Staff:** Patricia Williams, Sr.Libn.; Mayra Scarborough, Libn.; Emilia Ferguson, Asst.Libn.; Judith Sanford, Ed.; Mark Thompson, Asst.Libn., Ref.

★5691★
HOFFMANN-LA ROCHE, LTD. - CORPORATE LIBRARY (Med)
1000 Blvd. Roche　　　　　Phone: (514) 487-8425
Vaudreuil, PQ, Canada J7V 6B3　Mr. C.G.D. Hoare, Supv., Sci.Info.
Founded: 1956. **Staff:** Prof 2; Other 3. **Subjects:** Medicine, clinical pharmacology, toxicology, analytical chemistry, pharmaceutical technology, marketing. **Holdings:** 1200 books; 2036 bound periodical volumes; 18 VF drawers of product literature catalogs; pamphlets and brochures. **Subscriptions:** 274 journals and other serials; 5 newspapers. **Services:** Interlibrary loans; copying; library not open to public. **Computerized Information Services:** SDC, DIALOG, MEDLINE. **Staff:** Cecile Johnson, Libn.

★5692★
HOFFMANN-LA ROCHE, INC. - MISD TECHNICAL LIBRARY
Kingsland Rd., Bldg. 85
Nutley, NJ 07110
Defunct

★5693★
HOFFMANN-LA ROCHE, INC. - SCIENTIFIC LIBRARY (Med)
　　　　　　　　　　Phone: (201) 235-3091
Nutley, NJ 07110　　　　　Phyllis Deline, Mgr.
Founded: 1930. **Staff:** Prof 4; Other 8. **Subjects:** Organic chemistry, biochemistry, pharmacology, medicine, vitamins, chemotherapy. **Holdings:** 11,000 books; 19,000 bound periodical volumes; 400 pamphlets (cataloged); 1381 reels of microfilmed journals and 334 reels of microfilmed Chemical Abstracts in 16mm cartridges; 69,000 microfiche of Roche product reprint file. **Subscriptions:** 535 journals and other serials. **Services:** Interlibrary loans; copying; library open to Special Libraries Association members with permission. **Computerized Information Services:** DIALOG, SDC, MEDLARS; computerized book catalog. **Networks/Consortia:** Member of OCLC. **Publications:** Current Events, weekly; Periodicals/Serials List, annual; Publications List, annual - for internal distribution only. **Staff:** Margaret Corrado, Ref.Libn.; Margaret Elfner, ILL Libn.; Marian Koob, Tech.Serv.

★5694★
HOFFREL INSTRUMENTS, INC. - LIBRARY (Sci-Tech)†
345 Wilson Ave.
Box 825   Phone: (203) 866-9205
Norwalk, CT 06854   Donald P. Relyes, Hd.
Founded: 1963. **Subjects:** Electronics, acoustical physics. **Holdings:** 400 books; 1000 bound periodical volumes. **Services:** Library not open to public. **Networks/Consortia:** Member of Southwestern Connecticut Library Council (SCLC).

★5695★
HOFSTRA UNIVERSITY - LIBRARY - SPECIAL COLLECTIONS (Hum; Soc Sci)
1000 Fulton Ave.   Phone: (516) 560-3387
Hempstead, NY 11550   Marguerite Regan, Asst. to Dean
Staff: 2. **Subjects:** Humanities, social sciences. **Special Collections:** Author collections; Bloomsbury group; Georgian poets; New York State/Long Island History; Howard L. and Muriel Weingrow Collection of Avant-Garde Art and Literature; Nila Banton Smith Reading; Private Presses (Golden Cockerel, Hogarth, Mosher, Nonesuch & Overbrook); Utopian communities (Shakers, Oneida and Quakers); history of the book (fine printing, illustration, fine binding). **Holdings:** Figures not available. **Services:** Copying (limited); library open to public for reference use only. **Computerized Information Services:** Computerized cataloging and information service. **Networks/Consortia:** Member of SUNY/OCLC Library Network; Long Island Library Resources Council.

★5696★
HOFSTRA UNIVERSITY - SCHOOL OF LAW LIBRARY (Law)
                                           Phone: (516) 560-5900
Hempstead, NY 11550   Eugene M. Wypyski, Libn.
Staff: Prof 12; Other 8. **Subjects:** Law. **Holdings:** 216,000 volumes. **Services:** Library not open to public.

★5697★
HOGAN (Charles V.) REGIONAL CENTER - REGIONAL RESOURCE LIBRARY (Med)
Box A   Phone: (617) 774-5000
Hathorne, MA 01937   Bonnie Stecher, Libn.
Staff: Prof 1. **Subjects:** Mental retardation, special education. **Special Collections:** Games, toys, nonprint materials. **Holdings:** 150 books; 250 filmstrips; 200 cassettes; 350 nonprint items. **Services:** Library open to public within region. **Networks/Consortia:** Member of Essex County Cooperating Libraries. **Remarks:** Maintained by Massachusetts State Department of Mental Health. Figures include partial holdings of the former Danvers State Hospital - MacDonald Medical Library.

★5698★
HOGAN (Charles V.) REGIONAL CENTER - STAFF LIBRARY (Med)
Box A   Phone: (617) 774-5000
Hathorne, MA 01937   Bonnie Stecher, Libn.
Staff: Prof 1; Other 1. **Subjects:** Mental retardation, special education, medicine, rehabilitation, behavioral psychology, psychiatry, psychology, community mental health services. **Holdings:** 2000 books; 15 VF drawers of pamphlets, articles, booklets. **Subscriptions:** 100 journals and other serials. **Services:** Interlibrary loans; copying; library open to public with restrictions. **Networks/Consortia:** Member of Essex County Cooperating Libraries; Massachusetts Mental Health Librarians Consortium; Northeast Consortium for Health Information (NECHI). **Remarks:** Maintained by Massachusetts State Department of Mental Health. Figures include partial holdings of the former Danvers State Hospital - MacDonald Medical Library.

★5699★
HOGAN & HARTSON - LIBRARY (Law)
815 Connecticut Ave., N.W.   Phone: (202) 331-5799
Washington, DC 20006   R. Austin Doherty, Libn.
Founded: 1967. **Staff:** Prof 4; Other 9. **Subjects:** Law. **Holdings:** 37,500 books; 1400 bound periodical volumes. **Subscriptions:** 180 journals and other serials; 7 newspapers. **Services:** Interlibrary loans; library open to public with restrictions. **Computerized Information Services:** LEXIS, New York Times Information Service, DIALOG, SDC. **Networks/Consortia:** Member of D.C. Area Law Libraries. **Special Catalogs:** Listing of treatise holdings (card). **Staff:** Tom Pulver, Ref.Libn.; Ron Pramberger, Leg.Libn.

HOGAN (William Ransom) JAZZ ARCHIVE
See: Tulane University of Louisiana - William Ransom Hogan Jazz Archive

HOGG FOUNDATION FOR MENTAL HEALTH
See: University of Texas, Austin

HOLCOMB (T.L.) LIBRARY
See: American Baptist Theological Seminary - T.L. Holcomb Library

★5700★
HOLDEN ARBORETUM - WARREN H. CORNING LIBRARY (Sci-Tech)
Sperry Rd.   Phone: (216) 946-4400
Mentor, OH 44060   Paul C. Spector, Dir.
Staff: 1. **Subjects:** Horticulture, botany, environmental education. **Special Collections:** Warren H. Corning Collection of Horticultural Classics (1500 volumes). **Holdings:** 5500 books; 10 VF drawers. **Subscriptions:** 80 journals and other serials. **Services:** Library open to public.

HOLGATE (Thomas F.) LIBRARY
See: Bennett College - Thomas F. Holgate Library

★5701★
HOLIDAY INNS, INC. - RESEARCH SERVICES INFORMATION CENTER (Bus-Fin)
3742 Lamar Ave.   Phone: (901) 369-5993
Memphis, TN 38195   Vanessa Patterson, Supv., Res.Serv.
Founded: 1979. **Staff:** Prof 1; Other 1. **Subjects:** Strategic planning, hotel and restaurant management, casino gaming. **Special Collections:** SRI Business Intelligence Program reports (300 items); Conference Board reports (600 items). **Holdings:** 500 books; 3500 annual, quarterly and 10K reports of major American companies (microfiche and hard copy); 2500 in-house reports on microfilm. **Subscriptions:** 108 journals and other serials. **Services:** Library not open to public. **Computerized Information Services:** New York Times Information Service, BRS, SDC; computerized cataloging, acquisitions, serials and circulation.

★5702★
HOLLAND COMMUNITY HOSPITAL - HOSPITAL AND MEDICAL STAFF LIBRARY (Med)
602 Michigan Ave.   Phone: (616) 392-5141
Holland, MI 49423   Marge Kars, Dir.
Founded: 1968. **Staff:** Prof 1; Other 1. **Subjects:** Medicine, hospital administration, nursing. **Holdings:** 1600 books; 1500 bound periodical volumes. **Subscriptions:** 220 journals and other serials. **Services:** Interlibrary loans; copying; library open to public with restrictions. **Computerized Information Services:** MEDLINE, DIALOG; computerized cataloging. **Networks/Consortia:** Member of Ottagon Hospital Library Consortia.

★5703★
HOLLAND & HART - LIBRARY (Law)
Box 8749   Phone: (303) 575-8091
Denver, CO 80201   Connie M. Pirosko, Libn.
Staff: Prof 1; Other 4. **Subjects:** Law, business, environment, natural resources. **Holdings:** 18,000 volumes. **Services:** Interlibrary loans; copying; SDI; library open to professionals in related fields. **Computerized Information Services:** LEXIS; computerized cataloging. **Networks/Consortia:** Member of Bibliographic Center for Research, Rocky Mountain Region, Inc. (BCR).

HOLLAND (Mailande W.) LIBRARY
See: Pinellas County Juvenile Welfare Board - Mailande W. Holland Library

★5704★
HOLLAND SOCIETY OF NEW YORK - LIBRARY (Hist)
122 E. 58th St.   Phone: (212) 758-1675
New York, NY 10022   James E. Quackenbush, Pres.
Founded: 1885. **Staff:** 2. **Subjects:** Colonial history of the New Netherland Area (New York, New Jersey and Delaware) with emphasis on genealogical sources and cultural history; genealogies of families which settled there prior to 1675. **Special Collections:** Unpublished manuscript genealogies and Reformed Dutch Church records of New York and New Jersey. **Holdings:** 5000 volumes; 300 reels of microfilm. **Subscriptions:** 20 journals and other serials. **Services:** Copying; library open to the public on a limited schedule. **Publications:** de Halve Maen, quarterly - distributed to members and libraries. **Staff:** Patricia Bereday, Libn.; Barbara Stankowski, Exec.Sec.

★5705★
HOLLEY (A.G.) STATE HOSPITAL - BENJAMIN L. BROCK MEDICAL LIBRARY (Med)
Box 3084   Phone: (305) 582-5666
Lantana, FL 33462   Andree Sweek, Med.Rec.Libn.
Staff: 1. **Subjects:** Medicine. **Holdings:** 1276 books; 2100 bound periodical volumes. **Subscriptions:** 27 journals and other serials. **Services:** Interlibrary loans; copying; library open to health professionals.

★5706★
HOLLINGSWORTH (John D.) ON WHEELS, INC. - INFORMATION SERVICES
(Bus-Fin; Sci-Tech)†
Box 516 Phone: (803) 297-1000
Greenville, SC 29602 Rick Carter, Info.Spec.
Staff: Prof 1. **Subjects:** Textiles, engineering. **Holdings:** Figures not available.
Services: Interlibrary loans; copying; SDI; library not open to public.
Computerized Information Services: Online systems.

★5707★
HOLLINS COLLEGE - MUSIC DEPARTMENT - ERICH RATH LIBRARY - LISTENING CENTER (Mus)
Phone: (703) 362-6511
Hollins College, VA 24020 John Diercks, Chm.
Founded: 1971. **Subjects:** Music. **Holdings:** 4000 books; 200 bound periodical volumes; 150 tapes and 4300 phonograph records (cataloged); 19th-20th century American songs; piano and symphony scores; music textbooks; jazz record collection. **Services:** Library open to public with permission of chairman.

★5708★
HOLLISTER-STIER LABORATORIES - LIBRARY (Med)
Box 3145 Terminal Annex
Spokane, WA 99220 E.L. Foubert, Jr., Libn.
Staff: 1. **Subjects:** Allergy, immunology, biochemistry, immunochemistry, microbiology. **Holdings:** 640 books. **Subscriptions:** 39 journals and other serials. **Services:** Library open to public with restrictions.

HOLLOMAN AIR FORCE BASE (NM)
See: U.S. Air Force Base - Holloman Base Library

★5709★
HOLLYWOOD COMMUNITY HOSPITAL - MEDICAL STAFF LIBRARY (Med)
6245 DeLongpre Ave. Phone: (213) 462-2271
Hollywood, CA 90028 Beverly E. Carlton, Med.Libn.
Staff: Prof 1. **Subjects:** Clinical medicine, nursing. **Holdings:** 550 books; 96 Audio-Digest tapes; 162 NCME (Network for Continuing Medical Education) video cassettes. **Subscriptions:** 40 journals and other serials. **Services:** Interlibrary loans; copying; SDI; library open to public with restrictions.

★5710★
HOLLYWOOD FILM ARCHIVE - LIBRARY (Aud-Vis)
8344 Melrose Ave. Phone: (213) 933-3345
Hollywood, CA 90069 D. Richard Baer, Dir.
Staff: 3. **Subjects:** Motion pictures, television, video. **Special Collections:** Original synopses of 10,000 movies. **Holdings:** 1100 volumes; 3000 motion picture stills. **Services:** Library not open to public. **Computerized Information Services:** Hollywood Film Archive Reference Catalog (internal database). **Publications:** Movie World Almanac, biennial. **Special Indexes:** Hollywood Film Archive Reference Catalog (computer printout generated from magnetic tape).

★5711★
HOLLYWOOD PRESBYTERIAN MEDICAL CENTER - HEALTH SCIENCES LIBRARY (Med)
1300 N. Vermont Ave. Phone: (213) 660-3530
Los Angeles, CA 90027 Erika M. Hansen, Med.Libn.
Founded: 1924. **Staff:** Prof 2; Other 2. **Subjects:** Medicine, nursing, allied health sciences, hospital administration, health care. **Holdings:** 5300 books; 5000 bound periodical volumes; 640 AV items (cataloged); 1800 pamphlets and clippings. **Subscriptions:** 222 journals and other serials. **Services:** Interlibrary loans; copying; SDI; library open to public for reference use only on request. **Networks/Consortia:** Member of Pacific Southwest Regional Medical Library Service (PSRMLS).

HOLM (Irene) MEMORIAL LIBRARY
See: Ottawa Institute - Irene Holm Memorial Library

★5712★
HOLME ROBERTS & OWEN - LIBRARY (Law)
1700 Broadway, Suite 1800 Phone: (303) 861-7000
Denver, CO 80290 Mark E. Estes, Libn.
Staff: Prof 1; Other 4. **Subjects:** Law. **Holdings:** 11,000 volumes. **Services:** SDI; library not open to public. **Computerized Information Services:** Computerized cataloging. **Publications:** News from the Library - for attorneys and paralegal personnel.

★5713★
HOLMES COUNTY LAW LIBRARY (Law)
Court House Phone: (216) 674-5086
Millersburg, OH 44654 Thomas D. Gindlesberger, Law Libn.
Staff: Prof 1; Other 1. **Subjects:** Law. **Holdings:** 4600 volumes. **Services:** Library open to public.

HOLMES (John H.) LIBRARY
See: Westminster Presbyterian Church - John H. Holmes Library

HOLMES (Mary) COLLEGE
See: Mary Holmes College

★5714★
HOLMES & NARVER, INC. - TECHNICAL LIBRARY (Sci-Tech)
999 Town & Country Rd. Phone: (714) 973-1100
Orange, CA 92668 Connie Rickerson, Libn.
Staff: 1. **Subjects:** Nuclear safety, nuclear reactors, nuclear weapons, architectural engineering. **Holdings:** Figures not available. **Subscriptions:** 75 journals and other serials; 7 newspapers. **Services:** Interlibrary loans; copying; library open to public.

HOLMES (Oliver Wendell) LIBRARY
See: Phillips Academy - Oliver Wendell Holmes Library

★5715★
HOLOCAUST LIBRARY AND RESEARCH CENTER OF SAN FRANCISCO (Hist; Soc Sci)
601 14th Ave. Phone: (415) 751-6983
San Francisco, CA 94118 Elizabeth Houdek, Lib.Cons.
Staff: 1. **Subjects:** Nazi Germany, holocaust, modern Europe, Jews in Europe, survivors of concentration camps. **Holdings:** 5000 books; 2000 photographs; 50 oral history tapes. **Services:** Copying; library open to public for reference use only.

★5716★
HOLSTON VALLEY HOSPITAL AND MEDICAL CENTER - HEALTH SCIENCE LIBRARY (Med)†
Ravine St. Phone: (615) 246-3322
Kingsport, TN 37662 Angela C. England, Med.Libn.
Founded: 1953. **Staff:** Prof 1. **Subjects:** Medicine, nursing and allied health sciences. **Holdings:** 3107 books; 3668 bound periodical volumes. **Subscriptions:** 140 journals and other serials in library and 93 in hospital departments. **Services:** Interlibrary loans (limited); copying; library open to public for reference use only. **Computerized Information Services:** Computerized cataloging, acquisitions, serials and circulation. **Networks/Consortia:** Member of Tri-Cities Area Health Sciences Libraries Consortium.

HOLT-ATHERTON PACIFIC CENTER FOR WESTERN STUDIES
See: University of the Pacific - Stuart Library of Western Americana

★5717★
HOLY APOSTLES COLLEGE - LIBRARY (Rel-Theol)
33 Prospect Hill Rd.
Cromwell, CT 06416 Rev. Francis C. O'Hara, Dir., Lib.Serv.
Founded: 1957. **Subjects:** Religious studies, science, theology, sociology, philosophy, English literature and art. **Holdings:** 50,006 books; 400 bound periodical volumes; 424 phonograph records.

★5718★
HOLY CROSS COLLEGE - SCIENCE LIBRARY (Sci-Tech)
Phone: (617) 793-2643
Worcester, MA 01610 Tony Stankus, Sci.Libn.
Founded: 1958. **Staff:** Prof 1; Other 1. **Subjects:** Mathematics, biology, chemistry, physics, history of science, biographies of scientists, astronomy, earth science, physiological psychology, ethical and social implications of science and medicine. **Holdings:** 19,000 books; 26,000 bound periodical volumes. **Subscriptions:** 370 journals and other serials. **Services:** Interlibrary loans; copying; SDI; library open to public with restrictions. **Computerized Information Services:** BRS, DIALOG, SDC. **Networks/Consortia:** Member of OCLC through NELINET; Worcester Area Cooperating Libraries (WACL). **Also Known As:** Its O'Callahan Science Library.

HOLY CROSS GREEK ORTHODOX SCHOOL OF THEOLOGY
See: Hellenic College and Holy Cross Greek Orthodox School of Theology

★5719★
HOLY CROSS HOSPITAL OF CALGARY - DEPARTMENT OF LIBRARY SERVICES (Med)
2210 2nd St., S.W.   Phone: (403) 266-7231
Calgary, AB, Canada T2S 1S6   Mumtaz Jivraj, Hd.Libn.
Founded: 1976. **Staff:** Prof 1; Other 1. **Subjects:** Medicine, nursing, hospitals, allied health sciences. **Holdings:** 3000 books; 1000 bound periodical volumes; 700 cassette tapes; 137 video cassettes; 20 slide/tape programs. **Subscriptions:** 230 journals and other serials. **Services:** Interlibrary loans; library not open to public. **Formed by the Merger of:** Its Medical Library and its Nursing Library.

★5720★
HOLY CROSS HOSPITAL - HEALTH SCIENCE LIBRARY (Med)
2701 W. 68th St.   Phone: (312) 434-6700
Chicago, IL 60629   Olivija Fistrovic, Med.Libn.
Founded: 1962. **Staff:** Prof 1; Other 2. **Subjects:** Medicine, nursing, management. **Holdings:** 1600 books; 3125 bound periodical volumes; 8 VF drawers. **Subscriptions:** 123 journals and other serials. **Services:** Interlibrary loans; copying; library open to public. **Computerized Information Services:** MEDLINE. **Networks/Consortia:** Member of OCLC through ILLINET; Chicago and South Consortium; Regional Medical Library - Region 3. **Publications:** Scope: Health Science Library News.

★5721★
HOLY CROSS HOSPITAL - HEALTH SCIENCE LIBRARY (Med)
4777 E. Outer Dr.   Phone: (313) 369-9100
Detroit, MI 48234   Elaine Lynette Kissel, Mgr.
Staff: Prof 1. **Subjects:** Medicine and allied health sciences, health administration. **Holdings:** 500 books; 500 bound periodical volumes; 600 audio cassettes; 25 video cassettes; 2500 slides. **Subscriptions:** 125 journals and other serials. **Services:** Interlibrary loans; copying; library not open to public. **Computerized Information Services:** MEDLINE. **Networks/Consortia:** Member of Metropolitan Detroit Medical Library Group; Michigan Database Users Group.

★5722★
HOLY CROSS HOSPITAL - HEALTH SCIENCES LIBRARY (Med)
15031 Rinaldi St.   Phone: (213) 365-8051
San Fernando, CA 91345   Lucille R. Moss, Mgr., Health Sci.Lib.
Founded: 1973. **Staff:** Prof 2. **Subjects:** Clinical medicine, nursing, hospital administration. **Holdings:** 600 books; 600 bound periodical volumes. **Subscriptions:** 250 journals and other serials. **Services:** Interlibrary loans; copying; library open to public with restrictions. **Computerized Information Services:** MEDLINE. **Staff:** Nina M. Hull, Health Sci.Libn.

★5723★
HOLY CROSS HOSPITAL - MEDICAL LIBRARY (Med)†
1045 E. First South St.   Phone: (801) 350-4060
Salt Lake City, UT 84102   Sr. M. Fidelia, Med.Libn.
Founded: 1961. **Staff:** 1. **Subjects:** Medicine, surgery, nursing and allied health sciences. **Holdings:** 1000 books; 450 bound periodical volumes; 714 Audio-Digest tapes. **Subscriptions:** 95 journals and other serials. **Services:** Interlibrary loans (fee); copying; SDI; library open to staff and to medical and nursing students. **Computerized Information Services:** MEDLINE, MEDLARS; computerized cataloging (available through University of Utah Eccles Health Sciences Library). **Networks/Consortia:** Member of Utah Health Sciences Library Consortium.

★5724★
HOLY CROSS HOSPITAL OF SILVER SPRING - MEDICAL LIBRARY (Med)
1500 Forest Glen Road   Phone: (301) 565-1211
Silver Spring, MD 20910   Bernetta Payne, Libn.
Founded: 1963. **Staff:** Prof 1. **Subjects:** Medicine and allied sciences. **Holdings:** 1250 books; 450 bound periodical volumes; 400 Audio-Digest tapes. **Subscriptions:** 130 journals and other serials. **Services:** Interlibrary loans; copying; library open to public on request. **Computerized Information Services:** NLM. **Networks/Consortia:** Member of Maryland and D.C. Consortium of Resource Sharing (MADCORS).

HOLY CROSS PROVINCE - PROVINCIAL LIBRARY
See: Congregation of the Passion

★5725★
HOLY FAMILY COLLEGE - LIBRARY - SPECIAL COLLECTIONS (Area-Ethnic)†
Grant & Frankford Aves.   Phone: (215) 637-7703
Philadelphia, PA 19114   Sr. M. Kathryn Dobbs, C.S.F.N., Dir.
Founded: 1954. **Special Collections:** Collection of Polish literature and cultural history (3375 items). **Services:** Interlibrary loans; copying; library open to public for reference use only. **Computerized Information Services:** Access to DIALOG, SDC, BRS, New York Times Information Service; computerized cataloging. **Networks/Consortia:** Member of Tri-State College Library Cooperative (TCLC); Interlibrary Delivery Service of Pennsylvania (IDS); OCLC through PALINET & Union Library Catalogue of Pennsylvania.

★5726★
HOLY FAMILY COLLEGE - MOTHER DOLORES MEMORIAL LIBRARY (Rel-Theol)
159 Washington Blvd.
Box 3426   Phone: (415) 651-1639
Mission San Jose, CA 94539   Sr. Patricia Wittman, Libn.
Founded: 1946. **Staff:** Prof 1; Other 2. **Subjects:** Theology, catechetics, education, child psychology and development, early California history. **Special Collections:** Historical collections in religious education and kindergarten from 1850 to present; tapes on religious subjects. **Holdings:** 38,000 books; 2611 cassettes; 4000 pamphlets and church documents; 6 VF drawers. **Subscriptions:** 100 journals and other serials. **Services:** Interlibrary loans; copying; library open to public. **Computerized Information Services:** ONTYME. **Remarks:** Maintained by Sisters of the Holy Family.

★5727★
HOLY FAMILY CONVENT - LIBRARY (Rel-Theol)
    Phone: (414) 862-2010
Benet Lake, WI 53102   Sr. Maris Stella Doran, O.S.B., Libn.
Founded: 1949. **Staff:** Prof 1. **Subjects:** Theology, scripture, spiritual reading, biography, history, English, science. **Special Collections:** Benedictine collection (150 books). **Holdings:** 7000 books; 58 pamphlets; 500 cassette tapes; 50 reel-to-reel tapes. **Subscriptions:** 34 journals and other serials. **Services:** Interlibrary loans; library open to public with restrictions.

★5728★
HOLY FAMILY HOSPITAL - HEALTH SCIENCE LIBRARY (Med)
21st & Western Ave.   Phone: (414) 684-2260
Manitowoc, WI 54220   Dan Eckert, Libn.
Subjects: Medicine and nursing. **Holdings:** 1000 books. **Subscriptions:** 128 journals and other serials. **Services:** Interlibrary loans; copying; library open to public with restrictions. **Computerized Information Services:** MEDLINE. **Networks/Consortia:** Member of Fox River Valley Area Library Cooperative.

★5729★
HOLY LAND MUSEUM & LIBRARY (Rel-Theol)
Marble Collegiate Church
1 W. 29th St.   Phone: (212) 686-2770
New York, NY 10001   Dorothy Marsh, Cur.
Staff: 12. **Subjects:** Holy Land - history, archeology, people; religions; Bible; ecumenism. **Special Collections:** Artifacts from the Holy Land; rare books; slide collection of ancient and modern Holy Land. **Holdings:** 400 books; briefings for Holy Land tours; pamphlets; conversational Arabic and Hebrew booklets for travelers. **Services:** Provides speakers; tours; library open to public for reference use and research on a limited schedule. **Staff:** Isabelle Bacon, Founder; Cleo Monson, Asst.Cur.

★5730★
HOLY NAME HOSPITAL - MEDICAL LIBRARY (Med)
Teaneck Rd.   Phone: (201) 833-3014
Teaneck, NJ 07666   Leila M. Hover, Libn.
Founded: 1925. **Staff:** Prof 1; Other 3. **Subjects:** Medicine, nursing. **Holdings:** 6918 books; 3535 bound periodical volumes; 5 video cassettes; 1070 tape cassettes. **Subscriptions:** 160 journals and other serials. **Services:** Interlibrary loans; copying; library open to public with restrictions. **Computerized Information Services:** MEDLINE, DIALOG. **Networks/Consortia:** Member of Bergen/Passaic Health Sciences Library Consortium.

★5731★
HOLY NAME OF JESUS HOSPITAL - MEDICAL LIBRARY (Med)
600 S. 3rd St.   Phone: (205) 547-4911
Gadsden, AL 35901
Founded: 1965. **Staff:** 2. **Subjects:** Health sciences, medicine, anesthesiology, surgery. **Holdings:** 615 books; 586 bound periodical volumes; 182 tapes. **Subscriptions:** 60 journals and other serials. **Services:** Interlibrary loans; copying; library not open to public. **Publications:** New acquisition list, quarterly.

HOLY SPIRIT LIBRARY
See: Cabrini College

HOLY SPIRIT RESEARCH CENTER
See: Oral Roberts University - Library

★5732★
HOLY TRINITY LUTHERAN CHURCH - LIBRARY (Rel-Theol)
2730 E. 31st St.   Phone: (612) 729-8358
Minneapolis, MN 55406   Mae Cruys, Hd.Libn.
Founded: 1952. **Holdings:** 4000 books; 40 bound periodical volumes.
Services: Library open to church members.

★5733★
HOLZER MEDICAL CENTER - MEDICAL LIBRARY (Med)
385 Jackson Pike   Phone: (614) 446-5245
Gallipolis, OH 45631   Beverly J. Jackson, Lib.Ck.
Staff: 1. **Subjects:** Medicine, surgery, urology, pediatrics, diseases of the eye, ear, nose and throat. **Special Collections:** Nursing and Medical Archives. **Holdings:** 2500 books; 70 periodical titles. **Services:** Interlibrary loans; copying; library open to public with restrictions. **Computerized Information Services:** Online systems. **Networks/Consortia:** Member of Kentucky-Ohio-Michigan Regional Medical Library Network (KOMRML); Consortium for Health Education in Appalachian Ohio. **Publications:** Newsletter, quarterly. **Special Indexes:** Serials list. **Remarks:** Contains the holdings of the former School of Nursing Library.

★5734★
HOLZHEIMER INTERIORS - RESEARCH CENTER (Art)
10901 Carnegie Ave.   Phone: (216) 791-9292
Cleveland, OH 44106   Steven J. Grove, Hd.Libn.
Staff: Prof 1; Other 1. **Subjects:** Interior design. **Special Collections:** Fabric samples (200,000). **Holdings:** 2000 furniture catalogs; 2000 vertical files. **Subscriptions:** 10 journals and other serials. **Services:** Copying; center not open to public.

★5735★
HOME LIFE INSURANCE COMPANY - LIBRARY (Bus-Fin)
253 Broadway   Phone: (212) 233-6400
New York, NY 10007   Jeannette L. Secunda, Libn.
Founded: 1934. **Staff:** Prof 1; Other 1. **Subjects:** Life insurance, health insurance. **Holdings:** 2000 volumes; 86 VF drawers of unbound materials. **Subscriptions:** 130 journals and other serials. **Services:** Interlibrary loans to Special Libraries Association members only; library not open to public.

★5736★
HOME MISSIONERS OF AMERICA - GLENMARY NOVITIATE LIBRARY (Rel-Theol)
Box 46404   Phone: (513) 874-8900
Cincinnati, OH 45246   Thomas J. Meehan, Libn.
Founded: 1947. **Staff:** Prof 1. **Subjects:** Scripture, theology. **Holdings:** 3500 books and bound periodical volumes. **Subscriptions:** 15 journals and other serials. **Services:** Copying; library open to Glenmary students only. **Also Known As:** Glenmary Home Missioners.

★5737★
HOME OIL COMPANY, LTD. - LIBRARY (Energy)
2300 Home Oil Tower
324 8th Ave., S.W.   Phone: (403) 232-7207
Calgary, AB, Canada T2P 2Z5   R. Muir, Coord.
Staff: Prof 3; Other 2. **Subjects:** Geology, business, petroleum technology, computer science, energy resources. **Holdings:** 8000 books. **Subscriptions:** 400 journals and other serials. **Services:** Interlibrary loans; copying; library not open to public. **Computerized Information Services:** DIALOG, SDC, Info Globe, Dow Jones News Retrieval; computerized cataloging, acquisitions and serials. **Staff:** G.L. Fraser, Supv.

HOMER RESEARCH LABORATORIES
See: Bethlehem Steel Corporation - Technical Information

HOMESTEAD AIR FORCE BASE (FL)
See: U.S. Air Force Base - Homestead Base Library

HOMESTEAD NATL. MONUMENT
See: U.S. Natl. Park Service

HOMOPHILE RESEARCH LIBRARY
See: Church of the Beloved Disciple

★5738★
HOMOSEXUAL INFORMATION CENTER - TANGENT GROUP (Soc Sci)
6758 Hollywood Blvd., No. 208   Phone: (213) 464-8431
Hollywood, CA 90028   Leslie Colfax, Libn.
Founded: 1952. **Staff:** Prof 2; Other 2. **Subjects:** Homosexuality, civil liberties, censorship, sexual freedom, lesbiana. **Special Collections:** Homosexual Movement Collection. **Holdings:** 5050 books and bound periodical volumes; 32 VF drawers of manuscripts, clippings, pamphlets, documents; 60 legal briefs and court opinions; 30 boxes of material. **Subscriptions:** 12 journals and other serials; 25 newspapers. **Services:** Interlibrary loans; copying; center open to public with restrictions. **Publications:** Directory of Homosexual Organizations; Newsletter; selected bibliographies; reading lists; subject heading guides; list of other publications - available upon request. **Also Known As:** Tangent Group - Homosexual Information Center. **Staff:** Charles Lucas, Chm.

HONEY BEE PESTICIDES/DISEASES RESEARCH LABORATORY
See: U.S.D.A. - Agricultural Research Service

★5739★
HONEYWELL, INC. - COMMERCIAL DIVISION - LIBRARY (Sci-Tech)†
1500 W. Dundee   Phone: (312) 394-4000
Arlington Heights, IL 60004   Paul M. Klekner, Libn.
Staff: Prof 1. **Subjects:** Electrical engineering, computer programming, management. **Special Collections:** Energy management (500 unbound reports). **Holdings:** 500 books; 1000 internal documents. **Subscriptions:** 67 journals and other serials. **Services:** Interlibrary loans; copying; library open to public. **Computerized Information Services:** DIALOG; Honeywell MULTICS; Honeywell Computerized Library Catalog (HCLC; internal database); computerized serials. **Networks/Consortia:** Member of Honeywell Information Network. **Publications:** Honeywell Union List of Serials, annual - for internal distribution only. **Special Catalogs:** Union list of serials and conference proceedings for Honeywell Information Network.

★5740★
HONEYWELL, INC. - CORPORATE TECHNOLOGY CENTER LIBRARY (Sci-Tech)
10701 Lyndale Ave., S.   Phone: (612) 887-4321
Bloomington, MN 55420   Michael McClellan, Libn.
Staff: Prof 3. **Subjects:** Physics, chemistry, electrical engineering, computer science. **Holdings:** 5000 books; 6000 bound periodical volumes; government publications, patents and microfilm. **Subscriptions:** 200 journals and other serials. **Services:** Interlibrary loans; copying; library not open to public. **Computerized Information Services:** DIALOG, New York Times Information Service, Dow Jones News Retrieval, Mead Data Central; computerized cataloging. **Staff:** June Frehn, Asst.Libn.; Maggie Moffett, Asst.Libn.

★5741★
HONEYWELL, INC. - DEFENSE ELECTRONICS DIVISION, TRAINING AND CONTROL SYSTEMS OPERATION - TECHNICAL LIBRARY (Sci-Tech)
1200 E. San Bernardino Rd.   Phone: (213) 331-0011
West Covina, CA 91790   Emelie Goodridge, Libn.
Founded: 1962. **Staff:** Prof 1. **Subjects:** Training devices, ordnance, underwater acoustics, electronics, computer science, oceanography. **Holdings:** 3600 books; 5000 technical reports. **Subscriptions:** 165 journals and other serials. **Services:** Interlibrary loans; copying; library open to public with restrictions. **Computerized Information Services:** DIALOG, SDC - internal users only.

★5742★
HONEYWELL, INC. - DEFENSE SYSTEMS DIVISION - ENGINEERING LIBRARY (Sci-Tech)
600 Second St., N.   Phone: (612) 931-6603
Hopkins, MN 55343   Lawrence W. Werner, Libn.
Founded: 1957. **Staff:** Prof 1; Other 2. **Subjects:** Military ordnance, design engineering, electronics, controls, aerospace technology. **Holdings:** 4000 books; 950 bound periodical volumes; 125,000 engineering reports. **Subscriptions:** 200 journals and other serials. **Services:** Interlibrary loans; copying; library not open to public. **Computerized Information Services:** DIALOG, DTIC. **Publications:** Recent Acquisitions Bulletin, weekly - for internal distribution only.

★5743★
HONEYWELL, INC. - ELECTRO-OPTICS CENTER - TECHNICAL LIBRARY (Sci-Tech)
2 Forbes Rd.   Phone: (617) 863-3756
Lexington, MA 02173   Kathleen A. Long, Mgr., Tech.Info.Serv.
Founded: 1958. **Staff:** Prof 1; Other 2. **Subjects:** Optics, electro-optics, physics, infrared detection, aerospace technology. **Holdings:** 3000 books;

1000 bound periodical volumes; 400 technical reports (cataloged). **Subscriptions:** 203 journals and other serials. **Services:** Interlibrary loans; library open to public by appointment. **Computerized Information Services:** DIALOG, SDC, BRS, NASA/RECON; computerized cataloging. **Networks/Consortia:** Member of Honeywell Information Network (HIN); OCLC through NELINET. **Publications:** Monthly acquisition list.

★5744★
HONEYWELL, INC. - ENGINEERING LIBRARY (Sci-Tech)
10901 Malcolm McKinley Dr.
Box 17500   Phone: (813) 977-8511
Tampa, FL 33682   Betsy King, Libn.
Founded: 1981. **Staff:** Prof 1. **Subjects:** Electronics. **Holdings:** 300 books; 100 bound periodical volumes. **Subscriptions:** 30 journals and other serials. **Services:** Interlibrary loans; copying; library not open to public. **Computerized Information Services:** DIALOG.

★5745★
HONEYWELL, INC. - HONEYWELL INFORMATION SYSTEMS - INFORMATION AND LIBRARY SERVICES (Info Sci)
200 Smith St., MS 423   Phone: (617) 895-6370
Waltham, MA 02154   Melissa Brokalakis, Mgr., Info./Lib.Serv.
Staff: Prof 5; Other 2. **Subjects:** Computer science, data processing, computer marketing, electronics, engineering, business, accounting, management science. **Holdings:** 6000 books; technical reports; proceedings; 15,000 technical manuals; market studies; annual reports; bibliographic files. **Services:** Interlibrary loans; library open to public by appointment. **Computerized Information Services:** DIALOG, NEXIS; computerized serials and indexing. **Networks/Consortia:** Member of OCLC through NELINET; Wellesley-Lexington Area Consortium of Libraries (WELEXACOL). **Publications:** Acquisitions update, monthly. **Special Catalogs:** Union List of Journals - Waltham/Billerica/ Wellesley. **Remarks:** Branch libraries are maintained in Billerica and Wellesley, MA. **Staff:** Kathy Bell, Tech.Serv.Libn.; Eileen Ward, Res.Spec.; Judy Donovan; Mary Rezetka; Kathy Ott .

★5746★
HONEYWELL, INC. - HONEYWELL INFORMATION SYSTEMS - TECHNICAL LIBRARY (Sci-Tech; Info Sci)
Box 6000   Phone: (602) 866-4115
Phoenix, AZ 85005   Vera Minkel, Mgr., Lib.Serv.
Founded: 1958. **Staff:** Prof 2; Other 1. **Subjects:** Computer technology, electronics, electrical engineering, computer programming, information science, management. **Special Collections:** Computer science dissertations on microfilm (300 reels). **Holdings:** 12,000 books; 3000 bound periodical volumes; 8500 cataloged reports; 2500 company internal reports and customer software manuals; 1200 IEEE publications on microfiche; library collection on 20 magnetic tapes. **Subscriptions:** 220 journals and other serials; 6 newspapers. **Services:** Interlibrary loans; library not open to public. **Computerized Information Services:** DIALOG, Dow Jones News Retrieval; Honeywell MULTICS (internal database); computerized cataloging, acquisitions and circulation. **Networks/Consortia:** Member of Honeywell Information Network (HIN). **Publications:** Online News, quarterly. **Special Indexes:** Index of acquisitions, annual. **Staff:** Jackie Whitford, Libn.

★5747★
HONEYWELL, INC. - HONEYWELL MARINE SYSTEMS OPERATIONS - TECHNICAL INFORMATION CENTER (Sci-Tech)
5303 Shilshole Ave., N.W.   Phone: (206) 789-2000
Seattle, WA 98107   Christy Mackey, Tech.Libn.
Founded: 1956. **Staff:** 3. **Subjects:** Electronics, acoustics, communication systems, data processing, ship automation, ocean engineering, sonar devices. **Holdings:** 1600 books; 100 bound periodical volumes; 25,000 technical documents; 1500 microfiche of technical reports; visual search microfilm of all military and federal specifications and standards; industry specifications and standards. **Subscriptions:** 154 journals and other serials. **Services:** Library not open to public. **Computerized Information Services:** DIALOG, SDC; computerized circulation. **Publications:** Monthly Acquisitions Report - for internal distribution only.

★5748★
HONEYWELL, INC. - MICRO SWITCH ENGINEERING LIBRARY (Sci-Tech)
11 Spring St.   Phone: (815) 235-5609
Freeport, IL 61032   Mary Schneider, Libn.
Founded: 1960. **Staff:** Prof 1. **Subjects:** Electrical engineering, plastics, chemistry, business administration. **Holdings:** 2600 books; 1400 bound periodical volumes. **Subscriptions:** 300 journals and other serials. **Services:** Interlibrary loans; copying; library open to public with restrictions. **Computerized Information Services:** DIALOG.

★5749★
HONEYWELL, INC. - PROCESS CONTROLS DIVISION - INFORMATION CENTER, M.S. 221 (Sci-Tech)†
Industrial Rd.   Phone: (215) 641-3982
Fort Washington, PA 19034   Jean L. Hurd, Sr.Info.Sys.Spec.
Founded: 1935. **Staff:** Prof 2; Other 1. **Subjects:** Industrial instrumentation; control systems; engineering - electronic, electrical, mechanical, chemical; computers; marketing; business management. **Holdings:** 2800 books; 140 VF drawers of standards and specifications, technical reports, company reports and internal reports. **Subscriptions:** 256 journals and other serials. **Services:** Interlibrary loans; literature searches; library not open to public. **Publications:** Library Bulletin, monthly - for internal distribution only. **Staff:** Susan Plotkin, Info.Sys.Spec.

★5750★
HONEYWELL, INC. - RESIDENTIAL ENGINEERING RESOURCE AND LEARNING CENTER (Sci-Tech)
Mail Sta. Mn 52-1258, Parkdale Plaza
1660 S. Hwy. 100   Phone: (612) 542-6830
St. Louis Park, MN 55416   Elizabeth Hicks Howard, Tech.Libn.
Founded: 1944. **Staff:** Prof 1; Other 3. **Subjects:** Engineering, business. **Holdings:** 3500 books; 2500 periodical volumes; 70 VF drawers of miscellaneous material. **Subscriptions:** 150 journals and other serials. **Services:** Library open to public for reference use only, on request. **Computerized Information Services:** DIALOG. **Networks/Consortia:** Member of Honeywell Information Network (HIN). **Publications:** News & Views, monthly - for internal distribution only. **Formerly:** Its Residential Engineering Library.

★5751★
HONEYWELL, INC. - SOLID STATE ELECTRONICS DIVISION LIBRARY (Sci-Tech)
12001 Hwy. 55   Phone: (612) 541-2075
Plymouth, MN 55441   Kathleen M. Thompson, Res.Libn.
Founded: 1979. **Staff:** Prof 1. **Subjects:** Integrated circuits, semiconductors, electronics. **Special Collections:** Internal reports (100). **Holdings:** 200 books; 300 bound periodical volumes. **Subscriptions:** 75 journals and other serials. **Services:** Interlibrary loans; copying; library open to public. **Computerized Information Services:** DIALOG; computerized cataloging. **Publications:** Library Line, monthly - for internal distribution only.

★5752★
HONEYWELL, INC. - SYSTEMS & RESEARCH CENTER - LIBRARY (Sci-Tech)
2600 Ridgeway Pkwy.
Box 312   Phone: (612) 378-4238
Minneapolis, MN 55440   Maro Theologides, Supv., Lib.Info.Serv.
Founded: 1951. **Staff:** Prof 3; Other 3. **Subjects:** Aerospace technology, optical sciences, computer sciences, control systems technology, human factors engineering, information systems. **Special Collections:** 70,000 technical documents. **Holdings:** 8000 books; 7500 bound periodical volumes; 15,000 company internal reports. **Subscriptions:** 225 journals and other serials; 5 newspapers. **Services:** Interlibrary loans; SDI; library open to public with restrictions. **Computerized Information Services:** DIALOG, New York Times Information Service, NASA/RECON, DTIC; Honeywell MULTICS (interal database). **Networks/Consortia:** Member of Honeywell Information Network (HIN). **Publications:** Recent Acquisitions Bulletin, monthly; Infobriefs, monthly - both for internal distribution only. **Staff:** Vern Bartlett, Info.Spec.; Mary Miller, Cat.

★5753★
HONEYWELL, INC. - TECHNOLOGY STRATEGY CENTER - INFORMATION SERVICES (Sci-Tech)
400 Rosedale Towers
1700 W. Hwy. 36   Phone: (612) 378-5441
Roseville, MN 55113   Denise Cumming, Info.Spec.
Staff: Prof 2; Other 3. **Subjects:** Energy, engineering, processes and controls. **Holdings:** 1800 books; 15,000 government documents. **Subscriptions:** 150 journals and other serials; 10 newspapers. **Services:** Interlibrary loans; library open to public with restrictions. **Computerized Information Services:** DIALOG, DOE/RECON; Honeywell Conference Listings; computerized cataloging. **Networks/Consortia:** Member of Honeywell Library Network. **Formerly:** Located in Minneapolis, MN. **Staff:** Jane Kaufenberg, Acq.Asst.

★5754★
HONIGMAN MILLER SCHWARTZ & COHN - LAW LIBRARY (Law)
2290 First National Bldg.   Phone: (313) 871-5422
Detroit, MI 48202   Teresa N. Pritchard, Assoc./Law Libn.
Staff: Prof 3; Other 1. **Subjects:** Law - real estate, bankruptcy, corporate, environmental, hospital. **Holdings:** 6000 books; 500 bound periodical

volumes; 500 loose-leaf binders and reports; 1 VF drawer of legal briefs. **Subscriptions:** 200 journals and other serials; 5 newspapers. **Services:** Interlibrary loans; library not open to public. **Computerized Information Services:** LEXIS. **Staff:** Judy Floyd, Libn.; Sue Gruca, Asst.Libn.

★5755★
HONOLULU ACADEMY OF ARTS - ROBERT ALLERTON LIBRARY (Art)
900 S. Beretania St.
Honolulu, HI 96814
Phone: (808) 538-3693
Anne T. Seaman, Libn.
Founded: 1927. **Staff:** Prof 1; Other 1. **Subjects:** Art history, especially Chinese and Japanese art. **Special Collections:** Michigan archives of the Palace Museum, Taiwan (8000 mounted black/white photographs, 2000 2x2 color slides). **Holdings:** 30,000 books; 12,000 bound periodical volumes; 4000 pamphlets (cataloged); 12 VF drawers of clippings and announcements; 15 reels of microfilm. **Subscriptions:** 220 journals and other serials. **Services:** Interlibrary loans; copying; library open to members.

★5756★
HONOLULU ACADEMY OF ARTS - SLIDE COLLECTION (Art)
900 S. Beretania St.
Honolulu, HI 96814
Phone: (808) 538-3693
Doris Lutzky, Kpr.
Founded: 1972. **Staff:** Prof 1. **Subjects:** Art, architecture, crafts. **Holdings:** 40,000 slides. **Services:** Library open to public with restrictions.

★5757★
HONOLULU (City and County) - MUNICIPAL REFERENCE AND RECORDS CENTER (Soc Sci)
558 S. King St.
Honolulu, HI 96813
Phone: (808) 523-4577
Marsha C. Petersen, Dir.
Founded: 1929. **Staff:** Prof 3; Other 3. **Subjects:** Municipal government; urban planning, development and renewal; engineering and public works; traffic and transportation; public administration. **Special Collections:** Honolulu Ordinances File. **Holdings:** 43,000 books and pamphlets; 115 VF drawers of newspaper clippings. **Subscriptions:** 650 journals and other serials. **Services:** Interlibrary loans; copying; library open to public for reference use only. **Publications:** Bookshelf: A Selected Bibliography of Library Acquisitions, monthly - distributed to local libraries and government agencies. **Staff:** Kathleen S. Kudo, Libn.; Verna K. Miura, Libn.

HONOLULU HOUSE MUSEUM - MARSHALL ARCHIVES
See: Marshall Historical Society - Archives

★5758★
HOOD THEOLOGICAL SEMINARY - LIVINGSTONE COLLEGE - LIBRARY (Rel-Theol)†
W.J. Walls Ctr.
800 W. Thomas St.
Salisbury, NC 28144
Phone: (704) 633-7960
Mrs. Willie L. Aldrich, Hd.Libn.
Founded: 1880. **Staff:** Prof 2; Other 7. **Subjects:** Bible history, ethics, hymnology, homiletics, Christian education, theology, philosophy, Biblical languages, Church history. **Special Collections:** W.C. Brown Ecumenical Collection; Bible Collection; Jones Black Collection; Spots Collection; W.J. Walls Heritage Hall Archives. **Holdings:** 21,117 books; 1050 bound periodical volumes; 64 reels of microfilm; 231 microfiche; 265 tapes and filmstrips; archives. **Subscriptions:** 209 journals and other serials; 18 newspapers. **Services:** Interlibrary loans; copying; library open to public with restrictions. **Publications:** Student handbook, staff handbook. **Special Catalogs:** Tape catalog; AV catalog. **Staff:** Saeid Zehery, Cat.Libn.

★5759★
HOOKER CHEMICAL CORPORATION - TECHNICAL INFORMATION CENTER (Sci-Tech)
Box 8
Niagara Falls, NY 14302
Phone: (716) 773-8531
Dr. Irving Gordon, Supv.
Founded: 1916. **Staff:** Prof 5. **Subjects:** Organic chemistry, inorganic chemistry, polymers, textiles, physical chemistry. **Holdings:** 15,000 books; 20,000 bound periodical volumes; 90 VF drawers of technical reports; 10 cabinets of microforms. **Subscriptions:** 500 journals and other serials. **Services:** Interlibrary loans; copying; SDI; library open to public on request. **Computerized Information Services:** Online systems. **Networks/Consortia:** Member of Western New York Library Resources Council (WNYLRC). **Special Indexes:** Magnetic disc index of internal reports and patents. **Staff:** Jane Pattison, Sr.Res.Libn.

★5760★
HOOKER CHEMICAL & PLASTICS CORPORATION - DUREZ DIVISION - LABORATORY LIBRARY†
Walck Rd.
North Tonawanda, NY 14120
Founded: 1940. **Subjects:** Chemistry - general, organic, industrial; plastics.

Holdings: 2000 books; 1500 bound periodical volumes; 60 VF drawers of reports, technical data, PB reports, and reprints. **Remarks:** Presently inactive.

HOOKER (Ruth H.) TECHNICAL LIBRARY
See: U.S. Navy - Naval Research Laboratory - Ruth H. Hooker Technical Library

HOOKS (David Wayne) MEMORIAL LIBRARY
See: Psychical Research Foundation - David Wayne Hooks Memorial Library

HOOLE (William Stanley) SPECIAL COLLECTIONS LIBRARY
See: University of Alabama - William Stanley Hoole Special Collections Library

★5761★
HOOVER COMPANY - ENGINEERING DIVISION LIBRARY (Sci-Tech)
101 E. Maple St.
North Canton, OH 44720
Phone: (216) 499-9200
Founded: 1928. **Staff:** 1. **Subjects:** Engineering, chemistry, plastics, metallurgy, electronics, physics. **Holdings:** 1850 books; 500 bound periodical volumes; 2000 pamphlets; 1560 standards; 9550 notebooks; 5650 reports; 168 presenting books; 6 VF drawers of progress reports; 20 VF drawers of engineering reports. **Subscriptions:** 60 journals and other serials. **Special Indexes:** Card indexes to internal reports.

HOOVER (Herbert) LIBRARY
See: U.S. Presidential Libraries - Herbert Hoover Library

HOOVER INSTITUTION ON WAR, REVOLUTION AND PEACE
See: Stanford University

★5762★
HOPE LUTHERAN CHURCH - LIBRARY (Rel-Theol)
1115 N. 35th St.
Milwaukee, WI 53208
Esther Damkoehler, Libn.
Staff: 4. **Subjects:** Religion, sociology, history, psychology, children's literature. **Holdings:** 2930 books and bound periodical volumes; records; tapes. **Subscriptions:** 10 journals and other serials. **Services:** Library open to public.

★5763★
HOPEWELL MUSEUM - LIBRARY (Hist)
28 E. Broad St.
Hopewell, NJ 08525
Phone: (609) 466-0103
Beverly Weidl, Cur.
Staff: 2. **Subjects:** Local history, genealogy. **Holdings:** 300 books. **Services:** Library open to public with restrictions. **Publications:** Pioneers of Old Hopewell, 1963 reprint; Hopewell Valley Heritage, 1974; Medical Records of Benjamin VanKirk, 1768-1815. **Staff:** Betsy Errickson, Asst.Cur.

HOPEWELL VILLAGE NATL. HISTORIC SITE
See: U.S. Natl. Park Service

★5764★
HOPITAL DE CHICOUTIMI INC. - BIBLIOTHEQUE (Med)
305, rue St-Vallier
C.P. 5006
Chicoutimi, PQ, Canada G7H 5H6
Phone: (418) 549-2195
Angele Tremblay, Bibliothecaire
Staff: Prof 2; Other 3. **Subjects:** Medicine, public health. **Holdings:** 6300 books; 9100 bound periodical volumes; 15,000 slides and cassettes. **Subscriptions:** 100 journals and other serials. **Services:** Interlibrary loans; copying; library open to public. **Staff:** Rodrigue Girard, Bibliotechnicien.

★5765★
HOPITAL DE L'ENFANT-JESUS - BIBLIOTHEQUE MEDICALE (Med)
1401 18eme Rue
Quebec, PQ, Canada G1J 1Z4
Phone: (418) 694-5686
Madeleine Dumais, Responsable
Staff: Prof 1; Other 1. **Subjects:** Medicine. **Holdings:** 2768 books; 6133 bound periodical volumes. **Subscriptions:** 241 journals and other serials. **Services:** Interlibrary loans; copying; library not open to public. **Special Catalogs:** Catalogue collectif des periodiques dans les bibliotheques de sante de la region de Quebec.

HOPITAL GENERAL DE MONTREAL
See: Montreal General Hospital

HOPITAL GENERAL D'OTTAWA
See: Ottawa General Hospital

★5766★
HOPITAL DU HAUT-RICHELIEU - BIBLIOTHEQUE MEDICALE (Med)
920, boul. du Seminaire   Phone: (514) 348-6101
St-Jean, PQ, Canada J3A 1B7   Helene Heroux-Bouchard, Bibliotechnicienne
Staff: Prof 1. **Subjects:** Medicine, psychiatry, pediatrics, obstetrics and gynecology, surgery. **Holdings:** 1350 books; 816 bound periodical volumes. **Subscriptions:** 161 journals and other serials. **Services:** Interlibrary loans; copying; library not open to public.

HOPITAL HOTEL-DIEU...
See: Hotel-Dieu...

★5767★
HOPITAL JEAN-TALON - BIBLIOTHEQUE MEDICALE (Med)
1385 E. Jean-Talon   Phone: (514) 273-5151
Montreal, PQ, Canada H2E 1S6   Pierrette Galarneau, Med.Libn.
Founded: 1961. **Staff:** Prof 1. **Subjects:** Medicine. **Special Collections:** CIBA Collection (slides). **Holdings:** 1750 books; 3500 bound periodical volumes. **Subscriptions:** 160 journals and other serials. **Services:** Interlibrary loans; copying; manual bibliographic research for staff; library open to public for consultation only. **Also Known As:** Jean-Talon Hospital.

★5768★
HOPITAL LOUIS H. LAFONTAINE - BIBLIOTHEQUE (Med)
7401 Rue Hochelaga   Phone: (514) 253-8200
Montreal, PQ, Canada H1N 3M5   Camil Lemire, Med.Libn.
Founded: 1950. **Staff:** Prof 1; Other 7. **Subjects:** Psychology, psychiatry, psychoanalysis. **Holdings:** 6400 books; 2500 bound periodical volumes. **Subscriptions:** 280 journals and other serials. **Services:** Interlibrary loans; copying; library open to public with restrictions.

★5769★
HOPITAL MAISONNEUVE-ROSEMONT - SERVICE DES BIBLIOTHEQUES (Med)
5415 de l'Assomption Blvd.   Phone: (514) 254-8341
Montreal, PQ, Canada H1T 2M4   Helene Lauzon, Hd.Libn.
Staff: Prof 2; Other 3. **Subjects:** Medicine, surgery, psychiatry, pneumology, gynecology, pediatrics, hospital administration, nursing, medical technology. **Holdings:** 2165 books; 8529 bound periodical volumes. **Subscriptions:** 273 journals and other serials. **Services:** Interlibrary loans; copying; library open to public with restrictions. **Computerized Information Services:** MEDLINE. **Special Catalogs:** Periodical lists and basic volumes, annual.

★5770★
HOPITAL DE MONT-JOLI, INC. - BIBLIOTHEQUE (Med)
800 Sanatorium   Phone: (418) 775-7261
Mont-Joli, PQ, Canada G5H 3L6   Sylvie Dupuis, Lib.Techn.
Founded: 1974. **Staff:** Prof 1. **Subjects:** Psychiatry, psychology, medicine, health care. **Special Collections:** Psychiatry (150 volumes); medicine (300 volumes). **Holdings:** 4000 books; 180 bound periodical volumes. **Subscriptions:** 180 journals and other serials. **Services:** Interlibrary loans; copying; library not open to public. **Networks/Consortia:** Member of ASTED. **Publications:** Documentation et Bibliotheques, quarterly - by subscription.

★5771★
HOPITAL NOTRE DAME DE L'ESPERANCE - BIBLIOTHEQUE (Med)†
1275 Cote Vertu   Phone: (514) 747-4771
St. Laurent, PQ, Canada H4L 4V2   Sr. Gemma Emond, Med.Libn.
Founded: 1942. **Staff:** Prof 1; Other 1. **Subjects:** Medicine. **Holdings:** Figures not available. **Services:** Library not open to public.

★5772★
HOPITAL NOTRE DAME - MEDICAL LIBRARY (Med)
C.P. 1560, Succ. C.   Phone: (514) 876-6862
Montreal, PQ, Canada H2L 4K8   Marcelle L'Esperance, Chf.Libn.
Founded: 1935. **Staff:** Prof 1; Other 4. **Subjects:** Medicine and related subjects. **Holdings:** 26,000 books and bound periodical volumes. **Subscriptions:** 600 journals and other serials. **Services:** Interlibrary loans; copying; library open to public for reference use only. **Also Known As:** Notre Dame Hospital.

★5773★
HOPITAL REINE ELIZABETH - A. HOLLIS MARDEN BIBLIOTHEQUE (Med)
2100 Marlowe Ave.   Phone: (514) 488-2311
Montreal, PQ, Canada H4A 3L6   Ms. S.L. Mullan, Lib.Techn.
Founded: 1937. **Staff:** 2. **Subjects:** Medicine, nursing. **Holdings:** 11,400 books and bound periodical volumes. **Subscriptions:** 203 journals and other serials. **Services:** Interlibrary loans; copying; library not open to public. **Formerly:** Queen Elizabeth Hospital of Montreal.

★5774★
HOPITAL RIVIERE-DES-PRAIRIES - BIBLIOTHEQUE DU PERSONNEL (Med)†
7070, est Blvd. Perras   Phone: (514) 323-7260
Montreal, PQ, Canada H1E 1A4   Noella Martineau, Med.Libn.
Founded: 1966. **Staff:** Prof 2; Other 1. **Subjects:** Child psychiatry, pediatrics, special education, psychology, hospital administration, behavior modification. **Special Collections:** Freud: Collected Papers (23 volumes). **Holdings:** 5330 books; 398 bound periodical volumes; 200 AV items; 185 technical reports; 150 films; 2000 photographs; 100 cassettes; 1526 monographs. **Subscriptions:** 231 journals and other serials; 6 newspapers. **Services:** Interlibrary loans; copying; library open to public for reference use only. **Computerized Information Services:** MEDLINE. **Publications:** Monthly list of new books; annual report; bibliographies. **Staff:** Sylvie Fortin, Techn.

★5775★
HOPITAL DU SACRE COEUR - PAVILLON ALBERT-PREVOST - MEDICAL LIBRARY (Med)
6555 Gouin Blvd., W.   Phone: (514) 333-4284
Montreal, PQ, Canada H4K 1B3   Margareth Page, Techn., Docs.
Founded: 1962. **Staff:** Prof 1. **Subjects:** Psychiatry, psychoanalysis, psychology, child psychiatry. **Holdings:** 6000 books; Audio-Digest tapes on psychiatry. **Subscriptions:** 140 journals and other serials. **Services:** Interlibrary loans; copying; library open to public.

★5776★
HOPITAL ST-FRANCOIS D'ASSISE - BIBLIOTHEQUE MEDICALE ET ADMINISTRATIVE (Med)
10 rue de l'Espinay   Phone: (418) 529-7311
Quebec, PQ, Canada G1L 3L5   Ulric Lefebvre, Chief
Founded: 1959. **Staff:** 2. **Subjects:** Anesthesiology, pharmacology, geriatrics, pediatrics, gynecology, obstetrics, dermatology, surgery, orthopedics. **Holdings:** 4615 books; 4451 bound periodical volumes; annual reports; documents. **Subscriptions:** 291 journals and other serials. **Services:** Interlibrary loans; copying; Bibliotheque open to public with restrictions. **Computerized Information Services:** MEDLINE, Universite Laval. **Publications:** Liste de volume, periodiques, rapports. **Also Known As:** Hopital Generale. **Staff:** Denise Paquet Morin, Tech. en Doc.; Nicole Dion, Dir., Serv.Hosp.

★5777★
HOPITAL STE-JUSTINE - CENTRE D'INFORMATION SUR LA SANTE DE L'ENFANT (Med)†
3175, Chemin Cote Ste-Catherine   Phone: (514) 731-4931
Montreal, PQ, Canada H3T 1C5   Pierrette Bubuc, Hd.
Founded: 1962. **Staff:** Prof 7; Other 10. **Subjects:** Pediatrics, obstetrics and gynecology, nursing, child psychology and psychiatry, exceptional children, special education. **Special Collections:** Materiatheque (curriculum manuals and instructional materials for the special child; 3814 items); Renseignements (standing file on province-wide clinical and educational resources for the special child); ERIC microfiche collection on the special child. **Holdings:** 9946 books; 5577 reports, videotapes and other items. **Subscriptions:** 836 journals and other serials. **Services:** Interlibrary loans; copying; SDI; library open to public with restrictions. **Computerized Information Services:** DIALOG, MEDLINE, CAN/OLE, SABINE. **Networks/Consortia:** Member of Banque Quebecoise de Materiel Didactique (BQMD). **Publications:** Manual for the organization of small collections in the special child field; Services a l'enfance, regional clinical and educational resources for the child in Quebec. **Special Catalogs:** Materiatheque catalog; special child collection catalog; filmography, updated listing and analysis of films on child health available in Canada; catalog of Quebec hospital videotape productions on child health. **Staff:** Louise Jolin, Libn.; Louis-Luc Lecompte, Asst.; Carmen Dupuis, Materiatheque; Lise Leduc, Renseignements; Ginette Charest, Audiovideotheque; Lucienne Saint-Martin, Libn.

★5778★
HOPITAL ST-LUC - BIBLIOTHEQUE MEDICALE (Med)
1058 St. Denis St.   Phone: (514) 285-1525
Montreal, PQ, Canada H2X 3J4   Rene Cote, Chf.Libn.
Staff: Prof 3; Other 2. **Subjects:** Medicine, paramedicine, surgery, hospital administration, nursing. **Holdings:** 2332 books; 2268 bound periodical volumes. **Subscriptions:** 376 journals and other serials. **Services:** Interlibrary loans; copying; library open to medical personnel only. **Also Known As:** St. Luc Hospital.

★5779★
HOPITAL DU ST-SACREMENT - BIBLIOTHEQUE MEDICALE (Med)†
1050 Chemin Ste-Foy   Phone: (418) 688-7560
Quebec, PQ, Canada G1S 4L8   Bernadette Drolet, Chf.Libn.
Staff: Prof 1; Other 2. **Subjects:** Medicine. **Holdings:** 2642 books; 5091

bound periodical volumes. **Subscriptions:** 290 journals and other serials. **Services:** Interlibrary loans; copying; library open to public for reference use only.

★5780★
HOPKINS COUNTY - REGIONAL MEDICAL CENTER - LIBRARY (Med)†
Hospital Dr.   Phone: (502) 825-5100
Madisonville, KY 42431   Mark A. Ingram, Med.Libn.
Founded: 1969. **Staff:** Prof 1. **Subjects:** Medicine, surgery. **Holdings:** 820 books; 1765 bound periodical volumes; 840 audio cassettes; 4000 unbound journals; films; audiovisual material. **Subscriptions:** 173 journals and other serials. **Services:** Interlibrary loans; copying; library open to public with restrictions.

HOPKINS MARINE STATION
See: Stanford University

HOPWOOD ROOM
See: University of Michigan

HORMEL INSTITUTE
See: University of Minnesota

HORN LIBRARY
See: Babson College

HORNBAKE LIBRARY
See: University of Maryland, College Park - Libraries - Music Library - International Piano Archives at Maryland

HORNE (Marilyn) ARCHIVES
See: Long Beach Public Library - Fine Arts Department

★5781★
HORNER (Frank W.), LTD. - RESEARCH LIBRARY (Med)
5485 Ferrier St.   Phone: (514) 731-3931
Montreal, PQ, Canada H4P 1M6   Miss R. Robinson, Adm.Asst.
Staff: 1. **Subjects:** Medical sciences, analytical chemistry, biochemistry, pharmacology, sales. **Holdings:** 2000 books; 5000 bound periodical volumes. **Subscriptions:** 125 journals and other serials. **Services:** Copying; library not open to public.

HORNER (Joseph) MEMORIAL LIBRARY
See: German Society of Pennsylvania - Joseph Horner Memorial Library

HORNEY (Karen) CLINIC
See: Ivimey (Muriel) Library

HORRAX LIBRARY
See: New England Deaconess Hospital

HORRMANN LIBRARY
See: Wagner College

HORSEY (J. William) LIBRARY
See: Ontario Bible College/Ontario Theological Seminary - J. William Horsey Library

HORTICULTURAL RESEARCH INSTITUTE OF ONTARIO
See: Ontario - Ministry of Agriculture and Food

HORTICULTURAL RESEARCH LABORATORY LIBRARY
See: U.S.D.A. - Agricultural Research Service

★5782★
HORTICULTURAL SOCIETY OF NEW YORK - PUBLIC REFERENCE LIBRARY (Sci-Tech)
128 W. 58th St.   Phone: (212) 757-0915
New York, NY 10019   Lana Nguyen, Libn.
Founded: 1924. **Staff:** Prof 2. **Subjects:** Horticulture; landscape gardening; garden history; medical botany, including herbals; international floras; flower arrangement; nursery, seed and plant supply catalogs. **Special Collections:** Enid A. Haupt Young Peoples Collection of books in horticulture and gardening (100 volumes). **Holdings:** 20,000 books; 350 bound periodical volumes; biographical file on 400 botanists and horticulturists; VF material on 1800 subjects; slide collections. **Subscriptions:** 60 journals and other serials. **Services:** Copying; library open to public for reference use only. **Publications:** Garden Magazine, monthly; members newsletter, bimonthly. **Special Indexes:** Index to nursery, seed and plant suppliers. **Staff:** Elizabeth Hall, Libn.

Emeritus.

HORTON HEALTH SCIENCES LIBRARY
See: Providence Medical Center

★5783★
HORTON MEMORIAL HOSPITAL - MEDICAL LIBRARY (Med)
60 Prospect Ave.   Phone: (914) 342-5561
Middletown, NY 10940   Laura Leese, Med.Libn.
Staff: Prof 1; Other 1. **Subjects:** Medicine, surgery, nursing, allied health sciences. **Holdings:** 1000 books; 1500 bound periodical volumes; 50 pamphlets; 25 pamphlets (uncataloged); vertical file of 250 research topics; 500 audio cassette tapes. **Subscriptions:** 150 journals and other serials. **Services:** Interlibrary loans; library open to allied medical professionals and law enforcement personnel. **Networks/Consortia:** Member of New York State Interlibrary Loan Network (NYSILL); Southeastern New York Library Resources Council.

HOSPITAL ASSOCIATION OF NEW YORK STATE - HOSPITAL EDUCATIONAL AND RESEARCH FUND
See: Hospital Educational and Research Fund

★5784★
HOSPITAL ASSOCIATION OF PENNSYLVANIA - LIBRARY (Med)
Box 608   Phone: (717) 763-7053
Camp Hill, PA 17011   Katharine M. Silvasi, Libn.
Staff: Prof 1; Other 1. **Subjects:** Hospitals - administration, law, finance and economics; insurance; nursing administration; Medicare and Medicaid. **Holdings:** 2100 books; 100 bound periodical volumes; 70 internal publications; 45 AV titles. **Subscriptions:** 140 journals and other serials; 5 newspapers. **Services:** Interlibrary loans; copying; library open to public for reference use only. **Computerized Information Services:** MEDLARS. **Networks/Consortia:** Member of Central Pennsylvania Health Sciences Library Association (CPHSLA); Mideastern Regional Medical Library Service (MERMLS). **Publications:** Acquisitions List, quarterly.

★5785★
HOSPITAL CENTER AT ORANGE - WILLIAM PIERSON MEDICAL LIBRARY (Med)
188 S. Essex Ave.   Phone: (201) 266-2000
Orange, NJ 07051   Jeanette Merkl, Libn.
Staff: Prof 1. **Subjects:** Medicine. **Holdings:** 1497 books; 1502 bound periodical volumes. **Subscriptions:** 95 journals and other serials. **Services:** Interlibrary loans; copying; SDI; library not open to public. **Networks/Consortia:** Member of Cosmopolitan Biomedical Library Consortium.

★5786★
HOSPITAL CORPORATION OF AMERICA - RESEARCH/INFORMATION SERVICES (Med)
One Park Plaza
Box 550   Phone: (615) 327-9551
Nashville, TN 37202   Lisa Ogletree, Mgr., Strategic Res.
Founded: 1976. **Staff:** Prof 2; Other 1. **Subjects:** Health care industry, business management, hospital management. **Holdings:** 1000 volumes; 36 volumes of periodicals on microfilm; 7 VF drawers. **Subscriptions:** 120 journals and other serials; 6 newspapers. **Services:** Interlibrary loans; copying; library open to corporate personnel. **Computerized Information Services:** DIALOG, New York Times Information Service, SDC, BRS, Dow Jones News Retrieval. **Networks/Consortia:** Member of OCLC through SOLINET. **Staff:** Jane C. Butler, Tech.Serv.Libn.; Mary Wester-House, Info.Spec.

★5787★
HOSPITAL EDUCATIONAL AND RESEARCH FUND - LILLIAN R. HAYT MEMORIAL LIBRARY (Med)
Center for Health Initiatives
15 Computer Dr., W.   Phone: (518) 458-7940
Albany, NY 12205   Elaine C. Rotman, Libn.
Staff: Prof 1. **Subjects:** Hospital administration, management. **Holdings:** 2600 books; 18 VF drawers of pamphlets, reports. **Subscriptions:** 260 journals and other serials. **Services:** Interlibrary loans; copying; open to public by appointment. **Networks/Consortia:** Member of Capital District Library Council. **Remarks:** Parent organization is Hospital Association of New York State.

★5788★
HOSPITAL EQUITIES, INC. - MEDICAL WORLD NEWS - LIBRARY
211 E. 43rd St., Suite 401
New York, NY 10017
Founded: 1962. **Subjects:** Medicine, health, medical education, nursing,

pharmacology. **Holdings:** 4500 books; 30 bound periodical volumes; 30 VF drawers of pamphlets, clippings, medical school catalogs, and manuscripts. **Remarks:** Presently inactive.

★5789★
HOSPITAL OF THE GOOD SAMARITAN - MEDICAL LIBRARY (Med)
616 S. Witmer St.   Phone: (213) 977-2326
Los Angeles, CA 90017   Elizabeth Sherson, Med.Libn.
Staff: Prof 1; Other 1. **Subjects:** Medicine, nursing, hospital administration. **Holdings:** 2143 books; 5100 bound periodical volumes. **Subscriptions:** 180 journals and other serials. **Services:** Library not open to public.

HOSPITAL FOR JOINT DISEASES ORTHOPAEDIC INSTITUTE
See: Beth Israel Medical Center

★5790★
HOSPITAL OF ST. RAPHAEL - HEALTH SCIENCES LIBRARY (Med)
1450 Chapel St.   Phone: (203) 789-3330
New Haven, CT 06511   Patricia L. Wales, Dir., Lib.Serv.
Founded: 1942. **Staff:** Prof 3. **Subjects:** Medicine, nursing and allied health sciences. **Holdings:** 1100 books; 3000 bound periodical volumes; 2 VF drawers; AV materials. **Subscriptions:** 204 journals and other serials. **Services:** Interlibrary loans; copying; library open to public for reference use only. **Computerized Information Services:** NLM, BRS (through Yale Medical Library). **Networks/Consortia:** Member of Connecticut Association of Health Science Libraries (CAHSL); North Atlantic Health Sciences Libraries; Southwestern Connecticut Library Council. **Staff:** John Schilke, AV Coord.; Barbara M. Rosnagle, Lib.Asst.

★5791★
HOSPITAL FOR SICK CHILDREN - HOSPITAL LIBRARY (Med)
555 University Ave.   Phone: (416) 597-1500
Toronto, ON, Canada M5G 1X8   Irene Jeryn, Libn.
Founded: 1919. **Staff:** Prof 2; Other 4. **Subjects:** Pediatrics. **Special Collections:** Pediatric journals published in English from their inception. **Holdings:** 4840 books; 16,353 periodical volumes. **Subscriptions:** 487 journals and other serials. **Services:** Interlibrary loans (limited); library not open to public. **Publications:** Medical Library Bulletin (listing contents of some journals received).

★5792★
HOSPITAL FOR SPECIAL SURGERY - KIM BARRETT MEMORIAL LIBRARY (Med)
535 E. 70th St.   Phone: (212) 535-5500
New York, NY 10021   Munir U. Din, Med.Libn.
Founded: 1934. **Staff:** Prof 1. **Subjects:** Orthopedic surgery and rheumatic diseases. **Holdings:** 2229 books; 2306 bound periodical volumes; 2838 reprints; 174 video cassettes, slide programs and films. **Subscriptions:** 81 journals and other serials. **Services:** Library open to staff of hospital and affiliated institutions for reference use; service to researchers with restrictions. **Publications:** Library News; List of Journals.

★5793★
HOSPITAL OF THE UNIVERSITY OF PENNSYLVANIA - ROBERT DUNNING DRIPPS LIBRARY OF ANESTHESIA (Med)
Department of Anesthesia
3400 Spruce St.   Phone: (215) 662-3784
Philadelphia, PA 19104   Joan Meranze, Dir.
Staff: Prof 1; Other 2. **Subjects:** Anesthesia. **Special Collections:** History of anesthesia, 150 texts and transcripts. **Holdings:** 475 books; 31 bound periodical volumes; 60 videotape teaching cassettes. **Subscriptions:** 51 journals and other serials. **Services:** Interlibrary loans; copying; library open to area anesthesiologists only. **Computerized Information Services:** DIALOG. **Networks/Consortia:** Member of Mideastern Regional Medical Library Service.

HOTCHKIN (George W.) MEMORIAL LIBRARY
See: Rogers Environmental Education Center - George W. Hotchkin Memorial Library

★5794★
HOTEL-DIEU D'ARTHABASKA - MEDICAL LIBRARY-DOCUMENTATION SERVICE (Med)
5 Quesnel St.   Phone: (819) 357-2031
Arthabaska, PQ, Canada G6P 6N2   Micheline LeClair, Lib.Techn.
Founded: 1960. **Staff:** Prof 1. **Subjects:** Health sciences, nursing. **Holdings:** 2148 books; 2924 bound periodical volumes. **Subscriptions:** 100 journals and other serials. **Services:** Interlibrary loans; copying; SDI; library open to public.

HOTEL-DIEU DE GASPE
See: Centre Hospitalier de l'Hotel-Dieu de Gaspe

★5795★
HOTEL DIEU HOSPITAL - LIBRARY (Med)†
Box 61262   Phone: (504) 588-3000
New Orleans, LA 70161   Georgia Gwin Sewell, Libn.
Founded: 1972. **Staff:** Prof 1. **Subjects:** Medicine, surgery, hospital administration, nursing. **Holdings:** 1616 books; 2000 bound periodical volumes; 42 volumes of hospital archives. **Subscriptions:** 200 journals and other serials. **Services:** Interlibrary loans; copying; SDI; library open to hospital personnel. **Publications:** Column in hospital house organ, Esprit de Corps, quarterly. **Remarks:** Library is located at 2021 Perdido St., New Orleans, LA 70112.

★5796★
HOTEL-DIEU DE LEVIS - BIBLIOTHEQUE MEDICALE (Med)†
143 rue Wolfe   Phone: (418) 833-7121
Levis, PQ, Canada G6V 3Z1   Colette Pasquis-Audant, Libn.
Founded: 1950. **Staff:** Prof 1; Other 1. **Subjects:** Medicine. **Holdings:** 5394 books. **Subscriptions:** 278 journals and other serials. **Services:** Interlibrary loans; copying; library not open to public. **Networks/Consortia:** Member of ASTED.

★5797★
HOTEL-DIEU DE MONTREAL - CENTRE DE DOCUMENTATION (Med)
3840 Rue St-Urbain   Phone: (514) 844-0161
Montreal, PQ, Canada H2W 1T8   Ginette Boyer, Libn.
Founded: 1947. **Staff:** Prof 1; Other 3. **Subjects:** Medicine and nursing. **Holdings:** 2500 books; 17,000 bound periodical volumes; 50,000 slides. **Subscriptions:** 302 journals and other serials. **Services:** Interlibrary loans; copying; library open to public for reference use only. **Computerized Information Services:** MEDLINE. **Networks/Consortia:** Member of Association des Bibliotheques de la Sante Affiliees a l'Universite de Montreal (ABSAUM).

★5798★
HOTEL-DIEU DU SACRE-COEUR DE JESUS - BIBLIOTHEQUE MEDICALE (Med)†
1, Ave. du Sacre-Coeur   Phone: (418) 529-6851
Quebec, PQ, Canada G1N 2W1   Christian Martel, Lib.Techn.
Founded: 1968. **Staff:** Prof 1; Other 1. **Subjects:** Child psychiatry, neurology. **Holdings:** 3150 books. **Subscriptions:** 121 journals and other serials. **Services:** Interlibrary loans; copying; library open to public for reference use only.

★5799★
HOTEL-DIEU OF ST. JOSEPH HOSPITAL - MEDICAL LIBRARY (Med)
1030 Ouellette Ave.   Phone: (519) 252-3631
Windsor, ON, Canada N9A 1E1   Toni Janik, Hosp.Libn.
Staff: Prof 1. **Subjects:** Medicine and allied health fields. **Holdings:** 400 books; 2000 bound periodical volumes; 15 slide/tape programs; 30 video cassettes; 100 vertical files. **Subscriptions:** 112 journals and other serials. **Services:** Interlibrary loans; copying; library open to other librarians. **Networks/Consortia:** Member of Metropolitan Detroit Medical Library Group (MDMLG).

HOTEL-DIEU DE SHERBROOKE
See: Centre Hospitalier Hotel-Dieu de Sherbrooke

★5800★
HOTEL SALES MANAGEMENT ASSOCIATION - SALES RESEARCH LIBRARY (Bus-Fin)
1235 Jefferson Davis Hwy., Suite 610   Phone: (703) 521-6300
Arlington, VA 22202   Frank W. Berkman, Exec.Dir.
Subjects: Sales promotion, merchandising, public relations, marketing, direct mail, publicity, advertising, education work in sales. **Special Collections:** Compilation of hotel sales promotion material covering 30 years. **Holdings:** 200 books and bound periodical volumes; **Subscriptions:** 22 journals and other serials. **Services:** Library may be visited only by special arrangement. **Formerly:** Located in New York, NY.

HOUDRY LABORATORIES
See: Air Products and Chemicals, Inc. - Houdry Laboratories

★5801★
HOUGHTON COLLEGE - BUFFALO SUBURBAN CAMPUS - ADA M. KIDDER MEMORIAL LIBRARY (Rel-Theol)
910 Union Rd. Phone: (716) 674-6363
West Seneca, NY 14224 Ruth G. Butler, Libn.
Founded: 1938. **Staff:** Prof 1; Other 1. **Subjects:** Theology, missions, Christian education. **Holdings:** 31,000 books; 950 bound periodical volumes; 520 phonograph records; 120 cassettes; 150 filmstrips; 55 reels of microfilm. **Subscriptions:** 90 journals and other serials. **Services:** Interlibrary loans; copying; library open to public for reference use only. **Networks/Consortia:** Member of SUNY/OCLC; Western New York Library Resources Council (WNYLRC); Christian College Consortium.

★5802★
HOUGHTON COUNTY HISTORICAL SOCIETY - LIBRARY (Hist; Sci-Tech)
Highway M-26, Lock Box D Phone: (906) 296-4121
Lake Linden, MI 49945 Joseph H. Hawke, Cur.
Staff: 2. **Subjects:** Mining, transportation, engineering, forestry, industry, local history. **Special Collections:** Engineering and mining journals; copper handbooks; Lake Superior books. **Holdings:** Figures not available. **Services:** Library open to public with approval of Board of Directors.

★5803★
HOUGHTON (E.F.) TECHNICAL CENTER - LIBRARY (Sci-Tech)
Madison & Van Buren Aves. Phone: (215) 666-4000
Valley Forge, PA 19482 Margaret C. Schweitzer, Libn.
Staff: Prof 1. **Subjects:** Industrial oils, chemicals; metallurgy; organic chemistry; lubricants; hydraulics; paper and textiles. **Holdings:** 6000 books; 300 bound periodical volumes; 6 VF drawers of research reports; 8 VF drawers of patents; 20 VF drawers of catalogs and pamphlets. **Subscriptions:** 60 journals and other serials. **Services:** Interlibrary loans; copying; library not open to public. **Computerized Information Services:** DIALOG.

HOUGHTON LIBRARY
See: Harvard University

★5804★
HOUGHTON MIFFLIN COMPANY - LIBRARY (Publ)
One Beacon St. Phone: (617) 725-5270
Boston, MA 02107 Guest Perry, Libn.
Founded: 1966. **Staff:** Prof 2; Other 2. **Subjects:** Education, textbooks, publishing. **Holdings:** 15,000 books; 15 VF drawers of pamphlets; curricula guides; microfiche; competing textbooks. **Subscriptions:** 600 journals and other serials. **Services:** Interlibrary loans; research. **Computerized Information Services:** Online systems; computerized cataloging and ILL. **Publications:** Newsletter. **Staff:** Terry Moran, Assoc.Libn.

★5805★
HOULTON REGIONAL HOSPITAL - LIBRARY (Med)
20 Hartford St. Phone: (207) 532-9471
Houlton, ME 04730 Cathy Bates, Med.Libn.
Staff: Prof 1. **Subjects:** Medicine, nursing. **Holdings:** 150 books. **Subscriptions:** 75 journals and other serials. **Services:** Interlibrary loans; copying; SDI; library open to public for reference use only. **Networks/Consortia:** Member of Aroostook Health Information and Resources Consortium; Health Science Library and Information Cooperative of Maine.

★5806★
HOUSE BEAUTIFUL - STAFF LIBRARY (Art)†
1700 Broadway Phone: (212) 903-5241
New York, NY 10019 Carolyn E. Chesney, Libn.
Staff: 1. **Subjects:** Architecture, interior design, decorative arts. **Holdings:** 2000 books. **Subscriptions:** 100 journals and other serials. **Services:** Library not open to public. **Remarks:** House Beautiful is owned by the Hearst Corporation.

HOUSE OF THE BOOK
See: Brandeis-Bardin Institute

HOUSE MAGAZINE LIBRARY
See: Gebbie Press, Inc.

★5807★
HOUSEHOLD INTERNATIONAL - CORPORATE LIBRARY (Bus-Fin)
2700 Sanders Rd. Phone: (312) 564-5000
Prospect Heights, IL 60070 Win Sadecki, Corp.Libn.
Founded: 1930. **Staff:** Prof 1; Other 1. **Subjects:** Personal finance loans and companies; money management; consumer credit; installment finance; consumer education and protection. **Holdings:** 1000 books. **Subscriptions:**

300 journals and other serials; 4 newspapers. **Services:** Interlibrary loans; copying; library not open to public. **Computerized Information Services:** New York Times Information Service. **Formerly:** Household Finance Corporation.

★5808★
HOUSING ADVOCATES - LAW AND CONSUMER AFFAIRS LIBRARY (Soc Sci)
717 Citizens Bldg. Phone: (216) 579-0575
Cleveland, OH 44114 Jim Buchanan, Dir.
Staff: Prof 1. **Subjects:** Housing, law, consumer affairs. **Special Collections:** Mobile homes. **Holdings:** 1415 books; 38 bound periodical volumes; 2 VF drawers of clippings on housing and community development; 1 vertical file of investigatory material on General Revenue Sharing; 7 VF drawers plus 6 feet of legal brief files. **Subscriptions:** 57 journals and other serials. **Services:** Copying; SDI; library open for in-house use with some special lending permission given. **Remarks:** Library offers consumer service to Ohio libraries, foundations and government agencies through a statewide toll-free hotline during specific hours.

★5809★
HOUSING ASSOCIATION OF DELAWARE VALLEY - LIBRARY (Soc Sci)
1317 Filbert St., Suite 523 Phone: (215) 563-4050
Philadelphia, PA 19107 Anthony Lewis, Managing Dir.
Subjects: Housing, urban development, local government, community development, association history. **Special Collections:** HADV studies. **Holdings:** 1000 books; 2000 pamphlets. **Subscriptions:** 50 journals and other serials. **Services:** Copying; library open to public. **Remarks:** Most of collection is housed in the Temple University - Central Library System - Urban Archives. **Staff:** James Berry, Res.Coord.

★5810★
HOUSTON ACADEMY OF MEDICINE - TEXAS MEDICAL CENTER LIBRARY (Med)
Jesse H. Jones Lib. Bldg. Phone: (713) 797-1230
Houston, TX 77030 Richard Lyders, Exec.Dir.
Founded: 1915. **Staff:** Prof 23; Other 37. **Subjects:** Medicine, nursing, psychology, psychiatry, biological sciences, pharmacology. **Holdings:** 165,000 volumes. **Subscriptions:** 4300 journals and other serials. **Services:** Interlibrary loans; copying; SDI; library open to public on a fee basis. **Computerized Information Services:** DIALOG, SDC, BRS, NLM, Institute for Scientific Information (ISI); computerized cataloging and circulation. **Networks/Consortia:** Member of OCLC; Houston Area Research Library Consortium (HARLIC); TALON. **Publications:** New Titles and News, monthly - available by mail; Annual Statistics of Medical School Libraries in the United States and Canada. **Staff:** James Bingham, Asst.Dir./Adm.Aff.; Sara Jean Jackson, Assoc.Dir., Pub.Serv.

★5811★
HOUSTON CHRONICLE - EDITORIAL LIBRARY (Publ)
Box 4260 Phone: (713) 220-7313
Houston, TX 77210 Sherry Ray, Libn.
Staff: Prof 2; Other 10. **Subjects:** General news and biography, Texana, Houstoniana. **Holdings:** 2500 books; 2 million clippings; 300,000 photographs; VF drawers of pamphlets; 1300 reels of microfilm; 55,000 microfiche. **Subscriptions:** 20 journals and other serials; 15 newspapers. **Services:** Copying; photograph sales; microfilm reprints; library not open to public. **Computerized Information Services:** New York Times Information Service. **Staff:** Barbara Seebers, Asst.Libn.

★5812★
HOUSTON CITY AVIATION DEPARTMENT - LIBRARY (Trans)†
Box 60106 Phone: (713) 443-4361
Houston, TX 77205 Susan Terauds, Libn.
Founded: 1976. **Staff:** 1. **Subjects:** Aviation. **Holdings:** Figures not available for books; Aviation Daily/Airport Operators Council International (AOCI) reports; slides of airports; technical reports. **Subscriptions:** 18 journals and other serials. **Services:** Interlibrary loans; copying; library open to public by appointment.

★5813★
HOUSTON - CITY LEGAL DEPARTMENT - LAW LIBRARY (Law)
4th Fl. City Hall
Box 1562 Phone: (713) 222-5151
Houston, TX 77251 F.J. Coleman, Jr., City Att.
Founded: 1910. **Staff:** Prof 1. **Subjects:** Municipal law and jurisprudence. **Holdings:** 22,000 volumes. **Services:** Library not open to public. **Staff:** Nick C. Demeris, Adm.Asst.

HOUSTON DOW CENTER LIBRARY
See: Dow Chemical U.S.A.

★5814★
HOUSTON INTERNATIONAL MINERALS CORPORATION - LIBRARY (Sci-Tech)
3801 E. Florida Ave.
Box 10200
Denver, CO 80210
Phone: (303) 692-6200
Sara E. Martin, Hd.Libn.
Founded: 1977. Staff: Prof 1; Other 1. Subjects: Geology, mining, business. Holdings: 14,000 books; 200 bound periodical volumes; 20 VF drawers and 5 flat case drawers of maps. Subscriptions: 105 journals and other serials. Services: Interlibrary loans; library not open to public. Computerized Information Services: DIALOG, SDC, Computerized Resources Information Bank (CRIB); computerized cataloging. Publications: Information Services Update, monthly - for internal distribution only. Remarks: A subsidiary of Tenneco, Inc.

★5815★
HOUSTON LIGHTING & POWER COMPANY - LIBRARY (Sci-Tech; Energy)
Box 1700
Houston, TX 77001
Phone: (713) 228-9211
Alicia B. Quinn, Supv.
Founded: 1968. Staff: Prof 1; Other 2. Subjects: Power systems, business management, computer science, control systems, civil engineering. Holdings: 3000 books and 100 bound periodical volumes. Subscriptions: 154 journals and other serials. Services: Interlibrary loans; copying.

★5816★
HOUSTON MUSEUM OF NATURAL SCIENCE - REFERENCE LIBRARY (Sci-Tech)
1 Hermann Circle Dr.
Houston, TX 77030
Phone: (713) 526-4273
Carl H. Ailsen, Act.Dir.
Founded: 1970. Staff: 1. Subjects: Natural science and related topics. Holdings: 10,000 books and bound periodical volumes; slides and motion pictures. Subscriptions: 100 journals and other serials. Services: Interlibrary loans; library open to public for reference use only.

HOUSTON OIL & MINERALS CORPORATION
See: Tenneco, Inc. - Tenneco Oil Exploration and Production - Corporate Library

★5817★
HOUSTON POST - LIBRARY/INFORMATION CENTER (Publ)
Phone: (713) 840-5830
Houston, TX 77001
Kathy Foley, Chf.Libn.
Founded: 1954. Staff: Prof 3; Other 6. Subjects: Newspaper reference topics. Special Collections: Texana (250 volumes). Holdings: 3500 books; 3 million pictures; 5.5 million clippings; 2000 pamphlets (cataloged). Subscriptions: 150 journals and other serials. Services: Interlibrary loans; copying; library not open to public. Computerized Information Services: DIALOG, New York Times Information Service, NEXIS.

HOUSTON POWER LIBRARY
See: Bechtel Power Corporation - Library

★5818★
HOUSTON PUBLIC LIBRARY - ARCHIVES AND MANUSCRIPT DEPARTMENT (Hist)
500 McKinney St.
Houston, TX 77002
Phone: (713) 224-5441
Dr. Louis J. Marchiafava, Archv.
Founded: 1976. Staff: 9. Subjects: Houston institutional records, local government records. Special Collections: Houston Manuscript Collection; Houston Architectural Collection; Houston Oral History Interviews; Mexican American Collection. Holdings: Archival and manuscript material; 500 tapes of oral history interviews. Services: Copying; photographic laboratory; library open to public. Remarks: Operates in cooperation with the State Archives Division of the Texas State Library, a Regional Historical Resource Depository Program for a seven county area.

★5819★
HOUSTON PUBLIC LIBRARY - BUSINESS, SCIENCE & TECHNOLOGY DEPARTMENT (Bus-Fin; Sci-Tech)
500 McKinney Ave.
Houston, TX 77002
Phone: (713) 224-5441
Brenda Peabody Tirrell, Dept.Hd.
Founded: 1961. Staff: Prof 23; Other 11. Subjects: Geology, business, engineering, mathematics, labor and economics, science, commerce, public services and utilities, manufactures. Special Collections: Barton, Dumble, Dewolf, and Morrison Collections (petroleum geology). Holdings: 145,684 books and bound periodical volumes; industry, federal and military standards

and specifications; company annual, 10K and proxy reports; Texas Drillers Logs; Electric Well Logs (Gulf Coast area); Texas Railroad Commission Production Records (oil, gas and distillate). Subscriptions: 1200 journals and other serials. Services: Interlibrary loans; copying. Computerized Information Services: DIALOG, New York Times Information Service, SDC; computerized cataloging, acquisitions and circulation.

★5820★
HOUSTON PUBLIC LIBRARY - CLAYTON LIBRARY - CENTER FOR GENEALOGICAL RESEARCH (Hist)
5300 Caroline St.
Houston, TX 77004
Phone: (713) 524-0101
Maxine Alcorn, Hd., Clayton Lib.
Staff: Prof 4; Other 7. Subjects: Local history and genealogy. Special Collections: Federal census, 1790-1880, 1900; military records; state and colonial records; county records; family histories. Holdings: 26,000 books; 300 bound periodical volumes; 20,000 reels of microfilm; 20,000 microfiche; VF material. Subscriptions: 285 journals and other serials. Services: Copying; library open. Special Catalogs: Film catalog (computer). Staff: Margaret J. Harris, Asst.Libn.

★5821★
HOUSTON PUBLIC LIBRARY - FILM COLLECTION DEPARTMENT (Aud-Vis)
500 McKinney Ave.
Houston, TX 77002
Phone: (713) 224-5441
Syma Zerkow, Dept.Hd.
Staff: Prof 4; Other 6. Holdings: 4510 16mm films. Services: Department open to public.

★5822★
HOUSTON PUBLIC LIBRARY - FINE ARTS & RECREATION DEPARTMENT (Art; Rec)
500 McKinney Ave.
Houston, TX 77002
Phone: (713) 224-5441
John Harvath, Dept.Hd.
Staff: Prof 10; Other 5. Subjects: Art, oriental art, decorative and minor arts, architecture, landscaping, sculpture, drawing, handicrafts, costumes, antiques, furniture, painting, photography, music, entertainment, theater, dance, sports. Special Collections: Current and retrospective sheet music; auction and exhibition catalogs; artist information file (28,133 items). Holdings: 90,600 books; 630 framed reproductions; 2500 slides; 23 posters; 3829 auction catalogs; 9471 pieces of sheet music; 23,148 vertical files; 30 sculpture replicas; 20,000 phonograph records. Subscriptions: 525 journals and other serials. Services: Interlibrary loans; copying. Computerized Information Services: Computerized cataloging, acquisitions and circulation.

★5823★
HOUSTON PUBLIC LIBRARY - SPECIAL COLLECTIONS DEPARTMENT (Hum)
500 McKinney Ave.
Houston, TX 77002
Phone: (713) 224-5441
Donna Grove, Dept.Hd.
Staff: Prof 1; Other 1. Subjects: U.S. slavery and Civil War, Salvation Army, religious history, 19th century travel. Special Collections: Milsaps Collection (6102 volumes); Annette Finnigan Collection (60 volumes); fine press books; Mark Twain, limited editions; Historical Juvenile Literature Collection; Norma Meldrum Children's Collection; Harriet Dickson Reynolds Room. Holdings: 10,500 books; 483 bound periodical volumes. Services: Copying; library open to public by appointment. Networks/Consortia: Member of Houston Area Research Library Consortium (HARLIC).

★5824★
HOUSTON PUBLIC LIBRARY - TEXAS AND LOCAL HISTORY DEPARTMENT (Hist)
500 McKinney Ave.
Houston, TX 77002
Phone: (713) 224-5441
Dorothy Glasser, Dept.Hd.
Staff: Prof 4; Other 3. Subjects: Houstonia, Texana. Special Collections: Bank of the Southwest/Schlueter Photographic Collection; Maresh Files, consisting of typescript of original research done for Federal Writers Project and materials used in Texas and Houston Writers Projects. Holdings: 20,596 volumes; 19,500 Texas state government documents (cataloged); 3000 municipal documents; newspaper clippings on microfiche; scrapbooks, maps and pamphlets; photographs. Services: Interlibrary loans (limited); copying; library open to public. Networks/Consortia: Member of Texas State Library Communications Network.

HOUSTON (Sam) REGIONAL LIBRARY AND RESEARCH CENTER
See: Texas State Library - Texas Archives Division - Sam Houston Regional Library and Research Center

HOUSTON (Sam) STATE UNIVERSITY
See: Sam Houston State University

★5825★
HOUZE, SHOURDS & MONTGOMERY, INC. - RESEARCH LIBRARY (Bus-Fin)†
2029 Century Park East
Los Angeles, CA 90067
Phone: (213) 522-6027
Elaine Kuo, Res.Dir.
Staff: Prof 1; Other 1. **Subjects:** Business, management, communications. **Holdings:** 300 books; 200 directories; 5 binders of newspaper and magazine clippings; 5 VF drawers of annual reports. **Subscriptions:** 65 journals and other serials; 15 newspapers. **Services:** Interlibrary loans; copying; library open to public with restrictions. **Publications:** Microports, monthly - by request; New Acquisitions, monthly - for internal distribution only.

HOWARD AIR FORCE BASE (Panama)
See: U.S. Air Force Base - Howard Base Library

HOWARD (Catherine E.) MEMORIAL LIBRARY
See: Springfield Library and Museums Association - Catherine E. Howard Memorial Library

HOWARD-TILTON MEMORIAL LIBRARY
See: Tulane University of Louisiana

★5826★
HOWARD UNIVERSITY - ARCHITECTURE & PLANNING LIBRARY (Art; Plan)
6th St. & Howard Pl., N.W.
Washington, DC 20059
Phone: (202) 636-7773
Mod Mekkawi, Libn.
Staff: Prof 1; Other 3. **Subjects:** Architectural history, construction and design, city planning, environmental design. **Special Collections:** Dominick Collection of pre-1900 books and periodicals on architecture (350 volumes); K. Keith Collection of books and photographs on indigenous African architecture. **Holdings:** 18,755 books; 1900 bound periodical volumes; 600 planning documents (cataloged); 29,000 slides, filmstrips and lantern frames; 850 reels of microfilm; 200 maps. **Subscriptions:** 360 journals and other serials. **Services:** Interlibrary loans; library open to public for reference use only. **Computerized Information Services:** Computerized cataloging, acquisitions and serials; slide indexing and retrieval system. **Networks/Consortia:** Member of OCLC through CAPCON; Consortium of Universities of the Washington Metropolitan Area. **Publications:** SLIDEX, a system for indexing, filing and retrieving slides; About the A & P Library; Resources for Architects and Planners in Washington, DC and Metropolitan Area; recent acquisitions. **Special Catalogs:** Subject-classified slide viewing cabinets supplemented by KWOC multi-aspect printed catalog. **Special Indexes:** Architectural Graphic Representations Index; index to chairs by famous architects; building types index.

★5827★
HOWARD UNIVERSITY - BERNARD B. FALL COLLECTION (Area-Ethnic)
Founders Library, Room 300A
Washington, DC 20059
Phone: (202) 636-7261
Steven I. Yoon, Cur.
Founded: 1968. **Staff:** Prof 1; Other 1. **Subjects:** Southeast Asia, China, Korea and Japan. **Holdings:** 5228 books; 67 periodicals; 300 pamphlets; 2000 vertical file items; 1010 reels of microfilm of the Asian studies; 84 maps. **Services:** Copying; bibliographical search; subject consultation; collection open to public. **Networks/Consortia:** Member of OCLC through CAPCON; Consortium of Universities of the Washington Metropolitan Area.

★5828★
HOWARD UNIVERSITY - CHANNING POLLOCK THEATRE COLLECTION (Theater)
University Library
Washington, DC 20059
Phone: (202) 636-7259
Marilyn E. Mahanand, Cur.
Founded: 1950. **Staff:** Prof 2; Other 1. **Subjects:** Theatre, drama, performing arts. **Special Collections:** William Warren I journals, 1796-1831; William Warren II diaries, dramatic scrapbooks, letters and prompt books covering the American Stage and specifically the Boston Museum for the period 1847-1888 (4 diaries and 2 scrapbooks). **Holdings:** 15,131 books; 1039 bound periodical volumes; 1904 other cataloged items; 84,752 clippings; 35,348 articles; 1923 autograph letters; autograph letter signatures, card autographs and archive autographs; 12,377 Carte de visite/Cabinet photographs; 6603 photographs; 260 manuscripts; 1493 pieces of sheet music; 2240 prints; 12,056 playbills; 485 rare programs; 516 souvenir programs; 283 reels of microfilm; 5571 microcards; 720 microfiche. **Subscriptions:** 306 journals and other serials; 5 newspapers. **Services:** Copying; collection open to public with identification. **Networks/Consortia:** Member of OCLC through CAPCON; Consortium of Universities of the Washington Metropolitan Area. **Special Indexes:** Indexes to scrapbooks - Olga Nethersole Collection (9 volumes of scrapbooks), Percy G. Williams Collection (Novelty Theatre, Brooklyn, programs), Alfred H. Woods Collection (theatrical contracts), Roland Reed Collection (playbills), Albert Berkowitz

Collection (photographs of the Old Vic Company), Channing Pollock Collection (complete library and his writings).

★5829★
HOWARD UNIVERSITY - FINE ARTS LIBRARY (Mus; Art)
Washington, DC 20059
Phone: (202) 636-7071
Carrie M. Hackney, Libn.
Founded: 1960. **Staff:** Prof 1; Other 2. **Subjects:** Music, art, drama, dance. **Special Collections:** Jazz Collection; Research Collection on black artists, musicians, playwrights, actors, dancers. **Holdings:** 14,907 books; 5791 phonograph records; 440 art prints; 1769 pieces of sheet music; 3516 scores; 1391 reels of microfilm. **Subscriptions:** 514 journals and other serials. **Services:** Interlibrary loans; copying; library open to public. **Computerized Information Services:** Computerized cataloging, acquisitions and serials. **Networks/Consortia:** Member of OCLC through CAPCON; Consortium of Universities of the Washington Metropolitan Area.

★5830★
HOWARD UNIVERSITY - HEALTH SCIENCES LIBRARY (Med)
600 W St., N.W.
Washington, DC 20059
Phone: (202) 636-6433
Joseph Forrest, Assoc.Dir.
Founded: 1927. **Staff:** Prof 7; Other 14. **Subjects:** Medicine, dentistry, nursing and allied health sciences. **Special Collections:** Sickle cell anemia (2 drawers of clippings and pamphlets); Negroes in medicine, dentistry and psychiatry (2 drawers and 20 boxes). **Holdings:** 147,067 books; 80,266 bound periodical volumes; 500 bibliographies (cataloged); 50 shelves of AV items; 20 VF drawers of disease, health and medical vertical files; 6 VF drawers of biographical files; 85 drawers of microfilm. **Subscriptions:** 3077 journals and other serials. **Services:** Interlibrary loans; copying; SDI; library open to public for reference use only. **Computerized Information Services:** MEDLARS; computerized cataloging, acquisitions and serials. **Networks/Consortia:** Member of OCLC through CAPCON; Consortium of Universities of the Washington Metropolitan Area; District of Columbia Health Libraries Information Network (DOCHSIN); Consortium of the District of Columbia Academic Health Sciences Libraries. **Publications:** Acquisitions List, bimonthly - to faculty and network libraries; Serials Holdings, annual; special subject bibliographies. **Special Catalogs:** Sickle cell anemia; hypertension among Negroes (both card). **Staff:** Bettifae Fassler, Assoc.Libn.; Maceo McCray, Assoc.Libn.; Julia Player, Assoc.Libn.; Howertine Farrell-Duncan, Libn./Supv., Ref.; Lavonda Broadnax, Asst.Libn.; Sekum Boni-Awotwi, Asst.Libn.

★5831★
HOWARD UNIVERSITY - HEALTH SCIENCES LIBRARY - ANNEX (Pharmacy) (Sci-Tech; Med)
2300 4th St.
Washington, DC 20059
Phone: (202) 636-6545
Mr. Jei Whan Kim, Libn.
Staff: Prof 1; Other 2. **Subjects:** Pharmacy, pharmacology, pharmacognosy, biomedical chemistry, microbiology. **Holdings:** 12,159 books; 2900 bound periodical volumes; 609 reels of microfilm; 368 cassettes; 2940 slides; 13,600 microfiche. **Subscriptions:** 306 journals and other serials. **Services:** Interlibrary loans; copying; library open to public with restrictions. **Computerized Information Services:** Computerized cataloging, acquisitions and serials. **Networks/Consortia:** Member of OCLC through CAPCON; Consortium of Universities of the Washington Metropolitan Area.

★5832★
HOWARD UNIVERSITY - MOORLAND-SPINGARN RESEARCH CENTER - LIBRARY DIVISION (Area-Ethnic)†
500 Howard Pl., N.W.
Washington, DC 20059
Phone: (202) 636-7480
Michael R. Winston, Dir. of Ctr.
Founded: 1914. **Staff:** Prof 10. **Subjects:** Afro-America, Africa, Caribbean. **Holdings:** 91,112 books; 8359 bound periodical volumes; 9935 microforms (cataloged). **Subscriptions:** 501 journals and other serials; 94 newspapers. **Services:** Copying; SDI; library open to public. **Networks/Consortia:** Member of Consortium of Universities of the Washington Metropolitan Area. **Staff:** James P. Johnson, Chf.Libn.; Betty M. Culpepper, Bibliog./Hd., Ref.Dept.; Janet L. Sims-Wood, Ref.Libn.; Doris M. Hull, Ref.Libn.; Cornelia R. Stokes, Coord., Rd.Serv.; Ethel M. Ellis, Cat.; Kathy I. Jenkins, Acq.Libn.; Ruth H. Li, Cat.; Bessie Fowler, Cat.

★5833★
HOWARD UNIVERSITY - MOORLAND-SPINGARN RESEARCH CENTER - MANUSCRIPT DIVISION (Area-Ethnic)†
500 Howard Pl., N.W.
Washington, DC 20059
Phone: (202) 636-7480
Dr. Michael R. Winston, Dir. of Ctr.
Founded: 1914. **Staff:** Prof 9; Other 5. **Subjects:** Afro-Americana, Africana, Caribbeana. **Special Collections:** Ralph J. Bunche Oral History Collection (individuals involved in 1960s civil rights activities; 700 tapes and transcripts); Arthur B. Spingarn Music Collection (4000 sheet music items);

Prints and Photographs (14,000, including Rose McClendon Collection of Photographs of Celebrated Negroes by Carl Van Vechten); Mary O.H. Williamson Collection; Griffith Davis Collection. **Holdings:** 1700 linear feet of processed manuscripts; 4800 linear feet of unprocessed manuscripts. **Services:** Copying; library open to qualified researchers. **Networks/Consortia:** Member of Consortium of Universities of the Washington Metropolitan Area. **Staff:** Thomas C. Battle, Cur. of Mss.; Karen L. Jefferson, Sr.Mss.Libn.; Esme B. Bhan, Mss.Res.Assoc.; W. Paul Coates, Mss.Libn.; Wilda D. Logan, Mss.Libn.; Greta S. Wilson, Mss.Libn.; Maricia Bracey, Prts. & Photo Libn.; Elinor D. Sinnette, Oral Hist.Libn.; Deborra A. Richardson, Music Libn.

★5834★
HOWARD UNIVERSITY - SCHOOL OF BUSINESS AND PUBLIC ADMINISTRATION - LIBRARY (Bus-Fin)
2345 Sherman Ave., N.W.   Phone: (202) 636-5683
Washington, DC 20059   Lucille B. Smiley, Libn.
Staff: Prof 3; Other 4. **Subjects:** Business administration, public administration, health services administration, management, accounting, real estate, insurance, marketing, finance. **Special Collections:** Small Business and Minority Economic Development. **Holdings:** 33,514 books; 500 bound periodical volumes; 226 small business management research reports; 82 technical assistance reports; 3500 reels of microfilm; 63,600 10K reports on microfiche. **Subscriptions:** 2240 journals and other serials; 32 newspapers. **Services:** Interlibrary loans; copying; library open to public for reference use only. **Computerized Information Services:** Computerized cataloging, acquisitions and serials. **Networks/Consortia:** Member of OCLC through CAPCON; Consortium of Universities of the Washington Metropolitan Area. **Publications:** Accessions, 10/year; The Negro in the Field of Business, an annotated bibliography.

★5835★
HOWARD UNIVERSITY - SCHOOL OF DIVINITY LIBRARY (Rel-Theol)
1240 Randolph St. N.E.   Phone: (202) 636-7282
Washington, DC 20017   Irene Owens, Libn.
Founded: 1932. **Staff:** Prof 1; Other 3. **Subjects:** Theology. **Special Collections:** Afro-American religious studies. **Holdings:** 87,579 books; 10,225 bound periodical volumes. **Subscriptions:** 407 journals and other serials; 6 newspapers. **Services:** Interlibrary loans; copying; library open to public with restrictions (in-house circulation). **Computerized Information Services:** Computerized cataloging, acquisitions and serials. **Networks/Consortia:** Member of OCLC through CAPCON; Consortium of Universities of the Washington Metropolitan Area; Washington Theological Consortium. **Publications:** Biographical Directory of Negro Ministers, revised periodically; Afro-American Religious Studies, supplements issued periodically; The Howard University Bibliography of African and Afro-American Religious Studies, revised periodically. **Special Indexes:** Alphabetical name index of 1800 Negro ministers with addresses.

★5836★
HOWARD UNIVERSITY - SCHOOL OF LAW - ALLEN MERCER DANIEL LAW LIBRARY (Law)†
2900 Van Ness St., N.W.   Phone: (202) 686-6684
Washington, DC 20008   Judy Dimes-Smith, Dir.
Founded: 1867. **Staff:** Prof 6; Other 16. **Subjects:** Law. **Special Collections:** Civil rights, African customary law, English law. **Holdings:** 154,689 books and bound periodical volumes; 317,306 microforms; 44 motion pictures; 179 tape cassettes; 2 VF drawers of pamphlets. **Subscriptions:** 499 journals and other serials. **Services:** Interlibrary loans; copying; library open to public with restrictions. **Computerized Information Services:** LEXIS, WESTLAW. **Networks/Consortia:** Member of Consortium of Universities of the Washington Metropolitan Area. **Publications:** Periodical index, monthly - for internal distribution only. **Special Indexes:** Index of microform holdings (pamphlet); Checklist of U.S. Congress Committee Hearings & Committee Prints (pamphlet); Checklist of United Nations Documents (pamphlet); Legislative Research Documents: state (pamphlets); Subject List of Legal Lectures on Tape (pamphlet). **Staff:** Ms. Meera Kashyap, Circ./Tech.Serv.Libn.; Helen Miller, Ref./Cat.Libn.; Mrs. Myung-Jha Kim, AV Libn.

★5837★
HOWARD UNIVERSITY - SCIENCE AND TECHNOLOGY LIBRARY (Sci-Tech)
The Carnegie Bldg.   Phone: (202) 636-5744
Washington, DC 20059   Doris Mitchell, Sci. & Tech.Libn.
Founded: 1947. **Staff:** Prof 5; Other 5. **Subjects:** Engineering - civil, chemical, mechanical, electrical, urban systems; computer science; chemistry. **Holdings:** 91,842 books and bound periodical volumes; 2200 pamphlets and reports; 355 dissertations; 6302 reels of microfilm; 285,153 microfiche; 14 filmstrips; 11 motion pictures. **Subscriptions:** 854 journals and other serials.

Services: Interlibrary loans; copying; SDI; library open to public for reference use only. **Computerized Information Services:** DIALOG, SDC, BRS, MEDLARS; computerized cataloging, acquisitions and serials. **Networks/Consortia:** Member of OCLC through CAPCON; Consortium of Universities of the Washington Metropolitan Area. **Publications:** Black Engineers in the United States directory. **Formerly:** Its Chemistry Library and its Engineering Library. **Staff:** Mrs. Clemence Perslin, Assoc.Libn.; Ruth Hodges, Asst.Libn.; Mostassa Sadegh, Asst.Libn.

★5838★
HOWARD UNIVERSITY - SOCIAL WORK LIBRARY (Soc Sci)
6th St. & Howard Pl., N.W.   Phone: (202) 636-7316
Washington, DC 20059   Brenda J. Cox, Libn.
Founded: 1971. **Staff:** Prof 1; Other 3. **Subjects:** Social work theory and practice; social policy, planning and administration; social welfare problems of black community; urban-oriented problems; human development. **Holdings:** 22,360 books; 3061 bound periodical volumes. **Subscriptions:** 731 journals and other serials. **Services:** Interlibrary loans; copying; library open to public for reference use only. **Computerized Information Services:** Computerized cataloging, acquisitions and serials. **Networks/Consortia:** Member of OCLC through CAPCON; Consortium of Universities of the Washington Metropolitan Area.

★5839★
HOWARD YOUNG MEDICAL CENTER - HEALTH SCIENCE LIBRARY (Med)
Box 470   Phone: (715) 356-8000
Woodruff, WI 54568   Debra L. Nordgren, Libn.
Founded: 1973. **Staff:** Prof 1. **Subjects:** Medicine, nursing. **Holdings:** 1000 books and bound periodical volumes; 200 pamphlets (cataloged); 100 video cassettes; 500 audio cassettes. **Subscriptions:** 110 journals and other serials. **Services:** Interlibrary loans; copying; library open to public with restrictions. **Computerized Information Services:** MEDLINE. **Networks/Consortia:** Member of Northern Wisconsin Health Science Libraries Cooperative; Regional Medical Library - Region 3.

HOWE ARCHITECTURE LIBRARY
See: Arizona State University

HOWE LIBRARY
See: Shenandoah College & Conservatory of Music

HOWE (Lucien) LIBRARY OF OPHTHALMOLOGY
See: Harvard University - School of Medicine - Lucien Howe Library of Ophthalmology

HOWE (Percy) MEMORIAL LIBRARY
See: Forsyth Dental Center - Percy Howe Memorial Library

HRB-SINGER, INC.
See: Singer Company

HRIS
See: National Academy of Sciences - National Research Council - Highway Research Information Service

HRUSKA (Roman L.) U.S. MEAT ANIMAL RESEARCH CENTER
See: U.S.D.A. - Agricultural Research Service - Meat Animal Research Center

★5840★
HTB, INC. - TECHNICAL INFORMATION CENTER (Sci-Tech; Plan)
Box 1845   Phone: (405) 525-7451
Oklahoma City, OK 73101   Retha Robertson, Libn.
Staff: Prof 1; Other 2. **Subjects:** Architecture, engineering, planning. **Holdings:** 300 books; 50 bound periodical volumes; 200 government documents; 15,000 photographs; 15,000 slides; 50 filmstrips; 750 unbound reports. **Subscriptions:** 250 journals and other serials; 10 newspapers. **Services:** Interlibrary loans; library not open to public.

HUBBARD (Elbert) LIBRARY AND MUSEUM
See: Aurora Historical Society - Elbert Hubbard Library and Museum

★5841★
HUBBELL (Harvey), INC. - LIBRARY
584 Derby-Milford Rd.   Phone: (203) 789-1100
Orange, CT 06477   Roger M. Search, V.P.Indus.Rel.
Staff: 1. **Subjects:** Electricity. **Holdings:** Figures not available. **Services:** Library not open to public.

★5842★
HUBER (J.M.) CORPORATION - RESEARCH LIBRARY (Sci-Tech)†
Box 2831   Phone: (806) 274-6331
Borger, TX 79007   Phyllis Vaughn, Libn.
Subjects: Chemistry and engineering. **Holdings:** 1500 books; 2000 bound
periodical volumes. **Subscriptions:** 40 journals and other serials.

HUDELSON LIBRARY
See: First Meridian Heights Presbyterian Church

★5843★
HUDSON COUNTY LAW LIBRARY (Law)†
Hudson County Administration Bldg.
595 Newark Ave.   Phone: (201) 795-6629
Jersey City, NJ 07306
Staff: 1. **Subjects:** Law. **Holdings:** 19,000 volumes. **Services:** Library not
open to public.

★5844★
HUDSON ESSEX TERRAPLANE CLUB, INC. - LIBRARY (Rec)
5765 Munger Rd.   Phone: (313) 434-3289
Ypsilanti, MI 48197   Charles Liskow, Libn.
Staff: 1. **Subjects:** History and detail specifications of Hudson, Essex, and
Terraplane cars. **Special Collections:** 2000 original factory photos of Hudson
Motor Car Company. **Holdings:** Several hundred books, owners' manuals, shop
manuals, parts books, service and sales literature for Hudson, Essex and
Terraplane cars, 1909-1957. **Services:** Copying (fee); library not open to
public.

★5845★
HUDSON INSTITUTE - LIBRARY (Soc Sci)
Quaker Ridge Rd.   Phone: (914) 762-0700
Croton-On-Hudson, NY 10520   Mildred Schneck, Libn.
Founded: 1962. **Staff:** Prof 1; Other 1. **Subjects:** Possible world futures -
social, economic, political; public policy; military affairs; arms control.
Holdings: 12,000 books; 4000 reports; 700 reels of microfilm; 2 drawers of
microfiche. **Subscriptions:** 300 journals and other serials; 23 newspapers.
Services: Interlibrary loans; copying; library access by special arrangement
only. **Computerized Information Services:** DIALOG, New York Times
Information Service.

★5846★
HUDSON LIBRARY AND HISTORICAL SOCIETY (Hist)
22 Aurora St.   Phone: (216) 653-6658
Hudson, OH 44236   Thomas L. Vince, Libn. & Cur.
Founded: 1910. **Staff:** Prof 4; Other 6. **Subjects:** Hudson and Summit
County history, Ohio history and genealogy, John Brown. **Special Collections:**
Clarence Gee Collection and Clark-Brown Collection (John Brown Material).
Holdings: 54,060 books and bound periodical volumes; 8173 phonograph
records; 232 reels of microfilm; 531 microfiche; 82 slides; 94 boxes of
manuscripts. **Subscriptions:** 175 journals and other serials; 8 newspapers.
Services: Interlibrary loans; copying; library open to public. **Networks/
Consortia:** Member of Information and Referral Service of Los Angeles
County, Inc. (INFO); North Central Library Cooperative. **Publications:** Annual
Report; Ex Libris, monthly. **Staff:** Gail E. Dowell, Cat. & Music Libn.; Marjorie
Origlio, Children's Libn.; James F. Caccamo, Archv.

★5847★
HUDSON RIVER ENVIRONMENTAL SOCIETY - LIBRARY (Env-Cons)
675 West 252nd St.   Phone: (212) 884-4199
Bronx, NY 10471   Florence Smeraldi, Info.Off./Mgr., Oper.
Founded: 1978. **Staff:** 1. **Subjects:** Marine biology, regional planning, waste
treatment, toxicology. **Special Collections:** Hudson River Ecology (4 biennial
symposia). **Holdings:** 350 books. **Services:** Library open to public by
appointment.

HUDSON RIVER MUSEUM
See: Yonkers Historical Society - Library

★5848★
HUDSON RIVER PSYCHIATRIC CENTER - MEDICAL LIBRARY (Med)
                                            Phone: (914) 452-8000
Poughkeepsie, NY 12601   Joyce Cunningham, Libn.
Founded: 1970. **Staff:** Prof 1; Other 1. **Subjects:** Psychiatry, psychology,
medicine. **Holdings:** 6500 books; 12,000 bound periodical volumes;
Subscriptions: 200 journals and other serials. **Services:** Interlibrary loans;
copying; library open to public for reference use only. **Networks/Consortia:**
Member of Southeastern New York Library Resources Council (SENYLRC).
Formerly: New York School of Psychiatry and Hudson River Psychiatric Center

- Medical Library.

★5849★
**HUDSON VALLEY COMMUNITY COLLEGE - DWIGHT MARVIN LEARNING
   RESOURCES CENTER** (Sci-Tech)†
80 Vandenburgh Ave.   Phone: (518) 283-1100
Troy, NY 12180   James F. McCoy, Dir.
Founded: 1953. **Staff:** Prof 6; Other 25. **Subjects:** Literature, history,
business, engineering technology, nursing, automotive technology, dental
hygiene, community services, mortuary science. **Special Collections:**
Automobile service manuals (95 volumes); Microbook Library of American
Civilization and Library of English. **Holdings:** 91,037 books; 10,207 bound
periodical volumes; 12,457 monographs in microform; 5940 reels of
microfilmed periodicals; 3120 periodicals on microcards; 600 maps.
Subscriptions: 803 journals and other serials; 29 newspapers. **Services:**
Interlibrary loans; copying; library open to public. **Networks/Consortia:**
Member of Capital District Library Council for Reference & Research
Resources. **Publications:** News From the Library, bimonthly - faculty and staff
distribution. **Special Catalogs:** Periodicals and microfilms listing; periodical
indexes listing. **Staff:** John White, Pub.Serv.Libn.; Susan Blandy, Ref.Libn.; B.
Twiggs, Tech.Serv.Libn.; Kenneth Williams, Per.Libn.; Christine Root,
Coll.Dev.Libn.; Mary Kirsch, Spec. Projects; N. Longacker, AV Spec.

★5850★
HUDSON'S BAY COMPANY ARCHIVES (Hist)
Manitoba Archives Bldg.
200 Vaughan St.   Phone: (204) 944-4949
Winnipeg, MB, Canada R3C 0V8   Shirlee Anne Smith, Kpr.
Staff: Prof 6; Other 2. **Subjects:** History - Canadian Arctic, Canadian West,
northwestern United States, and Hudson's Bay Company; fur trade history.
Holdings: 3000 books; 3000 linear feet of classified documents. **Services:**
Library open to public. **Staff:** Judith Beattie, Hd., Res. & Ref.

★5851★
HUDSON'S BAY COMPANY - LIBRARY (Hist)
Hudson's Bay House
77 Main St.   Phone: (204) 943-0881
Winnipeg, MB, Canada R3C 2R1   Carol Preston, Libn.
Founded: 1920. **Staff:** Prof 1; Other 2. **Subjects:** History of Hudson's Bay
Company and Western Canada; history of Arctic exploration; Indians and
Inuit. **Holdings:** 7000 volumes; 200 vertical files; 25,000 photographs and
transparencies; 2000 pamphlets and reprints. **Subscriptions:** 100 journals
and other serials. **Services:** Copying (restricted); library open to public for
reference use only.

★5852★
HUDSON'S BAY OIL & GAS COMPANY, LTD. - CORPORATE LIBRARY
700 Second St., S.W.
Calgary, AB, Canada T2P 0X5
Defunct. Holdings absorbed by Dome Petroleum Limited.

★5853★
HUEBNER (S.S.) FOUNDATION FOR INSURANCE EDUCATION - LIBRARY
   (Bus-Fin)
W-145 Dietrich Hall
University of Pennsylvania   Phone: (215) 898-7621
Philadelphia, PA 19104   Elizabeth W. Gillies, Libn.
Founded: 1941. **Staff:** Prof 1. **Subjects:** Insurance, economics. **Holdings:**
5000 volumes; 12 VF drawers; 90 dissertations. **Subscriptions:** 80 journals
and other serials. **Services:** Interlibrary loans; copying (limited); library open to
public with restrictions.

HUEY (William P.) GRAPHIC ARTS LIBRARY
See: Tree of Life Press - Library and Archives

HUFELAND MEMORIAL LIBRARY
See: Huguenot-Thomas Paine Historical Association of New Rochelle

HUFF MEMORIAL LIBRARY
See: Bradford Hospital

★5854★
HUFFMAN MEMORIAL UNITED METHODIST CHURCH - LIBRARY (Rel-Theol)
2802 Renick   Phone: (816) 233-0239
St. Joseph, MO 64507   Dorothy Thomann, Libn.
Founded: 1958. **Subjects:** Religion. **Holdings:** 3444 books; 361 filmstrips,
tapes and records.

★5855★
HUGHES AIRCRAFT COMPANY - CANOGA PARK LIBRARY (Sci-Tech)
Bldg. CP-2, Mail Sta. T-10
8433 Fallbrook Ave.   Phone: (213) 833-2400
Canoga Park, CA 91304   Donald C. Paul, Libn.
Founded: 1966. **Staff:** Prof 2. **Subjects:** Electronics, physics, mathematics, missiles and rockets. **Holdings:** 9870 books; 925 bound periodical volumes; 56,000 microfiche reports. **Subscriptions:** 235 journals and other serials. **Services:** Library not open to public.

★5856★
HUGHES AIRCRAFT COMPANY - EL SEGUNDO LIBRARY (Sci-Tech)†
Bldg. 512, Mail Sta. V-311
Box 92919   Phone: (213) 648-4192
Los Angeles, CA 90009   Vicky S. Huang, Libn.
Founded: 1963. **Staff:** Prof 2. **Subjects:** Space sciences, electronics, telecommunications, radar, optics, physics. **Special Collections:** Satellite communications. **Holdings:** 8400 books; 160 bound periodical volumes; 6000 microfiche reports. **Subscriptions:** 161 journals and other serials. **Services:** Library not open to public. **Computerized Information Services:** DIALOG, SDC, DTIC, NASA/RECON; internal database. **Remarks:** Library is located at 1950 East Imperial Highway, Los Angeles, CA 90245. **Staff:** Susan G. Clifford, Libn.

★5857★
HUGHES AIRCRAFT COMPANY - ELECTRO-OPTICAL & DATA SYSTEMS GROUP - COMPANY TECHNICAL DOCUMENT CENTER (Sci-Tech)
2000 E. El Segundo Blvd.
Bldg. E1, Mail Sta. E110
Box 902   Phone: (213) 616-0414
El Segundo, CA 90245   Billy W. Campbell, Supv.
Founded: 1958. **Staff:** Prof 6; Other 8. **Subjects:** Aeronautics, electronics, engineering, missile technology, mathematics, physics, weapon systems. **Holdings:** 75,000 documents; 300,000 documents on microfiche. **Services:** Center open to public by appointment only. **Publications:** Library Information Bulletin, monthly - for internal distribution only. **Special Catalogs:** Hughes Document Catalog, hard copy and 16mm film, automated, on COM (computer output microfilm). **Staff:** Jeffrey A. Sevier, Tech.Proc.Libn.; Dorothy Webb, Pub.Serv.Libn.; Frederick W. Patten, Cat.Libn.; Daphne R. King, Cat.Libn.; Josephine V. Drong, Security & Storage.

★5858★
HUGHES AIRCRAFT COMPANY - ELECTRO-OPTICAL & DATA SYSTEMS GROUP - INFORMATION RESOURCES SECTION (Sci-Tech)
2000 E. El Segundo Blvd.
Bldg. E1, Mail Sta. J145
Box 902   Phone: (213) 616-8178
El Segundo, CA 90245   Clinton E. Merritt, Hd.
Founded: 1956. **Staff:** Prof 15; Other 17. **Subjects:** Electronics, aeronautics, missile technology, weapons systems, space sciences, physics, chemistry, mathematics, management. **Holdings:** 25,000 books; 30,000 bound periodical volumes; 75,000 technical documents; 300,000 technical documents on microfiche; 9500 microfiche journals. **Subscriptions:** 703 journals and other serials. **Services:** Interlibrary loans; copying; literature searching; bibliographic services (all for employees only); library open to public by appointment. **Publications:** Library Information Guide, irregular - for internal distribution only.

★5859★
HUGHES AIRCRAFT COMPANY - ELECTRO-OPTICAL & DATA SYSTEMS GROUP - TECHNICAL LIBRARY (Sci-Tech)
2000 E. El Segundo Blvd.,
Bldg. E1, Mail Sta. E117
Box 902   Phone: (213) 616-3333
El Segundo, CA 90245   Mr. Masse Bloomfield, Supv.
Founded: 1950. **Staff:** Prof 5; Other 7. **Subjects:** Electronics, mathematics, physics, chemistry, management. **Holdings:** 26,500 books; 22,000 bound periodical volumes; 19,120 journals on microfiche. **Subscriptions:** 700 journals and other serials. **Services:** Interlibrary loans; copying; literature searching and bibliographic services (all for employees only); library open to public by appointment only. **Staff:** Rose Konrath, Pub.Serv.Libn.; Annette Sterlin, Tech.Serv.Libn.; Marcia J. Williams, Per.Libn.; Howard Gantman, Acq.

★5860★
HUGHES AIRCRAFT COMPANY - ENGINEERING LIBRARY (Sci-Tech)
500 Superior Ave.   Phone: (714) 759-2492
Newport Beach, CA 92663   Barbara Squyres, Engr.Libn.
Founded: 1957. **Staff:** 1. **Subjects:** Solid state electronics, semiconductors, physics, crystallography, transistors, chemistry. **Holdings:** 4404 books; 2356

bound periodical volumes; 393 microfiche; 55 reels of microfilm. **Subscriptions:** 95 journals and other serials. **Services:** Copying; library not open to public.

★5861★
HUGHES AIRCRAFT COMPANY - GROUND SYSTEMS GROUP - TECHNICAL LIBRARY (Sci-Tech)
Bldg. 600, M.S. C-222   Phone: (714) 732-3506
Fullerton, CA 92633   Don H. Matsumiya, Libn.
Founded: 1957. **Staff:** Prof 2; Other 6. **Subjects:** Radar, sonar, military communications, command and control systems. **Holdings:** 9000 books; 5700 bound periodical volumes; 54,240 technical reports (cataloged); 1000 maps; 500 standards. **Subscriptions:** 220 journals and other serials; 5 newspapers. **Services:** Interlibrary loans; copying (limited); library open to public by appointment. **Computerized Information Services:** DTIC. **Networks/Consortia:** Member of Libraries of Orange County Network (LOCNET). **Publications:** Accessions List, monthly. **Staff:** Wilma Price, Acq.Libn.; Sophie Tung, ILL Libn.

★5862★
HUGHES AIRCRAFT COMPANY - HUGHES RESEARCH LABORATORIES LIBRARY (Sci-Tech)
3011 Malibu Canyon Rd.   Phone: (213) 456-6411
Malibu, CA 90265   Tobyann Mandel, Libn.
Founded: 1959. **Staff:** Prof 1; Other 1. **Subjects:** Theoretical and applied physics, electronics. **Holdings:** 15,000 books; 4000 bound periodical volumes. **Subscriptions:** 300 journals and other serials. **Services:** Interlibrary loans; copying; library open by appointment to qualified users. **Computerized Information Services:** DIALOG; internal database.

★5863★
HUGHES AIRCRAFT COMPANY - SANTA BARBARA RESEARCH CENTER - TECHNICAL LIBRARY (Sci-Tech)
75 Coromar Dr.   Phone: (805) 968-3511
Goleta, CA 93117   Susan K. Gentry, Tech.Libn.
Staff: Prof 1; Other 3. **Subjects:** Infrared technology, solid state electronics, electro-optics, space science and technology, solid state physics, astronomy. **Holdings:** 3000 books; 150 bound periodical volumes; 300 unbound volumes; 3000 microfiche reports. **Subscriptions:** 161 journals and other serials. **Services:** Interlibrary loans; library not open to public. **Computerized Information Services:** DIALOG, DTIC. **Publications:** Library Bulletin, bimonthly; Management Bulletin, bimonthly; Infrared Abstracts, bimonthly.

HUGHES HELICOPTERS
See: Summa Corporation

★5864★
HUGHES & HILL - LIBRARY (Law)
1000 Mercantile Dallas Bldg.   Phone: (214) 651-0477
Dallas, TX 75201   Ann Jeter, Libn.
Staff: Prof 1. **Subjects:** Law. **Holdings:** 8000 books. **Services:** Interlibrary loans; copying; SDI; library open to public by appointment. **Computerized Information Services:** LEXIS, New York Times Information Service. **Publications:** Library bulletin, weekly. **Special Indexes:** Index to in-house research.

★5865★
HUGHES, HUBBARD, AND REED - LIBRARY (Law)
One Wall St.   Phone: (212) 709-7777
New York, NY 10005   Laurie A. Hart, Libn.
Staff: Prof 2; Other 5. **Subjects:** Antitrust, securities, taxation, estates, wills, trusts. **Holdings:** 25,000 books. **Subscriptions:** 100 journals and other serials. **Services:** Interlibrary loans; copying. **Computerized Information Services:** DIALOG, SDC, LEXIS, WESTLAW. **Staff:** John Fitzgerald, Asst.Libn.

HUGHES (Langston) COMMUNITY LIBRARY AND CULTURAL CENTER
See: Queens Borough Public Library

HUGHES (Langston) MEMORIAL LIBRARY
See: Inner City Cultural Center - Langston Hughes Memorial Library

HUGHES (Langston) MEMORIAL LIBRARY
See: Lincoln University - Langston Hughes Memorial Library

HUGHES RESEARCH LABORATORIES LIBRARY
See: Hughes Aircraft Company

HUGHES (Thomas) CHILDREN'S LIBRARY
See: Chicago Public Library Cultural Center - Thomas Hughes Children's
Library

★5866★
HUGHES (Thomas) LIBRARY (Rare Book)
Box 8   Phone: (615) 628-2441
Rugby, TN 37733   Barbara Stagg Paylor, Exec.Dir.
Founded: 1882. **Subjects:** Victorian literature - novels, poetry, children's
literature. **Holdings:** 7000 books. **Services:** Library open to public for
research by request, and for viewing as part of guided tour of Rugby.
Remarks: Library contains original 7000 books and equipment unchanged
since it was built in 1882; maintained by Historic Rugby, Inc.

★5867★
HUGHES TOOL COMPANY - BUSINESS AND TECHNICAL LIBRARY (Sci-Tech)
Box 2539   Phone: (713) 924-2990
Houston, TX 77001   Marlene Shaughnessy, Libn.
Founded: 1948. **Staff:** Prof 1. **Subjects:** Metallurgy, rock mechanics,
chemistry. **Holdings:** 4000 volumes. **Subscriptions:** 175 journals and other
serials; 20 newspapers. **Services:** Interlibrary loans; copying; library not open
to public. **Computerized Information Services:** DIALOG, SDC. **Remarks:** The
library is located at 5425 Polk Ave., Houston, TX 77023.

HUGO MOORE PARK - CANAL MUSEUM
See: Pennsylvania Canal Society - Canal Museum

★5868★
HUGUENOT HISTORICAL SOCIETY, NEW PALTZ - LIBRARY (Hist)†
18 Brodhead Ave.
Box 339   Phone: (914) 255-1660
New Paltz, NY 12561   Kenneth E. Hasbrouck, Dir.
Founded: 1894. **Staff:** Prof 4; Other 15. **Subjects:** History and genealogy of
Ulster and Orange counties, history of New York State, Huguenots, Civil War.
Special Collections: Lincoln Collection. **Holdings:** 3000 books; 40 reports;
600 manuscripts; 2500 documents. **Subscriptions:** 10 journals and other
serials. **Services:** Copying; library open to public for reference use only by
appointment.

★5869★
HUGUENOT SOCIETY OF AMERICA - LIBRARY (Hist)
122 E. 58th St.   Phone: (212) 755-0592
New York, NY 10022   Mrs. Nicholas P. Christy, Exec.Sec.
Staff: 1. **Subjects:** French Huguenot migration to America, Huguenot history
in France and elsewhere, biography, genealogy. **Holdings:** 2035 books and
bound periodical volumes; 30 manuscripts; 20 autograph letters. **Services:**
Copying; library open to public with restrictions.

★5870★
HUGUENOT SOCIETY OF SOUTH CAROLINA - LIBRARY (Hist)†
25 Chalmers St.   Phone: (803) 723-3235
Charleston, SC 29401
Staff: Prof 2. **Subjects:** Genealogical data on Huguenots and allied families,
especially French Huguenots. **Special Collections:** Publications of the
Huguenot Society of London (England); Gorssline collection on Huguenot
subjects. **Holdings:** 1000 volumes; 4 VF drawers of genealogical data.
Subscriptions: 12 journals and other serials. **Services:** Library open to public
on a limited basis.

★5871★
**HUGUENOT-THOMAS PAINE HISTORICAL ASSOCIATION OF NEW
ROCHELLE - HUFELAND MEMORIAL LIBRARY (Hist)**
893 North Ave.   Phone: (914) 632-5376
New Rochelle, NY 10804   Ruth M. Phillips, Chm.
Staff: Prof 1. **Subjects:** Local history. **Special Collections:** Early Americana
with emphasis on lower Westchester County and upper Bronx. **Holdings:**
5000 books; maps; manuscripts. **Services:** Library open to scholars by
appointment.

HUIDEKOPER LIBRARY
See: Montana State University - Veterinary Research Laboratory

HULL (Cordell) LAW LIBRARY
See: Samford University - Cumberland School of Law - Cordell Hull Law
Library

HUMACAO UNIVERSITY COLLEGE
See: University of Puerto Rico

★5872★
HUMAN FACTORS RESEARCH, INC. - TECHNICAL LIBRARY (Soc Sci)†
5775 Dawson Ave.   Phone: (805) 964-0591
Goleta, CA 93117   Paulette Moggia, Libn.
Founded: 1967. **Staff:** 1. **Subjects:** Human factors, psychiatry, psychology,
biology, education, transportation, engineering. **Holdings:** 720 books; 600
bound periodical volumes; 195 reprints (cataloged); 125 bibliographies; 9400
reports; 103 microfiche. **Subscriptions:** 160 journals and other serials; 5
newspapers. **Services:** Interlibrary loans; copying; library open to public by
request. **Publications:** Accessions lists, semimonthly; company bibliography.

★5873★
HUMAN LACTATION CENTER, LTD. - LIBRARY (Soc Sci)
666 Sturges Hwy.   Phone: (203) 259-5995
Westport, CT 06880   Dana Raphael, Dir.
Founded: 1975. **Staff:** 5. **Subjects:** Breastfeeding, maternal and infant
nutrition, social science, demography, childbirth, women in development,
supportive behavior, mammalian reproduction. **Holdings:** 2000 volumes; 4 VF
drawers of reports, manuscripts and dissertations; 3 tapes; 1 film.
Subscriptions: 70 journals and other serials; 5 newspapers. **Publications:**
The Lactation Review, irregular - to friends of the center, and for sale.

★5874★
HUMAN RELATIONS AREA FILES, INC. (Soc Sci)
755 Prospect St.   Phone: (203) 777-2334
New Haven, CT 06511   Timothy J. O'Leary, Dir., File Res.
Founded: 1949. **Staff:** Prof 1. **Subjects:** Anthropology, ethnology,
geography. **Holdings:** 5000 books; 3 million file slips. **Subscriptions:** 25
journals and other serials. **Services:** Interlibrary loans; copying; library open to
public by advance arrangement. **Publications:** Behavior Science Research,
quarterly; monographs.

HUMAN RELATIONS RESEARCH CENTRE (Montreal, PQ)
See: Centre de Recherches en Relations Humaines - Bibliotheque

★5875★
HUMAN RESOURCES CENTER - RESEARCH LIBRARY (Soc Sci)
I.U. Willets & Searingtown Rds.   Phone: (516) 747-5400
Albertson, NY 11507   Ruth A. Velleman, Lib.Dir.
Founded: 1962. **Staff:** Prof 1; Other 1. **Subjects:** Vocational rehabilitation of
disabled, job placements, attitudes, career education, self sufficiency,
recreation, special education. **Holdings:** 2000 books; 45 VF drawers of
pamphlets; 715 microforms; 30 films and video cassettes; 300 volumes of
periodicals on microfilm. **Subscriptions:** 250 journals and other serials.
Services: Interlibrary loans; copying; library open to public by appointment.
Networks/Consortia: Member of Long Island Library Resources Council.

★5876★
HUMAN RESOURCES NETWORK - INFORMATION CENTER (Soc Sci)
2011 Chancellor St.   Phone: (215) 299-2920
Philadelphia, PA 19103   Eleanor Mitchell, Dir.
Staff: Prof 4; Other 2. **Subjects:** Corporate social responsibility, special
interest groups, public issues. **Special Collections:** Organization files (1000);
corporate social reports (100). **Holdings:** 5500 books and bound periodical
volumes; 1600 clipping files; 250 foundation files; 100 research
organizations files. **Subscriptions:** 500 journals and other serials; 10
newspapers. **Services:** Copying; SDI; library not open to public.
Computerized Information Services: Internal database. **Publications:** Public
Issues Index. **Staff:** Carla B. McLean, Asst.Dir.; Kathleen O'Donnell, Supv.
Indexer; Maureen Neville, Indexer; Deborah Staves, Indexer.

★5877★
HUMAN RESOURCES RESEARCH ORGANIZATION - CALIFORNIA LIBRARY
27857 Berwick Dr.
Carmel, CA 93923
Founded: 1952. **Subjects:** Military behavioral research, psychology,
sociology, education, mental health, management. **Holdings:** 1500 books;
850 bound periodical volumes; 12,500 technical reports (cataloged); 2000
microfiche; 10,000 unbound periodicals. **Networks/Consortia:** Member of
CIN. **Remarks:** Presently inactive.

★5878★
**HUMAN RESOURCES RESEARCH ORGANIZATION - VAN EVERA LIBRARY
(Soc Sci)**
300 N. Washington St.   Phone: (703) 549-3611
Alexandria, VA 22314   Josephine R. Hunter, Libn.
Founded: 1951. **Staff:** Prof 2. **Subjects:** Psychology, human engineering,

education, computer-assisted instruction. **Holdings:** 2500 books; 220 bound periodical volumes; 30,000 technical reports (cataloged); 11,000 microfiche. **Subscriptions:** 50 journals and other serials. **Services:** Interlibrary loans; copying (limited); library open to public by appointment. **Publications:** HumRRO Bibliography; HumRRO Reports. **Remarks:** Human Resources Research Organization has its central headquarters in Alexandria, Virginia.

★5879★
HUMAN RIGHTS INTERNET - LIBRARY (Soc Sci)
1502 Ogden St., N.W.　　　　　　　Phone: (202) 462-4320
Washington, DC 20010　　　　　　　Charles Lee Regan, Libn.
Staff: Prof 1. **Subjects:** International human rights. **Holdings:** 2000 books; newsletters; reports; periodicals; 50 VF drawers of pamphlets, clippings, documents. **Subscriptions:** 700 journals and other serials. **Services:** Interlibrary loans; copying; library open to public by appointment. **Publications:** Human Rights Internet Reporter, 5/year - distributed to contributors and subscribers. **Special Indexes:** Human Rights Directory: Latin America, Africa, Asia; North American Human Rights Directory; Human Rights Directory: Western Europe; Teaching Human Rights (a collection of course outlines and bibliographies).

★5880★
HUMBER COLLEGE OF APPLIED ARTS & TECHNOLOGY - LIBRARY - SPECIAL COLLECTIONS
205 Humber College Blvd.　　　　　Phone: (416) 675-3111
Rexdale, ON, Canada M9W 5L7　　　Audrey MacLellan, Chf.Libn.
Founded: 1967. **Special Collections:** Horsemanship; mortuary science; Canadiana; horticulture. **Holdings:** Figures not available. **Services:** Interlibrary loans; copying; library open to public with limited borrowing privileges. **Networks/Consortia:** Member of Bibliocentre.

★5881★
HUMBOLDT COUNTY LAW LIBRARY (Law)
Court House, 825 Fifth St.　　　　　Phone: (707) 445-7201
Eureka, CA 95501　　　　　　　　　Nancy A. Guy, Law Libn.
Founded: 1897. **Staff:** Prof 1. **Subjects:** Law. **Holdings:** 18,206 volumes. **Subscriptions:** 20 journals and other serials. **Services:** Interlibrary loans; copying; library open to public.

HUME LIBRARY
See: University of Florida

HUMMER LIBRARY
See: Meadville City Hospital

HUMPHREY (H.H.) MEMORIAL STAFF LIBRARY
See: Brown County Mental Health Center - H.H. Humphrey Memorial Staff Library

HUNGARIAN RESEARCH LIBRARY
See: Kossuth Foundation

HUNT (Henry Alexander) MEMORIAL LEARNING RESOURCES CENTER
See: Fort Valley State College - Henry Alexander Hunt Memorial Learning Resources Center

HUNT INSTITUTE FOR BOTANICAL DOCUMENTATION
See: Carnegie-Mellon University

HUNT LIBRARY
See: Carnegie-Mellon University

★5882★
HUNT MEMORIAL HOSPITAL - GEORGE B. PALMER MEMORIAL LIBRARY (Med)
75 Lindall St.　　　　　　　　　　　Phone: (617) 774-4400
Danvers, MA 01923　　　　　　　　Yvonne I. Cretecos, Med.Libn.
Founded: 1975. **Staff:** Prof 2; Other 5. **Subjects:** Medicine and nursing. **Holdings:** 666 books; 997 bound periodical volumes; 60 cassettes; 1 VF drawer of pamphlets. **Subscriptions:** 127 journals and other serials. **Services:** Interlibrary loans; copying; library open to public with restrictions. **Computerized Information Services:** MEDLINE, BRS. **Networks/Consortia:** Member of Northeast Consortium for Health Information (NECHI); Consortium for Information Resources; Massachusetts Health Sciences Library Network (MAHSLIN). **Staff:** Theresa Keane, Asst.Libn.

★5883★
HUNT-WESSON FOODS - INFORMATION CENTER (Food-Bev)
1645 W. Valencia Dr.　　　　　　　Phone: (714) 680-2158
Fullerton, CA 92634　　　　　　　　Joy Hastings, Mgr.
Founded: 1967. **Staff:** Prof 1; Other 2. **Subjects:** Food science, food technology, food packaging. **Holdings:** 2600 books; 1000 bound periodical volumes; patents, technical reports, market research reports, annual reports. **Subscriptions:** 430 journals and other serials. **Services:** Interlibrary loans; copying; library not open to public. **Computerized Information Services:** DIALOG, SDC.

HUNT (William Morris) MEMORIAL LIBRARY
See: Museum of Fine Arts - William Morris Hunt Memorial Library

★5884★
HUNTER COLLEGE OF THE CITY UNIVERSITY OF NEW YORK - HEALTH PROFESSIONS LIBRARY (Med)
440 E. 26th St.　　　　　　　　　　Phone: (212) 481-4326
New York, NY 10010　　　　　　　　Samuel J. Waddell, Chf.Libn.
Founded: 1909. **Staff:** Prof 3; Other 3. **Subjects:** Nursing, medicine, speech and hearing pathology, physical therapy, dance therapy, medical laboratory sciences, environmental health sciences, biomedical computers, community health education. **Holdings:** 12,000 books; 9000 bound periodical volumes; 1250 federal and state environmental reports. **Subscriptions:** 300 journals and other serials. **Services:** Interlibrary loans; copying; library open to public for reference use only. **Computerized Information Services:** MEDLINE. **Networks/Consortia:** Member of OCLC. **Publications:** Recent Acquisitions list, quarterly. **Staff:** Karen Barnett, Dp.Libn.

★5885★
HUNTER COLLEGE OF THE CITY UNIVERSITY OF NEW YORK - HUNTER COLLEGE SCHOOL OF SOCIAL WORK - LIBRARY (Soc Sci)
129 E. 79th St.　　　　　　　　　　Phone: (212) 570-5072
New York, NY 10021　　　　　　　　Charles W. Elder, Hd.Libn.
Founded: 1969. **Staff:** Prof 2; Other 10. **Subjects:** Social work, psychology, sociology, public administration, urban affairs, ethnology, education, law, health. **Special Collections:** Paul Schreiber Collection: History of Social Welfare, U.S. and Europe. **Holdings:** 35,000 books; 3900 bound periodical volumes; 480 volumes of masters' theses; 34 dissertations; 13 VF drawers; 1980 reels of microfilm; 1000 microfiche. **Subscriptions:** 404 journals and other serials. **Services:** Interlibrary loans; copying; library not open to public. **Computerized Information Services:** Computerized acquisitions. **Special Catalogs:** Theses and Dissertations Catalog (card). **Staff:** Vivian Balaban, Asst.Libn.

HUNTER MEMORIAL LIBRARY
See: Western Carolina University

HUNTER MEMORIAL PEDIATRIC LIBRARY
See: Rockford Memorial Hospital - Health Science Library

★5886★
HUNTER MUSEUM OF ART - REFERENCE LIBRARY (Art)
Bluff View　　　　　　　　　　　　Phone: (615) 267-0968
Chattanooga, TN 37403　　　　　　Diana W. Suarez, Cur. of Educ.
Founded: 1958. **Staff:** Prof 2; Other 3. **Subjects:** American art, antiques, architecture. **Holdings:** 1300 books; 13 VF drawers of sales and auction catalogs; 17 VF drawers of museum and exhibition catalogs. **Subscriptions:** 38 journals and other serials. **Services:** Library open to public by appointment and on a limited schedule. **Staff:** Keating Griffiss, Libn.

★5887★
HUNTERDON COUNTY HISTORICAL SOCIETY - HIRAM E. DEATS MEMORIAL LIBRARY (Hist)
114 Main St.　　　　　　　　　　　Phone: (201) 782-1091
Flemington, NJ 08822　　　　　　　Norman C. Wittwer, Chm., Lib.Comm.
Founded: 1885. **Staff:** 10. **Subjects:** Hunterdon County history and genealogy; New Jersey history and genealogy. **Special Collections:** Hiram E. Deats Genealogical Collection; Emley-Race manuscripts; Capner Family manuscripts; county newspaper files, 1825 to present. **Holdings:** 5000 books. **Services:** Copying; genealogical queries answered by mail; library open to public on a limited schedule and by appointment. **Publications:** Hunterdon Historical Newsletter, 3/year.

★5888★
HUNTERDON MEDICAL CENTER - MEDICAL LIBRARY (Med)
Rte. 31　　　　　　　　　　　　　　Phone: (201) 782-2121
Flemington, NJ 08822　　　　　　　Joyce G. White, M.D., Libn.
Founded: 1953. **Staff:** Prof 1. **Subjects:** Medicine, family practice.

Holdings: 2000 books; 2500 bound periodical volumes; 950 Audio-Digest tapes. **Subscriptions:** 180 journals and other serials. **Services:** Interlibrary loans; copying; library open to students. **Networks/Consortia:** Member of MEDCORE; Central Jersey Health Science Libraries Association.

★5889★
HUNTINGTON ALLOYS, INC. - TECHNOLOGY LIBRARY (Sci-Tech)
Guyan River Rd.
Box 1958   Phone: (304) 696-6260
Huntington, WV 25720   Lola W. McClure, Tech.Libn.
Staff: 2. **Subjects:** Alloys - nonferrous and nickel; metallurgical engineering; analytical chemistry; environment. **Holdings:** 4000 books; 2800 bound periodical volumes; 2000 government reports; 300 translations; 20 VF drawers of reports. **Subscriptions:** 250 journals and other serials; 5 newspapers. **Services:** Interlibrary loans; copying; library open to public by appointment.

HUNTINGTON (Collis P.) MEMORIAL LIBRARY
See: Hampton Institute - Collis P. Huntington Memorial Library

★5890★
**HUNTINGTON FREE LIBRARY - MUSEUM OF THE AMERICAN INDIAN -
    LIBRARY** (Area-Ethnic)
9 Westchester Sq.   Phone: (212) 829-7770
Bronx, NY 10461   Mary B. Davis, Libn.
Founded: 1930. **Staff:** Prof 2; Other 1. **Subjects:** Archeology and ethnology of the Indians of the Western Hemisphere; linguistics; anthropology; history. **Holdings:** 12,000 volumes; 100 VF drawers; 50 manuscripts. **Subscriptions:** 200 journals and other serials; 140 Indian newspapers. **Services:** Copying; library open to public by appointment. **Networks/Consortia:** Member of Consortium of Foundation Libraries. **Remarks:** The Museum of the American Indian, Heye Foundation also maintains archives. **Staff:** Rosina Romano, Asst.Libn.

★5891★
HUNTINGTON GALLERIES - REFERENCE LIBRARY (Art)
Park Hills   Phone: (304) 529-2701
Huntington, WV 25701
Staff: Prof 1. **Subjects:** Fine arts and crafts with emphasis on American art and glass. **Special Collections:** Antique firearms collection with supportive materials. **Holdings:** Museum bulletins, exhibition catalogs, arts newsletters. **Subscriptions:** 80 journals and other serials. **Services:** Library open to public for reference use only.

★5892★
**HUNTINGTON (Henry E.) LIBRARY, ART GALLERY AND BOTANICAL
    GARDENS** (Rare Book)
1151 Oxford Rd.   Phone: (213) 792-6141
San Marino, CA 91108   James Thorpe, Dir.
Founded: 1919. **Staff:** Prof 23; Other 23. **Subjects:** Incunabula, early English and American printed books, English and American literature, medieval English manuscripts, English history to 1837, American history to 1900, California history. **Holdings:** 334,262 rare books; 250,349 reference books; 2.5 million manuscripts; microforms. **Subscriptions:** 600 journals and other serials. **Services:** Interlibrary loans (photoduplications only); copying; library open to qualified scholars. **Publications:** Program Brochure; Huntington Library Press Publications; Huntington Library Quarterly; Calendar of Exhibitions. **Staff:** Carey S. Bliss, Cur., Rare Books; Mary Robertson, Cur. of Mss.; Faith Cornwall, Prin.Cat.; Virginia J. Renner, Rd.Serv.Libn.; Daniel H. Woodward, Libn.

★5893★
HUNTINGTON HISTORICAL SOCIETY - LIBRARY (Hist)
2 High St.   Phone: (516) 427-7045
Huntington, NY 11743   Agnes K. Packard, Libn.
Founded: 1909. **Staff:** Prof 1; Other 1. **Subjects:** Local history, genealogy, New York history, American crafts, American decorative arts. **Special Collections:** Nellie Rich Scudder Collection of Long Island Genealogical Records; Scudder (family) Association Genealogical Records; W. Wilton Wood Collection (business records and family papers, late 18th century through 1960s; 20 linear feet; Crossman Brickyard Records (19th century; 2 linear feet); The Long Islander (newspaper), 1839 to present. **Holdings:** 3000 books; 128 bound periodical volumes; 30 linear feet of manuscripts and archives; 8 files of clippings; 3000 photographs; 3800 slides. **Subscriptions:** 30 journals and other serials. **Services:** Copying; library open for research only. **Networks/Consortia:** Member of Long Island Library Resources Council. **Publications:** Huntington-Babylon Town History; Eaton's Neck; Index to the Long Islander; Marriages and Births 1839-1864; Huntington at the Turn of the Century; Huntington in Our Time; John Sloss Hobart, Forgotten

Patriot. **Special Indexes:** Index to the Long Islander, 1839-1842, 1843-1849 and 1850-1857.

★5894★
HUNTINGTON MEMORIAL HOSPITAL - HEALTH SCIENCES LIBRARY (Med)
100 Congress St.   Phone: (213) 258-7869
Pasadena, CA 91105   Samir Zeind, Dir.
Staff: Prof 1; Other 4. **Subjects:** Medicine, nursing, paramedicine, rehabilitation, neurosurgery. **Holdings:** 4000 books; 20,000 bound periodical volumes; 1000 audiotapes. **Subscriptions:** 617 journals and other serials. **Services:** Interlibrary loans; copying; SDI; library open to public with restrictions. **Computerized Information Services:** DIALOG, MEDLARS, SDC; computerized cataloging, serials and information retrieval. **Networks/Consortia:** Member of Pacific Southwest Regional Medical Library Services (PSRMLS). **Publications:** List of Periodicals; New Books List; Patient Education List.

★5895★
HUNTON & WILLIAMS - LAW LIBRARY (Law)
707 E. Main St.
Box 1535   Phone: (804) 788-8245
Richmond, VA 23212   Mr. Beverley Butler, Hd.Libn.
Staff: Prof 6. **Subjects:** Law - corporate, real estate, antitrust, tax, labor, environmental; litigation. **Holdings:** 45,150 books and bound periodical volumes. **Subscriptions:** 500 journals and other serials; 6 newspapers. **Services:** Copying; library not open to public. **Computerized Information Services:** Online systems.

★5896★
**HUNTSVILLE MEMORIAL HOSPITAL - SCHOOL OF VOCATIONAL NURSING -
    EARNESTINE CANNON MEMORIAL LIBRARY** (Med)
3000 I-45
Box 479   Phone: (713) 291-3411
Huntsville, TX 77340   J. Martin, Dir.
Founded: 1966. **Staff:** Prof 1; Other 1. **Subjects:** Professional and vocational nursing, medicine. **Special Collections:** Ciba Collection; reconstructive plastic surgery. **Holdings:** 450 books; 120 bound periodical volumes; 200 filmstrips (cataloged). **Subscriptions:** 13 journals and other serials. **Services:** Interlibrary loans; copying; library open to public with restrictions.

HUPP MEDICAL LIBRARY
See: Ohio Valley Medical Center

HURLEY (Captain Charles H.) LIBRARY
See: Massachusetts Maritime Academy - Captain Charles H. Hurley
    Library

★5897★
HURLEY MEDICAL CENTER - HAMADY HEALTH SCIENCES LIBRARY (Med)
One Hurley Plaza   Phone: (313) 766-0427
Flint, MI 48502   Anthos Hungerford, Dir.
Founded: 1976. **Staff:** Prof 7; Other 1. **Subjects:** Medicine, nursing, hospital administration. **Holdings:** 8622 books; 9000 bound periodical volumes and reels of microfilm; 1065 AV programs; hospital archives; pamphlets files. **Subscriptions:** 750 journals and other serials. **Services:** Interlibrary loans; copying; library open to college students and professionals for reference use only. **Computerized Information Services:** MEDLINE, DIALOG, NTIS; computerized cataloging. **Networks/Consortia:** Member of Flint Medline Consortium. **Publications:** Booklist; Newsletter - for internal distribution only. **Staff:** J. Raphelson, Tech.Serv.Libn.; M. Schleg, Pub.Serv.Libn.; N. Winslow, Health Educ.Libn.; M. Studaker, Tech.Serv.Libn.; S. Williams, Health Educ.Libn.; S. Sundeen, Tech.Serv.Libn.; G. Stoudamire, Pub.Serv.Libn.

★5898★
HURON COLLEGE - SILCOX MEMORIAL LIBRARY (Rel-Theol; Hum)
1349 Western Rd.   Phone: (519) 438-7224
London, ON, Canada N6G 1H3   Victoria Ripley, Chf.Libn.
Founded: 1863. **Staff:** Prof 3; Other 3. **Subjects:** Theology, English and French literature, history, philosophy, psychology. **Holdings:** 110,000 volumes; 8 linear feet of archives; 5 linear feet of manuscripts. **Subscriptions:** 250 journals and other serials; 5 newspapers. **Services:** Interlibrary loans; copying; SDI; library open to graduate students, clergy and alumni. **Staff:** Ms. P. MacKay, Cat.; Ms. M. Robertson, Lib.Asst., Acq.; Ms. P. Wilson, Circ.

★5899★
HURON ROAD HOSPITAL - LIBRARY AND AUDIOVISUAL CENTER (Med)
13951 Terrace Rd.   Phone: (216) 261-8106
Cleveland, OH 44112   Sara W. Baker, Dir., Lib.Serv.
Staff: Prof 3. **Subjects:** Medicine, nursing, hospital administration and allied health sciences. **Special Collections:** Marshall Research Foundation monographs on peptic ulcers; homeopathy. **Holdings:** 2000 books; 1800 bound periodical volumes; 4 VF drawers; cassette tapes. **Subscriptions:** 150 journals and other serials. **Services:** Interlibrary loans; copying; library open to public with restrictions. **Computerized Information Services:** MEDLINE, BRS. **Networks/Consortia:** Member of Kentucky-Ohio-Michigan Regional Medical Library Network (KOMRML). **Staff:** Mary Krichbaum, Asst.Libn.; Mary Ellen Jewell, Asst.Libn.

★5900★
HURONIA HISTORICAL PARKS - RESOURCE CENTRE (Hist)
P.O. Box 160   Phone: (705) 526-7838
Midland, ON, Canada L4R 4K8   Mrs. M. Quealey, Supv., Lib.Serv.
Founded: 1971. **Staff:** Prof 1; Other 1. **Subjects:** New France to 1660; Jesuit missions in North America; Iroquoian Indians in 17th century; British naval and military establishments in Upper Canada; Ontario social history, 1791 to 1867. **Holdings:** 5000 books; 35 bound periodical volumes; 2000 photocopied articles (cataloged); 4 drawers of manuscripts; 8 boxes of archival records; 600 sheets of maps; 3000 pictures; 3000 slides; 100 microforms. **Subscriptions:** 100 journals and other serials; 5 newspapers. **Services:** Copying; SDI; library open to public by appointment. **Publications:** Recent Acquisitions, irregular - for internal distribution only. **Special Indexes:** Manuscript file (cards). **Remarks:** Maintained by Ontario - Ministry of Citizenship and Culture - Ministry of Tourism and Recreation.

★5901★
HURONIA REGIONAL CENTRE - LIBRARY (Med)
Box 1000   Phone: (705) 326-7361
Orillia, ON, Canada L3V 6L2   Christie MacMillan, Libn.
Founded: 1974. **Staff:** Prof 1; Other 1. **Subjects:** Mental retardation. **Holdings:** 2500 books; 200 reports; 3 VF drawers of archival materials; 7 VF drawers of reports, pamphlets and articles. **Subscriptions:** 94 journals and other serials. **Services:** Interlibrary loans; copying; library open to public.

HURST LIBRARY
See: Northwest College of the Assemblies of God

HURST MEMORIAL LIBRARY
See: Pacific Christian College

HURST (R.O.) LIBRARY
See: University of Toronto - Faculty of Pharmacy - R.O. Hurst Library

★5902★
HURTY-PECK LIBRARY OF BEVERAGE LITERATURE (Food-Bev)†
5600 W. Raymond St.
Indianapolis, IN 46241
Founded: 1959. **Staff:** 1. **Subjects:** Beer and brewing, cider, cocktails and mixed drinks, coffee, drinks and drinking, flavorings, food and drink, inns, liquors, mineral waters, soft drinks, tea, temperance, wine and winemaking. **Holdings:** 6000 books; files on soft drinks and alcoholic beverages. **Subscriptions:** 15 journals and other serials. **Services:** Interlibrary loans; library open to public by appointment. **Publications:** Beverage Literature: A Bibliography (catalog of books in library), 1971.

★5903★
HUSSON COLLEGE - LIBRARY (Bus-Fin)†
One College Circle   Phone: (207) 945-5641
Bangor, ME 04401   Berneice Thompson, Libn.
Staff: Prof 2; Other 1. **Subjects:** Business, liberal arts. **Holdings:** 31,000 books; 1481 bound periodical volumes. **Subscriptions:** 407 journals and other serials. **Services:** Interlibrary loans; copying; library open to public.

HUSTEN (Harvey) JAZZ LIBRARY
See: Free Library of Philadelphia - Music Department

HUTCHINS LIBRARY
See: Berea College

★5904★
HUTCHINSON ROSS PUBLISHING COMPANY - REFERENCE LIBRARY
523 Sarah St.
Box 699
Stroudsburg, PA 18360
Founded: 1972. **Subjects:** Science, architecture, community planning, library

and general reference subjects. **Holdings:** 350 books. **Remarks:** Presently inactive. **Formerly:** Dowden, Hutchinson & Ross, Inc.

HUTTNER ABOLITION AND ANTI-SLAVERY COLLECTION
See: Minneapolis Public Library & Information Center

★5905★
HUTTON (E.F.) & COMPANY, INC. - LIBRARY (Bus-Fin)
One State Street Plaza, 19th Fl.   Phone: (212) 742-2970
New York, NY 10004   Sheila Sterling, Hd.Libn.
Founded: 1937. **Staff:** Prof 1; Other 8. **Subjects:** Corporation records, investments, finance, economics. **Holdings:** 1000 books; 200 bound periodical volumes; 280 VF drawers; microfiche. **Subscriptions:** 150 journals and other serials. **Services:** Interlibrary loans; library open to staff and other librarians.

★5906★
HUTZEL HOSPITAL - MEDICAL LIBRARY (Med)†
4707 St. Antoine   Phone: (313) 494-7179
Detroit, MI 48201   Caryl L. Scheuer, Dir., Lib.Serv.
Founded: 1936. **Staff:** Prof 2; Other 3. **Subjects:** Obstetrics and gynecology, internal medicine, surgery, pathology, radiology, health care and administration. **Holdings:** 2012 books; 5980 bound periodical volumes; 6 VF drawers; Audio-Digest tapes in surgery, internal medicine, obstetrics and gynecology. **Subscriptions:** 415 journals and other serials. **Services:** Interlibrary loans; copying; SDI; library open to hospital staff and students. **Computerized Information Services:** DIALOG, NLM. **Networks/Consortia:** Member of Pontiac-Allen Park-Detroit Consortium (PAD).

★5907★
HUXLEY COLLEGE OF ENVIRONMENTAL STUDIES - ENVIRONMENTAL RESOURCE LIBRARY (Env-Cons)
ESC 535, Huxley College   Phone: (206) 676-3974
Bellingham, WA 98225   Bill Taylor, Lib. Co-coord.
Founded: 1970. **Staff:** Prof 6. **Subjects:** Environmental education; human ecology; social science; environmental philosophy and ethics; environmental planning; terrestrial, fresh water and marine ecology; environmental health and toxicology; agriculture, nutrition and food supply; environmental technology and recycling; energy alternatives. **Holdings:** 2000 books; 3 files of pamphlets and clippings; 50 newsletters; 600 student reports; 12 tapes. **Subscriptions:** 32 journals and other serials. **Services:** Center open to public. **Publications:** The Monthly Planet, monthly. **Remarks:** Huxley College is a division of Western Washington University. The Environmental Resource Library is jointly maintained by Western Washington University and its Associated Students Environmental Center.

★5908★
HYDE COLLECTION (Hum)
161 Warren St.   Phone: (518) 792-1761
Glens Falls, NY 12801
Founded: 1952. **Subjects:** Art, local history, British poetry, old travel books. **Special Collections:** Nuremberg Chronicle, Augsberg Chronicle, Book of Hours. **Holdings:** 2600 volumes. **Subscriptions:** 10 journals and other serials. **Services:** Collection open for scholarly research only.

HYDE (Inez L.) MEMORIAL COLLECTION
See: Sequoia Genealogical Society - Inez L. Hyde Memorial Collection

HYDRAULIC ENGINEERING INFORMATION ANALYSIS CENTER
See: U.S. Army - Engineer Waterways Experiment Station

★5909★
HYDRO-QUEBEC - BIBLIOTHEQUE (Sci-Tech; Energy)
75 Dorchester Blvd., W.   Phone: (514) 289-2149
Montreal, PQ, Canada H2Z 1A4   Claude-Andre Bonin, Info.Mgr.
Founded: 1962. **Staff:** Prof 8; Other 10. **Subjects:** Electrical engineering, hydraulics, energy, management. **Holdings:** 15,000 books; 10 VF drawers of unbound documents and pamphlets; 60 VF drawers of electrical standards; 100 microfiche of technical reports. **Subscriptions:** 2000 journals and other serials. **Services:** Interlibrary loans; copying; library open to public with restrictions. **Computerized Information Services:** CAN/OLE, SABINE, DIALOG, SDC, CANSIM, QL Systems, MEDLINE, Info Globe; MINISIS-RIDAQ (internal database); computerized cataloging and routing of serials. **Networks/Consortia:** Member of UTLAS Inc; RIBLIN. **Publications:** Au Courant, library list of accessions, monthly - free upon request. **Special Catalogs:** COM Union catalog on microfiche.

★5910★

HYDRO-QUEBEC - DIRECTION RECHERCHE ECONOMIQUE - CENTRE DE DOCUMENTATION (Bus-Fin; Energy)†

870 Blvd. de Maisonneuve   Phone: (614) 289-6787
Montreal, PQ, Canada H2L 4S8   Sylvie Perron, Analyste
Founded: 1969. **Staff:** Prof 2. **Subjects:** Economics, politics of energy. **Holdings:** 500 books; 75 bound periodical volumes; 1000 international economic papers; Statistics Canada publications. **Subscriptions:** 25 journals and other serials; 8 newspapers. **Services:** Interlibrary loans; copying; library open to public with restrictions. **Computerized Information Services:** Computerized acquisitions. **Publications:** Dossier d'actualite (journal abstracts), weekly - for internal distribution only. **Staff:** Celine Bellerose, Documentaliste.

★5911★

HYDRO-QUEBEC - INSTITUT DE RECHERCHE - BIBLIOTHEQUE (Sci-Tech)

1800, Montee Ste-Julie   Phone: (514) 652-8324
Varennes, PQ, Canada J0L 2P0   Louise Pelletier, Hd.
Founded: 1967. **Staff:** Prof 2; Other 3. **Subjects:** Electricity, electrochemistry, energy. **Holdings:** 20,000 books; 70,000 bound periodical volumes; 5500 reports (cataloged); 25,000 microfiche. **Subscriptions:** 600 journals and other serials. **Services:** Interlibrary loans; copying; SDI; library open to public. **Computerized Information Services:** DIALOG, CAN/OLE, SDC; internal database; computerized cataloging and reference. **Special Indexes:** KWIC Index. **Staff:** Roger Drouin, Ref.Libn.

★5912★

HYDRO RESEARCH SCIENCE - LIBRARY (Sci-Tech)

3334 Victor Ct.   Phone: (408) 988-1027
Santa Clara, CA 95050   Judith C. Lee, Info.Rsrcs.Mgr.
Staff: Prof 1. **Subjects:** Fluid mechanics, experimental hydraulics, model studies in hydrology. **Special Collections:** Delft Hydraulics Laboratory Reports, 1967 to present. **Holdings:** 425 books; 82 bound periodical volumes; 1100 technical reports. **Subscriptions:** 49 journals and other serials. **Services:** Interlibrary loans; copying; library not open to public. **Computerized Information Services:** DIALOG. **Networks/Consortia:** Member of CIN; CLASS. **Publications:** Acquisitions list.

HYDROGRAPHIC/TOPOGRAPHIC CENTER
See: U.S. Defense Mapping Agency

★5913★

HYMN SOCIETY OF AMERICA - LIBRARY (Mus)

Wittenberg University   Phone: (513) 327-6308
Springfield, OH 45501   W. Thomas Smith, Exec.Dir.
Founded: 1922. **Staff:** 2. **Subjects:** Hymns and hymnology. **Holdings:** 3000 books. **Services:** Library open to public for reference use only. **Publications:** The Hymn, quarterly magazine distributed to members; The Stanza, semiannual newsletter. **Remarks:** Part of the library is housed and accessible at the Union Theological Seminary, New York.

HYPNOSIS TECHNICAL CENTER
See: American Hypnotists' Association

★5914★

HYSTER COMPANY - ENGINEERING LIBRARY (Sci-Tech)

2902 N.E. Clackamas   Phone: (503) 280-7405
Portland, OR 97208   Ruth Jahnke, Libn.
Founded: 1961. **Staff:** Prof 1. **Subjects:** Material handling, metallurgy and welding, safety and design standards, automotive engineering. **Special Collections:** Manufacturers catalogs (1851); annual reports (2600); society papers; legal publications. **Holdings:** 8249 books; Society of Automotive Engineers papers (cataloged); 1667 engineering test reports; 2 drawers of pamphlets; 6 shelves of archives. **Subscriptions:** 40 journals and other serials. **Services:** Interlibrary loans; library open to public with restrictions. **Computerized Information Services:** SDC. **Publications:** Library Bulletin, irregular. **Special Indexes:** Test reports (card). **Formerly:** Its Technical Information Services.

I

I TATTI ARCHIVES
See: New York University - Institute of Fine Arts - Photographic Archive

IAEWP CENTER OF INTERCULTURAL INFORMATION
See: International Association of Educators for World Peace

IAPG
See: U.S. Interagency Advanced Power Group

IBM CANADA, LTD. - DP CENTRAL LIBRARY
See: IBM Canada, Ltd. - Marketing Library

★5915★
IBM CANADA, LTD. - EASTERN REGION REFERENCE LIBRARY (Info Sci)†
5 Place Ville Marie, 2nd Fl.   Phone: (514) 874-6123
Montreal, PQ, Canada H3B 2G2   Catherine Bourgeois, Libn.
Founded: 1966. **Staff:** Prof 1. **Subjects:** Data processing, industrial management, pulp and paper. **Special Collections:** Share proceedings; IBM symposia; complete series of IBM publications. **Holdings:** 150 books. **Subscriptions:** 70 journals and other serials. **Services:** Interlibrary loans; library not open to public.

★5916★
IBM CANADA, LTD. - HEADQUARTERS LIBRARY (Bus-Fin; Sci-Tech)
31/761
3500 Steeles Ave. E.   Phone: (416) 474-2348
Markham, ON, Canada L3R 2Z1   Anne F. Martin, Libn.
Staff: Prof 1; Other 1. **Subjects:** Computers, office systems. **Holdings:** Figures not available for books; annual reports; IBM product literature; Canadian government documents and reports; videotapes; slides; photographs; clipping files. **Subscriptions:** 60 journals and other serials; 5 newspapers. **Services:** Interlibrary loans; copying; library open to library personnel only or by special appointment . **Computerized Information Services:** Info Globe; internal database. **Publications:** Newsletter.

★5917★
IBM CANADA, LTD. - LABORATORY LIBRARY (Sci-Tech)
1150 Eglinton Ave., E.   Phone: (416) 443-3136
Don Mills, ON, Canada M3C 1H7   Ms. R.H. Yan, Lab.Libn.
Founded: 1969. **Staff:** Prof 2. **Subjects:** Computer technology, management, programming, education. **Holdings:** 2000 books; microfiche of IBM reports and standards and miscellaneous external reports. **Subscriptions:** 120 journals and other serials; 10 newspapers. **Services:** Interlibrary loans; copying; library not open to public. **Computerized Information Services:** SDC, Info Globe; internal databases. **Publications:** Library News, monthly - for internal distribution only.

★5918★
IBM CANADA, LTD. - MARKETING LIBRARY (Sci-Tech; Bus-Fin)
Dept. 931
1150 Eglinton Ave. E.   Phone: (416) 443-2043
Don Mills, ON, Canada M3C 1H7   Marjorie Lauer, Libn.
Staff: Prof 1; Other 1. **Subjects:** Computers, business, management. **Special Collections:** IBM documentation/manuals. **Holdings:** 1000 books; 15,000 IBM documents (cataloged); 2000 clippings; 250 annual reports; 400 speeches; 600 items in IBM archive. **Subscriptions:** 65 journals and other serials. **Services:** Interlibrary loans; copying; library open to IBM personnel. **Publications:** Library Newsletter. **Special Indexes:** Index to speeches, books, clippings, product files (card). **Formerly:** Its DP Central Library.

★5919★
IBM CORPORATION - BOULDER LIBRARY (Sci-Tech)
Dept. 419, Box 1900
Boulder, CO 80302   Phone: (303) 447-5064
    Lyle Vigil, Lib.Mgr.
Founded: 1967. **Staff:** Prof 1; Other 1. **Subjects:** Optics, electronics, programming, management, copier systems and technology. **Holdings:** 10,000 volumes; 500,000 technical reports in microform. **Subscriptions:** 400 journals and other serials. **Services:** Interlibrary loans; copying; library not open to public. **Computerized Information Services:** DIALOG; computerized acquisitions and circulation. **Publications:** Periodical Subscription Holdings; Library Guide to IBM Boulder. **Staff:** Dean Butler, Sr.Libn.; Linda Kirklin, Jr.Libn.

★5920★
IBM CORPORATION - BUSINESS INFORMATION LIBRARY (Bus-Fin)
Parson's Pond Dr.
Franklin Lakes, NJ 07417   Ellen Lyons, Mgr.
Staff: Prof 3. **Subjects:** Business. **Holdings:** 2000 books; 523 cassettes. **Subscriptions:** 160 journals and other serials; 19 newspapers. **Services:** Interlibrary loans; library not open to public. **Computerized Information Services:** Computerized cataloging. **Staff:** Nellie W. Baker, Libn.; Betty Zidzik, Libn.

★5921★
IBM CORPORATION - COMMUNICATION PRODUCTS DIVISION - LIBRARY (Info Sci)
Dept. 609/Bldg. 060
Box 12195   Phone: (919) 543-5942
Research Triangle Park, NC 27709   Dorothy Huey, Libn.
Staff: 2. **Subjects:** Communications, teleprocessing, computer science. **Holdings:** 7000 books. **Subscriptions:** 400 journals and other serials. **Services:** Interlibrary loans; copying; library not open to public. **Formerly:** Its System Communications Division.

★5922★
IBM CORPORATION - DP COMMUNICATIONS LIBRARY (Info Sci)†
1133 Westchester Ave.   Phone: (914) 696-2382
White Plains, NY 10604   Anne A. Austin, Manager
Staff: Prof 4; Other 2. **Subjects:** Automation, computers, data processing, information retrieval, business management, marketing. **Special Collections:** Complete file of IBM annual reports; library of IBM publications. **Holdings:** 3500 books. **Subscriptions:** 250 journals and other serials. **Services:** Library not open to public. **Computerized Information Services:** Online systems. **Special Indexes:** Index of newspaper and periodical articles categorized by application; chronological listing of IBM product announcements.

IBM CORPORATION - DP LIBRARY
See: IBM Corporation - National Accounts Division - Library

★5923★
IBM CORPORATION - DSD SITE LIBRARY (Info Sci)
Dept. 65P/840
Neighborhood Rd.   Phone: (914) 383-3574
Kingston, NY 12401   Frank von Rekowski, Mgr.
Founded: 1956. **Staff:** Prof 5; Other 2. **Subjects:** Computers, data processing, computer graphics, display technology, software/hardware development, electronics, physics, mathematics, chemistry. **Holdings:** 12,000 books; 15,000 bound periodical volumes; 70,000 technical reports; 108,000 microfiche. **Subscriptions:** 556 journals and other serials. **Services:** Interlibrary loans; copying; visitors may consult books and periodicals by appointment. **Computerized Information Services:** BRS; ACQUARIUS (internal database); computerized cataloging, serials and circulation. **Staff:** Lillian Bosco, Libn.

★5924★
IBM CORPORATION - FEDERAL SYSTEMS DIVISION - AVIONICS SYSTEMS - LIBRARY (Sci-Tech; Info Sci)
    Phone: (607) 751-2721
Owego, NY 13827   Charles F. Balz, Project Mgr.
Founded: 1951. **Staff:** Prof 3; Other 3. **Subjects:** Aeronautics and astronautics, computers, electronics and electronic equipment, mathematics, nuclear sciences, physics, psychology and human engineering, space sciences, management and administration, documentation and information retrieval. **Special Collections:** Clippings on plant history. **Holdings:** 14,000 books; 4200 bound periodical volumes; 45,000 technical reports; 3000 slides; 16 VF drawers of pamphlets. **Subscriptions:** 350 journals and other serials; 5 newspapers. **Services:** Interlibrary loans. **Computerized Information Services:** Computerized cataloging, circulation and searches. **Publications:** Library Readings. **Special Indexes:** Cumulated KWIC indexes. **Staff:** Richard Duffy, Sr.Libn.

★5925★
IBM CORPORATION - GENERAL PRODUCTS DIVISION - INFORMATION/ LIBRARY/LEARNING CENTER (Info Sci)
Dept. J17/Bldg. K15
555 Baily Ave.   Phone: (408) 463-4259
San Jose, CA 95150   Karen Takle Quinn, Dir.
Founded: 1975. **Staff:** Prof 5; Other 10. **Subjects:** Programming, distributed processing, database systems, systems software, personal and career development. **Special Collections:** Self-Study and Computer Aided Instruction Courses (1000); System Reference Manuals (40,000); Study Reference Lists. **Holdings:** 12,000 books; 2000 bound periodical volumes;

3000 AV materials; microfilm and microfiche; computer programs. **Subscriptions:** 350 journals and other serials; 7 newspapers. **Services:** Interlibrary loans; copying; SDI; library not open to public. **Computerized Information Services:** Online systems; computerized cataloging, acquisitions, serials and circulation. **Publications:** Infoscan, monthly - for internal distribution only. **Special Catalogs:** Online internal catalog. **Staff:** Ellen Warneke, Ref./ILL; Carolyn Pendegrass, Ref./CAI; Lorraine Stribling, Ref./Cat.; Donna O'Connor, Ref./Circ.

★5926★

IBM CORPORATION - GENERAL PRODUCTS DIVISION - TECHNICAL INFORMATION CENTER (Info Sci)
G35/141
5600 Cottle Rd.   Phone: (408) 256-2908
San Jose, CA 95193   Ruth Winik, Mgr., Tech.Info.Ctr.
Founded: 1961. **Staff:** Prof 2; Other 3. **Subjects:** Data processing, electronics, computers, chemistry, physics, mathematics, electrical engineering. **Holdings:** 9000 books; 2500 bound periodical volumes. **Subscriptions:** 350 journals and other serials; 10 newspapers. **Services:** Interlibrary loans; copying; library open to public with restrictions. **Computerized Information Services:** DIALOG, BRS, Information Handling Services, MEDLARS, Source Telecomputing Corporation; IBM Technical Information Retrieval Center System (internal database); computerized cataloging, acquisitions and circulation. **Networks/Consortia:** Member of CLASS. **Staff:** Loren Molieri, Libn.

★5927★

IBM CORPORATION - GENERAL TECHNOLOGY DIVISION - EAST FISHKILL FACILITY - LIBRARY (Sci-Tech; Info Sci)
Rte. 52   Phone: (914) 897-6219
Hopewell Junction, NY 12533   Robert B. Murphy, Mgr.
Founded: 1964. **Staff:** Prof 2; Other 3. **Subjects:** Electronics, computers. **Holdings:** 27,000 books; 13,000 bound periodical volumes; 75,000 microforms. **Subscriptions:** 425 journals and other serials. **Services:** Interlibrary loans; copying; library not open to public. **Computerized Information Services:** BRS; IBM Technical Information Retrieval Center System (internal database); computerized cataloging. **Publications:** Library Bulletin, semimonthly - for internal distribution only. **Staff:** Karen Ashkar Murley, Tech.Libn.; A.H. Agajanian, Bibliog.

★5928★

IBM CORPORATION - GENERAL TECHNOLOGY DIVISION - INFORMATION CENTER/LEARNING CENTER (Info Sci; Sci-Tech)
                                         Phone: (802) 769-2331
Essex Junction, VT 05452   C. Allen Merritt, Mgr.
Founded: 1965. **Staff:** Prof 4; Other 1. **Subjects:** Computer science, chemistry, solid-state electronics, physics, programming, management science, mathematics. **Holdings:** 12,000 books; 1900 bound periodical volumes; 800 audio cassettes; 250,000 microfiche; 100 reels of microfilm; 25,000 IBM technical reports; 380 video cassettes; 130 specialized computer training courses; films. **Subscriptions:** 515 journals and other serials; 9 newspapers. **Services:** Interlibrary loans; library open to public with restrictions. **Computerized Information Services:** Computerized cataloging, serials, circulation. **Publications:** Current Awareness Bulletin - for internal distribution only. **Special Catalogs:** Computerized circulation and subject files; computerized periodical check-in file; Learning Center Directory of Services in Self Inquiry and Self Education; Audio Cassette Listing. **Staff:** Ruth Macek; Barbara Willard; Ron Gagner; Bob Pontbriand; Edith Feeley .

★5929★

IBM CORPORATION - GENERAL TECHNOLOGY DIVISION - LIBRARY (Sci-Tech)†
1701 North St.
Box 6   Phone: (607) 755-3223
Endicott, NY 13760   Shirley K. Manaley, Libn.
Founded: 1933. **Staff:** Prof 1; Other 2. **Subjects:** Mathematics, mechanics, electrical engineering, electronics, chemistry, computers. **Holdings:** 7000 books; 8000 bound periodical volumes. **Subscriptions:** 350 journals and other serials. **Services:** Interlibrary loans; copying; use of library for reference may be requested. **Computerized Information Services:** Computerized serials and circulation.

★5930★

IBM CORPORATION - INFORMATION CENTER/LIBRARY (Sci-Tech; Info Sci)
Dept. 205, Hwy. 52 & 37th St., N.W.   Phone: (507) 286-4462
Rochester, MN 55901   Ursula Shimek, Sr.Libn.
Staff: Prof 1; Other 2. **Subjects:** Programming, engineering, materials. **Special Collections:** Manufacturers' catalogs on microfilm (10,000). **Holdings:** 12,000 books; 4000 bound periodical volumes. **Subscriptions:**

450 journals and other serials. **Services:** Interlibrary loans; center open to public by request. **Computerized Information Services:** IBM Technical Information Retrieval Center System (internal database); computerized cataloging, acquisitions and circulation. **Publications:** Technical Report; Selected Resources in the IBM Rochester Information Center. **Special Catalogs:** Book catalog (also available in microfiche); COM Catalog. **Special Indexes:** KWIC index of book and journal collections.

★5931★

IBM CORPORATION - INFORMATION SYSTEMS DIVISION - TECHNICAL LIBRARY (Sci-Tech)†
Dept. 503, Bldg. 032
740 New Circle Rd.   Phone: (606) 232-6044
Lexington, KY 40507   Jewell C. Castle, Lib.Mgr.
Founded: 1959. **Staff:** Prof 1; Other 2. **Subjects:** Electronics, mechanics, chemistry, physics, mathematics, data processing, metallurgy, management, graphic arts. **Special Collections:** Programming; trade literature; product manuals; personal and technical vitality (books, video and audio cassettes). **Holdings:** 7800 books; 2500 bound periodical volumes; 7500 unbound reports; IBM document base, microfilm and microfiche; 2 files of archives; 150 cassettes. **Subscriptions:** 350 journals and other serials. **Services:** Interlibrary loans; copying; library open to public by appointment. **Computerized Information Services:** ACQUARIUS; computerized cataloging. **Networks/Consortia:** Member of IBM Technical Information Retrieval Center. **Publications:** Technical Reports Bulletin, biweekly; Current Technical Literature, monthly. **Special Catalogs:** Book catalog.

★5932★

IBM CORPORATION - LIBRARY (Info Sci)
Box 390   Phone: (914) 463-1630
Poughkeepsie, NY 12602   Gabrielle S. Nelson, Mgr.
Founded: 1957. **Staff:** 7. **Subjects:** Electronic computers, computer programming, physics, mathematics, information retrieval. **Holdings:** 25,000 books; 15,000 bound periodical volumes. **Subscriptions:** 750 journals and other serials. **Services:** Interlibrary loans; copying; literature searching; library open to public with written permission of library manager. **Computerized Information Services:** BRS; IBM Technical Information Retrieval Center System (internal database); computerized serials, circulation and retrieval. **Publications:** Library Bulletin, bimonthly - for internal distribution only. **Staff:** Betty B. Bateman, Ref.Libn.; Lorraine J. Solen, Ref.Libn.

★5933★

IBM CORPORATION - NATIONAL ACCOUNTS DIVISION - LIBRARY (Info Sci)
Two Riverway   Phone: (713) 940-2554
Houston, TX 77056   Agnete V. Katherman, Libn.
Founded: 1971. **Staff:** Prof 1; Other 1. **Subjects:** Electronic data processing, marketing, systems engineering. **Holdings:** 20,000 items, (cataloged); 350 35mm slide sets; 150 video cassettes; 65 audiotapes. **Subscriptions:** 10 journals and other serials. **Services:** Library not open to public. **Computerized Information Services:** SMART (internal database); computerized acquisitions and circulation. **Special Indexes:** Computerized audiovisual indexes.

★5934★

IBM CORPORATION - RESEARCH LIBRARY (Sci-Tech)†
Dept. K 25, Bldg. 281
5600 Cottle Rd.   Phone: (408) 256-2562
San Jose, CA 95193   W.T. Gallagher, Mgr.
Founded: 1952. **Staff:** Prof 3; Other 1. **Subjects:** Chemistry, physics, mathematics, computer science, engineering. **Holdings:** 24,000 books; 26,000 bound periodical volumes; 11,000 reports (cataloged); 30,000 microfiche; 3000 IBM reports (uncataloged); 40 reels of dissertation abstracts. **Subscriptions:** 700 journals and other serials; 10 newspapers. **Services:** Interlibrary loans; copying; library not open to public. **Computerized Information Services:** DIALOG; IBM Technical Information Retrieval Center System (internal database); computerized cataloging, circulation and serials. **Publications:** Directory of Publications, annual. **Staff:** Beverley Clarke, Sr.Libn.; Vilia Ma, Ref.Libn.

★5935★

IBM CORPORATION - SITE TECHNICAL LIBRARY/INFORMATION CENTER (Sci-Tech)
11400 Burnet Rd., Dept. 449 045-3
Austin, TX 78758   Maye A. Bartlett, Libn.
Founded: 1967. **Staff:** Prof 1; Other 2. **Subjects:** Computer science, electronics, management, technology, engineering. **Holdings:** 10,000 books; 1000 bound periodical volumes; 60 video cassettes; 500,000 microfiche. **Subscriptions:** 200 journals and other serials. **Services:** Library not open to public. **Computerized Information Services:** Online systems. **Staff:** Rose Haschle, Asst.Libn.

IBM CORPORATION - SYSTEM COMMUNICATIONS DIVISION - SITE LIBRARY
See: IBM Corporation - DSD Site Library

IBM CORPORATION - SYSTEM PRODUCTS DIVISION - LIBRARY
See: IBM Corporation - General Technology Division - Library

★5936★
IBM CORPORATION - THOMAS J. WATSON RESEARCH CENTER LIBRARY
(Sci-Tech)
Box 218   Phone: (914) 945-1415
Yorktown Heights, NY 10598   J.W. Leonard, Mgr.
Founded: 1952. **Staff:** Prof 2; Other 5. **Subjects:** Physics, chemistry, mathematics, computer science. **Holdings:** 35,000 books; 35,000 bound periodical volumes. **Subscriptions:** 1300 journals and other serials. **Services:** Interlibrary loans; copying; SDI; use of library for reference may be requested. **Computerized Information Services:** DIALOG; computerized acquisitions, serials and circulation.

ICC
See: U.S. Interstate Commerce Commission

ICD REHABILITATION AND RESEARCH CENTER
See: International Center for the Disabled

★5937★
ICI AMERICAS INC. - ATLAS LIBRARY (Sci-Tech)
                                                Phone: (302) 575-8231
Wilmington, DE 19897   Velga B. Rukuts, Libn.
Founded: 1913. **Staff:** Prof 6; Other 7. **Subjects:** Bio-medicine, chemistry, chemical technology, business economics, pharmaceuticals. **Holdings:** 24,000 volumes; 75 VF drawers of government documents; 150 VF drawers and 132 shelf feet of company technical reports; 60 shelf feet of patents; 7 VF drawers of specifications; 20 VF drawers of pamphlets; 53 VF drawers of catalogs; 35 VF drawers of Skeleton files; U.S. patents on microfilm from 1964; 100 titles on microfilm. **Subscriptions:** 1400 journals and other serials; 6 newspapers. **Services:** Interlibrary loans; copying; SDI; library open to local public on limited basis. **Computerized Information Services:** DIALOG, SDC, BRS, MEDLINE, New York Times Information Service; computerized circulation. **Networks/Consortia:** Member of Wilmington Area Biomedical Libraries Consortium. **Staff:** Sadako Orraca, Acq.; Shauna Bryson, Cat.; Karol Killinger, Bioscience Libn.; Karen Zeitler, Ref.; Nancy Thoman, Reports Libn.

★5938★
ICI AMERICAS INC. - DARCO EXPERIMENTAL LABORATORY LIBRARY (Sci-Tech)†
Box 790   Phone: (214) 938-9211
Marshall, TX 75670   S. Neafus, Libn.
Subjects: Activated carbons, chemical engineering, analytical and inorganic chemistry. **Holdings:** 2964 books; 2033 bound periodical volumes; 7 VF drawers of U.S. Government reports; 22 VF drawers of internal reports; 2 VF drawers of patents. **Subscriptions:** 16 journals and other serials. **Services:** Library not open to public.

★5939★
ICI AMERICAS INC. - PROCESS TECHNOLOGY DEPARTMENT LIBRARY (Sci-Tech)
Main St.   Phone: (617) 669-6731
Dighton, MA 02715   Candace A. Fish, Libn.
Staff: 1. **Subjects:** Organics, dyes, general chemistry. **Holdings:** 300 books; 280 bound periodical volumes. **Services:** Library open to public by permission. **Formerly:** Its Works Experimental Department Library.

ICPSR
See: University of Michigan - Inst. for Social Research - Inter-University Consortium for Political & Soc.Res.

★5940★
IDAHO FALLS CONSOLIDATED HOSPITALS - MEDICAL LIBRARY (Med)
2525 Boulevard   Phone: (208) 529-7128
Idaho Falls, ID 83401   Coleen C. Winward, Med.Libn.
Staff: Prof 1. **Subjects:** Medicine, nursing, hospital administration. **Holdings:** 460 books; 1509 bound periodical volumes; 3 vertical files; 200 cassettes. **Subscriptions:** 163 journals and other serials; 7 newspapers. **Services:** Interlibrary loans; copying; library open to health care professionals and upon physician recommendation. **Computerized Information Services:** MEDLINE, Ontyme. **Networks/Consortia:** Member of Southeast Idaho Area Resource Consortium; Idaho Health Libraries Network. **Formerly:** Consolidated Hospitals

of Idaho Falls.

IDAHO MUSEUM OF NATURAL HISTORY
See: Idaho State University

IDAHO NATIONAL ENGINEERING LABORATORY
See: EG&G, Inc.

★5941★
IDAHO STATE HISTORICAL SOCIETY - GENEALOGICAL LIBRARY (Hist)
610 N. Julia Davis Dr.   Phone: (208) 334-2305
Boise, ID 83706   Frieda O. March, Libn.
Staff: Prof 1; Other 2. **Subjects:** Genealogy. **Holdings:** 7500 books; 1850 films; microfiche. **Remarks:** The library is located at 325 State Street, Boise, ID 83702.

★5942★
IDAHO STATE HISTORICAL SOCIETY - LIBRARY AND ARCHIVES (Hist)
610 N. Julia Davis Dr.   Phone: (208) 334-3356
Boise, ID 83702   Karin E. Ford, Libn.
Founded: 1907. **Staff:** Prof 6; Other 2. **Subjects:** Idaho history - state government, irrigation, law, architecture, labor; genealogy; Pacific Northwest history. **Special Collections:** W.E. Borah manuscripts; J.H. Hawley manuscripts; Henry Dworshak manuscripts; Twin Falls Carey Act irrigation records; State Federation of Labor records; Boise-Cascade Lumber Company records; R.E. Smylie manuscripts; Orval Hansen manuscripts. **Holdings:** 5000 books; 3200 bound periodical volumes; 1520 cubic feet of manuscripts; 4800 maps; 9600 cubic feet of Idaho State archives; 50,000 photographs; 7000 reels of microfilm; 60 cubic feet of vertical file material. **Subscriptions:** 100 journals and other serials; 68 newspapers. **Services:** Interlibrary loans (limited to microfilm); copying; library and archives open to public. **Publications:** Idaho Yesterdays, quarterly - to members and subscribers; Reference Series, irregular - free upon request; Idaho Historical Series, irregular; Mountain Light, newsletter, quarterly. **Special Catalogs:** Manuscripts and pictures (card). **Staff:** Dr. Merle Wells, Hist. & Archv.; Gary Bettis, Archv.; Judith Austin, Ed./Res.Hist./Archv.; Larry Jones, Hist.; Elizabeth P. Jacox, Lib.Asst.

★5943★
IDAHO STATE LAW LIBRARY (Law)
Supreme Court Bldg.
451 W. State St.   Phone: (208) 334-3316
Boise, ID 83720   Laura M. Pershing, Law Libn.
Founded: 1870. **Staff:** Prof 2; Other 4. **Subjects:** Law; Idaho history. **Holdings:** 97,000 volumes; 4 VF drawers of pamphlets; unbound periodicals and loose-leaf services. **Subscriptions:** 230 journals and other serials. **Services:** Copying; library open to public. **Computerized Information Services:** Computerized cataloging. **Staff:** R. Scott Wrenn, Dp. Law Libn.

★5944★
IDAHO STATE LIBRARY (Info Sci)
325 W. State St.   Phone: (208) 334-2150
Boise, ID 83702   Charles Bolles, State Libn.
Founded: 1901. **Staff:** Prof 12; Other 20. **Subjects:** Idaho and Pacific Northwest; library science. **Special Collections:** Federal and state document depository. **Holdings:** 133,000 books; 3559 phonograph records and 1248 films (cataloged). **Subscriptions:** 350 journals and other serials. **Services:** Interlibrary loans; copying; library open to public for reference use only. **Computerized Information Services:** DIALOG, BRS; computerized cataloging. **Networks/Consortia:** Member of WLN; CLASS.

★5945★
IDAHO STATE LIBRARY - REGIONAL LIBRARY FOR THE BLIND AND PHYSICALLY HANDICAPPED (Aud-Vis)
325 W. State St.   Phone: (208) 334-2150
Boise, ID 83702   Evva L. Larson, Asst.State Libn.
Founded: 1973. **Staff:** Prof 2; Other 3. **Holdings:** 60,000 talking books. **Services:** Interlibrary loans; copying; library open to public. **Computerized Information Services:** BRS.

★5946★
IDAHO STATE UNIVERSITY - IDAHO MUSEUM OF NATURAL HISTORY - LIBRARY (Sci-Tech)
Campus Box 8096   Phone: (208) 232-3168
Pocatello, ID 83209   Lucille Harten, Pubn.Ed.
Founded: 1960. **Subjects:** Paleontology, anthropology, biology, geology. **Special Collections:** Stirton collection of paleontological publications. **Holdings:** 3000 volumes. **Subscriptions:** 30 journals and other serials. **Services:** Interlibrary loans; library not open to public. **Publications:** Tebiwa

(journal); occasional papers of the Idaho Museum of Natural History; special publications.

★5947★
IDAHO STATE UNIVERSITY - INSTRUCTIONAL MATERIALS CENTER (Educ)
College of Education   Phone: (208) 236-2652
Pocatello, ID 83209   Art Cullen, Asst.Prof.
Founded: 1953. **Staff:** Prof 1; Other 1. **Subjects:** Textbooks in all subjects for kindergarten through grade 12; professional books. **Holdings:** 10,378 books; 8 boxes of service bulletins; AV and media reference materials. **Services:** Instructional materials production area for student teachers and education students; center open to public.

★5948★
IDAHO STATESMAN - LIBRARY (Publ)
1200 N. Curtis Rd.
Box 40   Phone: (208) 377-6435
Boise, ID 83707   Nancy Van Dinter, Chf.Libn.
Founded: 1972. **Staff:** Prof 1; Other 1. **Subjects:** Newspaper reference topics. **Holdings:** 350 books; 250,000 newspaper clippings; 150,000 negatives; 20,000 photographs. **Subscriptions:** 10 journals and other serials; 30 newspapers. **Services:** Copying.

IDAHO WATER RESOURCES RESEARCH INSTITUTE
See: University of Idaho

★5949★
IDEAL BASIC INDUSTRIES - CEMENT DIVISION - RESEARCH DEPARTMENT - LIBRARY (Sci-Tech)
Box 1667   Phone: (303) 482-5600
Fort Collins, CO 80522
Founded: 1953. **Subjects:** Portland cement, concrete, inorganic chemistry, mineralogy. **Holdings:** 1600 books; 4 VF drawers of patents (U.S., British, Canadian); 1300 bulletins, reports, and translations. **Subscriptions:** 100 journals and other serials. **Services:** Interlibrary loans; library open to public by appointment.

IDS - INVESTMENT LIBRARY
See: Investors Diversified Services, Inc. - Investment Library

★5950★
IDS LIFE INSURANCE COMPANY - LIBRARY
IDS Tower
Minneapolis, MN 55402
Defunct

★5951★
IF EVERY FOOL, INC. - PERFORMING ARTS LIBRARY (Theater)
143 Chambers St.   Phone: (212) 964-7240
New York, NY 10007   Diane L. Goodman, Dir.
Staff: Prof 1; Other 1. **Subjects:** Circus, physical theater, comedy, clowns, pantomime, movement. **Holdings:** 2100 books and bound periodical volumes; 450 35mm slides; 56 cassettes; 24 8mm films; 300 hours of videotapes of performances; 100 folders of clippings, photographs and posters. **Services:** Copying; library open to public with restrictions.

★5952★
IFI/PLENUM DATA COMPANY - LIBRARY (Sci-Tech)
302 Swann Ave.   Phone: (703) 683-1085
Alexandria, VA 22301   Harry M. Allcock, V.P.
Founded: 1955. **Staff:** Prof 23; Other 10. **Subjects:** Chemistry, mechanics, electronics. **Special Collections:** U.S. Chemical Patent Index (1950 to present); U.S. Mechanical and Electrical Patent Bibliographic Data Collection, 1963. **Holdings:** Figures not available. **Services:** Copying; SDI; library open to public with restrictions, fee charged. **Computerized Information Services:** Online systems; computerized indexing. **Publications:** Uniterm Index to U.S. Chemical Patents-Magnetic Tape. **Remarks:** Maintained by Plenum Publishing Corporation. **Staff:** Harry Allcock, V.P.; John W. Lotz, Gen.Mgr.; Monica Rieder, Tech.Supv.; David Young, Mgr., Comp.Sys.

★5953★
IIT RESEARCH INSTITUTE - COMPUTER SEARCH CENTER (Sci-Tech)
10 W. 35th St.   Phone: (312) 567-4341
Chicago, IL 60616   Gerald J. Yucuis, Mgr.
Founded: 1968. **Staff:** Prof 3; Other 1. **Subjects:** Chemistry, engineering, physics, biology, education, electronics, database design. **Holdings:** 500 books; 1000 bound periodical volumes. **Subscriptions:** 75 journals and other serials. **Services:** Interlibrary loans; copying; SDI; retrospective searches; full document retrieval; information systems design; center open to public with

restrictions. **Computerized Information Services:** DIALOG, SDC, BRS, NLM, Control Data Corporation, DTIC, Institute for Scientific Information, Union Carbide Corporation; GACIAC (internal database); computerized cataloging, acquisitions, serials and circulation. **Networks/Consortia:** Member of OCLC through ILLINET. **Also Known As:** Illinois Institute of Technology. **Staff:** Rita DeLa Pena, Tech.Asst.; Jeanette Harlow, Libn.

★5954★
IIT RESEARCH INSTITUTE - ELECTROMAGNETIC COMPATIBILITY ANALYSIS CENTER - TECHNICAL INFORMATION SERVICES (Sci-Tech)
185 Admiral Cochrane   Phone: (301) 267-2251
Annapolis, MD 21402   Alison A. Storch, Mgr., Info.Serv.
Founded: 1961. **Staff:** Prof 4; Other 13. **Subjects:** Electromagnetic compatibility, radio frequency interference, communications equipment, electronics equipment, spectrum engineering, wave propagation, computer programming. **Special Collections:** Complete library of spectrum signatures; all Department of Defense frequency applications. **Holdings:** 6000 books; 35,000 technical reports; 9000 military and commercial equipment manuals; 25,000 microfiche of research & development reports; 300 military and commercials standards; 10,000 standards and specifications; back issues of periodicals, bound and on microform. **Subscriptions:** 300 journals and other serials. **Services:** Interlibrary loans; copying; SDI; library not open to public. **Computerized Information Services:** DTIC, BRS, DIALOG, SDC; Library Automated Information Retrieval (LAIR, internal database); computerized circulation. **Networks/Consortia:** Member of Interlibrary Users Association; FEDLINK. **Publications:** ECAC Info Center Bulletin, monthly - for internal distribution only. **Special Indexes:** Index of Spectrum Signature Data. **Also Known As:** U.S. Electromagnetic Compatibility Analysis Center. **Staff:** Ellen Huddleston, Info.Serv.Libn.; Ted Kruse, Tech.Serv.Libn.

★5955★
IIT RESEARCH INSTITUTE - ENGINEERING RESEARCH LIBRARY (Sci-Tech)
10 W. 35th St.   Phone: (312) 567-4802
Chicago, IL 60616   Jeanette Harlow, Tech.Libn.
Staff: Prof 1; Other 1. **Subjects:** Fire and explosion, structural engineering, transportation, safety, mechanical engineering. **Holdings:** 1200 books; 300 bound periodical volumes; 15,000 reports. **Subscriptions:** 50 journals and other serials. **Services:** Interlibrary loans; copying; library not open to public. **Computerized Information Services:** DIALOG, SDC. **Networks/Consortia:** Member of Chicago Library System; ILLINET.

★5956★
IIT RESEARCH INSTITUTE - GUIDANCE AND CONTROL INFORMATION ANALYSIS CENTER (GACIAC) (Sci-Tech)
10 W. 35th St.   Phone: (312) 567-4345
Chicago, IL 60616   Charles Smoots, Dir.
Founded: 1977. **Staff:** Prof 4; Other 2. **Subjects:** Tactical weapons - guidance and control systems; missiles, rockets, bombs. **Special Collections:** Machine-readable database of 28,000 citations. **Holdings:** Figures not available. **Services:** SDI; retrospective searches; information analysis; special studies; center open to public with restrictions. **Computerized Information Services:** Online systems through in-house and DTIC computers. **Publications:** GACIAC Bulletin, bimonthly; handbooks, state of the art reviews, technology assessments. **Special Indexes:** GACIAC Bibliography, quarterly; Annual Demand Bibliographies. **Staff:** Vakare Valaitis, Info.Sci.; Emily Swietek, GACIAC Coord.

★5957★
IIT RESEARCH INSTITUTE - RELIABILITY ANALYSIS CENTER (Sci-Tech)
RADC (RBRAC)
Griffiss Air Force Base   Phone: (315) 330-4151
Rome, NY 13441   H.A. Lauffenburger, Act.Tech.Dir.
Founded: 1968. **Staff:** Prof 14; Other 22. **Subjects:** Microcircuit, discrete semiconductor and nonelectric part reliability and technology. **Holdings:** 400 books; 5000 bound periodical volumes; 13,000 other cataloged items; reliability data; 5000 documents; 3 drawers of Government Industry Data Exchange Program microfilm files. **Services:** Consulting services and search services; library open to public with fee charged. **Computerized Information Services:** Internal databases. **Publications:** List of publications - available on request. **Remarks:** The Reliability Analysis Center has been established as a U.S. Department of Defense Information Analysis Center for the collection, analysis and dissemination of reliability and experience information on microcircuit devices. It features an analysis capability - producing output engineering information from raw input data.

ILGWU
See: International Ladies' Garment Workers Union

★5958★
ILIFF SCHOOL OF THEOLOGY - IRA J. TAYLOR LIBRARY (Rel-Theol)
2233 S. University Blvd.
Phone: (303) 744-1287
Denver, CO 80210-4796
Andrew D. Scrimgeour, Libn.
Founded: 1892. **Staff:** Prof 3; Other 5. **Subjects:** Bible, Christian history and missions, philosophy of religion, Christian theology and ethics, religious education, parish ministry, sociology of religion, psychology of religion, counseling. **Special Collections:** Hymnals (750 items covering many denominations); church histories of the Methodist Rocky Mountain Conference; denominational histories of the Rocky Mountain area. **Holdings:** 121,000 books and bound periodical volumes; 245 dissertations; 20 VF drawers of archives; 12,183 microforms; 560 cassette tapes; 218 reel-to-reel sermon tapes. **Subscriptions:** 900 journals and other serials; 7 newspapers. **Services:** Interlibrary loans; copying; library open to public. **Computerized Information Services:** Computerized cataloging, serials. **Networks/Consortia:** Member of Bibliographical Center for Research. **Staff:** Alice Runis, Tech.Serv.Libn.; Milton J. Coalter, Jr., Pub.Serv.Libn.

★5959★
ILLINOIS AGRICULTURAL ASSOCIATION - IAA AND AFFILIATED COMPANIES LIBRARY (Agri)
1701 Towanda Ave.
Box 2901
Phone: (309) 557-2550
Bloomington, IL 61701
Rue E. Olson, Libn.
Founded: 1957. **Staff:** Prof 3; Other 6. **Subjects:** Agriculture - economics, marketing, cooperatives, management, insurance. **Special Collections:** Alternative sources of energy. **Holdings:** 3000 books; 600 bound periodical volumes; 264 VF drawers of pamphlets including series (cataloged). **Subscriptions:** 600 journals and other serials. **Services:** Interlibrary loans; copying; literature searching, abstracting; library open to public for reference use only. **Computerized Information Services:** DIALOG, BRS, SDC, New York Times Information Service; computerized serials. **Networks/Consortia:** Member of OCLC through ILLINET. **Publications:** Acquisitions List, semimonthly; Library Newsletter, monthly - for internal distribution only. **Special Indexes:** Thesaurus covering collection's subject matter (typed list). **Staff:** Janice R. Metz, Asst.Libn.; Nancy Armstrong, Asst.Libn.

★5960★
ILLINOIS BELL TELEPHONE COMPANY - CORPORATE COMMUNICATION INFORMATION CENTER (Bus-Fin)
225 W. Randolph St., Rm. 30-B
Phone: (312) 727-2668
Chicago, IL 60606
Marguerite J. Krynicki, Hd.Libn.
Founded: 1927. **Staff:** Prof 1. **Subjects:** Business management, technology, telephone industry and history. **Special Collections:** Microfilm collection of documents and photographs on the history of the telephone and Illinois Bell Telephone Company; telephone journals. **Holdings:** 18,000 volumes. **Subscriptions:** 63 journals and other serials. **Services:** Interlibrary loans; copying; center open to employees only. **Publications:** List of new accessions, quarterly. **Formed by the Merger of:** Its Library and its Pioneer Historical Library.

★5961★
ILLINOIS BELL TELEPHONE COMPANY - PIONEER HISTORICAL LIBRARY
225 W. Randolph St.
Chicago, IL 60606
Defunct. Merged with its Library to form its Corporate Communication Information Center.

★5962★
ILLINOIS BENEDICTINE COLLEGE - THEODORE LOWNIK LIBRARY (Rel-Theol)
5700 College Rd.
Phone: (312) 960-1500
Lisle, IL 60532
Bert A. Thompson, Dir., Lib.Serv.
Founded: 1887. **Staff:** Prof 6; Other 8. **Subjects:** Theology, history, political science, science, sociology, literature. **Special Collections:** Lincolniana (2500 items); rare book collection; Slavic collection; Neuzil Memorial Sherlock Holmes Collection; college archives. **Holdings:** 122,640 books and bound periodical volumes; 7520 AV items; 2300 corporate annual reports; 14,000 government documents; 9638 microforms; 32 VF drawers. **Subscriptions:** 830 journals and other serials. **Services:** Interlibrary loans; copying; library open to public with restrictions. **Computerized Information Services:** Computerized cataloging; student terminals for computerized programs. **Networks/Consortia:** Member of LIBRAS Academic Library Cooperative; Suburban Library System (SLS); Metropolitan Chicago Library Assembly; Council of West Suburban Colleges. **Special Catalogs:** SLS/LIBRAS Union List of Serials (printout); catalog of AV sources. **Staff:** Rev. Mark Walz, O.S.B., Spec.Coll.Libn.; Joan Hopkins, Pub.Serv.Libn.; Richard H. Hansen, Info.Libn.; Mark Kroll, Tech.Serv.Libn.; Rev. Donald Hardesty, O.S.B., Circ.Asst.; Craig Eben, Instr.Dev.Div.; Mary Caron, Pub.Serv.Asst.; Joyce A. Speer,

Instr.Mtls.Libn.; William F. Sherman, Weekend Libn.

★5963★
ILLINOIS CANAL SOCIETY - LIBRARY (Trans)
1109 Garfield St.
Phone: (815) 838-7316
Lockport, IL 60441
John M. Lamb, Info.Dir.
Founded: 1977. **Staff:** 1. **Subjects:** Canals. **Special Collections:** Illinois and Michigan Canal manuscripts, photographs, maps and books. **Holdings:** 300 books; 230 photographs of canals; canal boat plans and maps; 2 VF drawers of manuscripts; 200 pamphlets. **Services:** Library open to public by appointment. **Publications:** Annual publication about canals.

★5964★
ILLINOIS COLLEGE OF OPTOMETRY - CARL F. SHEPARD MEMORIAL LIBRARY (Sci-Tech)†
3241 S. Michigan Ave.
Phone: (312) 225-1700
Chicago, IL 60616
Peter E. Weil, Libn.
Founded: 1955. **Staff:** Prof 2; Other 3. **Subjects:** Optometry, vision, vision malfunctions, optics, perception, eye diseases. **Holdings:** 11,000 books; 3100 bound periodical volumes; 3100 pamphlets and theses (cataloged); 6000 AV items; 750 microforms. **Subscriptions:** 130 journals and other serials. **Services:** Interlibrary loans; copying; library open to public for reference use only. **Computerized Information Services:** DIALOG. **Networks/Consortia:** Member of Metropolitan Chicago Library Assembly; OCLC through ILLINET; Regional Medical Library - Region 3. **Publications:** Acquisitions list, quarterly; subscription list, annual. **Staff:** Concepcion V. Gilliana, Asst.Libn.

ILLINOIS COLLEGE OF PODIATRIC MEDICINE
See: Scholl (Dr. William M.) College of Podiatric Medicine

ILLINOIS HISTORICAL SURVEY LIBRARY
See: University of Illinois

ILLINOIS INSTITUTE OF TECHNOLOGY - CENTER FOR THE STUDY OF ETHICS IN THE PROFESSIONS
See: Center for the Study of Ethics in the Professions

★5965★
ILLINOIS INSTITUTE OF TECHNOLOGY - CHICAGO KENT LAW SCHOOL - LIBRARY (Law)
77 S. Wacker Dr.
Phone: (312) 567-5014
Chicago, IL 60606
Georgia Strohm, Assoc.Libn.
Staff: Prof 5; Other 13. **Subjects:** Federal, Illinois and New York law; law and aging. **Holdings:** 65,000 books; 25,000 bound periodical volumes; 40,000 Congressional Information Service hearings and reports; 5000 state session laws; U.S. government documents. **Subscriptions:** 2532 journals and other serials. **Services:** Interlibrary loans; copying; library open to public. **Computerized Information Services:** LEXIS; computerized cataloging and circulation. **Staff:** Philip Maksymonko, Ref.Libn.; Virginia Thomas, Govt.Doc.Libn.; Helmut Reiter, Hd.Cat.; Kathy Camp, Asst.Cat.

★5966★
ILLINOIS INSTITUTE OF TECHNOLOGY - HAROLD LEONARD STUART SCHOOL OF MANAGEMENT & FINANCE - LIBRARY (Bus-Fin)
10 W. 31st St.
Phone: (312) 567-5136
Chicago, IL 60616
Jerome A. Lom, Stuart Libn.
Founded: 1972. **Staff:** Prof 1; Other 3. **Subjects:** Business, economics, labor relations, manpower, engineering economics, accounting, investment, organization theory. **Holdings:** 19,612 books; 4932 bound periodical volumes; 206 cassette tapes; 944 reels of microfilm; 19,424 microfiche; selected government and U.N. documents; reprints; pamphlets. **Subscriptions:** 441 journals and other serials. **Services:** Interlibrary loans; copying; library open to public. **Computerized Information Services:** Computerized circulation. **Networks/Consortia:** Member of Chicago Academic Library Council (CALC).

ILLINOIS INSTITUTE OF TECHNOLOGY - IIT RESEARCH INSTITUTE
See: IIT Research Institute

★5967★
ILLINOIS INSTITUTE OF TECHNOLOGY - INFORMATION AND LIBRARY RESOURCES CENTER (Bus-Fin; Sci-Tech)
3300 S. Federal St.
Phone: (312) 567-6846
Chicago, IL 60616
David R. Dowell, Dir.
Founded: 1892. **Staff:** Prof 9; Other 16. **Subjects:** Engineering, science, management, economics, design, architecture, city planning. **Special Collections:** Fire protection engineering. **Holdings:** 150,000 books; 50,000 bound periodical volumes; dissertations; 12 drawers of Department of

Housing and Urban Development 701 Depository documents; Defense Mapping Agency depository; Government Printing Office depository. **Subscriptions:** 3000 journals and other serials; 16 newspapers. **Services:** Interlibrary loans; copying; library open to public for reference use only. **Computerized Information Services:** DIALOG; internal database; computerized cataloging, serials, circulation and ILL. **Networks/Consortia:** Member of OCLC through ILLINET; Metropolitan Chicago Library Assembly; Chicago Academic Library Council (CALC). **Publications:** Newsletter; Library Handbook; Serial Publications Held in IIT Libraries. **Formerly:** Its James S. Kemper Library. **Staff:** Anita Anderson, Chf., Ref.Dept.; Susan Davis, Ser.Libn.; Pablo Barrera, Ref.Libn.; Nirmala Bangalore, Cat.Libn.; Jeannie Kim, Acq.Libn.

★5968★

ILLINOIS MASONIC MEDICAL CENTER - NOAH VAN CLEEF MEDICAL MEMORIAL LIBRARY (Med)†
836 W. Wellington Ave., Rm. 7470   Phone: (312) 975-1600
Chicago, IL 60657   Harriette M. Cluxton, Dir., Med.Lib.Serv.
Founded: 1963. **Staff:** Prof 1; Other 3. **Subjects:** Medicine, surgery, hospital administration. **Holdings:** 10,632 books; 3408 bound periodical volumes; 10 VF drawers of pamphlets; 2500 tapes; 72 records. **Subscriptions:** 426 journals and other serials. **Services:** Interlibrary loans; copying; library open to other health professionals for reference use only. **Networks/Consortia:** Member of Metropolitan Consortium; ILLINET; Chicago Library System; Regional Medical Library - Region 3. **Publications:** Noah's Ark, quarterly - internal and consortium distribution.

★5969★

ILLINOIS MASONIC MEDICAL CENTER - SCHOOL OF NURSING - DR. JOSEPH DEUTSCH MEMORIAL LIBRARY (Med)
826 W. Nelson   Phone: (312) 525-2300
Chicago, IL 60657   Ann Markham, Coord.
Staff: Prof 1; Other 6. **Subjects:** Nursing and allied health subjects. **Holdings:** 4000 books; 285 bound periodical volumes; 486 AV Lessons; 2 VF drawers of American Nurses Association pamphlets; 6 VF drawers of National League for Nursing pamphlets; 8 VF drawers of other pamphlets. **Subscriptions:** 106 journals and other serials. **Services:** Interlibrary loans; copying; library open to public for reference use only. **Networks/Consortia:** Member of Metropolitan Consortium. **Publications:** Collection News, quarterly; List of Periodicals & Audiovisuals, annual.

ILLINOIS ORAL HISTORY CLEARINGHOUSE
See: Sangamon State University - Oral History Office

★5970★

ILLINOIS RAILWAY MUSEUM - TECHNICAL LIBRARY (Trans; Hist)
Box 431   Phone: (815) 923-4391
Union, IL 60180   James E. Kehrein, Libn.
Founded: 1974. **Staff:** 2. **Subjects:** Railroad technology and history, steam locomotive technology, electric railroads, diesel locomotives. **Special Collections:** Railway Educational Bureau Collection (1000 books; 100 blueprints); T-Z Railway Equipment Company Collection (2000 blueprints); Brewster Company Blueprint Collection (500 blueprints). **Holdings:** 2000 books; 3000 blueprints; bound periodical volumes, pamphlets, maps, photographs (figures not available). **Services:** Library open to public with restrictions. **Computerized Information Services:** Computerized cataloging. **Remarks:** Library is in process of cataloging its collection. **Staff:** Lester Asher, Asst.Libn.

★5971★

ILLINOIS SCHOOL FOR THE DEAF - SCHOOL MEDIA CENTER (Educ)
125 Webster   Phone: (217) 245-5141
Jacksonville, IL 62650   Bill Stark, Dir.
Staff: Prof 3; Other 4. **Subjects:** Deafness and deaf education, curriculum supporting AV materials, high interest/low vocabulary materials, audiology, children's and adult books. **Special Collections:** Captioned films (1500); ISD Historical Picture File (700 photographs). **Holdings:** 10,000 books; 550 bound periodical volumes; 20,500 nonprint materials; 42 boxes of pamphlets. **Subscriptions:** 49 journals and other serials; 8 newspapers. **Services:** Library open to public with restrictions. **Networks/Consortia:** Member of Great River Library System. **Publications:** Sights and Sounds, 3/year - for internal distribution only. **Staff:** Mary Metcalf, Libn.; Carole Hack, Libn.

★5972★

ILLINOIS SCHOOL FOR THE VISUALLY IMPAIRED - LIBRARY (Educ)
658 E. State St.   Phone: (217) 245-4101
Jacksonville, IL 62650   Helen L. Curtis, Libn.
Staff: Prof 1; Other 1. **Subjects:** Blindness, education, child psychology, exceptional children, medicine, social work. **Holdings:** 10,704 books; 166

bound periodical volumes; 167 filmstrips; 379 tactile items; pamphlets; unbound periodicals; tapes; scrapbooks; braille, talking, large print and cassette books; phonograph records. **Subscriptions:** 96 journals and other serials. **Services:** Interlibrary loans; copying; library open to public.

★5973★

ILLINOIS STATE - APPELLATE COURT, 3RD DISTRICT - LIBRARY (Law)
1004 Columbus St.   Phone: (815) 434-5050
Ottawa, IL 61350   Sharon Smith, Libn.
Staff: 1. **Subjects:** Law. **Holdings:** 15,000 volumes, including journals of 7 Chicago area law schools. **Services:** Copying; library open to public for reference use only.

★5974★

ILLINOIS STATE - APPELLATE COURT, 5TH DISTRICT - LIBRARY (Law)†
14th & Main St.   Phone: (618) 242-3120
Mt. Vernon, IL 62864   Walter T. Simmons, Ck. of Court
Subjects: Law and government. **Holdings:** 16,733 volumes. **Services:** Library open to professionals only.

ILLINOIS STATE ARCHIVES
See: Illinois State - Office of the Secretary of State

★5975★

ILLINOIS STATE BOARD OF EDUCATION - MEDIA AND RESOURCES CENTER (Aud-Vis)
100 N. First St.   Phone: (217) 782-4433
Springfield, IL 62777   William E. Lohman, Mgr.
Staff: Prof 2; Other 1. **Subjects:** General and special education. **Holdings:** 5000 books; 3000 bound periodical volumes; 1700 16mm films and 1700 media kits (cataloged); ERIC microfiche collection. **Subscriptions:** 225 journals and other serials. **Services:** Interlibrary loans; copying; library open to Illinois residents. **Computerized Information Services:** DIALOG. **Publications:** Film catalog for Illinois teachers and multimedia catalog. **Staff:** Juanita S. Tripp, Libn.

★5976★

ILLINOIS STATE BUREAU OF THE BUDGET - ILLINOIS STATE DATA CENTER (Soc Sci)
524 S. 2nd St., Rm. 315   Phone: (217) 782-5414
Springfield, IL 62706   Paul Schnirring, Prog.Mgr.
Founded: 1980. **Subjects:** U.S. Census Bureau information. **Holdings:** 500 books; census maps, 1970-1980. **Services:** Interlibrary loans; copying; center open to public. **Networks/Consortia:** Member of Illinois State Data Center Cooperative. **Staff:** Rebecca Smith, Plan./Res.Anl.

★5977★

ILLINOIS STATE BUREAU OF EMPLOYMENT SECURITY - LABOR MARKET INFORMATION CENTER (Soc Sci)
910 S. Mighigan Ave., Rm. 1255   Phone: (312) 793-5277
Chicago, IL 60605   Eunice Choi, Libn.
Founded: 1976. **Staff:** Prof 1. **Subjects:** Illinois labor market data, state employment hours and earnings, labor turnover, occupational and wage data. **Holdings:** 2500 books. **Subscriptions:** 125 journals and other serials. **Services:** Interlibrary loans; center open to public. **Networks/Consortia:** Member of Chicago Library System. **Publications:** Guide to Labor Market Information Center. **Remarks:** Maintained by Illinois Department of Labor - Management Information Systems/Research and Analysis.

★5978★

ILLINOIS STATE DEPARTMENT OF COMMERCE & COMMUNITY AFFAIRS - OFFICE OF RESEARCH - LIBRARY (Bus-Fin)
222 S. College St.   Phone: (217) 782-1438
Springfield, IL 62706   W.W. Biermann, Chf., Res.
Staff: Prof 8; Other 3. **Subjects:** Economic development in Illinois. **Holdings:** 4000 volumes; 30 VF drawers of serials. **Subscriptions:** 65 journals and other serials. **Services:** Interlibrary loans; copying (both limited); library open to public for reference use only. **Publications:** Illinois Regional Economic Data Book, annual; County Profiles, biennial; Gross State Product, quarterly; Monthly Data Sheets.

ILLINOIS STATE DEPARTMENT OF CONSERVATION - FORT MASSAC HISTORIC SITE
See: Fort Massac Historic Site

★5979★
**ILLINOIS STATE DEPARTMENT OF ENERGY AND NATURAL RESOURCES -
ENERGY INFORMATION LIBRARY (Energy)**
325 W. Adams St., Rm. 300   Phone: (217) 785-2388
Springfield, IL 62706
Founded: 1977. **Staff:** Prof 1; Other 1. **Subjects:** Energy conservation;
biomass energy; coal; electric utilities; energy policy; natural resources;
nuclear, petroleum and power resources; solar energy; wind power. **Special
Collections:** Topographic quadrangles. **Holdings:** 3000 books and documents;
71 VF folders of newspaper clippings and pamphlets; 100 titles on microfiche.
Subscriptions: 275 journals and other serials. **Services:** Interlibrary loans;
copying; loan of 16mm films and slide shows; distribution of brochures and
departmental publications; library open to public for reference use only.
Computerized Information Services: DIALOG, DOE/RECON. **Networks/
Consortia:** Member of OCLC; Rolling Prairie Library System. **Formerly:** Illinois
State Institute of Natural Resources.

★5980★
**ILLINOIS STATE DEPARTMENT OF ENERGY AND NATURAL RESOURCES -
ENVIRONMENTAL INFORMATION CENTER (Env-Cons; Energy)**
309 W. Washington   Phone: (312) 793-7695
Chicago, IL 60606   Alice Lane, Lib.Assoc.
Founded: 1971. **Staff:** Prof 1; Other 1. **Subjects:** Environment; pollution -
air, water, noise, solid waste, thermal; environmental law and education;
energy crisis; land use; endangered species; economic impact studies.
Holdings: 8700 books; 20 VF drawers of newspaper clippings and pamphlets.
Services: Interlibrary loans; copying; library open to public for reference use
only. **Computerized Information Services:** DIALOG, DOE/RECON.
Networks/Consortia: Member of OCLC through ILLINET. **Publications:**
Library Acquisitions List, quarterly. **Special Catalogs:** Catalog of Solid Waste
Literature; Catalog of Environmental Literature (book). **Formerly:** Illinois State
Institute of Natural Resources.

**ILLINOIS STATE DEPARTMENT OF LABOR - MANAGEMENT INFORMATION
SYSTEMS/RESEARCH & ANALYSIS**
See: Illinois State Bureau of Employment Security - Labor Market
Information Center

**ILLINOIS STATE DEPARTMENT OF MENTAL HEALTH AND
DEVELOPMENTAL DISABILITIES**
See: Dixon Developmental Ctr.; Madden (John J.) Zone Ctr.; Mental
Health Centers located at Chicago-Read; Elgin; Galesburg; McFarland;
Manteno; Singer (H. Douglas); Tinley Park; Zeller (George A.)

★5981★
**ILLINOIS STATE DEPARTMENT OF TRANSPORTATION - TECHNICAL
REFERENCE LIBRARY (Trans; Law)**
338 Administration Bldg.
2300 S. Dirksen Pkwy.   Phone: (217) 782-6680
Springfield, IL 62764   Gisela Motzkus, Libn.
Founded: 1963. **Staff:** Prof 1; Other 1. **Subjects:** Transportation - planning,
economics, administration; traffic control and operations; urban transportation
administration and systems; maintenance; law. **Special Collections:** Complete
law library. **Holdings:** 503 textbooks; 148 bound periodical volumes; 5000
other cataloged items; 20 VF drawers of pamphlets, conference reports and
speeches; 15 shelves of Illinois documents. **Subscriptions:** 151 journals and
other serials. **Services:** Interlibrary loans; copying; library not open to public.
Publications: Library Newsletter, bimonthly.

★5982★
**ILLINOIS STATE ENVIRONMENTAL PROTECTION AGENCY - LIBRARY (Env-
Cons)**
2200 Churchill Rd.   Phone: (217) 782-9691
Springfield, IL 62706   Nancy Simpson, Libn.
Staff: Prof 1; Other 1. **Subjects:** Environmental pollution and protection,
environmental law and economics. **Holdings:** 12,000 books; 250 bound
periodical volumes; 1500 legal documents; 10,000 EPA technical reports on
microfiche. **Subscriptions:** 300 journals and other serials. **Services:**
Interlibrary loans; library open to public for reference use only. **Computerized
Information Services:** DIALOG, SDC. **Networks/Consortia:** Member of
ILLINET; Midwest Health Science Library Network (MHSLN). **Publications:**
Acquisitions list, monthly - for internal distribution only.

★5983★
ILLINOIS STATE GEOLOGICAL SURVEY - LIBRARY (Sci-Tech; Energy)
615 E. Peabody   Phone: (217) 344-1481
Champaign, IL 61820   Mary Krick, Libn.
Staff: Prof 1; Other 1. **Subjects:** Geology, stratigraphy, mineral economics,
fuel technology, paleontology, coal chemistry, analytical chemistry,

geochemistry, environmental geology and mineral resources of Illinois.
Special Collections: State geological survey publications. **Holdings:** 8000
books; 6100 bound periodical volumes; 16,000 documents (cataloged); 300
patents; 85 reels of microfilm; 6500 maps; 8 VF drawers. **Subscriptions:**
105 journals and other serials. **Services:** Interlibrary loans; library open to
public. **Computerized Information Services:** SDC. **Networks/Consortia:**
Member of Lincoln Trail Libraries System. **Publications:** Acquisition list,
monthly - for internal distribution only. **Staff:** Kristi Komadina, Asst.Libn.

★5984★
ILLINOIS STATE HISTORICAL LIBRARY (Hist)
Old State Capitol   Phone: (217) 782-4836
Springfield, IL 62706   Olive S. Foster, State Hist.
Founded: 1889. **Staff:** Prof 24; Other 49. **Subjects:** Illinois history,
Lincolniana, Civil War history, Midwest Americana, Mormon history, Indian
history, genealogy. **Special Collections:** Abraham Lincoln Collection (1425
manuscripts; 8000 books and pamphlets); Picture and Print Collection
(175,000 items). **Holdings:** 155,000 books and bound periodical volumes;
5.2 million manuscripts; 55,000 reels of microfilm; 2000 maps; 3000
broadsides (cataloged). **Subscriptions:** 600 journals and other serials; 300
newspapers. **Services:** Interlibrary loans (limited); copying; library open to
public. **Publications:** Illinois State Historical Society Journal, quarterly; Illinois
History, 8 times per year; Dispatch (newsletter), 6/year. **Staff:** William E.
Keller, Admin.Asst.; Maynard A. Crossland, Hd., Ext.Serv.; Dr. Roger D. Bridges,
Hd.Libn. & Dir., Res.; James T. Hickey, Cur., Lincoln Coll.; Laurel Bowen, Cur.
of Mss.; Sandra Stark, Newspaper Libn.; Mary Ellen McElligott, Supv.,
Ed.Sect.; Mary Michals, Iconographer; Daniel D. Holt, Acq.; Marianna Munyer,
Cur., Hist. Sites; Diane Wilhelm, Ref.Libn.; Jo Anne Nast, Supv., Sch.Serv.;
Blanche Burgess, Supv., Local Hist.; Bruce Cody, Pub.Info.Off.

ILLINOIS STATE INSTITUTE OF NATURAL RESOURCES
See: Illinois State Department of Energy and Natural Resources

★5985★
ILLINOIS STATE LEGISLATIVE REFERENCE BUREAU (Law)
State House, Rm. 112   Phone: (217) 525-6625
Springfield, IL 62706   Mary Louise McCreary, Libn.
Founded: 1913. **Staff:** Prof 1. **Subjects:** Legislation. **Special Collections:**
Illinois statutes and reports; statutes of all other states. **Holdings:** 5000
books; 150 bound periodical volumes; House and Senate Bills from 1877-
1970 on microfilm. **Subscriptions:** 15 journals and other serials. **Services:**
Copying; research work on out-of-state statutes for persons in the state;
library open to public. **Publications:** Legislative Digest, weekly when General
Assembly is in session - available for purchase. **Staff:** Stanley Johnston,
Exec.Sec.

★5986★
ILLINOIS STATE LIBRARY (Info Sci)†
Centennial Bldg.   Phone: (217) 782-2994
Springfield, IL 62756   Kathryn J. Gesterfield, Dir.
Founded: 1839. **Staff:** Prof 44; Other 69. **Subjects:** General nonfiction,
social sciences, Illinois state government, business, economics, science and
technology. **Special Collections:** State documents (268,349); federal
documents (1.6 million). **Holdings:** 1.9 million books; 988,906 microforms.
Subscriptions: 3083 journals and other serials; 35 newspapers. **Services:**
Interlibrary loans; copying; library open to public for reference use only.
Computerized Information Services: BRS; computerized cataloging,
acquisitions and circulation. **Networks/Consortia:** Headquarters of ILLINET;
member of Regional Medical Library - Region 3; CLENE, Inc. **Publications:**
Illinois Libraries, 10/year; Illinois Nodes, 12/year. **Staff:** Sherwood Kirk,
Assoc.Dir., Lib.Oper.; Bridget Lamont, Assoc.Dir., Lib.Dev.; Margaret Herman,
Coord., Coll.Dev.Serv.

★5987★
**ILLINOIS STATE MUSEUM OF NATURAL HISTORY AND ART - TECHNICAL
LIBRARY (Art; Sci-Tech)**
            Phone: (217) 782-6623
Springfield, IL 62706   Orvetta Robinson, Libn.
Staff: 2. **Subjects:** Anthropology, archeology, art, botany, geology, zoology.
Special Collections: R.M. Barnes Collection (ornithology); Benjamin S. Hunter
Collection (art); Raymond Janssen Collection (geology); Thorne Deuel
Collection (anthropology). **Holdings:** 10,000 volumes; 6 VF drawers of
pamphlets; 1000 maps. **Subscriptions:** 200 journals and other serials.
Services: Interlibrary loans; copying; library open to public for reference use
only. **Publications:** Living Museum, quarterly - free on request.

ILLINOIS STATE NATURAL HISTORY SURVEY
See: University of Illinois

★5988★

ILLINOIS STATE - OFFICE OF THE SECRETARY OF STATE - STATE ARCHIVES (Hist)
Illinois State Archives Bldg.   Phone: (217) 525-4682
Springfield, IL 62756   John Daly, Dir.
Founded: 1921. **Staff:** Prof 20; Other 24. **Subjects:** Illinois history and official records. **Special Collections:** Perrin Collection of early French records of St. Clair County, Illinois; Illinois and Michigan canal records. **Holdings:** 7250 volumes; 70,000 cubic feet of state agency reports, land patents, manuscript records, and county and state agency records. **Subscriptions:** 35 journals and other serials. **Services:** Copying; genealogical research; war records research; historical research; land record research; library open to public, some files closed by law. **Publications:** A Descriptive Inventory of the Archives of the State of Illinois; A Proposal for the Management of Judicial Records in Illinois; A Guide to Management of State Records and Services of the Archives-Records Management Division. **Special Indexes:** Name Index of individuals found in records prior to 1850; indexes to records of Illinois' participation in wars to 1900.

★5989★

ILLINOIS STATE PSYCHIATRIC INSTITUTE - PROFESSIONAL LIBRARY (Med)
1601 W. Taylor St.   Phone: (312) 996-1320
Chicago, IL 60612   Mrs. Kineret Lichtenstein, Libn.
Founded: 1959. **Staff:** Prof 1; Other 1. **Subjects:** Psychiatry, psychology, psychopharmacology. **Holdings:** 10,000 books; 270 audio cassettes; 15 videotapes. **Subscriptions:** 205 journals and other serials. **Services:** Interlibrary loans. **Networks/Consortia:** Member of Regional Medical Library - Region 3; Illinois Department of Mental Health and Developmental Disabilities Professional Libraries Consortium. **Publications:** Newsletter, bimonthly - for internal distribution only; Subject Bibliographies.

★5990★

ILLINOIS STATE - SUPREME COURT LIBRARY (Law)†
Supreme Court Bldg.   Phone: (217) 782-2424
Springfield, IL 62706   Catherine Bradley, Law Libn.
Staff: Prof 1; Other 2. **Subjects:** Law. **Special Collections:** Early English reports in folio; British materials; reports, statutes, laws and codes. **Holdings:** 78,000 books and bound periodical volumes. **Subscriptions:** 280 journals and other serials. **Services:** Library open to public.

★5991★

ILLINOIS STATE UNIVERSITY - MILNER LIBRARY - SPECIAL COLLECTIONS (Hum)
                                                  Phone: (309) 438-3675
Normal, IL 61761   Fred M. Peterson, Univ.Libn.
Special Collections: Circus and related arts; children's literature; American and English authors of the 19th and 20th century; private presses; university archives (1800 cubic feet). **Services:** Interlibrary loans; copying; library open to public. **Computerized Information Services:** DIALOG; computerized cataloging. **Networks/Consortia:** Member of OCLC through ILLINET; Library Computer System (LCS).

★5992★

ILLINOIS STATE WATER SURVEY - LIBRARY (Sci-Tech)
605 E. Springfield
Sta. A
Box 5050
Champaign, IL 61820   Phone: (217) 333-4956
                                              Marcia E. Nelson, Hd.Libn.
Founded: 1920. **Staff:** Prof 2; Other 1. **Subjects:** Hydrology, water resources, atmospheric and aquatic chemistry, water quality, meteorology, atmospheric sciences. **Special Collections:** State Water Survey Archives; Water Supply Papers of USGS (entire set); U.S. climatic data; HIPLEX reports. **Holdings:** 19,500 books; 1200 bound periodical volumes; 400 microfiche (cataloged). **Subscriptions:** 450 journals and other serials. **Services:** Interlibrary loans; SDI; library open to public. **Computerized Information Services:** DIALOG; internal databases; computerized serials and journal routing. **Networks/Consortia:** Member of Lincoln Trail Library System. **Publications:** Acquisition list, monthly - to researchers. **Special Indexes:** Illinois County Index to State Water Survey Publications (online). **Remarks:** Branch libraries maintained in Peoria and Warrenville, IL.

ILLINOIS SUPREME COURT - MC LEAN COUNTY BAR ASSOCIATION
See: Mc Lean County Bar Association

★5993★

ILLINOIS WESLEYAN UNIVERSITY - THORPE MUSIC LIBRARY (Mus)
                                                  Phone: (309) 556-3003
Bloomington, IL 61701   Robert C. Delvin, Fine Arts Libn.
Staff: Prof 1; Other 8. **Subjects:** Music, music education. **Holdings:** 14,000 books; 250 bound periodical volumes; 5000 recordings (cataloged); 145 masters theses; 110 reels of microfilm. **Subscriptions:** 42 journals and other serials. **Services:** Interlibrary loans; copying; library open to public. **Computerized Information Services:** DIALOG; computerized cataloging. **Networks/Consortia:** Member of OCLC through ILLINET. **Publications:** Monthly lists of new acquisitions - distributed to faculty.

★5994★

IMA INCORPORATED - LIBRARY (Sci-Tech)
15233 Ventura Blvd., Suite 500   Phone: (213) 783-4461
Sherman Oaks, CA 91403   Susan F. Sudduth, Libn.
Staff: Prof 1. **Subjects:** Electronics, military and medical electronics, engineering, marketing and sales. **Holdings:** 500 books; 2 file cabinets of unbound reports; 1 VF drawer of government documents. **Subscriptions:** 80 journals and other serials; 5 newspapers. **Services:** Copying; library not open to public.

IMAGE ARCHIVES
See: University of Calgary - Special Collections Division

★5995★

IMASCO FOODS, LTD. - LIBRARY (Food-Bev)
4945 Ontario St., E.   Phone: (514) 255-2811
Montreal, PQ, Canada H1V 1M2   Louise Pichet, Lib.Techn.
Founded: 1973. **Staff:** Prof 1. **Subjects:** Food, nutrition, legislation of food. **Holdings:** 470 books. **Subscriptions:** 100 journals and other serials. **Services:** Interlibrary loans; copying.

IMASCO LTD. - IMPERIAL TOBACCO LTD.
See: Imperial Tobacco Ltd.

IMC
See: International Minerals & Chemicals Corporation

IMF
See: International Monetary Fund

★5996★

IMMACULATE CONCEPTION SEMINARY - LIBRARY (Rel-Theol)
671 Ramapo Valley Rd.   Phone: (201) 327-0300
Mahwah, NJ 07430   Rev. James C. Turro, Dir., Lib.Serv.
Staff: Prof 2; Other 3. **Subjects:** Theology, philosophy, Catholic Church history, Bible. **Special Collections:** Sacred books (rare). **Holdings:** 69,282 books; 2938 bound periodical volumes; 175 other cataloged items; 431 reels of microfilm; 225 tapes and cassettes; 431 microforms. **Subscriptions:** 688 journals and other serials; 16 newspapers. **Services:** Interlibrary loans; library open to public. **Publications:** Bibliography of new titles in library, bimonthly. **Staff:** Enzo Prisco, Libn.

★5997★

IMMACULATE HEART COLLEGE - MUSIC LIBRARY (Mus)†
2021 N. Western Ave.   Phone: (213) 462-1301
Los Angeles, CA 90027
Founded: 1944. **Staff:** Prof 1. **Subjects:** Instrumental music, vocal music. **Holdings:** 4000 phonograph records; 4100 scores; 490 audiotapes and cassettes.

★5998★

IMMACULATE HEART OF MARY - PARISH LIBRARY (Rel-Theol)
3700 Canyon Rd.   Phone: (505) 662-6193
Los Alamos, NM 87544
Founded: 1961. **Staff:** 20. **Subjects:** Religion, religious education, theology, philosophy, marriage and family, psychology, socioeconomic concerns. **Holdings:** 4000 books; 20 bound periodical volumes; 200 pamphlets; 45 records and record-book sets; 25 reel-to-reel tapes; 500 cassette tapes. **Subscriptions:** 15 journals and other serials. **Services:** Interlibrary loans; library open to public by request. **Staff:** Marcella Backsen, Libn.; Ursula Hayter, Libn.

★5999★

IMMANUEL MEDICAL CENTER - PROFESSIONAL LIBRARY (Med)
6901 N. 72nd St.   Phone: (402) 572-2345
Omaha, NE 68122   Dorothy B. Willis, Media Rscrs.Coord.
Staff: 1. **Subjects:** Medicine, nursing and allied health sciences. **Holdings:**

375 books; 189 bound periodical volumes. **Subscriptions:** 52 journals and other serials. **Services:** Interlibrary loans; copying; library open with physician's permission.

IMMIGRATION APPEAL BOARD
See: Canada - Immigration Appeal Board

IMMIGRATION HISTORY RESEARCH CENTER COLLECTION
See: University of Minnesota

★6000★
IMODCO - BUSINESS LIBRARY (Sci-Tech)
10960 Wilshire Blvd., Suite 1100   Phone: (213) 477-1441
Los Angeles, CA 91405   Janice McKinney, Libn.
Staff: Prof 1. **Subjects:** Engineering, offshore oil industry. **Holdings:** 500 books; Offshore Technology Conference (OTC) proceedings; 460 catalogs; 400 files of technical reports. **Subscriptions:** 103 journals and other serials. **Services:** Library not open to public.

★6001★
IMPERIAL CLEVITE INC. - IC INFORMATION CENTER (Sci-Tech)
540 E. 105th St.   Phone: (216) 851-5500
Cleveland, OH 44108   Barbara Sanduleak, Supv.
Founded: 1954. **Staff:** Prof 1; Other 2. **Subjects:** Metals, powder metallurgy, materials, engineering, plastics and rubber. **Holdings:** 6500 books; 28 VF drawers of unbound reports; 24 VF drawers of clippings; 750 reels of microfilm; 6000 titles on microfiche; 4 VF drawers of patents; 6 VF drawers of archives. **Subscriptions:** 650 journals and other serials. **Services:** Interlibrary loans; copying; center open to public by appointment. **Computerized Information Services:** DIALOG, BRS, SDC; periodical holdings, search activities; computerized cataloging. **Networks/Consortia:** Member of OCLC; OHIONET. **Formerly:** Gould, Inc. - Gould Information Center.

★6002★
IMPERIAL COUNTY LAW LIBRARY (Law)†
Court House
939 Main St.   Phone: (619) 352-3610
El Centro, CA 92243   Mary Ann Azzarello, Law Libn.
Subjects: Law. **Holdings:** 10,700 volumes.

★6003★
IMPERIAL LIFE ASSURANCE COMPANY - LIBRARY (Bus-Fin)†
95 St. Clair Ave., W.   Phone: (416) 923-6661
Toronto, ON, Canada M4V 1N7   P. Stewart, Libn.
Founded: 1921. **Staff:** 1. **Subjects:** Insurance - proceedings, law and history; general and actuarial mathematics; life insurance and statistics; office management; investment; marketing; economics. **Holdings:** 4000 volumes; clippings, government documents; pamphlets. **Subscriptions:** 120 journals and other serials. **Services:** Library not open to public.

★6004★
IMPERIAL OIL, LTD. - BUSINESS INFORMATION CENTRE (Bus-Fin)
111 St. Clair Ave., W.   Phone: (416) 968-4111
Toronto, ON, Canada M5W 1K3   Susan McDonald, Mgr.
Founded: 1945. **Staff:** Prof 5; Other 6. **Subjects:** Petroleum industry, industrial relations, marketing, management, economics, public relations. **Holdings:** 15,000 books; 12 VF drawers and 84 shelving feet of Statistics Canada reports; 84 VF drawers of annual reports; 70 VF drawers of pamphlets and reports. **Subscriptions:** 650 journals and other serials. **Services:** Interlibrary loans; copying; SDI; library open to public by appointment. **Computerized Information Services:** DIALOG, SDC, CAN/OLE, Info Globe, QL Systems; internal database; computerized cataloging and serials. **Publications:** Business Information Alert, monthly - for internal distribution only. **Staff:** Frances Krayewski, Supv., Info.Serv.; Sarah Vanstone, Supv., Tech.Serv.; Kathryn Ryans, Info.Spec.

★6005★
IMPERIAL OIL, LTD. - RESEARCH TECHNICAL INFORMATION CENTRE (Sci-Tech; Energy)
Box 3022   Phone: (519) 339-2471
Sarnia, ON, Canada N7T 7M1   N.J. Gaspar, Hd., Info.Serv.
Staff: Prof 2; Other 3. **Subjects:** Chemistry, petroleum, petrochemicals, polymers, chemical engineering, energy. **Holdings:** 12,000 books; 10,000 bound periodical volumes; 40,000 company research reports; U.S. chemical patents; chemical abstracts, 1907-present; API literature and patents, 1964 to present. **Subscriptions:** 240 journals and other serials. **Services:** Interlibrary loans; copying; library not open to public. **Computerized Information Services:** DIALOG, SDC, QL Systems. **Staff:** D.E. Eagles, Chem.-Libn.

★6006★
IMPERIAL TOBACCO LTD. - CORPORATE LIBRARY (Bus-Fin)
P.O. Box 6500   Phone: (514) 932-6161
Montreal, PQ, Canada H3C 3L6   Yolande Mukherjee, Corp.Libn.
Founded: 1938. **Staff:** 6. **Subjects:** Tobacco, management. **Special Collections:** Tobacco nostalgia (20,000 ads, packages, paintings and other items). **Holdings:** 4000 books; 10,000 pamphlets (cataloged); 20 VF drawers of photographs. **Subscriptions:** 1000 journals and other serials. **Services:** Interlibrary loans; library open to public. **Computerized Information Services:** Computerized serials. **Publications:** What's New/Nouveautes, monthly - available on request; New Books, Lending Library, monthly - for internal distribution only. **Special Catalogs:** Books in the Library (book); About Tobacco: Books and Periodicals on Tobacco (book). **Special Indexes:** Canadian Cigar and Tobacco Journal Index (from 1898; card). **Remarks:** Maintained by Imasco Ltd.

★6007★
IMPERIAL TOBACCO LTD. - RESEARCH LIBRARY (Sci-Tech)
734 Bourget St.   Phone: (514) 932-6161
Montreal, PQ, Canada H4C 2M7   Miss R.A. Ayoung, Res.Libn.
Founded: 1954. **Staff:** Prof 1; Other 1. **Subjects:** Tobacco, chemistry of natural products, agricultural chemistry, biochemistry. **Holdings:** 1755 books; 1000 bound periodical volumes; 2 drawers of reports; 18 drawers of reprints and photocopies; 4 drawers and 25 boxes of pamphlets. **Subscriptions:** 115 journals and other serials. **Services:** Interlibrary loans; copying; library not open to public. **Publications:** Accession List, monthly.

★6008★
IN-FACT - RESEARCH AND INFORMATION SERVICE (Info Sci)
Righter Rd.
Box 151   Phone: (518) 797-5154
Rensselaerville, NY 12147   Katherine H. Storms, Info.Spec.
Founded: 1976. **Staff:** Prof 2. **Subjects:** Management - records, archives; genealogy; history. **Holdings:** 2000 books and bound periodical volumes. **Services:** Copying; information search service for a fee; copy editing; library not open to public. **Staff:** Kenneth Storms, Info.Spec.

★6009★
INA CORPORATION - LIBRARY (Bus-Fin)
1600 Arch St.   Phone: (215) 241-4677
Philadelphia, PA 19101   Joan C. Divor, Libn.
Founded: 1947. **Staff:** Prof 2; Other 3. **Subjects:** Insurance, management, occupational and environmental safety and health. **Holdings:** 23,000 books; 2100 bound periodical volumes; 70 VF drawers of pamphlets. **Subscriptions:** 300 journals and other serials. **Services:** Library open to public for reference use only. **Staff:** Marnie Louderback, Asst.Libn.

★6010★
INCARNATE WORD HOSPITAL - MEDICAL LIBRARY (Med)
3545 Lafayette Ave.   Phone: (314) 664-6500
St. Louis, MO 63104   Sr. Raymond Borgmeyer, Libn.
Founded: 1960. **Staff:** Prof 1; Other 4. **Subjects:** Medicine and allied sciences; staff development. **Holdings:** 2500 books; 1250 bound periodical volumes; 50 pamphlets (cataloged); reports and medical papers; 70 video cassettes. **Subscriptions:** 150 journals and other serials; 8 newspapers. **Services:** Interlibrary loans; copying; library open to medical and nursing students. **Networks/Consortia:** Member of Network for Continuing Medical Education (NCME); St. Louis Regional Library Network; Midcontinental Regional Medical Library Network.

★6011★
INCO METALS COMPANY - BUSINESS LIBRARY (Bus-Fin)
1 First Canadian Pl.
Box 44   Phone: (416) 361-7640
Toronto, ON, Canada M5X 1C4   Sheila Korom, Supv., Info.Serv.
Staff: 2. **Subjects:** Metal industry, economics. **Holdings:** 8000 books; 300 bound periodical volumes; 6500 annual reports; 2 VF drawers of pamphlets and clippings. **Subscriptions:** 603 journals and other serials; 15 newspapers. **Services:** Interlibrary loans; copying; library open to public by appointment only. **Computerized Information Services:** DIALOG, SDC, Info Globe; internal database; computerized cataloging, serials and circulation. **Publications:** Acquisitions list; Current Periodical Review, both monthly - both for internal distribution only. **Staff:** Neftalie Abrenica, Info.Spec.

★6012★
INCO METALS COMPANY - EXPLORATION LIBRARY (Energy)
1 First Canadian Place
Box 44   Phone: (416) 361-7511
Toronto, ON, Canada M5X 1C4   Neftalie Abrenica, Libn.
Founded: 1970. **Staff:** Prof 1. **Subjects:** Geology, mining, engineering,

mineral economics, remote sensing. **Special Collections:** Surveys and reports from Geological Survey of Canada, Ontario Ministry of Natural Resources, Geological Association of Canada, and Canadian Institute of Mining and Metallurgy. **Holdings:** 1200 books; 100 boxes of pamphlets and clippings; map collection; annual reports of 300 mining companies. **Subscriptions:** 35 journals and other serials. **Services:** Interlibrary loans; copying; library open to public with restrictions. **Computerized Information Services:** DIALOG, SDC, Info Globe. **Publications:** Accession lists; periodical contents lists.

★6013★
INCO METALS COMPANY - J. ROY GORDON RESEARCH LABORATORY (Energy)
Sheridan Park   Phone: (416) 822-3322
Mississauga, ON, Canada L5K 1Z9   L. Green, Libn.
Founded: 1966. **Staff:** Prof 2; Other 1. **Subjects:** Extractive metallurgy, electrochemistry, geology, mining, pollution control. **Holdings:** 3100 books; 6700 bound periodical volumes; 6000 patents; 7500 pamphlets; government documents. **Subscriptions:** 215 journals and other serials. **Services:** Interlibrary loans; copying; SDI; library open to public by appointment. **Computerized Information Services:** DIALOG, SDC, CAN/OLE, QL Systems, INFOLINE, BRS; internal database; computerized cataloging. **Networks/Consortia:** Member of Sheridan Park Association. **Publications:** Extramet Digest, semimonthly - for internal distribution only. **Special Indexes:** Index to Inco staff publications (book).

★6014★
INDEPENDENCE MENTAL HEALTH INSTITUTE - MEDICAL LIBRARY (Med)†
Box 111   Phone: (319) 334-2583
Independence, IA 50644   Lois J. Samek, Med.Libn.
Founded: 1880. **Staff:** Prof 1. **Subjects:** Psychiatry, medicine, psychiatric nursing. **Holdings:** 3500 books; 650 bound periodical volumes; 200 cassette tapes. **Subscriptions:** 48 journals and other serials. **Services:** Interlibrary loans; library not open to public.

INDEPENDENCE NATL. HISTORICAL PARK
See: U.S. Natl. Park Service

★6015★
INDEPENDENT PETROLEUM ASSOCIATION OF AMERICA - COMMUNICATIONS DEPARTMENT (Energy)
1101 16th St., N.W.
Washington, DC 20036
Subjects: Crude oil; natural gas; petroleum industry - taxation, public lands, environment and safety, supply and demand, cost-study. **Holdings:** Figures not available. **Services:** Department not open to public. **Formerly:** Its Information Service.

INDEX OF AMERICAN DESIGN
See: National Gallery of Art

INDEX OF CHRISTIAN ART
See: Princeton University - Department of Art & Archaeology

★6016★
INDIA - EMBASSY OF INDIA - LIBRARY OF THE INFORMATION SERVICE OF INDIA (Area-Ethnic)†
2107 Massachusetts Ave., N.W.   Phone: (202) 265-5050
Washington, DC 20008   Baburaj Stephen, Libn.
Staff: Prof 3. **Subjects:** India - philosophy, religion, history, geography, literature, food and agriculture, economics, political science. **Special Collections:** Rabindranath Tagore collection; Mahatma Gandhi collection; Sri Aurobindo collection. **Holdings:** 11,200 books and bound periodical volumes. **Subscriptions:** 110 journals and other serials; 40 newspapers. **Services:** Interlibrary loans; library open to public.

INDIAN ARTS AND CRAFTS BOARD
See: U.S. Dept. of the Interior

★6017★
INDIAN CENTER OF SAN JOSE, INC. - LIBRARY
3485 East Hills Dr.
San Jose, CA 95127
Subjects: American Indian. **Special Collections:** American Indian newspapers and language tapes. **Holdings:** 1700 books; 54 bound periodical volumes; phonograph records (cataloged); films; book and audiovisual teaching materials for and about Native Americans (cataloged); pamphlets; government documents; maps; charts; pictures; publications from Indian reservations. **Networks/Consortia:** Member of CIN. **Remarks:** Presently inactive.

★6018★
INDIAN AND COLONIAL RESEARCH CENTER, INC. - EVA BUTLER LIBRARY (Hist; Area-Ethnic)
Route 27   Phone: (203) 536-9771
Old Mystic, CT 06372   Kathleen Greenhalgh, Libn.
Founded: 1965. **Staff:** Prof 2; Other 15. **Subjects:** Indians, genealogy, colonial history. **Special Collections:** Elmer Waite collection of glass plate negatives of the area; rare American school books, 1700-1850 (300). **Holdings:** 2000 books; 954 manuscripts; 90 maps and atlases; 2000 early American notebooks; 69 boxes of bulletins and pamphlets; 2000 photographs. **Subscriptions:** 10 journals and other serials. **Services:** Copying; library open to public. **Remarks:** Also maintains a museum.

INDIAN HEAD COMPANY - INFORMATION HANDLING SERVICES - GLOBAL ENGINEERING DOCUMENTS
See: Global Engineering Documents

★6019★
INDIAN NATIONS COUNCIL OF GOVERNMENTS - LIBRARY
707 S. Houston
Tulsa, OK 74127
Defunct

INDIAN & NORTHERN AFFAIRS CANADA
See: Canada - Indian & Northern Affairs Canada

INDIAN RIGHTS COLLECTION
See: National Library of Canada - Canadian Indian Rights Collection

★6020★
INDIAN RIVER MEMORIAL HOSPITAL - PROFESSIONAL LIBRARY (Med)
1000 36th St.   Phone: (305) 567-4311
Vero Beach, FL 32860   Arna Lyons, Libn.
Staff: Prof 1; Other 4. **Subjects:** Medicine, emergency medical care, radiology. **Holdings:** 1263 books; 375 bound periodical volumes; 650 cassettes. **Subscriptions:** 85 journals and other serials. **Services:** Interlibrary loans; library open to public with permission.

★6021★
INDIANA ACADEMY OF SCIENCE - JOHN SHEPARD WRIGHT MEMORIAL LIBRARY (Sci-Tech)
State Library, 140 N. Senate Ave.   Phone: (317) 232-3685
Indianapolis, IN 46204   Lois Burton, Libn.
Founded: 1896. **Subjects:** Science and technology. **Holdings:** 11,000 volumes. **Services:** Interlibrary loans; copying; library open to public.

INDIANA COLLECTION
See: Allen County Public Library

★6022★
INDIANA COUNTY LAW LIBRARY (Law)†
Court House
Eighth & Philadelphia
Indiana, PA 15701   Phone: (412) 465-2661
       Bonnie Zich, Law Libn.
Staff: 1. **Subjects:** Law. **Holdings:** 11,000 volumes. **Subscriptions:** 10 journals and other serials **Services:** Copying; library open to county residents for reference use only.

★6023★
INDIANA HISTORICAL SOCIETY - WILLIAM HENRY SMITH MEMORIAL LIBRARY (Hist)
315 W. Ohio St.   Phone: (317) 232-1879
Indianapolis, IN 46202   Robert K. O'Neill, Dir.
Founded: 1934. **Staff:** Prof 12; Other 3. **Subjects:** History of Indiana and adjacent area. **Special Collections:** Architectural history (including Burns, Russ and Harrison, and Fernstermacher collections; 10,000 items); black history (including Mme. C.J. Walker, Elijah Roberts and Herbert Heller manuscript collections, Emmett Brown photograph collection; 6000 items); railroads (including Kauffman photograph collection and Preston collection; 6000 items); Indiana in the Civil War (including Lew Wallace, D.E. Beem and Jefferson C. Davis manuscript collections; 15,000 items); Indiana 19th century politics (including Charles Fairbanks, William H. English and John G. Davis manuscript collections; 10,000 items); Old Northwest Territory history (600 manuscripts); William Henry Harrison and Indiana Territory history (500 manuscripts); charitable organizations (including Family Service Association, Pleasant Run Children's Home and Jewish Welfare Federation manuscript collections; 85,000 items). **Holdings:** 12,500 books; 150 bound periodical volumes; 15,000 pamphlets; 2 million manuscripts; 650 maps; 1500 reels of microfilm; 150,000 pictures. **Services:** Copying; library open to public.

Networks/Consortia: Member of OCLC through INCOLSA. **Publications:** Indiana Historical Society, annual report (accessions); Black History News and Notes, quarterly. **Special Catalogs:** Manuscript catalog. **Special Indexes:** Picture index. **Staff:** Linda Carlson Sharp, Hd., Tech.Serv.; Helen Kahn, Ref.Libn.; Eric Pumroy, Hd., Mss.; Leigh Darbee, Hd., Ref.; Seth Rossman, Photographer; Chris Young, Hd., Cons.; Constance McBirney, Mss.Libn.; F. Gerald Handfield, Fld.Libn.; Tim Peterson, Hd., Photographic Coll.; Ramona Duncan, Cons.; Donald West, Prog.Archv.

★6024★
INDIANA INSTITUTE OF TECHNOLOGY - MC MILLEN LIBRARY (Sci-Tech)
1600 E. Washington Blvd.   Phone: (219) 422-5561
Fort Wayne, IN 46803   Jeanne Hickling, Libn.
Founded: 1932. **Staff:** Prof 1; Other 1. **Subjects:** Engineering, technology. **Holdings:** 35,826 books; 10,174 bound periodical volumes; 24 VF drawers of pamphlets; 2000 Society of Automotive Engineers papers; 1300 student seminar reports; 22,631 microfiche. **Subscriptions:** 200 journals and other serials; 5 newspapers. **Services:** Interlibrary loans; copying; library open to public.

★6025★
INDIANA LAW ENFORCEMENT ACADEMY - DAVID F. ALLEN MEMORIAL LEARNING RESOURCES CENTER (Soc Sci)
Box 313   Phone: (317) 839-5191
Plainfield, IN 46168   Donna K. Zimmerman, Libn.
Staff: Prof 1. **Subjects:** Police science, law enforcement, criminology, corrections, weapons, drugs. **Special Collections:** Law - U.S. Code Annotated; Supreme Court Reporter; Federal Reporter; Federal Supplement, Burn's Indiana Statutes Annotated; Indiana Code, NE2 - Indiana Cases; Law dictionaries and encyclopedias. **Holdings:** 5750 books; 36 bound periodical volumes; 648 cataloged pamphlets; 340 16mm films; 100 slide/tape series; 18 filmstrips. **Subscriptions:** 101 journals and other serials. **Services:** Interlibrary loans; copying; center open to public by appointment. **Networks/Consortia:** Member of Central Indiana Area Library Services Authority; National Criminal Justice Reference Service. **Special Catalogs:** AV Catalog (bound); subject bibliographies of library (looseleaf).

★6026★
INDIANA LIMESTONE INSTITUTE OF AMERICA, INC. - LIBRARY AND INFORMATION CENTER (Sci-Tech)†
Stone City Bank Bldg., Suite 400   Phone: (812) 275-4426
Bedford, IN 47421   William H. McDonald, Arch.Serv.Dir.
Subjects: Indiana limestone. **Holdings:** 300 books. **Services:** Technical and engineering aids.

★6027★
INDIANA NORTHERN GRADUATE SCHOOL OF PROFESSIONAL MANAGEMENT - LIBRARY (Bus-Fin)†
410 S. 10th St.
Box 1000   Phone: (317) 674-2900
Gas City, IN 46933   Viola M. Moore
Staff: 1. **Subjects:** Management - business, hospital, industry, hotel/motel; economics; security administration; energy conservation. **Holdings:** 8000 books; 50 bound periodical volumes; 650 dissertations; 100 reports; 1000 AV items. **Subscriptions:** 35 journals and other serials; 15 newspapers. **Services:** Interlibrary loans; library open to public. **Networks/Consortia:** Member of OCLC through INCOLSA.

★6028★
INDIANA STATE BOARD OF HEALTH - JACOB T. OLIPHANT LIBRARY (Med)†
1330 W. Michigan St.   Phone: (317) 633-8585
Indianapolis, IN 46206   Billy Smith, Dir.
Founded: 1950. **Staff:** Prof 1; Other 1. **Subjects:** Communicable disease, chronic disease, nursing, public health, health education, sanitation, pollution, drugs. **Holdings:** 3000 books; 3000 bound periodical volumes; 2 VF drawers of Board of Health archives. **Subscriptions:** 150 journals and other serials. **Services:** Interlibrary loans; copying; library open to public for reference use only. **Networks/Consortia:** Member of Central Indiana Area Library Services Authority. **Publications:** Annual Report; Monthly Bulletin.

★6029★
INDIANA STATE CHAMBER OF COMMERCE - RESEARCH LIBRARY (Bus-Fin)
One N. Capitol Ave., Suite 200   Phone: (317) 634-6407
Indianapolis, IN 46204   Max L. Moser, Dir., Res. & Spec.Proj.
Founded: 1939. **Staff:** 2. **Subjects:** Business, finance, labor relations, state government. **Services:** Copying; library not open to public, with occasional exceptions. **Publications:** Indiana Industrial Directory; Labor Laws of Indiana; Here is Your Indiana Government; Indiana Legislative Directory; research reports - all primarily for in-house and membership distribution.

★6030★
INDIANA STATE COMMISSION ON PUBLIC RECORDS - ARCHIVES DIVISION (Hist)
140 N. Senate Ave.   Phone: (317) 232-3737
Indianapolis, IN 46204   John J. Newman, Dp.Dir./Archv.
Founded: 1913. **Staff:** Prof 4; Other 4. **Subjects:** Indiana government; Indiana history - civil and military; natural resources; education; public utilities; taxation; finance; state institutional services; internal improvements; corrections. **Holdings:** 25,000 cubic feet of state archival records; 2000 cubic feet of county and municipal records; 20,000 reels of microfilmed archival materials. **Services:** Copying; division open to public. **Publications:** Guide Entries, published in Indiana History Bulletin. **Staff:** Lawrie G. Meldrum, Archv.; Kerry S. Bartels, Hd., Archv.Div.

★6031★
INDIANA STATE DEPARTMENT OF COMMERCE - ENERGY LIBRARY (Energy)
440 N. Meridian   Phone: (317) 232-8985
Indianapolis, IN 46204   Shaukat A. Naeem, Res.Anl.
Founded: 1977. **Staff:** Prof 1. **Subjects:** Energy - conservation, resource development, production and consumption, alternative sources. **Holdings:** 3800 volumes; 10 VF drawers of information files. **Subscriptions:** 71 journals and other serials. **Services:** Copying (limited); SDI; library open to public with restrictions. **Networks/Consortia:** Member of Central Indiana Area Library Services Authority (CIALSA).

★6032★
INDIANA STATE DEPARTMENT OF HIGHWAYS - PLANNING DIVISION - TECHNICAL REFERENCE LIBRARY (Trans; Plan)
State Office Bldg., Rm. 1205
100 N. Senate Ave.   Phone: (317) 232-5485
Indianapolis, IN 46204   Thomas E. Brethauer, Libn.
Founded: 1965. **Staff:** 1. **Subjects:** Highway engineering and planning; transportation and urban planning. **Special Collections:** Transportation research records published by Transportation Research Board. **Holdings:** 3000 volumes. **Subscriptions:** 10 journals and other serials. **Services:** Interlibrary loans; library open to public. **Publications:** Weekly Listings of New Material. **Special Catalogs:** Catalog (book). **Formerly:** Indiana State Highway Commission - Office of Highway Development.

★6033★
INDIANA STATE DEPARTMENT OF PUBLIC INSTRUCTION, DIVISION OF TITLE IV-C - NATIONAL MIDDLE SCHOOL RESOURCE CENTER (Educ)
901 N. Carrollton Ave.   Phone: (317) 266-4611
Indianapolis, IN 46202   Robert M. Malinka, Project Dir.
Staff: Prof 1; Other 1. **Subjects:** Middle schools - organization, programming. **Holdings:** Figures not available. **Services:** Interlibrary loans; copying; library open to public. **Publications:** Bibliography, annual; Middle School Position Paper; Middle School Guidelines; Middle School Surveys.

★6034★
INDIANA STATE DEPARTMENT OF PUBLIC INSTRUCTION - PROFESSIONAL LIBRARY (Educ)
229 State House   Phone: (317) 927-0295
Indianapolis, IN 46204   Phyllis M. Land, Dir. of Fed.Res.
Founded: 1965. **Staff:** Prof 1; Other 1. **Subjects:** Teacher education. **Holdings:** 3500 books; 150 16mm films; 18 VF drawers. **Subscriptions:** 203 journals and other serials. **Services:** Interlibrary loans; copying; library open to public with restrictions. **Staff:** Dorothy M. Everett, Libn.

INDIANA STATE HIGHWAY COMMISSION
See: Indiana State Department of Highways

★6035★
INDIANA STATE LEGISLATIVE SERVICES AGENCY - OFFICE OF CODE REVISION - LIBRARY (Law)
Rm. 302 State House   Phone: (317) 269-3728
Indianapolis, IN 46208   Nancy Thoms, Libn.
Staff: Prof 1. **Subjects:** Laws - statutes, court reports, legislative reports, Federal Register, Code of Federal Regulations. **Special Collections:** Records of the Indiana General Assembly; bills and journals. **Holdings:** 2000 books. **Services:** Copying; library not open to public. **Publications:** Indiana General Assembly papers.

★6036★
INDIANA STATE LIBRARY (Info Sci)
140 N. Senate Ave.
Indianapolis, IN 46204
Phone: (317) 232-3675
C. Ray Ewick, Dir.
Founded: 1825. **Staff:** Prof 36; Other 42. **Subjects:** Braille and talking books, genealogy, Indiana history, Indiana newspapers. **Special Collections:** Indiana Academy of Science Library; Library Science Collection. **Holdings:** 920,000 items; regional depository for federal documents. **Subscriptions:** 13,778 journals and other serials. **Services:** Interlibrary loans; copying; library open to public. **Computerized Information Services:** DIALOG, SDC; computerized cataloging. **Networks/Consortia:** Member of OCLC through INCOLSA. **Publications:** Indiana Libraries, quarterly; Focus on Indiana Libraries, monthly; Institutional Newsletter, quarterly. **Special Indexes:** Index of Indianapolis newspapers since 1898 (card); genealogical indexes; newspaper, picture and map holdings index (card). **Remarks:** The Indiana State Library is the regional library for the blind and physically handicapped. **Staff:** Jean Jose, Asst.Dir.; Mary Hartzler, Hd., Cat.Div.; Laura Johnson, Hd., Ext.Div.; Diane Sharp, Act.Hd., Genealogy Div; Barney McEwen, Hd., Div. For Blind; Robert Logsdon, Hd., Ref. & Loan/IN Div.; David Baker, Bus.Mgr.; Debora Shaw, Hd., Data Serv.Div.

★6037★
INDIANA STATE LIBRARY - INDIANA DIVISION (Hist)
140 N. Senate Ave.
Indianapolis, IN 46204
Phone: (317) 232-3668
Mary B. Burch, Act.Hd.
Staff: Prof 7; Other 5. **Subjects:** State and local history, books by Indiana authors, biography of Indiana persons, music by Indiana composers. **Holdings:** 54,538 books and bound periodical volumes; depository for state documents; 8644 maps (cataloged); 50,135 pamphlets (cataloged); 3.25 million manuscripts; 26 VF drawers of pictures; 22 VF drawers of programs; 1990 broadsides; 1758 reels of microfilm; 350 oral history tapes; 92 VF drawers of clippings. **Subscriptions:** 285 newspapers. **Services:** Interlibrary loans (limited); copying (limited); library open to public. **Computerized Information Services:** Computerized cataloging. **Publications:** Checklist of Indiana State Documents, quarterly - available on request. **Special Indexes:** Newspaper index (69,700 cards); biographical index (44,500 cards). **Staff:** Kathleen Bugman, Ref.Libn.; Diane Burnside, Ref.Libn.; Patricia Matkovic, State Doc.Libn.; Linda Walton, Ref.Libn.; Martha Wright, Ref.Libn.; John Selch, Newspaper Libn.

★6038★
INDIANA STATE PLANNING SERVICES AGENCY - LIBRARY
Harrison Bldg., 143 W. Market St.
Indianapolis, IN 46204
Defunct

★6039★
INDIANA STATE SCHOOL FOR THE DEAF - LIBRARY (Educ)
1200 E. 42nd St.
Indianapolis, IN 46205
Phone: (317) 924-4374
Irene Hodock, Libn.
Founded: 1935. **Staff:** Prof 1; Other 1. **Subjects:** Audiology, psychology of deafness, multiple-handicapped, special education. **Holdings:** 24,000 books and bound periodical volumes; 1000 other cataloged items. **Subscriptions:** 71 journals and other serials. **Services:** Interlibrary loans; library open to public with restrictions. **Networks/Consortia:** Member of Central Indiana Area Library Services Authority.

★6040★
INDIANA STATE SUPREME COURT - LAW LIBRARY (Law)
316 State House
Indianapolis, IN 46204
Phone: (317) 633-4640
Juanita A. Miller, Libn.
Founded: 1867. **Staff:** Prof 1; Other 3. **Subjects:** Law. **Special Collections:** English Commonwealth Series; early volumes of Indiana law. **Holdings:** 80,000 volumes. **Subscriptions:** 125 journals and other serials. **Services:** Copying; library open to public for reference use only.

★6041★
INDIANA STATE UNIVERSITY - CONTINUING EDUCATION AND EXTENDED SERVICES - LIBRARY (Educ)
Alumni Ctr.
Terre Haute, IN 47809
Phone: (812) 232-6311
Dr. Louis R. Jensen, Asst. Dean
Founded: 1964. **Staff:** Prof 1. **Subjects:** Education, psychology, humanities, literature, business. **Holdings:** 9405 books; 285 mental tests. **Subscriptions:** 59 journals and other serials.

★6042★
INDIANA STATE UNIVERSITY - DEPARTMENT OF RARE BOOKS AND SPECIAL COLLECTIONS (Rare Book)
Cunningham Memorial Library
Terre Haute, IN 47809
Phone: (812) 232-6311
Dr. Lawrence J. McCrank, Hd., Rare Bks./Spec.Coll.
Staff: Prof 3; Other 2. **Subjects:** Languages and lexicography; Eugene V. Debs and socioeconomic history; Indiana - regional history and literature; WPA Writers' Project; American education; travel, discovery and geography; university collections and archives. **Special Collections:** Cordell Collection of Rare and Early Dictionaries (10,000 pre-1900); Debs Collection (4250 letters and books); Indiana Collection (2500 books); Cunningham Classics of American Education (19th century; 1000 books and textbooks); travel, discovery and geography (400 items); rare books (6000). **Holdings:** 21,000 volumes. **Services:** Copying; exhibits; department open to public for reference and research. **Special Catalogs:** Printed short-title catalog of Cordell Collection (1975); Descriptive Catalog (in preparation); English and Foreign Language Dictionaries, Volumes 1 and 2. **Staff:** Robert L. Carter, Asst.Libn.; Frances Kepner, Cat.

★6043★
INDIANA STATE UNIVERSITY - SCIENCE LIBRARY (Sci-Tech)
Science Bldg.
Terre Haute, IN 47809
Phone: (812) 232-6311
Susan J. Thompson, Sci.Libn.
Founded: 1968. **Staff:** Prof 1; Other 2. **Subjects:** Chemistry, physics, life sciences, geography, geology. **Holdings:** 14,348 books; 35,129 bound periodical volumes; 160 microfilms; 12,606 microfiche. **Subscriptions:** 711 journals and other serials. **Services:** Interlibrary loans; copying; library open to public. **Computerized Information Services:** DIALOG, BRS.

★6044★
INDIANA STATE UNIVERSITY - SPECIAL SERVICES AREA (Hum)
Cunningham Memorial Library
Terre Haute, IN 47809
Phone: (812) 232-6311
Allen Keathley, Spec.Serv.Libn.
Staff: Prof 1; Other 2. **Subjects:** Education, English literature, history, music, art. **Holdings:** 488,261 microforms; 1406 phonograph records and tapes. **Services:** Copying; audiovisual listening center; area open to public.

★6045★
INDIANA STATE UNIVERSITY - TEACHING MATERIALS DIVISION (Educ)
Cunningham Memorial Library
Terre Haute, IN 47809
Phone: (812) 232-6311
Founded: 1944. **Staff:** Prof 2; Other 1. **Subjects:** Elementary and secondary school teaching. **Holdings:** 30,606 books; 6517 pamphlets; 1623 curriculum guides; 11,687 pictures; 1046 mental tests; 14,110 slides; 4842 recordings; 4100 filmstrips; 1209 charts; 504 exhibits; 193 maps; 727 publisher's catalogs; 2562 tapes; 187 transparencies; 80 kits; 144 art prints. **Subscriptions:** 21 journals and other serials. **Services:** Interlibrary loans; division open to public with a non-student card. **Staff:** Virginia Anderson, Asst.Libn.

★6046★
INDIANA STATE UNIVERSITY, EVANSVILLE - SPECIAL COLLECTIONS AND UNIVERSITY ARCHIVES (Hist)
8600 University Blvd.
Evansville, IN 47712-3595
Phone: (812) 464-1896
Gina R. Walker, Act.Archv.
Founded: 1972. **Staff:** Prof 1; Other 1. **Subjects:** Regional and university history, communal societies, petroleum, geology, theater and film, children's literature. **Special Collections:** University Archives (70 cubic feet); Center for Communal Studies (200 volumes and 34 tapes, 12 linear feet); Sun Oil Geology Collection (130 VF drawers); Mead Johnson Archives (75 linear feet); Indiana labor history (18 linear feet). **Holdings:** 3280 books; 1080 linear feet of manuscripts; 202 oral history tapes; archives; maps; photographs; slides. **Services:** Interlibrary loans; copying; library open to public. **Computerized Information Services:** Computerized cataloging. **Networks/Consortia:** Member of OCLC. **Publications:** A Preliminary Guide to the Special Collections of Indiana State University Evansville, 1975. **Special Catalogs:** Guides to collections (typescript, loose-leaf), with updates; selected holdings of I.S.U.E. and other area repositories. **Also Known As:** I.S.U.E.

INDIANA UNITED METHODIST CHURCH ARCHIVES
See: De Pauw University - Archives of De Pauw University and Indiana United Methodism

★6047★
INDIANA UNIVERSITY - AFRO-AMERICAN LEARNING RESOURCE CENTER (Area-Ethnic)
109 N. Jordan Ave.
Bloomington, IN 47405
Phone: (812) 335-3675
Leslie Denton, Supv.
Founded: 1972. **Staff:** Prof 1; Other 2. **Subjects:** Blacks - history, reference

works, music, literature, drama; black-oriented novels. **Special Collections:** The Arno Press Collection (200 titles). **Holdings:** 1000 books; 100 cassette tapes. **Subscriptions:** 19 journals and other serials; 10 newspapers. **Services:** Library open to public.

★6048★
INDIANA UNIVERSITY - ARCHIVES OF TRADITIONAL MUSIC (Mus)
Maxwell Hall 057   Phone: (812) 335-8632
Bloomington, IN 47405   Ronald R. Smith, Dir.
Founded: 1936. **Staff:** Prof 2; Other 7. **Subjects:** Ethnic music, folk music, oral data, ethnomusicology, discography. **Holdings:** 23,000 tape recordings; 6000 cylinder recordings; 35,000 disc recordings; 125 wire recordings. **Services:** Interlibrary loans; copying; library open to public. **Publications:** A Catalog of Phonorecordings of Music and Oral Data Held by the Archives of Traditional Music; African Music and Oral Data, 1902-1975; Native North American Music and Oral Data, A Catalogue of Sound Recordings, 1893-1976. **Special Indexes:** Indiana Folk Music and Oral Data (typescript). **Remarks:** The archives include the Center for African Oral Data. **Staff:** Louise S. Spear, Asst.Dir.

★6049★
INDIANA UNIVERSITY - BIOLOGY LIBRARY (Sci-Tech)
Jordan Hall   Phone: (812) 335-9791
Bloomington, IN 47405   Steven Sowell, Hd.
Staff: Prof 2; Other 3. **Subjects:** Microbiology, botany, zoology. **Holdings:** 47,778 books; 36,733 bound periodical volumes; 61,568 pamphlets and reprints (cataloged); 9483 microforms. **Subscriptions:** 1346 journals and other serials. **Services:** Interlibrary loans; copying; library open to public. **Computerized Information Services:** DIALOG. **Staff:** Carol Tullis, Ref.Libn.

★6050★
INDIANA UNIVERSITY - BUSINESS/SPEA LIBRARY (Bus-Fin; Soc Sci; Env-Cons)
Business Bldg.   Phone: (812) 335-1957
Bloomington, IN 47405   Nevin W. Raber, Hd.
Founded: 1926. **Staff:** Prof 4; Other 8. **Subjects:** Accounting, environment, energy, ecology, finance, insurance, management, marketing, public administration, social problems, urban affairs. **Special Collections:** History of management thought. **Holdings:** 94,000 books and bound periodical volumes; 40,000 pamphlets; 70,000 microforms; 11,000 annual reports. **Subscriptions:** 2200 journals and other serials; 30 newspapers. **Services:** Interlibrary loans; copying; library open to public. **Formed by the Merger of:** Its Business Library and its School of Public and Environmental Affairs Library. **Staff:** Michael Parrish, Hd.

INDIANA UNIVERSITY - CENTER FOR AFRICAN ORAL DATA
See: Indiana University - Archives of Traditional Music

★6051★
INDIANA UNIVERSITY - CHEMISTRY LIBRARY (Sci-Tech)
                                      Phone: (812) 335-9452
Bloomington, IN 47405   Gary Wiggins, Hd.
Founded: 1941. **Staff:** Prof 3; Other 2. **Subjects:** Chemistry and related subjects. **Holdings:** 48,000 books and bound periodical volumes; 1200 microforms. **Subscriptions:** 400 journals and other serials. **Services:** Interlibrary loans; copying; microfilming; SDI; table of contents service; library open to public. **Computerized Information Services:** Online retrospective searches; DIALOG, SDC, CIS, Cambridge Crystallographic Data Base. **Publications:** International Standard Interest Profiles on: Crystal Structure, biweekly; Charge, Spin and Momentum Density, every six weeks; Isotope Effects, Gas Phase Molecular Structure, monthly - all available by subscription.

★6052★
INDIANA UNIVERSITY - EAST ASIAN COLLECTION (Area-Ethnic)
                                      Phone: (812) 335-9695
Bloomington, IN 47405   Shizue Matsuda, Libn.
Staff: Prof 1; Other 2. **Subjects:** East Asian (Chinese, Japanese and Korean) humanities, social sciences, history. **Special Collections:** Ebara Bunko Literature Collection on microfilm (207 reels). **Holdings:** 102,853 books and bound periodical volumes; 906 reels of microfilm of newspapers, serials and books. **Subscriptions:** 344 journals and other serials; 13 newspapers. **Services:** Interlibrary loans; copying; collection open to public.

★6053★
INDIANA UNIVERSITY - EDUCATION LIBRARY (Educ)
                                      Phone: (812) 335-1798
Bloomington, IN 47405   Adele Dendy, Hd.
Founded: 1955. **Staff:** Prof 2; Other 5. **Subjects:** Education theory, practice and history; child development; guidance; educational psychology. **Special**

Collections: Curriculum materials. **Holdings:** 33,000 volumes; 23,572 AV units; 216,864 ERIC microfiche and other microforms. **Subscriptions:** 297 journals and other serials. **Services:** Interlibrary loans; copying; library open to public. **Computerized Information Services:** DIALOG, SDC.

★6054★
INDIANA UNIVERSITY - FINE ARTS LIBRARY (Art)
Fine Arts Ctr.   Phone: (812) 335-5743
Bloomington, IN 47405   Betty Jo Irvine, Hd.
Staff: Prof 3; Other 8. **Subjects:** Art, history of arts and crafts, photography. **Holdings:** 51,000 volumes; 695 reels of microfilm; 54,000 photographs. **Subscriptions:** 300 journals and other serials. **Services:** Interlibrary loans; copying; library open to public with limited circulation. **Staff:** Lynn Korenic, Libn.

★6055★
INDIANA UNIVERSITY - FINE ARTS SLIDE LIBRARY (Art)
Fine Arts 415   Phone: (812) 335-6717
Bloomington, IN 47405   Eileen Fry, Slide Libn.
Staff: Prof 1; Other 3. **Subjects:** Art history. **Special Collections:** Sieber African Slide Collection (11,000 slides of African and Third World art). **Holdings:** 220,000 slides. **Services:** Library not open to public.

★6056★
INDIANA UNIVERSITY - FOLKLORE ARCHIVES (Area-Ethnic)
510 N. Fess   Phone: (812) 335-3652
Bloomington, IN 47405   Timothy J. Kloberdanz, Hd.Archv.
Staff: Prof 2; Other 4. **Subjects:** Folklore, folksong, material culture. **Special Collections:** Joseph T. Hall Limerick Collection (5000); Roger Mitchell Collection of Micronesian Folktales (300). **Holdings:** 100 books; 40 bound periodical volumes; 200 dissertations; 40,000 folklore items; 500 cassettes; 80 tapes; 1000 slides. **Services:** Copying; open to public. **Publications:** Guide to the Indiana University Folklore Archives, 1979.

★6057★
INDIANA UNIVERSITY - FOLKLORE COLLECTION (Area-Ethnic)
10th and Jordan Sts.   Phone: (812) 335-1550
Bloomington, IN 47405   Polly S. Grimshaw, Libn./Cur.
Staff: Prof 1; Other 1. **Subjects:** Folk literature, ethnomusicology, material culture, ethnic and urban folklore, folk ritual, regional folklore. **Special Collections:** Stith Thompson Collection (8000 items); Henri Gaidoz Collection (6500 items). **Holdings:** 33,000 books; 632 titles of bound periodicals. **Subscriptions:** 211 journals and other serials. **Services:** Interlibrary loans; copying; SDI; library open to public. **Publications:** Acquisitions Lists, irregular - for internal distribution only, and to researchers on request; list of journals and monograph series in the Folklore Collection; Annotated Bibliography of Indiana Folklore, revised annually. **Special Catalogs:** Subject catalog of the Gaidoz Collection.

★6058★
INDIANA UNIVERSITY - GEOGRAPHY AND MAP LIBRARY (Geog-Map)
301 Kirkwood Hall   Phone: (812) 335-1108
Bloomington, IN 47405   Daniel Seldin, Hd.
Founded: 1946. **Staff:** Prof 1; Other 2. **Subjects:** Geography, cartography. **Special Collections:** Sanborn Fire Insurance maps of Indiana cities. **Holdings:** 7900 books and bound periodical volumes, including atlases; 250 gazetteers; 2736 government publications; 200,000 maps and charts. **Subscriptions:** 171 journals and other serials. **Services:** Interlibrary loans; copying; library open to public with limited circulation. **Publications:** Acquisitions List, monthly; Library Handbook.

★6059★
INDIANA UNIVERSITY - GEOLOGY LIBRARY (Sci-Tech)
Geology Bldg., 1005 E. Tenth St.   Phone: (812) 335-7170
Bloomington, IN 47405   Lois Heiser, Libn.
Founded: 1894. **Staff:** Prof 1; Other 2. **Subjects:** Geochemistry, geology, geomorphology, geophysics, mineral resources, mineralogy, paleontology, petrology, stratigraphy. **Holdings:** 65,000 books and bound periodical volumes; 4500 microforms; 1000 pamphlets; 19,582 reprints; 250,000 maps and charts. **Subscriptions:** 1100 journals and other serials. **Services:** Interlibrary loans; copying; SDI; library open to public. **Computerized Information Services:** DIALOG, SDC. **Remarks:** Also serves the Indiana Geological Survey.

★6060★
INDIANA UNIVERSITY - HEALTH, PHYSICAL EDUCATION & RECREATION LIBRARY (Educ)
HPER Bldg. 031   Phone: (812) 335-4420
Bloomington, IN 47401   John Curry, Hd.
Founded: 1978. **Staff:** 7. **Subjects:** Physical education, recreation and park

administration, health and safety, coaching, adapted physical education and therapeutic recreation, sports medicine and psychology. **Holdings:** 5200 monographs; 390 bound periodical volumes; 8 VF drawers; 700 dissertations; 6000 microforms. **Subscriptions:** 104 journals and other serials. **Services:** Interlibrary loans; copying; library open to public. **Computerized Information Services:** DIALOG, SDC, BRS; computerized cataloging. **Networks/ Consortia:** Member of Association of Research Libraries (ARL); OCLC through INCOLSA. **Publications:** New Books in HPER, quarterly; HPER Student Handbook.

★6061★
INDIANA UNIVERSITY - INSTITUTE FOR URBAN TRANSPORTATION - RESOURCE CENTER (Trans)
809 E. 9th St.   Phone: (812) 335-8143
Bloomington, IN 47401   Rachelle Reinhold, Sr. Staff Res.
Staff: 1. **Subjects:** Urban transportation. **Holdings:** 250 books; 7500 technical reports; 2000 microfiche; 36 VF drawers of maps, schedules, annual reports, reprints; 15 slide shows, video cassettes and films. **Subscriptions:** 140 journals and other serials. **Services:** Library open to public. **Computerized Information Services:** Computerized cataloging.

★6062★
INDIANA UNIVERSITY - JOURNALISM LIBRARY (Info Sci)
Ernie Pyle Hall, 7th St.   Phone: (812) 335-3517
Bloomington, IN 47405   Frances Wilhoit
Staff: Prof 1; Other 1. **Subjects:** Journalism; mass communication. **Special Collections:** Ernie Pyle. **Holdings:** 9000 volumes; 302 microfilms; 2030 slides and transparencies; 288 videotapes. **Subscriptions:** 227 journals and other serials. **Services:** Interlibrary loans; copying; library open to public. **Publications:** Mass Media Periodicals: an annotated bibliography (monograph) - for sale.

INDIANA UNIVERSITY - KINSEY INSTITUTE FOR RESEARCH IN SEX, GENDER & REPRODUCTION, INC.
See: Kinsey Institute for Research in Sex, Gender & Reproduction, Inc.

★6063★
INDIANA UNIVERSITY - LAW LIBRARY (Law)
School of Law   Phone: (812) 337-9666
Bloomington, IN 47405   Colleen K. Pauwels, Dir.
Founded: 1925. **Staff:** Prof 5; Other 8. **Subjects:** Law. **Special Collections:** U.S. government documents depository, U.S. and Indiana Supreme Court records and briefs depository. **Holdings:** 222,396 volumes; 86,953 microforms. **Subscriptions:** 3528 journals and other serials. **Services:** Interlibrary loans; copying; library open to public. **Computerized Information Services:** LEXIS; computerized cataloging. **Networks/Consortia:** Member of OCLC. **Staff:** Byron D. Cooper, Assoc.Dir.; Keith Buckley, Ref.Libn.; Linda Fariss, Pub.Serv.Libn.; Janis Johnston, Ser.Libn.

★6064★
INDIANA UNIVERSITY - LILLY LIBRARY (Hist; Hum)
                            Phone: (812) 335-2452
Bloomington, IN 47405   William R. Cagle, Libn.
Founded: 1960. **Staff:** Prof 8; Other 10. **Subjects:** British literature (especially Milton, Defoe, Wordsworth, 19th century British drama and modern literary manuscripts); American literature (especially Poe, Riley, Sinclair, Plath and the files of several American publishers and literary magazines); American history (especially discovery, American Revolution, U.S. Constitution, War of 1812, Lincoln, Indiana and Western expansion); European expansion (especially Spanish, Portuguese and Dutch colonial empires); history of science and medicine. **Special Collections:** Mendel Latin American Collection; Ellison Far West Collection; Oakleaf Lincoln Collection; J.K. Lilly Collection; Wendell Willkie papers; Orson Welles papers. **Holdings:** 314,000 bound volumes; 4 million manuscripts; 5750 pictures and prints; 1740 maps; 1400 radio, television and film scripts. **Services:** Copying; library open to public. **Publications:** Lilly Library Publications Series, irregular - distributed to Friends of the Lilly Library. **Special Catalogs:** Exhibition catalogs. **Staff:** Dr. L.C. Rudolph, Cur. of Books; Elizabeth Johnson, Cat.; Josiah Q. Bennett, Cat.; Miguel Solis, Ref.; Saundra Taylor, Cur. of Mss.; Virginia Mauck, Asst.Cur. of Mss.; Dr. Cecil K. Byrd, Cons.

★6065★
INDIANA UNIVERSITY - MEDICAL SCIENCES LIBRARY (Med)
251 Myers Hall   Phone: (812) 335-3347
Bloomington, IN 47405   Julia S. Carter, Libn.
Staff: Prof 1; Other 1. **Subjects:** Anatomy, physiology, pharmacology, pathology, medicine, biomedical computer science, biochemistry, immunology. **Holdings:** 25,000 bound volumes. **Subscriptions:** 291 journals and other serials. **Services:** Interlibrary loans; copying; library open to public.

★6066★
INDIANA UNIVERSITY - MUSEUM - MUSEUM LIBRARY (Area-Ethnic)
Student Bldg., Rm. 209   Phone: (812) 335-7224
Bloomington, IN 47405
Subjects: Indians of North America and South America, anthropology/ archeology, museums, U.S. history, Africa, conservation. **Special Collections:** Ross Stotter Collection (26 books on seashells). **Holdings:** 1600 books; 340 pamphlets (cataloged); catalogs; maps; manuscripts and reproductions. **Subscriptions:** 20 journals and other serials. **Services:** Library open to public for reference use only.

★6067★
INDIANA UNIVERSITY - MUSIC LIBRARY (Mus)
School of Music Library   Phone: (812) 335-8541
Bloomington, IN 47405   Dr. David Fenske, Hd.Libn.
Founded: 1939. **Staff:** Prof 5; Other 9. **Subjects:** Music. **Special Collections:** Apel Collection (photocopies of early keyboard music compiled by Professor Willi Apel, 200 volumes); black music; Latin American music; opera; piano pedagogy. **Holdings:** 42,996 books and bound periodical volumes; 247,544 music scores; 9806 microforms; 29,620 audio discs; 31,868 audio reels; 15 filmstrips; 140 slides; 58 videotapes; 39 media kits. **Subscriptions:** 592 journals and other serials. **Services:** Interlibrary loans; copying; library open to public. **Computerized Information Services:** Computerized cataloging. **Networks/Consortia:** Member of OCLC through INCOLSA. **Staff:** M. Fling, Ref.Libn.; K. Talalay, Ref.Libn.; A. Ralph Papakhian, Tech.Serv.Libn.; S. Stancu, Sound Recording Cat.

★6068★
INDIANA UNIVERSITY - NEAR EASTERN COLLECTION (Area-Ethnic)
                            Phone: (812) 335-3403
Bloomington, IN 47405
Staff: Prof 2; Other 2. **Subjects:** Arabic, Hebrew, Persian and Turkish languages and literatures. **Holdings:** 60,000 books; 6500 bound periodical volumes. **Subscriptions:** 230 journals and other serials; 12 newspapers. **Services:** Interlibrary loans; copying; collection open to public. **Staff:** James W. Pollock, Libn./Cat.; Seid Karic, Cat.

★6069★
INDIANA UNIVERSITY - OPTOMETRY LIBRARY (Med)
Optometry Bldg.   Phone: (812) 335-8629
Bloomington, IN 47405   Sabina Sinclair, Hd.
Founded: 1968. **Staff:** Prof 1; Other 1. **Subjects:** Vision, including all pertinent disciplines. **Holdings:** 12,000 books and bound periodical volumes; 6200 pamphlets; 3300 reprints; 1496 tests; 444 microforms; 1311 slides and transparencies; 104 audio discs; 100 audio cassettes; 1500 technical reports. **Subscriptions:** 264 journals and other serials. **Services:** Interlibrary loans; copying; library open to public. **Networks/Consortia:** Member of Regional Medical Library - Region 3; Association of Visual Science Librarians. **Publications:** List of acquisitions, monthly. **Special Indexes:** KWOC Index.

★6070★
INDIANA UNIVERSITY - ORAL HISTORY RESEARCH PROJECT - LIBRARY (Area-Ethnic)
512 N. Fess   Phone: (812) 335-2856
Bloomington, IN 47401   John Bodnar, Dir.
Staff: Prof 4; Other 1. **Subjects:** Indiana - history, industry, agriculture, politics. **Special Collections:** History of the Kinsey Institute for Sex Research, 27 interviews; Biography of Melvyn Douglas, 26 interviews; History of the Theater in the Twentieth Century, 10 interviews. **Holdings:** 50 books; 600 oral histories; clippings, 1 VF drawer. **Services:** Copying (with restrictions); library open to public. **Publications:** Guide to Indiana University Oral History Research Project and Related Studies, booklet, 1977.

★6071★
INDIANA UNIVERSITY - RESEARCH INSTITUTE FOR INNER ASIAN STUDIES - LIBRARY (Area-Ethnic)
Goodbody Hall 157   Phone: (812) 337-1605
Bloomington, IN 47405   Prof. Stephen Halkovic, Dir.
Founded: 1967. **Subjects:** Inner Asia - history, civilization, linguistics studies. **Holdings:** 5000 books; 250 Tibetan blockprints and manuscripts; 400,000 microfiche. **Subscriptions:** 25 journals and other serials. **Services:** Library open to public by appointment. **Staff:** Prof. Paul Draghi, Asst.Dir.

★6072★
INDIANA UNIVERSITY - SCHOOL OF LIBRARY AND INFORMATION SCIENCE LIBRARY (Info Sci)
                            Phone: (812) 335-5968
Bloomington, IN 47405   Patricia Steele, Hd.Libn.
Founded: 1947. **Staff:** Prof 1; Other 1. **Subjects:** Library and information

science. **Holdings:** 15,000 books and bound periodical volumes; 22,669 pamphlets; 2458 microforms; 20 motion pictures; 169 filmstrips; 1176 slides and transparencies; 18 film cartridges; 249 prints; 80 multimedia kits. **Subscriptions:** 271 journals and other serials. **Services:** Interlibrary loans; library open to public. **Computerized Information Services:** DIALOG.

★6073★
INDIANA UNIVERSITY - SCHOOL OF PUBLIC AND ENVIRONMENTAL AFFAIRS - LIBRARY
Poplars Research Ctr.
400 E. 7th St.
Bloomington, IN 47405
Defunct. Merged with its Business Library to form the Business/SPEA Library.

★6074★
INDIANA UNIVERSITY - SOCIAL STUDIES DEVELOPMENT CENTER - CURRICULUM RESOURCE CENTER (Educ)†
513 N. Park   Phone: (812) 337-3584
Bloomington, IN 47405   Linda Kelty, Libn.
Founded: 1974. **Staff:** 1. **Subjects:** Curriculum materials in pre-college social studies. **Holdings:** 8000 books; 1000 simulations, educational games, filmstrip sets, photographs, posters, educational kits. **Subscriptions:** 80 journals and other serials. **Services:** Library open to public with restrictions. **Networks/Consortia:** Member of Stone Hills Area Library Services Authority (SHALSA). **Publications:** Acquisitions list, monthly - for internal distribution only.

★6075★
INDIANA UNIVERSITY - SWAIN HALL LIBRARY (Sci-Tech)
                                               Phone: (812) 335-2758
Bloomington, IN 47405   Miriam Bonham, Act.Hd.
Founded: 1940. **Staff:** Prof 1; Other 3. **Subjects:** Physics, mathematics, astronomy, computer science. **Special Collections:** Astronomy Chart Room (300 volumes); Goethe Link Observatory (900 volumes); Cyclotron Facility (1500 volumes). **Holdings:** 71,000 volumes; 1800 pamphlets; 6700 preprints; 700 college catalogs; 3130 technical reports; 940 films and other visual materials. **Subscriptions:** 1200 journals and other serials. **Services:** Interlibrary loans; copying; SDI; library open to public. **Computerized Information Services:** DIALOG. **Publications:** Acquisition List, monthly; Annual Report - both free upon request.

★6076★
INDIANA UNIVERSITY - WORKSHOP IN POLITICAL THEORY & POLICY ANALYSIS - WORKSHOP LIBRARY (Soc Sci)
814 E. Third St.   Phone: (812) 335-0441
Bloomington, IN 47405   Susan G. Wynne, Libn.
Staff: 3. **Subjects:** Police services, public service delivery and evaluation, democratic theory, survey methods, neighborhood organization. **Holdings:** 300 books; 45 bound periodical volumes; 6000 journal articles and professional papers; 8 VF drawers of clippings; 1 shelf of dissertations. **Subscriptions:** 40 journals and other serials. **Services:** Copying; library open to public with restrictions. **Computerized Information Services:** DOCUDEX (internal database). **Publications:** Workshop working papers; technical reports. **Special Catalogs:** Content coded items of service delivery material (computer printout).

★6077★
INDIANA UNIVERSITY, INDIANAPOLIS - SCHOOL OF DENTISTRY LIBRARY (Med)
1121 W. Michigan St.   Phone: (317) 264-7204
Indianapolis, IN 46202   Marie Sparks, Lib.Dir.
Founded: 1929. **Staff:** Prof 2; Other 11. **Subjects:** Dentistry and allied medical subjects. **Holdings:** 45,000 books and bound periodical volumes; 106,744 pamphlets and other unbound material; 5350 nonprint items; 5402 unbound reports and manuscripts; 57,416 miscellaneous pieces. **Subscriptions:** 552 journals and other serials. **Services:** Interlibrary loans; copying; library open to public. **Computerized Information Services:** BRS; computerized cataloging. **Networks/Consortia:** Member of OCLC through INCOLSA; Central Indiana Health Sciences Consortium. **Publications:** New Book List, bimonthly. **Staff:** Monica A. Moffa, Pub.Serv.Libn.

★6078★
INDIANA UNIVERSITY, INDIANAPOLIS - SCHOOL OF LAW LIBRARY (Law)
735 W. New York St.   Phone: (317) 264-4028
Indianapolis, IN 46202   Prof. James F. Bailey, III, Dir. Law Lib.
Founded: 1944. **Staff:** Prof 6; Other 7. **Subjects:** Law - U.S., Commonwealth, international, comparative; jurisprudence; legal history. **Special Collections:** U.S. government publications depository, 1967 to present; United Nations publications depository, 1977 to present;

Organization of American States records, 1977 to present; law and law-related publications of European communities. **Holdings:** 310,000 volumes. **Subscriptions:** 5529 journals and other serials; 20 newspapers. **Services:** Interlibrary loans; copying; library open to public for reference use only. **Computerized Information Services:** LEXIS, Auto-Cite, Disclosure Inc.; computerized cataloging. **Networks/Consortia:** Member of Ohio Regional Association of Law Libraries; OCLC through INCOLSA. **Publications:** Recent Acquisitions List, monthly - for internal distribution only; Model Bibliography of Indiana Legal Materials. **Staff:** Kathy J. Welker, Asst.Dir.; Laura Kimberly, Acq./Ser.Libn.; Wendell E. Johnting, Tech.Serv.Libn.; Constance Matts, Readers Serv.Libn.; Christine L. Stevens, Ref.Libn.

★6079★
INDIANA UNIVERSITY, INDIANAPOLIS - SCHOOL OF MEDICINE LIBRARY (Med)
635 Barnhill Dr.   Phone: (317) 264-7182
Indianapolis, IN 46223   Mary Jane Laatz, Dir.
Founded: 1917. **Staff:** Prof 10; Other 15. **Subjects:** Medicine, nursing and allied health sciences. **Holdings:** 133,121 books and bound periodical volumes. **Subscriptions:** 1725 journals and other serials. **Services:** Interlibrary loans; library open to public for reference use only. **Computerized Information Services:** MEDLINE, BRS, SDC, DIALOG; computerized cataloging. **Networks/Consortia:** Member of OCLC through INCOLSA; Regional Medical Library - Region 3; statewide teletype network for interlibrary loans. **Publications:** Library Newsletter, quarterly; Booklist, quarterly; Library Brochure, annual; Health Science Serials in Indianapolis, annual. **Special Indexes:** KWIC indexes to various publications. **Staff:** Nina S. Campbell, Assoc.Lib.Dir.; Virginia Humnicky, Ext.Libn.; Lynn R. Smith, Acq.Libn.; Elaine H. Whitinger, Nursing Libn.; Harold Shaffer, Ser.Libn.; Ann Van Camp, Search Anl.; Jeanne G. Mueller, Tech.Serv.Libn.; Frances A. Brahmi, Med.Ref./Search Anl.; Scott S. Loman, Med.Ref./Circ.Libn.

★6080★
INDIANA UNIVERSITY, INDIANAPOLIS - UNIVERSITY LIBRARY/HERRON SCHOOL OF ART (Art)
1701 N. Pennsylvania   Phone: (317) 923-3651
Indianapolis, IN 46202   Maudine B. Williams, Hd.Libn.
Staff: Prof 2; Other 3. **Subjects:** Visual arts. **Holdings:** 13,200 books; 2000 bound periodical volumes; 65,000 35mm slides; 10,000 lantern slides; 30 VF drawers of clippings, exhibition catalogs and pictures. **Subscriptions:** 169 journals and other serials. **Services:** Interlibrary loans; copying; library open to public. **Computerized Information Services:** Computerized cataloging. **Networks/Consortia:** Member of OCLC through INCOLSA.

★6081★
INDIANA UNIVERSITY NORTHWEST - CALUMET REGIONAL ARCHIVES (Hist)
Library, 3400 Broadway   Phone: (219) 980-6628
Gary, IN 46408   Robert Moran
Staff: Prof 4. **Subjects:** Calumet Region - urban history, labor history, ethnic history, industrialization, education history, women's history. **Special Collections:** International Institute of Northwest Indiana (10 file cabinets); United States Steel photographs (2 file cabinets and 6 boxes); Hammond Oil, Chemical, and Atomic Workers' Union (8 boxes); Gary Historical Society papers (6 boxes); Bailly Alliance papers (5 boxes); Community Action to Reverse Pollution papers (4 boxes); Gary YWCA records (14 boxes); Lake County local government records, 1858-1961 (350 volumes). **Holdings:** 300 books; 200 linear feet of additional Calumet Region manuscript materials. **Services:** Copying; library open to public. **Remarks:** The Calumet Regional Archives collects any type of archival materials relating to the history of the Calumet Region, Indiana, 1850 to present. **Staff:** Ronald D. Cohen, Co-Dir.; James B. Lane, Co-Dir.; Stephen McShane, Archv./Cur.

★6082★
INDIANA UNIVERSITY OF PENNSYLVANIA - COGSWELL MUSIC LIBRARY (Mus)
Cogswell Hall   Phone: (412) 357-2892
Indiana, PA 15705   Calvin Elliker, Music Libn.
Founded: 1965. **Staff:** Prof 1; Other 14. **Subjects:** Music. **Holdings:** 5000 books; 30,000 music scores; 16,000 sound recordings. **Services:** Interlibrary loans; library open to public with restrictions. **Computerized Information Services:** Computerized cataloging. **Networks/Consortia:** Member of OCLC; Pittsburgh Regional Library Center.

★6083★
INDIANA UNIVERSITY OF PENNSYLVANIA - UNIVERSITY LIBRARY (Educ)
                                               Phone: (412) 357-2340
Indiana, PA 15705   William E. Lafranchi, Dir., Libs./Media Rsrcs.
Founded: 1875. **Staff:** Prof 21; Other 18. **Subjects:** U.S. public education,

Pennsylvania history, home economics, American and English literature, music, social studies, fine arts, Spain, Portugal and Latin America (culture and civilization). **Special Collections:** Curriculum materials; University School Library (4000 volumes). **Holdings:** 510,000 books; 65,000 bound periodical volumes; U.S. and Pennsylvania government document depository; pamphlets; clippings; pictures; 1.6 million microforms; slides; phonograph records. **Subscriptions:** 4000 journals and other serials; 13 newspapers. **Services:** Interlibrary loans; copying; library open to public. **Computerized Information Services:** DIALOG; computerized cataloging, serials and circulation. **Networks/Consortia:** Member of Pittsburgh Regional Library Center. **Staff:** Ronald Steiner, Assoc.Dir.; Richard Chamberlin, Asst.Libn.; Carol Connell, Asst.Libn.; Cynthia Creekmore, Asst.Libn.; John Grassinger, Asst.Libn.; Paul Hicks, Asst.Libn.; James Hooks, Asst.Libn.; David Kaufman, Asst.Libn.; Robert Kirby, Asst.Libn.; Lynn Lucas, Asst.Libn.; Kathryne Mallino, Asst.Libn.; Wanda Rife, Asst.Libn.; Martha Scheeren, Asst.Libn.; Daniel Shively, Asst.Libn.; Marie Snead, Asst.Libn.; Edward Wolf, Asst.Libn.; Calvin Elliker, Asst.Libn.; Walter Laude, Asst.Libn.; Philip Zorich, Asst.Libn.; Rosa Jen, Asst.Libn.

★6084★
INDIANA UNIVERSITY/PURDUE UNIVERSITY AT FORT WAYNE - FINE ARTS LIBRARY (Art)†
1026 W. Berry St.   Phone: (219) 482-5201
Fort Wayne, IN 46804   Marilyn L. Murphy, Libn.
Staff: Prof 1. **Subjects:** Fine arts. **Holdings:** 8000 books; 400 bound periodical volumes; 4878 mounted pictures; 2637 clippings and pamphlets; 18,900 slides. **Subscriptions:** 24 journals and other serials. **Services:** Interlibrary loans; copying; library open to public.

INDIANA UNIVERSITY/PURDUE UNIVERSITY AT INDIANAPOLIS - AEROSPACE RESEARCH APPLICATIONS CENTER
See: Indianapolis Center for Advanced Research

★6085★
INDIANA UNIVERSITY/PURDUE UNIVERSITY AT INDIANAPOLIS - 38TH STREET CAMPUS LIBRARY (Sci-Tech)
1201 E. 38th St.
Box 647   Phone: (317) 923-1325
Indianapolis, IN 46223   William F. Mayles, Act.Hd., Pub.Serv.
Founded: 1945. **Staff:** Prof 3; Other 2. **Subjects:** Biology, chemistry, computer science and technology, engineering, mathematics, physics, psychology. **Holdings:** 25,582 books; 20,403 bound periodical volumes; 348,980 STAR microfiche. **Subscriptions:** 829 journals and other serials; 9 newspapers. **Services:** Interlibrary loans; copying; library open to public. **Computerized Information Services:** BRS; computerized cataloging. **Networks/Consortia:** Member of OCLC through INCOLSA; Central Indiana Area Library Services Authority. **Staff:** Randi L. Stocker, Ref.Libn.; Marian C. Foley, Off.Mgr.

★6086★
INDIANA UNIVERSITY/PURDUE UNIVERSITY AT INDIANAPOLIS - UNIVERSITY LIBRARY (Soc Sci)
815 W. Michigan St.   Phone: (317) 264-4101
Indianapolis, IN 46202   Barbara B. Fischler, Dir. of Libs.
Founded: 1928. **Staff:** Prof 13; Other 22. **Subjects:** Social work, business, child welfare, community organization, criminology, public welfare. **Holdings:** 194,322 books and bound periodical volumes; 1.1 million archival items. **Subscriptions:** 3070 journals and other serials; 25 newspapers. **Services:** Interlibrary loans; copying; library open to public. **Computerized Information Services:** DIALOG, BRS; Indiana Information Retrieval System; computerized cataloging. **Networks/Consortia:** Member of OCLC through INCOLSA; Central Indiana Area Library Services Authority. **Publications:** Library Page, irregular - for internal distribution only. **Staff:** Frank Brey, Hd., Pub.Serv.; Jean M. Gnat, Hd., Tech.Serv.; Jeannette Matthew, Archv.; Ann Griffin, Adm.Asst.; Steven Schmidt, Circ./ILL Assoc.

★6087★
INDIANA VOCATIONAL-TECHNICAL COLLEGE - RESOURCE CENTER (Educ)
1440 E. 35th Ave.   Phone: (219) 981-1111
Gary, IN 46409   John M. Niemann, Dir.
Staff: Prof 1; Other 2. **Subjects:** Health occupations, industrial maintenance, fire science, business science, electronics, drafting. **Holdings:** 4000 books; 2000 other cataloged items; transparencies; slides; filmstrips; programmed materials; videotapes. **Subscriptions:** 89 journals and other serials. **Services:** Interlibrary loans; copying; instructional material developing; library open to public for reference use only. **Networks/Consortia:** Member of Northwest Indiana Area Library Service Authority. **Staff:** Nick P. Vasil, Tech.Serv.Supv.

★6088★
INDIANAPOLIS BAR ASSOCIATION - LIBRARY (Law)†
One Indiana Sq.   Phone: (317) 632-8240
Indianapolis, IN 46204   Mary Kramer, Libn.
Founded: 1878. **Subjects:** Law. **Holdings:** 20,000 volumes.

★6089★
INDIANAPOLIS CENTER FOR ADVANCED RESEARCH - ARAC - NASA TECHNICAL INFORMATION CENTER (Sci-Tech)†
611 N. Capitol   Phone: (317) 264-4507
Indianapolis, IN 46204   John M. Ulrich, Dir.
Founded: 1963. **Staff:** Prof 16. **Subjects:** Engineering and scientific research and its applications; applied science and technology. **Holdings:** Access to over 12 million articles, reports, and other documents by computer searching. **Services:** Retrospective search service; Current Awareness service; document acquisition and delivery; technical assistance. **Computerized Information Services:** DIALOG, SDC, NASA/RECON; computerized literature searches and current awareness announcements. **Remarks:** Center located at the Indiana University/Purdue University campus. **Also Known As:** Aerospace Research Applications Center (ARAC). **Staff:** Becky Weisman, Adm.Serv.Mgr.

★6090★
INDIANAPOLIS - DEPARTMENT OF METROPOLITAN DEVELOPMENT - DIVISION OF PLANNING AND ZONING - LIBRARY (Plan)
2041 City-County Bldg.   Phone: (317) 633-3331
Indianapolis, IN 46204   Elizabeth Simmons, Libn.
Founded: 1958. **Staff:** Prof 2. **Subjects:** Areawide planning, community services, land use, zoning, housing, energy, social and economic planning. **Special Collections:** Reports of the division. **Holdings:** 5000 books; 30 bound periodical volumes; 2 VF drawers. **Subscriptions:** 30 journals and other serials. **Services:** Interlibrary loans; copying; library open to public with permission of the administrator. **Computerized Information Services:** Computerized cataloging, acquisitions and serials. **Publications:** Library manual, annual - for internal distribution only. **Staff:** Larry Carroll, Asst.Adm.

★6091★
INDIANAPOLIS-MARION COUNTY PUBLIC LIBRARY - ARTS DIVISION (Art; Hum)
40 E. St. Clair St.   Phone: (317) 269-1764
Indianapolis, IN 46204   Daniel Gann, Div.Hd.
Founded: 1924. **Staff:** Prof 9. **Subjects:** Art, language, drama, sports, literature, music. **Special Collections:** Julia Conner Thompson Collection (books on the finer arts of homemaking); Lang Collection (books written or edited by Andrew Lang); James Whitcomb Riley Collection (1st editions and memorabilia); Philharmonic Symphony programs; choral music; music scores and parts; framed art collection. **Holdings:** 100,000 titles; 70 VF drawers of pamphlets, clippings and mounted pictures; 26,000 phonograph records; Schwann catalogs and New York Times Index on microfilm. **Subscriptions:** 280 journals and other serials. **Services:** Interlibrary loans; copying; listening facilities; concert series. **Publications:** Consolidated List of Choral Music, triennial. **Special Indexes:** Index to symphony program notes (card).

★6092★
INDIANAPOLIS-MARION COUNTY PUBLIC LIBRARY - BUSINESS, SCIENCE AND TECHNOLOGY DIVISION (Sci-Tech)
40 E. St. Clair St.   Phone: (317) 269-1741
Indianapolis, IN 46204   Mark Leggett, Div.Hd.
Founded: 1921. **Staff:** Prof 9. **Subjects:** Science, engineering, space science, agriculture, electronics, building, health, cookery, television, accounting, advertising, economics, insurance, investment management. **Special Collections:** Wright Marble collection of rare cook books; Arthur Stumpf collection of old menus. **Holdings:** 60,000 titles; 90 VF drawers. **Subscriptions:** 750 journals and other serials. **Services:** Interlibrary loans; copying. **Computerized Information Services:** Access to DIALOG, New York Times Information Service, Indiana Information Retrieval Service (INDIRS).

★6093★
INDIANAPOLIS-MARION COUNTY PUBLIC LIBRARY - FILM DIVISION (Aud-Vis)
1435 N. Illinois St.   Phone: (317) 269-1821
Indianapolis, IN 46202   Jacqueline Ek, Div.Hd.
Founded: 1948. **Staff:** Prof 2; Other 7. **Holdings:** 2691 films (16mm); 211 filmstrips; 1432 films (8mm); 995 art prints (framed); 200 videotapes. **Publications:** Film Catalog and supplement, irregular - for sale.

★6094★
INDIANAPOLIS-MARION COUNTY PUBLIC LIBRARY - NEWSPAPER AND PERIODICAL DIVISION (Info Sci)
40 E. St. Clair St.   Phone: (317) 269-1728
Indianapolis, IN 46204   Harriet Cohen, Div.Hd.
Founded: 1981. **Staff:** Prof 1; Other 6. **Subjects:** Newspapers, periodicals, government documents. **Holdings:** 57,228 bound periodical volumes; 16,456 government documents. **Subscriptions:** 1025 journals and other serials; 70 newspapers. **Services:** Interlibrary loans; copying; library open to public. **Computerized Information Services:** DIALOG, SDC; INDIRS (internal database).

★6095★
INDIANAPOLIS-MARION COUNTY PUBLIC LIBRARY - SOCIAL SCIENCE DIVISION (Soc Sci)
40 E. St. Clair St.   Phone: (317) 269-1733
Indianapolis, IN 46204   Lois Laube, Div.Hd.
Founded: 1960. **Staff:** Prof 7. **Subjects:** Bibliography, philosophy, religion, sociology, law, folklore, political science, education, travel, history, biography. **Special Collections:** Indiana and Indianapolis (75 VF drawers); Indiana county histories; Foundation Center Collection; college catalogs; college catalogs on microfiche; early American textbooks; adult education information files; club and organzation file. **Holdings:** 80,000 titles; 70 VF drawers of subject files; 16 VF drawers of miscellaneous costume, portrait, career and foundation files; microfilm. **Subscriptions:** 312 journals and other serials; 55 newspapers. **Services:** Interlibrary loans; copying.

★6096★
INDIANAPOLIS MOTOR SPEEDWAY HALL OF FAME MUSEUM - LIBRARY (Rec)
4790 W. 16th St.   Phone: (317) 241-2501
Indianapolis, IN 46222   Jack L. Martin, Dir.
Subjects: Auto racing, antique and classic cars. **Special Collections:** Auto racing films since 1909; complete network broadcast tapes of the Indianapolis 500 race since World War II. **Holdings:** 600 books; 3000 bound periodical volumes. **Services:** Copying; library open to public by appointment only.

★6097★
INDIANAPOLIS MUSEUM OF ART - REFERENCE LIBRARY (Art)†
1200 W. 38th St.   Phone: (317) 923-1331
Indianapolis, IN 46208   Martha G. Blocker, Hd.Libn.
Founded: 1907. **Staff:** Prof 2; Other 2. **Subjects:** Fine arts. **Special Collections:** Indiana artists (6 VF drawers of clippings, catalogs). **Holdings:** 22,000 books and bound periodical volumes; auction, sales and exhibition catalogs; 78 VF drawers of clippings and pamphlets. **Subscriptions:** 99 journals and other serials; 3 newspapers. **Services:** Interlibrary loans (limited); copying; library open to public. **Computerized Information Services:** Computerized cataloging. **Networks/Consortia:** Member of INCOLSA; Central Indiana Area Library Services Authority (CIALSA). **Staff:** Julie C. Su, Cat.

★6098★
INDIANAPOLIS MUSEUM OF ART - SLIDE COLLECTION (Art)
1200 W. 38th St.   Phone: (317) 923-1331
Indianapolis, IN 46208   Carolyn J. Metz, Dir., Vis.Rsrcs. & Serv.
Staff: Prof 1; Other 2. **Subjects:** Art history, painting, sculpture, minor arts, decorative arts, architecture. **Holdings:** 80,000 slides. **Services:** Copying (limited); collection open to public on a limited schedule. **Special Indexes:** Artist name card file; theme and subject guides.

★6099★
INDIANAPOLIS NEWSPAPERS, INC. - INDIANAPOLIS STAR AND INDIANAPOLIS NEWS - REFERENCE LIBRARY (Publ)
307 N. Pennsylvania St.   Phone: (317) 633-9293
Indianapolis, IN 46206   Sandra E. Fitzgerald, Hd.Libn.
Founded: 1912. **Staff:** Prof 2; Other 16. **Subjects:** General newspaper reference, especially Indiana and Indianapolis news. **Holdings:** 1200 books; Star and News, 1912 to present. **Services:** Interlibrary loans; copying (limited); library open to public on a limited basis. **Special Indexes:** Index to Star and News. **Staff:** Sally L. Adams, Day Supv.; M. Cathern Hess, Asst.Hd.Libn.

★6100★
INDIANAPOLIS POWER & LIGHT COMPANY - CORPORATE COMMUNICATIONS REFERENCE CENTER (Energy)
Box 1595B   Phone: (317) 261-8390
Indianapolis, IN 46206   Robert W. Golobish, Commun.Res.Coord.
Founded: 1980. **Staff:** Prof 1; Other 1. **Subjects:** Electric power. **Holdings:**

Figures not available. **Services:** Interlibrary loans; copying; library open to public with restrictions. **Networks/Consortia:** Member of Central Indiana Area Library Services Authority (CIALSA).

★6101★
INDIANAPOLIS PUBLIC SCHOOLS - KARL R. KALP LIBRARY (Educ)
120 E. Walnut St.   Phone: (317) 266-4499
Indianapolis, IN 46204   Marjorie Percival, Hd.Libn.
Founded: 1921. **Staff:** Prof 2; Other 1. **Subjects:** Education, child development. **Holdings:** 10,000 books; 1400 bound periodical volumes; 52 linear shelves of pamphlets and courses of study; microfilm; 2500 microfiche. **Subscriptions:** 160 journals and other serials. **Services:** Interlibrary loans; copying; bibliographic and research services for administrators and teachers in school system; library open to public but circulation only to Indianapolis Public Schools personnel and non-teaching students in Indianapolis colleges. **Publications:** Bookmark, monthly during the school year - distributed to administrators and teachers in the school system. **Formerly:** Its Teachers Library. **Staff:** Doris Thompson, Asst.Libn.

INDIANHEAD TECHNICAL INSTITUTE
See: Wisconsin Indianhead Technical Institute

★6102★
INDUSMIN, LTD. - TECHNICAL CENTRE LIBRARY (Sci-Tech)
1933 Leslie St.   Phone: (416) 445-6720
Don Mills, ON, Canada M3B 2M3   Yvonne Postill, Sec./Libn.
Founded: 1967. **Staff:** 1. **Subjects:** Metallurgy, geology, ceramics, glass. **Holdings:** 700 books; 300 bound periodical volumes. **Subscriptions:** 45 journals and other serials. **Services:** Interlibrary loans; copying.

★6103★
INDUSTRIAL ACCIDENT PREVENTION ASSOCIATION - LIBRARY (Soc Sci)
2 Bloor St., E.   Phone: (416) 965-8888
Toronto, ON, Canada M4W 3C2   Marion Frank, Libn.-in-Charge
Founded: 1977. **Staff:** Prof 3. **Subjects:** Accident prevention, occupational health, safety. **Holdings:** 3000 books and bound periodical volumes; 1500 pamphlets and reports. **Subscriptions:** 300 journals and other serials. **Services:** Interlibrary loans; library open to public for reference use only.

INDUSTRIAL ACCIDENT PREVENTION ASSOCIATION - TECHNICAL INFORMATION LIBRARY
See: Association Paritaire de Prevention pour la Sante et la Securite du Travail du Quebec

★6104★
INDUSTRIAL FORESTRY ASSOCIATION - LIBRARY (Env-Cons)
225 S.W. Broadway, Rm. 400   Phone: (503) 222-9505
Portland, OR 97205   Michael D. Sullivan, Dir., Pub.Aff.
Subjects: Forests - protection, reforestation, ecomonics, history; tree farming. **Holdings:** 10,000 books; 2000 bound periodical volumes; unbound reports. **Services:** Library not open to public.

★6105★
INDUSTRIAL GENERAL INSURANCE COMPANY - LIBRARY (Bus-Fin)
1080 St. Louis Rd.
Box 1907   Phone: (418) 688-8210
Quebec, PQ, Canada G1K 7M3   N. Demers, Sec.
Founded: 1961. **Staff:** 1. **Subjects:** Insurance, accounting, finance, salesmanship, psychology of selling, mathematics, office management, personnel management, economics, investments. **Holdings:** 5500 books; 1000 pamphlets. **Subscriptions:** 47 journals and other serials. **Services:** Copying; library open to qualified users.

★6106★
INDUSTRIAL GRAIN PRODUCTS, LTD. - RESEARCH & DEVELOPMENT LIBRARY (Food-Bev)†
995 Mill St.
P.O. Box 6089   Phone: (514) 866-1838
Montreal, PQ, Canada H3C 3H1   Muriel Henri, Libn.
Staff: 1. **Subjects:** Grain products research, food, nutrition. **Holdings:** 1916 books; 2000 bound periodical volumes; 260 NTIS reports. **Subscriptions:** 127 journals and other serials. **Services:** Interlibrary loans; copying; library open to public for consultation only.

★6107★
INDUSTRIAL HEALTH FOUNDATION, INC. - LIBRARY (Med)
5231 Centre Ave.   Phone: (412) 687-2100
Pittsburgh, PA 15232   Jane F. Brislin, Dir., Info.Serv.
Founded: 1969. **Staff:** Prof 2; Other 1. **Subjects:** Industrial hygiene,

toxicology. **Holdings:** 1800 books; 100 bound periodical volumes; 56,000 abstracts on industrial hygiene and toxicology; 20 VF drawers of pamphlets and reprints. **Subscriptions:** 60 journals and other serials. **Services:** Library open to members only. **Publications:** Industrial Hygiene Digest (abstract service), monthly - by subscription; Memos to Members (newsletter), quarterly; technical bulletins, subject bibliographies, symposia proceedings - all irregular and for sale. **Special Catalogs:** Publications Catalog (pamphlet) - free upon request. **Staff:** Jean L. Collins, Libn.

★6108★
INDUSTRIAL HOME FOR THE BLIND - NASSAU-SUFFOLK BRAILLE LIBRARY (Aud-Vis)
320 Fulton Ave.   Phone: (516) 485-1234
Hempstead, NY 11550   Helen Lomax, Libn.
Founded: 1956. **Staff:** 4. **Subjects:** Text books (elementary through high school); reading books in braille and large type. **Holdings:** 60,000 volumes. **Services:** Interlibrary loans; copying; library open to public. **Staff:** Beatrice Weinberg, Asst.Libn.; Edith Magee, Assignment Supv.

★6109★
INDUSTRIAL INDEMNITY COMPANY - LIBRARY (Bus-Fin)
255 California St.   Phone: (415) 986-3535
San Francisco, CA 94120   Louise R. Murata, Libn.
Founded: 1956. **Staff:** 1. **Subjects:** Californiana, insurance, business, technical subjects. **Holdings:** 17,000 books. **Subscriptions:** 92 journals and other serials.

★6110★
INDUSTRIAL MANAGEMENT SOCIETY - FILM LIBRARY
570 Northwest Hwy.
Des Plaines, IL 60016
Defunct. Holdings absorbed by Institute of Industrial Engineers - Film Library.

INDUSTRIAL MATERIALS RESEARCH INSTITUTE LIBRARY
See: Canada - National Research Council - CISTI

INDUSTRIAL PUBLISHING COMPANY
See: Penton/IPC

INDUSTRIAL RESEARCH CENTRE OF QUEBEC
See: Centre de Recherche Industrielle du Quebec

★6111★
INDUSTRIAL RISK INSURERS - IRI LIBRARY (Sci-Tech)
85 Woodland St.   Phone: (203) 525-2601
Hartford, CT 06102   Anne S. Grise, Libn.
Founded: 1952. **Staff:** Prof 1. **Subjects:** Fire protection engineering. **Holdings:** 825 volumes; 42 VF drawers of subjects files; 28 VF drawers of unbound company catalogs. **Subscriptions:** 40 journals and other serials; 10 newspapers. **Services:** Interlibrary loans; copying; library not open to public. **Publications:** Sentinel, quarterly - to underwriters.

★6112★
INDUSTRIAL UNION OF MARINE AND SHIPBUILDING WORKERS OF AMERICA - RESEARCH LIBRARY (Soc Sci)†
8121 Georgia Ave.   Phone: (301) 589-8820
Silver Spring, MD 20910
Subjects: Union history, collective bargaining. **Holdings:** 500 books; 1000 research reports; 5000 government documents; 200 VF drawers; 50,000 collective bargaining agreements. **Services:** Library open to qualified users.

★6113★
INDUSTRIAL WORKERS OF THE WORLD - LIBRARY (Soc Sci)
3435 N. Sheffield, Suite 202
Chicago, IL 60657   Phone: (312) 549-5045
Subjects: Labor history, economics, political science. **Holdings:** 200 volumes. **Remarks:** The library is inactive, but collection is open to public for reference use only.

INFORM
See: International Reference Organization in Forensic Medicine and Sciences

INFORM
See: University of Minnesota

INFORMATICS GENERAL CORPORATION - NATIONAL CLEARINGHOUSE FOR ALCOHOL INFORMATION
See: National Clearinghouse for Alcohol Information

★6114★
INFORMATICS INC. - ISG LIBRARY (Info Sci)†
6011 Executive Blvd.   Phone: (301) 770-3000
Rockville, MD 20852   Judy C. Huffman, Libn.
Founded: 1972. **Staff:** Prof 1; Other 1. **Subjects:** Computer, library and information sciences. **Holdings:** 1000 books; 500 analytics. **Subscriptions:** 100 journals and other serials. **Services:** Interlibrary loans; copying; SDI; library not open to public. **Computerized Information Services:** Online systems; computerized cataloging, acquisitions and serials. **Networks/Consortia:** Member of RLG.

★6115★
INFORMATION ACCESS CORPORATION - LIBRARY
404 Sixth Ave.
Menlo Park, CA 94025
Subjects: Library automation and instruction; information science; computers; publishing; online trends. **Special Collections:** Oil and gas reserves information (350 books, serials, pamphlets). **Holdings:** 400 books; 295 reports; 350 microforms; 50 magnetic tapes. **Remarks:** Presently inactive.

INFORMATION CENTER ON CHILDREN'S CULTURES
See: U.S. Committee for UNICEF

INFORMATION CENTER FOR GRAVITATION CHEMISTRY
See: Ensanian Physicochemical Institute

INFORMATION CENTER FOR THE HANDICAPPED
See: American Alliance for Health, Physical Education, Recreation & Dance

INFORMATION CENTER FOR INTERNAL EXPOSURE
See: Oak Ridge National Laboratory

INFORMATION CLEARING HOUSE, INC. - FIND/SVP
See: FIND/SVP

★6116★
INFORMATION CONNECTION - LIBRARY (Info Sci; Sci-Tech)
Box 6061   Phone: (805) 967-0922
Santa Barbara, CA 93111   Linda R. Phillips, Ph.D., Info.Dir.
Founded: 1979. **Staff:** Prof 2; Other 1. **Subjects:** Electronics, small computers, parapsychology. **Holdings:** 3000 volumes. **Subscriptions:** 30 journals and other serials. **Services:** Interlibrary loans; copying; SDI; library not open to public. **Computerized Information Services:** DIALOG, SDC, BRS, National CSS, Inc., NLM, Ontyme. **Networks/Consortia:** Member of CLASS.

★6117★
INFORMATION FUTURES - INFORMATION CENTER (Info Sci)
2217 College Station   Phone: (509) 332-5726
Pullman, WA 99163   Gerald R. Brong, Pres.
Founded: 1974. **Staff:** 4. **Subjects:** Educational technology, library/information service. **Holdings:** 300 books; 50 AV resources. **Subscriptions:** 17 journals and other serials. **Services:** Interlibrary loans; copying; center open to public by appointment. **Computerized Information Services:** Online systems. **Publications:** List of publications - free upon request. **Remarks:** Information Futures is a research and consulting organization with 30 associates in the U.S. and Canada. Its publications may be released as conference proceedings.

INFORMATION HANDLING SERVICES - GLOBAL ENGINEERING DOCUMENTS
See: Global Engineering Documents

★6118★
INFORMATION HANDLING SERVICES - LIBRARY (Info Sci)
15 Inverness Way E.   Phone: (303) 779-0600
Englewood, CO 80150   Rhea E. Johnson, Info.Spec.
Staff: Prof 1. **Subjects:** Information science, marketing, publishing. **Holdings:** 500 books; 250,000 microfiche. **Subscriptions:** 230 journals and other serials; 7 newspapers. **Services:** Library not open to public.

INFORMATION RESOURCES CENTER FOR MENTAL HEALTH & FAMILY LIFE EDUCATION
See: Mental Health Materials Center

INFORMATION SERVICE OF INDIA LIBRARY
See: Consulate General of India

★6119★
INFORMATION TECHNOLOGY CENTER - LIBRARY (Info Sci)*
One World Trade Center
New York, NY 10048   Richard VanAuken, Dir.
Founded: 1973. **Staff:** Prof 2; Other 2. **Subjects:** Information technology and information technology products; micrographics and data processing. **Special Collections:** Manufacturers product files in the information technology field, including corporate histories and financial statements; publications and technical reviews from associations and companies; calendars and literature on all national and international information technology events. **Holdings:** 5000 volumes; 2000 files; 35 microfiche (National Micrographics Association (NMA) proceedings, 1968-75, and Journal of Micrographics). **Subscriptions:** 50 journals and other serials; 5 newspapers. **Services:** Interlibrary loans; copying; library open to public. **Computerized Information Services:** Computerized cataloging, acquisitions, serials and circulation. **Publications:** Information technology product and service source lists; micrographics and data processing newsletter; workshop brochure. **Staff:** Carol Hendershot, D.P. Specialist.

INFORMATION & TECHNOLOGY TRANSFER RESOURCE CENTER
See: International Research & Evaluation (IRE)

★6120★
INFORMETRICA LTD. - BUSINESS LIBRARY (Bus-Fin)
350 Sparks, Suite 1007   Phone: (613) 238-4831
Ottawa, ON, Canada K1P 5P9   Diane Purdie, Libn.
Staff: Prof 1. **Subjects:** Economics, Canadian economy and government, statistics, energy, business, computer science. **Special Collections:** Informetrica publications; Candide documents. **Holdings:** 800 books; 3800 Canadian and foreign official documents; 5000 unbound reports, manuscripts, clippings. **Subscriptions:** 125 journals and other serials; 5 newspapers. **Services:** Interlibrary loans; copying; SDI; library open to public with restrictions. **Computerized Information Services:** CAN/SDI. **Publications:** Accessions list, monthly; Bulletin, monthly; bibliographies. **Special Catalogs:** Technical reports and document catalog (card); catalog of National Forecast Service publications (card).

★6121★
INFORONICS, INC. - TECHNICAL LIBRARY (Info Sci)
550 Newton Rd.   Phone: (617) 486-8976
Littleton, MA 01460   Sandra Dennis, Mgr., Lib.Serv.
Founded: 1962. **Staff:** Prof 2; Other 1. **Subjects:** Systems analysis, word and text processing, library automation, information retrieval, computer typesetting. **Holdings:** 300 books; 700 reports. **Subscriptions:** 50 journals and other serials. **Services:** Interlibrary loans; copying; library not open to public. **Computerized Information Services:** Online systems; computerized cataloging. **Staff:** Nancy Dennis, Coord., Lib.Serv.

INFRARED INFORMATION AND ANALYSIS CENTER
See: Environmental Research Institute of Michigan

★6122★
INGALLS MEMORIAL HOSPITAL - MEDICAL LIBRARY (Med)
One Ingalls Dr.   Phone: (312) 333-2300
Harvey, IL 60426   Carol Ross, Libn.
Founded: 1968. **Staff:** Prof 1; Other 1. **Subjects:** Medicine, nursing, health sciences. **Holdings:** 2000 books; 2500 bound periodical volumes; 4 VF drawers of pamphlets; 1000 cassette tapes; 500 slides, videotapes and films. **Subscriptions:** 200 journals and other serials; 5 newspapers. **Services:** Interlibrary loans; copying; library not open to public. **Networks/Consortia:** Member of Chicago and South Consortium; Suburban Library System (SLS).

★6123★
INGERSOLL-RAND COMPANY - ENGINEERING LIBRARY (Sci-Tech)
150 Burke St.   Phone: (603) 882-2711
Nashua, NH 03061   M.A. Doyle, Libn.
Founded: 1963. **Staff:** 1. **Subjects:** Engineering, pulp and paper industry, water pollution, solid-liquid separation. **Special Collections:** Trade catalogs; patents. **Holdings:** 2000 books; 5000 catalogs; 3000 trade pamphlets; 350 federal and military specifications; 8500 patents (pulp and paper), microfilm. **Subscriptions:** 170 journals and other serials; 15 newspapers. **Services:** Interlibrary loans; copying; library open to public after consultation with librarian. **Computerized Information Services:** Computerized cataloging. **Networks/Consortia:** Member of Nashua Area Materials Exchange (NAME). **Publications:** Notes from the Library, monthly - for internal distribution only. **Special Indexes:** Manufacturers and subject index to trade data (card); patent index (card).

★6124★
INGERSOLL-RAND COMPANY - TECHNICAL LIBRARY (Sci-Tech)
Memorial Pkwy.   Phone: (201) 859-8288
Phillipsburg, NJ 08865   Sharon L. Shiner, Libn.
Founded: 1950. **Staff:** Prof 1. **Subjects:** Engineering, metallurgy. **Holdings:** 3000 books and bound periodical volumes; paper file. **Subscriptions:** 150 journals and other serials. **Services:** Interlibrary loans; copying; library not open to public. **Computerized Information Services:** DIALOG. **Publications:** Monthly Library Bulletin.

★6125★
INGERSOLL-RAND RESEARCH, INC. - TECHNICAL LIBRARY (Sci-Tech)
Box 301   Phone: (609) 921-9103
Princeton, NJ 08540   Diane M. Kliminski, Tech.Libn.
Founded: 1964. **Staff:** Prof 1. **Subjects:** Mechanics, mathematics, business, management, materials, mining. **Holdings:** 5200 books; 200 bound periodical volumes; 750 internal reports; 6000 external reports, unbound. **Subscriptions:** 153 journals and other serials. **Services:** Interlibrary loans; copying; library not open to public. **Computerized Information Services:** DIALOG; computerized serials.

INGERSOLL (Roy C.) RESEARCH CENTER
See: Borg-Warner Corporation - Roy C. Ingersoll Research Center

★6126★
INGHAM MEDICAL CENTER - JOHN W. CHI MEMORIAL MEDICAL LIBRARY (Med)
401 West Greenlawn Ave.   Phone: (517) 374-2270
Lansing, MI 48909   David G. Keddle, Dir., Med.Lib.
Staff: Prof 1; Other 2. **Subjects:** Medicine, nursing, pharmacology, hospital administration, dentistry. **Holdings:** 3500 books; 3000 bound periodical volumes; 150 cassette tapes; 350 audiotapes. **Subscriptions:** 420 journals and other serials. **Services:** Interlibrary loans; copying; library open to health care personnel. **Computerized Information Services:** DIALOG, SDC, MEDLARS; computerized serials. **Networks/Consortia:** Member of Mid-Michigan Health Sciences Libraries Association; Kentucky-Ohio-Michigan Regional Medical Libraries (KOMRML); Michigan Area Serial Holdings Consortium. **Staff:** Rosalie Ray, Med.Lib.Techn.; Lorraine Myers, Med.Lib.Asst.

INGRAHAM (Edward) LIBRARY
See: American Clock and Watch Museum - Edward Ingraham Library

INGRAHAM LIBRARY
See: Litchfield Historical Society

INGRAM (Irvine Sullivan) LIBRARY
See: West Georgia College - Irvine Sullivan Ingram Library

INHALATION TOXICOLOGY RESEARCH INSTITUTE
See: Lovelace Biomedical & Environmental Research Institute, Inc.

INLAND LAKES YACHTING ASSOCIATION COLLECTION
See: Oshkosh Public Museum - Library & Archives

INLAND RIVERS LIBRARY
See: Public Library of Cincinnati and Hamilton County - Department of Rare Books & Special Collections

★6127★
INLAND STEEL COMPANY - INDUSTRIAL RELATIONS LIBRARY (Bus-Fin)
30 W. Monroe   Phone: (312) 346-0300
Chicago, IL 60603   Barbara G. Morton, Libn.
Founded: 1954. **Staff:** Prof 1. **Subjects:** Industrial relations - labor relations, management development, personnel administration, steel history and economics. **Holdings:** 2500 books and bound periodical volumes; 25 VF drawers of pamphlets. **Subscriptions:** 100 journals and other serials. **Services:** Interlibrary loans; library open to public by appointment. **Computerized Information Services:** SDC, BRS. **Networks/Consortia:** Member of Metropolitan Chicago Library Assembly; ILLINET.

★6128★
INLAND STEEL COMPANY - RESEARCH LABORATORIES - LIBRARY (Sci-Tech)
3001 E. Columbus Dr.   Phone: (219) 392-5824
East Chicago, IN 46312   Barbara Minne Banek, Libn.
Staff: Prof 1; Other 1. **Subjects:** Metallurgy and allied fields. **Holdings:** 4500 books; 5800 bound periodical volumes; 3200 government publications (pamphlets, reports, papers); 47 VF drawers translations; 15 VF drawers of

patents. **Subscriptions:** 200 journals and other serials. **Services:** Interlibrary loans; copying; computerized literature searching; library open to public if authorized by the Vice President of Research. **Computerized Information Services:** DIALOG, SDC; internal database. **Networks/Consortia:** Member of Indiana Cooperative Library Services Authority (INCOLSA); Metropolitan Chicago Library Assembly. **Publications:** General Acquisitions; Patent List; BISITS Translations List, all monthly - for internal distribution only. **Special Indexes:** Computerized index for company research and development reports.

★6129★
INLOW CLINIC - LIBRARY (Med)
Box 370
Shelbyville, IN 46176   Linda Stark, Libn.
Founded: 1923. **Subjects:** History and philosophy of medicine, medicine, social sciences, history. **Special Collections:** Indiana history. **Holdings:** 3500 books; 2500 bound periodical volumes; 4 VF drawers of pamphlets. **Services:** Interlibrary loans; copying; library open to public by appointment.

★6130★
INNER CITY CULTURAL CENTER - LANGSTON HUGHES MEMORIAL LIBRARY (Area-Ethnic)
1308 S. New Hampshire Ave.   Phone: (213) 387-1161
Los Angeles, CA 90006   Fred Beauford, Lib.Cons.
Founded: 1967. **Staff:** Prof 2; Other 2. **Subjects:** Ethnic groups, performing and visual arts. **Holdings:** 6500 books; 300 bound periodical volumes; 100 manuscripts and 100 recordings and tapes; 250 clippings; 175 reports; 200 photographs. **Subscriptions:** 10 journals and other serials. **Services:** Library open to public by request. **Remarks:** Inner City Cultural Center also has Inner City Press, which publishes Innerview (newsletter), books and recordings.

INNES (Campbell) MEMORIAL LIBRARY
See: Battleford National Historic Park - Campbell Innes Memorial Library

INRS - URBANISATION
See: Universite du Quebec a Montreal - Institut National de la Recherche Scientifique - Cartotheque

★6131★
INSECT CONTROL AND RESEARCH, INC. - LIBRARY (Sci-Tech)
1330 Dillon Heights Ave.   Phone: (301) 747-4500
Baltimore, MD 21228   Dr. Eugene J. Gerberg, Pres.
Founded: 1946. **Subjects:** Entomology, plant pathology, tropical diseases, pesticides, agriculture, food plant sanitation. **Holdings:** 1000 books; 600 bound periodical volumes; 5000 reprints. **Subscriptions:** 50 journals and other serials. **Services:** Library open to public.

★6132★
INSIDE SPORTS MAGAZINE - LIBRARY (Publ)
444 Madison Ave.
New York, NY 10022   Mary Bruno, Res.Libn.
Founded: 1980. **Staff:** 1. **Subjects:** Sports. **Holdings:** Newspaper clippings. **Subscriptions:** 20 journals and other serials; 10 newspapers. **Services:** Copying; library not open to public. **Special Indexes:** Index to Inside Sports (card). **Remarks:** Published by Newsweek, Inc.

INSTITUT CANADIEN DE CONSERVATION
See: Canada - National Museums of Canada - Canadian Conservation Institute

★6133★
INSTITUT CANADIEN D'EDUCATION DES ADULTES - CENTRE DE DOCUMENTATION (Educ)†
506 rue Ste-Catherine, Suite 800   Phone: (514) 842-2766
Montreal, PQ, Canada H2L 2C7   Micheline Seguin, Documentaliste
Founded: 1966. **Staff:** Prof 1; Other 1. **Subjects:** Adult and continuing education, community development, manpower, communication. **Holdings:** 5600 books; 28 VF drawers of pamphlets; 12 VF drawers of clippings. **Subscriptions:** 350 journals and other serials; 2 newspapers. **Services:** Interlibrary loans; copying; library open to public. **Also Known As:** Canadian Institute of Adult Education.

INSTITUT CANADIEN DU FILM
See: Canadian Film Institute

★6134★
INSTITUT CANADIEN-FRANCAIS D'OTTAWA - LIBRARY (Hist)†
316 Dalhousie St.   Phone: (613) 234-1288
Ottawa, ON, Canada K1N 7E7   Yves Franche, Libn.
Staff: Prof 1. **Subjects:** History, biography, science. **Special Collections:**

French (Paris) collection of l'Illustration, 1849-1940. **Holdings:** 4000 volumes. **Subscriptions:** 20 journals and other serials; 6 newspapers. **Services:** Library open to students, researchers and historians.

INSTITUT CANADIEN DE L'INFORMATION SCIENTIFIQUE ET TECHNIQUE
See: Canada - National Research Council - Canada Institute for Scientific and Technical Information

INSTITUT CANADIEN DE RECHERCHES SUR LES PATES ET PAPIERS
See: Pulp and Paper Research Institute of Canada

INSTITUT CANADO-AMERICAIN
See: Association Canado-Americaine

INSTITUT DE DIAGNOSTIC ET DE RECHERCHES CLINIQUES DE MONTREAL
See: Clinical Research Institute of Montreal

INSTITUT DE GENIE DES MATERIAUX
See: Canada - National Research Council - CISTI - Industrial Materials Research Institute Library

★6135★
INSTITUT D'HISTOIRE DE L'AMERIQUE FRANCAISE (1970) - RESEARCH CENTRE LIBRARY (Hist)
257-261 Ave. Bloomfield   Phone: (514) 271-4759
Montreal, PQ, Canada H2V 3R6   Jacques Mathieu, Pres.
Founded: 1947. **Staff:** 4. **Subjects:** History, Canadian history, French literature, methodology, pedagogy, sociology, philosophy. **Holdings:** 15,000 books; 454 unbound periodicals; 4000 small volumes or writings (classified and in envelopes). **Subscriptions:** 60 journals and other serials. **Services:** Copying; library open to public with restrictions. **Publications:** Revue d'histoire de l'Amerique francaise. **Staff:** Juliette Remillard; Lise McNicoll; Linda Beaudoin; Berthe Stapinsky .

INSTITUT MILITAIRE ET CIVIL DE MEDECINE DE L'ENVIRONNEMENT
See: Canada - Defence and Civil Institute of Environmental Medicine

INSTITUT NATIONAL CANADIEN POUR LES AVEUGLES
See: Canadian National Institute for the Blind

★6136★
INSTITUT NAZARETH ET LOUIS-BRAILLE - BIBLIOTHEQUE PUBLIQUE (Aud-Vis)
1255 Beauregard   Phone: (514) 463-1710
Longueuil, PQ, Canada J4K 2M3   Suzanne Olivier, Chief
Founded: 1911. **Staff:** Prof 1; Other 10. **Subjects:** Humanities. **Special Collections:** Braille books and talking books. **Holdings:** 10,000 books; 22,000 cassettes (talking books); 35,000 braille books; 1280 bound periodical volumes. **Subscriptions:** 80 journals and other serials (36 in braille). **Services:** Interlibrary loans; copying; library open to the visually handicapped only. **Publications:** Le Carrefour Braille, monthly. **Special Catalogs:** Ink print catalog (card); braille catalog (card and book).

★6137★
INSTITUT PHILIPPE PINEL - LIBRARY (Med)
10905 Henri-Bourassa Blvd., E.   Phone: (514) 648-8461
Montreal, PQ, Canada H1C 1H1   Normand Beaudet, Bibliotechnicien
Founded: 1970. **Staff:** 1. **Subjects:** Forensic psychiatry, mentally ill offenders. **Holdings:** 1000 books; 850 bound periodical volumes; 5 VF drawers of reprints and pamphlets. **Subscriptions:** 200 journals and other serials. **Services:** Interlibrary loans; copying; library not open to public. **Publications:** Pinel-Documentation, irregular - for internal distribution only.

★6138★
INSTITUT DE TECHNOLOGIE AGRICOLE - RESEARCH LIBRARY (Agri)
                                     Phone: (418) 856-1110
La Pocatiere, PQ, Canada G0R 1Z0   Rene-Daniel Langlois, Libn.
Founded: 1859. **Staff:** Prof 1; Other 2. **Subjects:** General agriculture, biochemistry, mineralogy, economics, statistics, botany, animal husbandry, field crops. **Holdings:** 25,000 books; 2160 bound periodical volumes; 100,000 reports and bulletins; 260 maps. **Subscriptions:** 300 journals and other serials. **Services:** Interlibrary loans; copying; library open to public for reference use only. **Computerized Information Services:** Online systems; computerized cataloging.

★6139★

INSTITUTE FOR ADVANCED PASTORAL STUDIES - REFERENCE LIBRARY (Rel-Theol)
29129 Southfield Rd.   Phone: (313) 569-1616
Southfield Hills, MI 48076
Subjects: Theology, personal and spiritual growth, organizational development. **Holdings:** Figures not available.

★6140★

INSTITUTE FOR ADVANCED PERCEPTION - LIBRARY (Hum)†
719 S. Clarence Ave.   Phone: (312) 386-1742
Oak Park, IL 60304   Donna Marie Schroeppel, Exec.Sec.
Founded: 1967. **Staff:** 2. **Subjects:** Occultism, yoga, E.S.P., astrology, psychology. **Holdings:** 1000 books; 3 VF drawers. **Services:** Library open to its students for a fee.

★6141★

INSTITUTE FOR ADVANCED STUDIES OF WORLD RELIGIONS - LIBRARY (Rel-Theol)
Melville Memorial Library, 5th Fl.
SUNY at Stony Brook   Phone: (516) 246-8366
Stony Brook, NY 11794   C.T. Shen, Pres.
Founded: 1970. **Staff:** Prof 10; Other 11. **Subjects:** Buddhism and related subjects in history, philosophy and culture; Hinduism and Indology; other religions of Asian origin; Christian pastoral theology, Islam. **Special Collections:** Richard A. Gard Collection (Buddhist and related subjects; 24,000 volumes); Ngiam Hoo-pang Collection of Chinese Buddhist Texts (9700 volumes); Christopher S. George Collection of Rare Nepalese Manuscripts (16 manuscripts); collection of Tibetan books published in India since 1963 (10,000 volumes); Sanskrit Collection (5000 volumes); other South Asia collections (mainly on Hinduism and Islam; 8000 volumes); G.E. Sargent Collection of Asian Studies (4000 volumes); D.D. Crescenzo, J.P. Mitton and D.B. Lefevre Collections in Pastoral Theology (8000 volumes). **Holdings:** 61,000 books; 5100 bound periodical volumes; 179 reels of microfilm of Chinese manuscripts from Tun-huang; 31,000 microfiche of Sanskrit, Tibetan and Chinese texts; 11 VF drawers of correspondence from U.S. and foreign religious and educational organizations. **Subscriptions:** 300 journals and other serials. **Services:** Copying; SDI; library open to public for reference use only. **Computerized Information Services:** Asiagraphics (internal database); computerized cataloging. **Networks/Consortia:** Member of Stony Brook Center for Religious Studies; New York Area Theological Library Association; Long Island Library Resources Council (LILRC); OCLC. **Publications:** IASWR Monograph Series: Buddhist Text Information, Buddhist Research Information, Hindu Text Information, Sikh Religious Studies Information; Basic Buddhism Series (booklets). **Special Catalogs:** A Classified Catalogue of Chinese Books in the Library of the IASWR (book). **Special Indexes:** IASWR Buddhist Sanskrit Manuscripts (microfiche). **Remarks:** The institute aims to preserve religious literature which has not received adequate attention from scholars and translators. It seeks to provide bibliographic information, as well as publish important religious materials in various languages and the translation of selected texts into English. In addition, the institute seeks to strengthen contacts and cooperation among those concerned with the academic study and practical applications of world religions. **Staff:** Hannah G. Robinson, Libn., S. Asia Coll./Lang; Lena L. Yang, Libn., E. Asia Coll.; June C. Kin, Ser./Cat.

★6142★

INSTITUTE FOR ADVANCED STUDY OF HUMAN SEXUALITY - RESEARCH LIBRARY (Soc Sci)†
1523 Franklin St.   Phone: (415) 928-1133
San Francisco, CA 94109   Dr. Erwin J. Haeberle, Dir.
Founded: 1976. **Subjects:** Human sexuality. **Special Collections:** Over 10,000 items of sexually explicit visual material (films, videotapes, slides) covering every aspect of human and animal sexuality. **Holdings:** 3000 books; videotapes of all lectures given at the institute; 10 unbound volumes of American and European journals on homosexuality. **Subscriptions:** 15 journals and other serials. **Services:** Library not open to public.

★6143★

INSTITUTE FOR ADVANCED STUDY - LIBRARIES (Educ)
                                        Phone: (609) 734-8000
Princeton, NJ 08540
Founded: 1940. **Staff:** Prof 6; Other 5. **Subjects:** Archeology; art history; astrophysics; classical, medieval and Renaissance studies; history; mathematics; theoretical physics; social sciences. **Special Collections:** History of science. **Holdings:** 100,000 volumes. **Services:** Library open to members only. **Staff:** Mrs. W.S. Agar, Hist.Stud.Libn.; Mrs. Rubby Sherr, Soc.Sci.Libn.; Mrs. Robert Evans, Math/Natural Sci.Libn.

★6144★

INSTITUTE OF THE AMERICAN MUSICAL, INC. - LIBRARY (Mus; Theater)
121 N. Detroit St.   Phone: (213) 934-1221
Los Angeles, CA 90036   Miles M. Kreuger, Cur.
Founded: 1972. **Staff:** Prof 2. **Subjects:** American musical theater, film, broadcasting, world's fairs and other allied areas of showmanship. **Special Collections:** Record catalogs and supplements (750); 200 unpublished screenplays. **Holdings:** 6000 books; over 35,000 phonograph records, tapes and cylinders dating back to the 1890s; theater and film playbills and programs, periodicals, sheet music and vocal scores dating back to 1844; motion picture press books; 200,000 stills from 1914 to present; extensive biographies; every musical comedy script published in America and dozens in manuscript form; original or photocopied materials from the archives of movie studios and recording companies, including discographies of many major Broadway and Hollywood stars. **Subscriptions:** 15 journals and other serials. **Services:** Library open to qualified scholars by appointment; produces film retrospectives and exhibitions for the public. **Publications:** Plans to publish quarterly of American musical theater, films and recordings.

★6145★

INSTITUTE OF ARAB STUDIES, INC. - LIBRARY (Area-Ethnic)
556 Trapelo Rd.   Phone: (617) 484-3262
Belmont, MA 02178
Staff: 1. **Subjects:** Arab World, Third World countries. **Holdings:** 1010 volumes; 75 volumes of clipping services; 6 boxes of U.N. documents; 3 boxes of newsletters; 6 boxes of research reports; 1 box of unpublished reports and papers. **Subscriptions:** 70 periodicals and journals; 5 newspapers. **Services:** Copying; library open to public.

INSTITUTE OF ARCTIC & ALPINE RESEARCH AT BOULDER
See: University of Colorado, Boulder

INSTITUTE FOR ASTRONOMY AT THE UNIVERSITY OF HAWAII
See: University of Hawaii

INSTITUTE FOR BASIC RESEARCH IN DEVELOPMENTAL DISABILITIES OF NEW YORK
See: New York State Institute for Basic Research in Developmental Disabilities

INSTITUTE OF BEHAVIORAL RESEARCH
See: Texas Christian University

★6146★

INSTITUTE FOR BEHAVIORAL RESEARCH - LIBRARY (Soc Sci)
3201 New Mexico Ave., N.W., Suite 250   Phone: (301) 585-3915
Washington, DC 20016   Ken Williams, Libn.
Staff: 1. **Subjects:** Behavioral science, psychology, education, design. **Holdings:** 2000 books; films; videotapes. **Subscriptions:** 60 journals and other serials. **Services:** Interlibrary loans; copying; library open to public with advance notification. **Formerly:** Located in Silver Springs, MD.

INSTITUTE FOR BEHAVIOURAL RESEARCH
See: York University

★6147★

INSTITUTE OF BUDDHIST STUDIES - LIBRARY (Rel-Theol)
2717 Haste St.   Phone: (415) 849-2383
Berkeley, CA 94704   Haruyoshi Kusada, Dir.
Staff: Prof 2; Other 2. **Subjects:** Buddhism, Japanese religion, oriental philosophy, Japanese in United States, Shin sect. **Holdings:** 31,000 books; 250 bound periodical volumes; 3500 clippings; 20 boxes of realia budistica. **Subscriptions:** 190 journals and other serials. **Services:** Interlibrary loans; copying; library open to serious researchers by appointment.

INSTITUTE FOR CANCER AND BLOOD RESEARCH
See: Loma Linda University

INSTITUTE OF CANCER RESEARCH
See: Columbia University Cancer Center

★6148★

INSTITUTE FOR CANCER RESEARCH - LIBRARY (Med)
Fox Chase Cancer Center   Phone: (215) 728-2711
Philadelphia, PA 19111   Jane M. Bosley, Libn.
Founded: 1926. **Staff:** Prof 2; Other 2. **Subjects:** Biochemistry, cancer, cell biology, chemistry, clinical research, experimental pathology. **Special Collections:** A.L. Patterson Collection on mathematics and crystallography (1100 volumes). **Holdings:** 4160 books; 17,600 bound periodical volumes;

641 reels of microfilm; 529 reports (cataloged). **Subscriptions:** 419 journals and other serials. **Services:** Interlibrary loans; copying (limited); library open to public for reference use only. **Computerized Information Services:** DIALOG, MEDLINE. **Networks/Consortia:** Member of Interlibrary Delivery Service of Pennsylvania. **Staff:** Ann M. Schifano, Asst.Libn.

★6149★
INSTITUTE FOR CENTRAL EUROPEAN RESEARCH - LIBRARY (Area-Ethnic)
2950 Warrensville Ctr. Rd.   Phone: (216) 752-9927
Shaker Heights, OH 44122   W.K. Von Uhlenhorst-Ziechmann, Dir.
Founded: 1945. **Staff:** 2. **Subjects:** Central Europe - history, literature, genealogy, heraldry. **Holdings:** 600 books; 25 bound periodical volumes; 200 manuscripts and periodicals (cataloged); 20 boxes and files of clippings and archival material. **Services:** Library not open to public.

★6150★
INSTITUTE OF CERTIFIED TRAVEL AGENTS - LIBRARY (Bus-Fin)
148 Linden St.   Phone: (617) 237-0280
Wellesley, MA 02181   Lois Tilles, Dir., Inst.Rel.
Subjects: Travel agency history and administration. **Special Collections:** Travel research papers. **Holdings:** 2000 books and papers. **Services:** Library not open to public.

★6151★
INSTITUTE OF CHARTERED ACCOUNTANTS OF ONTARIO - THE MERRILEES LIBRARY (Bus-Fin)
69 Bloor St., E.   Phone: (416) 962-1841
Toronto, ON, Canada M4W 1B3   Theresa Wolak, Libn.
Founded: 1881. **Staff:** Prof 1; Other 1. **Subjects:** Business administration and management, accounting, auditing, data processing, taxation, economics, law. **Special Collections:** Historical collection on accounting and allied subjects (800 items). **Holdings:** 2400 books; 595 bound periodical volumes; 403 pamphlets. **Subscriptions:** 45 journals and other serials. **Services:** Interlibrary loans; copying; library open for reference use only to certain selected nonmembers. **Publications:** Library catalog and supplement; List of Suggested Publications for a Chartered Accountant's Basic Library, annual - to members and students on request; Guidelines for Selection of Accounting and Related Materials Compiled for Public Libraries.

★6152★
INSTITUTE OF CHARTERED FINANCIAL ANALYSTS - LIBRARY (Bus-Fin)†
University of Virginia
Box 3668   Phone: (804) 977-6600
Charlottesville, VA 22903
Founded: 1962. **Subjects:** Security analysis, investments, finance. **Holdings:** 350 books and bound periodical volumes. **Subscriptions:** 60 journals and other serials. **Services:** Library open to staff. **Publications:** C.F.A. Digest, quarterly.

★6153★
INSTITUTE FOR CHILDHOOD RESOURCES - LIBRARY (Soc Sci; Educ)
1169 Howard St.   Phone: (415) 864-1169
San Francisco, CA 94103   Stevanne Auerbach, Ph.D., Dir.
Staff: Prof 1; Other 5. **Subjects:** Child care, early childhood, parent education, special education. **Holdings:** 5000 volumes; reports; manuscripts; clippings. **Services:** Copying; library open to public with restrictions. **Publications:** List of publications - available upon request.

INSTITUTE OF CHRISTIAN ORIENTAL RESEARCH
See: Catholic University of America - Semitics

★6154★
INSTITUTE ON THE CHURCH IN URBAN-INDUSTRIAL SOCIETY - LIBRARY (Soc Sci)
5700 S. Woodlawn   Phone: (312) 643-7111
Chicago, IL 60637   Richard P. Poethig, Dir.
Founded: 1967. **Staff:** 3. **Subjects:** Urban problems, urbanization, missions, community organization, international relations, economic development, social change, labor movement. **Special Collections:** Presbyterian Institute of Industrial Relations historical files; Urban Training Center historical files. **Holdings:** 1050 books; 50 bound periodical volumes; 7000 ICUIS abstract service documents; 30 drawers of project files, organization files and general information. **Subscriptions:** 100 journals and other serials. **Services:** Interlibrary loans; copying; library open to public with restrictions. **Publications:** Occasional Paper Series; Bibliography Series; Justice Ministries, quarterly.

INSTITUTE OF CISTERCIAN STUDIES LIBRARY
See: Western Michigan University

INSTITUTE OF COMMUNITY & FAMILY PSYCHIATRY
See: Sir Mortimer B. Davis Jewish General Hospital

INSTITUTE FOR THE CRIPPLED AND DISABLED
See: International Center for the Disabled

★6155★
INSTITUTE FOR DEFENSE ANALYSES - COMMUNICATIONS RESEARCH DIVISION - LIBRARY (Sci-Tech)
Thanet Rd.   Phone: (609) 924-4600
Princeton, NJ 08540   Jane P. Ciosek, Libn.
Founded: 1959. **Staff:** Prof 1; Other 1. **Subjects:** Mathematics, computer science, speech. **Holdings:** 10,000 books; 5000 bound periodical volumes; reprints and pamphlets. **Subscriptions:** 275 journals and other serials. **Services:** Library not open to public. **Computerized Information Services:** DIALOG.

★6156★
INSTITUTE FOR DEFENSE ANALYSES - TECHNICAL INFORMATION SERVICES (Sci-Tech)
1801 N. Beauregard St.   Phone: (703) 845-2043
Alexandria, VA 22311   Cathryn C. Lyon, Mgr., Tech.Info.Serv.
Founded: 1960. **Staff:** Prof 7; Other 19. **Subjects:** Aeronautical engineering, economics, mathematics, physics, political science, operations research. **Holdings:** 28,000 volumes; 82,500 documents. **Subscriptions:** 450 journals and other serials. **Services:** Interlibrary loans; library not open to public. **Staff:** Sarah H. Nash, Asst.Mgr.; Joan Sweeney, Res.Libn.; Ann Fleming, Res.Libn.; Thomasina Jones, Chf./Control & Distr.

★6157★
INSTITUTE FOR DEFENSE AND DISARMAMENT STUDIES - LIBRARY (Mil)
251 Harvard St.   Phone: (617) 734-4216
Brookline, MA 02146   Elizabeth Bernstein, Libn./Pub.Info.Coord.
Founded: 1980. **Staff:** Prof 1; Other 2. **Subjects:** Military forces and policies; disarmament and arms control efforts and policies; nuclear weapons and policies; peace and peace-related organizations. **Holdings:** Figures not available for books; government documents; documents from military and disarmament-related agencies; 500 files on U.S. peace-related organizations; newspaper clipping file. **Subscriptions:** 153 journals and other serials. **Services:** Copying (fee); library open to public for reference use only.

★6158★
INSTITUTE OF EARLY AMERICAN HISTORY AND CULTURE - KELLOCK LIBRARY (Hist)
Box 220   Phone: (804) 229-2771
Williamsburg, VA 23187   Patricia Higgs, Supv.
Staff: 2. **Subjects:** Early American history, book publication. **Holdings:** 4860 books; 750 bound periodical volumes; microforms. **Subscriptions:** 42 journals and other serials. **Services:** Library open to outside users with permission of director. **Remarks:** Institute is sponsored by the College of William and Mary and the Colonial Williamsburg Foundation.

INSTITUTE FOR ENERGY STUDIES
See: Stanford University

INSTITUTE OF ENVIRONMENTAL MEDICINE
See: New York University Medical Center

INSTITUTE FOR ENVIRONMENTAL RESEARCH
See: Kansas State University

★6159★
INSTITUTE OF ENVIRONMENTAL SCIENCES - LIBRARY (Env-Cons)
940 E. Northwest Hwy.   Phone: (312) 255-1561
Mt. Prospect, IL 60056   Betty L. Peterson, Exec.Dir.
Staff: 4. **Subjects:** Engineering, ecology and environment, contamination control. **Holdings:** Figures not available. **Publications:** List of publications - available on request.

INSTITUTE FOR FISHERIES RESEARCH
See: Michigan State Department of Natural Resources

★6160★

INSTITUTE OF GAS TECHNOLOGY - TECHNICAL INFORMATION CENTER (Energy)

3424 S. State St.
Chicago, IL 60616

Phone: (312) 567-3870
H.L. Mensch, Assoc.Dir.

Founded: 1941. Staff: Prof 8; Other 4. Subjects: Gas technology, kinetics, cryogenics, thermodynamics, mass transfer, energy. Holdings: 17,000 books; 15,000 bound periodical volumes; 249 VF drawers of patents, gas utility company annual reports, dissertations; 25,000 microfiche. Subscriptions: 500 journals and other serials. Services: Interlibrary loans; copying; library open to public for reference use only by appointment. Computerized Information Services: Online systems; computerized cataloging. Publications: Gas Abstracts, monthly; Energy Statistics, quarterly. Special Indexes: Gas Abstracts annual index. Staff: Elizabeth M. Van Ryzin, Sr.Libn.; George W. Price, Supv.Doc.Ctr.; John L. Schaeffer, Ed., Gas Abstracts; Anne C. Roess, Mgr., Tech.Info.Ctr.; Lawrence Dawson, Supv., Tech.Info.Ctr.; Dolores Rix, Tech.Libn.; Joanne V. McKenzie, Assoc.Ed.; Rebecca L. Bushy, Asst.Ed.

★6161★

INSTITUTE OF GERONTOLOGY - GERONTOLOGY LEARNING RESOURCES CENTER (Soc Sci)

Wayne State University
Knapp Bldg.
71-C East Ferry
Detroit, MI 48202

Phone: (313) 577-2221
H. Jean Owens, Dir.

Founded: 1968. Staff: Prof 1; Other 4. Subjects: All aspects of gerontology including aging, death, health, nursing homes, housing, retirement, social security. Special Collections: Historical collection on child and human development (17,000 items). Holdings: 8000 books; 50 bound periodical volumes; 3000 government documents (cataloged); clippings; pamphlets; bibliographies; tapes; newsletters. Subscriptions: 54 journals and other serials; 100 newsletters. Services: Interlibrary loans (fee); copying; library open to public with restrictions. Publications: Library News Notes, monthly. Remarks: Contains the holdings of the former Merrill Palmer Institute - Kresge Historical Library. The Institute of Gerontology is sponsored and funded by the state of Michigan and is housed at Wayne State University and the University of Michigan.

★6162★

INSTITUTE OF GERONTOLOGY - LEARNING RESOURCE CENTER (Soc Sci)

University of Michigan
300 N. Ingalls St., 9th Fl.
Ann Arbor, MI 48109

Phone: (313) 763-1325
Willie M. Edwards, Hd.Libn.

Founded: 1965. Staff: Prof 2; Other 7. Subjects: Gerontology - housing and environment, social policy, retirement, psychology, long-term care, social security/economics. Special Collections: International Aspects of Aging (1000 items); Pre-retirement Reference Desk (100 volumes); history collection (300 items); Susan Haas Humanities Collection; archival collection on social policy. Holdings: 10,000 books; 60 bound periodical volumes; 2000 unpublished research papers; 3100 microfiche; 360 newsletters; 52 VF drawers of census material. Subscriptions: 140 journals and other serials. Services: Copying; library open to public for reference use only. Computerized Information Services: Computerized cataloging. Networks/Consortia: Member of OCLC; RLIN. Publications: Acquisitions list, quarterly. Remarks: The Institute of Gerontology is sponsored and funded by the state of Michigan and is housed at the University of Michigan and Wayne State University. Staff: Jeanne Miller, Asst.Libn.

★6163★

INSTITUTE FOR GLAUCOMA RESEARCH, INC. - CARL C. SWISHER LIBRARY

667 Madison Ave.
New York, NY 10021

Founded: 1963. Subjects: Glaucoma, ophthalmic research, ophthalmology. Holdings: 2500 books; 1200 bound periodical volumes; 2000 feet of audiotape and film. Remarks: Presently inactive.

★6164★

INSTITUTE OF INDUSTRIAL ENGINEERS - FILM LIBRARY (Aud-Vis)

25 Technology Park/Atlanta
Norcross, GA 30092

Phone: (404) 449-0460
Greg Balestrero, Film Lib.Mgr.

Founded: 1982. Staff: Prof 1; Other 2. Subjects: Industrial engineering, work simplification techniques, performance rating, work sampling. Holdings: 100 films. Services: Library not open to public. Publications: Film Library Catalog - free upon request. Remarks: Contains the holdings of the former Industrial Management Society - Film Library.

INSTITUTE OF INDUSTRIAL RELATIONS
See: St. Joseph's University - Drexel Library

★6165★

INSTITUTE OF INTERNAL AUDITORS, INC. - LIBRARY (Bus-Fin)

International Headquarters
249 Maitland Ave.
Altamonte Springs, FL 32701

Phone: (305) 830-7600

Founded: 1941. Staff: 1. Subjects: Accounting, auditing, management. Holdings: 2000 volumes. Services: Interlibrary loans; library open to public. Publications: The Internal Auditor, bimonthly; EDPACS, monthly; IIA Today, bimonthly.

INSTITUTE FOR INTERNATIONAL COMMERCE
See: University of Michigan - Business Administration Library

INSTITUTE FOR INTERNATIONAL DEVELOPMENT
See: Harvard University

★6166★

INSTITUTE OF INTERNATIONAL EDUCATION - LIBRARY/ COMMUNICATIONS (Educ)

809 UN Plaza
New York, NY 10017

Phone: (212) 883-8470
Barbara Cahn Connotillo, Sr.Info.Adm.

Founded: 1919. Staff: 1. Subjects: International educational exchange of persons; higher education abroad and in the United States. Holdings: 2000 volumes; 40 VF drawers of information on fields of study in the U.S. and abroad, education systems abroad and related subject areas. Subscriptions: 100 journals and other serials. Services: Library not open to public.

INSTITUTE OF JAZZ STUDIES
See: Rutgers University, The State University of New Jersey

★6167★

INSTITUTE OF JUDICIAL ADMINISTRATION - LIBRARY (Law)

One Washington Sq. Village
New York, NY 10012

Phone: (212) 598-7721
Philip Klingle, Libn.

Founded: 1952. Staff: Prof 1; Other 1. Subjects: Administration of justice, courts and judges. Holdings: 12,000 books and reports; 2000 bound periodical volumes; 4 VF drawers of clippings. Subscriptions: 170 journals and other serials; 130 newsletters. Services: Copying; library open to public with restrictions. Publications: Acquisitions list, quarterly; IJA Report (newsletter), quarterly; irregular publications.

★6168★

INSTITUTE FOR JUVENILE RESEARCH - PROFESSIONAL LIBRARY (Soc Sci)

907 S. Wolcott
Chicago, IL 60612

Phone: (312) 996-1675
Flora L. Hawthorne, Hd.Libn.

Founded: 1928. Staff: Prof 1; Other 1. Subjects: Psychology, psychiatry, family studies, sociology, organization/administration, psychotherapy and mental health. Holdings: 5000 books; 7000 bound periodical volumes; archives; reprint collection. Subscriptions: 80 journals and other serials. Services: Interlibrary loans; library open to public by special arrangement. Publications: Acquisitions list. Staff: Nikki Holloway, Libn.; Estelle Marvel, Asst.Libn.

★6169★

INSTITUTE OF LAW RESEARCH AND REFORM - LIBRARY (Law)

402 Law Centre
University of Alberta
Edmonton, AB, Canada T6G 2H5

Phone: (403) 432-5291
Marlene Welton, Lib.Asst.

Staff: Prof 1; Other 1. Subjects: Law, law reform. Special Collections: Commonwealth Law Reform Publications (1600). Holdings: 1800 books; 3150 bound periodical volumes; 13 boxes of pamphlets. Subscriptions: 100 journals and other serials. Services: Copying; library open to public for reference use only. Networks/Consortia: Member of Canadian Association of Law Libraries. Publications: List of publications - available upon request.

★6170★

INSTITUTE OF LIVING - MEDICAL LIBRARY (Med)

400 Washington St.
Hartford, CT 06106

Phone: (203) 278-7950
Helen R. Lansberg, Dir.

Founded: 1822. Staff: Prof 4; Other 1. Subjects: Neurology, psychiatry, psychoanalysis, social sciences. Special Collections: Norman Collection (300 volumes, illustrating development of psychiatry and mental hospitals); Zilboorg Collection (290 rare books on medical psychology). Holdings: 24,000 books; 11,000 bound periodical volumes; 1200 pamphlets (cataloged); 30 boxes of hospital archives; 60 feet of shelving of asylum reports; 50 audiotapes; 200 audio cassettes; 8 video cassettes. Subscriptions: 375 journals and other serials. **Services:** Interlibrary loans; copying; SDI; library open to qualified professionals and college students for reference use only. **Computerized Information Services:** Online systems. **Networks/Consortia:** Member of Connecticut Association of Health Science Libraries (CAHSL); Capitol Area Health Consortium Libraries. **Publications:** Digest of Neurology and Psychiatry, 10/year - free to doctors and librarians who request it. **Special Indexes:** Computerized index to psychiatric and neurological literature. **Staff:** Norma A. Daugherty, Asst.Libn.; Elizabeth A. Fishe, Asst.Libn.; Jeanne D. Cantrell, Asst.Libn.

★6171★
INSTITUTE FOR LOCAL SELF-RELIANCE - LIBRARY (Env-Cons)
1717 18th St., N.W.						Phone: (202) 232-4108
Washington, DC 20009						David Morris, Dir.
Founded: 1974. **Subjects:** Energy, especially alternative sources; food, nutrition, agriculture; cities and neighborhoods; ecology and environment; housing; recycling and waste utilization; local economic development. **Holdings:** 1500 books; 6 VF drawers of material on communities and their development; 6 VF drawers of material on technology and its application; 6 VF drawers of geographic files. **Subscriptions:** 300 journals and other serials. **Services:** Library open to public. **Publications:** List of publications - available on request.

★6172★
INSTITUTE OF LOGOPEDICS - TECHNICAL LIBRARY (Med)
2400 Jardine Dr.						Phone: (316) 262-8271
Wichita, KS 67219						Clyde Cochran Berger, Tech.Libn.
Founded: 1934. **Staff:** Prof 2; Other 1. **Subjects:** Speech pathology, audiology, medicine, neurology, psychology, special education. **Special Collections:** Collections of rare books on speech pathology and audiology (200 volumes). **Holdings:** 7000 books; 832 bound periodical volumes; 15,000 reprints of scientific articles, government documents, pamphlets and other ephemera. **Subscriptions:** 70 journals and other serials. **Services:** Interlibrary loans; copying; library open to public. **Publications:** Bibliographies, occasional - prepared on request; new acquisitions lists, occasional. **Staff:** Rita Kunkel, Asst.Tech.Libn.

INSTITUTE OF MANAGEMENT/LABOR RELATIONS LIBRARY
See: Rutgers University, The State University of New Jersey

★6173★
INSTITUTE FOR MEDICAL RESEARCH - LIBRARY (Med)
Copewood St.							Phone: (609) 966-7377
Camden, NJ 08103						Dorothy H. Gruber, Libn.
Founded: 1968. **Staff:** Prof 1. **Subjects:** Cancer, virology, immunology, pediatrics, genetics, microbiology. **Holdings:** 5849 books and bound periodical volumes; 10 VF drawers of annual reports, newsletters, clippings, reprints. **Subscriptions:** 105 journals and other serials. **Services:** Interlibrary loans; copying; library open to public for reference use only. **Computerized Information Services:** MEDLINE. **Networks/Consortia:** Member of Southwest New Jersey Consortium for Health Information Services; New Jersey Health Sciences Network.

INSTITUTE OF MINERAL RESEARCH
See: Michigan Technological University

INSTITUTE FOR MINING AND MINERALS RESEARCH
See: University of Kentucky

★6174★
INSTITUTE OF NAVIGATION - LIBRARY (Trans)
815 15th St., N.W., Suite 832				Phone: (202) 783-4121
Washington, DC 20005						Frank B. Brady, Exec.Dir.
Subjects: Navigation and related subjects. **Holdings:** 200 books. **Subscriptions:** 50 journals and other serials.

INSTITUTE OF NORTHERN FORESTRY
See: U.S. Forest Service

★6175★
INSTITUTE OF OCCUPATIONAL AND ENVIRONMENTAL HEALTH - ARCHIVES (Med)
Crown Trust Bldg., Suite 410
1130 Sherbrooke St., W.
Montreal, PQ, Canada H3A 2M8				Phone: (514) 844-4955
								Therese Brien, Exec.Sec.
Founded: 1966. **Staff:** 4. **Subjects:** Biological effects of asbestos. **Holdings:** 515 books; 4165 documents. **Subscriptions:** 41 journals and other serials. **Services:** Library open to persons concerned with the problems of asbestos and health. **Remarks:** Maintained by Quebec Asbestos Mining Association.

★6176★
INSTITUTE OF OCEAN SCIENCES - LIBRARY (Sci-Tech)
9860 W. Saanich Rd.
Box 6000							Phone: (604) 656-8392
Sidney, BC, Canada V8L 4B2					Sharon Thomson, Libn.
Staff: Prof 1; Other 1. **Subjects:** Physical and chemical oceanography; hydrographic surveying; oil pollution; remote sensing; geophysics - applied, marine; marine geology; seismology. **Holdings:** 4200 books; 400 bound periodical volumes; 8500 technical documents (cataloged); 4320 microfiche; 520 microforms. **Subscriptions:** 430 journals and other serials. **Services:** Interlibrary loans; copying; library open to public with introduction from staff member. **Publications:** Canadian Reports of Hydrography and Ocean Sciences. **Also Known As:** Canada - Peches et Oceans. **Remarks:** Institute is funded by Canada - Fisheries and Oceans and Canada - Energy, Mines & Resources Canada.

INSTITUTE OF OUTDOOR DRAMA
See: University of North Carolina, Chapel Hill

★6177★
INSTITUTE OF PAPER CHEMISTRY - LIBRARY (Sci-Tech)
1043 E. South River St.
Box 1039							Phone: (414) 734-9251
Appleton, WI 54912						Craig S. Booher, Libn.
Staff: Prof 2; Other 4. **Subjects:** Technology of pulp and paper. **Special Collections:** Dard Hunter Collection on the history of papermaking (1300 books and 3000 documents). **Holdings:** 38,500 volumes; 149,500 patents on papermaking and related subjects; 1500 student reports; 7850 technical translations; 272,000 technical abstracts on 335 cards; 680 dissertations on microfilm; 71 VF drawers; 542 specialized bibliographies issued by the institute; 1718 government reports on microfiche; 25 journal titles on 1500 reels of microfilm. **Subscriptions:** 825 journals and other serials. **Services:** Copying; SDI; manual searches; custom translating service; library open to public for reference use only. **Computerized Information Services:** SDC; Paperchem (internal database). **Publications:** Abstract Bulletin of the Institute of Paper Chemistry (hard copy and microform), monthly. **Staff:** Linda M. Manwell, Asst.Libn.

INSTITUTE FOR PARAPSYCHOLOGY
See: Foundation for Research on the Nature of Man

★6178★
INSTITUTE OF THE PENNSYLVANIA HOSPITAL - MEDICAL LIBRARY (Med)
111 N. 49th St.							Phone: (215) 471-2013
Philadelphia, PA 19139					June M. Strickland, Libn.
Founded: 1841. **Staff:** Prof 1; Other 1. **Subjects:** Psychiatry, neurology, psychoanalysis, community mental health, religion, psychology. **Holdings:** 7128 books; 4613 bound periodical volumes; hospital reports; pamphlets. **Subscriptions:** 208 journals and other serials. **Services:** Interlibrary loans; copying; library open to public with restrictions.

INSTITUTE OF POLAR STUDIES
See: Ohio State University

INSTITUTE FOR POLICY RESEARCH AND EVALUATION
See: Pennsylvania State University

INSTITUTE OF PROCEDURAL ASPECTS OF INTERNATIONAL LAW
See: International Human Rights Law Group

INSTITUTE FOR PSYCHOANALYSIS
See: Chicago Institute for Psychoanalysis

★6179★
INSTITUTE OF PUBLIC ADMINISTRATION - LIBRARY (Soc Sci)
55 W. 44th St.							Phone: (212) 730-5632
New York, NY 10036						Xenia W. Duisin, Libn.
Founded: 1906. **Staff:** Prof 2; Other 2. **Subjects:** Public administration, public policy, metropolitan area problems, civil service, local government, housing, urban transportation, public finance. **Special Collections:** International material on urbanization, regional planning, metropolitan government. **Holdings:** 50,000 volumes; 120 VF drawers. **Subscriptions:** 320 journals and other serials. **Services:** Interlibrary loans; library open to scholars and students. **Publications:** Selected IPA Library Acquisitions, 6/year.

INSTITUTE OF PUBLIC AFFAIRS
See: Dalhousie University

INSTITUTE OF PUBLIC POLICY STUDIES COLLECTION
See: University of Michigan - Bureau of Government Library

★6180★
INSTITUTE FOR PUBLIC TRANSPORTATION - LIBRARY
211 E. 43rd St.
New York, NY 10017
Defunct

INSTITUTE OF PUERTO RICAN CULTURE
See: Puerto Rico - Institute of Puerto Rican Culture

★6181★
INSTITUTE FOR RATIONAL LIVING - RESEARCH LIBRARY (Soc Sci)
45 E. 65th St.   Phone: (212) 535-0822
New York, NY 10021   J. Wolf, Assoc.Dir.
Subjects: Rational-emotive psychotherapy, psychology, sexology. **Holdings:**
10,000 books; 3000 clippings. **Subscriptions:** 50 journals and other serials.
Services: Library open to researchers working in rational-emotive therapy and
cognitive behavior therapy. **Publications:** Rational Living (journal), semiannual
- by subscription.

★6182★
THE INSTITUTE FOR REHABILITATION AND RESEARCH (TIRR) -
INFORMATION SERVICES CENTER (Med)
1333 Moursund Ave.
Box 20025   Phone: (713) 797-1440
Houston, TX 77025   Kay Lindloff, Info.Sci.
Staff: Prof 1; Other 1. **Subjects:** Rehabilitation, medicine. **Holdings:** 2000
books; 550 bound periodical volumes. **Services:** Library open to public by
appointment.

★6183★
INSTITUTE FOR RESEARCH IN HYPNOSIS - BERNARD B. RAGINSKY
RESEARCH LIBRARY (Med)
10 W. 66th St.   Phone: (212) 874-5290
New York, NY 10023   Dr. Milton V. Kline, Dir. of Institute
Founded: 1965. **Subjects:** Hypnosis, hypnoanalysis and hypnotherapy -
clinical and experimental applications. **Special Collections:** Tape recordings of
the hypnotherapy of Bernard B. Raginsky. **Holdings:** 400 books; 2000
reprints; 500 tapes. **Services:** Copying; library not open to public.

INSTITUTE FOR RESEARCH ON LAND AND WATER RESOURCES
See: Pennsylvania State University

INSTITUTE FOR RESEARCH ON POVERTY
See: University of Wisconsin, Madison - Gerald G. Somers Graduate
Reference Room

★6184★
INSTITUTE FOR RESEARCH IN SOCIAL BEHAVIOR - LIBRARY (Soc Sci)
456 22nd St.   Phone: (415) 465-2791
Oakland, CA 94612   Patricia Chun-Spielberg, Libn.
Staff: Prof 1. **Subjects:** Drug use and abuse, stress and coping, faculty time
use, ethics and biomedical research, marriage and the family, opinion polls and
questionnaires. **Holdings:** 1000 books; 5000 unbound reports, manuscripts
and clippings. **Subscriptions:** 35 journals and other serials; 5 newspapers.
Services: Interlibrary loans; copying; library not open to public. **Publications:**
List of publications - available upon request.

INSTITUTE FOR RESEARCH IN SOCIAL SCIENCE
See: University of North Carolina, Chapel Hill

★6185★
INSTITUTE FOR SCIENTIFIC INFORMATION (Sci-Tech; Hum)†
3501 Market St.
University City Science Ctr.
Philadelphia, PA 19104   Phone: (215) 386-0100
                                              Susan S. Jones, Jrnl.Serv.Mgr.
Founded: 1960. **Subjects:** Life sciences; physical and chemical sciences;
clinical medicine; engineering and technology; agriculture; environmental,
social and behavioral sciences; arts and humanities. **Holdings:** Figures not
available. **Subscriptions:** 6500 journals and other serials. **Services:** SDI
including Automatic Subject Citation Alert (ASCA), ASCATOPICS, Automatic
New Structure Alert (ANSA); ISI Search Service (fee-based); Original Article
Tear Sheet (OATS) Service; online products including SCISEARCH, Social
SCISEARCH, ISI/BIOMED, ISI/CompuMath. **Publications:** Current Contents,
weekly - 7 editions covering the life sciences, clinical practice, physical,
chemical and earth sciences, social and behavioral sciences, computer
sciences and mathematics, engineering, technology and applied sciences,

agricultural, biological and environmental sciences, and arts and humanities;
Science Citation Index, bimonthly; Current Abstracts of Chemistry and Index
Chemicus, weekly; Chemical Substructure Index, monthly; Social Sciences
Citation Index, triannual with annual index; CompuMath Citation Index, annual;
Index to Scienctific Reviews, semiannual; Arts and Humanities Citation Index,
triannual with annual index; Journal Citation Reports, annual; Index to
Scientific and Technical Proceedings, monthly, with annual cumulation.
Remarks: ISI is said to be the world's largest independent, multidisciplinary
retriever of information from the world's professional journals.

INSTITUTE OF SEDIMENTARY & PETROLEUM GEOLOGY
See: Canada - Geological Survey of Canada

INSTITUTE FOR SEX RESEARCH, INC.
See: Kinsey Institute for Research in Sex, Gender, & Reproduction

INSTITUTE FOR SINO-SOVIET STUDIES LIBRARY
See: George Washington University

INSTITUTE FOR SOCIAL SCIENCE RESEARCH
See: University of California, Los Angeles

★6186★
INSTITUTE OF SOCIETY, ETHICS & THE LIFE SCIENCES - HASTINGS
CENTER (Soc Sci)
360 Broadway   Phone: (914) 478-0500
Hastings On Hudson, NY 10706   Marna Howarth, Libn.
Founded: 1969. **Staff:** 25. **Subjects:** Medical ethics, ethics, ethics/life
sciences, ethics/social sciences, congressional ethics, teaching of ethics,
population/abortion, behavior control, death/dying, genetics, public policy,
health policy. **Holdings:** 3500 books; 125 unbound journals; 25 VF drawers.
Subscriptions: 150 journals and other serials. **Services:** Library not open to
public. **Publications:** IRB: A Review of Human Subjects Research, 10/year;
Hastings Center Report, bimonthly. **Staff:** Daniel Callahan, Lib.Supv.

★6187★
INSTITUTE FOR STORM RESEARCH - LIBRARY (Sci-Tech)
4104 Mt. Vernon   Phone: (713) 529-4891
Houston, TX 77006   Dr. John C. Freeman, Hd.
Founded: 1966. **Staff:** Prof 1; Other 1. **Subjects:** Meteorology,
oceanography, physics, hydrology, climatology. **Holdings:** 1000 books;
government scientific publications; research papers; maps; microfilm.
Subscriptions: 11 journals and other serials. **Services:** Interlibrary loans;
copying; library open to public for reference use only. **Staff:** Lori Miller .

INSTITUTE FOR STUDIES IN AMERICAN MUSIC ARCHIVES
See: University of Missouri, Kansas City - Conservatory Library

★6188★
INSTITUTE FOR STUDIES OF DESTRUCTIVE BEHAVIORS AND THE SUICIDE
PREVENTION CENTER - HAROLD M. HILDRETH MEMORIAL LIB.
1041 S. Menlo Ave.
Los Angeles, CA 90006
Subjects: Behavioral sciences, suicide. **Holdings:** Figures not available.
Remarks: Presently inactive.

★6189★
INSTITUTE FOR THE STUDY OF LABOR AND ECONOMIC CRISIS - LIBRARY
AND DATABANK (Soc Sci)
608 Taraval St.   Phone: (415) 661-1850
San Francisco, CA 94116   Nancy P. Kelly, Libn.
Staff: Prof 1. **Subjects:** World systems, Marxist theory and methodology,
state and local politics, labor, crime. **Special Collections:** United Farm
Workers archives (1 file cabinet); crime archives (4 file cabinets). **Holdings:**
3000 books; 2 file cabinets of databank material. **Subscriptions:** 150
journals and other serials; 8 newspapers. **Services:** Interlibrary loans; copying;
library open to public by appointment. **Publications:** List of publications -
available on request.

★6190★
INSTITUTE OF TEXTILE TECHNOLOGY - TEXTILE INFORMATION SERVICES
- ROGER MILLIKEN TEXTILE LIBRARY (Sci-Tech)†
Rte. 250 W.
Box 391   Phone: (804) 296-5511
Charlottesville, VA 22902   Linda Justus, Libn.
Founded: 1944. **Staff:** Prof 1; Other 2. **Subjects:** Textile technology, dyeing,
polymers, apparel manufacture. **Holdings:** 12,000 books; 14,000 bound
periodical volumes; 3500 cataloged translations; 2000 technical reports;
65,000 patents; 25 shelves of reprints; 50 shelves of trade literature; 36 VF

drawers; 900 microforms. **Subscriptions:** 700 journals and other serials; 5 newspapers. **Services:** Interlibrary loans; copying; library open to public. **Computerized Information Services:** DIALOG; internal database. **Publications:** ITT Bibliography, irregular - free; New Additions to the Library, annual - free; Textile Library List - free upon request; Textile Technology Digest, monthly - by subscription; Keyterm Index, monthly - by subscription.

★6191★
INSTITUTE FOR THEOLOGICAL & PHILOSOPHICAL STUDIES - LIBRARY
(Rel-Theol)
Box 3563
Bloomington, IL 61701   Dr. James Kurtz, Dir.
Staff: Prof 1; Other 2. **Subjects:** Religion, philosophy, sociology. **Holdings:** Figures not available. **Subscriptions:** 10 journals and other serials. **Services:** Interlibrary loans; copying; library not open to public. **Publications:** Opinion, monthly - available by mail. **Staff:** Diana Kurtz, Assoc.; Joan Kurtz, Assoc.

★6192★
INSTITUTE OF TRANSPORTATION ENGINEERS - LIBRARY (Trans)
525 School St., S.W., Suite 410   Phone: (202) 554-8050
Washington, DC 20024   Thomas W. Brahms, Exec.Dir.
Founded: 1930. **Staff:** Prof 6; Other 3. **Subjects:** Traffic and transportation engineering, transportation planning, highway safety. **Special Collections:** ITE Journal, ITE publications and Institute of Transportation Engineers Technical Council Reports (complete file of back issues). **Services:** Copying; library open to public with restrictions. **Publications:** Publications list of Institute of Transportation Engineers. **Special Indexes:** Index to ITE Journal.

INSTITUTE FOR URBAN TRANSPORTATION
See: Indiana University

INSTITUTE OF WOOD RESEARCH INFORMATION CENTER
See: Michigan Technological University

★6193★
INSTITUTES OF RELIGION AND HEALTH - LIBRARY (Soc Sci)
3 W. 29th St.   Phone: (212) 725-7842
New York, NY 10001   Roslyn Roth, Chf.Libn.
Founded: 1961. **Staff:** Prof 1; Other 2. **Subjects:** Psychiatry, psychology, pastoral counseling, marriage counseling, psychotherapy. **Holdings:** 5000 books; 4 VF drawers of reports, pamphlets and dissertations. **Subscriptions:** 23 journals and other serials. **Services:** Interlibrary loans; copying; library not open to public.

★6194★
INSTITUTO INTERAMERICANO - LIBRARY
1133 N. Texas Sta.
Denton, TX 76203
Defunct

INSTITUTO ITALIANO DI CULTURA
See: Italian Cultural Service

★6195★
INSTRUMENT SOCIETY OF AMERICA - LIBRARY (Sci-Tech)
67 Alexander Dr.
Box 12277   Phone: (919) 549-8411
Research Triangle Park, NC 27709   Charles D. McAlister, Tech.Dir.
Founded: 1964. **Staff:** Prof 1; Other 1. **Subjects:** Automatic control, automation, instrumentation. **Holdings:** 1000 books; 60 bound periodical volumes. **Subscriptions:** 100 journals and other serials. **Services:** Library serves members of the Society. **Special Indexes:** Card index of films on automation.

★6196★
INSTRUMENTATION LABORATORY, INC. - ANALYTICAL INSTRUMENTS DIVISION - LIBRARY (Sci-Tech)
Jonspin Rd.   Phone: (617) 658-5125
Wilmington, MA 01887   Jacqueline R. Kates, Corp.Libn.
Staff: 1. **Subjects:** Atomic absorption spectrophotometry. **Holdings:** 65 books and bound periodical volumes. **Services:** Library not open to public, except by special arrangement. **Computerized Information Services:** DIALOG, BRS.

★6197★
INSTRUMENTATION LABORATORY, INC. - LIBRARY (Sci-Tech)
113 Hartwell Ave.   Phone: (617) 861-0710
Lexington, MA 02173   Jacqueline R. Kates, Corp.Libn.
Staff: Prof 1; Other 1. **Subjects:** Medicine, engineering, chemistry. **Holdings:**

5500 books and bound periodical volumes; 400 technical reports (paper and microfiche). **Subscriptions:** 200 journals and other serials. **Services:** Interlibrary loans; copying; SDI; library open by special arrangement to qualified researchers. **Networks/Consortia:** Member of Northeast Consortium for Health Information. **Publications:** New Books List, quarterly; Periodicals Holding List, annual.

★6198★
INSURANCE CORPORATION OF BRITISH COLUMBIA - LAW LIBRARY (Law)
1055 W. Georgia St.
Box 1131, Royal Centre   Phone: (604) 665-5976
Vancouver, BC, Canada V6E 3R4   Norman Churchland, Hd.Libn.
Staff: Prof 1; Other 1. **Subjects:** Law, traffic safety, insurance. **Holdings:** 6000 books and bound periodical volumes. **Services:** Library open to public with restrictions. **Special Catalogs:** ICBC Cases - list of decisions based on corporate decisions.

★6199★
INSURANCE INFORMATION INSTITUTE - LIBRARY (Bus-Fin)
110 William St.   Phone: (212) 669-9210
New York, NY 10038   Theresa D'Agostaro, Libn.
Staff: Prof 1; Other 1. **Subjects:** Insurance. **Holdings:** 1500 books; 600 reference files; annual reports. **Subscriptions:** 104 journals and other serials.

INSURANCE INSTITUTE OF AMERICA
See: American Institute for Property & Liability Underwriters

★6200★
INSURANCE INSTITUTE FOR HIGHWAY SAFETY - LIBRARY (Trans)
600 New Hampshire Ave., Suite 300   Phone: (202) 333-0770
Washington, DC 20037   Christine A. Pruzin, Libn.
Staff: 2. **Subjects:** Highway safety research, transportation, automotive engineering and medicine, traffic laws and implementation. **Holdings:** 600 books and bound periodical volumes; 3000 research reports; 350 institute publications; institute 16mm films. **Subscriptions:** 200 journals and other serials; 20 newspapers. **Services:** Interlibrary loans; copying; library open to public by appointment. **Computerized Information Services:** DIALOG, SDC. **Publications:** Status Report, fortnightly - upon request. **Special Indexes:** Status Report Index (book). **Staff:** Jacqui Hanser, Lib.Asst.

★6201★
INSURANCE INSTITUTE OF SOUTHERN ALBERTA - LIBRARY (Bus-Fin)
630 8th Ave., S.W., No. 601   Phone: (403) 266-3427
Calgary, AB, Canada T2P 1G6   Carolyn Geary, Sec.
Founded: 1953. **Staff:** 1. **Subjects:** Insurance. **Holdings:** 209 books and bound periodical volumes; 5 films and filmstrips. **Services:** Library open to public on a limited schedule.

★6202★
INSURANCE LIBRARY ASSOCIATION OF BOSTON (Bus-Fin)
156 State St.   Phone: (617) 227-2087
Boston, MA 02109   Jean E. Lucey, Dir.
Founded: 1887. **Staff:** Prof 3. **Subjects:** Insurance - fire, casualty, property, life and health. **Special Collections:** Sanborn Map Collection (New England); Henry Belknap Collection relating to fire insurance, fire prevention, and firemen. **Holdings:** 4000 books; 2700 bound periodical volumes; reports of insurance companies and insurance commissioners; pamphlets and pictures. **Subscriptions:** 75 journals and other serials. **Services:** Interlibrary loans; copying; library open to public. **Publications:** Quarterly Newsletter - to members. **Staff:** Sandra Ropper, Asst.Dir.; Mary Lou Cocci, Asst.Dir.

★6203★
INSURANCE SCHOOL OF CHICAGO - LIBRARY (Bus-Fin)
330 S. Wells   Phone: (312) 427-2520
Chicago, IL 60606
Founded: 1883. **Subjects:** Insurance - property, liability, life, fire; safety engineering; claims adjusting. **Holdings:** 2000 books; 80 boxes of unbound periodicals. **Subscriptions:** 50 journals and other serials. **Services:** Copying; library open to public for reference use only.

INSURANCE SOCIETY OF NEW YORK
See: College of Insurance

★6204★
INTEL CORPORATION - TECHNICAL INFORMATION CENTER (Sci-Tech)
3585 S.W. 198th   Phone: (503) 642-6598
Aloha, OR 97007   Jim Engiles, Tech.Info.Spec.
Staff: Prof 2; Other 8. **Subjects:** Microelectronics, semiconductors, computer science, solid state physics, chemistry, management. **Holdings:** 5000 books.

Subscriptions: 150 journals and other serials; 14 newspapers. **Services:** Interlibrary loans; copying; SDI; library open to public. **Computerized Information Services:** DIALOG, SDC, BRS, Source Telecomputing Corporation; internal database; computerized cataloging, acquisitions and serials. **Networks/Consortia:** Member of Research Libraries Group, Inc. **Publications:** Tic Talk, irregular - for internal distribution only. **Staff:** Trula Mugford, Asst.Info.Spec.

★6205★
INTEL-TECHNICAL INFORMATION CENTER (Info Sci)
2625 Walsh Ave. 4-106　　　　　　　　Phone: (408) 987-6014
Santa Clara, CA 95051　　　　　　　　　Marge Boyd, Mgr.
Founded: 1978. **Staff:** Prof 5; Other 4. **Subjects:** Semiconductors, microprocessors, microcomputers, integrated circuits. **Holdings:** 6500 books; 320 bound periodical volumes; 10,000 technical reports; 180 annual reports; 150 volumes of reports; 6 trays of microfiche on standards and specifications; industrial product catalog data. **Subscriptions:** 400 journals and other serials; 20 newspapers. **Services:** Interlibrary loans; SDI; library not open to public. **Computerized Information Services:** Online systems; computerized cataloging. **Networks/Consortia:** Member of CIN; CLASS. **Staff:** Linda Post, Info.Spec.; Colleen Sobieski, Info.Spec.; Clare Zazkowski, Info.Spec.; John McGorray, Info.Spec.

INTER AMERICA RESEARCH ASSOCIATES, INC.
See: Consumer Education Resource Network

★6206★
INTERAMERICA RESEARCH ASSOCIATES, INC. - NATIONAL CLEARINGHOUSE FOR BILINGUAL EDUCATION (Educ)
1300 B2-11 Wilson Blvd.　　　　　　　Phone: (703) 522-0710
Rosslyn, VA 22209　　　　　　　　Deborah Sauve, Info.Serv.Mgr.
Staff: Prof 3; Other 1. **Subjects:** Bilingual education, English as a second language. **Holdings:** 10,000 books; 300 reports; 400 dissertations; 2250 clippings; 500 reels of microfilm. **Subscriptions:** 250 journals and other serials; 2000 newspapers. **Services:** Interlibrary loans; library open to public for reference use only. **Computerized Information Services:** DIALOG, SDC, BRS, New York Times Information Service, Source Telecomputing Corporation, Data Use and Access Laboratories (DUALabs); internal database; computerized serials. **Publications:** Forum, monthly; Directory Series of Resources in Bilingual Education, irregular. **Remarks:** The toll-free telephone number for the clearinghouse is (800)336-4560. **Staff:** Tony Pien, Resource Coll.Coord.; John Doenges, Acq.Libn.

★6207★
INTER-AMERICAN DEFENSE BOARD - LIBRARY
2600 16th St., N.W. 6
Washington, DC 20441
Defunct

★6208★
INTER-AMERICAN DEFENSE COLLEGE - LIBRARY (Mil)
Fort McNair　　　　　　　　　　Phone: (202) 693-8154
Washington, DC 20319　　　　　　Mercedes M. Bailey, Chf.Libn.
Founded: 1962. **Staff:** Prof 2; Other 5. **Subjects:** Politics and governments of individual countries; military, social and economic topics; Inter-American system. **Holdings:** 12,000 books; 11,300 documents and pamphlets (cataloged). **Subscriptions:** 330 journals and other serials; 20 newspapers. **Services:** Interlibrary loans; library open to public with restrictions. **Staff:** Gioconda Vallarino, Cat.

★6209★
INTER-AMERICAN DEVELOPMENT BANK - TECHNICAL INFORMATION CENTER (Sci-Tech)
808 17th St., N.W.　　　　　　　　Phone: (202) 634-8385
Washington, DC 20577　　　　　　　　Ana I. Conde, Hd.
Staff: Prof 2; Other 2. **Subjects:** Economic and social development with emphasis on Latin America; agriculture; energy; industry; appropriate technology. **Special Collections:** Commodities; international agricultural centers. **Holdings:** 40,000 documents, periodicals and economic reports. **Subscriptions:** 1000 journals and other serials. **Services:** Interlibrary loans; copying; center open to public with restrictions. **Computerized Information Services:** Computerized circulation. **Networks/Consortia:** Member of OCLC. **Publications:** Conference and Seminars, every three months; selected list of acquisitions.

INTER-AMERICAN MUSIC ARCHIVE
See: University of Miami - School of Music - Albert Pick Music Library

INTER-AMERICAN TROPICAL TUNA COMMISSION COLLECTION
See: U.S. Natl. Marine Fisheries Service - Southwest Fisheries Center - Library

INTER-UNIVERSITY CONSORTIUM FOR POLITICAL & SOCIAL RESEARCH
See: University of Michigan - Institute for Social Research

INTERAGENCY ADVANCED POWER GROUP
See: U.S. Interagency Advanced Power Group

★6210★
INTERAMERICAN UNIVERSITY OF PUERTO RICO - SCHOOL OF LAW - DOMINGO TOLEDO ALAMO LAW LIBRARY (Law)
1610 Fernandez Juncos Ave.
Box 8897　　　　　　　　　　Phone: (809) 727-1930
Santurce, PR 00910　　　　　　Prof. Carlos J.R. Davis, Dir.
Founded: 1961. **Staff:** Prof 5; Other 12. **Subjects:** Law - criminal, constitutional, civil, international, environmental. **Special Collections:** Domingo Toledo Alamo Collection. **Holdings:** 82,028 books; 9475 bound periodical volumes; 3640 reels of microfilm; 81,802 microfiche; 350 tapes and cassettes; 120 video cassettes. **Subscriptions:** 635 journals and other serials; 7 newspapers. **Services:** Interlibrary loans; copying; library open to public with restrictions. **Publications:** List of New Acquisitions; List of Subject Headings. **Staff:** Odila Collazo, Asst. to Dir.; Gloria Mendez, Cat.; Martha Martinez, Cat.; Valentin Gonzalez, Coll.Dev. & Ref.Libn.; Alberto Guzman, Ref.Libn.

★6211★
INTERCOLLEGIATE CENTER FOR NURSING EDUCATION - LIBRARY (Med)
W. 2917 Ft. George Wright Dr.　　　Phone: (509) 326-7270
Spokane, WA 99204　　　　　Robert M. Pringle, Jr., Hd.Libn.
Founded: 1969. **Staff:** Prof 2; Other 4. **Subjects:** Nursing, allied health sciences. **Special Collections:** History of nursing. **Holdings:** 11,000 books; 500 bound periodical volumes; 25 VF drawers. **Subscriptions:** 380 journals and other serials. **Services:** Interlibrary loans; copying; library open to public for reference use only. **Computerized Information Services:** DIALOG. **Networks/Consortia:** Member of Washington Library Network. **Remarks:** Maintained by Washington State University.

★6212★
INTERDENOMINATIONAL THEOLOGICAL CENTER - LIBRARY (Rel-Theol)†
671 Beckwith St., S.W.　　　　　　Phone: (404) 522-1744
Atlanta, GA 30314　　　　　　Wilson N. Flemister, Libn.
Founded: 1958. **Staff:** Prof 2; Other 2. **Subjects:** Religion, theology, ecumenical studies, Afro-American studies, denominational history, black theology. **Special Collections:** Afro-American theology; church history. **Holdings:** 70,000 books; 10,000 bound periodical volumes; 250,000 items on Freedman's Aid Society; 300,000 items on black church leaders. **Subscriptions:** 375 journals and other serials; 25 newspapers. **Services:** Interlibrary loans; copying; library open to public for reference use only. **Special Catalogs:** Special Collections Catalog. **Remarks:** Includes the holdings of the Johnson C. Smith University Theological Seminary Library of Charlotte, NC. **Staff:** Sandra H. Beedles, Asst.Libn.

INTERFAITH CENTER ON CORPORATE RESPONSIBILITY
See: National Council of Churches

★6213★
INTERFAITH FORUM ON RELIGION, ART AND ARCHITECTURE - LIBRARY (Pict)†
1777 Church St., N.W.　　　　　　Phone: (202) 387-8333
Washington, DC 20036　　　　　Judith A. Miller, Exec.Dir.
Subjects: Churches - foreign, domestic, interiors and exteriors. **Holdings:** 5000 35mm slides (cataloged). **Services:** Library open to public. **Special Catalogs:** Catalog identifying slides by number available to those interested in renting slides (mimeographed).

★6214★
INTERGALACTIC CORP. - LIBRARY (Sci-Tech)†
3585 Via Terra
Box 15752　　　　　　　　　　Phone: (801) 262-0094
Salt Lake City, UT 84115　　　　Douglas MacGregor, Dir.
Staff: Prof 2; Other 4. **Subjects:** Testing procedures, chemistry, nuclear sciences, engineering. **Special Collections:** Antique scientific works prior to 1850. **Holdings:** 14,000 books; 12,000 bound periodical volumes; 12,000 items of product data; 13,000 technical reports; 6500 material science studies. **Subscriptions:** 235 journals and other serials. **Services:** Interlibrary loans; copying; library open to public with restrictions. **Publications:** Unilink Journal, by subscription. **Staff:** Pat Plese, Asst.Techn.

★6215★

INTERGOVERNMENTAL COMMITTEE ON URBAN & REGIONAL RESEARCH (ICURR) (Soc Sci; Plan)
123 Edward St., Suite 625
Toronto, ON, Canada M5G 1E2   Phone: (416) 966-5629
Tanya Wanio, Info.Coord.
Staff: 4. **Subjects:** Housing and building, municipal and urban affairs, rural and regional development, environment, transportation, recreation. **Special Collections:** Group of Experts on Urban & Regional Research, Economic Commission for Europe (41 documents). **Holdings:** 7000 documents; 1000 bound periodical volumes. **Subscriptions:** 250 journals and other serials; 6 newspapers. **Services:** Interlibrary loans; open to government personnel only. **Computerized Information Services:** Internal database. **Publications:** Interaction, bimonthly; Calendar, semiannual; Directory, updated annually; occasional papers. **Staff:** Ysolde Nott, Doc.; Monica Hope, Doc.

★6216★

INTERLOCHEN CENTER FOR THE ARTS - MUSIC LIBRARY (Mus)
Interlochen, MI 49643   Phone: (616) 276-9221
E. Delmer Weliver, Dir.
Staff: Prof 2; Other 20. **Subjects:** Music. **Holdings:** 10,000 orchestra titles; 5300 band titles; 2700 choir titles; 17,000 solo and small ensemble titles; 2000 recordings; 2500 study score titles. **Services:** Copying; library open to public for reference use only. **Staff:** Elizabeth Chryst; Janet Wild .

★6217★

INTERMEDICS, INC. - LIBRARY (Sci-Tech)
240 W. 2nd St.
Box 617
Freeport, TX 77541   Phone: (713) 233-8611
Mary Guilloud, Tech.Info.Spec.
Founded: 1979. **Staff:** Prof 1. **Subjects:** Bioengineering, electrical engineering, medicine. **Holdings:** Figures not available.

★6218★

INTERMETRICS INC. - LIBRARY (Sci-Tech)
733 Concord Ave.
Cambridge, MA 02138   Phone: (617) 661-1840
Ann M. Wilson, Libn.
Staff: Prof 2. **Subjects:** Computer science, mathematics, physics, aeronautics, astronautics, avionics. **Holdings:** 1000 books; 200 bound periodical volumes; 400 technical reports. **Subscriptions:** 125 journals and other serials. **Services:** Interlibrary loans; library not open to public. **Computerized Information Services:** DIALOG; computerized cataloging. **Publications:** Quarterly Bulletin.

INTERMOUNTAIN FOREST & RANGE EXPERIMENT STATION
See: U.S. Forest Service

INTERMOUNTAIN HEALTH CARE, INC.
See: L.D.S. Hospital

INTERNAL REVENUE SERVICE
See: U.S. Internal Revenue Service

★6219★

INTERNATIONAL ACADEMY AT SANTA BARBARA - LIBRARY (Env-Cons; Soc Sci)
2074 Alameda Padre Serra
Santa Barbara, CA 93103   Phone: (805) 965-5010
Helen K. Rocky, Dir.Lib.Serv.
Staff: 8. **Subjects:** Energy, environment, current world leaders. **Holdings:** Figures not available. **Services:** Library open to public. **Computerized Information Services:** DIALOG. **Publications:** Environmental Periodicals Bibliography, bimonthly; Energy Review, bimonthly; Current World Leaders, 8 issues; Almanac, 3/year; Biography & News/Speeches & Reports, 5/year.

★6220★

INTERNATIONAL ADVERTISING ASSOCIATION - LIBRARY (Bus-Fin)
475 Fifth Ave.
New York, NY 10017   Phone: (212) 684-1583
Subjects: Advertising and marketing. **Holdings:** General reference books; foreign advertising and marketing periodicals.

★6221★

INTERNATIONAL ASSOCIATION OF ASSESSING OFFICERS - RESEARCH AND TECHNICAL SERVICES DEPT. - LIBRARY (Law; Bus-Fin)
1313 E. 60th St.
Chicago, IL 60637   Phone: (312) 947-2050
Stuart W. Miller, Libn.
Staff: Prof 2; Other 1. **Subjects:** Property taxation, assessment administration, appraisal. **Special Collections:** Archive of IAAO publications. **Holdings:** 5500 volumes (collection is largely government publications); 25 linear feet of pamphlet and clipping files. **Subscriptions:** 600 journals and

other serials. **Services:** Interlibrary loans; copying; library open to public by application; information service available on subscription basis (Property Tax Information Service). **Networks/Consortia:** Member of OCLC; ILLINET. **Publications:** Bibliographic Series, irregular; Research and Information Series, irregular; selected recent acquisitions list, published bimonthly in Association's newsletter, Assessment Digest. **Remarks:** Affiliated with the Charles E. Merriam Center Library. **Staff:** Robert Clatanoff, Res.Assoc./Bibliog.

★6222★

INTERNATIONAL ASSOCIATION OF CHIEFS OF POLICE - CENTER FOR LAW ENFORCEMENT RESEARCH
11 Firstfield Rd.
Gaithersburg, MD 20760
Subjects: Criminal justice, law enforcement. **Special Collections:** Police department manuals (40). **Holdings:** 6000 volumes; FBI uniform crime reports; Police Chief magazine (1934 to present); Police Yearbook (1893 to present). **Remarks:** Presently inactive.

★6223★

INTERNATIONAL ASSOCIATION OF EDUCATORS FOR WORLD PEACE - IAEWP CENTER OF INTERCULTURAL INFORMATION (Soc Sci)
Blue Springs Sta.
Box 3282
Huntsville, AL 35810   Phone: (205) 539-7205
Charles Mercieca, Exec. V.P.
Founded: 1974. **Staff:** Prof 5. **Subjects:** Education, philosophy, sociology, history, literature, languages. **Holdings:** 150,000 volumes; 2200 slides and cassettes. **Subscriptions:** 30 journals and other serials. **Services:** Copying; library open to public with restrictions. **Computerized Information Services:** Online systems. **Networks/Consortia:** Member of International Association of Educators for World Peace (IAEWP). **Publications:** Education for Peace; Peace Progress; Peace Education; The Age of Trust; IAEWP Newsletter. **Special Catalogs:** Peace education literature. **Remarks:** The IAEWP Center incorporates private libraries of IAEWP officials around the country and across the world. The center is located at 2013 Orba Dr., N.E., Huntsville, AL 35811.

★6224★

INTERNATIONAL ASSOCIATION FOR IDENTIFICATION - LIBRARY (Soc Sci)
Box 139
Utica, NY 13503   Phone: (315) 732-2897
Walter G. Hoetzer, Sec./Treas.
Staff: 1. **Subjects:** Identification, criminalistics. **Holdings:** 500 books and bound periodical volumes. **Subscriptions:** 15 journals and other serials. **Services:** Interlibrary loans; copying; library open to public. **Publications:** Identification News.

★6225★

INTERNATIONAL ASSOCIATION OF INDEPENDENT PRODUCERS - LIBRARY (Aud-Vis)
Box 1933
Washington, DC 20013   Phone: (202) 638-5595
Dr. Edward Von Rothkirch, Dir.
Founded: 1960. **Staff:** Prof 1. **Subjects:** Films, record industry, production and distribution techniques. **Holdings:** 2400 volumes; 3100 clippings; 1800 photographs; 260 films. **Subscriptions:** 14 journals and other serials. **Services:** Copying; library not open to public.

★6226★

INTERNATIONAL ATLANTIC SALMON FOUNDATION - LIBRARY (Sci-Tech)
P.O. Box 429
St. Andrews, NB, Canada E0G 2X0   Phone: (506) 529-3818
Mrs. Lee Sochasky, Prog.Coord.
Staff: 5. **Subjects:** Atlantic salmon - general information, research and education programs, international programs. **Special Collections:** Rare fishing books and gear. **Holdings:** Books; periodical volumes; reprints; government reports. **Subscriptions:** 14 journals and other serials. **Services:** Copying; library open to public by request. **Publications:** Atlantic Salmon Journal; Atlantic Salmon Newsletter, both quarterly - by subscription; Special Publication Series - for sale.

★6227★

INTERNATIONAL BACKPACKERS ASSOCIATION - LIBRARY
Box 85
Lincoln Center, ME 04458
Defunct

★6228★

INTERNATIONAL BANK NOTE SOCIETY - LIBRARY (Bus-Fin)
Box 1222
Racine, WI 53405   Milan Alusic, Sec.
Founded: 1961. **Staff:** 1. **Subjects:** Bank note printing and collection, monetary systems. **Holdings:** 204 books and bound periodical volumes; 200

other cataloged items. **Services:** Interlibrary loans; library not open to public. **Special Indexes:** Indexes to subjects, photographs, authors, and book reviews in the society's quarterly journal.

★6229★
INTERNATIONAL BIRD RESCUE RESEARCH CENTER - LIBRARY (Env-Cons)†
Aquatic Pk.   Phone: (415) 841-9086
Berkeley, CA 94710   Alice Berkner, Dir.
Founded: 1971. **Staff:** Prof 4. **Subjects:** Avian physiology, pathology and behavior; effects of pollutants; oiled bird rehabilitation; contingency plans. **Holdings:** 100 books; 450 reprints; 20 microforms; 200 pages San Francisco Oil Spill records; 2500 IBM cards veterinary records (birds). **Subscriptions:** 22 journals and other serials. **Services:** Copying; library open to public for reference use only. **Publications:** International Bird Rescue Newsletter, quarterly - subscription. **Special Catalogs:** Thesaurus for avian biology. **Staff:** K. Loomis, Libn.

★6230★
INTERNATIONAL BROTHERHOOD OF OLD BASTARDS, INC. - SIR THOMAS CRAPPER MEMORIAL ARCHIVES (Hist)
2330 S. Brentwood Blvd., Suite 666   Phone: (314) 961-9825
St. Louis, MO 63144   Bro. Jose "Bat" Guano, O.B., Chf. of Archv. & Seals
Founded: 1869. **Staff:** 9. **Subjects:** Bastardy, genealogy, politics, royalty. **Holdings:** 9387 books; 649 bound periodical volumes; 487 archive reports (cataloged); 1172 maps; 6 tons of archival material and many boxes unopened from predecessor organizations in Spain and England; miscellaneous information. **Subscriptions:** 47 journals and other serials; 18 newspapers. **Services:** Interlibrary loans; copying; archives open to scholarly researchers subject to approval of the Board of Presiding Archbastards. **Publications:** Ye Olde Bastards Bulletin, semiannual; Archives Report, irregular; Emergency Bulletins, as needed; Special Research Reports, semimonthly. **Special Indexes:** Punched card index. **Staff:** Bro. Lewis N. Clarke; Bro. Cozen P. Bantling; Bro. Mike Hunt, O.B.

★6231★
INTERNATIONAL BROTHERHOOD OF TEAMSTERS, CHAUFFEURS, WAREHOUSEMEN AND HELPERS OF AMERICA - RES./EDUC. LIBRARY (Soc Sci)
25 Louisiana Ave., N.W.   Phone: (202) 624-6978
Washington, DC 20001   Betty Bourg, Libn.
Founded: 1955. **Staff:** Prof 2; Other 2. **Subjects:** Labor economics, transportation economics, labor law. **Special Collections:** Archives of IBT. **Holdings:** 7000 books; microfilm of union serial publications; pamphlets, tapes, films, photographs. **Subscriptions:** 650 journals and other serials; 22 newspapers. **Services:** Interlibrary loans; library not open to public. **Computerized Information Services:** New York Times Information Service, DIALOG, SDC, BRS, Dow Jones News Retrieval. **Special Indexes:** Index to nonwire service coverage on the Teamsters Union from March 1964 to April 1972 (card). **Staff:** William Wilkinson, Asst.Libn.; Vickie O'Coin, Ser.Techn.

★6232★
INTERNATIONAL BUSINESS FORMS INDUSTRIES/PRINTING INDUSTRIES OF AMERICA - LIBRARY
1730 N. Lynn St.
Arlington, VA 22209
Founded: 1953. **Subjects:** Business forms, paper, equipment. **Holdings:** 750 books; 500 bound periodical volumes; 200 cataloged items. **Remarks:** Presently inactive.

INTERNATIONAL BUSINESS MACHINES CANADA, LTD.
See: IBM Canada, Ltd.

INTERNATIONAL BUSINESS MACHINES CORPORATION
See: IBM Corporation

INTERNATIONAL CENTER FOR AQUACULTURE
See: Auburn University

★6233★
INTERNATIONAL CENTER FOR THE DISABLED (ICD) - BRUCE BARTON MEMORIAL LIBRARY (Med)
340 E. 24th St.   Phone: (212) 679-0100
New York, NY 10010   Helen Stonehill, Chf.Libn.
Founded: 1917. **Staff:** Prof 1; Other 1. **Subjects:** Rehabilitation, physical medicine, vocational training, psychology, psychiatry, psychopharmacology, job placement, speech and hearing, gerontology. **Special Collections:** McMurtrie Collection - early writings on rehabilitation (500 volumes). **Holdings:** 6000 books; 2000 bound periodical volumes; 78 VF drawers; 50 boxes of occupational materials; 4000 research reports on microfiche.

Subscriptions: 150 journals and other serials. **Services:** Interlibrary loans; copying; SDI; library open to public. **Computerized Information Services:** DIALOG, BRS. **Networks/Consortia:** Member of METRO; Manhattan-Bronx Health Sciences Library Group. **Publications:** Acquisitions List, quarterly. **Also Known As:** Institute for the Crippled and Disabled. **Formerly:** ICD Rehabilitation and Research Center - Library.

INTERNATIONAL CENTER FOR MARINE RESOURCE DEVELOPMENT
See: University of Rhode Island

★6234★
INTERNATIONAL CENTER OF PHOTOGRAPHY - ARCHIVES (Pict)
1130 Fifth Ave.
New York, NY 10028   Miles Barth, Cur.
Staff: Prof 2. **Subjects:** Photography. **Special Collections:** Camera and equipment collection; original manuscripts and letters of photographers. **Holdings:** 5000 photographs; 300 hours of audiotape interviews and lectures; 30 hours of film; 20 hours of videotape; catalogs of auctions and other photography collections. **Services:** Archives open to public by appointment.

★6235★
INTERNATIONAL CENTER OF PHOTOGRAPHY - LIBRARY RESOURCE CENTER (Pict)
1130 Fifth Ave.   Phone: (212) 860-1787
New York, NY 10028   Lee C. Sievan, Resource Libn.
Staff: Prof 2. **Subjects:** Photography. **Special Collections:** Literature of Photography series (58 volumes); complete set of Life Magazine; archives. **Holdings:** 3000 books; 1000 unbound volumes of American photography periodicals; 200 museum catalogs; 50 auction catalogs; 2000 folders of clippings; 10,000 slides; 5000 photographs; 300 audiotapes; 20 videotapes; 15 other AV items; 30 16mm films. **Services:** Copying; library open to public by appointment.

INTERNATIONAL CENTRE FOR COMPARATIVE CRIMINOLOGY
See: Universite de Montreal - Centre International de Criminologie Comparee

INTERNATIONAL CENTRE FOR RESEARCH ON BILINGUALISM
See: Universite Laval

★6236★
INTERNATIONAL CHRISTIAN GRADUATE UNIVERSITY - LIBRARY (Rel-Theol)
Arrowhead Springs   Phone: (714) 886-7876
San Bernardino, CA 92414   Dr. Cyril J. Barber, Dir.
Founded: 1965. **Staff:** Prof 1; Other 10. **Subjects:** Theology, Bible, counseling, pastoral studies, communication, management. **Holdings:** 35,000 books; 1200 bound periodical volumes; 1000 cassettes. **Subscriptions:** 402 journals and other serials. **Services:** Interlibrary loans; library open to public with permission. **Formerly:** International Christian School of Theology - Graduate University Library.

INTERNATIONAL CIRCULATING EXHIBITIONS ARCHIVE
See: Museum of Modern Art - Library

★6237★
INTERNATIONAL CITY MANAGEMENT ASSOCIATION - LIBRARY (Soc Sci)†
1120 G St., N.W.   Phone: (202) 626-4600
Washington, DC 20005   Mary Od'Neal, Libn.
Founded: 1972. **Staff:** Prof 1; Other 1. **Subjects:** Municipal government and management, public administration. **Special Collections:** City budgets; annual reports and comprehensive plans; ICMA Archives; council-manager form of government. **Holdings:** 3000 books; 2000 monographs and reports; 60 VF drawers. **Subscriptions:** 250 journals and other serials. **Services:** Interlibrary loans; copying; library open to public by appointment.

★6238★
INTERNATIONAL CIVIL AVIATION ORGANIZATION - LIBRARY (Trans)
Place De L'Aviation Internationale
1000 Sherbrooke St., W.
Box 400   Phone: (514) 285-8208
Montreal, PQ, Canada H3A 2R2   Mrs. Fathia Ismail, Libn.
Founded: 1947. **Staff:** Prof 2; Other 5. **Subjects:** Aeronautics, aviation medicine, airports, air law, international law, international organizations, telecommunications, meteorology, maps and charts. **Special Collections:** Academie de Droit International Recueil (1923 to present); Commission Internationale de Navigation Aerienne (1922-47); Institut du Transport Aerien (ITA) Collection; Royal Aeronautical Society Journal (1897 to present);

United Nations Treaty Series (1946 to present). **Holdings:** 15,500 volumes; United Nations and Specialized Agencies Documents (2-5 years); International Organizations Documents (2-5 years); Member-States Governments, Civil Aviation Economic and Technical Publications. **Subscriptions:** 198 journals and other serials; 11 newspapers. **Services:** Interlibrary loans; library open to public for reference use only. **Publications:** Library Information; Recent Accessions and Selected Articles, bimonthly. **Special Indexes:** Index of ICAO publications (annual cumulation).

★6239★

INTERNATIONAL CLARINET SOCIETY - BURNET C. TUTHILL RESEARCH LIBRARY (Mus)†
University of Denver   Phone: (303) 753-3691
Denver, CO 80210   Jerry Pierce, Pres.
Founded: 1973. **Staff:** Prof 1. **Subjects:** Clarinet music of all types. **Special Collections:** Burnet C. Tuthill Collection, Frederick E. Cohen Collection. **Holdings:** 1400 volumes. **Services:** Interlibrary loans; copying; library open to public for reference use only. **Publications:** Articles about the library appear in Clarinet Magazine, quarterly.

INTERNATIONAL CLARINET SOCIETY RESEARCH CENTER
See: University of Maryland, College Park - Libraries - Music Library

★6240★

INTERNATIONAL COLLEGE OF SURGEONS HALL OF FAME - DR. JOSEPH MONTAGUE PROCTOLOGIC LIBRARY (Med)
1524 N. Lake Shore Dr.   Phone: (312) 642-3555
Chicago, IL 60610   George F. Smith, M.D., Cur. & Dir.
Founded: 1955. **Staff:** Prof 1; Other 2. **Subjects:** History of medicine and surgery. **Holdings:** 7000 volumes; 250 manuscripts and letters. **Subscriptions:** 30 journals and other serials. **Services:** Interlibrary loans; library open to public for reference use only. **Remarks:** Includes the holdings of the Dr. Max Thorek Library and Manuscript Room.

INTERNATIONAL COMMUNICATION AGENCY
See: U.S. Information Agency

INTERNATIONAL COMMUNICATION AGENCY, UNITED STATES OF AMERICA
See: United States Information Service

★6241★

INTERNATIONAL CONSUMER CREDIT ASSOCIATION - DEPARTMENT OF EDUCATION LIBRARY (Bus-Fin)†
243 N. Lindbergh Blvd.   Phone: (314) 991-3030
St. Louis, MO 63141   Mary Alice Minney, Dir., Dept. of Educ.
Staff: Prof 1; Other 10. **Subjects:** Consumer credit and collections. **Holdings:** 800 books and bound periodical volumes. **Services:** Copying; library not open to public.

★6242★

INTERNATIONAL COPPER RESEARCH ASSOCIATION, INC. - LIBRARY (Sci-Tech)
708 Third Ave.   Phone: (212) 697-9355
New York, NY 10017
Founded: 1960. **Subjects:** Metallurgy, chemistry, mining. **Special Collections:** Complete set of the association's project reports (300 volumes). **Holdings:** Figures not available. **Services:** Library not open to public.

★6243★

INTERNATIONAL COUNCIL OF SHOPPING CENTERS - LIBRARY (Bus-Fin)
665 Fifth Ave.   Phone: (212) 421-8181
New York, NY 10022   Nancy G. Morley, Libn.
Staff: Prof 1; Other 1. **Subjects:** Shopping centers - development, management, marketing, law, design. **Holdings:** 1500 books; AV materials. **Subscriptions:** 50 journals and other serials; 8 newspapers. **Services:** Library open to public by appointment.

★6244★

INTERNATIONAL CRANE FOUNDATION - LIBRARY (Env-Cons)
City View Rd.   Phone: (608) 356-9462
Baraboo, WI 53913   Joan A. Fordham, Adm.
Founded: 1973. **Subjects:** Cranes, storks, ibises. **Holdings:** 2000 manuscripts; file of articles and clippings concerning crane research, captive propagation and habitat developments throughout the world. **Services:** Copying (fee); library open to public with permission of administrator. **Publications:** The Brolga Bugle, quarterly - with membership.

★6245★

INTERNATIONAL DATA CORPORATION - INFORMATION CENTER (Info Sci)
5 Speen St.   Phone: (617) 872-8200
Framingham, MA 01701   Mary Jo McSorley, Mgr.
Founded: 1970. **Staff:** Prof 1; Other 1. **Subjects:** Data processing, computer technology, finance. **Holdings:** 1000 annual reports; 4000 company files. **Subscriptions:** 300 journals and other serials; 25 newspapers. **Services:** Interlibrary loans; library open to clients only. **Computerized Information Services:** DIALOG, NEXIS. **Networks/Consortia:** Member of New England On-Line Users (NENON); Route 128 Librarians Group.

INTERNATIONAL & DEVELOPMENT EDUCATION PROGRAM CLEARINGHOUSE
See: University of Pittsburgh - School of Education

★6246★

INTERNATIONAL DEVELOPMENT RESEARCH CENTRE - LIBRARY (Soc Sci)
Box 8500   Phone: (613) 996-2321
Ottawa, ON, Canada K1G 3H9   Charles A. Godfrey, Assoc.Dir.
Founded: 1971. **Staff:** Prof 8; Other 15. **Subjects:** International development including agriculture, food, nutrition, population, health; information science; social sciences. **Holdings:** 35,000 books. **Subscriptions:** 4200 journals and other serials; 38 newspapers. **Services:** Interlibrary loans; copying; library open to public with restrictions. **Computerized Information Services:** DIALOG, SDC, QL Systems, MEDLINE, CAN/OLE, BRS, INFORMATECH, Info Globe, International Labour Office, United Nations Food and Agriculture Organization, United Nations Educational Scientific and Cultural Organization, United Nations Industrial Development Organization; internal databases; computerized cataloging, acquisitions and serials. **Publications:** Ex Libris, accessions list, monthly. **Staff:** Maureen Sly, Hd., Tech.Serv.; Susan Hodges, Acq.Libn.; Anne Simpson, Supv., Cat. & Indexing; Sharon Henry, Dp.Libn.; Margo Monteith, Hd., Pub.Serv.

INTERNATIONAL DRUG INFORMATION CENTER
See: Long Island University - Arnold & Mary Schwartz College of Pharmacy & Health Sciences

★6247★

INTERNATIONAL ENGINEERING COMPANY, INC. - LIBRARY (Sci-Tech)
180 Howard St.   Phone: (415) 442-7300
San Francisco, CA 94105   Louis I. Pigott, Jr., Libn.
Founded: 1964. **Staff:** Prof 1. **Subjects:** Civil engineering, soil mechanics, water resource development. **Holdings:** 6000 books; 1000 bound periodical volumes. **Subscriptions:** 150 journals and other serials. **Services:** Interlibrary loans; copying; library not open to public. **Computerized Information Services:** DIALOG.

★6248★

INTERNATIONAL FABRICARE INSTITUTE - RESEARCH CENTER LIBRARY (Sci-Tech)
12251 Tech Rd.   Phone: (301) 622-1900
Silver Spring, MD 20904   C. Busler, Res.Chem.
Staff: Prof 2. **Subjects:** Chemistry, textiles, dry-cleaning, laundering. **Special Collections:** Periodicals pertaining to drycleaning and laundry industries. **Holdings:** 2000 volumes; 700 slides. **Subscriptions:** 30 journals and other serials; 5 newspapers. **Services:** Library open to public by appointment. **Staff:** R. Reddon, Lab.Techn.

★6249★

INTERNATIONAL FEDERATION OF PETROLEUM AND CHEMICAL WORKERS - LIBRARY (Bus-Fin)
Box 6603   Phone: (303) 388-9237
Denver, CO 80206   Curtis J. Hogan, Gen.Sec.
Founded: 1964. **Staff:** 1. **Subjects:** International trade unions, petroleum unions, industrial relations and International Labor Organization (ILO). **Special Collections:** ILO publications. **Holdings:** 1500 books. **Subscriptions:** 12 journals and other serials; 38 newspapers. **Services:** Interlibrary loans; copying; library open to public by appointment.

★6250★

INTERNATIONAL FERTILITY RESEARCH PROGRAM - LIBRARY (Soc Sci)
Triangle Dr.   Phone: (919) 549-0517
Research Triangle Park, NC 27709   William Barrows, Info.Coord.
Staff: Prof 1; Other 1. **Subjects:** Population/family planning, contraceptive research, demography, statistics. **Holdings:** 2000 books; 600 unbound periodical volumes; 1700 reports; 6000 reprints and unpublished documents; 330 patents. **Subscriptions:** 150 journals and other serials; 119 newsletters. **Services:** Interlibrary loans; copying; SDI; library open to public with restrictions. **Computerized Information Services:** MEDLARS; computerized

serials. **Networks/Consortia:** Member of Association for Population/Family Planning Libraries and Information Centers - International (APLIC-Internatl.).

★6251★
INTERNATIONAL FESTIVALS ASSOCIATION - LIBRARY (Bus-Fin)
Commodore Court
702 Wayzata Blvd.   Phone: (612) 377-4621
Minneapolis, MN 55403   Ken Walstad, Mng.Dir.
Staff: Prof 1. **Subjects:** Management, civic and nonprofit organizations. **Holdings:** 40 books; 120 bound periodical volumes. **Services:** Copying; library not open to public. **Publications:** Listing of current and new offerings, annual - to members.

★6252★
INTERNATIONAL FLAVORS AND FRAGRANCES, INC. - TECHNICAL INFORMATION CENTER (Sci-Tech)
1515 Hwy. 36   Phone: (201) 264-4500
Union Beach, NJ 07735   Bernard J. Mayers, Supv.
Founded: 1952. **Staff:** Prof 2; Other 2. **Subjects:** Organic chemistry, essential oils, flavors, perfumery, spectroscopy. **Holdings:** 6000 volumes; 26 VF drawers of patents; 25 VF drawers of reprints and pamphlets; 5 VF drawers of manufacturers' literature; 316 VF drawers of internal research reports; 3500 reels of microfilm. **Subscriptions:** 200 journals and other serials. **Services:** Center not open to public. **Computerized Information Services:** DIALOG, SDC, NLM, New York Times Information Service. **Publications:** Research Bulletin, quarterly. **Staff:** Raymond Latendresse, Sr.Lit.Chem.

★6253★
INTERNATIONAL FOOD POLICY RESEARCH INSTITUTE - LIBRARY (Food-Bev; Agri)
1776 Massachusetts Ave., N.W.   Phone: (202) 862-5614
Washington, DC 20036   Patricia W. Klosky, Libn.
Staff: 1. **Subjects:** Food policy and research, developmental economics, international trade, agricultural economics and statistics. **Holdings:** 2000 books; 2600 research reports. **Subscriptions:** 160 journals and other serials. **Services:** Interlibrary loans; copying; library open to public.

★6254★
INTERNATIONAL FOOD SERVICE EXECUTIVES ASSOCIATION - LIBRARY
111 E. Wacker Dr., Suite 600
Chicago IL 60601
Subjects: Food service careers. **Holdings:** Figures not available. **Remarks:** Presently inactive.

★6255★
INTERNATIONAL FOODSERVICE MANUFACTURERS ASSOCIATION - INFORMATION SERVICE (Food-Bev)†
875 N. Michigan, Suite 3460   Phone: (312) 944-3838
Chicago, IL 60611   Michael Hoffman, Dir. of Marketing
Staff: Prof 1; Other 2. **Subjects:** Food away from home industry. **Holdings:** Books; publications; periodicals; statistics; training materials. **Subscriptions:** 36 journals and other serials; 5 newspapers. **Services:** Interlibrary loans; copying (fee); library open to prospective members. **Publications:** List of publications - available on request.

★6256★
INTERNATIONAL FORTEAN ORGANIZATION - INFO RESEARCH LIBRARY (Sci-Tech)
Box 367
Arlington, VA 22210-0367   Paul J. Willis, Archv.
Founded: 1965. **Staff:** Prof 1. **Subjects:** Exotic zoology, exobiology, natural history, unidentified aerial phenomena, archeology, anthropology, philosophy of science, Forteana, physical sciences, history of exploration. **Special Collections:** Letters of Charles Fort, 1873-1932. **Holdings:** 2000 books; 1000 bound periodical volumes; 50,000 reprints, clippings, and notes; 1000 slides and photographs. **Subscriptions:** 100 journals and other serials. **Services:** Copying; bibliographic research on specialized subjects (fee charged); library open to serious Fortean scholars. **Publications:** INFO Journal, quarterly - by subscription.

★6257★
INTERNATIONAL FOUNDATION OF EMPLOYEE BENEFIT PLANS - INFORMATION CENTER (Bus-Fin)
18700 W. Bluemound Rd.   Phone: (414) 786-6700
Brookfield, WI 53005   Jack Baltes, Dir., Info.Serv.
Founded: 1970. **Staff:** Prof 3; Other 2. **Subjects:** Employee benefits, insurance, investments, management, economics, collective bargaining. **Holdings:** 4000 books; 500 bound periodical volumes; 60 VF drawers of

documents, clippings; 45 VF drawers of archival materials. **Subscriptions:** 350 journals and other serials; 15 newspapers. **Services:** Copying; SDI; library open to public. **Networks/Consortia:** Member of Library Council of Metropolitan Milwaukee, Inc. (LCOMM). **Publications:** List of publications - available on request. **Special Indexes:** Index to Digest (card). **Staff:** Dee Birschel, Assoc.Dir.; Julia E. Miller, Libn.

★6258★
INTERNATIONAL FRANCHISE ASSOCIATION - LIBRARY (Bus-Fin)†
1025 Connecticut Ave., N.W.   Phone: (202) 659-0790
Washington, DC 20036   Nancy B. Shaver, Libn.
Staff: Prof 1. **Subjects:** Franchising. **Holdings:** 100 books; 3 shelves of legal reports and journal articles; 2 VF drawers of annual reports. **Subscriptions:** 50 journals and other serials. **Services:** Interlibrary loans; library open to public by appointment. **Publications:** Bibliographies for Potential Franchisees and Franchisors - free upon request.

★6259★
INTERNATIONAL GAME FISH ASSOCIATION - INTERNATIONAL LIBRARY OF FISHES (Rec)
3000 E. Las Olas Blvd.   Phone: (305) 467-0161
Fort Lauderdale, FL 33316   M.B. McCracken, Libn.
Founded: 1973. **Staff:** Prof 1; Other 2. **Subjects:** Fish, sport fishing. **Special Collections:** Michael Lerner Collection (photos, papers, films, memorabilia); Joe Brooks Collection (photos, paper prepared for a history of angling, rare books). **Holdings:** 5000 books; fishing club yearbooks and newsletters; fishing films; photographs; angling artifacts. **Subscriptions:** 500 journals and other serials. **Services:** Library open to public for reference use only. **Publications:** World Record Game Fishes, annual - free to members and available for sale; The International Angler, bimonthly - to members.

★6260★
INTERNATIONAL HARVESTER COMPANY - CORPORATE ARCHIVES (Bus-Fin)
401 N. Michigan, 15th Fl.   Phone: (312) 836-2149
Chicago, IL 60611   Gregory Lennes, Archv.
Staff: Prof 1; Other 2. **Subjects:** Trucks, agricultural equipment, construction equipment, business. **Holdings:** 2500 cubic feet of archives. **Services:** Interlibrary loans; archives open to qualified researchers. **Computerized Information Services:** Bowne Information Systems, Inc.; computerized cataloging. **Special Catalogs:** Keys to Archives.

INTERNATIONAL HEALTH PROGRAMS - RESOURCE CENTER
See: American Public Health Association

★6261★
INTERNATIONAL HIBERNATION SOCIETY (Sci-Tech)*
300 Dean Dr.
Rockville, MD 20851   Dr. Richard C. Simmonds, Exec.Sec.
Founded: 1960. **Staff:** Prof 1. **Subjects:** Mammalian hibernation. **Holdings:** Over 1200 references. **Services:** Copying (for members only); open to public through mail requests. **Publications:** Newsletter, bimonthly - to members.

INTERNATIONAL HORN SOCIETY ARCHIVES
See: Ball State University - Music Library

★6262★
INTERNATIONAL HOUSE LIBRARY (Soc Sci)
Box 52020   Phone: (504) 522-3591
New Orleans, LA 70152   Mina L. Crais, Libn.
Founded: 1946. **Staff:** Prof 1; Other 2. **Subjects:** Import and export trade, travel, international relations, economics, transportation. **Holdings:** 20,000 volumes; 350 foreign phone books; 700 U.S. phone books; 700 trade directories; 32 VF drawers of pamphlet material. **Subscriptions:** 400 journals and other serials. **Services:** Copying; library not open to public. **Remarks:** The library is located at 607 Gravier St., New Orleans, LA 70130.

★6263★
INTERNATIONAL HUMAN RIGHTS LAW GROUP - LIBRARY (Law)
1346 Connecticut Ave., N.W., Suite 502   Phone: (202) 659-5023
Washington, DC 20036   Marianne Dugan, Adm.Asst.
Founded: 1978. **Subjects:** International human rights law. **Special Collections:** United Nations Commission on Human Rights. **Holdings:** Books, newspaper clippings, reports, proceedings. **Services:** Interlibrary loans; copying; library open to public. **Remarks:** Associated with the Institute of Procedural Aspects of International Law.

★6264★

INTERNATIONAL INSTITUTE OF MUNICIPAL CLERKS - MANAGEMENT INFORMATION CENTER (Info Sci)

160 N. Altadena Dr.   Phone: (213) 795-6153
Pasadena, CA 91107   John J. Hunnewell, Exec.Dir.
Staff: Prof 2; Other 4. **Subjects:** Municipal ordinances, records management. **Special Collections:** Examples of agendas, minutes, filing systems, records, administration programs from U.S. and Canadian municipalities. **Holdings:** 500 books; 1000 file folders on sample ordinances. **Subscriptions:** 200 journals and other serials. **Services:** Copying; center not open to public.

★6265★

INTERNATIONAL INSTITUTE FOR RESOURCE ECONOMICS - LIBRARY (Bus-Fin)

6210 Massachusetts Ave.   Phone: (301) 229-6066
Bethesda, MD 20016
Subjects: Resource economics. **Special Collections:** International commodity agreements. **Holdings:** 300 books; 190 other cataloged items. **Services:** Library open to clients only.

★6266★

INTERNATIONAL INSTITUTE FOR ROBOTICS - LIBRARY

Box 210708
Dallas, TX 75211
Defunct

★6267★

INTERNATIONAL INSTITUTE OF STRESS - LIBRARY AND DOCUMENTATION CENTER (Med)

659 Milton St.   Phone: (514) 288-6665
Montreal, PQ, Canada H2X 1W6   Mrs. G. Larue, Chf.Libn.
Staff: Prof 2; Other 4. **Subjects:** Stress and related subjects. **Holdings:** 1800 books. **Services:** Interlibrary loans; copying; library open to public. **Remarks:** Contains part of the holdings of the Universite de Montreal - Institut de Medecine et de Chirurgie Experimentales - Bibliotheque. **Staff:** Mrs. M. Timm, Chf. Documentalist.

INTERNATIONAL INSTITUTE FOR THE STUDY OF HUMAN REPRODUCTION
See: Columbia University - Center for Population and Family Health

★6268★

INTERNATIONAL JOINT COMMISSION - GREAT LAKES REGIONAL OFFICE LIBRARY (Env-Cons)

100 Ouellette Ave., 8th Fl.   Phone: (519) 256-7821
Windsor, ON, Canada N9A 6T3   Patricia Murray, Libn./Tech.Ed.
Founded: 1975. **Staff:** Prof 1; Other 1. **Subjects:** Great Lakes water quality, resources management, land use, toxic substances, limnology, wastewater treatment. **Special Collections:** Pollution from Land Use Activities Research Group (PLUARG) reports (120); Pollution of Boundary Waters reports, 1951-1970. **Holdings:** 2500 books; 12 VF drawers of clippings and pamphlets; 40,000 technical reports; 1200 microfiche. **Subscriptions:** 300 journals and other serials. **Services:** Interlibrary loans; copying; library open to public by appointment. **Computerized Information Services:** Online systems. **Publications:** Reports issued under the Great Lakes Water Quality Agreement 1972, a Bibliography, issued annually; PLUARG Bibliography, 1980. **Remarks:** Contains the holdings of the Great Lakes Basin Commission - Great Lakes Basin Library.

★6269★

INTERNATIONAL JOINT COMMISSION - LIBRARY (Law; Sci-Tech)

100 Metcalfe St., 18th Fl.   Phone: (613) 995-2984
Ottawa, ON, Canada K1P 5M1   Dennis Quong, Asst.Sec.
Staff: 1. **Subjects:** Hydrology, law. **Special Collections:** International Joint Commission reports. **Holdings:** 1500 volumes. **Subscriptions:** 28 journals and other serials. **Services:** Interlibrary loans; copying; library open to public.

★6270★

INTERNATIONAL LABOR OFFICE - WASHINGTON BRANCH LIBRARY (Soc Sci)

1750 New York Ave., N.W.   Phone: (202) 376-2315
Washington, DC 20006   Patricia S. Hord, Libn.
Founded: 1920. **Staff:** Prof 1. **Subjects:** Social and economic development, world employment program, labor statistics, labor-management relations, vocational training and rehabilitation, occupational safety and health. **Special Collections:** ILO publications and documentation; Legislative Series, 1919 to present (laws and regulations on labor and social security of more than 100 nations in English translation). **Holdings:** 13,000 books; 3750 ILO documents (uncataloged). **Services:** Copying; library open to public. **Computerized Information Services:** SDC. **Publications:** International Labor Documentation

(bulletin form), 12/year. **Special Catalogs:** ILO Catalog of Publications in Print 1982 (book). **Remarks:** The main International Labor Office Library, located in Geneva, Switzerland, contains a worldwide collection of publications and prepares the publications and catalogs listed above.

★6271★

INTERNATIONAL LADIES' GARMENT WORKERS UNION - RESEARCH DEPARTMENT LIBRARY (Soc Sci)

1710 Broadway   Phone: (212) 265-7000
New York, NY 10019   Sue Barlach Derskowitz, Hd.
Founded: 1937. **Staff:** Prof 1. **Subjects:** Earnings and hours, employment and payrolls, fringe benefits, labor and labor statistics, old-age insurance, social insurance, trade unions, unemployment insurance, union agreements, wearing apparel industry, women's clothing industry. **Holdings:** 14,000 volumes; 75 VF drawers. **Subscriptions:** 155 journals and other serials; 6 newspapers. **Services:** Library open to public with restrictions.

★6272★

INTERNATIONAL LIBRARY, ARCHIVES & MUSEUM OF OPTOMETRY (Med)

243 N. Lindbergh Blvd.   Phone: (314) 991-0324
St. Louis, MO 63141   Maria Dablemont, Libn.
Founded: 1902. **Staff:** Prof 3; Other 2. **Subjects:** Vision, optometry, ophthalmology. **Special Collections:** Early optometric publications; Archives of the American Optometric Association (185 VF drawers); early eyeglasses and optical instruments. **Holdings:** 6000 books; 4000 bound periodical volumes; 350 file boxes of pamphlets and clippings; AV materials. **Subscriptions:** 500 journals and other serials. **Services:** Interlibrary loans; copying; library open to public. **Networks/Consortia:** Member of Association of Visual Science Librarians. **Staff:** Sandra Smith, Asst. to Libn.; Linda Draper, Hd., Tech.Serv.

INTERNATIONAL LIBRARY OF FISHES
See: International Game Fish Association

★6273★

INTERNATIONAL LONGSHOREMEN'S AND WAREHOUSEMEN'S UNION - ANNE RAND RESEARCH LIBRARY (Soc Sci)

1188 Franklin St.   Phone: (415) 775-0533
San Francisco, CA 94109   Carol Schwartz, Libn.
Founded: 1946. **Staff:** Prof 1. **Subjects:** Trade unions, longshoremen, shipping, sugar, collective bargaining, pension and welfare. **Special Collections:** Union archives. **Holdings:** 3000 books; 450 VF drawers; 300 boxes. **Subscriptions:** 100 journals and other serials; 65 newspapers. **Services:** Interlibrary loans; copying; library open to public with restrictions.

INTERNATIONAL MARINE ARCHIVES
See: Old Dartmouth Historical Society - Whaling Museum Library

★6274★

INTERNATIONAL MICROWAVE POWER INSTITUTE - REFERENCE LIBRARY (Sci-Tech)

301 Maple Ave., W., Tower Suite 520   Phone: (703) 281-1515
Vienna, VA 22180   Dan Lynch, Exec.Dir.
Founded: 1966. **Subjects:** Microwave power - industrial, scientific, medical, domestic; cooking. **Special Collections:** All publications of the IMPI. **Holdings:** 100 volumes. **Services:** Interlibrary loans; library not open to public. **Remarks:** This is a highly specialized reference center for members of the institute and major (national) libraries. **Formerly:** Located in New York, NY.

★6275★

INTERNATIONAL MILITARY ARCHIVES (Mil)*

Government Box 30051
Washington, DC 20014   Helga K. Knoeppel, Libn.
Founded: 1965. **Staff:** Prof 2. **Subjects:** Paramilitary and military politics, propaganda, history and biography, uniforms and insignia, colors and standards, aircraft and armored vehicles, psychological warfare, weapons systems. **Special Collections:** Elebaut Collection on Adolf Hitler; German World War II military and political photographs. **Holdings:** 600 rare books in German, several hundred in English; negatives and color slides; prints and maps; postage stamp issues; miscellaneous printed matter. **Services:** Historical research and searching service on a fee basis; picture editing; translation from German; library not open to public. **Publications:** Catalog of surplus books for sale; catalog of photographs available from archives. **Staff:** Lowell Anson Kenyon, Dir.

★6276★
INTERNATIONAL MINERALS & CHEMICALS CORPORATION - IMC RESEARCH & DEVELOPMENT LIBRARY (Sci-Tech)
1331 S. First St.
Box 207
Terre Haute, IN 47808   Phone: (812) 232-0121
    Mr. T.C. Shane, Jr., Dir., Info.Serv.
Founded: 1927. **Staff:** Prof 5; Other 3. **Subjects:** Chemistry, microbiology, nutrition, agriculture. **Holdings:** 15,000 books; 14,250 bound periodical volumes; 206 theses; 19,583 internal reports; 33 newsletters and bulletins; chemical patents in microform; microfilm. **Subscriptions:** 600 journals and other serials; 6 newspapers. **Services:** Interlibrary loans; copying; library open to public with restrictions. **Computerized Information Services:** DIALOG, SDC, NLM, BRS. **Networks/Consortia:** Member of Regional Medical Library - Region 3; OCLC through INCOLSA. **Special Indexes:** Index to internal reports (punched cards). **Also Known As:** IMC. **Staff:** Ruth Smedlund, Prin.Res.Libn.; Ruth Turner, Asst.Libn.; John A. Frump, Info.Spec.; William F. Phillips, Lit.Chem.; George Curran, Search Anl.

★6277★
INTERNATIONAL MINERALS & CHEMICAL CORPORATION - LIBRARY
421 E. Hawley St.
Mundelein, IL 60060
Defunct. Holdings absorbed by the International Minerals & Chemical Corporation - IMC Research & Development Library.

★6278★
INTERNATIONAL MONETARY FUND - LAW LIBRARY (Law)
700 19th St., N.W.
Washington, DC 20431   Phone: (202) 477-6148
    Eliana D. Prebisch, Libn.
Staff: Prof 1; Other 2. **Subjects:** Law - international, constitutional, commercial; conflict of laws; legislation and law reports of member countries. **Special Collections:** Central bank, banking and monetary laws of member countries. **Holdings:** 45,000 volumes; 122 binders of central bank and banking laws; 123 binders of monetary laws. **Subscriptions:** 220 journals and other serials; 6 newspapers. **Services:** Interlibrary loans; library not open to public. **Computerized Information Services:** LEXIS. **Publications:** Current accessions, monthly - available on request. **Special Catalogs:** Catalog of monographs, periodicals and law reports (card). **Special Indexes:** Legal journals and annuals currently received (card); banking and monetary laws of member countries (card and binders by country). **Also Known As:** IMF.

★6279★
INTERNATIONAL MONETARY FUND/WORLD BANK - JOINT BANK-FUND LIBRARY (Bus-Fin)
700 19th St., N.W.
Washington, DC 20431   Phone: (202) 477-3167
    Maureen M. Moore, Libn.
Founded: 1946. **Staff:** Prof 19; Other 25. **Subjects:** Economic development, international economics, international finance, money and banking. **Holdings:** 150,000 books and bound periodical volumes. **Subscriptions:** 3000 journals and other serials; 200 newspapers. **Services:** Interlibrary loans (limited); library open to public for reference use only by appointment. **Computerized Information Services:** DIALOG, BRS, SDC, New York Times Information Service, Dow Jones News Retrieval, Legi-Slate, NEXIS, MEDLARS, Business Information Display, Inc.; computerized cataloging, acquisitions, indexing and routing. **Networks/Consortia:** Member of OCLC; CAPCON. **Publications:** List of Recent Periodical Articles, monthly; List of Recent Additions, monthly - limited circulation. **Special Indexes:** Economics and Finance: Index to Periodical Articles, 1947-1971, published 1972 (4 volumes); First Supplement, 1972-1974; Second Supplement, 1975-1977; The Developing Areas, a Classified Bibliography of the Joint Bank-Fund Library, published 1975 (3 volumes); IMF Bibliography.

★6280★
INTERNATIONAL MUSEUM OF PHOTOGRAPHY AT GEORGE EASTMAN HOUSE - LIBRARY (Pict; Art)
900 East Ave.
Rochester, NY 14607   Phone: (716) 271-3361
    Rachel Stuhlman, Hd.Libn.
Founded: 1949. **Staff:** Prof 3; Other 1. **Subjects:** Photography and cinematography - history, science, aesthetics. **Special Collections:** 19th century books illustrated with photographs (1500 volumes); Sipley/3M Collection; Alvin Langdon Coburn Collection; Lewis W. Hine Collection. **Holdings:** 13,000 books; 12,000 bound periodical volumes; 25 VF drawers of history of photography and current activities; 600,000 photographic prints; 5000 letters and manuscripts; 8 taped interviews with photographers. **Subscriptions:** 300 journals and other serials. **Services:** Interlibrary loans; copying; mail reference. **Computerized Information Services:** Computerized cataloging. **Networks/Consortia:** Member of OCLC. **Publications:** IMAGE, quarterly - free to museum members. **Staff:** Gail McClain, Hd., Tech.Serv.; Judy Bloch, Cat.; Norma Feld, Ser.Libn.

★6281★
INTERNATIONAL NICKEL COMPANY, INC. - LIBRARY (Sci-Tech; Bus-Fin)
One New York Plaza
New York, NY 10004   Phone: (212) 742-4061
    Linda G. Doty, Lib.Adm.
Staff: Prof 1; Other 6. **Subjects:** Business, management, tax, law, processing and fabrication of nickel, metal and mineral statistics, corrosion. **Holdings:** 15,000 books. **Subscriptions:** 1000 journals. **Services:** Interlibrary loans; library not open to public. **Computerized Information Services:** New York Times Information Service, DIALOG, SDC, Dow Jones News Retrieval, Control Data Corporation; computerized cataloging and serials. **Publications:** Library Update, monthly - for internal distribution only.

★6282★
INTERNATIONAL NUMISMATIC SOCIETY - LIBRARY (Rec)
1100 17th St. N.W.
Box 19386
Washington, DC 20036   Phone: (202) 223-4496
    Charles R. Hoskins, Info.Dir.
Founded: 1976. **Staff:** Prof 2; Other 3. **Subjects:** Coins, currency, medals. **Holdings:** 800 books; 400 unbound numismatic publications, 1890-1978. **Services:** Copying; library open to public with restrictions. **Publications:** Numorum, quarterly - members only. **Staff:** Francis Fazzari, Asst.Libn.

★6283★
INTERNATIONAL OIL SCOUTS ASSOCIATION - LIBRARY (Sci-Tech)
Box 2121
Austin, TX 78768   Phone: (512) 472-3357
    Barbara Lockstedt, Mgr.
Founded: 1924. **Subjects:** Petroleum. **Holdings:** Figures not available. **Services:** Library for association use only. **Publications:** Yearbooks of Petroleum Exploration and Production Statistics - for sale; newsletter, quarterly. **Remarks:** Library located at 326 E. 5th St., Austin, TX 78701.

★6284★
INTERNATIONAL OMBUDSMAN INSTITUTE - I.O.I. LIBRARY (Soc Sci)
Faculty of Law
University of Alberta
Edmonton, AB, Canada T6G 2H5   Phone: (403) 432-3196
    Priscilla Kennedy, Asst. to Exec.Dir.
Staff: 2. **Subjects:** Ombudsmanship, human rights, administrative law. **Holdings:** 800 books; 100 pieces of legislation; 1000 annual reports. **Services:** Copying; library open to public. **Computerized Information Services:** Internal database; computerized cataloging and serials. **Publications:** List of publications - available on request.

★6285★
INTERNATIONAL PACIFIC SALMON FISHERIES COMMISSION - LIBRARY (Food-Bev)
Box 30
New Westminster, BC, Canada V3L 4X9   Phone: (604) 521-3771
    Mrs. Fumi Sato, Libn.
Staff: Prof 1. **Subjects:** Salmon research. **Holdings:** Figures not available. **Subscriptions:** 6 newspapers. **Services:** Interlibrary loans; library open to public with restrictions.

★6286★
INTERNATIONAL PAPER COMPANY - CORPORATE INFORMATION CENTER (Bus-Fin)
77 W. 45th St., 2nd Fl.
New York, NY 10036   Phone: (212) 536-5549
    Elizabeth Skerritt, Corp.Libn.
Founded: 1962. **Staff:** Prof 1; Other 2. **Subjects:** Pulp, paper and forest products, plastics, business, finance, marketing, economics, government, energy, communications. **Special Collections:** History of Papermaking collection. **Holdings:** 4500 books and bound periodical volumes; 115 VF drawers of annual reports, pamphlets and research material; 175 boxes of back periodicals and directories; 538 reels of microfilm; 9279 microfiche; 29 audio and visual cassettes; maps. **Subscriptions:** 490 journals; 17 newspapers. **Services:** Interlibrary loans; library open to Special Libraries Association members and by appointment. **Computerized Information Services:** DIALOG, SDC, New York Times Information Service, Dow Jones News Retrieval, NEXIS, LEXIS; computerized serials. **Networks/Consortia:** Member of METRO. **Publications:** Acquisitions List, quarterly; periodicals listing; Notes and Comments; Directory of Services.

★6287★
INTERNATIONAL PAPER COMPANY - CORPORATE RESEARCH & DEVELOPMENT DIVISION - TECHNICAL INFORMATION CENTER (Sci-Tech)
Box 797
Tuxedo, NY 10987   Phone: (914) 351-2101
    Bernadette Marasco, Sr.Tech.Info.Spec.
Founded: 1969. **Staff:** Prof 2; Other 3. **Subjects:** Pulp and paper, forestry, cellulose chemistry, environment, packaging. **Holdings:** 14,000 books and bound periodical volumes; 1500 documents; dissertations. **Subscriptions:**

500 journals and other serials. **Services:** Interlibrary loans; SDI; library open to public by appointment only. **Computerized Information Services:** DIALOG, SDC, NLM, New York Times Information Service. **Networks/Consortia:** Member of Southeastern New York Library Resources Council.

★6288★
INTERNATIONAL PAPER COMPANY - ERLING RIIS RESEARCH LABORATORY - INFORMATION SERVICES (Sci-Tech)
Box 2787   Phone: (205) 457-8911
Mobile, AL 36652   Janice T. Pope, Supv.
Staff: Prof 2. **Subjects:** Wood pulp, paper, cellulose, wood chemistry, forest products, chemical engineering, packaging, printing, pollution. **Holdings:** 5000 books; 1000 bound periodical volumes; 500 pamphlets and translations (cataloged); 300 technical reports of National Council of Paper Industry for Air and Stream Improvement; 3000 U.S. patents; 1000 Canadian patents; 200 folders of paper industry clippings; 3 shelves of pamphlets. **Subscriptions:** 250 journals and other serials. **Services:** Interlibrary loans; copying; SDI and retrospective searches; library not open to public. **Computerized Information Services:** DIALOG, SDC. **Publications:** Newsletter and acquisitions list, irregular - for internal distribution only. **Special Indexes:** Internal research reports index and technical reports index, both computer-produced annually with five-year cumulations, for company use only (book). **Staff:** Frances D. Row, Info.Spec.

★6289★
INTERNATIONAL PAPER COMPANY - FOREST PRODUCTIVITY & RESEARCH - FOREST RESEARCH LIBRARY (Env-Cons)
Box 2328   Phone: (205) 470-3376
Mobile, AL 36652   LaMerle C. Green, Act.Libn.
Founded: 1977. **Staff:** Prof 1. **Subjects:** Forestry. **Holdings:** 800 books; 58 bound periodical volumes; 8300 forestry publications; Forest Science (1955 to present); Forest Farmer (1952 to present); Journal of Forestry (1950 to present); New Zealand Journal of Forestry Science, volumes 1 to present; conference papers. **Subscriptions:** 59 journals and other serials. **Services:** Interlibrary loans; copying; SDI; library open to public with restrictions. **Computerized Information Services:** DIALOG. **Publications:** Monthly Acquisitions List.

INTERNATIONAL PERCUSSION REFERENCE LIBRARY
See: Arizona State University - Music Library

INTERNATIONAL PHARMACEUTIC & THERAPEUTIC DRUG INFORMATION CENTER
See: Long Island University - Arnold & Marie Schwartz College of Pharmacy & Health Sciences - Intl. Drug Info. Ctr.

INTERNATIONAL PIANO ARCHIVES
See: University of Maryland, College Park - Libraries - Music Library - International Piano Archives at Maryland

★6290★
INTERNATIONAL PLANNED PARENTHOOD FEDERATION - WESTERN HEMISPHERE REGION - LIBRARY (Soc Sci)
105 Madison Ave.   Phone: (212) 679-2230
New York, NY 10016   Helen Szterenfeld, Hd.
Staff: Prof 2. **Subjects:** Family planning, population, demography, biomedicine, health care. **Special Collections:** Population and family planning in Latin America and the Caribbean. **Holdings:** 15,000 books; AV materials. **Subscriptions:** 400 journals and other serials. **Services:** Interlibrary loans; copying; library open to public by appointment. **Networks/Consortia:** Member of Association for Population/Family Planning Libraries and Information Centers - International. **Publications:** FORUM - for family planners in Latin America and the Caribbean; occasional essays and other publications.

★6291★
INTERNATIONAL POSTCARD COLLECTORS ASSOCIATION, INC. - LIBRARY (Rec)†
Loyola/Marymount University
7101 W. 80th St.   Phone: (213) 642-2788
Los Angeles, CA 90045
Founded: 1968. **Staff:** Prof 5. **Subjects:** Postcards, viewcards, postal cards, cancellations. **Special Collections:** Worldwide postcard collection (over 1 million cards); books and periodicals of postcards and postcard collecting. **Holdings:** 500 books; 200 bound periodical volumes; 1 file cabinet of manuscripts and letters. **Subscriptions:** 20 journals and other serials. **Services:** Interlibrary loans; copying; library open to public by appointment. **Staff:** W. Von Boltenstern, Coord.

INTERNATIONAL QUICK PRINTING FOUNDATION LIBRARY
See: National Association of Quick Printers

★6292★
INTERNATIONAL RAILROAD & TRANSPORTATION POSTCARD COLLECTORS CLUB - LIBRARY (Trans; Rec)
Box 6782
Providence, RI 02940   Robert J. Andrews, Pres.
Staff: 2. **Subjects:** Transportation vehicles, postcards. **Holdings:** 1000 books and bound periodical volumes; bulletins. **Subscriptions:** 30 journals and other serials; 10 newspapers. **Services:** Copying; library open to public with restrictions. **Publications:** Transport World. **Special Indexes:** Checklist of transportation postcards.

★6293★
INTERNATIONAL READING ASSOCIATION - LIBRARY (Educ)
800 Barksdale Rd.
Box 8139   Phone: (302) 731-1600
Newark, DE 19711   Wendy Wei, Libn.
Founded: 1974. **Staff:** Prof 1; Other 1. **Subjects:** Teaching and remedial teaching of reading; elementary and secondary reading programs; children's literature; adult education. **Special Collections:** Nila Banton Smith Research Collection in Reading; William S. Gray Collection in Reading; Children's Choices Collection: Children's Literature. **Holdings:** 10,000 books and bound periodical volumes; 600 technical and annual reports; 6 VF drawers of clippings, pamphlets, brochures; 9000 microforms. **Subscriptions:** 287 journals and other serials. **Services:** Interlibrary loans; copying; library open to researchers. **Computerized Information Services:** Computerized cataloging. **Special Indexes:** IRA Literature Retrieval Index. **Also Known As:** IRA.

★6294★
INTERNATIONAL REFERENCE ORGANIZATION IN FORENSIC MEDICINE AND SCIENCES - LIBRARY AND REFERENCE CENTER (Med; Law)
Milton Helpern Center
Wichita State University
Box 95   Phone: (316) 262-6211
Wichita, KS 67208   Dr. William G. Eckert, Dir.
Founded: 1966. **Staff:** 2. **Subjects:** Abortion, accidents, alcohol, alcoholism, drugs and drug abuse, forensic sciences, history medicolegal, homicide, iatrogenic problems, legal medicine, pediatric medicine, poisoning, suicidology, sex problems, thanatology, toxicology, trauma, war crimes, war wounds. **Special Collections:** Texts in forensic medicine from 20 countries; journals in forensic and legal medicine from 20 countries; reference materials on forensic medical problems in 80 countries. **Holdings:** 1700 books; 1500 bound periodical volumes; 2000 cataloged papers; 2000 miscellaneous reports; 100 literature bibliographies; microfilms and magnetic tapes. **Subscriptions:** 30 journals and other serials. **Services:** Copying; sale of slide lectures; library open to public. **Computerized Information Services:** Computerized reference service (being developed). **Publications:** INFORM Newsletter, quarterly; list of publications - available on request. **Special Catalogs:** Special indexed compilations of subjects listed above. Special indexed compilations of the table of contents for the following - Journal of Forensic Sciences, Medicine, Science and the Law, Journal of Forensic Medicine, Journal of Indian Academy of Forensic Sciences, American Journal of Clinical Pathology (volumes 1-56). **Remarks:** The center acts as the Secretariat for the Pan-American Association of Forensic Sciences. **Also Known As:** INFORM.

INTERNATIONAL RESEARCH CENTER FOR VERBAL AGGRESSION, INC.
See: Maledicta

★6295★
INTERNATIONAL RESEARCH & EVALUATION (IRE) - INFORMATION & TECHNOLOGY TRANSFER RESOURCE CENTER (Env-Cons; Sci-Tech)
21098 IRE Control Ctr.   Phone: (612) 888-9635
Eagan, MN 55121   Randall L. Voight, Info.Dir.
Staff: Prof 12; Other 22. **Subjects:** Waste management and resources recovery, energy and environmental engineering, law enforcement and criminal justice, robotics, fiber optics and lasers. **Holdings:** 255,464 books; 5701 bound periodical volumes; 3.1 million microfiche; 513 ultrafiche; 631 videotapes; 3106 other microforms. **Subscriptions:** 5150 journals and other serials; 321 newspapers. **Services:** Interlibrary loans; copying; library open to clients and ITTD card owners. **Computerized Information Services:** DIALOG, BRS, SDC; Information & Technology Transfer Database (ITTD; internal database); computerized cataloging, acquisitions and serials. **Networks/Consortia:** Member of GTE Telenet; Martin Marietta Data Systems. **Publications:** Information Age, monthly - by subscription. **Special Indexes:** KWIC index (computer printout). **Staff:** George Franklin, Jr., Acq.Dir.

★6296★
INTERNATIONAL ROCK AND ROLL MUSIC ASSOCIATION, INC. - LIBRARY
(Mus)
Box 50111   Phone: (615) 352-1443
Nashville, TN 37025   Bernard G. Walters, Pres.
Staff: 3. **Subjects:** English and American rock and roll, Beatles, Rolling Stones. **Special Collections:** Early English rock periodicals, photographs, slides and posters. **Holdings:** 40 books; 1200 unbound periodicals; 2100 rock concert slides; 5000 rock photographs; 900 rock and roll phonograph records. **Services:** Library not open to public. **Publications:** Communique, 6/year - to members.

INTERNATIONAL RUNNING CENTER LIBRARY
See: New York Road Runners Club

★6297★
INTERNATIONAL SILVER COMPANY - HISTORICAL LIBRARY (Bus-Fin)†
550 Research Pkwy.   Phone: (203) 238-8058
Meriden, CT 06450   Ed P. Hogan, Hist.
Founded: 1938. **Remarks:** Library is described as a collection of old catalogs and historical records of I.S. Co. and its many predecessors, primarily for the use of International Silver Company, but open to serious researchers by appointment.

★6298★
INTERNATIONAL SKATEBOARD ASSOCIATION - LIBRARY
5466 Complex St., Unit 207
San Diego, CA 92123
Defunct

★6299★
INTERNATIONAL SOAP BOX DERBY - LIBRARY (Rec)
789 Derby Downs Dr.   Phone: (216) 733-8723
Akron, OH 44306   Jeff Iula, Asst.Gen.Mgr.
Founded: 1934. **Staff:** Prof 2; Other 5. **Subjects:** Soap Box Derby. **Special Collections:** History of past races. **Holdings:** 100 books; 40 films; heat records; pictures. **Services:** Library open to public with restrictions. **Computerized Information Services:** Online systems. **Publications:** Topside, bimonthly - free upon request.

INTERNATIONAL SOCIETY FOR OPTICAL ENGINEERING
See: SPIE - The International Society for Optical Engineering

★6300★
INTERNATIONAL SOCIETY FOR PHILOSOPHICAL ENQUIRY - ARCHIVES
(Hist)
307 Pleasant St.   Phone: (617) 489-3170
Belmont, MA 02178   Robert J. Davis, Hist.
Founded: 1977. **Staff:** Prof 1. **Subjects:** High IQ - societies, testing. **Special Collections:** Archives of the International Society for Philosophical Enquiry; complete collection of Telicom, the journal of the I.S.P.E. **Holdings:** 300 pages of archival material; microfiche. **Services:** Copying; archives not open to public. **Computerized Information Services:** Computerized cataloging and circulation. **Publications:** Telicom, 10/year. **Special Indexes:** Author index of Telicom.

★6301★
INTERNATIONAL SOCIETY FOR REHABILITATION OF THE DISABLED/ REHABILITATION INTERNATIONAL - LIBRARY (Med)
432 Park Ave., S.   Phone: (212) 679-6520
New York, NY 10016   Barbara Duncan, Dir. of Info.
Subjects: Disability - international aspects. **Special Collections:** Disabled children in developing countries; barrier free design; economics of disability. **Holdings:** Figures not available. **Services:** Library open to public by appointment. **Publications:** International Rehabilitation Review, quarterly. **Remarks:** The majority of the library's holdings have been transferred to the Rehabilitation International Information Service in Heidelberg, Germany. Basic references are still maintained. **Also Known As:** ISRD.

★6302★
INTERNATIONAL SWIMMING HALL OF FAME - MUSEUM & LIBRARY (Rec)
One Hall of Fame Dr.   Phone: (305) 462-6536
Fort Lauderdale, FL 33316   Marion Washburn, Libn.
Founded: 1968. **Subjects:** Swimming source books and instruction; sports medicine and psychology; swimming history and reference; pool care and management; diving and water polo; guidebooks; swimmers' biographies; swim officiating - games, charts, tables. **Special Collections:** Sports stamp collection; aquatic memorabilia; historical swimming and diving films and tapes; medals and trophies of major swimmers past and present. **Holdings:**

3000 books; 70 bound periodical volumes; 80 scrapbooks; 40 theses and dissertations. **Subscriptions:** 20 journals and other serials. **Services:** Library open to public. **Publications:** Yearbooks, annual; newsletters, annual - both distributed to membership list of contributors and honorees.

★6303★
INTERNATIONAL TENNIS HALL OF FAME AND TENNIS MUSEUM - LIBRARY
(Rec)
Newport Casino
194 Bellevue Ave.   Phone: (401) 846-4567
Newport, RI 02840   Jane G. Brown, Exec.Dir.
Founded: 1954. **Staff:** 7. **Subjects:** Lawn tennis and court tennis. **Holdings:** Books, periodicals, catalogs and photographs. **Services:** Museum open to public year around; library open to researchers for reference use. **Staff:** Mark L. Stenning, Cur.

★6304★
INTERNATIONAL THEATRE INSTITUTE OF THE UNITED STATES, INC. - INTERNATIONAL THEATRE COLLECTION (Theater)
1860 Broadway, Suite 1510   Phone: (212) 245-3950
New York, NY 10023   Elizabeth B. Burdick, Dir.
Founded: 1970. **Staff:** Prof 1; Other 1. **Subjects:** Contemporary international theatre. **Holdings:** 4300 books; 8000 plays; 205 periodicals on performing arts; theatres of 139 countries are represented by their yearbooks, newsletters, programs, house organs, press releases, production schedules, brochures, reviews, photographs. **Subscriptions:** 200 journals and other serials. **Services:** Copying; library open to public. **Publications:** Theatre Notes, 8/year - free upon request; International Directory of Theatre, Dance and Folklore Festivals, 1979 - for sale.

★6305★
INTERNATIONAL THESPIAN SOCIETY - LIBRARY (Theater)
3368 Central Pkwy.   Phone: (513) 559-1996
Cincinnati, OH 45225   Ronald L. Longstreth, Exec.Sec.
Founded: 1929. **Subjects:** Playscripts and theatre texts. **Holdings:** 14,000 scripts and theater textbooks. **Services:** Collection accessible only to membership.

★6306★
INTERNATIONAL THOMSON EDUCATIONAL PUBLISHING, INC. - EDITORIAL LIBRARY (Publ)
135 W. 50th St.   Phone: (212) 265-8700
New York, NY 10020   David Brown
Staff: Prof 1. **Subjects:** Education, history, science. **Holdings:** 5000 books. **Subscriptions:** 159 journals and other serials. **Services:** Interlibrary loans; copying; library open to public by appointment.

INTERNATIONAL TROMBONE ASSOCIATION RESOURCE LIBRARY
See: University of Arizona - Music Collection

★6307★
INTERNATIONAL TSUNAMI INFORMATION CENTER (Sci-Tech)
Box 50027   Phone: (808) 546-2847
Honolulu, HI 96850   Dr. George Pararas-Carayannis, Dir.
Founded: 1964. **Staff:** Prof 2; Other 3. **Subjects:** Tsunamis, earthquakes, oceanography. **Holdings:** 2000 volumes; 10 microforms, magnetic tapes. **Subscriptions:** 200 journals and other serials. **Services:** Interlibrary loans; copying; SDI; library open to public. **Publications:** International Tsunami Information Center Newsletter, quarterly; Tsunami Reports, annual; Director's Report, semiannual. **Remarks:** The center is maintained as a joint research collection by UNESCO-IOC member states which participate in the International Tsunami Warning System in the Pacific.

★6308★
THE INTERNATIONAL UNIVERSITY - INTERNATIONAL RELATIONS LIBRARY AND RESEARCH CENTER (Soc Sci)
1301 S. Noland Rd.   Phone: (816) 931-6374
Independence, MO 64055   Kathleen Thompson, Dir.
Founded: 1973. **Staff:** Prof 1; Other 2. **Subjects:** European studies, Latin American studies, international education, world community. **Special Collections:** Hibernian Collection (155 volumes). **Holdings:** 5120 books; 130 bound periodical volumes; 265 pamphlets (cataloged); 415 photocopies of documents; 3500 clippings; 16 dissertations. **Subscriptions:** 18 journals and other serials. **Services:** Library open to public with prior approval. **Also Known As:** TIU.

★6309★
INTERNATIONAL VISITORS INFORMATION SERVICE
801 19th St., N.W.   Phone: (202) 872-8747
Washington, DC 20006   Marianne H. Cruze, Exec.Dir.
Subjects: Foreign visitors. **Holdings:** Figures not available. **Staff:** Lisa S. Smith, Coord. of Vols.

INTERNATIONAL WOMEN'S HISTORY ARCHIVE
See: Women's History Research Center, Inc. - Women's History Library

★6310★
INTERNORTH - LAW LIBRARY (Law)†
2223 Dodge St.   Phone: (402) 633-4000
Omaha, NE 68102   Janet Geist, Libn.
Subjects: Law. **Holdings:** 3000 volumes. **Services:** Library open to public for reference use only.

★6311★
INTERNORTH - TECHNICAL INFORMATION CENTER (Energy)
2223 Dodge St.   Phone: (402) 633-4298
Omaha, NE 68102   Marvin E. Lauver, Hd.Libn.
Founded: 1959. **Staff:** Prof 2; Other 2. **Subjects:** Petroleum engineering, gas industry, public utilities, marketing, fuel and energy studies, area development, chemical engineering, synthetic fuels, coal and coal gasification. **Special Collections:** Early history of the gas industry. **Holdings:** 30,000 books; 10,000 bound periodical volumes; 380 slides; 125 VF drawers of keydexed reports; 20 reels of microfilm; 1200 reports on microfiche. **Subscriptions:** 400 journals and other serials; 8 newspapers. **Services:** Interlibrary loans; library open to public by appointment. **Computerized Information Services:** SDC, DIALOG; computerized acquisitions and serials. **Staff:** Ruby Mathison, Asst.Libn.

INTERSTATE COMMERCE COMMISSION
See: U.S. Interstate Commerce Commission

★6312★
INTERSTATE OIL AND GAS COMPACT COMMISSION - LIBRARY (Env-Cons; Energy)
900 N.E. 23rd St.
Box 53127
Oklahoma City, OK 73152   Phone: (405) 525-3556
                                     W. Timothy Dowd, Exec.Dir.
Subjects: Conservation of oil and gas. **Holdings:** 80 VF drawers; 10,000 file cards. **Subscriptions:** 50 journals and other serials.

★6313★
INTERTECHNOLOGY/SOLAR CORPORATION - LIBRARY (Energy)†
100 Main St.   Phone: (703) 347-7900
Warrenton, VA 22186   Sherry L. Crocker, Libn.
Founded: 1975. **Staff:** Prof 1. **Subjects:** Solar and alternate forms of energy. **Holdings:** 1300 books; 15 bound periodical volumes; 3000 documents. **Subscriptions:** 30 journals and other serials. **Services:** Interlibrary loans; copying; library not open to public.

INUVIK SCIENTIFIC RESOURCE CENTRE
See: Canada - Indian & Northern Affairs Canada

★6314★
INVENTORS CLUBS OF AMERICA - INVENTORS REFERENCE CENTER (Sci-Tech; Env-Cons)
121 Chestnut St.   Phone: (413) 737-0670
Springfield, MA 01103   Alexander T. Marinaccio, Supv., Lib./Tech.Serv.
Founded: 1970. **Staff:** Prof 1. **Subjects:** Inventions, solar and hydrogen technology, air and water purification, patent information. **Special Collections:** Solar Home Building Plans. **Holdings:** 350 books and bound periodical volumes; 200 technical reports. **Services:** Copying; library open to public with restrictions. **Publications:** Inventors News.

★6315★
INVESTIGATIVE REPORTERS AND EDITORS, INC. - PAUL WILLIAMS MEMORIAL RESOURCE CENTER (Publ)
Box 838
Columbia, MO 65205   Phone: (314) 882-2024
                                     John Ullmann, Exec.Dir.
Founded: 1969. **Staff:** 2. **Subjects:** Investigative reports in the U.S. and Canada published in newspapers and magazines or broadcast on radio and television. **Holdings:** 50 books; 1500 newspaper, magazine or broadcast clips. **Services:** Copying; library open to public with restrictions. **Remarks:** Center is associated with the Freedom of Information Center at the University of Missouri, Columbia.

★6316★
INVESTMENT COMPANY INSTITUTE - LIBRARY (Bus-Fin; Law)
1775 K St., N.W.   Phone: (202) 293-7700
Washington, DC 20006   Cut Parker, Libn.
Founded: 1970. **Staff:** Prof 1. **Subjects:** Investment, mutual funds, banking laws and regulations, economics. **Special Collections:** Investment materials; U.S. Securities & Exchange Commission No Action Letters (1971 to present). **Holdings:** 380 books; 200 bound periodical volumes; 150 other cataloged items; ICI historical data and publications. **Subscriptions:** 115 journals and other serials; 5 newspapers. **Services:** Copying; library open to public. **Publications:** Mutual Funds Forum, quarterly - by subscription.

★6317★
INVESTORS DIVERSIFIED SERVICES, INC. - INVESTMENT LIBRARY (Bus-Fin)†
IDS Tower   Phone: (612) 372-3429
Minneapolis, MN 55402   Mel Kirkpatrick, Libn.
Subjects: Investments. **Holdings:** 300 titles; corporation files on 3500 companies. **Services:** Library open to public for reference use only by appointment. **Computerized Information Services:** Dow Jones News Retrieval.

★6318★
INVISIBLE MINISTRY - LIBRARY (Rel-Theol)
Box 37   Phone: (714) 746-9430
San Marcos, CA 92069   A. Stuart Otto, Dir.
Staff: 3. **Subjects:** Religion, philosophy, metaphysics, science. **Holdings:** 500 books; 500 bound periodical volumes; 250 cassettes and other recordings. **Services:** Library open by appointment only. **Publications:** Tidings, bimonthly; Theologia 21, quarterly; Master Thoughts, weekly. All publications are distributed by mail. **Special Catalogs:** List of items available upon request. **Remarks:** Invisible Ministry is a California nonprofit religious corporation. It includes a publishing subsidiary, The Dominion Press.

★6319★
INYO COUNTY LAW LIBRARY (Law)†
168 N. Edwards
Drawer K
Independence, CA 93526   Phone: (714) 878-2411
Subjects: Law. **Holdings:** 2800 volumes. **Services:** Copying; library open to public.

INYO NATL. FOREST
See: U.S. Forest Service

ION KINETICS AND ENERGETICS DATA CENTER
See: U.S. Natl. Bureau of Standards

ION PHYSICS CORPORATION
See: High Voltage Engineering Corporation

★6320★
IONICS, INC. - RESEARCH DEPARTMENT LIBRARY (Sci-Tech)
65 Grove St.   Phone: (617) 926-2500
Watertown, MA 02172   Lorraine C. Baron, Libn.
Staff: Prof 1. **Subjects:** Ion exchange membranes, electrodialysis, electrochemistry, membrane processes. **Holdings:** Figures not available. **Subscriptions:** 149 journals and other serials. **Services:** Interlibrary loans; copying; library not open to public. **Computerized Information Services:** DIALOG.

★6321★
IOWA BEEF PROCESSORS, INC. - CORPORATE LIBRARY (Food-Bev)
Box 515   Phone: (402) 494-2061
Dakota City, NE 68731   Jane R. Reiling, Mgr., Printed Commun.
Founded: 1976. **Staff:** Prof 1; Other 3. **Subjects:** Meat industry and science, management, business. **Holdings:** 1600 books; 250 government and research reports; 10 drawers of clippings; 7 drawers of annual reports. **Subscriptions:** 400 journals and other serials; 6 newspapers. **Services:** Copying; SDI; library open to public by appointment. **Computerized Information Services:** DIALOG.

IOWA DRUG INFORMATION SERVICE
See: University of Iowa - College of Pharmacy

★6322★
IOWA GENEALOGICAL SOCIETY - LIBRARY (Hist)
6000 Douglas, Box 3815   Phone: (515) 276-0287
Des Moines, IA 50322   Carl W. Nissly, Pres.
Founded: 1966. **Subjects:** Genealogy, local history. **Special Collections:** Pioneer Certificate Collection; Iowa census records. **Holdings:** Figures not available. **Services:** Copying; library open to non-members for a fee. **Publications:** Hawkeye Heritage and newsletter, quarterly. **Special Indexes:** Surname index.

★6323★
IOWA GEOLOGICAL SURVEY - I.G.S. LIBRARY SERVICES
123 N. Capitol St.
Iowa City, IA 52242
Defunct. Holdings absorbed by University of Iowa - Geology Library.

IOWA HISTORICAL LIBRARY
See: Iowa State Department of History and Archives

★6324★
IOWA HOSPITAL ASSOCIATION - LIBRARY (Med)
600 5th Ave. Plaza.   Phone: (515) 288-1955
Des Moines, IA 50309   Deborah Van Egdom, Dir., Lib.Serv.
Founded: 1974. **Staff:** Prof 1. **Subjects:** Hospital administration, nursing, inservice training and education, standards and regulations. **Holdings:** 1300 books; 400 audiovisual items; 6 lateral file drawers of pamphlet material, education material, publications and bibliographies. **Subscriptions:** 150 journals and other serials. **Services:** Interlibrary loans; copying; literature searching; library open to public for reference use only. **Networks/Consortia:** Member of Polk County Biomedical Consortium.

★6325★
IOWA LAW ENFORCEMENT ACADEMY - LIBRARY (Soc Sci)
Camp Dodge
Box 130   Phone: (515) 278-9357
Johnston, IA 50131   Nancy O'Brien, Libn.
Founded: 1976. **Staff:** Prof 1. **Subjects:** Police, law enforcement, criminal justice, criminal law. **Holdings:** 2200 books; 500 documents and training materials; 321 films and slide programs; 3 VF drawers of clippings. **Subscriptions:** 57 journals and other serials. **Services:** Interlibrary loans; copying; SDI; library open to Iowa law enforcement personnel and to the public with permission. **Special Catalogs:** Film catalog (booklet).

★6326★
IOWA LUTHERAN HOSPITAL - DEPARTMENT OF LIBRARY SERVICES (Med)
University at Penn   Phone: (515) 263-5181
Des Moines, IA 50316   Wayne A. Pedersen, Dir. of Lib.Serv.
Founded: 1980. **Staff:** Prof 1; Other 1. **Subjects:** Medicine, nursing, health care administration. **Holdings:** 2453 books; 50 bound periodical volumes; 10 16mm films; 144 video cassettes; 387 audiotapes; 25 slide-tape kits; 1 VF drawer of pamphlets. **Subscriptions:** 138 journals and other serials. **Services:** Interlibrary loans; copying; SDI; library open to public for reference use only. **Computerized Information Services:** MEDLARS. **Networks/Consortia:** Member of Polk County Biomedical Consortium; Regional Medical Library - Region 3. **Publications:** Bibliophilia, bimonthly - for internal distribution only. **Special Indexes:** Uniterm index card system for indexing articles used by the Family Practice Residency Program; KWOC card index for Network for Continuing Medical Education (NCME) tapes. **Remarks:** Contains the holdings of the administrative and nursing libraries.

IOWA MASONIC LIBRARY
See: Grand Lodge of Iowa, A.F. and A.M.

★6327★
IOWA METHODIST MEDICAL CENTER - OLIVER J. FAY MEMORIAL LIBRARY (Med)
1200 Pleasant St.   Phone: (515) 283-6490
Des Moines, IA 50308   Mary Wegner, Dir., Med.Lib.
Founded: 1940. **Staff:** Prof 1; Other 1. **Subjects:** Medicine and allied sciences. **Holdings:** 3200 books; 3000 bound periodical volumes; 200 pamphlets and reprints; 1150 cassette tapes. **Subscriptions:** 250 journals and other serials. **Services:** Interlibrary loans; copying; library open to public with restrictions and to all health professionals engaged in medical research. **Computerized Information Services:** MEDLARS, BRS, DIALOG. **Networks/Consortia:** Member of Polk County Biomedical Consortium; Regional Medical Library - Region 3.

★6328★
IOWA METHODIST SCHOOL OF NURSING - MARJORIE GERTRUDE MORROW LIBRARY (Med)
1117 Pleasant St.   Phone: (515) 283-6453
Des Moines, IA 50309   Patricia Downey, Libn.
Founded: 1901. **Staff:** Prof 1; Other 1. **Subjects:** Nursing. **Holdings:** 5363 books; 295 bound periodical volumes; 12 VF drawers of clippings, brochures, pamphlets; 210 AV software items. **Subscriptions:** 147 journals and other serials. **Services:** Interlibrary loans (limited); library open to public for reference use only. **Networks/Consortia:** Member of Polk County Biomedical Consortium.

★6329★
IOWA STATE COMMISSION FOR THE BLIND - LIBRARY FOR THE BLIND & PHYSICALLY HANDICAPPED (Aud-Vis)
4th & Keosauqua Way   Phone: (515) 283-2601
Des Moines, IA 50309   Sine Olesen, Libn.
Founded: 1960. **Staff:** Prof 6; Other 24. **Holdings:** 93,000 braille books; 341 tapes; 75,000 cassettes; 111,000 talking books; 5200 large type books; 5100 print reference books. **Services:** Interlibrary loans; copying; library open to public. **Networks/Consortia:** Member of U.S. National Library Service for the Blind & Physically Handicapped (NLS). **Publications:** The Iowa Transcriber, annual - distributed to volunteer transcribers. **Special Catalogs:** Book lists. **Staff:** Jimmy Burns, Libn.; Karen Paloma, Libn.; Lorraine Rovig, Libn.; Elizabeth Sheets, Libn.; Carol Eckey, Libn.

★6330★
IOWA STATE DEPARTMENT OF ENVIRONMENTAL QUALITY - TECHNICAL LIBRARY (Env-Cons)
Henry A. Wallace Bldg.   Phone: (515) 281-8899
Des Moines, IA 50319   Cecilia Nelson, Rec.Ck.
Founded: 1973. **Staff:** 3. **Subjects:** Air and water quality, solid wastes, chemical technology, radiation, administration. **Holdings:** 1666 books; publications of Environmental Protection Agency. **Subscriptions:** 26 journals and other serials. **Services:** Library open to public for reference use only. **Staff:** Jim Combs, Chf./Off.Serv.Sect.; Laura Stephenson, Off.Serv.Supv.

★6331★
IOWA STATE DEPARTMENT OF HEALTH - FILM LIBRARY (Med)
State Historical Bldg.   Phone: (515) 281-4316
Des Moines, IA 50319   Eileen C. Devine, Dir.
Founded: 1950. **Staff:** Prof 1. **Subjects:** Human body, health, sex education, alcoholism, aging, nutrition, maternal and child health. **Holdings:** 510 16mm films (cataloged). **Services:** Interlibrary loans; library open to Iowa residents with restrictions. **Publications:** Catalog, annual update. **Remarks:** This special collection has been integrated into the State Library Commission public library film collection but has separate loan policies. Some of the films have been placed with Planned Parenthood of Iowa.

★6332★
IOWA STATE DEPARTMENT OF HEALTH - STATISTICAL SERVICES (Soc Sci)
Lucas State Office Bldg.   Phone: (515) 281-4945
Des Moines, IA 50319   Carson E. Whitlow, Dir.
Subjects: Vital statistics (general); statistical tabulations - Iowa births, marriages, divorces, deaths; health manpower statistics; statistical tabulations - location of Iowa dentists, dental hygienists, chiropractors, optometrists, physical therapists, physicians, podiatrists, nursing home administrators. **Services:** Center not open to public. **Computerized Information Services:** Mechanized retrieval. **Publications:** Annual Statistical Supplement to the Biennial Report of the Iowa State Department of Health - distributed to agencies and individuals indicating sustained interest; exchange upon request. **Remarks:** Unit is primarily a distributive center for data accumulated as an adjunct to a government registration unit. Services provided are basically the provision of tabulated distributions, incidental consultation and assistance.

★6333★
IOWA STATE DEPARTMENT OF HISTORY AND ARCHIVES - IOWA HISTORICAL LIBRARY (Hist)
E. 12th & Grand Ave.
Historical Bldg.   Phone: (515) 281-5472
Des Moines, IA 50319   Lowell R. Wilbur, Libn.
Staff: Prof 1; Other 2. **Subjects:** History - Iowa, Midwest, American; genealogy. **Special Collections:** Manuscript collections - Grenville Dodge, Charles Mason, Albert Cummins, William Boyd Allison, John A. Kasson and others; Aldrich Autograph Collection. **Holdings:** 62,000 volumes. **Subscriptions:** 160 journals and other serials. **Services:** Copying; library open to public. **Staff:** Phyllis McLaughlin, Mss.Div.; Virginia Dochterman .

★6334★

IOWA STATE DEPARTMENT OF PUBLIC INSTRUCTION - RESOURCE CENTER (Educ)
Grimes State Office Bldg.
Des Moines, IA 50319
Phone: (515) 281-3770
Lydia B. Thomas, Libn.
Founded: 1967. **Staff:** Prof 1; Other 2. **Subjects:** Education. **Special Collections:** ERIC documents. **Holdings:** 4100 books; 180 VF drawers of curriculum and educational materials; 6900 textbooks; trade books; 10 VF drawers of bibliographies. **Subscriptions:** 441 journals and other serials. **Services:** Interlibrary loans; copying; library open to public with restrictions. **Computerized Information Services:** DIALOG. **Networks/Consortia:** Member of State Agency Library Association (SALA).

★6335★

IOWA STATE DEPARTMENT OF SOCIAL SERVICES - LIBRARY (Soc Sci)
Hoover Bldg.
Des Moines, IA 50319
Phone: (515) 281-5925
Kay M. Elliott, Chf.Libn.
Founded: 1968. **Staff:** Prof 2; Other 2. **Subjects:** Social casework, public assistance, mental health and retardation, corrections, child abuse. **Holdings:** 7400 books; 100 bound periodical volumes; vertical file (1250 items); 360 AV materials. **Subscriptions:** 127 journals and other serials. **Services:** Interlibrary loans; copying; SDI; library open to public. **Publications:** New Books, monthly - for internal distribution only. **Staff:** Lila Feitler, Ref.Libn.; Robert C. Ferrier, AV Spec.

★6336★

IOWA STATE DEPARTMENT OF TRANSPORTATION - LIBRARY (Trans)
800 Lincoln Way
Ames, IA 50010
Phone: (515) 296-1200
Josephine Said, Libn.
Staff: Prof 2; Other 1. **Subjects:** Highways and transportation, road construction and materials, aeronautics, public transit, motor vehicle, railroads, rivers. **Special Collections:** Historic roads and trail files of Iowa (80 folders). **Holdings:** 8000 books; 346 bound periodical volumes. **Subscriptions:** 220 journals and other serials. **Services:** Interlibrary loans; copying; library open to public for reference use only. **Computerized Information Services:** DIALOG, BRS, SDC. **Publications:** Library Bulletin, semimonthly - for internal distribution only. **Staff:** Hank Zaletel, Ref.Libn.

IOWA STATE HISTORICAL SOCIETY
See: State Historical Society of Iowa

★6337★

IOWA STATE LAW LIBRARY (Law)
State House
Des Moines, IA 50319
Phone: (515) 281-5125
James H. Gritton, Law Libn.
Founded: 1838. **Staff:** Prof 1; Other 7. **Subjects:** Law. **Special Collections:** Iowa law. **Holdings:** 127,600 books; 11,000 bound periodical volumes; 56,400 documents (cataloged); 56 VF drawers of Iowa House and Senate bills. **Subscriptions:** 400 journals and other serials. **Services:** Library open to public for reference use only. **Staff:** Richard Schulze, Lib.Assoc.

★6338★

IOWA STATE LEGISLATIVE SERVICE BUREAU - LIBRARY (Soc Sci)
State House
Des Moines, IA 50319
Phone: (515) 281-3312
Serge H. Garrison, Bur.Dir.
Founded: 1962. **Staff:** Prof 1; Other 1. **Subjects:** Studies of other states; legislation introduced and enacted in Iowa. **Holdings:** 100 books; 100 bound periodical volumes; 7000 publications and documents (cataloged). **Subscriptions:** 20 journals and other serials. **Services:** Interlibrary loans; copying (limited); library open to public with restrictions. **Staff:** Ruth D. McGhee, Libn.

★6339★

IOWA STATE LIBRARY COMMISSION (Info Sci)
E. 12th & Grand
Des Moines, IA 50319
Phone: (515) 281-4103
Barry L. Porter, State Libn.
Staff: Prof 13; Other 23. **Subjects:** Management, corrections, budgeting, state government, library science. **Special Collections:** Iowa Collection; State Documents Archival Collection; Federal Documents Depository. **Holdings:** 93,669 books; 8 cabinets of vertical files about Iowa; 925 reels of microfilm; 156,337 microfiche. **Subscriptions:** 783 journals and other serials. **Services:** Interlibrary loans; copying; SDI; library open to public. **Computerized Information Services:** DIALOG, SDC, BRS, New York Times Information Service. **Networks/Consortia:** Member of Bibliographical Center for Research, Rocky Mountain Region, Inc. (BCR). **Publications:** Footnotes, monthly - to public libraries. **Staff:** Jack Hurkett, Asst.Dir.; Diane K. Johnson, Dir., Info.Serv.

★6340★

IOWA STATE MEDICAL LIBRARY (Med)†
Historical Bldg.
E. 12th & Grand Ave.
Des Moines, IA 50319
Phone: (515) 281-5772
Pamela Clark Rees, Dir.
Founded: 1919. **Staff:** Prof 1; Other 4. **Subjects:** Medicine, dentistry, nursing. **Special Collections:** Medical history. **Holdings:** 95,000 books and bound periodical volumes. **Subscriptions:** 600 journals and other serials. **Services:** Interlibrary loans (fee); copying; library open to public. **Computerized Information Services:** DIALOG, SDC, BRS; computerized cataloging. **Networks/Consortia:** Member of Regional Medical Library - Region 3; Polk County Biomedical Consortium. **Publications:** Serials lists. **Remarks:** Maintained by the State Library Commission of Iowa.

IOWA STATE MENTAL HEALTH INSTITUTE - CLARINDA MENTAL HEALTH INSTITUTION
See: Clarinda Mental Health Institution

IOWA STATE UNIVERSITY - AMES LABORATORY
See: Ames Laboratory

★6341★

IOWA STATE UNIVERSITY - ENERGY AND MINERAL RESOURCES RESEARCH INSTITUTE - RARE-EARTH INFORMATION CENTER (Sci-Tech)
Ames, IA 50011
Phone: (515) 294-2272
Karl A. Gschneidner, Jr., Dir.
Founded: 1966. **Staff:** Prof 2; Other 1. **Subjects:** Rare earth, metals, alloys and compounds; physical metallurgy; solid state physics; analytical, inorganic and physical chemistry; toxicity; technology; geochemistry; ceramics. **Holdings:** 16,350 books and bound periodical volumes; 2000 reports; 4000 abstracts. **Services:** Copying; inquiries, referrals, surveys and in-depth analyses, all on a fee basis; center open to public with prior notice. **Computerized Information Services:** Computer retrieval system. **Publications:** RIC Newsletter, quarterly - free to subscribers; Reviews, irregular - free. **Staff:** J.M. Capellen, Asst.Chem.II.

★6342★

IOWA STATE UNIVERSITY - LIBRARY - SPECIAL COLLECTIONS (Env-Cons; Hist)
Ames, IA 50011
Phone: (515) 294-1442
Stanley M. Yates, Spec.Coll.
Founded: 1870. **Special Collections:** Regional history; soil conservation; labor relations; The American Archives of the Factual Film (9500 documentary films); U.S. Government documents (180,000); aerial photographs (22,000). **Holdings:** Figures not available. **Services:** Interlibrary loans; copying; SDI; library open to public for reference use only. **Computerized Information Services:** BRS, DIALOG, SDC; computerized circulation. **Networks/Consortia:** Member of CRL; MIDLNET; Iowa Library Information Teletype Exchange (ILITE).

★6343★

IOWA STATE UNIVERSITY - VETERINARY MEDICAL LIBRARY (Med)
Ames, IA 50011
Phone: (515) 294-2225
Sara Peterson, Hd.Libn.
Staff: Prof 1; Other 3. **Subjects:** Veterinary and comparative medicine, anatomy, biomedical engineering, physiology, toxicology, clinical sciences, microbiology, preventive medicine, pathology, pharmacology. **Special Collections:** German theses (2300). **Holdings:** 12,769 books; 10,624 bound periodical volumes. **Subscriptions:** 626 journals and other serials. **Services:** Copying; library open to public for reference use only. **Computerized Information Services:** BRS, DIALOG, SDC, MEDLARS. **Networks/Consortia:** Member of Regional Medical Library - Region 3; Polk County Biomedical Consortium.

IOWA URBAN COMMUNITY RESEARCH CENTER
See: University of Iowa

IPC
See: Penton/IPC

IRA
See: International Reading Association

★6344★

IRELAND CONSULATE GENERAL - LIBRARY (Area-Ethnic)†
580 Fifth Ave.
New York, NY 10036
Phone: (212) 382-2525
Hon. Sean Oh'Uiginn, Consul Gen.
Subjects: Economic, social, political, and cultural information on Ireland. **Services:** Library open to public.

IRELAND (John) MEMORIAL LIBRARY
See: St. Paul Seminary - John Ireland Memorial Library

★6345★
IRELL & MANELLA - LIBRARY (Law)
1800 Ave. of the Stars, Suite 900
Los Angeles, CA 90067
Phone: (213) 277-1010
Louise Laughlin Lieb, Lib.Adm.
Staff: Prof 5; Other 4. **Subjects:** Law - civil, tax, corporate, entertainment, antitrust, labor; federal and state litigation; real estate. **Special Collections:** Tender and exchange offer files; Federal Trade Commission publications, 1979 to present. **Holdings:** 30,000 volumes; microfiche, videotapes, audiotapes, internal documents. **Subscriptions:** 465 journals and other serials; 25 newspapers. **Services:** Interlibrary loans; copying; SDI; library not open to public. **Computerized Information Services:** LEXIS; computerized serials. **Publications:** Newsletter. **Special Indexes:** Legal memo/opinion letter index; legal forms indexes and catalogs. MaryAnn Cappa-Rotunno, Supv., Tech.Proc.; Gabrielle Martin, Supv., Internal Doc.; Lee Nemchek, Asst.Libn.; Denise Grigst, Doc.Anl.

★6346★
IRI RESEARCH INSTITUTE, INC. - LIBRARY (Agri)†
One Rockefeller Plaza, Rm. 1401
New York, NY 10020
Phone: (212) 581-1942
Founded: 1950. **Staff:** Prof 4. **Subjects:** Agricultural research, animal nutrition, food technology, soil science. **Holdings:** 1000 books. **Subscriptions:** 150 journals and other serials; 10 newspapers. **Services:** Library open to public upon written request. **Publications:** IRI Research Institute Bulletin series published upon development of significant research findings.

★6347★
IRISH-AMERICAN CULTURAL ASSOCIATION - LIBRARY (Hum)
10415 S. Western
Chicago, IL 60643
Phone: (312) 239-6760
Cynthia L. Buescher, Libn.
Founded: 1974. **Staff:** Prof 3; Other 5. **Subjects:** Literature, history, biography, art, music. **Holdings:** 3000 books. **Services:** Copying; library not open to public. **Staff:** Richard T. Crowe, Dir.; Thomas R. McCarthy, Asst.Dir.

★6348★
IRISH FAMILY HISTORY SOCIETY - LIBRARY (Hist; Area-Ethnic)
173 Tremont St.
Newton, MA 02158
Phone: (617) 965-0939
Joseph M. Glynn, Jr., Dir./Libn.
Staff: Prof 1. **Subjects:** Ireland - genealogy, history, heraldry. **Special Collections:** Lewis's Topographical Dictionary of Ireland. **Holdings:** 200 volumes; 80 tapes on Irish genealogy; maps. **Services:** Library open to public by appointment. **Publications:** Newsletter, quarterly. **Special Indexes:** Surname index of members; Irish Family History Index (card).

★6349★
IRON COUNTY MUSEUM - ARCHIVES (Hist)
Box 272
Caspian, MI 49915
Phone: (906) 265-3942
Marcia Bernhardt, Exhibits Coord.
Founded: 1970. **Staff:** 1. **Subjects:** Local history, lumbering, mining. **Special Collections:** Letters of Carrie Jacobs Bond; manuscript of Iron County by Jack Hill; manuscript of Iron Country (Class of 44, paperback title) by Mary Jane Patterson. **Holdings:** 200 books; 300 other cataloged items; 3200 underground mining maps; 3200 photographs; 20,000 obituaries. **Services:** Archives open to researchers by request. **Publications:** Past-Present Prints, annual - free upon request; list of publications - available on request. **Remarks:** Maintained by Iron County Historical and Museum Society. The winter address for the archives is 233 Bernhardt Rd., Iron River, MI 49935.

★6350★
IRON RANGE RESEARCH CENTER (Hist)
Box 392
Chisholm, MN 55719
Phone: (218) 254-5733
Elizabeth Bright, Libn.
Founded: 1980. **Staff:** Prof 3; Other 2. **Subjects:** Mining, iron range history, ethnology, genealogy, labor history, peat resources, mineland reclamation. **Special Collections:** Peat Resource Reports; IRRRB administrative records; Hibbing Finnish Temperance Union records; Carl Pederson Photograph Collection; Jones & Laughlin Hill Annex Mining Operation Records; Chisholm School Superintendents' papers, 1903-1943; municipal court records for eight Iron Range cities, 1888-1973. **Holdings:** 600 books; 300 oral history tapes; 1350 reels of microfilm; 200 linear feet of public documents; manuscripts; maps; films; clippings; photographs. **Subscriptions:** 98 journals and other serials; 20 newspapers. **Services:** Interlibrary loans; copying; center open to public. **Networks/Consortia:** Member of OCLC; North Country Library Cooperative; MINITEX. **Special Catalogs:** Accession and inventory list of archives and manuscripts. **Remarks:** Maintained by the Minnesota State

Iron Range Resources & Rehabilitation Board. **Staff:** Edward Nelson, Archv.

★6351★
IROQUOIS COUNTY GENEALOGICAL SOCIETY - LIBRARY (Hist)
103 W. Cherry St.
Watseka, IL 60970
Roxanne Frey, Libn.
Founded: 1970. **Staff:** 1. **Subjects:** Local history. **Holdings:** 300 books; 250 county records; 300 reels of microfilm of census reports and newspapers; 25 family Bibles; 100 volumes of school reports; 25 VF drawers of historical pamphlets and leaflets of local interest. **Subscriptions:** 35 journals and other serials. **Services:** Copying; library open to public. **Publications:** Iroquois Stalker, quarterly - distributed to the membership. **Special Catalogs:** Catalog of local county records (card).

IRS
See: U.S. Internal Revenue Service

★6352★
IRVING TRUST COMPANY - BUSINESS LIBRARY (Bus-Fin)
One Wall St.
New York, NY 10015
Phone: (212) 487-6431
Susan Stewart, Asst.Sec./Hd.Libn.
Founded: 1920. **Staff:** Prof 2; Other 3. **Subjects:** Banking, economics, finance. **Holdings:** 4500 books; 2100 bound periodical volumes; 70 VF drawers; 930 reels of microfilm. **Subscriptions:** 142 journals and other serials. **Services:** Interlibrary loans; library open to public with restrictions.

IRWIN ARMY HOSPITAL
See: U.S. Army Hospitals

IRWIN (Forrest A.) LIBRARY
See: Jersey City State College - Forrest A. Irwin Library

IRWIN (Fred) MEDICAL LIBRARY
See: Hilo Hospital - Fred Irwin Medical Library

IRWIN LIBRARY
See: Butler University

★6353★
IRWIN MANAGEMENT COMPANY, INC. - LIBRARY (Bus-Fin)†
235 Washington St.
Columbus, IN 47201
Phone: (812) 376-3331
Shirley Brown, Libn.
Founded: 1964. **Subjects:** Business, finance, economics, philanthropy, education, urban affairs, architecture, Indiana. **Holdings:** 3500 books; 2000 bound periodical volumes; 2000 unbound periodicals and government serials (cataloged); 200 VF drawers of Company files and archives; 300 reels of microfilm; tapes; cassettes. **Services:** Library open to public by referral.

★6354★
ISHAM, LINCOLN & BEALE - LIBRARY (Law)
3 First National Plaza
Chicago, IL 60602
Phone: (312) 558-7488
Margaret Lundahl, Libn.
Staff: Prof 1; Other 3. **Subjects:** Law. **Holdings:** 20,000 books; 20 bound periodical volumes; 1500 microfiche; 1200 unbound periodicals. **Subscriptions:** 500 journals and other serials; 10 newspapers. **Services:** Interlibrary loans; copying; library open to public with permission of librarian. **Computerized Information Services:** Online systems; computerized cataloging. **Networks/Consortia:** Member of OCLC through ILLINET; Chicago Library System.

ISHAM MEMORIAL LIBRARY
See: Harvard University - Eda Kuhn Loeb Music Library

★6355★
ISI CORPORATION - RESEARCH LIBRARY (Bus-Fin)
Box 23330
Oakland, CA 94623
Phone: (415) 832-1400
Lynn Krekemeyer, Libn.
Staff: 1. **Subjects:** Business and economics. **Holdings:** 500 books; 40 bound periodical volumes. **Subscriptions:** 150 journals and other serials; 10 newspapers. **Services:** Library not open to public.

★6356★
ISLANDS RESEARCH FOUNDATION, INC. - INFORMATION CENTER*
108 Prospect Tower
45 Tudor City Pl.
New York, NY 10017
Founded: 1944. **Subjects:** Islandography, oceanography, archeology. **Special Collections:** Information on all named islands of the world. **Holdings:** 2000 books; maps, charts, regional directories, navigational data. **Remarks:**

Presently inactive.

★6357★

ISOCHEM RESINS COMPANY - TECHNICAL INFORMATION CENTER (Sci-Tech)
99 Cook St.
Lincoln, RI 02865
Phone: (401) 723-2100
Herman C. Selya, Pres.
Staff: Prof 2. **Subjects:** Adhesives, polyesters, silicones, epoxies, conductives. **Holdings:** 500 books; 200 bound periodical volumes. **Subscriptions:** 20 journals and other serials. **Services:** Center not open to public. **Staff:** Robert P. Glovin, Sales Mgr.

★6358★

ISOTTA FRASCHINI OWNERS ASSOCIATION - RESEARCH LIBRARY (Rec)
35 Ligonier Dr., N.E.
North Fort Meyers, FL 33903
H.B. Willis, Dir.
Founded: 1954. **Subjects:** History and technical information pertaining to Isotta Fraschini automobiles. **Holdings:** Books, bound periodical volumes, photographs, advertisements, catalogs, and pamphlets. **Services:** Interlibrary loans; copying; material available by special request only.

ISRD
See: International Society for Rehabilitation of the Disabled/Rehabilitation International

★6359★

ITALIAN CULTURAL INSTITUTE - LIBRARY (Area-Ethnic)
686 Park Ave.
New York, NY 10021
Phone: (212) 879-4242
Dr. Maria A. Gargotta, Hd.Libn.
Founded: 1959. **Staff:** 6. **Subjects:** Italy and Italian culture. **Holdings:** 32,600 books; 103 VF drawers of clippings; 228 slide sets; 123 containers of photographs. **Subscriptions:** 100 journals and other serials. **Services:** Interlibrary loans; copying; library open to public with card required for borrowing privileges. **Remarks:** This is a cultural agency of the Italian Government. **Also Known As:** Instituto Italiano di Cultura.

★6360★

ITALIAN CULTURAL SERVICE - LIBRARY (Area-Ethnic)
1200 Dr. Penfield Ave.
Montreal, PQ, Canada H3A 1A9
Phone: (514) 849-3473
Dr. Guido Bistolfi, Dir.
Founded: 1962. **Staff:** Prof 1; Other 1. **Subjects:** Italian culture, including art, theatre, cinema, literature, history, philosophy, music, social sciences. **Holdings:** 8593 books. **Subscriptions:** 119 journals and other serials. **Services:** Interlibrary loans; library open to public. **Also Known As:** Instituto Italiano di Cultura.

★6361★

ITALIAN FAMILY HISTORY SOCIETY - LIBRARY (Area-Ethnic)
173 Tremont St.
Newton, MA 02158
Phone: (617) 965-0939
Joseph M. Glynn, Jr., Dir./Libn.
Staff: Prof 1. **Subjects:** Italy - genealogy, history, heraldry. **Holdings:** 25 volumes; 10 tapes of lectures on Italian genealogy. **Publications:** Manual for Italian Genealogy.

★6362★

ITEK CORPORATION - APPLIED TECHNOLOGY DIVISION - TECHNICAL LIBRARY (Sci-Tech)†
645 Almanor Ave.
Sunnyvale, CA 94086
Phone: (408) 732-2710
Doron A. Dula, Tech.Libn.
Founded: 1964. **Staff:** Prof 1; Other 1. **Subjects:** Electronics, millimeter wave technology, radar and electronic countermeasures. **Holdings:** 5000 books; 528 bound periodical volumes; 540 pamphlets and 4000 technical reports (cataloged); 772 microfilm cartridges of vendor catalogs; 450 microfilm cartridges of military specifications and standards; 8 VF drawers of instruction manuals. **Subscriptions:** 176 journals and other serials. **Services:** Interlibrary loans; copying; SDI (limited to employees); library not open to public. **Networks/Consortia:** Member of CIN; South Bay Area Reference Network.

★6363★

ITEK CORPORATION - OPTICAL SYSTEMS DIVISION - LIBRARY (Sci-Tech)
10 Maguire Rd.
Lexington, MA 02173
Phone: (617) 276-2643
Dorothy B. Cowe, Sr.Tech.Libn.
Staff: Prof 2; Other 1. **Subjects:** Optics, photography, optical coatings, engineering - mechanical, electrical. **Holdings:** 4000 books; 500 bound periodical volumes; 1700 Itek reports; documents. **Subscriptions:** 190 journals and other serials. **Services:** Interlibrary loans; copying; library open to public. **Computerized Information Services:** SDC. **Publications:** Document catalog. **Staff:** Mary Latham, Libn.

ITT AVIONICS/DEFENSE COMMUNICATIONS DIVISION
See: ITT Corporation

★6364★

ITT CONTINENTAL BAKING COMPANY - RESEARCH LABORATORIES LIBRARY (Food-Bev)
Halstead Ave.
Box 731
Rye, NY 10580
Phone: (914) 899-0380
Jocelyn Rosen, Supv., Tech.Info.Serv.
Founded: 1958. **Staff:** Prof 1; Other 1. **Subjects:** Cereal chemistry, food technology, food analysis, nutrition. **Holdings:** 2600 books; 300 bound periodical volumes; 10,000 patents; 12 VF drawers. **Subscriptions:** 125 journals and other serials. **Services:** Interlibrary loans; copying; library not open to public. **Computerized Information Services:** DIALOG, SDC. **Publications:** Library Bulletin, irregular - for internal distribution only.

★6365★

ITT CORPORATION - AEROSPACE/OPTICAL DIVISION - INFORMATION SERVICES CENTER (Sci-Tech)
3700 E. Pontiac St.
Box 3700
Fort Wayne, IN 46801
Phone: (219) 423-9636
Cheryl A. Womack, Info. Data Spec.
Founded: 1977. **Staff:** 1. **Subjects:** Electronics, communications. **Holdings:** 250 books and bound periodical volumes; 16 VF drawers of specifications and documents. **Subscriptions:** 26 journals and other serials. **Services:** Library open to employees only. **Computerized Information Services:** DIALOG, DTIC; internal database; computerized cataloging.

★6366★

ITT CORPORATION - GILFILLAN ENGINEERING LIBRARY (Sci-Tech)†
7821 Orion Ave.
Box 7713
Van Nuys, CA 91409
Phone: (213) 988-2600
Dawn N. Villere, Sr.Tech.Libn.
Staff: Prof 2. **Subjects:** Radars, electronics, electrical engineering, navigation/communication, microwaves/filters, optics. **Special Collections:** Radars. **Holdings:** 10,000 books; 20,000 bound periodical volumes; 30,000 documents; complete AD microfiche file and NASA microfiche file; latest microfilm of all military specifications. **Subscriptions:** 250 journals and other serials. **Services:** Interlibrary loans; library open to public with restrictions. **Computerized Information Services:** DIALOG; computerized acquisitions, serials and circulation. **Publications:** Library Accessions Listings, monthly; ITTG Current Contents. **Remarks:** This library includes the technical library of the Electro-Optical Products Division. **Staff:** Juanita Lopez, Asst.Libn.

★6367★

ITT CORPORATION - HEADQUARTERS LIBRARY (Bus-Fin)
320 Park Ave.
New York, NY 10022
Phone: (212) 752-6000
Margaret M. DeLorme, Mgr.
Founded: 1947. **Staff:** 3. **Subjects:** Telecommunications, public relations, business. **Holdings:** 1000 books. **Subscriptions:** 200 journals and other serials; 5 newspapers. **Services:** Interlibrary loans; library open to public by appointment.

★6368★

ITT CORPORATION - ITT AVIONICS/DEFENSE COMMUNICATIONS DIVISION - TECHNICAL LIBRARY (Sci-Tech)†
492 River Rd., Dept. 39212
Nutley, NJ 07110
Phone: (201) 284-2096
Stephanie Pawelek, Tech.Ck.
Staff: 2. **Subjects:** Electronics, navigation, physics, data processing, astronautics. **Holdings:** 10,000 volumes; 1000 technical reports; 103 microforms. **Subscriptions:** 296 journals and other serials. **Services:** Interlibrary loans; copying; library open to public upon application. **Publications:** Recent Accessions, irregular - for internal distribution only.

★6369★

ITT CORPORATION - LEGAL DEPARTMENT LIBRARY (Law)
320 Park Ave.
New York, NY 10022
Beryl White, Law Libn.
Subjects: Law. **Holdings:** 5628 volumes.

★6370★

ITT NORTH - LIBRARY (Sci-Tech)
Box 20345
Columbus, OH 43220
Phone: (614) 548-4301
Gerald M. Hay, Libn.
Staff: Prof 1. **Subjects:** Telecommunications, electronics, computers, business management. **Special Collections:** Standards and other company publications. **Holdings:** 3000 books; 120 bound periodical volumes; 175 proceedings of conferences and symposia; 200 engineering reports. **Subscriptions:** 225 journals and other serials. **Services:** Interlibrary loans;

copying; library open to public by appointment. **Computerized Information Services:** DIALOG.

★6371★
ITT RAYONIER, INC. - RESEARCH CENTER - LIBRARY (Sci-Tech)
409 E. Harvard St.   Phone: (206) 426-4461
Shelton, WA 98584   Patricia A. Tostevin, Libn.
Staff: Prof 1; Other 2. **Subjects:** Pulp and paper, natural products chemistry, forests and forestry, chemical engineering. **Holdings:** 8000 books; 9000 bound periodical volumes; 13,000 patents; 500 translations; 50 cassette tapes; reports on microfiche. **Subscriptions:** 250 journals and other serials. **Services:** Library not open to public. **Computerized Information Services:** DIALOG, SDC, CIS. **Networks/Consortia:** Member of CLASS; Pacific Northwest Bibliographic Center (PNBC). **Formerly:** Its Olympic Research Division.

★6372★
IULIU MANIU AMERICAN ROMANIAN RELIEF FOUNDATION - LIBRARY
17 E. 79th St.
Box 1151
New York, NY 10028
Defunct

IVEY (Stinceon) MEMORIAL LIBRARY
See: First Baptist Church - Stinceon Ivey Memorial Library

★6373★
IVIMEY (Muriel) LIBRARY (Med)†
329 E. 62nd St.   Phone: (212) 752-5267
New York, NY 10021   Eleanor Yachnes, M.D., Chm., Lib.Comm.
Founded: 1962. **Staff:** Prof 1; Other 1. **Subjects:** Psychoanalysis. **Holdings:** 4000 books; 500 bound periodical volumes. **Subscriptions:** 35 journals and other serials. **Services:** Library not open to public. **Remarks:** Library formed by three member organizations: Association for the Advancement of Psychoanalysis, Karen Horney Clinic, and American Institute for Psychoanalysis.

IVORYDALE TECHNICAL CENTER
See: Procter & Gamble Company

★6374★
IZAAK WALTON KILLAM HOSPITAL FOR CHILDREN - MEDICAL STAFF LIBRARY (Med)
5850 University Ave.   Phone: (902) 424-3055
Halifax, NS, Canada B3J 3G9   Hilda van Rooyen, Med.Libn.
Founded: 1970. **Staff:** 1. **Subjects:** Pediatrics and other medical specialties. **Holdings:** 1300 books; 2300 bound periodical volumes. **Subscriptions:** 130 journals and other serials. **Services:** Library not open to public.

J

★6375★

J-B PUBLISHING COMPANY - RESEARCH LIBRARY (Hist)
430 Ivy Ave.   Phone: (402) 826-3356
Crete, NE 68333   William F. Rapp, Libn.
Staff: 1. **Subjects:** Railway and postal history, industrial archaeology. **Holdings:** 600 books and bound periodical volumes; 4000 photographs. **Subscriptions:** 10 journals and other serials. **Services:** Copying; library open to public by appointment. **Publications:** The Bulletin, Railroad Station Historical Society, Railway History Monographs, Postal History U.S.A.

★6376★

J.P. STEVENS AND CO., INC. - TECHNICAL LIBRARY (Sci-Tech)
400 E. Stone Ave.
Box 2850
Greenville, SC 29602   Phone: (803) 239-4211
Dr. William F. Grubb, III, Mgr., Project Anl.
Founded: 1948. **Staff:** Prof 2. **Subjects:** Textiles, chemistry. **Holdings:** 4000 books; 1700 bound periodical volumes; 8 VF drawers of U.S. government reports; 8 VF drawers of pamphlets and clippings; 100 microfiche. **Subscriptions:** 153 journals and other serials. **Services:** Copying; library open to public with permission. **Computerized Information Services:** DIALOG, SDC, BRS, QUESTEL. **Formerly:** Located in Garfield, NJ. **Staff:** Teresa M. Jaworski, Libn.

★6377★

JACK LONDON RESEARCH CENTER AND LIBRARY (Hum)
14300 Arnold Dr.
Box 337
Glen Ellen, CA 95442   Phone: (707) 996-2888
Winifred Kingman, Libn.
Staff: Prof 1. **Subjects:** Jack London. **Special Collections:** Jack London and early San Francisco Bay Area writers. **Holdings:** 500 books; 50 bound periodical volumes; 500 manuscripts and articles by Jack London; 750 pamphlets and dissertations; 35,000 file cards; 20,000 microforms and AV items. **Subscriptions:** 20 journals and other serials. **Services:** Copying; library open to public. **Remarks:** This is a private facility within a bookstore operation; the bookstore is also headquarters for the Jack London Foundation.

★6378★

JACKSON COUNTY HISTORICAL SOCIETY - RESEARCH LIBRARY & ARCHIVES (Hist)
Independence Sq. Courthouse, Rm.103   Phone: (816) 252-7454
Independence, MO 64050   Nancy M. Ehrlich, Dir.
Staff: Prof 1; Other 1. **Subjects:** Local history. **Holdings:** 600 books; manuscripts, business and organizational records. **Services:** Copying; library open to public. **Staff:** Marie Blackburn, Asst.Dir.

★6379★

JACKSON COUNTY LAW LIBRARY (Law)
Scarritt Bldg., 2nd Fl.
818 Grand Ave.
Kansas City, MO 64106   Phone: (816) 421-6115
Vivian Shaw, Libn.
Staff: 1. **Subjects:** Law. **Holdings:** 45,000 books and bound periodical volumes. **Subscriptions:** 15 journals and other serials. **Services:** Library not open to public.

★6380★

JACKSON COUNTY LAW LIBRARY (Law)*
Court House
Jackson, OH 45640   M. Murphy, Lib. Custodian
Subjects: Law. **Holdings:** 5000 volumes. **Services:** Library open to public.

★6381★

JACKSON COUNTY LAW LIBRARY (Law)
Jackson County Justice Bldg.
Medford, OR 97501   Phone: (503) 776-7214
Janet Hannaford, Libn.
Founded: 1931. **Staff:** 1. **Subjects:** Law. **Holdings:** 15,000 books. **Services:** Interlibrary loans; copying; library open to public for reference use only.

JACKSON (Grady) MEMORIAL LIBRARY
See: Georgia State Department of Human Resources - Georgia Mental Health Institute - Addison M. Duval Library

★6382★

JACKSON HOMESTEAD - LIBRARY & ARCHIVES (Hist)
527 Washington St.   Phone: (617) 552-7238
Newton, MA 02158   Duscha S. Scott, Dir.
Staff: Prof 2. **Subjects:** Newton, Massachusetts history, genealogy, architecture. **Holdings:** 450 volumes; 2000 letters and manuscripts; 5000 photographs and slides. **Services:** Copying; library and archives open to public by appointment. **Publications:** The Older Houses of Newton - Built Before 1855 and Still Standing, irregular. **Staff:** Lisa Gougian, Cur.

★6383★

JACKSON HOSPITAL & CLINIC, INC. - MEDICAL LIBRARY (Med)
1235 Forest Ave.   Phone: (205) 832-4000
Montgomery, AL 36106   Annelle Johnson, Med.Libn.
Founded: 1955. **Staff:** Prof 1. **Subjects:** Medicine, ophthalmology, otolaryngology. **Holdings:** 950 books; 2600 bound periodical volumes. **Subscriptions:** 100 journals and other serials. **Services:** Interlibrary loans; copying; library open to students and nurses.

JACKSON (J. Hugh) LIBRARY
See: Stanford University - J. Hugh Jackson Library

JACKSON (John Herrick) MUSIC LIBRARY
See: Yale University - John Herrick Jackson Music Library

★6384★

JACKSON, KELLY, HOLT & O'FARRELL - LIBRARY (Law)
1500 One Valley Sq.
Box 553
Charleston, WV 25322   Phone: (304) 347-7500
Kyle E. Fisher, Libn.
Staff: Prof 1. **Subjects:** Law. **Holdings:** 15,000 books; 120 bound periodical volumes. **Subscriptions:** 114 journals and other serials. **Services:** Copying; library open to attorneys. **Computerized Information Services:** LEXIS. **Special Indexes:** Brief bank of legal briefs, memoranda and opinion letters (card).

JACKSON LABORATORY LIBRARY
See: Du Pont de Nemours (E.I.) & Company, Inc. - Chemicals & Pigments Dept. - Jackson Laboratory Library

★6385★

JACKSON LABORATORY - RESEARCH LIBRARY (Sci-Tech)
Bar Harbor, ME 04609   Phone: (207) 288-3371
Joan Staats, Sr. Staff Sci./Libn.
Founded: 1929. **Staff:** Prof 1; Other 2. **Subjects:** Inbred strains of mice, genetics, cancer, growth, immunology, animal behavior, cell biology. **Special Collections:** Subject-strain bibliography of inbred strains of mice, named genes in mice, and named transplantable tumors in mice (65,000 items on magnetic tape). **Holdings:** 3000 books; 18,000 bound periodical volumes; 45,000 reprints (cataloged). **Subscriptions:** 250 journals and other serials. **Services:** Interlibrary loans; copying; literature searches on specific subjects above on a fee basis; library open to qualified scientists and students. **Computerized Information Services:** NLM, DIALOG. **Networks/Consortia:** Member of Health Science Library and Information Cooperative of Maine; New England Regional Medical Library Service (NERMLS). **Publications:** Bibliographic supplement to Mouse News Letter, semiannual; Inbred Strains of Mice, biennial.

JACKSON (Lambert L.) MEMORIAL LIBRARY
See: Mount Cuba Astronomical Observatory - Lambert L. Jackson Memorial Library

JACKSON LIBRARY
See: University of North Carolina, Greensboro

★6386★

JACKSON-MADISON COUNTY GENERAL HOSPITAL - LEARNING CENTER (Med)
708 W. Forest Ave.   Phone: (901) 424-0424
Jackson, TN 38301   Linda G. Farmer, Med.Libn.
Staff: Prof 1; Other 2. **Subjects:** Medicine, nursing, health. **Holdings:** 1500 books; 600 bound periodical volumes; 4 VF drawers of pamphlets; 200 filmstrip cassettes; 150 cassette tapes; 100 slide cassettes. **Subscriptions:** 192 journals and other serials. **Services:** Interlibrary loans; copying; center open to public with restrictions. **Networks/Consortia:** Member of Association of Memphis Area Health Sciences Libraries.

★6387★
JACKSON MEMORIAL HOSPITAL - SCHOOL OF NURSING LIBRARY (Med)
1611 N.W. 12th Ave.   Phone: (305) 325-6833
Miami, FL 33136   Lynn Towers, Libn.
Staff: Prof 1; Other 3. **Subjects:** Nursing, medicine, health. **Holdings:** 3200 books; 150 bound periodical volumes; 230 National League for Nursing reports and pamphlets; 80 video cassettes. **Subscriptions:** 67 journals and other serials. **Services:** Interlibrary loans; copying; library open to public for reference use only. **Networks/Consortia:** Member of Miami Health Sciences Library Consortium.

JACKSON MEMORIAL LIBRARY
See: Amelia Historical Library

★6388★
JACKSON METROPOLITAN LIBRARY - INFORMATION AND REFERENCE DIVISION
301 N. State St.   Phone: (601) 352-3677
Jackson, MS 39201   Jack Mulkey, Dir.
Founded: 1914. **Staff:** Prof 4; Other 2. **Subjects:** Biography, literature, business, cookery, gardening, applied and social sciences. **Special Collections:** Mississippi Collection including Jackson material (3000 volumes, current and back files of selected Mississippi periodicals, 25 VF drawers of clippings and pamphlets); Foundation Center, Regional Depository Library (IRS returns of state and national foundations on microfiche; Foundation Center publications and directories). **Holdings:** 795,000 books; 1000 bound periodical volumes; 45,213 reels of microfilm. **Subscriptions:** 550 journals and other serials; 41 newspapers. **Services:** Interlibrary loans; copying; library open to public. **Computerized Information Services:** Computerized cataloging. **Networks/Consortia:** Member of OCLC; Central Mississippi Library Council. **Staff:** Annetta Clark, Assoc.Dir.; Allan C. Hauth, Pub.Serv.Coord.; Margaret Dixon, ILL; Rosemary Landon, Found.Ctr.Coll.

★6389★
JACKSON PARK HOSPITAL - MEDICAL LIBRARY (Med)†
7531 South Stony Island Ave.   Phone: (312) 947-7653
Chicago, IL 60649   Syed A. Maghrabi, Med.Ref.Libn.
Staff: Prof 1. **Subjects:** Medicine. **Holdings:** 2000 books. **Subscriptions:** 175 journals and other serials. **Services:** Interlibrary loans; copying; SDI; library open to public with valid need. **Networks/Consortia:** Member of Chicago and South Consortium.

★6390★
JACKSONVILLE ART MUSEUM - LIBRARY
4160 Boulevard Center Dr.
Jacksonville, FL 32207
Founded: 1948. **Subjects:** Art. **Holdings:** 500 volumes. **Remarks:** Presently inactive.

★6391★
JACKSONVILLE HEALTH EDUCATION PROGRAMS, INC. - BORLAND HEALTH SCIENCES LIBRARY (Med)
580 W. 8th St.   Phone: (904) 359-6516
Jacksonville, FL 32209   Robert P. Hinz, Dir.
Founded: 1964. **Staff:** Prof 2; Other 4. **Subjects:** Medicine, psychiatry, public health, nursing, allied health sciences, dentistry. **Holdings:** 12,600 books; 12,300 bound periodical volumes. **Subscriptions:** 500 journals and other serials. **Services:** Interlibrary loans; copying. **Computerized Information Services:** MEDLINE. **Remarks:** Contains the holdings of the former Florida State Department of Health and Rehabilitative Services - HRS Resource Center.

★6392★
JACKSONVILLE MENTAL HEALTH AND DEVELOPMENTAL CENTER - LIBRARY (Med)
1201 S. Main St.   Phone: (217) 245-2111
Jacksonville, IL 62650
Staff: Prof 1. **Subjects:** Mental retardation, psychiatry, mental health, psychology, medicine, psychiatric nursing, sociology, fiction and nonfiction. **Holdings:** 6000 books; 7000 bound periodical volumes; 8 VF drawers of pamphlets and reprints. **Subscriptions:** 14 journals and other serials. **Services:** Library open to public. **Networks/Consortia:** Member of Illinois Department of Mental Health and Developmental Disabilities Consortium; Regional Medical Library - Region 3.

★6393★
JACKSONVILLE PUBLIC LIBRARY - FLORIDA COLLECTION (Hist)
122 N. Ocean St.   Phone: (904) 633-3305
Jacksonville, FL 32202   Mr. Carol Harris, Cur.
Founded: 1914. **Staff:** Prof 1. **Subjects:** Florida and Jacksonville - history, biography, description and travel, politics and government, plants and wildlife, fine arts, economics. **Special Collections:** Merritt Collection of Floridiana (500 rare books, maps and documents). **Holdings:** 13,000 books and cataloged pamphlets; 900 bound periodical volumes; 1811 reels of microfilm; 7730 checklisted Florida documents; 50 file boxes of Jacksonville documents; 155 file boxes of Florida documents; 11 VF drawers of uncataloged pamphlets; 17 VF drawers of newspaper clippings; 2 VF drawers of photographs; 472 maps; 196 microfiche. **Subscriptions:** 30 journals and other serials. **Services:** Copying; collection open to public for serious research with restrictions. **Computerized Information Services:** Computerized cataloging. **Networks/Consortia:** Member of OCLC through SOLINET. **Special Indexes:** Florida Times-Union Index, 1895-1979 (bound volumes and on microfilm); Jacksonville Journal Index, 1925-1938 (bound volume and on microfilm).

JACOB EDWARDS LIBRARY
See: Edwards (Jacob) Library

JACOBI HOSPITAL
See: Yeshiva University - Albert Einstein College of Medicine - Surgery Library

★6394★
JACOBS ENGINEERING GROUP - TECHNICAL INFORMATION SERVICES DEPARTMENT (Energy)
Box 53495   Phone: (713) 626-2020
Houston, TX 77052   Carolyn A. Meanley, Mgr., Tech.Info.
Founded: 1953. **Staff:** Prof 3. **Subjects:** Petroleum refining technology, petrochemical plant design, natural gas processing, environmental engineering, energy analysis and forecasting, business statistics. **Holdings:** 7000 books; 800 bound periodical volumes; 300 company reports; 1200 Bureau of Mines reports; 2500 microforms. **Subscriptions:** 300 journals and other serials. **Services:** Interlibrary loans; copying; department open to public by appointment. **Staff:** Sara Davis; Rena Wells .

JACOBSON (Jack) MEMORIAL LIBRARY
See: B'nai Jeshurun Temple on the Heights - Jack Jacobson Memorial Library

JAINSEN (Wilson C.) LIBRARY
See: St. Francis Hospital and Medical Center - Wilson C. Jainsen Library

★6395★
JAMAICA HOSPITAL - MEDICAL LIBRARY (Med)
89th Ave. & Van Wyck Expy.   Phone: (212) 657-1800
Jamaica, NY 11418   Carolyn Mansbach, Med.Libn.
Founded: 1963. **Staff:** Prof 1; Other 1. **Subjects:** Medicine. **Holdings:** 4990 books; 2927 bound periodical volumes; Audio-Digest cassettes. **Subscriptions:** 185 journals and other serials. **Services:** Interlibrary loans; copying; library open to students and visiting physicians with permission. **Networks/Consortia:** Member of Brooklyn-Queens-Staten Island Health Sciences Librarians (BQSI); Medical & Scientific Libraries of Long Island (MEDLI).

JAMES BAY DEVELOPMENT CORPORATION
See: Societe de Developpement de la Baie James

JAMES BAY ENERGY CORPORATION
See: Societe d'Energie de la Baie James

★6396★
JAMES BUCHANAN FOUNDATION FOR THE PRESERVATION OF WHEATLAND - LIBRARY (Hist)
1120 Marietta Ave.   Phone: (717) 392-8721
Lancaster, PA 17603   Sally S. Cahalan, Dir.
Founded: 1936. **Subjects:** 19th century American history. **Holdings:** Figures not available. **Remarks:** Wheatland, the restored 1828 mansion residence of President Buchanan (1857-1861), contains a library having books owned by James Buchanan. Wheatland is operated by the James Buchanan Foundation for the Preservation of Wheatland.

JAMES (Harry and Grace) RECORDED SOUND ARCHIVE
See: University of California, Riverside - Music Library

JAMES (M. Lucia) CURRICULUM LIBRARY
See: University of Maryland, College Park - M. Lucia James Curriculum Library

★6397★
JAMES RIVER CORPORATION - NEENAH TECHNICAL CENTER - TECHNICAL INFORMATION CENTER (Sci-Tech)
1915 Marathon Ave.
Box 899
Neenah, WI 54956
Phone: (414) 729-8169
Cheryl Lamb, Info.Sci.
Founded: 1937. Staff: Prof 1; Other 3. Subjects: Packaging technology, pulp and paper chemistry and technology, plastics, food technology, chemical engineering. Special Collections: All U.S. patents on microfilm, 1978 to present. Holdings: 6000 books; 250 bound periodical volumes; 10,000 technical documents; 175 VF drawers. Subscriptions: 455 journals and other serials. Services: Interlibrary loans; copying; SDI; library open to public with restrictions. Computerized Information Services: DIALOG, SDC; computerized cataloging. Networks/Consortia: Member of Fox Valley Library Council, Inc; Fox Valley On-line Users Group; OCLC; ILLINET; Library Council of Metropolitan Milwaukee, Inc. (LCOMM). Publications: Monthly Newsletter; Patent Alert; Information Update. Formerly: American Can Company - Neenah Technical Center - Technical Information Center.

★6398★
JAMESON MEMORIAL HOSPITAL - SCHOOL OF NURSING LIBRARY (Med)
W. Garfield Ave.
New Castle, PA 16105
Phone: (412) 658-9001
Joan T. Whitman, Libn.
Staff: Prof 1. Subjects: Medicine, surgery, nursing. Holdings: 3687 books; 300 bound periodical volumes. Subscriptions: 106 journals and other serials. Services: Interlibrary loans; copying; library open to public with approval of librarian.

JANE AUSTEN SOCIETY OF NORTH AMERICA
See: Austen (Jane) Society of North America

★6399★
JANEWAY (Dr. Charles A.) CHILD HEALTH CENTRE - JANEWAY MEDICAL LIBRARY (Med)
Pleasantville
St. John's, NF, Canada A1A 1R8
Phone: (709) 778-4344
Joan E. Wheeler, Med.Libn.
Founded: 1966. Staff: 1. Subjects: Pediatrics, medicine, surgery. Holdings: 3078 books; 2300 bound periodical volumes; 809 Audio-Digest tapes; 375 pamphlets. Subscriptions: 140 journals and other serials. Services: Interlibrary loans; copying; literature searches; library not open to public.

★6400★
JANUS FOUNDATION - LIBRARY (Med)
2420 Sutter St.
San Francisco, CA 94115
Phone: (415) 563-0344
Janet L. Bergman, Libn.
Staff: 1. Subjects: History of medicine and science; psychiatry. Holdings: 3193 titles including books, reprints, pamphlets and manuscripts. Services: Library open to public by appointment.

★6401★
JANUS INFORMATION FACILITY (Soc Sci)
1952 Union St.
San Francisco, CA 94123
Phone: (415) 567-0162
Paul A. Walker, Dir.
Founded: 1976. Staff: Prof 1; Other 1. Subjects: Transsexualism, transvestism. Holdings: 100 books. Services: Library not open to public.

★6402★
JAPAN ECONOMIC INSTITUTE OF AMERICA - LIBRARY (Bus-Fin)
1000 Connecticut Ave., N.W.
Washington, DC 20036
Phone: (202) 296-5633
Phyllis A. Genther, Res.
Founded: 1956. Subjects: Japanese economy, international trade. Holdings: 1800 books; Japanese language reference materials. Subscriptions: 131 journals and other serials; 8 newspapers. Services: Interlibrary loans; copying; library open to public for reference use only. Publications: Japan Insight; JEI Report, both weekly; Japan Report, monthly - all by subscription.

JAPAN INFORMATION CENTER
See: Consulate General of Japan

★6403★
JAPAN SOCIETY, INC. - LIBRARY (Area-Ethnic)
333 E. 47th St.
New York, NY 10017
Phone: (212) 832-1155
Tomie Mochizuki, Libn.
Staff: 2. Subjects: Art, business, history, economics, general (both English and Japanese language). Holdings: 6000 books; 1.5 VF drawers of clippings;

1.5 VF drawers of archives; 5 VF drawers of pamphlets. Subscriptions: 130 journals and other serials; 11 newspapers. Services: Copying (limited); library open to public by appointment. Staff: Reiko Sassa, Asst.Libn.

★6404★
JAPANESE-AMERICAN SOCIETY FOR PHILATELY - LIBRARY (Rec)
Box 1049
El Cerrito, CA 94530
George M. Baka, Libn.
Subjects: Philatelic history of the Japanese Empire and associated areas. Holdings: 75 books; maps, photographs. Services: Interlibrary loans; copying; library open to public. Special Catalogs: Printed catalog (every 3 years).

JAPANESE CONSULATE LIBRARY
See: Consulate-General of Japan

★6405★
JARDIN BOTANIQUE DE MONTREAL - BIBLIOTHEQUE (Sci-Tech)
4101 Sherbrooke St., E.
Montreal, PQ, Canada H1X 2B2
Phone: (514) 252-8765
Celine Arseneault, Botanist/Libn.
Staff: Prof 1. Subjects: Botany, horticulture. Special Collections: Botanical magazines, some dating back to the 18th century. Holdings: 8300 books; 2900 bound periodical volumes; 11,000 unbound periodicals; 23,500 reprints and pamphlets. Subscriptions: 100 journals and other serials. Services: Interlibrary loans; copying; library open to public. Publications: Publications au Jardin Botanique de Montreal, annual - distributed upon request. Also Known As: Montreal Botanical Garden.

★6406★
JARDIN ZOOLOGIQUE DE QUEBEC - BIBLIOTHEQUE (Sci-Tech)
8191 Ave. Du Zoo
Charlesbourg, PQ, Canada G1G 4G4
Phone: (418) 643-2310
Jeannine Gagne, Responsable
Founded: 1934. Staff: 1. Subjects: Zoology, mammalogy, ornithology, ichthyology, zoological gardens, horticulture, botany. Holdings: 6000 books and bound periodical volumes. Subscriptions: 30 journals and other serials. Services: Interlibrary loans; copying; library open to public. Also Known As: Quebec Zoological Garden.

JARRELL (Randall) COLLECTION
See: University of North Carolina, Greensboro - Randall Jarrell Collection

JARRETT (Mamye) LEARNING CENTER
See: East Texas Baptist College - Mayme Jarrett Learning Center

JAY (John) COLLEGE OF CRIMINAL JUSTICE OF THE CITY UNIVERSITY OF NEW YORK
See: John Jay College of Criminal Justice of the City University of New York

★6407★
JAY (John) HOMESTEAD - JAY LIBRARY (Hist)
Box A.H.
Katonah, NY 10536
Phone: (914) 232-5651
Lino S. Lipinsky de Orlov, Cur. of Hist.
Founded: 1959. Staff: Prof 4. Subjects: Jay Family, New York State history, antislavery, Westchester County history. Special Collections: Antislavery pamphlets of William Jay and John Jay II; archival material relating to the Jay family from the 18th through 20th centuries (5000 items). Holdings: 3000 volumes. Services: Special arrangements can be made for use of the material by qualified scholars at the site. Networks/Consortia: Member of Taconic State Park and Recreation Commission. Remarks: The bulk of this collection consists of the library of John Jay (first Chief Justice of the United States) and four generations of his descendants. The John Jay Homestead is a New York State Historic Site, maintained by New York State Parks and Recreation - Division for Historic Preservation.

JAY-ROLLINS LIBRARY
See: United Methodist Church - Northwest Texas Annual Conference - Commission on Archives and History

JAZZ ARCHIVE
See: Detroit Jazz Center

JEAN-TALON HOSPITAL
See: Hopital Jean-Talon

JEFFERSON COUNTY FREE LIBRARY
See: Birmingham Public and Jefferson County Free Library

★6408★
JEFFERSON COUNTY HISTORICAL SOCIETY - LIBRARY (Hist)
228 Washington St.   Phone: (315) 782-3491
Watertown, NY 13601   Margaret W.M. Shaeffer, Dir.
Subjects: Watertown and Jefferson County history. **Special Collections:** Papers of Governor R.P. Flower. **Holdings:** 750 volumes; pamphlets, ledgers, daybooks, account books and journals of 19th century country stores; 19th century bank record books and boxes of archival materials; current museum periodicals and directories. **Services:** Copying; library open to public for reference use only. **Publications:** Bulletin, quarterly - distributed to members.

★6409★
JEFFERSON COUNTY HISTORICAL SOCIETY - RESOURCE CENTER - VICTORIANA (Hist)
City Hall   Phone: (206) 385-0245
Port Townsend, WA 98368   Carol L. Yandell, Asst.Dir.
Founded: 1975. **Staff:** 1. **Subjects:** Jefferson County and regional history; biography; ships and shipping, 1874-1936; Indian lore; early Pacific Northwest histories; historic preservation and restoration. **Holdings:** 162 volumes; city, county and school records; Port Townsend Leader (weekly newspapers, bound, 1891-present); 100 maps and nautical charts; 33 manuscript cases of family histories. **Services:** Copying; center open to public for reference use only under supervision of research staff.

★6410★
JEFFERSON COUNTY LAW LIBRARY (Law)
900 Jefferson County Court House   Phone: (205) 325-5628
Birmingham, AL 35263   Linda M. Hand, Libn.
Staff: Prof 1; Other 3. **Subjects:** Law. **Holdings:** 42,911 volumes. **Subscriptions:** 115 journals and other serials. **Services:** Interlibrary loans; copying; library open to public for reference use only.

★6411★
JEFFERSON COUNTY LAW LIBRARY (Law)
Courthouse   Phone: (614) 283-4111
Steubenville, OH 43952   Christine K. Firm, Libn.
Founded: 1900. **Staff:** Prof 1; Other 1. **Subjects:** Law. **Holdings:** 16,500 volumes; 2600 volumes of microfiche reporters. **Subscriptions:** 31 journals and other serials. **Services:** Copying; library open to public for research only. **Remarks:** Maintained by Jefferson County Law Library Association.

★6412★
JEFFERSON COUNTY OFFICE OF HISTORIC PRESERVATION AND ARCHIVES (Hist)
Fiscal Court Bldg., Rm. 100   Phone: (502) 581-5761
Louisville, KY 40202   Olivia Frederick, Cons.Archv.
Staff: Prof 4; Other 1. **Subjects:** Jefferson County government and historic sites. **Holdings:** 14,000 official records. **Services:** Copying; office open to public. **Staff:** Elizabeth F. Jones, Adm.; Mary Jean Kinsman, Res.; David Morgan, Archv.Techn.

JEFFERSON COUNTY PLANNING COMMISSION
See: Louisville and Jefferson County Planning Commission

★6413★
JEFFERSON COUNTY PUBLIC LAW LIBRARY (Law)†
Old Louisville Trust Bldg.
200 S. Fifth St.   Phone: (502) 581-5943
Louisville, KY 40202   Kent E. Metcalf, Dir.
Founded: 1839. **Staff:** Prof 1; Other 7. **Subjects:** Law. **Special Collections:** Kentucky law. **Holdings:** 50,000 volumes. **Services:** Interlibrary loans; copying; library open to public for reference use only. **Networks/Consortia:** Member of Louisville Area Law Libraries (LALL).

★6414★
JEFFERSON COUNTY PUBLIC SCHOOLS R1 - PROFESSIONAL LIBRARY MEDIA CENTER (Educ)
1209 Quail St.   Phone: (303) 231-2309
Lakewood, CO 80215   Christa K. Coon, Exec.Dir., Lib.Serv.
Founded: 1962. **Staff:** Prof 1; Other 3. **Subjects:** Education, art, music, special education. **Holdings:** 12,814 books; 4437 phonograph records; 9404 AV materials; 39,111 uncataloged curriculum books; 1855 titles of sheet music; publishers' catalogs and pamphlet file. **Subscriptions:** 240 journals and other serials. **Services:** Interlibrary loans; preview; microprint library; center open to Jefferson County taxpayers. **Computerized Information Services:** Online systems. **Staff:** Roberta Ponis, Lib. Media Spec.

★6415★
JEFFERSON HISTORICAL SOCIETY AND MUSEUM - ARCHIVES (Hist)
223 Austin St.
Drawer G   Phone: (214) 665-2775
Jefferson, TX 75657   Mrs. Jack Bullard, Cur.
Subjects: Local history, Civil War, genealogy. **Special Collections:** Carl Hertzog Collection (his typography, arranging and printing). **Holdings:** Figures not available for books and bound periodical volumes; 35 manuscripts; 20 notebooks of clippings; several hundred documents; maps. **Services:** Archives open to public with restrictions.

JEFFERSON NATL. EXPANSION MEMORIAL
See: U.S. Natl. Park Service

JEFFERSON (Thomas) LIBRARY
See: National College - Thomas Jefferson Library; University of Missouri, St. Louis - Thomas Jefferson Library

★6416★
JEFFERSON (Thomas) RESEARCH CENTER - LIBRARY (Soc Sci)
1143 N. Lake Ave.   Phone: (213) 798-0791
Pasadena, CA 91104   Frank G. Goble, Pres.
Founded: 1963. **Staff:** Prof 4; Other 5. **Subjects:** Philosophy, psychology, social sciences, business, management, religion, history, mental health. **Holdings:** 1200 books; 8 VF drawers of pamphlets; 41 pamphlet boxes of organizations; 9 pamphlet boxes of foundations; 23 pamphlet boxes of magazines. **Subscriptions:** 15 journals and other serials. **Services:** Library not open to public. **Publications:** Research Letter, monthly; research reports, occasional.

★6417★
JEFFERSON (Thomas) UNIVERSITY - CARDEZA FOUNDATION - TOCANTINS MEMORIAL LIBRARY (Med)
1015 Walnut St.   Phone: (215) 928-8474
Philadelphia, PA 19107   Doris Riso, Sec.-Libn.
Founded: 1962. **Staff:** Prof 1; Other 1. **Subjects:** Hematology and related sciences. **Special Collections:** Leandro M. Tocantins, M.D., Publications; Carlos Finlay Collections. **Holdings:** 1000 books and bound periodical volumes. **Subscriptions:** 35 journals and other serials. **Services:** Library open to staff only.

★6418★
JEFFERSON (Thomas) UNIVERSITY - SCOTT MEMORIAL LIBRARY (Med)
11th & Walnut Sts.   Phone: (215) 928-6994
Philadelphia, PA 19107   John A. Timour, Libn.
Founded: 1896. **Staff:** Prof 13; Other 29. **Subjects:** Medicine and allied sciences. **Special Collections:** Bland Collection (history of obstetrics and gynecology). **Holdings:** 124,919 books and bound periodical volumes; 6452 microforms (104 periodical titles); 608 audio reels and cassettes; 1412 video cassettes, slide sets and multi-media kits. **Subscriptions:** 1601 journals and other serials. **Services:** Interlibrary loans; copying; SDI; library open to public with restrictions. **Computerized Information Services:** BRS, DIALOG, SDC, NTIS, MEDLINE; computerized cataloging. **Networks/Consortia:** Member of OCLC through PALINET & Union Library Catalogue of Pennsylvania; Interlibrary Delivery Service of Pennsylvania (IDS); Mideastern Regional Medical Library System (MERMLS). **Staff:** Samuel A. Davis, Evening Libn.; Alice O. Mackov, Ref.Libn.; Henry T. Armistead, Hd., Coll.Dept.; Elaine Spyker, AV Libn.; Rosalinda Ross, Online Ref.Libn.; Robert T. Lentz, Archv.; Robert Lee, Asst.Libn.; Barbara Laynor, Clinical Libn.; Margaret Devlin, Circ.Libn.; Marianne Fernandez-Caballero, Cat.Libn.; Nancy Calabretta, Ref.Libn.; Lillian Brazin, Res.Libn.

JENKINS (Arthur D.) LIBRARY
See: Textile Museum - Arthur D. Jenkins Library

JENKINS RESEARCH CENTER
See: Southern Baptist Convention - Foreign Mission Board

★6419★
JENKINS (Theodore F.) MEMORIAL LAW LIBRARY COMPANY - LIBRARY (Law)
Widener Bldg., 10th Fl.
1339 Chestnut St.   Phone: (215) 686-5692
Philadelphia, PA 19107   Regina A. Smith, Dir.
Staff: Prof 4; Other 7. **Subjects:** Law. **Special Collections:** John Marshall Gest Memorial Library (civil and canon law; 1900 volumes). **Holdings:** 200,000 books and bound periodical volumes; Pennsylvania state legislative material. **Subscriptions:** 750 journals and other serials. **Services:** Interlibrary loans; copying; library open to public for reference use only. **Computerized**

Information Services: WESTLAW, DIALOG, SDC, Tech-Net. **Networks/Consortia:** Member of Interlibrary Delivery Service of Pennsylvania (IDS). **Staff:** David Proctor, Asst.Libn., Pub.Serv.; Elsa B. Atson, Asst.Libn., Tech.Serv.; Phillip Meyer, Asst.Libn., Coll.Dev.

★6420★
JENKINTOWN LIBRARY - PENNSYLVANIA COLLECTION (Hist)
York & Vista Rds.   Phone: (215) 884-0593
Jenkintown, PA 19046   Joan Greenberg, Libn.
Founded: 1803. **Staff:** Prof 1; Other 4. **Subjects:** Local history. **Holdings:** 1000 volumes. **Services:** Interlibrary loans; copying; library open to public. **Remarks:** Maintained by the Abington Library Society.

JENKS MEMORIAL COLLECTION OF ADVENTUAL MATERIALS
See: Aurora College

JENNINGS (Andrew R.) COMPUTING CENTER
See: Case Western Reserve University - Andrew R. Jennings Computing Center

★6421★
JENNINGS LIBRARY (Info Sci)
437 Jennings Ave.   Phone: (216) 337-3348
Salem, OH 44460   Dale E. Shaffer, Lib.Cons. & Dir.
Staff: Prof 1. **Subjects:** Library management and consulting; bibliographies; teaching materials on library methods, training, and development of collections. **Holdings:** 3000 books; 300 audiotapes; 1000 pamphlets. **Services:** Copying; library open to public by appointment. **Publications:** List of publications for librarians and educators - available on request.

★6422★
JENSEN ASSOCIATES, INC. - LIBRARY (Energy)
84 State St.   Phone: (617) 227-8115
Boston, MA 02109   Janet C. Dwyer, Libn.
Staff: Prof 1; Other 1. **Subjects:** Energy economics, energy resources, petroleum, natural gas, electricity, coal. **Special Collections:** U.S. Government Committee Prints and Hearings on Energy Topics (200 volumes). **Holdings:** 3500 books; 100 bound periodical volumes; annual reports on 300 domestic and foreign companies; 20 VF drawers of clippings and papers; 200 maps. **Subscriptions:** 147 journals and other serials. **Services:** Library not open to public. **Publications:** New in the Library, monthly - for company personnel.

★6423★
JENSEN (Rolf) & ASSOCIATES - LIBRARY (Sci-Tech)
104 Wilmot Rd.   Phone: (312) 948-0700
Deerfield, IL 60015   Lois Gorr Rosenberg, Libn.
Staff: Prof 1. **Subjects:** Fire protection, building research, architectural design. **Holdings:** 340 books; 400 product catalogs; 16 VF drawers of technical data; 15 shelves of standards and codes; 4 shelves of technical reports; 100 reports on microfiche. **Subscriptions:** 101 journals and other serials. **Services:** Library open to public with restrictions.

JEPSON (Henry G.) MEMORIAL LIBRARY
See: Wheeling Hospital, Inc. - Henry G. Jepson Memorial Library

JEROME MEDICAL LIBRARY
See: St. Joseph's Hospital

★6424★
JERSEY CITY STATE COLLEGE - FORREST A. IRWIN LIBRARY (Educ)†
2039 Kennedy Blvd.   Phone: (201) 547-3026
Jersey City, NJ 07305   Robert S. Nugent, Dir.
Founded: 1927. **Special Collections:** Juvenile Collection; Curriculum Materials Center; Library of American Civilization (20,000 items); Library of English Literature (4522 items); Human Relations Area File (79, 086). **Services:** Interlibrary loans; copying; library open to adult public with identification. **Computerized Information Services:** Computerized cataloging. **Networks/Consortia:** Member of OCLC through PALINET & Union Library Catalogue of Pennsylvania. **Publications:** Ethnic Studies Bibliography; Guide to the Library for Students; Russian Area Studies Bibliography; New Jersey Bibliography.

★6425★
JERSEY SHORE MEDICAL CENTER - MEDICAL LIBRARY (Med)
1945 Corlies Ave.   Phone: (201) 775-5500
Neptune, NJ 07753   Mr. Gian C. Hasija, Med.Libn.
Staff: Prof 1; Other 1. **Subjects:** Medicine. **Holdings:** 1200 books; 7800 bound periodical volumes; 1000 AV materials. **Subscriptions:** 150 journals.

Services: Interlibrary loans; copying; library open to students. **Computerized Information Services:** MEDLINE. **Networks/Consortia:** Member of Monmouth- Ocean Biomedical Information Consortium; New York & New Jersey Regional Medical Library Program. **Publications:** Annotated List of Additions, quarterly.

★6426★
JERVIS PUBLIC LIBRARY (Hist)
613 N. Washington St.   Phone: (315) 336-4570
Rome, NY 13440   William A. Dillon, Dir.
Special Collections: John Jervis Library (railroads and canals): 2000 volumes; 900 reports, survey maps, engineering drawings; 30,000 broadly classified pages of correspondence; Huntington-Bright Collection of historical papers; 250 letters, broadsides from French and Indian and Revolutionary periods; Washington, Lafayette, Declaration Signers, generals. **Services:** Interlibrary loans; copying; library open to public with restrictions. **Networks/Consortia:** Member of Mid-York Library System. **Special Indexes:** Index to Jervis Papers (book).

JESUIT CENTER LIBRARY
See: California Province of the Society of Jesus

JESUIT SCHOOL OF THEOLOGY AT BERKELEY
See: Graduate Theological Union

★6427★
JESUIT SCHOOL OF THEOLOGY IN CHICAGO - LIBRARY (Rel-Theol)†
1100 E. 55th St.   Phone: (312) 667-3500
Chicago, IL 60615   Dr. W. Earle Hilgert, Act.Libn.
Founded: 1934. **Staff:** Prof 3; Other 1. **Subjects:** Theology, philosophy. **Holdings:** 82,951 books; 13,514 bound periodical volumes; 272 microfilm units. **Subscriptions:** 389 journals and other serials. **Services:** Interlibrary loans; copying; open to public for reference use only. **Computerized Information Services:** Computerized cataloging. **Networks/Consortia:** Member of Chicago Cluster of Theological Schools. **Remarks:** Shares facilities with the libraries of the McCormick Theological Seminary and Lutheran School of Theology at Chicago. **Staff:** Eileen Fitz Simmons, Libn.

JESUITS LIBRARY (St. Jerome, PQ)
See: Compagnie de Jesus

JET PROPULSION LABORATORY
See: California Institute of Technology

★6428★
JET RESEARCH CENTER, INC. - TECHNICAL INFORMATION AND SCIENCE LIBRARY (Sci-Tech)
Box 246   Phone: (817) 483-0933
Arlington, TX 76010   Karan Mathes, Engr.Sec.
Founded: 1958. **Staff:** 1. **Subjects:** Explosives, pyrotechnics. **Special Collections:** Patents and patent holdings (18 books). **Holdings:** 497 books; 83 bound periodical volumes; 804 vendor catalogs; 5 VF drawers of reports; military and federal specifications and standards; government documents. **Services:** Interlibrary loans; library not open to public.

JEWELL (William) COLLEGE - MISSOURI BAPTIST HISTORICAL COMMISSION LIBRARY
See: Missouri Baptist Historical Commission Library

JEWETT ARTS CENTER
See: Wellesley College

★6429★
JEWISH BOARD OF FAMILY & CHILDREN SERVICES - LIBRARY (Soc Sci)†
120 W. 57th St.   Phone: (212) 582-9100
New York, NY 10019   Teresa Kremer, Libn.
Staff: Prof 1; Other 1. **Subjects:** Child and adolescent psychology and psychiatry, social work, family therapy, psychoanalysis, psychiatry. **Special Collections:** The Charities (Hebrew charities), 1891-1907; Conference on Charities, 1896-1929, continued as National Conference of Social Work, 1930-1949, continued as Social Welfare Forum, 1950 to present. **Holdings:** 5000 books; 2000 bound periodical volumes; 8 VF drawers of manuscripts and dissertations. **Subscriptions:** 95 journals and other serials. **Services:** Interlibrary loans; copying; library not open to public.

★6430★

JEWISH BRAILLE INSTITUTE OF AMERICA, INC. - LIBRARY (Aud-Vis)
110 E. 30th St.   Phone: (212) 889-2525
New York, NY 10016   Richard Borgersen, Lib.Dir.
Founded: 1931. **Staff:** Prof 1; Other 6. **Subjects:** Judaica. **Special Collections:** English and Hebrew braille; English, Yiddish and Hebrew tapes; English and Hebrew large type. **Holdings:** 55,000 books; 40,000 tapes. **Services:** Library open to public. **Publications:** Jewish Braille Review; English braille monthly; JBI Voice: English record, monthly. **Special Catalogs:** Catalogs based on subject, language and medium (computer-generated).

★6431★

JEWISH COMMUNITY CENTER OF GREATER MINNEAPOLIS - LIBRARY (Rel-Theol)
4330 S. Cedar Lake Rd.   Phone: (612) 377-8330
Minneapolis, MN 55416   Sharon Perwien, Lib.Coord.
Founded: 1969. **Subjects:** Judaica, Israel, historical views of Jews and Christians, arts and sciences, American and European literature, Jewish reference material, Hebrew and Yiddish literature, social issues and ecology. **Holdings:** 3000 books; 200 unbound periodicals; 300 records. **Services:** Interlibrary loans; library open to public. **Publications:** Identity Magazine, 2/year. **Remarks:** Library maintained by National Council of Jewish Women Volunteers.

★6432★

JEWISH COMMUNITY CENTER OF GREATER WASHINGTON - KASS JUDAIC LIBRARY (Area-Ethnic)
6125 Montrose Rd.   Phone: (301) 881-0100
Rockville, MD 20852   T.K. Feldman, Dir., Literary Arts Dept.
Staff: Prof 1. **Subjects:** Bible, Israel, Zionism, religion, history, sociology, arts, Holocaust, biography. **Special Collections:** American Jewry; Jews in other countries; Jewish holidays; archeology. **Holdings:** 4000 books. **Subscriptions:** 24 journals and other serials. **Services:** Library open to public.

★6433★

JEWISH COMMUNITY CENTER - LIBRARY
525 14th St.
Sioux City, IA 51105
Founded: 1906. **Subjects:** Books of current interest in English, Hebrew and Yiddish. **Holdings:** 1500 books. **Remarks:** Presently inactive.

★6434★

JEWISH COMMUNITY CENTER - LIBRARY (Area-Ethnic)
3500 West End Ave.   Phone: (615) 297-3588
Nashville, TN 37205   Annette R. Levy, Libn.
Staff: Prof 1; Other 1. **Subjects:** Judaica; Israel; Holocaust; Hebrew, Russian and Yiddish languages. **Holdings:** 5200 books; unbound periodicals. **Subscriptions:** 23 journals and other serials. **Services:** Interlibrary loans; copying; library open to public. **Special Catalogs:** Joint catalog of books in West End Synagogue and Temple libraries.

★6435★

JEWISH COMMUNITY CENTER OF METROPOLITAN DETROIT - HENRY MEYERS MEMORIAL LIBRARY (Area-Ethnic)
6600 W. Maple Rd.   Phone: (313) 661-1000
West Bloomfield, MI 48033   Adele Silver, Cultural Arts Dir.
Founded: 1959. **Staff:** Prof 1; Other 2. **Subjects:** Judaica. **Special Collections:** Judaica and non-Judaica for children; newspapers and periodicals in English, Yiddish, and Hebrew. **Holdings:** 8500 volumes; 4 VF drawers. **Subscriptions:** 32 journals and other serials; 10 newspapers. **Services:** Interlibrary loans; library open to public.

★6436★

JEWISH COMMUNITY CENTER - SAMUEL & REBECCA ASTOR JUDAICA LIBRARY (Area-Ethnic)
4079 54th St.   Phone: (714) 583-3300
San Diego, CA 92105   Mollie S. Harris, Hd.Libn.
Founded: 1960. **Staff:** Prof 1; Other 1. **Subjects:** Judaica. **Special Collections:** Holocaust Collection. **Holdings:** 6500 volumes (includes books in Yiddish, Hebrew, German and Spanish); pamphlets; 24 videotapes and audiotapes. **Subscriptions:** 32 journals and other serials. **Services:** Interlibrary loans; copying; library open to public. **Publications:** Annual report, book lists, bibliographies, pamphlets - all free upon request to libraries.

★6437★

JEWISH COMMUNITY CENTERS ASSOCIATION (JCCA) - TANNIE LEWIN JUDAICA LIBRARY (Rel-Theol)
11001 Schuetz Rd.   Phone: (314) 432-5700
St. Louis, MO 63141   Lorraine K. Miller, Hd.Libn.
Founded: 1964. **Staff:** Prof 1; Other 2. **Subjects:** Jewish history, philosophy, religion, art, literature, Holocaust. **Special Collections:** Set of Jewish symbols in Roman-Grecian times. **Holdings:** 9000 books; tapes of speeches by nationally known personalities. **Subscriptions:** 50 journals and other serials; 5 newspapers. **Services:** Interlibrary loans; copying; library open to public with restrictions.

★6438★

JEWISH COMMUNITY CENTRE - LIBRARY (Rel-Theol)
151 Chapel St.   Phone: (613) 232-7306
Ottawa, ON, Canada K1N 7Y2   Miriam Paghis, Libn.
Founded: 1955. **Staff:** Prof 1; Other 1. **Subjects:** Judaica. **Holdings:** 6000 books; pamphlets. **Subscriptions:** 15 journals and other serials; 10 newspapers. **Services:** Library open to public.

★6439★

JEWISH COMMUNITY RELATIONS COUNCIL - ANTI-DEFAMATION LEAGUE OF MINNESOTA-DAKOTAS - LIBRARY (Soc Sci)
15 S. 9th St. Bldg., Suite 400   Phone: (612) 338-7816
Minneapolis, MN 55402   Morton W. Ryweck, Dir.
Founded: 1975. **Staff:** Prof 3; Other 2. **Subjects:** Anti-Semitism, prejudice and discrimination, Judaism, Soviet Jewry, Israel, teacher education in human relations, the Holocaust, minority studies. **Holdings:** 1000 books; 16 VF drawers; 85 films. **Subscriptions:** 10 journals and other serials. **Services:** Library open to public. **Publications:** List of publications and films - available on request.

★6440★

JEWISH CONVALESCENT HOSPITAL CENTRE - HEALTH SCIENCES INFORMATION CENTRE (Med)
3205 Alton Goldbloom   Phone: (514) 688-9550
Chomedey, Laval, PQ, Canada H7V 1R2   Irene Deborah Shanefield, Med.Libn.
Founded: 1979. **Staff:** Prof 1. **Subjects:** Medicine, speech therapy, physiotherapy, rehabilitation, occupational therapy, nursing. **Special Collections:** Travel guides for the disabled (500). **Holdings:** 800 books; 400 bound periodical volumes. **Subscriptions:** 83 journals and other serials. **Services:** Interlibrary loans; copying; library open to public by appointment. **Computerized Information Services:** MEDLINE; computerized acquisitions. **Networks/Consortia:** Member of McGill Medical and Health Libraries Association. **Publications:** Information Package, quarterly.

★6441★

JEWISH EDUCATION SERVICE OF NORTH AMERICA, INC. - LIBRARY (Educ)†
114 Fifth Ave.   Phone: (212) 675-5656
New York, NY 10011   Dr. Shimon Frost, Dir.
Subjects: Jewish education. **Holdings:** 4000 volumes.

★6442★

JEWISH EDUCATION SERVICE OF NORTH AMERICA, INC. - NATIONAL EDUCATIONAL RESOURCE CENTER (Area-Ethnic)
114 Fifth Ave.   Phone: (212) 675-5656
New York, NY 10011   Carolyn S. Hessel, Coord.
Founded: 1978. **Staff:** Prof 2; Other 1. **Subjects:** Jewish education, Holocaust, Israel, Bible, Jewish life cycle, youth movements. **Special Collections:** Uncopyrighted teacher-designed classroom materials. **Holdings:** 1000 boxes of educational materials. **Subscriptions:** 35 journals and other serials; 35 newspapers. **Services:** Copying; center open to public by appointment. **Networks/Consortia:** Member of Association of Jewish Libraries. **Publications:** Printed subject bibliographies. **Formerly:** American Association for Jewish Education.

★6443★

JEWISH FEDERATION COUNCIL OF GREATER LOS ANGELES - PETER M. KAHN JEWISH COMMUNITY LIBRARY (Area-Ethnic)
6505 Wilshire Blvd.   Phone: (213) 663-8484
Los Angeles, CA 90048   Mrs. Hava Ben-Zvi, Libn.
Founded: 1947. **Staff:** Prof 1; Other 2. **Subjects:** Jewish culture - education, sociology, history, life in America; Israel and Zionism; Yiddish and Hebrew literature. **Special Collections:** Historical documents and pictures pertaining to the history of the Jewish community in Los Angeles and vicinity. **Holdings:** 46,000 books; 4000 bound periodical volumes; 20 cases of pamphlets; 69 reels of microfilm; archives of the parent organization. **Subscriptions:** 200 journals and other serials; 35 newspapers. **Services:** Interlibrary loans; copying; library open to public, deposit required for borrowing. **Publications:** Acquisitions lists; bibliographies as needed.

★6444★
JEWISH FEDERATION OF NASHVILLE AND MIDDLE TENNESSEE - ARCHIVES (Rel-Theol)
3500 West End Ave.   Phone: (615) 297-3588
Nashville, TN 37205   Annette R. Levy, Dir.
Founded: 1979. **Staff:** Prof 2. **Special Collections:** Archives of the Nashville Jewish community (95 linear feet). **Holdings:** 3 record groups; 43 manuscript collections; 60 small collections; Jewish newspapers on microfilm. **Services:** Interlibrary loans; archives open to public with restrictions. **Staff:** Ferd Engel, Archv.

★6445★
JEWISH FEDERATION OF OMAHA - LIBRARY (Rel-Theol)
333 S. 132nd St.   Phone: (402) 334-8200
Omaha, NE 68154   Edythe Wolf, Dir.
Founded: 1928. **Staff:** Prof 1; Other 2. **Subjects:** Jewish religion and philosophy, Biblical commentary and research, history, Jewish literature and art, Israel, Holocaust, fiction. **Special Collections:** Marc Chagall; Rabbi Moses Maimonides; Saul Raskin; comparative religion. **Holdings:** 18,000 books; 1100 bound periodical volumes; 2500 records (cataloged); 1000 pamphlets; 600 films, 1000 filmstrips; 60 audio-slide presentations. **Subscriptions:** 75 journals and other serials. **Services:** Interlibrary loans; copying; library open to public. **Special Indexes:** Index to Omaha Jewish Press (book).

★6446★
JEWISH GUILD FOR THE BLIND - YOUNG MEN'S PHILANTHROPIC LEAGUE - CASSETTE LIBRARY (Aud-Vis)
15 W. 65th St.   Phone: (212) 595-2000
New York, NY 10023   Bruce E. Massis, Dir.
Founded: 1974. **Staff:** Prof 1; Other 2. **Subjects:** Best sellers. **Holdings:** 30,000 cassettes (590 titles). **Services:** Interlibrary loans; library open to the blind and physically handicapped. **Remarks:** Entire collection is on standard compact cassettes; books are circulated, by mail, without charge to blind persons in the United States and foreign countries.

★6447★
JEWISH HISTORICAL SOCIETY OF NEW YORK, INC. - LIBRARY (Hist; Area-Ethnic)
8 W. 70th St.   Phone: (212) 873-0300
New York, NY 10023   Steven W. Siegel, Exec.Sec.
Founded: 1973. **Staff:** Prof 1. **Subjects:** American and New York Jewish history. **Holdings:** 300 books. **Services:** Provides telephone and mail reference service.

★6448★
JEWISH HOSPITAL OF CINCINNATI - MEDICAL LIBRARY (Med)
3200 Burnet Ave.   Phone: (513) 569-2014
Cincinnati, OH 45229   Melanie F. McGuire, Med.Libn.
Founded: 1959. **Staff:** Prof 1; Other 2. **Subjects:** Medicine. **Special Collections:** History of medicine (1004 volumes); Heritage file (1042 cataloged journal articles written by members of the hospital staff); medical rare books (374); Robert C. Rothenberg shelf for leisurely medical reading (146 volumes). **Holdings:** 3401 books; 5238 bound periodical volumes; 230 video cassettes; 870 audio cassettes; 200 slides. **Subscriptions:** 180 journals and other serials. **Services:** Interlibrary loans; copying; library open to public for reference use only. **Computerized Information Services:** NLM, BRS. **Networks/Consortia:** Member of Cincinnati Area Health Sciences Libraries Association; Kentucky-Ohio-Michigan Regional Medical Library Network (KOMRML); Cincinnati Online Consortium for Life Sciences.

★6449★
JEWISH HOSPITAL OF CINCINNATI SCHOOL OF NURSING - NURSE'S REFERENCE LIBRARY (Med)
3161 Harvey Ave.   Phone: (513) 872-3534
Cincinnati, OH 45229   Alice W. Neumann, Instr./Media Coord.
Staff: Prof 1. **Subjects:** Nursing, medicine, psychology, education. **Holdings:** 3700 books; 261 bound periodical volumes; 200 boxes of unbound periodicals; 125 files of pamphlets. **Subscriptions:** 87 journals and other serials. **Services:** Interlibrary loans; library open to alumni and hospital personnel.

★6450★
JEWISH HOSPITAL AND MEDICAL CENTER OF BROOKLYN - GREENPOINT HOSPITAL AFFILIATION - MEDICAL LIBRARY (Med)†
300 Skillman Ave.   Phone: (212) 387-3010
Brooklyn, NY 11211   Leon Elveson, Med.Libn.
Founded: 1950. **Staff:** Prof 1; Other 1. **Subjects:** Medicine and allied sciences. **Holdings:** 2000 books; 500 bound periodical volumes; 3 VF drawers of unbound materials. **Subscriptions:** 160 journals and other serials.

Services: Interlibrary loans; copying; library not open to public.

★6451★
JEWISH HOSPITAL AND MEDICAL CENTER OF BROOKLYN - MEDICAL & NURSING LIBRARY (Med)
555 Prospect Pl.   Phone: (212) 240-1795
Brooklyn, NY 11238   Sharon R. Peterson, Med.Libn.
Founded: 1896. **Staff:** Prof 1; Other 4. **Subjects:** Medicine and allied sciences; nursing. **Holdings:** 7920 books; 2500 bound periodical volumes; 6 VF drawers; 4 drawers of audiotapes. **Subscriptions:** 250 journals and other serials. **Services:** Interlibrary loans; copying; library not open to public. **Networks/Consortia:** Member of Medical Library Center of New York; Brooklyn-Queens-Staten Island Health Science Librarians; METRO. **Special Catalogs:** Periodical articles. **Staff:** Ida Greenberg, Asst.Per.

★6452★
JEWISH HOSPITAL OF ST. LOUIS - ROTHSCHILD MEDICAL LIBRARY (Med)†
216 S. Kingshighway   Phone: (314) 454-7208
St. Louis, MO 63110   Ruth Kelly, Libn.
Founded: 1930. **Staff:** Prof 1; Other 2. **Subjects:** Medicine. **Holdings:** 2262 books; 5634 bound periodical volumes. **Subscriptions:** 167 journals and other serials. **Services:** Interlibrary loans; copying; library open to medical personnel.

★6453★
JEWISH HOSPITAL OF ST. LOUIS - SCHOOL OF NURSING - MOSES SHOENBERG MEMORIAL LIBRARY (Med)
306 S. Kingshighway   Phone: (314) 454-8474
St. Louis, MO 63110   Alice Bruenjes, Hd.Libn.
Founded: 1920. **Staff:** Prof 1; Other 3. **Subjects:** Nursing and nursing education; medicine. **Holdings:** 2300 books; VF materials. **Subscriptions:** 52 journals and other serials. **Services:** Interlibrary loans; library open to persons in the health sciences field for limited use.

JEWISH INSTITUTE OF RELIGION
See: Hebrew Union College

★6454★
JEWISH MEMORIAL HOSPITAL - IRVING DORFMAN MEMORIAL MEDICAL LIBRARY (Med)
4600 Broadway   Phone: (212) 569-4700
New York, NY 10040   Theodora L.D. Lindt, Dir.
Founded: 1934. **Staff:** Prof 1. **Subjects:** Medicine and allied sciences. **Special Collections:** History of medicine. **Holdings:** 3650 books; 3780 bound periodical volumes; 6 VF drawers; 250 audiotapes; 150 manuscripts. **Subscriptions:** 63 journals and other serials. **Services:** Interlibrary loans; copying; library open to public with restrictions.

★6455★
JEWISH MUSEUM - LIBRARY (Area-Ethnic; Art)
1109 Fifth Ave.   Phone: (212) 860-1888
New York, NY 10028   Beverly Franco, Libn.
Founded: 1947. **Subjects:** Jewish art, architecture, decorative arts, history, religion, archeology, coins. **Holdings:** 1500 books; 1000 other cataloged items. **Subscriptions:** 30 journals and other serials. **Services:** Library open to scholars and students by appointment. **Remarks:** Library is under the auspices of the Jewish Theological Seminary of America.

JEWISH PRESS - BROOKLYN DAILY LIBRARY
See: Brooklyn Daily Library

★6456★
JEWISH PUBLIC LIBRARY OF MONTREAL (Area-Ethnic)
5151 Cote St. Catherine Rd.   Phone: (514) 735-6535
Montreal, PQ, Canada H3W 1M6 Zipporah Dunsky-Shnay, Dir.
Founded: 1914. **Staff:** Prof 4; Other 13. **Subjects:** Judaica and Hebraica. **Special Collections:** Jewish Canadiana; archives; vertical file on world Jewry; rare books; Holocaust Collection. **Holdings:** 105,000 books; 5000 bound periodical volumes; 400 tapes; phonograph records. **Subscriptions:** 250 journals and other serials (in 4 languages). **Services:** Interlibrary loans; copying; library open to public. **Publications:** JPL News (bulletin), quarterly - community-wide distribution. **Special Catalogs:** Holocaust Bibliography. **Remarks:** Also maintains a Branch Library in Laval and a Children's Library. **Staff:** Naomi Caruso, Coord.

★6457★
JEWISH PUBLIC LIBRARY OF TORONTO (Area-Ethnic)
22 Glen Park Ave.   Phone: (416) 781-6282
Toronto, ON, Canada M6B 2B9   Rabbi Z. Wolkenstein, Exec.Dir.
Founded: 1939. **Staff:** Prof 3; Other 1. **Subjects:** Bible and Talmud,
Rabbinics and Hassidism, Holocaust, Israel and Zionism, history, language and
literature. **Special Collections:** Judaica and Hebraica. **Holdings:** 30,000
volumes. **Subscriptions:** 50 journals and other serials. **Services:** Interlibrary
loans; copying; library open to public. **Remarks:** Maintained by Toronto Jewish
Congress. **Staff:** Rose Miskin, Libn.; Helena Isenberg, Libn.; Jeannette Blatt,
Asst.Libn.

★6458★
JEWISH THEOLOGICAL SEMINARY OF AMERICA - LIBRARY (Rel-Theol)
3080 Broadway   Phone: (212) 749-8000
New York, NY 10027   Dr. Menahem Schmelzer, Libn.
Founded: 1903. **Staff:** Prof 16; Other 14. **Subjects:** Bible, rabbinics,
theology, Jewish history, liturgy, Hebrew literature, early Yiddish writings,
science, medicine. **Special Collections:** Haggadahs, Megillot (Esther scrolls),
Ketuboth Incunabula (marriage contracts); L. Ginzberg microfilm collection
(Hebrew manuscripts). **Holdings:** 240,000 volumes; 10,000 manuscripts.
Subscriptions: 500 journals and other serials. **Services:** Interlibrary loans;
copying; library open to public for on-site use. **Computerized Information
Services:** Computerized cataloging. **Networks/Consortia:** Member of SUNY/
OCLC Library Network; New York Area Theological Library Association.
Publications: Selected list of recent acquisitions, monthly. **Staff:** Edith
Degani, Adm.Libn.

★6459★
JEWISH VOCATIONAL SERVICE - LIBRARY (Soc Sci)
1 S. Franklin   Phone: (312) 346-6700
Chicago, IL 60606
Founded: 1935. **Staff:** Prof 1. **Subjects:** Social services, vocational
rehabilitation, educational counseling, psychology. **Holdings:** 2500 books;
350 bound periodical volumes; 75 VF drawers of pamphlets. **Subscriptions:**
90 journals and other serials. **Services:** Interlibrary loans; library open to
qualified users in social work and related fields.

JFK CENTER FOR THE PERFORMING ARTS - AMERICAN FILM INSTITUTE
See: American Film Institute

★6460★
JHK & ASSOCIATES - TECHNICAL LIBRARY - EAST (Trans)
4660 Kenmore Ave.   Phone: (703) 370-2411
Alexandria, VA 22304   Richard Presby, Dir.
Founded: 1975. **Staff:** Prof 2; Other 1. **Subjects:** Traffic engineering,
transportation, regional and environmental studies. **Holdings:** 7800 books;
1500 bound periodical volumes; 25,000 items in vertical file; 1000
microfiche; 1800 slides and maps. **Subscriptions:** 210 journals and other
serials; 15 newspapers. **Services:** Interlibrary loans; copying; library open to
public by appointment. **Computerized Information Services:** TRIS; internal
database; computerized acquisitions, serials and circulation. **Publications:**
Acquisition list, quarterly; annual report. **Staff:** Kay Hathaway, Asst.Libn.

★6461★
JHK & ASSOCIATES - TECHNICAL LIBRARY - WEST (Trans)
5801 Christie Ave., No. 220   Phone: (415) 428-2550
Emeryville, CA 94608   Richard Presby, Dir. of Libs.
Founded: 1971. **Staff:** Prof 2; Other 1. **Subjects:** Traffic engineering,
transportation, environmental studies, defense-crisis studies, management.
Special Collections: Motorist Aid Systems Studies File (1400 items).
Holdings: 12,500 books; 1000 bound periodical volumes; 280 linear feet of
vertical files; 7500 company files; 3200 microforms. **Subscriptions:** 230
journals and other serials; 16 newspapers. **Services:** Interlibrary loans;
copying; library open to public with restrictions. **Publications:** Acquisition list,
quarterly; annual report.

★6462★
JIM WALTER RESEARCH CORPORATION - LIBRARY (Sci-Tech)
10301 9th St., N.   Phone: (813) 576-4171
St. Petersburg, FL 33702   Jane E. Mueller, Chf.Libn.
Founded: 1966. **Subjects:** Building materials research and development,
polymer science, chemical engineering, pulp and paper products, acoustics,
insulation. **Holdings:** 3000 books; 600 bound periodical volumes.
Subscriptions: 150 journals and other serials. **Services:** Interlibrary loans;
copying; library not open to public. **Computerized Information Services:**
DIALOG.

★6463★
JOCKEY CLUB - LIBRARY (Rec)
380 Madison Ave.   Phone: (212) 599-1919
New York, NY 10017   Robert L. Melican, Exec.Dir.
Subjects: Thoroughbred breeding and racing. **Special Collections:** Stud books
of many countries. **Holdings:** 2000 books; 500 bound periodical volumes.

JOHN CARROLL UNIVERSITY
See: Carroll (John) University

JOHN CRERAR LIBRARY
See: Crerar (John) Library

★6464★
JOHN DEERE PRODUCT ENGINEERING CENTER - LIBRARY (Sci-Tech)
Box 8000   Phone: (319) 236-8020
Waterloo, IA 50704   YangHoon Rhee, Libn.
Staff: Prof 2; Other 1. **Subjects:** Applied mechanics, internal combustion
engines, fuels and lubricants, materials. **Holdings:** 3000 volumes; technical
reports and manuals; patents. **Subscriptions:** 200 journals and other serials.
Services: Interlibrary loans; copying; library open to public with restrictions.
Computerized Information Services: DIALOG, Tech-Net. **Networks/
Consortia:** Member of OCLC. **Staff:** Millicent Williams, Libn.

★6465★
**JOHN HANCOCK MUTUAL LIFE INSURANCE COMPANY - COMPANY
LIBRARY** (Bus-Fin)
John Hancock Pl.
Box 111   Phone: (617) 421-4524
Boston, MA 02117   Amy C. Wang, Libn.
Founded: 1949. **Staff:** Prof 3; Other 4. **Subjects:** Life and health insurance,
pensions, business, management. **Special Collections:** Company archives;
memorablilia relating to John Hancock, the Patriot; old insurance books.
Holdings: 18,000 books; 276 VF drawers of unbound material; microfilm.
Subscriptions: 500 journals and other serials; 6 newspapers. **Services:**
Interlibrary loans; copying; SDI; library open to public with restrictions.
Computerized Information Services: DIALOG, BRS, New York Times
Information Service; computerized serials. **Publications:** What's New in the
Company Library, monthly - for internal distribution only. **Special Indexes:**
Index of pertinent articles from publications received.

★6466★
**JOHN JAY COLLEGE OF CRIMINAL JUSTICE OF THE CITY UNIVERSITY OF
NEW YORK - REISMAN MEMORIAL LIBRARY** (Law)†
445 W. 59th St.   Phone: (212) 489-5169
New York, NY 10019   Professor Eileen Rowland, Chf.Libn.
Founded: 1965. **Staff:** Prof 10; Other 12. **Subjects:** Criminal justice,
government, fire science, forensic science, forensic psychology, public
administration, police science. **Special Collections:** John Howard Collection
(prison reform; 100 volumes); Theater for the Forgotten Workshops (30
videotapes); New York City criminal courts trial transcripts, 1890-1920
(1000 volumes); Lewis E. Lawes (warden of Sing Sing Prison) papers, 1883-
1947 (13 boxes). **Holdings:** 115,000 books; 14,000 bound periodical
volumes. **Subscriptions:** 1200 journals and other serials. **Services:**
Interlibrary loans; copying; library open to public for reference use only.
Computerized Information Services: DIALOG; computerized cataloging.
Networks/Consortia: Member of METRO. **Staff:** Professor D. Grande, Hd.,
Tech.Serv.; Professor M. Lutzker, Hd., Rd.Serv.

★6467★
JOHN MARSHALL LAW SCHOOL - LIBRARY (Law)
315 S. Plymouth Ct.   Phone: (312) 427-2737
Chicago, IL 60604   Randall T. Peterson, Dir.
Founded: 1899. **Staff:** Prof 8; Other 12. **Subjects:** Law, taxation, intellectual
property. **Holdings:** 185,000 volumes; 66,363 volumes on microform; 24
sets of federal administrative documents; NRS ultrafiche (1st series);
Congressional Information Service (CIS) publications (1970 to present);
Congressional Record (1873 to present); Code of Federal Regulations (CFR)
microfiche edition (1938 to present); IHS microfiche of legislative histories
(10 subject areas); CCH Tax Library; U.S. Supreme Court Records and Briefs
(1930 to present); Federal Register (1936 to present). **Subscriptions:** 1917
journals and other serials; 12 newspapers. **Services:** Interlibrary loans;
copying; circulation privileges to current faculty and students only.
Computerized Information Services: LEXIS; WESTLAW; computerized
cataloging. **Networks/Consortia:** Member of Metropolitan Chicago Library
Assembly; OCLC through ILLINET; Chicago Library System. **Staff:** Carole
Levitt Axelrod, Hd., Pub.Serv.; Dorothy In-Lan Wang Li, Hd., Tech.Serv.;
Hazel Hill, Acq.; Kathleen Powers, Cat.Libn; Judy DeGarmo, Asst.Cat.Libn.;
Ruth Nelson, Ref.Libn.; Kelly Warnken, Ref.Libn.; Sarah Goenne, Circ.Mgr.;

Laura Hyzy, Ser.Mgr.

★6468★

JOHN MUIR MEMORIAL HOSPITAL - HEALTH SCIENCES LIBRARY (Med)
1601 Ygnacio Valley Rd.   Phone: (415) 939-3000
Walnut Creek, CA 94598   Helen M. Reyes, Libn.
Founded: 1967. **Staff:** Prof 1; Other 6. **Subjects:** Health sciences, medicine, dentistry, nursing, pharmacy, hospital administration, psychiatry and allied health sciences. **Holdings:** 1650 books; 1450 bound periodical volumes. **Subscriptions:** 210 journals and other serials. **Services:** Interlibrary loans; copying; SDI; library open to qualified health science personnel. **Computerized Information Services:** MEDLARS. **Networks/Consortia:** Member of Pacific Southwest Regional Medical Library Service (PSRMLS); East Bay Medical Library Group; Northern California Medical Library Group; Bay Area Library and Information System (BALIS). **Publications:** New Acquisitions, monthly; Serials Titles List.

★6469★

JOHN PETER SMITH HOSPITAL - MARIETTA MEMORIAL MEDICAL LIBRARY (Med)
1500 S. Main   Phone: (817) 921-3431
Fort Worth, TX 76104   Sharon Louise McAllister, Med.Libn.
Founded: 1963. **Staff:** Prof 1; Other 2. **Subjects:** Medicine, nursing, and related subjects. **Holdings:** 3500 books; 8000 bound periodical volumes; 800 audiotapes. **Subscriptions:** 282 journals and other serials. **Services:** Interlibrary loans (limited); copying; complete services to the personnel of the Tarrant County Hospital District and the Tarrant County Medical Society; library open to public but services available to health professionals only. **Computerized Information Services:** NLM, MEDLINE. **Networks/Consortia:** Member of Metroplex Council of Health Science Librarians; Dallas-Tarrant County Consortium of Health Science Libraries. **Publications:** Union List of Serials, biennial - to members; Acquisitions List, bimonthly.

★6470★

JOHN XXIII ECUMENICAL CENTER, INC. - CENTER FOR EASTERN CHRISTIAN STUDIES (Rel-Theol)
2502 Belmont Ave.   Phone: (212) 298-8752
Bronx, NY 10458   Rev. Thomas F. Sable, S.J., Dir.
Staff: Prof 1; Other 1. **Subjects:** Eastern theology, art, liturgy, Church history, Russian history, literature. **Special Collections:** Tyskiewich Collection (Russian books on Russian theology; 850 books); John Ryder, S.J. manuscripts (23 boxes); Walter Ciszek, S.J. manuscripts (12 boxes). **Holdings:** 6600 books; 400 bound periodical volumes; 20 boxes of unbound periodicals. **Subscriptions:** 60 journals and other serials; 20 newspapers.

★6471★

JOHNS HOPKINS HOSPITAL - DEPARTMENT OF RADIOLOGY - LIBRARY (Med)
601 N. Broadway   Phone: (301) 955-6029
Baltimore, MD 21205   Elaine Pinkney, Libn.
Staff: Prof 1; Other 1. **Subjects:** Radiology, sonography, computed tomography, nuclear medicine. **Holdings:** 1700 books; 5000 bound periodical volumes; 10,000 X-ray films. **Subscriptions:** 54 journals and other serials. **Services:** Interlibrary loans; copying; library open to public with restrictions.

★6472★

JOHNS HOPKINS UNIVERSITY - APPLIED PHYSICS LABORATORY - CHEMICAL PROPULSION INFORMATION AGENCY (Sci-Tech)†
Johns Hopkins Rd.   Phone: (301) 953-7100
Laurel, MD 20810   Ronald D. Brown, Group Supv.
Founded: 1946. **Staff:** Prof 10; Other 11. **Subjects:** Chemical rockets, chemical propellants, solid rocket motors, liquid rocket engines, ramjet engines, gun propellants. **Holdings:** 50,000 chemical propulsion research, development, test and evaluation reports. **Services:** Agency open to outside users who have security clearance and a need-to-know; payment of annual service charge required. **Computerized Information Services:** Internal database. **Publications:** List of publications - available upon request.

★6473★

JOHNS HOPKINS UNIVERSITY - APPLIED PHYSICS LABORATORY - R.E. GIBSON LIBRARY (Sci-Tech)
Johns Hopkins Rd.   Phone: (301) 953-7100
Laurel, MD 20810   Linda J. Kosmin, Act.Dir.
Founded: 1946. **Staff:** Prof 5; Other 21. **Subjects:** Physics, electronics, space research, mathematics, computing sciences, mechanical engineering, biophysics. **Holdings:** 41,500 books; 20,000 bound periodical volumes; 40,000 technical reports on microfiche (cataloged); 137,000 hard copy technical reports. **Subscriptions:** 1042 journals and other serials. **Services:** Interlibrary loans; copying; mechanized literature searches; SDI; library open to public with restrictions. **Computerized Information Services:** DIALOG, SDC, BRS, New York Times Information Service, NASA/RECON; acquisitions and circulation. **Networks/Consortia:** Member of Interlibrary Users Association. **Publications:** APL Library Bulletin, irregular - for internal distribution only; Guide to the Abstracting and Indexing Journals in the APL Libraries, triennial; APL Journal List-Holdings in the Libraries of the Applied Physics Laboratory, biennial - both available on request. **Special Indexes:** Technical Report Index (KWIC title, author/title, corporate author/report number). **Staff:** Hattie T. Anderson, Contracts Info.; DeAnna Jones, Asst.Supv., Tech.Serv.; Mary E. Brown, Online Search Serv.; Zoe Carpenter, Cat.Libn.; Amy Debrower, Ref.Libn.

★6474★

JOHNS HOPKINS UNIVERSITY - CENTER FOR METROPOLITAN PLANNING AND RESEARCH - LIBRARY (Plan)
Shriver Hall   Phone: (301) 338-7169
Baltimore, MD 21218   Deniz Bilgin
Founded: 1968. **Staff:** Prof 1. **Subjects:** Urban planning and architecture, law, social studies. **Special Collections:** Occasional Papers of the Center (50 titles). **Holdings:** 3000 books; 100 bound periodical volumes; foreign publications; selected local, state and federal government agency reports. **Subscriptions:** 15 journals and other serials. **Services:** Copying; library open to public.

★6475★

JOHNS HOPKINS UNIVERSITY - DEPARTMENT OF EARTH AND PLANETARY SCIENCES - SINGEWALD READING ROOM (Sci-Tech)
                    Phone: (301) 366-3300
Baltimore, MD 21218   Dr. George W. Fisher, Chm.
Founded: 1966. **Staff:** Prof 1; Other 1. **Subjects:** Chemistry, mineralogy, economic geology, paleontology, sedimentology, structural geology, regional geology, petrology, geophysics. **Special Collections:** Geological theses. **Holdings:** 300 books; 850 bound periodical volumes; 200 dissertations. **Subscriptions:** 30 journals and other serials. **Services:** Interlibrary loans; copying; library not open to public.

★6476★

JOHNS HOPKINS UNIVERSITY - FERDINAND HAMBURGER, JR. ARCHIVES (Hist)
3400 North Charles St.   Phone: (301) 338-8323
Baltimore, MD 21218   Julia B. Morgan, Archv.
Founded: 1971. **Staff:** Prof 1; Other 2. **Subjects:** Johns Hopkins University. **Holdings:** 1500 linear feet of archives. **Subscriptions:** 10 journals and other serials. **Services:** Copying; archives open to public by appointment. **Remarks:** This is the official archival repository for the nonmedical divisions of the university.

★6477★

JOHNS HOPKINS UNIVERSITY - JOHN WORK GARRETT LIBRARY (Rare Book)
Evergreen House
4545 N. Charles St.   Phone: (301) 338-7641
Baltimore, MD 21218   Ann Gwyn, Asst.Univ.Lib.Dir.
Founded: 1952. **Staff:** Prof 1. **Subjects:** 16th and 17th century English literature, 15th century books, early travel exploration, architecture, Bibles. **Special Collections:** Books printed before 1700 relating to Maryland; Lawrence H. Fowler Architectural Collection; Hofmann Bible Collection; letters and papers of A.C Pugin (35 pieces), Ignacio Zuloaga (100 pieces), Edith Wharton (64 pieces), Leon Bakst (30 pieces), Signers of the Constitution (75 pieces). **Holdings:** 20,000 books; 500 bound periodical volumes. **Services:** Interlibrary loans; copying (limited); library open to public with restrictions. **Computerized Information Services:** Computerized cataloging. **Networks/Consortia:** Member of RLG. **Special Catalogs:** The Fowler Architectural Catalog, compiled by Laurence Hall Fowler and Elizabeth Baer, 1961; Medals Relating to Medicine and Allied Sciences in the Numismatic Collection of the Johns Hopkins University, a catalog compiled by Sarah Elizabeth Freeman, 1964. **Special Indexes:** Seventeenth Century Maryland: A Bibliography, compiled by Elizabeth Baer, 1949. **Remarks:** The John Work Garrett Library is a part of The Milton S. Eisenhower Library, Special Collections Department. **Staff:** Jane Katz, Libn.

★6478★

JOHNS HOPKINS UNIVERSITY - MILTON S. EISENHOWER LIBRARY - GEORGE PEABODY COLLECTION (Hist; Hum)
17 E. Mt. Vernon Pl.   Phone: (301) 396-5540
Baltimore, MD 21202   Lyn Hart, Dept.Hd.
Founded: 1857. **Staff:** Prof 2; Other 4. **Subjects:** English and American history, genealogy, languages and literature (especially English, Romance, Classical), art and architecture, cartography/exploration and travel, natural

history, history of science. **Special Collections:** John Pendleton Kennedy Manuscript Collection. **Holdings:** 215,000 books; 40,000 bound periodical volumes. **Subscriptions:** 140 journals and other serials. **Services:** Interlibrary loans; copying; collection open to public for reference use only. **Networks/Consortia:** Member of Maryland Interlibrary Loan Organization (MILO). **Special Catalogs:** Catalog of the Peabody Institute Library. **Formerly:** Enoch Pratt Free Library - George Peabody Department. **Staff:** Robert Bartram, Ref.Libn.

★6479★

JOHNS HOPKINS UNIVERSITY - MILTON S. EISENHOWER LIBRARY - GOVERNMENT PUBN./MAPS/LAW LIBRARY (Info Sci; Geog-Map)
Charles & 34th Sts.   Phone: (301) 338-8360
Baltimore, MD 21218   Diane K. Harvey, Libn.
Staff: Prof 2; Other 4. **Special Collections:** U.S. Government documents (1882 to present); U.N. documents (1945 to present); international documents; technical reports (Atomic Energy Commission, NASA, RAND Corporation); League of Nations documents; U.S. Geological Survey maps. **Holdings:** 183,000 books and bound periodical volumes; 180,000 maps; 300 atlases; state and federal legal materials. **Services:** Interlibrary loans; copying; library open to public upon application. **Computerized Information Services:** DIALOG, BRS, SDC; computerized circulation. **Networks/Consortia:** Member of RLG; Maryland Interlibrary Loan Organization (MILO). **Staff:** James Gillispie, Asst.Libn.

★6480★

JOHNS HOPKINS UNIVERSITY - POPULATION INFORMATION PROGRAM (Soc Sci)
624 N. Broadway   Phone: (301) 955-8200
Baltimore, MD 21205   Dr. Phyllis T. Piotrow, Dir.
Founded: 1972. **Staff:** Prof 13; Other 13. **Subjects:** Population, family planning, human fertility, contraception and related health, law and policy issues. **Holdings:** 3000 books; 1000 VF items. **Subscriptions:** 500 journals and other serials. **Services:** Interlibrary loans; copying; SDI; center open to public by appointment. **Computerized Information Services:** POPLINE. **Publications:** Population Reports, bimonthly - 80,000 mailing list distribution worldwide; POPLINE Thesaurus; annual index to Population Reports. **Remarks:** The purpose of the program is to provide accurate, continuing, systematic and up-to-date information on new developments in population, family planning and related issues. The program is supported by the United States Agency for International Development. **Staff:** Walter W. Stender, Assoc.Dir.; Anne Comptor, Coord.; Ward Rinehart, Ed.

★6481★

JOHNS HOPKINS UNIVERSITY - RESEARCH & DEVELOPMENT CENTER - CENTER FOR SOCIAL ORGANIZATION OF SCHOOLS (Educ)
3505 N. Charles St.   Phone: (301) 338-7570
Baltimore, MD 21218   John H. Hollifield, Asst.Dir.
Founded: 1966. **Staff:** 25. **Subjects:** School organization, desegregation, delinquency and schools, career guidance. **Holdings:** 300 research reports. **Services:** Interlibrary loans; center open to public by appointment. **Publications:** Annual Publications, Abstracts, research reports, - free upon request.

★6482★

JOHNS HOPKINS UNIVERSITY - SCHOOL OF ADVANCED INTERNATIONAL STUDIES - SYDNEY R. & ELSA W. MASON LIBRARY (Soc Sci)
1740 Massachusetts Ave., N.W.   Phone: (202) 785-6296
Washington, DC 20036   Peter J. Promen, Libn.
Founded: 1943. **Staff:** Prof 3; Other 7. **Subjects:** International affairs since 1945, international economics and law, history, politics, sociology. **Holdings:** 77,000 books; 10,000 bound periodical volumes; 4600 reels of microfilm; 6000 microfiche. **Subscriptions:** 850 journals and other serials; 35 newspapers. **Services:** Interlibrary loans; copying; library open to public with registration and fee. **Computerized Information Services:** Computerized cataloging. **Networks/Consortia:** Member of OCLC through PALINET & Union Library Catalogue of Pennsylvania. **Staff:** Linda Carlson, Rd.Serv.Libn.; Sabiha Famularo, Cat.Libn.

★6483★

JOHNS HOPKINS UNIVERSITY - SCHOOL OF HYGIENE AND PUBLIC HEALTH - INTERDEPARTMENTAL LIBRARY (Med)
615 N. Wolfe St.   Phone: (301) 955-3028
Baltimore, MD 21205   Edward S. Terry, Dir.
Founded: 1963. **Staff:** Prof 3; Other 4. **Subjects:** Health services administration, epidemiolgy, mental hygiene, international health, behavioral sciences, sociology. **Holdings:** 10,500 books and bound periodical volumes; 5500 Department of Health, Education and Welfare publications; 10 VF drawers and 114 pamphlet boxes of state health department reports and special health reports. **Subscriptions:** 250 journals and other serials. **Services:** Library open to health professionals and researchers in the Baltimore area. **Computerized Information Services:** BRS, DIALOG. **Publications:** List of selected acquisitions, monthly - for internal distribution only. **Staff:** Barbara L. Zelnik, Asst.Dir.; Chris Ikehara, Ref.Libn.

★6484★

JOHNS HOPKINS UNIVERSITY-SCHOOL OF HYGIENE & PUBLIC HEALTH- MATERNAL & CHILD HEALTH/POPULATION DYNAMICS LIB. (Soc Sci)
615 N. Wolfe St.   Phone: (301) 955-3573
Baltimore, MD 21205   Linda Knarr, Libn.
Staff: Prof 2; Other 2. **Subjects:** Population dynamics, maternal and child health, family planning, physiology of reproduction, nurse-midwifery, pediatrics. **Special Collections:** U.S. Census publications, 1790 to present; U.S. vital and health statistics, 1935 to present. **Holdings:** 7000 books; 600 bound periodical volumes; 150 theses (cataloged); 600 pamphlets of the National Center for Health Statistics; 100 documents in bibliography file; 500 documents of the Population Association of America. **Subscriptions:** 157 journals and other serials. **Services:** Interlibrary loans; library open to public. **Computerized Information Services:** POPLINE, DIALOG, MEDLINE; computerized cataloging. **Networks/Consortia:** Member of Association for Population/Family Planning Libraries and Information Centers - International (APLIC-Internatl.). **Publications:** Current contents of journals received, bimonthly - to faculty and students; acquisitions list, monthly - to students, faculty, and university libraries; serials holdings list. **Special Catalogs:** Reprints and working papers catalog (card). **Staff:** Susan Leibtag, Cat.

★6485★

JOHNS HOPKINS UNIVERSITY - SCHOOL OF MEDICINE - DEPARTMENT OF PEDIATRICS - BAETJER MEMORIAL LIBRARY (Med)
CMSC 2-104 Johns Hopkins Hospital   Phone: (301) 955-3124
Baltimore, MD 21205   Patricia A. Nulle, Libn.
Founded: 1963. **Subjects:** Pediatrics, general medicine. **Special Collections:** Transactions of the American Pediatric Society; Archives of Pediatrics, 1884-1922; Dr. Edwards A. Park Medical Notes, 1927-1955 (26 notebooks). **Holdings:** 400 books; 2200 bound periodical volumes. **Subscriptions:** 53 journals and other serials. **Services:** Copying; library not open to public. **Publications:** Department of Pediatrics Collected Reprints, semiannual.

★6486★

JOHNS HOPKINS UNIVERSITY - SCHOOL OF MEDICINE - JOSEPH L. LILIENTHAL LIBRARY (Med)
Blalock Bldg., 10th Fl.
601 N. Broadway   Phone: (301) 955-6641
Baltimore, MD 21205   Robin A. Kroft, Libn.
Staff: Prof 1. **Subjects:** Internal medicine. **Holdings:** 500 books; 2000 bound periodical volumes; slide/tape Postgraduate Course in Internal Medicine. **Subscriptions:** 45 journals and other serials. **Services:** Copying; library open to public with restrictions.

★6487★

JOHNS HOPKINS UNIVERSITY - WILLIAM H. WELCH MEDICAL LIBRARY (Med)
1900 E. Monument St.   Phone: (301) 955-3411
Baltimore, MD 21205   Richard A. Polacsek, M.D., Dir./Libn.
Founded: 1929. **Staff:** Prof 13; Other 37. **Subjects:** Life sciences, public health, history of medicine. **Special Collections:** Institute of the History of Medicine (40,000 volumes); Henry Jacobs Collection (history of the diseases of the chest and vaccination); Florence Nightingale Collection (history of nursing); Emory H. Niles Collection (legal medicine). **Holdings:** 145,000 books; 112,500 bound periodical volumes; 1800 AV items. **Subscriptions:** 2300 journals and other serials. **Services:** Interlibrary loans; copying; library not open to public. **Computerized Information Services:** BRS, SDC, NLM, Control Data Corporation; retrospective and SDI computer-based retrieval; computerized cataloging, serials and interlibrary loans. **Networks/Consortia:** Member of OCLC. **Publications:** Recent Acquisitions, monthly. **Staff:** Robert Gresehover, Assoc.Dir.; Karen Higgins, Asst.Dir.; Gloria Lyles, Adm.; Gretchen Naisawald, Hd. of Ref.

★6488★

JOHNS HOPKINS UNIVERSITY - WILMER OPHTHALMOLOGICAL INSTITUTE - JONAS S. FRIEDENWALD LIBRARY (Med)†
Johns Hopkins Hospital
601 N. Broadway   Phone: (301) 955-3127
Baltimore, MD 21205   Maria Tama Maggio, Lib.Techn.
Founded: 1925. **Staff:** 1. **Subjects:** Ophthalmology. **Holdings:** 6135 books; 6500 bound periodical volumes. **Subscriptions:** 110 journals and other serials. **Services:** Library open to public for reference use only.

JOHNS-MANVILLE CORPORATION
See: Manville Service Corporation

JOHNSON (A.M.) MEMORIAL MEDICAL LIBRARY
See: St. Luke's Memorial Hospital - A.M. Johnson Memorial Medical Library

JOHNSON (Andrew) NATL. HISTORIC SITE
See: U.S. Natl. Park Service - Andrew Johnson Natl. Historic Site

★6489★
JOHNSON (Bernard) INC. - TECHNICAL LIBRARY (Sci-Tech)
5050 Westheimer
Houston, TX 77056
Phone: (713) 622-1400
C. David Rushbrook, Libn.
Founded: 1975. **Staff:** Prof 1; Other 1. **Subjects:** Engineering, architecture, environment, land development. **Special Collections:** History of architecture. **Holdings:** 5000 books; 79 bound periodical volumes; 750 VF drawers of company archives; 4 VF drawers of clippings; 20 VF drawers of maps. **Subscriptions:** 302 journals and other serials. **Services:** Interlibrary loans; copying; library open to public by appointment. **Computerized Information Services:** DIALOG, SDC; internal database. **Publications:** New at the Library, monthly - free upon request.

★6490★
JOHNSON BIBLE COLLEGE - GLASS MEMORIAL LIBRARY (Rel-Theol)
Kimberlin Heights, TN 37920
Phone: (615) 573-4517
Helen E. Lemmon, Libn.
Founded: 1893. **Staff:** Prof 1; Other 20. **Subjects:** Theology, church history, literature. **Holdings:** 53,000 books; 3300 bound periodical volumes; 14 VF drawers of pamphlets; 6 VF drawers of mission letters; 200 reels of microfilm. **Subscriptions:** 265 journals and other serials; 5 newspapers. **Services:** Interlibrary loans; copying; library open to public with restrictions.

★6491★
JOHNSON CONTROLS - BATTERY DIVISION - TECHNICAL LIBRARY (Sci-Tech)†
5757 N. Green Bay Ave.
Milwaukee, WI 53201
Phone: (414) 228-2382
Marian Rauch, Tech.Libn.
Founded: 1952. **Subjects:** Electronics, chemistry, batteries, business management, ceramics, physics. **Holdings:** Figures not available. **Services:** Interlibrary loans; library open to public on request.

★6492★
JOHNSON CONTROLS, INC. - CORPORATE INFO. CTR./LIBRARY M47 (Sci-Tech)
507 E. Michigan St.
Box 423
Milwaukee, WI 53201
Phone: (414) 274-4687
Mary F. Kaczmarek, Libn.
Founded: 1973. **Staff:** Prof 2. **Subjects:** Electronics, computers, heating, ventilating, air conditioning, energy conservation, management. **Holdings:** 5200 books; 130 bound periodical volumes; 8250 technical reports; 1000 standards and specifications. **Subscriptions:** 350 journals and other serials. **Services:** Interlibrary loans; SDI; library open to public with restrictions. **Computerized Information Services:** DIALOG, SDC. **Networks/Consortia:** Member of Library Council of Metropolitan Milwaukee, Inc. (LCOMM). **Publications:** JCI Technical Library News, bimonthly - for internal distribution only; serials list. **Staff:** Mary Beth Allsop, Asst.Libn.

★6493★
JOHNSON COUNTY HISTORICAL SOCIETY - HERITAGE LIBRARY (Hist)
135 E. Pine St.
Warrensburg, MO 64093
Phone: (816) 747-3381
Leona J. Sisson, Libn.
Founded: 1968. **Subjects:** History of townships; genealogy; business; transportation. **Holdings:** 500 volumes; 3 VF drawers of papers of U.S. Senator Cockrell; Smiser Collection; directories; census records; diaries; cemetery records; documents; manuscripts; photographs; early county newspapers; 75 tapes. **Subscriptions:** 30 journals and other serials. **Services:** Library open to public for reference use only. **Publications:** Bulletin, semiannual - to membership.

★6494★
JOHNSON COUNTY LAW LIBRARY (Law)
Courthouse
Olathe, KS 66061
Phone: (913) 782-5000
J.W. Breyfogle, III, Libn.
Staff: Prof 1; Other 1. **Subjects:** Law. **Holdings:** 14,000 books; 25 bound periodical volumes; cassettes. **Subscriptions:** 40 journals and other serials; 5 newspapers. **Services:** Interlibrary loans; copying; library open to public.

★6495★
JOHNSON COUNTY MENTAL HEALTH CENTER - JOHN R. KEACH MEMORIAL LIBRARY (Med)
6000 Lamar Ave.
Mission, KS 66202
Phone: (913) 384-1100
Heidi Simpson, Libn.
Founded: 1963. **Staff:** 1. **Subjects:** Mental health, psychology, psychiatry, social work. **Holdings:** 1712 books; 199 bound periodical volumes; 8 VF drawers. **Subscriptions:** 25 journals and other serials. **Services:** Interlibrary loans; copying; open to Johnson County residents. **Networks/Consortia:** Member of Midcontinental Regional Medical Library Program.

★6496★
JOHNSON (George) ADVERTISING - LIBRARY (Bus-Fin)
763 New Ballas Rd., S.
St. Louis, MO 63141
Phone: (314) 569-3440
Marianne C. Goedeker, Libn.
Founded: 1965. **Staff:** Prof 1. **Subjects:** Advertising, management, marketing. **Holdings:** 261 volumes; 16 VF drawers of clippings. **Subscriptions:** 65 journals and other serials; 5 newspapers. **Services:** Interlibrary loans; copying; library open to public with restrictions.

★6497★
JOHNSON & HIGGINS - EBP RESEARCH LIBRARY (Bus-Fin)
95 Wall St.
New York, NY 10005
Phone: (212) 482-6570
Renee Sanders, Libn.
Staff: Prof 1; Other 1. **Subjects:** Pensions, Social Security, group insurance, health care. **Holdings:** 1000 books; 20 VF drawers of annual reports; 17 VF drawers of clippings. **Subscriptions:** 37 journals and other serials. **Services:** Copying; library open to public with restrictions. **Publications:** Monthly Acquisitions List; subject heading list, annual - both for internal distribution only.

JOHNSON AND JOHNSON - CHICOPEE, INC.
See: Chicopee, Inc.

JOHNSON AND JOHNSON - PERSONAL PRODUCTS COMPANY
See: Personal Products Company

★6498★
JOHNSON & JOHNSON PRODUCTS INC. - RESEARCH INFORMATION SERVICES (Sci-Tech; Med)
New Brunswick, NJ 08903
Phone: (201) 524-5563
Claire R. McDonnell, Mgr., Info.Serv.
Founded: 1948. **Staff:** Prof 5; Other 1. **Subjects:** Chemistry, textiles, biology, medicine and dentistry. **Holdings:** 8000 volumes. **Subscriptions:** 400 journals and other serials. **Services:** Interlibrary loans; library open to public with restrictions. **Computerized Information Services:** DIALOG, SDC, NLM, BRS; computerized circulation. **Networks/Consortia:** Member of Medical Resources Consortium of Central New Jersey (MEDCORE). **Staff:** Charlotte Finneran, Assoc.Libn.; Dorothy Whateley, Info.Sci.

★6499★
JOHNSON AND JOHNSON, INC. - RESEARCH LIBRARY (Sci-Tech)
7101 Notre Dame St., E.
Montreal, PQ, Canada H1N 2G4
Phone: (514) 252-5029
Lilian Smyth, Res.Libn.
Founded: 1954. **Staff:** 1. **Subjects:** Toiletries, adhesives, textiles, chemistry, pulp and paper, plastics. **Holdings:** 1200 books; patents and reprints. **Subscriptions:** 87 journals and other serials. **Services:** Interlibrary loans; copying; library not open to public.

JOHNSON AND JOHNSON - SURGIKOS - TECHNICAL INFORMATION CENTER
See: Surgikos - Technical Information Center

JOHNSON LIBRARY
See: Bergen County Historical Society

JOHNSON (Lyndon B.) LIBRARY
See: U.S. Presidential Libraries - Lyndon B. Johnson Library

JOHNSON (Lyndon B.) NATL. HISTORICAL PARK
See: U.S. Natl. Park Service - Lyndon B. Johnson Natl. Historical Park

JOHNSON (Lyndon B.) SCHOOL OF PUBLIC AFFAIRS LIBRARY
See: University of Texas, Austin - Lyndon B. Johnson School of Public Affairs Library

JOHNSON (Lyndon B.) SPACE CENTER
See: U.S. NASA - Lyndon B. Johnson Space Center

JOHNSON (Martin and Osa) SAFARI MUSEUM
See: Martin and Osa Johnson Safari Museum

JOHNSON (Mildred) LIBRARY
See: North Dakota State School of Science - Mildred Johnson Library

★6500★
JOHNSON PUBLISHING COMPANY, INC. - LIBRARY (Area-Ethnic; Publ)
820 S. Michigan Ave.   Phone: (312) 322-9320
Chicago, IL 60605   Pamela J. Cash, Libn.
Founded: 1949. **Staff:** Prof 2; Other 2. **Subjects:** Afro-Americana; black history, literature, biography; Africa. **Special Collections:** Newspaper clippings that date from the 1940s; black newspapers from 1846 (microfilm). **Holdings:** 8000 books; 600 bound periodical volumes; 300 drawers of newspaper clippings; pamphlets, company publications. **Subscriptions:** 150 journals and other serials; 50 newspapers. **Services:** Library not open to public.

JOHNSON RESEARCH FOUNDATION LIBRARY
See: University of Pennsylvania

★6501★
JOHNSON (Robert Wood) FOUNDATION - LIBRARY (Med; Educ)
Box 2316   Phone: (609) 452-8701
Princeton, NJ 08540   Philip J. Gallagher, Libn.
Founded: 1972. **Staff:** Prof 1; Other 1. **Subjects:** Health care, health economics, medical education, higher education, philanthropy. **Holdings:** 3600 books; 200 annual reports of foundations; 15 films; 28 cassettes; 17 maps; 170 health school catalogs. **Subscriptions:** 165 journals and other serials; 7 newspapers. **Services:** Interlibrary loans; copying; library open to public with restrictions. **Networks/Consortia:** Member of Consortium of Foundation Librarians; Central Jersey Health Science Libraries Association.

JOHNSON (Roswell H.) RESEARCH LIBRARY
See: American Institute of Family Relations - Roswell H. Johnson Research Library

★6502★
JOHNSON (S.C.) AND SON, INC. - TECHNICAL & BUSINESS INFORMATION CENTER (Sci-Tech)
1525 Howe St.   Phone: (414) 554-2372
Racine, WI 53403   E.L. Schaut, Tech.Mgr.
Staff: Prof 2; Other 1. **Subjects:** Chemistry, biology, physics, business. **Holdings:** 14,000 books; 7500 bound periodical volumes. **Subscriptions:** 600 journals and other serials. **Services:** Interlibrary loans; library open to public by appointment. **Computerized Information Services:** DIALOG, SDC. **Publications:** Activity and acquisitions list - for internal distribution only. **Staff:** Mara Teranis, Info.Sci.

★6503★
JOHNSON & SWANSON - LIBRARY (Law)
4700 First International Bldg.   Phone: (214) 746-7059
Dallas, TX 75270   Catherine Pennington, Law Libn.
Founded: 1975. **Staff:** Prof 4; Other 2. **Subjects:** Law - taxation, banking, labor; international securities; oil and gas. **Holdings:** 20,000 books; 1100 bound periodical volumes; microfiche; 35 volumes of bound transactions; 6000 volumes in microform; collection of bills introduced before the 69th Texas legislative session. **Subscriptions:** 450 journals and other serials; 14 newspapers. **Services:** Interlibrary loans; copying (fee); library open to public with introduction. **Computerized Information Services:** LEXIS; computerized cataloging and serials. **Networks/Consortia:** Member of Dallas Association of Law Librarians; OCLC. **Publications:** Library Newsletter listing new acquisitions; Labor & International Law Watch Service. **Special Catalogs:** Catalog of inhouse opinions and memoranda (card); catalog for bound transactions (card). **Remarks:** Maintains a branch library of 5000 volumes in Austin, TX. **Formerly:** Johnson Swanson & Barbee. **Staff:** Betty Dewberry, Assoc.Libn.; Diane Gates, Asst.Libn./Tech.Serv.; Catherine Pogue, Br.Libn.

★6504★
JOHNSON & WALES COLLEGE - PAUL FRITZSCHE LIBRARY (Food-Bev)
1150 Narragansett Blvd.   Phone: (401) 456-1174
Cranston RI 02905   David B. Puffer, Lib.Dir.
Founded: 1979. **Staff:** Prof 1; Other 1. **Subjects:** Cookbooks, menu planning, nutrition, hostessing and party giving, household manuals, canning, preserving and freezing. **Special Collections:** Church and civic group cookbooks and pamphlets (1500). **Holdings:** 6500 books; 300 bound periodical volumes; 200 menus. **Services:** Library open to public with restrictions.

JOHNSTON MEMORIAL LIBRARY
See: Virginia State University

★6505★
JOHNSTONE (E.R.) TRAINING & RESEARCH CENTER - PROFESSIONAL LIBRARY (Med)
Burlington St.   Phone: (609) 298-2500
Bordentown, NJ 08505   Herman H. Spitz, Dir. of Res.
Staff: 2. **Subjects:** Mental retardation, psychology. **Holdings:** 2775 books; 1280 bound periodical volumes; 100 Johnstone bulletins; 75 research reports. **Subscriptions:** 72 journals and other serials. **Services:** Interlibrary loans; copying; library open to public.

★6506★
JOHNSTOWN HISTORICAL SOCIETY - LIBRARY REFERENCE CENTER (Hist)
17 N. William St.   Phone: (518) 762-7076
Johnstown, NY 12095   Dr. Charles J. Noxon, Cur.
Staff: 1. **Subjects:** Local history, Sir William Johnson, Elizabeth Cady Stanton. **Special Collections:** Keck Zouaves; Knox Gelatine; Grace Livingston Hill; Brigadier-General Edgar S. Dudley. **Holdings:** 700 books; 50 bound periodical volumes; 250 booklets and pamphlets; 2000 photographs; 1000 documents; 3 files of clippings; 32 old maps. **Services:** Library open to public. **Computerized Information Services:** Computerized cataloging and acquisitions.

JOINT BANK-FUND LIBRARY
See: International Monetary Fund/World Bank

★6507★
JOINT DISEASES/NORTH GENERAL HOSPITAL - MEDICAL LIBRARY (Med)
1919 Madison Ave.   Phone: (212) 650-4000
New York, NY 10035   Jana Martin, Med.Libn.
Staff: Prof 1; Other 1. **Subjects:** Medicine. **Holdings:** 2200 monographs; 4200 bound periodical volumes. **Subscriptions:** 146 journals and other serials. **Services:** Interlibrary loans; copying; library open to public by appointment. **Networks/Consortia:** Member of Medical Library Center of New York (MLCNY). **Formerly:** North General Hospital.

JOINT DISTRIBUTION COMMITTEE - LIBRARY
See: American Jewish Joint Distribution Committee - Library

★6508★
JOINT EDUCATIONAL CONSORTIUM - ARCHIVES (Soc Sci)
Box 499   Phone: (501) 246-9283
Arkadelphia, AR 71923   Dolphus Whitten, Jr., Exec.Dir.
Staff: Prof 1; Other 2. **Subjects:** Oral history of Arkansas, rural studies, community development. **Holdings:** 500 tapes of oral history interviews; 14 tapes from conferences on problems on rural America; 150 tapes of community opinion interviews; 900 historical photographs. **Services:** Archives open to public.

JOINT INSTITUTE FOR LABORATORY ASTROPHYSICS (Boulder, CO)
See: University of Colorado, Boulder

JONAS (Oswald) MEMORIAL ARCHIVE
See: University of California, Riverside - Music Library

JONES (Bayard Hale) LITURGICAL LIBRARY
See: University of the South - School of Theology Library

★6509★
JONES, BIRD & HOWELL, ATTORNEYS AT LAW - LIBRARY
75 Poplar St., N.W.
Haas-Howell Bldg.
Atlanta, GA 30335
Defunct. Merged with Alston, Miller and Gaines to form Alston and Bird.

JONES (Bob) UNIVERSITY
See: Bob Jones University

★6510★
JONES, DAY, REAVIS & POGUE - LAW LIBRARY (Law)
2001 Bryan Tower, Suite 2700   Phone: (214) 748-3939
Dallas, TX 75201   Mary Guittard Voegtle, Libn.
Founded: 1981. **Staff:** Prof 1; Other 2. **Subjects:** Law - antitrust, real estate, tax, corporate, securities, contract. **Holdings:** 20,000 books; 133 bound periodical volumes; 9 pamphlet files of annual reports; 5 VF drawers of government releases and ephemera; Federal Register on microfiche, 1977-1980; Price-Waterhouse and Ernst & Whinney Information Guides.

Subscriptions: 232 journals and other serials; 13 newspapers. **Services:** Interlibrary loans; copying; library open to public with restrictions. **Computerized Information Services:** LEXIS. **Publications:** Library acquisitions lists.

★6511★
JONES, DAY, REAVIS & POGUE - LIBRARY (Law)
1700 Union Commerce Bldg.
Cleveland, OH 44115   Phone: (216) 696-3939
     Sharon R. McIntyre, Libn.
Staff: Prof 2; Other 4. **Subjects:** Law. **Holdings:** 32,000 books; 1500 bound periodical volumes. **Subscriptions:** 160 journals and other serials. **Services:** Interlibrary loans; library not open to public. **Computerized Information Services:** DIALOG, SDC, New York Times Information Service, LEXIS. **Staff:** Timothy Petty, Asst.Libn.

JONES (James A.) LIBRARY
See: Brevard College - James A. Jones Library

★6512★
JONES AND LAUGHLIN STEEL CORPORATION - COMMERCIAL LIBRARY (Bus-Fin)
1600 W. Carson St.   Phone: (412) 227-4354
Pittsburgh, PA 15263   Nancy Winstanley, Libn.
Staff: Prof 1. **Subjects:** Steel industry, marketing. **Holdings:** 700 books; 8 VF drawers of government documents; 16 VF drawers of annual reports; 4 VF drawers of business services; 10 VF drawers of clippings. **Subscriptions:** 50 journals and other serials. **Services:** Interlibrary loans; copying; library open to public by appointment. **Computerized Information Services:** DIALOG, SDC. **Publications:** Holdings list, irregular.

★6513★
JONES AND LAUGHLIN STEEL CORPORATION - GRAHAM LIBRARY (Sci-Tech)
900 Agnew Rd.   Phone: (412) 884-1000
Pittsburgh, PA 15227   Joanne S. Klein, Tech.Libn.
Founded: 1955. **Staff:** Prof 1; Other 1. **Subjects:** Metallurgy, chemistry, engineering, instrumentation, electronics. **Holdings:** 6000 books; 7500 bound periodical volumes; 13,000 translations; 30 VF drawers of U.S. patents (indexed); 5000 government reports (indexed); 150 microforms. **Subscriptions:** 300 journals and other serials; 5 newspapers. **Services:** Interlibrary loans; translation (limited); literature searching; SDI; library not open to public. **Computerized Information Services:** DIALOG, SDC, BRS. **Publications:** Current Information Alert, biweekly. **Special Indexes:** Computer-produced index to internal research reports.

JONES LAW INSTITUTE
See: University of Alabama

★6514★
JONES LIBRARY, INC. - SPECIAL COLLECTIONS (Hist)
43 Amity St.   Phone: (413) 256-0246
Amherst, MA 01002   Daniel J. Lombardo, Cur. of Spec.Coll.
Founded: 1921. **Staff:** Prof 1; Other 3. **Subjects:** Local and regional history, Amherst authors, genealogy. **Special Collections:** Robert Frost Collection; Emily Dickinson Collection; Ray Stannard Baker Collection. **Holdings:** Figures not available. **Services:** Interlibrary loans; copying; special collections open to public. **Special Catalogs:** Finding aids.

JONES (Nettie Marie) FINE ARTS LIBRARY
See: Lake Placid Association for Music, Drama & Art - Nettie Marie Jones Fine Arts Library

JONES (Perrie) MEMORIAL ROOM
See: St. Paul Public Library - Highland Park Branch - Perrie Jones Memorial Room

JONES (Seby) LIBRARY
See: Toccoa Falls College - Seby Jones Library

JONES (T.J.) MEMORIAL LIBRARY
See: North Central Bible College - T.J. Jones Memorial Library

★6515★
JONES (W. Alton) CELL SCIENCE CENTER - GEORGE AND MARGARET GEY LIBRARY (Med)
Old Barn Rd.   Phone: (518) 523-2427
Lake Placid, NY 12946   A. Kathleen Bonham, Libn.
Staff: Prof 1. **Subjects:** Cell culture, organ culture, cytology, cancer research, virology, biochemistry, immunology. **Special Collections:** Plant tissue culture.

Holdings: 3100 books; 4500 bound periodical volumes; 50,000 reprints on tissue culture. **Subscriptions:** 100 journals and other serials. **Services:** Interlibrary loans; copying; library open to public. **Computerized Information Services:** MEDLINE, DIALOG. **Formerly:** Tissue Culture Association - W. Alton Jones Cell Science Center.

★6516★
JONES, WALKER, WAECHTER, POITEVENT, CARRERE & DENEGRE - LAW LIBRARY (Law)
225 Baronne St.   Phone: (504) 581-6641
New Orleans, LA 70112   Deborah A. Sabalot, Libn.
Staff: Prof 1; Other 2. **Subjects:** Law, Louisiana law. **Special Collections:** Oil and gas law. **Holdings:** 21,000 books; 1000 bound periodical volumes; 5000 other cataloged items. **Subscriptions:** 200 journals and other serials; 12 newspapers. **Services:** Interlibrary loans; copying; library open to public with restrictions. **Computerized Information Services:** LEXIS.

JORDAN (Barbara) ARCHIVES
See: Texas Southern University - Library - Heartman Collection

JORDAN COLLEGE OF FINE ARTS MUSIC LIBRARY
See: Butler University

★6517★
JORDAN (Edward C.) CO., INC. - LIBRARY (Env-Cons)
Box 7050   Phone: (207) 775-5401
Portland, ME 04112   Jane Weeks, Libn.
Staff: Prof 1. **Subjects:** Water pollution control, engineering, planning, architecture. **Holdings:** 3000 books; 48 bound periodical volumes. **Subscriptions:** 240 journals and other serials; 12 newspapers. **Services:** Copying; library open to public by referral and appointment.

JORDAN (L.R.) LIBRARY
See: Baptist Medical Centers-Samford University - Ida V. Moffett School of Nursing - L.R. Jordan Library

JORGENSEN (Niels Bjorn) MEMORIAL LIBRARY
See: Loma Linda University - Niels Bjorn Jorgensen Memorial Library

★6518★
JOSEPHINE COUNTY HISTORICAL SOCIETY - RESEARCH LIBRARY (Hist)
716 N.W. A St.
Box 742   Phone: (503) 479-7827
Grants Pass, OR 97526   Pauline Shier, Libn.
Staff: 2. **Subjects:** Local history. **Special Collections:** Newspaper microfilm collection (198 reels); original county tax records (1856-1953). **Holdings:** 150 books; 27 VF drawers of pamphlets; 3 VF drawers of photographs; 2000 slides. **Services:** Copying; library open to public. **Networks/Consortia:** Member of Southern Oregon Library Federation (SOLF). **Publications:** The Oldtimer, quarterly - for members only.

★6519★
JOSEPHINE COUNTY LAW LIBRARY (Law)
Courthouse   Phone: (503) 474-5181
Grants Pass, OR 97526   A.M. Foster, County Ck.
Founded: 1939. **Staff:** 1. **Subjects:** State and federal law, bankruptcy, eminent domain, mining laws, municipal corporations, laws of evidence, automobile law. **Holdings:** 5270 books; 2060 bound periodical volumes. **Services:** Library open to public for reference use only.

JOSEY MEMORIAL MEDICAL LIBRARY
See: Richland Memorial Hospital

★6520★
JOSLIN DIABETES CENTER, INC. - MEDICAL LIBRARY (Med)
One Joslin Pl.   Phone: (617) 723-9065
Boston, MA 02215   Greene Havener, Libn.
Staff: Prof 1. **Subjects:** Diabetes mellitus, endocrinology, metabolism, life sciences. **Special Collections:** Archives (400 volumes); reprint collection of papers by the staff of the Joslin Research Laboratory (1000). **Holdings:** 950 books; 5000 bound periodical volumes; 75 VF folders. **Subscriptions:** 70 journals and other serials. **Services:** Interlibrary loans; copying; library open to public with librarian's approval. **Networks/Consortia:** Member of Boston Biomedical Library Consortium. **Publications:** Acquisitions list, monthly. **Special Catalogs:** Catalog of papers published by Joslin Research Laboratory staff.

★6521★
JOSLYN ART MUSEUM - ART REFERENCE LIBRARY (Art)
2200 Dodge   Phone: (402) 342-3300
Omaha, NE 68102   Ann E. Birney, Libn.
Founded: 1931. Staff: Prof 3. Subjects: Art - native American, Western, Oriental; architecture; impressionism. Special Collections: Western Americana: Frontier History of the Trans-Mississippi West, 1550-1900 (7000 volumes on microfilm). Holdings: 17,000 books; 2750 bound periodical volumes; 140 VF drawers of clippings; 500 bound bulletins, annual reports; 800 reports; 20,000 slides. Subscriptions: 96 journals and other serials. Services: Interlibrary loans; copying; library open to public. Staff: Marie Sedlacek, Cat.; Grace G. Keenan, Asst.Libn.

JOSTEN (Werner) LIBRARY FOR THE PERFORMING ARTS
See: Smith College - Werner Josten Library for the Performing Arts

★6522★
JOURNAL OF COMMERCE - EDITORIAL LIBRARY (Bus-Fin)
110 Wall St.   Phone: (212) 425-1616
New York, NY 10005   Christine Karpevych, Info.Serv.Mgr.
Staff: Prof 1; Other 1. Subjects: World trade, shipping, aviation and surface transportation, oil, gas, coal, banking and international finance, insurance, commodoties, plastics and chemicals. Holdings: 150 books; 32 VF drawers of Journal of Commerce clippings; 9 VF drawers of annual reports and current information files. Subscriptions: 75 journals and other serials; 11 newspapers. Services: Interlibrary loans; copying; library open to public by appointment. Publications: Voice from the Morgue (newsletter) - for internal distribution only.

JOURNAL COMPANY - NEWSPAPERS, INC.
See: Newspapers, Inc.

JOYCE RESEARCH CENTER
See: SCM Corporation - Glidden Coatings & Resins Div./Durkee Foods Division - Technical Information Services

★6523★
JRB ASSOCIATES, INC. - OCCUPATIONAL HEALTH & SAFETY LIBRARY (Sci-Tech)
8400 Westpark Dr.   Phone: (703) 827-8108
McLean, VA 22102   Madeleine Hahn, Libn.
Subjects: Safety, health. Holdings: 80 books; 70 journals; 1000 Occupational Safety and Health Administration and National Institute for Occupational Safety and Health publications; 3500 documents, articles, patents, dissertations and archival materials. Subscriptions: 50 journals and other serials. Services: Interlibrary loans; copying; library not open to public. Computerized Information Services: Online systems; computerized acquisitions. Networks/Consortia: Member of Interlibrary Users Association.

JUBILEE FOUNDATION FOR AGRICULTURAL RESEARCH
See: Christian Farmers Federation of Ontario

JUDAICA MUSIC LIBRARY
See: Temple Beth Israel - Library

JUDGE BAKER GUIDANCE CENTER - GARDNER LIBRARY - REGION I CHILD ABUSE AND NEGLECT RESOURCE CENTER
See: National Center on Child Abuse and Neglect - Region I Child Abuse and Neglect Resource Center

★6524★
JUILLIARD SCHOOL - LILA ACHESON WALLACE LIBRARY (Mus)
Lincoln Center Plaza   Phone: (212) 799-5000
New York, NY 10023   Brinton Jackson, Libn.
Founded: 1945. Staff: Prof 5; Other 2. Subjects: Music, drama, theatre, dance. Special Collections: 19th century opera scores and librettos; first and rare editions of scores; chamber music. Holdings: 16,000 books; 23,000 AV items; 32,000 circulating scores; 9500 non-circulating scores; 500 choral scores. Subscriptions: 101 journals and other serials. Services: Interlibrary loans; copying; library open to public for reference use by arrangement only. Networks/Consortia: Member of METRO. Staff: Deborah Davis, Asst.Libn.

★6525★
JULIEN, SCHLESINGER & FINZ, P.C., ATTORNEYS-AT-LAW - LIBRARY (Law)†
2 Lafayette St., Suite 1006   Phone: (212) 962-8020
New York, NY 10007
Subjects: Law, products liability, malpractice, negligence tort. Holdings: 5000 volumes. Subscriptions: 30 journals and other serials. Services: Interlibrary loans; copying; library not open to public.

JUSTICE AND PEACE CENTER, MILWAUKEE ARCHIVES
See: Marquette University - Department of Special Collections and University Archives

★6526★
JUNG (C.G.) INSTITUTE OF LOS ANGELES, INC. - LIBRARY (Soc Sci)
10349 West Pico Blvd.   Phone: (213) 556-1193
Los Angeles, CA 90064   Claire Oksner, Dir.
Staff: Prof 3. Subjects: Analytical psychology (Jungian psychology), general and children's psychology, religion, mythology. Special Collections: ARAS (Archive for Research in Archetypal Symbolism) pictorial archive. Holdings: 4000 books, cassettes, theses, papers. Subscriptions: 12 journals and other serials. Services: Library open to public by membership. Publications: Psychological Perspectives, semiannual - by subscription. Staff: Eloise Schlesinger, Libn.; Lore Zeller, Libn.

★6527★
JUSTICE SYSTEM TRAINING ASSOCIATION - PSYCHO-MOTOR SKILL DESIGN ARCHIVE (Soc Sci)
Box 356   Phone: (414) 731-8893
Appleton, WI 54912   Kevin Parsons, Dir.
Staff: Prof 7. Subjects: Physical training, defensive tactics, rape prevention. Special Collections: Police self defense (3000 volumes). Holdings: 8000 books; 100 bound periodical volumes. Subscriptions: 50 journals and other serials. Services: Copying; library not open to public. Publications: Column in Law and Order Magazine, monthly - nationally to law enforcement agencies. Special Catalogs: Bibliographies on specific topics.

K

★6528★
K.K. BENE ISRAEL/ROCKDALE TEMPLE - SIDNEY G. ROSE MEMORIAL LIBRARY (Rel-Theol)
8501 Ridge Rd.   Phone: (513) 891-9900
Cincinnati, OH 45236   Mrs. Seymour Miller, Libn.
Staff: Prof 2. **Subjects:** Judaica. **Holdings:** 6000 books. **Subscriptions:** 9 journals and other serials. **Services:** Library open to public.

★6529★
KADISON, PFAELZER, WOODARD, QUINN & ROSSI - LAW LIBRARY (Law)
707 Wilshire Blvd., 40th Fl.   Phone: (213) 688-9000
Los Angeles, CA 90017   Diane G. Sapienza, Law Libn.
Staff: Prof 1; Other 1. **Subjects:** Law, business. **Holdings:** 15,000 books; 250 bound periodical volumes. **Subscriptions:** 50 journals and other serials; 12 newspapers. **Services:** Interlibrary loans; library not open to public. **Computerized Information Services:** LEXIS, New York Times Information Service.

KAHLER LIBRARY
See: Rochester Methodist Hospital - Methodist Kahler Library

KAHN (Albert) ARCHITECTURE LIBRARY
See: Detroit Institute of Arts - Research Library

KAHN (Peter M.) JEWISH COMMUNITY LIBRARY
See: Jewish Federation Council of Greater Los Angeles - Peter M. Kahn Jewish Community Library

★6530★
KAISER ALUMINUM & CHEMICAL CORPORATION - TECHNICAL INFORMATION CENTER (Sci-Tech)
Center for Technology
6177 Sunol Blvd.
Box 877
Pleasanton, CA 94566   Phone: (415) 462-1122
                                 Gary Gerard, Mgr.
Staff: Prof 4; Other 5. **Subjects:** Aluminum, refractories, chemistry, metallurgy, nonferrous metals, aluminas, extractive metallurgy, ores. **Holdings:** 20,000 books; 15,000 bound periodical volumes; 30,000 reports and reprints (cataloged). **Subscriptions:** 650 journals and other serials; 5 newspapers. **Services:** Interlibrary loans; copying; center not open to public. **Publications:** Current Awareness Bulletin, semimonthly; Library Accessions List, biweekly. **Special Catalogs:** Computer-produced book catalogs of book and periodical holdings, documents, and KACC company reports. **Staff:** Fred Farhat, Mgr., Lib.Serv.

★6531★
KAISER ENGINEERS, INC. - ENGINEERING LIBRARY (Sci-Tech)
300 Lakeside Dr.
Box 23210
Oakland, CA 94623   Phone: (415) 271-4375
                           Elaine Zacher, Tech.Libn.
Founded: 1951. **Staff:** Prof 1; Other 2. **Subjects:** Engineering - hydraulic, mechanical, mining and metallurgy, sanitary, structural. **Holdings:** 5500 books; 500 pamphlets. **Subscriptions:** 153 journals and other serials. **Services:** Interlibrary loans; library open to public for reference use only by request. **Computerized Information Services:** DIALOG, SDC, DOE/RECON; computerized serials.

★6532★
KAISER FOUNDATION HOSPITAL - MANAGEMENT EFFECTIVENESS LIBRARY (Med)†
4747 Sunset Blvd.   Phone: (213) 667-5460
Los Angeles, CA 90027   Frances E. Beattie, Libn.
Founded: 1976. **Staff:** Prof 2. **Subjects:** Hospital administration, health laws. **Holdings:** 2800 books; 150 bound periodical volumes. **Subscriptions:** 77 journals and other serials. **Services:** Interlibrary loans; copying; library open to public with restrictions. **Computerized Information Services:** DIALOG, BRS; internal database; computerized cataloging and circulation. **Networks/Consortia:** Member of Kaiser Permanente Library System (KPLS). **Staff:** Jim Faryar, Libn.

★6533★
KAISER FOUNDATION HOSPITALS - HEALTH SERVICES RESEARCH CENTER LIBRARY (Soc Sci; Med)
4610 S.E. Belmont St.   Phone: (503) 233-5631
Portland, OR 97215   Leslie Webb Wykoff, Libn.
Staff: Prof 1; Other 2. **Subjects:** Health maintenance organizations (HMO), quality of care, health care utilization, manpower, health behavior, group practice. **Holdings:** 3200 books; 27 VF drawers of material; 30,000 microfiche. **Subscriptions:** 175 journals and other serials. **Services:** Interlibrary loans; copying; SDI; library open to public with restrictions. **Computerized Information Services:** DIALOG, BRS, MEDLARS; computerized cataloging. **Networks/Consortia:** Member of Oregon Health Information Network (OHIN).

★6534★
KAISER FOUNDATION HOSPITALS - MEDICAL LIBRARY (Med)
11203 Fairhill Rd.   Phone: (216) 795-8000
Cleveland, OH 44104   Marlene Saul, Med.Libn.
Staff: Prof 1. **Subjects:** Medicine, nursing, ancillary health care. **Holdings:** 188 books; 286 bound periodical volumes; pamphlets; medical literature. **Subscriptions:** 76 journals and other serials. **Services:** Interlibrary loans; copying; library not open to public.

★6535★
KAISER FOUNDATION HOSPITALS - MEDICAL LIBRARY (Med)
12301 Snow Rd.   Phone: (216) 362-2086
Parma, OH 44130   Dianne McCutcheon, Med.Libn.
Staff: 1. **Subjects:** Medicine, nursing and ancillary health services. **Holdings:** 385 books; 550 bound periodical volumes; pamphlets, medical literature. **Subscriptions:** 76 journals and other serials; 9 Audio-Digest series. **Services:** Library not open to public.

KAISER FOUNDATION HOSPITALS - MEDICAL LIBRARY (Honolulu, HI)
See: Kaiser Medical Center - Medical Library

KAISER FOUNDATION HOSPITALS - MEDICAL LIBRARY (Los Angeles, CA)
See: Kaiser Permanente Medical Center - Kaiser Foundation Hospital Medical Library

KAISER (Georg) ARCHIV
See: University of Alberta - Special Collections

★6536★
KAISER MEDICAL CENTER - MEDICAL LIBRARY (Med)
1697 Ala Moana Blvd.   Phone: (808) 944-6149
Honolulu, HI 96815   Janice Varner Nakagawara, Med.Libn.
Staff: Prof 1. **Subjects:** Medicine, surgery and related fields. **Holdings:** 1500 books. **Subscriptions:** 160 journals and other serials. **Services:** Interlibrary loans; copying; SDI; library not open to public. **Computerized Information Services:** MEDLINE. **Formerly:** Kaiser Foundation Hospitals.

★6537★
KAISER-PERMANENTE MEDICAL CENTER - HEALTH EDUCATION CENTER (Med)
27400 Hesprian Blvd.
Hayward, CA 94545   Alice Pipes, Libn.
Subjects: Health information for the layman. **Holdings:** Books, medical reference texts, pamphlets and AV materials. **Services:** Center open to members and the general public.

★6538★
KAISER-PERMANENTE MEDICAL CENTER - HEALTH LIBRARY (Med)†
280 W. MacArthur Blvd.   Phone: (415) 428-5000
Oakland, CA 94611   Eileen McAdam, Libn.
Staff: Prof 1; Other 3. **Subjects:** Health maintenance, prenatal care, nutrition, family planning, child care, cancer, medicine. **Holdings:** 1097 books; 407 pamphlet titles; 200 films; 120 AV programs. **Services:** Library open to public. **Publications:** Book List, annual; Equipment, Sources & Software - free upon request; Pamphlet List.

★6539★
KAISER-PERMANENTE MEDICAL CENTER - HEALTH SCIENCES LIBRARY (Med)
27400 Hesperian Blvd.   Phone: (415) 784-5298
Hayward, CA 94545   Alice Pipes, Med.Libn.
Staff: Prof 1. **Subjects:** Medicine and medical specialities, nursing and allied health sciences. **Holdings:** 1500 volumes. **Subscriptions:** 100 journals and other serials. **Services:** Interlibrary loans; copying; library open to public for reference use only by referral.

★6540★

KAISER-PERMANENTE MEDICAL CENTER - HEALTH SCIENCES LIBRARY (Med)
2025 Morse Ave.
Box 254999   Phone: (916) 486-5813
Sacramento, CA 95825   Michael W. Bennett, Health Sci.Libn.
Staff: Prof 1; Other 2. **Subjects:** Medicine, nursing, allied health sciences, health care administration. **Holdings:** 2000 books; 2500 bound periodical volumes; 780 Audio-Digest tapes; 135 audiotapes. **Subscriptions:** 200 journals and other serials. **Services:** Interlibrary loans; copying; library open to health care professionals for reference use only. **Computerized Information Services:** NLM; computerized cataloging. **Networks/Consortia:** Member of Pacific Southwest Regional Medical Library Service (PSRMLS).

★6541★

KAISER-PERMANENTE MEDICAL CENTER - HEALTH SCIENCES LIBRARY (Med)
4647 Zion Ave.   Phone: (714) 563-2190
San Diego, CA 92120   Sheila Latus, Med.Libn.
Founded: 1967. **Staff:** Prof 2; Other 2. **Subjects:** Medicine, nursing, allied health professions. **Holdings:** 3500 books; 5000 bound periodical volumes; 2000 audiotapes. **Subscriptions:** 350 journals and other serials. **Services:** Interlibrary loans; copying; SDI; library open to public with restrictions. **Computerized Information Services:** MEDLINE, BRS; internal database; computerized cataloging, serials and circulation. **Networks/Consortia:** Member of Kaiser Permanente Library System (KPLS). **Staff:** Laurel Windrem, Med.Libn.

★6542★

KAISER-PERMANENTE MEDICAL CENTER - HEALTH SCIENCES LIBRARY (Med)
Box 7612   Phone: (415) 929-4101
San Francisco, CA 94120   Vincent Lagano, Med.Libn.
Founded: 1955. **Staff:** Prof 1; Other 1. **Subjects:** Clinical sciences. **Holdings:** 3500 books; 8000 bound periodical volumes; 1000 pamphlets; 2 file boxes of staff reprints. **Subscriptions:** 190 journals. **Services:** Interlibrary loans; library not open to public. **Publications:** Recent Acquisitions; Current Journals. **Special Catalogs:** Staff publications.

★6543★

KAISER-PERMANENTE MEDICAL CENTER - KAISER FOUNDATION HOSPITAL MEDICAL LIBRARY (Med)
4867 Sunset Blvd.   Phone: (213) 667-8568
Los Angeles, CA 90027   Judith A. Dowd, Dept.Hd.
Founded: 1956. **Staff:** Prof 3; Other 4. **Subjects:** Clinical medicine, nursing, health administration, health media. **Special Collections:** Health Management (3239 books); media center (1116 items). **Holdings:** 4815 books; 6000 bound periodical volumes; 1000 audiotapes. **Subscriptions:** 350 journals and other serials. **Services:** Interlibrary loans; copying; SDI; library not open to public. **Computerized Information Services:** MEDLARS, DIALOG; internal database; computerized circulation. **Networks/Consortia:** Member of Kaiser-Permanente Library System (KPLS). **Publications:** Acquisitions lists, wants lists, exchange lists. **Special Catalogs:** Local and regional catalogs of holdings (book). **Formerly:** Kaiser Foundation Hospitals - Medical Library. **Staff:** Linda Yamamoto, Asst.Med.Libn.; Frances Beattie, Mgt.Libn.

★6544★

KAISER-PERMANENTE MEDICAL CENTER - MEDICAL LIBRARY (Med)†
280 W. MacArthur Blvd.   Phone: (415) 428-5033
Oakland, CA 94611   Helen C. Sheward, Libn.
Founded: 1946. **Staff:** Prof 1; Other 1. **Subjects:** Medicine, psychiatry, administration. **Holdings:** 3500 books; 9000 bound periodical volumes. **Subscriptions:** 209 journals and other serials. **Services:** Interlibrary loans; library not open to public. **Computerized Information Services:** MEDLARS. **Networks/Consortia:** Member of Pacific Southwest Regional Medical Library Service (PSRMLS).

★6545★

KAISER-PERMANENTE MEDICAL CENTER - MEDICAL LIBRARY (Med)
5055 N. Greeley Ave.   Phone: (503) 285-9321
Portland, OR 97217   Patricia Hanley, Med.Libn.
Staff: Prof 1. **Subjects:** Medicine. **Holdings:** 700 books; 400 bound periodical volumes. **Subscriptions:** 203 journals and other serials. **Services:** Interlibrary loans; copying; library not open to public. **Computerized Information Services:** MEDLINE, DIALOG.

★6546★

KAISER-PERMANENTE MEDICAL CENTER - PANORAMA CITY HEALTH SCIENCE LIBRARY (Med)
13652 Cantara St.   Phone: (213) 781-2361
Panorama City, CA 91402   Winnie Yu, Hd.Libn.
Founded: 1962. **Staff:** 4. **Subjects:** Medicine. **Holdings:** 1800 books; 2500 bound periodical volumes; 200 cassettes. **Subscriptions:** 225 journals and other serials. **Services:** Interlibrary loans; copying; library open to staff and employees only. **Computerized Information Services:** MEDLINE; computerized cataloging, serials and circulation. **Networks/Consortia:** Member of Kaiser Permanente Library System (KPLS). **Staff:** Donna Neves, Asst.Libn.

★6547★

KAISER-PERMANENTE MEDICAL CENTER - SOUTH SAN FRANCISCO HEALTH SCIENCES LIBRARY (Med)†
1200 El Camino Real   Phone: (415) 876-0408
South San Francisco, CA 94080   Ysabel R. Bertolucci, Health Sci.Libn.
Staff: Prof 1. **Subjects:** Medicine and nursing. **Holdings:** 1000 books; 2000 bound periodical volumes; 350 audiotapes. **Subscriptions:** 140 journals and other serials. **Services:** Interlibrary loans; copying; library not open to public.

★6548★

KAISER-PERMANENTE MEDICAL CENTERS, NORTHERN CALIFORNIA REGION - REGIONAL HEALTH LIBRARY SERVICES (Med)
3451 Piedmont Ave.   Phone: (415) 428-7176
Oakland, CA 94611   Caren K. Quay, Regional Cons.
Staff: Prof 1; Other 1. **Subjects:** Patient and health education. **Holdings:** Figures not available for catalogs and files. **Services:** Consultation and staff training for Kaiser-Permanente Medical Centers, Northern California Region.

KAISER-RAMAKER LIBRARY
See: North American Baptist Seminary

★6549★

KAISER SUNNYSIDE MEDICAL CENTER - LIBRARY (Med)
10180 S.E. Sunnyside Rd.
Clackamas, OR 97015   Ann H. Haines, Med.Libn.
Staff: Prof 1. **Subjects:** Medicine, nursing. **Holdings:** 450 books. **Subscriptions:** 125 journals and other serials. **Services:** Interlibrary loans; copying; bibliographic searching; library open to public with permission of librarian. **Computerized Information Services:** MEDLINE.

★6550★

KALAMAZOO COUNTY LAW LIBRARY - JUDGE RAYMOND FOX MEMORIAL LIBRARY (Law)
227 W. Michigan Ave.   Phone: (616) 383-8950
Kalamazoo, MI 49007   Jeffrey C. Brennan, Law Lib./Bar Assn.Dir.
Staff: Prof 1. **Subjects:** Law. **Holdings:** 15,000 books; 100 bound periodical volumes; federal and state statutes; reporters. **Services:** Copying; library open to public for reference use only.

★6551★

KALAMAZOO INSTITUTE OF ARTS - ART CENTER LIBRARY (Art)
314 S. Park St.   Phone: (616) 349-7775
Kalamazoo, MI 49007   Helen Sheridan, Hd.Libn.
Founded: 1961. **Staff:** Prof 2. **Subjects:** American art, photography, art history, painting, architecture, drawing, prints, sculpture. **Holdings:** 5500 books; 220 bound periodical volumes; exhibition and sales catalogs; 9500 slides; 32 VF drawers on artists and art-related subjects. **Subscriptions:** 55 journals and other serials. **Services:** Copying; circulation of books to members of Kalamazoo Institute of Arts; slide loans to schools and other established groups; library open to public during gallery hours; reference service. **Networks/Consortia:** Member of Kalamazoo et al (KETAL); Southwest Michigan Library Cooperative (SMLC). **Staff:** Wendy Gadd, Assoc.Libn.; Connie Reik, Asst.Libn.

★6552★

KALAMAZOO NATURE CENTER - REFERENCE LIBRARY (Env-Cons)
7000 N. Westnedge Ave.   Phone: (616) 381-1575
Kalamazoo, MI 49007   Linda Ormond, Libn.
Founded: 1962. **Staff:** Prof 1; Other 1. **Subjects:** Ornithology, natural history, pollution, environmental education, alternative energies, citizen action. **Special Collections:** Collection of VF materials on environmental groups and education facilities (8000 items). **Holdings:** 6200 books; 165 bound periodical volumes; 48 VF drawers of clippings, pamphlets and documents (cataloged); 3 VF drawers of student papers; 3000 units of microfiche. **Subscriptions:** 250 journals and other serials. **Services:** Interlibrary loans; copying; current awareness to staff; bibliography on request; library open to

public for reference use only, circulation to members. **Networks/Consortia:** Member of Kalamazoo et al (KETAL); Great Lakes Environmental Information Sharing (GLEIS). **Publications:** Acquisitions List, bimonthly; cumulative bibliography on earthworm research; directory of Michigan environmental education facilities - all free upon request. **Special Indexes:** Index of National Pollutant Discharge Elimination System permit applications in lower Michigan.

KALAMAZOO SPICE EXTRACTION COMPANY
See: Kalsec, Inc.

★6553★
KALBA BOWEN ASSOCIATES - LIBRARY (Info Sci)
12 Arrow St. Phone: (617) 661-2624
Cambridge, MA 02138 John Adams, Libn./Info.Spec.
Staff: Prof 1; Other 1. **Subjects:** Communications research and technology, information science and services, public policy. **Holdings:** 1000 books; 1500 reports; vertical file of clippings. **Subscriptions:** 126 journals and other serials. **Services:** Library not open to public. **Computerized Information Services:** DIALOG.

KALES (Carl) MEMORIAL LIBRARY
See: Beth El Temple Center - Carl Kales Memorial Library

★6554★
KALISPELL REGIONAL HOSPITAL - MEDICAL LIBRARY (Med)
310 Sunnyview Ln. Phone: (406) 755-5111
Kalispell, MT 59901 Susan Long, Med.Libn.
Staff: Prof 1. **Subjects:** Medicine, surgery, nursing. **Holdings:** 344 books; 502 bound periodical volumes; 150 video cassettes. **Subscriptions:** 80 journals and other serials. **Services:** Interlibrary loans; copying; library open to public for reference use only by appointment. **Computerized Information Services:** MEDLARS. **Networks/Consortia:** Member of Montana Health Sciences Information Network.

★6555★
KALMBACH PUBLISHING COMPANY - INFORMATION CENTER (Trans; Publ)
1027 N. Seventh St. Phone: (414) 272-2060
Milwaukee, WI 53233 George H. Drury, Info.Chf.
Staff: Prof 1. **Subjects:** Railroads, model railroading. **Holdings:** 6000 books; 2000 bound periodical volumes; documents and manuscripts; photographs. **Subscriptions:** 200 journals and other serials. **Services:** Library not open to public. **Remarks:** A research library used by the staffs of Model Railroader, FineScale Modeler and Trains magazines, Kalmbach Books and Kalmbach Video.

KALP (Karl R.) LIBRARY
See: Indianapolis Public Schools - Karl R. Kalp Library

★6556★
KALSEC, INC. - LIBRARY (Food-Bev)
3713 W. Main Phone: (616) 349-9711
Kalamazoo, MI 49005 Mary Sagar, Libn.
Founded: 1972. **Staff:** Prof 1. **Subjects:** Chemistry, food technology, business. **Holdings:** 1000 books; 500 bound periodical volumes; 1000 annual reports, patents, pamphlets, reprints, tapes, microfiche and clippings. **Subscriptions:** 70 journals and other serials. **Services:** Interlibrary loans; library open to employees only. **Also Known As:** Kalamazoo Spice Extraction Company - Library.

★6557★
KAMAN SCIENCES CORPORATION - LIBRARY (Sci-Tech)
1500 Garden of the Gods Rd.
Box 7463
Colorado Springs, CO 80933 Phone: (303) 599-1777
 Barbara A. Kinslow, Libn.
Founded: 1963. **Staff:** 2. **Subjects:** Chemistry, mechanical and nuclear engineering, electronics, instrumentation, materials, mathematics, meteorology, physics. **Holdings:** 5500 books; 15,000 technical reports (cataloged); 800 Kaman reports. **Subscriptions:** 200 journals and other serials. **Services:** Interlibrary loans; copying; library open to public with restrictions.

★6558★
KAMAN-TEMPO - METAL MATRIX INFORMATION ANALYSIS CENTER (Sci-Tech)
816 State St.
Drawer QQ
Santa Barbara, CA 93102 Phone: (805) 963-6497
 Louis Gonzalez, Dir.
Staff: Prof 5; Other 1. **Subjects:** Continuous fibers, wires - manufacturing, defense systems applications, cost, test and evaluation methods, properties,

serviceability/repairs. **Holdings:** Figures not available. **Services:** Center open to Department of Defense contractors. **Computerized Information Services:** DIALOG, DTIC; computerized cataloging and acquisitions. **Publications:** Bibliographies; newsletter. **Remarks:** The Metal Matrix Information Analysis Center (MMC) collects, reviews, analyzes, appraises, summarizes and stores information from Department of Defense technical reports, other government agencies, industry, academic institutions, open literature, including foreign and unpublished sources. **Staff:** Roberta Young, Info.Spec.

★6559★
KAMAN-TEMPO - TECHNICAL INFORMATION CENTER (Sci-Tech)
Drawer QQ Phone: (805) 965-0551
Santa Barbara, CA 93102 Sara B. Ellinwood, Libn.
Founded: 1971. **Staff:** 1. **Subjects:** Physics, mathematics, military science, engineering, astronautics, environment. **Holdings:** 2000 books; 1800 bound periodical volumes; 7 VF drawers of pamphlets; 200 maps. **Subscriptions:** 80 journals and other serials. **Services:** Interlibrary loans; copying.

KAMLOOPS COURTHOUSE LIBRARY
See: British Columbia Law Library Foundation

KAMMANDALE LIBRARY
See: Orphan Voyage

KANANASKIS ENVIRONMENTAL SCIENCES CENTRE
See: University of Calgary

★6560★
KANDIYOHI COUNTY HISTORICAL SOCIETY - VICTOR E. LAWSON RESEARCH LIBRARY (Hist)†
610 NE Hwy. 71 Phone: (612) 235-1881
Willmar, MN 56201 Mona R. Nelson, Program Coord.
Subjects: History - local, state, and U.S. **Special Collections:** Augustana Lutheran Synod minutes (92 volumes). **Holdings:** 1100 books; 500 bound periodical volumes; 297 volumes and 67 linear feet of archives and manuscripts. **Subscriptions:** 30 journals and other serials; 5 newspapers. **Services:** Copying; library open to public. **Publications:** Newsletter, quarterly. **Special Indexes:** Newspaper index (card); archives & manuscripts guide and index (card).

★6561★
KANKAKEE COUNTY HISTORICAL SOCIETY - LIBRARY (Hist)
Eighth & Water St. Phone: (815) 932-5279
Kankakee, IL 60901 Don Des Lauriers, Cur.
Founded: 1906. **Staff:** Prof 1. **Subjects:** County and state history. **Special Collections:** Local newspapers from 1870. **Holdings:** 4000 books; genealogies; city directories; manuscripts; documents; clippings; Civil War volumes. **Services:** Library open to public for reference use only. **Staff:** Genevieve Kusche, Libn.

★6562★
KANKAKEE DAILY JOURNAL - LIBRARY (Publ)
8 Dearborn Sq. Phone: (815) 937-3378
Kankakee, IL 60901 Kay Belletete, Hd.Libn.
Staff: Prof 1; Other 2. **Subjects:** Newspaper reference topics. **Holdings:** Bound volumes of newspapers; newspapers on microfilm, 1854 to present. **Services:** Library open to public when staff member is present.

★6563★
KANSAS CITY ART INSTITUTE - LIBRARY (Art)
4415 Warwick Blvd.
Box 10360 Phone: (816) 561-4852
Kansas City, MO 64111 Ellen Lignell, Lib.Dir.
Staff: Prof 2; Other 3. **Subjects:** Visual arts, humanities. **Special Collections:** Limited editions; decorative arts; ceramics; textiles; photography. **Holdings:** 32,000 books; 2800 bound periodical volumes; 36 file drawers of pamphlets and pictures; 13 file drawers of archives. **Subscriptions:** 110 journals and other serials. **Services:** Interlibrary loans; copying; library open to public for reference use only. **Networks/Consortia:** Member of Kansas City Regional Council for Higher Education; Union of Independent Art Colleges. **Publications:** Accessions list, each semester. **Staff:** May Gamer, Cat.; Joe Fennewald, Circ.; Joyce Peitso, Ser.; Leonard Webers, Circ.

★6564★
KANSAS CITY - CITY DEVELOPMENT DEPARTMENT - LIBRARY (Plan)
City Hall, 414 E. 12th St. Phone: (816) 274-1864
Kansas City, MO 64106 Alma Lee, Libn.
Staff: Prof 2. **Subjects:** Area plans, master plans, housing, environmental quality, census materials. **Holdings:** 5000 books. **Subscriptions:** 100 journals

and other serials. **Services:** Interlibrary loans; library open to public.

★6565★
KANSAS CITY LIFE INSURANCE COMPANY - GENERAL LIBRARY AND ARCHIVES (Bus-Fin)†
3520 Broadway
Kansas City, MO 64111
Phone: (816) 753-7000
Wanda L. Burks, Libn.
Founded: 1957. **Staff:** 1. **Subjects:** Insurance, finance. **Special Collections:** Archives pertaining to company history. **Holdings:** 3000 books. **Services:** Interlibrary loans; library not open to public.

★6566★
KANSAS CITY MUSEUM OF HISTORY AND SCIENCE - ARCHIVES (Hist)
3218 Gladstone Blvd.
Kansas City, MO 64123
Phone: (816) 483-8300
Barbara M. Gorman, Cur. of Hist.
Staff: Prof 1. **Subjects:** History of Kansas City, Missouri. **Special Collections:** Manuscript collections relating to the history of the Kansas City region. **Holdings:** 5000 books; 90 bound periodical volumes; 5000 photographs; 100 paintings. **Subscriptions:** 76 journals and other serials. **Services:** Copying; archives open to public by appointment. **Publications:** Museum Magazine, bimonthly - distributed to Museum Association members.

★6567★
KANSAS CITY PUBLIC LIBRARY - ART AND MUSIC COLLECTION (Art; Mus)
311 E. 12th St.
Kansas City, MO 64106
Phone: (816) 221-2685
Subjects: Art, music. **Holdings:** Figures not available. **Services:** Interlibrary loans; copying.

★6568★
KANSAS CITY PUBLIC LIBRARY - BUSINESS AND TECHNICAL COLLECTION (Bus-Fin; Sci-Tech)
311 E. 12th St.
Kansas City, MO 64106
Phone: (816) 221-2685
Subjects: Economics, business administration, insurance, commerce, science, engineering, agriculture, industrial technology. **Special Collections:** Directories (trade and telephone, U.S. and foreign); annual reports of companies. **Holdings:** 33,000 books; 55 VF drawers of pamphlets; 47,000 maps; 95 reels of microfilm; 85,000 documents; 6 VF drawers of clippings. **Services:** Interlibrary loans; copying. **Remarks:** This collection is now accessed through Central Reference.

★6569★
KANSAS CITY PUBLIC LIBRARY - MISSOURI VALLEY ROOM (Hist)
311 E. 12th St.
Kansas City, MO 64106
Phone: (816) 221-2685
Subjects: Local and Western history, genealogy. **Holdings:** Figures not available.

★6570★
KANSAS CITY PUBLIC LIBRARY - PERIODICAL-MICROFILM COLLECTION (Aud-Vis)
311 E. 12th St.
Kansas City, MO 64106
Holdings: Bound periodical volumes and reels of microfilm. **Subscriptions:** 1082 journals and other serials. **Services:** Interlibrary loans; copying.

★6571★
KANSAS CITY TIMES-STAR - LIBRARY (Publ)
1729 Grand Ave.
Kansas City, MO 64108
John J. Springer, Libn.
Subjects: Newspaper reference topics. **Holdings:** 500,000 photographs; 1.5 million clippings and film records. **Staff:** Patricia S. Smith, Asst.Libn.

★6572★
KANSAS ENERGY EXTENSION SERVICE (Energy)
Ward Hall
Kansas State University
Manhattan, KS 66506
Dr. Dick Hayter, Dir.
Founded: 1978. **Staff:** Prof 3; Other 1. **Subjects:** Energy. **Holdings:** 1500 books; 50 bound periodical volumes; 500 reports on surface mining; 50 Kansas Energy Reports; 10,000 posters and pamphlets; microfilm. **Subscriptions:** 20 journals and other serials; 10 newspapers. **Services:** Copying; library open to public. **Computerized Information Services:** Computerized cataloging. **Publications:** Various publications on energy - to state residents. **Remarks:** The in-state toll-free phone number is 1-800-332-0036. **Formerly:** Kansas State Energy Office, located in Topeka, KS.

★6573★
KANSAS HERITAGE CENTER - LIBRARY (Hist)
Box 1275
Dodge City, KS 67801
Phone: (316) 227-2823
Jeanie Covalt, Res.Libn.
Founded: 1966. **Staff:** 4. **Subjects:** Frontier and pioneer life, Kansas, the West, Indians of North America, cowboys, cattle trade, transportation, agricultural history, folklore. **Special Collections:** Historical collections from the states of Kansas, Oklahoma, Nebraska, Arizona, Missouri, Colorado and New Mexico. **Holdings:** 10,000 books and bound periodical volumes; VF drawers of clippings and pamphlets; microfilm; filmstrips; slides; tapes and phonograph records; 16mm films. **Services:** Interlibrary loans; copying; assembles mini-kits on various subjects; bibliographies; arranges programs and workshops; library open to public. **Publications:** Reference Materials and Resources (catalog, 1970, 1973, 1975, 1979, 1981, 1982); Museums of Southwest Kansas (1969); Trails of Kansas, a Bibliography (1969); Sentinel to the Cimarron; The Frontier Experience of Fort Dodge, Kansas (1970); Up From the Prairie (1974); The Process of Oral History (1976); Dodge City maps (1982). **Staff:** Betty Braddock, Dir.; Noel Ary, Asst.Dir.

KANSAS LUNG ASSOCIATION
See: American Lung Association of Kansas

KANSAS MUSIC TEACHERS' ASSOCIATION ARCHIVES
See: Wichita State University - Thurlow Lieurance Memorial Music Library

KANSAS STATE BUREAU OF CHILD RESEARCH - PARSONS STATE HOSPITAL AND TRAINING CENTER
See: Parsons State Hospital and Training Center

★6574★
KANSAS STATE DEPARTMENT OF HEALTH & ENVIRONMENT - BUREAU OF HEALTH & ENVIRONMENTAL EDUCATION LIBRARY (Med)
Forbes AFB, Bldg. 321
Topeka, KS 66620
Phone: (913) 296-3571
Virginia Lockhart, Dir.
Founded: 1936. **Staff:** Prof 8; Other 8. **Subjects:** All aspects of health and safety, including mental and environmental health. **Special Collections:** Annual reports of the department from 1885. **Holdings:** 900 books; 290 bound periodical volumes; 2200 films (cataloged); 40 filmstrips; 1000 health, safety and environmental pamphlets. **Subscriptions:** 25 journals and other serials. **Services:** Library open to Kansas residents. **Special Catalogs:** Film and literature catalog.

★6575★
KANSAS STATE DEPARTMENT OF SOCIAL & REHABILITATION SERVICES - STAFF DEVELOPMENT TRAINING CENTER LIBRARY (Soc Sci)†
2700 W. 6th St.
Topeka, KS 66606
Phone: (913) 296-4327
Frank Roth, Lib.Asst.
Founded: 1935. **Staff:** Prof 1. **Subjects:** Social service and welfare, personnel, staff development. **Holdings:** 2600 books; 295 bound periodical volumes; 8400 cataloged reports and pamphlets; films and tapes. **Subscriptions:** 39 journals and other serials. **Services:** Interlibrary loans; consultation services to librarians from other agency libraries; library open to public. **Publications:** Acquisitions List, quarterly - distribution to all state staff.

KANSAS STATE ENERGY OFFICE
See: Kansas Energy Extension Service

★6576★
KANSAS STATE GEOLOGICAL SURVEY - MOORE HALL LIBRARY (Sci-Tech; Energy)
1930 Ave. A, Campus W
Lawrence, KS 66044
Phone: (913) 864-3965
Janice H. Sorensen, Libn.
Staff: Prof 1. **Subjects:** Geology, Kansas geology, mineral resources, oil and gas, well logs, environmental geology, geochemistry, water resources, geomathematics, geologic research. **Special Collections:** U.S. Dept. of Energy Uranium Studies. **Holdings:** 5000 books; 380 bound periodical volumes; 1000 open file reports; 200 reels of microfilm; 200 computer contributions; 8000 slides and photographs. **Subscriptions:** 40 journals and other serials. **Services:** Interlibrary loans; copying; library open to public with restrictions. **Computerized Information Services:** Data storage and retrieval. **Special Catalogs:** List of publications published by Kansas Geological Survey.

★6577★
KANSAS STATE GEOLOGICAL SURVEY - WICHITA WELL SAMPLE LIBRARY (Sci-Tech)
4150 Monroe St.
Wichita, KS 67209
Phone: (316) 943-2343
Lawrence H. Skelton, Geologist & Mgr.
Founded: 1938. **Staff:** Prof 1; Other 7. **Subjects:** Wellbore sample cuttings. **Holdings:** Drill cuttings from 115,000 wells, primarily from Kansas; 85,000

microfiche copies of wireline logs. **Services:** Copying; library open to public. **Remarks:** All Kansas Geological Survey publications and maps are available for reference; in-print copies are for sale.

★6578★
KANSAS STATE HISTORICAL SOCIETY - LIBRARY (Hist)
120 W. 10th St.   Phone: (913) 296-3251
Topeka, KS 66612   Portia Allbert, Lib.Dir.
Founded: 1875. **Staff:** Prof 6; Other 5. **Subjects:** Kansas history, local history of other states, genealogy, American Indians, the West, American biography. **Special Collections:** Kansas (17,355 books, 122,060 pamphlets); genealogy and local history (15,820 books, 5785 pamphlets); American Indians and the West (3754 books, 1864 pamphlets). **Holdings:** 116,118 books; 23,391 bound periodical volumes; 1689 volumes of clippings (cataloged); 30,204 reels of microfilm (including newspapers, archives); 194 microcards (titles). **Subscriptions:** 300 journals and other serials. **Services:** Interlibrary loans; copying (both limited); library open to public. **Staff:** Margaret Briggs, Asst.Libn.; Sara Judge, Doc.Cat.; Susan Forbes, West.Hist.Cat.; Roberta Pray, Res.Libn.; Jane Journot, Genealogy Cat.

★6579★
KANSAS STATE LIBRARY (Info Sci)†
State Capitol, 3rd Fl.   Phone: (913) 296-3296
Topeka, KS 66612   Duane F. Johnson, State Libn.
Founded: 1855. **Staff:** Prof 12; Other 12. **Subjects:** Legislative reference, government. **Special Collections:** Federal and state documents depository. **Holdings:** 43,000 books; 150,000 government documents (microfilm). **Subscriptions:** 150 journals and other serials; 10 newspapers. **Services:** Interlibrary loans; copying; library open to public with restrictions. **Computerized Information Services:** DIALOG, SDC, New York Times Information Service, BRS; Kansas State legislative online data information; computerized cataloging and serials. **Networks/Consortia:** Member of Bibliographical Center for Research, Rocky Mountain Region, Inc. (BCR). **Publications:** Kansas Public Library Statistics, annual - distributed to all public libraries and regional systems. **Special Indexes:** Kansas State Documents Catalog and Index. **Remarks:** Part of the library is located at 529 Kansas Ave., Topeka, KS 66603. **Staff:** Sheila Merrell, Dir., Div. for Blind; Marc Galbraith, Dir. of Ref.

★6580★
KANSAS STATE SUPREME COURT - LAW LIBRARY (Law)
Judicial Center
301 West 10th   Phone: (913) 296-3257
Topeka, KS 66612   Fred W. Knecht, Law Libn.
Staff: Prof 4; Other 5. **Subjects:** Law - federal, state and foreign. **Special Collections:** Rare Book Collection (400 titles of English materials). **Holdings:** 185,000 books; 21,000 bound periodical volumes. **Subscriptions:** 3000 journals and other serials; 5 newspapers. **Services:** Interlibrary loans; copying; library open to public. **Publications:** Court Related Acquisitions List, quarterly - to all state judges; Recent Acquisitions List, quarterly - to law schools and Kansas Bar Associations. **Staff:** Janice L. Cook, Tech.Serv.Libn.; Claire E. Vincent, Asst. Law Libn.; Sandra I. Stoller, Legal Lit.Libn.

KANSAS STATE UNIVERSITY - ARCHITECTURE AND DESIGN LIBRARY
See: Kansas State University - Paul Weigel Library of Architecture and Design

★6581★
KANSAS STATE UNIVERSITY - CHEMISTRY LIBRARY (Sci-Tech)
     Phone: (913) 532-6530
Manhattan, KS 66506   Pat Parris, Libn.
Founded: 1881. **Staff:** 1. **Subjects:** Chemistry, biochemistry. **Special Collections:** Sadtler Standard Spectra (168 volumes). **Holdings:** 8152 books; 5475 bound periodical volumes. **Subscriptions:** 370 journals and other serials. **Services:** Interlibrary loans; copying; library open to public. **Formerly:** Its Willard Library.

★6582★
KANSAS STATE UNIVERSITY - FARRELL LIBRARY (Agri; Sci-Tech)
     Phone: (913) 532-6516
Manhattan, KS 66506   Brice C. Hobrock, Dean of Libs.
Founded: 1863. **Staff:** Prof 37; Other 94. **Subjects:** Physical sciences, agriculture, engineering, applied science and technology, natural sciences, veterinary medicine, home economics. **Special Collections:** Department of Energy/Energy Research and Development Administration/Atomic Energy Commission Collection (26,000 paper titles; 92,000 microcards; 430,000 microfiche); ERIC Collection (complete); Minorities Resource Research Center Collection (3500 volumes, 175 films and filmstrips); Juvenile Literature Collection (15,000 volumes); Curriculum Materials Collection (10,000 units of

print and nonprint materials specializing in environmental education); Physical Fitness Collection (1600 microfiche); Human Relations Area Files (19,000 microfiche); Travels in the West and Southwest. **Holdings:** 900,000 books and bound periodical volumes; 594,000 government documents; 100,000 maps; 26,405 reels of microfilm; 1.2 million microfiche; 18,000 microcards; 130,135 microprints; 10,000 phonograph records; 5500 slides; 2300 tapes; 215 filmstrips; 8000 scores. **Subscriptions:** 11,161 journals and other serials; 200 newspapers. **Services:** Interlibrary loans; copying; library open to public. **Computerized Information Services:** DIALOG, SDC, MEDLINE; computerized cataloging and circulation. **Networks/Consortia:** Member of OCLC; Bibliographical Center for Research, Rocky Mountain Region, Inc.; CRL; Kansas Information Circuit. **Publications:** Kansas State University Library Bibliography Series, irregular - distributed on exchange and sold on request; KSU Library Cassette Series on Library Technology, irregular - sold on request. **Staff:** Virginia M. Quiring, Assoc. Dean, Pub.Serv.; Leslie A. Manning, Assoc. Dean, Tech.Serv.; Meredith C. Litchfield, Asst.Dir., Adm.; Sue Williams, ILL; Diana Farmer, Acq. & Ser.; Charlene Grass, Cat.; Rachel Moreland, Circ.; Lucy Wilde, Gen.Ref.; Robert Klapthor, Sci.; James Lu, Soc.Sci./Hum.; John Johnson, Doc.; Ann Scott, Educ./Online Search Serv.; John J. Vander Velde, Spec.Coll.; Antonia Pigno, Spec.Coll./Archv.; Cherie Geiser, Post-Harvest Doc.Serv.

★6583★
KANSAS STATE UNIVERSITY - FOOD AND FEED GRAIN INSTITUTE - SWANSON MEMORIAL LIBRARY (Food-Bev)
     Phone: (913) 532-6161
Manhattan, KS 66506   Dr. Charles Deyoe
Founded: 1950. **Staff:** Prof 1. **Subjects:** Milling technology, feed technology, baking technology, grain handling and storage, cereal chemistry, biochemistry, food technology, nutrition. **Holdings:** 2000 books; 1000 bound periodical volumes; 2500 pamphlets and bulletins; 1500 reprints. **Subscriptions:** 28 journals and other serials. **Services:** Copying; library not open to public.

★6584★
KANSAS STATE UNIVERSITY - HERBARIUM LIBRARY (Sci-Tech)
Bushnell Hall   Phone: (913) 532-6619
Manhattan, KS 66506   T.M. Barkley, Cur. of Herbarium
Founded: 1870. **Staff:** Prof 3; Other 1. **Subjects:** Flora of the Central Prairies and Plains. **Holdings:** 1500 books; 2500 monographs and pamphlets (cataloged). **Subscriptions:** 12 journals and other serials. **Services:** Interlibrary loans; copying; library open to public.

★6585★
KANSAS STATE UNIVERSITY - INSTITUTE FOR ENVIRONMENTAL RESEARCH - LIBRARY (Env-Cons)
Dept. of Mechanical Engineering   Phone: (913) 532-5620
Manhattan, KS 66506   Dr. F.H. Rohles
Founded: 1963. **Subjects:** Environmental control, bioinstrumentation, human factors. **Special Collections:** Effects of environment on comfort, health, productivity and learning. **Holdings:** 1000 technical articles; 700 categorized references. **Services:** Copying; library open to public.

KANSAS STATE UNIVERSITY - KANSAS ENERGY EXTENSION SERVICE
See: Kansas Energy Extension Service

★6586★
KANSAS STATE UNIVERSITY - PAUL WEIGEL LIBRARY OF ARCHITECTURE AND DESIGN (Art)
     Phone: (913) 532-5968
Manhattan, KS 66506   Patricia Weisenburger, Libn.
Founded: 1920. **Staff:** 2. **Subjects:** Architecture, city planning, architectural history, historic preservation, landscape architecture, structures, building construction. **Holdings:** 21,855 books; 4312 bound periodical volumes; 2300 pamphlets and reports on planning. **Subscriptions:** 223 journals and other serials. **Services:** Interlibrary loans; copying; AV equipment available; library open to public. **Staff:** Dorothy Barnett, Asst.

★6587★
KANSAS STATE UNIVERSITY - PHYSICS LIBRARY (Sci-Tech)
     Phone: (913) 532-6827
Manhattan, KS 66506   Bernice Bartel, Libn.
Founded: 1963. **Staff:** 1. **Subjects:** Physics - atomic, molecular, nuclear, particle, general; condensed matter. **Special Collections:** World Meteorological Organization publications. **Holdings:** 5500 books; 4200 bound periodical volumes. **Subscriptions:** 289 journals and other serials. **Services:** Interlibrary loans; copying; library open to public.

★6588★
KANSAS STATE UNIVERSITY - POPULATION RESEARCH LABORATORY - LIBRARY (Soc Sci)
Manhattan, KS 66506
Phone: (913) 532-5984
Donald J. Adamchak, Act.Dir.
Founded: 1967. **Staff:** Prof 1. **Subjects:** Demography. **Holdings:** 600 books; 50 other cataloged items; Census of Population, 1940-1980; Census of Agriculture, 1930, 1950-1960, 1969, 1974. **Subscriptions:** 10 journals and other serials. **Services:** Library open to public.

★6589★
KANSAS STATE UNIVERSITY - RESOURCES ON DEVELOPING COUNTRIES (Area-Ethnic)
Farrell Library
Manhattan, KS 66506
Phone: (913) 532-6516
Sylvia J. Blanding, Libn.
Founded: 1979. **Staff:** Prof 2. **Subjects:** South Asia - history, economics, sociology, politics, languages, literature, religion, philosophy; elementary and high school level teaching materials; other developing countries; bibliography; agriculture and related social sciences. **Special Collections:** Pre-1900 History of India Collection (400 volumes). **Holdings:** 12,200 books; 1400 bound periodical volumes; microfiche of Indian Census, 1881-1951; 960 reels of microfilm including South Asian newspapers in English. **Subscriptions:** 120 journals; 24 newspapers. **Services:** Interlibrary loans; library open to public. **Networks/Consortia:** Member of CRL; South Asia Microforms Project (SAMP). **Staff:** Susan Casement, Libn.

★6590★
KANSAS STATE UNIVERSITY - SPECIAL COLLECTIONS DEPARTMENT & UNIVERSITY ARCHIVES (Hum)
Farrell Library
Manhattan, KS 66506
Phone: (913) 532-6516
Velde Vander, Spec.Coll.
Founded: 1966. **Staff:** Prof 1; Other 1. **Subjects:** Kansas, Kansas State University. **Special Collections:** Cookbook Collection (2800 volumes; earliest imprint, 1541); Linnaeus (1280 volumes); Robert Graves (180 volumes); Dan Casement (2500 manuscripts); Papers of Harold Ralph Fatzer, retired Chief Justice of Kansas Supreme Court (5000 manuscripts). **Holdings:** 20,000 books; 100 bound periodical volumes; 8000 Kansas State University dissertations, theses and masters' reports; 60 VF drawers of archives; 6000 photographs in Kansas State University Photo Collections. **Services:** Copying; collections open to public. **Special Indexes:** Historical Index of Kansas State University; Kansas State University Photo Index - both on cards; Indexed Register to Fatzer Papers, 1934-1977.

★6591★
KANSAS STATE UNIVERSITY - VETERINARY MEDICAL LIBRARY (Med)
Manhattan, KS 66506
Phone: (913) 532-6006
E. Guy Coffee, Hd.Libn.
Founded: 1936. **Staff:** Prof 1; Other 2. **Subjects:** Veterinary medicine, comparative medicine, preclinical science, internal medicine, pharmacology, toxicology. **Special Collections:** Faculty reprints (350). **Holdings:** 10,000 books; 11,000 bound periodical volumes. **Subscriptions:** 690 journals and other serials. **Services:** Interlibrary loans; copying; SDI; library open to public. **Computerized Information Services:** DIALOG, SDC, MEDLINE; computerized cataloging. **Networks/Consortia:** Member of OCLC. **Publications:** Acquisitions List, semimonthly.

KANSAS STATE UNIVERSITY - WILLARD LIBRARY
See: Kansas State University - Chemistry Library

★6592★
KANSAS TECHNICAL INSTITUTE - TULLIS RESOURCE CENTER (Sci-Tech)
1831 Crompton Rd.
Salina, KS 67401
Phone: (913) 825-0275
Eleen M. Owen, Libn.
Founded: 1965. **Staff:** Prof 1; Other 2. **Subjects:** Computers, electronics, aeronautics, civil and mechanical engineering. **Special Collections:** Computer programming, management, applied engineering. **Holdings:** 18,000 books; 20 VF drawers; 6 VF drawers of archival materials. **Subscriptions:** 175 journals and other serials; 5 newspapers. **Services:** Interlibrary loans; copying; library open to public with restrictions. **Computerized Information Services:** Computerized acquisitions. **Networks/Consortia:** Member of Salina College Consortium.

KANSAS YEARLY MEETING OF FRIENDS ARCHIVES
See: Friends University - Edmund Stanley Library

★6593★
KAPIOLANI-CHILDREN'S MEDICAL CENTER - KCMC MEDICAL LIBRARY (Med)
1319 Punahou St.
Honolulu, HI 96826
Phone: (808) 947-8573
Ikuko Uesato, Libn.
Staff: Prof 1. **Subjects:** Obstetrics and gynecology, pediatrics. **Holdings:** 1000 books; 550 bound periodical volumes; 3 VF drawers of reprints, pamphlets. **Subscriptions:** 100 journals and other serials. **Services:** Interlibrary loans; copying; library open to public for reference use only. **Publications:** PAULMS 1978.

★6594★
KAPLAN, LIVINGSTON, GOODWIN BERKOWITZ & SELVIN - LIBRARY (Law)
450 N. Roxbury Dr.
Beverly Hills, CA 90210
Phone: (213) 274-8011
Robert Fortin Richards, Libn.
Staff: Prof 1; Other 2. **Subjects:** California and federal law. **Holdings:** 11,000 books; 4000 bound periodical volumes. **Subscriptions:** 177 journals and other serials. **Services:** Library not open to public. **Computerized Information Services:** Mead Data Central.

KAPLAN (Louis S.) MEMORIAL LIBRARY
See: Philadelphia Association for Psychoanalysis - Louis S. Kaplan Memorial Library

KAPLAN (Mordecai M.) LIBRARY
See: Reconstructionist Rabbinical College - Mordecai M. Kaplan Library

KARDATZKE (Carl) MEMORIAL LIBRARY
See: Park Place Church of God - Carl Kardatzke Memorial Library

KARESH (Coleman) LAW LIBRARY
See: University of South Carolina - Coleman Karesh Law Library

KARNOSH LIBRARY
See: Cleveland Psychiatric Institute

KARRMANN LIBRARY
See: University of Wisconsin, Platteville

KARTH (Joseph E.) RESEARCH CENTER
See: Ramsey County Historical Society - Joseph E. Karth Research Center

KASAK (Michael) LIBRARY
See: Milwaukee County Mental Health Complex - Michael Kasak Library

KASS JUDAIC LIBRARY
See: Jewish Community Center of Greater Washington

KATKOWSKY (Joseph) LIBRARY
See: Congregation Beth Achim - Joseph Katkowsky Library

★6595★
KATTEN, MUCHIN, ZAVIS, PEARL & GALLER - LIBRARY (Law)
55 E. Monroe, Suite 4100
Chicago, IL 60603
Phone: (312) 346-7400
Susan P. Spector, Libn.
Staff: Prof 1; Other 2. **Subjects:** Law, taxation, securities law. **Holdings:** 14,000 books; 150 bound periodical volumes. **Subscriptions:** 150 journals and other serials; 5 newspapers. **Services:** Interlibrary loans; library open to public with restrictions. **Computerized Information Services:** LEXIS, New York Times Information Service.

★6596★
KAYE, SCHOLER, FIERMAN, HAYS & HANDLER - LAW LIBRARY (Law)
425 Park Ave.
New York, NY 10022
Phone: (212) 407-8312
Gerald Goodhartz, Libn.
Staff: Prof 4; Other 9. **Subjects:** Law. **Special Collections:** Law - antitrust, tax, trademark, corporate, real estate, banking, bankruptcy. **Holdings:** 33,700 books; 750 bound periodical volumes. **Subscriptions:** 1894 journals and other serials; 30 newspapers. **Services:** Interlibrary loans; copying; SDI; library open to public by appointment. **Computerized Information Services:** LEXIS, New York Times Information Service, SDC, DIALOG, Info Globe, NEXIS. **Staff:** Ewa Rozmyslowska, Cat.; John S. Kostecky, Asst.Libn.; German B. Compas, Ref.Libn.

KEACH (John R.) MEMORIAL LIBRARY
See: Johnson County Mental Health Center - John R. Keach Memorial Library

★6597★
KEAN ARCHIVES (Pict)
1320 Locust St.   Phone: (215) 735-1812
Philadelphia, PA 19107   Manuel Kean, Owner
Founded: 1939. **Staff:** Prof 1; Other 1. **Subjects:** General pictorial scenes, views, portraits, popular American sheet music. **Special Collections:** David Edwin, 1st American engraver; Alexander Anderson, 1st American wood engraver; Rosenthals, lithographers, artists, engravers; Sartains, engravers; history of photography; Bible illustrations; Civil War. **Holdings:** 100,000 books; 350 bound periodical volumes; over 3 million pictures; engravings, lithographs, woodcuts, photographs. **Subscriptions:** 10 journals and other serials. **Services:** Copying; library open to public by appointment. **Special Indexes:** Authority index; birthday and date file; chronological and title popular music file.

★6598★
KEAN COLLEGE OF NEW JERSEY - EVE ADULT ADVISORY SERVICES (Educ)
                                         Phone: (201) 527-2210
Union, NJ 07083   Phyllis Shaunesey, Info.Rsrcs.Coord.
Staff: 1. **Subjects:** Vocational information, careers, job hunting, education, employment references, women. **Holdings:** 300 books; 3 file drawers of vocational information; 3 drawers of general information files; 3 shelves of college catalogs. **Subscriptions:** 5 newspapers. **Services:** Library open to public. **Publications:** EVE Adult Advisory Services newsletter, semiannual - to mailing list. **Remarks:** EVE is an acronym for Education, Vocation and Employment.

★6599★
KEAN COLLEGE OF NEW JERSEY - INSTRUCTIONAL RESOURCE CENTER (Educ)
Morris Ave.   Phone: (201) 527-2073
Union, NJ 07083   Vincent V. Merlo, Dir., Media & Tech.
Founded: 1958. **Staff:** Prof 4; Other 5. **Special Collections:** Nonprint media representative of each of the major disciplines represented in the curriculum. **Holdings:** 354 books; 8000 nonprint items (cataloged). **Services:** Center provides instructional materials for use by faculty and students of the college. **Publications:** Circular, monthly - newsletter to faculty; instructional materials - to faculty.

★6600★
KEAN COLLEGE OF NEW JERSEY - NANCY THOMPSON LIBRARY (Educ)
                                         Phone: (201) 527-2017
Union, NJ 07083   Dr. Louis N. Nagy, Dir.
Staff: Prof 16; Other 17. **Subjects:** Education, humanities, sciences. **Special Collections:** Dwyers Papers. **Holdings:** 240,000 books; 14,300 bound periodical volumes; 1980 reels of microfilm; 110 VF drawers. **Subscriptions:** 1980 journals and other serials. **Services:** Interlibrary loans; copying; library open to public for reference use only. **Computerized Information Services:** DIALOG, SDC; computerized cataloging. **Networks/Consortia:** Member of Consortium of East New Jersey; OCLC through PALINET & Union Library Catalogue of Pennsylvania. **Staff:** Dr. Barna Csuros, Assoc.Dir.; Mark M. Ferrara, Assoc.Dir.; Gloria Valone, Asst.Dir.; Tamara Avdzej, Acq.Libn.; Kevork Berberian, Cat.Libn.; Schi-Zhin Rhie, Cat.Libn.; Phyllis M. Tallerico, Cat.Libn.; Joan De Crenascol, Ref.Libn.; Rena Rogge, Ref.Libn.; Edwin Erbe, Per.Libn.; Yvonne McCray, Educ.Libn.

★6601★
KEARNEY (A.T.), INC. - INFORMATION CENTER (Bus-Fin)
222 S. Riverside Plaza   Phone: (312) 648-0111
Chicago, IL 60606   Kathryn Sheehan, Mgr., Info.Ctr.
Staff: Prof 2; Other 1. **Subjects:** Management systems, finance, health services, marketing, organization, personnel administration, production and operations, transportation. **Holdings:** 5000 books; 45 VF drawers of pamphlets; 25 VF drawers of annual reports; microfiche file of client reports. **Subscriptions:** 280 journals and other serials. **Services:** Interlibrary loans; copying; center not open to public. **Computerized Information Services:** DIALOG, SDC, New York Times Information Service, Control Data Corporation. **Networks/Consortia:** Member of OCLC through ILLINET. **Publications:** Acquisition List, monthly. **Staff:** Linda Larsen, Res.Assoc.

★6602★
KEARNEY STATE COLLEGE - CALVIN T. RYAN LIBRARY - SPECIAL COLLECTIONS (Hist)†
905 W. 25th   Phone: (308) 236-4218
Kearney, NE 68847   John Mayeski, Dir. of Lib.
Founded: 1906. **Special Collections:** Nebraska history (1631 volumes); Autograph Collection (331 volumes); local history (7900 items); Curriculum laboratory (7853 items). **Services:** Interlibrary loans; copying; library open to public. **Computerized Information Services:** DIALOG. **Networks/Consortia:**

Member of OCLC.

KEARNY INFORMATION RESOURCE CENTER
See: Western Electric Company, Inc.

KEENA (Martin J.) MEMORIAL LIBRARY
See: American Stock Exchange - Martin J. Keena Memorial Library

★6603★
KEENE STATE COLLEGE - WALLACE E. MASON LIBRARY (Educ)
Appian Way   Phone: (603) 352-1909
Keene, NH 03431   Clifford S. Mead, Libn.
Founded: 1909. **Staff:** Prof 5; Other 7. **Subjects:** Teacher education, liberal arts. **Special Collections:** Preston Collection, New Hampshire materials (2000 volumes). **Holdings:** 130,000 books; 20,000 microfiche of American civilization; 5000 microfiche of English literature; 12 VF drawers of pamphlets. **Subscriptions:** 1200 journals and other serials; 40 newspapers. **Services:** Interlibrary loans; copying; library open to public for reference use only. **Networks/Consortia:** Member of New Hampshire College and University Council, Library Policy Committee (NHCUC).

★6604★
KEENELAND ASSOCIATION - LIBRARY (Rec)
Keeneland Race Course
Box 1690   Phone: (606) 254-3412
Lexington, KY 40592   Doris Jean Waren, Libn.
Founded: 1939. **Staff:** Prof 2. **Subjects:** Thoroughbred horse racing and breeding; horse sports. **Special Collections:** Photographic negatives of American racing. **Holdings:** 5550 books; 1175 bound periodical volumes; 200,000 photographic negatives; 36 VF drawers of clippings; pamphlet file. **Subscriptions:** 45 journals and other serials. **Services:** Library open to public for reference use only. **Special Catalogs:** The Keeneland Association Library, Guide to the Collection by Amelia King Buckley, published in Lexington, University of Kentucky Press, 1958. **Staff:** Cathy Cooper, Assoc.Libn.

KEESLER AIR FORCE BASE (MS)
See: U.S. Air Force Base - Keesler Base; U.S. Air Force Hospital Medical Center - Medical Library (MS-Keesler AFB); U.S. Air Force - Keesler Technical Training Center

KEGOAYAH KOZGA LIBRARY
See: Nome Library/Kegoayah Kozga Library

KEISER (George Camp) LIBRARY
See: Middle East Institute - George Camp Keiser Library

KEITH LIBRARY
See: College of Physicians and Surgeons of British Columbia

KELLAR LIBRARY
See: Baptist Missionary Association Theological Seminary

KELLER (Helen) NATIONAL CENTER
See: Helen Keller National Center

★6605★
KELLER (J.J.) & ASSOCIATES, INC. - RESEARCH & TECHNICAL LIBRARY (Trans)
145 W. Wisconsin Ave.   Phone: (414) 722-2848
Neenah, WI 54956   John K. Breese, Mgr., RTL
Founded: 1958. **Staff:** Prof 4; Other 2. **Subjects:** Transportation, motor carrier regulations, occupational safety, hazardous materials and waste, law. **Holdings:** 4100 books; 2100 pamphlets (cataloged); Department of Transportation and Environmental Protection Agency documents. **Subscriptions:** 214 journals and other serials. **Services:** Interlibrary loans; copying; library open to public with referral. **Computerized Information Services:** DIALOG, SDC. **Networks/Consortia:** Member of Fox Valley Library Council, Inc. **Publications:** Library Bulletin, monthly. **Staff:** Colleen Olmsted, Res.Asst.; Betty Bartel, Rec.Mgmt.Asst.; Frank Hollenback, Sci.Anl.

★6606★
KELLEY, DRYE & WARREN - LAW LIBRARY (Law)
101 Park Ave.   Phone: (212) 808-7800
New York, NY 10178   Martha Goldman, Libn.
Staff: Prof 2; Other 5. **Subjects:** Law - banking, transportation, corporate, securities, trusts and estates, labor, tax. **Holdings:** 20,000 books. **Subscriptions:** 110 journals and other serials; 10 newspapers. **Services:** Interlibrary loans (limited); library not open to public. **Computerized Information Services:** Mead Data Central, New York Times Information

Service. **Networks/Consortia:** Member of Law Library Association of Greater New York. **Publications:** Library Bulletin, monthly - for internal distribution only.

KELLOCK LIBRARY
See: Institute of Early American History and Culture

★6607★
KELLOGG COMPANY - TECHNICAL LIBRARY SERVICES (Food-Bev)
235 Porter St.   Phone: (616) 966-2291
Battle Creek, MI 49016   Emily Weingartz, Tech.Info.Spec.
Subjects: Food science and technology, nutrition, chemistry, microbiology. **Holdings:** 1000 books; 3000 bound periodical volumes; 120 reports (cataloged); laboratory notebooks; microfiche. **Subscriptions:** 124 journals and other serials. **Services:** Interlibrary loans; copying; SDI; library not open to public. **Computerized Information Services:** DIALOG, SDC.

★6608★
KELLOGG (M.W.) - RESEARCH INFORMATION DIVISION (Sci-Tech)
16200 Park Row
Industrial Park Ten   Phone: (713) 492-2500
Houston, TX 77084   Una M. Gourlay, Mgr.
Founded: 1936. **Staff:** Prof 2; Other 2. **Subjects:** Engineering - petroleum, chemical, mechanical; chemistry. **Special Collections:** Technical Oil Mission microfilms. **Holdings:** 10,000 books; 8000 bound periodical volumes; 4 VF drawers; 49 drawers of microfilm; government reports and patents. **Subscriptions:** 300 journals and other serials. **Services:** Copying; library open to public by appointment. **Computerized Information Services:** SDC, DIALOG, DOE/RECON, SRI World Petrochemicals; ISTAR - internal reports and memo database. **Publications:** Book List, monthly.

KELLOGG (W.K.) BIOLOGICAL STATION
See: Michigan State University - W.K. Kellogg Biological Station

KELLOGG (W.K.) HEALTH SCIENCES LIBRARY
See: Dalhousie University - W.K. Kellogg Health Sciences Library

KELLOGG (W.K.) SOCIAL SCIENCE RESEARCH CENTER
See: Norfolk State College - W.K. Kellogg Social Science Research Center

KELLY AIR FORCE BASE (TX)
See: U.S. Air Force Base - Kelly Base

KELLY (James A.) INSTITUTE FOR LOCAL HISTORICAL STUDIES
See: St. Francis College - James A. Kelly Institute for Local Historical Studies

KELLY (John M.) LIBRARY
See: University of Toronto - St. Michael's College - John M. Kelly Library

★6609★
KELSEY INSTITUTE OF APPLIED ARTS AND SCIENCES - LEARNING RESOURCES CENTRE (Sci-Tech)
P.O. Box 1520   Phone: (306) 664-6417
Saskatoon, SK, Canada S7K 3R5   D.F. Robertson, Dir.
Founded: 1963. **Staff:** Prof 3; Other 8. **Subjects:** Applied sciences, health sciences, industrial arts, service programs. **Holdings:** 35,000 books; 8428 AV items; 317 reels of microfilm; 150 maps. **Subscriptions:** 660 journals and other serials. **Services:** Interlibrary loans; copying; centre open to public for reference use only. **Staff:** E. Crosthwaite, Hd., AV Area; T. Harrison, Hd., Print Area.

★6610★
KEMPER GROUP - LIBRARY (Bus-Fin)
Library, F-5   Phone: (312) 540-2229
Long Grove, IL 60049   Evelyn Giannini, Libn.
Founded: 1926. **Staff:** Prof 3; Other 1. **Subjects:** Insurance law, general law, insurance. **Holdings:** 25,000 books; 40 VF drawers of pamphlets. **Subscriptions:** 400 journals and other serials; 4 newspapers. **Services:** Interlibrary loans; copying; library open to public for reference use only on request. **Computerized Information Services:** DIALOG, New York Times Information Service, SDC, Dow Jones News Retrieval. **Networks/Consortia:** Member of Lake County Consortium; North Suburban Library System; Metropolitan Chicago Library Assembly. **Publications:** Between the Bookends, quarterly - for internal distribution only. **Staff:** Anne Coonce, Asst.Libn.; Mary Wilson, Ref.Libn.

★6611★
KEMPTVILLE COLLEGE OF AGRICULTURAL TECHNOLOGY - LIBRARY (Agri)
                                 Phone: (613) 258-3414
Kemptville, ON, Canada K0G 1J0   Alison Meikle, Libn.
Founded: 1946. **Staff:** Prof 1; Other 2. **Subjects:** Agriculture, home economics. **Holdings:** 9500 books. **Subscriptions:** 125 journals and other serials; 14 newspapers. **Services:** Interlibrary loans; copying; library open to public.

KENAN CHEMISTRY LIBRARY
See: University of North Carolina, Chapel Hill

★6612★
KENDALL SCHOOL OF DESIGN - LEARNING RESOURCE CENTER (Art)
1110 College N.E.   Phone: (616) 451-2787
Grand Rapids, MI 49503   Ruth Hornbach, Hd.Libn.
Founded: 1929. **Staff:** Prof 3; Other 2. **Subjects:** Art history, furniture, interior design, advertising, illustration. **Special Collections:** Furniture collection. **Holdings:** 8000 books; 900 bound periodical volumes; 26,000 slides. **Subscriptions:** 95 journals and other serials. **Services:** Center open to public. **Staff:** Diane Gunn, Slide Libn.; Janet Hook, Circ.Libn.

★6613★
KENDALL WHALING MUSEUM - LIBRARY (Hist)
27 Everett St.
Box 297   Phone: (617) 784-5642
Sharon, MA 02067   Stuart M. Frank, Dir.
Staff: Prof 4; Other 2. **Subjects:** Whaling; art inspired by the whaling industry. **Holdings:** 4500 books; 520 log books (indexed); 25 cases of pamphlets; 175 account books; 2000 photographs of whaleships and whaling; 1500 prints; 375 paintings; clippings. **Services:** Library open to public for reference use only. **Staff:** Robert H. Ellis, Jr.,Cur.; Robert L. Webb, Res.Assoc.; Gare B. Reid, Mgr.

★6614★
KENILWORTH HISTORICAL SOCIETY - KILNER LIBRARY (Hist)
415 Kenilworth Ave.   Phone: (312) 251-2565
Kenilworth, IL 60043   George A. Veeder, Pres.
Staff: 2. **Subjects:** Local history. **Holdings:** 500 books; 200 bound periodical volumes. **Services:** Library open to public for reference use only.

★6615★
KENMORE MERCY HOSPITAL - HEALTH SCIENCES RESOURCE CENTER (Med)
2950 Elmwood Ave.   Phone: (716) 879-6253
Kenmore, NY 14217   Susan N. Craft, Libn.
Staff: Prof 1. **Subjects:** Medicine, nursing. **Holdings:** 550 books; 400 bound periodical volumes. **Subscriptions:** 60 journals and other serials. **Services:** Interlibrary loans; copying; center not open to public. **Networks/Consortia:** Member of Western New York Library Resources Council.

★6616★
KENNEBEC COUNTY LAW LIBRARY (Law)†
95 State St.   Phone: (207) 622-9357
Augusta, ME 04330   Matthew F. Dyer, Libn.
Founded: 1915. **Staff:** 1. **Subjects:** Law. **Holdings:** 11,000 volumes. **Services:** Library open to area attorneys.

★6617★
KENNEBEC VALLEY MEDICAL CENTER - MEDICAL LIBRARY (Med)
6 E. Chestnut St.   Phone: (207) 623-4711
Augusta, ME 04330   Mrs. Gabriel W. Kirkpatrick, Med.Libn.
Founded: 1968. **Staff:** Prof 1; Other 1. **Subjects:** Medicine, surgery, nursing, health sciences. **Special Collections:** History and Biography of Medicine (300 volumes). **Holdings:** 3100 books and bound periodical volumes; 6 VF drawers of reprints; 4 VF drawers of pamphlets; 2600 audiotapes; 313 filmstrips; 450 video cassettes; 275 slide sets; 55 16mm films. **Subscriptions:** 162 journals and other serials. **Services:** Interlibrary loans; copying; literature and AV searches. **Networks/Consortia:** Member of Health Science Library and Information Cooperative of Maine. **Publications:** LRC Bulletin, monthly - for library users. **Special Catalogs:** Audiovisual Holdings catalog (book).

★6618★
KENNECOTT CORPORATION - CARBORUNDUM COMPANY - INFORMATION CENTER
Buffalo Ave.
Box 1054
Niagara Falls, NY 14302
Defunct

★6619★
KENNECOTT CORPORATION - CORPORATE PLANNING LIBRARY (Sci-Tech)†
10 Stamford Forum   Phone: (203) 964-3481
Stamford, CT 06940   Dina Lokets, Libn.
Staff: Prof 1; Other 1. **Subjects:** Business, management, finance, statistics, mining, metals, minerals. **Holdings:** 1000 books; 9 file drawers of company annual reports; 4 file drawers of market studies. **Subscriptions:** 106 journals and other serials. **Services:** Interlibrary loans; copying; library not open to public. **Computerized Information Services:** DIALOG, Dun & Bradstreet, Inc. **Networks/Consortia:** Member of Southwestern Connecticut Library Council (SCLC). **Publications:** Guide to Business Information, semiannual.

KENNEDY CENTER - GEORGE PEABODY COLLEGE FOR TEACHERS OF VANDERBILT UNIVERSITY
See: Peabody (George) College for Teachers of Vanderbilt University

★6620★
KENNEDY GALLERIES - ART LIBRARY (Art)
40 W. 57th St.   Phone: (212) 541-9600
New York, NY 10019   Cynthia Seibels, Libn.
Staff: Prof 1. **Subjects:** American painting and sculpture, fine prints. **Holdings:** 6500 books; 2 drawers of microfilm of early 20th century art periodicals; 1 drawer of microfilm of Ph.D. dissertations on American art; 10 VF drawers of clippings on American artists. **Subscriptions:** 25 journals and other serials. **Services:** Library open to public with restrictions. **Publications:** American Art Journal. **Special Catalogs:** Exhibition catalogs; 18th, 19th and 20th century American Masters catalogs; Marine and Western artists' catalogs; Fine Print catalog; profiles of American artists.

KENNEDY INSTITUTE OF ETHICS
See: Georgetown University

★6621★
KENNEDY/JENKS ENGINEERS, INC. - LIBRARY (Sci-Tech)
657 Howard St.   Phone: (415) 362-6065
San Francisco, CA 94105   Verda M. Hawkins, Libn.
Founded: 1979. **Staff:** Prof 1. **Subjects:** Engineering - civil, sanitary, environmental, hydraulic; hydrology; biological sciences. **Holdings:** 1800 books; 1500 technical reports; 2500 pamphlets, annual reports, reprints. **Subscriptions:** 80 journals and other serials. **Services:** Interlibrary loans; library open to public with restrictions. **Publications:** Current Awareness Bulletin, monthly - for internal distribution only. **Special Catalogs:** Technical Reports Catalog (card).

KENNEDY (John F.) CENTER FOR THE PERFORMING ARTS
See: Library of Congress - John F. Kennedy Center for the Performing Arts

★6622★
KENNEDY (John F.) INSTITUTE - INTERDISCIPLINARY MULTI-MEDIA LIBRARY (Med; Educ)†
707 North Broadway   Phone: (301) 955-4240
Baltimore, MD 21205
Staff: Prof 1; Other 1. **Subjects:** Mental retardation, birth defects, cerebral palsy, epilepsy, developmental disability, special education, audiology, child psychology. **Special Collections:** Cerebral Palsy reprints. **Holdings:** 4500 books and bound periodical volumes; 15 VF drawers; 300 videotapes; 370 audio cassettes; 15 teaching packages. **Subscriptions:** 115 journals and other serials. **Services:** Interlibrary loans; copying; open to public for reference use only. **Publications:** Production of video cassettes and audio cassettes relating to developmental disabilities.

KENNEDY (John F.) LIBRARY
See: U.S. Presidential Libraries - John F. Kennedy Library

★6623★
KENNEDY (John F.) MEDICAL CENTER - LIBRARY (Med)
James St.   Phone: (201) 321-7181
Edison, NJ 08817   Roberta Tipton, Med.Libn.
Founded: 1974. **Staff:** Prof 1. **Subjects:** Clinical medicine, family practice, rehabilitation. **Holdings:** 500 books; 1000 bound periodical volumes. **Subscriptions:** 200 journals and other serials. **Services:** Interlibrary loans; copying; library open to public by appointment. **Networks/Consortia:** Member of Medical Resources Consortium of Central New Jersey (MEDCORE).

KENNEDY (John F.) MEMORIAL HOSPITAL
See: New Jersey School of Osteopathic Medicine - Dr. Jerrold S. Schwartz Memorial Library

★6624★
KENNEDY (John F.) MEMORIAL HOSPITAL - CHERRY HILL DIVISION - DR. BARNEY A. SLOTKIN MEMORIAL LIBRARY (Med)
Chapel Ave. & Cooper Landing Rd.   Phone: (609) 665-2000
Cherry Hill, NJ 08002   Amy Kaplan, Libn.
Founded: 1974. **Staff:** Prof 1. **Subjects:** Medicine, nursing. **Holdings:** 1148 books; 1710 bound periodical volumes. **Subscriptions:** 130 journals and other serials. **Services:** Interlibrary loans; library open to public by request. **Networks/Consortia:** Member of Southwest New Jersey Consortium for Health Information Services; New Jersey Health Sciences Network.

KENNEDY (John F.) MEMORIAL LIBRARY
See: California State University, Los Angeles - Science and Technology Reference Room

KENNEDY (John F.) SPACE CENTER
See: U.S. NASA - John F. Kennedy Space Center

KENNEDY (John Fitzgerald) SCHOOL OF GOVERNMENT
See: Harvard University - John Fitzgerald Kennedy School of Government

★6625★
KENNEDY (Joseph P., Jr.) MEMORIAL HOSPITAL FOR CHILDREN - MEDICAL LIBRARY (Med)
30 Warren St.   Phone: (617) 254-3800
Brighton, MA 02135   Barbara L. McMurrough, Libn.
Staff: 1. **Subjects:** Pediatrics, child development, developmental disorders, nursing, therapies, handicapped children, rehabilitation. **Special Collections:** Charities Research Collection on Autism (50 books, journals and proceedings); Human Ethics Collection (20 books, journals and proceedings). **Holdings:** 576 books; 1494 unbound and bound periodical volumes; 11 annuals (72 volumes, cataloged). **Subscriptions:** 90 journals and other serials. **Services:** Interlibrary loans; copying; searching; library open to public with permission. **Networks/Consortia:** Member of Massachusetts Health Sciences Library Network (MAHSLIN).

★6626★
KENNEDY-KING COLLEGE - LIBRARY (Soc Sci)
6800 S. Wentworth   Phone: (312) 962-3200
Chicago, IL 60621   Mrs. Noel R. Grego, Hd.
Founded: 1934. **Staff:** Prof 6; Other 6. **Subjects:** Black studies - history, sociology, current issues, nursing. **Holdings:** 42,000 volumes. **Subscriptions:** 400 journals and other serials; 12 newspapers. **Services:** Interlibrary loans; copying; library open to public with restrictions. **Networks/Consortia:** Member of OCLC through ILLINET; Metropolitan Chicago Library Assembly. **Staff:** James B. Osgood, Asst.Hd./Cat.; Ora Anders, Ref.; Salvatore J. Attinello, Ref.; Annette Figatner, Per.; Mary Jane Rudolph, Acq.

KENNEDY (Robert E.) LIBRARY
See: California Polytechnic State University - Robert E. Kennedy Library

KENNER ARMY HOSPITAL
See: U.S. Army Hospitals

KENNESAW MOUNTAIN NATL. BATTLEFIELD PARK
See: U.S. Natl. Park Service

KENNGOTT (Margaret A.) MEMORIAL LIBRARY OF THE HEALTH SCIENCES
See: Craig Developmental Center - Margaret A. Kenngott Memorial Library of the Health Sciences

KENNY (Sister) INSTITUTE
See: Abbott-Northwestern Hospital Corporation

★6627★
KENOSHA ACHIEVEMENT CENTER - LIBRARY (Educ)†
1218 79th St.   Phone: (414) 658-1687
Kenosha, WI 53140   Betty Anderson
Staff: 1. **Subjects:** Mental retardation, mental illness, counseling, learning disabilities, behavioral management, special education, chronic disabilities, job skills. **Holdings:** 200 books. **Subscriptions:** 10 journals and other serials. **Services:** Interlibrary loans; copying; library open to public.

★6628★
KENOSHA COUNTY HISTORICAL MUSEUM - HISTORICAL RESEARCH LIBRARY (Hist)
6300 Third Ave.   Phone: (414) 654-5770
Kenosha, WI 53140   Phil Sander, Musm.Dir.
Founded: 1878. **Staff:** 8. **Subjects:** Local and state history, genealogy.

Holdings: 2000 books; 250 bound periodical volumes; local newspapers (cataloged); 9 VF drawers of documents and clippings; file on death notices. **Services:** Library open to public for research work only.

★6629★
KENOSHA MEMORIAL HOSPITAL - HEALTH SCIENCES LIBRARY (Med)
6308 Eighth Ave. Phone: (414) 656-2120
Kenosha, WI 53140 Esther L. Puhek, Libn.
Founded: 1970. **Staff:** Prof 1. **Subjects:** Medicine and nursing. **Holdings:** 2000 books; 250 tape cassettes; 270 video cassettes. **Subscriptions:** 120 journals and other serials. **Services:** Interlibrary loans; copying (limited); library open to staff, students and persons referred by doctors. **Networks/Consortia:** Southeastern Wisconsin Health Science Library Consortium; Regional Medical Library - Region 3.

★6630★
KENOSHA NEWS - NEWSPAPER LIBRARY (Publ)†
715 58th St. Phone: (414) 657-1000
Kenosha, WI 53141 Bernice L. Nagy, Libn.
Staff: Prof 1. **Subjects:** Newspaper reference topics. **Holdings:** 200 books; 84 drawers of clippings and photographs; 320 reels of microfilm. **Subscriptions:** 19 newspapers. **Services:** Library open to public for reference use only.

★6631★
KENOSHA PUBLIC MUSEUM - LIBRARY (Art; Hist)
Civic Center, 5608 10th Ave. Phone: (414) 656-6026
Kenosha, WI 53140 Stephen H. Schwartz, Dir.
Subjects: Art, natural history. **Holdings:** 1590 books; 50 bound periodical volumes. **Subscriptions:** 10 journals and other serials. **Services:** Library open to public for reference use only.

★6632★
KENRICK SEMINARY LIBRARY (Rel-Theol)
7800 Kenrick Rd. Phone: (314) 961-4320
St. Louis, MO 63119 Rev. Myron Gohmann, C.P., Hd.Libn.
Founded: 1893. **Staff:** Prof 1; Other 6. **Subjects:** Roman Catholic theology, scripture, patristics. **Special Collections:** Thomas Merton Collection; Official Catholic Directory; cuneiform tablets; rare books (1780). **Holdings:** 63,314 books and bound periodical volumes; 3125 nonbook materials. **Subscriptions:** 360 journals and other serials; 8 newspapers. **Services:** Interlibrary loans; copying; library open to public for reference use only. **Networks/Consortia:** Member of St. Louis Theological Consortium. **Publications:** Handbook, annual. **Staff:** Terese K. Wiley, Acq.Libn.; Dorothy Kaiser, Tech.Serv./Archv.; Janet Moenster, Tech.Serv.

★6633★
KENT COUNTY MEMORIAL HOSPITAL - MEDICAL LIBRARY (Med)
455 Toll Gate Rd. Phone: (401) 737-7000
Warwick, RI 02886 Jo-Anne M. Aspry, Libn.
Staff: Prof 1. **Subjects:** Surgery, medicine, nursing. **Holdings:** 500 books; 850 bound periodical volumes; 105 audio cassettes. **Subscriptions:** 126 journals and other serials. **Services:** Interlibrary loans; copying; SDI; library open to area professionals and students in the health field. **Computerized Information Services:** MEDLINE. **Networks/Consortia:** Member of Association of Rhode Island Health Sciences Librarians.

KENT LIBRARY
See: East Stroudsburg State College

★6634★
KENT MEMORIAL LIBRARY - HISTORICAL ROOM (Hist)
50 N. Main St. Phone: (203) 668-2325
Suffield, CT 06078 Anne W. Borg, Asst.Dir.
Staff: Prof 3; Other 4. **Subjects:** Local history, genealogy. **Holdings:** 300 books; 50 bound periodical volumes; 100 diaries; 10,000 clippings, photograph albums, newspapers. **Services:** Interlibrary loans; copying; library open to public for reference use only. **Networks/Consortia:** Member of Capitol Regional Library Council. **Staff:** Eugene Biggio, Dir.; Francine Aloisa, Asst.Dir.

★6635★
KENT STATE UNIVERSITY - AMERICAN HISTORY RESEARCH CENTER (Hist)
Library Phone: (216) 672-2411
Kent, OH 44242 Stephen C. Morton, Dir.
Founded: 1970. **Staff:** Prof 2; Other 1. **Subjects:** Ohio, local and labor history; religion; social service organizations. **Special Collections:** Records of the International Brotherhood of Pottery and Allied Workers (194 cubic feet);

county records from Portage, Mahoning and Jefferson counties (280 linear feet); papers of Giles Hooker Cowles (6 cubic feet); papers of Charles Mosher, Ohio congressman (225 cubic feet); papers of Fuller Family (2 cubic feet); papers of Betsey Mix Cowles (3 cubic feet); papers of John A. Begala (15 cubic feet); photograph collection of Arthur J. Trory (29 cubic feet); records of Carpenters Local Union No. 186 (5 cubic feet); records of East Liverpool Trade and Labor Council (1.5 cubic feet); papers of Stephen B. Harbourt (2 cubic feet); records of Kent Bicentennial Commission (1.5 cubic feet); records of Columbiana County Nursing Home (1.5 cubic feet); records of Jefferson County Court (1.5 cubic feet); records of the Diocese of Youngstown (80 cubic feet); papers of James Towner (1 cubic foot); papers of Roger Wolcott - Edward Parsons (1 cubic foot); records of Voices in Vital America (51 cubic feet); records of Trumbull County Mental Health Center (1 cubic foot); records of Warren Trumbull Urban League (6 cubic feet); records of Rebecca Williams Community House (8 cubic feet); records of the Trumbull County Federation of Labor (1 cubic foot); and records of International Union of Electrical, Radio and Machine Workers Local No. 7-17 (17 cubic feet). **Holdings:** 2500 books and publications. **Services:** Copying; library open to public. **Networks/Consortia:** Member of Ohio Network of American History Research Centers. **Special Catalogs:** Inventories to all major collections. **Staff:** Dr. Robert J. Dodge, Local Govt.Rec.Spec.

★6636★
KENT STATE UNIVERSITY - ARCHIVES (Hist)
Library Phone: (216) 672-2411
Kent, OH 44242 Stephen C. Morton, Univ.Archv.
Founded: 1910. **Staff:** Prof 1; Other 1. **Subjects:** University archives. **Special Collections:** May 4 Collection (60 cubic feet); papers of George A. Bowman (10 cubic feet); papers of Florence Beall (2 cubic feet); papers of Joseph N. Begala (18 cubic feet). **Holdings:** 600 books and publications; 320 linear feet of dissertations and theses; 650 cubic feet of manuscripts, clippings and correspondence; 65 cubic feet of photographs. **Services:** Copying; archives open to public. **Special Catalogs:** May 4 Central Catalog; box inventories for all large collections.

★6637★
KENT STATE UNIVERSITY - AUDIOVISUAL SERVICES (Aud-Vis)
330 University Library Phone: (216) 672-3456
Kent, OH 44242 Charles Hunger, Dir., AV Serv.
Founded: 1948. **Staff:** Prof 6; Other 26. **Subjects:** Elementary through higher education. **Holdings:** 9500 films; 50 videotapes; 150 AV reference tools. **Subscriptions:** 20 journals and other serials. **Services:** Interlibrary loans (rental basis); center open to public. **Computerized Information Services:** Computerized cataloging and circulation. **Networks/Consortia:** Member of Consortium of University Film Centers (CUFC). **Publications:** Educational Rental Films, every 3 years with annual supplements - distributed to all customers in continental U.S., schools and colleges of Ohio and to campus faculty. **Staff:** Robert A. Yoder, Supv., Film Ctr.; Paul G. Sisamis, Supv., Mtls.; John P. Kerstetter, Supv., Acq./Cat.; Norman Reynolds, Supv., Campus Serv.; Larry Rubens, Mgr./Photography.

★6638★
KENT STATE UNIVERSITY - CENTER FOR THE STUDY OF ETHNIC PUBLICATIONS (Area-Ethnic)
University Library, Rm. 318 Phone: (216) 672-2782
Kent, OH 44242 Dr. Lubomyr Wynar, Dir.
Staff: 2. **Subjects:** Ethnic - bibliography, history, education, press. **Special Collections:** Ethnic group archives. **Holdings:** 1000 books; 500 pamphlets. **Subscriptions:** 200 journals and other serials. **Services:** Center open to public. **Publications:** Ethnic Forum: Bulletin of Ethnic Studies and of Ethnic Bibliography, 2/year - by subscription; Ethnic, Nationality, and Foreign-Language Broadcasting and Telecasting in Ohio, 1981; Guide to Ethnic Museums, Libraries and Archives in the United States, 1978.

★6639★
KENT STATE UNIVERSITY - CHEMISTRY/PHYSICS LIBRARY (Sci-Tech)
312 Williams Hall Phone: (216) 672-2532
Kent, OH 44242 Julia Cannan, Supv.
Founded: 1942. **Staff:** 1. **Subjects:** Biochemistry, chemistry, physics. **Holdings:** 30,000 volumes. **Subscriptions:** 450 journals and other serials. **Services:** Interlibrary loans; copying; library open to public.

★6640★
KENT STATE UNIVERSITY - DEPARTMENT OF SPECIAL COLLECTIONS (Hum; Hist)
University Library Phone: (216) 672-2270
Kent, OH 44242 Dean H. Keller, Cur.
Staff: Prof 3. **Subjects:** American and English literature, American history, cryptography, history of printing, performing arts. **Holdings:** 20,000 books;

589 boxes of manuscripts. **Services:** Copying; library open to public. **Staff:** Alex Gildzen, Assoc.Cur.; Neal Edgar, Assoc.Cur.

★6641★

KENT STATE UNIVERSITY - DOCUMENTS UNIT (Info Sci**)**
370 Library   Phone: (216) 672-2388
Kent, OH 44242
Staff: Prof 1; Other 3. **Subjects:** Government and political science, economics, business, geology, health and welfare, education, agriculture, science. **Holdings:** 306,000 documents. **Services:** Interlibrary loans; copying; library open to public. **Computerized Information Services:** Computerized cataloging, acquisitions and serials. **Networks/Consortia:** Member of NEOMAL; OHIONET.

★6642★

KENT STATE UNIVERSITY - MAP LIBRARY (Geog-Map**)**
406 McGilvery Hall   Phone: (216) 672-2017
Kent, OH 44242   Julia Cannan, Supv.
Founded: 1968. **Staff:** 1. **Subjects:** Topography, soils, geology, climate. **Holdings:** 250 books; 150,000 maps; 75 relief models; depository for U.S. Geological Survey topographic and geological maps; 25 VF drawers of U.S.G.S. publications. **Services:** Copying; library open to public with KSU courtesy card.

★6643★

KENT STATE UNIVERSITY - MUSIC LIBRARY (Mus**)**
D5 Music & Speech Bldg.   Phone: (216) 672-2004
Kent, OH 44242   Judith B. McCarron, Music Lib.Supv.
Founded: 1967. **Staff:** 1. **Subjects:** Music. **Special Collections:** Choralist (9800 items). **Holdings:** 11,650 books; 2210 bound periodical volumes; 18,285 scores (cataloged); 17,000 scores and sheet music (unbound and uncataloged); 600 publishers' and record catalogs; 20,250 tapes, cassettes and phonograph records; 486 reels of microfilm. **Subscriptions:** 95 journals and other serials. **Services:** Interlibrary loans; copying; library open to public. **Computerized Information Services:** Multiple-index listing of choral scores.

KENT STATE UNIVERSITY - NATIONAL ASSOCIATION FOR CORE CURRICULUM, INC.
See: National Association for Core Curriculum, Inc.

★6644★

KENT STATE UNIVERSITY - SELF INSTRUCTION CENTER (Hum**)**
265 Library   Phone: (216) 672-2889
Kent, OH 44242   Patrick C. Boyden, Dir.
Founded: 1958. **Staff:** Prof 3; Other 1. **Subjects:** Foreign languages, music, English literature. **Special Collections:** School of Music Recital tapes (1200); Ohio History tapes (1200). **Holdings:** 2410 reel tapes; 6421 cassettes; 21 phonograph records. **Services:** Copying; library open to public. **Formerly:** Its Computer Assisted and Self-Instruction Center.

★6645★

KENTON COUNTY PUBLIC LIBRARY - KENTUCKY & LOCAL HISTORY DEPARTMENT (Hist**)**
5th & Scott Sts.   Phone: (606) 491-0799
Covington, KY 41011   Mike Averdick, Assoc.Dir.
Staff: Prof 5; Other 4. **Subjects:** Kentucky genealogy, local history. **Special Collections:** Old photograph collection (5000). **Holdings:** 3000 books; 150 bound periodical volumes; 4000 reels of microfilm; 1100 local history files; 468 family files; 1200 maps. **Subscriptions:** 9 journals and other serials. **Services:** Copying; library open to public. **Special Indexes:** Index to local newspapers, 1834-1910, and to Kentucky genealogical magazines (card). **Staff:** Linda Bailey, Ref.Libn.; Don W. Barlow, Sr. Indexer.

★6646★

KENTUCKY CHRISTIAN COLLEGE - MEDIA CENTER (Rel-Theol**)†**
College Ave.   Phone: (606) 474-6613
Grayson, KY 41143   Kenneth L. Beck, Libn.
Staff: Prof 2; Other 14. **Subjects:** Religion, Restoration history, psychology, philosophy, education. **Special Collections:** Restoration history books and writers, including first editions. **Holdings:** 24,989 books; 923 bound periodical volumes; 100 microforms of journals; 444 cassette tapes; 295 filmstrips; 184 phonograph records. **Subscriptions:** 147 journals and other serials; 5 newspapers. **Services:** Interlibrary loans; copying; library open to public. **Staff:** Ruth Gemeinhart, Clerk.

★6647★

KENTUCKY COVERED BRIDGE ASSOCIATION - LIBRARY (Hist**)**
62 Miami Pkwy.   Phone: (606) 441-7000
Fort Thomas, KY 41075   L.K. Patton, Exec.Dir.
Founded: 1964. **Staff:** 3. **Subjects:** Covered bridges of Kentucky and other states. **Special Collections:** Dr. J. Winston Coleman's covered bridge picture collection from his Kentuckiana Collection. **Holdings:** 400 volumes; 1000 newspaper clippings (in scrapbooks); 50 archive records; 3000 pictures of covered bridges; 60 maps and blueprints; 10 State Highway Department reports. **Subscriptions:** 8 journals and other serials. **Services:** Copying; library open to public for reference use only. **Publications:** Timbered Tunnel Talk, monthly - distributed free to members and also through various Chambers of Commerce. **Special Indexes:** Existing (17) bridges indexed and material pertaining to them (card).

KENTUCKY ENERGY RESEARCH LABORATORY - INSTITUTE FOR MINING AND MINERALS RESEARCH
See: University of Kentucky - Institute for Mining and Minerals Research

★6648★

KENTUCKY HISTORICAL SOCIETY - LIBRARY (Hist**)†**
Broadway, Old Capitol Annex
Box H   Phone: (502) 564-3016
Frankfort, KY 40601   Anne McDonnell, Lib.Mgr.
Staff: Prof 4; Other 6. **Subjects:** History, including Kentucky history; genealogy; folklore; religion. **Special Collections:** Collins Collection (Kentucky history). **Holdings:** 50,000 books; 7000 bound periodical volumes; 4000 documents; 1000 VF drawers of governors' papers; 100 volumes of governors' journals; 1200 manuscripts; 250 VF drawers of clippings, correspondence and family files; 2000 reels of microfilm; 500 maps. **Subscriptions:** 150 journals and other serials. **Services:** Copying; library open to public for research.

★6649★

KENTUCKY MOUNTAIN BIBLE INSTITUTE - GIBSON LIBRARY (Rel-Theol**)†**
     Phone: (606) 666-5000
Vancleve, KY 41385   Ava Smith, Libn.
Founded: 1939. **Staff:** Prof 1. **Subjects:** Bible, theology, Christian education, religious history, Christian missions, history, religions, sermons. **Special Collections:** Christian Holiness (467 volumes). **Holdings:** 13,548 books; 975 pamphlets (cataloged); 169 maps. **Subscriptions:** 70 journals and other serials. **Services:** Library open to public with permission.

KENTUCKY REGIONAL LIBRARY FOR THE BLIND & PHYSICALLY HANDICAPPED
See: Kentucky State Department for Libraries and Archives

★6650★

KENTUCKY STATE DEPARTMENT OF COMMERCE - DIVISION OF RESEARCH - MAP LIBRARY (Geog-Map**)**
133 Holmes St.   Phone: (502) 564-4715
Frankfort, KY 40601   Bill Howard, Chf.
Founded: 1958. **Staff:** Prof 4. **Subjects:** Maps - topographic, geologic, city, county; geologic and industrial publications. **Special Collections:** Original control photographs and topographic manuscripts. **Holdings:** 12,000 books; 5680 bound periodical volumes; aerial photographs; maps. **Services:** Library open to public.

★6651★

KENTUCKY STATE DEPARTMENT OF ECONOMIC DEVELOPMENT - RESEARCH & PLANNING DIVISION - LIBRARY (Bus-Fin**)**
Capitol Plaza Office Tower   Phone: (502) 564-4886
Frankfort, KY 40601   Doris Arnold, Libn.
Founded: 1966. **Staff:** Prof 1; Other 1. **Subjects:** Government statistics, economics, economic development, industrial geology. **Holdings:** 5000 volumes. **Subscriptions:** 125 journals and other serials; 8 newspapers. **Services:** Copying (limited); library open to public for reference use only. **Formerly:** Kentucky State Department of Commerce.

★6652★

KENTUCKY STATE DEPARTMENT OF EDUCATION - RESOURCE CENTER (Educ**)**
Capital Plaza Tower   Phone: (502) 564-5385
Frankfort, KY 40601   Melissa Briscoe, Dir.
Staff: Prof 3; Other 4. **Subjects:** Education. **Special Collections:** Educational archival collection. **Holdings:** 6104 books; 3890 media kits; complete set of ERIC documents on microfiche. **Subscriptions:** 189 journals and other serials; 15 newspapers. **Services:** Interlibrary loans; copying; library open to public. **Computerized Information Services:** DIALOG. **Publications:** List of

media kits and films, annual - distributed to local school districts; list of new materials, quarterly - for internal distribution only. **Staff:** Donna Swanson; Larry Davis; Anne Hamilton.

★6653★

KENTUCKY STATE DEPARTMENT FOR HUMAN RESOURCES - LIBRARY (Med; Soc Sci)
275 E. Main St.
Frankfort, KY 40621
Phone: (502) 564-4530
Douglas Raisor, Supv./Acq./ILL
Founded: 1960. **Staff:** Prof 2; Other 2. **Subjects:** Public health, social welfare, social work, child welfare. **Holdings:** 27,500 books; 10,000 unbound periodicals; 3000 pamphlets. **Subscriptions:** 223 journals and other serials. **Services:** Interlibrary loans; copying; library open to public for reference use only. **Computerized Information Services:** BRS. **Staff:** Deborah Robb, Cat./ Ser./Ref.

★6654★

KENTUCKY STATE DEPT. FOR LIBRARIES & ARCHIVES - KENTUCKY REGIONAL LIB. FOR THE BLIND & PHYSICALLY HANDICAPPED (Aud-Vis)
300 Coffee Tree Rd.
Box 818
Frankfort, KY 40602
Phone: (502) 875-7000
Richard Feindel, Br.Mgr.
Staff: Prof 5; Other 9. **Subjects:** General collection. **Special Collections:** Kentucky Collection (300 volumes). **Holdings:** 150,000 volumes. **Services:** Interlibrary loans; library open to eligible blind and physically handicapped persons. **Networks/Consortia:** Member of National Library Service for the Blind & Physically Handicapped. **Publications:** Newsletter, quarterly. **Staff:** Adam Ruschival, Regional Libn.; Judy Baron, Sr.Libn.; Lisa Lowry, Sr.Libn.; Wendy Hatfield, Sr.Libn.

★6655★

KENTUCKY STATE DEPARTMENT FOR LIBRARIES & ARCHIVES - PUBLIC RECORDS DIVISION - ARCHIVES BRANCH (Hist)
300 Coffee Tree Rd.
Box 537
Frankfort, KY 40602
Phone: (502) 875-7000
Dr. Lewis Bellardo, Dir.
Staff: Prof 15; Other 20. **Subjects:** Kentucky - state and local government records. **Holdings:** 80,000 cubic reet of records; 25,000 reels of microfilm; 2000 microfiche. **Services:** Copying; archives open to public. **Networks/ Consortia:** Member of SPINDEX Users Network (SUN); internal database. **Publications:** List of publications - available upon request. **Formerly:** Kentucky State Department of Library & Archives - Kentuckiana Collection. **Staff:** Edna M. Milliken, Archv.Br.Mgr.; Jeffrey Duff, Asst. State Archv.; Dr. Walter Place, Sr.Archv.; Jerry Carlton, Local Rec.Archv.; Frances Coleman, Sr.Archv.; Jean Rudloff, Archv.

★6656★

KENTUCKY STATE DEPARTMENT FOR LIBRARIES AND ARCHIVES - STATE LIBRARY SERVICES DIVISION (Info Sci)
300 Coffee Tree Rd.
Box 537
Frankfort, KY 40602
Phone: (502) 875-7000
Suzanne LeBarron, Dir.
Staff: Prof 17; Other 19. **Subjects:** Kentucky, arts, social science. **Holdings:** 120,000 books; 38,000 documents; 16mm films. **Subscriptions:** 575 journals and other serials; 6 newspapers. **Services:** Interlibrary loans; copying; division open to public. **Computerized Information Services:** DIALOG, INFO-KY; computerized cataloging. **Networks/Consortia:** Member of Kentucky Cooperative Library Information Project (KENCLIP). **Publications:** Keynote, bimonthly - to Kentucky libraries and to other state libraries. **Staff:** Sharon Breeding, Sr.Libn.; Charlene E. Davis, Br.Mgr., Tech.Supp.; Eloise Duvall, Prin.Libn.; Jane Easley, Sr.Libn.; Brenda Fuller, Sr.Libn.; Martha Gregory, Br.Mgr., Pub.Serv.; Annie Harrison, Sr.Libn.; Ressie Johnson, Sr.Libn., KENCLIP; Mary Mattingly, Sr.Libn., KENCLIP; Gerald Miller, Sr.Libn., KENCLIP; Ruth Pierce, Sr.,Libn., KENCLIP; Myra Prewitt, Sr.Libn.; Gloria "Jo" Rawlings, Sr.Libn.; Linda L. Sherrow, Br.Mgr., Network; Linda Stith, AV Coord.; Sarah Taylor, Prin.Libn.

★6657★

KENTUCKY STATE EXECUTIVE DEPARTMENT FOR FINANCE LIBRARY - OFFICE FOR POLICY AND MANAGEMENT (Soc Sci)
Capitol Annex, Rm. 200
Frankfort, KY 40601
Phone: (502) 564-7300
Founded: 1965. **Staff:** 1. **Subjects:** Budgeting, planning and development, grants information. **Special Collections:** Background information on budgeting. **Holdings:** 4500 volumes; 5 drawer information file. **Subscriptions:** 63 journals and other serials. **Services:** Interlibrary loans; copying; library open to public.

★6658★

KENTUCKY STATE LAW LIBRARY (Law)
State Capitol, Rm. 200
Frankfort, KY 40601
Phone: (502) 564-4848
Wesley Gilmer, Jr., State Law Libn.
Founded: 1954. **Staff:** Prof 4; Other 4. **Subjects:** American law. **Special Collections:** Published legal material relating to the past and present practice of law in Kentucky. **Holdings:** 40,000 books; 30,000 bound periodical volumes. **Subscriptions:** 250 journals and other serials. **Services:** Interlibrary loans; copying; library open to public. **Computerized Information Services:** LEXIS (available to Court of Justice only). **Publications:** Guide to Kentucky Legal Research: A State Bibliography, 1979 - for sale. **Remarks:** Maintained by the Kentucky Court of Justice, Administrative Office of the Courts. **Staff:** Evelyn Lockwood, Cat.; Vivian Beasley, Ref.; Sallie M. Howard, Staff Att.; Barbara Kibler, Staff Att.

★6659★

KENTUCKY STATE LEGISLATIVE RESEARCH COMMISSION - LIBRARY (Law; Soc Sci)
State Capitol, 4th Fl.
Frankfort, KY 40601
Phone: (502) 564-8100
Peggy King, Leg.Libn.
Founded: 1950. **Staff:** Prof 2; Other 2. **Subjects:** Law, government, public administration. **Holdings:** 18,000 volumes; 280 pamphlet boxes of state publications. **Subscriptions:** 276 journals and other serials. **Services:** Interlibrary loans; copying; SDI; library open to public. **Special Indexes:** Index of legislation and legislators since 1948 (card).

★6660★

KENWORTH TRUCK CO. - DIVISION LIBRARY (Trans)†
Box 1000
Kirkland, WA 98033
Phone: (206) 828-5255
Maureen McCrea, Libn.
Founded: 1977. **Staff:** Prof 1; Other 1. **Subjects:** Mechanical engineering, trucks and trucking. **Special Collections:** Papers of Society of Automotive Engineers. **Holdings:** 1000 books; 20 VF drawers of vendor drawings on microfilm; 15 VF drawers of vendor literature. **Subscriptions:** 100 journals and other serials. **Services:** Interlibrary loans; library not open to public. **Computerized Information Services:** DIALOG. **Publications:** Monthly Newsletter - for internal distribution only.

KENYA NATIONAL ARCHIVES
See: Michigan State University - International Library

★6661★

KENYON & ECKHARDT ADVERTISING - INFORMATION CENTER (Bus-Fin)†
200 Park Ave.
New York, NY 10017
Phone: (212) 880-2361
Aina Geske, Hd.Libn.
Founded: 1947. **Staff:** Prof 2. **Subjects:** Advertising, marketing. **Special Collections:** Chrysler Corporation. **Holdings:** 700 books; 200 bound periodical volumes; 500 annual reports. **Subscriptions:** 200 journals and other serials; 5 newspapers. **Services:** Interlibrary loans; copying; library open to public at discretion of librarian. **Staff:** Barbara Pomerantz, Asst.Libn.

★6662★

KERN COUNTY HEALTH DEPARTMENT - DR. MYRNIE A. GIFFORD PUBLIC HEALTH LIBRARY
1700 Flower St.
Bakersfield, CA 93305
Defunct

★6663★

KERN COUNTY LAW LIBRARY (Law)
Courts & Administration Bldg., Rm. 301
Bakersfield, CA 93301
Phone: (805) 861-2379
Marian N. Smrekar, Law Libn.
Founded: 1891. **Staff:** Prof 1; Other 2. **Subjects:** Law. **Special Collections:** State depository (selective). **Holdings:** 24,254 books; Federal Register since 1945; 674 CEB tapes; pamphlets. **Subscriptions:** 120 journals and other serials. **Services:** Interlibrary loans (limited); copying; library open to public for reference use only.

★6664★

KERN COUNTY MUSEUM - LIBRARY (Hist)
3801 Chester Ave.
Bakersfield, CA 93301
Phone: (805) 861-2132
Christopher D. Brewer, Musm.Techn.
Subjects: Local history. **Holdings:** 2000 volumes. **Services:** Library open to staff and researchers, with permission of director and appointment.

★6665★
KERN COUNTY SUPERINTENDENT OF SCHOOLS OFFICE - INSTRUCTIONAL RESOURCES CENTER (Educ)
5801 Sundale
Bakersfield, CA 93309
Phone: (805) 861-2446
Karl R. Hardin, Libn.
Founded: 1935. **Staff:** Prof 2; Other 12. **Subjects:** Education. **Holdings:** 20,000 books; 5000 bound periodical volumes; 14,000 films and slides; 1300 microforms; 2000 curriculum guides (cataloged). **Subscriptions:** 225 journals and other serials. **Services:** Library open to public. **Computerized Information Services:** Computerized circulation.

★6666★
KERN MEDICAL CENTER - KERN HEALTH SCIENCES LIBRARY (Med)
1830 Flower St.
Bakersfield, CA 93305-4197
Phone: (805) 326-2227
L.L. Rizzo, Health Sci.Libn.
Staff: Prof 1; Other 2. **Subjects:** Clinical medicine, nursing, hospital administration. **Holdings:** 2500 books; 10,500 bound periodical volumes; 300 audiotapes; 200 slides. **Subscriptions:** 255 journals and other serials. **Services:** Interlibrary loans; copying; SDI; library open by referral from another library and to Kern County residents. **Computerized Information Services:** MEDLINE, BRS. **Networks/Consortia:** Member of Kern Health Sciences Library Consortium.

KERR INDUSTRIAL APPLICATIONS CENTER
See: Southeastern Oklahoma State University

★6667★
KERR-MC GEE CORPORATION - MC GEE LIBRARY (Sci-Tech; Energy)
Box 25861
Oklahoma City, OK 73125
Phone: (405) 270-3358
Tom W. Harrison, Mgr.
Founded: 1948. **Staff:** Prof 5; Other 3. **Subjects:** Geology, energy, mineral deposits, petroleum technology, economics, business. **Holdings:** 10,000 books; 12,000 documents. **Subscriptions:** 600 journals and other serials. **Services:** Library not open to public. **Computerized Information Services:** DIALOG, SDC, New York Times Information Service, Dow Jones News Retrieval, NLM, RLIN, U.S. Geological Survey; computerized cataloging. **Staff:** Vicki Vann, Libn.; Virginia Barnes, Info.Spec.; Ernest Albright, Info.Spec.; Becky Marks, Asst.Libn.

KERR (Robert S.) ENVIRONMENTAL RESEARCH CENTER
See: Environmental Protection Agency - Robert S. Kerr Environmental Research Center

KERR (William Jasper) LIBRARY
See: Oregon State University - William Jasper Kerr Library

★6668★
KESHER ZION SYNAGOGUE SISTERHOOD - LIBRARY (Rel-Theol)
Perkiomen & Hill Aves.
Reading, PA 19602
Phone: (215) 372-3818
Rachel Yaffee, Libn.
Staff: 1. **Subjects:** Judaica and related subjects. **Holdings:** 2000 books. **Services:** Library open to public with restrictions.

KESLER CIRCULATING LIBRARY
See: Vanderbilt University Library - Divinity Library

KETCHIKAN LAW LIBRARY
See: Alaska State Court System

KETCHUM (M.B.) MEMORIAL LIBRARY
See: Southern California College of Optometry - M.B. Ketchum Memorial Library

★6669★
KETTERING (Charles F.) RESEARCH LABORATORY - LIBRARY (Sci-Tech)†
150 E. South College St.
Yellow Springs, OH 45387
Phone: (513) 767-7271
Janice Williams, Libn.
Founded: 1954. **Staff:** Prof 1. **Subjects:** Biochemistry - photosynthesis, enzymology, nitrogen fixation, cell differentiation; related technology and instrumentation. **Holdings:** 7000 books; 6000 bound periodical volumes; U.S. government technical reports; yearbooks and annual reports from other scientific institutions. **Subscriptions:** 152 journals and other serials. **Services:** Interlibrary loans; copying; library open to public for reference use only. **Computerized Information Services:** DIALOG. **Networks/Consortia:** Member of Dayton-Miami Valley Consortium.

★6670★
KETTERING COLLEGE OF MEDICAL ARTS - LEARNING RESOURCES CENTER (Med)
3737 Southern Blvd.
Kettering, OH 45429
Phone: (513) 296-7201
Edward Collins, Libn.
Staff: Prof 2; Other 6. **Subjects:** Medicine and allied health fields. **Holdings:** 50,430 books and bound periodical volumes; 6289 AV materials. **Subscriptions:** 892 journals and other serials; 9 newspapers. **Services:** Interlibrary loans; copying; library open to public. **Computerized Information Services:** Online systems. **Networks/Consortia:** Member of Dayton-Miami Valley Consortium (Library Division); Kentucky-Ohio-Michigan Regional Medical Library Network (KOMRML). **Staff:** Joseph Stoia, Med.Libn.

KETTERING LABORATORY LIBRARY
See: University of Cincinnati - Department of Environmental Health Library

★6671★
KETTERING MEMORIAL HOSPITAL - MEDICAL LIBRARY (Med)
3535 Southern Blvd.
Kettering, OH 45429
Phone: (513) 298-4331
Joseph P. Stoia, Med.Libn.
Founded: 1964. **Staff:** Prof 1; Other 3. **Subjects:** Medicine and allied health. **Special Collections:** Health education collection. **Holdings:** 5500 books; 15,400 bound periodical volumes; 2063 AV items. **Subscriptions:** 587 journals and other serials; 6 newspapers. **Services:** Interlibrary loans; copying; SDI; library open to area health professionals. **Computerized Information Services:** MEDLINE, BRS. **Networks/Consortia:** Member of Miami Valley Association of Health Science Libraries. **Publications:** Union list of serials; union list of audiovisuals.

★6672★
KEUFFEL AND ESSER COMPANY - CHEMICAL RESEARCH AND DEVELOPMENT LIBRARY (Sci-Tech)
20 Whippany Rd.
Morristown, NJ 07960
Phone: (201) 285-5530
Gloria Hickey, Libn.
Staff: Prof 1. **Subjects:** Chemistry, photography. **Holdings:** 700 books; 350 bound periodical volumes. **Subscriptions:** 56 journals and other serials. **Services:** Interlibrary loans; library not open to public.

★6673★
KEY BANK N.A. - INFORMATION CENTER (Bus-Fin)
60 State St.
Albany, NY 12207
Phone: (518) 447-3594
Joy Longo, Libn.
Founded: 1963. **Staff:** 1. **Subjects:** Business, finance, management. **Holdings:** 4800 books; 12 VF drawers of clippings and pamphlets. **Subscriptions:** 74 journals and other serials. **Services:** Interlibrary loans; center open to public with limited circulation of materials.

★6674★
KEYES ASSOCIATES - LIBRARY (Sci-Tech)
321 S. Main St.
Providence, RI 02903
Phone: (401) 861-2900
Carole E. Twombly, Libn.
Staff: Prof 1. **Subjects:** Engineering - sanitary, environmental, civil, structural, mechanical, electrical; architecture; landscape and interior design. **Holdings:** 2200 books; 650 specifications and reports; 128 VF drawers of project files. **Subscriptions:** 200 journals and other serials. **Services:** Interlibrary loans; library open to public by permission of librarian. **Publications:** Current Acquisitions List, monthly - for internal distribution only.

★6675★
KEYSTONE CUSTODIAN FUNDS, INC. - LIBRARY (Bus-Fin)
99 High St.
Boston, MA 02104
Phone: (617) 338-3435
Kathleen Young, Libn.
Staff: 1. **Subjects:** Business and statistics. **Holdings:** 300 books. **Subscriptions:** 100 journals and other serials; 11 newspapers. **Services:** Library not open to public.

★6676★
KEYSTONE PRESS AGENCY, INC. - PICTURE LIBRARY (Pict)
156 Fifth Ave.
New York, NY 10010
Phone: (212) 924-8123
Brian F. Alpert, Mng.Ed.
Founded: 1914. **Staff:** Prof 1; Other 1. **Subjects:** Photographs of all aspects of life with worldwide coverage. **Special Collections:** Picture material for educational publications. **Holdings:** Several million black/white and color photographs. **Services:** Library not open to public. **Staff:** Satoko Alpert, Photo Libn.

★6677★
KHD (Canada) LTD. - DEUTZ DIESEL (Canada) LIMITED - ENGINEERING LIBRARY (Sci-Tech)
4660 Hickmore Ave.
Montreal, PQ, Canada H4T 1K2
Phone: (514) 735-4411
Sharon E. McKay, Info.Dir.
Founded: 1976. Staff: 1. Subjects: Engineering. Holdings: 2000 books; 1500 bound periodical volumes; 1000 other cataloged items. Subscriptions: 212 journals and other serials. Services: Interlibrary loans; copying; library not open to public. Computerized Information Services: Micromedia Ltd.

KIDDER (Ada M.) MEMORIAL LIBRARY
See: Houghton College - Buffalo Suburban Campus - Ada M. Kidder Memorial Library

★6678★
KIDDER, PEABODY AND COMPANY, INC. - LIBRARY (Bus-Fin)
10 Hanover Sq., 21st Fl.
New York, NY 10005
Phone: (212) 747-2504
Joanne Ultang, Libn.
Founded: 1962. Staff: Prof 2; Other 8. Subjects: Corporation records, business conditions, finance, investments, economics. Special Collections: Corporation files. Holdings: Figures not available. Services: Interlibrary loans; copying (both limited); library open to members of Special Libraries Association by appointment. Computerized Information Services: DIALOG, New York Times Information Service, NEXIS, Dow Jones News Retrieval, Computer Directions Advisors, Inc., Finsbury Data Services, Ltd.; computerized acquisitions, serials and corporation files. Staff: Nancy Sheridan, Ref.Libn.

KIDENEY HEALTH SCIENCES LIBRARY
See: Fillmore (Millard) Hospital

KIEF (Ella P.) MEMORIAL LIBRARY
See: New Mexico State Department of Hospitals - State Hospital - Ella P. Kief Memorial Library

KIEHLE LIBRARY
See: University of Minnesota, Crookston

KIENBUSCH LIBRARY OF ARMS AND ARMOR
See: Philadelphia Museum of Art - Library

KILLAM (Izaak Walton) HOSPITAL FOR CHILDREN
See: Izaak Walton Killam Hospital for Children

KILNER LIBRARY
See: Kenilworth Historical Society

★6679★
KILPATRICK & CODY - LIBRARY (Law)
3100 Equitable Bldg.
100 Peachtree St.
Atlanta, GA 30303
Phone: (404) 572-6397
Peggy Martin, Libn.
Founded: 1904. Staff: Prof 2. Subjects: Law. Holdings: 30,000 books; 2000 bound periodical volumes; 10,000 microfiche; 300 reels of microfilm. Subscriptions: 240 journals and other serials; 10 newspapers. Services: Library not open to public. Special Catalogs: Union Catalogue of the Atlanta-Athens Area.

KIMBALL (Fiske) FINE ARTS LIBRARY
See: University of Virginia - Fiske Kimball Fine Arts Library

★6680★
KIMBELL ART MUSEUM - LIBRARY (Art)
Will Rogers Rd., W.
Box 9440
Fort Worth, TX 76107
Phone: (817) 332-8451
Erika Esau, Libn.
Founded: 1967. Staff: Prof 2; Other 3. Subjects: Art (excluding contemporary and American). Holdings: 23,000 books; 925 bound periodical volumes; 35,000 slides; 1100 microforms. Subscriptions: 130 journals and other serials. Services: Interlibrary loans; copying; library open to public for scholarly use on request. Networks/Consortia: Member of RLG. Staff: Chia-Chun Shih, Asst.Cat.

★6681★
KIMBERLY-CLARK CORPORATION - LIBRARY (Sci-Tech)
2100 Winchester Rd.
Box 999
Neenah, WI 54956
Phone: (414) 721-5261
Mary E. Sutliff, Tech.Libn.
Staff: Prof 1; Other 3. Subjects: Paper technology and chemistry, engineering, biomedical sciences, business and management. Holdings: 6500 books; 3000 bound periodical volumes; 7500 pamphlets. Subscriptions: 450 journals and other serials; 10 newspapers. Services: Copying; library not open to public. Computerized Information Services: SDC, New York Times Information Service, Pergamon International Information Corporation.

★6682★
KIMBERLY-CLARK CORPORATION - TECHNICAL LIBRARY (Sci-Tech)
1400 Holcomb Bridge Rd.
Roswell, GA 30076
Phone: (404) 587-8479
Judy C. Dyer, Tech.Libn.
Founded: 1981. Staff: Prof 1. Subjects: Nonwoven fabrics, polypropylene. Holdings: 1200 books. Subscriptions: 356 journals and other serials. Services: Interlibrary loans; copying; library not open to public. Networks/Consortia: Member of Georgia Library Information Network (GLIN).

★6683★
KINDEL & ANDERSON - LIBRARY (Law)
555 S. Flower St., 26th Fl.
Los Angeles, CA 90071
Phone: (213) 680-2222
Marie Wallace, Law Libn.
Staff: 3. Subjects: Law - corporate, probate, state and federal trial practice and tax, labor, securities. Holdings: 22,000 books; 400 bound periodical volumes. Services: Copying; library not open to public. Computerized Information Services: LEXIS, New York Times Information Service.

★6684★
KING COUNTY LAW LIBRARY (Law)
601 County Courthouse
Seattle, WA 98104
James J. McArdle, Libn.
Founded: 1915. Staff: Prof 3; Other 2. Subjects: Law. Holdings: 85,000 books; 4700 bound periodical volumes. Subscriptions: 200 journals and other serials. Services: Copying; library open to public. Staff: Alan B. Anderson, Asst.Libn.; Mary Lou Duvall, Ref.Libn.

★6685★
KING COUNTY MASONIC LIBRARY ASSOCIATION - LIBRARY (Rec)†
Harvard & E. Pine St.
Seattle, WA 98122
Phone: (206) 322-9535
Erwin L. Hippe, Libn.
Staff: 2. Subjects: Freemasonry, philosophy, biography, literature. Special Collections: Proceedings of Grand Lodges throughout the world; complete set of proceedings of Ars Quatuor Cornatorum - Premier Lodge of Research in World (London, England). Holdings: 12,000 books; 2500 bound periodical volumes; Short Talk Bulletins, 1923 to present. Subscriptions: 60 journals and other serials. Services: Library open to public with restrictions. Special Indexes: Index of Philalethes Magazine from 1946 to present (card).

★6686★
KING COUNTY YOUTH SERVICE CENTER - LIBRARY (Soc Sci)
1211 E. Alder
Seattle, WA 98122
Phone: (206) 323-9500
Julie Ann Oiye, Libn.
Founded: 1972. Staff: Prof 1; Other 1. Subjects: Juvenile delinquency and justice, adolescent psychology, volunteers in corrections. Holdings: 8000 books; 800 cassettes, phonograph records, filmstrips; 250 reports on microfiche. Subscriptions: 106 journals and other serials. Services: Interlibrary loans; copying; library open to public with restrictions. Computerized Information Services: Computerized cataloging and acquisitions. Remarks: This program is jointly funded by the King County Library System and the King County Juvenile Court.

KING (Emma B.) LIBRARY
See: Shaker Museum Foundation - Emma B. King Library

KING LIBRARY
See: Miami University - Walter Havighurst Special Collections Library

KING (Margaret I.) LIBRARY
See: University of Kentucky - Margaret I. King Library

★6687★
KING (Martin Luther, Jr.) CENTER FOR SOCIAL CHANGE - KING LIBRARY AND ARCHIVES (Soc Sci)
449 Auburn Ave.
Atlanta, GA 30312
Phone: (404) 524-1956
D. Louise Cook, Dir.
Founded: 1968. Staff: Prof 2; Other 4. Subjects: Martin Luther King, Jr., civil rights, black history, black politics, black religion, nonviolence. Special Collections: Bilingual materials by Martin Luther King, Jr. Holdings: Over a million documents in archives, related primarily to the American civil rights movement. Services: Copying; library open to public. Publications: Martin Luther King Center Newsletter, quarterly; library holdings and services brochures. Remarks: These archives are dedicated to the documentation of

the post-1954 Civil Rights Movement with emphasis on the life and work of Martin Luther King, Jr. and the nonviolent movement which continues. **Staff:** Cynthia P. Lewis, Archv./Libn.

KING (Martin Luther, Jr.) GENERAL HOSPITAL
See: Los Angeles County/Martin Luther King, Jr. General Hospital

KING (Martin Luther) MEMORIAL LIBRARY
See: District of Columbia Public Library

KING (Mary Ann) HEALTH SCIENCES LIBRARY
See: Fairview Southdale Hospital - Mary Ann King Health Sciences Library

★6688★
KING RESEARCH, INC. - CENTER FOR QUANTITATIVE SCIENCES - LIBRARY (Info Sci)
6000 Executive Blvd.   Phone: (301) 881-6766
Rockville, MD 20852   Mary K. Yates, Libn.
Founded: 1975. **Staff:** Prof 1; Other 1. **Subjects:** Science/technology communication, journal publishing, information retrieval systems, planning, analysis, design and evaluation of information systems, libraries and library networks, survey and socioeconomic research. **Holdings:** 300 books; 1500 other cataloged items. **Subscriptions:** 30 journals and other serials. **Services:** Interlibrary loans; copying (limited); library accessible to researchers in information sciences. **Computerized Information Services:** DIALOG.

★6689★
KING & SPALDING - LAW LIBRARY (Law)
2500 Trust Company Tower   Phone: (404) 572-4808
Atlanta, GA 30303   Mary Anne C. Fry, Libn.
Subjects: Law - corporate, antitrust, real estate, tax, banking, labor, international. **Holdings:** 22,000 volumes. **Subscriptions:** 400 journals and other serials. **Services:** Interlibrary loans; copying; library open to public on request. **Computerized Information Services:** LEXIS; internal database; computerized cataloging, acquisitions, serials and circulation. **Staff:** Kayron F. Bearden, Asst.; Jean Nicholson, Ref.; Peggy Bennett, Circ.

★6690★
KINGMAN MUSEUM OF NATURAL HISTORY - LIBRARY (Sci-Tech)
West Michigan Ave. at 20th St.   Phone: (616) 965-5117
Battle Creek, MI 49017   Robert Learner, Musm.Dir.
Staff: Prof 5. **Subjects:** Ecology, geology, astronomy, ethnology. **Holdings:** 837 books. **Subscriptions:** 64 journals and other serials. **Staff:** Allison Van Nocker, Cur. of Coll.; D. Thomas Johnson, Cur./Exhibits; Paul Rheaume, Cur./ Prog.

★6691★
KING'S COLLEGE - D. LEONARD CORGAN LIBRARY (Hist)
14 W. Jackson St.   Phone: (717) 824-9931
Wilkes-Barre, PA 18711   Judith Tierney, Spec.Coll.Libn.
Founded: 1946. **Staff:** Prof 4; Other 12. **Subjects:** Folklore, coal mines and mining, Wyoming Valley, PA history. **Special Collections:** The George Korson Folklore Archive (books, records, 42 linear feet of personal papers, 107 reels of tape); Daniel J. Flood Collection (600 linear feet of public and private papers); John F. Kennedy Collection (books, records); collections on Wyoming Valley, PA. **Holdings:** Figures not available. **Services:** Library open to public by appointment. **Networks/Consortia:** Headquarters of Northeastern Pennsylvania Bibliographic Center. **Publications:** A Description of the George Korson Folklore Archive; Daniel J. Flood, A Register of his Papers.

KING'S COLLEGE LIBRARY
See: University of King's College

KINGS COUNTY HOSPITAL - PSYCHIATRY LIBRARY
See: SUNY - Downstate Medical Center - Department of Psychiatry Library

★6692★
KINGS COUNTY LAW LIBRARY (Law)
County Government Ctr.
Hanford, CA 93230   Jean H. Borraccino, Law Libn.
Founded: 1893. **Subjects:** Law. **Holdings:** 11,650 volumes. **Services:** Library open to public for reference use only.

KINGS MOUNTAIN NATL. MILITARY PARK
See: U.S. Natl. Park Service

★6693★
KINGS PARK PSYCHIATRIC CENTER - LIBRARY (Med)
Box A   Phone: (516) 544-2671
Kings Park, NY 11754   James W. Macinick, Sr.Libn.
Founded: 1959. **Staff:** Prof 1; Other 3. **Subjects:** Psychiatry, nursing, medicine and allied sciences. **Special Collections:** Collection in psychiatry. **Holdings:** 7000 books; 1000 bound periodical volumes; 15 VF drawers of pamphlets; 750 audiotapes. **Subscriptions:** 70 journals and other serials. **Services:** Interlibrary loans; copying; library open to staff. **Networks/ Consortia:** Member of Suffolk Cooperative Library System.

★6694★
KINGSBORO PSYCHIATRIC CENTER - MEDICAL LIBRARY (Med)
681 Clarkson Ave.   Phone: (212) 735-1273
Brooklyn, NY 11203   Olga K. Heisler, Sr.Libn.
Founded: 1895. **Staff:** Prof 1; Other 1. **Subjects:** Psychiatry, medicine, psychology, rehabilitation, social service, nursing. **Holdings:** 3000 books; 4 VF files of pamphlets and clippings; 258 tape cassettes. **Subscriptions:** 144 journals and other serials. **Services:** Interlibrary loans; copying; library open to public for reference use only. **Networks/Consortia:** Member of Brooklyn-Queens-Staten Island Health Sciences Librarians (BQSI).

★6695★
KINGSBOROUGH COMMUNITY COLLEGE - KINGSBOROUGH HISTORICAL SOCIETY (Hist)†
2001 Oriental Blvd.   Phone: (212) 934-5417
Brooklyn, NY 11235   John B. Manbeck, Archv.
Founded: 1970. **Staff:** Prof 2; Other 2. **Subjects:** Brooklyn, New York history. **Special Collections:** Old and new photographs of Coney Island and Manhattan Beach. **Holdings:** 100 books; photographs; clippings; newspapers; pamphlets; color slides; films music. **Subscriptions:** 18 journals and other serials. **Services:** Interlibrary loans; library open to public. **Staff:** Lorraine Tondi, Dir./Res.

★6696★
KINGSBROOK JEWISH MEDICAL CENTER - MEDICAL LIBRARY (Med)†
585 Schenectady Ave.   Phone: (212) 756-9700
Brooklyn, NY 11203   Mary E. Buchheit, Dir. of Med.Lib.
Founded: 1925. **Staff:** Prof 1; Other 3. **Subjects:** Pathology, neurology, orthopedics, rehabilitative medicine, clinical medicine, dentistry. **Holdings:** 4900 books; 7200 bound periodical volumes; 10 VF drawers of pamphlets and clippings. **Subscriptions:** 272 journals and other serials. **Services:** Interlibrary loans; copying; library not open to public.

★6697★
KINGSTON GENERAL HOSPITAL - MEDICAL LIBRARY (Med)
Stuart St.   Phone: (613) 547-5023
Kingston, ON, Canada K7L 2V7   Enid M. Scott, Libn.
Founded: 1961. **Staff:** 2. **Subjects:** Medicine, surgery, nursing, nutrition, laboratory technology, rehabilitative medicine, administration. **Special Collections:** Books and articles written by staff doctors; patient handbooks and literature; pharmacy literature for interns. **Holdings:** 2620 books; 2970 bound periodical volumes; AV items. **Subscriptions:** 160 journals and other serials. **Services:** Interlibrary loans (local only); copying; library open to medical students and professionals.

★6698★
KINGSTON HOSPITAL - LIBRARY (Med)
396 Broadway   Phone: (914) 331-3131
Kingston, NY 12401   Linda Stopard, Libn.
Staff: Prof 1. **Subjects:** Medicine. **Holdings:** 800 books; 2 VF drawers of pamphlets and pictures. **Subscriptions:** 94 journals and other serials. **Services:** Interlibrary loans; copying; library open to public with restrictions. **Computerized Information Services:** BRS, MEDLINE. **Networks/Consortia:** Member of Southeastern New York Library Resources Council (SENYLRC); Health Information Libraries of Westchester (HILOW).

★6699★
KINGSTON PSYCHIATRIC HOSPITAL - STAFF LIBRARY (Med)
Bag 603   Phone: (613) 546-1101
Kingston, ON, Canada K7L 4X3   Mae Morley, Libn.
Staff: Prof 1; Other 1. **Subjects:** Psychiatry, psychology, medicine, nursing, social sciences. **Holdings:** 3353 books; 2753 bound periodical volumes; 4 VF drawers of clippings and pamphlets; 198 cassettes. **Subscriptions:** 125 journals and other serials. **Services:** Interlibrary loans; copying; library open to public.

★6700★
KINGWOOD CENTER - LIBRARY (Sci-Tech)
900 Park Ave. W.   Phone: (419) 522-0211
Mansfield, OH 44906
Founded: 1953. **Staff:** 1. **Subjects:** Horticulture, natural history. **Special Collections:** Significant 17th, 18th, 19th century herbals and gardening books; current literature. **Holdings:** 8200 books; 500 bound periodical volumes; 12 VF drawers of pamphlets, pictures and clippings; 600 current seed and nursery catalogs. **Subscriptions:** 180 journals and other serials. **Services:** Interlibrary loans; copying; an extensive lending collection is available for public use; library open to public. **Publications:** Kingwood Center News.

★6701★
KINNEY (A.M.) INC. - LIBRARY (Sci-Tech)
2900 Vernon Place   Phone: (513) 281-2900
Cincinnati, OH 45219   Donna L. Middendorf, Libn.
Founded: 1929. **Staff:** Prof 1. **Subjects:** Chemistry, engineering, architecture. **Holdings:** 10,000 books and bound periodical volumes. **Subscriptions:** 200 journals and other serials. **Services:** Interlibrary loans; copying; information services to the staff; library not open to public. **Computerized Information Services:** Computerized circulation.

★6702★
KINO COMMUNITY HOSPITAL - LIBRARY (Med)†
2800 E. Ajo Way   Phone: (602) 294-4471
Tucson, AZ 85713   Connie Skinner, Libn.
Founded: 1959. **Staff:** Prof 1. **Subjects:** Medicine. **Holdings:** 1329 books. **Subscriptions:** 81 journals and other serials. **Services:** Interlibrary loans; copying; library open to public for reference use only by request. **Computerized Information Services:** Online systems.

★6703★
KINSEY INSTITUTE FOR RESEARCH IN SEX, GENDER & REPRODUCTION, INC. - LIBRARY AND INFORMATION SERVICE (Soc Sci)
416 Morrison Hall
Indiana University   Phone: (812) 335-7686
Bloomington, IN 47405   Susan Matusak, Hd.Libn.
Founded: 1947. **Staff:** Prof 2. **Subjects:** Sex behavior and attitudes, erotic literature and art. **Special Collections:** Multimedia (nonbook) sex related materials; unpublished behavioral data. **Holdings:** 54,000 books and bound periodical volumes; 39 VF drawers; 209 reels of microfilm; 105 tapes; 108 phonograph records; 1300 objects; 55,000 pictures; 5000 slides; 1700 films. **Subscriptions:** 90 journals and other serials. **Services:** Copying (limited); literature searches; bibliography preparation; library open to qualified scholars. **Computerized Information Services:** Internal database; computerized cataloging. **Publications:** Sources of Information and Materials Related to Human Sexuality, annual. **Special Indexes:** Master index for all collections. **Formerly:** Institute for Sex Research, Inc. **Staff:** Joan Scherer Brewer, Info.Serv.Off.

KIPLING COLLECTION
See: Dalhousie University

KIRBY LIBRARY OF GOVERNMENT AND LAW
See: Lafayette College

★6704★
KIRKLAND & ELLIS - LIBRARY (Law)
1776 K St., N.W.   Phone: (202) 857-5109
Washington, DC 20006   George B. Kirlin, Libn.
Founded: 1951. **Staff:** Prof 3; Other 4. **Subjects:** Law, communications, antitrust law and trade regulations, energy, environment, food and drugs, labor, taxation, securities regulation. **Special Collections:** Bound volumes of the U.S. Court of Appeals, DC Circuit, opinions and briefs of Federal Communications Commission cases since 1934, Legislative Library Collection. **Services:** Interlibrary loans; library open to public by appointment. **Computerized Information Services:** LEXIS, SDC, BRS, New York Times Information Service. **Networks/Consortia:** Member of OCLC. **Publications:** Washington Update, weekly - for internal distribution only. **Special Catalogs:** Catalog of bound hearings and reports re communications from 1929 to present; catalog of Federal Trade Commission dockets; catalog of Department of Justice antitrust complaints, orders and stipulations. **Staff:** Janet L. Crowther, Asst.Libn.; W. Jeffery Tacy, Leg.Spec.

★6705★
KIRKLAND & ELLIS - LIBRARY (Law)
200 E. Randolph Dr., 60th Fl.   Phone: (312) 861-3200
Chicago, IL 60601   Charles E. Kregel, Jr., Info.Mgr.
Staff: Prof 5; Other 5. **Subjects:** Law, business. **Holdings:** Figures not available. **Services:** Library not open to public. **Computerized Information Services:** LEXIS, New York Times Information Service, SDC, DIALOG, BRS, Dow Jones News Retrieval, Control Data Corporation, Dun & Bradstreet, Inc.; computerized cataloging. **Networks/Consortia:** Member of OCLC through ILLINET. **Staff:** Mary Ann Miya, Asst.Libn.; Mary K. Salovaara, Asst.Libn.; Rebecca Schroff, Asst.Libn.

★6706★
KIRKSVILLE COLLEGE OF OSTEOPATHIC MEDICINE - A.T. STILL MEMORIAL LIBRARY (Med)
       Phone: (816) 626-2345
Kirksville, MO 63501   Georgia Walter, Dir. of Lib.
Founded: 1897. **Staff:** Prof 2; Other 2. **Subjects:** Osteopathic medicine, medicine, psychology, basic sciences. **Special Collections:** Osteopathic medicine. **Holdings:** 53,000 books and bound periodical volumes; 3000 AV software items; 400 osteopathic materials (cataloged); 8 VF drawers of osteopathic pamphlets. **Subscriptions:** 745 journals and other serials; 5 newspapers. **Services:** Interlibrary loans; copying; library open to public with restrictions. **Computerized Information Services:** MEDLINE, OCTANET. **Networks/Consortia:** Member of Northeast Missouri Library Network; Midcontinental Regional Medical Library Program. **Publications:** Recent Acquisitions, quarterly - to other osteopathic libraries; Audiovisual Materials, annual. **Staff:** Jean Lewis, Ref./Circ.Libn.

★6707★
KIRKSVILLE COLLEGE OF OSTEOPATHIC MEDICINE - LAUGHLIN OSTEOPATHIC HOSPITAL - PROFESSIONAL LIBRARY (Med)
900 E. La Harpe   Phone: (816) 665-5171
Kirksville, MO 63501   Andrea Lyons, Dir.
Staff: 1. **Subjects:** Medicine. **Special Collections:** Osteopathic medicine. **Holdings:** 1050 books. **Subscriptions:** 45 journals and other serials. **Services:** Interlibrary loans; copying; library not open to public.

KIRSTEIN BUSINESS BRANCH
See: Boston Public Library

KIRTLAND AIR FORCE BASE (NM)
See: U.S. Air Force Base - Kirtland Base Library; U.S. Air Force Hospital - Medical Library (NM-Kirtland AFB); U.S. Air Force Weapons Laboratory

KISTLER (Gertrude) MEMORIAL LIBRARY
See: Rosemont College - Gertrude Kistler Memorial Library

★6708★
KITCHENER-WATERLOO ART GALLERY - ELEANOR CALVERT MEMORIAL LIBRARY (Art)
101 Queen St. N.   Phone: (519) 579-5860
Kitchener, ON, Canada N2H 6P7   Nancy Francis, Libn.
Founded: 1968. **Staff:** 1. **Subjects:** Fine arts. **Holdings:** 3000 books; 3500 files of artist biographical information; 12 books of clippings; 19 carousels of slides-sound lecture series; 4000 slides; gallery archives; reproduction files. **Subscriptions:** 20 journals and other serials. **Services:** Interlibrary loans; copying; library open to public for reference use only. **Special Catalogs:** 12 slide catalogues.

★6709★
KITCHENER-WATERLOO HOSPITAL - HEALTH SCIENCES LIBRARY (Med)
835 King St., W.   Phone: (519) 742-3611
Kitchener, ON, Canada N2G 1G3   Thelma Bisch, Libn.
Founded: 1954. **Staff:** Prof 1; Other 2. **Subjects:** Medicine, nursing, hospital administration, paramedicine. **Special Collections:** Ethical and religious collection donated by hospital's Chapel Committee (500 books). **Holdings:** 2700 books; 3500 bound periodical volumes; 500 AV items. **Subscriptions:** 200 journals and other serials. **Services:** Interlibrary loans; copying; library open to public for reference use only.

★6710★
KITCHENER-WATERLOO OVERSEAS AID INC. - GLOBAL COMMUNITY CENTRE - LIBRARY (Soc Sci)
94 Queen St. S.   Phone: (519) 743-7111
Kitchener, ON, Canada N2G 1V9   Stephen Allen, Resource Coord.
Staff: Prof 1. **Subjects:** Development, aid, trade, food and agriculture, Southern Africa, Latin and Central America, disarmament, Christianity and justice, technology, employment and labor. **Holdings:** 300 volumes.

Subscriptions: 130 journals and other serials. Services: Library open to Waterloo County residents. Publications: Newsletter, 4/year. Special Catalogs: AV catalog.

★6711★
KITCHENER-WATERLOO RECORD - LIBRARY (Publ)
225 Fairway Rd., S.   Phone: (519) 579-2231
Kitchener, ON, Canada N2G 4E5   Penny Coates, Libn.
Founded: 1972. Staff: Prof 2; Other 1. Subjects: General reference, biography. Special Collections: Waterloo regional material. Holdings: 300 books; 1000 pamphlets (cataloged); 6500 subject files; 40,000 personal biographies. Subscriptions: 30 newspapers. Services: Interlibrary loans; copying; library open to public by appointment. Staff: Clifford Cunningham, Asst.Libn.

★6712★
KITSAP COUNTY HISTORICAL MUSEUM - LIBRARY (Hist)
3343 N.W. Byron St.   Phone: (206) 692-1949
Silverdale, WA 98383   Mrs. Sigurd Olsen, Musm.Dir.
Founded: 1948. Subjects: Local history, agriculture and forestry. Holdings: 500 books and bound periodical volumes. Services: Library open to public with restrictions.

★6713★
KITSAP COUNTY LAW LIBRARY (Law)
614 Division St.   Phone: (206) 876-7140
Port Orchard, WA 98366
Founded: 1947. Subjects: Law. Holdings: 9000 volumes. Services: Library open to public for reference use only.

★6714★
KITT PEAK NATIONAL OBSERVATORY - LIBRARY (Sci-Tech)
Box 26732   Phone: (602) 327-5511
Tucson, AZ 85726   Cathaleen Van Atta, Libn.
Founded: 1959. Staff: Prof 1; Other 1. Subjects: Astronomy, physics, mathematics. Holdings: 25,000 volumes. Subscriptions: 275 journals and other serials. Services: Interlibrary loans (limited); library open to public with restrictions. Computerized Information Services: Computerized cataloging. Networks/Consortia: Member of OCLC through FEDLINK. Also Known As: Association of Universities for Research in Astronomy (AURA, Inc.). Remarks: Library located at 950 N. Cherry Ave., Tucson, AZ 85716.

KITTLESON WORLD WAR II COLLECTION
See: Minneapolis Public Library & Information Center

KITTYHAWK CENTER
See: U.S. Air Force Base - Wright-Patterson General Library

★6715★
KLAMATH COUNTY - LOYD DELAP LAW LIBRARY (Law)
Court House   Phone: (503) 882-2501
Klamath Falls, OR 97601   Ruth Rice, Law Libn.
Founded: 1930. Staff: 1. Subjects: Law. Holdings: 15,000 volumes; 74 bound periodical volumes. Subscriptions: 18 journals and other serials. Services: Interlibrary loans; copying; library open to public. Remarks: Library is under the direction of the Klamath County Library.

KLANWATCH
See: Southern Poverty Law Center

KLAPPER (Paul) LIBRARY
See: Queens College of the City University of New York - Paul Klapper Library

KLAU LIBRARY
See: Hebrew Union College - Jewish Institute of Religion (New York and Cincinnati)

KLAUBER (L.) HERPETOLOGICAL LIBRARY
See: San Diego Society of Natural History - Natural History Museum Library

★6716★
KLAUDER (Louis T.) & ASSOCIATES - LIBRARY (Trans)
2000 Philadelphia Natl. Bank Bldg.   Phone: (215) 563-2570
Philadelphia, PA 19107   Nancy C. Todd, Libn.
Founded: 1974. Staff: Prof 1. Subjects: Transportation engineering; urban transportation; railcar design; railway construction, maintenance and operation. Holdings: 4000 books and unbound reports; 10 VF drawers of

annual reports, specifications, state and federal laws pertaining to transportation. Subscriptions: 80 journals and other serials. Services: Interlibrary loans; library open to public for reference use only, by appointment. Publications: Accession list, monthly - for internal distribution only.

★6717★
KLD ASSOCIATES, INC. - LIBRARY (Trans)
300 Broadway   Phone: (516) 549-9803
Huntington Station, NY 11746
Founded: 1973. Staff: 2. Subjects: Traffic engineering, transportation, computer programming. Holdings: 150 books; 35 bound periodical volumes; 2000 papers; 2000 microfiche. Subscriptions: 35 journals and other serials. Services: Library not open to public. Networks/Consortia: Member of Long Island Library Resources Council (LILRC).

★6718★
KLEIN (B.) PUBLICATIONS - RESEARCH LIBRARY (Publ)
Box 8503   Phone: (305) 752-1708
Coral Springs, FL 33065   B. Stecher, Libn.
Staff: Prof 1. Subjects: Social studies, history, business, research. Holdings: 2000 books. Subscriptions: 20 journals and other serials. Services: Library not open to public.

KLINCK MEMORIAL LIBRARY
See: Concordia College

KLINE SCIENCE LIBRARY
See: Yale University

KLIPPLE (Margaret) MEMORIAL ARCHIVES OF AFRICAN FOLKTALES
See: Cleveland Public Library - John G. White Collection of Folklore, Orientalia, & Chess

★6719★
KLOCKNER STADLER HURTER, LTD. - LIBRARY (Sci-Tech)
1600 Dorchester Blvd., W.   Phone: (514) 932-4611
Montreal, PQ, Canada H3H 1P9
Founded: 1976. Subjects: Engineering, pulp and paper. Holdings: 1500 books; 495 bound periodical volumes; 300 reprints; 750 technical reports; 600 standards. Publications: Acquisitions list. Services: Library not open to public.

KLUTZNICK LIBRARY
See: Creighton University - Law School

★6720★
KM&G INTERNATIONAL INC. - KETCHUM LIBRARY SERVICES (Bus-Fin)
Four Gateway Ctr.   Phone: (412) 456-3600
Pittsburgh, PA 15222   Florence V. Merkel, Lib.Supv.
Founded: 1949. Staff: Prof 3; Other 1. Subjects: Advertising, marketing, general reference. Holdings: 1100 books; 40 VF drawers of marketing material; 2000 complimentary periodicals (unbound); reference collection; annual reports. Subscriptions: 400 journals and other serials. Computerized Information Services: DIALOG, New York Times Information Service. Staff: Beth Churchfield, Info.Spec. II; Betsy Feldman, Info.Spec. I.

★6721★
KMS FUSION, INC. - FUSION LIBRARY (Sci-Tech)†
3941 Research Park Dr.
Box 1567   Phone: (313) 769-8500
Ann Arbor, MI 48106   Christine Bennet, Tech.Libn.
Founded: 1974. Staff: Prof 1. Subjects: Fusion, lasers, optics, radiation effects, atomic physics. Special Collections: Radiation applications reprint file (50 VF drawers). Holdings: 2624 books; 750 technical reports; 9000 reports on microfiche. Subscriptions: 52 journals and other serials. Services: Interlibrary loans; copying; SDI; library open to public with restrictions. Computerized Information Services: Online systems.

★6722★
KNIGHT (Lester B.) & ASSOCIATES, INC. - MANAGEMENT CONSULTING LIBRARY (Bus-Fin)
549 W. Randolph St.   Phone: (312) 346-2100
Chicago, IL 60606   Clarita M. Generao, Libn.
Founded: 1970. Staff: Prof 1. Subjects: Management consulting, business, physical distribution, materials requirements, industrial engineering. Special Collections: Annual reports, proxies and 10Ks of leading U.S. and international industrial companies. Holdings: 400 titles; business directories; reports; proposals. Subscriptions: 96 journals and other serials. Services: Copying;

library open to those known by company executives. **Computerized Information Services:** DIALOG, New York Times Information Service, Predicast Inc., Data Courier Inc.

KNIGHT PUBLISHING COMPANY - CHARLOTTE OBSERVER AND THE CHARLOTTE NEWS
See: Charlotte Observer and the Charlotte News

KNIGHTS OF COLUMBUS VATICAN FILM LIBRARY
See: St. Louis University

KNIGHTS TEMPLAR, U.S.A. - LIBRARY OF THE GRAND ENCAMPMENT
See: Red Cross of Constantine - United Grand Imperial Council - Edward A. Glad Memorial Library

★6723★
KNOEDLER (M.) AND COMPANY, INC. - LIBRARY (Art)
19 E. 70th St.   Phone: (212) 794-0569
New York, NY 10021   Nancy C. Little, Libn.
Founded: 1846. **Staff:** Prof 2. **Special Collections:** Exhibition and art auction catalogs. **Holdings:** Microfiche of 26,000 volumes of catalogs; archives. **Services:** Library open to public by appointment for a nominal fee. **Staff:** Caroline Hyman, Asst.Libn.

★6724★
KNOLL PHARMACEUTICAL COMPANY - RESEARCH LIBRARY (Sci-Tech)
30 N. Jefferson Rd.   Phone: (201) 887-8300
Whippany, NJ 07981   Kerry L. Kushinka, Mgr., Med./Sci.Info.
Founded: 1938. **Staff:** Prof 3; Other 1. **Subjects:** Pharmacology, chemistry, medicine, marketing. **Holdings:** 1500 books; 2500 bound periodical volumes; 30 VF drawers of unpublished reports and manuscripts; foreign and domestic patents. **Subscriptions:** 120 journals and other serials; 10 newspapers. **Services:** Interlibrary loans; SDI; bibliographic and reference services for members of the medical and allied professions; library open to public with restrictions. **Computerized Information Services:** DIALOG, SDC, MEDLARS; in-house database on products. **Networks/Consortia:** Member of Medical Resources Consortium of New Jersey (MEDCORE). **Publications:** Digest, irregular - for internal distribution only. **Special Catalogs:** Cross-referenced card catalog detailing published materials on this company's products. **Staff:** Carolyn J. Welch, Med.Libn.; Joanne Lustig, Info.Spec.

★6725★
KNOLLS ATOMIC POWER LABORATORY - LIBRARIES (Sci-Tech; Energy)
Box 1072   Phone: (518) 393-6611
Schenectady, NY 12301   J. Olivia Yunker, Supv.
Founded: 1946. **Staff:** Prof 3; Other 5. **Subjects:** Nuclear science and engineering, chemistry, physics, mathematics, metallurgy. **Special Collections:** U.S. Navy specifications, standards, handbooks, and manuals; naval nuclear propulsion engineering support documents (100,000). **Holdings:** 34,000 books and bound periodical volumes; 5000 pamphlets (cataloged); 300,000 research and development reports. **Subscriptions:** 500 journals and other serials. **Services:** Interlibrary loans; libraries not open to public. **Computerized Information Services:** DOE/RECON; TIGIR computerized information retrieval system for internal documentation. **Publications:** Book Shelf, bimonthly; Listing of New Reports, bimonthly; Latest Issue List of Specifications and Standards, monthly - all for internal distribution only. **Remarks:** The Knolls Atomic Power Laboratory operates under contract to the U.S. Department of Energy. **Staff:** Helyn M. Walton, Tech.Libn.; Elizabeth A. DeSimone, Ref.Libn.

★6726★
KNOW, INC. (Soc Sci)
Box 86031   Phone: (412) 241-4844
Pittsburgh, PA 15221   F. Black, Educ.Dir.
Founded: 1969. **Subjects:** Feminist literature. **Holdings:** 40 file drawers of feminist publications and newsletters. **Services:** Library open to public with staff present. **Publications:** KNOW NEWS, quarterly - free to members; Books of Interest to Feminists (bibliography with periodic updating); Female Studies Series; list of additional publications - free upon request. **Remarks:** This nonprofit, tax exempt corporation was founded by Pittsburgh NOW (National Organization of Women) members to disseminate literature concerning the women's movement.

KNOX COLLEGE
See: University of Toronto

★6727★
KNOX COMMUNITY HOSPITAL - MEDICAL LIBRARY (Med)
117 E. High St.   Phone: (614) 397-5555
Mount Vernon, OH 43050   Havilah Phelps, Libn.
Staff: Prof 1. **Subjects:** Medicine, surgery. **Holdings:** 1250 books; 300 bound periodical volumes. **Subscriptions:** 30 journals and other serials. **Services:** Interlibrary loans; copying; library not open to public. **Networks/Consortia:** Member of Central Ohio Hospital Library Consortium.

★6728★
KNOX COUNTY GOVERNMENTAL LIBRARY (Law)
M - 47, City-County Bldg.
Main Ave.   Phone: (615) 521-2368
Knoxville, TN 37902   Meredith Douglas, Libn.
Founded: 1955. **Staff:** Prof 1. **Subjects:** Law. **Holdings:** 12,000 books; 66 bound periodical volumes. **Services:** Copying; library open to public.

★6729★
KNOX COUNTY HISTORICAL SOCIETY - LIBRARY (Hist)
                                  Phone: (816) 397-2346
Edina, MO 63537   Brenton Karhoff, Pres.
Founded: 1966. **Staff:** 1. **Subjects:** Local and state history, genealogy. **Holdings:** 120 books; 45 bound periodical volumes; 4 scrapbooks; clippings. **Services:** Copying; library open to public with restrictions.

★6730★
KNOX COUNTY LAW LIBRARY (Law)
62 Union St.   Phone: (207) 594-2254
Rockland, ME 04841   Connie Campbell, Libn.
Founded: 1860. **Staff:** 1. **Subjects:** Law. **Holdings:** 8500 volumes. **Subscriptions:** 10 journals and other serials. **Services:** Library open to public.

KNOX (Dudley) LIBRARY
See: U.S. Navy - Naval Postgraduate School - Dudley Knox Library

★6731★
KNOXVILLE-KNOX COUNTY METROPOLITAN PLANNING COMMISSION - LIBRARY (Plan)
City-County Bldg., Suite 403   Phone: (615) 521-2500
Knoxville, TN 37902   Gretchen F. Beal, Libn.
Staff: Prof 1. **Subjects:** Urban planning, economic development, transportation, housing, environment, land use/zoning. **Holdings:** 5857 volumes; 1244 local documents; 4 VF drawers of clippings; dissertations; manuscripts; archives. **Subscriptions:** 152 journals and other serials; 6 newspapers. **Services:** Interlibrary loans; copying; library open to public. **Publications:** Acquisitions List, monthly - for internal distribution only.

★6732★
KNOXVILLE-KNOX COUNTY PUBLIC LIBRARY SYSTEM - MC CLUNG HISTORICAL COLLECTION (Hist)
East Tennessee Historical Center
600 Market St.   Phone: (615) 523-0781
Knoxville, TN 37902   William J. MacArthur, Jr., Hd.
Founded: 1921. **Staff:** Prof 4; Other 6. **Subjects:** History and genealogy of Knoxville, Tennessee and the southeastern states. **Special Collections:** Knoxville and Tennessee newspapers, 1791 to present. **Holdings:** 22,450 books; 3420 bound periodical volumes; 350,000 manuscripts; 500 maps; 5937 reels of microfilm; 12,012 microfiche; 62 VF drawers of photographs and clippings. **Subscriptions:** 175 journals and other serials; 11 newspapers. **Services:** Copying; collection open to public. **Networks/Consortia:** Member of SOLINET. **Publications:** Occasional publications. **Special Catalogs:** A Guide to the Manuscript Collections of the Calvin M. McClung Historical Collection by Linda L. Posey (book). **Remarks:** East Tennessee Historical Society, organized in 1925, makes its headquarters in the McClung Collection; the society's library is part of the collection. **Staff:** Linda L. Posey, Asst.Hd.Libn.; Steve Cotham, Tech.Serv./Ref.Libn.; Sally K. Ripatti, Spec.Mtls.Libn.

★6733★
KOBE, INC. - ENGINEERING LIBRARY (Sci-Tech)†
3040 E. Slauson Ave.   Phone: (213) 588-1271
Huntington Park, CA 90255   Zenny Mamdani, Engr.Adm.Asst.
Founded: 1952. **Staff:** 1. **Subjects:** Hydraulic oil well pumping, hydraulics, mechanical engineering, chemical engineering, petroleum production, acetylene manufacture. **Holdings:** 3000 volumes; 1500 patents; 7000 clippings. **Subscriptions:** 10 journals and other serials. **Services:** Library not open to public.

KODAK COMPANY
See: Eastman Kodak Company

KOHLER ART LIBRARY
See: University of Wisconsin, Madison

KOHLER (Herbert V.) SCIENCE LIBRARY
See: Beloit College - Herbert V. Kohler Science Library

KOHN (Blanche Wolf) LIBRARY
See: Settlement Music School - Blanche Wolf Kohn Library

KOHN (Harold) MEMORIAL VISUAL SCIENCE LIBRARY
See: SUNY - College of Optometry - Harold Kohn Memorial Visual Science Library

★6734★
KOKOMO TRIBUNE - LIBRARY (Publ)
300 N. Union   Phone: (317) 459-3121
Kokomo, IN 46901   Janice Johnson, Libn.
Founded: 1976. **Staff:** 1. **Subjects:** Newspaper reference topics. **Holdings:** 200 books; 8 VF drawers of pamphlets; 26 VF drawers of clippings; 4 VF drawers of historical photographs; photographic file (1976 to present); negative file (1958 to present); microfilm of Tribune from 1868 to present; 4 VF drawers of backlog clippings (1970-76). **Subscriptions:** 30 journals and other serials. **Services:** Interlibrary loans; library not open to public.

★6735★
KOLLSMAN INSTRUMENT COMPANY - KIC LIBRARY (Sci-Tech)
Daniel Webster Hwy., S.   Phone: (603) 889-2500
Merrimack, NH 03054   Gerald W. Rice, Info.Spec.
Staff: Prof 1. **Subjects:** Aeronautics, optics, electronics, engineering, mathematics, management, marketing, accounting. **Holdings:** 4000 books; 5 volumes of patents. **Subscriptions:** 123 journals and other serials. **Services:** Interlibrary loans; copying; library not open to public. **Computerized Information Services:** DIALOG. **Remarks:** Kollsman Instrument Company is a subsidiary of Sun Chemical Corporation.

KONOLD (W.S.) MEMORIAL LIBRARY
See: Doctors Hospital - W.S. Konold Memorial Library

★6736★
KOOCHICHING COUNTY HISTORICAL SOCIETY - MUSEUM (Hist)
Smokey Bear Park
214 6th St.
Box 1147
International Falls, MN 56649   Phone: (218) 283-4316
                                       Mary Hilke, Exec.Sec. & Cur.
Founded: 1967. **Staff:** 2. **Subjects:** History - Koochiching County, Boise Cascade, personal; logging. **Special Collections:** Mando photograph collection (10 VF drawers); International Lumber Company & Bussman papers; Harold Reich papers; S.F. Plummer diaries; early county records; post office records; Hadler collection; women's clubs records. **Holdings:** 600 books and bound periodical volumes; 21 VF drawers and 15 boxes of records and manuscripts; 15 VF drawers of photographs. **Services:** Copying; library open to public by appointment. **Publications:** Gesundheit, monthly - distributed to members.

★6737★
KOOTENAY LAKE HISTORICAL SOCIETY - LIBRARY (Hist)
Box 537   Phone: (604) 353-2525
Kaslo, BC, Canada V0G 1M0   June Griswold, Cur.
Staff: 2. **Subjects:** Local history. **Special Collections:** History of transportation in the Kootenays. **Holdings:** 300 books; 50 other cataloged items; textbooks, society records, journals, newspapers, photographs. **Services:** Copying; library open to public for reference use only. **Staff:** Edna Haw, Cur.

★6738★
KOPPERS COMPANY, INC. - ENGINEERING AND CONSTRUCTION DIVISION - INFORMATION SERVICE - LIBRARY (Sci-Tech; Energy)†
C806 Chamber of Commerce Bldg.   Phone: (412) 355-6517
Pittsburgh, PA 15219   Catherine A. Emish, Coord., Info.Serv.
Staff: Prof 1; Other 1. **Subjects:** Specialized coal and coke production, specialized steel production, engineering and construction. **Special Collections:** Coke-making patents; coal and ore resources; German and Russian periodicals. **Holdings:** 1200 books; 450 bound periodical volumes; 25 3-foot shelves of pamphlets and public documents; 20,000 U.S., British and German patents; 55 file drawers of unbound materials. **Subscriptions:** 200 journals and other serials. **Services:** Interlibrary loans; copying; library open to public with restrictions.

★6739★
KOPPERS COMPANY, INC. - TECHNICAL INFORMATION GROUP (Sci-Tech)
440 College Park Dr.   Phone: (412) 327-3000
Monroeville, PA 15146   Eugene P. Meckly, Libn.
Founded: 1915. **Staff:** Prof 3; Other 3. **Subjects:** Polymers, coal tar chemistry, coke ovens. **Holdings:** 9000 books; 19,000 bound periodical volumes. **Subscriptions:** 500 journals and other serials. **Services:** Library not open to public.

★6740★
KORN/FERRY INTERNATIONAL - LIBRARY (Sci-Tech; Bus-Fin)†
1100 Milam, Suite 3400   Phone: (713) 651-1834
Houston, TX 77002   Laura L. Sorrell, Dir. of Res.
Staff: Prof 2; Other 2. **Subjects:** Executive search, energy, finance, chemistry. **Holdings:** Figures not available. **Subscriptions:** 13 journals and other serials. **Services:** Copying; library open to public with restrictions. **Staff:** Marlene Briski, Res.Assoc.

★6741★
KORN/FERRY INTERNATIONAL - RESEARCH LIBRARY (Bus-Fin)†
120 S. Riverside Plaza, Suite 918   Phone: (312) 726-1841
Chicago, IL 60606   Margaret A. French, Dir. of Res./Midwest
Founded: 1979. **Staff:** Prof 2; Other 2. **Subjects:** Executive search, business reference. **Holdings:** 200 books. **Subscriptions:** 11 journals and other serials. **Services:** Copying; SDI; library not open to public. **Computerized Information Services:** Online systems. **Special Indexes:** Index to resumes.

KORNHAUSER HEALTH SCIENCES LIBRARY
See: University of Louisville

KORSON (George) FOLKLORE ARCHIVE
See: King's College - D. Leonard Corgan Library

★6742★
KOSAIR CRIPPLED CHILDREN HOSPITAL - LIBRARY
982 Eastern Pkwy.
Louisville, KY 40217
Defunct. Merged with Norton-Children's Hospitals Library to form NKC, Inc. Medical Library.

★6743★
KOSCIUSZKO FOUNDATION - REFERENCE LIBRARY
15 E. 65th St.
New York, NY 10021
Founded: 1946. **Subjects:** Polish history, art, music, literature; Polish-American history. **Holdings:** 5000 books. **Remarks:** Presently inactive.

★6744★
KOSSUTH FOUNDATION - HUNGARIAN RESEARCH LIBRARY (Area-Ethnic)
Butler University
Indianapolis, IN 46208   Dr. Janos Horvath, Pres.
Founded: 1957. **Staff:** Prof 1; Other 1. **Subjects:** Hungary, Hungarian culture, social sciences, American-Hungarian relations. **Special Collections:** Hungarica-Americana; the Hungarian Revolution in 1956 and 1848; Hungarian scholars, scientists and artists in the United States. **Holdings:** 1600 books; 70 bound periodical volumes; 500 pamphlets; newspaper clippings; manuscripts; documents; photographs; maps; tapes. **Subscriptions:** 20 journals and other serials; 15 newspapers. **Services:** Interlibrary loans.

★6745★
KRAFT, INC. - BUSINESS RESEARCH CENTER (Food-Bev)
Kraft Ct.   Phone: (312) 998-2951
Glenview, IL 60025   Dorothy Schmidt, Coord.
Founded: 1972. **Staff:** Prof 1; Other 1. **Subjects:** Food industry, business, finance and management. **Special Collections:** History of Kraft and National Dairy Products. **Holdings:** 3500 books; 1000 annual reports of companies. **Subscriptions:** 500 journals and other serials; 8 newspapers. **Services:** Interlibrary loans; copying; library open to public with restrictions. **Computerized Information Services:** DIALOG, SDC, New York Times Information Service, Dow Jones News Retrieval.

★6746★
KRAFT, INC. - RESEARCH & DEVELOPMENT LIBRARY (Food-Bev)
801 Waukegan Rd.   Phone: (312) 998-3707
Glenview, IL 60025   Helen Pettway, Libn.
Founded: 1938. **Staff:** Prof 2; Other 4. **Subjects:** Food technology, dairy science, marketing, nutrition, microbiology, packaging. **Holdings:** 8150 books; 2700 bound periodical volumes; 21,350 patents; 3600 reels of microfilm; 91 boxes of bulletins; pamphlets; 21,000 research reports; 1 drawer of clippings.

Subscriptions: 556 journals and other serials. **Services:** Interlibrary loans; copying; SDI; library not open to public. **Computerized Information Services:** DIALOG, SDC; computerized serials and circulation. **Networks/Consortia:** Member of Metropolitan Chicago Library Assembly; North Suburban Library System. **Staff:** Marquerite Schutten, Ref.Spec.

★6747★
KRAMER CHIN AND MAYO INC. - LIBRARY (Sci-Tech)
1917 First Ave. Phone: (206) 447-5301
Seattle, WA 98101 Gretchen K. Leslie, Libn.
Staff: Prof 1; Other 1. **Subjects:** Water and sewer engineering, land planning and water resources, environmental engineering, aquaculture and fisheries, transportation. **Special Collections:** Aquaculture and fisheries research. **Holdings:** 1500 books; 2000 reports; extensive newsletter file. **Subscriptions:** 150 journals and other serials. **Services:** Interlibrary loans; copying; SDI; library not open to public. **Computerized Information Services:** Online systems. **Networks/Consortia:** Member of Seattle Engineering Librarians Roundtable. **Publications:** Accessions list, monthly - for internal distribution only.

KRANNERT GRADUATE SCHOOL OF MANAGEMENT - LIBRARY
See: Purdue University - Management and Economics Library

KRASKER MEMORIAL FILM LIBRARY
See: Boston University

KRATTER (Marvin & Lillian) LAW LIBRARY
See: University of San Diego - Marvin & Lillian Kratter Law Library

★6748★
KRAUSE MILLING COMPANY - TECHNICAL LIBRARY (Sci-Tech)
4222 W. Burnham St. Phone: (414) 272-6200
Milwaukee, WI 53215 Virginia M. Gamache, Lib.Asst.
Founded: 1965. **Staff:** Prof 1; Other 1. **Subjects:** Agriculture, chemistry, food, engineering. **Holdings:** 1500 books and bound periodical volumes; 500 pamphlets; 4000 reprints. **Subscriptions:** 200 journals and other serials. **Services:** Copying (limited); library not open to public. **Networks/Consortia:** Member of Library Council of Metropolitan Milwaukee, Inc. (LCOMM).

KRAUSKOPF (Joseph) MEMORIAL LIBRARY
See: Delaware Valley College of Science and Agriculture - Joseph Krauskopf Memorial Library

KRAUSS LIBRARY
See: Lutheran School of Theology at Chicago

KRAUSZ (Charles E.) LIBRARY
See: Pennsylvania College of Podiatric Medicine - Charles E. Krausz Library

KRAUTH MEMORIAL LIBRARY
See: Lutheran Theological Seminary

KRESGE MEDICAL LIBRARY
See: Scripps Clinic & Research Foundation

KRESGE PHYSICAL SCIENCES LIBRARY
See: Dartmouth College

KRESGE (Sebastian S.) ENGINEERING LIBRARY
See: University of California, Berkeley - Sebastian S. Kresge Engineering Library

KRESGE (Sebastian S.) NATURAL SCIENCE LIBRARY
See: University of Louisville - Sebastian S. Kresge Natural Science Library

KRESS LIBRARY
See: Harvard University - Graduate School of Business Administration - Baker Library

KROHN MEMORIAL LIBRARY
See: Good Samaritan Hospital

★6749★
KROTONA INSTITUTE OF THEOSOPHY - KROTONA LIBRARY - BETTY WARRINGTON MEMORIAL (Rel-Theol)
Krotona 2 Phone: (805) 646-2653
Ojai, CA 93023 Erna Achenbach, Hd.Libn.
Founded: 1912. **Staff:** 6. **Subjects:** Theosophy, philosophy, religions,

philosophy of science, art. **Holdings:** 13,500 books and bound periodical volumes. **Subscriptions:** 12 journals and other serials. **Services:** Copying; library open to public.

★6750★
KRUPNICK & ASSOCIATES, INC. - INFORMATION CENTER (Bus-Fin)†
135 N. Meramec Phone: (314) 862-9393
St. Louis, MO 63105 Jacque Sturm, Libn.
Founded: 1944. **Staff:** 1. **Subjects:** Advertising, marketing, management. **Holdings:** 200 books; 65 VF drawers of clippings (cataloged). **Subscriptions:** 150 journals and other serials; 10 newspapers. **Services:** Interlibrary loans; copying; library open to public on request.

★6751★
KRUPP WILPUTTE CORPORATION - LIBRARY (Sci-Tech)
152 Floral Ave. Phone: (201) 464-5900
Murray Hill, NJ 07974 Roberta K. Sager, Supv.
Founded: 1972. **Staff:** Prof 1; Other 1. **Subjects:** Coke technology, coal by-product plants, air pollution emission control, coal gasification. **Holdings:** 500 books; 40 VF drawers; 250 research reports (cataloged); 150 standards and building codes; 200 company reports; 1500 patents for coke technology. **Subscriptions:** 100 journals and other serials. **Services:** Interlibrary loans; copying; library not open to public. **Publications:** Acquisitions list - for internal distribution only. **Formerly:** Wilputte Corporation - Library.

★6752★
KTA-TATOR, INC. - LIBRARY (Sci-Tech)
115 Technology Dr. Phone: (412) 788-1300
Pittsburgh, PA 15275 Dr. Thor Johndahl, Lab.Dir.
Founded: 1947. **Staff:** Prof 25; Other 10. **Subjects:** Organic coatings, industrial paint performances, industrial color, thermal insulation, industrial maintenance. **Holdings:** Case histories of performances in industrial exposures (35,000 punched information cards keyed to original data sources in record and microfilm files). **Services:** Use of data restricted to clients; reviews or reports made by staff on a fee basis.

KUEHNE (John M.) LIBRARY
See: University of Texas, Austin - Physics-Mathematics-Astronomy Library

KUEHNER MEMORIAL LIBRARY
See: Reformed Episcopal Church - Theological Seminary

KULIS AIR NATL. GUARD BASE
See: Alaska Air National Guard

KULOW (Don L.) MEMORIAL LIBRARY
See: U.S. Geological Survey - EROS Data Center - Don L. Kulow Memorial Library

★6753★
KUTAK ROCK & HUIE, ATTORNEYS AT LAW - LAW LIBRARY (Law)
1200 Standard Federal Bldg. Phone: (404) 522-8700
Atlanta, GA 30303 Yvonne J. Chandler, Libn.
Staff: Prof 1; Other 1. **Subjects:** Law. **Holdings:** 8000 books; 1500 bound periodical volumes; 500 other cataloged items. **Subscriptions:** 90 journals and other serials; 6 newspapers. **Services:** Interlibrary loans; copying; SDI; library open to public with restrictions. **Computerized Information Services:** LEXIS.

★6754★
KUTAK, ROCK & HUIE - LAW LIBRARY (Law)
1650 Farnam St. Phone: (402) 346-6000
Omaha, NE 68102 Avis B. Forsman, Libn.
Staff: 5. **Subjects:** Law. **Holdings:** 18,000 books; 500 bound periodical volumes; 2500 pamphlets. **Subscriptions:** 175 journals and other serials. **Services:** Library open to public by appointment. **Computerized Information Services:** DIALOG, SDC, LEXIS. **Staff:** Angie Lange, Asst.Libn./Tech.Serv.; Catherine Ciacco, Ref.; Susan Rock, Ref.; Marian Nielsen, Abstractor.

★6755★
KUTZTOWN STATE COLLEGE - ROHRBACH LIBRARY (Educ)
Phone: (215) 683-3511
Kutztown, PA 19530 John K. Amrhein, College Libn.
Founded: 1915. **Staff:** Prof 12; Other 11. **Subjects:** Education, art, library science, literature, history. **Special Collections:** Russian Culture Center Collection; Curriculum Materials Center; Pennsylvania Collection. **Holdings:** 273,772 books; 36,417 bound periodical volumes; 820,341 microforms; 13,319 maps; 12,000 pamphlets; 2800 college catalogs; 400 telephone

directories. **Subscriptions:** 1989 periodicals and newspapers. **Services:** Interlibrary loans; copying; library open to public. **Computerized Information Services:** Computerized cataloging. **Networks/Consortia:** Member of OCLC through PALINET & Union Library Catalogue of Pennsylvania. **Staff:** Helen I. Berg, Circ.Libn.; Paul M. Apostolos, Evening Libn.; Curt S. Goldstaub, Cat.Libn.; Janet Bond, Asst.Cat.Libn.; Margaret M. Apostolos, Microforms & Per.Libn.; Claire Andrews, Ref.Libn.; Linda Halma, Ref.Libn.; Elsie Kennet, Ref.Libn.; Anita T. Sprankle, Non-Bk.Mtls.Libn.; Linda A. Woods, Ref.Libn.; Charles McFadden, Acq.Libn.

★6756★
KXE6S VEREIN CHESS SOCIETY - SPECIAL/RESEARCH LIBRARY - EAST DIVISION (Rec)†
Box 2204
Chapel Hill, NC 27514   Steven Leslie Buntin, Bibliothecar
Founded: 1977. **Staff:** Prof 2; Other 3. **Subjects:** Chess. **Special Collections:** Vertical file of the 1972 Fischer/Spassky match; master rating list of all North Carolina chessplayers. **Holdings:** 2000 books; 4000 magazine and newspaper articles. **Subscriptions:** 30 journals and other serials; 15 newspapers. **Services:** Interlibrary loans; copying; SDI; library open to public with restrictions. **Publications:** Newsletter; list of publications - available upon request. **Special Indexes:** Bibliography of the AIPE Chess News; index of

chess column in North Carolina Anvil; index of Carolina Gambit. **Remarks:** The name of this society, Kxe6s Verein, is a registered trademark. **Also Known As:** Chess Press Syndicate. **Staff:** Hans Laf Offe, Ref.Libn.; Arthur A.A. Goldstein, Chf.Cat.

KYNE (William P.) MEMORIAL LIBRARY
See: California Jockey Club at Bay Meadows - William P. Kyne Memorial Library

★6757★
KZF, INC. - KZF LIBRARY (Sci-Tech; Plan)
2830 Victory Pkwy.   Phone: (513) 281-7723
Cincinnati, OH 45206   Dennis O. Hamilton, Lib.Dir.
Founded: 1974. **Staff:** Prof 1. **Subjects:** Architecture; engineering - civil, mechanical, structural; environmental sciences; planning. **Holdings:** 2000 books; 2000 specifications; 200 company reports; 9 VF drawers of pamphlets; 40 cassettes. **Subscriptions:** 240 journals and other serials. **Services:** Interlibrary loans; copying; library open to public for reference use only.

L

★6758★
L.D.S. HOSPITAL - MEDICAL LIBRARY (Med)
325 Eighth Ave. Phone: (801) 350-1054
Salt Lake City, UT 84143 Mr. Terry L. Heyer, Lib.Dir.
Founded: 1957. **Staff:** Prof 1; Other 1. **Subjects:** Medicine and nursing.
Holdings: 1200 books; 4000 bound periodical volumes; 175 pamphlets; 900
audiotape cassettes. **Subscriptions:** 200 journals and other serials. **Services:**
Interlibrary loans; copying; library open to public. **Computerized Information
Services:** MEDLINE, CANCERLINE. **Networks/Consortia:** Member of Utah
Health Sciences Library Consortium. **Remarks:** Maintained by Intermountain
Health Care, Inc.

★6759★
L-5 SOCIETY - LIBRARY (Sci-Tech)
1060 E. Elm Phone: (602) 622-6351
Tucson, AZ 85719 Philip Chapman, Pres.
Founded: 1975. **Staff:** 4. **Subjects:** Space - colonization, industries,
transportation; solar power satellites. **Holdings:** 50 books; 200 papers.
Services: Copying; library open to public. **Publications:** L-5 NEWS, monthly -
for sale to members.

★6760★
LA CROSSE LUTHERAN HOSPITAL - HEALTH SCIENCES LIBRARY (Med)
1910 South Ave. Phone: (608) 785-0530
La Crosse, WI 54601 LaVerne Samb, Libn.
Founded: 1961. **Staff:** Prof 2; Other 3. **Subjects:** Medical sciences, nursing,
administration, pastoral care. **Special Collections:** March of Dimes software.
Holdings: 7000 books; 14,000 bound periodical volumes; 250 software
programs. **Subscriptions:** 400 journals and other serials. **Services:**
Interlibrary loans; copying; library open to public with restrictions.
Computerized Information Services: MEDLINE. **Networks/Consortia:**
Member of Western Wisconsin Consortium; Regional Medical Library - Region
3; Midwest Regional Medical Library Service. **Publications:** Medical staff and
nursing bulletins. **Special Catalogs:** Contributor to Wisconsin Union List of
Biomedical Serials.

LA FORTE (Benoist) ARCHIVES
See: Cornell University - History of Science Collections

LA JOLLA LIBRARY ASSOCIATION
See: Library Association of La Jolla

★6761★
**LA JOLLA MUSEUM OF CONTEMPORARY ART - HELEN PALMER GEISEL
LIBRARY** (Art)
700 Prospect St. Phone: (714) 454-3541
La Jolla, CA 92037 Gail Richardson, Libn.
Subjects: Contemporary art. **Holdings:** 2500 books; 189 bound periodical
volumes; 80 file boxes of monographs on artists; 10 VF drawers of clippings;
4809 slides. **Subscriptions:** 39 journals and other serials; 8 newspapers.
Services: Interlibrary loans; copying; library open to public by appointment.

★6762★
LA PRESSE, LTEE. - CENTRE DE DOCUMENTATION (Publ)
7 Ouest, Rue St-Jacques Phone: (514) 285-7007
Montreal, PQ, Canada H2Y 1K9 Fernand Drouin, Dir.
Founded: 1969. **Staff:** Prof 3; Other 12. **Subjects:** Statistics, political
science, economics, public administration, technology, literature, history.
Special Collections: Le Nouveau Journal, 1961-62 (complete collection); La
Presse, 1884 to present (945 reels of microfilm); La Patrie, 1879 to present
(662 reels of microfilm). **Holdings:** 5000 books; clippings on 25,000
subjects (Montreal region and others, 1962-78); 1.5 million photographs
dating back to 1900. **Subscriptions:** 200 journals and other serials; 20
newspapers. **Services:** Centre not open to public. **Staff:** Louise Audet, Asst.
to Dir.; Gerard Monette, Asst. to Dir.

★6763★
LA PURISIMA MISSION - ARCHIVES (Hist)
La Purisima Mission State Historic Pk.
R.F.D. Box 102 Phone: (805) 733-3713
Lompoc, CA 93436 Ronald J. Dupuy, Interpretive Ranger
Founded: 1936. **Staff:** Prof 2; Other 9. **Subjects:** Spanish Colonial Period
including artifacts. **Special Collections:** Edith Webb Collection (personal
papers pertaining to the mission); Harrington Collection. **Holdings:** 60 books;
300 blueprint drawings; restoration material; 600 pieces of correspondence
(indexed). **Services:** Archives open to public with a resume. **Remarks:**
Maintained by State Parks System of California. **Staff:** John Hillerman, Mgr.

★6764★
**LA RABIDA CHILDREN'S HOSPITAL AND RESEARCH CENTER - LAWRENCE
MERCER PICK MEMORIAL LIBRARY** (Med)
E. 65th St. at Lake Michigan Phone: (312) 363-6700
Chicago, IL 60649 Dr. Burton J. Grossman, Chf. of Med. Staff
Founded: 1959. **Staff:** 1. **Subjects:** Biomedical research, medicine,
dentistry, nursing. **Holdings:** 920 books; 508 bound periodical volumes.
Subscriptions: 49 journals and other serials. **Services:** Library not open to
public.

★6765★
LA SALLE STEEL COMPANY - RESEARCH AND DEVELOPMENT LIBRARY
(Sci-Tech)†
1412 150th St. Phone: (219) 853-6000
Hammond, IN 46327 Marianne Rosiles, Libn.
Founded: 1950. **Staff:** 1. **Subjects:** Metallurgy. **Special Collections:** La Salle
research reports. **Holdings:** 1000 books; 500 reports, clippings (cataloged).
Subscriptions: 85 journals and other serials. **Services:** Library not open to
public.

★6766★
LA SOCIETE LA HAYE OUELLET - LIBRAIRIE (Art; Plan)
2500 Bates Rd.
Montreal, PQ, Canada H3S 1A6 Claude La Haye, Documentaliste
Staff: Prof 1. **Subjects:** Architecture, city planning, landscape architecture.
Holdings: 1000 books; 50 bound periodical volumes; 800 reports; 1000
clippings; 1000 maps; 3000 microfilms. **Subscriptions:** 10 journals and other
serials; 5 newspapers. **Services:** Interlibrary loans; copying; library open to
public. **Networks/Consortia:** Member of Council of Planning Librarians (CPL);
Consortium Canadien de Recherches Urbaines et Regionales. **Formerly:**
Urbarc Canada Library.

★6767★
LA VINA HOSPITAL FOR RESPIRATORY DISEASES - MEDICAL LIBRARY
(Med)†
3900 N. Lincoln Ave. Phone: (213) 791-1241
Altadena, CA 91001 Grace M. Waser, Lib.Dir.
Founded: 1971. **Staff:** Prof 1. **Subjects:** Respiratory and cardiopulmonary
diseases, tuberculosis, nursing. **Holdings:** 1074 books; 740 bound periodical
volumes; 10 VF drawers of pamphlets and reprints (uncataloged).
Subscriptions: 62 journals. **Services:** Interlibrary loans; copying; library open
to public for reference use only.

★6768★
LABATT BREWING COMPANY LIMITED - CENTRAL RESEARCH LIBRARY
(Food-Bev; Sci-Tech)
150 Simcoe St.
Box 5050 Phone: (519) 673-5324
London, ON, Canada N6A 4M3 Marliese Lehwaldt, Hd.Libn.
Staff: Prof 1; Other 1. **Subjects:** Chemistry - general, physical, inorganic,
analytical; general science; microbiology. **Holdings:** 6000 books; 3000 bound
periodical volumes. **Subscriptions:** 450 journals and other serials; 10
newspapers. **Services:** Interlibrary loans; copying; library open to public with
restrictions. **Computerized Information Services:** Computerized cataloging.

★6769★
LABOR RESEARCH ASSOCIATION - LIBRARY (Soc Sci)
80 E. 11th St. Phone: (212) 473-1042
New York, NY 10003 Dr. Joseph Harris, Res.Dir.
Staff: 1. **Subjects:** Economics, labor and labor problems, social conditions,
peace and anti-war action, civil rights and civil liberties. **Holdings:** 5000
books; 8500 pamphlets. **Subscriptions:** 200 journals and other serials; 50
newspapers. **Services:** Library open to subscribers of Economic Notes,
readers of Labor Fact Book and members of unions that take the association's
services.

LABORATORY OF BIOMEDICAL AND ENVIRONMENTAL SCIENCES
See: University of California, Los Angeles

LABOUR AGREEMENTS DATA BANK
See: Mc Gill University

LABOUR CANADA
See: Canada - Labour Canada

★6770★
LABRADOR CITY COLLEGIATE - LIBRARY (Hum)
213 Matthew Ave.   Phone: (709) 944-2232
Labrador City, NF, Canada A2V 2J9   Bruce Dyer, Libn.
Founded: 1963. **Staff:** Prof 1. **Subjects:** English literature, social sciences, history, chemistry, physics, French literature. **Holdings:** 16,000 books; 91 videotapes; 350 16mm films. **Subscriptions:** 64 journals and other serials. **Services:** Interlibrary loans; library open to area teachers.

★6771★
LAC QUI PARLE COUNTY HISTORICAL SOCIETY - HISTORIC CENTER (Hist)
408 Park Ave., No. 2.   Phone: (612) 598-7678
Madison, MN 56256   Melvin S. Wroolie, Cur.
Staff: Prof 1; Other 2. **Subjects:** Local and county history, genealogy. **Special Collections:** Old editions of the Bible; Indian history (14 books). **Holdings:** 150 books; 25 other cataloged items; newspaper file; obituaries; scrapbooks; pioneer stories; territorial and statehood centennials. **Publications:** Annual Report.

LACEY ARCHITECTURAL ARCHIVES
See: Broome County Historical Society - Research Center - Josiah T. Newcomb Library

★6772★
LACKAWANNA BAR ASSOCIATION - LAW LIBRARY (Law)
Court House   Phone: (717) 342-8089
Scranton, PA 18503   Marita E. Paparelli, Law Libn.
Staff: Prof 1. **Subjects:** Law. **Holdings:** 17,000 volumes. **Services:** Interlibrary loans; copying; library open to public.

★6773★
LACKAWANNA HISTORICAL SOCIETY - LIBRARY AND ARCHIVES (Hist)
232 Monroe Ave.   Phone: (717) 344-3841
Scranton, PA 18510   William P. Lewis, Exec.Dir.
Founded: 1886. **Staff:** Prof 1; Other 1. **Subjects:** Local history and genealogy. **Holdings:** 3000 books; 100 bound periodical volumes; 48 VF drawers of manuscripts, clippings, pamphlets, documents, photographs and maps. **Subscriptions:** 13 journals and other serials. **Services:** Copying; library open to public with research fee. **Publications:** Lackawanna Historical Society Bulletin, bimonthly.

LACKLAND AIR FORCE BASE (TX)
See: U.S. Air Force Medical Center - Wilford Hall U.S.A.F. Medical Center

★6774★
LADISH CO. - METALLURGICAL DEPARTMENT LIBRARY (Sci-Tech)
5481 S. Packard Ave.
Cudahy, WI 53110   Patrick Berry, Libn.
Founded: 1942. **Staff:** Prof 1. **Subjects:** Metalworking technology, chemical analysis, metal cleaning and testing, mechanical and physical properties, metallography, corrosion, industrial environment. **Holdings:** 3500 volumes; 13,000 unbound reports. **Subscriptions:** 300 journals and other serials. **Services:** Library not open to public.

LADY DAVIS INSTITUTE FOR MEDICAL RESEARCH
See: Sir Mortimer B. Davis Jewish General Hospital

★6775★
LAFAYETTE CLINIC - LIBRARY (Med)
951 E. Lafayette   Phone: (313) 256-9596
Detroit, MI 48207   Nancy E. Ward, Libn.
Founded: 1956. **Staff:** Prof 1. **Subjects:** Psychiatry, psychology, psychopharmacology, geriatrics, neurology, behavioral aspects of social and medical problems, allied health sciences. **Holdings:** 4439 books; 2659 bound periodical volumes; 3 years of unbound periodicals. **Subscriptions:** 201 journals and other serials. **Services:** Interlibrary loans; library open to public for reference use only. **Computerized Information Services:** DIALOG, MEDLINE. **Networks/Consortia:** Member of Metropolitan Detroit Medical Library Group (MDMLG).

★6776★
LAFAYETTE COLLEGE - AMERICAN FRIENDS OF LAFAYETTE COLLECTION (Hist)
David Bishop Skillman Library   Phone: (215) 253-6281
Easton, PA 18042   Robert G. Gennett, Spec.Coll.Libn.
Subjects: Marquis de Lafayette, American Revolutionary War, George Washington. **Special Collections:** Hubbard Collection of Lafayette letters to Washington. **Holdings:** 4000 books and manuscripts; 636 engravings of Lafayette. **Services:** Copying; library open to public by appointment.

★6777★
LAFAYETTE COLLEGE - KIRBY LIBRARY OF GOVERNMENT AND LAW (Law)†
Kirby Hall   Phone: (215) 250-5399
Easton, PA 18042   Mercedes Benitez Sharpless, Libn.
Founded: 1930. **Staff:** Prof 1; Other 5. **Subjects:** Political science, international law and relations, constitutional law, urban organization. **Special Collections:** British Parliamentary Debates, 1st through 5th series (1468 volumes). **Holdings:** 20,400 books; 2200 bound periodical volumes; 3 VF drawers of pamphlets. **Subscriptions:** 130 journals and other serials. **Services:** Interlibrary loans; copying; library open to public for reference use only. **Networks/Consortia:** Member of OCLC through PALINET & Union Library Catalogue of Pennsylvania; Lehigh Valley Association of Independent Colleges, Inc. **Remarks:** Includes the holdings of the Kirby Library of Civil Rights.

★6778★
LAFAYETTE JOURNAL AND COURIER - LIBRARY (Publ)†
217 N. 6th St.   Phone: (317) 423-5511
Lafayette, IN 47901   Marlene Bailey, Libn.
Founded: 1964. **Staff:** Prof 4. **Subjects:** Newspaper reference topics. **Holdings:** The newspaper on microfilm, 1950 to present. **Services:** Library open to public with restrictions. **Special Indexes:** Index to the newspaper (card). **Staff:** Eva Goodman, Asst.Libn.; Kathleen Bricker, Asst.Libn.

★6779★
LAHEY CLINIC MEDICAL CENTER - RICHARD B. CATTELL MEMORIAL LIBRARY (Med)
41 Mall Rd.   Phone: (617) 273-8253
Burlington, MA 01805   Carol Spencer, Med.Libn.
Founded: 1965. **Staff:** Prof 1; Other 1. **Subjects:** Medicine. **Holdings:** 1500 books; 5200 bound periodical volumes. **Subscriptions:** 246 journals and other serials. **Services:** Interlibrary loans; copying; library open to public with permission of librarian. **Networks/Consortia:** Member of New England Regional Medical Library Service (NERMLS); Boston Biomedical Library Consortium; Massachusetts Health Sciences Library Network.

LAHONTAN BASIN MEDICAL LIBRARY
See: Carson-Tahoe Hospital

LAIRD (R.C.) HEALTH SCIENCES LIBRARY
See: Toronto Western Hospital - R.C. Laird Health Sciences Library

★6780★
LAKE CIRCUIT COURT - LIBRARY (Law)†
2293 N. Main St.   Phone: (219) 663-0760
Crown Point, IN 46307   Beth Henderson, Libn.
Staff: Prof 1. **Subjects:** Law. **Holdings:** 9000 volumes. **Services:** Library open to public for reference use only.

★6781★
LAKE COUNTY DEPARTMENT OF PLANNING, ZONING & ENVIRONMENTAL QUALITY - LIBRARY (Plan)
803 County Bldg., Rm. A   Phone: (312) 689-6350
Waukegan, IL 60085   Nancy B. Ross, Libn.
Founded: 1977. **Staff:** 1. **Subjects:** Land use planning, planning law, housing, natural environment, census, municipal information. **Holdings:** 200 books and bound periodical volumes; 500 brochures and manuscripts; 500 pamphlets. **Subscriptions:** 45 journals and other serials; 5 newspapers. **Services:** Copying; library open to public for reference use only. **Formerly:** Lake County Regional Planning Commission.

★6782★
LAKE COUNTY FOREST PRESERVE DISTRICT - RYERSON NATURE LIBRARY (Env-Cons)
2000 N. Milwaukee Ave.   Phone: (312) 948-7750
Libertyville, IL 60048   Steven E. Meyer, Supv. of Educ.
Founded: 1976. **Staff:** Prof 1. **Subjects:** Botany, zoology, ecology, environmental education, agriculture, forestry. **Holdings:** 2000 books; 4 VF

drawers of pamphlets and clippings. **Services:** Interlibrary loans (limited); library open to public for reference use only.

★6783★
LAKE COUNTY HISTORICAL SOCIETY - LIBRARY (Hist)
115 N. New Hampshire Ave.
Tavares, FL 32778   Mrs. M. Brownberger, Sec./Libn.
Staff: 1. **Subjects:** Local history and affairs. **Holdings:** Figures not available. **Services:** Library open to public for reference use only. **Publications:** Lake County - Now and Then, 1956-1959, 1962, 1966.

★6784★
LAKE COUNTY HISTORICAL SOCIETY - PERCY KENDALL SMITH LIBRARY FOR HISTORICAL RESEARCH (Hist)
8095 Mentor Ave.   Phone: (216) 255-8722
Mentor, OH 44060   Carl Thomas Engel, Libn.
Staff: Prof 1; Other 1. **Subjects:** Local history and genealogy, President James A. Garfield. **Holdings:** 2375 books; manuscripts; clippings; 100 years of Painesville Telegraph on microfilm; 10 reels of microfilm of Federal Census, 1820-1900; Lake County and Geauga County marriages, to 1900; Common Pleas, probate court and deeds to 1840; obituaries to 1900. **Subscriptions:** 20 journals and other serials. **Services:** Copying; library open to older students and adults. **Publications:** Lake County Historical Society, quarterly; Here is Lake County, Ohio, 1964 (hardbound). **Special Indexes:** Genealogy Index (70,000; card).

★6785★
LAKE COUNTY LAW LIBRARY (Law)
315 W. Main St.
Lake County Courthouse
Tavares, FL 32278   Phone: (904) 343-9730
                                        Pamela L. Woodworth, Libn.
Staff: Prof 1. **Subjects:** Law. **Holdings:** 12,000 volumes. **Services:** Copying; library open to public for reference use only.

★6786★
LAKE COUNTY LAW LIBRARY (Law)
18 N. County St.   Phone: (312) 689-6654
Waukegan, IL 60085   Joanne T. Baker, Law Libn.
Staff: 1. **Subjects:** Law. **Holdings:** 15,000 books; Illinois Appellate Court Briefs, 2nd district, 1964 to present. **Subscriptions:** 145 journals and other serials. **Services:** Interlibrary loans; copying; library open to public for reference use only.

★6787★
LAKE COUNTY MEMORIAL HOSPITAL - MEDICAL LIBRARIES (East and West) (Med)
Washington at Liberty   Phone: (216) 354-2400
Painesville, OH 44077   Vicki Kresak, Health Sci.Libn.
Staff: Prof 1; Other 1. **Subjects:** Medicine, nursing, health administration. **Holdings:** 1200 books; 2200 bound periodical volumes. **Subscriptions:** 105 journals and other serials. **Services:** Interlibrary loans; library not open to public. **Computerized Information Services:** Online systems. **Formed by the Merger of:** Lake County Memorial Hospital East - Medical Library and Lake County Memorial Hospital West - Medical Library.

★6788★
LAKE COUNTY MEMORIAL HOSPITAL WEST - MEDICAL LIBRARY
36000 Euclid Ave.
Willoughby, OH 44094
Defunct. Merged with Lake County Memorial Hospital East - Medical Library to form Lake County Memorial Hospital - Medical Libraries (East and West).

★6789★
LAKE COUNTY MUSEUM - LIBRARY AND INFORMATION CENTER (Hist)
Lakewood Forest Preserve
Rte. 176 & Fairfield Rd.   Phone: (312) 526-7878
Wauconda, IL 60084   Rebecca Goldberg, Dir.
Founded: 1957. **Staff:** 4. **Subjects:** Lake County, Chicago and Illinois history; Civil War history. **Holdings:** 1500 books; pamphlets; 14 VF cabinets; maps. **Subscriptions:** 25 journals and other serials. **Services:** Copying; library open to public with restrictions.

★6790★
LAKE COUNTY PUBLIC LIBRARY - SPECIAL COLLECTIONS (Hist)
1115 Harrison Ave.   Phone: (303) 486-0569
Leadville, CO 80461   David R. Parry, Dir.
Founded: 1903. **Staff:** Prof 1; Other 4. **Subjects:** Colorado Mountain History Collection, Leadville-Lake County history. **Holdings:** 300 titles; 1865 historic local photographs. **Services:** Interlibrary loans; copying; special collections

open to public for reference use only. **Computerized Information Services:** Computerized cataloging. **Networks/Consortia:** Member of Three Rivers Regional Library Service System. **Special Catalogs:** Special subject bibliographies.

★6791★
LAKE COUNTY SUPERIOR COURT LIBRARY (Law)
400 Broadway, Rms. 3 & 4   Phone: (219) 886-3621
Gary, IN 46402-1286   Birdie Witson, Libn.
Staff: Prof 2. **Subjects:** Law. **Holdings:** 16,280 volumes. **Services:** Library not open to public. **Staff:** Willie M. Julkes, Libn.

LAKE ERIE PROGRAM LIBRARY
See: Ohio State University - Center for Lake Erie Area Research

★6792★
LAKE FOREST COLLEGE - DONNELLEY LIBRARY - SPECIAL COLLECTIONS (Hum; Hist)
College & Sheridan Rds.   Phone: (312) 234-3100
Lake Forest, IL 60045   Arthur H. Miller, Jr., Coll.Libn.
Staff: Prof 4; Other 3. **Subjects:** American and English literature, art and art history, American and British history, political science, psychology, Afro-American studies. **Special Collections:** Hamill Collection (6000 rare books); Scotiana Collection (Scottish history; 3000 volumes); Garrett Leverton collection (development of theater in the U.S.; 5000 volumes); railroad history collection; library of Elliott Donnelley and Munson Paddock (6000 items). **Services:** Interlibrary loans; copying; library open to public with restrictions. **Computerized Information Services:** DIALOG, SDC; computerized cataloging. **Networks/Consortia:** Member of North Suburban Library Systems; ILLINET; LIBRAS Academic Library Cooperative; Regional Medical Library - Region 3.

★6793★
LAKE FOREST COLLEGE - THOMAS OSCAR FREEMAN MEMORIAL LIBRARY (Sci-Tech)
                                        Phone: (312) 234-3100
Lake Forest, IL 60045   Arthur H. Miller, Jr., Coll.Libn.
Founded: 1962. **Subjects:** Biology, chemistry, physics. **Holdings:** 7000 books; 3500 bound periodical volumes; 101 volumes on microcards; 380 reels of microfilm. **Subscriptions:** 50 journals and other serials. **Services:** Interlibrary loans; copying; library open to persons who cannot be served by their public library; letter of reference required. **Computerized Information Services:** DIALOG, SDC, BRS; computerized cataloging and circulation. **Staff:** Joann H. Lee, Hd., Rd.Serv.

LAKE MEAD NATL. RECREATION AREA
See: U.S. Natl. Park Service

★6794★
LAKE MICHIGAN FEDERATION - ENVIRONMENTAL LIBRARY (Env-Cons; Energy)
53 W. Jackson, No. 1710   Phone: (312) 427-5121
Chicago, IL 60604   Judy Kiriazis, Exec.Dir.
Founded: 1970. **Staff:** Prof 1; Other 5. **Subjects:** Lake Michigan, water quality, land use planning, land disposal, energy, nuclear power production, power plant siting, thermal pollution, erosion-shoreland management. **Holdings:** 2500 books; 476 bound periodical volumes. **Services:** Interlibrary loans; copying; library open to public for reference use only. **Networks/Consortia:** Member of ILLINET; Chicago Library System. **Publications:** Lake Michigan, quarterly - to members and libraries in Illinois, Indiana, Michigan and Wisconsin; list of other publications - available on request.

★6795★
LAKE PLACID ASSOCIATION FOR MUSIC, DRAMA & ART - NETTIE MARIE JONES FINE ARTS LIBRARY (Art; Music)
Saranac Ave. at Fawn Ridge   Phone: (518) 523-2512
Lake Placid, NY 12946   Suellen Linn, Lib.Dir.
Founded: 1975. **Staff:** Prof 1; Other 1. **Subjects:** Fine arts, performing arts, architecture. **Special Collections:** Victor Herbert Memorial Collection; Stedman and Moses glass negative collections; Wilford T. Getman Adirondack Collection. **Holdings:** 7500 books; 100 bound periodical volumes; 8000 slides; 10,000 glass negatives. **Subscriptions:** 130 journals and other serials; 10 newspapers. **Services:** Interlibrary loans; copying; library open to public with restrictions. **Networks/Consortia:** Member of North Country Reference & Research Resources Council (NCRRRC).

★6796★

LAKE SUPERIOR STATE COLLEGE - MICHIGAN & MARINE COLLECTIONS (Hist)

Sault Ste. Marie, MI 49783

Phone: (906) 635-2402
Dr. Frederick A. Michels, Dir.

Founded: 1946. **Staff:** Prof 4; Other 6. **Subjects:** History of Michigan's Upper Peninsula; Indians of Michigan's Upper Peninsula; local history of Sault Ste. Marie, Michigan. **Special Collections:** Special editions and sources of Longfellow's "Hiawatha"; Marine-Laker Collection. **Holdings:** 1400 books; Sault Evening News on microfilm; 16 VF drawers of pamphlets concerned with local and area history. **Services:** Copying; library open to public for reference use only. **Networks/Consortia:** Member of Sault Area International Library Association; Michigan Library Consortium. **Publications:** History - Hiawatha: Michigan Collection - distributed to libraries in immediate service area free. **Staff:** Charles E. Nairn, Ref.Libn.

★6797★

LAKEHEAD UNIVERSITY - CHANCELLOR PATERSON LIBRARY (Sci-Tech; Bus-Fin)

Oliver Rd.
Thunder Bay, ON, Canada P7B 5E1

Phone: (807) 345-2121
Marshall Clinton, Chf.Libn.

Staff: Prof 8; Other 33. **Subjects:** Arts and pure science, forestry, engineering, physical education, outdoor recreation, business administration, nursing, library technology. **Special Collections:** Seaway Collection (500 books, pamphlets and reports); Finnish (local) collection (550 books, 24 linear feet of manuscripts and archives); forestry pamphlet collection (25,000 pamphlets and documents, some on microfiche). **Holdings:** 300,000 books; 65,000 bound periodical volumes; 1000 linear feet of documents; 100,000 volumes on microfiche; 150 linear feet of manuscripts and archives. **Subscriptions:** 2800 journals and other serials; 49 newspapers. **Services:** Interlibrary loans; copying; library open to public with a deposit required for borrowing. **Computerized Information Services:** DIALOG, MEDLINE, QL Systems, CAN/OLE; computerized cataloging and serials. **Publications:** Readers' Guide, annual - local distribution. **Staff:** Anne Deighton, Acq.Libn.; Shirley Bonoca, Ref.Libn.; Joan Seeley, Hd., Circ.Serv.; Don Sharp, Tech.Serv.Libn.; Bryce Allen, Coll.Dev.Libn.

★6798★

LAKEHEAD UNIVERSITY - EDUCATION LIBRARY (Educ)

Oliver Road
Thunder Bay, ON, Canada P7B 5E1

Phone: (807) 345-2121
Mr. J. Arnot, Educ.Libn.

Founded: 1960. **Staff:** Prof 1; Other 6. **Subjects:** Special education, school administration, curriculum, school and community, philosophy and psychology of education, personnel service in education, tests and measurements. **Holdings:** 33,000 books; 600 bound periodical volumes; 800 reels of microfilm; 17,000 microfiche; 650 tapes; 350 multimedia kits; 1100 filmstrips; 64 slide sets; 8 VF drawers of pamphlets. **Subscriptions:** 352 journals and other serials; 5 newspapers. **Services:** Interlibrary loans; copying; library open to public with restrictions. **Computerized Information Services:** DIALOG (through main library); computerized cataloging and acquisitions.

★6799★

LAKELAND COUNSELING CENTER - LIBRARY (Soc Sci)

Hwy. NN
Box 1005
Elkhorn, WI 53121

Phone: (414) 723-5400
Ruby Bill, Libn.

Staff: Prof 1. **Subjects:** Alcoholism, drug abuse, social work, mental health, psychology, psychotherapy, emotional problems. **Holdings:** 3025 books; 2 file drawers of clippings; 20 reels of films. **Subscriptions:** 75 journals and other serials; 5 newspapers. **Services:** Interlibrary loans; copying; library open to residents of Walworth county, Wisconsin. **Networks/Consortia:** Member of Tri-County Library Council; Regional Medical Library - Region 3; Southeastern Wisconsin Health Science Libraries Consortium (SWHSL). **Remarks:** Maintained by Walworth County.

★6800★

LAKELAND GENERAL HOSPITAL - MEDICAL LIBRARY (Med)

Lakeland Hills Blvd.
Drawer 448
Lakeland, FL 33802

Phone: (813) 683-0411
Cheryl R. Dee, Med.Libn.

Founded: 1959. **Subjects:** Medicine, nursing, medical administration. **Holdings:** 1400 books; 4000 bound periodical volumes; AV programs. **Subscriptions:** 103 journals and other serials. **Services:** Interlibrary loans; copying; library open to public by doctor's permission. **Computerized Information Services:** MEDLINE.

★6801★

LAKELAND HOSPITAL - MEDICAL LIBRARY (Med)

Hwy. NN
Box 1002
Elkhorn, WI 53121

Phone: (414) 723-2960
Mary Bray, Libn.

Founded: 1974. **Staff:** Prof 1. **Subjects:** Medicine, nursing. **Holdings:** 497 books. **Subscriptions:** 68 journals and other serials. **Services:** Interlibrary loans; copying; library open to public by appointment. **Networks/Consortia:** Member of Regional Medical Library - Region 3; Southeastern Wisconsin Health Science Libraries Consortium (SWHSL).

LAKES (Arthur) LIBRARY
See: Colorado School of Mines - Arthur Lakes Library

LAKESIDE HOSPITAL MEDICAL LIBRARY
See: U.S. Veterans Administration (IL-Chicago)

★6802★

LAKEVIEW MEDICAL CENTER - MEDICAL/NURSING LIBRARY (Med)

812 N. Logan Ave.
Danville, IL 61832

Phone: (217) 443-5000
Donna Judd, Libn.

Staff: Prof 1; Other 2. **Subjects:** Nursing, medicine. **Holdings:** 3015 books; 785 bound periodical volumes; 8 VF drawers of pamphlets. **Subscriptions:** 172 journals and other serials. **Services:** Interlibrary loans; copying; library open to allied health professionals.

★6803★

LAKEVILLE HOSPITAL - HEALTH SCIENCES LIBRARY (Med)

Main St.
Lakeville, MA 02346

Phone: (617) 947-1231
Janet Doherty, Libn.

Founded: 1910. **Staff:** 1. **Subjects:** Medicine, nursing, rehabilitation, orthopedics and orthopedic surgery, birth defects and crippling conditions. **Holdings:** 1500 books; 1520 bound periodical volumes; pamphlet file; 125 AV materials. **Subscriptions:** 103 journals and other serials. **Services:** Interlibrary loans; copying; library open to public with restrictions. **Computerized Information Services:** Online systems. **Networks/Consortia:** Member of Southeastern Massachusetts Health Sciences Libraries. **Publications:** Newsletter, semiannual - local distribution. **Remarks:** Maintained by Massachusetts State Department of Public Health.

★6804★

LAKEWOOD HISTORICAL SOCIETY - LIBRARY (Hist)

14710 Lake Ave.
Lakewood, OH 44107

Phone: (216) 221-7343
Bertha M. Noe, Cur.

Founded: 1952. **Subjects:** History - Western Reserve, Ohio, Lakewood, Rockport. **Special Collections:** Early school books. **Holdings:** Figures not available. **Services:** Library open to members of the society. **Publications:** Pictorial History of the Western Reserve. **Staff:** Mrs. Robert Folsom, Libn.

★6805★

LAKEWOOD HOSPITAL - MEDICAL LIBRARY (Med)

14519 Detroit Ave.
Lakewood, OH 44107

Phone: (216) 521-4200
Dorothy Jorgens, Dir.

Staff: Prof 1; Other 1. **Subjects:** Medicine, nursing, hospital administration, sciences. **Holdings:** 6605 books; 4787 bound periodical volumes; pamphlet files. **Subscriptions:** 352 journals and other serials; 5 newspapers. **Services:** Interlibrary loans; copying; library open to public by permission. **Computerized Information Services:** Computerized cataloging. **Publications:** LibGuide, Acquisition List, Biomedical Serials List - all for internal distribution only. **Special Indexes:** Special Bibliographies.

LAL
See: Oakland Public Library - Latin American Library

★6806★

LAMB-WESTON - BUSINESS RESEARCH CENTER (Bus-Fin)

Box 23517
Portland, OR 97223

Phone: (503) 639-8612
Anne Vixie, Bus.Res.Spec.

Founded: 1978. **Staff:** Prof 1; Other 1. **Subjects:** Marketing, food processing. **Holdings:** 1000 books. **Subscriptions:** 200 journals and other serials. **Services:** Interlibrary loans; copying; SDI; library not open to public. **Computerized Information Services:** Online systems. **Networks/Consortia:** Member of Washington County Cooperative Library Service. **Publications:** Newsletter, monthly.

LAMBDA CORPORATION
See: General Research Corporation

★6807★
LAMBERT (Harold M.) STUDIOS - LIBRARY (Pict)
2801 W. Cheltenham Ave.
Box 27310   Phone: (215) 224-1400
Philadelphia, PA 19150   Raymond Lambert, Owner
Founded: 1936. **Holdings:** 1 million color transparencies and black and white prints. **Services:** Stock photographs available on a fee basis.

LAMONT-DOHERTY GEOLOGICAL OBSERVATORY
See: Columbia University

LAMP GLASS & COMPONENTS LIBRARY
See: General Electric Company

LAMSON (Herbert H.) LIBRARY
See: Plymouth State College - Herbert H. Lamson Library

★6808★
LANCASTER BIBLE COLLEGE - STOLL MEMORIAL LIBRARY (Rel-Theol)
901 Eden Rd.   Phone: (717) 569-7071
Lancaster, PA 17601   Mary L. Walters, Lib.Dir.
Founded: 1933. **Staff:** Prof 3; Other 1. **Subjects:** Bible, theology, missions, Christian education, music, liberal arts, pastoral studies. **Holdings:** 34,000 books; 728 bound periodical volumes; 1755 AV items (cataloged); 5 file drawers of pamphlets and clippings; 3 file drawers of missions materials; microforms. **Subscriptions:** 339 journals and other serials. **Services:** Interlibrary loans; copying; library open to public. **Computerized Information Services:** Computerized cataloging. **Staff:** Fred W. Pearson, Ref.Libn.; Deborah Hunt, Asst.Libn./Circ.; Sharon L. Gordon, Tech.Serv.

★6809★
LANCASTER COUNTY HISTORICAL SOCIETY - LIBRARY (Hist)
Willson Bldg.
230 N. President Ave.   Phone: (717) 392-4633
Lancaster, PA 17603   Salinda M. Matt, Chf.Libn.
Founded: 1886. **Staff:** 3. **Subjects:** History of Southeastern Pennsylvania and Lancaster County. **Special Collections:** Jasper Yeates Law Library Collection (1043 volumes on English law assembled by Judge Yeates in the 1760s and 1770s, being virtually every work on law published in England between 1600 and 1800). **Holdings:** 8500 books; 1500 bound periodical volumes; 740 bound newspaper volumes; 37 cubic feet and 98 cases of manuscripts. **Subscriptions:** 27 journals and other serials. **Services:** Copying; library open to public. **Staff:** Arthur C. Lord, Chm., Lib.Comm.; William Luck, Assoc.Libn.

★6810★
LANCASTER GENERAL HOSPITAL - MUELLER HEALTH SCIENCES LIBRARY (Med)†
555 N. Duke St.   Phone: (717) 299-5511
Lancaster, PA 17604   Virginia H. Engle, Libn.
Founded: 1967. **Staff:** Prof 1; Other 1. **Subjects:** Medicine, nursing, allied health sciences, hospital administration. **Holdings:** 4431 books; 787 bound periodical volumes; 746 reels of microfilm; 720 cassettes; 2 VF drawers of pamphlets. **Subscriptions:** 205 journals and other serials. **Services:** Interlibrary loans; copying; will answer brief inquiries and make referrals; library open to public for reference use only. **Networks/Consortia:** Member of Central Pennsylvania Health Sciences Library Association (CPHSLA). **Publications:** New titles listing, monthly - for internal distribution only.

★6811★
LANCASTER LAW LIBRARY (Law)
50 N. Duke St.
Box 3480   Phone: (717) 299-8090
Lancaster, PA 17604   Eleanor Lloyd, Libn.
Staff: Prof 1; Other 1. **Subjects:** Law. **Holdings:** 21,000 volumes. **Subscriptions:** 24 journals and other serials. **Services:** Interlibrary loans; copying; SDI; library open to public.

★6812★
LANCASTER MENNONITE HISTORICAL SOCIETY - LIBRARY (Rel-Theol; Hist)
2215 Millstream Rd.   Phone: (717) 393-9745
Lancaster, PA 17602   Carolyn C. Wenger, Dir.
Founded: 1958. **Staff:** Prof 2; Other 4. **Subjects:** History - local and denominational; genealogy, especially Pennsylvania German names; theology. **Special Collections:** Mennonitica; Amishana. **Holdings:** 55,000 books and bound periodical volumes; 3000 archive boxes; 200,000 vital statistics cards; 100 maps; 10,000 pamphlets; 250 reels of microfilm. **Subscriptions:** 100 journals and other serials. **Services:** Translation; copying; library open to

public. **Publications:** Pennsylvania Mennonite Heritage, quarterly - subscription; Mirror, bimonthly - direct mailing; Used Book Sales, Brochure - subscription. **Special Catalogs:** Genealogical catalog of abstracted vital statistics (card); cemetery files. **Staff:** Lloyd R. Zeager, Libn.

★6813★
LANCASTER NEWSPAPERS - LIBRARY (Publ)
8 W. King St.   Phone: (717) 291-8773
Lancaster, PA 17603   Helen L. Everts, Libn.
Founded: 1952. **Staff:** 5. **Subjects:** State, county and city government events and personalities; current events. **Special Collections:** Local newspapers, 1795 to present. **Holdings:** 500 books; Remington Rand Lektriever, 27 carriers, 9 drawers per carrier, subject file; Linedex subject index with 15,500 subject headings; Remington Rand Lektriever, 21 carriers, 9 drawers per carrier - 6 carriers with velox negatives of personalities; 15 filing cabinets of pictures, pamphlets and maps. **Services:** Library open to public with permission. **Remarks:** Library serves staffs of Lancaster Sunday News, Intelligencer-Journal, and Lancaster New Era.

LANCASTER THEOLOGICAL SEMINARY - EVANGELICAL AND REFORMED HISTORICAL SOCIETY
See: Evangelical and Reformed Historical Society - Lancaster Central Archives and Library

★6814★
LANCASTER THEOLOGICAL SEMINARY OF THE UNITED CHURCH OF CHRIST - PHILIP SCHAFF LIBRARY (Rel-Theol)
555 W. James St.   Phone: (717) 393-0654
Lancaster, PA 17603   Anne-Marie Salgat, Dir. of Lib.Serv.
Founded: 1825. **Staff:** Prof 2; Other 2. **Subjects:** Biblical studies, theology, pastoral counseling, church history, Christian education, church and society. **Special Collections:** Albright Collection of German Religious Books printed in America (7500 volumes). **Holdings:** 129,000 books; 10,300 bound periodical volumes. **Subscriptions:** 455 journals and other serials. **Services:** Interlibrary loans; library open to public. **Networks/Consortia:** Member of Southeastern Pennsylvania Theological Libraries Association (SEPTLA).

★6815★
LAND, INC. - LIBRARY (Energy; Soc Sci)
Route 1
525 River Rd.   Phone: (715) 423-7996
Rudolph, WI 54475   Naomi Jacobson, Co-Chm.
Staff: 1. **Subjects:** Anti-nuclear side of the nuclear power plant controversy. **Holdings:** 25 books; pamphlets, reprints, research on low-level radiation and cancer; films; testimony of PSC hearings. **Services:** Library open to public with restrictions. **Publications:** Methodologies for the Study of Low-Level Radiation in the Midwest - available for sale. **Also Known As:** League Against Nuclear Dangers, Inc.

LAND TENURE CENTER - LIBRARY
See: University of Wisconsin, Madison

★6816★
LANDAUER ASSOCIATES, INC. - INFORMATION CENTER (Bus-Fin; Plan)
200 Park Ave., Suite 3710   Phone: (212) 687-2323
New York, NY 10166   Therese E. Byrne, Dir., Info.Serv.
Founded: 1974. **Staff:** Prof 2; Other 1. **Subjects:** Real estate, finance, marketing, land use, development, property acquisition and management. **Holdings:** 280 books; 100 VF drawers of reports; 16,000 clippings, offerings, brochures and statistical data; 125 VF drawers of research materials; U.S. maps; annual reports; 1980, 1970 and 1960 census publications. **Subscriptions:** 180 journals and other serials; 20 newspapers. **Services:** Center open to public by special permission. **Computerized Information Services:** DIALOG, New York Times Information Service, Dun & Bradstreet, Inc., Marshall & Swift Publication Company; internal database; computerized cataloging and circulation. **Publications:** Landauer Library Letter, biweekly - for internal distribution only and monthly - external distribution. **Special Indexes:** Index to Landauer Library Letter; index to all real estate events covered by Landauer Library Letter and trade publications (card). **Staff:** Robin Sanders, Asst.Libn.

★6817★
LANDELS, RIPLEY & DIAMOND - LIBRARY (Law)
450 Pacific Ave.   Phone: (415) 788-5000
San Francisco, CA 94133   Jeanette S. Lizotte, Libn.
Staff: Prof 1; Other 1. **Subjects:** Law. **Holdings:** 15,000 books; 200 bound periodical volumes. **Subscriptions:** 150 journals and other serials; 5 newspapers. **Services:** Interlibrary loans; library not open to public. **Computerized Information Services:** LEXIS, DIALOG.

LANDER (Clara) LIBRARY
See: Winnipeg Art Gallery - Clara Lander Library

★6818★
**LANDMARK CONSERVATORS - CABOTS OLD INDIAN PUEBLO MUSEUM
    LIBRARY** (Hist; Area-Ethnic)
67-616 E. Desert View Ave.   Phone: (714) 329-7610
Desert Hot Springs, CA 92240   Colbert H. Eyraud, Pres./Cur.
Founded: 1968. **Staff:** 2. **Subjects:** Indians, history, business. **Special
Collections:** City Council and Planning Commission agenda and actions, 1968-
1982; Desert Sentinel newpaper, 1946-1981 (microfilm); Earthquake Watch
newsletter, 1980-1982. **Holdings:** 3000 books; 50 bound periodical
volumes; 8 VF drawers of clippings; 4 boxes of old newspapers; 1500 78rpm
records (Edison cylinders). **Subscriptions:** 18 journals and other serials.
Services: Library open to public for reference use only. **Staff:** Grace
Tarbutton, Lib.Archv.

★6819★
**LANDMARK SOCIETY OF WESTERN NEW YORK - WENRICH MEMORIAL
    LIBRARY** (Hist; Plan)
130 Spring St.   Phone: (716) 546-7029
Rochester, NY 14608   Ann B. Parks, Asst.Dir.
Staff: Prof 2. **Subjects:** Architecture, state and local history, historic
preservation and restoration techniques, decorative arts, landscape
architecture, planning. **Special Collections:** John Wenrich Collection
(architectural and locomotive renderings); Walter Cassebeer Collection
(lithographs of area buildings and historic scenes). **Holdings:** 2500 books; 70
bound periodical volumes; 6000 slides; 5500 photographs; 100 drawings.
Subscriptions: 38 journals and other serials. **Services:** Interlibrary loans;
copying; library open to public with restrictions. **Networks/Consortia:**
Member of Rochester Regional Research Library Council (RRRLC).
Publications: Newsletter; Landmark Exchange - both bimonthly - distributed
to members and available to public on request; listing of area buildings for sale
that are of architectural and/or historical interest. **Staff:** Cynthia Howk,
Res.Coord.

LANDOWNE-BLOOM COLLECTION
See: Yeshiva University - Pollack Library - Landowne-Bloom Collection

LANDSMANSHAFT ARCHIVE
See: Yivo Institute for Jewish Research - Library and Archives

★6820★
LANE COUNCIL OF GOVERNMENTS - LIBRARY (Plan)†
Public Service Bldg.
125 E. 8th   Phone: (503) 687-4283
Eugene, OR 97401   JoAnn McCauley, Info.Coord.
Staff: 1. **Subjects:** City planning; regional planning; zoning; housing; population
- census, social services, transportation. **Holdings:** 1700 books.
Subscriptions: 9 journals and other serials; 7 newspapers. **Services:** Library
open to public for reference use only. **Special Catalogs:** Punched card
catalog.

★6821★
LANE COUNTY LAW LIBRARY (Law)
Courthouse   Phone: (503) 687-4337
Eugene, OR 97401   Mary E. Clayton, Law Libn.
Founded: 1948. **Staff:** Prof 1; Other 1. **Subjects:** Law. **Holdings:** 15,500
books; 500 bound periodical volumes; Oregon Supreme Court briefs, 1955 to
present; Oregon Court of Appeals briefs, 1969 to present. **Subscriptions:** 25
journals. **Services:** Library open to lawyers at all times; to public when
courthouse is open. **Computerized Information Services:** WESTLAW.

★6822★
LANE COUNTY MUSEUM - SPECIAL COLLECTIONS & ARCHIVES (Hist)
740 W. 13th Ave.   Phone: (503) 687-4239
Eugene, OR 97402   Edward W. Nolan, Archv.
Founded: 1971. **Staff:** Prof 1. **Subjects:** Lane County history and
settlement. **Special Collections:** William Kyle and Sons (24 linear feet);
Eugene Woolen Mills (10 linear feet); Central Lane League of Women Voters
(20 linear feet); Oregon Repertory Theater (5 linear feet); American
Rhododendron Society, Eugene Chapter (4 linear feet); H.H. Waechter
(architect), 35 linear feet; Willamette Peoples Co-op (15 linear feet).
Holdings: 1100 books; 40,000 photographs; 75 linear feet of Lane County
archives; 125 maps; 27 reels of microfilm; 10 VF drawers of ephemera and
clippings; 200 architectural drawings. **Services:** Copying; library open to
public by appointment. **Computerized Information Services:** Computerized
index of photographs. **Publications:** Exhibit catalogs, irregular; Catalogue of
Manuscript Collections (1980). **Special Catalogs:** A Piece of the Old Tent

(artifact catalog).

LANE HALL MEMORIAL LIBRARY
See: Notre Dame College

LANE MEDICAL LIBRARY
See: Stanford University

★6823★
LANE & MITTENDORF - LAW LIBRARY (Law)
26 Broadway   Phone: (212) 943-3000
New York, NY 10004   Joel L. Solomon, Libn.
Founded: 1952. **Staff:** Prof 1. **Subjects:** Law. **Holdings:** 10,500 books.
Services: Interlibrary loans; copying; library not open to public. **Formerly:**
Casey, Lane & Mittendorf.

★6824★
LANGE, SIMPSON, ROBINSON & SOMERVILLE - LIBRARY (Law)
1700 First Alabama Bank Bldg.   Phone: (205) 252-7000
Birmingham, AL 35203   Angela J. Wier, Libn.
Staff: Prof 1; Other 1. **Subjects:** Law - securities, corporate, banking,
antitrust. **Holdings:** 20,000 books; 100 bound periodical volumes; 780 briefs
and memorandum; 220 form files; 80 expert witness files; 100 pamphlets
files. **Subscriptions:** 25 journals and other serials; 6 newspapers. **Services:**
Interlibrary loans; copying; SDI; library open to public for reference use only.
Computerized Information Services: DIALOG, WESTLAW. **Publications:**
Annotated bibliography to new titles. **Special Indexes:** Index to briefs and
memorandum; index to expert witness file.

LANGLEY AIR FORCE BASE (VA)
See: U.S. Air Force Base - Langley Base Library; U.S. Air Force - Tactical
    Air Command

★6825★
LANGLEY PORTER PSYCHIATRIC INSTITUTE - PROFESSIONAL LIBRARY
    (Med)
University of California
401 Parnassus Ave.
Box 13-B/C   Phone: (415) 681-8080
San Francisco, CA 94143   Lisa M. Dunkel, Libn.
Founded: 1943. **Staff:** Prof 1; Other 2. **Subjects:** Psychiatry,
psychoanalysis, clinical psychology, allied mental health subjects. **Holdings:**
6575 books; 4145 bound periodical volumes; pamphlets (cataloged).
Subscriptions: 200 journals and other serials. **Services:** Interlibrary loans;
library open to mental health professionals. **Computerized Information
Services:** MEDLARS, DIALOG, BRS.

LANGLEY RESEARCH CENTER
See: U.S. NASA

★6826★
LANGLEY SCHOOL DISTRICT - RESOURCE CENTRE (Educ)
19740 32nd Ave.   Phone: (604) 530-5151
Langley, BC, Canada V3A 4S1   Shirley D. Fisher-Fleming, Educ. Media Coord.
Founded: 1963. **Staff:** Prof 1; Other 9. **Subjects:** Education. **Holdings:** 250
books; 1460 16mm films; 600 8mm films; 700 cassette tapes; 500 picture
sets; 500 transparencies; 2837 filmstrips; 1650 programmed videotapes;
models, media kits. **Subscriptions:** 80 journals and other serials. **Services:**
Copying; cassette and video cassette copying; centre open to teachers.
Publications: Content, bimonthly. **Special Catalogs:** Catalogue of resources
(book); list of periodical contents. **Remarks:** Resource Centre comprises an
Educational Media Nonprint Collection and a Teachers' Professional Collection.

★6827★
LANGSTON UNIVERSITY - MELVIN B. TOLSON BLACK HERITAGE CENTER
    (Area-Ethnic)
2nd Fl., Page Hall Annex   Phone: (405) 466-2231
Langston, OK 73050   Rosalind Savage, Cur.
Founded: 1969. **Staff:** Prof 1. **Subjects:** Afro-American experience in the
U.S.; Afro-Americans in the humanities and arts since 1900; African history.
Special Collections: African Art Collection (93 items); Langston University
Archives (brochures, programs, yearbooks, presidential papers); Melvin B.
Tolson Collection (books, personal items, pictures, awards). **Holdings:** 7500
books; 800 bound periodical volumes; 400 recordings; 350 audio cassettes;
60 video cassettes; 48 films; 8000 VF items. **Subscriptions:** 70 journals and
other serials; 20 newspapers. **Services:** Interlibrary loans; copying; library
open to public. **Publications:** Acquisitions List, monthly; newsletter, quarterly.
Special Indexes: Biography index; periodical articles index.

LANGSTON (Wann) MEMORIAL LIBRARY
See: Baptist Medical Center - Wann Langston Memorial Library

LANGUAGE INSTITUTE
See: U.S. Dept. of Defense

★6828★
LANKENAU HOSPITAL - MEDICAL LIBRARY (Med)
Lancaster & City Line Aves.   Phone: (215) 645-2698
Philadelphia, PA 19151   Loann Scarpato, Med.Lbn.
Founded: 1860. **Staff:** Prof 1. **Subjects:** Medicine, medical research. **Special Collections:** Collected papers of the Lankenau Hospital Department of Research. **Holdings:** 2000 books; 7800 bound periodical volumes; 350 audio cassettes. **Subscriptions:** 200 journals and other serials. **Services:** Interlibrary loans; copying; library open to public for reference use only. **Networks/Consortia:** Member of Mideastern Regional Medical Library Service (MERMLS); Delaware Valley Information Consortium.

★6829★
LANKENAU HOSPITAL - SCHOOL OF NURSING LIBRARY (Med)
City Ave. & 64th St.   Phone: (215) 642-3931
Philadelphia, PA 19151   Sr. Alma Koder, Lbn.
Staff: Prof 1. **Subjects:** Nursing and nursing history, medicine, public health, microbiology, chemistry, psychology, sociology. **Special Collections:** First editions of nursing textbooks; Lankenau historical collection. **Holdings:** 3960 books and bound periodical volumes; 5 VF drawers of illustrations, clippings, pamphlets, reports and archives. **Subscriptions:** 100 journals and other serials. **Services:** Interlibrary loans (except historical items); copying; library open to public by appointment.

★6830★
LANSING COMMUNITY COLLEGE - PROFESSIONAL RESOURCE CENTER
(Educ)
419 N. Capitol Ave.
Box 40010   Phone: (517) 373-7274
Lansing, MI 48901   James P. Platte, Dean/Div.Lrng.Rsrcs.
Founded: 1974. **Staff:** Prof 1; Other 2. **Subjects:** Higher education - administration, teaching, financial support; community colleges. **Special Collections:** Lansing Community College Archives (800 titles, over 120 titles of current journals in the field of higher education). **Holdings:** 2200 books; 4 VF drawers of unbound reports, documents, articles and ephemera. **Subscriptions:** 120 journals and other serials. **Services:** Interlibrary loans; copying; SDI; library open to students, and others by appointment. **Computerized Information Services:** Online systems; computerized cataloging and acquisitions. **Networks/Consortia:** Member of Michigan Data Base Users Group; Michigan Library Consortium. **Publications:** Acquisitions Announcement, semiannual. **Remarks:** The LCC Professional Resource Center serves as a clearinghouse on the subject of higher education for staff members of LCC.

★6831★
LANSING GENERAL HOSPITAL - OSTEOPATHIC - K.M. BAKER MEMORIAL LIBRARY (Med)
2800 Devonshire Ave.   Phone: (517) 377-8389
Lansing, MI 48909   Bethany A. Heinlen, Med.Lbn.
Founded: 1969. **Staff:** Prof 1. **Subjects:** Medicine, nursing, osteopathic medicine, hospital management. **Holdings:** 1250 books; 1000 bound periodical volumes; 800 Audio-Digest tapes; 75 slide/tape programs; 8 VF drawers of pamphlets. **Subscriptions:** 172 journals and other serials. **Services:** Interlibrary loans; copying; library not open to public. **Computerized Information Services:** MEDLINE. **Networks/Consortia:** Member of Mid-Michigan Health Sciences Libraries; Michigan Health Sciences Libraries Association.

★6832★
LANTERMAN (Frank J.) STATE HOSPITAL - STAFF LIBRARY (Med)
3530 W. Pomona Blvd.
Box 100   Phone: (714) 595-1221
Pomona, CA 91769   Eleanor E. Wash, Sr.Lbn.
Founded: 1954. **Staff:** Prof 2. **Subjects:** Mental retardation, child psychology, medicine. **Holdings:** 11,364 books and bound periodical volumes; 15 VF drawers of pamphlets. **Subscriptions:** 202 journals and other serials. **Services:** Interlibrary loans (fee); copying; library open to public. **Staff:** Laurie Piccolotti, Lbn.

LARAMIE ENERGY TECHNOLOGY CENTER LIBRARY
See: U.S. Dept. of Energy

★6833★
LARAMIE PLAINS MUSEUM ASSOCIATION - LIBRARY (Hist)
603 Ivinson   Phone: (307) 742-4448
Laramie, WY 82070   Murray L. Carroll, Ph.D., Dir.
Staff: 3. **Subjects:** History. **Holdings:** 1000 volumes; bound manuscripts; newspapers. **Services:** Library open to public for reference use only, on the premises.

★6834★
LARNED STATE HOSPITAL - J.T. NARAMORE LIBRARY (Med)
Route 3, Box 89   Phone: (316) 285-2131
Larned, KS 67550   Martha Zook, Dir., Nursing Educ.
Staff: Prof 1; Other 1. **Subjects:** Psychiatry, psychiatric nursing, psychology, mental health, medicine. **Special Collections:** J.T. Naramore Collection (525 books). **Holdings:** 4700 books. **Subscriptions:** 65 journals and other serials. **Services:** Interlibrary loans; library open to local students.

LARSON (A.C.) LIBRARY
See: Hinsdale Sanitarium and Hospital - A.C. Larson Library

LAS CAMPANAS OBSERVATORY - LIBRARY
See: Carnegie Institution of Washington - Mount Wilson & Las Campanas Observatories - Library

★6835★
LAS VEGAS - CITY MANAGER'S LIBRARY (Soc Sci; Plan)
City Hall, 10th Fl.
400 E. Stewart Ave.   Phone: (702) 386-6501
Las Vegas, NV 89101   Diane Ortiz, Mgt.Anl./Rec.Mgt.Coord.
Staff: Prof 1; Other 1. **Subjects:** Public administration, local politics and government, state legislative materials, urban and regional planning, environmental quality. **Holdings:** 2500 books; 8 VF drawers of newspaper clippings; 55 titles of newsletters; archives and records. **Subscriptions:** 89 journals and other serials. **Services:** Interlibrary loans (limited); copying; library open to public by special arrangement.

★6836★
LAS VEGAS REVIEW-JOURNAL - LIBRARY (Publ)
Box 70   Phone: (702) 383-0269
Las Vegas, NV 89125   Glenda Harris, Lbn.
Founded: 1960. **Staff:** Prof 1; Other 1. **Subjects:** Nevada history, current history. **Holdings:** 115 bound periodical volumes; microfilm of newspaper from 1905 to present. **Services:** Library not open to public. **Remarks:** Library located at 1111 W. Bonanza, Las Vegas, NV 89106.

LASKER MEMORIAL LIBRARY
See: Temple B'nai Israel

LASKEY (Virginia Davis) LIBRARY
See: Scarritt College for Christian Workers - Virginia Davis Laskey Library

LASSITER LIBRARY
See: Mint Museum of History

★6837★
LATAH COUNTY HISTORICAL SOCIETY - LIBRARY (Hist)
110 S. Adams   Phone: (208) 882-1004
Moscow, ID 83843   Kit Freudenberg, Dir.
Founded: 1968. **Staff:** Prof 2. **Subjects:** Local history. **Special Collections:** Oral history collection (700 hours of tape, 150 transcripts); technical library on historic preservation (100 volumes). **Holdings:** 350 books; 300 feet of boxes of manuscripts; 16 boxes of pamphlets; 4 reels of microfilm; 1 file drawer of clippings and ephemera; 4000 photographs. **Subscriptions:** 15 journals and other serials. **Services:** Copying; library open to public. **Publications:** Guide to The Latah County, Idaho, Oral History Collection by Sam Schrager (book); Guide to the Local History Library at the Latah County Historical Society by Keith Petersen (book); Guide to Historical & Genealogical Records in Latah County, Idaho by Nancy Luebbert, Bette Meyer and Keith Petersen. **Staff:** Karen Broenneke, Cur.

★6838★
LATHAM & WATKINS - LAW LIBRARY (Law)
555 S. Flower St.   Phone: (213) 485-1234
Los Angeles, CA 90071   Marie G. Wallace, Law Lbn.
Founded: 1962. **Staff:** Prof 3; Other 2. **Subjects:** Law. **Holdings:** 25,000 volumes; microforms. **Subscriptions:** 250 journals and other serials; 7 newspapers. **Services:** Interlibrary loans; library not open to public. **Computerized Information Services:** LEXIS, New York Times Information Service. **Publications:** Library Bulletin, monthly.

★6839★
LATHROP, KOONTZ, RIGHTER, CLAGETT & NORQUIST - LIBRARY (Law)
2600 Mutual Benefit Life Bldg.
2345 Grand Ave.   Phone: (816) 842-0820
Kansas City, MO 64108   Mary Ann Leahy, Libn.
Founded: 1890. **Staff:** Prof 1. **Subjects:** Law - corporate, real estate, tax, Securities and Exchange Commission, banking. **Holdings:** 15,000 volumes. **Subscriptions:** 10 journals and other serials. **Services:** Library not open to public.

★6840★
LATHROP (Norman) ENTERPRISES - LIBRARY (Publ; Rec)
2342 Star Dr.
Box 198   Phone: (216) 262-5587
Wooster, OH 44691   Mary Lou Lathrop, Mgr.
Staff: Prof 1; Other 1. **Subjects:** Newspaper and periodical indexing, arts and crafts. **Holdings:** 99 periodical titles in craft, hobby and model making; 5 VF drawers of descriptive information and samples of over 500 North American newspaper indexes. **Subscriptions:** 103 journals and other serials. **Services:** Copying; library not open to public. **Publications:** Lathrop Reports on Newspaper Indexing. **Special Indexes:** Index to How to do it Information, 1963 to present.

LATHROPE HEALTH SCIENCES LIBRARY
See: Morristown Memorial Hospital

★6841★
LATROBE AREA HOSPITAL - MEDICAL & NURSING LIBRARIES (Med)
W. Second Ave.   Phone: (412) 537-1275
Latrobe, PA 15650   Marsha E. Gelman, Med.Libn.
Staff: Prof 1; Other 1. **Subjects:** Medicine, nursing, medical technology. **Holdings:** 1600 books; 420 bound periodical volumes; 12 VF drawers of pamphlets and clippings; 2 VF drawers of Patient Education materials. **Subscriptions:** 147 journals and other serials. **Services:** Interlibrary loans; copying; library open to public with permission. **Computerized Information Services:** MEDLINE, BRS; computerized cataloging. **Networks/Consortia:** Member of Southeast Pittsburgh Consortium. **Publications:** Library Newsletter, monthly; Current Contents of Journals, monthly - distributed to health professionals.

LATTIN (Berton) MEMORIAL MEDICAL LIBRARY
See: White Plains Hospital - Berton Lattin Memorial Medical Library

★6842★
LAUBACH LITERACY INTERNATIONAL, INC. - LIBRARY (Educ)
1320 Jamesville Ave.
Box 131   Phone: (315) 422-9121
Syracuse, NY 13210   Jenny L. Ryan, Libn.
Founded: 1959. **Staff:** Prof 1. **Subjects:** Adult literacy education, English as a second language. **Special Collections:** International simplified reading materials of historical value for adult new readers (141 languages); books for new readers developed by U.S. literacy programs (412 items); resource material for volunteer tutors (810 items); writings of Frank C. Laubach (101 volumes and 2 VF drawers). **Holdings:** 4639 books; 24 VF drawers of pamphlets, unbound reports, clippings, dissertations and other documents; 50 slide/tape sets; 4 video cassettes. **Subscriptions:** 98 journals and other serials; 128 local U.S. literacy group newsletters. **Services:** Interlibrary loans; copying (limited); library open to public with interest in adult literacy. **Special Indexes:** Catalog of the LLA Collection (resources for U.S. volunteer tutors); Index of the Laubach Collection at Bird Library, Syracuse University (book). **Remarks:** Includes collections of the Laubach Literacy Action and New Readers Press; Frank C. Laubach Collection housed at Bird Library, Syracuse University.

LAUGHLIN AIR FORCE BASE (TX)
See: U.S. Air Force Base - Laughlin Base Library

LAUGHLIN (Matthew) MEMORIAL LIBRARY
See: Chicago Academy of Sciences - Matthew Laughlin Memorial Library

LAUGHLIN OSTEOPATHIC HOSPITAL
See: Kirksville College of Osteopathic Medicine

LAUINGER MEMORIAL LIBRARY
See: Georgetown University - Special Collection Division

★6843★
LAUREL GROVE HOSPITAL - MEDICAL & DENTAL STAFF LIBRARY (Med)†
19933 Lake Chabot Rd.
Castro Valley, CA 94546   Phone: (415) 538-6464
                                         Marie Culwell, Staff Sec.
Subjects: Medicine and surgery. **Holdings:** 125 books. **Subscriptions:** 10 journals and other serials. **Services:** Interlibrary loans; copying; library not open to public.

★6844★
LAURELTON CENTER - LIBRARY (Med)
                                         Phone: (717) 922-3311
Laurelton, PA 17835   Jane G. Slack, Libn.
Founded: 1913. **Staff:** Prof 1. **Subjects:** Mental retardation, psychology, special education, social service. **Holdings:** 4825 volumes. **Subscriptions:** 76 journals and other serials. **Services:** Interlibrary loans; copying; library not open to public.

★6845★
LAUREN ROGERS LIBRARY AND MUSEUM OF ART (Art; Hist)
5th Ave. at 7th St.   Phone: (601) 428-4875
Laurel, MS 39440   Betty Mulloy, Libn.
Founded: 1922. **Staff:** Prof 1; Other 1. **Subjects:** Fine arts, genealogy, Mississippiana. **Holdings:** 15,620 books; 1185 bound periodical volumes. **Subscriptions:** 87 journals and other serials. **Services:** Interlibrary loans; copying; library open to public. **Remarks:** Maintained by the Eastman Memorial Foundation.

LAURENTIAN FOREST RESEARCH CENTRE
See: Canada - Canadian Forestry Service

★6846★
LAURENTIAN HOSPITAL - MEDICAL LIBRARY (Med)
41 Ramsey Lake Rd.   Phone: (705) 522-2200
Sudbury, ON, Canada P3E 5J1   Simone Hamilton, Supv.
Staff: 1. **Subjects:** Medicine and allied health sciences. **Holdings:** 1000 books; 4500 bound periodical volumes; 185 cassettes. **Subscriptions:** 90 journals and other serials. **Services:** Interlibrary loans; copying; library open to public with restrictions.

★6847★
LAURENTIAN UNIVERSITY - MAIN LIBRARY (Soc Sci; Hum)
Ramsey Lake Rd.   Phone: (705) 675-1151
Sudbury, ON, Canada P3E 2C6   Andrzej H. Mrozewski, Chf.Libn.
Founded: 1960. **Staff:** Prof 9; Other 32. **Subjects:** Social sciences, humanities, social work, psychology, nursing, business and commerce, Native Studies (Canadian Indians). **Special Collections:** Finnish Studies (5000 volumes); Estonian Studies (1500 volumes); Northeastern Ontario Collection (1000 volumes); Northeastern Ontario Labor-Industrial Archives (NOLIA). **Holdings:** 313,555 books and bound periodical volumes; 9000 maps; 283,077 public documents; 11,591 reels of microfilm; 51,330 microfiche and microcards; 1931 filmstrips; 8000 slides; 639 transparencies; 663 tapes. **Subscriptions:** 2505 journals and other serials. **Services:** Interlibrary loans; copying; SDI; library open to public. **Computerized Information Services:** Infomart, DIALOG; computerized cataloging. **Networks/Consortia:** Member of UTLAS Inc. **Staff:** Glen Kelly, Hd., Acq.; Chuck Wong, Cat.; Eileen Goltz, Hd., Pub.Docs.; Annette Bradley, Hd., Ser.; Suvakorn Vongpaisal, Ref. & Circ.; Ronald Slater, Cat.; Ashley Thomson, Hd., Ref. & Circ.

★6848★
LAURENTIAN UNIVERSITY - SCHOOL OF EDUCATION - LIBRARY (Educ)
Ramsey Lake Rd.   Phone: (705) 675-1151
Sudbury, ON, Canada P3E 2C6   Lionel Bonin, Libn.
Founded: 1963. **Staff:** Prof 1; Other 1. **Subjects:** Education and educational psychology. **Holdings:** 20,700 books; 390 bound periodical volumes; 908 filmstrips; 442 slide sets; 300 reels of microfilm; 2500 microfiche; 367 phonograph records; 282 cassettes; 10,053 slides; 568 transparencies. **Subscriptions:** 137 journals and other serials. **Services:** Interlibrary loans; copying; library open to public. **Computerized Information Services:** Computerized cataloging. **Networks/Consortia:** Member of UTLAS Inc.

★6849★
LAURENTIAN UNIVERSITY - SCIENCE AND ENGINEERING LIBRARY (Sci-Tech)
Ramsey Lake Rd.   Phone: (705) 675-1151
Sudbury, ON, Canada P3E 2C6   Robert M. Wilson, Sci. & Engr.Libn.
Founded: 1965. **Staff:** Prof 1; Other 3. **Subjects:** Geology, chemistry, biology, physics, mathematics, astronomy, engineering, computer science. **Special Collections:** C.I.M.M. Collection (an extensive collection of Canadian and American mining and metallurgical books, periodicals and technical

reports); Snyder Collection (ornithology); Gardner Northern Collection (an extensive collection on the Arctic and Subarctic; 2400 monographs; 75 subscriptions; 1500 maps and photographs; extensive biological and mineralogical specimens; herbarium; 65,000 clippings). **Holdings:** 15,535 books; 15,350 bound periodical volumes; 1670 bound abstracts and indexes; government documents (mainly mining and metallurgical); 95 videotapes. **Subscriptions:** 760 journals and other serials. **Services:** Interlibrary loans; copying; SDI; library open to public on payment of registration fee. **Computerized Information Services:** Infomart, DIALOG; computerized cataloging. **Networks/Consortia:** Member of UTLAS, Inc. **Remarks:** Contains the holdings of the Universite du Quebec a Montreal - Arctic and Subarctic Research Services - Library.

★6850★
LA LAURENTIENNE COMPAGNIE D'ASSURANCES GENERALES - LIBRARY (Bus-Fin)†
425 St-Amable   Phone: (418) 647-5151
Quebec, PQ, Canada G1K 7X5   Louise de Bellefeville, Tech.Libn.
Staff: Prof 1; Other 1. **Subjects:** Insurance, management, psychology, business, administration. **Holdings:** 5000 books; 180 bound periodical volumes. **Subscriptions:** 170 journals and other serials; 8 newspapers. **Services:** Interlibrary loans (fee); copying; library open to public with restrictions. **Networks/Consortia:** Member of ASTED. **Publications:** Biblio - for internal distribution only.

LAURIER (Wilfrid) UNIVERSITY
See: Wilfrid Laurier University

LAURITSEN (Charles C.) LIBRARY
See: Aerospace Corporation - Charles C. Lauritsen Library

LAUTERMAN LIBRARY OF ART
See: Mc Gill University - Blackader Library of Architecture/Lauterman Library of Art

★6851★
LAUTZE & LAUTZE ACCOUNTANCY CORPORATION - RESOURCES DEVELOPMENT CENTER (Bus-Fin)
100 Pine St.   Phone: (415) 362-1970
San Francisco, CA 94111   Linda Marion Feingold, Sr.Cons., Info.
Founded: 1979. **Staff:** Prof 1; Other 1. **Subjects:** Accounting and auditing, organization development, taxation. **Holdings:** 1860 books and bound periodical volumes; 1000 professional development brochures and course materials. **Subscriptions:** 38 journals and other serials. **Services:** Interlibrary loans; copying; SDI; center open to public with fee for services. **Computerized Information Services:** Online systems. **Publications:** Information Resources Guide; Staff Guide; other manuals and publications - all for sale.

LAVA BEDS NATL. MONUMENT
See: U.S. Natl. Park Service

LAVAL UNIVERSITY
See: Universite Laval

LAVOISIER LIBRARY
See: Du Pont de Nemours (E.I.) & Company, Inc.

★6852★
LAW LIBRARY ASSOCIATION OF ST. LOUIS (Law)
1300 Civil Courts Bldg.   Phone: (314) 622-4386
St. Louis, MO 63101   Rosa Gahn Wright, Libn.
Founded: 1838. **Staff:** Prof 1; Other 6. **Subjects:** Law. **Holdings:** 80,637 volumes. **Subscriptions:** 180 journals and other serials. **Services:** Library not open to public.

LAW LIBRARY IN BROOKLYN
See: New York State Supreme Court - 2nd Judicial District - Law Library

★6853★
LAW LIBRARY OF LOUISIANA (Law)
100 Supreme Court Bldg.
301 Loyola Ave.   Phone: (504) 568-5705
New Orleans, LA 70112   Carol D. Billings, Dir.
Staff: Prof 4; Other 4. **Subjects:** Law. **Holdings:** 115,000 volumes. **Services:** Interlibrary loans; copying; library open to public. **Computerized Information Services:** Computerized cataloging. **Networks/Consortia:** Member of OCLC through SOLINET. **Staff:** Patsy Brautigam, Ref.Libn.; Sarah Churney, Cat.; Betty Kern, Acq. & Ser.

LAW REFORM COMMISSION OF CANADA
See: Canada - Law Reform Commission of Canada

★6854★
LAW SOCIETY OF ALBERTA - CALGARY LIBRARY (Law)
Court House
611 4th St., S.W.   Phone: (403) 261-6148
Calgary, AB, Canada T2P 1T5   Melody M. Hainsworth, Libn.
Founded: 1910. **Staff:** Prof 1; Other 4. **Subjects:** Law. **Holdings:** 47,300 volumes; 2 VF drawers of pamphlets; 2 cabinets of unreported Alberta judgements. **Subscriptions:** 650 journals and other serials. **Services:** Interlibrary loans; copying; library open to public for reference use only. **Computerized Information Services:** QL Systems. **Special Indexes:** Index and Biographies of all Alberta Federally Appointed Judiciary (book; card). **Special Catalogs:** Energy Law Sources (book). **Remarks:** Housed with the Alberta Department of the Attorney General - Judges' Law Library.

★6855★
LAW SOCIETY OF ALBERTA - EDMONTON LIBRARY (Law)
Law Courts Bldg., 1A Churchill Sq.   Phone: (403) 423-7601
Edmonton, AB, Canada T5J 0R2   Shih-Sheng Hu, Chf.Prov. Law Libn.
Founded: 1908. **Staff:** Prof 2; Other 5. **Subjects:** Law. **Holdings:** 41,000 volumes; reports, statutes, government documents. **Subscriptions:** 300 journals and other serials. **Services:** Library open to public for reference use only. **Remarks:** Branch of the Alberta Department of the Attorney General. Housed with the Judges' Law Library.

★6856★
LAW SOCIETY OF MANITOBA - LIBRARY (Law)†
Law Courts Bldg.
Broadway & Kennedy   Phone: (204) 943-5277
Winnipeg, MB, Canada R3C 0V7   Garth Niven, Chf.Libn.
Founded: 1877. **Staff:** Prof 1; Other 2. **Subjects:** Law. **Holdings:** 30,000 volumes. **Subscriptions:** 70 journals and other serials. **Services:** Library not open to public.

★6857★
LAW SOCIETY OF NEWFOUNDLAND - LIBRARY (Law)
Court House, Duckworth St.
P.O. Box 1028   Phone: (709) 753-7770
St. John's, NF, Canada A1C 5M3   Suzanna P. Duke, Libn.
Founded: 1836. **Staff:** Prof 1; Other 1. **Subjects:** Law. **Holdings:** 10,000 volumes. **Subscriptions:** 110 journals and other serials. **Services:** Copying; library not open to public.

★6858★
LAW SOCIETY OF SASKATCHEWAN - BARRISTERS LIBRARY (Law)
Court House
520 Spadina Crescent, E.   Phone: (306) 664-5141
Saskatoon, SK, Canada S7K 3G7   Peta Bates, Libn.
Staff: Prof 1; Other 1. **Subjects:** Law. **Holdings:** 12,000 books; 150 bound periodical volumes. **Services:** Interlibrary loans; copying; SDI; library open to public with librarian's permission. **Computerized Information Services:** QL Systems; computerized serials control. **Special Indexes:** Computer search index; Saskatchewan regulation index.

★6859★
LAW SOCIETY OF SASKATCHEWAN - LIBRARY (Law)
2425 Victoria Ave.
P.O. Box 5032   Phone: (306) 569-8020
Regina, SK, Canada S4P 3M3   Douglass T. MacEllven, Dir.
Founded: 1907. **Staff:** Prof 3; Other 6. **Subjects:** Law. **Holdings:** 20,000 volumes. **Services:** Interlibrary loans; copying; reference assistance provided to public libraries. **Computerized Information Services:** QL Systems, Info Globe, WESTLAW; SASKLAW (internal database); computerized acquisitions and circulation. **Publications:** Law Society of Saskatchewan Practitioners' Journal, quarterly - distributed to lawyers in Canada and some libraires; This Week's Law - online and by subscription. **Remarks:** The Law Society of Saskatchewan maintains branches in the courthouses of Saskatoon, Moose Jaw, Prince Albert, Battleford, Estevan, Yorkton, Swift Current, Melville, Melfort, Weyburn, Humboldt, Lloydminster, Kerrobert, Meadow Lake, La Ronge, Wynyard, Gravelbourg, Assiniboia, Moosomin, Shaunavon and Nipawin, SK.

★6860★
LAW SOCIETY OF UPPER CANADA - GREAT LIBRARY (Law)
Osgoode Hall, 130 Queen St., W.   Phone: (416) 362-5811
Toronto, ON, Canada M5H 2N6   Glen W. Howell, Chf.Libn.
Founded: 1827. **Staff:** Prof 7; Other 16. **Subjects:** Law, legislation and

reports (Canadian, British, Commonwealth and American). **Special Collections:** Riddell Collection of Canadiana (6000 volumes). **Holdings:** 140,000 books and bound periodical volumes; 4000 government documents; 1500 rare books. **Subscriptions:** 500 journals and other serials. **Services:** Interlibrary loans (limited); copying; research assistance for lawyers; library open to public for research only, by arrangement with chief librarian. **Publications:** Special One-day Programme - Developing and Using Law Libraries (new edition in progress); Working Library List for County and District Law Libraries, annually from 1971; Acquisition List, 9/year. **Special Indexes:** Index to Applications Disposed of by the Ontario Municipal Board and the Land Compensation Board; Index to Summaries of Reasons for Judgment, Ontario Court of Appeals, 11/year with annual cumulation, publication for sale suspended February, 1977; up-to-date and available for use in library; Index to Private Bills, Canada and Ontario, 1916 to present (to be published).

★6861★

LAWLER, FELIX & HALL - LAW LIBRARY (Law)
700 S. Flower St.   Phone: (213) 629-9513
Los Angeles, CA 90017   Frank Houdek, Libn.
Staff: Prof 2; Other 2. **Subjects:** Law. **Holdings:** 28,000 books. **Subscriptions:** 50 journals and other serials. **Services:** Library not open to public. **Computerized Information Services:** LEXIS, New York Times Information Service. **Staff:** Nancy Brundige, Asst.Libn.

★6862★

LAWLER MATUSKY & SKELLY ENGINEERS - LIBRARY (Env-Cons)
One Blue Hill Plaza   Phone: (914) 735-8300
Pearl River, NY 10965   Katharine S. Thomas, Info.Sci.
Staff: Prof 1; Other 1. **Subjects:** Environment, water supply, wastewater treatment, ecology, aquatic biology, limnology. **Special Collections:** LMSE reports (650). **Holdings:** 3500 books; 9000 cataloged items; 30,000 documents on microfiche; 82 reels of microfilm; 4 VF drawers of clippings. **Subscriptions:** 161 journals and other serials. **Services:** Interlibrary loans; copying; library open to public with restrictions. **Computerized Information Services:** DIALOG, SDC, NIH-EPA Chemical Information System. **Special Indexes:** LMSE Reports Index (card).

★6863★

LAWRENCE BERKELEY LABORATORY - GEOTHERMAL RESOURCE AREAS DATABASE (Sci-Tech)
University of California, Bldg. 90H   Phone: (415) 486-4294
Berkeley, CA 94720   Winifred Yen, Prin. Investigator
Staff: Prof 2; Other 2. **Subjects:** Geothermal development. **Holdings:** 15 books; 700 laboratory technical reports; unbound journals; 20 files of computer tapes and files. **Services:** Center not open to public. **Computerized Information Services:** Internal database. **Staff:** J. Dennis Lawrence, Prin. Investigator.

★6864★

LAWRENCE BERKELEY LABORATORY - LIBRARY (Sci-Tech; Energy)
University of California
Bldg. 50B, Rm. 4206   Phone: (415) 486-4626
Berkeley, CA 94720   Gloria Haire, Hd.Libn.
Founded: 1946. **Staff:** Prof 14; Other 8. **Subjects:** Energy, environment, nuclear physics, nuclear chemistry, electronics, mathematics, computing, biology, medicine, biochemistry, materials, mechanical engineering. **Holdings:** 52,700 books; 15,315 bound periodical volumes; 80,000 titles of unbound reports. **Subscriptions:** 1500 journals and other serials. **Services:** Interlibrary loans; SDI; library not open to public. **Computerized Information Services:** DIALOG, SDC, BRS, MEDLINE, New York Times Information Service, DOE/RECON, NASA/RECON, SPIRES; computerized cataloging, acquisitions and serials. **Publications:** Berkeley New Titles, monthly - for internal distribution only; Energinfo Newsletter, monthly - to DOE/RECON users. **Remarks:** The Lawrence Berkeley Laboratory operates under contract to the U.S. Department of Energy. **Staff:** Maria Feder, Tech. Processes; Dorothy Denney, Biomed.Libn.; Josephine Robinson, Hd., Info. & Res.; John Rollefson, Acq.Libn.; Richard Robinson, Ref.Libn.; Carol Backhus, Engr.Libn.; Dennis Lawrence, Prin. Investigator.

LAWRENCE (Carl G.) LIBRARY
See: **University of South Dakota, Springfield - Carl G. Lawrence Library**

LAWRENCE (Cyrus J.), INC.
See: **Cyrus J. Lawrence, Inc.**

★6865★

LAWRENCE EAGLE TRIBUNE - LIBRARY (Publ)
Box 100   Phone: (617) 685-1000
Lawrence, MA 01842   Cheryl Lynch, Libn.
Staff: Prof 1; Other 1. **Subjects:** Newspaper reference topics. **Holdings:** 100 books; the newspaper on microfilm; 40,000 clipping files. **Services:** Copying; library open to public with permission of librarian; telephone requests are accepted.

★6866★

LAWRENCE GENERAL HOSPITAL - HEALTH SCIENCE LIBRARY (Med)
One General Street   Phone: (617) 683-4000
Lawrence, MA 01842   Carmel M. Gram, Dir. of Lib.Serv.
Staff: Prof 1; Other 2. **Subjects:** Clinical medicine, nursing. **Holdings:** 1500 books; 156 bound periodical volumes. **Subscriptions:** 156 journals and other serials. **Services:** Interlibrary loans; copying; SDI; library open to public with permission. **Computerized Information Services:** MEDLINE. **Networks/Consortia:** Member of Northeast Consortium for Health Information.

★6867★

LAWRENCE HOSPITAL - ASHLEY BAKER MORRILL LIBRARY (Med)
   Phone: (914) 337-7300
Bronxville, NY 10708   Judith M. Topper, Med.Libn.
Staff: Prof 1; Other 1. **Subjects:** Medicine, nursing, hospital administration. **Special Collections:** Health information for laymen. **Holdings:** 6500 volumes; 9 VF drawers. **Subscriptions:** 180 journals and other serials. **Services:** Interlibrary loans; copying; library open to public. **Computerized Information Services:** MEDLINE. **Networks/Consortia:** Member of Health Information Libraries of Westchester.

★6868★

LAWRENCE LAW LIBRARY (Law)
Superior Court House
Appleton Way   Phone: (617) 687-7608
Lawrence, MA 01840   Natalie C. Ballard, Libn.
Staff: 1. **Subjects:** Law. **Holdings:** 28,000 books; 15 bound periodical volumes. **Subscriptions:** 15 journals and other serials. **Services:** Interlibrary loans; copying; library open to public. **Remarks:** This library is maintained by the Commonwealth of Massachusetts.

★6869★

LAWRENCE LIVERMORE NATIONAL LABORATORY - TECHNICAL INFORMATION DEPARTMENT LIBRARY (Sci-Tech; Energy)
Box 808   Phone: (415) 422-5277
Livermore, CA 94550   John B. Verity, Lib.Mgr.
Staff: Prof 15; Other 32. **Subjects:** Nuclear science, physics, chemistry, mathematics, electronics, engineering, biology, medicine, materials, energy. **Holdings:** 58,000 books; 112,000 bound periodical volumes; 236,000 technical reports (cataloged); 480,000 microfiche. **Subscriptions:** 6800 journals and other serials. **Services:** Interlibrary loans; SDI; library not open to public. **Computerized Information Services:** DIALOG, SDC, MEDLINE, RLIN, New York Times Information Service, BRS, TECHNET, Source Telecomputing Corporation, CAS Online, DARC/QUESTEL, Institute for Scientific Information; computerized cataloging, acquisitions and serials. **Publications:** New Titles: technical reports, books, journals, translations, biweekly; literature searches and bibliographies occasionally published as part of UCRL series of reports. **Remarks:** The Lawrence Livermore National Laboratory operates under contract to the U.S. Department of Energy. **Staff:** Marie Cushing, Hd., Branches; Berta Keizur, Hd., Info.Proc.; H. Leonard Fisher, Hd., Res.Info. Group; Barbara Ingram, Hd., Circ.; Robert Lormand, Staff Asst., Lib.Oper.

★6870★

LAWRENCE MEMORIAL HOSPITAL OF MEDFORD - HEALTH SCIENCES LIBRARY (Med)
170 Governors Ave.   Phone: (617) 396-9250
Medford, MA 02155   Elaine V. LeGendre, Health Sci.Libn.
Staff: Prof 1. **Subjects:** Nursing, medicine, hospital administration. **Special Collections:** Helene Fuld Audio-Visual Center. **Holdings:** 4000 books; 600 bound periodical volumes; 550 filmstrip cassettes and videotapes; 200 subject pamphlet file; 450 paperbacks. **Subscriptions:** 114 journals and other serials. **Services:** Interlibrary loans; copying; library open to public with restrictions. **Computerized Information Services:** BRS available through Tufts University for a fee. **Networks/Consortia:** Member of Northeastern Consortium for Health Information (NECHI).

LAWRENCE (Walter) MEMORIAL LIBRARY
See: **West Suburban Hospital - Walter Lawrence Memorial Library**

★6871★
LAWRY'S FOODS, INC. - LIBRARY (Food-Bev)
570 West Ave. 26   Phone: (213) 225-2491
Los Angeles, CA 90065   Susan Newcomer, Corp.Libn.
Staff: Prof 1. **Subjects:** Food science, microbiology, chemistry, cookbooks. **Special Collections:** Photographic archives. **Holdings:** Figures not available for books; films and clipping files. **Services:** Interlibrary loans; copying; SDI; library not open to public.

LAWSON INDIAN LIBRARY
See: Southwestern Art Association - Philbrook Art Center - Library

LAWSON (Victor E.) RESEARCH LIBRARY
See: Kandiyohi County Historical Society - Victor E. Lawson Research Library

LAWTON (George) MEMORIAL LIBRARY
See: National Psychological Association for Psychoanalysis - George Lawton Memorial Library

★6872★
LAWYERS' JOINT LAW LIBRARY (Law)
3930 IDS Tower   Phone: (612) 338-4320
Minneapolis, MN 55402   Barbara E. Schmidt, Libn.
Staff: Prof 1; Other 2. **Subjects:** Law. **Holdings:** 20,600 books; 400 bound periodical volumes; 4 VF drawers of pamphlets; 4 plat books of maps. **Subscriptions:** 39 journals and other serials; 7 newspapers. **Services:** Copying (limited); library not open to public. **Publications:** Library Guide; Lawyers' Joint Law Library Newsletter, irregular.

★6873★
LAZARD FRERES AND COMPANY - FINANCIAL LIBRARY (Bus-Fin)
One Rockefeller Plaza   Phone: (212) 489-6600
New York, NY 10020   Anne Mintz, Libn.
Staff: Prof 1; Other 4. **Subjects:** Finance, investment, corporate records. **Holdings:** 500 books and bound periodical volumes; 15,000 microfiche; 400 VF drawers. **Subscriptions:** 600 journals and other serials. **Services:** Library open to Special Libraries Association members only. **Computerized Information Services:** DIALOG, SDC, Dow Jones News Retrieval, New York Times Information Service, Spectrum Data Base, COMPUSTAT Services, Inc.

LAZARO (Jose M.) MEMORIAL LIBRARY
See: University of Puerto Rico - General Library

LAZRUS (Paula K.) LIBRARY OF INTERGROUP RELATIONS
See: National Conference of Christians and Jews - Paula K. Lazrus Library of Intergroup Relations

★6874★
LE BEACON PRESSE - SMALL PRESS COLLECTION (Publ)
2921 E. Madison St., Suite 7   Phone: (206) 322-1431
Seattle, WA 98112-4237   Keith S. Gormezano, Dir./Coord.
Founded: 1979. **Staff:** Prof 1; Other 2. **Subjects:** Small press publications. **Holdings:** 900 books; 50 bound periodical volumes; 10 files of miscellaneous materials; 2 VF drawers. **Subscriptions:** 35 journals and other serials. **Services:** Interlibrary loans; library open to public with restrictions. **Publications:** Le Beacon Review, quarterly - by subscription. **Formerly:** Located in Iowa City, IA.

★6875★
LE BONHEUR CHILDREN'S MEDICAL CENTER - HEALTH SCIENCES LIBRARY (Med)
One Children's Plaza   Phone: (901) 522-3167
Memphis, TN 38103   Jan Hawkins, Libn.
Staff: Prof 1. **Subjects:** Pediatrics. **Holdings:** 1128 books; 1418 bound periodical volumes; 1 shelf of faculty reprints; 2 shelves of patient education materials. **Subscriptions:** 138 journals and other serials. **Services:** Interlibrary loans; copying; library open to public. **Networks/Consortia:** Member of Association of Memphis Area Health Sciences Libraries. **Publications:** Guide for Users, bimonthly newsletter - free upon request. **Special Catalogs:** References from Morning Report, Grand Rounds, Nursing Grand Rounds and Journal Club (card).

LE BRUN LIBRARY
See: Montclair Art Museum

★6876★
LE DEVOIR - CENTRE DE DOCUMENTATION (Publ)
211, Rue du St-Sacrement   Phone: (514) 844-3361
Montreal, PQ, Canada H2Y 1X1   Gilles Pare, Libn.
Staff: Prof 1; Other 2. **Subjects:** Politics, economy, social problems. **Holdings:** 2000 books; 150 bound periodical volumes; 5000 files of clippings; 30,500 files of photographs; 200 reels of microfilm. **Subscriptions:** 120 journals and other serials; 30 newspapers. **Services:** Interlibrary loans; copying; centre not open to public.

★6877★
LE DROIT - CENTRE DE DOCUMENTATION (Publ)
375, Rue Rideau   Phone: (613) 237-3050
Ottawa, ON, Canada K1N 5Y7   Alice Mimeault, Documentaliste
Founded: 1971. **Staff:** Prof 1; Other 1. **Subjects:** Local, regional and international news. **Holdings:** 500 books; 100,000 clippings; 15,000 documents; 1000 color slides. **Subscriptions:** 20 journals and other serials; 30 newspapers. **Services:** Copying; centre open to public. **Computerized Information Services:** Computerized cataloging and acquisitions. **Special Catalogs:** Subject catalog for clipping collection and color slides (card).

LE MOYNE HOUSE LIBRARY
See: Washington County Historical and Museum Society

★6878★
LE ROY HISTORICAL SOCIETY - LIBRARY (Hist)
23 E. Main St.
Box 176   Phone: (716) 768-7433
Le Roy, NY 14482   Wesley G. Balla, Dir./Cur.
Founded: 1940. **Staff:** Prof 1. **Subjects:** Local history and genealogy. **Special Collections:** Morganville Pottery; Le Roy Family; Daniel Webster material; Ingham University; works of local artists; Henry Wyckoff papers; Miles P. Lampson papers. **Holdings:** 900 books; 10 bound periodical volumes; 5 VF drawers of reports, clippings and scrapbooks; family photographs; local family manuscripts. **Services:** Interlibrary loans; copying; library open to public on limited schedule. **Publications:** Annual Report.

LE SEURE (Oscar) PROFESSIONAL LIBRARY
See: Harper-Grace Hospitals - Grace Hospital Division - Oscar Le Seure Professional Library

★6879★
LE SUEUR COUNTY HISTORICAL SOCIETY MUSEUM - LIBRARY (Hist)
Box 557   Phone: (507) 267-4620
Elysian, MN 56028   Caroline Roessler, Asst.Cur.
Staff: Prof 2; Other 1. **Subjects:** Local and state histories, county church records, state laws and statistics, county cemetery records, local store ledgers, county tax receipts. **Special Collections:** Books, sketches, and works of artist Adolf Dehn; books, articles, and works of wildlife artist Roger Preuss; articles and works of wildlife artist David Maass; artifacts and works of artist Lloyd Herfendahl; silhouettes and works of artist Earle Swaine. **Holdings:** 1405 volumes; 60 interview tapes of older citizens; 200 reels of microfilmed newspapers; 1 volume of obituary clippings. **Subscriptions:** 5 newspapers. **Services:** Library open to public for reference use only by request and on a limited schedule. **Staff:** Dorothy Hruska, Co-Dir. & Cur.

★6880★
LE TOURNEAU COLLEGE - MARGARET ESTES LIBRARY (Sci-Tech)
Box 7001   Phone: (214) 753-0231
Longview, TX 75607   Rachel Miley, Act.Dir., Lib.Serv.
Founded: 1946. **Staff:** Prof 2; Other 7. **Subjects:** Liberal arts, engineering, technology. **Special Collections:** R.G. LeTourneau Collection; Billy Sunday Collection; Abraham Lincoln Collection; Rare Book Collection. **Holdings:** 77,946 books; 11,872 bound periodical volumes; 54,711 microforms; 2764 AV items; 13,532 clippings and pictures. **Subscriptions:** 358 journals and other serials; 13 newspapers. **Services:** Interlibrary loans; copying; library open to public, deposit required. **Also Known As:** Longview Citizens' Resource Center. **Staff:** Nah Lin Yeh, Hd., Tech.Serv.; Wynona Prince, Supv., Day Circ.; Patricia Olsen, Ser.; Helen Miller, Night Supv.

LEA (Henry Charles) LIBRARY
See: University of Pennsylvania - Henry Charles Lea Library

LEACH (Ann Bates) EYE HOSPITAL
See: University of Miami - School of Medicine - Bascom Palmer Eye Institute

★6881★
LEACOCK (Stephen) MEMORIAL HOME - LIBRARY (Hum)
Old Brewery Bay
P.O. Box 625   Phone: (705) 324-9357
Orillia, ON, Canada L3V 6K5   Jay Cody, Dir./Cur.
Founded: 1957. **Staff:** Prof 1; Other 6. **Subjects:** Stephen Leacock (personal library, correspondence, documents). **Holdings:** 5000 books; 15,000 letters; 311 manuscripts; 500 contemporary review clippings of Leacock's books; 200 documents. **Services:** Copying; research inquiries answered; library open to scholars with credentials for reference use.

LEAGUE AGAINST NUCLEAR DANGERS, INC.
See: LAND, Inc.

★6882★
LEAGUE OF ARAB STATES - ARAB INFORMATION CENTER (Area-Ethnic)†
747 Third Ave.   Phone: (212) 838-8700
New York, NY 10017   Marwan Kanafani, Info.Off.
Staff: Prof 3; Other 2. **Subjects:** Arab countries - political, social and economic conditions. **Special Collections:** Arab League documents (40 file cabinets); U.N. documents (15 file cabinets). **Holdings:** 7000 books; 500 bound periodical volumes; 7 file cabinets of pamphlets and newspaper clippings; 25 films. **Subscriptions:** 200 journals and other serials; 35 newspapers, including 25 current Arabic newspapers. **Services:** Center not open to public. **Publications:** Palestine Digest; Arab Report; booklets and other publications on the 20 Arab countries. **Staff:** Mahmoud Farghal, U.N. Spec.

★6883★
LEAGUE OF ARIZONA CITIES AND TOWNS - LIBRARY (Soc Sci)
1820 W. Washington St.   Phone: (602) 258-5786
Phoenix, AZ 85007   John J. DeBolske, Exec.Dir.
Staff: Prof 7; Other 5. **Subjects:** Municipal government. **Holdings:** Figures not available. **Subscriptions:** 100 journals and other serials; 75 newspapers. **Services:** Interlibrary loans; library not open to public. **Publications:** Legislative Bulletin; various annual publications.

★6884★
LEAGUE FOR INTERNATIONAL FOOD EDUCATION - LIBRARY (Food-Bev; Soc Sci)
915 15th St., N.W., Suite 915   Phone: (202) 331-1658
Washington, DC 20005   Margaret Fowles, Libn.
Staff: 1. **Subjects:** Nutrition, food science and technology, international development programs. **Holdings:** 650 books; 10,000 reprints and reports. **Subscriptions:** 302 journals and other serials. **Services:** Library open to public by appointment. **Publications:** L.I.F.E. Newsletter, monthly - free to people working on food and nutrition problems in developing countries.

★6885★
LEAGUE OF IOWA MUNICIPALITIES - LIBRARY (Soc Sci)
900 Des Moines St., Suite 100   Phone: (515) 265-9961
Des Moines, IA 50316   Robert W. Harpster, Exec.Dir.
Staff: 10. **Subjects:** Municipal government. **Special Collections:** Codes of Iowa cities. **Holdings:** 1150 volumes; 10 VF drawers; informational booklets and fact sheets; model ordinances. **Services:** Copying; library open to public with consent of director. **Special Catalogs:** Listing of municipal officials of Iowa.

★6886★
LEAGUE OF MINNESOTA CITIES - LIBRARY (Law)
183 University Ave., E.   Phone: (612) 227-5600
St. Paul, MN 55101   Peter Tritz, Res.Dir.
Staff: Prof 2; Other 5. **Subjects:** Ordinance codes of many cities, Minnesota Statutes and Session laws, municipal government. **Special Collections:** City charters of all 104 home rule cities. **Holdings:** 1000 books; 300 bound periodical volumes; 600 memorandums (cataloged). **Subscriptions:** 150 journals and other serials; 12 newspapers. **Services:** Interlibrary loans; copying; library open to public with restrictions. **Publications:** Minnesota Cities, monthly - to members and by subscription; Legislative Bulletin, weekly during Session (20 issues); City Handbook, revised annually; Directory of Minnesota City Officials, revised annually; Local and Regional Planning in Minnesota; research memorandums, as needed. **Staff:** Louise Kuderling, Pubn.Mgr.

LEAGUE OF UNITED LATIN AMERICAN CITIZENS - ARCHIVE
See: University of Texas, Austin - Mexican American Library Program

★6887★
LEAGUE FOR YIDDISH - LIBRARY (Area-Ethnic)
200 W. 72nd St.   Phone: (212) 787-6675
New York, NY 10023   Leybl Kahn, Libn.
Subjects: Yiddish culture, Judaica, colonization. **Holdings:** 1500 books; documents and correspondence. **Subscriptions:** 50 journals and other serials. **Formerly:** Yiddish League.

LEAHI HOSPITAL
See: Hawaii State Department of Health - Hastings H. Walker Medical Library

★6888★
LEAR SIEGLER, INC. - ASTRONICS DIVISION - TECHNICAL LIBRARY (Sci-Tech)
3171 S. Bundy Dr.   Phone: (213) 391-7211
Santa Monica, CA 90406   Karen Flanders, Tech.Info.Coord.
Founded: 1981. **Staff:** Prof 1. **Subjects:** Flight control, digital avionics, computer management, electronics. **Holdings:** 400 books; 20 bound periodical volumes; 1000 technical reports. **Subscriptions:** 40 journals and other serials; 5 newspapers. **Services:** Copying; library not open to public. **Computerized Information Services:** DIALOG; computerized cataloging.

★6889★
LEAR SIEGLER, INC. - INSTRUMENT DIVISION - ENGINEERING LIBRARY (Sci-Tech)
4141 Eastern Ave., S.E.   Phone: (616) 241-7467
Grand Rapids, MI 49508   N. Scott Brackett, Tech.Libn.
Founded: 1959. **Staff:** Prof 1; Other 2. **Subjects:** Electronics, electrical engineering, computer technology, aeronautics, aerospace, management. **Holdings:** 6000 books; 1000 bound periodical volumes; 600 microforms; 100,000 specifications and standards; 6000 government technical reports. **Subscriptions:** 300 journals and other serials. **Services:** Interlibrary loans; copying; library open to public by prior arrangement. **Computerized Information Services:** DIALOG, DTIC, NASA/RECON; computerized serials and circulation. **Publications:** Recent Acquisitions Bulletin, monthly - for internal distribution only.

LEARNING CENTER FOR LUNG HEALTH
See: American Lung Association of Hawaii

★6890★
LEARNING INCORPORATED - LIBRARY (Educ)
Learning Place   Phone: (207) 244-5015
Manset-Seawall, ME 04656   A.L. Welles, Dir.
Subjects: Learning handicaps, teaching spelling and reading, teaching those with learning disabilities and dyslexia. **Holdings:** 15,000 volumes. **Services:** Library open to public by appointment. **Publications:** Learning Incorporated Dictionary of Learning Handicaps - for sale.

★6891★
LEARNING RESOURCES NETWORK - PUBLICATIONS AND RESOURCES (Educ; Publ)
1221 Thurston   Phone: (913) 539-5376
Manhattan, KS 66502   William A. Draves, Natl.Coord.
Founded: 1974. **Staff:** Prof 3; Other 1. **Subjects:** Lifelong education, noncredit programming, technical assistance. **Services:** Workshops; national conferences; consulting; memberships. **Publications:** Adult and Continuing Education Today, biweekly newsletter; Resources, monthly newsletter; The Learning Connection, quarterly magazine; Course Trends in Adult Learning, quarterly noncredit course trend analysis. List of additional publications - available on request. **Formerly:** Free University Network. **Staff:** Karen Stevenson, Asst. to Dir.; Lori Bergen, Mng.Ed.

★6892★
LEBANON COUNTY HISTORICAL SOCIETY - LIBRARY (Hist; Area-Ethnic)
924 Cumberland St.   Phone: (717) 272-1473
Lebanon, PA 17042
Founded: 1898. **Staff:** 3. **Subjects:** History of Lebanon County and Pennsylvania, local genealogy, Germans in Pennsylvania. **Special Collections:** Bibles; hymn books; school books; Coleman Collection (housed at the Pennsylvania Historical and Museum Commission). **Holdings:** 2500 books; 1500 pictures, archives and 1000 files (cataloged); 1000 deeds; 700 reels of microfilm. **Subscriptions:** 14 journals and other serials. **Services:** Copying; genealogical searching (fee basis); library open to public with restrictions. **Publications:** Papers of the Lebanon County Historical Society - distributed to members, for sale to others; History of Dauphin and Lebanon Counties (index to Lebanon County included); reprint of 1875 Lebanon County Atlas (index separate). **Special Indexes:** Papers of the Lebanon County Historical Society

(card); 1904 Biographical Annals of Lebanon County (book). **Staff:** Mrs. Weaver, Genealogist; Mrs. Kelley, Asst. Genealogist; William Smith, Asst.Libn.

LEBANON VALLEY COLLEGE - GOSSARD MEMORIAL LIBRARY - EVANGELICAL UNITED BRETHREN CHURCH
See: Evangelical United Brethren Church

★6893★
LEBER KATZ, INC. - MARKETING INFORMATION CENTER LIBRARY (Bus-Fin)
767 Fifth Ave.   Phone: (212) 826-5892
New York, NY 10022   Gretchen Freeman, Mgr., Info.Serv.
Staff: 1. **Subjects:** Advertising, marketing, market research. **Holdings:** Figures not available. **Subscriptions:** 30 journals and other serials. **Services:** Library open to clients only.

★6894★
LEBHAR-FRIEDMAN, INC. - CHAIN STORE AGE - READER SERVICE RESEARCH LIBRARY (Publ)
425 Park Ave.   Phone: (212) 689-4800
New York, NY 10022   Ruth Weselteer, Libn.
Founded: 1948. **Staff:** 1. **Subjects:** Chain stores - retailing, personnel, sales promotion, merchandising methods, store location, construction and equipment, warehousing, public relations, shopping centers, discount houses, home centers, restaurants, drugstores. **Holdings:** 300 books; 200 bound periodical volumes; 1500 pamphlets; 11 VF drawers. **Subscriptions:** 97 journals and other serials. **Services:** Interlibrary loans; copying (both limited); library open to public.

★6895★
LEBOEUF, LAMB, LEIBY & MAC RAE - LIBRARY (Law)
140 Broadway, 31st Fl.   Phone: (212) 269-1100
New York, NY 10005   Ruth V. Mortensen, Libn.
Founded: 1929. **Staff:** Prof 2; Other 5. **Subjects:** Law, public utilities, taxation, energy, insurance, securities, municipal bonds, banking, environment. **Holdings:** 23,000 books; 34 VF drawers. **Subscriptions:** 500 journals and other serials; 10 newspapers. **Services:** Interlibrary loans; copying; library open to clients and other libraries. **Networks/Consortia:** Member of Law Library Association of Greater New York; American Association of Law Libraries. **Staff:** Rita Conway, Asst.Libn.; Suzanne Fuchs, ILL Libn.

LEDERLE LABORATORIES DIVISION
See: American Cyanamid Company

★6896★
LEE COUNTY LAW LIBRARY (Law)
Courthouse   Phone: (813) 335-2230
Fort Myers, FL 33901   Owen Grant, Libn.
Staff: Prof 1. **Subjects:** Law. **Holdings:** 14,000 books. **Services:** Copying; library open to public.

LEE (Jeremiah) MANSION - LIBRARY
See: Marblehead Historical Society - Jeremiah Lee Mansion - Library

LEE (Joseph) MEMORIAL LIBRARY AND INFORMATION CENTER
See: National Recreation and Park Association - Joseph Lee Memorial Library and Information Center

LEE (Lawrence) MEMORIAL LIBRARY
See: National Railway Historical Society - Mohawk and Hudson Chapter - Lawrence Lee Memorial Library

LEE LIBRARY
See: Don Bosco Technical Institute

★6897★
LEE PHARMACEUTICALS - LIBRARY
1444 Santa Anita Ave.
South El Monte, CA 91733
Subjects: Polymer chemistry, biomedical polymers, dentistry. **Holdings:** 2000 books. **Remarks:** Presently inactive.

LEE (Robert E.) MEMORIAL
See: U.S. Natl. Park Service - Arlington House, The Robert E. Lee Memorial

LEE (Robert E.) MEMORIAL ASSOCIATION, INC.
See: Stratford Hall Plantation

LEE SCHOOL MUSEUM
See: Schuyler County Historical Society

★6898★
LEEDS, HILL & JEWETT, INC. - LIBRARY (Sci-Tech)
1275 Market St.   Phone: (415) 626-2070
San Francisco, CA 94103   Gregory B. Sedgwick, Tech.Libn.
Founded: 1968. **Staff:** Prof 1. **Subjects:** Water resources, hydraulics, mining engineering, rock mechanics, environmental sciences, geology. **Special Collections:** U.S. Geological Survey: Water-supply Papers (almost complete series); California Department of Water Resources Bulletins (almost complete series). **Holdings:** 18,000 books; 35 boxes of pamphlets; professional papers, circulars, company reports; miscellaneous standards, specifications; 6 flat files of maps. **Subscriptions:** 72 journals and other serials. **Services:** Interlibrary loans; copying; library open to public on request. **Computerized Information Services:** DIALOG.

★6899★
LEEDS AND NORTHRUP COMPANY - TECHNICAL CENTER LIBRARY (Sci-Tech)
Dickerson Rd.   Phone: (215) 643-2000
North Wales, PA 19454   Adina Zupanick, Mgr., Lib.Serv.
Founded: 1920. **Staff:** Prof 1; Other 1. **Subjects:** Instrumentation and control systems. **Holdings:** 5000 books; 5500 bound periodical volumes; 36 VF drawers of trade catalogs. **Subscriptions:** 200 journals and other serials. **Services:** Interlibrary loans; copying; library open to public by appointment. **Computerized Information Services:** DIALOG, SDC.

★6900★
LEESONA CORPORATION - LIBRARY (Sci-Tech)†
333 Strawberry Field Rd.   Phone: (401) 737-7000
Warwick, RI 02887   Madeline Johansen, Libn.
Founded: 1948. **Staff:** 1. **Subjects:** Engineering, management, machinery design, textiles, corporation law. **Holdings:** 3000 books. **Subscriptions:** 150 journals and other serials. **Services:** Interlibrary loans; copying (both limited); library open to public with restrictions.

★6901★
LEEWARD COMMUNITY COLLEGE LIBRARY - SPECIAL COLLECTIONS (Area-Ethnic)
96-045 Ala Ike   Phone: (808) 455-0210
Honolulu, HI 96782   Muriel Y. King, Lib.Div.Adm.Comm.
Founded: 1968. **Special Collections:** Hawaii/Pacific Collection; government documents (7674). **Services:** Interlibrary loans; copying; library open to public. **Networks/Consortia:** Member of Community College Film Consortium. **Publications:** Student Handbook, annual; Faculty Handbook, annual; Periodical and Newspaper List, annual; Bibliographic Reporter; Current Awareness Paper; Occasional Paper, all irregular.

LEFFINGWELL INN LIBRARY
See: Society of the Founders of Norwich, Connecticut

★6902★
LEGAL AID SOCIETY OF HAWAII - LIBRARY (Law)
1164 Bishop St., Suite 1100   Phone: (808) 536-4302
Honolulu, HI 96813   Thomas P. Churma, Libn.
Staff: Prof 1. **Subjects:** Law, poverty law. **Holdings:** 1500 books; 1600 bound periodical volumes; 125 newspaper clippings. **Subscriptions:** 41 journals and other serials. **Services:** SDI; library open to public for reference use only.

★6903★
LEGAL AID SOCIETY - LIBRARIES (Law)†
15 Park Row   Phone: (212) 577-3333
New York, NY 10038   David Donaldson, Hd.Libn.
Staff: Prof 1. **Subjects:** Law - criminal, civil, juvenile rights. **Holdings:** Figures not available. **Services:** Copying; libraries not open to public. **Remarks:** "The Legal Aid Society has no central library, rather a system of libraries throughout the city in more than 35 offices."

★6904★
LEGAL AID SOCIETY OF WESTCHESTER - LIBRARY (Law)
1 North Broadway   Phone: (914) 682-0250
White Plains, NY 10601   Mina Pease, Dir.
Staff: Prof 2; Other 1. **Subjects:** Law - criminal, matrimonial, administrative. **Holdings:** 4000 books and bound periodical volumes; 10 audio cassettes. **Subscriptions:** 10 journals and other serials; 5 newspapers. **Services:** Copying; library not open to public. **Special Indexes:** Morgue clipping file index (MorClip) - from local newspapers.

★6905★
LEGAL ASSISTANCE FOUNDATION OF CHICAGO - LIBRARY (Law)
343 S. Dearborn   Phone: (312) 341-1070
Chicago, IL 60604   Herbert L. Ho, Law Libn.
Staff: Prof 2. **Subjects:** Welfare law. **Holdings:** 12,000 books; 300 bound periodical volumes; 300 other cataloged items; 200 legal documents. **Subscriptions:** 80 journals and other serials; 6 newspapers. **Services:** Library open to public for reference use only. **Computerized Information Services:** LEXIS. **Networks/Consortia:** Member of ILLINET; Chicago Library System. **Publications:** LAFC Library Bulletin. **Staff:** Freda Davidson, Asst. Law Libn.

★6906★
LEGAL SERVICES OF EASTERN MISSOURI, INC. - LIBRARY (Law)
625 N. Euclid Ave.
Field Sta., Box 4999A
St. Louis, MO 63108   Phone: (314) 367-1700
Staff: Prof 1. **Subjects:** Law - federal and Missouri; poverty law. **Holdings:** 6000 volumes. **Subscriptions:** 90 journals and other serials. **Services:** Interlibrary loans; copying; library open to public with restrictions.

LEGAL SERVICES ORGANIZATION OF INDIANA, INC. - DELAWARE COUNTY OFFICE
See: East Central Legal Services

★6907★
LEGAL SERVICES ORGANIZATION OF INDIANA, INC. - LIBRARY (Law)
222 N.W. 3rd St.   Phone: (812) 426-1295
Evansville, IN 47708   Carol Sanders, Off.Mgr.
Founded: 1978. **Staff:** 1. **Subjects:** Law. **Holdings:** 2509 books; 41 bound periodical volumes. **Subscriptions:** 59 journals and other serials. **Services:** Interlibrary loans; copying; library not open to public. **Networks/Consortia:** Member of Four Rivers Area Library Services Authority.

★6908★
LEGAL SERVICES ORGANIZATION OF INDIANA, INC. - LIBRARY (Law)
107 N. Pennsylvania, Suite 800   Phone: (317) 639-4151
Indianapolis, IN 46204   Sherry Englehart, Libn.
Founded: 1973. **Staff:** Prof 1. **Subjects:** Law - federal, state, welfare, consumer. **Holdings:** 8000 books; 4 VF drawers of periodicals; 6 VF drawers of briefs; 1 VF drawer of hearings, government documents. **Subscriptions:** 67 journals and other serials. **Services:** Library not open to public. **Publications:** You and the Law, annual - free upon request. **Special Catalogs:** Brief bank - file holding internal briefs by attorneys and cataloged by subject, client and author.

LEGISLATIVE ASSEMBLY OF ALBERTA
See: Alberta - Legislative Assembly of Alberta

★6909★
LEHIGH COUNTY HISTORICAL SOCIETY - SCOTT ANDREW TREXLER II MEMORIAL LIBRARY (Hist)
Old Court House
Fifth & Hamilton Sts.
Allentown, PA 18101   Phone: (215) 435-1072
                                         Anna Foster Allen, Libn.
Founded: 1904. **Staff:** Prof 1; Other 1. **Subjects:** Pennsylvania and Lehigh County history, Allentown imprints, native Indians. **Special Collections:** Allentown Newspapers (1810-1916); family genealogies; pictures of Allentown and people. **Holdings:** 6000 books; 200 newspaper volumes; 2000 pamphlets; 35 document boxes of family papers; deeds, maps, manuscripts and church records. **Subscriptions:** 12 journals and other serials. **Services:** Copying; library open to public with payment of fee. **Publications:** Proceedings, biennial.

★6910★
LEHIGH COUNTY LAW LIBRARY (Law)
County Court House
5th & Hamilton Sts.
Box 1548
Allentown, PA 18105   Phone: (215) 820-3308
                                         James L. Weirbach, Esq., Law Libn.
Founded: 1869. **Staff:** Prof 1; Other 1. **Subjects:** Law, Pennsylvania history and statutes. **Holdings:** 28,000 books; 1750 bound periodical volumes; 2 VF drawers of local municipal ordinances; 2 VF drawers of local, historical maps. **Subscriptions:** 60 journals and other serials. **Services:** Interlibrary loans; copying; library open to public. **Computerized Information Services:** LEXIS. **Publications:** Acquisitions list. **Special Indexes:** Wheel-index: subject, author and title (co-ordinate index).

★6911★
LEHIGH-NORTHAMPTON COUNTIES JOINT PLANNING COMMISSION - LIBRARY (Plan)
Allentown-Bethlehem-Easton Airport
Government Bldg.   Phone: (215) 264-4544
Lehigh Valley, PA 18103   Penn Clissold, Libn.
Founded: 1961. **Staff:** 1. **Subjects:** Architecture, engineering and design, census and statistics, economics and finance, governmental legislation, housing, transportation, urban analysis, planning theory, land use, recreation. **Special Collections:** Joint Planning Commission Reports on various municipalities in Lehigh-Northampton Counties; initial housing element, recreation reports. **Holdings:** 2000 volumes; slides, pictures and maps. **Subscriptions:** 25 journals and other serials; 6 newspapers. **Services:** Library open to public for reference use only. **Staff:** Michael N. Kaiser, Exec.Dir.

★6912★
LEHIGH UNIVERSITY - MART SCIENCE AND ENGINEERING LIBRARY (Sci-Tech)
15 East Packer Ave., Bldg. 8   Phone: (215) 861-3075
Bethlehem, PA 18015   Sharon Siegler, Hd., Pub.Serv.
Founded: 1968. **Staff:** Prof 3; Other 8. **Subjects:** Science, engineering, mathematics. **Special Collections:** Wiswesser Line Notation File. **Holdings:** 140,000 volumes; reports, pamphlets, microforms. **Subscriptions:** 2300 journals and other serials. **Services:** Interlibrary loans; copying; library open to public with restrictions. **Computerized Information Services:** DIALOG, SDC, BRS, New York Times Information Service; computerized cataloging, acquisitions, circulation and bibliographic searching. **Staff:** William Jarvis, Asst.Ref.Libn.

★6913★
LEHIGH VALLEY COMMITTEE AGAINST HEALTH FRAUD, INC. - LIBRARY (Soc Sci)
Box 1602   Phone: (215) 437-1795
Allentown, PA 18105   Dr. Stephen Barrett
Staff: 1. **Subjects:** Quackery and health frauds, consumer health, chiropractic, health food industry, consumer protection. **Holdings:** 350 books; 950 unbound magazines and journals; 12 VF drawers of documents and clippings; 75 cassette tapes; 50 reprinted articles. **Subscriptions:** 31 journals and other serials. **Services:** Copying; library open to public with restrictions.

LEHIGH VALLEY TRANSPORTATION RESEARCH CENTER
See: Railways to Yesterday, Inc.

★6914★
LEHMAN BROTHERS, KUHN, LOEB, INC. - LIBRARY (Bus-Fin)
55 Water St.   Phone: (212) 558-2134
New York, NY 10041   Louise Stoops, Chf.Libn.
Founded: 1930. **Staff:** Prof 5; Other 8. **Subjects:** Finance. **Special Collections:** Annual reports. **Holdings:** 1000 volumes; 350 VF drawers of pamphlets, 10K and 10Q reports, 1968 to present. **Subscriptions:** 700 journals and other serials; 20 newspapers. **Services:** Interlibrary loans; copying; library not open to public. **Computerized Information Services:** DIALOG, New York Times Information Service, Dow Jones News Retrieval, Mead Data Central; computerized serials and circulation. **Staff:** Louise Gent-Sandford, Libn.; Norman Clemens, Libn.; Harriet Wisner, Libn.; Martha Keller, Libn.

LEHMAN (Ezra) MEMORIAL LIBRARY
See: Shippensburg State College - Ezra Lehman Memorial Library

LEHMAN (Herbert H.) LIBRARY
See: Columbia University - Herbert H. Lehman Library

LEHMAN (Mme. Lotte) ARCHIVE
See: University of California, Santa Barbara - Department of Special Collections

LEHMAN (Robert) COLLECTION
See: Metropolitan Museum of Art - Robert Lehman Collection

LEHMAN (S.A.) MEMORIAL LIBRARY
See: Fort Wayne Bible College - S.A. Lehman Memorial Library

★6915★
LEHN & FINK PRODUCTS GROUP - LIBRARY (Sci-Tech)
225 Summit Ave.   Phone: (201) 573-5339
Montvale, NJ 07645   Eileen M. Matthews, Libn.
Staff: Prof 1. **Subjects:** Business management, cosmetics, dermatology, microbiology, detergents, disinfectants, floor waxes. **Holdings:** 1000 books;

600 bound periodical volumes; 1 VF drawer of annual reports; 1 VF drawer of patents; 8 VF drawers of pamphlets, articles; 100 reels of microfilm. **Subscriptions:** 177 journals and other serials. **Services:** Interlibrary loans; copying; library open to public with restrictions. **Computerized Information Services:** DIALOG, SDC. **Remarks:** Company is a division of Sterling Drug, Inc.

★6916★
LEIBIGER (O.W.) RESEARCH LABORATORIES, INC. - TECHNICAL INFORMATION CENTER (Sci-Tech)*
48 Classic St.
Box 10
Hoosick Falls, NY 12090   I. Leibiger, Hd.
Founded: 1936. **Staff:** Prof 4; Other 3. **Subjects:** Atomic physics, space aeronautics, nuclear physics, chemistry, electronic engineering, computers, medicine. **Holdings:** 2800 books; 150 bound periodical volumes; 800 translations; 500 unbound foreign scientific documents. **Subscriptions:** 27 journals and other serials. **Services:** Translating; literature searches; evaluation of foreign documents; abstracting; library not open to public.

★6917★
LEIGH INSTRUMENTS, LTD. - ENGINEERING & AEROSPACE DIVISION - TECHNICAL LIBRARY (Sci-Tech)
P.O. Box 82   Phone: (613) 257-3883
Carleton Place, ON, Canada K7C 3P3   Betty G. Robertson, Info.Sec.
Founded: 1965. **Staff:** Prof 1; Other 1. **Subjects:** Electronics, aeronautics, aerodynamics, quality control, management, plastics. **Holdings:** 850 books and bound periodical volumes; 1900 Leigh technical publications; 40 VF drawers of research papers and technical articles; 65 VF drawers and 21 shelving feet of military and commercial specifications and standards; 32 VF drawers and 69 shelving feet of suppliers' catalogs; 463 NTIS microfiche documents. **Subscriptions:** 138 journals and other serials. **Services:** Interlibrary loans; copying; library open to public for telephone or written requests only.

★6918★
LEILA HOSPITAL AND HEALTH CENTER - MEDICAL LIBRARY (Med)†
300 North Ave.   Phone: (616) 962-8551
Battle Creek, MI 49016   Sr. Mary Georgia Brown, Libn.
Staff: Prof 1. **Subjects:** Medicine, nursing. **Holdings:** 2139 volumes; 130 tapes and filmstrips. **Subscriptions:** 141 journals and other serials. **Services:** Interlibrary loans; library open to public on request. **Publications:** New Books List, quarterly.

★6919★
LENAWEE COUNTY HISTORICAL MUSEUM - LIBRARY (Hist)
110 E. Church
Box 511   Phone: (517) 265-6071
Adrian, MI 49221   Charles N. Lindquist, Cur.
Staff: 1. **Subjects:** County history. **Special Collections:** Elmer D. Smith Collection (500 glass negatives); complete holding of Official Records of Civil War. **Holdings:** County tax records, 1845-1900; portraits, photographs, tintypes; early deeds, miscellaneous artifacts. **Subscriptions:** 13 journals and other serials. **Services:** Library open to public with restrictions.

LENKE INSURANCE LIBRARY
See: Public Library of Cincinnati and Hamilton County - Government and Business Department

★6920★
LENNOX AND ADDINGTON COUNTY MUSEUM - LIBRARY & ARCHIVES (Hist)
97 Thomas St., E.
Postal Bag 1000   Phone: (613) 354-3027
Napanee, ON, Canada K7R 3S9   Jane Foster, Dir.
Founded: 1907. **Staff:** Prof 1; Other 3. **Subjects:** Local history and genealogy. **Holdings:** 300 linear feet of bound volumes; 40,000 documents; 150 linear feet of manuscripts and miscellanea; 75 linear feet of newspapers; 20 linear feet of photographs. **Services:** Genealogical research; copying; library open to public. **Special Indexes:** Cemetery Index for Lennox and Addington (card); Birth/Marriage/Death newspaper index (card); Preliminary Inventory of Collections of Lennox and Addington Historical Society, 1959 (book).

★6921★
LENOX HILL HOSPITAL - HEALTH SCIENCES LIBRARY (Med)
100 E. 77th St.   Phone: (212) 794-4266
New York, NY 10021   Shirley E. Dansker, Dir.
Founded: 1925. **Staff:** Prof 2; Other 2. **Subjects:** Medicine and medical

specialties, surgery, nursing, history of medicine. **Holdings:** 2500 books; 11,000 bound periodical volumes. **Subscriptions:** 330 journals and other serials. **Services:** Interlibrary loans; copying; library open to public with permission of hospital administrator. **Networks/Consortia:** Member of New York and Northern New Jersey Regional Medical Library; Manhattan Bronx Consortia; Medical Library Center of New York. **Staff:** Ruth Hoffenberg, Asst. Libn.

LENSKI (Lois) COLLECTION
See: University of North Carolina, Greensboro - Lois Lenski Collection

LENTZ HEALTH CENTER LIBRARY
See: Nashville - Metropolitan Department of Public Health

LEONARD (Ada I.) MEMORIAL LIBRARY
See: Middletown Hospital Association - Ada I. Leonard Memorial Library

LEONARD LIBRARY
See: University of Toronto - Wycliffe College

★6922★
LEONARD MORSE HOSPITAL - MEDICAL LIBRARY (Med)
67 Union St.   Phone: (617) 653-3400
Natick, MA 01760   M. Margaret Cheney, Med.Libn.
Founded: 1965. **Staff:** Prof 1; Other 2. **Subjects:** Medicine, nursing, hospital administration. **Holdings:** 1200 books; 2600 bound periodical volumes; 147 AV aids. **Subscriptions:** 121 journals and other serials. **Services:** Interlibrary loans; library open to public during regular library hours only. **Computerized Information Services:** MEDLINE, BRS; computerized cataloging and acquisitions. **Networks/Consortia:** Member of Consortium for Information Resources (CIR).

★6923★
LESSER (Robert Charles) AND COMPANY - RESOURCE DEPARTMENT (Bus-Fin)
8484 Wilshire Blvd., 3rd Fl.   Phone: (213) 658-7600
Beverly Hills, CA 90211   Katherine Hanson, Mgr.
Staff: Prof 1; Other 6. **Subjects:** Real estate, housing. **Holdings:** 300 books. **Subscriptions:** 112 journals and other serials. **Services:** Interlibrary loans; copying; library open to public by appointment. **Computerized Information Services:** DIALOG, SDC, New York Times Information Service, National CSS, Inc.

★6924★
LETCHWORTH VILLAGE DEVELOPMENTAL CENTER - ISAAC N. WOLFSON LIBRARY (Med)
                                          Phone: (914) 947-1000
Thiells, NY 10984   Cherie Werbel, Sr.Libn.
Staff: Prof 1; Other 2. **Subjects:** Mental retardation, special education. **Holdings:** 10,000 books; 75 reports on microfiche; 30 cassettes; 8 VF drawers of pamphlets. **Subscriptions:** 70 journals and other serials. **Services:** Interlibrary loans; copying; library open to public. **Networks/Consortia:** Member of Southeastern New York Library Resources Council (SENYLRC); Health Information Libraries of Westchester (HILOW).

LETTERMAN ARMY MEDICAL CENTER
See: U.S. Army Hospitals

LEUTHOLD (Walter M.) MEDICAL LIBRARY
See: Eisenhower Medical Center - Walter M. Leuthold Medical Library

★6925★
LEVENTHAL (Kenneth) & COMPANY - LIBRARY (Bus-Fin)
2049 Century Park E., 17th Fl.   Phone: (213) 277-0880
Los Angeles, CA 90067   Linda Nauman, Natl.Libn.
Founded: 1972. **Staff:** Prof 1; Other 2. **Subjects:** Accounting, auditing, taxation. **Special Collections:** Housing and real estate. **Holdings:** 3000 books; 60 bound periodical volumes; accounting materials; 2 VF drawers of clippings and pamphlets; 2 VF drawers of tax research; 15 VF drawers of accounting research. **Subscriptions:** 92 journals and other serials. **Services:** Library not open to public. **Computerized Information Services:** NAARS, LEXIS, DIALOG.

★6926★
LEVER BROTHERS COMPANY - RESEARCH AND DEVELOPMENT DIVISION - RESEARCH LIBRARY (Sci-Tech)
45 River Rd.   Phone: (201) 943-7100
Edgewater, NJ 07020   Terry Hauerstein, Info.Serv.Coord.
Founded: 1950. **Staff:** Prof 2; Other 1. **Subjects:** Detergents, soaps,

toiletries, fats and oils, chemistry. **Holdings:** 6000 books; 12,000 bound periodical volumes; 65 VF drawers of U.S. and foreign pamphlets, reports, government documents. **Subscriptions:** 275 journals and other serials. **Services:** Interlibrary loans; library not open to public. **Staff:** Karin Nazaruk, libn.

★6927★
LEVERE MEMORIAL FOUNDATION - LIBRARY
1856 Sheridan Rd.   Phone: (312) 475-1856
Evanston, IL 60201   Kenneth D. Tracey, Exec.Dir.
Founded: 1930. **Staff:** Prof 1. **Subjects:** Fraternity and sorority journals. **Special Collections:** Complete collection of all fraternity and sorority journals; Sigma Alpha Epsilon books, authors and papers. **Holdings:** 225 books; 4000 bound periodical volumes; 407 Chapter scrapbooks (cataloged). **Services:** Library open to public for reference use only.

LEVI MEMORIAL LIBRARY
See: **University of Cincinnati - Medical Center Libraries - College of Nursing & Health**

★6928★
LEVI STRAUSS & COMPANY - CORPORATE LAW LIBRARY (Law)
1155 Battery St.   Phone: (415) 544-7676
San Francisco, CA 94106   Yvonne B. Marty, Legal Info.Sys.Adm.
Staff: 2. **Subjects:** Antitrust law, trademarks, copyrights. **Holdings:** 3500 books; 2000 bound periodical volumes; 25 cassettes; 45 loose-leaf services; worldwide listing of trademarks and copyrights. **Subscriptions:** 15 journals and other serials; 14 newspapers. **Services:** Interlibrary loans; copying; library open to members of private law libraries. **Computerized Information Services:** Online systems.

★6929★
LEVI STRAUSS & COMPANY - CORPORATE MARKETING INFORMATION CENTER (Bus-Fin)
1155 Battery St.
Box 7215
San Francisco, CA 94120-6935   Catherine Rock, Adm.
Founded: 1978. **Staff:** Prof 4; Other 1. **Subjects:** Apparel industry, marketing, retailing, advertising, demographics. **Holdings:** 500 books; 1100 reports; 2000 clippings; 100 microfiche; 200 newsletters. **Subscriptions:** 203 journals and other serials. **Services:** Interlibrary loans; copying; SDI; center not open to public. **Computerized Information Services:** Online systems. **Staff:** Michelle Ridgway, Sys.Info.Spec.; Jan Hewitt, Mktg.Info.Spec.; Andrea Gonzales, Mktg.Info.Spec.

LEVIN (Louis R.) MEMORIAL LIBRARY
See: **Curry College - Louis R. Levin Memorial Library**

LEVITAS LIBRARY
See: **Temple Emanu - el of Yonkers**

LEVITT HEALTH SCIENCES LIBRARY
See: **Mercy Hospital**

LEVY (Austin T. and June Rockwell) LIBRARY
See: **Bradley (Emma Pendleton) Hospital - Austin T. and June Rockwell Levy Library**

LEVY (Gustave L. & Janet W.) LIBRARY
See: **Mount Sinai School of Medicine of the City University of New York - Gustave L. & Janet W. Levy Library**

LEVY (Leon) LIBRARY
See: **University of Pennsylvania - School of Dental Medicine - Leon Levy Library**

★6930★
LEVY (W.J.) CONSULTANTS CORPORATION - RESEARCH LIBRARY (Bus-Fin)
30 Rockefeller Plaza   Phone: (212) 586-5263
New York, NY 10020   Ilse E. Kagan, Libn.
Staff: Prof 2; Other 1. **Subjects:** Economics and policy of oil, international relations. **Holdings:** 10,000 books; 200 bound periodical volumes. **Services:** Library not open to public.

LEWIN (Elizabeth) BUSINESS LIBRARY & INFORMATION CENTER
See: **National Chamber of Commerce for Women - Elizabeth Lewin Business Library & Information Center**

LEWIN (Tannie) JUDAICA LIBRARY
See: **Jewish Community Centers Association (JCCA) - Tannie Lewin Judaica Library**

LEWIS (Byron R.) HISTORICAL LIBRARY
See: **Vincennes University - Byron R. Lewis Historical Library**

★6931★
LEWIS AND CLARK LAW SCHOOL - NORTHWESTERN SCHOOL OF LAW - PAUL L. BOLEY LAW LIBRARY (Law)
10015 S.W. Terwilliger Blvd.   Phone: (503) 244-1181
Portland, OR 97219   Professor Peter S. Nycum, Law Libn.
Founded: 1884. **Staff:** Prof 7; Other 5. **Subjects:** Law. **Holdings:** 26,423 books; 77,996 bound periodical volumes; 66,920 microforms. **Services:** Interlibrary loans; copying; library open to public for reference use only. **Computerized Information Services:** LEXIS, WESTLAW, DIALOG; computerized cataloging. **Staff:** Lauri R. Flynn, Asst.Libn.; Lynn Williams, Circ.Libn.; Kathy Faust, Cat.Libn.; Joe K. Stephens, Act.Pub.Serv.Libn.; Roberta Studwell, Ref.Libn.

★6932★
LEWIS COUNTY HISTORICAL MUSEUM - LIBRARY (Hist)
599 N.W. Front St.   Phone: (206) 748-0831
Chehalis, WA 98532   Jill Kangas, Musm.Dir.
Staff: Prof 1; Other 4. **Subjects:** History of Lewis County, Chehalis Indians, genealogy. **Special Collections:** St. Helens Club (minutes and scrapbooks); Chehalis Bee-Nuggett, 1883-1930; Lewis County cemetery history; Chehalis Indian Archival Files; genealogy research books and records; Ernst Bechley History Collection; Lewis County voting records, 1870-1930; Daily Chronicle newspapers, 1930-1964. **Holdings:** 5000 photographs; 525 oral history cassette tapes; 36 feet of archival papers and newspaper clippings; 3 feet of family histories; 200 maps. **Services:** Family research upon request; copies and transcripts of oral history tapes; library open to public for research by appointment only. **Publications:** Periodical Genealogy & History books. **Special Indexes:** Photograph index by subject and index of oral histories by subject (both card).

★6933★
LEWIS COUNTY LAW LIBRARY (Law)
Box 357   Phone: (206) 748-9121
Chehalis, WA 98532   Jan Draper, Act.Libn.
Staff: 1. **Subjects:** Law. **Holdings:** 6000 volumes. **Services:** Library open to public for reference use only.

★6934★
LEWIS (Elma) SCHOOL OF FINE ARTS - LIBRARY (Art; Area-Ethnic)
122 Elm Hill Ave.   Phone: (617) 442-8820
Dorchester, MA 02121
Founded: 1969. **Staff:** Prof 4; Other 3. **Subjects:** Dance, art, drama, music, costuming, wardrobe, Afro-American and African history, Third World. **Special Collections:** African, Afro-American and Caribbean art (3000 slides); African artifacts. **Holdings:** Figures not available. **Subscriptions:** 120 journals and other serials; 6 newspapers. **Services:** Interlibrary loans; library open to public.

★6935★
LEWIS (Frederic) INC. - PHOTOGRAPHIC LIBRARY (Pict)
15 W. 38th St.   Phone: (212) 921-2850
New York, NY 10018   David Perton, Pres.
Founded: 1940. **Staff:** Prof 2; Other 1. **Subjects:** Photographs of many subjects including people in different situations, industry, sports, architecture, landscapes, railroads, U.S.A., farming, interiors. **Special Collections:** Historical aviation, ships and sports; World War I; Americana; historical New York City. **Holdings:** 1 million photographs, color transparencies, black and white prints and engravings. **Services:** Library open by appointment and with possible fee. **Publications:** Frederick Lewis Picture Index - free to publishers.

LEWIS (G. Pillow) MEMORIAL LIBRARY
See: **Memphis Academy of Arts - G. Pillow Lewis Memorial Library**

★6936★
LEWIS-GALE HOSPITAL CORPORATION - LEWIS-GALE MEDICAL LIBRARY (Med)
1900 Electric Rd.   Phone: (703) 989-4261
Salem, VA 24153   Audrey D. Lachowicz, Med.Libn.
Staff: Prof 1; Other 1. **Subjects:** Medicine and surgery. **Holdings:** 1200 books; 5000 bound periodical volumes; vertical file of staff publications. **Subscriptions:** 125 journals and other serials. **Services:** Interlibrary loans; copying; bibliographic searches; library open to public. **Networks/Consortia:**

Member of Virginia Union List of Biomedical Serials.

LEWIS (Julia Deal) LIBRARY
See: Loyola University of Chicago - Julia Deal Lewis Library

LEWIS (Logan) LIBRARY
See: Carrier Corporation - Logan Lewis Library

LEWIS (Nolan D.C.) LIBRARY
See: Carrier Foundation - Nolan D.C. Lewis Library

LEWIS RESEARCH CENTER
See: U.S. NASA

★6937★
LEWIS, RICE, TUCKER, ALLEN AND CHUBB - LAW LIBRARY (Law)
1400 Railway Exchange Bldg.
611 Olive St. Phone: (314) 231-5833
St. Louis, MO 63101 Nancy M. Wiegand, Libn.
Staff: Prof 1. **Subjects:** U.S. law. **Holdings:** 10,000 volumes. **Subscriptions:** 200 journals and other serials; 6 newspapers. **Services:** Interlibrary loans; library open to public with restrictions. **Computerized Information Services:** LEXIS.

★6938★
LEWIS (Sinclair) INFORMATION & INTERPRETIVE CENTRE (Hum)
Box 222 Phone: (612) 352-5201
Sauk Centre, MN 56378 Janet Campbell, Mgr.
Founded: 1978. **Subjects:** Sinclair Lewis - life, books, literary criticism of his works. **Special Collections:** Foreign editions (30 copies); letters (8 originals); memorabilia (Boyhood Home). **Services:** Open to outside users with restrictions. **Remarks:** Jointly maintained by the Sinclair Lewis Foundation, Inc. and the Sauk Centre Area Chamber of Commerce. The Boyhood Home is a state historic site and a National Historic Landmark.

★6939★
LEWIS UNIVERSITY - LIBRARY
Rte. 53 Phone: (815) 838-0500
Romeoville, IL 60441 Fredereike A. Moskal, Lib.Dir.
Founded: 1952. **Staff:** Prof 3; Other 5. **Subjects:** Business and economics, political science, mathematics, nursing, English and American literature. **Special Collections:** Federal government documents (35,000); Contemporary Print Archives (800 original graphic art items produced 1960 to present). **Holdings:** 95,000 books; 17,500 bound periodical volumes; 12 VF drawers of pamphlets; 1252 records (cataloged); 24,708 books on microfiche; 7000 microfiche; 3050 boxes of periodicals and newspapers on microfilm. **Subscriptions:** 550 journals and other serials; 6 newspapers. **Services:** Interlibrary loans; copying; library open to public for reference use only. **Computerized Information Services:** Computerized cataloging. **Networks/ Consortia:** Member of OCLC through ILLINET; LIBRAS Academic Library Cooperative; Metropolitan Chicago Library Assembly. **Staff:** Laura Patterson, AV/Per.Libn; Michele Cash, Ref./ILL.

LEWISOHN (Irene) COSTUME REFERENCE LIBRARY
See: Metropolitan Museum of Art - Irene Lewisohn Costume Reference Library

LEWISOHN (Irene) LIBRARY
See: Neighborhood Playhouse School of the Theatre - Irene Lewisohn Library

LEWISOHN MEMORIAL LIBRARY
See: Mount Sinai Hospital Medical Center

★6940★
LEWISTON TRIBUNE LIBRARY (Publ)
505 C St. Phone: (208) 743-9411
Lewiston, ID 83501 Lynn King, Libn.
Founded: 1950. **Staff:** Prof 1. **Subjects:** Area events and history. **Holdings:** Newspaper on microfilm, 1892 to present. **Subscriptions:** 10 newspapers. **Services:** Interlibrary loans; copying; library open to public for reference use only. **Special Catalogs:** Key to pictures (book); organizations and historical files (card); obituary file, 1962 to present.

★6941★
LEWISTOWN HOSPITAL - MEDICAL LIBRARY (Med)
Highland Ave. Phone: (717) 248-5411
Lewistown, PA 17044 Jane B. Karn, Med.Libn.
Staff: Prof 1; Other 1. **Subjects:** Medicine, nursing, hospital administration.

Holdings: 800 books. **Subscriptions:** 100 journals and other serials; 7 newspapers. **Services:** Interlibrary loans; copying; SDI; library open to public with restrictions. **Networks/Consortia:** Member of Mideastern Regional Medical Library Service (MERMLS); Central Pennsylvania Health Sciences Library Association.

★6942★
LEXINGTON-FAYETTE URBAN COUNTY PLANNING COMMISSION - TECHNICAL INFORMATION LIBRARY (Plan)†
227 N. Upper St. Phone: (606) 252-8808
Lexington, KY 40507 Phil Choma, Exec.Dir.
Founded: 1961. **Subjects:** Community planning - administration, theory, practice. **Holdings:** 400 books; 1500 reports. **Subscriptions:** 13 journals and other serials. **Services:** Interlibrary loans; copying; library open to public. **Publications:** Agency reports, monthly.

★6943★
LEXINGTON HERALD-LEADER - LIBRARY (Publ)
Main & Midland Ave. Phone: (606) 231-3334
Lexington, KY 40507 Linda L. Smith, Libn.
Founded: 1946. **Staff:** Prof 2. **Subjects:** Newspaper reference topics. **Holdings:** 700 books; 76,144 subject clips (indexed); 17,200 photographs; microfilm from 1875 to present; 30,000 veloxes; biographical and news clippings. **Subscriptions:** 15 journals and other serials. **Services:** Copying; library open to business and professional community; prints made from negatives. **Computerized Information Services:** Internal database. **Networks/Consortia:** Member of Knight-Ridder Newspaper Library Network. **Staff:** Kathy Hensel, Asst.Libn.

★6944★
LEXINGTON HISTORICAL SOCIETY, INC. - LIBRARY (Hist)
Box 514 Phone: (617) 861-0928
Lexington, MA 02173 S. Lawrence Whipple, Archv.
Staff: 1. **Subjects:** Lexington history. **Special Collections:** Burr Church Photographic Collection (250 negatives, 8x10). **Holdings:** 500 books; documents, manuscripts, photographs, 40 hours of oral history tapes. **Services:** Library open to public by appointment. **Publications:** Newsletter.

★6945★
LEXINGTON PUBLIC SCHOOLS - CURRICULUM RESOURCE CENTER (Educ)
9 Philip Rd. Phone: (617) 862-7500
Lexington, MA 02173 Martha Stanton, Coord.
Founded: 1978. **Staff:** Prof 9; Other 4. **Subjects:** Education, elementary curriculum. **Holdings:** 13,000 books and bound periodical volumes; films, records, filmstrips, activity cards, and transparencies (cataloged). **Subscriptions:** 100 journals and other serials. **Services:** Center open to public for reference use only. **Computerized Information Services:** Online systems.

★6946★
LEXINGTON SCHOOL FOR THE DEAF - LIBRARY MEDIA CENTER (Educ)†
26-26 75th St. Phone: (212) 899-8800
Jackson Heights, NY 11370 Marie-Ann Marchese, Lib.Coord.
Staff: Prof 3; Other 2. **Subjects:** Audiology, behavior modification, deafness education, language, child study, exceptional children, psychology, reading, speech. **Holdings:** 1800 books and bound periodical volumes. **Subscriptions:** 78 journals and other serials. **Staff:** Benjamin Grant, Supv., Lib. Media Ctr.; Kenneth Tremaine, Coord. of Media.

★6947★
LEXINGTON TECHNICAL INSTITUTE - LIBRARY (Sci-Tech)
Cooper Dr., Oswald Bldg. Phone: (606) 258-4919
Lexington, KY 40506 Martha J. Birchfield, Dir.
Staff: Prof 2; Other 2. **Subjects:** Associated health technologies, engineering, data processing, business technology. **Holdings:** 6000 volumes. **Subscriptions:** 200 journals and other serials; 5 newspapers. **Services:** Interlibrary loans; copying; library open to public. **Computerized Information Services:** DIALOG; computerized cataloging. **Networks/Consortia:** Member of OCLC through SOLINET. **Publications:** Guide to the L.I.I. Library, annual - for sale.

★6948★
LEXINGTON THEOLOGICAL SEMINARY - BOSWORTH MEMORIAL LIBRARY (Rel-Theol)
S. Limestone St. Phone: (606) 252-0361
Lexington, KY 40508 Roscoe M. Pierson, Libn.
Founded: 1865. **Staff:** Prof 3; Other 4. **Subjects:** Christian theology, American church history, Disciples of Christ, Biblical studies, Southern states, Biblical archeology. **Holdings:** 100,000 volumes; 150 volumes of manuscripts

of missionaries and ministers; 90 VF drawers of pamphlets; 500 reels of microfilm. **Services:** Interlibrary loans; copying; library open to those engaged in scholarly research. **Staff:** Deloris A. Turner, Pub.Serv.Libn.

★6949★
LIBBEY-OWENS-FORD COMPANY - CORPORATE LIBRARY (Bus-Fin)
811 Madison Ave.   Phone: (419) 247-4862
Toledo, OH 43695   Patricia B. Jones, Corp.Libn.
Founded: 1960. **Staff:** Prof 1; Other 1. **Subjects:** Business, glass. **Special Collections:** Libbey-Owens-Ford Company history. **Holdings:** 300 books; 3000 unbound periodical volumes; 5000 annual reports. **Services:** Interlibrary loans; copying; SDI; library open to public with restrictions. **Publications:** Special News Briefings, daily.

★6950★
LIBBEY-OWENS-FORD COMPANY - TECHNICAL CENTER LIBRARY (Sci-Tech)
1701 E. Broadway   Phone: (419) 247-4367
Toledo, OH 43605   Jeanne M. Keogh, Tech.Libn.
Founded: 1946. **Staff:** Prof 1; Other 2. **Subjects:** Glass, optics, physics, chemistry, engineering. **Holdings:** 6000 books; 12,000 bound periodical volumes; 75 VF drawers of manufacturers' catalogs; 30 VF drawers of government documents. **Subscriptions:** 170 journals and other serials; 10 newspapers. **Services:** Interlibrary loans; copying; library open to public with special permission. **Computerized Information Services:** DIALOG.

LIBERATION NEWS SERVICE ARCHIVE
See: Temple University - Central Library System - Contemporary Culture Collection

★6951★
LIBERTY MEMORIAL MUSEUM - LIBRARY (Hist)
100 W. 26th St.   Phone: (816) 221-1918
Kansas City, MO 64108   Susan C. Wilkerson, Libn./Archv.
Staff: Prof 1. **Subjects:** World War I, history of Liberty Memorial. **Special Collections:** World War I posters (850); archives of Women's Overseas Service League (28 feet); World War I archival material (maps, letters, films, photographs; 800 feet). **Holdings:** 700 books; 100 Hollinger boxes and 35 volumes of Liberty Memorial Association archives. **Subscriptions:** 20 journals and other serials. **Services:** Library open to public by appointment. **Special Catalogs:** Posters and sheet music catalogs (card).

★6952★
LIBERTY MUTUAL INSURANCE COMPANY - BUSINESS REFERENCE LIBRARY (Bus-Fin)
600 Grant St.   Phone: (412) 391-6555
Pittsburgh, PA 15219   Dorothy Fornof, Supv., Lib.Serv.
Staff: Prof 1. **Subjects:** Insurance, management. **Holdings:** 1300 books. **Subscriptions:** 78 journals and other serials. **Services:** Interlibrary loans; copying. **Networks/Consortia:** Member of Liberty Mutual Library System. **Publications:** Book Shelf, biweekly - for internal distribution only.

★6953★
LIBERTY MUTUAL INSURANCE COMPANY - EDUCATION/INFORMATION RESOURCES (Bus-Fin)
175 Berkeley St.   Phone: (617) 357-9500
Boston, MA 02117   Ann M. McDonald, Mgr.
Staff: Prof 4; Other 2. **Subjects:** Insurance, management, business, training, data processing. **Holdings:** 15,000 books; 1000 periodical volumes; 10 VF drawers of pamphlets (uncataloged). **Subscriptions:** 250 journals and other serials. **Services:** Interlibrary loans; current awareness service; copying; library open to public for reference use only on request. **Publications:** Book Notes, weekly - distributed outside on request. **Staff:** Linda E. Peterson, Dir., Lib.Serv.; Ruth D. Haugen, Tech.Serv.Supv.; Evalyn A. Tyson, Ref.Serv.Supv.

★6954★
LIBERTY MUTUAL INSURANCE COMPANY - LAW LIBRARY (Law)
175 Berkeley St.   Phone: (617) 357-9500
Boston, MA 02117   C.E. Procopio, Dir. of Law Libs.
Staff: Prof 1; Other 1. **Subjects:** Insurance, law, medicine. **Holdings:** 20,000 volumes. **Subscriptions:** 99 journals and other serials. **Services:** Library not open to public. **Computerized Information Services:** WESTLAW. **Remarks:** Company has 34 branch law libraries with a total of 65,000 volumes.

LIBRARY OF AMERICAN TRANSPORTATION
See: National Railway Historical Society

★6955★
LIBRARY ASSOCIATION OF LA JOLLA - ATHENAEUM MUSIC AND ARTS LIBRARY (Art; Mus)
1008 Wall St.   Phone: (714) 454-5872
La Jolla, CA 92037   Evelyn Neumann, Lib.Adm.
Staff: Prof 1; Other 3. **Subjects:** Fine arts, music, drama. **Special Collections:** Bach Gesellschaft (47 volumes). **Holdings:** 3288 books and bound periodical volumes; 3100 phonograph records (cataloged); cassettes. **Subscriptions:** 44 journals and other serials. **Services:** Library open to public for reference use only.

★6956★
LIBRARY ASSOCIATION OF PORTLAND - ART AND MUSIC DEPARTMENT (Art; Mus)
801 S.W. Tenth Ave.   Phone: (503) 223-7201
Portland, OR 97205   Barbara K. Padden, Hd.
Founded: 1936. **Staff:** Prof 4; Other 8. **Subjects:** Antiques, architecture, costume, dance, fine arts, handicrafts, interior decorating, moving pictures, music, photography. **Holdings:** 27,500 books; 22,000 sheet music scores (cataloged); 17,595 phonograph records; 134 cassette tapes; 11,992 color slides; 2 million picture clippings; 663 color reproductions. **Subscriptions:** 188 journals and other serials. **Services:** Interlibrary loans; copying; department open to public. **Computerized Information Services:** Computerized circulation. **Special Catalogs:** Catalogs for phonograph records, art and music (card). **Special Indexes:** Song index to library's song books (card); film review index to library's movie books and periodicals (card).

★6957★
LIBRARY ASSOCIATION OF PORTLAND - GENERAL INFORMATION DEPARTMENT - FOUNDATION CENTER (Soc Sci)
801 S.W. 10th Ave.   Phone: (503) 223-7201
Portland, OR 97205   Ann Austin, Dept.Hd.
Founded: 1972. **Staff:** 1. **Subjects:** Foundations. **Special Collections:** Regional depository of Foundation Center, New York, NY; annual reports and Internal Revenue Service reports of foundations in Oregon; foundation newsletter and periodicals; federal government fundings sources. **Holdings:** Figures not available for books; 1524 microfiche; 36,042 aperture cards. **Services:** Interlibrary loans; copying; department open to public.

★6958★
LIBRARY ASSOCIATION OF PORTLAND - LITERATURE AND HISTORY DEPARTMENT (Hum)
801 S.W. Tenth Ave.   Phone: (503) 223-7201
Portland, OR 97205   Barbara J. Kahl, Dept.Hd.
Staff: Prof 8. **Subjects:** Philosophy, psychology, religion, languages, theater, literature, geography, travel, history, biography, general works, genealogy. **Holdings:** Figures not available for books; 64,481 maps; 1551 spoken records; 179 cassette sets. **Services:** Interlibrary loans; copying; department open to public.

★6959★
LIBRARY ASSOCIATION OF PORTLAND - OREGON COLLECTION (Hist)
801 S.W. Tenth Ave.   Phone: (503) 223-7201
Portland, OR 97205   Barbara J. Kahl
Staff: Prof 2. **Subjects:** Oregon, the Oregon Territory, and the early northwest. **Holdings:** Figures not available for books, documents, serials, bound periodicals and maps. **Services:** Interlibrary loans; copying; collection open to public for reference use only. **Special Indexes:** Newspaper and microfiche index of articles in Portland newspapers pertaining to Oregon and Oregonians.

★6960★
LIBRARY ASSOCIATION OF PORTLAND - SOCIAL SCIENCE AND SCIENCE DEPARTMENT (Sci-Tech; Soc Sci)
801 S.W. Tenth Ave.   Phone: (503) 223-7201
Portland, OR 97205   Jim Takita, Dept.Hd.
Staff: Prof 7. **Subjects:** Business, science, technology, social sciences, education. **Special Collections:** Thomas Newton Cook Rose Library; Jesse Currey Memorial Rose Collection (306 volumes). **Holdings:** Figures not available for books; U.S. documents, Oregon documents. **Services:** Interlibrary loans; copying; department open to public.

LIBRARY OF THE BOSTON AUTHORS CLUB
See: Boston Public Library - Rare Books and Manuscripts

LIBRARY OF THE BROWNING SOCIETY
See: Boston Public Library - Rare Books and Manuscripts

★6961★

LIBRARY COMPANY OF THE BALTIMORE BAR - LIBRARY (Law)†
618 Court House West   Phone: (301) 727-0280
Baltimore, MD 21202   Kai-Yun Chiu, Law Libn.
Founded: 1840. **Staff:** Prof 2; Other 15. **Subjects:** Law. **Special Collections:** Trials; Maryland law and briefs. **Holdings:** 140,000 volumes; U.S. legislative histories on microfiche; 12 drawers of microfiche; 4 drawers of microfilm; 5 drawers of cassettes. **Subscriptions:** 350 journals and other serials; 5 newspapers. **Services:** Interlibrary loans; copying; library not open to public. **Computerized Information Services:** LEXIS. **Staff:** L. Pachoca, Cat./Acq.Libn.

★6962★

LIBRARY COMPANY OF PHILADELPHIA (Hist)
1314 Locust St.   Phone: (215) 546-3181
Philadelphia, PA 19107   Edwin Wolf, II, Libn.
Founded: 1731. **Staff:** Prof 6; Other 7. **Subjects:** Pre-1860 Americana; Philadelphia and Pennsylvania; pre-1820 medical material; black history before 1906. **Special Collections:** Early printed books from Girard College and Christ Church (on deposit). **Holdings:** 400,000 volumes; 30,000 prints and photographs; 132,000 manuscripts. **Subscriptions:** 200 journals and other serials. **Services:** Interlibrary loans; copying; library open to public for research. **Publications:** Annual reports; newsletters - both free to libraries and individuals on request; occasional catalogs of special exhibitions. **Special Catalogs:** Catalog of the holdings of the Library Company and the Historical Society of Pennsylvania relating to black history (published); The Library of James Logan (published); Quarter of a Millennium: The Library Company of Philadelphia, 1731-1981 (published). **Remarks:** Holdings of the Bray Library, Christ Church in Philadelphia, are housed here. **Staff:** Gordon M. Marshall, Asst.Libn.; Phillip Lapsansky, Ref.Libn.; Kenneth Finkel, Cur., Prints/Photographs; Marie E. Korey, Cur./Printed Books.

★6963★

LIBRARY OF CONGRESS - AFRICAN & MIDDLE EASTERN DIVISION (Area-Ethnic)
John Adams Bldg., Rm. 1040C   Phone: (202) 287-7937
Washington, DC 20540   Dr. Julian W. Witherell, Chf.
Remarks: The Library of Congress has extensive holdings of books, newspapers, manuscripts, periodicals, and other material relating to nations of Africa and the Middle East. Detailed reference services on the 550,000 western-language volumes relating to this area in the library's general collections are provided by the division's African, Hebraic, and Near East sections. In addition, the Hebraic Section has custody of over 117,000 volumes in Hebrew, Yiddish, and cognate languages covering such topics as the Bible, ancient Middle East, and Jews and Judaism throughout the world. The Near East Section has holdings of more than 115,000 volumes in Arabic, Turkish, Persian, and other languages of an area of responsibility that extends from Afghanistan to Morocco, excluding Israel. The African Section, with primary responsibility for Africa south of the Sahara, has a small reference collection and extensive pamphlet files. Both the Hebraic and Near East sections maintain union catalogs relating to their respective areas of responsibility, while the African Section has a card index of citations to Africana periodical literature. The phone numbers for the 3 sections of this Division are as follows: African Section (202)287-5528; Hebraic Section (202)287-5422; Near East Section (202)287-5421. **Staff:** Beverly A. Gray, Hd., African Sect.; Myron Weinstein, Hd., Hebraic Sect.; George N. Atiyeh, Hd., Near East Sect.

★6964★

LIBRARY OF CONGRESS - AMERICAN FOLKLIFE CENTER (Area-Ethnic)
Thomas Jefferson Bldg. - G104D   Phone: (202) 287-6590
Washington, DC 20540   Alan Jabbour, Dir.
Founded: 1976. **Staff:** Prof 6; Other 4. **Subjects:** American folklife with emphasis on research, public programs and technical assistance; oral history and the Federal Cylinder Project. **Holdings:** Contains the results of current research projects including fieldnotes, sound recordings, photographs and videotapes. **Publications:** Folklife Center News, quarterly; mailing list composed of folklife organizations, institutions and individuals; additions upon request; Folklife and the Federal Government, a guide to the U.S. Government's role in folk culture; Folklife and the Library of Congress; list of additional publications - available upon request. **Staff:** Ray Dockstader, Dp.Dir.; Elena Bradunas, Folklife Spec.; Carl Fleischhauer, Folklife Spec.; Mary Hofford, Folklife Spec.; Peter Bartis, Folklife Res.

★6965★

LIBRARY OF CONGRESS - AMERICAN FOLKLIFE CENTER - ARCHIVE OF FOLK CULTURE (Mus; Area-Ethnic)
Thomas Jefferson Bldg. - G152   Phone: (202) 287-5505
Washington, DC 20540   Joseph C. Hickerson, Hd.
Founded: 1928. **Staff:** Prof 2; Other 2. **Subjects:** Folksong, folk music, folklore, folklife, ethnomusicology, oral history. **Special Collections:** Manuscript collections (50,000 pages); Smithsonian Institution/Frances Densmore American Indian Collection (3700 cylinders). **Holdings:** 3000 books; 800 bound periodical volumes; 2000 unbound serials; 22,000 hours of unpublished field recordings; 9000 cylinder recordings; 12,000 disc recordings; 10,000 tape recordings. **Subscriptions:** 500 journals and other serials. **Services:** Copying (limited); reading room open to public; listening by appointment; correspondence and telephone inquiries; an intern program is operated for the interested public. **Publications:** LC recordings of folk music and lore; 190 reference and finding aids available on request. **Special Catalogs:** Catalog of issued LPs (pamphlet); catalog of recorded collections (card); catalog of individual titles on some recordings (card); catalog of manuscript and microform collections (card). **Formerly:** Known as the Archive of Folk Song.

★6966★

LIBRARY OF CONGRESS - ASIAN DIVISION (Area-Ethnic)
John Adams Bldg., Rm. 1024   Phone: (202) 287-5420
Washington, DC 20540   Dr. Richard C. Howard, Act.Chf.
Subjects: Asian Division contains over 1.3 million volumes in Asian languages. Chinese: 461,000 volumes, especially strong in local histories, rare books, and materials of the Ch'ing period (1644-1911), and post 1949 periodical publications; Japanese: 634,000 volumes, especially strong in social sciences and modern history; Korean: 72,000 volumes with emphasis on historical works and current publications; Southern Asia: 165,000 volumes of research literature from Pakistan to Philippines, especially Bengali, Punjabi, Gujarati, Marathi, Hindi, Tamil, Telugu, Malayalam, Oriya, Kannada, Urdu, Sindhi, Nepali, Newari, Assamese, Indonesian, Vietnamese, Thai, Malaysian, Burmese. **Remarks:** The Hebraic and Near East Sections, formerly a part of this division, have merged with the African and Middle Eastern Division of the Library of Congress. **Staff:** Chi Wang, Hd., Chinese/Korean Sect.; Hisao Matsumoto, Hd., Japanese Sect.; Louis A. Jacob, Hd., Southern Asia Sect.

★6967★

LIBRARY OF CONGRESS - CHILDREN'S LITERATURE CENTER (Hum)
Thomas Jefferson Bldg., Rm. 140H   Phone: (202) 287-5535
Washington, DC 20540   Margaret N. Coughlan, Act.Chf.
Remarks: The Library of Congress has more than 200,000 volumes of children's literature, including its rare and old children's books and those in foreign languages. The Children's Literature Center has a 1300 volume reference collection and 50 current periodicals; a card catalog for children's books published since 1965 and earlier in-print titles, with separate illustrator index; and an LC classification shelf list of the library's fiction and nonfiction holdings in children's literature since 1957.

★6968★

LIBRARY OF CONGRESS - CONGRESSIONAL RESEARCH SERVICE (Soc Sci)
James Madison Memorial Bldg., LM213   Phone: (202) 287-5735
Washington, DC 20540   Gilbert Gude, Dir.
Founded: 1914. **Remarks:** The Congressional Research Service provides research and analytical, consultative and informational services exclusively to the members and committees of Congress in connection with their official business. In addition, it publishes, at regular intervals, the Digest of Public General Bills and Resolutions, and the Biennial Constitution of the U.S. - Analysis and Interpretation. The service is organized into divisions, established along broad subject field lines, as follows: (1) an American Law Division, which provides research in the fields of federal, state, county, and municipal law and prepares for publication the Digest of Public General Bills; (2) an Economics Division covering the fields of money and banking, housing and community development, transportation and communications, labor, industrial organization and corporation finance, international trade, and economic geography; (3) an Environment and Natural Resources Policy Division, covering agriculture, mineral economics, forestry and lumber, energy resources, environmental protection, pollution and the fields of water, irrigation, reclamation, and land use; (4) a Foreign Affairs and National Defense Division, covering international relations, regional affairs, and national defense; (5) an Education and Public Welfare Division, covering education, social security, retirement systems, problems of the aging, some areas of criminology and immigration; (6) a Government Division, covering political science and public administration, the general field of history, civil rights, governmental organization and operations, governmental procedures and Indian Affairs; and (7) a Science Policy Research Division, covering public policy and legislative problems relating to science and technology. The service also has an Office of Senior Specialists, providing authoritative, consultative and analytical research services, primarily to Congressional committees. A Congressional Reference Division, which responds to general reference questions, conducts magazine and newspaper searches, and operates a rush telephone response service, also operates reference centers in the House and Senate office buildings and maintains two Congressional Reading Rooms for the exclusive use of

Members of Congress, their families, and official staff. A Library Services Division is responsible for the acquisition, processing and servicing of research materials for the research and reference staff of the service as well as the provision of bibliographies and SDI services and the distribution of CRS reports to Congressional staff members. In addition to publications and other research products, the service provides numerous seminars, workshops, and institutes for members and staff of Congress on topics of current legislative concern and maintains extensive automated data resources for Congressional use.

★6969★

LIBRARY OF CONGRESS - COPYRIGHT PUBLIC INFORMATION OFFICE (Info Sci)
James Madison Memorial Bldg., LM-401
101 Independence Ave., S.E.   Phone: (202) 287-8700
Washington, DC 20559   Victor Marton, Supv., Info. Unit
Staff: Prof 14. **Subjects:** Copyright. **Holdings:** Copyright Card Catalog (40 million cards). **Services:** Copying (limited; fee). **Publications:** Circulars, application forms - free upon request. **Special Catalogs:** Catalog of Copyright Entries (book). **Staff:** Joseph G. Ross, Jr., Hd., Info./Pubn.; Michael Keplinger, Chf., Info./Ref.Div.

★6970★

LIBRARY OF CONGRESS - EUROPEAN DIVISION (Area-Ethnic)
John Adams Bldg., Rm. 5244   Phone: (202) 287-5413
Washington, DC 20540   Clara M. Lovett, Chf.
Remarks: The European Division provides specialized reference and bibliographic services, is responsible for the development of the collections within its area and subject specialization, and maintains liaison with governmental and academic specialists in the field. A staff of area specialists and librarians, supported by pertinent reference files and tools, render these services with respect to the past and present of the following areas, countries and peoples: Albania, Austria, Belgium, Bulgaria, Cyprus, Czechoslovakia, Denmark, Estonia, Finland, France, Germany, Greece, Hungary, Iceland, Italy, Latvia, Lithuania, Luxembourg, Monaco, Netherlands, Norway, Poland, Romania, San Marino, Sweden, Switzerland, the USSR, Vatican City, and Yugoslavia. Reading, study, and reference facilities, the latter including a reference collection of about 9000 volumes on the Soviet Union and Eastern Europe, are available in the division's European Reading Room, which has custody of current Slavic and Baltic periodicals and newspapers. The general collection of the Library of Congress includes close to 4.5 million volumes of monographs and several tens of thousands of periodical and newspaper titles in the languages of or pertaining to the countries covered by the division. **Staff:** David H. Kraus, Asst.Chf.; Robert V. Allen, Sr. Slavic Spec.

★6971★

LIBRARY OF CONGRESS - GEN. READING ROOMS DIV. (Info Sci)
Thomas Jefferson Bldg. - GRR B144   Phone: (202) 287-5530
Washington, DC 20540   Ellen Hahn, Chf.
Remarks: The division is responsible for providing direct service to users of the general, Local History and Genealogy and microform reading rooms, telephone reference and reference correspondence services. Reference librarians in the Main Reading Room, with its extensive collection of 45,000 reference volumes, provide orientation to the library, reference service in a broad range of subjects, and guidance in using the library's main catalog - the index to its resources. The staff helps readers select materials from the library's collections, prepares reference aids, and assists readers in using SCORPIO and MUMS, the library's automated bibliographic systems which provide access to books cataloged after 1968 and selected in-house databases. **Staff:** Winston Tabb, Asst.Chf.; Gary Jensen, Hd., Main Reading Rm.

★6972★

LIBRARY OF CONGRESS - GEN. READING ROOMS DIV. - LOCAL HISTORY & GENEALOGY READING ROOM SECTION (Hist)
Thomas Jefferson Bldg., Rm. 5010   Phone: (202) 287-5537
Washington, DC 20540   Judith P. Austin, Hd.
Remarks: The Library of Congress has more than 400,000 volumes of U.S. and European genealogy, heraldry, and U.S. local history, including compiled genealogies, city directories, published vital statistics, military records, and church registers. Local History and Genealogy Room has a 6000 volume reference collection, 40 current periodicals, and several card catalogs, including a 200,000 entry index to biographical histories from 50 states and a 42,000 card index to illustrations of coats of arms. **Formerly:** Its Thomas Jefferson Reading Rooms Section.

★6973★

LIBRARY OF CONGRESS - GEN. READING ROOMS DIV. - MICROFORM READING ROOM SECTION
Thomas Jefferson Bldg. - GRR 140B   Phone: (202) 287-5471
Washington, DC 20540   Robert V. Gross, Hd.
Subjects: Early state records; early English and American periodicals; American fiction to 1905; dime novels; American and British black journals; underground newspapers; oral histories; U.S. nondepository documents; U.S. Office of Education ERIC Reports; copyright records of the U.S. District Courts, 1790-1870; U.S. city directories to 1901; Barbour Collection of Connecticut vital records; State labor reports, 1865-1900; American labor union constitutions and proceedings; English books to 1700; architectural books, 15th-19th centuries; English and American plays, 1516-1830; Cabinet reports by British foreign ministers, 1837-1916; Journals and Sessional Papers of the British Parliament; papers of the Parliament of Northern Ireland, 1921-1972; manuscripts of American interest filmed by the American Council of Learned Societies; English parish registers, 16th to 19th centuries; Irish genealogical records; British radical periodicals; Modern Language Association reproductions of manuscripts and rare books; manuscripts in St. Catherine's Monastery on Mt. Sinai, in the libraries of the Greek and Armenian Patriarchates in Jerusalem and in the monasteries of Mt. Athos; early editions of Petrarch and Ronsard; pandects of the Notaries of Genoa to 1300; minutes of the Senate of the Venetian Republic; inventories from the Archives Nationales (Paris) and of numerous German, Austrian and Italian archives and libraries; Archives of the Austrian Foreign Office, 1848-1918; Spanish drama; early Latin American imprints; papers of Simon Bolivar; Mexican provincial and local archives from Jalisco, Oaxaca, Parral, Pueblo, and other cities; 16th and 17th century Russian imprints; 19th and 20th century Russian history and culture; archives of the Japanese Ministry of the Foreign Affairs and other ministries, 1868-1945; ULTRA intelligence messages, 1939-1945; summaries and translations of world broadcasts since World War II; press summaries and translations from Mainland China, Japan, Indonesia and Yugoslavia; economic literature prior to 1830; social and economic plans of developing countries; League of Nations documents; United Nations documents; Human Relations Area Files; corporation annual reports; doctoral dissertations; books from the library's general collections copied for preservation purposes. **Holdings:** 2.2 million reels and strips of microfilm, microfiche and micro-opaques.

★6974★

LIBRARY OF CONGRESS - GEOGRAPHY & MAP DIVISION (Geog-Map)
James Madison Memorial Bldg., LMB01   Phone: (202) 287-6277
Washington, DC 20540   Dr. John A. Wolter, Chf.
Founded: 1897. **Subjects:** Cartography; geography; maps, charts, atlases, globes, models, and other cartographic forms covering more than 700 subjects. **Holdings:** 46,000 atlases; 3.8 million maps. **Subscriptions:** 200 journals and other serials. **Services:** Interlibrary loans; copying. **Publications:** Bibliographies, irregular. **Staff:** Ralph E. Ehrenberg, Asst.Chf.; David K. Carrington, Hd., Tech.Serv.; Richard W. Stephenson, Hd., Ref.Sect.

★6975★

LIBRARY OF CONGRESS - HISPANIC DIVISION (Area-Ethnic)
Thomas Jefferson Bldg., Rm. 239E   Phone: (202) 287-5256
Washington, DC 20540   William E. Carter, Chf.
Remarks: Formerly known as the Hispanic Foundation, this center for the pursuit of studies in Spanish, Portuguese, Brazilian, Spanish-American, and Caribbean cultures was established in 1939 with the cooperation of the Hispanic Society of America. The library's Hispanic and Portuguese collections are among the finest in the world and represent resources that have been increasing for more than a century and a half. Primary and secondary source materials are available for the study of all periods, from pre-Columbian to the present. All major subject areas are represented; the collections are especially strong in history, literature, and the social sciences. Of the more than 19 million volumes in the general book collections of the library, nearly two million volumes are concerned with Hispanic and Portuguese cultures. The collections include 20,000 pamphlets; 8000 Spanish plays; Archives of Hispanic Literature representing 450 authors; 4500 volumes and clippings files of reference material. The collections are not housed in the Hispanic Division but are in the general and special collections of the Library of Congress. The division's primary roles are to develop the library's collections relating to Latin America, Spain, and Portugal; to assist scholars, officials, and the general public in the use of these materials; and to describe and interpret Hispanic Library resources through published guides and bibliographies. It compiles the annual Handbook of Latin American Studies. The division also maintains liaison and shares information with individuals and organizations with similar concerns. **Staff:** John R. Hebert, Asst.Chf.; Georgette M. Dorn, Spec./Hispanic Culture; Dolores M. Martin, Ed.

★6976★
LIBRARY OF CONGRESS - JOHN F. KENNEDY CENTER FOR THE PERFORMING ARTS - THE PERFORMING ARTS LIBRARY (Art; Mus)
John F. Kennedy Ctr.   Phone: (202) 287-6245
Washington, DC 20566   Peter J. Fay, Hd.Libn.
Staff: Prof 3; Other 1. **Subjects:** Music, film, theater, dance, broadcasting, performing arts. **Special Collections:** The White House Record Library donated by the Recording Industry Association of America which duplicates the collection given to the White House (2800 phonograph records). **Holdings:** 5000 books; 30 bound periodical volumes; 200 audio cassettes; 20 VF drawers of clippings; Stage Bill, an almost complete collection since the establishment of the Kennedy Center. **Subscriptions:** 300 journals and other serials, newsletters and bulletins of professional organizations; 10 newspapers. **Services:** Copying; library open to public. **Computerized Information Services:** Online systems; computerized acquisitions. **Publications:** The Performing Arts Library, an information brochure; An Introduction to the Performing Arts Collections of the Library of Congress - free upon request. **Staff:** Cynthia Barkley, Ref.Libn./Dance; Walter Zvonchenko, Ref.Libn./Theater.

★6977★
LIBRARY OF CONGRESS - LAW LIBRARY (Law)
James Madison Memorial Bldg., Rm. 240   Phone: (202) 287-5065
Washington, DC 20540   Carleton W. Kenyon, Law Libn.
Subjects: All legal systems - secular, religious, and historic - as well as international law, comparative law, general law, jurisprudence, philosophy of law and legal history. **Special Collections:** Microtext collection of primary and secondary American and foreign legal sources (25,000 reels of microfilm; 535,000 microfiche cards). **Holdings:** 1.8 million volumes. **Remarks:** Figures include holdings of all divisions of the Law Library.

★6978★
LIBRARY OF CONGRESS - LAW LIBRARY - AMERICAN-BRITISH LAW DIVISION (Law)
James Madison Memorial Bldg., Rm. 235   Phone: (202) 287-5077
Washington, DC 20540   Marlene C. McGuirl, Chf.
Subjects: American federal and state law, British Commonwealth law. **Special Collections:** American colonial and early state law; U.S. court records and briefs; early British law; American and English trials; U.S. legislative publications and Congressional documents. **Remarks:** This division administers the Law Library Reading Room and the Law Library in the Capitol (reserved for Congressional use only).

★6979★
LIBRARY OF CONGRESS - LAW LIBRARY - EUROPEAN LAW DIVISION (Law)
James Madison Memorial Bldg., Rm. 240   Phone: (202) 287-5088
Washington, DC 20540   Ivan Sipkov, Chf.
Subjects: Legal materials on all subjects covering the nations of continental Europe and their possessions, excluding Portugal and Spain. **Special Collections:** European country collections; ancient law; feudal law; foreign trials; Germanic law; Holy Roman Empire; incunabula; manuscripts; medieval law; war crimes.

★6980★
LIBRARY OF CONGRESS - LAW LIBRARY - FAR EASTERN LAW DIVISION (Law)
James Madison Memorial Bldg., Rm. 235   Phone: (202) 287-5085
Washington, DC 20540   Tao-Tai Hsia, Chf.
Subjects: Legal materials on all subjects covering the nations of East and Southeast Asia, including China, Taiwan, Indonesia, Japan, Korea, Thailand, and former British and French possessions in the area.

★6981★
LIBRARY OF CONGRESS - LAW LIBRARY - HISPANIC LAW DIVISION (Law)
James Madison Memorial Bldg., Rm. 235   Phone: (202) 287-5070
Washington, DC 20540   Rubens Medina, Chf.
Subjects: Legal materials on all subjects covering the Latin American republics, Spain and Portugal with possessions, Philippines and Puerto Rico. **Special Collections:** Roman Law; canon law; collections for Mexico, Argentina and Brazil are very comprehensive, for both national and state materials.

★6982★
LIBRARY OF CONGRESS - LAW LIBRARY - NEAR EASTERN AND AFRICAN LAW DIVISION (Law)
James Madison Memorial Bldg., Rm. 240   Phone: (202) 287-5073
Washington, DC 20540   Zuhair E. Jwaideh, Chf.
Subjects: Legal materials on all subjects covering the Middle Eastern countries; law of the North African countries; British-African law; French-African law; Roman-Dutch-African law; religious law (Jewish, Christian and

Islamic); tribal and customary African law.

★6983★
LIBRARY OF CONGRESS - LOAN DIVISION
Thomas Jefferson Bldg. - G151   Phone: (202) 287-5441
Washington, DC 20540   Olive C. James, Chf.
Remarks: The Loan Division provides bibliographic searching, verifying and document delivery to Congress, federal agencies and to scholars nationally and internationally through interlibrary loan. This service is available through academic, public or special libraries in the U.S. and major libraries throughout the world under the guidelines of the 1980 (U.S.) Interlibrary Loan Code and "International Lending: Principles and Guidelines... (1978)." It is intended to supplement the resources of other libraries by making available unusual materials not readily accessible elsewhere; but not to provide the major part of items needed for extended research. Local, state and regional libraries are expected to serve as the primary sources of research materials, while the Library of Congress serves as a library of last resort. Incorporating the former Union Catalog Reference Service, the division also attempts to provide libraries with locations for materials not found through standard bibliographic sources.

★6984★
LIBRARY OF CONGRESS - MANUSCRIPT DIVISION (Hist)
James Madison Memorial Bldg., Rms. 101-102   Phone: (202) 287-5388
Washington, DC 20540   James H. Hutson, Chf.
Subjects: Collections of the papers of most of the Presidents, from George Washington through Calvin Coolidge, of many other statesmen, military, scientific, and literary leaders and of numerous enterprises and institutions, totaling more than 40 million pieces. Among them: Records of the Virginia Company of London, the American Colonization Society, National Association for the Advancement of Colored People, National Urban League, American Federation of Labor, the League of Women Voters, Russian Church Records from Alaska, Kraus Collection (Latin America), Harkness Collection (Mexico and Peru), Herndon-Weik Collection (Lincolniana); Papers of Henry H. Arnold, Newton D. Baker, Nathaniel P. Banks, Clara Barton, Alexander Graham Bell, Albert J. Beveridge, Nicholas Biddle, Hugo Black, James G. Blaine, Gutzon Borglum, Huntington Cairns, Andrew Carnegie, Charlotte S. Cushman, Jo Davidson, Frederick Douglass, Ira C. Eaker, James A. Farley, Felix Frankfurter, Benjamin Franklin, Daniel Chester French, Sigmund Freud, Lillian Gish, Alexander Hamilton, B.W. Huebsch, Charles Evans Hughes, Cordell Hull, Harold Ickes, John Paul Jones, Ernest J. King, Frank Knox, Robert M. LaFollette Family Papers, Jacques Loeb, Henry R. and Clare Boothe Luce, Archibald MacLeish, William McAdoo, Edna St. Vincent Millay, Ogden Mills, William (Billy) Mitchell, Samuel F.B. Morse, Reinhold Niebuhr, J. Robert Oppenheimer, George S. Patton, Jr., John J. Pershing, Gifford Pinchot, A. Philip Randolph, Whitelaw Reid Family, William T. Sherman, Carl Spaatz, Arthur Spingarn, Harlan Fiske Stone, William Styron, Robert A. Taft, Joseph M. Toner, Booker T. Washington, Daniel Webster, James A. McNeill Whistler, Walt Whitman, Owen Wister, Wilbur and Orville Wright; reproductions of manuscripts in European archives that relate to American history.

★6985★
LIBRARY OF CONGRESS - MOTION PICTURE, BROADCASTING & RECORDED SOUND DIVISION (Aud-Vis)
James Madison Memorial Bldg., Rm. 338   Phone: (202) 287-5840
Washington, DC 20540   Paul Spehr, Act.Chf.
Subjects: International archival collection of over 300,000 motion picture reels and over 75,000 videotape titles, including films made from earliest paper prints deposited for copyright; 1.2 million sound recordings on disc, tape, wire, and cylinder, and including radio programs from 1924 to present; television programs on tape and film from 1948 to present. **Services:** Holdings are not for loan, but many items are available for individual study on library premises by advanced researchers. Reservations must be made in advance. Copies may be ordered, subject to considerations of copyright and other restrictions. **Publications:** Film and Television; Sound Recordings; information brochures - free upon request.

★6986★
LIBRARY OF CONGRESS - MUSIC DIVISION (Mus)
Thomas Jefferson Bldg., Rm. G144   Phone: (202) 287-5507
Washington, DC 20540   Donald L. Leavitt, Chf.
Subjects: Music and music literature of the world. Includes: Elizabeth Sprague Coolidge Foundation Collection (modern musical holographs, correspondence, and photographs); Serge Koussevitzky Music Foundation Collection (modern musical holographs, correspondence, papers); McKim Fund (holograph violin-piano music); Dayton C. Miller Flute Collection (instruments, music, and literature); Rachmaninoff Archives (musical holographs, correspondence, photographs, and memorabilia); Albert Schatz Collection (opera librettos and documentation); Gertrude Clarke Whittall Foundation Collection (musical

holographs, music imprints, objets d'art); Gertrude Clarke Whittall Collection of Stradivari instruments; Geraldine Farrar Collection (correspondence and memorabilia); musical manuscripts of Bach, Barber, Beethoven, L. Bernstein, Brahms, Haydn, Mendelssohn, Mozart, Schubert, R. Schumann, William Schuman, Rachmaninoff, Gershwin, R. Rodgers, Sousa, Schoenberg, Herbert, R. Harris, Korngold, Liszt, Delibes, Copland, Carter, Stravinsky, Bartok, Britten, Block, MacDowell, and extensive collections of American popular music and film scores.

LIBRARY OF CONGRESS - MUSIC DIVISION - AMERICAN HARP SOCIETY
See: American Harp Society Repository

LIBRARY OF CONGRESS - MUSIC DIVISION - ARCHIVE OF FOLK CULTURE
See: Library of Congress - American Folklife Center - Archive of Folk Culture

★6987★
LIBRARY OF CONGRESS - NATIONAL LIBRARY SERVICE FOR THE BLIND AND PHYSICALLY HANDICAPPED (Aud-Vis)
Taylor St. Annex
1291 Taylor St., N.W.   Phone: (202) 287-5100
Washington, DC 20542   Frank Kurt Cylke, Dir.
Remarks: The National Library Service for the Blind and Physically Handicapped administers a library program that provides recorded and braille books and magazines through 156 regional and subregional libraries located in all parts of the United States. The collection of approximately 19,000 titles in recorded form (disc and cassette) and 17,000 titles in braille may be borrowed from any network library by persons who are unable to read standard printed material because of visual or physical impairment. Special playback equipment is also part of this free library service. A collection of over 30,000 music scores, textbooks and instructional materials in braille, large type, and recorded form is available on loan directly from the National Library Service for the Blind and Physically Handicapped. Through the efforts of volunteer braille transcribers and tape narrators additional titles are provided in limited copies. Reference and information services on all aspects of handicapping conditions are available to libraries, organizations and the public by telephone or mail correspondence. A list of publications is available on request.

★6988★
LIBRARY OF CONGRESS - NATIONAL REFERRAL CENTER (Sci-Tech)
John Adams Bldg., Rm. 5228   Phone: (202) 287-5670
Washington, DC 20540   Edward N. MacConomy, Chf.
Founded: 1962. **Staff:** 20. **Subjects:** All subject areas, ranging from science and technology to the arts and humanities. **Holdings:** Database containing descriptions of information resources (13,000 items). **Services:** Center provides lists of knowledgeable organizations in response to questions on any subject; center open to public. **Publications:** General and special directories of information resources, irregular. **Remarks:** The center was previously a part of the Science & Technology Division.

★6989★
LIBRARY OF CONGRESS - PRESERVATION OFFICE (Rare Book)
James Madison Memorial Bldg., Rm. G-21   Phone: (202) 287-5213
Washington, DC 20540   Peter G. Sparks, Dir. for Preservation
Founded: 1967. **Staff:** Prof 31; Other 74. **Subjects:** Preservation, paper technology. **Special Collections:** Library and archival preservation (900 items relating to the field). **Holdings:** 1500 books; 95 bound periodical volumes; 3 films; 1 slide set. **Subscriptions:** 50 journals and other serials. **Services:** Library open to public. **Publications:** Procedures for Salvage of Water-Damaged Library Materials; Polyester Film Encapsulation; Matting and Hinging of Works of Art on Paper; Bookbinding and the Conservation of Books: A Dictionary of Descriptive Terminology; Boxes for the Protection of Rare Books: Their Design and Construction; Preservation Leaflet No.1: Selected References in the Literature of Conservation; No. 2: Environmental Protection of Books and Related Materials; No.3: Preserving Leather Bookbindings; No.4: Marking Manuscripts; No.5: Newsprint and Its Preservation. **Remarks:** This office provides reference service on preservation and conservation problems which can be answered without extensive and original research not already undertaken. **Staff:** Prentiss L. Gillespie, Libn.

★6990★
LIBRARY OF CONGRESS - PRINTS & PHOTOGRAPHS DIVISION (Pict)
James Madison Memorial Bldg., Rm. LM 339   Phone: (202) 287-5836
Washington, DC 20540   Oliver Jensen, Chf.
Subjects: J. and E.R. Pennell Collection (modern and contemporary fine prints, Pennelliana, Whistleriana); Gardiner Greene Hubbard Collection (fine prints, 15th-19th century), George Lothrop Bradley Collection (fine prints); 19th-century American lithographs by Currier and Ives and other printmakers;

Cabinet of American Illustration (original drawings); Civil War drawings by Edwin Forbes, A.R. Waud and others (originals); American political cartoons; the Caroline and Erwin Swann Collection of cartoons and caricatures; New Yorker cartoons (originals); American and British satirical prints from the 18th and 19th centuries; the Willard D. Straight Collection of French and American World War II prints; the Yanker Collection (political propaganda, mainly posters, 1965-1980); the WPA Collections (Work Projects Administration posters, architectural records, and fine prints); the Carnegie Survey of the Architecture of the South (pictorial archives of early American architecture); approximately 125,000 stereoscopic photoprints; documentary photographs, mainly American scenes; photographic collections; geographic collection; Mathew B. Brady and the Brady-Handy Collection (Civil War, portraits, the American scene); portrait collections; documentary photographers: Frances Benjamin Johnston, Lewis Hine, Roger Fenton, Arnold Genthe; George Grantham Bain (news photographs, 1898-1926); Detroit Photographic Company (archive of views, events and Americana, 1898-1914); Alexander Graham Bell Collection; Herbert E. French (news photographs, Washingtoniana, 1910-1935); American Red Cross (1900 through 1930s); Erwin Evans Smith Collection (cowboys and the western ranges); photographic survey of America made by the Office of War Information and the Farm Security Administration (1935-1945); Historic American Buildings Survey, Historic American Engineering Record (measured drawings, photographs, negatives); Archive of Hispanic Culture (photographs of Latin American art and architecture); Toni Frissell Collection (fashion and personalities); Matson Collection (Near East, 1898-1946); Seagram County Court House Collection (1100 buildings in 48 states). **Holdings:** 190,000 prints and drawings; 70,000 posters; 8.5 million photographic prints and negatives, daguerrotypes and slides. **Remarks:** The division houses 10 million images of all sorts other than painting and sculpture.

★6991★
LIBRARY OF CONGRESS - RARE BOOK & SPECIAL COLLECTIONS DIVISION (Rare Book)
Thomas Jefferson Bldg., Rm. 256   Phone: (202) 287-5434
Washington, DC 20540   William Matheson, Chf.
Subjects: Aeronautics and ballooning; Americana (almanacs, 1646-1900; American imprints, 1640-1800; books from Peter Force's library; Confederate States of America Collection, 1860-1865; documents of the first 14 Congresses; genealogical manuscripts of Charles Edward Banks; Hawaiian Collection; Joseph Meredith Toner Collection of Medicine and 19th Century Local History; Daniel Murray Collection of pamphlets by Negro Authors; Shakers; Wagner-Camp Collection; writings of Henry Harrisse); Anarchism; Bacon-Shakespeare controversy and cryptography (George Fabyan gift); Benjamin Franklin (books by, about, printed by, and part of personal library); Bibles; books designed by Bruce Rogers; bound pamphlets collection; broadsides, 15th century to present; "Bulgarian Renaissance" imprints; children's literature; collections of the printed output of individual publishers, some received as archival sets from the publishers (Armed Forces Editions, Big Little Books, Bollingen Foundation, Dell paperbacks, Franklin Book Program, Little Blue Books, Stone and Kimball); copyright records, 1790-1870; copyright title pages; dime novels, 1860-1910; Don Quixote Collection (Leonard Kebler gift); early English plays (Francis Longe Collection); early printing 1501-1520; English printing, 1478-1640; Frederic W. Goudy's library; gastronomy and nutrition (Katherine Golden Bitting and Elizabeth Pennell Collections); Hans and Hanni Kraus Sir Francis Drake Collection; Harrison Elliott Collection of Paperiana; Henry James; Hunting Library of Theodore Roosevelt; Jean Hersholt Collections of Hans Christian Andersen, Sinclair Lewis, and Hugh Walpole; John Boyd Thacher Collection (incunabula, discovery of the Americas, history of the French Revolution, autographs of European notables); John Davis Batchelder Collection of first editions and association copies; Justice Oliver Wendell Holmes' library; Lessing J. Rosenwald Collection of incunabula, illustrated books, and rare books; Lincolniana (Alfred Whital Stern gift); magic and the occult (Harry Houdini and McManus-Young Collections); manuscript plays received as copyright deposits; Martin Luther Collection; Medieval and Renaissance manuscripts; miniature books; Otto H. Vollbehr Collection of incunabula and 16th-18th century continental title pages and printers' marks; playbills; private press books; Reformation Collection; Rudyard Kipling (Adm. Lloyd H. Chandler and William M. Carpenter Collections); Russian Imperial Collection; Sigmund Freud Collection, including books from Freud's library; Spanish-American Imprints, 1543-1820; Third Reich Collection; Thomas Jefferson's library; Walt Whitman (Carolyn Wells Houghton, Charles Feinberg and Thomas B. Harned Collections); women's suffrage (Susan B. Anthony's library, Carrie Chapman Catt and National American Woman Suffrage Association Collection); Woodrow Wilson's library. **Holdings:** 510,000 items, including the largest collection of incunabula (more than 5600) in the Western Hemisphere.

★6992★
LIBRARY OF CONGRESS - SCIENCE & TECHNOLOGY DIVISION (Sci-Tech)
John Adams Bldg., Rm. 5112   Phone: (202) 287-5639
Washington, DC 20540   Joseph W. Price, Chf.
Staff: 35. **Publications:** Bibliographies; LC Science Tracer Bullet series; chronologies. **Remarks:** Within the Library of Congress, the Science and Technology Division has acquisition-recommending responsibility for the science and technology collections; provides reference and bibliographic services on these collections to the scientific community, other government agencies, and the general public; prepares and issues various special bibliographies and other documents; and carries on a limited number of special bibliographic projects under transfer-of-funds arrangements with other agencies. Its services are based on the library's collections in science and technology which include more than three million books, over 60,000 journals and other serial titles, and three million unclassified (as to security) technical reports. The last-named category includes comprehensive holdings of the unclassified outputs of the Department of Energy, the National Aeronautics and Space Administration, and the Department of Defense and its contractors (mainly in microform). Computer terminals in Science Reading Room provide online bibliographic access to the emerging Library of Congress machine-readable catalogs.

★6993★
LIBRARY OF CONGRESS - SERIAL AND GOVERNMENT PUBLICATIONS DIVISION
James Madison Memorial Bldg., Rm. LM-133   Phone: (202) 287-5647
Washington, DC 20540   Donald F. Wisdom, Chf.
Subjects: Unbound serial publications, both official and nonofficial, including periodicals, journals of learned societies, and government serials (approximately 70,000 titles) and unbound issues, bound volumes, and microfilm of domestic and foreign newspapers in Western and Cyrillic alphabets, current and retrospective from the 17th century (approximately 12,000 titles, including over 1600 domestic and foreign titles received currently).

LIBRARY OF ESOTERIC STUDIES
See: Philosophical Heritage Institute

★6994★
LIBRARY OF HENRY J. GRUND (Hist)
4897 Corduroy Rd.
Mentor Headlands
Mentor, OH 44060   Henry J. Grund, II, Dir.
Staff: Prof 1; Other 1. **Subjects:** Ohio history, railroads, agriculture, outdoor life, North American history, art, literature. **Special Collections:** Ohio Collection (1075 volumes); Railroads Collection (600 volumes); Rare Book Collection (1315 volumes). **Holdings:** 12,027 books; 102 bound periodical volumes; 60 volumes of Pennsylvania County histories; 20 volumes of New York State county histories. **Services:** Interlibrary loans (limited); library open to public with written approval.

LIBRARY & HOUSING INFORMATION CENTER
See: Action-Housing, Inc.

LIBRARY OF THE IMMACULATE HEART OF MARY
See: Carmelite Monastery

LIBRARY OF INDIVIDUAL BUSINESS HISTORIES
See: Lincoln Educational Foundation

★6995★
LIBRARY OF INTERNATIONAL RELATIONS (Soc Sci)
666 Lake Shore Dr.   Phone: (312) 787-7928
Chicago, IL 60611   Eloise ReQua, Dir.
Founded: 1932. **Staff:** Prof 4; Other 1. **Subjects:** Economics; political science; geography; sociology; international relations, organizations, trade and law. **Special Collections:** Latin America, Asia, Africa, underdeveloped areas; U.N. depository; complete U.N. and League of Nations Treaty Series. **Holdings:** 306,000 books; 40,000 unbound periodical volumes; pamphlets and documents (cataloged); 800 maps; 15 VF drawers of information files on nongovernmental organizations. **Subscriptions:** 1000 journals and other serials. **Services:** Interlibrary loans (limited); copying; library open to public. **Special Catalogs:** Catalog of articles in foreign published materials. **Staff:** Jonas Dainauskas, Cat. & Ref.Libn.; Yoon S. Park, Cat.

LIBRARY OF THE ITALIAN RISORGIMENTO
See: Garibaldi and Meucci Memorial Museum

LIBRARY AT LINCOLN CENTER
See: Fordham University

LIBRARY OF NATURAL SOUNDS
See: Cornell University - Laboratory of Ornithology

LIBRARY OF PARLIAMENT
See: Canada - Library of Parliament

LIBRARY OF THE UNITED STATES COURTS
See: William J. Campbell Library of the United States Courts

★6996★
LIBRARY OF VEHICLES (Trans)
12172 Sheridan Ln.   Phone: (714) 636-9517
Garden Grove, CA 92640   W. Everett Miller, Libn. & Owner
Founded: 1914. **Staff:** Prof 1. **Subjects:** Automobiles, trucks, motorcycles, bicycles, sleighs, carriages, wagons. **Special Collections:** Automobile sales catalogs (16,000); J. Frank Duryea Collection. **Holdings:** 8250 books; 75 bound periodical volumes; 15,000 vendors catalogs; 275 file drawers of manuscripts, patents, clippings, archives, and documents; 3000 negatives. **Subscriptions:** 40 journals and other serials. **Services:** Literature searching in automotive engineering; copying; library open to public by appointment on a fee basis. **Publications:** America's First Gasoline Automobile by J. Frank Duryea. **Special Catalogs:** Roster of American automobiles.

LICHTENSTEIN (Grace & Philip) SCIENTIFIC LIBRARY
See: AMC Cancer Research Center and Hospital - Grace & Philip Lichtenstein Scientific Library

LICK OBSERVATORY LIBRARY
See: University of California, Santa Cruz - Science Library

★6997★
LICKING COUNTY LAW LIBRARY ASSOCIATION (Law)†
22 1/2 N. Second St.   Phone: (614) 345-6400
Newark, OH 43055   Hon. Virginia Weiss, Libn.
Founded: 1896. **Subjects:** Law. **Holdings:** 30,000 books; 350 bound periodical volumes. **Services:** Copying; library not open to public.

★6998★
LICKING MEMORIAL HOSPITAL - MEDICAL LIBRARY (Med)
1320 W. Main St.   Phone: (614) 344-0331
Newark, OH 43055   Kathleen M. Martin, Lib.Asst.
Founded: 1966. **Staff:** Prof 1; Other 3. **Subjects:** Clinical medicine, nursing. **Holdings:** 600 books; 300 bound periodical volumes; tapes. **Subscriptions:** 32 journals. **Services:** Interlibrary loans; copying; library not open to public. **Networks/Consortia:** Member of Central Ohio Hospital Library Consortium.

LIEURANCE (Thurlow) MEMORIAL MUSIC LIBRARY
See: Wichita State University - Thurlow Lieurance Memorial Music Library

★6999★
LIFE INSURANCE MARKETING AND RESEARCH ASSOCIATION - LIBRARY (Bus-Fin)
Box 208   Phone: (203) 677-0033
Hartford, CT 06141   William J. Mortimer, Mgr., Lib./Ref.Serv.
Founded: 1926. **Staff:** Prof 2; Other 3. **Subjects:** Life insurance, industrial psychology, statistical methods. **Holdings:** 5000 books; 215 file drawers of clippings, pamphlets, and documents. **Subscriptions:** 125 journals and other serials. **Services:** Interlibrary loans; open to member companies of the association and to others upon application. **Computerized Information Services:** SDC. **Special Indexes:** LIMRA publication index, annual (book). **Remarks:** The library is located at 8 Farm Springs, Farmington, CT 06032. **Staff:** Anita Morency, Asst.Libn.

★7000★
LIFE OFFICE MANAGEMENT ASSOCIATION - INFORMATION CENTER (Bus-Fin)
100 Colony Sq.   Phone: (404) 892-7272
Atlanta, GA 30361   Patricia A. Toups, Libn.
Founded: 1925. **Staff:** Prof 1; Other 3. **Subjects:** Life insurance, office management, statistics, life insurance company history, finance, personnel management, accounting. **Holdings:** 1200 books; 15,000 reports (cataloged); 3 VF drawers of pamphlets. **Subscriptions:** 300 journals and other serials. **Services:** Interlibrary loans (to member companies); use of library for reference may be requested. **Also Known As:** LOMA.

★7001★

LIFE PLANNING/HEALTH SERVICES - LIBRARY/MEDIA SERVICES (Soc Sci)
2727 Oaklawn, Suite 228   Phone: (214) 522-0290
Dallas, TX 75219   Martha Brewer, Dp.Dir.
Staff: Prof 1; Other 1. **Subjects:** Birth control, family planning, sex education, population data, general health services. **Holdings:** 1100 books; 75 bound periodical volumes; 150 films; unbound reports; clippings; monographs. **Subscriptions:** 77 journals and other serials. **Services:** Interlibrary loans; copying; library open to public. **Networks/Consortia:** Member of Dallas/Fort Worth Health Science Consortium; Dallas Area Metroplex Project (DAMP); Association for Population/Family Planning Libraries and Information Centers - International (APLIC); TALON. **Special Catalogs:** Film listing.

★7002★

LIFE SAVERS, INC. - RESEARCH AND DEVELOPMENT DIVISION - TECHNICAL INFORMATION CENTER (Food-Bev)
N. Main St.   Phone: (914) 937-3200
Port Chester, NY 10573   Clare Adamo, Libn.
Founded: 1964. **Staff:** Prof 1; Other 1. **Subjects:** Food processing, analytical methodology, confections, gum, packaging. **Holdings:** 2000 books; 980 bound periodical volumes; 10 VF drawers of patents; 8 VF drawers of photoprints; 50 VF drawers of manuscripts; lab notebooks; technical reports; project folders. **Subscriptions:** 90 journals and other serials. **Services:** Interlibrary loans; copying; center open to public for reference use only on request. **Computerized Information Services:** DIALOG.

★7003★

LIFWYNN FOUNDATION, INC. - LIBRARY (Soc Sci)
30 Turkey Hill Rd., S.   Phone: (203) 227-4139
Westport, CT 06880   Alfreda S. Galt, Sec.
Founded: 1927. **Staff:** 2. **Subjects:** Behavioral science, psychiatry and psychology, sociology. **Holdings:** 2500 books (one-fourth in German); 500 bound periodical volumes; 5000 reprints of published articles; 1000 unbound journals. **Subscriptions:** 30 journals and other serials. **Services:** Library open to qualified persons by appointment.

★7004★

LIGGETT & MYERS TOBACCO CO. - INFORMATION SERVICES (Sci-Tech)
Research Department
Box 1572   Phone: (919) 683-8985
Durham, NC 27702   Sandra S. Harris, Libn.
Founded: 1947. **Subjects:** Tobacco technology, chemistry, engineering, medicine. **Holdings:** 1500 books; 300 bound periodical volumes. **Subscriptions:** 40 journals and other serials. **Special Indexes:** Indexes to Registry Systems.

LIGHTHOUSE LIBRARY
See: New York Association for the Blind

LILIENTHAL (Joseph L.) LIBRARY
See: Johns Hopkins University - School of Medicine - Joseph L. Lilienthal Library

★7005★

LILLICK MC HOSE & CHARLES, ATTORNEYS AT LAW - LAW LIBRARY (Law)†
707 Wilshire Blvd., 45th Fl.   Phone: (213) 620-9000
Los Angeles, CA 90017   Luramay Ellsworth, Law Libn.
Staff: Prof 1; Other 1. **Subjects:** Law. **Special Collections:** Maritime law (800 items). **Holdings:** 15,000 books; 500 bound periodical volumes; 1500 legal memoranda and loose-leaf items. **Subscriptions:** 220 journals and other serials; 9 newspapers. **Services:** Interlibrary loans; not open to public. **Publications:** Acquisitions List, bimonthly - for internal distribution only.

LILLY ARCHIVES
See: Eli Lilly and Company

LILLY (Eli) AND COMPANY
See: Eli Lilly and Company

LILLY LIBRARY
See: Earlham College - Quaker Collection

LILLY LIBRARY
See: Indiana University

LILRC
See: Long Island Library Resources Council, Inc.

★7006★

LIMA MEMORIAL HOSPITAL - HEALTH SCIENCES LIBRARY (Med)
Linden & Mobel Sts.   Phone: (419) 228-3335
Lima, OH 45804   Margaret S. Cutter, Libn.
Founded: 1972. **Staff:** Prof 1. **Subjects:** Medicine, nursing, pharmacology, hospital administration. **Holdings:** 1010 books; 682 bound periodical volumes; 1 drawer of clippings, pamphlets, documents. **Subscriptions:** 50 journals and other serials. **Services:** Interlibrary loans; copying; library open to public with restrictions.

LIMA (Oliveira) LIBRARY
See: Catholic University of America - Oliveira Lima Library

★7007★

LIMA STATE HOSPITAL - FORENSIC PSYCHIATRY LIBRARY (Soc Sci)†
North West St. Rd.
Drawer Q   Phone: (419) 227-4631
Lima, OH 45801   Charles W. Lee, Dir.
Founded: 1961. **Staff:** Prof 2; Other 2. **Subjects:** Philosophy and psychology, religion, social service, science, psychiatry. **Holdings:** 14,000 books; 78 bound periodical volumes; 2500 tapes (cataloged). **Subscriptions:** 32 journals and other serials; 14 newspapers. **Services:** Interlibrary loans; copying; library open to public with restrictions. **Networks/Consortia:** Member of Western Ohio Regional Library Development System (WORLDS); OCLC. **Publications:** Habilitator; Bridgebuilder. **Special Catalogs:** Catalog of cassette tapes. **Staff:** David Goldsmith, Asst.

LINCOLN (Abraham) BIRTHPLACE NATL. HISTORIC SITE
See: U.S. Natl. Park Service - Abraham Lincoln Birthplace Natl. Historic Site

LINCOLN (Abraham) LIBRARY AND MUSEUM
See: Lincoln Memorial University - Abraham Lincoln Library and Museum

LINCOLN BOYHOOD NATL. MEMORIAL VISITOR CENTER
See: U.S. Natl. Park Service

★7008★

LINCOLN CHRISTIAN COLLEGE & SEMINARY - JESSIE C. EURY LIBRARY (Rel-Theol)
Keokuk & Limit Sts.   Phone: (217) 732-3168
Lincoln, IL 62656   Thomas M. Tanner, Libn.
Founded: 1944. **Staff:** Prof 2; Other 5. **Subjects:** Biblical studies, Restoration movement, religion, philosophy, ministry. **Special Collections:** Enos E. Dowling Rare Book Room (2000 hymnbooks). **Holdings:** 64,000 books; 5000 bound periodical volumes; 4750 volumes in microform (cataloged); 14,000 AV units **Subscriptions:** 470 journals and other serials; 6 newspapers. **Services:** Interlibrary loans; copying; library open to public. **Computerized Information Services:** Computerized cataloging. **Networks/Consortia:** Member of Sangamon Valley Academic Consortium (SVAL); Rolling Prairie Library System; OCLC. **Staff:** Ann Spellman, Media Ctr.Libn.

LINCOLN COLLECTIONS
See: Bradley University - Virginius H. Chase Special Collections Center

★7009★

LINCOLN COUNTY LAW LIBRARY (Law)†
                    Phone: (207) 882-7517
Wiscasset, ME 04578   George A. Cowan, Libn.
Staff: 1. **Subjects:** Law. **Holdings:** 10,200 volumes. **Services:** Library open to public with permission.

★7010★

LINCOLN EDUCATIONAL FOUNDATION - LIBRARY OF INDIVIDUAL BUSINESS HISTORIES (Bus-Fin; Hist)
299 Madison Ave., Rm. 503   Phone: (212) 697-2236
New York, NY 10017   Frank Wetzel, Libn.
Founded: 1951. **Staff:** Prof 2. **Subjects:** Industrial history of America. **Holdings:** 3000 volumes. **Services:** Free lending library to scholars, writers and researchers.

★7011★

LINCOLN FIRST BANK, NA, INC. - LINCOLN FIRST LIBRARY (Bus-Fin)
One Lincoln First Square   Phone: (716) 258-6460
Rochester, NY 14643   Alla F. Levi, Dir. of Lib.Serv.
Founded: 1972. **Staff:** Prof 1; Other 1. **Subjects:** Banking, finance, management, personnel. **Special Collections:** Annual reports from savings and loans associations, commercial banks and bank holding companies; New York State statistics. **Holdings:** 3574 books; 1500 other cataloged items; 17

file drawers of other material; annual reports on microfiche; Fortune 500 on microfiche. **Subscriptions:** 300 journals and other serials; 10 newspapers. **Services:** Interlibrary loans; copying; SDI; library open to public by appointment. **Networks/Consortia:** Member of Rochester Regional Research Library Council. **Publications:** Lincoln First Library Acquisitions List, quarterly.

★7012★
LINCOLN GENERAL HOSPITAL - MEDICAL LIBRARY (Med)
2300 S. 16th St.   Phone: (402) 473-5332
Lincoln, NE 68502   Lucille Rosenberg, Libn.
Founded: 1976. **Staff:** Prof 1. **Subjects:** Medicine, oncology, orthopedics, psychiatry, nursing, trauma and related health sciences and professions. **Special Collections:** Winett Orr orthopedic books. **Holdings:** 625 books; 90 bound periodical volumes. **Subscriptions:** 225 journals and other serials. **Services:** Interlibrary loans; copying; library open to health professionals or students for reference use only. **Computerized Information Services:** MEDLINE; computerized cataloging. **Networks/Consortia:** Member of Lincoln Area Health Science Libraries Group. **Publications:** News in General; House Call; Generally Speaking. **Special Catalogs:** Union List of Journals (ring bound book).

★7013★
LINCOLN HOSPITAL - MEDICAL LIBRARY (Med)
234 E. 149th St.   Phone: (212) 579-5745
Bronx, NY 10451   Miss Milagros M. Paredes, Med.Libn.
Staff: Prof 1; Other 3. **Subjects:** Medicine, surgery, pediatrics, obstetrics/gynecology, nursing. **Holdings:** 2000 books; 6923 bound periodical volumes. **Subscriptions:** 300 journals and other serials. **Services:** Interlibrary loans; copying; library not open to public.

★7014★
LINCOLN INSTITUTE OF LAND POLICY - LIBRARY (Env-Cons)
26 Trowbridge St.   Phone: (617) 661-3016
Cambridge, MA 02138   Mary J. O'Brien, Libn.
Staff: Prof 1; Other 1. **Subjects:** Land reform in developing countries, land use, land taxation, urban renewal, economics and public finance, land economics. **Holdings:** 2590 books; 3127 VF drawers of pamphlets. **Subscriptions:** 125 journals and other serials; 5 newspapers. **Services:** Interlibrary loans; library open to qualified researchers. **Publications:** List of publications - available upon request.

★7015★
LINCOLN JOURNAL-STAR - LIBRARY (Publ)
926 P St.
Box 81709   Phone: (402) 473-7293
Lincoln, NE 68501   Patricia R. Loos, Dir.
Founded: 1951. **Staff:** Prof 2; Other 3. **Subjects:** Clipping files on people and subjects. **Special Collections:** Microfilm of newspaper clippings of Starkweather-Fugate murder spree and follow-up, 1957-1973. **Holdings:** 2500 books; 1400 reels of microfilm of Journal-Star newspapers and other subjects; 500,000 pictures. **Subscriptions:** 25 journals and other serials; 20 newspapers. **Services:** Copying; library open to public for a fee. **Special Indexes:** Index of all historical issues of Journal-Star.

LINCOLN LABORATORY LIBRARY
See: Massachusetts Institute of Technology

LINCOLN LIBRARY AND MUSEUM
See: Lincoln National Life Foundation - Louis A. Warren Lincoln Library and Museum

★7016★
LINCOLN LIBRARY - SANGAMON VALLEY COLLECTION (Hist)
326 S. 7th St.   Phone: (217) 753-4910
Springfield, IL 62701   Edward J. Russo, Hd.
Founded: 1972. **Staff:** Prof 2; Other 2. **Subjects:** Local history, genealogy. **Special Collections:** Vachel Lindsay Collection (4 VF drawers). **Holdings:** 4800 books; 200 bound periodical volumes; 6000 local photographs. **Subscriptions:** 159 journals and other serials. **Services:** Interlibrary loans; copying; library open to public. **Publications:** Bulletin, monthly. **Special Indexes:** Local obituary index; current index to Illinois State Journal-Register.

LINCOLN MEMORIAL LIBRARY
See: Veterans Home of California

LINCOLN MEMORIAL LIBRARY (Essex Fells, NJ)
See: Northeastern Bible College

★7017★
LINCOLN MEMORIAL SHRINE - LIBRARY (Hist)
120 4th St.
Box 751   Phone: (714) 793-6622
Redlands, CA 92373   Dr. Larry E. Burgess, Cur.
Founded: 1932. **Staff:** Prof 1; Other 1. **Subjects:** Abraham Lincoln, Civil War. **Special Collections:** Rare pamphlet collection of Civil War and Lincoln (3000 items); Gideon Welles manuscript collection (120 items). **Holdings:** 4000 books; 750 unbound periodicals (cataloged); 1000 manuscripts; 350 photographs; 3000 clippings. **Services:** Copying; library open to public. **Special Catalogs:** A Selective Bibliography of the Holdings of the Lincoln Memorial Shrine; yearly keepsake publications. **Remarks:** Maintained by A.K. Smiley Public Library.

★7018★
LINCOLN MEMORIAL UNIVERSITY - ABRAHAM LINCOLN LIBRARY AND MUSEUM (Hist)
Harrogate, TN 37752   Edgar G. Archer, Dir.
Staff: Prof 1; Other 14. **Subjects:** Abraham Lincoln, Civil War, Cumberland Gap, Lincoln Memorial University. **Special Collections:** Presidential Signatures Collection. **Holdings:** 8500 books; 15,000 pamphlets; 20,000 clippings; 250,000 artifacts, archival and manuscript material; War between the States sheet music; Lincoln sheet music; manuscripts - Abraham Lincoln, Civil War, Cassius M. Clay, O.O. Howard; microfilm; scrapbooks. **Subscriptions:** 49 journals and other serials. **Services:** Copying; library open to public for reference use only and under supervision; museum/archives conservation laboratory and museum consulting service available. **Publications:** Lincoln Herald, quarterly - for sale by subscription. **Remarks:** Includes holdings of National Lincoln-Civil War Council Library and the Society of Civil War Surgeons Library.

★7019★
LINCOLN NATIONAL CORPORATION - LAW LIBRARY (Law)
1300 S. Clinton St., 7th Fl.
Box 1110   Phone: (219) 427-3870
Fort Wayne, IN 46801   Mary A. McDonald, Adm., Info.Serv.
Staff: Prof 1; Other 1. **Subjects:** Law. **Holdings:** 22,000 volumes. **Services:** Copying; library open to professionals for research use only. **Computerized Information Services:** LEXIS; internal database; computerized acquisitions, serials and legal memoranda index. **Networks/Consortia:** Member of TRI-ALSA (Area 3 Library Services Authority); OCLC; INCOLSA. **Formerly:** Lincoln National Life Insurance Company.

★7020★
LINCOLN NATIONAL LIFE FOUNDATION - LOUIS A. WARREN LINCOLN LIBRARY AND MUSEUM (Hist)
1300 S. Clinton St.
Box 1110   Phone: (219) 427-3864
Fort Wayne, IN 46801   Mark E. Neely, Jr., Dir.
Founded: 1928. **Staff:** Prof 2; Other 2. **Subjects:** Lincolniana; 19th century American history, biography, politics; Civil War; slavery; reconstruction. **Special Collections:** Association books (books similar to those Lincoln read); manuscripts; philatelic Lincolniana; metallic Lincolniana; pictorial Lincolniana - original paints, rare lithographs, engravings, original photographs, prints. **Holdings:** 18,000 volumes; 10,000 items of Lincolniana; 400 association books; 7600 collateral books. **Services:** Interlibrary loans (by special request); copying; library open to public. **Publications:** Lincoln Lore, monthly; R. Gerald McMurty Lecture, annual - available on request. **Staff:** Mary Jane Hubler, Asst. to Dir.

★7021★
LINCOLN PARK ZOOLOGICAL GARDENS - LIBRARY (Sci-Tech)
2200 N. Cannon Dr.   Phone: (312) 294-4640
Chicago, IL 60614   Louise Bower, Libn.
Staff: 1. **Subjects:** Zoology, animal behavior and care, wildlife conservation, management of captive wild animals, natural history, zoos. **Special Collections:** Zoo archives; international zoo posters. **Holdings:** 1400 books; 450 newsletters, inventories; 200 journals and reprints. **Subscriptions:** 45 journals and other serials. **Services:** Interlibrary loans; copying; library open to public by appointment. **Networks/Consortia:** Member of Metropolitan Chicago Library Assembly; ILLINET. **Publications:** Acquisitions list - on request.

★7022★
LINCOLN UNIVERSITY - LANGSTON HUGHES MEMORIAL LIBRARY - SPECIAL COLLECTIONS (Area-Ethnic)
                                     Phone: (215) 932-8300
Lincoln University, PA 19352   Sophy H. Cornwell, Spec.Coll.Libn.
Staff: Prof 1; Other 2. **Subjects:** Black Studies - especially fine arts, history,

civil rights and education; African Studies - especially economics, history, political science, language and literature. **Special Collections:** Personal library of Langston Hughes (3300 items); manuscripts of Pennsylvania Colonization Society and Young Men's Colonization Society (6 volumes); rare books (850); rare antislavery pamphlets (200). **Holdings:** 18,350 books; 1060 bound periodical volumes; 772 reels of microfilm and 100 phonograph records (cataloged); 250 pictures (black performers, historical); 6000 unbound periodicals; 1595 microfiche (antislavery); 1300 African government documents; 2500 VF items; 6000 items of archives and miscellany. **Subscriptions:** 180 journals and other serials; 7 newspapers. **Services:** Interlibrary loans; copying; library open to public for reference use only. **Computerized Information Services:** Computerized cataloging and ILL. **Networks/Consortia:** Member of OCLC through PALINET & Union Library Catalogue of Pennsylvania; Tri-State College Library Cooperative (TCLC). **Publications:** Catalog of the Special Negro and African Collection, 2 volumes and supplement, 1970; Computer Output Microfilm Catalog, July 1970 - June 1977; A Survey of the Special Negro Collections by Donald C. Yelton; Reference Handbook of Special Collections - all four for sale; selected bibliography on Malcolm X, bimonthly accessions lists - both free on request. **Special Catalogs:** Catalog of the Special Negro and African Collection; mimeographed list of periodicals in the African collection; mimeographed reference handbook. **Staff:** Emery Wimbish, Jr., Hd.Libn.

★7023★
LINCOLN UNIVERSITY - LAW LIBRARY (Law)
281 Masonic Ave.　　　　　　　Phone: (415) 221-1212
San Francisco, CA 94118　　　　　Andrea Segall, Law Libn.
Staff: Prof 1; Other 3. **Subjects:** Law. **Holdings:** 20,000 books; 700 bound periodical volumes. **Subscriptions:** 66 journals and other serials. **Services:** Copying; library open to public with restrictions. **Computerized Information Services:** WESTLAW.

★7024★
LINCOLN UNIVERSITY OF MISSOURI - INMAN E. PAGE LIBRARY (Educ)
　　　　　　　　　　　　　　　Phone: (314) 751-2325
Jefferson City, MO 65101　　　　Catherine Long, Act.Libn.
Founded: 1866. **Staff:** Prof 2; Other 8. **Subjects:** Liberal arts; education - elementary and secondary; nursing; corrections and law enforcement. **Special Collections:** Pro-slavery and antislavery tracts; pre- and post-Civil War period; black and ethnic collections (6000 books). **Holdings:** 139,873 books; 8819 bound periodical volumes; 10,374 government documents (cataloged); 42,657 government documents; 225 theses and dissertations; 30 VF drawers; 4 VF drawers of pictures; 51,615 titles on microforms. **Subscriptions:** 1168 journals and other serials; 43 newspapers. **Services:** Interlibrary loans; copying; library open to public with restrictions. **Networks/Consortia:** Member of Mid-Missouri Library Network. **Publications:** Lincoln's Page, irregular; Bibliography of Books By and About Blacks, annual supplement; Monthly Checklist (selected); newsletter; students handbook; Library Manual. **Staff:** Fay T. Carter, Acq.Libn.

★7025★
LINDA HALL LIBRARY (Sci-Tech)
5109 Cherry St.　　　　　　　Phone: (816) 363-4600
Kansas City, MO 64110　　　　　Larry X. Besant, Dir.
Founded: 1946. **Staff:** Prof 18; Other 38. **Subjects:** Mathematics, astronomy, physics, chemistry, geology, biology, pharmacy, agriculture, engineering. **Special Collections:** History of science; standards and specifications of over 300 governmental and professional organizations. **Holdings:** 520,400 books and bound periodical volumes; U.S. patent specifications, July 1946 to present; 738,500 microforms. **Subscriptions:** 15,600 journals and other serials. **Services:** Interlibrary loans; copying; library open to public. **Networks/Consortia:** Member of OCLC. **Publications:** Serials Holdings in the L.H.L., annual. **Staff:** Siegfried Ruschin, Libn., Coll.Dev.; Wilma L. Hartman, Libn., Pub.Serv.

LINDBERG (Ralph F.) MEMORIAL LIBRARY
See: Riverside Osteopathic Hospital - Ralph F. Lindberg Memorial Library

★7026★
LINDEMANN (Erich) MENTAL HEALTH CENTER - LIBRARY (Med; Soc Sci)†
25 Staniford St.　　　　　　　Phone: (617) 727-7280
Boston, MA 02114　　　　　　Elizabeth Jones, Libn.
Staff: Prof 1. **Subjects:** Psychology, psychiatry, community mental health, mental retardation, drug rehabilitation. **Special Collections:** Documents and archives of Massachusetts Department of Mental Health (1000 items). **Holdings:** 3000 books; 300 bound periodical volumes; 500 documents; 16 VF drawers of pamphlets. **Subscriptions:** 20 journals and other serials. **Services:** Interlibrary loans; library open to public for reference use only. **Networks/Consortia:** Member of CHAMELEON; Boston Group of Government

Libraries (BOGGL). **Remarks:** Maintained by Massachusetts State Department of Mental Health.

LINDGREN LIBRARY
See: Massachusetts Institute of Technology

★7027★
LINDSAY LAW LIBRARY (Law)†
Widener Univ.
Wolfgram Memorial Library　　　Phone: (215) 499-4087
Chester, PA 19013　　　　　　Theresa Taborsky, Hd.
Staff: 1. **Subjects:** Law. **Holdings:** 12,000 volumes. **Subscriptions:** 10 journals and other serials. **Services:** Library open to public for reference use only.

LINEBERGER MEMORIAL LIBRARY
See: Lutheran Theological Southern Seminary

LINGEMAN (Leslie R.) MEMORIAL MEDICAL LIBRARY
See: Blount Memorial Hospital - Leslie R. Lingeman Memorial Medical Library

LINK LIBRARY
See: Concordia Teachers College

★7028★
LINN COUNTY BAR ASSOCIATION - LAW LIBRARY (Law)
Linn County Court House　　　　Phone: (319) 398-3449
Cedar Rapids, IA 52401　　　　Betty Dye, Law Libn.
Founded: 1907. **Staff:** 1. **Subjects:** Law. **Holdings:** 11,000 volumes. **Services:** Copying; library open to public for reference use only. **Remarks:** Operates under the auspices of the Linn County Board of Supervisors.

★7029★
LINN COUNTY HISTORICAL SOCIETY - LIBRARY (Hist)
Box 137　　　　　　　　　　Phone: (913) 352-8739
Pleasanton, KS 66075　　　　　Ola May Earnest, Pres.
Founded: 1973. **Staff:** 3. **Subjects:** Local history and genealogy, state history, agriculture. **Special Collections:** Linn County photographs. **Holdings:** 600 books; 30 manuscripts; 8 VF drawers; newspapers on microfilm. **Subscriptions:** 35 journals and other serials. **Services:** Copying; library open to public for reference use only. **Publications:** Linn County Historical News, quarterly; list of additional publications - available upon request. **Staff:** ; Jean Sylvester, Musm. Docent

LINN (Otto F.) LIBRARY
See: Warner-Pacific College - Otto F. Linn Library

★7030★
LIONEL D. EDIE AND COMPANY, INC. - LIBRARY (Bus-Fin)†
530 Fifth Ave., 4th Fl.　　　　Phone: (212) 957-1400
New York, NY 10036　　　　　Kay Stock, Sr.Lib.Asst.
Founded: 1949. **Staff:** Prof 1; Other 2. **Subjects:** Finance, economics, business. **Special Collections:** Corporation records. **Holdings:** 2000 books; 200 bound periodical volumes; 280 linear feet of corporation material; 70 linear feet of subject files; U.S. government and association materials. **Subscriptions:** 750 journals and other serials. **Services:** Interlibrary loans; library open to clients and SLA members. **Computerized Information Services:** Computerized serials.

★7031★
LIONS GATE HOSPITAL - DR. H. CARSON GRAHAM MEMORIAL LIBRARY (Med)
230 E. 13th St.　　　　　　　Phone: (604) 988-3131
North Vancouver, BC, Canada V7L 2L7　　Myrra N. Marshall, Libn.
Founded: 1961. **Staff:** 2. **Subjects:** Medicine. **Holdings:** 2500 books. **Subscriptions:** 170 journals and other serials. **Services:** Interlibrary loans; copying; literature searches; library not open to public.

LIPPINCOTT LIBRARY
See: University of Pennsylvania

★7032★
LIPTON (Thomas J.) INC. - RESEARCH LIBRARY (Food-Bev)
800 Sylvan Ave.　　　　　　　Phone: (201) 567-8000
Englewood Cliffs, NJ 07632　　Gloria S. Bernstein, Mgr., Lib.Info.Serv.
Staff: Prof 2; Other 1. **Subjects:** Tea, food technology. **Holdings:** 5000 books; 3500 bound periodical volumes; U.S. chemical patents from 1970 to present on microfilm. **Subscriptions:** 250 journals and other serials.

Services: Interlibrary loans; library not open to public. **Computerized Information Services:** DIALOG, SDC, MEDLINE, New York Times Information Service. **Networks/Consortia:** Member of Bergen/Passaic Health Sciences Library Consortium. **Publications:** Bulletin, monthly; KWAC Index of Tea Technology, from 1965 to present. **Staff:** Carol Kornfeld, Lib.Info.Spec.

★7033★
LIQUID CARBONIC CORPORATION - LIBRARY (Sci-Tech)
3740 W. 74th St.   Phone: (312) 855-2500
Chicago, IL 60629   M.A. Armstrong, Libn.
Founded: 1959. **Staff:** Prof 1. **Subjects:** Chemistry, engineering. **Holdings:** 1500 books; 1000 bound periodical volumes; 300 microforms. **Subscriptions:** 192 journals and other serials. **Services:** Interlibrary loans; library open to public with restrictions. **Computerized Information Services:** New England Research Application Center (NERAC). **Networks/Consortia:** Member of ILLINET; Chicago Library System. **Formerly:** Its Research and Development Library.

★7034★
LIQUID PAPER CORPORATION - EMPLOYEE LIBRARY (Sci-Tech; Bus-Fin)*
9130 Markville
Box 225909
Dallas, TX 75265   Emily C. Lin, Libn.
Staff: Prof 1; Other 1. **Subjects:** Pigments, plastics, management, women. **Holdings:** 1000 books. **Subscriptions:** 255 journals and other serials.

LISFORR (Library and Information Service for Rubber)
See: American Chemical Society, Inc. - Rubber Division - John H. Gifford Memorial Library & Information Ctr.

LISTER HILL LIBRARY OF THE HEALTH SCIENCES
See: University of Alabama in Birmingham

LISWOOD (Sidney) LIBRARY
See: Mount Sinai Hospital - Sidney Liswood Library

★7035★
LITCHFIELD HISTORICAL SOCIETY - INGRAHAM LIBRARY (Hist)
Box 385   Phone: (203) 567-5862
Litchfield, CT 06759   Robert G. Carroon, Dir.
Founded: 1856. **Staff:** Prof 1; Other 2. **Subjects:** Local history, genealogy, local authors, early American law. **Special Collections:** Manuscript collections; graphic archives. **Holdings:** 12,000 books and bound periodical volumes; 40,000 manuscripts (cataloged); 300 account books; 20 cartons of almanacs; 70 volumes of Ransom autograph materials; 40 cartons of pamphlets. **Subscriptions:** 15 journals and other serials. **Services:** Copying; genealogical research; library open to public. **Special Catalogs:** Manuscript card catalog.

★7036★
LITERACY VOLUNTEERS OF AMERICA, INC. - LIBRARY (Educ)
404 Oak St.   Phone: (315) 474-7039
Syracuse, NY 13203   Frances J. Farnsworth, Supv.
Staff: 1. **Subjects:** Teaching reading to adults, teaching English as a second language. **Special Collections:** Humanistic reading for grades 1-8 (219 titles). **Holdings:** 1725 books; clippings; picture file. **Services:** Copying; library open to public with restrictions. **Publications:** The Reader, quarterly newsletter. **Special Catalogs:** Bibliography of Basic Materials for Reading; English as a Second Language, Humanities, 1980.

★7037★
LITERARY AND HISTORICAL SOCIETY OF QUEBEC - LIBRARY (Hist)†
44 St. Stanislas St.   Phone: (418) 694-9147
Quebec, PQ, Canada G1R 4H3   Cynthia Dooley, Libn.
Staff: Prof 1; Other 2. **Subjects:** Quebec history. **Holdings:** 25,000 books. **Services:** Library open to public (full use entails annual subscription).

★7038★
LITERATURE SERVICE ASSOCIATES (Info Sci)*
Rd. 3
Box 352 B
Lehighton, PA 18235
Staff: 1. **Subjects:** Indexing, documentation, library science. **Special Collections:** Abstract and periodical indexes to all fields of literature. **Holdings:** 500 books; 800 bound periodical volumes. **Subscriptions:** 125 journals and other serials. **Services:** Searches and translations on fee basis; not open to public. **Computerized Information Services:** DIALOG, SDC.

LITHIUM CORPORATION OF AMERICA, INC.
See: Gulf Resources and Chemical Corporation

LITHIUM INFORMATION CENTER
See: University of Wisconsin, Madison - Department of Psychiatry

★7039★
LITHUANIAN AMERICAN COMMUNITY OF THE U.S.A. - LITHUANIAN WORLD ARCHIVES (Area-Ethnic)
5620 S. Claremont
Chicago, IL 60636   Ceslovas V. Grincevicius, Dir.
Staff: 2. **Subjects:** Lithuanica. **Holdings:** 15,000 books; 500 bound periodical volumes; manuscripts. **Subscriptions:** 50 journals and other serials; 12 newspapers. **Services:** Library open to public.

LITMAN (Rose M.) RESEARCH LABORATORY
See: University of Colorado, Boulder - Institute of Arctic & Alpine Research - Library

LITTAUER LIBRARY
See: Harvard University

LITTLE (Arthur D.), INC.
See: Arthur D. Little, Inc.

★7040★
LITTLE COMPANY OF MARY HOSPITAL - EDUCATION BUILDING LIBRARY (Med)
2800 W. 95th St.   Phone: (312) 422-6200
Evergreen Park, IL 60642   Rita Karner, Libn.
Founded: 1950. **Staff:** Prof 1; Other 2. **Subjects:** Nursing and medicine. **Holdings:** 3000 books; 40 bound periodical volumes; 9 VF drawers of pamphlets. **Subscriptions:** 50 journals and other serials. **Services:** Library not open to public.

LITTLE (Ilah Dunlap) MEMORIAL LIBRARY
See: University of Georgia - Department of Records Management & University Archives

LITTLE MUSEUM
See: Cameron County Historical Society

LITTLE ROCK AIR FORCE BASE (AR)
See: U.S. Air Force Base - Little Rock Base Library

★7041★
LITTLE WHITE HOUSE HISTORIC SITE - ARCHIVES (Hist)
Drawer 68   Phone: (404) 655-3511
Warm Springs, GA 31830   Norman Edwards, Supt.
Staff: 1. **Subjects:** Historical and biographical material relating to career of President Franklin D. Roosevelt, especially his life as part-time resident of Georgia and originator and developer of Georgia Warm Springs Foundation. **Holdings:** 200 books; archives; documents. **Services:** Archives open to scholars by appointment. **Formerly:** Roosevelt's (Franklin D.) Little White House and Museum - Archives.

LITTLEJOHN RARE BOOK ROOM
See: Wofford College - Sandor Teszler Library

★7042★
LITTLETON AREA HISTORICAL MUSEUM - LIBRARY (Hist)†
6028 S. Gallup   Phone: (303) 795-3850
Littleton, CO 80120   Robert J. McQuarie, Dir.
Staff: Prof 4; Other 9. **Subjects:** Local history including agriculture and railroad. **Special Collections:** Photograph collection of local subjects (4000 pictures). **Holdings:** 500 books; 175 bound periodical volumes; 5000 other cataloged items (related museum artifacts); 60 boxes of public records and city council data; 50 reels of microfilm of newspapers; 30 maps. **Subscriptions:** 12 journals and other serials. **Services:** Copying; library open to public with restrictions.

★7043★
LITTON BIONETICS, INC. - SCIENTIFIC LIBRARY (Sci-Tech)
5516 Nicholson Lane   Phone: (301) 881-5600
Kensington, MD 20895   E.M. Henderson, Libn.
Founded: 1963. **Staff:** Prof 1; Other 1. **Subjects:** Clinical chemistry, primates, veterinary research, pharmacology, life sciences, toxicology. **Holdings:** 2900 books; 150 bound periodical volumes. **Subscriptions:** 165 journals and other serials. **Services:** Interlibrary loans; copying; library not

open to public. **Publications:** Library Acquisitions List, quarterly - for internal distribution only.

★7044★
LITTON INDUSTRIES - DATA SYSTEMS DIVISION - ENGINEERING LIBRARY (Sci-Tech)
8000 Woodley Ave.   Phone: (213) 781-8211
Van Nuys, CA 91409   Joe Ann Clifton, Mgr., Tech.Libs.
Founded: 1958. **Staff:** Prof 2. **Subjects:** Electronics, engineering, computer technology, communications, management. **Holdings:** 10,000 books; 1000 bound periodical volumes. **Services:** Interlibrary loans; copying; library open to public by appointment. **Staff:** Tallulah Frederick, Tech.Libn.

★7045★
LITTON INDUSTRIES - ELECTRON TUBE DIVISION - LIBRARY (Sci-Tech)
960 Industrial Rd.   Phone: (415) 591-8411
San Carlos, CA 94070   Anne Vaughan, Libn.
Staff: Prof 1; Other 1. **Subjects:** Electronics, physics. **Holdings:** 4000 books; 300 bound periodical volumes. **Subscriptions:** 30 journals and other serials. **Services:** Interlibrary loans; copying; library not open to public. **Computerized Information Services:** DIALOG. **Publications:** Monthly bulletin.

★7046★
LITTON INDUSTRIES - GUIDANCE AND CONTROL SYSTEMS - LIBRARY (Sci-Tech)
5500 Canoga Ave.   Phone: (213) 887-3867
Woodland Hills, CA 91364   Joe Ann Clifton, Mgr., Info.Serv.
Founded: 1954. **Subjects:** Computer technology; electrical and mechanical engineering; electronics; inertial guidance; management, mathematics, physics. **Holdings:** 30,000 books; 3500 bound periodical volumes; pamphlets and reports. **Subscriptions:** 520 journals and other serials. **Services:** Interlibrary loans; copying; library open to public by appointment. **Computerized Information Services:** DIALOG. **Publications:** New Holdings List, quarterly.

★7047★
LITTON INDUSTRIES - LAW LIBRARY (Law)
360 N. Crescent Dr.   Phone: (213) 859-5102
Beverly Hills, CA 90210   W. Thomas Johnson, Law Libn.
Staff: Prof 1. **Subjects:** Law. **Holdings:** 6000 volumes. **Subscriptions:** 20 journals and other serials. **Services:** Copying; library not open to public. **Computerized Information Services:** LEXIS.

★7048★
LITTON MELLONICS - PROGRAM LIBRARY (Sci-Tech)†
1001 W. Maude Ave.   Phone: (408) 245-0795
Sunnyvale, CA 95070   Cynthia Rimbach, Software Libn.
Founded: 1977. **Staff:** Prof 1; Other 1. **Subjects:** Computer software and hardware, aerospace, business, automation. **Holdings:** 500 books; 200 magnetic tapes; 30 disks. **Subscriptions:** 25 journals and other serials; 5 newspapers. **Services:** Interlibrary loans; copying; library open to public by appointment. **Computerized Information Services:** Computerized cataloging. **Networks/Consortia:** Member of CIN. **Special Indexes:** Online indexes to in-house programs.

LITZENBERG-LUND LIBRARY
See: University of Minnesota

★7049★
LIVESTOCK FEED BOARD OF CANADA - LIBRARY (Agri)
Snowdon Sta., P.O. Box 177   Phone: (514) 283-7505
Montreal, PQ, Canada H3X 3T4   A. Douglas Mutch
Staff: Prof 2; Other 1. **Subjects:** Canadian and U.S. agriculture, economic policy, farm produce, marketing, grain, transportation, government information. **Holdings:** 1800 books. **Subscriptions:** 400 journals and other serials. **Services:** Interlibrary loans; library open to public. **Remarks:** Library is located at 5180 Queen Mary Rd., Suite 400, Montreal, PQ H3W 3E7.

★7050★
LIVING DESERT RESERVE - HAYNES MEMORIAL LIBRARY (Sci-Tech)†
Box 1775
Palm Desert, CA 92261   Phone: (619) 346-5694
Founded: 1973. **Subjects:** Desert ecology, herpetology, mammalogy, birds, invertebrates, North American ecology, botany, Indian history, local history. **Holdings:** 500 books; 10 bound periodical volumes; 20 manuscripts; 2 dissertations; 1 VF drawer of clippings; 4 VF drawers of unbound periodicals. **Subscriptions:** 14 journals and other serials. **Services:** Library open to public with restrictions.

★7051★
LIVINGSTON COUNTY LAW LIBRARY (Law)
2 Court St.   Phone: (716) 243-2500
Geneseo, NY 14454   Alice Esposito, Libn.
Staff: 1. **Subjects:** Law. **Holdings:** 5000 volumes. **Services:** Library open to public with restrictions.

LIVINGSTON LIBRARY
See: Webb Institute of Naval Architecture

LIVINGSTONE COLLEGE
See: Hood Theological Seminary

★7052★
LIVONIA PUBLIC SCHOOLS - CURRICULUM STUDY CENTER
18000 Newburgh Rd.
Livonia, MI 48152
Subjects: Education, psychology, social work. **Holdings:** 8750 books; microfilm (cataloged). **Remarks:** Presently inactive.

★7053★
LIZZADRO MUSEUM OF LAPIDARY ART - LIBRARY (Art)
220 Cottage Hill Ave.   Phone: (312) 833-1616
Elmhurst, IL 60126   Judith Greene, Exec.Sec.
Subjects: Engraved stones, mineralogy, paleontology. **Holdings:** 750 volumes. **Publications:** Newsletter, semiannual - distributed to members, also for sale.

LLEWELLYN PUBLICATIONS - CARL L. WESCHCKE LIBRARY
See: Weschcke (Carl L.) Library

★7054★
LLOYD (Alice) COLLEGE - APPALACHIAN ORAL HISTORY PROJECT (Area Ethnic)
                                        Phone: (606) 368-2101
Pippa Passes, KY 41844   Katherine R. Martin, Dir.
Staff: Prof 2. **Special Collections:** Oral history interviews concerning Appalachian life and culture, folklore, history, music (emphasis on coal and the Depression). **Holdings:** 650 transcripts; 1850 cassettes (cataloged); reel-to-reel recordings of music and lectures. **Services:** Copying; library open to public (limited). **Publications:** Mountain Memories. **Special Catalogs:** Catalog of manuscripts. **Special Indexes:** Index to tapes.

LLOYD HOUSE
See: Alexandria Library

★7055★
LLOYD LIBRARY AND MUSEUM (Sci-Tech)†
917 Plum St.   Phone: (513) 721-3707
Cincinnati, OH 45202   John B. Griggs, Libn.
Staff: Prof 3; Other 4. **Subjects:** Botany, pharmacy, biology, chemistry, natural science, zoology, entomology, mycology, eclectic medicine. **Special Collections:** Pharmacopoeias, dispensatories, formularies, eclectic medicine and herbals. **Holdings:** 65,000 books; 100,000 bound periodical volumes; 120,000 pamphlets. **Subscriptions:** 1500 journals and other serials. **Services:** Copying; library open to public with restrictions. **Networks/Consortia:** Member of Kentucky-Ohio-Michigan Regional Medical Library Network (KOMRML); OCLC. **Publications:** The Journal of Natural Products (LLOYDIA), bimonthly - by subscription.

★7056★
LOCARE MOTION PICTURE RESEARCH GROUP - LIBRARY (Theater)
910 N. Fairfax Ave.   Phone: (213) 656-4420
Los Angeles, CA 90046   Bebe Bergsten, Libn.
Staff: Prof 1. **Subjects:** Motion picture history and photography prior to 1920. **Holdings:** 500 books; 50 bound periodical volumes. **Subscriptions:** 10 journals and other serials. **Services:** Library not open to public.

★7057★
LOCK HAVEN STATE COLLEGE - GEORGE B. STEVENSON LIBRARY - ARCHIVES
                                        Phone: (717) 893-2371
Lock Haven, PA 17745   Charles Kent, Archv.
Founded: 1876. **Special Collections:** Eden Phillpotts Works (260 volumes); college archives. **Services:** Interlibrary loans; copying; library open to public with restrictions. **Computerized Information Services:** DIALOG; computerized cataloging. **Networks/Consortia:** Member of OCLC through PALINET and Union Library Catalogue of Pennsylvania; Council of Pennsylvania State College and University Library Directors (COPSCAULD); Susquehanna

Library Cooperative.

★7058★

LOCKHEED-CALIFORNIA COMPANY - TECHNICAL INFORMATION CENTER (Sci-Tech)
Dept. 82-40, Bldg. U-51, Plant B-1
Box 551   Phone: (213) 847-5646
Burbank, CA 91520   Stanley A. Elman, Mgr.
Founded: 1937. **Staff:** Prof 8; Other 15. **Subjects:** Aerospace systems; airplane structures and materials; aero- and thermodynamics; avionics. **Holdings:** 46,000 books; 11,000 bound periodical volumes; 350,000 microfiche; 300,000 technical reports (cataloged). **Subscriptions:** 1400 journals and other serials. **Services:** Interlibrary loans; copying; translation; literature searching; center open to U.S. citizens. **Computerized Information Services:** DIALOG, BRS, New York Times Information Service, DTIC, NASA/RECON; DIALTEC (internal database). **Publications:** Technical Information Center Bulletin - for internal distribution only. **Remarks:** The Technical Information Center consists of a (1) Central Library which provides all technical processing as well as library service; (2) Microform viewing stations for locations remote from the Central Library; (3) Technical Data Services; (4) various staff functions such as literature search and publications; (5) reports services for control and distribution of company reports. **Staff:** Renee Evans, Supv., Current Awareness; Cliff C. Butterfield, Supv., Tech.Data/Rpt.Serv; Ferne C. Allan, Supv., Acq.; Joyce Shields, Lit. Searcher; Norm Crum, Supv., Online Res.; Ann Voigt, Cat.; Charlene M. Baldwin, Supv., Ref./Circ.

★7059★

LOCKHEED CORPORATION - INTERNATIONAL MARKETING LIBRARY (Bus-Fin)
Bldg. 61
Box 551   Phone: (213) 847-6527
Burbank, CA 91520   Betty Scanlon, Libn.
Staff: Prof 1. **Subjects:** International business, foreign trade. **Holdings:** Figures not available. **Subscriptions:** 50 journals and other serials. **Services:** Library not open to public.

★7060★

LOCKHEED ELECTRONICS COMPANY, INC. - TECHNICAL INFORMATION CENTER (Sci-Tech)
1501 U.S. Hwy. 22, C.S. No. 1   Phone: (201) 757-1600
Plainfield, NJ 07061   Marie L. Knight, Sr.Tech.Libn.
Founded: 1950. **Staff:** 1. **Subjects:** Electronics, radar, sonar, data systems, computers. **Holdings:** 3000 books; 2000 bound periodical volumes and indexes; 85 drawers of technical reports; 4000 microfiche. **Subscriptions:** 300 journals and other serials. **Services:** Interlibrary loans; copying; library not open to public. **Computerized Information Services:** DIALOG. **Special Indexes:** Uniterm card and micro file to 1000 reports. **Formerly:** Its Technical Document Center and Library.

★7061★

LOCKHEED-GEORGIA COMPANY - TECHNICAL INFORMATION DEPARTMENT (Sci-Tech)
86 S. Cobb Dr.   Phone: (404) 424-2928
Marietta, GA 30063   C. David Rife, Mgr.
Founded: 1951. **Staff:** Prof 7; Other 11. **Subjects:** Aeronautics, astronautics, operations research, engineering, human factors, ordnance, propulsion, marketing, management, materials. **Holdings:** 40,000 books; 6000 bound periodical volumes; 140,000 technical reports; 10 VF drawers of pamphlets; 1100 maps; 350,000 microfiche; 50,000 specifications and standards; cassettes; annual reports; Government-Industry Data Exchange Program (GIDEP) reports. **Subscriptions:** 1200 journals and other serials. **Services:** Interlibrary loans; copying; SDI; library open to public by appointment. **Computerized Information Services:** DIALOG, DTIC, NASA/RECON; computerized cataloging. **Networks/Consortia:** Member of Georgia Library Information Network (GLIN). **Publications:** Accession List (computer-prepared), bimonthly; bibliographies; journal subscription lists. **Special Catalogs:** Gelac Authors in Print, 1963-1968 (book); update, 1969-1980, in preparation. **Special Indexes:** Computer-prepared indexes to all material added to the collection since 1963. **Staff:** T.J. Kopkin, Res.Info.Spec.; F.J. Cronin, Res.Info.Spec.; Jan Edwards, Tech.Libn.; B.A. McAdams, Tech.Libn.; L.W. Kimbro, Tech.Libn.; D.K. Patterson, Tech.Libn.

LOCKHEED MISSILES & SPACE COMPANY, INC. - LOCKHEED INFORMATION SYSTEMS
See: DIALOG Information Services, Inc.

★7062★

LOCKHEED MISSILES & SPACE COMPANY, INC. - TECHNICAL INFORMATION CENTER (Sci-Tech)
3251 Hanover St.   Phone: (415) 493-4411
Palo Alto, CA 94304   Arthur N. Fried, Mgr.
Founded: 1954. **Staff:** Prof 15; Other 7. **Subjects:** Aerospace sciences, missile and space vehicles, electronics, materials and structures, data processing, information sciences, laser systems, energy systems, physics, chemistry, engineering. **Special Collections:** Archives of company documents. **Holdings:** 35,000 books; 27,000 bound periodical volumes; 125,000 technical reports (cataloged); 2400 periodical volumes on microfilm; 208 books in microform; 65,000 reports on microfiche; 175,000 technical data. **Subscriptions:** 650 journals and other serials. **Services:** Interlibrary loans; copying; center not open to public. **Computerized Information Services:** Online systems; computerized cataloging and circulation. **Networks/Consortia:** Member of CIN. **Special Catalogs:** Catalog in microfiche format, monthly cumulative supplements; monthly KWIT of new accessions. **Remarks:** Maintains a branch library in Sunnyvale, CA. **Staff:** E.B. Leong, Sr.Libn.; B.B. LeBaron, Tech. Data Libn.; J.E. Conahan, Acq.Libn.; J.A. Wagner, Reports Acq.Libn.; S. Stanek, Clas. Reports Libn.

LOCKHEED PETROLEUM SERVICES LTD.
See: CanOcean Resources Ltd.

★7063★

LOCKWOOD, ANDREWS & NEWNAM, INC. - INFORMATION CENTER (Sci-Tech)
1500 CityWest Blvd.   Phone: (713) 266-6900
Houston, TX 77042   Diane E. Walker, Info.Ctr.Coord.
Founded: 1977. **Staff:** Prof 1; Other 2. **Subjects:** Engineering - civil, mechanical, electrical; architecture; energy. **Holdings:** 1820 books and bound periodical volumes; 2000 reels of microfilm; 1000 company records and manuscripts; 1600 archival records and books. **Subscriptions:** 200 journals and other serials; 10 newspapers. **Services:** Interlibrary loans; copying; center not open to public. **Computerized Information Services:** Internal database; computerized cataloging and acquisitions.

LOCKWOOD MEMORIAL LIBRARY
See: Research Medical Center

★7064★

LOCTITE CORPORATION - INFORMATION CENTER (Sci-Tech)
705 N. Mountain Rd.   Phone: (203) 278-1280
Newington, CT 06001   Laurice Von Daacke, Libn.
Staff: Prof 1; Other 1. **Subjects:** Polymer chemistry, adhesives, organic chemistry, management, marketing. **Holdings:** 10,000 volumes; 4 VF drawers of patents; 4 VF drawers of technical reports. **Subscriptions:** 150 journals and other serials; 5 newspapers. **Services:** Interlibrary loans; copying; SDI; library not open to public. **Computerized Information Services:** DIALOG, SDC; Technical Report Index (internal database).

LODGE (Miriam) PROFESSIONAL LIBRARY
See: Rosewood Center - Miriam Lodge Professional Library

LOEB (Eda Kuhn) MUSIC LIBRARY
See: Harvard University - Eda Kuhn Loeb Music Library

LOEB (Frances) LIBRARY
See: Harvard University - Graduate School of Design - Frances Loeb Library

★7065★

LOEB AND LOEB - LAW LIBRARY (Law)†
One Wilshire Bldg., Suite 1600   Phone: (213) 629-0200
Los Angeles, CA 90017   Nella L. Jarett, Libn.
Staff: Prof 1; Other 3. **Subjects:** Law. **Holdings:** 24,000 volumes. **Subscriptions:** 200 journals and other serials; 6 newspapers. **Services:** Library not open to public. **Computerized Information Services:** LEXIS. **Publications:** Union list of periodicals; Monthly Memo.

LOEWS THEATRES, INC. - LORILLARD DIVISION
See: Lorillard Research Center Library

★7066★

LOGAN COLLEGE OF CHIROPRACTIC - LIBRARY (Med)
1851 Schoettler Rd.
Box 100   Phone: (314) 227-2100
Chesterfield, MO 63107   Harriett Hirschfeld, Hd.Libn.
Founded: 1935. **Staff:** Prof 4; Other 4. **Subjects:** Chiropractic, histology,

anatomy, clinical medicine, pathology, physical therapy. **Special Collections:** Osseous material, individual bones and full skeletons (600 items). **Holdings:** 15,000 books; 250 bound periodical volumes; 95 tapes; 222 slide sets; newspaper clippings. **Subscriptions:** 160 journals and other serials. **Services:** Interlibrary loans (fee); copying; binding machines are available; library open to public with restrictions. **Computerized Information Services:** NLM. **Networks/Consortia:** Member of St. Louis Regional Library Network. **Staff:** Mary Ann Hoeman, Asst.Lbn.; Donnan Duncan, Circ.Lbn.; Patricia Woods, Media Lbn.

LOGAN (John A.) LIBRARY
See: Rose-Hulman Institute of Technology - John A. Logan Library

LOGAN MUSEUM OF ANTHROPOLOGY
See: Beloit College

★7067★
LOGANSPORT STATE HOSPITAL - MEDICAL LIBRARY (Med)†
R.R. 2   Phone: (219) 722-4141
Logansport, IN 46947   Terra Newton, Lbn.
Founded: 1938. **Staff:** Prof 1. **Subjects:** Medicine, psychiatry, psychology, social service, drug abuse, alcoholism, geriatrics. **Holdings:** 4340 books. **Subscriptions:** 30 journals and other serials. **Services:** Interlibrary loans; copying; library not open to public.

★7068★
LOGETRONICS, INC. - INFORMATION CENTER (Sci-Tech)†
7001 Loisdale Rd.   Phone: (703) 971-1400
Springfield, VA 22150   Janet Duckworth, Lbn.
Staff: 1. **Subjects:** Science and technology. **Holdings:** 1000 books; archives; manufacturing literature; abstracts; proceedings; telephone directories; reports. **Subscriptions:** 150 journals and other serials; 5 newspapers. **Services:** Interlibrary loans; copying; library open to public with restrictions.

★7069★
LOGICON, INC. - INFORMATION CENTER (Sci-Tech)
255 W. 5th St.
Box 471   Phone: (213) 831-0611
San Pedro, CA 90731   Constance B. Davenport, Info.Mgr.
Staff: Prof 1; Other 2. **Subjects:** Systems engineering, programming languages, inertial navigation, ballistic missiles, mathematics, computers, guidance and control, software. **Special Collections:** Military standards. **Holdings:** 2500 books; 920 boxes of periodicals; 5000 documents (cataloged); 750 standards and specifications; 10,000 microfiche. **Subscriptions:** 241 journals and other serials; 9 newspapers. **Services:** Interlibrary loans; copying; SDI; center open to public with appropriate clearance. **Computerized Information Services:** DIALOG, BRS, SDC; computerized cataloging. **Special Catalogs:** Computer printout catalog.

★7070★
LOGICON, INC. - TACTICAL & TRAINING SYSTEMS DIVISION LIBRARY (Sci-Tech)
Box 80158   Phone: (714) 455-1330
San Diego, CA 92138   Paula Oquita, Lbn.
Staff: Prof 1; Other 2. **Subjects:** Tactical systems; command, control and communications systems; training systems; simulated training; simulation and simulators; system engineering; computer image generation; speech recognition and generation; database management. **Holdings:** 2200 books; 15,000 reports; 250 VF drawers of classified and company reports; military specifications and standards. **Subscriptions:** 250 journals and other serials. **Services:** Interlibrary loans; copying; library open to public with restrictions. **Networks/Consortia:** Member of METRO. **Publications:** Accessions list, monthly; subject bibliographies, irregular. **Remarks:** Library is located at 4010 Sorrento Valley Blvd., San Diego, CA 92121.

★7071★
LOGISTICS MANAGEMENT INSTITUTE - LIBRARY (Mil)
4701 Sangamore Rd.
Box 9489   Phone: (301) 229-1000
Washington, DC 20016   Ms. Omah H. Mondello, Lbn.
Staff: Prof 1; Other 1. **Subjects:** Logistics, defense, manpower, defense procurement. **Holdings:** 2000 books; 2000 reports; 200 manuals and newsletters in binders. **Subscriptions:** 51 journals and other serials. **Services:** Library not open to public. **Computerized Information Services:** DIALOG.

LOMA
See: Life Office Management Association

★7072★
LOMA LINDA UNIVERSITY - DEL E. WEBB MEMORIAL LIBRARY (Med)
     Phone: (714) 824-4550
Loma Linda, CA 92350   H. Maynard Lowry, Dir.
Founded: 1907. **Staff:** Prof 14; Other 35. **Subjects:** Medicine, nursing, dentistry, religion, health, allied health professions. **Special Collections:** Nineteenth Century Health Reform in America; Remondino Collection (history of medicine); C. Burton Clark Collection (history of Seventh-Day Adventist Church). **Holdings:** 147,181 books; 78,238 bound periodical volumes; 37,994 microforms; 4317 tapes and phonodiscs; 2387 filmstrips, films, slides; 278 AV kits; 200 feet of archival material. **Subscriptions:** 2345 journals and other serials; 13 newspapers. **Services:** Interlibrary loans; copying; computerized bibliographic searches; library open to qualified users. **Computerized Information Services:** SDI-line; computerized serials. **Networks/Consortia:** Member of Inland Empire Academic Libraries Cooperative (IEALC); San Bernardino, Inyo, Riverside County United Library Services (SIRCULS); Pacific Southwest Regional Medical Library Service (PSRMLS); OCLC. **Publications:** SDA Periodical Index. **Staff:** George L. McAlister, Assoc.Dir.; Carroll Westermeyer, Chm., Tech.Serv.; Helen Chinn, Chm., Coll.Dev.; Gudrun Williams, Chm., Pub.Serv.; James R. Nix, Chm., Archv./Res.; Jerry Daly, Chm., Media Serv.; Shirley Graves, Chm., Ser.

★7073★
LOMA LINDA UNIVERSITY - INSTITUTE FOR CANCER AND BLOOD RESEARCH - LIBRARY (Med)
140 N. Robertson Blvd.   Phone: (213) 655-4706
Beverly Hills, CA 90211   Belle Gould, Lbn.
Founded: 1967. **Staff:** 1. **Subjects:** Hematology, oncology. **Holdings:** 300 books; 30 bound periodical volumes. **Subscriptions:** 35 journals and other serials. **Services:** Library not open to public.

★7074★
LOMA LINDA UNIVERSITY - NIELS BJORN JORGENSEN MEMORIAL LIBRARY (Med)
School of Dentistry   Phone: (714) 796-0141
Loma Linda, CA 92350   Carol Richardson, Lbn.
Founded: 1978. **Staff:** Prof 1; Other 6. **Subjects:** Dentistry, dental anesthesiology and pain control. **Special Collections:** Archival material of the American Dental Society of Anesthesiology. **Holdings:** 264 books and bound periodical volumes; 150 video cassettes; 50 self-study units; 115 microfiche sets; 25 boxes of archives. **Subscriptions:** 120 journals and other serials. **Services:** Interlibrary loans; copying; SDI; computerized bibliographic searches; library open to public. **Publications:** Bibliography for the Control of Anxiety, Fear and Pain in Dentistry, semiannual - by subscription.

LOMBARD THEOLOGICAL SCHOOL
See: Meadville/Lombard Theological School

★7075★
LOMBARDY HALL FOUNDATION - LIBRARY (Hist; Rec)
1611 Concord Pike
Box 7036   Phone: (302) 772-4286
Wilmington, DE 19803   Harold J. Littleton, Pres./Cur.
Staff: 1. **Subjects:** Freemasonry, Gunning Bedford, Jr., Delaware history. **Holdings:** Figures not available. **Services:** Library open to public with restrictions.

LOMMEN (Christian P.) HEALTH SCIENCES LIBRARY
See: University of South Dakota - Christian P. Lommen Health Sciences Library

★7076★
LOMPOC MUSEUM - LIBRARY (Area-Ethnic)†
200 South H St.   Phone: (805) 736-3888
Lompoc, CA 93436   Lucille Christie, Dir.
Founded: 1972. **Staff:** Prof 1. **Subjects:** Chumash Indians, Indians of Southern California, Lompoc natural history, Lompoc history, archeology. **Special Collections:** Manuscripts; historical photographs. **Holdings:** 800 books; 4 VF drawers; 150 maps; 350 slides. **Services:** Interlibrary loans; library open to public for reference use only on request.

★7077★
LONDON CLUB - ARCHIVES (Soc Sci)
Box 4527
Topeka, KS 66604   L.D. Baranski, Archv.
Founded: 1975. **Staff:** Prof 1. **Subjects:** Criminology, criminal investigation. **Holdings:** 1500 books; 500 bound periodical volumes; 150 maps; 60 tapes. **Subscriptions:** 7 journals and other serials; 4 newspapers. **Services:** Archives not open to public. **Publications:** London Club Journal - to active club

members. **Remarks:** London Club is currently in the process of building the collection and may open a segment of it to researchers from outside the organization in the near future.

★7078★
LONDON FREE PRESS PUBLISHING COMPANY, LTD. - EDITORIAL LIBRARY (Publ)
369 York St.
London, ON, Canada N6A 4G1
Phone: (519) 679-1111
Edythe Cusack, Libn.
Founded: 1940. **Staff:** Prof 3; Other 2. **Subjects:** Newspaper reference topics. **Holdings:** 600 books; 100 bound periodical volumes; 940 reels of microfilm; clippings and pictures. **Subscriptions:** 50 journals and other serials. **Services:** Interlibrary loans (limited); copying; library open to other newspapers and libraries only. **Special Catalogs:** Historic and features catalogs (both in card form).

LONDON (Jack) RESEARCH CENTER AND LIBRARY
See: Jack London Research Center and Library

LONDON (Meyer) MEMORIAL LIBRARY OF THE RAND SCHOOL OF SOCIAL SCIENCE
See: New York University - Tamiment Library

★7079★
LONDON PUBLIC LIBRARIES AND MUSEUMS - CFPL NEWSCLIPS
305 Queens Ave.
London, ON, Canada N6B 3L7
Defunct. Holdings absorbed by London Public Libraries and Museums - London Room.

★7080★
LONDON PUBLIC LIBRARIES AND MUSEUMS - LONDON ROOM (Hist)
305 Queens Ave.
London, ON, Canada N6B 3L7
Phone: (519) 432-7166
W. Glen Curnoe, Libn.
Founded: 1967. **Staff:** Prof 1; Other 1. **Subjects:** London and London area - history, family genealogy, local buildings and objects; London Public Library history. **Special Collections:** Edwin Seaborn Collection (Western Ontario history, with emphasis on the medical; 56 volumes and index); Orlo Miller Collection (genealogical card file and Miller's correspondence); Looking Over Western Ontario (newspaper references to landmarks and history of London). **Holdings:** Microfilm of theses, newspapers and books; unbound reports; scrapbooks; family manuscripts; clippings (1940 to present); documents. **Services:** Interlibrary loans (of second copies only); copying; library open to public. **Networks/Consortia:** Member of Lake Erie Regional Library System. **Publications:** Occasional papers, irregular - available for purchase. **Special Indexes:** Card indexes to local history events, scrapbooks and city directories (1856-1864). **Remarks:** Collection is extensive and still in process of being organized and enlarged. Contains holdings of the former London Public Libraries and Museums - CFPL Newsclips.

LONDON RESEARCH CENTRE LIBRARY
See: Canada - Agriculture Canada

★7081★
LONE STAR GAS COMPANY - RESEARCH LIBRARY (Energy)
301 S. Harwood St.
Dallas, TX 75201
Phone: (214) 741-3711
Charlotte W. Vinson, Chf.Libn.
Founded: 1956. **Staff:** Prof 2; Other 1. **Subjects:** Oil and gas industry, chemistry, business and finance, geology. **Holdings:** 2000 books; 500 bound periodical volumes. **Subscriptions:** 40 journals and other serials; 5 newspapers. **Services:** Interlibrary loans; library open to public by appointment. **Computerized Information Services:** DIALOG, SDC, New York Times Information Service. **Staff:** Constance Lawson, Res.Libn.

★7082★
LONG, ALDRIDGE, HEINER, STEVENS & SUMNER - LAW LIBRARY (Law)
1900 Rhodes-Haverty Bldg.
134 Peachtree St.
Atlanta, GA 30043
Phone: (404) 681-3000
Ms. Marty Mulinix, Lib./Rec.Mgr.
Staff: Prof 1; Other 2. **Subjects:** Law. **Holdings:** 4500 books; 300 bound periodical volumes; 20 cassettes. **Subscriptions:** 85 journals and other serials; 5 newspapers. **Services:** Interlibrary loans; copying; library open to public with restrictions. **Publications:** Library Newsletter, quarterly.

★7083★
LONG BEACH CITY COLLEGE - PACIFIC COAST CAMPUS LIBRARY (Educ)
1305 E. Pacific Coast Hwy.
Long Beach, CA 90806
Phone: (213) 420-4548
John L. Ayala, Lib.Dir./Assoc.Prof.
Founded: 1947. **Staff:** Prof 3; Other 1. **Special Collections:** Vocational

education; ethnic materials (Chicano, black, American Indian); English as a second language. **Holdings:** 15,000 books; 86 bound periodical volumes. **Subscriptions:** 129 journals and other serials; 10 newspapers. **Services:** Interlibrary loans; copying; library open to public for reference use only. **Staff:** Robin Nordee, Ref.

★7084★
LONG BEACH COMMUNITY HOSPITAL - MEDICAL LIBRARY (Med)
1720 Termino Ave.
Long Beach, CA 90801
Phone: (213) 597-6655
Lois O. Clark, Med.Libn.
Staff: Prof 1; Other 1. **Subjects:** Medicine, nursing and hospital administration. **Holdings:** 1950 books; 1500 bound periodical volumes; Audio-Digest tapes. **Subscriptions:** 289 journals and other serials. **Services:** Interlibrary loans; copying; library open to public for reference use only. **Publications:** Newsletter, monthly - for internal distribution only.

LONG BEACH GENERAL HOSPITAL
See: Los Angeles County/Long Beach General Hospital

★7085★
LONG BEACH MUSEUM OF ART - LIBRARY (Art)
2300 E. Ocean Blvd.
Long Beach, CA 90803
Phone: (213) 439-2119
Russell J. Moore, Dir.
Staff: Prof 10; Other 3. **Subjects:** Art history (all periods). **Holdings:** 1550 books; 25 bound periodical volumes; 750 exhibition catalogs (cataloged). **Services:** Library open to museum members and docent council by appointment.

★7086★
LONG BEACH PRESS-TELEGRAM - LIBRARY (Publ)
604 Pine Ave.
Long Beach, CA 90844
Phone: (213) 435-1161
Violet R. Phillips, Hd.Libn.
Staff: Prof 1; Other 2. **Subjects:** Newspaper reference topics. **Holdings:** 3 million clippings; 350,000 photographs; 1600 reels of microfilm. **Services:** Library not open to public. **Formerly:** Long Beach Independent, Press-Telegram.

★7087★
LONG BEACH PUBLIC LIBRARY - CALIFORNIA PETROLEUM INDUSTRY COLLECTION (Sci-Tech; Hist)
101 Pacific Ave.
Long Beach, CA 90802
Phone: (213) 437-2949
James Jackson, Dept.Libn.
Founded: 1959. **Staff:** Prof 1. **Subjects:** History of California petroleum industry. **Holdings:** 1700 books; 200 bound periodical volumes; 3050 pictures; 850 tool catalogs and brochures; 500 pamphlets; 1700 government publications. **Services:** Copying; library open to public by appointment. **Computerized Information Services:** DIALOG. **Networks/Consortia:** Member of Metropolitan Cooperative Library System (MCLS).

★7088★
LONG BEACH PUBLIC LIBRARY - FINE ARTS DEPARTMENT (Art)
101 Pacific Ave.
Long Beach, CA 90802
Phone: (213) 437-2949
Natalee Collier, Dept.Hd.
Founded: 1926. **Staff:** Prof 2. **Subjects:** Art history and techniques, music history and scores, dance, sports, flower arranging, antiques, theater, moving pictures. **Special Collections:** Marilyn Horne Archives (recordings, pictures, press clippings); Miller Fine Arts Collection; Bertram Smith Collection. **Holdings:** 34,103 books; 8624 bound scores; 7099 pieces of sheet music; 203 framed pictures; 91,043 mounted pictures. **Services:** Interlibrary loans; copying; library open to public with restrictions. **Computerized Information Services:** DIALOG; computerized cataloging. **Networks/Consortia:** Member of SCAN; SCILL. **Special Indexes:** Song, dance and piano music, artist, mounted picture subject indexes (all on cards).

★7089★
LONG BEACH PUBLIC LIBRARY - LITERATURE AND HISTORY DEPARTMENT (Hum)
101 Pacific Ave.
Long Beach, CA 90802
Phone: (213) 437-2949
Helene A. Silver, Dept.Hd.
Staff: Prof 3; Other 1. **Subjects:** Fiction, literature, foreign languages, travel, biography, history. **Special Collections:** Long Beach Historical Collection; genealogy. **Holdings:** 78,500 books; 70 VF drawers. **Services:** Interlibrary loans. **Computerized Information Services:** DIALOG. **Networks/Consortia:** Member of Southern California Answering Network (SCAN); Southern California Interlibrary Loan Network (SCILL); Long Beach Consortium for Local and Community History. **Special Indexes:** Local newspaper index (card).

★7090★
LONG BEACH PUBLIC LIBRARY - RANCHO LOS CERRITOS MUSEUM - LIBRARY (Hist)
4600 Virginia Rd.
Long Beach, CA 90807
Phone: (213) 424-9423
Keith Foster, Cur.
Founded: 1955. **Staff:** Prof 2; Other 1. **Subjects:** History - local, California, Southwest. **Special Collections:** Jonathan Temple Collection; Bixby-Hathaway Family Collection, both archival/manuscript collections. **Holdings:** 3037 books; 235 bound periodical volumes; pictorial and topographical maps; local history picture file; scrapbooks. **Services:** Interlibrary loans (limited); library open to public for reference use only. **Networks/Consortia:** Member of Long Beach Consortium for Local and Community History. **Remarks:** Rancho Los Cerritos Museum and Library are owned by the City of Long Beach and operated as an agency of the Long Beach Public Library. It was designated a National Historic Landmark in 1970.

★7091★
LONG BEACH UNIFIED SCHOOL DISTRICT - PROFESSIONAL LIBRARY†
701 Locust Ave.
Long Beach, CA 90813
Phone: (213) 436-9931
Subjects: Education. **Holdings:** 7239 books; 187 bound periodical volumes. **Services:** Interlibrary loans; copying; library open to public for reference use only.

LONG (Crawford W.) MEMORIAL HOSPITAL
See: Crawford W. Long Memorial Hospital

★7092★
LONG (Earl K.) MEMORIAL HOSPITAL - MEDICAL LIBRARY (Med)
5825 Airline Highway
Baton Rouge, LA 70805
Phone: (504) 358-1089
Elaine P. O'Connor, Dir.
Staff: Prof 3; Other 2. **Subjects:** Medicine. **Holdings:** 1850 books; 2600 bound periodical volumes; 700 AV items; 20 VF drawers of articles. **Subscriptions:** 230 journals and other serials. **Services:** Interlibrary loans; copying; library open to health scientists. **Computerized Information Services:** MEDLINE, DIALOG. **Networks/Consortia:** Headquarters for Community Medical Library Consortium.

LONG (Huey P.) MEMORIAL LAW LIBRARY
See: Louisiana State Department of Justice - Office of the Attorney General - Huey P. Long Memorial Law Library

★7093★
LONG ISLAND CATHOLIC - RESEARCH LIBRARY (Publ; Rel-Theol)
Box 700
Hempstead, NY 11551
Phone: (516) 538-8800
Doris S. Bader, Libn.
Founded: 1962. **Staff:** Prof 1; Other 2. **Subjects:** World affairs, religious affairs, Catholic Church. **Holdings:** 1974 books; 32 VF drawers of pictures; 28 VF drawers of subject files; 6 VF drawers of foreign files; 8 VF drawers of biographical files; 118 reels of microfilm; 185 maps. **Subscriptions:** 104 journals and other serials; 119 newspapers. **Services:** Copying; library not open to public. **Special Indexes:** Index to The Long Island Catholic (card). **Remarks:** Established by the Catholic Press Association of Rockville Centre Inc. to serve reference and research needs of the newspaper; also serves the Bureau of Public Information and the Diocesan Commission for Ecumenism of the Catholic Diocese of Rockville Centre.

★7094★
LONG ISLAND COLLEGE HOSPITAL - HOAGLAND MEDICAL LIBRARY (Med)
340 Henry St.
Brooklyn, NY 11201
Phone: (212) 780-1077
Gabriel Bakcsy, Dir.
Founded: 1880. **Staff:** Prof 2; Other 3. **Subjects:** Medicine, nursing, basic sciences, social sciences, education. **Holdings:** 20,000 volumes; 60 linear feet of archives; 3 VF drawers of National League for Nursing pamphlets; 600 audio cassettes. **Subscriptions:** 377 journals and other serials. **Services:** Interlibrary loans; copying; library open to public with restrictions. **Networks/Consortia:** Member of Medical Library Center of New York. **Staff:** Roslyn S. Glassman.

★7095★
LONG ISLAND HISTORICAL SOCIETY - LIBRARY (Hist)
128 Pierrepont St.
Brooklyn, NY 11201
Phone: (212) 624-0890
Patricia A. Flavin, Libn.
Founded: 1863. **Staff:** Prof 4; Other 4. **Subjects:** Brooklyn, Long Island and New York State - local history, biography, genealogy; American history. **Special Collections:** Bookplate collection; scrapbook collection (165 indexed volumes of local history); black studies (1200 items). **Holdings:** 125,000 volumes; Long Island newspapers, maps, documents, pictures, portraits, archives, manuscripts, microfilm, and microcards. **Subscriptions:** 140

journals and other serials; 27 newspapers. **Services:** Copying; library open to public. **Publications:** Journal of Long Island History, twice a year - distributed free to members; Newsletter; Catalogue of American Genealogies in the Library of the Long Island Historical Society, book. **Special Catalogs:** Catalogue of American Revolutionary Manuscripts (1980; K. Mango); Checklist of Long Island Printing (1977; Doggett); A Guide to Brooklyn Manuscripts in the Long Island Historical Society (1980; R. Sink); Brooklyn Before the Bridge: American Paintings from the Long Island Historical Society (1982; The Brooklyn Museum). **Staff:** Judy Metzger, Asst.Libn.

★7096★
LONG ISLAND JEWISH-HILLSIDE MEDICAL CENTER - HEALTH SCIENCES LIBRARY (Med)
270-05 76th Ave.
New Hyde Park, NY 11042
Phone: (212) 470-2673
Norma Frankel, Dir., Lib.Serv.
Founded: 1954. **Staff:** Prof 2; Other 3. **Subjects:** Medicine, dentistry and related sciences. **Holdings:** 4500 books; 21,700 bound periodical volumes. **Subscriptions:** 504 journals and other serials. **Services:** Interlibrary loans; copying; library open to public for reference use only. **Computerized Information Services:** BRS. **Networks/Consortia:** Member of Medical Library Center of New York (MLCNY). **Staff:** Esther King, Med.Libn., ILL.

★7097★
LONG ISLAND JEWISH-HILLSIDE MEDICAL CENTER - HILLSIDE DIVISION - HEALTH SCIENCES LIBRARY (Med)
Box 38
Glen Oaks, NY 11004
Phone: (212) 470-4406
Joan L. Kauff, Chf.Med.Libn.
Founded: 1943. **Staff:** Prof 1; Other 3. **Subjects:** Psychiatry, psychoanalysis, psychology, nursing, social work, hospital administration. **Holdings:** 8000 books; 5500 bound periodical volumes; 36 VF drawers of reprints, dissertations, pamphlets; 250 audio cassettes. **Subscriptions:** 250 journals and other serials. **Services:** Interlibrary loans; copying; SDI; specialized bibliographies; library open to public for reference use only. **Computerized Information Services:** BRS. **Networks/Consortia:** Member of Medical Library Center of New York (MLCNY); Long Island Library Resources Council (LILRC).

★7098★
LONG ISLAND JEWISH-HILLSIDE MEDICAL CENTER - QUEENS HOSPITAL CENTER - HEALTH SCIENCE LIBRARY (Med)
82-68 164th St.
Jamaica, NY 11432
Phone: (212) 990-2795
Helen M. Pilikian, Chf.Med.Libn.
Staff: Prof 2; Other 1. **Subjects:** Medicine, social services, public health. **Holdings:** 5649 books; 6357 bound periodical volumes. **Subscriptions:** 300 journals and other serials. **Services:** Interlibrary loans; copying; library open to public for reference use only. **Computerized Information Services:** Online systems. **Networks/Consortia:** Member of Medical Library Center of New York (MLCNY). **Special Catalogs:** Union catalog of journal holdings of 4 libraries in Long Island Jewish-Hillside Medical Center consortia. **Staff:** Vivian Frankel, Med.Libn.

★7099★
LONG ISLAND LIBRARY RESOURCES COUNCIL, INC. (LILRC) (Info Sci)
Box 31
Bellport, NY 11713
Phone: (516) 286-0400
Herbert Biblo, Dir.
Founded: 1967. **Staff:** Prof 3; Other 6. **Publications:** A Directory of Government Documents Collections in Nassau and Suffolk Counties, 2nd edition, 1982; Resource Guide: a composite subject profile of Long Island libraries, 1981. **Special Catalogs:** Nassau-Suffolk Union List of Serials; Serials in Long Island Health Science Libraries: a Union List. **Remarks:** "LILRC, a New York State 3 R's Agency, maintains an office to develop and implement cooperative use of 138 member libraries by researchers from any member institution. The office operates a service locating and delivering materials." **Staff:** Judith Neufeld, Asst. to the Dir.; Helen Pagels, Regional Input Ctr., Ser.

★7100★
LONG ISLAND LIGHTING COMPANY - CORPORATE LIBRARY (Sci-Tech)†
175 E. Old Country Rd.
Hicksville, NY 11801
Phone: (516) 733-4264
Patricia Clancy, Libn.
Founded: 1958. **Staff:** 1. **Subjects:** Engineering - nuclear, power; gas and electric operations; management; finance. **Special Collections:** Long Island history (100 titles). **Holdings:** 5000 books; engineering standards on microfiche. **Subscriptions:** 250 journals and other serials; 6 newspapers. **Services:** Interlibrary loans; copying; library not open to public. **Computerized Information Services:** Computerized cataloging.

★7101★

LONG ISLAND UNIV. - ARNOLD & MARIE SCHWARTZ COLLEGE OF PHARMACY & HEALTH SCIENCES - INTL. DRUG INFO. CTR. (Med)

81 DeKalb Ave. at University Plaza   Phone: (212) 403-1064
Brooklyn, NY 11201   Jack M. Rosenberg, Dir.
Founded: 1973. **Staff:** Prof 7; Other 7. **Subjects:** Drug therapy. **Special Collections:** Foreign drug compendia. **Holdings:** 150 books; 30 bound periodical volumes; 8000 microfiche (Iowa Drug Information System); 50,000 3x5 cards (deHaen Drug Information System); deHaen Collections of Drug Development and Drugdex; 10 other cataloged items. **Subscriptions:** 35 journals and other serials. **Services:** Library open to health professionals. **Computerized Information Services:** MEDLINE, TOXLINE. **Publications:** Monthly Question and Answer column published in Apothecary, Journal of the Medical Society, New Jersey; New York State Journal of Medicine; New York State Pharmacist, Lippincott's Hospital Pharmacy; Poisindex Company; Yakugyo Jiho Co., Ltd. Japanese Drug Information Service. **Remarks:** This Drug Information Center is also known as the International Pharmaceutic & Therapeutic Drug Information Center. **Staff:** Harold L. Kirschenbaum, Asst.Dir.; Jayne Ritz, Drug Info. Resident; Ghazala Chishti, Clinical Assoc.

★7102★

LONG ISLAND UNIV. - ARNOLD & MARIE SCHWARTZ COLLEGE OF PHARMACY & HEALTH SCIENCES - PHARMACEUTICAL STUDY CENTER (Med)

75 DeKalb Ave.   Phone: (212) 834-6000
Brooklyn, NY 11201   Lisa M. Livingston, Dir.
Staff: Prof 1. **Subjects:** Pharmacy, pharmacology, pharmacy administration, hospital pharmacy. **Special Collections:** Pharmacy AV items; masters' theses from the graduate school; computer-assisted instruction files (10). **Holdings:** 30 books; 250 current periodicals; 500 AV items. **Subscriptions:** 225 journals and other serials. **Services:** Center open to public. **Publications:** New Pharmacy Acquisitions.

★7103★

LONG ISLAND UNIVERSITY - C.W. POST CENTER - CENTER FOR ECONOMIC RESEARCH (Bus-Fin)

B. Davis Schwartz Memorial Library   Phone: (516) 299-2932
Greenvale, NY 11548   Mary McNierney Grant, Mgr.
Staff: Prof 5; Other 4. **Subjects:** Business, finance, industry, marketing, management, accounting and taxation. **Special Collections:** Disclosure microfiche; DUNS Account Identification Service; Conference Board papers. **Holdings:** 7300 books; 1000 bound periodical volumes; 11,800 reels of microfilm; 10 VF drawers of subject files; 5 VF drawers of Long Island and New York subject files; state industrial directories. **Subscriptions:** 1507 journals and other serials. **Services:** Copying; SDI; library open to public. **Computerized Information Services:** DIALOG; computerized cataloging and circulation. **Networks/Consortia:** Member of Long Island Library Resources Council (LILRC); OCLC. **Staff:** Carole Ottenheimer Cohen, Info.Spec.; Anne Donnellan, Libn.; Lise Rasmussen, Libn.; Richard Reid, Libn.

★7104★

LONG ISLAND UNIVERSITY - C.W. POST CENTER - PALMER SCHOOL OF LIBRARY AND INFORMATION SCIENCE - LIBRARY (Info Sci)

B. Davis Schwartz Memorial Library   Phone: (516) 299-2826
Greenvale, NY 11548   Ellen Weinstein, Hd.
Founded: 1955. **Staff:** Prof 1; Other 8. **Subjects:** Library and information science, history of books and printing, children's literature, bibliography. **Special Collections:** Historical children's literature. **Holdings:** 14,800 books; 4285 periodical volumes; 884 theses (cataloged); 823 dissertations on microfilm; 10 files of library annual reports. **Subscriptions:** 835 journals, 339 serials. **Services:** Interlibrary loans; copying; library open to public for reference use only. **Computerized Information Services:** Computerized cataloging, acquisitions and circulation. **Networks/Consortia:** Member of Long Island Library Resources Council. **Publications:** Acquisitions list, 6/year - to faculty and students.

LONGFELLOW NATL. HISTORIC SITE
See: U.S. Natl. Park Service

LONGVIEW CITIZENS' RESOURCE CENTER
See: Le Tourneau College - Margaret Estes Library

★7105★

LONGWOOD GARDENS, INC. - LIBRARY (Sci-Tech)

    Phone: (215) 388-6741
Kennett Square, PA 19348   Enola Jane N. Teeter, Libn.
Founded: 1961. **Staff:** Prof 1; Other 3. **Subjects:** Botany, horticulture and allied fields. **Special Collections:** Curtis' Botanical Magazine (volume 1, 1787 to present); nursery catalogs. **Holdings:** 14,348 volumes; 10 VF drawers of pamphlets and clippings on plant material; 4 VF drawers of information on botanical gardens and arboreta; 26 VF drawers of information on horticulture and allied fields; 5 VF drawers on geographical information; unbound periodicals; microforms. **Subscriptions:** 200 journals and other serials. **Services:** Interlibrary loans; copying; library open to public with restrictions. **Networks/Consortia:** Member of OCLC through PALINET and Union Library Catalogue of Pennsylvania. **Special Indexes:** Index to collection of nursery catalogs.

LONGYEAR (J.M.) RESEARCH LIBRARY
See: Marquette County Historical Society - J.M. Longyear Research Library

★7106★

LOO MERIDETH & MC MILLAN - LAW LIBRARY (Law)

1800 Century Park East, Suite 200   Phone: (213) 277-0300
Los Angeles, CA 90067   Susan A. Miller, Libn.
Staff: Prof 1. **Subjects:** Law - corporate, real estate, probate, international, taxation; securities. **Holdings:** 6000 books; 105 bound periodical volumes. **Subscriptions:** 103 journals and other serials. **Services:** Interlibrary loans; library not open to public.

★7107★

LORAIN COMMUNITY HOSPITAL - MEDICAL STAFF LIBRARY (Med)

3700 Kolbe Rd.   Phone: (216) 282-9121
Lorain, OH 44053   Mrs. Tory Wagner, Med.Libn.
Staff: Prof 1; Other 1. **Subjects:** Medicine, nursing, psychiatry, alcoholism. **Holdings:** 1200 books; 150 bound periodical volumes; 1500 unbound journals; 50 government documents. **Subscriptions:** 140 journals and other serials. **Services:** Interlibrary loans; copying; SDI; library open to public for reference use only.

★7108★

LORAIN COUNTY HISTORICAL SOCIETY - GERALD HICKS MEMORIAL LIBRARY (Hist)

509 Washington Ave.   Phone: (216) 322-3341
Elyria, OH 44035   Mary Jeffries, Cat.
Founded: 1975. **Subjects:** Local, state and national history, genealogy. **Special Collections:** Ely Family Papers, 1790-1900; early local city directories (75 volumes); Lorain County Manuscript collection (150 items). **Holdings:** 623 volumes. **Services:** Library open to public for reference use only. **Special Indexes:** Index of Lorain County, OH histories and cemeteries (card).

★7109★

LORAIN COUNTY LAW LIBRARY ASSOCIATION - LIBRARY (Law)†

3rd Fl., Courthouse   Phone: (216) 322-5024
Elyria, OH 44035   Eleanor E. Pietch, Libn.
Staff: Prof 1. **Subjects:** Law. **Holdings:** 24,000 books; 379 bound periodical volumes; 78 cassette tapes; 350 microfiche. **Subscriptions:** 25 journals and other serials. **Services:** Copying; library open to judges, county officals, Ohio legislators, attorneys and law students residing in Lorain County.

★7110★

LORAL ELECTRONIC SYSTEMS - TECHNICAL INFORMATION CENTER (Sci-Tech; Mil)

999 Central Park Ave.   Phone: (914) 968-2500
Yonkers, NY 10704   Terry Mozorosky, Mgr.
Staff: Prof 1; Other 1. **Subjects:** Electronic countermeasures, radar, electronic warfare, defense industry management. **Holdings:** 4000 books; 250 bound periodical volumes; 1000 microfiche; 1000 U.S. Defense Department reports; 10,000 drawings. **Subscriptions:** 85 journals and other serials. **Services:** Interlibrary loans; copying; SDI; library not open to public. **Computerized Information Services:** DIALOG. **Publications:** Online, monthly.

★7111★

LORD, BISSELL AND BROOK - LAW LIBRARY (Law)

115 S. LaSalle St.   Phone: (312) 443-0647
Chicago, IL 60603   Jane L. Gaddis, Libn.
Staff: Prof 2; Other 4. **Subjects:** Law - insurance, maritime, corporate, aviation. **Holdings:** 25,000 books; 27 bound periodical volumes. **Subscriptions:** 60 journals and other serials. **Services:** Interlibrary loans; copying; library not open to public.

★7112★

LORD CORPORATION - INFORMATION CENTERS (Sci-Tech)
Box 10039   Phone: (814) 456-8511
Erie PA 16514   Mary F. Calvano, Info.Spec.
Staff: Prof 3; Other 2. **Subjects:** Rubber technology, noise and vibration control, materials science, coatings technology, adhesives technology. **Holdings:** 10,000 books; 5000 bound periodical volumes; technical reports and papers. **Subscriptions:** 540 journals and other serials; 10 newspapers. **Services:** Interlibrary loans; copying; SDI; library open to public by appointment. **Computerized Information Services:** DIALOG, New England Research Application Center (NERAC); TISR System (internal database); computerized circulation. **Networks/Consortia:** Member of Northwest Interlibrary Cooperative of Pennsylvania (NICOP). **Publications:** Acquisitions List, monthly; Digest of Engineering and Technology, monthly; Digest of Macromolecular Technology, bimonthly - all distributed internally by request. **Remarks:** Center is located at 1635 W. 12th St., Erie, PA 16512. A second information center is located at 2000 W. Grandview, Erie, PA 16512. Its telephone number is (814) 868-3611. **Staff:** Elizabeth J. Critchfield, Supv.Info.Acq. & Dissem.; L. Dianne Howard, Lit. Searcher.

★7113★

LORD, DAY & LORD - LIBRARY (Law)
25 Broadway   Phone: (212) 344-8480
New York, NY 10004   Laurie A. Hart, Libn.
Staff: Prof 3; Other 5. **Subjects:** Law - corporate, maritime. **Holdings:** 30,000 volumes. **Services:** Interlibrary loans; library not open to public. **Computerized Information Services:** LEXIS, New York Times Information Service. **Staff:** Timothy J. Hanley, Asst.Libn.; Pamela Sue Brown-Inz, Asst.Libn.

LORENZ (Walter) MEMORIAL LIBRARY
See: Westwood First Presbyterian Church - Walter Lorenz Memorial Library

★7114★

LORETTO HEIGHTS COLLEGE - MAY BONFILS STANTON LIBRARY (Soc Sci)
3001 S. Federal Blvd.   Phone: (303) 936-8441
Denver, CO 80236   Richard Ban Wye, Dir.
Founded: 1963. **Staff:** Prof 1; Other 4. **Subjects:** Literature, history, social sciences, education, nursing, philosophy, theology. **Special Collections:** Role of woman in today's world. **Holdings:** 107,000 books and bound periodical volumes; 4 VF cabinets and 50 boxes of archival materials. **Subscriptions:** 650 journals and other serials; 8 newspapers. **Services:** Interlibrary loans; copying; library open to public on a fee basis. **Computerized Information Services:** Computerized cataloging. **Networks/Consortia:** Member of Bibliographical Center for Research, Rocky Mountain Region, Inc. (BCR). **Staff:** Michael Furuli, Coord., Media; JoElla Russell, Coord., Tech.Proc.

★7115★

LORETTO HOSPITAL - HEALTH SCIENCES LIBRARY (Med)†
645 S. Central Ave.   Phone: (312) 626-4300
Chicago, IL 60644   Dimiter Etimov, Dir.
Founded: 1939. **Staff:** Prof 1. **Subjects:** Medicine, nursing, health administration. **Holdings:** 1250 books; 1010 bound periodical volumes. **Subscriptions:** 145 journals and other serials. **Services:** Interlibrary loans; copying; library not open to public. **Networks/Consortia:** Member of Metropolitan Consortium. **Publications:** Serials List.

★7116★

LORILLARD RESEARCH CENTER LIBRARY (Sci-Tech)
420 English St.
Box 21688
Greensboro, NC 27420   Phone: (919) 373-6895
                                                 Lawrence M. Skladanowski, Lib.Supv.
Founded: 1959. **Staff:** Prof 4; Other 2. **Subjects:** Tobacco products and manufacturing, tobacco chemistry. **Holdings:** 4750 books; 5380 bound periodical volumes; 1000 boxes of unbound periodicals. **Subscriptions:** 149 journals and other serials. **Services:** Interlibrary loans; copying; library open to public by appointment. **Computerized Information Services:** DIALOG, SDC, NLM. **Remarks:** Lorillard is a division of Loews Theatres, Inc.

LORING AIR FORCE BASE (ME)
See: U.S. Air Force Base - Loring Base Library

★7117★

LOS ALAMOS COUNTY HISTORICAL MUSEUM - ARCHIVES (Hist)
Fuller Lodge Cultural Ctr.
Box 43
Los Alamos, NM 87544   Phone: (505) 662-6272
                                                 Thera Joyce Hunn, Archv.
Founded: 1978. **Staff:** Prof 2. **Subjects:** Los Alamos history, history and archeology of Northern New Mexico. **Special Collections:** Photographs of Los Alamos Ranch School by T.H. Parkhurst (56 photographs) and Laura Gilpin (110 photographs); Manhattan Project Collection (building of the atom bomb; books; photographs; memorabilia). **Holdings:** 500 books; 16 serial titles; 114 oral history tapes; unpublished manuscripts; 6 films; 200 projection slides; 87 maps; 5 videotapes; local newspapers and clippings. **Services:** Archives available for research; assistance available upon request. **Publications:** When Los Alamos was a Ranch School (1974); A Los Alamos Reader (1976); Inside Box 1663 (1977); Los Alamos Outdoors (1981). **Special Indexes:** Materials indexed by topic. **Staff:** Hedy M. Dunn, Musm.Mgr.

LOS ALAMOS NATIONAL LABORATORY
See: University of California

★7118★

LOS ANGELES BAPTIST COLLEGE - ROBERT L. POWELL MEMORIAL LIBRARY (Rel-Theol)
21726 W. Placerita Canyon Rd.
Box 878   Phone: (805) 259-3540
Newhall, CA 91322   Agnes M. Holt, Libn.
Staff: Prof 1; Other 2. **Subjects:** Religion. **Special Collections:** Biblical theology; Mormonism; Jehovah's Witnesses. **Holdings:** 33,000 books; 2000 AV items. **Subscriptions:** 400 journals and other serials; 10 newspapers. **Services:** Interlibrary loans; copying; library open to public.

★7119★

LOS ANGELES CENTER FOR PHOTOGRAPHIC STUDIES - RESOURCE CENTER (Art)
814 S. Spring St., 3rd Fl.   Phone: (213) 623-9410
Los Angeles, CA 90014   Darryl Curran, Pres.
Founded: 1974. **Staff:** Prof 1; Other 1. **Subjects:** Photographic art. **Special Collections:** Southern California Photography (1000 slides and biographical information on local artists). **Holdings:** 150 volumes; slides; 1 box of clippings; 2 boxes of ephemera. **Subscriptions:** 12 journals and other serials. **Services:** Center open to public. **Publications:** Photo calendar, monthly (lists gallery and museum exhibitions, lectures in area) - samples on request; OBSCURA, quarterly. **Special Catalogs:** Paul Outerbridge, Jr. (1976); Photographic Directions; Los Angeles (1979); William Mortensen (1979); Multicultural Focus, a photography exhibition for the Los Angeles Bicentennial (1981); L.A. as Subject Matter (1982) - all for sale. **Staff:** Carol Flax, Resource Ctr.Dir.

★7120★

LOS ANGELES CHAMBER OF COMMERCE - ECONOMIC INFORMATION & RESEARCH DEPARTMENT LIBRARY (Bus-Fin)†
404 S. Bixel
Box 3696   Phone: (213) 629-0711
Los Angeles, CA 90051   Harry H. Hamparzumian, Mgr.
Founded: 1923. **Staff:** Prof 2. **Subjects:** Population characteristics, employment and earnings, construction and real estate, retail and wholesale trade, income, manufacturing, industrial growth. **Special Collections:** Census information from 1890; government publications. **Holdings:** 500 books. **Services:** Interlibrary loans; copying; library open to public with restrictions.

★7121★

LOS ANGELES CITY ATTORNEY - LAW LIBRARY (Law)
200 N. Main, Rm. 1700   Phone: (213) 485-5400
Los Angeles, CA 90012   Sandee Mirell, Libn.
Founded: 1925. **Staff:** Prof 1; Other 1. **Subjects:** California and federal legislation; judicial rules and decisions; administrative rules and decisions; legislative history; tax services; municipal law and liability; economic and labor relations and environmental services. **Special Collections:** Los Angeles City Charter and Revisions, 1854 to present (17 volumes); statutes and amendments of California Codes, 1854 to present (84 volumes); California Constitutional Convention, 1880 (3 volumes); Los Angeles City Attorney Opinions, 1939 to present (425 volumes); City Attorney Criminal Appeals Cases (14 volumes). **Holdings:** 35,000 books; 300 bound periodical volumes; 1 file cabinet of City Attorney legal memos, letters. **Subscriptions:** 30 journals and other serials; 6 newspapers. **Services:** Copying; library not open to public. **Publications:** Opinions and Index, 3/year - local distribution. **Special Indexes:** Index to legal memoranda (card).

LOS ANGELES CITY - GRIFFITH OBSERVATORY
See: Griffith Observatory

★7122★
LOS ANGELES COLLEGE OF CHIROPRACTIC - HENRY G. HIGHLY LIBRARY (Med)
16200 E. Amber Valley Dr.
Whittier, CA 90604
Phone: (213) 947-8755
Robin L. Lober, Dir.
Founded: 1948. **Staff:** Prof 1; Other 6. **Subjects:** Human spine and related structures; chiropractic medicine; basic and clinical sciences; naturopathy. **Special Collections:** Chiropractic History. **Holdings:** 17,500 books; 3000 bound periodical volumes; VF materials; 300 AV items. **Subscriptions:** 256 journals and other serials. **Services:** Interlibrary loans; copying; library open to public for reference use only. **Networks/Consortia:** Member of Pacific Southwest Regional Medical Library Service (PSRMLS); CLASS; Chiropractic Library Consortium. **Formerly:** Located in Glendale, CA.

★7123★
LOS ANGELES COUNTY DEPARTMENT OF ARBORETA AND BOTANIC GARDENS - PLANT SCIENCE LIBRARY (Agri)
301 N. Baldwin Ave.
Arcadia, CA 91006-2697
Phone: (213) 446-8251
Joan DeFato, Plant Sci.Libn.
Founded: 1948. **Staff:** Prof 1; Other 1. **Subjects:** Botany, horticulture, plant pathology, medicinal and poisonous plants, landscape architecture. **Special Collections:** Rare books; nursery catalogs. **Holdings:** 23,000 books and bound periodical volumes; 340 boxes of nursery catalogs; microfiche; maps. **Services:** Interlibrary loans; copying; library open to public. **Also Known As:** Los Angeles State and County Arboretum Plant Science Library.

★7124★
LOS ANGELES COUNTY - DEPARTMENT OF DATA PROCESSING - TECHNICAL LIBRARY (Bus-Fin; Sci-Tech)
9150 E. Imperial Hwy., Rm. R-118
Downey, CA 90242
Phone: (213) 771-5421
Millie Jones, Tech.Libn.
Founded: 1969. **Staff:** Prof 1. **Subjects:** Computer programming, management science, personnel training. **Holdings:** 2000 books; 1000 bound periodical volumes; 500 pamphlets (cataloged); 6000 technical computer manuals; 70 programmed instruction courses; 80 videotape training materials; 50 cassette lectures; 16 16mm films. **Subscriptions:** 53 journals and other serials. **Services:** Copying; library not open to public. **Publications:** Guide to Educational Services, updated as needed - for internal distribution only.

★7125★
LOS ANGELES COUNTY DEPARTMENT OF HEALTH SERVICES-PREVENTIVE PUBLIC HEALTH - JOHN L. POMEROY MEMORIAL LIBRARY (Med)
313 N. Figueroa St., Rm. Mz1
Los Angeles, CA 90012
Phone: (213) 974-7780
Agnes Imbrie, Libn.
Founded: 1928. **Staff:** Prof 1. **Subjects:** Public health, preventive medicine. **Holdings:** 3000 volumes; 9 VF drawers of pamphlets. **Subscriptions:** 165 journals and other serials. **Services:** Interlibrary loans; copying; library open to public for reference use only. **Networks/Consortia:** Member of Pacific Southwest Regional Medical Library Service (PSRMLS). **Publications:** Recent Book List; Periodicals Currently Received.

★7126★
LOS ANGELES COUNTY - DEPARTMENT OF MENTAL HEALTH - LIBRARY (Soc Sci)
2415 W. Sixth St.
Los Angeles, CA 90057
Phone: (213) 738-4730
Edward E. Asawa, Libn.
Founded: 1962. **Staff:** Prof 1; Other 1. **Subjects:** Community mental health services. **Holdings:** 2000 books and periodicals. **Services:** Library not open to public.

★7127★
LOS ANGELES COUNTY HARBOR-UCLA MEDICAL CENTER - A.F. PARLOW LIBRARY OF HEALTH SCIENCES (Med)
1000 W. Carson St.
Box 18
Torrance, CA 90509
Phone: (213) 377-0108
Mary Ann Berliner, Dir., Lib.Serv.
Founded: 1946. **Staff:** Prof 4; Other 8. **Subjects:** Medicine, nursing, dentistry, patient education, administration. **Holdings:** 13,850 books; 18,520 bound periodical volumes; 3000 titles of pamphlets; 453 reels of microfilm; 850 AV items. **Subscriptions:** 747 journals and other serials. **Services:** Interlibrary loans; copying library open to public with restrictions. **Computerized Information Services:** BRS, NLM; CAI (Computer Assisted Instruction, online system); computerized cataloging. **Publications:** Journal holdings, annual; AV holdings, annual; Serials Holdings List.

★7128★
LOS ANGELES COUNTY LAW LIBRARY (Law)
301 W. First St.
Los Angeles, CA 90012
Phone: (213) 629-3531
Richard T. Iamele, Libn.
Founded: 1891. **Staff:** Prof 15; Other 44. **Subjects:** Law. **Holdings:** 671,967 volumes; 5225 reels of microfilm; 283,612 microforms. **Subscriptions:** 9546 journals and other serials. **Services:** Interlibrary loans; copying; library open to public. **Computerized Information Services:** WESTLAW; computerized cataloging. **Networks/Consortia:** Member of RLG. **Publications:** Bibliographies, irregular. **Remarks:** Maintains branch libraries in the following cities: Beverly Hills, Compton, Long Beach, Norwalk, Pasadena, Pomona, Santa Monica, Torrance and Van Nuys.

★7129★
LOS ANGELES COUNTY/LONG BEACH GENERAL HOSPITAL - MEDICAL LIBRARY (Med)
2597 Redondo Ave.
Long Beach, CA 90806
Phone: (213) 636-0784
Thomas P. Dengler, Med.Libn.
Staff: Prof 1; Other 1. **Subjects:** Medicine. **Holdings:** 500 books. **Subscriptions:** 100 journals and other serials. **Services:** Interlibrary loans; copying; library open to public with restrictions.

★7130★
LOS ANGELES COUNTY/MARTIN LUTHER KING, JR. GENERAL HOSPITAL - MEDICAL LIBRARY (Med)
12021 S. Wilmington Ave., Rm. 1070
Los Angeles, CA 90059
Phone: (213) 603-4068
Ms. M. Moss Humphrey, Sr.Med.Libn.
Staff: Prof 2; Other 3. **Subjects:** Medicine. **Holdings:** 5000 books; 6000 bound periodical volumes; 16 drawers of audio cassettes. **Subscriptions:** 552 journals and other serials. **Services:** Interlibrary loans; copying (staff only); library open to public. **Computerized Information Services:** MEDLINE, SDC. **Staff:** Elaine L. Wells, Med.Libn.

★7131★
LOS ANGELES COUNTY MEDICAL ASSOCIATION - LIBRARY (Med)
634 S. Westlake Ave.
Los Angeles, CA 90057
Phone: (213) 483-4555
Elizabeth S. Crahan, Dir., Lib.Serv.
Founded: 1891. **Staff:** Prof 5; Other 6. **Subjects:** Medicine, history of medicine. **Special Collections:** Dr. George Dock Collection; local medical memorabilia; Osleriana; medical Californiana; history of medicine collection; rare books collection. **Holdings:** 81,320 books; 48,384 bound periodical volumes; 1 room of AV items; 2 rooms of medical artifacts; boxed archival material; 2 VF drawers of pamphlets. **Subscriptions:** 1146 journals and other serials. **Services:** Interlibrary loans; copying; library open to public with restrictions. **Computerized Information Services:** MEDLINE, DIALOG; computerized cataloging. **Networks/Consortia:** Member of OCLC. **Staff:** James J. Ochoa, Hd., Tech.Proc.; Sheri Kruyer, Hd., Ref.

★7132★
LOS ANGELES COUNTY MUSEUM OF ART - RESEARCH LIBRARY (Art)
5905 Wilshire Blvd.
Los Angeles, CA 90036
Phone: (213) 857-6118
Eleanor C. Hartman, Musm.Libn.
Founded: 1963. **Staff:** Prof 3; Other 4. **Subjects:** Art. **Special Collections:** Textiles and costumes; prints and drawings. **Holdings:** 61,000 books; 9000 bound periodical volumes; 25,000 sales and auction catalogs; 100 VF drawers of exhibition catalogs. **Subscriptions:** 337 journals and other serials. **Services:** Interlibrary loans; copying; library open to qualified researchers for reference use upon request. **Networks/Consortia:** Member of OCLC. **Staff:** Eleanor D. Riley, Asst.Libn.; Carl R. Baker, Cat.

★7133★
LOS ANGELES COUNTY MUSEUM OF NATURAL HISTORY - RESEARCH LIBRARY (Sci-Tech; Hist)
900 Exposition Blvd.
Los Angeles, CA 90007
Phone: (213) 744-3387
Katharine E. Donahue, Musm.Libn.
Founded: 1921. **Staff:** Prof 2; Other 2. **Subjects:** History - California, natural, Southwest; industrial technology; mammalogy; malacology; mineralogy; paleontology; ornithology; archeology; anthropology; entomology; herpetology. **Special Collections:** Los Angeles Theatre programs (pre-1900); Southern California newspaper collection (pre-1900; 350 titles). **Holdings:** 92,000 volumes; 20,000 maps, 5000 pamphlets, manuscripts; 250 Environmental Impact Reports for Los Angeles County. **Subscriptions:** 950 journals and other serials. **Services:** Interlibrary loans; copying; library open to public with restrictions. **Computerized Information Services:** Computerized cataloging and serials. **Networks/Consortia:** Member of OCLC; CLASS; Southern California Answering Network (SCAN); Southern California Interlibrary Loan Network (SCILL). **Special Indexes:** Chronological index to newspapers. **Staff:** Kathryn E. King, Libn.

★7134★

LOS ANGELES COUNTY/OLIVE VIEW MEDICAL CENTER - HEALTH SCIENCES LIBRARY (Med)
7533 Van Nuys Blvd.
Rm. 303, South Tower   Phone: (213) 997-1800
Van Nuys, CA 91405   Miriam Kafka, Act.Libn.
Founded: 1920. **Staff:** 3. **Subjects:** Mental health, medicine, pediatrics, surgery. **Special Collections:** Emil Bogen Memorial Collection. **Holdings:** 2200 books; 2800 bound periodical volumes; 2 VF drawers of pamphlets; audiotapes; 8 audio cassettes. **Subscriptions:** 400 journals and other serials. **Services:** Interlibrary loans; copying; SDI; library not open to public. **Computerized Information Services:** MEDLINE. **Networks/Consortia:** Member of San Fernando Valley Health Sciences Library Group; Southern California Interlibrary Loan Network (SCILL).

★7135★

LOS ANGELES COUNTY SUPERINTENDENT OF SCHOOLS - PROFESSIONAL REFERENCE CENTER (Educ)
9300 E. Imperial Hwy.   Phone: (213) 922-6359
Downey, CA 90242   Margaret Marquette, Coord.
Staff: Prof 1; Other 5. **Subjects:** Education. **Special Collections:** Los Angeles County Education Center publications; Adult Basic Education-English as a Second Language collection. **Holdings:** 7500 books; ERIC microfiche collection, 1966 to present. **Subscriptions:** 500 journals and other serials; 5 newspapers. **Services:** Interlibrary loans; copying; center open to public with restrictions. **Computerized Information Services:** Los Angeles Center for Education Resources (LANCERS); computerized cataloging and acquisitions.

★7136★

LOS ANGELES COUNTY/UNIVERSITY OF SOUTHERN CALIFORNIA MEDICAL CENTER - MEDICAL LIBRARIES (Med)
1200 N. State St.   Phone: (213) 226-7006
Los Angeles, CA 90033   Alice Reinhardt, Chf., Lib.Serv.
Founded: 1914. **Staff:** Prof 5; Other 8. **Subjects:** Medicine, nursing and allied health professions. **Holdings:** 24,000 books; 29,500 bound periodical volumes; 10,000 pamphlets; 2800 audio cassettes; 192 motion picture films; 55 slide sets; 697 transparencies and filmstrips. **Subscriptions:** 1030 journals and other serials. **Services:** Interlibrary loans; copying; SDI; bibliographies; translations; briefing and abstracting; library open to hospital employees; libraries not open to public. **Computerized Information Services:** NLM, DIALOG, SDC; computerized cataloging. **Networks/Consortia:** Member of Los Angeles County Health Sciences Librarians Group; CLASS. **Remarks:** The figures given above comprise the holdings of the three medical center libraries - General Hospital, Women's Hospital, and the Nursing Library. **Staff:** Bella Kwong, Women's Hosp.Libn.; Christina Chen, Tech.Serv.Libn.; Sharon Pruhs, Ref.Libn.

★7137★

LOS ANGELES COUNTY/UNIVERSITY OF SOUTHERN CALIFORNIA MEDICAL CENTER - PEDIATRICS LIBRARY
1129 N. State St.
Los Angeles, CA 90033
Subjects: Pediatrics. **Holdings:** 463 books; 373 bound periodical volumes; 4 drawers of audio cassettes. **Remarks:** Presently inactive.

LOS ANGELES DAILY NEWS
See: Van Nuys Publishing Company

★7138★

LOS ANGELES - DEPARTMENT OF RECREATION AND PARKS - CABRILLO MARINE MUSEUM - LIBRARY (Sci-Tech)
3720 Stephen White Dr.   Phone: (213) 548-7562
San Pedro, CA 90731   Dr. Susanne Lawrenz-Miller, Assoc.Dir.
Founded: 1935. **Staff:** Prof 3; Other 2. **Subjects:** Marine biology, maritime history, aquariums, whaling. **Holdings:** 1300 volumes; unbound periodical volumes; pictures. **Subscriptions:** 15 journals and other serials. **Services:** Library open to public for reference use only. **Staff:** Emmanuel N. Rosales, Cur.

★7139★

LOS ANGELES - DEPARTMENT OF WATER AND POWER - LEGAL DIVISION - LAW LIBRARY (Law)†
1520 General Office Bldg.
111 N. Hope St.
Los Angeles, CA 90012   Phone: (213) 481-6309
    Ethel Hardy
Staff: 1. **Subjects:** Law. **Holdings:** 11,500 books; 750 bound periodical volumes. **Subscriptions:** 250 journals and other serials. **Services:** Library not open to public.

★7140★

LOS ANGELES HERALD-EXAMINER - NEWSPAPER LIBRARY (Publ)
1111 S. Broadway   Phone: (213) 744-8420
Los Angeles, CA 90015   Ann E. Sausedo, Lib.Dir.
Staff: Prof 1; Other 8. **Subjects:** Newspaper reference topics. **Holdings:** Newspaper clippings; Herald-Examiner pictures, wire services pictures; microfilmed copies of Herald-Examiner. **Services:** Library not open to public.

★7141★

LOS ANGELES INSTITUTE OF CONTEMPORARY ART - LIBRARY (Art)
2020 S. Robertson Blvd.   Phone: (213) 559-5033
Los Angeles, CA 90034   Debra Burchett, Cur.
Subjects: Contemporary art. **Special Collections:** Original artists' books; exhibition catalogs. **Holdings:** 500 books. **Services:** Copying; library open to public for reference use only.

LOS ANGELES MUNICIPAL REFERENCE DEPARTMENT
See: Los Angeles Public Library - Municipal Reference Department

LOS ANGELES POWER CORPORATION LIBRARY
See: Bechtel Power Corporation - Library

★7142★

LOS ANGELES PSYCHOANALYTIC SOCIETY AND INSTITUTE - SIMMEL-FENICHEL LIBRARY (Med)
2014 Sawtelle Blvd.   Phone: (213) 478-6851
Los Angeles, CA 90025   Kathleen Matson, Libn.
Founded: 1953. **Staff:** Prof 1. **Subjects:** Psychoanalysis and psychiatry, the behavioral sciences. **Special Collections:** Freudiana, including books, articles, letters, photographs and other items. **Holdings:** 4900 books; 760 bound periodical volumes; 800 unbound periodicals (cataloged); 14 VF drawers of reprints and pamphlets; 550 unpublished papers; 2 phonograph records and 300 tapes. **Subscriptions:** 25 journals and other serials. **Services:** Interlibrary loans; copying; library open to public with guest membership. **Special Indexes:** Chicago Psychoanalytic Literature Index, pertaining to psychoanalysis and psychiatry, psychosomatic medicine and related areas of the behavioral sciences (card file up to 1974; bound volumes from 1920-1981).

★7143★

LOS ANGELES PUBLIC LIBRARY - ART, MUSIC & RECREATION DEPARTMENT (Art; Mus)
630 W. Fifth St.   Phone: (213) 626-7461
Los Angeles, CA 90071   Judy M. Horton, Dept.Mgr.
Staff: Prof 7; Other 9. **Subjects:** Art, music, sports and recreation, film, photography, dance, costume, urban planning, circus. **Special Collections:** Japanese prints (300 items); Art in Los Angeles Scrapbooks (1938 to present); Dance in Los Angeles Scrapbooks (1955 to present); Music in Los Angeles Scrapbooks (1894 to present); orchestral scores and parts (1800 items); chess; bullfighting; circus. **Holdings:** 203,633 volumes; 150,000 clippings; 45,000 scores; 569 unbound periodicals. **Subscriptions:** 569 journals and other serials. **Services:** Interlibrary loans; copying. **Computerized Information Services:** Computerized acquisitions. **Special Catalogs:** Catalog of orchestral scores and parts. **Special Indexes:** Art Biography Index; Film Index; Index to Musicians; Symphony Program Notes; Song Index; Sports Files; Circus Index; Architecture Index; Costume Index; Dance Index - all on cards.

★7144★

LOS ANGELES PUBLIC LIBRARY - AUDIO-VISUAL DEPARTMENT (Aud-Vis)
630 W. Fifth St.   Phone: (213) 626-7461
Los Angeles, CA 90071   Richard V. Partlow, Dept.Mgr.
Staff: Prof 2; Other 11. **Holdings:** 16mm films; videotapes; mounted pictures and clippings; phonograph records; filmstrips; slides; audio cassettes. **Special Catalogs:** Film catalog. **Staff:** Bronislaw M. Sokol, Asst.Dept.Mgr.

★7145★

LOS ANGELES PUBLIC LIBRARY - BUSINESS & ECONOMICS DEPARTMENT (Bus-Fin)
630 W. Fifth St.   Phone: (213) 626-7461
Los Angeles, CA 90071   Joan Bartel, Dept.Mgr.
Staff: Prof 8; Other 11. **Subjects:** Management, investment, international trade, transportaton, economics, media, commercial law, labor, taxes, real estate. **Holdings:** 158,639 volumes; corporate annual reports; Securities and Exchange Commission 10K reports, 1970 to present, on microfiche; depository for U.S., California and U.N. documents; trade and business specialty directories; telephone books. **Subscriptions:** 4000 journals and other serials. **Services:** Interlibrary loans; copying; in-person and telephone reference. **Computerized Information Services:** DIALOG, New York Times

Information Service. **Publications:** Investment Information Sources: Los Angeles Public Library Investment Collection - free upon request.

★7146★
LOS ANGELES PUBLIC LIBRARY - CHILDREN'S LITERATURE DEPARTMENT (Hum)
630 W. Fifth St.   Phone: (213) 626-7461
Los Angeles, CA 90071   Serenna Day, Sr.Libn.
Staff: Prof 4; Other 2. **Subjects:** Children's literature. **Special Collections:** Folk and fairy tales (2520 volumes); foreign language children's books (4355 volumes); Mother Goose (300 volumes); poetry. **Holdings:** 116,500 books; 820 bound periodical volumes. **Subscriptions:** 93 journals and other serials. **Services:** Interlibrary loans; copying; library open to public. **Computerized Information Services:** Computerized acquisitions. **Special Indexes:** Author and illustrator biographies; fiction; folktales and short stories; illustrations; picture books; plays; songs.

★7147★
LOS ANGELES PUBLIC LIBRARY - FICTION DEPARTMENT (Hum)
630 W. Fifth St.   Phone: (213) 626-7461
Los Angeles, CA 90071   Helene G. Mochedlover, Dept.Mgr.
Staff: Prof 4; Other 4. **Subjects:** Fiction in general, foreign translations. **Special Collections:** California in fiction; black fiction. **Holdings:** 207,302 volumes. **Subscriptions:** 23 journals and other serials. **Services:** Interlibrary loans; copying. **Computerized Information Services:** Computerized acquisitions. **Special Indexes:** Balzac Index; biographical index; California in Fiction; California Locale Index; California Chronological Index; Detectives; Fiction Book Review File; Index of Filmed Books; Maupassant Index; Prize Novels Index; Serials and Sequels Index; Short Story Index; Subject Index to Fiction; Title Derivation Index; Jules Verne Index.

★7148★
LOS ANGELES PUBLIC LIBRARY - FOREIGN LANGUAGES DEPARTMENT (Hum)
630 W. Fifth St.   Phone: (213) 626-7461
Los Angeles, CA 90071   Sylva N. Manoogian, Prin.Libn.
Founded: 1920. **Staff:** Prof 4; Other 5. **Subjects:** Books in 28 modern languages (primarily history, literature, drama, poetry, biography, fiction). **Special Collections:** Multilingual health materials (400 volumes in 12 languages); language instructional materials (5000 volumes in 28 languages, including English as a second language). **Holdings:** 165,683 books; 150 bound periodical volumes; 500 reels of microfilmed retrospective periodical titles in French, German and Spanish. **Subscriptions:** 150 journals and other serials. **Services:** Interlibrary loans; multilingual reference and reader's advisory service. **Publications:** Special bibliographies. **Special Indexes:** Drama and Short Story Indexes in French, German, Italian, Russian, Spanish; Short Story Collections in French, German, Italian, Russian, Swedish and Yiddish; Spanish Poetry Index; Spanish Literary Criticism File; Multilingual Fiction Subject Index.

★7149★
LOS ANGELES PUBLIC LIBRARY - HISTORY DEPARTMENT (Hist)
630 W. Fifth St.   Phone: (213) 626-7461
Los Angeles, CA 90071   Mary S. Pratt, Dept.Mgr.
Staff: Prof 11; Other 15. **Subjects:** History, travel, biography, Californiana, genealogy, local history, heraldry. **Special Collections:** Genealogy (28,000 volumes); Californiana (10,000 items); maps and atlases; American Indians; World Wars I and II; travel. **Holdings:** 275,000 volumes; 80,000 maps; 240,000 photographs. **Subscriptions:** 1300 journals and other serials. **Services:** Interlibrary loans; copying (limited). **Computerized Information Services:** Computerized acquisitions. **Special Indexes:** California biography; California subject; Western outlaws and sheriffs; collected biography; American Indians; family history; local history; coats of arms - all on cards.

★7150★
LOS ANGELES PUBLIC LIBRARY - LITERATURE & PHILOLOGY DEPARTMENT (Hum)
630 W. Fifth St.   Phone: (213) 626-7461
Los Angeles, CA 90071   Helene Mochedlover, Dept.Mgr.
Staff: Prof 7; Other 9. **Subjects:** Bibliography, library science, printing, philology, drama and the theater, poetry, literary history and criticism, public speaking, authorship, classical languages and literature, humor. **Special Collections:** Dobinson Collection of Theatre Memorabilia. **Holdings:** 245,000 volumes. **Subscriptions:** 1300 journals and other serials. **Services:** Interlibrary loans; copying; library open to public. **Computerized Information Services:** Computerized acquisitions. **Special Indexes:** Arabian Nights Index; ; Argosy Magazine Index; author clippings (45,000); Index to Works of Robert Benchley; Don Blanding Index; Cosmopolitan Magazine Index; Thomas Augustine Daly Index; Index to Dialect Readings; Drama Clippings Index; Drama in Los Angeles Scrapbook; Edgar A. Guest Index; Holiday Index; Liberty Magazine Index; Index to Monologs; Index to New York Dramatic Mirror; Alfred Noyes Index; obituary file; play review file; printing analytics; subject index to plays; subject index to poetry; supplemental essay index; television reviews scrapbook index; Theatre Program Index; James Thurber Index; True Magazine Index; Mark Twain Index; unpublished play index; Ella Wheeler Wilcox Index.

★7151★
LOS ANGELES PUBLIC LIBRARY - MUNICIPAL REFERENCE DEPARTMENT (Soc Sci)
530 City Hall E.
200 N. Main St.   Phone: (213) 485-3791
Los Angeles, CA 90012   Wilma J. Dewey, Prin.Libn.
Staff: Prof 3; Other 6. **Subjects:** Public administration, municipal government, municipal finance, fire, recreation and parks, public works, civil service, personnel. **Special Collections:** Municipal documents from large cities; biography file of Los Angeles officials. **Holdings:** 43,212 volumes. **Subscriptions:** 591 journals. **Services:** Specialized reference service for city officials and employees; library open to public for reference use only.

★7152★
LOS ANGELES PUBLIC LIBRARY - MUNICIPAL REFERENCE DEPARTMENT - PLANNING DIVISION (Plan)
City Hall, Rm. 618
200 N. Spring St.   Phone: (213) 485-5077
Los Angeles, CA 90012   Sarah D. Wolf, Libn.
Founded: 1968. **Staff:** Prof 1; Other 1. **Subjects:** City planning, regional planning, housing, transportation, environment zoning, energy. **Special Collections:** Los Angeles City Planning Department reports; American Society of Planning Officials reports. **Holdings:** 8500 volumes. **Subscriptions:** 200 journals and other serials. **Services:** Library open to public for reference use only.

★7153★
LOS ANGELES PUBLIC LIBRARY - MUNICIPAL REFERENCE DEPARTMENT - POLICE LIBRARY
150 N. Los Angeles St., Rm. 503
Los Angeles, CA 90012
Defunct

★7154★
LOS ANGELES PUBLIC LIBRARY - MUNICIPAL REFERENCE DEPARTMENT - WATER & POWER LIBRARY (Sci-Tech)
Rm. 518 GOB
Box 111   Phone: (213) 481-4610
Los Angeles, CA 90051   Donald F. Hinrichs, Sr.Libn.
Staff: Prof 4; Other 7. **Subjects:** Electrical and civil engineering, water, public utilities. **Holdings:** 20,000 volumes. **Subscriptions:** 600 journals and other serials. **Services:** Library open to public for reference use only.

★7155★
LOS ANGELES PUBLIC LIBRARY - NEWSPAPER ROOM
630 W. Fifth St.   Phone: (213) 646-7461
Los Angeles, CA 90071   Dan Strehl, Libn.
Founded: 1872. **Staff:** Prof 2; Other 10. **Subjects:** Newspapers. **Holdings:** 20,000 reels of microfilm, indexes, directories; 300 bound volumes; 800 historical newspaper titles. **Subscriptions:** 25 journals and other serials; 65 newspapers. **Services:** Copying; library open to public. **Computerized Information Services:** Computerized acquisitions and circulation. **Networks/Consortia:** Member of Southern California Answering Network; Metropolitan Cooperative Library System. **Publications:** Holdings list, annual - available upon request. **Special Indexes:** alphabetical file of newspaper holdings by cities, chronologically by year (card).

★7156★
LOS ANGELES PUBLIC LIBRARY - PHILOSOPHY & RELIGION DEPARTMENT (Rel-Theol)
630 W. Fifth St.   Phone: (213) 626-7461
Los Angeles, CA 90071   Marilyn C. Wherley, Dept.Hd.
Staff: Prof 3; Other 4. **Subjects:** Philosophy, religion, psychology. **Holdings:** 130,260 volumes. **Subscriptions:** 350 journals and other serials. **Services:** Interlibrary loans; copying. **Special Indexes:** Superstitions; Mythology; Metaphysical Societies; Cults and Sects; Psychics - all on cards.

★7157★
LOS ANGELES PUBLIC LIBRARY - SCIENCE & TECHNOLOGY DEPARTMENT (Sci-Tech)
630 W. Fifth St.   Phone: (213) 626-7461
Los Angeles, CA 90071   Billie M. Connor, Prin.Libn.
Staff: Prof 9; Other 17. **Subjects:** Physical and biological sciences, public

health, industrial standards, earth and natural sciences, applied technology, ecology. **Special Collections:** U.S. patents (complete set); cookery; automotive history and repair; specifications and standards. **Holdings:** 319,739 volumes; documents. **Subscriptions:** 2000 journals and other serials. **Services:** Interlibrary loans; copying; library open to public. **Computerized Information Services:** Computerized acquisitions. **Publications:** Periodical Holdings of the Science & Technology Department, 1981 (quarterly supplements) - available for sale. **Special Indexes:** Colored plates of wild flowers, fish, birds, reptiles, antique automoblies, trees, animals, butterflies; Ship Index by type and name; Anthropology Index by tribe; Consumer Index; Automotive Repair Index.

★7158★
LOS ANGELES PUBLIC LIBRARY - SOCIAL SCIENCES DEPARTMENT (Soc Sci)
630 W. Fifth St.   Phone: (213) 626-7461
Los Angeles, CA 90071   Marilyn C. Wherley, Dept.Hd.
Staff: Prof 7; Other 10. **Subjects:** Social problems, government, foreign affairs, international relations, law, criminology, education, women's movements, family relations, ethnic groups, child and adolescent psychology, interpersonal relations. **Special Collections:** U.S. and U.N. documents depository; black history; Mexican-American Affairs; women. **Holdings:** 231,421 volumes. **Subscriptions:** 2500 journals and other serials. **Services:** Interlibrary loans; copying. **Special Indexes:** Crime, current affairs, elections, statistics.

LOS ANGELES STATE AND COUNTY ARBORETUM PLANT SCIENCE LIBRARY
See: Los Angeles County Department of Arboreta and Botanic Gardens - Plant Science Library

★7159★
LOS ANGELES TIMES - EDITORIAL LIBRARY (Publ)
Times-Mirror Square   Phone: (213) 972-7181
Los Angeles, CA 90053   Cecily J. Surace, Lib.Dir.
Founded: 1905. **Staff:** Prof 23; Other 30. **Subjects:** Newspaper reference topics. **Special Collections:** Photographs (over 1 million). **Holdings:** Books, newspapers, pamphlets, clippings, photographs, negatives, microfilm. **Subscriptions:** 200 journals and other serials. **Services:** Interlibrary loans; library not open to public. **Computerized Information Services:** DIALOG, Data Resources, Inc. (DRI), International Data Corporation (IDC), Legitech, SDC, New York Times Information Service, BRS, Mead Data Central, MEDLINE, Dow Jones News Retrieval; internal database. **Networks/Consortia:** Member of CLASS. **Publications:** New Materials; Library Information Notes, irregular.

★7160★
LOS ANGELES TRADE-TECHNICAL COLLEGE - LIBRARY (Sci-Tech)
400 W. Washington Blvd.   Phone: (213) 746-0800
Los Angeles, CA 90015   Harold Eckes, Coord., LRC
Staff: Prof 6; Other 21. **Subjects:** Trades - aircraft, apparel, art, automotive, building, cosmetology, culinary arts, drafting, electricity, electronics, metal, printing, vocational nursing, registered nursing, business education, librarianship. **Special Collections:** Apprenticeship training books. **Holdings:** 80,000 volumes. **Subscriptions:** 750 journals and other serials; 14 newspapers. **Services:** Interlibrary loans; copying; library open to public. **Publications:** Learning Resources Newsletter. **Staff:** J. McTyre, Acq.Libn.; D. Ramey, Per.Libn.; J. Livingston, Ref.Libn.; M. Hochman, Cat.Libn.

★7161★
LOS ANGELES UNIFIED SCHOOL DISTRICTS - WEST VALLEY OCCUPATIONAL CENTER - LEARNING CENTER
6200 Winnetka Ave.
Woodland Hills, CA 91364
Founded: 1967. **Subjects:** Technology, occupations, arts. **Holdings:** 8500 books; 1500 filmstrips; 500 slides; 800 cassettes, tapes, records. **Remarks:** Presently inactive.

LOS ANGELES ZOO ASSOCIATION
See: Greater Los Angeles Zoo Association

★7162★
LOS ENCINOS DOCENT ASSOCIATION - LOS ENCINOS STATE HISTORIC PARK - LIBRARY (Hist)
16756 Moorpark St.   Phone: (213) 784-4849
Encino, CA 91436
Founded: 1949. **Staff:** 3. **Subjects:** History - local, state, Indian; missions. **Special Collections:** Los Encinos State Historic Park Archives; genealogies of former ranch owners. **Holdings:** 200 books; clippings, reports, documents.

Subscriptions: 12 journals and other serials; 10 newspapers. **Services:** Library open to public for reference use only. **Formerly:** Encino Historical Society, Inc.

★7163★
LOS LUNAS HOSPITAL AND TRAINING SCHOOL - LIBRARY AND RESOURCE CENTER (Med)
Box 1269   Phone: (505) 865-9611
Los Lunas, NM 87031   Sarah Knox Morley, Libn.
Founded: 1969. **Staff:** Prof 1; Other 2. **Subjects:** Mental retardation, developmental disabilities, psychology, medicine, nursing, education, social services. **Holdings:** 1600 books; 15 dissertations; 40 reports; 80 films; 20 microfiche; 100 filmstrips; 60 filmstrip/audio packs; 35 puppets; 100 toys; 15 videotapes. **Subscriptions:** 70 journals and other serials. **Services:** Interlibrary loans; copying; SDI; library open to public. **Computerized Information Services:** BRS. **Networks/Consortia:** Member of TALON; New Mexico Information System (NEMISYS); New Mexico Consortium of Biomedical Libraries. **Also Known As:** New Mexico Mental Retardation and Developmental Disabilities Library and Resource Center.

LOUCHHEIM (Henry S.) LIBRARY
See: Eagleville Hospital - Henry S. Louchheim Library

LOUIS A. WARREN LINCOLN LIBRARY AND MUSEUM
See: Lincoln National Life Foundation

LOUIS HARRIS & ASSOCIATES, INC.
See: Harris (Louis) & Associates, Inc.

LOUISIANA HISTORICAL CENTER
See: Louisiana State Museum

★7164★
LOUISIANA STATE DEPT. OF COMMERCE - OFFICE OF COMMERCE & INDUSTRY - INDUSTRIAL DEVELOPMENT REFERENCE LIBRARY (Bus-Fin)†
Box 44185   Phone: (504) 342-5383
Baton Rouge, LA 70804   Doyle Ray Bellotte, Libn.
Founded: 1979. **Staff:** Prof 1; Other 1. **Subjects:** Economics, business, statistics. **Holdings:** 350 volumes; 14 shelves of Louisiana state agency publications; 7 shelves of other states' state agency publications; 6 linear shelf feet of vertical file material; 20 shelves of federal government publications. **Subscriptions:** 112 journals and other serials. **Services:** Copying; library open to public with restrictions. **Networks/Consortia:** Member of Louisiana Government Information Network (LaGIN).

LOUISIANA STATE DEPARTMENT OF CULTURE, RECREATION & TOURISM - LOUISIANA STATE LIBRARY
See: Louisiana State Library

★7165★
LOUISIANA STATE DEPT. OF CULTURE, RECREATION & TOURISM - MANSFIELD STATE COMMEMORATIVE AREA - MUSEUM & LIB. (Hist)
Rte. 2, Box 252   Phone: (318) 872-1474
Mansfield, LA 71052   Ernestiene Roundtree, Cur.
Founded: 1957. **Staff:** Prof 2. **Subjects:** History of the War Between the States, especially the Red River Campaign. **Special Collections:** War of the Rebellion, Union and Confederate Armies (129 volumes); Louisiana Soldiers and Commands (4 volumes); Official Records of Union and Confederate Navies (10 volumes); Photographic History of the Civil War, by Miller (6 volumes); Letters of Captain Petty. **Holdings:** 221 books; 304 bound periodical volumes; 6000 pamphlets (cataloged); 8 soldiers' diaries; 20 maps; 12 scrapbooks. **Services:** Library open to public for reference use only. **Remarks:** This library is part of the Office of State Parks. **Staff:** Goode B. Edge, Hist. Site Mgr.

★7166★
LOUISIANA STATE DEPARTMENT OF JUSTICE - OFFICE OF THE ATTORNEY GENERAL - HUEY P. LONG MEMORIAL LAW LIBRARY (Law)†
State Capitol, 25th Fl. W.
Box 44005   Phone: (504) 342-7013
Baton Rouge, LA 70804   Freda Jackson, Intern in Charge
Founded: 1932. **Subjects:** Law, especially Louisiana law. **Special Collections:** Personal collection of Senator Huey Pierce Long. **Holdings:** 3000 books and bound periodical volumes. **Services:** Library open to public for reference use only.

★7167★

LOUISIANA STATE DEPARTMENT OF NATURAL RESOURCES - RESEARCH AND DEVELOPMENT LIBRARY (Energy)

Box 44156   Phone: (504) 342-4498
Baton Rouge, LA 70804   Duchamp Smith, Info.Dir.
Staff: Prof 2. **Subjects:** Energy - conservation, alternative sources, solar, economics, statistics, oil, gas. **Holdings:** 200 books; 4000 documents; 1000 unbound periodicals; 8 films and videotapes. **Subscriptions:** 24 journals and other serials; 30 newsletters. **Services:** Copying (limited); library open to public for reference use only. **Networks/Consortia:** Member of Louisiana Government Information Network (LaGIN). **Publications:** Louisiana Energy Conservation Update, quarterly newsletter. **Staff:** Grace A. Fitzgerald, Libn.

★7168★

LOUISIANA STATE DEPARTMENT OF TRANSPORTATION DEVELOPMENT - OFFICE OF PUBLIC WORKS - TECHNICAL LIBRARY (Sci-Tech)

Capitol Sta., Box 44155   Phone: (504) 342-7566
Baton Rouge, LA 70804   Dorothy D. McConnell, Libn.
Founded: 1941. **Staff:** Prof 1. **Subjects:** Hydrology, hydraulic engineering, water resources and related subjects. **Special Collections:** High altitude aerial photography of Louisiana (microfiche); current and historic topographic map coverage of Louisiana. **Holdings:** 20,000 volumes; specifications; reports; Congressional and U.S. Corps of Engineers documents. **Subscriptions:** 43 journals and other serials. **Services:** Copying; library open to public for reference use only.

★7169★

LOUISIANA STATE HOUSE OF REPRESENTATIVES LEGISLATIVE SERVICES - RESEARCH LIBRARY (Law)

Box 44012   Phone: (504) 342-2431
Baton Rouge, LA 70804   Suzanne Hughes, Adm.
Founded: 1981. **Staff:** Prof 5; Other 5. **Subjects:** Legislative procedure, law, government administration, constitutional and legal issues, energy and environment, health and welfare, business and industry. **Special Collections:** Louisiana legislative archives (special committees, studies, projects). **Holdings:** 3000 books; 200 bound periodical volumes; 10,000 speeches, copies of other state laws, staff memoranda, committee reports. **Subscriptions:** 250 journals and other serials; 5 newspapers. **Services:** Copying; PULS Line (public legislative information during sessions); library open to public with administrator's permission when materials cannot be found elsewhere. **Computerized Information Services:** Computer indexing and citation of bills; internal database for bill status information; computerized 50 state legislative bibliographic search. **Publications:** Directory for Louisiana Legislators. **Special Indexes:** Calendar index of bills; journal index; citation report; Resume index of acts. **Formerly:** Louisiana State Legislative Council - Division of Information Services. **Staff:** Kate Lemon, Info.Spec.; Sharon Eaton, Info.Spec.; Margo Kasprowicz, Info.Spec.; Denise Uzee, Info.Spec.

LOUISIANA STATE LEGISLATIVE COUNCIL - DIVISION OF INFORMATION SERVICES

See: Louisiana State House of Representatives Legislative Services - Research Library

★7170★

LOUISIANA STATE LIBRARY (Hist; Info Sci)

Box 131   Phone: (504) 342-4923
Baton Rouge, LA 70821   Thomas F. Jaques, State Libn.
Founded: 1925. **Staff:** Prof 29; Other 50. **Special Collections:** Louisiana (48,790 cataloged items; 2866 state documents); genealogy (1075 items); U.S. government documents. **Holdings:** 322,418 volumes; 10,147 reels of microfilm. **Subscriptions:** 1575 journals and other serials; 25 newspapers. **Services:** Interlibrary loans; copying; library open to public. **Computerized Information Services:** Computerized cataloging. **Networks/Consortia:** Member of OCLC through SOLINET. **Publications:** Public Libraries in Louisiana (statistics). **Special Catalogs:** Louisiana Union Catalog (card, microfiche). **Remarks:** Library is operated by Louisiana State Department of Culture, Recreation & Tourism. **Staff:** Harriet Callahan, Hd., Louisiana Dept.; Elizabeth S. Roundtree, Coord., Tech.Serv.; Blanche Cretini, Coord., User Serv.

★7171★

LOUISIANA STATE MUSEUM - LOUISIANA HISTORICAL CENTER (Hist)

751 Chartres St.   Phone: (504) 568-8214
New Orleans, LA 70116   Rose Lambert, Libn.
Staff: Prof 6; Other 2. **Subjects:** New Orleans and Louisiana history. **Special Collections:** Judicial records of French Superior Council, 1714-1769, and Spanish Regime, 1769-1804; 19th and 20th century family and commercial papers; 19th century personal manuscript collection; 18th and 19th century maps. **Holdings:** 30,000 books; 2000 bound periodical volumes. **Services:** Copying (limited); library open to public for reference use only. **Remarks:**

Library is located at 400 Esplanade Ave., New Orleans, LA 70116. **Staff:** Edward F. Haas, Dir.; Stephen Webre, Cur., Spanish Mss.; Julie Barrois, Libn.; Steven Reinhardt, French Mss.; Joseph Castle, Spanish Mss. & Maps.

★7172★

LOUISIANA STATE OFFICE OF THE SECRETARY OF STATE - STATE ARCHIVES AND RECORDS SERVICE (Hist)

Capitol Sta., Box 44125   Phone: (504) 342-5440
Baton Rouge, LA 70804   Dr. Donald J. Lemieux, State Archv./Dir.
Founded: 1956. **Staff:** Prof 8; Other 2. **Subjects:** State government records, Louisiana history, genealogy. **Special Collections:** Louisiana Confederate government records (80 volumes and 8 cubic feet); Records of Board of Confederate Pension Commissioners (147 cubic feet); Louisiana Legal Archives (85 cubic feet); original acts of the Louisiana Legislature, 1804-1964 (121 bound volumes); Louisiana Long Leaf Lumber Company (276 cubic feet and 50 volumes); Louisiana Hayride tapes (300); oral history tape library (50); graphics collection (1000 images). **Holdings:** 800 books; 20,000 cubic feet of government records; 6000 reels of microfilm. **Subscriptions:** 19 journals and other serials. **Services:** Copying; microfilming; conservation laboratory; archives open to public. **Computerized Information Services:** Louisiana Information Processing Authority (internal database). **Networks/Consortia:** Member of Louisiana State Archival System. **Publications:** Legacy, bimonthly newsletter - free upon request. **Special Indexes:** 1898 and 1913 Louisiana Voter Registration index (book); Records of the Opelousas Post, 1766-1803 (book); Confederate pension applicants index (book; in progress); collections indexes (card). **Staff:** Mable T. Combouzou, Assoc.Dir.; Claudia F. Racca, Rec.Mgt.Off.; Theron D. Hinton, Jr., Archv.; Rose M. Angelle, Archv.; Charlene C. Cain, Archv.; Lewis Morris, Archv.; Ruth Mansur, Rec.Mgt.Cons.; Nancy B. Vezinat, Rec.Mgt.Cons.; Arlette K. Dickerson, Consrv.

★7173★

LOUISIANA STATE PLANNING OFFICE - LIBRARY (Plan)

Box 44426   Phone: (504) 342-7428
Baton Rouge, LA 70804   Kay W. McGinnis, Adm.Libn./Info.Res.Spec.
Staff: Prof 2; Other 2. **Subjects:** Planning, information dissemination, economic and social indicators, land use, environmental quality, census data. **Special Collections:** Louisiana Planning Districts planning reports; Louisiana comprehensive planning reports; census data; Low-Altitude RADAR Interface System (LARIS) land use statistics. **Holdings:** 7000 books; maps; vertical file materials; statistical bulletins; 750 microfiche. **Subscriptions:** 228 journals and other serials. **Services:** Interlibrary loans; copying; library open to public for reference use only. **Publications:** Acquisitions list, monthly. **Remarks:** By legislative mandate, this library houses the archives for all state planning information as well as those planning reports from the eight planning districts.

LOUISIANA STATE SUPREME COURT - LAW LIBRARY OF LOUISIANA
See: Law Library of Louisiana

★7174★

LOUISIANA STATE UNIVERSITY - BUSINESS ADMINISTRATION/GOVERNMENT DOCUMENTS DEPARTMENT (Bus-Fin)

Troy H. Middleton Library   Phone: (504) 388-2570
Baton Rouge, LA 70803   Jimmie H. Hoover, Hd.
Staff: Prof 5; Other 4. **Subjects:** Business administration. **Special Collections:** U.S. and United Nations documents depository. **Holdings:** 250,000 volumes; 500,000 microforms; 10K reports. **Services:** Interlibrary loans; copying; library open to public. **Staff:** Roberta A. Scull, Libn.; Milt Ternburg, Asst.Libn.; Deborah J. Pitcher, Lib.Asst.

★7175★

LOUISIANA STATE UNIVERSITY - CENTER FOR ENGINEERING & BUSINESS ADMINISTRATION READING ROOM (Sci-Tech; Bus-Fin)

    Phone: (504) 388-8221
Baton Rouge, LA 70803   J.H. Hoover, Hd., Bus.Adm./Govt.Doc.
Founded: 1979. **Staff:** Prof 1; Other 1. **Subjects:** Business, engineering. **Special Collections:** School of Banking collection. **Holdings:** 450 books. **Subscriptions:** 63 journals and other serials. **Services:** Library open to public.

★7176★

LOUISIANA STATE UNIVERSITY - CHEMISTRY LIBRARY (Sci-Tech)

Virginia Williams Hall   Phone: (504) 388-2530
Baton Rouge, LA 70803   Barbara R. Biggs, Libn.
Founded: 1930. **Staff:** Prof 1; Other 5. **Subjects:** Chemistry, biochemistry, chemical engineering. **Holdings:** 39,000 volumes; U.S. chemical patents from January 1955 to 1975 on microcards and microfiche. **Subscriptions:** 648 journals and other serials. **Services:** Interlibrary loans; copying; collection open to public. **Computerized Information Services:** DIALOG, BRS. **Publications:** List of serials, irregular; recent acquisitions list, irregular.

★7177★

LOUISIANA STATE UNIVERSITY - COASTAL INFORMATION REPOSITORY (Sci-Tech)

Center for Wetland Resources   Phone: (504) 388-8265
Baton Rouge, LA 70803   Norman Howden, Prog.Dir.
Staff: Prof 2; Other 5. **Subjects:** Geology, marine science, ecology, meteorology, wetland soil, chemistry, ports and waterways. **Special Collections:** Richard J. Russell Collection (geomorphology, earth sciences); Goes Satellite Photographs (current 3 years); Marine Education Microfilm Series (MEMS). **Holdings:** 2500 books; 50,000 microforms; data tape library; maps; archives. **Subscriptions:** 10 serials. **Services:** Interlibrary loans; copying; repository open to public with restrictions. **Computerized Information Services:** DIALOG; internal database; computerized cataloging. **Publications:** Annual bibliography. **Staff:** Judy Henderson, Tech.Serv.Coord.; Rowena Hill, Bibliog.Spec.

★7178★

LOUISIANA STATE UNIVERSITY - COLLEGE OF DESIGN - DESIGN RESOURCE CENTER (Art)

136 Atkinson Hall   Phone: (504) 388-2665
Baton Rouge, LA 70803   Doris A. Wheeler, Design Libn.
Founded: 1959. **Staff:** Prof 1; Other 8. **Subjects:** Architecture, interior design, landscape architecture, planning, restoration and preservation. **Holdings:** 7600 books; 10,100 architecture slides; 12 VF drawers of clippings; 211 blueprints. **Subscriptions:** 90 journals and other serials. **Services:** Center open to public with restrictions.

★7179★

LOUISIANA STATE UNIVERSITY - DEPARTMENT OF ARCHIVES AND MANUSCRIPTS (Hist)

Troy H. Middleton Library, Rm. 202   Phone: (504) 388-2240
Baton Rouge, LA 70803   M. Stone Miller, Jr., Hd.
Founded: 1936. **Staff:** Prof 2; Other 2. **Subjects:** Louisiana and Southern history; slavery; Civil War; agriculture; politics; literature; history - banking, business, lumber, steamboat and travel; university archives. **Holdings:** 4 million items; 600 reels of microfilm; 3400 photographs; 500 maps. **Services:** Copying; department open to public.

★7180★

LOUISIANA STATE UNIVERSITY - E.A. MC ILHENNY NATURAL HISTORY COLLECTION (Sci-Tech)

Library   Phone: (504) 388-6934
Baton Rouge, LA 70803   Kathryn Morgan, Cur.
Founded: 1971. **Staff:** Prof 1; Other 2. **Subjects:** Natural history, especially rare and/or finely illustrated books, ornithology and botany. **Holdings:** 6000 books; porcelain and metal sculptures, wood and stone carvings, paintings, prints and other art objects pertaining to natural history. **Services:** Interlibrary loans; copying; collection open to public.

★7181★

LOUISIANA STATE UNIVERSITY - GOVERNMENTAL SERVICES INSTITUTE - LIBRARY (Bus-Fin)

385 Pleasant Hall   Phone: (504) 388-6746
Baton Rouge, LA 70803   Judith D. Smith, Libn.
Founded: 1981. **Staff:** Prof 1. **Subjects:** Management training, personnel management, public policy and administration, financial management, data and statistical services. **Holdings:** 600 books; GSI technical assistance reports. **Subscriptions:** 21 journals and other serials. **Services:** Interlibrary loans; copying; SDI; library open to public. **Publications:** Acquisitions list, monthly - for internal distribution only.

★7182★

LOUISIANA STATE UNIVERSITY - LAW LIBRARY (Law)

                                Phone: (504) 388-8802
Baton Rouge, LA 70803-1010   Lance E. Dickson, Dir.
Founded: 1906. **Staff:** Prof 12; Other 12. **Subjects:** Law - Anglo-American, Louisiana, comparative, foreign, international. **Special Collections:** Civil law; French, German and Roman Law; Louisiana Courts of Appeal and Supreme Court Records. **Holdings:** 300,000 books and bound periodical volumes; 150,000 microforms. **Subscriptions:** 3600 journals and other serials. **Services:** Interlibrary loans; copying; library open to public. **Computerized Information Services:** DIALOG, SDC, LEXIS, New York Times Information Service, WESTLAW; computerized cataloging and acquisitions. **Networks/Consortia:** Member of OCLC through SOLINET. **Special Indexes:** Index to Louisiana Courts of Appeal and Supreme Court Records (card). **Staff:** Charlotte Corneil, Pub.Serv.; Deborah Mann, Ref.; Ana Litvinoff, Acq.; Charlotte Melius, Circ.; Tran Van Linh, Comparative Law; Joseph Simpson, Tech.Serv.; Isabel Wingerter, Media.

★7183★

LOUISIANA STATE UNIVERSITY - LIBRARY SCHOOL LIBRARY (Info Sci)

Library, Rm. 263 Coates Hall   Phone: (504) 388-4576
Baton Rouge, LA 70803   D.W. Schneider, Assoc.Dir.
Founded: 1925. **Staff:** Prof 1; Other 6. **Subjects:** Library and information science. **Special Collections:** Young Peoples Collection (10,000 volumes); Historical Young Peoples Collection (2500 items); Cataloging Workshop Collection (581 items). **Holdings:** Figures not available for books and bound periodical volumes; 7 VF drawers of annual reports; 3 VF drawers of library newsletters; 5 drawers of VF materials; 376 dissertations on microfilm; media collection. **Services:** Interlibrary loans; copying; library open to public with restrictions. **Networks/Consortia:** Member of OCLC through SOLINET. **Publications:** Acquisitions lists, annual - for internal distribution only.

★7184★

LOUISIANA STATE UNIVERSITY - LISTENING ROOMS (Aud-Vis)

Library   Phone: (504) 388-2900
Baton Rouge, LA 70803   Glenn Walden, Hd.
Founded: 1958. **Staff:** 7. **Subjects:** Music - medieval to present; jazz and related areas; Acadian folk; spoken word materials; American music including movie and musical soundtracks. **Holdings:** 17,000 sound recordings (9500 titles). **Services:** Rooms open to public with restrictions.

★7185★

LOUISIANA STATE UNIVERSITY - LOUISIANA ROOM (Hist)

Library   Phone: (504) 388-2575
Baton Rouge, LA 70803   Evangeline Mills Lynch, Libn./Hd.
Founded: 1927. **Staff:** Prof 2. **Subjects:** Louisiana - history, description and travel, biography, agriculture, literature, politics and government, folklore, anthropology, geography, geology, education, language, music, natural history. **Special Collections:** Louisiana State documents; Louisiana State University Press and faculty collections. **Holdings:** 32,000 books and bound periodical volumes; 1300 maps; dissertations; 104 VF drawers of newspaper clippings; 250 pamphlet boxes of uncataloged pamphlets. **Services:** Interlibrary loans; copying (both limited); room open to public with identification. **Special Catalogs:** Subject Heading List for clipping file. **Remarks:** Housed with the Rare Book Collection.

★7186★

LOUISIANA STATE UNIVERSITY - MAP LIBRARY (Geog-Map)

School of Geoscience
313 Geology Bldg.   Phone: (504) 388-5318
Baton Rouge, LA 70803   Joyce Nelson, Map Cur.
Staff: Prof 1; Other 4. **Subjects:** Cartography, geography. **Holdings:** 400,000 maps. **Services:** Library open to public.

★7187★

LOUISIANA STATE UNIVERSITY MEDICAL CENTER - LIBRARY (Med)

1542 Tulane Ave.   Phone: (504) 568-6100
New Orleans, LA 70112   John P. Ische, Dir.
Founded: 1931. **Staff:** Prof 12; Other 16. **Subjects:** Medicine, dentistry, nursing, allied health fields. **Special Collections:** Yellow fever; Louisiana medicine. **Holdings:** 135,000 volumes. **Subscriptions:** 1760 journals and other serials. **Services:** Interlibrary loans; copying; library open to public with specific need. **Computerized Information Services:** BRS, SDC, DIALOG, MEDLINE; computerized serials. **Networks/Consortia:** Member of OCLC through SOLINET; TALON; Southeastern Louisiana Library Network Cooperative (SEALLINC). **Publications:** Library Bulletin, quarterly. **Remarks:** Includes the holdings of the School of Dentistry Library and the Education Building Library. **Staff:** Ann Hodge Macomber, Libn.; M. Jean Rouse, Cat.; Elizabeth R. Ashin, Dental Ref.Libn.; Judith A. Caruthers, Ref.Libn.; Robert Skinner, Ref., Educ.Bldg.Lib.

★7188★

LOUISIANA STATE UNIVERSITY MEDICAL CENTER - SCHOOL OF MEDICINE IN SHREVEPORT - LIBRARY (Med)

Box 33932   Phone: (318) 674-5446
Shreveport, LA 71130   Mr. Mayo Drake, Libn.
Founded: 1968. **Staff:** Prof 9; Other 10. **Subjects:** Medicine, nursing. **Holdings:** 23,000 books; 50,000 bound periodical volumes; 300 reels of microfilm; 3 VF drawers of pamphlets; 600 video cassettes. **Subscriptions:** 1700 journals and other serials. **Services:** Interlibrary loans; copying; SDI; library open to public. **Computerized Information Services:** MEDLINE. **Networks/Consortia:** Member of TALON. **Staff:** Marilyn Miller, Ref.Libn.; Marianne Puckett, Circ.Libn.; Pamela Ashley, ILL; Walter Morton, Cat.Libn.; Elizabeth Peatross, Requisitions Libn.; Marilyn Rogers, Ser.Libn.; Billy Triplett, AV Libn.

★7189★
LOUISIANA STATE UNIVERSITY - MICROFORM ROOM
Phone: (504) 388-4662
Baton Rouge, LA 70803 Deborah Honeychurch, Hd.
Staff: 1. **Special Collections:** American Periodical Series; Early American Imprints; Early English books; Louisiana newspapers; L.S.U. theses and dissertations; crime and juvenile delinquency; documents on contemporary China; ERIC; health and physical education; presidential papers; Spanish drama; Russian historical sources; underground newspapers; women's history; Energyfiche; Envirofiche; William S. Gray Research Collection. **Holdings:** 65,317 reels of microfilm; 1.1 million microfiche; 164,000 microcards; 41,520 microprints; theses; dissertations; current newspapers - local, state, out-of-state, foreign. **Subscriptions:** 185 newspapers. **Services:** Interlibrary loans; copying; room open to public.

★7190★
LOUISIANA STATE UNIVERSITY - RARE BOOK COLLECTION (Rare Book)
Library Phone: (504) 388-2575
Baton Rouge, LA 70803 Evangeline M. Lynch, Libn./Hd.
Founded: 1927. **Staff:** Prof 2. **Subjects:** All subject divisions of the library except natural history. **Special Collections:** Bruce Rogers Collection; Richard T. Ely Collection (economics). **Holdings:** 17,000 volumes. **Services:** Copying (limited); collection available to public with identification. **Remarks:** Housed with the Louisiana Room Collection.

★7191★
LOUISIANA STATE UNIVERSITY - REFERENCE SERVICES (Sci-Tech; Soc Sci)
Phone: (504) 388-8875
Baton Rouge, LA 70803 Joyce C. Werner, Hd.
Staff: Prof 8; Other 4. **Subjects:** Reference, all subjects. **Holdings:** 19,000 volumes. **Services:** Interlibrary loans; copying; SDI; services open to public. **Computerized Information Services:** DIALOG, SDC, BRS, NIH-EPA Chemical Information System, Tulsa City-County Library System. **Networks/Consortia:** Member of OCLC through SOLINET. **Staff:** Carrie Streb; Silvia Espinosa; Paul Wank; Edith Sims; Sandra Mooney; Jane Kleiner; Doris Dantin .

★7192★
LOUISIANA STATE UNIVERSITY - SCHOOL OF VETERINARY MEDICINE - LIBRARY (Med)
Phone: (504) 346-3173
Baton Rouge, LA 70803 Sue Loubiere, Libn.
Founded: 1974. **Staff:** Prof 2; Other 5. **Subjects:** Veterinary medicine, medicine. **Holdings:** 5000 books; 15,000 bound periodical volumes. **Subscriptions:** 1000 journals and other serials; 10 newspapers. **Services:** Interlibrary loans; copying; library open to public. **Computerized Information Services:** DIALOG, NLM. **Networks/Consortia:** Member of TALON.

★7193★
LOUISIANA TECH UNIVERSITY - COLLEGE OF EDUCATION - EDUCATIONAL RESEARCH LIBRARY (Educ)
Tech Sta., Box 10108 Phone: (318) 257-4683
Ruston, LA 71272 Jeannette Robinson, Sec.
Founded: 1971. **Staff:** 3. **Subjects:** Education. **Holdings:** 500 cataloged items including staff publications, Department of Health, Education and Welfare publications, ERIC directories, program announcements. **Subscriptions:** 10 journals and other serials. **Publications:** Filmstrips, conference reports - all irregular.

★7194★
LOUISIANA TECH UNIVERSITY - RESEARCH DIVISION/COLLEGE OF ADMINISTRATION AND BUSINESS - LIBRARY (Bus-Fin)
Tech Sta., Box 10318 Phone: (318) 257-3701
Ruston, LA 71272 Dr. James Robert Michael, Dir., Bus.Res.
Founded: 1948. **Staff:** Prof 4; Other 2. **Subjects:** Business, economics. **Holdings:** 3000 books; 13,000 periodical volumes (bound and unbound). **Subscriptions:** 284 journals and other serials. **Services:** Library not open to public. **Publications:** The Louisiana Economy, quarterly. **Staff:** Edward J. O'Boyce, Res.Assoc.

★7195★
LOUISVILLE ACADEMY OF MUSIC - LIBRARY (Mus)†
2740 Frankfort Ave. Phone: (502) 893-7885
Louisville, KY 40206 Robert B. French, Pres.
Subjects: Music, photography, literature, biography, United States. **Special Collections:** Music, recordings and written material by and about American composer Roy Harris; Robert Crone; Clifford Shaw; biographical information on 1000 local musicians; local histories. **Holdings:** 3000 books, including rare books; 3000 phonograph records; 60 recital reel tapes; 243 piano rolls; 20 VF drawers of periodicals; 28 VF drawers of music. **Services:** Library not

open to public; archives open to qualified researchers.

★7196★
LOUISVILLE BAPTIST HOSPITALS, INC. - HAGAN LIBRARY (Med)
Highlands Baptist Hospital
810 Barret Ave. Phone: (502) 566-3108
Louisville, KY 40204 Garry Johnson, Dir.
Staff: Prof 2. **Subjects:** Medicine. **Holdings:** 1000 books. **Subscriptions:** 162 journals and other serials. **Services:** Interlibrary loans; copying; SDI; library open to public with director's permission. **Computerized Information Services:** Online systems. **Networks/Consortia:** Member of Kentucky Health Sciences Library Consortium; Kentucky Society of Health Sciences Librarians. **Remarks:** Holdings and services include Louisville Baptist Hospitals, Inc. - Pedigo Library, Baptist Hospital East, 400 Kresge Way, Louisville, KY 40207. **Staff:** Ronda Straub, Asst.Libn.

★7197★
LOUISVILLE DEPARTMENT OF LAW - LIBRARY (Law)
6th & Jefferson, Rm. 200 Phone: (502) 587-3511
Louisville, KY 40202 Marynell Haas, Libn.
Staff: 1. **Subjects:** Law - municipal, Kentucky, federal. **Holdings:** 1000 books. **Subscriptions:** 30 journals and other serials. **Services:** Interlibrary loans; library open to public with restrictions.

★7198★
LOUISVILLE FREE PUBLIC LIBRARY - FILM SERVICES (Aud-Vis)
301 W. York St. Phone: (502) 584-4154
Louisville, KY 40203 Barbara Pickett, Mgr.
Staff: Prof 1; Other 5. **Holdings:** 2603 film titles on 3519 reels; 1517 filmstrip canisters containing 1496 titles; 113 sets of slides with 4533 individual frames; 87 video cassettes. **Services:** Library open to public. **Staff:** Mary Winn Reider, Film Serv.Supv.

★7199★
LOUISVILLE FREE PUBLIC LIBRARY - GOVERNMENT DOCUMENTS DIVISION (Info Sci)
Fourth & York Sts. Phone: (502) 584-4154
Louisville, KY 40203 Kathleen Bullard, Hd.
Staff: Prof 1; Other 3. **Subjects:** U.S. Government publications, 1904 to present. **Holdings:** 803,363 items; 32,333 microfiche. **Services:** Copying; library open to public. **Computerized Information Services:** Computerized cataloging. **Special Catalogs:** Documents shelflist.

★7200★
LOUISVILLE FREE PUBLIC LIBRARY - KENTUCKY DIVISION (Hist)
Fourth & York Sts. Phone: (502) 584-4154
Louisville, KY 40203 Mark Harris, Hd.
Staff: Prof 1; Other 3. **Subjects:** Kentucky and Louisville history and current events. **Special Collections:** Books by Kentucky authors. **Holdings:** 11,500 books; 2200 bound periodical volumes; 38 VF drawers of clippings; 22 shelves of pamphlets; 75 shelves of scrapbooks; 55 shelves of documents; 5180 reels of microfilm. **Subscriptions:** 140 journals and other serials; 25 newspapers. **Services:** Interlibrary loans; copying; library open to public. **Special Indexes:** Index to Courier-Journal, 1917 to present (card).

★7201★
LOUISVILLE FREE PUBLIC LIBRARY - LIBRARY BROADCASTING (Aud-Vis)
301 W. York St.
Louisville, KY 40203 Thomas A. Donoho, Dept.Hd.
Holdings: 4200 discs of 15-inch transcriptions; 51,000 12-inch discs; 65,000 titles of tape recordings on 103,000 reels. **Services:** LP phonograph records, transcriptions and tapes are used for broadcasting on the library's two public FM stations and do not circulate.

★7202★
LOUISVILLE AND JEFFERSON COUNTY PLANNING COMMISSION - LOUISVILLE METROPOLITAN PLANNING LIBRARY (Plan)
900 Fiscal Court Bldg. Phone: (502) 581-5860
Louisville, KY 40202 Biljon Slifer, Adm.Asst.
Founded: 1962. **Staff:** 1. **Subjects:** Planning, transit, housing, schools, land use, census studies, recreation and parks, urban studies. **Holdings:** 800 books; 2550 municipal reports; 2100 technical bulletins; 17 VF drawers; 5 VF drawers of newspaper clippings; zoning maps; regulations; plan maps - 500 scale; aerial photos of the area - school sites (1970 pictures). **Subscriptions:** 60 journals and other serials; 7 newspapers. **Services:** Interlibrary loans; copying; library open to public with special permission or to government agencies. **Special Catalogs:** Vertical File Sheet Listing.

★7203★
LOUISVILLE PRESBYTERIAN THEOLOGICAL SEMINARY - LIBRARY (Rel-Theol)
1044 Alta Vista Rd.   Phone: (502) 895-3411
Louisville, KY 40205   Ernest M. White, Libn.
Founded: 1853. **Staff:** Prof 1; Other 4. **Subjects:** Theology and related subjects, Biblical studies, church history, systematic theology, Christian education. **Special Collections:** Presbyterian Church history; Emmett C. McKowen rare Bible collection. **Holdings:** 92,000 volumes. **Subscriptions:** 350 journals and other serials; 8 newspapers. **Services:** Interlibrary loans; copying; library open to public. **Networks/Consortia:** Member of Team-A Librarians; Kentucky Educational/Career Information Center (KEIC).

★7204★
LOUISVILLE SCHOOL OF ART - LIBRARY & MEDIA RESOURCE CENTER (Art)
The Cloister
806 E. Chestnut   Phone: (502) 245-8836
Anchorage, KY 40204   Peggy A. Wagner, Libn.
Founded: 1960. **Subjects:** Creative applied arts, art history, literature. **Special Collections:** History of arts in Louisville. **Holdings:** 7458 books; 249 bound periodical volumes; 9000 slides; 12 VF drawers of clippings on art and artists. **Subscriptions:** 63 journals and other serials. **Services:** Copying; library open to public. **Special Indexes:** Art Center Association Scrapbooks (card).

LOUISVILLE TIMES
See: Courier-Journal and Louisville Times

★7205★
LOURDES HOSPITAL - HEALTH SCIENCES LIBRARY (Med)
1530 Lone Oak Rd.   Phone: (502) 444-2138
Paducah, KY 42001   Betsy Fusco, Libn.
Staff: Prof 1. **Subjects:** Medicine, nursing, allied health sciences. **Holdings:** 600 books; 6 file drawers of patient education materials; 300 AV programs. **Subscriptions:** 75 journals and other serials. **Services:** Interlibrary loans; copying; SDI; library open to students in affiliated schools. **Computerized Information Services:** MEDLARS; computerized cataloging and reference. **Networks/Consortia:** Member of Kentucky Health Sciences Library Consortium.

LOVE LIBRARY
See: University of Nebraska, Lincoln

LOVE (Malcolm A.) LIBRARY
See: San Diego State University - Malcolm A. Love Library

LOVEJOY LIBRARY
See: Southern Illinois University, Edwardsville

★7206★
LOVELACE BIOMEDICAL & ENVIRONMENTAL RESEARCH INSTITUTE, INC. - INHALATION TOXICOLOGY RESEARCH INST. - LIB. (Med)
Box 5890   Phone: (505) 844-2600
Albuquerque, NM 87115   Julia D. Grimes, Libn.
Staff: Prof 1; Other 1. **Subjects:** Inhalation toxicology, aerosol physics, radiobiology, biophysics, veterinary medicine, comparative medicine. **Holdings:** 8000 books; 4650 bound periodical volumes; 3000 documents on microform; 8000 technical reports. **Subscriptions:** 585 journals and other serials. **Services:** Interlibrary loans; copying; SDI; library open to researchers. **Computerized Information Services:** DIALOG, SDC, DOE/RECON, MEDLARS; computerized cataloging and ILL. **Networks/Consortia:** Member of TALON; New Mexico Consortium of Biomedical Libraries.

★7207★
LOVELL LITHO & PUBLICATIONS INC. - LIBRARY (Bus-Fin)
423 St. Nicholas St.
Montreal, PQ, Canada H2Y 2P4
Holdings: City directories.

LOVELY LANE MUSEUM LIBRARY
See: United Methodist Historical Society - Baltimore Annual Conference

LOW (Juliette Gordon) GIRL SCOUT NATIONAL CENTER
See: Girl Scouts of the USA - Juliette Gordon Low Girl Scout National Center

LOW MEMORIAL LIBRARY
See: Columbia University - Columbiana

LOWE ART MUSEUM LIBRARY
See: University of Miami

★7208★
LOWELL GENERAL HOSPITAL - HEALTH SCIENCE LIBRARY (Med)
295 Varnum Ave.   Phone: (617) 454-0411
Lowell, MA 01854   Joan Kaiser, Med.Libn.
Founded: 1960. **Staff:** Prof 1; Other 1. **Subjects:** Basic sciences, nutrition, medicine, nursing, psychology, psychiatry, sociology. **Holdings:** 3945 books; AV items. **Subscriptions:** 183 journals and other serials. **Services:** Interlibrary loans; copying; library open to public with restricted borrowing. **Networks/Consortia:** Member of Northeast Consortium for Health Information (NECHI); New England Regional Medical Library Service (NERMLS).

LOWELL HISTORICAL SOCIETY COLLECTION
See: University of Lowell, North Campus - University Libraries - Special Collections

★7209★
LOWELL OBSERVATORY - LIBRARY (Sci-Tech)
                                            Phone: (602) 774-3358
Flagstaff, AZ 86002
Subjects: Physics, astronomy, photography, mathematics. **Holdings:** 10,000 volumes. **Services:** Library not open to public.

★7210★
LOWENSTEIN (M.) CORPORATION - DESIGN RESEARCH LIBRARY (Art)
1430 Broadway   Phone: (212) 930-5610
New York, NY 10018   Colleen A. Ryan-McIntyre, Libn.
Founded: 1934. **Staff:** Prof 1. **Subjects:** Textile design; decorative arts - design, ornament, handicrafts, tapestry, carpets; children's picture books; plantlife. **Special Collections:** Textile swatch collection, 1800-1982 (1 million swatches). **Holdings:** 2500 books; 100 map drawers of original painted designs; 19 drawers of picture collection; 500 VF drawers of textile swatch cards; 150 scrapbook volumes of fabric. **Subscriptions:** 42 journals and other serials. **Services:** Copying; library open to customers, clients and studio staff. **Special Indexes:** Index of picture collection.

★7211★
LOWNDES COUNTY LAW LIBRARY (Law)†
County Courthouse, Rm. 210   Phone: (601) 328-1056
Columbus, MS 39701   Shirlee Harvey, Libn.
Staff: Prof 1. **Subjects:** Law. **Holdings:** 5000 volumes. **Services:** Copying; library open to public.

LOWNIK (Theodore) LIBRARY
See: Illinois Benedictine College - Theodore Lownik Library

LOWRY AIR FORCE BASE (CO)
See: U.S. Air Force Base - Lowry Base Library

LOWRY NATURE CENTER
See: Hennepin County Park Reserve District

★7212★
LOYALIST COLLEGE OF APPLIED ARTS & TECHNOLOGY - ANDERSON RESOURCE CENTRE (Sci-Tech; Med)
Loyalist-Wallbridge Rd.
Box 4200   Phone: (613) 962-9501
Belleville, ON, Canada K8N 5B9   Ronald H. Boyce, Hd., Lib.Serv.
Founded: 1967. **Staff:** Prof 1; Other 11. **Subjects:** Science and technology, behavioral sciences, health sciences. **Holdings:** 45,000 books; 2600 bound periodical volumes; 12,000 AV software items. **Subscriptions:** 500 journals and other serials. **Services:** Interlibrary loans; copying; centre open to public. **Networks/Consortia:** Member of Bibliocentre.

★7213★
LOYOLA LAW SCHOOL - LIBRARY (Law)
1440 W. 9th St.   Phone: (213) 736-1120
Los Angeles, CA 90015-1295   Frederica M. Sedgwick, Dir.
Founded: 1920. **Staff:** Prof 8; Other 11. **Subjects:** Law - civil, federal, state, international. **Holdings:** 260,000 volumes. **Subscriptions:** 5000 journals and other serials. **Services:** Interlibrary loans; copying; library open to public with restrictions. **Computerized Information Services:** LEXIS. **Staff:** Laszlo Szegedi, Cat.Libn.; Karen Verdugo, Pub.Serv.; Barbara Huff, Acq.Libn.;

Demetrio Orlino, Evening Pub.Serv.; Carol Petrowski, Ser.; Cecilia Wong, Asst.Cat.

★7214★
LOYOLA MARYMOUNT UNIVERSITY - ORANGE CAMPUS LIBRARY (Rel-Theol)
480 S. Batavia St.   Phone: (714) 633-8121
Orange, CA 92668   Sr. Therese Zickgraf, C.S.J., Libn.
Founded: 1952. **Staff:** Prof 1. **Subjects:** Religion, philosophy, Christian ethics, social issues, literature, history, psychology, art. **Holdings:** 38,000 books; 5200 bound periodical volumes; 1550 recordings (cataloged); 320 cassette/reel programs. **Subscriptions:** 78 journals and other serials. **Services:** Interlibrary loans; copying; library open to public with user fee. **Remarks:** Includes the holdings of St. Joseph College of Orange.

★7215★
LOYOLA REFERENCE LIBRARY (Rel-Theol)
Fordham University
Keating Hall   Phone: (212) 579-2499
Bronx, NY 10458   Rev. Theodore Cunnion, S.J., Libn.
Staff: Prof 1; Other 1. **Subjects:** Philosophy, theology, Latin and Greek classics, church and Jesuit history. **Holdings:** 165,000 books and bound periodical volumes. **Subscriptions:** 120 journals and other serials. **Services:** Interlibrary loans; library open to public for reference use only. **Publications:** Classified list of acquisitions, quarterly. **Remarks:** Maintained by the Society of Jesus, New York Province.

★7216★
LOYOLA UNIVERSITY OF CHICAGO - CUDAHY MEMORIAL LIBRARY - UNIVERSITY ARCHIVES (Hist)
6525 Sheridan Rd.   Phone: (312) 274-3000
Chicago, IL 60626   Michael J. Grace, S.J., Univ.Archv.
Staff: Prof 2; Other 2. **Subjects:** Local and social history. **Special Collections:** University archives; Samuel Insull Papers; Catholic Church Extension Society papers; Theater Collection (playbills, autographs); Chicago Inter-Student Catholic Actions papers; social topics pamphlet collection, 1902-1930. **Holdings:** Figures not available. **Services:** Copying; library open to public by appointment. **Formerly:** Its Special Collections.

★7217★
LOYOLA UNIVERSITY OF CHICAGO - JULIA DEAL LEWIS LIBRARY (Educ; Bus-Fin)
820 N. Michigan Ave.   Phone: (312) 670-2875
Chicago, IL 60611   Genevieve Delana, Hd.Libn.
Staff: Prof 4; Other 16. **Subjects:** Education, social work, business. **Holdings:** 114,675 books; 20,992 bound periodical volumes; 148,445 microforms. **Subscriptions:** 1308 journals and other serials; 23 newspapers. **Services:** Interlibrary loans; copying; library open to public. **Computerized Information Services:** BRS, DIALOG. **Networks/Consortia:** Member of ILLINET; MIDLNET; OCLC; Chicago Consortium of Colleges and Universities; Chicago Academic Library Council (CALC). **Staff:** Yolande Wersching, Bibliog. Educ./Soc. Work; Jack Jochim, Bibliog. Bus./Urban Stud.; Eleanor Kennedy, Curric.Libn.

★7218★
LOYOLA UNIVERSITY OF CHICAGO - LAW LIBRARY (Law)
1 E. Pearson St.   Phone: (312) 670-2952
Chicago, IL 60611   Francis R. Doyle, Law Libn.
Founded: 1908. **Staff:** Prof 5; Other 12. **Subjects:** Law. **Holdings:** 83,418 books; 14,235 bound periodical volumes; 26,211 volumes in microform. **Subscriptions:** 1001 journals and other serials; 5 newspapers. **Services:** Interlibrary loans; copying; library open to public for legal research only. **Computerized Information Services:** LEXIS. **Staff:** Nancy Tuohy, Asst.Libn.; Alexander Sved, Asst.Libn.; Dorothy Cox, Asst.Libn.; Karen Hayward, Asst.Libn.

★7219★
LOYOLA UNIVERSITY OF CHICAGO - MEDICAL CENTER LIBRARY (Med)
2160 S. First Ave.   Phone: (312) 531-3192
Maywood, IL 60153   James C. Cox, Chf.Libn.
Founded: 1968. **Staff:** Prof 5; Other 12. **Subjects:** Biomedicine, dentistry, nursing, health sciences. **Holdings:** 34,282 books; 65,215 bound periodical volumes; 723 theses; 14,047 AV materials. **Subscriptions:** 1674 journals and other serials; 5 newspapers. **Services:** Interlibrary loans; library open to public with restrictions. **Computerized Information Services:** DIALOG, MEDLARS, BRS; computerized cataloging. **Networks/Consortia:** Member of Regional Medical Library - Region 3; OCLC through ILLINET; Metropolitan Chicago Library Assembly. **Publications:** Acquisitions list, quarterly. **Staff:** Dorothy Burns, Ser.Libn.; Janet K. Mixter, Coord., Bibliog.Serv.; Dianne Olson,

Cat./Acq.Libn.

★7220★
LOYOLA UNIVERSITY (New Orleans) - LAW LIBRARY (Law)
6363 St. Charles Ave.   Phone: (504) 865-3426
New Orleans, LA 70118   Win-Shin S. Chiang, Law Libn.
Founded: 1914. **Staff:** Prof 7; Other 9. **Subjects:** Law. **Holdings:** 120,000 volumes. **Services:** Interlibrary loans; copying; library open to law students and attorneys. **Computerized Information Services:** LEXIS. **Networks/Consortia:** Member of OCLC through SOLINET. **Staff:** Marguerite A. Rey, Hd., Tech.Serv.; Margaret D. Benetz, Circ.; Joan Pelland, Doc.; J. Wesley Cochran, Hd., Pub.Serv.

★7221★
LUBBOCK CHRISTIAN COLLEGE - MOODY LIBRARY (Rel-Theol)
5601 W. 19th St.   Phone: (806) 792-3221
Lubbock, TX 79407
Founded: 1957. **Staff:** Prof 2; Other 4. **Subjects:** Religion, liberal arts, teacher education. **Special Collections:** Materials regarding the Church of Christ. **Holdings:** 85,000 books; 4193 bound periodical volumes; 5 VF drawers of archives; 5 VF drawers; 3265 reels of microfilm; 110 reel-to-reel tapes; 441 cassette tapes. **Subscriptions:** 590 journals and other serials; 7 newspapers. **Services:** Interlibrary loans; copying; library open to public for reference use only. **Staff:** Rebecca Vickers, Assoc.Dir./Tech.Serv.; Paula Gannaway, Assoc.Dir./Ref.Libn.

★7222★
LUBRIZOL CORPORATION - CHEMICAL LIBRARY (Sci-Tech)
29400 Lakeland Blvd.   Phone: (216) 943-4200
Wickliffe, OH 44092   Dr. Horton Dunn, Jr., Supv., Info.Serv.
Founded: 1946. **Staff:** Prof 2; Other 2. **Subjects:** Chemistry - organic, petroleum, polymer. **Holdings:** 5000 books; 4800 bound periodical volumes; 8300 lubrication papers; 1528 clippings; 7 VF drawers of technical papers. **Subscriptions:** 200 journals and other serials. **Services:** Library not open to public. **Computerized Information Services:** SDC, DIALOG. **Publications:** Lubrizol Periodical Abstracts, semimonthly.

LUCAS COUNTY PUBLIC LIBRARY
See: Toledo-Lucas County Public Library

LUCAS (Vane B.) MEMORIAL LIBRARY
See: American College - Vane B. Lucas Memorial Library

★7223★
LUCE, FORWARD, HAMILTON & SCRIPPS - LIBRARY (Law)
110 West A St.   Phone: (714) 236-1414
San Diego, CA 92101   June B. Williams, Libn.
Staff: Prof 1; Other 1. **Subjects:** Law - taxation, securities, corporate, labor, commercial. **Holdings:** 15,000 books; 1000 bound periodical volumes. **Subscriptions:** 106 journals and other serials. **Services:** Copying; library not open to public. **Computerized Information Services:** LEXIS.

LUCE (Stephen B.) LIBRARY
See: SUNY - Maritime College - Stephen B. Luce Library

LUCIDOL DIVISION - RESEARCH LIBRARY
See: Pennwalt Corporation

LUCKETT (James D.) MEMORIAL ARCHIVES
See: Geneva Historical Society and Museum - James D. Luckett Memorial Archives

★7224★
LUDLOW (Fitz Hugh) MEMORIAL LIBRARY
Box 99346
San Francisco, CA 94109
Founded: 1970. **Subjects:** Psychoactive drugs - history, literature, research; drug-related art and artifacts; drug culture. **Special Collections:** California Marijuana Initiative Archives. **Holdings:** 6000 books; drug-related manuscripts, illustrations, research papers, phonograph records, artifacts. **Remarks:** Presently inactive.

LUFKIN (Richard H.) LIBRARY
See: Tufts University - Richard H. Lufkin Library

LUFKIN (Richard H.) MEMORIAL LIBRARY
See: Wentworth Institute of Technology - Library

LUKE AIR FORCE BASE (AZ)
See: U.S. Air Force Base - Luke Base Library

LUKEN HEALTH SCIENCES LIBRARY
See: St. Elizabeth's Hospital

★7225★
LUKENS STEEL COMPANY - TECHNICAL LIBRARY (Sci-Tech)
Phone: (215) 383-2675
Coatesville, PA 19320   Gloria R. Hartley, Tech.Libn.
Founded: 1942. **Staff:** Prof 1. **Subjects:** Steel making, steel fabrication, management. **Holdings:** 2500 books; 45 VF drawers of pamphlets. **Subscriptions:** 480 journals and other serials. **Services:** Interlibrary loans; copying; library open to public for reference use only. **Computerized Information Services:** DIALOG. **Publications:** What's New, quarterly.

★7226★
LUM, BIUNNO & TOMPLINS - LAW LIBRARY (Law)
550 Broad St.   Phone: (201) 622-2300
Newark, NJ 07102   Tae J. Yoo, Libn.
Staff: Prof 1; Other 1. **Subjects:** Law - taxation, securities, corporate, banking, trust and estates. **Holdings:** 15,000 volumes. **Subscriptions:** 25 journals and other serials; 5 newspapers. **Services:** Interlibrary loans; library not open to public. **Computerized Information Services:** WESTLAW.

★7227★
LUMMUS COMPANY - LUMMUS TECHNICAL CENTER - TECHNICAL INFORMATION DEPARTMENT (Sci-Tech)
1515 Broad St.   Phone: (201) 893-2251
Bloomfield, NJ 07003   Mary A. Ciaramella, Chf.Libn.
Founded: 1939. **Staff:** Prof 2; Other 4. **Subjects:** Chemical engineering, petroleum refining, petrochemicals. **Special Collections:** Crude oil manuals (8 VF drawers). **Holdings:** 8586 books; 2510 bound periodical volumes; 30 3-foot shelves of technical standards; 34 3-foot shelves of technical society publications; 17 3-foot shelves of government reports; 32,070 microfiche. **Subscriptions:** 262 journals and other serials. **Services:** Interlibrary loans; copying; library open to local public only. **Computerized Information Services:** DIALOG, SDC. **Publications:** New Acquisitions List, monthly - for internal distribution only. **Special Indexes:** Index of company manuals and confidential documents (computer printed). **Staff:** Susan Davis, Asst.Libn.

★7228★
LUMMUS COMPANY - TECHNICAL LIBRARY
3000 S. Post Oak Rd.
Box 22105
Houston, TX 77227
Subjects: Chemical engineering, petrochemicals, petroleum refining. **Holdings:** 600 books; 325 bound periodical volumes; standards and technical publications; government reports. **Remarks:** Presently inactive.

★7229★
LUNAR AND PLANETARY INSTITUTE - LIBRARY/INFORMATION CENTER (Sci-Tech)
3303 NASA Rd., No. 1   Phone: (713) 486-2135
Houston, TX 77058   Frances B. Waranius, Lib./Info.Ctr.Mgr.
Founded: 1968. **Staff:** Prof 1; Other 1. **Subjects:** Selenology, planetology, lunar geology, lunar geophysics, applications of space data to terrestrial problems. **Holdings:** 5000 books; 7500 bound periodical volumes; 500 documents (cataloged); 1000 reels of microfilmed geophysical data resulting from Apollo program. **Subscriptions:** 180 journals and other serials. **Services:** Interlibrary loans; copying (limited); search on demand; library open to public by appointment. **Computerized Information Services:** Computerized serials; online bibliography of lunar and planetary science, Antarctic meteorites. **Publications:** Lunar and Planetary Information bulletin, quarterly - mailing list.

★7230★
LUNAR AND PLANETARY INSTITUTE - PLANETARY IMAGE CENTER (Sci-Tech; Pict)
3303 NASA Rd., No. 1   Phone: (713) 486-2172
Houston, TX 77058   Ron Weber, Mgr.
Staff: Prof 2; Other 1. **Subjects:** Planetary photography and maps. **Special Collections:** Spacecraft photography and maps of Earth, Moon, Mercury, Mars, and satellites of Jupiter and Saturn. **Holdings:** 230,000 photographs; 2500 maps; 6000 slides; 215 films; 1700 microforms. **Services:** Interlibrary loans; library open to public by appointment. **Computerized Information Services:** Online systems. **Staff:** Mary Ann Hager, Photo/Cart.Spec.

LUND MUSIC LIBRARY
See: Gustavus Adolphus College

★7231★
LUNDEBERG MARYLAND SEAMANSHIP SCHOOL - PAUL HALL LIBRARY AND MARITIME MUSEUM (Hist)
Phone: (301) 994-0010
Piney Point, MD 20674   Janice McAteer Smolek, Lib.Dir.
Founded: 1970. **Staff:** Prof 2; Other 8. **Subjects:** Maritime history, union history. **Special Collections:** Manuscripts of union meetings, 1891-1907. **Holdings:** 14,000 books; 200 bound periodical volumes; 8 VF drawers; 650 16mm films; 500 filmstrips; 300 cassettes; 1500 slides; 60 videotapes. **Subscriptions:** 250 journals and other serials; 9 newspapers. **Services:** Library open to public on a limited schedule. **Special Indexes:** Index to Seafarers Log. **Staff:** Zenaida Schuffels, Cat.; Kaye Assenmacher, Archv.

LUNDELL RARE BOOK LIBRARY
See: University of Texas, Austin - Humanities Research Center

LUOKIN (Samuel S.) MEMORIAL MUSIC REFERENCE LIBRARY
See: Temple Beth El of Greater Buffalo - Library

LURA HEALTH SCIENCES LIBRARY
See: Greater Southeast Community Hospital

LURIA MEDICAL LIBRARY
See: Einstein (Albert) Medical Center - Northern Division

LURIE LIBRARY
See: Rogers Corporation

★7232★
LUTHER COLLEGE - PREUS LIBRARY (Area-Ethnic)
Phone: (319) 387-1163
Decorah, IA 52101   Leigh D. Jordahl, Hd.Libn.
Staff: Prof 6. **Subjects:** Liberal arts. **Special Collections:** Norwegian-American newspapers (685 reels of microfilm); Scandinavian Collection (Norwegian history, culture and literature; Norwegians in America; Norwegian-Lutheran Church in America. **Holdings:** 254,525 books, bound periodical volumes, microforms and AV materials; 337 cataloged manuscript collections in the Luther College Archives (325,649 pieces); 2503 pictures; 93 cataloged collections in the Winneshiek County Archives (39,419 pieces). **Subscriptions:** 1802 journals and other serials; 33 newspapers. **Services:** Interlibrary loans; copying; library open to public. **Computerized Information Services:** Computerized cataloging. **Networks/Consortia:** Member of Northeast Iowa Academic Libraries; Iowa Library Information Teletype Exchange (ILITE); OCLC; Bibliographical Center for Research, Rocky Mountain Region, Inc. (BCR). **Special Catalogs:** Norwegian-American Newspapers in Luther College Library, 1976 (book). **Staff:** Debra Hartley, Ref.Libn.; Elizabeth Kaschsins, Hd.Ref.Libn.; Harlan Sanderson, AV Libn.; Duane Fenstermann, Hd., Tech.Serv.; Jane Kemp, Circ.Libn.

★7233★
LUTHER HOSPITAL - LIBRARY SERVICES (Med)
1221 Whipple St.   Phone: (715) 839-3248
Eau Claire, WI 54701   Eileen Emberson, Dir., Lib.Serv.
Founded: 1938. **Staff:** Prof 1; Other 3. **Subjects:** Nursing and clinical medicine, hospital administration. **Special Collections:** Consumer health information; Hospital Historical Archives. **Holdings:** 3141 books; 4523 bound periodical volumes; 6 VF drawers of pamphlets; 547 AV materials. **Subscriptions:** 403 journals and other serials. **Services:** Interlibrary loans; copying; library open to public. **Computerized Information Services:** DIALOG, NLM; internal database. **Networks/Consortia:** Member of West Central Wisconsin Hospital Library Consortium. **Publications:** Newsletter, quarterly. **Remarks:** This library serves as area resource library for consortium.

★7234★
LUTHER NORTHWESTERN SEMINARY - LIBRARY (Rel-Theol)
2375 Como Ave.   Phone: (612) 641-3225
St. Paul, MN 55108   Norman G. Wente, Libn.
Founded: 1876. **Staff:** Prof 5; Other 4. **Subjects:** Biblical studies, theology, church history, missions and related subjects, records of all Norwegian antecedents of the American Lutheran Church. **Special Collections:** Carl Doving Hymnology Collection; Jacob Tanner Catechism Collection (Martin Luther); Missionary Research Center archival and library resources relating to China, Madagascar and Cameroon. **Holdings:** 176,000 books. **Subscriptions:** 674 journals and other serials. **Services:** Interlibrary loans; copying; extension loans direct to pastors of the synod; library open to public. **Networks/**

Consortia: Member of Minnesota Consortium of Theological Schools. **Remarks:** Holdings include some of the Archives of the American Lutheran Church and Northwestern Lutheran Theological Seminary. Others are housed in the Wartburg Theological Seminary, Dubuque, IA. **Staff:** Ray A. Olson, Act.Libn.; Agnes Kerr, Cat.Libn.; Carol Olson, Order Libn.; Sulamit Ozolins, Tech.Serv.Libn.; Allan Krahn, Automation Libn.

LUTHER NORTHWESTERN SEMINARY - MIDWEST CHINA CENTER
See: Midwest China Center

★7235★
LUTHER RICE SEMINARY - BERTHA SMITH LIBRARY (Rel-Theol)
1050 Hendricks Ave.   Phone: (904) 396-2316
Jacksonville, FL 32207   David Rhew, Libn.
Founded: 1972. **Staff:** Prof 1; Other 1. **Subjects:** Christian education. **Special Collections:** Dissertations on religious topics (1406 volumes). **Holdings:** 28,856 books; 3527 AV items. **Subscriptions:** 91 journals and other serials. **Services:** Interlibrary loans; copying; library open to public with annual fee.

LUTHERAN ARCHIVES CENTER AT PHILADELPHIA COLLECTION
See: Lutheran Theological Seminary - Krauth Memorial Library

★7236★
LUTHERAN BIBLE INSTITUTE - LIBRARY (Rel-Theol)
Providence Heights   Phone: (206) 392-0400
Issaquah, WA 98027   Mary E. Porter, Hd.Libn.
Founded: 1960. **Staff:** Prof 1; Other 4. **Subjects:** Old and New Testaments, religion and science, theology, philosophy and ethics, religions, Christian church, psychology, social sciences. **Holdings:** 19,407 books; 598 bound periodical volumes; 4 VF drawers of pamphlets; 501 cassette tapes; 80 filmstrips; 550 microfiche. **Subscriptions:** 160 journals and other serials. **Services:** Copying; library open to church leaders on a limited basis.

★7237★
LUTHERAN BRETHREN SCHOOLS - BIBLE COLLEGE AND SEMINARY LIBRARY (Rel-Theol)
815 W. Vernon Ave.   Phone: (218) 739-3373
Fergus Falls, MN 56537   Donald W. Brue, Libn.
Founded: 1903. **Staff:** Prof 1; Other 1. **Subjects:** Bible study, theology, church history, Christian biography and education, missions. **Holdings:** 14,000 books; 1000 audiotapes. **Subscriptions:** 100 journals and other serials. **Services:** Interlibrary loans; copying; library open to public on a limited basis.

★7238★
LUTHERAN BROTHERHOOD INSURANCE SOCIETY - LB LIBRARY (Rel-Theol; Bus-Fin)
625 Fourth Ave., S.   Phone: (612) 340-7269
Minneapolis, MN 55415   Grete Hanson, Libn.
Founded: 1957. **Staff:** Prof 1. **Subjects:** Martin Luther, Lutheran Church history and doctrine, insurance, business, religion. **Special Collections:** Rare Bible collection; Martin Luther (microfilm). **Holdings:** 3500 books. **Subscriptions:** 100 journals and other serials. **Services:** Interlibrary loans; copying (limited); library open to employees.

★7239★
LUTHERAN CHURCH IN AMERICA - ARCHIVES (Rel-Theol)
Lutheran School of Theology at Chicago
1100 E. 55th St.   Phone: (312) 667-3500
Chicago, IL 60615   Joel W. Lundeen, Assoc.Archv.
Founded: 1860. **Staff:** Prof 1; Other 1. **Subjects:** Lutheran Church history, immigration to America, biography, history of theology, World Missions. **Special Collections:** Official records of the Lutheran Church in America and its predecessors (Augustana Lutheran Church, American Evangelical Lutheran Church, United Lutheran Church, Finnish Lutheran Church - Suomi Synod). **Holdings:** 2075 shelf feet of manuscripts and unbound books; records of Swedish Lutheran congregations to 1930 on microfilm; 200 shelf feet of personal papers of church leaders (cataloged); picture files of historical interest (prints, slides, movies). **Subscriptions:** 85 journals and other serials. **Services:** Interlibrary loans; copying; archives open to public with permission of archivist. **Publications:** Preserving Yesterday for Tomorrow: A Guide to the Archives of the Lutheran Church in America, 1977. **Special Catalogs:** Printed catalog of holdings to 1977.

★7240★
LUTHERAN CHURCH IN AMERICA - BOARD OF PUBLICATION - LIBRARY (Rel-Theol)
2900 Queen Ln.   Phone: (215) 848-6800
Philadelphia, PA 19129   Rev. Frederick C. Watson, Libn.
Staff: 1. **Subjects:** Theology and religion. **Special Collections:** Books published by Fortress Press and by previous publication houses now a part of the Lutheran Church in America. **Holdings:** 3000 books; 50 bound periodical volumes. **Subscriptions:** 30 journals and other serials. **Services:** Library not open to public. **Remarks:** Library is for editors and copyreaders working with the Board of Publication.

★7241★
LUTHERAN CHURCH IN AMERICA - FLORIDA SYNOD - MULTI-MEDIA LIBRARY (Aud-Vis; Rel-Theol)
3838 W. Cypress St.   Phone: (813) 876-7660
Tampa, FL 33607   Grace Little, Libn.
Staff: 1. **Subjects:** Christian education, stewardship, missions. **Holdings:** 25 books; 50 films; 310 filmstrips; 50 cassettes; 65 phonograph records. **Services:** Library open to public with restrictions.

★7242★
LUTHERAN CHURCH IN AMERICA - NORTH CAROLINA SYNOD - ARCHIVES (Rel-Theol)
Box 2049   Phone: (704) 633-4861
Salisbury, NC 28144   Rev. David L. Martin, Sec./Archv.
Staff: 1. **Subjects:** Lutheran Church. **Special Collections:** Congregation records; Papers of Pastors Collection; Synod proceedings for the North Carolina and Tennessee Synods, 1803 to present. **Holdings:** 300 volumes; 55 linear feet of archives; 4 VF drawers of historical files; 65 reels of microfilm. **Services:** Copying; archives open to public.

★7243★
LUTHERAN CHURCH - MISSOURI SYNOD - CALIFORNIA, NEVADA AND HAWAII DISTRICT ARCHIVES (Rel-Theol)
465 Woolsey St.   Phone: (415) 468-2336
San Francisco, CA 94134   Rev. Karl H. Wyneken
Founded: 1887. **Staff:** Prof 1. **Subjects:** History of Lutheran Church work on the Pacific Coast and in Hawaii. **Holdings:** 614 volumes; 60 VF drawers of archival material. **Services:** Archives open to qualified users.

★7244★
LUTHERAN CHURCH - MISSOURI SYNOD - COLORADO DISTRICT ARCHIVES (Rel-Theol)
1591 Fulton St.
Box 488   Phone: (303) 364-9148
Aurora, CO 80010   Lyle Schaefer, District Archv.
Founded: 1921. **Staff:** 1. **Subjects:** Lutheran archives for Colorado, New Mexico, and Utah. **Holdings:** Archives, records, periodicals, photographs. **Services:** Materials available to researchers in church history.

★7245★
LUTHERAN CHURCH - MISSOURI SYNOD - COMMISSION ON WORSHIP LIBRARY (Rel-Theol)
1333 S. Kirkwood Rd.   Phone: (314) 965-9000
St. Louis, MO 63122   Rev. Dr. Fred L. Precht, Exec.Sec.
Founded: 1965. **Staff:** Prof 1; Other 1. **Subjects:** Liturgiology, hymnology, church music, church art. **Special Collections:** Rare volumes in hymnody and liturgy. **Holdings:** 2000 books; 147 bound periodical volumes; 250 pieces of choral music; 300 pamphlets (cataloged); 6000 other volumes used in service to headquarters personnel. **Subscriptions:** 18 journals and other serials. **Services:** Interlibrary loans; library open to public for reference use only on request. **Publications:** News bulletin, 3/year.

LUTHERAN CHURCH - MISSOURI SYNOD - CONCORDIA HISTORICAL INSTITUTE
See: Concordia Historical Institute

★7246★
LUTHERAN CHURCH - MISSOURI SYNOD - LUTHERAN LIBRARY FOR THE BLIND (Rel-Theol)†
3558 S. Jefferson Ave.   Phone: (314) 664-7000
St. Louis, MO 63118   Francine Lieneke, Serv.Dir.
Founded: 1951. **Staff:** 3. **Subjects:** Christian literature. **Holdings:** 3000 braille books; 500 talking book titles; 600 cassette tapes. **Services:** Library open to the blind. **Publications:** The Lutheran Messenger; Portals of Prayer; My Devotions; Teen Time.

★7247★
LUTHERAN CHURCH - MISSOURI SYNOD - MICHIGAN DISTRICT ARCHIVES (Rel-Theol)
4090 Geddes Rd.   Phone: (313) 665-3691
Ann Arbor, MI 48105   Rev. Edwin A. Mueckler, Archv.
Founded: 1854. **Staff:** Prof 1; Other 1. **Subjects:** Lutheran churches in Michigan (Missouri Synod). **Holdings:** Historical records; reports; minutes;

clippings; pictures; slides. **Remarks:** Archives are housed in the library of Concordia College, Ann Arbor, MI.

★7248★
LUTHERAN CHURCH - MISSOURI SYNOD - NORTH WISCONSIN DISTRICT ARCHIVES (Rel-Theol)
3103 Seymour Ln.   Phone: (715) 845-8241
Wausau, WI 54401   Rev. Ronald W. Goetsch, Archv.
Founded: 1916. **Staff:** Prof 1; Other 1. **Subjects:** History and biography of the Lutheran church. **Holdings:** 145 books; 45 VF drawers and 150 feet of proceedings, minutes, documents, histories, sketches, blueprints, and pamphlets. **Subscriptions:** 6 journals and other serials. **Services:** Copying; archives open to public with restrictions.

★7249★
LUTHERAN CHURCH - MISSOURI SYNOD - SOUTHERN ILLINOIS DISTRICT ARCHIVES (Rel-Theol)†
2408 Lebanon Ave.   Phone: (618) 234-4767
Belleville, IL 62221
Founded: 1927. **Subjects:** History and publications of the Southern Illinois District. **Holdings:** Figures not available. **Services:** Interlibrary loans; archives open to public on a limited basis.

★7250★
LUTHERAN COUNCIL IN THE U.S.A. - RECORDS AND INFORMATION CENTER - REFERENCE LIBRARY (Rel-Theol)
360 Park Ave., S.   Phone: (212) 532-6350
New York, NY 10010   Alice M. Kendrick, Dir.
Founded: 1918. **Staff:** Prof 2; Other 3. **Subjects:** History of American Lutheranism, Biblical theology, dogmatic theology, ecumenism, current theology, sociology, church welfare work, devotional liturgics. **Special Collections:** Archives of Cooperative Lutheranism in America; Lutheran World Convention Archives; Oral History Collection (96 memoirs). **Holdings:** 4200 books; 450 bound periodical volumes; 200 bound reports, minutes (cataloged); 30 closed shelf-cases of archives; 12 VF drawers of photographs; 66 reels of microfilm; 400 boxes of pamphlets, reports, minutes, directories; 52 VF drawers of reference materials; 176 linear feet and 23 VF drawers of central records; 20 VF drawers of biographical material. **Subscriptions:** 305 journals and other serials; 22 newspapers. **Services:** Interlibrary loans; copying; library open to qualified students, scholars and officials. **Special Catalogs:** The Oral History Collection of the Archives of Cooperative Lutheranism; Guide to Lutheran Archives and Manuscript Collections. **Special Indexes:** Master name and subject indexes to the Oral History Collection of the Archives of Cooperative Lutheranism. **Staff:** Helen Knubel, Archv.Cons.

★7251★
LUTHERAN DEACONESS ASSOCIATION - DEACONESS HALL LIBRARY (Rel-Theol)
Deaconess Hall, E. Union St.   Phone: (219) 464-5033
Valparaiso, IN 46383   Deaconess Louise Williams, Dir. of Serv.
Founded: 1961. **Staff:** Prof 2; Other 4. **Subjects:** Theology, Christian education, pastoral care and counseling, women in the church, history of diaconate. **Holdings:** 850 books and bound periodical volumes. **Subscriptions:** 30 journals and other serials; 10 newspapers. **Services:** Library open to public by special request.

LUTHERAN DEACONESS COMMUNITY LIBRARY
See: Deaconess Community Lutheran Church of America

LUTHERAN DEACONESS HOSPITAL
See: Fairview Deaconess Hospital

★7252★
LUTHERAN GENERAL HOSPITAL - LIBRARY (Med)
1775 Dempster St.   Phone: (312) 696-5494
Park Ridge, IL 60068   Joanne Crispen, Dir. of Lib.Serv.
Founded: 1966. **Staff:** Prof 6; Other 9. **Subjects:** Clinical medicine, nursing education, nursing, pastoral psychology, social work, nutrition, physical rehabilitation. **Holdings:** 19,975 books; 11,357 bound periodical volumes; 4400 AV items. **Subscriptions:** 440 journals and other serials. **Services:** Interlibrary loans; copying; library open to public for reference use only. **Computerized Information Services:** MEDLINE; computerized cataloging. **Networks/Consortia:** Member of Regional Medical Library - Region 3; North Suburban Library System (NSLS). **Staff:** Gertrude Curran, Asst.Libn.; Judith Degenhardt, Asst.Libn.

LUTHERAN HISTORICAL SOCIETY LIBRARY
See: Lutheran Theological Seminary - A.R. Wentz Library

★7253★
LUTHERAN HOSPITAL OF FORT WAYNE, INC. - HEALTH SCIENCES LIBRARY (Med)
3024 Fairfield Ave.   Phone: (219) 458-2277
Fort Wayne, IN 46807   Raisa Cherniv, Dir.
Founded: 1978. **Staff:** Prof 1; Other 2. **Subjects:** Nursing, medicine, hospital administration, health subjects. **Special Collections:** Orthopedics. **Holdings:** 2500 books; 60 titles of audio cassettes on management; 5 years of audio cassette series in cardiology, internal medicine and pediatrics. **Subscriptions:** 165 journals and other serials; 5 newspapers. **Services:** Interlibrary loans; copying; library open to public for reference use only by appointment. **Computerized Information Services:** BRS; computerized cataloging. **Networks/Consortia:** Member of Northeast Indiana Health Sciences Libraries Consortium.

★7254★
LUTHERAN HOSPITAL OF MARYLAND - CHARLES G. REIGNER MEDICAL LIBRARY (Med)†
730 Ashburton St.   Phone: (301) 945-1600
Baltimore, MD 21216   Sharon Morris, Hd.Libn.
Founded: 1948. **Staff:** Prof 1. **Subjects:** Internal medicine, surgery, gynecology, podiatry, hospital administration. **Holdings:** 1500 books; 3800 bound periodical volumes. **Subscriptions:** 140 journals and other serials. **Services:** Interlibrary loans; copying; library is open to health professionals.

★7255★
LUTHERAN HOSPITAL - MEDICAL STAFF LIBRARY AND SCHOOL FOR NURSES LIBRARY (Med)
501 10th Ave.   Phone: (309) 757-2912
Moline, IL 61265   Jeanne A. Gittings, Libn.
Staff: Prof 3. **Subjects:** Medicine, nursing. **Holdings:** 5615 books, bound periodical volumes and media. **Subscriptions:** 166 journals and other serials; 5 newspapers. **Services:** Interlibrary loans; copying; library open to public for reference use only. **Computerized Information Services:** MEDLINE. **Networks/Consortia:** Member of ILLINET. **Remarks:** Library also serves the RN completion program of the University of Illinois, Quad City Campus. **Staff:** Evelyn Page, Asst.Libn.; Carol Boykin, Asst.Libn.

LUTHERAN HOSPITAL SCHOOL FOR NURSES LIBRARY
See: Lutheran Hospital - Medical Staff Library and School for Nurses Library

★7256★
LUTHERAN HOSPITALS AND HOMES SOCIETY OF AMERICA - LIBRARY (Med)
Box 2087   Phone: (701) 293-9053
Fargo, ND 58107   Mary L. Littlefield, Sec., Lib.Comm.
Subjects: Hospital management, hospital law, human resources development, rehabilitation. **Holdings:** 400 books; 250 reports, manuals, and pamphlets. **Subscriptions:** 102 journals and other serials.

LUTHERAN LIBRARY FOR THE BLIND
See: Lutheran Church - Missouri Synod

★7257★
LUTHERAN MEDICAL CENTER - C.W. NEVEL MEMORIAL LIBRARY (Med)
2609 Franklin Blvd.   Phone: (216) 696-4300
Cleveland, OH 44113   Rosary H. Martin, Med.Libn.
Staff: Prof 3; Other 2. **Subjects:** Medicine, nursing, allied health sciences. **Holdings:** 7000 volumes; 4 VF drawers of articles; 500 cassettes and filmstrips. **Subscriptions:** 152 journals and other serials. **Services:** Interlibrary loans; copying; library not open to public. **Networks/Consortia:** Member of Kentucky-Ohio-Michigan Regional Medical Library Program (KOMRML); Medical Library Association of Northeast Ohio (MLANO). **Staff:** Irene Szentkiralyi, Lib.Techn.; Dorothy Malburg, Lib.Techn.

★7258★
LUTHERAN MEDICAL CENTER - MEDICAL LIBRARY (Med)
8300 W. 38th Ave.   Phone: (303) 425-8662
Wheat Ridge, CO 80033   Susan B. Higginbotham, Med.Libn.
Founded: 1961. **Staff:** Prof 1; Other 1. **Subjects:** Medicine, nursing, health management. **Holdings:** 1000 books; 1600 bound periodical volumes; 500 audiotapes. **Subscriptions:** 150 journals and other serials. **Services:** Interlibrary loans; copying; library not open to public. **Computerized Information Services:** MEDLINE; computerized cataloging and ILL. **Networks/Consortia:** Member of Denver Area Health Science Library

Consortia; OCLC.

★7259★
LUTHERAN MEDICAL CENTER - MEDICAL LIBRARY (Med)
2639 Miami St.   Phone: (314) 772-1456
St. Louis, MO 63118   Jean Monsivais, Sec.
Staff: 2. **Subjects:** Medicine. **Holdings:** 310 books; 1134 bound periodical volumes; 175 cassette tapes. **Subscriptions:** 73 journals and other serials. **Services:** Interlibrary loans; copying; library not open to public.

★7260★
LUTHERAN MEDICAL CENTER - MEDICAL LIBRARY (Med)
150 55th St.   Phone: (212) 630-7200
Brooklyn, NY 11220   Mary Fugle, Libn.
Staff: Prof 2; Other 1. **Subjects:** Pathology, medicine, surgery, gynecology, obstetrics, pediatrics, radiology, family health, anesthesiology. **Holdings:** 6000 books; 2000 AV programs; 235 videotapes. **Subscriptions:** 195 journals and other serials. **Services:** Interlibrary loans; copying; library not open to public. **Computerized Information Services:** Online systems. **Networks/Consortia:** Member of Brooklyn-Queens-Staten Island Health Sciences Group (BQSI).

★7261★
LUTHERAN SCHOOL OF THEOLOGY AT CHICAGO - KRAUSS LIBRARY (Rel-Theol)†
1100 E. 55th St.   Phone: (312) 667-3500
Chicago, IL 60615   Rev. Lowell Albee, Jr., Libn.
Staff: Prof 3; Other 4. **Subjects:** Theology, church history, pastoral care, Lutheran orthodoxy and pietism, Scandinavian and German theology. **Special Collections:** L. Franklin Gruber Collection (150 items); German Bibles. **Holdings:** 113,172 books; 350 bound periodical volumes. **Subscriptions:** 450 journals and other serials; 10 newspapers. **Services:** Interlibrary loans; copying; library open to local clergy and serious scholars. **Networks/Consortia:** Member of OCLC; Chicago Cluster of Theological Schools. **Remarks:** Housed with Jesuit School of Theology in Chicago and McCormick Theological Seminary. **Staff:** Brian Helge, Assoc.Libn.

LUTHERAN THEOLOGICAL SEMINARY
See: University of Saskatchewan

★7262★
LUTHERAN THEOLOGICAL SEMINARY - A.R. WENTZ LIBRARY (Rel-Theol)
66 W. Confederate Ave.   Phone: (717) 334-6286
Gettysburg, PA 17325   Donald N. Matthews, Libn.
Founded: 1826. **Staff:** Prof 2; Other 5. **Subjects:** American Lutheranism. **Holdings:** 125,000 books and bound periodical volumes; 1193 microforms. **Subscriptions:** 432 journals and other serials. **Services:** Interlibrary loans; copying; library open to public for limited circulation. **Networks/Consortia:** Member of Washington Theological Consortium; Southeastern Pennsylvania Theological Libraries Association (SEPTLA). **Remarks:** Includes the holdings of the Lutheran Historical Society and Archives of the Central Pennsylvania Synod. **Staff:** Ethel V. Shaffer, Cat.Libn.

★7263★
LUTHERAN THEOLOGICAL SEMINARY - KRAUTH MEMORIAL LIBRARY (Rel-Theol)
7301 Germantown Ave.   Phone: (215) 248-4616
Philadelphia, PA 19119   Rev. David J. Wartluft, Lib.Dir.
Founded: 1864. **Staff:** Prof 4; Other 3. **Subjects:** Theology, Martin Luther, U.S. Lutheran colonial history, hymnody and liturgy, Protestant Reformation, patristics, religious art and architecture, urbanism and religion. **Special Collections:** Archives of Pennsylvania Ministerium, New Jersey Synod, Slovak Zion Synod, Northeastern Pennsylvania, Southeastern Pennsylvania, and Upper New York Synods. **Holdings:** 135,000 books and bound periodical volumes; 7100 unbound periodicals; 5000 AV materials. **Subscriptions:** 550 journals and other serials. **Services:** Interlibrary loans; copying; library open to public for reference use only. **Computerized Information Services:** Computerized cataloging. **Networks/Consortia:** Member of American Theological Library Association; Southeastern Pennsylvania Theological Library Association (SEPTLA); OCLC through PALINET and Union Library Catalogue of Pennsylvania; Cooperative Microfilm Project on Religion and Theology (COMPORT). **Publications:** Library List, monthly - to selected libraries, and by request for payment of postage. **Remarks:** The Lutheran Archives Center at Philadelphia Collection is included in the Krauth Memorial Library's holdings. **Staff:** Lillian Scoggins, Asst.Libn., Tech.Serv.; John Peterson, Cur. of the Archv.; Ruth Missfeldt, Pub.Serv.Libn./ILL; Jeffrey Davis, Media Spec.

★7264★
LUTHERAN THEOLOGICAL SOUTHERN SEMINARY - LINEBERGER MEMORIAL LIBRARY (Rel-Theol)
4201 Main St.   Phone: (803) 786-5150
Columbia, SC 29203   William Richard Fritz, Sr., Libn.
Founded: 1830. **Staff:** Prof 2; Other 1. **Subjects:** Theology, religion and allied subjects. **Special Collections:** 17th-18th century German Pietism (1000 volumes); German hymn books and catechisms (300). **Holdings:** 81,000 books; 5500 bound periodical volumes; 575 tapes; 9000 microforms; 10 boxes of archives. **Subscriptions:** 563 journals and other serials. **Services:** Interlibrary loans; copying; library open to public with registration and I.D. **Special Catalogs:** Catalog of Older Books (book). **Staff:** Linda B. Puckett, Asst.Libn.

LUTHERANS ALERT NATIONAL
See: Faith Evangelical Lutheran Seminary

★7265★
LYCOMING COUNTY LAW LIBRARY (Law)†
Court House, 3rd Fl.   Phone: (717) 327-2475
Williamsport, PA 17701   Charles Hunt, Law Libn.
Staff: Prof 1. **Subjects:** Law. **Holdings:** 13,950 volumes; 2950 volumes on ultrafiche. **Subscriptions:** 13 journals and other serials. **Services:** Interlibrary loans; copying; library open to public.

LYDON LIBRARY
See: University of Lowell, North Campus - Alumni/Lydon Library

LYLE (Kathryn E.) MEMORIAL LIBRARY
See: Lyman House Memorial Museum - Kathryn E. Lyle Memorial Library

LYMAN ALLYN MUSEUM
See: Allyn (Lyman) Museum

★7266★
LYMAN HOUSE MEMORIAL MUSEUM - KATHRYN E. LYLE MEMORIAL LIBRARY (Area-Ethnic)
276 Haili St.   Phone: (808) 935-5021
Hilo, HI 96720   Christina R.N. Lothian, Archv./Libn.
Staff: Prof 1; Other 1. **Subjects:** Hawaii - history including prehistory, volcanology, flora and fauna, mythology and legends, religions, geology, agriculture; local family genealogies; Pacific islands; missionaries in Hawaii. **Special Collections:** Lyman Family; Hilo Boarding School; sugar industry. **Holdings:** 5500 volumes; 11,000 photographs; 10 VF drawers of manuscripts, paintings, maps; other historical items of early Hawaii; 5850 pamphlets, booklets and ephemera; 900 newspapers and clippings; 450 New England newspapers, early to middle 1800s. **Subscriptions:** 34 journals and other serials. **Services:** Copying; library open to public for reference use only. **Publications:** The Lymans of Hilo, published in 1979 - for sale.

★7267★
LYME HISTORICAL SOCIETY, INC. - ARCHIVES (Hist)
Lyme St.   Phone: (203) 434-5542
Old Lyme, CT 06371   Jeffrey W. Andersen, Dir.
Founded: 1955. **Staff:** Prof 2. **Subjects:** Local history and art. **Special Collections:** The Art Colony at Old Lyme Archives (photographs of artists, paintings); exhibition records and correspondence. **Holdings:** 9000 manuscripts and documents (cataloged); 400 photographs; 4 boxes of clippings. **Services:** Copying; library open to public. **Special Indexes:** Archives (card); each record group (book). **Staff:** Bonnie MacAdam, Cur.

★7268★
LYNCHBURG TRAINING SCHOOL AND HOSPITAL - PROFESSIONAL LIBRARY (Med)†
Box 1098   Phone: (804) 528-6104
Lynchburg, VA 24505   Barbara Elliott, Libn.
Founded: 1941. **Staff:** 1. **Subjects:** Mental retardation, epilepsy, psychology, medicine, special education. **Holdings:** 4035 books; 1884 bound periodical volumes; reports, articles, clippings. **Subscriptions:** 148 journals and other serials. **Services:** Interlibrary loans; copying; library open to public for reference use only. **Computerized Information Services:** Online systems. **Networks/Consortia:** Member of Virginia Extension Service (VES); Virginia Union List of Biomedical Serials (VULBS); Lynchburg Area Library Cooperative. **Publications:** List of journal holdings with subject index, annual - for internal distribution only.

★7269★

LYNN HISTORICAL SOCIETY, INC. - LIBRARY (Hist)
125 Green St.   Phone: (617) 592-2465
Lynn, MA 01902   Miss Ludovine Hamilton, Libn.
Staff: Prof 3. **Subjects:** Lynn and Essex County history, genealogy. **Holdings:** 5000 books; 3000 photographs (cataloged); 37 VF drawers of unbound books, manuscripts, clippings, records; newspapers. **Subscriptions:** 10 journals and other serials. **Services:** Copying; library open to public. **Publications:** Town Meeting Records of Lynn, 1691 through 1783 (7 volumes). **Staff:** Faith Magoun, Archv./Dir.

★7270★

LYNN HOSPITAL - HEALTH SCIENCES LIBRARY (Med)
212 Boston St.   Phone: (617) 598-5100
Lynn, MA 01904   Midge DeSimone, Health Sci.Libn.
Staff: Prof 1; Other 2. **Subjects:** Medicine, surgery, nursing. **Holdings:** 871 books; 2225 bound periodical volumes; 80 video cassettes; 125 audio cassettes; 6 16mm films; 12 filmstrips and slide/tape programs. **Subscriptions:** 208 journals and other serials. **Services:** Interlibrary loans; copying; SDI; library open to public with restrictions. **Computerized Information Services:** MEDLINE, BRS; computerized cataloging. **Networks/Consortia:** Member of Northeastern Consortium for Health Information; Essex County Cooperating Libraries. **Special Indexes:** Patient and consumer health information index (card); bibliographies index (card).

★7271★

LYON ASSOCIATES, INC. - BELT, COLLINS AND ASSOCIATES DIVISION - INFORMATION SERVICES
745 Fort St., 5th Fl.
Honolulu, HI 96813
Defunct

LYONS (Harrye) DESIGN LIBRARY
See: North Carolina State University - Harrye Lyons Design Library

★7272★

LYON'S SCHOOL OF BUSINESS - LIBRARY (Bus-Fin)
316 Rhodes Pl.   Phone: (412) 658-9066
New Castle, PA 16103   Grace Lyon, Hd.Libn.
Subjects: Business administration, accounting, executive secretarial work, marketing, sales. **Holdings:** 3830 books; slides, tapes, and filmstrips. **Subscriptions:** 100 journals and other serials. **Services:** Interlibrary loans; library not open to public.

LYSTER ARMY COMMUNITY HOSPITAL
See: U.S. Army Hospitals

M

M.I.T....
See: Massachusetts Institute of Technology...

★7273★
M.P.K. OMEGA COMPANY - B.O.T.I. SPECIAL RESEARCH COLLECTION
(Sci-Tech)
3615 Carson — Phone: (806) 355-9369
Amarillo, TX 79109 — Jacques Cantrell, Libn.
Staff: Prof 1; Other 1. **Subjects:** Bio-omega transintegration, biophysics, space physics, genetics. **Holdings:** 25 books; 100 technical reports; 200 archival documents. **Services:** Interlibrary loans; copying; SDI; library not open to public. **Computerized Information Services:** Online systems. **Special Catalogs:** Catalog to B.O.T.I. papers (card).

★7274★
M.P.K. OMEGA COMPANY - BIOSCIENCE LIBRARY (Sci-Tech)
3615 Carson — Phone: (806) 355-9369
Amarillo, TX 79109 — Jacques Cantrell, Corp.Libn.
Founded: 1970. **Staff:** Prof 3; Other 3. **Subjects:** Biology, biochemistry, chemistry, biophysics, physics, geology. **Special Collections:** "Accelerator" biology; genetic engineering; experimental hypnosis; biohypnosis. **Holdings:** 600 books; 10 bound periodical volumes; 100 technical reports; 500 slides and cassettes; 100 motion pictures; 10,000 archival documents. **Subscriptions:** 12 journals and other serials. **Services:** Interlibrary loans; copying; SDI; library not open to public. **Computerized Information Services:** Online systems. **Publications:** "In" Biological Science Magazine, monthly - by subscription. **Special Indexes:** MPKO Research Papers (card). **Staff:** Duncan Lawrence, Tech.Libn.; Ralph Morrison, Tech.Libn.

★7275★
M AND T CHEMICALS, INC. - TECHNICAL & BUSINESS INFORMATION CENTER (Sci-Tech)
Box 1104 — Phone: (201) 499-2437
Rahway, NJ 07065 — Marguerite K. Moran, Dir.
Founded: 1942. **Staff:** Prof 4; Other 5. **Subjects:** Chemistry, ceramics, plastics, organometallic chemistry. **Holdings:** 30,000 volumes; 70,000 reports, patents, pamphlets, dissertations, reprints, microfilm and microcards. **Subscriptions:** 400 journals and other serials. **Services:** Interlibrary loans; patent and literature searching; translation; center not open to public. **Computerized Information Services:** DIALOG, SDC.

★7276★
MAASS (Clara) MEDICAL CENTER - DOCTORS' LIBRARY (Med)
Franklin Ave. — Phone: (201) 751-1000
Belleville, NJ 07109 — Betty L. Garrison, Libn.
Staff: 1. **Subjects:** Medicine, surgery. **Holdings:** 1488 books; 3000 bound periodical volumes. **Subscriptions:** 100 journals and other serials. **Services:** Interlibrary loans; copying; library not open to public. **Networks/Consortia:** Member of Cosmopolitan Biomedical Library Consortium; Health Sciences Library Association of New Jersey.

★7277★
MAASS (Clara) MEDICAL CENTER - RADIOGRAPHY PROGRAM LIBRARY
(Med)
1 Franklin Ave. — Phone: (201) 751-1000
Belleville, NJ 07109 — Willard Bell
Staff: 1. **Subjects:** Anatomy and physiology, radiographic physics, x-ray procedures, radiation protection, patient care. **Holdings:** 800 books; 20 bound periodical volumes; 25 visual aids; 58 radiography tapes; 23 volumes of A Stereoscopic Atlas of Human Anatomy; 30 unbound periodicals. **Services:** Library not open to public. **Computerized Information Services:** Computerized cataloging, acquisitions and circulation.

★7278★
MC ADAMS, WILLIAM DOUGLAS, INC. - MEDICAL LIBRARY (Med)
110 E. 59th St. — Phone: (212) 759-6300
New York, NY 10022 — Molly Garfin, Mgr., Lib.
Staff: Prof 2. **Subjects:** Medicine, pharmacology, biological sciences, drugs and therapeutics, advertising. **Holdings:** 1500 books; 10,000 bound periodicals; 50 VF drawers. **Subscriptions:** 500 journals and other serials. **Services:** Interlibrary loans; copying; library open to SLA members only. **Computerized Information Services:** BRS, MEDLINE. **Networks/Consortia:** Member of Manhattan-Bronx Health Sciences Libraries Group. **Staff:** Marilyn

Kahn, Libn.

MC ALISTER LIBRARY
See: Fuller Theological Seminary

★7279★
MAC ARTHUR (General Douglas) MEMORIAL - LIBRARY AND ARCHIVES
(Hist)
MacArthur Sq. — Phone: (804) 441-2965
Norfolk, VA 23510 — Lyman H. Hammond, Jr., Dir.
Staff: 3. **Subjects:** Occupation of Japan, Korean War, World War II (Pacific), life of General MacArthur, East Asia. **Holdings:** 4000 books; 600 shelf-feet of files from personal headquarters of General MacArthur. **Services:** Copying; library open to public with restrictions. **Staff:** E.J. Boone, Archv.

MC ATEER LIBRARY
See: American Association of Variable Star Observers

MC BRAYER LIBRARY
See: West Coast Bible College

★7280★
MC BRIDE AND BAKER - LAW LIBRARY (Law)
Three First National Plaza, Suite 3800 — Phone: (312) 346-6191
Chicago, IL 60602 — Mary Ann Alfonsi-Gini, Libn.
Staff: Prof 2. **Subjects:** Law - corporate, tax; litigation. **Special Collections:** Admiralty and international law. **Holdings:** 15,000 books and bound periodical volumes. **Services:** Interlibrary loans; library open to other law firms. **Computerized Information Services:** LEXIS. **Staff:** Susan Bogner, Libn.

MC BRIDE LIBRARY
See: Grand Rapids Art Museum

MC BRIDE LIBRARY
See: U.S. Air Force Base - Keesler Base

MC CABE LIBRARY
See: Swarthmore College - Friends Historical Library - Peace Collection

MC CAIN (John Sidney) AMPHIBIOUS WARFARE LIBRARY
See: U.S. Navy - Naval Amphibious School - John Sidney Mc Cain Amphibious Warfare Library

MC CAIN LIBRARY
See: University of Southern Mississippi

★7281★
MC CANN-ERICKSON, INC. - LIBRARY (Bus-Fin)†
485 Lexington Ave. — Phone: (212) 697-6000
New York, NY 10017 — Katherine Dodge, Supv., Lib.Serv.
Founded: 1924. **Staff:** 6. **Subjects:** Advertising. **Holdings:** 2000 books; 158 VF drawers of pamphlets, clippings, annual reports, advertisements, pictures. **Subscriptions:** 210 journals and other serials. **Services:** Library open to clients and SLA members.

MC CARDLE LIBRARY
See: Vicksburg & Warren County Historical Society

★7282★
MC CARTER & ENGLISH - LAW LIBRARY (Law)
550 Broad St. — Phone: (201) 622-4444
Newark, NJ 07102 — Carol Lee Discavage, Libn.
Founded: 1870. **Staff:** Prof 1; Other 2. **Subjects:** Law. **Special Collections:** English Law Reports (complete set). **Holdings:** 20,000 volumes. **Subscriptions:** 103 journals and other serials. **Services:** Interlibrary loans; SDI; library not open to public. **Computerized Information Services:** LEXIS.

★7283★
MC CARTHY AND MC CARTHY - LIBRARY (Law)
Toronto Dominion Ctr.
P.O. Box 48 — Phone: (416) 362-1812
Toronto, ON, Canada M5K 1E6 — Mary Percival, Libn.
Staff: Prof 1; Other 2. **Subjects:** Law. **Holdings:** 11,000 books and bound periodical volumes; legislation from provincial and federal government. **Subscriptions:** 130 journals and other serials. **Services:** Interlibrary loans; copying; library open to public by referral. **Computerized Information Services:** QL Systems. **Staff:** Mary-Jane Oussoren, Asst.Libn.

★7284★
MC CARTHY (Walter T.) LAW LIBRARY (Law)
1400 N. Courthouse Rd.
Court House, Rm. 501   Phone: (703) 558-2243
Arlington, VA 22201   Betty J. Waldow, Exec.Dir.
Staff: 2. **Subjects:** Law. **Special Collections:** Maintains comprehensive collection of Virginia law-related volumes. **Holdings:** 12,000 volumes. **Services:** Copying; library open to public with restrictions.

MC CHORD AIR FORCE BASE (WA)
See: U.S. Air Force Base - Mc Chord Base Library

MC CLELLAN AIR FORCE BASE (CA)
See: U.S. Air Force Base - Mc Clellan Base Library

★7285★
MC CLELLAND ENGINEERS, INC. - CORPORATE TECHNICAL LIBRARY (Sci-Tech)
6100 Hillcroft
Box 740010   Phone: (713) 772-3700
Houston, TX 77274   Pat M. Johnson, Sr.Libn.
Founded: 1966. **Staff:** Prof 2; Other 2. **Subjects:** Geotechnical engineering, geology, marine geotechnology, marine geophysics, civil engineering, computer science. **Holdings:** 12,000 books; 350 bound periodical volumes; 12,000 company reports, 1946-1982, in 700 volumes; 15 VF drawers of technical files (2500 documents); 200 issues of unbound serials; microfiche; 200 microfilm cartridges; 2000 aerial photographs; trade brochures. **Subscriptions:** 227 journals and other serials. **Services:** Interlibrary loans; copying; library open to public by appointment with permission of senior librarian. **Computerized Information Services:** DIALOG, SDC; ME-INDEX (internal database); computerized cataloging and ILL. **Networks/Consortia:** Member of OCLC through AMIGOS Bibliographic Council, Inc. **Publications:** New...in the Library, biweekly - for internal distribution only. **Special Indexes:** MEI Index (in microform). **Special Catalogs:** McClelland Bibliographic Union List of Holdings (in microform). **Remarks:** Library serves 15 company divisions and subsidiaries in the U.S., Canada, Europe, Saudi Arabia and Southeast Asia. **Staff:** Karen Ainslie, Asst.Libn.

MC CLELLAND AND STEWART LTD. PUBLISHING ARCHIVES
See: Mc Master University - Archives and Research Collections Division

MC CLUNG HISTORICAL COLLECTION
See: Knoxville-Knox County Public Library System

★7286★
MC COLLISTER, MC CLEARY, FAZIO, MIXON, HOLLIDAY & HICKS - LAW LIBRARY (Law)
One American Place, Suite 1800
Box 2706   Phone: (504) 387-5961
Baton Rouge, LA 70821   Anne Slaughter Towles, Law Libn.
Staff: Prof 1. **Subjects:** Law. **Holdings:** 5000 volumes. **Services:** Interlibrary loans; copying; library not open to public.

MC COLLOUGH (Alameda) RESEARCH & GENEALOGY LIBRARY
See: Tippecanoe County Historical Association - Alameda Mc Collough Research & Genealogy Library

MC CONNELL AIR FORCE BASE (KS)
See: U.S. Air Force Base - Mc Connell Base Library

MC CORD THEATER COLLECTION
See: Southern Methodist University

★7287★
MC CORMICK & CO. - R & D INFORMATION CENTER (Sci-Tech; Food-Bev)
202 Wight Ave.   Phone: (301) 667-7485
Hunt Valley, MD 21031   Merle I. Eiss, Mgr.
Founded: 1968. **Staff:** Prof 2; Other 3. **Subjects:** Food technology, chemistry. **Special Collections:** Spices. **Holdings:** 2500 books; 1800 bound periodical volumes. **Subscriptions:** 195 journals and other serials. **Services:** Interlibrary loans; copying; SDI; center open to public by special request only. **Computerized Information Services:** DIALOG, MEDLINE; internal database.

MC CORMICK (Katharine Dexter) LIBRARY
See: Planned Parenthood Federation of America, Inc. - Katharine Dexter Mc Cormick Library

★7288★
MC CORMICK THEOLOGICAL SEMINARY - LIBRARY (Rel-Theol)†
5555 S. Woodlawn Ave.   Phone: (312) 241-7800
Chicago, IL 60637   Elvire R. Hilgert, Libn.
Founded: 1829. **Staff:** Prof 5; Other 3. **Subjects:** Bible, Biblical archeology, theology, patristics, the Reformation, church history, early Americana. **Special Collections:** Presbyteriana - Historical Record, Synod of Illinois, UPCUSA; Lane Theological Seminary archives; Church Federation of Chicago Archives prior to 1969; USA imprints of the Bible. **Holdings:** 170,457 books and bound periodical volumes; 70,000 microtexts (cataloged). **Subscriptions:** 611 journals and other serials. **Services:** Interlibrary loans; copying; library open to public with letter of introduction. **Networks/Consortia:** Member of OCLC; Chicago Cluster of Theological Schools. **Remarks:** Shares facilities with the libraries of the Jesuit School of Theology in Chicago and the Lutheran School of Theology at Chicago. **Staff:** Janet Davidson, Relg.Educ.Libn.; Earle Hilgert, Coll.Dev.; Judy Knop, Cat.; Charmain Kuhr, Circ.Asst.

MC CRACKEN (Harold) RESEARCH LIBRARY
See: Buffalo Bill Historical Center - Harold Mc Cracken Research Library

MAC CRACKEN (William P., Jr.) MEMORIAL LIBRARY
See: Southern College of Optometry - William P. Mac Cracken, Jr. Memorial Library

★7289★
MC CRONE (Walter C.) ASSOCIATES - LIBRARY (Sci-Tech)
2820 S. Michigan   Phone: (312) 842-7100
Chicago, IL 60616   Juliet Robinson, Libn.
Staff: 1. **Subjects:** Microscopy, analytical chemistry, microanalysis, crystallography. **Holdings:** 4000 books; 1000 bound periodical volumes; 1000 other items; 100 chemical and optical catalogs; 30 reprints. **Subscriptions:** 130 journals and other serials. **Services:** Interlibrary loans; copying; library open to public with restrictions.

★7290★
MC CUTCHEN, BLACK, VERLEGER AND SHEA - LAW LIBRARY (Law)
600 Wilshire Blvd.   Phone: (213) 624-2400
Los Angeles, CA 90017   Stewart Annand, Libn.
Subjects: Law. **Holdings:** 22,000 volumes. **Subscriptions:** 50 journals and other serials. **Services:** Library not open to public.

★7291★
MC CUTCHEN, DOYLE, BROWN & ENERSEN - LAW LIBRARY (Law)
3 Embarcadero Ctr.   Phone: (415) 393-2198
San Francisco, CA 94111   Elizabeth S. Nicholson, Libn.
Staff: Prof 1; Other 3. **Subjects:** Law. **Holdings:** 40,000 volumes. **Services:** Interlibrary loans; library not open to public. **Computerized Information Services:** DIALOG, LEXIS. **Networks/Consortia:** Member of CLASS.

MC DERMOTT INC. - BABCOCK AND WILCOX COMPANY
See: Babcock and Wilcox Company

★7292★
MC DERMOTT INC. - CORPORATE INFORMATION CENTER (Bus-Fin; Energy)
1010 Common St.   Phone: (504) 587-5799
New Orleans, LA 70112   Karen L. Furlow, Corp.Libn.
Founded: 1907. **Staff:** Prof 1; Other 1. **Subjects:** Management, economics, statistics, engineering, oil and gas, energy. **Holdings:** 2500 books; 600 bound periodical volumes. **Services:** Interlibrary loans; center open to public. **Computerized Information Services:** SDC, DIALOG; internal database. **Special Catalogs:** Union list of serials of Babcock & Wilcox.

★7293★
MC DERMOTT, WILL & EMERY - LIBRARY (Law)
111 W. Monroe St.   Phone: (312) 372-2000
Chicago, IL 60603   Louis J. Covotsos, Hd.Libn.
Founded: 1934. **Staff:** Prof 3; Other 3. **Subjects:** Federal, state and foreign tax materials; American and English probate materials; litigation, pension and real estate materials. **Special Collections:** Legislative histories of Federal Tax Reform Hearings. **Holdings:** 24,000 books. **Subscriptions:** 60 journals and other serials. **Services:** Interlibrary loans to librarians only; copying; library not open to public; books loaned to law firms only. **Computerized Information Services:** LEXIS, WESTLAW, Dow Jones News Retrieval. **Networks/Consortia:** Member of Metropolitan Chicago Library Assembly. **Staff:** Susan Bresciano, Asst.Libn.; Terry Sklair, Asst.Libn.

MAC DILL AIR FORCE BASE (FL)
See: U.S. Air Force Base - Mac Dill Base Library

MAC DONALD (A.E.) OPHTHALMIC LIBRARY
See: University of Toronto - A.E. Mac Donald Ophthalmic Library

MC DONALD (Dr. James E.) LIBRARY
See: University of Arizona - Institute of Atmospheric Physics Library

MC DONALD USA COMMUNITY HOSPITAL
See: U.S. Army Hospitals

MC DONALD (Worden) LIBRARY
See: Southern Bible College - Worden Mc Donald Library

MAC DONELL (Elizabeth M.) MEMORIAL LIBRARY
See: Allen County Historical Society - Elizabeth M. Mac Donell Memorial
Library

MC DONNELL DOUGLAS ASTRONAUTICS COMPANY
See: Mc Donnell Douglas Corporation

★7294★
**MC DONNELL DOUGLAS AUTOMATION COMPANY - MCAUTO CAMPUS
LIBRARY** (Info Sci)
Dept. K222/300/2
Box 516   Phone: (314) 233-5194
St. Louis, MO 63166   Jenny Preston, Sr.Libn.
Founded: 1981. **Staff:** Prof 2; Other 2. **Subjects:** Data processing,
management. **Holdings:** 4000 books. **Subscriptions:** 250 journals and other
serials; 10 newspapers. **Services:** Interlibrary loans; computerized; library
open to public with librarian's approval. **Computerized Information Services:**
DIALOG; computerized cataloging. **Networks/Consortia:** Member of St. Louis
Regional Library Network; OCLC. **Staff:** Stephanie D. Tolson, Asst.Libn.

★7295★
MC DONNELL DOUGLAS CORPORATION - ACTRON TECHNICAL LIBRARY
(Sci-Tech)†
700 Royal Oaks Dr.   Phone: (213) 359-8216
Monrovia, CA 91016   Stella A. Medigovich, Libn.
Staff: Prof 1. **Subjects:** Optical systems, computer-aided design and
manufacturing, reconnaissance systems, microprocessors, communications
systems, information display systems, microcomputers. **Holdings:** 7000
books; specifications on microfilm; 1500 patents. **Subscriptions:** 415
journals and other serials; 5 newspapers. **Services:** Library not open to public.
Computerized Information Services: Internal database; computerized
acquisitions. **Publications:** Accessions list, monthly.

★7296★
**MC DONNELL DOUGLAS CORPORATION - DOUGLAS AIRCRAFT COMPANY
- TECHNICAL LIBRARY** (Sci-Tech)
3855 Lakewood Blvd.   Phone: (213) 593-9541
Long Beach, CA 90846   P.M. Ackerman, Sect.Mgr.
Founded: 1937. **Staff:** Prof 5; Other 8. **Subjects:** Aeronautical engineering,
electronics, power plants, management. **Special Collections:** National
Advisory Committee for Aeronautics (NACA) documents. **Holdings:** 20,000
books; 200,000 reports (cataloged); 700,000 documents on microfiche.
Subscriptions: 1066 journals and other serials. **Services:** Interlibrary loans;
SDI (services are for employees only); library not open to public.
Computerized Information Services: Mechanized literature searching;
computerized cataloging. **Special Indexes:** Microfiche index of holdings.
Staff: M.M. Smith, Supv., User Serv.; J.J. Weigel, Supv., Automated Oper.

★7297★
**MC DONNELL DOUGLAS CORPORATION - MC DONNELL AIRCRAFT
LIBRARY** (Sci-Tech)
Dept. 022, Box 516   Phone: (314) 232-6134
St. Louis, MO 63166   C.E. Zoller, Mgr.
Founded: 1945. **Staff:** Prof 6; Other 23. **Subjects:** Aeronautics,
astronautics, electronics, engineering. **Holdings:** 19,056 books; 7112 bound
periodical volumes; 173,450 documents (cataloged); 186,200 NASA and
DTIC microfiche copies of technical reports. **Subscriptions:** 988 journals and
other serials. **Services:** Interlibrary loans; copying; library open to public with
security clearance by prior arrangement. **Computerized Information
Services:** DIALOG; internal database; computerized reference retrieval.
Publications: Accession Notice, weekly; Acronyms, Abbreviations and
Initialisms, annual - both for internal distribution only. **Remarks:** This library
contains holdings of the Mc Donnell Douglas Electronics Company Library and
Mc Donnell Douglas Research Laboratories. **Staff:** R.D. Detrich, Abstractor;

C.F. Lauer, Ref.; P.A. Fischer, Res.Libn.

★7298★
**MC DONNELL DOUGLAS CORPORATION - MC DONNELL DOUGLAS
ASTRONAUTICS COMPANY - TECHNICAL LIBRARY SERVICES** (Sci-Tech)
5301 Bolsa Ave.   Phone: (714) 896-2317
Huntington Beach, CA 92647   E.G. Reed, Sect.Mgr.
Founded: 1958. **Staff:** Prof 4; Other 4. **Subjects:** Aerospace technology,
defense systems, space sciences, thermodynamics, electronics, propulsion,
materials, life sciences, communications. **Holdings:** 27,000 books; 6500
bound periodical volumes; 150,000 technical reports (cataloged); 150,000
titles of microfiche of technical reports; 1500 government and commercial
specifications and standards. **Subscriptions:** 653 journals and other serials.
Services: Interlibrary loans; SDI; library not open to public. **Computerized
Information Services:** DIALOG; computerized cataloging, acquisitions, serials
and circulation.

MC DONNELL DOUGLAS ELECTRONICS COMPANY - LIBRARY
See: Mc Donnell Douglas Corporation - Mc Donnell Aircraft Library

MC DONNELL DOUGLAS RESEARCH LABORATORIES
See: Mc Donnell Douglas Corporation - Mc Donnell Aircraft Library

★7299★
MC DONNELL PLANETARIUM - LIBRARY (Sci-Tech)
5100 Clayton Rd., Forest Pk.   Phone: (314) 535-5811
St. Louis, MO 63110   Richard W. Heuermann, Lib.Info.Dir.
Founded: 1963. **Staff:** Prof 2. **Subjects:** Astronomy, astronautics,
astrophysics. **Holdings:** 1500 books; 15 bound periodical volumes; selected
NASA reports. **Subscriptions:** 15 journals and other serials. **Services:** Library
open to public for reference use only. **Staff:** Ronald R. Sutherland, Dir.

MC DOWELL (C. Blake) LAW LIBRARY
See: University of Akron - School of Law - C. Blake Mc Dowell Law Library

MC DOWELL MICROFILM ARCHIVES
See: Ohio State University - Theatre Research Institute

MC ENERNEY (Garret W.) LAW LIBRARY
See: University of California, Berkeley - Law Library

★7300★
MC FARLAND MENTAL HEALTH CENTER - STAFF LIBRARY (Med)†
901 Southwind Rd.   Phone: (217) 786-6861
Springfield, IL 62703   Marie Rine, Libn.
Founded: 1968. **Staff:** Prof 1. **Subjects:** Behavior therapy, psychology,
psychiatry, psychotherapy, social psychiatry, family psychodynamics,
addiction, mental retardation, psychiatric nursing. **Holdings:** 2500 books; 200
bound periodical volumes; 4 drawers of pamphlets; 3 drawers of journal
reprints; 3 drawers of Department of Mental Health documents; psychological
testing materials; 8 shelves of special education textbooks. **Subscriptions:**
130 journals and other serials. **Services:** Interlibrary loans; copying (limited);
library open to public with restrictions on some materials. **Remarks:**
Maintained by Illinois State Department of Mental Health & Developmental
Disabilities.

★7301★
**MAC FARLANE & COMPANY, INC. - FRY CONSULTANTS INCORPORATED -
MANAGEMENT CENTRE, INC.** (Bus-Fin)
One Park Place, Suite 450   Phone: (404) 352-2293
Atlanta, GA 30318   Beth Clark, Mgr.
Staff: Prof 3. **Subjects:** Management consulting, marketing, executive
search, industry. **Holdings:** 1000 books; 500 bound periodical volumes;
articles, speeches, and books on management consultancy; 1000 client
reports dating from 1942. **Subscriptions:** 25 journals and other serials; 5
newspapers. **Services:** Copying; library open to clients and potential clients.
Staff: Judy Cone, Libn.; Linda K. Short, Libn.

★7302★
MC GEAN-ROHCO, INC. - RESEARCH LIBRARY (Sci-Tech)
2910 Harvard Ave.
Box 09087   Phone: (216) 441-4900
Cleveland, OH 44109   Charlotte L. Conklin, Libn.
Staff: 1. **Subjects:** Metallurgy, organic and inorganic chemistry,
electroplating, ceramics. **Special Collections:** Plating information. **Holdings:**
500 books; 1600 bound periodical volumes; 4000 patents; 4 VF drawers of
pamphlets; 4 VF drawers of catalogs; 2 VF drawers of articles. **Subscriptions:**
23 journals and other serials. **Services:** Interlibrary loans; copying; library
open to public with restrictions. **Computerized Information Services:**

DIALOG, SDC; computerized acquisitions. **Publications:** CA Bulletin. **Special Indexes:** Indexes to pamphlets, catalogs and articles. **Formed by the Merger of:** McGean Chemical Company, Inc. and R.O. Hull Co. (ROHCO).

MC GEE (Dean A.) EYE INSTITUTE
See: University of Oklahoma - Dean A. Mc Gee Eye Institute

MC GEE LIBRARY
See: Kerr-Mc Gee Corporation

MC GEHEE (John L.) LIBRARY
See: Baptist Memorial Hospital - John L. Mc Gehee Library

★7303★
MC GEORGE SCHOOL OF LAW - LAW LIBRARY (Law)
University of the Pacific
3282 Fifth Ave.
Sacramento, CA 95817   Alice J. Murray, Law Libn.
Founded: 1924. **Staff:** Prof 9; Other 13. **Subjects:** Law. **Holdings:** 185,000 volumes. **Services:** Interlibrary loans; copying; library not open to public. **Computerized Information Services:** LEXIS, RLIN, WESTLAW. **Networks/Consortia:** Member of CLASS; Interuniversity Communications Council (EDUCOM). **Staff:** Katherine Henderson, Asst. Law Libn.; Robert Owens, Asst. Law Libn.; Marian Spittler, Asst. Law Libn.

★7304★
MC GILL & SMITH ENGINEERS, ARCHITECTS & PLANNERS - LIBRARY (Sci-Tech; Plan)†
119 W. Main St.   Phone: (513) 753-4430
Amelia, OH 45102   Patricia A. Cutrell, Lib. Media Tech.Asst.
Founded: 1978. **Staff:** 1. **Subjects:** Sanitary and civil engineering, architecture, planning, zoning, subdivisions. **Special Collections:** Original tracings (4000); aerial photographs (500); U.S. Geological Survey maps (107). **Holdings:** 700 books; 450 maps and reports; 2000 articles in VF drawers; manufacturers' catalogs. **Subscriptions:** 136 journals and other serials. **Services:** Interlibrary loans; copying; library not open to public.

★7305★
MC GILL UNIVERSITY - ALLAN MEMORIAL INSTITUTE OF PSYCHIATRY - LIBRARY (Med)†
1025 Pine Ave., W.   Phone: (514) 842-1251
Montreal, PQ, Canada H3A 1A1   Felicitas Kirchenberger, Act.Libn.
Founded: 1946. **Staff:** Prof 1; Other 1. **Subjects:** Psychiatry, psychology, psychopharmacology, biochemistry, social work. **Holdings:** 4000 books; 2300 bound periodical volumes; 1200 unbound journals; 850 pamphlets. **Subscriptions:** 53 journals and other serials. **Services:** Interlibrary loans; copying; library open to professional staff and McGill medical students. **Staff:** Dr. D. Pivnicki, Chm., Lib.Comm.

★7306★
MC GILL UNIVERSITY - BLACKADER LIBRARY OF ARCHITECTURE/LAUTERMAN LIBRARY OF ART (Art; Plan)
3459 McTavish St.   Phone: (514) 392-4960
Montreal, PQ, Canada H3A 1Y1
Founded: 1922. **Staff:** Prof 1; Other 2. **Subjects:** Architecture, urban planning, fine arts, landscape architecture, decorative and industrial arts. **Special Collections:** Old Canadian Architecture (measured original drawings and photographs; 6000 items). **Holdings:** 37,999 books; 12,863 bound periodical volumes; 2423 boxes of exhibition catalogs. **Subscriptions:** 268 journals and other serials. **Services:** Interlibrary loans; copying.

★7307★
MC GILL UNIVERSITY - BLACKER/WOOD LIBRARY OF ZOOLOGY AND ORNITHOLOGY (Sci-Tech)
Redpath Library Bldg.
3459 McTavish St.   Phone: (514) 392-4955
Montreal, PQ, Canada H3A 1Y1   Eleanor MacLean, Libn.
Founded: 1920. **Staff:** Prof 1; Other 2. **Subjects:** Ornithology, zoology, natural history. **Special Collections:** Naturalists' letters; Robert Gurney Collection (reprints on crustacea); Ivanow Collection of Oriental Manuscripts. **Holdings:** 39,844 books; 36,135 bound periodical volumes; 8028 paintings, drawings and photographs; 98 records and cassettes; 3332 manuscripts. **Subscriptions:** 680 journals and other serials. **Services:** Interlibrary loans (via McLennan Library); library open to public for consultation only. **Computerized Information Services:** DIALOG.

MC GILL UNIVERSITY - B'NAI BRITH HILLEL FOUNDATION
See: B'nai Brith Hillel Foundation at Mc Gill University

★7308★
MC GILL UNIVERSITY - BOTANY-GENETICS LIBRARY (Sci-Tech)
Stewart Biological Sciences Bldg.
1205 Dr. Penfield Ave.   Phone: (514) 392-5829
Montreal, PQ, Canada H3A 1B1   Wendy Patrick, Libn.
Founded: 1970. **Staff:** Prof 1; Other 2. **Subjects:** Botany, genetics, cell and molecular biology. **Holdings:** 11,115 books; 9154 bound periodical volumes. **Subscriptions:** 247 journals and other serials. **Services:** Interlibrary loans; copying; library open to public for consultation.

★7309★
MC GILL UNIVERSITY - CENTRE FOR DEVELOPING AREA STUDIES - DOCUMENTATION CENTRE (Soc Sci)
815 Sherbrooke St. W.   Phone: (514) 392-5342
Montreal, PQ, Canada H3A 2K6   Marjorie Neilson, Documentalist
Founded: 1963. **Staff:** Prof 1. **Subjects:** Economic, social and political development of Third World countries. **Special Collections:** Government documents from Third World countries. **Holdings:** 1106 books; monographs and research papers from 269 universities and research foundations; 241 pamphlet boxes of reprints and pamphlets. **Subscriptions:** 181 journals and other serials. **Services:** Centre open to public through referral. **Publications:** List of publications - available on request.

MC GILL UNIVERSITY - CURRICULUM LABORATORY
See: Mc Gill University - Education Library

★7310★
MC GILL UNIVERSITY - DENTISTRY LIBRARY (Med)
Strathcona Anatomy & Dentistry Bldg.
3640 University St.   Phone: (514) 392-4926
Montreal, PQ, Canada H3A 2B2   Jean Fensom, Libn.
Founded: 1965. **Staff:** Prof 1; Other 1. **Subjects:** Dentistry, mouth diseases. **Holdings:** 5291 books; 5005 bound periodical volumes; 1870 AV items; 121 audio cassettes. **Subscriptions:** 243 journals and other serials. **Services:** Interlibrary loans; copying; library open to public for consultation only. **Publications:** Accessions list.

★7311★
MC GILL UNIVERSITY - DEPARTMENT OF RARE BOOKS & SPECIAL COLLECTIONS (Rare Book; Hist)
McLennan Library Bldg.
3459 McTavish St.   Phone: (514) 392-4973
Montreal, PQ, Canada H3A 1Y1   Elizabeth Lewis, Rare Book Libn.
Founded: 1965. **Staff:** Prof 3; Other 7. **Subjects:** Canadiana, printing, history of the book, exploration, voyages and travel. **Special Collections:** Lande Canadiana (12,000 items); Joubert Collection on French Canada (3000 volumes); Colgate Printing (13,000 items); Lande Blake (1600 items); Redpath British Historical Tracts (20,000 items); David Hume (490 items); Rousseau (560 items); Kierkegaard (1500 volumes); Napoleon (4000 prints; 2000 books); Stearn Puppet Theatre (2600 books; 150 puppets). **Holdings:** 155,976 books and bound periodical volumes; 4361 manuscripts; 6500 maps, atlases, charts and globes; 7000 Canadian pamphlets; 77,505 items of printed ephemera and exhibition material; 18,300 prints and other illustrative materials; 12,000 McGill theses. **Subscriptions:** 1932 journals and other serials. **Services:** Copying; library open to public. **Publications:** Departmental Brochure, annual - for local distribution. **Special Catalogs:** European and American Manuscripts (book); Rosalynde Stearn Puppet Collection (book); McGill University Libraries Special Collections: Lande Canadiana and Redpath British Historical Tracts (book). **Staff:** Nellie Reiss, Lande Libn.; Carol Marley, Map Cur.-Libn.; Gary Tynski, Print Cur.

★7312★
MC GILL UNIVERSITY - EDUCATION LIBRARY (Educ)
3700 McTavish St.   Phone: (514) 392-8849
Montreal, PQ, Canada H3A 1Y2   Joan Gagne, Educ.Libn.
Founded: 1970. **Staff:** Prof 3; Other 6. **Subjects:** Education, special education, teaching methods, psychology of education, psychology, art, religion (particularly Catholicism), women. **Special Collections:** Audiovisual teaching aids (in Curriculum Laboratory); Physical Education Collection (in Physical Education Library); ERIC microfiche from 1973; Fearon Pitman Curriculum Development Library; Canadian curriculum guides; Canadex. **Holdings:** 80,688 books; 10,795 bound periodical volumes; 1538 microfilms of theses on education; 199,052 microfiche. **Subscriptions:** 675 journals and other serials. **Services:** Interlibrary loans (from Education Library and Physical Education Library, but not Curriculum Laboratory); library open to public for reference use only. **Remarks:** Above data also includes the Curriculum Laboratory (392-8896) and the Physical Education Library (392-8893). **Staff:** Elizabeth Mennie, Ref.Libn.; Gloria Hall, Curric.Lab.Supv.

★7313★
MC GILL UNIVERSITY - EDUCATION LIBRARY - SAM RABINOVITCH MEMORIAL COLLECTION (Educ)
3700 McTavish St.   Phone: (514) 392-8849
Montreal, PQ, Canada H3A 1Y2   Joan Gagne, Educ.Libn.
Founded: 1969. **Staff:** Prof 3; Other 6. **Subjects:** Psychology, sociology, reading and remedial reading, child study, teacher training, diagnosis and remediation, special education. **Holdings:** 2012 books; 231 bound periodical volumes. **Subscriptions:** 32 journals and other serials. **Services:** Copying; library open to public. **Remarks:** Transferred to present location in 1977.

★7314★
MC GILL UNIVERSITY - ENGINEERING LIBRARY
Macdonald Engineering Bldg.
817 Sherbrooke St. W.
Montreal, PQ, Canada H3A 2K6
Defunct. Merged with its Physical Sciences Library to form the Physical Sciences & Engineering Library.

★7315★
MC GILL UNIVERSITY - EXPERIMENTAL SURGERY LIBRARY (Med)
Donner Bldg.
740 Dr. Penfield Ave.   Phone: (514) 392-4858
Montreal, PQ, Canada H3A 1A4   Brenda Bewick, Libn.
Staff: Prof 1. **Subjects:** Immunology. **Holdings:** 1550 books and bound periodical volumes; 275 theses. **Subscriptions:** 20 journals and other serials. **Services:** Interlibrary loans; copying; library open to public for reference use only.

★7316★
MC GILL UNIVERSITY - FRENCH CANADA STUDIES PROGRAMME - REFERENCE LIBRARY (Soc Sci; Area-Ethnic)
3475 Peel St.   Phone: (514) 392-5200
Montreal, PQ, Canada H3A 1W7   Professor Yvan Lamonde, Dir.
Founded: 1963. **Staff:** Prof 1; Other 1. **Subjects:** Quebec and Canadian social sciences (research tools and reference works). **Holdings:** 1200 books. **Services:** Copying; library open to public by permission.

★7317★
MC GILL UNIVERSITY - HOWARD ROSS LIBRARY OF MANAGEMENT (Bus-Fin)
Bronfman Bldg.
1001 Sherbrooke St., W.   Phone: (514) 392-5795
Montreal, PQ, Canada H3A 1G5   Marjorie Judah, Libn.
Founded: 1943. **Staff:** Prof 2; Other 5. **Subjects:** Management, marketing, accounting, finance, statistics, operations research, industrial relations, international business. **Holdings:** 30,378 books; 26,284 bound periodical volumes; 2522 other cataloged items; 18,356 corporate reports; 707 reels of microfilm; 48 microfiche. **Subscriptions:** 426 journals and other serials. **Services:** Interlibrary loans; copying; library open to public for consultation only.

★7318★
MC GILL UNIVERSITY - ISLAMIC STUDIES LIBRARY (Area-Ethnic)
Stephen Leacock Bldg., 9th Fl.
855 Sherbrooke St. W.   Phone: (514) 392-5197
Montreal, PQ, Canada H3A 2T7   Raja Dirlik, Libn.
Founded: 1952. **Staff:** Prof 2; Other 3. **Subjects:** Islamic religion, philosophy, civilization, culture, history, language, literature. **Holdings:** 66,480 books; 9142 bound periodical volumes; 533 reels of microfilm; 161 volumes of manuscripts; 699 AV items. **Subscriptions:** 237 journals and other serials. **Services:** Interlibrary loans; library open to public for reference use only. **Publications:** Occasional brochures and guides.

★7319★
MC GILL UNIVERSITY - LABOUR AGREEMENTS DATA BANK (Soc Sci)
1001 Sherbrooke St., W.   Phone: (514) 392-3076
Montreal, PQ, Canada H3A 1G5   Dr. Charles Steinberg, Dir.
Founded: 1968. **Staff:** Prof 2; Other 3. **Subjects:** Labour agreements analyses. **Holdings:** Over 7000 current labour agreements from all economic sectors across Canada; 175 U.S. and Canadian higher education collective agreements. **Services:** Copying; documentation relating to wages, hours of work and other working conditions; creation and maintenance of specialized databases of labour agreement provisions; data bank open to public on a fee basis. **Computerized Information Services:** STARS (internal database); computerized analysis of labour agreements. **Staff:** Mr. J. Zackon, Asst.Dir./Mgr.; Ms. C. Cossette, Res.Anl.

★7320★
MC GILL UNIVERSITY - LAW LIBRARY (Law)
New Chancellor Day Hall
3644 Peel St.   Phone: (514) 392-5060
Montreal, PQ, Canada H3A 1W9   Michael Renshawe, Law Libn.
Founded: 1890. **Staff:** Prof 5; Other 11. **Subjects:** Law and common law. **Special Collections:** Air/Space Law (6000 volumes); Wainwright Collection (French legal history; 2550 volumes). **Holdings:** 58,856 books; 54,145 bound periodical volumes; 118,880 government documents; 7432 pamphlets. **Subscriptions:** 2741 journals and other serials. **Services:** Interlibrary loans; copying; library open to public by special arrangement.

★7321★
MC GILL UNIVERSITY - LIBRARY SCIENCE LIBRARY (Info Sci)
McLennan Library Bldg.
3459 McTavish St.   Phone: (514) 392-5931
Montreal, PQ, Canada H3A 1Y1   Stephanie Both, Libn.
Founded: 1927. **Staff:** Prof 1; Other 2. **Subjects:** Library science; information science; bibliography; documentation; history of books and printing; cataloging and classification; book trade; children's and young adult literature. **Special Collections:** Children's Literature; Young Adult Literature; Rare Books. **Holdings:** 32,160 books; 5449 bound periodical volumes; 18,504 pamphlets and clippings; 8721 annual reports; 6563 publishers' catalogs; 1621 accessions lists; 2434 microforms; 1888 library school calendars; 21,886 library newsletters. **Subscriptions:** 352 journals and other serials. **Services:** Interlibrary loans; copying; library open to public upon registration.

★7322★
MC GILL UNIVERSITY - MACDONALD CAMPUS - BRACE RESEARCH INSTITUTE LIBRARY (Energy)
P.O. Box 900   Phone: (514) 457-2000
Ste. Anne Bellevue, PQ, Canada H9X 1C0   Mrs. A. Ives, Adm. & Info.Serv.
Subjects: Arid zone development, saline water conversion, solar energy utilization, wind energy utilization, controlled environment agriculture. **Holdings:** 1000 books; 50 bound periodical volumes; 4200 articles and reports; 300 conference proceedings. **Subscriptions:** 290 journals and other serials. **Services:** Library open to public by appointment. **Publications:** List of publications - available upon request.

★7323★
MC GILL UNIVERSITY - MACDONALD CAMPUS - LIBRARY (Agri)
Barton Bldg.
2111 Lakeshore Rd.   Phone: (514) 457-2000
Ste. Anne Bellevue, PQ, Canada H9X 1C0   Janet Finlayson, Hd.Libn.
Founded: 1907. **Staff:** Prof 3; Other 9. **Subjects:** Environmental, food and agricultural sciences. **Special Collections:** F.A.O. Depository Collection (840 volumes); Lyman Entomological Collection (9600 volumes, including rare books). **Holdings:** 48,127 books; 32,978 bound periodical volumes; 136,927 government documents. **Subscriptions:** 991 journals and other serials. **Services:** Interlibrary loans; copying; library open to public for consultation only. **Computerized Information Services:** DIALOG, CAN/OLE. **Publications:** Accession List, monthly - for internal distribution only. **Staff:** Mr. B. Grainger, Pub.Serv.Libn.; Mrs. V. Fortin, Tech.Serv.Libn.

★7324★
MC GILL UNIVERSITY - MAP AND AIR PHOTO LIBRARY (Geog-Map)
524 Burnside Hall
805 Sherbrooke St., W.   Phone: (514) 392-5492
Montreal, PQ, Canada H3A 2K6   Lorraine Dubreuil, Map Cur.
Founded: 1945. **Staff:** Prof 1; Other 1. **Subjects:** Cartography, geography. **Holdings:** 136,805 maps; 615 atlases; 165 gazetteers; 29,546 air photographs. **Services:** Interlibrary loans; library open to public with restrictions. **Publications:** Bibliographies.

MC GILL UNIVERSITY - MARINE SCIENCES LIBRARY
Mc Gill University - Oceanography Library

★7325★
MC GILL UNIVERSITY - MARVIN DUCHOW MUSIC LIBRARY (Mus)
Strathcona Music Bldg.
555 Sherbrooke St., W.   Phone: (514) 392-4530
Montreal, PQ, Canada H3A 1E3   Kathleen M. Toomey, Libn.
Founded: 1965. **Staff:** Prof 1; Other 4. **Subjects:** Music. **Holdings:** 13,288 books; 3363 bound periodical volumes; 12,789 recordings; 16,715 scores; 222 reels of microfilm; 1462 microfiche; 121 open reel tapes; 3 audio cassettes. **Subscriptions:** 187 journals and other serials. **Services:** Interlibrary loans; copying; library open to public for consultation only.

★7326★

MC GILL UNIVERSITY - MATHEMATICS LIBRARY (Sci-Tech)
1105 Burnside Hall
805 Sherbrooke St., W.   Phone: (514) 392-8273
Montreal, PQ, Canada H3A 2K6   Allan Youster, Lib.Supv.
Staff: 1. **Subjects:** Mathematics, statistics. **Holdings:** 7944 volumes.
Subscriptions: 247 journals and other serials. **Services:** Copying; library open
to public with restrictions.

★7327★

MC GILL UNIVERSITY - MEDICAL LIBRARY (Med)
McIntyre Medical Sciences Bldg.
3655 Drummond St.   Phone: (514) 392-3056
Montreal, PQ, Canada H3G 1Y6   Frances Groen, Life Sci. Area Libn.
Founded: 1823. **Staff:** Prof 6; Other 15. **Subjects:** Medicine and related
topics. **Special Collections:** Dr. Casey A. Wood Ophthalmology Collection.
Holdings: 54,626 books; 116,686 bound periodical volumes; 6536 slides.
Subscriptions: 2075 journals and other serials. **Services:** Interlibrary loans;
copying; library open to public for consultation only. **Computerized
Information Services:** CAN/OLE, DIALOG, SDC, NLM; computerized
cataloging. **Networks/Consortia:** Member of UTLAS, Inc. **Publications:**
Subject bibliographies; library guides; accessions list. **Staff:** David S.
Crawford, Asst. Area Libn.; B. LeSieur, Acq. & Coll.Libn.; H. Waluzyniec, Cat. &
Proc.Libn.; W. Patrick, Pub.Serv.Libn.

★7328★

MC GILL UNIVERSITY - METEOROLOGY LIBRARY (Sci-Tech)
704 Burnside Hall
805 Sherbrooke St. W.   Phone: (514) 392-8237
Montreal, PQ, Canada H3A 2K6   Keston Forde, Lib.Supv.
Founded: 1961. **Staff:** 1. **Subjects:** Meteorology, climatology, Arctic studies,
mathematics. **Special Collections:** Stormy Weather Group Scientific MW
reports; Arctic Meteorology Research Group publications; Andrew Thomson
Memorial Arctic Collection; theses of meteorology students. **Holdings:** 1919
books; 888 bound periodical volumes; 9839 government documents.
Subscriptions: 88 journals and other serials. **Services:** Interlibrary loans;
library open to public with restrictions.

★7329★

MC GILL UNIVERSITY - NORTHERN STUDIES LIBRARY (Area-Ethnic; Sci-
Tech)
1020 Pine Ave., W.   Phone: (514) 392-8233
Montreal, PQ, Canada H3A 1A2   Louise Nadeau, Lib.Supv.
Founded: 1976. **Staff:** 1. **Subjects:** Regions north of the 60th degree
latitude; Quebec north of 49th degree latitude; Labrador. **Holdings:** 11,622
books; 2349 bound periodical volumes; 6607 government documents; 6204
reprints; 3978 pamphlets. **Subscriptions:** 346 journals and other serials.
Services: Interlibrary loans; library open to public. **Computerized
Information Services:** DIALOG, SDC, CAN/OLE; computerized cataloging.
Networks/Consortia: Member of Reseau INQ.

★7330★

MC GILL UNIVERSITY - NURSING/SOCIAL WORK LIBRARY (Med)
Wilson Hall
3506 University St.   Phone: (514) 392-5027
Montreal, PQ, Canada H3A 2A7   Wendy Patrick, Hd.Libn.
Founded: 1920. **Staff:** Prof 1; Other 4. **Subjects:** Nurses and nursing,
nursing education, health care, human development, behavioral science, social
welfare. **Special Collections:** Workshop Travelling Collection on Family Health
Education (800 volumes; 50 journals); Info Corner. **Holdings:** 26,638 books;
8085 bound periodical volumes; 1375 slides; 197 filmstrips; 314 audio
cassettes; 86 video cassettes; 200 nursing studies; 5125 government
documents; 9363 pamphlets. **Subscriptions:** 500 journals and other serials.
Services: Interlibrary loans; copying; library open to nurses in affiliated
hospitals and open to public for reference use only. **Publications:** Accessions
list. **Special Catalogs:** Info Corner catalogue (card). **Formed by the Merger
of:** Its Nursing and Social Work Libraries.

★7331★

MC GILL UNIVERSITY - OCEANOGRAPHY LIBRARY (Sci-Tech)
3620 University St.   Phone: (514) 392-5723
Montreal, PQ, Canada H3A 2B2   Yvonne Barrington, Lib.Supv.
Founded: 1963. **Staff:** 1. **Subjects:** Biological and physical oceanography,
geology and geophysics of the sea floor, polar regions, pollution. **Holdings:**
1298 books; 2815 bound periodical volumes; 11,310 government
documents. **Subscriptions:** 254 journals and other serials. **Services:**
Interlibrary loans; library open to public with restrictions. **Special Catalogs:**
Theses & Publications of the Insitute of Oceanography, 1964-1979.
Formerly: Its Marine Sciences Library **Staff:** Robert Freese, Area Libn.

★7332★

MC GILL UNIVERSITY - OSLER LIBRARY (Med)
McIntyre Medical Sciences Bldg.
3655 Drummond St.   Phone: (514) 392-4329
Montreal, PQ, Canada H3G 1Y6   Philip Teigen, Osler Libn.
Founded: 1929. **Staff:** Prof 3; Other 3. **Subjects:** History of medicine.
Special Collections: E.W. Archibald Collection; Worthington Family Collection;
D. Sclater Lewis Collection; Evans Collection of Pathological Illustrations;
Griffith Collection of Homoeopathy; Antonio Cantero; McGill Medical Library
Archives; Cushing Papers; H.E. MacDermot; C.A. Wood Ophthalmic Collection;
medical artifacts; Casey A. Wood Historical Collection of Sinhalese Materia
Medica; manuscript collections of Sir William Osler, C.K. Russel, Norman
Bethune, Maude Abbott, Boris Babkin, and W.H. Drummond; Osler Society
Papers; Medical Portrait Collection; Harold N. Segall Collection; Canadian
Dermatological Association archives; Homoeopathy collection from library of
Queen Elizabeth Hospital, Montreal; A.D. Blackader Collection. **Holdings:**
29,839 books; 1637 bound periodical volumes. **Subscriptions:** 127 journals
and other serials. **Services:** Interlibrary loans; copying; microfilming
photography; library open to public. **Publications:** The Osler Library (1979);
Osler Library Newsletter. **Special Indexes:** Index to early Canadian Medical
Journals, 1844-1883. **Staff:** M. Fransiszyn, Hd., Pub.Serv.; O. Werbowyj,
Hd., Tech.Serv.

MC GILL UNIVERSITY - PHYSICAL EDUCATION LIBRARY
See: Mc Gill University - Education Library

★7333★

MC GILL UNIVERSITY - PHYSICAL SCIENCES AND ENGINEERING LIBRARY
(Sci-Tech)
809 Sherbrooke St., W.   Phone: (514) 392-5914
Montreal, PQ, Canada H3A 2K6   Robert Freese, Area Libn.
Founded: 1956. **Staff:** Prof 5; Other 12. **Subjects:** Chemistry; physics;
geology; engineering - chemical, civil, mechanical, aeronautical, environmental,
industrial, metallurgical, mining; automatic control; computer science;
mathematics. **Special Collections:** NASA technical reports and translations.
Holdings: 64,887 books; 52,240 bound periodical volumes; 102,702
government documents. **Subscriptions:** 1862 journals and other serials.
Services: Interlibrary loans; copying; library open to public with restrictions.
Computerized Information Services: DIALOG, SDC, CAN/OLE, QL Systems.
Formed by the Merger of: Its Physical Sciences and Engineering Libraries.
Staff: Mrs. Rohini Adam, Pub.Serv.Libn.; Brenda Hurst, Ref.Libn.; Mrs.
Jadwiga Wygnanski, Tech.Serv.Libn.; Joanna Andrews, Cat.

MC GILL UNIVERSITY - POLISH LIBRARY
See: Polish Institute of Arts and Sciences in Canada

★7334★

MC GILL UNIVERSITY - RELIGIOUS STUDIES LIBRARY (Rel-Theol)
William & Henry Birks Bldg.
3520 University St.   Phone: (514) 392-4832
Montreal, PQ, Canada H3A 2A7   Norma Johnston, Hd.Libn.
Founded: 1948. **Staff:** Prof 1; Other 3. **Subjects:** Historical theology, Old
and New Testament, church history, philosophy of religion and ethics,
comparative religion, pastoral psychology, practical theology, homiletics.
Special Collections: Montreal Diocesan Theological College Collection,
including the Jeannie Willis Memorial Library; United Theological College
Collection. **Holdings:** 57,263 books; 6911 bound periodical volumes; 8870
microforms; 1198 slides; 901 pamphlets; 9 films; 9 audiotapes; 59 audio
cassettes; 16 phonograph records; 8 filmstrips. **Subscriptions:** 164 journals
and other serials. **Services:** Interlibrary loans; copying; library open to public
for reference use only; borrowing to professional ministry.

★7335★

MC GILL UNIVERSITY - RUTHERFORD PHYSICS LIBRARY (Sci-Tech)
3600 University St.   Phone: (514) 392-4785
Montreal, PQ, Canada H3A 2T8   Violet Stewart, Lib.Supv.
Founded: 1970. **Staff:** 1. **Subjects:** Physics - solid state, nuclear, high
energy. **Holdings:** 761 books; 1582 bound periodical volumes; published
papers of Atomic Energy of Canada; 291 theses on solid state physics and
nuclear physics. **Subscriptions:** 21 journals and other serials. **Services:**
Interlibrary loans; copying; library open to public with restrictions.

★7336★

**MC GILL UNIVERSITY - SCHOOL OF HUMAN COMMUNICATION DISORDERS
- LIBRARY** (Sci-Tech)†
1266 Pine Ave., W.   Phone: (514) 392-5966
Montreal, PQ, Canada H3G 1A8   Dr. James C. McNutt, Assoc.Prof.
Staff: 1. **Subjects:** Speech pathology, audiology, language development,
speech and hearing science. **Holdings:** 1500 books; 500 bound periodical

volumes; 200 other cataloged items. **Services:** Library open to public with restrictions.

★7337★
MC GILL UNIVERSITY - SOCIAL WORK LIBRARY
Wilson Hall
3506 University
Montreal, PQ, Canada H3A 2A7
Defunct. Merged with its Nursing Library to form the Nursing/Social Work Library.

★7338★
MC GILL UNIVERSITY - SUB-ARCTIC RESEARCH STATION LIBRARY (Sci-Tech)
Box 790
Schefferville, PQ, Canada G0G 2T0
Phone: (418) 585-2489
Douglas R. Barr, Mgr.
Founded: 1954. **Staff:** 1. **Subjects:** Arctic and subarctic, environmental studies. **Special Collections:** McGill Sub-Arctic Research Papers (36 volumes); manuscript theses by students at the McGill Station (50 volumes). **Holdings:** 500 books and bound periodical volumes. **Subscriptions:** 130 journals and other serials. **Services:** Interlibrary loans; copying; library open to qualified users. **Publications:** McGill Sub-Arctic Research Papers, irregular - for sale or exchange, through the Centre for Northern Studies & Research, McGill University, 1020 Pine Ave., W., Montreal, PQ H3A 1A2.

★7339★
MC GLADREY HENDRICKSON & COMPANY, C.P.A. - CENTRAL LIBRARY (Bus-Fin)†
1017 Davenport Bank Bldg.
Davenport, IA 52801
Phone: (319) 326-5111
Carol Boykin, Libn.
Founded: 1973. **Staff:** Prof 1; Other 1. **Subjects:** Accounting, business, management. **Holdings:** 1500 books; 200 bound periodical volumes; 700 files of annual reports; 60,000 microfiche. **Subscriptions:** 100 journals and other serials. **Services:** Interlibrary loans; copying; SDI; library open to public with restrictions. **Publications:** Acquisitions list - for internal distribution only.

MC GLANNAN MEMORIAL LIBRARY
See: Mercy Hospital

MC GOOGAN LIBRARY OF MEDICINE
See: University of Nebraska Medical Center

★7340★
MC GRAW-HILL, INC. - BUSINESS WEEK MAGAZINE LIBRARY (Bus-Fin)†
1221 Ave. of the Americas
New York, NY 10020
Phone: (212) 997-3297
Tessie Mantzoros, Libn.
Founded: 1929. **Staff:** Prof 1. **Subjects:** Business conditions, prices, agriculture, commodities, foreign trade, railroads, department store sales, cost of living. **Holdings:** 800 volumes; 73 VF drawers of pamphlets. **Subscriptions:** 250 journals and other serials. **Services:** Interlibrary loans.

MC GRAW-HILL/CTB
See: CTB/Mc Graw-Hill

★7341★
MC GRAW-HILL, INC. - LIBRARY (Publ)
1221 Ave. of the Americas
New York, NY 10020
Phone: (212) 997-6829
George W. Barlow, Chf.Libn.
Founded: 1926. **Staff:** Prof 8; Other 6. **Subjects:** Business, economics, industry, science, technology, engineering, publishing. **Holdings:** 30,000 books and bound periodical volumes; 135 VF drawers of subject file material; 85 VF drawers of current government reports; microfilm of McGraw-Hill magazines. **Subscriptions:** 600 journals and other serials. **Services:** Interlibrary loans; library open to selected outside users, with limitations. **Computerized Information Services:** DIALOG, SDC, New York Times Information Service, NEXIS. **Publications:** What's New in the Library, monthly - for internal distribution only. **Staff:** Ruth Cangialosi, Asst.Libn.; Judy Benyey, Cat.; Helen Schaefer, Chf. Indexer; Carol Rankin, Ref.Libn.; Frances Narducci, Ref.Libn.; Maria Garcia, Indexer.

★7342★
MC GRAW-HILL PUBLICATIONS COMPANY - MARKETING INFORMATION CENTER (Bus-Fin)
1221 Ave. of the Americas
New York, NY 10020
Phone: (212) 997-3222
Ranulph F. Norman, Dir.
Staff: Prof 1; Other 3. **Subjects:** Administration, advertising, marketing, selling techniques, markets (products and industries). **Special Collections:** Abstracts of 20,000 books, articles, and studies covering over 1000 advertising and marketing topics, 1946-1982. **Holdings:** 1000 books and bound periodical volumes; 20,000 articles and studies on the techniques of industrial advertising and marketing; 175,000 articles, studies and reports on markets for 2000 products and industries. **Subscriptions:** 385 journals and other serials. **Services:** Copying (limited); center open only to staff and staff referrals, McGraw-Hill advertisers and advertising agencies, B/PAA members. **Special Catalogs:** Subject headings for an industrial advertising/marketing library. **Remarks:** Functions also as the marketing library of the Business/Professional Advertising Association (B/PAA). **Staff:** Shirley Keating, Asst.Dir.

MC GREGOR (Tracy W.) LIBRARY
See: University of Virginia - Tracy W. Mc Gregor Library

★7343★
MC GUFFEY (William Holmes) HOUSE AND MUSEUM - LIBRARY (Hist; Educ)
Spring & Oak Sts.
Oxford, OH 45056
Phone: (513) 529-4917
Sterling Cook, Cur.
Founded: 1961. **Staff:** Prof 1; Other 2. **Subjects:** McGuffey Readers, 19th century textbooks in all subject categories. **Holdings:** 3500 books; 6 boxes of photographs; manuscripts; McGuffey letters on microfilm. **Services:** Copying; library open to public on a limited schedule and by appointment. **Publications:** Pamphlets on the House-Museum and on W.H. McGuffey. **Remarks:** Maintained by Miami University.

MC GUIRE AIR FORCE BASE (NJ)
See: U.S. Air Force Base - Mc Guire Base Library

MC GUIRE MEMORIAL LIBRARY
See: St. Catherine Hospital

★7344★
MC GUIRE, WOODS AND BATTLE - LAW LIBRARY (Law)
1400 Ross Bldg.
Richmond, VA 23219
Phone: (804) 644-4131
Ann B. Roberts, Libn.
Staff: Prof 1; Other 3. **Subjects:** Law. **Holdings:** 18,000 books; 1000 bound periodical volumes; 2 VF drawers of microfilm. **Subscriptions:** 100 journals and other serials. **Services:** Copying; library not open to public. **Computerized Information Services:** LEXIS, New York Times Information Service, DIALOG, Dow Jones News Retrieval, Computer Directions Advisors, Inc., WESTLAW.

MC HENRY (Dean E.) LIBRARY
See: University of California, Santa Cruz - Dean E. Mc Henry Library

★7345★
MC HENRY MUSEUM - LIBRARY (Hist)
1402 I St.
Modesto, CA 95354
Phone: (209) 577-5366
Heidi L. Warner, Cur.
Staff: Prof 2. **Subjects:** Stanislaus County history. **Holdings:** City and county records, oral history tapes, school records, court records, diaries, photographs (figures not available). **Publications:** Quarterly Newsletter. **Remarks:** Maintained by the city of Modesto.

MC ILHENNY (E.A.) NATURAL HISTORY COLLECTION
See: Louisiana State University - E.A. Mc Ilhenny Natural History Collection

MC INTYRE LIBRARY
See: University of Wisconsin, Eau Claire

MC KAMY (David Knox) MEDICAL LIBRARY
See: Noland (Lloyd) Hospital - David Knox Mc Kamy Medical Library

★7346★
MC KAY DEE HOSPITAL CENTER - EDUCATIONAL MEDIA CENTER (Med)
3939 Harrison Blvd.
Ogden, UT 84409
Phone: (801) 399-4141
Mark Meldrum, Lib.Dir.
Staff: Prof 1; Other 1. **Subjects:** Medicine, hospital administration, nursing. **Holdings:** 2300 books; 2000 bound periodical volumes; Audio-Digest tapes; 6 nursing masters' theses. **Subscriptions:** 230 journals and other serials. **Services:** Interlibrary loans; copying; library open to public. **Computerized Information Services:** MEDLINE. **Networks/Consortia:** Member of Utah Health Sciences Library.

MC KAY (Gordon) LIBRARY
See: Harvard University - Gordon Mc Kay Library

MC KAY MEMORIAL LIBRARY
See: Community Memorial Hospital of Menomonee Falls

★7347★
MC KEAN COUNTY LAW LIBRARY (Law)
Court House
Smethport, PA 16749
Phone: (814) 887-5571
Phyllis P. Anderson, Libn.
Staff: 1. **Subjects:** Law. **Holdings:** 10,000 volumes. **Services:** Library open to public.

★7348★
MC KEE (Davy) CORPORATION - INFORMATION RESOURCE CENTER (Sci-Tech)
6200 Oak Tree Blvd.
Cleveland, OH 44131
Phone: (216) 524-9300
Ruth W. Parratt, Libn.
Staff: Prof 1; Other 1. **Subjects:** Petrochemicals, ferrous metals, management, corporation law. **Holdings:** 16,000 books; 90 bound periodical volumes; vendors' catalogs on microfilm; Bureau of Mines publications on microfiche; industry standards; clippings. **Subscriptions:** 1000 journals and other serials; 25 newspapers. **Services:** Interlibrary loans; library open to public by appointment. **Computerized Information Services:** Online systems.

MC KEE LIBRARY
See: Southern Missionary College

★7349★
MC KEESPORT HOSPITAL - HEALTH SERVICES LIBRARY (Med)
1500 Fifth Ave.
McKeesport, PA 15132
Phone: (412) 664-2363
Kate Kearney, Dir.
Staff: Prof 1; Other 2. **Subjects:** Medicine, lab sciences, nursing. **Holdings:** 4800 books; 4700 bound periodical volumes; 8 series of Audio-Digest tapes; 8 VF drawers of pamphlets. **Subscriptions:** 260 journals and other serials. **Services:** Interlibrary loans; copying; SDI; library open to public with restrictions. **Computerized Information Services:** NLM. **Networks/Consortia:** Member of Southeast Pittsburgh Consortium. **Publications:** Booklist, bimonthly. **Remarks:** Includes partial holdings of McKeesport Hospital School of Nursing Library and Learning Resources Center.

MC KELDIN LIBRARY
See: University of Maryland, College Park

★7350★
MC KENNAN HOSPITAL - MEDICAL LIBRARY (Med)
800 E. 21st St.
Sioux Falls, SD 57101
Phone: (605) 339-8088
Frances Ellis Rice, Med.Libn.
Staff: Prof 1. **Subjects:** Medicine, nursing, allied health sciences. **Special Collections:** Clinical Pastoral Education Collection (200 items). **Holdings:** 3000 books; 750 bound periodical volumes; 200 microforms; 2 VF drawers. **Subscriptions:** 180 journals and other serials. **Services:** Interlibrary loans; copying; LATCH; library open to public for reference use only. **Computerized Information Services:** MEDLINE. **Networks/Consortia:** Member of Midcontinental Regional Medical Library Program. **Publications:** The Resource, quarterly - hospital-wide.

MAC KENZIE ENVIRONMENTAL EDUCATION CENTER
See: Wisconsin State Department of Natural Resources

MC KENZIE MEMORIAL LIBRARY
See: Rowan Memorial Hospital

MC KENZIE (R. Tait) RESEARCH LIBRARY
See: Mississippi Valley Conservation Authority - R. Tait Mc Kenzie Research Library

★7351★
MAC KENZIE, SMITH, LEWIS, MICHELL & HUGHES - LAW LIBRARY (Law)
600 Onondaga Savings Bank Bldg.
Syracuse, NY 13202
Phone: (315) 474-7571
Cynthia J. Kesler, Libn.
Staff: Prof 1. **Subjects:** Law - tax, labor, corporation, real estate, medical. **Holdings:** 9000 books; 50 cassettes (cataloged); 800 law briefs; 300 memoranda of law. **Subscriptions:** 29 journals and other serials. **Services:** Interlibrary loans; library open to public with restrictions. **Computerized Information Services:** WESTLAW, DIALOG.

MC KEON MEMORIAL LIBRARY
See: St. Patrick's Seminary

MC KIBBIN (H.B.) HEALTH SCIENCE LIBRARY
See: Wesley Medical Center - H.B. Mc Kibbin Health Science Library

★7352★
MC KIM ADVERTISING, LTD. - RESEARCH SERVICES LIBRARY (Bus-Fin)
Commerce Court East
P.O. Box 99
Toronto, ON, Canada M5L 1E1
Phone: (416) 863-5471
Patricia L. Petruga, Libn.
Founded: 1961. **Staff:** Prof 1. **Subjects:** Marketing, marketing research, advertising. **Holdings:** 300 books; Statistics Canada and census publications. **Subscriptions:** 30 journals and other serials. **Services:** Copying; library open to students only. **Computerized Information Services:** DIALOG, Info Globe.

MC KINLEY (Lloyd) MEMORIAL CHEMISTRY LIBRARY
See: Wichita State University - Department of Chemistry - Lloyd Mc Kinley Memorial Chemistry Library

★7353★
MC KINLEY MUSEUM OF HISTORY, SCIENCE AND EDUCATION - RALPH K. RAMSAYER, M.D. LIBRARY (Hist)
749 Hazlett Ave., N.W.
Box 483
Canton, OH 44701
Phone: (216) 455-7043
Eva Sparrowgrove
Subjects: State and local history, Civil War. **Special Collections:** McKinleyana collection (9 VF drawers); letters and reports of Captain W.F. Raynolds; Civil War letters; Stark County Clipping files (19 VF drawers). **Holdings:** 3000 books; 300 bound periodical volumes; 30 VF drawers of photographs, maps and papers; 255 boxes of pamphlets and articles; cemetery records; roster of Ohio soldiers, sailors and marines. **Services:** Copying; library open to public for research. **Remarks:** Contains the holdings of the Stark County Historical Society Library.

★7354★
MC KINNEY JOB CORPS - LIBRARY (Educ)
1501 N. Church St.
Box 750
McKinney, TX 75069
Phone: (214) 542-2623
Lois Stewart, Libn.
Founded: 1964. **Staff:** Prof 1; Other 1. **Subjects:** Negro history, special education, self-improvement, psychology, careers, guidance and counseling. **Holdings:** 10,500 books; 390 phonograph records. **Subscriptions:** 19 journals and other serials. **Services:** Library not open to public.

MC KINNEY LIBRARY
See: Albany Institute of History and Art

MC KINNEY (Richard W.) LIBRARY
See: University of Texas, Austin - Engineering Library

★7355★
MC KINNON, ALLEN & ASSOCIATES (Western), LTD. - RESEARCH LIBRARY (Agri)
1115 46th Ave., S.E.
Calgary, AB, Canada T2G 2A5
Phone: (403) 243-4345
Janice Lore, Res.Assoc.
Founded: 1960. **Staff:** 1. **Subjects:** Agricultural economics, animal science, field crops, soils, diseases and pests, horticulture, agricultural engineering, forestry, rural land appraisal. **Special Collections:** Effects of airborne pollutants on crops and animals; agricultural extension education. **Holdings:** 500 books and bound periodical volumes; 4500 annual reports, maps, clippings, government releases. **Subscriptions:** 48 journals and other serials. **Services:** Interlibrary loans; copying; library not open to public.

★7356★
MC KINNON (I.N.) MEMORIAL LIBRARY (Sci-Tech)
3512 33rd St., N.W.
Calgary, AB, Canada T2L 2A6
Phone: (403) 282-1211
L. Nugent, Libn.
Staff: Prof 1; Other 1. **Subjects:** Petroleum engineering, energy economics. **Holdings:** 3500 books. **Subscriptions:** 54 journals and other serials. **Services:** Interlibrary loans; copying; SDI; library open to public. **Computerized Information Services:** DIALOG, SDC, CAN/OLE, QL Systems, Info Globe, SPIRES; computerized cataloging. **Publications:** New Book List, monthly - free upon request. **Remarks:** The library is maintained jointly by the Canadian Energy Research Institute, the Computer Modelling Group and the Petroleum Recovery Institute.

★7357★
MC KINSEY & COMPANY, INC. - INFORMATION CENTER (Bus-Fin)
611 W. Sixth St.
Los Angeles, CA 90017
Phone: (213) 624-1414
Doreen A. Welborn, Mgr., Info.Serv.
Staff: Prof 2. **Subjects:** Management, finance. **Holdings:** 1500 books; 50 bound periodical volumes; 1500 pamphlets (cataloged); 2000 corporate files. **Subscriptions:** 175 journals and other serials; 15 newspapers. **Services:** Center not open to public. **Computerized Information Services:** Online

systems. **Staff:** Beverly Wong, Info.Spec.

★7358★
MC KINSEY & COMPANY, INC. - INFORMATION SERVICES (Bus-Fin)
55 E. 52nd St.   Phone: (212) 909-8400
New York, NY 10022   Ellen Shedlarz, Mgr.
Staff: Prof 12; Other 6. **Subjects:** Business, finance. **Holdings:** 6000 books.
Subscriptions: 300 journals and other serials; 25 newspapers. **Services:**
Interlibrary loans; library not open to public. **Computerized Information
Services:** DIALOG, NEXIS, New York Times Information Service, Standard &
Poor's Corporation, Computer Directions Advisors, Inc., Finsbury Data
Services Ltd., Dow Jones News Retrieval. **Staff:** Valerie Knupp, Supv.,
Info.Serv.

★7359★
MC KINSEY & COMPANY, INC. - LIBRARY (Energy; Bus-Fin)
555 California St., Suite 4800   Phone: (415) 981-0250
San Francisco, CA 94104   Linda L. Kraemer, Mgr., Info.Serv.
Staff: Prof 2; Other 2. **Subjects:** Forest products, energy, management
consulting. **Holdings:** Figures not available. **Subscriptions:** 225 journals and
other serials. **Services:** Interlibrary loans; copying; library not open to public.
Computerized Information Services: DIALOG, SDC, Dow Jones News
Retrieval, New York Times Information Service. **Staff:** Marsha Wyler,
Ref.Spec.

★7360★
MC KINSEY & COMPANY, INC. - LIBRARY (Bus-Fin)
1700 Pennsylvania Ave., N.W.   Phone: (202) 393-6820
Washington, DC 20006   Ann Robertson, Mgr., Info. & Anl.Serv.
Staff: Prof 4; Other 1. **Subjects:** Business management, energy, industries,
government. **Holdings:** In-house reports; clippings; corporate files; subject
files. **Subscriptions:** 100 journals and other serials; 4 newspapers. **Services:**
Interlibrary loans; copying; SDI; library not open to public. **Computerized
Information Services:** Online systems. **Staff:** Adrienne Eng, Info.Anl.;
Frances Gotkowitz, Info.Spec.; Terry Ann Toch, Energy Info.Anl.

★7361★
MC KINSEY & COMPANY, INC. - LIBRARY (Bus-Fin)†
Two First National Plaza   Phone: (312) 368-0600
Chicago, IL 60603   L. Smith, Mgr., Info.Serv.
Subjects: Management. **Holdings:** Figures not available.

★7362★
MC KINSEY & COMPANY, INC. - RESEARCH LIBRARY (Bus-Fin)
80 Bloor St., W.   Phone: (416) 922-2200
Toronto, ON, Canada M5S 2V1   Lorraine Mazzocato, Lib.Asst.
Staff: Prof 2. **Subjects:** Banking, insurance, food industry, management,
health care. **Holdings:** 2000 books; 2000 in-house documents; 600 annual
reports; 200 subject files; 8000 microfiche; 1100 Statistics Canada.
Subscriptions: 54 journals and other serials; 6 newspapers. **Services:**
Interlibrary loans; copying; library open to public with restrictions. **Staff:**
Catherine Myers, Lib.Asst.

MAC KOWN LIBRARY
See: New Hampshire Hospital

MC KUSICK LAW LIBRARY
See: University of South Dakota

★7363★
MC LAREN GENERAL HOSPITAL - MEDICAL LIBRARY (Med)
401 Ballenger Hwy.   Phone: (313) 762-2141
Flint, MI 48502   Lea Ann McGaugh, Med.Libn.
Staff: 3. **Subjects:** Medicine, nursing, allied health sciences. **Holdings:** 1200
books; 2700 bound periodical volumes. **Subscriptions:** 260 journals and
other serials. **Services:** Interlibrary loans; copying; library open to public for
reference use only. **Computerized Information Services:** MEDLARS,
DIALOG.

MC LAUGHLIN LIBRARY
See: Seton Hall University

MC LAUGHLIN LIBRARY
See: University of Guelph

★7364★
MC LAWS & COMPANY - LIBRARY (Law)
407 8th Ave., S.W.   Phone: (403) 264-0580
Calgary, AB, Canada T2P 1E6   Susan L. Ross, Libn.
Staff: Prof 1. **Subjects:** Law. **Holdings:** Figures not available. **Services:**
Interlibrary loans; copying; library open to public with restrictions.
Computerized Information Services: Computerized cataloging.

★7365★
**MC LEAN COUNTY BAR ASSOCIATION - ILLINOIS SUPREME COURT -
LIBRARY** (Law)
300 Peoples Bank Bldg.   Phone: (309) 827-8009
Bloomington, IL 61701   Loretta I. Talley
Staff: 1. **Subjects:** Law. **Holdings:** 6000 volumes. **Subscriptions:** 20
journals and other serials. **Services:** Copying; library open to public for
reference use only.

★7366★
MC LEAN COUNTY HISTORICAL SOCIETY - MUSEUM AND LIBRARY (Hist)
201 E. Grove St.   Phone: (309) 827-0428
Bloomington, IL 61701   Barbara Dunbar, Dir.
Founded: 1892. **Staff:** 3. **Subjects:** McLean County, Central Illinois and
Illinois history, Civil War. **Holdings:** 3000 books; 200 historical journals
(cataloged); 197 bound newspaper volumes (cataloged); papers of locally and
militarily important people; 200 linear feet of archives. **Subscriptions:** 6
journals and other serials. **Services:** Copying; library open to public for
reference use only. **Publications:** Transactions, irregular. **Special Indexes:**
Daily Pantagraph indexed, 1854-1940; index to archives (card).

★7367★
MC LEAN HOSPITAL - MEDICAL LIBRARY (Med)†
115 Mill   Phone: (617) 855-2000
Belmont, MA 02178   Hector Bossange, Dir.
Founded: 1811. **Staff:** Prof 2; Other 2. **Subjects:** Mental health, behavioral
sciences, alcoholism, drug abuse, geriatrics, psychiatry, psychoanalysis,
psychology, sociology, psychosomatics, neurology, psychopharmacology,
psychotherapy, schizophrenia, psychobiology, child and adolescent psychiatry;
forensic psychiatry. **Holdings:** 13,200 books; 12,800 bound periodical
volumes. **Subscriptions:** 294 journals and other serials. **Services:** Interlibrary
loans; copying; reference; library open to qualified persons.

MC LEAN LIBRARY
See: Chicago Institute for Psychoanalysis

MAC LEISH (Archibald) COLLECTION
See: Greenfield Community College Foundation - Archibald Mac Leish
Collection

★7368★
MC LENNAN COUNTY LAW LIBRARY (Law)
Box 1606   Phone: (817) 753-7341
Waco, TX 76703   Mary Padgett
Founded: 1928. **Subjects:** Law. **Holdings:** 11,000 volumes. **Services:**
Copying; library open to public for reference use only. **Remarks:** This library
also serves the state's 10th Judicial District of the Court of Civil Appeals.

MC LEOD REGIONAL MEDICAL CENTER
See: Pee Dee Area Health Education Center Library

★7369★
MC LEOD YOUNG WEIR LIMITED - INFORMATION CENTRE (Bus-Fin)†
Commercial Union Tower
Toronto-Dominion Centre, Box 433   Phone: (416) 863-7737
Toronto, ON, Canada M5K 1M2   Marie Gadula, Libn.
Founded: 1979. **Staff:** Prof 1; Other 3. **Subjects:** Investments, finance,
security analysis, economics. **Special Collections:** Toronto Stock Exchange
Monthly Review (1960 to present); Toronto Stock Exchange Daily Record
(1973 to present); Ontario Securities Commission Bulletin (1967 to present);
Financial Post Surveys; Ontario Securities Commission Filings (microfiche);
Toronto Stock Exchange 10 year Company Performance Summaries.
Holdings: 1000 books; 150 bound periodical volumes; 20,000 microfiche;
130 Statistics Canada titles; 211 VF drawers. **Subscriptions:** 220 journals
and other serials; 6 newspapers. **Services:** Interlibrary loans; copying; library
open to librarians and clients by appointment. **Computerized Information
Services:** Online systems. **Publications:** Information Centre Periodical
Holdings, annual.

MC LOUTH MEMORIAL HEALTH SCIENCE LIBRARY
See: Oakwood Hospital

MC LURE EDUCATION LIBRARY
See: University of Alabama

MAC MANUS COLLECTION
See: Seton Hall University

MC MASTER DIVINITY COLLEGE - CANADIAN BAPTIST ARCHIVES
See: Baptist Convention of Ontario and Quebec

★7370★
MC MASTER UNIVERSITY - ARCHIVES AND RESEARCH COLLECTIONS DIVISION (Rare Book; Hist)
Mills Memorial Library
Hamilton, ON, Canada L8S 4L6
Phone: (416) 525-9140
Mr. G.R. Hill, Chf.Libn.
Staff: Prof 4; Other 8. **Subjects:** Eighteenth-century British literature and history, Canadian social history, Canadian literature, 20th century British pacifism, Bertrand Russell, McMaster University archives. **Special Collections:** Archival collections of Bertrand Russell, Pierre Berton, Farley Mowat, Austin Clarke, Thomas Carlyle, Vera Brittain, George Catlin, J.W. Bengough, Matt Cohen, Margaret Laurence, Canadian Union of Students, Peter Newman, Susan Musgrave, Mulberry papers, Charles Kingsley, John Connell, Copeau-Obey correspondence, John Coulter, General Steel Wares Archive; Hamilton and District Labour Council; U.S.W.A. Local 1005; U.S.W.A. District 6; McClelland and Stewart Ltd. and Macmillan of Canada publishing archives; book collections of Jonathan Swift, Daniel Defoe and Samuel Beckett. **Holdings:** 50,000 books and bound periodical volumes; 5000 feet of archives and manuscripts; 1000 maps; 5000 pamphlets (Canadiana); 700 tapes. **Subscriptions:** 50 journals and other serials; 9 newspapers. **Services:** Interlibrary loans; copying (both limited); answers correspondence requests for bibliographical information; library open to public with restrictions on archives. **Publications:** McMaster University Library Research News, 2/year; Russell: The Journal of the Bertrand Russell Archives, 2/year. **Remarks:** Library sponsors lectures, exhibits, tours and contributes to some loan exhibitions. **Staff:** Charlotte Stewart, Dir., Res.Coll.

★7371★
MC MASTER UNIVERSITY - BUSINESS LIBRARY (Bus-Fin)
Innis Room, Mills Memorial Library
Hamilton, ON, Canada L8S 4L6
Phone: (416) 525-9140
Sheila Pepper, Bus.Libn.
Staff: Prof 1; Other 6. **Subjects:** Business administration. **Special Collections:** Economics Working Papers; American Enterprise Institute publications; company and industry files; labour union materials (6 drawers). **Holdings:** 9000 books; 1000 documents; 15 drawers of company, industry and subject files. **Subscriptions:** 431 journals and other serials. **Services:** Interlibrary loans (through main library); copying; library open to public for reference use only. **Computerized Information Services:** Online systems; computerized cataloging, serials and circulation. **Publications:** Accession list, monthly; bibliographies, irregular.

★7372★
MC MASTER UNIVERSITY - HEALTH SCIENCES LIBRARY (Med)
1400 Main St., W.
Hamilton, ON, Canada L8N 3Z5
Phone: (416) 525-9140
Elizabeth Uleryk, Act.Libn.
Staff: Prof 6; Other 21. **Subjects:** Basic medical sciences, clinical medicine, nursing. **Holdings:** 36,800 books; 45,625 bound periodical volumes; 4329 slide-tape programs (cataloged); 207 16mm films; 477 video cassettes; 818 audio cassettes; 425 pathological specimens. **Subscriptions:** 1325 journals and other serials. **Services:** Interlibrary loans; copying; library open to public for reference use only. **Computerized Information Services:** LEXIS, NLM, Institute for Scientific Information. **Networks/Consortia:** Member of Hamilton/Wentworth District Health Library Network. **Special Catalogs:** Learning Resources, a printed catalog of nonprint material, periodically revised. **Staff:** Joanne Marshall, Pub.Serv.Libn.; Sharon Branton, Hd. of Cat.; Linda Panton, Hosp.Lib.Coord.; Mary Anne Trainor, Ser. & Acq.Libn.

★7373★
MC MASTER UNIVERSITY - MAP LIBRARY (Geog-Map)
Burke Science Bldg.
Hamilton, ON, Canada L8S 4K1
Phone: (416) 525-9140
Kate Donkin, Map Cur.
Founded: 1947. **Staff:** Prof 1; Other 1. **Subjects:** Geography, geology, history. **Special Collections:** Wentworth County History; World Settlements; Canadian history; rare maps; survey notes of Upper Canada to 1850. **Holdings:** 307 books; 1411 atlases; 189 serial volumes; 424 government documents; 93,373 maps; 172 reels of microfilm; 41,810 aerial photographs; 17,420 satellite images. **Services:** Interlibrary loans; copying; library open to public with restrictions. **Computerized Information Services:**

Computerized cataloging. **Networks/Consortia:** Member of Association des Cartotheques Canadiennes. **Special Catalogs:** Chronological and area catalogs of World Settlements and rare maps collections.

★7374★
MC MASTER UNIVERSITY - THODE LIBRARY OF SCIENCE & ENGINEERING (Sci-Tech)
Hamilton, ON, Canada L8S 4P5
Phone: (416) 525-9140
Harold Siroonian, Sci. & Engr.Libn.
Staff: Prof 3; Other 13. **Subjects:** General science, mathematics, physics, chemistry, geology, biology, engineering. **Holdings:** 78,470 books; 78,635 bound periodical volumes; 36,924 hardcopy technical reports; 26,463 hard copy government documents; 296,194 microforms of technical reports, documents and journals; 8630 AV items. **Subscriptions:** 2821 journals and other serials. **Services:** Interlibrary loans; library open to public for reference use only. **Computerized Information Services:** CAN/SDI, CAN/OLE, DIALOG, QL Systems; computerized circulation. **Staff:** Elaine Tooke, Ref.Libn.; Peggy Findlay, Info.Serv.Libn.

★7375★
MC MASTER UNIVERSITY - URBAN DOCUMENTATION CENTRE (Soc Sci; Plan)
1200 Main St. West
Hamilton, ON, Canada L8S 4K1
Phone: (416) 525-9140
Cathy Moulder, Documentalist
Founded: 1968. **Staff:** Prof 1. **Subjects:** Urban affairs, regional development and planning, environmental issues, urban transportation, economics and social problems, urban research and methodology. **Special Collections:** University Collection (working and discussion papers, reports, reprints and bibliographies from universities in Canada, U.S. and Europe; 8000 items). **Holdings:** 200 books; 18,000 documents (10,000 cataloged); 250 subject files of newspaper clippings. **Subscriptions:** 125 journals and other serials. **Services:** Interlibrary loans; centre open to public. **Publications:** Some Recent Acquisitions of the Urban Documentation Centre, bimonthly; UDC newsletter, quarterly. **Special Indexes:** Periodicals index (card and paper).

★7376★
MC MILLAN, BINCH - LIBRARY (Law)
Royal Bank Plaza
P.O. Box 38
Toronto, ON, Canada M5J 2J7
Phone: (416) 865-7031
Staff: 2. **Subjects:** Law, legislation, taxation. **Holdings:** 8000 books. **Subscriptions:** 84 journals and other serials. **Services:** Interlibrary loans; copying; library open to public with permission of librarian. **Publications:** What's Up, weekly - for internal distribution only.

★7377★
MAC MILLAN BLOEDEL RESEARCH LIMITED - LIBRARY (Sci-Tech)
3350 E. Broadway
Vancouver, BC, Canada V5M 4E6
Phone: (604) 254-5151
Diana Wilimovsky, Supv., Info.Serv.
Founded: 1966. **Staff:** Prof 1; Other 1. **Subjects:** Pulp and paper technology, wood and wood products, building materials, forest chemicals. **Holdings:** 7000 books; 1500 bound periodical volumes; 5 VF drawers of patents; 3 VF drawers of translations; 400 pamphlet boxes of government and professional publications; 325 reels of microfilm. **Subscriptions:** 400 journals and other serials; 10 newspapers. **Services:** Interlibrary loans; copying; library open to public for reference use only by request. **Computerized Information Services:** DIALOG, SDC; internal database; computerized serials.

MAC MILLAN FORESTRY/AGRICULTURE LIBRARY
See: University of British Columbia

MC MILLAN (Ida J.) LIBRARY
See: Baptist Bible Institute - Ida J. Mc Millan Library

MAC MILLAN LIBRARY
See: Ellis Hospital

MC MILLAN LIBRARY
See: New York City Human Resources Administration

MC MILLEN LIBRARY
See: Indiana Institute of Technology

★7378★
MC NAMEE, PORTER & SEELEY - MPS ENGINEERING LIBRARY (Sci-Tech)
3131 S. State St.
Ann Arbor, MI 48104
Phone: (313) 665-6000
Elizabeth G. Brennan, Libn.
Founded: 1980. **Staff:** Prof 1. **Subjects:** Wastewater treatment, potable water, water pollution, highway and bridge construction, hydraulics and

hydrology, environmental engineering, architecture, drainage. **Holdings:** 1312 books; 170 bound periodical volumes; 380 Environmental Protection Agency reports; 357 U.S. Geological Survey Water Supply papers. **Subscriptions:** 129 journals and other serials. **Services:** Interlibrary loans; library open to public with restrictions. **Publications:** Accessions list, bimonthly - for internal distribution only.

★7379★
MC NAY (Marion Koogler) ART INSTITUTE - LIBRARY (Art)
Box 6069   Phone: (512) 824-5368
San Antonio, TX 77509   Mrs. John P. Leeper, Libn.
Staff: Prof 1; Other 14. **Subjects:** Art - European and American (late 19th to 20th centuries), Japanese (18th to 20th centuries). **Special Collections:** Books related to Japanese wood-block prints (400 books); actual-size reproductions of Japanese wood-block prints (500). **Holdings:** 11,000 books; 26 bound periodical volumes; 14,500 museum bulletins, pamphlets, and art dealers and auction catalogs (cataloged); 10,000 entries in biographical file of artists, mostly contemporary (cataloged). **Subscriptions:** 24 journals and other serials; 5 newspapers. **Services:** Interlibrary loans only under special circumstances; copying; library open to public. **Remarks:** Library is located at 6000 N. New Braunfels Ave., San Antonio, TX 78209.

★7380★
MAC NEAL MEMORIAL HOSPITAL - HEALTH SCIENCES RESOURCE CENTER
  (Med)
3249 S. Oak Park Ave.   Phone: (312) 797-3089
Berwyn, IL 60402   Rya Ben-Shir, Mgr.
Founded: 1982. **Staff:** Prof 1; Other 1. **Subjects:** Medicine and nursing. **Holdings:** 2562 books; 1827 bound periodical volumes; cassette tapes. **Subscriptions:** 150 journals and other serials. **Services:** Interlibrary loans; copying; bibliographies prepared; center not open to public. **Computerized Information Services:** BRS. **Networks/Consortia:** Member of Metropolitan Consortium; Suburban Library System; Regional Medical Library - Region 3. **Formerly:** Its Frank C. Becht Memorial Library.

★7381★
MC NEES, WALLACE AND NURICK - LIBRARY (Law)
100 Pine St.
Box 1166   Phone: (717) 232-8000
Harrisburg, PA 17108   Mary E. Rinesmith, Libn.
Staff: Prof 1. **Subjects:** Law. **Holdings:** 8500 books. **Services:** Library not open to public.

★7382★
MC NEIL LABORATORIES (Canada) LIMITED - LIBRARY (Med)
600 Main St., W.   Phone: (416) 640-6900
Stouffville, ON, Canada L0H 1L0   Karen Connell, Libn.
Staff: Prof 1; Other 1. **Subjects:** Medicine, pharmaceuticals, marketing, business, chemistry. **Holdings:** 600 books; 15 VF drawers of documents. **Subscriptions:** 302 journals and other serials. **Services:** Interlibrary loans; copying; SDI; library not open to public. **Computerized Information Services:** DIALOG, MEDLARS.

★7383★
MC NEIL LABORATORIES - LIBRARY (Med)
Camp Hill Rd.
Fort Washington, PA 19034   M.E. Rountree, Hd.Libn.
Founded: 1879. **Staff:** Prof 3; Other 6. **Subjects:** Chemistry, pharmacology, biochemistry, clinical medicine, toxicology, technology. **Holdings:** 3000 books; 12,000 bound periodical volumes. **Subscriptions:** 550 journals and other serials. **Services:** Interlibrary loans; SDI; library open to public by appointment only. **Computerized Information Services:** DIALOG, SDC, NLM, BRS; computerized circulation and serials. **Networks/Consortia:** Member of Delaware Valley Information Consotium. **Staff:** R. Fullam, Asst.Libn.

★7384★
MC PHERSON COLLEGE - MILLER LIBRARY (Hist; Rel-Theol)†
1600 E. Euclid   Phone: (316) 241-0731
McPherson, KS 67460   Rowena Olsen, Libn.
Staff: Prof 3; Other 1. **Subjects:** Church of the Brethren, McPherson College, local history. **Holdings:** 800 books; 280 bound periodical volumes; 5 filing cabinets of historical and governmental records; 4500 slides; 12 cassette tapes. **Services:** Interlibrary loans; copying; library open to public. **Computerized Information Services:** Computerized cataloging. **Networks/Consortia:** Member of Associated Colleges of Central Kansas (ACCK); South Central Kansas Library System. **Staff:** Joan Johnson, Asst.Libn.; Herb Johnson, Dir., Media Ctr.

MC PHERSON LIBRARY
See: University of Victoria

★7385★
MACALESTER COLLEGE - OLIN SCIENCE LIBRARY (Sci-Tech)
1600 Grand Ave.   Phone: (612) 696-6344
St. Paul, MN 55105   Rosemary Salscheider, Supv.
Staff: 1. **Subjects:** Astronomy, mathematics, physics, chemistry. **Holdings:** 8300 books; 4140 bound periodical volumes. **Subscriptions:** 80 journals and other serials. **Services:** Interlibrary loans; library open to public for reference use only.

★7386★
MACALESTER COLLEGE - WEYERHAEUSER LIBRARY (Hum)
Grand & Macalester Sts.   Phone: (612) 696-6345
St. Paul, MN 55105   Jean K. Archibald, Dir.
Staff: Prof 6; Other 6. **Subjects:** Economics and finance, English literature, North American history and geography, European history and geography, American literature. **Special Collections:** Edward D. Neill Collection of Americana; Sinclair Lewis; Arthur Billings Hunt Collection of American Hymnology; Stella Louise Wood Collection of Juvenile Literature; Mosher Imprints (325 imprints); Curriculum Laboratory; Rare Book Collection; Great Books; Macalester Archives. **Holdings:** 240,322 books; 33,847 bound periodical volumes; 3250 government documents; 7245 microforms; pamphlets file; 6677 phonograph records and tapes. **Subscriptions:** 1085 journals and other serials; 56 newspapers. **Services:** Interlibrary loans; copying; literature searches; library open to public for reference use only. **Computerized Information Services:** DIALOG; computerized cataloging and acquisitions. **Networks/Consortia:** Member of OCLC; Cooperating Libraries in Consortium (CLIC). **Special Catalogs:** Catalogs to Neill Collection, Hunt Collection, Curriculum Laboratory, government documents, and Macalester Archives. **Staff:** Karen S. Oakes, Hd., Circ.; Peggy Feldick, Ref. & ILL; Bruce C. Willms, Hd., Tech.Serv.; Mary Lou Steiner, Cat.; Bob Di Giusto, Cat.

MACDONALD SCIENCE LIBRARY
See: Dalhousie University

★7387★
MACEDONIAN ETHNIC LIBRARY (Area-Ethnic)
920 Shoreham Rd.   Phone: (313) 886-3361
Grosse Pointe Woods, MI 48236   Adrijana Panoska Randolph, Dir./Libn.
Founded: 1975. **Staff:** Prof 1. **Subjects:** Macedonia - language and literature, politics and government; Yugoslavian statistics; Yugoslavian art; Serbo-Croation language. **Special Collections:** Complete collection of books in all subjects studied in Macedonia from 1st to 4th grades elementary; books on the system of education in Macedonia. **Holdings:** 1000 books; Macedonian songs; Macedonian and Yugoslavian tapes and records; maps, clippings and pictures. **Services:** Interlibrary loans; library open to public by appointment. **Publications:** Macedonian Word, monthly - by subscription. **Remarks:** The Macedonian Ethnic Library is a nonprofit organization formed for the purpose of collecting, preserving and disseminating the Macedonian culture.

MACHINABILITY DATA CENTER
See: Metcut Research Associates, Inc.

MACK (Alexander) MEMORIAL LIBRARY
See: Bridgewater College - Alexander Mack Memorial Library

MACK MEMORIAL HEALTH SCIENCES LIBRARY
See: Salem Hospital

★7388★
MACK TRUCKS, INC. - TECHNICAL INFORMATION CENTER - ENGINEERING
  DIVISION LIBRARY (Sci-Tech)
1999 Pennsylvania Ave.   Phone: (301) 733-8308
Hagerstown, MD 21740   E.E. Stout, Engr.Adm.Coord.
Founded: 1959. **Staff:** Prof 1; Other 1. **Subjects:** Automotive engineering, metallurgy, chemistry, diesel engines. **Holdings:** 4500 books; 100 bound periodical volumes; 5800 internal engineering reports. **Subscriptions:** 75 journals and other serials. **Services:** Interlibrary loans; copying; library open to public with prior approval. **Computerized Information Services:** SDC. **Publications:** Library Bulletin, bimonthly - for internal distribution only.

MACKAY SCHOOL OF MINES LIBRARY
See: University of Nevada, Reno

★7389★
MACKAY - SHIELDS FINANCIAL CORPORATION - RESEARCH LIBRARY
(Bus-Fin)
551 Fifth Ave.   Phone: (212) 986-1100
New York, NY 10017   Hertha Ketcham, Libn.
Staff: 2. **Subjects:** Finance. **Holdings:** 40 books; 185 bound periodical
volumes. **Subscriptions:** 60 journals and other serials. **Services:** Library not
open to public.

★7390★
MACKINAC ISLAND STATE PARK COMMISSION - HISTORICAL RESEARCH
   COLLECTION (Hist)
Box 30028   Phone: (517) 322-1319
Lansing, MI 48909   Keith R. Widder, Cur.
Staff: Prof 1; Other 1. **Subjects:** History and archeology of Mackinac Island
and Fort Michilimackinac. **Holdings:** 2500 books and bound periodical
volumes; 4000 photographs; 100 maps; 50 building plans; 200 reels of
microfilm. **Subscriptions:** 20 journals and other serials. **Services:** Copying;
library open to public by appointment. **Remarks:** Library is open between
October 15 and May 15.

MACLAREN ENGINEERS PLANNERS & SCIENTISTS INC.
See: Fenco Engineers, Inc.

★7391★
MACLEAN-HUNTER, LTD. - LIBRARY (Bus-Fin; Publ)
481 University Ave.   Phone: (416) 596-5244
Toronto, ON, Canada M5W 1A7   Marian Duncan, Lib.Mgr.
Founded: 1938. **Staff:** Prof 2; Other 2. **Subjects:** Canadian business, finance
and investment. **Special Collections:** Maclean-Hunter publications. **Holdings:**
10,000 current Canadian corporation files; government and economic
research studies. **Services:** Library not open to public.

MACLEAN (James) TECHNICAL LIBRARY
See: Burns and Roe, Inc. - James Maclean Technical Library

MACMILLAN OF CANADA PUBLISHING ARCHIVES
See: Mc Master University - Archives and Research Collections Division

MACODRUM LIBRARY
See: Carleton University

★7392★
MACOMB INTERMEDIATE SCHOOL DISTRICT - BEAL LIBRARY (Educ)
44001 Garfield Rd.   Phone: (313) 286-8800
Mt. Clemens, MI 48044   Richard J. Palmer, Libn.
Founded: 1973. **Staff:** Prof 1; Other 7. **Subjects:** Education. **Special
Collections:** ERIC microfiche (1970 to present); curriculum guides on
microfilm (1500). **Holdings:** 37,000 books; 2100 periodicals on microfilm.
Subscriptions: 475 journals and other serials. **Services:** Interlibrary loans;
copying; SDI; library open to public for reference use only. **Computerized
Information Services:** DIALOG; computerized circulation. **Publications:**
Periodical List, annual; Media Messenger, 5/year.

★7393★
MACON COUNTY LAW LIBRARY (Law)
County Bldg.   Phone: (217) 422-7441
Decatur, IL 62523   Norman C. Higgs, Libn.
Subjects: Law. **Holdings:** 6630 volumes.

★7394★
MACON TELEGRAPH AND NEWS - LIBRARY (Publ)
Broadway & Riverside Dr.   Phone: (912) 744-4328
Macon, GA 31208   Harriet Comer, Libn.
Founded: 1935. **Subjects:** Newspaper material. **Special Collections:** Macon
Telegraph Civil War editions, 1861-1865. **Holdings:** 200 books; clippings;
photographs; newspapers on microfilm (921 reels). **Services:** Library not open
to public. **Special Catalogs:** Macon history card catalog.

★7395★
MACRAE, MONTGOMERY & CUNNINGHAM - LIBRARY
555 Burrard St., No. 1585
Vancouver, BC, Canada V7N 2A5
Defunct

★7396★
MADDEN (John J.) ZONE CENTER - PROFESSIONAL LIBRARY (Med)†
1200 S. 1st Ave.   Phone: (312) 531-5653
Hines, IL 60141   Flora L. Hawthorne, Libn.
Founded: 1965. **Staff:** Prof 1. **Subjects:** Psychiatry, administration, nursing,
medicine, mental health, social work. **Holdings:** 3200 books; 50 bound
periodical volumes; 60 videotapes. **Subscriptions:** 55 journals and other
serials. **Remarks:** Maintained by Illinois State Department of Mental Health &
Developmental Disabilities.

MADER (Clarence V.) ARCHIVE
See: University of California, Los Angeles - Music Library

★7397★
MADERA COUNTY HISTORICAL SOCIETY - MUSEUM/LIBRARY (Hist)
210 W. Yosemite Ave.
Box 478   Phone: (209) 673-0291
Madera, CA 93639   Rintha Robbins, Libn.
Founded: 1974. **Staff:** Prof 1. **Subjects:** Madera County history, California
history, old textbooks and early periodicals. **Special Collections:** Madera
Mercury, bound copies 1913-1925; Madera Tribune, bound copies 1913-
1959. **Holdings:** Figures not available; photographs, diaries, clippings, maps,
charts, documents, scrapbooks. **Services:** Library open to qualified
researchers on a limited basis. **Publications:** Madera County Historian, 2/
year; newsletter, quarterly. **Staff:** Bud Richards, Cur.

MADIGAN ARMY MEDICAL CENTER
See: U.S. Army Hospitals

★7398★
MADISON AREA TECHNICAL COLLEGE - TECHNICAL CENTER LIBRARY
   (Sci-Tech)
2125 Commercial Ave.   Phone: (608) 266-5025
Madison, WI 53704   Janet B. Jeffcott, Tech.Libn.
Founded: 1968. **Staff:** Prof 1; Other 3. **Subjects:** Automotive technology,
wood construction, printing, welding, electronics, surveying, fire science.
Special Collections: Repair manuals (automotive, television and radio).
Holdings: 20,000 books; 1500 reels of microfilm of periodicals; 3000
pamphlets; 500 tapes and cassettes; 1000 films; filmloops; filmstrips; 1000
slide series, transparency series. **Subscriptions:** 265 journals and other
serials. **Services:** Interlibrary loans; copying; library open to public.
Computerized Information Services: DIALOG. **Networks/Consortia:**
Member of Madison Area Library Council (MALC). **Publications:** Annotated
new booklist, weekly; Library Handbook. **Special Catalogs:** Computer
produced catalog (book); energy catalog. **Special Indexes:** KWIC index of
periodical article titles, pamphlets, monographs, numerous keyword indexes
from local online databases.

★7399★
MADISON BUSINESS COLLEGE - LIBRARY (Bus-Fin)
1110 Spring Harbor Dr.   Phone: (608) 238-4266
Madison, WI 53705   Mary T. Boyd, Libn.
Founded: 1958. **Staff:** Prof 1. **Subjects:** Business administration,
accounting, sales and marketing, shorthand, court reporting, secretarial
sciences, government, economics, management. **Holdings:** 7600 books;
clipping file; tapes. **Subscriptions:** 42 journals and other serials. **Services:**
Interlibrary loans; library open to public with restrictions. **Networks/
Consortia:** Member of Madison Area Library Council.

MADISON CHAMBER OF COMMERCE
See: Greater Madison Chamber of Commerce

★7400★
MADISON COMMUNITY HOSPITAL - HEALTH-SCIENCE LIBRARY (Med)
917 N. Washington Ave.   Phone: (605) 256-6551
Madison, SD 57042   Donna Sullivan, Lib.Mgr.
Subjects: Nursing, medicine, paramedicine. **Holdings:** 500 books; 82
unbound periodicals; 100 cassette tapes. **Subscriptions:** 20 journals and
other serials. **Services:** Copying; library open to health professionals only.

★7401★
MADISON COUNTY - ELBERT H. PARSONS PUBLIC LAW LIBRARY (Law)
205 East Side Sq.   Phone: (205) 536-5911
Huntsville, AL 35801   Cleo S. Cason, Libn.
Staff: Prof 1. **Subjects:** Law. **Holdings:** 12,000 books; 1000 bound
periodical volumes. **Subscriptions:** 54 journals and other serials. **Services:**
Copying; library open to public.

★7402★

MADISON COUNTY HISTORICAL SOCIETY, INC. - LIBRARY (Hist)*
101 W. Irvine St.   Phone: (606) 623-1720
Richmond, KY 40475   Mrs. Neal Colyer
Founded: 1933. **Staff:** 1. **Subjects:** Local and state history. **Special Collections:** Papers of the Boonesborough Chapter of the Daughters of the American Revolution (on loan); Fort Boonesborough (1775) Bicentennial Commission papers; Society of Boonesborough papers. **Holdings:** 100 volumes; 10 scrapbooks; 200 newspaper articles; 50 items in Kentucky Bicentennial Series. **Services:** Library open to public by appointment. **Publications:** Kentucky Pioneer, 2/year - distributed to members and for sale.

★7403★

MADISON COUNTY HISTORICAL SOCIETY - LIBRARY (Hist)
435 Main St.
Box 415   Phone: (315) 363-4136
Oneida, NY 13421   John H. Braunlein, Dir.
Staff: 2. **Subjects:** Local history, genealogy, traditional crafts. **Special Collections:** Traditional Craft Archive; Historic Resource File; 19th century business ledgers; local architectural surveys. **Holdings:** 1850 books; 150 bound periodical volumes; 650 pamphlets, brochures, 19th century newspapers, maps, broadsides; 90 tapes; 50 films; 13 VF drawers of slides. **Services:** Copying; library open to public for reference use only. **Special Catalogs:** Guide to Holdings MCHS Library, 1977; Guide to Holdings of the Traditional Craft Archive, 1979; Historic Resource File; Vital Statistics File.

★7404★

MADISON COUNTY HISTORICAL SOCIETY - MUSEUM LIBRARY (Hist)
715 N. Main St.   Phone: (618) 656-7562
Edwardsville, IL 62025   Anna Symanski, Supt.
Founded: 1924. **Staff:** Prof 1; Other 3. **Subjects:** Illinois and Madison County history. **Holdings:** 1146 books; 675 manuscripts, documents, diaries, secretarial books, county papers; 28 reels of microfilm of special editions of Madison County newspapers; county cemetery inventories. **Subscriptions:** 5 newspapers. **Services:** Copying; library open to public for reference use only. **Publications:** Newsletter, quarterly - area distribution. **Special Indexes:** Two county newpapers and cemetery surname index; indexes to manuscripts, clippings, schools, historic houses and pictures (card); History of St. Clair County, Illinois; History of Madison County, Illinois, published in 1882 (book); Gazetteer of Madison County, Illinois (1866). **Staff:** Katharine Moorhead, Libn.; Cynthia Hill Longwisch, Asst.Libn.

★7405★

MADISON COUNTY LAW LIBRARY (Law)
Court House
Wampsville, NY 13163
Subjects: Law. **Holdings:** 10,000 volumes. **Services:** Library open to public for reference use only.

★7406★

MADISON COUNTY LAW LIBRARY (Law)
Court House   Phone: (614) 852-9515
London, OH 43140   Diane H. Pickens, Libn.
Staff: Prof 1. **Subjects:** Law. **Holdings:** 10,000 volumes of Federal and Ohio State law statutes, treatises and texts; 50 bound periodical volumes; 2300 volumes on microfilm. **Services:** Copying; library not open to public. **Networks/Consortia:** Member of Ohio Regional Association of Law Libraries.

★7407★

MADISON GENERAL HOSPITAL - MEDICAL LIBRARY (Med)
202 South Park St.   Phone: (608) 267-6234
Madison, WI 53715   Dona Bowman, Med.Libn.
Staff: Prof 2. **Subjects:** Medicine. **Holdings:** 1772 books; 1878 bound periodical volumes; 162 Audio-Digest tapes. **Subscriptions:** 133 journals and other serials. **Services:** Interlibrary loans; copying; library open to public. **Computerized Information Services:** MEDLINE. **Networks/Consortia:** Member of South Central Wisconsin Health Planning Area Cooperative. **Publications:** Library Guide. **Staff:** Glen Salter, Med.Libn.

MADISON GENERAL HOSPITAL - NURSING EDUCATION - MAUDE WEBSTER MIDDLETON LIBRARY
See: Edgewood College - Maude Webster Middleton Nursing Library

★7408★

MADISON HISTORICAL SOCIETY, INC. - LIBRARY (Hist)
853 Boston Post Rd.
Box 17   Phone: (203) 245-4567
Madison, CT 06443   William T. Mills, Pres.
Founded: 1920. **Staff:** Prof 1. **Subjects:** Local history, genealogy, religion, arts. **Special Collections:** Library of Daniel Hand. **Holdings:** 850 books and bound periodical volumes; 6 VF drawers of manuscripts, sermons, photographs, clippings, reports, and pamphlets. **Services:** Library open to public by appointment. **Publications:** Society Newsletter, quarterly. **Staff:** Robert W. Carder, Libn.

★7409★

MADISON METROPOLITAN SCHOOL DISTRICT - EDUCATION REFERENCE LIBRARY (Educ)
545 W. Dayton St.   Phone: (608) 266-6188
Madison, WI 53703   Maryfaith Fox, Ref.Libn.
Founded: 1966. **Staff:** Prof 1; Other 1. **Subjects:** Education. **Special Collections:** Education journals on microfilm. **Holdings:** 10,000 books and bound periodical volumes; 16 VF drawers of reports, pamphlets, bibliographies; microfilm, filmstrips, tapes; ERIC microfiche, 1971 to present. **Subscriptions:** 225 journals and other serials. **Services:** Interlibrary loans; copying; library open to public for reference use only. **Computerized Information Services:** DIALOG; ERIC searches via WISE-ONE, free to primary clientele. **Publications:** HELPS (new acquisitions), bimonthly; bibliographies.

★7410★

MADISON PUBLIC LIBRARY - ART AND MUSIC DIVISION (Art; Mus)
201 W. Mifflin St.   Phone: (608) 266-6311
Madison, WI 53703   Beverly Brager, Supv.
Staff: Prof 4; Other 1. **Subjects:** Art and architecture, music, antiques, theater, photography, coins and stamps. **Special Collections:** Hathaway Collection. **Holdings:** 37,000 books; 90 bound and unbound periodical volumes; 15,000 phonograph records (cataloged); 1000 16mm films; 500 8mm films; 80 video cassettes; 900 audio cassettes; 520 framed reproductions. **Subscriptions:** 90 journals and other serials. **Services:** Interlibrary loans; copying; library open to public. **Computerized Information Services:** Computerized cataloging and circulation. **Networks/Consortia:** Member of WILS. **Special Catalogs:** 16mm film catalog; super 8mm film catalog; Art to Go (framed picture catalog); video cassette catalog, all annual. **Special Indexes:** Song Index; Handicraft Index. **Staff:** Vada Mayfield, Music Libn.; Ann Michalski, AV Libn.

★7411★

MADISON PUBLIC LIBRARY - BUSINESS AND SCIENCE DIVISION (Bus-Fin; Sci-Tech)
201 W. Mifflin St.   Phone: (608) 266-6333
Madison, WI 53703   Philip Sullivan, Supv.
Staff: Prof 4; Other 2. **Subjects:** Investment and consumer information, industrial arts, home economics, pure sciences. **Special Collections:** Madison and Dane County documents. **Holdings:** 62,639 books; 3800 bound periodical volumes; industrial directories; 800 clipping folders of Madison and Dane County industries. **Subscriptions:** 565 journals and other serials; 8 newspapers. **Services:** Interlibrary loans; copying; library open to public. **Staff:** Lee Hayden, Asst.Supv.; Vivian Sweet, Libn.; Romeo Dais, Libn.

★7412★

MADISON PUBLIC LIBRARY - LITERATURE AND SOCIAL SCIENCES (Soc Sci)
201 W. Mifflin St.   Phone: (608) 266-6350
Madison, WI 53703   Natalie Tinkham, Supv.Libn.
Staff: Prof 9; Other 3. **Subjects:** Literature, social sciences, history, travel, sports, languages, philosophy, religion. **Special Collections:** Local materials (3000 items); low vision collection (2500 titles, 75 aids). **Holdings:** 214,824 books; 4890 bound periodical volumes; 20 VF drawers of local newspaper clippings; 45 VF drawers of pamphlets. **Subscriptions:** 390 journals and other serials; 40 newspapers. **Services:** Interlibrary loans; copying; library open to public. **Special Indexes:** Wisconsin State Journal Index (card); index to local magazines (card); index of Madison Associations.

★7413★

MADISON PUBLIC LIBRARY - MUNICIPAL REFERENCE SERVICE (Soc Sci)
City-County Bldg., Rm. 230
210 Monona Ave.   Phone: (608) 266-6316
Madison, WI 53710   Ann Waidelich, Libn.
Staff: Prof 2; Other 1. **Subjects:** Municipal government. **Special Collections:** City of Madison and Dane County government documents (2800). **Holdings:** 1100 books. **Subscriptions:** 31 journals and other serials. **Services:** Interlibrary loans; copying; SDI; library open to public. **Publications:** A Bibliography of Government Publications by and about Madison and Dane County, 2nd edition 1977, updated daily in office copy - free upon request.

★7414★

MADISON STATE HOSPITAL - CRAGMONT MEDICAL LIBRARY (Med)†

Phone: (812) 265-2611

Madison, IN 47250   Lloyd Roberts, Libn.

Founded: 1956. **Staff:** Prof 1. **Subjects:** Medicine, psychiatry, psychology, social work. **Special Collections:** Collections housed in 15 hospital departments including dental, occupational therapy, nursing, addiction. **Holdings:** 3824 books and bound periodical volumes; 1750 clippings; 56 boxes of pamphlets. **Subscriptions:** 58 journals and other serials. **Services:** Interlibrary loans; reference; library open to hospital staff and qualified students. **Networks/Consortia:** Member of Southeastern Indiana Area Library Services Authority (SIALSA).

★7415★

MADISON TOWNSHIP HISTORICAL SOCIETY - THOMAS WARNE HISTORICAL MUSEUM AND LIBRARY (Hist)*

RD 1, Box 150   Phone: (201) 566-0348

Matawan, NJ 07747   Alvia D. Martin, Cur.

Staff: 10. **Subjects:** Local history, genealogy. **Special Collections:** Sheet music, 1840-1920; Edison Cylinder records; diaries; social and church records. **Holdings:** 500 books; photographs; albums; postcards; newspapers; pamphlets; maps. **Services:** Library open to public. **Publications:** At the Headwaters of Cheesequake Creek. **Remarks:** The library is located on Route 516, in Old Bridge Township, NJ 08857.

★7416★

MADONNA COLLEGE - CURRICULUM LIBRARY (Educ)

36600 Schoolcraft Rd.   Phone: (313) 591-5149

Livonia, MI 48150   Sr. M. Martina, Dir.

Founded: 1937. **Staff:** Prof 2; Other 1. **Subjects:** Reading, language arts, literature, mathematics, science, social science, foreign languages, music, religion. **Special Collections:** Multicultural books and pamphlets (71 items); children's literature (995 volumes). **Holdings:** 8460 books; 1 VF drawer of publishers' catalogs; 6 VF drawers of testing materials; 465 filmstrips; 86 transparencies, cassettes, phonograph records. **Services:** Interlibrary loans; copying; library open to teachers of immediate school districts. **Networks/Consortia:** Member of Michigan Association of Curriculum Libraries. **Staff:** Carol Schmidt, Tech.Asst.

★7417★

MAGAZINE PUBLISHERS ASSOCIATION - MAGAZINE INFORMATION CENTER (Publ)

575 Lexington Ave.   Phone: (212) 752-0055

New York, NY 10022   Annmaria Di Cesare, Mgr., Info.Serv.

Founded: 1940. **Staff:** Prof 2; Other 1. **Subjects:** Magazine publishing and advertising. **Holdings:** 850 books; magazine publishers research reports, circulation reports, magazine advertising expenditures statistics; 50 vertical files of information on markets and media. **Subscriptions:** 150 journals and other serials. **Services:** Copying (limited); center open to public by referral.

MAGCOBAR RESEARCH LIBRARY

See: Dresser Industries, Inc.

★7418★

MAGEE MEMORIAL REHABILITATION HOSPITAL - MAGEE MEMORIAL MEDICAL LIBRARY (Med)

1513 Race St.

Philadelphia, PA 19102   Phone: (215) 864-7100

Subjects: Physical medicine and rehabilitation; nursing; therapy - physical, vocational, occupational, speech; hospital administration. **Holdings:** 257 books; 70 bound periodical volumes; 600 unbound periodicals; 40 cassette tapes; 30 bulletins and newsletters. **Subscriptions:** 61 journals and other serials. **Services:** Interlibrary loans; library not open to public.

★7419★

MAGEE-WOMENS HOSPITAL - HOWARD ANDERSON POWER MEMORIAL LIBRARY (Med)

Forbes Ave. & Halket St.   Phone: (412) 647-4288

Pittsburgh, PA 15213   Velma Axelrod, Med.Libn.

Founded: 1964. **Staff:** Prof 1; Other 1. **Subjects:** Medicine, obstetrics, gynecology, neonatology, human sexuality. **Holdings:** 1000 books; 470 bound periodical volumes; 200 pamphlets and documents. **Subscriptions:** 75 journals and other serials. **Services:** Interlibrary loans; library open to public for reference use only.

★7420★

MAGNAVOX GOVERNMENT & INDUSTRIAL ELECTRONICS COMPANY - ADVANCED PRODUCTS DIVISION - LIBRARY (Sci-Tech)†

2829 Maricopa Ave.   Phone: (213) 328-0770

Torrance, CA 90503   Janet L. Gutheim

Founded: 1958. **Staff:** Prof 1. **Subjects:** Physics, electronics, engineering. **Holdings:** 1200 books; 500 bound periodical volumes; 5000 technical reports. **Subscriptions:** 180 journals and other serials. **Services:** Interlibrary loans; library not open to public.

★7421★

MAGNAVOX GOVERNMENT & INDUSTRIAL ELECTRONICS COMPANY - ENGINEERING LIBRARY (Sci-Tech)

1313 Production Rd.   Phone: (219) 429-6000

Fort Wayne, IN 46808   Lydia Peralta, Libn.

Staff: Prof 2. **Subjects:** Astronautics, mechanics, management, mathematics, physics, chemistry, sonar, electronics, radar, computer science. **Holdings:** 5000 books and bound periodical volumes; 7 VF drawers of engineering literature reports; 2 VF drawers of reliability files; 2 VF drawers of house organs; 18 VF drawers of miscellaneous material. **Subscriptions:** 125 journals and other serials. **Services:** Interlibrary loans (limited); copying; library primarily for company personnel. **Computerized Information Services:** DIALOG; computerized cataloging. **Staff:** Lynda Fulkerson, Asst.Libn.

★7422★

MAGNES (Judah L.) MEMORIAL MUSEUM - MORRIS GOLDSTEIN LIBRARY (Rel-Theol; Area-Ethnic)

2911 Russell St.   Phone: (415) 849-2710

Berkeley, CA 94705   Jane Levy, Libn./Archv.

Founded: 1967. **Staff:** 2. **Subjects:** Jewish history and art, Yiddish literature, Soviet Jewry. **Special Collections:** S. Belkin Papers. **Holdings:** 11,000 books; 3000 documents; 300 manuscripts; 30 maps; 500 rare books. **Subscriptions:** 10 journals and other serials. **Services:** Interlibrary loans; copying; library open to public for reference use only.

★7423★

MAGNES (Judah L.) MEMORIAL MUSEUM - WESTERN JEWISH HISTORY CENTER (Hist; Area-Ethnic)

2911 Russell St.   Phone: (415) 849-2710

Berkeley, CA 94705   Ruth K. Rafael, Archv./Libn.

Founded: 1967. **Staff:** Prof 2; Other 1. **Subjects:** History of Jews in the Western United States. **Special Collections:** Judah L. Magnes Collection; memoirs, oral histories and genealogy of Western Jews; Jewish congregational archives; archives of Committee for the Preservation of Jewish Cemeteries and Landmarks; Western Jewish newspapers from the 19th and 20th centuries; secular Jewish institutions; oral histories; David Lubin Harris Weinstock collection; Jewish Welfare Federation of San Francisco, Marin County and the Peninsula; Jewish Community Center, San Francisco; Rosalie Meyer Stern papers; Eureka Benevolent Society - Jewish Family Service Archives, San Francisco. **Holdings:** 500 books; 30 bound periodical volumes; 650 boxes of manuscript material (cataloged); 40 titles on microfilm; 10 VF drawers of pamphlets, family biographies and other material; 5000 photographs; 30 tapes and cassettes. **Subscriptions:** 11 journals and other serials; 20 newspapers. **Services:** Interlibrary loans (limited); photocopying of rare materials; center open to public for reference use only. **Networks/Consortia:** Member of Committee of Archives and Research Libraries in Jewish Studies; Bay Area Reference Center (BARC). **Publications:** List of publications - available upon request. **Special Indexes:** Analytical book index to manuscripts; Index to Emanu-el, San Francisco. **Staff:** Lynn Fonfa, Asst.Archv.

★7424★

MAGUIRE, VOORHIS AND WELLS - LIBRARY (Law)

2 S. Orange Plaza

Orlando, FL 32801   John D. Vanston, Law Libn.

Staff: Prof 1. **Subjects:** Law. **Holdings:** 12,700 volumes. **Subscriptions:** 20 journals and other serials; 5 newspapers. **Services:** Library not open to public.

★7425★

MAHARISHI INTERNATIONAL UNIVERSITY - SCIENCE OF CREATIVE INTELLIGENCE COLLECTION (Soc Sci)

Phone: (515) 472-5301

Fairfield, IA 52556   Gloria Watterson Foster, Libn.

Founded: 1974. **Staff:** Prof 3; Other 8. **Subjects:** Consciousness, Transcendental Meditation Program, Science of Creative Intelligence. **Holdings:** 200 volumes; 6000 audiotapes and videotapes. **Services:** Interlibrary loans; copying; collection open to public with restrictions. **Computerized Information Services:** Computerized cataloging. **Networks/Consortia:** Member of Bibliographical Center for Research, Rocky Mountain

Region, Inc. (BCR); OCLC; Iowa Private Academic Library Consortium (IPAL); Southeast Iowa Academic Libraries (SIAL); CRL. **Special Catalogs:** Online catalog of the Science of Creative Intelligence Collection. **Staff:** Carol Royce, Libn.; Martha Bright, Asst.Libn.

MAHONING COUNTY PUBLIC LIBRARY
See: Public Library of Youngstown and Mahoning County

★7426★
MAHONING LAW LIBRARY (Law)
Court House
120 Market St.   Phone: (216) 747-2000
Youngstown, OH 44503   Lucille G. DeMoss, Law Libn.
Founded: 1906. **Staff:** 3. **Subjects:** Law. **Holdings:** 65,000 volumes.
Subscriptions: 100 journals and other serials. **Services:** Copying.
Computerized Information Services: WESTLAW.

MAILLIARD (J.W., Jr.) LIBRARY
See: California Academy of Sciences - J.W. Mailliard, Jr. Library

★7427★
MAIMONIDES HOSPITAL GERIATRIC CENTRE - POLLACK LIBRARY (Med)
5795 Caldwell Ave.   Phone: (514) 483-2121
Montreal, PQ, Canada H4W 1W3   Sheindel Bresinger, Libn.
Founded: 1965. **Staff:** 1. **Subjects:** Geriatrics, gerontology, medicine, social work, nursing, psychiatry. **Holdings:** 1155 books; 633 bound periodical volumes; 260 photocopies on Parkinsonism; 5 years of Audio-Digest tapes; 65 reprints of staff articles; 3 drawers of current topics in geriatrics and gerontology. **Subscriptions:** 77 journals and other serials. **Services:** Interlibrary loans; copying; library open to public with restrictions.

★7428★
MAIMONIDES MEDICAL CENTER - MEDICAL LIBRARY (Med)
4802 Tenth Ave.   Phone: (212) 270-7679
Brooklyn, NY 11219   Lydia Friedman, Chf.Med.Libn.
Founded: 1952. **Staff:** Prof 1; Other 1. **Subjects:** Medicine, dentistry, gynecology, surgery, pediatrics, obstetrics, pharmacology, psychiatry, anatomy, physiology. **Holdings:** 2524 books; 7713 bound periodical volumes; 1314 audio cassettes; **Subscriptions:** 187 journals and other serials. **Services:** Interlibrary loans; copying; library open to hospital's health care staff. **Networks/Consortia:** Member of Brooklyn-Queens-Staten Island Health Sciences Librarians.

★7429★
MAIN (Chas. T.), INC. - LIBRARY (Sci-Tech)
Southeast Tower, Prudential Ctr.   Phone: (617) 262-3200
Boston, MA 02199   Hayden Mason, Libn.
Founded: 1893. **Staff:** Prof 1; Other 3. **Subjects:** Engineering, architecture, business, construction management, economics, environment, pulp and paper, water supply and soils, energy resources, power systems. **Special Collections:** Archives (10,000 items); standards and specifications. **Holdings:** 15,000 books; 360 bound periodical volumes; 5000 technical reports (cataloged); 15 VF drawers of map collection; 70 cassettes and 5000 volumes of U.S. Geological Survey Water-Supply Papers and Water-Data Reports. **Subscriptions:** 250 journals and other serials. **Services:** Interlibrary loans; copying; library open to public by special arrangement. **Publications:** Library Accessions, quarterly.

★7430★
MAIN HURDMAN - LIBRARY (Bus-Fin)
Two Embarcadero, 25th Fl.   Phone: (415) 981-7720
San Francisco, CA 94111   Carolyn Weirich, Libn.
Founded: 1970. **Staff:** Prof 1. **Subjects:** Accounting, auditing, tax services. **Holdings:** 2000 books; 2400 annual reports. **Subscriptions:** 100 journals and other serials; 5 newspapers. **Services:** Interlibrary loans; copying; library open to public with permission. **Publications:** New books/materials list, irregular.

★7431★
MAIN HURDMAN - LIBRARY (Bus-Fin)
55 E. 52nd St.   Phone: (212) 909-5600
New York, NY 10055   Marjorie Moyal, Libn.
Founded: 1946. **Staff:** Prof 2; Other 2. **Subjects:** Accounting. **Special Collections:** 3000 annual reports. **Holdings:** 2000 books; 300 bound periodical volumes; 200 pamphlets (cataloged). **Subscriptions:** 150 journals and other serials. **Services:** Interlibrary loans; library not open to public. **Computerized Information Services:** LEXIS. **Publications:** Book Ends, quarterly - to all personnel.

★7432★
MAIN LINE REFORM TEMPLE - LIBRARY (Rel-Theol)
410 Montgomery Ave.   Phone: (215) 649-7800
Wynnewood, PA 19096   Betty Graboyes, Libn.
Founded: 1961. **Staff:** Prof 1; Other 1. **Subjects:** Judaica. **Holdings:** 5700 books; 500 records and filmstrips (cataloged); clippings and reviews. **Services:** Library open to public with special permission. **Publications:** Acquisitions List, monthly - faculty and staff distribution. **Special Indexes:** Index of periodicals and book reviews.

★7433★
MAINE AUDUBON SOCIETY - ENVIRONMENTAL INFORMATION SERVICE (Env-Cons)†
Gilsland Farm
118 U.S. Rte. 1   Phone: (207) 781-2330
Falmouth, ME 04105   Miriam Schneider, Libn.
Founded: 1843. **Staff:** Prof 1. **Subjects:** Environment. **Holdings:** 3000 books; 300 environment childrens books; 9 VF drawers Maine environmental file; 300 curriculum guides; 20 films and slides. **Subscriptions:** 75 journals and other serials. **Services:** Interlibrary loans; copying; service open to public. **Publications:** Maine Audubon News. **Special Catalogs:** Maine Audubon Quarterly.

★7434★
MAINE CHARITABLE MECHANIC ASSOCIATION - LIBRARY (Hist)†
519 Congress St.   Phone: (207) 773-8396
Portland, ME 04111   Edith M. Riley, Libn.
Founded: 1820. **Staff:** Prof 1. **Subjects:** Travel, biography, fiction, history. **Special Collections:** Material dealing with the history of the association and books pertaining to Maine and to Portland. **Holdings:** 30,896 books. **Subscriptions:** 23 journals and other serials. **Services:** Library open to members and their families.

★7435★
MAINE CRIMINAL JUSTICE ACADEMY - MEDIA RESOURCES (Law)
93 Silver St.   Phone: (207) 873-2651
Waterville, ME 04901   Linda J. Dwelley, Media Resource Supv.
Founded: 1976. **Staff:** Prof 1; Other 2. **Subjects:** Criminal justice, corrections, police, law enforcement, prisons, rehabilitation. **Special Collections:** Law enforcement/corrections training films (169) and slide/cassette programs (104); probation/parole officers training video cassettes (39); highway safety films (258). **Holdings:** 2100 books and government publications; 51 bound periodical volumes. **Subscriptions:** 50 journals and other serials. **Services:** Interlibrary loans; copying; library open to public. **Computerized Information Services:** Computerized cataloging. **Networks/Consortia:** Member of OCLC through NELINET. **Publications:** Newsletter, quarterly - to mailing list. **Special Catalogs:** Media catalog.

★7436★
MAINE HISTORICAL SOCIETY - LIBRARY (Hist)
485 Congress St.   Phone: (207) 774-1822
Portland, ME 04101   William H. Toner, Jr., Dir.
Founded: 1822. **Staff:** Prof 4; Other 4. **Subjects:** Maine history and biography, New England history and genealogy. **Holdings:** 60,000 books; newspapers; documents, records, manuscripts and maps. **Subscriptions:** 97 journals and other serials. **Services:** Library open to public.

★7437★
MAINE MARITIME ACADEMY - NUTTING MEMORIAL LIBRARY (Sci-Tech)†
                                        Phone: (207) 326-4311
Castine, ME 04421   Kenneth H. Anthony, LCDR, Hd.Libn.
Founded: 1941. **Staff:** Prof 3; Other 3. **Subjects:** Navigation, seamanship, marine engineering, maritime industry. **Special Collections:** Admiral Nimitz Collection (75 volumes); Betty Land Collection (182 volumes); Sailing Memorial Collection (200 volumes); selective depository for government document publications. **Holdings:** 50,400 books; 2930 bound periodical volumes; 800 NTIS fiche; 700 maps and charts; 18,000 microforms; 750 audio cassettes; 191 film loops; 1160 phonograph records; 1100 video cassettes. **Subscriptions:** 959 journals and other serials; 20 newspapers. **Services:** Interlibrary loans; copying; library open to public (must obtain ID card). **Computerized Information Services:** Computerized cataloging. **Networks/Consortia:** Member of OCLC through NELINET. **Staff:** Marjorie T. Harrison, Asst.Libn.; Willard H. Gilmore, Asst.Libn.; Libby Rosemeier, Per. & Govt.Doc.Libn.; Barbara Churchill, Acq.Libn.; H. Brent Hall, Ref.Supv. & ILL.

★7438★
MAINE MARITIME MUSEUM - LIBRARY/ARCHIVES (Trans)
963 Washington St.   Phone: (207) 443-6311
Bath, ME 04530   Kathy Hudson, Adm.Asst.
Founded: 1964. **Staff:** 10. **Subjects:** Maine and American maritime history; shipbuilding in Maine; local history and genealogy. **Special Collections:** Sewall ship papers (325 document boxes). **Holdings:** 5000 books; 800 bound periodical volumes; 1000 pamphlets (cataloged); 250 navigation charts; 20 unbound journals; 30 filing drawers of photographs of vessels; 500 ship plans; 800 ships' logs, account books, ledgers; 250 document boxes. **Subscriptions:** 10 journals and other serials. **Services:** Copying; library open to public by appointment with fee. **Publications:** List of publications - available upon request. **Special Catalogs:** Maine ship captains and Maine built vessels (card). **Staff:** Nathan Lipfert, Asst.Cur.Res.; Harold Brown, Cur. Emeritus.

★7439★
MAINE MEDICAL CENTER - LIBRARY (Med)
22 Bramhall St.   Phone: (207) 871-2201
Portland, ME 04102   Robin M. Rand, Dir., Lib.Serv.
Founded: 1874. **Staff:** Prof 3; Other 5. **Subjects:** Medicine, public health, nursing, medical education, hospital administration. **Special Collections:** Archives and History of Medicine (especially Maine). **Holdings:** 5539 books; 9776 bound periodical volumes. **Subscriptions:** 572 journals and other serials. **Services:** Interlibrary loans (fee); copying; library open to health professionals in Maine. **Computerized Information Services:** NLM, DIALOG. **Networks/Consortia:** Member of New England Regional Medical Library Service (NERMLS). **Publications:** Holdings List, annual; Accessions list, quarterly. **Staff:** Diane Winand, Pub.Serv.Libn.; Rose F. Thompson, Tech.Serv.Libn.

★7440★
MAINE STATE DEPARTMENT OF ENVIRONMENTAL PROTECTION & DEPARTMENT OF CONSERVATION - DEP-DOC JOINT LIBRARY (Env-Cons)
State House, Station 17   Phone: (207) 289-2811
Augusta, ME 04333   Priscilla Bickford, Libn.
Founded: 1975. **Staff:** Prof 1. **Subjects:** Air, water and land quality; forestry; land use; geology; recreation planning; natural resources. **Holdings:** 2200 books; U.S.G.S. maps; Maine Soil Surveys. **Subscriptions:** 50 journals and other serials; 6 newspapers. **Services:** Interlibrary loans; copying; library open to public for reference use only. **Computerized Information Services:** Computerized cataloging. **Networks/Consortia:** Member of OCLC. **Publications:** Maine Environ News, monthly - to mailing list.

★7441★
MAINE STATE DEPARTMENT OF HUMAN SERVICES - DEPARTMENTAL LIBRARY (Soc Sci)
State House   Phone: (207) 289-3055
Augusta, ME 04333   Mary J. Wandersee, Libn.
Founded: 1970. **Staff:** Prof 1; Other 1. **Subjects:** Health, welfare, medicine. **Special Collections:** State of Maine reports and documents. **Holdings:** 1217 books. **Subscriptions:** 130 journals and other serials; 8 newspapers. **Services:** Interlibrary loans; copying; SDI; library open to public. **Computerized Information Services:** Computerized cataloging. **Networks/ Consortia:** Member of Health Science Library and Information Cooperative of Maine. **Publications:** HSLIC Newsletter, monthly - for internal distribution only.

★7442★
MAINE STATE DEPARTMENT OF MARINE RESOURCES - FISHERIES RESEARCH STATION - LIBRARY (Sci-Tech)
                                        Phone: (207) 633-5572
West Boothbay Harbor, ME 04575   Kimberly Douglas, Libn.
Staff: Prof 1; Other 1. **Subjects:** Marine biology, fisheries, oceanography, marine chemistry, marine ecology, zoology. **Special Collections:** Government and institutional documents (5000). **Holdings:** 2000 books; 3000 bound periodical volumes; 5000 government documents 6 filing drawers of reprint collection. **Subscriptions:** 200 journals and other serials. **Services:** Interlibrary loans; copying; library open to public with restrictions, short term loans only. **Computerized Information Services:** DIALOG. **Networks/ Consortia:** Member of OCLC through NELINET. **Special Indexes:** Index of publications of the Maine Department of Marine Resources, 1964-1978, Fisheries Information Series Number 3. **Remarks:** The Bigelow Laboratory for Ocean Sciences of the Northeastern Research Foundation, Inc. shares the library holdings with the Maine State Department of Marine Resources.

★7443★
MAINE STATE DEPARTMENT OF TRANSPORTATION - LIBRARY (Trans)
Child St.   Phone: (207) 289-2681
Augusta, ME 04333   Richard Siroin, Libn.
Subjects: Engineering - traffic, highway, bridge; public transportation; traffic safety. **Special Collections:** Maine Traffic Studies; Transportation Research Board publications (1600). **Holdings:** 2200 books; 129 bound periodical volumes; 210 documents, Maine statutes, standards. **Services:** Library open to public for reference use only.

★7444★
MAINE STATE LAW AND LEGISLATIVE REFERENCE LIBRARY (Law)
State House, Station 43   Phone: (207) 289-2648
Augusta, ME 04333   Martha L. Palmer, State Law Libn.
Founded: 1971. **Staff:** Prof 4; Other 3. **Subjects:** Anglo-American law, American state government. **Special Collections:** Legislative reference material; Maine Supreme Judicial Court records and briefs 1957 to present. **Holdings:** 86,048 volumes; 14 VF drawers of news clippings; current Congressional Bills; U.S. Senate and House documents and reports (unbound). **Services:** Interlibrary loans; copying (limited); library open to public. **Computerized Information Services:** LEGIST (Maine current legislation; internal database). **Special Indexes:** Index to legislators of Maine, 1820 to present (card); Index to Resolves, 1820-1949 (card). **Staff:** Lynn E. Randall, Assoc.Libn.; David L. Rabasca, Assoc.Libn.; Paul A. D'Alessandro, Assoc.Libn.

★7445★
MAINE STATE LIBRARY (Hist)
Station 64   Phone: (207) 289-3561
Augusta, ME 04333   J. Gary Nichols, State Libn.
Founded: 1839. **Staff:** Prof 20; Other 37. **Subjects:** Maine - history, genealogy, state, county and local histories. **Special Collections:** Maine Author Collection (4000 volumes); Baxter Collection (personal papers of Governor Percival P. Baxter); Avery Collection (photos and paintings of Mt. Katahdin); Maine music; maps; manuscripts; federal and state government documents. **Holdings:** 400,000 volumes. **Subscriptions:** 200 journals and other serials; 25 newspapers. **Services:** Interlibrary loans; copying; library open to Maine state residents. **Computerized Information Services:** DIALOG; computerized cataloging. **Networks/Consortia:** Member of OCLC through NELINET. **Publications:** Downeast Libraries, quarterly.

★7446★
MAINE STATE MUSEUM - RESOURCE CENTER (Hist)
State House, Station 83   Phone: (207) 289-2301
Augusta, ME 04333   Jane E. Radcliffe, Musm. Registrar
Staff: 1. **Subjects:** Museology, archeology, Maine history, Americana, conservation, education. **Holdings:** 1300 books; 80 boxes of archival papers; 10 shelves of albums and journals. **Subscriptions:** 50 journals and other serials. **Services:** Copying; library open to public for reference use only.

★7447★
MAINE STATE OFFICE OF ENERGY RESOURCES - LIBRARY (Energy)†
State House Sta. 53   Phone: (207) 289-3811
Augusta, ME 04330   Robert Michaud, Libn.
Founded: 1979. **Staff:** Prof 1. **Subjects:** Energy. **Holdings:** 300 books; 4700 cataloged items. **Subscriptions:** 10 journals and other serials. **Services:** Interlibrary loans; copying; library not open to public. **Computerized Information Services:** Computerized cataloging.

★7448★
MAISON BELLARMIN LIBRARY (Rel-Theol; Soc Sci)
25 W. Jarry   Phone: (514) 387-2541
Montreal, PQ, Canada H2P 1S6   Edmond E. Desrochers, Dir.
Founded: 1935. **Staff:** Prof 1; Other 2. **Subjects:** Religion, social sciences, industrial relations. **Holdings:** 81,000 books and bound periodical volumes; 5500 unbound periodicals; 3000 pamphlets; 15,000 documents. **Subscriptions:** 306 journals and other serials; 43 newspapers. **Services:** Copying; library open to public with approval of director.

MAIZE VIRUS INFORMATION SERVICE
See: Ohio State Agricultural Research and Development Center

MAKAPUU OCEANIC CENTER
See: Oceanic Institute Library

MALCHO (Dr. Thomas J.) MEMORIAL LIBRARY
See: York-Finch General Hospital - Dr. Thomas J. Malcho Memorial Library

★7449★
MALCOLM PIRNIE, INC. - TECHNICAL LIBRARY (Env-Cons)
2 Corporate Park Dr.
Box 751   Phone: (914) 694-2100
White Plains, NY 10602   Myron E. Menewitch, Tech.Libn.
Staff: Prof 1; Other 1. **Subjects:** Environmental engineering, water - supply and treatment, pollution control. **Holdings:** 10,000 books and bound periodical volumes; 1000 U.S. Environmental Protection Agency reports. **Subscriptions:** 150 journals and other serials. **Services:** Copying; requests for library access individually evaluated. **Computerized Information Services:** DIALOG.

★7450★
MALDEN HISTORICAL SOCIETY - LIBRARY (Hist)
36 Salem St.   Phone: (617) 324-0220
Malden, MA 02148   Dorathy L. Rothe, Cur.
Founded: 1887. **Subjects:** Maldeniana. **Holdings:** 2000 books. **Services:** Copying; library not open to public. **Publications:** Register of Malden Historical Society.

★7451★
MALDEN HOSPITAL - MEDICAL LIBRARY (Med)
Hospital Rd.   Phone: (617) 322-7560
Malden, MA 02148   Denise Corless, Libn.
Staff: Prof 1. **Subjects:** Medicine and allied sciences. **Special Collections:** History of medicine (20 volumes). **Holdings:** 640 books; 2000 bound periodical volumes; 125 pamphlets; 2 boxes of AV catalogs. **Subscriptions:** 109 journals and other serials. **Services:** Interlibrary loans; copying; SDI; library open to public for reference use only with permission of librarian. **Computerized Information Services:** MEDLARS. **Networks/Consortia:** Member of New England Regional Medical Library Service (NERMLS); Boston Biomedical Library Consortium; Massachusetts Health Science Library Network (MAHSLIN). **Publications:** Monthly column in Medical Staff Newsletter. **Special Indexes:** Pamphlet file index (card); journal holdings index (card); AV catalog file (card).

★7452★
MALDEN HOSPITAL - SCHOOL OF NURSING LIBRARY (Med)
Hospital Rd.   Phone: (617) 322-7560
Malden, MA 02148   Phyllis M. McAuliffe, Libn.
Founded: 1939. **Staff:** Prof 1; Other 1. **Subjects:** Nursing, medicine, surgery, biological and social sciences. **Special Collections:** Recreational/Cultural Collection (396); Historical Collection (156). **Holdings:** 3259 books; 138 bound periodical volumes; 8 VF drawers. **Subscriptions:** 52 journals and other serials. **Services:** Interlibrary loans; copying; SDI; library open to public for reference use only. **Networks/Consortia:** Member of CHAMELEON. **Remarks:** An Autotutorial Laboratory equipped with hardware and software is housed in the library.

★7453★
MALEDICTA: INTERNATIONAL RESEARCH CENTER FOR VERBAL AGGRESSION, INC. - ARCHIVES (Soc Sci)
331 S. Greenfield Ave.   Phone: (414) 542-5853
Waukesha, WI 53186   Dr. Reinhold A. Aman, Pres.
Founded: 1965. **Staff:** Prof 1. **Subjects:** Verbal aggression, slurs, insults, name-calling, blasphemy, scatology, sexual terminology, value judgements, language. **Holdings:** 800 books; 14,000 pages of book and article manuscripts; 2500 newspaper clippings; 4 theses and dissertations; 5000 bibliography cards. **Subscriptions:** 20 journals and other serials. **Services:** Archives not open to public. **Publications:** Maledicta: International Journal of Verbal Aggression, annual - subscription; Maledicta Press Publications (books).

MALLET (John W.) CHEMISTRY LIBRARY
See: University of Texas, Austin - Chemistry Library

MALLET LIBRARY
See: Union Saint-Jean-Baptiste

MALLINCKRODT (Edward) INSTITUTE OF RADIOLOGY LIBRARY
See: Washington University - Edward Mallinckrodt Institute of Radiology Library

★7454★
MALLINCKRODT, INC. - LIBRARY (Sci-Tech)
Box 5439   Phone: (314) 695-5514
St. Louis, MO 63147   Juanita McCarthy, Corp.Libn.
Founded: 1867. **Staff:** Prof 2; Other 2. **Subjects:** Chemistry and pharmacology. **Holdings:** 7000 books; 15,000 bound periodical volumes. **Subscriptions:** 400 journals and other serials. **Services:** Interlibrary loans;

copying; library open to public. **Computerized Information Services:** DIALOG, SDC, New York Times Information Service, BRS, Dow Jones News Retrieval. **Networks/Consortia:** Member of St. Louis Regional Library Network. **Publications:** Library Bulletin, monthly.

MALLOY (Sybile) MEMORIAL LIBRARY
See: Memphis Botanic Garden Foundation, Inc. - Goldsmith Civic Garden Ctr. - Sybile Malloy Memorial Library

MALMSTROM AIR FORCE BASE (MT)
See: U.S. Air Force Base - Malmstrom Base Library

MALTWOOD (Katharine) COLLECTION
See: University of Victoria - Katharine Maltwood Collection

MALY (Eugene H.) MEMORIAL LIBRARY
See: Mount St. Mary's Seminary of the West - Eugene H. Maly Memorial Library

MANAGEMENT INFORMATION CONSULTING LIBRARY
See: Arthur Andersen & Co. - Library (Hartford, CT)

★7455★
MANALYTICS, INC. - LIBRARY (Trans)
625 Third St.   Phone: (415) 788-4143
San Francisco, CA 94107   Deus Petrites, Libn.
Staff: Prof 1. **Subjects:** Maritime, truck, rail, and air freight transportation and distribution. **Holdings:** 4000 books. **Subscriptions:** 110 journals and other serials. **Services:** Interlibrary loans (limited); copying; library not open to public.

MANASSAS NATL. BATTLEFIELD PARK
See: U.S. Natl. Park Service

★7456★
MANATEE COUNTY BAR ASSOCIATION - LAW LIBRARY (Law)
County Court House
Box 1000   Phone: (813) 748-4501
Bradenton, FL 33506   L. Marie Ingram, Law Libn.
Founded: 1950. **Staff:** Prof 1. **Subjects:** Law, taxation, medical jurisprudence. **Holdings:** 15,000 volumes. **Services:** Interlibrary loans; copying; library open to public for reference use only.

★7457★
MANATEE COUNTY PLANNING AND DEVELOPMENT DEPARTMENT - TECHNICAL REFERENCE LIBRARY (Plan; Env-Cons)
212 6th Ave., E.   Phone: (813) 748-4501
Bradenton, FL 33506   Carol B. Clarke
Subjects: Planning and land use; conservation and environment; housing and population; highways, streets, roads; water supply; coastal zone management; local government. **Holdings:** 1200 reports and technical material; 30 categories of clippings; 904 photographs of Manatee County. **Subscriptions:** 23 journals and other serials. **Services:** Interlibrary loans; library open to public.

★7458★
MANATEE MEMORIAL HOSPITAL - WENTZEL MEDICAL LIBRARY (Med)
206 2nd St., E.   Phone: (813) 746-5111
Bradenton, FL 33508   Jeanette Mosher, Med.Libn.
Staff: 1. **Subjects:** Medicine, nursing. **Holdings:** 2500 books and bound periodical volumes. **Services:** Interlibrary loans; library open to public with restrictions.

★7459★
MANCHESTER CITY LIBRARY - FINE ARTS DEPARTMENT (Art)
405 Pine St.   Phone: (603) 625-6485
Manchester, NH 03104   Theresa Snow Toy, Fine Arts Libn.
Founded: 1914. **Staff:** Prof 1; Other 1. **Subjects:** Art, music, architecture, painting, photography, crafts, needlework, antiques, drawing, printing, textiles, glass. **Holdings:** 10,000 art volumes; 5000 music volumes; picture collection; recordings; films; cassettes; framed prints and photographs (for loan to public). **Subscriptions:** 27 journals and other serials. **Services:** Interlibrary loans; copying; library open to public. **Networks/Consortia:** Member of Urban Public Library Consortium.

★7460★

MANCHESTER CITY LIBRARY - NEW HAMPSHIRE ROOM (Hist)†
405 Pine St.   Phone: (603) 625-6485
Manchester, NH 03104
Staff: Prof 1; Other 1. **Subjects:** New Hampshire - state and local history, biography, genealogy; history of Amoskeag Corporation. **Holdings:** 5000 books; 750 bound periodical volumes; 140 scrapbooks (Manchester news clips, 1840-1942); 1367 photographs of Amoskeag mills and millyards. **Subscriptions:** 22 journals and other serials. **Services:** Interlibrary loans; copying; genealogical and state historical research and reference; library open to public. **Networks/Consortia:** Member of Urban Public Library Consortium.

★7461★

MANCHESTER HISTORIC ASSOCIATION - LIBRARY (Hist)
129 Amherst St.   Phone: (603) 622-7531
Manchester, NH 03104   Elizabeth Lessard, Libn.
Founded: 1896. **Staff:** Prof 1. **Subjects:** Local history. **Special Collections:** Business archives of Amoskeag Manufacturing Company; textile designers files; 19th century music. **Holdings:** 10,000 books, pamphlets, manuscripts, prints and maps; diaries, letters and account books. **Services:** Copying; library open to public for serious research.

★7462★

MANCHESTER HISTORICAL SOCIETY - LIBRARY (Hist)†
10 Union St.   Phone: (617) 526-7230
Manchester, MA 01944   Esther W. Proctor, Libn.
Staff: 2. **Subjects:** Local history. **Holdings:** 400 books; 15 bound periodical volumes; 4 drawers of photographs of local homes and people; old local maps; genealogy manuscripts. **Services:** Copying (limited); library open to public with restrictions.

★7463★

MANCHESTER MEMORIAL HOSPITAL - LIBRARY (Med)
71 Haynes St.   Phone: (203) 646-1222
Manchester, CT 06040   Anna B. Salo
Founded: 1955. **Subjects:** Medicine. **Holdings:** 900 books; 300 bound periodical volumes; audio cassettes. **Subscriptions:** 75 journals and other serials. **Services:** Interlibrary loans; copying; library not open to public. **Computerized Information Services:** Computerized serials.

MANHATTAN COLLEGE - AMERICAN TEILHARD ASSOCIATION FOR THE FUTURE OF MAN
See: American Teilhard Association for the Future of Man

★7464★

MANHATTAN COLLEGE - GROVER M. HERMANN ENGINEERING LIBRARY (Sci-Tech)
Corlear Ave. & 238th St.   Phone: (212) 920-0165
Bronx, NY 10471   Richard A. Barry, Libn.
Founded: 1964. **Staff:** Prof 1; Other 2. **Subjects:** Engineering - chemical, civil, electrical, mechanical and environmental, radiology. **Holdings:** 22,105 books; 1843 bound periodical volumes; 300 maps; 7 VF cabinets; 68 journal titles on microfilm. **Subscriptions:** 268 journals and other serials. **Services:** Interlibrary loans; copying; library open to public for reference use only. **Computerized Information Services:** DIALOG.

★7465★

MANHATTAN COLLEGE - SONNTAG LIBRARY (Sci-Tech)†
Engineering Bldg.
Corlear Ave. & 238th St.   Phone: (215) 920-0266
Bronx, NY 10471   Bro. Philip Dowd, Lib.Dir.
Founded: 1964. **Staff:** 1. **Subjects:** Plant cancer, plant morphogenesis, plant physiology, microbiology. **Special Collections:** Klein Collection of papers on Crown Gall. **Holdings:** 702 books; 1997 bound periodical volumes; 6 reels of microfilm. **Subscriptions:** 28 journals and other serials. **Services:** Interlibrary loans; copying; library open to public for reference use only.

★7466★

MANHATTAN SCHOOL OF MUSIC - FRANCES HALL BALLARD LIBRARY (Mus)
120 Claremont Ave.   Phone: (212) 749-2802
New York, NY 10027   Nina Davis-Millis, Libn.
Founded: 1925. **Staff:** Prof 3; Other 3. **Subjects:** Music. **Holdings:** 15,000 academic books; 8700 books on music; 26,800 phonograph records; 56,500 music scores and pieces. **Subscriptions:** 68 journals and other serials. **Services:** Interlibrary loans; copying; library open to public with METRO card or by arrangement. **Staff:** Richard Presser, Ref.Libn.; Christine Hoffman, Cat.

★7467★

MANISTEE COUNTY HISTORICAL MUSEUM - FORTIER MEMORIAL LIBRARY (Hist)
425 River St.   Phone: (616) 723-5531
Manistee, MI 49660   Steve Harold, Musm.Dir.
Founded: 1954. **Subjects:** Manistee County - history, logging and lumbering, early industries, pioneer families, transportation. **Special Collections:** Hanselman, Russel, and Short photographic collections; Manistee City newspapers dating from 1871. **Holdings:** Photographs, reports, pamphlets, programs, clippings and other miscellaneous materials. **Services:** Museum and collections open to public. **Publications:** Manistee Museum Log, 3/year.

★7468★

MANITOBA ASSOCIATION OF REGISTERED NURSES - LIBRARY (Med)
647 Broadway   Phone: (204) 774-3477
Winnipeg, MB, Canada R3C 0X2   Eleanor Gowerluk, Lib.Techn.
Staff: Prof 1. **Subjects:** Nursing and related topics. **Holdings:** 700 books; 80 bound periodical volumes; 350 pamphlets; 10 file boxes of archives; 15 file boxes of MARN documents. **Subscriptions:** 27 journals and other serials. **Services:** Interlibrary loans; copying; library open to nurses, nursing students and allied health personnel. **Publications:** Nurscene, 6-8/year - to active and nonpracticing registered nurses of Manitoba.

★7469★

MANITOBA CANCER TREATMENT AND RESEARCH FOUNDATION - LIBRARY (Med)
700 Bannatyne Ave.   Phone: (204) 787-2136
Winnipeg, MB, Canada R3C 1N7   Isobel M. Steedman, Libn.
Staff: 1. **Subjects:** Medicine, basic sciences. **Holdings:** 4251 books and bound periodical volumes. **Subscriptions:** 105 journals and other serials. **Services:** Interlibrary loans (local only); library open to professionals for reference use only. **Publications:** Annual Report.

MANITOBA - CENTRE DE RESSOURCES EDUCATIVES FRANCAISES DU MANITOBA
See: Centre de Ressources Educatives Francaises

★7470★

MANITOBA - DEPT. OF CONSUMER & CORPORATE AFFAIRS & ENVIRONMENT - DEPT. REFERENCE SERV. - CONSUMER AFF. LIB. (Bus-Fin)
1023-405 Broadway Ave.   Phone: (204) 944-3319
Winnipeg, MB, Canada R3C 3L6   S. Norma Godavari, Libn.
Founded: 1972. **Staff:** Prof 1. **Subjects:** Consumer education, protection and law. **Holdings:** 2000 volumes. **Subscriptions:** 115 journals and other serials. **Services:** Interlibrary loans; copying; library open to public for reference use only. **Publications:** Accessions lists; bibliographies; consumer affairs clippings service.

★7471★

MANITOBA - DEPT. OF CONSUMER & CORPORATE AFFAIRS & ENVIRONMENT - DEPT. REF. SERV. - ENVIRONMENTAL MGT. LIB. (Env-Cons)
139 Tuxedo Ave.
Box 7
Winnipeg, MB, Canada R3N 0H6   S. Norma Godavari, Libn.
Founded: 1972. **Subjects:** Environmental pollution and protection. **Holdings:** 16,000 volumes. **Subscriptions:** 180 journals and other serials. **Services:** Interlibrary loans; Manitoba Environmental clippings service; library serves government departments primarily; open to public for reference use only. **Publications:** Accessions lists; bibliographies; newsletter, quarterly. **Staff:** Pat Collins, Lib.Techn.

★7472★

MANITOBA - DEPARTMENT OF ECONOMIC DEVELOPMENT AND TOURISM - BUSINESS LIBRARY (Bus-Fin)
648-155 Carlton St.   Phone: (204) 944-2036
Winnipeg, MB, Canada R3C 3H8   F. Helen Paine, Libn.
Founded: 1960. **Staff:** Prof 2; Other 2. **Subjects:** Business management, economics, ecology, industrial technology, engineering, marketing, industrial development, public policy. **Special Collections:** Publications on industrial development in Manitoba. **Holdings:** 14,000 books. **Subscriptions:** 325 journals and other serials; 15 newspapers. **Services:** Interlibrary loans; copying; library open to public. **Computerized Information Services:** DIALOG. **Staff:** John W. Giesbrecht, Asst.Libn.; Myrna Baker, Techn.; Moyra Harrington, Techn.

★7473★
MANITOBA - DEPARTMENT OF EDUCATION - LIBRARY (Educ)
1181 Portage Ave., Main Fl.
Box 3   Phone: (204) 786-0218
Winnipeg, MB, Canada R3G 0T3   John Tooth, Chf.Libn.
Staff: Prof 5; Other 21. **Subjects:** Education, native studies. **Special Collections:** Rare textbook collection. **Holdings:** 60,000 books; 1300 phonograph records; 1500 kits; 293,436 microfiche; 13,500 16mm films. **Subscriptions:** 950 journals and other serials. **Services:** Interlibrary loans; copying; library open to public for reference use only. **Computerized Information Services:** DIALOG; internal database. **Networks/Consortia:** Member of UTLAS, Inc. **Publications:** List of publications and special catalogs - available upon request. **Staff:** Phyllis Barich, Hd. Film Booking/Ref.Serv.; Atarrha Wallace, Hd., Tech.Serv.

★7474★
MANITOBA - DEPARTMENT OF FINANCE - FEDERAL-PROVINCIAL RELATIONS AND RESEARCH DIVISION LIBRARY (Bus-Fin)
Legislative Bldg., Rm. 4   Phone: (204) 944-3757
Winnipeg, MB, Canada R3C OV8   Beatrice Miller, Lib.Ck.
Staff: 1. **Subjects:** Finance, taxation, economics. **Holdings:** 2500 books; 1000 federal and provincial government reports. **Subscriptions:** 55 journals and other serials; 6 newspapers. **Services:** Interlibrary loans; copying; library not open to public.

★7475★
MANITOBA - DEPARTMENT OF HEALTH - ANNA E. WELLS MEMORIAL LIBRARY (Med; Soc Sci)
202-880 Portage Ave.   Phone: (204) 786-5867
Winnipeg, MB, Canada R3G 0P1   Marilyn J. Hernandez, Health Libn.
Founded: 1921. **Staff:** Prof 2; Other 2. **Subjects:** Public health, preventive medicine, public welfare, social service, health education, sociology, medicine, nursing, mental health. **Holdings:** 18,000 books; 1000 bound periodical volumes; 5000 pamphlets; 28,000 unbound periodicals; 12,000 government publications; 75 reels of microfilm; miscellaneous annual reports, statistics, statutes and calendars. **Subscriptions:** 235 journals and other serials. **Services:** Interlibrary loans; copying; library open to public with restrictions on borrowing. **Networks/Consortia:** Member of Manitoba Health Libraries Association. **Publications:** Quarterly and Annual Reports; quarterly list of new additions to the collection; annual journals list; bibliographies on selected subjects - for department staff and others working in related fields in the province. **Staff:** Susan Rogers, Asst.Libn.

★7476★
MANITOBA - DEPARTMENT OF HEALTH - MANITOBA SCHOOL - MEMORIAL LIBRARY (Med)
Box 1190   Phone: (204) 239-6435
Portage La Prairie, MB, Canada R1N 3C6   Mrs. P. Calder, Lib.Supv.
Staff: 1. **Subjects:** Mental retardation, psychology, nursing, sociology, behavioral science. **Holdings:** 1500 books; 20 dissertations and theses; 1000 slides; 60 videotapes. **Subscriptions:** 104 journals and other serials and newspapers. **Services:** Interlibrary loans; library open to public.

★7477★
MANITOBA - DEPARTMENT OF MUNICIPAL AFFAIRS - LIBRARY (Plan)
1436-405 Broadway   Phone: (204) 944-4129
Winnipeg, MB, Canada R3C 3L6   Judy Stephenson, Libn.
Subjects: Land use, regional planning, community planning and housing, municipal government, statistics. **Holdings:** 5000 books; 22 bound periodical volumes; 700 microfiche; 3000 microfilmed aerial photographs; 3 VF drawers of documents. **Subscriptions:** 52 journals and other serials; 12 newspapers. **Services:** Interlibrary loans; copying; SDI; library open to public. **Publications:** Municipal Informat, quarterly - to all elected and appointed officials in Manitoba and other interested parties.

★7478★
MANITOBA - DEPARTMENT OF NATURAL RESOURCES - LIBRARY (Env-Cons)
1495 St. James St.
Box 26   Phone: (204) 786-9299
Winnipeg, MB, Canada R3H 0W9   Irene Hamerton, Libn.
Staff: Prof 1; Other 3. **Subjects:** Fisheries, forests, wildlife, water resources, land use, park planning. **Holdings:** 8500 books; 1000 bound periodical volumes; 9500 pamphlets; 21,000 reports; 3500 slides; 10,300 microfiche. **Subscriptions:** 326 journals and other serials. **Services:** Interlibrary loans; copying; library open to public by request. **Computerized Information Services:** CISTI, QL Systems. **Publications:** Annotated bibliography of publications, annual; Accessions List, monthly - both distributed to interested libraries and individuals.

★7479★
MANITOBA - HEALTH SERVICES COMMISSION - LIBRARY (Med)
599 Empress St.   Phone: (204) 786-7398
Winnipeg, MB, Canada R3C 2T6   Vera Ott, Libn.
Founded: 1972. **Staff:** Prof 1. **Subjects:** Medicine, health services administration, laboratory technology. **Holdings:** 2145 books; 180 items of Statistics Canada material (hospital-related); 240 annual reports (provincial medical plans); 450 pamphlets. **Subscriptions:** 181 journals and other serials; 6 newspapers. **Services:** Interlibrary loans; copying; library open to department personnel and personnel in health-related fields. **Publications:** List of periodicals and new additions, quarterly - for internal distribution only.

★7480★
MANITOBA HYDRO - LIBRARY (Sci-Tech; Bus-Fin)
Box 815   Phone: (204) 474-3614
Winnipeg, MB, Canada R3C 2P4   Rhona A. Wright, Libn.
Founded: 1957. **Staff:** Prof 1; Other 4. **Subjects:** Engineering - electrical, mechanical, hydraulic, civil; marketing and sales; management and personnel; accounting. **Special Collections:** Corporation historical material. **Holdings:** 10,000 books; 500 bound periodical volumes; 20 shelves of Statistics Canada material; 35 VF drawers of technical data; 160 shelf feet of annual reports and standards; 2800 feet of unbound periodicals; 110 feet of government documents. **Subscriptions:** 400 journals and other serials. **Services:** Interlibrary loans; copying; library open to public with restrictions.

★7481★
MANITOBA INDIAN CULTURAL EDUCATION CENTRE - PEOPLES LIBRARY (Area-Ethnic)
119 Sutherland Ave.   Phone: (204) 942-0228
Winnipeg, MB, Canada R2W 3C9   V.J. Chalmers, Lib.Dir.
Staff: 2. **Subjects:** Native peoples. **Holdings:** 3500 books; 2000 vertical files; 75 kits; 60 books of clippings; 7 films; 43 videotapes; 67 cassettes of Indian music; 24 tapes; 4 slide presentations. **Subscriptions:** 50 journals and other serials. **Services:** Interlibrary loans; copying; library open to public. **Publications:** Listing of material, annual. **Staff:** Marie Rose Spence .

★7482★
MANITOBA - LEGISLATIVE LIBRARY (Soc Sci)
200 Vaughan St., Main Fl.   Phone: (204) 946-7214
Winnipeg, MB, Canada R3C 0P8   Joyce Irvine, Leg.Libn.
Founded: 1884. **Staff:** Prof 9; Other 7. **Subjects:** Political science, economics, history, Western Canadiana. **Special Collections:** Statutes, journals, gazettes, and debates of Canadian legislative bodies; government and U.N. documents; documents of British and American governments and international bodies; Manitoba local history; Manitoba rural newspapers. **Holdings:** 90,000 books; 1.4 million documents; microforms. **Subscriptions:** 350 journals and other serials; 140 newspapers. **Services:** Interlibrary loans; library open to public for reference use only. **Publications:** Annual Reports; Selected New Titles, monthly; Checklist of Manitoba government publications, monthly; Checklist cumulation, annual.

★7483★
MANITOBA MUSEUM OF MAN AND NATURE - LIBRARY (Sci-Tech)
190 Rupert Ave.   Phone: (204) 956-2830
Winnipeg, MB, Canada R3B 0N2   Valerie Hatten, Libn.
Founded: 1967. **Staff:** Prof 1; Other 1. **Subjects:** Natural history, Manitoba history, museology, ethnology, archeology, geology, astronomy. **Holdings:** 19,500 books and bound periodical volumes; 3700 pamphlets; 725 oral history tapes; 27 microforms; 8000 pictures. **Subscriptions:** 250 journals and other serials. **Services:** Interlibrary loans; copying; library open to public for reference use only.

★7484★
MANITOBA - PROVINCIAL ARCHIVES OF MANITOBA (Hist)
Manitoba Archives Bldg.
200 Vaughan St.   Phone: (204) 944-3971
Winnipeg, MB, Canada R3C 1T5   Peter Bower, Prov.Archv.
Founded: 1884. **Staff:** Prof 18; Other 10. **Subjects:** History of Manitoba and the Canadian West (including Red River Settlement records, Riel Family papers, lieutenant-governors papers, Indian treaty negotiations, Winnipeg General Strike manuscripts). **Special Collections:** Archives of the Hudson's Bay Company, 1670-1920 (5200 linear feet). **Holdings:** 2900 linear feet of manuscripts; 3550 linear feet of government records; 100,000 photographs; 4000 maps; 300 paintings. **Services:** Copying; archives open to public. **Remarks:** Houses the Anglican Church of Canada - Ecclesiastical Province of Rupert's Land - Archives. **Staff:** Barry E. Hyman, Asst.Prov.Archv.; Shirlee A. Smith, Kpr. Hudson's Bay Archv.; Charles A.E. Brandt, Chf.Consrv.; Gordon Dodds, Chf., Govt.Rec.

MANITOBA SCHOOL - MEMORIAL LIBRARY
See: Manitoba - Department of Health

★7485★
MANITOWOC MARITIME MUSEUM - LIBRARY (Hist)
809 S. 8th St.   Phone: (414) 684-0218
Manitowoc, WI 54220   David Pamperin, Dir.
Staff: 2. **Subjects:** Submarine and other vessels, marine construction, Great Lakes history, vessel construction. **Special Collections:** Carus collection (3000 items); Captain Tim Kelley Log (10 volumes). **Holdings:** 6000 books and bound periodical volumes; 8 VF drawers of information; 48 boxes of clippings; 24 boxes of loose manuscripts; 100 films and filmstrips; 12,000 photographs and negatives; 1000 postcards; 5 VF drawers of blueprints. **Subscriptions:** 35 journals and other serials; 6 newspapers. **Services:** Copying; library open to public for reference use only. **Publications:** Anchor News, bimonthly.

★7486★
MANKATO AREA VOCATIONAL-TECHNICAL INSTITUTE - LIBRARY (Sci-Tech)†
1920 Lee Blvd.   Phone: (507) 625-3441
North Mankato, MN 56001
Founded: 1946. **Staff:** 1. **Subjects:** Business - trade and industrial, technical; health food service; agri-business; distributive education. **Holdings:** 5000 books; 300 bound periodical volumes; AV materials (cataloged); professional collection. **Subscriptions:** 300 journals and other serials; 10 newspapers. **Services:** Interlibrary loans (limited); library open to public. **Networks/Consortia:** Member of Southcentral Minnesota Interlibrary Exchange (SMILE). **Special Catalogs:** Professional Library catalog in cooperation with other school libraries. **Remarks:** Maintained by Independent School District 77, Mankato, MN.

★7487★
MANKATO STATE UNIVERSITY - BUREAU OF BUSINESS AND ECONOMIC RESEARCH - LIBRARY (Bus-Fin)
                                               Phone: (507) 389-2963
Mankato, MN 56001   Dr. Yvonne Nyman, Dir.
Staff: Prof 1; Other 1. **Subjects:** Business. **Holdings:** Government publications; business annual reports; local business indicators; theses. **Subscriptions:** 40 journals and other serials. **Services:** Library open to faculty and graduate students. **Publications:** Mankato-North Mankato Business and Economic Indicators.

★7488★
MANKATO STATE UNIVERSITY - LIBRARY - SPECIAL COLLECTIONS (Educ)
Memorial Library   Phone: (507) 389-6201
Mankato, MN 56001   Dale K. Carrison, Dean of Lib.
Special Collections: Center for Minnesota Studies; curriculum guides and materials; urban studies; maps and aerial photographs (85,968); U.S. Government Printing Office depository library. **Services:** Interlibrary loans; copying; library open to public. **Computerized Information Services:** DIALOG, SDC, New York Times Information Service; computerized cataloging, acquisitions and serials. **Networks/Consortia:** Member of MINITEX; Southcentral Minnesota Inter-Library Exchange (SMILE); Minnesota State University System Project for Automated Library Systems (MSUS/PALS). **Special Catalogs:** Computer-produced book catalogs for curriculum guides and state and urban publications.

MANKATO STATE UNIVERSITY - SOUTHERN MINNESOTA HISTORICAL CENTER
See: Southern Minnesota Historical Center

MANN (Albert R.) LIBRARY
See: Cornell University - Albert R. Mann Library

MANN (Horace) LEARNING CENTER
See: Northwest Missouri State University - Horace Mann Learning Center

MANN (Kristine) LIBRARY
See: Analytical Psychology Club of New York

★7489★
MANNES COLLEGE OF MUSIC - HARRY SCHERMAN LIBRARY (Mus)
157 E. 74th St.   Phone: (212) 737-0700
New York, NY 10021   Barbara Railo, Hd.Libn.
Founded: 1954. **Staff:** Prof 2; Other 1. **Subjects:** Music. **Special Collections:** Leopold Mannes manuscript collection; Carlos Salzedo Memorial Collection of Annotated Harp Music. **Holdings:** 5700 books; 22,200 music scores; 2970 phonograph record albums. **Subscriptions:** 47 journals and

other serials. **Services:** Library open to public for reference use only upon application for specific materials. **Networks/Consortia:** Member of METRO.

MANNING (Cardinal Henry Edward) LIBRARY
See: Emory University - Pitts Theology Library

MANNING (Warren) COLLECTION
See: Harvard University - Graduate School of Design - Frances Loeb Library

★7490★
MANOR JUNIOR COLLEGE - BASILEIAD LIBRARY - SPECIAL COLLECTIONS (Area-Ethnic)
Fox Chase Manor   Phone: (215) 885-2360
Jenkintown, PA 19046   Sr. Mary Anne, O.S.B.M., Libn.
Staff: Prof 1; Other 2. **Special Collections:** The Ukraine - history, culture, literature. **Holdings:** Figures not available. **Services:** Copying; library open to public for reference use only.

★7491★
MANSFIELD HISTORICAL SOCIETY - EDITH MASON LIBRARY (Hist)†
954 Storrs Rd.
Box 145   Phone: (203) 429-9789
Storrs, CT 06268   Roberta Smith, Pres.
Founded: 1957. **Subjects:** Local Mansfield history. **Special Collections:** Account books of Edwin Fitch, noted local architect. **Holdings:** 400 books; 4 VF drawers of photographs; 1790 manuscripts, account books, scrapbooks, diaries. **Services:** Genealogical searching (limited); library open to public with restrictions from May to October. **Staff:** Randall Jimerson, Libn./Archv.

MANSFIELD (Maureen & Mike) LIBRARY
See: University of Montana - Maureen & Mike Mansfield Library

★7492★
MANSFIELD STATE COLLEGE - AUDIO VISUAL CENTER (Aud-Vis)
Retan, Rm. G-1   Phone: (717) 662-4138
Mansfield, PA 16933   Ronald E. Remy, Dir.
Founded: 1965. **Staff:** Prof 2; Other 5. **Subjects:** Education, special education, science, art, biology, communications. **Holdings:** 800 films and other AV materials. **Subscriptions:** 21 journals and other serials. **Services:** Copying; center open to public. **Publications:** Media catalog, yearly. **Staff:** Gene Fessler, AV Techn.

★7493★
MANSFIELD STATE COLLEGE - BUTLER CENTER LIBRARY (Mus)
                                               Phone: (717) 662-4365
Mansfield, PA 16933   Holly Gardinier, Music Libn.
Founded: 1969. **Staff:** Prof 1; Other 1. **Subjects:** Music, music therapy, music education, music merchandising, jazz. **Special Collections:** Historical sets and monuments of music; old popular sheet music. **Holdings:** 6500 books; 1230 bound periodical volumes; 8500 scores; 9500 phonograph records; 130 titles in microforms; 175 kits; 30 tapes; 14 filmstrips; 2 videotapes; 355 cassettes; 4 transparencies. **Subscriptions:** 47 journals and other serials. **Services:** Interlibrary loans; copying; library open to public with restrictions. **Computerized Information Services:** DIALOG, SDC; computerized cataloging and ILL. **Networks/Consortia:** Member of OCLC through PALINET & Union Library Catalogue of Pennsylvania; Susquehanna Library Cooperative. **Staff:** Gwen Sumner, Media Techn.

MANSFIELD STATE COMMEMORATIVE AREA
See: Louisiana State Dept. of Culture, Recreation and Tourism

★7494★
MANSFIELD TRAINING SCHOOL - MEDICAL LIBRARY
Box 51
Mansfield Depot, CT 06251
Defunct

MANSHIP (Luther) MEDICAL LIBRARY
See: St. Dominic-Jackson Memorial Hospital - Luther Manship Medical Library

MANSION MUSEUM LIBRARY
See: Oglebay Institute

★7495★
MANTELL (C.L.) AND ASSOCIATES - LIBRARY (Sci-Tech)†
447 Ryder Rd.   Phone: (516) 627-1472
Manhasset, NY 11030
Founded: 1924. **Subjects:** Electrochemistry, chemical engineering, nonferrous metallurgy. **Holdings:** 3500 books; 200 bound periodical volumes. **Services:** Library not open to public.

★7496★
MANTENO MENTAL HEALTH CENTER - STAFF LIBRARY (Med)
100 Barnard Rd.   Phone: (815) 468-3451
Manteno, IL 60950   Charlotte M. Morgan, Libn.
Staff: Prof 1; Other 1. **Subjects:** Psychiatry, psychology, medicine, nursing, social work, hospital administration. **Holdings:** 7757 books; 118 shelves of unbound journals; 5 VF drawers. **Subscriptions:** 172 journals and other serials. **Services:** Interlibrary loans; copying; library open to public by appointment. **Networks/Consortia:** Member of Chicago and South Consortium; Illinois Department of Mental Health and Developmental Disabilities Library Services Network (DMHDD/LISN); Bur Oak Library System. **Remarks:** Maintained by Illinois State Department of Mental Health & Developmental Disabilities.

MANTOR LIBRARY
See: University of Maine, Farmington

MANUEL (George M.) MEMORIAL LIBRARY
See: Piedmont Bible College - George M. Manuel Memorial Library

★7497★
MANUFACTURERS ASSOCIATION OF CENTRAL NEW YORK - LIBRARY (Bus-Fin)
770 James St.   Phone: (315) 474-4201
Syracuse, NY 13203   Mary F. Pennock, Lib.Assoc.
Founded: 1947. **Staff:** 1. **Subjects:** Industrial relations, labor laws and interpretations, personnel management, wage and salary surveys, employment. **Holdings:** 1100 books; 14 VF cabinets of reports, clippings, and pamphlets. **Subscriptions:** 75 journals and other serials. **Services:** Library open to public, some materials are confidential.

★7498★
MANUFACTURERS HANOVER TRUST COMPANY - CORPORATE LIBRARY/ FINANCIAL LIBRARY DIVISION (Bus-Fin)
350 Park Ave.   Phone: (212) 350-4733
New York, NY 10022   Ann Little, Libn.
Founded: 1975. **Staff:** Prof 1; Other 6. **Subjects:** Banking, finance, economics. **Holdings:** 8583 books; 868 bound periodical volumes; 157 unbound periodical titles; 35 VF drawers of periodical releases; 55 VF drawers of subject/industry files; 2342 reels of microfilm. **Subscriptions:** 592 journals and other serials; 6 newspapers. **Services:** Interlibrary loans; copying; library open to public by referral of a company officer. **Computerized Information Services:** New York Times Information Service, DIALOG, Finsbury Data Services Ltd. **Publications:** Reviews of recent corporate library acquisitions, monthly - for internal distribution only. **Special Indexes:** Periodic releases by subject (loose-leaf format). **Staff:** Mary Mannion, Asst.Libn.

★7499★
MANUFACTURERS HANOVER TRUST COMPANY - CORPORATE LIBRARY/ INVESTMENT LIBRARY DIVISION (Bus-Fin)
600 Fifth Ave.   Phone: (212) 957-1356
New York, NY 10020   Ann Little, Libn.
Staff: 2. **Subjects:** Trusts, estates and investments. **Holdings:** 350 books; 70 bound periodical volumes; 40 unbound periodical titles; 7 VF drawers of periodical releases; 45 VF drawers of municipal files; 20 VF drawers of subject/industry files of clippings; 135 VF drawers of corporate files. **Services:** Interlibrary loans; copying; library open to public by recommendation of company officer. **Staff:** Madeline Keller, Ref.Libn.

★7500★
MANUFACTURERS HANOVER TRUST COMPANY - INTERNATIONAL ECONOMICS DEPARTMENT - LIBRARY (Bus-Fin)
46 E. 52nd St., 5th Fl.   Phone: (212) 350-5829
New York, NY 10022   Halina Osysko, Libn.
Founded: 1971. **Staff:** Prof 1; Other 2. **Subjects:** International economics, business, trade, banking, industry and energy, finance and commodities. **Holdings:** 2000 books; 80 bound periodical volumes; 20,000 files on 1100 countries. **Subscriptions:** 100 journals and other serials; 11 newspapers. **Services:** Copying; library not open to public. **Computerized Information Services:** Data Resources, Inc. **Publications:** International Digest. **Special Catalogs:** Subject catalogs.

★7501★
MANUFACTURERS LIFE INSURANCE COMPANY - BUSINESS LIBRARY (Bus-Fin)
200 Bloor St., E.   Phone: (416) 928-4104
Toronto, ON, Canada M4W 1E5   Oriole Anderson, Libn.
Founded: 1925. **Staff:** Prof 2; Other 1. **Subjects:** Life insurance, management, behavioural sciences, economics, banking and investments, legislation, human resources. **Holdings:** 3000 books; 325 subject files of pamphlets and other items. **Subscriptions:** 350 journals and other serials; 9 newspapers. **Services:** Interlibrary loans; copying; SDI; library open to public with permission from librarian. **Computerized Information Services:** SDC, Info Globe. **Publications:** Profile (SDI to management); Acquisitions List, monthly. **Staff:** Marsha Shapiro, Asst.Libn.

★7502★
MANVILLE SERVICE CORPORATION - CORPORATE INFORMATION CENTER
Ken-Caryl Ranch
Box 5108
Denver, CO 80217
Defunct

★7503★
MANVILLE SERVICE CORPORATION - HEALTH, SAFETY & ENVIRONMENT LIBRARY & INFORMATION CENTER (Med; Sci-Tech)
Box 5108   Phone: (303) 978-2580
Denver, CO 80217   Kathy Hodges, Coord.Info.Serv.
Founded: 1974. **Staff:** Prof 1; Other 1. **Subjects:** Occupational health, toxicology, industrial hygiene and safety, pollution, carcinogens. **Special Collections:** Asbestos, silica and man-made vitreous fibers, medical-scientific papers (38 lateral file drawers). **Holdings:** 5000 books. **Subscriptions:** 193 journals and other serials. **Services:** Interlibrary loans; copying; library open to public with restrictions. **Computerized Information Services:** NLM, DIALOG; internal database. **Networks/Consortia:** Member of Colorado Council of Medical Librarians. **Publications:** Health, Safety & Environment Publications Information Sheet, semiweekly - for internal distribution only. **Formerly:** Johns-Manville Corporation.

★7504★
MANVILLE SERVICE CORPORATION - RESEARCH INFORMATION CENTER (Sci-Tech)
Box 5108   Phone: (303) 978-5477
Denver, CO 80217   Judy Gerber, Chf.Libn., R & D
Founded: 1946. **Staff:** Prof 2; Other 2. **Subjects:** Chemistry, engineering, building materials, mining. **Special Collections:** Diatomite; asbestos. **Holdings:** 7000 books and government agency reports; internal reports; 18 VF drawers of patents; 26 VF drawers. **Subscriptions:** 400 journals and other serials. **Services:** Interlibrary loans; library open to public with restrictions. **Computerized Information Services:** DIALOG, SDC; computerized retrieval system for internal reports (TRS). **Publications:** Bulletin, weekly - to research center professional staff. **Remarks:** The library is located at 10100 W. Ute Ave., Littleton, CO 80123.

MANWILLER (Lloyd V.) CURRICULUM LABORATORY
See: Glassboro State College - Savitz Library - Lloyd V. Manwiller Curriculum Laboratory

MAP LIBRARY
See: New York City Human Resources Administration - Medical Assistance Program - Medicaid Library

MAPS
See: University of Minnesota - Agricultural Extension Service - Minnesota Analysis & Planning System

★7505★
MARATHON COUNTY HISTORICAL MUSEUM - LIBRARY (Hist)
403 McIndoe St.   Phone: (715) 848-6143
Wausau, WI 54401   Maryanne C. Norton, Libn.
Founded: 1952. **Staff:** Prof 1; Other 1. **Subjects:** State and county history, antiques, logging, Indian lore. **Special Collections:** Books published by Van Vechten and Ellis at the Philosopher Press in Wausau (20 volumes); John D. Mylrea Journals (15). **Holdings:** 6000 books; 5000 maps and photographs (cataloged); 80 manuscripts; 14 VF drawers of clippings. **Subscriptions:** 11 journals and other serials. **Services:** Copying; library open to public during regular hours of museum.

★7506★
MARATHON OIL COMPANY - LAW LIBRARY (Law)
539 S. Main St., Rm. 854-M   Phone: (419) 422-2121
Findlay, OH 45840   Durand S. Dudley, Sr. Law Libn.
Staff: Prof 1; Other 1. **Subjects:** Law, petroleum industry. **Holdings:** 15,000 books; 200 bound periodical volumes. **Subscriptions:** 50 journals and other serials. **Services:** Interlibrary loans; copying; library open to public by permission. **Computerized Information Services:** LEXIS.

★7507★
MARATHON OIL COMPANY - RESEARCH TECHNICAL INFORMATION CENTER (Energy)
Box 269   Phone: (303) 794-2601
Littleton, CO 80160   Clarence A. Sturdivant, Supv.
Founded: 1956. **Staff:** Prof 7; Other 2. **Subjects:** Petroleum - exploration, refining, production, engineering; mining geology and engineering; petrochemicals. **Holdings:** 90,000 books; periodicals, documents and patent specifications; 70,000 maps and charts; 1 million computerized data records; 1500 technical reports (hard copy and microfiche); 3000 laboratory notebooks; technical correspondence. **Services:** Interlibrary loans; center not open to public. **Computerized Information Services:** Online systems.

★7508★
MARBLEHEAD HISTORICAL SOCIETY - JEREMIAH LEE MANSION - LIBRARY (Hist)
161 Washington St.
Box 1048   Phone: (617) 631-1069
Marblehead, MA 01945
Subjects: Local history and genealogy. **Holdings:** Figures not available for documents. **Services:** Library open to public by appointment.

MARCH AIR FORCE BASE (CA)
See: U.S. Air Force Base - March Base Library

MARCH (Clarence E.) LIBRARY
See: Androscoggin Historical Society - Clarence E. March Library

★7509★
MARCH OF DIMES BIRTH DEFECTS FOUNDATION - REFERENCE ROOM (Med)
1275 Mamaroneck Ave.   Phone: (914) 428-7100
White Plains, NY 10605   Sandra Schepis, Libn.
Founded: 1958. **Staff:** Prof 1. **Subjects:** Birth defects, pediatrics, obstetrics, maternal and child health. **Special Collections:** Reprints of March of Dimes Grantees. **Holdings:** 2200 books; 1722 bound periodical volumes; 5 VF drawers. **Subscriptions:** 115 journals and other serials. **Services:** Interlibrary loans; library open to public by appointment only. **Networks/Consortia:** Member of Health Information Libraries of Westchester. **Publications:** Monthly acquisitions list; semiannual journal holdings list.

★7510★
MARCHAIS (Jacques) CENTER OF TIBETAN ARTS, INC. - LIBRARY (Rel-Theol)
338 Lighthouse Ave.   Phone: (212) 987-3478
Staten Island, NY 10306   Sigrid Sidrow, Libn.
Founded: 1946. **Staff:** Prof 1. **Subjects:** Buddhist art, philosophy and religion with emphasis on Tibetan Buddhism. **Services:** Library open to public with restrictions.

MARCY PSYCHIATRIC CENTER
See: Utica/Marcy Psychiatric Center

MARDEN (A. Hollis) BIBLIOTHEQUE
See: Hopital Reine Elizabeth - A. Hollis Bibliotheque

MARIAN LIBRARY
See: University of Dayton

★7511★
MARIANJOY REHABILITATION HOSPITAL - MEDICAL LIBRARY (Med)
Roosevelt Rd.
Box 795   Phone: (312) 653-7600
Wheaton, IL 60187   Sr. Louise Ebel, Dir.
Staff: Prof 1; Other 1. **Subjects:** Rehabilitation, neurology, orthopedics, pain, biofeedback. **Holdings:** 286 books. **Subscriptions:** 35 journals and other serials. **Services:** Interlibrary loans; library open to public with restrictions. **Networks/Consortia:** Member of Fox Valley Health Science Library Consortium; DuPage Library System.

★7512★
MARIANOPOLIS COLLEGE - LIBRARY - SPECIAL COLLECTIONS (Hum)
3880 Cote des Neiges Rd.   Phone: (514) 931-8792
Montreal, PQ, Canada H3H 1W1   Dr. Roman R. Grodzicky, Chf.Libn.
Founded: 1908. **Special Collections:** Canadiana and rare books (150). **Services:** Interlibrary loans; copying; library open to professors and alumni.

★7513★
MARICOPA COUNTY GENERAL HOSPITAL - MEDICAL LIBRARY (Med)
2601 E. Roosevelt St.   Phone: (602) 267-5197
Phoenix, AZ 85008   Fernande Hebert, Med.Libn.
Founded: 1958. **Staff:** Prof 1; Other 2. **Subjects:** Medicine, surgery, nursing, hospital administration. **Special Collections:** Audiotapes in medicine and its specialities. **Holdings:** 3700 books; 6500 bound periodical volumes. **Subscriptions:** 275 journals and other serials. **Services:** Interlibrary loans; copying.

★7514★
MARICOPA COUNTY LAW LIBRARY (Law)
East Court Bldg., 2nd Fl.
101 W. Jefferson St.   Phone: (602) 262-3461
Phoenix, AZ 85003   Elizabeth Kelley, Dir.
Founded: 1912. **Staff:** Prof 4; Other 6. **Subjects:** Law and related subjects. **Holdings:** 100,000 books and bound periodical volumes. **Subscriptions:** 350 journals and other serials. **Services:** Interlibrary loans; copying (both limited); library open to public. **Computerized Information Services:** WESTLAW. **Staff:** Bruce Naegeli, Pub.Ser.; Patricia Higgins, Cat.Libn.; Richard Teenstra, Ref./Assoc.Dir.

★7515★
MARICOPA MEDICAL SOCIETY - LIBRARY (Med)†
2025 N. Central Ave.   Phone: (602) 258-6461
Phoenix, AZ 85004
Founded: 1923. **Subjects:** Medicine, surgery and allied fields on a clinical level. **Holdings:** 25,000 volumes.

★7516★
MARICOPA TECHNICAL COMMUNITY COLLEGE - INDUSTRY EDUCATION CENTER LIBRARY
108 N. 40th St.
Phoenix, AZ 85034
Defunct. Holdings absorbed by Maricopa Technical Community College - Library Resource Center.

★7517★
MARICOPA TECHNICAL COMMUNITY COLLEGE - LIBRARY RESOURCE CENTER (Educ)
108 N. 40th St.   Phone: (602) 257-8500
Phoenix, AZ 85034   Peg Smith, Dir.
Founded: 1969. **Staff:** Prof 3; Other 5. **Subjects:** Business, graphic communications, data processing, Indian history and culture, black studies, nursing and allied health, industrial arts. **Holdings:** 45,000 books; 7000 programmed materials and media kits (cataloged); 6873 microfiche; 395 reels of microfilm; 1393 titles on cassette tapes; 864 titles of filmstrips and filmloops. **Subscriptions:** 350 journals and other serials; 10 newspapers. **Services:** Interlibrary loans; copying; library open to public with proper identification. **Publications:** Acquisitions List, monthly - for internal distribution only; bibliographies. **Special Catalogs:** Special Materials (card). **Remarks:** Contains the holdings of its former Industry Education Center Library. **Staff:** Fran Johnson, Ref.Libn.; Bruce Stasium, Circ.Asst.; Sue Thomas, Circ.Asst.; Amanda Rathbun, Acq.Tech.; David Schmidt, Mechanical Techn.; Larry Wild, Coord., Bus./Tech.Serv.

MARIETTA MEMORIAL MEDICAL LIBRARY
See: John Peter Smith Hospital

★7518★
MARIN COUNTY HISTORICAL SOCIETY - LIBRARY (Hist)
1125 B St.   Phone: (415) 454-8538
San Rafael, CA 94901   Elsie P. Mazzini, Dir./Pres.
Founded: 1935. **Staff:** Prof 10; Other 5. **Subjects:** History of Marin County and California, history of coastal Indians. **Special Collections:** Marin Journal newspapers, 1861-1947; photographs of Marin County. **Holdings:** 1000 volumes; 100 bound manuscripts and studies; 2 VF drawers of source material; 3 scrapbooks of clippings. **Subscriptions:** 10 journals and other serials. **Services:** Copying; library open to public for reference use only. **Publications:** Bulletin; Newsletter, bimonthly.

★7519★

MARIN COUNTY LAW LIBRARY (Law)
Hall of Justice, C-33
San Rafael, CA 94903   Phone: (415) 499-6355
    Meyer W. Halpern, Hd. Law Libn.
Founded: 1891. **Staff:** Prof 1; Other 4. **Subjects:** Law. **Holdings:** 22,600 books; 1800 bound periodical volumes; cassettes; California State Law Library publications. **Subscriptions:** 35 journals and other serials. **Services:** Interlibrary loans; copying; library open to public.

★7520★

MARIN GENERAL HOSPITAL - LIBRARY (Med)
Box 2129
San Rafael, CA 94901   Phone: (415) 461-0100
    Julie Kahl, Libn.
Staff: 1. **Subjects:** Medicine, psychiatry, nursing. **Holdings:** 800 books; 2800 bound periodical volumes; 1 VF cabinet of pamphlets; 8 shelves of documents. **Subscriptions:** 123 journals and other serials. **Services:** Interlibrary loans; copying; library open to public with restrictions.

★7521★

MARIN WILDLIFE CENTER - LIBRARY (Sci-Tech)
76 Albert Park Lane
Box 957
San Rafael, CA 94915   Phone: (415) 454-6961
    Alice C. Katzung, Dir.
Subjects: Natural history; California botany, mammals, reptiles and birds; marine and aquatic biology. **Holdings:** 1000 books. **Services:** Library open to public with restrictions.

MARINE AWARENESS CENTER
See: **University of Rhode Island, Narragansett Bay - Division of Marine Resources**

MARINE BAND LIBRARY
See: **U.S. Marine Corps**

★7522★

MARINE BIOLOGICAL LABORATORY - LIBRARY (Sci-Tech)
    Phone: (617) 548-3705
Woods Hole, MA 02543   Jane Fessenden, Libn.
Founded: 1888. **Staff:** 11. **Subjects:** Marine biology, biochemistry, physiology, oceanography, meteorology, ecology, paleontology, physics, marine botany, invertebrate zoology, chemistry, geology. **Holdings:** 30,000 books; 187,000 bound periodical volumes; 300,000 reprints (cataloged). **Subscriptions:** 5000 journals and other serials. **Services:** Interlibrary loans; copying; library not open to public. **Computerized Information Services:** DIALOG, MEDLINE, SDC. **Networks/Consortia:** Member of Southeastern Massachusetts Health Sciences Libraries (SEMCO). **Publications:** 1983 Serial Publications - for sale. **Remarks:** Figures listed above include the books and serials of the Woods Hole Oceanographic Institution - Research Library. **Staff:** Catherine Norton, Asst.Libn.

MARINE BIOLOGICAL SOCIETY
See: **Western Canadian Universities**

MARINE CORPS
See: **U.S. Marine Corps**

MARINE CORPS DEVELOPMENT & EDUCATION COMMAND
See: **U.S. Marine Corps - Education Center - James Carson Breckinridge Library**

★7523★

MARINE ENVIRONMENTAL SCIENCES CONSORTIUM - LIBRARY (Sci-Tech)
Dauphin Island Sea Lab
Box 386
Dauphin Island, AL 36528   Phone: (205) 861-2141
    Judy Stout, Libn.
Founded: 1971. **Staff:** Prof 2. **Subjects:** Marine biology, oceanography, marine geology, ecology. **Holdings:** 3250 books; 5500 unbound reprints and reports; 60 volumes of bound reprints and collections; 50 volumes of cruise reports. **Subscriptions:** 140 journals and other serials. **Services:** Interlibrary loans; copying; library open to public. **Publications:** Journal of Marine Science; Northeast Gulf Science. **Staff:** Connie Mallon, Asst.Libn.

★7524★

MARINE MIDLAND BANK - LIBRARY (Bus-Fin)
140 Broadway, 22nd Fl.
New York, NY 10015   Phone: (212) 797-6473
    Joan W. Glazier, Lib.Off.
Founded: 1968. **Staff:** Prof 2; Other 4. **Subjects:** Banking, finance, investments, management. **Special Collections:** Moody's Manuals from 1930. **Holdings:** 7000 books; 95 VF drawers; Wall Street Journal from 1947 (microfilm); American Banker from 1971 (microfilm); New York Times from 1967 (microfilm). **Subscriptions:** 600 journals and other serials; 10 newspapers. **Services:** Interlibrary loans; copying; library open to SLA members and clients. **Computerized Information Services:** DIALOG, Dow Jones News Retrieval. **Publications:** Acquisitions list, monthly - by request. **Staff:** Colleen Byrne, Asst.Libn.

★7525★

MARINE MIDLAND BANK - TECHNICAL INFORMATION CENTER (Bus-Fin)
One Marine Midland Ctr., 4th Fl., W. Wing   Phone: (716) 843-5011
Buffalo, NY 14240   Eva M. Saintcross, Stat.Libn.
Founded: 1973. **Subjects:** Computers, computer programs, management, systems analysis, banks and banking, programming languages. **Special Collections:** Papers and theses (120). **Holdings:** 2731 books; 1427 periodical volumes; 84 microfiche; 35 cassettes; 727 reports; 120 papers and theses; 7 shelves and 2 VF drawers of uncataloged materials. **Subscriptions:** 140 journals and other serials; 7 newspapers. **Services:** Interlibrary loans; copying; center open to public. **Computerized Information Services:** Computerized cataloging and circulation. **Networks/Consortia:** Member of Western New York Library Resources Council. **Publications:** Acquisition list, monthly. **Special Indexes:** Index of Marine Midland Bank papers and theses, 1950-1979; bibliographies.

★7526★

MARINE MUSEUM AT FALL RIVER, INC. - LIBRARY (Hist)
70 Water St.
Fall River, MA 02722   Phone: (617) 674-3533
    John F. Gosson, Cur.
Founded: 1968. **Staff:** 3. **Subjects:** History of power-driven water craft; arctic exploration. **Special Collections:** William King Covell Collection; James S. Hart Collection. **Holdings:** 1100 books; 125 bound periodical volumes; 5000 photographic plates; 1000 glass slides. **Services:** Library open to public with restrictions.

★7527★

MARINE PRODUCTS COMPANY - LIBRARY (Sci-Tech)
333 W. First St.
Boston, MA 02127   Phone: (617) 268-0758
    Dr. E. James Iorio, Mgr.
Staff: Prof 7; Other 6. **Subjects:** Organic chemicals, pharmacology, toxicology. **Holdings:** 200 books; 630 bound periodical volumes; 139 suppliers' catalogs. **Services:** Copying; library not open to public. **Computerized Information Services:** Online systems. **Publications:** Tableting and Coating - 3/year. **Staff:** Prof. George Krause, Dir. of Res.

MARINE SCIENCE AND MARITIME STUDIES CENTER
See: **Northeastern University**

★7528★

MARINELAND, INC. - RESEARCH LABORATORY (Sci-Tech)
Route 1, Box 122
St. Augustine, FL 32084   Phone: (904) 829-5607
    Robert L. Jenkins, Cur.
Staff: 2. **Subjects:** Marine biology, marine mammals, animal husbandry, oceanology, water testing. **Holdings:** 550 books and bound periodical volumes; 1000 other periodicals; 1000 reprints; 12 films. **Services:** Interlibrary loans; copying; library open to public for reference use only. **Publications:** Curator's Notebook.

★7529★

MARINERS MUSEUM - LIBRARY (Trans)
    Phone: (804) 595-0368
Newport News, VA 23606   Ardie L. Kelly, Libn.
Founded: 1933. **Staff:** Prof 2; Other 2. **Subjects:** Shipping, shipbuilding, navigation, merchant marine, navies, exploration and travel, whaling, yachting. **Holdings:** 60,000 volumes; 150,000 photographs; logbooks, journals and ships' papers; microfilm, tape, maps and charts. **Subscriptions:** 200 journals and other serials. **Services:** Copying; library open to public.

★7530★

MARINETTE COUNTY LAW LIBRARY (Law)†
Court House
1926 Hall Ave.
Marinette, WI 54143   Phone: (715) 735-3371
    Don E. Phillips, Ck. of Court
Founded: 1880. **Staff:** 1. **Subjects:** Law. **Holdings:** 7000 volumes. **Services:** Library open to public.

★7531★

MARION COUNTY LAW LIBRARY (Law)
602 City County Bldg.
Indianapolis, IN 46204   Phone: (317) 633-3643
    Lynn S. Connor, Libn.
Founded: 1963. **Staff:** Prof 1; Other 2. **Subjects:** Law. **Holdings:** 14,550

books; 197 bound periodical volumes; 1400 volumes on microfiche. **Subscriptions:** 35 journals and other serials. **Services:** Interlibrary loans; copying; library open to public. **Computerized Information Services:** WESTLAW. **Networks/Consortia:** Member of Central Indiana Area Library Services Authority. **Publications:** Annual Report - for internal distribution only; Worth Reading, weekly - for internal distribution only. **Staff:** Bonnie J. Warren, Asst.Libn.

★7532★
MARION COUNTY LAW LIBRARY (Law)
Court House
Marion, OH 43302
Phone: (614) 387-5871
Hazel Aldrich, Ck.
Subjects: Law. **Holdings:** 14,000 volumes.

★7533★
MARION COUNTY MEMORIAL HOSPITAL - LIBRARY (Med)
1108 N. Main St.
Marion, SC 29571
Phone: (803) 423-3210
Ann Finney, Educ.Dir.
Staff: Prof 1. **Subjects:** Medicine, surgery and nursing. **Holdings:** 602 books; 220 bound periodical volumes. **Subscriptions:** 22 journals and other serials. **Services:** Library not open to public. **Networks/Consortia:** Member of Health Communications Network.

MARION COUNTY PUBLIC LIBRARY
See: Indianapolis-Marion County Public Library

★7534★
MARION GENERAL HOSPITAL - MEDICAL LIBRARY (Med)†
Wabash & Euclid Avenues
Marion, IN 46952
Phone: (317) 662-4607
Kay Lake, Dir., Educ.Servs.
Staff: 1. **Subjects:** Medicine, nursing, management. **Holdings:** 1100 books; 225 bound periodical volumes; 118 video cassettes. **Subscriptions:** 138 journals and other serials. **Services:** Interlibrary loans; copying; library open to students and professionals only.

★7535★
MARION LABORATORIES, INC. - R & D LIBRARY (Med)
10236 Bunker Ridge Rd.
Kansas City, MO 64137
Phone: (816) 761-2500
Jane Stehlik-Kokker, Mgr., Sci.Info.Serv.
Founded: 1967. **Staff:** Prof 2; Other 2. **Subjects:** Medicine, pharmacology, pharmaceutical technology. **Holdings:** 1900 books; 100 bound periodical volumes; 800 reels of microfilm (109 titles). **Subscriptions:** 320 journals and other serials. **Services:** Interlibrary loans; copying; translations; SDI; library not open to public. **Computerized Information Services:** DIALOG, SDC, BRS, NLM. **Networks/Consortia:** Member of Kansas City Library Network, Inc. (KCLN). **Publications:** Marion Library Alert, monthly - for internal distribution only. **Staff:** Flo Jordan, Lib.Assoc.; Sarah Weitzel, Info.Sci.

MARISKA ALDRICH MEMORIAL FOUNDATION, INC.
See: Aldrich (Mariska) Memorial Foundation, Inc.

★7536★
MARISSA HISTORICAL & GENEALOGICAL SOCIETY - LIBRARY (Hist)
Box 27
Marissa, IL 62257
Doris Steele, Libn.
Founded: 1973. **Staff:** 3. **Subjects:** Genealogy, local history. **Special Collections:** Family and church histories. **Holdings:** Scrapbooks, area histories, rare books, ledgers, autographs, microfilm and microfiche. **Subscriptions:** 50 journals and other serials. **Services:** Copying; library open to public. **Publications:** Branching Out From St. Clair County, quarterly.

★7537★
MARIST COLLEGE - LIBRARY (Rel-Theol)
220 Taylor St., N.E.
Washington, DC 20017
Phone: (202) 529-2821
Paul M. Cabrita, Hd.Libn.
Founded: 1898. **Staff:** Prof 3. **Subjects:** Philosophy, theology, scripture, canon law, pastoral theology. **Holdings:** 19,700 books; 5500 bound periodical volumes. **Subscriptions:** 69 journals and other serials. **Services:** Library open to public by appointment. **Networks/Consortia:** Member of Washington Theological Consortium. **Staff:** Lewis F. Luks, Cons.; Timothy Keating, Asst.Libn.

MARITIME COLLEGE
See: SUNY

MARITIME CONFERENCE ARCHIVES
See: United Church of Canada

★7538★
MARITIME MUSEUM (Allen Knight) - LIBRARY (Hist)
550 Calle Principal
Box 805
Monterey, CA 93940
Phone: (408) 375-2553
G. Robert Giet, Libn.
Founded: 1970. **Staff:** 2. **Subjects:** Ships and shipping - American and foreign. **Holdings:** 1197 books; 193 special collections (cataloged); list of merchant vessels; Lloyd's Registers; photographs of ships. **Services:** Library open to public for reference use only.

★7539★
MARITIME MUSEUM OF BRITISH COLUMBIA - LIBRARY (Hist)
28-30 Bastion Square
Victoria, BC, Canada V8W 1H9
Phone: (604) 385-4222
C.H. Shaw, Dir.
Founded: 1965. **Staff:** 2. **Subjects:** Maritime history, West Coast shipping. **Special Collections:** Collection of ship's models and marine artifacts. **Holdings:** 8000 books; 150 bound periodical volumes; 10,000 pamphlets and documents (cataloged). **Subscriptions:** 15 journals and other serials. **Services:** Copying; library open to public by prior arrangement only. **Publications:** Newsletter, quarterly. **Staff:** A.K. Cameron, Cur.

★7540★
MARITIME RESOURCE MANAGEMENT SERVICE - INFORMATION CENTRE (Plan)†
16 Station St.
P.O. Box 310
Amherst, NS, Canada B4H 3H3
Phone: (902) 667-7231
C. Bradley Fay, Mgr.
Staff: Prof 1; Other 3. **Subjects:** Atlantic and Maritime Provinces: resources, planning, engineering, land use, environment, community development. **Holdings:** 8000 books. **Subscriptions:** 50 journals and other serials; 10 newspapers. **Services:** Interlibrary loans; copying; centre open to public. **Computerized Information Services:** Online systems. **Staff:** M.E. Campbell, Libn.

MARITIME SCHOOL OF SOCIAL WORK
See: Dalhousie University

★7541★
MARITIME TELEGRAPH & TELEPHONE CO. LTD. - INFORMATION RESOURCE CENTRE (Sci-Tech)
P.O. Box 880
Halifax, NS, Canada B3J 2W3
Phone: (902) 421-4570
Joan E. Fage, Libn.
Founded: 1979. **Staff:** Prof 1; Other 2. **Subjects:** Telecommunications, business. **Holdings:** 2500 books; 500 periodical volumes; 10 VF drawers of annual reports, pamphlets and clippings; 4000 reports on microfiche; 100 serial titles in microform. **Subscriptions:** 400 journals and other serials. **Services:** Interlibrary loans; copying; library open to public with restrictions. **Computerized Information Services:** Online systems; computerized cataloging and serials. **Networks/Consortia:** Member of Nova Scotia On-Line Consortium. **Publications:** General Circular, 1979; Current Awareness Bibliography, semiannual; New Publications List, bimonthly - all for internal distribution only.

MARITIMES FOREST RESEARCH CENTRE
See: Canada - Canadian Forestry Service

★7542★
MARITZ, INC. - LIBRARY (Bus-Fin)
1355 N. Highway Dr.
Fenton, MO 63026
Phone: (314) 225-4000
Patty S. Slocombe, Libn.
Founded: 1968. **Staff:** 1. **Subjects:** Marketing, psychology, travel, art. **Holdings:** 1450 books; 33 drawers of pamphlets and clippings; archives. **Subscriptions:** 120 journals and other serials. **Services:** Library open to public with restrictions. **Computerized Information Services:** DIALOG. **Networks/Consortia:** Member of St. Louis Regional Library Network.

★7543★
MARITZ TRAVEL COMPANY - TRAVEL LIBRARY (Rec)
1385 N. Highway Dr.
Fenton, MO 63026
Phone: (314) 225-4000
Sue Hamilton, Libn.
Founded: 1969. **Staff:** 1. **Subjects:** Travel data - hotels, restaurants, sightseeing, steamships, countries and cities. **Holdings:** 300 books; 177 bound periodical volumes; 49 VF drawers of travel-related brochures and reports. **Subscriptions:** 35 journals and other serials. **Services:** Interlibrary loans; library not open to public. **Publications:** Subscription Content Update - for internal distribution only.

★7544★
MARK TWAIN BIRTHPLACE MUSEUM - RESEARCH LIBRARY (Hist)
Box 54   Phone: (314) 565-3449
Stoutsville, MO 65283   Stanley Fast, Adm.
Founded: 1960. **Staff:** Prof 2. **Subjects:** Samuel L. Clemens (Mark Twain) -
life and family. **Special Collections:** Manuscript used for the first printing of
The Adventures of Tom Sawyer and associated letters and documents.
Holdings: 400 books. **Services:** Library open to public for reference use only.
Remarks: Maintained by the Missouri State Department of Natural Resources.

★7545★
MARK TWAIN MEMORIAL - LIBRARY (Hum)
351 Farmington Ave.   Phone: (203) 247-0998
Hartford, CT 06105   Mr. Wynn Lee, Dir.
Founded: 1929. **Subjects:** Samuel L. Clemens and family. **Special
Collections:** Samuel L. Clemens manuscript material, letters, clippings,
pamphlets, documents and photographs. **Services:** Copying; library open to
public by appointment.

★7546★
MARK TWAIN MUSEUM - LIBRARY (Hum)
208 Hill St.   Phone: (314) 221-9010
Hannibal, MO 63401   Henry Sweets, Cur.
Founded: 1937. **Staff:** Prof 2; Other 3. **Subjects:** Mark Twain. **Special
Collections:** Norman Rockwell paintings (15); first editions of Twain's works.
Holdings: 400 books; 8 bound periodical volumes; booklets and pamphlets;
scrapbooks of clippings; manuscript letters; 1 moving picture of Mark Twain.
Services: Copying; library only open to special students with permission of
curator. **Remarks:** Maintained by Mark Twain Home Board.

★7547★
MARK TWAIN RESEARCH FOUNDATION - LIBRARY (Hum)
    Phone: (314) 565-3570
Perry, MO 63462   Chester L. Davis, Exec.Sec.
Founded: 1939. **Subjects:** Items related to the life and writings of Mark
Twain. **Services:** Open to foundation members only. **Publications:** The
Twainian, bimonthly - to members.

★7548★
MARKEM CORPORATION - LIBRARY (Sci-Tech)
150 Congress St.   Phone: (603) 352-1130
Keene, NH 03431   Adrienne Johnson, Libn.
Founded: 1966. **Staff:** 1. **Subjects:** Mechanics, chemistry, graphic arts,
business management, data processing, statistics, language aides, economics,
sociology. **Holdings:** 2250 books; 11 volumes of credit ratings; 5 VF drawers
of patents; 100 U.S. government census reports. **Subscriptions:** 300
journals and other serials. **Services:** Library open to families of employees.

MARKET PATHOLOGY RESEARCH LIBRARY
See: U.S.D.A. - Agricultural Research Service - North Central Region

★7549★
**MARKETING INFORMATION INSTITUTE - SELECTED INFORMATION
    LIBRARY CENTER** (Bus-Fin)
861 Sixth Ave., Suite 510   Phone: (714) 231-8939
San Diego, CA 92101   Angela M. Nossal, Libn.
Staff: Prof 1; Other 2. **Subjects:** Marketing. **Holdings:** 10,000 books; 1980
census on magnetic tapes; San Diego real estate ownership records on
microfilm. **Subscriptions:** 44 journals and other serials. **Services:** Copying;
library open to public with approval of executive officer. **Computerized
Information Services:** New York Times Information Service, DIALOG, SDC,
BRS; computerized cataloging. **Publications:** Pace Newsletter, quarterly - on
request.

MARKOWITZ (Jewel K.) LIBRARY
See: Beth David Reform Congregation - Jewel K. Markowitz Library

MARKS (Max B. & Louisa S.) MEMORIAL MEDICAL LIBRARY
**See: Metropolitan Jewish Geriatric Center - Max B. & Louisa S. Marks
    Memorial Medical Library**

★7550★
MARLBOROUGH GALLERY - LIBRARY (Art)
40 W. 57th St.   Phone: (212) 541-4900
New York, NY 10019   Dorothy W. Herman, Libn.
Staff: Prof 1. **Subjects:** Modern painting, sculpture, drawings; graphics;
American painting, sculpture, drawings, photography. **Special
Collections:** Auction catalogs from American and European auction-houses.
Holdings: 7500 volumes; exhibition catalogs. **Subscriptions:** 15 journals and

other serials. **Services:** Copying; library open to public with restrictions.
Publications: Catalogs for exhibitions held at gallery.

★7551★
MARLBOROUGH HOSPITAL - HEALTH SCIENCE LIBRARY (Med)
57 Union St.   Phone: (617) 485-1121
Marlborough, MA 01752   Eleanor Kunen, Libn.
Staff: Prof 1. **Subjects:** Medicine, nursing and allied sciences. **Holdings:** 800
books; 1000 bound periodical volumes; audiovisuals. **Subscriptions:** 160
journals and other serials. **Services:** Interlibrary loans; copying; library open to
public for reference use only. **Computerized Information Services:**
MEDLINE. **Networks/Consortia:** Member of Consortium for Information
Resources (CIR).

MARMION LIBRARY
See: Church of the Incarnation

MARQUAND LIBRARY
See: Princeton University

★7552★
**MARQUANDIA SOCIETY FOR STUDIES IN HISTORY AND LITERATURE -
    LIBRARY** (Hum)
421 Scotland St., No. 6   Phone: (804) 229-7049
Williamsburg, VA 23185   John Thelin, Dir.
Founded: 1976. **Staff:** Prof 1. **Subjects:** John P. Marquand, New England,
fine printing. **Holdings:** 300 books. **Services:** Library not open to public.
Publications: Newsletter, irregular. **Formerly:** Located in Santa Ana, CA.

MARQUAT MEMORIAL LIBRARY
See: U.S. Army Institute for Military Assistance

★7553★
MARQUETTE COPPERSMITHING COMPANY - LIBRARY (Sci-Tech)
Box 4584   Phone: (215) 877-9362
Philadelphia, PA 19131   T. T. Hill, Libn.
Founded: 1946. **Staff:** Prof 1. **Subjects:** Applied mechanics,
thermodynamics, chemical and metallurgical engineering, nuclear physics.
Holdings: 1900 books; 3000 bound periodical volumes; 800 other volumes.
Subscriptions: 46 journals and other serials. **Services:** Library serves
company technical personnel only.

★7554★
**MARQUETTE COUNTY HISTORICAL SOCIETY - J.M. LONGYEAR RESEARCH
    LIBRARY** (Hist)
213 N. Front St.   Phone: (906) 226-3571
Marquette, MI 49855   Frank O. Paull, Jr., Dir.
Founded: 1918. **Staff:** 8. **Subjects:** History of Great Lakes area and
Michigan - shipping, railroads, industries, ethnic groups. **Special Collections:**
Charles Thompson Harvey Papers; Burt family papers; J.M. Longyear papers;
E.N. Breitung papers; local newspapers, bound and on microfilm; business and
organization records. **Holdings:** 8000 books; 2000 pamphlets (cataloged); 35
VF drawers of letters, manuscripts, maps, photographs, and documents; all
known copies of local newspaper, Lake Superior Journal, Lake Superior News,
and Mining Journal, July 1846 to present, available on microfilm.
Subscriptions: 25 journals and other serials; 6 newspapers. **Services:** Library
open to qualified researchers. **Publications:** Harlow's Wooden Man, quarterly
- to members or by subscription.

★7555★
**MARQUETTE GENERAL HOSPITAL - KEVIN F. O'BRIEN HEALTH SCIENCES
    LIBRARY** (Med)
420 W. Magnetic   Phone: (906) 228-9440
Marquette, MI 49855   Mildred E. Kingsbury, Lib.Dir.
Founded: 1974. **Staff:** Prof 1; Other 1. **Subjects:** Medicine, nursing and
related fields. **Holdings:** 5555 books; 500 bound periodical volumes; 4 VF
drawers of pamphlets; 3000 slides. **Subscriptions:** 185 journals and other
serials. **Services:** Interlibrary loans; library open to public. **Computerized
Information Services:** MEDLINE. **Networks/Consortia:** Member of
Kentucky-Ohio-Michigan Regional Medical Library Network (KOMRML);
Michigan Area Serial Holdings Consortium (MASH); Upper Peninsula of
Michigan Hospital Libraries Consortium (UPHLC).

★7556★
**MARQUETTE UNIVERSITY - DEPARTMENT OF SPECIAL COLLECTIONS AND
    UNIVERSITY ARCHIVES** (Hist)
Memorial Library
1415 W. Wisconsin Ave.   Phone: (414) 224-7256
Milwaukee, WI 53233   Charles B. Elston, Dept.Hd.
Founded: 1961. **Staff:** Prof 4; Other 4. **Subjects:** Catholic social thought and

action, Catholic Indian missions, Marquette University history, sociology of religion, recent U.S. political history. **Special Collections:** National Catholic Conference for Interracial Justice Collection, 1956 to present (300 feet); Project Equality, Inc. Collection, 1971 to present (60 feet); Sr. Margaret Ellen Traxler Papers, 1909-1919, 1950 to present (55 feet); National Coalition of American Nuns Collection, 1969 to present (16 feet); Sister Formation Movement Records, 1954 to present (40 feet); The Madonna Center Records, 1865-1964 (10 feet); Council on Urban Life Records, 1965 to present (52 feet); The Dorothy Day - Catholic Worker Collection, 1933 to present (100 feet); Catholic Association for International Peace Archives, 1926-1970 (45 feet); Monsignor Luigi G. Ligutti Papers, 1915 to present (40 feet); Brother Leo V. Ryan Papers, 1956 to present (30 feet); President's Committee on Employment of the Handicapped Archives, 1946 to present (82 feet); John L. and Barbara B. Hammond Papers, 1898-1961 (8 feet); Joseph R. McCarthy Papers, 1930-1957 (100 feet); Charles J. Kersten Papers, 1946-1971 (20 feet); Donald T. McNeill Collection, 1933-1968 (70 feet); Citizens for Educational Freedom Records, 1959 to present (20 feet); Sociology of Religion Collections, 1938 to present (21 feet); H. Herman Rauch Labor Arbitration Case Files, 1940-1978 (42 feet); John Ronald Reuel Tolkien Manuscript Collection, 1930 to present (10 feet); Elizabeth Whitcomb Houghton Collection, 1900-1945 (10 feet); Karl J. Priebe Papers, 1900-1978 (15 feet); National Catholic Rural Life Conference Archives, 1923 to present (88 feet); Justice and Peace Center (Milwaukee) Archives, 1970 to present (36 feet). **Holdings:** 15,000 volumes; 2140 cubic feet of archival and manuscript collections relating primarily to Catholic social action, 1890 to present; 2120 cubic feet of Marquette University Archives, 1881 to present; 475 cubic feet of records of Bureau of Catholic Indian Missions and other missions. **Subscriptions:** 22 journals and other serials; 7 newspapers. **Services:** Copying; library open to public. **Networks/Consortia:** Member of Library Council of Metropolitan Milwaukee, Inc. (LCOMM). **Staff:** Rev. Robert V. Callen, S.J., Univ. Archv.; Philip C. Bantin, Asst.Archv.; Phillip M. Runkel, Asst.Archv.; Mark G. Thiel, Project Archv.

★7557★
MARQUETTE UNIVERSITY - FOUNDATION CENTER REGIONAL REFERENCE COLLECTION (Soc Sci)
Memorial Library
1415 W. Wisconsin Ave.   Phone: (414) 224-1515
Milwaukee, WI 53233   Susan Hopwood, Found.Coll.Libn.
Staff: Prof 1. **Subjects:** Fundraising, proposal writing, philanthropy. **Holdings:** 300 books; publications of the Foundation Center; foundation annual reports; Internal Revenue Service Information Returns (3300 Midwest foundations); 1000 pamphlets; 10,000 microfiche. **Subscriptions:** 25 journals and other serials. **Services:** Copying; collection open to public. **Computerized Information Services:** DIALOG. **Publications:** Foundations in Wisconsin: A Directory, biennial.

★7558★
MARQUETTE UNIVERSITY - LEGAL RESEARCH CENTER (Law)
1103 W. Wisconsin Ave.   Phone: (414) 224-7031
Milwaukee, WI 53233   Robert L. Starz, Law Libn.
Founded: 1908. **Staff:** Prof 4; Other 4. **Subjects:** Law. **Holdings:** 100,522 books and bound periodical volumes; 23 VF drawers of pamphlets; 120 linear feet of unbound periodicals; 8159 volumes in microform. **Subscriptions:** 1969 journals and other serials; 15 newspapers. **Services:** Interlibrary loans; copying; library open to Marquette students, faculty, judges and lawyers. **Computerized Information Services:** LEXIS. **Publications:** New Titles, quarterly. **Staff:** Sue Khavari, Hd.Cat; Mildred Strawn, Hd., Tech.Serv.

★7559★
MARQUETTE UNIVERSITY - MEMORIAL LIBRARY (Hum)
1415 W. Wisconsin Ave.   Phone: (414) 224-7214
Milwaukee, WI 53233   William M. Gardner, Dir. of Libs.
Founded: 1881. **Staff:** Prof 25; Other 40. **Subjects:** Philosophy, theology, humanities, history. **Special Collections:** Lester W. Olson Lincoln Collection; Jesuitica. **Holdings:** 560,606 books and bound periodical volumes; 217,587 pieces of microtext; 1010 audio recordings. **Subscriptions:** 7076 journals and other serials; 100 newspapers. **Services:** Interlibrary loans; copying; library open to public with restrictions. **Computerized Information Services:** BRS; computerized cataloging and serials. **Networks/Consortia:** Member of WILS; Library Council of Metropolitan Milwaukee, Inc. (LCOMM); CRL; OCLC. **Special Catalogs:** Computerized serials record on microfiche. **Special Indexes:** Index to University Archives, Manuscript and Archival Collections. **Staff:** David J. Farley, Asst.Dir. for Adm.; Olive S. Caulker, Asst.Dir./ Tech.Serv.; Robert J. Haertle, Hd., Coll.Dept.; Rev. J. Philip Talmage, Hd., Ref.Dept.; Michele M. Plewa, Adm.Asst.; Charles Elston, Hd., Spec.Coll.; Rev. Robert V. Callen, S.J., Univ.Archv.; Mary J. Cronin, Asst.Dir., Pub.Serv.; Kathleen Frymark, Circ.Libn.

★7560★
MARQUETTE UNIVERSITY - SCIENCE LIBRARY (Sci-Tech)
560 N. Sixteenth St.   Phone: (414) 224-3396
Milwaukee, WI 53233   Jay H. Kirk, Hd., Sci.Lib.
Staff: Prof 4; Other 6. **Subjects:** Human biology, dentistry, nursing, engineering, chemistry, mathematics, physics. **Holdings:** 55,000 books; 51,000 bound periodical volumes. **Subscriptions:** 2000 journals and other serials. **Services:** Interlibrary loans (fee); copying; library open to public. **Computerized Information Services:** DIALOG, BRS, MEDLINE; computerized cataloging and serials. **Networks/Consortia:** Member of Regional Medical Library - Region 3; Library Council of Metropolitan Milwaukee, Inc. (LCOMM); WILS; OCLC. **Staff:** Patricia Berge, Asst.Sci.Libn.; Gwendolyn Goldbeck, Asst.Sci.Libn.; Ljudmila Mursec, Asst.Sci.Libn.; Keven Riggle, Operational Serv.Supv.

★7561★
MARQUIS BIOGRAPHICAL LIBRARY SOCIETY, INC.
2810 E. Oakland Park Blvd., Suite 210
Fort Lauderdale, FL 33306
Defunct

★7562★
MARQUIS WHO'S WHO, INC. - RESEARCH DEPARTMENT LIBRARY (Hist)
200 E. Ohio St.   Phone: (312) 787-2008
Chicago, IL 60611   Adele Hast, Editor-in-Chief
Founded: 1974. **Staff:** Prof 2. **Subjects:** Biography, company history. **Special Collections:** Contemporary biographical directories. **Holdings:** 3000 books; 5 VF drawers of company archives. **Subscriptions:** 185 journals and other serials; 10 newspapers. **Services:** Library open to Marquis staff. **Networks/Consortia:** Member of Chicago Library System. **Staff:** Paul Bralower, Mng.Ed. for Res.

★7563★
MARRIAGE COUNCIL OF PHILADELPHIA - DIVISION OF FAMILY STUDY AND MARRIAGE COUNCIL LIBRARY (Soc Sci)
4025 Chestnut St., 2nd Fl.   Phone: (215) 382-6680
Philadelphia, PA 19104   Ellen M. Berman, Dir. of Clinical Trng.
Founded: 1932. **Subjects:** Marriage and family relationships, marriage counseling, human sexuality and sex therapy, mental health, religion and marriage. **Holdings:** 1000 books. **Subscriptions:** 16 journals and other serials. **Services:** Library not open to public. **Remarks:** Affiliated with the University of Pennsylvania.

MARRINER LIBRARY
See: Thomas College

MARRIOTT LIBRARY
See: University of Utah

★7564★
MARSCHALK COMPANY, INC. - LIBRARY (Bus-Fin)†
1345 Ave. of the Americas   Phone: (212) 708-8800
New York, NY 10019
Founded: 1955. **Staff:** Prof 1. **Subjects:** Advertising. **Holdings:** 200 volumes; 20 VF drawers of reports; 3 VF drawers of clippings; 1 VF drawer of maps; 35 VF drawers of company information; 1 VF drawer of pictures. **Subscriptions:** 1500 journals and other serials. **Services:** Interlibrary loans; library not open to public.

★7565★
MARSCHALK COMPANY, INC. - LIBRARY (Bus-Fin)
601 Rockwell Ave.   Phone: (216) 687-8859
Cleveland, OH 44114   Mildred Mitchell, Libn.
Staff: Prof 1. **Subjects:** Advertising, market research, information pertaining to clients' and prospective clients' businesses. **Holdings:** 200 books; 36 VF drawers of clippings, pamphlets, pictures. **Subscriptions:** 500 journals and other serials. **Services:** Library not open to public.

★7566★
MARSH AND MC LENNAN, INC. - INFORMATION CENTER (Bus-Fin)
1221 Ave. of the Americas   Phone: (212) 997-7800
New York, NY 10020   Susan Kucsma, Mgr.
Founded: 1970. **Staff:** Prof 3; Other 3. **Subjects:** Property and casualty insurance, risk management, safety engineering, maritime law, finance. **Holdings:** 7000 books; 250 periodical titles; 30 VF drawers of pamphlets; 1000 annual reports; back issue periodicals in microform. **Subscriptions:** 300 journals and other serials; 7 newspapers. **Services:** Interlibrary loans; SDI. **Computerized Information Services:** New York Times Information Service, DIALOG, SDC, Dow Jones News Retrieval; internal database; computerized

circulation. **Publications:** At a Glance, monthly. **Staff:** Julia Blanchard; Pamela Cook .

★7567★
MARSH & MC LENNAN - INFORMATION CENTRE (Bus-Fin)
1 First Canadian Pl.
P.O. Box 58
Toronto, ON, Canada M5X 1G2
Phone: (416) 868-2623
Angela Agostino, Libn.
Founded: 1976. **Staff:** Prof 1. **Subjects:** Insurance, insurance law, management theory, finance. **Holdings:** 700 books. **Subscriptions:** 105 journals and other serials; 5 newspapers. **Services:** Interlibrary loans; copying; SDI; library open only to other librarians and company clients. **Publications:** Acquisition list, monthly - for internal distribution only.

MARSH AND MC LENNAN, INC. - PUTNAM COMPANIES
See: Putnam Companies

MARSH (W. Ward) CINEMA ARCHIVES
See: Cleveland Public Library - Literature Department

★7568★
MARSHALL, BRATTER, GREENE, ALLISON & TUCKER - LIBRARY
430 Park Ave.
New York, NY 10022
Defunct

MARSHALL (C.J.) MEMORIAL LIBRARY
See: University of Pennsylvania - School of Veterinary Medicine - C.J.
Marshall Memorial Library

★7569★
MARSHALL COUNTY HISTORICAL SOCIETY MUSEUM - LIBRARY (Hist)
317 W. Monroe St.
Plymouth, IN 46563
Phone: (219) 936-2306
Mary L. Durnan, Dir.
Staff: 2. **Subjects:** Marshall County and Indiana history, genealogy. **Holdings:** 225 books; 350 reels of microfilm of Marshall County newspapers; 15 tapes of oral history. **Services:** Copying; library open to public. **Publications:** Marshall County Historical Society Quarterly. **Special Indexes:** Surname Index.

★7570★
MARSHALL (George C.) RESEARCH FOUNDATION - GEORGE C. MARSHALL RESEARCH LIBRARY (Hist)
Box 1600
Lexington, VA 24450
Phone: (703) 463-7103
Dr. Fred L. Hadsel, Dir.
Staff: Prof 8; Other 6. **Subjects:** Life, times and career of General George C. Marshall, 1880-1959; 20th century military and diplomatic history, including World War I and World War II; Marshall Plan; propaganda; international foreign relations and economics. **Special Collections:** General Marshall's personal files (400 linear feet); copies and microfilm of selected items from official State and War Department files pertaining to General Marshall; William F. Friedman Cryptologic Collection; Francis Pickens Miller World War II Intelligence Collection; selected papers of General Lucian K. Truscott, General Marshall S. Carter, General Lucius D. Clay, Frank McCarthy, and over 100 persons. **Holdings:** 25,500 books; 725 bound periodical volumes; 30,000 photographs of World War II and General Marshall; 150 tape recordings of interviews with General Marshall and his associates; 700 posters from World War I and World War II; 1500 maps from World War I and World War II. **Subscriptions:** 45 journals and other serials. **Services:** Copying; library open to public. **Publications:** Topics, irregular. **Staff:** Royster Lyle, Cur. of Coll.; John Jacob, Archv.Larry Bland, Ed.; Sharon Ritenour, Asst.Ed.

★7571★
MARSHALL HISTORICAL SOCIETY - ARCHIVES (Hist)
Box 68
Marshall, MI 49068
Phone: (616) 781-8544
James Bryant, Pres.
Founded: 1917. **Staff:** Prof 1. **Subjects:** Marshall history and pioneers, Marshall homes and views, Calhoun County history, railroads. **Special Collections:** Martin F. Ryan Railroad Collection; Amelia Frink Redfield Collection (genealogy and family scrapbooks); Mabel Cooper Skjelver research on Marshall homes; Johnson, Johnson and Roy research on architectural survey of Marshall. **Holdings:** 300 books; 9 boxes of photographs; 28 boxes of manuscripts and documents; 30 boxes of clippings and unbound periodicals; 4 boxes of maps. **Services:** Copying; answers public inquiries by mail; archives open to public by appointment. **Remarks:** Archives located in Honolulu House Museum, West Michigan Ave. and North Kalamazoo Ave., Marshall, MI. **Staff:** Carol B. Lovett, Archv.

MARSHALL (John) LAW SCHOOL
See: John Marshall Law School

MARSHALL LABORATORY LIBRARY
See: Du Pont de Nemours (E.I.) & Company, Inc.

MARSHALL LAW LIBRARY
See: University of Maryland, Baltimore - School of Law

★7572★
MARSHALL MACKLIN MONAGHAN LIMITED - LIBRARY
275 Duncan Mill Rd.
Don Mills, ON, Canada M3B 2Y1
Founded: 1975. **Subjects:** Planning - environment, recreation, transportation, land use; urban design. **Special Collections:** National Research Council, Transportation Research Board and National Cooperative Highway Research Program reports (500). **Holdings:** 1100 books; 400 bound periodical volumes; 2030 company reports, official plans, zoning by-laws; 70 archival items. **Remarks:** Presently inactive.

★7573★
MARSHALL, MELHORN, COLE, HUMMER & SPITZER - LIBRARY (Law)
1434 Natl. Bank Bldg.
Toledo, OH 43604
Phone: (419) 243-4200
Deborah Elkins, Libn.
Staff: Prof 1. **Subjects:** Corporate law, taxation, labor law, federal practice and procedure. **Holdings:** 15,000 volumes. **Subscriptions:** 29 journals and other serials. **Services:** Interlibrary loans; copying; library open to attorneys and librarians known to firm members. **Computerized Information Services:** LEXIS.

MARSHALL RESEARCH FOUNDATION
See: Huron Road Hospital

MARSHALL (S.L.A.) MILITARY HISTORY COLLECTION
See: University of Texas, El Paso - S.L.A. Marshall Military History Collection

MARSHALL SPACE FLIGHT CENTER
See: U.S. Army - Missile Command & Marshall Space Flight Center; U.S. NASA - MSFC Library

★7574★
MARSHALL UNIVERSITY - JAMES E. MORROW LIBRARY - SPECIAL COLLECTIONS (Hist)
Huntington, WV 25701
Phone: (304) 696-2320
Lisle G Brown, Cur.
Founded: 1972. **Staff:** Prof 3; Other 2. **Subjects:** West Virginiana, Civil War, Appalachian studies, history of medicine. **Special Collections:** Regional manuscripts collections; WSAZ-TV News Film Archive, 1952-1976; Charles A. Hoffman Library of the History of Medical Sciences; Appalachian Oral History Collection. **Holdings:** 12,000 books; 250 bound periodical volumes; 700 linear feet of manuscripts; 18,000 West Virginia state documents; 550 cubic feet of university archives; 22 linear feet of additional materials. **Subscriptions:** 130 journals and other serials; 10 newspapers. **Services:** Interlibrary loans; copying; library open to public. **Computerized Information Services:** DIALOG; computerized cataloging. **Networks/Consortia:** Member of OCLC. **Publications:** A Guide to Local History and Genealogy in the Special Collections Department; A Guide to the Manuscript Collections in the Special Collections Department. **Staff:** Cora Teel, Archv.; Nancy Whear, Asst.Libn.

★7575★
MARSHALL UNIVERSITY - RESEARCH COORDINATING UNIT FOR VOCATIONAL EDUCATION (Educ)
Huntington, WV 25701
Phone: (304) 696-3180
Kristine Standifur, Res.Asst.
Staff: 1. **Subjects:** Educational, research, and instructional materials. **Special Collections:** Complete collection of ERIC microfiche. **Holdings:** 20 bound periodical volumes. **Subscriptions:** 10 journals and other serials. **Services:** Interlibrary loans; copying; library open to public.

★7576★
MARSHALL UNIVERSITY - SCHOOL OF MEDICINE - HEALTH SCIENCE LIBRARIES (Med)
Marshall University Campus
Huntington, WV 25701
Phone: (304) 696-6426
Ann Howard, Dir.
Founded: 1975. **Staff:** Prof 4; Other 2. **Subjects:** Clinical medicine, basic sciences, nursing, allied health sciences. **Special Collections:** Esposito Collection in Ophthalmology (150 books). **Holdings:** 16,000 books; 185 slide sets; 350 video cassettes; 22 16mm films; 45 audio cassettes.

Subscriptions: 770 journals and other serials. Services: Interlibrary loans; copying; libraries open to public. Computerized Information Services: Online systems. Networks/Consortia: Member of Huntington Health Science Library Consortium; West Virginia Biomedical Information Network; Mid-Atlantic Regional Medical Library Program. Publications: Guide to the Health Science Libraries, annual - distributed on campus. Special Catalogs: Serial Holdings List 1981 - Huntington (computer printout); Audiovisual Catalog 1981 (computer printout). Staff: Mildred Hildreth, Ref.Libn.; Carlyle Mallory, Ref.Libn.; Phoebe Randall, Circ.Libn.

MARSHALL-WYTHE LAW LIBRARY
See: College of William and Mary

★7577★
MARSHFIELD CLINIC - MEDICAL CENTER LIBRARY (Med)
1000 N. Oak   Phone: (715) 387-5183
Marshfield, WI 54449   Albert Zimmermann, Libn./Med.Ed.
Founded: 1975. Staff: Prof 2. Subjects: Medicine, clinical chemistry. Holdings: 1776 books; 9899 bound periodical volumes. Subscriptions: 430 journals and other serials. Services: Interlibrary loans; copying; library open to public for reference use only. Computerized Information Services: MEDLARS. Networks/Consortia: Member of Northern Wisconsin Health Science Libraries Cooperative; Regional Medical Library - Region 3. Staff: Alana Ziaya, Asst.Libn.

★7578★
MARSTELLER, INC. - INFORMATION SERVICES (Bus-Fin)
One E. Wacker Dr.   Phone: (312) 329-1100
Chicago, IL 60601   Ellen Steininger, Mgr., Info.Serv.
Founded: 1967. Staff: Prof 4; Other 3. Subjects: Advertising, public relations. Holdings: 2000 books; 1000 internal reports; 20 VF drawers of clippings; 20,000 pictures. Subscriptions: 2500 journals and other serials; 11 newspapers. Services: Interlibrary loans; copying; library open to public by appointment. Computerized Information Services: DIALOG, SDC, New York Times Information Service, Dow Jones News Retrieval, Mead Data Central, Computer Directions Advisors, Inc. Networks/Consortia: Member of Metropolitan Chicago Library Assembly; ILLINET. Publications: News Summary, biweekly - for internal distribution only. Staff: Joyce Rowe, Info.Spec.; Dwayne Nelson, Info.Spec.

MARSTON MEMORIAL HISTORICAL LIBRARY
See: Free Methodist Church of North America

MART SCIENCE AND ENGINEERING LIBRARY
See: Lehigh University

★7579★
MARTIN (Albert C.) & ASSOCIATES - INFORMATION RESEARCH CENTER (Sci-Tech)†
445 S. Figueroa St.   Phone: (213) 683-1900
Los Angeles, CA 90071   Millie Nicholson, Libn.
Founded: 1967. Staff: 1. Subjects: Architecture, civil and structural engineering, city planning, interior design. Special Collections: Albert C. Martin, Sr., Collections (1014 items on history of architecture). Holdings: 1500 books; 42 bound periodical volumes; 3240 outside reports, documents and pamphlets; 10 VF drawers of clippings; 1520 company reports, proposals and programs; 20 drawers of microfilm of company projects (aperture cards). Subscriptions: 75 journals and other serials. Services: Interlibrary loans; copying; center open to public on request.

MARTIN ARMY COMMUNITY HOSPITAL
See: U.S. Army Hospitals

★7580★
MARTIN COUNTY HISTORICAL SOCIETY - PIONEER MUSEUM - LIBRARY (Hist)
304 E. Blue Earth Ave.   Phone: (507) 235-5178
Fairmont, MN 56031   Catherine Harber, Supt.
Founded: 1929. Staff: 1. Subjects: American Indian, Civil War, Minnesota history. Special Collections: Local newspaper file, 1874 to present. Holdings: 4 cases of pamphlets and letters; 4 VF drawers of photographs; Civil War letters. Services: Library open to public with restrictions.

MARTIN (John) LIBRARY
See: Gallery/Stratford - John Martin Library

★7581★
MARTIN MARIETTA CHEMICALS - SODYECO DIVISION - TECHNICAL LIBRARY (Sci-Tech)
Box 33429   Phone: (704) 827-4351
Charlotte, NC 28233   Jacqueline N. Kirkman, Tech.Libn.
Founded: 1963. Staff: Prof 1. Subjects: Dyestuffs, organic chemistry. Holdings: 1215 books; 1420 bound periodical volumes; 4000 patents; 165 P.B. reports. Subscriptions: 89 journals and other serials. Services: Interlibrary loans; library open to public with restrictions.

★7582★
MARTIN MARIETTA CORPORATION - DENVER DIVISION - RESEARCH LIBRARY (Sci-Tech)
Box 179   Phone: (303) 977-5512
Denver, CO 80201   Jay R. McKee, Chf.Libn.
Founded: 1955. Staff: Prof 3; Other 3. Subjects: Aerospace technology, guided missiles, launch vehicles, propulsion, mathematics, space electronics, explosive forming, cryogenics, reliability. Holdings: 18,000 books; 5000 bound periodical volumes; 65,000 NASA, DTIC and contractor documents; 60,000 NASA, AIAA, AAS microfiche. Subscriptions: 277 journals and other serials. Services: Library not open to public. Publications: Report Index, monthly with cumulations - for internal distribution only. Special Indexes: Computer-produced index to technical reports and documents. Staff: Mel Coffman, Supv.Clas. Loan Ctr.; Newton P. Clark, Rec. Retention Ctr.; Carol Robbins, Acq.; Shari Braly, Ref.; Linda Running, Ref.

★7583★
MARTIN MARIETTA CORPORATION - ORLANDO AEROSPACE DIVISION - INFORMATION CENTER (Sci-Tech)
Box 5837 MP-30   Phone: (305) 352-2051
Orlando, FL 32855   Morton Meltzer, Mgr.
Founded: 1957. Staff: Prof 6; Other 5. Subjects: Aerospace, electronics. Holdings: 25,000 books and bound periodical volumes; 150,000 technical reports; 55,000 microfiche. Subscriptions: 300 journals and other serials. Services: Interlibrary loans; center not open to public. Computerized Information Services: DIALOG, SDC. Staff: Mona C. Griffith, Chf.Libn.

★7584★
MARTIN MARIETTA LABORATORIES - LIBRARY (Sci-Tech)
1450 S. Rolling Rd.   Phone: (301) 247-0700
Baltimore, MD 21227-3898   Rosalind P. Cheslock, Mgr., Tech.Info.Serv.
Staff: Prof 3; Other 2. Subjects: Chemistry, physics, bioscience, environmental science, metallurgy, fluid mechanics, computer science, materials science. Holdings: 12,000 books; 5000 bound periodical volumes; 5000 documents; 2000 reels of microfilm; 1000 microfiche. Subscriptions: 600 journals and other serials. Services: Interlibrary loans; SDI; library open to public by appointment. Computerized Information Services: DIALOG, SDC, BRS, New York Times Information Service, QL Systems, DOE/RECON, DTIC. Networks/Consortia: Member of Interlibrary Users Association; Interlibrary Network of Baltimore County; Metropolitan Washington Library Council. Staff: Margaret M. Carr, Info.Spec.; Eleanor C. Feldman, Bibliog.Serv.

★7585★
MARTIN AND OSA JOHNSON SAFARI MUSEUM - STOTT EXPLORERS LIBRARY (Area-Ethnic)
16 S. Grant St.   Phone: (316) 431-2730
Chanute, KS 66720   Sondra Alden, Musm.Dir.
Founded: 1980. Staff: Prof 1; Other 4. Subjects: Natural history, exploration, photography. Special Collections: Complete set of materials by Martin and Osa Johnson, including some unpublished material; Martin and Osa Johnson Photographic Collection (several films and several thousand photographs). Holdings: 6000 books; reprint file. Subscriptions: 15 journals and other serials. Services: Interlibrary loans (limited); copying; library open to public for scholarly research, with appointment. Publications: The Cultural Heritage of Africa (Museum catalog) - for sale; Exploring with Osa and Martin Johnson (biography) - for sale; The Johnson Safari Wait-a-bit News, quarterly - sent to members, museums and libraries. Staff: Barbara Henshall, Cur.

MARTIN (Paul) LAW LIBRARY
See: University of Windsor - Paul Martin Law Library

MARTIN (Thomas W.) MEMORIAL LIBRARY
See: Southern Research Institute - Thomas W. Martin Memorial Library

★7586★
MARTIN/WILLIAMS ADVERTISING AGENCY - LIBRARY/INFORMATION CENTER (Bus-Fin)
10 S. 5th St.   Phone: (612) 340-0800
Minneapolis, MN 55402   L. Bock, Dir., Info.Serv.
Founded: 1977. Staff: Prof 1. Subjects: Advertising, marketing, business.

Holdings: 100 books; 200 unbound reports. **Subscriptions:** 500 journals and other serials. **Services:** Library open to agency employees and clients, and open to public with special permission. **Computerized Information Services:** DIALOG, New York Times Information Service.

MARVIN (Dwight) LEARNING RESOURCES CENTER
See: Hudson Valley Community College - Dwight Marvin Learning Resources Center

MARX (Robert S.) LAW LIBRARY
See: University of Cincinnati - Robert S. Marx Law Library

★7587★
MARY BALL WASHINGTON MUSEUM AND LIBRARY, INC. (Hist)
Box 97   Phone: (804) 462-7280
Lancaster, VA 22503   Ann Lewis Burrows, Exec.Dir.
Founded: 1958. **Staff:** Prof 3; Other 15. **Subjects:** U.S. and Virginia history; county histories; genealogy. **Holdings:** 6000 books; 200 bound periodical volumes; historical research and family papers. **Subscriptions:** 10 journals and other serials. **Services:** Copying; library open to public. **Publications:** Newsletter, quarterly.

★7588★
MARY COLLEGE - LIBRARY (Hum)
Apple Creek Rd.   Phone: (701) 255-4681
Bismarck, ND 58501   Cheryl M. Bailey, Dir.
Founded: 1959. **Staff:** Prof 2; Other 3. **Subjects:** Theology, philosophy, education, music, history, nursing, business. **Holdings:** 42,000 books; 7000 bound periodical volumes; 5300 records, films, tapes, maps and related material (cataloged); 850 reels of microfilm of back files of magazines. **Subscriptions:** 375 journals and other serials; 15 newspapers. **Services:** Interlibrary loans; copying; library open to public with restrictions. **Networks/Consortia:** Member of North Dakota Network for Knowledge; Northern Plains Consortium for Education; MINITEX; OCLC.

★7589★
MARY HOLMES COLLEGE - BARR LIBRARY - ORAL HISTORY COLLECTION (Hist)†
                                               Phone: (601) 494-6820
West Point, MS 39773
Subjects: History, sociology, folklore. **Special Collections:** Taped interviews and transcriptions of conversations with rural black Mississippians 70 years of age and older (600). **Holdings:** 14 volumes. **Services:** Interlibrary loans; copying; library open to public for reference use only.

★7590★
MARY IMMACULATE SEMINARY - LIBRARY (Rel-Theol)
R.D. 1, Cherryville Rd.
Box 27   Phone: (215) 262-7866
Northampton, PA 18067   Rev. Michael V. Thornton, C.M., Libn.
Staff: Prof 1; Other 2. **Subjects:** Bible, liturgy, theology, church history, patristics, canon law. **Special Collections:** Vincentiana Collection. **Holdings:** 47,253 books; 11,487 bound periodical volumes; 64 cassettes; 34 filmstrips; 300 phonograph records; 784 other cataloged items. **Subscriptions:** 376 journals and other serials; 6 newspapers. **Services:** Interlibrary loans; copying; library open to public with restrictions. **Networks/Consortia:** Member of Southeastern Pennsylvania Theological Libraries Association.

★7591★
MARY KAY COSMETICS, INC. - TECHNICAL INFORMATION CENTER (Sci-Tech)
1330 Regal Row   Phone: (214) 638-6750
Dallas, TX 75247   Susan M. Wilson, Tech.Info.Coord.
Founded: 1976. **Staff:** Prof 1; Other 1. **Subjects:** Cosmetics, dermatology, business. **Holdings:** 825 books; 300 bound periodical volumes. **Subscriptions:** 200 journals and other serials. **Services:** Interlibrary loans; copying; SDI; library open to public with restrictions. **Computerized Information Services:** DIALOG, MEDLARS. **Networks/Consortia:** Member of Dallas-Tarrant County Consortium of Health Science Libraries. **Publications:** Information Bulletin, monthly.

★7592★
MARYCREST COLLEGE - CONE LIBRARY (Educ)
1607 West 12th St.   Phone: (319) 326-9254
Davenport, IA 52804   Sr. Joan Sheil, Dir., Lib.Serv.
Founded: 1939. **Staff:** Prof 6; Other 3. **Subjects:** Education, social sciences, nursing, language and literature, art, music. **Holdings:** 100,000 books; 47,000 other cataloged items (curriculum guides and textbooks, microforms,

films, records, slides, tapes, transparencies, kits). **Subscriptions:** 770 journals and other serials; 7 newspapers. **Services:** Interlibrary loans; copying; library open to public. **Computerized Information Services:** DIALOG; computerized cataloging and circulation. **Networks/Consortia:** Member of Bi-State Academic Libraries (BISAL); Iowa Private Academic Libraries (IPAL). **Publications:** General information sheets. **Special Indexes:** Computerized index to nonprint materials. **Staff:** James A. Weeg, Cat.; Sr. Mary Edith Kane, Curric.Libn.; Sue Sellers, Circ.; Jane Weech, Media Libn.; Sr. Annette Gallagher, Ref.; Harold O'Dell, Libn.; Sr. Harriett Ping, Acq.

★7593★
MARYKNOLL FATHERS - PHOTO LIBRARY (Pict)
Pines Bridge Rd.   Phone: (914) 941-7590
Maryknoll, NY 10545   Penny Ann Sandoval, Photo Libn.
Founded: 1911. **Staff:** 1. **Subjects:** Third World, poverty, hunger, socioeconomic conditions, anthropology. **Special Collections:** China, 1918-1948 (3000 items). **Holdings:** 3 VF drawers of art files; 116 VF drawers of photographs; 1000 large prints; 95,000 color slides. **Services:** Copying; library open to public by appointment. **Publications:** Maryknoll Magazine, monthly; Revista Maryknoll, monthly (Spanish/English).

★7594★
MARYKNOLL SEMINARY - LIBRARY (Rel-Theol)
Maryknoll, P.O.   Phone: (914) 941-7590
Maryknoll, NY 10545   Rev. Arthur E. Brown, M.M., Libn.
Founded: 1928. **Staff:** Prof 3; Other 2. **Subjects:** Theology, missions, Maryknoll history and biography. **Special Collections:** Maryknoll (Field Afar) Archives. **Holdings:** 90,000 books; 20,000 bound periodical volumes. **Subscriptions:** 500 journals and other serials. **Services:** Interlibrary loans; copying; library open to public. **Special Indexes:** Index to Maryknoll Magazine (cards). **Remarks:** The official name of the organization is Maryknoll Fathers (Catholic Foreign Mission Society of America). The Maryknoll Information Library is maintained as an information bureau within this library. **Staff:** Peggy Mayti, Hd. of Info. Bureau.

★7595★
MARYLAND CRIMINAL JUSTICE COORDINATING COUNCIL - LIBRARY (Law)
One Investment Pl., Suite 700
Towson, MD 21204   Patricia M. Donaho, Lib.Supv.
Founded: 1969. **Subjects:** Crime, juvenile delinquency, police, corrections, criminal justice planning. **Holdings:** 3300 books; microfiche of 3270 Law Enforcement Assistance Administration grants, 1969-1979. **Subscriptions:** 20 journals and other serials; 5 newspapers. **Services:** Interlibrary loans; copying; library open to public by appointment. **Formerly:** Maryland State Governor's Commission on Law Enforcement.

★7596★
MARYLAND GENERAL HOSPITAL - MEDICAL STAFF LIBRARY (Med)
827 Linden Ave.   Phone: (301) 728-7900
Baltimore, MD 21201   Monica Yang, Coord., Lib.Serv.
Staff: Prof 2; Other 2. **Subjects:** Medicine. **Holdings:** 2000 books; 1600 bound periodical volumes; 7 Audio-Digest subscriptions; 1000 tapes; 3000 slides; slide/tape, video-disc and video cassette programs. **Subscriptions:** 100 journals and other serials. **Services:** Interlibrary loans; library not open to public. **Computerized Information Services:** MEDLINE. **Networks/Consortia:** Member of Maryland Health Care System, Inc.

★7597★
MARYLAND HISTORICAL SOCIETY - LIBRARY (Hist)
201 W. Monument St.   Phone: (301) 685-3750
Baltimore, MD 21201   William B. Keller, Hd.Libn.
Founded: 1844. **Staff:** Prof 7; Other 7. **Subjects:** Maryland history and genealogy; United States history. **Special Collections:** Manuscript collections: Calvert, Latrobe, Carroll, Wirt, Howard, Ridgley, Lloyd; Maryland biographical index (1 million cards); sheet music (Maryland); World War II records. **Holdings:** 80,000 books; 1500 newspaper volumes; 3 million manuscripts; 10,000 pamphlets; 1700 reels of microfilm; 200,000 prints, photographs, and maps; 26 VF drawers of clippings. **Subscriptions:** 400 journals and other serials. **Services:** Copying; library open to public with fee charged for nonmembers. **Publications:** Maryland Historical Magazine, quarterly - available by subscription; News and Notes, monthly - to members; Maryland Magazine of Genealogy, semiannual. **Special Catalogs:** Obituary file, 1794 to present; manuscript collections - both on cards. **Staff:** A. Hester Rich, Libn.; Paula Velthuys, Prints & Photographs; Donna Burns Ellis, Mss.Libn.; Dr. Gary Browne, Ed.; Betty Key, Oral Hist.Dir.; Mary K. Meyer, Genealogical Libn.

★7598★

MARYLAND INSTITUTE, COLLEGE OF ART - DECKER LIBRARY (Art)
1400 Cathedral St.   Phone: (301) 669-9200
Baltimore, MD 21201   John Stoneham, Dir.
Founded: 1826. **Staff:** Prof 4; Other 6. **Subjects:** Art, crafts, theater, cinema, photography. **Special Collections:** Lucas Collection (books and prints). **Holdings:** 45,000 books; 2000 bound periodical volumes; 60,000 slides (cataloged); 9 VF drawers of plates; 18 VF drawers of pamphlets. **Subscriptions:** 200 journals and other serials. **Services:** Interlibrary loans; library open to public. **Staff:** Pamela A. Potter, Slide Libn.; Robin Klein, Cat.

★7599★

MARYLAND MUNICIPAL LEAGUE - LIBRARY (Soc Sci)
76 Maryland Ave.   Phone: (301) 268-5514
Annapolis, MD 21401   Jon C. Burrell, Exec.Dir.
Staff: Prof 7; Other 2. **Subjects:** Municipal administration, law, finance, personnel. **Holdings:** 1000 volumes. **Subscriptions:** 25 journals and other serials; 10 newspapers. **Services:** Copying; library not open to public. **Publications:** Municipal Maryland, monthly; periodic surveys and reports.

★7600★

MARYLAND NATIONAL CAPITAL PARK AND PLANNING COMMISSION - LIBRARY (Plan)
8787 Georgia Ave.   Phone: (301) 565-7507
Silver Spring, MD 20907   Janice C. Holt, Hd.Libn.
Founded: 1961. **Staff:** Prof 2. **Subjects:** Urban and regional planning, parks, land use, population, housing, environment, transportation, recreation, public facilities. **Holdings:** 6000 books; 500 bound periodical volumes; 9000 technical reports. **Subscriptions:** 300 journals and other serials. **Services:** Interlibrary loans; copying; library not open to public. **Computerized Information Services:** DIALOG. **Networks/Consortia:** Member of Metropolitan Washington Library Council; Interlibrary Users Association. **Publications:** Library Newsletter - for internal distribution only. **Remarks:** Maintains branch libraries at Brookside Gardens, Meadowside Nature Center and Brookside Nature Center. **Staff:** Marion Goodman, Libn.

MARYLAND NATURAL HISTORY SOCIETY
See: Natural History Society of Maryland

★7601★

MARYLAND PHARMACEUTICAL ASSOCIATION - LIBRARY (Med)
Kelly Memorial Bldg.
650 W. Lombard St.   Phone: (301) 727-0746
Baltimore, MD 21201   David A. Banta, Exec.Dir.
Subjects: Pharmacy and allied subjects. **Special Collections:** Library of E.F. Kelly. **Holdings:** 1000 volumes.

MARYLAND PSYCHIATRIC RESEARCH CENTER
See: University of Maryland - School of Medicine - Dept. of Psychiatry - Helen C. Tingley Memorial Library

★7602★

MARYLAND STATE DEPARTMENT OF EDUCATION - DIVISION OF LIBRARY DEVELOPMENT & SERVICES - MEDIA SERVICES CENTER (Educ)†
200 W. Baltimore St.   Phone: (301) 659-2113
Baltimore, MD 21201   Elsie A. Leonard, Sect.Chf.
Founded: 1960. **Staff:** Prof 3; Other 3. **Subjects:** Education, library science. **Special Collections:** History of education in Maryland; U.S. Office of Education publications; complete ERIC collection; course of study resource guides. **Holdings:** 7500 volumes; 9 VF drawers; 800 films; 200 audiotapes; 20 slide sets; 300 filmstrip sets; 10 phonograph records; 400 videotapes. **Subscriptions:** 400 journals and other serials. **Services:** Interlibrary loans; copying; center open to Maryland educators. **Computerized Information Services:** DIALOG, BRS. **Publications:** Maryland Curriculum Materials; selected bibliographies of curriculum materials. **Special Catalogs:** AV materials (book). **Staff:** C. Ira Stancil, Info.Spec.; William A. Streamer, Jr., Info.Spec.

MARYLAND STATE DEPARTMENT OF HEALTH & MENTAL HYGIENE - EASTERN SHORE HOSPITAL CENTER
See: Eastern Shore Hospital Center

★7603★

MARYLAND STATE DEPARTMENT OF HEALTH & MENTAL HYGIENE - LIBRARY (Med)†
201 W. Preston St.   Phone: (301) 383-2634
Baltimore, MD 21201   Yvette Dixon, Assoc.Libn.
Founded: 1960. **Staff:** Prof 2; Other 2. **Subjects:** Health, mental health, mental retardation, drug abuse, environmental health, clinical medicine and other health related subjects. **Special Collections:** Departmental reports and publications. **Holdings:** 5000 volumes. **Subscriptions:** 250 journals and other serials. **Services:** Interlibrary loans; copying; library open to public, but borrowing is restricted to staff. **Computerized Information Services:** MEDLARS. **Staff:** Brenda Scott, Supv., Lib. & Files.

★7604★

MARYLAND STATE DEPARTMENT OF LEGISLATIVE REFERENCE - LIBRARY (Soc Sci)
Legislative Services Bldg.
90 State Circle   Phone: (301) 841-3810
Annapolis, MD 21401   Lynda C. Davis, Chf., Lib.Div.
Founded: 1966. **Staff:** Prof 9; Other 7. **Subjects:** Laws and codes, legislative reports. **Holdings:** 44,000 books; 805 bound periodical volumes; microfilm of newspapers and house and senate journals; General Assembly committee bill file, 1975 to present. **Subscriptions:** 273 journals and other serials; 9 newspapers. **Services:** Interlibrary loans; copying; library open to public. **Computerized Information Services:** DIALOG, LEXIS; Bill Status System (internal database); computerized cataloging. **Networks/Consortia:** Member of OCLC. **Publications:** Legislative Policy Committee Reports; Bound and Advance Sheets Session Laws; Synopsis of Laws, annual - distributed to members of General Assembly and interested public. **Special Indexes:** Legislative Bills and indexes by subject, sponsor, number, statute and committee from 1918 to present. **Staff:** Lynda S. Cunningham, Tech.Serv./Hd.; Georgeann Waller, Leg.Libn.; Carolyn Delavan, Leg.Libn.; David Warner, Leg.Libn.; Rita Newnham, Leg.Libn.; Lorretta Turnage, Leg.Libn.; Carol Carman, Leg.Libn.; Mary Ruland, Leg.Libn.

★7605★

MARYLAND STATE DEPARTMENT OF NATURAL RESOURCES - LIBRARY (Env-Cons)
Tawes State Office Bldg.   Phone: (301) 269-3015
Annapolis, MD 21401   Shashi P. Thaper, Hd.Libn.
Founded: 1971. **Staff:** Prof 1; Other 1. **Subjects:** Maryland - natural resources, geology, water quality, Chesapeake Bay conditions, environment. **Special Collections:** Chesapeake Bay Institute; U.S. Environmental Protection Agency; U.S.Geological Survey Interstate Commission of Potomac River publications; Ohio River and Susquehanna River Basin Commissions publications; Maryland Geological Survey publications. **Holdings:** 14,000 books; 25 bound periodical volumes; 1100 department documents; 6 drawers of microfiche; 50 films; 9 VF drawers. **Subscriptions:** 75 journals and other serials; 6 newspapers. **Services:** Interlibrary loans; copying; library open to public with restrictions. **Publications:** Library Newsletter, monthly - for internal distribution only. **Special Indexes:** DNR Publications List; periodicals and serials holdings list; film list; DNR Library pamphlet.

★7606★

MARYLAND STATE DEPARTMENT OF STATE PLANNING - LIBRARY (Plan)
State Office Bldg., Rm. 1101
301 W. Preston St.   Phone: (301) 383-2439
Baltimore, MD 21201   Edlea K. Jones, Libn.
Staff: Prof 1; Other 2. **Subjects:** Urban affairs, planning, land use. **Special Collections:** Planning Advisory Service Reports; depository of state, regional, county, municipal and interstate plans pertaining to Maryland. **Holdings:** 10,000 books and bound periodical volumes; 10 drawers of unbound pamphlets and periodicals; AV materials. **Subscriptions:** 486 journals and other serials; 20 newspapers. **Services:** Interlibrary loans; copying; library open to public for reference use only. **Computerized Information Services:** Computerized cataloging. **Networks/Consortia:** Member of State Agency Library Association of Maryland.

★7607★

MARYLAND STATE ENERGY OFFICE - LIBRARY (Energy)
301 W. Preston St., Suite 903   Phone: (301) 383-6810
Baltimore, MD 21201   Jane Frye, Libn./Mgr.
Founded: 1975. **Staff:** 1. **Subjects:** Energy conservation and management, alternate fuels, transportation. **Holdings:** 7500 books; newsletters. **Subscriptions:** 55 journals and other serials. **Services:** Interlibrary loans; copying; library open to public.

MARYLAND STATE GOVERNOR'S COMMISSION ON LAW ENFORCEMENT
See: Maryland Criminal Justice Coordinating Council

★7608★

MARYLAND STATE HALL OF RECORDS COMMISSION - LIBRARY (Hist)
College Ave. & St. John's St.   Phone: (301) 269-3915
Annapolis, MD 21404   Dr. Edward C. Papenfuse, Archv.
Founded: 1935. **Subjects:** State, county and local history records; genealogy. **Special Collections:** Records and publications of Maryland state, county and

local agencies. **Holdings:** 12,000 books; 320 bound periodical volumes; reports, manuscripts, archives; Works Progress Administration (WPA) Survey Files. **Subscriptions:** 87 journals and other serials. **Services:** Copying; library open to public. **Computerized Information Services:** Computerized cataloging. **Publications:** Irregular publications; Maryland Manual, biennial; accessions list of state publications and reports, monthly. **Staff:** Dr. Gregory A. Stiverson, Asst.Archv.; Douglas P. McElrath, Archv./Libn.

★7609★
MARYLAND STATE HIGHWAY ADMINISTRATION - LIBRARY (Trans)
707 Calvert St. Phone: (301) 659-1420
Baltimore, MD 21202 Ruby D. Weston, Libn.
Founded: 1963. **Staff:** Prof 2. **Subjects:** Traffic; highways - construction, maintenance, design; programming. **Special Collections:** State Specifications Reports; Highway Research Board Papers; Maryland State Highway Administration Annual Reports. **Holdings:** 8000 books; 5 VF drawers of Maryland State Highway Administration reports; 16 VF drawers of pamphlets; 200 periodicals. **Subscriptions:** 75 journals and other serials. **Services:** Will answer brief inquiries and make referrals; library open to public for reference use only on request. **Publications:** Annual report of Commission; Library Acquisitions, quarterly.

★7610★
MARYLAND STATE LAW DEPARTMENT - ATTORNEY GENERAL'S OFFICE - LIBRARY (Law)
7 N. Calvert St., 1st Fl. Phone: (301) 576-6300
Baltimore, MD 21202 Natalie S. Paymer, Law Libn.
Staff: Prof 1; Other 2. **Subjects:** Law - state and federal. **Special Collections:** National Reporter System (1st series on microfilm); laws of Maryland from 1680. **Holdings:** 18,000 books; 200 bound periodical volumes; National Association of Attorneys General publications (cataloged). **Subscriptions:** 20 journals and other serials. **Services:** Interlibrary loans; copying; SDI; library open to public with prior appointment. **Networks/Consortia:** Member of Law Library Association of Maryland.

★7611★
MARYLAND STATE LAW LIBRARY (Law; Hist)
361 Rowe Blvd. Phone: (301) 269-3395
Annapolis, MD 21401 Michael S. Miller, Dir.
Founded: 1826. **Staff:** Prof 5; Other 3. **Subjects:** Law, Marylandia, genealogy. **Special Collections:** Early English Reports and Statutes; Maryland census records (1790-1910); Maryland state documents depository; select U.S. government documents depository. **Holdings:** 130,000 books; 8500 bound periodical volumes; newspapers; 3300 reels of microfilm. **Subscriptions:** 475 journals and other serials. **Services:** Interlibrary loans; copying; library open to public. **Computerized Information Services:** LEXIS; computerized cataloging. **Networks/Consortia:** Member of OCLC through CAPCON; **Publications:** Catalog of Law Books in the Maryland State Library; History of Maryland State Library; selected recent acquisitions list, bimonthly; F.Y.I., The Maryland State Law Library; Maryland State Law Library: A Guide to Resources and Services. **Staff:** Bernice G. Bernstein, Asst.Libn.; Shirley A. Rittenhouse, Ref.Libn.; Dee T. Van Nest, Asst. Law Libn.; Shirley C. Aronson, Doc.Libn.

MARYLAND STATE MEDICAL AND CHIRURGICAL FACULTY
See: Medical and Chirurgical Faculty of the State of Maryland

MARYLAND STATE NATIONAL CAPITAL PARK AND PLANNING COMMISSION
See: Maryland National Capital Park and Planning Commission

★7612★
MARY'S HELP HOSPITAL - LIBRARY (Med)†
1900 Sullivan Ave. Phone: (415) 992-4000
Daly City, CA 94015 Marie Grace Abbruzzese, Libn.
Staff: Prof 1. **Subjects:** Medicine, nursing and hospital administration. **Holdings:** 2000 books; 2000 bound periodical volumes; 8 shelves of audio cassettes and tapes. **Subscriptions:** 125 journals and other serials. **Services:** Interlibrary loans; copying; library open to professionals and referrals. **Publications:** Acquisitions List, irregular - for internal distribution only.

★7613★
MARYVIEW HOSPITAL - HEALTH SCIENCES LIBRARY (Med)
3636 High St. Phone: (804) 398-2330
Portsmouth, VA 23707 Katherine A. Yatrofsky, Libn.
Founded: 1956. **Staff:** Prof 1; Other 1. **Subjects:** Medicine. **Holdings:** 1000 books; 1065 bound periodical volumes. **Subscriptions:** 91 journals and other serials. **Services:** Interlibrary loans; library open to public for reference use only. **Computerized Information Services:** MEDLINE.

★7614★
MARYWOOD COLLEGE - LEARNING RESOURCES CENTER (Educ)
2300 Adams Ave. Phone: (717) 348-6260
Scranton, PA 18509 James P. Clarke, Lib.Dir.
Founded: 1915. **Staff:** Prof 9; Other 10. **Subjects:** Education, library science, social sciences, music, art, literature, philosophy. **Special Collections:** Library science. **Holdings:** 165,000 volumes; 8100 microfiche; 7158 reels of microfilm; 4138 phonograph records; 2870 audiotapes; 342 film loops; 543 filmstrips; 2767 sound filmstrip sets; 11,099 slides; 188 sound slidesets; 257 art prints; 71 transparencies. **Subscriptions:** 1191 journals and other serials; 20 newspapers. **Services:** Interlibrary loans; copying; center open to public with restrictions. **Computerized Information Services:** Computerized cataloging and ILL. **Networks/Consortia:** Member of Northeastern Pennsylvania Bibliographic Center; Northeastern Pennsylvania Independent Colleges; PALINET & Union Library Catalogue of Pennsylvania. **Publications:** Media Holdings, irregular - for internal distribution only. **Staff:** Mary Ann Cooney, Circ.Libn.; Irene Munchak, ILL & Ref.Libn.; Sr. M. Theron Mack, I.H.M., Cat.Libn.; Sr. Catherine Donnegan, I.H.M., Acq.Libn.; Sr. Gilmary Speirs, I.H.M., Commun.Libn.; Elma Anderson, Ser.Libn.; Margaret Philbin, Media Cat.Libn.; Annette Hizny, Assoc.Ser.Libn.

★7615★
MASARYK MEMORIAL INSTITUTE INC. - LIBRARY
450 Scarborough Golf Club Rd.
Scarborough, ON, Canada M1G 1H1
Subjects: Czech and Slovak language material. **Special Collections:** Jirasek, Neruda, Nemcova, Hviezdoslav, Razus. **Holdings:** 2000 books. **Remarks:** Presently inactive.

MASCARELLO LIBRARY OF CRIMINAL JUSTICE
See: Crime & Justice Foundation

★7616★
MASON COUNTY HISTORICAL SOCIETY - ROSE HAWLEY MUSEUM AND HISTORICAL LIBRARY (Hist)
305 E. Filer St. Phone: (616) 843-2001
Ludington, MI 49431 Virginia Gaines, Cur.
Staff: Prof 2. **Subjects:** History - Mason County, marine, Indian; biography. **Holdings:** 1500 books; 20 VF drawers of clippings, photographs, legal documents, brochures, and newspapers. **Services:** Copying; library open to public. **Publications:** Mason Memories, quarterly; Epoch (newsletter), monthly; Historic Mason County (book). **Staff:** Lucille Lake, Libn.

MASON (Edith) LIBRARY
See: Mansfield Historical Society - Edith Mason Library

MASON (George) UNIVERSITY
See: George Mason University

★7617★
MASON & HANGER-SILAS MASON COMPANY, INC. - PANTEX PLANT - TECHNICAL LIBRARY (Sci-Tech)
Box 30020 Phone: (806) 381-3547
Amarillo, TX 79177 Sue Sutphin, Tech.Libn.
Staff: Prof 2. **Subjects:** High explosives. **Holdings:** 6000 volumes. **Subscriptions:** 250 journals and other serials. **Services:** Library not open to public. **Remarks:** Plant is operated under a U.S. Department of Energy contract.

★7618★
MASON, MAC LEOD, LYLE, SMITH - BARRISTERS AND SOLICITORS - LIBRARY (Law)
2200 Bow Valley Sq. IV
205 6th Ave., S.W. Phone: (403) 263-2190
Calgary, AB, Canada T2P 3H7 Grace Sardo, Libn.
Founded: 1977. **Staff:** Prof 1; Other 1. **Subjects:** Law. **Holdings:** 5000 books; 1000 bound periodical volumes. **Subscriptions:** 200 journals and other serials. **Services:** Interlibrary loans; library open to other librarians. **Computerized Information Services:** QL Systems. **Formed by the Merger of:** Mason and Company and Lyle, Smith, Davison.

MASON RESEARCH INSTITUTE
See: EG&G, Inc.

MASON (Sydney R. & Elsa W.) LIBRARY
See: Johns Hopkins University - School of Advanced International Studies - Sydney R. & Elsa W. Mason Library

MASON (Wallace E.) LIBRARY
See: Keene State College - Wallace E. Mason Library

★7619★
MASONIC GRAND LODGE LIBRARY AND MUSEUM OF TEXAS (Rec)
Box 446   Phone: (817) 753-7395
Waco, TX 76703   Janet Melton, Libn.
Founded: 1873. **Staff:** 2. **Subjects:** Masonic Order - philosophy, history and biography; Texana. **Special Collections:** Manuscript collection of Masonic and Texas material (4210 items). **Holdings:** 32,100 books and bound periodical volumes; 10,420 pamphlets; 1425 pictures. **Services:** Interlibrary loans; copying; library open to public for reference use only. **Staff:** Emery Stewart, Museum Cur.

★7620★
MASONIC MEDICAL RESEARCH LABORATORY - LIBRARY (Med)
2150 Bleecker St.   Phone: (315) 735-2217
Utica, NY 13501   Irma S. Tuttle, Libn.
Staff: Prof 2; Other 1. **Subjects:** Biochemistry, pharmacology, physiology, gerontology, vision research, biorheology. **Special Collections:** Biochemical gerontology. **Holdings:** 6200 books; 9000 bound periodical volumes; 500 films (cataloged); 300 microcards; 250 reels of microfilm. **Subscriptions:** 225 journals and other serials. **Services:** Interlibrary loans; copying; Russian and Polish translations; library open to public with restrictions. **Publications:** Holdings list, bimonthly.

★7621★
MASONIC SERVICE ASSOCIATION OF THE UNITED STATES - LIBRARY (Rec)†
8120 Fenton St.   Phone: (301) 588-4010
Silver Spring, MD 20910   Stewart M.L. Pollard, Exec.Sec.
Subjects: Masonic history, symbolism and criticism. **Special Collections:** Masonic Grand Lodge proceedings; Masonic publications. **Holdings:** 4500 volumes; clippings, reports and manuscripts. **Subscriptions:** 10 journals and other serials; 50 newspapers. **Services:** Library open to public by appointment. **Special Indexes:** Cumulative index of nearly 100,000 entries giving information on Masonic topics, lodge names and numbers.

★7622★
MASSACHUSETTS AUDUBON SOCIETY - BERKSHIRE SANCTUARIES - LIBRARY (Env-Cons)†
Pleasant Valley Wildlife Sanctuary   Phone: (413) 637-0320
Lenox, MA 01240   Lowell McAllister, Dir.
Founded: 1929. **Staff:** 3. **Subjects:** Natural history, environmental politics, alternative lifestyles, agriculture. **Special Collections:** Reports on natural science in Berkshire County, Massachusetts. **Holdings:** 500 books; 100 bound periodical volumes; 1000 35mm color slides; 2 16mm sound color films of birds; 15 phonograph records; field guides. **Services:** Library open to public with restrictions. **Publications:** Berkshire Seasons.

★7623★
MASSACHUSETTS AUDUBON SOCIETY - HATHEWAY ENVIRONMENTAL EDUCATION INSTITUTE (Env-Cons)
Lincoln, MA 01773   Phone: (617) 259-9500
                                           Louise Maglione, Dir.
Founded: 1967. **Staff:** Prof 1; Other 2. **Subjects:** Air and water pollution, environment, conservation, environmental education, natural resources, wildlife management, careers. **Special Collections:** Natural history; environmental affairs; curriculum. **Holdings:** 9000 books; 4000 pamphlets; 15 VF drawers of curriculum guides, filmstrips, charts, records, slides, tapes, films, pictures, newsletters. **Subscriptions:** 100 journals and other serials. **Services:** Copying; library open to public. **Remarks:** This library has the most extensive collection of its kind in the Northeastern United States.

MASSACHUSETTS BIBLE SOCIETY LIBRARY
See: Boston University - School of Theology Library

★7624★
MASSACHUSETTS CENTRAL TRANSPORTATION PLANNING STAFF - LIBRARY AND PRODUCTION SERVICES (Trans; Plan)
27 School St., 2nd Fl.   Phone: (617) 451-5785
Boston, MA 02108   Ms. Toby Pearlstein, Libn.
Founded: 1974. **Staff:** Prof 3. **Subjects:** Transportation and urban planning. **Special Collections:** Archives of Boston Transportation Planning Review, 1969-1975 (7 cubic feet). **Holdings:** 6500 books; 5 VF drawers. **Subscriptions:** 50 journals and other serials. **Services:** Interlibrary loans; copying; library open to public for reference use only. **Computerized Information Services:** DIALOG. **Publications:** List of Selected Acquisitions, quarterly - mailed to interested parties. **Remarks:** The Central Transportation

Planning Staff Library is sponsored by the following agencies of the Commonwealth of Massachusetts: Executive Office of Transportation and Construction; Department of Public Works; Massachusetts Bay Transportation Authority (MBTA); MBTA Advisory Board; Metropolitan Area Planning Council; Massachusetts Port Authority. **Staff:** Leland Morrison, Tech.Ed.; Diane McHenry, Graphic Designer.

★7625★
MASSACHUSETTS COLLEGE OF ART - LIBRARY (Art)
364 Brookline Ave.   Phone: (617) 731-2340
Boston, MA 02215   Benjamin Hopkins, Hd.Libn.
Founded: 1873. **Staff:** Prof 2; Other 3. **Subjects:** Fine arts; art education; design - graphic, industrial and fashion; photography. **Special Collections:** Art Education in Massachusetts (200 items). **Holdings:** 69,000 books; 6000 bound periodical volumes; 24 VF drawers of pictures; 65,000 slides; 3000 children's books; 800 phonograph records; 550 films. **Subscriptions:** 400 journals and other serials; 4 newspapers. **Services:** Interlibrary loans; copying; library open to public. **Computerized Information Services:** Computerized cataloging. **Networks/Consortia:** Member of Fenway Library Consortium; NELINET; Massachusetts Conference of Chief Librarians in Public Higher Educational Institutions (MCCLPHEI). **Special Indexes:** Fenway Union List of Serials. **Staff:** Charles Churchill, Ref.Libn./Tech.Serv.; Torrey Burnett, Slides & Media; Linda Savage, Circ.; Helen Donovan, Circ.; John Keating, Cat.

★7626★
MASSACHUSETTS COLLEGE OF PHARMACY & ALLIED HEALTH SCIENCES - HAMPDEN CAMPUS LIBRARY (Med)
Churchill Library
1215 Wilbraham Rd.
Western New England College   Phone: (413) 782-3111
Springfield, MA 01119   Mark J. Gazillo, Pharmacy Libn.
Founded: 1949. **Staff:** 10. **Subjects:** Pharmacy. **Holdings:** 6200 books; 1000 bound periodical volumes; Iowa Drug Information Service, 1975 to present; microforms. **Services:** Interlibrary loans; copying; library open to public. **Networks/Consortia:** Member of Western Massachusetts Health Information Consortium.

★7627★
MASSACHUSETTS COLLEGE OF PHARMACY & ALLIED HEALTH SCIENCES - SHEPPARD LIBRARY (Sci-Tech)
179 Longwood Ave.   Phone: (617) 732-2810
Boston, MA 02115   Barbara M. Hill, Libn.
Founded: 1823. **Staff:** Prof 4; Other 7. **Subjects:** Pharmacy, biological sciences, chemistry, medical botany, drug abuse, drug interactions. **Special Collections:** College archives. **Holdings:** 55,000 volumes; 28 VF drawers of pamphlets, clippings, documents, advertising materials, reprints; audio and video cassettes; phonograph records; microfilms; slides. **Subscriptions:** 655 journals and other serials. **Services:** Interlibrary loans; copying; library open to public for reference use only. **Computerized Information Services:** MEDLARS, DIALOG. **Networks/Consortia:** Member of Fenway Library Consortium. **Publications:** Acquisitions list, irregular - available on request. **Staff:** David E. Rush, Assoc.Libn.; Barbara L. Greehey, Asst.Libn.; Mary G. Chitty, Asst.Libn.; Edward T. O'Dwyer, Jr., Media Serv.Coord.

★7628★
MASSACHUSETTS COMPUTER ASSOCIATES, INC. - LIBRARY (Sci-Tech)
26 Princess St.   Phone: (617) 245-9540
Wakefield, MA 01880   Arlene M. McGrane, Libn.
Founded: 1961. **Staff:** Prof 1; Other 2. **Subjects:** Computers, mathematics of computation. **Holdings:** 550 books; 1156 bound periodical volumes; 117 volumes and 9 VF drawers of documents; 243 microfiche; 300 computer vendor manuals; 116 volumes of conferences, proceedings and tutorials. **Subscriptions:** 52 journals and other serials. **Services:** Interlibrary loans; copying; library not open to public. **Publications:** Bibliography of Selected Publications.

★7629★
MASSACHUSETTS FINANCIAL SERVICES, INC. - BUSINESS LIBRARY (Bus-Fin)†
200 Berkeley St.   Phone: (617) 423-3500
Boston, MA 02116   Mrs. Kit Danskey, Libn.
Founded: 1924. **Staff:** 1. **Subjects:** Business and industry. **Holdings:** 500 books; 1000 bound periodical volumes. **Subscriptions:** 25 journals and other serials; 8 newspapers. **Services:** Library not open to public.

★7630★

MASSACHUSETTS GENERAL HOSPITAL - MGH HEALTH SCIENCES LIBRARIES (Med)
Fruit St.   Phone: (617) 726-8600
Boston, MA 02114   Jacqueline Bastille, Dir.
Founded: 1848. **Staff:** Prof 9; Other 12. **Subjects:** Medicine, biochemistry, health care, nursing and allied health subjects. **Holdings:** 17,984 books; 34,000 bound periodical volumes. **Subscriptions:** 1000 journals and other serials. **Services:** Interlibrary loans (fee); copying; SDI; libraries open to public with restrictions. **Computerized Information Services:** DIALOG, Faxon Company, Inc.; computerized cataloging and serials. **Networks/Consortia:** Member of New England Regional Medical Library Service (NERMLS); OCLC. **Formerly:** Its Treadwell and Palmer-Davis Library. **Staff:** Helene Leighton, Hd., Comp.Serv.; Mark Taylor, Hd., Tech.Serv.; Katherine Button, MEDLINE Anl.; Ellen Westling, Hd., Info.Serv.; Patricia Ryan, Hd., Lib.Cons.Serv.; Carole Mankin, Res. Project Libn.; Elizabeth Schneider, Coll.Org.Libn.; Rhonda Rios Kravitz, Ref.Libn.

★7631★

MASSACHUSETTS HISTORICAL SOCIETY - RESEARCH LIBRARY (Hist)
1154 Boylston St.   Phone: (617) 536-1608
Boston, MA 02215   John D. Cushing, Libn.
Founded: 1791. **Staff:** Prof 6; Other 9. **Subjects:** Massachusetts history, New England history to 1820, Americana. **Special Collections:** American imprints. **Holdings:** 500,000 volumes; manuscripts, maps, prints. **Subscriptions:** 712 journals and other serials. **Services:** Copying; library open to public. **Computerized Information Services:** Computerized cataloging. **Networks/Consortia:** Member of OCLC.

★7632★

MASSACHUSETTS HORTICULTURAL SOCIETY - LIBRARY (Sci-Tech)
300 Massachusetts Ave.   Phone: (617) 536-9280
Boston, MA 02115   Judith Weinberg, Libn.
Founded: 1829. **Staff:** Prof 1. **Subjects:** Ornamental horticulture, garden history, pomology, floras of the world, landscape design, floral arrnagement. **Special Collections:** Print collection covering 6 centuries; nursery catalog collection dating back to 1771. **Holdings:** 37,000 books and bound periodical volumes; 24 VF drawers of pamphlets and clippings; 2000 documents. **Subscriptions:** 241 journals and other serials. **Services:** Interlibrary loans; copying; library open to public for reference use only. **Publications:** Dictionary Catalog of the Library of the Massachusetts Horticultural Society, 1962, Supplement 1962/1971.

★7633★

MASSACHUSETTS INSTITUTE OF TECHNOLOGY - AERONAUTICS AND ASTRONAUTICS LIBRARY (Sci-Tech)
Rm. 33-316   Phone: (617) 253-5665
Cambridge, MA 02139
Founded: 1941. **Staff:** Prof 1; Other 1. **Subjects:** Mechanics and physics of fluids; computational fluids; instrumentation, guidance and control; energy conversion and propulsion; materials, structures and aeroelasticity; aeronautical and astronautical systems (including flight transportation). **Special Collections:** Publications of National Advisory Committee for Aeronautics and National Aeronautics and Space Administration from the beginning in 1915; complete set of Institute of the Aeronautical/Aerospace Sciences, American Rocket Society, American Institute of Aeronautics and Astronautics technical papers. **Holdings:** 6500 books; 3200 bound periodical volumes; 70,000 technical reports; 25,500 bound serial volumes (cataloged); 375 M.I.T. theses; 215,000 microfiche sheets. **Subscriptions:** 475 journals and other serials. **Services:** Interlibrary loans; copying; library open to public for reference use only; fee for borrowing. **Computerized Information Services:** Online systems; computerized cataloging. **Networks/Consortia:** Member of OCLC through NELINET; Boston Library Consortium.

★7634★

MASSACHUSETTS INSTITUTE OF TECHNOLOGY - BARKER ENGINEERING LIBRARY (Sci-Tech)
Rm. 10-500   Phone: (617) 253-5663
Cambridge, MA 02139   James M. Kyed, Hd., Engr.Libs.
Staff: Prof 7; Other 16. **Subjects:** Engineering - electrical, mechanical, civil, ocean, materials and environmental; bioengineering; transportation; energy; mineral resources; computer science and applied mathematics. **Holdings:** 56,000 books; 27,000 bound periodical volumes; 61,000 bound serial volumes; 14,000 M.I.T. theses; 2200 pamphlets; 64,000 technical reports; 178,000 microfiche sheets; 700 reels of microfilm; 450 audio cassettes. **Services:** Interlibrary loans; copying; library open to public for brief room use; fee for borrowing. **Computerized Information Services:** Online systems; computerized cataloging. **Networks/Consortia:** Member of OCLC through NELINET; Boston Library Consortium. **Publications:** Barker Engineering

Library Bulletin, biweekly - mailing list, by subscription for mailing outside M.I.T.

★7635★

MASSACHUSETTS INSTITUTE OF TECHNOLOGY - CENTER FOR POLICY ALTERNATIVES - DOCUMENTS COLLECTION (Sci-Tech)
Rm. E40-216   Phone: (617) 253-1659
Cambridge, MA 02139   Eileen B. Callum, Libn./Doc.Coord.
Staff: Prof 1. **Subjects:** Science and technology policy - U.S. and international; professional manpower; engineering education; industrial innovation; natural resources and energy; occupational health and safety; consumer policy. **Special Collections:** Foreign government documents on science and technology policy. **Holdings:** 5400 books. **Subscriptions:** 85 journals and other serials. **Services:** Collection open to public for reference use only by prior telephone arrangement. **Publications:** List of center-produced publications, annual - with updates.

★7636★

MASSACHUSETTS INSTITUTE OF TECHNOLOGY - CENTER FOR SPACE RESEARCH - READING ROOM (Sci-Tech)
Rm. 37-582   Phone: (617) 253-3746
Cambridge, MA 02139
Founded: 1965. **Subjects:** Astrophysics, astronomy, nuclear physics, astronautics. **Special Collections:** Center for Space Research technical reports. **Holdings:** 2750 books; 517 bound periodical volumes; 210 bound serial volumes; 3506 technical reports; 210 pamphlets; selected bibliographies and NASA reports. **Services:** Interlibrary loans; copying; reading room open to public for brief room use. **Computerized Information Services:** Online systems; computerized cataloging. **Networks/Consortia:** Member of OCLC through NELINET; Boston Library Consortium.

★7637★

MASSACHUSETTS INSTITUTE OF TECHNOLOGY - CHEMISTRY READING ROOM (Sci-Tech)
Rm. 18-480   Phone: (617) 253-1891
Cambridge, MA 02139
Founded: 1970. **Staff:** Prof 1; Other 1. **Subjects:** Chemistry - organic, inorganic, physical; biochemistry. **Holdings:** 2500 books and bound serial volumes (cataloged); 2800 reels of microfilm; Sadtler Spectra. **Subscriptions:** 85 journals. **Services:** Reading room open to public for brief room use. **Computerized Information Services:** Online systems; computerized cataloging. **Networks/Consortia:** Member of OCLC through NELINET; Boston Library Consortium.

★7638★

MASSACHUSETTS INSTITUTE OF TECHNOLOGY - CIVIL ENGINEERING DEPT. - RALPH M. PARSONS LABORATORY - REF. RM. (Sci-Tech)
Bldg. 48-411   Phone: (617) 253-2994
Cambridge, MA 02139   Chiang C. Mei, Prof.Civ.Engr.
Staff: 1. **Subjects:** Hydrodynamics, hydrostatics, water resources, hydraulic machinery and structures, flow measurement, hydrology, environmental engineering, force resistance, aquatic chemistry, coastal engineering, ecology. **Holdings:** 300 books; 90 VF drawers of technical reports; 600 theses. **Subscriptions:** 30 journals and other serials. **Services:** Interlibrary loans; room open to public for reference use only.

★7639★

MASSACHUSETTS INSTITUTE OF TECHNOLOGY - DEPARTMENT OF CHEMICAL ENGINEERING READING ROOM (Sci-Tech)
Room 66-365   Phone: (617) 253-6521
Cambridge, MA 02139
Founded: 1930. **Staff:** 1. **Subjects:** Chemical engineering. **Special Collections:** Theses and Chemical Engineering course solution books. **Holdings:** 1200 books. **Services:** Reading room reserved for department use only.

★7640★

MASSACHUSETTS INSTITUTE OF TECHNOLOGY - DEPARTMENT OF NUTRITION AND FOOD SCIENCE - READING ROOM (Food-Bev)
Rm. 20A-213   Phone: (617) 253-7994
Cambridge, MA 02139   Margaret Mubirumusoke, Info.Spec.
Staff: Prof 1. **Subjects:** Nutrition - international, clinical, policy and planning. **Holdings:** Over 3000 books, theses and pamphlets; area files on 200 countries and subject files (unbound and/or unpublished reports, documents, clippings, reprints). **Subscriptions:** 80 journals and other serials. **Services:** Copying; reading room open to public for reference use only.

★7641★

MASSACHUSETTS INSTITUTE OF TECHNOLOGY - DEWEY LIBRARY (Bus-Fin)
Hermann Bldg., E53-138　　Phone: (617) 253-5677
Cambridge, MA 02139　　Edgar W. Davy, Dewey Libn.
Founded: 1938. **Staff:** Prof 6; Other 15. **Subjects:** Economics, political science, management and finance, sociology, psychology, law. **Special Collections:** Industrial Relations (66,000 pamphlets and special materials); United Nations documents; corporate financial reports. **Holdings:** 160,000 books; 34,000 bound periodical volumes; 172,000 bound serial volumes (cataloged); 122,500 pamphlets (cataloged); 20,000 technical reports; 4200 M.I.T. theses; 66,500 microfiche; 3500 reels of microfilm. **Services:** Interlibrary loans; copying; library open to public for brief room use; fee for borrowing. **Computerized Information Services:** Online systems; computerized cataloging and literature searching. **Networks/Consortia:** Member of OCLC through NELINET; Boston Library Consortium. **Publications:** Industrial Relations Accessions Lists, bimonthly. **Special Indexes:** Index to Working Papers, Sloan School of Management, 1962-1969.

★7642★

MASSACHUSETTS INSTITUTE OF TECHNOLOGY - DIVISION FOR STUDY AND RESEARCH IN EDUCATION - READING ROOM
Rm. 20C-117
Cambridge, MA 02139
Defunct

★7643★

MASSACHUSETTS INSTITUTE OF TECHNOLOGY - DYNAMICS OF ATMOSPHERES AND OCEANS LIBRARY (Sci-Tech)
Rm. 54-1427　　Phone: (617) 253-2450
Cambridge, MA 02139　　Jule G. Charney, Prof.
Founded: 1958. **Staff:** 1. **Subjects:** Meteorology, oceanography, geophysics, applied mathematics, physics, astrophysics. **Holdings:** 350 books; 40 bound periodical volumes; 43 dissertations; 118 unbound reports. **Subscriptions:** 50 journals and other serials. **Services:** Library open to public for reference use only.

★7644★

MASSACHUSETTS INSTITUTE OF TECHNOLOGY - ENVIRONMENTAL MEDICAL SERVICE - LIBRARY (Env-Cons)
77 Massachusetts Ave., Rm. 20B-23B　　Phone: (617) 253-7983
Cambridge, MA 02139　　Amy J. Knutson, Libn.
Staff: 1. **Subjects:** Industrial hygiene and toxicology, radiation protection, clinical toxicology. **Holdings:** 9 VF drawers of clippings and reprints. **Subscriptions:** 30 journals and other serials. **Services:** Library open to public with approval. **Publications:** Lead as an Environmental Poison - available on request; Biohazards Assessment.

★7645★

MASSACHUSETTS INSTITUTE OF TECHNOLOGY - FRANCIS HART NAUTICAL MUSEUM - LIBRARY
Room 5-329
Cambridge, MA 02139
Defunct. Merged into the M.I.T. Museum and Historical Collections.

★7646★

MASSACHUSETTS INSTITUTE OF TECHNOLOGY - HUMANITIES LIBRARY (Hum)
Rm. 14S-200　　Phone: (617) 253-5683
Cambridge, MA 02139　　David S. Ferriero, Libn.
Staff: Prof 5; Other 8. **Subjects:** Anthropology, archeology, education, foreign languages, history, history of science and technology, library and information science, linguistics, literature, philosophy, psychology, religion, women's and men's studies. **Holdings:** 130,000 books; 21,000 bound periodical volumes; 77,000 bound serial volumes (cataloged); 300 M.I.T. theses; 2200 technical reports; 2000 pamphlets; 4000 reels of microfilm; 4500 microfiche; 200 maps and plans. **Subscriptions:** 3700 journals and other serials. **Services:** Interlibrary loans; copying; library open to public for brief room use. **Computerized Information Services:** Computerized cataloging. **Networks/Consortia:** Member of OCLC through NELINET; Boston Library Consortium.

★7647★

MASSACHUSETTS INSTITUTE OF TECHNOLOGY - INFORMATION PROCESSING SERVICES - READING ROOM (Info Sci)
Rm. 39-233　　Phone: (617) 253-4105
Cambridge, MA 02139　　Richard D. Scott, Mgr.
Founded: 1956. **Staff:** 1. **Subjects:** Manuals for operating system utility software and application software available at Information Processing

Services. **Holdings:** 800 manuals; IPS memos and newsletters. **Services:** Reading room open to public but preference given to users of IPS Computing Services.

★7648★

MASSACHUSETTS INSTITUTE OF TECHNOLOGY - INSTITUTE ARCHIVES AND SPECIAL COLLECTIONS (Hist; Sci-Tech)
Hayden Library, Rm. 14N-118　　Phone: (617) 253-5688
Cambridge, MA 02139　　Helen W. Slotkin, Archv./Spec.Coll.Hd.
Founded: 1961. **Staff:** Prof 5; Other 2. **Subjects:** Archival and manuscript collections concerning M.I.T. and science and technology in the 19th and 20th centuries. **Special Collections:** Rare book collection on engineering, animal magnetism, chemistry, electricity and other branches of science and technology; books and periodicals about M.I.T. and/or by M.I.T. alumni and staff; oral history collection. **Holdings:** 3500 cubic feet of manuscripts and archives; 46,000 theses; 15,400 books. **Subscriptions:** 70 journals and other serials. **Services:** Copying. **Special Catalogs:** Finding aids and guides to manuscript and archival collections available.

★7649★

MASSACHUSETTS INSTITUTE OF TECHNOLOGY - LABORATORY FOR COMPUTER SCIENCE - READING ROOM (Sci-Tech)
545 Technology Sq., Rm. 114　　Phone: (617) 253-5896
Cambridge, MA 02139　　Maria Sensale, Lib.Asst.
Staff: 2. **Subjects:** Computer science. **Holdings:** 1225 books; 6000 technical reports; 590 dissertations; 225 microfiche reports. **Subscriptions:** 155 journals and other serials. **Services:** Interlibrary loans; reading room not open to public. **Computerized Information Services:** Computerized cataloging. **Publications:** Computer Science Technical Reports - for sale; Computer Science Technical Memos - free upon request; Newsletter - for internal distribution only.

★7650★

MASSACHUSETTS INSTITUTE OF TECHNOLOGY - LINCOLN LABORATORY LIBRARY (Sci-Tech)
244 Wood St.　　Phone: (617) 863-5500
Lexington, MA 02173　　Jane H. Katayama, Lib.Mgr.
Founded: 1957. **Staff:** Prof 6; Other 12. **Subjects:** Electronics, physics, mathematics, astronomy, space science, engineering, chemistry, computer technology. **Holdings:** 60,000 books; 10,000 bound periodical volumes; 150,000 technical reports; 3000 maps; 1500 volumes of journals on microfilm. **Subscriptions:** 1500 journals and other serials. **Publications:** Documents Accessions List, semimonthly; Scanner, weekly; Lincoln Laboratory Supplement to Current Contents, irregular - all for internal distribution only. **Staff:** Mary Granese, Supv./Doc. & Archv.; Carolyn Greenberg, Supv./Rd.Serv.; Janice Bower, Info.Sci.; Hema Viswanatha, Info.Spec.; Richard Burnes, Supv., Tech.Proc.

★7651★

MASSACHUSETTS INSTITUTE OF TECHNOLOGY - LINDGREN LIBRARY (Sci-Tech)
Rm. 54-200　　Phone: (617) 253-5679
Cambridge, MA 02139　　Jean Eaglesfield, Lindgren Libn.
Founded: 1964. **Staff:** Prof 1; Other 2. **Subjects:** Geology, meteorology, oceanography, geophysics, geochemistry, planetary sciences, seismology. **Holdings:** 12,000 books; 8300 bound periodical volumes; 16,000 bound serial volumes (cataloged); 11,000 maps; 330 pamphlets; 900 M.I.T. theses; 1200 technical reports; 5000 microforms. **Services:** Interlibrary loans; copying; SDI; library open to public for brief room use; fee for borrowing. **Computerized Information Services:** Online systems; computerized cataloging. **Networks/Consortia:** Member of OCLC through NELINET; Boston Library Consortium.

★7652★

MASSACHUSETTS INSTITUTE OF TECHNOLOGY - M.I.T. MUSEUM AND HISTORICAL COLLECTIONS (Hist)
Bldg. N52　　Phone: (617) 253-4444
Cambridge, MA 02139　　Warren A. Seamans, Dir.
Founded: 1971. **Staff:** Prof 6; Other 2. **Special Collections:** Nautical collections (books, drawings, prints); Radiation Laboratory photographs (40,000) and instruments (100); H.H. Young Globe Collection (35); Wente Collection of Meters and Motors (78); Draper Laboratory Historical Collection (600 square feet). **Holdings:** 1200 books; 533,000 photographs; 3000 instruments; 12,000 student architectural drawings (1873-1968); 145 portraits including 20 busts; 200 19th and 20th century works of art; 800 motion films; videotapes and AV material; a large and varied collection of decorative art. **Services:** Copying; graphic arts service; collections open to public. **Networks/Consortia:** Member of Boston Library Consortium. **Publications:** MIT in Perspective in The M.I.T. Museum gathers, conserves,

catalogues and exhibits the visual and biographical material documenting the development of the Institute and of 19th and 20th century science, engineering and architecture. Contains the holdings of the Francis Hart Nautical Museum Library. **Staff:** Marcia E. Conroy, Cur. of Educ.; Barbara Linden, Adm.Asst.; Joan Loria, Cur. of Exhibits; Michael W. Yeates, Registrar; John Waterhouse, Act.Cur., Hart Coll.

★7653★
MASSACHUSETTS INSTITUTE OF TECHNOLOGY - MUSIC LIBRARY (Mus)
Rm. 14E-109   Phone: (617) 253-5689
Cambridge, MA 02139   Linda I. Solow, Music Libn.
Staff: Prof 1; Other 2. **Subjects:** Music. **Special Collections:** Music, recordings and biographies of composers associated with M.I.T. **Holdings:** 8650 books; 1350 bound periodical volumes; 12,600 sound recordings; 19,850 scores; 80 microforms; 1250 audiotapes (uncataloged). **Services:** Interlibrary loans; copying; library open to public for brief room use; fee for borrowing; phonodisc, open reel and cassette tape listening facilities. **Computerized Information Services:** DIALOG; computerized cataloging. **Networks/Consortia:** Member of OCLC through NELINET; Boston Library Consortium; Boston Area Music Libraries. **Publications:** Music Library Newsletter, quarterly.

MASSACHUSETTS INSTITUTE OF TECHNOLOGY - NEUROSCIENCES RESEARCH PROGRAM
See: Rockefeller University - Neurosciences Research Program

★7654★
MASSACHUSETTS INSTITUTE OF TECHNOLOGY - PHYSICS READING ROOM (Sci-Tech)
Rm. 26-152   Phone: (617) 253-1791
Cambridge, MA 02139
Founded: 1949. **Staff:** 2. **Subjects:** Physics, astrophysics, biophysics, astronomy. **Holdings:** 5000 books; 6500 bound periodical volumes; 750 theses; 6000 preprints; 900 technical reports. **Subscriptions:** 100 journals and other serials. **Services:** Copying.

★7655★
MASSACHUSETTS INSTITUTE OF TECHNOLOGY - PSYCHOLOGY LIBRARY (Soc Sci)
Rm. E10-030   Phone: (617) 253-5755
Cambridge, MA 02139   Catherine Gibbes, Ph.D., Libn.
Founded: 1962. **Staff:** 1. **Subjects:** Neurophysiology and neuroanatomy; psychology - physiological, experimental, comparative, developmental; cognitive science; psycholinguistics; language and communication; mathematical psychology. **Holdings:** 5000 books; 3800 bound periodical volumes; 1000 reprints; 70 bound doctoral theses of psychology department graduates. **Subscriptions:** 65 journals and other serials. **Services:** Library open to M.I.T.-affiliated persons with written permission from a faculty member of the Psychology Department.

★7656★
MASSACHUSETTS INSTITUTE OF TECHNOLOGY - PURE MATHEMATICS READING ROOM (Sci-Tech)
Rm. 2-285
Cambridge, MA 02139
Subjects: Pure Mathematics. **Holdings:** 4000 books. **Subscriptions:** 34 journals and other serials. **Services:** Reading room not open to public.

★7657★
MASSACHUSETTS INSTITUTE OF TECHNOLOGY - RESEARCH LABORATORY OF ELECTRONICS - DOCUMENT ROOM (Sci-Tech)
Rm. 36-412   Phone: (617) 253-2566
Cambridge, MA 02139
Founded: 1946. **Staff:** 2. **Subjects:** Biophysics, neurophysiology, cognitive information processing, plasma dynamics, radio astronomy, lasers, molecular beams, microwave electronics. **Special Collections:** Radiation Laboratory reports. **Holdings:** 2200 books; 2700 bound periodical volumes; 1000 scientific technical reports; 2500 dissertations. **Subscriptions:** 200 journals and other serials. **Services:** Interlibrary loans; room open to public with limited borrowing. **Publications:** Accessions list in plasma physics, monthly; Publications of RLE: 1946-1966, and Supplements: 1966-1976. **Special Indexes:** Author and subject indexes for RLE theses; author, subject, source and equipment number indexes for progress and technical reports.

★7658★
MASSACHUSETTS INSTITUTE OF TECHNOLOGY - ROTCH LIBRARY OF ARCHITECTURE AND PLANNING (Art; Plan)
Rm. 7-238   Phone: (617) 253-7052
Cambridge, MA 02139   Margaret DePopolo, Rotch Libn.
Founded: 1868. **Staff:** Prof 6; Other 12. **Subjects:** Architectural history and design, urban and environmental studies, regional planning, 20th century art, film and photography. **Holdings:** 81,000 books; 9500 bound periodical volumes; 10,500 bound serial volumes (cataloged); 34,100 pamphlets (cataloged); 5700 maps and plans; 2000 M.I.T. theses; 1500 technical reports; 33,000 microfiche; 800 reels of microfilm. **Subscriptions:** 7 newspapers. **Services:** Interlibrary loans; copying; library open to public for brief room use. **Networks/Consortia:** Member of OCLC through NELINET; Boston Library Consortium. **Staff:** Micheline E. Jedrey, Assoc.Libn.

★7659★
MASSACHUSETTS INSTITUTE OF TECHNOLOGY - ROTCH LIBRARY VISUAL COLLECTIONS - LOUIS SKIDMORE ROOM (Pict)
Room 7-304   Phone: (617) 253-7098
Cambridge, MA 02139   Merrill W. Smith, Libn.
Founded: 1976. **Staff:** Prof 1; Other 3. **Subjects:** Architecture, archeology, art history, environmental and urban design. **Special Collections:** Photostats of drawings by Bullfinch and Latrobe; photographs of drawings by Bertram G. Goodhue; Lynch-Kepes Collection of photographs of Boston in the 1950s; Aga Khan Program for Islamic Architecture visual archives; Skidmore, Owings and Merrill work, 1950-1970 (4681 slides); federal architecture (1400 slides). **Holdings:** 200,000 slides; 43,000 photographs; 145 videotapes and films. **Services:** Open to scholars and researchers for brief room use.

★7660★
MASSACHUSETTS INSTITUTE OF TECHNOLOGY - SCHERING-PLOUGH LIBRARY (Med)
Rm. E25-131
Cambridge, MA 02139
Staff: 1. **Subjects:** Health sciences, technology and management. **Holdings:** 700 volumes. **Services:** Interlibrary loans; library open to public for brief room use; fee for borrowing. **Computerized Information Services:** Computerized cataloging. **Networks/Consortia:** Member of OCLC through NELINET; Boston Library Consortium.

★7661★
MASSACHUSETTS INSTITUTE OF TECHNOLOGY - SCIENCE FICTION SOCIETY - LIBRARY (Rec)
Rm. W20-421   Phone: (617) 253-1000
Cambridge, MA 02139
Founded: 1949. **Subjects:** Science fiction, fantasy literature. **Special Collections:** Bound professional science fiction magazines (almost complete set of major American and British); large collection of foreign science fiction; Science Fiction Writers of America - New England Depository. **Holdings:** 20,000 books; 800 bound periodical volumes; foreign magazines (cataloged); 4 filing cabinets of science fiction fan magazines, published by individuals; microfilm of Analog, Astounding (in process). **Subscriptions:** 20 journals and other serials. **Services:** Library open to public, fee for borrowing privileges. **Publications:** Twilight Zine, irregular - mailed upon request for a small fee. **Remarks:** World's largest library of science fiction open to the general public; staffed by student volunteers.

★7662★
MASSACHUSETTS INSTITUTE OF TECHNOLOGY - SCIENCE LIBRARY (Sci-Tech)
Rm. 14S-100   Phone: (617) 253-5680
Cambridge, MA 02139   Irma Y. Johnson, Science Libn.
Staff: Prof 6; Other 4. **Subjects:** Biology, biochemistry, chemical engineering, chemistry, nutrition and food science, medicine, neuroscience, materials science, mathematics, nuclear engineering, physics, astronomy. **Special Collections:** Derr collection of early works in mathematics and physics; Eastham collection of books on microscopy; Gaffield collection of materials on glass manufacture; Kayser collection of pamphlets on spectroscopy. **Holdings:** 115,000 books; 82,000 bound periodical volumes; 55,000 bound serial volumes (cataloged); 53,000 technical reports; 63,000 maps; 5200 M.I.T. theses; 137,670 microcards; 234,000 microfiche; 1700 reels of microfilm. **Services:** Interlibrary loans; copying; SDI; library open to public for brief room use; fee for borrowing. **Computerized Information Services:** Online systems; computerized cataloging. **Networks/Consortia:** Member of OCLC through NELINET; Boston Library Consortium.

★7663★
MASSACHUSETTS INSTITUTE OF TECHNOLOGY - SEA GRANT PROGRAM - SEA GRANT INFORMATION CENTER (Sci-Tech)
E38-320, 292 Main St.   Phone: (617) 253-5944
Cambridge, MA 02139   Barbara Steen-Elton, Info.Spec.
Staff: Prof 1. **Subjects:** Ocean engineering, oil spills, fisheries, aquaculture, ocean mining, coastal zone management. **Special Collections:** Sea Grant Technical Reports (2000 volumes). **Holdings:** 3000 books; 12 VF drawers of pamphlets and topical files; 20 VF drawers of M.I.T. Sea Grant Program

archives; 40 Sea Grant newsletters. **Subscriptions:** 122 journals and other serials.

★7664★

MASSACHUSETTS INSTITUTE OF TECHNOLOGY - TRI-SERVICE LIBRARY (Mil)
U.S. AFROTC DET 365
Rm. 20E-122   Phone: (617) 253-4472
Cambridge, MA 02139
Staff: 3. **Subjects:** Military history. **Holdings:** 3000 books. **Subscriptions:** 80 journals and other serials. **Services:** Interlibrary loans; library open to public.

★7665★

MASSACHUSETTS INSTITUTE OF TECHNOLOGY - VON HIPPEL MATERIALS CENTER READING ROOM (Sci-Tech)
Rm. 13-2137   Phone: (617) 253-6840
Cambridge, MA 02139   Polly Baslock, Sr.Lib.Asst.
Founded: 1965. **Staff:** 1. **Subjects:** Chemical and solid state physics; electronic, magnetic and optical properties of materials and device applications; metallurgy and materials science; materials engineering. **Holdings:** 1173 books; **Networks/Consortia:** Member of OCLC through NELINET; Boston Library Consortium. **Publications:** Von Hippel Reading Room Bulletin, bimonthly. 370 bound serial volumes (cataloged); 50 technical reports; 88 annual reports from materials research centers; 1558 cataloged archive papers. **Subscriptions:** 84 journals and other serials. **Services:** Copying; SDI; open to public for brief room use. **Computerized Information Services:** Online systems; computerized cataloging.

★7666★

MASSACHUSETTS MARITIME ACADEMY - CAPTAIN CHARLES H. HURLEY LIBRARY (Sci-Tech)
Taylor's Point
Box D
Buzzards Bay, MA 02532   Phone: (617) 759-5761
     Maurice H. Bosse, Dir. of Lib.Serv.
Founded: 1970. **Staff:** Prof 2; Other 2. **Subjects:** Marine and ocean engineering, marine transportation, fisheries, oceanography, navigation, seamanship, merchant marine operations, meteorology, nautical astronomy, radar, cargo handling, naval architecture, fishing gear and vessel operation, marine and naval science, law of the sea, admiralty law. **Special Collections:** Rare books dealing with maritime history (350 volumes); Cape Cod Canal Collection - August Belmont papers, original documents and facsimiles (5 reels of microfilm). **Holdings:** 36,000 books; 25,000 reels of microfilm; National Ocean Survey chart depository; Defense Mapping Agency depository (maps). **Subscriptions:** 368 journals and other serials; 10 newspapers. **Services:** Interlibrary loans; copying; library open to public for reference use only. **Computerized Information Services:** Computerized cataloging. **Networks/Consortia:** Member of OCLC through NELINET.

★7667★

MASSACHUSETTS MENTAL HEALTH CENTER - CHARLES MAC FIE CAMPBELL MEMORIAL LIBRARY (Med)
74 Fenwood Rd.   Phone: (617) 734-1300
Boston, MA 02115   Alice H. Wolpert, Act.Libn.
Founded: 1912. **Staff:** Prof 1. **Subjects:** Psychiatry, neurology, occupational therapy, law, nursing, psychology. **Holdings:** 13,500 books and bound periodical volumes; reprints. **Subscriptions:** 72 journals and other serials. **Services:** Interlibrary loans; library open to qualified users.

★7668★

MASSACHUSETTS MUNICIPAL ASSOCIATION - RESEARCH LIBRARY (Soc Sci)
131 Tremont St.   Phone: (617) 426-7272
Boston, MA 02111   James Segel, Exec.Dir.
Founded: 1961. **Subjects:** Municipal government, city ordinances, town bylaws, annual municipal reports; state legislative documents. **Holdings:** 300 books. **Services:** Interlibrary loans; copying; library open to public.

★7669★

MASSACHUSETTS MUTUAL LIFE INSURANCE COMPANY - LAW LIBRARY (Law)
1295 State St.   Phone: (413) 788-8411
Springfield, MA 01111   Joyce H. Beaton, Legal Serv.Techn.
Staff: 2. **Subjects:** Insurance, taxation, litigation, securities, real estate, pensions. **Holdings:** 9300 books; 2000 bound periodical volumes; 1300 other cataloged items. **Subscriptions:** 42 journals and other serials. **Services:** Interlibrary loans; library open to public with prior approval on request.

★7670★

MASSACHUSETTS MUTUAL LIFE INSURANCE COMPANY - LIBRARY (Bus-Fin)†
1295 State St.   Phone: (413) 788-8411
Springfield, MA 01111   Yvette M. Jensen, Libn.
Founded: 1929. **Staff:** 2. **Subjects:** Insurance, office management, economics, travel, biography, investment. **Holdings:** 13,500 books; 3 VF drawers of pamphlets. **Subscriptions:** 75 journals and other serials. **Services:** Interlibrary loans; library open to qualified persons.

MASSACHUSETTS NEW CHURCH UNION - SWEDENBORG LIBRARY AND BOOKSTORE
See: Swedenborg Library and Bookstore

★7671★

MASSACHUSETTS REHABILITATION COMMISSION - LIBRARY (Soc Sci)
20 Providence St.   Phone: (617) 727-1140
Boston, MA 02116   June C. Holt, Libn.
Founded: 1963. **Staff:** 2. **Subjects:** Physical impairments, mental problems, severely disabled, counseling techniques, vocational rehabilitation, social problems, disability, independent living, psychological rehabilitation, staff development. **Holdings:** 20,000 books; 1200 microfiche (cataloged); 56 VF drawers; 20 16mm films; 34 audiotapes; Social and Rehabilitation Service (SRS) research information system. **Subscriptions:** 100 journals and other serials. **Services:** Interlibrary loans; copying; library open to public. **Computerized Information Services:** BRS. **Networks/Consortia:** Member of Boston Group of Government Libraries; Boston Biomedical Library Consortium. **Publications:** A Model Library - Community and Commission Benefit, Journal of Rehabilitation, March-April, 1973; A Special Vocational Rehabilitation Library - the Massachusetts Rehabilitation Commission, revised 1972, written for distribution to rehabilitation agencies throughout country through Oklahoma Clearing House, Oklahoma University; Massachusetts Rehabilitation Commission Library, Boston Chapter News Bulletin, Special Libraries Association, March 1975; Bits and Pieces, bimonthly; newsletter - acquisitions listings. **Special Indexes:** Subject Index to Rehabilitation Literature published by the National Easter Seal Society for Crippled Children and Adults. **Staff:** Maya De, Ref.Asst.

MASSACHUSETTS STATE ARCHIVES DIVISION
See: Massachusetts State Office of the Secretary of State - Archives Division

★7672★

MASSACHUSETTS STATE BOARD OF LIBRARY COMMISSIONERS - REFERENCE AND RESEARCH LIBRARY (Info Sci)
648 Beacon St.   Phone: (617) 267-9400
Boston, MA 02215   Roland Piggford, Act.Dir.
Founded: 1890. **Staff:** Prof 21; Other 23. **Subjects:** Library and information science, management. **Special Collections:** Library science (3780 volumes); education (300 volumes). **Holdings:** 10,000 books; 425 bound periodical volumes; 242 reels of microfilm; 128 films, filmstrips and cassettes; ERIC/CLIS (Clearinghouse for Library and Information Science) microfiche collection, 1968 to present; 26 VF drawers. **Subscriptions:** 354 journals and other serials. **Services:** Interlibrary loans; copying; library open to public with restrictions. **Publications:** List of publications - available on request. **Staff:** Catherine McCarthy, Hd., Ref. & Res.Lib.

★7673★

MASSACHUSETTS STATE DEPARTMENT OF THE ATTORNEY GENERAL - LIBRARY (Law)
McCormack Bldg., 20th Fl.
One Ashburton Pl.   Phone: (617) 727-1036
Boston, MA 02108   Ruth G. Matz, Chf.Libn.
Staff: Prof 1; Other 2. **Subjects:** Law. **Special Collections:** Approved town by-law amendments and zoning maps (12 VF drawers and 4 microfiche drawers). **Holdings:** 20,000 books; 150 bound periodical volumes; 34 microform drawers of legal periodicals; 23 microfiche drawers of other legal material; 43 videotapes of legal programs and other material. **Subscriptions:** 135 journals and other serials. **Services:** Interlibrary loans; copying; library open to public with restrictions. **Computerized Information Services:** Internal database. **Publications:** Library Bulletin, monthly - in-house and by request. **Special Indexes:** Index to Attorney General Opinions (card). **Staff:** Norma M. Taylor, Assoc.Libn.

★7674★

MASSACHUSETTS STATE DEPARTMENT OF COMMERCE AND DEVELOPMENT - RESEARCH LIBRARY (Bus-Fin)†
100 Cambridge St.   Phone: (617) 727-3206
Boston, MA 02202   Abbe Stepheson, Libn.
Staff: Prof 1. **Subjects:** Business, economics, planning, tourism,

transportation, marine resources, industry, finance, foreign trade. **Special Collections:** U.S. Census, 1850-1960 censuses; reports of the New England Regional Commission; Federal Reserve Bank research reports; small business management reports, 1960-1965; annual reports of Massachusetts cities and towns. **Holdings:** 5000 volumes; 32 VF drawers. **Subscriptions:** 100 journals and other serials. **Services:** Library open to public. **Computerized Information Services:** Computerized cataloging and acquisitions.

★7675★
MASSACHUSETTS STATE DEPARTMENT OF COMMUNITY AFFAIRS - LIBRARY*
100 Cambridge St.
Boston, MA 02202
Founded: 1970. **Subjects:** Urban affairs; city, state and regional planning; municipal government and finance; housing; land use and zoning; transportation. **Special Collections:** Dime-File Tapes for Massachusetts; Massachusetts Supreme Court decisions, 1923 to present. **Holdings:** 4000 books; Massachusetts General Laws, annotated; annual town reports; 8 book cases of town master plans; 4 VF drawers; 1 file cabinet of pamphlets. **Remarks:** Presently inactive.

★7676★
MASSACHUSETTS STATE DEPARTMENT OF CORRECTION - CENTRAL OFFICE STAFF LIBRARY (Soc Sci)
State Office Bldg., 22nd Fl.
100 Cambridge St.   Phone: (617) 727-3312
Boston, MA 02202   Daniel P. LeClair, Dp.Dir.
Founded: 1964. **Staff:** 1. **Subjects:** Criminology, sociology, social work, psychology. **Holdings:** 600 volumes; unbound periodicals (cataloged); 15 VF drawers of reports, research studies, pamphlets, and proceedings. **Subscriptions:** 12 journals and other serials; 8 newspapers. **Services:** Interlibrary loans; library open to public with identification. **Publications:** Department of Correction Research Reports, 15/yr.

★7677★
MASSACHUSETTS STATE DEPARTMENT OF EDUCATION - OPERATIONS AND SUPPORT - LIBRARY (Educ)
1385 Hancock   Phone: (617) 727-5792
Boston, MA 02169
Founded: 1968. **Staff:** Prof 1. **Subjects:** Educational research. **Holdings:** 200 volumes. **Subscriptions:** 100 journals and other serials. **Services:** Library open to Department of Education staff only.

★7678★
MASSACHUSETTS STATE DEPARTMENT OF LABOR & INDUSTRIES - DIV. OF OCCUPATIONAL HYGIENE - SPECIAL TECHNICAL LIBRARY (Med)
39 Boylston St.   Phone: (617) 727-3982
Boston, MA 02116   Mary Lim, Libn.
Founded: 1934. **Staff:** Prof 1. **Subjects:** Chemistry, radiation, engineering, nursing, occupational medicine. **Holdings:** 500 books; 120 bound periodical volumes; 180 pamphlets. **Subscriptions:** 28 journals and other serials. **Services:** Interlibrary loans; copying; library open to public for reference use only. **Publications:** List of publications - available on request.

★7679★
MASSACHUSETTS STATE DEPARTMENT OF LABOR & INDUSTRIES - REFERENCE LIBRARY
Leverett Saltonstall Bldg., Rm. 1101
100 Cambridge St.
Boston, MA 02202
Defunct

MASSACHUSETTS STATE DEPARTMENT OF MENTAL HEALTH - CHARLES V. HOGAN REGIONAL CENTER
See: Hogan (Charles V.) Regional Center

MASSACHUSETTS STATE DEPARTMENT OF MENTAL HEALTH - ERICH LINDEMANN MENTAL HEALTH CENTER
See: Lindemann (Erich) Mental Health Center

★7680★
MASSACHUSETTS STATE DEPARTMENT OF PUBLIC HEALTH - CENTRAL LIBRARY (Med)
600 Washington St., Rm. 608   Phone: (617) 727-7170
Boston, MA 02111   Catherine Moore, Libn.
Staff: Prof 1; Other 1. **Subjects:** Public health, health care planning and administration. **Special Collections:** U.S. government documents (250); Massachusetts government documents (150); Massachusetts Health Department annual reports, 1871 to present; state cities and towns annual

reports (75). **Holdings:** 400 books; 2640 unbound periodicals. **Subscriptions:** 36 journals and other serials. **Services:** Interlibrary loans; copying; current awareness; library open to public for reference use only. **Computerized Information Services:** NLM. **Networks/Consortia:** Member of Boston Group of Government Librarians (BOGGL); New England Regional Medical Library Service (NERMLS).

MASSACHUSETTS STATE DEPARTMENT OF PUBLIC HEALTH - LAKEVILLE HOSPITAL
See: Lakeville Hospital

★7681★
MASSACHUSETTS STATE DISTRICT COURT - FOURTH EASTERN MIDDLESEX DIVISION - LIBRARY (Law)
30 Pleasant St.   Phone: (617) 935-4000
Woburn, MA 01801   Gertrude M. Allen, Libn.
Founded: 1967. **Staff:** Prof 1. **Subjects:** Massachusetts law. **Holdings:** 3000 books; U.S. Supreme Court reports and digest. **Subscriptions:** 30 journals and other serials. **Services:** Copying; library open to lawyers and students.

MASSACHUSETTS STATE DIVISION OF OCCUPATIONAL HYGIENE
See: Massachusetts State Department of Labor & Industries

★7682★
MASSACHUSETTS STATE HOSPITAL SCHOOL - MEDICAL LIBRARY (Med)
Randolph St.   Phone: (617) 828-2440
Canton, MA 02021   Caroline Cento, Med.Rec.Techn.
Staff: Prof 1; Other 1. **Subjects:** Orthopedics, pediatrics, neurology, anatomy, psychology, nursing. **Special Collections:** Exceptional children (100 books). **Holdings:** 1500 books; 375 bound periodical volumes; videotapes. **Subscriptions:** 55 journals and other serials. **Services:** Interlibrary loans; copying; library open to public with restrictions. **Networks/Consortia:** Member of Southeastern Massachusetts Health Sciences Libraries (SEMCO).

MASSACHUSETTS STATE - LAWRENCE LAW LIBRARY
See: Lawrence Law Library

★7683★
MASSACHUSETTS STATE LIBRARY (Hist; Law)
341 State House   Phone: (617) 727-2590
Boston, MA 02133   Gasper Caso, Act.State Libn.
Founded: 1826. **Staff:** Prof 9; Other 23. **Subjects:** Public law, public affairs, government, politics, U.S. and Massachusetts history. **Special Collections:** Boston newspaper collection from 1700; early Massachusetts school reports; Massachusetts directories; state documents, reports; early 19th century tax lists and legislative, judicial and executive documents from all states. **Holdings:** 822,000 books and bound periodical volumes; 256,000 microforms. **Subscriptions:** 1904 journals and other serials. **Services:** Interlibrary loans; copying; library open to public for reference use only. **Computerized Information Services:** Computerized cataloging and ILL. **Networks/Consortia:** Member of Boston Library Consortium; OCLC through NELINET. **Publications:** Commonwealth of Massachusetts Publications Received, annual and quarterly. **Staff:** Brenda Howitson, Chf., Spec.Coll.; Charles Lumpkins, Chf., Tech.Serv.; Kenneth Flower, Chf., Ref.Serv.; Mary McLellan, Legislative Ref.; Mary Ann Neary, Doc.Libn.

★7684★
MASSACHUSETTS STATE OFFICE OF THE SECRETARY OF STATE - ARCHIVES DIVISION (Hist)
55 State House   Phone: (617) 727-2816
Boston, MA 02133   Albert H. Whitaker, Jr., Archv.
Staff: Prof 5; Other 3. **Subjects:** Massachusetts state and local government and history. **Special Collections:** Massachusetts Archives (328 volumes of colonial and Revolutionary-era manuscripts); legislative documents, 1630 to present; gubernatorial records. **Holdings:** 6000 cubic feet of archival records; 8000 microforms; 24,000 photographs. **Services:** Copying; archives open to public with restrictions. **Publications:** Signature (newsletter), biennial; collections bulletins. **Staff:** Robert W. McDonnell, Cur. of Archv.

MASSACHUSETTS STATE SUPREME JUDICIAL COURT - THORNDIKE LIBRARY
See: Thorndike Library

MASSACHUSETTS STATE - TRIAL COURT - BRISTOL COUNTY LAW LIBRARY
See: Bristol County Law Library

★7685★
MASSACHUSETTS STATE TRIAL COURT - FRANKLIN COUNTY LAW LIBRARY (Law)
Court House
Greenfield, MA 01301
Phone: (413) 772-6580
Marilyn M. Lee, Law Libn.
Founded: 1814. **Staff:** Prof 1. **Subjects:** Law. **Special Collections:** Early English law; Massachusetts statute law, 1692 to present. **Holdings:** 26,000 volumes; 18 tapes. **Subscriptions:** 25 journals and other serials. **Services:** Copying; library open to public for reference use only. **Special Indexes:** Index to legal periodicals, subject and author (card file).

★7686★
MASSACHUSETTS TAXPAYERS FOUNDATION, INC. - LIBRARY (Soc Sci)
One Federal St.
Boston, MA 02110
Phone: (617) 357-8500
Vicky J. Slavin, Libn.
Founded: 1945. **Staff:** Prof 1. **Subjects:** Public administration, Massachusetts state and local government, taxation. **Special Collections:** Massachusetts town reports, legislative journals, bills and bulletins. **Holdings:** 4000 books; 3500 pamphlets (cataloged); 30 VF drawers of pamphlets (uncataloged). **Subscriptions:** 160 journals and other serials. **Services:** Interlibrary loans; copying; library open to public. **Computerized Information Services:** Internal database.

★7687★
MASSACHUSETTS VOCATIONAL CURRICULUM RESOURCE CENTER - MVCRC LIBRARY (Educ)
758 Marrett Rd.
Lexington, MA 02173-7398
Phone: (617) 863-1863
Susan N. Bjorner, Libn.
Founded: 1980. **Staff:** Prof 1; Other 1. **Subjects:** Education - vocational, special, bilingual; microcomputers in education. **Special Collections:** Microcomputer software (40 packages). **Holdings:** 2000 books; microfiche; 2 VF drawers of pamphlets. **Subscriptions:** 20 journals and other serials. **Services:** Interlibrary loans; copying; library open to public with restrictions. **Computerized Information Services:** BRS; computerized cataloging. **Networks/Consortia:** Member of National Network for Curriculum Coordination in Vocational and Technical Education. **Publications:** Catalog of materials, annual; bibliographies, irregular - to state vocational Educators.

MASSEY (Alyne Queener) LAW LIBRARY
See: Vanderbilt University - Alyne Queener Massey Law Library

★7688★
MASSEY COLLEGE - ROBERTSON DAVIES LIBRARY (Info Sci; Hum)
4 Devonshire Place
Toronto, ON, Canada M5S 2E1
Phone: (416) 978-2893
Desmond G. Neill, Libn.
Founded: 1963. **Staff:** Prof 1; Other 1. **Subjects:** Bibliography (calligraphy to typography); Canadian fiction and poetry. **Special Collections:** McLean Collection of 19th century printing (1900 items); Carl Dair Archive; papers of Vincent Massey (access controlled). **Holdings:** 41,000 volumes. **Subscriptions:** 93 journals and other serials; 10 newspapers. **Services:** Interlibrary loans; copying; library open to public for reference use only, on request.

MASSEY LIBRARY & SCIENCE/ENGINEERING LIBRARY
See: Royal Military College of Canada

MATAS (Rudolph) MEDICAL LIBRARY
See: Tulane University of Louisiana - School of Medicine - Rudolph Matas Medical Library

MATERIEL DEVELOPMENT & READINESS COMMAND (DARCOM)
See: U.S. Army

MATERNAL & CHILD HEALTH/POPULATION DYNAMICS LIBRARY
See: Johns Hopkins University - School of Hygiene & Public Health

★7689★
MATERNITY CENTER ASSOCIATION - REFERENCE LIBRARY (Soc Sci)
48 E. 92nd St.
New York, NY 10028
Phone: (212) 369-7300
Esther Hanchett, Act.Libn.
Founded: 1940. **Staff:** Prof 1. **Subjects:** Obstetrics, maternal and infant care, family life, nurse-midwifery, preparation for child-bearing. **Holdings:** 2000 books. **Subscriptions:** 31 journals and other serials. **Services:** Copying; library open to public by appointment to professionals, students and writers.

★7690★
MATHEMATICAL REVIEWS - LIBRARY (Sci-Tech)
611 Church St.
Ann Arbor, MI 48104
Phone: (313) 764-7228
Janice Seidler, Hd.Libn.
Staff: Prof 6; Other 6. **Subjects:** Mathematics. **Holdings:** 100 reference volumes; 10,000 unbound periodicals; 225 reels of microfilm. **Subscriptions:** 1500 journals and other serials. **Services:** Library not open to public. **Publications:** Mathematical Reviews, monthly; Index of Mathematical Publications, yearly; Current Mathematical Publications, biweekly - all by subscription. **Staff:** Bonita Ross, Western Bk.Acq.Libn.; Sharon Heller, Western Jnl.Acq.Libn.; Judith Harvey, Ref.Libn.; Margaret Pooler, Ref.Libn.; Barbara Diatchun, Ref.Libn.

MATHER AIR FORCE BASE (CA)
See: U.S. Air Force Base - Mather Base Library; U.S. Air Force Hospital - Medical Library (CA-Mather AFB)

MATHER (Harriet L.) ARCHIVES
See: Southern Baptist Hospital - Learning Resource Center

★7691★
MATSUSHITA INDUSTRIAL COMPANY - TECHNICAL INFORMATION SERVICES LIBRARY (Sci-Tech)
9401 W. Grand Ave.
Franklin Park, IL 60131
Phone: (312) 451-1200
Ted Rzeszewski, Mgr.
Founded: 1957. **Staff:** Prof 1. **Subjects:** Technical information, TV electronics, cable TV and scrambling systems, video recording, laser application, semiconductors. **Special Collections:** National Television System Committee (NTSC) Reports (17 volumes); Hazeltine Bulletin (4 volumes); RCA Bulletin (12 volumes); RCA Review (19 volumes); Institute of Electrical and Electronics Engineers (IEEE) bound editions, 1943 to present; Sams Photofacts, Range Number 2000; Bell Laboratory journals, 1948-1979; Electronics Magazine, all editions 1943. **Holdings:** 1250 books; 175 bound periodical volumes; 59 standards (cataloged); 8 VF drawers of reports, clippings, archives, pamphlets and documents. **Subscriptions:** 110 journals and other serials. **Services:** Copying; library not open to public. **Publications:** Book Reviews Bulletin, Periodicals Contents, monthly or bimonthly. **Staff:** Diane Grajek, Libn.

MATTACHINE SOCIETY INC. OF NEW YORK
See: Church of the Beloved Disciple - Homophile Research Library

MATTHAEI BOTANICAL GARDENS
See: University of Michigan

★7692★
MATTHEWS & BRANSCOMB - LIBRARY (Law)
One Alamo Center
106 S. St. Mary's St.
San Antonio, TX 78205
Phone: (512) 226-4211
Noreen McGee, Libn.
Founded: 1874. **Staff:** Prof 1. **Subjects:** Law. **Holdings:** 20,000 books; 285 bound periodical volumes; 75 tapes (cataloged); 200 briefs, memoranda. **Subscriptions:** 45 journals and other serials; 5 newspapers. **Services:** Copying; SDI; library open to other law firms. **Computerized Information Services:** Online systems. **Publications:** Pocketparts, every 2 months - for internal distribution only. **Formerly:** Matthews & Nowlin.

★7693★
MAUI HISTORICAL SOCIETY - RESEARCH LIBRARY (Hist)
2375 A Main St.
Box 1018
Wailuku, HI 96793
Phone: (808) 244-3326
Virginia Wirtz, Musm.Dir.
Founded: 1975. **Staff:** Prof 1. **Subjects:** Hawaiiana. **Holdings:** 300 books; 6 VF drawers of mounted clippings; 2 VF drawers of photographs. **Services:** Library open to public when director is present.

MAUNA KEA OBSERVATORY
See: University of Hawaii - Institute for Astronomy

MAURY (Matthew Fontaine) MEMORIAL LIBRARY
See: U.S. Navy - Naval Observatory - Matthew Fontaine Maury Memorial Library

★7694★
MAX FACTOR & COMPANY - R & D LIBRARY (Sci-Tech)
1655 N. McCadden Pl.
Hollywood, CA 90028
Phone: (213) 856-6648
Dawn A. Wingate, Tech.Libn.
Founded: 1954. **Staff:** Prof 1. **Subjects:** Cosmetics, dermatology, perfumes, microbiology, bacteriology, mycology. **Holdings:** 3500 books; 2450 bound

periodical volumes; 1 VF drawer of U.S. and foreign patents; 1 VF drawer plus 2 stacks of trade catalogs; 5 VF drawers of literature and reports. **Subscriptions:** 80 journals and other serials. **Services:** Interlibrary loans; copying; bibliographic and reference service for staff, and for others on a referral basis; library open to public if referred by a staff member. **Publications:** New Books Received, irregular; R&D News Update, monthly - for internal distribution only.

★7695★
MAXIMA CORPORATION - TECHNICAL INFORMATION CENTER - FILM LIBRARY (Aud-Vis; Energy)
Box 62
Oak Ridge, TN 37830
Phone: (615) 576-1287
Terri Alexander, Tech.Coord.
Founded: 1972. **Staff:** Prof 2; Other 1. **Subjects:** Energy conservation, solar and geothermal energy, environment, oil, technology. **Holdings:** 5000 prints of 40 titles. **Services:** Films may be rented at a nominal fee. **Formerly:** U.S. Dept. of Energy - Technical Information Center - Film Library.

MAXWELL AIR FORCE BASE (AL)
See: U.S. Air Force Hospital - Medical Library (AL-Montgomery)

MAXWELL (Clement C.) LIBRARY
See: Bridgewater State College - Clement C. Maxwell Library

MAXWELL MUSIC LIBRARY
See: Tulane University of Louisiana

★7696★
MAY DEPARTMENT STORES COMPANY - INFORMATION CENTER (Bus-Fin; Law)
611 Olive St., Suite 1350
St. Louis, MO 63101
Phone: (314) 247-0329
Julia O'Neil, Dir.
Founded: 1969. **Staff:** Prof 4; Other 4. **Subjects:** Retail trade, law, business and finance. **Special Collections:** Corporate archives. **Holdings:** 15,000 books; 800 bound periodical volumes; 20 files of corporate reports; 1 file of pamphlets. **Subscriptions:** 750 journals and other serials; 20 newspapers. **Services:** Interlibrary loans; copying; center open to public with the permission of the manager. **Computerized Information Services:** DIALOG, SDC, BRS, New York Times Information Service, Dow Jones News Retrieval, LEXIS; computerized cataloging. **Networks/Consortia:** Member of MIDLNET; St. Louis Regional Library Network. **Publications:** Bulletin, monthly. **Special Catalogs:** Catalog of archival materials (card). **Staff:** Sara R. Beck, Mgr., Corp.Lib.; Linda G. Duval, Law/Tax Libn.; Patricia A. Stephenson, Indexer; Kathleen A. Nystrom, Hd., Tech.Serv.

MAY (Louis E.) MUSEUM
See: Dodge County Historical Society - Louis E. May Museum

★7697★
MAYER, BROWN & PLATT - LIBRARY (Law)
231 S. LaSalle St.
Chicago, IL 60604
Phone: (312) 782-0600
Janice B. Bentley, Libn.
Staff: Prof 3; Other 6. **Subjects:** Law - corporations, securities, tax, banking. **Special Collections:** English and Irish law. **Holdings:** 40,000 volumes. **Services:** Interlibrary loans; library open to public with restrictions. **Computerized Information Services:** LEXIS, New York Times Information Service, WESTLAW. **Staff:** Bobby Towns, Asst.Libn.; Gail Munden, Ref.Libn.

MAYER (Louis B.) LIBRARY
See: American Film Institute - Louis B. Mayer Library

MAYER (Norman) LIBRARY
See: Tulane University of Louisiana - School of Business Administration - Norman Mayer Library

★7698★
MAYER (Oscar) FOODS CORPORATION - R&D LIBRARY (Food-Bev)
Box 7188
Madison, WI 53707
Phone: (608) 241-3311
Thomas R. Whitemarsh, R&D Libn.
Subjects: Food science and technology, package engineering, meat science. **Holdings:** 1500 books; 500 bound periodical volumes; patents; pamphlets. **Subscriptions:** 150 journals and other serials. **Services:** Interlibrary loans; copying; information services to company R&D personnel; library open to public by appointment. **Computerized Information Services:** DIALOG.

MAYFIELD LIBRARY
See: Syracuse University - George Arents Research Library for Special Collections

★7699★
MAYO FOUNDATION - MAYO CLINIC LIBRARY (Med)
200 First St., S.W.
Rochester, MN 55905
Phone: (507) 284-2061
Jack D. Key, Libn.
Founded: 1907. **Staff:** Prof 14; Other 21. **Subjects:** Medicine, basic sciences. **Special Collections:** Rare books in the history of medicine; History of Mayo Clinic. **Holdings:** 55,235 books; 177,350 bound periodical volumes; 2000 dissertations, translations and pamphlets (cataloged). **Subscriptions:** 3369 journals and other serials. **Services:** Interlibrary loans; copying; library open to professionals in medicine and allied sciences. **Computerized Information Services:** DIALOG, SDC, NLM, BRS, Control Data Corporation; computerized cataloging. **Networks/Consortia:** Member of Regional Medical Library - Region 3; MINITEX; OCLC. **Publications:** Mayo Clinic Proceedings - available from library through exchange. **Special Catalogs:** Mayo Foundation theses (card and book form); Mayo Author Bibliography (book form); List of Serial Holdings (book and card). **Staff:** Betty Sande, Lib.Spec.Proj.Coord.; Marjorie Ginn, Acq.Libn.; Theodore Caron, Hd.Cat.; Paula Burich, Comp. Applications; Anita Terry, Hd., Info.Serv.; John Kopper, Hd., Tech.Proc.; Ruth Mann, Hist. of Med.Libn.; Patricia Erwin, Ref.Libn.; Judith Lorrig, Mayo Med.Sch.Libn.; Joy Cornwell, Cat.; Clark Nelson, ILL Libn.; Dottie Hawthorne, Ref.Libn.; Suei An, Monograph Cat.; Joyce Kao, Ser.Cat.

MAYTAG (Mary Louise) MEMORIAL LIBRARY
See: St. John Vianney College Seminary - Mary Louise Maytag Memorial Library

★7700★
MAYVILLE HISTORICAL MUSEUM - LIBRARY (Hist)
22 Turner
Mayville, MI 48744
Phone: (517) 843-6429
Mrs. Willard Phelps, Dir. & Cur.
Staff: Prof 1; Other 1. **Subjects:** Local history, rare books. **Special Collections:** Portrait collection. **Holdings:** Figures not available for books; photographs, clippings, old local newspapers. **Services:** Library open to public. **Publications:** History of Mayville & Surrounding Townships. **Special Indexes:** Local obituaries.

★7701★
MAZAMAS - LIBRARY (Geog-Map)
909 N.W. Nineteenth Ave.
Portland, OR 97209
Phone: (503) 227-2345
Founded: 1916. **Subjects:** Mountaineering, exploration, history of northwestern United States. **Special Collections:** Journals of other mountaineering clubs, U.S. and foreign. **Holdings:** 2500 books; maps, periodicals and exchanges. **Subscriptions:** 25 journals and other serials. **Services:** Library open to public with restrictions.

MC...
Entries beginning "Mc" are interfiled with entries beginning "Mac."

★7702★
MEAD CORPORATION - CORPORATE LIBRARY (Bus-Fin)
Corporate Plaza N.E.
Dayton, OH 45463
Phone: (513) 222-6323
Susan Kremer, Corp.Libn./Anl.
Founded: 1970. **Staff:** Prof 1; Other 1. **Subjects:** Finance, marketing. **Holdings:** 3000 volumes (cataloged). **Services:** Interlibrary loans; library not open to public. **Computerized Information Services:** DIALOG, SDC, MEDLARS, LEXIS, NEXIS, Info Globe, Finsbury Data Services Ltd., Dun & Bradstreet, Inc.

★7703★
MEAD CORPORATION - LIBRARY (Sci-Tech)
Central Research Laboratories
8th & Hickory Sts.
Chillicothe, OH 45601
Phone: (614) 772-3524
Sheldon T. Miller, Supv., Lib.Serv.
Founded: 1930. **Staff:** Prof 2. **Subjects:** Pulp, paper and board; chemistry; chemical engineering; engineering; physics. **Special Collections:** Dard Hunter books on papermaking by hand. **Holdings:** 7300 books; 4700 bound periodical volumes; 17,000 corporation technical reports; 1000 pamphlets; 1000 manufacturers' trade catalogs; 150 reels of microfilm. **Subscriptions:** 200 journals and other serials. **Services:** Interlibrary loans; copying; library open to public with restrictions. **Computerized Information Services:** DIALOG, SDC; computerized cataloging. **Networks/Consortia:** Member of OHIONET; OCLC. **Publications:** Accessions list, bimonthly - for internal distribution only. **Staff:** Jane M. White, Libn.

★7704★

MEAD CORPORATION - MEAD PAPERS - MEAD LIBRARY OF IDEAS
Courthouse Plaza, N.E.
Dayton, OH 45463
Defunct

★7705★

MEAD JOHNSON AND COMPANY - MEAD JOHNSON INSTITUTE - LIBRARY
(Bus-Fin)
2404 Pennsylvania   Phone: (812) 426-7042
Evansville, IN 47721   Larry H. Higgins, Mgr., Educ.
Founded: 1957. **Staff:** Prof 2; Other 1. **Subjects:** General business, management, economics, psychology, human behavior, marketing, finance. **Holdings:** 5500 books. **Subscriptions:** 40 journals and other serials. **Services:** Library not open to public. **Publications:** Bibliography, annual. **Staff:** Loretta Sweeney, Libn.

MEAD JOHNSON AND COMPANY - MEAD JOHNSON RESEARCH CENTER
See: Bristol-Myers Company - Pharmaceutical Research & Development Division - Research Library - Evansville

MEAD LIBRARY
See: University of Florida - P.K. Yonge Laboratory School

★7706★

MEADVILLE CITY HOSPITAL - HUMMER LIBRARY (Med)
751 Liberty St.   Phone: (814) 336-3121
Meadville, PA 16335   Barbara Ewing, Libn.
Founded: 1971. **Staff:** Prof 1. **Subjects:** Nursing, medicine, pre-medical sciences, allied health sciences. **Holdings:** 1228 books; 101 bound periodical volumes; 14 cassette/slide educational programs; 21 video cassettes; 13 anatomical models; 11 wall charts. **Subscriptions:** 22 journals and other serials. **Services:** Interlibrary loans; copying; library open to employees and related allied health agencies; restricted use to students. **Networks/Consortia:** Member of Mideastern Regional Medical Library Service (MERMLS); Erie Area Health Information Library Cooperative.

★7707★

MEADVILLE/LOMBARD THEOLOGICAL SCHOOL - LIBRARY (Rel-Theol)
5701 S. Woodlawn Ave.   Phone: (312) 753-3196
Chicago, IL 60637   Rev. Neil W. Gerdes, Libn.
Staff: Prof 1; Other 5. **Subjects:** Unitarian Universalism, social ethics, history of religions. **Special Collections:** Jenkin Lloyd Jones, A. Powell Davies papers; some William Ellery Channing original manuscripts. **Holdings:** 94,000 books. **Subscriptions:** 145 journals and other serials. **Services:** Interlibrary loans; copying; library not open to public. **Computerized Information Services:** Computerized cataloging. **Networks/Consortia:** Member of Chicago Cluster of Theological Schools (CCTS).

★7708★

MEALS FOR MILLIONS/FREEDOM FROM HUNGER FOUNDATION - LIBRARY
(Food-Bev; Soc Sci)
1800 Olympic Blvd.   Phone: (213) 829-5337
Santa Monica, CA 90406   Patricia Butzer Larson, Dir., Resource Ctr.
Founded: 1967. **Staff:** Prof 1. **Subjects:** Small-scale food technology, nutrition, international development. **Holdings:** 600 books; 7 VF drawers of technical reports; 3 VF drawers of annual reports and pamphlets. **Subscriptions:** 120 journals and other serials. **Services:** Interlibrary loans; library open to public.

MEAT ANIMAL RESEARCH CENTER
See: U.S.D.A. - Agricultural Research Service

MEAT INDUSTRY INFORMATION CENTER
See: National Livestock and Meat Board

★7709★

MECHANICS' INSTITUTE LIBRARY (Sci-Tech; Hist)
57 Post St.   Phone: (415) 421-1750
San Francisco, CA 94104   Kathleen T. Pabst, Lib.Dir.
Founded: 1854. **Staff:** Prof 5; Other 14. **Subjects:** Engineering, art, art history, geology, mining, American history (Civil War), Californiana, American and English literature. **Holdings:** 180,000 books; 21,000 bound periodical volumes; 7 VF drawers of clippings, reports, abstracts, ephemera. **Subscriptions:** 550 journals and other serials; 40 newspapers. **Services:** Interlibrary loans; copying (members only); reference service for sale - only U.S. Document section open to public. **Special Indexes:** Index to U.S. Patents, 1906 to present. **Networks/Consortia:** Member of Bay Area Reference Center (BARC). **Publications:** Monthly Booklist; Newsletter,

irregular - distributed to members. **Special Catalogs:** Catalog of bound institute annual reports. **Staff:** Marylou Pierce, Ref.Libn.; Ann Brady, Hd., Bibliog.Serv.

★7710★

MECHANICS' INSTITUTE OF MONTREAL - ATWATER LIBRARY (Sci-Tech; Hum)
1200 Atwater Ave.   Phone: (514) 935-7344
Montreal, PQ, Canada H3Z 1X4   Heather Connolly, Chf.Libn.
Founded: 1828. **Staff:** Prof 1; Other 13. **Subjects:** Engineering, arts, history, literature, science and technology. **Holdings:** 58,000 volumes. **Subscriptions:** 155 journals and other serials. **Services:** Interlibrary loans; copying; books by mail; library open to public. **Publications:** Annual report.

MECKLENBURG COUNTY MEDICAL LIBRARY
See: Charlotte Memorial Hospital and Medical Center

★7711★

MEDFIELD HISTORICAL SOCIETY - LIBRARY (Hist)
6 Pleasant St.
Box 233
Medfield, MA 02052   Connie Sabbag, Libn.
Subjects: Local history and genealogy. **Holdings:** Figures not available. **Services:** Library open to public by permission.

★7712★

MEDFIELD STATE HOSPITAL - MEDICAL LIBRARY (Med)
Hospital Rd.   Phone: (617) 359-7312
Medfield, MA 02052   Jeanne Migliacci, Sr.Libn.
Founded: 1951. **Staff:** Prof 1. **Subjects:** Psychiatry, nursing, neurology, psychology. **Holdings:** 2214 books; 1615 bound periodical volumes; 165 pamphlets (cataloged); 108 cassettes; 3 drawers of pamphlets (uncataloged). **Subscriptions:** 21 journals and other serials. **Services:** Interlibrary loans; library open to public for reference use only by request. **Networks/Consortia:** Member of New England Regional Medical Library Service (NERMLS). **Remarks:** Includes the holdings of the Nursing Library.

★7713★

MEDFORD HISTORICAL SOCIETY - LIBRARY (Hist)
10 Governor's Ave.   Phone: (617) 395-7863
Medford, MA 02155   Michael Bradford, Treas./Libn.
Founded: 1896. **Staff:** Prof 1. **Subjects:** Local history. **Special Collections:** Lydia Maria Child collection; Civil War Collection. **Holdings:** Figures not available for books, manuscripts, letters. **Services:** Library open to public for reference use only. **Publications:** Medford on the Mystic, 1980.

★7714★

MEDFORD MAIL TRIBUNE - LIBRARY (Publ)
Box 1108   Phone: (503) 776-4493
Medford, OR 97501   Kathryn Harper, Libn.
Founded: 1975. **Staff:** Prof 1. **Subjects:** Newspaper reference topics. **Special Collections:** Newspaper on microfilm from 1895 to present. **Holdings:** 1000 books and bound periodical volumes; 28 VF drawers of clippings, photographs, maps and pamphlets. **Subscriptions:** 15 journals and other serials; 27 newspapers. **Services:** Interlibrary loans; copying; library open to public with restrictions.

★7715★

MEDIC ALERT FOUNDATION INTERNATIONAL - CENTRAL REFERENCE FILE OF MEMBERSHIP (Med)
2323 Colorado Ave.
Box 1009   Phone: (209) 668-3333
Turlock, CA 95381   Alfred A. Hodder, Pres.
Founded: 1956. **Staff:** Prof 5; Other 90. **Remarks:** Maintains a central file with emergency medical information, addresses of physician and nearest relative of all members. Information is crossfiled under name and serial number which appears on the member's Medic Alert Emblem worn around the wrist or neck, and is available to physicians and other authorized personnel on a 24 hour, collect telephone call basis in emergencies.

★7716★

MEDICAL ASSOCIATES - HEALTH CENTER - LIBRARY (Med)
W180 N7950 Town Hall Rd.   Phone: (414) 255-2500
Menomonee Falls, WI 53051   Carol J. McIlveen, Libn.
Founded: 1971. **Staff:** Prof 1. **Subjects:** Medicine. **Holdings:** 350 books; 400 bound periodical volumes; 5 VF drawers of pamphlets; 360 cassette tapes. **Subscriptions:** 80 journals and other serials. **Services:** Library not open to public. **Networks/Consortia:** Member of Southeastern Wisconsin Health Science Library Consortium (SWHSLC).

★7717★
MEDICAL CARE DEVELOPMENT, INC. - LIBRARY (Med)
11 Parkwood Dr. Phone: (207) 622-7566
Augusta, ME 04330 Mary Anne Spindler, Libn.
Staff: Prof 1. **Subjects:** Health - planning, policy, manpower, rural. **Holdings:** 300 books. **Subscriptions:** 25 journals and other serials. **Services:** Interlibrary loans; SDI; library open to Maine health institutions. **Networks/Consortia:** Member of Health Sciences Library and Information Cooperative of Maine.

★7718★
MEDICAL CENTER OF BEAVER COUNTY - HEALTH SCIENCES LIBRARY (Med)†
1000 Dutch Ridge Rd. Phone: (412) 728-7000
Beaver, PA 15009 Patricia M. Coghlan, Dir.
Staff: Prof 1; Other 1. **Subjects:** Medicine, nursing, hospital administration. **Holdings:** 1400 books; 6000 bound periodical volumes; Audio-Foundation tapes (3 years back holdings). **Subscriptions:** 207 journals and other serials. **Services:** Interlibrary loans; copying; library open to outside users for research purposes only. **Computerized Information Services:** MEDLINE.

★7719★
MEDICAL CENTER HOSPITAL - BELL-MARSH MEMORIAL LIBRARY (Med)†
1000 Beckham Ave.
Box 4600 Phone: (214) 597-0357
Tyler, TX 75701 Mrs. Rae Dowdy, Med. Staff Sec.
Founded: 1951. **Staff:** 1. **Subjects:** Medicine. **Holdings:** 188 books; 447 bound periodical volumes. **Subscriptions:** 19 journals and other serials. **Services:** Interlibrary loans; copying; library open only to medical staff.

★7720★
MEDICAL CENTER HOSPITAL OF OROVILLE - EDWARD P. GODDARD, M.D., MEMORIAL LIBRARY (Med)
2767 Olive Hwy. Phone: (916) 533-8500
Oroville, CA 95965 Gertrude N. Bartley, Libn.
Staff: Prof 1. **Subjects:** Medicine. **Holdings:** 269 books; 110 bound periodical volumes. **Subscriptions:** 22 journals and other serials. **Services:** Interlibrary loans; copying; library not open to public. **Networks/Consortia:** Member of Pacific Southwest Regional Medical Library Service (PSRMLS).

★7721★
MEDICAL CENTER AT PRINCETON - MEDICAL CENTER LIBRARY (Med)
253 Witherspoon St. Phone: (609) 921-7700
Princeton, NJ 08540 Louise M. Yorke, Med.Libn.
Staff: Prof 2; Other 10. **Subjects:** Medicine, surgery, nursing, and allied health sciences. **Holdings:** 2050 books; 2300 bound periodical volumes; 3 drawers of pamphlets; 20 video cassettes; 330 audio cassettes; 40 slide sets and filmstrips. **Subscriptions:** 209 journals and other serials. **Services:** Interlibrary loans; copying; bibliographies; LATCH; library open to public for reference use only. **Computerized Information Services:** MEDLARS. **Networks/Consortia:** Member of Medical Resources Consortium of Central New Jersey (MEDCORE); Central Jersey Health Science Libraries Association. **Publications:** Guide to the Library, annual - to all new employees. **Special Catalogs:** AV catalog; Periodicals Holdings List. **Staff:** Joan Loughran, Dir., Med.Rec. & Lib.

★7722★
MEDICAL CENTER - SIMON SCHWOB MEDICAL LIBRARY (Med)
710 Center St. Phone: (404) 324-4711
Columbus, GA 31902 Opal Bartlett, Libn.
Founded: 1949. **Staff:** 3. **Subjects:** Medicine, surgery, nursing. **Holdings:** 2950 books; 7300 bound periodical volumes; 275 tapes. **Subscriptions:** 215 journals. **Services:** Interlibrary loans; copying; library open to public with restrictions. **Computerized Information Services:** MEDLINE. **Networks/Consortia:** Member of Health Science Libraries of Central Georgia.

★7723★
MEDICAL AND CHIRURGICAL FACULTY OF THE STATE OF MARYLAND - LIBRARY (Med)
1211 Cathedral St. Phone: (301) 539-0872
Baltimore, MD 21201 Joseph E. Jensen, Libn.
Founded: 1830. **Staff:** Prof 5; Other 5. **Subjects:** Medicine and allied sciences, medical history. **Special Collections:** Krause Collection (History of Medicine); Ruhrah Collection (pediatrics); Osler Collection (297 items by and about Osler). **Holdings:** 120,000 books and bound periodical volumes; 300 manuscripts; Audio-Digest tapes; American College of Pathology videotapes. **Subscriptions:** 700 journals and other serials. **Services:** Interlibrary loans (fee); copying; SDI; library open to public for reference use only. **Computerized Information Services:** MEDLARS, BRS. **Networks/Consortia:**

Member of Mid-Atlantic Regional Medical Library Program. **Publications:** Library page in Maryland State Medical Journal, monthly; The Library, brochure on services. **Special Catalogs:** Current periodicals list. **Staff:** Adam Szczepaniak, Assoc.Libn.; Patricia Munoz, Cat. & Acq.Libn.; Susan Harman, Ref. & Circ.Libn.; Eleanor Mason, Hist. of Med./Archv.Libn.

★7724★
MEDICAL COLLEGE OF GEORGIA - LIBRARY (Med)
1120 15th St. Phone: (404) 828-3441
Augusta, GA 30912 Thomas G. Basler, Dir. of Libs.
Founded: 1828. **Staff:** Prof 9; Other 30. **Subjects:** Medicine, dentistry, nursing, allied health sciences. **Special Collections:** The original library of the Medical College of Georgia and other 19th century books. **Holdings:** 115,000 volumes. **Subscriptions:** 1600 journals and other serials; 7 newspapers. **Services:** Interlibrary loans; copying; library open to public. **Computerized Information Services:** MEDLINE; computerized cataloging. **Networks/Consortia:** Member of SOLINET; Augusta Area Committee for Health Information Resources; Southeastern Regional Medical Library Program (SERMLP). **Publications:** Annual Report. **Staff:** Linda M. Flavin, Hd.Cat.; Mary K. Mosner, ILLDorothy H. Mims, Spec.Coll.Libn.; Gail C. Anderson, Search Anl.; Mary Louise Turner, Chf.Educ./Info.Serv.Dept.; Samille J. Smoot, Hd., Circ.Serv.; Jacquelyn L. Dennison, Coll.Dev.Libn.

★7725★
MEDICAL COLLEGE OF OHIO AT TOLEDO - RAYMON H. MULFORD LIBRARY (Med)
3000 Arlington Ave. Phone: (419) 381-4223
Toledo, OH 43614 R.M. Watterson, Libn.
Founded: 1967. **Staff:** Prof 5; Other 13. **Subjects:** Medicine, dentistry, nursing, animal medicine. **Holdings:** 32,898 books; 51,262 bound periodical volumes; 6 VF drawers of archival material. **Subscriptions:** 2002 journals and other serials. **Services:** Interlibrary loans; copying; literature searches; SDI; library open to public for reference use only. **Computerized Information Services:** NLM, BRS, Birth Defects Information System (BDIS); computerized cataloging and serials. **Networks/Consortia:** Member of Biomedical Communications Network; Kentucky-Ohio-Michigan Regional Medical Libraries (KOMRML); Committee on Library Cooperation (CLC). **Special Catalogs:** List of Serials Held; Subject List of Serials. **Remarks:** Contains the holdings of its former Doctors Library. **Staff:** Florence Hidalgo, Hd., Pub.Serv.

★7726★
MEDICAL COLLEGE OF PENNSYLVANIA - ARCHIVES AND SPECIAL COLLECTIONS ON WOMEN IN MEDICINE (Med)
3300 Henry Ave. Phone: (215) 842-7124
Philadelphia, PA 19129 Sandra L. Chaff, Dir.
Founded: 1977. **Staff:** Prof 3; Other 1. **Subjects:** Women physicians, health care for women, Medical College of Pennsylvania, education, medicine. **Special Collections:** College archives; women in medicine. **Holdings:** 500 books; 6000 reprints; 10,000 photographs; 700 linear feet of archives and manuscripts; memorabilia. **Services:** Copying (fee); photo reproduction; slide reproduction; archives open to public. **Computerized Information Services:** Computerized cataloging. **Publications:** Newsletter, semiannual - available on request. **Special Catalogs:** Inventories available for individual collections. **Staff:** Margaret Jerrido, Archv.

★7727★
MEDICAL COLLEGE OF PENNSYLVANIA - EASTERN PENNSYLVANIA PSYCHIATRIC INSTITUTE - LIBRARY (Med)
Henry Ave. & Abbottsford Rd. Phone: (215) 842-4510
Philadelphia, PA 19129 Etheldria Templeton, Dir.
Founded: 1956. **Staff:** Prof 4; Other 3. **Subjects:** Psychiatry, psychoanalysis, behavioral sciences, biological sciences. **Holdings:** 14,000 books; 11,000 bound periodical volumes; 2500 pamphlets (cataloged); 213 audiotapes. **Subscriptions:** 380 journals and other serials. **Services:** Interlibrary loans; copying; library open to mental health professionals and to students by referral. **Computerized Information Services:** DIALOG, BRS. **Networks/Consortia:** Member of Mideastern Regional Medical Library Service (MERMLS). **Staff:** Terry Wiggins, Ref.; John Barr, Cat.; Frieda Liem, ILL.

MEDICAL COLLEGE OF VIRGINIA
See: Virginia Commonwealth University

★7728★
MEDICAL COLLEGE OF WISCONSIN - TODD WEHR LIBRARY (Med)
8701 Watertown Plank Rd.
Box 26509 Phone: (414) 257-8323
Milwaukee, WI 53226 Marilyn Sullivan, Act.Dir.
Founded: 1913. **Staff:** Prof 12; Other 15. **Subjects:** Medicine and allied

health fields. **Special Collections:** History of Medicine (4000 volumes). **Holdings:** 38,140 books; 65,879 bound periodical volumes; 1289 AV items. **Subscriptions:** 1768 journals and other serials. **Services:** Interlibrary loans; copying; SDI; library open to public with restrictions. **Computerized Information Services:** DIALOG, SDC, BRS; computerized cataloging. **Networks/Consortia:** Member of Regional Medical Library - Region 3; Library Council of Metropolitan Milwaukee, Inc. (LCOMM); Wisconsin Interlibrary Services (WILS). **Publications:** Acquisitions list, monthly; Holdings list, annual - both to local and regional libraries and others on request. **Staff:** Helen Ehrke, Acq.Libn.; Susan O'Neill, Cat.Libn.Linda Oddan, Assoc.Dir./Info.Serv.; Darel J. Robb, Assoc.Dir./Coll.Dev.; Neil Hootkin, Spec.Coll.Libn.; Martha Eberhart, ILL Libn.; Mary Ellen Baas, Ref.Libn.; Mary Blackwelder, Ref.Libn.; Jacqueline Glick, Ref.Libn.; Jody Sussman, Ref.Libn.

★7729★

MEDICAL GROUP MANAGEMENT ASSOCIATION - INFORMATION SERVICE (Med)
4101 E. Louisiana Ave.   Phone: (303) 753-1111
Denver, CO 80222   Barbara U. Hamilton, Dir.
Staff: Prof 2; Other 1. **Subjects:** Group practice administration and statistics; health maintenance organizations; ambulatory care administration; medical clinic architectural design and construction; health manpower. **Special Collections:** Information Exchange Collection - data from existing medical group practices; MGMA Archives; American College of Medical Group Administrators Professional Papers. **Holdings:** 3000 books; 270 folders of VF material. **Subscriptions:** 157 journals and other serials. **Services:** Interlibrary loans; copying; literature searches, demand reference service (fee for all services); Bibliography Series (94 bibliographies); open to public with restrictions. **Computerized Information Services:** MEDLARS; computerized cataloging. **Networks/Consortia:** Member of Colorado Council of Medical Librarians. **Publications:** Comprehensive Bibliography on Health Maintenance Organizations: 1970-1973; Administrator's Bookshelf, annual; Digest of Job Descriptions for Medical Group Administrators, 1978. **Special Indexes:** In-house index to all current literature on management aspects of medical group practice and other types of ambulatory care administration. **Staff:** Linda Elinoff Murray, Asst.Dir.

★7730★

MEDICAL LETTER - LIBRARY (Med)
56 Harrison St.   Phone: (914) 235-0500
New Rochelle, NY 10801   Donna Goodstein, Libn.
Founded: 1959. **Staff:** 1. **Subjects:** Drugs, therapeutic agents. **Holdings:** Figures not available for books, reprints and advertisements. **Services:** Library not open to public except in special circumstances. **Computerized Information Services:** MEDLARS, DIALOG, SDC. **Networks/Consortia:** Member of Medical Library Center of New York (MLCNY); Health Information Libraries of Westchester (HILOW).

★7731★

MEDICAL LIBRARY CENTER OF NEW YORK (Med)
5 E. 102nd St.   Phone: (212) 427-1630
New York, NY 10029   William D. Walker, Dir.
Founded: 1959. **Staff:** Prof 7; Other 15. **Subjects:** Medicine and allied sciences, nursing, dentistry. **Special Collections:** Biomedical dissertations from universities throughout the world; U.S. Government Printing Office Depository Library (selected). **Holdings:** 77,793 bound periodical volumes; 160,156 unbound periodical issues; 37,632 textbooks and monographs; 214,000 dissertations; 6735 government documents. **Services:** Interlibrary loans; copying; messenger service for network libraries; serials rationalization program for member libraries; library not open to public. **Computerized Information Services:** NLM, BRS; internal database; computerized cataloging and serials. **Networks/Consortia:** The Medical Library Center provides cooperative housing and acquisition of less-used materials in medicine and its allied sciences for the health science libraries in the New York Metropolitan area. **Publications:** Union Catalog of Medical Periodicals; UCMP/Quarterly; Union Catalog of Medical Monographs; Union Catalog of Medical Audiovisuals - available for purchase. **Staff:** Shifra Atik, Hd., Tech.Serv.; Narciso Rodriguez, Hd., Circ.; Don Potts, Hd., Automation Serv.; Robert Dempsey, Hd., Ser.

MEDICAL LIBRARY OF MECKLENBURG COUNTY/LRC OF CHARLOTTE AHEC
See: **Charlotte Memorial Hospital and Medical Center**

MEDICAL LITERATURE INFORMATION CENTER
See: **St. Mary's Hospital Medical Education Foundation**

★7732★

MEDICAL PLANNING ASSOCIATES - LIBRARY (Med)
1601 Rambla Pacifico   Phone: (213) 456-2084
Malibu, CA 90265   David C. Lennartz, Libn.
Founded: 1970. **Staff:** Prof 1. **Subjects:** Hospital design and planning, architecture. **Holdings:** 250 books; 250 unbound periodicals; 1700 monographs; VF drawers of cataloged journal articles, newspaper clippings (4800 items). **Subscriptions:** 30 journals and other serials. **Services:** Interlibrary loans. **Computerized Information Services:** MEDLINE.

★7733★

MEDICAL RESEARCH LABORATORIES - LIBRARY (Sci-Tech)†
7450 Natchez Ave.   Phone: (312) 792-2666
Niles, IL 60648   Patrick Murphy, Libn.
Founded: 1975. **Staff:** Prof 1. **Subjects:** Medical electronics. **Holdings:** 253 books. **Subscriptions:** 6 journals and other serials. **Services:** Interlibrary loans; copying; library not open to public. **Publications:** Service manuals; Field Service bulletins.

MEDICAL RESEARCH LIBRARY OF BROOKLYN
See: **SUNY - Downstate Medical Center**

★7734★

MEDICAL UNIVERSITY OF SOUTH CAROLINA - ARTHRITIS CENTER LIBRARY (Med)
Division of Rheumatology and Immunology
171 Ashley Ave.   Phone: (803) 792-2001
Charleston, SC 29464   E.C. LeRoy, M.D., Dir.
Staff: 1. **Subjects:** Rheumatology; immunology; medicine - internal, physical. **Special Collections:** Rheumatology Patient Education Library (30 pamphlets and several AV programs). **Holdings:** 200 books; 100 bound periodical volumes. **Subscriptions:** 25 journals and other serials. **Services:** Library not open to public. **Publications:** Patient booklets - available to patients seeking information.

★7735★

MEDICAL UNIVERSITY OF SOUTH CAROLINA - LIBRARY (Med)
171 Ashley Ave.   Phone: (803) 792-2374
Charleston, SC 29425   Warren A. Sawyer, Dir.
Founded: 1824. **Staff:** Prof 12; Other 27. **Subjects:** Medicine, dentistry, nursing, pharmacy, allied health sciences, history of medicine, pharmacology. **Special Collections:** History of Medicine (5000 volumes). **Holdings:** 66,800 books; 76,360 bound periodical volumes; 12 VF drawers of pamphlets, clippings and South Carolina material; 2037 titles of AV materials, self-instructional programs, videotapes, audio cassettes, slides. **Subscriptions:** 2200 journals and other serials; 13 newspapers. **Services:** Interlibrary loans; copying; SDI; library open to public with restrictions. **Computerized Information Services:** BRS, DIALOG, SDC, MEDLARS; computerized cataloging. **Networks/Consortia:** Member of Charleston Consortium Library Committee; OCLC through SOLINET. **Publications:** Library Notes, monthly. **Staff:** Anne W. Kabler, Assoc.Dir. of Libs.; Anne Donato, Cur., Waring Lib.; Desmond Koster, Ref.Libn.; Ann Resch, ILL; Virginia Miller, Computerized Serv.; Robert Poyer, Coord., Pub.Serv.; Nancy McKeehan, Coord., Tech.Serv.; Patti Fields, Cat.Libn.; Elizabeth Burkhart, Coord., LRC; Ellen T. Reinig, Ext.Libn.

★7736★

MEDINA COUNTY LAW LIBRARY ASSOCIATION (Law)
Court House, 93 Public Sq.   Phone: (216) 723-3641
Medina, OH 44256   Stan Scheetz, Libn.
Staff: 1. **Subjects:** Law. **Holdings:** 23,000 books; 8000 bound periodical volumes. **Services:** Copying; library not open to public.

MEDI-PHYSICS, INC. - CINTICHEM, INC.
See: **Cintichem, Inc.**

★7737★

MEDTRONIC, INC. - LIBRARY (Med; Sci-Tech)
3055 Old Hwy. 8
Box 1453
          Phone: (612) 574-3154
Minneapolis, MN 55440   Leonard Bigelow, Mgr. of Lib.Serv.
Founded: 1965. **Staff:** Prof 3; Other 3. **Subjects:** Biomedical engineering, pacemaking (cardiac), medical electronics, electrical stimulation, cardiology. **Special Collections:** Copies from journals of pacemaking articles in all languages; copies of electrical stimulation articles. **Holdings:** 10,000 books; 5000 bound periodical volumes; 8000 pacemaker papers (cataloged); 1000 government documents (mainly medicine). **Subscriptions:** 350 journals and other serials; 5 newspapers. **Services:** Interlibrary loans; information retrieval for pacemaking papers; library open to public with restrictions. **Publications:**

Cardiac Pacing Abstract Bulletin; Neuro/stimulation Abstract Bulletin. **Staff:** Cheryl Schwichtenberg, Libn.; Steve Rasmussen, Lit. Searcher; Maryanne Lo, Libn.

MEEK (Mary) SCHOOL OF NURSING
See: Hendrick Medical Center - Mary Meek School of Nursing

★7738★
MEETING HOUSE GREEN MEMORIAL AND HISTORICAL ASSOCIATION, INC. - TUCK MEMORIAL MUSEUM - LIBRARY (Hist)
Meeting House Green
40 Park Ave.
Hampton, NH 03842   John M. Holman, Cur.
Founded: 1925. **Subjects:** History, biography and autobiography, genealogy. **Special Collections:** Post card collections of Hampton and Hampton Beach subjects. **Holdings:** 300 volumes; photographs of Hampton area; scrapbooks, New Hampshire Marine Memorial Album, Edward Tuck Memorial Album. **Services:** Library open to public by appointment. **Also Known As:** Hampton Historical Society.

★7739★
MEHARRY MEDICAL COLLEGE - MEDICAL LIBRARY - LEARNING RESOURCES CENTER (Med)
1005 18th Ave., N.   Phone: (615) 327-6319
Nashville, TN 37208   Bernice Armstead, Lib.Dir.
Founded: 1942. **Staff:** Prof 7; Other 10. **Subjects:** Medicine, dentistry, medical technology, health care administration. **Special Collections:** Black Medical History Collection (457 books, 12 manuscripts); Meharry Archives Collection (172 books, 44 dissertations, 60 boxes of manuscripts, 10 VF drawers). **Holdings:** 77,000 volumes; 2068 audio cassettes; 361 video cassettes; 305 slide-tape sets; 3 VF drawers of clippings; 3 cabinets and 6 VF drawers of pamphlets. **Subscriptions:** 1130 journals and other serials. **Services:** Interlibrary loans (fee); copying (fee); center open to public. **Computerized Information Services:** MEDLINE, DIALOG; computerized cataloging and serials. **Networks/Consortia:** Member of OCLC. **Publications:** Print Out, quarterly - to medical libraries. **Staff:** Connie McKissack, Archv.; Mattie McHollin, Ser.Libn.; Cheryl Hamberg, Ref.Libn. & ILL; Mickey Hill-Masey, Acq.Libn.; Susan Way, Media Libn.; Julie Julian, Cat.Libn.

★7740★
MEIDINGER, INC. - INFORMATION CENTER (Soc Sci; Bus-Fin)
2600 Meidinger Tower, Louisville Galeria   Phone: (502) 561-4500
Louisville, KY 40202   Albertha Jacob, Mgr.
Staff: Prof 2; Other 3. **Subjects:** Employee benefits, compensation administration, human resources management, pensions, profit sharing, communications, retirement. **Special Collections:** Actuarial annual proceedings. **Holdings:** 1500 books; 75 cassettes; 800 in-house reports, surveys, proposals; unbound periodicals. **Subscriptions:** 165 journals and other serials. **Services:** Interlibrary loans; copying; library open to public with restrictions. **Computerized Information Services:** DIALOG; internal database; computerized cataloging, acquisitions and circulation. **Networks/Consortia:** Member of LOCOLS. **Publications:** Meidinger Abstracts, monthly; Awareness Bulletin Index, quarterly; Readers Service list, monthly; monthly releases of acquisitions. **Special Indexes:** Legal department publications index. **Staff:** Herbert Miller, Sr.Libn.

★7741★
MEIGS COUNTY LAW LIBRARY (Law)†
Court House   Phone: (614) 992-7430
Pomeroy, OH 45769   Karen Story, Libn.
Subjects: Law. **Holdings:** 3950 volumes.

★7742★
MEIKLEJOHN CIVIL LIBERTIES INSTITUTE - LIBRARY (Law)
Box 673   Phone: (415) 848-0599
Berkeley, CA 94701   Ann Fagan Ginger, Pres.
Founded: 1965. **Staff:** Prof 3; Other 4. **Subjects:** Civil rights and liberties, due process, sex discrimination, juries, police misconduct. **Special Collections:** Angela Davis case (20,000 pages); Pentagon Papers Case (35,000 pages); official repository for National Lawyers Guild archives; Draft and Military Law Collection (188 microfiche). **Holdings:** 200 books; legal documents from over 9000 cases. **Subscriptions:** 130 journals and other serials; 20 newspapers. **Services:** Copying; library open to public. **Publications:** Human Rights Docket; Human Rights Organizations and Periodicals Directory, biennial - for sale; Alexander Meiklejohn: Teacher of Freedom, 1981; list of other publications - available upon request. **Special Catalogs:** Pentagon Papers Case Collection (book); Angela Davis Collection (book). **Special Indexes:** Meiklejohn Library Acquisitions Index, 1968-1972; Human Rights Casefinder, 1953-1969; index to National Lawyers Guild

Periodicals, 1937-1970; The Legal Struggle to Abolish the House Un-American Activities Committee. **Staff:** David Christiano, Libn.

MEIR (Golda) LIBRARY
See: American Geographical Society Collection of the University of Wisconsin, Milwaukee - Golda Meir Library

MEIR (Golda) LIBRARY - CURRICULUM COLLECTION
See: University of Wisconsin, Milwaukee - Golda Meir Library - Curriculum Collection

MELCHER (Frederic G.) LIBRARY
See: Bowker (R.R.) Company - Frederic G. Melcher Library

MELCHIOR (Lauritz) MEMORIAL
See: Dana College - C.A. Dana-Life Library

★7743★
MELDRUM AND FEWSMITH, INC. - BUSINESS INFORMATION LIBRARY (Bus-Fin)
1220 Huron Rd.   Phone: (216) 241-2141
Cleveland, OH 44115   Laura Gusky, Supv.
Founded: 1944. **Staff:** Prof 1; Other 2. **Subjects:** Advertising, marketing, media, communications. **Special Collections:** Industrial advertising. **Holdings:** 1550 books; 16 VF drawers of pamphlets; 22 VF drawers of media data; 18 boxes of annual reports. **Subscriptions:** 3000 journals and other serials; 25 newspapers. **Services:** Library not open to public. **Computerized Information Services:** SDC; computerized cataloging and acquisitions. **Publications:** M & F Library News, monthly - to members of the organization and clients. **Special Catalogs:** Art and media files.

MELLANDER LIBRARY
See: North Park College and Theological Seminary

★7744★
MELLON BANK, N.A. - LIBRARY (Bus-Fin)†
Mellon Sq.   Phone: (412) 234-4100
Pittsburgh, PA 15230   Patricia H. Riordan, Libn.
Founded: 1943. **Staff:** Prof 4; Other 8. **Subjects:** Banking, finance, economics, data processing, insurance, international banking. **Special Collections:** Mellon Historical File - Mellon Family historical and current information and also various Mellon family foundations. **Holdings:** 5500 books; 600 bound periodical volumes; 170 VF drawers of clippings and pamphlets. **Subscriptions:** 550 journals and other serials; 8 newspapers. **Services:** Interlibrary loans; library open to public with restrictions. **Computerized Information Services:** DIALOG, SDC, New York Times Information Service, Dow Jones News Retrieval. **Publications:** Library Bulletin. **Staff:** Gertrude M. Kneil, Asst.Libn./Cat.; Richard McConnville, Res.Libn.; Josephine Thornton, Transl.

MELLON INSTITUTE LIBRARY
See: Carnegie-Mellon University

MELLON (M.G.) LIBRARY OF CHEMISTRY
See: Purdue University - Chemistry Library

MELTON (Arthur W.) LIBRARY
See: American Psychological Association - Arthur W. Melton Library

MELVILLE MEMORIAL LIBRARY
See: Institute for Advanced Studies of World Religions

MELVILLE WHALING ROOM
See: New Bedford Free Public Library

★7745★
MEMOREX CORPORATION - TECHNICAL INFORMATION CENTER (Sci-Tech)†
San Tomas at Central Expy., M/S14-05   Phone: (408) 987-3599
Santa Clara, CA 95052   Paula Rand, Libn.
Founded: 1977. **Staff:** Prof 2; Other 3. **Subjects:** Magnetism, video recording, paints, polymers, chemistry, optics, computer equipment, physics, management. **Holdings:** 10,000 books and bound periodical volumes; 3000 patent files; 1000 annual reports. **Subscriptions:** 300 journals and other serials. **Services:** Interlibrary loans; copying; library open to public with restrictions. **Computerized Information Services:** DIALOG, SDC, New York Times Information Service; computerized cataloging. **Networks/Consortia:** Member of Bay Area Reference Center (BARC); CIN; RLG. **Publications:** Acquisitions list; patent scan sheet.

★7746★

MEMORIAL HOSPITAL AND BETH-EL SCHOOL OF NURSING - MEDICAL-NURSING LIBRARY (Med)†

1400 E. Boulder   Phone: (303) 475-5182
Colorado Springs, CO 80901   Frances Meese, Libn.
Founded: 1950. **Staff:** Prof 1; Other 1. **Subjects:** Medicine, nursing, psychology, sociology, education, psychiatry, therapeutics, physical medicine, medical and nursing history. **Special Collections:** Medical and nursing rare book collection. **Holdings:** 4111 books; 6000 bound periodical volumes; 2 VF cabinets of ephemeral materials. **Subscriptions:** 175 journals and other serials. **Services:** Interlibrary loans; copying; library open to public.

★7747★

MEMORIAL HOSPITAL OF DU PAGE COUNTY - MEDICAL & HEALTH SCIENCES LIBRARY (Med)

200 Berteau Ave.   Phone: (312) 833-1400
Elmhurst, IL 60126   Pauline Ng, Dir.
Staff: Prof 1; Other 3. **Subjects:** Medicine and allied health sciences. **Holdings:** 600 books; 840 audiotapes (cataloged); 159 videotapes (cataloged); 250 files of pamphlets. **Subscriptions:** 116 journals and other serials. **Services:** Interlibrary loans; copying; SDI; library not open to public. **Computerized Information Services:** MEDLARS. **Networks/Consortia:** Member of Regional Medical Library - Region 3; Suburban Library System (SLS). **Publications:** New Acquisitions, monthly - for internal distribution only.

★7748★

MEMORIAL HOSPITAL - HEALTH SCIENCES LIBRARY (Med)

S. Washington St.   Phone: (301) 822-1000
Easton, MD 21601   Maureen Molter, Libn.
Founded: 1929. **Staff:** Prof 1; Other 3. **Subjects:** Medicine, nursing, and allied health fields. **Holdings:** 4000 books; 1900 bound periodical volumes; microfilm, AV materials. **Subscriptions:** 240 journals and other serials. **Services:** Interlibrary loans; copying; library open to public for reference use only with permission. **Computerized Information Services:** MEDLINE. **Networks/Consortia:** Member of Mid-Atlantic Regional Medical Library Program; Maryland Association of Health Science Libraries; Consortium of Health Sciences Libraries of the Eastern Shore. **Publications:** Recent Acquisiitions, monthly - for internal distribution only.

★7749★

MEMORIAL HOSPITAL - HOMER GAGE LIBRARY (Med)

119 Belmont St.   Phone: (617) 793-6421
Worcester, MA 01605   Alberta T. Franke, Libn.
Staff: Prof 1; Other 1. **Subjects:** Medicine, nursing. **Holdings:** 4000 books; 1083 bound periodical volumes. **Subscriptions:** 250 journals and other serials. **Services:** Interlibrary loans; library open to public. **Networks/Consortia:** Member of Central Massachusetts Consortium of Health Related Libraries.

★7750★

MEMORIAL HOSPITAL OF MARTINSVILLE - MEDICAL LIBRARY (Med)

Commonwealth Blvd.   Phone: (703) 632-2911
Martinsville, VA 24112   Mary Alice Sherrard, Libn.
Staff: Prof 1. **Subjects:** Medicine, nursing and allied health sciences. **Holdings:** 2000 books; 3000 bound periodical volumes. **Subscriptions:** 115 journals and other serials. **Services:** Interlibrary loans; copying; library open to public with permission.

★7751★

MEMORIAL HOSPITAL MEDICAL CENTER OF LONG BEACH - MEDICAL LIBRARY (Med)

2801 Atlantic Ave.
Box 1428
Long Beach, CA 90801   Phone: (213) 595-3841
                                     Frances Lyon, Dir. of Lib.Serv.
Founded: 1923. **Staff:** Prof 2; Other 3. **Subjects:** Medicine, hospitals, nursing, allied health sciences. **Holdings:** 10,573 books; 11,076 bound periodical volumes. **Subscriptions:** 1100 journals and other serials. **Services:** Interlibrary loans; copying; SDI; library open to public with restrictions. **Computerized Information Services:** BRS, MEDLARS, SDC. **Networks/Consortia:** Member of Pacific Southwest Regional Medical Library Service (PSRMLS); CLASS. **Staff:** Emi Kosaka, Med.Libn.

★7752★

MEMORIAL HOSPITAL - MEDICAL LIBRARY (Med)

1901 Arlington St.   Phone: (813) 953-1238
Sarasota, FL 33579   Doris Marose, Dir., Med.Lib.
Staff: Prof 1. **Subjects:** Medicine, nursing. **Holdings:** 2500 books; 8710 bound periodical volumes; 400 audio- and videotapes. **Subscriptions:** 400 journals; 6 newspapers. **Services:** Interlibrary loans; copying; library open to public.

★7753★

MEMORIAL HOSPITAL - MEDICAL LIBRARY (Med)

Northern Blvd.   Phone: (518) 471-3264
Albany, NY 12204   G.A. McNamara, Libn.
Founded: 1960. **Staff:** Prof 1; Other 1. **Subjects:** Medicine, nursing. **Holdings:** 3200 books; 300 bound periodical volumes; tapes and films (cataloged). **Subscriptions:** 105 journals and other serials. **Services:** Interlibrary loans; library not open to public. **Networks/Consortia:** Member of Capital District Library Council for Reference and Research Resources.

★7754★

MEMORIAL HOSPITAL - MEDICAL LIBRARY (Med)

Box 1447   Phone: (713) 634-8111
Lufkin, TX 75902   Nancy Anderson, Dir., Med.Rec.
Staff: 1. **Subjects:** Medicine, obstetrics and gynecology, surgery, pediatrics. **Holdings:** 500 books; 20 bound periodical volumes. **Services:** Library not open to public.

★7755★

MEMORIAL HOSPITAL - MEDICAL LIBRARY (Med)

142 S. Main St.   Phone: (804) 799-4418
Danville, VA 24541   Ann B. Sasser, Med.Libn.
Staff: Prof 1. **Subjects:** Medicine, surgery, basic and clinical sciences, hospital administration. **Holdings:** 2756 books; 1500 bound periodical volumes; 4 VF drawers of pamphlets, pictures, clippings, manuals. **Subscriptions:** 87 journals and other serials. **Services:** Interlibrary loans; copying; translation; library open to public by appointment. **Networks/Consortia:** Member of Virginia Medical Information Services.

★7756★

MEMORIAL HOSPITAL - MEDICAL AND NURSING LIBRARY (Med)

Memorial Ave.   Phone: (301) 777-4027
Cumberland, MD 21502   Mary E. Courtney, Libn.
Staff: 1. **Subjects:** Medicine, surgery, nursing. **Holdings:** 1146 books; 40 bound periodical volumes. **Subscriptions:** 60 journals and other serials. **Services:** Interlibrary loans; library open to public with restrictions.

★7757★

MEMORIAL HOSPITAL OF NATRONA COUNTY - MEDICAL LIBRARY (Med)

1233 E. 2nd St.   Phone: (307) 577-2450
Casper, WY 82601   Jeanette Murrell, Med.Libn.
Staff: Prof 1. **Subjects:** Medicine. **Holdings:** 660 books; 1121 bound periodical volumes. **Subscriptions:** 91 journals and other serials. **Services:** Interlibrary loans; copying; library open to public. **Computerized Information Services:** MEDLARS. **Networks/Consortia:** Member of Muddy Mountain Health Sciences Library Consortium. **Publications:** New book list, monthly - for internal distribution only.

★7758★

MEMORIAL HOSPITAL AT OCONOMOWOC - HEALTH SCIENCES LIBRARY (Med)

791 East Summit Ave.   Phone: (414) 567-0371
Oconomowoc, WI 53066   Mary Kaye Lintner, Health Sci.Libn.
Founded: 1970. **Staff:** Prof 1. **Subjects:** Medicine, nursing, dentistry. **Holdings:** 1426 books and AV items; 1265 bound periodical volumes; 6 VF drawers; 5 VF drawers of patient education pamphlets; 59 audiotapes; 192 videotapes; teaching materials. **Subscriptions:** 200 journals and other serials. **Services:** Interlibrary loans; copying; literature searches; library open to public by appointment. **Networks/Consortia:** Member of Southeastern Wisconsin Health Science Libraries Consortium (SWHSL); Library Council of Metropolitan Milwaukee, Inc. (LCOMM). **Publications:** Monthly and annual reports; bibliographies for new materials; newsletter, semiannual - for internal distribution only.

★7759★

MEMORIAL HOSPITAL - SCHOOL OF PROFESSIONAL NURSING - LIBRARY (Med)

Simpson Hall
Danville, VA 24541   Edith K. Ledford, Libn.
Staff: Prof 1. **Subjects:** Nursing. **Holdings:** 2100 books; 100 audio cassettes. **Subscriptions:** 31 journals and other serials. **Services:** Library open to public.

★7760★

MEMORIAL MEDICAL CENTER - HEALTH SCIENCES LIBRARY (Med)†
2606 Hospital Blvd.
Box 5280
Corpus Christi, TX 78405
Phone: (512) 881-4197
Charles A. Brown, Dir. of Lib.
Founded: 1945. **Staff:** Prof 1; Other 2. **Subjects:** Medicine, nursing, pre-clinical sciences. **Holdings:** 3000 books; 5000 bound periodical volumes; 1 VF drawer of pamphlets; 660 cataloged AV materials; 500 audio cassettes; 35 video cassettes; 25 slide-tape sets. **Subscriptions:** 300 journals and other serials. **Services:** Interlibrary loans; copying; SDI; translation; library open to health professionals. **Computerized Information Services:** MEDLINE. **Networks/Consortia:** Member of Coastal Bend Health Sciences Library Consortium. **Special Catalogs:** Union list of serials of Consortium Institutions; Union catalog of Consortium Institutions; AV Union Catalog, 1978. **Staff:** Sue Floerke, Consortium Coord.

★7761★

MEMORIAL MEDICAL CENTER OF WEST MICHIGAN - LIBRARY (Med)
One Atkinson Dr.
Ludington, MI 49431
Phone: (616) 843-2591
Linda L. Glocheski, Dir. of Med.Rec.
Subjects: Medicine. **Holdings:** 400 books; 500 bound periodical volumes. **Subscriptions:** 72 journals and other serials. **Services:** Interlibrary loans; library open to public with the approval of the hospital administrator. **Computerized Information Services:** Computerized cataloging.

★7762★

MEMORIAL PRESBYTERIAN CHURCH - LIBRARY (Rel-Theol)
1310 Ashman St.
Midland, MI 48640
Phone: (517) 835-6759
Florence E. Hazlett, Chm., Lib.Bd.
Founded: 1945. **Staff:** Prof 3. **Subjects:** Bible interpretation, church history, Christian education, prayer. **Holdings:** 4500 books; phonograph records (cataloged); archives; films, filmstrips, tapes and audiovisual materials. **Services:** Interlibrary loans; copying; library not open to public. **Staff:** Alberta Scheffler, Adult Serv.Libn.; Marjorie Pochert, Children's Libn.

★7763★

MEMORIAL SLOAN-KETTERING CANCER CENTER - LEE COOMBE MEMORIAL LIBRARY (Med)
1275 York Ave.
New York, NY 10021
Phone: (212) 794-7439
Angelina Harmon, Libn.
Founded: 1945. **Staff:** Prof 4; Other 8. **Subjects:** Cancer and allied diseases, cytology, general medicine, radiobiology, biochemistry. **Special Collections:** Hayes Martin collection on history of cancer; MSKCC Archives; James Ewing Society, 1936-1974. **Holdings:** 15,500 books; 13,000 bound periodical volumes; 15 VF drawers of reports, reprints, pamphlets; 18 drawers of microforms. **Subscriptions:** 650 journals and other serials. **Services:** Interlibrary loans; copying; SDI; library open to qualified users under certain conditions. **Computerized Information Services:** MEDLINE, BRS, DIALOG; computerized cataloging. **Networks/Consortia:** Member of Medical Library Center of New York (MLCNY); OCLC; Cornell Media Consortium for Education and Training. **Publications:** Library News, biweekly; Staff Bibliography, annual. **Staff:** Linda Gleason, Acq.Libn.; Arsenia Avetria, Cat.; M. Catherine Ruggieri, Info.Serv.Libn.; D. Rosenwasser-Skalak, Archv.

★7764★

MEMORIAL UNIVERSITY OF NEWFOUNDLAND - EDUCATION LIBRARY
Elizabeth Ave.
St. John's, NF, Canada A1C 5S7
Defunct. Holdings absorbed by Memorial University of Newfoundland - University Library.

★7765★

MEMORIAL UNIVERSITY OF NEWFOUNDLAND - FOLKLORE AND LANGUAGE ARCHIVE (Area-Ethnic)
St. John's, NF, Canada A1C 5S7
Phone: (709) 737-8401
Neil V. Rosenberg, Dir.
Founded: 1968. **Staff:** Prof 4; Other 20. **Subjects:** Newfoundland, Labrador and the Maritime Provinces - folklore, folklife, language, oral history. **Special Collections:** MacEdward Leach Newfoundland, Labrador and Nova Scotia field recordings; Maude Karpeles Newfoundland field notes; Newbell Niles Puckett Ontario field recordings; E.R. Seary Newfoundland genealogy files. **Holdings:** 6000 manuscripts; 70,000 5x8 Folklore Survey Cards; 5000 tape recordings; 8000 photographs. **Services:** Copying (limited); archive open for scholarly research. **Special Indexes:** Card indexes for some of the special collections. **Also Known As:** MUNFLA. **Staff:** Peter Narvaez, Archv.; Philip Hiscock, Asst.Archv.

★7766★

MEMORIAL UNIVERSITY OF NEWFOUNDLAND - OCEAN ENGINEERING INFORMATION CENTRE (Sci-Tech)
St. John's, NF, Canada A1B 3X5
Phone: (709) 737-8377
Judith A. Whittick, Info.Res.
Founded: 1976. **Staff:** Prof 1; Other 3. **Subjects:** Engineering - ice and cold ocean; offshore technology. **Special Collections:** Technical reports relating to offshore hydrocarbon development in the Arctic and Canadian offshore. **Holdings:** 19,000 technical reports and conference papers; 2000 maps and charts; 4000 microfiche of satellite imagery. **Subscriptions:** 140 journals and other serials. **Services:** Interlibrary loans; copying; centre open to public for reference use only. **Computerized Information Services:** Online systems (through University Library). **Publications:** Monthly Information Bulletin. **Special Indexes:** KWOC Index of holdings (microfiche).

★7767★

MEMORIAL UNIVERSITY OF NEWFOUNDLAND - UNIVERSITY LIBRARY - CENTRE FOR NEWFOUNDLAND STUDIES (Area-Ethnic)
Elizabeth Ave.
St. John's, NF, Canada A1B 3Y1
Phone: (709) 753-1200
Anne Hart, Hd.
Staff: Prof 2; Other 11. **Subjects:** Newfoundland and Labrador. **Holdings:** 35,000 books and pamphlets; 750 bound periodical volumes; 2000 microforms; 350 maps; 500 linear meters of archives; 8000 rare books. **Subscriptions:** 400 journals and other serials; 20 newspapers. **Services:** Interlibrary loans; copying; library open to public for reference use only. **Special Catalogs:** Bibliography of Newfoundland, chronological (card). **Special Indexes:** Index to the Newfoundland Quarterly (in progress).

★7768★

MEMORIAL UNIVERSITY OF NEWFOUNDLAND - UNIVERSITY LIBRARY - HEALTH SCIENCES LIBRARY (Med)
Health Science Centre
300 Prince Philip Dr.
St. John's, NF, Canada A1B 3V6
Phone: (709) 737-6672
Isabel Hunter, Hd.Libn.
Founded: 1969. **Staff:** Prof 5; Other 16. **Subjects:** Medicine, history of medicine, nursing, pharmacy, dentistry and allied health professions. **Holdings:** 32,182 books; 32,745 bound periodical volumes; 15,674 slides; 3083 audiotapes; 1050 reels of microfilm; 151 motion pictures; 530 videotapes. **Subscriptions:** 1642 journals and other serials. **Services:** Interlibrary loans; copying; SDI; library open to public. **Computerized Information Services:** MEDLINE, TOXLINE, CANCERLINE, DIALOG; computerized cataloging and circulation. **Networks/Consortia:** Member of UTLAS, Inc. **Publications:** Library Guide, annual. **Staff:** Shelagh Wotherspoon, Hd. of Pub.Serv.; Lai-Ying Hsiung, Hd. of Tech.Serv.; G. Moores, Cat.; Catherine Sheehan, Ref.Libn.

★7769★

MEMORIAL UNIVERSITY OF NEWFOUNDLAND - UNIVERSITY LIBRARY - INFORMATION SERVICES DIVISION - MAP LIBRARY (Geog-Map)
St. John's, NF, Canada A1B 3Y1
Phone: (709) 737-8892
Gladys Deutsch, Lib.Asst. IV/Supv.
Staff: 4. **Subjects:** Canada, North America, North Atlantic, Western Europe. **Special Collections:** Depository for NTS (Canada). **Holdings:** 740 atlases; 375 books; 40,000 maps; 2 globes. **Services:** Copying; library open to public.

★7770★

MEMORY SHOP, INC. - MOVIE MEMORABILIA STILLS (Pict)
109 E. 12th St.
New York, NY 10003
Phone: (212) 473-2404
Mark Ricci, Mgr.
Subjects: Memorabilia from 1910 to present pertaining to movies, television, theatre, rock music, music. **Holdings:** 7 million photographs; posters; pressbooks; lobby cards; magazines.

★7771★

MEMPHIS ACADEMY OF ARTS - G. PILLOW LEWIS MEMORIAL LIBRARY (Art)†
Overton Pk.
Memphis, TN 38112
Phone: (901) 726-4085
Robert M. Scarlett, Libn.
Founded: 1937. **Staff:** Prof 2. **Subjects:** Art history, painting, sculpture, art crafts, photography, printmaking, drawing, art education. **Holdings:** 14,300 books; 575 bound periodical volumes; 24 VF drawers of clippings, and pamphlet material; 1000 matted prints; 7700 mounted prints; 21,500 glass mounted slides. **Subscriptions:** 100 journals and other serials. **Services:** Interlibrary loans; library open to public for reference use only. **Networks/Consortia:** Member of Greater Memphis Consortium. **Staff:** Bette R. Callow, Slide Libn.

★7772★
MEMPHIS BOTANIC GARDEN FOUNDATION, INC. - GOLDSMITH CIVIC GARDEN CTR. - SYBILE MALLOY MEMORIAL LIBRARY (Sci-Tech)
750 Cherry Rd.   Phone: (901) 685-1566
Memphis, TN 38117   Clara M. Wright, Adm.Ck.
Founded: 1964. **Staff:** 2. **Subjects:** Horticulture, gardening, flower arranging, environmental science, botany, agriculture. **Holdings:** 3500 books; 10 bound periodical volumes; 500 horticultural magazines and pamphlets. **Subscriptions:** 37 journals and other serials. **Services:** Copying; library open to public for reference use only. **Publications:** Bulletin, monthly - distributed to members of Memphis Botanic Garden Foundation and free to libraries on request. **Remarks:** Memphis Park Commission cooperates with Memphis Botanic Garden Foundation, Inc. in maintaining this library. **Staff:** Phillip Norfleet, Botanist

MEMPHIS CITY DEPARTMENT OF RECREATION - PINK PALACE MUSEUM
See: Memphis Pink Palace Museum

★7773★
MEMPHIS COMMERCIAL APPEAL - LIBRARY (Publ)
495 Union Ave.   Phone: (901) 529-2781
Memphis, TN 38101   Eugene G. Brady, Jr., Libn.
Founded: 1920. **Staff:** Prof 3; Other 2. **Subjects:** Current events. **Holdings:** 170 VF drawers of newspaper clippings; 104 VF drawers of photographs, drawings, maps; 1240 reels of microfilm. **Subscriptions:** 20 newspapers. **Services:** Interlibrary loans; copying; library open to public with approval. **Staff:** Dollie Gandy, Libn.; George L. Dunn, Jr., Libn.

★7774★
MEMPHIS MENTAL HEALTH INSTITUTE - JAMES A. WALLACE LIBRARY (Med)
865 Poplar Ave.
Box 4966   Phone: (901) 529-7768
Memphis, TN 38104   Josephine Maddry, Lib.Techn.
Founded: 1963. **Staff:** Prof 1. **Subjects:** Psychiatry, psychology, nursing, social work and activity therapy, medicine. **Holdings:** 2430 books and bound periodical volumes; 103 tapes. **Subscriptions:** 118 journals and other serials. **Services:** Interlibrary loans; copying; library open to public with restrictions. **Networks/Consortia:** Member of Association of Memphis Area Health Sciences Libraries.

★7775★
MEMPHIS PINK PALACE MUSEUM - LIBRARY (Hist)
3050 Central Ave.   Phone: (901) 454-5600
Memphis, TN 38111   Coralu D. Buddenbohm, Libn.
Founded: 1967. **Staff:** 1. **Subjects:** Regional history, geology, archeology and biology; natural history; museums. **Special Collections:** Shiloh Trails, Inc. (121 Civil War, 125 regional history). **Holdings:** 3000 books; 246 bound periodical volumes; 7 scrapbooks of clippings of history of Memphis Pink Palace Museum. **Subscriptions:** 36 journals and other serials; 47 newspapers. **Services:** Library open to public for reference use only on request. **Publications:** Monitor, monthly except July and August - distributed to city and county schools, Friends of Museum and Foundation Board members and for exchange. **Remarks:** Maintained by Recreation Department of City of Memphis.

MEMPHIS PINK PALACE MUSEUM LIBRARY - SHILOH MILITARY TRAIL, INC.
See: Shiloh Military Trail, Inc. - Library

★7776★
MEMPHIS PRESS-SCIMITAR - LIBRARY (Publ)
495 Union Ave.   Phone: (901) 529-2535
Memphis, TN 38101   Janet Rowe, Hd.Libn.
Staff: Prof 1; Other 2. **Subjects:** Newspaper reference topics. **Special Collections:** Photographs. **Holdings:** Figures not available for books, photographs, clippings, reports. **Services:** Copying; library open to public with restrictions and with permission of managing editor.

★7777★
MEMPHIS-SHELBY COUNTY BAR ASSOCIATION LIBRARY (Law)
Court House   Phone: (901) 527-7041
Memphis, TN 38103   Mary Sue Boushe, Law Libn.
Subjects: Law. **Holdings:** 45,000 volumes.

★7778★
MEMPHIS-SHELBY COUNTY OFFICE OF PLANNING AND DEVELOPMENT - LIBRARY (Plan)
City Hall, Rm. 419
125 N. Main St.   Phone: (901) 528-2601
Memphis, TN 38103   Marilyn A. Meeks, Libn.
Founded: 1978. **Staff:** Prof 1. **Subjects:** Planning - economic, transportation, environmental, community, land use. **Holdings:** 4500 books; 76 bound periodical volumes. **Subscriptions:** 58 journals and other serials. **Services:** Copying (limited); SDI; library open to public with restrictions. **Publications:** New book list - for internal distribution only. **Remarks:** Library is now a State Data Center Affiliate and maintains a small statistical collection for reference use.

★7779★
MEMPHIS-SHELBY COUNTY PUBLIC LIBRARY AND INFORMATION CENTER - MEMPHIS ROOM COLLECTIONS (Hist)†
1850 Peabody Ave.   Phone: (901) 528-2961
Memphis, TN 38104   James R. Johnson, Hd., Hist. & Travel
Staff: Prof 7; Other 4. **Subjects:** Memphis/Shelby County, genealogy, Mardi Gras/Cotton Carnival, yellow fever, Blues & Beale Street, Mississippi steamboats. **Special Collections:** Memphis-Shelby County Archives (17,000 volumes); K.D. McKellar Collection; mayor's letterbooks (60,000 items). **Holdings:** 10,371 books; 1200 bound periodical volumes; 900 maps (cataloged); 500,000 newspaper clippings; 6000 photographs; 3000 pages of oral history transcripts. **Subscriptions:** 120 journals and other serials; 15 newspapers. **Services:** Interlibrary loans; copying; library open to public. **Publications:** Senator Kenneth Douglas McKellar: A Register of His Papers, by Retha Farr Weiss, 1974 - for sale. **Special Catalogs:** A McKellar Calendar of Speeches 1928-1940, by Joseph H. Riggs, 1962; Nathan Bedford Forrest and the Civil War in Memphis: A Subject Bibliography; John Ogden Curley Papers; The Reverend George H. Harris Letters; Yellow Fever Collections of the Memphis Room; The Captain Rees V. Downs River Collection; The Everett R. Cook Oral History Collection. **Staff:** Robert Miller, First Asst.; Josiah B. Brady, Libn.II; Stephen Findlay, Libn.I; Delanie M. Ross, Libn.I; David Feinberg, Libn.I; John Harkins, Archv.

★7780★
MEMPHIS-SHELBY COUNTY PUBLIC LIBRARY AND INFO. CTR. - SCIENCE/ BUSINESS/SOCIAL SCIENCES DEPT. (Soc Sci; Sci-Tech)
1850 Peabody Ave.   Phone: (901) 528-2984
Memphis, TN 38104   Barbara C. Shultz, Dept.Hd.
Founded: 1893. **Staff:** Prof 12; Other 3. **Subjects:** Business, science, technology, social science. **Holdings:** Figures not available. **Subscriptions:** 3000 journals and other serials; 84 newspapers. **Services:** Interlibrary loans; copying; library open to public. **Computerized Information Services:** DIALOG; computerized cataloging and acquisitions. **Networks/Consortia:** Member of OCLC through SOLINET. **Staff:** Reba Orman, First Asst.; Frances French, Libn.; David Feinberg, Libn.; Ava Hicks, Libn.; David Mays, Libn.; Allison Pitcock, Libn.; Dennis Smith, Libn.; Rosemary Nelms, Libn.; Carol McCarley, Libn.; Ken Potts, Libn.; Pat Wood, Libn.

MEMPHIS STATE UNIVERSITY - AMERICAN BLAKE FOUNDATION
See: American Blake Foundation

★7781★
MEMPHIS STATE UNIVERSITY - GRADUATE DEPT. OF PLANNING & REGIONAL ECONOMIC DEVELOPMENT CTR. - PLANNING LIBRARY (Plan)
226 Johnson Hall   Phone: (901) 454-2056
Memphis, TN 38152   Luchy S. Burrell, Supv.
Staff: Prof 1; Other 4. **Subjects:** Comprehensive physical planning, economic and developmental planning, housing, law, natural resources. **Special Collections:** Russell Van Ness Black Collection (300 volumes); Memphis and Shelby County Collection (500 items). **Holdings:** 2100 books; 4700 local government publications; 475 U.S. government documents; 1 vertical file; 34 titles of unbound periodicals; 1 drawer of newsletters. **Subscriptions:** 61 journals and other serials. **Services:** Library open to public for reference use only.

★7782★
MEMPHIS STATE UNIVERSITY LIBRARIES - ART SLIDE LIBRARY (Art; Aud-Vis)
Department of Art
Jones Hall, Rm. 220   Phone: (901) 454-2216
Memphis, TN 38152   Belinda C. Patterson, Slide Cur.
Founded: 1954. **Staff:** Prof 1; Other 4. **Subjects:** Architecture, sculpture, painting, decorative arts, archeology, photography. **Holdings:** 120 books; 88,000 slides (cataloged); 77 sets of filmstrips; 100 theses and slides of work; 50 cassettes. **Services:** Library open to other organizations with

restrictions.

★7783★
MEMPHIS STATE UNIVERSITY LIBRARIES - BUREAU OF EDUCATIONAL RESEARCH AND SERVICES - LIBRARY (Educ)
College of Education
302 Ball Bldg.   Phone: (901) 454-2362
Memphis, TN 38152   John R. Petry, Res.Assoc./Assoc.Prof.
Founded: 1966. **Staff:** Prof 1; Other 2. **Subjects:** Educational research, statistics, education, disadvantaged persons, adult basic education. **Holdings:** 600 books; 3000 items in Princeton file; 20 drawers of reports and proposals; 1500 microfiche. **Subscriptions:** 8 journals and other serials. **Services:** Copying; library open to public. **Publications:** BERS Newsletter, periodically; COE Events.

★7784★
MEMPHIS STATE UNIVERSITY LIBRARIES - C.H. NASH MUSEUM LIBRARY (Sci-Tech)
1987 Indian Village Dr.   Phone: (901) 785-3160
Memphis, TN 38109   Gerald P. Smith, Cur.
Founded: 1968. **Staff:** 3. **Subjects:** Eastern North American archeology and ethnology; physical anthropology; geology of southeastern United States. **Holdings:** 1500 books. **Subscriptions:** 10 journals and other serials. **Services:** Library open to public for reference use only. **Staff:** John A. Hesse, Assoc.Cur.; Melissa Lehman, Libn./Educ.Rep.

★7785★
MEMPHIS STATE UNIVERSITY LIBRARIES - CHEMISTRY LIBRARY (Sci-Tech)
      Phone: (901) 454-2625
Memphis, TN 38152   Joan Fiveash, Lib.Asst.
Founded: 1966. **Staff:** 2. **Subjects:** Chemistry. **Holdings:** 7024 books; 14,833 bound periodical volumes; 376 reels of microfilm; 2535 microforms. **Subscriptions:** 194 journals and other serials. **Services:** Interlibrary loans; copying; library open to public. **Computerized Information Services:** DIALOG, MEDLINE, BRS, SDC.

★7786★
MEMPHIS STATE UNIVERSITY LIBRARIES - ENGINEERING LIBRARY (Sci-Tech)
Central Ave.   Phone: (901) 454-2179
Memphis, TN 38152   Sue Ward, Libn.
Founded: 1964. **Staff:** Prof 1; Other 1. **Subjects:** Engineering, geology, technology. **Holdings:** 30,642 books; 8438 bound periodical volumes; 5556 maps (cataloged); 10,572 microforms. **Subscriptions:** 535 journals and other serials. **Services:** Interlibrary loans; copying; library open to public. **Computerized Information Services:** DIALOG, MEDLINE, BRS, SDC.

★7787★
MEMPHIS STATE UNIVERSITY LIBRARIES - MISSISSIPPI VALLEY COLLECTION (Hist)
      Phone: (901) 454-2210
Memphis, TN 38152   Eleanor McKay, Cur.
Founded: 1964. **Staff:** 5. **Subjects:** Lower Mississippi Valley - history, culture, literature. **Special Collections:** Memphis multi-media project (race relations); Grundstein Collection on Public Management Sciences; sanitation strike of Memphis, 1968 (55 cubic feet); Robert R. Church Family, 1870-1980 (61 cubic feet); U.S. circus, 1890-1970; university archives (250,000 items); assassination of Martin Luther King, Jr. **Holdings:** 20,000 books; 5000 periodical volumes; 1700 pamphlets; 2.5 million manuscripts; 750,000 photographs; 7000 items of sheet music; 1000 maps; 1000 audio- and videotapes; 464 oral history tapes; 552 oral history transcripts; 120 films. **Subscriptions:** 350 journals and other serials. **Services:** Copying; collection open to public. **Computerized Information Services:** Computerized cataloging and acquisitions. **Networks/Consortia:** Member of OCLC through SOLINET. **Publications:** Brister Library Monograph; Campus Tower News - both irregular and available through exchange. **Special Catalogs:** Registers and inventories to collections. **Staff:** John Terreo, Lib.Asst.

★7788★
MEMPHIS STATE UNIVERSITY LIBRARIES - MUSIC LIBRARY (Mus)
Central Ave.   Phone: (901) 454-2556
Memphis, TN 38152   Ann Viles, Music Libn.
Founded: 1967. **Staff:** Prof 1; Other 2. **Subjects:** Music. **Special Collections:** Sound recordings (7709). **Holdings:** 10,867 books; 1923 bound periodical volumes; 16,645 performance music and scores; 2141 microforms. **Subscriptions:** 77 journals and other serials. **Services:** Interlibrary loans; copying; library open to public. **Staff:** Anna Neal, Libn.

★7789★
MEMPHIS STATE UNIVERSITY LIBRARIES - SCHOOL OF LAW LIBRARY (Law)
      Phone: (901) 454-2426
Memphis, TN 38152   Sara Turley Cole, Law Libn.
Founded: 1961. **Staff:** Prof 5; Other 6. **Subjects:** Law. **Holdings:** 140,000 volumes. **Subscriptions:** 2200 journals and other serials. **Services:** Library open to attorneys. **Computerized Information Services:** LEXIS, WESTLAW. **Staff:** Marianne C. Mussett, Asst.Libn.

★7790★
MEMPHIS STATE UNIVERSITY LIBRARIES - SPEECH AND HEARING CENTER LIBRARY (Med)
807 Jefferson Ave.   Phone: (901) 525-2682
Memphis, TN 38104   Edwin Frank, Lib.Asst.
Founded: 1965. **Staff:** 1. **Subjects:** Audiology, speech pathology. **Holdings:** 2800 books; 950 bound periodical volumes; film and filmstrips; recordings. **Subscriptions:** 90 journals and other serials. **Services:** Interlibrary loans; copying; library open to public. **Computerized Information Services:** DIALOG, MEDLINE.

★7791★
MEMPHIS THEOLOGICAL SEMINARY - LIBRARY (Rel-Theol)
168 E. Pkwy. S.   Phone: (901) 458-8232
Memphis, TN 38104   Bobbie E. Oliver, Adm.Libn.
Founded: 1956. **Staff:** Prof 2; Other 1. **Subjects:** Theology, church history, missions, homiletics, Old Testament, Christian education, New Testament, sociology of religion. **Special Collections:** R. Pierce Beaver Missions Library (5000 volumes and 8 VF drawers). **Holdings:** 70,295 books and bound periodical volumes; 372 reels of microfilm; 2500 microfiche; 12 VF drawers. **Subscriptions:** 603 journals and other serials. **Services:** Interlibrary loans; copying; library open to ministers for reference use. **Staff:** Harold Chandler, Acq.Libn.

MENDEL ART GALLERY
See: Saskatoon Gallery and Conservatory Corporation

★7792★
MENDOCINO ART CENTER - ART LIBRARY (Art)
Box 765   Phone: (707) 937-5818
Mendocino, CA 95460   Joan Burleigh, Libn.
Staff: 3. **Subjects:** Art. **Holdings:** 1500 books; 200 bound periodical volumes. **Subscriptions:** 18 journals and other serials. **Services:** Library open to public for reference use only.

MENDOCINO COUNTY HISTORICAL SOCIETY
See: Held-Poage Memorial Home & Research Library

★7793★
MENDOCINO COUNTY LAW LIBRARY (Law)
Courthouse, Rm. 207   Phone: (707) 468-4481
Ukiah, CA 95482   Ginny Holmen, Law Libn.
Staff: 1. **Subjects:** Law. **Holdings:** 8000 books. **Services:** Library open to public with restrictions.

★7794★
MENDOTA MENTAL HEALTH INSTITUTE - LIBRARY MEDIA CENTER (Med)
301 Troy Dr.   Phone: (608) 244-2411
Madison, WI 53704   Margaret Tielke Grinnell, Act.Dir.
Founded: 1955. **Staff:** Prof 2; Other 2. **Subjects:** Clinical psychology and psychiatry including psychiatric nursing and social work; mental health - training, research, consultation; psychiatry for the deaf; forensic psychiatry. **Holdings:** 16,372 books; 967 bound periodical volumes; 12 VF drawers of specialized reprints and reports; 131 titles of films and videotapes; AV catalogs relevant to subject area; 102 newsletters. **Subscriptions:** 205 journals and other serials. **Services:** Interlibrary loans; copying; SDI; library open to state residents. **Computerized Information Services:** Access to online systems. **Networks/Consortia:** Member of Madison Area Library Council (MALC); South Central Health Planning Area Cooperative. **Publications:** Library News and List of Newly Cataloged Books and AVs. **Staff:** Marijane Reich, Patients' Libn.

★7795★
MENNINGER FOUNDATION - ARCHIVES (Med)
Box 829   Phone: (913) 234-9566
Topeka, KS 66601   Verne B. Horne, Archv.
Founded: 1960. **Staff:** Prof 1; Other 1. **Subjects:** Psychiatry, psychoanalysis, clinical psychology, psychiatric social work, medical history. **Special Collections:** Dr. C.F. Menninger Collection; Mrs. Flo. V. Menninger

Bible Study Collection; Dr. Karl Menninger Collection; Dr. William C. Menninger Collection; Sigmund Freud Collection; Dorothea Lynde Dix Collection; George III Collection; Dr. Emil Oberholzer Collection; Dr. Ugo Carletti Collection. **Holdings:** 1800 pamphlets; 700 manuscript boxes; 400 VF drawers; 30,000 clippings; 12,000 photographs; 2500 tapes. **Services:** Copying; use of archives for research may be requested. **Staff:** Dr. Robert G. Menninger, Dir. of Musm.

★7796★
MENNINGER FOUNDATION - PROFESSIONAL LIBRARY (Med)
Box 829
Topeka, KS 66601
Phone: (913) 273-7500
Alice Brand, Chf.Libn.
Founded: 1930. **Staff:** Prof 3; Other 3. **Subjects:** Clinical psychiatry, psychoanalysis, clinical psychology, family therapy, forensic psychiatry, related fields. **Holdings:** 22,700 books; 13,400 bound periodical volumes. **Subscriptions:** 347 journals and other serials. **Services:** Interlibrary loans; copying; SDI; library open to mental health professionals. **Computerized Information Services:** NLM, DIALOG, BRS. **Special Catalogs:** Catalog of the Menninger Clinic Library (book and supplement). **Staff:** Rebecca Breeden, Asst.Libn.

MENNINGER (Dr. Karl A.) MEDICAL LIBRARY
See: U.S. Veterans Administration (KS-Topeka)

MENNONITE ARCHIVES OF ONTARIO
See: Conrad Grebel College

MENNONITE BIBLICAL SEMINARY
See: Associated Mennonite Biblical Seminaries

★7797★
MENNONITE BRETHREN BIBLE COLLEGE - LIBRARY (Rel-Theol)
77 Henderson Hwy.
Winnipeg, MB, Canada R2L 1L1
Phone: (204) 667-9560
Herbert Giesbrecht, College Libn.
Founded: 1944. **Staff:** Prof 1; Other 1. **Subjects:** Theology, humanities, music. **Special Collections:** Mennonitica and Anabaptistica. **Holdings:** 28,500 books; 1350 bound periodical volumes; 150 educational and theological pamphlets; 50 dissertations and theses; 60 VF drawers of Mennonite Brethren archives; 600 phonograph records. **Subscriptions:** 259 journals and other serials. **Services:** Interlibrary loans; copying; library open to public upon registration. **Publications:** Library Leaves, monthly - distributed to college faculty and friends. **Special Catalogs:** Winnipeg Union List of Periodicals in Religion. **Special Indexes:** Index to Archives (Mennonite Brethren) Collection; contributes to Christian Periodical Index.

★7798★
MENNONITE BRETHREN BIBLICAL SEMINARY - HIEBERT LIBRARY (Rel-Theol)
1717 S. Chestnut Ave.
Fresno, CA 93702
Phone: (209) 251-7194
Steven Brandt, Libn.
Founded: 1955. **Staff:** Prof 3; Other 2. **Subjects:** Theology, Bible, Christian education, missions, evangelism, Biblical languages, church history. **Special Collections:** Mennonite Brethren Historical Documents. **Holdings:** 82,134 books and bound periodical volumes; 5716 AV items. **Subscriptions:** 713 journals and other serials; 12 newspapers. **Services:** Interlibrary loans; copying; library open to public for reference use only. **Publications:** Annual report; accession list, monthly.

★7799★
MENNONITE CHURCH - WESTERN DISTRICT CONFERENCE - WESTERN DISTRICT LOAN LIBRARY (Rel-Theol)
Box 66
North Newton, KS 67117
Mrs. J. Lloyd Spaulding, Libn.
Founded: 1936. **Staff:** 1. **Subjects:** Religion, children's collection, fiction and biography. **Holdings:** 6000 books.

★7800★
MENNONITE HISTORICAL LIBRARY (Rel-Theol)
Goshen College
Goshen, IN 46526
Phone: (219) 533-3161
John S. Oyer, Dir.
Founded: 1907. **Staff:** Prof 2; Other 3. **Subjects:** Anabaptist and Mennonite writings and history, genealogy, limited materials relating to the Church of the Brethren, the Society of Friends, and regional history. **Special Collections:** John Horsch Research Collection (Anabaptist, Mennonite, and related Reformation materials). **Holdings:** 25,000 books; 10,000 bound periodical volumes; 105 VF drawers of unpublished treatises, archival materials, pamphlets, folders, maps, photographs and photocopies; microforms, phonograph records. **Subscriptions:** 300 journals and other serials. **Services:** Interlibrary loans (fee for frequent requests); copying; library open to public.

Computerized Information Services: Computerized cataloging and interlibrary loans. **Networks/Consortia:** Member of OCLC through INCOLSA. **Staff:** Nelson P. Springer, Cur.

MENNONITE HISTORICAL LIBRARY (Bluffton, OH)
See: Bluffton College

★7801★
MENNONITE HISTORICAL LIBRARY OF EASTERN PENNSYLVANIA (Hist; Rel-Theol)
1000 Forty Foot Rd.
Lansdale, PA 19446
Phone: (215) 362-2675
Joseph S. Miller, Adm.
Staff: Prof 1. **Subjects:** Church history. **Special Collections:** Jacob B. Mench collection; 30 manuscript collections of Mennonite persons. **Holdings:** 4000 books; 60 bound periodical volumes; 10 manuscripts. **Services:** Copying; library open to public. **Publications:** MHEP Newsletter, monthly - by subscription.

★7802★
MENNONITE HOSPITAL AND SCHOOL OF NURSING - HEALTH SCIENCES LIBRARY (Med)
807 N. Main St.
Bloomington, IL 61701
Phone: (309) 827-4321
Sue Stroyan, Dir.
Founded: 1973. **Staff:** Prof 1; Other 1. **Subjects:** Medicine, geriatrics, nursing, ophthalmology, hospital administration. **Special Collections:** McLean County Medical Society Collection. **Holdings:** 6000 books; 400 bound periodical volumes; 530 AV titles; 100 boxes of archival material; 2 drawers of pamphlets. **Subscriptions:** 288 journals and other serials. **Services:** Interlibrary loans; copying; SDI; library open to public for reference use only by appointment. **Networks/Consortia:** Member of Corn Belt Library System; OCLC through ILLINET; Regional Medical Library - Region 3; Central Illinois Consortium of Health Science Libraries. **Publications:** Serials holdings list, annual; acquisitions list, monthly; introductory brochure. **Staff:** Gerrie Godwin, Asst.Libn.

MENNONITE LIBRARY AND ARCHIVES
See: Bethel College

★7803★
MENNONITE VILLAGE MUSEUM (Canada) INC. - LIBRARY (Area-Ethnic; Rel-Theol)
Box 1136
Steinbach, MB, Canada R0A 2A0
Phone: (204) 326-9661
Peter Goertzen, Mgr.
Staff: Prof 1. **Subjects:** Mennonites in U.S.S.R. and Canada; German-language Mennonitica. **Holdings:** 4000 books; 2000 archival items (cataloged). **Services:** Library open to public.

MENOMONEE FALLS COMMUNITY MEMORIAL HOSPITAL
See: Community Memorial Hospital of Menomonee Falls

★7804★
MENORAH INSTITUTE - LIBRARY (Rel-Theol)
1533 60th St.
Box FF
Brooklyn, NY 11219
Phone: (212) 435-0500
Rabbi N. Halberstam, Libn.
Staff: 1. **Subjects:** Judaica. **Holdings:** 10,000 books. **Services:** Copying; library open to public with restrictions. **Publications:** Bibliography and biography journal devoted to genealogy.

★7805★
MENORAH MEDICAL CENTER - ROBERT UHLMAN MEDICAL LIBRARY (Med)
4949 Rockhill Rd.
Kansas City, MO 64110
Phone: (816) 276-8172
Marjorie L. Terrill, Med.Libn.
Staff: Prof 1; Other 1. **Subjects:** Medicine, surgery, psychiatry, nursing, microbiology, pharmacology, nutrition, pediatrics, neurology. **Special Collections:** Slide collection (pathology; 17,500 slides). **Holdings:** 16,000 books; 6000 bound periodical volumes; 15 boxes of pamphlets; 1500 tapes. **Subscriptions:** 110 journals and other serials. **Services:** Interlibrary loans; copying; library not open to public. **Computerized Information Services:** MEDLINE. **Publications:** New book lists, 4/year.

★7806★
MEN'S RIGHTS, INC. - READING CENTER (Soc Sci)
Rindge Towers - 402, Suite 8J
Cambridge, MA 02140
Phone: (617) 547-5054
Fredric Hayward, Dir.
Founded: 1977. **Staff:** Prof 1. **Subjects:** Sexism and men's problems. **Holdings:** 40 books; clippings; periodicals. **Services:** Library open to public for reference use only. **Publications:** News Releases.

★7807★
MENTAL HEALTH ASSOCIATION OF WESTCHESTER COUNTY - LIBRARY
(Med)
29 Sterling Ave.   Phone: (914) 949-6741
White Plains, NY 10606   Mary H. Johnson, Libn.
Founded: 1950. **Staff:** Prof 1. **Subjects:** Mental health, psychiatry, psychology, drugs, graduate social work. **Holdings:** 3150 books and bound periodical volumes; 150 VF drawers of pamphlets and clippings. **Subscriptions:** 25 journals and other serials. **Services:** Interlibrary loans; copying; library open to public.

★7808★
MENTAL HEALTH INSTITUTE - HEALTH SCIENCE LIBRARY (Med)†
1200 W. Cedar St.   Phone: (712) 225-2594
Cherokee, IA 51012   Tom Folkes, Health Sci.Libn.
Staff: Prof 1. **Subjects:** Psychiatry, psychology, neurology, nursing, social service, medicine. **Holdings:** 2500 books; 300 cassette tapes. **Subscriptions:** 45 journals and other serials. **Services:** Interlibrary loans; copying; library open to public for reference use only. **Networks/Consortia:** Member of Siouxland Health Science Library Consortium.

★7809★
MENTAL HEALTH MATERIALS CENTER - INFORMATION RESOURCES CENTER FOR MENTAL HEALTH & FAMILY LIFE EDUCATION (Med)
30 E. 29th St.   Phone: (212) 889-5760
New York, NY 10016
Founded: 1953. **Staff:** Prof 1. **Subjects:** Child growth and development, mental health for all age levels, marriage and family life, mental illness, community mental health programs and resources. **Holdings:** 700 books; 65 VF drawers of pamphlets. **Subscriptions:** 157 journals and other serials. **Services:** Under contract to governmental and other agencies, the center engages in the preparation of selective guides to literature and AV aids; center is open to subscribers only. **Publications:** Selective Guide to Materials for Mental Health and Family Life Education; Sneak Previews; Best in Print, all quarterly; other books and pamphlets in the field of mental health and family life.

★7810★
MENTAL HEALTH AND MENTAL RETARDATION AUTHORITY OF HARRIS COUNTY - INFORMATION RESOURCE CENTER (Med)
2850 Fannin   Phone: (713) 759-1010
Houston, TX 77002   Jacqueline M. Woods, Adm.Techn. III
Staff: Prof 1. **Subjects:** Mental health, mental retardation. **Holdings:** 450 books; 1000 pamphlets; 400 unbound journals; 100 reports. **Subscriptions:** 17 journals and other serials. **Services:** Interlibrary loans; copying; center open to public for reference use only.

MENTAL HEALTH RESEARCH INSTITUTE
See: University of Michigan

MENTAL HEALTH STUDY CENTER LIBRARY
See: U.S. Public Health Service - Natl. Institute of Mental Health

★7811★
MERCANTILE LIBRARY ASSOCIATION - MERCANTILE LIBRARY (Hum)
17 E. 47th St.   Phone: (212) 755-6710
New York, NY 10017   Claire J. Roth, Lib.Dir.
Founded: 1820. **Staff:** Prof 5; Other 5. **Subjects:** 19th and 20th century literature, biography. **Special Collections:** 19th century fiction and nonfiction (55,000 volumes). **Holdings:** 185,000 books. **Subscriptions:** 66 journals and other serials. **Services:** Library open to public with restrictions. **Publications:** Annual Report; New Arrivals List, monthly; newsletter, monthly. **Staff:** Joni Cassidy, Pub.Serv.Libn.; Nora Donegan, Tech.Serv.Libn.

★7812★
MERCANTILE TRUST COMPANY - INTERNATIONAL LIBRARY (Bus-Fin)
Box 14881   Phone: (314) 425-2867
St. Louis, MO 67178   Carrie L. Sallwasser, Libn.
Staff: Prof 1. **Subjects:** International economics and affairs; trade and finance; banking. **Holdings:** 200 books; 150 international bank newsletters; 6 VF drawers of country files; 20 VF drawers. **Subscriptions:** 104 journals and other serials; 16 newspapers. **Services:** Copying; library open to public for reference use only.

★7813★
MERCED COMMUNITY MEDICAL CENTER - MEDICAL LIBRARY (Med)
290 E. 15th St.
Box 231   Phone: (209) 723-2861
Merced, CA 95340   Betty Maddalena, Med.Libn.
Founded: 1965. **Staff:** Prof 1; Other 2. **Subjects:** Medicine, nursing.

Holdings: 680 books; 1800 bound periodical volumes; 301 Audio-Digest tapes. **Subscriptions:** 83 journals and other serials. **Services:** Interlibrary loans; copying; library open to medical and health professionals and students only. **Computerized Information Services:** MEDLINE, BRS. **Networks/Consortia:** Member of Pacific Southwest Regional Medical Library Service (PSRMLS); Merced County Health Information Consortium.

★7814★
MERCER COUNTY HISTORICAL SOCIETY - LIBRARY AND ARCHIVES (Hist)
119 S. Pitt St.   Phone: (412) 662-3490
Mercer, PA 16137   Mark Brown, Pres.
Staff: 2. **Subjects:** Mercer County history. **Special Collections:** Dr. Goodsell's Collection. **Holdings:** 2500 books; 200 bound periodical volumes; newspapers; maps; surveys; microfilm. **Services:** Copying; library open to public for reference use only. **Publications:** Mercer County History, annual journal; newsletter, quarterly. **Staff:** Orvis Anderson, Cur.; Viola Lowry, Asst.Cur.

★7815★
MERCER COUNTY LAW LIBRARY (Law)
Court House   Phone: (419) 586-2122
Celina, OH 45822   Carolyn Leffler, Law Libn.
Staff: 1. **Subjects:** Law. **Holdings:** 5500 volumes. **Services:** Library open to public for reference use only; bar association members have borrowing privileges.

★7816★
MERCER COUNTY LAW LIBRARY (Law)
Court House
Mercer, PA 16137   Olive L. Griffin, Libn.
Founded: 1912. **Subjects:** Law, especially Pennsylvania law and federal law. **Holdings:** 8000 volumes. **Services:** Library open to bar associations and law students, and open to public for reference use only.

★7817★
MERCER COUNTY REGIONAL PLANNING COMMISSION - LIBRARY (Plan)
Sharpsville Ctr. Plaza
94 E. Shenango St.   Phone: (412) 962-5787
Sharpsville, PA 16150   Leslie B. Spaulding, Libn.
Staff: Prof 6; Other 5. **Subjects:** Planning, transportation, environment. **Holdings:** 300 books. **Subscriptions:** 10 journals and other serials. **Services:** Library open to public.

★7818★
MERCER (George, Jr.) SCHOOL OF THEOLOGY - LIBRARY (Rel-Theol)
65 Fourth St.   Phone: (516) 248-4800
Garden City, NY 11530   Elizabeth D. Dupont, Libn.
Founded: 1955. **Staff:** Prof 2; Other 2. **Subjects:** Religion, church history, theology, ethics, philosophy. **Holdings:** 25,500 books and bound periodical volumes; 452 cassettes; 735 microforms; 500 pamphlets. **Subscriptions:** 149 journals. **Services:** Interlibrary loans; copying; library open to public. **Networks/Consortia:** Member of Long Island Library Resources Council (LILRC).

★7819★
MERCER MEDICAL CENTER - DAVID B. ACKLEY MEDICAL LIBRARY (Med)
446 Bellevue Ave.
Box 1658   Phone: (609) 394-4125
Trenton, NJ 08607   Catherine W. Marchok, Lib.Dir.
Founded: 1947. **Staff:** Prof 1; Other 1. **Subjects:** Medicine. **Special Collections:** 19th century medical books. **Holdings:** 1820 books; 690 bound periodical volumes; 5 VF drawers of clippings and pamphlets; 1 VF drawer of pictures; 400 audiotapes; 1455 slides. **Subscriptions:** 125 journals and other serials. **Services:** Interlibrary loans; copying; library open to public for reference use only. **Networks/Consortia:** Member of New York & New Jersey Regional Medical Library Program; Central Jersey Health Science Libraries Association.

MERCER UNIVERSITY - GEORGIA BAPTIST HISTORICAL SOCIETY
See: Georgia Baptist Historical Society

★7820★
MERCER UNIVERSITY - LAW SCHOOL - HALLIBURTON LAW LIBRARY (Law)
                                          Phone: (912) 744-2612
Macon, GA 31201   Leah F. Chanin, Dir., Law Lib.
Founded: 1874. **Staff:** Prof 4; Other 6. **Subjects:** Law. **Holdings:** 134,000 books. **Subscriptions:** 800 journals and other serials; 8 newspapers. **Services:** Interlibrary loans; copying; library open to public with restrictions. **Computerized Information Services:** LEXIS; computerized cataloging.

Networks/Consortia: Member of OCLC through SOLINET. **Publications:** Acquisition List. **Staff:** Steve Thorpe, Cat.; Reynold Kosek, Assoc.Libn.; Pat O'Neal, Circ.Libn.

★7821★
MERCER UNIVERSITY - MEDICAL SCHOOL LIBRARY (Med)
Macon, GA 31207

Phone: (912) 744-2519
Jocelyn Rankin, Dir., Med.Lib.

Founded: 1974. **Staff:** Prof 5; Other 6. **Subjects:** Medicine. **Holdings:** 4800 books; 15,500 bound periodical volumes; 4047 microfiche; 3227 government documents; 321 AV materials. **Subscriptions:** 842 journals and other serials. **Services:** Interlibrary loans; copying; SDI; library open to public. **Computerized Information Services:** BRS, MEDLINE; computerized cataloging. **Networks/Consortia:** Member of OCLC through SOLINET; Health Science Libraries of Central Georgia; Southeastern Regional Medical Library Program (SERMLP). **Publications:** Library Guide, irregular; acquisitions list, bimonthly. **Staff:** Jean Williams, Asst.Dir.; Fred Bush, Ref.Libn.; Elaine Woods, Cat.; Karen Guth, Night Supv.

★7822★
MERCER UNIVERSITY - SOUTHERN COLLEGE OF PHARMACY - H. CUSTER NAYLOR LIBRARY (Sci-Tech; Med)
345 Boulevard, N.E.
Atlanta, GA 30312

Phone: (404) 688-6291
Elizabeth Christian Jackson, Libn.

Founded: 1948. **Staff:** Prof 2. **Subjects:** Pharmacy, medicine, chemistry, biological sciences, cosmetics, business. **Holdings:** 3500 books; 3500 bound periodical volumes; Iowa Drug Information Service (cards and microfiche). **Subscriptions:** 250 journals and other serials. **Services:** Interlibrary loans; copying; library open to health professionals. **Networks/Consortia:** Member of OCLC through CCLC; Atlanta Health Science Libraries Consortium; Georgia Library Information Network (GLIN). **Publications:** Atlanta-Athens Union Catalog. **Staff:** Sandra Gallop Franklin, Asst.Libn.

★7823★
MERCER (William M.), INC. - LIBRARY INFORMATION CENTER (Bus-Fin)
3303 Wilshire Blvd.
Los Angeles, CA 90010

Phone: (213) 386-7840
Robert C. Costello

Subjects: Employee benefits, health insurance, life insurance, social security, disability insurance, pensions. **Special Collections:** Employee Benefit Collection. **Holdings:** 300 books; 50 VF drawers of reports, clippings and legal documents. **Subscriptions:** 640 journals and other serials; 25 newspapers. **Services:** Interlibrary loans; library open to public with restrictions. **Computerized Information Services:** DIALOG; MRLIN (internal database). **Publications:** Library Browser, monthly.

★7824★
MERCER (William M.), INC. - LIBRARY/INFORMATION CENTER (Soc Sci)
200 Clarendon St.
Boston, MA 02116

Phone: (617) 421-0367
Holly W. Garner, Mgr., Info.Serv.

Staff: Prof 2; Other 1. **Subjects:** Pensions, health care benefits, compensation, consulting. **Holdings:** 450 books; 500 bound periodical volumes; 18 VF drawers of subject files; reports. **Subscriptions:** 100 journals and other serials; 10 newspapers. **Services:** Interlibrary loans; library open to other librarians. **Computerized Information Services:** DIALOG. **Publications:** Library Browser, monthly - to consultants and clients; Of Interest, bimonthly - to consultants. **Special Indexes:** Computerized Report Index.

★7825★
MERCER (William M.) LTD. - LIBRARY/INFORMATION CENTRE (Bus-Fin)
1 First Canadian Pl., 56th Fl.
P.O. Box 59
Toronto, ON, Canada M5X 1G3

Phone: (416) 868-2989
Laurence Pellan, Libn.

Staff: Prof 2. **Subjects:** Employee benefits, pensions, financial planning, salary administration, executive compensation, group insurance benefits. **Holdings:** 2000 books. **Subscriptions:** 250 journals and other serials; 5 newspapers. **Computerized Information Services:** Infomart; computerized serials circulation lists.

MERCHANT MARINE LIBRARY ASSOCIATION
See: American Merchant Marine Library Association

★7826★
MERCHANTS NATIONAL BANK OF MOBILE - EMPLOYEES LIBRARY (Bus-Fin)†
58 St. Francis St.
Box 2527
Mobile, AL 36622

Phone: (205) 690-1139
Pat Looney, Libn.

Staff: Prof 1. **Subjects:** Banking, fiction and nonfiction, children's books.

Holdings: 5000 books; 150 bound periodical volumes. **Services:** Interlibrary loans; not open to public.

★7827★
MERCK & COMPANY, INC. - CALGON CORPORATION - INFORMATION CENTER (Sci-Tech)
Box 1346
Pittsburgh, PA 15230

Phone: (412) 777-8203
Marie Louise Stonehouse, Mgr.

Founded: 1937. **Staff:** Prof 3; Other 4. **Subjects:** Industrial and municipal water treatment and reclamation, chemistry of water soluble polymers, activated carbon technology. **Holdings:** 50,000 books; 100 bound periodical volumes; 1000 reels of microfilm; 20,000 Environmental Protection Agency (EPA) reports; patents; newsletters. **Subscriptions:** 600 journals and other serials; 15 newspapers. **Services:** Interlibrary loans; copying; SDI; center open to public by appointment. **Computerized Information Services:** DIALOG, CAS, New York Times Information Service, BRS, SDC, NLM, INFO, BI/DATA; internal database; computerized cataloging. **Networks/Consortia:** Member of Pittsburgh Regional Library Center. **Publications:** Acquisitions list, monthly - for internal distribution only. **Staff:** Betty Ann Schwarz, Info.Sci.; Josephine Quartey, Info.Ret.Spec.

★7828★
MERCK & COMPANY, INC. - KELCO DIVISION - LITERATURE AND INFORMATION SERVICES (Sci-Tech)
8355 Aero Dr.
San Diego, CA 92123

Phone: (714) 292-4900
Ann A. Jenkins, Mgr.

Staff: Prof 2; Other 3. **Subjects:** Chemistry, microbiology, food, industrial applications of polysaccharides, rheology, biochemistry, marine botany. **Holdings:** 2500 books; periodicals in microform and bound volumes; patents; reprints; photographs; pamphlets; internal research records. **Services:** Interlibrary loans (limited); copying. **Computerized Information Services:** DIALOG, BRS, SDC; internal databases. **Publications:** Monthly patent bulletin - for internal distribution only; SDI profiles; monthly scientific information bulletin; literature surveys; bibliographies. **Staff:** Susan J. Shepherd, Info.Spec.

★7829★
MERCK & COMPANY, INC. - LAW LIBRARY (Law)
Box 2000
Rahway, NJ 07065

Phone: (201) 574-5805
Elizabeth H. Penman, Libn.

Founded: 1959. **Staff:** Prof 1; Other 1. **Subjects:** Law, patents, trademarks, copyright. **Holdings:** 11,500 books; 300 bound periodical volumes. **Subscriptions:** 231 journals and other serials. **Services:** Library not open to public.

★7830★
MERCK & COMPANY, INC. - MERCK SHARP & DOHME RESEARCH LABORATORIES - LITERATURE RESOURCES (Sci-Tech)
Rahway, NJ 07065

Phone: (201) 574-6713
Jerome E. Holtz, Mgr.

Founded: 1933. **Staff:** Prof 4; Other 6. **Subjects:** Chemistry, biochemistry, pharmacology, biomedical sciences, science and technology. **Holdings:** 46,000 books and bound periodical volumes; 1000 reels of U.S. chemical patents on microfilm; 25 periodicals on microfilm. **Subscriptions:** 800 journals and other serials. **Services:** Interlibrary loans. **Computerized Information Services:** Online systems. **Networks/Consortia:** Member of OCLC through PALINET & Union Library Catalogue of Pennsylvania. **Staff:** Helen Hester, Res.Libn.; Ilona Giedrys, Res.Libn.; Pat Levan, Assoc.Libn.

★7831★
MERCK & COMPANY, INC. - MERCK SHARP & DOHME RESEARCH LABORATORIES - LITERATURE RESOURCES (Sci-Tech)
West Point, PA 19486

Phone: (215) 661-6026
Karen J. Messick, Supv.

Founded: 1921. **Staff:** Prof 1; Other 6. **Subjects:** Organic chemistry, biochemistry, immunology, pharmacology, medicine. **Holdings:** 3000 books; 20,000 bound periodical volumes; 2000 reels of microfilm. **Subscriptions:** 1000 journals and other serials. **Services:** Interlibrary loans; library open to medical and allied professions. **Computerized Information Services:** Online systems. **Networks/Consortia:** Member of OCLC through PALINET and Union Library Catalogue of Pennsylvania.

★7832★
MERCK & COMPANY, INC. - MERCK SHARP & DOHME RESEARCH LABORATORIES - RESEARCH INFORMATION SYSTEMS (Sci-Tech)
126 E. Lincoln Ave.
Rahway, NJ 07065

Phone: (201) 574-4726
Arlene C. Peterson, Mgr., Res.Info.Sys.

Founded: 1938. **Staff:** Prof 6; Other 11. **Subjects:** Chemistry, biology, medicine, pharmaceuticals, veterinary medicine. **Holdings:** Unpublished research reports; manuscripts. **Services:** Information center not open to public. **Computerized Information Services:** Internal database. **Special Indexes:** Computer-stored subject and contact indexes. **Staff:** Jacqueline Algon, Sr.Pubn.Coord.; Frances Keresztesy, Sect.Hd., Res.Info.; Mary Schulz, Group Leader; Paula Heck, Sr.Res.Info.Anl.; Mary Carol Scully, Info.Anl.

★7833★
MERCK FROSST LABORATORIES - RESEARCH LIBRARY (Med)
P.O. Box 1005   Phone: (514) 695-7920
Pointe Claire-Dorval, PQ, Canada H9R 4P8   Claire B. Kelly, Res.Libn.
Founded: 1937. **Staff:** Prof 1; Other 1. **Subjects:** Medicine, chemistry, pharmacy, general science, radioisotopes. **Holdings:** 2000 books; 25,000 bound periodical volumes. **Subscriptions:** 250 journals and other serials. **Services:** Interlibrary loans; copying; library not open to public. **Computerized Information Services:** MEDLARS, DIALOG. **Publications:** Monthly Library Bulletin.

MERCK SHARP & DOHME RESEARCH LABORATORIES
See: Merck & Company, Inc.

★7834★
MERCURY ARCHIVES (Pict)
1574 Crossroads of the World   Phone: (213) 463-8000
Hollywood, CA 90028   Herbert L. Kornfeld, Dir.
Staff: 2. **Special Collections:** 1850-1900 steel and wood engravings on all subjects (1 million). **Holdings:** 5000 books; 500 bound periodical volumes. **Services:** Archives open to public by appointment. **Special Indexes:** Index to pictures in books (card). **Staff:** Joelle McGonagle, Cur.

★7835★
MERCY CATHOLIC MEDICAL CENTER - HEALTH SCIENCES LIBRARY (Med)
Lansdowne & Baily Rd.   Phone: (215) 586-2050
Darby, PA 19023   Janet Clinton, Chf. of Lib.Serv.
Founded: 1933. **Staff:** Prof 1; Other 5. **Subjects:** Medicine, nursing, surgery and allied health sciences, psychiatry, religion and medical ethics. **Holdings:** 4500 books; 6000 bound periodical volumes; 278 folders of pamphlets, bibliographies, unbound reports, video cassettes, audio cassettes, filmstrips and slides. **Subscriptions:** 300 journals. **Services:** Interlibrary loans; copying; libraries open to public for reference use only. **Networks/Consortia:** Member of Consortium for Health Information and Library Services; Mideastern Regional Medical Library Service (MERMLS). **Remarks:** Mercy Catholic Medical Center Health Sciences Libraries are administered as one collection. The larger collection is located at the Fitzgerald Mercy Division in Darby, PA, with a core collection at the Misericordia Division, 54th & Cedar Ave., Philadelphia, PA 19143.

★7836★
MERCY CENTER FOR HEALTH CARE SERVICES - MEDICAL LIBRARY (Med)
1325 N. Highland Ave.   Phone: (312) 859-2222
Aurora, IL 60506   Mary P. Murray, Libn.
Founded: 1965. **Staff:** Prof 2; Other 2. **Subjects:** Medicine, psychiatry, nursing. **Holdings:** 6300 books; 216 bound periodical volumes; 12 VF drawers of pamphlets; 400 audiovisual items. **Subscriptions:** 260 journals and other serials. **Services:** Interlibrary loans; copying; library open to public. **Networks/Consortia:** Member of Fox Valley Health Science Library Consortium.

★7837★
MERCY HEALTH CENTER - ANTHONY C. PFOHL HEALTH SCIENCE LIBRARY (Med)
Mercy Dr.   Phone: (319) 589-8000
Dubuque, IA 52001   James H. Lander, Lib.Mgr.
Founded: 1973. **Staff:** Prof 2; Other 3. **Subjects:** Medicine, patient education, management. **Holdings:** 5000 monographs; 250 bound periodical volumes; 1500 pamphlets (65 titles); AV software; 10 anatomical charts, graphs. **Subscriptions:** 220 journals and other serials. **Services:** Interlibrary loans; library open to public. **Computerized Information Services:** BRS. **Networks/Consortia:** Member of Dubuque Area Library Consortium. **Publications:** New Holdings, monthly - for internal distribution only; Library Lines, bimonthly. **Special Catalogs:** Tri-Hospital Library Catalog (AV only); Union List of Serials (consortia list). **Remarks:** Contains the holdings of the former Xavier Hospital - Doctor's Library.

★7838★
MERCY HEALTH CENTER - MEDICAL LIBRARY (Med)
4300 W. Memorial Rd.   Phone: (405) 755-1515
Oklahoma City, OK 73118   Sr. Mary Eileen Durnell, Hd.Libn.
Founded: 1947. **Staff:** Prof 2; Other 1. **Subjects:** Medicine, nursing, allied health sciences. **Holdings:** 728 books; 3560 bound periodical volumes.

Subscriptions: 179 journals and other serials. **Services:** Interlibrary loans; copying; library open to public for reference use only. **Computerized Information Services:** MEDLINE; computerized serials. **Networks/Consortia:** Member of Greater Oklahoma City Area Health Sciences Library Consortium (GOAL). **Staff:** May Whelpley, Libn.

★7839★
MERCY HOSPITAL - EDWARD L. BURNS HEALTH SCIENCES LIBRARY (Med)
2200 Jefferson Ave.   Phone: (419) 259-1327
Toledo, OH 43624   Thomas R. Sink, Dir. of Lib.Serv.
Founded: 1940. **Staff:** Prof 1; Other 2. **Subjects:** Medicine, nursing, and allied health sciences. **Holdings:** 6000 volumes; AV and VF items. **Subscriptions:** 120 journals and other serials. **Services:** Interlibrary loans; copying; library open to public with restrictions. **Computerized Information Services:** MEDLINE. **Networks/Consortia:** Member of Health Science Librarians of Northwest Ohio; Kentucky-Ohio-Michigan Regional Medical Libraries (KOMRML).

★7840★
MERCY HOSPITAL - HEALTH SCIENCES LIBRARY (Med)
144 State St.   Phone: (207) 774-1461
Portland, ME 04101   Mary Jane Geer, Libn.
Founded: 1956. **Subjects:** Medicine, surgery, nursing. **Special Collections:** CIBA Collection of Medical Illustration (1855 slides). **Holdings:** 750 books. **Subscriptions:** 85 journals and other serials. **Services:** Interlibrary loans; copying; library open to selected college and paramedical students. **Networks/Consortia:** Member of Health Science Library and Information Cooperative of Maine; Health and Medical Information Cooperative of Southern Maine.

★7841★
MERCY HOSPITAL - HEALTH SCIENCES LIBRARY (Med)
1500 E. Sherman Blvd.   Phone: (616) 739-9341
Muskegon, MI 49443   Jean Parker, Libn.
Founded: 1950. **Staff:** Prof 1; Other 1. **Subjects:** Medicine, nursing, allied health sciences. **Holdings:** 600 books; 3275 bound periodical volumes; 300 pamphlets. **Subscriptions:** 143 journals and other serials. **Services:** Interlibrary loans; copying; library not open to public. **Computerized Information Services:** MEDLINE.

★7842★
MERCY HOSPITAL - HEALTH SERVICES LIBRARY (Med)
701 Tenth St., S.E.   Phone: (319) 398-6165
Cedar Rapids, IA 52403   Linda Miller, Libn.
Founded: 1970. **Staff:** Prof 1; Other 1. **Subjects:** Medicine, nursing, hospital administration. **Holdings:** 2200 books; 2500 bound periodical volumes; 8 VF drawers of clippings and pamphlets. **Subscriptions:** 300 journals and other serials; 6 newspapers. **Services:** Interlibrary loans; copying; SDI; library open to public with referral from a librarian. **Computerized Information Services:** BRS, DIALOG. **Networks/Consortia:** Member of Cedar Rapids Area Cooperative; Regional Medical Library - Region 3; Linn County Library Consortium.

★7843★
MERCY HOSPITAL - LEVITT HEALTH SCIENCES LIBRARY (Med)
1165 5th Ave.   Phone: (515) 247-4189
Des Moines, IA 50314   Lenetta Atkins, Libn.
Founded: 1960. **Staff:** Prof 1; Other 2. **Subjects:** Health sciences. **Holdings:** 2097 books; 121 bound periodical volumes; 96 filmstrips; 61 slides, tapes, film loops; 8 16mm sound filmstrips. **Subscriptions:** 128 journals and other serials. **Services:** Interlibrary loans; copying; library open to special classes or by doctor recommendation. **Networks/Consortia:** Member of Polk County Biomedical Consortium. **Staff:** Deloras Sloan, Asst.Libn.

★7844★
MERCY HOSPITAL - LIBRARY (Med)
1400 W. Park St.   Phone: (217) 337-2283
Urbana, IL 61801   Harriet Williamson, Dir.
Staff: Prof 1; Other 1. **Subjects:** Clinical medicine, nursing, allied health sciences. **Holdings:** 1000 books; 150 bound periodical volumes; 500 unbound periodicals; 6 archival boxes of material. **Subscriptions:** 175 journals and other serials; 7 newspapers. **Services:** Interlibrary loans; copying; SDI; literature searches; library open to public for reference use only. **Computerized Information Services:** MEDLARS, DIALOG, BRS; CLSI (internal database); computerized cataloging. **Networks/Consortia:** Member of OCLC through ILLINET; Regional Medical Library - Region 3; Champaign-Urbana Consortium.

★7845★

MERCY HOSPITAL - MC GLANNAN MEMORIAL LIBRARY (Med)
301 St. Paul Pl.   Phone: (301) 727-5400
Baltimore, MD 21202   Eileen W. Gillis, Libn.
Staff: 2. **Subjects:** Medicine and medical specialties. **Special Collections:** Rare books on medical subjects. **Holdings:** 3850 books; 5750 bound periodical volumes; 6 VF drawers of pamphlets and reprints. **Subscriptions:** 145 journals and other serials; 6 newspapers. **Services:** Interlibrary loans; copying; library not open to public.

★7846★

MERCY HOSPITAL AND MEDICAL CENTER - JEAN FARB MEDICAL LIBRARY (Med)
4077 Fifth Ave.   Phone: (714) 294-8024
San Diego, CA 92103   Anna M. Habetler, Lib.Dir.
Staff: Prof 1; Other 3. **Subjects:** Medicine, nursing, basic sciences, hospital management, psychology and psychiatry. **Holdings:** 1457 books; 4800 bound periodical volumes. **Subscriptions:** 429 journals and other serials. **Services:** Interlibrary loans; copying; library open to health professionals and students for reference use only. **Computerized Information Services:** BRS, MEDLARS.

★7847★

MERCY HOSPITAL & MEDICAL CENTER - MEDICAL LIBRARY (Med)
2510 S. King Dr.   Phone: (312) 567-2364
Chicago, IL 60616   Timothy T. Oh, Dir. of Lib.
Founded: 1940. **Staff:** Prof 1; Other 3. **Subjects:** Medicine, surgery, pediatrics, obstetrics-gynecology, radiology, pathology. **Holdings:** 5800 books; 7200 bound periodical volumes; 620 AV items (cataloged). **Subscriptions:** 385 journals and other serials. **Services:** Interlibrary loans; copying; library open to public for reference use only. **Computerized Information Services:** MEDLINE. **Networks/Consortia:** Member of Regional Medical Library - Region 3; Chicago Metropolitan Consortium. **Special Catalogs:** Audiovisual Resources (book); Serial Holdings List (book).

★7848★

MERCY HOSPITAL - MEDICAL & HOSPITAL INSERVICE LIBRARIES (Med)†
233 Carew St.   Phone: (413) 781-9100
Springfield, MA 01104   Mary G. Manning, Libn.
Staff: Prof 1. **Subjects:** Medicine, nursing and allied health services. **Holdings:** 1939 books and bound periodical volumes. **Subscriptions:** 81 journals and other serials. **Services:** Interlibrary loans; copying; literature searches; libraries open to area college students.

★7849★

MERCY HOSPITAL - MEDICAL LIBRARY (Med)
2215 Truxtun Ave.   Phone: (805) 327-3371
Bakersfield, CA 93301   Melanie Nathan, Med.Libn.
Staff: 1. **Subjects:** Medicine, gastroenterology, pediatrics, surgery, physical therapy, internal medicine. **Holdings:** 368 books; 451 bound periodical volumes; 5 boxes of Hospital Abstract Service materials. **Subscriptions:** 110 journals and other serials. **Services:** Interlibrary loans; copying; SDI; library open to public for reference use only. **Computerized Information Services:** MEDLINE **Networks/Consortia:** Member of 49-99 Cooperative Library System; Central California Medical Library Group; Kern Health Sciences Library Consortium.

★7850★

MERCY HOSPITAL - MEDICAL LIBRARY (Med)†
3663 S. Miami Ave.
Miami, FL 33133   Phone: (305) 854-4400
                                                  Cornelia C. Pope, Libn.
Founded: 1954. **Staff:** Prof 1; Other 1. **Subjects:** Cardiology, internal medicine, nursing. **Holdings:** 1500 books; 4000 bound periodical volumes; 200 video cassettes; 2500 cassettes; pamphlets; videotapes; audiotapes; slide-tape synchronizations. **Subscriptions:** 213 journals and other serials. **Services:** Interlibrary loans; copying; SDI; library open to public with restrictions. **Computerized Information Services:** MEDLARS. **Networks/Consortia:** Member of Miami Health Sciences Library Consortium. **Publications:** Newsletter; journal holdings list.

★7851★

MERCY HOSPITAL - MEDICAL LIBRARY (Med)†
565 Abbott Rd.
Buffalo, NY 14220   Phone: (716) 826-7000
                                                  Linda S. Karch, Libn.
Staff: Prof 1; Other 1. **Subjects:** Medicine, nursing and allied health sciences. **Special Collections:** Research Symposium Collection, 1968 to present. **Holdings:** 2300 books; 5500 bound periodical volumes; 2500 AV cassettes, films, tapes. **Subscriptions:** 150 journals and other serials. **Services:** Interlibrary loans; copying; library open to students for reference service by request. **Networks/Consortia:** Member of Western New York Health

Sciences Librarians; Western New York Library Resources Council.

★7852★

MERCY HOSPITAL - MEDICAL LIBRARY (Med)
746 Jefferson Ave.   Phone: (717) 348-7800
Scranton, PA 18510   Sr. Elizabeth Anne Brandreth, Libn.
Staff: Prof 2. **Subjects:** Medicine and allied health sciences. **Holdings:** 2265 books; 2872 bound periodical volumes; 1907 microfiche. **Subscriptions:** 190 journals and other serials. **Services:** Interlibrary loans; copying; library open to public for reference use only. **Computerized Information Services:** MEDLARS. **Networks/Consortia:** Member of Health Information Library Network of Northeastern Pennsylvania. **Staff:** Eloise Bartosh, Asst.Libn.

★7853★

MERCY HOSPITAL - MEDICAL LIBRARY (Med)
25 Church St.   Phone: (717) 826-3699
Wilkes-Barre, PA 18765   Barbara Nanstiel, Dir. of Lib.Serv.
Staff: Prof 1; Other 1. **Subjects:** Medicine, nursing, hospital administration. **Holdings:** 1600 books; 750 journal volumes on microfilm; 450 Audio-Digest cassettes; 440 other AV items (cataloged). **Subscriptions:** 185 journals and other serials. **Services:** Interlibrary loans; copying; SDI; library open to qualified users. **Computerized Information Services:** MEDLARS. **Networks/Consortia:** Member of Health Information Library Network of Northeast Pennsylvania. **Staff:** Sr. Ann Marie Austin, R.S.M., Asst.Libn.

★7854★

MERCY HOSPITAL - MEDICAL LIBRARY (Med)
1000 Mineral Point   Phone: (608) 756-6749
Janesville, WI 53545   Lois J. Zuehlke, Lib.Dir.
Founded: 1925. **Subjects:** Medicine. **Special Collections:** Nursing Service Library (500 books and journals). **Holdings:** 756 books; 70 bound periodical volumes. **Subscriptions:** 35 journals and other serials. **Services:** Interlibrary loans; copying; library open to public for reference use only. **Networks/Consortia:** Member of Southeastern Wisconsin Health Science Library Consortium.

★7855★

MERCY HOSPITAL - MEDICAL/NURSING LIBRARY (Med)
1000 N. Village Ave.   Phone: (516) 255-2255
Rockville Centre, NY 11570   Carol L. Reid, Med./Nursing Libn.
Staff: Prof 1; Other 1. **Subjects:** Medicine, surgery, nursing. **Holdings:** 1983 books; 2850 bound periodical volumes; 1100 audio cassette tapes. **Subscriptions:** 151 journals and other serials. **Services:** Interlibrary loans; copying; library open to public by appointment. **Networks/Consortia:** Member of Long Island Library Resources Council (LILRC).

★7856★

MERCY HOSPITAL - MEDICAL STAFF LIBRARY (Med)†
Pride & Locust Sts.   Phone: (412) 232-7520
Pittsburgh, PA 15219   Suzanne A. Gabarry, Libn.
Founded: 1921. **Staff:** Prof 1; Other 4. **Subjects:** Internal medicine, surgery, surgical specialties, anesthesia, obstetrics, pediatrics. **Holdings:** 3000 books; 9000 bound periodical volumes; Audio-Digest tapes. **Subscriptions:** 215 journals and other serials. **Services:** Interlibrary loans; copying; library not open to public. **Computerized Information Services:** MEDLINE. **Networks/Consortia:** Member of Mideastern Regional Medical Library Service (MERMLS); Pittsburgh-East Hospital Library Cooperative. **Publications:** Latest from the Library, bimonthly.

★7857★

MERCY HOSPITAL OF NEW ORLEANS - MEDICAL LIBRARY (Med)†
301 N. Jefferson Davis Pkwy.   Phone: (504) 486-7361
New Orleans, LA 70119   Jean Leonard, Med.Libn.
Staff: Prof 1. **Subjects:** Medicine, nursing, management. **Holdings:** 907 books; 500 bound periodical volumes. **Subscriptions:** 55 journals and other serials. **Services:** Interlibrary loans; copying; library open to public with permission of librarian.

★7858★

MERCY HOSPITAL, INC. - NURSING LIBRARY (Med)
301 St. Paul Pl.   Phone: (301) 332-9228
Baltimore, MD 21202   Dolores H. Kaisler, Libn.
Founded: 1901. **Staff:** Prof 1; Other 1. **Subjects:** Nursing and related subjects. **Holdings:** 4073 books; 1305 bound periodical volumes; 16 VF drawers; 980 pamphlets. **Subscriptions:** 102 journals and other serials. **Services:** Interlibrary loans; library open to public with restrictions.

★7859★
MERCY HOSPITAL - SCHOOL OF NURSING LIBRARY (Med)
2621 8th Ave.   Phone: (814) 944-1681
Altoona, PA 16602   Patricia Shirley, Libn.
Founded: 1935. Staff: Prof 1. Subjects: Nursing, medicine, natural sciences, psychology, sociology, education. Holdings: 3161 books; 929 bound periodical volumes; 7 VF drawers and 15 boxes of pamphlets and clippings. Subscriptions: 42 journals and other serials. Services: Interlibrary loans; library open to public.

★7860★
MERCY HOSPITAL - SCHOOL OF NURSING LIBRARY (Med)
1401 Blvd. of the Allies   Phone: (412) 232-7963
Pittsburgh, PA 15219   Veronica C. Harrison, Libn.
Founded: 1920. Staff: Prof 2. Subjects: Nursing, medicine, religion, psychology, sociology, ethics. Holdings: 4360 books; 1327 bound periodical volumes; 9 VF drawers of archival material, history of the school and Mercy Hospital; AV materials. Subscriptions: 93 journals and other serials. Services: Interlibrary loans; copying; library open to public with approval of librarian. Publications: Acquisitions Lists, monthly; Current Periodical Bibliography Lists, monthly. Staff: Sr. Gertrude Butler, Asst.Libn.

★7861★
MERCY HOSPITAL - SCHOOL OF NURSING - LIBRARY (Med)
520 Jefferson Ave.   Phone: (717) 344-8571
Scranton, PA 18501   Marie McAndrew, Libn.
Staff: Prof 1; Other 1. Subjects: Nursing, medicine, sociology, psychology. Holdings: 6500 books and bound periodical volumes; National League for Nursing publications. Subscriptions: 61 journals and other serials. Services: Interlibrary loans; copying; library open to public with restrictions. Networks/Consortia: Member of Health Information Library Network of Northeast Pennsylvania (HILNNEP). Special Catalogs: Union List of Serials - biennial.

★7862★
MERCY HOSPITAL OF WATERTOWN - HEALTH SCIENCE LIBRARY (Med)
218 Stone St.   Phone: (315) 782-7400
Watertown, NY 13601   Jeffrey M. Garvey, Libn.
Founded: 1970. Staff: Prof 1; Other 1. Subjects: Medicine, nursing, mental health, hospital management. Holdings: 2100 books; 4000 bound periodical volumes; 800 AV items; 1 VF drawer of pamphlets (uncataloged); 82 reels of microfilm. Subscriptions: 200 journals and other serials. Services: Interlibrary loans; copying; SDI; library open to public. Networks/Consortia: Member of North Country Research and Reference Resources; Northern New York Health Information Cooperative; Health Resources Council of Central New York. Publications: Mercy Hospital Library Newsletter, quarterly - by request.

★7863★
MERCY MEDICAL CENTER - HEALTH SCIENCES LIBRARY (Med)
1343 Fountain   Phone: (513) 390-5000
Springfield, OH 45501   Marietta Wilson, Libn.
Founded: 1952. Staff: 1. Subjects: Clinical medicine and related subjects. Holdings: 800 books; 1000 bound periodical volumes; 300 pamphlets. Subscriptions: 125 journals and other serials. Services: Interlibrary loans; library open to students and research workers. Computerized Information Services: NLM, BRS. Networks/Consortia: Member of Miami Valley Association of Health Science Libraries.

★7864★
MERCY MEDICAL CENTER - LIBRARY AND MEDIA RESOURCES DEPARTMENT (Med)
1619 Milwaukee St.   Phone: (303) 393-3296
Denver, CO 80206   Rosalind Dudden, Dir. of Lib.Serv.
Founded: 1936. Staff: Prof 1; Other 1. Subjects: Medicine, nursing. Holdings: 1200 books; 1400 bound periodical volumes. Subscriptions: 181 journals and other serials. Services: Interlibrary loans; copying; SDI; library open to health professionals. Networks/Consortia: Member of Colorado Council of Medical Librarians.

★7865★
MERCY NORTH HOSPITAL - HEALTH SCIENCES LIBRARY (Med)
116 Dayton St.   Phone: (513) 867-6458
Hamilton, OH 45011   Frances McCullough, Libn.
Founded: 1956. Staff: Prof 1. Subjects: Medicine, nursing, hospital administration, allied health sciences. Holdings: 5000 books; 830 bound periodical volumes; 16 VF drawers of pamphlets, clippings; films, slides, filmstrips, charts, models, records. Subscriptions: 250 journals and other serials. Services: Interlibrary loans; copying; library open to public for reference use only. Publications: List of acquisitions, irregular - for internal distribution only.

★7866★
MERCY REGIONAL MEDICAL CENTER LIBRARY (Med)
100 McAuley Dr.
Box 271   Phone: (601) 636-2131
Vicksburg, MS 39180   Frances Betts, Libn.
Founded: 1900. Staff: Prof 2; Other 1. Subjects: Medicine, surgery, obstetrics, gynecology, allied fields. Special Collections: Rare medical books. Holdings: 712 books; 3532 periodical volumes (bound and unbound). Subscriptions: 60 journals and other serials; 12 newspapers. Services: Interlibrary loans; copying; library open to public with restrictions. Networks/Consortia: Member of Central Mississippi Council of Medical Libraries; Southeastern Regional Medical Library Program (SERMLP). Publications: Echoes of Mercy, 3/year. Staff: Becky McCormick, Asst.Libn.

★7867★
MERCY SCHOOL OF NURSING OF DETROIT - LIBRARY (Med)
660 Clinton St.   Phone: (313) 923-5700
Detroit, MI 48226   Mary Jo Wyels, Libn.
Staff: Prof 1. Subjects: Nursing, surgery, pediatrics, behavioral sciences. Holdings: 2117 books; 15 bound periodical volumes. Subscriptions: 40 journals and other serials. Services: Interlibrary loans; copying; library not open to public. Computerized Information Services: MEDLINE.

★7868★
MERCY SCHOOL OF NURSING - E.O. MORROW LIBRARY (Med)
1320 Timken Mercy Dr., N.W.   Phone: (216) 489-1140
Canton, OH 44708   Jane L. Clark, Dir.
Founded: 1940. Staff: Prof 1; Other 1. Subjects: Nursing, medicine. Holdings: 4444 books; 372 bound periodical volumes; 1300 AV items; 3 VF drawers of pamphlets and clippings. Subscriptions: 65 journals and other serials. Services: Interlibrary loans; copying; library open to public for reference use only with permission from director. Computerized Information Services: BRS; computerized cataloging. Networks/Consortia: Member of Northeastern Ohio Universities, College of Medicine (NEOUCOM).

★7869★
MERCY SCHOOL OF NURSING - LIBRARY (Med)
1921 Vail Ave.   Phone: (704) 379-5845
Charlotte, NC 28207   Barbara Duval, Libn.
Staff: Prof 1; Other 1. Subjects: Nursing, medicine. Holdings: 4705 books; 430 bound periodical volumes; 114 AV titles; 4 VF drawers. Subscriptions: 74 journals and other serials. Services: Interlibrary loans; copying; library open to public for reference use only.

★7870★
MERCYHURST COLLEGE - LEARNING RESOURCE CENTER - ARCHIVES (Hist)
501 E. 38th St.   Phone: (814) 825-4000
Erie, PA 16546   Joanne S. Cooper, Dir.
Staff: Prof 3; Other 4. Subjects: Mercyhurst College Archives; Erie County - industries, societies, history and churches; ethnic history. Special Collections: Erie County Commissioners' Records, 1937-1971 (15 cartons); Erie County Government Study Commission Collection 1972-1976 (12 legal-size boxes); oral history tape collection (175 cassettes). Holdings: 595 books; 193 bound periodical volumes; 265 accessions; 3 files of oversize maps, charts, blueprints; 247 reels of microfilm; 2240 slides. Services: Interlibrary loans (limited); copying; archives open to public. Networks/Consortia: Member of Northwest Interlibrary Cooperative of Pennsylvania; Interlibrary Delivery Service of Pennsylvania (IDS). Publications: Journal of Erie Studies, semiannual - to members of Erie County Historical Society. Staff: Sr. Mary Lawrence Franklin, Archv.; Judith Bradley, Ref., ILL; Richard Kubiak, Hist.

MERIAM LIBRARY
See: California State University, Chico

★7871★
MERIDEN-WALLINGFORD HOSPITAL - HEALTH SCIENCES LIBRARY (Med)
181 Cook Ave.   Phone: (203) 238-0771
Meriden, CT 06450   Patricia C. Westbrook, Libn.
Staff: Prof 1; Other 1. Subjects: Medicine, nursing. Holdings: 2082 books; 1037 bound periodical volumes; 6 VF drawers of pamphlets; 1000 AV items. Subscriptions: 107 journals and other serials. Services: Interlibrary loans; copying; library open to public for reference use only. Computerized Information Services: MEDLARS, MEDLINE. Networks/Consortia: Member of Connecticut Association of Health Science Libraries (CAHSL). Special Catalogs: Subject catalog of audiovisuals (book). Staff: Loretta Saviteer,

Asst.Libn.

MERRELL DOW PHARMACEUTICALS, INC.
See: Dow Chemical Company

★7872★
MERRIAM CENTER LIBRARY (Soc Sci)
Charles E. Merriam Center
for Public Administration
1313 E. 60th St.   Phone: (312) 947-2162
Chicago, IL 60637   Patricia Coatsworth, Hd.Libn.
Founded: 1932. **Staff:** Prof 3; Other 4. **Subjects:** Public administration, city
and regional planning, public finance, energy and the environment, criminal
justice, building and housing, land use. **Holdings:** 40,000 books; 1000 bound
periodical volumes; 150,000 pamphlets. **Subscriptions:** 1000 journals and
other serials. **Services:** Interlibrary loans; copying; library open to research
personnel. **Computerized Information Services:** DIALOG. **Networks/
Consortia:** Member of Metropolitan Chicago Library Assembly; ILLINET.
Publications: Recent Publications on governmental problems, bimonthly with
annual cumulation. **Remarks:** The Merriam Library serves the following
organizations housed at the Charles E. Merriam Center for Public
Administration: American Planning Association, American Public Works
Association, Council of Planning Librarians, International Association of
Assessing Officials, Public Administration Service, University of Chicago
Computation Center, and the Academy for Interscience Methodologies. **Staff:**
Sue Lannin, Ref.Libn.; Joseph Wilson, Cat.Libn.; Diane Rudall, Mng.Ed.

MERRIAM (Charles E.) CENTER LIBRARY
See: International Association of Assessing Officers - Research and
   Technical Services Dept.

★7873★
MERRICK COUNTY HISTORICAL MUSEUM - ARCHIVES (Hist)
                                         Phone: (308) 946-3309
Central City, NE 68826   T.C. Reeves, Pres.
Subjects: Local history. **Holdings:** 300 books; photographs; atlases;
newspapers since 1876. **Services:** Archives open to public with restrictions.
Publications: County History Book, 1981.

THE MERRILEES LIBRARY
See: Institute of Chartered Accountants of Ontario - The Merrilees
   Library

★7874★
MERRILL (Charles E.) PUBLISHING COMPANY - LIBRARY (Publ)
1300 Alum Creek Dr.   Phone: (614) 258-8441
Columbus, OH 43216   Marcia Earnest, Libn.
Staff: 1. **Subjects:** Textbooks, state and local curriculum guides. **Holdings:**
7500 books; 4 VF drawers in information file; 3 VF drawers in state and
country file; 1 VF drawer of newsletters; 2 VF drawers in photo source file; 3
VF drawers of publishers' catalogs. **Services:** Library not open to public.

★7875★
MERRILL LYNCH PIERCE FENNER & SMITH, INC. - LIBRARY (Bus-Fin)
One Liberty Plaza
165 Broadway   Phone: (212) 637-7420
New York, NY 10080   Rita A. Hughes, Chf. Libn.
Founded: 1941. **Staff:** Prof 3; Other 15. **Subjects:** Industries, economics,
commodities, business, investment. **Holdings:** 8000 books; microfiche
(corporate files); 1100 feet of files. **Subscriptions:** 1300 journals and other
serials. **Services:** Library not open to public.

★7876★
MERRILL LYNCH WHITE WELD - CAPITAL MARKETS GROUP - LIBRARY
(Bus-Fin)
One Liberty Plaza, 42nd Fl.   Phone: (212) 637-2085
New York, NY 10080   Eva Vanek, Mgr., Lib.Serv.
Founded: 1978. **Staff:** Prof 5; Other 9. **Subjects:** Finance - corporate,
municipal, international. **Holdings:** 750 books; 200 bound periodical volumes;
7000 corporate files (7000 companies); Securities and Exchange Commission
(SEC) files on microfiche; 25 VF drawers of general business and corporate
finance information; 300 reels of microfilm. **Subscriptions:** 350 journals and
other serials and newspapers. **Services:** Interlibrary loans; library not open to
public. **Computerized Information Services:** DIALOG, New York Times
Information Service, BRS, NEXIS; New Issues (internal database);
computerized serials. **Remarks:** This organization is part of Merrill Lynch &
Company, Inc. **Staff:** Alice Scherer, Libn.; Rita Schaffer, Libn.; Jill Weinstein,
Libn., Intl.; Susan Adinolfi, Database Mgr.

★7877★
MERRILL-PALMER INSTITUTE - EDNA NOBLE WHITE LIBRARY
71 E. Ferry Ave.
Detroit, MI 48202
Defunct

★7878★
MERRILL-PALMER INSTITUTE - KRESGE HISTORICAL LIBRARY
71 E. Ferry Ave.
Detroit, MI 48202
Defunct. Merged into Institute of Gerontology - Gerontology Learning
Resources Center.

★7879★
MERRIMACK VALLEY TEXTILE MUSEUM - LIBRARY (Sci-Tech)
800 Massachusetts Ave.   Phone: (617) 686-0191
North Andover, MA 01845   Helena Wright, Libn.
Founded: 1960. **Staff:** Prof 3. **Subjects:** Textile technology and
manufacturing; water power. **Special Collections:** Archives of textile
businesses (1800 shelf feet); trade catalogs; cloth labels; insurance surveys.
Holdings: 35,000 books and bound periodical volumes; 25,000 maps, prints
and photographs; 150 audiovisual materials; 1800 feet of manuscripts.
Subscriptions: 20 journals and other serials. **Services:** Interlibrary loans;
copying; library open to public for reference use only. **Special Catalogs:**
Checklists of study collections, artifacts, manuscripts, prints, textiles.
Remarks: Holdings of the North Andover Historical Society are also housed in
the Museum Library. **Staff:** Eartha Dengler, Ser.; Patricia Markey, Cat.

★7880★
MERRITT (Samuel) HOSPITAL - MEDICAL LIBRARY (Med)
Hawthorne & Webster Sts.   Phone: (415) 655-4000
Oakland, CA 94609   Linda Charlmyra Thomas, Med.Libn.
Staff: Prof 1; Other 1. **Subjects:** Nursing, medicine, social science, education.
Holdings: 3200 books; 300 bound periodical volumes; 4 VF drawers of
pamphlets. **Subscriptions:** 183 journals and other serials. **Services:**
Interlibrary loans; copying; library not open to public. **Computerized
Information Services:** MEDLARS. **Networks/Consortia:** Member of Pacific
Southwest Regional Medical Library Service (PSRMLS). **Staff:** Ruth Leeper,
Lib.Asst.

★7881★
MERSHON, SAWYER, JOHNSTON, DUNWODY & COLE - LIBRARY (Law)
100 S. Biscayne Blvd., Suite 1600   Phone: (305) 358-5100
Miami, FL 33131   Jean Snyder, Libn.
Staff: Prof 1. **Subjects:** Law. **Holdings:** 14,000 books; 200 bound periodical
volumes; 19 binders of law memoranda. **Subscriptions:** 245 journals and
other serials; 5 newspapers. **Services:** Library open to public with librarian's
permission. **Computerized Information Services:** LEXIS. **Special Catalogs:**
Memorandum of Law Catalog (card).

MERTLE LIBRARY
See: 3M

MERTON (Thomas) STUDIES CENTER
See: Bellarmine College - Thomas Merton Studies Center

MERYMAN LIBRARY OF AQUATIC RESEARCH
See: Fish Doctor Clinical Center, Inc.

★7882★
MESA COUNTY MEDICAL SOCIETY - DR. E.H. MUNRO MEDICAL LIBRARY
(Med)
St. Mary's Hospital & Medical Ctr.   Phone: (303) 244-2171
Grand Junction, CO 81501   Cynthia M. Tharaud, Med.Libn.
Staff: Prof 1; Other 1. **Subjects:** Medicine, nursing. **Holdings:** 783 books;
320 audio cassettes. **Subscriptions:** 161 journals and other serials.
Services: Interlibrary loans; copying; library open to allied health professionals
and nursing students. **Computerized Information Services:** MEDLARS.
Networks/Consortia: Member of Midcontinental Regional Medical Library
Program; Colorado Council of Medical Librarians.

★7883★
**MESA COUNTY VALLEY SCHOOL DISTRICT 51 - DEPARTMENT OF
RESOURCES, RESEARCH AND DEVELOPMENT** (Educ)
410 Hill Ave.   Phone: (303) 245-1788
Grand Junction, CO 81501   Tedd S. Brumbaugh, Dir.
Subjects: Education. **Special Collections:** Special services media materials.
Holdings: 5500 books. **Subscriptions:** 134 journals and other serials.
Networks/Consortia: Member of Pathfinder Library System.

MESA LIBRARY
See: National Center for Atmospheric Research

MESA VERDE NATL. PARK
See: U.S. Natl. Park Service

MESSIAH COLLEGE - BRETHREN IN CHRIST CHURCH
See: Brethren in Christ Church and Messiah College

MESSICK (John) LEARNING RESOURCE CENTER
See: Oral Roberts University - Graduate Theology Library - John Messick Learning Resource Center

MESSLER LIBRARY
See: Fairleigh Dickinson University

★7884★
METAL LATH/STEEL FRAMING ASSOCIATION - LIBRARY (Sci-Tech)
221 N. La Salle St. Phone: (312) 346-1600
Chicago, IL 60601 Durward Humes, Mng.Dir.
Subjects: Metal lathing and furring, light-gage steel framing. **Holdings:** Press releases, special reports, engineering data, slides and photographs. **Subscriptions:** 33 journals and other serials. **Services:** Information available to public.

METAL MATRIX INFORMATION ANALYSIS CENTER
See: Kaman-Tempo

★7885★
METAL POWDER INDUSTRIES FEDERATION - TECHNICAL INFORMATION CENTER (Sci-Tech)
105 College Rd., E. Phone: (609) 452-7700
Princeton, NJ 08540 Kempton H. Roll, Exec.Dir.
Founded: 1943. **Subjects:** Metal powders; powder metallurgy products, processes and equipment. **Holdings:** Books; periodicals; standards; slides; photographs. **Services:** Center not open to public. **Publications:** P/M Technology Newsletter, monthly; International Journal of Powder Metallurgy, quarterly.

METALLURGICAL AND MATERIALS LIBRARY
See: Combustion Engineering, Inc.

METALS AND CERAMICS INFORMATION CENTER
See: Battelle-Columbus Laboratories

METALS INFORMATION
See: American Society for Metals

★7886★
METASCIENCE FOUNDATION - LIBRARY (Rec)
Box 32 Phone: (401) 783-8683
Kingston, RI 02881 Marc Seifer, Dir.
Founded: 1970. **Staff:** Prof 3. **Subjects:** Parapsychology, graphology, palmistry, UFO, synchronicity, astrology, tarot. **Special Collections:** Rare books on occult sciences; Nikola Tesla (10 volumes); Gurdjieff and Ouspensky (10 volumes). **Holdings:** 400 books; 100 bound periodical volumes; research papers. **Subscriptions:** 10 journals and other serials. **Services:** Copying (fee); library open to public by appointment. **Publications:** MetaScience Quarterly. **Staff:** Monica Schaeffer, Libn.; Lois Pazienza, Libn.

METCALF (Clarence) RESEARCH LIBRARY
See: Great Lakes Historical Society - Clarence Metcalf Research Library

★7887★
METCALF & EDDY, INC. - LIBRARY (Env-Cons)
50 Staniford St. Phone: (617) 367-4087
Boston, MA 02114 Mary E. Lydon, Corp.Libn.
Founded: 1913. **Staff:** 2. **Subjects:** Environmental engineering. **Holdings:** 6000 books; 700 bound periodical volumes; trade catalogs; photographs. **Subscriptions:** 200 journals and other serials. **Services:** Interlibrary loans; library open to public by appointment. **Computerized Information Services:** SDC, DIALOG. **Publications:** New Book List, monthly; Company Reports.

★7888★
METCO INC. - ENGINEERING LIBRARY (Sci-Tech)
1101 Prospect Ave. Phone: (516) 334-1300
Westbury, NY 11590 Peter H. Leonard, Dir.
Founded: 1965. **Staff:** 3. **Subjects:** Engineering - chemical, ceramic, electrical, mechanical, metallurgical. **Holdings:** 610 volumes; standards;

handbooks; technical research and development reports. **Subscriptions:** 150 journals and other serials. **Services:** Interlibrary loans; copying; library not open to public. **Networks/Consortia:** Member of Long Island Library Resources Council (LILRC).

★7889★
METCUT RESEARCH ASSOCIATES, INC. - MACHINABILITY DATA CENTER (Sci-Tech)
3980 Rosslyn Dr. Phone: (513) 271-9510
Cincinnati, OH 45209 John F. Kahles, Dir.
Founded: 1964. **Staff:** Prof 6; Other 5. **Subjects:** Machinability, material removal, metallurgy, surface integrity. **Special Collections:** Metallurgical Technical File (6000 documents). **Holdings:** 1700 books; 97 bound periodical volumes; 35,000 documents. **Subscriptions:** 90 journals and other serials. **Services:** Interlibrary loans; literature searching; center open to public by appointment. **Computerized Information Services:** Mechanized retrieval. **Publications:** Machining Briefs; Machining Data Handbook; MDC Reports, irregular. **Special Indexes:** Machining and material removal document file. **Staff:** Susan M. Harvey, Corp.Libn.

METHODIST CHURCH
See: United Methodist Church...

METHODIST HISTORICAL COLLECTIONS
See: Southern Methodist University - Bridwell Library

★7890★
METHODIST HOSPITAL - HEALTH SCIENCES LIBRARY (Med)
506 6th St. Phone: (212) 780-3368
Brooklyn, NY 11215 Martha E. Lynch, Dir. of Libs.
Staff: Prof 2; Other 2. **Subjects:** Medicine, surgery, nursing and allied subjects. **Special Collections:** Methodist Hospital annual reports, 1887 to present. **Holdings:** 2300 books; 4033 bound periodical volumes; 352 videotapes; 104 slide/tape programs; 17 films; 5 audio cassette subject series. **Subscriptions:** 300 journals and other serials. **Services:** Interlibrary loans; copying; library not open to public. **Computerized Information Services:** MEDLINE. **Networks/Consortia:** Member of Medical Library Center of New York (MLCNY); New York State Interlibrary Loan Network (NYSILL). **Publications:** New Arrivals, weekly. **Staff:** June Burroughs, Asst.Med.Libn.

★7891★
METHODIST HOSPITAL OF INDIANA, INC. - LIBRARY SERVICES (Med)
1604 N. Capitol Ave. Phone: (317) 924-8021
Indianapolis, IN 46202 Joyce S. Allen, Lib.Mgr.
Founded: 1947. **Staff:** Prof 3; Other 5. **Subjects:** Medicine, nursing, administration, health education, recreation, psychology and allied health fields. **Holdings:** 8911 books; 3492 bound periodical volumes; 577 AV materials; 8 VF drawers of pamphlets; 16 audiotape journal subscriptions. **Subscriptions:** 867 journals and other serials. **Services:** Interlibrary loans; copying; SDI; LATCH; library open to public for reference use only. **Computerized Information Services:** MEDLINE, BRS. **Networks/Consortia:** Member of Central Indiana Health Sciences Consortium; Central Indiana Area Library Services Authority (CIALSA); INCOLSA. **Publications:** Library Handbook; Library Newsletter. **Special Catalogs:** Media Center Catalog (book). **Special Indexes:** Medical Information Systems Bibliography file (card). **Remarks:** Includes the holdings of the Professional Collection, Recreation Collection and Media Center. **Staff:** Gary B. Gray, Asst.Lib.Mgr./Media Ctr.; Christine Oler, Ref.Libn.

★7892★
METHODIST HOSPITAL - LIBRARY (Med)
2301 S. Broad St. Phone: (215) 952-9404
Philadelphia, PA 19148 Sara J. Richardson, Libn.
Staff: Prof 1; Other 1. **Subjects:** Nursing, medicine, hospital administration, pre-clinical sciences. **Holdings:** 2500 books; 100 bound periodical volumes; 6 VF drawers of pamphlets; 400 titles of AV software. **Subscriptions:** 171 journals and other serials. **Services:** Interlibrary loans; copying; library not open to public. **Computerized Information Services:** DIALOG. **Networks/Consortia:** Member of Mideastern Regional Medical Library Service (MERMLS). **Publications:** Booklist, bimonthly - for internal distribution only.

★7893★
METHODIST HOSPITAL - LIBRARY (Med)
309 W. Washington Ave.
Madison, WI 53703 Mary Alice Kuehling, Libn.
Staff: 1. **Subjects:** Medicine, nursing. **Holdings:** 1405 books; 1293 bound periodical volumes. **Subscriptions:** 143 journals and other serials. **Services:** Interlibrary loans; copying; library not open to public. **Networks/Consortia:** Member of South Central Wisconsin Health Planning Area Cooperative.

★7894★

METHODIST HOSPITAL - MEDICAL LIBRARY (Med)†
6500 Excelsior Blvd.   Phone: (612) 932-5451
St. Louis Park, MN 55426   Pearly Rudin, Med.Libn.
Founded: 1959. **Staff:** Prof 1; Other 1. **Subjects:** Clinical medicine, nursing. **Holdings:** 1500 books and bound periodical volumes. **Subscriptions:** 100 journals and other serials. **Services:** Interlibrary loans; copying; library open to medical personnel and other librarians. **Computerized Information Services:** MEDLINE. **Networks/Consortia:** Member of Twin Cities Biomedical Consortium (TCBC).

★7895★

METHODIST HOSPITAL AND SCHOOL OF NURSING - LIBRARY (Med)
3615 19th St.   Phone: (806) 793-4180
Lubbock, TX 79410   June Rayburn, Libn.
Founded: 1960. **Staff:** Prof 1; Other 2. **Subjects:** Medicine, nursing. **Holdings:** 3500 books; 4000 bound periodical volumes; 10 boxes of pamphlets; 14 VF drawers of information material. **Subscriptions:** 200 journals and other serials. **Services:** Interlibrary loans; copying; library open to public for reference use only.

★7896★

METHODIST HOSPITALS OF DALLAS - MEDICAL LIBRARY (Med)
301 W. Colorado   Phone: (214) 946-8181
Dallas, TX 75222   Mary J. Jarvis, Med.Libn.
Staff: Prof 1. **Subjects:** Medicine, nursing. **Holdings:** 1900 books; 3700 bound periodical volumes; 1000 medical cassette tapes; pamphlets; clippings; reports. **Subscriptions:** 165 journals and other serials. **Services:** Interlibrary loans; copying; library not open to public. **Computerized Information Services:** MEDLARS. **Networks/Consortia:** Member of Dallas-Tarrant County Consortium of Health Science Libraries; Metroplex Council of Health Science Librarians. **Remarks:** Library serves hospital's internship program and nursing staff as well as nursing classes from area's colleges.

METHODIST KAHLER LIBRARY
See: Rochester Methodist Hospital

★7897★

METHODIST MEDICAL CENTER OF ILLINOIS - LEARNING RESOURCE CENTER (Med)
221 N.E. Glen Oak   Phone: (309) 672-5570
Peoria, IL 61636   Dorothy Mortimer, Libn.
Founded: 1950. **Staff:** Prof 1; Other 2. **Subjects:** Nursing, nursing education. **Holdings:** 5000 books; 190 bound periodical volumes; 6 VF drawers of pamphlets; 4400 unbound periodicals; 350 AV items. **Subscriptions:** 100 journals and other serials. **Services:** Interlibrary loans; copying; center open to public with restrictions. **Networks/Consortia:** Member of Heart of Illinois Consortium; Regional Medical Library - Region 3; Illinois Valley Library System; Health Science Librarians of Illinois. **Publications:** Periodicals Holdings List, annual; Book Acquisitions List, bimonthly.

★7898★

METHODIST MEDICAL CENTER OF ILLINOIS - MEDICAL LIBRARY (Med)
221 N.E. Glen Oak   Phone: (309) 672-4937
Peoria, IL 61636   Trudy Landwirth, Dir.
Staff: Prof 2; Other 3. **Subjects:** Medicine. **Holdings:** 2000 books; 3500 bound periodical volumes. **Subscriptions:** 250 journals and other serials. **Services:** Interlibrary loans; copying; library not open to public. **Computerized Information Services:** MEDLARS, MEDLINE; computerized cataloging. **Networks/Consortia:** Member of Heart of Illinois Library Consortium; Illinois Valley Library System; OCLC. **Staff:** Brenda Grove, Asst.Med.Libn.

★7899★

METHODIST MEDICAL CENTER - SCHOOL OF NURSING LIBRARY (Med)
9th & Faraon Sts.   Phone: (816) 271-7280
St. Joseph, MO 64501   Sherril Garner, Libn.
Subjects: Nursing. **Holdings:** 4500 books. **Subscriptions:** 146 journals and other serials. **Services:** Interlibrary loans; copying; SDI; library open to public with permission of director.

★7900★

METHODIST THEOLOGICAL SCHOOL IN OHIO - JOHN W. DICKHAUT LIBRARY (Rel-Theol)
Box 1204   Phone: (614) 363-1146
Delaware, OH 43015   John B. McTaggart, Dir., Lib.Serv.
Staff: Prof 2; Other 3. **Subjects:** Religion, theology, Bible, church history. **Special Collections:** Irenaeus, Schleiermacher, Justin Martyr collections. **Holdings:** 80,000 volumes. **Subscriptions:** 325 journals and other serials; 8 newspapers. **Services:** Interlibrary loans; copying; library open to public.

Computerized Information Services: Computerized cataloging. **Staff:** M. Edward Hunter, Libn.

METRIC COMMISSION
See: Canada - Metric Commission

★7901★

METRO-GOLDWYN-MAYER, INC. - PICTURE RESEARCH LIBRARY (Art)
10202 W. Washington Blvd.   Phone: (213) 558-5518
Culver City, CA 90230   Bonnie Rothbart, Mgr.
Founded: 1925. **Staff:** Prof 1. **Subjects:** Architecture, costume, social life and customs. **Special Collections:** Trade catalogs; 19th-century illustrated periodicals; location photographs taken in connection with various movie productions. **Holdings:** 27,000 books; 3000 maps; 502 VF drawers of prints, photographs, clippings. **Subscriptions:** 60 journals and other serials. **Services:** Copying; research and reference service for independent motion picture and television companies available on a fee basis; library not open to public. **Special Indexes:** Index to illustrations and articles useful in motion picture and television production in current periodicals has been maintained for over thirty years.

★7902★

METROMEDIA INC. - CORPORATE RESEARCH LIBRARY (Bus-Fin)
205 E. 67th St.   Phone: (212) 682-9100
New York, NY 10021   Francine Holzer, Hd.Libn.
Founded: 1966. **Staff:** Prof 1. **Subjects:** Advertising, marketing, media research, television, radio, publishing. **Holdings:** 110 VF drawers of clippings, pamphlets, audience rating reports; government documents. **Subscriptions:** 100 journals and other serials. **Services:** Interlibrary loans; library not open to public.

METROPARKS ZOOLOGICAL PARK
See: Cleveland Metroparks Zoological Park

★7903★

METROPLAN, A COUNCIL OF GOVERNMENTS - PLANNING LIBRARY (Plan)
800 Wallace Bldg.
105 Main St.   Phone: (501) 372-3300
Little Rock, AR 72201   Joyce Messer, Dir., Finance/Adm.
Founded: 1955. **Staff:** 19. **Subjects:** Planning, land use and controls, housing and urban renewal, land economics, social and economic planning, neighborhood studies, public administration and finance, community facilities, transportation, air and water quality. **Holdings:** 500 books; 250 past publication of Metroplan. **Subscriptions:** 7 newspapers. **Services:** Interlibrary loans; copying; library open to public. **Publications:** Metroplanner, monthly newspaper.

★7904★

METROPOLITAN ATLANTA RAPID TRANSIT AUTHORITY - LIBRARY
2200 Peachtree Summit
401 W. Peachtree St., N.E.
Atlanta, GA 30308
Founded: 1966. **Subjects:** Engineering, construction, transportation, urban planning. **Holdings:** 1500 books; 30 bound periodical volumes; 1200 other cataloged items; authority reports; minutes, resolutions and progress reports. **Remarks:** Presently inactive. **Also Known As:** MARTA.

★7905★

METROPOLITAN COUNCIL FOR EDUCATIONAL OPPORTUNITY - LIBRARY (Soc Sci)†
55 Dimock St.   Phone: (617) 427-1545
Roxbury, MA 02119   Marcus J. Mitchell, Pub.Rel.Dir.
Founded: 1966. **Staff:** Prof 1. **Subjects:** Quality integrated education, Afro-American history. **Special Collections:** 40 scrapbooks of clippings on Greater Boston school systems and Boston's desegregation case. **Holdings:** 1000 books; dissertations; 12 annual financial reports; 10 unpublished reports; films and photographs. **Subscriptions:** 20 journals and other serials; 10 newspapers. **Services:** Copying; library open to public. **Computerized Information Services:** Online systems; computerized cataloging. **Publications:** Images Newsletter, monthly; METCO Parent Handbook. **Special Catalogs:** Student enrollment, transportation and routes (both computer printouts).

★7906★

METROPOLITAN COUNCIL OF THE TWIN CITIES AREA - LIBRARY (Plan)
300 Metro Sq.   Phone: (612) 227-9421
St. Paul, MN 55101   Mary D. Adams, Libn.
Founded: 1963. **Staff:** Prof 1; Other 1. **Subjects:** Metropolitan planning in general and in the specific areas of transportation, housing, health, criminal

justice, parks and open space, water and sewers; local government and politics. **Holdings:** 1122 books; 3500 reports (cataloged); 15,000 planning reports and government documents; 6 VF drawers of clippings; 300 microfiche. **Subscriptions:** 250 journals and other serials; 8 newspapers. **Services:** Interlibrary loans; copying; library open to public for reference use only. **Computerized Information Services:** DIALOG; computerized cataloging and circulation. **Publications:** Recent Additions to the Library, monthly - for internal distribution only.

★7907★
METROPOLITAN DADE COUNTY PLANNING DEPARTMENT - LIBRARY/INFORMATION CENTER (Plan)
909 S.E. 1st Ave., Suite 900   Phone: (305) 579-2869
Miami, FL 33131
Staff: Prof 1. **Subjects:** Dade County demographics, planning. **Special Collections:** Dade County Planning Department reports (275). **Holdings:** 700 books; 400 bound periodical volumes; 6500 soft cover reports (cataloged). **Subscriptions:** 140 journals and other serials. **Services:** Interlibrary loans; copying; library open to public for reference use only. **Publications:** Department publications list. **Special Catalogs:** Metropolitan Dade County Planning Department Publications (mimeo).

★7908★
METROPOLITAN EDISON COMPANY - SYSTEM LIBRARY (Sci-Tech; Bus-Fin)†
2800 Pottsville Pike   Phone: (215) 929-3601
Reading, PA 19605
Staff: Prof 1. **Subjects:** Engineering - electrical, environmental; business. **Special Collections:** Electric Power Research Institute Reports (720); Edison Electric Institute Reports (250); Pennsylvania Electric Association Minutes (85). **Holdings:** 1680 books; 150 bound periodical volumes; 52 films; 420 annual reports; topographic maps. **Subscriptions:** 400 journals and other serials; 5 newspapers. **Services:** Interlibrary loans; copying; library open to public with restrictions. **Computerized Information Services:** Computerized cataloging and serials. **Publications:** Library Bulletin, monthly.

★7909★
METROPOLITAN HOSPITAL CENTER - DRAPER HALL LIBRARY (Med)†
1918 First Ave.   Phone: (212) 360-6957
New York, NY 10029   Walter Klivcks, Libn.
Staff: Prof 1. **Subjects:** Nursing, medicine. **Holdings:** 2050 books; 300 bound periodical volumes; 10 VF drawers of pamphlets; 103 envelopes of clippings. **Services:** Library not open to public.

★7910★
METROPOLITAN HOSPITAL CENTER - FREDERICK M. DEARBORN MEDICAL LIBRARY (Med)†
1901 First Ave.   Phone: (212) 360-6270
New York, NY 10029   Vivienne Whitson, Chf.Libn.
Founded: 1894. **Staff:** Prof 2; Other 1. **Subjects:** Medicine and related fields. **Holdings:** 5630 books; 7800 bound periodical volumes; 150 pamphlets (cataloged); 800 Audio-Digest tapes. **Subscriptions:** 404 journals and other serials. **Services:** Interlibrary loans; copying; library not open to public. **Networks/Consortia:** Member of Manhattan-Bronx Consortium. **Publications:** Acquisitions List, quarterly - for internal distribution only.

★7911★
METROPOLITAN HOSPITAL - CENTRAL DIVISION LIBRARY (Med)
201 N. Eighth St.   Phone: (215) 238-2312
Philadelphia, PA 19106-1098   Marjorie Greenfield, Libn.
Staff: Prof 1. **Subjects:** Medicine, nursing, surgery. **Holdings:** 2200 books and bound periodical volumes; audio cassettes. **Subscriptions:** 100 journals and other serials. **Services:** Interlibrary loans; copying; library not open to public. **Networks/Consortia:** Member of Mideastern Regional Medical Library Service (MERMLS).

★7912★
METROPOLITAN HOSPITAL - MEDICAL LIBRARY (Med)
1800 Tuxedo Ave.   Phone: (313) 869-3600
Detroit, MI 48206   William F. McQueen, Med.Libn.
Founded: 1955. **Staff:** Prof 1. **Subjects:** Medicine, nursing, alcohol, patient education, hospital administration. **Holdings:** 2010 books; 4490 bound periodical volumes; 51 reels of microfilm; 945 audio cassettes; 49 microfiche. **Subscriptions:** 287 journals and other serials. **Services:** Interlibrary loans; copying; library open to public for reference use only.

★7913★
METROPOLITAN HOSPITAL - PARKVIEW DIVISION - MEDICAL LIBRARY (Med)
1331 E. Wyoming Ave.   Phone: (215) 537-7684
Philadelphia, PA 19124   Grace Toll, Libn.
Founded: 1957. **Staff:** Prof 1; Other 1. **Subjects:** Osteopathy, medicine, nursing. **Holdings:** 1220 books; 357 bound periodical volumes; 335 cassettes; 300 slides. **Subscriptions:** 124 journals and other serials. **Services:** Interlibrary loans; copying; SDI; library open to public with permission of hospital administrator. **Networks/Consortia:** Member of Mideastern Regional Medical Library System (MERMLS). **Formerly:** Parkview Hospital - Library.

★7914★
METROPOLITAN HOSPITAL - SPRINGFIELD DIVISION - MEDICAL LIBRARY (Med)
Sproul & Thomson Rds.
Springfield, PA 19064   Barbara Rivers, Libn.
Staff: Prof 1. **Subjects:** Medicine, nursing. **Holdings:** 1000 books; 100 bound periodical volumes; 1 VF drawer; 900 cassette tapes; slides. **Subscriptions:** 80 journals and other serials. **Services:** Interlibrary loans; copying; library open to public with restrictions. **Networks/Consortia:** Member of Consortium for Health Information & Library Services (CHI). **Formerly:** Tri-County Hospital - Medical Library.

★7915★
METROPOLITAN JEWISH GERIATRIC CENTER - MAX B. & LOUISA S. MARKS MEMORIAL MEDICAL LIBRARY (Med)
4915 Tenth Ave.   Phone: (212) 853-2800
Brooklyn, NY 11219   Gracie Cooper, Libn.
Founded: 1955. **Staff:** Prof 1; Other 1. **Subjects:** Geriatrics, gerontology. **Holdings:** 780 books; 942 bound periodical volumes; 4 VF drawers of pamphlets (uncataloged). **Subscriptions:** 20 journals and other serials; 6 newspapers. **Services:** Interlibrary loans; copying; library not open to public.

★7916★
METROPOLITAN LIFE INSURANCE COMPANY - CORPORATE INFORMATION CENTER AND LIBRARY (Bus-Fin)
One Madison Ave., 1 M-R   Phone: (212) 578-3700
New York, NY 10010   Elizabeth McCloat, Libn.
Founded: 1909. **Staff:** Prof 8; Other 9. **Subjects:** Insurance, management, medicine and medical economics. **Special Collections:** Company archives. **Holdings:** 126,000 books and bound periodical volumes. **Subscriptions:** 574 journals and other serials. **Services:** Interlibrary loans; library open to public by appointment. **Computerized Information Services:** DIALOG, New York Times Information Service. **Publications:** Library Bulletin, monthly - for internal distribution only. **Staff:** Rosemary Stevens, Asst.Libn.; Natalie Kupferberg, Res.Libn., Med.; Kevin Barry, Res.Libn., Mgt.; Andrea McElrath, Res.Libn., Med.; Marianne Stolp, Cat.Libn.; Bonnie Chernin, Archv.Libn.

★7917★
METROPOLITAN LIFE INSURANCE COMPANY - LAW LIBRARY (Law)
One Madison Ave.   Phone: (212) 578-3111
New York, NY 10010   Rita Barone, Law Libn.
Founded: 1910. **Staff:** Prof 2; Other 1. **Subjects:** Law. **Holdings:** 24,000 volumes. **Services:** Interlibrary loans; library not open to public.

★7918★
METROPOLITAN LIFE INSURANCE COMPANY - LIBRARY (Bus-Fin)
99 Bank St.   Phone: (613) 231-3531
Ottawa, ON, Canada K1P 5A3   Marjorie A. Purvis, Commun.Res.Supv.
Staff: Prof 1; Other 2. **Subjects:** Life insurance, business, statistics, art, civilization, history, politics, management, taxation. **Special Collections:** Prints, engravings and photographs; rare maps dating back to the 17th century (46). **Holdings:** 10,000 books; 300 bound periodical volumes; 25,000 pieces of archival materials; 12 VF drawers of clippings; 300 volumes of company organs; Superintendent of Insurance Reports Canada, 1872 to present. **Subscriptions:** 250 journals and other serials; 10 newspapers. **Services:** Interlibrary loans; copying; library and archives open to public with restrictions. **Publications:** Library Services, quarterly list of acquisitions and reports - for internal distribution only.

METROPOLITAN MONTREAL CENTRE OF SOCIAL SERVICES
See: Centre de Services Sociaux du Montreal Metropolitain (CSSMM)

★7919★
METROPOLITAN MUSEUM OF ART - CLOISTERS LIBRARY (Art)
Fort Tryon Pk.   Phone: (212) 923-3700
New York, NY 10040   Suse Childs, Libn.
Staff: Prof 1; Other 1. **Subjects:** Medieval art history. **Special Collections:** George Grey Barnard Archive. **Holdings:** 6250 books; 850 bound periodical volumes; 14,000 color slides; 5500 photographs; 25 boxes of pamphlet material. **Subscriptions:** 46 journals and other serials. **Services:** Library open to qualified researchers.

★7920★
METROPOLITAN MUSEUM OF ART - DEPARTMENT OF PRINTS AND PHOTOGRAPHS (Art)
Fifth Ave. & 82nd St.   Phone: (212) 879-5500
New York, NY 10028   Colta Ives, Cur.
Founded: 1916. **Staff:** Prof 6; Other 5. **Subjects:** Art prints, illustrated books, architectural and ornamental drawings, photographs. **Holdings:** 12,000 books; 1 million prints and photographs. **Services:** Open to public by appointment only.

★7921★
METROPOLITAN MUSEUM OF ART - IRENE LEWISOHN COSTUME REFERENCE LIBRARY (Art)
Fifth Ave. & 82nd St.   Phone: (212) 879-5500
New York, NY 10028   Gordon Stone, Assoc.Musm.Libn.
Staff: Prof 1; Other 1. **Subjects:** History of costume. **Special Collections:** Original fashion sketches of Mainbocher, 1940-1970. **Holdings:** 78,000 items - swatch books, fashion sketches, fashion plates (cataloged). **Subscriptions:** 52 journals and other serials. **Services:** Copying; library open to professional designers and research scholars by appointment.

★7922★
METROPOLITAN MUSEUM OF ART - PHOTOGRAPH AND SLIDE LIBRARY (Art)
Fifth Ave. & 82nd St.   Phone: (212) 879-5500
New York, NY 10028   Margaret P. Nolan, Chf.Libn.
Staff: Prof 7; Other 13. **Subjects:** Art, art history, architecture, sculpture, painting, decorative arts, prints and photographs. **Special Collections:** William Keighley Color Slide Collection of Art and Architecture (70,000 slides). **Holdings:** 203,500 color slides; 168,000 black/white slides; 252,000 black/white reference photographs; 6000 color prints; 21,000 color transparencies of the museum collection; black/white photographic records of the museum collection. **Services:** Copying (with restriction); slides are available for rental to public; photographs of objects in the museum are for sale; color transparencies are available for rental for publication; library open to public. **Special Catalogs:** Color Transparencies for rental. **Staff:** Priscilla Farah, Musm.Libn.; Mary F. Doherty, Assoc.Musm.Libn.; Donna C. Smidt, Assoc.Musm.Libn.

★7923★
METROPOLITAN MUSEUM OF ART - ROBERT GOLDWATER LIBRARY (Art)
Fifth Ave. & 82nd St.   Phone: (212) 879-5500
New York, NY 10028   Allan D. Chapman, Musm.Libn.
Founded: 1957. **Staff:** Prof 2; Other 4. **Subjects:** Primitive art, archeology, ethnology, anthropology, art. **Special Collections:** Photographs of primitive art objects (125,000). **Holdings:** 26,000 books and bound periodical volumes. **Subscriptions:** 175 journals and other serials. **Services:** Copying; library open to graduate students and qualified researchers. **Staff:** Jean C. Wagner, Libn.

★7924★
METROPOLITAN MUSEUM OF ART - ROBERT LEHMAN COLLECTION - LIBRARY (Art)
Fifth Ave. & 82nd St.   Phone: (212) 879-5500
New York, NY 10028   Victoria S. Galban, Asst.Cur., Res.
Staff: Prof 2; Other 1. **Subjects:** Western European Arts, 13th-20th centuries, with special emphasis on the art of Siena; Old Master drawings; Renaissance decorative arts. **Holdings:** 10,000 volumes; Archives of the Robert Lehman Collection, including autograph letters of connoisseurs and art historians; 5000 mounted photographs. **Services:** Library open to public by appointment.

★7925★
METROPOLITAN MUSEUM OF ART - THOMAS J. WATSON LIBRARY (Art)
Fifth Ave. & 82nd St.   Phone: (212) 879-5500
New York, NY 10028   William B. Walker, Chf.Libn.
Founded: 1880. **Staff:** Prof 12; Other 17. **Subjects:** Art, art history, archeology, painting, sculpture, medieval art, decorative arts. **Special Collections:** Art auction catalogs. **Holdings:** 240,000 books and bound

periodical volumes; 99 VF drawers; 375 reels of microfilm. **Subscriptions:** 1400 journals and other serials. **Services:** Copying; library open to graduate students and qualified researchers. **Computerized Information Services:** RLIN; computerized cataloging. **Publications:** Selected New Accessions List, monthly. **Special Catalogs:** Continuing printed library catalog (published). **Staff:** Dobrila-Donya Schimansky, Musm.Libn.; Patricia Barnett, Assoc.Musm.Libn.; Lucy Ho, Assoc.Musm.Libn.; Doralynn Pines, Assoc.Musm.Libn.; Edward K. Werner, Libn.; Celine Palatsky, Assoc.Musm.Libn.; Patrick Coman, Supv.Dept.Asst.; Ljuba Backovsky, Assoc.Musm.Libn.; Kathryn Deiss, Asst.Musm.Libn.; Paula Frosch, Libn.; Ayako Nakada, Res.Asst.; Richard W. Arnold, Libn.

★7926★
METROPOLITAN MUSEUM OF ART - URIS LIBRARY AND RESOURCE CENTER (Art)
Fifth Ave. & 82nd St.   Phone: (212) 879-5500
New York, NY 10028   Roberta M. Paine, Musm. Educator
Founded: 1941. **Staff:** Prof 1; Other 1. **Subjects:** Arts, crafts, archeology, history, biography, mythology, religion. **Holdings:** 5200 volumes. **Services:** Library open to public for reading and reference. **Publications:** Book lists for students - art, archeology, bi-annual; others on special occasions. **Formerly:** Its Junior Museum Library.

★7927★
METROPOLITAN OPERA ASSOCIATION - ARCHIVES (Theater)
Lincoln Ctr. Plaza   Phone: (212) 799-3100
New York, NY 10023   Heloise L. Pressey, Asst.Archv.
Staff: Prof 1; Other 6. **Subjects:** Metropolitan Opera - programs, photographs and slides, biographies, newspaper clippings of reviews, 1880 to present. **Special Collections:** Historic costumes and artifacts. **Holdings:** Figures not available for books; bound programs, 1883 to present; bound Opera News magazine, 1935 to present. **Services:** Copying; archives open by appointment to qualified researchers. **Special Catalogs:** Card files of all performances given by Metropolitan Opera singers (1883 to present); card files of orchestra, ballet and chorus personnel (1910 to present).

METROPOLITAN OPERA - INFORMATION CENTER AND LIBRARY
See: Central Opera Service

★7928★
METROPOLITAN PITTSBURGH PUBLIC BROADCASTING, INC. - WQED LIBRARY (Info Sci)
4802 Fifth Ave.   Phone: (412) 622-1524
Pittsburgh, PA 15213   Deborah Barrett, Libn.
Staff: 1. **Subjects:** Public broadcasting, television programming. **Holdings:** 600 books; 27 bound periodical volumes. **Subscriptions:** 77 journals and other serials; 15 newspapers. **Services:** Library not open to public.

★7929★
METROPOLITAN PROPERTY & LIABILITY INSURANCE COMPANY - LAW & BUSINESS LIBRARY (Law)
700 Quaker Ln.   Phone: (401) 827-2658
Warwick, RI 02886   Kevin J. Carty, Libn.
Founded: 1976. **Staff:** Prof 1; Other 2. **Subjects:** Insurance, law. **Holdings:** 10,000 books; 4 VF drawers of subject files. **Subscriptions:** 60 journals and other serials; 5 newspapers. **Services:** Interlibrary loans; copying; SDI; library open to attorneys and other professionals with librarian's permission. **Publications:** Library Listings, monthly - for internal distribution only; Media Update, monthly - for internal distribution only.

★7930★
METROPOLITAN SANITARY DISTRICT OF GREATER CHICAGO - TECHNICAL LIBRARY (Sci-Tech)
100 E. Erie St.   Phone: (312) 751-5782
Chicago, IL 60611   Rudolph C. Ellsworth, Libn.
Founded: 1966. **Staff:** Prof 1; Other 1. **Subjects:** Wastewater treatment, engineering, management, soil mechanics, water resources and development. **Special Collections:** Archival collection. **Holdings:** 3000 books; 50 bound periodical volumes; 3500 technical reports; district proceedings and internal reports; reprints; 350 microfiche. **Subscriptions:** 235 journals and other serials. **Services:** Interlibrary loans; copying; library open to public for reference use only. **Networks/Consortia:** Member of Metropolitan Chicago Library Assembly. **Publications:** Information packet, updated yearly. **Also Known As:** Chicago Metropolitan Sanitary District.

★7931★

METROPOLITAN STATE HOSPITAL - STAFF LIBRARY (Med)
11400 Norwalk Blvd. Phone: (213) 863-7011
Norwalk, CA 90650 G. Calvin Tooker, Libn.
Founded: 1953. **Staff:** Prof 1; Other 2. **Subjects:** Psychiatry, psychology, psychiatric social work, psychiatric nursing. **Holdings:** 7697 books; 1593 bound periodical volumes; 691 audio cassettes. **Subscriptions:** 120 journals and other serials. **Services:** Interlibrary loans; copying; library open to public for reference use only. **Networks/Consortia:** Member of Pacific Southwest Regional Medical Library Service (PSRMLS). **Remarks:** Maintained by California State Department of Mental Health.

★7932★

METROPOLITAN TORONTO ASSOCIATION FOR THE MENTALLY RETARDED - HOWARD E. BACON MEMORIAL LIBRARY (Med)
8 Spadina Rd. Phone: (416) 968-0650
Toronto, ON, Canada M5R 2S7 Adrienne Wykes, Lib.Asst.
Staff: Prof 1; Other 1. **Subjects:** Mental retardation. **Holdings:** 1200 books; 4 drawers of pamphlets. **Subscriptions:** 15 journals and other serials. **Services:** Library open to public.

★7933★

METROPOLITAN TORONTO LIBRARY - AUDIO VISUAL SERVICES (Aud-Vis)
789 Yonge St. Phone: (416) 928-5185
Toronto, ON, Canada M4W 2G8 Laura Murray, AV Coord.
Staff: Prof 2; Other 13. **Holdings:** 8300 16mm films; 600 videotapes. **Services:** Interlibrary loans; projectionist training classes; film previews before booking; equipment and technicians' services; talking books services - all for area public library systems only. **Staff:** Christine Hoyland, Film Depot; Bruce Fairley, AV Equip. & Prod.; Maureen Donaldson, Talking Bks.Serv.

★7934★

METROPOLITAN TORONTO LIBRARY - BIBLIOGRAPHIC CENTRE & INTERLOAN (Info Sci)
789 Yonge St. Phone: (416) 928-5182
Toronto, ON, Canada M4W 2G8 Robert H.S. Yu, Hd.
Founded: 1960. **Staff:** Prof 3; Other 21. **Subjects:** National and general bibliography; book trade. **Holdings:** 5547 volumes. **Subscriptions:** 49 journals and other serials. **Services:** Interlibrary loans; copying; telephone and telex reference service for identification and/or location of books; centre open to public. **Special Catalogs:** Union catalog of the holdings of the Metropolitan Toronto Library, the Toronto Public Library and five metropolitan borough libraries.

★7935★

METROPOLITAN TORONTO LIBRARY - BUSINESS DEPARTMENT (Bus-Fin)
789 Yonge St. Phone: (416) 928-5256
Toronto, ON, Canada M4W 2G8 Patricia Dye, Hd.
Founded: 1941. **Staff:** Prof 7; Other 10. **Subjects:** Business, economics, finance, management, labour, corporate history, accounting, advertising, commerce, transportation, insurance. **Special Collections:** Canadian corporation annual reports; Statistics Canada. **Holdings:** 67,000 books; 13,000 bound periodical volumes; 180,000 microfiche. **Subscriptions:** 955 journals and other serials; 7 newspapers. **Services:** Interlibrary loans; copying; department open to public. **Computerized Information Services:** Metropolitan Toronto Library Board (Metroline); computerized cataloging. **Publications:** New acquisitions list, monthly; Pathfinders, irregular. **Special Indexes:** Magazine index (card) covering Canadian business periodicals not elsewhere indexed, 1941-1975.

★7936★

METROPOLITAN TORONTO LIBRARY - CANADIAN HISTORY DEPARTMENT (Hist)
Baldwin Room, 789 Yonge St. Phone: (416) 928-5275
Toronto, ON, Canada M4W 2G8 David B. Kotin, Hd.
Founded: 1883. **Staff:** Prof 6; Other 8. **Subjects:** Canadian history and travel; Canadian books published before 1868. **Holdings:** 51,300 books; 2500 bound periodical volumes; 4059 bound newspapers; 237 meters of manuscripts; 78,000 pictures; 10,114 pieces of printed ephemera; 25,000 microforms. **Subscriptions:** 295 journals and other serials. **Services:** Interlibrary loans; copying; department open to public.

★7937★

METROPOLITAN TORONTO LIBRARY - FINE ART DEPARTMENT (Art)
789 Yonge St. Phone: (416) 928-5214
Toronto, ON, Canada M4W 2G8 Alan Suddon, Hd.
Founded: 1960. **Staff:** Prof 4; Other 10. **Subjects:** Fine and decorative arts; printing and publishing; costume. **Special Collections:** Private press and fine printing; Hector Bolitho Victoriana; 19th and 20th-century Canadian, English

and American trade catalogs. **Holdings:** 38,283 books; 9514 bound periodical volumes; 671,284 circulating picture clippings; 98,670 reference picture clippings including early postcards; 8044 VF folders. **Subscriptions:** 378 journals and other serials. **Services:** Interlibrary loans; copying; department open to public. **Special Indexes:** Canadian artists' index (card). **Staff:** George Grant, Libn.; Milena McGuigan, Libn.; Murray Waddington, Libn.; Patricia Rogal, Pict.Coll.

★7938★

METROPOLITAN TORONTO LIBRARY - GENERAL REFERENCE DEPARTMENT (Info Sci)
789 Yonge St. Phone: (416) 928-5211
Toronto, ON, Canada M4W 2G8 Anne Mack, Hd.
Founded: 1966. **Staff:** Prof 4; Other 10. **Subjects:** Library science, museums. **Holdings:** 21,124 books; 4843 bound periodical volumes; 13,157 microforms (cataloged); 3379 VF folders of clippings. **Subscriptions:** 559 journals and other serials. **Services:** Interlibrary loans; copying; department open to public. **Publications:** Selected List of New Titles. **Staff:** Lesya Jones, Libn.; Donald Watt, Libn.

★7939★

METROPOLITAN TORONTO LIBRARY - HISTORY DEPARTMENT (Hist)
789 Yonge St. Phone: (416) 928-5267
Toronto, ON, Canada M4W 2G8 Michael Pearson, Hd.
Staff: Prof 6; Other 9. **Subjects:** World history, with emphasis on modern period; topography and regional geography; travel and exploration, including guidebooks, timetables and directories; heraldry and genealogy; collective biography; military art and science; military history and uniforms. **Holdings:** 133,000 books; 8800 bound periodical volumes; 38,700 maps; 1450 VF folders. **Subscriptions:** 1749 journals and other serials. **Services:** Interlibrary loans; copying; department open to public. **Staff:** Marion Addison, Libn.; Susanne Balpataky, Libn.; Alice Wong, Libn.; Freda Zych, Libn.; Nancy Biehl, Map Rm.; Dennis Joyes, The Americas; Gwen Manning, Libn.

★7940★

METROPOLITAN TORONTO LIBRARY - LANGUAGES CENTRE (Hum)
789 Yonge St. Phone: (416) 928-5280
Toronto, ON, Canada M4W 2G8 Barbara Gunther, Hd.
Founded: 1957. **Staff:** Prof 6; Other 13. **Subjects:** Language; literature in languages other than English. **Special Collections:** North American Indian and Eskimo linguistics; Canadian ethnica. **Holdings:** 89,564 books; 2493 bound periodical volumes; 7792 language and spoken word records, tapes, and cassettes; 270 VF folders. **Subscriptions:** 226 journals and other serials; 74 newspapers. **Services:** Interlibrary loans; copying; language teaching with record players, video and tape machines. **Publications:** List of Additions, quarterly - distributed to mailing list; occasional bibliographies - available upon request. **Remarks:** All staff are language specialists, with 30-40 languages covered. **Staff:** Mrs. Harcharan Grewal, Second-in-Charge.

★7941★

METROPOLITAN TORONTO LIBRARY - LITERATURE DEPARTMENT (Hum)
789 Yonge St. Phone: (416) 928-5284
Toronto, ON, Canada M4W 2G8 Katherine McCook, Hd.
Founded: 1967. **Staff:** Prof 7; Other 8. **Subjects:** Creative writing - Canada (comprehensive), England (especially 19th and 20th century), United States; German, Italian and Spanish creative writing in English translation; literary criticism, biography and other secondary sources; linguistics; journalism; mystery stories. **Special Collections:** Maria Chapdelaine Collection (70 editions); Rasselas Collection (200 editions); Arthur Conan Doyle Collection (3000 volumes; 2000 pamphlets, magazines, records, letters); Literary Reference File (3600 files containing clippings and copies of critical articles and essays). **Holdings:** 132,000 books; 6769 bound periodical volumes; 1089 audiotapes and phonograph records. **Subscriptions:** 814 journals and other serials. **Services:** Interlibrary loans; copying; department open to public. **Publications:** Checklist of Arthur Conan Doyle Collection. **Special Indexes:** Sherlock Holmes Index; Bigelow on Holmes; Fiction Subject Index (card). **Staff:** Ellen Pilon, English Lit.Spec.; Rosalind Taitt, Linguistics Spec.; Sheila Latham, Canadian Lit.Spec.; Olga Pavlovsky, European Lit.Spec.; Cameron Hollyer, Doyle/Am.Lit.Spec.; Osyp Goshulak, Classics/Oriental Lit.

★7942★

METROPOLITAN TORONTO LIBRARY - MUNICIPAL REFERENCE LIBRARY (Soc Sci)
City Hall, Nathan Phillips Square Phone: (416) 928-5357
Toronto, ON, Canada M5H 2N1 Margot Hewings, Hd.
Founded: 1965. **Staff:** Prof 4; Other 7. **Subjects:** Municipal affairs, municipal finance, traffic and transit, urban sociology, municipal government, municipal services, pollution (urban aspects), housing, municipal institutions, urban planning, urban geography. **Special Collections:** Metropolitan Toronto area

documents depository. **Holdings:** 54,323 books; 4831 bound periodical volumes; 1264 VF folders of local committee reports, pamphlets and clippings; 83,508 microforms; 3402 maps; 2002 slides; 288 pictures; 113 cassettes. **Subscriptions:** 737 journals and other serials; 24 newspapers. **Services:** Interlibrary loans; copying; library open to public. **Publications:** Acquisitions, monthly; Memo from Municipal, quarterly; brochure on the collections and services. **Special Indexes:** Subject index to VF material (card); subject/geographic index to magazines (book); map catalog (card); Quick Reference Index (card); Index to Campaign Literature (book). Janet Hall, Libn.; Judy Curry, Libn.; Dale Moore, Libn.

★7943★

METROPOLITAN TORONTO LIBRARY - MUSIC DEPARTMENT (Mus)
789 Yonge St.   Phone: (416) 928-5224
Toronto, ON, Canada M4W 2G8   Isabel Rose, Hd.
Founded: 1915. **Staff:** Prof 3; Other 8. **Subjects:** Music. **Special Collections:** Retrospective Canadian sheet music. **Holdings:** 52,000 books, scores, and bound periodical volumes; 14,700 phonograph records; 15,000 programs; 8300 VF folders; 500 microforms. **Subscriptions:** 189 journals and other serials. **Services:** Interlibrary loans; copying (limited); department open to public. **Publications:** Acquisitions, monthly.

★7944★

METROPOLITAN TORONTO LIBRARY - NEWSPAPER UNIT (Publ)
789 Yonge St.   Phone: (416) 928-5254
Toronto, ON, Canada M4W 2G8   Alan Suddon, Hd. of Unit
Staff: 5. **Subjects:** Newspapers. **Holdings:** 20,249 reels of microfilm. **Subscriptions:** 74 newspapers. **Services:** Interlibrary loans; copying; unit open to public. **Computerized Information Services:** Computerized cataloging. **Special Catalogs:** Newspapers on microfilm (loose-leaf). **Staff:** Norma Dainard, Asst. in Charge.

★7945★

METROPOLITAN TORONTO LIBRARY - SCIENCE & TECHNOLOGY DEPARTMENT (Sci-Tech)
789 Yonge St.   Phone: (416) 928-5234
Toronto, ON, Canada M4W 2G8   Margaret Walshe, Hd.
Founded: 1963. **Staff:** Prof 7; Other 13. **Subjects:** Physical and biological sciences, engineering sciences, natural history, horticulture, technology and food technology, cookery, sports and recreation. **Special Collections:** Geological Survey of Canada publications; Atomic Energy of Canada publications; workshop manuals for motor vehicles and household appliances. **Holdings:** 113,898 books; 30,935 bound periodical volumes; 5875 volumes of patent abstracts (Canadian, American and British); 12,000 volumes of standards; 4250 volumes of radio and television schematics (Canadian and American); 7907 VF folders; 3882 maps. **Subscriptions:** 1053 journals and other serials. **Services:** Interlibrary loans; copying; department open to public. **Computerized Information Services:** DIALOG, MEDLARS, Info Globe, SDC. **Special Indexes:** Shop manual index; map index; vertical file index to science and sports.

★7946★

METROPOLITAN TORONTO LIBRARY - SOCIAL SCIENCES DEPARTMENT (Soc Sci)
789 Yonge St.   Phone: (416) 928-5246
Toronto, ON, Canada M4W 2G8   Abdus Salam, Hd.
Founded: 1966. **Staff:** Prof 9; Other 10. **Subjects:** Sociology, foreign relations, political science, law, philosophy and religion, social welfare, folklore and mythology, anthropology, psychology, education, women's studies. **Special Collections:** Canadian federal and Ontario provincial government publications (depository); Canadian census since 1851; Canadian congregational and denominational histories; immigration to Canada. **Holdings:** 190,456 books; 11,475 bound periodical volumes; 20,780 microcards and microfiche; 3569 microfilms; 927 tapes, records and cassettes; 2000 university and college calendars; 1911 vertical files. **Subscriptions:** 2400 journals and other serials. **Services:** Interlibrary loans; copying; department open to public. **Publications:** Social Sciences Department Acquisitions, monthly; Bibliographies in Social Sciences, No. 1, 1975 to present. **Special Indexes:** Index to current Canadian federal and Ontario provincial bills (card); Index of Current Canadian Conferences in the field of social sciences. **Staff:** Ross Anderson, Libn.; Janice Denyer, Libn.; Melanie Milanich, Libn.; Margaret Keefe, Libn.; Judy McCann, Libn; Pierre Mercier, Libn.; Paul Pilon, Libn.; Joseph Romain, Libn.

★7947★

METROPOLITAN TORONTO LIBRARY - THEATRE DEPARTMENT (Theater)
789 Yonge St.   Phone: (416) 928-5230
Toronto, ON, Canada M4W 2G8   Heather McCallum, Hd.
Founded: 1961. **Staff:** Prof 3; Other 7. **Subjects:** Theater/drama, motion

pictures, dance, radio and television, music hall, vaudeville, circus, puppetry, magic. **Special Collections:** Canadian touring companies and personalities: Taverner Touring Company; Thomas Scott Collection (Grand Opera House, Toronto); Marks Brothers; Princess Theatre (Toronto); Ned Sparks; Judith Evelyn scrapbooks; Canadian Players; Canadian Repertory Theatre (Ottawa); Crest Theatre (Toronto); Toronto Children's Players; Ralph Hicklin Collection; Boris Volkoff Collection; Studio Lab Theatre (Toronto); Cosette Lee Collection; John Fraser Collection (Toronto theater and dance critic); The Dumbells Collection; Bettina Byers Collection; Mae Edwards Collection; Jupiter Theatre (Toronto) acting scripts; London Theatre Company (Newfoundland); Ramona McBean Collection; E.A. McDowell Company photographs and programmes; Charles Manny Collection (vaudeville); Jack Karr Collection (Toronto theater and film critic); Nancy Pyper Collection; Walker Theatre (Winnipeg) photograph collection. **Holdings:** 28,504 books; 1852 bound periodical volumes; 1782 microforms; 1278 spoken word recordings, tapes, cassettes; 1009 files (Canadian theater and film, personalities, companies and theaters); 19,216 theater programs; 404 19th-century Canadian playbills; 4522 posters; 2137 original Canadian stage designs; 1713 theatrical prints; 229 theater plans; 51,769 photographs; 3320 slides; 75 rare court festival books; 104 Japanese woodblock prints. **Subscriptions:** 152 journals and other serials. **Services:** Interlibrary loans; copying; department open to public. **Publications:** Acquisitions list, monthly - free upon request. **Special Indexes:** Title index to plays performed professionally in Canada (card); title index to plays in collections (card); FIAF film index (card); biographical/critical index (card); subject index to newspaper clippings files (card/microfiche); index to newspaper files and photographs for Canadian personalities; index to film stills. **Staff:** Glen Hunter, Libn.; Annette Wengle, Libn.

★7948★

METROPOLITAN TORONTO PLANNING DEPARTMENT - LIBRARY (Plan)
City Hall, 11th Fl., East Tower   Phone: (416) 367-8101
Toronto, ON, Canada M5H 2N1   Pamela J. Smith, Libn.
Founded: 1954. **Staff:** Prof 1; Other 4. **Subjects:** Planning - urban, regional, environmental, social; housing; transportation; urban renewal. **Special Collections:** Metropolitan Toronto Planning Board agendas; Metropolitan Toronto Executive Council minutes. **Holdings:** 5000 books. **Subscriptions:** 103 journals and other serials. **Services:** Interlibrary loans; copying; library open to public by appointment. **Publications:** The Planning Post, monthly.

★7949★

METROPOLITAN TORONTO SCHOOL BOARD - LIBRARY (Educ)
155 College St., 3rd Fl.   Phone: (416) 598-4620
Toronto, ON, Canada M5T 1P6   Carol Williams, Libn.
Staff: Prof 1. **Subjects:** Education. **Special Collections:** Educational research; Study of Educational Facilities (SEF); education of the mentally handicapped. **Holdings:** 500 books; 18 VF drawers. **Subscriptions:** 150 journals and other serials. **Services:** Interlibrary loans; copying; library open to public by appointment. **Computerized Information Services:** DIALOG, ISIS.

★7950★

METROPOLITAN (Toronto) SEPARATE SCHOOL BOARD - CATHOLIC EDUCATION CENTRE LIBRARY (Educ)
80 Sheppard Ave., E.   Phone: (416) 222-8282
Toronto, ON, Canada M2N 6E8   Rev. William J. Brown, Asst.Supt., Curric.
Founded: 1966. **Staff:** Prof 2; Other 5. **Subjects:** Elementary and secondary education, religious education, philosophy of education, teaching, methodology, curriculum, child development services, special education, innovations in education. **Special Collections:** Historical Collection (400 textbooks and other materials); art slide collection (1500 titles). **Holdings:** 19,400 books, AV materials, cataloged reports and documents; 82 bound periodical volumes; 4 boxes of MSSB reports; 565 files of pamphlets and clippings; 2670 reels of microfilm; 182,720 ERIC titles on microfiche. **Subscriptions:** 682 journals and other serials; 11 newspapers. **Services:** Interlibrary loans; SDI (for administrators and subject coordinators); library open to public by special arrangement. **Computerized Information Services:** INFOMART, DIALOG. **Networks/Consortia:** Member of Library Resource Sharing Committee. **Publications:** Under/Cover, monthly journal content information service published in three editions. **Formerly:** Its Professional Library. **Staff:** Lynn Poth, Libn.; Duncan MacPhee, Libn.

★7951★

METROPOLITAN TRANSPORTATION COMMISSION - ASSOCIATION OF BAY AREA GOVERNMENTS (ABAG) - LIBRARY (Plan; Trans)
Hotel Claremont   Phone: (415) 849-3223
Berkeley, CA 94705   Dian Gillmar, Info.Coord.
Founded: 1972. **Staff:** Prof 1; Other 1. **Subjects:** Regional planning, housing, urban development policy, environmental resources, transportation. **Special Collections:** General plans of local jurisdictions in 9-county Bay area; 1980 census depository. **Holdings:** 7000 volumes; 294 sheets. **Subscriptions:**

104 journals and other serials. **Services:** Interlibrary loans; copying; library open to public for reference use only with appointment. **Computerized Information Services:** DIALOG; computerized cataloging. **Networks/Consortia:** Member of OCLC; Bay Area Transportation Information Network. **Publications:** TransAction; Recent Accessions.

★7952★
METROPOLITAN WASHINGTON COUNCIL OF GOVERNMENTS - LIBRARY
(Plan)
1875 Eye St., N.W.   Phone: (202) 223-6800
Washington, DC 20006
Founded: 1967. **Subjects:** Council of governments, intergovernmental relations, local governments, air pollution, transportation, regional planning, public safety, community resources, water quality. **Special Collections:** Maps of local area (10,000). **Holdings:** 5000 books; 3000 documents published by member governments; 200 pamphlets; 200 reports; 200 reels of microfilm (local clippings); 250 microfiche; 3000 archives and local governments items. **Subscriptions:** 200 journals and other serials; 25 newspapers. **Services:** Interlibrary loans; copying; reference service to member governments; will answer brief inquiries and make referrals; library open to public by appointment. **Also Known As:** District of Columbia - Metropolitan Council of Governments Library.

MEXICAN AMERICAN ARCHIVAL COLLECTION
See: University of Texas, Austin - Benson Latin American Collection

★7953★
MEXICAN AMERICAN LEGAL DEFENSE AND EDUCATIONAL FUND - LIBRARY (Law)†
28 Geary St., 6th Fl.   Phone: (415) 981-5800
San Francisco, CA 94108   Tyler Kelly, Libn.
Subjects: Law. **Special Collections:** Mexican-American civil rights and sociology (200 books). **Holdings:** 2000 books. **Services:** Library open to public by appointment.

MEXICAN AMERICAN LIBRARY PROGRAM
See: University of Texas, Austin

★7954★
MEXICAN-AMERICAN OPPORTUNITY FOUNDATION - INFORMATION AND REFERRAL SERVICE - RESOURCE CENTER (Educ)
664 Monterey Pass Rd.   Phone: (213) 289-0286
Monterey Park, CA 91754   Gloria Cortez, Info. & Referral Coord.
Staff: Prof 2; Other 1. **Subjects:** Infant development, parenting, domestic and child abuse, self-esteem, handicap - emotional and physical, displaced homemaker. **Special Collections:** Mayan & Aztec History; Mexican History; Child Psychology and Development. **Holdings:** 1500 books; filmstrips; cassettes; records; audiophonic media cards; arts and crafts materials. **Services:** Interlibrary loans; library open to licensed providers of child care. **Networks/Consortia:** Member of Southern California Information and Referral Network; Southern California Association for Education of Young Children. **Publications:** Newsletter, bimonthly - distributed by mailing list and public contact. **Remarks:** The Information and Referral Service is funded by the Office of Child Development/State Department of Education. This program is geared for the needs of the Hispanic community of East Los Angeles and surrounding communities.

MEYER (John E.) EYE FOUNDATION LIBRARY
See: Eye Foundation Hospital - John E. Meyer Eye Foundation Library

MEYER LIBRARY
See: California College of Arts and Crafts

MEYERCORD (Madeline Roach) LIBRARY
See: Highland Park Presbyterian Church - Madeline Roach Meyercord Library

MEYERHOFF (Joseph) LIBRARY
See: Baltimore Hebrew College - Joseph Meyerhoff Library

MEYERS (Henry) MEMORIAL LIBRARY
See: Jewish Community Center of Metropolitan Detroit

MEYERS LIBRARY
See: Reform Congregation Keneseth Israel

★7955★
MGIC INVESTMENT CORPORATION - CORPORATE LIBRARY (Bus-Fin)
MGIC Plaza   Phone: (414) 347-6409
Milwaukee, WI 53202   Peg Peterson, Corp.Libn.
Founded: 1973. **Staff:** Prof 2. **Subjects:** Mortgage insurance, housing, insurance statistics and law, real estate statistics, banking, finance. **Holdings:** Figures not available. **Subscriptions:** 300 journals and other serials; 10 newspapers. **Services:** Interlibrary loans; copying; library open to public with restrictions.

MGM, INC.
See: Metro-Goldwyn-Mayer, Inc.

★7956★
MIAMI COUNTY LAW LIBRARY (Law)
201 W. Main St.   Phone: (513) 335-8341
Troy, OH 45373   Carolyn Bolin, Libn.
Staff: 2. **Subjects:** Law. **Holdings:** 20,000 volumes. **Services:** Interlibrary loans; copying; library not open to public.

★7957★
MIAMI-DADE PUBLIC LIBRARY - ART AND MUSIC DIVISION (Art; Mus)
1 Biscayne Blvd.   Phone: (305) 579-5001
Miami, FL 33132   Barbara Edwards, Hd.
Staff: Prof 4; Other 3. **Subjects:** Art, music, theater, motion pictures, television. **Holdings:** 22,405 books; 3 VF drawers of clippings; 4 VF drawers of contemporary artist files; 133,000 pictures; 31,000 phonograph records; 4500 cassettes; 1495 music scores; 8252 pieces of sheet music; 1663 framed pictures. **Subscriptions:** 140 journals and other serials. **Services:** Interlibrary loans (limited); copying; library open to public. **Staff:** Kenneth Benoit; Rebecca Powell; Dorothy Donio.

★7958★
MIAMI-DADE PUBLIC LIBRARY - AUDIO/VISUAL DEPARTMENT (Aud-Vis)
1 Biscayne Blvd.   Phone: (305) 579-5001
Miami, FL 33132
Staff: Prof 1; Other 3. **Holdings:** 4366 16mm films; 141 8mm films; 540 filmstrips; 2117 slides; 1645 filmstrip/cassette units; 7 videotapes.

★7959★
MIAMI-DADE PUBLIC LIBRARY - BUSINESS, SCIENCE AND TECHNOLOGY DEPARTMENT (Sci-Tech; Bus-Fin)
1 Biscayne Blvd.   Phone: (305) 579-5001
Miami, FL 33132   Louise Maurer, Sci.Libn.
Staff: Prof 3; Other 5. **Subjects:** Business, economics, international trade, investments, laymen's medical reference, pure and applied sciences. **Special Collections:** Annual reports of companies and Florida corporations; manufacturing, specialized and foreign business directories (600); microfiche collection. **Holdings:** 80 VF drawers of pamphlets. **Subscriptions:** 700 journals and other serials. **Services:** Interlibrary loans (limited); copying; library open to public. **Computerized Information Services:** DIALOG. **Staff:** Edward Oswald, Bus.Libn.

★7960★
MIAMI-DADE PUBLIC LIBRARY - FEDERAL DOCUMENTS DIVISION (Info Sci)
1 Biscayne Blvd.   Phone: (305) 579-3555
Miami, FL 33132   Eva Conrad, Fed.Doc.Libn.
Founded: 1952. **Staff:** Prof 1. **Subjects:** U.S. government, federal laws, history, statistics, military, Library of Congress. **Special Collections:** Annual and statistical reports (bound); State Department papers; President's Commission reports (bound); Serial Set (selective); Smithsonian reports and bulletins. **Holdings:** 47,000 books; 85,000 bound periodical volumes; 103,000 U.S. government publications (selective); Supreme Court Reports; treaties; registers; gazetteers, almanacs. **Subscriptions:** 350 journals and other serials. **Services:** Copying; division open to public for reference use only.

★7961★
MIAMI-DADE PUBLIC LIBRARY - FLORIDA COLLECTION (Hist)
1 Biscayne Blvd.   Phone: (305) 579-5189
Miami, FL 33132   Sam J. Boldrick, Libn.
Staff: Prof 2; Other 3. **Subjects:** Florida history, local, state and regional. **Special Collections:** Florida Author Collection; Foundation Center Regional Collection; Romer Photograph Collection. **Holdings:** 5514 books; 40,000 documents; 11,324 photographs; 2300 maps; 17,500 photographic negatives; 700,000 newspaper clippings; microforms; 195 reels of microfilm; 500 pamphlets. **Subscriptions:** 66 journals and other serials; 33 newspapers. **Services:** Interlibrary loans (limited); copying; library open to public. **Computerized Information Services:** Internal database. **Special Indexes:**

Miami Newspapers Index, monthly. **Staff:** Norman Gillespie, Asst.Libn.

★7962★
MIAMI-DADE PUBLIC LIBRARY - FOREIGN LANGUAGES DIVISION (Hum)
1 Biscayne Blvd.   Phone: (305) 579-5001
Miami, FL 33132   Alicia Godoy, Lang.Libn.
Staff: Prof 2; Other 1. **Subjects:** Books in 29 foreign languages, mainly Spanish: fiction; technical books; biography; history and travel; literature for high school, college and university level; mysteries; westerns; science fiction; grammars; Latin America; heraldry; Spanish surnames. **Special Collections:** Spanish Reference Collection; Spanish, French, German, Italian and Basque Encylopedias; foreign and bilingual dictionaries and atlases of the Caribbean countries. **Holdings:** 30,000 books; 2000 paperbacks (cataloged); 250 language records; 4 turntables and 30 cassettes for language learning in various languages, especially English, French and Spanish; 2 file drawers of clippings on 60 subjects. **Subscriptions:** 40 journals and other serials; 20 newspapers, mainly foreign. **Services:** Interlibrary loans; copying; translations in any language other than English at the desk and by phone; library open to public.

★7963★
MIAMI-DADE PUBLIC LIBRARY - GENEALOGY ROOM (Hist)
1 Biscayne Blvd.   Phone: (305) 579-5015
Miami, FL 33132   Edward F. Sintz, Dir.
Staff: 1. **Subjects:** Genealogy and heraldry. **Holdings:** 5000 volumes; 8606 reels of census microfilm; 960 reels of microfilmed directories (1861-1900); 1647 entries on microfiche of American directories through 1860. **Subscriptions:** 42 journals and other serials. **Services:** Copying; room open to public. **Staff:** Lucretia D. Warren, Libn.

★7964★
MIAMI-DADE PUBLIC LIBRARY - URBAN AFFAIRS LIBRARY (Plan)
1 Biscayne Blvd.   Phone: (305) 579-5487
Miami, FL 33132   Richard G. Frow, Libn.
Founded: 1960. **Staff:** Prof 1. **Subjects:** City planning, local government administration. **Holdings:** 2785 books; unbound reports of non-Florida cities and counties; pamphlets on city planning, administration, local government and regional planning; 8405 pamphlets. **Subscriptions:** 98 journals and other serials. **Services:** Interlibrary loans; copying; library open to public. **Publications:** Urban Affairs Newsletter, monthly - to city and county officials.

★7965★
MIAMI HEART INSTITUTE HOSPITAL - MEDICAL LIBRARY (Med)
4701 N. Meridian Ave.   Phone: (305) 672-1111
Miami Beach, FL 33140   Bronia Barbash, Libn.
Founded: 1966. **Staff:** Prof 1; Other 1. **Subjects:** Medicine, medical research. **Holdings:** 3700 books; 4300 bound periodical volumes; AV material; pamphlets; heart reports; bulletins; research. **Subscriptions:** 73 journals and other serials. **Services:** Interlibrary loans; copying; library not open to public. **Computerized Information Services:** MEDLINE; internal database. **Networks/Consortia:** Member of Southeastern Regional Medical Library Program (SERMLP); Miami Health Sciences Library Consortium (MHSLC).

★7966★
MIAMI HERALD - LIBRARY (Publ)
One Herald Plaza   Phone: (305) 350-2418
Miami, FL 33101   Nora Medley, Lib.Dir.
Founded: 1940. **Staff:** Prof 5; Other 5. **Subjects:** Newspaper reference topics. **Special Collections:** Historical pictures of Miami. **Holdings:** 2000 books; photographs; microfilm of the Herald. **Subscriptions:** 40 journals and other serials; 20 newspapers. **Services:** Interlibrary loans; copying (for news agencies only); library open to public by mailed request only. **Computerized Information Services:** New York Times Information Service, SDC, BRS, NEXIS; internal database. **Staff:** Luis Bueno, Hd.Libn.; Elisabeth Donovan, Online Res.

★7967★
MIAMI NEWS - LIBRARY (Publ)
One Herald Plaza   Phone: (305) 350-2189
Miami, FL 33101   Joseph F. Wright, Hd.Libn.
Staff: Prof 2; Other 3. **Subjects:** Newspaper reference topics. **Special Collections:** Historical photographs of Miami. **Holdings:** 400 books; 277 VF drawers of newspaper clippings; 237 drawers of black/white photographs; Miami News on microfilm from its beginning in 1896 to present; 9 drawers of pamphlets. **Services:** Library not open to public. **Computerized Information Services:** Internal database. **Staff:** Dorothy McDermott, Asst.Libn.

★7968★
MIAMI PURCHASE ASSOCIATION FOR HISTORIC PRESERVATION - LIBRARY AND INFORMATION CENTER (Hist)
812 Dayton St.   Phone: (513) 721-4506
Cincinnati, OH 45214   Cecelia S. Grineff, Registrar
Founded: 1964. **Staff:** 1. **Subjects:** Preservation, restoration, history of Cincinnati and Southwestern Ohio, 19th-century decorative arts. **Special Collections:** 19th-century Ohio and Cincinnati history and literature (200 volumes). **Holdings:** 400 books; 25 boxes of ephemeral material. **Subscriptions:** 16 journals and other serials. **Services:** Copying; library open to public for reference use only. **Publications:** Newsletter, quarterly - for members only.

★7969★
MIAMI UNIVERSITY - ART AND ARCHITECTURE LIBRARY (Art)
Alumni Hall   Phone: (513) 529-3219
Oxford, OH 45056   Joann Olson, Hum.Libn.
Founded: 1952. **Staff:** Prof 1; Other 1. **Subjects:** Architecture, art, city planning, art education, landscape design and allied subjects. **Holdings:** 30,000 books; 3200 bound periodical volumes; pamphlets and catalogs. **Subscriptions:** 120 journals and other serials. **Services:** Interlibrary loans; copying; library open to public.

★7970★
MIAMI UNIVERSITY - BRILL SCIENCE LIBRARY (Sci-Tech)
                                             Phone: (513) 529-7527
Oxford, OH 45056   Marian C. Winner, Hd.Sci.Libn.
Founded: 1978. **Staff:** Prof 4; Other 6. **Subjects:** Science - biological, physical, earth; mathematics; technology; medicine. **Special Collections:** Paper Science (1000 books, 2500 bound periodicals). **Holdings:** 115,000 books; 65,000 bound periodical volumes; 30,000 microforms; 15,000 specialized maps; 20,000 U.S. Defense Mapping Agency/Army Map Service maps; 26,000 U.S. Geological Survey maps; 8 VF drawers of pamphlets. **Subscriptions:** 1600 journals and other serials. **Services:** Interlibrary loans; copying; library open to public. **Computerized Information Services:** DIALOG, SDC, BRS; computerized cataloging. **Networks/Consortia:** Member of OCLC; OHIONET. **Special Catalogs:** Subject bibliographies. **Staff:** Nancy Moeckel, Sci.Libn.

★7971★
MIAMI UNIVERSITY - MUSIC LIBRARY (Mus)
Ctr. for Performing Arts   Phone: (513) 529-2017
Oxford, OH 45056   Edith Miller, Hum.Libn.
Founded: 1969. **Staff:** Prof 1; Other 2. **Subjects:** Music. **Holdings:** 21,000 books; 1200 bound periodical volumes; 11,500 phonograph records; 3000 sound recordings. **Subscriptions:** 105 journals and other serials. **Services:** Interlibrary loans; copying; library open to public.

★7972★
MIAMI UNIVERSITY - SCRIPPS FOUNDATION FOR RESEARCH IN POPULATION PROBLEMS & GERONTOLOGY CENTER - LIBRARY
Hoyt Library
Oxford, OH 45056
Defunct

★7973★
MIAMI UNIVERSITY - WALTER HAVIGHURST SPECIAL COLLECTIONS LIBRARY (Hist)
King Library   Phone: (513) 529-2537
Oxford, OH 45056   Helen Ball, Cur. of Spec.Coll.
Staff: Prof 2; Other 1. **Subjects:** Early children's books, Ohio Valley history, Walt Whitman, Henrik Ibsen, J.T. Farrell, Willa Cather, Christopher Morley, George Orwell, William Dean Howells, William H. McGuffey, folklore. **Special Collections:** King Collection (early juveniles, 7500 volumes); Covington Collection (Ohio Valley history, 5700 volumes); William H. McGuffey Manuscript Letters (150); William Dean Howells Manuscript Letters (133); 19th-century botanical medicine and older herbals (250 volumes); Jefferson Davis papers (491); Working Library of Louise Bogan (1772 items). **Holdings:** 22,000 books; 1000 bound periodical volumes; literary annuals and gift books. **Subscriptions:** 12 journals and other serials. **Services:** Interlibrary loans (limited); library open to public for reference use only with identification. **Staff:** Catherine De Saint-Rat, Asst.Cur.

MIAMI UNIVERSITY - WILLIAM HOLMES MC GUFFEY HOUSE AND MUSEUM
See: Mc Guffey (William Holmes) House and Museum

★7974★
MIAMI VALLEY HOSPITAL - EDUCATIONAL RESOURCES CENTER - MEDICAL LIBRARY (Med)
One Wyoming St.
Dayton, OH 45409
Phone: (513) 223-6192
Margaret C. Hardy, Dir.
Founded: 1944. **Staff:** Prof 2; Other 4. **Subjects:** Medicine, nursing, allied health sciences. **Holdings:** 5000 books; 13,500 bound periodical volumes; 12 VF drawers of pamphlets; 12 VF drawers of hospital archives. **Subscriptions:** 600 journals and other serials. **Services:** Interlibrary loans; library open to qualified persons with permission. **Computerized Information Services:** NLM, BRS, DIALOG. **Networks/Consortia:** Member of MIDLNET; West Central Ohio Online Users Group (WCOOUG).

MIAMI VALLEY LABORATORIES
See: Procter & Gamble Company

★7975★
MIAMI VALLEY REGIONAL PLANNING COMMISSION - LIBRARY (Plan)
117 S. Main St., Suite 200
Dayton, OH 45402
Phone: (513) 223-6323
Nora Lake, Exec.Dir.
Founded: 1968. **Staff:** Prof 2. **Subjects:** Transportation, planning, housing, land use, economics, population, government, water. **Special Collections:** Data file on 5 county region - Greene, Montgomery, Miami, Darke and Preble counties (10 VF drawers). **Holdings:** 12,000 books; 3000 bound periodical volumes; 5 VF drawers of clippings. **Subscriptions:** 166 journals and other serials; 17 newspapers. **Services:** Interlibrary loans; copying; library open to public for reference use only by request. **Publications:** Planning Notes, monthly - mailout listings; Technical Bulletins. **Staff:** Karen Burns, Info.Spec.

★7976★
MICHAEL, BEST & FRIEDRICH - LAW LIBRARY (Law)
250 E. Wisconsin Ave.
Milwaukee, WI 53202
Phone: (414) 271-6560
Betty Hertel, Libn.
Staff: Prof 2; Other 1. **Subjects:** Law - tax, labor, patent, corporate. **Holdings:** 1,000 books. **Subscriptions:** 202 journals and other serials. **Services:** Interlibrary loans (limited); copying (limited); library open to public by appointment. **Computerized Information Services:** LEXIS. **Networks/Consortia:** Member of Library Council of Metropolitan Milwaukee, Inc. (LCOMM). **Staff:** Mary Wood, Asst.Libn.

MICHAEL (Marie) LIBRARY
See: St. Francis Xavier University - Coady International Institute - Marie Michael Library

★7977★
MICHAEL REESE HOSPITAL & MEDICAL CENTER - DEPARTMENT OF LIBRARY & MEDIA RESOURCES (Med)
2908 S. Ellis Ave.
Chicago, IL 60616
Phone: (312) 791-2474
Dr. George Mozes, Dir.
Founded: 1935. **Staff:** Prof 4; Other 9. **Subjects:** Medicine, dentistry, nursing. **Special Collections:** History of medicine (450 books). **Holdings:** 12,000 books; 18,000 bound periodical volumes; 500 audio- and videotapes. **Subscriptions:** 380 journals and other serials. **Services:** Interlibrary loans; computer assisted instruction; library open to public for reference use only. **Computerized Information Services:** NLM, SDC, DIALOG; computerized cataloging.

★7978★
MICHENER CENTRE - STAFF LIBRARY (Med; Soc Sci)
Box 5002
Red Deer, AB, Canada T4N 5Y5
Phone: (403) 343-5936
Judith Benson, Libn.
Founded: 1973. **Staff:** Prof 1. **Subjects:** Mental retardation, behavior modification, sociology, psychology. **Holdings:** 3062 volumes. **Subscriptions:** 130 journals and other serials. **Services:** Interlibrary loans; copying; computer searches; library open to public with restrictions.

★7979★
MICHIE/BOBBS-MERRILL LAW PUBLISHERS - MICHIE COMPANY LIBRARY (Publ; Law)
914 Emmet St.
Charlottesville, VA 22903
Phone: (804) 295-6171
Marion J. Samuels, Libn.
Staff: Prof 1; Other 1. **Subjects:** Law and legal publishing. **Holdings:** 25,000 books. **Subscriptions:** 2000 journals and other serials. **Services:** Interlibrary loans; copying; library open to public for reference use only.

MICHIGAN ARCHIVES OF THE PALACE MUSEUM, TAIWAN
See: Honolulu Academy of Arts - Robert Allerton Library

MICHIGAN ART ARCHIVES
See: Battle Creek Art Center

★7980★
MICHIGAN AUDUBON SOCIETY - EDITH MUNGER LIBRARY (Sci-Tech)
7000 N. Westnedge Ave.
Kalamazoo, MI 49007
Phone: (616) 344-8648
Patricia L. Adams, Off.Mgr.
Founded: 1904. **Staff:** 1. **Subjects:** Ornithology, natural history. **Holdings:** 120 books; 162 bound periodical volumes; 61 serials (cataloged); 2 VF drawers of pamphlet material; 2045 slides. **Subscriptions:** 180 journals and other serials. **Services:** Library open to public. **Remarks:** Interested parties should contact Roger Sutherland or Grover Niegarth at Schoolcraft College, Livonia, MI.

★7981★
MICHIGAN BELL TELEPHONE COMPANY - CORPORATE REFERENCE CENTER (Bus-Fin)
1365 Cass Ave., Rm. 1200
Detroit, MI 48226
Phone: (313) 223-8040
Karol S. Sprague, Human Rsrcs.Supv.
Staff: Prof 2; Other 2. **Subjects:** Personnel management, management, telecommunications, applied psychology, computer science, communication skills, mathematics, statistics, marketing. **Special Collections:** Telephone history. **Holdings:** 6000 books; 100 bound periodical volumes; 400 videotapes; 100 audiotapes; 80 16mm films; 700 AMA and Conference Board papers (cataloged); 48 VF drawers of unbound pamphlets, reports and clippings. **Subscriptions:** 400 journals and other serials; 5 newspapers. **Services:** Interlibrary loans; copying; center open to public with permission. **Staff:** Kelly Hollosy, Asst. to Libn.

★7982★
MICHIGAN CANCER FOUNDATION - LEONARD N. SIMONS RESEARCH LIBRARY (Med)
110 E. Warren
Detroit, MI 48201
Phone: (313) 833-0710
C.J. Glodek, Dir.
Founded: 1949. **Staff:** Prof 2. **Subjects:** Cancer research and related topics. **Holdings:** 3000 books; 700 bound periodical volumes; 500 pamphlets and reprints. **Subscriptions:** 115 journals and other serials. **Services:** Interlibrary loans; copying; library open to public with restrictions. **Computerized Information Services:** MEDLINE, DIALOG.

★7983★
MICHIGAN CONSOLIDATED GAS COMPANY - CORPORATE LIBRARY (Energy)
One Woodward Ave.
Detroit, MI 48226
Phone: (313) 965-2430
Kay L. Ames, Corp.Libn.
Staff: Prof 2. **Subjects:** Natural gas, energy, business. **Holdings:** 750 books; 15 VF drawers of clippings and pamphlets. **Subscriptions:** 80 journals and other serials; 12 newspapers. **Services:** Interlibrary loans; copying; library not open to public. **Computerized Information Services:** SDC, DIALOG, DOE/RECON. **Publications:** Corporate Library Update, monthly - to management personnel. **Staff:** Karen M. Dahl, Asst.Libn.

★7984★
MICHIGAN EDUCATION ASSOCIATION - LIBRARY
Box 673
East Lansing, MI 48823
Subjects: Education and labor relations. **Special Collections:** Old textbooks. **Holdings:** Figures not available. **Remarks:** Presently inactive.

MICHIGAN EMPLOYMENT SECURITY COMMISSION
See: Michigan State Department of Labor

MICHIGAN INFORMATION TRANSFER SOURCE
See: University of Michigan

★7985★
MICHIGAN LUTHERAN SEMINARY - LIBRARY (Rel-Theol)
2128 Court
Saginaw, MI 48602
Phone: (517) 793-1041
Milton P. Spaude, Libn. & Professor
Founded: 1952. **Staff:** Prof 2; Other 1. **Subjects:** History, religion, education. **Holdings:** 10,000 books; 100 bound periodical volumes. **Subscriptions:** 48 journals and other serials. **Services:** Library not open to public.

★7986★
MICHIGAN MUNICIPAL LEAGUE - LIBRARY (Soc Sci)
1675 Green Rd.
Box 1487
Ann Arbor, MI 48106
Phone: (313) 662-3246
Carol Genco, Coord.Lib./Inquiry Serv.
Founded: 1928. **Staff:** Prof 2; Other 1. **Subjects:** Municipal government, city

charters, ordinances, Michigan Statutes, Michigan legislation. **Special Collections:** Charters of all Michigan home rule cities and villages (365 items). **Holdings:** 8000 books; 35 VF drawers of unbound reports, manuscripts, clippings, pamphlets and documents. **Subscriptions:** 200 journals and other serials; clipping service for all Michigan dailies and weeklies. **Services:** Interlibrary loans; copying; SDI to staff; library open to public. **Publications:** List of Publications of the Michigan Municipal League.

★7987★
MICHIGAN OSTEOPATHIC MEDICAL CENTER, INC. - HEALTH SCIENCE LIBRARY (Med)
2700 Martin Luther King Jr. Blvd.   Phone: (313) 494-0470
Detroit, MI 48208   Carolyn A. Hough, Mgr., Lib.Serv.
Founded: 1971. **Staff:** Prof 4; Other 4. **Subjects:** Medicine, osteopathy, psychiatry. **Holdings:** 3000 books; 1200 bound periodical volumes; 350 video cassettes; 600 audio cassettes. **Subscriptions:** 300 journals and other serials. **Services:** Interlibrary loans; copying; library open to medical staff of other medical institutions. **Computerized Information Services:** MEDLINE, DIALOG. **Networks/Consortia:** Member of Metropolitan Detroit Medical Library Group. **Staff:** Becky Huang, Tech.Serv.Libn.; Judy Schram, AV Coord.

★7988★
MICHIGAN PSYCHOANALYTIC INSTITUTE - IRA MILLER MEMORIAL LIBRARY (Med)
16310 W. 12 Mile Rd., Suite 204   Phone: (313) 559-5855
Southfield, MI 48076   Alan Krohn, Ph.D., Chm., Lib.Comm.
Founded: 1962. **Staff:** 2. **Subjects:** Psychoanalysis, psychotherapy, psychiatry. **Holdings:** 1000 books; 400 bound periodical volumes. **Services:** Interlibrary loans; copying; library open to individuals in the mental health professions.

MICHIGAN STATE BAR ASSOCIATION
See: State Bar of Michigan

★7989★
MICHIGAN STATE DEPARTMENT OF AGRICULTURE - LIBRARY (Agri)
1615 S. Harrison Rd.   Phone: (517) 373-6410
East Lansing, MI 48823   Kathleen E. Callahan, Lib.Asst.
Founded: 1957. **Staff:** Prof 1. **Subjects:** Agriculture, food and dairy products analysis, liquors and wines, veterinary medicine. **Special Collections:** National Bureau of Standards Publications (7 complete series); American Standard Testing Materials (40 volumes). **Holdings:** 1500 books; 1000 bound periodical volumes. **Subscriptions:** 90 journals and other serials. **Services:** Library not open to public.

★7990★
MICHIGAN STATE DEPARTMENT OF LABOR - MICHIGAN EMPLOYMENT SECURITY COMMISSION - LIBRARY (Bus-Fin; Soc Sci)
7310 Woodward Ave., Rm. 5   Phone: (313) 876-5597
Detroit, MI 48202   Richard L. Daoust, Hd.Libn.
Staff: 2. **Subjects:** Employment services for general population and for veterans, women, rural employment, handicapped, youth, and minorities; job interviewing, counseling and testing; employment programs; unemployment insurance law, regulations, research, theory, practice; occupational information and research; labor market research and statistics; personnel/administrative management; job analysis. **Holdings:** 7300 books; 17,000 bound periodical volumes; 15,500 files; 40 16mm films; 15 Fairchild cassettes; 55 video cassettes. **Subscriptions:** 150 journals and other serials. **Services:** Interlibrary loans; copying; library open to Commission employees and other state agencies, professionals and students. **Publications:** Brochure. **Special Catalogs:** Catalog of Promotional and Informational Material. **Special Indexes:** AV catalog (annotated, indexed). **Staff:** Lena Wolk, Lib.Asst.

★7991★
MICHIGAN STATE DEPARTMENT OF MENTAL HEALTH - LIBRARY (Med)†
Lewis Cass Bldg., 6th Fl.   Phone: (517) 373-0408
Lansing, MI 48926   Laurel Minott, Libn.
Staff: Prof 1; Other 2. **Subjects:** Mental health and mental retardation services in Michigan and the U.S. **Holdings:** 1000 books; 160 16mm films; 12 VF drawers of departmental documents; 6 VF drawers of state and local agency files; 6 VF drawers of subject files. **Subscriptions:** 181 journals and other serials. **Services:** Interlibrary loans; copying; library open to public for reference use only. **Publications:** Special reports.

★7992★
MICHIGAN STATE DEPARTMENT OF NATURAL RESOURCES - GEOLOGICAL SURVEY DIVISION - LIBRARY
Box 30028
Lansing, MI 48909
Subjects: Geological surveys - U.S., Michigan, Canada. **Holdings:** Geological

survey publications. **Special Catalogs:** Michigan Geology Bibliography (card). **Remarks:** Presently inactive.

★7993★
MICHIGAN STATE DEPARTMENT OF NATURAL RESOURCES - INSTITUTE FOR FISHERIES RESEARCH - LIBRARY (Sci-Tech)
Univ. Musms. Annex,
University of Michigan   Phone: (313) 663-3554
Ann Arbor, MI 48109   Grace M. Zurek, Libn.
Staff: 1. **Subjects:** Fisheries biology and management. **Special Collections:** Great Lakes bibliography; Michigan Climatological Data. **Holdings:** 600 books and bound periodical volumes; 10,000 reprints; 1900 reports; 105 theses; 2400 lake maps. **Subscriptions:** 42 journals and other serials. **Services:** Library open to public for reference use only.

★7994★
MICHIGAN STATE DEPARTMENT OF PUBLIC HEALTH - LIBRARY (Med)
3500 N. Logan St.   Phone: (517) 373-1359
Lansing, MI 48909   Bill Nelton, Libn.
Founded: 1873. **Staff:** Prof 1; Other 2. **Subjects:** Public health, law. **Holdings:** 15,000 bound periodical volumes; 4 VF drawers of pamphlets and documents; 600 16mm films. **Subscriptions:** 400 journals and other serials. **Services:** Interlibrary loans; SDI; library open to public for reference use only.

★7995★
MICHIGAN STATE DEPARTMENT OF TRANSPORTATION - TRANSPORTATION LIBRARY (Trans)†
400 W. Ottawa
Box 30050   Phone: (517) 373-1545
Lansing, MI 48909   Norman J. Bunker, Libn.
Founded: 1964. **Staff:** Prof 1; Other 2. **Subjects:** Highways - design, construction, engineering, materials, safety; transportation planning; traffic and environmental engineering; mass transit. **Special Collections:** MDSHT publications; Transportation Research Board publications; Highway Research Information Service publications. **Holdings:** 5000 books; 300 bound periodical volumes; 120,000 unbound reports. **Subscriptions:** 340 journals and other serials. **Services:** Interlibrary loans; copying; library open to public. **Publications:** Monthly Acquisition List; Journal Highlights. **Special Indexes:** Documentary retrieval system; computer printout of indexed abstracts, Highway Research Information Service.

★7996★
MICHIGAN STATE HISTORY DIVISION - ARCHIVES (Hist)
3405 N. Logan   Phone: (517) 373-0512
Lansing, MI 48918   David J. Johnson, State Archv.
Staff: Prof 5; Other 2. **Subjects:** Official Michigan archives. **Holdings:** 17,000 cubic feet of state, local and private records; 200,000 photographic items. **Services:** Copying; abstracting; archives open to public. **Publications:** List of publications - available upon request.

★7997★
MICHIGAN STATE LEGISLATIVE COUNCIL - LEGISLATIVE SERVICE BUREAU LIBRARY (Soc Sci)
125 W. Allegan
Box 30036   Phone: (517) 373-0472
Lansing, MI 48909   Elliott Smith, Dir.
Founded: 1941. **Staff:** Prof 1; Other 1. **Subjects:** State government, law. **Special Collections:** Michigan manuals since 1873; Michigan Supreme Court cases since 1843; legislative journals since 1897; Michigan Statutes since 1837. **Holdings:** 7800 books; 20 VF drawers. **Subscriptions:** 95 journals and other serials; 6 newspapers. **Services:** Copying. **Computerized Information Services:** DIALOG; National Conference of State Legislatures Legislative Information System (internal database); computerized cataloging. **Publications:** Recent Acquisitions in the Legislative Service Bureau Library, monthly - for internal distribution only. **Staff:** Anne T. Bautista, Libn.

★7998★
MICHIGAN STATE LIBRARY SERVICES (Educ)
Box 30007   Phone: (517) 373-1580
Lansing, MI 48909   Francis X. Scannell, State Libn.
Founded: 1828. **Staff:** Prof 38; Other 56. **Special Collections:** Bower and Averbach (fish); Michigan newspapers; special Michigan collection; regional depository for federal documents; official depository for State of Michigan documents. **Holdings:** 1.4 million volumes. **Services:** Interlibrary loans; copying; library open to public. **Publications:** State Library Newsletter, monthly; Michigan in Books, quarterly; Michigan in Documents, quarterly; Family Trails, semiannual. **Remarks:** The library is located at 735 E. Michigan Ave., Lansing, MI, 48913. **Staff:** Donald Leaf, Hd., Tech.Proc.; R. Mahoney, Hd./Pub.Lib. Program; Julie Nicol, Libn. for the Blind.

★7999★
MICHIGAN STATE LIBRARY SERVICES - LAW LIBRARY (Law)
Law Bldg.
Box 30012   Phone: (517) 373-0630
Lansing, MI 48909   Charles B. Wolfe, State Law Libn.
Founded: 1828. **Staff:** Prof 3; Other 4. **Subjects:** Law. **Special Collections:** Michigan Records and Briefs (1874 to present); United States Records and Briefs (1870 to present). **Holdings:** 120,000 volumes; 3 VF drawers of clippings; 13 VF drawers of documents and reports. **Subscriptions:** 380 journals. **Services:** Interlibrary loans; copying. **Computerized Information Services:** WESTLAW. **Remarks:** Statistics given are also included in entry for Michigan State Library Services (see above). **Staff:** Duncan C. Webb, Asst. State Law Libn.

★8000★
MICHIGAN STATE UNIVERSITY - AGRICULTURAL ECONOMICS REFERENCE ROOM (Agri)
29 Agriculture Hall   Phone: (517) 355-6650
East Lansing, MI 48824   Pauline Sondag, Libn.
Staff: 2. **Subjects:** Economic aspects of agriculture, agricultural business, rural manpower, public affairs, food systems. **Special Collections:** Agricultural Economics Department publications. **Holdings:** 1200 books; 440 bound periodical volumes; 2000 U.S. documents (cataloged); 200 U.N. and international documents; 50 boxes of State Experiment Station publications; 16 VF drawers. **Subscriptions:** 250 journals and other serials.

★8001★
MICHIGAN STATE UNIVERSITY - ANIMAL INDUSTRIES REFERENCE ROOM (Sci-Tech)
208 Anthony Hall   Phone: (517) 355-8483
East Lansing, MI 48824   Carole S. Armstrong, Sci.Br.Coord.
Founded: 1956. **Staff:** 1. **Subjects:** Physiology, biochemistry, nutrition, food science, animal breeding and production. **Holdings:** 7800 volumes; 540 theses; 20 VF drawers of pamphlets. **Subscriptions:** 87 journals and other serials. **Services:** Interlibrary loans.

★8002★
MICHIGAN STATE UNIVERSITY - ART/MAPS DIVISION (Art; Geog-Map)
                                             Phone: (517) 353-4593
East Lansing, MI 48824   Shirlee A. Studt, Art Libn.
Founded: 1973. **Staff:** 4. **Subjects:** Art, architecture, painting, sculpture, graphic and applied arts, photography. **Holdings:** 43,000 volumes including 9000 exhibition catalogs; picture file including reproductions of art works, portraiture and general subjects; vertical file for local artists, art organizations; 134,000 sheet maps; 2100 atlases. **Subscriptions:** 175 journals and other serials. **Services:** Interlibrary loans; copying; library open to public. **Computerized Information Services:** DIALOG.

★8003★
MICHIGAN STATE UNIVERSITY - BUSINESS LIBRARY (Bus-Fin)
21 Eppley Ctr.   Phone: (517) 355-3380
East Lansing, MI 48824   William S. Stoddard, Bus.Libn.
Founded: 1962. **Staff:** Prof 1; Other 3. **Subjects:** Business; accounting; finance; economics; taxation; transportation; hotel, restaurant, personnel and institutional management; tourism; marketing; real estate; operations research; business history. **Special Collections:** Annual reports and 10K reports of major American and foreign corporations, including early railroad reports; brokerage house reports, New York and American Stock Exchanges listing statements; collection of dissertations. **Holdings:** 60,000 books and bound periodical volumes; dissertations. **Subscriptions:** 900 journals and other serials; 30 newspapers. **Services:** Interlibrary loans; copying; library open to public. **Computerized Information Services:** Management Contents, ABI/Inform, Predicasts, LEXIS. **Networks/Consortia:** Member of OCLC. **Publications:** Accessions list, monthly; subject bibliographies.

★8004★
MICHIGAN STATE UNIVERSITY - C.W. BARR PLANNING AND DESIGN LIBRARY (Plan)
                                             Phone: (517) 353-3941
East Lansing, MI 48824   Dale E. Casper, Libn.
Founded: 1964. **Staff:** Prof 1; Other 1. **Subjects:** Planning, landscape architecture, design. **Special Collections:** Local Michigan planning documents. **Holdings:** 3500 books; 1000 bound periodical volumes; 9000 reports; 3000 pamphlets; 1000 maps. **Subscriptions:** 36 journals and other serials. **Services:** Interlibrary loans; library open to public.

★8005★
MICHIGAN STATE UNIVERSITY - CHEMISTRY LIBRARY (Sci-Tech)
426 Chemistry Bldg.   Phone: (517) 355-8512
East Lansing, MI 48824   Bernice Wallace, Libn.
Staff: Prof 1; Other 15. **Subjects:** Chemistry, chemical engineering, biochemistry, food science, medicine, technology. **Special Collections:** Gmelin; Beilstein; Landolt-Bornstein; Chemical Abstracts; Science Citation Index; Sadtler Spectra. **Holdings:** 43,700 volumes; 2850 microfiche; 690 reels of microfilm; 15,031 theses (masters' and doctoral). **Subscriptions:** 650 journals and other serials. **Services:** Interlibrary loans; copying; information retrieval program for faculty and limited use for graduate students; AV instruction for use of major reference texts; computerized literature searching for faculty and students. **Computerized Information Services:** DIALOG, BRS, MERIT Computer Network; computerized cataloging and circulation. **Publications:** Serials Listings.

★8006★
MICHIGAN STATE UNIVERSITY - DOCUMENTS DEPARTMENT (Info Sci)
                                             Phone: (517) 353-8707
East Lansing, MI 48824   Eleanor J. Boyles, Doc.Libn.
Founded: 1949. **Staff:** Prof 2; Other 3. **Subjects:** Documents - U.S. (depository and nondepository), U.N., UNESCO, Pan American Union, International Organizations, Canada. **Holdings:** 23,000 books; 8100 bound periodical volumes; 381,101 bound and unbound documents; Congressional Serial set (1st Congress to present); 634,265 microforms. **Services:** Interlibrary loans; copying; library open to public. **Staff:** Marillyn Owens .

★8007★
MICHIGAN STATE UNIVERSITY - ENGINEERING LIBRARY (Sci-Tech)
308 Engineering Bldg.   Phone: (517) 355-8536
East Lansing, MI 48824   Jackson Yang, Engr./Sci.Libn.
Founded: 1963. **Staff:** Prof 1; Other 4. **Subjects:** Engineering - chemical, civil, transportation, environmental, electrical, mechanical; electronics; metallurgy; materials science. **Holdings:** 51,089 volumes. **Subscriptions:** 604 journals and other serials. **Services:** Interlibrary loans; copying; library open to public. **Computerized Information Services:** DIALOG, BRS. **Networks/Consortia:** Member of OCLC. **Publications:** New books list.

★8008★
MICHIGAN STATE UNIVERSITY - EXTERNAL COURSES AND PROGRAMS LIBRARY (Educ; Bus-Fin)
Main Library, Rm. WG-5   Phone: (517) 355-2345
East Lansing, MI 48824   Frank C. MacDougall, Libn.
Founded: 1952. **Staff:** 1. **Subjects:** Education, business. **Holdings:** 11,500 volumes; 750 periodicals on microfilm. **Subscriptions:** 32 journals and other serials. **Services:** Interlibrary loans; library open to extension faculty and students only. **Remarks:** Maintained as a part of the Michigan State University Lifelong Education Library. **Formerly:** Its University Extension Library.

★8009★
MICHIGAN STATE UNIVERSITY - G. ROBERT VINCENT VOICE LIBRARY (Hum)
Main Library Bldg., W433-W437   Phone: (517) 335-5122
East Lansing, MI 48824   Dr. Maurice A. Crane, Hd.
Staff: Prof 1; Other 7. **Subjects:** Historical sound recordings of voices and events in all fields of human endeavor; media history; literature and theater; classical jazz. **Holdings:** 4600 items; 4000 tape recordings. **Services:** Copying; library open to public for educational research only. **Special Catalogs:** Dictionary Catalog (book); Descriptive Guide, annual.

★8010★
MICHIGAN STATE UNIVERSITY - GEOLOGY LIBRARY (Sci-Tech)
5 Natural Sciences Bldg.   Phone: (517) 353-7988
East Lansing, MI 48824   Carole S. Armstrong, Sci.Br.Coord.
Founded: 1967. **Staff:** 1. **Subjects:** Geology. **Holdings:** 17,000 volumes; 3300 maps. **Subscriptions:** 134 journals and other serials. **Services:** Interlibrary loans; copying; library open to public.

★8011★
MICHIGAN STATE UNIVERSITY - HIGHWAY TRAFFIC SAFETY AND COMMUNITY DEVELOPMENT - LIBRARY (Trans)
University Library   Phone: (517) 353-9309
East Lansing, MI 48824   Frank C. MacDougall, Libn.
Founded: 1956. **Staff:** Prof 1; Other 1. **Subjects:** Traffic safety, driver education and behavior, law enforcement, police administration, traffic engineering, crash studies, highway accident statistics, community development, urban and rural sociology, state and local government. **Holdings:** 21,500 books and report literature; 1400 periodical volumes; 3400 Highway Research Board publications. **Subscriptions:** 468 journals and other serials.

Services: Interlibrary loans; copying; library open to public. **Remarks:** Maintained as a part of Michigan State University Lifelong Education Library.

★8012★
MICHIGAN STATE UNIVERSITY - INSTRUCTIONAL MEDIA CENTER - FILM LIBRARY (Aud-Vis)
East Lansing, MI 48824
Phone: (517) 353-7850
Sue Ann Wilt, Libn.
Founded: 1955. **Staff:** Prof 1; Other 2. **Holdings:** 4100 16mm films. **Services:** Film service to the campus; rental to all states; library open to public. **Networks/Consortia:** Member of Consortium of University Film Centers (CUFC). **Publications:** MSU Film Rental Catalog, published every 3 years with periodic supplements.

★8013★
MICHIGAN STATE UNIVERSITY - INTERNATIONAL LIBRARY (Area-Ethnic)
W310-316 University Library
Phone: (517) 355-2366
East Lansing, MI 48824
Dr. Eugene de Benko, Hd., Intl.Lib.
Founded: 1964. **Staff:** Prof 3; Other 4. **Subjects:** Sub-Saharan Africa, Sahel Zone of West Africa, South and Southeast Asia, Latin America, East Asia. **Special Collections:** African languages, linguistics and literature; Congo (Zaire) Collection; archival resources on the slave trade; British Colonial and Foreign Office archival materials on Africa (microform); Kenya National Archives (microform); PL-480 collection on South Africa. **Holdings:** 226,400 books and bound periodical volumes; 33,100 pamphlets (cataloged); 17,140 sheet maps; 39,600 titles on microforms. **Subscriptions:** 5980 journals and other serials; 11 newspapers. **Services:** Interlibrary loans; library open to public. **Publications:** Africana - Select Recent Acquisitions, 4/year; Sahel Bibliographic Bulletin/Bulletin Bibliographique 4/year - both distributed by mail. **Special Catalogs:** Card catalogs for Africa, Asia, and Latin America; card catalog of area studies pamphlet collections; Research Sources for African Studies: A Checklist of Relevant Serial Publications Based on Library Collections at Michigan State University, compiled by Eugene de Benko and Patricia L. Butts, 1969; Current Periodicals: A Select Bibliography in the Area of Latin American Studies, compiled by Tamara Brunnschweiler, 1968; Research Sources for South Asian Studies in Economic Development: A Select Bibliography of Serial Publications, compiled by Eugene de Benko and V.N. Krishnan, 1966; On Mao-Tse-tung: A Bibliographical Guide, compiled by Austin Chi-wei Shu, 1972; A Guide to Africana Materials in the Michigan State University Libraries, compiled by Joseph J. Lauer, 1982. **Remarks:** Except for the Area Files (pamphlet collection) of over 33,000 pieces, the International Library does not house the holdings indicated above. These materials are shelved according to their classification in the stacks or in special areas (e.g. Special Collections; Maps and Microfilms; Periodicals Reading Room). The International Library is responsible for the development of the collections for African, Asian and Latin American studies needed for teaching and research; provides bibliographic advisory service to faculty and students engaged in the study of these areas; and provides consultation service for the University's several overseas projects. **Staff:** Mrs. Onuma Ezera, Bibliog. Africa Stud.; Dr. Tamara Brunnschweiler, Bibliog.Lat.Amer.Stud.

★8014★
MICHIGAN STATE UNIVERSITY - INTERNATIONAL LIBRARY - SAHEL DOCUMENTATION CENTER (Area-Ethnic)
W-312 University Library
Phone: (517) 355-2397
East Lansing, MI 48824
Dr. Eugene de Benko, Act.Ed. & Libn.
Founded: 1976. **Staff:** Prof 1; Other 2. **Subjects:** Socio-economic development of the Sahel region of West Africa. **Holdings:** 11,000 books, bound periodical volumes and pamphlets. **Services:** Interlibrary loans; copying; library open to public. **Computerized Information Services:** Computerized circulation. **Publications:** Sahel: Bibliographic Bulletin/Bulletin Bibliographique, quarterly - distributed by mail. **Special Indexes:** Title index for all materials listed in the Sahel Bibliographic Bulletin; comprehensive author index. **Remarks:** Except for the area files of pamphlets and ephemera, the Sahel Documentation Center does not house the materials mentioned above, which are kept in the appropriate place in the University Library. The Sahel Documentation Center is also responsible for serving and maintaining links with documentation centers in the Sahelian countries of West Africa.

★8015★
MICHIGAN STATE UNIVERSITY - LABOR AND INDUSTRIAL RELATIONS LIBRARY (Soc Sci)
Library E109
Phone: (517) 355-4647
East Lansing, MI 48824
Martha Jane Soltow, Libn.
Founded: 1956. **Staff:** Prof 1; Other 2. **Subjects:** Labor unions, public employee unionism, labor law, manpower, minorities. **Special Collections:** Union constitutions and proceedings; public sector agreements for State of Michigan. **Holdings:** 50,000 books; 5000 bound periodical volumes; 200 VF drawers by subject of pamphlets, mimeographed materials. **Subscriptions:**

125 journals and other serials; 75 newspapers. **Services:** Interlibrary loans; copying; library open to public. **Computerized Information Services:** Computerized cataloging. **Staff:** Nancy Barkey Young, Asst.Libn.

MICHIGAN STATE UNIVERSITY - LIFELONG EDUCATION LIBRARY
See: Michigan State University - External Courses and Programs Library; Michigan State University - Highway Traffic Safety and Community Development Library

★8016★
MICHIGAN STATE UNIVERSITY - MICROFORMS LIBRARY (Soc Sci; Hum)
East Lansing, MI 48824
Phone: (517) 353-3120
Sally A. Hiddinga, Br.Lib.Ck.
Founded: 1978. **Staff:** 3. **Subjects:** American and English history, literature and culture, foreign imprints, African and Asian source documents, newspapers. **Holdings:** 900,000 microforms, bibliographic aids. **Services:** Interlibrary loans; copying; library open to public.

★8017★
MICHIGAN STATE UNIVERSITY - MUSIC LIBRARY (Mus)
East Lansing, MI 48824-1043
Phone: (517) 355-7660
Roseann Hammill, Music Libn.
Staff: Prof 1. **Subjects:** Music. **Holdings:** 17,147 music scores; 5667 recordings. **Subscriptions:** 101 journals and other serials. **Services:** Interlibrary loans; copying; library open to public.

★8018★
MICHIGAN STATE UNIVERSITY - NONFORMAL EDUCATION INFORMATION CENTER (Educ)
College of Education
513 Erickson Hall
Phone: (517) 355-5522
East Lansing, MI 48824
Joan M. Claffey, Dir.
Staff: Prof 6; Other 4. **Subjects:** Nonformal education - theory, development, women in development. **Holdings:** 1500 books; 5500 fugitive documents; 200 periodicals. **Subscriptions:** 110 journals and other serials. **Services:** Copying; library open to public. **Publications:** The NFE Exchange, 3/year; annotated bibliographies; occasional papers - all free upon request to development planners and practitioners.

★8019★
MICHIGAN STATE UNIVERSITY - PHYSICS-ASTRONOMY LIBRARY (Sci-Tech)
Rm. 229, Physics-Astronomy Bldg.
Phone: (517) 355-9704
East Lansing, MI 48824
Carole S. Armstrong, Sci.Br.Coord.
Founded: 1967. **Staff:** 1. **Subjects:** Physics, astronomy. **Holdings:** 23,000 volumes. **Subscriptions:** 370 journals and other serials. **Services:** Interlibrary loans; library open to public.

★8020★
MICHIGAN STATE UNIVERSITY - SCIENCE LIBRARY (Sci-Tech)
East Lansing, MI 48824
Phone: (517) 355-2347
Carole S. Armstrong, Hd.
Founded: 1955. **Staff:** Prof 8; Other 4. **Subjects:** Medicine, biological sciences, agriculture, veterinary medicine, nursing, technology, human ecology, history of science. **Holdings:** 350,000 books and bound periodical volumes. **Subscriptions:** 6000 journals and other serials. **Services:** Interlibrary loans; copying; library open to public. **Computerized Information Services:** MEDLINE, BRS, DIALOG. **Networks/Consortia:** Member of Kentucky-Ohio-Michigan Regional Medical Library Program (KOMRML). **Remarks:** Library is a depository for U.S. Dept. of Agriculture documents. **Staff:** Leslie Behm, Clinical Ctr./Sci.Libn.; Mr. Carol D. Jones, Sci.Libn.; Jan Rice, Sci.Libn.; Chris J. Miko, Vet.Med./Sci.Libn.; Judy Coppola, Sci.Libn.; Janet Parsch, Asst.Hd.; Jackson Yang, Engr./Sci.Libn.

★8021★
MICHIGAN STATE UNIVERSITY - SPECIAL COLLECTIONS DIVISION
University Library
Phone: (517) 355-3770
East Lansing, MI 48824
Jannette Fiore, Libn.
Founded: 1960. **Staff:** Prof 1; Other 1. **Subjects:** American radicalism; veterinary medicine (history); literary collections - U.S., England, Ireland; American popular culture; French monarchy (history); botany; entomology; agriculture; apiculture; cookery. **Special Collections:** American Radicalism (10,600); veterinary medicine (1600); Popular Culture (34,000). **Holdings:** 134,000 volumes. **Subscriptions:** 150 journals and newspapers. **Services:** Copying; library open to public with required identification.

★8022★

MICHIGAN STATE UNIVERSITY - SPECIAL COLLECTIONS DIVISION - RUSSEL B. NYE POPULAR CULTURE COLLECTION (Hum)

University Library
East Lansing, MI 48824

Phone: (517) 355-3770
Jannette Fiore, Libn.

Staff: Prof 1; Other 1. **Subjects:** Comic art, popular fiction, juvenile fiction, performing arts and information. **Holdings:** 34,000 volumes. **Services:** Copying; library open to public with required identification. **Publications:** The Russel B. Nye Popular Culture Collection, A Descriptive Guide (pamphlet).

★8023★

MICHIGAN STATE UNIVERSITY - UNIVERSITY ARCHIVES AND HISTORICAL COLLECTIONS (Hist)

Phone: (517) 355-2330
East Lansing, MI 48824
Dr. Frederick L. Honhart, Dir.

Staff: Prof 3; Other 2. **Subjects:** University archives, Michigan automobile industry, lumbering, agriculture and rural life, civil war. **Special Collections:** Samaritan Manuscripts (Biblical and liturgical texts, 1470-1927; 2 cubic feet); Ransom E. Olds Papers (5 cubic feet); John Harvey Kellogg Papers (26 cubic feet); Charles Hackley and Thomas Hume Papers (83 cubic feet); John A. Hannah Papers (100 cubic feet); Reo Motor Car Company Records, 1905-1961 (216 cubic feet); American Agri-Women Records, 1970-1981 (6 cubic feet). **Services:** Copying; library open to public. **Publications:** Guide to Michigan State University Archives and Historical Collections. **Special Catalogs:** Inventories available for processed collections. **Staff:** Richard Harms, Spec.; Mary Patton, Spec.

★8024★

MICHIGAN STATE UNIVERSITY - UNIVERSITY CENTER FOR INTERNATIONAL REHABILITATION (UCIR) - RESOURCE LIBRARY (Soc Sci)

513 Erickson Hall
East Lansing, MI 48824

Phone: (517) 355-1824
James J. Mullin, Sr.Res.Assoc.

Founded: 1978. **Staff:** 1. **Subjects:** World-wide rehabilitation and special education. **Special Collections:** International Labour Office Legislative Series, 1942-1978. **Holdings:** 2500 books. **Subscriptions:** 45 journals and other serials; 70 newsletters. **Services:** Library open to public for reference use only. **Computerized Information Services:** Computerized cataloging. **Remarks:** The University Center for International Rehabilitation is maintained by the College of Education and funded by the National Institute for Handicapped Research, U.S. Department of Education.

MICHIGAN STATE UNIVERSITY - UNIVERSITY EXTENSION LIBRARY
See: Michigan State University - External Courses and Programs Library

★8025★

MICHIGAN STATE UNIVERSITY - URBAN POLICY AND PLANNING LIBRARY (Plan)

University Library
East Lansing, MI 48824

Phone: (517) 353-9304
Dale E. Casper, Soc.Sci.Coord.

Founded: 1969. **Staff:** Prof 1; Other 1. **Subjects:** Urban policy and planning, housing, municipal finance, transportation. **Special Collections:** H.U.D. 701 Collection (16,700 volumes); Non-701 planning reports (8200 volumes). **Holdings:** 560 books; 4500 pamphlets and clippings in VF drawers. **Subscriptions:** 65 journals and other serials. **Services:** Interlibrary loans; SDI; library open to public. **Computerized Information Services:** DIALOG, SDC, BRS. **Publications:** Recent Books, monthly; This Is the Way Series (one each on Revenue Sharing and New Towns); A Bibliographic Guide to Environmental Impact Statements; Policy and Planning Related Courses at Michigan State University; A Guide to Policy and Planning Resources in the Michigan State University Libraries - all publications distributed free to the university community. **Staff:** Sandra Parks, Lib.Techn.

★8026★

MICHIGAN STATE UNIVERSITY - V.G. GROVE RESEARCH LIBRARY OF MATHEMATICS-STATISTICS (Sci-Tech)

101-D Wells Hall
East Lansing, MI 48824

Phone: (517) 353-8852
Berle Reiter, Libn.

Founded: 1967. **Staff:** Prof 1; Other 1. **Subjects:** Pure and applied mathematics, statistics, probability, mathematics education. **Holdings:** 30,245 volumes; 150 reels of microfilm; 245 microfiche cards. **Subscriptions:** 470 journals and other serials. **Services:** Interlibrary loans; library open to public for room use only; special permit may be obtained from Circulation department, Main Library.

★8027★

MICHIGAN STATE UNIVERSITY - W.K. KELLOGG BIOLOGICAL STATION - WALTER F. MOROFSKY MEMORIAL LIBRARY (Sci-Tech)

3700 E. Gull Lake Dr.
Hickory Corners, MI 49060

Phone: (616) 671-5117
Carolyn Hammarskjold, Libn.

Founded: 1966. **Staff:** Prof 1; Other 1. **Subjects:** Aquatic ecology, terrestrial ecology, limnology, botany, zoology, ornithology, entomology. **Holdings:** 3969 books; 3809 bound periodical volumes. **Subscriptions:** 157 journals and other serials. **Services:** Interlibrary loans; copying; library open to graduate students and other researchers. **Computerized Information Services:** BRS.

★8028★

MICHIGAN TECHNOLOGICAL UNIVERSITY - FORD FORESTRY CENTER - LIBRARY (Env-Cons)†

Phone: (906) 524-6181
L'Anse, MI 49946
Stephen Shetron, Sr.Res.Sci.

Staff: Prof 1. **Subjects:** Forestry, botany, ecology. **Special Collections:** History of forests in the Upper Peninsula, Michigan. **Holdings:** 1000 books. **Subscriptions:** 15 journals and other serials.

★8029★

MICHIGAN TECHNOLOGICAL UNIVERSITY - INSTITUTE OF MINERAL RESEARCH (Sci-Tech)

Phone: (906) 487-2600
Houghton, MI 49931
C.W. Schultz, Dir.

Subjects: Metallurgy, geophysics, mineral beneficiation, mineralogy, mining methods, nonmetalic mineral resources. **Holdings:** Figures not available. **Subscriptions:** 10 journals and other serials. **Services:** Literature searches and analyses on a fee basis.

★8030★

MICHIGAN TECHNOLOGICAL UNIVERSITY - INSTITUTE OF WOOD RESEARCH INFORMATION CENTER (Sci-Tech)

Phone: (906) 487-2464
Houghton, MI 49931
Nina A. Ridge, Res.Info.Serv.

Founded: 1947. **Staff:** 1. **Subjects:** Forest products industries, wood science and technology. **Holdings:** 1000 books and bound periodical volumes; 20,000 documents. **Subscriptions:** 102 journals and other serials. **Services:** Interlibrary loans; copying; library open to public with prior permission. **Computerized Information Services:** DIALOG, SDC, NLM, NIH/EPA Chemical Information System, TECHNOTEC, Information Handling Service, New York Times Information Service; computerized cataloging and circulation.

★8031★

MICHIGAN TECHNOLOGICAL UNIVERSITY - LIBRARY (Sci-Tech)

Phone: (906) 487-2500
Houghton, MI 49931
Lee J. Lebbin, Dir.

Founded: 1885. **Staff:** Prof 12; Other 21. **Subjects:** Geology, metallurgy, biology, mathematics, mining, engineering, forestry, chemistry. **Special Collections:** Spitzbergen Collection (75 books, maps, clippings and articles); Foundation Library Center Regional Collection; Copper Country Historical Collection; depository for U.S. Government documents; university archives; regional depository for Michigan State Archives; U.S. Bureau of Mines Maps of Michigan Collection. **Holdings:** 514,163 volumes; 89,236 maps; 68,233 microforms. **Subscriptions:** 9415 journals and other serials; 36 newspapers. **Services:** Interlibrary loans; copying; library open to public with first priority to students. **Computerized Information Services:** DIALOG, SDC; computerized cataloging, serials and ILL. **Networks/Consortia:** Member of OCLC; Michigan Library Consortium; Upper Peninsula Region of Library Cooperation. **Publications:** Serials Holdings List, irregular; Theses and Dissertations, irregular; Guide to the Library, irregular. **Staff:** Robert Patterson, Hd., Pub.Serv.; Janet Locatelli, ILL; David H. Thomas, Hd., Tech.Serv.; Laszlo Velics, Univ.Bibliog.

★8032★

MICHIGAN WISCONSIN PIPELINE COMPANY - LIBRARY (Env-Cons)

5075 Westheimer, Suite 1100 W.
Houston, TX 77056

Phone: (713) 623-0300
Donna Heard, Rec.Supv.

Founded: 1978. **Staff:** 2. **Subjects:** Geology. **Holdings:** 1500 books; 400 bound periodical volumes. **Subscriptions:** 62 journals and other serials.

MICMAC-MALISEET INSTITUTE
See: University of New Brunswick - Education Resource Centre

★8033★

MICRODOC - TECHNICAL DOCUMENTATION COLLECTION (Info Sci)

815 Carpenter Ln.
Philadelphia, PA 19119

Phone: (215) 848-4545
Thomas F. Deahl, Info.Sys.Engr.

Staff: Prof 1. **Subjects:** Micrographics technology, micropublishing, thesaurus construction, indexing and abstracting, information storage and retrieval, linguistics. **Special Collections:** Micro-equipment, software and small computer vendor specifications. **Holdings:** 300 books; 6000 other cataloged items. **Services:** Customized literature searches and analyses; collection not open to public.

★8034★
MICROMEDEX, INC. - PAUL DE HAEN DRUG INFORMATION SYSTEMS (Med)
2750 S. Shoshone St.   Phone: (303) 781-6683
Englewood, CO 80110
Founded: 1956. **Staff:** Prof 3. **Subjects:** Drugs. **Holdings:** 500 books; 200,000 scientific reports from international biomedical literature. **Subscriptions:** 1000 journals and other serials. **Services:** Indexing; literature translations. **Computerized Information Services:** DIALOG, SDC, MEDLINE, TOXLINE. **Publications:** List of publications - available upon request. **Staff:** Paul E. Groth, Vice Pres.

MICRONESIAN AREA RESEARCH CENTER - PACIFIC COLLECTION
See: University of Guam

★8035★
MICROTEL PACIFIC RESEARCH LTD. - TECHNICAL LIBRARY (Sci-Tech)
8999 Nelson Way   Phone: (604) 294-1471
Burnaby, BC, Canada V5A 4B5   V. Renzetti, Tech.Libn.
Founded: 1960. **Staff:** 1. **Subjects:** Telecommunications, engineering, microwave, video voice and data communication, management. **Holdings:** 900 volumes. **Subscriptions:** 200 journals and other serials. **Services:** Interlibrary loans; copying; library not open to public. **Computerized Information Services:** DIALOG; MILS, MIC (internal databases).

★8036★
MICROWAVE ASSOCIATES, INC. - LIBRARY (Sci-Tech)
South Ave.   Phone: (617) 272-3000
Burlington, MA 01803   Christine S. Coburn, Libn.
Founded: 1960. **Staff:** 1. **Subjects:** Electrical and electronics engineering, microwaves, communication, solid state physics. **Holdings:** 1500 books; 1000 bound periodical volumes; 255 pamphlet boxes of company contract reports; 60 pamphlet boxes of patents. **Subscriptions:** 100 journals and other serials. **Services:** Interlibrary loans; copying; library not open to public.

MID ATLANTIC CENTER FOR COMMUNITY EDUCATION
See: University of Virginia

★8037★
MIDDLE EAST INSTITUTE - GEORGE CAMP KEISER LIBRARY (Area-Ethnic)
1761 N St., N.W.   Phone: (202) 785-1141
Washington, DC 20036   Lois M. Khairallah, Libn.
Founded: 1946. **Staff:** Prof 2; Other 2. **Subjects:** North Africa and Middle East - history, culture, religion, economics, philosophy, language and literature, sociology, law. **Special Collections:** George Camp Keiser Collection of the art of the Middle East; Richard D. Robinson Collection of books and documents relating to the development of modern Turkey; U.S. government documents relating to the Middle East. **Holdings:** 12,000 books; 3000 bound periodical volumes; 3 VF cases; 50 drawer files of newsletters. **Subscriptions:** 150 journals and other serials. **Services:** Interlibrary loans; copying; library open to public; only institute members may borrow materials. **Staff:** Ruth K. Baacke, Asst.Libn.

★8038★
MIDDLE GEORGIA REGIONAL LIBRARY - WASHINGTON MEMORIAL LIBRARY - GENEALOGICAL & HISTORICAL ROOM (Hist)
1180 Washington Ave.   Phone: (912) 744-0821
Macon, GA 31201   Nancy C. Watson, Chf. of Genealogy
Founded: 1923. **Staff:** Prof 2; Other 5. **Subjects:** Genealogy, history, county histories, heraldry, British genealogies. **Special Collections:** Stevens-Davis Memorial Collection (British and pre-Colonial); Georgia authors. **Holdings:** 13,504 books; 60 bound periodical volumes; 569 bound volumes of newspapers; 177 city directories; 3598 reels of microfilm (cataloged); 361 microfiche; 259 maps; 26 drawers of architectural drawings; 52 boxes of county and family histories. **Subscriptions:** 37 journals and other serials. **Services:** Copying; library open to public for reference use only. **Special Indexes:** Index to History of Jones County, Georgia. **Remarks:** An additional telephone number is (912)744-0820. **Staff:** Willard L. Rocker, Genealogy Libn.

★8039★
MIDDLEBURY HISTORICAL SOCIETY - MIDDLEBURY ACADEMY MUSEUM LIBRARY (Hist)
22 S. Academy St.   Phone: (716) 495-6495
Wyoming, NY 14591   Mary D. Wilson, Sec.
Founded: 1951. **Subjects:** Middlebury Academy. **Special Collections:** History of Wyoming County and environs; some deeds and documents concerned with academy and locality from 1818. **Holdings:** 750 volumes. **Services:** Library open to public by appointment on a limited schedule.

★8040★
MIDDLESEX COUNTY HISTORICAL SOCIETY - LIBRARY (Hist)†
151 Main St.   Phone: (203) 346-0746
Middletown, CT 06457
Founded: 1901. **Subjects:** Connecticut history, genealogy and town histories. **Holdings:** 2000 books; archives, manuscripts, letters, notebooks and records. **Services:** Library open to public on request. **Publications:** Activity report, irregular.

★8041★
MIDDLESEX COUNTY LAW LIBRARY (Law)
County Court House, 2nd Fl., E. Wing
1 Kennedy Square   Phone: (201) 745-3357
New Brunswick, NJ 08901   Roland A. Winter, Libn.
Staff: Prof 2. **Subjects:** Law. **Holdings:** 12,000 volumes. **Services:** Interlibrary loans; copying; library open to public. **Staff:** Pat Kennedy, Asst.Libn.

★8042★
MIDDLESEX COUNTY PLANNING BOARD - LIBRARY (Plan)†
40 Livingston Ave.   Phone: (201) 745-3062
New Brunswick, NJ 08901   Marla Kalaitzis, Libn.
Founded: 1972. **Staff:** Prof 1. **Subjects:** Natural resources and environment, land use and comprehensive planning, transportation, urban studies, planning. **Holdings:** 10,000 books; 125 periodical volumes; master plans and other data covering New Jersey counties and municipalities. **Subscriptions:** 100 journals and other serials. **Services:** Copying; library open to public for reference use only.

★8043★
MIDDLESEX LAW ASSOCIATION - LIBRARY (Law)
80 Dundas St.
Box 5600   Phone: (519) 679-7046
London, ON, Canada N6A 2P3   J.V. Gulliver, Libn./Adm.
Staff: Prof 1; Other 1. **Subjects:** Law. **Holdings:** 12,000 volumes. **Subscriptions:** 100 journals and other serials. **Services:** Copying; library open to public for reference use only. **Publications:** Newsletter, monthly.

★8044★
MIDDLESEX LAW LIBRARY (Law)
40 Thorndike St.   Phone: (617) 494-4148
Cambridge, MA 02141   Sandi Lindheimer, Lib.Dir.
Founded: 1815. **Staff:** Prof 1; Other 2. **Subjects:** Law - state and federal. **Holdings:** 75,000 books; 4500 bound periodical volumes. **Subscriptions:** 150 journals and other serials. **Services:** Library open to public.

★8045★
MIDDLESEX LAW LIBRARY ASSOCIATION - LIBRARY (Law)†
Superior Court House
360 Gorham St.   Phone: (617) 452-9301
Lowell, MA 01852   Madeline M. Corey, Libn.
Subjects: Law. **Holdings:** 77,685 volumes. **Staff:** Sharon A. Conley, Asst.Libn.

★8046★
MIDDLESEX MEMORIAL HOSPITAL - HEALTH SCIENCES LIBRARY (Med)
28 Crescent St.   Phone: (203) 347-9471
Middletown, CT 06457   Evelyn M. Breck, Dir.
Founded: 1972. **Staff:** Prof 1; Other 1. **Subjects:** Medicine, nursing. **Holdings:** 2000 books; 1400 bound periodical volumes; 6 VF drawers of clippings, catalogs. **Subscriptions:** 135 journals and other serials. **Services:** Interlibrary loans; copying; library open to public for reference use only. **Computerized Information Services:** MEDLINE. **Networks/Consortia:** Member of Connecticut Association of Health Sciences Libraries (CAHSL).

MIDDLETON (Maude Webster) NURSING LIBRARY
See: Edgewood College - Maude Webster Middleton Nursing Library

MIDDLETON (Troy H.) LIBRARY
See: Louisiana State University - Department of Archives and Manuscripts

MIDDLETON (William S.) HEALTH SCIENCES LIBRARY
See: University of Wisconsin, Madison - Center for Health Sciences Libraries

MIDDLETON (William S.) MEMORIAL VETERANS HOSPITAL
See: U.S. Veterans Administration (WI-Madison) - William S. Middleton Memorial Veterans Hospital

★8047★
MIDDLETOWN HOSPITAL ASSOCIATION - ADA I. LEONARD MEMORIAL LIBRARY (Med)
105 McKnight Dr.
Middletown, OH 45042
Phone: (513) 422-2111
Ursula S. Boettcher, Libn.
Founded: 1957. **Staff:** Prof 1. **Subjects:** Medicine, nursing, and allied health sciences. **Special Collections:** Anne Middlemiss Memorial Collection (500 volumes). **Holdings:** 900 books; 400 bound periodical volumes; 600 AV items; 1000 items in health information pamphlet file. **Subscriptions:** 110 journals and other serials. **Services:** Interlibrary loans; copying; library open to public for reference use only. **Computerized Information Services:** MEDLINE; computerized cataloging. **Networks/Consortia:** Member of Kentucky-Ohio-Michigan Regional Medical Library Program (KOMRML); Cincinnati Area Health Sciences Library Association (CAHSLA); Miami Valley Health Sciences Libraries Association.

★8048★
MIDDLETOWN PSYCHIATRIC CENTER - MEDICAL LIBRARY (Med)
141 Monhagen Ave.
Box 1453
Middletown, NY 10940
Phone: (914) 342-5511
Frank C. Appell, Jr., Asst.Libn.
Founded: 1880. **Staff:** Prof 1; Other 1. **Subjects:** Psychiatry, medicine, nursing. **Special Collections:** Extensive collection on homeopathy. **Holdings:** 4500 books; 1943 bound periodical volumes. **Subscriptions:** 110 journals and other serials. **Services:** Interlibrary loans; copying; library open to public with restrictions. **Networks/Consortia:** Member of Southeastern New York Library Resources Council (SENYLRC).

★8049★
MIDLAND COUNTY HISTORICAL SOCIETY - ARCHIVES (Hist)
1801 W. St. Andrews Dr.
Midland, MI 48640
Phone: (517) 835-7401
Kathryn Cummins, Dir.
Founded: 1952. **Staff:** 1. **Subjects:** History and genealogy - Midland, Michigan. **Holdings:** 1000 books; local newspapers on microfilm (1870 to present); maps, slides, pictures. **Services:** Copying; archives open to public by permission.

★8050★
MIDLAND COUNTY PUBLIC LIBRARY - PETROLEUM DEPARTMENT LIBRARY (Sci-Tech)
Box 1191
Midland, TX 79702
Phone: (915) 683-2708
Sandra Wegner, Petroleum Dept.Libn.
Founded: 1935. **Staff:** Prof 1; Other 2. **Subjects:** Geology, petroleum engineering, geophysics. **Special Collections:** Geological Society guidebooks; U.S. Geological Survey publications; state surveys. **Holdings:** 27,100 books; 950 bound periodical volumes; 7300 maps; 300 items in VF drawers; 6 file drawers of driller's logs; 17 shelves of Scout tickets; 340 reels of microfilm. **Subscriptions:** 58 journals and other serials. **Services:** Interlibrary loans; copying; library open to public. **Formerly:** Midland County Public Library - Sci-Tech Section Library. **Remarks:** Library is located at 301 W. Missouri, Midland, TX.

★8051★
MIDLAND DOHERTY, LTD. - LIBRARY (Bus-Fin)
Box 25, Commercial Union Tower
Toronto Dominion Centre
Toronto, ON, Canada M5K 1B5
Phone: (416) 361-6063
Ilme Regina, Hd.
Founded: 1977. **Staff:** Prof 1; Other 1. **Subjects:** Investments, economics, finance. **Holdings:** 900 books; 3500 corporation files; reports; clippings; periodicals; Statistics Canada. **Subscriptions:** 7 newspapers. **Services:** Copying; library open to public by appointment only. **Computerized Information Services:** Online systems.

★8052★
MIDLAND HOSPITAL CENTER - HEALTH SCIENCES LIBRARY (Med)
4005 Orchard Dr.
Midland, MI 48640
Phone: (517) 631-7700
Carole Colter, Health Sci.Libn.
Founded: 1979. **Staff:** 1. **Subjects:** Medicine, nursing, family practice, allied health sciences. **Holdings:** 2000 books; 7000 bound periodical volumes. **Subscriptions:** 200 journals and other serials. **Services:** Interlibrary loans; copying; library open to public. **Computerized Information Services:** MEDLINE. **Networks/Consortia:** Member of Valley Regional Health Science Librarians; Michigan Area Serial Holdings Consortium; Kentucky-Ohio-Michigan Regional Medical Library Program (KOMRML).

★8053★
MIDLAND-ROSS CORPORATION - LIBRARY (Bus-Fin)
20600 Chagrin Blvd.
Cleveland, OH 44122
Phone: (216) 491-8400
Diane Greenbaum, Libn.
Staff: Prof 1; Other 1. **Subjects:** Business, personnel, law, labor relations, management. **Holdings:** 4600 volumes; 35 file drawers of pamphlets and clippings; 7 file drawers of annual reports; 85 microfilm reels of periodicals. **Subscriptions:** 165 journals and other serials. **Services:** Interlibrary loans; copying; SDI; library open to public with restrictions. **Computerized Information Services:** DIALOG, SDC, New York Times Information Service, Dow Jones News Retrieval; computerized cataloging. **Networks/Consortia:** Member of OCLC through OHIONET. **Publications:** New Book List, quarterly.

★8054★
MIDLAND-ROSS CORPORATION - THERMAL SYSTEMS TECHNICAL CENTER - LIBRARY (Sci-Tech)
900 N. Westwood Ave.
Box 985
Toledo, OH 43696
Phone: (419) 537-6449
Jean Raynock, Libn.
Founded: 1935. **Staff:** 1. **Subjects:** Industrial furnaces, engineering, chemistry, environmental control equipment. **Holdings:** 1000 books; 5000 patents, articles, company reports. **Subscriptions:** 50 journals and other serials. **Services:** Library not open to public. **Special Catalogs:** Reports and article catalogs (card).

MIDLANDS CENTER LIBRARY
See: South Carolina State Department of Mental Retardation

★8055★
MIDLANTIC NATIONAL BANK - TRUST DEPARTMENT LIBRARY (Bus-Fin)
Metro Park Plaza
Box 600
Edison, NJ 08818
Phone: (201) 266-6355
Eileen Y. Logan, Hd.
Founded: 1971. **Staff:** Prof 1. **Subjects:** Business, finance, investments. **Holdings:** 300 books; company files on 3500 companies including annual reports, interim statements. **Subscriptions:** 18 journals and other serials. **Services:** Library not open to public.

★8056★
MID-MAINE MEDICAL CENTER - CLARA HODGKINS MEMORIAL HEALTH SCIENCES LIBRARY (Med)
Phone: (207) 873-0621
Waterville, ME 04901
Cora M. Damon, Libn.
Staff: Prof 1; Other 1. **Subjects:** Medicine and related subjects. **Special Collections:** F.T. Hill Historical Collection. **Holdings:** 850 books; 1000 bound periodical volumes; 3 VF drawers of bibliographies, articles, pamphlets. **Subscriptions:** 175 journals and other serials. **Services:** Interlibrary loans; copying; library open to public with legitimate need for biomedical information - reference use only. **Networks/Consortia:** Member of Health Science Library and Information Cooperative.

MID-MANHATTAN LIBRARY
See: New York Public Library

MIDMARCH ASSOCIATES - WOMEN ARTISTS NEWS
See: Women Artists News

★8057★
MIDRASHA COLLEGE OF JEWISH STUDIES - LIBRARY (Area-Ethnic; Rel-Theol)
21550 W. Twelve Mile Rd.
Southfield, MI 48076
Phone: (313) 354-3130
Sarah Bell, Libn.
Founded: 1952. **Staff:** Prof 1; Other 3. **Subjects:** Judaica, Hebraica, Israel and Zionism, Jewish and general education. **Holdings:** 36,000 books; 900 bound periodical volumes; 27 VF drawers; 45 pamphlet boxes; 500 filmstrips. **Subscriptions:** 150 journals and other serials. **Services:** Interlibrary loans; copying; library open to public. **Networks/Consortia:** Member of Wayne/Oakland Library Federation.

★8058★

MIDREX CORPORATION - LIBRARY (Sci-Tech)

One NCNB Plaza   Phone: (704) 373-1600

Charlotte, NC 28280   Josef Schmid, Jr., Libn.

Staff: Prof 1; Other 1. **Subjects:** Engineering, management. **Special Collections:** Iron and steel direct reduction. **Holdings:** 2300 books; 500 bound periodical volumes; 500 technical reports. **Subscriptions:** 100 journals and other serials; 5 newspapers. **Services:** Interlibrary loans; copying; SDI; library open to public with restrictions.

★8059★

MID-VALLEY HOSPITAL ASSOCIATION - PHYSICIAN'S MEDICAL LIBRARY (Med)

1400 Main St.   Phone: (717) 489-7546

Peckville, PA 18452   Arline Ham, Med.Rec.Adm.

Staff: 6. **Subjects:** Medicine. **Holdings:** 608 books; 190 cassettes; 30 manuals; 6 audiovisual cassettes. **Subscriptions:** 56 journals and other serials. **Services:** Library not open to public.

★8060★

MIDWAY HOSPITAL - HEALTH SCIENCES LIBRARY (Med)

1700 University Ave.   Phone: (612) 641-5234

St. Paul, MN 55104   Carol Windham, Hd.Libn.

Founded: 1907. **Staff:** Prof 2. **Subjects:** Medicine and nursing. **Holdings:** 5000 books; 72 bound periodical volumes; 360 films, loops and filmstrips; 10,240 slides; 908 transparencies; 1123 tapes; 385 records. **Subscriptions:** 100 journals and other serials. **Services:** Interlibrary loans; copying; library not open to public. **Networks/Consortia:** Member of Twin Cities Biomedical Consortium (TCBC); Regional Medical Library - Region 3. **Publications:** RC Line-5234. **Staff:** Lorraine Lilja, R.N. in AV Lab.

MIDWEST ARCHEOLOGICAL CENTER

See: U.S. Natl. Park Service

★8061★

MIDWEST CHINA CENTER - MIDWEST CHINA ORAL HISTORY ARCHIVES AND MUSEUM COLLECTION (Hist)

2375 Como Ave.   Phone: (612) 641-3238

St. Paul, MN 55108   Jane Baker Koons, Dir.

Staff: Prof 1; Other 2. **Subjects:** Sino-American relations, 1900-1952; China mission history, 1900-1952; modern China, 1900-1952. **Special Collections:** Oral history collection (10,000 pages in bound volumes). **Holdings:** 60 linear feet of archival documents; slides; movies; photographs; posters; museum artifacts. **Services:** Interlibrary loans; library open to public. **Publications:** China Perspectives, irregular - by request. **Remarks:** The Collection is housed at Luther-Northwestern Seminary.

★8062★

MIDWEST CHINA STUDY RESOURCE CENTER (Hist)

2375 Como Ave., W.

Gullixson Hall, Rm. 308   Phone: (612) 641-3238

St. Paul, MN 55108   P. Richard Bohr, Dir.

Founded: 1975. **Staff:** 4. **Subjects:** China - religion, history, economics, arts, science, political science. **Holdings:** 1600 books; 1000 unbound periodical volumes; 600 newsletters; 100 dissertations and reports; 100 pamphlets and articles; 25 archival documents. **Subscriptions:** 130 journals and other serials; 6 newspapers. **Services:** Interlibrary loans; library open to public. **Computerized Information Services:** Computerized cataloging. **Networks/Consortia:** Member of MINITEX. **Publications:** China Spectrum, 3/year - by subscription.

★8063★

MIDWEST COLLEGE OF ENGINEERING - JOSEPH M. HARRER LIBRARY (Sci-Tech)

440 S. Finley Rd.

Box 127   Phone: (312) 627-6851

Lombard, IL 60148   Margot Fruehe, Libn.

Founded: 1967. **Staff:** 1. **Subjects:** Science, technology. **Holdings:** 8000 volumes; Institute of Electrical and Electronics Engineers (IEEE) Transactions and Proceedings on microfiche. **Subscriptions:** 135 journals and other serials; 6 newspapers. **Services:** Library open to public with restrictions.

★8064★

MIDWEST HISTORICAL & GENEALOGICAL SOCIETY, INC. - LIBRARY (Hist)

Box 1121

Wichita, KS 67201   Beverly Malone, Libn.

Founded: 1966. **Subjects:** Genealogy, local history. **Special Collections:** Printed personal histories and family records. **Holdings:** 2331 books; 2604 bound periodical volumes; 550 unbound archives; 116 Kansas cemetery references; 100 scrapbooks of obituaries and golden anniversaries; 33 reels of microfilm; card files for surnames, place cards; 7 VF drawers. **Subscriptions:** 400 journals and other serials. **Services:** Copying; library open to public with restrictions. **Publications:** The Register, quarterly - for members and other libraries; Alert, monthly. **Special Indexes:** Surname indexes (card); pedigree charts (book). **Remarks:** The library is located at Old Cowtown Museum, 1871 Sim Park Dr., Wichita, KS 67203.

★8065★

MIDWEST OLD SETTLERS AND THRESHERS ASSOCIATION - OLD THRESHERS OFFICE - LIBRARY (Hist)†

R.R. 1   Phone: (319) 385-9432

Mount Pleasant, IA 52641   Lennis Moore, Adm.

Founded: 1976. **Staff:** Prof 4; Other 4. **Subjects:** Steam engines and trains, gas engines and tractors, agricultural and American history. **Special Collections:** Traction steam engines. **Holdings:** 1000 books; 100 manufacturers' reprints. **Services:** Interlibrary loans; copying; library open to public. **Publications:** Threshers Chaff.

★8066★

MIDWEST RESEARCH INSTITUTE - PATTERSON REFERENCE LIBRARY AND ECONOMICS REFERENCE CENTER (Sci-Tech)

425 Volker Blvd.   Phone: (816) 753-7600

Kansas City, MO 64110   Marsha Cole, Hd.Libn.

Founded: 1946. **Staff:** Prof 2; Other 2. **Subjects:** Biology, chemistry, chemical engineering, environmental sciences, economics, management science. **Special Collections:** American Economic Development Council Collection; Traffic Systems and Safety. **Holdings:** 5000 volumes. **Subscriptions:** 600 journals and other serials. **Services:** Interlibrary loans; library open to public for reference use only and by appointment. **Computerized Information Services:** DIALOG, Chemical Abstract Services (CAS), SDC, NLM, DOE/RECON. **Networks/Consortia:** Member of Kansas City Metropolitan Library Network.

★8067★

MIDWEST STOCK EXCHANGE, INC. - LISTINGS DEPARTMENT

120 S. LaSalle St., Rm. 1200

Chicago, IL 60603

Special Collections: Financial, proxy and registration statements for approximately 400 corporations. **Remarks:** Presently inactive.

★8068★

MIDWESTERN BAPTIST THEOLOGICAL SEMINARY - LIBRARY (Rel-Theol)

5001 N. Oak St. Trafficway   Phone: (816) 453-4600

Kansas City, MO 64118   Dr. K. David Weekes, Dir.

Founded: 1958. **Staff:** Prof 1; Other 3. **Subjects:** Theology, Bible, biblical archeology, missions, Christian education, Christian ethics. **Holdings:** 80,000 books; 1500 bound periodical volumes; 100 sermon tapes; 100 filmstrips; 250 reels of microfilm - Early English Baptist. **Subscriptions:** 300 journals and other serials. **Services:** Interlibrary loans (fee); copying; library not open to public. **Computerized Information Services:** Computerized cataloging. **Staff:** Susan Booker, Tech.Serv.Libn.

★8069★

MIFFLIN COUNTY HISTORICAL SOCIETY - LIBRARY AND MUSEUM (Hist)

The McCoy House

17 N. Main St.

Lewistown, PA 17044   Helen McNitt, Libn.

Staff: 1. **Subjects:** History of central Pennsylvania and Mifflin County. **Holdings:** 1000 books; manuscripts, maps, pictures. **Services:** Library open to public with restrictions. **Publications:** Nine pamphlet publications - price list on request.

★8070★

MIFFLIN COUNTY LAW LIBRARY (Law)

20 N. Wayne St.   Phone: (717) 248-7332

Lewistown, PA 17044

Founded: 1890. **Staff:** 2. **Subjects:** Law. **Special Collections:** Early English law cases. **Holdings:** 5100 books. **Subscriptions:** 50 journals and other serials. **Services:** Library open to public for reference use only.

MIGEL (M.C.) MEMORIAL LIBRARY

See: American Foundation for the Blind - M.C. Migel Memorial Library

★8071★

MIGRAINE FOUNDATION - LIBRARY (Med)

390 Brunswick Ave.   Phone: (416) 920-4916

Toronto, ON, Canada M5R 2Z4   David Jones, Chm., Lib.Comm.

Staff: Prof 1; Other 1. **Subjects:** Migraine; cluster headache. **Special**

Collections: Migraine data retrieval file of 5000 citations, 1969 to present. **Holdings:** 300 books; 200 bound periodical volumes; clippings, documents, tapes, films. **Subscriptions:** 20 journals and other serials; 10 newspapers. **Services:** Interlibrary loans; copying; library open to health care professionals, medical journalists, and related personnel. **Computerized Information Services:** MEDLINE. **Publications:** Information kit for migraine sufferers; information kit for health care professionals.

★8072★

MILBANK, TWEED, HADLEY & MC CLOY - LIBRARY (Law)
1 Chase Manhattan Plaza   Phone: (212) 530-5200
New York, NY 10005   Gina Resnick, Libn.
Staff: Prof 6; Other 10. **Subjects:** Law, taxation, corporate banking. **Special Collections:** Federal and New York State legislation. **Holdings:** 35,000 volumes. **Services:** Interlibrary loans; library not open to public. **Computerized Information Services:** LEXIS, New York Times Information Service; computerized circulation. **Networks/Consortia:** Member of Law Library Association of Greater New York; METRO. **Publications:** Contents library newsletter, monthly. **Staff:** Henry Haywood, Ref. Supv.; Dwight Brown, Tax Libn.; Georgia Alexander, Tech.Ser.Libn.; Lorna Cohen, Libn.

★8073★

MILBOURNE & TULL RESEARCH CENTER - LIBRARY (Hist)
10605 Lakespring Way   Phone: (301) 628-2490
Cockeysville, MD 21030   Willis Clayton Tull, Jr., Libn.
Founded: 1971. **Staff:** Prof 1; Other 1. **Subjects:** Tull family, Milbourne family. **Holdings:** 267 books; 12,412 dossiers containing ancestor charts and photocopies of birth records, marriage notices, wills and obituaries which have appeared in books, newspapers, magazines and other printed sources of public record; 4 microfilms of census records. **Subscriptions:** 14 journals and other serials. **Services:** Copying; library open to subscribers. **Publications:** Tull Tracing; By the Mill Born, both quarterly - annual subscription. **Remarks:** A private library whose purpose is to collect, organize and publish genealogical information on the Milbourne and the Tull families. Membership is granted to subscribers to its publications who have furnished the library with information on any line of either family.

★8074★

MILES LABORATORIES, INC.- DELBAY PHARMACEUTICALS - RESEARCH LIBRARY (Med)†
400 Morgan Lane   Phone: (203) 934-9221
West Haven, CT 06516   J.P. Fatcheric, Mgr., Info./Doc.
Staff: Prof 1. **Subjects:** Medicine, clinical research. **Holdings:** 1000 books; 8000 bound periodical volumes. **Subscriptions:** 95 journals and other serials. **Services:** Interlibrary loans; copying; library open to public with advance approval.

★8075★

MILES LABORATORIES, INC. - LIBRARY RESOURCES AND SERVICES (Sci-Tech; Bus-Fin)
1127 Myrtle St.   Phone: (219) 264-8341
Elkhart, IN 46515   Alan K.E. Hagopian, Ph.D., Mgr.
Founded: 1940. **Staff:** Prof 10; Other 9. **Subjects:** Chemistry, microbiology, medicine, pharmacology, business. **Holdings:** 16,000 books; 32,000 bound periodical volumes; 25 shelves of product literature; 10 microfilm drawers of microfilm; 13 VF drawers of company reports. **Subscriptions:** 650 journals and other serials. **Services:** Interlibrary loans; library open to public by appointment. **Computerized Information Services:** DIALOG, SDC, BRS, MEDLARS, New York Times Information Service, Dow Jones News Retrieval, Chemical Abstract Services (CAS), NIH-EPA Chemical Information System; Product Literature (internal database); computerized cataloging and acquisitions. **Networks/Consortia:** Member of OCLC; INCOLSA; Area 2 Library Services Authority (ALSA-2); Regional Medical Library - Region 3. **Publications:** LRS Media, irregular; Current Notice Product Literature, monthly; ADLIB, quarterly - all for internal distribution only. **Staff:** Robert G. Meade, Bus.Libn.; Charles A. LeGuern, Tech.Serv.Libn.; Shannon J. Clever, Sci Libn.; George A. Foster, Jr., Supv., Product Lit.; David S. Saari, Info.Spec.; George W. Thompson, Info.Spec.; Nelson Weindling, Info.Spec.

MILBANK MEMORIAL LIBRARY
See: Teachers College

MILITARY COLLEGE OF SOUTH CAROLINA
See: Citadel - The Military College of South Carolina

MILITARY ORDER OF THE LOYAL LEGION OF THE UNITED STATES - MASSACHUSETTS COMMANDERY LIBRARY
See: U.S. Army Military History Institute

★8076★

MILITARY ORDER OF THE LOYAL LEGION OF THE UNITED STATES - WAR LIBRARY AND MUSEUM (Hist)
1805 Pine St.   Phone: (215) 735-8196
Philadelphia, PA 19103   Russ A. Pritchard, Dir.
Founded: 1888. **Staff:** Prof 2. **Subjects:** Civil War, Abraham Lincoln. **Special Collections:** Regimental histories. **Holdings:** 10,000 books; pamphlets; manuscripts; photographs; archives; portraits. **Services:** Copying; library open to public for reference use only. **Publications:** Loyal Legion Historical Journal. **Staff:** Karla Steffen, Libn.

MILLER (Alden E.) LAW LIBRARY
See: Clackamas County, Oregon - Alden E. Miller Law Library

MILLER (Anna) MUSEUM
See: Weston County Historical Society - Anna Miller Museum

★8077★

MILLER BREWING COMPANY - SCIENTIFIC TECHNICAL INFORMATION FACILITY (Food-Bev)
3939 W. Highland Blvd.   Phone: (414) 931-3640
Milwaukee, WI 53201   Joanne L. Schwarz, Supv., Info.Serv.
Staff: Prof 2; Other 2. **Subjects:** Brewing, chemistry, microbiology, chemical engineering, genetics, enzymology. **Special Collections:** Brewing science. **Holdings:** 500 books; 1500 bound periodical volumes; 10,000 patents; 80 reels of microfilm; 2000 microfiche; 200 research reports. **Subscriptions:** 170 journals and other serials. **Services:** Interlibrary loans; copying; library open to public with restrictions. **Computerized Information Services:** SDC, DIALOG, RLIN, MEDLINE; internal database; computerized cataloging and circulation. **Networks/Consortia:** Member of RLG. **Publications:** Research Bulletin, monthly; Patent and Translation Alert Bulletin; Checklist of current information, weekly. **Staff:** Patricia Krajnak, Info.Anl.

★8078★

MILLER, CANFIELD, PADDOCK & STONE - LIBRARY (Law)
2500 Detroit Bank & Trust Bldg.   Phone: (313) 963-6420
Detroit, MI 48226   Katherine A. Green, Hd.Libn.
Staff: Prof 1; Other 1. **Subjects:** Law - federal, state, tax, maritime, banking, labor. **Holdings:** 5000 books; 25 bound periodical volumes. **Subscriptions:** 1200 journals and other serials; 10 newspapers. **Services:** Interlibrary loans; copying; library not open to public. **Computerized Information Services:** LEXIS.

★8079★

MILLER-DWAN MEDICAL CENTER - TILDERQUIST MEMORIAL MEDICAL LIBRARY (Med)
502 E. Second St.   Phone: (218) 727-8762
Duluth, MN 55805   Annelie Sober, Dir., Med.Lib.
Founded: 1973. **Staff:** Prof 1. **Subjects:** Medicine and related fields. **Holdings:** 790 books; 2070 bound periodical volumes. **Subscriptions:** 165 journals and other serials. **Services:** Interlibrary loans; copying; library open to public by request. **Computerized Information Services:** MEDLINE, BRS. **Networks/Consortia:** Member of Arrowhead Professional Libraries Association (APLA); Regional Medical Library - Region 3; North Country Library Cooperative.

MILLER (Herman), INC.
See: Herman Miller, Inc.

MILLER (Hugh Thomas) RARE BOOK ROOM
See: Butler University - Irwin Library - Hugh Thomas Miller Rare Book Room

MILLER (Ira) MEMORIAL LIBRARY
See: Michigan Psychoanalytic Institute - Ira Miller Memorial Library

MILLER (J. Hillis) HEALTH CENTER LIBRARY
See: University of Florida - J. Hillis Miller Health Center Library

MILLER (Jean) LIBRARY
See: Riverside Presbyterian Church - Jean Miller Library

MILLER LIBRARY
See: Colby College

MILLER LIBRARY
See: Mc Pherson College

★8080★
MILLER, NASH, YERKE, WIENER & HAGER - LIBRARY (Law)
900 S.W. Fifth Ave.   Phone: (503) 224-5858
Portland, OR 97204   Leslie Meserve, Libn.
Staff: Prof 1; Other 1. **Subjects:** Law. **Holdings:** 15,142 volumes.
Subscriptions: 273 journals and other serials. **Services:** Interlibrary loans;
copying; library not open to public.

MILLER (Ralph W.) GOLF LIBRARY
See: City of Industry - Ralph W. Miller Golf Library

MILLER (Sam and Emma) LIBRARY
See: Fairmount Temple - Sam and Emma Miller Library

MILLER (Steve) LIBRARY OF AMERICAN ARCHAEOLOGY
See: World Archeological Society - Information Center

★8081★
MILLERSVILLE STATE COLLEGE - HELEN A. GANSER LIBRARY - SPECIAL
    COLLECTIONS (Educ)
                                                 Phone: (717) 872-3607
Millersville, PA 17551   Robert E. Colby, Hd., Archv./Spec.Coll.
Special Collections: Pennsylvaniana (8000 titles); Wickerham Pedagogical
Collection (1900 titles); Pennsylvania Imprint Collection (1500 titles); Rare
Book Collection (800 titles); College Archives (3000 linear feet and 300
volumes); Archives of the American Industrial Arts Association (300 linear
feet); Leo Ascher Collection for the Study of Operetta Music (4000 items);
Myers Oriental Collection (500 items); Amish and Mennonites. **Services:**
Interlibrary loans; copying; library open to public from the surrounding
geographical area of Lancaster, PA. **Computerized Information Services:**
DIALOG; internal database; computerized cataloging and ILL. **Networks/**
Consortia: Member of OCLC through PALINET & Union Library Catalogue of
Pennsylvania. **Staff:** Marjorie Markoff, Cat., Spec.Coll.

★8082★
MILLHOUSE BUNDY PERFORMING & FINE ARTS CENTER - LIBRARY (Art)†
                                                 Phone: (802) 496-3713
Waitsfield, VT 05673
Founded: 1962. **Subjects:** Modern art, painting, sculpture, architecture,
history of art, art education. **Holdings:** 400 books; 100 catalogs of
exhibitions in museums and galleries. **Services:** Library open to public with
restrictions.

MILLIKAN LIBRARY
See: California Institute of Technology - Millikan Library

★8083★
MILLIKEN RESEARCH CORPORATION - RESEARCH LIBRARY (Sci-Tech)
Box 1927   Phone: (803) 573-2340
Spartanburg, SC 29304   Don Miles, Res.Libn.
Founded: 1960. **Staff:** Prof 2; Other 2. **Subjects:** Textiles, chemistry,
engineering, physics. **Holdings:** 10,000 books; 3500 bound periodical
volumes; 175 films (cataloged). **Subscriptions:** 300 journals and other
serials; 10 newspapers. **Services:** Interlibrary loans; copying; SDI; library
open to public by appointment. **Computerized Information Services:**
DIALOG, SDC, MEDLINE, NIH-EPA Chemical Information System. **Networks/**
Consortia: Member of OCLC through SOLINET. **Staff:** Trudy W. Craven,
Asst.Libn.

MILLIKEN (Roger) TEXTILE LIBRARY
See: Institute of Textile Technology - Textile Information Services -
    Roger Milliken Textile Library

★8084★
MILLIKIN UNIVERSITY - STALEY LIBRARY - SPECIAL COLLECTIONS (Hum)
1184 W. Main St.   Phone: (217) 424-6214
Decatur, IL 62522   Dr. Charles E. Hale, Lib.Dir.
Special Collections: Bookplate collection; Alice-in-Wonderland collection.
Services: Interlibrary loans; copying; library open to public for reference use
only. **Computerized Information Services:** University of Illinois Libraries
Library Computer System (LCS); computerized cataloging, circulation and ILL.
Networks/Consortia: Member of ILLINET; Sangamon Valley Academic
Library Consortium; OCLC.

★8085★
MILLIPORE CORPORATION - INFORMATION CENTER (Sci-Tech)
Ashby Rd.   Phone: (617) 275-9200
Bedford, MA 01730   Leslie R. Jacobs, Info.Spec.
Founded: 1970. **Staff:** Prof 2; Other 1. **Subjects:** Microbiology, health and

environmental sciences, pharmaceutical technology, analytical chemistry.
Special Collections: Filtration technology (10 VF drawers of clippings).
Holdings: 3500 books; 9500 unbound journals and newsletters; 475
technical reports; 235 microforms. **Subscriptions:** 210 journals and other
serials. **Services:** Interlibrary loans; library not open to public. **Computerized**
Information Services: DIALOG, New York Times Information Service, Dow
Jones News Retrieval, SDC, BRS; computerized cataloging. **Networks/**
Consortia: Member of OCLC through NELINET. **Publications:** Newsletter,
bimonthly - for internal distribution only. **Special Indexes:** Bibliography of
journal articles dealing with filtration technology.

★8086★
MILLS COLLEGE - MARGARET PRALL MUSIC LIBRARY (Mus)†
5000 MacArthur Blvd.
Oakland, CA 94613   Gerald Gabel, Coord.
Founded: 1852. **Staff:** Prof 1; Other 1. **Subjects:** Music. **Special**
Collections: All published works of Darius Milhaud; scores, critical works by
and about Milhaud, manuscripts, source materials. **Holdings:** 4000 books;
2500 records (cataloged); 9000 scores. **Subscriptions:** 20 journals and
other serials. **Services:** Copying; library open to public with restrictions.
Computerized Information Services: Computerized cataloging. **Networks/**
Consortia: Member of RLG. **Special Indexes:** Index to Darius Milhaud
Collection (card). **Remarks:** Milhaud Collection and all books concerning music
theory are housed in the Main Library.

MILLS MEMORIAL LIBRARY
See: Mc Master University

MILLS MUSIC LIBRARY
See: University of Wisconsin, Madison

MILLS (Randall V.) ARCHIVES OF NORTHWEST FOLKLORE
See: University of Oregon - Department of English - Randall V. Mills
    Archives of Northwest Folklore

MILLSAPS COLLEGE LIBRARY - J.B. CAIN ARCHIVES OF MISSISSIPPI
    METHODISM AND MILLSAPS COLLEGE
See: Cain (J.B.) Archives of Mississippi Methodism and Millsaps College

MILNE (James M.) LIBRARY
See: SUNY - College at Oneonta - James M. Milne Library

MILNER LIBRARY
See: Illinois State University

★8087★
MILNER & STEER, BARRISTERS & SOLICITORS - LAW LIBRARY (Law)
10040 104th St., 9th Fl.   Phone: (403) 425-8830
Edmonton, AB, Canada T5J 0Z7   Janet M. Darby, Libn.
Staff: Prof 1; Other 1. **Subjects:** Law. **Holdings:** 1000 books; 550 bound
periodical volumes; 4300 law reports; 200 looseleaf services; 835 statutes
and regulations; 900 legal digests and encyclopedias; 200 files of pamphlets;
200 files of precedents. **Subscriptions:** 171 journals and other serials.
Services: Interlibrary loans; copying; SDI; library open to public by
appointment. **Computerized Information Services:** QL Systems, DIALOG,
INFOMART; computerized cataloging. **Publications:** Legislative Update,
weekly; Legislative Summary, semiannual - both to members of firm and to
clients. **Special Indexes:** KWOC library catalog; manual of precedents.

★8088★
MILWAUKEE ACADEMY OF MEDICINE - LIBRARY (Med)*
8701 Watertown Plank Rd.
Box 26509
Milwaukee, WI 53226   John P. Mullooly, M.D., Libn.
Founded: 1886. **Staff:** Prof 1. **Subjects:** Medical history. **Special**
Collections: Horace Manchester Brown Collection. **Holdings:** 2000 books.
Services: Library open to physicians.

★8089★
MILWAUKEE AREA TECHNICAL COLLEGE - RASCHE MEMORIAL LIBRARY
    (Sci-Tech)
1015 N. Sixth St.   Phone: (414) 278-6205
Milwaukee, WI 53203   Richard E. Meerdink, District Libn.
Staff: Prof 11. **Subjects:** Applied science and technology. **Special**
Collections: Voigt Graphic Arts Collection. **Holdings:** 40,000 books and
bound periodical volumes. **Subscriptions:** 360 journals and other serials; 15
newspapers. **Services:** Interlibrary loans; copying; library open to public.
Networks/Consortia: Member of Library Council of Metropolitan Milwaukee
(LCOMM). **Staff:** Mariellen E. Evenson, Tech.Serv.Libn.; Mary E. Landeck,

Pub.Serv.Libn.; Margaret Lutovsky, Lrng.Res.Libn.

★8090★

MILWAUKEE AREA TECHNICAL COLLEGE - SOUTH CAMPUS LIBRARY (Sci-Tech)
6665 S. Howell Ave.   Phone: (414) 762-2500
Oak Creek, WI 53154   Louise Weber, Lib.Techn.
Staff: 4. **Subjects:** Applied science and technology. **Holdings:** 4831 titles; 10 drawers of pamphlets. **Subscriptions:** 111 journals and other serials; 12 newspapers. **Services:** Interlibrary loans; copying; library open to public with restrictions on circulation.

★8091★

MILWAUKEE ART CENTER - LIBRARY (Art)
750 N. Lincoln Memorial Dr.   Phone: (414) 271-9508
Milwaukee, WI 53202   Betty Karow, Libn.
Founded: 1962. **Staff:** Prof 1. **Subjects:** Visual arts in all forms including painting, graphic arts, sculpture, drawing and design, photography. **Special Collections:** Art museum exhibition catalogs (fully cataloged); art auction catalogs and price lists. **Holdings:** 4000 books; 250 bound periodical volumes; 4000 exhibition catalogs; 25 VF drawers; 10,000 slides; archive material; 80 tapes of art lectures. **Subscriptions:** 28 journals and other serials. **Services:** Interlibrary loans; library open to public for reference use only.

★8092★

MILWAUKEE CHILDREN'S HOSPITAL - HEALTH SCIENCES LIBRARY (Med)†
Box 1997   Phone: (414) 931-4121
Milwaukee, WI 53201   Margaret Wold, Health Sci.Libn.
Staff: Prof 1; Other 1. **Subjects:** Pediatrics, nursing, medicine. **Holdings:** 1300 books; 2300 bound periodical volumes. **Subscriptions:** 150 journals and other serials. **Services:** Interlibrary loans; copying. **Computerized Information Services:** BRS. **Networks/Consortia:** Member of Southeastern Wisconsin Health Science Library Consortium (SWHSL).

★8093★

MILWAUKEE COUNTY BOARD OF SUPERVISORS - RESEARCH LIBRARY
901 N. 9th St., Rm. 201   Phone: (414) 278-4952
Milwaukee, WI 53233
Founded: 1972. **Subjects:** Welfare, mass transit, health, housing. **Holdings:** 2000 books; 5 bound periodical volumes; 12 VF drawers of pamphlet material; 3500 county reports; 150 microfiche of county documents and NTIS publications. **Remarks:** Presently inactive.

★8094★

MILWAUKEE COUNTY HISTORICAL SOCIETY - LIBRARY AND ARCHIVES (Hist)
910 N. Third St.   Phone: (414) 273-8288
Milwaukee, WI 53203   Charles W. Cooney, Jr., Cur., Res.Coll.
Founded: 1935. **Staff:** Prof 9. **Subjects:** History of Milwaukee County, history of socialist movements, German and other immigrant groups. **Holdings:** 5200 books; 75 bound periodical volumes; 60 bound volumes of government proceedings; manuscript collection; iconographic material. **Subscriptions:** 20 journals and other serials; 12 newspapers. **Services:** Copying; library open to registered visitors. **Publications:** Milwaukee History. **Special Catalogs:** Research Guide 1, German-American Studies; Research Guide 2, Bibliography of Milwaukee History; Historical Resources in Milwaukee Area Archives.

★8095★

MILWAUKEE COUNTY LAW LIBRARY (Law)
Rm. 307, Courthouse
901 N. 9th St.   Phone: (414) 278-4321
Milwaukee, WI 53233   Divinia J. Astraquillo, Law Libn.
Founded: 1932. **Staff:** Prof 3; Other 3. **Subjects:** Law, county government. **Special Collections:** Briefs of cases argued before the Wisconsin Supreme Court from volume 1, Wisconsin Reports, 1st series to present. **Holdings:** 64,733 books; 4320 bound periodical volumes; 9 VF drawers of newspaper clippings; 6 catalog drawers of microcards. **Subscriptions:** 330 journals and other serials. **Services:** Copying; library open to public. **Networks/Consortia:** Member of Library Council of Metropolitan Milwaukee (LCOMM). **Staff:** Kathryn Barbasiewicz, Libn. I.

★8096★

MILWAUKEE COUNTY MENTAL HEALTH COMPLEX - MICHAEL KASAK LIBRARY (Med; Soc Sci)†
9455 Watertown Plank Rd.   Phone: (414) 257-7381
Milwaukee, WI 53226   Anna M. Green, Libn.
Founded: 1941. **Staff:** Prof 1. **Subjects:** Psychology, mental health, psychiatry, psychoanalysis. **Holdings:** 7900 books; 3300 bound periodical volumes; 110 video cassette tapes; 425 audio cassette tapes; 40 filmstrips. **Subscriptions:** 289 journals and other serials. **Services:** Interlibrary loans; copying; library open to public with permission from medical director. **Computerized Information Services:** BRS. **Networks/Consortia:** Member of Southeastern Wisconsin Health Science Library Consortium.

★8097★

MILWAUKEE INSTITUTE OF ART & DESIGN - LIBRARY (Art)
207 N. Milwaukee St.   Phone: (414) 276-7889
Milwaukee, WI 53202   Terry Marcus, Libn.
Founded: 1977. **Staff:** Prof 1; Other 4. **Subjects:** Artists, graphic design, art history, aesthetics, decorative arts, advertising, photography. **Holdings:** 9000 books; 1000 bound periodical volumes; 3600 art reproductions (postcards); clipping file of visual aids covering 50 subjects; 11,000 slides. **Subscriptions:** 45 journals and other serials. **Services:** Interlibrary loans; copying; library open to public with restrictions. **Networks/Consortia:** Member of Library Council of Metropolitan Milwaukee, Inc. (LCOMM); ARLIS/NA.

MILWAUKEE JOURNAL
See: Newspapers, Inc.

★8098★

MILWAUKEE - LEGISLATIVE REFERENCE BUREAU - LEGISLATIVE LIBRARY (Soc Sci)
City Hall, Rm. 404
200 E. Wells St.   Phone: (414) 278-2295
Milwaukee, WI 53202   Ronald D. Leonhardt, Dir.
Founded: 1908. **Staff:** Prof 9; Other 18. **Subjects:** City government, revenue and planning; housing; crime; intergovernmental relations; Wisconsin state and local government; public administration; urban affairs. **Special Collections:** Official depository for current city documents. **Holdings:** 49,530 books and bound periodical volumes; 6500 reels of microfilm; 6 VF drawers of pamphlets; newspaper clippings from 1908. **Subscriptions:** 226 journals and other serials. **Services:** Interlibrary loans; copying; library open to public with restrictions. **Computerized Information Services:** Access to parent organization's computerized information. **Remarks:** When the Municipal Reference Library was reorganized in 1970 it was divided into 3 sections: the Legislative Library, the City Records Center which is the official depository of the city for noncurrent historical, confidential and valuable records, and the Ordinance Drafting and Research Section which performs in-depth research on major urban problems affecting the city and conducts legislative research for the City Common Council. **Staff:** David Hall, Libn., Leg.Lib.; Bert Hartinger, Mgr., City Rec.Ctr.; Jean Zabel, Libn., Leg.Lib.; Barry Zalben, Res.Coord.; Doris Gantner, Code.

★8099★

MILWAUKEE PSYCHIATRIC HOSPITAL - LIBRARY (Med)
1220 Dewey Ave.   Phone: (414) 258-2600
Wauwatosa, WI 53213   Darlyne Ritter, Libn.
Staff: 1. **Subjects:** Psychiatry, mental disorders, psychology, mental healing. **Holdings:** 1413 books; 20 pamphlets. **Subscriptions:** 20 journals and other serials. **Services:** Library not open to public.

★8100★

MILWAUKEE PUBLIC LIBRARY - ART, MUSIC AND RECREATION SECTION (Art; Mus)
814 W. Wisconsin Ave.   Phone: (414) 278-3043
Milwaukee, WI 53233   June M. Edlhauser, Coord. of Fine Arts
Subjects: Art and music history, aesthetics, architecture, sculpture, antiques, interior decoration, crafts, music theory and techniques, biographies of artists, musicians, actors and sportspersons, painting, drawing, print-making, photography, sports and games, theater, cinema, dance, numismatics and postage stamps. **Special Collections:** Historical record collection; auction and exhibition catalogs; poster collection; framed art; mounted prints; picture file; sculpture reproductions; theater and concert programs; art and music clipping file; historic popular song collection; W.P.A. copied music collection. **Holdings:** Figures not available. **Services:** Interlibrary loans; copying; library open to nonresident public for reference use with purchase of fee card. **Computerized Information Services:** Computerized cataloging and circulation. **Networks/Consortia:** Member of Library Council of Metropolitan Milwaukee (LCOMM). **Publications:** New Books list (includes new recordings), weekly. **Special Indexes:** Song title index; film review file.

★8101★

MILWAUKEE PUBLIC LIBRARY - HUMANITIES DIVISION - LOCAL HISTORY AND MARINE ROOM (Hum)
814 W. Wisconsin Ave.   Phone: (414) 278-3074
Milwaukee, WI 53233   Paul Woehrmann, Local Hist.Libn.
Founded: 1953. **Staff:** Prof 1. **Subjects:** Local history, Great Lakes history, history of Wisconsin and surrounding states, genealogy. **Special Collections:** Marine Collections - Runge and Nelson; data on Great Lakes ships (22,000 photographs); local history collection; Milwaukee-related political manuscripts, including those of Daniel Hoan, F.P. Zeidler and Socialist Party - Social Democratic Federation (200 linear feet). **Holdings:** 30,000 books; 1200 bound periodical volumes; theses; 165 boxes of pamphlets; 120 file drawers of photographs; 500 linear feet of manuscripts. **Subscriptions:** 320 journals and other serials. **Services:** Interlibrary loans; copying (limited); library open to nonresident public for reference use with purchase of fee card. **Computerized Information Services:** Computerized cataloging, acquisitions, serials and circulation. **Networks/Consortia:** Member of Library Council of Metropolitan Milwaukee, Inc. (LCOMM); OCLC. **Publications:** Acquisitions list, monthly; selected manuscript and genealogical finding aids. **Special Catalogs:** Subject catalogs to photograph and pamphlet collections (card); Milwaukee area manuscript guide. **Special Indexes:** Index to Milwaukee Sentinel Newspaper for state news, 1837-1890. **Staff:** Orval Liljequist, Coord. of Hum.

★8102★

MILWAUKEE PUBLIC LIBRARY - SCIENCE & BUSINESS DIVISION (Sci-Tech)
814 W. Wisconsin Ave.   Phone: (414) 278-3043
Milwaukee, WI 53233   Theodore Cebula, Coord.Sci./Bus.Div.
Subjects: Agriculture, business, census, chemistry, economics, engineering, industrial labor, natural and physical sciences, physics, statistics. **Special Collections:** U.S. and British patents; industrial standards. **Holdings:** Figures not available. **Services:** Interlibrary loans; copying; library open to nonresident public for reference use with purchase of fee card. **Computerized Information Services:** Computerized cataloging and circulation. **Computerized Information Services:** USPATENTS (USPO); computerized circulation. **Networks/Consortia:** Member of Library Council of Metropolitan Milwaukee, Inc. (LCOMM); OCLC.

★8103★

MILWAUKEE PUBLIC LIBRARY - WISCONSIN ARCHITECTURAL ARCHIVE (Art)
814 W. Wisconsin Ave.   Phone: (414) 278-3897
Milwaukee, WI 53233   June Edlhauser, Coord. of Fine Arts
Staff: 1. **Subjects:** Architecture. **Special Collections:** Collection of 3100 projects representing over 200 architects primarily from Wisconsin. **Holdings:** Figures not available for books; drawings, specifications, documents. **Services:** Copying; library open to public by appointment.

★8104★

MILWAUKEE PUBLIC MUSEUM - REFERENCE LIBRARY (Sci-Tech)
800 W. Wells St.   Phone: (414) 278-2736
Milwaukee, WI 53233   Judith Campbell Turner, Sect.Hd., Libn.
Founded: 1883. **Staff:** Prof 2; Other 1. **Subjects:** Anthropology, botany, geology, zoology, history, museology. **Holdings:** 45,062 books and bound periodical volumes; 37,402 pamphlets (cataloged); microforms; museology clipping file; maps. **Subscriptions:** 900 journals and other serials. **Services:** Interlibrary loans; copying; library open to public. **Networks/Consortia:** Member of Library Council of Metropolitan Milwaukee, Inc. (LCOMM); WILS. **Special Catalogs:** Tribal File (card). **Staff:** Patricia Laughlin, Libn.

★8105★

MILWAUKEE SCHOOL OF ENGINEERING - WALTER SCHROEDER LIBRARY (Sci-Tech)
500 E. Kilbourn Ave.
Box 644   Phone: (412) 277-7180
Milwaukee, WI 53201   Mary Ann Schmidt, Lib.Dir.
Staff: Prof 2; Other 3. **Subjects:** Engineering - electrical, mechanical, biomechanical, computer, architectural, building and construction, industrial management, fluid power. **Holdings:** 30,000 books; 9600 bound periodical volumes; 20 VF drawers of pamphlets. **Subscriptions:** 362 journals and other serials; 21 newspapers. **Services:** Interlibrary loans; copying; library open to students and to the business and industrial community. **Networks/Consortia:** Member of Library Council of Metropolitan Milwakee, Inc. (LCOMM). **Publications:** Library handbook; new books list; periodicals list. **Staff:** Dr. Constantin Popescu, Assoc.Libn.

MILWAUKEE SENTINEL
See: Newspapers, Inc.

★8106★

MILWAUKEE URBAN OBSERVATORY - URBAN INFORMATION CENTER (Plan)
University Of Wisconsin, Milwaukee
Box 413   Phone: (414) 963-4271
Milwaukee, WI 53201   Miriam Palay, Assoc.Dir.
Staff: Prof 2. **Subjects:** Urban planning and housing in the Milwaukee area, education, housing, statistics, transportation, minorities, cable television. **Holdings:** 300 books; 12,000 unbound reports and documents (cataloged); 350 boxes of clippings. **Subscriptions:** 20 journals and other serials; 5 newspapers. **Services:** Copying; library open to public for reference use only. **Computerized Information Services:** Data Lab (internal database); computerized cataloging. **Networks/Consortia:** Member of Library Council of Metropolitan Milwaukee, Inc. (LCOMM). **Publications:** Milwaukee Observer, irregular - to urban affairs interest groups in Milwaukee area. **Special Catalogs:** Milwaukee Report, union list of reports on area; Faculty Interest File; Agency and Organization File - all three computer files.

★8107★

MINE SAFETY APPLIANCES COMPANY - BUSINESS LIBRARY (Bus-Fin)
600 Penn Ctr. Blvd.   Phone: (412) 273-5131
Pittsburgh, PA 15235   Hilda M. Reitzel, Libn.
Founded: 1972. **Staff:** Prof 1; Other 1. **Subjects:** Management, marketing, sales, personnel. **Holdings:** 2500 books; 30 VF drawers of pamphlets. **Subscriptions:** 250 journals and other serials. **Services:** Interlibrary loans; library not open to public. **Publications:** Recent Accessions.

★8108★

MINE SAFETY APPLIANCES COMPANY - MSA RESEARCH CORPORATION - CALLERY CHEMICAL COMPANY - LIBRARY (Sci-Tech)
                                    Phone: (412) 538-3510
Evans City, PA 16033   Barbara Boutwell, Libn.
Founded: 1959. **Staff:** Prof 1; Other 1. **Subjects:** Chemistry - boron and organometallic; alkali metals; nuclear engineering; rare metals. **Holdings:** 3000 books; 4500 bound periodical volumes. **Subscriptions:** 327 journals and other serials. **Services:** Interlibrary loans. **Computerized Information Services:** DIALOG, CAS ONLINE, SDC, NLM. **Special Indexes:** Patent index (card).

★8109★

MINE SAFETY APPLIANCES COMPANY - TECHNICAL LIBRARY (Sci-Tech)
201 N. Braddock Ave.   Phone: (412) 273-5600
Pittsburgh, PA 15208   Hilda M. Reitzel, Libn.
Founded: 1936. **Staff:** Prof 1; Other 1. **Subjects:** Industrial and mining safety and hygiene. **Holdings:** 5000 books; 1000 bound periodical volumes; 24 VF drawers of pamphlets. **Subscriptions:** 100 journals and other serials. **Services:** Interlibrary loans; library not open to public. **Publications:** Recent Accessions.

MINE SAFETY & HEALTH ADMINISTRATION
See: U.S. Dept. of Labor

★8110★

MINER (Alice T.) COLONIAL COLLECTION - LIBRARY (Hist)
Box 330   Phone: (518) 846-7336
Chazy, NY 12921   Lucille L. Czarnetzky, Cur.
Subjects: Art and paintings, colonial furniture, household goods, silver, chinaware, artifacts of Abraham Lincoln. **Holdings:** 250 books. **Services:** Library open to public.

MINER (Edward G.) LIBRARY
See: University of Rochester - School of Medicine & Dentistry - Edward G. Miner Library

★8111★

MINER INSTITUTE FOR MAN AND ENVIRONMENT - MINER CENTER LIBRARY (Env-Cons)
SUNY College at Plattsburgh   Phone: (518) 564-2178
Chazy, NY 12921   Linda J. Masters, Lib.Tech.Asst.
Founded: 1972. **Subjects:** Human ecology, air and water pollution, alternative energy sources, environmental sciences, wildlife ecology, rural sociology, land use planning, environmental economics. **Holdings:** 3800 books; 24 VF drawers; 825 government documents (environmental issues). **Subscriptions:** 155 journals and other serials. **Services:** Interlibrary loans; copying; library open to public for reference use only.

★8112★

MINERAL SPRINGS HOSPITAL - MEDICAL LIBRARY (Med)
Box 1050 Phone: (403) 762-2222
Banff, AB, Canada T0L 0C0 Mrs. E. Heikkila, Dir., Med.Rec.
Founded: 1957. **Subjects:** Medicine, administration. **Holdings:** 75 books; 100 Medifact tapes. **Subscriptions:** 30 journals and other serials. **Services:** Library not open to public.

MINI EMPLOYMENT INFORMATION CENTER (MEIC)
See: District of Columbia Public Library - Business, Economics & Vocations Division

★8113★

MINITEX (Info Sci)
30 Wilson Library, Univ. of Minnesota
309 19th Ave. S. Phone: (612) 376-3925
Minneapolis, MN 55455 Alice E. Wilcox, Dir.
Founded: 1969. **Staff:** Prof 5; Other 30. **Services:** MINITEX is a network of libraries which facilitates sharing of resources and services among and between libraries by providing the following: document delivery; a communications system; maintenance of machine-readable bibliographic databases; support for online cataloging through OCLC; computerized and manual literature searching; reference and referral services; a periodical exchange; and workshops and skills development programs for librarians. **Computerized Information Services:** DIALOG, SDC, BRS, NLM, RLIN. **Networks/Consortia:** Member of MIDLNET; OCLC. **Publications:** MINITEX Messenger; manuals and reports - for participants only. **Special Catalogs:** MULS: A Union List of Serials. **Remarks:** Contractual and reciprocal arrangements with North Dakota State Library, South Dakota State Library, and Wisconsin Interlibrary Services provide access to material in those states. **Also Known As:** Minnesota Interlibrary Telecommunications Exchange. **Staff:** Anita Anker, MULS Coord.; Julia Blixrud, OCLC Coord.; M.J. Dustin, Ref.Coord.; Mark Eckes, Adm.Coord.

MINKLER (F.W.) LIBRARY
See: North York Board of Education - F.W. Minkler Library

MINNEAPOLIS ATHENAEUM LIBRARY
See: Minneapolis Public Library & Information Center

★8114★

MINNEAPOLIS COLLEGE OF ART AND DESIGN - LIBRARY AND MEDIA CENTER (Art)
200 E. 25th St. Phone: (612) 870-3291
Minneapolis, MN 55404 Richard Kronstedt, Hd.Libn.
Founded: 1960. **Staff:** Prof 4; Other 4. **Subjects:** Art - painting, architecture, sculpture, graphic arts, history; design; films and film making; photography; video; fashion and costume. **Holdings:** 49,000 books and bound periodical volumes; 165 artists' books; 200 videotapes; 5 films; 62,000 slides; 69 VF cabinets of clippings, pamphlets, maps, brochures, artists catalogs; 378 audio cassettes; 298 phonograph records; 378 microfiche. **Subscriptions:** 177 journals and other serials. **Services:** Interlibrary loans (limited); copying; library open to public for reference use only. **Networks/Consortia:** Member of Union of Independent Colleges (UICA); MINITEX. **Remarks:** Maintained by the Minneapolis Society of Fine Arts. **Staff:** Timothy Perkins, Media Ctr.Dir.; Mary Miller, Asst.Libn.; Peggy Rudberg, Slide Libn.

★8115★

MINNEAPOLIS INSTITUTE OF ARTS - ARTS RESOURCE AND INFORMATION CENTER (Art)
2400 Third Ave., S. Phone: (612) 870-3131
Minneapolis, MN 55404 Robert C. Booker, Supv.
Founded: 1973. **Staff:** Prof 3. **Subjects:** Arts organizations in Minnesota, metropolitan arts activities, art classes, speakers on the arts. **Holdings:** Figures not available. **Services:** Library open to public. **Publications:** Nonprofit Arts Organizations in Minnesota; Exhibition and Performing Spaces in the Twin Cities; Minnesota Art Fairs - for sale; Collecting, Identifying, Pricing Art. **Special Indexes:** Indexes of art classes, art activities, arts organizations and speakers (Kardex). **Remarks:** Maintained by the Minneapolis Society of Fine Arts.

★8116★

MINNEAPOLIS INSTITUTE OF ARTS - LIBRARY - EDITORIAL DEPARTMENT (Art)
2400 Third Ave., S. Phone: (612) 874-0200
Minneapolis, MN 55404 Harold Peterson, Libn./Ed.-in-Chf.
Staff: Prof 2; Other 2. **Subjects:** General art history, European painting, decorative arts. **Special Collections:** Leslie Collection of Fine Books (fine printing). **Holdings:** 30,000 books and bound periodical volumes; auction

catalogs; exhibition catalogs. **Subscriptions:** 100 journals and other serials. **Services:** Copying; library open to public. **Publications:** The Minneapolis Institute of Arts Bulletin. **Special Catalogs:** Museum exhibition catalogs. **Remarks:** Maintained by the Minneapolis Society of Fine Arts. **Staff:** Barbara Lassonde, Asst.Libn.

★8117★

MINNEAPOLIS PUBLIC LIBRARY & INFORMATION CENTER - ART, MUSIC & FILMS DEPARTMENT (Art; Mus; Aud-Vis)
300 Nicollet Mall Phone: (612) 372-6520
Minneapolis, MN 55401 Marlea R. Warren, Dept.Hd.
Staff: Prof 6; Other 12. **Subjects:** Art, music, architecture, sculpture, painting, music theory and practice, art and music biographies, drawing, prints, decorative arts, films. **Special Collections:** Bookplates; advertising cards; Christmas cards; band parts; old songs and popular songs since 1900; Koussevitsky tapes; music scrapbooks; WPA art. **Holdings:** 94,200 books; 6746 bound periodical volumes; 1450 phonotapes, 15,000 78 RPM albums, 31,732 LP discs, 34,750 pieces of sheet music (all cataloged); 30,790 pieces of sheet music (uncataloged); over 1 million mounted and unmounted pictures; 102 vertical file drawers; 2891 films; 1907 filmstrips; 15,811 2x2 slides; 26,190 3 1/4x4 slides; 10,650 stereographs; 376 projected books on film; 383 video cassettes. **Subscriptions:** 415 journals and other serials. **Services:** Interlibrary loans; copying (limited). **Networks/Consortia:** Member of Metropolitan Library Services Agency (MELSA); MINITEX. **Special Catalogs:** Film Catalog, annual supplements. **Special Indexes:** Popular song index; Song index (both on cards). **Remarks:** Telephone number for Films Department is (612) 372-6558. **Staff:** Richard Zgodava, Asst.Dept.Hd.; Janet Hennesy, Prof.Asst.; Darryl Barrett, Prof.Asst.; Elizabeth Bingaman, Films Spec.; Thomas Smisek, Lib.Asst. Films.

★8118★

MINNEAPOLIS PUBLIC LIBRARY & INFORMATION CENTER - BUSINESS AND SCIENCE DEPARTMENT (Bus-Fin; Sci-Tech)
300 Nicollet Mall Phone: (612) 372-6552
Minneapolis, MN 55401 Leonard J. Pignatello, Dept.Hd.
Founded: 1973. **Staff:** Prof 8; Other 11. **Subjects:** Natural sciences, applied sciences, business, economics, labor, statistics. **Special Collections:** Business directories (1000); telephone directories (1200); 35 VF drawers of local company histories; auto repair manuals (2500); tax services; 10Ks on microfiche for Minnesota corporations. **Holdings:** 200,000 books; 18,006 bound periodical volumes; 20 VF drawers of corporation annual reports; Patent Depository Library; Official Gazette, U.S. Patent and Trademark Office, volume 1 to present; SAMS Photofact Service, volume 1 to present; U.S. Patents, 1790 to present (microfilm). **Subscriptions:** 1365 journals and other serials; 9 newspapers. **Services:** Interlibrary loans; copying. **Computerized Information Services:** Online systems; computerized cataloging. **Networks/Consortia:** Member of Metropolitan Library Service Agency (MELSA); MINITEX. **Publications:** Books for Business, quarterly - mailed free to businessman. **Staff:** Mary Zeimetz, Asst.Dept.Hd.; Edythe Abrahamson, Libn.; Walter Carlock, Libn.; Kathryn Kohli, Libn.; Mary Lawson, Libn.; Irving Robbins, Libn.; Roberta Ratcliff, Libn.

★8119★

MINNEAPOLIS PUBLIC LIBRARY & INFORMATION CENTER - ENVIRONMENTAL CONSERVATION LIBRARY OF MINNESOTA (Env-Cons)
300 Nicollet Mall Phone: (612) 372-6609
Minneapolis, MN 55401 Julia Copeland, Env.Consrv.Libn.
Founded: 1972. **Staff:** Prof 2; Other 2. **Subjects:** Environmental policy, conservation, pollution, environmental education, natural resources, energy. **Special Collections:** Documents relating to Minnesota Regional Copper-Nickel Project; Reserve Mining Company Trials; Minnesota power plant siting program; U.S. Nuclear Regulatory Commission Public Documents Room (nuclear power plants in Minnesota). **Holdings:** 15,500 books; 162 bound periodical volumes; 25 VF drawers of pamphlets and clippings; 2000 environmental impact statements (paper and microfiche); 38,000 microfiche. **Subscriptions:** 375 journals and other serials. **Services:** Interlibrary loans; copying; library open to public. **Computerized Information Services:** DIALOG, SDC, BRS. **Publications:** ECOL News, irregular - free upon request. **Remarks:** This collection is a state center for environmental information. **Staff:** Elizabeth Frisbie, Hd., Spec.Serv.Dept.

★8120★

MINNEAPOLIS PUBLIC LIBRARY & INFORMATION CENTER - GOVERNMENT DOCUMENTS (Info Sci)
300 Nicollet Mall Phone: (612) 372-6534
Minneapolis, MN 55401 Helen E. Garnaas, Doc.Libn.
Founded: 1893. **Staff:** Prof 3; Other 2. **Subjects:** Federal documents. **Special Collections:** City of Minneapolis and Minnesota State publications. **Holdings:** 500,000 documents; Congressional hearings, 1869-1938, on

microfiche; serial set 1817-1879, microprint; U.S. Supreme Court reports, 1887 to present (microfiche and paper). **Subscriptions:** 200 journals and other serials. **Special Catalogs:** In-house subject catalog of government publications. **Staff:** Gregor Henrikson, Libn.

★8121★

MINNEAPOLIS PUBLIC LIBRARY & INFORMATION CENTER - HISTORY DEPARTMENT (Hist)
300 Nicollet Mall   Phone: (612) 372-6537
Minneapolis, MN 55401   Robert K. Bruce, Dept.Hd.
Staff: Prof 7; Other 6. **Subjects:** History, travel and description, government, politics, biography, genealogy, coins, law. **Special Collections:** Minneapolis History Collection (4000 volumes, periodicals, pictures, maps and VF holdings). **Holdings:** 186,500 books; 26,600 bound periodical volumes; 700 other cataloged items; 7900 reels of microfilm; 830 records and tapes; 48 VF drawers; U.S. Geological Survey maps. **Subscriptions:** 750 journals and other serials; 67 newspapers. **Services:** Interlibrary loans; copying. **Computerized Information Services:** Online systems; computerized cataloging. **Networks/Consortia:** Member of Metropolitan Library Services Agency (MELSA); MINITEX. **Special Indexes:** Index to Minneapolis Star and Minneapolis Tribune, monthly printed with cumulated index every six months. **Staff:** Doris Skalstad, Asst.Hd.; Dorothy Burke, Spec.Coll.Libn.; Audrey Canelake, Libn.; Anna Hobbs, Lib.Asst.; Judith Mosiniak, Lib.Asst.; Jeanette Thompson-Larsen, Libn.

★8122★

MINNEAPOLIS PUBLIC LIBRARY & INFORMATION CENTER - HUTTNER ABOLITION AND ANTI-SLAVERY COLLECTION (Soc Sci)
300 Nicollet Mall   Phone: (612) 372-6522
Minneapolis, MN 55401   Richard Hofstad, Athenaeum Libn.
Founded: 1974. **Staff:** Prof 1; Other 2. **Subjects:** Abolitionist movement, slavery, black writers and reformers. **Holdings:** 550 books; 50 letters and documents; 250 pamphlets, broadsides, newspapers. **Services:** Copying.

★8123★

MINNEAPOLIS PUBLIC LIBRARY & INFORMATION CENTER - KITTLESON WORLD WAR II COLLECTION (Mil)
300 Nicollet Mall   Phone: (612) 372-6522
Minneapolis, MN 55401   Richard Hofstad, Athenaeum Libn.
Founded: 1945. **Staff:** Prof 1; Other 2. **Subjects:** World War II - military and naval operations, social and economic aspects, personal narratives, Antisemitism and the Holocaust. **Holdings:** 6722 books; 400 pamphlets (cataloged); 14 volumes of scrapbooks; 3 VF drawers of clippings; 2000 posters; 400 unbound periodicals; 1500 leaflets and pictures. **Services:** Copying.

★8124★

MINNEAPOLIS PUBLIC LIBRARY & INFORMATION CENTER - LITERATURE AND LANGUAGE DEPARTMENT (Hum)
300 Nicollet Mall   Phone: (612) 372-6540
Minneapolis, MN 55401   Dorothy D. Thews, Dept.Hd.
Founded: 1958. **Staff:** Prof 4; Other 5. **Subjects:** Literary criticism and history, fiction, poetry, drama, film, foreign languages and literatures. **Holdings:** 210,000 books; 11,500 bound periodical volumes; 50 VF drawers; 1800 phonograph records; 850 audio cassettes. **Subscriptions:** 350 journals and other serials. **Services:** Interlibrary loans; copying; translation. **Computerized Information Services:** DIALOG, SDC, BRS, New York Times Information Service; computerized cataloging. **Publications:** New Books in Theatre, quarterly - handout. **Staff:** Carol Van Why, Asst.Dept.Hd.; Renee Reed, Libn.; Gloria Rohman, Libn.

★8125★

MINNEAPOLIS PUBLIC LIBRARY & INFORMATION CENTER - MINNEAPOLIS ATHENAEUM LIBRARY (Hist)
300 Nicollet Mall   Phone: (612) 372-6522
Minneapolis, MN 55401   Richard Hofstad, Athenaeum Libn.
Founded: 1859. **Staff:** Prof 1; Other 2. **Subjects:** North American Indians; natural history; early American travel and exploration; art; colorplate books; music. **Holdings:** 100,000 books and bound periodical volumes. **Services:** Interlibrary loans (limited); copying.

★8126★

MINNEAPOLIS PUBLIC LIBRARY & INFORMATION CENTER - MUNICIPAL INFORMATION LIBRARY (Soc Sci; Plan)
City Hall, Rm. 302   Phone: (612) 348-8139
Minneapolis, MN 55415   Sylvia Frisch, Libn.
Founded: 1972. **Staff:** Prof 1. **Subjects:** Urban affairs, cable television, planning, public administration, police, local government. **Holdings:** 35,000 volumes; 32 VF drawers. **Subscriptions:** 65 journals and other serials; 15 newspapers. **Services:** Interlibrary loans; copying; SDI; library open to public. **Computerized Information Services:** DIALOG, Local Government Information Network (LOGIN), SDC, New York Times Information Service. **Publications:** Selected Bibliography on the City of Minneapolis, irregular.

★8127★

MINNEAPOLIS PUBLIC LIBRARY & INFORMATION CENTER - 19TH CENTURY AMERICAN STUDIES COLLECTION (Hum)
N. Regional Library, Emerson Rm.
1315 Lowry Ave., N.   Phone: (612) 522-3333
Minneapolis, MN 55411
Founded: 1970. **Subjects:** Materials by and about 19th century American writers; anti-slavery movement; New England - descriptive and historical writings. **Special Collections:** Truman Nelson letters; John Greenleaf Whittier - Evelina Bray Downey correspondence; manuscript "Ode to France," James Russell Lowell. **Holdings:** 4500 books; 200 bound periodical volumes; 150 pamphlets (cataloged); 140 autograph letters; 150 pictures; 250 unbound periodicals, pamphlets, newspapers; 1 VF drawer of clippings. **Services:** Copying.

★8128★

MINNEAPOLIS PUBLIC LIBRARY & INFORMATION CENTER - SOCIOLOGY DEPARTMENT (Soc Sci)
300 Nicollet Mall   Phone: (612) 372-6555
Minneapolis, MN 55401   Eileen Schwartzbauer, Dept.Hd.
Staff: Prof 4; Other 5. **Subjects:** Psychology, philosophy, religion, education, social sciences (except economics and history), anthropology, folklore, manners and customs, recreation. **Special Collections:** College catalogs from major colleges and universities in the United States (microfiche); Foundation Center Regional Collection; Adult Basic Education Collection. **Holdings:** 90,000 books; 7800 bound periodical volumes; 76 VF drawers of pamphlets and clippings; records and cassettes; periodicals on microfilm. **Subscriptions:** 472 journals and other serials. **Computerized Information Services:** DIALOG, BRS, SDC, New York Times Information Service. **Networks/Consortia:** Member of MINITEX; Metropolitan Library Services Agency (MELSA); METRONET. **Staff:** Helen J. Gilbertson, Asst.Dept.Hd.

★8129★

MINNEAPOLIS PUBLIC SCHOOLS - SPECIAL SCHOOL DISTRICT 1 - BOARD OF EDUCATION LIBRARY (Educ)
807 N.E. Broadway   Phone: (612) 348-6048
Minneapolis, MN 55413   Phyllis Thornley, Asst.Dir.
Staff: Prof 1; Other 1. **Subjects:** Education, preschool through 12th grade; educational psychology; disadvantaged children and youth; child and adolescent psychology; sociology; minorities; school media centers. **Special Collections:** Archives of School District publications; Indian education (200 titles). **Holdings:** 8000 books; 160 archival materials (cataloged); 24 VF drawers of pamphlets. **Subscriptions:** 125 journals and other serials; 4 newspapers. **Services:** Interlibrary loans; copying; library open to public for reference use only. **Networks/Consortia:** Member of METRONET. **Special Catalogs:** Union List of Serials in Minneapolis Public Schools, annual.

MINNEAPOLIS SOCIETY OF FINE ARTS - MINNEAPOLIS COLLEGE OF ART AND DESIGN
See: Minneapolis College of Art and Design

MINNEAPOLIS SOCIETY OF FINE ARTS - MINNEAPOLIS INSTITUTE OF ARTS
See: Minneapolis Institute of Arts

★8130★

MINNEAPOLIS STAR AND TRIBUNE - LIBRARY (Publ)
Fifth & Portland
Minneapolis, MN 55488   Robert H. Jansen, Hd.Libn.
Founded: 1946. **Staff:** Prof 3; Other 13. **Subjects:** Newspaper reference topics. **Holdings:** 1500 books; 6 million clippings; 4 million pictures. **Services:** Library open to public with special permission only. **Staff:** Linda L. James, Asst.Libn.; William L. Rafferty, Ref.Libn.

★8131★

MINNEAPOLIS TECHNICAL INSTITUTE/MINNEAPOLIS COMMUNITY COLLEGE - LIBRARY (Sci-Tech)
1415 Hennepin Ave. S.   Phone: (612) 341-7219
Minneapolis, MN 55403   David L. Jenson, Libn.
Staff: Prof 1; Other 1. **Subjects:** Vocational-technical material in 27 trade areas. **Services:** Only currently enrolled students may borrow materials. **Formerly:** Minneapolis Technical Institute - Library.

MINNESOTA ANALYSIS AND PLANNING SYSTEM
See: University of Minnesota - Agricultural Extension Service

★8132★
MINNESOTA BIBLE COLLEGE - LIBRARY (Rel-Theol)
920 Mayowood Rd., S.W.   Phone: (507) 288-4563
Rochester, MN 55901   Ardis C. Sawyer, Libn.
Founded: 1913. Staff: Prof 2; Other 2. Subjects: Bible, theology, social
sciences, philosophy, history. Holdings: 20,500 books; 3010 bound
periodical volumes; 170 cassette tapes; 200 phonograph records; 635 AV
resource items. Subscriptions: 100 journals and other serials. Services:
Library open to public.

MINNESOTA CENTER FOR PHILOSOPHY OF SCIENCE
See: University of Minnesota

★8133★
MINNESOTA GAS COMPANY - LIBRARY (Energy; Bus-Fin)
201 S. 7th St.   Phone: (612) 372-4824
Minneapolis, MN 55402   Virginia B. Shirk, Libn.
Founded: 1959. Staff: Prof 1; Other 1. Subjects: Gas industry, sales and
marketing, management, household appliance merchandising, public utilities,
peat gasification. Holdings: 5000 volumes; 300 annual reports of utility
companies; 17 VF drawers of information files. Subscriptions: 300 journals
and other serials. Services: Interlibrary loans; copying; library open to public
with restrictions. Computerized Information Services: DIALOG.
Publications: Library Bulletin, monthly - for internal distribution only.

★8134★
MINNESOTA GEOLOGICAL SURVEY - LIBRARY (Sci-Tech)
University of Minnesota
1633 Eustis St.   Phone: (612) 373-3372
St. Paul, MN 55108   Lynn Swanson, Sr.Lib.Asst.
Founded: 1970. Staff: Prof 1. Subjects: Minnesota and U.S. geology.
Holdings: 1400 books; 250 bound periodical volumes; 3300 unbound serials;
90 theses; 3450 maps; 6 VF drawers of reprints; 3 VF drawers of pamphlets
and clippings. Subscriptions: 50 journals and other serials. Services: Copying;
library open to public with restrictions.

MINNESOTA HIGHER EDUCATION COORDINATING BOARD
See: Minnesota State Department of Education - Interagency Resource
and Information Center

**MINNESOTA HISTORICAL SOCIETY - CENTRAL MINNESOTA HISTORICAL
CENTER**
See: Central Minnesota Historical Center

★8135★
**MINNESOTA HISTORICAL SOCIETY - DIVISION OF ARCHIVES AND
MANUSCRIPTS (Hist)**
1500 Mississippi St.   Phone: (612) 296-6980
St. Paul, MN 55101   Sue E. Holbert, State Archv.
Founded: 1849. Staff: Prof 18; Other 7. Subjects: Local, state, national
politics; travel (Western); immigration; labor; business; transportation;
conservation; religion; diplomacy; genealogy; Minnesota territorial, state and
local census records; Minnesota territorial, state and local public records.
Special Collections: Allyn K. Ford Manuscript Collection; Public Affairs Center
Collections; Great Northern and Northern Pacific Railways Collection.
Holdings: 30,000 linear feet of state archives; 40,000 linear feet of
manuscripts; 4000 reels of microfilm; additional holdings in 8 state regional
research centers. Services: Interlibrary loans of microfilmed collections and
state census records; copying; library open to public. Publications: Periodic
guides, guides to microfilm editions. Special Catalogs: Catalogs of
manuscript collections, public affairs collections, regional center collections,
public records. Staff: James E. Fogerty, Dp. State Archv.; Lydia Lucas, Hd.,
Tech.Serv.; Duane P. Swanson, Archv., Govt.Rec.; Dallas R. Lindgren, Hd.,
Ref.Serv.; Richard A. Cameron, Field Dir.

★8136★
**MINNESOTA HISTORICAL SOCIETY - FORT SNELLING BRANCH LIBRARY
(Hist)**
Fort Snelling History Center   Phone: (612) 726-1171
St. Paul, MN 55111
Founded: 1970. Staff: 1. Subjects: History - Minnesota, regional, military;
American Indians; American and regional archeology; 19th century America.
Holdings: 6000 volumes; 1500 other items. Services: Copying; library open
to public for reference use only.

**MINNESOTA HISTORICAL SOCIETY - NORTH CENTRAL MINNESOTA
HISTORICAL CENTER**
See: North Central Minnesota Historical Center

**MINNESOTA HISTORICAL SOCIETY - NORTHEAST MINNESOTA
HISTORICAL CENTER**
See: Northeast Minnesota Historical Center

**MINNESOTA HISTORICAL SOCIETY - NORTHWEST MINNESOTA
HISTORICAL CENTER**
See: Northwest Minnesota Historical Center

★8137★
MINNESOTA HISTORICAL SOCIETY - REFERENCE LIBRARY (Hist)
690 Cedar St.   Phone: (612) 296-2143
St. Paul, MN 55101   Patricia C. Harpole, Chf. of Ref.Lib.
Founded: 1849. Staff: Prof 9; Other 8. Subjects: Minnesota, Upper
Midwest, United States history, travel, genealogy, Scandinavians in North
America, nationality groups in U.S., Canada. Special Collections: Minnesota
newspapers 1849 to present. Holdings: 350,000 books, bound periodical
volumes and newspaper volumes; 103,000 government documents; 800
microcards; 6000 microfiche; 44,000 reels of microfilm (primarily Minnesota
newspapers); 172 VF drawers of pamphlets and clippings (primarily on
Minnesota). Subscriptions: 1300 journals and other serials. Services:
Interlibrary loans; copying; library open to public for reference use only.
Special Catalogs: Dakota and Chippewa Indians: a subject catalog (book).
Staff: Alice B. Grygo, Ser.Libn.; Faustino Avaloz, Newspaper Cur.; Alissa
Wiener, ILL Asst.; Brigid Shields, Newspaper Ref.Libn.; Edward Swanson, Hd.,
Tech.Serv.; Marlin L. Heise, Hd.Cat.Libn.; Margaret J. Habermann, Cat.Libn.;
Wiley R. Pope, Ref.Libn.

**MINNESOTA HISTORICAL SOCIETY - SOUTHEAST MINNESOTA
HISTORICAL SOCIETY**
See: Southeast Minnesota Historical Society

**MINNESOTA HISTORICAL SOCIETY - SOUTHERN MINNESOTA HISTORICAL
CENTER**
See: Southern Minnesota Historical Center

**MINNESOTA HISTORICAL SOCIETY - SOUTHWEST MINNESOTA
HISTORICAL CENTER**
See: Southwest Minnesota Historical Center

★8138★
MINNESOTA HISTORICAL SOCIETY - SPECIAL LIBRARIES (Aud-Vis)
690 Cedar St.   Phone: (612) 296-2489
St. Paul, MN 55101   Bonnie Wilson, Hd.
Staff: Prof 5; Other 3. Subjects: Minnesota, transportation, agriculture, arts,
commerce, family life, industry, Indians. Special Collections: Hubert H.
Humphrey Photograph Collection (25,000); Norton & Peel Commercial
Photograph Collection (75,000). Holdings: 250,000 photographs; 2000 art
works; 2000 films, tapes and videotapes; 2000 35mm slides; 16,000 maps;
3000 posters. Services: Copying; department open to public for reference
use only. Staff: Nancy Erickson, Cat.Libn.; Elizabeth Hall, Chf. Photographer;
Tracey Baker, Asst.Libn.; Jon Walstrom, Map Libn.

**MINNESOTA HISTORICAL SOCIETY - WEST CENTRAL MINNESOTA
HISTORICAL CENTER**
See: West Central Minnesota Historical Center

MINNESOTA INTERLIBRARY TELECOMMUNICATIONS EXCHANGE
See: MINITEX

★8139★
**MINNESOTA LIBRARY FOR THE BLIND AND PHYSICALLY HANDICAPPED
(Aud-Vis)**
                                               Phone: (507) 332-3279
Faribault, MN 55021   Myrna Wright, Libn.
Founded: 1933. Staff: Prof 2; Other 10. Holdings: 38,000 talking book
records; 20,000 volumes in braille; 12,000 open reel tapes; 600 large print
books. Services: Interlibrary loans; tapes copied from masters; library serves
the legally blind and physically handicapped.

★8140★
MINNESOTA MUSEUM OF ART - LIBRARY (Art)
St. Peter St. at Kellogg Blvd.   Phone: (612) 292-4350
St. Paul, MN 55102   Leanne A. Klein, Libn.
Staff: Prof 1. Subjects: Asian art; 20th century American and European
painting, graphics, sculpture. Holdings: 1000 books; 2000 exhibit catalogs

from other museums; 1000 slides of permanent collection art objects; 4 VF drawers of art clippings; Sotheby Parke Bernet and Christies auction catalogs. **Subscriptions:** 10 journals and other serials. **Services:** Interlibrary loans; library open to public for reference use only. **Publications:** Minnesota Museum of Art exhibition catalogs; list of other publications - available upon request.

MINNESOTA ORCHESTRA ARCHIVES
See: University of Minnesota - Manuscripts Division

★8141★
MINNESOTA ORCHESTRA - MUSIC LIBRARY (Mus)
1111 Nicollet Mall   Phone: (612) 371-5622
Minneapolis, MN 55403   James N. Berdahl, Libn.
Staff: Prof 2. **Subjects:** Orchestral music. **Holdings:** Figures not available. **Services:** Library not open to public. **Staff:** Eric A. Sjostrom, Asst.Libn.

MINNESOTA ROOM
See: Stillwater Public Library

★8142★
MINNESOTA SCIENCE FICTION SOCIETY - LIBRARY†
Loop Sta., Box 2128   Phone: (612) 722-5217
Minneapolis, MN 55402   Dennis Lien, Contact Person
Founded: 1970. **Subjects:** Science fiction, fantasy. **Holdings:** 1200 books. **Services:** Library open to public upon application.

★8143★
MINNESOTA STATE ATTORNEY GENERAL - LAW LIBRARY (Law)
102 State Capitol Bldg.   Phone: (612) 296-8152
St. Paul, MN 55155   Anita Anderson, Libn.
Staff: Prof 1. **Subjects:** Law. **Holdings:** 4.5 feet of microfiche; 30 VF drawers of attorney general opinions. **Subscriptions:** 370 journals and other serials; 20 newspapers. **Services:** Interlibrary loans; copying; library not open to public. **Computerized Information Services:** WESTLAW, DIALOG; computerized cataloging. **Networks/Consortia:** Member of MINITEX; Capitol Area Library Consortium (CALCO).

★8144★
MINNESOTA STATE BOARD OF ANIMAL HEALTH - LIBRARY (Agri)
LL-70, Metro Square Bldg.
7th & Robert Sts.   Phone: (612) 296-2942
St. Paul, MN 55101   J.G. Flint, Sec.
Subjects: Minutes of board meetings since 1903. **Holdings:** Textbooks on various diseases of animals and poultry. **Services:** Library open to public for reference use only.

MINNESOTA STATE CRIMINAL JUSTICE PROGRAM
See: Minnesota State Department of Energy Planning and Development - Criminal Justice Program

★8145★
MINNESOTA STATE DEPARTMENT OF ECONOMIC SECURITY - LIBRARY (Soc Sci)
690 American Center Bldg.   Phone: (612) 296-8810
St. Paul, MN 55101   Linda Woodstrom, Libn.
Staff: Prof 1; Other 1. **Subjects:** Poverty program and manpower reports, poverty statistics for Minnesota. **Holdings:** 3000 books; training films and materials; government reports. **Subscriptions:** 142 journals and other serials. **Services:** Interlibrary loans; library open to public with restrictions. **Computerized Information Services:** DIALOG; computerized cataloging. **Networks/Consortia:** Member of MINITEX; OCLC; Capitol Area Library Consortium (CALCO). **Formerly:** Minnesota State Office of Economic Opportunity.

★8146★
MINNESOTA STATE DEPARTMENT OF EDUCATION - INTERAGENCY RESOURCE AND INFORMATION CENTER (Educ)
401-A Capitol Square Bldg.   Phone: (612) 296-6684
St. Paul, MN 55101   Pat Tupper, Lib.Prog.Dir.
Founded: 1970. **Staff:** Prof 3; Other 2. **Subjects:** Education - elementary, secondary and higher; vocational rehabilitation; disabled and handicapped employment; adult basic education; planning. **Special Collections:** Abledata - assistive devices for the handicapped. **Holdings:** 5000 books; 2000 Minnesota State documents on microfiche; ERIC microfiche collection. **Subscriptions:** 500 journals and other serials. **Services:** Interlibrary loans; center open to public for reference use only. **Computerized Information Services:** BRS, DIALOG, Control Data Corporation; internal database; computerized cataloging. **Networks/Consortia:** Member of MINITEX; OCLC; Capitol Area Library Consortium (CALCO); METRONET. **Special Indexes:**

KWIC index to vocational rehabilitation. **Remarks:** Includes holdings of Minnesota State Department of Energy, Planning and Development, Minnesota State Division of Vocational Rehabilitation, Minnesota State University Board and Higher Education Coordinating Board. **Staff:** Lois Byrum, Sr.Libn.; Pat Fenton, Ref.Libn.

★8147★
MINNESOTA STATE DEPARTMENT OF EDUCATION - OFFICE OF PUBLIC LIBRARIES AND INTERLIBRARY COOPERATION (Info Sci)
301 Hanover Bldg.
480 Cedar St.   Phone: (612) 296-2821
St. Paul, MN 55101   William G. Asp, Dir.
Founded: 1901. **Staff:** Prof 6; Other 5. **Subjects:** Professional library materials, information science. **Holdings:** 10,000 volumes; 30 VF drawers of pamphlets and clippings; 85 16mm films; 225 reels of microfilm; 2200 microfiche; 300 audio cassettes; 100 video cassettes and slide-tape sets. **Subscriptions:** 250 journals and other serials. **Services:** Interlibrary loans; copying; in-depth reference services; open for use and loan to all interested persons; mail and phone requests accepted. **Computerized Information Services:** DIALOG; computerized cataloging. **Networks/Consortia:** Member of MINITEX; METRONET; Capitol Area Library Consortium (CALCO). **Publications:** Minnesota Libraries, quarterly - free to libraries in Minnesota, other states on exchange; Public Library Newsletter, Resources in Library and Information Science - both monthly and distributed to public libraries within state; Look & Listen, annual AV catalog - to Minnesota libraries. **Also Known As:** OPLIC. **Staff:** Alan Lewis, Asst.Dir.; Darlene Arnold, Sr.Libn.

★8148★
MINNESOTA STATE DEPARTMENT OF ENERGY, PLANNING AND DEVELOPMENT - CRIMINAL JUSTICE PROGRAM - LIBRARY (Law)
100 Hanover Bldg.
480 Cedar St.   Phone: (612) 296-2771
St. Paul, MN 55101   Marcia Anderson Reeve
Staff: 1. **Subjects:** Criminal justice. **Special Collections:** Internally produced publications. **Holdings:** 3000 books; 1000 reports; unbound periodicals. **Subscriptions:** 58 journals and other serials. **Services:** Interlibrary loans; copying; SDI; library open to public. **Computerized Information Services:** DIALOG. **Networks/Consortia:** Member of MINITEX; Capitol Area Library Consortium; Criminal Justice Information Exchange. **Formerly:** Crime Control Planning Board.

★8149★
MINNESOTA STATE DEPARTMENT OF ENERGY, PLANNING AND DEVELOPMENT - ENERGY LIBRARY (Energy)
150 E. Kellogg Blvd., Rm. 980   Phone: (612) 296-8902
St. Paul, MN 55101   Donna Slamkowski, Res.Libn.
Staff: Prof 2; Other 1. **Subjects:** Energy conservation, electricity, alternative sources of energy, energy policy and modeling. **Special Collections:** NTIS - SRIM energy microfiche (80,000 items). **Holdings:** 12,000 books. **Subscriptions:** 250 journals and other serials; 6 newspapers. **Services:** Interlibrary loans; copying; library open to public. **Computerized Information Services:** DIALOG, BRS, DOE/RECON; computerized journal circulation. **Networks/Consortia:** Member of MINITEX; METRONET; Capitol Area Library Consortium (CALCO); Minnesota Online Users Group. **Remarks:** Maintains an energy information telephone service for Minnesota residents. The toll-free number is 800-652-9747. **Formerly:** Minnesota State Energy Agency - Library. **Staff:** Roberta Hovde, Libn.

★8150★
MINNESOTA STATE DEPARTMENT OF HEALTH - ROBERT N. BARR PUBLIC HEALTH LIBRARY (Med)
717 Delaware St., S.E.   Phone: (612) 296-5240
Minneapolis, MN 55440   Lynne Siemers, Libn.
Founded: 1872. **Staff:** Prof 1; Other 2. **Subjects:** Public health; health planning, promotion, statistics and administration; disease prevention. **Special Collections:** Annual reports of other state (and provincial) health departments. **Holdings:** 15,000 books; 5000 bound periodical volumes; 48 VF drawers of pamphlets. **Subscriptions:** 275 journals and other serials. **Services:** Interlibrary loans; library open to public for reference use only. **Computerized Information Services:** BRS, DIALOG, NLM. **Networks/Consortia:** Member of Capitol Area Library Consortium (CALCO); METRONET; Regional Medical Library - Region 3; MINITEX; Twin Cities Biomedical Consortium (TCBC).

★8151★
MINNESOTA STATE DEPARTMENT OF PUBLIC SAFETY - FILM LIBRARY (Aud-Vis)
Griggs Midway Bldg., Rm. 180 S.
1821 University Ave.   Phone: (612) 482-5925
St. Paul, MN 55104   Janet Weber, Libn.
Founded: 1955. **Staff:** Prof 1; Other 3. **Subjects:** Safety - traffic, highway,

public, bicycle, pedestrian; driver education; alcohol and drug abuse; police training. **Holdings:** 2000 traffic safety movie films; crime watch and emergency service films. **Services:** Library open to public. **Computerized Information Services:** Computerized cataloging. **Special Catalogs:** Film Catalog. **Formerly:** Its State Patrol Film Library.

★8152★

MINNESOTA STATE DEPARTMENT OF PUBLIC WELFARE - LIBRARY (Soc Sci)†

Centennial Bldg., 1st Floor   Phone: (612) 296-1548
St. Paul, MN 55155   William G. McCarthy, Lib.Prog.Dir.
Founded: 1934. **Staff:** Prof 3; Other 3. **Subjects:** Public welfare, public administration, mental illness, psychology, social work, child welfare, hospital administration. **Holdings:** 4000 books; 5000 pamphlets (cataloged); 700 16mm films on social welfare. **Subscriptions:** 200 journals and other serials. **Services:** Interlibrary loans; copying; library open to public for reference use only. **Computerized Information Services:** DIALOG. **Networks/Consortia:** Member of Minnesota Department of Public Welfare Library Consortium; MINITEX; Capitol Area Library Consortium (CALCO). **Publications:** Film Catalog, biennial - Minnesota residents only; monthly bibliography. **Staff:** Margaret Olson, Libn.; Henry Wagener, Media Cons.

MINNESOTA STATE DEPARTMENT OF PUBLIC WELFARE - OAK TERRACE NURSING HOME
See: Oak Terrace Nursing Home

★8153★

MINNESOTA STATE DEPARTMENT OF REVENUE - TAX LIBRARY (Bus-Fin)
Centennial Office Bldg.
658 Cedar St.   Phone: (612) 296-1022
St. Paul MN 55145
Subjects: Taxes, accounting, state statutes. **Holdings:** 5000 books; 1000 tax reports. **Subscriptions:** 8 journals and other serials. **Services:** Library not open to public.

★8154★

MINNESOTA STATE DEPARTMENT OF TRANSPORTATION - LIBRARY AND INFORMATION SERVICES SECTION (Trans)
B-26A State Transportation Bldg.
St. Paul, MN 55155   Phone: (612) 296-2385
                              Jerome C. Baldwin, Dir., Lib./Info.Serv.
Founded: 1957. **Staff:** Prof 1; Other 2. **Subjects:** Transportation planning and engineering. **Holdings:** 2000 books; 500 bound periodical volumes; 4000 reports (cataloged); 100 pamphlets; 7000 microfiche. **Subscriptions:** 300 journals and other serials. **Services:** Interlibrary loans; copying; library open to public. **Computerized Information Services:** DIALOG, SDC, BRS. **Networks/Consortia:** Member of MINITEX; METRONET; Capital Area Library Consortium (CALCO).

MINNESOTA STATE DIVISION OF VOCATIONAL REHABILITATION
See: Minnesota State Department of Education - Interagency Resource and Information Center

MINNESOTA STATE ENERGY AGENCY
See: Minnesota State Department of Energy, Planning and Development

★8155★

MINNESOTA STATE HORTICULTURAL SOCIETY - LIBRARY (Sci-Tech)
161 Alderman Hall
1970 Folwell Ave.   Phone: (612) 373-1031
St. Paul, MN 55108   Glenn Ray, Exec.Dir.
Staff: 1. **Subjects:** Gardening, natural history, botany. **Holdings:** 1500 volumes. **Services:** Library open to public for reference use only.

★8156★

MINNESOTA STATE INFORMATION SYSTEMS DIVISION - LIBRARY (Info Sci)
Centennial Office Bldg., 5th Fl.   Phone: (612) 296-4621
St. Paul, MN 55155   Arlene Kromminga, Libn.
Founded: 1972. **Staff:** 1. **Holdings:** 135 shelves of program listings and documents. **Subscriptions:** 225 journals and other trade publications. **Services:** Library not open to public.

MINNESOTA STATE IRON RANGE RESOURCES & REHABILITATION BOARD - IRON RANGE RESEARCH CENTER
See: Iron Range Research Center

★8157★

MINNESOTA STATE LAW LIBRARY (Law)
117 University Ave.   Phone: (612) 296-2775
St. Paul, MN 55155   Marvin Roger Anderson, State Law Libn.
Staff: Prof 5; Other 4. **Subjects:** Law. **Special Collections:** Trial transcripts for cases decided by the Minnesota Supreme Court. **Holdings:** 200,000 volumes; Minnesota Supreme Court briefs and records on microfiche, 1981 to present. **Subscriptions:** 675 journals and other serials; 7 newspapers. **Services:** Interlibrary loans; copying; library open to public for reference use only. **Computerized Information Services:** Computerized cataloging. **Networks/Consortia:** Member of MINITEX; OCLC. **Publications:** Miscellaneous checklist, annual - to other law libraries. **Staff:** Shirley H. David, Asst. State Law Libn.; Elizabeth Peterson, Hd., Tech.Serv.; Daniel Lunde, Hd., Pub.Serv.

★8158★

MINNESOTA STATE LEGISLATIVE REFERENCE LIBRARY (Soc Sci)
State Capitol, Rm. 111   Phone: (612) 296-3398
St. Paul, MN 55155   Linda F. Montgomery, Dir.
Staff: Prof 5; Other 5. **Subjects:** Legislatures, government, politics. **Holdings:** 15,000 volumes; Minnesota government publications on microfiche, 1974 to present; legislative debate on tape, 1973 to present. **Subscriptions:** 600 journals and other serials; 50 newspapers. **Services:** Interlibrary loans; library open to public for reference use only. **Computerized Information Services:** DIALOG, New York Times Information Service; computerized cataloging. **Networks/Consortia:** Member of MINITEX; OCLC. **Publications:** LRL Checklist, monthly - by subscription. **Special Indexes:** Statutory Compliance Index. **Staff:** Patricia Conley, Ref.Libn.; Zona DeWitt, Libn.; Dan Gjelten, Ref.Libn.

MINNESOTA STATE OFFICE OF ECONOMIC OPPORTUNITY
See: Minnesota State Department of Economic Security

★8159★

MINNESOTA STATE POLLUTION CONTROL AGENCY - LIBRARY (Env-Cons)
1935 W. County Road B-2   Phone: (612) 296-7719
Roseville, MN 55113   Elizabeth C. Gelbmann, Libn.
Staff: Prof 1. **Subjects:** Water and air pollution control, solid wastes pollution, hazardous waste. **Special Collections:** NTIS Environmental Pollution & Control Selected Research in Microfiche (SRIM) series (1976-present). **Holdings:** 1000 books. **Subscriptions:** 116 journals and other serials. **Services:** Interlibrary loans; library open to public for reference use only. **Computerized Information Services:** DIALOG. **Networks/Consortia:** Member of MINITEX.

★8160★

MINNESOTA STATE SERVICES FOR THE BLIND AND VISUALLY HANDICAPPED - COMMUNICATION CENTER (Aud-Vis)
1745 University Ave.   Phone: (612) 296-6723
St. Paul, MN 55104   Joanne Jonson, Dir.
Founded: 1953. **Staff:** Prof 12; Other 16. **Subjects:** General, with all books on tape or in braille. **Holdings:** 5000 titles on tape; 4000 titles in braille. **Subscriptions:** 120 journals and other serials; 5 newspapers. **Services:** Copying; center open to public but is for use only by eligible clients; circulates on loan without charge tapes and braille books; provides on loan without charge phonograph and cassette equipment and closed-circuit radio receivers. **Publications:** Radio Talking Book calendar of programming, monthly. **Staff:** Ellie Seudy, Supv. Tape Textbook Sect.; Judy Normandin, Supv. Braille Sect.; Marilynn Alcott, Supv. Radio Talking Bks.; Robert Watson, Supv./Chf.Engr.,Engr.Sec.

MINNESOTA STATE UNIVERSITY BOARD
See: Minnesota State Department of Education - Interagency Resource and Information Center

★8161★

MINNESOTA STATE WATER RESOURCES BOARD - LIBRARY (Env-Cons)
555 Wabasha St.   Phone: (612) 296-2840
St. Paul, MN 55102   Mel Sinn, Dir.
Subjects: Watershed districts; water and soil erosion. **Special Collections:** Watershed District Establishment File (maps, statements, photographs). **Holdings:** 250 volumes. **Services:** Copying; library open to public for reference use only.

★8162★

MINNESOTA WOMEN'S CENTER - RESOURCE COLLECTION
University of Minnesota
324 Walter Library
117 Pleasant St., S.E.
Minneapolis, MN 55455
Defunct

★8163★
MINNESOTA ZOOLOGICAL GARDEN - LIBRARY (Sci-Tech)
12101 Johnny Cake Ridge Rd.   Phone: (612) 432-9010
Apple Valley, MN 55124   Angie Norell, Libn.
Founded: 1977. **Staff:** Prof 1. **Subjects:** Natural history, animal
management, veterinary medicine, zoology, horticulture. **Special Collections:**
Publications of the International Union for the Conservation of Nature and
Natural Resources; zoo newsletters. **Holdings:** 2000 books; 45 bound
periodical volumes; 1 filing cabinet of 35mm slides. **Subscriptions:** 80
journals and other serials. **Services:** Interlibrary loans; copying; library open to
public for reference use only. **Computerized Information Services:** DIALOG.
Networks/Consortia: Member of Capitol Area Library Consortium (CALCO);
MINITEX; OCLC. **Publications:** New Books at the Zoo, irregular - for internal
distribution only.

MINOR SWARTHOUT MEMORIAL LIBRARY
See: Curtiss (Glenn H.) Museum of Local History - Minor Swarthout
   Memorial Library

★8164★
MINORITY BUSINESS INFORMATION INSTITUTE, INC. - LIBRARY (Bus-Fin)
295 Madison Ave., 12th Fl.   Phone: (212) 889-8220
New York, NY 10017   Eleanor M. Hurka, Info.Spec.
Founded: 1971. **Staff:** Prof 1; Other 1. **Subjects:** Minority economic
development, minority groups, business. **Special Collections:** Directories of
minority businesses. **Holdings:** 2100 books and bound periodical volumes; 14
VF drawers of pamphlets and clippings. **Subscriptions:** 110 journals and other
serials. **Services:** Copying; library open to public by appointment. **Networks/
Consortia:** Member of METRO. **Publications:** MBII Newsletter, irregular.
Special Indexes: Black Business Development, complete index to Black
Enterprise magazine (card).

MINOT AIR FORCE BASE (ND)
See: U.S. Air Force Base - Minot Base Library

★8165★
MINOT DAILY NEWS - LIBRARY (Publ)
301-303 Fourth St., S.E.   Phone: (701) 852-3341
Minot, ND 58701   Betty Rogstad, Libn.
Staff: Prof 3. **Subjects:** Newspaper reference topics. **Holdings:** Figures not
available; newspaper clippings, photographs. **Services:** Copying; library open
to public for reference use only. **Staff:** Foli Taylor, Photograph Libn.; Correne
Fossum, Asst.Libn.

★8166★
MINOT STATE COLLEGE - MEMORIAL LIBRARY - SPECIAL COLLECTIONS
   (Area-Ethnic)
                                               Phone: (701) 857-3200
Minot, ND 58701   Ronald Rudser, Act.Dir.
Special Collections: North Dakota Collection; Indians of the North Central
States; government documents (600 shelves). **Services:** Interlibrary loans;
copying; library open to public. **Networks/Consortia:** Member of MINITEX;
North Dakota State Library Teletype Network.

★8167★
MINT MUSEUM OF ART - LIBRARY (Art)†
501 Hempstead Pl.
Box 6011
Charlotte, NC 28207   Phone: (704) 334-9723
                                               Sara H. Wolf, Libn.
Founded: 1958. **Staff:** 1. **Subjects:** Ceramics; decorative arts; fine arts -
history and techniques. **Special Collections:** Delhom-Gambrell Reference
Library (1639 volumes). **Holdings:** 5790 books; 698 bound periodical
volumes; auction catalogs, collections (cataloged); 5 shelves of exhibition
catalogs; 2 shelves of museum newsletters; 41 shelves of sales catalogs.
Subscriptions: 58 journals and other serials. **Services:** Library open to public
for reference use only.

★8168★
MINT MUSEUM OF HISTORY - LASSITER LIBRARY (Hist)
3500 Shamrock Dr.   Phone: (704) 568-1774
Charlotte, NC 28215   Phyllis Russell, Libn.
Founded: 1980. **Staff:** Prof 2. **Subjects:** American history, decorative arts,
American ceramics, local and state history, local genealogy. **Special
Collections:** Local archival collection. **Holdings:** 400 books; 50 VF drawers of
local family papers; 10 VF drawers of Charlotte Fire Department papers and
photographs. **Subscriptions:** 25 journals and other serials. **Services:** Copying;
library open to public for reference use only.

★8169★
MINTZ, LEVIN, COHN, FERRIS, GLOVSKY AND POPEO, P.C. - LAW LIBRARY
   (Law)
One Center Plaza   Phone: (617) 742-5800
Boston, MA 02108   Judy Rosen, Libn.
Staff: Prof 1; Other 2. **Subjects:** Federal and Massachusetts law. **Holdings:**
7000 books; 112 bound periodical volumes; 500 unbound periodicals and
pamphlets. **Subscriptions:** 100 journals and other serials. **Services:**
Interlibrary loans; library open to public with special permission.
Computerized Information Services: LEXIS. **Networks/Consortia:** Member
of Association of Boston Law Librarians.

★8170★
MIRAMICHI HOSPITAL - HEALTH SCIENCES LIBRARY (Med)
P.O. Box 420   Phone: (506) 622-1340
Newcastle, NB, Canada E1V 3M5   Audrey D. Somers, Educ.Coord.
Founded: 1974. **Staff:** 1. **Subjects:** Medicine, nursing, administration,
patient education, allied health subjects. **Holdings:** 800 books; 30 bound
periodical volumes; 10 AV hardware items; 3 cabinets of AV materials.
Subscriptions: 46 journals and other serials. **Services:** Interlibrary loans;
copying; library open to public with restrictions.

★8171★
MIRIAM HOSPITAL - MEDICAL LIBRARY (Med)
164 Summit Ave   Phone: (401) 274-3700
Providence, RI 02906   Ann LeClaire, Dir., Lib.Serv.
Staff: Prof 1; Other 1. **Subjects:** Clinical medicine, surgery, biomedical
research. **Special Collections:** Nephrology and cardiology. **Holdings:** 2347
books; 7489 bound periodical volumes; 676 cassettes (cataloged); 5 VF
drawers of unbound reports, archives, pamphlets, published articles by staff;
2 16mm films; 16 tape reels; LATCH Program; 24 microfiche programs.
Subscriptions: 341 journals and other serials. **Services:** Interlibrary loans;
copying. **Computerized Information Services:** MEDLINE. **Networks/
Consortia:** Member of Association of Rhode Island Health Science Librarians.
Publications: Annual report, Newsletter, Acquisitions Lists, Journal Titles List.

MIRROR LAKE/TOMLINSON EDUCATION CENTER - LIBRARY/MEDIA
CENTER
See: Pinellas County School Board

★8172★
MISERICORDIA GENERAL HOSPITAL - HOSPITAL LIBRARY (Med)
99 Cornish Ave.   Phone: (204) 774-6581
Winnipeg, MB, Canada R3C 1A2   Sharon Allentuck, Hosp.Libn.
Founded: 1974. **Staff:** 3. **Subjects:** Nursing, medicine and allied health fields.
Holdings: 4100 books and bound periodical volumes. **Subscriptions:** 324
journals and other serials. **Services:** Interlibrary loans; copying; library· not
open to public.

★8173★
MISERICORDIA HOSPITAL - MEDICAL LIBRARY (Med)
600 E. 233rd St.   Phone: (212) 920-9869
Bronx, NY 10466   Denise L. Kirk, Dir., Libs.
Staff: Prof 1; Other 2. **Subjects:** Medicine. **Holdings:** 1673 books; 5425
bound periodical volumes; 64 volumes of microforms. **Subscriptions:** 300
journals and other serials. **Services:** Interlibrary loans; copying; library open to
health care personnel. **Computerized Information Services:** BRS.
Networks/Consortia: Member of Medical Library Center of New York
(MLCNY); Manhattan-Bronx Health Sciences Library Group.

★8174★
MISERICORDIA HOSPITAL - SCHOOL OF NURSING LIBRARY
4401 Bronx Blvd.
Bronx, NY 10470
Defunct

★8175★
MISERICORDIA HOSPITAL - WEINLOS MEDICAL LIBRARY (Med)
16940 87th Ave.   Phone: (403) 484-8811
Edmonton, AB, Canada T5R 4H5   Francine Lapointe, Med.Libn.
Founded: 1969. **Staff:** Prof 1; Other 8. **Subjects:** Medicine, surgery, nursing,
health sciences. **Holdings:** 6000 books and bound periodical volumes;
microforms. **Subscriptions:** 250 journals and other serials. **Services:**
Interlibrary loans; copying; current awareness; library not open to public.

★8176★
MISSION RESEARCH CORPORATION - TECHNICAL LIBRARY (Sci-Tech)
735 State St.
P.O. Drawer 719
Santa Barbara, CA 93102
Phone: (805) 963-8761
Elaine Messier, Libn.
Staff: Prof 1. **Subjects:** Atmospheric physics and chemistry, radar studies, computer programming, physical security. **Holdings:** 2700 books; 85 titles of bound periodical volumes; 4000 technical reports; 50 dissertations; 200 microfiche; 12 reels of microfilm; 50 patents. **Subscriptions:** 73 journals and other serials. **Services:** Library not open to public. **Computerized Information Services:** DIALOG, DTIC. **Publications:** MRC New Acquisitions, monthly. **Special Catalogs:** Thesaurus of MRC Subject Headings (book).

MISSIONARIES OF THE SACRED HEART - MSC CENTER LIBRARY
See: MSC Center Library

MISSIONARY ORIENTATION LIBRARY
See: Southern Baptist Convention - Foreign Mission Board

MISSIONARY RESEARCH CENTER ARCHIVES
See: Luther Northwestern Seminary

MISSIONARY RESEARCH LIBRARY COLLECTION
See: Union Theological Seminary - Library

★8177★
MISSISQUOI HISTORICAL SOCIETY - CORNELL MILL MUSEUM - REFERENCE LIBRARY & ARCHIVES (Hist)
Box 186
Stanbridge East, PQ, Canada J0J 2H0
Margaret Ellis, Archv.
Founded: 1964. **Staff:** Prof 1; Other 5. **Subjects:** Eastern Townships of Quebec - genealogy, history, biography, geography; Canadiana; antiques. **Special Collections:** Missisquoi Historical Society Histories and Reports. **Holdings:** 4000 books; 50 bound periodical volumes; 693 reports, manuscripts, clippings, documents, maps, oral history tapes. **Services:** Interlibrary loans; copying; library open to public for reference use only. **Publications:** Missisquoi Historical Society reports. **Special Catalogs:** Catalog of archives material (book form with indexes); catalogs of reports, documents, artifacts and cemeteries. **Remarks:** The society provides a genealogical research service by mail, and provides research assistance for a fee.

★8178★
MISSISSIPPI BAPTIST CONVENTION BOARD - MISSISSIPPI BAPTIST HISTORICAL COMMISSION (Rel-Theol)
Box 51
Clinton, MS 39056
Phone: (601) 924-6172
Alice G. Cox, Libn.
Founded: 1926. **Staff:** Prof 1; Other 2. **Subjects:** Mississippi Baptist history including convention minutes, association minutes, church minutes. **Holdings:** 1450 volumes; 433 reels of microfilm; 165 slides; 6 manuscripts; 118 cassette tapes; 32 VF drawers of subjects related to Mississippi Baptist history. **Services:** Copying; library open to public. **Publications:** A History of Mississippi Baptists, 1780-1970; Highlights of Mississippi Baptist History. **Special Indexes:** Index to Mississippi Baptist Record. **Remarks:** Collection is housed in Mississippi College Library.

★8179★
MISSISSIPPI COLLEGE SCHOOL OF LAW - LAW LIBRARY (Law)
151 E. Griffith St.
Jackson, MS 39201
Phone: (601) 944-1970
Carol C. West, Dir./Professor of Law
Staff: Prof 5; Other 4. **Subjects:** Law. **Holdings:** 115,000 volumes. **Services:** Interlibrary loans; copying; library not open to public. **Computerized Information Services:** Computerized cataloging. **Networks/Consortia:** Member of OCLC through SOLINET. **Staff:** Judith F. Anspaugh, Pub.Serv.Libn.; John Paul Laughlin, Night Ref.Libn.; Carnette McMillan, Acq.Libn.; Vickey Baggott, Cat.Libn.

★8180★
MISSISSIPPI MUSEUM OF NATURAL SCIENCE - LIBRARY (Sci-Tech)
111 N. Jefferson St.
Jackson, MS 39202
Phone: (601) 354-7303
Mary P. Stevens, Musm.Libn.
Founded: 1973. **Staff:** Prof 1. **Subjects:** Ornithology, ichthyology, herpetology, mammology, botany, invertebrata, paleontology. **Special Collections:** Fannye A. Cook Collection (500 books, 1500 periodicals, 500 reprints); rare book collection (26 items). **Holdings:** 2500 books; 200 bound periodical volumes; 12 VF drawers; 500 reprints. **Subscriptions:** 102 journals and other serials. **Services:** Interlibrary loans; copying; library open to public with permission of director. **Computerized Information Services:** DIALOG; computerized cataloging.

MISSISSIPPI RIVER COMMISSION TECHNICAL LIBRARY
See: U.S. Army - Corps of Engineers - Lower Mississippi Valley Division

★8181★
MISSISSIPPI STATE AGRICULTURAL & FORESTRY EXPERIMENT STATION - DELTA BR. EXPERIMENT STA. LIBRARY (Sci-Tech; Agri)
Phone: (601) 686-9311
Stoneville, MS 38776
Charlotte G. Pierce, Libn.
Founded: 1966. **Staff:** Prof 1; Other 1. **Subjects:** Agriculture, botany, chemistry, economics, mathematics, mechanical engineering, meteorology, zoology. **Special Collections:** Complete holdings of Mississippi Agricultural and Forestry Experiment Station publications; U.S. Department of Agriculture publications. **Holdings:** 13,500 books; 4500 bound periodical volumes; 348 reels of microfilm; 25,000 pamphlets. **Subscriptions:** 222 journals and other serials; 10 newspapers. **Services:** Interlibrary loans; library open to public. **Publications:** New Books List, irregular. **Special Indexes:** Subject and author indexes of publications of staff members; chronological index of publications of the Agricultural and Forestry Experiment Station.

★8182★
MISSISSIPPI STATE BOARD OF HEALTH - FILM LIBRARY (Aud-Vis)
Box 1700
Jackson, MS 39205
Phone: (601) 354-6639
Nancy Kay Sullivan, Dir., Pub.Rel.
Founded: 1940. **Staff:** Prof 1; Other 2. **Subjects:** Alcohol, dental health, diseases, drug addiction and narcotics, family planning, nursing, nutrition. **Holdings:** 1800 16mm films; 300 35mm filmstrips (cataloged). **Services:** Library open to Mississippi residents only. **Staff:** Mrs. Gena R. Henson, Film Libn.

★8183★
MISSISSIPPI STATE BOARD OF HEALTH - LIBRARY
2423 N. State St.
Box 1700
Jackson, MS 39205
Defunct

★8184★
MISSISSIPPI STATE BUREAU OF GEOLOGY - LIBRARY (Sci-Tech; Energy)
2525 N. West St.
Box 5348
Jackson, MS 39216
Phone: (601) 354-6228
Carolyn Woodley, Libn.
Founded: 1906. **Staff:** Prof 1. **Subjects:** Geology, paleontology, mineralogy, geohydrology, geophysics, foreign geology. **Special Collections:** U.S. Geological Survey depository; state Geological Survey publications; Geological Society guidebooks. **Holdings:** 30,000 volumes; dissertations; topographic maps; microforms; government documents. **Subscriptions:** 80 journals and other serials. **Services:** Interlibrary loans; copying; library open to public. **Computerized Information Services:** SDC, DOE/RECON; computerized cataloging.

★8185★
MISSISSIPPI STATE DEPARTMENT OF ARCHIVES AND HISTORY - ARCHIVES AND LIBRARY DIVISION (Hist)
100 S. State St.
Box 571
Jackson, MS 39205
Phone: (601) 354-6218
Mrs. Madel J. Morgan, Dir., Archv. & Lib.Div.
Founded: 1902. **Staff:** Prof 14; Other 7. **Subjects:** Mississippiana, genealogy, Confederate history. **Holdings:** 37,000 volumes; 1547 collections of manuscripts; 6509 cubic feet of official archives; 7095 maps; 12,500 reels of microfilm; 11,587 photographs; 2203 architectural drawings; 158 VF drawers. **Subscriptions:** 370 journals and other serials; 137 newspapers. **Services:** Copying; library open to public for reference use only. **Publications:** Guide to Official Records in the Mississippi Department of Archives and History; list of other publications available. **Staff:** William Hanna, Archv., Spec.Coll.; Anne Lipscomb, Libn.; Dwight Harris, Archv., Govt.Rec.

★8186★
MISSISSIPPI STATE DEPARTMENT OF PUBLIC WELFARE - JEAN GUNTER SOCIAL WELFARE LIBRARY (Soc Sci)
515 E. Amite St.
Box 352
Jackson, MS 39205
Phone: (601) 354-0341
Mary Ellen Simpson, Welfare Libn.
Founded: 1951. **Staff:** Prof 2. **Subjects:** Public welfare, social work, child welfare, psychology, administration, group work, aging, management. **Holdings:** 5600 volumes; 10,000 pamphlets, booklets and brochures; 55 videotapes. **Subscriptions:** 72 journals and other serials. **Services:** Interlibrary loans; copying; library open to public with priority to Mississippi social workers. **Special Catalogs:** Author-title analytics of bound periodicals, proceedings and compilations; author-title analytics to contents of pamphlet

file. **Staff:** Cindy McLemare, Asst.Libn.

★8187★
MISSISSIPPI STATE LAW LIBRARY (Law)
Gartin Justice Bldg.
Box 1040   Phone: (601) 354-7113
Jackson, MS 39205   Merle Buckley Allen, Libn.
Founded: 1821. **Staff:** Prof 4; Other 2. **Subjects:** Law. **Holdings:** 80,000 volumes. **Subscriptions:** 199 journals and other serials; 93 newspapers. **Services:** Copying; library open to public. **Staff:** B. Susan Upton, Asst.Libn.

★8188★
MISSISSIPPI STATE LIBRARY COMMISSION (Info Sci)
Box 3260   Phone: (601) 354-6369
Jackson, MS 39207   David M. Woodburn, Dir.
Founded: 1926. **Staff:** Prof 36; Other 49. **Subjects:** General, library science. **Special Collections:** Mississippi; materials for the handicapped. **Holdings:** 310,501 books; 78 bound periodical volumes; 18,582 AV items; vertical files of Mississippi materials; 116,735 recordings and tapes for the handicapped; 3265 braille volumes. **Subscriptions:** 510 journals and other serials; 6 newspapers. **Services:** Interlibrary loans; copying; library open to state employees for job-related purposes. **Computerized Information Services:** Computerized cataloging and acquisitions. **Publications:** Mississippi State Government Publications: A KWIC Index; The Packet, monthly - primarily to public libraries; The Reading Light, quarterly - to handicapped patrons and to public libraries. **Special Catalogs:** Union catalog (microfiche). **Staff:** Gerald Buchanan, Asst.Dir., Lib.Oper.; Linda Gates, Asst.Dir., Lib.Dev.; James S. Progar, Asst.Dir., Adm.

★8189★
MISSISSIPPI STATE MEDICAL ASSOCIATION - LIBRARY (Med)
735 Riverside Dr.   Phone: (601) 354-5433
Jackson, MS 39216
Founded: 1856. **Subjects:** Medical socioeconomics and related fields pertinent to medical organization and policies. **Holdings:** 5000 volumes. **Subscriptions:** 50 journals and other serials. **Services:** Library not open to public.

★8190★
MISSISSIPPI STATE RESEARCH AND DEVELOPMENT CENTER - INFORMATION SERVICES DIVISION (Bus-Fin)
3825 Ridgewood Rd.
Drawer 2470   Phone: (601) 982-6324
Jackson, MS 39205   Natelle Isley, Mgr.
Founded: 1960. **Staff:** Prof 6; Other 8. **Subjects:** Economics, statistics, Mississippi economic data, technology, management, community planning, industrial development, community appearance, engineering. **Special Collections:** Newspaper clippings for 6 months; collection of audiovisual aids available on loan in fields of supervisory training, management, community planning, merchandising, salesmanship, technology (160). **Holdings:** 10,000 books; Data Bank of pamphlets and unbound reports; printouts and publications of census data; telephone directories; archives of center publications; maps. **Subscriptions:** 504 journals and other serials; 53 newspapers. **Services:** Interlibrary loans; copying; telephone inquiries; center open to public with restrictions. **Computerized Information Services:** DIALOG; Audiovisual Aids scheduler, shipper and management reports; Mississippi County Data Bank. **Publications:** Recently Published Materials of Interest to Mississippi Businessmen, bimonthly; Catalog of Audiovisual Aids Available on Loan, irregular; Mississippi Community Data, annual; Mississippi Labor Supply Data, annual; Quick Reference Data Summary, annual. **Staff:** Marilyn Moore, Coord., Ref.Serv.; Martha Ann Lee, Mgr., Tech.Proc.; Polly Shanks, Mgr., S.D.I.; Mary Evelyn Tomlin, Ref. & Data Serv. Unit; Nan Vodde, Coord., Data Serv.

★8191★
MISSISSIPPI STATE UNIVERSITY - MITCHELL MEMORIAL LIBRARY - SPECIAL COLLECTIONS (Hist)†
Drawer 5408   Phone: (601) 325-4225
Mississippi State, MS 39762   Frances N. Coleman, Act.Hd., Spec.Coll.
Staff: Prof 4; Other 3. **Subjects:** State and local history, John C. Stennis, Southern history and politics. **Special Collections:** John C. Stennis Collection (1298 linear feet); David Bowen Collection; Mississippi politics (250,000 items); Hodding and Betty Werlein Carter papers (85 linear feet); Turner Catledge papers; Gil Carmichael Papers; Delta and Pineland Company Records: Minor Gray Addition; Mississippi Republican Party Papers. **Holdings:** 21,614 books; 1153 bound periodical volumes; 837 titles in microform; 62 VF drawers; 3500 linear feet of manuscripts. **Subscriptions:** 1077 journals and other serials; 65 newspapers. **Services:** Interlibrary loans; copying; library open to public for reference and research. **Computerized Information**

Services: DIALOG, SDC, MEDLINE, New York Times Information Service; computerized cataloging, serials and circulation. **Networks/Consortia:** Member of OCLC through SOLINET. **Publications:** Guide to the Public Series in the John C. Stennis Collection; Guide to Manuscript Holdings at Mississippi State University. **Staff:** Hilda B. Scholtes, Univ.Archv.; Anne S. Wells, Mss.Libn.; Lynne Mueller, Ref.Libn.

★8192★
MISSISSIPPI UNIVERSITY FOR WOMEN - SCHOOL OF EDUCATION - LIBRARY SCIENCE DIVISION (Info Sci)
    Phone: (601) 328-9100
Columbus, MS 39701   Dr. Maude Yow, Hd.
Founded: 1930. **Staff:** Prof 3; Other 1. **Subjects:** Library science, adult reading, cataloging and classification, library organization, practice work, public library, reference, school library, children's literature, young adult literature. **Special Collections:** Arthur Rackham (32 volumes). **Holdings:** 10,000 books; 164 audiovisual items (cataloged). **Services:** Library open to public for reference use only. **Staff:** Jamie S. Mills, Asst.Prof.

MISSISSIPPI VALLEY COLLECTION
See: Memphis State University Libraries

★8193★
MISSISSIPPI VALLEY CONSERVATION AUTHORITY - R. TAIT MC KENZIE RESEARCH LIBRARY (Art)
R.R. 1, The Mill of Kintail   Phone: (613) 256-3610
Almonte, ON, Canada K0A 1A0
Founded: 1977. **Staff:** Prof 1. **Subjects:** Sculpture - original plaster, records, bronze; pioneer artifacts. **Special Collections:** Original sculptures by Dr. R. Tait McKenzie. **Holdings:** Figures not available. **Services:** Library open to researchers only.

★8194★
MISSISSIPPI VALLEY STATE UNIVERSITY - JAMES HERBERT WHITE LIBRARY (Educ)†
    Phone: (601) 254-9041
Itta Bena, MS 38941   Dr. Robbye R. Henderson, Hd.Libn.
Founded: 1952. **Special Collections:** Education; Martin Luther King, Jr. Collection; Mississippi history. **Services:** Interlibrary loans; copying; library open to public for reference use only. **Publications:** Current Acquisitions List, monthly.

★8195★
MISSOURI BAPTIST HISTORICAL COMMISSION LIBRARY (Hist)†
William Jewell College Library   Phone: (816) 781-3806
Liberty, MO 64068
Founded: 1885. **Staff:** 1. **Subjects:** Church records, church histories, biography. **Holdings:** 1579 books; 178 bound periodical volumes; 406 manuscripts and pictures; 7 VF drawers of metal cuts, photographs, clippings and reports. **Services:** Copying; library open to public for reference use only.

★8196★
MISSOURI BAPTIST HOSPITAL - MEDICAL LIBRARY (Med)
3015 N. Ballas Rd.   Phone: (314) 432-1212
St. Louis, MO 63131   Mildred Schupmann, Med.Libn.
Founded: 1966. **Staff:** Prof 1; Other 1. **Subjects:** Medicine and related subjects. **Holdings:** 603 books; 1794 bound periodical volumes; 504 audiotapes (cataloged). **Subscriptions:** 81 journals and other serials. **Services:** Interlibrary loans; copying; library open to public with permission of the Director of Medical Education. **Networks/Consortia:** Member of Midcontinental Regional Medical Library Program.

★8197★
MISSOURI BAPTIST HOSPITAL - SCHOOL OF NURSING LIBRARY (Med)
3015 N. Ballas Rd.   Phone: (314) 432-1212
St. Louis, MO 63131   Helen J. Seaton, Libn.
Founded: 1921. **Staff:** Prof 1. **Subjects:** Nursing, medicine, psychology. **Holdings:** 2000 books; AV material (cataloged). **Subscriptions:** 55 journals and other serials. **Services:** Interlibrary loans; copying; library not open to public.

★8198★
MISSOURI BOTANICAL GARDEN - LIBRARY (Sci-Tech)
Box 299   Phone: (314) 577-5155
St. Louis, MO 63166   James R. Reed, Dir. of Lib.
Founded: 1859. **Staff:** Prof 5; Other 9. **Subjects:** Plant taxonomy, plant geography, horticulture, botanical history. **Special Collections:** Sturtevant pre-Linnaean library, and subsequent additions (1000 items); Linnaeana (1830 items); illustrated flower books (750 items); Engelmann correspondence

(6000 letters); Engelmann notes and drawings (5000 pieces); W.C. Steere Bryological Collection (mosses and liverworts; 1000 volumes, 5000 pamphlets). **Holdings:** 47,000 books; 49,000 bound periodical volumes; 100,000 pamphlets (cataloged); 500 slides (cataloged); 6500 vegetation and topographic maps; 140,000 manuscripts; 15,000 microfiche of herbaria; 6000 art works. **Subscriptions:** 1500 journals and other serials. **Services:** Interlibrary loans; copying; library open to public. **Networks/Consortia:** Member of OCLC; St. Louis Regional Library Network. **Publications:** Monthly accessions list. **Remarks:** The library is located at 2345 Tower Grove Ave., St. Louis, MO 63110. **Staff:** Carla Lange, Asst.Libn.; Harva Kennedy, Cat.; Morton Deutch, Hand Binder; Barbara Mykrantz, Archv.

★8199★
MISSOURI COUNCIL FOR HANDGUN CONTROL - LIBRARY (Law)
7207 Pershing Ave. Phone: (314) 727-7563
University City, MO 63130 Eugene P. Schwartz, Chm.
Subjects: Police standards and code of ethics, handgun violence. **Holdings:** Figures not available. **Services:** Interlibrary loans; library open to public. **Publications:** Police Code of Ethical Standards; Police Attitudes on Handgun Control; Service to the Mentally Retarded Offender - Instructor's Manual.

★8200★
MISSOURI HISTORICAL SOCIETY - ARCHIVES AND MANUSCRIPTS (Hist)†
Jefferson Memorial Bldg.
Forest Park Phone: (314) 361-1424
St. Louis, MO 63112
Subjects: St. Louis history and culture, Missouri, Mississippi Valley, American West, Thomas Jefferson, Abraham Lincoln, Ulysses S. Grant, Charles Lindbergh, General William T. Sherman. **Special Collections:** Diary, journals and field notes of William Clark from his expedition with Meriwether Lewis; Louisiana Territory documents; papers of Walt Whitman, Eugene Field, Kate Chopin; manuscripts of Frederic Remington and Thomas Hart Benton; Aaron Burr; George Rogers Clark; black history; French settlement; German immigrants; Mexican and Civil Wars; colonial business and commerce in the Missouri area; Women's Suffrage Movement; William Torrey Harris (founder of the St. Louis Philosophical Society); Russian Revolution; American fur trade. **Holdings:** 2 million items.

★8201★
MISSOURI HISTORICAL SOCIETY - PICTORIAL HISTORY COLLECTION (Pict)†
Jefferson Memorial Bldg.
Forest Park Phone: (314) 361-1424
St. Louis, MO 63112 Judy Ciampoli, Cur.
Subjects: Missouri and Western life - buildings, street scenes, Indians, theater, music, transportation, valentines, steamboats, aviation, Lindbergh pictures. **Holdings:** 200,000 items: photographs, postcards, prints, paintings, sketches, daguerreotypes, tintypes, ambrotypes, advertising material. **Services:** Print and reproduction services available on a fee basis; use of archives for reference may be requested.

★8202★
MISSOURI HISTORICAL SOCIETY - RESEARCH LIBRARY (Hist)†
Jefferson Memorial Bldg.
Forest Park Phone: (314) 361-1424
St. Louis, MO 63112 Anthony R. Crawford, Asst.Dir./Lib. & Archv.
Founded: 1866. **Staff:** Prof 2; Other 2. **Subjects:** History - St. Louis, Missouri, Western, Missouri and Mississippi Rivers; fur trade; biography; genealogy; theater; music; Thomas Jefferson; early Mississippi travel; steamboats; Lewis and Clark expedition; American Indians. **Special Collections:** Mississippi River Collection; rare Western Americana; music collection (5000 pieces of sheet music; 500 volumes); theater collection (10,000 programs dating from 1817); scrapbook collection; 1904 World's Fair; Missouri Gazette collection (complete file). **Holdings:** 120,000 titles of books, pamphlets and periodicals; 2000 volumes of bound newspapers. **Subscriptions:** 241 journals and other serials. **Services:** Copying; library open to public with research fee for nonmembers. **Networks/Consortia:** Member of St. Louis Regional Library Network. **Publications:** Gateway Heritage, quarterly. **Staff:** Deborah W. Bolas, Assoc.Libn.; Beth Wilson, Asst.Libn.

★8203★
MISSOURI INSTITUTE OF PSYCHIATRY LIBRARY (Med)†
5400 Arsenal St. Phone: (314) 644-8838
St. Louis, MO 63139 Connie Wolf, Libn.
Founded: 1962. **Staff:** Prof 1; Other 7. **Subjects:** Psychiatry, pharmacology, neurology, biochemistry, psychology, physiology, sociology, nursing. **Holdings:** 9000 books; 9000 bound periodical volumes; 2 VF drawers; 90 films; 200 tape recordings; 50 microforms. **Subscriptions:** 470 journals and other serials. **Services:** Interlibrary loans; copying; SDI; library open to qualified

users. **Computerized Information Services:** DIALOG, BRS. **Networks/Consortia:** Member of Midcontinental Regional Medical Library Program. **Publications:** MIP Faculty Publications.

★8204★
MISSOURI SCHOOL OF RELIGION - LIBRARY
100 Hitt St.
Columbia, MO 65201
Defunct

★8205★
MISSOURI STATE CHEST HOSPITAL - MEDICAL LIBRARY (Med)
Phone: (417) 466-3711
Mount Vernon, MO 65712 Shirley Boucher, Libn.
Founded: 1948. **Staff:** Prof 1. **Subjects:** Chest and pulmonary diseases, allergies, medicine, surgery. **Holdings:** 1412 books; 1263 bound periodical volumes; 93 published articles by staff doctors; 402 tapes; 1434 slides; 41 microfiche. **Subscriptions:** 49 journals and other serials; 20 newspapers. **Services:** Interlibrary loans; copying; library open to area physicians and technicians.

★8206★
MISSOURI STATE COURT OF APPEALS, SOUTHERN DISTRICT - LAW LIBRARY (Law)
1018 Woodruff Bldg. Phone: (417) 862-6314
Springfield, MO 65806 Carole Wingert, Law Libn.
Founded: 1909. **Staff:** 1. **Subjects:** Law. **Holdings:** 15,086 volumes; microfiche. **Subscriptions:** 32 law journals. **Services:** Copying (limited). **Remarks:** Poplar Bluff branch contains 10,232 volumes.

★8207★
MISSOURI STATE COURT OF APPEALS, WESTERN DISTRICT - LIBRARY (Law)
1300 Oak St. Phone: (816) 474-5511
Kansas City, MO 64106 Vickie Selby, Libn.
Staff: Prof 1. **Subjects:** Law. **Holdings:** 35,000 volumes. **Subscriptions:** 152 journals and other serials. **Services:** Copying; library not open to public. **Computerized Information Services:** LEXIS.

MISSOURI STATE DEPARTMENT OF NATURAL RESOURCES - MARK TWAIN BIRTHPLACE MUSEUM
See: Mark Twain Birthplace Museum

★8208★
MISSOURI STATE DIVISION OF COMMUNITY AND ECONOMIC DEVELOPMENT - RESEARCH LIBRARY (Bus-Fin; Soc Sci)
1014 Madison St.
Box 118 Phone: (314) 751-3674
Jefferson City, MO 65102
Founded: 1962. **Staff:** Prof 6; Other 2. **Subjects:** Labor/manpower, economics, taxation/financing, manufacturing, agriculture, industry, natural resources, regional studies, transportation/energy, education, population. **Special Collections:** Missouri Community Profiles (300); State and other Area Manufacturer Directories (50); Missouri Industrial Sites (250). **Holdings:** 2000 books and bound periodical volumes; 32 VF drawers of unbound reports and articles; tapes. **Subscriptions:** 50 journals and other serials. **Services:** Library open to public on request and approval. **Publications:** Missouri New and Expanding Manufacturers, annual; Missouri Corporate Planner, periodically updated. **Staff:** John Kleindienst, Sr.Res.Assoc.; Don Smith, Res.Assoc.; John Hobbs, Res.Assoc.; Linda Lewis, Sr.Res.Assoc.; Kathy Fannin, Res.Assoc.; Earl Cannon, Mgr., Res.

★8209★
MISSOURI STATE DIVISION OF GEOLOGY AND LAND SURVEY - LIBRARY (Sci-Tech)
Box 250 Phone: (314) 364-1752
Rolla, MO 65401 Marcia Cussins, Libn.
Founded: 1853. **Staff:** 1. **Subjects:** Geology, geological engineering, water resources, mineral resources. **Holdings:** 25,000 books; 1000 bound periodical volumes; 6000 geological manuscripts, maps and charts. **Subscriptions:** 135 journals and other serials. **Services:** Interlibrary loans; library open to public for reference use only.

MISSOURI STATE DIVISION OF PARKS & HISTORIC PRESERVATION - WATKINS WOOLEN MILL
See: Watkins Woolen Mill State Historic Site

MISSOURI STATE HISTORICAL SOCIETY
See: State Historical Society of Missouri

★8210★

MISSOURI STATE LEGISLATIVE LIBRARY (Soc Sci)
State Capitol Bldg.   Phone: (314) 751-4633
Jefferson City, MO 65101   Anne Rottman, Libn.
Founded: 1909. Staff: Prof 1; Other 1. Subjects: Legislative problems, U.S.
and state government, law. Special Collections: Missouri legislation, 1804 to
present (350 volumes); Missouri House and Senate Journals, 1837 to present
(250 volumes). Holdings: 6500 books and bound periodical volumes; 33 VF
drawers of miscellaneous subjects. Subscriptions: 70 journals and other
serials. Services: Copying; library open to public. Computerized Information
Services: Missouri Bill Status Tracking System Inquiry (internal database).

★8211★

MISSOURI STATE LIBRARY (Info Sci)
308 E. High St.
Box 387
Jefferson City, MO 65102   Phone: (314) 751-4214
                                             Charles O'Halloran, State Libn.
Founded: 1907. Staff: Prof 12; Other 23. Subjects: State government,
history. Holdings: 179,500 books; 3500 bound periodical volumes; 60,000
microforms. Subscriptions: 1118 journals and other serials. Services:
Interlibrary loans; copying; library open to public with restrictions.
Publications: Newsletter, monthly; Directory of Missouri Libraries, annual.
Staff: Alan Engelbert, Coord., Spec.Lib.Serv.; Patricia Behler, Ch. & Young
Adult; John Finley, Ref.Bibliog.;; Jon Harrison, Fed.Doc.Libn.; Bob Nedderman,
State Doc.Libn.; Karen Hicklin, Ref.Libn.; Madeline Matson, Coord., Pubn.;
Richard Miller, Projects Coord.; Darla Parkes, Ref.Libn.; Frank Pascoe, Ref. &
Loan Serv.; Elaine Harrison, Ref.Libn.

★8212★

**MISSOURI STATE LIBRARY - WOLFNER MEMORIAL LIBRARY FOR THE
   BLIND & PHYSICALLY HANDICAPPED** (Aud-Vis)†
1221 Locust St.   Phone: (314) 241-4227
St. Louis, MO 63103   Pennie D. Peterson, Coord.
Founded: 1924. Staff: Prof 2; Other 15. Subjects: General. Holdings: 7124
braille books; 63,806 talking books; 62,232 cassette books. Services:
Interlibrary loans; library open to public and to legally blind and physically
handicapped readers in Missouri, also to persons, institutions, and
organizations working with the legally blind and physically handicapped.
Computerized Information Services: Computerized cataloging and
circulation.

★8213★

MISSOURI STATE SUPREME COURT LIBRARY (Law)
Supreme Court Bldg., High St.   Phone: (314) 751-2636
Jefferson City, MO 65101   D.A. Divilbiss, Hd.Libn.
Founded: 1829. Staff: Prof 3; Other 2. Subjects: Law. Holdings: 100,000
volumes; microfiche of Session Laws to 1900; 800 reels of microfilm of
Congressional Record, 1789-1972, and the Federal Register. Subscriptions:
150 journals and other serials; 15 newspapers. Services: Interlibrary loans;
copying; library open to public. Computerized Information Services: LEXIS.
Publications: The Summary - distributed within the building only. Staff:
Sandy Schroeder, Asst.Libn.

MITCHELL ARCHIVES
See: Historic Mobile Preservation Society

MITCHELL (D.W.) MEMORIAL LIBRARY
See: American Management Associations - D.W. Mitchell Memorial
   Library

MITCHELL (John and Mary) LIBRARY
See: Multnomah School of the Bible - John and Mary Mitchell Library

MITCHELL (Maria) ASSOCIATION OF NANTUCKET
See: Nantucket Maria Mitchell Association

MITCHELL MEMORIAL LIBRARY
See: Mississippi State University

MITCHELL MEMORIAL LIBRARY
See: U.S. Air Force Base - Travis Base Library

★8214★

MITCHELL (William) COLLEGE OF LAW - JOHN B. SANBORN LIBRARY
(Law)
871 Summit Ave.   Phone: (612) 227-9171
St. Paul, MN 55105   Madeleine J. Wilken, Lib.Dir.
Founded: 1900. Staff: Prof 5; Other 4. Subjects: Law. Holdings: 159,000
volumes. Subscriptions: 2000 journals and other serials. Services:
Interlibrary loans; copying; library open to public. Computerized Information
Services: DIALOG, WESTLAW; computerized cataloging. Networks/
Consortia: Member of MINITEX. Staff: Pat Creamer, Ser.; Patricia Dolan,
Evening Ref.; Ursula Allard, Cat.; Barbara Kallusky, Ref.

★8215★

MITRE CORPORATION - CORPORATE LIBRARY (Env-Cons)
Box 208   Phone: (617) 271-7834
Bedford, MA 01730   Mary F. Leahy, Supv./Libn.
Founded: 1959. Staff: Prof 3; Other 6. Subjects: Systems engineering,
electrical and electronic engineering, mathematics, computer technology.
Holdings: 64,277 books; 1794 bound periodical volumes; 839 tape
cassettes. Subscriptions: 1794 journals and other serials; 17 newspapers.
Services: Interlibrary loans; copying; library open to public. Computerized
Information Services: Online systems; computerized serials. Publications:
Weekly Review, abstracts journal articles and lists selective new book titles;
Computer Review, monthly - both for internal distribution only. Staff: Mary
Lou Cocci, Ref.Libn.; Joseph Rush, ILL Libn.; Betsy Cogliano, Cat.

★8216★

MITRE CORPORATION - LIBRARY (Env-Cons)
1820 Dolley Madison Blvd.   Phone: (703) 827-6484
McLean, VA 22102   Paula M. Strain, Mgr., Info.Serv.
Founded: 1964. Staff: Prof 6; Other 7. Subjects: System engineering (as a
methodology); communications systems (including military communications,
command and control); environmental problems; energy; mass and urban
transportation; air traffic systems; other civil systems. Holdings: 10,000
books; 1800 bound periodical volumes; 1500 reels of microfilm (each reel
representing one year's issues of a periodical); 75,000 technical reports
(microfiche). Subscriptions: 1035 journals and other serials; 25 newspapers.
Services: Interlibrary loans; copying; library open to public by appointment.
Computerized Information Services: DIALOG, SDC, MEDLINE, DOE/
RECON, New York Times Information Service, BRS, Source Telecomputing
Corporation, Integrated Library System. Networks/Consortia: Member of
Committee on Information Hang-ups; Interlibrary Users Association;
Metropolitan Washington Library Council; Consortium for Continuing Higher
Education in Northern Virginia; Library Networking Committee. Publications:
Accessions Bulletin, monthly; InforMITRE (newsletter, irregular). Staff: Sherri
Lieberman, Ref.Libn.; JoAnne Reid, Ref.Libn.; Mary Coyle, Ref.Libn.; David
Shumaker, Ref.Libn.; Jill Hanna, Ref.Libn.

★8217★

MITRE CORPORATION - TECHNICAL REPORT CENTER (Sci-Tech)
Box 208   Phone: (617) 271-2351
Bedford, MA 01730   Patricia J. McNulty, Supv.
Founded: 1977. Staff: Prof 4; Other 13. Subjects: Command control,
communications, computer technology, electrical and electronic engineering.
Special Collections: Air Force regulations, manuals and technical orders;
Department of Defense instructions, directives, specifications and standards.
Holdings: 125,000 technical reports; 50,000 reports on microfiche.
Services: Library not open to public. Computerized Information Services:
DTIC, BRS, DIALOG; internal database. Publications: Weekly Abstracts of
Selected Reports - for internal distribution only. Special Indexes: Computer
prepared report indexes. Staff: Susan Cornet, Info.Spec.; Frank Mastrovita,
Ref.; Hank Robinson, Info.Sys.Spec.

★8218★

MITTELHAUSER CORPORATION - LIBRARY (Energy)
5120 Belmont Rd., Suite G   Phone: (312) 964-8164
Downers Grove, IL 60515   Dorothy Allen, Libn.
Staff: Prof 1. Subjects: Coal conversion technologies, oil production and
utilization, waste treatment processes, synthetic fuels. Holdings: 5000
volumes. Subscriptions: 81 journals and other serials. Services: Interlibrary
loans; library not open to public. Computerized Information Services: DOE/
RECON.

★8219★

MIXING EQUIPMENT COMPANY, INC. - MIXCO R&D LIBRARY (Env-Cons)
135 Mt. Read Blvd.   Phone: (716) 436-5550
Rochester, NY 14611   Maryann Kerwin, Libn.
Staff: 2. Subjects: Mixing technology, chemical and mechanical engineering,
waste and water treatment, product, plant and machine design, marketing,

sales. **Holdings:** 950 books; 55 VF drawers of R&D reports; 30 VF drawers of articles; 5 VF drawers of patents; 100 theses. **Subscriptions:** 100 journals and other serials. **Services:** Interlibrary loans; copying; library not open to public. **Computerized Information Services:** DIALOG, BRS.

★8220★
MOBAY CHEMICAL CORPORATION - AGRICULTURAL CHEMICALS DIVISION - LIBRARY (Agri)†
Hawthorne Rd.
Box 4913
Kansas City, MO 64120
Phone: (816) 242-2236
Cheryl Postlewait, Libn.
Staff: Prof 1. **Subjects:** Agriculture, chemistry, botany, entomology, law, mechanical engineering, management. **Special Collections:** State Agricultural Experiment Station publications. **Holdings:** 2000 books; 3500 bound periodical volumes; 500 government documents (cataloged); quarterly reports; 7800 patents. **Subscriptions:** 350 journals and other serials. **Services:** Interlibrary loans; library open to public by appointment. **Computerized Information Services:** DIALOG, SDC, NLM. **Networks/Consortia:** Member of Kansas City Library Network, Inc.; Kansas City Metropolitan Library Network.

★8221★
MOBAY CHEMICAL CORPORATION - RESEARCH CENTER LIBRARY (Sci-Tech)†
Penn Lincoln Pkwy., W.
Pittsburgh, PA 15205
Phone: (412) 777-2782
Nancy R. Alstadt, Libn.
Founded: 1954. **Staff:** Prof 1; Other 1. **Subjects:** Marketing, chemical plastics, polymers, business, engineering, coatings. **Holdings:** 6000 books; 3000 bound periodical volumes; market studies; AV material. **Subscriptions:** 340 journals and other serials; 12 newspapers. **Services:** Interlibrary loans; copying; center open to public by appointment. **Computerized Information Services:** Online systems. **Publications:** Library Newsletter, quarterly; Periodicals Listing, annual; Report Index, annual. **Special Indexes:** Market studies (card).

★8222★
MOBAY CHEMICAL CORPORATION - RESEARCH LIBRARY (Sci-Tech)
New Martinsville, WV 26155
Phone: (304) 455-4400
Douglas A. Portmann, Tech.Libn.
Founded: 1955. **Staff:** Prof 1; Other 1. **Subjects:** Polymer and organic chemistry, chemical engineering. **Holdings:** 2000 books; 7300 bound periodical volumes. **Subscriptions:** 100 journals and other serials. **Services:** Interlibrary loans; copying; library open to public with restrictions.

★8223★
MOBIL CHEMICAL COMPANY - PLASTICS DIVISION - INFORMATION CENTER (Sci-Tech; Bus-Fin)
Technical Center
Macedon, NY 14502
Phone: (315) 986-6375
Violanda O. Burns, Info.Anl.
Founded: 1963. **Staff:** Prof 1; Other 1. **Subjects:** Polymer science, plastics technology, business. **Holdings:** 1200 books; 800 bound periodical volumes. **Subscriptions:** 145 journals and other serials; 5 newspapers. **Services:** Interlibrary loans; copying; center open to public by appointment. **Computerized Information Services:** DIALOG, SDC, BRS. **Networks/Consortia:** Member of Rochester Regional Research Library Council (RRRLC). **Publications:** Management Summary, biweekly; Bulletin, monthly.

★8224★
MOBIL CHEMICAL COMPANY - RESEARCH & DEVELOPMENT - TECHNICAL INFORMATION CENTER (Sci-Tech)
Box 240
Edison, NJ 08817
Phone: (201) 321-6229
Claire A. Holden, Supv., Info.Serv.
Founded: 1961. **Staff:** Prof 3; Other 2. **Subjects:** Polymer chemistry and physics, plastics technology, petrochemicals, paints and coatings, chemical engineering, agricultural chemistry, information science. **Holdings:** 10,000 books; 20,000 bound periodical volumes; 1000 government documents (cataloged); 500 VF drawers of company research reports and materials; U.S. chemical patents from 1967 to present; 3000 reels of microfilmed journals, patents, company research reports and laboratory notebooks. **Subscriptions:** 450 journals and other serials. **Services:** Interlibrary loans; copying; center open to qualified researchers upon application to laboratory management. **Computerized Information Services:** DIALOG, SDC, Chemical Abstract Services (CAS); computerized circulation, retrieval of company records and journal routing. **Publications:** New Technical Titles, monthly; Patent News, weekly; listing of internal and contract reports, quarterly. **Remarks:** Division of Mobil Oil Corporation. **Staff:** William Melnizek, Jr., Res.Lit.Chem.; Susan Avers-Fejes, Libn.

★8225★
MOBIL EXPLORATION AND PRODUCING SERVICES INC. - MEPSI LIBRARY (Sci-Tech)
Box 900
Dallas, TX 75221
Phone: (214) 658-4779
Mary Lee Freeman, Libn.
Founded: 1977. **Staff:** Prof 1; Other 1. **Subjects:** Geology, geophysics. **Holdings:** 11,400 books; 1600 bound periodical volumes; 2000 maps; 9300 microforms. **Subscriptions:** 296 journals and other serials. **Services:** Interlibrary loans; library open to public by appointment. **Computerized Information Services:** Computerized cataloging. **Networks/Consortia:** Member of OCLC through AMIGOS Bibliographic Council, Inc. **Staff:** Barbara D. Farrell, Coord.

★8226★
MOBIL LAND DEVELOPMENT CORPORATION - LIBRARY (Plan)
3 Twin Dolphin Dr., Suite 200
Redwood City, CA 94065
Phone: (415) 594-4200
Barbara Bernhart, Libn.
Founded: 1972. **Staff:** Prof 1. **Subjects:** Land use, demography, planning and architecture, project development and control. **Special Collections:** Metropolitan area information for California, Arizona and Colorado. **Holdings:** 1200 books. **Subscriptions:** 75 journals and other serials. **Services:** Copying; library open to SLA members and Mobil Corporation affiliates.

★8227★
MOBIL OIL CANADA, LTD. - LIBRARY (Sci-Tech)
P.O. Box 800
Calgary, AB, Canada T2P 2J7
Phone: (403) 268-7785
Kathleen V. McNeely, Libn.
Staff: 2. **Subjects:** Geology, geophysics and related topics. **Holdings:** 4200 books; 630 bound periodical volumes; 3580 government publications; 2100 maps. **Subscriptions:** 200 journals and other serials. **Services:** Interlibrary loans; copying; library not open to public. **Publications:** Monthly listings of new acquisitions; Weekly Journal Contents Pages.

★8228★
MOBIL OIL CORPORATION - E & P DIVISION LIBRARY (Energy)
Box 5444, Terminal Annex
Denver, CO 80217
Phone: (303) 572-2287
M.G. Harris, Division Libn.
Founded: 1972. **Staff:** Prof 1; Other 1. **Subjects:** Geology; geophysics; oil, gas and uranium exploration, engineering and production; petroleum and uranium industry. **Holdings:** 20,000 books; 500 bound periodical volumes; 7000 government documents; 5000 journal issues; 11,000 maps; 600 in-house reports. **Subscriptions:** 148 journals and other serials. **Services:** Interlibrary loans; library not open to public. **Publications:** Contents of Recent Journal Acquisitions, bimonthly; New Publications Received, monthly - both for internal distribution only.

MOBIL OIL CORPORATION - MOBIL CHEMICAL COMPANY
See: Mobil Chemical Company

★8229★
MOBIL OIL CORPORATION - PUBLIC AFFAIRS SECRETARIAT (Bus-Fin)
150 E. 42nd St., Rm. 606
New York, NY 10017
Phone: (212) 883-2155
E. Holmes Bearden, Mgr.
Founded: 1930. **Staff:** Prof 6; Other 7. **Subjects:** Energy industries, finance, corporations, management. **Special Collections:** Petroleum industry economics and history (2000 volumes). **Holdings:** 10,000 books; 500 bound periodical volumes; 2000 pamphlets; 40 VF drawers of newspaper clippings; 200 periodical backruns in microform; 30,000 microfiche. **Subscriptions:** 480 journals and other serials; 20 newspapers. **Services:** Interlibrary loans; SDI; library open to public with restrictions. **Computerized Information Services:** DIALOG, SDC, BRS, New York Times Information Service, Mead Data Central, Dow Jones News Retrieval, Info Globe, I.P. Sharp Associates Limited; Mobil Public Statements & Documents (internal database). **Publications:** New Materials List, monthly. **Staff:** Patricia K. Marshall, Mgr., Res.Serv.; Irene R. Pierce, Mgr., News Serv.; Margret Brennan, Supv., News Serv.; Elizabeth Hale, Archv.; David Newman, Res.Assoc; Kathleen Miller, Res.Assoc.

★8230★
MOBIL PIPE LINE COMPANY - ENGINEERING LIBRARY (Sci-Tech)
Box 900
Dallas, TX 75221
Phone: (214) 658-2039
K.E. Anderson, Mgr. of Engr.
Founded: 1955. **Staff:** 1. **Subjects:** Crude, LPG, and refined products; pipeline transportation; pipeline construction, maintenance, and operation. **Holdings:** 1200 volumes. **Subscriptions:** 44 journals and other serials. **Services:** Interlibrary loans; library open to public.

★8231★
MOBIL PRODUCING TEXAS & NEW MEXICO INC. - INFORMATION RESOURCE CENTER (Sci-Tech; Energy)
Nine Greenway Plaza, Suite 2700   Phone: (713) 871-5621
Houston, TX 77046   Melody M. Morningstar, Info.Rsrcs.Coord.
Founded: 1979. **Staff:** Prof 1; Other 2. **Subjects:** Geology, engineering, petroleum industry, business. **Holdings:** 6000 books and bound periodical volumes; 450 proprietary reports; vendor catalogs. **Subscriptions:** 224 journals and other serials. **Services:** Interlibrary loans; center open to public with restrictions. **Computerized Information Services:** DIALOG, SDC; computerized cataloging and ILL. **Networks/Consortia:** Member of OCLC through AMIGOS Bibliographic Council, Inc. **Special Indexes:** Index to proprietary reports (card).

★8232★
MOBIL RESEARCH & DEVELOPMENT CORPORATION - CENTRAL RESEARCH DIVISION LIBRARY (Energy)
Box 1025   Phone: (609) 737-4328
Princeton, NJ 08540   Jean B. Clarke, Libn.
Staff: Prof 1; Other 1. **Subjects:** Petroleum refining technology, chemistry, chemical engineering, energy. **Holdings:** 12,000 books; 10,000 bound periodical volumes. **Subscriptions:** 350 journals and other serials. **Services:** Interlibrary loans; copying; library open to public on request.

★8233★
MOBIL RESEARCH & DEVELOPMENT CORPORATION - ENGINEERING DEPARTMENT - INFORMATION CENTER (Sci-Tech)
Box 1026   Phone: (609) 737-3000
Princeton, NJ 08540   Elizabeth N. Mailloux, Mgr.
Staff: Prof 6; Other 8. **Subjects:** Petroleum refining, mechanical and chemical engineering. **Holdings:** 4000 books; indexed documents on microfilm; engineering drawings. **Subscriptions:** 325 journals and other serials. **Services:** Interlibrary loans; copying; center open to qualified researchers by appointment. **Computerized Information Services:** SDC, DIALOG; internal databases; computerized cataloging. **Networks/Consortia:** Member of OCLC through PALINET and Union Library Catalogue of Pennsylvania. **Publications:** Bulletin, monthly - to Engineering Department. **Staff:** Usok Pak, Info.Rsrcs.Coord.; Shirley Mungro, Doc.Anl.; Dorothy McLaughlin, Tech.Libn.; Beryl Heisman, Lit.Spec.

★8234★
MOBIL RESEARCH & DEVELOPMENT CORPORATION - FIELD RESEARCH LABORATORY LIBRARY (Energy)
Box 900   Phone: (214) 333-6111
Dallas, TX 75221   Ammarette Roberts, Mgr., Tech.Info.Serv.
Founded: 1945. **Staff:** Prof 5; Other 3. **Subjects:** Petroleum exploration and production; basic sciences. **Holdings:** 35,000 books; 30,000 bound periodical volumes; 1200 maps; U.S. patents on microfilm; U.S. Bureau of Mines documents on microfilm. **Subscriptions:** 600 journals and other serials. **Services:** Interlibrary loans; library open to public by appointment. **Computerized Information Services:** DIALOG, BRS, SDC; computerized cataloging. **Networks/Consortia:** Member of OCLC through AMIGOS Bibliographic Council, Inc. **Staff:** Ruth L. Keefer, Lit.Spec.; Dudley B. Schoolfield, Cat.; Janet Wolford, Tech.Libn.; Jacque Kyle, Ref.Libn.

★8235★
MOBIL RESEARCH & DEVELOPMENT CORPORATION - OFFSHORE ENGINEERING INFORMATION CENTER (Sci-Tech)
Box 900   Phone: (214) 333-6312
Dallas, TX 75221   R.S. Thomson, Tech.Info.Spec.
Founded: 1980. **Staff:** Prof 1. **Subjects:** Engineering - structural, geotechnical, marine; oceanography. **Holdings:** 400 books. **Subscriptions:** 75 journals and other serials. **Services:** Interlibrary loans; copying; library not open to public.

★8236★
MOBIL RESEARCH & DEVELOPMENT CORPORATION - PAULSBORO LABORATORY - TECHNICAL INFORMATION SERVICES (Energy)
Box 300   Phone: (609) 423-1040
Paulsboro, NJ 08066   Phillip Q. Stumpf, Jr., Mgr.
Founded: 1931. **Staff:** Prof 6; Other 5. **Subjects:** Petroleum refining technology, petroleum products and related technology, chemistry, chemical engineering. **Holdings:** 15,000 books; 15,000 bound periodical volumes; U.S. chemical patents on microfilm; 64 VF drawers of pamphlets. **Subscriptions:** 650 journals and other serials. **Services:** Interlibrary loans; SDI; open to public by application. **Computerized Information Services:** DIALOG, SDC; computerized circulation. **Networks/Consortia:** Member of OCLC through PALINET and Union Library Catalogue of Pennsylvania. **Publications:** Periodic patent summaries in specific areas; list of searches performed, annual with

quarterly updating; MRDC Eastern Laboratories Reports, monthly list and yearly index; Technical Library Bulletin - all distributed internally. **Staff:** Jane L. Bitter, Tech.Libn.

★8237★
MOBIL TYCO SOLAR ENERGY CORPORATION - LIBRARY (Energy)
16 Hickory Dr.   Phone: (617) 890-0909
Waltham, MA 02254   Dorothy O. Bergin, Libn.
Founded: 1975. **Staff:** Prof 1; Other 1. **Subjects:** Photovoltaics; solar energy conversion (silicon solar cells); crystal growth by edge-defined, film-fed growth; materials science; solar energy. **Holdings:** 2000 books; 800 bound periodical volumes; 40 VF drawers of government contract reports; 17 VF drawers of reports on microfiche. **Subscriptions:** 125 journals and other serials; 5 newspapers. **Services:** Interlibrary loans; library not open to public. **Computerized Information Services:** DIALOG.

★8238★
MOBILE COUNTY PUBLIC LAW LIBRARY (Law)
County Court House   Phone: (205) 690-8436
Mobile, AL 36602   May Lowe, Libn.
Founded: 1947. **Staff:** 2. **Subjects:** Law - civil, criminal, business, tax. **Special Collections:** English Chancery Court books. **Holdings:** 25,000 books; 17 bound periodical volumes. **Subscriptions:** 59 journals and other serials. **Services:** Copying; library open to public for reference use only.

MOBILE GENERAL HOSPITAL - CHARLES A. MOHR MEDICAL LIBRARY
See: University of South Alabama - College of Medicine - Biomedical Library

★8239★
MOBILE PUBLIC LIBRARY - SPECIAL COLLECTIONS DIVISION (Hist)
704 Government St.   Phone: (205) 438-7094
Mobile, AL 36602   Robert J. Zietz, Hd.
Founded: 1961. **Staff:** Prof 3; Other 1. **Subjects:** Local history, genealogy. **Special Collections:** Panton-Leslie colonial trade papers, 1770-1840; Waterman Steamship Company papers; Hunley Civil War papers. **Holdings:** 12,750 books; 1125 bound periodical volumes; 590 reels of Mobile newspapers, 2220 reels of federal census records, 50 reels of French and Spanish colonial records, (all on microfilm). **Subscriptions:** 10 journals and other serials. **Services:** Copying; library open to public (fee for out of town users and for staff research). **Special Indexes:** Vertical file index (card); map index (card). **Staff:** Jay Higginbotham, Local Hist.Spec.; George Schroeter, Assoc.Libn.

★8240★
MODERN HANDCRAFT, INC. - RESEARCH LIBRARY (Rec)
4251 Pennsylvania Ave.   Phone: (816) 531-5730
Kansas City, MO 64111
Subjects: Horticulture, needlework and home arts, wood working, home improvement. **Holdings:** 2000 volumes. **Subscriptions:** 50 journals and other serials. **Services:** Library not open to public. **Publications:** Workbench, bimonthly; Workbasket, 10/year; Flower and Garden, bimonthly.

★8241★
MODERN LANGUAGE ASSOCIATION - CENTER FOR BIBLIOGRAPHICAL SERVICES (Hum)
62 Fifth Ave.   Phone: (212) 741-5590
New York, NY 10011   Eileen M. Mackesy, Dir./Mng.Ed.
Staff: Prof 12; Other 5. **Subjects:** Language, literature, linguistics, folklore. **Holdings:** Figures not available. **Subscriptions:** 1100 journals and other serials. **Services:** Interlibrary loans; copying; center not open to public. **Computerized Information Services:** DIALOG, BRS. **Publications:** MLA International Bibliography, annual; MLA Directory of Periodicals. **Staff:** Jane Matsinger, Index Ed.; Karen Mateyak, Ser.Ed.

★8242★
MODESTO BEE - EDITORIAL LIBRARY (Publ)†
Box 3928   Phone: (209) 578-2101
Modesto, CA 95352   Lillian Wendt, Libn.
Founded: 1944. **Staff:** 2. **Subjects:** Newspaper reference topics. **Holdings:** Books; clippings; pictures; pamphlets; microfilm; microfiche. **Services:** Library not open to public. **Networks/Consortia:** Member of 49-99 Cooperative Library System.

MOFFATT (Dr. Garfield) HEALTH SCIENCES LIBRARY
See: Chalmers (Dr. Everett) Hospital - Dr. Garfield Moffatt Health Sciences Library

MOFFETT (Ida V.) SCHOOL OF NURSING
See: Baptist Medical Centers-Samford University - Ida V. Moffett School of Nursing

MOFFETT TECHNICAL LIBRARY
See: CPC International

★8243★
MOHAVE MUSEUM OF HISTORY AND ARTS - LIBRARY (Hist)
400 W. Beale St.   Phone: (602) 753-3195
Kingman, AZ 86401   Norma Hughes, Dir.
Founded: 1960. **Subjects:** History of Mohave County and Arizona, Indian lore, arts and craft, mining history, genealogy. **Holdings:** 550 books; 100 bound periodical volumes; 350 manuscripts; 25 maps; 30 reels of microfilm. **Subscriptions:** 10 journals and other serials. **Services:** Interlibrary loans (fee); copying; library open to public for reference use only. **Remarks:** Maintained by the Mohave County Historical Society.

★8244★
MOHAWK-CAUGHNAWAGA MUSEUM - LIBRARY (Hist)†
R.D. 1
Box 6
Fonda, NY 12068   Wayne Lenig, Musm.Adm.
Staff: Prof 1; Other 1. **Subjects:** Archeology, Colonial and Revolutionary history of Northeastern North America, museology, 17th and 18th century Euro-American culture. **Special Collections:** 16th, 17th and 18th century maps of North America; 18th and 19th century Mohawk Valley history (manuscripts); archives of the Mohawk Valley Historical Association, 1920-1940; museum archives, 1949 to present; archives of the Van Epps-Hartley Chapter of the New York State Archaeological Association, 1933 to present; papers of Edward J. Sheehan, historian and archivist, 1920-1960. **Holdings:** 4000 books; 2000 pamphlets and brochures; periodicals, manuscripts, maps and atlases. **Services:** Copying; library open for serious historical research. **Networks/Consortia:** Member of Mohawk Valley Museum Consortium.

★8245★
MOHAWK COLLEGE OF APPLIED ARTS AND TECHNOLOGY - HEALTH SCIENCES LIBRARY RESOURCE CENTRE (Med)
P.O. Box 2034   Phone: (416) 389-4461
Hamilton, ON, Canada L8N 3T2   June Shore, Libn.
Founded: 1964. **Staff:** Prof 1; Other 3. **Subjects:** Nursing, medical and laboratory technology, radiography, physiotherapy, occupational therapy. **Holdings:** 16,366 books; 1323 bound periodical volumes; 2089 AV items. **Subscriptions:** 205 journals and other serials. **Services:** Interlibrary loans; copying; centre open to public. **Networks/Consortia:** Member of Hamilton District Health Council, McMaster University.

★8246★
MOHAWK COLLEGE OF APPLIED ARTS AND TECHNOLOGY - MOHAWK LIBRARY RESOURCE CENTRE (Sci-Tech)
P.O. Box 2034   Phone: (416) 389-4461
Hamilton, ON, Canada L8N 3T2   Sandra M. Black, Chf.Libn.
Founded: 1967. **Staff:** Prof 6; Other 14. **Subjects:** Business, technology, architecture, textile technology, early childhood education, manpower retraining. **Holdings:** 96,000 books; 7000 periodical volumes; 17,306 AV items; 1400 microforms; 4317 government documents; 439 maps; 948 clipping file folders; 1513 uncataloged items. **Subscriptions:** 1030 journals and other serials; 15 newspapers. **Services:** Interlibrary loans; copying; library open to public. **Networks/Consortia:** Member of Hamilton/Wentworth District Health Library Network; Bibliocentre. **Staff:** Helen Shaver, Resource Ctr.Supv.; Glenna Grantham, ILL; Marilyn McDermott, Ref. & Circ.Libn.; Irene Fenton, Saltfleet Supv.; Gail Sekine, Braneida Supv.; Joan Redmond, Nursing Lib.Supv.

★8247★
MOHAWK VALLEY COMMUNITY COLLEGE LIBRARY - SPECIAL COLLECTIONS (Soc Sci)
1101 Sherman Dr.   Phone: (315) 792-5408
Utica, NY 13501   Alice B. Griffith, Lib.Dir.
Founded: 1946. **Special Collections:** Women's Resource Collection (500 titles); Technical Information Center (machine tooling and metal working); Minorities Study Center. **Services:** Interlibrary loans; copying; library open to public. **Computerized Information Services:** Computerized cataloging. **Networks/Consortia:** Member of Central New York Library Resources Council (CENTRO); OCLC. **Staff:** Joanne Werner, Cat./Women's Rsrcs.Coll.

MOHAWK VALLEY HISTORICAL ASSOCIATION ARCHIVES
See: Mohawk-Caughnawaga Museum - Library

MOHR (Charles A.) MEDICAL LIBRARY
See: University of South Alabama - College of Medicine - Biomedical Library

★8248★
MOHYLA INSTITUTE - LIBRARY AND ARCHIVES (Area-Ethnic)
1240 Temperance St.   Phone: (306) 653-1944
Saskatoon, SK, Canada S7N 0P1   F.J. Kindrachuk, Rector
Founded: 1916. **Staff:** 1. **Subjects:** Ukrainian studies (in Ukrainian, English, Russian and other languages). **Holdings:** 6000 books; 1000 bound periodical volumes; 800 Ukrainian Voice; 1000 pamphlets. **Subscriptions:** 10 journals and other serials; 15 newspapers. **Services:** Library open to public with restrictions. **Publications:** Mohyla Institute Newsletter.

★8249★
MOLDENHAUER ARCHIVES (Mus)
1011 Comstock Ct.   Phone: (509) 747-4555
Spokane, WA 99203   Dr. Hans Moldenhauer, Dir.
Staff: 6. **Subjects:** Music and music history. **Special Collections:** Webern and other comprehensive archives. **Holdings:** Autograph music manuscripts, letters, and documents, 10th to 20th centuries; reference library of facsimile scores, books, recordings. **Remarks:** Branches of the Moldenhauer Archives are located at Northwestern University, Evanston, IL; Washington State University, Pullman, WA; Bayrische Staatsbibliothek, Munich, West Germany; Wiener Stadtbibliothek, Vienna, Austria and at the Zentralbibliothek, Zurich, Switzerland.

★8250★
MOLESWORTH INSTITUTE - LIBRARY AND ARCHIVES (Hist; Rec)
143 Hanks Hill Rd.   Phone: (203) 486-2220
Storrs, CT 06268   Cecily Cardew, Lib.Dir. & Archv.
Staff: Prof 2; Other 3. **Subjects:** Library humor and history, treens. **Special Collections:** Timothy J. Peason Collection of Library Humor (1500 items); Basil Fotherington-Thomas Collection of Library Postcards and Commemoratives (9000 items); Molesworth Institute Archives (3333 items). **Holdings:** 5500 books and bound periodical volumes. **Subscriptions:** 99 journals and other serials; 13 newspapers. **Services:** Library not open to public. **Computerized Information Services:** CALP computerized information base for 7500 library postcards (internal database); computerized cataloging and acquisitions. **Networks/Consortia:** Headquarters of MOLENET. **Publications:** The Librarians' Record, quarterly. **Staff:** Janice Merrill-Oldham, Preservation Spec.

★8251★
(Moline) DAILY DISPATCH - LIBRARY (Publ)
1720 5th Ave.   Phone: (309) 764-4344
Moline, IL 61265   Marlene Gantt, Libn.
Staff: Prof 1; Other 1. **Subjects:** Newspaper reference topics. **Special Collections:** Local Historical Book Collection; local historical news (newspaper clipping file); biography file. **Services:** Copying; library open to public by appointment.

MOLINE PUBLIC LIBRARY - BLACKHAWK GENEALOGICAL SOCIETY - LIBRARY
See: Blackhawk Genealogical Society - Library

★8252★
MOLLOY, JONES, DONAHUE, TRACHTA, CHILDERS & MALLAMO - LIBRARY (Law)
Arizona Bank Plaza
Box 2268   Phone: (602) 622-3531
Tucson, AZ 85702   Paula H. Nordin, Libn.
Staff: Prof 1; Other 1. **Subjects:** Bankruptcy; law - tax, litigation, commercial, estate planning. **Holdings:** 10,000 books, pamphlets, periodicals and newspapers. **Services:** Copying; library not open to public. **Networks/Consortia:** Member of Arizona On-Line Users' Group.

★8253★
MOLSON BREWERIES OF CANADA, LTD. - INFORMATION CENTRE (Food-Bev)
1555 Notre Dame St., E.   Phone: (514) 527-5151
Montreal, PQ, Canada H2L 2R5   Sheila Globus, Res.Libn.
Founded: 1967. **Staff:** Prof 1. **Subjects:** Brewing, chemistry, microbiology, engineering. **Special Collections:** Historical brewing books (private collection). **Holdings:** 1000 books and bound periodical volumes; 7000 microfilm cards; newspaper clippings; patents; pamphlets. **Subscriptions:** 50 journals and other serials. **Services:** Interlibrary loans; copying (limited); centre open to public by appointment. **Also Known As:** Brasseries Molson du Canada, Ltee.

★8254★
MOLYCORP, INC. - LIBRARY (Sci-Tech)
Box 54945   Phone: (213) 977-6932
Los Angeles, CA 90054   Jean K. Martin, Lib.Mgr.
Staff: Prof 2; Other 1. Subjects: Geology, mineralogy, mining, metallurgy. Holdings: 3000 books; 200 bound periodical volumes; 18,000 government documents. Subscriptions: 350 journals and other serials. Services: Interlibrary loans; copying; library open to public by appointment. Computerized Information Services: DIALOG, New York Times Information Service, SDC; computerized cataloging. Networks/Consortia: Member of CLASS; OCLC. Remarks: Library located at 461 South Boylston, Los Angeles, CA 90017. Staff: Estella Castillo, Info.Spec.

★8255★
MONARCH MARKING SYSTEMS - TECHNICAL LIBRARY (Sci-Tech; Bus-Fin)
1 Kohnle Dr.   Phone: (513) 865-2082
Miamisburg, OH 45342   Mrs. Artence Walton, Tech.Dir.
Founded: 1975. Staff: Prof 2; Other 1. Subjects: Chemistry, business, physics, English, sales and marketing. Holdings: 3200 books; 35 bound periodical volumes; 16 VF drawers of conference reports, R&D patents, clippings, microfilm, cassettes. Subscriptions: 240 journals and other serials. Services: Interlibrary loans; copying; library not open to public. Computerized Information Services: Online systems. Networks/Consortia: Member of Miami Valley Library Organization (MILO). Publications: Acquisitions list, quarterly - for internal distribution only. Staff: Ernie Garbade, Info.Libn.

★8256★
MONASTERE DES PERES REDEMPTORISTES - BIBLIOTHEQUE (Rel-Theol)†
871 Rue Ontario   Phone: (819) 562-2677
Sherbrooke, PQ, Canada J1J 3S1   Laurent Tousegnant, Libn.
Founded: 1912. Staff: Prof 2. Subjects: Theology. Holdings: 37,600 books; 1700 cases of documents, manuscripts and maps.

★8257★
MONASTERE DES URSULINES - ARCHIVES DES URSULINES DE QUEBEC (Hist)†
C.P. 760   Phone: (418) 692-2523
Quebec, PQ, Canada G1R 4T1
Staff: Prof 2; Other 3. Subjects: Canadiana. Special Collections: Old and rare books and periodicals from France and the U.S.; regional historical reviews. Holdings: 10,000 books; 300 bound periodical volumes. Services: Archives open to serious researchers for reference use only, by appointment. Remarks: Archives are located at 18 Donnacona St., Quebec, PQ, G1R 3Y7.

MONCHANIN INTERCULTURAL CENTRE
See: Centre Interculturel Monchanin

★8258★
MONCTON HOSPITAL - HEALTH SCIENCES LIBRARY (Med)
135 MacBeath Ave.   Phone: (506) 855-1600
Moncton, NB, Canada E1C 6Z8   Mrs. I.W. Wallace, Libn.
Staff: Prof 1; Other 1. Subjects: Medicine, nursing, physiotherapy, education. Holdings: 2300 books and bound periodical volumes; 100 videotapes; 500 slides and cassettes. Subscriptions: 150 journals and other serials. Services: Interlibrary loans; copying; library open to public with restrictions. Computerized Information Services: Online systems. Publications: W.K. Kellogg list of recent acquisitions, monthly; listing of videotape and other AV material programs, weekly.

MONELL (Ambrose) ENGINEERING LIBRARY
See: Columbia University - Ambrose Monell Engineering Library

★8259★
MONELL CHEMICAL SENSES CENTER - LIBRARY (Sci-Tech)
3500 Market St.   Phone: (215) 243-6666
Philadelphia, PA 19104
Founded: 1965. Staff: 1. Subjects: Taste, olfaction and related neurosciences. Holdings: 300 books; 400 bound periodical volumes; reprint files and unbound periodicals (cataloged). Subscriptions: 25 journals and other serials. Services: Library open to public by appointment.

MONENCO LTD.
See: Montreal Engineering Company, Ltd.

MONEY MUSEUM LIBRARY
See: National Bank of Detroit

★8260★
MONKMEYER PRESS PHOTO SERVICE (Pict)
118 E. 28th St.   Phone: (212) 689-2242
New York, NY 10016   Hilde R. Monkmeyer, Hd.
Subjects: Photographs and color transparencies. Services: Photographs available on a fee basis.

★8261★
MONMOUTH COUNTY HISTORICAL ASSOCIATION - LIBRARY (Hist)
70 Court St.   Phone: (201) 462-1466
Freehold, NJ 07728   Barbara Carver Smith, Act.Libn.
Staff: Prof 1. Subjects: Monmouth County history and genealogy, church and Bible records. Special Collections: James P. Allaire Papers; records of the North American Phalanx; Philip Freneau; Cherry Hall Papers; Battle of Monmouth. Holdings: 3000 books; 870 bound periodical volumes; 28 VF drawers of newspaper clippings; pamphlets; programs; manuscript collections; microfilm; photographs; maps; extensive newspaper collection. Subscriptions: 12 journals and other serials. Services: Copying; library open to public. Publications: Monmouth County in Print; Bibliography - Monmouth County; Cemetery Holdings; Genealogical Holdings in Library; Library Acquisitions, November 1974 to present; Local History Collections. Special Indexes: Index to Early Dutch Settlers of Monmouth County.

★8262★
MONMOUTH COUNTY LAW LIBRARY (Law)
Court House   Phone: (201) 431-7079
Freehold, NJ 07728   Carolyn S. Geiling, Law Libn.
Staff: Prof 1. Subjects: Law. Holdings: Figures not available. Services: Library open to public. Remarks: Library is maintained by Board of Freeholders, County of Monmouth.

★8263★
MONMOUTH COUNTY SOCIAL SERVICES - LIBRARY (Soc Sci)
Box 3000   Phone: (201) 431-6011
Freehold, NJ 07728   Francine Scheier, Libn.
Founded: 1971. Staff: Prof 1; Other 1. Subjects: Social work, public welfare, psychiatry, psychology. Holdings: 3000 books; 40 VF drawers of noncataloged pamphlets, reports, government documents, clippings. Subscriptions: 140 journals and other serials. Services: Interlibrary loans; copying; library open to public with restrictions. Networks/Consortia: Member of Monmouth Biomedical Information Consortium. Publications: Library News, monthly - for internal distribution only.

★8264★
MONMOUTH MEDICAL CENTER - ALTSCHUL MEDICAL LIBRARY (Med)
Third & Pavilion Aves.   Phone: (201) 870-5170
Long Branch, NJ 07740   John Conway, Dir.
Founded: 1959. Staff: Prof 1; Other 3. Subjects: Medicine, nursing, dentistry, pediatrics, obstetrics, neurology, psychiatry. Holdings: 3200 books; 2100 bound periodical volumes; 2800 reels of microfilm. Subscriptions: 350 journals and other serials. Services: Interlibrary loans; copying; library open to public for reference use only. Computerized Information Services: MEDLARS, DIALOG, BRS. Networks/Consortia: Member of Monmouth-Ocean Biomedical Information Consortium; New Jersey Health Sciences Network. Publications: Acquisitions List, quarterly - for internal distribution only.

MONOGRAM FILM LIBRARY
See: University of Wisconsin, Madison - Wisconsin Center for Film and Theater Research

★8265★
MONROE COMMUNITY HOSPITAL - HEALTH SCIENCES LIBRARY (Med)
435 E. Henrietta Rd.   Phone: (716) 473-4080
Rochester, NY 14603   Elinor Reynolds, Med.Lib.Dir.
Staff: Prof 1. Subjects: Medicine, geriatrics. Holdings: 883 books; 130 bound periodical volumes. Subscriptions: 60 journals and other serials. Services: Interlibrary loans; library open to public for reference use only. Networks/Consortia: Member of Rochester Regional Research Library Council.

MONROE COUNTY - DEPARTMENT OF PARKS - HIGHLAND PARK HERBARIUM
See: Highland Park Herbarium

★8266★

MONROE COUNTY HISTORIAN'S DEPARTMENT - LIBRARY (Hist)
115 South Ave.
Rochester, NY 14604 Shirley C. Husted, County Hist.
Staff: Prof 1. **Subjects:** County history, city of Rochester history, Erie and Barge canals, genealogy. **Holdings:** 1000 volumes; 30,000 items including newspapers, photographs, clippings, manuscripts, census data. **Services:** Copying; library open to public by appointment. **Publications:** Books & Booklets, annual. **Special Indexes:** Index to history of Monroe County, 1877 and 1895 (card and book).

★8267★

MONROE COUNTY HISTORICAL MUSEUM - ARCHIVES (Hist)
126 S. Monroe St. Phone: (313) 243-7137
Monroe, MI 48161 Christine L. Kull, Archv.
Staff: Prof 1. **Subjects:** Civil War, George A. Custer, Michigan and Monroe history, local genealogy. **Special Collections:** War of the Rebellion. **Holdings:** 1120 books; 136 bound periodical volumes; 64 other cataloged items; 4 VF drawers of photographs; 19 tapes; 10 drawers of maps; 130 linear feet of manuscript collections. **Subscriptions:** 15 journals and other serials. **Services:** Copying; archives open to public.

★8268★

MONROE COUNTY HISTORICAL SOCIETY - LIBRARY AND MUSEUM (Hist)
Ninth & Main Sts.
Stroud Community House
Box 488 Phone: (717) 421-7703
Stroudsburg, PA 18360 Vertie Knapp, Cur./Libn.
Founded: 1921. **Staff:** Prof 1. **Subjects:** Monroe County history and genealogy. **Special Collections:** Family histories; county maps; church histories. **Holdings:** 900 books; newspapers, clippings, records, and maps. **Services:** Library open to public on limited schedule.

★8269★

MONROE COUNTY LAW LIBRARY (Law)
Court House
Monroe, MI 48161 Margaret Weipert, Sec.
Subjects: American law - civil and criminal. **Holdings:** 5745 volumes.

★8270★

MONROE COUNTY LAW LIBRARY (Law)
Court House Phone: (717) 424-5100
Stroudsburg, PA 18360 Kennard Lewis, Esq., Chm., Lib.Comm.
Subjects: Law. **Holdings:** 8000 volumes. **Services:** Library open to public. **Staff:** Janeth L. Pensyl, Libn.

★8271★

MONROE COUNTY LIBRARY SYSTEM - GENERAL GEORGE ARMSTRONG CUSTER COLLECTION (Hist)
3700 S. Custer Phone: (313) 241-5277
Monroe, MI 48161 Karen Stoll, Cur.
Staff: Prof 1; Other 1. **Subjects:** General George A. Custer, Battle of Little Big Horn, American Indians, Indian wars, the West. **Special Collections:** Custer Collection; Dr. Lawrence A. Frost Collection of Custeriana. **Holdings:** 2930 books; 17 bound periodical volumes; 1435 unbound periodicals; 163 newspapers; 110 books on microfilm; 150 slides; 35 maps; 48 pictures; 150 pamphlets; 8 original manuscripts. **Services:** Interlibrary loans (of duplicates only); copying; library open to public by appointment for reference use only. **Publications:** Custeriana Monographs. **Special Catalogs:** Bibliography of cataloged materials in special collections of the Billings Public Library and Monroe County Library System. **Staff:** Bernard Margolis, Dir., Lib.Sys.

★8272★

MONROE COUNTY LOCAL HISTORY ROOM & LIBRARY (Hist)
Community Services Bldg.
Rte. 2, Box 21 Phone: (608) 269-8680
Sparta, WI 54656 Audrey Johnson, Act. County Hist.
Founded: 1977. **Staff:** Prof 1; Other 15. **Subjects:** Local history, genealogy. **Special Collections:** All census and newspapers through 1910; church, school and logging history; manuscripts of business history and early letters. **Holdings:** 120 books; 15 bound periodical volumes; 64 reels of microfilm; 2 VF drawers of clippings; 12 VF drawers of cemeteries; 5000 documents. **Subscriptions:** 7 journals and other serials. **Services:** Interlibrary loans; copying; library open to public. **Publications:** Monroe County Pictorial History (published 1976). **Special Indexes:** Genealogy card file of Monroe County; cemetery index. **Staff:** Carolyn Habelman, Supv.; Alice Schaller, Asst.Supv.

★8273★

MONROE DEVELOPMENTAL CENTER - STAFF/PARENT LIBRARY (Med)
620 Westfall Rd. Phone: (716) 461-2800
Rochester, NY 14620 Mary Ann Hryvniak, Staff Libn.
Founded: 1974. **Staff:** Prof 1; Other 1. **Subjects:** Mental retardation, developmental disabilities. **Holdings:** 2200 books; 20 bound periodical volumes; 1000 reprints; 300 bibliographies; 2 VF drawers of pamphlets. **Subscriptions:** 40 journals and other serials. **Services:** Interlibrary loans; copying; library open to public by appointment. **Computerized Information Services:** Access to online systems through New York State Library. **Networks/Consortia:** Member of Rochester Regional Research Library Council (RRRLC). **Special Catalogs:** Indexed catalog of reprints, bibliographies, and significant book chapters (card). **Remarks:** This library attempts to serve as a regional resource on mental retardation for the local community, both lay and professional. Parent agency is the New York State Department of Mental Hygiene.

★8274★

MONROE (James) MUSEUM AND MEMORIAL LIBRARY (Hist)
908 Charles St. Phone: (703) 373-8426
Fredericksburg, VA 22401 Donald W. Baldwin, Chm., Bd. of Regt.
Founded: 1928. **Staff:** 8. **Subjects:** James Monroe, Monroe Doctrine, Americana, Virginiana. **Special Collections:** Private correspondence of James Monroe. **Holdings:** 10,000 books; 2500 bound periodical volumes; 2000 pamphlets, documents and manuscripts; largest known collection of likenesses of James Monroe; slides and films. **Services:** Library open to public by special appointment only; museum open to public. **Remarks:** Museum-Library is owned by Commonwealth of Virginia and administered through Mary Washington College. **Staff:** Paulette Skirbunt Watson, Dir.

★8275★

MONROE, JUNEAU, JACKSON COUNTY, WISCONSIN GENEALOGY WORKSHOP - LIBRARY (Hist)
Rte. 3, Box 253 Phone: (608) 378-4388
Black River Falls, WI 54615 Carolyn Habelman, Pres.
Staff: 1. **Subjects:** Local history, genealogy. **Holdings:** 500 books; 300 bound periodical volumes; 100 cemetery and church records; 300 biographical family charts; census and newspapers on microfilm; maps. **Subscriptions:** 15 journals and other serials; 7 newspapers. **Services:** Copying; library open to public by appointment. **Publications:** Annual Surname Query Index, of members. **Special Indexes:** Church Vital records; 1905 census; cemetery index.

★8276★

MONSANTO COMPANY - ENGINEERING INFORMATION CENTER - F1EE (Sci-Tech)
800 N. Lindbergh Blvd. Phone: (314) 694-7133
St. Louis, MO 63166 Frank L. Reynard, Libn.
Founded: 1965. **Staff:** Prof 1; Other 3. **Subjects:** Chemical and mechanical engineering. **Special Collections:** Vendor catalogs (4000). **Holdings:** 3000 books; 2000 bound periodical volumes; 3000 standards (cataloged). **Subscriptions:** 150 journals and other serials. **Services:** Interlibrary loans; copying; center open to public by application. **Computerized Information Services:** DIALOG; computerized cataloging and serials. **Publications:** Quarterly Interpretations of Engineering Literature - for internal distribution only. **Special Catalogs:** Computer-produced listings of vendor holdings and standards.

★8277★

MONSANTO COMPANY - FISHER CONTROLS COMPANY - R.A. ENGEL TECHNICAL LIBRARY (Sci-Tech)
R.A. Engel Technical Center, Box 11 Phone: (515) 754-2161
Marshalltown, IA 50158 Mark Heindselman, Tech.Libn.
Staff: Prof 1; Other 1. **Subjects:** Automatic control, instrumentation, process control, computer science, mechanical engineering, materials science. **Holdings:** 1600 books; 100 bound periodical volumes; 3000 standards; 2000 vendor catalogs; 5000 technical and marketing papers. **Subscriptions:** 300 journals and other serials; 10 newspapers. **Services:** Interlibrary loans; copying; SDI; library open to public by appointment. **Computerized Information Services:** DIALOG, SDC, Control Data Corporation; internal database; computerized cataloging. **Publications:** Control Chronicle, quarterly.

★8278★

MONSANTO COMPANY - INFORMATION CENTER (Sci-Tech)
800 N. Lindbergh Blvd.
Box 7090 Phone: (314) 694-4778
St. Louis, MO 63177 William A. Wilkinson, Mgr.
Founded: 1961. **Staff:** Prof 14; Other 5. **Subjects:** Chemicals, business, agriculture, biology, engineering, plastics, electronics, fibers, science.

Holdings: 40,000 books; 40,000 bound periodical volumes; 4000 directories (cataloged); 30 VF drawers of trade literature; 75 VF drawers of annual reports; 55,000 technical reports; 600,000 U.S. chemical patents; 60 VF drawers of pamphlets; 12,000 translations. **Subscriptions:** 1500 journals and other serials; 10 newspapers. **Services:** Interlibrary loans; copying; reference/searching; translating; alerting; center open to public by application. **Computerized Information Services:** DIALOG, SDC, BRS, NLM; Technical Reports Index (internal database); computerized cataloging, acquisitions, serials and circulation. **Networks/Consortia:** Member of St. Louis Area Library Network. **Special Catalogs:** Computer-produced and computer-searchable catalogs and indexes. **Staff:** Margaret E. Madden, Reports Libn.; Shirley Evans, Bus.Libn.; Jan Williams, Tech.Libn.

★8279★
MONSANTO COMPANY - LAW LIBRARY (Law)
800 N. Lindbergh Blvd.					Phone: (314) 694-4306
St. Louis, MO 63166					Bette M. Buffa, Sr. Law Libn.
Staff: Prof 1; Other 1. **Subjects:** Law, legal services. **Holdings:** 25,000 books; 1000 bound periodical volumes; statutes. **Subscriptions:** 203 journals and other serials. **Services:** Interlibrary loans; copying; library not open to public. **Computerized Information Services:** LEXIS, Mead Data Central.

★8280★
MONSANTO COMPANY - RUBBER CHEMICALS RESEARCH LIBRARY (Sci-Tech)
260 Springside Dr.					Phone: (216) 666-4111
Akron, OH 44313					Paul Ferrin, Libn.
Founded: 1940. **Staff:** Prof 1; Other 1. **Subjects:** Organic synthesis, rubber and plastics, tire technology. **Holdings:** 2300 books; 4000 bound periodical volumes; 25 VF drawers of reports; 4 VF drawers of papers; 10 VF drawers of commercial literature; microfilm. **Subscriptions:** 140 journals and other serials. **Services:** Library not open to public. **Computerized Information Services:** DIALOG.

★8281★
MONSANTO COMPANY - TRIANGLE PARK DEVELOPMENT CENTER, INC. - LIBRARY (Sci-Tech)
Box 12274					Phone: (919) 549-8111
Research Triangle Park, NC 27709					Teresa Reams, Act.Libn.
Founded: 1952. **Staff:** Prof 1; Other 1. **Subjects:** Textiles, polymers, materials. **Holdings:** 28,000 volumes; 165 VF drawers of archives. **Subscriptions:** 300 journals and other serials. **Services:** Interlibrary loans; copying; library not open to public. **Computerized Information Services:** DIALOG, SDC; computerized cataloging.

★8282★
MONSANTO CORPORATION - FABRICATED PRODUCTS DIVISION - TECHNICAL INFORMATION CENTER (Sci-Tech)
101 Granby St.					Phone: (203) 242-6221
Bloomfield, CT 06002					D.R. Kiley, Adm.Mgr.
Subjects: Polymer science, chemistry, food technology, plastics. **Holdings:** 800 books; 50 bound periodical volumes. **Subscriptions:** 80 journals and other serials. **Services:** Library not open to public.

★8283★
MONSANTO FIBERS & INTERMEDIATES COMPANY - PROCESS TECHNOLOGY DEPARTMENT - LIBRARY (Sci-Tech)
Box 1311					Phone: (713) 945-4431
Texas City, TX 77590					Effie N. Birdwell, Sr.Libn.
Founded: 1948. **Staff:** Prof 1; Other 1. **Subjects:** Chemistry, physics, chemical engineering, mathematics. **Holdings:** 4050 books; 4900 bound periodical volumes; company reports; pamphlets and government documents; trade literature; microforms. **Subscriptions:** 85 journals and other serials. **Services:** Interlibrary loans; copying; library open to public by appointment. **Computerized Information Services:** Internal database. **Publications:** Library Bulletin, monthly - to company technical personnel. **Formerly:** Monsanto Chemical Intermediates Company.

★8284★
MONSANTO PLASTICS & RESINS COMPANY - PLASTICS DIV. - SPRINGFIELD PLANT - TECHNOLOGY LIBRARY (Sci-Tech)†
730 Worcester St.					Phone: (413) 788-2532
Indian Orchard, MA 01151					Lorraine M. Daudelin, Libn.
Founded: 1937. **Staff:** Prof 1; Other 1. **Subjects:** Plastics technology, chemistry, physics, mathematics, engineering, safety, toxicology, personnel training, management. **Special Collections:** Company research reports; government standards and specifications. **Holdings:** 6500 books; 8000 bound periodical volumes. **Subscriptions:** 150 journals and other serials. **Services:** Interlibrary loans. **Staff:** Betty Moutinho, ILL.

★8285★
MONSANTO PLASTICS & RESINS COMPANY - RESINS DIVISION - TECHNOLOGY LIBRARY (Sci-Tech)
190 Grochmal Ave.					Phone: (413) 788-6911
Indian Orchard, MA 01151					Mary H. Sheehan, Libn.
Staff: Prof 1. **Subjects:** Polymer chemistry, organic chemistry, plastics, chemical engineering, mathematics and statistics. **Holdings:** 3000 books; 700 bound periodical volumes. **Subscriptions:** 140 journals and other serials. **Services:** Interlibrary loans; copying; library open to public with restrictions. **Computerized Information Services:** DIALOG, NLM. **Networks/Consortia:** Member of Greater Springfield Area Union List of Serials.

★8286★
MONSANTO RESEARCH CORPORATION - DAYTON LABORATORY LIBRARY (Sci-Tech)†
1515 Nicholas Rd.
Sta. B, Box 8					Phone: (513) 268-3411
Dayton, OH 45407					Dorothy T. Crabtree, Libn.
Staff: Prof 1; Other 1. **Subjects:** Chemistry, physics, engineering. **Holdings:** Figures not available.

★8287★
MONSANTO RESEARCH CORPORATION - MOUND FACILITY - TECHNICAL INFORMATION CENTER (Sci-Tech)
Box 32					Phone: (513) 865-3942
Miamisburg, OH 45342					Hermina Brinkmeier, Supv., Lib. & Rec.
Staff: Prof 2; Other 2. **Subjects:** Chemistry, physics, engineering, nuclear energy, mathematics. **Special Collections:** Nuclear energy documents issued by U.S. Atomic Energy Commission since 1964 (400,000 titles on microfiche). **Holdings:** 22,160 books; 10,600 bound periodical volumes; 350,000 government reports on microfiche; 3000 laboratory originated reports; 2000 volumes of technical journals on 16mm microfilm. **Subscriptions:** 600 journals and other serials. **Services:** Interlibrary loans; copying; SDI; center not open to public. **Computerized Information Services:** DIALOG, SDC, DOE/RECON, DTIC.

★8288★
MONSANTO TEXTILES COMPANY - LIBRARY (Sci-Tech)†
Box 1057					Phone: (803) 223-4241
Greenwood, SC 29646					Mildred Upton, Libn.
Staff: 1. **Subjects:** Nylon manufacturing. **Holdings:** 800 books; 1200 reports. **Subscriptions:** 30 journals and other serials. **Services:** Library not open to public.

★8289★
MONSANTO TEXTILES COMPANY - TECHNICAL CENTER LIBRARY (Sci-Tech)†
					Phone: (205) 552-2223
Decatur, AL 35601					Betty H. Patterson, Libn.
Founded: 1952. **Staff:** Prof 1; Other 1. **Subjects:** Textile technology, chemistry, chemical engineering, business and personnel administration. **Holdings:** 3300 books; 3100 bound periodical volumes; 35 pamphlets; 13,000 technical reports; 10 VF drawers of clippings; 177 reels of microfilm. **Subscriptions:** 240 journals and other serials. **Services:** Interlibrary loans; use of library for reference may be requested. **Publications:** Book list, monthly - for internal distribution only. **Special Catalogs:** Periodical Holdings List.

★8290★
MONSANTO TEXTILES COMPANY - TECHNICAL LIBRARY (Sci-Tech)
Box 12830					Phone: (904) 968-8248
Pensacola, FL 32575					Farrell J. Allen, Supv., Lib.Sys.
Founded: 1953. **Staff:** Prof 2; Other 2. **Subjects:** Chemistry, chemical engineering, polymer chemistry, textile technology, quality control. **Holdings:** 12,275 books; 3000 bound periodical volumes; 700 pamphlets (cataloged); 760 reels of microfilm; 500 VF drawers of company generated technical reports. **Subscriptions:** 290 journals and other serials; 10 newspapers. **Services:** Interlibrary loans; copying; SDI; library open to public by appointment. **Computerized Information Services:** DIALOG, BRS, SDC; internal database. **Publications:** New Books Purchased, Technical Reports Issued, Selected Patent & Technical Abstracts, monthly - for internal distribution only. **Special Catalogs:** Computer print-out of technical reports, index and book catalog.

★8291★
MONSOUR MEDICAL CENTER - HEALTH SERVICES LIBRARY (Med)
70 Lincoln Way, East					Phone: (412) 527-1511
Jeannette, PA 15644					Edith Gross, Med.Libn.
Founded: 1972. **Staff:** Prof 1. **Subjects:** Medicine, nursing, hospital

management, social work, pharmacology. **Holdings:** 868 books; 500 bound periodical volumes; 378 audiotapes, 26 audiotape-slide systems. **Subscriptions:** 120 journals and other serials. **Services:** Interlibrary loans; copying; library open to public with restrictions. **Networks/Consortia:** Member of Southeast Pittsburgh Consortium; Mideastern Regional Medical Library Service.

MONTAGUE (Dr. Joseph) PROCTOLOGIC LIBRARY
See: International College of Surgeons Hall of Fame - Dr. Joseph Montague Proctologic Library

★8292★
MONTANA COLLEGE OF MINERAL SCIENCE AND TECHNOLOGY - LIBRARY (Sci-Tech)
W. Park St.   Phone: (406) 496-4281
Butte, MT 59701   Elizabeth Morrissett, Hd.Libn.
Staff: Prof 2; Other 7. **Subjects:** Geology, mining, engineering, petroleum, metallurgy, industrial safety and health. **Special Collections:** Mineral industries; regional geology; history of science; mineral, geological and mines maps. **Holdings:** 74,000 volumes; microforms; archives; government documents; maps. **Subscriptions:** 700 journals and other serials; 7 newspapers. **Services:** Interlibrary loans; copying; library open to public. **Computerized Information Services:** DIALOG, SDC, DOE/RECON; internal databases; computerized serials. **Networks/Consortia:** Member of University of Washington Libraries Resource Sharing Program (UWRSP); WLN; CLASS. **Special Catalogs:** Montana geology bibliography. **Staff:** Dena Echard, Ref.Libn.; Jean Bishop, Circ./ILL Libn.; Ilen Stoll, Tech.Serv.Libn.; Laurel Egan, Docs.Libn.

MONTANA ENVIRONMENTAL LIBRARY
See: Western Montana Scientists' Committee for Public Information

★8293★
MONTANA HISTORICAL SOCIETY - LIBRARY/ARCHIVES (Hist)†
225 N. Roberts   Phone: (406) 449-2681
Helena, MT 59620
Founded: 1865. **Staff:** Prof 8; Other 4. **Subjects:** Lewis and Clark Expedition; Custer; Charles M. Russell; military history - Montana Indians; Montana biography/genealogy; mining; cattle and range; homesteading. **Special Collections:** T.C. Power papers; Senator Lee Metcalf papers; Thomas Teakle Collection of books on western cattle and range subjects (2300 books and periodicals); F.J. and Jack Ellis Haynes Photograph Collection; state archives (4900 cubic feet). **Holdings:** 30,000 books; 5000 bound periodical volumes; 50,000 state publications; 20,000 government documents; 9000 cubic feet of archives of private papers and state records; 90,000 photographs; 10,000 reels of microfilm of Montana newspapers. **Subscriptions:** 300 journals and other serials; 106 newspapers. **Services:** Interlibrary loans (limited); copying (limited); library open to public for research and reference use only. **Special Indexes:** History of Montana, 1739-1885; Montana obituary index, 1864-1950 (card). **Staff:** Robert Clark, Hd.Libn.; Dave Walter, Ref.Libn.; Brian Cockhill, State Archv.; Gordon Brown, Asst.Archv.; Ellie Arguimbau, Asst.Archv.; Sue Jackson, Asst.Archv.; Lory Morrow, Photo Archv.; David Girshick, Cat.Libn.

★8294★
MONTANA STATE DEPARTMENT OF ADMINISTRATION - CENSUS & ECONOMIC INFORMATION CENTER LIBRARY (Plan)
Mitchell Bldg., Rm. 108
Capitol Sta.   Phone: (406) 449-2896
Helena, MT 59620   Patricia A.B. Roberts, Res.Spec.
Founded: 1970. **Staff:** Prof 1. **Subjects:** Montana - demography, census, economics. **Holdings:** 4000 books; 4000 maps; 300 microfiche. **Subscriptions:** 221 journals and other serials. **Services:** Interlibrary loans; copying; SDI; library open to public for reference use only. **Computerized Information Services:** Computerized cataloging. **Formerly:** Its Research & Information Systems Division - Resource Center.

★8295★
MONTANA STATE DEPARTMENT OF COMMERCE - TRAVEL PROMOTION BUREAU (Pict)
                                             Phone: (406) 449-2654
Helena, MT 59620   John Wilson, Chf.
Founded: 1935. **Subjects:** Tourist information and photo library of tourist attractions. **Services:** Films for loan; free literature.

★8296★
MONTANA STATE DEPARTMENT OF NATURAL RESOURCES & CONSERVATION - RESEARCH & INFORMATION CENTER (Env-Cons; Energy)
32 S. Ewing   Phone: (406) 449-3647
Helena, MT 59601   Mildred Sullivan, Res.Spec.
Staff: Prof 1. **Subjects:** Planning - water resource and energy; land use and conservation; forests; geology; Missouri, Columbia and Yellowstone River Basins. **Special Collections:** MWRB Water Resources survey reports; departmental publications. **Holdings:** 1000 documents; geological maps of Montana; minutes of River Basin meetings. **Subscriptions:** 250 journals and other serials. **Services:** Interlibrary loans; copying; library not open to public.

★8297★
MONTANA STATE LAW LIBRARY (Law)
State Capitol Bldg.   Phone: (406) 449-3660
Helena, MT 59620   Claire Engel, State Law Libn.
Founded: 1873. **Staff:** Prof 2; Other 4. **Subjects:** Law. **Holdings:** 51,000 books; 4000 bound periodical volumes; 82,000 microfiche. **Subscriptions:** 400 journals and other serials. **Services:** Interlibrary loans; copying; library open to public. **Computerized Information Services:** Computerized cataloging.

★8298★
MONTANA STATE LEGISLATIVE COUNCIL - RESEARCH DIVISION - REFERENCE LIBRARY (Law)
State Capitol, Rm. 101   Phone: (406) 449-3064
Helena, MT 59601   Janice C. Bacino, Res.Libn.
Staff: Prof 1; Other 1. **Subjects:** Laws and legislation, legislatures, state and local government, public administration. **Special Collections:** Montana constitutional and legislative history (350 volumes); Montana State Commission on Local Government Collection (160 volumes). **Holdings:** 4000 books; 12 VF drawers of newspaper clippings; 175 microfiche of Montana Legislative Council reports; 40 boxes of workpapers of legislative interim studies. **Subscriptions:** 128 journals and other serials. **Services:** Interlibrary loans; copying; SDI; library open to public for reference use only. **Computerized Information Services:** DIALOG, SDC, BRS (available through Montana State Library). **Networks/Consortia:** Member of Montana Information Network Exchange (MINE).

★8299★
MONTANA STATE LIBRARY COMMISSION - LIBRARY (Info Sci)
930 E. Lyndale   Phone: (406) 449-3004
Helena, MT 59620   Alma S. Jacobs, State Libn.
Staff: Prof 10; Other 15. **Subjects:** General subjects. **Special Collections:** Federal government publications (59,000); state government publications (8300). **Holdings:** 80,000 books. **Subscriptions:** 400 journals and other serials; 8 newspapers. **Services:** Interlibrary loans; copying; library open to public. **Computerized Information Services:** DIALOG, SDC, BRS; computerized cataloging. **Networks/Consortia:** Member of Pacific Northwest Bibliographic Center; CLASS. **Publications:** Montana Newsletter, irregular; Montana Library Directory, annual - both distributed to all Montana libraries and interested persons. **Staff:** Alene Cooper, Coord., Lib.Dev.; Beth Givens, Coord., Lib.Dev.

★8300★
MONTANA STATE OFFICE OF PUBLIC INSTRUCTION - RESOURCE CENTER (Educ)
State Capitol, Rm. 106   Phone: (406) 449-2082
Helena, MT 59620   Cheri Bergeron, Libn.
Staff: Prof 1; Other 1. **Subjects:** Education. **Special Collections:** Archives of the Office of Public Instruction. **Holdings:** 1200 books; complete collection of ERIC microfiche. **Subscriptions:** 1000 journals and other serials. **Services:** Copying; library open to school personnel only. **Computerized Information Services:** DIALOG, SDC; internal database.

★8301★
MONTANA STATE UNIVERSITY - ROLAND R. RENNE LIBRARY - SPECIAL COLLECTIONS (Hist)
                                         Phone: (406) 994-4242
Bozeman, MT 59717   Minnie Paugh, Spec.Coll.Libn.
Staff: Prof 1; Other 1. **Subjects:** Montana and Northwest history, Yellowstone National Park, agricultural history, Native Americans, Abraham Lincoln. **Special Collections:** Haynes Yellowstone National Park Library and business archive; Leggat-Donahoe Northwest Book and Manuscript Collection; M.L. Wilson Agricultural History Collection; Abraham Lincoln collections. **Holdings:** 20,000 books; 100 bound periodical volumes; 1400 manuscripts and manuscript sets; 100 slides and cassettes. **Subscriptions:** 10 journals and other serials; 10 newspapers. **Services:** Interlibrary loans; copying; library

open to public. **Computerized Information Services:** Computerized cataloging and acquisitions. **Networks/Consortia:** Member of WLN.

★8302★
MONTANA STATE UNIVERSITY - VETERINARY RESEARCH LABORATORY - HUIDEKOPER LIBRARY (Med)
Phone: (406) 994-4705
Bozeman, MT 59717　　Kathryn Klingensmith, Libn.
Founded: 1929. **Staff:** Prof 1. **Subjects:** Veterinary science and related subjects. **Holdings:** 3300 books; 3100 bound periodical volumes; 6000 pamphlets and reprints. **Subscriptions:** 120 journals and other serials. **Services:** Interlibrary loans; copying (limited); library open to public.

★8303★
MONTCLAIR ART MUSEUM - LE BRUN LIBRARY (Art)
3 S. Mountain Ave.
Box 1582　　Phone: (201) 746-5555
Montclair, NJ 07042　　Edith A. Rights, Libn.
Staff: Prof 1. **Subjects:** Arts (major and minor), American Indians. **Holdings:** 10,000 books; 3000 bound periodical volumes; museum bulletins and catalogs of exhibitions; posters; 116 VF drawers of clippings, pictures, and pamphlets; 15,000 slides; 44 VF drawers of mounted reproductions; 8000 bookplates; 50 tapes of museum programs and lectures. **Subscriptions:** 50 journals and other serials. **Services:** Copying; library open to public by appointment.

★8304★
MONTCLAIR PUBLIC LIBRARY - LOCAL HISTORY FILE (Hist)
50 S. Fullerton Ave.　　Phone: (201) 744-0500
Montclair, NJ 07042　　Michael Connell, Dir.
Subjects: Local history. **Holdings:** 16 VF drawers of mounted pictures; programs; club rosters, diaries, and maps. **Services:** Interlibrary loans; copying; library open to public for reference use only. **Special Catalogs:** Index to the Montclair Times (card).

MONTCLAIR STATE COLLEGE - EDUCATIONAL FOUNDATION FOR HUMAN SEXUALITY
See: Educational Foundation for Human Sexuality

★8305★
MONTCLAIR STATE COLLEGE - HARRY A. SPRAGUE LIBRARY - SPECIAL COLLECTIONS (Hum)
Phone: (201) 893-4291
Upper Montclair, NJ 07035　　Blanche W. Haller, Dir. of Lib.Serv.
Founded: 1908. **Special Collections:** Modern poetry - Sullivan Collection, Webster Collection, William Carlos Williams Collection; government documents (60,958). **Holdings:** 1357 volumes. **Services:** Interlibrary loans; copying; library open to public for reference use only. **Computerized Information Services:** BRS; internal database; computerized cataloging and circulation. **Networks/Consortia:** Member of OCLC through PALINET and Union Library Catalogue of Pennsylvania; METRO.

★8306★
MONTCLAIR STATE COLLEGE - NATIONAL ADULT EDUCATION CLEARINGHOUSE/MULTIMEDIA CENTER (Educ)
Montclair State College　　Phone: (201) 893-4353
Upper Montclair, NJ 07043　　Frances M. Spinelli, Dir.
Founded: 1970. **Staff:** Prof 2; Other 1. **Subjects:** Education - adult, community, career, consumer; aging; professional development. **Special Collections:** Adult Basic Education; English as a Second Language; Adult High School; Competency-Based Adult Education; Leisure Reading; Mathematics (designed for adults). **Holdings:** 20,000 books; 10 VF drawers of reports and clippings. **Subscriptions:** 55 journals and other serials. **Services:** Copying; library open to public. **Networks/Consortia:** Member of Coalition of Adult Education Organizations. **Publications:** List of publications - available upon request. **Special Indexes:** Quarterly Index of Informational Abstracts; bibliographies. **Remarks:** The clearinghouse is a nonprofit organization, supported by the services provided.

★8307★
MONTCLAIR STATE COLLEGE - WOMEN'S CENTER LIBRARY (Soc Sci)
Phone: (201) 893-5106
Upper Montclair, NJ 07043　　Dr. Constance Waller, Dir.
Staff: 3. **Subjects:** Women - legal rights, career information, health, literature. **Holdings:** 550 books; 5 VF drawers of clippings. **Services:** Library open to public.

★8308★
MONTEFIORE MEDICAL CENTER - KARL CHERKASKY SOCIAL MEDICINE LIBRARY (Med)
111 E. 210th St.　　Phone: (212) 920-5508
Bronx, NY 10467　　Dr. Victor W. Sidel, Chm., Dept.Soc.Med.
Founded: 1970. **Subjects:** Social medicine, epidemiology, community and international health, occupational health. **Holdings:** 350 volumes. **Subscriptions:** 15 journals and other serials. **Services:** Library open to public with restrictions.

★8309★
MONTEFIORE MEDICAL CENTER - MEDICAL LIBRARY (Med)
111 E. 210 St.　　Phone: (212) 920-4666
Bronx, NY 10467　　Debra Cassel, Act.Dir.
Founded: 1900. **Staff:** Prof 3; Other 4. **Subjects:** Medicine, biochemistry, orthopedics, plastic surgery, surgery, pathology, psychology, psychiatry, pediatrics, physical medicine, sociology. **Holdings:** 45,000 books. **Subscriptions:** 700 journals and other serials. **Services:** Interlibrary loans; copying; library open to public by appointment. **Computerized Information Services:** BRS, DIALOG; computerized cataloging. **Networks/Consortia:** Member of OCLC; Medical Library Center of New York (MLCNY). **Staff:** Vernon Bruette, Ref.Libn.

MONTEREY CITY - COLTON HALL MUSEUM
See: Colton Hall Museum

★8310★
MONTEREY COUNTY LAW LIBRARY (Law)
Courthouse
Salinas, CA 93901　　Nancy Yuenger, Libn.
Staff: Prof 1; Other 2. **Subjects:** Law. **Holdings:** 27,000 volumes. **Services:** Interlibrary loans; copying; library open to public.

★8311★
MONTEREY HISTORY & ART ASSOCIATION - MAYO HAYES O'DONNELL LIBRARY (Hist)
155 Van Buren St.
Box 805
Monterey, CA 93940　　Mrs. Charles M. Bentley, Lib.Chm.
Staff: Prof 1; Other 4. **Subjects:** California, Monterey, Western United States. **Holdings:** 2500 books; archives; photographs. **Services:** Copying (limited); library open to public for reference use only.

★8312★
MONTEREY INSTITUTE OF INTERNATIONAL STUDIES - LIBRARY (Area-Ethnic)
425 Van Buren St.
Box 1978　　Phone: (408) 649-3113
Monterey, CA 93940　　Dr. Glynn Wood, Dir.
Founded: 1961. **Staff:** Prof 3; Other 3. **Subjects:** Language and area studies, translation and interpretation, international management, international economics, education, international studies. **Holdings:** 41,046 books; 377 MIFS masters' theses (cataloged); 1279 pamphlets; 630 phonograph records; 293 microforms. **Subscriptions:** 181 journals and other serials; 12 newspapers. **Services:** Interlibrary loans; copying; library open to public with payment of fee. **Networks/Consortia:** Member of CIN. **Staff:** Dr. Barron G. Holland, Asst.Libn., Pub.Serv.; Doris J. Seely, Asst.Libn., Cat.

MONTEREY PENINSULA COMMUNITY HOSPITAL
See: Community Hospital of the Monterey Peninsula

★8313★
MONTGOMERY ADVERTISER AND ALABAMA JOURNAL - LIBRARY (Publ)†
200 Washington Ave.　　Phone: (205) 262-1611
Montgomery, AL 36104　　Peggy Ross, Libn.
Staff: Prof 1. **Subjects:** Newspaper reference topics. **Holdings:** 300 books; 330 drawers of clippings; 68 drawers of photographs; microfilm of both newspapers from 1940 to present. **Subscriptions:** 43 newspapers. **Services:** Library open to outside users with approval of managing editor.

★8314★
MONTGOMERY COUNTY CIRCUIT COURT - LAW LIBRARY (Law)
Judicial Center
50 Courthouse Sq., Rm. 326　　Phone: (301) 251-7165
Rockville, MD 20850　　Karen D.M. Smith, Law Libn.
Staff: Prof 1; Other 4. **Subjects:** Law. **Holdings:** 30,000 volumes. **Services:** Interlibrary loans; copying; library open to lawyers and Montgomery County residents. **Computerized Information Services:** WESTLAW.

★8315★
MONTGOMERY COUNTY - DEPARTMENT OF HISTORY AND ARCHIVES (Hist)
Old Court House
Fonda, NY 12068
Phone: (518) 853-3431
Anita A. Smith, County Hist.
Staff: 2. **Subjects:** Local and state history. **Holdings:** 9300 books; 1200 maps; county documents; will abstracts; deeds; church and cemetery records. **Services:** Copying; library open to Montgomery County residents and with restrictions to others. **Computerized Information Services:** Computerized acquisitions. **Special Catalogs:** Catalog of historical and genealogical materials. **Special Indexes:** Family Files Index; map index. **Staff:** Violet Fallone, Hist.Archv.Asst.

★8316★
MONTGOMERY COUNTY HISTORICAL SOCIETY - LIBRARY (Hist)
103 W. Montgomery Ave.
Rockville, MD 20850
Phone: (301) 762-1492
Jane C. Sween, Libn.
Staff: 5. **Subjects:** History, biography, genealogy. **Holdings:** 1000 books; information files on history of Montgomery County, Maryland; photographs; plats; card files of some early court records; church records; marriage records; newspaper abstracts; census and tax assessment records. **Services:** Copying; library open to public with fee. **Publications:** Montgomery County Story, quarterly - mailed to members, for sale to nonmembers.

MONTGOMERY COUNTY INTERMEDIATE UNIT LIBRARY
See: Research & Information Services for Education

★8317★
MONTGOMERY COUNTY LAW LIBRARY (Law)
Box 1667
Montgomery, AL 36192
Phone: (205) 832-4950
Jean M. Bowar, Law Libn.
Founded: 1958. **Staff:** 3. **Subjects:** Law. **Holdings:** 12,500 books and bound periodical volumes. **Subscriptions:** 10 journals and other serials. **Services:** Library open to outside users for reference with borrowing privileges for attorneys. **Staff:** Judge Perry O. Hooper, Dir.

★8318★
MONTGOMERY COUNTY LAW LIBRARY (Law)
Court House
Norristown, PA 19404
Phone: (215) 278-3806
Arthur S. Zanan, Law Libn.
Founded: 1869. **Staff:** Prof 2; Other 3. **Subjects:** Law, with emphasis on Pennsylvania law. **Special Collections:** Ordinances of Montgomery County Municipalities. **Holdings:** 37,000 books; 700 bound periodical volumes; 6 VF drawers of municipal ordinances; 50 audio cassettes; 10 video cassettes. **Subscriptions:** 92 journals and other serials. **Services:** Interlibrary loans; copying; library open to public with restrictions. **Computerized Information Services:** WESTLAW. **Publications:** Newsletter, monthly - to members of Montgomery Bar Association. **Remarks:** Maintained by Montgomery County Commissioners. **Staff:** Bruce S. Piscadlo, Asst. Law Libn.

★8319★
MONTGOMERY COUNTY PLANNING COMMISSION - RESEARCH LIBRARY (Plan)
Court House
Norristown, PA 19404
Phone: (215) 278-3726
Florence Bailey, Supv.
Subjects: Practical urban planning, transportation, sanitary engineering, land use, housing, social and economic statistics. **Holdings:** 3500 books and bound periodical volumes; 2000 documents, reports (cataloged); 4000 slides; 60 boxes of microfilm; 30 binders of computer printouts; VF drawers of newspaper clippings, correspondence, pamphlets. **Subscriptions:** 70 journals and other serials; 15 newspapers. **Services:** Interlibrary loans (limited); copying; SDI (for staff); library open to public with restrictions.

★8320★
MONTGOMERY COUNTY PUBLIC SCHOOLS - PROFESSIONAL LIBRARY (Educ)†
850 N. Hungerford Dr.
Rockville, MD 20850
Phone: (301) 279-3227
Karen Dowling, Curric.Libn.
Founded: 1961. **Staff:** 5. **Subjects:** Education. **Special Collections:** Complete ERIC collection; Montgomery County Public Schools' curriculum guides; dissertations by MCPS employees. **Holdings:** 30,000 books; 1000 nonprint items (cataloged). **Subscriptions:** 500 journals and other serials; 14 newspapers. **Services:** Interlibrary loans; copying; SDI; library open to public for reference use only. **Computerized Information Services:** DIALOG, New York Times Information Service. **Publications:** Bibliographies.

★8321★
MONTGOMERY HOSPITAL - MEDICAL LIBRARY (Med)
Powell & Fornance St.
Norristown, PA 19401
Phone: (215) 631-3232
Alberta T. O'Brien, Med.Libn.
Staff: Prof 1; Other 1. **Subjects:** Medicine, surgery, drugs, nursing, basic sciences. **Holdings:** 1500 books; 599 bound periodical volumes; 220 AV items. **Subscriptions:** 98 journals and other serials. **Services:** Interlibrary loans; copying; library open to public with special permission from the administration. **Networks/Consortia:** Member of Delaware Valley Information Consortium (DEVIC). **Staff:** Dr. Robert Perch, Lib.Chm.

★8322★
MONTGOMERY (James M.), CONSULTING ENGINEERS - LIBRARY (Sci-Tech)
555 E. Walnut St.
Pasadena, CA 91101
Phone: (213) 796-9141
Marjorie M. Ford, Libn.
Staff: Prof 1; Other 1. **Subjects:** Water quality, effluents, drinking water, wastewater. **Holdings:** 500 books; 300 bound periodical volumes; 1000 bound and unbound reports and specifications; 2 VF drawers of reprints; 100 specifications and standards; 1000 archival items in microform. **Subscriptions:** 100 journals and other serials. **Services:** Interlibrary loans; copying; library not open to public. **Computerized Information Services:** DIALOG; internal database.

MONTGOMERY LIBRARY
See: Fairchild Tropical Garden

MONTGOMERY LIBRARY
See: Westminster Theological Seminary

★8323★
MONTGOMERY, MC CRACKEN, WALKER & RHOADS - LIBRARY (Law)
3 Pkwy.
Philadelphia, PA 19102
Phone: (215) 563-0650
G.H. Brown, Libn.
Staff: Prof 1; Other 1. **Subjects:** Law. **Holdings:** 11,000 volumes. **Computerized Information Services:** LEXIS.

★8324★
MONTGOMERY MUSEUM OF FINE ARTS - ART RESEARCH LIBRARY (Art)
440 S. McDonough St.
Montgomery, AL 36104
Phone: (205) 834-3490
Barbara Magan, Pubns.Libn.
Subjects: American painting, sculpture, contemporary art, decorative art, photography, European art. **Holdings:** 4000 books; 1200 bound periodical volumes; 49 Montgomery Museum scrapbooks; 3000 slides of American and European art. **Subscriptions:** 28 journals and other serials. **Services:** Copying; library open to public for reference use only. **Publications:** Calendar of Events, bimonthly; exhibition catalogs.

★8325★
MONTGOMERY TECHNICAL INSTITUTE - LEARNING RESOURCES CENTER (Sci-Tech)
Drawer 487
Troy, NC 27371
Phone: (919) 572-3691
Gay R. Russell, Libn.
Staff: Prof 1; Other 7. **Subjects:** Gunsmithing, taxidermy, business administration, beekeeping, pottery, law enforcement, automotive mechanics, history. **Holdings:** 10,000 books; 4 VF drawers of pamphlets; 290 reels of microfilm. **Subscriptions:** 117 journals and other serials; 12 newspapers. **Services:** Interlibrary loans; copying; library open to public. **Networks/Consortia:** Member of In-Watts; Consortium for Sharing Instructional Materials (CSIM).

★8326★
MONTGOMERY WARD AND CO. - INFORMATION SERVICES (Bus-Fin)
One Montgomery Ward Plaza
Chicago, IL 60671
Phone: (312) 467-2334
Barbara J. Burnett, Mgr.
Founded: 1965. **Staff:** Prof 3. **Subjects:** Retailing. **Holdings:** 1500 books; 16 shelving sections of government documents; 60 VF drawers of pamphlets; Montgomery Ward catalogs. **Subscriptions:** 100 journals and other serials; 10 newspapers. **Services:** Interlibrary loans; services not open to public. **Formerly:** Its Corporate Library.

★8327★
MONTICELLO MEDICAL CENTER - MEDICAL STAFF LIBRARY (Med)
Box 638
Longview, WA 98632
Phone: (206) 423-5850
Margaret B. Geering, Coord., Med. Staff Serv.
Staff: Prof 1. **Subjects:** Medicine. **Holdings:** 400 books. **Services:** Interlibrary loans; copying; library is open to nursing and paramedical personnel.

★8328★
MONTREAL ASSOCIATION FOR THE MENTALLY RETARDED -
    DOCUMENTATION CENTRE (Med)
8605 rue Berri
Bureau 300   Phone: (514) 381-2307
Montreal, PQ, Canada H2P 2G5   Michelle Jacques, Documentalist
Founded: 1969. **Staff:** Prof 1. **Subjects:** Mental retardation. **Holdings:** 1200
books; 41 bound periodical volumes; pamphlets; vertical files; AV material.
Subscriptions: 75 journals and other serials. **Services:** Interlibrary loans;
copying; centre open to public. **Publications:** The Rights of the Mentally
Handicapped in Quebec; Educational Facilities for Mentally Handicapped
Children in Greater Montreal - both available from the documentation centre.
Also Known As: Association de Montreal pour les Deficients Mentaux.

★8329★
MONTREAL BOARD OF TRADE - INFORMATION CENTRE (Bus-Fin)
1080 Beaver Hall Hill, 7th Fl.   Phone: (514) 878-4651
Montreal, PQ, Canada H2Z 1S9   Carole Peters, Mgr., Info.Serv.
Staff: 4. **Subjects:** International trade, civic development, research,
employee relations, statistics, legislation, taxation, trade and commerce,
transportation, salary surveys. **Holdings:** 2000 books and bound periodical
volumes; 110 telephone directories; 200 foreign custom tariffs.
Subscriptions: 80 journals and other serials. **Services:** Copying; library open
to public.

MONTREAL BOTANICAL GARDEN
See: Jardin Botanique de Montreal

★8330★
MONTREAL CANCER INSTITUTE - LIBRARY (Med)
1560 Sherbrooke St., E.   Phone: (514) 876-7078
Montreal, PQ, Canada H2L 4M1   Dr. Roger Daoust, Info.Dir.
Staff: Prof 1; Other 1. **Subjects:** Cellular biology, virology, genetics,
molecular biology, biochemistry, cancer. **Holdings:** 600 books; 3500 bound
periodical volumes; 50 scientific reports; 50 annual reports; 20 theses.
Subscriptions: 74 journals and other serials; 5 newspapers. **Services:**
Interlibrary loans; copying; library open to qualified researchers only.

★8331★
MONTREAL CHEST HOSPITAL CENTRE - MEDICAL LIBRARY (Med)
3650 St. Urbain St.   Phone: (514) 849-5201
Montreal, PQ, Canada H2X 2P4   Marianne Constantine, Med.Libn.
Founded: 1965. **Staff:** Prof 1. **Subjects:** Chest medicine, thoracic surgery.
Holdings: 1800 books and bound periodical volumes. **Subscriptions:** 100
journals and other serials. **Services:** Interlibrary loans; copying; library open to
public by permission only. **Networks/Consortia:** Member of McGill Medical
and Health Libraries Association. **Also Known As:** Centre Hospitalier
Thoracique de Montreal.

★8332★
MONTREAL CHILDREN'S HOSPITAL - MEDICAL LIBRARY (Med)
2300 Tupper St.   Phone: (514) 937-8511
Montreal, PQ, Canada H3H 1P3   Dorothy Sirois, Med.Libn.
Founded: 1946. **Staff:** Prof 2; Other 2. **Subjects:** Pediatrics, pediatric
surgery, child psychiatry, nursing. **Holdings:** 18,000 books and bound
periodical volumes. **Subscriptions:** 350 journals and other serials. **Services:**
Interlibrary loans; copying; library open to public with restrictions. **Staff:**
Angella Lambrou, Asst.Med.Libn.

MONTREAL CITY LIBRARY - GAGNON COLLECTION
See: Bibliotheque de la Ville de Montreal

★8333★
MONTREAL CITY PLANNING DEPARTMENT - LIBRARY
85 Notre-Dame St., E.
Montreal, PQ, Canada H2Y 1B5
Founded: 1963. **Subjects:** Town planning, urban studies, urban statistics,
housing, architecture, geography, transportation, historic preservation.
Holdings: 7000 books; 500 bound periodical volumes. **Remarks:** Presently
inactive. **Also Known As:** Ville de Montreal - Service de l'Urbanisme.

MONTREAL CONSERVATORY OF MUSIC - DOCUMENTATION CENTRE
See: Conservatoire de Musique de Montreal - Centre de Documentation

MONTREAL DIOCESAN ARCHIVES
See: Anglican Church of Canada - Diocese of Montreal - Archives

★8334★
MONTREAL ENGINEERING COMPANY, LTD. - CALGARY LIBRARY (Sci-
    Tech)
900 One Palliser Sq.
125 9th Ave. S.E.   Phone: (403) 263-1680
Calgary, AB, Canada T2G 0P6   Beverley Bendell, Libn.
Staff: Prof 1; Other 3. **Subjects:** Engineering - electrical, mechanical, civil;
mining; environmental assessments. **Special Collections:** Trade catalogs
(microfilm). **Holdings:** 8000 books; 2000 other cataloged items.
Subscriptions: 200 journals and other serials. **Services:** Interlibrary loans;
copying; library open to public with restrictions. **Computerized Information
Services:** Online systems; computerized cataloging and serials distribution.
Publications: Library News. **Also Known As:** Monenco Ltd.

★8335★
MONTREAL ENGINEERING COMPANY, LTD. - LIBRARY (Sci-Tech)
Sta. A, Box 6088   Phone: (514) 286-3519
Montreal, PQ, Canada H3C 3Z8   Penelope H. Kamichaitis, Libn.
Founded: 1960. **Staff:** Prof 1; Other 2. **Subjects:** Power engineering, water
resources, electric utilities, hydrology, electric transmission. **Holdings:**
10,000 books; 20 VF drawers of topographical maps of Canada; 40 VF
drawers; 2000 engineering standards. **Subscriptions:** 400 journals and other
serials; 5 newspapers. **Services:** Interlibrary loans; copying; library open to
public for reference use only. **Publications:** Accessions list, quarterly -
distributed internally and to selected outside firms and libraries. **Also Known
As:** Monenco Ltd.

★8336★
MONTREAL GAZETTE - LIBRARY (Publ)
250 St. Antoine St. W.
P.O. Box 4300, Place d'Armes   Phone: (514) 282-2771
Montreal, PQ, Canada H2Y 3S1   Agnes McFarlane, Libn.
Staff: 6. **Subjects:** Newspaper reference topics. **Holdings:** Newspaper
clipping files, photographs. **Services:** Library open to public by appointment
with payment of fee; mail inquiries accepted.

★8337★
MONTREAL GENERAL HOSPITAL - MEDICAL LIBRARY (Med)
1650 Cedar Ave.   Phone: (514) 937-6011
Montreal, PQ, Canada H3G 1A4   Kathryn Vaughn, Chf.Med.Libn.
Staff: Prof 2; Other 3. **Subjects:** Medicine, surgery, gynecology, pathology,
radiology, anaesthesia. **Holdings:** 3000 books; 12,000 bound periodical
volumes; 1 VF drawer of pamphlets. **Subscriptions:** 300 journals and other
serials. **Services:** Interlibrary loans; copying; library open to public by
appointment. **Computerized Information Services:** MEDLARS. **Networks/
Consortia:** Member of McGill Medical and Health Libraries Association.
Publications: New Acquisitions, bimonthly - local distribution and available
upon request. **Also Known As:** Hopital General de Montreal - Bibliotheque
Medicale. **Staff:** Gary Lee Kober, Asst.Libn.

★8338★
MONTREAL GENERAL HOSPITAL - NURSES LIBRARY (Med)
Room 3808   Phone: (514) 937-6011
Montreal, PQ, Canada H3G 1A4   Mrs. B.A. Covington, Lib.Techn.
Staff: 1. **Subjects:** Nursing. **Holdings:** 8000 books; 150 bound periodical
volumes. **Subscriptions:** 40 journals and other serials. **Services:** Library open
to nursing staff and visiting nurses. **Networks/Consortia:** Member of McGill
Medical and Health Libraries Association.

MONTREAL MILITARY AND MARITIME MUSEUM
See: St. Helen's Island Museum Montreal

★8339★
THE MONTREAL MUSEUM OF FINE ARTS - LIBRARY (Art)
3400 Ave. du Musee   Phone: (514) 285-1600
Montreal, PQ, Canada H3G 1K3   Juanita M. Toupin, Libn.
Founded: 1882. **Staff:** Prof 2; Other 5. **Subjects:** Fine arts, sculpture,
ceramics, decorative arts, costume, silver, painting, furniture, textiles,
architecture. **Special Collections:** Files on Canadian art and artists. **Holdings:**
36,600 books and bound periodical volumes; 16,250 exhibition catalogs;
36,170 sales catalogs; 52 VF drawers. **Subscriptions:** 477 journals and
other serials. **Services:** Interlibrary loans (limited); copying; library open to
public for reference use only. **Also Known As:** Musee des beaux-arts de
Montreal.

★8340★

MONTREAL NEUROLOGICAL INSTITUTE - LIBRARY (Med)
3801 University St.	Phone: (514) 284-4651
Montreal, PQ, Canada H3A 2B4	Marina M. Boski, Libn.
Founded: 1934. **Staff:** Prof 1; Other 1. **Subjects:** Neurosciences. **Holdings:** 3200 books; 3100 bound periodical volumes; 300 theses and reprints. **Subscriptions:** 75 journals and other serials. **Services:** Interlibrary loans; library not open to public.

★8341★

MONTREAL URBAN COMMUNITY TRANSIT COMMISSION - LIBRARY (Trans)
159 St. Antoine St., W., Rm. 912	Phone: (514) 877-6046
Montreal, PQ, Canada H2Z 1H3	Victor Itesco, Hd.Libn.
Staff: Prof 2. **Subjects:** Urban transit, engineering, management, law, finance. **Special Collections:** Urban transit history of Montreal (thousands of clippings and 200 other items). **Holdings:** 4500 books; 300 bound periodical volumes; 1200 technical reports on microfiche; 7 VF drawers of pamphlets; 40 reels of microfilm. **Subscriptions:** 255 journals and other serials; 5 newspapers. **Services:** Interlibrary loans; copying; library open to public for reference use only. **Also Known As:** Commission de Transport de la Communaute Urbaine de Montreal (CTCUM). **Staff:** Louis Beaupre; Jocelyne Trauquille; Helene Leclerc.

★8342★

MONTREAL YOUNG WOMEN'S CHRISTIAN ASSOCIATION - LIBRARY (Soc Sci)†
1355 Dorchester Blvd., W.	Phone: (514) 866-9941
Montreal, PQ, Canada H3G 1T3
Founded: 1874. **Subjects:** Social group work, roles of women in society (emphasis in education and employment). **Special Collections:** Grace Childs Collection (analytical psychology). **Holdings:** 4000 books; pamphlets and clippings. **Subscriptions:** 27 journals and other serials. **Services:** Interlibrary loans; library open to public by permission. **Publications:** Bibliography on Roles of Women, annual.

MOODY AIR FORCE BASE (GA)
See: U.S. Air Force Base - Moody Base Library

★8343★

MOODY BIBLE INSTITUTE - LIBRARY (Rel-Theol)
820 N. LaSalle St.	Phone: (312) 329-4139
Chicago, IL 60610	Richard G. Schock, Dir.
Founded: 1890. **Staff:** Prof 5; Other 6. **Subjects:** Bible, missions, church history, theology, church music, Christian education, homiletics, evangelism and pastoral training, communications. **Holdings:** 100,000 books; 4500 bound periodical volumes; 6500 other cataloged items; 525 reels of microfilm; 25 lateral file drawers of unbound catalogs, reports, brochures and organization files; 28 VF drawers of curriculum laboratory materials; 60 VF drawers of classified pamphlets. **Subscriptions:** 607 journals and other serials; 6 newspapers. **Services:** Interlibrary loans; copying; library open to public. **Publications:** Periodic Acquisitions List - distributed to faculty and institute department heads; MBI Library Manual - to faculty and students. **Special Indexes:** Sermon index; subject and title index to periodical holdings. **Staff:** Henrietta Watts, Cat.Libn.; Karen Simpson, Per.Libn.; Brien Belangar, Circ.Libn.; Walter Osborn, Ref.Libn.

★8344★

MOODY BIBLE INSTITUTE - MOODYANA COLLECTION (Rel-Theol)
820 N. LaSalle St.	Phone: (312) 329-4140
Chicago, IL 60610	Richard G. Schock, Dir.
Founded: 1936. **Staff:** Prof 3; Other 1. **Subjects:** Life and work of D.L. Moody, including documents and photographs; history of Moody Bible Institute; biographical data of notables connected with MBI; early Bibles and rare theology books. **Special Collections:** Books by and about D.L. Moody and MBI presidents. **Holdings:** 450 books; 195 bound periodical volumes; 25 dissertations and theses on D.L. Moody and revivalism, and 500 pamphlets (cataloged); 1000 pieces of correspondence; 1000 clipping accounts of D.L. Moody's evangelistic campaigns and 2000 tributes and obituary notices; 600 manuscript notes of notable MBI instructors; 50 VF drawers and 10 oversized drawers of photographs. **Services:** Copying; collection open to public for reference and research. **Publications:** Bibliography of books and dissertations by and about D.L. Moody. **Special Indexes:** Name and place index to Moody's letters; index to comprehensive itinerary of Moody's travels. **Remarks:** A permanent Moodyana Exhibit (artifacts) is located at the Institute in Smith Hall. **Staff:** Henrietta Watts, Cat.Libn.; Walter Osborn, Ref.Libn.

MOODY LIBRARY
See: Baylor University

MOODY LIBRARY
See: Lubbock Christian College

MOODY MEDICAL LIBRARY
See: University of Texas Medical Branch

★8345★

MOODY'S INVESTORS SERVICE, INC. - INFORMATION CENTER (Bus-Fin)†
99 Church St.	Phone: (212) 553-0525
New York, NY 10007	Angelica Carroll, Mgr.
Founded: 1900. **Staff:** Prof 1; Other 12. **Subjects:** Publicly held corporations, governments and municipalities. **Holdings:** 1400 VF drawers of annual reports, interim reports, prospectuses, news releases; Moody's manuals, 1909 to present (microfiche); U.S. Securities and Exchange Commission documents for 11,000 publicly held companies (microfiche). **Services:** Copying; library open to public. **Special Catalogs:** Catalog of companies covered in Moody's publications (card).

MOON (F. Franklin) LIBRARY
See: SUNY - College of Environmental Science and Forestry - F. Franklin Moon Library

★8346★

MOORE BUSINESS FORMS, INC. - RESEARCH CENTER LIBRARY (Bus-Fin; Sci-Tech)
300 Lang Blvd.	Phone: (716) 773-0557
Grand Island, NY 14072	Betsy M. Waters, Lib.Supv.
Staff: Prof 1; Other 2. **Subjects:** Pulp and paper products, graphic arts, chemistry, electronics, marketing. **Holdings:** 3500 books; 1000 microfiche; 200 reels of microfilm; 60 cassettes; 6 VF drawers of annual reports and pamphlets. **Subscriptions:** 400 journals and other serials. **Services:** Interlibrary loans; copying; library open to public with prior arrangement. **Computerized Information Services:** DIALOG, SDC; computerized cataloging, acquisitions, serials and circulation. **Networks/Consortia:** Member of Western New York Library Resources Council.

MOORE (Claude) HEALTH SCIENCES LIBRARY
See: University of Virginia - Medical Center - Claude Moore Health Sciences Library

★8347★

MOORE COLLEGE OF ART - LIBRARY (Art)
20th & Race Sts.	Phone: (215) 568-4515
Philadelphia, PA 19103	Deborah Alterman, Lib.Dir.
Staff: Prof 2; Other 4. **Subjects:** Fine arts, professional arts, art education, art history, humanities. **Special Collections:** John Sartain Collection (engravings and prints); Sartain family correspondence and miscellaneous objects (one drawer). **Holdings:** 33,000 books; 1500 bound periodical volumes; 400 folios; 112 VF drawers of pictures, prints, clippings, plates; 73,000 slides; 1100 phonograph records. **Subscriptions:** 340 journals and other serials; 10 newspapers. **Services:** Interlibrary loans; copying; library open to public by permission. **Networks/Consortia:** Member of OCLC through PALINET & Union Library Catalogue of Pennsylvania. **Staff:** Karin Lazarus, Cat.

★8348★

MOORE-COTTRELL SUBSCRIPTION AGENCIES - SERIALS REFERENCE LIBRARY
North Cohocton, NY 14868
Defunct

MOORE (Franklin F.) LIBRARY
See: Rider College - Franklin F. Moore Library

★8349★

MOORE, GARDNER & ASSOCIATES, INC. - LIBRARY (Sci-Tech)†
Box 728	Phone: (919) 625-6111
Asheboro, NC 27203	Louise C. Johnston, Libn.
Founded: 1975. **Staff:** Prof 1. **Subjects:** Sanitary and civil engineering. **Holdings:** 600 books; 650 technical reports. **Subscriptions:** 100 journals and other serials. **Services:** Interlibrary loans; library open to public with restrictions. **Special Indexes:** KWIC index to technical reports.

MOORE HALL LIBRARY
See: Kansas State Geological Survey

MOORE (Joseph A.) LIBRARY
See: Society of California Pioneers - Joseph A. Moore Library

MOORE (Joseph) MUSEUM
See: Earlham College - Joseph Moore Museum

★8350★
MOORE (Julie) & ASSOCIATES - LIBRARY (Sci-Tech)
6130 Camino Real, No. 225
Box 5156   Phone: (714) 684-0441
Riverside, CA 92517-5156   Julie L. Moore, Bibliog.
Staff: Prof 2; Other 1. **Subjects:** Game mammals and birds, marine mammals and birds, bats, endangered species, fisheries, fauna, taxonomy. **Special Collections:** Hard copy files of all SDI profiles created for the databases; retrospective hard copy files for game, mammals and birds, 1934-1981. **Holdings:** 425 books; microfilm copy of Zoological Record 1864-1948; Aves and Mammalia; database tapes of SDI files; biological and technical dictionaries. **Services:** SDI; retrospective searches; library not open to public. **Subscriptions:** 14 journals and other serials. **Computerized Information Services:** Online systems; HERMAN (Wildlife and Marine Mammals; internal database).

MOORE LIBRARY
See: University of Pennsylvania - School of Engineering and Applied Science

MOORE (Marianne) ARCHIVE
See: Rosenbach Museum & Library

★8351★
MOORE (Walter P.) & ASSOCIATES - LIBRARY (Sci-Tech)
3203 W. Alabama
Houston, TX 77098   Dottie Collins, Libn.
Staff: Prof 1. **Subjects:** Structural engineering, architecture, traffic and transportation, waste water, steel and concrete structures. **Holdings:** 1000 books. **Subscriptions:** 32 journals and other serials. **Services:** Interlibrary loans; library open to public by appointment.

MOORES CREEK NATL. BATTLEFIELD
See: U.S. Natl. Park Service

MOORHEAD STATE UNIVERSITY - NORTHWEST MINNESOTA HISTORICAL CENTER
See: Northwest Minnesota Historical Center

MOORLAND-SPINGARN RESEARCH CENTER
See: Howard University

MOORMAN MEMORIAL LIBRARY
See: Eastern Virginia Medical School

★8352★
MOOSE JAW LAW SOCIETY - LIBRARY (Law)†
Court House
64 Ominica St., W.   Phone: (306) 693-6105
Moose Jaw, SK, Canada S6H 4P1   Lola Sharp, Libn.
Subjects: Law. **Holdings:** 6000 volumes. **Services:** Library not open to public. **Computerized Information Services:** Computerized acquisitions, serials and circulation.

★8353★
MOOSE LAKE STATE HOSPITAL - STAFF LIBRARY (Med)†
1000 Lake Shore Dr.   Phone: (218) 485-4411
Moose Lake, MN 55767   John C. Flynn, Libn.
Staff: Prof 1; Other 1. **Subjects:** Psychiatry, mental retardation, chemical dependency. **Holdings:** 500 books. **Subscriptions:** 26 journals and other serials. **Services:** Interlibrary loans; library open to local and Midwest regional consortia. **Networks/Consortia:** Member of Regional Medical Library - Region 3; Minnesota Department of Public Welfare Library Consortium.

★8354★
MORAGA HISTORICAL SOCIETY - ARCHIVES (Hist)
St. Mary's College Library   Phone: (415) 376-4411
Moraga, CA 94575   Bro. L. Dennis Goodman, F.S.C.
Staff: 3. **Subjects:** Moraga Rancho area history; Moraga family history and genealogy; history of communities of Orinda, Lafayette and Canyon. **Holdings:** 18 oral history tapes; 20 VF drawers of clippings; 6 volumes of land title abstracts; 150 files of court cases; photographs; 300 maps; 60 reels of microfilm of San Francisco Bay Area missions and parishes, to 1900; tax

assessor's records. **Services:** Interlibrary loans; copying; archives open to public under supervision. **Publications:** El Rancho (historical journal); Newsletter. **Special Indexes:** 10 year index to El Rancho.

★8355★
MORAINE PARK TECHNICAL INSTITUTE - LEARNING RESOURCE CENTER (Bus-Fin; Sci-Tech)
235 N. National Ave.   Phone: (414) 922-8611
Fond Du Lac, WI 54935   Judy Denor, Lib.Spec.
Founded: 1965. **Staff:** Prof 3; Other 4. **Subjects:** Health occupations; business and marketing; trade, police and fire science; home economics; agri-bio-technology. **Holdings:** 20,000 books; 650 bound periodical volumes; 2000 pamphlets; 600 microforms; 10,000 slides; 9000 audio and video cassettes; 200 tapes; 2000 16mm films. **Subscriptions:** 500 journals and other serials; 25 newspapers. **Services:** Interlibrary loans; copying; library open to public. **Networks/Consortia:** Member of Mid-Wisconsin Multitype Library Association. **Publications:** New Book List, monthly; Library Handbook, annual. **Staff:** Carol Boede, Cat.; Charlene Pettit, Cat.

★8356★
MORAVIAN CHURCH IN AMERICA - NORTHERN PROVINCE - MORAVIAN ARCHIVES (Rel-Theol)†
41 W. Locust St.   Phone: (215) 866-3255
Bethlehem, PA 18018   Vernon H. Nelson, Archv.
Founded: 1751. **Staff:** Prof 2; Other 2. **Subjects:** Moravian Church history - general and American; history of Bethlehem and area; biography; hymnody; Moravian missions. **Holdings:** 5600 books; 1550 bound periodical volumes; manuscripts and documents. **Subscriptions:** 12 journals and other serials. **Services:** Library open to public; manuscripts may be consulted by special arrangement.

★8357★
MORAVIAN CHURCH IN AMERICA - SOUTHERN PROVINCE - MORAVIAN ARCHIVES (Rel-Theol)
Salem Sta., Drawer M   Phone: (919) 722-1742
Winston-Salem, NC 27108   Mary Creech, Archv.
Staff: Prof 1; Other 2. **Subjects:** Moravian Church history, Moravian missions, North Carolina. **Holdings:** 2000 volumes; 10,000 pages of manuscripts, 1753 to present, relating chiefly to the Moravian settlement in North Carolina (known as Wachovia). **Services:** Copying (limited); archives open to public, with fee for services of archivist. **Remarks:** Much of material has been published by the State Department of Archives and History in Records of the Moravians in North Carolina. Archives are located at 4 E. Bank St., Winston-Salem, NC 27101.

★8358★
MORAVIAN COLLEGE - REEVES LIBRARY (Rel-Theol)
Main St. at Elizabeth Ave.   Phone: (215) 865-0741
Bethlehem, PA 18018   Henry L. Williams, Libn.
Founded: 1807. **Staff:** Prof 4; Other 6. **Subjects:** Liberal arts, theology. **Special Collections:** Moravian Church collection; Moraviana (2800 volumes). **Holdings:** 165,000 volumes; microprint; cassettes and recordings. **Subscriptions:** 1003 journals and other serials; 25 newspapers. **Services:** Interlibrary loans; copying; library open to public. **Computerized Information Services:** Computerized cataloging and ILL. **Networks/Consortia:** Member of OCLC; Lehigh Valley Association of Independent Colleges. **Staff:** Mary Louise Bross, Circ.; Ruth P. D'Aleo, Ref.Libn.; Roma Ziegler, Cat.Libn.

★8359★
MORAVIAN MUSIC FOUNDATION, INC. - PETER MEMORIAL LIBRARY (Mus)
20 Cascade Ave.   Phone: (919) 725-0651
Winston-Salem, NC 27108   James Boeringer, Dir.
Founded: 1956. **Staff:** Prof 2. **Subjects:** Sacred anthems and arias, hymnological materials and books, American music of 18th and 19th centuries, symphonies and music of 18th and 19th centuries, music and religious history and biography. **Special Collections:** Irving Lowens Musical Americana Collection (1500 items). **Holdings:** 5500 books; 10,000 manuscripts and early printed music editions; 3000 items of American and European music of 18th and 19th centuries; 7000 items of American and European manuscripts of 18th and 19th centuries; 200 tape recordings of Moravian music; programs; pictures; clippings. **Subscriptions:** 12 journals and other serials. **Services:** Copying (limited); mail inquiries; library open to public. **Publications:** Journal, quarterly - available for sale. **Special Catalogs:** Catalog of the Johannes Herbst Collection by M. Gombosi; Catalog of the Music of the Salem Congregation by F. Cumnock; Catalog of the Lititz Congregation Collection by R. Steelman; other catalogs to manuscript collections in preparation.

★8360★
MOREAU SEMINARY - LIBRARY (Rel-Theol)
Congregation of Holy Cross
Notre Dame, IN 46556
Phone: (219) 239-5046
Rev. Joseph A. Rogusz, C.S.C., Libn.
Staff: Prof 1; Other 7. **Subjects:** Theology and philosophy. **Holdings:** 53,469 books; 5799 bound periodical volumes. **Subscriptions:** 200 journals and other serials; 8 newspapers. **Services:** Library open to public for reference use only.

MOREELL LIBRARY
See: U.S. Navy - Naval School - Civil Engineer Corps Officers

MOREHEAD (Albert H.) MEMORIAL LIBRARY
See: American Contract Bridge League - Albert H. Morehead Memorial
Library

★8361★
MOREHEAD STATE UNIVERSITY - CAMDEN-CARROLL LIBRARY (Educ)
Phone: (606) 783-2142
Morehead, KY 40351
Dr. Jack D. Ellis, Dir. of Libs.
Founded: 1922. **Staff:** Prof 22; Other 18. **Subjects:** Education, science, industrial arts, history, literature, music, art, philosophy, Spanish and other foreign languages. **Special Collections:** Kentucky Collection (5464 volumes); Learning Resource Center (94,552 items); Appalachian Collection (1447 items); Microform Collection (54,131 volumes); Jesse Stuart Collection (315 items); James Still Collection; rare books (1018). **Holdings:** 442,128 books; 40,882 bound periodical volumes; 29,504 documents; 3412 curriculum guides and courses of study; 2842 pictures, art objects, models and displays; 2856 programmed learning materials, kits, games; 14,904 recordings; 1415 maps, charts and globes; 43,907 films, filmstrips, slides and transparencies. **Subscriptions:** 2240 journals and other serials; 35 newspapers. **Services:** Interlibrary loans; copying; library open to public. **Computerized Information Services:** BRS; computerized cataloging. **Networks/Consortia:** Member of State Assisted Academic Library Council of Kentucky (SAALCK); Kentucky Cooperative Library Information Project (KENCLIP); East Kentucky Health Science Information Network (EKHSIN); OCLC through SOLINET. **Staff:** Faye Belcher, Assoc.Dir.; Margaret Stone, Hd., Ref. & Info.; Juanita Hall, Hd., Tech.Serv.; Al Evans, Lrng.Rsrcs.Libn.

★8362★
MOREHOUSE COLLEGE - SCHOOL OF MEDICINE - MULTI-MEDIA CENTER
(Med)
830 Westview Dr., S.W.
Atlanta, GA 30314
Phone: (404) 681-2800
Beverly E. Allen, Dir.
Staff: Prof 4; Other 5. **Subjects:** Medical and life sciences. **Holdings:** 3573 books; 3450 bound periodical volumes. **Subscriptions:** 467 journals and other serials. **Services:** Interlibrary loans; library not open to public. **Networks/Consortia:** Member of OCLC through SOLINET. **Staff:** Cassandra M. Norman, Asst.Dir.; Barbara H.S. Martin, Cat.Libn.; Joe Swanson, Jr., Acq.Libn.

MORGAN (Charles S.) TECHNICAL LIBRARY
See: National Fire Protection Association - Charles S. Morgan Technical
Library

★8363★
MORGAN COUNTY BAR ASSOCIATION - LIBRARY (Law)
Court House
McConnelsville, OH 43756
Mary Woodward, Libn.
Staff: 1. **Subjects:** Law. **Holdings:** 8000 books. **Services:** Library not open to public.

★8364★
MORGAN COUNTY HISTORICAL SOCIETY - LIBRARY (Hist)
120 N. Monroe St.
Versailles, MO 65084
Mrs. Preston Hutchison, Supv.
Staff: 2. **Subjects:** Local history. **Special Collections:** Morgan County Newspapers, 1897 to present; tombstone inscriptions. **Holdings:** Figures not available. **Services:** Library open to public with restrictions. **Publications:** Morgan County History Book, 1979.

★8365★
MORGAN GUARANTY TRUST COMPANY OF NEW YORK - REFERENCE LIBRARY (Bus-Fin)†
23 Wall St.
New York, NY 10015
Phone: (212) 483-2180
J. Robert Reuter, Libn.
Founded: 1918. **Staff:** Prof 3; Other 3. **Subjects:** Banking, international finance, economics, business statistics, investments, commerce, foreign trade. **Special Collections:** Moody's Manuals, 1928 to present. **Holdings:** 25,500 books and bound periodical volumes; 16 VF drawers of pamphlets. **Subscriptions:** 2050 journals and other serials; 40 newspapers. **Services:**

Interlibrary loans; copying; library open to SLA members and others by appointment through their library. **Computerized Information Services:** New York Times Information Service. **Staff:** Mary DePasquale, Ref.Libn.; Lucia Hsieh, Cat.

★8366★
MORGAN (J. Harris) LAW OFFICE - LAW LIBRARY (Law)
Box 556
Greenville, TX 75401
Phone: (214) 455-3183
Almarine Morgan, Libn.
Staff: Prof 1. **Subjects:** Law. **Holdings:** 2675 books; 130 bound periodical volumes; 1100 pamphlets (cataloged); 450 cassettes; 25 boxes of unbound reports, clippings and manuscripts. **Subscriptions:** 60 journals and other serials. **Services:** Interlibrary loans; copying; library open to local attorneys.

★8367★
MORGAN, LEWIS & BOCKIUS - LIBRARY (Law)
1800 M St., N.W.
Washington, DC 20036
Phone: (202) 872-7691
Victoria M. Ward, Law Libn.
Staff: Prof 4; Other 6. **Subjects:** Law. **Holdings:** 20,000 volumes. **Services:** Interlibrary loans; library open to outside researchers by appointment. **Computerized Information Services:** LEXIS, New York Times Information Service.

★8368★
MORGAN, LEWIS & BOCKIUS - LIBRARY (Law)
9 W. 57th St.
New York, NY 10019
Phone: (212) 980-4562
Janice E. Henderson, Libn.
Staff: Prof 1; Other 2. **Subjects:** Law - corporate, labor, tax. **Holdings:** 12,000 books; corporate file. **Subscriptions:** 65 journals and other serials. **Services:** Interlibrary loans; library open to members of the Law Library Association of Greater New York. **Computerized Information Services:** LEXIS.

★8369★
MORGAN, LEWIS & BOCKIUS - LIBRARY (Law)
123 S. Broad St.
Philadelphia, PA 19109
Phone: (215) 491-9633
Linda C. Roach, Libn.
Staff: Prof 4; Other 7. **Subjects:** Law. **Holdings:** 30,000 volumes. **Services:** Interlibrary loans; copying; library open to public. **Computerized Information Services:** DIALOG, New York Times Information Service, IN/FORM Data Services, Dow Jones News Retrieval, LEXIS, WESTLAW. **Publications:** Monthly Library Bulletin, monthly - for internal distribution only. **Special Indexes:** Index to memos, opinion letters and briefs. **Staff:** Ellen Silverstein, Asst.Libn.; Judith Hill, Asst.Libn.; B. Beardwood, Asst.Libn.

MORGAN (Pierpont) LIBRARY
See: Pierpont Morgan Library

★8370★
MORGAN STANLEY & COMPANY, INC. - LIBRARY (Bus-Fin)
1251 Ave. of the Americas
New York, NY 10020
Phone: (212) 974-4369
Sarah C. Jones, Dir., Lib.Serv.
Founded: 1935. **Staff:** Prof 17; Other 17. **Subjects:** Investment banking, capital markets. **Holdings:** 7200 volumes; 1.1 million microfiche of corporate disclosure; 2000 reels of microfilm of business and financial periodicals. **Subscriptions:** 500 journals and other serials. **Services:** Interlibrary loans; library not open to public. **Computerized Information Services:** DIALOG, SDC, New York Times Information Service, Dow Jones News Retrieval, Dun & Bradstreet, Inc., ABI/Inform, NEXIS, Computer Directions Advisors, Inc., Finsbury Data Services Ltd. **Staff:** Barbara Ormerod, Res./Data Mgt.Mgr.; Sandra Bonner, Tech.Serv.Mgr.; John Grundman, Rec.Mgr.

MORGAN (William E.) LIBRARY
See: Colorado State University - William E. Morgan Library

MORGANTOWN ENERGY TECHNOLOGY CENTER
See: U.S. Dept. of Energy

★8371★
MORIKAMI MUSEUM OF JAPANESE CULTURE - DONALD B. GORDON MEMORIAL LIBRARY (Area-Ethnic)
4000 Morikami Park Rd.
Delray Beach, FL 33446
Phone: (305) 495-0233
Larry Rosensweig, Cur.
Staff: 1. **Subjects:** Japan - art, culture; Japanese-American history. **Holdings:** 800 books; 100 bound periodical volumes; 12 video cassettes. **Subscriptions:** 12 journals and other serials. **Services:** Library open to public by appointment. **Staff:** Tobie Heller, Libn.

MORINI MEMORIAL COLLECTION
See: Order of Servants of Mary - Eastern Province Library

MORISSET LIBRARY
See: University of Ottawa

★8372★
MORITZ COMMUNITY HOSPITAL - DEAN PIEROSE MEMORIAL HEALTH SCIENCES LIBRARY (Med)†
Box 86   Phone: (208) 622-3323
Sun Valley, ID 83353   Margaret McNamara, Libn.
Subjects: Orthopedics, emergency medicine, general surgery and medicine, allied health professions. **Holdings:** 200 books; 800 bound periodical volumes; 24 pamphlets. **Subscriptions:** 35 journals and other serials. **Services:** Interlibrary loans; copying; SDI; library open to public on request. **Computerized Information Services:** DIALOG, MEDLINE; computerized cataloging (through Idaho's Health Information Retrieval Center). **Networks/Consortia:** Member of Ida-Heal-Net; Southeast Idaho Health Information Consortium.

MOROFSKY (Walter F.) MEMORIAL LIBRARY
See: Michigan State University - W.K. Kellogg Biological Station - Walter F. Morofsky Memorial Library

MORRILL (Ashley Baker) LIBRARY
See: Lawrence Hospital - Ashley Baker Morrill Library

MORRILL BIOLOGICAL & GEOLOGICAL SCIENCES LIBRARY
See: University of Massachusetts, Amherst

★8373★
MORRIS ANIMAL FOUNDATION - LIBRARY (Med)
45 Inverness Dr., E.   Phone: (303) 779-8867
Englewood, CO 80123   Dorothy Biggs, Libn.
Founded: 1978. **Subjects:** Veterinary medicine, zoo medicine. **Special Collections:** MAF Fellows Reports (400 reports of foundation-sponsored research on the health of companion animals); Sam Sheer Cat Collection (300 books and pamphlets). **Holdings:** 350 books. **Subscriptions:** 75 journals and other serials; 5 newspapers. **Services:** Interlibrary loans; copying; library open to public by special arrangement.

MORRIS ARBORETUM LIBRARY
See: University of Pennsylvania

MORRIS (Arthur J.) LAW LIBRARY
See: University of Virginia - Arthur J. Morris Law Library

★8374★
MORRIS CERULLO WORLD EVANGELISM, INC. - SCHOOL OF MINISTRY LIBRARY
Box 700
San Diego, CA 92101
Defunct

★8375★
MORRIS COUNTY FREE LIBRARY - NEW JERSEY ROOM (Hist)
30 East Hanover Ave.   Phone: (201) 285-6130
Whippany, NJ 07981   Evelyn L. Klingler, Ref.Libn.
Staff: Prof 1. **Subjects:** State and local history, genealogy. **Special Collections:** Master Plans and Ordinances for Morris County Municipalities; Early American Imprints, 1639-1800; manuscript collection of Morristown National Historical Park (69 reels of microfilm); New Jersey maps - historical and current; New Jersey Federal Census Schedules, 1830-1900 (microfilm). **Holdings:** 4000 books; 90 bound periodical volumes; 16 VF drawers; 300 reels of microfilm. **Subscriptions:** 30 journals and other serials. **Services:** Copying; library open to public. **Computerized Information Services:** Computerized cataloging and circulation. **Networks/Consortia:** Member of OCLC. **Publications:** Acquisitions Lists; The History of the Public Monuments and Sculpture of Morris County, New Jersey; The Public Monuments and Sculpture of Morristown, New Jersey. **Staff:** Linda Ott, Hd., Ref.Dept.

★8376★
MORRIS COUNTY HISTORICAL SOCIETY - VICTORIAN RESOURCE LIBRARY (Hist)
68 Morris Ave.   Phone: (201) 267-3465
Morristown, NJ 07960   J.H. Watson, Dir.
Founded: 1979. **Subjects:** Social and cultural history of the Victorian-Edwardian periods, especially local. **Special Collections:** Hone-Leonard-Weis Collection of 19th and early 20th century children's books and related

materials (200 volumes). **Holdings:** 1200 books; 130 bound periodical volumes; 20 boxes of manuscripts; 900 photographs. **Subscriptions:** 15 journals and other serials. **Services:** Library open to public by appointment.

★8377★
MORRIS COUNTY LAW LIBRARY (Law)
Morris County Court House
Washington St.   Phone: (201) 285-6497
Morristown, NJ 07960   Karen B. Brunner, Law Libn.
Staff: Prof 1; Other 1. **Subjects:** Law. **Special Collections:** Pilch Library (a four-generation collection of the Henry Pilch family in the practice of law). **Holdings:** 20,000 books; 2450 volumes on microfiche. **Subscriptions:** 26 journals and other serials. **Services:** Interlibrary loans; copying; library open to Morris County residents, as well as to lawyers, law students and pro se litigants. **Special Indexes:** Index by subject and case name to all current decisions by New Jersey courts (card).

MORRIS (Hugh M.) LIBRARY
See: University of Delaware, Newark - Hugh M. Morris Library

MORRIS LIBRARY
See: Southern Illinois University, Carbondale

★8378★
MORRIS MUSEUM OF ARTS AND SCIENCE - REFERENCE LIBRARY (Art; Sci-Tech)
Morristown, NJ 07960   Mrs. James C. Pitney
Staff: 1. **Subjects:** Fine and decorative arts, earth sciences, astronomy. **Holdings:** 2200 books; 1500 art slides. **Subscriptions:** 12 journals and other serials. **Services:** Library not open to public.

★8379★
MORRIS (Robert) ASSOCIATES - LIBRARY (Bus-Fin)
1616 Philadelphia Natl. Bank Bldg.   Phone: (215) 665-2850
Philadelphia, PA 19107   Susan M. Kelsay, Asst.Dir.
Staff: Prof 1. **Subjects:** Lending/credit, finance, economics, banking, industry analyses. **Holdings:** 500 books; 25 periodical volumes. **Subscriptions:** 53 journals and other serials. **Services:** Interlibrary loans; library not open to public.

MORRIS (William) LIBRARY ON FORGERY OF WORKS OF ART
See: University of Virginia - Fiske Kimball Fine Arts Library

MORRISON COUNTY HISTORICAL SOCIETY - CHARLES A. WEYERHAEUSER MEMORIAL MUSEUM
See: Weyerhaeuser (Charles A.) Memorial Museum

★8380★
MORRISON AND FOERSTER - BRANCH LAW LIBRARY (Law)
1920 N St., N.W., Suite 800   Phone: (202) 466-6060
Washington, DC 20036   Jane Amon, Libn.
Founded: 1979. **Staff:** Prof 1; Other 1. **Subjects:** Law - American, Californian, energy, tax, business and corporate; banking. **Holdings:** 3012 books and bound periodical volumes. **Subscriptions:** 35 journals and other serials; 7 newspapers. **Services:** Interlibrary loans; library not open to public. **Computerized Information Services:** LEXIS. **Remarks:** The firm's main law library is located in San Francisco. **Staff:** Gina Rabai Clair, Leg.Libn.

★8381★
MORRISON & FOERSTER - LAW LIBRARY (Law)†
One Market Plaza
Spear St. Tower   Phone: (415) 777-6000
San Francisco, CA 94105   Carl Whitaker, Law Libn.
Founded: 1925. **Staff:** Prof 1; Other 4. **Subjects:** Law. **Holdings:** 50,000 volumes. **Services:** Interlibrary loans; library not open to public. **Computerized Information Services:** DIALOG, LEXIS, WESTLAW, New York Times Information Service. **Networks/Consortia:** Member of RLG. **Staff:** Teresa Oppedal, Assoc. Law Libn.

★8382★
MORRISON & FOERSTER - LIBRARY (Law)
601 W. 5th St., 5th Fl.   Phone: (213) 626-3800
Los Angeles, CA 90017   Karen A. Mayers, Libn.
Founded: 1975. **Staff:** 1. **Subjects:** Law - banking, corporate, state and federal, tax, real estate. **Holdings:** 7550 books; 500 bound periodical volumes. **Subscriptions:** 60 journals and other serials; 10 newspapers. **Services:** Interlibrary loans; copying; SDI; library open to public by appointment; 24 hour loan. **Computerized Information Services:** LEXIS.

★8383★

MORRISON-KNUDSEN CO., INC. - INFORMATION RESEARCH CENTER (Bus-Fin)

Box 7808
Boise, ID 83729

Phone: (206) 386-7039
John Tribby, Supv.

Founded: 1975. **Staff:** Prof 2; Other 1. **Subjects:** Corporate reports, construction management, business. **Holdings:** Figures not available. **Services:** Center not open to public. **Computerized Information Services:** DIALOG, SDC, Dow Jones News Retrieval, BRS. **Publications:** Information & Search Service News, irregular - for internal distribution only. **Formerly:** Its Records and Micrographics Center. **Staff:** ; Carla Brunn, Search Coord.; Yung Harbison, Search Coord.

★8384★

MORRISTOWN JEWISH COMMUNITY CENTER - THE LIBRARY (Area-Ethnic)

177 Speedwell Ave.
Morristown, NJ 07960

Phone: (201) 538-9292
Frances Tillinger, Libn.

Founded: 1967. **Staff:** Prof 1; Other 3. **Subjects:** Judaica, Israel, Jewish art, religious studies, history, languages. **Holdings:** 5900 books; 420 bound periodical volumes; 50 pamphlets; 15 documents. **Subscriptions:** 10 journals and other serials. **Services:** Interlibrary loans; library open to public for reference use only.

★8385★

MORRISTOWN MEMORIAL HOSPITAL - LATHROPE HEALTH SCIENCES LIBRARY (Med)

100 Madison Ave., Rm. JB-80
Morristown, NJ 07960

Phone: (201) 540-5657
JoAnne M. Searle, Dir.

Staff: Prof 1; Other 2. **Subjects:** Medicine, dentistry, nursing. **Special Collections:** Consumer health. **Holdings:** 2593 books; 4611 bound periodical volumes; 55 slide/cassette sets; 127 video cassettes. **Subscriptions:** 420 journals and other serials. **Services:** Interlibrary loans; copying; library open to public for reference use only. **Computerized Information Services:** DIALOG, NLM. **Networks/Consortia:** Member of Medical Resources Consortium of Central New Jersey (MEDCORE); Central Jersey Health Science Libraries Association; Cosmopolitan Biomedical Library Consortium (CBLC).

MORRISTOWN NATIONAL HISTORICAL PARK
See: U.S. Natl. Park Service

MORROW (E.O.) LIBRARY
See: Mercy School of Nursing - E.O. Morrow Library

MORROW (James E.) LIBRARY
See: Marshall University - James E. Morrow Library

MORROW (Marjorie Gertrude) LIBRARY
See: Iowa Methodist School of Nursing - Marjorie Gertrude Morrow Library

MORSE (Leonard) HOSPITAL
See: Leonard Morse Hospital

MORSE MUSIC LIBRARY
See: Harvard University - Radcliffe College

★8386★

MORSE SCHOOL OF BUSINESS - LIBRARY (Bus-Fin)

275 Asylum St.
Hartford, CT 06103

Phone: (203) 522-2261
Joanne Rees Kaczor, Libn.

Founded: 1968. **Staff:** Prof 1. **Subjects:** Management, accounting, economics, fashion merchandising, office procedures, data processing. **Holdings:** 3000 books; 4 VF drawers of pamphlets. **Subscriptions:** 38 journals and other serials. **Services:** Library not open to public.

MORSE-SLANGER LIBRARY
See: Boston City Hospital - Nursing

★8387★

MORTGAGE BANKERS ASSOCIATION OF AMERICA - LIBRARY (Bus-Fin)

1125 15th St., N.W.
Washington, DC 20005

Phone: (202) 861-6580
Timothy S. Wolf, Libn.

Staff: Prof 1; Other 1. **Subjects:** Mortgage finance, investment, housing, real estate, statistics. **Holdings:** 6000 books. **Subscriptions:** 250 journals and other serials; 6 newspapers. **Services:** Interlibrary loans (limited); library open to public by appointment, for reference use only. **Publications:** Subject bibliographies.

MORTGAGE AND HOUSING CORPORATION
See: Canada - Mortgage and Housing Corporation

★8388★

MORTON ARBORETUM - STERLING MORTON LIBRARY (Sci-Tech)

Lisle, IL 60532

Phone: (312) 968-0074
Ian MacPhail, Libn.

Founded: 1922. **Staff:** Prof 3; Other 2. **Subjects:** Botany, horticulture, dendrology, arboriculture, landscape architecture, natural history, ecology and the environment. **Special Collections:** Rare books in botany, horticulture and landscape architecture; botanical prints and drawings; Jens Jensen archive. **Holdings:** 22,000 books and bound periodical volumes; 20 VF drawers of nursery and seed catalogs; 1500 pamphlets. **Subscriptions:** 500 journals and other serials. **Services:** Interlibrary loans; copying; library open to public. **Computerized Information Services:** DIALOG. **Networks/Consortia:** Member of Metropolitan Chicago Library Assembly. **Staff:** Peter Wang, Cat.; Douglas Ritchey, Ref.Libn.

MORTON COLLECTANEA
See: University of Miami

★8389★

MORTON-NORWICH PRODUCTS, INC. - LIBRARY (Food-Bev)

110 N. Wacker Dr.
Chicago, IL 60606

Phone: (312) 621-5244
Mary Beth Van Cura, Libn.

Staff: 1. **Subjects:** Salt and its uses. **Special Collections:** Historical archives of the Morton Salt Company. **Holdings:** 3000 books; 300 bound periodical volumes. **Subscriptions:** 920 journals and other serials. **Services:** Interlibrary loans; library open to public with restrictions.

MORTON-NORWICH PRODUCTS, INC. - NORWICH-EATON
See: Norwich-Eaton

MORTON-NORWICH PRODUCTS, INC. - NORWICH PHARMACAL COMPANY
See: Norwich-Eaton Pharmaceuticals, Inc.

★8390★

MORTON-NORWICH PRODUCTS, INC. - WOODSTOCK RESEARCH INFORMATION CENTER (Sci-Tech)

1275 Lake Ave.
Woodstock, IL 60098

Phone: (815) 338-1800
Valentina M. Woodruff, Info.Sci.

Founded: 1954. **Staff:** Prof 1; Other 1. **Subjects:** Chemistry - inorganic, organic, polymer. **Holdings:** 1000 books; 2200 bound periodical volumes; 1000 pamphlets (cataloged); 3 drawers of pamphlets; 150 reels of microfilm. **Subscriptions:** 400 journals and other serials. **Services:** Library open to outside users with an Infopass. **Computerized Information Services:** DIALOG, SDC, NIH-EPA Chemical Information System. **Networks/Consortia:** Member of Northern Illinois Library System.

MORTON (Sterling) LIBRARY
See: Morton Arboretum - Sterling Morton Library

MOSHER (Ina) HEALTH SCIENCES LIBRARY
See: Newport Hospital - Ina Mosher Health Sciences Library

MOSHER LIBRARY
See: Dallas Theological Seminary

★8391★

MOSS ARCHIVES (Hist)

Box 336
Sea Bright, NJ 07760

Phone: (201) 842-0336
George H. Moss, Jr.

Subjects: Monmouth County and New Jersey history. **Holdings:** 5000 glass negatives; 1000 photographs; 4000 other items including pictures, maps, logbooks, ledgers and letters. **Services:** Archives open to public with restrictions. **Remarks:** The archives are located at 39 Rumson Rd., Rumson, NJ.

MOSS LANDING MARINE LABORATORIES
See: California State University and Colleges

★8392★

MOTE MARINE LABORATORY - DAVIS LIBRARY (Sci-Tech)

1600 City Island Pk.
Sarasota, FL 33577

Phone: (813) 388-4441
Mary A. Parks, Libn.

Founded: 1978. **Staff:** Prof 1. **Subjects:** Marine biology, estuarine ecology. **Holdings:** 2000 books; 725 bound periodical volumes; 15,000 reprints (cataloged). **Subscriptions:** 178 journals and other serials. **Services:** Interlibrary loans; copying; library open to public by appointment.

Computerized Information Services: DIALOG. Networks/Consortia: Member of Florida Library Information Network (FLIN). Publications: Collected Papers of Mote Marine Laboratory, biennial; Contributions from Mote Marine Laboratory, irregular; MML Newsletter, quarterly - all distributed to marine research centers internationally.

MOTHER DOLORES MEMORIAL LIBRARY
See: Holy Family College

MOTHER MACARIA HEALTH SCIENCE LIBRARY
See: St. Francis Medical Center

★8393★
MOTION PICTURE ASSOCIATION OF AMERICA - LIBRARY (Rec)
522 Fifth Ave.   Phone: (212) 840-6161
New York, NY 10036   Robert A. Franklin, Ph.D., Dir. of Res.
Founded: 1946. Staff: Prof 1; Other 2. Subjects: Theatrical motion pictures - history, finance, censorship, content. Holdings: 3000 volumes. Subscriptions: 20 journals and other serials. Services: Library available to qualified persons for consultation by mail or telephone.

★8394★
MOTION PICTURE SERVICES (Aud-Vis)
Box 252   Phone: (201) 992-8194
Livingston, NJ 07039   Murray Mankowitz, Dir.
Founded: 1960. Staff: Prof 2; Other 2. Subjects: Health, science, safety education, human relations, travel, driver education. Special Collections: Steel construction. Holdings: 650 16mm films; film brochures; video cassettes. Services: Open to schools, institutions, industry, community groups, churches, adult groups, clubs. Films on health and science are free and open for distribution throughout the United States. Other subjects are open for distribution only in the State of New Jersey. Staff: Gloria Mankowitz, Assoc.Dir.

★8395★
MOTOR BUS SOCIETY, INC. - LIBRARY (Trans; Hist)
Box 7058
Trenton, NJ 08628   Gerald L. Squier, Pres.
Subjects: Motor bus transportation history. Special Collections: Greyhound historical collection. Holdings: 2000 bound periodical volumes; 90,000 photographs; 500 catalogs and bus specifications. Subscriptions: 11 journals and other serials. Services: Library open to public by appointment. Publications: Motor Coach Age, monthly; Over the Road, hardcover book.

MOTOR VEHICLE EMISSION LABORATORY
See: Environmental Protection Agency

★8396★
MOTOR VEHICLE MANUFACTURERS ASSOCIATION (MVMA) - COMMUNICATIONS LIBRARY (Trans)
300 New Center Bldg.   Phone: (313) 872-4311
Detroit, MI 48202   Christina C. Kanabrodzki, Commun.Libn.
Founded: 1971. Staff: Prof 1. Subjects: Auto industry, transportation, safety, air pollution, energy. Special Collections: Automotive photograph collection. Holdings: 100 VF drawers of clippings. Subscriptions: 36 journals and other serials; 5 newspapers. Services: Copying; library open to public with restrictions.

★8397★
MOTOR VEHICLE MANUFACTURERS ASSOCIATION (MVMA) - PATENT RESEARCH LIBRARY (Sci-Tech)
320 New Center Bldg.   Phone: (313) 872-4311
Detroit, MI 48202   James A. Wren, Mgr.
Founded: 1919. Staff: Prof 3; Other 2. Subjects: Automotive patents; technology; automotive history. Special Collections: Patents specifically related to motor vehicle technology (one million); foreign and U.S. automotive sales brochures dating back to pre-1900s. Holdings: 13,000 bound periodical volumes; 1000 textbooks; manufacturers' brochures and instruction books. Subscriptions: 100 journals and other serials. Services: Copying; library open to public by special permission. Staff: Otto Merte, Sr.Res.Supv.

★8398★
MOTOR VEHICLE MANUFACTURERS ASSOCIATION (MVMA) - STATISTICS INFORMATION CENTER (Trans)
300 New Center Bldg.   Phone: (313) 872-4311
Detroit, MI 48202   Jacques J. Evers, Mgr.
Founded: 1965. Staff: 6. Subjects: Transportation. Holdings: National and international vehicle-related statistical materials.

★8399★
MOTOR VEHICLE MANUFACTURERS ASSOCIATION (MVMA) - TECHNICAL LIBRARY (Trans; Env-Cons)
300 New Center Bldg.   Phone: (313) 872-4311
Detroit, MI 48202   M. Neil Massong, Info.Assoc.
Founded: 1968. Staff: Prof 1. Subjects: Vehicle safety, air quality, fuel economy, alternative fuels, environment, emissions, energy, industrial relations, electromagnetic compatibility, trucks and buses, economics. Special Collections: All National Highway Traffic Safety Administration (NHTSA) safety docket material (microfiche). Holdings: 200 books; 12,000 reports, papers, government documents, proceedings. Subscriptions: 40 journals and other serials. Services: Interlibrary loans (limited); library open to public with restrictions. Computerized Information Services: DIALOG, SDC; computerized cataloging. Publications: Technical Library Acquisitions List, monthly - to members.

★8400★
MOTOROLA, INC. - COMMUNICATIONS SECTOR LIBRARY (Sci-Tech)
1301 E. Algonquin Rd.   Phone: (312) 576-5949
Schaumburg, IL 60196   Bonnie Hohhof, Mgr.
Founded: 1930. Staff: Prof 1; Other 2. Subjects: Electronics, mathematics, communications. Holdings: 6500 books; 825 bound periodical volumes. Subscriptions: 500 journals and other serials. Services: Interlibrary loans; copying; SDI; library open to public on request. Computerized Information Services: DIALOG, SDC; computerized cataloging. Networks/Consortia: Member of North Suburban Library System; Metropolitan Chicago Library Assembly. Publications: Monthly acquisition list; general brochure (unlimited distribution); Patents. Special Catalogs: Computerized book catalog. Special Indexes: Report index.

★8401★
MOTOROLA, INC. - GOVERNMENT ELECTRONICS DIVISION - TECHNICAL LIBRARY (Sci-Tech)
8201 E. McDowell Rd.   Phone: (602) 949-3471
Scottsdale, AZ 85252   A.J. Kordalewski, Mgr., Tech.Info.Ctr.
Founded: 1951. Staff: Prof 1; Other 6. Subjects: Communications, radar, navigation, control systems, digital systems, physics, electronics, space science, mathematics. Holdings: 4700 books; 120,000 technical reports (100,000 in microform). Subscriptions: 200 journals and other serials. Services: Interlibrary loans; copying; advanced information retrieval system; library not open to public. Computerized Information Services: DIALOG, SDC, DTIC. Staff: Ann Biermacher, Libn.

★8402★
MOTOROLA, INC. - INTEGRATED CIRCUITS DIVISION - TECHNICAL LIBRARY (Sci-Tech)
Box 20906   Phone: (602) 962-2157
Phoenix, AZ 85036   C. Denise Ashford, Sr.Libn. & Mgr.
Founded: 1973. Staff: Prof 3. Subjects: Physics, chemistry. Special Collections: Lockheed Bibliography Searches (125 bound volumes). Holdings: 10,000 books; 5000 bound periodical volumes. Subscriptions: 288 journals and other serials; 5 newspapers. Services: Interlibrary loans; copying; library open to public by appointment. Computerized Information Services: Online system. Remarks: The library is located at 2200 W. Broadway, Mesa, AZ 85202. Staff: Lois Woll, Libn.

★8403★
MOTOROLA, INC. - MOS INTEGRATED CIRCUITS GROUP - INFORMATION CENTER (Sci-Tech)
3501 Ed Bluestein Blvd.   Phone: (512) 928-6089
Austin, TX 78721   Jacqueline Baas Davis, Dir., Info.Serv.
Founded: 1980. Staff: Prof 1; Other 2. Subjects: Electronics, computer design, semiconductors, engineering. Holdings: 3000 books and bound periodical volumes. Subscriptions: 235 journals and other serials; 15 newspapers. Services: Interlibrary loans; copying; SDI; library open to public by appointment. Computerized Information Services: Online systems; computerized circulation. Networks/Consortia: Member of Motorola Information Services Facilities.

★8404★
MOTOROLA, INC. - PORTABLE PRODUCTS DIVISION - TECHNICAL LIBRARY (Sci-Tech)
8000 W. Sunrise Blvd.   Phone: (305) 475-5049
Fort Lauderdale, FL 33322   Mary Anne Foley, Tech.Libn.
Founded: 1971. Staff: Prof 1. Subjects: Electrotechnology, electrical and mechanical engineering, business. Holdings: 700 books; 200 bound periodical volumes; computer searches; company reports and patents. Subscriptions: 83 journals and other serials. Services: SDI; library not open to public. Formerly: Its Communication Products Division.

★8405★
MOTOROLA, INC. - SEMICONDUCTOR PRODUCTS SECTOR - TECHNICAL LIBRARY (Sci-Tech)
Box 2953   Phone: (602) 244-6065
Phoenix, AZ 85062   C. Denise Ashford, Sr.Libn. & Mgr.
Founded: 1958. **Staff:** Prof 1. **Subjects:** Semiconductors, fiber optics, photovoltaics, electronics, engineering, material science, computer programming, mathematics, business. **Holdings:** 5000 books; 3500 bound periodical volumes; 500 technical reports (cataloged). **Subscriptions:** 250 journals and other serials. **Services:** Interlibrary loans; copying; library not open to public. **Computerized Information Services:** DIALOG. **Publications:** Government Contract Reports, irregular - for internal distribution only; New Acquisitions, bimonthly - distributed internally and on request. **Special Indexes:** Coordinate index for reports (card); list of computer searches done in library. **Remarks:** Library is located at 5005 E. McDowell Rd., Phoenix, AZ 85036. **Staff:** Deirdre A. Irvine, Libn.

★8406★
MOTOROLA, INC. - SYSTEMS DIVISION - TECHNICAL LIBRARY (Sci-Tech)
2553 N. Edgington St.   Phone: (312) 451-1000
Franklin Park, IL 60131   Rose Marie Bowsher, Libn.
Founded: 1978. **Staff:** 1. **Subjects:** Quartz crystal design, vacuum technology. **Holdings:** 550 books; 1000 slides; 40 periodicals on microfiche. **Subscriptions:** 125 journals and other serials; 11 newspapers. **Services:** Interlibrary loans to other libraries considered on an individual basis; copying; library open to public with restrictions.

★8407★
MOTT (Charles Stewart) FOUNDATION - LIBRARY (Soc Sci)
Mott Foundation Bldg.   Phone: (313) 238-5651
Flint, MI 48502   Eve Brown, Rec.Mgt.Supv.
Founded: 1974. **Staff:** Prof 1; Other 2. **Subjects:** Community education, philanthropy. **Special Collections:** Historical documents of the Mott Foundation (50 VF drawers and microfilm). **Holdings:** 2000 books; 190 VF drawers of reference files, grant related material, and correspondence. **Subscriptions:** 100 journals and other serials; 48 newspapers. **Services:** Library not open to public. **Publications:** Acquisitions list - for internal distribution only. **Special Catalogs:** Microfilm index for historical documents.

★8408★
MOTT RESEARCH GROUP - LIBRARY (Soc Sci)
3220 Rittenhouse St., N.W.   Phone: (202) 363-3809
Washington, DC 20015   Dorothy Williams Mott, Libn./Cur.
Founded: 1954. **Staff:** Prof 2. **Subjects:** Transportation, political science, public administration, municipal and state government, journalism and public affairs, history, psychology, sociology, Western and Far Eastern literature, higher education, management sciences, law. **Special Collections:** Korean affairs since 1945 - original document collection (3793 items); public affairs reports and evaluation studies (932 items); children's books, mid-19th century to present (463 items). **Holdings:** 9425 books; 56 bound periodical volumes; 876 pamphlets; 15 VF drawers of miscellaneous pamphlets, reports and magazines (worldwide, especially Korea). **Subscriptions:** 16 journals and other serials; 7 newspapers. **Services:** Library not open to public. **Remarks:** Affiliated with Mott of Washington and Associates Research and Information Center.

MOULTON LIBRARY
See: Bangor Theological Seminary

★8409★
MOULTRIE COUNTY HISTORICAL & GENEALOGICAL SOCIETY - MOULTRIE COUNTY HERITAGE CENTER (Hist)
117 E. Harrison St.
Box MM   Phone: (217) 728-4085
Sullivan, IL 61951   Mary L. Storm, Libn.
Founded: 1974. **Staff:** 7. **Subjects:** Local history and genealogy. **Holdings:** 595 books; 4 VF drawers of family surname folders; 8 VF drawers of official county records; 35 reels of newspapers and census on microfilm. **Services:** Library open to public. **Publications:** Moultrie County Heritage, quarterly - to membership. **Special Indexes:** Obituaries (card); marriages (card); family record files.

MOUND CITY GROUP NATL. MONUMENT
See: U.S. Natl. Park Service

★8410★
MOUNT ALLISON UNIVERSITY - ALFRED WHITEHEAD MEMORIAL MUSIC LIBRARY (Mus)
                                         Phone: (506) 536-2040
Sackville, NB, Canada E0A 3C0   Gwendolyn Creelman
Founded: 1967. **Staff:** Prof 1; Other 2. **Subjects:** Music - theory, history, criticism, biography; musicology; music education. **Special Collections:** Twentieth century Canadian music scores and recordings. **Holdings:** 5800 books; 840 bound periodical volumes; 9200 scores (cataloged); 84 reels of microfilm (34 titles); 3287 microfiche (99 titles); 9 films; 5000 recordings (3500 titles); 450 tapes. **Subscriptions:** 110 journals and other serials. **Services:** Interlibrary loans; copying; SDI; library open to public. **Computerized Information Services:** Computerized cataloging and acquisitions (through main library). **Publications:** Canadian Music Scores & Recordings (holdings of Mount Allison libraries); Sources in Canadian Music, 2nd edition (bibliography) - available for purchase.

★8411★
MOUNT ALLISON UNIVERSITY - WINTHROP P. BELL COLLECTION OF ACADIANA (Area-Ethnic)
Ralph Pickard Bell Library   Phone: (506) 536-2040
Sackville, NB, Canada E0A 3C0   Margaret Fancy, Spec.Coll.Libn.
Subjects: Acadiana (historical material relating to Nova Scotia, New Brunswick, Prince Edward Island and Maine). **Holdings:** 5400 volumes; 800 slides. **Subscriptions:** 23 journals and other serials. **Services:** Copying; library open to public. **Computerized Information Services:** Computerized acquisitions (through main library). **Publications:** Catalogue of the Bell Collection of Acadiana, 1972 - free upon request.

★8412★
MOUNT AUBURN HOSPITAL - HEALTH SCIENCES LIBRARY (Med)
330 Mt. Auburn St.   Phone: (617) 492-3500
Cambridge, MA 02138   M. Cherie Haitz, Dir.
Staff: Prof 1; Other 2. **Subjects:** Medicine, nursing, pathology, administration, consumer health and allied health sciences. **Holdings:** 2000 books; 3000 bound periodical volumes; audiovisual material (cataloged); 4 VF drawers of pamphlets. **Subscriptions:** 270 journals and other serials; 3 newspapers. **Services:** Interlibrary loans; copying; orientations; SDI; library open to public for reference use only. **Computerized Information Services:** BRS, NLM; Paper Chase (internal database). **Networks/Consortia:** Member of Boston Biomedical Library Consortium; Community Health Information Network.

★8413★
MOUNT CARMEL LUTHERAN CHURCH - LIBRARY (Rel-Theol)†
8424 W. Center St.   Phone: (414) 771-1270
Milwaukee, WI 53222   Verna A. Weller, Libn.
Founded: 1947. **Staff:** 2. **Subjects:** Bible study, devotions, missions. **Holdings:** 4300 volumes; 2 VF drawers of clippings; 3000 mounted pictures; 3 films; 300 filmstrips; 145 recordings; 80 flannelgraphs; 76 costumes. **Subscriptions:** 10 journals and other serials. **Services:** Interlibrary loans; library open to other church groups.

★8414★
MOUNT CARMEL MEDICAL CENTER - MOTHER M. CONSTANTINE MEMORIAL LIBRARY (Med)
793 W. State St.   Phone: (614) 225-5214
Columbus, OH 43222   Pamela M. Elwell, Libn.
Staff: Prof 1; Other 6. **Subjects:** Medicine, nursing, allied health sciences, health administration. **Holdings:** 3000 books; 12,000 bound periodical volumes; kits, slides, audio cassettes (cataloged). **Subscriptions:** 300 journals and other serials. **Services:** Interlibrary loans; copying; SDI; library open to public for reference use only. **Computerized Information Services:** MEDLINE. **Networks/Consortia:** Member of OCLC; Central Ohio Hospital Consortium.

★8415★
MOUNT CARMEL MERCY HOSPITAL - MEDICAL LIBRARY (Med)
6071 W. Outer Dr.   Phone: (313) 927-7073
Detroit, MI 48235   Joan Luksik, Dir.
Founded: 1939. **Staff:** Prof 1; Other 3. **Subjects:** Medicine, surgery, obstetrics, gynecology, radiology, pathology, pediatrics, nursing. **Special Collections:** Ethel Wiener Memorial Collection on allergy and related subjects. **Holdings:** 5100 books; 6000 bound periodical volumes; 900 Audio-Digest tapes. **Subscriptions:** 375 journals and other serials. **Services:** Interlibrary loans; copying; SDI; library not open to public. **Computerized Information Services:** DIALOG, MEDLARS. **Networks/Consortia:** Member of Kentucky-Ohio-Michigan Regional Medical Library Network (KOMRML).

★8416★

MOUNT CARMEL SPIRITUAL CENTER - TOELLE MEMORIAL LIBRARY (Rel-Theol)†

Box 767   Phone: (416) 356-4113
Niagara Falls, NY 14302
Subjects: Theology, philosophy, history, biography, Carmelite Order. **Special Collections:** Carmelitana Collection. **Holdings:** 22,557 books; 300 bound periodical volumes; 100 documents. **Services:** Library not open to public. **Remarks:** A document depository for the Carmelite Institute of Rome, Italy. Library is located at Fallsview, Niagara Falls, ON.

★8417★

MOUNT CLEMENS GENERAL HOSPITAL - STUCK MEDICAL LIBRARY (Med)

1000 Harrington Blvd.   Phone: (313) 466-8147
Mt. Clemens, MI 48043   Lynne L. Coles, Med.Libn.
Founded: 1956. **Staff:** Prof 1. **Subjects:** Medicine, nursing. **Holdings:** 2000 books; 2000 bound periodical volumes; 1300 Audio-Digest tapes; 300 audio cassettes; 100 videotapes; 150 slide-tape sets; 4 VF drawers of pamphlets. **Subscriptions:** 120 journals and other serials. **Services:** Interlibrary loans; copying; library open to public for reference use only. **Networks/Consortia:** Member of Metropolitan Detroit Medical Library Group.

★8418★

MOUNT CUBA ASTRONOMICAL OBSERVATORY - LAMBERT L. JACKSON MEMORIAL LIBRARY (Sci-Tech)

Greenville, Box 3915   Phone: (302) 654-6407
Wilmington, DE 19807   Leo G. Glasser, Dir.
Founded: 1963. **Staff:** Prof 1; Other 1. **Subjects:** Observational astronomy, astrophysics. **Special Collections:** National Geographic and Mt. Palomar Sky Survey, White Oak Zones; Lick Observatory Sky Atlas. **Holdings:** 850 books; 707 bound periodical volumes; 1000 other cataloged items; reprints and pamphlets. **Subscriptions:** 40 journals and other serials. **Services:** Library open to public by special arrangements. **Staff:** L.E. Wade, Adm.

★8419★

MOUNT DESERT ISLAND BIOLOGICAL LABORATORY - LIBRARY (Sci-Tech)

                                          Phone: (207) 288-3605
Salsbury Cove, ME 04672
Subjects: Biology. **Holdings:** Figures not available for books; reprint collection of laboratory research. **Services:** Interlibrary loans; copying; library open to public for reference use only. **Publications:** Bulletin, annual - to members and academic libraries.

★8420★

MOUNT DIABLO UNIFIED SCHOOL DISTRICT - TEACHERS' PROFESSIONAL LIBRARY

Willow Creek Center
1026 Mohr Lane
Concord, CA 94518
Founded: 1960. **Subjects:** Professional materials for teachers. **Holdings:** 9299 books. **Remarks:** Presently inactive.

★8421★

MOUNT OLIVE COLLEGE - FREE WILL BAPTIST HISTORICAL COLLECTION (Hist)

Moye Library   Phone: (919) 658-2502
Mount Olive, NC 28365   Gary Fenton Barefoot, Libn.
Staff: Prof 2; Other 1. **Subjects:** Free Will Baptist history. **Holdings:** 750 books; 1250 bound periodical volumes; 47 manuscript collections; 2000 clippings and brochures; 500 photographs; 100 reels of microfilm, audiotapes, films. **Subscriptions:** 10 journals and other serials. **Services:** Copying; library open to public. **Special Indexes:** Card indexes to manuscripts, clippings, photographs, printed obituaries; Index to Free Will Baptist (card). **Staff:** Pamela R. Wood, Asst.Libn.

★8422★

MOUNT OLIVET LUTHERAN CHURCH - LIBRARY (Rel-Theol)

5025 Knox Ave., S.   Phone: (612) 926-7651
Minneapolis, MN 55419   Bonnie Morris, Lib.Adm.
Founded: 1950. **Staff:** Prof 1; Other 70. **Subjects:** Religion, theology and doctrine, Bible, Lutheran Church history, psychology (family life), children's and juvenile literature. **Special Collections:** Les Rouba wildlife paintings (30). **Holdings:** 9000 books; 250 pictures (cataloged); 500 cassette tapes (cataloged); clipping file of 125 subjects; 10 boxes of church archives. **Subscriptions:** 30 journals and other serials. **Services:** Copying; library open to public.

★8423★

MOUNT PLEASANT MENTAL HEALTH INSTITUTE - PROFESSIONAL LIBRARY (Med)

1200 E. Washington St.   Phone: (319) 385-7231
Mount Pleasant, IA 52641   James Sommerville, Libn.
Founded: 1963. **Staff:** Prof 1. **Subjects:** Psychiatry, nursing, psychology, social work, pharmacology, nutrition, medicine. **Holdings:** 2000 books; 800 periodical volumes. **Subscriptions:** 75 professional journals. **Services:** Interlibrary loans; copying; library open to public.

MOUNT PROSPECT PUBLIC LIBRARY - NORTHWEST MUNICIPAL CONFERENCE
See: Northwest Municipal Conference

★8424★

MOUNT ST. ALPHONSUS THEOLOGICAL SEMINARY - LIBRARY (Rel-Theol)†

                                          Phone: (914) 384-6550
Esopus, NY 12429   Joan W. Durand, Libn.
Staff: Prof 1; Other 3. **Subjects:** Theology, ecclesiastical history, church law, liturgy, sacred scripture. **Special Collections:** Redemptoristica (3000 volumes); Wuenschel Collection of Holy Shroud (800 volumes). **Holdings:** 74,000 books; 10,410 bound periodical volumes; 2900 units of micromaterials; 300 tapes of audio recordings; 30 units of slides. **Subscriptions:** 600 journals and other serials; 10 newspapers. **Services:** Interlibrary loans; copying; library open to public. **Networks/Consortia:** Member of Southeastern New York Library Resources Council (SENYLRC); New York Area Theological Library Association. **Publications:** Handbook - distributed to all students. **Staff:** Ceil Perry, ILL Libn.

MOUNT ST. MARY RESEARCH CENTER
See: Sisters of St. Mary of Namur

★8425★

MOUNT ST. MARY'S COLLEGE - NEWMAN SEMINAR (Rel-Theol)

Coe Memorial Library
12001 Chalon Rd.   Phone: (213) 476-2237
Los Angeles, CA 90049   Erika Condon, Lib.Dir.
Founded: 1960. **Staff:** Prof 1. **Subjects:** Cardinal Newman and the Oxford Movement. **Holdings:** 269 books. **Services:** Interlibrary loans; copying; library open to public.

★8426★

MOUNT ST. MARY'S SEMINARY OF THE WEST - EUGENE H. MALY MEMORIAL LIBRARY (Rel-Theol)

6616 Beechmont Ave.   Phone: (513) 231-1516
Cincinnati, OH 45230   Sr. Deborah Harmeling, O.S.B., Hd.Libn.
Founded: 1829. **Staff:** Prof 1; Other 4. **Subjects:** Biblical studies, sacred theology, pastoral theology, ecclesiastical history, dogmatic theology, ethics. **Special Collections:** Rare books and Bibles pertaining to history of the Archdiocese of Cincinnati (archdiocesan archives); American Church History. **Holdings:** 46,306 books; 10,295 bound periodical volumes; 407 rare books (cataloged); 2500 cassettes and tapes; 1400 theses; 50 manuscripts; 1100 microforms. **Subscriptions:** 350 journals and other serials; 16 newspapers. **Services:** Interlibrary loans; copying; library is open with restrictions to priests and religious of the archdiocese and members of consortia institutions. **Computerized Information Services:** Computerized cataloging. **Networks/Consortia:** Member of OCLC; Greater Cincinnati Library Consortium (GCLC); Consortium for Higher Education Religion Studies. **Remarks:** Maintained by Athenaeum of Ohio - Archdiocese of Cincinnati. **Staff:** Bro. Timothy Miskowski, Cat./AV Libn.; James Hurtt, Circ./ILL Libn.; Ann C. Jansen, Per.Libn.

★8427★

MOUNT SAINT VINCENT UNIVERSITY - LIBRARY (Bus-Fin; Educ)

166 Bedford Hwy.   Phone: (902) 443-4450
Halifax, NS, Canada B3M 2J6   Mr. L. Bianchini, Hd.Libn.
Founded: 1925. **Staff:** Prof 4; Other 16. **Subjects:** Home economics, business administration, education, English literature (19th and early 20th century), religious studies, children's literature. **Special Collections:** MacDonald Collection (literature); Women's Studies (16,000 microfiche; 600 reels of microfilm). **Holdings:** 110,000 books; 22,000 bound periodical volumes. **Subscriptions:** 872 journals and other serials; 22 newspapers. **Services:** Interlibrary loans; copying; library open to public for reference use only. **Computerized Information Services:** SDC; computerized cataloging. **Special Catalogs:** Periodical Holdings, updated yearly (book). **Staff:** Peter Glenister, Cat.; Terry Paris, Circ. & Ref.; Kathleen Currie, Acq. & Spec. Coll.

★8428★

MOUNT SINAI HOSPITAL - HEALTH SCIENCES LIBRARY (Med)†
500 Blue Hills Ave. Phone: (203) 242-4431
Hartford, CT 06112 Nancy B. Cohen, Dir.
Founded: 1948. **Subjects:** Clinical medicine, nursing and allied health sciences. **Holdings:** 1100 books; 2000 bound periodical volumes; AV collection; microfilm. **Subscriptions:** 216 journals and other serials. **Services:** Interlibrary loans; copying; library open to public by appointment. **Networks/ Consortia:** Member of Connecticut Association of Health Science Libraries (CAHSL); Capitol Area Health Consortium Libraries.

★8429★

MOUNT SINAI HOSPITAL MEDICAL CENTER - LEWISOHN MEMORIAL LIBRARY (Med)
California Ave. at 15th St. Phone: (312) 542-2056
Chicago, IL 60608 Emily Sobkowiak, Med.Libn.
Founded: 1942. **Subjects:** Medicine. **Holdings:** 8500 books; 6800 bound periodical volumes. **Subscriptions:** 300 journals and other serials. **Services:** Interlibrary loans; copying; library not open to public.

★8430★

MOUNT SINAI HOSPITAL - MEDICAL LIBRARY (Med)
2215 Park Ave. Phone: (612) 871-3700
Minneapolis, MN 55404 Susan J. McIntyre, Med.Libn.
Founded: 1951. **Staff:** Prof 1; Other 1. **Subjects:** Medicine, nursing, allied health sciences. **Holdings:** 5000 books; 3700 bound periodical volumes; 90 cassette tape/slide learning programs. **Subscriptions:** 300 journals and other serials. **Services:** Interlibrary loans; copying; library open to hospital medical staff and personnel. **Computerized Information Services:** MEDLINE, BRS. **Networks/Consortia:** Member of Twin Cities Biomedical Consortium (TCBC).

★8431★

MOUNT SINAI HOSPITAL SERVICES - CITY HOSPITAL CENTER AT ELMHURST - MEDICAL LIBRARY (Med)
79-01 Broadway Phone: (212) 830-1538
Elmhurst, NY 11373 Stacey Saley, Chf.Med.Libn.
Staff: Prof 1; Other 4. **Subjects:** Basic sciences, health sciences. **Holdings:** 8000 books; 13,500 bound periodical volumes; pamphlets; AV materials. **Subscriptions:** 340 journals and other serials. **Services:** Interlibrary loans; copying; library open to public with restrictions. **Computerized Information Services:** Online systems. **Networks/Consortia:** Member of Medical Library Center of New York. **Publications:** Newsletter, bimonthly. **Staff:** Guillermo Rivas, Asst.Libn.

★8432★

MOUNT SINAI HOSPITAL - SIDNEY LISWOOD LIBRARY (Med)†
600 University Ave. Phone: (416) 596-4614
Toronto, ON, Canada M6S 4C6 Eleanor Hayes, Libn.
Staff: 3. **Subjects:** Medicine. **Holdings:** Figures not available. **Services:** Library open to public with restrictions.

★8433★

MOUNT SINAI MEDICAL CENTER OF CLEVELAND - GEORGE H. HAYS MEMORIAL LIBRARY (Med)
University Circle Phone: (216) 795-6000
Cleveland, OH 44106 Pamela Alderman, Chf.Med.Libn.
Founded: 1961. **Staff:** Prof 1; Other 5. **Subjects:** Medicine, nursing, hospital administration, allied health sciences. **Special Collections:** Staff Reprint Collection; AV collection. **Holdings:** 3000 books; 2500 bound periodical volumes; 8 VF drawers of pamphlets. **Subscriptions:** 260 journals and other serials. **Services:** Interlibrary loans; copying; library open to institutions and allied health professionals. **Computerized Information Services:** MEDLINE. **Formerly:** Mount Sinai Hospital of Cleveland.

★8434★

MOUNT SINAI MEDICAL CENTER OF GREATER MIAMI - MEDICAL LIBRARY (Med)†
4300 Alton Rd. Phone: (305) 674-2840
Miami Beach, FL 33139 Isabel Ezquerra, Chf.Med.Libn.
Founded: 1950. **Staff:** Prof 2; Other 3. **Subjects:** Medicine, nursing, hospital administration, allied health sciences. **Holdings:** 9000 books; 9000 bound periodical volumes; 400 audiotape cassettes; 200 videotape cassettes; 3000 slides. **Subscriptions:** 450 journals and other serials. **Services:** Interlibrary loans; copying; library restricted to physicians, staff and students on affiliated programs. **Computerized Information Services:** NLM; computerized cataloging. **Networks/Consortia:** Member of Southeastern Regional Medical Library Program (SERMLP); Miami Health Sciences Library Consortium (MHSLC). **Publications:** Library/Audiovisual Services Book Catalog. **Staff:** Mildred Karukin, Assoc.Libn.

★8435★

MOUNT SINAI MEDICAL CENTER - MEDICAL LIBRARY (Med)
Box 342 Phone: (414) 289-8318
Milwaukee, WI 53201 Deborah A. Hall, Dir.
Founded: 1957. **Staff:** Prof 2. **Subjects:** Clinical medicine, surgery, obstetrics and gynecology. **Holdings:** 3000 books; 3110 bound periodical volumes; 250 audiotapes. **Subscriptions:** 360 journals and other serials. **Services:** Interlibrary loans; copying; current awareness; library open to public on request. **Computerized Information Services:** BRS, NLM. **Networks/ Consortia:** Member of Southeastern Wisconsin Health Science Libraries Consortium (SWHSL); Library Council of Metropolitan Milwaukee, Inc. (LCOMM). **Publications:** Acquisitions list; serials list, both annual. **Remarks:** Library is located at 950 N. 12th St., Milwaukee, WI 53233. **Staff:** Janice Curnes, Asst.Libn.

★8436★

MOUNT SINAI SCHOOL OF MEDICINE OF THE CITY UNIVERSITY OF NEW YORK - GUSTAVE L. & JANET W. LEVY LIBRARY (Med)
One Gustave L. Levy Pl. Phone: (212) 650-7793
New York, NY 10029 Jane S. Port, Dir.
Staff: Prof 11; Other 24. **Subjects:** Clinical medicine, nursing, basic sciences. **Holdings:** 32,000 books; 66,000 bound periodical volumes; 3300 AV programs. **Subscriptions:** 1775 journals and other serials. **Services:** Interlibrary loans; copying; SDI; library not open to public. **Computerized Information Services:** BRS, DIALOG, SDC, NLM; computerized cataloging and serials. **Networks/Consortia:** Member of Medical Library Center of New York (MLCNY); OCLC. **Publications:** Faculty Bibliography, annual - distributed to faculty and libraries, and available on request. **Staff:** Dorothy Hill, Hd., Acq; Robert Culp, ILL Libn.; Harriet Meiss, Res.Libn.; Doris Jaeger, Ser.Libn.; Janet Cowen, AV/CAI Libn.; James E. Raper, Jr., Tech.Serv.Libn.; Merril Schindler, Sys.Coord.

★8437★

MOUNT UNION COLLEGE - STURGEON MUSIC LIBRARY (Mus)
Cope Music Hall Phone: (216) 823-3206
Alliance, OH 44601 Becky C. Thomas, Music Libn.
Founded: 1964. **Staff:** Prof 1; Other 12. **Subjects:** Music history and theory, vocal methods, instrumental methods, music education, musical instruments, vocal music, instrumental music, American music. **Special Collections:** Collegium Musicum collection; hymnal collection. **Holdings:** 1000 books; 10,700 pieces of music and scores (cataloged); 4850 recordings; 300 pamphlets; 400 music publishers' catalogs; 300 college catalogs; 2300 recital tapes; complete works of Schumann, Liszt, and Mendelssohn on microfiche; complete works of Bach, Beethoven, Brahms, Chopin, Schubert, Mozart, Schuetz, Schoenberg and Hindemith (bound). **Subscriptions:** 55 journals and other serials. **Services:** Library open to public with restrictions. **Special Indexes:** Art Song Index (computer tape); index to poets of art songs.

★8438★

MOUNT VERNON HOSPITAL - LIBRARY AND INFORMATION SERVICES (Med)
12 N. Seventh Ave.
Mount Vernon, NY 10550 Mary L. Coan, Dir.
Staff: Prof 1; Other 1. **Subjects:** Health sciences, medicine, nursing. **Holdings:** 2815 books; 317 bound periodical volumes; 12 VF drawers; 656 AV programs. **Subscriptions:** 112 journals and other serials. **Services:** Interlibrary loans (limited to HILOW members); copying; SDI; library open to public with restrictions. **Computerized Information Services:** NLM. **Networks/Consortia:** Member of Health Information Libraries of Westchester and Lower Connecticut (HILOW).

★8439★

MOUNT VERNON LADIES' ASSOCIATION OF THE UNION - RESEARCH AND REFERENCE LIBRARY (Hist)
Phone: (703) 780-2000
Mount Vernon, VA 22121 Ellen McCallister, Libn.
Founded: 1858. **Staff:** Prof 2. **Subjects:** Domestic life of George and Martha Washington; history of Mount Vernon, 1674 to present; history of the Mount Vernon Ladies' Association of the Union. **Special Collections:** Manuscript collection; Washington eulogies; early views of Mount Vernon; Mansion Library (books owned by George Washington or duplicates). **Holdings:** 12,000 books; 400 bound periodical volumes; 350,000 other items. **Subscriptions:** 20 journals and other serials. **Services:** Copying; library open to public by appointment to qualified researchers. **Publications:** Annual Report. **Staff:** John Rhodehamel, Archv.

★8440★

MOUNT VERNON PLACE UNITED METHODIST CHURCH - DESSIE M. HALLETT LIBRARY (Rel-Theol)

900 Massachusetts Ave., N.W.
Washington, DC 20001
Phone: (202) 347-9620
Dessie M. Hallett, Libn.

Staff: 2. **Subjects:** Religion, psychology, family life, Bible, fiction, biography. **Special Collections:** Large print devotionals (12). **Holdings:** 1600 books; clippings, pamphlets. **Subscriptions:** 17 journals and other serials. **Services:** Library open to public. **Staff:** G. Ruth Wright, Chm., Lib.Comm.

★8441★

MOUNT WASHINGTON OBSERVATORY - LIBRARY (Sci-Tech)

Gorham, NH 03581
Phone: (603) 466-3388
Guy Gosselin, Dir.

Staff: Prof 4; Other 1. **Subjects:** Icing; atmospheric electricity; atmospheric physics; White Mountain history (science and fiction). **Holdings:** 200 books; 30 feet of bound and unbound scientific papers; guidebooks; hiking material. **Staff:** Hope Hamlin, Musm.Cur.

MOUNT WILSON & LAS CAMPANAS OBSERVATORIES - LIBRARY
See: Carnegie Institution of Washington

★8442★

MOUNT ZION HEBREW CONGREGATION - TEMPLE LIBRARY (Rel-Theol)

1300 Summit Ave.
St. Paul, MN 55105
Phone: (612) 698-3881
Janice Leichter, Libn.

Founded: 1928. **Staff:** Prof 2. **Subjects:** Jews - history, religion, literature, biography, philosophy; Israel. **Holdings:** 6000 books; 125 phonograph records; 30 cassette tapes. **Subscriptions:** 20 journals and other serials. **Services:** Interlibrary loans; copying; library open to public with restrictions. **Staff:** Donald Singerman, Cat.

★8443★

MOUNT ZION HOSPITAL AND MEDICAL CENTER - HARRIS M. FISHBON MEMORIAL LIBRARY (Med)

Box 7921
San Francisco, CA 94120
Phone: (415) 567-6600
Angela Green Wesling, Med.Libn.

Staff: Prof 1; Other 5. **Subjects:** Medicine, nursing and allied health sciences; hospital administration; history of medicine. **Special Collections:** History of Medicine (3000 volumes). **Holdings:** 7219 books; 24,500 bound periodical volumes; AV items (cataloged). **Subscriptions:** 485 journals and other serials. **Services:** Interlibrary loans; current awareness; library not open to public. **Computerized Information Services:** MEDLARS. **Networks/Consortia:** Member of San Francisco Biomedical Library Network.

★8444★

MOUNTAIN AREA HEALTH EDUCATION CENTER - HEALTH SCIENCES LIBRARY (Med)

501 Biltmore Ave.
Asheville, NC 28801
Phone: (704) 258-0881
Linda C. Butson, Health Sci.Libn.

Staff: Prof 2; Other 3. **Subjects:** Health sciences. **Holdings:** 3500 books; 8000 bound and unbound periodicals; 300 AV programs; slides; filmstrips. **Subscriptions:** 210 journals and other serials. **Services:** Interlibrary loans; copying; library open to public for reference use only. **Computerized Information Services:** NLM; computerized cataloging. **Networks/Consortia:** Member of Area Health Education Center of North Carolina; MEDLINE.

★8445★

MOUNTAIN BELL TELEPHONE COMPANY - LIBRARY (Sci-Tech)

1005 17th St., Rm. 180
Denver, CO 80202
Phone: (303) 624-4607
Ida M. Hooker, Libn.

Founded: 1953. **Staff:** Prof 1; Other 1. **Subjects:** Communications, management and economics, fiction, hobbies. **Holdings:** 8000 books; 500 bound periodical volumes; pamphlets; Bell Laboratory records; Bell technical journals; maps. **Subscriptions:** 84 journals and other serials. **Services:** Interlibrary loans; copying; library not open to public. **Staff:** Beverly Wheeler, Lib.Ck.

★8446★

MOUNTAIN STATES EMPLOYERS COUNCIL - INFORMATION CENTER (Bus-Fin)

1790 Logan St.
Denver, CO 80203
Phone: (303) 839-5177
Joy Sandberg, Info.Ctr.Mgr.

Staff: Prof 1; Other 1. **Subjects:** Labor law, personnel, management, business, industrial relations. **Holdings:** 10,000 volumes; newspaper clipping files. **Subscriptions:** 85 journals and other serials. **Services:** Copying (limited); library open to special students; library serves mainly member companies. **Computerized Information Services:** Computerized cataloging. **Publications:** New Acquisitions letter, monthly.

★8447★

MOUNTAIN STATES ENERGY, INC. - CDIF TECHNICAL LIBRARY (Sci-Tech)

Box 3767
Butte, MT 59702
Phone: (406) 494-7386
Marilyn Patrick, Lib.Ck.

Staff: 1. **Subjects:** Magnetohydrodynamics. **Holdings:** 1000 books; 100 bound periodical volumes; 2500 technical reports; 5000 manufacturing standards and specifications. **Subscriptions:** 33 journals and other serials. **Services:** Interlibrary loans; copying; library not open to public. **Computerized Information Services:** Online systems. **Networks/Consortia:** Member of Montana Information Network Exchange (MINE). **Remarks:** CDIF is an acronym for Component Development and Integration Facility.

MOUNTAIN STATES TUMOR INSTITUTE - HEALTH INFORMATION RETRIEVAL CENTER
See: St. Luke's Regional Medical Center - Medical Library

★8448★

MOUNTAIN VIEW BIBLE COLLEGE - LIBRARY (Rel-Theol)

Box 190
Didsbury, AB, Canada T0M 0W0
Phone: (403) 335-3337
A. Chris Beldan, Libn.

Staff: 3. **Subjects:** Bible, Christian education, missions, theology, church history. **Holdings:** 8250 books. **Subscriptions:** 85 journals and other serials. **Services:** Copying; library open to ministers and laymen.

★8449★

MOUNTAINSIDE HOSPITAL - SCHOOL OF NURSING LIBRARY (Med)

School of Nursing
Bay & Highland Aves.
Montclair, NJ 07042
Phone: (201) 746-6000
Ann Vreeland, Libn.

Staff: Prof 1; Other 2. **Subjects:** Nursing and allied subjects. **Special Collections:** History of nursing. **Holdings:** 3000 books; 98 bound periodical volumes. **Subscriptions:** 110 journals and other serials. **Services:** Interlibrary loans; library not open to public.

MOVIE MEMORABILIA STILLS
See: Memory Shop, Inc.

★8450★

MOVIE STAR NEWS - PHOTOGRAPH COLLECTION (Pict)

212 E. 14th St.
New York, NY 10003
Phone: (212) 777-5564
Paula Klaw, Pres.

Founded: 1937. **Staff:** Prof 2; Other 2. **Subjects:** Movie stars. **Special Collections:** Movie stills (1920-1981); pressbooks; movie magazines; lobby cards; movie posters; Damsels in Distress (Hollywood). **Holdings:** Ten million movie star photographs (1918-1981). **Services:** Open to public; photographs leased for reproduction and available for purchase by mail order.

MOYE LIBRARY
See: Mount Olive College

★8451★

MPR ASSOCIATES, INC. - LIBRARY (Sci-Tech)

1140 Connecticut Ave., N.W.
Washington, DC 20036
Phone: (202) 659-2320
Alice McNamara, Libn.

Founded: 1964. **Staff:** Prof 2; Other 1. **Subjects:** Engineering - nuclear, mechanical, marine, electrical. **Holdings:** 1000 books; 75,000 NRC/DOE microfiche and full-size reports; 2500 standards and codes; 4 sets of published abstracts and indexes; 2000 theses, pamphlets, conference papers and speeches. **Subscriptions:** 100 journals and other serials. **Services:** Interlibrary loans; copying; library not open to public. **Computerized Information Services:** DIALOG, SDC. **Publications:** Library Bulletin, monthly. **Staff:** Maryrita Guay, Libn.

MRI
See: Midwest Research Institute

MSA RESEARCH CORPORATION
See: Mine Safety Appliances Company

★8452★

MSC CENTER LIBRARY (Rel-Theol)

Route 4
Shelby, OH 44875
Phone: (419) 747-4772
Rev. Mark McDonald, m.s.c., Dir.

Founded: 1934. **Staff:** Prof 1. **Subjects:** Religion, Bible, theology, prayer. **Special Collections:** M.S.C. Province Archives. **Holdings:** 5000 books; 1000 bound periodical volumes. **Subscriptions:** 48 journals and other serials. **Services:** Copying; library open to public. **Remarks:** The MSC Center Library is maintained by the Missionaries of the Sacred Heart.

MSFC LIBRARY
See: U.S. NASA

★8453★
MTS SYSTEMS CORPORATION - INFORMATION SERVICES (Sci-Tech)
8055 Mitchell Rd.   Phone: (612) 937-4000
Eden Prairie, MN 55344   Kathleen M. Warner, Supv.
Founded: 1967. Staff: Prof 3; Other 1. Subjects: Electronics, materials, testing, hydraulics, fatigue, business management. Holdings: 3000 books; 1000 pamphlets, documents and reports; 5 drawers of engineering standards. Subscriptions: 300 journals and other serials. Services: Interlibrary loans; copying; SDI; library open to public. Computerized Information Services: DIALOG, SDC, SBC, TECHNOTEC. Special Indexes: Standards Cross Reference List, biennial. Staff: Agnes Schepers, Libn. II; Judith Rogers, Libn. I.

MUDD (Harvey) COLLEGE - NORMAN F. SPRAGUE MEMORIAL LIBRARY
See: Claremont Colleges - Norman F. Sprague Memorial Library

MUDD (Seeley G.) LIBRARY FOR SCIENCE AND ENGINEERING
See: Northwestern University - Seeley G. Mudd Library for Science and Engineering

MUDD (Seeley G.) SCIENCE LIBRARY
See: Claremont Colleges - Seeley G. Mudd Science Library

★8454★
MUDGE, ROSE, GUTHRIE & ALEXANDER - LIBRARY (Law)
20 Broad St.   Phone: (212) 701-1535
New York, NY 10005   Mrs. C. Alvy, Libn.
Subjects: Law. Holdings: 19,000 volumes.

MUELLER HEALTH SCIENCES LIBRARY
See: Lancaster General Hospital

MUELLER (Joseph M.) LIBRARY
See: St. Mary Seminary - Joseph M. Mueller Library

★8455★
MUHLENBERG COLLEGE - JOHN A.W. HAAS LIBRARY (Soc Sci)
                                                         Phone: (215) 433-3191
Allentown, PA 18104   Patricia Ann Sacks, Dir. of Libs.
Staff: Prof 9; Other 21. Subjects: Sciences, social sciences, humanities. Special Collections: Pennsylvania German (2000 items); 19th century African Exploration and Travel (300 titles); fencing (200 titles). Holdings: 180,000 volumes; 60,000 U.S. government documents (depository); 3500 reels of microfilm; 11,900 microfiche. Subscriptions: 857 journals and other serials. Services: Interlibrary loans; copying; library open to public with restrictions on borrowing. Networks/Consortia: Member of Lehigh Valley Association of Independent Colleges; OCLC through PALINET & Union Library Catalogue of Pennsylvania. Publications: Acquisitions List, monthly; bibliography series, occasional; Serials Holdings List. Special Catalogs: Pennsylvania German collection (card). Remarks: Affiliated with Cedar Crest College. Staff: Linda Bowers, Hd.Cat.; Dianne Melnychuk, Ser.; Dennis J. Phillips, Pub.Serv.; Nan Flautz, Acq.; Christine Fiedler, Ref.; Mary Beth Freeh, Ref.; Sara Swijter, Ref.

★8456★
MUHLENBERG HOSPITAL - E. GORDON GLASS, M.D., MEMORIAL LIBRARY (Med)
Park Ave. & Randolph Rd.   Phone: (201) 668-2005
Plainfield, NJ 07061   Jane McCarthy, Libn.
Founded: 1955. Staff: Prof 1; Other 4. Subjects: Medicine, nursing, hospital management. Holdings: 5800 books; 3000 bound periodical volumes. Subscriptions: 200 journals and other serials. Services: Interlibrary loans; copying; library open to public. Computerized Information Services: DIALOG, MEDLINE, SDC.

★8457★
MUHLENBERG MEDICAL CENTER - MEDICAL LIBRARY (Med)
Schoenersville Rd.   Phone: (215) 861-2237
Bethlehem, PA 18017   Mary Moran, Libn.
Staff: Prof 1. Subjects: Medicine, nursing, dentistry. Holdings: 680 books; unbound periodicals. Subscriptions: 90 journals and other serials. Services: Interlibrary loans; copying; library not open to public. Computerized Information Services: MEDLINE. Networks/Consortia: Member of Cooperating Hospital Libraries of the Lehigh Valley Area.

MUIR (John) MEMORIAL HOSPITAL
See: John Muir Memorial Hospital

MUIR WOODS NATL. MONUMENT
See: U.S. Natl. Park Service

MULCAHY SCIENCE LIBRARY
See: Fordham University

MULFORD (Raymon H.) LIBRARY
See: Medical College of Ohio at Toledo - Raymon H. Mulford Library

MULLEN LIBRARY
See: Catholic University of America

MULTILINGUAL BIBLIOSERVICE
See: National Library of Canada

MULTISTATE CENTER FOR THE BLIND
See: Florida State Division of Blind Services

★8458★
MULTITECH - INFORMATION CENTER (Sci-Tech)
225 S. Idaho
Box 3809
Butte, MT 59701   Eveline T. Micone, Libn.
Staff: Prof 1. Subjects: Magnetohydrodynamics, alternative technology, ceramic engineering, environmental concerns. Holdings: 500 books; 3000 reports on microfiche; 1000 unbound reports; newspaper clippings. Subscriptions: 125 journals and other serials; 9 newspapers. Services: Interlibrary loans; copying; library not open to public. Computerized Information Services: DOE/RECON, DIALOG. Formerly: Its Merdi Technical Library.

★8459★
MULTNOMAH LAW LIBRARY (Law)
Court House   Phone: (503) 248-3394
Portland, OR 97204   Jacquelyn J. Jurkins, Law Libn.
Founded: 1890. Staff: Prof 2; Other 2. Subjects: Law. Holdings: 165,000 volumes. Services: Interlibrary loans; copying; library open to public for reference use only.

★8460★
MULTNOMAH SCHOOL OF THE BIBLE - JOHN AND MARY MITCHELL LIBRARY (Rel-Theol)
8435 N.E. Glisan St.   Phone: (503) 255-0332
Portland, OR 97220   James F. Scott, Lib.Dir.
Founded: 1936. Staff: Prof 2; Other 4. Subjects: Bible doctrine, missions, Christian education, New Testament Greek, journalism, music, women's ministries. Holdings: 31,884 books; 1030 bound periodical volumes; 4029 AV items (cataloged); 1218 microforms. Subscriptions: 432 journals and other serials. Services: Interlibrary loans; copying; library open to public. Staff: Susan E. Johnson, Asst.Libn.

★8461★
MUNCIE STAR-PRESS LIBRARY (Publ)
High & Jackson Sts.   Phone: (317) 747-5767
Muncie, IN 47302   Breena L. Wysong, Libn.
Founded: 1950. Staff: Prof 1; Other 1. Subjects: Newspaper reference topics. Holdings: 70 VF drawers of newspaper clippings; 10 VF drawers of photographs. Services: Copying; library open to public.

★8462★
MUNCY HISTORICAL SOCIETY AND MUSEUM OF HISTORY - HISTORICAL LIBRARY (Hist)
40 N. Main St.   Phone: (717) 546-6172
Muncy, PA 17756   Thomas J. Clegg, Pres.
Founded: 1936. Staff: 1. Subjects: Local history. Special Collections: Samuel Wallis Papers (10,000 documents on microfilm). Holdings: 1000 books. Subscriptions: 15 journals and other serials. Services: Copying; collections may be consulted by appointment. Publications: The Now and Then, quarterly historical magazine.

MUNDT (Karl E.) LIBRARY
See: Dakota State College - Karl E. Mundt Library

MUNFLA
See: Memorial University of Newfoundland - Folklore and Language Archive

MUNGER AFRICANA LIBRARY
See: California Institute of Technology

MUNGER (Edith) LIBRARY
See: Michigan Audubon Society - Edith Munger Library

★8463★
MUNGER, TOLLES & RICKERSHAUSER - LIBRARY (Law)
612 S. Flower St., 5th Fl.   Phone: (213) 683-9100
Los Angeles, CA 90017   Helen Kim, Libn.
Subjects: Law. **Holdings:** 11,500 books; 500 bound periodical volumes.
Subscriptions: 40 journals and other serials; 10 newspapers. **Services:** Copying; library not open to public. **Computerized Information Services:** LEXIS.

★8464★
MUNICIPAL ART SOCIETY OF NEW YORK - INFORMATION EXCHANGE (Art)
457 Madison Ave.   Phone: (212) 935-3960
New York, NY 10022   Darlene McCloud, Dir.
Staff: Prof 2; Other 3. **Subjects:** Built environment; New York City history and architecture; urban parks and open spaces; historic preservation; architects. **Holdings:** 1100 books; 2500 folders of organizations and reports; 500 folders of clippings. **Subscriptions:** 120 journals and other serials; 40 newspapers. **Services:** Interlibrary loans; copying; SDI; library open to public by appointment. **Networks/Consortia:** Member of METRO. **Staff:** Shirley Secunda, Libn.

★8465★
MUNICIPAL ASSOCIATION OF SOUTH CAROLINA - LIBRARY AND REFERENCE CENTER (Soc Sci)†
1529 Washington
Box 11558   Phone: (803) 799-9574
Columbia, SC 29201   Edward J. Kinghorn, Jr., Staff Assoc.
Founded: 1975. **Staff:** Prof 1; Other 1. **Subjects:** Finance, municipal government administration, public policy. **Special Collections:** Code of ordinances; association publications. **Holdings:** 1200 books; 300 bound periodical volumes; budgets; municipal financial statements; clippings; documents. **Subscriptions:** 204 journals and other serials. **Services:** Interlibrary loans; copying; library open to public. **Publications:** Directory; Compensation Study. **Remarks:** Association is the clearinghouse for local and municipal government information in the state.

★8466★
MUNICIPAL RESEARCH AND SERVICES CENTER OF WASHINGTON - LIBRARY (Soc Sci)
4719 Brooklyn Ave., N.E.   Phone: (206) 543-9050
Seattle, WA 98105   Lynne DeMerritt, Libn.
Founded: 1970. **Staff:** Prof 1; Other 1. **Subjects:** Municipal government, finance, planning and law; public works and personnel; public safety. **Special Collections:** Municipal ordinances of state of Washington. **Holdings:** Figures not available for books; 2500 subject files on municipal government administration containing articles, clippings, manuscripts, pamphlet materials, technical reports, and city ordinances. **Subscriptions:** 300 journals and other serials. **Services:** Interlibrary loans; usage restricted to public officials.

★8467★
MUNICIPAL TECHNICAL ADVISORY SERVICE - LIBRARY (Soc Sci)
     Phone: (615) 974-5301
Knoxville, TN 37996-4400   Carol C. Hewlett, Libn.
Founded: 1950. **Staff:** Prof 1; Other 3. **Subjects:** Municipal government, finance, public works and law; local government problems; city ordinances. **Special Collections:** Municipal law; States' Municipal League Publications. **Holdings:** 4000 books; 13,000 pamphlets, unbound reports, sample ordinances; 64 VF drawers of newspaper clippings. **Subscriptions:** 300 journals and other serials. **Services:** Copying (limited); library open to public for reference use only. **Remarks:** The Municipal Technical Advisory Service is an agency of University of Tennessee - Institute for Public Service.

MUNK LIBRARY OF ARIZONIANA
See: Southwest Museum - Research Library

MUNRO (Dr. E.H.) MEDICAL LIBRARY
See: Mesa County Medical Society - Dr. E.H. Munro Medical Library

★8468★
MUNSON-WILLIAMS-PROCTOR INSTITUTE - ART REFERENCE AND MUSIC LIBRARY (Art; Mus)
310 Genesee St.   Phone: (315) 797-0000
Utica, NY 13502   Linda Lott, Libn.
Founded: 1940. **Staff:** Prof 1; Other 2. **Subjects:** American art, architecture,

decorative arts, music. **Special Collections:** Fountain Elms Collection (family library; 1000 volumes); autographs (950); book plates; 19th century pictorial sheet music covers; artists' books. **Holdings:** 13,000 books; 342 bound periodical volumes; 15,000 slides; 5000 phonograph records; 150 scores. **Subscriptions:** 74 journals and other serials. **Services:** Interlibrary loans; copying; library open to public for reference use only. **Networks/Consortia:** Member of Central New York Library Resources Council (CENTRO).

MURAKAMI LIBRARY OF MEIJI LITERATURE
See: University of California, Berkeley - East Asiatic Library

MURPHY (Beatrice) FOUNDATION
See: District of Columbia Public Library - Black Studies Division

MURPHY LIBRARY
See: University of Wisconsin, La Crosse

MURPHY LIBRARY OF ART HISTORY
See: University of Kansas

★8469★
MURPHY OIL CORPORATION - LAW DEPARTMENT LIBRARY (Law)
200 Jefferson St.   Phone: (501) 862-6411
El Dorado, AR 71730   Ann Ripley, Asst.
Staff: 1. **Subjects:** Corporation law (including antitrust, labor), state statutes, regional reporters, oil and gas law. **Holdings:** 9000 books; 172 bound periodical volumes; 26 loose-leaf services. **Services:** Library open to public.

★8470★
MURPHY OIL CORPORATION - LIBRARY (Energy)
200 Jefferson St.   Phone: (501) 862-6411
El Dorado, AR 71730   Peggy H. Makepeace, Libn.
Founded: 1955. **Staff:** Prof 1; Other 1. **Subjects:** Petroleum geology, petroleum industry, business, geology, statistics, management. **Holdings:** 5900 books and bound periodical volumes. **Subscriptions:** 115 journals and other serials. **Services:** Interlibrary loans; copying; library open to public for reference use only.

★8471★
MURPHY OIL CORPORATION - TAX LIBRARY (Bus-Fin)
200 Jefferson St.   Phone: (501) 862-6411
El Dorado, AR 71730   Harry Bain, Tax Mgr.
Staff: 1. **Subjects:** Taxation - federal, state and foreign. **Holdings:** 870 volumes. **Services:** Interlibrary loans; library not open to public.

MURPHY (Richard J.) MEMORIAL LIBRARY
See: Baptist Bible College of Pennsylvania - Richard J. Murphy Memorial Library

MURRAY (Henry A.) RESEARCH CENTER
See: Radcliffe College - Henry A. Murray Research Center

★8472★
MURRAY PROPERTIES COMPANY - RESOURCE CENTER (Bus-Fin)
5520 LBJ Fwy., Suite 600   Phone: (214) 385-2637
Dallas, TX 75240   Joan Davis, Rsrcs.Ctr.Mgr.
Staff: Prof 1. **Subjects:** Real estate. **Holdings:** 65 books; 75 prospectuses; 25 reports. **Subscriptions:** 110 journals and other serials; 10 newspapers. **Services:** Library not open to public. **Computerized Information Services:** Internal database.

★8473★
MURRAY STATE UNIVERSITY - LIBRARY (Educ)
     Phone: (502) 762-2291
Murray, KY 42071   Edwin C. Strohecker, Dean
Founded: 1923. **Staff:** Prof 17; Other 22. **Subjects:** Education, business, law, liberal arts. **Special Collections:** Jesse Stuart Literary Collection (780 linear feet); Regional Politics and Government (2525 linear feet); Regional History and Culture (115 linear feet); TVA Land Between the Lakes (100 volumes); Jack London, first editions (87 volumes). **Holdings:** 298,698 books; 68,488 bound periodical volumes; 223,425 other cataloged items; 22,550 reels of microfilm; 215 linear feet of university archives; 306,558 microfiche and microcards; 28,036 media resource materials. **Subscriptions:** 1977 journals and other serials; 25 newspapers. **Services:** Interlibrary loans; copying; library open to public. **Computerized Information Services:** Online systems; computerized cataloging and circulation. **Networks/Consortia:** Member of OCLC through SOLINET. **Special Catalogs:** Special Collections (book); periodical holdings (print-out). **Staff:** Keith M. Heim, Hd., Spec.Coll.; Quava Honchub, Hd., Legal Rsrcs.; Marilyn McFadden, Hd., Cat.; Jetta

Culpepper, Hd., Acq.

★8474★
MURRAY (Warren G.) DEVELOPMENTAL CENTER - LIBRARY (Med)
1717 W. Broadway
Centralia, IL 62801
Phone: (618) 532-1811
Edith Jacke, Libn.
Founded: 1965. **Staff:** 1. **Subjects:** Mental retardation, medicine, nursing, psychology, special education, speech pathology. **Holdings:** 1400 books and bound periodical volumes; 550 phonograph records; 2100 slides, filmstrips, cassette tapes and prints. **Subscriptions:** 20 journals and other serials. **Services:** Interlibrary loans; library open to public. **Networks/Consortia:** Member of Cumberland Trails Library System; DMHDD Professional Library Services Consortium. **Publications:** Information sheets, irregular.

★8475★
MUSCATATUCK STATE HOSPITAL & TRAINING CENTER - RESIDENT AND STAFF DEVELOPMENT LIBRARY (Med)
Box 77
Butlerville, IN 47223
Phone: (812) 346-4401
William Bohall, Info.Spec.
Staff: Prof 1; Other 1. **Subjects:** Medicine, staff development, nursing, behavior modification, supervision and management, mental retardation. **Holdings:** 3000 books; 200 filmstrips, phonograph records and transparencies; videotapes. **Subscriptions:** 23 journals and other serials. **Services:** Interlibrary loans; copying; library open to public. **Networks/Consortia:** Member of Southeastern Indiana Area Library Services Authority (SIALSA). **Publications:** Mirror, quarterly - to staff and families of residents.

★8476★
MUSCULAR DYSTROPHY ASSOCIATION - LIBRARY (Med)
810 Seventh Ave.
New York, NY 10019
Phone: (212) 586-0808
Founded: 1978. **Staff:** Prof 1; Other 1. **Subjects:** Neuromuscular disease, neurology, biochemistry, pharmacology, voluntary health agencies, grantmanship. **Holdings:** 200 books; 5 VF drawers of grant information, bibliographies, university research center materials. **Subscriptions:** 18 journals and other serials. **Services:** Interlibrary loans; copying; SDI; library not open to public. **Computerized Information Services:** Online systems; in-house computerized data bank. **Publications:** Pamphlets, annual reports. **Remarks:** The Muscular Dystrophy Association has one of the largest voluntary health organization programs; 20 million dollars was allocated to research in 1981.

★8477★
MUSEE D'ART CONTEMPORAIN - CENTRE DE DOCUMENTATION (Art)
Cite Du Havre
Montreal, PQ, Canada H3C 3R4
Phone: (514) 873-2878
Isabelle Montplaisir, Libn.
Founded: 1967. **Staff:** Prof 1; Other 1. **Subjects:** Contemporary art. **Special Collections:** Paul-Emile Borduas (12,500 documents). **Holdings:** 5378 books; 635 bound periodical volumes; 7987 exhibition catalogs (cataloged); 25,541 slides; 19,850 photographs; 2756 artist, gallery and museum files; 180 tapes and films; 1020 microforms. **Subscriptions:** 186 journals and other serials. **Services:** Copying; library open to public. **Networks/Consortia:** Member of ASTED. **Remarks:** Maintained by Quebec Province Ministere des Affaires Culturelles.

★8478★
MUSEE D'ART DE JOLIETTE - BIBLIOTHEQUE (Art)
145 rue Wilfrid-Corbeil
Joliette, PQ, Canada J6E 3Z3
Phone: (514) 756-0311
Carmen Delorme Toupin, Animator
Staff: Prof 1. **Subjects:** Art, architecture. **Holdings:** 1000 books; 500 bound periodical volumes; 100 museum catalogs. **Services:** Library open to public for consultation only.

MUSEE DES BEAUX-ARTS DE MONTREAL
See: The Montreal Museum of Fine Arts

MUSEE CANADIEN DE LA GUERRE
See: Canada - National Museums of Canada - Canadian War Museum

★8479★
MUSEE DU QUEBEC - BIBLIOTHEQUE (Art)
Parc des Champs de Bataille
Quebec, PQ, Canada G1S 1C8
Phone: (418) 643-7134
Francois Lafortune, Chf.Libn.
Staff: Prof 1; Other 5. **Subjects:** Art. **Holdings:** 27,099 books; 1500 bound periodical volumes; 68,000 slides; 17,000 clippings; 6661 photographs; 2600 negatives; 154 phonograph records; 2112 microforms; 20 magnetic tapes; 95 videotapes. **Subscriptions:** 250 journals and other serials; 27 newspapers. **Services:** Library open to public with restrictions. **Publications:** Bibliographies; press releases. **Remarks:** Museum is maintained by Quebec

Province Ministere des Affaires Culturelles.

MUSEES NATIONAUX CANADA
See: Canada - National Museums of Canada

MUSEUM OF AFRICAN ART
See: Smithsonian Institution Libraries

★8480★
MUSEUM OF THE AMERICAN CHINA TRADE - ARCHIVES (Hist)
215 Adams St.
Milton, MA 02186
Phone: (617) 696-1815
Dana D. Ricciardi, Registrar/Cur.
Staff: 1. **Subjects:** American-China trade, Chinese history and art. **Special Collections:** Forbes Papers (collection of the Forbes Family, especially Robert Bennet Forbes, 1804-1889; 30,000 pages); documents relating to other China traders, including the journals and correspondence of Samuel Shaw. **Holdings:** 2500 books and pamphlets. **Subscriptions:** 25 journals and other serials. **Services:** Copying; archives open to public by appointment. **Special Indexes:** Microfilm Guide to the Forbes Collection (in conjunction with the Massachusetts Historical Society); index to documents.

★8481★
MUSEUM OF AMERICAN FLY FISHING, INC. - LIBRARY (Rec)
Manchester, VT 05254
Phone: (802) 362-3300
JoAnna Sheridan, Registrar
Founded: 1968. **Staff:** 4. **Subjects:** Fly fishing; history, lore and literature of angling; entomology. **Special Collections:** File of patent applications relating to fly fishing from mid-19th century to present. **Holdings:** 1000 volumes; articles, memorabilia, original manuscripts. **Services:** Library open to public on request. **Publications:** The American Fly Fisher, quarterly - available to members. **Special Catalogs:** A Bibliography of American Sporting Periodicals (book).

MUSEUM OF THE AMERICAN INDIAN
See: Huntington Free Library

★8482★
MUSEUM OF THE AMERICAS - LIBRARY (Art)
Brookfield, VT 05036
Phone: (802) 276-3386
Earle W. Newton, Dir.
Founded: 1972. **Staff:** Prof 1. **Subjects:** Art and architecture - English, American, Spanish, Latin American. **Special Collections:** Pre-Columbian art; English paintings and engravings; Spanish decorative arts; Latin American folk art. **Holdings:** 3000 books. **Subscriptions:** 12 journals and other serials. **Remarks:** Maintained in connection with College of the Americas. The library is partly in storage, having been moved from Florida, and is available by appointment.

MUSEUM OF ANESTHESIOLOGY
See: American Society of Anesthesiologists - Wood Library-Museum of Anesthesiology

MUSEUM & ARCHIVES OF CANADIAN SCOUTING
See: Boy Scouts of Canada

★8483★
MUSEUM OF ARTS AND SCIENCES - BRUCE EVERETT BATES MEMORIAL LIBRARY (Sci-Tech; Art)
1040 Museum Blvd.
Daytona Beach, FL 32014
Phone: (904) 255-0285
Marjorie L. Sigerson, Libn.
Founded: 1954. **Staff:** Prof 1. **Subjects:** Birds, shells, fish and marine life, biology, art, archeology, whaling. **Special Collections:** Cuban Collection (500 items); books about birds (400). **Holdings:** 2800 books. **Subscriptions:** 16 journals and other serials. **Services:** Library open to public with restrictions.

★8484★
MUSEUM OF CARTOON ART - LIBRARY (Art; Rec)
Comly Ave.
Port Chester, NY 10573
Phone: (914) 939-0234
Ellen J. Armstrong, Mgr.
Founded: 1972. **Staff:** 4. **Subjects:** Comic strip art, political/editorial cartooning, caricature, animation, panel cartoons. **Special Collections:** Original artwork by over 1000 different artists (over 50,000 pieces). **Holdings:** 300 books; 100 bound periodical volumes; 3 VF drawers of clippings; 800 animated cartoons. **Subscriptions:** 5 journals and other serials. **Services:** Copying; library open to public by appointment. **Staff:** Chuck Green, Dir.; Brian Walker, Dir.

★8485★
MUSEUM OF THE CITY OF NEW YORK - LIBRARY (Hist)
Fifth Ave. at 103rd St.
New York, NY 10029   Phone: (212) 534-1672
                                         Nancy Kessler-Post, Libn.
Subjects: Local history. **Special Collections:** Manuscripts of New Yorkers
(17th century to present; 15,000 pieces). **Holdings:** 8000 books.
Subscriptions: 11 journals and other serials. **Services:** Library not open to
public but the manuscript collection is open to public by appointment.

★8486★
MUSEUM OF THE CITY OF NEW YORK - THEATRE COLLECTION (Theater)
103rd St. & Fifth Ave.
New York, NY 10029   Phone: (212) 534-1672
                                         Dr. Mary C. Henderson, Cur.
Founded: 1926. **Staff:** Prof 5. **Subjects:** History of performing arts in New
York City - illustrated by paintings, prints, books, objects, printed and written
material; costumes; scene and costume designs. **Special Collections:** Dazian
Library of Theatrical Design; Howard Dietz Collection; George M. Cohan
Collection; Betty Comden-Adolph Green Collection; George and Ira Gershwin
Collection; Mary Martin Collection; Yiddish Theatre Collection. **Holdings:** 4000
books; 2000 manuscripts; clippings, documents, prints, photographs, and
paintings; sheet music; recordings. **Subscriptions:** 10 journals and other
serials. **Services:** Copying; collection open only to qualified scholars and
researchers by appointment. **Publications:** Catalogs on major exhibitions.
Staff: Wendy Warnken, Assoc.Cur.; Maryann D. Smith, Asst.Cur.

MUSEUM OF COMPARATIVE ZOOLOGY
See: Harvard University

MUSEUM OF THE CONFEDERACY
See: Confederate Memorial Literary Society

★8487★
MUSEUM OF CONTEMPORARY ART - LIBRARY (Art)
237 E. Ontario St.
Chicago, IL 60611   Phone: (312) 943-7755
                                         Kathryn Vaughn, Libn.
Founded: 1967. **Staff:** Prof 1; Other 1. **Subjects:** Twentieth-century art.
Special Collections: Complete collection of 35mm color slides of every item
in exhibits since opening of museum; videotapes of contemporary artists
discussing their work. **Holdings:** 3500 books; 52 VF drawers of museum
catalogs, exhibit brochures, brochures and clippings on individual artists.
Subscriptions: 70 journals and other serials. **Services:** Copying; library open
to public for reference use only by appointment.

MUSEUM OF EARLY SOUTHERN DECORATIVE ARTS (MESDA)
See: Old Salem, Inc.

★8488★
MUSEUM OF FINE ARTS - ART REFERENCE LIBRARY (Art)
255 Beach Dr., N.
St. Petersburg, FL 33701   Phone: (813) 896-2667
                                         Muriel S. Kirk, Coord. for Lib.
Founded: 1962. **Staff:** 6. **Subjects:** Oriental art, architecture, decorative
arts, history of art. **Special Collections:** 900 old engravings, etchings and
prints. **Holdings:** 6000 books; 522 bound periodical volumes; 39 files of
museum reports and bulletins, art auction and sales catalogs; 700 museum
catalogs; 6000 art reproductions; 400 glass architectural slides; 15,000
slides on art history. **Subscriptions:** 28 journals and other serials. **Services:**
Interlibrary loans; library open to students and scholars by appointment.
Special Indexes: Card index to paintings in American museums.

★8489★
MUSEUM OF FINE ARTS - DEPARTMENT OF PHOTOGRAPHIC SERVICES -
  SLIDE & PHOTOGRAPH LIBRARY (Art; Pict)
465 Huntington Ave.
Boston, MA 02115   Phone: (617) 267-9300
                                         Janice Sorkow, Mgr., Photographic Serv.
Founded: 1922. **Staff:** Prof 1; Other 6. **Subjects:** Eastern and Western
painting, architecture, sculpture, prints, decorative arts, photography. **Special
Collections:** Slides and photographs of works in collections of Museum of Fine
Arts; videodisc of selected museum objects. **Holdings:** 90,000 slides
(cataloged); 38,000 black and white negatives. **Services:** Duplicate slides of
museum objects available for sale; library open to public except
undergraduates. **Publications:** Information packet available by mail. **Special
Catalogs:** Catalog of slide sets - available for sale; detailed slide set lists -
available on request.

★8490★
MUSEUM OF FINE ARTS, HOUSTON - HIRSCH LIBRARY (Art)
1001 Bissonnet
Houston, TX 77005   Phone: (713) 526-1361
                                         Nelson Shearouse, Libn.
Staff: Prof 1; Other 3. **Subjects:** Art history, photography. **Holdings:** 14,000

books; 1200 bound periodical volumes; 81 VF drawers of exhibition catalogs;
56 VF drawers of auction catalogs. **Subscriptions:** 72 journals and other
serials. **Services:** Interlibrary loans; copying; library open to public.

★8491★
MUSEUM OF FINE ARTS - SCHOOL LIBRARY (Art)
230 The Fenway
Boston, MA 02115   Phone: (617) 267-9300
                                         Carol Bjork, Libn.
Founded: 1928. **Staff:** Prof 1; Other 6. **Subjects:** Art. **Holdings:** 8400
books; 300 bound periodical volumes; 44,000 slides; 27 VF drawers of
clippings and pictures. **Subscriptions:** 75 journals and other serials. **Services:**
Copying; library not open to public.

★8492★
MUSEUM OF FINE ARTS - WILLIAM MORRIS HUNT MEMORIAL LIBRARY
  (Art)
465 Huntington Ave.
Boston, MA 02115   Phone: (617) 267-9300
                                         Nancy S. Allen, Libn.
Founded: 1879. **Staff:** Prof 2; Other 3. **Subjects:** Classical, Egyptian and
Oriental art; textiles; civic heraldry; European and American decorative arts.
Special Collections: Chapin Collection of Civic Heraldry. **Holdings:** 120,000
books and bound periodical volumes; 127,000 pamphlets and auction catalogs
(cataloged). **Subscriptions:** 599 journals and other serials. **Services:**
Interlibrary loans (limited); copying; library open to public for reference use
only. **Computerized Information Services:** Computerized cataloging.
Networks/Consortia: Member of Fenway Library Consortium. **Special
Catalogs:** Chronological list of Museum of Fine Arts exhibitions, 1872 to
present. **Staff:** Deirdre Lawrence, Cat.

★8493★
MUSEUM OF THE GREAT PLAINS - GREAT PLAINS RESEARCH LIBRARY
  AND ARCHIVES (Hist)
601 Ferris
Box 68   Phone: (405) 353-5675
Lawton, OK 73502   Peggy Fuller, Cur., Spec.Coll.
Founded: 1960. **Staff:** Prof 1; Other 1. **Subjects:** Great Plains - history,
natural history, archaeology, anthropology. **Special Collections:** Original
documents and photographs dealing with the settlement of southwestern
Oklahoma and Southern Plains. **Holdings:** 17,000 books; 725 bound periodical
volumes; 600 cases of manuscripts, 1880-1940, Comanche County
newspapers, 1901 to present and City of Lawton Journals; 12,000
photographs. **Subscriptions:** 100 journals and other serials. **Services:**
Interlibrary loans; copying; library and archives open to public. **Publications:**
Great Plains Journal, annual; Museum of the Great Plains Newsletter, irregular.
Special Indexes: Index to photograph collections (card); index to articles in
regional journals.

★8494★
MUSEUM OF INDEPENDENT TELEPHONY - ARCHIVES COLLECTION (Hist)
412 S. Campbell   Phone: (913) 263-2681
Abilene, KS 67410   Peg Chronister, Cur.
Staff: Prof 1. **Subjects:** Telephone history and technology. **Special
Collections:** Early telephone trade magazines; historical photograph collection;
antique telephone catalogs. **Holdings:** 500 books; 750 bound periodical
volumes; 1000 other cataloged items; 500 manuscripts; 120 boxes of loose
periodicals; 150 tapes. **Subscriptions:** 10 journals and other serials.
Services: Copying; library open to public.

★8495★
MUSEUM OF INDIAN HERITAGE - LIBRARY (Area-Ethnic)†
Eagle Creek Park
6040 DeLong Rd.   Phone: (317) 293-4488
Indianapolis, IN 46254   P.A. Lawton, Registrar
Founded: 1967. **Subjects:** American Indian. **Holdings:** 3000 volumes and
films. **Subscriptions:** 10 journals and other serials. **Services:** Library not open
to public.

MUSEUM OF INTERNATIONAL FOLK ART
See: Museum of New Mexico

★8496★
MUSEUM OF MODERN ART - DEPARTMENT OF RIGHTS AND
  REPRODUCTIONS - AUDIOVISUAL ARCHIVES (Pict)
11 W. 53rd St.   Phone: (212) 956-7255
New York, NY 10019   Esther M. Carpenter, Archv.
Founded: 1932. **Staff:** Prof 1. **Subjects:** Modern art, 1890 to present.
Special Collections: Curt Valentin Archive (120 albums of photographs).
Holdings: 130 albums of photographs of works in museum collection; 680
albums of photographs of works in museum exhibitions; 178,000

photographs; 2000 slides; 56,000 negatives. **Services:** Archives open to public by appointment only; slide collection not open to public.

★8497★

MUSEUM OF MODERN ART - FILM STUDY CENTER (Theater)
11 W. 53rd St.   Phone: (212) 956-4212
New York, NY 10019   Charles Silver, Supv.
Founded: 1968. **Staff:** Prof 2. **Subjects:** Cinema. **Special Collections:** D.W. Griffith Papers and Scrapbooks; Merritt Crawford Papers on early cinema. **Holdings:** 10,000 films; 300,000 clippings; 1400 scripts; 3 million stills (housed separately); 100 reference books; 1000 pressbooks; 30,000 posters. **Subscriptions:** 50 journals and other serials. **Services:** Interlibrary loans (restricted); copying; center open to bonafide film scholars by appointment. **Staff:** Mary Corliss, Cur.Asst., Stills; Ronald S. Magliozzi, Asst. to Supv.

★8498★

MUSEUM OF MODERN ART - LIBRARY (Art)
11 W. 53rd St.   Phone: (212) 956-7236
New York, NY 10019   Clive Phillpot, Dir.
Founded: 1929. **Staff:** Prof 6; Other 3. **Subjects:** Modern art since 1880, including architecture, photography and film. **Special Collections:** International Circulating Exhibitions Archive; Hans Richter Archives; Curt Valentin albums and files. **Holdings:** 40,000 books; 6000 bound periodical volumes; 50,000 exhibition catalogs (cataloged); 80,000 other items. **Subscriptions:** 250 journals and other serials. **Services:** Interlibrary loans (limited); copying; library open to staff, members, and serious art researchers. **Networks/Consortia:** Member of METRO; RLG. **Publications:** List of Acquisitions; Art Bibliographies. **Special Catalogs:** Catalog of the Library of the Museum of Modern Art, 1976 (book). **Staff:** Janis Ekdahl, Asst.Dir.; Daniel A. Starr, Sr.Cat.

★8499★

MUSEUM OF NEW MEXICO - HISTORY LIBRARY (Hist)
Box 2087   Phone: (505) 827-2343
Santa Fe, NM 87503   Marcia Muth Miller, Libn.
Founded: 1880. **Staff:** Prof 1. **Subjects:** New Mexico and Southwest history. **Holdings:** 12,000 books; 837 reels of microfilm; 3000 maps; 180 linear feet of manuscripts; newspapers. **Subscriptions:** 115 journals and other serials; 5 newspapers. **Services:** Interlibrary loans; copying; library open to public for reference use only.

★8500★

MUSEUM OF NEW MEXICO - LABORATORY OF ANTHROPOLOGY - LIBRARY (Sci-Tech)
Box 2087   Phone: (505) 827-3241
Santa Fe, NM 87503   Laura J. Holt, Libn.
Staff: Prof 1. **Subjects:** Southwestern anthropology, archeology, botany, ethnology. **Special Collections:** Sylvanus G. Morley Collection (Meso American archaeology and ethnohistory). **Holdings:** 4000 books; maps; 1000 serial titles; 300 dissertations in microform. **Services:** Interlibrary loans; copying; library open to public for reference use only. **Special Indexes:** Index of articles on southwestern anthropology (card).

★8501★

MUSEUM OF NEW MEXICO - MUSEUM OF FINE ARTS - LIBRARY (Art)
Box 2087   Phone: (505) 827-3165
Santa Fe, NM 87501   Alberta F. Donlan, Hd.Libn.
Founded: 1917. **Staff:** Prof 1; Other 4. **Subjects:** Art and artists - American, Southwestern, European, world; art history; photography. **Special Collections:** Files of individual artists. **Holdings:** 4000 books; 369 bound periodical volumes; 1740 artists' catalogs; 7564 unbound periodicals; 1740 exhibit catalogs of New Mexico Museum of Fine Arts; 1300 museum exchange catalogs; 2400 slides (uncataloged). **Subscriptions:** 63 journals and other serials. **Services:** Interlibrary loans; copying; library open to public for reference use only. **Computerized Information Services:** Access to DIALOG. **Networks/Consortia:** Member of OCLC (through New Mexico State Library). **Publications:** Museum of Fine Arts Handbook of the Collections; Light and Color: Images from New Mexico; Larry Bell: The Sixties. **Special Catalogs:** File of catalogs of individual artists, especially Southwestern artists (card).

★8502★

MUSEUM OF NEW MEXICO - MUSEUM OF INTERNATIONAL FOLK ART - LIBRARY (Art)
Box 2087   Phone: (505) 827-2544
Santa Fe, NM 87504-2087   Judith Sellars, Libn.
Founded: 1953. **Staff:** Prof 1. **Subjects:** International folk art, costume, Spanish colonial art, New Mexico religious folk art, textiles. **Special Collections:** Folk literature and music of the Spanish Colonist in New Mexico,

1800-1971. **Holdings:** 7500 books; 1300 bound periodical volumes; 5000 slides; 250 tapes; 200 phonograph records; postcards. **Subscriptions:** 94 journals and other serials. **Services:** Interlibrary loans; copying; library open to public for reference use only. **Computerized Information Services:** Computerized cataloging and ILL.

★8503★

MUSEUM OF NEW MEXICO - PHOTOGRAPHIC ARCHIVES (Pict)
Box 2087   Phone: (505) 827-2559
Santa Fe, NM 87503   Arthur L. Olivas, Photographic Archv.
Staff: Prof 3. **Subjects:** New Mexico, Indians, southwest states, railroads, mining, archeology, anthropology, ethnology. **Special Collections:** G. Ben Wittick; T. Harmon Parkhurst; William Henry Jackson; Jesse L. Nusbaum; John K. Hillers; Charles F. Lummis; H.F. Robinson; D.B. Chase; Timithy O'Sullivan; Nicholas Brown; Emerson A. Plunkett; George C. Bennett; J.R. Riddle; Tyler Dingee; Harold Kellogg; Philip E. Harroun; Edward A. Kemp; Fereuz Fedor; Keystone View Co.; J.S. Wooley; Royal A. Prentice; Henry A. Schmidt; Joseph E. Smith. **Holdings:** 600 books; 100 bound periodical volumes; 130,000 photographs; 70,000 negatives. **Subscriptions:** 20 journals and other serials. **Services:** Copying; library open to public. **Publications:** List of publications - available upon request. **Staff:** Richard Rudisill, Hist.; Arthur Taylor, Photographer.

★8504★

MUSEUM OF NORTHERN ARIZONA - HAROLD S. COLTON MEMORIAL LIBRARY (Hist; Sci-Tech)
Rte. 4, Box 720   Phone: (602) 774-5211
Flagstaff, AZ 86001   Dorothy A. House, Libn.
Founded: 1928. **Staff:** Prof 1; Other 1. **Subjects:** American Southwest - archeology, geology, paleontology, ethnology, natural history, history, art. **Special Collections:** Southwestern archeology; Navajo and Hopi Indians; geology of the Colorado Plateau. **Holdings:** 19,000 books; 400 periodical titles; 25,000 pamphlets; maps and manuscript collections. **Subscriptions:** 300 journals and other serials; 6 newspapers. **Services:** Interlibrary loans; copying; library open to public for reference use only.

MUSEUM RESOURCES AND INFORMATION SERVICE
See: American Association of Museums

★8505★

MUSEUM OF SCIENCE & INDUSTRY - LIBRARY (Sci-Tech; Trans)
57th St. & Lake Shore Dr.   Phone: (312) 684-1414
Chicago, IL 60637   Bernice Richter, Libn.
Founded: 1928. **Staff:** Prof 2; Other 1. **Subjects:** Science, technology, museology, expositions, science education, children's nonfiction. **Special Collections:** Travel in the U.S., 1680-1910; Dunbar Collection (1741 prints and drawings). **Holdings:** 28,450 books; 4906 bound periodical volumes; 2753 bound documents; 196 VF drawers of pamphlets, trade catalogs and museology material; miscellaneous 19th century maps, almanacs and travelers guides; 308 photographs, engravings and locomotive drawings; 7.5 cubic feet of Huegely Mill records. **Subscriptions:** 200 journals and other serials; 6 newspapers. **Services:** Interlibrary loans; copying; library open to members and by special request to public. **Networks/Consortia:** Member of Chicago Library System. **Publications:** Book Notes, quarterly accessions list - for internal distribution only; Children's Science Books, annual - available for sale.

★8506★

MUSEUM OF SCIENCE - LIBRARY (Sci-Tech)
Science Pk.   Phone: (617) 723-2500
Boston, MA 02114   Edward D. Pearce, Libn.
Founded: 1831. **Staff:** Prof 2; Other 1. **Subjects:** Science, natural history, science education. **Special Collections:** Publications, corporate records and some of the holdings of the Boston Society of Natural History. **Holdings:** 35,000 books; manuscripts related to 19th century natural history. **Subscriptions:** 200 journals and other serials. **Services:** Interlibrary loans; copying; library open to public. **Publications:** Recent Additions, weekly - for in-house use but available to others. **Staff:** Barbara R. Wiseman, Ref.Libn.

★8507★

MUSEUM OF SCIENCE AND NATURAL HISTORY - LIBRARY (Sci-Tech)
2 Oak Knoll Pk.   Phone: (314) 726-2888
St. Louis, MO 63105   Dwight S. Crandell, Dir.
Founded: 1856. **Subjects:** General science, natural history. **Holdings:** 810 books and bound periodical volumes. **Services:** Library for use of museum staff only.

★8508★

MUSEUM OF WESTERN COLORADO - ARCHIVES (Hist)
4th & Ute Sts.   Phone: (303) 242-0971
Grand Junction, CO 81501   John Brumgardt, Musm.Dir.
Founded: 1965. **Staff:** 8. **Subjects:** History of western Colorado, Mesa County and Grand Junction; anthropology of southwestern Indians; Colorado railroad history. **Special Collections:** Wilson Rockwell Collection of Western Colorado History (300 items); Al Look Collection of Frank Dean photographs and negatives (200); Moore Family Collection of Frank Dean plate glass negatives (600); Palisade Library Collection (150 items); Warren Kiefer Railroad Collection (1300 items); Don Winslow Collection of Comic Art (113 items). **Holdings:** 950 books; 350 manuscripts and documents; 10,000 photographs and negatives; 550 tapes; 200 maps. **Subscriptions:** 11 journals and other serials. **Services:** Copying; photographic reproduction; archives open to public by appointment only. **Publications:** Museum Notes, quarterly; Mesa County Cooking with History. **Staff:** Judy Prosser, Archv./Registrar.

★8509★

MUSEUM OF YORK COUNTY - EDUCATIONAL LIBRARY (Sci-Tech)
Mt. Gallant Rd.
Rte. 4, Box 211
Rock Hill, SC 29730   Charles W. Hall, Exec.Dir.
Founded: 1950. **Subjects:** African animals, western hemisphere African artifacts, natural history. **Special Collections:** F. Delano Collection on African animals and life (95 books); videotape library. **Holdings:** 925 books; 1010 bound periodical volumes; 2500 other items (cataloged); 300 National Geographic maps. **Services:** Library open to staff, museum members and approved researchers. **Remarks:** Maintains a planetarium.

★8510★

MUSEUMS OF THE CITY OF MOBILE - MUSEUM REFERENCE LIBRARY (Hist)
355 Government St.   Phone: (205) 438-7569
Mobile, AL 36602   Caldwell Delaney, Musm.Dir.
Founded: 1964. **Staff:** Prof 4; Other 11. **Subjects:** Mobile history, Gulf Coast history, Civil War, American art, Indian culture, fire service. **Special Collections:** Julian Lee Rayford Folklore Collection; Mary Fenollosa Collection; negatives (6000); riverboat waybills (150 items). **Holdings:** 3000 books; 50 bound periodical volumes; 200 pamphlets (cataloged); 300 historic newspapers; 300 Volunteer Fire Company records; 1400 colonial and Confederate manuscript documents; 500 historic mercantile invoices. **Subscriptions:** 12 journals and other serials. **Services:** Library open to public on request. **Publications:** Military Buttons of the Gulf Coast; Journal of a Voyage to Dauphin Island, 1720; Phoenix Volunteer Fire Company of Mobile; Old Mobile, Fort Louis de la Louisiane, 1702-1711; Raphael Semmes: Rear Admiral, Confederate States Navy, Brigadier General, Confederate States Army; Iron Ore to Iron Lace.

★8511★

MUSEUMS AT STONY BROOK - KATE STRONG HISTORICAL LIBRARY (Trans)
Rte. 25A   Phone: (516) 751-0066
Stony Brook, NY 11790   Janice Gray Armstrong, Libn.
Founded: 1951. **Staff:** Prof 1; Other 1. **Subjects:** Horse-drawn vehicles; Long Island history. **Special Collections:** 19th and early 20th century carriage books; William S. Mount and family archives; archives of local Long Island material. **Holdings:** 2500 books; 500 bound periodical volumes; 500 catalogs (cataloged) 100 boxes of archives; photographs. **Subscriptions:** 10 journals and other serials. **Services:** Interlibrary loans; copying; bibliographic and reference services for carriage collectors and research workers; library open to public for reference use only by appointment.

★8512★

MUSIC AND ARTS INSTITUTE OF SAN FRANCISCO - COLLEGE LIBRARY (Mus)
2622 Jackson St.   Phone: (415) 567-1445
San Francisco, CA 94115   Ross McKee, Dir.
Founded: 1934. **Subjects:** Music, fine arts, English literature and drama, foreign languages, government and history, religion and philosophy. **Holdings:** 12,000 books and scores; 1000 bound periodical volumes; 4000 recordings (cataloged). **Subscriptions:** 8 journals and other serials. **Services:** Library open to public with restrictions.

★8513★

MUSIC CENTER OPERATING COMPANY - ARCHIVES (Mus; Theater)
135 N. Grand Ave.   Phone: (213) 972-7499
Los Angeles, CA 90012   Joel M. Pritkin, Cur.
Founded: 1969. **Staff:** Prof 1; Other 2. **Subjects:** Music center history, performing arts - music, theater, dance. **Special Collections:** Early history of

the Los Angeles Philharmonic Orchestra and the Los Angeles and New York Theatre. **Holdings:** 400 books; archival items; programs and playbills; photographs. **Subscriptions:** 20 journals and other serials; 6 newspapers. **Services:** Copying; archives open to public by appointment. **Networks/Consortia:** Member of Southern California Answering Network (SCAN).

MUSIC EDUCATORS NATL. CONFERENCE HISTORICAL CENTER
See: **University of Maryland, College Park - Libraries - Music Library**

MUSIC LIBRARY ASSOCIATION ARCHIVES
See: **University of Maryland, College Park - Libraries - Music Library**

MUSICAL FUND SOCIETY OF PHILADELPHIA LIBRARY
See: **Free Library of Philadelphia - Music Department**

★8514★

MUSICAL INSTRUMENT MUSEUM - LIBRARY (Mus)
1124 Dionne St.   Phone: (612) 488-4303
St. Paul, MN 55113   William J. Kugler, Pres.
Subjects: Organology, history of musical instruments and mechanical and electronic musical instruments, music reference. **Holdings:** 700 books; dissertations; pamphlets; bulletins; periodicals; memorabilia; catalogs; clippings; slides; films; all National Geographics with music articles. **Subscriptions:** 20 journals and other serials. **Services:** Library open to public with restrictions.

★8515★

MUSICAL MUSEUM - RESEARCH LIBRARY (Mus)
Main St.   Phone: (315) 841-8774
Deansboro, NY 13328   Arthur H. Sanders, Cur.
Founded: 1948. **Staff:** 5. **Subjects:** Musical antiques with emphasis on mechanical musical antiques - music boxes, grind organs, nickelodeons, melodeons. **Special Collections:** Welte Mignon piano rolls. **Holdings:** 150 volumes. **Services:** Copying; library not open to general public; research done by library on advance fee basis.

MUSICIENS AMATEURS DU CANADA
See: **Canadian Amateur Musicians-Musiciens Amateurs du Canada**

★8516★

MUSKEGON BUSINESS COLLEGE - LIBRARY (Bus-Fin)
145 Apple Ave.   Phone: (616) 726-4904
Muskegon, MI 49442   Margaret Moon, Libn.
Founded: 1885. **Staff:** 3. **Subjects:** Business management, economics and accounting. **Holdings:** 3100 books. **Subscriptions:** 62 journals and other serials. **Services:** Library not open to public. **Staff:** Josephine Pavlich, Asst.Libn.

★8517★

MUSKEGON CHRONICLE - EDITORIAL LIBRARY (Publ)
981 Third St.   Phone: (616) 722-3161
Muskegon, MI 49443   Linda S. Thompson, Libn.
Staff: 1. **Subjects:** Local history, newspaper reference topics. **Special Collections:** Muskegon history (Charles Yates weekly series of articles). **Holdings:** 500 books; 450,000 news clippings; 85,000 photos and pictures; 770 reels of microfilm. **Subscriptions:** 8 journals and other serials; 10 newspapers. **Services:** Copying; library not open to public.

★8518★

MUSKINGUM LAW LIBRARY (Law)
Court House   Phone: (614) 452-9143
Zanesville, OH 43701   Helen Porter, Libn.
Subjects: Law. **Holdings:** 15,000 volumes; 3000 volumes on ultrafiche.

MUSLIM BIBLIOGRAPHIC CENTER
See: **American Institute of Islamic Studies**

MUSLIM LIBRARY
See: **Ahmadiyya Movement in Islam**

MUSSALLEM (Helen K.) LIBRARY
See: **Canadian Nurses Association - Helen K. Mussallem Library**

MUSSELMAN LIBRARY
See: **Gettysburg College**

★8519★
MUTUAL LIFE ASSURANCE COMPANY OF CANADA - LIBRARY (Bus-Fin)
227 King St.   Phone: (519) 888-2262
Waterloo, ON, Canada N2J 1R2   Leslie Day, Libn.
Founded: 1948. **Subjects:** Life insurance, management, business communication, interpersonal relationships, fitness and health, self-improvement. **Holdings:** 1500 books; 16 self-study courses. **Subscriptions:** 170 journals and other serials; 5 newspapers. **Services:** Interlibrary loans; library not open to public. **Publications:** Newsletter - for internal distribution only.

★8520★
MUTUAL OF NEW YORK - LAW LIBRARY (Bus-Fin; Law)
1740 Broadway   Phone: (212) 708-2235
New York, NY 10019   Janet Stoller, Libn.
Staff: Prof 1; Other 1. **Subjects:** Life insurance, accident and health insurance, pensions, law. **Special Collections:** Statutes and laws of New York from 1664. **Holdings:** 26,000 volumes. **Services:** Interlibrary loans; library not open to public.

★8521★
MUTUAL OF NEW YORK - LIBRARY/INFORMATION SERVICE (Bus-Fin)
1740 Broadway   Phone: (212) 708-2139
New York, NY 10019   Marion Koshar, Corp.Libn.
Founded: 1945. **Staff:** Prof 1; Other 1. **Subjects:** Life insurance, management, social insurance, business, accident and health insurance, finance, pensions. **Holdings:** 6000 books; 55 VF drawers of pamphlets and clippings; 500 reels of microfilm; microfiche. **Subscriptions:** 300 journals and other serials. **Services:** Interlibrary loans; library open to public for reference use only on request. **Computerized Information Services:** DIALOG.

★8522★
MUTUAL OF OMAHA/UNITED OF OMAHA - LIBRARY (Bus-Fin)
Mutual of Omaha Plaza   Phone: (402) 978-2002
Omaha, NE 68175   Elizabeth Bremer, Hd.
Founded: 1941. **Staff:** 2. **Subjects:** Insurance. **Holdings:** 5500 books; 110 bound periodical volumes. **Subscriptions:** 153 journals and other serials; 7 newspapers. **Services:** Interlibrary loans; library open to public with restrictions. **Staff:** Seeta Persaud, Asst.Libn.

MVMA
See: Motor Vehicle Manufacturers Association

MYRTLE BEACH AIR FORCE BASE (SC)
See: U.S. Air Force Base - Myrtle Beach Base Library

★8523★
MYSTERY WRITERS OF AMERICA, INC. - MYSTERY LIBRARY (Rec)
150 Fifth Ave.   Phone: (212) 255-7005
New York, NY 10011   Harold Q. Masur, Exec. V.P.
Founded: 1945. **Subjects:** Mystery and crime. **Holdings:** Figures not available. **Services:** Library not open to public. **Publications:** The Third Degree, 10 times a year - to all members.

★8524★
MYSTIC SEAPORT, INC. - G.W. BLUNT WHITE LIBRARY (Hist)
                                         Phone: (203) 536-2631
Mystic, CT 06355   Gerald E. Morris, Libn.
Founded: 1965. **Staff:** Prof 4; Other 5. **Subjects:** American maritime history, shipbuilding, vessel registration, yachting, naval architecture, fisheries. **Special Collections:** American Maritime History Manuscript Collection (400,000 items). **Holdings:** 40,000 books; 4000 bound periodical volumes; 1000 logbooks; 1000 reels of microfilm; 5000 charts; 45,000 ships' plans; 4000 government documents (limited depository). **Subscriptions:** 392 journals and other serials. **Services:** Interlibrary loans; library open to public for research and reference use only. **Publications:** Manuscript inventories, irregular - free. **Staff:** Douglas L. Stein, Mss.Libn.; Lisa Halttunen, Ref.Libn.; Susan M. Filupeit, Tech.Proc.Libn.; Virginia M. Allen, Ships Plans Libn.

N

★8525★

NABISCO BRANDS, INC. - FAIR LAWN TECHNICAL CENTER LIBRARY (Food-Bev)
2111 Rte. 208   Phone: (201) 797-6800
Fair Lawn, NJ 07410   Sonia D. Meurer, Libn.
Staff: Prof 1; Other 1. **Subjects:** Food, nutrition, chemistry. **Holdings:** 1200 books; 1500 other cataloged items; 4000 patents; 300 company reports and notebooks. **Subscriptions:** 250 journals and other serials. **Services:** Interlibrary loans; copying; library open to public by appointment. **Computerized Information Services:** DIALOG, SDC, BRS, New York Times Information Service. **Publications:** Guide to Current Technical Literature, weekly; Library Bulletin, monthly. **Formed by the Merger of:** Nabisco, Inc. and Standard Brands Inc.

★8526★

NABISCO BRANDS, INC. - TECHNICAL INFORMATION CENTER (Food-Bev)
15 River Rd.   Phone: (203) 762-2500
Wilton, CT 06897   Melanie C. Sze, Libn.
Founded: 1922. **Staff:** Prof 1; Other 1. **Subjects:** Nutrition, chemistry, microbiology, food science, computer science. **Holdings:** 9000 books; 2800 bound periodical volumes; 200 technical reports. **Subscriptions:** 270 journals. **Services:** Interlibrary loans; copying; SDI; library open to public. **Computerized Information Services:** DIALOG, SDC, Control Data Corporation, Dun & Bradstreet, Inc., Chemical Abstracts Service, Data Resources, Inc. **Networks/Consortia:** Member of Southwestern Connecticut Library Council. **Publications:** Periodicals Holdings List, annual; New Acquisitions List, quarterly. **Formed by the Merger of:** Nabisco, Inc. and Standard Brands Inc.

NABOW (David) LIBRARY
See: Duke Power Company - David Nabow Library

★8527★

NAISMITH MEMORIAL BASKETBALL HALL OF FAME - EDWARD J. AND GENA G. HICKOX LIBRARY (Rec)
460 Alden St.
Highland Sta., Box 175   Phone: (413) 781-6500
Springfield, MA 01109   June Harrison Steitz, Subject Spec.
Staff: Prof 1. **Subjects:** Basketball (men's and women's) - amateur, scholastic, collegiate, professional. **Special Collections:** William G. Mokray Collection (691 books, guides, scrapbooks). **Holdings:** 2627 books; 24 VF drawers of photographs; 68 VF drawers of news clippings, pamphlets, reports and statistics; 12 VF drawers of collegiate, professional and international game programs, including all-star and tournament games. complete set of basketball guides. **Subscriptions:** 16 journals and other serials. **Services:** Copying; library open to public by appointment. **Publications:** Official Hall of Fame Book - for sale; Newsletter, quarterly.

★8528★

NALCO CHEMICAL COMPANY - TECHNICAL CENTER - INFORMATION SERVICES (Sci-Tech)
1801 Diehl Rd.   Phone: (312) 961-9500
Naperville, IL 60540   Marie Tashima, Supv.
Founded: 1928. **Staff:** Prof 3; Other 2. **Subjects:** Chemistry, water treatment, pulp and paper chemistry. **Holdings:** 7000 books; 8000 bound periodical volumes; 28 VF drawers of bulletins, reprints, photocopies; 12 VF drawers of internal research reports; 20 VF drawers of technical data; 24 VF drawers of patents; 4000 unbound journals; microfilm. **Subscriptions:** 425 journals and other serials. **Services:** Library open to public for reference use only.

★8529★

NANAIMO AND DISTRICT MUSEUM SOCIETY - ARCHIVES (Hist)
100 Cameron Rd.   Phone: (604) 753-1821
Nanaimo, BC, Canada V9R 2X1 Dick Ferre, Supv.
Founded: 1967. **Staff:** Prof 3. **Subjects:** Coal mining, American Indians and other ethnic groups, local history, colonial history, fashion. **Special Collections:** Local historical photographs; diorama depicting traditional Indian life style; restored and fully furnished miner's cottage. **Holdings:** 4000 volumes; 4000 photographs; 150 maps; 2000 archival items. **Services:** Interlibrary loans; archives open to public for reference use only. **Publications:** Nanaimo Scenes from the Past, published 1965. **Staff:** Meg Rintoul, Educ.Prog.Coord.; Kelly Clarkson, Display Techn.

★8530★

NANTUCKET HISTORICAL ASSOCIATION - PETER FOULGER LIBRARY (Hist)
Broad St.
Nantucket, MA 02554   Edourd A. Stackpole, Hist.
Founded: 1894. **Staff:** Prof 2. **Subjects:** History of whaling, whaling implements, whaling and marine fiction, topics of local interest. **Special Collections:** Log books; account and letter books; original documents connected with whaling; Nantucket and maritime history. **Holdings:** 5600 volumes; pamphlets; 200 log books on microfilm. **Services:** Library open to public with entrance fee or membership card.

★8531★

NANTUCKET MARIA MITCHELL ASSOCIATION - LIBRARY (Hist; Sci-Tech)
Vestal St.   Phone: (617) 228-9198
Nantucket, MA 02554   Dr. M. Jane Stroup, Libn.
Founded: 1902. **Staff:** Prof 1; Other 1. **Subjects:** Astronomy, biology, chemistry, general science, mathematics, biography, Nantucket topics. **Special Collections:** Maria Mitchell Memorabilia (Maria Mitchell's personal library). **Holdings:** 12,000 books; 1236 bound periodical volumes; 338 boxes of pamphlets. **Subscriptions:** 49 journals and other serials. **Services:** Interlibrary loans; library open to public.

★8532★

NAPA COUNTY HISTORICAL SOCIETY - GOODMAN LIBRARY (Hist)
1219 First St.   Phone: (707) 224-1739
Napa, CA 94558   Jess Doud, Exec.Dir./Archv.
Founded: 1975. **Staff:** Prof 3; Other 12. **Subjects:** Napa County history. **Holdings:** 900 books; 10 bound periodical volumes; 700 pictures; 174 boxes of newspaper clippings and ephemera; 15 linear feet of scrapbooks, diaries, manuscripts; artifacts and tools; Napa Register (1954 to present); Napa Journal (1890-1960). **Services:** Copying; library open to public. **Publications:** Gleanings, annual - to members or for sale. **Staff:** Dorothy Donahoe, Tech.Serv.; Ruth Marra, Asst.Archv.; Dolly Prchal, Photo Serv.; Ruth B. Northrop, Oral Hist.

★8533★

NAPA STATE HOSPITAL - WRENSHALL A. OLIVER PROFESSIONAL LIBRARY (Med)
Box A   Phone: (707) 253-5477
Imola, CA 94558   Margaret L. Buss, Sr.Libn.
Founded: 1875. **Staff:** Prof 1. **Subjects:** Psychiatry, psychiatric social work, psychiatric nursing, neurology, clinical psychology, mental retardation. **Special Collections:** Argens Memorial Collection (history of psychiatry and psychology). **Holdings:** 9000 books; 901 bound periodical volumes; 800 tape cassettes. **Subscriptions:** 175 journals and other serials. **Services:** Interlibrary loans; library not open to public. **Networks/Consortia:** Member of Pacific Southwest Regional Medical Library Service (PSRMLS). **Publications:** Recent Additions to the Library; News and Reviews, monthly.

★8534★

NAPA VALLEY WINE LIBRARY ASSOCIATION - LIBRARY (Food-Bev)
Box 328   Phone: (707) 963-5244
St. Helena, CA 94574   Mrs. Clayla Davis, Lib.Dir.
Staff: Prof 1; Other 1. **Subjects:** Brewing, cookery, drinks and drinking, gastronomy, grapes, viticulture, wine and winemaking. **Special Collections:** Wine labels (1500). **Holdings:** 3000 books; 150 bound periodical volumes; 4 VF drawers; 99 reels of microfilm. **Subscriptions:** 43 journals and other serials. **Services:** Interlibrary loans; copying; library open to public. **Computerized Information Services:** RLIN. **Networks/Consortia:** Member of North Bay Cooperative Library System. **Publications:** Napa Valley wine library bibliography. **Remarks:** Library is part of St. Helena Public Library and is located at 1492 Library Lane, St. Helena, CA 94574.

NAPPS (National Association for the Preservation & Perpetuation of Storytelling)
See: National Storytelling Resource Center

NARAMORE (J.T.) LIBRARY
See: Larned State Hospital - J.T. Naramore Library

★8535★

NARCOTICS EDUCATION, INC. - SCHARFFENBERG MEMORIAL LIBRARY (Soc Sci)
6830 Laurel St., N.W.
Box 4390   Phone: (202) 722-6739
Washington, DC 20012   James Ford, Libn.
Staff: Prof 1. **Subjects:** Drug problems, alcoholism, tobacco and health. **Special Collections:** Joseph T. Zottoli Collection (personal papers of Judge Zottoli of Boston on the Prohibition period in U.S.); rare books on alcoholism

and temperance (500). **Holdings:** 2400 books; 10 bound periodical volumes; 1300 pamphlets. **Subscriptions:** 80 journals and other serials; 5 newspapers. **Services:** Library open to public by special request. **Staff:** F.A. Soper, Dir.

NARMIC
See: National Action/Research on the Military-Industrial Complex

NASA
See: U.S. NASA

NASH (C.H.) MUSEUM LIBRARY
See: Memphis State University Libraries - C.H. Nash Museum Library

★8536★
NASHOBA COMMUNITY HOSPITAL - MEDICAL LIBRARY (Med)
200 Groton Rd.   Phone: (617) 772-0200
Ayer, MA 01432   Patricia Payton, Libn.
Staff: Prof 1; Other 2. **Subjects:** Medicine and nursing. **Special Collections:** Patient education pamphlets. **Holdings:** 500 books; 400 bound periodical volumes. **Subscriptions:** 40 journals and other serials. **Services:** Interlibrary loans; copying; library open to local health professionals and students only. **Networks/Consortia:** Member of Consortium of Central Massachusetts Health Related Libraries.

★8537★
NASHOTAH HOUSE - LIBRARY (Rel-Theol)
                                   Phone: (414) 646-3371
Nashotah, WI 53058   James Dunkly, Libn.
Founded: 1842. **Staff:** Prof 2; Other 3. **Subjects:** Theology, Bible, church history. **Holdings:** 68,000 books; 1450 bound periodical volumes. **Subscriptions:** 580 journals and other serials. **Services:** Interlibrary loans; copying; library open to public. **Computerized Information Services:** Computerized cataloging. **Networks/Consortia:** Member of Wisconsin Library Consortium; OCLC; American Theological Library Association; Chicago Area Theological Library Association (CATLA); Library Council of Metropolitan Milwaukee, Inc. (LCOMM). **Staff:** Evelyn Payson, Asst.Libn.

★8538★
NASHUA CORPORATION - TECHNICAL LIBRARY (Sci-Tech)
44 Franklin St.   Phone: (603) 880-2537
Nashua, NH 03061   Kay Marquis, Tech.Lib.Supv.
Founded: 1918. **Staff:** 3. **Subjects:** Discrete particle technology - formulation and application of chemical coatings to paper and other substrates; chemistry; physics; reprography. **Holdings:** 3900 books and bound periodical volumes; 15 VF drawers of U.S. and foreign patents. **Subscriptions:** 150 journals and other serials. **Services:** Interlibrary loans; library not open to public.

★8539★
NASHVILLE BANNER - LIBRARY (Publ)
1100 Broadway   Phone: (615) 255-5401
Nashville, TN 37202   Sally P. Moran, Libn.
Founded: 1938. **Staff:** Prof 1; Other 2. **Subjects:** Newspaper reference topics. **Holdings:** 1500 books; clippings (cataloged); 50,000 photographs. **Subscriptions:** 15 journals and other serials. **Services:** Library open to public with permission from editor.

★8540★
NASHVILLE AND DAVIDSON COUNTY METROPOLITAN PLANNING COMMISSION - LIBRARY (Plan)†
Lindsley Hall
730 Second Ave. S.   Phone: (615) 259-6268
Nashville, TN 37201   Wanda Lucia Moore, Libn./Ed.
Staff: Prof 1. **Subjects:** Urban planning, demography, economics, environment, transportation, zoning. **Special Collections:** Commission archives; Citizen's Resource Center. **Holdings:** 6500 books; 45 bound periodical volumes; 250 documents and archival items. **Subscriptions:** 214 journals and other serials. **Services:** Interlibrary loans; library open to public. **Computerized Information Services:** Internal database. **Publications:** Acquisition List, monthly; Agency Books and Reports.

NASHVILLE AND DAVIDSON COUNTY PUBLIC LIBRARY
See: Public Library of Nashville and Davidson County

★8541★
NASHVILLE - METROPOLITAN DEPARTMENT OF PUBLIC HEALTH - LENTZ HEALTH CENTER LIBRARY (Med)
311 23rd Ave., N.   Phone: (615) 327-9313
Nashville, TN 37203   Jenny Patterson, Libn.
Founded: 1967. **Staff:** Prof 1. **Subjects:** Internal medicine, public health,

nursing, environmental health. **Holdings:** 2000 volumes. **Subscriptions:** 230 journals and other serials. **Services:** Interlibrary loans; copying; library not open to public. **Computerized Information Services:** DIALOG. **Networks/Consortia:** Member of Mid-Tennessee Health Sciences Librarian Group; Tennessee Health Science Library Association.

★8542★
NASHVILLE METROPOLITAN GENERAL HOSPITAL - HEALTH SCIENCE LIBRARY (Med)†
72 Hermitage Ave.   Phone: (615) 259-5657
Nashville, TN 37210   Stephanie Towle, Libn.
Staff: Prof 1. **Subjects:** Medicine, surgery, nursing. **Holdings:** 1000 books; 1000 bound periodical volumes. **Subscriptions:** 125 journals and other serials. **Services:** Interlibrary loans; copying; library open to public with restrictions.

★8543★
NASHVILLE STATE TECHNICAL INSTITUTE - EDUCATIONAL RESOURCE CENTER (Sci-Tech)
120 White Bridge Rd.   Phone: (615) 741-1229
Nashville, TN 37209   Carolyn Householder, Hd.
Founded: 1970. **Staff:** Prof 7; Other 4. **Subjects:** Engineering technology, science, business. **Holdings:** 24,300 books; 825 bound periodical volumes; 1020 AV items; 1100 microforms; 500 solar energy items on microfiche; 875 video and cassette tapes; 201 16mm films; 3 VF drawers. **Subscriptions:** 250 journals and other serials; 8 newspapers. **Services:** Interlibrary loans; copying; library open to public. **Staff:** James R. Veatch, Professor; Charles May, Assoc. Professor; Harriet Dunn, Asst. Professor; Jack Smith, AV Spec.; Joe Rogers, Tech. Illustrator; Betty Renfro, Learning Lab.Coord.

NASHVILLE TENNESSEAN
See: Tennessean

NASPE
See: National Association for Sport & Physical Education

NASSAU ACADEMY OF MEDICINE - JOHN N. SHELL LIBRARY
See: Nassau County Medical Society

★8544★
NASSAU COUNTY DEPARTMENT OF HEALTH - DIVISION OF LABORATORIES & RESEARCH - MEDICAL LIBRARY (Med)
209 Main St.   Phone: (516) 483-9158
Hempstead, NY 11550   Madeline H. Burston, Pub. Health Adm.
Founded: 1959. **Staff:** Prof 1; Other 2. **Subjects:** Laboratory diagnosis, communicable diseases, pathology, public health. **Holdings:** 1227 books; 4700 microfilmed and bound periodical volumes; 125 miscellaneous books. **Subscriptions:** 75 journals and other serials; 10 newspapers. **Services:** Interlibrary loans; copying; library not open to public. **Networks/Consortia:** Member of Medical & Scientific Librarians of Long Island. **Staff:** Beatrice R. Sewald, Asst.Libn.

★8545★
NASSAU COUNTY DEPARTMENT OF HEALTH - OFFICE OF PUBLIC HEALTH - LIBRARY (Med)
240 Old Country Rd., Rm. 613   Phone: (516) 535-3368
Mineola, NY 11501   Irena Robkoff, Lib.Asst.
Staff: 1. **Subjects:** Public health. **Holdings:** 6000 books; 413 bound periodical volumes; 288 reels of microfilmed journals; Nassau County Department of Health publications, monthly and yearly reports. **Subscriptions:** 225 journals and other serials; 165 newsletters. **Services:** Interlibrary loans (limited); copying (limited); library open to public for reference use only. **Publications:** Content Collection of Public Health Oriented Periodicals, monthly - distributed to staff members and others by approval only. **Formerly:** Nassau County Department of Health - Central Research Library.

NASSAU COUNTY DEPARTMENT OF RECREATION AND PARKS - TACKAPAUSHA MUSEUM
See: Tackapausha Museum

★8546★
NASSAU COUNTY MEDICAL CENTER - HEALTH SCIENCES LIBRARY (Med)
2201 Hempstead Turnpike   Phone: (516) 542-3542
East Meadow, NY 11554   Paul G. Merrigan, Libn.
Founded: 1952. **Staff:** Prof 1; Other 5. **Subjects:** Medicine, nursing and allied health sciences. **Holdings:** 6000 books; 6000 bound periodical volumes; 3000 AV materials (cataloged). **Subscriptions:** 520 journals and other serials. **Services:** Interlibrary loans; library open to public for reference use only.

Networks/Consortia: Member of Medical Library Center of New York (MLCNY); Long Island Library Resources Council (LILRC).

★8547★

NASSAU COUNTY MEDICAL SOCIETY - NASSAU ACADEMY OF MEDICINE - JOHN N. SHELL LIBRARY (Med)
1200 Stewart Ave.   Phone: (516) 832-2320
Garden City, NY 11530   Mary L. Westermann, Med.Libn.
Staff: Prof 1; Other 2. **Subjects:** Medicine, psychiatry, nursing. **Holdings:** 8000 books; 45,000 bound periodical volumes; 3 VF drawers; 2500 tapes. **Subscriptions:** 400 journals and other serials. **Services:** Interlibrary loans to medical libraries only; copying; library open to public for reference use only. **Computerized Information Services:** MEDLINE.

★8548★

NASSAU COUNTY MUSEUM REFERENCE LIBRARY (Hist)
Dwight D. Eisenhower Memorial Pk.   Phone: (516) 542-4516
East Meadow, NY 11554   Edward J. Smits, Dir.
Founded: 1961. **Staff:** Prof 2; Other 1. **Subjects:** Nassau County and Long Island history, anthropology, archeology, botany, zoology. **Holdings:** 7000 books; 1500 bound periodical volumes; 100,000 documents; 32 VF drawers; 800 maps; 3000 reels of microfilmed local newspapers; 2500 pamphlets; 10,000 clippings; 15,000 photographs. **Subscriptions:** 100 journals and other serials. **Services:** Interlibrary loans; copying; library open to public for reference use only. **Staff:** Richard A. Winsche, Hist.; Monica Albala, Musm.Cur.

★8549★

NASSAU COUNTY PLANNING COMMISSION - LIBRARY (Plan; Env-Cons)
222 Willis Ave.   Phone: (516) 535-2244
Mineola, NY 11501   Adele Falco Siedlecki, Libn.
Founded: 1950. **Staff:** Prof 1. **Subjects:** Planning, population, environment, industry, zoning, land use, conservation, transportation, history. **Special Collections:** Census computer printouts (60). **Holdings:** 4000 books and bound periodical volumes. **Services:** Copying; library open to public for reference use only. **Publications:** Annual Report; Data Book; Census volumes; professional reports.

★8550★

NASSAU COUNTY SUPREME COURT - LAW LIBRARY (Law)
100 Supreme Court Dr.   Phone: (516) 535-3883
Mineola, NY 11501   James J. Lodato, Prin. Law Libn.
Founded: 1968. **Staff:** Prof 3; Other 8. **Subjects:** Law. **Holdings:** 164,000 volumes; 3183 reels of microfilm; 6073 microfiche; 12,795 microcards. **Subscriptions:** 958 journals and other serials; 6 newspapers. **Services:** Library open to public. **Publications:** Ex Libris, Nassau Lawyer, (new acquisitions for Nassau County Bar Journal), monthly. **Staff:** Barbara Oberlander, Law Libn.

NASSAU EDUCATIONAL RESOURCES CENTER (NERC)
See: Board of Cooperative Educational Services of Nassau County (BOCES)

★8551★

NASSAU HOSPITAL - BENJAMIN WHITE SEAMAN MEDICAL LIBRARY (Med)
259 First St.   Phone: (516) 663-2280
Mineola, NY 11501   Virginia I. Cook, Med.Libn.
Staff: Prof 1; Other 2. **Subjects:** Medicine, nursing, surgery. **Holdings:** 2100 books; 5000 bound periodical volumes; 70 AV materials. **Subscriptions:** 232 journals and other serials. **Services:** Interlibrary loans; copying; library not open to public. **Computerized Information Services:** NLM.

NASSAU-SUFFOLK BRAILLE LIBRARY
See: Industrial Home for the Blind

NATCHEZ TRACE PARKWAY - LIBRARY & VISITOR CENTER
See: U.S. Natl. Park Service

★8552★

NATHAN (Robert R.) ASSOCIATES, INC. - LIBRARY (Bus-Fin; Energy)
1301 Pennsylvania Ave., N.W.   Phone: (202) 393-2700
Washington, DC 20004   Joan Bow, Libn.
Staff: Prof 1; Other 1. **Subjects:** Economics - national and international, social research, transportation and communication, antitrust, energy. **Holdings:** 2000 books; 10,000 pamphlets and government documents. **Subscriptions:** 150 journals and other serials. **Services:** Interlibrary loans; copying; library not open to public. **Computerized Information Services:** Online systems.

★8553★

NATICK HISTORICAL SOCIETY - LIBRARY (Hist)
Bacon Free Library Bldg.   Phone: (617) 653-6730
South Natick, MA 01760   Iola Scheufele, Dir.
Founded: 1870. **Staff:** Prof 1. **Subjects:** Local history, vital records of Massachusetts towns. **Special Collections:** Harriet Beecher Stowe Collection; John Eliot Indian Bible; Horatio Alger Collection; Henry Wilson Collection, U.S. Vice-President under Ulysses S. Grant; old natural history books. **Services:** Library open to public for reference use only.

NATICK RESEARCH AND DEVELOPMENT LABORATORIES
See: U.S. Army

NATIONAL... OF CANADA
See also: Canada - National...

★8554★

NATIONAL ACADEMY OF DESIGN - LIBRARY AND ARCHIVES (Art)
1083 Fifth Ave.   Phone: (212) 369-4880
New York, NY 10028   Abigail Booth Gerdts, Archv.
Founded: 1825. **Subjects:** American art, art history. **Holdings:** 3000 volumes. **Services:** Copying; library and archives open to students and scholars by appointment.

NATIONAL ACADEMY OF ENGINEERING
See: National Academy of Sciences

NATIONAL ACADEMY OF RECORDING ARTS & SCIENCES
See: Country Music Foundation

NATIONAL ACADEMY OF SCIENCES - INTERNATIONAL GEOPHYSICAL YEAR ARCHIVES
See: World Data Center A - Solar-Terrestrial Physics

★8555★

NATIONAL ACADEMY OF SCIENCES - NATIONAL ACADEMY OF ENGINEERING - LIBRARY (Sci-Tech)
2101 Constitution Ave., N.W.   Phone: (202) 334-2125
Washington, DC 20418   James L. Olsen, Jr., Libn.
Staff: Prof 5; Other 2. **Special Collections:** Publications of the National Academy of Sciences - National Research Council, National Academy of Engineering and Institute of Medicine. **Holdings:** Figures not available. **Subscriptions:** 500 journals and other serials. **Services:** Interlibrary loans; copying; library open to public by appointment. **Computerized Information Services:** DIALOG, SDC, New York Times Information Service, BRS, DOE/RECON, Dow Jones News Retrieval; computerized cataloging and serials. **Networks/Consortia:** Member of Interlibrary Users Associaton; Metropolitan Washington Library Council. **Special Catalogs:** Bibliographic Record of NAS-NAE, -IOM, -NRC reports in 42x microfiche (1970 to present). **Staff:** Barbara Kratz, ILL Libn.; Helene Goldstein, Reports Libn.; Rosalyn Leiderman, Info.Serv.Libn.; Audrey Ward, Leg.Ref.Spec.

★8556★

NATIONAL ACADEMY OF SCIENCES - NATIONAL RESEARCH COUNCIL - HIGHWAY RESEARCH INFORMATION SERVICE (Trans)
Transportation Research Bd.
2101 Constitution Ave., N.W.   Phone: (202) 334-3250
Washington, DC 20418   Arthur B. Mobley, HRIS Mgr.
Founded: 1967. **Staff:** Prof 3; Other 5. **Subjects:** Highway transport, nonrail mass transit, operations, planning, design and maintenance, construction. **Holdings:** 85,000 machine readable abstracts of technical literature; 4000 machine readable resumes of ongoing research projects. **Services:** SDI; library open to public. **Computerized Information Services:** DIALOG, TRIS On-Line; Batch-Mode Retrieval HRIS Data Base (internal database). **Networks/Consortia:** Member of International Road Federation (IRF). **Publications:** HRIS Abstracts, quarterly; Current Awareness Service. **Also Known As:** HRIS. **Staff:** Nancy Dagenhart, Info.Spec.; Curtis Antos, Info.Spec.

★8557★

NATIONAL ACADEMY OF SCIENCES - NATIONAL RESEARCH COUNCIL - MARITIME RESEARCH INFORMATION SERVICE
Maritime Transportation Research Board
2101 Constitution Ave., N.W.
Washington, DC 20418
Defunct

★8558★
NATIONAL ACADEMY OF SCIENCES - NATIONAL RESEARCH COUNCIL - RAILROAD RESEARCH INFORMATION SERVICE
Transportation Research Bd.
2101 Constitution Ave., N.W.
Washington, DC 20418
Defunct

★8559★
NATIONAL ACADEMY OF SCIENCES - NATIONAL RESEARCH COUNCIL - TRANSPORTATION RESEARCH BOARD LIBRARY (Trans)
2101 Constitution Ave., N.W.　　　　Phone: (202) 334-2989
Washington, DC 20418　　　　Lisbeth L. Luke, Libn.
Founded: 1946. **Staff:** Prof 1; Other 2. **Subjects:** Transportation - engineering, planning, geology, law, safety, economics, environment; traffic engineering. **Special Collections:** Transportation Research Board publications (complete collection). **Holdings:** 17,000 books, bound periodical volumes and reports; VF drawers. **Subscriptions:** 300 journals and other serials. **Services:** Interlibrary loans; copying (fee); library open to research workers. **Computerized Information Services:** DIALOG, SDC. **Publications:** Periodicals List, annual - free upon request.

★8560★
NATIONAL ACTION/RESEARCH ON THE MILITARY-INDUSTRIAL COMPLEX - LIBRARY (Mil)
1501 Cherry St.　　　　Phone: (215) 241-7175
Philadelphia, PA 19102　　　　David Goodman
Founded: 1969. **Staff:** 5. **Subjects:** U.S. weapons systems, U.S. military contracts, U.S. policy and human rights, U.S. military aid in Central America, Southern Africa, multinational corporations, nuclear energy. **Holdings:** Figures not available for books; slides of nuclear weapons. **Subscriptions:** 50 journals and other serials. **Services:** Copying; library not open to public. **Publications:** List of publications - available upon request. **Remarks:** This is a project of the American Friends Service Committee. **Also Known As:** NARMIC.

NATIONAL ADULT EDUCATION CLEARINGHOUSE/MULTIMEDIA CENTER
See: Montclair State College

★8561★
NATIONAL AERONAUTIC ASSOCIATION - LIBRARY (Sci-Tech)
821 15th St., N.W.　　　　Phone: (202) 347-2808
Washington, DC 20005　　　　Milton M. Brown, Sec.
Staff: Prof 1; Other 3. **Subjects:** Aviation. **Special Collections:** World and U.S. aviation records. **Holdings:** 75 annuals; 15 filing cabinets of completed dossiers on record flights. **Subscriptions:** 12 journals and other serials. **Services:** Copying; library open to public by appointment. **Publications:** NAA Magazine, bimonthly - to members and by subscription.

NATIONAL AERONAUTICS AND SPACE ADMINISTRATION
See: U.S. NASA

NATIONAL AGRICULTURAL LIBRARY
See: U.S.D.A.

NATIONAL AIR PHOTO LIBRARY
See: Canada - Energy, Mines & Resources Canada - Surveys & Mapping Branch

NATIONAL AIR AND SPACE MUSEUM
See: Smithsonian Institution Libraries

★8562★
NATIONAL ALLIANCE FOR OPTIONAL PARENTHOOD - NAOP RESOURCE CENTER (Soc Sci)
2010 Massachusetts Ave., N.W.　　　　Phone: (202) 296-7474
Washington, DC 20036　　　　Ann Ulmschneider, Prog.Dir.
Founded: 1979. **Staff:** 1. **Subjects:** Voluntary childlessness, parenthood decision making, pronatalism, sexuality, family. **Special Collections:** Research studies on voluntary childlessness (197). **Holdings:** 115 books; 32 curriculum guides; 21 reports; 2 VF drawers of clippings. **Subscriptions:** 20 newspapers. **Services:** Copying; library open to public by appointment. **Publications:** A Decade of Voluntary Childlessness: A Bibliography - for sale. **Special Catalogs:** Catalog of research studies on voluntary childlessness (card).

★8563★
NATIONAL ALLIANCE OF SENIOR CITIZENS - LIBRARY (Soc Sci)
101 Park Washington Ct.　　　　Phone: (703) 241-9181
Falls Church, VA 22046　　　　C.C. Clinkscales, III, Natl.Dir.
Staff: 3. **Subjects:** Aging, economics, political theory, reference. **Holdings:**

1850 books; 100 bound periodical volumes; extensive governmental hearings. **Subscriptions:** 6 journals and other serials. **Services:** Library not open to public. **Publications:** The Senior Guardian; The Senior Services Manual.

NATIONAL ANIMAL DISEASE CENTER LIBRARY
See: U.S.D.A. - Agricultural Research Service

NATIONAL ANTHROPOLOGICAL ARCHIVES
See: Smithsonian Institution

★8564★
NATIONAL ANTI-VIVISECTION SOCIETY - LIBRARY (Env-Cons)
100 E. Ohio St.
Chicago, IL 60611
Subjects: Vivisection. **Holdings:** Figures not available.

NATIONAL ARCHIVES & RECORDS SERVICE
See: U.S. Natl. Archives & Records Service

★8565★
NATIONAL ASSOCIATION OF ACCOUNTANTS - LIBRARY (Bus-Fin)
919 Third Ave.　　　　Phone: (212) 754-9736
New York, NY 10022　　　　Miriam J. Redrick, Mgr., Lib.Serv.
Founded: 1920. **Staff:** Prof 1; Other 1. **Subjects:** Management accounting, financial accounting, data processing, management and financial management. **Special Collections:** Trade association accounting manuals (150). **Holdings:** 8000 books; 450 bound periodical volumes; 25 VF drawers. **Subscriptions:** 70 journals and other serials. **Services:** Interlibrary loans (limited); copying (limited); library open to public for reference use only. **Publications:** The Bookshelf, irregular; Industry Accounting Manuals, biennial - both for sale.

★8566★
NATIONAL ASSOCIATION OF ANIMAL BREEDERS - LIBRARY (Agri)
401 Bernadette Dr.
Box 1033　　　　Phone: (314) 445-4406
Columbia, MO 65205　　　　Richard Antweiler, Dir. of Info.
Subjects: Cattle breeding, artificial breeding, physiology of reproduction, artificial insemination industry. **Holdings:** 300 books; 40 bound periodical volumes. **Subscriptions:** 50 journals and other serials. **Services:** Library not open to public.

★8567★
NATIONAL ASSOCIATION OF ANOREXIA NERVOSA AND ASSOCIATED DISORDERS, INC. (ANAD) - LIBRARY (Med)
Box 271　　　　Phone: (312) 831-3438
Highland Park, IL 60035　　　　June Garland, Adm.Dir.
Founded: 1976. **Subjects:** Anorexia nervosa, bulimia, bulimarexia, other eating disorders. **Holdings:** Figures not available. **Services:** Library not open to public. **Publications:** Quarterly newsletter.

★8568★
NATIONAL ASSOCIATION OF BOARDS OF PHARMACY - LIBRARY
One E. Wacker Dr., Suite 2210
Chicago, IL 60601
Founded: 1904. **Subjects:** Pharmacy - law and regulation, education, licensure. **Remarks:** Presently inactive.

★8569★
NATIONAL ASSOCIATION OF BROADCASTERS - LIBRARY (Info Sci)
1771 N St., N.W.　　　　Phone: (202) 293-3578
Washington, DC 20036　　　　Susan M. Hill, Libn.
Founded: 1946. **Staff:** Prof 2; Other 1. **Subjects:** Radio and television broadcasting and related topics. **Holdings:** 6200 volumes. **Subscriptions:** 225 journals and other serials. **Services:** Library open to public by appointment. **Computerized Information Services:** New York Times Information Service, DIALOG, SDC, NewsNet. **Staff:** Ann Cardace, Asst.Libn.

NATIONAL ASSOCIATION OF BROADCASTERS - TELEVISION INFORMATION OFFICE
See: Television Information Office of the National Association of Broadcasters

NATIONAL ASSOCIATION OF COLLEGE WIND AND PERCUSSION INSTRUCTORS RESEARCH CENTER
See: University of Maryland, College Park - Libraries - Music Library

★8570★

NATIONAL ASSOCIATION FOR CORE CURRICULUM, INC. - LIBRARY (Educ)
Kent State University
407 D White Hall   Phone: (216) 672-7977
Kent, OH 44242   Dr. Gordon F. Vars, Exec.Sec.-Treas.
Staff: 1. **Subjects:** Core curriculum, interdisciplinary studies, block-time programs, humanities programs, education. **Holdings:** 50 books; 1 file drawer of clippings; 150 curriculum guides. **Services:** Library open to public by appointment. **Publications:** The Core Teacher, quarterly newsletter, Core Today; curriculum guides and bulletins. **Special Indexes:** Selected References on Block-Time, Core and Interdisciplinary Programs, 1981; A Bibliography of Research on the Effectiveness of Block-Time, Core and Interdisciplinary Programs, 1981.

★8571★

NATIONAL ASSOCIATION FOR CREATIVE CHILDREN AND ADULTS (NACCA) - LIBRARY (Soc Sci)
8080 Springvalley Dr.   Phone: (513) 631-1777
Cincinnati, OH 45236   Ann Fabe Isaacs, Hd.
Subjects: Creativity, giftedness, talent, art, music, writing. **Holdings:** Figures not available. **Subscriptions:** 30 journals and other serials. **Services:** Library open to public by appointment. **Publications:** The Creative Child and Adult Quarterly - to members and by subscription.

NATIONAL ASSOCIATION FOR HISPANIC ELDERLY
See: Asociacion Nacional Pro Personas Mayores

★8572★

NATIONAL ASSOCIATION OF HOME BUILDERS - NATIONAL HOUSING CENTER LIBRARY (Sci-Tech)
15th & M Sts., N.W.   Phone: (202) 822-0203
Washington, DC 20005   Margery M. Clark, Chf.Libn.
Staff: Prof 2; Other 2. **Subjects:** All aspects of homebuilding (technical, social, financial). **Holdings:** 10,000 books; 20,000 pamphlets and trade catalogs. **Subscriptions:** 200 journals and other serials. **Services:** Interlibrary loans; copying; library open to public. **Publications:** Library Bulletin, bimonthly; bibliographies. **Staff:** Doris Campbell, Asst.Libn.

★8573★

NATIONAL ASSOCIATION OF HOSIERY MANUFACTURERS - LIBRARY (Bus-Fin)
Box 35098   Phone: (704) 372-4200
Charlotte, NC 28235   Sid Smith, Sr. V.P.
Subjects: Hosiery - statistics, industry standards, newsletters and regulatory bulletins. **Holdings:** Figures not available. **Services:** Library is maintained for use of association staff and members. **Remarks:** Library is located at Charlottetown Office Gallery at Outlet Square, Suite 516, Charlotte, NC.

★8574★

NATIONAL ASSOCIATION OF HOUSING AND REDEVELOPMENT OFFICIALS - RESOURCE CENTER
2600 Virginia Ave., N.W., Suite 404
Washington, DC 20037
Defunct

★8575★

NATIONAL ASSOCIATION OF INSURANCE COMMISSIONERS - NAIC INFORMATION CENTER (Bus-Fin)
350 Bishops Way   Phone: (414) 784-9540
Brookfield, WI 53005   Jean DeLauche, Libn.
Founded: 1970. **Staff:** Prof 1; Other 1. **Subjects:** Insurance - regulation, law, business; insurance company profitability and solvency; actuarial science. **Special Collections:** NAIC Proceedings since 1871; annual reports of state insurance departments (250 volumes). **Holdings:** 7000 books; 200 bound periodical volumes; 300 files of clippings, reports, correspondence; annual statement data in time-sharing storage. **Subscriptions:** 150 journals and other serials; 5 newspapers. **Services:** Copying; SDI; library open to public for reference use only by appointment. **Computerized Information Services:** DIALOG; Statistical Reporting Service (internal database); computerized cataloging. **Networks/Consortia:** Member of Library Council of Metropolitan Milwaukee, Inc. (LCOMM). **Publications:** Proceedings of the NAIC, semiannual - for sale (legislative history of insurance law). **Remarks:** The association is not concerned with individual companies or information useful to investors; its purpose relates to state regulation only.

★8576★

NATIONAL ASSOCIATION OF LIFE UNDERWRITERS - LIBRARY (Bus-Fin)†
1922 F St., N.W.   Phone: (202) 331-6001
Washington, DC 20006   Jack E. Bobo, Exec.V.P.
Subjects: Life insurance. **Holdings:** 400 books; 200 bound periodical volumes; 2 VF drawers.

★8577★

NATIONAL ASSOCIATION OF MUTUAL SAVINGS BANKS - LIBRARY AND CENTRAL FILES (Bus-Fin)
200 Park Ave.   Phone: (212) 973-4704
New York, NY 10166   Elizabeth Riera Cohn, Libn.
Founded: 1920. **Staff:** Prof 1; Other 1. **Subjects:** Mutual savings banking, housing, bank operations, general banking. **Special Collections:** Publications of National Association of Mutual Savings Banks, 1920 to present (bound and unbound). **Holdings:** 4000 books; 480 bound periodical volumes; 225 boxes of archives; 170 boxes of magnetic tapes; 55 drawers of clippings, unbound reports, pamphlets and documents. **Subscriptions:** 72 journals and other serials. **Services:** Interlibrary loans; library open to public by appointment. **Publications:** Publications Received in the Library, quarterly - for internal distribution only.

★8578★

NATIONAL ASSOCIATION OF PARLIAMENTARIANS - TECHNICAL INFORMATION CENTER (Law)†
3706 Broadway, Suite 300   Phone: (816) 531-1735
Kansas City, MO 64111   Elaine Fulton, Exec.Sec.
Staff: Prof 1. **Subjects:** Parliamentary procedure. **Holdings:** 500 books; 200 bound periodical volumes; reports. **Services:** Center open to public for reference use only.

★8579★

NATIONAL ASSOCIATION OF PHYSICAL THERAPISTS - LIBRARY
Box 367
West Covina, CA 91793
Defunct

★8580★

NATIONAL ASSOCIATION OF PRECANCEL COLLECTORS, INC. - CHESTER DAVIS MEMORIAL LIBRARY (Rec)
5121 Park Blvd.   Phone: (609) 522-2569
Wildwood, NJ 08260   Glenn W. Dye, Sec.-Tres.
Subjects: Precancelled stamps of the United States, Canada, Great Britain and Europe; birds and wild flowers of the United States; color photographs of wild flowers in the Bert Hoover Arboretum and others. **Holdings:** 5000 books; 2000 bound periodical volumes; 500 3x5 color prints; 5000 negatives; 100 black/white negatives of early New Jersey post offices. **Services:** Library open to public by appointment. **Computerized Information Services:** Access to online systems. **Publications:** List of publications - available on request.

NATIONAL ASSOCIATION FOR THE PRESERVATION & PERPETUATION OF STORYTELLING
See: National Storytelling Resource Center

★8581★

NATL. ASSN. OF PRIVATE, NONTRADITIONAL SCHOOLS & COLLEGES - ACCREDITING COMMN. ON POSTSECONDARY EDUC. - LIB. (Educ)
1129 Colorado Ave., Suite 320   Phone: (303) 243-5441
Grand Junction, CO 81501   Jacquelyn Luster, Staff Sec./Treas.
Staff: Prof 1. **Subjects:** Education, accreditation. **Special Collections:** Council on Postsecondary Accreditation (COPA; 12 reports); Criteria and Standards for Regional and National Specialized Accrediting Agencies and Associations (15 reports). **Holdings:** 62 books. **Subscriptions:** 15 journals and other serials. **Services:** Copying; library open to public for reference use only. **Publications:** List of publications - available upon request. **Special Indexes:** Index of COPA Project Findings.

★8582★

NATIONAL ASSOCIATION OF PURCHASING MANAGEMENT, INC. - PURCHASING INFORMATION CENTER (Bus-Fin)
496 Kinderkamack Rd.
Box 418
Oradell, NJ 07649   Phone: (201) 967-8585
    Michael Brent, Libn.
Founded: 1968. **Staff:** 1. **Subjects:** Industrial purchasing, materials management, inventory management, cost reduction, value analysis, vendors relations. **Special Collections:** Doctoral dissertations on aspects of purchasing; NAPM and other archives on purchasing. **Holdings:** 1000 books; 14 VF drawers of clippings, reports, serials of NAPM and related publications on purchasing. **Subscriptions:** 190 journals and other serials; 5 newspapers.

Services: Copying; library open to public by appointment. **Formerly:** Located in New York, NY.

★8583★

NATIONAL ASSOCIATION OF QUICK PRINTERS - INTERNATIONAL QUICK PRINTING FOUNDATION LIBRARY (Publ)†
111 E. Wacker Dr., Suite 600
Chicago, IL 60601
Phone: (312) 644-6610
Barbara Chalik, Exec.Dir.
Staff: Prof 1. **Subjects:** Printing Industry Computer Associates, Inc. (PICA) programs, typesetting, printing, marketing. **Holdings:** 200 books; 100 bound periodical volumes; 10 management reports; 40 tapes and slides; 100 other cataloged items; association literature; technical publications. **Subscriptions:** 12 journals and other serials. **Publications:** Newsletter, monthly; Products & Services Catalog, annual - to NAQP members and other quick printers. **Formerly:** Located in Lafayette, IN.

★8584★

NATIONAL ASSOCIATION OF REALTORS - HERBERT U. NELSON MEMORIAL LIBRARY (Bus-Fin)
430 N. Michigan Ave.
Chicago, IL 60611
Phone: (312) 329-8292
Mabel K. Wong, Chf.Libn.
Founded: 1923. **Staff:** Prof 3; Other 2. **Subjects:** Real estate, architecture, city planning. **Holdings:** 16,000 books and bound periodical volumes; 127 shelves of pamphlets (75,000 items). **Subscriptions:** 425 journals and other serials. **Services:** Interlibrary loans; library open to public on request for reference use. **Staff:** Beverly F. Dordick, Libn.

★8585★

NATIONAL ASSOCIATION OF RETAIL GROCERS OF THE U.S., INC. - LIBRARY (Bus-Fin)
Box 17208
Washington, DC 20041
Phone: (703) 437-5300
Jane Arnwine, Info.Mgr.
Staff: Prof 1. **Subjects:** Food store operation. **Holdings:** 700 books and bound periodical volumes; 6 VF drawers. **Services:** Library not open to public.

★8586★

NATIONAL ASSOCIATION OF SELF-INSTRUCTIONAL LANGUAGE PROGRAMS - NASILP INFORMATION CENTER & ARCHIVES (Educ)
Temple University
Critical Languages 022-38
Philadelphia, PA 19122
Phone: (215) 787-1715
Dr. John B. Means, Exec.Dir.
Staff: Prof 1; Other 1. **Subjects:** Foreign language self-instruction - methodology, procedures, guidelines. **Holdings:** Audio-lingual materials (textbooks and audio cassettes). **Services:** Copying; center open to NASILP members only. **Publications:** NASILP Bulletin, quarterly.

★8587★

NATIONAL ASSOCIATION OF SOCIAL WORKERS - RESOURCE CENTER (Soc Sci)
7981 Eastern Ave.
Silver Spring, MD 20910
Phone: (301) 565-0333
David N. Weber, Info./Res.Ctr.Coord.
Staff: Prof 1. **Subjects:** Social work practice, administration, education and related areas. **Special Collections:** Complete sets of Social Work Journal; Health and Social Work; Social Work Research and Abstracts; Social Work in Education. **Holdings:** 900 books; 100 bound periodical volumes; 2000 other items (cataloged). **Subscriptions:** 150 journals and other serials. **Services:** Interlibrary loans; copying; library open to public by appointment. **Formerly:** Located in Washington, DC.

★8588★

NATIONAL ASSOCIATION FOR SPORT & PHYSICAL EDUCATION (NASPE) - MEDIA RESOURCE CENTER (Educ)
University of South Carolina
Dept. of Physical Education
Columbia, SC 29208
Phone: (803) 777-3172
Dr. Richard C. Hohn, Dir.
Subjects: Physical education, sport, physical fitness, intramurals, career information. **Holdings:** 200 audio- and videotapes. **Services:** Copying; library open to public for reference use only. **Remarks:** Affiliated with the American Alliance for Health, Physical Education, Recreation & Dance.

★8589★

NATIONAL ASSOCIATION OF SUGGESTION SYSTEMS - LIBRARY (Bus-Fin)
230 N. Michigan Ave., Suite 1200
Chicago, IL 60601
Phone: (312) 372-1770
Founded: 1942. **Subjects:** Suggestion systems and promotional programs. **Holdings:** Manuals; employee booklets; special studies and reports. **Services:** Library open on a limited basis to members interested in studying or setting up suggestion programs.

★8590★

NATIONAL ASSOCIATION OF WATCH AND CLOCK COLLECTORS MUSEUM - LIBRARY (Rec)
514 Poplar St.
Box 33
Columbia, PA 17512
Phone: (717) 684-8261
W.H. Francillon, Pres.
Staff: Prof 1. **Subjects:** Horology. **Special Collections:** Hamilton Watch Company business records (58 volumes). **Holdings:** 2800 books; 486 bound periodical volumes; 100 reels of microfilm. **Subscriptions:** 33 journals and other serials. **Services:** Copying; library open to public for reference use only. **Also Known As:** NAWCC. **Staff:** Donald J. Summar, Libn.

NATIONAL ASTHMA CENTER
See: National Jewish Hospital & Research Center/National Asthma Center

NATIONAL AUDIOVISUAL CENTER
See: U.S. Natl. Archives & Records Service

★8591★

NATIONAL AUDUBON SOCIETY - LIBRARY (Env-Cons)
950 Third Ave.
New York, NY 10022
Phone: (212) 832-3200
Michelle I. Epstein, Libn.
Staff: Prof 2; Other 1. **Subjects:** Ornithology, conservation of natural resources, natural history. **Special Collections:** Publications of local Audubon societies and bird clubs; Audubon manuscripts (38 items); archives of National Audubon Society. **Holdings:** 20,000 books and bound periodical volumes; 1000 manuscripts. **Subscriptions:** 250 journals and other serials. **Services:** Interlibrary loans; copying; library open to public by appointment. **Staff:** Barbara Linton, Assoc.Libn.

NATIONAL AUTOMOTIVE HISTORY COLLECTION
See: Detroit Public Library

★8592★

NATIONAL BANK OF ALASKA - HERITAGE LIBRARY AND MUSEUM (Hist)
Box 600
Anchorage, AK 99510
Phone: (907) 276-1132
Vanny Davenport, Libn. & Cur.
Founded: 1968. **Staff:** Prof 1. **Subjects:** Alaska - history, geography, anthropology, resources. **Special Collections:** Alaska Collection (400 volumes of old reference books and early maps). **Holdings:** 1500 books; 200 bound periodical volumes. **Subscriptions:** 6 journals and other serials. **Services:** Library open to public.

★8593★

NATIONAL BANK OF DETROIT - MONEY MUSEUM LIBRARY (Rec)*
200 Renaissance Center, Street Level
Detroit, MI 48243
Phone: (313) 446-0713
Susan E. Cherry, Mgr.
Founded: 1960. **Staff:** Prof 2. **Subjects:** Ancient coinage, modern foreign coinage, U.S. coinage, foreign paper currency, U.S. paper currency, medals, tokens, primitive forms of money. **Holdings:** 700 books; 200 slides. **Subscriptions:** 11 journals and other serials. **Services:** Information about old coins and currency; library open to public for reference use only, on request. **Publications:** The World of Money; The Money Museum. **Staff:** Sharon J. Treumuth, Adm.Asst.

★8594★

NATIONAL BANK OF DETROIT - RESEARCH LIBRARY (Bus-Fin)
Box 116
Detroit, MI 48232
Phone: (313) 225-2840
Steven Wecker, Mgr., Lib.Serv.
Founded: 1955. **Staff:** Prof 2; Other 2. **Subjects:** Banking, finance, economics, business and management. **Holdings:** 5000 books; 115 VF drawers of pamphlets and clippings; 500 reels of microfilm; 500 theses. **Subscriptions:** 1000 journals and other serials; 15 newspapers. **Services:** Interlibrary loans; library open to Special Libraries Association members. **Computerized Information Services:** DIALOG, SDC, New York Times Information Service, Dow Jones News Retrieval.

★8595★

NATIONAL BASEBALL HALL OF FAME AND MUSEUM - NATIONAL BASEBALL LIBRARY (Rec)
Cooperstown, NY 13326
Phone: (607) 547-9988
Clifford Kachline, Hist.
Founded: 1968. **Staff:** Prof 2; Other 3. **Subjects:** Baseball. **Special Collections:** August Herrmann correspondence; A.G. Mills correspondence; official records of the major leagues. **Holdings:** 1300 books; 600 bound periodical volumes; 900 pamphlets; 120,000 player data cards; 185 VF drawers of clippings and photographs; 360 reels of microfilm; 200 reels of motion pictures. **Subscriptions:** 7 journals and other serials; 5 newspapers.

Services: Copying; inquiries answered; library open to public for serious research only. **Staff:** John F. Redding, Libn.

★8596★
NATIONAL BIOMEDICAL RESEARCH FOUNDATION - LIBRARY (Med)
Georgetown University Medical Ctr.
3900 Reservoir Rd., N.W.   Phone: (202) 625-2121
Washington, DC 20007   Doris K. Mela, Libn.
Founded: 1960. **Staff:** Prof 1. **Subjects:** Biochemistry, evolution, proteins, nucleic acid research, origins of life, pattern recognition, biomedical computing, mathematics, computer science, radiology, computed tomography, health operations research. **Holdings:** 3000 books; 8 VF drawers of staff publications reprints. **Subscriptions:** 115 journals and other serials. **Services:** Interlibrary loans; library open to public with permission. **Remarks:** Affiliated with Georgetown University Medical School.

★8597★
NATIONAL BROADCASTING COMPANY, INC. - INFORMATION SERVICES - RESEARCH DEPARTMENT (Bus-Fin; Info Sci)
30 Rockefeller Plaza, Rm. 1640   Phone: (212) 664-4243
New York, NY 10020   Doris B. Katz, Mgr.
Founded: 1953. **Staff:** Prof 1; Other 1. **Subjects:** Broadcasting companies - radio, television, cable, satellites; economic/social conditions; marketing/advertising. **Holdings:** 400 books; 90 VF drawers of clippings, pamphlets, studies. **Subscriptions:** 50 journals and other serials. **Services:** Interlibrary loans; copying (limited); library open to staff, clients, scholars, students and librarians by appointment.

★8598★
NATIONAL BROADCASTING COMPANY, INC. - NEWS ARCHIVAL SERVICES LIBRARY (Aud-Vis)
30 Rockefeller Plaza   Phone: (212) 664-3271
New York, NY 10020   Michael Francaviglia, Mgr.
Staff: Prof 8; Other 20. **Subjects:** Current and historic events. **Holdings:** 200 million feet of newsfilm; 50 million feet of stock shot footage; news video cassettes; NBC news documentaries. **Subscriptions:** 12 journals and other serials. **Services:** Library open to purchasers of newsfilm/tape. **Computerized Information Services:** Internal database; computerized information storage, cataloging and retrieval.

★8599★
NATIONAL BROADCASTING COMPANY, INC. - RECORDS ADMINISTRATION INFORMATION AND ARCHIVES (Info Sci)
30 Rockefeller Plaza, Rm. 2M1W   Phone: (212) 664-2690
New York, NY 10020   Vera Mayer, V.P., Info. & Archv.
Staff: Prof 3; Other 2. **Subjects:** NBC radio and television broadcast history. **Special Collections:** Radio masterbooks and logs; television masterbooks. **Holdings:** 2000 bound periodical volumes; 6800 reels of microfilm; 34 VF drawers of broadcasting indexes; 5900 audiotapes; 3000 radio and television audio cassettes. **Services:** Copying; archives open to public with restrictions. **Staff:** Marilyn C. Dean, Mgr.; Joan Mitchell, Adm.

★8600★
NATIONAL BROADCASTING COMPANY, INC. - REFERENCE LIBRARY (Info Sci)
30 Rockefeller Plaza   Phone: (212) 664-5307
New York, NY 10020   Vera Mayer, V.P., Info. & Archv.
Founded: 1930. **Staff:** Prof 8; Other 3. **Subjects:** Broadcasting, politics and government, history and travel, current events, biography, New York City. **Holdings:** 12,500 books; 495 bound periodical volumes; 5200 reels of microfilm; 65 VF drawers of clippings. **Subscriptions:** 170 journals and other serials; 15 newspapers. **Services:** Copying; SDI; library open to NBC and RCA employees, professional librarians, and to the public for special projects by appointment. **Computerized Information Services:** New York Times Information Service, DIALOG, BRS, NEXIS. **Staff:** Judy Friedman, Mgr./Lib. & Ref.Serv.; Debra Levinson, Mgr./Info.Ret.Serv.; Ernest Angstadt, Res.Libn.; Karen Botkin, Res.Libn.; Barbara Ladley, Res.Libn.; Scott Lewis, Res.Libn.; Robert Meyer, Res.Libn.

NATIONAL BUREAU OF STANDARDS
See: U.S. Natl. Bureau of Standards

★8601★
NATIONAL CABLE TELEVISION INSTITUTE - LIBRARY (Sci-Tech)
Box 27277   Phone: (303) 761-8554
Denver, CO 80227   Roland D. Hieb, Exec.Dir.
Subjects: Technical careers in cable television, satellite earth station technology. **Holdings:** Figures not available. **Services:** Copying; library not open to public. **Publications:** CATV Installer; CATV Technician; CATV Chief

Technician Training Materials; Introduction to CATV; CATV Testing.

★8602★
NATIONAL CAPITAL HISTORICAL MUSEUM OF TRANSPORTATION - LIBRARY (Trans)
Colesville Branch, Box 4007   Phone: (301) 384-9797
Silver Spring, MD 20904   Edmond Henderer, Libn.
Founded: 1979. **Staff:** 1. **Subjects:** Railroads, transportation. **Holdings:** 100 books. **Services:** Library open to public with restrictions.

NATIONAL CAPITAL PARK-EAST - DOUGLASS PRIVATE COLLECTION
See: U.S. Natl. Park Service - Frederick Douglass Home and Visitor Center

NATIONAL CAPITAL REGION - ROCK CREEK NATURE CENTER
See: U.S. Natl. Park Service

★8603★
NATIONAL CAR RENTAL SYSTEM, INC. - BUSINESS INFORMATION CENTER (Bus-Fin)
7700 France Ave. S.   Phone: (612) 893-6382
Minneapolis, MN 55435   Holly Hupfer, Info.Coord.
Founded: 1977. **Staff:** Prof 1; Other 1. **Subjects:** Data processing, travel, business, telecommunications. **Holdings:** 150 books; 200 bound periodical volumes; 350 technical manuals. **Subscriptions:** 150 journals and other serials; 25 newspapers. **Services:** Interlibrary loans; copying; library not open to public. **Computerized Information Services:** DIALOG; computerized circulation. **Publications:** MIS Bimonthly Newsletter.

NATIONAL CARTOGRAPHIC INFORMATION CENTER
See: U.S. Geological Survey - Natl. Cartographic Information Center

NATIONAL CASH REGISTER COMPANY
See: NCR Corporation

NATIONAL CATHOLIC PRESS AND LIBRARY FOR THE VISUALLY HANDICAPPED
See: Xavier Society for the Blind

NATIONAL CATHOLIC RURAL LIFE CONFERENCE ARCHIVES
See: Marquette University - Department of Special Collections and University Archives

★8604★
NATIONAL CATHOLIC STEWARDSHIP COUNCIL - INFORMATION CENTER (Rel-Theol)
1 Columbia Place   Phone: (518) 465-0233
Albany, NY 12207   Rev. James M. Mackey, Exec.Dir.
Staff: 2. **Subjects:** Stewardship-ministries; fundraising; data for diocesan/parish councils, finance committees, stewardship committees. **Holdings:** 125 books; 70 diocesan folders (cataloged). **Services:** Copying; library open to public for reference use only. **Publications:** Newsletter, quarterly; Stewardship of Time and Talent; Stewardship of Money; Annual Stewardship Conference presentations/cassettes.

NATIONAL CENTER FOR AMERICAN HORTICULTURE
See: American Horticultural Society - Harold B. Tukey Memorial Library

★8605★
NATIONAL CENTER FOR APPROPRIATE TECHNOLOGY - RESEARCH LIBRARY (Energy)†
3040 Continental Dr.
Box 3838   Phone: (406) 494-4572
Butte, MT 59702   Raelen Williard, Libn.
Founded: 1977. **Staff:** Prof 1; Other 1. **Subjects:** Appropriate technology, solar and wind energy, community energy planning, agriculture, biomass, community and economic development. **Holdings:** 2000 books; 12 VF drawers; 1 cabinet of blueprints. **Subscriptions:** 300 journals and other serials; 5 newspapers. **Services:** Library open to public. **Publications:** List of publications - available upon request. **Staff:** Carmela A. Conning, Libn.

★8606★
NATIONAL CENTER FOR ATMOSPHERIC RESEARCH - HIGH ALTITUDE OBSERVATORY LIBRARY (Sci-Tech)
Box 3000   Phone: (303) 494-5151
Boulder, CO 80307   Kathryn Strand, Libn.
Founded: 1960. **Staff:** Prof 1. **Subjects:** Astronomy, astrophysics, geophysics, solar physics, mathematics, physics. **Holdings:** 5500 books; 5000 bound periodical volumes; reports. **Subscriptions:** 160 journals and other serials. **Services:** Interlibrary loans; copying; library open to public for

reference use only.

★8607★
NATIONAL CENTER FOR ATMOSPHERIC RESEARCH - MESA LIBRARY (Sci-Tech)
Box 3000   Phone: (303) 494-5151
Boulder, CO 80307   Charles B. Wenger, Chf.Libn.
Founded: 1962. **Staff:** Prof 2; Other 6. **Subjects:** Meteorology, physics, mathematics, computer science, chemistry, oceanography. **Holdings:** 15,000 books; 13,000 bound periodical volumes; 16,000 indexed technical reports (hard copy); 22,000 indexed technical reports (microfiche). **Subscriptions:** 550 journals and other serials. **Services:** Interlibrary loans; copying; SDI; current awareness; library open to public with permission. **Computerized Information Services:** DIALOG, SDC, NASA/RECON, Information Handling Services (IHS); computerized cataloging, acquisitions, serials and circulation. **Networks/Consortia:** Member of OCLC. **Publications:** Weekly bulletin of acquisitions. **Special Catalogs:** Author, corporate author, title and subject catalogs in book form for technical reports; monthly serials record. **Special Indexes:** KWIC Index to books, journals, climate data, atlases, and microfiche. **Remarks:** Maintains four branch libraries. **Staff:** Gayl Gray, Ref.Libn.

NATIONAL CENTER FOR AUDIO TAPES
See: University of Colorado, Boulder - Educational Media Center

NATIONAL CENTER ON CHILD ABUSE AND NEGLECT - CLEARINGHOUSE ON CHILD ABUSE AND NEGLECT INFORMATION
See: Clearinghouse on Child Abuse and Neglect Information

★8608★
NATIONAL CENTER ON CHILD ABUSE AND NEGLECT - REGION I CHILD ABUSE AND NEGLECT RESOURCE CENTER (Soc Sci)
Judge Baker Guidance Center - Gardner Library
295 Longwood Ave.   Phone: (617) 232-8390
Boston, MA 02115   Mary Lee Cox, Info.Spec.
Staff: Prof 1; Other 1. **Subjects:** Child abuse and neglect, child welfare. **Holdings:** 120 books; 20 bound periodical volumes; 214 unbound reports and curricula; 3000 reprints. **Subscriptions:** 12 journals and other serials. **Services:** Copying; library open to public. **Computerized Information Services:** DIALOG. **Publications:** List of publications - available upon request. **Remarks:** Funded by U.S. Dept. of Health and Human Services.

★8609★
NATIONAL CENTER ON CHILD ABUSE AND NEGLECT - REGION II CHILD ABUSE AND NEGLECT RESOURCE CENTER (Soc Sci)
Cornell University
E200 MVR Hall   Phone: (607) 256-7794
Ithaca, NY 14853   Ellen Ehrenreich, Rsrcs.Libn./Adm.
Staff: Prof 1; Other 8. **Subjects:** Child abuse and neglect, child welfare and protection services, family, parenting. **Holdings:** 1400 books; 400 bound periodical volumes; 71 films; 60 filmstrips and audio cassettes; 11 VF drawers of clippings. **Subscriptions:** 75 newsletters. **Services:** Copying; library open to public with restrictions. **Computerized Information Services:** Access to DIALOG, BRS. **Networks/Consortia:** Member of South Central Research Library Council (SCRLC). **Publications:** Family Life Developments, bimonthly - to professionals and general audience in Region II. **Special Indexes:** Index to newsletter articles. **Remarks:** The center is based at Cornell University as part of the Human Development and Family Studies Department, one of the departments of the New York State College of Human Ecology. It is funded by U.S. Dept. of Health and Human Services.

THE NATIONAL CENTER FOR CITIZEN INVOLVEMENT
See: VOLUNTEER/The National Center for Citizen Involvement

★8610★
NATIONAL CENTER FOR COMPUTER CRIME DATA (Soc Sci)
2700 N. Cahuenga Blvd., Suite 2113   Phone: (213) 874-8233
Los Angeles, CA 90068   Jay J. BloomBecker, Dir.
Founded: 1978. **Staff:** 4. **Subjects:** Computer crime, computer security. **Special Collections:** Case histories of computer crimes (800 files). **Holdings:** 200 books; legal documents. **Subscriptions:** 20 journals and other serials; 5 newspapers. **Services:** Interlibrary loans; copying; library open to public.

★8611★
NATIONAL CENTER FOR HEALTH STATISTICS - CLEARINGHOUSE ON HEALTH INDEXES (Soc Sci)
3700 East West Hwy., Rm. 2-27   Phone: (301) 436-7035
Hyattsville, MD 20782   Pennifer Erickson, Chf.
Staff: Prof 2; Other 1. **Subjects:** Health statistics, health economics.

Holdings: 3000 reprints and original manuscripts. **Services:** SDI; library open to public by appointment. **Computerized Information Services:** NLM; Health Index Info (internal database). **Publications:** Bibliography on Health Indexes. **Staff:** Anita Powell, Lib.Serv. & Tech.Info.

NATIONAL CENTER FOR HEALTH STATISTICS MORTALITY DATA
See: Duke University - Center for Demographic Studies

NATIONAL CENTER FOR HIGHER EDUCATION
See: American Council on Education

★8612★
NATIONAL CENTER FOR HOUSING MANAGEMENT - TECHNICAL INFORMATION CENTER (Soc Sci)†
1228 M St., N.W.   Phone: (202) 872-1717
Washington, DC 20005   Beth A. Brown, Dir., Tech.Info.Ctr.
Staff: Prof 1; Other 1. **Subjects:** Housing management, real estate, housing, management, curriculum development, urban planning. **Special Collections:** Housing (5000 items). **Holdings:** 5000 books; 300 bound periodical volumes; 3000 research documents (cataloged). **Subscriptions:** 300 journals and other serials. **Services:** Interlibrary loans; copying; library open to public by phone request.

NATIONAL CENTER FOR RESEARCH IN VOCATIONAL EDUCATION
See: ERIC Clearinghouse on Adult, Career and Vocational Education

NATIONAL CENTER FOR STANDARDS AND CERTIFICATION INFORMATION
See: U.S. Natl. Bureau of Standards

★8613★
NATIONAL CENTER FOR STATE COURTS - LIBRARY (Law)
300 Newport Ave.   Phone: (804) 253-2000
Williamsburg, VA 23185   Erick Baker Low, Libn.
Founded: 1973. **Staff:** Prof 3; Other 1. **Subjects:** Judicial administration, state courts, criminal justice. **Holdings:** 11,000 books and pamphlets (cataloged); 1700 microforms. **Subscriptions:** 350 journals and other serials. **Services:** Interlibrary loans; copying; library open to public by request. **Computerized Information Services:** DIALOG; computerized cataloging, acquisitions and ILL. **Networks/Consortia:** Member of Bibliographic Center for Research, Rocky Mountain Region, Inc. (BCR); OCLC. **Staff:** Peggy W. Rogers, Cat.

★8614★
NATIONAL CENTER FOR THE STUDY OF CORPORAL PUNISHMENT & ALTERNATIVES IN THE SCHOOLS - LIBRARY (Educ)
822 Ritter Annex   Phone: (215) 787-6091
Philadelphia, PA 19122   Irwin A. Hyman, Dir.
Subjects: Corporal punishment, discipline, classroom management. **Holdings:** 1000 books, pamphlets and research reports; 2000 clippings; 20 dissertations. **Services:** Copying; library open to members. **Publications:** Discipline, 3/year - by subscription.

NATIONAL CENTER FOR TOXICOLOGICAL RESEARCH
See: U.S. Food & Drug Administration

★8615★
NATIONAL CENTER ON WOMEN AND FAMILY LAW, INC. - INFORMATION CENTER (Law)
799 Broadway, Rm. 402   Phone: (212) 674-8200
New York, NY 10003   Laurie Woods, Exec.Dir.
Subjects: Battered women and law, marital rape, rape, single mothers, divorce, custody, child snatching, child and wife support. **Holdings:** 100 books; 20 VF drawers of material. **Subscriptions:** 25 journals and other serials. **Services:** Copying; library open to public with director's approval. **Publications:** Newsletter, quarterly.

★8616★
NATIONAL CHAMBER OF COMMERCE FOR WOMEN - ELIZABETH LEWIN BUSINESS LIBRARY & INFORMATION CENTER (Bus-Fin)
Box 1132   Phone: (212) 532-6408
New York, NY 10159   Madeline Reynolds, Dir.
Founded: 1977. **Staff:** 2. **Subjects:** Law and women, labor - management relations, small business, consumerism, women in education. **Holdings:** 1800 books; 650 bound periodical volumes; 100 cassette tapes; 800 market research reports and proposals; 500 annual reports and quarterly brochures; 2 VF drawers of press clippings. **Subscriptions:** 10 journals and other serials. **Services:** Special reports and clippings; library not open to public. **Publications:** National Chamber of Commerce for Women Research Digest, monthly - to members.

NATIONAL CLEARINGHOUSE ON AGING - SERVICE CENTER FOR AGING INFORMATION (SCAN)
See: District One Technical Institute - Library - Educational Resource Center

★8617★
NATIONAL CLEARINGHOUSE FOR ALCOHOL INFORMATION - LIBRARY (Med; Soc Sci)
Box 2345
Rockville, MD 20852
Phone: (301) 468-2600
Sean O'Rourke, Dir.
Founded: 1972. **Staff:** Prof 3; Other 1. **Subjects:** Alcohol abuse and alcoholism. **Special Collections:** Classified Abstract Archives of the Alcohol Literature (20,000 abstracts). **Holdings:** 1345 books; 55,000 accessioned items. **Subscriptions:** 363 journals and other serials. **Services:** SDI; library open to public for reference use only. **Computerized Information Services:** Online systems. **Publications:** NIAAA/Information and Feature Service - monthly newsletter; Alcohol Health and Research World - quarterly journal for alcoholism professionals; subject area bibliographies; selected translations of international alcoholism research; law and legislative summaries; guide to audiovisual materials; directories of state alcoholism treatment facilities; alcohol awareness service, bimonthly. **Special Indexes:** Computer-produced index to NCALI Database. **Remarks:** The clearinghouse is a branch of the U.S. Public Health Service - National Institute on Alcohol Abuse & Alcoholism and is operated under contract by Informatics General Corporation. **Staff:** Carol Jelich, Mgr., Lib.

NATIONAL CLEARINGHOUSE FOR BILINGUAL EDUCATION
See: InterAmerica Research Associates, Inc.

NATIONAL CLEARINGHOUSE FOR COMMUTER PROGRAMS
See: University of Maryland, College Park

NATIONAL CLEARINGHOUSE ON ELECTION ADMINISTRATION
See: Federal Election Commission

★8618★
NATIONAL CLEARINGHOUSE FOR FAMILY PLANNING INFORMATION (Soc Sci)
Box 2225
Rockville, MD 20852
Phone: (301) 881-9400
Anita P. Cowan, Dir.
Founded: 1976. **Subjects:** Contraception, family planning, reproductive health, patient education. **Holdings:** Figures not available. **Subscriptions:** 60 journals and other serials. **Computerized Information Services:** DIALOG, SDC, BRS, MEDLINE. **Remarks:** The clearinghouse was created to serve federally supported service agencies. It provides information to family-planning workers, educators and trainers.

★8619★
NATIONAL CLEARINGHOUSE FOR LEGAL SERVICES - LIBRARY (Soc Sci)
500 N. Michigan Ave., Suite 1940
Chicago, IL 60611
Phone: (312) 353-2566
Katherine Stevenson, Libn.
Founded: 1967. **Staff:** Prof 1. **Subjects:** Legal services, public welfare, housing, employment, schools and education, mental health, public utilities, consumer law, juveniles. **Holdings:** 500 books; 32,000 cases of litigation materials; 3000 nonlitigation materials. **Subscriptions:** 150 journals and other serials. **Services:** Copying; library open to public by appointment. **Publications:** Clearinghouse Review, 12/year and index - free to Legal Services attorneys. **Special Catalogs:** Clearinghouse Publications in Print, 13/year.

NATIONAL CLEARINGHOUSE ON MARITAL RAPE
See: Women's History Research Center, Inc.

★8620★
NATIONAL CLEARINGHOUSE FOR MENTAL HEALTH INFORMATION (Med)
5600 Fishers Lane, Rm. 11A-33
Rockville, MD 20857
Phone: (301) 443-4517
Carrie Lee Rothgeb, Act.Chf.
Founded: 1963. **Staff:** Prof 9; Other 13. **Subjects:** Mental illness, psychiatry, psychopharmacology, psychology, crime and delinquency, social studies. **Special Collections:** Archival file of NIMH publications. **Holdings:** 7000 books; 150 bound periodical volumes; 450,000 machine-readable abstracts (with 40,000 added annually); 2000 unbound reports; 6.5 cabinets of microfilmed journals. **Subscriptions:** 1600 journals and other serials. **Services:** Interlibrary loans; copying; bibliography preparation; consultation; public inquiries; referrals; clearinghouse open to public for reference use only; borrowing privileges reserved for staff. **Computerized Information Services:** Online systems; computerized cataloging and acquisitions. **Networks/Consortia:** Member of Mid Atlantic Regional Medical Library; Mental Health Librarians Group; Maryland Interlibrary Loan Organization (MILO).

Publications: Psychopharmacology Abstracts; list of free NIMH publications - available on request; Monthly Acquisitions List from Library; computer-generated bibliographies. **Remarks:** Clearinghouse is a branch of the U.S. Public Health Service - National Institute of Mental Health. **Staff:** Angela Sirrocco, Chf., Commun.Ctr.; Joan Abell, Chf., Info.Sys.Sec.; Edith Tyler, Chf., Pub. Inquiries.

NATIONAL CLEARINGHOUSE FOR MENTAL HEALTH INFORMATION - NATL. INSTITUTE OF MENTAL HEALTH - COMMUNICATION CENTER
See: U.S. Public Health Service - Natl. Institute of Mental Health - Communication Center

NATIONAL CLEARINGHOUSE FOR POISON CONTROL CENTERS
See: U.S. Food & Drug Administration

★8621★
NATIONAL CLEARINGHOUSE OF REHABILITATION TRAINING MATERIALS - REFERENCE COLLECTION (Soc Sci)
Oklahoma State University
115 Old USDA Bldg.
Stillwater, OK 74074
Phone: (405) 624-7650
Paul Gaines, Proj.Dir.
Subjects: Rehabilitation, staff development, inservice training, continuing education, vocational rehabilitation. **Special Collections:** Publications of the Institute on Rehabilitation Issues. **Holdings:** 3000 titles in hard copy or microfiche format; AV materials. **Services:** Copying (fee); service available to the public. **Publications:** NCHRTM Memorandum, an annotated bibliographic newsletter, quarterly. **Also Known As:** NCHRTM.

NATIONAL CLIMATIC CENTER
See: U.S. Natl. Oceanic & Atmospheric Administration - Environmental Data & Information Service

★8622★
NATIONAL COAL ASSOCIATION - LIBRARY (Bus-Fin)
Coal Bldg.
1130 17th St., N.W.
Washington, DC 20036
Phone: (202) 463-2641
Richard E. Niswander, Dir., Lib.Serv.
Subjects: Coal - technology, transportation, economics, research, environment, use, and history. **Holdings:** Books, journals, reports and nonprinted data. **Services:** Library open to public by appointment.

★8623★
NATIONAL COLLEGE OF CHIROPRACTIC - LEARNING RESOURCE CENTER (Med)
200 E. Roosevelt Rd.
Lombard, IL 60148
Phone: (312) 629-2000
Joyce Whitehead, Dir.
Founded: 1963. **Staff:** Prof 3; Other 4. **Subjects:** Chiropractic, manipulation, anatomy, radiology, physiology, orthopedics. **Special Collections:** Chiropractic Archives (400 volumes; 6 VF drawers of pamphlets and reprints). **Holdings:** 12,300 books; 8300 bound periodical volumes; 16 VF drawers of pamphlets. **Subscriptions:** 432 journals and other serials; 30 newspapers. **Services:** Interlibrary loans; copying; library open to public. **Computerized Information Services:** BRS, DIALOG, MEDLINE. **Networks/Consortia:** Member of Regional Medical Library - Region 3; Chiropractic Library Consortium. **Publications:** Catalog of Audiovisual Materials, annual. **Staff:** Catherine Marathas, AV Libn.; Russell Iwami, Libn.

★8624★
NATIONAL COLLEGE OF DISTRICT ATTORNEYS - RESOURCE CENTER (Law)
College of Law
University of Houston
Houston, TX 77004
Phone: (713) 749-1571
Mary Ann Freeman, Commun.Mgr.
Staff: Prof 1; Other 1. **Subjects:** Constitutional law, functions of the prosecutor, trial techniques, scientific evidence. **Holdings:** Figures not available. **Services:** Center open to prosecuting attorneys.

★8625★
NATIONAL COLLEGE OF EDUCATION - LEARNING RESOURCE CENTERS (Educ)
2840 Sheridan Rd.
Evanston, IL 60201
Phone: (312) 256-5150
Marilyn A. Lester, Dir. of Lrng.Rsrcs.
Staff: Prof 10; Other 8. **Subjects:** Education, child psychology, children's literature. **Holdings:** 107,825 books; 123,160 other cataloged items. **Subscriptions:** 549 journals and other serials; 15 newspapers. **Services:** Interlibrary loans; copying; library open to public for reference use only. **Computerized Information Services:** DIALOG; computerized cataloging. **Networks/Consortia:** Member of Metropolitan Chicago Library Assembly; ILLINET; North Suburban Library System. **Staff:** Judith Ream, Assoc.Dir.;

Dennis Strasser; Gertrude Weinstein; Anne Hoskins; Norman Weston; Rose Novil; Benjamin Schapiro; William Jesse; Elizabeth Smith.

★8626★

NATIONAL COLLEGE OF EDUCATION - URBAN CAMPUS LEARNING RESOURCE CENTER (Educ)
18 S. Michigan Ave. Phone: (312) 621-9676
Chicago, IL 60603 Dennis Strasser, Coord.
Founded: 1971. **Staff:** Prof 1; Other 6. **Subjects:** Elementary, teacher and childhood education. **Special Collections:** K-8 curriculum collection; educational test materials. **Holdings:** 10,000 books; 200 bound periodical volumes. **Subscriptions:** 202 journals and other serials. **Services:** Interlibrary loans; copying; library open to public for reference use only. **Computerized Information Services:** DIALOG; computerized cataloging. **Networks/Consortia:** OCLC through ILLINET; Chicago Library System.

★8627★

NATIONAL COLLEGE OF NATUROPATHIC MEDICINE - LIBRARY (Med)
510 S.W. 3rd Ave. Phone: (503) 226-3745
Portland, OR 97204 Friedhelm Kirchfeld, Libn.
Staff: Prof 1. **Subjects:** Naturopathy, homeopathy, nutrition, physiotherapy, botanical medicine, acupuncture, clinical and basic sciences. **Holdings:** 4000 books; 400 bound periodical volumes. **Subscriptions:** 85 journals and other serials. **Services:** Interlibrary loans; copying; library open to public with restrictions.

★8628★

NATIONAL COLLEGE - THOMAS JEFFERSON LIBRARY (Bus-Fin)
Box 1780 Phone: (605) 394-4943
Rapid City, SD 57709 Linda L. Watson, Dir.
Founded: 1964. **Staff:** Prof 2; Other 2. **Subjects:** Accounting, word processing, electronics, management, finance, taxation, data processing, marketing, economics, animal health, airlines, travel, fashion merchandising, medical assistance. **Special Collections:** American Enterprise Institute depository. **Holdings:** 24,000 books; 150 bound periodical volumes; 625 AV items; 16 VF drawers of pamphlets; microforms. **Subscriptions:** 475 journals and other serials; 35 newspapers. **Services:** Interlibrary loans; copying; library open to public. **Computerized Information Services:** Computerized cataloging. **Networks/Consortia:** Member of OCLC. **Remarks:** Library located at 321 Kansas City St. & 400 3rd St., Rapid City, SD 57701. **Staff:** Janet Mastalir, Cat./Asst.Libn.; Laurie Kershner, AV Techn.; Amy Johnson, Acq.Techn.

★8629★

NATIONAL COMMISSION ON RESOURCES FOR YOUTH, INC. - NCRY CLEARINGHOUSE (Soc Sci)
36 W. 44th St., Rm. 1314 Phone: (212) 840-2844
New York, NY 10036 Ellen Lippmann, Coord.
Staff: Prof 1; Other 1. **Subjects:** Youth participation. **Holdings:** 1600 files on youth participation programs. **Subscriptions:** 65 journals and other serials; 5 newspapers. **Services:** Copying; clearinghouse open to public with restrictions. **Publications:** Resources for Youth, quarterly - by subscription; list of additional publications - available upon request.

★8630★

NATIONAL COMMISSION ON WORKING WOMEN - RESOURCE CENTER (Soc Sci)
2000 P St., N.W., Suite 508 Phone: (202) 466-6770
Washington, DC 20036 Sally Steenland, Info.Spec.
Founded: 1977. **Staff:** Prof 3. **Subjects:** Women - nonprofessional employment, education, equal pay, child care, career counseling, women's organizations. **Holdings:** Technical reports. **Services:** Center open to public by appointment. **Remarks:** The NCWW Resource Center compiles data, materials and publications concerning the problems of nonprofessional working women.

★8631★

NATIONAL CONFECTIONERS ASSOCIATION OF THE U.S. - LIBRARY (Food-Bev)
36 S. Wabash Ave., Suite 1300 Phone: (312) 372-1492
Chicago, IL 60603 Richard T. O'Connell, Exec.Dir.
Subjects: Candy - production, selling, merchandising, ingredients. **Holdings:** 2500 books; 200 bound periodical volumes; 180 VF drawers.

★8632★

NATIONAL CONFERENCE OF CHRISTIANS AND JEWS - PAULA K. LAZRUS LIBRARY OF INTERGROUP RELATIONS (Soc Sci)
43 W. 57th St. Phone: (212) 688-7530
New York, NY 10019 Edith G. Selig, Adm.Asst.
Staff: Prof 1. **Subjects:** Intergroup relations, interreligious relations, religion and public affairs, race relations. **Special Collections:** Early works on intergroup relations; materials from the presidential election of 1960. **Holdings:** 3500 books; 500 pamphlets (cataloged); 1000 archival documents; 16 VF drawers of clippings, magazine articles, manuscripts, reports; 75 boxes of unbound periodical volumes. **Subscriptions:** 50 journals and other serials. **Services:** Interlibrary loans; copying; lending services to college workshops; library open to public for reference use only. **Publications:** The Human Family...Understanding Other People, annual; paperbacks on intergroup relations. **Remarks:** Archival material housed at University of Minnesota - Social Welfare History Archives, c/o Wilson Library, Minneapolis, MN 55455.

★8633★

NATIONAL CONFERENCE ON MINISTRY TO THE ARMED FORCES - CHAPLAINS MEMORIAL LIBRARY
5100 Wisconsin Ave., N.W., Suite 310
Washington, DC 20016
Founded: 1963. **Subjects:** Military chaplaincy; religion in the armed forces; church and state relations and the chaplaincy. **Holdings:** 655 volumes; 85 journals and publications. **Remarks:** Presently inactive. **Formerly:** General Commission on Chaplains and Armed Forces Personnel.

★8634★

NATIONAL CONFERENCE ON SOVIET JEWRY (NCSJ) - RESEARCH BUREAU (Area-Ethnic)
10 E. 40th St., Suite 907 Phone: (212) 679-6122
New York, NY 10016 Myrna Shinbaum, Assoc.Dir.
Founded: 1975. **Subjects:** Soviet Jewry - emigration, culture; U.S.-U.S.S.R. relations. **Special Collections:** Case histories of individual Soviet Jewish refuseniks and prisoners of conscience. **Holdings:** 100 books; periodical volumes; 32 VF drawers of files and clippings and 30 loose-leaf books. **Subscriptions:** 45 journals and other serials; 35 newspapers. **Services:** Copying; library open to public with restrictions. **Publications:** Emigration Update and Statistics Press Service, weekly - by subscription.

NATIONAL CONGRESS OF PARENTS AND TEACHERS
See: National Parent Teacher Association

★8635★

NATIONAL COTTON COUNCIL OF AMERICA - LIBRARY (Agri)
1918 N. Parkway Phone: (901) 274-9030
Memphis, TN 38112 Carolyn Robertson, Libn.
Founded: 1946. **Staff:** Prof 1. **Subjects:** Cotton. **Holdings:** 935 books; 136 bound periodical volumes; 72 VF drawers of unbound material. **Subscriptions:** 125 journals and other serials. **Services:** Copying; library open to public by appointment.

★8636★

NATIONAL COUNCIL ON THE AGING - LIBRARY (Soc Sci)
600 Maryland Ave., S.W. Phone: (202) 223-6250
Washington, DC 20024 Dorothy M. Gropp, Libn.
Founded: 1950. **Staff:** Prof 1; Other 1. **Subjects:** Aging, retirement, economics, employment, community organization, legislation, nursing homes, senior centers, health care. **Special Collections:** Ollie A. Randall Collection. **Holdings:** 12,000 books; 450 bound periodical volumes; 30 VF drawers (cataloged); 32 VF drawers of archives. **Subscriptions:** 371 journals and other serials. **Services:** Interlibrary loans; copying; library open to public. **Publications:** Current Literature on Aging, quarterly - by subscription; bibliographies, available for purchase.

★8637★

NATIONAL COUNCIL ON ALCOHOLISM, INC. - YVELIN GARDNER ALCOHOLISM LIBRARY (Soc Sci)†
733 Third Ave. Phone: (212) 986-4433
New York, NY 10017 Betty Gold, Libn.
Founded: 1957. **Staff:** 1. **Subjects:** Alcoholism - nature of the disease, scope, treatment, resources for therapy, educational and research programs, industrial programs, community programs. **Special Collections:** Quarterly Journal of Studies on Alcohol; Classified Abstract Archive of the Alcohol Literature; publications of Alcoholics Anonymous, Al-Anon Family Groups, Alateen; publications of state and local public and voluntary alcoholism agencies in U.S.A., Canada, and foreign countries. **Holdings:** 2000 books; pamphlets, reprints and periodicals. **Subscriptions:** 300 journals and other serials. **Services:** Interlibrary loans; copying; library open to public by appointment.

★8638★
NATIONAL COUNCIL OF CHURCHES - INTERFAITH CENTER ON CORPORATE RESPONSIBILITY (Soc Sci)
475 Riverside Dr., Rm. 566   Phone: (212) 870-2293
New York, NY 10115   Valerie Heinonen, Res.Mgr.
Founded: 1970. Staff: 15. Subjects: Corporate responsibility, South Africa, Latin America, infant formula, community reinvestment, economic conversion, nuclear weapons production, affirmative action, full employment, pension fund investments, plant closings, alternate investments, energy and environment, pharmaceutical marketing. Holdings: 20 VF cabinets of corporate annual reports, newsletters of action groups on corporate responsibility issues, newspaper clippings on corporate social issues. Subscriptions: 50 journals and other serials. Services: Library open to public by appointment with research manager. Publications: Corporate Examiner, monthly - for sale (sample copy free upon request); studies and CIC briefs. Staff: Diane Bratcher, Ed.; Timothy H. Smith, Exec.Dir.

★8639★
NATIONAL COUNCIL ON CRIME AND DELINQUENCY - LIBRARY (Soc Sci)
Continental Plaza
411 Hackensack Ave.   Phone: (201) 488-0400
Hackensack, NJ 07601   Phyllis A. Schultze, Libn.
Founded: 1921. Staff: Prof 1. Subjects: Crime and juvenile delinquency - prevention, control, and treatment; criminology and correction. Holdings: 6700 books; 500 bound periodical volumes; 33,000 unpublished and published reports, studies, monographs, letters, clippings and pictures. Subscriptions: 200 journals and other serials; 5 newspapers. Services: Interlibrary loans to organizations only; telephone information service.

★8640★
NATIONAL COUNCIL ON FAMILY RELATIONS - FAMILY RESOURCE & REFERRAL CENTER (Soc Sci)
1219 University Ave., S.E.   Phone: (612) 331-2774
Minneapolis, MN 55414   Margaret J. Bodley, Dir.
Founded: 1979. Staff: Prof 1; Other 2. Subjects: All aspects of family life including history, family life in foreign countries, relationships, marriage and divorce, issues related to reproduction, sexual attitudes and behavior, minority groups; families with special problems; organizations and services for families. Holdings: 40,000 volumes of books, government documents, pamphlets, manuscripts, newsletters, reports, essays. Subscriptions: 1000 journals and other serials. Services: Center open to public for reference use only. Computerized Information Services: BRS; NCFR Family Resources Database (internal database). Publications: Guide to Family Literature, Services and Programs.

★8641★
NATIONAL COUNCIL OF SENIOR CITIZENS, INC. - LIBRARY (Soc Sci)
925 15th St., N.W.   Phone: (202) 347-8800
Washington, DC 20005   Teman Treadway, Lib.Serv.Coord.
Staff: Prof 1. Subjects: Gerontology. Holdings: 2000 books; 24 VF cabinets. Subscriptions: 150 journals and other serials. Services: Interlibrary loans; copying; library open to public.

★8642★
NATIONAL COUNCIL OF TEACHERS OF ENGLISH - CURRICULUM LIBRARY (Educ)
1111 Kenyon Rd.   Phone: (217) 328-3870
Urbana, IL 61801   Carolyn H. McMahon, Libn.
Founded: 1912. Staff: Prof 1. Subjects: English language teaching, curriculum, language, education, communication, teacher training, teaching English as a second language, speech. Special Collections: Porter Perrin Collection (3500 volumes); NCTE monographs (1300 titles); ERIC microfiche. Holdings: 4500 books; 225 bound periodical volumes; 136 boxes of pamphlets; 100 boxes of filmstrips; 200 boxes of archival material; 250 tape cassettes. Subscriptions: 300 journals and other serials. Services: Interlibrary loans; copying; library open to public for reference use only. Computerized Information Services: DIALOG, SDC. Networks/Consortia: Member of Lincoln Trail Library System.

NATIONAL COUNCIL OF TEACHERS OF ENGLISH - ERIC CLEARINGHOUSE ON READING AND COMMUNICATIONS SKILLS
See: ERIC Clearinghouse on Reading and Communications Skills

★8643★
NATIONAL COUNCIL OF TEACHERS OF MATHEMATICS - TEACHER/ LEARNING CENTER (Educ)†
1906 Association Dr.   Phone: (703) 620-9840
Reston, VA 22091   Joseph R. Caravella, Dir., Prof.Serv.
Staff: 3. Subjects: Mathematics. Holdings: 2003 books and bound periodical

volumes; 4 drawers of reports on microfiche; 62 AV items; 100 games and other instructional aids. Services: Copying; library open to public. Staff: Betty A. Rollins, Program Asst.

★8644★
NATIONAL COUNCIL FOR U.S.-CHINA TRADE - LIBRARY (Bus-Fin)
1050 17th St., N.W., Suite 350   Phone: (202) 828-8375
Washington, DC 20036   Marianna Graham, Libn.
Staff: Prof 2; Other 1. Subjects: China - economy, trade, industry; U.S-foreign trade. Special Collections: Chinese export catalogs; trip reports. Holdings: 800 books; periodicals; 2000 microfiche; 35 VF drawers of clippings, reports and papers. Subscriptions: 75 journals and other serials. Services: Copying; library open to qualified researchers by appointment. Special Indexes: Book index to China Business Review. Staff: Jennifer L. Little, Asst.Libn.

★8645★
NATIONAL COUNCIL FOR YEAR-ROUND EDUCATION - LIBRARY (Educ)
6401 Linda Vista Rd.
San Diego, CA 92111   Dr. Pius Lacher, Pres.
Founded: 1971. Staff: 1. Subjects: Year-round education - research, feasibility studies, legislation, models, curriculum, program. Holdings: Books, pamphlets, brochures, unbound periodicals, clippings. Services: Library open to public by arrangement. Publications: The Year-Rounder, quarterly; proceedings of annual seminars; Annual Directory; occasional papers. Remarks: The aim of the council is "to aid and assist local, state and national organizations in the research, collection, evaluation, design and implementation of year-round education." Staff: Dr. Charles E. Ballinger, Exec.Sec.

★8646★
NATIONAL COUNCIL OF THE YOUNG MEN'S CHRISTIAN ASSOCIATIONS OF THE U.S. - YMCA HISTORICAL LIBRARY (Soc Sci)†
291 Broadway   Phone: (212) 406-0090
New York, NY 10007   Ellen Sowchek, Libn.
Founded: 1880. Staff: Prof 1; Other 1. Subjects: History of the YMCA movement in the United States, Canada, and abroad; religion; social group work; religious education; physical education. Special Collections: Early Young Men's Societies, 1712 to 1850. Holdings: 6000 books; 2000 bound periodical volumes; 3000 reports, manuscripts, dissertations; 5000 pamphlets; 2.5 million boxed documents; 125 reels of microfilm; 3000 photographs; bibliographical notes prepared for YMCA histories. Subscriptions: 35 journals and other serials. Services: Interlibrary loans; copying; bibliographic services for researchers; library open to persons engaged in legitimate research projects.

★8647★
NATIONAL COWBOY HALL OF FAME & WESTERN HERITAGE CENTER - RESEARCH LIBRARY OF WESTERN AMERICANA (Hist)†
1700 N.E. 63rd St.   Phone: (405) 478-2250
Oklahoma City, OK 73111   Mr. A.J. Tytgat, Educ.Dir.
Founded: 1965. Subjects: Cowboys and Western history. Holdings: 4000 volumes. Services: Library open to public for reference use only.

★8648★
NATIONAL CRIME PREVENTION INSTITUTE - INFORMATION CENTER (Soc Sci)
University of Louisville, Shelby Campus   Phone: (502) 588-6987
Louisville, KY 40292   Barbara R. Bomar, Info.Mgr.
Founded: 1973. Staff: Prof 1. Subjects: Crime prevention, security systems, community participation. Holdings: 1200 books; 300 bound periodical volumes; 2000 crime prevention programs; 50,000 brochures; 50 films. Subscriptions: 100 journals and other serials. Services: Copying; library open to public with restrictions. Special Indexes: Selected bibliography of crime prevention and security; crime prevention film list.

NATIONAL CRIMINAL JUSTICE REFERENCE SERVICE
See: U.S. Dept. of Justice - National Institute of Justice

★8649★
NATIONAL DAIRY COUNCIL - LIBRARY (Food-Bev)
6300 N. River Rd.   Phone: (312) 696-1020
Rosemont, IL 60018   Diana Culbertson, Libn.
Founded: 1929. Staff: Prof 3; Other 2. Subjects: Human nutrition, dairy foods. Holdings: 6000 books; 4000 microforms; 45 VF drawers of reprints and pamphlets; 240 linear feet of internal records; 3200 slides. Subscriptions: 600 journals and other serials. Services: Interlibrary loans; copying; library open to public with prior arrangements. Computerized Information Services: DIALOG, MEDLARS; Verfile (internal database).

Networks/Consortia: Member of Illinois Health Libraries Consortium; Metropolitan Chicago Library Assembly; North Suburban Library System; Regional Medical Library - Region 3. **Publications:** Dairy Council Digest, bimonthly; New Acquisitions List, monthly; Serials Holdings List, irregular. **Staff:** Barbara Blatecky, Asst.Libn.; Patricia Harnett, Rec.Mgr.

NATIONAL DEFENCE
See: Canada - National Defence

NATIONAL DEFENCE COLLEGE OF CANADA & CANADIAN LAND FORCES COMMAND AND STAFF COLLEGE
See: Canada - National Defence - Fort Frontenac Library

NATIONAL DEFENCE MEDICAL CENTRE
See: Canada - National Defence

NATIONAL DEFENSE UNIVERSITY
See: U.S. Natl. Defense University

NATIONAL ECONOMIC DEVELOPMENT AND LAW CENTER
See: National Housing Law Project/National Economic Development and Law Center

★8650★
NATIONAL ECONOMIC RESEARCH ASSOCIATES, INC. - LIBRARY (Soc Sci)
555 S. Flower St.   Phone: (213) 628-0131
Los Angeles, CA 90071   Ellyn Sato, Res.Libn.
Staff: Prof 1. **Subjects:** Economics, antitrust law, public utilities. **Holdings:** 2000 books; 8 VF drawers of internal reports and testimonies; 2 VF drawers of trade regulation case decisions. **Subscriptions:** 94 journals and other serials. **Services:** Interlibrary loans; copying; SDI; library not open to public. **Computerized Information Services:** DIALOG. **Also Known As:** NERA.

★8651★
NATIONAL ECONOMIC RESEARCH ASSOCIATES, INC. - LIBRARY (Energy; Law)
1800 M St., N.W.   Phone: (202) 466-3510
Washington, DC 20036   Jane Platt-Brown, Libn.
Founded: 1965. **Staff:** Prof 1; Other 1. **Subjects:** Petroleum, natural gas, energy, economics, antitrust, public utilities. **Holdings:** 4000 books; 1600 congressional economic and energy hearings; Wall Street Journal on microfilm, 1973 to present. **Subscriptions:** 300 journals and other serials. **Services:** Interlibrary loans; copying; library open to public with restrictions. **Computerized Information Services:** DIALOG, SDC, LEXIS. **Publications:** Library Acquisitions, bimonthly - for internal distribution only.

★8652★
NATIONAL ECONOMIC RESEARCH ASSOCIATES, INC. - LIBRARY (Bus-Fin; Energy)
5 World Trade Ctr., 8th Fl.   Phone: (212) 524-7800
New York, NY 10048   Dolores Colgan, Libn.
Founded: 1960. **Staff:** Prof 2; Other 1. **Subjects:** Energy, public utilities, economics, environmental studies, antitrust. **Holdings:** 3500 books; U.S. Government documents; annual reports on microfiche of New York Stock Exchange and American Stock Exchange Companies from 1977. **Subscriptions:** 500 journals and other serials. **Services:** Interlibrary loans; copying; library open to public with restrictions. **Computerized Information Services:** DIALOG, SDC, Mead Data Central. **Staff:** Debra Gaffey, Asst.Libn.

★8653★
NATIONAL ECUMENICAL COALITION, INC. - LIBRARY (Rel-Theol; Soc Sci)†
Georgetown Sta., Box 3554   Phone: (202) 833-2616
Washington, DC 20007   Bro. Scott Desmond, F.O.C., Libn.
Staff: Prof 27. **Subjects:** Civil and constitutional rights, ecumenical programs, juvenile delinquency, drug abuse, law, gay rights, human rights, Equal Rights Amendment (ERA), refugee programs. **Holdings:** 4100 books; 5000 bound periodical volumes; 69 boxes of civil rights archives; 17 boxes of gay rights archives; 14 boxes of ecumenical archives; U.N. publications. **Subscriptions:** 436 journals and other serials; 55 newspapers. **Services:** Copying; library not open to public. **Computerized Information Services:** Computerized cataloging and serials. **Publications:** N.E.C. Today, monthly - by subscription. **Special Catalogs:** Bibliography on civil rights, gay rights, ecumenical organizations, and drug abuse (computer printout). **Remarks:** Library is located at 2059 N. Woodstock St., Suite 305, Arlington, VA 22207. An additional phone number is (703)522-7127. **Staff:** Norma LaVigne, Asst.Libn.

★8654★
NATIONAL EDUCATION RESEARCH - INFORMATION CENTER (Educ)
1201 16th St., N.W.   Phone: (202) 822-7400
Washington, DC 20036   Donald Walker, Mgr., Info.Serv.
Founded: 1942. **Subjects:** Education, labor relations. **Special Collections:** Publications produced by the NEA and its affiliates. **Holdings:** 20,000 volumes. **Services:** Center not open to public.

NATIONAL ELECTRONIC INJURY SURVEILLANCE SYSTEM
See: National Injury Information Clearinghouse

★8655★
NATIONAL EMERGENCY TRAINING CENTER - LIBRARY (Sci-Tech)
16825 S. Seton Ave.   Phone: (301) 447-6771
Emmitsburg, MD 21727   Adele M. Chiesa, Chf., Lrng.Rsrcs.Ctr.
Founded: 1980. **Staff:** Prof 1; Other 5. **Subjects:** Fire science, civil defense, emergency preparedness, management, education. **Holdings:** 19,700 books; 300 bound periodical volumes; 15,000 technical reports; 5000 nonprint materials. **Subscriptions:** 150 journals and other serials; 9 newspapers. **Services:** Interlibrary loans; copying; library open to public by appointment. **Computerized Information Services:** SDC. **Networks/Consortia:** Member of OCLC through FEDLINK. **Formerly:** National Fire Academy Library.

★8656★
NATIONAL EMPLOYEE SERVICES & RECREATION ASSOCIATION - INFORMATION CENTER (Rec)
20 N. Wacker Dr.   Phone: (312) 346-7575
Chicago, IL 60606   Patrick B. Stinson, Exec.Dir.
Founded: 1941. **Subjects:** Employee activities, sports, facilities, travel, physical fitness. **Holdings:** 23 books and bound periodicals. **Services:** Center open to public for reference use only. **Computerized Information Services:** Computerized circulation. **Publications:** List of publications - available upon request. **Formerly:** National Industrial Recreation Association.

★8657★
NATIONAL EMPLOYMENT LAW PROJECT, INC. - LIBRARY (Law)
475 Riverside Dr., Suite 240   Phone: (212) 870-2121
New York, NY 10027   Andrue Scott, Lib.Info.Mgr.
Staff: Prof 1; Other 1. **Subjects:** Employment law. **Holdings:** 3000 books and bound periodical volumes; 12 filing cases of case materials (legal). **Subscriptions:** 50 journals and other serials. **Services:** Library open to legal services personnel only. **Special Catalogs:** Employment law dealing with employment problems of the poor (card).

★8658★
NATIONAL ENDOWMENT FOR THE ARTS - ARTS LIBRARY/INFORMATION CENTER (Art)
2401 E St., N.W., Rm. 1256   Phone: (202) 634-7640
Washington, DC 20506   M. Christine Morrison, Hd.
Staff: Prof 1. **Subjects:** Crafts, dance, design, arts in education, literature, museums, music, public policy and arts, theater, visual arts, arts management, law and art, history of government and the arts, history of the National Endowment for the Arts. **Holdings:** 6000 books; 10 VF drawers of pamphlets (uncataloged). **Subscriptions:** 175 journals and other serials. **Services:** Interlibrary loans; library open to public for reference use only. **Networks/Consortia:** Member of Metropolitan Washington Library Council. **Publications:** Periodicals List, annual.

★8659★
NATIONAL ENDOWMENT FOR THE ARTS - LAW LIBRARY (Law)†
Office of the General Counsel
2401 E St., N.W.   Phone: (202) 634-6588
Washington, DC 20506   Susan Liberman, Asst. to Gen. Counsel
Founded: 1973. **Staff:** 1. **Subjects:** Law. **Holdings:** 800 books and bound periodical volumes. **Subscriptions:** 10 journals and other serials. **Services:** Library open to public for reference use only.

★8660★
NATIONAL ENDOWMENT FOR THE HUMANITIES - LIBRARY (Hum)
806 15th St., N.W.   Phone: (202) 724-0360
Washington, DC 20506   Jeannette D. Coletti, Libn.
Staff: Prof 1; Other 1. **Subjects:** Humanities, higher education, American history, contemporary culture, biography, politics and government. **Special Collections:** Books resulting from National Endowment for the Humanities' funding; documents relating to the history of the Endowment. **Holdings:** 6000 books; 3000 college and university catalogs. **Subscriptions:** 425 journals and other serials; 7 newspapers. **Services:** Interlibrary loans; copying; library open to public by appointment. **Publications:** Acquisitions list, bimonthly; periodicals list, irregular.

NATIONAL ENERGY BOARD
See: Canada - National Energy Board

★8661★
NATIONAL ENERGY FOUNDATION - ENERGY REFERENCE AND RESOURCE CENTER (Energy)
366 Madison Ave., Rm. 705   Phone: (212) 697-2920
New York, NY 10017   Ann Borden, Exec.V.P.
Staff: 14. **Subjects:** Energy - forms, sources and education. **Holdings:** 500 books; 200 pamphlets and teaching aids; 10 AV items. **Services:** Copying; library open to public. **Publications:** Energy Guide; Outlook, bimonthly; In Search of Energy (textbook). **Special Catalogs:** NEF Annotated Bibliography of Energy & Energy Education Materials. **Remarks:** The National Energy Foundation is a nonprofit organization specializing in promoting energy education among junior and senior high school students. **Staff:** Susan Dashnaw, Dir., Prog. & Proj.

NATIONAL ENERGY SOFTWARE CENTER
See: Argonne National Laboratory

NATIONAL ENFORCEMENT INVESTIGATIONS
See: Environmental Protection Agency

★8662★
NATIONAL ENQUIRER - RESEARCH DEPARTMENT LIBRARY (Publ)
600 Southeast Coast Ave.   Phone: (305) 586-1111
Lantana, FL 33464   Martha Moppett, Res.Libn.
Founded: 1956. **Staff:** Prof 3. **Holdings:** 1300 books; back issues of the Enquirer, 1926 to present (microfilm). **Services:** Library open to staff only. **Special Indexes:** Index to National Enquirer.

★8663★
NATIONAL EPILEPSY LIBRARY AND RESOURCE CENTER (Med)
4351 Garden City Dr.   Phone: (301) 459-3700
Landover, MD 20785   Sr. Ann Vivia Walton, Dir.
Founded: 1982. **Staff:** Prof 2; Other 2. **Subjects:** Social, psychological and medical aspects of epilepsy; neurology. **Special Collections:** Archives of the Epilepsy Movement. **Holdings:** 1000 books; 60,000 microfiche; 200 reports. **Subscriptions:** 30 journals and other serials. **Services:** Interlibrary loans; copying; library open to public by appointment. **Computerized Information Services:** DIALOG, NLM, Source Telecomputing Corporation; TEXTRACT (internal database). **Remarks:** NELRC is a service of the Epilepsy Foundation of America. **Staff:** Cynthia W. Shockley, Asst.Dir.

NATIONAL ETHNIC ARCHIVES
See: Canada - Public Archives of Canada

NATIONAL EVANGELICAL LUTHERAN CHURCH ARCHIVES
See: Concordia Historical Institute

NATIONAL FARMERS UNION ARCHIVES
See: University of Colorado, Boulder - Western Historical Collection & University Archives

★8664★
NATIONAL FEDERATION OF ABSTRACTING AND INFORMATION SERVICES (Info Sci)
112 S. 16th St.   Phone: (215) 563-2406
Philadelphia, PA 19102   M. Lynne Neufeld, Exec.Dir.
Founded: 1958. **Staff:** Prof 1; Other 3. **Subjects:** Information science. **Publications:** NFAIS Newsletter, bimonthly; irregular reports, free to members and available on subscription to nonmembers; special publications on abstracting and indexing. **Remarks:** The federation is a group of member organizations which publish abstracting and indexing services and other information services in all subject areas in print and computer-readable forms. The purpose of the federation is to foster, encourage and improve the documentation of the world literature through editing, research and publication, and foster the interchange of information between the U.S. and foreign countries.

★8665★
NATIONAL FEDERATION OF LOCAL CABLE PROGRAMMERS - LIBRARY (Info Sci)
906 Pennsylvania Ave., S.E.   Phone: (202) 544-7272
Washington, DC 20003   Sue Miller Buske, Exec.Dir.
Staff: Prof 2. **Subjects:** Cable television. **Special Collections:** Community access programs from across the country (150 videotapes). **Holdings:** Figures not available. **Subscriptions:** 18 journals and other serials. **Publications:** Community Television Review, quarterly; NFLCP Newsletter,

bimonthly. **Formerly:** Located in Kettering, Ohio. **Staff:** Joan Gudgel, Asst. to Dir.

NATIONAL FERTILIZER DEVELOPMENT CENTER
See: Tennessee Valley Authority - Technical Library (Muscle Shoals, AL)

NATIONAL FILM BOARD OF CANADA
See: Canada - National Film Board of Canada

★8666★
NATIONAL FILM BOARD OF CANADA - FILM LIBRARY (Aud-Vis)
1251 Ave. of the Americas, 16th Fl.   Phone: (212) 586-5131
New York, NY 10020   Ken Shere, U.S. Gen.Mgr.
Staff: 13. **Subjects:** Film. **Holdings:** 4300 16mm films; 1000 video cassettes. **Services:** Audiovisual distributor; maintains collection of films, and videotapes available for preview, rental and purchase in the United States. **Special Catalogs:** Catalog of current titles. **Staff:** A.G. Whalen, Chf.Libn.; Karen Capen, Distr.Rep.; Jane Gutteridge, Distr.Rep.; Mary Jane Terrell, Distr.Rep.

NATIONAL FILM, TELEVISION & SOUND ARCHIVES
See: Canada - Public Archives of Canada

NATIONAL FIRE ACADEMY
See: National Emergency Training Center

★8667★
NATIONAL FIRE PROTECTION ASSOCIATION - CHARLES S. MORGAN TECHNICAL LIBRARY (Sci-Tech)
Batterymarch Park   Phone: (617) 328-9290
Quincy, MA 02269   Nancy Corrin, Mgr.
Founded: 1945. **Staff:** Prof 2; Other 1. **Subjects:** Fire prevention and protection, fire protection engineering and research, arson investigation, fire services management, flammability of materials, model building codes. **Special Collections:** NFPA Published Archives, (includes the National Fire Codes historical file; 192 shelf feet); voluntary industrial standards (43 shelf feet). **Holdings:** 4900 books; 11,300 technical reports; 129 film titles; 11,000 microfiche; 210 reels and cartridges of microfilm; 325 tapes; 36 VF drawers of pamphlets, reprints and clippings. **Subscriptions:** 450 journals and other serials. **Services:** Copying; library open to public by appointment. **Computerized Information Services:** DIALOG. **Publications:** Information Dialog, semimonthly - for internal distribution only. **Staff:** Dorinda Fergason, Fire Info.Spec.

NATIONAL FISHERIES CENTER
See: U.S. Fish & Wildlife Service

NATIONAL FISHERY RESEARCH LABORATORY LIBRARY
See: U.S. Fish & Wildlife Service

★8668★
NATIONAL FLAG FOUNDATION - FLAG PLAZA LIBRARY (Soc Sci)
Flag Plaza   Phone: (412) 261-1776
Pittsburgh, PA 15219   George F. Cahill, Pres.
Founded: 1968. **Staff:** Prof 1. **Subjects:** History of the American flag, flag courtesy and display. **Special Collections:** Historic Flags of America (original art and text; 42 scenes); Bicentennial salutes by preeminent Americans (65 pieces); Bicentennial salutes by America's great cartoonists (50 pieces); One Hundred Years Ago (painting, c. 1876). **Holdings:** 100 books; 15 bound periodical volumes; 10 charts (cataloged); 75 pamphlets (cataloged); 15 35mm films. **Services:** Designing flag related programs; research inquiries on flag history and flag display; library open to public by special request. **Publications:** Our Flag: How to Honor It, How to Display It (brochure); You Are the Flag; Flags of America (books and charts); Broad Stripes and Bright Stars (book); The New Constellation, A Flag for Every Star - all available for purchase; Flag Plaza Standard, 3/year and special editions - sent to members.

★8669★
NATIONAL FLUID POWER ASSOCIATION - FLUID POWER NATIONAL INFORMATION CENTER (Sci-Tech)
3333 N. Mayfair Rd.   Phone: (414) 259-0990
Milwaukee, WI 53222   Ruth Falatyk, Libn.
Founded: 1980. **Staff:** Prof 1. **Subjects:** Industrial fluid power; communication; fluid, lubricants and sealing devices; pressure rating; pumps, motors, power units and reservoirs; filtration and contamination. **Special Collections:** Proceedings of National Conferences on Fluid Power, 1955 to present. **Holdings:** 400 books; 145 National Fluid Power standards; 500 International Standard Organization publications; 20 standards of the American Society for Testing and Materials. **Subscriptions:** 50 journals and other serials; 5 newspapers. **Services:** Interlibrary loans; copying; library open

to association members.

NATIONAL FLUTE ASSOCIATION COLLECTION
See: University of Arizona - Music Collection

NATIONAL FOOTBALL MUSEUM
See: Pro Football Hall of Fame - Library/Research Center

★8670★
NATIONAL FOREST PRODUCTS ASSOCIATION - INFORMATION CENTER (Env-Cons)
1619 Massachusetts Ave., N.W.　　Phone: (202) 797-5836
Washington, DC 20036　　Barbara A. Beall, Mgr.
Founded: 1962. Staff: Prof 1; Other 1. Subjects: Forest management and economics, wood construction, wood technology, forest products industry. Holdings: 5000 books; 80 bound periodical volumes; 24 VF drawers of pamphlets and documents; 1500 scientific and technical reports. Subscriptions: 300 journals and other serials. Services: Interlibrary loans; copying; center open to public by appointment; some files are for internal use only. Networks/Consortia: Member of Metropolitan Washington Library Council. Publications: Monthly Acquisitions List; Periodicals Digest, monthly - for staff and association members and by exchange.

NATIONAL FOUNDATION ON THE ARTS AND THE HUMANITIES
See: National Endowment for the Arts; National Endowment for the Humanities

★8671★
NATIONAL FOUNDATION FOR CONSUMER CREDIT - LIBRARY (Bus-Fin)
8701 Georgia Ave., Suite 601　　Phone: (301) 589-5600
Silver Spring, MD 20910
Subjects: Consumer credit; credit counseling; credit research and education. Services: Library not open to public. Formerly: Located in Washington, DC.

★8672★
NATIONAL FOUNDATION OF FUNERAL SERVICE - BERYL L. BOYER LIBRARY (Soc Sci)
1600-1612 Central St.　　Phone: (312) 328-6545
Evanston, IL 60201　　Dr. Joe A. Adams, Dir.
Founded: 1945. Subjects: Funeral service, mortuary management, death customs, burial, bereavement, embalming, mortuary science, restorative art. Special Collections: Frank K. Fairchild Collection; Clarence E. Smith Collection; Dr. Charles A. Renouard Collection; Harry G. Samson Collection. Holdings: 2800 books; 300 bound periodical volumes; 300 prints and pamphlets (cataloged). Subscriptions: 48 journals and other serials. Services: Library open to responsible adults for reference only.

★8673★
NATIONAL FOUNDATION FOR GIFTED AND CREATIVE CHILDREN - LIBRARY (Soc Sci; Educ)
395 Diamond Hill Rd.　　Phone: (401) 942-2253
Warwick, RI 02886　　Marie Friedel, Exec.Dir.
Staff: Prof 1; Other 1. Subjects: Gifted children, creative children, misuse of prescription drugs, physical chemistry and biology, science, humanities, music, art, creative writing. Special Collections: Case histories of individual gifted and creative children; statistical studies. Holdings: 2500 books; 1000 unbound periodicals (cataloged); 45 notebooks of newspaper clippings from 1968; test scores of 800 children; 200 records of prescription drugs given to children. Subscriptions: 10 journals and other serials. Services: Library open to parents and professionals. Publications: Newsletter, bimonthly.

★8674★
NATIONAL 4-H COUNCIL - COMMUNICATIONS DIVISION (Soc Sci)
7100 Connecticut Ave.
Chevy Chase, MD 20815　　Mary Bedford, Rsrcs./Reporting Coord.
Founded: 1977. Subjects: Citizenship, leadership, youth development, current 4-H projects. Special Collections: Foreign youth programs. Holdings: Reports, clippings, photographs, slides, tapes, films, printed educational materials.

★8675★
NATIONAL GALLERY OF ART - DEPARTMENT OF EXTENSION PROGRAMS (Art; Aud-Vis)
Sixth and Constitution Ave., N.W.　　Phone: (202) 737-4215
Washington, DC 20565　　Ruth R. Perlin, Cur.-in-Charge
Staff: Prof 5; Other 8. Subjects: Western European and American painting, sculpture, decorative arts and folk arts; themes of temporary exhibitions. Holdings: 40 slide lecture titles; 11 videotapes; 38 film titles. Services: Slide programs, films and video cassettes - distributed on a free-loan basis to

schools, colleges, libraries, civic groups and individuals. Publications: Catalog - free upon request. Staff: Laura T. Schneider, Supv., Ext.Serv.; Phyllis Meltzer, Regional Loan Coord.

★8676★
NATIONAL GALLERY OF ART - EDUCATION DIVISION SLIDE LIBRARY (Art; Aud-Vis)
Sixth and Constitution Ave., N.W.　　Phone: (202) 842-6100
Washington, DC 20565　　Anne von Rebhan, Chf. Slide Libn.
Staff: Prof 2; Other 1. Subjects: Western European and American painting and sculpture; graphic arts. Holdings: 120,000 slides. Services: Interlibrary loans; library open to public. Publications: Lantern Slide Manual.

★8677★
NATIONAL GALLERY OF ART - INDEX OF AMERICAN DESIGN (Art)
Sixth and Constitution Ave., N.W.　　Phone: (202) 737-4215
Washington, DC 20565　　Lina Steele, Cur.
Staff: Prof 1. Subjects: Renderings of decorative and folk arts of the United States. Holdings: 17,000 water colors; photographs. Services: Extension service; collection of slides and color microfiche of the watercolors open to public by appointment.

★8678★
NATIONAL GALLERY OF ART - LIBRARY (Art)
Sixth and Constitution, N.W.　　Phone: (202) 737-4215
Washington, DC 20565　　J.M. Edelstein, Chf.Libn.
Founded: 1941. Staff: Prof 10; Other 18. Subjects: Art, architecture, decorative arts, European and American painting and sculpture, drawing, prints. Special Collections: Artist biographies; sale catalogs; exhibition catalogs; Leonardo da Vinci; museum and private collection catalogs. Holdings: 100,000 books; 14,802 bound periodical volumes; 150 VF drawers; 24,320 microform titles. Subscriptions: 822 journals and other serials. Services: Interlibrary loans; copying; library open to graduate students and qualified researchers. Computerized Information Services: DIALOG, RLIN; computerized cataloging and ILL. Networks/Consortia: Member of OCLC through FEDLINK. Staff: Celine Alvey, Assoc.Libn.; Caroline H. Backlund, Hd., Rd.Serv.; Lamia Doumato, Ref.Libn.; Margot E. Grier, Per.Libn.; Jane Collins, Hd.Cat.; Roger Lawson, Cat.; Trudy Olivetti, Cat.; Catherine Quinn, Hd.Cat.; Marsha Spieth, Cat.

★8679★
NATIONAL GALLERY OF ART - PHOTOGRAPHIC ARCHIVES (Art; Pict)
Sixth and Constitution Ave., N.W.　　Phone: (202) 737-4215
Washington, DC 20565　　Ruth R. Philbrick, Cur.
Staff: Prof 6; Other 2. Subjects: Western European art, early Christian era to present; American art, 17th century to present; ancient art. Holdings: 950,000 photographs; 170,000 negatives; 2.5 million microforms. Services: Archives open to graduate students and qualified researchers. Staff: Jerry Mallick, Cat./Adm.; Richard Hutton, Chf.Cat.; Andrea Gibbs, Cat.; Karen Horn, Cat.; William Harkins, Cat.; Stacy Belkind, Cat.

NATIONAL GALLERY OF CANADA
See: Canada - National Gallery of Canada

★8680★
NATIONAL GASOHOL COMMISSION - LIBRARY
521 S. 14th St., Suite 5
Lincoln, NE 68508
Defunct

★8681★
NATIONAL GENEALOGICAL SOCIETY - LIBRARY (Hist)
1921 Sunderland Pl., N.W.　　Phone: (202) 785-2123
Washington, DC 20036　　Joyce Page, Libn.
Founded: 1912. Staff: Prof 3. Subjects: Genealogy, local history, bibliography, biography. Special Collections: Manuscript collections of former members. Holdings: 15,000 books; 2000 bound periodical volumes; 100 boxes of manuscript materials; 40 VF drawers of documents, clippings, pamphlets; microfilm. Subscriptions: 20 journals and other serials. Services: Copying; library open to public for reference use only with fee for nonmembers. Publications: National Genealogical Society Quarterly; National Genealogical Society Newsletter, bimonthly; 48 special publications, book list revised 1978.

★8682★
NATIONAL GEOGRAPHIC SOCIETY - AUDIOVISUAL LIBRARY (Aud-Vis)
17th and M Sts., N.W.　　Phone: (202) 857-7691
Washington, DC 20036　　Betty Kotcher, AV Libn.
Founded: 1972. Staff: Prof 2; Other 4. Subjects: Wildlife, animal behavior,

lands and peoples of the world, science, exploration, recreational activities. **Special Collections:** National Geographic research grant documentaries (film); NGS television productions (64 titles); NGS educational films (118 titles); stock film (out-takes from NGS's television and educational film productions; over 2 million feet); magnetic sound tapes (cataloged). **Services:** Copying; library open to public by appointment. **Staff:** Laura Painter, Asst.Libn.

★8683★
NATIONAL GEOGRAPHIC SOCIETY - CARTOGRAPHIC DIVISION - MAP LIBRARY (Geog-Map)
17th & M Sts., N.W.   Phone: (301) 921-1401
Washington, DC 20036   Margery K. Barkdull, Map Libn.
Staff: Prof 1; Other 2. **Subjects:** Topography, political and physical geography. **Holdings:** 105,000 items. **Services:** Interlibrary loans (limited); library not open to public.

★8684★
NATIONAL GEOGRAPHIC SOCIETY - ILLUSTRATIONS LIBRARY (Pict)
17th & M Sts., N.W.   Phone: (202) 857-7000
Washington, DC 20036   Fern Shrewsberry Dame, Illus.Libn.
Founded: 1919. **Staff:** Prof 10; Other 23. **Subjects:** Photographs, transparencies and artwork of subjects suitable for use in National Geographic publications. **Special Collections:** Herbert G. Ponting (Antarctic); George Shiras 3rd (wildlife); Joseph F. Rock (China); Robert F. Griggs (Mt. Katmai, Alaska); Hiram Bingham (Machu Picchu, Peru); Bradford Washburn (Yukon); Society's Space Collection of NASA space probe and Skylab missions. **Holdings:** 8 million published and indexed transparencies, photographs and original paintings. **Services:** Library for the exclusive use of the society and its publications. **Special Catalogs:** Thesaurus (book), created by the Illustrations Library to fulfill its unique needs. **Staff:** Carolyn J. Harrison, Asst.Libn.; M. Scott Bolden, Asst.Libn.; Ilona S. Gants, Supv., Res./Cat.; R. Gary Colbert, Asst.Libn./Circ.; Margaret C. Allen, Supv., Unpubl.Pict.; Scott W. Maker, Supv., Publ.Pict.; Joyce C. Betsill, Supv., Proc.; Alphonso B. Petteway, Supv., Ref./Cat.; Richard A. White, Supv., Archv.; Robin E. Siegel, Cons.

★8685★
NATIONAL GEOGRAPHIC SOCIETY - LIBRARY (Geog-Map)
16th & M Sts., N.W.   Phone: (202) 857-7787
Washington, DC 20036   Virginia Carter Hills, Libn.
Founded: 1920. **Staff:** Prof 9; Other 19. **Subjects:** Geography and allied sciences, description and travel, natural history. **Special Collections:** General A.W. Greely's Polar Library; complete set of Hakluyt Society publications. **Holdings:** 70,000 books; 4299 bound periodical volumes; 430 VF drawers of clippings, pamphlets and documents. **Subscriptions:** 1442 journals and other serials. **Services:** Interlibrary loans (limited); library open to public. **Staff:** Patricia M. Smith, Asst.Libn.; Susan Fifer, Asst.Libn./Circ.Libn.; Carolyn Locke, Ref.Libn.; Louise Robinson, Chf., Clipping Serv.; Susan Dempsey, Bibliog.; Karen Al-Kinani, Per.; Dorothy Bricker, Acq.; Marta Strada, Dir., Cat.; Carol Stroud, Acq.

NATIONAL GEOPHYSICAL DATA CENTER
See: World Data Center A - Solar-Terrestrial Physics

NATIONAL GERONTOLOGY RESOURCE CENTER
See: American Association of Retired Persons

NATIONAL GROUND WATER INFORMATION CENTER
See: National Water Well Association

★8686★
NATIONAL GUARD ASSOCIATION OF THE UNITED STATES - LIBRARY (Mil)
One Massachusetts Ave., N.W.
Washington, DC 20001   Cpt. Thomas M. Weaver, Res.Asst./Libn.
Staff: Prof 1. **Holdings:** Military histories including works relating to the National Guard and state militia. **Services:** Library not open to public.

★8687★
NATIONAL HAMILTONIAN PARTY - HAMILTONIAN LIBRARY (Hist)
434 Chalmers St.   Phone: (313) 234-5552
Flint, MI 48503   Albert Victor, Libn.
Staff: Prof 1; Other 5. **Subjects:** American political history, National Hamiltonian Party, American political campaigns, minor political parties, Alexander Hamilton. **Special Collections:** Kelly Collection (political documents and campaign material from American presidential campaigns, 1824 to present). **Holdings:** 2340 books; 20,000 items of political memorabilia. **Subscriptions:** 17 journals and other serials. **Services:** Interlibrary loans; library open to public by appointment.

NATIONAL HANSEN'S DISEASE CENTER
See: U.S. Public Health Service Hospital

NATIONAL HEALTH STANDARDS AND QUALITY INFORMATION CLEARINGHOUSE
See: Capital Systems Group, Inc.

NATIONAL HIGHWAY TRAFFIC SAFETY ADMINISTRATION
See: U.S. Natl. Highway Traffic Safety Administration

NATIONAL HISTORICAL FIRE FOUNDATION - HALL OF FLAME
See: Hall of Flame

★8688★
NATIONAL HOME STUDY COUNCIL - LIBRARY (Educ)
1601 18th St., N.W.   Phone: (202) 234-5100
Washington, DC 20009   Michael P. Lambert
Subjects: Home study, correspondence and vocational education. **Holdings:** 500 books. **Services:** Copying; library open to public.

NATIONAL HOUSING CENTER LIBRARY
See: National Association of Home Builders

★8689★
NATIONAL HOUSING LAW PROJECT/NATIONAL ECONOMIC DEVELOPMENT AND LAW CENTER - LIBRARY (Law; Soc Sci)
1950 Addison St.   Phone: (415) 548-2600
Berkeley, CA 94704   Katherine Parkes, Libn.
Founded: 1969. **Staff:** Prof 1; Other 1. **Subjects:** Housing, community economic development, health services, law. **Holdings:** 5000 books; 8000 handbooks, regulations and government documents. **Subscriptions:** 150 journals and other serials; 5 newspapers. **Services:** Copying; library open to public by appointment for reference use only.

★8690★
NATIONAL HUMANITIES CENTER - LIBRARY (Hum)
Box 12256   Phone: (919) 549-0661
Research Triangle Park, NC 27709   Walter Alan Tuttle, Libn.
Staff: Prof 2; Other 1. **Subjects:** Humanities. **Holdings:** 900 volumes. **Services:** Copying; library not open to public. **Computerized Information Services:** DIALOG; computerized cataloging and serials. **Networks/Consortia:** Member of OCLC through SOLINET. **Staff:** Rebecca B. Sutton, Asst.Libn.

NATIONAL IMMIGRATION ARCHIVES
See: Temple University - Central Library System

★8691★
NATIONAL INDIAN EDUCATION ASSOCIATION - LIBRARY (Area-Ethnic)†
Ivy Tower Bldg., 2nd Fl.
1115 Second Ave., S.   Phone: (612) 333-5341
Minneapolis, MN 55403   Joyce Yellowhammer, Libn./Data Anl.
Founded: 1970. **Subjects:** Native Americans - history, customs, art, religion, education, music. **Holdings:** 4000 books; 300 films and filmstrips (cataloged); 20 microfiche; 150 reel to reel magnetic tapes; 100 cassette tapes; 150 phonograph records. **Subscriptions:** 20 journals and other serials; 20 newspapers. **Services:** SDI; library open to public for reference use only. **Special Indexes:** Index to bibliographies and resource materials.

NATIONAL INDIAN LAW LIBRARY
See: Native American Rights Fund

NATIONAL INDUSTRIAL RECREATION ASSOCIATION
See: National Employee Services & Recreation Association

NATIONAL INFORMATION CENTER ON DEAFNESS
See: Gallaudet College

★8692★
NATIONAL INFORMATION CENTER FOR EDUCATIONAL MEDIA (NICEM) (Educ)
University of Southern California
University Park
Los Angeles, CA 90007   Phone: (213) 743-6681
                                       M. Thomas Risner, Ph.D., Dir.
Staff: Prof 5; Other 7. **Subjects:** Educational media. **Holdings:** 500,000 abstracts. **Services:** Center open to public with restrictions. **Computerized Information Services:** DIALOG, BRS. **Special Indexes:** List of indexes available on request.

★8693★

NATIONAL INFORMATION CENTER FOR SPECIAL EDUCATION MATERIALS (NICSEM) (Educ)
University of Southern California
University Park
Los Angeles, CA 90007
Subjects: Special education. **Holdings:** 40,000 abstracts. **Services:** Center open to public with restrictions. **Computerized Information Services:** DIALOG, BRS. **Special Indexes:** List of indexes available on request.

★8694★

NATIONAL INJURY INFORMATION CLEARINGHOUSE (Med)
5401 Westbard Ave.
Westwood Towers Bldg., Rm. 625   Phone: (301) 492-6424
Washington, DC 20207   Edward A. Pascarella, Ph.D., Dir.
Founded: 1973. **Staff:** Prof 4; Other 3. **Subjects:** Injury data from accidents associated with consumer products; epidemiology of accidents. **Special Collections:** Injury data from one million consumer product-associated accidents reported through the National Electronic Injury Surveillance System (NEISS); 55,000 reports of in-depth investigations of accidents associated with consumer products. **Holdings:** 100 staff studies and special reports on consumer product-associated injuries. **Services:** Interlibrary loans; copying. **Computerized Information Services:** Online systems. **Publications:** NEISS Data Highlights, quarterly - currently free upon request. **Remarks:** Maintained by U.S. Consumer Product Safety Commission, Hazard Identification and Analysis. **Staff:** Cathleen A. Irish, Tech.Info.Spec.; Joel I. Friedman, Tech.Info.Spec.

★8695★

NATIONAL INSTITUTE ON AGING - GERONTOLOGY RESEARCH CENTER (Soc Sci)
4940 Eastern Ave.   Phone: (301) 396-9403
Baltimore, MD 21224   Doris M. Hilferty, Act.Chf., Lib.Serv.
Founded: 1977. **Staff:** Prof 1; Other 5. **Subjects:** Gerontology, aging, geriatrics, chemistry, psychology, sociology. **Holdings:** 6200 books; 7000 bound periodical volumes; 260 unbound reports and documents; 120 microforms. **Subscriptions:** 415 journals and other serials. **Services:** Interlibrary loans; library open to public for reference use only. **Computerized Information Services:** Online systems.

NATIONAL INSTITUTE ON ALCOHOL ABUSE & ALCOHOLISM
See: National Clearinghouse for Alcohol Information

NATIONAL INSTITUTE OF ALLERGY & INFECTIOUS DISEASES
See: U.S. Natl. Institutes of Health

NATIONAL INSTITUTE OF ARTHRITIS, DIABETES, DIGESTIVE AND KIDNEY DISEASES - ARTHRITIS INFORMATION CLEARINGHOUSE
See: Arthritis Information Clearinghouse

★8696★

NATIONAL INSTITUTE OF ARTHRITIS, METABOLISM & DIGESTIVE DISEASES - OFFICE OF HEALTH RESEARCH REPORTS (Med)†
Phone: (301) 496-3583
Bethesda, MD 20205   Betsy Singer, Chf.
Staff: Prof 4; Other 3. **Subjects:** Clinical and laboratory research dealing with the various arthritic, rheumatic and collagen diseases, the metabolic diseases including diabetes, digestive diseases, orthopedics, dermatology, hematology, nutrition, endocrine disorders, urology and renal disease including research and development of the artificial kidney. Basic research includes biochemistry, nutrition, pathology, histochemistry, chemistry, pharmacology, toxicology, and physical, chemical and molecular biology. **Services:** Office of Health Research Reports collects and disseminates scientific information about current research carried on at the institute and by its grantees in nonfederal research centers. **Remarks:** Institute is a branch of U.S. Public Health Service - National Institutes of Health.

NATIONAL INSTITUTE OF CORRECTIONS
See: U.S. Dept. of Justice

★8697★

NATIONAL INSTITUTE OF DENTAL RESEARCH - DENTAL RESEARCH DATA OFFICE (Med)
Phone: (301) 496-7220
Bethesda, MD 20205   Kenneth C. Lynn, Data Off.
Staff: Prof 1; Other 1. **Subjects:** Dental research. **Holdings:** 10,000 project summaries; 1500 technical reports on microfiche. **Services:** Copying; office open to public with restrictions. **Computerized Information Services:** Internal database. **Publications:** List of publications - available upon request.

Remarks: Institute is a branch of U.S. Public Health Service - National Institutes of Health.

★8698★

NATIONAL INSTITUTE ON DRUG ABUSE - RESOURCE CENTER (Med; Soc Sci)
5600 Fishers Lane, Rm. 10A54   Phone: (301) 443-6614
Rockville, MD 20857   Ilse Vada, Libn.
Founded: 1974. **Staff:** Prof 1; Other 2. **Subjects:** Drug abuse. **Special Collections:** Grant/Contract final reports. **Holdings:** 10,000 books; 35,000 microfiche; AV materials. **Subscriptions:** 300 journals and other serials. **Services:** Interlibrary loans; copying; library open to public. **Computerized Information Services:** DIALOG, NLM. **Publications:** New Acquisitions Listing, monthly - to mailing list; Journal Holdings, biennial - by request. **Special Catalogs:** Audiovisual Catalog, biennial - by request. **Remarks:** The resource center provides library and bibliographic services to staff and the public through interlibrary loan.

★8699★

NATIONAL INSTITUTE OF EDUCATION - EDUCATIONAL RESEARCH LIBRARY (Educ)
1200 - 19th St., N.W., 2nd Fl.   Phone: (202) 254-5060
Washington, DC 20208   Charles D. Missar, Supv.Libn.
Staff: Prof 2; Other 2. **Subjects:** Education, psychology, management, educational statistics, information science. **Special Collections:** Rare Book Collection (education); American Textbook Collection, 1786-1940; William S. Gray Reading Collection (on microfiche); U.S. Office of Education Historical Collection, 1870-1980; Elaine Exton's papers; historical foreign language periodicals. **Holdings:** 150,000 books; 42,000 bound periodical volumes; 300,000 ERIC microfiche; 500 NIE archives collection; 500 NIE reports collection; 2000 reels of microfilm; 35,000 microfiche. **Subscriptions:** 1000 journals and other serials. **Services:** Interlibrary loans; copying; library open to public with restrictions. **Computerized Information Services:** Online systems; computerized cataloging. **Networks/Consortia:** Member of OCLC through FEDLINK. **Publications:** Acquisitions list, monthly. **Special Catalogs:** Periodical Holdings List; Catalog of Rare Books on Education; Early American Textbook Catalog; NIE Products Catalog. **Staff:** Jo Anne S. Cassell, Asst.Libn.; James P. Josey, Ref.Libn.

NATIONAL INSTITUTE OF EDUCATION - ERIC PROCESSING AND REFERENCE FACILITY
See: ERIC Processing and Reference Facility

★8700★

NATIONAL INSTITUTE OF ENVIRONMENTAL HEALTH SCIENCES - ENVIRONMENTAL TERATOLOGY INFORMATION CENTER (Med; Env-Cons)
Box 122233   Phone: (919) 541-3214
Research Triangle Park, NC 27709   Florence E. Jordan, Tech.Info.Spec.
Founded: 1975. **Staff:** Prof 1; Other 3. **Subjects:** Teratology, environment. **Holdings:** 26,000 microfiche of teratology studies reports. **Services:** Library open to public. **Computerized Information Services:** TOXLINE, DOE/RECON. **Special Catalogs:** Computer printout of the following: species studies (common and taxonomic name); agent studied (chemical, drug, biological, physical); Chemical Abstract Service Registry Number; bibliography (author, title, source).

★8701★

NATIONAL INSTITUTE OF ENVIRONMENTAL HEALTH SCIENCES - LIBRARY (Sci-Tech)
Box 12233   Phone: (919) 541-3426
Research Triangle Park, NC 27709   W. Davenport Robertson, Hd.Libn.
Founded: 1966. **Staff:** Prof 3; Other 4. **Subjects:** Pharmacology, toxicology, mutagenesis, teratogenesis, cell biology, carcinogenesis. **Holdings:** 8685 books; 1800 bound periodical volumes; 7500 unbound periodical volumes; 1305 reels of microfilm; 3500 microfiche; 6 VF drawers of manuscripts; 500 technical reports; 200 microfiche reports; 4 file drawers of in-house reprints. **Subscriptions:** 665 journals and other serials. **Services:** Interlibrary loans; copying; SDI; library open to public. **Computerized Information Services:** DIALOG, BRS, Chemical Abstracts Service (CAS), SDC, NLM; computerized cataloging. **Networks/Consortia:** Member of OCLC through FEDLINK. **Publications:** NIEHS Library Newsletter, monthly - for internal distribution only; NIEHS Bibliography, annual - free upon request. **Special Catalogs:** Reports Collection Catalog (computer printout). **Remarks:** Institute is a branch of U.S. Public Health Service - National Institutes of Health and also serves the National Toxicology Program. **Staff:** Ralph Hester, Tech.Info.Spec.; Christine Chastain, Ref.Libn.

NATIONAL INSTITUTE OF JUSTICE
See: U.S. Dept. of Justice

NATIONAL INSTITUTE OF MENTAL HEALTH
See: U.S. Public Health Service - Natl. Institute of Mental Health

★8702★
NATIONAL INSTITUTE ON MENTAL RETARDATION - NATIONAL REFERENCE SERVICE LIBRARY (Med)
Kinsmen Bldg., York University
4700 Keele St.   Phone: (416) 661-9611
Downsview, ON, Canada M3J 1P3 Mrs. Edward Armour, Coord.Natl.Ref.Serv.
Founded: 1964. **Staff:** Prof 3; Other 2. **Subjects:** Mental retardation, developmental disabilities, rehabilitation, special education, community organization. **Holdings:** 12,000 books; 12 VF drawers of pamphlets and reprints; 222 films. **Subscriptions:** 100 journals and other serials. **Services:** Interlibrary loans; copying; library open to public for reference use only. **Special Catalogs:** Specialized bibliographies; film and videotape catalog. **Remarks:** Library is sponsored by the Canadian Association for the Mentally Retarded. **Formerly:** Its John Orr Foster National Reference Library. **Staff:** Mary Ann Hutton, Libn.

★8703★
NATIONAL INSTITUTE OF MUNICIPAL LAW OFFICES - LIBRARY (Law)
1000 Connecticut Ave., N.W., Suite 800
Washington, DC 20036   Charles S. Rhyne, Gen.Couns.
Subjects: City codes, ordinances, briefs and opinions, and other specialized municipal law material. **Services:** Library open to members only.

NATIONAL INSTITUTE FOR OCCUPATIONAL SAFETY AND HEALTH
See: U.S. Natl. Institute for Occupational Safety and Health

NATIONAL INSTITUTES OF HEALTH
See: U.S. Natl. Institutes of Health

★8704★
NATIONAL INTERFRATERNITY CONFERENCE - LIBRARY (Educ)
3901 W. 86th St.   Phone: (317) 297-1112
Indianapolis, IN 46268   Jack L. Anson, Exec.Dir.
Founded: 1956. **Staff:** 1. **Subjects:** College fraternities, scholarship programs, fraternity statistics, fraternity operational procedures. **Holdings:** 500 books. **Subscriptions:** 50 journals and other serials. **Services:** Library open to public by appointment.

★8705★
NATIONAL INVESTIGATIONS COMMITTEE ON AERIAL PHENOMENA - INFORMATION CENTER (Sci-Tech)
2926 Applegate Rd.
Glenview, IL 60025   Sherman J. Larsen, Pres.
Founded: 1956. **Subjects:** Unidentified flying objects (UFOs), extraterrestrial life, space exploration and travel. **Special Collections:** UFO Reports and Photographs (1900 to present); aerial and terrestrial phenomena; special files on investigations and evaluations. **Holdings:** 300 books; 10 file cabinets of unbound periodicals, news clippings, technical reports, articles and papers, private correspondence and tape recordings. **Services:** Center open to qualified researchers for a fee. **Formerly:** Located in Gaithersburg, MD.

★8706★
NATIONAL INVESTIGATIONS COMMITTEE ON UFOS - NEW AGE CENTER (Sci-Tech)
7970 Woodman Ave., No. 103   Phone: (213) 781-7704
Van Nuys, CA 91402   Madeleine Udin, Mgr.
Staff: Prof 1; Other 3. **Subjects:** Unidentified flying objects, space, science, law, religion, astronomy. **Holdings:** 10 manuscripts; 4 16mm films; 500 slides; clippings. **Subscriptions:** 12 journals and other serials.

★8707★
NATIONAL INVESTMENT LIBRARY (Bus-Fin)
80 Wall St.   Phone: (212) 254-1700
New York, NY 10005   Kathe Engro, Asst.Dir.
Founded: 1970. **Staff:** 28. **Subjects:** Business, finance, stock market. **Holdings:** All copies of 10Ks, 10Qs, 8Ks, 13 Ds, annual reports, registrations, prospectuses and proxies filed with the Securities and Exchange Commission. **Subscriptions:** 25 journals and other serials. **Services:** Copying; research. **Computerized Information Services:** Mechanized services. **Staff:** Linda Rosenberg, Asst.Dir./Res.

★8708★
NATIONAL INVESTMENT SERVICES OF AMERICA, INC. - LIBRARY (Bus-Fin)
815 E. Mason St.
Box 2143   Phone: (414) 271-6540
Milwaukee, WI 53201   Debbie Chapin, Libn.
Founded: 1976. **Staff:** Prof 1. **Subjects:** Corporate profiles, economics, investment strategy. **Holdings:** 150 books; 50 bound periodical volumes; 3000 subject files. **Subscriptions:** 60 journals and other serials. **Services:** Library not open to public.

★8709★
NATIONAL JEWISH HOSPITAL & RESEARCH CTR/NATIONAL ASTHMA CTR - GERALD TUCKER MEMORIAL - MEDICAL LIBRARY (Med; Sci-Tech)
3800 E. Colfax Ave.   Phone: (303) 388-4461
Denver, CO 80206   Helen-Ann Brown, Med.Libn.
Staff: Prof 1; Other 2. **Subjects:** Molecular and cellular biology, immunology, allergy, asthma, tuberculosis. **Holdings:** 1500 books; 10,500 bound periodical volumes; 200 reprints; 12 boxes of hospital archives. **Subscriptions:** 237 journals and other serials. **Services:** Interlibrary loans; copying; library open to public with restrictions. **Computerized Information Services:** BRS, NLM; computerized cataloging and ILL. **Networks/Consortia:** Member of Denver Area Health Sciences Library Consortium; Colorado Council of Medical Librarians.

★8710★
NATIONAL JEWISH INFORMATION SERVICE FOR THE PROPAGATION OF JUDAISM - RESEARCH LIBRARY AND ARCHIVES (Rel-Theol)
5174 W. 8th St.   Phone: (213) 936-6033
Los Angeles, CA 90036   Rachel D. Maggal, P.R. Dir.
Founded: 1960. **Staff:** 2. **Subjects:** Propagation of Judaism, Jewish missionary activities, Judaica, comparative religion. **Special Collections:** Conversions to Judaism in history and literature. **Holdings:** 1000 books. **Subscriptions:** 12 journals and other serials. **Services:** Translation of periodical articles from major European magazines; questions on Judaism answered through the mail; library open to public by appointment for reference use only. **Publications:** Voice of Judaism, annual - available to members and by donation. **Staff:** Rabbi Moshe M. Maggal, Founder & Pres.

★8711★
NATIONAL JUDICIAL COLLEGE - LAW LIBRARY (Law)
University of Nevada   Phone: (702) 784-6747
Reno, NV 89557   Kathleen Dion, Libn.
Founded: 1965. **Staff:** Prof 1; Other 4. **Subjects:** Law, judicial administration and education. **Special Collections:** Judges' manuals and benchbooks; pattern jury instructions; court rules; U.S. depository library. **Holdings:** 55,000 books and bound periodical volumes. **Subscriptions:** 506 journals and other serials. **Services:** Interlibrary loans; copying. **Computerized Information Services:** WESTLAW.

NATIONAL LABOR RELATIONS BOARD
See: U.S. Natl. Labor Relations Board

NATIONAL LAW CENTER
See: George Washington University

NATIONAL LAWYERS GUILD ARCHIVES
See: Meikeljohn Civil Liberties Institute - Library

★8712★
NATIONAL LEAGUE OF CITIES - MUNICIPAL REFERENCE SERVICE (Soc Sci)
1301 Pennsylvania Ave., N.W.   Phone: (202) 626-3210
Washington, DC 20004   Olivia Kredel, Mgr.
Founded: 1924. **Staff:** Prof 2; Other 2. **Subjects:** Municipal government and administration, citizen participation, community development, environmental quality, housing, intergovernmental relations, manpower, public revenue and finance, urban affairs, transportation. **Special Collections:** Reports of state leagues of cities; city codes, reports, and ordinances. **Holdings:** 20,000 books; 600 bound periodical volumes; censuses (cataloged); 42 shelves of archives. **Subscriptions:** 825 journals and other serials; 5 newspapers. **Services:** Interlibrary loans; copying (limited); library open to public with restrictions. **Computerized Information Services:** DIALOG. **Publications:** Urban Affairs Abstracts, weekly - available by subscription. **Remarks:** Contains the holdings of Public Technology Inc. - Information Center. **Staff:** Nancy Minter, Ed.

★8713★
NATIONAL LEAGUE FOR NURSING, INC. - LIBRARY/RECORDS CENTER
(Med)
10 Columbus Circle   Phone: (212) 582-1022
New York, NY 10019   Beryl Gilkes, Supv.
Staff: Prof 1; Other 1. **Subjects:** Nursing education and administration, health manpower, nursing statistics. **Special Collections:** Archives of the National League for Nursing Education et al, 1894-1952. **Holdings:** 1200 books; 135 bound periodical volumes; 4000 NLN publications; 10,000 NTIS reports on microfiche. **Subscriptions:** 20 journals and other serials. **Services:** Copying; library open to masters or doctoral nursing students with prior written permission, by appointment. **Special Indexes:** Index of microfilmed records: schools and agencies (binder); index of NLN publications (card); index of U.S. government publications (card).

★8714★
NATIONAL LEGAL AID AND DEFENDER ASSOCIATION - LIBRARY
1625 K St., N.W.
Washington, DC 20006
Subjects: Legal aid and defender - history, status, commentaries, law and social welfare. **Remarks:** Presently inactive.

NATIONAL LEGAL SERVICES CORPORATION
See: Center on Social Welfare Policy and Law

★8715★
NATIONAL LIBRARY OF CANADA
395 Wellington St.   Phone: (613) 995-9481
Ottawa, ON, Canada K1A 0N4   Dr. J.G. Sylvestre, Natl.Libn.
Founded: 1953. **Staff:** Prof 180; Other 320. **Subjects:** Canadiana, humanities, social sciences, music, children's literature, library science, Judaica and Hebraica. **Holdings:** 896,406 volumes; 45,000 Canadian sound recordings; 1.5 million microforms. **Subscriptions:** 23,521 journals and other serials; 280 newspapers. **Services:** Interlibrary loans; copying; SDI; Multilingual Biblioservice; publishes national bibliography; library open to public, but material does not circulate. **Computerized Information Services:** DOBIS. **Publications:** Publications Catalog; CAN/MARC: authorities, quarterly with cumulative biweekly supplements (1977 to 1979) continued by Canadiana authorities (1979 to present); Canadian Theses, (1947-1960; annual 1960/61 to present); Canadian Theses on Microfiche: Catalogue (1974 to present); Canadiana, monthly (1950 to present; on microfiche, 1978 to present); Canadiana 1867-1900: Monographs, quarterly (September 1980 to present); CONSER Microfiche, annual supplements (1975/78 to present); National Library News, monthly (1969 to present); Report of the National Librarian, annual (1953 to present); Research Collections in Canadian Libraries (1972 to present); Repertoire de vedettes-matiere: supplement, quarterly (1978 to present). **Special Catalogs:** Union List of Serials in the Social Sciences and the Humanities Held by Canadian Libraries (1981, first segment, on microfiche); Checklist of Canadian Ethnic Serials; Checklists of Law Reports and Statutes in Canadian Law Libraries. **Staff:** Hope Clement, Assoc.Natl.Libn.; Flora E. Patterson, Dir., Pub.Serv.; Louis Forget, Dir., Lib.Sys.Ctr.; Andre Preibish, Dir., Coll.Dev.; Mr. A.C. Taylor, Exec.Dir., Dept.Adm.; Barrie Burns, Dir., Cat.; Cynthia Durance, Dir., Off. Network Dev.; Michel Schryer, Fed.Lib. Liaison Off.; Richard Carver, Chf., P.R. Off.

★8716★
NATIONAL LIBRARY OF CANADA - CANADIAN BOOK EXCHANGE CENTRE
(Hum; Sci-Tech)
85 Bentley Ave.   Phone: (613) 995-2317
Ottawa, ON, Canada K2E 6T7   Ergun Camlioglu, Chf.
Staff: Prof 1; Other 14. **Subjects:** Social sciences, humanities, science, technology, medicine, Canadian history and literature. **Holdings:** 80,000 books; 30,000 bound periodical volumes. **Services:** Centre open to member institutions. **Publications:** Canadian Book Exchange Centre (booklet) - by request. **Special Catalogs:** Monographs exchange lists; periodicals exchange lists; Canadian official publications exchange list; foreign and international official publications exchange list. **Staff:** Rick Bluoin, Hd., Official Pubn.Sect.; Yvonne Charbonneau, Hd., Per. Unit; Richard Milne, Hd., Canadian Pubn.Sect.; Greg Stanton, Hd., Foreign & Intl.Pubn.

★8717★
NATIONAL LIBRARY OF CANADA - CANADIAN INDIAN RIGHTS COLLECTION (Area-Ethnic; Law)
395 Wellington St.   Phone: (613) 992-6628
Ottawa, ON, Canada K1A 0N4   Alfred Fisher, Hd.
Founded: 1970. **Staff:** 2. **Subjects:** Native claims in Canada - historical, parliamentary, legal and socioeconomic documentation; comparative materials from comparable areas, especially the U.S., Australia and New Zealand. **Holdings:** 12,000 volumes. **Services:** Interlibrary loans; copying; collection

open to public.

★8718★
NATIONAL LIBRARY OF CANADA - COMPUTER-BASED REFERENCE SERVICES (Info Sci)
395 Wellington   Phone: (613) 992-5190
Ottawa, ON, Canada K1A 0N4   Missy Hillman, Chf.
Founded: 1973. **Staff:** Prof 4; Other 2. **Subjects:** Social and behavioral sciences, humanities. **Holdings:** 5000 magnetic tapes. **Services:** SDI; retrospective literature searches (fee); services open to public with restrictions. **Computerized Information Services:** DIALOG, SDC, CAN/OLE, New York Times Information Service, QL Systems, BADADUQ, Informatech France-Quebec, Info Globe, CAN/SDI, CAN/MARC, MINISIS, Bookline. **Publications:** Publicity brochures and manuals. **Special Catalogs:** Guide to Canadian Machine-Readable Databases. **Staff:** Louis Belanger, Act.Hd.

★8719★
NATIONAL LIBRARY OF CANADA - LIBRARY DOCUMENTATION CENTRE
(Info Sci)
395 Wellington   Phone: (613) 995-8717
Ottawa, ON, Canada K1A 0N4   Beryl L. Anderson, Chf.
Founded: 1970. **Staff:** Prof 4; Other 2. **Subjects:** Library science, information science, Canadian libraries. **Special Collections:** Papers of the International Federation of Libraries Association (IFLA) conferences, 1972 to present. **Holdings:** 125 VF drawers of unbound reports, pamphlets, offprints, clippings, unpublished speeches and papers, tearsheets. **Services:** Interlibrary loans; copying; center open to public. **Computerized Information Services:** DIALOG, DOBIS. **Publications:** Accession list - distribution limited; Guide to Provincial Library Agencies in Canada, annual; list of Canadian library/information science research projects, annual; selective bibliographies. **Special Indexes:** ISORID file (library research in Canada).

★8720★
NATIONAL LIBRARY OF CANADA - LITERARY MANUSCRIPTS COLLECTION
(Hum)
395 Wellington St.   Phone: (613) 995-3364
Ottawa, ON, Canada K1A 0N4   Claude LeMoine, Cur.
Staff: Prof 2. **Subjects:** Literature, librarianship, publishing, Canadian writers. **Holdings:** 70 collections of manuscripts. **Services:** Copying; collection open to public. **Staff:** Linda Hoad, Mss.Libn.

★8721★
NATIONAL LIBRARY OF CANADA - MULTILINGUAL BIBLIOSERVICE (Hum)
                                             Phone: (819) 997-9930
Ottawa, ON, Canada K1A 0N4   Marie F. Zielinska, Chf.
Founded: 1973. **Staff:** Prof 3; Other 6. **Subjects:** Fiction, biographies, children's literature, travel, poetry, folklore. **Holdings:** 200,000 volumes. **Subscriptions:** 100 journals and other serials. **Services:** Library not open to public; long-term loans to Canadian public libraries through designated deposit centres - 27 languages available. **Special Catalogs:** Author, title, shelflist catalog in each language (card). **Remarks:** The Multilingual Biblioservice also employs 16 part-time language specialists. It is located at 25 Eddy St., 2nd Fl., Hull, PQ. **Staff:** Irena L. Bell, Asst.Chf.; Mrs. Truus Plaskacz, Hd., Cat. Unit.

★8722★
NATIONAL LIBRARY OF CANADA - MUSIC DIVISION (Mus)
395 Wellington   Phone: (613) 996-3377
Ottawa, ON, Canada K1A 0N4   Dr. Helmut Kallmann, Chf.
Founded: 1970. **Staff:** Prof 4; Other 3. **Subjects:** Music. **Special Collections:** Percy Scholes Collection (200 linear feet of clippings, pamphlets and pictures); Percival Price Campanology Collection (200 linear feet). **Holdings:** 24,000 books and scores; 800 bound periodical volumes; 45,000 Canadian sound recordings; 32 VF drawers of files on Canadian music and musicians; 1300 linear feet of manuscript and archival collections; 52,000 pieces of sheet music. **Subscriptions:** 250 journals and other serials. **Services:** Interlibrary loans; copying; dubbing of sound recordings; division open to public. **Special Catalogs:** Union catalog of Canadian music, pre-1950 (data sheets). **Staff:** Dr. Stephen Willis, Hd., Mss.Coll.; C. Gerald Parker, Hd., Sound Coll.; Maria Bryce, Hd., Printed Coll.

★8723★
NATIONAL LIBRARY OF CANADA - NEWSPAPER DIVISION (Info Sci)
395 Wellington   Phone: (613) 996-3515
Ottawa, ON, Canada K1A 0N4   Lois Burrell, Chf.
Staff: Prof 4; Other 6. **Subjects:** Canadian and foreign newspapers, Canadian ethnic newspapers and serials. **Holdings:** 50,000 reels of microfilm of newspapers; 18,000 original newspapers. **Subscriptions:** 280 newspapers. **Services:** Interlibrary loans; copying; division open to public. **Special**

Catalogs: Union list of Canadian newspapers held by Canadian libraries, 1977; union list of non-Canadian newspapers held by Canadian libraries, 1966 (under revision); Checklist of Canadian Ethnic Serials, 1981. **Staff:** Sabine Sonnemann, Asst.Chf.

★8724★
NATIONAL LIBRARY OF CANADA - OFFICIAL PUBLICATIONS DIVISION (Info Sci)
395 Wellington   Phone: (613) 996-3842
Ottawa, ON, Canada K1A 0N4   Doreen Guentner, Chf.
Founded: 1965. **Staff:** Prof 7; Other 16. **Special Collections:** Depository for Canadian Federal and Provincial publications; sales publications of Great Britain, Belgium, Germany, India, France, U.S. Congressional and statistical microform sets, Alaska, New York, UNESCO, European Communities, OECD, League of Nations, U.N., OAS, Pan American Institute of Geography and History, WIPO. **Holdings:** 2 million government documents in hard copy and microform (Canadian, foreign countries, international government organizations). **Services:** Interlibrary loans; copying; division open to public. **Staff:** Elizabeth Deavy, Hd., Pub.Serv.; Alice Guay, Hd., Coll. Organization.

★8725★
NATIONAL LIBRARY OF CANADA - RARE BOOK DIVISION (Rare Book)
395 Wellington   Phone: (613) 996-1318
Ottawa, ON, Canada K1A 0N4   Liana Van der Bellen, Chf.
Staff: Prof 3; Other 1. **Subjects:** Rare Canadiana, Canadian writers, conservation. **Special Collections:** Jacob M. Lowy collection of rare Hebraic and Judaic books; Saul Hayes Hebraic microfilm collection; manuscripts of Canadian authors. **Holdings:** 15,386 items. **Services:** Copying; division open to public. **Special Catalogs:** Subject catalog to the collection of native North American language books. **Staff:** Brad S. Hill, Cur., Lowy Coll.; Joyce Banks, Rare Bks./Cons.Libn.

★8726★
NATIONAL LIBRARY OF CANADA - REFERENCE SERVICES SECTION (Info Sci)
395 Wellington   Phone: (613) 995-9481
Ottawa, ON, Canada K1A 0N4   Missy Hillman, Chf.
Founded: 1972. **Staff:** Prof 10; Other 2. **Subjects:** Canadian studies, humanities, social sciences. **Holdings:** 30,000 volumes. **Services:** Copying; section open to public. **Computerized Information Services:** DIALOG, BRS, SDC, Info Globe, CAN/OLE, New York Times Information Service, DOBIS, Informatech France-Quebec; computerized cataloging and serials. **Publications:** Guide for researchers, 1978; Theses in Canada: A Guide to Sources of Information about Theses Completed or in Preparation, 1978; National Library of Canada: Publications, 1980; Books About Canada (in Canada yearbook), annual; Index translationum (Canada's contribution); Bibliografia de historia de America. **Formerly:** Its Reference and Bibliography Section. **Staff:** Irma Larouche, Bibliog.

★8727★
NATIONAL LIBRARY OF MEDICINE (Med; Sci-Tech)
    Phone: (301) 496-6308
Bethesda, MD 20209   Martin M. Cummings, M.D., Dir.
Founded: 1836. **Staff:** Prof 269; Other 203. **Subjects:** Medicine, health sciences, dentistry, public health, nursing, biomedical research. **Special Collections:** History of medicine. **Holdings:** 500,000 bound monographs; 660,000 bound periodical volumes; 215,000 AV items, reels of microfilm and prints (cataloged); 454,000 theses and pamphlets; 1.1 million manuscripts. **Subscriptions:** 25,000 journals and other serials. **Services:** Interlibrary loans; library open to public. **Computerized Information Services:** MEDLINE. **Networks/Consortia:** Headquarters of Regional Medical Library Networks. **Publications:** Index Medicus, monthly.

★8728★
NATIONAL LIBRARY OF MEDICINE - TOXICOLOGY DATA BANK (Med)
Oak Ridge Natl. Laboratory   Phone: (615) 574-7805
Oak Ridge, TN 37830   Dr. Po-Yung Lu, Dir.
Founded: 1974. **Staff:** Prof 4; Other 11. **Subjects:** Toxicology, pharmacology, environmental sciences, chemical safety, antidote and emergency treatment, manufacturing information. **Holdings:** Information on 3000 completed compounds. **Computerized Information Services:** MEDLARS. **Publications:** Update public file records, quarterly - distributed through MEDLARS.

NATIONAL LIBRARY OF MEDICINE - TOXICOLOGY INFORMATION PROGRAM
See: Oak Ridge National Laboratory - Toxicology Information Response Center

NATIONAL LIBRARY SERVICE FOR THE BLIND AND PHYSICALLY HANDICAPPED
See: Library of Congress

★8729★
NATIONAL LIBRARY OF SPORTS (Rec)
San Jose Public Library
180 W. San Carlos St.   Phone: (408) 287-0993
San Jose, CA 95113   Wes Mathis, Lib.Dir.
Founded: 1929. **Staff:** Prof 1; Other 1. **Subjects:** Sports. **Special Collections:** Reach and Spalding Baseball Guides from 1871 to present; sports guides. **Holdings:** 3000 books; 10,000 bound periodical volumes; 18,000 personality packets; 45,000 college and pro football programs; 18,000 college brochures; 2000 pro sports brochures; 300 personally prepared sports histories. **Subscriptions:** 59 journals and other serials. **Services:** Copying; library open to public. **Special Indexes:** 175,000 cards with 1.5 million references for 95 sports. **Staff:** Mike Stevens, Supv. of Res.

★8730★
NATIONAL LIFE INSURANCE COMPANY - LIBRARY (Bus-Fin)
National Life Dr.   Phone: (802) 229-3278
Montpelier, VT 05602   Saba L. Foster, Chf.Libn.
Staff: Prof 1; Other 2. **Subjects:** Law, insurance, business, economics. **Special Collections:** Archives (historical material relating to company). **Holdings:** 16,500 books; 225 bound periodical volumes; 32 VF drawers of pamphlets and clippings. **Subscriptions:** 289 journals and other serials; 7 newspapers. **Services:** Interlibrary loans; copying; library open to public.

NATIONAL LINCOLN-CIVIL WAR COUNCIL - LIBRARY
See: Lincoln Memorial University - Abraham Lincoln Library and Museum

★8731★
NATIONAL LIVESTOCK AND MEAT BOARD - MEAT INDUSTRY INFORMATION CENTER (Food-Bev)
444 N. Michigan Ave.   Phone: (312) 467-5520
Chicago, IL 60611   William D. Siarny, Jr., Dir.
Founded: 1976. **Staff:** Prof 1; Other 1. **Subjects:** Meat, nutrition, food economics, cookery. **Special Collections:** Publications of members of the American Meat Science Association; Meat Board Archives. **Holdings:** 3500 books; 200 bound periodical volumes; 600 reports; 8 VF drawers of reprints, clippings, government documents; 6 VF drawers of archives. **Subscriptions:** 275 journals and other serials; 5 newspapers. **Services:** Interlibrary loans; copying; library open to public by appointment. **Computerized Information Services:** Online systems. **Networks/Consortia:** Member of ILLINET; Metropolitan Chicago Library Assembly; Regional Medical Library - Region 3; Illinois Health Libraries Consortium. **Publications:** Information in Action, monthly bulletin and accession list.

NATIONAL MAPPING DIVISION ASSISTANCE FACILITY
See: U.S. Geological Survey

NATIONAL MARINE FISHERIES SERVICE
See: U.S. Natl. Marine Fisheries Service

NATIONAL MARINE MAMMAL LABORATORY
See: U.S. Natl. Marine Fisheries Service

★8732★
NATIONAL MARINE MANUFACTURERS ASSOCIATION - INFORMATION CENTER (Rec)†
401 N. Michigan Ave.   Phone: (312) 836-4747
Chicago, IL 60611   John A. Lamont, Info.Mgr.
Founded: 1963. **Staff:** Prof 1. **Subjects:** Recreational pleasure craft design, construction and maintenance; recreational boating statistics; marina design, construction, maintenance and operation; history of recreational boating and yachting. **Special Collections:** Lloyd's Register of American Yachts 1911 to present. **Holdings:** 700 books; 120 bound periodical volumes; 4500 photographs and slides; 2000 newspaper clippings; 225 government reports. **Subscriptions:** 80 journals and other serials. **Services:** Interlibrary loans; copying; library open to public for reference use only by appointment. **Publications:** Boating Registration Statistics, annual; Boat Show Calendar, annual; Boating Statistical Pamphlet, annual; Boating Information Guide, annual; Inter/Port, weekly; Boating Films Directory; Annual Market Research Notebook; Directory of Marina Architects & Engineers. **Formerly:** Located in New York, NY.

★8733★

NATIONAL MARITIME MUSEUM - J. PORTER SHAW LIBRARY (Hist)
Foot of Polk St.　　　　　　　　　　　Phone: (415) 556-8177
San Francisco, CA 94109　　　　　　　　David Hull, Prin.Libn.
Founded: 1956. **Staff:** Prof 6; Other 2. **Subjects:** Maritime history, especially Pacific Ocean; local history; nautical technology; navigation. **Special Collections:** Oral histories (285 taped interviews); John Lyman Maritime Collection; San Francisco Marine Exchange vessel movement records, 1903-1960 (75,000 cards; 80 ledgers); photographic collection of sailing ships from 1885 to 1935 (150,000 images); ship plans. **Holdings:** 12,000 books; 450 logbooks (24 cataloged); 650 nautical charts and maps; archival material (66 linear feet); 700 cataloged documents; 70 VF drawers of reports, pamphlets, clippings. **Subscriptions:** 90 journals and other serials; 150 discontinued journal runs. **Services:** Interlibrary loans; copying; library open to public for reference use only. **Publications:** Sea Letter. **Remarks:** Maintained by U.S. National Park Service, Golden Gate National Recreation Area. **Staff:** Herbert H. Beckwith, Cat.; Justine Schulz, Ref.Libn.; John Maonnis, Photo Libn.; Daniel Keller, Photo Cat.; Judith Cohen, Oral Hist.Libn.

NATIONAL MARITIME RESEARCH CENTER
See: U.S. Maritime Administration

★8734★

NATIONAL MENTAL HEALTH ASSOCIATION - CLIFFORD BEERS MEMORIAL LIBRARY (Soc Sci; Med)
1800 N. Kent St.　　　　　　　　　　　Phone: (703) 528-6405
Arlington, VA 22209　　　　　　　　Joshua Hammond, Dir., Commun.
Founded: 1950. **Staff:** Prof 1; Other 1. **Subjects:** Mental health for laymen, voluntary public agencies. **Holdings:** 1500 books. **Subscriptions:** 40 journals and other serials; 100 newspapers and newsletters. **Services:** Interlibrary loans; library open to public by appointment only.

NATIONAL METRIC COUNCIL
See: American National Metric Council

★8735★

NATIONAL MICROGRAPHICS ASSOCIATION - RESOURCE CENTER (Aud-Vis)
8719 Colesville Rd.　　　　　　　　　　　Phone: (301) 587-8202
Silver Spring, MD 20910　　　　　　　　Nila Zynjuk, Info.Coord.
Staff: Prof 1. **Subjects:** Micrographics, computer output microfilm (COM), related technologies. **Holdings:** NMA publications; microfiche collection. **Subscriptions:** 80 journals and other serials. **Services:** Center open to public. **Computerized Information Services:** Internal database. **Also Known As:** NMA.

NATIONAL MIDDLE SCHOOL RESOURCE CENTER
See: Indiana State Department of Public Instruction, Division of Title IV-C

NATIONAL MILITARY COMMAND SYSTEM SUPPORT CENTER
See: U.S. Defense Communications Agency

★8736★

NATIONAL MULTIPLE SCLEROSIS SOCIETY - MEDICAL LIBRARY (Med)
205 E. 42nd St.　　　　　　　　　　　Phone: (212) 986-3240
New York, NY 10017　　　　　　　Margaret Calvano, Med.Info.Spec.
Founded: 1946. **Staff:** Prof 1; Other 2. **Subjects:** All medical aspects of multiple sclerosis. **Holdings:** 200 books; 10,000 reprints (indexed); patient service materials; 1000 clippings and pamphlets. **Subscriptions:** 47 journals and other serials. **Services:** Interlibrary loans; copying (limited); library not open to public.

NATIONAL MUNICIPAL LEAGUE, INC.
See: Citizens Forum on Self-Government/National Municipal League, Inc.

NATIONAL MUSEUM OF AMERICAN ART
See: Smithsonian Institution

NATIONAL MUSEUM OF AMERICAN ART/NATIONAL PORTRAIT GALLERY
See: Smithsonian Institution

NATIONAL MUSEUM OF AMERICAN HISTORY
See: Smithsonian Institution Libraries

NATIONAL MUSEUM OF NATURAL HISTORY
See: Smithsonian Institution Libraries

★8737★

NATIONAL MUSEUM OF TRANSPORT - TRANSPORTATION REFERENCE LIBRARY (Trans)
3015 Barrett Station Rd.　　　　　　　　Phone: (314) 965-6885
St. Louis, MO 63122　　　　　　　　Dr. John P. Roberts, Sec.
Founded: 1944. **Staff:** Prof 1; Other 4. **Subjects:** Transportation and communication. **Holdings:** 10,000 books; 6000 bound periodical volumes; 2000 pamphlets (cataloged); 9 VF drawers of pamphlets (uncataloged); extensive collection of photographs, blueprints, phonograph records, movie films and slides. **Subscriptions:** 200 journals and other serials. **Services:** Library open to qualified users by appointment. **Publications:** Occasional papers.

NATIONAL MUSEUMS OF CANADA
See: Canada - National Museums of Canada

NATIONAL NATURAL RESOURCES LIBRARY
See: U.S. Dept. of the Interior - Natural Resources Library

NATIONAL NAVAL MEDICAL CENTER - ARMED FORCES RADIOBIOLOGY RESEARCH INSTITUTE
See: U.S. Armed Forces Radiobiology Research Institute (AFRRI)

NATIONAL NAVAL MEDICAL CENTER - NAVAL SCHOOL OF HEALTH SCIENCES
See: U.S. Navy - Naval School of Health Sciences

★8738★

NATIONAL NETWORK OF YOUTH ADVISORY BOARDS, INC. - TECHNICAL ASSISTANCE LIBRARY (Soc Sci)
Ocean View Branch
Box 402036　　　　　　　　　　　Phone: (305) 532-2607
Miami Beach, FL 33140　　　　　　Stuart Alan Rado, Exec.Dir.
Staff: 1. **Subjects:** Youth involvement and employment, child abuse, juvenile justice, substance abuse, education. **Holdings:** 250 books; manuals. **Services:** Copying; library not open to public. **Publications:** Resources list giving information on organizations concerned with all aspects of youth - available on request.

NATIONAL NUCLEAR DATA CENTER
See: Brookhaven National Laboratory

NATIONAL OCEAN SURVEY
See: U.S. Natl. Oceanic & Atmospheric Administration

NATIONAL OCEANIC & ATMOSPHERIC ADMINISTRATION
See: U.S. Natl. Oceanic & Atmospheric Administration

NATIONAL OCEANOGRAPHIC DATA CENTER
See: U.S. Natl. Oceanic & Atmospheric Administration - Environmental Data and Information Service

NATIONAL OPINION RESEARCH CENTER
See: University of Chicago

★8739★

NATIONAL ORGANIZATION FOR WOMEN (NOW) - ACTION CENTER LIBRARY (Soc Sci)†
425 13th St., N.W., No. 1048　　　　　　Phone: (202) 347-2279
Washington, DC 20004　　　　　　　　Jenny Tipton, Libn.
Founded: 1978. **Staff:** Prof 1; Other 1. **Subjects:** Women's issues. **Special Collections:** History of National Organization for Women; history of women's movement. **Holdings:** 650 books and bound periodical volumes; 18 VF drawers of clippings, reports, statistics; 40 videotapes. **Subscriptions:** 130 journals and other serials; 7 newspapers. **Services:** Library open to public by appointment.

★8740★

NATIONAL OUTDOOR LEADERSHIP SCHOOL - OUTDOOR EDUCATION RESOURCE LIBRARY (Rec)
Box AA　　　　　　　　　　　　　Phone: (307) 332-4381
Lander, WY 82520　　　　　　　　Kevin Hildebrant, Chf.Instr.
Staff: Prof 1; Other 1. **Subjects:** Outdoor education skills and programs, natural history, recreation, climbing. **Holdings:** 500 books; 100 journals and other serials; films, slides. **Subscriptions:** 10 journals and other serials. **Services:** Library open to public with restrictions.

★8741★

NATIONAL PAINT AND COATINGS ASSOCIATION - TECHNICAL LIBRARY (Sci-Tech)†
1500 Rhode Island Ave., N.W.   Phone: (202) 462-6272
Washington, DC 20005   Donna Kordoski, Libn.
Staff: 1. **Subjects:** Paints, lacquers, printing inks, fats and oils, chemistry, industrial hazards, coatings. **Holdings:** 3000 books; 300 bound periodical volumes; 30,000 patents, documents, pamphlets, and reports. **Subscriptions:** 146 journals and other serials; 5 newspapers. **Services:** Copying; library open to public with permission. **Publications:** Abstract Review, monthly - to association members or by annual subscription.

★8742★

NATIONAL PARENT TEACHER ASSOCIATION - INFORMATION RESOURCE CENTER (Educ)
700 N. Rush St.
Chicago, IL 60611   Dr. Lenore Glanz, Mgr.
Staff: Prof 1; Other 1. **Subjects:** Parental involvement in education. **Special Collections:** National Congress of Parents and Teachers records, publications and archives (1000 volumes and 100 boxes). **Holdings:** 2500 books; 30 VF drawers of pamphlets and clippings; 5 VF drawers of photographs. **Subscriptions:** 575 journals and other serials; 5 newspapers. **Services:** Copying; library not open to public.

NATIONAL PARK SERVICE
See: U.S. Natl. Park Service

★8743★

NATIONAL PARKS AND CONSERVATION ASSOCIATION - LIBRARY (Env-Cons)
1701 18th St., N.W.
Washington, DC 20009
Subjects: National parks, conservation. **Services:** Library open to members only.

★8744★

NATIONAL PASSENGER RAILROAD CORPORATION (AMTRAK) - COMPUTER SERVICES DEPARTMENT LIBRARY
400 North Capitol St., N.W.
Washington, DC 20001
Defunct

NATIONAL PEKING LIBRARY - RARE BOOK COLLECTION ON MICROFILM
See: University of Michigan - Asia Library

NATIONAL PERSONNEL RECORDS CENTER
See: U.S. Natl. Archives & Records Service

NATIONAL PORTRAIT GALLERY
See: Smithsonian Institution - Natl. Museum of American Art/National Portrait Gallery

★8745★

NATIONAL PRESBYTERIAN CHURCH - WILLIAM S. CULBERTSON LIBRARY (Rel-Theol)
4101 Nebraska Ave., N.W.   Phone: (202) 537-0800
Washington, DC 20016   Muriel M. Kirk, Libn.
Founded: 1966. **Staff:** Prof 2; Other 1. **Subjects:** Religion, theology. **Holdings:** 4000 books; 136 bound periodical volumes; 278 cassettes (cataloged). **Subscriptions:** 45 journals and other serials. **Services:** Interlibrary loans; copying; library open to public. **Staff:** Parkash Samuel, Chm., Lib.Comm.

★8746★

NATIONAL PSYCHOLOGICAL ASSOCIATION FOR PSYCHOANALYSIS - GEORGE LAWTON MEMORIAL LIBRARY (Med)
150 W. 13th St.   Phone: (212) 924-7440
New York, NY 10011   Annabella B. Nelken, Exec.Adm.
Founded: 1958. **Staff:** Prof 1. **Subjects:** Psychoanalysis, psychology, and allied subjects. **Holdings:** 2000 volumes. **Subscriptions:** 25 journals and other serials. **Services:** Library not open to public.

★8747★

NATIONAL PUBLIC RADIO - PROGRAM LIBRARY & AUDIO ARCHIVE (Info Sci)†
2025 M St., N.W.   Phone: (202) 822-2000
Washington, DC 20036   Susan T. Bau, Prog.Libn.
Founded: 1973. **Staff:** Prof 4; Other 1. **Subjects:** Radio programs, production materials. **Holdings:** 8000 radio programs. **Subscriptions:** 25

journals and other serials; 5 newspapers. **Services:** Copying (limited); library open to public with restrictions. **Computerized Information Services:** Computerized cataloging. **Remarks:** After 5 years NPR transfers its programs to the Library of Congress and the National Archives.

★8748★

NATIONAL PUBLICATIONS LIBRARY (Soc Sci)
7611 Oakland Ave.   Phone: (612) 861-2162
Minneapolis, MN 55423   Elmer Josephs, Libn.
Founded: 1945. **Staff:** 1. **Subjects:** The physically handicapped and their organizations, affirmative action, civil rights. **Holdings:** 550 volumes. **Subscriptions:** 50 journals and other serials; 100 newspapers. **Services:** Library not open to public.

★8749★

NATIONAL RADIO ASTRONOMY OBSERVATORY - LIBRARY (Sci-Tech)
Edgemont Rd.   Phone: (804) 296-0211
Charlottesville, VA 22901   Sarah S. Stevens-Rayburn, Libn.
Founded: 1957. **Staff:** Prof 2. **Subjects:** Astronomy, physics, mathematics, engineering, computer science, general science. **Holdings:** 5800 books; 10,300 bound periodical volumes; 650 linear feet of observatory publications; 340 reels of microfilm; 4800 microfiche; 3 VF drawers of reprints; 2200 photographs (star charts). **Subscriptions:** 300 journals and other serials. **Services:** Interlibrary loans; copying; library open to qualified users. **Computerized Information Services:** DIALOG, BRS; internal database; computerized cataloging. **Networks/Consortia:** Member of OCLC through FEDLINK. **Publications:** Acquisitions list, monthly; NRAO reprint series list, irregular; RAPsheet, biweekly - all available to qualified users. **Remarks:** Library also maintains small collections in Green Bank, WV, Tucson, AZ and Socorro, NM.

★8750★

THE NATIONAL RAILROAD CONSTRUCTION AND MAINTENANCE ASSOCIATION, INC. - TECHNICAL REFERENCE LIBRARY (Trans)
9331 Waymond Ave.   Phone: (219) 924-1709
Highland, IN 46322   larry shields, Exec.Dir.
Staff: 1. **Subjects:** Railroad - construction, maintenance, rehabilitation, removal. **Holdings:** 2000 volumes. **Subscriptions:** 27 journals and other serials; 7 newspapers. **Services:** Interlibrary loans; copying; library open to members only. **Publications:** Directory and Buyer's Guide, annual; Clear Track (monthly except December/January and June/July, combined).

★8751★

NATIONAL RAILWAY HISTORICAL SOCIETY - LIBRARY OF AMERICAN TRANSPORTATION (Trans)
Box 7   Phone: (609) 829-5204
Jobstown, NJ 08041   Earle P. Finkbiner, Libn.
Founded: 1977. **Staff:** Prof 2. **Subjects:** Railroads, trolleys, transportation. **Special Collections:** Negatives of American Locomotive Works. **Holdings:** 1600 books; 90 bound periodical volumes. **Services:** Library open to public for reference use only.

★8752★

NATIONAL RAILWAY HISTORICAL SOCIETY - MOHAWK AND HUDSON CHAPTER - LAWRENCE LEE MEMORIAL LIBRARY (Trans)
Union College Library
Schenectady, NY 12308   Clarence Langley, Jr., Libn.
Staff: Prof 1. **Subjects:** Railroads. **Holdings:** 300 books; 75 bound periodical volumes. **Services:** Library not open to public.

★8753★

NATIONAL RECORDS MANAGEMENT COUNCIL - LIBRARY (Info Sci)
60 E. 42nd St.   Phone: (212) 697-0290
New York, NY 10165   Robert A. Shiff, Pres.
Services: Maintains speakers bureau and research material relating to information retrieval, micrographics, records management, office automation, word processing and administrative support systems; library not open to public.

★8754★

NATIONAL RECREATION AND PARK ASSOCIATION - JOSEPH LEE MEMORIAL LIBRARY AND INFORMATION CENTER (Rec)
3101 Park Ctr. Dr., 12th Fl.
Alexandria, VA 22209   Madeleine J. Wilkins, Ph.D., Mgr.
Founded: 1980. **Subjects:** Public recreation, park services, leisure time use, conservation, therapeutic recreation. **Special Collections:** Archives of recreation and park movement in U.S. **Services:** Interlibrary loans; copying; information center open to public. **Remarks:** The information center is being developed into a national clearinghouse for current and retrospective historical

information. It can be reached by calling (703) 820-4940. **Formerly:** Located in Arlington, VA.

NATIONAL REFERRAL CENTER
See: Library of Congress

★8755★
NATIONAL REHABILITATION INFORMATION CENTER (Soc Sci)
4407 8th St., N.E.
Catholic University of America   Phone: (202) 635-5826
Washington, DC 20017   Eleanor Biscoe, Dir.
Founded: 1977. **Staff:** Prof 8; Other 6. **Subjects:** Rehabilitation of the physically and mentally disabled, handicapped individuals. **Special Collections:** RSA/NIHR Collection (700 print and AV items prepared under grants from Rehabilitation Services Administration/Department of Education and the National Institute of Handicapped Research/HEW, 1958 to present). **Holdings:** 7000 books; 3000 microfiche. **Subscriptions:** 250 journals and other serials. **Services:** Copying; SDI; library open to public. **Computerized Information Services:** DIALOG, SDC, BRS; ABLEDATA (internal database); computerized cataloging. **Publications:** Pathfinder, bimonthly; Thesaurus. **Remarks:** The number for TDD users is (202) 635-5884. **Staff:** Sharon McFarland, Hd., Lib.Serv.; Mark Odum, Info.Off.; Joan Appel, Info.Spec.; Elizabeth Thorton, Info.Spec.; Nancy Colligan, Info.Spec.; Cindy Tipple, Info.Spec.

NATIONAL RESEARCH COUNCIL
See: National Academy of Sciences

NATIONAL RESEARCH COUNCIL (Canada)
See: Canada - National Research Council

NATIONAL RESERVOIR RESEARCH LIBRARY
See: U.S. Fish & Wildlife Service

★8756★
NATIONAL RESOURCE CENTER FOR CONSUMERS OF LEGAL SERVICES - CLEARINGHOUSE (Law)
1302 18th St., N.W., Suite 303   Phone: (202) 659-8514
Washington, DC 20036   Shelley Benson, Clghse.Dept.
Staff: Prof 2. **Subjects:** Group and prepaid legal services; paralegals; lawyer advertising; legal clinics; consumer education. **Holdings:** 803 books and bound periodical volumes; 34 VF drawers of documents and clippings. **Subscriptions:** 32 journals and other serials. **Services:** Copying; library open to public with restrictions. **Publications:** Legal Plan Letter, biweekly; list of additional publications - available on request. **Staff:** Bill Bolger, Dir.

★8757★
NATIONAL RESTAURANT ASSOCIATION - INFORMATION SERVICE AND LIBRARY (Food-Bev)
311 First St., N.W.   Phone: (202) 638-6100
Washington, DC 20001   Joan E. Campbell, Mgr.
Staff: Prof 3; Other 1. **Subjects:** Foodservice industry, restaurants, cookery, public health. **Holdings:** 3500 books; 400 subject clipping file; annual reports; 50 film cassettes. **Subscriptions:** 95 journals and other serials. **Services:** Copying; library open to public by appointment. **Staff:** Laurie A. Barbuschak, Tech.Serv.Spec.; Kimberly J. Walker, Info.Spec.

NATIONAL RETIRED TEACHERS ASSOCIATION
See: American Association of Retired Persons

★8758★
NATIONAL RIFLE ASSOCIATION - TECHNICAL LIBRARY (Rec)†
1600 Rhode Island Ave., N.W.   Phone: (202) 828-6227
Washington, DC 20036   Joe Roberts, Ed.
Staff: Prof 1. **Subjects:** Firearms, ammunition and their use; hunting and target shooting. **Holdings:** 1100 volumes. **Subscriptions:** 20 journals and other serials. **Services:** Library not open to public. **Remarks:** Technical data for NRA membership only. Mr. Roberts is research editor of NRA publications.

★8759★
NATIONAL RURAL ELECTRIC COOPERATIVE ASSOCIATION - NORRIS MEMORIAL LIBRARY (Law; Energy)
1800 Massachusetts Ave., N.W.   Phone: (202) 857-9788
Washington, DC 20036   Chuck Rice, Lib.Serv.Spec.
Founded: 1963. **Staff:** Prof 1; Other 1. **Subjects:** Rural electrification, electric power, energy policy. **Special Collections:** Congressional documents; Electric Power Research Institute reports (320; cataloged). **Holdings:** 22,000 volumes; 800 subject files (in 2 collections); 315 reels of microfilm; 15 drawers of microfiche. **Subscriptions:** 450 journals and other serials.

Services: Interlibrary loans (limited); copying; library open to public by appointment.

★8760★
NATIONAL SAFETY COUNCIL - LIBRARY (Soc Sci)
444 N. Michigan Ave.   Phone: (312) 527-4800
Chicago, IL 60611   Ruth K. Hammersmith, Dir.
Founded: 1913. **Staff:** Prof 7; Other 2. **Subjects:** Accident prevention, industrial health, all aspects of safety and safety research. **Special Collections:** Who's Who in Safety (48 binders); National Safety Council Archives. **Holdings:** 7500 books; 700 bound periodical volumes; 100,000 other cataloged items; 700 reels of microfilm; 1000 microfiche. **Subscriptions:** 700 journals and other serials. **Services:** Interlibrary loans; copying; library open to public on a limited basis with prior contact suggested. **Computerized Information Services:** NSCL Database (internal database). **Networks/Consortia:** Member of Regional Medical Library - Region 3; Metropolitan Chicago Library Assembly. **Publications:** Library Bulletin, monthly; columns in National Safety News, Traffic Safety, and Journal of Safety Research. **Special Indexes:** Indexes to 6 National Safety Council publications. **Remarks:** Includes holdings of its Safety Research Information Service. **Staff:** Nancy Pruter, Supv., Cat.; William Nisbet, Supv., Ref.; Robert Maracek, Coord., ILL.

NATIONAL SCHOLASTIC PRESS ASSOCIATION
See: Associated Collegiate Press/National Scholastic Press Association

★8761★
NATIONAL SCHOOL BOARDS ASSOCIATION - RESOURCE CENTER (Educ)
1055 Thomas Jefferson St., N.W.   Phone: (202) 337-7666
Washington, DC 20007   Eve Shepard, Info.Coord.
Staff: Prof 1; Other 2. **Subjects:** Clearinghouse of local school district policies and regulations and state school boards association management. **Special Collections:** State School Board Association publications. **Holdings:** 2000 books; 6 VF drawers of current information on issues in public elementary and secondary education; speaker services file. **Subscriptions:** 158 journals and other serials; 13 newspapers. **Services:** Interlibrary loans; library open to public by appointment.

NATIONAL SCIENCE FILM LIBRARY
See: Canadian Film Institute

★8762★
NATIONAL SCIENCE FOUNDATION - LIBRARY (Sci-Tech)
1800 G St., N.W.   Phone: (202) 632-4070
Washington, DC 20550   Herman Fleming, Rec./Rpt.Off.
Founded: 1951. **Staff:** Prof 4; Other 2. **Subjects:** Basic and applied science and technology; biological sciences; environmental policy; physics; computer science; mathematics; astronomical, atmospheric, earth, ocean and polar science; chemistry; engineering; science education. **Special Collections:** Summary Technical Report of the National Defense Research Committee of the Office of Scientific Research and Development (72 volumes). **Holdings:** 15,000 books; 650 bound periodical volumes. **Subscriptions:** 500 journals and other serials. **Services:** Interlibrary loans; copying; library open to public with restrictions. **Computerized Information Services:** DIALOG. **Networks/Consortia:** Member of OCLC through FEDLINK. **Publications:** Periodicals Received, annual; Library Reading List, quarterly. **Staff:** Richard P. Scott, Cat.; Florence E. Heckman, Ref.Libn.

★8763★
NATIONAL SCIENCE TEACHERS ASSOCIATION - GLENN O. BLOUGH LIBRARY (Sci-Tech; Educ)
1742 Connecticut Ave., N.W.   Phone: (202) 265-4150
Washington, DC 20009   Phyllis Marcuccio, Chf.Libn.
Founded: 1978. **Staff:** Prof 1; Other 2. **Subjects:** Science, curriculum materials. **Special Collections:** Glenn O. Blough Science Textbook Collection (75 sets of textbooks and curriculum guides). **Holdings:** 2145 books; 21 bound periodical volumes; 10 boxes of archival material; 1000 other cataloged items. **Subscriptions:** 60 journals and other serials. **Services:** Interlibrary loans; library open to public by appointment. **Staff:** Ellie Snyder, Info.Spec.

★8764★
NATIONAL SHARECROPPERS FUND/RURAL ADVANCEMENT FUND - F.P. GRAHAM RESOURCE CENTER (Agri)†
Rte. 3, Box 95   Phone: (704) 851-9346
Wadesboro, NC 28170   Cary Fowler, Prog.Dir.
Founded: 1979. **Staff:** Prof 2. **Subjects:** Agriculture/farming, gardening, rural political movements, agricultural political economy. **Special Collections:** Organic agriculture; agricultural materials for new readers. **Holdings:** 4000

books; 8 VF drawers of subject files and clippings; 75 instructional tape recordings. **Subscriptions:** 125 journals and other serials; 5 newspapers. **Services:** Library open to public with advance notice and approval. **Special Indexes:** Indexes to subject files and AV materials. **Staff:** Hope Shand, Res.Assoc.

★8765★

NATIONAL SHERIFFS' ASSOCIATION - EDUCATION AND RESOURCE CENTER
1250 Connecticut Ave., N.W., Suite 320
Washington, DC 20036
Subjects: Law enforcement, corrections, jail administration, court security, contract law enforcement, team policing. **Special Collections:** Jail policy manuals and contract law enforcement. **Holdings:** 5500 books. **Remarks:** Presently inactive.

★8766★

NATIONAL SISTERS VOCATION CONFERENCE - LIBRARY (Rel-Theol)
1307 S. Wabash Ave.   Phone: (312) 939-6180
Chicago, IL 60605   Sr. Gertrude Wemhoff, O.S.B., Exec.Dir.
Founded: 1968. **Staff:** 3. **Subjects:** Church-related careers for women. **Special Collections:** Brochures that are specific to the various religious communities of women in the United States. **Holdings:** 8 VF drawers of pamphlets; 50 statistical studies and research. **Subscriptions:** 13 journals and other serials. **Services:** Interlibrary loans; copying; library open to public. **Publications:** News/Views, bimonthly.

★8767★

NATIONAL SKI HALL OF FAME AND MUSEUM - ROLAND PALMEDO NATIONAL SKI LIBRARY (Rec)
Box 191   Phone: (906) 486-9281
Ishpeming, MI 49849   Dr. Russell Magnaghi, Archv.
Founded: 1954. **Staff:** Prof 1; Other 2. **Subjects:** Skiing. **Special Collections:** Roland Palmedo Collection (300 volumes). **Holdings:** 650 books and bound periodical volumes; 20 VF drawers of reports, pamphlets and clippings; 50 films. **Subscriptions:** 5 journals and other serials. **Services:** Library open to public for reference use only. **Staff:** Deborah Nelson, Libn.

★8768★

NATIONAL SOARING MUSEUM - LIBRARY & ARCHIVES (Rec)†
Harris Hill, R.D. 3   Phone: (607) 734-3128
Elmira, NY 14903   Shirley Sliwa, Dir.
Founded: 1972. **Staff:** Prof 3; Other 4. **Subjects:** Soaring, aviation. **Special Collections:** Joseph C. Lincoln Collection (166 books and papers on soaring). **Holdings:** 200 books; 90 bound periodical volumes; 5 manuscripts; 4 document sets (cataloged); 2 files of papers and related documents on sailplanes; 2 boxes of Mountain Wave Project manuscripts; 1 case of Warren Eaton documents and newsclips; 2 cases of historical soaring photographs. **Subscriptions:** 75 journals and other serials. **Services:** Interlibrary loans; copying; library open to public for reference use only by request. **Networks/ Consortia:** Member of Regional Conference of Historical Agencies. **Publications:** NSM, quarterly - to Soaring Society of America members and National Soaring Museum members. **Staff:** Mary Dwyer, Musm.Serv.

★8769★

NATIONAL SOCIETY FOR CHILDREN AND ADULTS WITH AUTISM - INFORMATION & REFERRAL SERVICE (Soc Sci)
1234 Massachusetts Ave., N.W., Suite 1017   Phone: (202) 783-0125
Washington, DC 20005   Frank Warren, Exec.Dir.
Founded: 1970. **Staff:** Prof 7. **Subjects:** Autism and related subjects. **Holdings:** 200 books; 500 bound periodical volumes; 40 VF drawers of articles, lists, pamphlets, reports, bibliographies. **Subscriptions:** 12 journals and other serials. **Services:** Copying; library open to public for reference use only. **Publications:** Reports, irregular. **Formerly:** National Society for Autistic Children.

★8770★

NATIONAL SOCIETY, DAUGHTERS OF THE AMERICAN REVOLUTION - ALOHA CHAPTER - MEMORIAL LIBRARY (Hist)
1914 Makiki Heights Dr.
Honolulu, HI 96822   Florine H. Greenwood, Libn.
Founded: 1961. **Staff:** Prof 1; Other 8. **Subjects:** Family genealogies, state and regional archives, lineage books of national societies, census records, histories of early settlements. **Holdings:** 5500 books; 350 bound periodical volumes. **Subscriptions:** 10 journals and other serials. **Services:** Copying; library open to public.

★8771★

NATIONAL SOCIETY, DAUGHTERS OF THE AMERICAN REVOLUTION - HANNAH WESTON CHAPTER - BURNHAM TAVERN MUSEUM (Hist)
Main & Free Sts.   Phone: (207) 255-4432
Machias, ME 04654   Valdine C. Atwood, Chm.
Subjects: Local history. **Special Collections:** Machias Valley area collection (records; ledgers; daybooks; chapter books since 1901). **Holdings:** 300 books and bound periodical volumes. **Services:** Library open to public.

★8772★

NATIONAL SOCIETY, DAUGHTERS OF THE AMERICAN REVOLUTION - LIBRARY (Hist)
1776 D St., N.W.   Phone: (202) 628-1776
Washington, DC 20006   Carolyn Leopold Michaels, Staff Libn.
Staff: Prof 5; Other 10. **Subjects:** Genealogies; state, county and local histories; published rosters of Revolutionary War soldiers; published vital records; cemetery inscriptions; Bible records. **Special Collections:** Transcripts of various county records (such as wills), compiled by the Genealogical Records Committees of DAR; published archives of some of the thirteen original states; abstracts of some Revolutionary War pension files. **Holdings:** 70,000 books; 170 drawers of file case material; genealogical periodicals; pamphlets. **Services:** Copying; library open to public with fee charged. **Publications:** Family Histories and Genealogies, Volume 1, 1982. **Staff:** Kathryn Scott, Chf.Cat.

★8773★

NATIONAL SOCIETY FOR MEDICAL RESEARCH - NSMR DATA BANK (Med)
1029 Vermont Ave., N.W.   Phone: (202) 347-9565
Washington, DC 20005   William M. Samuels, Exec.Dir.
Staff: Prof 2; Other 3. **Subjects:** Laboratory animals, technical information on medical research subjects, historical references. **Holdings:** 500 books; 20 bound periodical volumes. **Subscriptions:** 28 journals and other serials. **Services:** Open to press researchers and staff members of member organizations. **Publications:** Bulletin; Unraveling Viruses; Untouchable Heart; Animals in Biology.

★8774★

NATIONAL SOCIETY TO PREVENT BLINDNESS - CONRAD BERENS LIBRARY (Med)
79 Madison Ave.   Phone: (212) 684-3505
New York, NY 10016   Dede Silverston, Med.Libn.
Staff: Prof 1; Other 2. **Subjects:** Ophthalmology, eye health, eye safety. **Holdings:** 3000 volumes; 21 VF drawers of reports, pamphlets, clippings, association reports, bulletins, and state health reports. **Subscriptions:** 500 journals and other serials. **Services:** Library open to researchers, health professionals and public by appointment.

★8775★

NATIONAL SOCIETY OF PROFESSIONAL ENGINEERS - INFORMATION CENTER (Sci-Tech)
2029 K St., N.W.   Phone: (202) 463-2300
Washington, DC 20006   Donald G. Weinert, Exec.Dir.
Staff: 3. **Subjects:** Engineering (nontechnical) - manpower, salary, ethics, registration, legislation, and related subjects. **Holdings:** 1500 books; 35 VF drawers of documents and reports. **Subscriptions:** 60 journals and other serials. **Services:** Center open to public. **Staff:** Jean Robertson, Dir., Info.Ctr.

★8776★

NATIONAL SOCIETY OF THE SONS OF THE AMERICAN REVOLUTION - GENEALOGY LIBRARY (Hist)
1000 S. 4th St.   Phone: (502) 589-1776
Louisville, KY 40203   Alice Faye Glover, Libn./Cat.
Founded: 1926. **Staff:** Prof 1. **Subjects:** American genealogy and biography, Revolutionary and state history. **Special Collections:** Genealogy of signers of the Declaration of Independence; Daughters of the American Revolution Lineage Book Collection; state census record indexes. **Holdings:** 12,500 books; 2400 periodicals; 1400 pamphlets. **Subscriptions:** 12 journals and other serials. **Services:** Copying; library open to public with restrictions. **Also Known As:** Sons of the American Revolution.

NATIONAL SPACE SCIENCE DATA CENTER (NSSDC)
See: World Data Center A - Rockets & Satellites - National Space Science Data Center (NSSDC)

NATIONAL SPACE TECHNOLOGY LABORATORIES
See: U.S. NASA - Natl. Space Technology Laboratories

NATIONAL SPACE TECHNOLOGY LABS - NATL. MAPPING DIVISION ASSISTANCE FACILITY
See: U.S. Geological Survey - Natl. Mapping Division Assistance Facility

★8777★
NATIONAL SPELEOLOGICAL SOCIETY - NSS LIBRARY (Sci-Tech)
1 Cave Ave.   Phone: (205) 852-1300
Huntsville, AL 35810   William W. Torode, Libn.
Staff: 1. **Subjects:** Speleology, geology, cave exploration, biospeleology, archeology. **Special Collections:** Foreign publications on speleology; "largest collection of American Cave Club literature in the world"; collection of foreign cave club newsletters. **Holdings:** 1500 books; 1000 periodical volumes; 2000 items in author reprint file; newspaper clippings, pamphlets, abstracts, paperbacks about speleology (recreational and scientific). **Subscriptions:** 150 exchange publications. **Services:** Interlibrary loans; copying; library not open to public. **Special Catalogs:** Bibliography of American speleology.

★8778★
NATIONAL SPORTING LIBRARY, INC. (Rec)
Box 1335   Phone: (703) 687-6542
Middleburg, VA 22117   Judith Ozment, Libn.
Founded: 1954. **Staff:** Prof 2. **Subjects:** Field sports - thoroughbred racing and breeding, foxhunting, beagling, polo, horse shows and allied activities, fishing, shooting, falconry, cockfighting. **Special Collections:** Thomas Holden White Polo Collection; Huth-Lonsdale-Arundel Collection of 16th-19th century books on horses; H.T. Peters' American Sporting Art Books. **Holdings:** 12,000 books; 1500 bound periodical volumes; 20 boxes of Harry Worcester Smith Papers; sporting paintings and prints; 120 microfilms of sporting periodicals. **Services:** Interlibrary loans; copying; library open to public for reference use only. **Publications:** National Sporting Library Newsletter, 2/year - issued to membership of Friends of the National Sporting Library. **Special Indexes:** Indexes of N.Y. Sporting Magazine, U.S. Sporting Magazine, Spirit of the Times, 1831-1861 (in progress), American Turf Register, 1829-1844. **Staff:** A. Mackay-Smith, Cur. & Chm. of Bd.

★8779★
NATIONAL STANDARDS ASSOCIATION, INC. - TECHINFO (Sci-Tech)
5161 River Rd.   Phone: (301) 951-1319
Washington, DC 20016   Sonja Young, Mgr.
Staff: Prof 3; Other 4. **Subjects:** Standards and specifications; government standards; industry standards; high technology. **Special Collections:** National Aerospace Standards (2500); Department of Defense Index of Specifications and Standards documents (44,000). **Holdings:** 250,000 specifications and standards; government and industrial technical documents. **Services:** Library open to public with restrictions. **Computerized Information Services:** Online systems; computerized cataloging and acquisitions. **Publications:** National Aerospace Standards (NAS), 10/year; AN, AND & MS, monthly; Metric National Aerospace Standards, 6/year; Standards and Specifications Information Bulletin, weekly; Metric Log, semiannual. **Special Indexes:** Indexes and supplements to NAS, NA, AN, AND & MS; Identified Sources of Supply. **Remarks:** Provides one of the databases for DIALOG. **Staff:** Robert B. Toth, Standards Engr./Pres.; Mrs. Renate Allsafar, Tech.Info.Spec.; Jan Heflin, Libn.

★8780★
NATIONAL STANDARDS COUNCIL OF AMERICAN EMBROIDERERS - NSCAE LIBRARY (Art; Rec)
Carnegie Office Park
600 Bell Ave.   Phone: (412) 279-0299
Carnegie, PA 15106   June H. Haulk, Libn.
Founded: 1969. **Staff:** Prof 1. **Subjects:** Embroidery, art, color, crafts, design, quilting, lace, needle arts and allied areas. **Holdings:** 1200 books; slides; study samplers; VF drawers. **Services:** Copying; library open to members of organization and serious researchers. **Computerized Information Services:** Computerized cataloging, acquisitions, serials and circulation.

★8781★
NATIONAL STARCH AND CHEMICAL CORPORATION - LIBRARY (Sci-Tech)
10 Finderne Ave.
Box 6500   Phone: (201) 685-5082
Bridgewater, NJ 08807   Marianne Vago, Libn.
Founded: 1954. **Staff:** Prof 1; Other 1. **Subjects:** Organic chemistry, physical chemistry, inorganic chemistry, chemical technology, physics. **Holdings:** 4000 books; 7000 bound periodical volumes; 25 VF drawers of patents and technical reports. **Subscriptions:** 200 journals and other serials. **Services:** Interlibrary loans; copying; library open to public by special arrangement. **Computerized Information Services:** DIALOG.

★8782★
NATIONAL STEEL CORPORATION - RESEARCH CENTER LIBRARY (Sci-Tech)
   Phone: (304) 797-2837
Weirton, WV 26062   Elizabeth W. Fulton, Sr.Res.Libn.
Founded: 1960. **Staff:** Prof 2; Other 1. **Subjects:** Steel, metallurgy, aluminum. **Holdings:** 2100 books; 2300 bound periodical volumes; unbound reports, pamphlets, documents, translations, patents (40 card catalog drawers). **Subscriptions:** 300 journals and other serials; 6 newspapers. **Services:** Interlibrary loans; library open to public with restrictions. **Computerized Information Services:** DIALOG. **Staff:** Sara J. Hair, Asst.Libn.

★8783★
NATIONAL STORYTELLING RESOURCE CENTER (Hum)
Box 112   Phone: (615) 753-2171
Jonesboro, TN 37659   Jean Smith, Adm.Asst.
Founded: 1977. **Staff:** Prof 2. **Subjects:** Storytelling. **Holdings:** 150 audiotapes; 180 videotapes. **Services:** Library open to public. **Special Indexes:** Index of storytelling recordings. **Also Known As:** National Association for the Preservation & Perpetuation of Storytelling (NAPPS).

★8784★
NATIONAL TAX EQUALITY ASSOCIATION - LIBRARY (Bus-Fin)
1000 Connecticut Ave. Bldg.   Phone: (202) 296-5424
Washington, DC 20036   Ray M. Stroupe, Pres.
Subjects: Taxation, economics, government. **Holdings:** 3000 books; selected periodicals. **Services:** Library open to public with advance notice and purpose. **Staff:** Jeffrey De Boer, Res.Dir.

NATIONAL TECHNICAL INFORMATION SERVICE
See: U.S. Dept. of Commerce

NATIONAL TECHNICAL INSTITUTE FOR THE DEAF
See: Rochester Institute of Technology

★8785★
NATIONAL THEATRE SCHOOL OF CANADA - THEATRICAL LIBRARY (Theater)
5030 St. Denis St.   Phone: (514) 842-7954
Montreal, PQ, Canada H2J 2L8   Beatrice De-Vreeze, Hd.Libn.
Founded: 1941. **Staff:** Prof 1; Other 2. **Subjects:** Plays in French and English, theater. **Holdings:** 35,000 books and bound periodical volumes; 100 VF drawers; records and slides. **Subscriptions:** 60 journals and other serials. **Services:** Interlibrary loans; copying; library open to public.

NATIONAL TILLAGE MACHINERY LABORATORY LIBRARY
See: U.S.D.A. - Agricultural Research Service

★8786★
NATIONAL TOBACCO-TEXTILE MUSEUM - LIBRARY AND INFORMATION CENTER (Hist; Sci-Tech)
614 Lynn St.   Phone: (804) 797-9437
Danville, VA 24541   Samuel W. Price, Dir.
Founded: 1971. **Staff:** 1. **Subjects:** Tobacco, textiles. **Holdings:** 1100 books; reports (cataloged); 500 unbound reports; 250 pamphlets; 1300 slides. **Subscriptions:** 30 journals and other serials; 5 newspapers. **Services:** Library open to public for reference use only.

★8787★
NATIONAL TRACK AND FIELD HALL OF FAME OF THE U.S.A. - LIBRARY (Rec)
1524 Kanawha Blvd., E.   Phone: (304) 345-0087
Charleston, WV 25311   Jack W. Rose, Exec.Dir.
Founded: 1974. **Staff:** Prof 1. **Subjects:** Track and field sports; olympic games. **Special Collections:** Track and field displays. **Holdings:** 38 hours of videotapes; 5000 35mm slides; 8 hours of magnetic tapes. **Services:** Library open to public.

★8788★
NATIONAL TRAINING CENTER OF POLYGRAPH SCIENCE - LIBRARY (Sci-Tech)
200 W. 57th St.
New York, NY 10019   Richard O. Arther, Pres.
Staff: Prof 1; Other 1. **Subjects:** Polygraphs, lie detection. **Special Collections:** All issues of the Journal of Polygraph Science. **Holdings:** Figures not available. **Services:** Copying; library not open to public. **Publications:** Journal of Polygraph Science, bimonthly.

★8789★
NATIONAL TRANSLATIONS CENTER (Sci-Tech; Info Sci)†
John Crerar Library
35 W. 33rd St.   Phone: (312) 225-2526
Chicago, IL 60616   Mrs. Ildiko D. Nowak, Chf.
Founded: 1949. **Staff:** Prof 2; Other 2. **Special Collections:** Collection of translations covering all fields of theoretical and applied sciences. **Holdings:** 260,000 volumes. **Services:** Interlibrary loans; copying; center open to public with services on a fee basis. **Publications:** SLA Author List of Translations, 1953; Supplement to Author List, 1954; Translation Monthly, volumes 1-4, 1955-1958; Bibliography of Translations from Russian Scientific and Technical Literature, October 1953-December 1956; Translations Register-Index, volume 1, 1967 to present, monthly - available by subscription; Consolidated Index of Translations into English, 1953-1966, published 1969. **Remarks:** Since 1967 the center has been collecting and processing translations from all domestic and foreign sources, including U.S. government agencies. In 1970 the center established exchange agreements with other English-speaking countries by which translations produced in the respective countries are available to U.S. users directly from the center. Starting in 1967 translations available from any known source (including those listed in U.S. Government Reports Announcements) are announced in the center's translations accession bulletin, Translations Register-Index. **Staff:** Donald D. Hinton, Jnl.Prod.Mgr.

NATIONAL TRUST FOR HISTORIC PRESERVATION - CHESTERWOOD
See: Chesterwood

NATIONAL TRUST FOR HISTORIC PRESERVATION - CLIVEDEN
See: Cliveden

★8790★
NATIONAL TRUST FOR HISTORIC PRESERVATION - INFORMATION SERVICES (Hist; Art)
1785 Massachusetts Ave., N.W.   Phone: (202) 673-4000
Washington, DC 20036   Susan Shearer, Info.Serv.Coord.
Staff: Prof 3; Other 1. **Subjects:** Historic preservation, preservation law, U.S. architecture and decorative arts, restoration of buildings, conservation of building materials. **Holdings:** 9500 books; 25 films; 100 audio- and videotapes; 13,000 vertical files; 600 microfiche of newspaper clippings; 34,000 black/white photographs and color slides of American architecture. **Subscriptions:** 200 journals and other serials. **Services:** Interlibrary loans; copying; open to members by appointment. **Publications:** List of publications - available on request. **Staff:** Alyce Morgan, Asst.Libn.; Hope Headley, Info.Serv.Asst.

★8791★
NATIONAL UNIVERSITY - LAW LIBRARY (Law)
3580 Aero Ct.   Phone: (714) 563-7318
San Diego, CA 92123   Lynne Potter
Founded: 1979. **Staff:** Prof 1; Other 3. **Subjects:** Law - California, federal. **Services:** Interlibrary loans; library open to public. **Computerized Information Services:** Computerized cataloging. **Publications:** Beginner's Guide to the Law Library.

★8792★
NATIONAL VIDEO CLEARINGHOUSE, INC. - NVC LIBRARY AND INFORMATION SERVICE (Aud-Vis)
100 Lafayette Dr.   Phone: (516) 364-3686
Syosset, NY 11791   Maxine K. Reed, Dir.
Founded: 1979. **Staff:** Prof 1; Other 2. **Subjects:** Video - film programs, equipment, products; advertising and marketing; book trade; publishing; broadcasting. **Special Collections:** National Video Clearinghouse publications; Board for International Broadcasting publications; collected material relating to Public Domain; Motion Picture Association of America ratings; copyright; movie industry; educational films; video industry. **Holdings:** 200 books; 120 bound periodical volumes; 20 bound newsletters; U.S. video information on microfiche; United Kingdom video information on microfiche; French video information on microfiche. **Subscriptions:** 67 journals and other serials. **Services:** Library not open to public. **Computerized Information Services:** Internal databases. **Publications:** List of publications - available on request. **Special Indexes:** Video Tape/Disc Guides, annual - to home consumer; Video Programs Update, annual; Video Source Book - United Kingdom, annual.

NATIONAL WATER DATA STORAGE & RETRIEVAL SYSTEM
See: U.S. Geological Survey - Water Resources Division

★8793★
NATIONAL WATER WELL ASSOCIATION - NATIONAL GROUND WATER INFORMATION CENTER (Sci-Tech)
500 W. Wilson Bridge Rd.   Phone: (614) 846-9355
Worthington, OH 43085   Valerie J. Orr, Info.Dir.
Founded: 1980. **Staff:** Prof 2. **Subjects:** Ground water, water well technology, hydrogeology, environmental pollution. **Holdings:** 12,000 books; 50 bound periodical volumes. **Subscriptions:** 120 journals and other serials. **Services:** Interlibrary loans; copying; library open to public. **Computerized Information Services:** DIALOG, SDC; internal database; computerized cataloging. **Networks/Consortia:** Member of OHIONET. **Staff:** Claire M. Fohl, Asst.Libn.

NATIONAL WEIGHTS AND MEASURES ARCHIVAL LIBRARY
See: U.S. Natl. Bureau of Standards - Library

★8794★
NATIONAL WILDLIFE FEDERATION - FRAZIER MEMORIAL LIBRARY (Env-Cons)
1412 16th St., N.W.   Phone: (202) 797-6828
Washington, DC 20036   Jay D. Hair, Exec. V.P.
Founded: 1960. **Staff:** Prof 2. **Subjects:** Wildlife, natural resources, conservation, ecology, environment. **Holdings:** 6000 books; 150 theses. **Subscriptions:** 300 journals and other serials. **Services:** Interlibrary loans; library open to public for reference use only. **Staff:** Jenafred J. Shore, Libn.; April Bohannan, Asst.Libn.

★8795★
NATIONAL WOMAN'S CHRISTIAN TEMPERANCE UNION - FRANCES E. WILLARD MEMORIAL LIBRARY (Soc Sci)
1730 Chicago Ave.   Phone: (312) 864-1396
Evanston, IL 60201   Rosalita J. Leonard, Libn.
Staff: Prof 2; Other 1. **Subjects:** History of temperance, biographies of temperance leaders, influence of alcohol and tobacco and narcotics on the human body, history of prohibition, alcohol education, history of women's movement, social reform history. **Special Collections:** Works by and about Frances Willard - correspondence, journals, scrapbooks. **Holdings:** 3500 books; 500 bound periodical volumes; photographs; archives; song books; reports; documents. **Subscriptions:** 110 journals and other serials. **Services:** Research by mail; library open to public with restrictions. **Staff:** Martha Edgar, Pres.

★8796★
NATIONAL WOMAN'S PARTY - FLORENCE BAYARD HILLES LIBRARY (Hist)
144 Constitution Ave., N.E.   Phone: (202) 546-1210
Washington, DC 20002   Elizabeth L. Chittick, Dir.
Staff: Prof 1. **Subjects:** Suffrage. **Special Collections:** Susan B. Anthony rare books. **Holdings:** 4000 volumes; suffrage archival material, 1913-1920, on microfilm; equal right archival material, 1920-1927. **Services:** Library open to history students for serious research only.

★8797★
NATIONAL WRESTLING HALL OF FAME - LIBRARY (Rec)
405 W. Hall of Fame Ave.   Phone: (405) 377-5243
Stillwater, OK 74074   Tereasa Stewart, Libn.
Founded: 1976. **Subjects:** Wrestling history, Olympics, sports medicine, biographies of wrestlers and coaches. **Holdings:** 161 books; 5 bound periodical volumes. **Services:** Copying; library open to museum visitors.

★8798★
NATIONAL WRITERS CLUB - LIBRARY (Hum)
1450 S. Havana, Suite 620   Phone: (303) 751-7844
Aurora, CO 80012   Donald E. Bower, Dir.
Founded: 1940. **Staff:** 3. **Subjects:** Writing, biographies of writers, markets for written work. **Special Collections:** Retrospective collection of "little" magazines. **Holdings:** 3000 books. **Subscriptions:** 20 journals and other serials. **Services:** Interlibrary loans; library open to public by appointment.

★8799★
NATIONAL YIDDISH BOOK EXCHANGE, INC. - LIBRARY (Area-Ethnic)
Box 969   Phone: (413) 584-1142
Amherst, MA 01004   Aaron Lansky, Exec.Dir.
Founded: 1980. **Staff:** Prof 4; Other 5. **Subjects:** Yiddish literature. **Special Collections:** Aliza Greenblatt Collection (women Yiddish writers); Sandler Collection (American Jewish experience); Flexer Collection (Russian socialist literature); Jakob Rosner Collection (100 photographs). **Holdings:** 100,000 books; 500 bound periodical volumes. **Services:** Interlibrary loans; copying; world-wide distribution of out-of-print Yiddish books; library open to public. **Publications:** Newsletter, quarterly; The Book Peddlar. **Special Catalogs:**

Published catalog of duplicate holdings. **Staff:** Francine Krasno, Asst.Dir.; Nansi Glick, Staff Asst.; Patricia Myerson, Staff Asst.

★8800★
NATIONAL YOUTH ORCHESTRA ASSOCIATION OF CANADA - LIBRARY (Mus)
76 Charles St., W. Phone: (416) 922-5031
Toronto, ON, Canada M5S 1K8 John Pellerin, Gen.Dir.
Subjects: Music - orchestra, chamber, scores. **Special Collections:** National Youth Orchestra performance tapes and video cassettes; historic orchestral recordings. **Holdings:** 4200 books; 40 bound periodical volumes; 2000 European concert programs; 1000 Asian and American concert programs; 150 shelf feet of scores, sheet music and performance materials; 200 shelf feet of recordings, tapes and cassettes. **Subscriptions:** 24 journals and other serials. **Services:** Copying; library open to public with restrictions. **Publications:** Who We Are And What We Do, information booklet.

★8801★
NATIONAL YOUTH WORK ALLIANCE, INC. - CLEARINGHOUSE/LIBRARY (Soc Sci)
1346 Connecticut Ave., N.W. Phone: (202) 785-0764
Washington, DC 20036 Thomas R. McCarthy, Dir.
Staff: Prof 1; Other 2. **Subjects:** Youth programs and problems, juvenile justice, youth alcohol and drug abuse, youth employment. **Holdings:** 1800 books; 9 VF drawers of pamphlets and clippings; 4 VF drawers of descriptions of local and national youth programs; 5 VF drawers of newsletters. **Subscriptions:** 45 journals and other serials. **Services:** Interlibrary loans; copying; library open to public with restrictions. **Publications:** Youth Alternatives, monthly newsletter - by subscription; 10 books and manuals.

NATIONAL ZOOLOGICAL PARK
See: Smithsonian Institution Libraries

★8802★
NATIONWIDE MUTUAL INSURANCE COMPANY - LIBRARY (Bus-Fin)
1 Nationwide Plaza Phone: (614) 227-6154
Columbus, OH 43216 Jean French, Chf.Libn.
Staff: Prof 1; Other 2. **Subjects:** Business management, insurance, cooperative movement. **Holdings:** 6000 books; 12 VF drawers. **Subscriptions:** 200 journals and other serials. **Services:** Use of library for reference may be requested. **Computerized Information Services:** DIALOG. **Networks/Consortia:** Member of CALICO.

★8803★
NATIVE AMERICAN EDUCATIONAL SERVICES - NAES LIBRARY AND RESOURCE CENTER (Educ)
4550 N. Hermitage Phone: (312) 728-1662
Chicago, IL 60640 Armin Beck, Dean
Staff: 1. **Subjects:** Indian community development, education, human services, history, culture and religion. **Holdings:** 750 books; 200 articles, studies and papers. **Services:** Library open to public with restrictions.

NATIVE AMERICAN INFORMATION & REFERRAL CENTER
See: Chicago Public Library Central Library

NATIVE AMERICAN RESEARCH LIBRARY
See: Navajo Nation Library

★8804★
NATIVE AMERICAN RIGHTS FUND - NATIONAL INDIAN LAW LIBRARY (Law)
1506 Broadway Phone: (303) 447-8760
Boulder, CO 80302 Diana Lim Garry, Libn.
Staff: Prof 2; Other 2. **Subjects:** American Indian law, U.S. government - Indian relations, federal law. **Holdings:** 633 books; 36 bound periodical volumes; 3400 legal documents, law reviews, studies, legislative histories; 48 file pockets of Indian topics; 13 binders of Bureau of Indian Affairs Manual; 2 binders of Indian Health Service Manual. **Subscriptions:** 50 journals and other serials; 89 newspapers. **Services:** Interlibrary loans (limited); copying; library open to public with restrictions. **Computerized Information Services:** WESTLAW. **Special Indexes:** Index to Indian legal materials and resources (book); index to the Indian Claims Commission decisions (book); bibliography of selected areas of Indian law (book). **Staff:** Bryce M. Wildcat, Res.Asst.

NATIVE AMERICAN STUDIES LIBRARY
See: University of California, Berkeley

NATRIUM RESEARCH AND DEVELOPMENT LIBRARY
See: PPG Industries, Inc. - Chemical Division

NATURAL FIBERS INFORMATION CENTER
See: University of Texas, Austin

★8805★
NATURAL HISTORY SOCIETY OF MARYLAND - LIBRARY (Sci-Tech)†
2643 N. Charles St. Phone: (301) 235-6116
Baltimore, MD 21218 C. Haven Kolb, Sec.
Founded: 1929. **Subjects:** Natural history and biology. **Special Collections:** Bird books. **Holdings:** Figures not available. **Subscriptions:** 40 journals and other serials. **Services:** Interlibrary loans; library open to members and others with professional interest.

★8806★
NATURE CENTER FOR ENVIRONMENTAL ACTIVITIES - REFERENCE LIBRARY (Env-Cons)
10 Woodside Ln. Phone: (203) 227-7253
Westport, CT 06880 Mrs. Robert J. Amirault, Libn.
Staff: Prof 1; Other 3. **Subjects:** Natural history, environment, ecology. **Holdings:** 3000 books; 150 bound periodical volumes; unbound periodicals; 6 VF drawers of pamphlets on natural history; 9 VF drawers of pamphlets on environment. **Subscriptions:** 65 journals and other serials. **Services:** Library not open to public.

★8807★
NATURE CONSERVANCY - LONG ISLAND CHAPTER - UPLANDS FARM ENVIRONMENTAL CENTER (Env-Cons)
Lawrence Hill Rd.
Box 72 Phone: (516) 367-3281
Cold Spring Harbor, NY 11724 Margo S. Myles, Dir.
Staff: Prof 1; Other 2. **Subjects:** Conservation, land preservation, natural history, terrestrial and freshwater ecology, endangered species, Long Island environment. **Special Collections:** Natural Diversity Collection; Long Island Freshwater and Terrestrial Ecology Collection. **Holdings:** 1000 books; 500 bound periodical volumes; 1000 documents; 2000 technical reports; 1000 slides; 500 vertical files. **Subscriptions:** 20 journals and other serials. **Services:** Copying; library open to public. **Networks/Consortia:** Member of Long Island Library Resources Council (LILRC). **Special Catalogs:** Long Island Environmental Council Documents Collection catalog (card); reprints catalog (card); registry of environmental resource people (card).

NATWA
See: North American Tiddlywinks Association

★8808★
NAVAJO NATION LIBRARY (Area-Ethnic; Hist)
Box K Phone: (602) 871-4941
Window Rock, AZ 86515 Jan Wright, Libn.
Founded: 1961. **Staff:** Prof 2; Other 3. **Subjects:** Navajos, Indians of the Southwest, Indians of America, archeology, Arizona history. **Special Collections:** Navajo History; Native American Research Library. **Holdings:** 4200 books; 1000 manuscripts; 60 films; 250 tape recordings; microfilm. **Subscriptions:** 68 journals and other serials. **Services:** Interlibrary loans; copying; library open to public. **Staff:** Deborah McBeth, Co-Libn.

NAVAL AEROSPACE MEDICAL INSTITUTE
See: U.S. Navy

★8809★
NAVY LEAGUE OF CANADA - NATIONAL OFFICE - LIBRARY (Mil)
4 Queen Elizabeth Dr. Phone: (613) 232-2784
Ottawa, ON, Canada K2P 2H9 W.J. Hodge, Gen.Mgr.
Founded: 1970. **Staff:** 1. **Subjects:** Maritime defense, marine-based industry, marine environment and training. **Holdings:** Figures not available. **Subscriptions:** 20 journals and other serials. **Services:** Library open to members or affiliated organizations. **Remarks:** The Navy League of Canada Library is mainly a collection of current reference materials for use in the league's publications, briefs and submissions.

NAWCC
See: National Association of Watch and Clock Collectors

NAYLOR (H. Custer) LIBRARY
See: Mercer University - Southern College of Pharmacy - H. Custer Naylor Library

★8810★
NAZARENE BIBLE COLLEGE - TRIMBLE LIBRARY (Rel-Theol)
Box 15749   Phone: (303) 596-5110
Colorado Springs, CO 80935   Roger M. Williams, Libn./Archv.
Staff: Prof 1; Other 5. **Subjects:** Bible, Christian education, music, theology. **Special Collections:** Wesley Collection. **Holdings:** 31,422 books; 2159 bound periodical volumes; 1553 books on microfiche; 2318 cassettes, phonograph records, slides and filmstrips; 8 VF drawers of pamphlets. **Subscriptions:** 192 journals and other serials; 5 newspapers. **Services:** Interlibrary loans (fee); copying; SDI; library open to alumni, pastors, student families.

★8811★
NAZARENE THEOLOGICAL SEMINARY - WILLIAM BROADHURST LIBRARY (Rel-Theol)
1700 E. Meyer Blvd.   Phone: (816) 333-6255
Kansas City, MO 64131   William C. Miller, Libn.
Founded: 1945. **Staff:** Prof 2; Other 6. **Subjects:** Theology, Christian education, missions, practics, philosophy, church history, philology. **Special Collections:** History of the Church of the Nazarene; Wesleyana-Methodism. **Holdings:** 62,500 books and bound periodical volumes; 1848 microforms. **Subscriptions:** 400 journals and other serials. **Services:** Interlibrary loans; copying; library open to public. **Computerized Information Services:** Computerized cataloging. **Networks/Consortia:** Member of MIDLNET; Kansas City Theological Library Association; Kansas City Metropolitan Library Network. **Staff:** Jean Amundson, Cat.

★8812★
NAZARETH HOSPITAL - MEDICAL LIBRARY (Med)
2601 Holme Ave.   Phone: (215) 335-6000
Philadelphia, PA 19152   Shirley M. Betz, Dir.
Founded: 1940. **Staff:** Prof 1; Other 1. **Subjects:** Medicine, surgery and allied subjects. **Holdings:** 3731 books; 2767 bound periodical volumes; 180 items of nursing materials; 125 pamphlets; 30 VF drawers; 684 cassettes. **Subscriptions:** 87 journals and other serials; 10 newspapers. **Services:** Interlibrary loans (fee); copying; library not open to public. **Computerized Information Services:** Computerized acquisitions, serials and circulation.

NBC
See: National Broadcasting Company, Inc.

NBS
See: U.S. Natl. Bureau of Standards

NCCAN (National Center on Child Abuse and Neglect)
See: Clearinghouse on Child Abuse and Neglect Information

NCHRTM
See: National Clearinghouse of Rehabilitation Training Materials

NCIC
See: U.S. Geological Survey - Natl. Cartographic Information Center (NCIC)

★8813★
NCNB - LIBRARY (Bus-Fin)†
One NCNB Plaza
Box 120   Phone: (704) 374-5842
Charlotte, NC 28255   Lisa Klien, Libn.
Staff: 1. **Subjects:** Banking and finance, business and economics, marketing; the Carolinas. **Holdings:** 100 books; 50 pamphlet boxes of files; 25 maps; 8 VF drawers of annual reports. **Subscriptions:** 105 journals and other serials. **Services:** Interlibrary loans (limited); copying; library open to public on request. **Also Known As:** North Carolina National Bank.

★8814★
NCR CANADA LTD. - MIRS LIBRARY (Bus-Fin)
6865 Century Ave.   Phone: (416) 826-9000
Mississauga, ON, Canada L5N 2E2   Ms. Tye Hofmeister, MIRS Libn.
Founded: 1975. **Staff:** Prof 1; Other 1. **Subjects:** Data processing and communications, business. **Holdings:** 600 books; 4 VF drawers of annual reports and pamphlets. **Subscriptions:** 155 journals and other serials. **Services:** Interlibrary loans; copying; library open to public by appointment. **Networks/Consortia:** Member of Sheridan Park Library Association.

★8815★
NCR CORPORATION - TECHNICAL LIBRARY (Bus-Fin)
Engineering & Manufacturing-Dayton
Building 28, 3rd Fl.   Phone: (513) 445-7032
Dayton, OH 45479   Vicki Stouder, Libn.
Founded: 1958. **Staff:** 1. **Subjects:** Computers, data processing, electronics, engineering, management, banking. **Special Collections:** Management and computer literature (250 items). **Holdings:** 7500 books; 4200 bound periodical volumes; 300 other cataloged items. **Subscriptions:** 160 journals and other serials. **Services:** Interlibrary loans; copying; library open to public by request. **Networks/Consortia:** Member of Dayton-Miami Valley Consortium. **Also Known As:** National Cash Register Company.

NDHQ LIBRARY
See: Canada - National Defence

NEATBY LIBRARY
See: Canada - Agriculture Canada

NEBRASKA ARCHIVES OF MEDICINE
See: University of Nebraska Medical Center - Mc Googan Library of Medicine

★8816★
NEBRASKA METHODIST HOSPITAL - LIBRARY (Med)
8303 Dodge St.   Phone: (402) 390-4611
Omaha, NE 68114   Angela Armer, Libn.
Founded: 1951. **Staff:** Prof 1; Other 2. **Subjects:** Medicine, nursing and allied health sciences. **Special Collections:** American Journal of Nursing, volume 1, 1900, to present. **Holdings:** 6059 books; 1949 bound periodical volumes; 10 VF drawers of pamphlets and reprints. **Subscriptions:** 226 journals and other serials. **Services:** Interlibrary loans; copying; library open to public for reference use only. **Computerized Information Services:** NLM. **Publications:** Library Memo, bimonthly, and Library Information Sheet - both for internal distribution only. **Remarks:** Contains holdings of former Children's Memorial Hospital, Medical Library.

★8817★
NEBRASKA PSYCHIATRIC INSTITUTE - LIBRARY (Med)
602 S. 45th St.   Phone: (402) 559-5000
Omaha, NE 68106   Pauline B. Allen, Libn.
Founded: 1955. **Staff:** Prof 1; Other 1. **Subjects:** Psychiatry, psychoanalysis, clinical psychology, mental retardation, social service, psychiatric nursing, special education, rehabilitation, biochemistry, neurology, neuropsychology, neurophysiology, psychophysiology, psychopharmacology. **Special Collections:** Historical collection (19th and early 20th century behavioral science; 125 books and reports, including early reports of state hospitals). **Holdings:** 7775 books; 480 bound periodical volumes; 220 tapes of academic lectures; 810 cassette tapes; 48 bound field studies for Masters' Degree Program; uncataloged pamphlets. **Subscriptions:** 220 journals and other serials. **Services:** Interlibrary loans; library open to public. **Publications:** List of new acquisitions, quarterly.

★8818★
NEBRASKA STATE DEPARTMENT OF PUBLIC WELFARE - LIBRARY (Soc Sci)
301 Centennial Mall S., 5th Fl.
Box 95026   Phone: (402) 471-3121
Lincoln, NE 68509   LeeAnn Zach, Sec./Libn.
Founded: 1943. **Staff:** 1. **Subjects:** Public welfare, social services. **Holdings:** 834 books. **Subscriptions:** 69 journals. **Services:** Library open to public for reference use only.

★8819★
NEBRASKA STATE GAME AND PARKS COMMISSION - LIBRARY (Sci-Tech)
2200 N. 33rd St.
Box 30370   Phone: (402) 464-0641
Lincoln, NE 68503   Carol A. Krueger, Agency Libn.
Founded: 1970. **Staff:** Prof 1. **Subjects:** Wildlife, fishery management, recreation. **Holdings:** 5000 books; 500 bound periodical volumes; 5000 cataloged reprints and pamphlets; 8000 uncataloged reprints and pamphlets; 1200 maps. **Subscriptions:** 60 journals and other serials. **Services:** Copying; library open to public with limited circulation periods. **Publications:** Booklist, bimonthly - for internal distribution only.

★8820★
NEBRASKA STATE HISTORICAL SOCIETY - ARCHIVES (Hist)
1500 R St. Phone: (402) 471-3270
Lincoln, NE 68508 James E. Potter, State Archv.
Founded: 1905. **Staff:** Prof 5; Other 7. **Subjects:** Nebraska - history, politics, agriculture, Western Indians. **Holdings:** 13,500 cubic feet of state and local archives; 4000 cubic feet of manuscripts; 20,000 reels of microfilmed newspapers (1854-1982). **Services:** Copying; archives open to public. **Publications:** Guides to the State Archives, series issued periodically. **Remarks:** The Archives and the Library of the society are separate departments but they function together as an information center. **Staff:** Donald D. Snoddy, Asst. State Archv.; Andrea I. Paul, Mss.Cur.; Anne P. Diffendal, Mss.Cur.

★8821★
NEBRASKA STATE HISTORICAL SOCIETY - FORT ROBINSON MUSEUM - RESEARCH LIBRARY (Hist)
Box 304 Phone: (308) 665-2852
Crawford, NE 69339 Vance E. Nelson, Cur.
Founded: 1970. **Subjects:** Western Americana - Indian ethnology, guns and U.S. military, wagons and automobiles, railroad, pioneers, Nebraska state government. **Special Collections:** Fort Robinson Medical Library. **Holdings:** Microfilm records of Fort Robinson; Red Cloud and Spotted Tail Agency records; diaries and interview manuscripts; newspapers of Crawford and Chadron, Nebraska. **Services:** Library open to public for reference use only.

★8822★
NEBRASKA STATE HISTORICAL SOCIETY - LIBRARY (Hist)
1500 R St. Phone: (402) 471-3270
Lincoln, NE 68508 Ann Reinert, Libn.
Founded: 1878. **Staff:** Prof 3; Other 8. **Subjects:** Nebraska history, Indians of the Great Plains, archeology, trans-Missouri history, genealogy. **Holdings:** 80,000 volumes; 590 Sanborn maps of Nebraska; 2200 other maps; 2500 photographs in Solomon D. Butcher Photograph Collection of Sod Houses; 465 photographs in John A. Anderson Photograph Collection of Brule Sioux; 90,000 other photographs; Nebraska state publications security repository. **Subscriptions:** 230 journals and other serials. **Services:** Copying; library open to public. **Publications:** Nebraska History, quarterly; Newsletter - by subscription. **Staff:** John E. Carter, Cur., Photographs.

★8823★
NEBRASKA STATE HISTORICAL SOCIETY - WILLA CATHER HISTORICAL CENTER - ARCHIVES (Hum)
Phone: (402) 746-3285
Red Cloud, NE 68970 Ann E. Billesbach, Cur.
Founded: 1955. **Staff:** Prof 1. **Subjects:** Willa Cather's life, art and the lives of real people who are prototypes of Cather's characters. **Holdings:** 400 books; 20 bound periodical volumes; 200 periodicals containing articles dealing with Cather and her works; 250 letters; 10 rare manuscripts about Cather; 1000 photographs; 700 pages of clippings; 80 reels of microfilm. **Services:** Copying; museum and archives open to public with advance notice.

★8824★
NEBRASKA STATE LIBRARY (Law)
3rd. Floor S., Statehouse Phone: (402) 432-2922
Lincoln, NE 68509 Reta Johnson, Dp.Libn.
Founded: 1854. **Staff:** Prof 1; Other 3. **Subjects:** Law, current Nebraska census. **Holdings:** 124,000 volumes; state and federal documents pertaining to law. **Subscriptions:** 220 journals and other serials. **Services:** Copying; mail service to attorneys and judges; library open to public for reference use only. **Publications:** Nebraska Statutes; Session Laws; Supreme Court Reports; Legislative Journals - on exchange and for sale. **Remarks:** Library is under the direction of the Nebraska State Supreme Court and serves the court, state agencies and attorneys.

★8825★
NEBRASKA STATE LIBRARY COMMISSION (Info Sci)
1420 P St. Phone: (402) 471-2045
Lincoln, NE 68508 John Kopischke, Dir.
Founded: 1901. **Staff:** Prof 24; Other 25. **Subjects:** General library reference and bibliographic research. **Holdings:** 37,000 books; 4119 films and AV items; 78,363 talking books and cassettes; 243,743 U.S. government documents (depository library); 28,907 Nebraska document titles. **Subscriptions:** 465 journals and other serials; 5 newspapers. **Services:** Interlibrary loans; copying; library open to public. **Computerized Information Services:** DIALOG, SDC, Source Telecomputing Corporation, BRS; computerized cataloging. **Networks/Consortia:** Member of NEBASE; Bibliographical Center for Research, Rocky Mountain Region, Inc. (BCR). **Publications:** Nebraska State Publications Checklist, bimonthly; Overtones,

13/year; Annual Report. **Special Catalogs:** Nebraska Film Services Catalog (computer produced); Network Services Manual (book); List of Reference Tools (book). **Staff:** Rod Wagner, Dp.Dir.; Susan Kling, Hd., Ref./Info.Serv.; Sandra Scott, Hd., Spec.Lib.Serv.; Mona Jeanne Easter, Hd., Tech.Serv.; Morel Fry, Hd., Adm.Serv.

★8826★
NEBRASKA TESTING LABORATORIES - LIBRARY (Sci-Tech)†
Elmwood Park Sta., Box 6075 Phone: (402) 331-4453
Omaha, NE 68117 Dan McCarthy, Pres.
Staff: 1. **Subjects:** Soils engineering, materials testing, chemical analysis, nondestructive and environmental testing. **Holdings:** 200 books; 500 bound periodical volumes; 1000 pamphlets (cataloged); 20 volumes of Air Pollution Abstracts; current Commerce Business Daily (6 months); 6 sets of filmstrips of soils testing. **Subscriptions:** 30 journals and other serials. **Services:** Interlibrary loans; copying; library open to public with permission. **Remarks:** Library located at 4453 S. 67th St., Omaha, NE 68117.

NEBRASKA WESLEYAN UNIVERSITY - UNITED METHODIST CHURCH - NEBRASKA CONFERENCE
See: United Methodist Church - Nebraska Conference - Historical Center

★8827★
NEC AMERICA - SWITCHING SYSTEMS DIVISON - LIBRARY (Sci-Tech)
1525 Walnut Hill Lane Phone: (214) 257-9100
Irving, TX 75062 Michiko K. Adams, Pubn.Coord.
Founded: 1980. **Staff:** Prof 1; Other 1. **Subjects:** Telecommunications. **Special Collections:** Technical publications in Japanese. **Holdings:** Figures not available. **Subscriptions:** 50 journals and other serials; 7 newspapers. **Services:** Library not open to public.

★8828★
NEEDHAM, HARPER & STEERS ADVERTISING, INC. - INFORMATION SERVICES (Bus-Fin)
303 E. Wacker Dr. Phone: (312) 861-0200
Chicago, IL 60601 Belle Mest, Mgr., Info.Serv.
Founded: 1938. **Staff:** Prof 4; Other 1. **Subjects:** Advertising, marketing, statistics. **Holdings:** 1500 books; 100 VF drawers of pamphlets, brochures and clippings; 25 VF drawers of corporation files; 100 pamphlet boxes of consumer analysis material. **Subscriptions:** 250 journals and other serials. **Services:** Copying; library open to company clients. **Computerized Information Services:** Online systems. **Networks/Consortia:** Member of Metropolitan Chicago Library Assembly; ILLINET. **Staff:** Marilyn Mack, Supv., Info.Serv.; Ruth Kobylecky, Libn.

★8829★
NEEDHAM, HARPER & STEERS ADVERTISING, INC. - RESEARCH LIBRARY (Bus-Fin)†
909 Third Ave., 18th Fl. Phone: (212) 758-7600
New York, NY 10022 Alice Vallinos, Res.Libn.
Founded: 1944. **Staff:** Prof 2. **Subjects:** Advertising, marketing, merchandising, commodities, industries. **Holdings:** 200 books; publication survey files; data file; picture collection. **Subscriptions:** 140 journals and other serials. **Services:** Interlibrary loans; copying; library not open to public.

★8830★
NEEDHAM, HARPER & STEERS OF CANADA, LTD. - INFORMATION SERVICES CENTRE (Bus-Fin)
130 Adelaide St., W. Phone: (416) 364-1492
Toronto, ON, Canada M5H 3P5 Linda Dominitz, Res.Asst.
Founded: 1977. **Staff:** Prof 1. **Subjects:** Advertising, media research, marketing. **Holdings:** 300 books; 400 research reports; 70 subject files; 120 annual reports. **Subscriptions:** 38 journals and other serials. **Services:** Interlibrary loans; SDI; library not open to public.

NEEF (Arthur) LAW LIBRARY
See: Wayne State University - Arthur Neef Law Library

NEFCO
See: Northeast Ohio Four County Regional Planning & Development Organization

NEFF (Joseph and Benjamin) MEMORIAL LIBRARY
See: Tri-City Jewish Center - Joseph and Benjamin Neff Memorial Library

★8831★

NEIGHBORHOOD PLAYHOUSE SCHOOL OF THE THEATRE - IRENE LEWISOHN LIBRARY (Theater)†
340 E. 54th St.   Phone: (212) 688-3770
New York, NY 10022   Alice G. Owen, Libn.
Founded: 1945. **Staff:** Prof 1. **Subjects:** Drama, theater, biography, literature. **Special Collections:** Neighborhood Playhouse-iana (12 books; 2 VF drawers; file of photographs). **Holdings:** 5323 books and bound periodical volumes; 573 typescripts and 870 music scores (cataloged); 3 VF drawers of pamphlets, clippings and pictures; 4 VF drawers of scenes; 1 VF drawer of sheet music. **Subscriptions:** 15 journals and other serials. **Services:** Permission may be requested to consult material not available elsewhere. **Publications:** Reading List, Memo from the Librarian, both irregular - for internal distribution only. **Special Indexes:** Scene index on cards.

NEILLY (Balmer) LIBRARY
See: Connaught Laboratories, Ltd. - Balmer Neilly Library

NELLIS AIR FORCE BASE (NV)
See: U.S. Air Force Base - Nellis Base Library

NELSON (Florence L.) MEMORIAL LIBRARY
See: Trinity Lutheran Hospital - Florence L. Nelson Memorial Library

NELSON FOREST REGION LIBRARY
See: British Columbia - Ministry of Forests

★8832★

NELSON GALLERY-ATKINS MUSEUM - SLIDE LIBRARY (Aud-Vis)
4525 Oak St.   Phone: (816) 561-4000
Kansas City, MO 64111   Jan McKenna, Slide Libn.
Staff: Prof 1. **Subjects:** Oriental and Occidental art - history, painting, sculpture, architecture, gardens. **Holdings:** 45,000 slides. **Services:** Library open to public with restrictions.

★8833★

NELSON GALLERY-ATKINS MUSEUM - SPENCER ART REFERENCE LIBRARY (Art)
4525 Oak St.   Phone: (816) 561-4000
Kansas City, MO 64111   Stanley W. Hess, Libn.
Founded: 1962. **Staff:** Prof 2; Other 2. **Subjects:** Art history, both Oriental and Occidental art with emphasis on Chinese painting; decorative arts; artists. **Special Collections:** John H. Bender Library of Prints and Drawings; Oriental Library; auction and sales catalogs. **Holdings:** 32,000 books and bound periodical volumes. 56 VF drawers of material by artist and subject; 750 periodical titles. **Subscriptions:** 375 journals and other serials. **Services:** Interlibrary loans; copying; library open to public for research purposes. **Networks/Consortia:** Member of Kansas City Metropolitan Library Network. **Staff:** Mrs. H.J. Cheng, Asst.Libn.

NELSON (Herbert U.) MEMORIAL LIBRARY
See: National Association of Realtors - Herbert U. Nelson Memorial Library

NELSON (Dr. Kenneth O.) LIBRARY OF THE HEALTH SCIENCES
See: Perry Memorial Hospital - Dr. Kenneth O. Nelson Library of the Health Sciences

NELSON LIBRARY
See: Freeborn County Historical Society

NELSON (P.C.) MEMORIAL LIBRARY
See: Southwestern Assemblies of God College - P.C. Nelson Memorial Library

★8834★

NEPTUNE MICROFLOC, INC. - RESEARCH AND TECHNICAL LIBRARY (Sci-Tech)
Box 612   Phone: (503) 754-7654
Corvallis, OR 97339   Marilyn Curteman, Doc.Coord.
Founded: 1981. **Staff:** 1. **Subjects:** Engineering. **Holdings:** 3000 books; 30 VF drawers of reports, vendor data and Environmental Protection Agency publications. **Subscriptions:** 243 journals and other serials. **Services:** Copying; library not open to public. **Remarks:** Library is located at 1965 Airport Rd., Corvallis, OR 97333.

★8835★

NER ISRAEL RABBINICAL COLLEGE - LIBRARY (Rel-Theol)†
400 Mt. Wilson Lane   Phone: (301) 484-7200
Baltimore, MD 21208   Rabbi Jakowiski, Libn.
Staff: Prof 2. **Subjects:** Religion, theology, sociology, education. **Special Collections:** Ancient religious tomes. **Holdings:** 15,582 volumes. **Subscriptions:** 20 journals and other serials; 5 newspapers. **Services:** Copying (limited); library open to public with special permission, but books do not circulate.

NERA
See: National Economic Research Associates, Inc.

★8836★

NERCO - LIBRARY (Energy)
111 S.W. Columbia, Suite 800   Phone: (503) 796-6631
Portland, OR 97201   Stewart W. Richards, Libn.
Staff: Prof 1. **Subjects:** Coal mining, energy, corporate development. **Holdings:** 3000 books. **Subscriptions:** 227 journals and other serials; 5 newspapers. **Services:** Interlibrary loans; library open to public for reference use only.

★8837★

NESBITT MEMORIAL HOSPITAL - LIBRARY (Med)
562 Wyoming Ave.   Phone: (717) 288-1411
Kingston, PA 18704   Katherine L. McCrea, Libn.
Staff: Prof 1. **Subjects:** Medicine, nursing, paramedical fields. **Holdings:** 2500 books; 380 bound periodical volumes. **Subscriptions:** 120 journals and other serials. **Services:** Interlibrary loans; copying; SDI; library open to public with permission. **Computerized Information Services:** DIALOG, NLM. **Networks/Consortia:** Member of Health Information Library Network of Northeast Pennsylvania; Mideast Regional Medical Library Service (MERMLS); Northeastern Pennsylvania Bibliographic Center. **Remarks:** Library includes the holdings of the Dr. E.C.O. Wagner Library.

★8838★

NESBITT, THOMSON AND COMPANY, LTD. - RESEARCH LIBRARY (Bus-Fin)
355 St. James St., W.   Phone: (514) 844-0131
Montreal, PQ, Canada H2Y 1P1   Ms. L. Cahill, Libn.
Founded: 1920. **Staff:** Prof 1; Other 1. **Subjects:** Stocks and bonds, investments, corporation and government finance, money market. **Holdings:** 400 books; 200 bound periodical volumes; 35 VF drawers of annual reports, prospectuses, trust deeds; 50 VF drawers of company files, clippings, pamphlets, government documents and studies. **Subscriptions:** 100 journals and other serials; 20 newspapers. **Services:** Interlibrary loans; library open to public by appointment only. **Publications:** Research studies.

★8839★

NESTE, BRUDIN & STONE, INC. - CORPORATE LIBRARY (Sci-Tech)
Box 28100   Phone: (714) 485-1500
San Diego, CA 92128   Joan J. Sierecki, Corp.Libn.
Founded: 1980. **Staff:** Prof 1. **Subjects:** Wastewater treatment, water systems, land development, flood control. **Holdings:** 1000 books; 50 bound periodical volumes; 5000 government documents; 50 maps; 1600 in-house publications. **Subscriptions:** 140 journals and other serials. **Services:** Interlibrary loans; library open to public with restrictions. **Computerized Information Services:** DIALOG; internal database; computerized cataloging, acquisitions, serials and circulation. **Publications:** In-house reports, specifications and proposals; New Publications List, quarterly - for internal distribution only.

★8840★

NESTLE COMPANY, INC. - TECHNICAL SERVICE DIVISION - LIBRARY (Food-Bev)
555 S. Fourth St.   Phone: (315) 598-1234
Fulton, NY 13069   Janice Burns, Libn.
Founded: 1955. **Staff:** Prof 1. **Subjects:** Confectionery industry; food processing; chemistry - industrial, physical, analytical; chemical engineering. **Special Collections:** Chocolate; cocoa. **Holdings:** 1095 books; 10,000 unbound periodical volumes; 17 VF drawers of pamphlets, articles, clippings and newsletters. **Subscriptions:** 40 journals and other serials. **Services:** Interlibrary loans; copying; library not open to public.

★8841★

NET ENERGY - DEMONSTRATION CENTER - APPROPRIATE TECHNOLOGY LIBRARY (Energy)
539 T St.   Phone: (707) 445-3004
Eureka, CA 95501   Brenda Todaro, Info.Spec.
Founded: 1977. **Staff:** Prof 1; Other 1. **Subjects:** Passive solar energy,

energy conservation, weatherization, solar retrofits, wind energy, wood stoves. **Holdings:** 1000 books; 18 bound periodical volumes; 2 shelves of energy policy and planning documents; 2 shelves of California Energy Commission reports; 1 shelf of energy curriculum; 3 VF drawers of general information files; 1 VF drawer of organization and agency files. **Subscriptions:** 50 journals and other serials; 20 newspapers. **Services:** Copying; library open to public for reference use only. **Special Catalogs:** Appropriate technology card catalog. **Formerly:** Net Energy - Alternative Energy Library.

★8842★

NETHERLANDS EMBASSY - REFERENCE ROOM LIBRARY (Area-Ethnic)
4200 Linnean Ave., N.W.   Phone: (202) 244-5300
Washington, DC 20008
Subjects: Netherlands, United States. **Holdings:** Figures not available. **Services:** Library open to public.

★8843★

NETHERLANDS MUSEUM - ARCHIVES AND LIBRARY (Hist; Area-Ethnic)
City Hall, 3rd Fl.   Phone: (616) 392-3129
Holland, MI 49423   Dr. Willard Wichers, Musm.Dir.
Staff: 1. **Subjects:** Dutch in Western Michigan and the United States; local history. **Holdings:** 500 books; Dutch newspapers; manuscripts; clippings; dissertations. **Services:** Copying; library open to public with restrictions. **Publications:** Guide to the Archives of the Netherlands Museum, 1978. **Staff:** Barbara Lampen, Archv.

★8844★

THE NETWORK, INC. - INFORMATION CENTER (Educ)
290 S. Main St.   Phone: (617) 470-1080
Andover, MA 01810   Ellen Messing, Info.Spec.
Staff: 1. **Subjects:** Education. **Holdings:** 2500 books; complete set of ERIC microfiche; reports; vertical files; proposals. **Subscriptions:** 50 journals; 50 newsletters. **Services:** Interlibrary loans; copying; SDI; center open to public for reference use only. **Computerized Information Services:** DIALOG. **Publications:** List of publications - available upon request. **Special Catalogs:** Catalog of Special Education (notebook).

★8845★

NEUROPSYCHIATRIC INSTITUTE - LIBRARY (Med)
700 1st Ave. S.   Phone: (701) 235-5354
Fargo, ND 58103   Diane Nordeng, Libn.
Founded: 1977. **Staff:** Prof 1. **Subjects:** Neurosurgery, neurology, psychiatry, neuropsychology. **Holdings:** 200 books; 1069 bound periodical volumes. **Subscriptions:** 47 journals and other serials. **Services:** Interlibrary loans; copying; library open to allied medical personnel. **Networks/Consortia:** Member of Valley Medical Network.

★8846★

NEUROPSYCHIATRIC INSTITUTE - MENTAL HEALTH INFORMATION SERVICE (Med)
University of California, Los Angeles
Center for the Health Sciences
760 Westwood Plaza   Phone: (213) 825-0597
Los Angeles, CA 90024   Sherry Terzian, Dir.
Founded: 1961. **Staff:** Prof 1; Other 9. **Subjects:** Biobehavioral sciences, psychiatry, psychoanalysis, clinical psychology, mental retardation, nursing, social work, specialized resources. **Special Collections:** Professional Staff Library; Mindlin Collection of historical holdings; Rose Reading Room in the Reed Neurological Institute. **Holdings:** 15,000 books and bound periodical volumes; 500 cassette tapes; 80,000 documents. **Subscriptions:** 300 current journals and other serials. **Services:** Service open to public with restrictions. **Publications:** Recent Acquisitions. **Special Catalogs:** Master Catalog to Professional Library. **Special Indexes:** Indexes of journal holdings, current and retrospective.

NEVADA ARCHITECTURAL ARCHIVES
See: University of Nevada, Reno - Special Collections Department/ University Archives

★8847★

NEVADA COUNTY HISTORICAL SOCIETY - SEARLS HISTORICAL LIBRARY (Hist)
214 Church St.
Nevada City, CA 95959   Edwin L. Tyson, Libn.
Subjects: Nevada County history. **Holdings:** 3465 books; 50 bound periodical volumes; 350,000 documents, pamphlets, vertical file items; 240 maps and charts; 50 tape recordings; 2415 photographs. **Services:** Copying; library open to public with restrictions. **Computerized Information Services:**

Mechanized services.

★8848★

NEVADA COUNTY LAW LIBRARY (Law)
Courthouse Annex   Phone: (916) 265-2461
Nevada City, CA 95959   Letha Baker, Law Libn.
Staff: Prof 1. **Subjects:** Law. **Holdings:** 5000 books. **Subscriptions:** 4 journals and other serials. **Services:** Interlibrary loans; copying; library open to public with restrictions.

★8849★

NEVADA HISTORICAL SOCIETY - LIBRARY (Hist)
1650 N. Virginia St.   Phone: (702) 784-6397
Reno, NV 89503   Peter L. Bandurraga, Dir.
Founded: 1904. **Staff:** 7. **Subjects:** Nevada history including mining, Indians, agriculture, and other topics. **Holdings:** 10,000 books; 5000 bound periodical volumes; 18,000 items in manuscript collections; 3500 reels of microfilm. **Subscriptions:** 260 journals and other serials. **Services:** Interlibrary loans (limited); copying; limited written research by mail; library open to public. **Publications:** Nevada Historical Society Quarterly. **Special Indexes:** An Index to the Publications of the Nevada Historical Society, 1907-1971; Guide to the Manuscript Collections at the Nevada Historical Society (1975).

★8850★

NEVADA MENTAL HEALTH INSTITUTE - MEDICAL LIBRARY (Med)
Box 2460   Phone: (702) 322-6961
Reno, NV 89505   Alice L. Lohse, Libn.
Founded: 1968. **Staff:** Prof 1; Other 1. **Subjects:** Psychiatry, psychology, mental retardation, mental health, psychiatric nursing. **Holdings:** 2500 books; 500 government documents; 2000 pamphlets and reports; 300 audio cassettes. **Subscriptions:** 65 journals and other serials; 6 newspapers. **Services:** Interlibrary loans; copying; library open to health professionals. **Networks/Consortia:** Member of Pacific Southwest Regional Medical Library Service (PSRMLS); Information Nevada. **Special Catalogs:** Developmental disabilities resource collection catalog.

★8851★

NEVADA STATE DEPARTMENT OF TRANSPORTATION - MAP INFORMATION LIBRARY (Geog-Map)
1263 S. Stewart St.   Phone: (702) 885-5400
Carson City, NV 89712   Jack Slansky, Chf. Cartographer
Subjects: Maps, geographic names. **Holdings:** Figures not available. **Services:** Library not open to public. **Special Indexes:** Map indexes - available upon request.

★8852★

NEVADA STATE LIBRARY (Info Sci)
Capitol Complex   Phone: (702) 885-5130
Carson City, NV 89710   Joseph J. Anderson, State Libn.
Founded: 1859. **Staff:** Prof 11; Other 25. **Subjects:** Public administration, history of Nevada, library science, mining in Nevada. **Special Collections:** Nevada Collection; state, county and municipal archives; Regional Library for the Blind and Physically Handicapped. **Holdings:** 65,000 books; 12,400 bound periodical volumes; 250,000 U.S. government publications; 55,000 Nevada state, city and county publications; 10,000 reels of microfilm of Nevada newspapers; 10 VF drawers of Nevada and local history. **Subscriptions:** 300 journals and other serials; 60 newspapers. **Services:** Interlibrary loans; copying; library open to public. **Computerized Information Services:** SDC, DIALOG, RLIN; state and local documents from internal databases; computerized cataloging. **Networks/Consortia:** Member of Information Nevada; CLASS. **Publications:** Dateline, Government Issues, Official Publications List, all monthly; Inventory of Research Activities in the Lake Tahoe Area, irregular (basic list covers 1845-1976). **Special Catalogs:** Nevada in Print, 1964; Nevada Union Catalog (card); statewide COM catalog; Index to Nevada Census of 1862 and 1875 (microfiche); Nevada Government Documents Microfiche Catalog. **Staff:** Oscar Ford, Asst. to the State Libn.; Joan G. Kerschner, Asst. State Libn/Pub.Serv; Jeanne Goodrich, Asst.St.Libn./Plan & Dev.; Ann Brinkmeyer, Coll.Libn.; Joyce Lee, Hd., Pub.Serv.; Larry Calkins, Doc.Libn.; Ann Brady, Cons.; Mark Fox, Cat.Libn.; Valerie Anderson, Ref.Libn.; Dana Sturm, ILL.

★8853★

NEVADA STATE LIBRARY - DIVISION OF ARCHIVES (Info Sci)
101 S. Fall St.   Phone: (702) 885-5210
Carson City, NV 89710   Guy L. Rocha, State Archv.
Founded: 1965. **Staff:** Prof 1; Other 2. **Subjects:** Nevada state and local records. **Special Collections:** Territorial and State Supreme Court Record Collection; various state archival records; records center for state government. **Holdings:** 500 books; 20,000 cubic feet of records;

photographs; portraits; maps; drawings; sketches. **Services:** Copying; archives open to public.

★8854★
NEVADA STATE MUSEUM - LIBRARY (Sci-Tech)
Capitol Complex
600 N. Carson St.   Phone: (702) 885-4810
Carson City, NV 89710   Dorothy Paulsen, Acq.Reg.
Founded: 1939. **Subjects:** Nevada history, historical artifacts. **Special Collections:** Site files on threatened and endangered plants of Nevada; anthropological papers; Virginia & Truckee Railroad ledgers and reports. **Holdings:** 650 volumes. **Subscriptions:** 20 journals and other serials. **Services:** Copying; library open to students and researchers by appointment. **Publications:** Newsletter, quarterly; Popular Series, irregular.

★8855★
NEVADA STATE SUPREME COURT - LIBRARY (Law)
Supreme Court Bldg., Capitol Complex   Phone: (702) 885-5140
Carson City, NV 89710   Catherine Finnegan, Law Libn.
Staff: Prof 2; Other 3. **Subjects:** Law. **Holdings:** 60,000 books and bound periodical volumes. **Subscriptions:** 220 journals and other serials. **Services:** Interlibrary loans; copying; library open to public with restrictions. **Publications:** New Titles List, irregular.

NEVEL (C.W.) MEMORIAL LIBRARY
See: Lutheran Medical Center - C.W. Nevel Memorial Library

★8856★
NEVILLE PUBLIC MUSEUM - LIBRARY (Art)
210 Museum Pl.   Phone: (414) 497-3767
Green Bay, WI 54303
Subjects: Art, earth sciences, and history with regional and state emphasis. **Holdings:** Figures not available. **Services:** Library open to public for reference use only.

NEVITT (George P.) LIBRARY
See: Paine Art Center and Arboretum - George P. Nevitt Library

NEW AGE CENTER
See: National Investigations Committee on UFOs

★8857★
NEW ALMADEN MERCURY MINING MUSEUM - LIBRARY (Hist)
21570 Almaden Rd.
Box 1   Phone: (408) 268-7869
New Almaden, CA 95042   Constance B. Perham, Owner-Dir.
Staff: 1. **Subjects:** New Almaden history. **Holdings:** 500 books; 300 bound periodical volumes; pamphlets, documents, clippings, manuscripts and photographs; displays and records of mines from early civilization to present; 100 mine maps; comprehensive collection of Yokut and local Indian materials. **Services:** Library open to public for small fee by arrangement. **Remarks:** This is said to be the only mercury mining museum in the United States.

★8858★
NEW BEDFORD FREE PUBLIC LIBRARY - GENEALOGY ROOM (Hist)
613 Pleasant St.   Phone: (617) 999-6291
New Bedford, MA 02740   Paul Cyr, Libn.
Staff: Prof 1; Other 1. **Subjects:** Genealogy of New England, Massachusetts town histories, history of New Bedford and vicinity, French-Canadian and Acadian genealogy. **Special Collections:** Leonard Papers (Dartmouth Genealogy); Pierce Papers (Bristol Genealogy); Paul Cuffe Papers; Quakeriana. **Holdings:** 5000 books; 500 bound periodical volumes; 1250 reels of microfilm of New Bedford newspapers and city documents. **Subscriptions:** 18 journals and other serials. **Services:** Interlibrary loans (microfilm); copying; library open to public for reference use only. **Publications:** Paul Cuffe Papers (on microfilm only). **Special Indexes:** New Bedford newspaper index (card). **Staff:** Susan Kelly, Ref.Dept.Hd.

★8859★
NEW BEDFORD FREE PUBLIC LIBRARY - MELVILLE WHALING ROOM (Hist)
613 Pleasant St.   Phone: (617) 999-6291
New Bedford, MA 02740   Paul Cyr, Cur.
Founded: 1962. **Staff:** Prof 1; Other 1. **Subjects:** Whaling - New Bedford, New England, and United States. **Special Collections:** Whaling logs of 495 voyages; J. & W.R. Wing Collection (business records 1840-1920); C.W. Morgan Collection (business records 1818-1850); C.R. Tucker Collection (1838-1867); G.H. Hussey Collection (1845-1865). **Holdings:** 650 books; 35 bound periodical volumes; 120 pamphlets (cataloged); 1025 volumes of whaling manuscripts (logs, journals, account books); 6700 crew lists; 11,000

custom house records; 300 reels of microfilm; 100 photographs, prints, paintings. **Services:** Interlibrary loans (limited); copying; literature searching; research in depth; library open to public for reference use only. **Publications:** Birth of a Whaleship; Addendum to Starbuck and Whaling Masters. **Special Indexes:** Card index of men who signed on whaleships (200,000 entries); voyage abstracts (37,000 entries) - index to whaling manuscripts (microfilm).

★8860★
NEW BEDFORD LAW LIBRARY (Law)
441 County St.   Phone: (617) 992-8077
New Bedford, MA 02740   Margaretha E.H. Birknes, Law Libn.
Staff: Prof 1. **Subjects:** Law. **Holdings:** 35,000 volumes. **Services:** Interlibrary loans; library open to outside users for research only. **Remarks:** Maintained by the Commonwealth of Massachusetts Trial Court.

★8861★
NEW BEDFORD STANDARD-TIMES LIBRARY (Publ)
555 Pleasant St.   Phone: (617) 997-7411
New Bedford, MA 02740   Maurice G. Lauzon, Libn.
Founded: 1890. **Staff:** Prof 1; Other 1. **Subjects:** Local history, newspaper reference topics. **Holdings:** Clippings; local newspapers. **Services:** Interlibrary loans; copying; library open to public for reference use only.

★8862★
NEW BERLIN MEMORIAL HOSPITAL - LIBRARY (Med)
13750 W. National Ave.   Phone: (414) 782-2700
New Berlin, WI 53151   June Regis, Staff Libn.
Staff: Prof 1. **Subjects:** Medicine, nursing. **Special Collections:** Podiatry; osteopathy. **Holdings:** 600 books; 435 bound periodical volumes; 400 audiotapes. **Subscriptions:** 133 journals and other serials. **Services:** Interlibrary loans; copying; SDI; library open to public for reference use only. **Networks/Consortia:** Member of Regional Medical Library - Region 3; Library Council of Metropolitan Milwaukee, Inc. (LCOMM); Southeastern Wisconsin Health Science Library Consortium.

NEW BOLTON CENTER
See: University of Pennsylvania

★8863★
NEW BRITAIN GENERAL HOSPITAL - HEALTH SCIENCE LIBRARY (Med)
100 Grand St.   Phone: (203) 224-5122
New Britain, CT 06050   Debora K. Stenberg, Lib.Dir.
Founded: 1946. **Staff:** Prof 1; Other 2. **Subjects:** Medicine, surgery, obstetrics and gynecology, pediatrics and cardiology. **Special Collections:** History of Medicine Collection (130 texts); History of Nursing; patient education. **Holdings:** 2000 books; 7500 bound periodical volumes; pamphlets; videotapes; films; slides; Audio-Digest tapes. **Subscriptions:** 180 journals and other serials. **Services:** Interlibrary loans (fee); library open to public by appointment. **Computerized Information Services:** MEDLARS; computerized cataloging. **Networks/Consortia:** Member of OCLC; Capitol Area Health Consortium Libraries; Connecticut Association of Health Science Libraries (CAHSL).

NEW BRITAIN HERALD
See: Herald Publishing Company

★8864★
NEW BRITAIN MUSEUM OF AMERICAN ART - LIBRARY (Art)
56 Lexington St.   Phone: (203) 229-0257
New Britain, CT 06052   Lois L. Blomstrann, Asst. to Dir.
Subjects: American art. **Holdings:** 600 books. **Services:** Library open to public for reference use only. **Remarks:** Maintained by New Britain Institute.

★8865★
NEW BRITAIN YOUTH MUSEUM - RESOURCE CENTER (Sci-Tech)
30 High St.   Phone: (203) 225-3020
New Britain, CT 06051   Alan J. Krauss, Musm.Dir.
Staff: 2. **Subjects:** Natural sciences, circus history. **Special Collections:** William Judd Collection of circus books and films (300 volumes; 18 films; posters). **Holdings:** 1000 books; 1000 slides (of wildlife); 250 loan kits of artifacts on American history, American Indians and world culture. **Subscriptions:** 20 journals and other serials. **Services:** Center open to public.

★8866★
NEW BRUNSWICK ASSOCIATION OF REGISTERED NURSES - LIBRARY (Med)
231 Saunders St.   Phone: (506) 454-5591
Fredericton, NB, Canada E3B 1N6   Barbara Thompson, Libn.
Staff: 1. **Subjects:** Nursing and nursing education. **Holdings:** 600 books; 150

bound periodical volumes; 4 VF drawers; 5 VF drawers of archives. **Subscriptions:** 50 journals and other serials. **Services:** Library not open to public.

NEW BRUNSWICK BARRISTERS' SOCIETY
See: Barristers' Society of New Brunswick

★8867★
NEW BRUNSWICK - DEPARTMENT OF AGRICULTURE & RURAL DEVELOPMENT - LIBRARY (Agri)
P.O. Box 6000   Phone: (506) 453-2258
Fredericton, NB, Canada E3B 5H1
Founded: 1966. **Subjects:** Agriculture science and industry; statistics. **Holdings:** Figures not available. **Special Catalogs:** Agdex catalog of documents. **Services:** Library not open to public.

★8868★
NEW BRUNSWICK - DEPARTMENT OF COMMERCE & DEVELOPMENT - LIBRARY (Bus-Fin)
P.O. Box 6000   Phone: (506) 453-3608
Fredericton, NB, Canada E3B 5H1   Pamela M. Spinney, Libn.
Staff: 1. **Subjects:** Foreign and domestic trade, statistics. **Holdings:** 1500 books; 1450 bound periodical volumes. **Subscriptions:** 62 journals and other serials; 55 newspapers. **Services:** Library open to public for reference use only. **Computerized Information Services:** Computerized cataloging and circulation.

★8869★
NEW BRUNSWICK - DEPARTMENT OF EDUCATION - LIBRARY (Educ)
3rd Fl., King's Place
P.O. Box 6000   Phone: (506) 453-3739
Fredericton, NB, Canada E3B 5H1   Germaine Burns, Supv.
Founded: 1979. **Staff:** 2. **Subjects:** Education, administration. **Holdings:** 3000 books; 1300 reports and studies; 1800 curriculum guides; 4 VF drawers of pamphlets; 200 government documents. **Subscriptions:** 820 journals and other serials; 8 newspapers. **Services:** Library open to public for reference use only.

★8870★
NEW BRUNSWICK - DEPARTMENT OF THE ENVIRONMENT - LIBRARY (Env-Cons)†
P.O. Box 6000   Phone: (506) 453-3700
Fredericton, NB, Canada E3B 5H1   Geraldine L. King, Libn.
Founded: 1972. **Staff:** 1. **Subjects:** Industrial waste, sewage treatment, air pollution, water resources, environmental impact assessment, pesticides. **Special Collections:** New Brunswick government reports related to environmental subjects. **Holdings:** 3000 books; 240 bound periodical volumes; 5 VF drawers of articles; 2 VF drawers of Canadian and American legislation. **Subscriptions:** 115 journals and other serials. **Services:** Interlibrary loans; library open to public for reference use only. **Publications:** Monthly Accessions List - to staff, other departments and interested firms.

★8871★
NEW BRUNSWICK - DEPARTMENT OF HEALTH - LIBRARY (Med)
Centennial Bldg., Rm. 349   Phone: (506) 453-2536
Fredericton, NB, Canada E3B 5H1   Margaret Cooper, Libn.
Founded: 1982. **Staff:** Prof 1. **Subjects:** Health, medicine, social services. **Holdings:** 1000 books; 100 bound periodical volumes. **Subscriptions:** 100 journals and other serials; 14 newspapers. **Services:** Interlibrary loans; copying; library open to public. **Publications:** New Library Additions, bimonthly.

★8872★
NEW BRUNSWICK - DEPARTMENT OF NATURAL RESOURCES - FORESTS BRANCH LIBRARY (Sci-Tech)†
P.O. Box 6000   Phone: (506) 453-2485
Fredericton, NB, Canada E3B 5H1   Irma R. Long, Lib.Asst.
Founded: 1957. **Subjects:** Forestry. **Holdings:** 500 books; 3000 bound periodical volumes; 200 annual reports; 40 shelf units of pamphlets; 60 shelf units of special reports. **Subscriptions:** 50 journals and other serials. **Services:** Library not open to public.

★8873★
NEW BRUNSWICK - DEPARTMENT OF YOUTH, RECREATION & CULTURAL RESOURCES - NEW BRUNSWICK LIBRARY SERVICE (Info Sci)†
P.O. Box 6000   Phone: (506) 453-2928
Fredericton, NB, Canada E3B 5H1   Rino Levesque
Staff: Prof 4; Other 10. **Subjects:** Library science, bibliography. **Holdings:** Figures not available. **Services:** Interlibrary loans; library not open to public.

Computerized Information Services: Computerized cataloging. **Special Catalogs:** Union catalog of public library holdings in the province. **Remarks:** Acts as a central cataloging office and clearinghouse for New Brunswick public libraries. Library is located at York Tower, King's Place, Fredericton, NB.

★8874★
NEW BRUNSWICK ELECTRIC POWER COMMISSION - REFERENCE CENTER (Sci-Tech; Energy)
527 King St.
P.O. Box 2000   Phone: (506) 453-4353
Fredericton, NB, Canada E3B 4X1   Aileen W. Humes, Libn.
Founded: 1965. **Staff:** 1. **Subjects:** Engineering, accounting, management, psychology, law, economics, energy. **Holdings:** 6400 books; 70 bound periodical volumes. **Subscriptions:** 447 journals and other serials; 43 newspapers. **Services:** Interlibrary loans; library open to public. **Also Known As:** Commission d'Energie Electrique du Nouveau Brunswick.

★8875★
NEW BRUNSWICK - LEGISLATIVE LIBRARY (Info Sci)†
Legislative Bldg.
P.O. Box 6000   Phone: (506) 453-2338
Fredericton, NB, Canada E3B 5H1   Jocelyn LeBel, Dir.
Founded: 1841. **Staff:** Prof 4; Other 3. **Subjects:** Legislative reference, government documents. **Special Collections:** New Brunswickana. **Holdings:** 37,500 volumes. **Subscriptions:** 500 journals and other serials. **Services:** Interlibrary loans; copying; library open to public. **Publications:** New Brunswick Government Documents, a checklist, annual - free upon request. **Staff:** Eric L. Swanick, Doc.Libn.; Richard Anderson, Cat.; Margaret Pacey, Ref. & Ser.Libn.

NEW BRUNSWICK LIBRARY SERVICE
See: New Brunswick - Department of Youth, Recreation & Cultural Resources

★8876★
NEW BRUNSWICK MUSEUM - LIBRARY AND ARCHIVES DEPARTMENT (Art; Hist)
277 Douglas Ave.   Phone: (506) 693-1196
Saint John, NB, Canada E2K 1E5   Carol Rosevear, Hd.
Founded: 1842. **Staff:** Prof 2; Other 4. **Subjects:** Fine arts, New Brunswick history, shipping, natural science, genealogy. **Special Collections:** Ganong Library (1000 volumes); Webster Canadiana Collection (10,000 volumes). **Holdings:** 55,000 books and bound periodical volumes; 200 linear meters of manuscripts; 3000 maps; 2000 reels of microfilm. **Subscriptions:** 200 journals and other serials. **Services:** Interlibrary loans (limited); copying; library and archives open to public.

★8877★
NEW BRUNSWICK - PROVINCIAL ARCHIVES OF NEW BRUNSWICK (Hist)†
Box 6000   Phone: (506) 453-2637
Fredericton, NB, Canada E3B 5H1   Marion Beyea, Prov.Archv.
Founded: 1968. **Staff:** Prof 10; Other 14. **Subjects:** Government, lumbering, business, judiciary, genealogy. **Holdings:** 13,500 cubic feet of government records and private manuscripts in the Historical Division; 25,000 cubic feet of government records in the Records Center; 25,000 photographs; 25,000 maps; 125,000 plans and architectural drawings. **Services:** Interlibrary loans; copying; archives open to public. **Staff:** Burton Glendenning, Coord., Hist.Div.; F.U. Le Blanc, Hd., Rec.Mgt.Div.; Harold Holland, Hd., Consrv.Div.; Mark Fallon, Hd., Microfilm Div.

★8878★
NEW BRUNSWICK RESEARCH AND PRODUCTIVITY COUNCIL - LIBRARY (Sci-Tech; Energy)†
P.O. Box 6000   Phone: (506) 455-8994
Fredericton, NB, Canada E3B 5H1   April L. James
Founded: 1965. **Staff:** 1. **Subjects:** Management and business administration, geology and mineralogy, food science, mechanical engineering, chemistry, metallurgy, nondestructive testing, energy conservation. **Holdings:** 8000 books; 3200 bound periodical volumes; 25 VF drawers of government documents; 70 reels of microfilm; 2000 microfiche; 4 VF drawers of trade publications; 750 journal titles with back issues. **Subscriptions:** 295 journals and other serials; 7 newspapers. **Services:** Interlibrary loans; copying; library open to public with restrictions. **Computerized Information Services:** SDC. **Special Catalogs:** Library Serials Holdings (book).

★8879★

NEW BRUNSWICK TELEPHONE COMPANY, LTD. - EDUCATIONAL LIBRARY (Bus-Fin)
One Brunswick Sq.
Box 1430
Saint John, NB, Canada E2L 4K2   Phone: (506) 693-6845
Patricia J. Blenkhorn, Libn.
Staff: 1. **Subjects:** Business, telephony, history. **Special Collections:** Senator Frank Bunting Black Memorial Collection (New Brunswick history; 200 rare books). **Holdings:** 5500 books. **Subscriptions:** 220 journals and other serials; 27 newspapers. **Services:** Library not open to public. **Remarks:** Company also maintains an Historical Museum, open to the public on request, which holds all telephone directories for the company since its incorporation, as well as magazine articles pertaining to the company.

★8880★

NEW BRUNSWICK THEOLOGICAL SEMINARY - GARDNER A. SAGE LIBRARY (Rel-Theol)
21 Seminary Pl.   Phone: (201) 247-5243
New Brunswick, NJ 08901   D. LeRoy Engelhardt, Libn.
Founded: 1784. **Staff:** Prof 2; Other 2. **Subjects:** Theology, church history, Biblical studies, classics. **Special Collections:** Vedder Art Collection; Dutch Church Collection; archives of Reformed Church in America; Leiby Collection. **Holdings:** 135,691 books and bound periodical volumes. **Subscriptions:** 346 journals and other serials. **Services:** Interlibrary loans; copying; library open to public with permission of librarian. **Staff:** Lynn Fetherston, Tech.Serv.; Carol Kinsey, Circ./ILL.

★8881★

NEW CANAAN HISTORICAL SOCIETY - LIBRARY (Hist)
13 Oenoke Ridge   Phone: (203) 966-1776
New Canaan, CT 06840   Mary C. Durbrow, Libn.
Founded: 1889. **Staff:** 1. **Subjects:** History of New Canaan, Fairfield County, and Connecticut; genealogy. **Special Collections:** Noyes Papers, 1750-1900 (10,000 cataloged items); Silliman Papers, 1792-1972 (750 cataloged items); Hoyt Papers, 1823-1971. **Holdings:** 4000 books; 300 bound periodical volumes; local newspapers, 1868 to present, on microfilm; 4000 biography cards; 852 manuscripts. **Subscriptions:** 31 journals and other serials. **Services:** Copying; library open to public for reference use only. **Networks/Consortia:** Member of Southwestern Connecticut Library Council. **Publications:** Annuals, 1943 to present; Portrait of New Canaan, the History of a Connecticut Town. **Special Indexes:** Subject index to local newspapers (card); file of names New Canaan early settlers and later residents (card). **Staff:** David Evans, Chm., Lib.Comm.

★8882★

NEW CASTLE COUNTY LAW LIBRARY (Law)
Public Bldg./Courthouse   Phone: (302) 571-2437
Wilmington, DE 19801   Rene Yucht, Hd.Libn.
Staff: Prof 1. **Subjects:** Law. **Holdings:** 30,000 books and bound periodical volumes. **Subscriptions:** 35 journals and other serials. **Services:** Copying; library open to public.

★8883★

NEW CASTLE PUBLIC LIBRARY - PENNSYLVANIA HISTORY ROOM (Hist)
207 E. North St.   Phone: (412) 658-6659
New Castle, PA 16101   Helen M. Roux, Dir.
Subjects: Pennsylvania history and genealogy. **Special Collections:** Pennsylvania census 1790 through 1910 on microfilm. **Holdings:** 6763 volumes. **Services:** Interlibrary loans; copying; library open to public with identification. **Computerized Information Services:** Computerized cataloging. **Networks/Consortia:** Member of OCLC.

★8884★

NEW CASTLE STATE HOSPITAL - MEDICAL LIBRARY (Med)
100 Van Nuys Rd.
Box 34
New Castle, IN 47362   Phone: (317) 529-0900
Jann Swinford, Media Dir.
Staff: 1. **Subjects:** Psychiatry, neurology, general medicine, physiology, nursing. **Holdings:** 600 books. **Subscriptions:** 25 journals and other serials. **Services:** Library open to public for reference use only.

NEW CHURCH THEOLOGICAL SCHOOL
See: Swedenborg School of Religion

★8885★

NEW ENGLAND AQUARIUM - LIBRARY (Sci-Tech)
Central Wharf   Phone: (617) 742-8830
Boston, MA 02110   Marilyn Murphy, Libn.
Staff: Prof 1. **Subjects:** Marine sciences, ecology, oceanography, limnology

(K-college levels). **Holdings:** 1500 books. **Subscriptions:** 200 journals and other serials. **Services:** Library open to public with permission.

★8886★

NEW ENGLAND BAPTIST HOSPITAL - HELENE FULD LIBRARY (Med)
220 Fisher Ave.   Phone: (617) 738-5800
Boston, MA 02120   Elizabeth Guiu, Libn.
Founded: 1931. **Staff:** Prof 1. **Subjects:** History of nursing, education, science. **Holdings:** 5800 books. **Subscriptions:** 69 journals and other serials. **Services:** Interlibrary loans; library not open to public. **Networks/Consortia:** Member of Libraries for Nursing Consortium (LINC). **Formerly:** Its School of Nursing Library.

★8887★

NEW ENGLAND BAPTIST HOSPITAL - MEDICAL STAFF LIBRARY (Med)
91 Parker Hill Ave.   Phone: (617) 738-5800
Boston, MA 02120   Dr. Paul E. Woodard, Chf.Libn.
Founded: 1963. **Staff:** Prof 1; Other 1. **Subjects:** Medicine, orthopedics, and history of medicine. **Special Collections:** M.N. Smith - Peterson Collection (48 volumes on orthopedics and the history of medicine). **Holdings:** 500 books; 2000 bound periodical volumes; 100 other cataloged items. **Subscriptions:** 70 journals and other serials. **Services:** Interlibrary loans; library open to medical librarians and visiting doctors only. **Networks/Consortia:** Member of Boston Biomedical Library Consortium; New England Regional Medical Library Service.

★8888★

NEW ENGLAND BOARD OF HIGHER EDUCATION - LIBRARY (Educ)
School St.   Phone: (617) 468-7341
Wenham, MA 01984   Elizabeth Craig, Libn./Archv.
Staff: Prof 1. **Subjects:** Higher education, New England economy. **Holdings:** 500 volumes. **Subscriptions:** 70 journals and other serials. **Services:** Interlibrary loans; library open to public with restrictions. **Networks/Consortia:** Member of Merrimack Interlibrary Cooperative.

★8889★

NEW ENGLAND COLLEGE OF OPTOMETRY - LIBRARY (Med)
420 Beacon St.   Phone: (617) 266-2030
Boston, MA 02115   F. Eleanor Warner, Hd.Libn.
Founded: 1894. **Staff:** Prof 3; Other 3. **Subjects:** Optometry, ophthalmology. **Holdings:** 6500 books; 2431 bound periodical volumes; 4 VF drawers of pamphlets; 6 VF drawers of reprints; 65 35mm color slides; 100 microforms; 346 audiotape cassettes; 71 video cassettes; 72 slide/tape units; 16 slide sets; 4 motion pictures; 15 realia. **Subscriptions:** 273 journals and other serials. **Services:** Interlibrary loans; copying; SDI to faculty members; library open to public with restrictions. **Computerized Information Services:** DIALOG. **Publications:** Acquisitions List, irregular - distributed within college and to other optometry libraries. **Staff:** Elizabeth Andrews, Asst.Libn.; Mary Steigner, Evening Supv.

★8890★

NEW ENGLAND CONSERVATORY OF MUSIC - HARRIET M. SPAULDING LIBRARY (Mus)
33 Gainsborough St.   Phone: (617) 262-1120
Boston, MA 02115   Geraldine Ostrove, Dir.
Founded: 1959. **Staff:** Prof 4; Other 4. **Subjects:** Music and music literature, acoustics, humanities and social sciences. **Special Collections:** Americana (music, manuscripts, Boston Classicists, letters, memorabilia, 18th century psalmody); Preston Collection of letters of great musicians; Elise Hall Collection of French music manuscripts; A.G. Morse Collection of opera piano scores; Voice of Firestone kinescopes and performance materials. **Holdings:** 46,000 books; 13,500 sound recordings; 240 theses; 200 reels of microfilm; publications and documents on Boston musical life and history of the conservatory. **Subscriptions:** 280 journals and other serials. **Services:** Interlibrary loans; copying; library open to public for reference use. **Publications:** Recently Cataloged, quarterly; reproduction of typescript. **Networks/Consortia:** Member of Fenway Library Consortium. **Remarks:** The Idabelle Firestone Audio Library is located at 290 Huntington Ave., Boston, MA 02115. **Staff:** Jean Morrow, Libn.; Mary Ellen Sweeney, Hd. of Circ.; Kenneth Pristash, Audio Libn.

★8891★

NEW ENGLAND DEACONESS HOSPITAL - HORRAX LIBRARY (Med)†
185 Pilgrim Rd.   Phone: (617) 732-8311
Boston, MA 02215   Paul Vaiginas, Libn.
Founded: 1959. **Staff:** Prof 1; Other 3. **Subjects:** General medicine, diabetes, cancer, renal disease, cardiology, surgery. **Special Collections:** Horrax Collection on Neurosurgery (212 books). **Holdings:** 3300 books; 3500 bound periodical volumes; 850 audio cassettes. **Subscriptions:** 252 journals

and other serials. **Services:** Interlibrary loans; library open with permission. **Networks/Consortia:** Member of Boston Biomedical Library Consortium.

★8892★

NEW ENGLAND DEPOSIT LIBRARY, INC. (Info Sci)
135 Western Ave.   Phone: (617) 782-8441
Allston, MA 02134   Edward J. Sweny, Libn.
Founded: 1942. **Staff:** Prof 1; Other 3. **Holdings:** Figures not available. **Services:** Library open to public with permission. **Remarks:** This is a depository for research and reference materials from 12 contributing libraries in the greater Boston area.

★8893★

NEW ENGLAND FIRE & HISTORY MUSEUM - LIBRARY AND ARCHIVE (Hist)
1439 Main St., Rte. 6A   Phone: (617) 896-5711
Brewster, MA 02631   Helen Berrien, Libn.
Founded: 1973. **Staff:** Prof 1; Other 1. **Subjects:** Fire history, fire insurance history, blacksmithing. **Special Collections:** Principles of Fire Rating & Analysis of Risks (25 volumes). **Holdings:** 600 books; 100 bound periodical volumes; 100 booklets and newspapers. **Services:** Interlibrary loans; library open to public by appointment.

★8894★

NEW ENGLAND GOVERNORS CONFERENCE - REFERENCE LIBRARY (Energy; Bus-Fin)
156 State St., 4th Fl.   Phone: (617) 720-4606
Boston, MA 02109   Shirley M. Raynard, Ref.Libn.
Staff: Prof 1; Other 2. **Subjects:** Energy, transportation, economic development, hazardous waste, tourism. **Special Collections:** New England Regional Commission reports (2000); New England River Basins Commission reports (complete set). **Holdings:** 10,000 volumes; 100 bound periodical volumes. **Subscriptions:** 28 journals and other serials. **Services:** Interlibrary loans; copying; library open to public for reference use only. **Formerly:** New England Regional Commission (NERCOM).

★8895★

NEW ENGLAND HISTORIC GENEALOGICAL SOCIETY - LIBRARY (Hist)
101 Newbury St.   Phone: (617) 536-5740
Boston, MA 02116   Dr. Ralph J. Crandall, Dir./Ed.
Founded: 1845. **Staff:** 16. **Subjects:** Genealogy and family history, local history, vital records, heraldry. **Special Collections:** New England family and local histories. **Holdings:** 150,000 books and bound periodical volumes; 1200 reels of microfilm; 3500 linear feet of manuscripts; city directories; biographies; diaries; regimental histories; church histories. **Subscriptions:** 420 periodicals. **Services:** Copying; lectures and seminars; library open to public with restrictions (daily fee charged). **Publications:** New England Historical and Genealogical Register, quarterly; Newsletter, quarterly; monographs. **Staff:** David C. Dearborn, Ref.Libn.; Gary B. Roberts, Res.Libn.; Nathaniel S. Shipton, Cur. of Mss.; James C. Agnew, Tech.Serv.

★8896★

NEW ENGLAND INSTITUTE - LIBRARY (Sci-Tech)†
90 Grove St.
Box 308
Norwalk, CT 06877   Phone: (203) 762-7369
    M. Vaccaro, Asst.Libn.
Founded: 1954. **Staff:** 1. **Subjects:** Biology, medicine, physics, chemistry, genetics, biochemistry. **Holdings:** 4000 books. **Subscriptions:** 140 journals and other serials. **Services:** Interlibrary loans; copying; library open to public by appointment only.

NEW ENGLAND MERCHANTS NATIONAL BANK
See: Bank of New England

★8897★

NEW ENGLAND MUTUAL LIFE INSURANCE COMPANY - BUSINESS LIBRARY (Bus-Fin)
501 Boylston St.   Phone: (617) 578-2306
Boston, MA 02117   Agnes Brite, Libn.
Founded: 1935. **Staff:** Prof 2; Other 7. **Subjects:** Life insurance, employee benefit plans, financial products, statistics, economics, marketing. **Holdings:** 8200 books; 150 VF drawers of pamphlets and reports. **Subscriptions:** 550 journals and other serials. **Services:** Interlibrary loans; library not open to public. **Computerized Information Services:** DIALOG, New York Times Information Service; computerized acquisitions, circulation and periodical receipt record. **Publications:** Selected Readings, weekly - for internal distribution only. **Special Catalogs:** Data from Selected Readings. **Staff:** Joann Huddleston, Asst.Libn.; Jean Poldoian, Supv.

★8898★

NEW ENGLAND NUCLEAR CORPORATION - TECHNICAL LIBRARY (Sci-Tech)
549 Albany St.   Phone: (617) 482-9595
Boston, MA 02118   Pauline R. Leeds, Libn.
Founded: 1964. **Staff:** Prof 2; Other 3. **Subjects:** Chemistry, nuclear medicine, pharmacology, metallurgy. **Holdings:** 11,500 books; 10,000 bound periodical volumes; 2500 reports (cataloged). **Subscriptions:** 310 journals and other serials. **Services:** Interlibrary loans; copying; library open to public by appointment. **Computerized Information Services:** DIALOG, SDC. **Staff:** Margaret Hanson, ILL Libn.

★8899★

NEW ENGLAND POWER COMPANY - TECHNICAL INFORMATION CENTER (Sci-Tech; Energy)
25 Research Dr.   Phone: (617) 366-9011
Westborough, MA 01581   William J. McCall, Sr.Tech.Libn.
Founded: 1947. **Staff:** Prof 1; Other 1. **Subjects:** Engineering, environmental sciences, alternative energy sources, management, economics. **Special Collections:** Alternative energy forms - biomass, hydro, solar, wind. **Holdings:** 4000 books; 10,000 technical reports (cataloged); 50 VF drawers; 35,000 microfiche. **Subscriptions:** 300 journals and other serials; 6 newspapers. **Services:** Interlibrary loans; copying (limited); SDI; center open to public by appointment. **Computerized Information Services:** DIALOG; computerized cataloging, serials and circulation. **Special Indexes:** KWIC index of all cataloged items (card).

NEW ENGLAND REGIONAL COMMISSION
See: New England Governors Conference

NEW ENGLAND REGIONAL PRIMATE RESEARCH CENTER
See: Harvard University

★8900★

NEW ENGLAND SCHOOL OF LAW - LIBRARY (Law)
154 Stuart St.   Phone: (617) 451-0010
Boston, MA 02116   Frank S.H. Bae, Law Libn.
Founded: 1908. **Staff:** Prof 5; Other 2. **Subjects:** Law. **Special Collections:** U.S. and Massachusetts legal materials from 17th century to present. **Holdings:** 130,000 books and bound periodical volumes. **Subscriptions:** 2042 journals and other serials. **Services:** Library open to qualified users for reference on request. **Computerized Information Services:** WESTLAW; computerized cataloging. **Publications:** New England School of Law Library Guide. **Staff:** Richard Ducey, Asst.Libn./Rd.Serv.; Phyllis Ansel, Govt.Docs./Circ.Libn.; Anne Acton, Asst.Libn.; Margaret Reiners, Ser. & AV Libn.

★8901★

NEW ENGLAND SOLAR ENERGY ASSOCIATION - LIBRARY (Energy)
14 Green St.
Box 541
Brattleboro, VT 05301   Phone: (802) 254-2386
    Larry Sherwood, Assoc.Dir.
Founded: 1976. **Staff:** 1. **Subjects:** Solar energy. **Holdings:** Figures not available. **Subscriptions:** 30 journals and other serials. **Services:** Copying; library open to public for reference use only. **Publications:** Newsletter, bimonthly - to members.

★8902★

NEW ENGLAND TELEPHONE LEARNING CENTER - RESOURCE CENTER (Bus-Fin)
280 Locke Dr.   Phone: (617) 480-2331
Marlborough, MA 01572   Mark F. Mancevice, Dir., Resource Ctr.
Founded: 1973. **Staff:** Prof 1; Other 5. **Subjects:** Training for management, instructional systems and techniques, management. **Holdings:** 4000 books; 10,000 microfiche; company documents; 8 VF drawers of pamphlets; 400 videotapes and films (cataloged); 60 audiotapes. **Subscriptions:** 200 journals and other serials; 12 newspapers. **Services:** Interlibrary loans; copying; SDI; center open to public by appointment. **Computerized Information Services:** DIALOG, New York Times Information Service. **Publications:** Bibliography series; News Notes; Course Lists - all for internal distribution plus other Bell System libraries.

★8903★

NEW ENGLAND WILD FLOWER SOCIETY, INC. - LAWRENCE NEWCOMB LIBRARY (Sci-Tech)
Hemenway Rd.   Phone: (617) 877-7630
Framingham, MA 01701   Mary M. Walker, Libn.
Staff: Prof 2. **Subjects:** Native plants, botany, natural history, wild flower gardening. **Holdings:** 2500 books; pamphlets; 8 VF drawers; 15,000 slides of Wild Flower Slide Collection. **Subscriptions:** 20 journals and other serials.

Services: Interlibrary loans; copying; SDI; slide set loans and sales; library open to public for reference use only, loans to members only. **Publications:** Wild Flowers Notes and News, 3/year. **Staff:** Iola Scheufele, Cat., Proc.

★8904★

NEW ENGLAND WIRELESS & STEAM MUSEUM, INC. - LIBRARY (Sci-Tech)
697 Tillinghast Rd.   Phone: (401) 884-1710
East Greenwich, RI 02818   Robert W. Merriam, Dir.
Staff: 1. **Subjects:** Wireless, telegraph, early electricity, telephone, steam engineering, gas/hot air engines. **Special Collections:** Lloyd Espensheid collection of textbooks (wireless and telegraph). **Holdings:** Figures not available. **Services:** Library not open to public. **Publications:** 1876-1976 Corliss Centennial folder.

NEW ENGLAND YEARLY MEETING OF FRIENDS
See: Society of Friends

★8905★

NEW HAMPSHIRE ANTIQUARIAN SOCIETY - LIBRARY (Hist)*
Route 1 (Main St. Hopkinton)
Concord, NH 03301   Rachael Johnson, Cur.
Founded: 1875. **Subjects:** New Hampshire - specifically Hopkinton and adjacent towns. **Special Collections:** Music books, 1722-1860; complete file of Hopkinton town reports; New Hampshire registers and almanacs; file of Hopkinton vital records, 1737 to present (6000 cards). **Holdings:** 1400 volumes; deeds, military records, town warrants, early sermons and newspapers, revolutionary diaries, manuscripts. **Services:** Library open to public by special permission from curator.

★8906★

NEW HAMPSHIRE COLLEGE - SHAPIRO LIBRARY (Bus-Fin)
2500 N. River Rd.   Phone: (603) 668-2211
Manchester, NH 03104   Richard Pantano, Dir.
Founded: 1963. **Staff:** Prof 5; Other 1. **Subjects:** Economics, accounting, computer sciences, business management, finance, taxes, marketing and retailing, hotel/resort/tourism, human services, mathematics, fashion merchandising, social sciences. **Special Collections:** Business Teacher Education (800 items); New Hampshiriana (100 volumes); federal and state documents depository (23,000 items). **Holdings:** 63,349 books; 667 bound periodical volumes; 1630 recordings; 500 art slides; 175 prints and posters (cataloged); 3984 reels of microfilm; 6 VF drawers of archives of New Hampshire College; 72,610 microfiche; 245 videotapes and films. **Subscriptions:** 763 journals and other serials; 11 newspapers. **Services:** Interlibrary loans; copying; library open to public. **Networks/Consortia:** Member of New Hampshire College and University Council, Library Policy Committee (NHCUC). **Publications:** Acquisitions list - for internal distribution only and consortium use: standing order list. **Remarks:** All holdings in computerized Union List of Periodicals (NHCUC). **Staff:** Patricia A. Beaton, Ref./Govt.Doc.; Camille Ahern, Ref./Ser.; Deborah Ross, Tech.Serv.Libn.; Karin Caruso, Dir., AV Serv.; John Measell, Asst. AV Dir.; Carol West, Circ., Desk Supv./ILL.

★8907★

NEW HAMPSHIRE GOVERNOR'S COUNCIL ON ENERGY - ENERGY INFORMATION CENTER (Energy)†
2 1/2 Beacon St.   Phone: (603) 271-2711
Concord, NH 03301   Carol Waters, Dir. of Educ.
Founded: 1977. **Staff:** 2. **Subjects:** Energy - data, policy and conservation. **Special Collections:** Solar energy information. **Holdings:** 500 books; 20 binders; reports and manuscripts. **Subscriptions:** 25 journals and other serials. **Services:** Library open to public with prior approval.

★8908★

NEW HAMPSHIRE HISTORICAL SOCIETY - LIBRARY (Hist)
30 Park St.   Phone: (603) 225-3381
Concord, NH 03301   John F. Page, Dir.
Founded: 1823. **Staff:** Prof 3. **Subjects:** New Hampshire history, New England history and genealogy, architecture and decorative arts of New England. **Special Collections:** Eighteenth and nineteenth century account books and diaries; papers of Daniel Webster, Franklin Pierce, General John Sullivan, William E. Chandler, Josiah Bartlett; New Hampshire maps. **Holdings:** 75,000 books and bound periodical volumes; 2000 volumes of early New Hampshire newspapers; 20,000 photographs of New Hampshire towns and people. **Subscriptions:** 150 journals and other serials. **Services:** Interlibrary loans (limited to duplicate copies in the collection); copying; library open to public. **Publications:** Historical New Hampshire, quarterly; Newsletter, quarterly. **Special Catalogs:** Manuscript catalog; genealogy index; New Hampshire Notables card index. **Staff:** William Copeley, Assoc.Libn.; Katherine Morrill, Asst.Libn.; R. Stuart Wallace, Mss.Libn.

★8909★

NEW HAMPSHIRE HOSPITAL - MAC KOWN LIBRARY (Med)†
105 Pleasant St.   Phone: (603) 224-6531
Concord, NH 03301   Marion Pierce, Prof. Staff Libn.
Founded: 1880. **Staff:** Prof 1; Other 1. **Subjects:** Psychiatry, psychology and allied health fields. **Holdings:** 1400 books; 1000 bound periodical volumes; reports of the hospital to the Governor and Council (1843-1956). **Subscriptions:** 135 journals and other serials. **Services:** Interlibrary loans; copying; library open to public. **Computerized Information Services:** MEDLINE, National Clearinghouse for Mental Health Information (NCMHI). **Networks/Consortia:** Member of Hospital Library Development Service (HLDS); New England Regional Medical Library Service (NERMLS).

★8910★

NEW HAMPSHIRE HOSPITAL - SCHOOL OF NURSING REFERENCE LIBRARY
105 Pleasant St.
Concord, NH 03301
Defunct

★8911★

NEW HAMPSHIRE MUNICIPAL ASSOCIATION - LIBRARY (Soc Sci)†
Box 617   Phone: (603) 224-7447
Concord, NH 03301   John B. Andrews, Exec.Dir.
Subjects: Local and state government. **Holdings:** 400 volumes. **Subscriptions:** 52 journals and other serials. **Services:** Library open to public.

★8912★

NEW HAMPSHIRE PUBLIC UTILITIES COMMISSION - LIBRARY (Energy)
8010 Suncook Rd.   Phone: (603) 271-2452
Concord, NH 03301   Paula Lebrocoguy, Rec.Ck.
Founded: 1980. **Staff:** Prof 1. **Subjects:** Energy - policies, resources, research and development. **Special Collections:** Electric Power Research Institute Rate Design Study. **Holdings:** 1000 books; 350 bound periodical volumes; 300 Interstate Commerce Commission reports; U.S. Nuclear Regulatory Commission releases and rulings; New Hampshire Supreme Court decisions. **Subscriptions:** 30 journals and other serials; 7 newspapers. **Services:** Interlibrary loans; copying; library open to public with restrictions.

★8913★

NEW HAMPSHIRE STATE DEPARTMENT OF EDUCATION - EDUCATIONAL INFORMATION OFFICE AND LIBRARY (Educ)
State House Annex, Rm. 410P   Phone: (603) 271-2778
Concord, NH 03301   Bruce G. Ryan, Asst.Chf.
Staff: 1. **Subjects:** New Hampshire education and comparative education statistics. **Holdings:** 3500 bound volumes; Federal and compiled state reports; microfiche. **Services:** Copying; library open to public. **Publications:** Annual statistics of New Hampshire Public Schools.

★8914★

NEW HAMPSHIRE STATE DEPARTMENT OF HEALTH & WELFARE - OFFICE OF ALCOHOL & DRUG ABUSE PREVENTION - LIBRARY (Med)
Health & Welfare Bldg.
Hazen Dr.   Phone: (603) 271-4630
Concord, NH 03301   Barry Rhodes, Dp.Dir.
Founded: 1966. **Staff:** Prof 1; Other 1. **Subjects:** Alcohol and drug abuse, medical research, statistical research, psychology, sociology, criminal justice. **Special Collections:** Classified Abstract Archive of the Alcohol Literature (maintained by the Quarterly Journal of Studies on Alcohol). **Holdings:** 1500 books; 400 bound periodical volumes; 6 VF drawers of unpublished research; 500 documents on microfiche. **Services:** Library open to public with restrictions.

★8915★

NEW HAMPSHIRE STATE DEPARTMENT OF PUBLIC WORKS AND HIGHWAYS - LIBRARY (Sci-Tech)
State Office Bldg.
Box 483   Phone: (603) 271-2515
Concord, NH 03301-0483   William L. Rollins, Pub.Info.
Staff: 1. **Subjects:** Civil engineering, highway research, traffic engineering. **Holdings:** Figures not available. **Services:** Library open to public.

★8916★

NEW HAMPSHIRE STATE DEPARTMENT OF STATE - DIVISION OF RECORDS MANAGEMENT & ARCHIVES (Hist)
71 S. Fruit St.   Phone: (603) 271-2236
Concord, NH 03301   Frank C. Mevers, Archv./Dir.
Staff: Prof 2. **Subjects:** State and county archives. **Services:** Copying; archives open to public for reference use. **Staff:** Andrew S. Taylor, Rec.Mgr.

★8917★

NEW HAMPSHIRE STATE DIVISION OF FORESTS AND LANDS - FOX FOREST LIBRARY (Sci-Tech)
Fox State Forest
Hillsboro, NH 03244
Phone: (603) 464-3453
J.B. Cullen, Chf., Forest Info. & Plan
Founded: 1933. **Staff:** Prof 1. **Subjects:** Forestry, entomology, fire, ecology. **Special Collections:** Herbarium. **Holdings:** Figures not available. **Subscriptions:** 5 journals and other serials. **Services:** Library not open to public. **Publications:** Fox Forest Notes, Fox Forest Bulletins, both occasional.

★8918★

NEW HAMPSHIRE STATE FISH AND GAME DEPARTMENT - MANAGEMENT AND RESEARCH DIVISION - LIBRARY (Sci-Tech)
Phone: (603) 271-2462
Concord, NH 03301
Founded: 1938. **Staff:** 2. **Subjects:** Wildlife management, ornithology, mammalogy, ecology, zoology. **Holdings:** 625 books; 150 bound periodical volumes; 9800 reprints and reports. **Subscriptions:** 17 journals and other serials. **Services:** Interlibrary loans; library open to public for reference use only. **Special Indexes:** Index to reprints and reports in computer printout form. **Staff:** Howard C. Nowell, Jr., Div.Chf.

★8919★

NEW HAMPSHIRE STATE LIBRARY (Hist)
20 Park St.
Concord, NH 03301
Phone: (603) 271-2392
Shirley G. Adamovich, State Libn.
Staff: Prof 18; Other 31. **Subjects:** History, government documents, political science, law. **Special Collections:** New Hampshire history and genealogy. **Holdings:** 624,897 books; 16,011 manuscripts; 5271 music scores; 10,096 reels of microfilm; 71,770 microcards; 27,316 microfiche; 653 motion pictures; 701 recordings. **Subscriptions:** 850 journals and other serials; 35 newspapers. **Services:** Interlibrary loans; copying; library open to public. **Computerized Information Services:** DIALOG; internal database; computerized cataloging and serials. **Networks/Consortia:** Member of New Hampshire College and University Council, Library Policy Committee (NHCUC); OCLC through NELINET; New England Library Board (NELB).

★8920★

NEW HAMPSHIRE STATE LIBRARY - DIVISION OF LAW AND LEGISLATIVE REFERENCE SERVICE (Law)
Supreme Court Bldg.
Loudon Rd.
Concord, NH 03301
Phone: (603) 271-3777
Constance T. Rinden, Law Libn.
Staff: Prof 3; Other 2. **Subjects:** Law, legislative reference. **Holdings:** 81,000 books and bound periodicals; 350 boxes of pamphlets; 10 VF drawers of reports and clippings. **Subscriptions:** 105 journals and other serials. **Services:** Copying; division open to public. **Staff:** Norma Jane Lyman, Asst. Law Libn.; Mrs. Pat Busselle, Leg.Ref.Libn.

★8921★

NEW HAMPSHIRE STATE WATER SUPPLY AND POLLUTION CONTROL COMMISSION - LIBRARY (Env-Cons)
Health and Welfare Bldg., Hazen Dr.
Box 95
Concord, NH 03301
Phone: (603) 271-3503
Terrence P. Frost
Subjects: Water - pollution, biology and quality; industrial wastes, waste treatment, lakes, New Hampshire, pesticides, chemistry. **Special Collections:** Water Pollution Control Research Series (316 issues). **Holdings:** 2500 books; 271 bound periodical volumes; pamphlets. **Services:** Interlibrary loans; copying (limited); library open to public. **Publications:** Library Manual. **Special Indexes:** Index to journal articles.

★8922★

NEW HAMPSHIRE VOCATIONAL-TECHNICAL COLLEGE - LIBRARY (Sci-Tech)
Hanover St. Extension
Claremont, NH 03743
Phone: (603) 542-7744
Phil Prever, Libn.
Founded: 1968. **Staff:** Prof 1; Other 1. **Subjects:** Technology, basic health sciences. **Special Collections:** New Hampshire history (146 volumes). **Holdings:** 9000 books; filmloops, filmstrips, records, cassettes. **Subscriptions:** 85 journals and other serials; 10 newspapers. **Services:** Interlibrary loans; library open to public with restrictions.

★8923★

NEW HAMPSHIRE VOCATIONAL-TECHNICAL COLLEGE - LIBRARY (Sci-Tech)
Prescott Hill
Laconia, NH 03246
Phone: (603) 524-8084
Patty Miller, Libn.
Founded: 1968. **Staff:** Prof 1. **Subjects:** Drafting, industrial electricity,

industrial electronics, graphic arts, fire protection, internal combustion engines, secretarial science, residential electricity. **Holdings:** 8383 books; 250 cassettes; 131 filmloops; 10 16mm films; 154 filmstrips; 899 microfiche; 152 reels of microfilm; 147 overhead transparencies; 6 phonograph records; 4120 slides. **Subscriptions:** 79 journals and other serials; 6 newspapers. **Services:** Interlibrary loans; copying; library open to public.

★8924★

NEW HAMPSHIRE VOCATIONAL-TECHNICAL COLLEGE - LIBRARY (Sci-Tech)†
505 Amherst St.
Nashua, NH 03063
Phone: (603) 882-6923
William A. McIntyre, Libn.
Staff: Prof 1. **Subjects:** Business, electronics, machine tools, secretarial studies, police science, automotive technology. **Holdings:** 7500 books. **Subscriptions:** 125 journals and other serials. **Services:** Library open to public.

★8925★

NEW HAMPSHIRE VOCATIONAL-TECHNICAL COLLEGE - LIBRARY (Med; Sci-Tech)
277R Portsmouth Ave.
Stratham, NH 03885
Nancy L. Dodge, Libn.
Founded: 1970. **Staff:** Prof 1. **Subjects:** Nursing, applied sciences. **Holdings:** 8500 books; 9600 microfiche. **Subscriptions:** 90 journals and other serials. **Services:** Interlibrary loans; copying; library open to public with restrictions.

NEW HAMPSHIRE WATER RESOURCE RESEARCH CENTER
See: University of New Hampshire

★8926★

NEW HARMONY WORKINGMEN'S INSTITUTE - LIBRARY AND MUSEUM (Hist)
407 W. Tavern St.
Box 368
New Harmony, IN 47631
Phone: (812) 682-4806
Mary Aline Cook, Libn.
Founded: 1838. **Subjects:** Owen Community and history of New Harmony, Indiana. **Special Collections:** Manuscript Collection, 1814-1940. **Holdings:** 20,000 books. **Services:** Archives open to researchers with restrictions and by appointment. **Staff:** Rosemary Alsop, Asst.Libn.

★8927★

NEW HAVEN COLONY HISTORICAL SOCIETY - LIBRARY (Hist)
114 Whitney Ave.
New Haven, CT 06510
Phone: (203) 562-4183
Ottilia Koel, Libn. & Cur. of Mss.
Founded: 1862. **Staff:** Prof 5. **Subjects:** Local history and genealogy. **Special Collections:** Dana Scrapbooks of New Haven (150 volumes). **Holdings:** 25,000 books and bound periodical volumes; 500 maps (cataloged); processed manuscript collection including New Haven County Superior Court documents (1789-1905); New Haven Clock Company papers (1853-1946); New Haven Water Company papers (1820-1895); United Church papers (1742-1970); Woman's Seamen's Friend Society of Connecticut records (1859-1968); papers of the Ingersoll, Morris & Twining families; New Haven City & Co. Documents (1648-1900); New Haven City records (1794-present); New Haven Board of Education records (1799-1970); School records (1715-1963); New Haven YWCA records (1880 to present); Maritime Collection (1721-1887); Harbor Collection (1750-1925); Military Collection (1737-1945); Civil War Collection (1861-1931); family papers; corporate records; national and historic figures A-Z (1638-1976). **Services:** Copying; library open to adults for research only. **Publications:** Monthly report to membership in News & Notes. **Special Indexes:** Finding aids to manuscript collection. **Staff:** Ruth Knowlton, Cat.; Anne Willard, Archv.; William A. Wiedersheim, Archv.; Lysbeth Andrews-Zike, Ref.Libn.

NEW HAVEN COUNTY LAW LIBRARY
See: Connecticut State Library - Law Library at New Haven

★8928★

NEW JERSEY EDUCATION ASSOCIATION - RESEARCH LIBRARY (Educ)
180 W. State St.
Box 1211
Trenton, NJ 08607
Phone: (609) 599-4561
E. Lynne Van Buskirk, Assoc.Dir.
Staff: Prof 1; Other 1. **Subjects:** New Jersey education including statistics and school law; school finance, teacher negotiations, collective bargaining. **Special Collections:** George H. Reavis Reading Area (complete set of Phi Delta Kappa materials); **Holdings:** 1000 books; National Education Association publications; 60 VF drawers of pamphlets; NJEA research bulletins and circulars; 512 New Jersey school contracts. **Subscriptions:** 250 journals

and other serials. **Services:** Interlibrary loans (limited); copying; library open to public. **Publications:** Index to the NJEA Review (book); Subject Index to New Jersey Commissioner of Education Decisions (loose-leaf notebook).

★8929★

NEW JERSEY GEOLOGICAL SURVEY - INFORMATION CENTER (Env-Cons)
CN 029   Phone: (609) 292-2576
Trenton, NJ 08625   Ian R. Walker, Adm.
Subjects: Geology, topography, ground water, geodetic control, mineral resources, fossils. **Holdings:** Geologic reports and open report files; survey publications since 1835. **Services:** Center open to public under staff supervision. **Formerly:** New Jersey State Department of Environmental Protection - Geological Survey.

★8930★

NEW JERSEY HISTORICAL SOCIETY - LIBRARY (Hist)
230 Broadway   Phone: (201) 483-3939
Newark, NJ 07104   Barbara Smith Irwin, Lib.Dir.
Founded: 1845. **Staff:** Prof 5; Other 2. **Subjects:** New Jersey history, genealogy of New Jersey and neighboring states. **Holdings:** 60,000 books; 3000 bound periodical volumes; 1100 manuscript groups. **Subscriptions:** 150 journals and other serials. **Services:** Copying; library open to public for reference use only. **Special Indexes:** Guide to Manuscript Collections of the New Jersey Historical Society, 1979 (book). **Staff:** Kathleen Stavec, Ref.Libn.; Carl Lane, Keeper of Mss.; Cynthia E. Browne, Cat.; Janet W. Koch, Conservator.

★8931★

NEW JERSEY INSTITUTE OF TECHNOLOGY - ROBERT W. VAN HOUTEN LIBRARY (Sci-Tech)
323 High St.   Phone: (201) 645-5306
Newark, NJ 07102   Morton Snowhite, Libn.
Founded: 1881. **Staff:** Prof 7; Other 9. **Subjects:** Engineering, physical sciences, management, architecture. **Holdings:** 103,000 books; 26,000 bound periodical volumes; 3200 reels of microfilm. **Subscriptions:** 1900 journals and other serials; 7 newspapers. **Services:** Interlibrary loans; copying; library open to public. **Computerized Information Services:** DIALOG. **Networks/Consortia:** Member of OCLC through PALINET & Union Library Catalogue of Pennsylvania. **Publications:** List of periodicals, annual. **Special Catalogs:** Catalog of dissertations and theses. **Staff:** Christine Zembicki, Ref.Dept.Hd.; Mari M. Linnamaa, Cat.Dept.Hd.; Charles F. Healey, Asst.Libn.; Janet Samet, Per.Libn.; Michele Reid, Circ.Libn.; Diana Skierski, Ref./Cat.

★8932★

NEW JERSEY NEURO-PSYCHIATRIC INSTITUTE - PROFESSIONAL LIBRARY (Med)
Box 1000   Phone: (609) 466-0400
Princeton, NJ 08540   Donald W. Biggs, Sr.Libn.
Founded: 1955. **Staff:** Prof 1. **Subjects:** Psychiatry, psychology, neurology, mental retardation, medicine. **Holdings:** 9000 books; 3000 bound periodical volumes. **Subscriptions:** 55 journals and other serials. **Services:** Interlibrary loans; copying; library open to specialists in library's fields of interest. **Networks/Consortia:** Member of Library of the College of Physicians of Philadelphia; Central Jersey Health Science Libraries Association. **Special Catalogs:** National Library of Medicine Classification.

★8933★

NEW JERSEY OPTOMETRIC ASSOCIATION - DR. E.C. NUROCK LIBRARY (Med)†
684 Whitehead Rd.   Phone: (609) 695-3456
Trenton, NJ 08648   David L. Knowlton, Exec.Dir.
Founded: 1970. **Staff:** Prof 2; Other 3. **Subjects:** Optometry, ophthalmology, health services. **Holdings:** 365 books; American Optometric Association reports; 200 pamphlets; 10 cassette tapes. **Services:** Library open to public.

★8934★

NEW JERSEY SCHOOL OF OSTEOPATHIC MEDICINE - DR. JERROLD S. SCHWARTZ MEMORIAL LIBRARY (Med)
John F. Kennedy Memorial Hospital
18 E. Laurel Rd.   Phone: (609) 784-4000
Stratford, NJ 08084   Judith Schuback, Med.Libn. & Lib.Coord.
Staff: Prof 2; Other 2. **Subjects:** Clinical medicine, nursing, hospital administration, allied health. **Holdings:** 2000 books; 5000 bound periodical volumes; 200 in-house produced videotapes; 250 government documents; 2 vertical files; 100 reels of microfilm. **Subscriptions:** 400 journals and other serials. **Services:** Interlibrary loans; copying; SDI; library open to public by appointment. **Computerized Information Services:** MEDLINE. **Networks/Consortia:** Member of Southwest New Jersey Consortia for Health

Information Services. **Publications:** Selected Acquisitions, quarterly - for internal distribution only. **Staff:** Carol Eisenbaum, Asst.Libn.

NEW JERSEY STATE DATA CENTER - CUMBERLAND COUNTY PLANNING BOARD
See: Cumberland County Planning Board

NEW JERSEY STATE DEPARTMENT OF EDUCATION - DIVISION OF THE STATE LIBRARY, ARCHIVES AND HISTORY
See: New Jersey State Library

★8935★

NEW JERSEY STATE DEPARTMENT OF ENVIRONMENTAL PROTECTION - DIVISION OF WATER RESOURCES - LIBRARY (Env-Cons)
1474 Prospect St.
Box CN029   Phone: (609) 292-5519
Trenton, NJ 08625   Angelo R. Papa, Lib.Techn.
Founded: 1974. **Staff:** 1. **Subjects:** Water pollution; water and wastewater treatment; water law and regulation; sanitary engineering. **Holdings:** 700 books; 100 bound periodical volumes; 2500 technical reports. **Subscriptions:** 30 journals and other serials. **Services:** Interlibrary loans; copying; library open to public with restrictions.

NEW JERSEY STATE DEPARTMENT OF ENVIRONMENTAL PROTECTION - GEOLOGICAL SURVEY
See: New Jersey Geological Survey

★8936★

NEW JERSEY STATE DEPARTMENT OF HEALTH - LIBRARY (Med)
CN 360   Phone: (609) 292-5693
Trenton, NJ 08625   Cathy A. Stout, Libn.
Founded: 1965. **Staff:** Prof 1. **Subjects:** Chemistry, dentistry, drug abuse, hospitals, microbiology, nursing, nutrition and diet, pediatrics, public health. **Holdings:** 2650 bound periodical volumes; 2450 pamphlets (cataloged); 182 reels of microfilmed journals; 200 bound indexes; 90 bibliographies. **Subscriptions:** 150 journals and other serials. **Services:** Interlibrary loans; copying; library open to public for reference use only. **Networks/Consortia:** Member of Central Jersey Health Science Libraries Association. **Publications:** Circulation Rules; List of Periodical Holdings; Union List of Medical Journals in the Trenton Area.

★8937★

NEW JERSEY STATE DEPARTMENT OF LABOR - LIBRARY (Soc Sci)
CN 110   Phone: (609) 292-2035
Trenton, NJ 08625   Stuart H. Anderson, Libn.
Founded: 1967. **Staff:** Prof 1; Other 3. **Subjects:** Vocational rehabilitation, employment and training, unemployment. **Holdings:** 540 books; 167 bound periodical volumes; 800 U.S. documents; 1200 state documents; 33 VF drawers of pamphlets, reports and reprints. **Subscriptions:** 300 journals and other serials. **Services:** Interlibrary loans; copying; all library services available to state employees; others may use the library for reference use only.

★8938★

NEW JERSEY STATE DEPARTMENT OF LAW AND PUBLIC SAFETY - ATTORNEY GENERAL'S LIBRARY (Law)
Hughes Justice Complex, CN115   Phone: (609) 292-4958
Trenton, NJ 08625   Moira O. Strong, Chf.Libn.
Staff: Prof 3; Other 2. **Subjects:** Law, especially New Jersey. **Holdings:** 30,000 volumes. **Services:** Library not open to public. **Special Indexes:** Brief Index; Legal Memoranda Index; Opinion Index.

★8939★

NEW JERSEY STATE LEAGUE OF MUNICIPALITIES - LIBRARY (Plan)
407 W. State St.   Phone: (609) 695-3481
Trenton, NJ 08618   Jeanne G. Helmstetter, Bureau Chf.
Staff: Prof 2; Other 1. **Subjects:** City planning, zoning, transportation. **Holdings:** Figures not available. **Services:** Library open to members only. **Publications:** New Jersey Municipalities Magazine, monthly. **Staff:** John E. Trafford, Exec.Dir.

★8940★

NEW JERSEY STATE LIBRARY (Info Sci)
185 W. State St.
Box 1898   Phone: (609) 292-6220
Trenton, NJ 08625   Barbara F. Weaver, State Libn.
Founded: 1945. **Staff:** Prof 58; Other 94. **Subjects:** Law; New Jersey history, archives and newspapers; political science; public administration; genealogy. **Special Collections:** Library for the Blind and Handicapped; New Jerseyana; manuscripts. **Holdings:** 750,000 volumes. **Subscriptions:** 2800

journals and other serials. **Services:** Interlibrary loans; copying; consultant services for libraries; library open to adults with restrictions. **Computerized Information Services:** Online systems; computerized cataloging. **Networks/Consortia:** The State Library coordinates the New Jersey Library System, a three level network of local public, area, and research libraries. **Publications:** New Jersey Bibliographer, bimonthly - limited distribution; Impressions, monthly newsletter. **Special Catalogs:** Catalog of New Jersey State Library on microfiche (on deposit at area libraries throughout the state); New Jersey Documents card catalog. **Remarks:** A division of the State Department of Education. **Staff:** Elizabeth Breedlove, Hd., Tech.Serv.; Henry J. Michniewski, Hd., Lib.Dev.; Marya Hunsicker, Lib. for the Blind; David C. Palmer, Asst. State Libn.; Oliver Gillock, Jr., Coord., Plan. & Dev.

★8941★
NEW JERSEY STATE LIBRARY - BUREAU OF LAW AND REFERENCE (Law; Soc Sci)
185 W. State St.
Box 1898   Phone: (609) 292-6210
Trenton, NJ 08625   Susan Roumfort, Hd.
Founded: 1945. **Staff:** Prof 24; Other 26. **Subjects:** Law, political science, social science, New Jerseyana, library science. **Special Collections:** New Jersey documents. **Holdings:** 511,000 volumes; 10,000 cubic feet of archives; 30 file cabinets of pamphlets and clippings; 19 microfilm cabinets; 16,500 reels of microfilm. **Subscriptions:** 2750 journals and other serials; 50 newspapers. **Services:** Interlibrary loans; copying; library open to public. **Computerized Information Services:** DIALOG, SDC, New York Times Information Service. **Publications:** New Jersey Bibliographer, bimonthly; Accessions List, biweekly. **Special Indexes:** Index to Supreme and Superior Court Cases. **Remarks:** A division of the State Department of Education. Contains the holdings of the state archives section. **Staff:** Dr. William Wright, Hd., Rec.Mgt.

★8942★
NEW JERSEY STATE MUSEUM - LIBRARY (Hist; Sci-Tech)
State Cultural Ctr., W. State St.
CN 530   Phone: (609) 292-6308
Trenton, NJ 08625   Leah P. Sloshberg, Dir. of Musm.
Founded: 1890. **Subjects:** New Jersey, history, archeology, art, natural science. **Holdings:** 2600 volumes. **Services:** Students and researchers may study books on museum premises only by advance reservation. **Staff:** Allen C. Hilborn, Pub.Info.Off.

★8943★
NEW LONDON COUNTY HISTORICAL SOCIETY - LIBRARY (Hist)
11 Blinman St.   Phone: (203) 443-1209
New London, CT 06320   Elizabeth B. Knox, Sec./Libn./Cur.
Founded: 1871. **Staff:** Prof 1. **Subjects:** Local history and genealogy. **Special Collections:** Shaw Collection (Revolutionary period); Caulkins Collection. **Holdings:** 5000 books; 400 antique newspapers; 50 early town and county records; 3000 pieces of family correspondence; 15 whaling logs; 15 ships' logs; 50 feet of bound manuscripts; 25 early account books. **Services:** Library open to public for reference use only. **Special Catalogs:** Shaw Collection (card); manuscripts (card).

★8944★
NEW MEXICO INSTITUTE OF MINING AND TECHNOLOGY - MARTIN SPEARE MEMORIAL LIBRARY (Sci-Tech)
Campus Station   Phone: (505) 835-5614
Socorro, NM 87801   Betty Reynolds, Dir.
Founded: 1889. **Staff:** Prof 2; Other 7. **Subjects:** Physics, mathematics, petroleum, ground-water hydrology, geology, geophysics, chemistry, mining. **Special Collections:** Depository for U.S. Geological Survey and U.S. Bureau of Mines publications. **Holdings:** 64,000 books; 15,000 bound periodical volumes; 6000 other cataloged items; 16,000 unbound volumes; 1500 maps; theses. **Subscriptions:** 650 journals and other serials; 10 newspapers. **Services:** Interlibrary loans; copying; library open to public for reference use only. **Computerized Information Services:** SDC; computerized cataloging. **Networks/Consortia:** Member of OCLC through AMIGOS Bibliographic Council, Inc. **Staff:** George Zamora, Acq.; Marty Gilmore, Tech.Serv.; Kathy LeFebre, Tech.Serv.; Beverly Hawles, ILL; Tony Telles, Ser.; Sharon Wooldridge, Circ.

NEW MEXICO MENTAL RETARDATION AND DEVELOPMENTAL DISABILITIES LIBRARY
See: Los Lunas Hospital and Training School

★8945★
NEW MEXICO SCHOOL FOR THE VISUALLY HANDICAPPED - LIBRARY (Aud-Vis)
1900 White Sands Blvd.   Phone: (505) 347-3505
Alamogordo, NM 88310   Wanda West, Libn.
Staff: Prof 1; Other 2. **Special Collections:** Visually handicapped. **Holdings:** 9500 books in braille and print; 2500 AV items. **Subscriptions:** 46 journals and other serials. **Services:** Library open to public with restrictions. **Staff:** Bill Davis, Media Spec.

★8946★
NEW MEXICO STATE DEPARTMENT OF HOSPITALS - STATE HOSPITAL - ELLA P. KIEF MEMORIAL LIBRARY (Med)
Hot Springs Blvd.
Box 1388   Phone: (505) 425-6711
Las Vegas, NM 87701   Hazel Hurley, Libn.
Founded: 1964. **Staff:** 1. **Subjects:** Medicine, psychiatry, psychoanalysis and therapy, theology, business. **Holdings:** 5000 books and bound periodical volumes; 100 cassette tapes. **Subscriptions:** 60 journals and other serials. **Services:** Interlibrary loans; copying; library not open to public. **Computerized Information Services:** Medical Center Library, UNM (internal database). **Networks/Consortia:** Member of TALON. **Publications:** Synergy, monthly - to TALON members.

★8947★
NEW MEXICO STATE ENERGY AND MINERALS DEPARTMENT - LIBRARY (Energy)
525 Camino de los Marquez   Phone: (505) 827-2471
Santa Fe, NM 87501   Kathleen LaPlante, Libn.
Staff: Prof 1; Other 1. **Subjects:** Energy. **Holdings:** Figures not available. **Subscriptions:** 206 journals and other serials. **Services:** Interlibrary loans; copying; SDI; library open to public. **Computerized Information Services:** Online systems.

★8948★
NEW MEXICO STATE LEGISLATIVE COUNCIL SERVICE - LIBRARY (Soc Sci)
334 State Capitol   Phone: (505) 827-3141
Santa Fe, NM 87503   E. Jean Peters, Hd.Libn.
Staff: Prof 1; Other 1. **Subjects:** Government, taxation, public finance, law. **Holdings:** 3000 books; 25 bound periodical volumes; 6000 pamphlets (cataloged); 6 VF drawers of pamphlets; clippings. **Subscriptions:** 27 journals and other serials. **Services:** Interlibrary loans; library open to public. **Publications:** Biennial Report - free upon request.

★8949★
NEW MEXICO STATE LIBRARY (Info Sci)
325 Don Gaspar   Phone: (505) 827-2033
Santa Fe, NM 87503   Paul A. Agriesti, Act. State Libn.
Founded: 1929. **Staff:** Prof 18; Other 54. **Subjects:** Management, education, literature, history, biography. **Special Collections:** Southwest Literature Collection; Southwest Historical Collection; Professional Library Science material; ERIC collection on microfiche (includes holdings of regional libraries). **Holdings:** 200,000 books; 650 music items (cataloged); 500,000 federal and state documents (Federal Regional Depository). **Subscriptions:** 262 journals and other serials; 44 newspapers. **Services:** Interlibrary loans; copying; library open to public. **Computerized Information Services:** DIALOG, SDC; computerized cataloging and ILL. **Networks/Consortia:** Member of New Mexico Information System (NEMISYS); OCLC through AMIGOS Bibliographic Council, Inc. **Publications:** Hitchhiker, weekly; series of Occasional Papers, irregular. **Staff:** Jane Gillentine, Assoc. State Libn.; Sandra Esquibel, Assoc. State Libn.Harold Bogart, Assoc. State Libn.

★8950★
NEW MEXICO STATE RECORDS AND ARCHIVES - ARCHIVAL SERVICES DIVISION (Hist)
404 Montezuma St.   Phone: (505) 827-2321
Santa Fe, NM 87567   Bryan M. Miller, Chf., Archv.Serv.
Founded: 1962. **Staff:** Prof 4; Other 2. **Subjects:** New Mexico state history, Southwestern history. **Special Collections:** Spanish and Mexican Archives of New Mexico. **Holdings:** 4000 books; 300 bound periodical volumes. **Services:** Copying; division open to public. **Publications:** Spanish, Mexican, Territorial Archives of New Mexico. **Special Indexes:** Photograph index. **Staff:** Lou Ellen Martinez, Archv.; Kay Dorman, Archv.; Mary Brecht, Archv.

★8951★
NEW MEXICO STATE SUPREME COURT - LAW LIBRARY (Law)
Supreme Court Bldg.
Drawer L   Phone: (505) 827-2515
Santa Fe, NM 87501   John P. Blum, Dir.
Founded: 1852. **Staff:** Prof 3; Other 5. **Subjects:** Law. **Special Collections:**

Spanish and Mexican colonial laws. **Holdings:** 105,650 books; 20,000 bound periodical volumes; 50 reels of microfilm of territorial land claim cases; 20,000 microfiche. **Subscriptions:** 2000 journals and other serials. **Services:** Interlibrary loans; copying; library open to public. **Computerized Information Services:** WESTLAW; STAIRS-LAW (internal database). **Staff:** John R. Eichstadt, Assoc. Law Libn.; Kevin Lancaster, Asst. Law Libn.

NEW MEXICO STATE UNIVERSITY - ERIC CLEARINGHOUSE ON RURAL EDUCATION AND SMALL SCHOOLS
See: ERIC Clearinghouse on Rural Education and Small Schools

★8952★
NEW MEXICO STATE UNIVERSITY - PHYSICAL SCIENCE LABORATORY - TECHNICAL LIBRARY
Box 3 PSL
Las Cruces, NM 88003
Defunct

★8953★
NEW ORLEANS BAPTIST THEOLOGICAL SEMINARY - JOHN T. CHRISTIAN LIBRARY (Rel-Theol)
4110 Seminary Pl.   Phone: (504) 282-4455
New Orleans, LA 70126   Dr. Paul Gericke, Dir. of Lib.
Founded: 1917. **Staff:** Prof 3; Other 15. **Subjects:** Bible, theology, Baptists, religious education, church music. **Special Collections:** Robert G. Lee Collection; William Carey Library (microfilm); Keith Collection (church music). **Holdings:** 156,000 books; 7500 bound periodical volumes; 25,000 Baptist annuals and minutes; 8000 VF materials; 10,000 pamphlets, tracts and manuscripts; 3200 reels of microfilm; 13,500 AV materials. **Subscriptions:** 807 journals and other serials; 5 newspapers. **Services:** Interlibrary loans; copying; library open to public for reference use only. **Staff:** Janette Griffin, Cat.; Irvin Murrell, Circ.-Ref.Libn.; Doris Freeman, Per. & ILL Libn.

★8954★
NEW ORLEANS MUSEUM OF ART - FELIX J. DREYOUS LIBRARY (Art)
City Park
Box 19123   Phone: (504) 488-2631
New Orleans, LA 70179   Jeannette D. Downing, Libn.
Founded: 1971. **Staff:** Prof 1; Other 6. **Subjects:** Photography, African art, Japanese painting, glass, American and European 19th and 20th century painting, pre-Columbian art. **Holdings:** 10,000 books; 900 bound periodical volumes; 7000 auction catalogs and museum publications; 300 file boxes of pamphlets; 2000 35mm slides; 23 VF drawers of living artist files. **Subscriptions:** 123 journals and other serials. **Services:** Interlibrary loans; copying; library open to museum members and general public by appointment. **Computerized Information Services:** Computerized cataloging. **Special Indexes:** Index to New Orleans Artists, 1805-1940 (15 volumes).

★8955★
NEW ORLEANS PSYCHOANALYTIC INSTITUTE, INC. - LIBRARY (Med)
3624 Coliseum St.   Phone: (504) 899-5815
New Orleans, LA 70115   Dr. Samuel Rubin, Chm.
Founded: 1950. **Staff:** 1. **Subjects:** Psychoanalysis. **Holdings:** 650 books; 500 bound periodical volumes. **Subscriptions:** 13 journals and other serials. **Services:** Library not open to public.

★8956★
NEW ORLEANS PUBLIC LIBRARY - ART, MUSIC & RECREATION DIVISION (Art; Mus; Rec)
219 Loyola Ave.   Phone: (504) 586-4938
New Orleans, LA 70140   Marilyn Wilkins, Div.Hd.
Staff: Prof 1; Other 7. **Subjects:** Fine arts, costume, music, sports, recreation. **Special Collections:** Early U.S. sheet music; Fischer Collection of Early Vocal Recordings. **Holdings:** 45,100 books; 4 VF drawers of film catalogs; 4 VF drawers of pamphlets; 75,000 mounted pictures in 11 file cabinets; 20,000 phonograph records; 500 framed art prints. **Services:** Interlibrary loans; copying.

★8957★
NEW ORLEANS PUBLIC LIBRARY - BUSINESS AND SCIENCE DIVISION (Bus-Fin; Sci-Tech)
219 Loyola Ave.   Phone: (504) 586-4917
New Orleans, LA 70140   Elizabeth O. Bedikian, Div.Hd.
Founded: 1958. **Staff:** Prof 3; Other 6. **Subjects:** Business, consumerism, science, technology, education, careers, social sciences. **Special Collections:** Federal document depository collection (800,000 items); Louisiana Cooperating Collection of Foundation Center (350 items). **Holdings:** 72,000 volumes; 3000 college catalogs on microfiche; 2500 annual and 10K reports; 2000 business, consumer and career pamphlets; 2000 industry standards.

Services: Interlibrary loans; copying; division open to public. **Computerized Information Services:** Computerized cataloging, acquisitions and circulation. **Networks/Consortia:** Member of OCLC through SOLINET; Louisiana Numerical Register. **Staff:** Katherine Nachod, Govt.Doc.Libn.

★8958★
NEW ORLEANS PUBLIC LIBRARY - FOREIGN LANGUAGE DIVISION (Hum)
219 Loyola Ave.   Phone: (504) 586-4943
New Orleans, LA 70140   Norka Diaz, Div.Hd.
Founded: 1972. **Staff:** Prof 1; Other 3. **Subjects:** Spanish, French, German, Vietnamese, Latin American popular and classical literature. **Special Collections:** Applied sciences in Spanish (600 volumes); children's books in Spanish (600 volumes). **Holdings:** 10,000 books; 100 bound periodical volumes; 30 filmstrips in Spanish. **Subscriptions:** 19 journals and other serials; 5 newspapers. **Services:** Interlibrary loans; library open to nonresidents on a fee basis.

★8959★
NEW ORLEANS PUBLIC LIBRARY - LOUISIANA DIVISION (Hist)
219 Loyola Ave.   Phone: (504) 524-7382
New Orleans, LA 70140   Collin B. Hamer, Jr., Div.Hd.
Founded: 1946. **Staff:** Prof 2; Other 9. **Subjects:** New Orleans archives, 1769 to present; New Orleans newspapers, 1802 to present; Louisiana state documents; books by Louisianians; books on Louisiana subjects. **Special Collections:** Mardi Gras Collection (10,800 items); Genealogy Collection (2176 volumes; 5500 reels of microfilm); City Archives Collection (15,900 volumes; 4400 reels of microfilm). **Holdings:** 15,800 books; 2200 bound newspapers; 9500 reels of microfilm; 30,000 Louisiana and New Orleans photographs; 24,000 Louisiana state documents. **Subscriptions:** 210 journals and other serials; 23 newspapers. **Services:** Interlibrary loans; copying; microfilming; library open to public. **Computerized Information Services:** Computerized cataloging, acquisitions and circulation. **Networks/Consortia:** Member of OCLC. **Special Indexes:** Louisiana Biography Index containing obituaries appearing in New Orleans newspapers, 1804 to present and biographies appearing in books (700,000 cards); News Index to news items in local papers concerning Louisiana and Louisianians (600,000 cards); Index of Picture File and Blueprints (famous buildings and houses).

NEW PLACE RARE BOOK LIBRARY
See: Shakespeare Society of America

★8960★
NEW PROVIDENCE HISTORICAL SOCIETY - LIBRARY (Hist)
1350 Springfield Ave.   Phone: (201) 464-5798
New Providence, NJ 07974   Dorothy Mason, Hd.Libn.
Staff: 3. **Subjects:** Local history and current events. **Holdings:** 67 loose-leaf binders; 29 loose-leaf photograph albums; VF drawers. **Subscriptions:** 5 journals and other serials. **Services:** Library open to public for reference use only. **Publications:** Turkey Tracks, quarterly. **Staff:** Elizabeth Newell; Josephine Westbrook .

NEW READERS PRESS COLLECTION
See: Laubach Literacy International, Inc.

★8961★
NEW ROCHELLE HOSPITAL MEDICAL CENTER - J. MARSHALL PERLEY HEALTH SCIENCE LIBRARY (Med)
Iselin Hall   Phone: (914) 632-5000
New Rochelle, NY 10802   Helene D. Lambert, Med.Libn.
Founded: 1950. **Staff:** Prof 1; Other 2. **Subjects:** Medicine and nursing. **Special Collections:** Nursing history; hospital archives. **Holdings:** 2200 books; 8000 bound periodical volumes; 300 tapes (cataloged); 100 AV materials; staff reprints; 8 VF drawers. **Subscriptions:** 300 journals and other serials. **Services:** Interlibrary loans; copying; library open to public by appointment. **Computerized Information Services:** MEDLINE. **Networks/Consortia:** Member of Health Information Libraries of Westchester (HILOW); Medical Library Center of New York (MLCNY); New York & New Jersey Regional Medical Library Program. **Publications:** Quarterly Library Newsletter. **Remarks:** This library contains School of Nursing Library holdings.

★8962★
NEW SCHOOL OF MUSIC, INC. - ALICE TULLY LIBRARY (Mus)
301 S. 21st St.   Phone: (215) 732-3966
Philadelphia, PA 19103   Susan L. Koenig, Libn.
Staff: Prof 1; Other 3. **Subjects:** Music, music literature. **Holdings:** 1791 books; 5551 scores (cataloged); 1800 phonograph records; 232 tapes. **Subscriptions:** 15 journals and other serials. **Services:** Copying; library not open to public.

NEW SCHOOL FOR SOCIAL RESEARCH - PARSONS SCHOOL OF DESIGN
See: Parsons School of Design

★8963★
NEW SCHOOL FOR SOCIAL RESEARCH - RAYMOND FOGELMAN LIBRARY (Soc Sci)†
65 Fifth Ave. Phone: (212) 741-7902
New York, NY 10003 Michael Lordi, Lib.Dir.
Founded: 1919. **Staff:** Prof 4; Other 8. **Subjects:** Psychology, political science, economics, sociology, philosophy, anthropology. **Holdings:** 112,797 books; 12,949 bound periodical volumes. **Subscriptions:** 2000 journals and other serials. **Services:** Library not open to public. **Computerized Information Services:** Computerized circulation. **Networks/Consortia:** Member of New York University, New School, Cooper Union Consortium.

NEW THOUGHT ARCHIVE
See: Southern Methodist University - Perkins School of Theology

★8964★
NEW TRANSCENTURY FOUNDATION - SECRETARIAT FOR WOMEN IN DEVELOPMENT - DOCUMENTATION CENTER (Soc Sci)†
1789 Columbia Rd., N.W. Phone: (202) 328-4400
Washington, DC 20009 Patricia Harlan McClure, Dir.
Staff: Prof 1; Other 1. **Subjects:** Women - in developing countries, law and politics, rural development, culture and society, and socioeconomic participation. **Holdings:** 1300 documents. **Subscriptions:** 100 journals and other serials. **Services:** Copying; center open to public. **Networks/Consortia:** Member of Information Network for Materials Effecting Development (INFORMED). **Publications:** Women in Development: A Resource List - for sale.

NEW VIRGINIA REVIEW LIBRARY
See: Virginia Commonwealth University - James Branch Cabell Library - Special Collections

★8965★
NEW WESTERN ENERGY SHOW - RENEWABLE ENERGY LIBRARY (Energy)
601 Power Block Phone: (406) 443-7272
Helena, MT 59601 Maureen Shaughnessy, Libn.
Staff: Prof 1; Other 2. **Subjects:** Renewable energy, energy conservation, appropriate technology. **Holdings:** 350 books; 2 file drawers of fact sheets, brochures and catalogs. **Subscriptions:** 20 journals and other serials; 8 newspapers. **Services:** Library open to public for reference use only. **Publications:** Get Your Hands on Energy; The Energy Show - both for sale.

NEW WESTMINSTER SCHOOL BOARD
See: Burnaby and New Westminster School Boards

★8966★
NEW YORK ACADEMY OF MEDICINE - LIBRARY (Med)
2 E. 103rd St. Phone: (212) 876-8200
New York, NY 10029 Brett A. Kirkpatrick, Libn.
Founded: 1847. **Staff:** Prof 19; Other 25. **Subjects:** Medicine and allied sciences. **Special Collections:** Medical Americana; history of medicine; medical biography; rare books; health reports; food and cookery. **Holdings:** 464,168 bound volumes; 180,981 pamphlets; 139 incunabula; 2227 manuscripts; 494 reels of microfilm; 250,043 portraits (cataloged); 25,412 illustrations (cataloged); 14,429 separate portraits. **Subscriptions:** 4012 journals and other serials. **Services:** Interlibrary loans (fee); copying; library open to public for reference use only; Fellows of the Academy and library subscribers may borrow. **Computerized Information Services:** NLM, BRS, SDC, DIALOG, Union Catalog of Medical Periodicals; Union Catalog of Monographs; computerized cataloging. **Networks/Consortia:** Headquarters of New York & New Jersey Regional Medical Library Program; member of Medical Library Center of New York; SUNY/OCLC Library Network; New York State Interlibrary Loan Network (NYSILL). **Publications:** History of Medicine Series; Portrait Catalog of the Library; Illustration Catalog of the Library; Catalog of Biographies in the Library; Newsletter and Selected Acquisitions List, monthly - on request. **Special Catalogs:** Author Catalog of the Library; Author Catalog - First and Second Supplements; Subject Catalog of Library; Subject Catalog - First Supplement. **Staff:** Lynn Kasner, Assoc.Libn.; Anne M. Pascarelli, Asst.Libn.

NEW YORK AQUARIUM LIBRARY
See: Osborn Laboratories of Marine Sciences

★8967★
NEW YORK ASSOCIATION FOR THE BLIND - LIGHTHOUSE LIBRARY (Aud-Vis)
111 E. 59th St. Phone: (212) 355-2200
New York, NY 10022 Agnes Beck, Coord., Ancillary Serv.
Staff: Prof 2; Other 1. **Subjects:** Blindness and visual impairment; handicaps. **Holdings:** 2000 books; 2000 volumes in Braille; 375 large print books; 1700 talking books on disc and cassette; 8 VF drawers. **Subscriptions:** 110 journals and other serials. **Services:** Library open to public. **Publications:** Popular Books on Cassette, irregular. **Staff:** Leslie Davis, Libn.

★8968★
NEW YORK BARTOK ARCHIVE (Mus)
301 Mill Rd., Suite U6 Phone: (516) 569-1468
Hewlett, NY 11557 Dr. Benjamin Suchoff, Trustee
Staff: Prof 1; Other 3. **Subjects:** Bela Bartok, musicology, enthnomusicology, computerized music research. **Special Collections:** Bartok compositions and folk music in manuscript, recordings, correspondence, iconographic materials, programs, press releases. **Holdings:** 6000 books; sheet music, theses, photographs, films. **Services:** Archive open to qualified scholars. **Computerized Information Services:** Internal database. **Publications:** The New York Bartok Archive Studies in Musicology Series (15 volumes); The Bartok Archive Edition: Series I and II. **Special Indexes:** Indexes to books, manuscripts, letters, journals, published music and folk music collections.

★8969★
NEW YORK BOTANICAL GARDEN - CARY ARBORETUM - LIBRARY (Sci-Tech; Env-Cons)
Box AB Phone: (914) 677-5343
Millbrook, NY 12545 Charles R. Long, Adm.Libn.
Founded: 1972. **Staff:** Prof 1. **Subjects:** Botany of woody plants, horticulture, environmental studies, plant nutrition. **Holdings:** 7850 books; 1650 bound periodical volumes; 3000 items in vertical files. **Subscriptions:** 165 journals and other serials. **Services:** Interlibrary loans; copying; library open to public. **Networks/Consortia:** Member of Southeastern New York Library Resources Council (SENYLRC). **Remarks:** Information and queries regarding Cary Arboretum should be directed to C.R. Long, Director of Library and Plant Information Services, Bronx, NY, 10458. **Staff:** Betsy Calvin, Asst.Libn.

★8970★
NEW YORK BOTANICAL GARDEN - LIBRARY (Sci-Tech; Env-Cons)
 Phone: (212) 220-8749
Bronx, NY 10458 Charles R. Long, Dir.
Founded: 1896. **Staff:** Prof 7; Other 16. **Subjects:** Systematic botany, horticulture, environmental sciences. **Special Collections:** Manuscripts, letters, archives (380,000 items). **Holdings:** 188,000 books and bound periodical volumes; 206,000 unbound items; 7000 nursery catalogs and seed lists; 82,000 scientific reprints; 4500 items on microfiche. **Subscriptions:** 2050 journals and other serials. **Services:** Copying; library open to public. **Computerized Information Services:** Online systems; computerized cataloging. **Networks/Consortia:** Member of OCLC. **Publications:** Bibliographies and indexes. **Staff:** Lothian Lynas, Assoc.Libn.; Rose Li, Assoc.Libn.; Gerard McKiernan, Asst.Libn.; Jane Brennan, Asst.Libn.; Katy Enders, Asst.Libn.; Grace Courtney, Cat.

★8971★
NEW YORK CHIROPRACTIC COLLEGE - LIBRARY (Med)
255 Valentines Ln., Old Brookville Phone: (516) 686-7657
Glen Head, NY 11545 Lorraine Palmer, Libn.
Founded: 1919. **Staff:** Prof 1; Other 2. **Subjects:** Health sciences, basic sciences; chiropractic. **Special Collections:** Palmer Series and other rare chiropractic material (150 volumes). **Holdings:** 3000 books; 390 bound periodical volumes. **Subscriptions:** 90 journals and other serials. **Services:** Interlibrary loans; library open to public for reference use only. **Computerized Information Services:** DIALOG, BRS. **Networks/Consortia:** Member of Chiropractic Library Consortium.

NEW YORK CITY BAR ASSOCIATION LIBRARY
See: Association of the Bar of the City of New York

★8972★
NEW YORK CITY BOARD OF EDUCATION - DIVISION OF SPECIAL EDUCATION - INSTRUCTIONAL SUPPORT UNIT (Educ)
400 First Ave. Phone: (212) 686-6120
New York, NY 10010 Roberta Berger, Asst.Libn.
Founded: 1971. **Staff:** Prof 2; Other 8. **Subjects:** Special education. **Special Collections:** Instructional materials and equipment. **Holdings:** 1000 books; reports, clippings, pamphlets. **Subscriptions:** 20 journals and other serials.

Services: Interlibrary loans; copying; library open to public. Staff: Frank Rubino, Media Coord.

★8973★

NEW YORK CITY BOARD OF EDUCATION - RESOURCE CENTER - CURRICULUM LIBRARY
131 Livingston St.
Brooklyn, NY 11201
Defunct

★8974★

NEW YORK CITY COMMISSION ON HUMAN RIGHTS - LIBRARY (Soc Sci)†
52 Duane St.   Phone: (212) 233-4410
New York, NY 10007   Laura Fisher, Libn.
Founded: 1972. Staff: 1. Subjects: Discrimination in employment, housing and public accommodations, public education integration, women's rights, blacks, Puerto Ricans, white ethnic groups, handicapped. Holdings: 300 books; 20 VF drawers of pamphlets and clippings. Subscriptions: 50 journals and other serials; 15 newspapers. Services: Library open to public with restrictions. Publications: New Acquisitions List - for internal distribution only.

★8975★

NEW YORK CITY - DEPARTMENT OF RECORDS AND INFORMATION SERVICES - MUNICIPAL ARCHIVES (Hist)
52 Chambers St.   Phone: (212) 566-5292
New York, NY 10007   Idilio Gracia-Pena, Dir.
Staff: Prof 6; Other 4. Subjects: New York City history. Special Collections: Brooklyn Bridge collection (12,000 drawings); New York Building Record collection (2000 cubic feet; 4000 drawings). Holdings: 75,000 cubic feet of archives; 12,000 photographs; 25,000 architectural and engineering records. Services: Copying; archives open to public. Staff: Anne M. Gordon, Dp.Dir.; Kenneth R. Cobb, Asst.Dir.; Linda Sommer, Asst.Dir.

★8976★

NEW YORK CITY HUMAN RESOURCES ADMINISTRATION - MC MILLAN LIBRARY (Soc Sci)
109 E. 16th St.   Phone: (212) 420-7652
New York, NY 10003   Harold W. Benson, Libn.
Founded: 1945. Staff: Prof 2; Other 3. Subjects: Public welfare, social work, child welfare, poverty, ethnic studies, public administration, employment, income maintenance. Holdings: 14,000 books and bound periodical volumes; 32 VF drawers; 5000 titles of uncataloged reports and pamphlets. Subscriptions: 200 journals and other serials; 6 newspapers. Services: Interlibrary loans; copying; library open to public. Computerized Information Services: DIALOG. Publications: McMillan Library Bulletin, bimonthly. Staff: Mary Gaydos, Ref.Libn.

★8977★

NEW YORK CITY HUMAN RESOURCES ADMINISTRATION - MEDICAL ASSISTANCE PROGRAM - MEDICAID LIBRARY (Med; Soc Sci)
330 W. 34th St., 10th Fl. South   Phone: (212) 790-2811
New York, NY 10001   Barry L. Cohen, MAP Libn.
Staff: Prof 1. Subjects: Medicaid, long-term care, health care management, HMOs (Health Maintenance Organizations), social services, Medicare. Special Collections: Monthly MARS Statistical Reports (New York State Department of Social Services: Management Analysis Reporting Subsystem); New York State Medical Handbook; Medicaid Management Information System Provider Handbooks (Bradford Administrative Services Inc.). Holdings: 200 books; 250 binders; 4 VF drawers of portfolios of New York City Planning Corporation Community Districts; 20 VF drawers of reports, studies, documents, pamphlets and clippings. Subscriptions: 6 journals and other serials; 15 newsletters. Services: Interlibrary loans (limited); copying; library open to public for reference use only. Computerized Information Services: Internal database. Publications: MAP Library Bulletin, monthly - for internal distribution only. Special Catalogs: Alphabetic card files of file subjects and sources of materials received. Also Known As: MAP Library.

★8978★

NEW YORK CITY - LAW DEPARTMENT - CORPORATION COUNSEL'S LIBRARY (Soc Sci)
100 Church St., Rm. 6B1   Phone: (212) 566-4418
New York, NY 10007   Jacob Wexler, Libn.
Staff: Prof 1; Other 6. Subjects: Federal, state and municipal government. Holdings: 66,000 volumes; microfilm, ultrafiche. Subscriptions: 30 journals and other serials. Services: Library not open to public. Computerized Information Services: LEXIS.

★8979★

NEW YORK CITY - MUNICIPAL REFERENCE AND RESEARCH CENTER (Soc Sci)
31 Chambers St.   Phone: (212) 566-4285
New York, NY 10007   Solomon Jacobson, Dir.
Founded: 1913. Staff: Prof 7; Other 3. Subjects: New York City - history, government, laws, politics, finance, economy, sociology. Special Collections: Civil service (40 VF drawers); public health; neighborhood information files (8 VF drawers); street name file (18 VF drawers); legislative reference collection. Holdings: 77,500 books; 4200 bound periodical volumes; 30,000 VF materials (cataloged); 55 drawers of microfilm and microfiche; 20 VF drawers of political information files; 4 VF drawers of New York State materials. Subscriptions: 200 journals and other serials. Services: Interlibrary loans; copying; center open to public for reference use only. Special Indexes: Index to local laws; index to departmental rules and regulations.

★8980★

NEW YORK CITY - MUNICIPAL REFERENCE AND RESEARCH CENTER - HAVEN EMERSON PUBLIC HEALTH LIBRARY (Med)
125 Worth St., Rm. 223   Phone: (212) 566-5169
New York, NY 10013   Shirley Paris, Chf.Libn.
Founded: 1916. Staff: Prof 1; Other 1. Subjects: Public health, hospitals, mental hygiene, vital statistics, medical sociology, nutrition. Special Collections: Official depository collection of documents pertaining to public health issued by New York City governmental agencies. Holdings: 14,000 books; 2200 bound periodical volumes; 5000 municipal documents. Subscriptions: 141 journals and other serials. Services: Interlibrary loans; library open to public for reference use only.

★8981★

NEW YORK CITY - OFFICE OF CHIEF MEDICAL EXAMINER - MILTON HELPERN LIBRARY OF LEGAL MEDICINE (Law; Med)
520 First Ave.   Phone: (212) 340-0102
New York, NY 10016   Ellen R. Brenner, Libn.
Founded: 1962. Staff: Prof 1. Subjects: Legal medicine, forensic pathology, forensic toxicology, forensic serology, criminology, forensic immunology. Special Collections: Papers of Dr. Milton Helpern; forensic and legal dentistry collection (books and articles). Holdings: 3250 books; 928 bound periodical volumes; 480 microfiche; 58 reels of microfilm; 16 VF drawers; 136 AV tapes; vertical files. Subscriptions: 56 serials. Services: Copying; library open to public for reference use by appointment. Publications: International Microform Journal of Legal Medicine and Forensic Sciences, quarterly.

★8982★

NEW YORK CITY POLICE DEPARTMENT - POLICE ACADEMY LIBRARY (Soc Sci)
235 E. 20th St.   Phone: (212) 477-9723
New York, NY 10003   John D. Preston, Libn.
Staff: Prof 1. Subjects: Criminal justice, police science. Holdings: 7600 books; 380 bound periodical volumes; 78 N.Y.C.P.D. annual reports, 1892-1969; 25 VF drawers of pamphlets and clippings; 320 masters' theses; 3 VF drawers of N.Y.C.P.D. crime statistics. Subscriptions: 12 journals and other serials. Services: Interlibrary loans; copying; library open to public for reference use only.

★8983★

NEW YORK CITY - PUBLIC HEALTH LABORATORIES - WILLIAM HALLOCK PARK MEMORIAL LIBRARY (Med)
455 First Ave.   Phone: (212) 340-4700
New York, NY 10016   Shirley Chapin, Libn.
Founded: 1900. Staff: Prof 1; Other 1. Subjects: Virology, applied immunology, biochemistry, bacteriology, genetics, laboratory diagnosis, microbiology, cytobiology, toxicology. Special Collections: New York City health reports from inception of Board of Health in 1866. Holdings: 5900 books; 42,000 bound periodical volumes; microcards; 10 VF drawers of archives; 150 boxes of Public Health Service Publications. Subscriptions: 265 journals and other serials. Services: Interlibrary loans; copying; library not open to public. Networks/Consortia: Member of Medical Library Center of New York (MLCNY).

NEW YORK CITY TECHNICAL COLLEGE LIBRARY/LEARNING RESOURCE CENTER
See: CUNY

★8984★
NEW YORK CITY TRANSIT AUTHORITY - LAW LIBRARY (Law)
370 Jay St., Rm. 1333   Phone: (212) 330-4330
Brooklyn, NY 11201   James P. McMahon, Asst.Gen. Counsel
Staff: Prof 1; Other 1. **Subjects:** Law. **Holdings:** 10,000 volumes. **Services:** Library not open to public.

★8985★
NEW YORK COLLEGE OF PODIATRIC MEDICINE - DR. SIDNEY DRUSKIN MEMORIAL LIBRARY (Med)†
53-55 E. 124th St., 3rd Fl.   Phone: (212) 427-8400
New York, NY 10035   Oksana Karaczewsky, Hd.Libn.
Founded: 1930. **Staff:** Prof 2. **Subjects:** Podiatry, medicine, orthopedics, physical medicine, basic sciences. **Holdings:** 5300 books and bound periodical volumes; reprints of journal articles; slides; audiotapes; video cassettes; microfilm; pamphlets. **Subscriptions:** 190 journals and other serials. **Services:** Interlibrary loans; copying; library open to public for reference use only by request. **Networks/Consortia:** Member of New York & Northern New Jersey Regional Medical Library Program; Manhattan/Bronx Health Sciences Library Group. **Publications:** Acquisitions lists, journals holdings list. **Staff:** Marshall Giannotti, AV Libn.

★8986★
NEW YORK COUNTY - DISTRICT ATTORNEY'S OFFICE LIBRARY (Law)
One Hogan Pl.   Phone: (212) 553-9344
New York, NY 10013   Madeleine Fenster, Libn.
Founded: 1905. **Staff:** Prof 1; Other 1. **Subjects:** Criminal law. **Holdings:** 19,110 books; 600 bound periodical volumes. **Subscriptions:** 35 journals and other serials. **Services:** Library not open to public. **Computerized Information Services:** LEXIS. **Publications:** Current Articles in Criminal Law and Procedure, monthly - for internal distribution only. **Special Indexes:** Subject index to U.S. and New York Court of Appeals cases (card).

★8987★
NEW YORK COUNTY LAWYERS' ASSOCIATION - LIBRARY (Law)
14 Vesey St.   Phone: (212) 267-6646
New York, NY 10007   Edward M. O'Connell, Law Libn.
Staff: Prof 4; Other 11. **Subjects:** Law. **Special Collections:** Latin American and international law, American constitutional law, American citizenship. **Holdings:** 170,000 volumes. **Subscriptions:** 300 journals and other serials. **Services:** Copying; library not open to public. **Staff:** Barbara Tanzer, Asst.Libn.; Nancy Meyrich, Cat.

★8988★
NEW YORK COUNTY SURROGATE'S COURT - LAW LIBRARY (Law)†
31 Chambers St., Rm. 401   Phone: (212) 374-8275
New York, NY 10007   Nadine A. Dubson, Libn.
Staff: Prof 1. **Subjects:** Law. **Holdings:** 12,500 volumes. **Services:** Library not open to public.

★8989★
NEW YORK DAILY NEWS - LIBRARY (Publ)
220 E. 42nd St.   Phone: (212) 949-3569
New York, NY 10017   John C. Hodgson, Chf.Libn.
Founded: 1919. **Staff:** Prof 1; Other 15. **Subjects:** Newspaper reference topics. **Holdings:** 5000 books; 20,000 microfiche; 2000 pamphlets; 10 million clippings; over 5 million pictures; 600,000 negatives; New York Daily News, 1919 to present (microfilm); New York Times, 1951 to present (microfilm). **Subscriptions:** 27 journals and other serials. **Services:** Library not open to public.

★8990★
NEW YORK EYE AND EAR INFIRMARY - BERNARD SAMUELS LIBRARY (Med)
310 E. 14th St.   Phone: (212) 598-1431
New York, NY 10003   Miriam Adorno, Med.Libn.
Founded: 1950. **Staff:** Prof 1. **Subjects:** Ophthalmology, otolaryngology. **Holdings:** 2000 books; pamphlets; 300 Audio-Digest tapes. **Subscriptions:** 34 journals and other serials. **Services:** Interlibrary loans; copying; library not open to public. **Computerized Information Services:** Computerized cataloging, acquisitions, serials and circulation.

NEW YORK FOUNDATION CENTER
See: Foundation Center - New York

★8991★
NEW YORK GENEALOGICAL AND BIOGRAPHICAL SOCIETY - GENEALOGICAL RESEARCH LIBRARY (Hist)
122 E. 58th St.   Phone: (212) 755-8532
New York, NY 10022   James P. Gregory, Libn.
Founded: 1869. **Staff:** 3. **Subjects:** Genealogy, biography, local history. **Special Collections:** New York State church records; family Bible records. **Holdings:** 62,000 volumes, including manuscripts; 2000 reels of microfilm. **Subscriptions:** 750 journals and other serials. **Services:** Library open to public with restrictions. **Staff:** Carol S. Day, Assoc.Libn.

★8992★
NEW-YORK HISTORICAL SOCIETY - LIBRARY (Hist)
170 Central Park W.   Phone: (212) 873-3400
New York, NY 10024   Dr. Larry E. Sullivan, Libn.
Founded: 1804. **Staff:** Prof 14; Other 3. **Subjects:** New York State and City history, American history, Civil War (Northern side), naval history to 1898, genealogy, art and museum reference, American painting, decorative arts. **Special Collections:** 18th century newspapers; Bella C Landauer Collection (one million pieces of printed ephemera). **Holdings:** 620,000 books; 1.5 million manuscripts; 150,000 pamphlets; 25,000 broadsides; 750,000 photographs; 10,000 prints; 30,000 maps. **Subscriptions:** 360 journals and other serials. **Services:** Copying; library open to adult public with daily fee for nonmembers. **Special Catalogs:** Manuscript catalog. **Staff:** Katherine Richards, Asst.Libn.

★8993★
NEW YORK HOSPITAL-CORNELL MEDICAL CENTER - MEDICAL ARCHIVES (Med; Hist)
1300 York Ave.   Phone: (212) 472-5759
New York, NY 10021   Adele A. Lerner, Archv.
Staff: Prof 2. **Subjects:** Medical education; health care; history of medicine, nursing and psychiatry; women's history. **Special Collections:** American Medical Women's Association collection (15.3 linear feet). **Holdings:** 2700 linear feet of archives and manuscripts; 28 linear feet of photographs; 200 instruments and artifacts; 212 reels of microfilm. **Subscriptions:** 14 journals and other serials (for archival reference). **Services:** Copying; archives open to qualified researchers. **Special Catalogs:** Finding aids; Guide to the Collection.

★8994★
NEW YORK HOSPITAL-CORNELL MEDICAL CENTER - OSKAR DIETHELM HISTORICAL LIBRARY (Med)
525 E. 68th St.   Phone: (212) 472-6434
New York, NY 10021   Phyllis Rubinton, Libn.
Founded: 1936. **Staff:** Prof 2. **Subjects:** History of psychiatry; philosophy; psychology. **Special Collections:** Early doctoral dissertations on psychiatric topics (241); hospital annual reports (2590); mental health archival and manuscript material. **Holdings:** 17,000 books; 3850 bound periodical volumes; 673 philosophy and psychology items; 200 cubic feet of archives and manuscripts; 123 reels of microfilm. **Subscriptions:** 55 journals and other serials. **Services:** SDI; library open to public for reference use only on application. **Staff:** Mary Mylenki, Sr.Asst.Libn.

★8995★
NEW YORK HOSPITAL-CORNELL MEDICAL CENTER, WESTCHESTER DIVISION - MEDICAL LIBRARY (Med)
21 Bloomingdale Rd.   Phone: (914) 682-9100
White Plains, NY 10605   Lillian A. Wahrow, Med.Libn.
Founded: 1823. **Staff:** Prof 2; Other 1. **Subjects:** Psychiatry, clinical psychology, psychoanalysis. **Holdings:** 4970 books; 4354 bound periodical volumes; 19 VF drawers of reprints and pamphlets. **Subscriptions:** 196 journals and other serials. **Services:** Interlibrary loans; copying; library open to local professionals. **Special Indexes:** Specialized indexes to literature of psychiatry and psychoanalysis. **Staff:** Marcia A. Miller, Asst.Libn.

NEW YORK HOSPITAL - PAYNE WHITNEY PSYCHIATRIC CLINIC LIBRARY
See: Payne Whitney Psychiatric Clinic Library

★8996★
NEW YORK INFIRMARY BEEKMAN DOWNTOWN HOSPITAL - ELISHA WALKER STAFF LIBRARY (Med)
170 William St.   Phone: (212) 233-5300
New York, NY 10038   Lois Sook, Med.Libn.
Staff: Prof 1. **Subjects:** Medicine, surgery, nursing. **Holdings:** 4500 volumes; 105 bound journals; reprints; catalogs; reports. **Subscriptions:** 145 journals and other serials. **Services:** Interlibrary loans; copying; library open to doctors and other authorized personnel on request.

★8997★

NEW YORK INSTITUTE FOR THE EDUCATION OF THE BLIND - WALTER BROOKS LIBRARY (Educ; Aud-Vis)

999 Pelham Pkwy.
Bronx, NY 10469
Phone: (212) 547-1234
Helen C. Isherwood, Libn.

Founded: 1832. **Staff:** Prof 1. **Special Collections:** Special education. **Holdings:** 22,000 books (6600 ink-print, 14,750 braille, 650 talking books); 5000 pamphlets; 10 VF drawers; 205 filmstrips; 200 tapes. **Subscriptions:** 66 journals and other serials. **Services:** Library open to graduate students.

★8998★

NEW YORK INSTITUTE OF TECHNOLOGY - CENTER FOR ENERGY POLICY AND RESEARCH - ENERGY INFORMATION CENTER (Energy)

Phone: (516) 686-7765
Old Westbury, NY 11568   Mickie Watterson, Assoc.Dir., Info.Sys.

Staff: Prof 2; Other 6. **Subjects:** Energy conservation and legislation, alternative energy systems, public policy developments. **Special Collections:** Solar energy (250 books, documents, journals). **Holdings:** 1160 books; 12,000 documents, reports, manuscripts, pamphlets, clippings, and catalogs. **Subscriptions:** 250 journals and other serials. **Services:** Copying; SDI; center open to public by appointment. **Computerized Information Services:** DIALOG, BRS, DOE/RECON. **Networks/Consortia:** Member of Long Island Library Resources Council (LILRC); Long Island Regional Advisory Council on Higher Education. **Staff:** Carol Spencer, Asst.Libn.

★8999★

NEW YORK INSTITUTE OF TECHNOLOGY - LIBRARY (Sci-Tech)

Wheatley Rd.
Old Westbury, NY 11568
Phone: (516) 686-7657
Dr. Constance Woo, Act.Dir. of Libs.

Staff: Prof 13; Other 15. **Subjects:** Business, technology, architecture, fine arts, electrical and computer technology, communication arts. **Special Collections:** ERIC Documents. **Holdings:** 80,000 books; 21,000 bound periodical volumes; 13,000 reels of microfilm; 29 VF cabinets. **Subscriptions:** 1000 journals and other serials. **Services:** Interlibrary loans (fee); copying; library open to public for reference use only. **Computerized Information Services:** DIALOG, BRS. **Networks/Consortia:** Member of Long Island Library Resources Council (LILRC); METRO. **Publications:** Library Guide. **Remarks:** Maintains branch libraries at 1855 Broadway, New York, NY 10023 and at 6350 Jericho Turnpike, Commack, NY 11725. **Staff:** Marjorie Shapiro, Tech.Serv.Div.; Ethel Gold, Ref.; Jane Barry, Acq.Libn.; Stephen Van Dyk, Art/Arch.Libn.

★9000★

NEW YORK LAW INSTITUTE - LIBRARY (Law)

120 Broadway, Rm. 932
New York, NY 10005
Phone: (212) 732-8720
Sieglinde H. Rothschild, Libn.

Founded: 1828. **Staff:** Prof 5; Other 12. **Subjects:** Law. **Special Collections:** Records and briefs of the New York Court of Appeals and Supreme Court, Appelate Division, 1st, 2nd and 3rd departments; legal Americana and incunabula. **Holdings:** 210,000 books; 22,820 bound periodical volumes; loose-leaf serials; microfilm; microfiche; periodicals. **Services:** Library open to public with restrictions. **Computerized Information Services:** Computerized cataloging. **Staff:** James C. Backes, Asst.Libn.; Stanley J. Walag, Asst.Libn.; Nancy G. Joseph, Asst.Libn.

★9001★

NEW YORK LAW SCHOOL - LIBRARY (Law)

57 Worth St.
New York, NY 10013
Phone: (212) 966-3500
Roy M. Mersky, Lib.Dir.

Founded: 1891. **Staff:** Prof 6; Other 8. **Subjects:** Law. **Special Collections:** Olin Collection (law periodicals). **Holdings:** 200,000 books; 11,000 bound periodical volumes. **Subscriptions:** 848 journals and other serials. **Services:** Interlibrary loans; copying; library not open to public. **Computerized Information Services:** LEXIS; computerized cataloging. **Networks/Consortia:** Member of OCLC. **Staff:** Joyce Saltalamachia, Assoc.Libn.

★9002★

NEW YORK LIFE INSURANCE COMPANY - LAW LIBRARY (Law)

51 Madison Ave., Rm. 10SB
New York, NY 10010
Phone: (212) 576-6458
Margaret Butler, Law Libn.

Founded: 1946. **Staff:** Prof 1; Other 2. **Subjects:** Law. **Holdings:** 25,000 volumes. **Services:** Interlibrary loans; library not open to public.

★9003★

NEW YORK LIFE INSURANCE COMPANY - MEDICAL DEPARTMENT LIBRARY (Med)

51 Madison Ave.
New York, NY 10010
Phone: (212) 576-6246
Thomas Jernigan, M.D., Med.Dir.

Founded: 1900. **Staff:** Prof 1; Other 1. **Subjects:** Medicine and surgery.

Holdings: 400 books; 900 bound periodical volumes. **Subscriptions:** 20 journals and other serials. **Services:** Library is open to New York Life employees.

★9004★

NEW YORK LIFE INSURANCE COMPANY - NEW YORK LIFE LIBRARY (Bus-Fin)

51 Madison Ave.
New York, NY 10010
Phone: (212) 576-6738
Gail W. Johnson, Sr.Libn.

Founded: 1938. **Staff:** Prof 2; Other 1. **Subjects:** Life insurance, economics, business management, statistics. **Holdings:** 7000 books; 200 pamphlets (cataloged). **Subscriptions:** 280 journals and other serials; 5 newspapers. **Services:** Interlibrary loans; copying; library open to SLA members. **Staff:** Judy L. Wallach, Asst.Libn.

NEW YORK MEDICAL COLLEGE - COLER MEMORIAL HOSPITAL
See: Coler Memorial Hospital

★9005★

NEW YORK MEDICAL COLLEGE - DEPARTMENT OF PSYCHIATRY - LIBRARY (Med)

Metropolitan Hospital Ctr.
1901 First Ave., Rm. 10M13
New York, NY 10029
Phone: (212) 360-7285
Lorna Macdonald, Libn.

Founded: 1961. **Staff:** Prof 1. **Subjects:** Psychiatry, psychoanalysis. **Holdings:** 6400 volumes; 3 VF drawers of reprints; 21 films. **Subscriptions:** 66 journals and other serials. **Services:** Library not open to public.

★9006★

NEW YORK MEDICAL COLLEGE AND THE WESTCHESTER ACADEMY OF MEDICINE - WESTCHESTER MEDICAL CENTER LIBRARY (Med)

New York Medical College
Basic Sciences Bldg.
Valhalla, NY 10595
Phone: (914) 347-5237
Donald E. Roy, Dir.

Founded: 1972. **Staff:** Prof 7; Other 8. **Subjects:** Basic science, clinical medicine. **Special Collections:** History of medicine; rare books in medicine and science. **Holdings:** 32,000 books; 85,000 bound periodical volumes; 60 VF drawers; 616 microfiche; 410 reels of microfilm; 32 audiotapes; 210 videotapes. **Subscriptions:** 1458 journals and other serials; 5 newspapers. **Services:** Interlibrary loans; copying; library open to health professionals only or to those who purchase a special membership. **Computerized Information Services:** MEDLARS, DIALOG, BRS; computerized cataloging and serials. **Networks/Consortia:** Member of OCLC; Medical Library Center of New York (MLCNY). **Publications:** Center News, 6/year - internal distribution and to 250 libraries in a nine-county area. **Staff:** Luiza Balthazar, Hd., ILL; Rosalie Stone, Hd., Tech.Serv.; Maureen Czujak, Hd., Rd.Serv.; Rita Lee, ILL Coord.; Arlene Miller, Hd., Circ.; Judith Myers, Acq.

NEW YORK MEDICAL LIBRARY CENTER
See: Medical Library Center of New York

★9007★

NEW YORK METROPOLITAN TRANSPORTATION COUNCIL - LIBRARY

One World Trade Ctr., 82nd Fl.
New York, NY 10048
Founded: 1961. **Subjects:** Regional planning, transportation, economic development, census, grants, ecology, air pollution, land use, open space, master plans. **Holdings:** 7000 books; 10,000 technical reports. **Remarks:** Presently inactive. **Formerly:** Tri-State Regional Planning Commission.

NEW YORK OFFICE OF TECHNOLOGY TRANSFER - REFERENCE COLLECTION
See: U.S. Veterans Administration (NY-New York) - Office of Technology Transfer - Reference Collection

★9008★

NEW YORK ORTHOPAEDIC HOSPITAL - RUSSELL A. HIBBS LIBRARY (Med)†

622 W. 168th St.
New York, NY 10032
Phone: (212) 694-3294
Jack E. Termine, Med.Libn.

Staff: Prof 1. **Subjects:** Orthopedics. **Special Collections:** Anatomical and surgical incunabula (16th, 17th, and 18th centuries). **Holdings:** 5500 volumes; staff papers from 1866 to present; slide/tape programs; video cassette recordings. **Subscriptions:** 45 journals and other serials. **Services:** Interlibrary loans; copying; library open to public by appointment, all services are fee-based. **Computerized Information Services:** MEDLARS. **Publications:** Library Newsletter, monthly; Bulletin of the New York Orthopaedic Hospital. **Special Catalogs:** Catalog of classical and rare books of the collection (in progress).

★9009★
NEW YORK POST - LIBRARY (Publ)†
210 South St.   Phone: (212) 349-5000
New York, NY 10002   Merrill F. Sherr, Hd.Libn.
Founded: 1920. **Staff:** Prof 4; Other 6. **Subjects:** Newspaper reference topics. **Holdings:** 5000 books; 10,000 pamphlets; 5 million clippings; 600,000 pictures. **Services:** Library not open to public.

★9010★
NEW YORK PSYCHOANALYTIC INSTITUTE - ABRAHAM A. BRILL LIBRARY
  (Med)
247 E. Eighty-Second St.   Phone: (212) 879-6900
New York, NY 10028   Ellen Gilbert, Asst.Libn.
Founded: 1932. **Staff:** Prof 1; Other 2. **Subjects:** Psychoanalysis, psychiatry. **Special Collections:** Works of Sigmund Freud in all available translations; Kris Memorial Collection (books in allied fields); archives and oral history. **Holdings:** 20,000 volumes. **Subscriptions:** 100 journals and other serials. **Services:** Interlibrary loans; copying; special permission to use library may be requested.

★9011★
**NEW YORK PUBLIC LIBRARY - ANNEX SECTION - NEWSPAPERS AND
  OTHER RESEARCH MATERIALS COLLECTION** (Info Sci)
521 W. 43rd St.   Phone: (212) 930-0847
New York, NY 10036   Richard L. Hill, First Asst., Annex
Founded: 1911. **Staff:** Prof 1; Other 12. **Subjects:** Extensive coverage of New York City newspapers (English and foreign language); selective coverage for U.S. and principal foreign countries. **Holdings:** 700,000 city directories, telephone directories, periodicals, public documents and other material; 23,400 bound volumes of newspapers; 59,200 reels of microfilm. **Subscriptions:** 164 newspapers. **Services:** Copying. **Networks/Consortia:** Member of RLG; METRO; New York State Interlibrary Loan Network (NYSILL).

★9012★
NEW YORK PUBLIC LIBRARY - ANNEX SECTION - PATENTS COLLECTION
  (Sci-Tech)
521 W. 43rd St.   Phone: (212) 930-0850
New York, NY 10036   Richard L. Hill, First Asst., Annex
Founded: 1911. **Staff:** 3. **Subjects:** Complete U.S. and British patents, extensive holdings from France, Germany, Belgium, Denmark and Sweden, abstracts from other nations, complete files of U.S. indexes. **Holdings:** 86,800 volumes; 4200 reels of microfilm; 4800 microfiche. **Services:** Copying; collection open to public. **Computerized Information Services:** CASSIS. **Networks/Consortia:** Member of RLG; METRO; New York State Interlibrary Loan Network (NYSILL).

★9013★
**NEW YORK PUBLIC LIBRARY - ARENTS COLLECTION OF BOOKS IN PARTS
  AND ASSOCIATED MATERIALS** (Hum)
Fifth Ave. & 42nd St., Rm. 324   Phone: (212) 930-0801
New York, NY 10018   Bernard McTigue, Cur.
Founded: 1957. **Staff:** 1. **Subjects:** Books issued in installments or parts in original format, unbound parts as issued. **Holdings:** 1000 books; autograph letters, original drawings and manuscripts related to works issued in parts. **Services:** Open to qualified researchers by card of admission secured in Special Collections Office.

★9014★
NEW YORK PUBLIC LIBRARY - ARENTS TOBACCO COLLECTION (Agri)
Fifth Ave. & 42nd St., Rm. 324   Phone: (212) 930-0801
New York, NY 10018   Bernard McTigue, Cur.
Founded: 1944. **Staff:** 1. **Subjects:** Tobacco, herbals, history, medicine, law. **Special Collections:** Autograph letters; manuscripts; first editions of English and American drama, poetry, prose containing mention of tobacco; selected tobacco ephemera. **Holdings:** 9000 items. **Services:** Open to qualified researchers by card of admission secured in Special Collections Office.

★9015★
**NEW YORK PUBLIC LIBRARY - ART, PRINTS & PHOTOGRAPHS DIVISION -
  ART AND ARCHITECTURE COLLECTION** (Art)
Fifth Ave. & 42nd St., Rm. 313   Phone: (212) 930-0834
New York, NY 10018   Joseph T. Rankin, Chf.
Staff: Prof 6. **Subjects:** Architecture, painting, drawing, sculpture, costume, applied arts, ceramics, interior decoration, Oriental art, photography. **Holdings:** 100,000 volumes and pamphlets; 500,000 clippings (arranged by name of artist). **Services:** Collection open to public for reference use only. **Networks/Consortia:** Member of RLG; METRO; New York State Interlibrary Loan Network (NYSILL).

★9016★
**NEW YORK PUBLIC LIBRARY - ART, PRINTS & PHOTOGRAPHS DIVISION -
  PRINT ROOM** (Pict)
Fifth Ave. & 42nd St., Rm. 308   Phone: (212) 930-0817
New York, NY 10018   Robert Rainwater, Kpr. of Prints
Founded: 1900. **Staff:** Prof 2. **Subjects:** Rare and fine prints from the 15th century to the present, with emphasis on 19th century French and American; representative examples of contemporary printmakers, American and international. **Special Collections:** Stokes and Eno Collections (American views); Japanese prints; books on printmaking, print collecting, and graphic arts. **Holdings:** 160,000 prints. **Services:** Room open to qualified researchers by card of admission secured in Special Collections Office.

★9017★
**NEW YORK PUBLIC LIBRARY - BELMONT REGIONAL LIBRARY - ENRICO
  FERMI CULTURAL CENTER** (Area-Ethnic)
610 E. 186th St.   Phone: (212) 933-6410
Bronx, NY 10458   Theresa K. Casile, Principal Libn.
Founded: 1981. **Staff:** Prof 5; Other 7. **Subjects:** Italian heritage and contribution to American ideals; immigration. **Special Collections:** Italian language books (2800); Italian/American biographies from newspapers and periodicals. **Holdings:** 32,000 books; filmstrips; recordings. **Subscriptions:** 102 journals and other serials; 10 newspapers. **Services:** Library open to public. **Staff:** Michela Lichtenstein, Asst.Libn.; Marisa Parish, Children's Libn.; Debra Aguece, Ref.Libn.

★9018★
NEW YORK PUBLIC LIBRARY - BERG COLLECTION (Rare Book)
Fifth Ave. & 42nd St., Rm. 318, 320   Phone: (212) 930-0802
New York, NY 10018   Dr. Lola L. Szladits, Cur.
Founded: 1940. **Subjects:** English and American literature of 15th to 20th centuries. **Holdings:** 25,000 books; 60,000 letters and manuscripts. **Services:** Library open by card of admission only. **Networks/Consortia:** Member of RLG; METRO; New York State Interlibrary Loan Network (NYSILL). **Special Catalogs:** Five-volume catalog published in 1969 with a one-volume supplement in 1975. **Remarks:** Incorporates libraries of Dr. Albert A. Berg, W.T.H. Howe, and Owen D. Young.

★9019★
NEW YORK PUBLIC LIBRARY - DONNELL LIBRARY CENTER
20 W. 53rd St.   Phone: (212) 621-0613
New York, NY 10019   Philip Gerrard, Prin.Coord.Libn.
Remarks: "Donnell Library Center provides extensive reference, advisory and lending services. It provides the most extensive service to children and young adults within The New York Public Library, through its Central Children's Room and Nathan Straus Young Adult Library. The system's major holdings in film and video and in foreign language materials are contained in Donnell's A/V Center and in the Foreign Language Library. The Donnell Library Center also includes a large Adult Lending Library, Reference Library and a large collection of recordings in the A/V Center. An auditorium offers a wide diversity of programs without charge to persons of all ages."

★9020★
**NEW YORK PUBLIC LIBRARY - DONNELL LIBRARY CENTER - AUDIO-VISUAL
  CENTER - FILM/VIDEO COLLECTION** (Aud-Vis)
20 W. 53rd St.   Phone: (212) 621-0609
New York, NY 10019   Marie Nesthus, Principal Libn.
Founded: 1958. **Staff:** Prof 4; Other 4. **Subjects:** General collection of short documentary and feature-length films for children, young adults and adults. **Special Collections:** Pamphlet collection of filmographies and sources of 16mm films. **Holdings:** 500 books; 5000 pamphlets; 5000 16mm sound films; 500 video cassettes. **Subscriptions:** 34 journals and other serials. **Services:** Films and video cassettes loaned to nonprofit organizations (not schools) and individuals in New York City; reference materials available for use within the library; Film/Video Study Center for viewing video cassettes; viewing equipment available for use by appointment. **Publications:** Film Catalog, Video Catalog - available for purchase.

★9021★
**NEW YORK PUBLIC LIBRARY - DONNELL LIBRARY CENTER - AUDIO-VISUAL
  CENTER - RECORD COLLECTION** (Aud-Vis; Mus)
20 W. 53rd St.   Phone: (212) 621-0624
New York, NY 10019   Louise Spain, Supv.Libn.
Founded: 1956. **Staff:** Prof 2. **Subjects:** Recordings of classical music, jazz, musical comedy and folk music; recordings of drama, poetry, speeches, documentaries in English and in some languages other than English; instructional recordings for learning English and over 40 European, African and Oriental languages; instructional recordings for steno-dictation, typing, spelling, Morse code, yoga and dance. **Holdings:** 24,000 phonograph records;

cassette and 8-track tape collection of classical and international popular music, language instruction and literature.

★9022★
NEW YORK PUBLIC LIBRARY - DONNELL LIBRARY CENTER - CENTRAL CHILDREN'S ROOM (Hum)
20 W. 53rd St.   Phone: (212) 621-0636
New York, NY 10019   Angeline Moscatt, Supv.Libn.
Founded: 1911. **Staff:** Prof 3; Other 1. **Subjects:** 20th century fiction and nonfiction, folklore, histories of children's literature, foreign languages. **Special Collections:** Historical collection of children's literature; Mary Gould Davis - Folklore; Erica Davies - autographed copies. **Holdings:** 95,000 books; 600 bound periodical volumes; phonograph records; cassettes; filmstrips; vertical files of clippings and pamphlets. **Services:** Copying; library open to public; appointment must be made to use rare book collection.

★9023★
NEW YORK PUBLIC LIBRARY - DONNELL LIBRARY CENTER - FOREIGN LANGUAGE LIBRARY (Hum)
20 W. 53rd St.   Phone: (212) 621-0641
New York, NY 10019   Bosiljka Stevanovic, Supv.Libn.
Founded: 1955. **Staff:** Prof 4; Other 3. **Subjects:** Books in foreign languages with emphasis on classical and contemporary literature in the languages represented. **Holdings:** Bilingual dictionaries, foreign language grammars and encyclopedias (for reference only); magazines of general interest. **Services:** Interlibrary loans; telephone reference.

★9024★
NEW YORK PUBLIC LIBRARY - DONNELL LIBRARY CENTER - NATHAN STRAUS YOUNG ADULT LIBRARY (Hum)
20 W. 53rd St.   Phone: (212) 621-0633
New York, NY 10019   Beryl Eber, Supv.Libn.
Founded: 1941. **Staff:** Prof 4. **Subjects:** Young adult literature. **Special Collections:** Historical collection of young adult books; reference copies of books appearing on New York Public Library's Books for the Teenage list (1250); Learners Advisory Service for Teenagers. **Holdings:** 10,063 books; posters; 119 filmstrips; 8 VF drawers of pamphlets; recreational materials; games. **Subscriptions:** 67 journals and other serials. **Services:** Interlibrary loans; library open to public. **Computerized Information Services:** Computerized cataloging.

★9025★
NEW YORK PUBLIC LIBRARY - EARLY CHILDHOOD RESOURCE AND INFORMATION CENTER (Educ)
66 Leroy St.   Phone: (212) 929-0815
New York, NY 10014   Hannah Nuba Scheffler, Dir.
Founded: 1978. **Staff:** Prof 2; Other 2. **Subjects:** Early childhood and parent education, pre-natal care, parent-child activities, language and intellectual development, multicultural and multilingual education, adoption and foster care. **Special Collections:** Adult collection on child development, parenting, education and special needs; browsing collection of children's books and puzzles. **Holdings:** 8500 books; 75 filmstrips; 43 noncirculating films; toys; pamphlets. **Subscriptions:** 125 journals and other serials. **Services:** Library open to public; offers 160 free workshops per year. **Computerized Information Services:** Computerized cataloging and acquisitions.

★9026★
NEW YORK PUBLIC LIBRARY - ECONOMIC AND PUBLIC AFFAIRS DIVISION (Bus-Fin; Soc Sci)
Fifth Ave. & 42nd St., Rm. 228   Phone: (212) 930-0750
New York, NY 10018   Edward Di Roma, Div.Chf.
Staff: Prof 12; Other 13. **Subjects:** Business and the social sciences (except history) with special emphasis on advertising, banking, demography, finance, government, industrial relations, insurance, international relations, marketing, public administration, sociology and statistics. **Special Collections:** Government publications of national, state and municipal jurisdictions throughout the world and of intergovernmental organizations; proceedings of conferences and symposia. **Holdings:** 1.35 million volumes; 950,000 micro-opaques; 272,000 microfiche; 91,000 reels of microfilm. **Subscriptions:** 12,000 journals and other serials. **Services:** Copying; open to public. **Computerized Information Services:** Computerized cataloging. **Networks/Consortia:** Member of RLG; METRO; New York State Interlibrary Loan Network (NYSILL). **Remarks:** Public Affairs Information Service is housed in this division but is not part of the library. **Staff:** Shirley L. Spranger, Hd., Pub.Serv.Sect.; Irene Itina, Hd., Govt.Doc.Sect.

★9027★
NEW YORK PUBLIC LIBRARY - GENERAL LIBRARY OF THE PERFORMING ARTS (Mus; Theater)
111 Amsterdam Ave.   Phone: (212) 870-1630
New York, NY 10023   George L. Mayer, Coord.
Founded: 1965. **Staff:** Prof 15; Other 10. **Subjects:** Music, drama, dance, other performing arts. **Special Collections:** Orchestra Collection (1500 sets); Children's Collection; museum which mounts special exhibits, but does not comprise a permanent collection. **Holdings:** 161,319 books; 2250 bound periodical volumes; 96 VF drawers; 96,488 music scores (cataloged); 41,509 recordings (cataloged). **Subscriptions:** 274 journals and other serials. **Services:** Copying; library open to public. **Computerized Information Services:** Computerized cataloging and acquisitions. **Networks/Consortia:** Member of METRO; Library Information and Online Network (LIONS). **Special Indexes:** Song index (card); play analytics; special subject bibliographies and discographies. **Staff:** Alan H. Sattler, Supv.Libn.; Lawrence Cioppa, Supv. Drama Libn.; John L. Hildreth, Supv.Rec.Libn.; Carlotta Gary, Sr. Orchestra Libn.; Elsie Peck, Sr. Dance Libn.; Elizabeth Long, Sr. Children's Libn.; Kristen Shuman, Supv. Music Libn.

★9028★
NEW YORK PUBLIC LIBRARY - GENERAL RESEARCH DIVISION (Hum)
Fifth Ave. & 42nd St.   Phone: (212) 930-0831
New York, NY 10011   Rodney Phillips, Chf.
Staff: Prof 28; Other 18. **Subjects:** American history, anthropology, archeology, bibliography, biography, geography, history, languages and literatures of the world (except collections in Jewish, Slavonic and Oriental Divisions), philology, philosophy, printing, publishing, psychology, religion, sports. **Special Collections:** Spaulding and Goulston Collections (baseball); David McKelvy White Collection (Spanish Civil War); folklore of the Americas; Indians of the Western Hemisphere; chess collections; small press poetry. **Holdings:** Over 2 million volumes. **Subscriptions:** 9000 journals and other serials. **Services:** Copying; open to public for reference use only. **Networks/Consortia:** Member of RLG; METRO; New York State Interlibrary Loan Network (NYSILL). **Remarks:** Contains holdings of the former American History Division, General Research & Humanities Division and the Periodicals Section.

★9029★
NEW YORK PUBLIC LIBRARY - JEWISH DIVISION (Area-Ethnic)
Fifth Ave. & 42nd St., Rm. 84   Phone: (212) 930-0601
New York, NY 10018   Leonard S. Gold, Div.Chf.
Founded: 1897. **Staff:** Prof 6; Other 6. **Subjects:** General works in Hebrew and Yiddish; Jewish history, literature and traditions (in various languages). **Special Collections:** Rare Hebrew books including 40 incunabula; early kabbalistic and ethical tracts; illuminated Ketubot (marriage contracts). **Holdings:** 190,000 volumes; newspapers, periodicals, microfilm, microfiche. **Networks/Consortia:** Member of RLG; METRO; New York State Interlibrary Loan Network (NYSILL).

★9030★
NEW YORK PUBLIC LIBRARY - MAP DIVISION (Geog-Map)
Fifth Ave. & 42nd St., Rm. 117   Phone: (212) 930-0587
New York, NY 10018   Alice C. Hudson, Div.Chf.
Staff: Prof 4; Other 2. **Subjects:** History of cartography, techniques of map making; gazetteers; state, county, historical and real estate atlases; city plans; travel. **Special Collections:** Scrapbook collection of small-size sheet maps. **Holdings:** 10,000 atlases and folded maps in binders; 2500 volumes; 350,000 sheet maps. **Subscriptions:** 110 journals and other serials. **Services:** Copying. **Computerized Information Services:** Computerized cataloging. **Networks/Consortia:** Member of RLG; METRO; New York State Interlibrary Loan Network (NYSILL). **Staff:** Robert B. Sperling, Asst.Chf.; Nancy A. Kandoian, Map Cat.; Edith Ostrowsky, Ref.Spec.

★9031★
NEW YORK PUBLIC LIBRARY - MICROFORMS DIVISION
Fifth Ave. & 42nd St.   Phone: (212) 930-0838
New York, NY 10018   Thomas Bourke, Chf.
Founded: 1980. **Staff:** Prof 1; Other 5. **Subjects:** Literature, psychology, social science, science. **Special Collections:** FBI files on the Assassination of President Kennedy; American Civil Liberties Union papers; history of women collection; papers pertaining to the Amistad Schooner case. **Holdings:** 125,000 reels of microfilm; 150,000 microfiche; 6000 microcards; city directories; newspapers. **Subscriptions:** 4000 journals and other serials; 200 newspapers. **Services:** Interlibrary loans (limited); copying; library open to public. **Computerized Information Services:** DIALOG, RLIN; computerized cataloging and acquisitions. **Networks/Consortia:** Member of RLG; METRO; New York State Interlibrary Loan Network (NYSILL).

★9032★
NEW YORK PUBLIC LIBRARY - MID-MANHATTAN LIBRARY
455 Fifth Ave.   Phone: (212) 340-0833
New York, NY 10016   Julia J. Brody, Chf.
Staff: Prof 66; Other 93. **Holdings:** 722,211 books; 38,000 bound periodical volumes. **Subscriptions:** 4500 journals and other serials; 45 newspapers. **Services:** Interlibrary loans; copying; library open to public. **Computerized Information Services:** Computerized cataloging and acquisitions. **Networks/Consortia:** Member of METRO. **Remarks:** "The Mid-Manhattan Library, which opened on October 26, 1970, is the central library of the New York Public Library's Branch Library System. It provides a needed transition between the level of service provided by the neighborhood branches and library centers and that provided through the vast scholarly collections of the Research Libraries of the New York Public Library. Mid-Manhattan Library's primary function is to serve, through open shelf collections, the serious adult reader and the college undergraduate and masters level student. The collections of the library are housed in a History and Social Science Department, a Literature and Language Department, a Science and Business Department, and the General Reference Service/Education (see entries below). The departments contain both reference and circulating materials. The library has strong holdings in serials, especially those appearing in the standard indexes. Its catalog is computer-produced and in book form." **Staff:** Robert M. Thomas, Asst.Chf.

★9033★
NEW YORK PUBLIC LIBRARY - MID-MANHATTAN LIBRARY - ART LIBRARY
   (Art)
455 Fifth Ave.   Phone: (212) 340-0871
New York, NY 10016   Rebecca Siekevitz, Supv.Libn.
Founded: 1956. **Staff:** Prof 3. **Subjects:** Fine arts, architecture, graphic art, photography. **Holdings:** 17,000 books; 1400 bound periodical volumes; 150 reels of microfilmed periodicals; 20 VF drawers of clippings and catalogs. **Subscriptions:** 75 journals and other serials. **Services:** Copying; library open to public. **Remarks:** Library is part of the Literature, Language and Art Department.

★9034★
NEW YORK PUBLIC LIBRARY - MID-MANHATTAN LIBRARY - GENERAL
   REFERENCE SERVICE/EDUCATION (Educ)
455 Fifth Ave.   Phone: (212) 340-0861
New York, NY 10016   Eleanor Radwan, Sr. Principal Libn.
Founded: 1970. **Staff:** Prof 15; Other 11. **Special Collections:** College catalogs, U.S. and foreign (4000); ERIC microfiche from 1966. **Holdings:** 43,706 books; 7987 bound periodical volumes. **Subscriptions:** 642 journals and other serials; 39 newspapers. **Services:** Copying; library open to public. **Remarks:** This department provides general reference services, telephone reference service, and specialized service in the field of education. **Staff:** Evelyn Williams, First Asst., Gen.Ref.; Dorothy Fludd, Educ.Libn.; Mary Brady, Telephone Ref.Serv.

★9035★
NEW YORK PUBLIC LIBRARY - MID-MANHATTAN LIBRARY - HISTORY AND
   SOCIAL SCIENCES DEPARTMENT (Hist; Soc Sci)
455 Fifth Ave.   Phone: (212) 340-0890
New York, NY 10016   Robert C. Sheehan, Sr. Principal Libn.
Founded: 1970. **Staff:** Prof 9; Other 5. **Subjects:** History, psychology, sociology, law, religion, philosophy. **Special Collections:** New York City history (3000 volumes); Microbook Library of American Civilization (ultrafiche). **Holdings:** 225,000 books; 10,000 bound periodical volumes; 60 VF drawers of pamphlets; selective government depository. **Subscriptions:** 2000 journals and other serials. **Services:** Interlibrary loans; copying; library open to public. **Staff:** Shirley Quement, First Asst.; Doris Neville, Supv.Libn.; Phyllis Current, Supv.Libn.

★9036★
NEW YORK PUBLIC LIBRARY - MID-MANHATTAN LIBRARY - LEARNER'S
   ADVISORY SERVICE (Educ)
455 Fifth Ave.   Phone: (212) 340-0835
New York, NY 10016   Barbara Shapiro, Supv.Libn.
Founded: 1975. **Staff:** Prof 5. **Subjects:** Educational and career guidance. **Holdings:** 300 books. **Subscriptions:** 12 journals and other serials. **Services:** Service open to public by appointment.

★9037★
NEW YORK PUBLIC LIBRARY - MID-MANHATTAN LIBRARY - LITERATURE,
   LANGUAGE & ART DEPARTMENT (Hum)
455 Fifth Ave.   Phone: (212) 340-0875
New York, NY 10016   Eric Steele, Sr. Principal Libn.
Founded: 1970. **Staff:** Prof 8; Other 3. **Subjects:** English and American

literature; French and Spanish literature; other foreign literatures in translation; linguistics; languages and language learning. **Holdings:** 97,500 books; 3000 bound periodical volumes; 4500 language and nonmusic phonodiscs and tape cassettes; 10,000 volumes of English literature on microfiche; 7000 periodical volumes in microform. **Subscriptions:** 375 journals and other serials. **Services:** Interlibrary loans; copying; closed circuit television enlarger; library open to public.

★9038★
NEW YORK PUBLIC LIBRARY - MID-MANHATTAN LIBRARY - PICTURE
   COLLECTION (Pict)
455 Fifth Ave.   Phone: (212) 340-0878
New York, NY 10016   Lenore Cowan, Cur.
Founded: 1915. **Staff:** Prof 8; Other 6. **Subjects:** Comprehensive subject coverage in the following areas: costume, flora and fauna, history, geographic views, design. **Holdings:** Over 2.5 million classified pictures. **Services:** Copying; library open to public with valid library card, except for classroom use or exhibition.

★9039★
NEW YORK PUBLIC LIBRARY - MID-MANHATTAN LIBRARY - PROJECT
   ACCESS (Aud-Vis)
455 Fifth Ave.   Phone: (212) 340-0843
New York, NY 10016   Diane Wolfe, Sr.Libn.
Staff: Prof 1; Other 1. **Subjects:** The disabled - blind, deaf, learning and mobility impaired. **Special Collections:** Directory collection of organizations, services, equipment and information sources for the disabled; access guides. **Holdings:** 10 VF drawers of pamphlet material concerning the disabled; career information on cassettes. **Services:** Library open to public by appointment; special equipment available for use. **Publications:** Bibliographies available on request. **Special Indexes:** Subject index to organizations, services, equipment, information sources and AV materials for and about the disabled (card). **Remarks:** The Telecommunications Device for the Deaf (TDD) telephone number is 340-0931.

★9040★
NEW YORK PUBLIC LIBRARY - MID-MANHATTAN LIBRARY - READERS'
   ADVISER'S OFFICE (Educ)
455 Fifth Ave.   Phone: (212) 340-0866
New York, NY 10016   Adele Greenberg, Rd.Adv.
Founded: 1929. **Staff:** Prof 1. **Subjects:** Individual reading guidance, library orientation. **Holdings:** 900 books. **Subscriptions:** 11 journals and other serials. **Services:** Library open to public. **Computerized Information Services:** Computerized cataloging.

★9041★
NEW YORK PUBLIC LIBRARY - MID-MANHATTAN LIBRARY - SCIENCE/
   BUSINESS DEPARTMENT (Sci-Tech; Bus-Fin)
455 Fifth Ave.   Phone: (212) 340-0882
New York, NY 10016   Frederick Dusold, Sr. Principal Libn.
Founded: 1970. **Staff:** Prof 10; Other 6. **Subjects:** Life sciences, pure and applied sciences, mathematics, economics, insurance, management. **Holdings:** 140,000 books; 15,000 bound periodical volumes; 12,000 volumes of periodicals in microform; 1700 phonograph records and cassettes. **Subscriptions:** 1440 journals and other serials; 6 newspapers. **Services:** Interlibrary loans; copying; library open to public. **Computerized Information Services:** Computerized cataloging. **Staff:** Natalie Rubenstein, Supv.Libn./Sci.Coll.; Donald G. Alexis, Supv.Libn./Bus.Coll.

★9042★
NEW YORK PUBLIC LIBRARY - ORIENTAL DIVISION (Area-Ethnic)
Fifth Ave. & 42nd St., Rm. 219   Phone: (212) 930-0716
New York, NY 10018   E. Christian Filstrup, Div.Chf.
Founded: 1897. **Staff:** Prof 5; Other 10. **Subjects:** Oriental languages and literature, Oriental religions, archeology of the Orient. **Special Collections:** Arabic manuscripts; Japanese technical periodicals. **Holdings:** 120,000 books; 11,000 bound periodical volumes; 650 pamphlets. **Services:** Open to public for reference use only. **Networks/Consortia:** Member of RLG; METRO; New York State Interlibrary Loan Network (NYSILL).

★9043★
NEW YORK PUBLIC LIBRARY - PERFORMING ARTS RESEARCH CENTER -
   BILLY ROSE THEATRE COLLECTION (Theater)
111 Amsterdam Ave.   Phone: (212) 870-1639
New York, NY 10023   Dorothy L. Swerdlove, Cur.
Founded: 1931. **Staff:** Prof 6; Other 17. **Subjects:** Stage, cinema, marionettes and puppets, industrial shows, circus, amusement parks, fairs, carnivals, night club and cabaret, radio and television. **Special Collections:** Robinson Locke Collection; Hiram Stead Collection; Henin Collection;

Chamberlain and Lyman Brown Theatrical Agency Collection; Archives of the Vandamm and White Studios; Society of American Magicians; Universal Pictures Still Books; Townsend Walsh Collection; George Becks Collection; Archives of Jules Irving's period of management, Vivian Beaumont Theater, NY; Archives of Lambs Club, NY; scrapbooks, office records, memorabilia of performing artists, writers and professional organizations, including: Brooks Atkinson, David Belasco, Katharine Cornell, Helen Hayes, Klaw and Erlanger, R.H. Burnside, Burl Ives, Maurice Evans, Jerome Lawrence and Robert E. Lee, Harold Clurman, Edward Albee, The Living Theatre, The Actor's Workshop (San Francisco), Leland Hayward, Sophie Tucker, Playwrights Company, Clifford Odets, Alexander H. Cohen, Neighborhood Playhouse (New York), Group Theatre, Montgomery Clift, John Golden, Hallie Flanagan, Elliott Nugent, Israel Horovitz, Jean Dalrymple, Paul Muni. The theatre collection maintains active clipping files on the personnel in all the areas of the performing arts within its purview, on theatre buildings, producing organizations, corporate bodies, amateur theatre and cinema groups, college and university theatre and cinema organizations and under several hundred subject headings (1000 VF drawers). Original designs for stage, cinema and television by famous designers including: Jo Mielziner, Ladislaus Czettel, Robert Edmond Jones, Bonnie Cashin, Lucinda Ballard, Aline Bernstein, John Boyt, Claude Bragdon, Mstislav Dobujinsky, Alexandra Exter, David Ffolkes, Simon Lissim, Norman Bel Geddes, Donald Oenslager, Irene Sharaff, Sergei Soudeikine; original drawings by Alex Gard, Al Frueh, Al Hirschfeld, Milton Marx, Bert Green. An additional dimension has been added to the collection through an archive of productions and dialogues on videotape. Collection has acquired production texts for most of the Hallmark Television specials; several years of the daily installments of Elaine Sterne Carrington's radio serials: Pepper Young's Family, When a Girl Marries, and Rosemary. **Holdings:** 70,000 books; 36,000 bound periodical volumes; 30,000 scrapbooks and portfolios; 2000 microforms; 2 million photographs and cinema stills; 800 reels of videotape and film; prompt books and typescripts; shooting scripts of motion pictures; radio and television production scripts; 1000 VF drawers of clippings and programs; 25 VF drawers of letters, business papers. **Subscriptions:** 500 journals and other serials. **Services:** Interlibrary loans, copying (both limited); collection open to public. **Networks/Consortia:** Member of RLG; METRO; New York State Interlibrary Loan Network (NYSILL). **Publications:** Printed book catalog and nonbook catalog.

★9044★
NEW YORK PUBLIC LIBRARY - PERFORMING ARTS RESEARCH CENTER - DANCE COLLECTION (Art)
111 Amsterdam Ave.   Phone: (212) 870-1657
New York, NY 10023   Genevieve Oswald, Cur.
Founded: 1944. **Staff:** Prof 8; Other 5. **Subjects:** All forms of dance. **Special Collections:** Jerome Robbins Archive of dance films and videotapes; Cia Fornaroli Toscanini (rare ballet history; 15,000 items); Lincoln Kirstein (rare dance history); Fania Marinoff (5000 photographs by Carl Van Vechten); Roger Pryor Dodge (Nijinsky photographs); George Platt Lynes (American ballet; 3000 negatives); Robert W. Dowling (Albert E. Kahn photographs of Galina Ulanova); Constantine (American ballet; 2300 photographs and negatives); Denishawn (American dance; 50,000 items); Ruth St. Denis (10,000 items); Ted Shawn (8000 items); Humphrey-Weidman (modern dance; 5000 items); Doris Humphrey (7000 items); Jose Limon Collection; Helen Tamiris Collection; Hanya Holm (modern dance in Europe and America; 1200 items); Irma Duncan (Isadora Duncan memorabilia); Craig-Duncan Collection (400 Isadora Duncan manuscripts); Loie Fuller Collection; American Ballet Theatre Archives; Ballet Russe de Monte Carlo-Serge Denham Collection; Astruc-Dyagilev (Dyagilev Ballets Russes; 1300 documents); Irving Deakin (American ballet); Ruth Page Collection; Claire Holt Collection on Asian dance (9000 items). **Holdings:** 40,000 books; 2000 original drawings and stage designs; 355,000 manuscripts; 750 reels of microfilm; 3200 reels of videotape (1642 titles); over 2.6 million feet of motion picture film (2166 titles); 1535 oral history tapes; 2190 scrapbooks; 200,000 clippings and reviews; 249,000 photographs; 150,400 photographic negatives; 4400 posters; 6000 prints; 92,000 programs. **Subscriptions:** 75 journals and other serials. **Services:** Copying; collection open to public. **Networks/Consortia:** Member of RLG; METRO; New York State Interlibrary Loan Network (NYSILL). **Publications:** Dictionary Catalog of the Dance Collection, 10 volumes, 1974 (annual supplements); The Dance Collection: Descriptive Leaflet; Isadora Duncan, Pioneer in the Art of Dance, by Irma Duncan, 1958; When All the World was Dancing: Rare and Curious Books from the Cia Fornaroli Collection, by Marian Eames, 1958 (2nd ed. 1971); Famed for Dance: Essays on the Theory and Practice of Theatrical Dancing in England, 1660-1740, by Ifan Kyrle Fletcher, Selma Jeanne Cohen, and Roger Lonsdale, 1960; New York's First Ballet Season, 1792, by Lillian Moore, 1961; The Professional Appearances of Ruth St. Denis and Ted Shawn: a Chronology and an Index of Dances, 1906-1932, by Christena L. Schlundt, 1962; Stravinsky and the Dance: a Survey of Ballet Productions, 1910-1962, by Selma Jeanne Cohen, introduction by Herbert Read, 1962; Stravinsky and

the Theatre: a Catalog of Decor and Costume Designs for Stage Productions of his Works, 1910-1962, 1963; Dancing in Prints, a Portfolio of Twelve Etchings, Engravings and Lithographs, 1634-1870, with Commentary by Marian Eames, 1964; Bournonville's London Spring, by Lillian Moore, 1965; Images of the Dance, Historical Treasures of the Dance Collection, 1581-1861, by Lillian Moore, 1965; The Professional Appearances of Ted Shawn & His Men Dancers: a Chronology and an Index of Dances, 1933-1940, by Christena L. Schlundt, 1967; The Papers of Gabriel Astruc, 1864-1938, a Register, by Nicki N. Ostrom, 1971; Tamiris, a Chronicle of Her Dance Career, 1927-1955, by Christena L. Schlundt, 1972; Your Isadora, by Francis Steegmuller, 1974; The Doris Humphrey Collection: an Introduction and Guide, by Andrew Wentink, 1973; Asian Dance Images from the Spencer Collection: an Exhibition ...at Lincoln Center, New York, 1977; the Ruth Page Collection: an Introduction and Guide to Manuscript Materials through 1970, by Andrew Wentink, 1980 (in Bulletin of Research in the Humanities, NYPL, 83:1, Spring 1980). **Special Catalogs:** WPA Card Index of Ethnic and Folkdance Material, circa 1936; International Dance Film and Videotape Festival Catalog, 1981.

★9045★
NEW YORK PUBLIC LIBRARY - PERFORMING ARTS RESEARCH CENTER - MUSIC DIVISION (Mus)
111 Amsterdam Ave.   Phone: (212) 870-1650
New York, NY 10023   Frank C. Campbell, Chf.
Founded: 1911. **Staff:** Prof 8; Other 10. **Subjects:** Opera, orchestra and chamber music, folk music, complete works of standard composers, monumenta devoted to special schools, theory, harmony, criticism, instruments, libretti, sheet music, music of the dance. **Special Collections:** Drexel Collection and Rare Book and Manuscript Collection; Americana Collection; Beethoven Collection; Toscanini Memorial Archives comprising microfilm reproductions of European composers' manuscripts. **Holdings:** 325,000 books; 5200 bound periodical volumes; 325,000 scores (cataloged); 700,000 pieces of sheet music; 2 million clippings, programs, iconography. **Subscriptions:** 750 journals. **Services:** Library open to adults. **Networks/Consortia:** Member of RLG; METRO; New York State Interlibrary Loan Network (NYSILL). **Publications:** Printed book catalogs. **Special Catalogs:** Song Index; biographical file; program note and first performance index; instrumental title file - all on cards.

★9046★
NEW YORK PUBLIC LIBRARY - PERFORMING ARTS RESEARCH CENTER - RODGERS & HAMMERSTEIN ARCHIVES OF RECORDED SOUND (Mus)
111 Amsterdam Ave.   Phone: (212) 870-1663
New York, NY 10023   David Hall, Cur.
Founded: 1963. **Staff:** Prof 4; Other 6. **Subjects:** Sound and video recordings and related materials. **Special Collections:** Benedict Stambler Memorial Collection of Recorded Jewish Music (5000 items); Jan Holcman Collection of Recorded Piano Music (2200 items); Rosalyn Tureck Archives (500 hours of tape); Metropolitan Opera Archives. **Holdings:** 1000 books; 1200 bound periodical volumes; 2000 phonograph record and manufacturers' catalogs and notebooks (cataloged); 150 linear feet of unbound periodicals, catalogs and notebooks; 396,000 phonograph records, including discs, tapes, cylinder and wire recordings; 300 reels of microfilm; 80 VF drawers of clippings and phonorecord catalog materials; videotapes. **Subscriptions:** 120 journals and other serials. **Services:** Library open to public for professional or serious research. **Networks/Consortia:** Member of RLG; METRO; New York State Interlibrary Loan Network (NYSILL). **Special Indexes:** Discography index (card); musical theater recordings (inventory list). **Staff:** Donald McCormick, First Asst.; Gary G. Gisondi, Libn.; Tom Owen, Audio Engr.

★9047★
NEW YORK PUBLIC LIBRARY - RARE BOOKS & MANUSCRIPTS DIVISION - MANUSCRIPTS AND ARCHIVES COLLECTION (Hist)
476 Fifth Ave., Rm. 319   Phone: (212) 930-0804
New York, NY 10018   Susan E. Davis, Cur. of Mss.
Staff: Prof 4; Other 4. **Subjects:** American source materials; representative holdings of all forms of handwritten (and modern typewritten) materials, from the clay tablet through the medieval illuminated manuscript to present day forms of author originals. **Special Collections:** American Revolutionary sources; colonial Americana; 19th and 20th century political, literary, and personal collections of correspondence; extensive collection of diaries; early merchants account-books; papers of engineers and inventors of the late 19th century; Shakers and Shaker communities; editorial files of periodicals published in New York City; New York World's Fairs, 1939-1940 and 1964-1965. **Holdings:** Over 9 million manuscript pieces. **Services:** Open to qualified researchers by card of admission secured in Special Collections Office.

★9048★

NEW YORK PUBLIC LIBRARY - RARE BOOKS & MANUSCRIPTS DIVISION - RARE BOOK COLLECTION (Rare Book)
Fifth Ave. & 42nd St. Phone: (212) 930-0820
New York, NY 10018 Francis O. Mattson, Cur. of Rare Bks.
Staff: Prof 3; Other 1. **Subjects:** Early voyages and travels; Americana, particularly before 1800. **Special Collections:** Early Bibles, including Gutenberg Bible; Bunyan's Pilgrim's Progress; Oscar Lion Collection of Walt Whitman; broadsides; 18th century American newspapers; modern fine printing. **Holdings:** 100,000 books; 2350 bound periodical volumes; 1750 volumes of bound newspapers; 20,000 broadsides; type facsimiles, bindings and ephemera. **Services:** Open to qualified researchers by card of admission secured in Special Collections office. **Publications:** Studies, bibliographies, and lists, irregular.

★9049★

NEW YORK PUBLIC LIBRARY - REGIONAL LIBRARY FOR THE BLIND AND PHYSICALLY HANDICAPPED (Aud-Vis)
166 Ave. of the Americas Phone: (212) 925-1014
New York, NY 10013 Barbara Nugent, Regional Br.Libn.
Founded: 1895. **Staff:** Prof 7; Other 14. **Holdings:** 7713 Braille books; 218,885 recorded books. **Services:** A designated Regional Library of the National Library Service for the Blind and Physically Handicapped for readers residing in New York City and Long Island. Materials and appropriate equipment loaned to eligible individuals and institutions. Bibliographic, reference, consultant, reader guidance, outreach and agency referral services. Message recording service, 24 hours a day at (212) 925-9699. Training and assistance in the use of the Kurzweil Reading Machine and other aids by appointment, Audio Book studio. **Computerized Information Services:** Computerized circulation. **Publications:** Informational brochures, quarterly newsletter in large-print and Braille, bibliographies on request.

★9050★

NEW YORK PUBLIC LIBRARY - SCHOMBURG CENTER FOR RESEARCH IN BLACK CULTURE (Area-Ethnic)
515 Lenox Ave. Phone: (212) 862-4000
New York, NY 10037 Wendell Wray, Chf.
Founded: 1925. **Staff:** Prof 14; Other 42. **Subjects:** Social sciences, humanities, the black experience throughout the world. **Special Collections:** Haitian Collection; African and Caribbean music; works of authors and artists of the Harlem Renaissance. **Holdings:** 85,000 books and bound periodical volumes; 200 archival record groups; 10,000 recordings; 60,000 photographs; 300 motion pictures; 300 videotapes; 5000 hours of oral history; 30,000 reels of microfilm; 18,000 microfiche; paintings, sculpture, drawings and prints; African artifacts. **Subscriptions:** 1000 journals and other serials. **Services:** Center open to adults for reference use. **Networks/Consortia:** Member of RLG; CRL; METRO; New York State Interlibrary Loan Network (NYSILL). **Special Indexes:** Index to articles in black periodical literature, 1948 to present (card); vertical file holdings, 1925-1974 (microfiche).

★9051★

NEW YORK PUBLIC LIBRARY - SCIENCE AND TECHNOLOGY RESEARCH CENTER (Sci-Tech)
Fifth Ave. & 42nd St., Rm. 121 Phone: (212) 930-0573
New York, NY 10018 Vitaut Kipel, Act.Chf.
Founded: 1911. **Staff:** Prof 6; Other 17. **Subjects:** Aeronautics, astronautics, astronomy, automobiles, chemistry, communications, earth sciences, electricity, electronics, engineering (all branches), industrial arts, mathematics, metallurgy, meteorology, mining, navigation, paper, petroleum, physics, plastics, radio, railroads, rubber, science history, shipbuilding, technology history, textiles. **Special Collections:** William B. Parsons Transportation Engineering (1200 titles of early works). **Holdings:** 900,000 books and bound periodical volumes; 50,000 pamphlet sets and reports. **Subscriptions:** 4900 journals and other serials. **Services:** Reference service by phone and letter; center open to public for reference use only. **Networks/Consortia:** Member of RLG; METRO; New York State Interlibrary Loan Network (NYSILL). **Publications:** New Technical Books, 10/year - available by subscription. **Remarks:** Science-technology materials in Oriental or Slavonic languages are available in the Oriental Division (room 219) or in the Slavonic Division (room 216); current government publications in science-technology generally are available in the Economic and Public Affairs Division (room 225).

★9052★

NEW YORK PUBLIC LIBRARY - SLAVONIC DIVISION (Area-Ethnic)
Fifth Ave. & 42nd St., Rm. 216, 223 Phone: (212) 930-0714
New York, NY 10018 Dr. Victor Koressaar, Div.Chf.
Founded: 1899. **Staff:** Prof 6; Other 7. **Subjects:** Slavic and Baltic literatures and linguistics, history (especially Russian Imperial regimental histories and history of Russian revolutionary movements, history of Alaska and her peoples), economics and political science, philosophy, archeology, folk-lore, art and architecture, ethnology of Baltic, Slavic and Soviet Central Asian peoples. **Special Collections:** Slavic rare books, including early Polonicas; especially strong in Russian 18th century imprints, many of which came from the Russian Imperial collections, including the library in Tsarskoye Selo. **Holdings:** 250,000 books and bound periodical volumes; 9700 reels of microfilm. **Subscriptions:** 1400 journals and other serials; 150 newspapers. **Services:** Copying; replies to written inquiries; division open to public for reference use only. **Networks/Consortia:** Member of RLG; METRO; New York State Interlibrary Loan Network (NYSILL). **Special Catalogs:** Dictionary Catalog of the Slavonic Collection, 1974.

★9053★

NEW YORK PUBLIC LIBRARY - SPENCER COLLECTION (Rare Book)
Fifth Ave. & 42nd St., Rm. 308 Phone: (212) 930-0818
New York, NY 10018 Joseph T. Rankin, Cur.
Subjects: Rare, illustrated books and illuminated manuscripts in fine bindings, showing the history of book illustration and the book arts from the Middle Ages to the present time; illustrative source material from China, Japan, India, Arabia, Persia. **Services:** Collection open to public for reference use only and by card of admission secured in Special Collections Office.

★9054★

NEW YORK PUBLIC LIBRARY - UNITED STATES HISTORY, LOCAL HISTORY AND GENEALOGY DIVISION (Hist)
Fifth Ave. & 42nd St., Rm. 315N Phone: (212) 930-0828
New York, NY 10018 Gunther E. Pohl, Div.Chf.
Staff: Prof 4; Other 6. **Subjects:** U.S. history; county, city and town histories of the United States; European and American genealogy and heraldry; works on names and flags of the world. **Special Collections:** Photographic views of New York City (100,000); postcards and scrapbooks of U.S. local views. **Holdings:** 102,000 volumes. **Networks/Consortia:** Member of RLG; METRO; New York State Interlibrary Loan Network (NYSILL).

★9055★

NEW YORK ROAD RUNNERS CLUB - INTERNATIONAL RUNNING CENTER LIBRARY (Rec)
FDR Sta., Box 881 Phone: (212) 860-4455
New York, NY 10150 Mimi Fahnestock, Libn.
Subjects: Running, sports medicine. **Special Collections:** Ted Corbitt Archives (papers of the first president of the New York Road Runners Club). **Holdings:** 200 books; American and international running publications; medical journals. **Services:** Copying (fee); library open to public.

NEW YORK SCHOOL OF PSYCHIATRY AND HUDSON RIVER PSYCHIATRIC CENTER
See: Hudson River Psychiatric Center

★9056★

NEW YORK SOCIETY LIBRARY (Hist)
53 E. 79th St. Phone: (212) 288-6900
New York, NY 10021 Mark Piel, Libn.
Founded: 1754. **Staff:** Prof 8; Other 6. **Subjects:** Fiction, Americana, New York City history and early newspaper files, 19th century travel, biography. **Special Collections:** John Winthrop collection of medicine and alchemy; Goodhue Papers (letters and documents of distinguished Americans, early 19th century); Hammond collection of American novels, 1750-1830. **Holdings:** 184,000 books; 1100 bound periodical volumes. **Subscriptions:** 80 journals. **Services:** Copying; library open to nonmembers for reading and reference. **Publications:** Annual Report; Monthly New Books. **Staff:** Sharon Brown, Asst.Libn.

★9057★

NEW YORK SOCIETY OF MODEL ENGINEERS - LIBRARY (Rec)†
341 Hoboken Rd. Phone: (201) 939-9212
Carlstadt, NJ 07072 Stephen Szewczuk, Libn.
Staff: 1. **Subjects:** Railroading and model railroading. **Holdings:** Magazines about railroading. **Services:** Library not open to public.

NEW YORK STATE AGRICULTURAL EXPERIMENT STATION
See: Cornell University

★9058★

NEW YORK STATE ARCHEOLOGICAL ASSOCIATION - LIBRARY (Soc Sci)
657 East Ave.
Box 1480 Phone: (716) 271-4320
Rochester, NY 14603 Charles F. Hayes, III, Res.Dir.
Subjects: Archeology, anthropology. **Special Collections:** Regional Northeast

archeology. **Holdings:** 3000 books. **Subscriptions:** 50 journals and other serials. **Services:** Copying; library for use of association members; open to public with restrictions. **Publications:** The Bulletin and Journal of Archeology for New York State, 3/year - for members. **Remarks:** Housed at the Lower Hudson Chapter, NYSAA, c/o MALFA, Muscoot Park, Route 100, Katonah, NY 10536. Library volumes up to 1950 are housed at the Rochester Museum and Science Center Library.

NEW YORK STATE ARCHEOLOGICAL ASSOCIATION - VAN EPPS-HARTLEY CHAPTER ARCHIVES
See: Mohawk-Caughnawaga Museum - Library

NEW YORK STATE COLLEGE OF AGRICULTURE & LIFE SCIENCES
See: Cornell University

★9059★
NEW YORK STATE COLLEGE OF CERAMICS AT ALFRED UNIVERSITY - SAMUEL R. SCHOLES LIBRARY OF CERAMICS (Sci-Tech; Art)
Harder Hall   Phone: (607) 871-2492
Alfred, NY 14802   Mr. Robin R.B. Murray, Dir.
Founded: 1947. **Staff:** Prof 6; Other 7. **Subjects:** Ceramics, engineering and science, pottery, glass, ceramic art, fine art, sculpture, materials, design. **Special Collections:** Hostetter Collection (glass); Barringer Collection (ceramics); Bancroft Collection (science and engineering); Silverman Collection (ceramic art); McBurney Collection (brick); Shand Collection (glass); Spretnac Collection (metallurgy). **Holdings:** 42,500 books; 24,500 bound periodical volumes; 8000 other cataloged items; 41,000 government documents (hardcopy and microfiche); 445 microtext; 4000 serial monographs; 80,000 slides. **Subscriptions:** 900 journals and other serials. **Services:** Interlibrary loans; copying; library open to public. **Computerized Information Services:** DIALOG; computerized cataloging, serials and ILL. **Networks/Consortia:** Member of South Central Research Library Council (SCRLC); SUNY/OCLC Library Network. **Publications:** Books, Reports, and Other Publications Received, bimonthly; Library Notes, bimonthly. **Special Indexes:** Card indexes to ceramics, glass, materials and science and engineering. **Staff:** Bruce E. Connolly, Hd., Tech.Serv.; Paul T. Culley, Hd., Tech.Ref.; Martha A. Mueller, Hd., Rd.Serv./ILL; Susan S. Strong, Hd., AV & Art Ref./Archv.; Linda L. Cannon, Sec.

NEW YORK STATE COLLEGE OF HUMAN ECOLOGY
See: Cornell University - Albert R. Mann Library

NEW YORK STATE COLLEGE OF VETERINARY MEDICINE AT CORNELL UNIVERSITY
See: Cornell University - Flower Veterinary Library

★9060★
NEW YORK STATE CONFERENCE OF MAYORS AND MUNICIPAL OFFICIALS - LIBRARY (Soc Sci)
119 Washington Ave.   Phone: (518) 463-1185
Albany, NY 12210   Gordon C. Perry, Exec.Dir.
Founded: 1908. **Staff:** Prof 6; Other 6. **Subjects:** New York municipal law, labor relations (public sector), cable television regulations, statistics. **Special Collections:** Proceedings of annual meetings of New York Conference of Mayors, 1908 to present; reports on subjects of local government concern from 1908 to present. **Holdings:** Figures not available; New York State government publications. **Subscriptions:** 100 journals and other serials. **Services:** Copying; library open to public with restrictions. **Publications:** New York Municipal Bulletin; Legal Bulletin; Across the Table; For Your Information. **Staff:** Donald A. Walsh, Gen. Counsel; John Galligan, Municipal Prog.Spec.; Donald F. Larson, Counsel; Cecilia M. Tyman, Municipal Prog.Spec.; Ross E. Muth, Municipal Prog.Spec.

★9061★
NEW YORK STATE COURT OF APPEALS - LIBRARY (Law)
Eagle St.   Phone: (518) 474-3624
Albany, NY 12207   Francis B. Waters, Libn.
Staff: Prof 1. **Subjects:** Law. **Holdings:** 70,000 volumes. **Subscriptions:** 91 journals and other serials. **Services:** Library not open to public.

★9062★
NEW YORK STATE DEPARTMENT OF AUDIT CONTROL - LIBRARY (Bus-Fin; Law)
Alfred E. Smith Office Bldg.   Phone: (518) 474-3419
Albany, NY 12236   Rita Wiers, Sr. Typist
Founded: 1948. **Staff:** 1. **Subjects:** Law, statistics, finance, accounting. **Holdings:** 3300 books; 420 bound periodical volumes; 1500 pamphlets and department reports (cataloged). **Subscriptions:** 25 journals and other serials. **Services:** Interlibrary loans; copying; library open to public for reference use

only.

★9063★
NEW YORK STATE DEPARTMENT OF CIVIL SERVICE - LIBRARY (Soc Sci)
State Office Bldg. Campus, Bldg. No. 1   Phone: (518) 457-6494
Albany, NY 12239   Virginia McCarthy, Libn.
Founded: 1950. **Staff:** Prof 1. **Subjects:** Public administration, management, training, testing, recruitment. **Holdings:** 8500 books; 4 VF drawers of pamphlets; college catalogs; telephone directories. **Subscriptions:** 400 journals and other serials. **Services:** Interlibrary loans; library not open to public.

★9064★
NEW YORK STATE DEPARTMENT OF COMMERCE - LIBRARY (Bus-Fin)
99 Washington Ave.   Phone: (518) 474-5664
Albany, NY 12245   John J. Kilrain, Libn.
Founded: 1943. **Staff:** Prof 1; Other 2. **Subjects:** Economic research. **Special Collections:** Census reports. **Holdings:** Figures not available. **Subscriptions:** 350 journals and other serials; 6 newspapers. **Services:** Library open to public for reference use only. **Computerized Information Services:** DIALOG, New York Times Information Service.

NEW YORK STATE DEPARTMENT OF EDUCATION - NORTH COUNTRY REFERENCE & RESEARCH RESOURCES COUNCIL
See: North Country Reference & Research Resources Council

★9065★
NEW YORK STATE DEPARTMENT OF ENVIRONMENTAL CONSERVATION - OFFICE OF EDUC. SERV. - INFORMATION SERVICE (Env-Cons)
50 Wolf Rd.   Phone: (518) 457-3720
Albany, NY 12233   Robert Budliger, Dir., Env.Educ.
Staff: Prof 2. **Subjects:** Environmental conservation. **Holdings:** 200 films; 20,000 photographs and slides; 3000 manuscripts; pamphlets and brochures relating to environmental topics. **Services:** Film loans and publications available to residents by mail; others by visit only.

★9066★
NEW YORK STATE DEPARTMENT OF HEALTH - CENTER FOR LABORATORIES AND RESEARCH LIBRARY (Med)
Empire State Plaza   Phone: (518) 474-6172
Albany, NY 12201   Thomas Flynn, Dir.
Founded: 1914. **Staff:** Prof 5; Other 5. **Subjects:** Public health, bacteriology, biochemistry, birth defects, child health, clinical labs, communicable diseases, cytology, environmental health, epidemiology, laboratory animals, mycology, pathology, radiology, sanitary engineering, toxicology, veterinary medicine, virology, zoonoses. **Special Collections:** Bibliographies on Coxsackie virus; nystatin. **Holdings:** 20,500 books; 33,500 bound periodical volumes; 600 linear feet of U.S. and New York State government publications; 180 linear feet of reference material. **Subscriptions:** 1200 journals and other serials. **Services:** Interlibrary loans; copying; library open to health professionals by permission. **Computerized Information Services:** BRS, NLM; computerized cataloging. **Networks/Consortia:** Member of OCLC. **Publications:** Library Information Bulletin, monthly - for internal distribution only. **Staff:** Dagmar Michalova, Assoc.Libn./Br.Lib.Supv; Jane D. Allen, Sr.Libn., Rd.Serv.; Rae Clark, Sr.Libn., Tech.Serv.; Kathleen McNamara, Asst.Libn.

NEW YORK STATE DEPARTMENT OF HEALTH - ROSWELL PARK MEMORIAL INSTITUTE
See: Roswell Park Memorial Institute

★9067★
NEW YORK STATE DEPARTMENT OF LABOR - LABOR STAFF ACADEMY LIBRARY
2 World Trade Ctr., Rm. 34-18
New York, NY 10047
Defunct. Merged with its Research Library to form its Library.

★9068★
NEW YORK STATE DEPARTMENT OF LABOR - LIBRARY (Soc Sci)
2 World Trade Ctr., Rm. 6826   Phone: (212) 488-6295
New York, NY 10047   Gloria Weinrich, Sr.Libn.
Founded: 1907. **Staff:** Prof 2; Other 3. **Subjects:** Economic and business conditions, personnel management, unions, radiological health, fringe benefits, unemployment insurance, wages and hours, labor legislation, vocational education and guidance, interviewing and counseling, occupational health and safety, women in industry, apprenticeship. **Special Collections:** Women's Trade Union League; releases of state labor departments; state labor laws; industrial code rules of New York State; publications of International Labour Office; publications of Canadian departments of labor. **Holdings:** 44,450

books; 1545 bound periodical volumes; 10,000 government documents; 3000 pamphlets; 275 reels of microfilm; 2700 microfiche; 408 VF drawers. **Subscriptions:** 175 journals and other serials; 350 trade union newspapers. **Services:** Interlibrary loans; copying; SDI; library open to public for materials not available in public or college libraries. **Publications:** Library Notes, irregular - available on request; Selected Additions List, monthly - for internal distribution only. **Remarks:** Includes holdings of the former New York State Department of Labor - Labor Staff Academy Library. **Staff:** R. Ashley Hibbard, Asst.Libn.

★9069★
NEW YORK STATE DEPARTMENT OF LABOR - WORKERS' COMPENSATION BOARD - LIBRARY (Soc Sci)
2 World Trade Ctr.
39th Fl., Rm. 3901   Phone: (212) 488-3103
New York, NY 10047   Donald H. Holley, Assoc. Attorney
Founded: 1944. **Staff:** Prof 2. **Subjects:** Workers' Compensation Law - legislation, statistics, and medical aspects. **Special Collections:** Workers' Compensation Laws of other states. **Holdings:** 5000 books; 100 bound periodical volumes. **Services:** Library open to attorneys and Board staff for reference use only. **Publications:** Workers' Compensation Board Decisions; Workers' Compensation Law; Compensation Court Decisions; Volunteer Firemen's Benefit Law; Disability Benefits Law Decisions. **Staff:** Olga Waron, Assoc. Examiner.

★9070★
NEW YORK STATE DEPARTMENT OF LAW - LIBRARY (Law)
The Capitol   Phone: (518) 474-3840
Albany, NY 12224   Thomas R. Heitz, Chf., Lib.Serv.
Staff: Prof 4; Other 7. **Subjects:** Law. **Holdings:** 60,000 volumes. **Subscriptions:** 250 journals and other serials. **Services:** Interlibrary loans; copying; library open to public with restrictions; personnel from other state agencies may use library; other law and non-law professionals by special permission. **Computerized Information Services:** WESTLAW; internal database. **Networks/Consortia:** Member of LAWNET. **Publications:** WESTLAW Training Guide for New York State Users. **Special Catalogs:** Department of Law briefs and records. **Remarks:** There are also branch libraries in Auburn, Binghamton, Buffalo, Garden City, Hauppauge, Monticello, New York City, Plattsburgh, Poughkeepsie, Rochester, Syracuse, Utica and Watertown. **Staff:** Lily Kouo, Asst.Libn.; Tina Reepmeyer, Asst.Libn.

★9071★
NEW YORK STATE DEPARTMENT OF LAW - NEW YORK CITY LIBRARY (Law)
2 World Trade Center, Rm. 4749   Phone: (212) 488-7445
New York, NY 10047   Fran Sheinwald, Sr.Libn.
Staff: Prof 1; Other 2. **Subjects:** Law. **Special Collections:** Opinions of the Attorney General of New York, 1892 to present. **Holdings:** 16,623 volumes; 22 VF drawers. **Subscriptions:** 30 journals and other serials. **Services:** Interlibrary loans; library open to members of the Law Department for reference and research. **Computerized Information Services:** WESTLAW.

NEW YORK STATE DEPARTMENT OF MENTAL HYGIENE - MONROE DEVELOPMENTAL CENTER
See: Monroe Developmental Center

NEW YORK STATE DEPARTMENT OF MENTAL HYGIENE - NEW YORK STATE OFFICE OF MENTAL HEALTH
See: New York State Office of Mental Health

★9072★
NEW YORK STATE DEPARTMENT OF MOTOR VEHICLES - RESEARCH LIBRARY (Trans)
Swan St. Bldg., Empire State Plaza   Phone: (518) 474-0684
Albany, NY 12228   Frances A. Miller, Sr.Libn.
Founded: 1961. **Staff:** Prof 1; Other 5. **Subjects:** Traffic safety, transportation, administration, management and personnel, medical sciences, vital statistics as related to traffic safety, electronic data processing, business. **Holdings:** 42,000 books, reports, documents, manuscripts and pamphlets; 71 bound periodical volumes; 284 film titles; 1000 microforms; 503 maps, charts and prints; 81 VF drawers. **Subscriptions:** 78 journals and other serials. **Services:** Interlibrary loans; copying (fee); library open to qualified users. **Networks/Consortia:** Member of Capital District Library Council for Reference and Research Resources. **Publications:** Selected New Holdings, monthly.

★9073★
NEW YORK STATE DEPARTMENT OF STATE - FIRE ACADEMY LIBRARY (Sci-Tech)
600 College Ave.
Box K   Phone: (607) 535-7136
Montour Falls, NY 14865   Diana Zell, Asst.Libn.
Staff: Prof 1. **Subjects:** Fire protection, prevention, control and equipment use and maintenance; occupational safety; fire department administration and management, including codes, standards, regulations, emergency medical services. **Special Collections:** Consumer safety; hazardous materials; arson prevention and control; history of fire service in New York State. **Holdings:** 2000 books; 50 bound periodical volumes; 8 VF drawers; 9 microfiche. **Subscriptions:** 86 journals and other serials. **Services:** Interlibrary loans; copying; library open to public for reference use only. **Networks/Consortia:** Member of South Central Research Library Council (SCRLC). **Publications:** Acquisitions list. **Special Catalogs:** Bibliographies.

★9074★
NEW YORK STATE DEPARTMENT OF STATE - LIBRARY (Soc Sci; Plan)
162 Washington Ave.   Phone: (518) 474-4324
Albany, NY 12231   David R. Cole, Asst.Libn.
Founded: 1975. **Staff:** Prof 2; Other 2. **Subjects:** Municipal, county, and state government; intergovernmental relations; planning for localities and regions; fire training; economic opportunity; municipal management; personnel training; labor relations management; historic and neighborhood preservation; economic development; community development; coastal zone management. **Special Collections:** New York State Community File. **Holdings:** 50,241 books, New York State and U.S. government documents; 32,541 pamphlets and vertical file materials; 334 microfiche. **Subscriptions:** 399 journals and other serials; 9 newspapers. **Services:** Interlibrary loans; copying; library open to public for reference use only. **Networks/Consortia:** Member of Capital District Library Council for Reference and Research Resources (CDLC).

★9075★
NEW YORK STATE DEPARTMENT OF TAXATION & FINANCE - TAX LIBRARY (Bus-Fin)
Bureau of Research & Statistics
Taxation & Finance Bldg.   Phone: (518) 457-3512
Albany, NY 12227   Janet Snay, Act.Libn.
Founded: 1946. **Staff:** 2. **Subjects:** Taxation, public finance. **Holdings:** 8148 books; 4671 bound periodical volumes; 100 VF drawers. **Subscriptions:** 104 journals and other serials. **Services:** Library not open to public.

★9076★
NEW YORK STATE DEPARTMENT OF TRANSPORTATION - MAP INFORMATION UNIT (Geog-Map)
State Office Campus
Bldg. 4, Rm. 105   Phone: (518) 457-3555
Albany, NY 12232   Paul McElligott, Assoc.Cartographer
Staff: Prof 2; Other 3. **Subjects:** Maps, aerial photography. **Holdings:** 100,000 aerial photographs; 3500 maps. **Services:** Unit open to public. **Publications:** Inventory of Aerial Photography & Other Remotely Sensed Imagery of New York State, 1979. **Special Indexes:** Map indexes. **Staff:** Kathy Ford, Cartographer.

★9077★
NEW YORK STATE DEPARTMENT OF TRANSPORTATION - PLANNING DIVISION - LIBRARY (Trans)
1220 Washington Ave.
Bldg. 4, Rm. 209   Phone: (518) 457-6143
Albany, NY 12232   Carol R. Olson, Asst.Libn.
Founded: 1962. **Staff:** Prof 3. **Subjects:** Transportation planning. **Holdings:** 20,000 books; 400 unbound periodical volumes. **Subscriptions:** 100 journals and other serials. **Services:** Interlibrary loans; copying; library open to public with restrictions. **Staff:** David T. Hartgen, Hd., Data Anl.Bur.; Alfred J. Neveu, Hd., Plan.Res. Unit.

★9078★
NEW YORK STATE DIVISION OF HOUSING AND COMMUNITY RENEWAL - REFERENCE ROOM (Soc Sci)
2 World Trade Center, 60th Fl.   Phone: (212) 488-4968
New York, NY 10047   William T. Mikell, Sr. Clerk
Founded: 1941. **Staff:** 1. **Subjects:** Housing - laws and titles, building codes, mobile housing, housing for elderly, neighborhood preservation. **Holdings:** 2000 books; slides, microfilm, microfiche. **Subscriptions:** 25 journals and other serials; 10 newspapers. **Services:** Reference room open to public for reference use only.

★9079★
NEW YORK STATE DIVISION OF HUMAN RIGHTS - REFERENCE LIBRARY
(Soc Sci)†
2 World Trade Center, Rm.5356   Phone: (212) 488-5372
New York, NY 10047
Staff: Prof 1; Other 1. **Subjects:** Human rights and civil liberties; intergroup relations; ethnic and minority organizations; discrimination in employment, education and housing; anti-poverty efforts; urban unrest; integration. **Special Collections:** Reports and laws of state and city Human Agencies (2000 items). **Holdings:** 3000 books; 50 bound periodical volumes; 4000 pamphlets; 17 VF drawers of clippings and documents; 859 reels of tape recordings. **Subscriptions:** 25 journals and other serials; 7 newspapers. **Services:** Library open to researchers and students. **Computerized Information Services:** Online systems. **Publications:** Bibliography of Housing and Urban Renewal, 1970; Bibliography on Education, 1971; Bibliography of Publications by and about New York State Division of Human Rights, 1971; Bibliography on Employment and Related Subjects, 1972; Bibliography on Equal Employment Opportunity and Affirmative Action Programs, 1974; Bibliography on the Disabled, 1974. **Staff:** J. George Longworth, Asst.Commnr.

★9080★
NEW YORK STATE DIVISION OF SUBSTANCE ABUSE SERVICES - BUREAU OF TRAINING & RESOURCE DEVELOPMENT - RESOURCE CENTER (Med)
350 Broadway, 4th Fl.   Phone: (212) 966-7600
New York, NY 10013   Binu Chaudhuri, Res.Ctr.Coord.
Founded: 1976. **Staff:** Prof 1; Other 1. **Subjects:** Drug abuse, addiction treatment, pharmacology, counseling, training. **Special Collections:** NIDA pamphlets and reports; Training Manuals from National Training System. **Holdings:** 1500 books; 6000 items in VF drawers; 100 computer searches. **Subscriptions:** 40 journals and other serials; 15 newspapers. **Services:** Interlibrary loans; copying; SDI; library open to public for reference use only. **Computerized Information Services:** DIALOG. **Networks/Consortia:** Member of Drug Abuse Communications Network (DRACON). **Publications:** Monthly Newsletter.

★9081★
NEW YORK STATE ELECTRIC AND GAS CORPORATION - CORPORATE LIBRARY (Sci-Tech; Energy)
4500 Vestal Pkwy., E.   Phone: (607) 729-2551
Binghamton, NY 13902   Melba H. Lewis, Libn.
Founded: 1954. **Staff:** Prof 1; Other 1. **Subjects:** Public utility regulation, nuclear and solar energy, environment, statistics, electrical engineering, mechanical engineering, management, finance, coal, mining. **Holdings:** 1978 books; 205 periodicals; 1000 pamphlets (cataloged); 16 VF drawers of newspaper clippings, pamphlets and annual reports. **Subscriptions:** 217 journals and other serials; 47 newspapers. **Services:** Interlibrary loans; copying; library not open to public. **Publications:** Tie Lines News, monthly - for internal distribution only.

★9082★
NEW YORK STATE HISTORICAL ASSOCIATION - LIBRARY (Hist)
                                        Phone: (607) 547-2509
Cooperstown, NY 13326   Wendell Tripp, Chf., Lib.Serv.
Founded: 1899. **Staff:** Prof 3; Other 5. **Subjects:** New York State history, 19th century arts and architecture. **Special Collections:** New York State Folklife Archives; American murder pamphlets; local and regional photographic archives; trade catalogs; Barriskill Theatre Collection (6 VF cabinets); central New York genealogy. **Holdings:** 60,000 books; 10,000 bound periodical volumes; 850 linear feet of manuscripts; 40 VF cabinets of New York State historical archives. **Subscriptions:** 400 journals and other serials. **Services:** Interlibrary loans; copying; genealogical and general reference; library open to public. **Networks/Consortia:** Member of South Central Regional Library Council (SCRLC). **Special Indexes:** Historical Resources Center, Cornell University; various local history card indexes, including cabinetmakers, imprints, place names, and taverns. **Staff:** Adele Johnson, Acq.Libn.; Wayne Wright, Rd.Serv.; Lois McAllister, Cat.; Amy Barnum, Spec.Coll.

★9083★
NEW YORK STATE INSTITUTE FOR BASIC RESEARCH IN DEVELOPMENTAL DISABILITIES - LIBRARY (Med)
1050 Forest Hill Rd.   Phone: (212) 494-5119
Staten Island, NY 10314   Lawrence Black, Sr.Libn.
Founded: 1968. **Staff:** Prof 1; Other 1. **Subjects:** Neurology, neurophysiology, neurochemistry, neuropathology, genetics, virology, immunology. **Holdings:** 5131 books and bound periodical volumes; 1 VF drawer of pamphlets. **Subscriptions:** 200 journals and other serials. **Services:** Library not open to public. **Networks/Consortia:** Member of Medical Library Center of New York; SUNY/OCLC Library Network. **Formerly:** New York State

Institute for Basic Research in Mental Retardation.

★9084★
NEW YORK STATE LIBRARY (Info Sci)
Cultural Education Center
Empire State Plaza   Phone: (518) 474-7646
Albany, NY 12230   Peter Paulson, Dir.
Founded: 1818. **Staff:** Prof 102; Other 152. **Subjects:** Education, science, technology, art, architecture, economics, sociology, current affairs, bibliography, New York State documents, New York State newspapers, law, medicine, state and local history, genealogy, heraldry. **Special Collections:** Almanacs; American imprints, bookplates; Fourth of July orations; World War posters; Shakers; New York State documents; Washington eulogies. **Holdings:** 3.5 million books, bound periodical volumes, manuscripts, and pamphlets; patents, microfilms, microcards, pictures, maps. **Subscriptions:** 27,000 journals and other serials; 205 newspapers. **Services:** Interlibrary loans; copying; library open to public. **Computerized Information Services:** BRS, New York Times Information Service, MEDLARS, MEDLINE; computerized cataloging and serials. **Networks/Consortia:** Member of New York State Interlibrary Loan Network (NYSILL). **Publications:** Bookmark, monthly - distributed free upon request; checklist of official publications of the state of New York. **Staff:** Joseph F. Shubert, Asst.Commnr.; William DeAlleaume, Hd., Coll.Acq.; J. Vanderveer Judd, Hd., Coll.Mgmt.; Henry Ilnicki, Hd., Gift Sect.; Barbara Rice, Hd., Ref.; Mary Redmond, Hd., Leg./Govt.Serv.

★9085★
NEW YORK STATE LIBRARY FOR THE BLIND AND VISUALLY HANDICAPPED (Aud-Vis)
Cultural Education Center
Empire State Plaza   Phone: (518) 474-5935
Albany, NY 12230   Audrey Smith, Assoc.Libn.
Founded: 1896. **Staff:** Prof 5; Other 25. **Subjects:** Recreational and informational reading materials in special media collections. **Holdings:** Figures not available. **Services:** Postage free mail circulation service of books and magazines in Braille and recorded on disc and cassette with loan of player machines with which to read books recorded on disc and cassette. Reader Advisory, Reference and Referral Services by telephone and mail. Deposit collection service to institutions having eligible patrons. **Computerized Information Services:** Computerized circulation. **Publications:** NYSLBVH News, bimonthly. **Remarks:** Persons certified as being eligible for the national program of the Library of Congress National Library Service for the Blind and Physically Handicapped because of visual or physical disability preventing use of standard print materials are eligible for this service which extends to New York State exclusive of New York City and Long Island. **Staff:** Frank Conron, Sr.Libn.; Peter Douglas, Asst.Libn.; Evelyn Galante, Asst.Libn.; Cassandra Hamm, Asst.Libn.

★9086★
NEW YORK STATE LIBRARY - HUMANITIES REFERENCE SECTION (Info Sci)
Cultural Education Center
Empire State Plaza   Phone: (518) 474-5958
Albany, NY 12230   Mildred Ledden, Assoc.Libn.
Staff: Prof 6; Other 1. **Subjects:** General works including bibliography, history, literature, fine arts, New York State local history, genealogy, philosophy, religion, philology, grantsmanship. **Special Collections:** Early New York State newspapers; descriptions and travel in the various states; directory collection (mostly New York State localities). **Holdings:** Figures not available. **Services:** Interlibrary loans; copying; reference service for Legislature, courts, state departments, libraries of the state and for any library or adult. **Computerized Information Services:** DIALOG, BRS, NLM, New York Times Information Service; computerized cataloging and serials. **Networks/Consortia:** Member of New York State Interlibrary Loan Network; OCLC. **Staff:** Melinda Yates, Sr.Libn.; Lee Stanton, Sr.Libn.; Sheila Ostrander, Sr.Libn.; Rise Rothbart, Asst.Libn.; Linda Braun, Asst.Libn.; Paul Mercer, Newspaper Proj.Coord.

★9087★
NEW YORK STATE LIBRARY - LAW/SOCIAL SCIENCE REFERENCE SERVICES (Law; Soc Sci)
Cultural Education Center
Empire State Plaza   Phone: (518) 474-5943
Albany, NY 12230   Stephanie Welden, State Law Libn.
Founded: 1818. **Staff:** Prof 10; Other 6. **Subjects:** Law, including the laws of the federal government, all states, and foreign governments; political science, public administration, legislative organization, intergovernmental relations, state and regional planning, education. **Special Collections:** Legislative background material; individual and collected trials; constitutional convention material of all 50 states; records and briefs of U.S. Supreme Court, 1874 to present; early rare books; virtually complete collection of Blackstone and Kent commentaries; session laws of all 50 states complete;

appeal records of all appellate courts of New York State; Bill Jacket Collection (laws of New York) 1921-1974; New York State publications; New York State Legislative Bills, 1830 to present (microfilm). **Holdings:** 240,000 volumes. **Subscriptions:** 500 journals and other serials including most English language legal periodicals. **Services:** Interlibrary loans; copying; research on legislative intent and background of legislation; library open to public. **Networks/Consortia:** Member of OCLC. **Publications:** Annual reports; bibliographies on special collections. **Staff:** Sally Legendre, Sr.Libn.; Michael Esposito, Sr.Libn.; Nancy Horan, Asst.Libn.; Mary Woodward, Asst.Libn.; Elaine Clark, Asst.Libn.; Claire Eberhardt, Asst.Libn.; Constance Ryan Alesse, Asst.Libn.; Dawn Tybur, Asst.Libn.; Karley Pillai, Asst.Libn.

★9088★

NEW YORK STATE LIBRARY - LEGISLATIVE AND GOVERNMENTAL SERVICES (Soc Sci)
Cultural Education Center
Empire State Plaza
Albany, NY 12230

Phone: (518) 474-3940
Mary Redmond, Principal Libn.

Staff: Prof 5; Other 5. **Services:** Provides special and enhanced services, bibliographic research and other publications to the legislature and state government. **Publications:** Legislative Trends, monthly annotated listing of selected recent acquisitions; Topic, highly selective subject reading lists; Target, short fact sheets on specific subjects; Spotlight, one page subject researchers' guides; Sources, lists of special/specialized materials and formats available; bibliographies on subjects of legislative interest for the legislature. **Remarks:** Operates a service point for the legislature in the Legislative Office Building. **Staff:** Robert Allan Carter, Sr.Libn.; Jean Hargrave, Sr.Libn.

★9089★

NEW YORK STATE LIBRARY - MANUSCRIPTS AND SPECIAL COLLECTION (Hist)
Cultural Education Center
Empire State Plaza
Albany, NY 12230

Phone: (518) 474-4461
Peter R. Christoph, Assoc.Libn.

Founded: 1818. **Staff:** Prof 4; Other 3. **Subjects:** New York, U.S. and local history; cartography; historic iconography. **Special Collections:** Historic manuscripts (4.5 million items); rare books (35,000). **Holdings:** 3500 books; 200 bound periodical volumes; 4800 posters; 3500 broadsides; 75,000 prints, glass negatives, pictures; 20,000 pieces of sheet music; 150,000 maps; 3400 reels of microfilm; 1000 atlases. **Services:** Interlibrary loans; copying; exhibits; collection open to public with restrictions. **Computerized Information Services:** Computerized cataloging for books and serials. **Networks/Consortia:** Member of New York State Interlibrary Loan Network (NYSILL). **Publications:** Brochures on collections and services. **Staff:** James Corsaro, Sr.Libn.; Jamie Messmer, Asst.Libn.; Christine Beauregard, Asst.Libn.

★9090★

NEW YORK STATE LIBRARY - SCIENCES/HEALTH SCIENCES/ TECHNOLOGY REFERENCE SERVICES (Med)
Cultural Education Center
Empire State Plaza
Albany, NY 12230

Phone: (518) 474-7040
Christine A. Bain, Assoc.Libn.

Founded: 1891. **Staff:** Prof 7; Other 1. **Subjects:** Science, medicine and allied health sciences, technology. **Special Collections:** National Technical Information Service (NTIS) reports (microfiche); all U.S. patents (depository library); Department of Energy reports (microfiche); U.S. Government Printing Office publications (depository and non-depository); Rand reports; standards and specifications. **Holdings:** 59,000 titles in the health sciences collection; 174,000 titles in the science and technology collections; microform collection. **Subscriptions:** 7400 journals and other serials. **Services:** Interlibrary loans; copying; reference services and borrowing privileges extended to state government libraries and certain qualified individuals; library open to adult public for reference use only. **Computerized Information Services:** BRS, DIALOG, NLM; computerized cataloging and serials. **Networks/Consortia:** Member of New York State Interlibrary Loan Network (NYSILL); New York & New Jersey Regional Medical Library Program; OCLC. **Publications:** Brochures on health information services and the patent collection. **Staff:** Alta Beach, Sr.Libn.; Florence Coonrod, Sr.Libn.; Soumaya Baaklini, Asst.Libn.; Campbell Lathey, Asst.Libn.; Allan Raney, Asst.Libn.; Theresa Strasser, Asst.Libn.

★9091★

NEW YORK STATE METROPOLITAN TRANSPORTATION AUTHORITY - LIBRARY (Trans)
347 Madison Ave., 10th Fl.
New York, NY 10017

Phone: (212) 878-7414
Carlotta Rossi, Libn.

Founded: 1967. **Staff:** Prof 1; Other 1. **Subjects:** Transportation, rail transportation, rapid transit, aviation, airports, bridges, tunnels, surface transportation. **Holdings:** 300 books; 5000 reports, pamphlets, brochures and clippings. **Subscriptions:** 100 journals and other serials. **Services:** Copying; library open to public by appointment.

★9092★

NEW YORK STATE MUSEUM AND SCIENCE SERVICE - MUSEUM LIBRARY (Sci-Tech)
State Education Dept., Rm.3128 CEC
Empire State Plaza
Albany, NY 12230

Phone: (518) 474-5878
Eleanor A. Gossen, Libn.

Founded: 1932. **Staff:** Prof 1. **Subjects:** General science, geology, paleontology, biology, anthropology. **Special Collections:** John M. Clarke Collection; Winifred Goldring Collection. **Holdings:** 1970 volumes; museum reports, government documents and society publications (3300 annually). **Subscriptions:** 90 journals and other serials. **Services:** Copying; library not open to public.

★9093★

NEW YORK STATE NURSES ASSOCIATION - LIBRARY (Med)
2113 Western Ave.
Guilderland, NY 12084

Phone: (518) 456-5371
Barbara Van Nortwick, Lib.Dir.

Founded: 1972. **Staff:** Prof 2; Other 1. **Subjects:** Nursing and allied health fields, labor, collective bargaining. **Special Collections:** Association archival materials. **Holdings:** 3000 books; 429 bound periodical volumes; complete New York State nursing school catalogs; 4 VF drawers of pamphlets. **Subscriptions:** 247 journals and other serials. **Services:** Interlibrary loans; copying; bibliographic instruction; library open to public with restrictions. **Networks/Consortia:** Member of Capital District Library Council for Reference and Research Resources; New York and New Jersey Regional Medical Library Program. **Publications:** Memorandum to Staff, irregular - for internal distribution only. **Staff:** Warren G. Hawkes, Assoc.Libn.

★9094★

NEW YORK STATE OFFICE OF COURT ADMINISTRATION - BRONX CRIMINAL-FAMILY COURT - LIBRARY (Law)
215 E. 161st St., Rm. 9-5A
Bronx, NY 10451

Phone: (212) 590-2931
Mary T. Rooney, Libn.

Staff: Prof 1; Other 1. **Subjects:** Criminal and family law. **Holdings:** 11,000 books. **Subscriptions:** 173 journals and other serials. **Services:** Interlibrary loans; library open to public with restrictions.

NEW YORK STATE OFFICE OF MENTAL HEALTH - CREEDMOOR PSYCHIATRIC CENTER
See: Creedmoor Psychiatric Center

★9095★

NEW YORK STATE OFFICE OF MENTAL HEALTH - NEW YORK STATE PSYCHIATRIC INSTITUTE - LIBRARY (Med)
722 W. 168 St.
New York, NY 10032

Phone: (212) 568-4000
James W. Montgomery, Dir.

Founded: 1896. **Staff:** Prof 3; Other 3. **Subjects:** Psychiatry, neurology, psychology, neuropathology. **Special Collections:** Sigmund Freud Memorial Collection (800 volumes). **Holdings:** 20,000 books; 21,000 bound periodical volumes; 300 dissertations and theses (paper copies); 500 dissertations on microfilm; 1000 microfiche reports and journal volumes. **Subscriptions:** 600 journals and other serials. **Services:** Interlibrary loans; copying (limited); in-house SDI; orientation lectures; library open to public with restrictions. **Computerized Information Services:** DIALOG, BRS, SDC, MEDLARS, Lithium Librarian, ISI. **Networks/Consortia:** Member of Medical Library Center of New York (MLCNY). **Publications:** ReLPI Bulletin, 1980, irregular; ReLPI Handbook - controlled distribution. **Staff:** David T. Lane, Adm.Asst./ Info.Spec.; John Harrison, ILL.

★9096★

NEW YORK STATE OFFICE OF MENTAL HEALTH - RESEARCH RESOURCE CENTER (Med)
44 Holland Ave.
Albany, NY 12229

Phone: (518) 474-7167
Paul G. Hillengas, Libn.

Staff: Prof 1; Other 1. **Subjects:** Psychiatry, psychology, mental hygiene, sociology. **Holdings:** 4000 books; 8000 unbound periodicals; 2258 reprints of articles. **Subscriptions:** 103 journals and other serials. **Services:** Interlibrary loans; copying; library open to public for reference use only. **Networks/Consortia:** Member of Capital District Library Council for Reference and Research Resources.

★9097★
NEW YORK STATE OFFICE OF MENTAL HEALTH - ST. LAWRENCE PSYCHIATRIC CENTER - LIBRARY (Med)
Station A
Ogdensburg, NY 13669
Phone: (315) 393-3000
Wayne Miller, Libn.
Staff: Prof 1; Other 1. **Subjects:** Nursing, psychiatry, general medicine. **Holdings:** 5493 volumes; 110 VF folders of clippings; 1100 items of non-print materials. **Subscriptions:** 125 journals and other serials. **Services:** Interlibrary loans; copying; library open to public. **Networks/Consortia:** Member of Northern New York Health Information Cooperative; North Country Reference and Research Resources Council; Health Resources Council of Central New York.

NEW YORK STATE OFFICE OF MENTAL RETARDATION/DEVELOPMENTAL DISABILITIES
See: Craig Developmental Center

★9098★
NEW YORK STATE PARKS AND RECREATION - DIVISION FOR HISTORIC PRESERVATION - FIELD SERVICES BUREAU - LIBRARY (Hist)
Agencies Tower No. 1
Empire State Plaza
Albany, NY 12238
Phone: (518) 474-0479
Kathleen LaFrank, Libn.
Staff: Prof 1. **Subjects:** Architectural history, historic preservation, historic archeology, New York State and local history. **Holdings:** Figures not available for books. **Services:** Library open to public with restrictions. **Staff:** Steven J. Raiche, Dir.

NEW YORK STATE PARKS AND RECREATION - JOHN JAY HOMESTEAD
See: Jay (John) Homestead

NEW YORK STATE PSYCHIATRIC INSTITUTE
See: New York State Office of Mental Health

NEW YORK STATE SCHOOL OF INDUSTRIAL AND LABOR RELATIONS AT CORNELL UNIVERSITY
See: Cornell University - Martin P. Catherwood Library of Industrial and Labor Relations

★9099★
NEW YORK STATE SUPREME COURT - APPELLATE DIVISION, 1ST JUDICIAL DEPARTMENT - LAW LIBRARY (Law)
27 Madison Ave.
New York, NY 10010
Phone: (212) 532-1000
Stephen R. Grotsky, Libn.
Subjects: Law. **Holdings:** 75,000 volumes. **Staff:** Robert C. Gelber, Asst.Libn.

★9100★
NEW YORK STATE SUPREME COURT - APPELLATE DIVISION, 2ND JUDICIAL DEPARTMENT - LAW LIBRARY (Law)
45 Monroe Pl.
Brooklyn, NY 11202
Albert Esselborn, Esq., Libn.
Subjects: Law. **Holdings:** 24,000 volumes. **Services:** Library not open to public.

★9101★
NEW YORK STATE SUPREME COURT - APPELLATE DIVISION, 3RD JUDICIAL DEPARTMENT - LAW LIBRARY (Law)
Justice Bldg., Empire State Plaza
Capitol Station, Box 7288
Albany, NY 12224
Ronald J. Milkins
Subjects: Law. **Holdings:** 50,000 volumes. **Services:** Library not open to public.

★9102★
NEW YORK STATE SUPREME COURT - APPELLATE DIVISION, 4TH JUDICIAL DEPARTMENT - LAW LIBRARY (Law)
525 Hall of Justice
Rochester, NY 14614
Phone: (716) 428-5480
Joseph T. Pascucci, Libn.
Founded: 1829. **Staff:** Prof 3; Other 4. **Subjects:** Law. **Special Collections:** Briefs and records in the Court of Appeals and the four departments of the Appellate Division of the State of New York and in the U.S. Court of Appeals for the 2nd Circuit. **Holdings:** 180,000 volumes. **Services:** Interlibrary loans; library open to public. **Staff:** Robert R. Gutz, Asst.Libn.; Maryanne Clark, Asst.Libn.

★9103★
NEW YORK STATE SUPREME COURT - APPELLATE DIVISION, 4TH JUDICIAL DEPARTMENT - LAW LIBRARY (Law)
500 Court House
Syracuse, NY 13202
Phone: (315) 425-2063
Susan M. Wood, Prin. Law Libn.
Founded: 1849. **Staff:** Prof 4; Other 1. **Subjects:** Law. **Special Collections:** Records and briefs of Appeals and Appellate Divisions, 1900 to present; English, Scottish and Irish case law. **Holdings:** 88,606 books; 5000 bound periodical volumes. **Subscriptions:** 300 journals and other serials; 6 newspapers. **Services:** Interlibrary loans; copying; library open to public. **Computerized Information Services:** Computerized cataloging. **Networks/Consortia:** Member of Central New York Library Resources Council (CENTRO); SUNY/OCLC Library Network. **Staff:** Carmen E. Brigandi, Law Libn.; Mary Anthony, Law Libn.; Mary B. Dunn, Law Libn.

★9104★
NEW YORK STATE SUPREME COURT - 2ND JUDICIAL DISTRICT - LAW LIBRARY (Law)
360 Adams St.
Brooklyn, NY 11201
Phone: (212) 643-8080
Libby F. Jessup, Prin. Law Libn.
Staff: 5. **Subjects:** Law. **Special Collections:** Forensic medicine; records and briefs of cases in New York Court of Appeals and all appellate divisions. **Holdings:** 250,000 books and bound periodical volumes; 1650 boxes of microfilm; 8632 microfiche cards; 3146 ultrafiche cards; 150 cassettes. **Subscriptions:** 600 journals and other serials. **Services:** Interlibrary loans; copying; library open to public on a limited basis. **Also Known As:** Law Library in Brooklyn. **Staff:** David Turiel, Sr. Law Libn.; Mary Jane Parmenter, Law Libn.; George E. Dobbs, Law Libn.; Paul Henrich, Law Libn.

★9105★
NEW YORK STATE SUPREME COURT - 2ND JUDICIAL DISTRICT - LAW LIBRARY (Law)
County Court House
Staten Island, NY 10301
Phone: (212) 447-4748
Philip A. Klingle, Libn.
Founded: 1920. **Staff:** Prof 1; Other 1. **Subjects:** Law. **Holdings:** 60,000 books; 185 feet of vertical files of reports, pamphlets and clippings. **Subscriptions:** 53 journals and other serials. **Services:** Interlibrary loans; copying; library open to public for reference use only.

★9106★
NEW YORK STATE SUPREME COURT - 3RD JUDICIAL DISTRICT - EMORY A. CHASE MEMORIAL LIBRARY (Law)
Greene County Court House, Main St.
Box 65
Catskill, NY 12414
Phone: (518) 943-3130
Mrs. Armida M. Marafioti, Libn.
Staff: Prof 1. **Subjects:** Law. **Holdings:** 12,000 volumes. **Services:** Interlibrary loans; copying; library open to public for reference use only. **Networks/Consortia:** Member of Association of Law Libraries of Upstate New York; American Association of Law Libraries. **Publications:** Law Library Journal, 4/year.

★9107★
NEW YORK STATE SUPREME COURT - 3RD JUDICIAL DISTRICT - HAMILTON ODELL LIBRARY (Law)
Sullivan County Court House
Monticello, NY 12701
Edith Schop, Libn.
Staff: Prof 1. **Subjects:** Law. **Holdings:** 9000 volumes. **Services:** Library open to public.

★9108★
NEW YORK STATE SUPREME COURT - 3RD JUDICIAL DISTRICT - LAW LIBRARY (Law)
Court House
Hudson, NY 12534
Emily M. Wildey, Libn.
Staff: Prof 1. **Subjects:** Law. **Holdings:** 5000 volumes. **Services:** Library open to public for reference use only.

★9109★
NEW YORK STATE SUPREME COURT - 3RD JUDICIAL DISTRICT - LAW LIBRARY (Law)
Court House
Kingston, NY 12401
Harriett Straus, Libn.
Staff: Prof 1. **Subjects:** Law. **Holdings:** 12,000 volumes. **Services:** Copying; library open to public.

★9110★
NEW YORK STATE SUPREME COURT - 3RD JUDICIAL DISTRICT - LAW LIBRARY (Law)
Court House, 2nd St. Annex
Rensselaer County   Phone: (518) 270-5238
Troy, NY 12180   Barbara P. Norelli, Law Libn.
Founded: 1908. **Staff:** Prof 1; Other 1. **Subjects:** Law including New York State law. **Holdings:** 35,000 volumes; 10,000 volumes in microform. **Services:** Copying; library service to prisoners; open to students, judges, Bar Association members and public.

★9111★
NEW YORK STATE SUPREME COURT - 4TH JUDICIAL DISTRICT - LAW LIBRARY (Law)*
Warren County Municipal Ctr.   Phone: (518) 761-6443
Lake George, NY 12845   Marjorie P. Potter, Law Lib.Ck.
Founded: 1923. **Subjects:** Law. **Holdings:** 31,000 books. **Services:** Copying; library open to public.

★9112★
NEW YORK STATE SUPREME COURT - 4TH JUDICIAL DISTRICT - LAW LIBRARY (Law)
Court House, E. Oneida St.   Phone: (315) 342-0550
Oswego, NY 13126   Janice Drumm Matthews, Law Lib.Ck.
Founded: 1920. **Staff:** Prof 1. **Subjects:** Law - Federal, state, county, city; medicine. **Special Collections:** New York State Reporters, 1891; Series Law of New York, 1853-1899 (Session Laws). **Holdings:** 20,000 books; periodicals. **Services:** Library open to public for reference use only; attorneys may borrow.

★9113★
NEW YORK STATE SUPREME COURT - 4TH JUDICIAL DISTRICT - LAW LIBRARY (Law)
2 City Hall   Phone: (518) 584-4862
Saratoga Springs, NY 12866   Linda E. Macica, Sr. Law Lib.Ck.
Founded: 1866. **Staff:** Prof 1. **Subjects:** Law. **Holdings:** 15,000 volumes. **Services:** Library open to public with restrictions.

★9114★
NEW YORK STATE SUPREME COURT - 4TH JUDICIAL DISTRICT - LAW LIBRARY (Law)
612 State St.   Phone: (518) 382-3310
Schenectady, NY 12307   Patricia L. North, Law Libn.
Staff: Prof 1. **Subjects:** Law. **Holdings:** 26,000 books; 2000 bound periodical volumes. **Services:** Copying; library open to public with restrictions.

★9115★
NEW YORK STATE SUPREME COURT - 5TH JUDICIAL DISTRICT - LAW LIBRARY (Law)†
Oneida County Court House   Phone: (315) 798-5703
Utica, NY 13501   Constance Zogby, Libn.
Founded: 1875. **Staff:** Prof 1; Other 2. **Subjects:** Law. **Special Collections:** Special Trials of the Century; history of law. **Holdings:** 40,000 books; 2000 bound periodical volumes; official documents from New York and the federal government; advance sheets from the courts. **Subscriptions:** 252 journals and other serials; 6 newspapers. **Services:** Interlibrary loans; copying; library open to public. **Publications:** Annual report.

★9116★
NEW YORK STATE SUPREME COURT - 5TH JUDICIAL DISTRICT - WATERTOWN LAW LIBRARY (Law)
Court House   Phone: (315) 782-9100
Watertown, NY 13601   Patrica B. Donaldson, Libn.
Subjects: Law. **Holdings:** 24,000 volumes. **Subscriptions:** 14 journals and other serials. **Services:** Interlibrary loans; library open to public for reference use only.

★9117★
NEW YORK STATE SUPREME COURT - 6TH JUDICIAL DISTRICT - LAW LIBRARY (Law)
107 Court House   Phone: (607) 772-2119
Binghamton, NY 13901   Judy A. Lauer, Law Libn.
Founded: 1911. **Staff:** Prof 1; Other 1. **Subjects:** Law. **Special Collections:** British law. **Holdings:** 46,100 volumes. **Subscriptions:** 19 journals and other serials. **Services:** Interlibrary loans; library open to judges, attorneys and legal researchers.

★9118★
NEW YORK STATE SUPREME COURT - 6TH JUDICIAL DISTRICT - LAW LIBRARY (Law)
Court House   Phone: (607) 746-2603
Delhi, NY 13753   Barbara B. Lewis, Lib.Ck.
Staff: 1. **Subjects:** Law. **Holdings:** 11,000 volumes. **Services:** Library open to public for reference use only.

★9119★
NEW YORK STATE SUPREME COURT - 6TH JUDICIAL DISTRICT - LAW LIBRARY (Law)
Hazlett Bldg.   Phone: (607) 737-2983
Elmira, NY 14901   Julie H. McDowell, Libn.
Staff: Prof 1. **Subjects:** Law. **Holdings:** 25,000 volumes. **Services:** Library open to public.

★9120★
NEW YORK STATE SUPREME COURT - 6TH JUDICIAL DISTRICT - LAW LIBRARY (Law)
West Park Pl.
Norwich, NY 13815   Bethany L. Ginther, Libn.
Staff: 1. **Subjects:** Law. **Holdings:** 9790 volumes. **Services:** Library open to public for reference use only.

★9121★
NEW YORK STATE SUPREME COURT - 7TH JUDICIAL DISTRICT - LAW LIBRARY (Law)
Cayuga County Court House   Phone: (315) 253-1279
Auburn, NY 13021
Staff: Prof 1. **Subjects:** Law. **Holdings:** 19,000 volumes. **Subscriptions:** 12 journals and other serials. **Services:** Library open to public with restrictions.

★9122★
NEW YORK STATE SUPREME COURT - 7TH JUDICIAL DISTRICT - LAW LIBRARY (Law)†
13 Surrogates Court
Pulteney Sq.
Bath, NY 14810   Phone: (607) 776-7126
                                      Ethel M. Lewis, Law Libn.
Founded: 1940. **Staff:** 1. **Subjects:** Law. **Holdings:** 12,000 volumes. **Services:** Library not open to public.

★9123★
NEW YORK STATE SUPREME COURT - 8TH JUDICIAL DISTRICT - LAW LIBRARY (Law)
92 Franklin St.   Phone: (716) 852-0712
Buffalo, NY 14202   James R. Sahlem, Principal Law Libn.
Founded: 1863. **Staff:** Prof 2; Other 4. **Subjects:** Law. **Holdings:** 124,000 volumes. **Subscriptions:** 180 journals and other serials. **Services:** Interlibrary loans; copying; library open to public.

★9124★
NEW YORK STATE SUPREME COURT - 9TH JUDICIAL DISTRICT - JOSEPH F. BARNARD MEMORIAL LAW LIBRARY ASSOCIATION (Law)
Court House
10 Market St.   Phone: (914) 485-9874
Poughkeepsie, NY 12601   Catherine A. Maher, Sr. Law Lib.Ck.
Founded: 1904. **Staff:** 1. **Subjects:** Law. **Holdings:** 19,000 books. **Services:** Library open to public.

★9125★
NEW YORK STATE SUPREME COURT - 9TH JUDICIAL DISTRICT - LAW LIBRARY (Law)
104 Second St.
Newburgh, NY 12550   Ann McClean, Law Lib.Ck.
Staff: 1. **Subjects:** Law. **Holdings:** Figures not available. **Services:** Library not open to public. **Remarks:** The Orange County Government Center, a branch library at 265 Main St., Goshen, NY 10924 is open to qualified researchers and may be reached by phone at 914-294-5151.

★9126★
NEW YORK STATE SUPREME COURT - 9TH JUDICIAL DISTRICT - LAW LIBRARY (Law)
Westchester County Court House
111 Grove St., 9th Fl.   Phone: (914) 682-2574
White Plains, NY 10601   Harriet E. Smith, Principal Law Libn.
Founded: 1908. **Staff:** Prof 2; Other 2. **Subjects:** Law. **Holdings:** 136,500 volumes; Records on Appeal of 4 Appellate Departments and Court of Appeals. **Subscriptions:** 135 journals and other serials. **Services:** Copying; library open to public. **Staff:** B. Sherman, Law Libn.

★9127★
NEW YORK STATE SUPREME COURT - 10TH JUDICIAL DISTRICT - LAW LIBRARY (Law)†
Court House, Rm. 210
Griffing Ave.   Phone: (516) 727-4700
Riverhead, NY 11901   Lynn C. Fullshire, Sr. Law Libn.
Staff: Prof 2; Other 2. **Subjects:** Law - federal, state, Suffolk County, town. **Holdings:** 70,000 volumes; microfilm of New York Law Journal, 1956 to present; checklist of official publications of New York State (microfilm of all publications), 1975, volume 29, number 1, to present; New York Court of Appeals Records and Briefs, 36 NY 2nd to present (microfilm). **Services:** Copying; library open to public. **Remarks:** The Criminal Court Law Library is located at Center Dr.; it is not open to the public. **Staff:** Dorothy B. McMeekan, Asst. Law Libn.

★9128★
NEW YORK STATE SUPREME COURT - 11TH JUDICIAL DISTRICT - LAW LIBRARY (Law)
General Court House
88-11 Sutphin Blvd.   Phone: (212) 520-3140
Jamaica, NY 11435   Andrew J. Tschinkel, Prin. Law Libn.
Founded: 1911. **Staff:** Prof 2; Other 2. **Subjects:** Law. **Holdings:** 90,000 books; 10,000 bound periodical volumes; New York state document depository; 800 reels of microfilmed legislative documents. **Subscriptions:** 104 journals and other serials. **Services:** Interlibrary loans; library open to public.

★9129★
NEW YORK STATE SUPREME COURT - 11TH JUDICIAL DISTRICT - LAW LIBRARY (Law)
Supreme Court Bldg.
125-01 Queens Blvd.   Phone: (212) 520-3541
Kew Gardens, NY 11415   Raymond Murphy, Esq., Sr. Law Libn.
Subjects: Law. **Holdings:** 20,000 volumes. **Services:** Library open to judges, staff and attorneys.

★9130★
NEW YORK STATE SUPREME COURT - 11TH JUDICIAL DISTRICT - LAW LIBRARY (Law)
Supreme Court Bldg.
25-10 Court Sq.   Phone: (212) 520-3921
Long Island City, NY 11101
Subjects: Law . **Holdings:** 1500 volumes. **Services:** Library open to judges, staff and attorneys.

★9131★
NEW YORK STATE TRIAL LAWYERS ASSOCIATION - LIBRARY (Law)
132 Nassau St., Suite 200
New York, NY 10038   Anne J. Quashen, Exec.Dir.
Founded: 1953. **Subjects:** Law. **Holdings:** Figures not available. **Services:** Copying; library not open to public.

★9132★
NEW YORK STOCK EXCHANGE - RESEARCH LIBRARY (Bus-Fin)†
11 Wall St., Rm. 1702   Phone: (212) 623-5049
New York, NY 10005   Jean E. Tobin, Libn.
Founded: 1935. **Staff:** Prof 1; Other 1. **Subjects:** Banking and finance, business and economics. **Special Collections:** Publications of other exchanges, domestic and foreign. **Holdings:** 4000 books; 3000 pamphlets; 75 VF drawers. **Subscriptions:** 75 journals and other serials. **Services:** Interlibrary loans; library not open to public.

★9133★
NEW YORK TELEPHONE COMPANY - LEGAL DEPARTMENT LIBRARY (Law)†
1095 Ave. of the Americas   Phone: (212) 395-6158
New York, NY 10036   Cornelia E. Mahon, Law Libn.
Staff: Prof 1. **Subjects:** Law, communications. **Holdings:** 17,500 volumes. **Subscriptions:** 20 journals and other serials. **Services:** Library not open to public. **Computerized Information Services:** LEXIS.

★9134★
NEW YORK THEOLOGICAL SEMINARY - LIBRARY (Rel-Theol)
5 W. 29th St.   Phone: (212) 532-4012
New York, NY 10001   Eleanor Soler, Libn.
Founded: 1902. **Staff:** Prof 1. **Subjects:** Bible, theology, pastoral counseling, parish ministry, black studies, women. **Holdings:** 16,000 books and bound periodical volumes; 400 cassettes. **Subscriptions:** 30 journals and other serials. **Services:** Interlibrary loans; copying; library open to public for

reference use only.

★9135★
NEW YORK TIMES - MUSEUM OF THE PRINTED WORD
229 W. 43rd St.
New York, NY 10036
Defunct

★9136★
NEW YORK UNIVERSITY - COURANT INSTITUTE OF MATHEMATICAL SCIENCES - LIBRARY (Sci-Tech)†
251 Mercer St.   Phone: (212) 460-7301
New York, NY 10012   Nancy Gubman, Dir.
Founded: 1954. **Staff:** Prof 1; Other 5. **Subjects:** Mathematics, computer science, mathematical physics. **Special Collections:** R. Courant Collection; H. Bohr Collection; K. Friedrichs Collection. **Holdings:** 33,400 books; 14,700 bound periodical volumes; CIMS reports; 1200 microfiche; 600 reels of microfilm. **Subscriptions:** 500 journals and other serials. **Services:** Interlibrary loans; copying; library not open to public. **Publications:** Library Bulletin, monthly - free upon request. **Special Indexes:** Geographic index of conferences and symposia in mathematics and computer science.

★9137★
NEW YORK UNIVERSITY - DENTAL CENTER - JOHN & BERTHA E. WALDMANN MEMORIAL LIBRARY (Med)
345 E. 24th St.   Phone: (212) 481-5874
New York, NY 10010   Roy C. Johnson, Libn.
Staff: Prof 2; Other 8. **Subjects:** Dentistry and allied sciences. **Special Collections:** Weinberger, Blum, Mestal Collection on Dental History. **Holdings:** 25,000 volumes; 88 volumes of master's dissertations; 4 VF drawers of archives. **Subscriptions:** 300 journals and other serials. **Services:** Interlibrary loans; copying; library not open to public. **Computerized Information Services:** Computerized cataloging. **Networks/Consortia:** Member of Medical Library Center of New York. **Special Catalogs:** Audiovisual Materials Catalog - booklet. **Staff:** Raouf Ghali, Assoc.Libn.

★9138★
NEW YORK UNIVERSITY - ELMER HOLMES BOBST LIBRARY - FROST LIBRARY (Hum)
70 Washington Square South   Phone: (212) 598-3756
New York, NY 10012   Frank Walker, Cur.
Staff: Prof 1. **Special Collections:** Personal library of American poet Robert Frost (1874-1963), from his residence at 35 Brewster St., Cambridge, MA. **Holdings:** 3200 books. **Services:** Library not open to public.

★9139★
NEW YORK UNIVERSITY - FALES LIBRARY - DIVISION OF SPECIAL COLLECTIONS (Rare Book)
Bobst Library
70 Washington Sq., S.   Phone: (212) 598-3756
New York, NY 10012   Frank Walker, Cur.
Founded: 1957. **Staff:** Prof 1. **Subjects:** British and American literature. **Holdings:** 141,610 books; 2000 bound periodical volumes; 21,000 manuscripts. **Subscriptions:** 10 journals and other serials. **Services:** Library not open to public.

★9140★
NEW YORK UNIVERSITY - FILM LIBRARY (Aud-Vis)
26 Washington Pl.   Phone: (212) 598-2251
New York, NY 10003   Daniel Lesser, Dir.
Founded: 1940. **Staff:** Prof 2; Other 6. **Subjects:** Teacher education, child development and psychology, over 80 categories emphasizing adult education. **Holdings:** 1500 film titles. **Services:** Library open to public; video cassettes available for rental and sale.

★9141★
NEW YORK UNIVERSITY - GRADUATE SCHOOL OF BUSINESS ADMINISTRATION - LIBRARY (Bus-Fin)
100 Trinity Pl.   Phone: (212) 285-6230
New York, NY 10006   Ronald F. Dow, Dir.
Founded: 1920. **Staff:** Prof 5; Other 18. **Subjects:** Finance, accounting, taxation, management, international business, computer applications. **Holdings:** 100,000 volumes; 424,000 microfiche of corporate financial reports; 5400 reels of microfilm; 4000 corporate annual reports; 50,000 government documents; 5000 bank economic newsletters. **Subscriptions:** 1500 journals and other serials. **Services:** Interlibrary loans; library open to SLA members by arrangement only. **Computerized Information Services:** BRS, DIALOG, New York Times Information Service; computerized cataloging and circulation. **Networks/Consortia:** Member of RLG; METRO. **Publications:**

Acquisitions list. **Remarks:** This Library contains holdings of the former Devine Institute of Finance Library. **Staff:** Melanie A. Hewitt, Tech.Serv.Libn.; Joseph J. Fletcher, Ref.Libn.; James L. Coen, Ref.Libn.; Patricia Radigan, Ref.Libn.; Richard Paul, Circ.

★9142★
NEW YORK UNIVERSITY - INSTITUTE OF FINE ARTS - PHOTOGRAPHIC ARCHIVE (Art)
1 East 78th St.   Phone: (212) 772-5800
New York, NY 10021   Suzanne Babineau-Simenauer, Cur.
Staff: Prof 1; Other 2. **Subjects:** European drawing, painting, sculpture, architecture; art of the Low Countries; antique art known to the Renaissance. **Special Collections:** Offner (Florentine painting); Coor (Sienese painting); Berenson (Italian painting); D.I.A.L. (art of the Low Countries; 11,000 items); I Tatti Archive (13,000 items); Gernsheim corpus (60,000 drawings); Bartsch prints (10,000); Offner corpus (50,000 items). **Holdings:** Figures not available. **Services:** Copying; library open to qualified researchers.

★9143★
NEW YORK UNIVERSITY MEDICAL CENTER - FREDERICK L. EHRMAN MEDICAL LIBRARY (Med)
550 First Ave.   Phone: (212) 340-5393
New York, NY 10016   Gilbert J. Clausman, Libn.
Staff: Prof 7; Other 18. **Subjects:** Medicine and allied sciences. **Special Collections:** Heaton Collection on the history of medicine. **Holdings:** 137,000 volumes. **Subscriptions:** 1475 journals and other serials. **Services:** Interlibrary loans; copying; library not open to public. **Computerized Information Services:** BRS, MEDLINE; computerized cataloging. **Networks/Consortia:** Member of Medical Library Center of New York (MLCNY); OCLC. **Staff:** Burton M. Blechman, Ref.Asst.; Joy G. Wofse, Ref.Asst.; Francis J. Thiegs, Hd., Tech.Serv.; Paul Wrynn, Per.Libn.; Eleonor E. Pasmik, Assoc.Libn., Hd.Ref.

★9144★
NEW YORK UNIVERSITY MEDICAL CENTER - INSTITUTE OF ENVIRONMENTAL MEDICINE - LIBRARY (Med)
Long Meadow Rd., Sterling Forest   Phone: (914) 351-4232
Tuxedo, NY 10987   Christine M. Singleton, Res.Libn.
Staff: Prof 1; Other 1. **Subjects:** Environmental medicine and science, cancer research, air and water pollution, industrial health, radiobiology and toxicology. **Holdings:** 5000 books; 5000 bound periodical volumes; 10,000 USAEC, ERDA and DOE reports (mainly on microfiche). **Subscriptions:** 175 journals and other serials. **Services:** Interlibrary loans; copying; library not open to public. **Computerized Information Services:** DIALOG, SDC, NLM, DOE/RECON. **Networks/Consortia:** Member of Southeastern New York Library Resources Council (SENYLRC).

★9145★
NEW YORK UNIVERSITY - SCHOOL OF LAW LIBRARY (Law)
40 Washington Sq., S.   Phone: (212) 598-3040
New York, NY 10012   Julius J. Marke, Law Libn.
Founded: 1860. **Staff:** Prof 11; Other 39. **Subjects:** Law. **Special Collections:** Frederick Bosch Collection on Spanish-American law; Frederick Brown Collection of ancient legal documents. **Holdings:** 567,507 volumes; cassettes, microforms. **Services:** Interlibrary loans (limited); library not open to public; however special requests for research will be considered.

NEW YORK UNIVERSITY - SEX INFORMATION & EDUCATION COUNCIL OF THE U.S.
See: Sex Information & Education Council of the U.S.

★9146★
NEW YORK UNIVERSITY - STEPHEN CHAN LIBRARY OF FINE ARTS (Art)†
1 E. 78th St.   Phone: (212) 988-5550
New York, NY 10021   Evelyn Samuel, Hd.Libn.
Founded: 1938. **Staff:** Prof 2; Other 4. **Subjects:** History of art, architectural history, archeology, art technology and conservation of art. **Holdings:** 80,409 books; 10,000 bound periodical volumes; 10,000 microforms. **Subscriptions:** 676 journals and other serials. **Services:** Interlibrary loans; library open to scholars by arrangement. **Networks/Consortia:** Member of RLG. **Special Catalogs:** Library Catalog of the Conservation Center of the Institute of Fine Arts, New York University.

★9147★
NEW YORK UNIVERSITY - TAMIMENT LIBRARY (Soc Sci)
70 Washington Sq., S.   Phone: (212) 598-3708
New York, NY 10012   Dorothy Swanson, Libn.
Founded: 1956. **Staff:** Prof 1; Other 4. **Subjects:** History of labor and unionism; radical and reform movements. **Special Collections:** Meyer London Memorial Library of the Rand School of Social Science; Eugene V. Debs Collection; American Socialist Society Collection; B. Charney Vladeck papers; Fund for the Republic Communism Collection; Robert F. Wagner Labor Archives; Oral History of the American Left (OHAL). **Holdings:** 44,027 books and bound periodical volumes; 2765 reels of microfilm; 500,000 items in special collections; 165 VF drawers of pamphlets; 1060 linear feet of manuscript collections. **Subscriptions:** 427 journals and other serials. **Services:** Interlibrary loans; library open to public for research. **Publications:** Tamiment Library Bulletin; New York Labor Heritage; OHAL Newsletter.

★9148★
NEW YORK UNIVERSITY - UNITED NATIONS COLLECTION (Soc Sci)
Bobst Library
70 Washington Sq., S.   Phone: (212) 598-3609
New York, NY 10012   Peter B. Allison, Hd., Soc.Sci./Docs.
Founded: 1946. **Staff:** Prof 1; Other 2. **Subjects:** United Nations and League of Nations; Specialized Agencies of the United Nations; other international organizations. **Holdings:** 3474 bound volumes of printed UN official records and sales publications; 5940 bound volumes of UN mimeographed documents; 16,265 current unbound UN mimeographed documents; 9650 volumes of UN Specialized Agencies, League of Nations and other international organizations; 7084 vertical file items; 1600 microfiche of OAS items; 4848 microfiche of UNCTAD items; 1892 microfiche of National Statistical Compendium items; 547 reels of microfilm of League of Nations documents; 6 reels of microfilm of IMF items. **Services:** Copying; library open to public.

NEW YORK YEARLY MEETING (Friends)
See: Society of Friends

★9149★
NEW YORK ZOOLOGICAL SOCIETY - LIBRARY (Sci-Tech)
185th St. & Southern Blvd.   Phone: (212) 220-5125
Bronx, NY 10460   Steven P. Johnson, Archv.-Libn.
Founded: 1899. **Staff:** Prof 1. **Subjects:** Vertebrate zoology, management of captive wildlife, natural history. **Holdings:** 10,000 books; 2000 bound periodical volumes; 240 bound volumes of official society publications and books by society authors; 1000 linear feet of archives. **Subscriptions:** 250 journals and other serials. **Services:** Interlibrary loans; copying; library open to public by appointment. **Networks/Consortia:** Member of METRO.

NEW YORK ZOOLOGICAL SOCIETY - NEW YORK AQUARIUM LIBRARY
See: Osborn Laboratories of Marine Sciences - New York Aquarium Library

★9150★
NEW ZEALAND CONSULATE GENERAL - LIBRARY (Area-Ethnic)
630 Fifth Ave., Suite 530   Phone: (212) 586-0060
New York, NY 10111   Nicholas Lorimer, Info. Officer
Staff: Prof 1. **Subjects:** New Zealand - history, government, foreign affairs, fiction; Maori culture. **Special Collections:** New Zealand statutes and statutory regulations; journals of the New Zealand Parliament. **Holdings:** 1720 books and bound periodical volumes; VF drawers of clippings. **Subscriptions:** 58 journals and other serials. **Services:** Copying; library open to public with restrictions.

★9151★
NEW ZEALAND EMBASSY - LIBRARY (Area-Ethnic)
37 Observatory Circle, N.W.   Phone: (202) 328-4800
Washington, DC 20008   Robert Hole, Second Sec.
Founded: 1953. **Staff:** Prof 3. **Subjects:** New Zealand - history, literature, geography, foreign policy, Polynesian peoples. **Special Collections:** Maori people; South Pacific Islands. **Holdings:** 2100 volumes. **Subscriptions:** 43 New Zealand journals and other serials. **Services:** Interlibrary loans; library open to public. **Publications:** New Zealand Update, monthly. **Staff:** Patricia Golden; Robyn Harrison .

★9152★
NEWARK BETH ISRAEL MEDICAL CENTER - DR. VICTOR PARSONNET MEMORIAL LIBRARY (Med)
201 Lyons Ave.   Phone: (201) 926-7233
Newark, NJ 07112   Lillian Bernstein, Libn.
Staff: Prof 1; Other 1. **Subjects:** Medicine, surgery, cardiology, oncology, pediatrics, dentistry. **Special Collections:** Dr. Victor Parsonnet rare book collection. **Holdings:** 1700 books; 5000 bound periodical volumes; 500 cassettes; 125 pamphlets; 150 slides. **Subscriptions:** 195 journals and other serials. **Services:** Interlibrary loans; copying; library open to public for reference use only. **Computerized Information Services:** Online systems (through University of Medicine & Dentistry of New Jersey). **Networks/Consortia:** Member of Cosmopolitan Biomedical Library Consortium.

★9153★

NEWARK BOARD OF EDUCATION - TEACHERS' PROFESSIONAL LIBRARY
(Educ)
2 Cedar St.   Phone: (201) 733-7136
Newark, NJ 07102   Elberta H. Stone, Libn.
Staff: Prof 1; Other 1. **Subjects:** Education. **Special Collections:** Textbook Education Center Library (approved textbooks for Newark Schools, grades K-12). **Holdings:** 4000 books; minutes and reports of Board of Education. **Subscriptions:** 113 journals and other serials. **Services:** Library open to public with restrictions. **Publications:** Read, See and Hear - distributed to Newark teachers; School Library Notes - distributed to Newark librarians.

★9154★

NEWARK MUSEUM ASSOCIATION - MUSEUM LIBRARY (Art; Sci-Tech)
49 Washington St.
Box 540   Phone: (201) 733-6640
Newark, NJ 07101   Margaret Di Salvi, Libn.
Founded: 1926. **Staff:** Prof 1; Other 1. **Subjects:** American painting and sculpture; decorative arts; Oriental arts; classical art; ethnological materials; natural sciences. **Holdings:** 22,000 books and bound periodical volumes; 10,000 pamphlets; 25,000 black/white photographs; 3000 slides; 102 color transparencies. **Subscriptions:** 200 journals and other serials. **Services:** Interlibrary loans; copying; library open to public for reference use only.

★9155★

NEWARK PUBLIC LIBRARY - ART AND MUSIC DEPARTMENT (Art; Mus)†
5 Washington St.
Box 630   Phone: (201) 733-7840
Newark, NJ 07101-0630   William J. Dane, Supv.
Staff: Prof 8; Other 7. **Subjects:** Art and art history, architecture, decorative arts, photography, music history, music theory and practice. **Special Collections:** R.C. Jenkinson Collection (fine printing); John Tasker Howard Collection (American music); Japanese prints and books of design; Bruce Rogers Collection; Posters (4000); Shopping Bag Collection (300 pieces); Illustrated books (1000). **Holdings:** 50,000 books; 11,000 music scores; 1600 portfolios of design; 1500 circulating prints; 13,000 fine prints; 1 million pictures; 15,000 slides; 6500 music recordings; 33,000 clippings; 980 autographs. **Subscriptions:** 300 journals and other serials. **Services:** Interlibrary loans; copying; photo lab service. **Computerized Information Services:** Computerized cataloging. **Networks/Consortia:** Member of OCLC; New Jersey Library Network Services; METRO. **Special Catalogs:** Picture Collection Subject Headings (book); Jenkinson Collection Catalogs I and II (books). **Special Indexes:** New Jersey Architectural Index (microfiche); Index to "Cartoonists Profile," "Old Print Shop Portfolio" (typescripts). **Staff:** Joan E. Burns, Principal Art Libn.

★9156★

NEWARK PUBLIC LIBRARY - BUSINESS LIBRARY (Bus-Fin)
34 Commerce St.   Phone: (201) 733-7849
Newark, NJ 07102   Leslie P. Rupprecht, Supv.
Founded: 1904. **Staff:** Prof 6; Other 4. **Subjects:** Business, accounting, insurance, advertising and marketing, investment, money and banking, industrial management. **Special Collections:** Directories (city, trade, telephone, foreign); business histories; W. Paul Stillman Collection of Books on Insurance and Finance. **Holdings:** 9000 books; 995 bound periodical volumes; 7238 directories; 1256 volumes of services; 162 bound newspaper volumes; 3530 other volumes; 104 VF drawers of clippings, pamphlets, reports, documents, maps, corporation annual reports, and house organs. **Services:** Interlibrary loans (limited); copying. **Publications:** Business Literature.

★9157★

NEWARK PUBLIC LIBRARY - EDUCATION DIVISION (Educ)
5 Washington St.
Box 630   Phone: (201) 733-7793
Newark, NJ 07101-0630   Frances Beiman, Prin.Libn.
Founded: 1929. **Staff:** Prof 4; Other 2. **Subjects:** Education, including psychology and philosophy of education; teaching methods; special education; guidance; child psychology; history of education. **Special Collections:** Career Information (books, pamphlets and clippings); Dissertation Abstracts (bound volumes and microfilm); Job Information Center (videotapes). **Holdings:** 10,000 books; 2466 bound periodical volumes; 500 pamphlets; 24 file cabinets of clippings, uncataloged pamphlets and leaflets; 7200 college catalogs on microfiche. **Subscriptions:** 143 journals and other serials. **Services:** Interlibrary loans; copying; reference assistance to groups from job-training programs; TTY machine; resume preparation assistance; career programs held 4 times a year. **Computerized Information Services:** DIALOG, BRS, New York Times Information Service. **Networks/Consortia:** Member of OCLC; New Jersey Library Network Services; METRO. **Publications:** Booklists - distributed to Newark schools, nonprofit agencies in New Jersey and library

patrons. **Special Indexes:** Career materials, lesson plans, case studies of exceptional children, specialized courses in the New York-Northern New Jersey metropolitan area.

★9158★

NEWARK PUBLIC LIBRARY - HUMANITIES DIVISION (Hum)
5 Washington St.
Box 630   Phone: (201) 733-7820
Newark, NJ 07101-0630   Sallie Hannigan, Prin.Libn., Ref.
Staff: Prof 5. **Subjects:** Literature, language and criticism, biography, bibliography, religion, philosophy, history, geography, psychology, librariana. **Special Collections:** Black literature, history and biography; Granger Collection of Poetry Anthologies; Puerto Rican Reference Collection; Travel Collection (books, pamphlets, clippings). **Holdings:** 65,000 books; 550 bound periodical volumes; 1000 maps; 11,000 volumes in Spanish; dictionaries and encyclopedias in Spanish, Italian, French, German and Russian; information file. **Subscriptions:** 630 journals and other serials. **Services:** Telephone and in-person reference available in Spanish. **Computerized Information Services:** BRS, New York Times Information Service. **Networks/Consortia:** Member of OCLC; New Jersey Library Network Services; METRO.

★9159★

NEWARK PUBLIC LIBRARY - NEW JERSEY REFERENCE DIVISION (Hist)
5 Washington St.
Box 630   Phone: (201) 733-7776
Newark, NJ 07101-0630   Charles F. Cummings, Supv.Libn.
Staff: Prof 7; Other 6. **Subjects:** New Jersey, Newark, and Essex County history and laws; current affairs; travel and description; biography (genealogy excluded). **Special Collections:** New Jersey Author-Imprints; Stephen Crane Collection (388 secondary source items relating to Crane and the Stephen Crane Association, defunct 1941); DeLagerberg Collection (manuscript drawings and newspaper clippings relating to New Jersey architecture); New Jersey and Newark Picture Collection (15,000 photographs of buildings and people; 2500 postal cards); Berg Collection (1800 photographs of Newark Street scenes); Dorer Collection (3000 negatives from Newark newspapers, recently microfilmed for preservation); HABS drawings (includes entire state); Newark Evening News photograph collection (entire newspaper photographic morgue, count in process); Newark Evening News archives. **Holdings:** 25,000 books; 550 bound periodical volumes; 2300 bound documents; 8200 unbound periodical volumes; 5000 reels of New Jersey newspapers and miscellaneous microfilm; 40 VF drawers of clippings (4000 subject folders); 24,000 documents; 1600 maps. **Subscriptions:** 100 journals and other serials; 12 newspapers. **Services:** Interlibrary loans (limited); copying (hard copy and microfilm); photo lab copies of prints owned by institution. **Publications:** Occasional booklist; librarians edit "New Jersey Bibliographer;" local subject list; compilation of walk tour guides. **Special Indexes:** New Jersey Periodical Notes (periodical index); New Jersey Illustration Index (160,000 card picture index to loose pictures and pictures in books); Star Ledger (Newark, NJ) Index, 1971 to present (60,000 card index); New Jersey Folklore Index; New Jersey Law Journal Index (biographical entries); Newark and New Jersey Association File; New Jersey Dissertation Index; New Jersey Author File; New Jersey Television News Index; New Jersey Abbreviation Index; New Jersey Lake File.

★9160★

NEWARK PUBLIC LIBRARY - SCIENCE AND TECHNOLOGY DIVISION (Sci-Tech)
5 Washington St.
Box 630   Phone: (201) 733-7815
Newark, NJ 07101-0630   Nicholas W. Patton, Prin.Libn.
Founded: 1879. **Staff:** Prof 2; Other 1. **Subjects:** Science and technology. **Special Collections:** U.S. patent specifications and drawings, 1790 to present; American National Standards Institute (ANSI) standards. **Holdings:** 70,000 books; 60,000 bound periodical volumes; 10 VF drawers of standards. **Subscriptions:** 430 journals and other serials. **Services:** Interlibrary loans; copying. **Computerized Information Services:** DIALOG, BRS, New York Times Information Service, U.S. Patent Office; computerized cataloging and serials. **Networks/Consortia:** Member of OCLC; New Jersey Library Network Services; METRO.

★9161★

NEWARK PUBLIC LIBRARY - SOCIAL SCIENCE DIVISION (Soc Sci)
5 Washington St.
Box 630   Phone: (201) 733-7782
Newark, NJ 07101-0630   Donald Fostel, Prin.Libn.
Staff: Prof 4. **Subjects:** Labor, international relations, black studies, consumer affairs, women's studies, economics, sociology, political science, housing. **Special Collections:** Pan American Union publications; Organization of American States official records; statistical yearbooks of foreign countries

(125); U.S. Government document depository; Service Center for Aging Information (SCAN) Microfiche Library. **Holdings:** 45,000 books; 48 VF drawers of pamphlets, clippings, and documents. **Subscriptions:** 270 journals and other serials. **Services:** Interlibrary loans; copying; division open to public. **Computerized Information Services:** DIALOG, BRS, New York Times Information Service. **Networks/Consortia:** Member of OCLC; New Jersey Library Network Services; METRO.

★9162★
NEWBERRY LIBRARY (Hum)
60 W. Walton St.   Phone: (312) 943-9090
Chicago, IL 60610   Lawrence W. Towner, Pres./Libn.
Founded: 1887. **Staff:** Prof 44; Other 73. **Subjects:** European, English and American history and literature; local and family history; church history; Italian Renaissance; expansion of Europe; philology; bibliography; history and theory of music; history of cartography. **Special Collections:** History of Printing; Western Americana; American Indian; Midwest manuscripts; Sherwood Anderson; music; Melville Collection; railroad archives. **Holdings:** 1.3 million books and bound periodical volumes; 5 million manuscripts; 225,000 units of microforms; 150,000 pieces of sheet music and music scores. **Subscriptions:** 1000 journals and other serials. **Services:** Copying; library open to public with identification. **Networks/Consortia:** Member of Independent Research Library Association; OCLC through ILLINET; Association of Research Libraries (ARL). **Publications:** General Guide to the Collections in the Newberry Library; An Uncommon Collection of Uncommon Collections; newsletter, bulletins. **Staff:** James M. Wells, V.P.; Joel L. Samuels, Dir., Lib.Serv.; Richard H. Brown, Dir., Res. & Educ.; Lawrence C. Hodapp, Controller; Victor B. Weber, Dir., Dev.

NEWBURGH BAY HISTORICAL SOCIETY
See: Historical Society of Newburgh Bay and the Highlands

NEWCOMB (Lawrence) LIBRARY
See: New England Wild Flower Society, Inc. - Lawrence Newcomb Library

★9163★
NEWCOMEN SOCIETY IN NORTH AMERICA - THOMAS NEWCOMEN LIBRARY IN STEAM TECHNOLOGY & INDUSTRIAL HISTORY (Hist; Sci-Tech)
412 Newcomen Rd.   Phone: (215) 363-6600
Exton, PA 19335   Nancy Arnold, Libn./Cur.
Founded: 1965. **Staff:** Prof 1. **Subjects:** History of steam and steam technology; business and industrial history. **Holdings:** 4500 books; 300 bound periodical volumes; 1100 trade catalogs. **Subscriptions:** 59 journals and other serials. **Services:** Interlibrary loans; copying; library open to public for reference use only.

NEWFOUNDLAND - DEPARTMENT OF CULTURE, RECREATION AND YOUTH - PROVINCIAL ARCHIVES OF NEWFOUNDLAND AND LABRADOR
See: Newfoundland - Provincial Archives of Newfoundland and Labrador

★9164★
NEWFOUNDLAND - DEPARTMENT OF EDUCATION - INSTRUCTIONAL MATERIALS LIBRARY (Aud-Vis; Educ)
Bldg. 951, Pleasantville   Phone: (709) 737-2619
St. John's, NF, Canada A1A 1R2   D. Nanayakkara, Libn.
Founded: 1946. **Staff:** Prof 6; Other 10. **Subjects:** All subjects relative to K-11 curriculum. **Holdings:** 12,000 films; 10,000 filmstrips; 5000 tape recordings. **Services:** Copying (audiotape and videotape); filmstrips and slide-tape presentations; materials available to public, priority given to schools. **Staff:** N. Harris, Asst.Dir. of Instr.

★9165★
NEWFOUNDLAND - DEPARTMENT OF JUSTICE - LAW LIBRARY (Law)
Confederation Bldg.   Phone: (709) 737-2861
St. John's, NF, Canada A1C 5T7   Mona B. Pearce, Libn.
Staff: Prof 1. **Subjects:** Law. **Holdings:** 18,000 books. **Subscriptions:** 90 journals and other serials. **Services:** Interlibrary loans; copying; library not open to public. **Remarks:** This library is the central reference library for all Newfoundland court libraries, which maintain small working collections.

★9166★
NEWFOUNDLAND - DEPARTMENT OF MINES AND ENERGY - MINERAL DEVELOPMENT DIVISION - LIBRARY (Energy)
95 Bonaventure Ave.   Phone: (709) 737-3159
St. John's, NF, Canada A1C 5T7   Genie Power, Lib.Techn.
Founded: 1950. **Staff:** 1. **Subjects:** Earth sciences, mining. **Holdings:** 250 textbooks; 3000 technical reports; 8000 geological documents (technical files on Newfoundland); 2000 maps. **Subscriptions:** 80 journals and other

serials; 6 newspapers. **Services:** Library not open to public.

★9167★
NEWFOUNDLAND - DEPARTMENT OF RURAL DEVELOPMENT - RESOURCE CENTRE (Soc Sci)
Atlantic Place   Phone: (709) 737-3172
St. John's, NF, Canada A1C 5T7   Philip I. Mullett, Info.Spec.
Founded: 1973. **Staff:** Prof 1. **Subjects:** Rural development, handcrafts, programs information. **Holdings:** 100 books; 1200 studies and reports. **Subscriptions:** 8 journals and other serials. **Services:** Centre open to Newfoundland regional development associations.

NEWFOUNDLAND FOREST RESEARCH CENTRE
See: Canada - Canadian Forestry Service

★9168★
NEWFOUNDLAND AND LABRADOR DEVELOPMENT CORPORATION LTD. - LIBRARY (Bus-Fin)†
44 Torbay Rd.
P.O. Box 9548   Phone: (709) 753-3560
St. John's, NF, Canada A1A 2Y4   Heddy M. Peddle, Libn.
Founded: 1973. **Staff:** Prof 1; Other 1. **Subjects:** Marketing, small business, natural resources, food service industry, accommodation, finance. **Holdings:** 2500 books; 17 VF drawers of subject files; Standard Industrial Classification (SIC) manufacturers' catalogs; annual reports. **Subscriptions:** 200 journals and other serials; 40 newspapers. **Services:** Interlibrary loans; copying; SDI; library open to public. **Publications:** Catalog of Selected Library Holdings, semiannual.

NEWFOUNDLAND LAW SOCIETY
See: Law Society of Newfoundland

★9169★
NEWFOUNDLAND - LEGISLATIVE LIBRARY (Soc Sci)
House of Assembly, Confederation Bldg.
P.O. Box 4750   Phone: (709) 737-3604
St. John's, NF, Canada A1C 5T7   N.J. Richards, Legislative Libn.
Staff: 2. **Special Collections:** Government documents; Newfoundlandiana. **Holdings:** Figures not available. **Services:** Library open to public if material not available elsewhere, with special permission. **Remarks:** This is a small library set up to provide assistance to the House of Assembly and the cabinet.

★9170★
NEWFOUNDLAND LIGHT & POWER COMPANY, LTD. - CENTRAL RECORDS LIBRARY (Bus-Fin)
P.O. Box 8910, Kenmount Road   Phone: (709) 737-5645
St. John's, NF, Canada A1B 3P6   Cyril C. Morgan, Supv.
Staff: 4. **Subjects:** Transportation, safety, Canadian statistics, finance, accounting. **Holdings:** 500 books; company annual reports from 1924; 500 reels of microfilm (company records); newspaper clippings. **Subscriptions:** 95 journals and other serials; 10 newspapers. **Services:** Library not open to public.

★9171★
NEWFOUNDLAND - PROVINCIAL ARCHIVES OF NEWFOUNDLAND AND LABRADOR (Hist)†
Colonial Bldg., Military Rd.   Phone: (709) 753-9390
St. John's, NF, Canada A1C 2C9   David J. Davis, Prov.Archv.
Founded: 1956. **Staff:** Prof 4; Other 5. **Subjects:** Newfoundland - history, economic history, folklore, sociology, geography, genealogy. **Special Collections:** Parish registers from churches throughout Newfoundland; British and French records relating to Newfoundland (586 reels of microfilm). **Holdings:** 180 linear feet of books and booklets; 1200 bound periodical volumes; 2000 linear feet of archival materials (manuscripts, maps, government documents); 10,000 photographs. **Subscriptions:** All newspapers published in Newfoundland. **Services:** Copying; archives open to public. **Special Catalogs:** Inventories; finding aids. **Remarks:** Administered by the Newfoundland Department of Culture, Recreation and Youth. **Staff:** Margaret Chang, Archv.; Howard C. Brown, Archv.

★9172★
NEWFOUNDLAND - PUBLIC LIBRARY SERVICES (Soc Sci)
Arts & Culture Centre
Allandale Rd.   Phone: (709) 737-3964
St. John's, NF, Canada A1B 3A3   Pearce J. Penney, Chf.Prov.Libn.
Founded: 1936. **Staff:** Prof 17; Other 96. **Special Collections:** Newfoundlandiana (16,000 items). **Holdings:** 731,946 volumes. **Subscriptions:** 800 journals and other serials; 40 newspapers. **Services:** Interlibrary loans; copying; library open to public. **Computerized Information**

Services: Computerized cataloging. **Networks/Consortia:** Member of UTLAS Inc. **Publications:** Provincial library newsletter, quarterly; Annual Report of the Newfoundland Public Libraries Board. **Special Catalogs:** Newfoundland newspaper index. **Remarks:** Above data includes 3 branch libraries and the Provincial Reference & Resource Library in St. John's, 105 libraries elsewhere in the province and bookmobiles - all operated by Public Library Services.

NEWHOUSE (Samuel I.) CENTER FOR LAW AND JUSTICE
See: Rutgers University, The State University of New Jersey - Justice Henry Ackerson Lib. of Law & Criminal Justice

★9173★
NEWINGTON CHILDREN'S HOSPITAL - PROFESSIONAL LIBRARY (Med)
181 E. Cedar St.   Phone: (203) 666-2461
Newington, CT 06111   Jean Long, Med.Libn.
Founded: 1970. **Staff:** Prof 1; Other 1. **Subjects:** Orthopedics, pediatrics, nursing. **Holdings:** 2300 books; 2500 bound periodical volumes; 800 reprints; 350 items in research file; 109 alumni presentations. **Subscriptions:** 125 journals and other serials. **Services:** Interlibrary loans; copying; library open to public with restrictions. **Computerized Information Services:** MEDLARS; computerized cataloging and serials. **Networks/Consortia:** Member of Capitol Area Health Consortium Libraries; Connecticut Association of Health Science Libraries (CAHSL).

NEWMAN (Carol M.) LIBRARY
See: Virginia Polytechnic Institute and State University - Carol M. Newman Library

NEWMAN CATHOLIC STUDENT CENTER
See: St. Thomas More Center - Timothy Parkman Memorial Library

NEWMAN CENTER LIBRARY
See: University of Minnesota

NEWMAN SEMINAR
See: Mount St. Mary's College

★9174★
NEWMAN THEOLOGICAL COLLEGE - LIBRARY (Rel-Theol)†
R.R. 8   Phone: (403) 459-6656
Edmonton, AB, Canada T5L 4H8   Shirley Anne Threndyle, Libn.
Founded: 1917. **Staff:** Prof 1; Other 4. **Subjects:** Roman Catholic theology, Christian authors, scripture studies, church law, Canadiana, philosophy. **Holdings:** 22,000 books; 5000 bound periodical volumes. **Subscriptions:** 110 journals and other serials. **Services:** Copying; library open to public with approval of librarian.

★9175★
NEWMONT MINING CORPORATION - TECHNICAL ENGINEERING LIBRARY (Sci-Tech)
300 Park Ave.   Phone: (212) 980-1111
New York, NY 10022   Loretta Herrmann, Libn.
Founded: 1920. **Staff:** Prof 1. **Subjects:** Metals (especially copper), geology, exploration, mining, energy. **Special Collections:** Mining in the Old West; U.S. Bureau of Mines publications; geological bulletins from the 1800s. **Holdings:** 1504 books; 12 bound periodical volumes; 2100 geology pamphlets (cataloged); 1000 annual reports; 31 VF drawers of commodity and photograph files; patents; reports. **Subscriptions:** 175 journals and other serials; 12 newspapers. **Services:** Interlibrary loans; library not open to public.

★9176★
NEWPORT AERONAUTICAL SALES (NAS) - LIBRARY (Sci-Tech)
4020 Birch St., No. 105   Phone: (714) 975-0545
Newport Beach, CA 92660   George M. Posey, III, V.P., Res.
Staff: Prof 2; Other 3. **Subjects:** Military and commercial aircraft. **Special Collections:** U.S. Air Force, Navy and Army aircraft technical manuals on early and late revision aircraft and systems. **Holdings:** 25,000 manuals on microfiche. **Subscriptions:** 25 journals and other serials. **Services:** Copying; library open to public.

NEWPORT (Christopher) COLLEGE - CHESAPEAKE & OHIO HISTORICAL SOCIETY, INC.
See: Chesapeake & Ohio Historical Society, Inc.

★9177★
NEWPORT HARBOR ART MUSEUM - LIBRARY (Art)
850 San Clemente Dr.   Phone: (714) 759-1122
Newport Beach, CA 92660   Ruth E. Roe, Libn.
Staff: Prof 1. **Subjects:** Art. **Holdings:** 200 books; 1000 art exhibition

catalogs (cataloged); 4 VF drawers of clippings and ephemera in field of art. **Subscriptions:** 12 journals and other serials. **Services:** Library not open to public.

★9178★
NEWPORT HISTORICAL SOCIETY - LIBRARY (Hist)†
82 Touro St.   Phone: (401) 846-0813
Newport, RI 02840   Madeline H. Wordell, Libn.
Subjects: Newport and Rhode Island history and genealogy. **Special Collections:** Manuscript material relating to 18th century colonial merchants; church records; records of the Newport Town Council. **Holdings:** 8900 books; 200 boxes of manuscripts; 100 scrapbooks; newspapers on microfilm. **Services:** Interlibrary loans (limited); copying; library open to public.

★9179★
NEWPORT HOSPITAL - INA MOSHER HEALTH SCIENCES LIBRARY (Med)
Friendship St.   Phone: (401) 846-6400
Newport, RI 02840   Tosca N. Carpenter, Hd.Libn.
Founded: 1958. **Staff:** Prof 1; Other 2. **Subjects:** Health sciences. **Holdings:** 5602 books and bound periodical volumes; 56 newsletters; 15 VF drawers; 10 tape journals. **Subscriptions:** 138 journals and other serials. **Services:** Interlibrary loans; copying; library open to public for reference use only. **Networks/Consortia:** Member of Association of Rhode Island Health Sciences Librarians. **Publications:** Newsletter, monthly.

★9180★
NEWPORT NEWS DAILY PRESS, INC. - LIBRARY (Publ)
7505 Warwick Blvd.
Box 746   Phone: (804) 244-8421
Newport News, VA 23607   Theresa M. Hammond, Dir., Lib.Serv.
Founded: 1961. **Staff:** Prof 2; Other 8. **Subjects:** Newspaper reference topics. **Holdings:** 1300 books; 96 VF drawers of clippings; 12 VF drawers of reports and pamphlets; 1320 reels of microfilm of the newspaper; 62 VF drawers of photograph files. **Subscriptions:** 25 journals and other serials; 14 newspapers. **Services:** Interlibrary loans; copying; library open to public with restrictions. **Computerized Information Services:** Internal database. **Publications:** Quarterly Library Memo - for internal distribution only.

★9181★
NEWPORT NEWS SHIPBUILDING AND DRY DOCK COMPANY - LIBRARY SERVICES DEPARTMENT (Sci-Tech)
     Phone: (804) 380-2610
Newport News, VA 23607   S.A. Orr, Lib.Supv.
Founded: 1947. **Staff:** Prof 3; Other 2. **Subjects:** Oceanography, management, naval architecture, marine engineering, mathematics. **Holdings:** 30,000 books; 9000 bound periodical volumes; 100,000 research reports and documents. **Subscriptions:** 850 journals and other serials. **Services:** Interlibrary loans; library open to public with security clearance.

★9182★
NEWS AND OBSERVER PUBLISHING COMPANY - LIBRARY (Publ)
215 S. McDowell St.   Phone: (919) 821-1234
Raleigh, NC 27602   Lany W. McDonald, Libn.
Founded: 1870. **Staff:** Prof 1; Other 6. **Subjects:** Newspaper reference topics. **Holdings:** Figures not available for books, news clippings, photographic files. **Services:** Copying; library not open to public.

★9183★
NEWSDAY, INC. - LIBRARY (Publ)
235 Pinelawn Rd.   Phone: (516) 454-2335
Melville, NY 11747   Andrew V. Ippolito, Dir. of Lib. & Res.
Staff: Prof 5; Other 18. **Subjects:** Queens, Nassau and Suffolk Counties records and history. **Holdings:** 9000 books; Newsday clippings, photographs, negatives. **Subscriptions:** 125 journals and other serials (microfilm); 5 newspapers. **Services:** Remington Rand mechanical files for clippings and Supreme Conservatrieve file for photographs; library not open to public. **Computerized Information Services:** SDC, Mead Data Central, New York Times Information Service; computerized acquisitions. **Staff:** David Hoffman, Chf.Libn.; Mary Ann Skinner, Libn.; Karen Van Rossem, Res.

★9184★
NEWSOM (Earl) & COMPANY, INC. - LIBRARY (Bus-Fin)
10 East 53rd St.   Phone: (212) 755-4664
New York, NY 10022   Joan M. Reicherter, Libn.
Founded: 1953. **Staff:** Prof 1; Other 2. **Subjects:** Business, public relations, environment, energy. **Holdings:** 2000 books; 700 pamphlets; 8 VF drawers of clippings; 24 VF drawers of reports. **Subscriptions:** 90 journals and other serials; 5 newspapers. **Services:** Interlibrary loans; library open to public by appointment.

★9185★
NEWSPAPER ADVERTISING BUREAU, INC. - INFORMATION CENTER (Bus-Fin)
485 Lexington Ave.   Phone: (212) 557-1822
New York, NY 10017   Ann Brady, Hd., Info.Ctr.
Staff: 2. **Subjects:** Advertising, marketing, newspapers. **Holdings:** 580 books; 48 bound periodical volumes; 18 shelves of government publications; 22 VF drawers of clippings and pamphlets. **Subscriptions:** 80 journals and other serials. **Services:** Interlibrary loans; center open to public for reference use only on request. **Staff:** Susan Hyer, Asst.Libn.

★9186★
NEWSPAPER COMICS COUNCIL - LIBRARY INFORMATION CENTER (Art)
Ward Castle
Comly Ave.   Phone: (914) 939-3919
Port Chester, NY 10573   Catherine T. Prentice, Libn.
Subjects: Comics. **Holdings:** 350 books; 4 VF drawers of comics and photographs of cartoonists. **Services:** Library not open to public.

★9187★
NEWSPAPER GUILD - HEYWOOD BROUN LIBRARY (Soc Sci)
1125 15th St., N.W.   Phone: (202) 296-2990
Washington, DC 20005   David J. Eisen, Dir. of Res. & Info.
Founded: 1957. **Subjects:** Works of Heywood Broun, labor relations, labor unions, newspaper industry; First Amendment. **Holdings:** 750 books. **Subscriptions:** 90 journals and other serials. **Services:** Copying; library open to public by appointment.

★9188★
NEWSPAPERS, INC. - EDITORIAL LIBRARY (Publ)
333 W. State St.   Phone: (414) 224-2376
Milwaukee, WI 53203   Jo Reitman, Libn.
Staff: Prof 1. **Subjects:** Newspaper reference topics. **Holdings:** 3500 books; 150 bound periodical volumes; 2.5 million clippings; 1.5 million photographs. **Services:** Copying; library open to public for reference use only. **Remarks:** Part of the Journal Company, the library serves the Milwaukee Journal and Milwaukee Sentinel newspapers.

NEWSWEEK, INC. - INSIDE SPORTS MAGAZINE
See: Inside Sports Magazine

★9189★
NEWSWEEK, INC. - LIBRARY (Publ)
444 Madison Ave.   Phone: (212) 350-2494
New York, NY 10022   Ted Slate, Lib.Dir.
Founded: 1933. **Staff:** Prof 12; Other 15. **Subjects:** Current affairs; history; biography; politics; statistics; international affairs; specific departmental subject fields, as music, press, religion, education, entertainment, science, art, books, business, medicine, and sports. **Holdings:** 34,000 books; 475 bound periodical volumes; 650 pamphlets (cataloged); 1600 VF drawers of biographical and subject material; 3200 reels of microfilm. **Subscriptions:** 420 journals and other serials; 45 newspapers. **Services:** Interlibrary loans (limited); copying; library not open to public. **Computerized Information Services:** DIALOG, New York Times Information Service, NEXIS. **Networks/Consortia:** Member of METRO. **Publications:** Weekly Acquisitions List. **Staff:** Nancy Loewenberg, Ref.Libn.; Cynthia Rigg, Ref.Libn.; Peter Salber, Asst.Lib.Dir.; Ron Wilson, Ref.Libn.; Lynn Seiffer, Ref.Libn.; Betsy Staller, Ref.Libn.; Marilyn Souders, Chf. of Acq.; Aidan Mooney, Chf. Indexer.

★9190★
NEWSWEEK, INC. - WASHINGTON BUREAU LIBRARY (Soc Sci; Publ)
1750 Pennsylvania Ave., N.W.
Suite 1220   Phone: (202) 626-2040
Washington, DC 20006   F. Joseph McHugh, Bureau Libn.
Founded: 1963. **Staff:** Prof 1; Other 2. **Special Collections:** Original reporting by bureau reporters dating back to late 1960s (140 linear feet of VF drawers). **Holdings:** 1400 books; 600 bound periodical volumes; 273 linear feet of clipping files. **Subscriptions:** 80 journals and other serials; 7 newspapers. **Services:** Interlibrary loans; copying; library not open to public. **Computerized Information Services:** Online systems.

NEWTON (Andover) THEOLOGICAL SCHOOL
See: Andover Newton Theological School

NEWTON (Sir Isaac) LIBRARY
See: Babson College - Horn Library

★9191★
NEWTON PUBLIC SCHOOLS - TEACHERS' PROFESSIONAL LIBRARY (Educ)
100 Walnut St.   Phone: (617) 552-7630
Newton, MA 02160   David S. Whiting, Coord.Libn./Media
Staff: Prof 1; Other 1. **Subjects:** Children's literature, education. **Special Collections:** Sample trade books for kindergarten through 10th grade. **Holdings:** 5500 books; ERIC resources in education; 400 items of AV software. **Subscriptions:** 30 journals and other serials. **Services:** Library not open to public. **Publications:** In-house catalog of professional books and reference collection. **Staff:** Evelyn N. Moreau, Sec.

★9192★
NEWTON-WELLESLEY HOSPITAL - PAUL TALBOT BABSON MEMORIAL LIBRARY (Med)
2014 Washington St.   Phone: (617) 964-2800
Newton Lower Falls, MA 02162   Christine L. Bell, Dir., Lib.Serv.
Founded: 1945. **Staff:** Prof 1; Other 4. **Subjects:** Medicine, surgery, nursing, health care administration, psychiatry, allied health sciences. **Special Collections:** Nursing and medicine historical collections. **Holdings:** 4500 books; 7000 bound periodical volumes; 220 AV aids (cataloged); 7 VF drawers of pamphlets; hospital archives. **Subscriptions:** 316 journals and other serials; 7 newspapers. **Services:** Interlibrary loans; copying; library open to public for reference use only. **Computerized Information Services:** MEDLARS; computerized cataloging. **Networks/Consortia:** Member of Consortium for Information Resources (CIR). **Publications:** The Bookmark (acquisitions); Administrative Information Packet (current awareness); Nursing Information Packet; all monthly - for internal distribution only.

★9193★
NEWTOWN HISTORIC ASSOCIATION, INC. - LIBRARY (Hist)†
Centre Ave. & Court St.   Phone: (215) 968-4004
Newtown, PA 18940   Claire Hennessy, Dir.
Staff: 2. **Subjects:** Local history - Bucks County and Pennsylvania. **Special Collections:** Original deeds of local properties (200); Edward Hicks reference collection. **Holdings:** 80 books; 60 pamphlets; 4 volumes of newspaper clippings; 1 postmark collection; maps. **Services:** Library open to public with restrictions. **Publications:** Brochures.

★9194★
NEZ PERCE COUNTY LAW LIBRARY (Law)
Court House
Box 896   Phone: (208) 799-3040
Lewiston, ID 83501   Judge John Maynard, Sr. District Judge
Subjects: Law. **Holdings:** 10,000 volumes.

NEZ PERCE NATL. HISTORICAL PARK
See: U.S. Natl. Park Service

★9195★
NIAGARA COLLEGE OF APPLIED ARTS AND TECHNOLOGY - LEARNING RESOURCE CENTRE (Sci-Tech)
Woodlawn Rd.
Box 1005   Phone: (416) 735-2211
Welland, ON, Canada L3B 5S2   Stephen J. Kees, Chf.Libn.
Founded: 1967. **Staff:** Prof 1; Other 8. **Subjects:** Applied arts, business, technology, health. **Holdings:** 30,748 books; 914 bound periodical volumes; 15,740 slides; 562 reels of microfilm; 327 titles on microfiche. **Subscriptions:** 586 journals and other serials; 13 newspapers. **Services:** Interlibrary loans; copying; library open to public. **Networks/Consortia:** Member of Bibliocentre.

★9196★
NIAGARA COUNTY HISTORICAL SOCIETY - LIBRARY AND ARCHIVES (Hist)
215 Niagara St.   Phone: (716) 434-7433
Lockport, NY 14094   Jan J. Losi, Cur.
Founded: 1954. **Subjects:** Local and state history, Indians, antiques. **Holdings:** 900 volumes; 25 VF drawers of clippings, pamphlets and other ephemera. **Services:** Library open to public for reference use only.

★9197★
NIAGARA HISTORICAL SOCIETY - LIBRARY (Hist)†
43 Castlereagh St.
Box 208   Phone: (416) 468-3912
Niagara on the Lake, ON, Canada L0S 1J0   Liza Whealy, Cur.
Staff: Prof 1; Other 1. **Subjects:** Genealogy, land grants. **Special Collections:** Secord family (8 volumes); pamphlets published by the society. **Holdings:** 2090 books; 285 bound periodical volumes. **Subscriptions:** 11 journals and other serials. **Services:** Library open to public. **Staff:** Lois Hiscott, Libn.

★9198★
NIAGARA PARKS COMMISSION - SCHOOL OF HORTICULTURE - HORTICULTURAL LIBRARY (Sci-Tech)
P.O. Box 150
Niagara Falls, ON, Canada L2E 6T2

Phone: (416) 356-8554
Ruth Stoner, Lib.Techn.

Founded: 1936. **Staff:** Prof 1; Other 1. **Subjects:** Horticulture. **Holdings:** 1274 books and bound periodical volumes; 12 VF drawers of clippings, theses, reports and pamphlets. **Subscriptions:** 65 journals and other serials. **Services:** Library not open to public.

★9199★
NICHOLS COLLEGE - CONANT LIBRARY (Bus-Fin)
Dudley, MA 01570

Phone: (617) 943-1560
Cheryl S. Nelson, Act.Lib.Dir.

Staff: Prof 2; Other 4. **Subjects:** Management, advertising, finance and accounting, small business, marketing, economics, international trade, humanities. **Holdings:** 65,000 books and bound periodical volumes; 110 Princeton files of pamphlets; conference proceedings. **Subscriptions:** 450 journals and other serials. **Services:** Interlibrary loans; copying; library open to public. **Networks/Consortia:** Member of Worcester Area Cooperating Libraries (WACL). **Staff:** Rochelle Rosen, Ref.Libn.

★9200★
NICHOLS MUSEUM - LIBRARY
400 E. Scenic Dr.
The Dalles, OR 97058

Founded: 1966. **Subjects:** Geology, paleontology, mineralogy, ethnology. **Holdings:** 550 books; 15 bound periodical volumes. **Remarks:** Library has merged with the Judson Baptist College Library and is presently inactive; the museum is separate.

NICHOLS PROFESSIONAL LIBRARY
See: Alexandria City Public Schools - Educational Media Center

★9201★
NICOLLET COUNTY HISTORICAL SOCIETY - MUSEUM (Hist)
400 S. 3rd St.
St. Peter, MN 56082

Phone: (507) 931-2160
Marjorie A. Schmidt, Sec.

Founded: 1928. **Staff:** 2. **Subjects:** County and town history, genealogy. **Holdings:** 750 books; 30 microfilms of newspapers; newspapers; dissertations. **Services:** Library open to public.

★9202★
NIELSEN ENGINEERING & RESEARCH, INC. - NEAR TECHNICAL LIBRARY (Sci-Tech)
510 Clyde Ave.
Mountain View, CA 94043

Phone: (415) 968-9457
Judy Faltz, Libn.

Staff: Prof 1. **Subjects:** Aerodynamics, fluid dynamics. **Holdings:** 720 books; 250 bound periodical volumes; 45,100 technical reports; 2100 microfiche. **Subscriptions:** 75 journals and other serials. **Services:** Interlibrary loans; copying; library not open to public. **Computerized Information Services:** DIALOG; computerized cataloging. **Networks/Consortia:** Member of CLASS; South Bay Cooperative Library System (SBCLS). **Publications:** In the Library, semimonthly - for internal distribution only.

NIEMAN-GRANT JOURNALISM READING ROOM
See: University of Wisconsin, Madison

NIFTAL INFORMATION CENTER
See: Nitrogen Fixation by Tropical Agricultural Legumes

NIMH
See: U.S. Public Health Service - Natl. Institute of Mental Health

NIMITZ LIBRARY
See: U.S. Navy - Naval Academy

19TH CENTURY AMERICAN STUDIES COLLECTION
See: Minneapolis Public Library & Information Center

★9203★
NINETY-NINES, INC. - LIBRARY (Soc Sci; Sci-Tech)
Will Rogers World Airport
Box 59965
Oklahoma City, OK 73159

Phone: (405) 685-7969
Dorothy Niekamp, Libn.

Staff: Prof 1; Other 2. **Subjects:** Aviation, women in aviation. **Special Collections:** Archives of the Ninety-Nines; records from the Powder Puff Derby. **Holdings:** 300 books. **Services:** Library open to public on request. **Publications:** 99 News.

★9204★
92ND STREET YOUNG MEN'S AND YOUNG WOMEN'S HEBREW ASSOCIATION - ARCHIVES (Area-Ethnic)
1395 Lexington Ave.
New York, NY 10028

Phone: (212) 427-6000
Steven W. Siegel, Archv.

Founded: 1979. **Staff:** Prof 2. **Subjects:** American Jewish History; Jewish social welfare; performing arts history; amateur athletics; poetry and literature; philanthropy. **Special Collections:** Records of Young Men's Hebrew Association, Young Women's Hebrew Association, Clara de Hirsch Home for Working Girls, Surprise Lake Camp and 92nd Street Young Men's and Young Women's Hebrew Association (800 cubic feet). **Holdings:** 1000 sound recordings. **Services:** Copying; library open to public. **Networks/Consortia:** Member of Council of Archives and Research Libraries in Jewish Studies. **Special Indexes:** Finding aids for archival holdings. **Staff:** Dr. John Ruskay, Educ.Dir.

★9205★
92ND STREET YOUNG MEN'S AND YOUNG WOMEN'S HEBREW ASSOCIATION - BUTTENWIESER LIBRARY (Area-Ethnic)
1395 Lexington Ave.
New York, NY 10028

Phone: (212) 427-6000
Susan Vogelstein, Lib.Dir.

Founded: 1898. **Staff:** Prof 2; Other 16. **Subjects:** Judaica, literature. **Special Collections:** Moses Crystal Judaica Collection (9000 items); Poetry Collection (2500 items); Frederick William Greenfield Young People's Library (3500 items); teen collection; senior adult, large print book and parent-child collections; foreign language collection (Hebrew, German, Yiddish). **Holdings:** 30,000 volumes. **Subscriptions:** 50 journals and other serials. **Services:** Library open to members; open to public for reference use only with fee.

NIOSH
See: U.S. Natl. Institute for Occupational Safety and Health

NIPISSING COLLEGE LIBRARY
See: North Bay College Education Centre - Library

★9206★
NISSAN MOTOR CORPORATION - CORPORATE LIBRARY (Trans; Bus-Fin)
18501 S. Figueroa St.
Box 191
Carson, CA 90247

Phone: (213) 532-3111
Moon H. Kim, Libn.

Founded: 1972. **Staff:** Prof 1; Other 1. **Subjects:** Automobiles, automobile industry, business management, economics, international relations, Japan. **Special Collections:** Complete set of service and owners' manuals for all makes of Nissan. **Holdings:** 2000 books; 220 bound periodical volumes; 300 catalogs and 150 pamphlets (cataloged); monthly automotive press clippings; 40 audio cassettes; video cassettes. **Subscriptions:** 70 journals and other serials. **Services:** Interlibrary loans; copying; Japanese translation; library open to public for reference use only. **Publications:** Library Angle, monthly - for internal distribution only; NMC-USA Weekly News Digest. **Remarks:** This is the only library in the company meeting needs of employees located throughout the U.S.

★9207★
NITROGEN FIXATION BY TROPICAL AGRICULTURAL LEGUMES - NIFTAL INFORMATION CENTER (Agri)
Box O
Paia, HI 96779

Phone: (808) 579-9568
James W. King, Info.Spec.

Staff: Prof 1; Other 1. **Subjects:** Rhizobium, legumes, soil conditions. **Special Collections:** Legume/Rhizobium symbiosis (5000 articles). **Holdings:** 100 books. **Subscriptions:** 10 journals and other serials. **Services:** Copying; library open to public by appointment. **Computerized Information Services:** Standards Information Service (SIS); computerized cataloging. **Remarks:** Information center is under the sponsorship of the University of Hawaii and U.S. Agency for International Development.

★9208★
NIXON, HARGRAVE, DEVANS & DOYLE - LAW LIBRARY (Law)†
Lincoln First Tower
Box 1051
Rochester, NY 14603

Phone: (716) 546-8000
Sharon A. Hayden, Libn.

Subjects: Law. **Holdings:** 14,000 volumes.

★9209★
NKC, INC. - MEDICAL LIBRARY (Med)
Box 35070
Louisville, KY 40232

Phone: (502) 589-8171
Holly S. Buchanan, Dir.

Founded: 1958. **Staff:** Prof 3; Other 4. **Subjects:** Medicine, nursing, hospital administration, psychiatry, pediatrics. **Special Collections:** Flexner Historical Collection. **Holdings:** 4000 books; pamphlets; audio and video cassettes.

Subscriptions: 310 journals and other serials. Services: Interlibrary loans; copying; AV production services; library open to public for reference use only. Computerized Information Services: MEDLINE, BRS; computerized cataloging. Networks/Consortia: Member of Kentucky Health Sciences Library Consortium; OCLC. Formed by the Merger of: Norton-Children's Hospitals' Medical Library and the Kosair Crippled Children Hospital Library.

★9210★
NL BAROID/NL INDUSTRIES, INC. - TECHNICAL LIBRARY (Sci-Tech)
2404 Southwest Freeway
Box 1675   Phone: (713) 527-1282
Houston, TX 77001   Bilha Wieczner, Info.Rsrcs.Supv.
Founded: 1930. **Staff:** Prof 1; Other 1. **Subjects:** Chemistry, physics, engineering sciences, business management, petroleum technology, economics, geology. **Special Collections:** Professional papers and clippings from trade literature on oil well drilling fluids technology; economic geology of barite and clay minerals. **Holdings:** 21,500 volumes; 36 legal file drawers of clippings. **Services:** Interlibrary loans; library not open to public. **Computerized Information Services:** DIALOG, SDC, BRS, NLM.

★9211★
NL INDUSTRIES, INC. - MARKETING & TECHNICAL INFORMATION SERVICE (Sci-Tech)
Box 700   Phone: (609) 448-3200
Hightstown, NJ 08520   Halina Kan, Libn.
Founded: 1920. **Staff:** Prof 1; Other 3. **Subjects:** Chemistry, chemical technology, paint technology, metals, plastics. **Holdings:** 10,000 books; 2500 bound periodical volumes; microfilm (cataloged). **Subscriptions:** 545 journals and other serials; 7 newspapers. **Services:** Interlibrary loans; copying; library not open to public.

NLM
See: National Library of Medicine

★9212★
NLO, INC. - LIBRARY (Sci-Tech)
Box 39158   Phone: (513) 738-1151
Cincinnati, OH 45239   Rosemary H. Gardewing, Lib.Asst.
Founded: 1951. **Staff:** 2. **Subjects:** Atomic energy, chemistry, metallurgy. **Holdings:** 6000 books; 2000 bound periodical volumes; 15,000 technical reports; 200,000 microcopies of technical reports. **Subscriptions:** 132 journals and other serials; 5 newspapers. **Services:** Interlibrary loans; copying; library not open to public. **Publications:** Library Accessions, bimonthly - for internal distribution only.

NMA
See: National Micrographics Association

NO MAN'S LAND HISTORICAL MUSEUM
See: Panhandle State University

NOAA
See: U.S. Natl. Oceanic & Atmospheric Administration

NOAH WEBSTER FOUNDATION & HISTORICAL SOCIETY OF WEST HARTFORD
See: Webster (Noah) Foundation & Historical Society of West Hartford

NOBLE ARMY HOSPITAL
See: U.S. Army Hospitals

NOBLE (Daniel E.) SCIENCE AND ENGINEERING LIBRARY
See: Arizona State University - Daniel E. Noble Science and Engineering Library

NOBLE (Samuel Roberts) FOUNDATION, INC.
See: Samuel Roberts Noble Foundation, Inc.

★9213★
NOLAND (Lloyd) HOSPITAL - DAVID KNOX MC KAMY MEDICAL LIBRARY (Med)†
701 Ridgeway Rd.   Phone: (205) 783-5121
Fairfield, AL 35064   Elisabeth Burton, Libn.
Founded: 1957. **Staff:** 2. **Subjects:** Medicine and related subjects. **Holdings:** 1500 volumes. **Subscriptions:** 147 journals and other serials. **Services:** Interlibrary loans; copying; library not open to public.

★9214★
NOME LIBRARY/KEGOAYAH KOZGA LIBRARY (Hist)
Box 1168   Phone: (907) 443-5133
Nome, AK 99762   Dee McKenna, Libn.
Founded: 1905. **Staff:** 3. **Subjects:** Alaska, including Eskimo and Gold Rush artifacts. **Special Collections:** Alaskana (75 rare volumes). **Holdings:** 10,000 books; 3000 cassette tapes; 1200 other AV materials; 800 paperback books; old photographs; bilingual and oral history materials; large print materials. **Subscriptions:** 70 journals and other serials. **Services:** Interlibrary loans; copying; library open to public.

NONDESTRUCTIVE TESTING INFORMATION ANALYSIS CENTER
See: Southwest Research Institute

NON-FORMAL EDUCATION INFORMATION CENTER
See: Michigan State University

★9215★
NOOTER CORPORATION - TECHNICAL LIBRARY (Sci-Tech)
Box 451   Phone: (314) 621-6000
St. Louis, MO 63166   Barry Heuer, Libn.
Subjects: Metals - properties, fabrication methods. **Holdings:** 500 volumes. **Subscriptions:** 20 journals and other serials. **Services:** Library not open to public.

★9216★
NORANDA MINES LTD. - CCR DIVISION - PROCESS DEVELOPMENT LIBRARY (Sci-Tech)
Place D'Armes
P.O. Box 338   Phone: (514) 645-8861
Montreal, PQ, Canada H2Y 3H2   Pierce Frattolillo, Process Dev.Supt.
Founded: 1940. **Staff:** Prof 2. **Subjects:** Chemical engineering, metallurgy, extractive and physical metallurgy, environmental control, health, safety and toxicology. **Holdings:** 2000 volumes; reports; patents. **Subscriptions:** 40 journals and other serials. **Services:** Interlibrary loans; copying; library open to members of Noranda Group only. **Special Indexes:** Patent index.

★9217★
NORANDA RESEARCH CENTRE - LIBRARY (Sci-Tech)
240 Hymus Blvd.   Phone: (514) 697-6640
Pointe Claire, PQ, Canada H9R 1G5   Shirley Courtis, Libn.
Founded: 1963. **Staff:** Prof 1; Other 2. **Subjects:** Metallurgy, inorganic chemistry, mining, mineral dressing, chemical engineering, environment, occupational health and safety. **Holdings:** 8000 books. **Subscriptions:** 250 journals and other serials. **Services:** Interlibrary loans; copying; library open to public for reference use only on introduction from another library. **Computerized Information Services:** DIALOG, SDC, CAN/OLE.

★9218★
NORANDA SALES CORPORATION, LTD. - SALES LIBRARY (Bus-Fin)
Commerce Court W.
Box 45   Phone: (416) 867-7036
Toronto, ON, Canada M5L 1B6   Karen L. Hammond, Libn.
Founded: 1973. **Staff:** 2. **Subjects:** Resource marketing, nonferrous metals, statistics, economics, finance. **Special Collections:** Conference Board publications; C.D. Howe Research Institute publications; Fraser Institute publications; Queens University Centre for Resource Studies publications. **Holdings:** 5000 books; 1129 slides; 1260 annual reports. **Subscriptions:** 276 journals and other serials; 10 newspapers. **Services:** Interlibrary loans; copying; library open to public with restrictions. **Computerized Information Services:** DIALOG; computerized cataloging. **Publications:** Noranda Sales Communique, weekly - for internal distribution only; Noranda Sales Library Acquisitions List, irregular - internal distribution and to others upon request.

★9219★
NORCEN ENERGY RESOURCES LIMITED - LIBRARY (Energy)
715 5th Ave., S.W.   Phone: (403) 231-0887
Calgary, AB, Canada T2P 2X7   Gwendolyn Cameron, Libn.
Founded: 1975. **Staff:** 2. **Subjects:** Petroleum exploration, geology, coal. **Holdings:** 2000 books; 3000 government documents (cataloged). **Subscriptions:** 350 journals and other serials; 20 newspapers. **Services:** Interlibrary loans; library open to public with restrictions. **Computerized Information Services:** DIALOG, SDC; computerized cataloging and circulation. **Publications:** Library bulletin - for internal distribution only.

★9220★

NORCLIFF THAYER MFG. FACILITY - DIVISION OF REVLON, INC. - LIBRARY (Sci-Tech)
319 S. 4th St.　　　　　　　　　　　Phone: (314) 621-2304
St. Louis, MO 63102　　　　　　　Joann Aldridge, R.N., Libn.
Founded: 1964. Staff: 1. Subjects: Pharmacy, chemistry, medicine, mathematics, plant management, Federal Drug Administration regulations. Holdings: 1180 books; 1562 bound periodical volumes; 20 VF drawers of pamphlets. Subscriptions: 97 journals and other serials; 12 newspapers. Services: Library open to public for reference use only on request.

NORD LIBRARY
See: American Swedish Historical Museum

★9221★

NORDEN SYSTEMS, INC. - TECHNICAL LIBRARY (Sci-Tech)
Norden Pl.　　　　　　　　　　　　Phone: (203) 852-4724
Norwalk, CT 06856　　　　　　　Bernice Astheimer, Br.Libn.
Founded: 1943. Staff: Prof 1. Subjects: Electronics, electrical engineering, physics, mathematics, business management, computers, metallurgy. Holdings: 7000 books; 2000 bound periodical volumes; 7000 documents; 4000 patents; 3000 pamphlets, reprints, photostats; 100 VF drawers of technical reports. Services: Interlibrary loans; copying; library not open to public. Computerized Information Services: DIALOG. Remarks: Norden Systems, Inc. is a subsidiary of United Technologies Corporation.

★9222★

NORDSON CORPORATION - TECHNICAL INFORMATION DEPARTMENT (Sci-Tech)
555 Jackson St.　　　　　　　　　Phone: (216) 988-9411
Amherst, OH 44001　　　　　　　Susan K. Smith, Corp.Libn.
Founded: 1974. Staff: Prof 1; Other 1. Subjects: Adhesives, coatings, paint, packaging machinery, fluid mechanics, robotics. Holdings: 2700 books; 250 bound periodical volumes; 25 VF drawers of internal reports; 16 VF drawers pamphlets; 250 reels of microfilm. Subscriptions: 175 journals and other serials. Services: Interlibrary loans; copying; SDI; translations; literature searches; open to public with restrictions. Computerized Information Services: SDC, DIALOG, Control Data Corporation. Networks/Consortia: Member of North Central Library Cooperative. Publications: Current Awareness Bulletin, Current Topics Bulletin, News Clips.

★9223★

NORFOLK BOTANICAL GARDENS - LIBRARY (Sci-Tech)
Airport Rd.　　　　　　　　　　　Phone: (804) 855-0194
Norfolk, VA 23518　　　　　　　Betty J. Sadler, Libn./Ck.
Founded: 1962. Staff: 1. Subjects: Horticulture, landscaping, insects, wildflowers. Holdings: 1801 books; 33 bound periodical volumes. Subscriptions: 33 journals and other serials. Services: Library open to public for reference use only. Publications: Norfolk Botanical Gardens Society Newsletter, monthly.

★9224★

NORFOLK COUNTY LAW LIBRARY (Law)
Superior Court House
650 High St.　　　　　　　　　　　Phone: (617) 326-1600
Dedham, MA 02026　　　　　　　Lois B. Russell, Libn.
Staff: Prof 1. Subjects: Law. Holdings: 12,000 books; 250 bound periodical volumes; 50 other cataloged items. Subscriptions: 18 journals and other serials. Services: Copying; library open to public.

★9225★

NORFOLK LAW LIBRARY (Law)
43 Clark St.　　　　　　　　　　　Phone: (617) 668-0800
Norfolk, MA 02067　　　　　　Sandra K. Lindheimer, Law Libn.
Staff: Prof 1; Other 6. Subjects: Law. Holdings: 2800 books. Services: Interlibrary loans; copying; library not open to public.

★9226★

NORFOLK AND PORTSMOUTH BAR ASSOCIATION - LAW LIBRARY (Law)
1105 Virginia National Bank Bldg.　　Phone: (804) 622-3152
Norfolk, VA 23510　　　　　　William J. Davis, Exec.Dir.
Founded: 1900. Staff: Prof 1; Other 1. Subjects: Law. Holdings: 24,000 books; 500 bound periodical volumes; 21 linear feet of legal periodicals. Subscriptions: 15 journals and other serials. Services: Copying; library not open to public.

★9227★

NORFOLK PUBLIC LIBRARY - SARGEANT MEMORIAL ROOM (Hist)
301 City Hall Ave.
Norfolk, VA 23510　　　　　　Lucile B. Portlock, Hd.
Staff: Prof 1; Other 3. Subjects: Norfolk and Virginia history and genealogy. Holdings: 15,561 books; 1010 bound periodical volumes; 63 drawers of newspaper articles, original manuscripts, 19th century local business ledgers, letters, autographs and rare pamphlets; 3042 reels of microfilm of local newspapers, census records, cemetery and church records; 1280 postcards; 5000 photographs; 1651 topographic and historic maps. Subscriptions: 41 journals and other serials; 6 newspapers. Services: Copying; library open to public.

★9228★

NORFOLK REGIONAL CENTER AND NORTHEAST MENTAL HEALTH CLINIC - STAFF LIBRARY (Med)
Box 1209　　　　　　　　　　　Phone: (402) 371-4343
Norfolk, NE 68701　　　　　　Muriel V. Hillson, Libn.
Founded: 1954. Staff: 1. Subjects: Clinical psychology, psychiatry, medicine, social work. Holdings: 2000 books; 175 bound periodical volumes. Subscriptions: 45 journals and other serials. Services: Interlibrary loans; copying; library open to students and health science professionals in community. Networks/Consortia: Member of Northern Library Network.

★9229★

NORFOLK STATE COLLEGE - W.K. KELLOGG SOCIAL SCIENCE RESEARCH CENTER - LIBRARY (Soc Sci)*
2401 Corprew Ave.　　　　　　Phone: (804) 623-8435
Norfolk, VA 23504　　　　　　　Angela Perkins
Founded: 1971. Staff: Prof 1; Other 2. Subjects: Urban economics, urban affairs. Special Collections: Data bank of 12 research studies carried out by laboratory related to adoption, criminal justice, community studies, health assessibility, college students and voting behavior. Holdings: 1525 books; 102 bound periodical volumes; 2000 newspaper clippings. Subscriptions: 4 journals and other serials; 10 newspapers. Services: Interlibrary loans; copying; library open to public with special permission granted on an individual basis.

★9230★

NORLAND CORPORATION - TECHNICAL LIBRARY (Sci-Tech)
R4 Norland Dr.　　　　　　　　Phone: (414) 563-8456
Fort Atkinson, WI 53538　　　　Jean Badura, Tech.Libn.
Staff: Prof 1; Other 1. Subjects: Product engineering, materials for design, manufacturing modes, mechanical design, electrical design, supplier catalogs. Holdings: 300 books; 4000 supplier catalogs (cataloged); 285 UL listings - Standards for Safety; 4 file drawers of unbound technical data. Subscriptions: 30 journals and other serials. Services: Library not open to public. Computerized Information Services: Computerized cataloging and circulation.

NORLIN LIBRARY
See: University of Colorado, Boulder

★9231★

NORMAN COUNTY HISTORICAL SOCIETY - MEMORIAL MUSEUM LIBRARY (Hist)
404 W. 5th Ave.　　　　　　　Phone: (218) 784-4911
Ada, MN 56510　　　　　　　Lenora I. Johnson, Musm.Dir.
Founded: 1957. Staff: Prof 2. Subjects: State and local history and biography. Special Collections: Norwegian, Swedish and German rare books; rare textbooks used in rural schools; county and state publications; family histories (25); government publications, 1890-1920; photograph collections (3500 items). Holdings: 2500 books; 50 bound periodical volumes; 72 boxes of newspapers, documents, local records, music texts. Subscriptions: 15 journals and other serials. Services: Library open to public for reference use only. Networks/Consortia: Member of Northern Lights Library Network. Publications: History of Ada; Family Histories of Norman County.

★9232★

NORMAN MUNICIPAL HOSPITAL - HEALTH SCIENCE LIBRARY (Med)
901 N. Porter
Box 1308　　　　　　　　　　　Phone: (405) 321-1700
Norman, OK 73070　　　　　　Jacalyn E. Mosnat, Libn.
Staff: 1. Subjects: Medicine, nursing. Holdings: 600 books. Subscriptions: 75 journals and other serials. Services: Interlibrary loans; literature searches; library open to health-related personnel. Networks/Consortia: Member of Greater Oklahoma City Area Health Sciences Library Consortium.

★9233★
NORMANDALE BAPTIST CHURCH - MEDIA CENTER (Rel-Theol)
Box 2615   Phone: (205) 288-6190
Montgomery, AL 36105   Mrs. A.L. Brannen, Co-Dir.
Staff: 8. **Subjects:** Religion, biography, philosophy, social studies. **Holdings:** 5700 books; 317 filmstrips; 290 cassettes; vertical file of 200 subjects; 20 Bible land maps. **Subscriptions:** 25 journals and other serials. **Services:** Center open to public with restrictions. **Publications:** Mediagraphy, quarterly - distributed to teachers and leaders. **Staff:** Mrs. Paul Slaughter, Co-Dir.

NORRIS MEDICAL LIBRARY
See: University of Southern California - Health Sciences Campus

NORRIS MEMORIAL LIBRARY
See: National Rural Electric Cooperative Association

NORRISTOWN STATE HOSPITAL
See: Pennsylvania State Department of Public Welfare

★9234★
NORTH ADAMS STATE COLLEGE - EUGENE L. FREEL LIBRARY - SPECIAL COLLECTIONS (Educ)†
Church St.   Phone: (413) 664-4511
North Adams, MA 01247
Founded: 1894. **Staff:** Prof 5; Other 3. **Special Collections:** Teacher Resources Center (6000 items); Specimen Test File (345 tests); Hoosac Valley Collection for Local History (200 items); College History Collection (150 items); McFarlin Printing Collection (375 items). **Services:** Interlibrary loans; copying; library open to public. **Staff:** Charles A. McIsaac, Dir., Lib.Serv.; Suzanne W. Kemper, Acq. & Ref.; Sarah H. Clarke, Circ./ Tchg.Res.Ctr.; Ann B. Terryberry, Cat./Order.

★9235★
NORTH AMERICAN BAPTIST COLLEGE AND DIVINITY SCHOOL - LIBRARY (Rel-Theol)
11523 23rd Ave.   Phone: (403) 988-5571
Edmonton, AB, Canada T6J 4T3   Arnold Rapske, Libn.
Staff: Prof 1; Other 2. **Subjects:** Theology, Christianity. **Special Collections:** North American Baptist Historical Collection. **Holdings:** 32,000 books and bound periodical volumes; 500 recordings; microforms. **Subscriptions:** 300 journals and other serials. **Services:** Copying.

★9236★
NORTH AMERICAN BAPTIST SEMINARY - KAISER-RAMAKER LIBRARY (Rel-Theol)
1321 W. 22nd St.   Phone: (605) 336-6805
Sioux Falls, SD 57105   George W. Lang, Lib.Adm.
Staff: Prof 2; Other 2. **Subjects:** Theology, Baptist Church history, pastoral administration and counseling, Biblical literature, evangelism and missions. **Special Collections:** North American Baptist General Conference Archives. **Holdings:** 57,038 books and bound periodical volumes; 849 filmstrips; 80 boxes of archives; 6 VF drawers of pamphlets; 8586 slides; 455 microforms; 919 phonograph records; 322 reels of tape; 149 maps and charts; 646 flat pictures; 1364 cassettes. **Subscriptions:** 345 journals and other serials. **Services:** Interlibrary loans; copying; library open to public. **Networks/ Consortia:** Member of North Central University Center; Bibliographical Center for Research, Rocky Mountain Region, Inc.; OCLC; MINITEX. **Staff:** Bruce Eldevik, Asst.Libn.

★9237★
NORTH AMERICAN ISLAMIC TRUST, INC. - LIBRARY (Rel-Theol)
10900 W. Washington St.   Phone: (317) 839-9248
Indianapolis, IN 46231   Muhammad Badr, Gen.Mgr.
Founded: 1973. **Subjects:** Islam. **Holdings:** Figures not available for Arabic and English works on Islam. **Publications:** List of publications - available on request.

★9238★
NORTH AMERICAN JEWISH STUDENTS' NETWORK - LIBRARY (Area-Ethnic)
1 Park Ave., Suite 418   Phone: (212) 689-0790
New York, NY 10016   Eric L. Jacobs, Dir.
Founded: 1970. **Staff:** Prof 2. **Subjects:** Israel, Diaspora Jewry, oppression, current events, Jewish student activism, campus programming. **Special Collections:** Jewish student and independent films; multimedia projects (25). **Holdings:** 10 file cabinets of reports, clippings, articles; 5 radio tapes; 20 films; 5 slide/tape programs; update file on Jewish films. **Subscriptions:** 150 journals and other serials; 50 newspapers. **Services:** Copying; library open to public. **Publications:** Network Spectrum, monthly; Guide to Jewish Student

Groups, biennial - both available by subscription. **Special Catalogs:** Guide to Jewish Student Groups (book); Media Catalog (pamphlet); numerous topical Information Packets. **Staff:** Joyce Lempel, Resource Coord.

★9239★
NORTH AMERICAN LIFE ASSURANCE COMPANY - LIBRARY (Bus-Fin)
105 Adelaide St., W.   Phone: (416) 362-6011
Toronto, ON, Canada M5H 1R1   Katie McMillan, Libn.
Subjects: Life insurance. **Holdings:** 8000 books; 24 VF drawers.

★9240★
NORTH AMERICAN PHILIPS CORPORATION - LIBRARY
100 E. 42nd St.
New York, NY 10017
Defunct

★9241★
NORTH AMERICAN PHILIPS CORPORATION - PHILIPS LABORATORIES RESEARCH LIBRARY (Sci-Tech)
345 Scarborough Rd.   Phone: (914) 762-0300
Briarcliff Manor, NY 10510   Betsy McIlvaine, Hd.Libn.
Founded: 1945. **Staff:** Prof 1; Other 3. **Subjects:** Electron optics, material sciences, optical physics, physics, computer sciences, cryogenics. **Holdings:** 6000 books; 5000 bound periodical volumes; 5000 company reports; 205 microfiche. **Subscriptions:** 200 journals and other serials. **Services:** Interlibrary loans; copying; library not open to public. **Computerized Information Services:** DIALOG, BRS, NASA/RECON, Questel, EMIS.

★9242★
NORTH AMERICAN RADIO ARCHIVES (NARA) - LENDING LIBRARY (Theater)*
Box 11962
Reno, NV 89510   S. Bland, Tape Libn.
Staff: 4. **Subjects:** Radio - history, programming, broadcasting, scripts, publications; television broadcasting. **Holdings:** 220 books; 600 tapes; 150 scripts; 300 slides; 300 magazines; 50 reprints of articles. **Services:** Library open to members only. **Publications:** Journal; newsletter, both quarterly. **Staff:** G. Bland, Libn.

★9243★
NORTH AMERICAN RADIO ARCHIVES (NARA) - LIBRARY (Theater)
4418 Irvington Ave.   Phone: (415) 656-6436
Fremont, CA 94538   Steven K. Ham, Pres.
Founded: 1973. **Staff:** 12. **Subjects:** Radio - drama, comedy, entertainment, news, documentary; radio programming. **Holdings:** 200 books; 25,000 radio programs on tape, 1926-1965; slides of radio personalities; radio scripts and magazines; reproduced articles on radio. **Services:** Copying; library open to members of NARA who may borrow its material. **Publications:** NARA News, a quarterly journal; bimonthly magazine; copies may be obtained by request with fee on a one-time basis. **Formerly:** Located in Tucson, AZ.

★9244★
NORTH AMERICAN STUDENTS OF COOPERATION - LIBRARY (Soc Sci)
Box 7293   Phone: (313) 663-0889
Ann Arbor, MI 48107   Bill Van Dore, Adm.Coord.
Founded: 1970. **Staff:** 5. **Subjects:** Cooperatives, communities. **Special Collections:** Files on North American student co-ops. **Holdings:** Figures not available. **Services:** Copying; library open to public with advance reservation. **Special Catalogs:** Directory of Campus-Based Co-ops (printed, bound directory). **Remarks:** Library is located at Michigan Union Bldg. no. 4312, 530 S. State St., Ann Arbor.

★9245★
NORTH AMERICAN TIDDLYWINKS ASSOCIATION - ARCHIVES (Rec)
2701 Woodedge Rd.   Phone: (301) 933-3840
Silver Spring, MD 20906   Richard W. Tucker, Archv.
Founded: 1978. **Staff:** 2. **Subjects:** Tiddlywinks - origins and history, tournament. **Holdings:** 50 journals; 1100 clippings and citations; 70 patents; statistics on 106 tournaments. **Services:** Library open to public by appointment. **Special Catalogs:** Tiddlywinks References List (pamphlet). **Also Known As:** NATwA. **Staff:** Fred R. Shapiro, Hist.

★9246★
NORTH AMERICAN WEATHER CONSULTANTS - TECHNICAL LIBRARY (Sci-Tech)
1141 E. 3900 S. A230
Salt Lake City, UT 84117   Carol Robinson Simpson, Libn.
Founded: 1955. **Staff:** Prof 1. **Subjects:** Meteorology, climatology, weather modification, air pollution meteorology, hydrology, synoptic meteorology.

Special Collections: Northern Hemisphere synoptic maps dating back to 1899. **Holdings:** 2500 books; 700 bound periodical volumes; 2100 volumes of historical synoptic charts and climate data; 800 volumes of historical hydrologic data (surface water, snow surveys); 6000 technical reports; 7000 technical reports on microfiche; 100 reels of microfilm; 2 motion pictures. **Subscriptions:** 100 journals and other serials. **Services:** Interlibrary loans; copying; SDI (in-house only); library open to public. **Computerized Information Services:** DIALOG; computerized cataloging. **Publications:** Quarterly Report; Recent Acquisitions, monthly; serials holdings list, annual; occasional memoranda.

★9247★
NORTH AMERICAN YOUTH SPORT INSTITUTE - INFORMATION CENTER (Rec)
4985 Oak Garden Dr.   Phone: (919) 784-4926
Kernersville, NC 27284   Dr. Jack Hutslar, Exec.Dir.
Subjects: Youth sport, sport sociology, physical education, recreation, sociology, teacher education. **Holdings:** 1000 books; manuscripts, clippings and reports. **Subscriptions:** 10 journals and other serials. **Services:** Library open to public when director is present. **Publications:** Sport Scene, quarterly.

★9248★
NORTH ANDOVER HISTORICAL SOCIETY - LIBRARY (Hist)
Merrimack Valley Textile Museum
800 Massachusetts Ave.   Phone: (617) 686-0191
North Andover, MA 01845   Mary Flinn, Soc.Adm.
Staff: Prof 2. **Subjects:** Local history and architecture, genealogy. **Special Collections:** Early town meeting records on microfilm; early church and town government records on microfilm (27 reels). **Holdings:** 1200 books; manuscripts, prints and photographs (cataloged). **Subscriptions:** 8 journals and other serials. **Services:** Interlibrary loans; copying; library open to public for reference use only.

★9249★
NORTH BAY COLLEGE EDUCATION CENTRE - LIBRARY (Educ)
Box 5001, Gormanville Rd.   Phone: (705) 474-7600
North Bay, ON, Canada P1B 8K9   J.G. Poff, Hd.Libn.
Founded: 1972. **Staff:** Prof 2; Other 7. **Subjects:** Education, nursing and general topics. **Holdings:** 105,000 books and bound periodical volumes; microfilm of 250 periodicals; VF drawers, government documents and pictures. **Subscriptions:** 550 journals and other serials; 10 newspapers. **Services:** Interlibrary loans; copying; library open to public for reference use only. **Special Indexes:** Education Index (card). **Remarks:** Includes the holdings of the libraries of Canadore College and Nipissing College. **Staff:** C. Gunning, Asst.Libn.

★9250★
NORTH CAROLINA AGRICULTURAL & TECHNICAL STATE UNIVERSITY - F.D. BLUFORD LIBRARY (Sci-Tech)
312 Market St.   Phone: (919) 379-7783
Greensboro, NC 27411   Alene C. Young, Act.Dir., Lib.Serv.
Founded: 1894. **Staff:** Prof 13; Other 26. **Subjects:** Agriculture, nursing, engineering, education. **Special Collections:** Collections of Black Studies; Film Collection; Chemistry Collection. **Holdings:** 312,774 volumes; archival materials; government documents; theses, pictures, maps, modules; 150,030 microforms. **Subscriptions:** 1500 journals and other serials. **Services:** Interlibrary loans; copying; cooperative lending; library open to public. **Computerized Information Services:** Online systems. **Networks/Consortia:** Member of OCLC through SOLINET. **Publications:** Newsletter; The Handbook; Quarterly Bibliography in Subject Fields. **Staff:** Sadie Smith, Act.Hd., Rd.Serv.; B.C. Crews, Hd., Tech.Serv.; John Akanful, Hd., Adm.Serv.

★9251★
NORTH CAROLINA CENTRAL UNIVERSITY - LAW LIBRARY (Law)
     Phone: (919) 683-6244
Durham, NC 27707   Douglas W. Martin, Law Libn.
Founded: 1941. **Staff:** Prof 5; Other 5. **Subjects:** Law. **Holdings:** 51,173 books; 34,196 bound periodical volumes. **Subscriptions:** 1164 journals and other serials; 15 newspapers. **Services:** Interlibrary loans; copying; library open to public. **Staff:** Hazel Lumpkin, Acq.Libn.; Carol Avery, Cat.; Adrine Atkinson, Ser./Circ.Libn.

★9252★
NORTH CAROLINA CENTRAL UNIVERSITY - SCHOOL OF LIBRARY SCIENCE - LIBRARY (Info Sci)
J.E. Shepard Library
Durham, NC 27707   Phone: (919) 683-6400
     Alice S. Richmond, Libn.
Staff: Prof 2; Other 1. **Subjects:** Librarianship, children's literature. **Special Collections:** William Tucker Collection (materials for children by black authors

and illustrators, 141 items and 173 volumes); Black Librarians' Collection (1200 items). **Holdings:** 20,481 books; 3092 bound periodical volumes; 434 reels of microfilm; 12,952 microfiche; 8065 AV items; 15 VF drawers. **Subscriptions:** 420 journals and other serials. **Services:** Interlibrary loans; library open to public with restrictions. **Computerized Information Services:** Online systems; computerized cataloging. **Networks/Consortia:** Member of OCLC through SOLINET. **Publications:** Acquisitions list, irregular - for internal distribution only. **Staff:** Virginia Purefoy Jones, Asst.Libn.

NORTH CAROLINA FOLK MUSIC ARCHIVE
See: University of North Carolina, Chapel Hill - Music Library

NORTH CAROLINA FOREIGN LANGUAGE CENTER
See: Cumberland County Public Library

★9253★
NORTH CAROLINA GEOLOGICAL SURVEY - LIBRARY (Sci-Tech)
Box 27687   Phone: (919) 733-2424
Raleigh, NC 27611   Alberta McKay, Libn.
Staff: 1. **Subjects:** Geology, especially in North Carolina. **Holdings:** Figures not available. **Services:** Copying; library open to public. **Publications:** North Carolina Geological Survey Publications. **Remarks:** Section maintained by the North Carolina State Department of Natural Resources & Community Development.

NORTH CAROLINA LIBRARY FOR THE BLIND AND PHYSICALLY HANDICAPPED
See: North Carolina State Department of Cultural Resources - Library for the Blind and Physically Handicapped

★9254★
NORTH CAROLINA MUSEUM OF ART - ART REFERENCE LIBRARY (Art)
Cultural Resources Dept.
2110 Blue Ridge Blvd.   Phone: (919) 833-1935
Raleigh, NC 27607   Dr. Anna Dvorak, Libn.
Founded: 1956. **Staff:** Prof 1; Other 1. **Subjects:** Painting, sculpture, costume, architecture, drawing, prints, decorative arts, graphics, pre-Columbian and African art. **Holdings:** 16,500 books and bound periodical volumes; 15,000 slides of museum's holdings; 58 VF drawers of artist clippings; 25 VF drawers of museum and subject files. **Subscriptions:** 50 journals and other serials. **Services:** Interlibrary loans; copying; library open to public.

NORTH CAROLINA NATIONAL BANK
See: NCNB

★9255★
NORTH CAROLINA STATE DEPT. OF CULTURAL RESOURCES - DIV. OF ARCHIVES AND HISTORY - ARCHIVES & RECORDS SECTION (Hist)
109 E. Jones St.   Phone: (919) 733-3952
Raleigh, NC 27611   David J. Olson, State Archv.
Founded: 1903. **Staff:** Prof 38; Other 39. **Subjects:** Official records of the state of North Carolina and its subdivisions. **Special Collections:** Manuscript collections from colonial times to present; maps; microfilms. **Services:** Copying; search room and archives open to public. **Staff:** Frank D. Gatton, Hd., Archival Serv.; Ronald E. Youngquist, Hd., Rec.Serv.; Roger C. Jones, Hd., Tech.Serv.Br.

★9256★
NORTH CAROLINA STATE DEPARTMENT OF CULTURAL RESOURCES - DIVISION OF THE STATE LIBRARY (Info Sci)
109 E. Jones St.   Phone: (919) 733-2570
Raleigh, NC 27611   David N. McKay, Dir./State Libn.
Founded: 1812. **Staff:** Prof 33; Other 79. **Subjects:** Southern history, library science, American literature, general nonfiction. **Special Collections:** Genealogy; books for the blind. **Holdings:** 227,321 books and bound periodical volumes; 422,553 state and U.S. documents; 8380 microcards; 22,542 reels of microfilm; 33,350 microfiche; 173,957 containers of talking books; 5322 16mm films. **Subscriptions:** 609 journals and other serials; 107 newspapers. **Services:** Interlibrary loans; copying; library open to public with circulation of materials limited to state employees. **Computerized Information Services:** DIALOG; computerized cataloging. **Networks/Consortia:** Member of OCLC through SOLINET. **Publications:** Recent Acquisitions; News Letter; Checklist of Official North Carolina State Publications. **Special Catalogs:** North Carolina Union Catalog (microfilm and card). **Also Known As:** North Carolina State Library. **Staff:** Jane Williams, Asst. State Libn.; Diana Young, Lib.Cons., Ch.Serv.; Nancy Wallace, Lib.Cons., Young Adult; John Welch, Gen.Cons.; Marjorie Lindsey, Cons., Multitype Lib.Serv; David Bevan, Dir., Info.Serv.Div.; Ophelia M. Irving, Asst.Dir.,

Info.Serv.; Sue Farr, ILL Serv.; Nancy Albright, Genealogy Ref.Libn.; Doris Holloway, Doc.Libn.; Angie Suhr, AV Spec.; Marion Johnson, Dir., Pub.Lib.Dev.; Eunice Drum, Dir., Tech.Serv.

★9257★
NORTH CAROLINA STATE DEPARTMENT OF CULTURAL RESOURCES - LIBRARY FOR THE BLIND AND PHYSICALLY HANDICAPPED (Aud-Vis)
1811 North Blvd.   Phone: (919) 733-4376
Raleigh, NC 27635   Charles H. Fox, Chf., Spec.Serv.Sect.
Founded: 1958. **Staff:** Prof 4; Other 25. **Holdings:** 160,634 books, including talking books, braille books, taped books and large type books. **Services:** Library open to legally eligible users. **Publications:** Newsletter, 5/year. **Remarks:** Maintained by Division of State Library. **Staff:** Penelope Hornsby, Asst. Regional Libn.; Sue Scott, Circ.Libn.; Bonnie Peele, Spec. Projects Libn.

★9258★
NORTH CAROLINA STATE DEPARTMENT OF CULTURAL RESOURCES - TRYON PALACE RESTORATION - LIBRARY (Hist)
613 Pollock St.
Box 1007   Phone: (919) 638-5109
New Bern, NC 28560   Donald R. Taylor, Adm.
Staff: Prof 6. **Subjects:** History, literature, antiques. **Special Collections:** Collection of original editions similar to those owned by Royal Governor William Tryon. **Holdings:** 3000 books; manuscripts; documents, clippings; Tryon Palace Commission records. **Services:** Library open to scholars with prior written approval.

★9259★
NORTH CAROLINA STATE DEPARTMENT OF HUMAN RESOURCES - DIVISION OF HEALTH SERVICES - PUBLIC HEALTH LIBRARY (Med)
Bath Bldg., Rm. 215
306 N. Wilmington St.
Box 2091   Phone: (919) 733-7389
Raleigh, NC 27602   Elnora H. Turner, Pub. Health Libn.
Founded: 1954. **Staff:** Prof 1. **Subjects:** Health sciences, medicine, nursing, social sciences, environmental sciences. **Holdings:** 15,500 books; 2500 bound periodical volumes; 12 VF drawers of pamphlets and booklets on health. **Subscriptions:** 186 journals and other serials; 7 newspapers. **Services:** Interlibrary loans; copying; library open to public with restrictions. **Computerized Information Services:** Computerized cataloging through State Library. **Publications:** Journals Listing; newsletters on new acquisitions - for internal distribution only.

★9260★
NORTH CAROLINA STATE DEPT. OF NATURAL RESOURCES & COMMUNITY DEVELOPMENT - DIV. OF COMMUNITY ASSISTANCE LIB. (Plan)
Box 27687   Phone: (919) 733-2850
Raleigh, NC 27611   Christine Coxe, Libn.
Founded: 1958. **Staff:** Prof 1. **Subjects:** Planning, housing, city and county management, land use, community development. **Special Collections:** Reports published by the division (30 VF drawers); North Carolina Collection (5 VF drawers). **Holdings:** 2500 books; 3000 bound periodical volumes; 347 planning advisory reports; 60 Urban Land Institute Special Reports; 500 color slides; 9 films; 6 slide-tape presentations. **Subscriptions:** 30 journals and other serials. **Services:** Copying; library open to public at discretion of librarian. **Publications:** Downtown North Carolina (newsletter), quarterly; What's New in the Library, irregular. **Special Catalogs:** Film bibliography (book).

★9261★
NORTH CAROLINA STATE DEPT. OF NATURAL RESOURCES & COMMUNITY DEVELOPMENT - ENVIRONMENTAL MGT. LIBRARY (Env-Cons)
512 N. Salisbury St., Rm. 702
Box 27687   Phone: (919) 733-5064
Raleigh, NC 27611   Jane Basnight, Libn.
Founded: 1969. **Staff:** Prof 1. **Subjects:** Water and air resources and related environmental subjects. **Holdings:** 10,000 volumes. **Subscriptions:** 125 journals and other serials. **Services:** Library open to public.

NORTH CAROLINA STATE DEPT. OF NATURAL RESOURCES & COMMUNITY DEVELOPMENT - GEOLOGICAL SURVEY
See: North Carolina Geological Survey

★9262★
NORTH CAROLINA STATE DEPARTMENT OF PUBLIC INSTRUCTION - EDUCATION INFORMATION CENTER (Educ)
Education Bldg.   Phone: (919) 733-7094
Raleigh, NC 27611   Ann Fowler, Coord.
Founded: 1960. **Staff:** Prof 1; Other 2. **Subjects:** Elementary and secondary education. **Special Collections:** Attorney General rulings; ERIC. **Holdings:** 5200 books; 1000 reels of periodicals on microfilm; 1000 topics in information files. **Subscriptions:** 250 journals and other serials; 12 newspapers. **Services:** Interlibrary loans; copying; center open to public for reference use only. **Computerized Information Services:** ERIC microfiche reproduction; computer searching. **Publications:** FOCUS; annotated bibliographies.

★9263★
NORTH CAROLINA STATE JUSTICE ACADEMY - LEARNING RESOURCE CENTER (Law)
Drawer 99   Phone: (919) 525-4151
Salemburg, NC 28385   Donald K. Stacy, Libn.
Founded: 1973. **Staff:** Prof 1; Other 4. **Subjects:** Law enforcement, juvenile delinquency, corrections. **Holdings:** 10,000 books; 4000 microfiche; 700 AV materials. **Subscriptions:** 137 journals and other serials; 12 newspapers. **Services:** Interlibrary loans; copying; library open to public. **Publications:** Acquisitions list, monthly; AV catalog, annual.

★9264★
NORTH CAROLINA STATE LEGISLATIVE LIBRARY (Law)
Legislative Bldg.   Phone: (919) 733-7778
Raleigh, NC 27611   Vivian Payne Halperen, Libn.
Staff: Prof 1; Other 4. **Subjects:** Legislative law. **Holdings:** 11,065 books; legislative bills. **Subscriptions:** 21 journals and other serials. **Services:** Library open to public for reference use only. **Computerized Information Services:** Internal database.

NORTH CAROLINA STATE LIBRARY
See: North Carolina State Department of Cultural Resources - Division of the State Library

★9265★
NORTH CAROLINA STATE MUSEUM OF NATURAL HISTORY - H.H. BRIMLEY MEMORIAL LIBRARY (Sci-Tech)
102 N. Salisbury St.
Box 27647   Phone: (919) 733-7450
Raleigh, NC 27611   Ray E. Ashton, Dir. of Educ.
Founded: 1877. **Staff:** 7. **Subjects:** Natural history, emphasis on North Carolina and Eastern United States. **Holdings:** 6000 volumes; 12,000 pamphlets and other unbound items. **Subscriptions:** 12 journals and other serials. **Services:** Copying; library open to public; Natural History Informational Resource Center for educators and researchers. **Publications:** Scientific and Popular Works on North Carolina Natural History.

★9266★
NORTH CAROLINA STATE SCIENCE AND TECHNOLOGY RESEARCH CENTER (Sci-Tech)
Box 12235   Phone: (919) 549-0671
Research Triangle Park, NC 27709   Dr. James E. Vann, Dir.
Founded: 1964. **Staff:** Prof 9; Other 8. **Subjects:** Applied sciences, government, engineering chemistry, life sciences, business, management, economics, social sciences, education, humanities, textile technology. **Holdings:** NASA announced report literature on 250,000 microfiche; abstract journals; 80 million documents. **Services:** Interlibrary loans; copying; SDI; library open to public. **Computerized Information Services:** DIALOG, SDC, BRS, NLM, NASA/RECON. **Publications:** Tech Topics; Tech Bulletin - free upon request. **Remarks:** NC/STRC is part of the Business Assistance Division, North Carolina Department of Commerce. It receives support from NASA as one of 6 Industrial Application Centers. It is a computerized information and technical assistance center. A toll-free telephone number for out-of-state residents is 800-334-8561. **Staff:** J. Graves Vann, Jr., Asst.Dir./Marketing; T.R. Potter, Mgr., Info.Serv.; A.W. Lockwood, Info.Spec.; E.A. Evans, Info.Spec.; M.J. Pugh, Info.Spec.

★9267★
NORTH CAROLINA STATE SUPREME COURT LIBRARY (Law)
Box 28006   Phone: (919) 733-3425
Raleigh, NC 27611   Frances H. Hall, Libn.
Founded: 1812. **Staff:** Prof 2; Other 3. **Subjects:** Law. **Special Collections:** North Carolina legal materials; U.S. government publications depository. **Holdings:** 95,000 volumes. **Subscriptions:** 375 journals and other serials. **Services:** Copying; library open to public. **Remarks:** Library is located at 500

Justice Bldg., 2 E. Morgan St., Raleigh, NC 27601. **Staff:** Alice Cameron Reaves, Asst.Libn.

★9268★

NORTH CAROLINA STATE UNIVERSITY - BURLINGTON TEXTILES LIBRARY
(Sci-Tech)
Box 5006   Phone: (919) 737-3231
Raleigh, NC 27650   Georgia H. Rodeffer, Textiles Libn.
Founded: 1941. **Staff:** Prof 2; Other 2. **Subjects:** Textile technology (fiber and yarn), textile chemistry, polymer chemistry, fabric design, textiles. **Holdings:** 11,073 books; 8054 bound periodical volumes; 400 reels of microfilm; 42 film loops; 20 VF drawers of pamphlets and clippings; 20 VF drawers of textile machinery trade catalogs; 3519 fabric samples. **Subscriptions:** 745 journals and other serials; 12 newspapers. **Services:** Interlibrary loans; copying; library open to public with restrictions. **Computerized Information Services:** DIALOG, SDC. **Networks/Consortia:** Member of OCLC through SOLINET; Triangle Universities Libraries Cooperative Committee; North Carolina Interlibrary Loan Network. **Publications:** Annual Serial Holdings List; Monthly Acquisitions List; NCSU School of Textiles Library Bibliography Series, irregular; Textile Pathfinders, irregular; NCSU School of Textiles List of Theses and Dissertations (1979).

★9269★

NORTH CAROLINA STATE UNIVERSITY - D.H. HILL LIBRARY (Agri; Sci-Tech)
Box 5007   Phone: (919) 737-2843
Raleigh, NC 27650   Isaac T. Littleton, Dir.
Founded: 1899. **Staff:** Prof 35; Other 110. **Subjects:** Engineering, agriculture, forestry, textiles, architecture, biological sciences, genetics, statistics. **Special Collections:** Tippmann Collection (entomology); Schenck Collection (forestry); textiles; history and technology of railroads. **Holdings:** 710,220 books; 337,760 bound periodical volumes; 28,150 maps and plans; 1.8 million microforms; 628,368 U.S. government publications; 23,770 slides. **Subscriptions:** 16,494 journals and other serials; 66 newspapers. **Services:** Interlibrary loans; copying; library open to public for reference use only with limited borrowing privileges. **Computerized Information Services:** DIALOG, SDC; computerized cataloging. **Networks/Consortia:** Member of OCLC through SOLINET; Cooperating Raleigh Colleges Consortium (CRCC); Triangle Universities Libraries Cooperative Committee (TULCC). **Publications:** FOCUS, irregular - free upon request. **Special Catalogs:** Serials catalog on microfiche. **Staff:** Walter M. High, Hd. Monographic Cat.; William C. Horner, Systems Libn.; Gloria W. Houser, Hd., Ser.Dept.; Donald S. Keener, Asst.Dir.Gen.Serv.; Cyrus B. King, Asst.Dir.Coll.Dev.; William C. Lowe, Asst.Dir.Ref.Serv.; Linda P. Fuller, Gen.Serv.Libn.; W. Robert Pollard, Hd., Ref.Dept.; Jean M. Porter, Hd., Doc.Dept.; M. Ronald Simpson, Hd., Tech.Info.Ctr.; Ann S. Smith, Hd., ILL Ctr.; Nell L. Waltner, Hd., Acq.Dept.

★9270★

NORTH CAROLINA STATE UNIVERSITY - D.H. HILL LIBRARY - TECHNICAL INFORMATION CENTER (Sci-Tech; Bus-Fin)
Box 5007   Phone: (919) 737-2830
Raleigh, NC 27650   M. Ronald Simpson, Hd.
Staff: Prof 1; Other 2. **Subjects:** Science, technology, business, management, marketing. **Holdings:** 154 books. **Services:** Interlibrary loans; copying; center open to public. **Computerized Information Services:** DIALOG, SDC. **Publications:** Furniture Industry Information Guide, 1981; subject bibliographies. **Remarks:** The Technical Information Center provides reference and literature searching services to business and industrial firms in North Carolina.

★9271★

NORTH CAROLINA STATE UNIVERSITY - FOREST RESOURCES LIBRARY
(Sci-Tech)
4012 Biltmore Hall   Phone: (919) 737-2306
Raleigh, NC 27650   Pamela E. Puryear, Libn.
Staff: Prof 1; Other 2. **Subjects:** Forestry, Recreation Resources Administration, pulp and paper technology. **Holdings:** 7473 books; 1230 bound periodical volumes; 30 AV materials; 46 filing cabinet drawers of U.S.D.A. Forest Service Experiment Station publications and Forest Products Labs publications. **Subscriptions:** 441 journals and other serials. **Services:** Interlibrary loans; copying; library open to those with borrower's card. **Computerized Information Services:** Online systems.

★9272★

NORTH CAROLINA STATE UNIVERSITY - HARRYE LYONS DESIGN LIBRARY
(Art)
209 Brooks Hall
Box 5398   Phone: (919) 737-2207
Raleigh, NC 27650   Maryellen LoPresti, Libn.
Founded: 1942. **Staff:** Prof 1; Other 3. **Subjects:** Architecture, landscape architecture, urban design, visual design, product design. **Special Collections:** Art and architectural history slide collection (46,416 cataloged slides). **Holdings:** 20,292 books; 5588 bound periodical volumes; 2842 vertical file materials; 2224 items of manufacturers' trade literature; 370 mounted prints; 458 maps and plans; 23 films; 21 recordings; 125 student theses. **Subscriptions:** 250 journals and other serials. **Services:** Interlibrary loans; copying; subject bibliographies; library open to public with restrictions. **Computerized Information Services:** DIALOG, SDC; computerized cataloging and serials. **Networks/Consortia:** Member of OCLC. **Special Catalogs:** Slide catalog (punched card); artists and paintings index - 6900 entries; 380 subject bibliographies compiled by staff. **Special Indexes:** Index to the Student Publication of the School of Design.

★9273★

NORTH CAROLINA STATE UNIVERSITY - SOUTHERN WATER RESOURCES SCIENTIFIC INFORMATION CENTER (Env-Cons)
D.H. Hill Library
Box 5007   Phone: (919) 737-2683
Raleigh, NC 27650   Jean M. Porter, Supv.
Founded: 1972. **Staff:** Prof 1. **Subjects:** Water quality management, protection and control; water cycle; water resources planning; engineering; nature of water; water supply augmentation and conservation; manpower, grants and facilities. **Subscriptions:** On mailing list for publications of Water Resources Scientific Information Center (WRSIC), an agency of the U.S. Department of the Interior, and those of the Water Resources Research Institute of the University of North Carolina. **Services:** Center searches selected Water Resources Abstracts; open to public in its geographical area; fee charged. **Computerized Information Services:** DOE/RECON. **Remarks:** SWRSIC is a joint project of the Water Resources Research Institute of the University of North Carolina and the D.H. Hill Library of North Carolina State University. Although housed in D.H. Hill Library, it is separate from the library. It is one of several regional centers in the United States which formerly comprised the Water Resources Information Network sponsored by WRSIC.

★9274★

NORTH CAROLINA STATE UNIVERSITY - TOBACCO LITERATURE SERVICE
(Agri)
2314 D.H. Hill Library
Box 5007   Phone: (919) 737-2837
Raleigh, NC 27650   Carmen M. Marin, Dir.
Founded: 1956. **Staff:** Prof 2; Other 2. **Subjects:** Tobacco. **Holdings:** 70,500 tobacco abstracts. **Services:** Interlibrary loans; copying. **Publications:** Tobacco Abstracts, bimonthly - subscription or exchange; Tobacco reprint series, irregular; Tobacco: Bibliography of Books at the D.H. Hill Library, 1968; Tobacco Translations, 1969; Tobacco Literature: A Bibliography of Publications in the U.S. Library of Congress, 1970; Tobacco Literature, a Bibliography, 1979. **Special Catalogs:** Tobacco science and technology in book form. **Staff:** Paul A. Suhr, Libn.

★9275★

NORTH CAROLINA STATE UNIVERSITY - VETERINARY MEDICAL LIBRARY
(Med)
School of Veterinary Medicine   Phone: (919) 737-3910
Raleigh, NC 27650   Thea J. Fischer, Veterinary Med.Libn.
Founded: 1981. **Staff:** Prof 1; Other 2. **Subjects:** Veterinary medicine, medicine, biology, biochemistry, pharmacology, toxicology. **Holdings:** 2500 books; 2000 bound periodical volumes; 75 autotutorial programs. **Subscriptions:** 404 journals and other serials. **Services:** Interlibrary loans; copying; SDI; library open to public. **Computerized Information Services:** NLM, DIALOG; computerized cataloging, acquisitions and serials. **Networks/Consortia:** Member of OCLC through SOLINET.

★9276★

NORTH CENTRAL ALABAMA REGIONAL COUNCIL OF GOVERNMENTS - LIBRARY (Plan)
City Hall Tower, 5th Fl.
Box C   Phone: (205) 355-4515
Decatur, AL 35602
Founded: 1966. **Staff:** Prof 10; Other 9. **Subjects:** Planning, education, housing, transportation, finance, drainage, parks, advertisements. **Holdings:** 2000 books; 1000 bound periodical volumes; 1000 other cataloged items. **Subscriptions:** 20 journals and other serials. **Services:** Library open to tri-county area citizens.

★9277★

NORTH CENTRAL BIBLE COLLEGE - T.J. JONES MEMORIAL LIBRARY (Rel-Theol)
910 Elliot Ave., S.   Phone: (612) 332-3491
Minneapolis, MN 55404   Marvin Smith, Lib.Dir.
Founded: 1930. **Staff:** Prof 2; Other 11. **Subjects:** Bible, theology, sacred

music, behavioral science. **Special Collections:** Archives of Assemblies of God movement, including materials on the Holy Spirit and Divine Healing. **Holdings:** 31,000 books; 137 bound periodical volumes; pamphlets; filmstrips; recordings; cassettes. **Subscriptions:** 231 journals and other serials; 5 newspapers. **Services:** Interlibrary loans (fee); copying; library open to public for research only. **Networks/Consortia:** Member of OCLC; MINITEX. **Staff:** Michelle Johns, Asst.Libn.

★9278★
NORTH CENTRAL BRONX HOSPITAL - HEALTH SCIENCES LIBRARY (Med)†
3424 Kossuth Ave.   Phone: (212) 920-7865
Bronx, NY 10467   Ms. Padma Chittampalli, Med.Libn.
Staff: Prof 1; Other 3. **Subjects:** Medicine and related health subjects; hospital administration. **Holdings:** 3500 books; 5000 bound periodical volumes; 1500 slides. **Subscriptions:** 258 journals and other serials; 14 newspapers. **Services:** Interlibrary loans; copying; library open to public with permission from administration and librarian. **Computerized Information Services:** MEDLINE. **Networks/Consortia:** Member of Manhattan-Bronx Health Sciences Library Group. **Publications:** Library Awareness Bulletin - for internal distribution only.

★9279★
NORTH CENTRAL COLLEGE - LIBRARY - SPECIAL COLLECTIONS (Hum)
320 E. School Ave.   Phone: (312) 355-0597
Naperville, IL 60566   Harriet Arklie, Dir.
Founded: 1861. **Special Collections:** Lincoln Collection (711 titles); Haven Hubbard Collection of English Literature (889 titles); Sang Jazz Collection (249 titles); Sang Limited Editions (88 titles). **Services:** Interlibrary loans; copying; SDI; library open to public with restrictions. **Computerized Information Services:** Computerized cataloging, interlibrary loan. **Networks/Consortia:** Member of LIBRAS Academic Library Cooperative; OCLC through ILLINET; DuPage Library System.

NORTH CENTRAL FOREST EXPERIMENT STATION LIBRARY
See: U.S. Forest Service

★9280★
NORTH CENTRAL MINNESOTA HISTORICAL CENTER - LIBRARY (Hist)
Bemidji State University   Phone: (218) 755-3349
Bemidji, MN 56601   Judith McDonald, Dir.
Staff: Prof 2; Other 1. **Subjects:** Minnesota politics and government, forestry, local and regional public records, local histories and biographies, school district records, Ojibwe Tribal history. **Special Collections:** Ah-Gwah-Ching State Sanitorium; Minnesota State Senator Gerald L. Willet Papers; Beltrami County records; J. Neils Lumber Company; U.S. Representative Coya Knutson papers; Kenfield Lumber Company; Star Island Cass Lake Oral Interview Project. **Holdings:** 58 books; 28 bound periodical volumes; 387 boxes of manuscripts, documents, papers; 296 volumes of public records; 217 audiotapes; 34 reels of microfilm. **Services:** Copying; archives open to public. **Remarks:** The center is maintained by Bemidji State University. **Formerly:** Minnesota Historical Society - North Central Minnesota Historical Center. **Staff:** Ardis Wilander, Coll. Preservation Libn.

★9281★
NORTH CENTRAL TEXAS COUNCIL OF GOVERNMENTS - REGIONAL INFORMATION SERVICE CENTER (Plan)
Drawer COG
1201 N. Watson Rd., Suite 270   Phone: (817) 640-3300
Arlington, TX 76011   Teri S. Wiseman
Founded: 1972. **Staff:** 1. **Subjects:** Regional and urban planning. **Special Collections:** Publications from the various governmental bodies within the North Central Texas Region (700 items). **Holdings:** 5000 books; 885 issues of the Council of Planning Librarians exchange bibliographies; 361 topographical and aerial maps. **Subscriptions:** 110 journals and other serials; 5 newspapers. **Services:** Interlibrary loans; copying; library open to public for reference use only. **Computerized Information Services:** Computerized cataloging. **Publications:** Publications List. **Special Catalogs:** Books and reports in agency (print-outs).

★9282★
NORTH CHARLES GENERAL HOSPITAL - MEDICAL STAFF LIBRARY (Med)
2724 N. Charles St.   Phone: (301) 338-2306
Baltimore, MD 21218   Bertha J. Shub, Libn.
Founded: 1958. **Staff:** Prof 1. **Subjects:** Medicine and surgery. **Holdings:** 400 books; Audio-Digests. **Subscriptions:** 65 journals and other serials. **Services:** Library not open to public.

★9283★
NORTH COLORADO MEDICAL CENTER - MEDICAL LIBRARY (Med)
1801 16th St.
Greeley, CO 80631   Meta Shore, Libn.
Staff: 3. **Subjects:** Medicine. **Holdings:** 800 books; 565 bound periodical volumes. **Subscriptions:** 80 journals and other serials; 5 newspapers. **Services:** Library open to public for reference use only. **Formerly:** Weld County General Hospital.

★9284★
NORTH COUNTRY HOSPITAL AND HEALTH CENTER, INC. - INFORMATION CENTER (Med)†
Prouty Dr.
Box 625   Phone: (802) 334-7331
Newport, VT 05855   Estelle Raymond, Info.Ctr.Techn.
Founded: 1971. **Staff:** 1. **Subjects:** Medicine and allied sciences. **Holdings:** 300 books. **Services:** Center open to those in medical fields.

★9285★
NORTH COUNTRY REFERENCE & RESEARCH RESOURCES COUNCIL - LIBRARY (Info Sci)
Box 568   Phone: (315) 386-4569
Canton, NY 13617   Richard H. Kimball, Exec.Dir.
Staff: Prof 2; Other 5. **Subjects:** Library networking, bibliographic access. **Special Collections:** Specialized bibliographic tools for interlibrary loan. **Holdings:** 500 books; library catalogs on 500 microfiche. **Subscriptions:** 15 journals and other serials. **Services:** Interlibrary loans; copying; library not open to public. **Computerized Information Services:** BRS, Compiled Literature Access Search Service (CLASS); computerized serials. **Publications:** Newsletter, quarterly; Union List of Serials. **Special Catalogs:** Catalogs of regional holdings; North Country Historical Materials. **Remarks:** Council is one of 9 systems providing reference and research services to New York state libraries and their patrons. It is supported by funds from New York State Department of Education and member libraries. **Staff:** Thomas Blauvelt, Hd., Ref.Serv.

★9286★
NORTH DAKOTA FARMERS UNION - LULU EVANSON RESOURCE LIBRARY (Agri)
Box 651   Phone: (701) 252-2340
Jamestown, ND 58401   Mildred Hofstad Ingebo, Resource Libn.
Staff: Prof 2. **Subjects:** Agricultural and land use policy, cooperatives, North Dakota Legislature, transportation, social concerns. **Special Collections:** Farmers Union historical materials. **Holdings:** 3100 books and bound periodical volumes; 25 slide programs. **Subscriptions:** 52 journals and other serials; 60 newspapers. **Services:** Interlibrary loans; library open to public with restrictions.

NORTH DAKOTA INSTITUTE FOR REGIONAL STUDIES
See: North Dakota State University - Institute for Regional Studies

★9287★
NORTH DAKOTA STATE DEPARTMENT OF HEALTH - HEALTH MEDIA CENTER (Med)
Capitol Bldg.
Judicial Wing, 2nd Fl.   Phone: (701) 224-2367
Bismarck, ND 58505   Judith Axtman, Libn.
Staff: Prof 1; Other 2. **Subjects:** Health. **Special Collections:** Health resource books for parents of handicapped children. **Holdings:** 350 books; 700 16mm films; 1200 pamphlet titles. **Subscriptions:** 16 journals and other serials. **Services:** Interlibrary loans; film distribution throughout state; center open to health professionals. **Special Catalogs:** Parent Resource Library Catalog; Health Media Catalog; Health Services Inventory. **Formed by the Merger of:** North Dakota State Department of Health - Health Education Film & Staff Journal Library and North Dakota State Department of Human Services - Health Media Center.

NORTH DAKOTA STATE FILM LIBRARY
See: North Dakota State University - Division of Independent Study - Film Library

★9288★
NORTH DAKOTA STATE HIGHWAY DEPARTMENT - LIBRARY (Trans)
North Dakota State Capitol Grounds   Phone: (701) 224-2490
Bismarck, ND 58505   Ruth Mahan, State Libn.
Founded: 1969. **Staff:** 1. **Subjects:** Highway technology and research. **Holdings:** 23,000 books and bound periodical volumes. **Subscriptions:** 40 journals and other serials. **Services:** Interlibrary loans; copying; library open to public for reference use only. **Publications:** In-house reports.

NORTH DAKOTA STATE HISTORICAL SOCIETY
See: State Historical Society of North Dakota

★9289★
NORTH DAKOTA STATE HOSPITAL - DEPARTMENT OF LIBRARY SERVICES - HEALTH SCIENCE LIBRARY (Med)
Box 476   Phone: (701) 253-2679
Jamestown, ND 58401   L. Fay Domek, Lib.Dir.
Founded: 1959. **Staff:** Prof 2; Other 6. **Subjects:** Psychiatry, psychology, nursing, medicine, social work, alcoholism and addiction. **Special Collections:** Biennial Reports, 1890 to present; Tunnel Tidbits (employee magazine), 1953 to present. **Holdings:** 10,000 books; 3200 bound periodical volumes; 291 therapy cassettes; 42 biennial reports; 35 cases of miscellaneous material and pamphlets; 22 therapy films; 14 AV items. **Subscriptions:** 150 journals and other serials; 65 newspapers. **Services:** Interlibrary loans (fee); copying; library open to college students. **Computerized Information Services:** Computerized serials. **Networks/Consortia:** Member of Valley Medical Network. **Publications:** Communique; periodical review list. **Special Catalogs:** Periodical Catalog (card). **Remarks:** Also maintains an Adult Reference Library and Adolescent Library. **Staff:** Denise Pahl, Asst.Lib.Dir.

★9290★
NORTH DAKOTA STATE LIBRARY (Info Sci)
Liberty Memorial Bldg.
Capitol Grounds   Phone: (701) 224-2490
Bismarck, ND 58505   Ruth Mahan, State Libn.
Founded: 1907. **Staff:** Prof 4; Other 19. **Subjects:** North Dakota, state government, library science, music, education. **Special Collections:** State documents since 1904. **Holdings:** 100,000 books; 20,000 tape cassettes; 4000 filmstrip/cassette sets. **Subscriptions:** 100 journals and other serials; 15 newspapers. **Services:** Interlibrary loans; copying; library open to public. **Computerized Information Services:** DIALOG; computerized cataloging. **Networks/Consortia:** Member of North Dakota Network for Knowledge; MINITEX. **Publications:** Flickertale Newsletter, monthly; North Dakota State Publications, monthly. **Staff:** Darrell McNamara, Dir., Lib.Serv.; Mary Braaten, Fld.Libn.

★9291★
NORTH DAKOTA STATE SCHOOL OF SCIENCE - MILDRED JOHNSON LIBRARY (Sci-Tech)
     Phone: (701) 671-2298
Wahpeton, ND 58075   Jerald Stewart, Lib.Dir.
Founded: 1903. **Staff:** Prof 4; Other 5. **Subjects:** Vocational education and technology, auto mechanics, electronics, dental hygiene, business. **Holdings:** 58,000 books; 2800 bound periodical volumes; 12 drawers of major U.S. corporation reports and information; 60 VF drawers of pamphlets; 450 videotapes; 10 file drawers of microfiche; 700 non-print kits; 1200 cassettes and recordings. **Subscriptions:** 925 journals and other serials; 138 newspapers. **Services:** Interlibrary loans; library open to public with restrictions.

★9292★
NORTH DAKOTA STATE SUPREME COURT LAW LIBRARY (Law)
State Capitol, 2nd Fl.   Phone: (701) 224-2227
Bismarck, ND 58505   Elmer J. Dewald, Law Libn.
Founded: 1889. **Staff:** Prof 3; Other 1. **Subjects:** Law. **Special Collections:** U.S. government depository (3310 bound volumes; 7580 paperbacks). **Holdings:** 53,740 bound volumes; 7633 paperbacks. **Subscriptions:** 44 journals and other serials. **Services:** Interlibrary loans; copying; library open to public for reference use only; only an attorney, judge or state department head may check out material. **Staff:** Marcella Kramer, Asst. Law Libn.; Sheryl Christensen, Cat.Libn.

★9293★
NORTH DAKOTA STATE UNIVERSITY - ARCHITECTURE RESOURCE CENTER (Art)
University Sta.   Phone: (701) 237-8616
Fargo, ND 58105
Staff: 1. **Subjects:** Architecture. **Special Collections:** Slide collection (18,000). **Holdings:** 6600 books. **Subscriptions:** 111 journals and other serials. **Services:** Interlibrary loans; copying; library open to public with restrictions.

★9294★
NORTH DAKOTA STATE UNIVERSITY - BOTTINEAU BRANCH AND INSTITUTE OF FORESTRY - LIBRARY (Agri)†
First & Simrall Blvd.   Phone: (701) 228-2277
Bottineau, ND 58318   Mary Claire Thorleifson, Libn.
Founded: 1907. **Staff:** Prof 1; Other 5. **Subjects:** Forestry, botany,

horticulture. **Special Collections:** Fossum Foundation Collection (horticulture, 500 volumes). **Holdings:** 28,000 books. **Subscriptions:** 195 journals and other serials; 43 newspapers. **Services:** Interlibrary loans; copying; library open to public. **Networks/Consortia:** Member of MINITEX.

★9295★
NORTH DAKOTA STATE UNIVERSITY - CHEMISTRY RESOURCE CENTER (Sci-Tech)
University Sta.   Phone: (701) 237-8293
Fargo, ND 58105   Linda Schultz, Supv.
Staff: 1. **Subjects:** Chemistry. **Holdings:** 3300 books. **Subscriptions:** 210 journals and other serials. **Services:** Interlibrary loans; copying; library open to public with restrictions.

★9296★
NORTH DAKOTA STATE UNIVERSITY - DIVISION OF INDEPENDENT STUDY - FILM LIBRARY (Aud-Vis)
State University Sta.
Box 5036   Phone: (701) 237-8907
Fargo, ND 58105   Lillian M. Wadnizak, Lib.Mgr.
Staff: Prof 1; Other 9. **Holdings:** 7000 16mm films. **Special Catalogs:** Film catalog, biennial. **Also Known As:** North Dakota State Film Library.

★9297★
NORTH DAKOTA STATE UNIVERSITY - INSTITUTE FOR REGIONAL STUDIES (Hist)
University Dr. & 12th Ave., N.   Phone: (701) 237-8914
Fargo, ND 58105   John E. Bye, Archv.
Founded: 1950. **Staff:** Prof 1. **Subjects:** Bonanza farming, land development, Nonpartisan League, Fargo city records, pioneer reminiscences. **Special Collections:** Hultstrand History in Pictures Collection of over 500 photographs of sod houses and pioneer life in North Dakota. **Holdings:** 2500 books; 200 bound periodical volumes; 1500 linear feet of manuscripts; 35,000 photographs; 200 linear feet of university archives; 300 maps. **Subscriptions:** 20 journals and other serials. **Services:** Copying; library open to public. **Special Catalogs:** Guide to the Small Collection Manuscripts of the North Dakota Institute for Regional Studies. **Special Indexes:** North Dakota Biography Index (card).

★9298★
NORTH DAKOTA STATE UNIVERSITY - PHARMACY RESOURCE CENTER (Med)
University Sta.   Phone: (701) 237-7748
Fargo, ND 58105   Linda Schultz, Supv.
Staff: 2. **Subjects:** Pharmacy. **Holdings:** 3600 books. **Subscriptions:** 312 journals and other serials. **Services:** Interlibrary loans; copying; library open to public with restrictions. **Networks/Consortia:** Member of Valley Medical Network.

★9299★
NORTH DAKOTA STATE UNIVERSITY - UPPER GREAT PLAINS TRANSPORTATION INSTITUTE - INFORMATION CENTER (Trans)
     Phone: (701) 237-7767
Fargo, ND 58105   Gene C. Griffin, Dir.
Founded: 1967. **Subjects:** Transportation - economics, planning, regulations. **Holdings:** 50 books; 2000 bound periodical volumes.

NORTH ENGINEERING LIBRARY
See: University of Michigan

NORTH GENERAL HOSPITAL
See: Joint Diseases/North General Hospital

★9300★
NORTH HILLS PASSAVANT HOSPITAL - MEDICAL LIBRARY (Med)
9100 Babcock Blvd.   Phone: (412) 367-6320
Pittsburgh, PA 15237   Margaret U. Trevanion, Med.Libn.
Staff: Prof 1; Other 6. **Subjects:** Medicine, nursing. **Holdings:** 1418 books; 2620 bound periodical volumes; 4 VF drawers of pamphlets. **Subscriptions:** 192 journals and other serials. **Services:** Interlibrary loans; copying; SDI; bibliographies; library open to public for reference use only. **Computerized Information Services:** NLM. **Networks/Consortia:** Member of Pittsburgh-East Hospital Library Cooperative; Mideastern Regional Medical Library Service (MERMLS). **Publications:** Medical Library News, monthly.

★9301★
NORTH MEMORIAL MEDICAL CENTER - MEDICAL LIBRARY (Med)
3300 Oakdale N.   Phone: (612) 520-5673
Robbinsdale, MN 55422   Sherry A. Oleson, Dir.Med.Lib.Serv.
Founded: 1968. **Staff:** Prof 3; Other 3. **Subjects:** Medicine, nursing, dentistry, paramedical sciences. **Special Collections:** Health Information Collection (250 books; 13 magazine titles, 685 pamphlets). **Holdings:** 2300 books; 5100 bound periodical volumes; 722 audiotape cassettes; 925 pamphlets; 218 items in journal review article file. **Subscriptions:** 390 journals and other serials. **Services:** Interlibrary loans; copying; SDI; library is open for professional reference use by permission. **Computerized Information Services:** BRS, MEDLARS. **Networks/Consortia:** Member of Twin Cities Biomedical Consortium (TCBC); METRONET. **Publications:** Contributor to Med. Staff Newsletter, monthly; Northern Lights, monthly; Capsule News, monthly. **Staff:** Donna Barbour-Talley, Libn.; Jacqueline Wulff, Libn.; Sylvia Timian, Libn.

★9302★
NORTH MISSISSIPPI MEDICAL CENTER - RESOURCE CENTER (Med)
830 S. Gloster St.   Phone: (601) 842-3632
Tupelo, MS 38801   Audra Castles, Libn.
Staff: Prof 1; Other 1. **Subjects:** Medicine, nursing, health care administration. **Holdings:** 1000 books; 1000 bound periodical volumes; 500 pamphlet files. **Subscriptions:** 137 journals and other serials. **Services:** Interlibrary loans; copying; SDI; library open to health care students. **Computerized Information Services:** BRS, MEDLARS. **Networks/Consortia:** Member of Southeastern Regional Medical Library Program (SERMLP).

★9303★
NORTH OAKLAND GENEALOGICAL SOCIETY - LIBRARY (Hist)
845 S. Lapeer Rd.   Phone: (313) 693-1888
Lake Orion, MI 48035   Betty Guziak, Pres.
Subjects: Local history, genealogy. **Holdings:** 1200 books; microfiche; ancestral charts of members; census records, tax records, cemetery documentations. **Services:** Interlibrary loans; copying; library open to public. **Publications:** Heir-Lines, quarterly - by membership or subscription. **Special Indexes:** Surname index (book). **Remarks:** The genealogy collection is housed at the Orion Township Public Library. **Staff:** Linda Sickles, Dir.

★9304★
NORTH OLYMPIC LIBRARY SYSTEM - PORT ANGELES BRANCH - PACIFIC NORTHWEST ROOM (Hist)
207 S. Lincoln St.   Phone: (206) 452-9253
Port Angeles, WA 98362   Peggy M. Brady, Hd., Ref.Dept.
Staff: Prof 2; Other 3. **Subjects:** Local history. **Special Collections:** Kellogg Photo Collection (5213 negatives, 1106 prints); oral history tapes on Clallam County people and industries (55 tapes). **Services:** Library open to public. **Networks/Consortia:** Member of WLN. **Staff:** Elaine Laessle, Ref.Libn.

★9305★
NORTH PARK BAPTIST CHURCH - LIBRARY (Rel-Theol)
2605 Rex Cruse Dr.   Phone: (214) 892-8429
Sherman, TX 75090   Mrs. Jack Raidt, Dir. of Lib.Serv.
Founded: 1958. **Staff:** 4. **Subjects:** Baptist doctrine, Bible, Christian life, meditations, missions, history and travel. **Holdings:** 4500 books; recordings, filmstrips, slides and VF items (all cataloged); 8 8mm and 16mm movies; 40 cassette tapes. **Subscriptions:** 31 journals and other serials. **Services:** Interlibrary loans; library open to public.

★9306★
NORTH PARK COLLEGE AND THEOLOGICAL SEMINARY - MELLANDER LIBRARY (Rel-Theol)
5125 N. Spaulding Ave.   Phone: (312) 583-2700
Chicago, IL 60625   Norma S. Goertzen, Dir.
Founded: 1958. **Staff:** Prof 1; Other 3. **Subjects:** Theology. **Special Collections:** Evangelical Covenant Church of America archives; Swedish Pioneer Society archives. **Holdings:** 55,981 books and bound periodical volumes; 348 tapes; 639 microforms. **Subscriptions:** 312 journals and other serials. **Services:** Interlibrary loans; copying; library open to Chicago clergy. **Computerized Information Services:** Computerized cataloging. **Networks/Consortia:** Member of OCLC through ILLINET; Chicago Area Theological Library Association.

★9307★
NORTH SHORE CONGREGATION ISRAEL - ROMANEK LIBRARY (Rel-Theol)
1185 Sheridan Rd.   Phone: (312) 835-0724
Glencoe, IL 60022   Matalie Cohen, Libn.
Founded: 1952. **Staff:** Prof 1; Other 3. **Subjects:** Religions, philosophy and ethics, the Bible, Torah, prophets, writings and Apocrypha, sociology, rabbinic literature, history of the Jews, Zionism and Israel. **Special Collections:** Archeology (160 books); Jewish art books. **Holdings:** 17,850 books; 150 bound periodical volumes; tapes, film and scripts; pamphlets, clippings, archives. **Subscriptions:** 85 journals and other serials; 10 newspapers. **Services:** Library open to public.

★9308★
NORTH SHORE MEDICAL CENTER - MEDICAL LIBRARY (Med)
1100 N.W. 95th St.   Phone: (305) 835-6000
Miami, FL 33150   Linda Day, Libn.
Subjects: Surgery, pathology, thoracic medicine, cancer, dermatology, pharmacology. **Holdings:** 250 books; 44 bound periodical volumes; 30 pamphlets; 47 films. **Subscriptions:** 26 journals and other serials. **Services:** Copying; library not open to public. **Staff:** Jesse G. Keshin, Dir./ Cont.Med.Educ.

★9309★
NORTH SHORE SYNAGOGUE - CHARLES COHN MEMORIAL LIBRARY (Rel-Theol)
83 Muttontown Rd.   Phone: (516) 921-2282
Syosset, NY 11791   Elaine Charnow, Libn.
Staff: Prof 1; Other 2. **Subjects:** Jewish history, religion and culture. **Special Collections:** Juvenile books on topics above. **Holdings:** 3700 books and bound periodical volumes; phonograph records; 80 sound filmstrips; 150 silent filmstrips; VF drawers. **Subscriptions:** 20 journals and other serials. **Services:** Library not open to public.

★9310★
NORTH SHORE UNIVERSITY HOSPITAL - DANIEL CARROLL PAYSON MEDICAL LIBRARY (Med)
Community Dr.   Phone: (516) 562-4324
Manhasset, NY 11030   Elsie Wilensky, Med.Libn.
Staff: Prof 3; Other 1. **Subjects:** Medicine, nursing. **Holdings:** 4000 books; 11,000 bound periodical volumes; slides, films and audio cassettes (cataloged). **Subscriptions:** 350 journals and other serials. **Services:** Interlibrary loans; copying; library open to local professionals. **Computerized Information Services:** NLM. **Networks/Consortia:** Member of Medical Library Center of New York. **Publications:** Book lists, bimonthly; special reports. **Staff:** Joan Napolitano, Asst.Libn.; Katherine Zippert, Asst.Libn.

NORTH STAR LIBRARY
See: Sons of Norway

★9311★
NORTH SUBURBAN LIBRARY SYSTEM - PROFESSIONAL INFORMATION CENTER (Info Sci)
200 W. Dundee   Phone: (312) 459-1300
Wheeling, IL 60090   Dr. Elliott E. Kanner, Rsrcs.Coord./Info.Libn.
Staff: Prof 1; Other 1. **Subjects:** Library science, information science, adult and continuing education. **Holdings:** 5235 volumes; 75 annual and technical reports; policy and procedure manuals; microfiche, kits, cassettes. **Subscriptions:** 200 journals and other serials. **Services:** Interlibrary loans; copying; center open to public by appointment. **Computerized Information Services:** Internal database; computerized cataloging and circulation. **Networks/Consortia:** Member of OCLC; North Suburban Library System. **Publications:** Nor'easter, monthly; Bulletin Board, weekly; special reports and bibliographies prepared on request.

★9312★
NORTH SUBURBAN LIBRARY SYSTEM & SUBURBAN LIBRARY SYSTEM - SUBURBAN AV SERVICE (Aud-Vis)
920 Barnsdale Rd.   Phone: (312) 352-7671
La Grange Park, IL 60525   Leon L. Drolet, Jr., Dir.
Founded: 1970. **Staff:** Prof 2; Other 45. **Subjects:** Motion picture - history and industry; AV technology; consumer electronics - video and home computers. **Holdings:** 3000 books; film bibliographies; files of media distributors and producers. **Subscriptions:** 160 journals and other serials. **Services:** Interlibrary loans; copying; SDI; centralized purchasing; tape duplication; equipment repair; library open to public with restrictions. **Computerized Information Services:** Computerized cataloging and circulation. **Networks/Consortia:** Member of OCLC through ILLINET. **Publications:** SAVS Short Subjects, monthly - for internal distribution only. **Remarks:** SAVS is a support service for 226 public and 24 academic libraries providing AV materials and reference service. It is a video resource center for the state of Illinois. **Staff:** Alora Cope, Asst.Dir.

★9313★

NORTH SUBURBAN SYNAGOGUE BETH EL - MAXWELL ABBELL LIBRARY
(Rel-Theol)
1175 Sheridan Rd.   Phone: (312) 432-8900
Highland Park, IL 60035   Patricia Cohler, Libn.
Founded: 1952. **Staff:** Prof 1. **Subjects:** Judaica. **Holdings:** 10,000 books;
100 bound periodical volumes; 350 phonograph records; 3 VF drawers of
pamphlets; 150 filmstrips. **Subscriptions:** 50 journals and other serials.
Services: Interlibrary loans; library open to public.

★9314★

NORTH TEXAS STATE UNIVERSITY LIBRARIES - MEDIA LIBRARY (Aud-Vis)
Box 12898   Phone: (817) 565-2691
Denton, TX 76203   George D. Mitchell, III, Media Lib.Dir.
Staff: Prof 2; Other 8. **Subjects:** Gerontology, education. **Special
Collections:** Gerontological Film Collection (225 titles). **Holdings:** 1500 films.
Services: Interlibrary loans (Gerontological Film Collection only); library open
to public for reference use only. **Computerized Information Services:**
Computerized circulation. **Networks/Consortia:** Member of Association for
Higher Education of North Texas. **Special Catalogs:** Gerontological Film
Collection catalog, biennial - free upon request. **Staff:** Darrel Pope, Asst.
Media Libn.

★9315★

**NORTH TEXAS STATE UNIVERSITY LIBRARIES - ORAL HISTORY
COLLECTION (Hist)**
University Sta., Box 13734   Phone: (817) 788-2558
Denton, TX 76203   Dr. Ronald E. Marcello, Coord.
Founded: 1963. **Staff:** Prof 1; Other 1. **Subjects:** Texas governors and
legislators, World War II, New Deal, business history, politics. **Holdings:** 560
books; 600 oral history tapes. **Services:** Copying; library open to public with
restrictions. **Publications:** Bulletin, Oral History Collection.

★9316★

**NORTH TEXAS STATE UNIVERSITY LIBRARIES - RARE BOOK ROOM (Rare
Book)**
North Texas Sta.
Box 5188   Phone: (817) 788-2411
Denton, TX 76203   Dr. Kenneth Lavender, Univ.Bibliog.
Founded: 1981. **Staff:** Prof 1; Other 3. **Subjects:** Travel, children's
literature, Texana, 18th century English literature. **Special Collections:** Larry
McMurtry (73 manuscripts); Mary Webb (38 editions; photographs); Anson
Jones (133 volumes); Willa Cather (49 first editions). **Holdings:** 5014 books;
75 manuscripts. **Services:** Library open to public with restrictions. **Networks/
Consortia:** Member of AMIGOS; Association for Higher Education of North
Texas. **Special Catalogs:** Catalogue of Webb Collection; Printers' File; catalog
of children's literature (all on cards).

★9317★

NORTH UNITED PRESBYTERIAN CHURCH - LIBRARY (Rel-Theol)†
3410 W. Silver Spring Dr.   Phone: (414) 466-1870
Milwaukee, WI 53209
Founded: 1960. **Staff:** 1. **Subjects:** Religion, Bible, children's books,
biographies. **Holdings:** 1000 books. **Services:** Library not open to public.

★9318★

NORTH YORK BOARD OF EDUCATION - F.W. MINKLER LIBRARY (Educ)
Education Administration Ctr.
5050 Yonge St.   Phone: (416) 225-4661
Willowdale, ON, Canada M2N 5N8   H.P. Greaves, Chf.Libn.
Founded: 1957. **Staff:** Prof 4; Other 4. **Subjects:** Education, psychology,
sociology. **Special Collections:** Board Archives (24 drawers); F.W. Minkler
Historical Text Collection (1000 volumes). **Holdings:** 22,000 books;
complete ERIC microfiche since 1971; 32 drawers of clippings and
pamphlets. **Subscriptions:** 500 journals and other serials; 5 newspapers.
Services: Interlibrary loans; copying; SDI; library open to public for reference
use only. **Computerized Information Services:** SDC, ONTERIS.
Publications: Current Awareness Bulletin, monthly; newsletters and
bibliographies, irregular. **Special Catalogs:** Where to look for VF material
(card).

★9319★

NORTH YORK GENERAL HOSPITAL - W. KEITH WELSH LIBRARY (Med)
4001 Leslie St.   Phone: (416) 492-4748
Willowdale, ON, Canada M2K 1E1   Marianne E. Brett, Hosp.Libn.
Founded: 1968. **Staff:** Prof 1; Other 1. **Subjects:** Medicine, nursing,
administration. **Special Collections:** History of medicine. **Holdings:** 6000
books; 340 bound periodical volumes; 700 cassettes; 1 file drawer of
government documents. **Subscriptions:** 305 journals and other serials.

Services: Interlibrary loans; copying; library open to medical students and
students doing medical projects.

★9320★

NORTH YORK PUBLIC LIBRARY - CANADIANA COLLECTION (Area-Ethnic)
35 Fairview Mall Dr.   Phone: (416) 494-6838
Willowdale, ON, Canada M2J 4S4   Ian Ross, Hd.
Founded: 1961. **Staff:** Prof 4; Other 2. **Subjects:** Ontario history and
genealogy, Canadian history, literature and culture. **Special Collections:**
Newton MacTavish Collection (150 books, 2 linear feet of manuscripts); Star
Weekly Papers (3 linear feet of manuscripts); John A. Cooper Papers (12
linear feet of manuscripts and photographs); Ontario Genealogical Society
library (1500 books and pamphlets). **Holdings:** 50,000 books; 700 bound
periodical volumes; 50,000 microforms; 34 VF drawers; North York Public
Library Archives. **Subscriptions:** 150 journals and other serials. **Services:**
Copying; library open to public. **Computerized Information Services:**
Computerized cataloging. **Publications:** Reader, Lover of Books: The Book
Arts in Ontario; Genealogy and Family History Catalogue. **Special Catalogs:**
Native Peoples Checklist; Newton MacTavish Collection Finding Aid; John A.
Cooper Collection Finding Aid. **Staff:** Adrienne Taylor, Ref.Libn.; Diana Fink,
Cat./Libn.; Patricia Stone, Libn./Archv.

★9321★

**NORTH YORK PUBLIC LIBRARY - MULTILINGUAL MATERIALS
DEPARTMENT (Hum)**
120 Martin Ross Ave.   Phone: (416) 667-1060
North York, ON, Canada M3J 2L4   Diane Dragasevich, Libn./Supv.
Founded: 1965. **Staff:** Prof 1. **Subjects:** Fiction and popular nonfiction in 26
languages; children's literature in 15 languages. **Holdings:** 77,000 volumes;
records; cassettes. **Subscriptions:** 237 journals and other serials. **Services:**
Interlibrary loans; copying; department open to public.

★9322★

NORTH YORK PUBLIC LIBRARY - URBAN AFFAIRS SECTION (Plan)
5126 Yonge St.   Phone: (416) 487-3145
North York, ON, Canada M2N 5N9   Clara J. Stacey, Libn.Supv.
Founded: 1977. **Staff:** Prof 1; Other 1. **Subjects:** Urban and regional
planning, municipal government and finance, urban transportation, housing,
municipal services, zoning and land use. **Special Collections:** North York Parks
and Recreation Department scrapbooks, 1957-1971 (9 volumes). **Holdings:**
15,000 books; 175 bound periodical volumes; 8 VF drawers; 1000
microfiche on Urban Canada; 125 scrapbooks. **Subscriptions:** 352 journals
and other serials. **Services:** Interlibrary loans; copying; section open to public
for reference use only. **Computerized Information Services:** Computerized
cataloging and circulation. **Publications:** Selected Acquisitions Relating to
Urban Affairs, 10/year - to mailing list. **Special Indexes:** Index to North York
Planning Board Agendas, 1977 to present (card).

★9323★

**NORTHAMPTON COUNTY HISTORICAL AND GENEALOGICAL SOCIETY -
HISTORICAL MUSEUM AND LIBRARY (Hist)**
101 S. Fourth St.   Phone: (215) 253-1222
Easton, PA 18042   Bruce Drinkhouse, Pres.
Staff: Prof 1; Other 3. **Subjects:** Local history and genealogy. **Holdings:**
3000 books, manuscripts, deeds, letters, maps, pictures. **Services:** Copying;
genealogical research (fee); library open to public on a limited schedule and by
appointment. **Publications:** List of books and pamphlets for sale furnished on
request. **Staff:** Mrs. Roland S. Moyer, Libn.

★9324★

NORTHAMPTON COUNTY LAW LIBRARY (Law)
7th & Washington Sts.   Phone: (215) 253-4111
Easton, PA 18042   George A. Gollub, Law Libn.
Founded: 1861. **Staff:** Prof 1. **Subjects:** Law, taxes, labor, business.
Holdings: 20,150 books and bound periodical volumes. **Subscriptions:** 25
journals and other serials. **Services:** Copying; library open to public for
reference use only.

★9325★

NORTHAMPTON HISTORICAL SOCIETY - HISTORICAL COLLECTION (Hist)
46 Bridge St.   Phone: (413) 584-6011
Northampton, MA 01060   Ruth E. Wilbur, Dir.
Founded: 1905. **Subjects:** Local history and biography. **Holdings:**
Documents, letters, diaries, manuscripts, account books, ephemera,
photographs, clippings, oral histories. **Services:** Collection open to researchers
only.

★9326★

NORTHEAST ALABAMA REGIONAL MEDICAL CENTER - MEDICAL LIBRARY (Med)
400 East Tenth St.
Box 2208   Phone: (205) 235-5877
Anniston, AL 36202   Priscilla Lloyd, Med.Libn.
Founded: 1961. **Staff:** Prof 1. **Subjects:** Medicine and allied sciences. **Holdings:** 200 books; 800 bound periodical volumes. **Subscriptions:** 66 journals and other serials. **Services:** Interlibrary loans; copying; library open to public for reference use only. **Computerized Information Services:** Computerized cataloging, serials and circulation. **Networks/Consortia:** Member of Alabama Hospital Association Medical Library Consortium.

NORTHEAST ARCHIVES OF FOLKLORE AND ORAL HISTORY
See: University of Maine, Orono

NORTHEAST FISHERIES CENTER
See: U.S. Natl. Marine Fisheries Service

★9327★

NORTHEAST GEORGIA MEDICAL CENTER AND HALL SCHOOL OF NURSING/BRENAU COLLEGE - LIBRARY (Med)
741 Spring St.   Phone: (404) 536-1114
Gainesville, GA 30505   Caroline Alday, Libn.
Founded: 1963. **Staff:** Prof 2. **Subjects:** Nursing, medicine. **Holdings:** 4179 books; 1980 bound periodical volumes; 4 VF drawers. **Subscriptions:** 112 journals and other serials. **Services:** Interlibrary loans; copying; library open to public for reference use only. **Computerized Information Services:** MEDLINE. **Staff:** Mary Gilbert, Libn.

NORTHEAST MENTAL HEALTH CLINIC
See: Norfolk Regional Center and Northeast Mental Health Clinic

★9328★

NORTHEAST MINNESOTA HISTORICAL CENTER - LIBRARY (Hist)
Library 375
University of Minnesota, Duluth   Phone: (218) 726-8526
Duluth, MN 55812   Pat Maus, Adm.
Founded: 1976. **Staff:** Prof 1. **Subjects:** Regional history, transportation, iron mining technology, environmental issues, social service and civic agencies and organizations, business and industry, women. **Special Collections:** Great Lakes-St. Lawrence Tidewater Association Records (39 linear feet); St. Louis County Social Service Department Records (38 linear feet); Julius Barnes papers (13 linear feet); Save Lake Superior Association Records (11 linear feet); Duluth Transit Authority Records (180 linear feet); Oliver Iron Mining Company Records; Merritt Family papers; Duluth Board of Trade Records; Seaway Port Authority of Duluth Records; Anderson Hilding papers; Reserve Mining Company Legal References. **Holdings:** 2000 books; 2000 linear feet of manuscripts; clippings; oral history tapes; 30,000 photographs; blueprints; maps. **Subscriptions:** 100 journals and other serials. **Services:** Copying; library open to public. **Networks/Consortia:** Member of Minnesota Regional Research Centers Network. **Special Catalogs:** Genealogical Resources Available at the Northeast Minnesota Historical Center; A Bibliography of Books and Pamphlets Held in the Northeast Minnesota Historical Center. **Remarks:** The Northeast Minnesota Historical Center at the University of Minnesota, Duluth is one of eight regional research centers and archives. It is jointly operated by the University of Minnesota, Duluth and the St. Louis County Historical Society. **Formerly:** Minnesota Historical Society - Northeast Minnesota Historical Center.

★9329★

NORTHEAST MISSOURI STATE UNIVERSITY - PICKLER MEMORIAL LIBRARY - SPECIAL COLLECTIONS (Hum)
                                            Phone: (816) 785-4526
Kirksville, MO 63501   George N. Hartje, Dir. of Lib.
Staff: Prof 9; Other 14. **Special Collections:** Missouriana (6543 volumes); Fred and Ethel Schwengel Lincoln Collection (books, paintings, artifacts); Glenn Frank (60 cubic feet); Laughlin Collection (22 cubic feet); government documents. **Services:** Interlibrary loans; copying; library open to public. **Computerized Information Services:** Online systems; computerized serials. **Networks/Consortia:** Member of Mississippi Valley Cooperative Library Service; Northeast Missouri Library Network; OCLC; MIDLNET.

★9330★

NORTHEAST OHIO AREAWIDE COORDINATING AGENCY - RESEARCH LIBRARY (Plan)†
1501 Euclid Ave.   Phone: (216) 241-2414
Cleveland, OH 44115   Lee Wachtel, Res.Libn.
Founded: 1972. **Staff:** 3. **Subjects:** Transportation, land use, housing,

demographics, water quality, environmental planning, community involvement. **Holdings:** 15,000 books, monographs and bound periodical volumes; 2000 unbound reports and specialized studies; subject files; 300 microfiche units. **Subscriptions:** 200 journals and other serials; 14 newspapers. **Services:** Interlibrary loans; copying; library open to public for reference use only.

★9331★

NORTHEAST OHIO FOUR COUNTY REGIONAL PLANNING & DEVELOPMENT ORGANIZATION - TECHNICAL INFORMATION CENTER (Plan)
137 S. Main St.   Phone: (216) 253-4196
Akron, OH 44308
Founded: 1956. **Subjects:** Urban planning, land use, community facilities, housing, environmental planning, economic development. **Special Collections:** American Society of Planning Officials; census depository for reports. **Holdings:** 3500 books and bound periodical volumes; pamphlet supplements to library (cataloged). **Subscriptions:** 10 journals and other serials; 10 newspapers. **Services:** Copying; library open to public. **Also Known As:** NEFCO.

★9332★

NORTHEAST UTILITIES SERVICE COMPANY - LIBRARY (Energy)†
Box 270   Phone: (203) 666-6911
Hartford, CT 06101   Joan N. Terry, Libn.
Staff: Prof 1; Other 1. **Subjects:** Public utilities, electric engineering, utility economics. **Holdings:** 1594 books; 610 bound periodical volumes; 600 volumes of transactions and proceedings of technical and engineering societies; 6 shelves of standards; 6 drawers of subject material. **Subscriptions:** 160 journals and other serials. **Services:** Interlibrary loans; copying; library open to public. **Remarks:** Library is located at 107 Selden St., Berlin, CT 06037.

★9333★

NORTHEAST WISCONSIN TECHNICAL INSTITUTE - LEARNING RESOURCE CENTER (Sci-Tech; Bus-Fin)
2740 W. Mason   Phone: (414) 497-3190
Green Bay, WI 54303   Mary Hein, Libn.
Founded: 1966. **Staff:** Prof 4; Other 6. **Subjects:** Health occupations, trade and industry, business and marketing, education, police science, agriculture, home economics, fire science. **Holdings:** 15,600 books; 3000 AV materials; 2500 reels of microfilm; 600 microfiche; 1000 video cassettes. **Subscriptions:** 600 journals and other serials; 30 newspapers. **Services:** Interlibrary loans; copying; library open to public. **Networks/Consortia:** Member of Northeast Wisconsin Intertype Libraries (NEWIL); Fox River Valley Area Library Cooperative (FRVALC). **Publications:** Yearly Student & Staff Handbooks; monthly print-out of holdings; yearly update of computerized union list of periodicals for FRVALC. **Staff:** D.W. Rowling, LRC Spec.; Jerry Turba, Media Techn.

★9334★

NORTHEASTERN BIBLE COLLEGE - LINCOLN MEMORIAL LIBRARY (Rel-Theol)
12 Oak Lane   Phone: (201) 226-1074
Essex Fells, NJ 07021   Shirley N. Wood, Act.Dir.
Founded: 1952. **Staff:** Prof 2. **Subjects:** Bible, religion, general and elementary education. **Holdings:** 56,000 books; 800 bound periodical volumes; 3045 pamphlets; 617 phonograph records; 200 filmstrips; 2400 cassette tapes; 40 microfilm reels. **Subscriptions:** 700 journals and other serials; 8 newspapers. **Services:** Interlibrary loans; copying; library open to public. **Networks/Consortia:** Member of County of Essex Cooperating Libraries. **Staff:** Charmaine L. MacMullen, Asst.Dir.

NORTHEASTERN FOREST EXPERIMENT STATION LIBRARY
See: U.S. Forest Service

★9335★

NORTHEASTERN HOSPITAL - SCHOOL OF NURSING LIBRARY (Med)
2301 E. Allegheny Ave.   Phone: (215) 291-3168
Philadelphia, PA 19134   James W. Osborne, Libn.
Founded: 1924. **Staff:** Prof 1. **Subjects:** Nursing, medicine, natural sciences, psychology, sociology. **Holdings:** 1500 books; 120 bound periodical volumes; filmstrips; videotapes; cassettes (cataloged); 6 VF boxes. **Subscriptions:** 40 journals and other serials. **Services:** Interlibrary loans; library not open to public.

★9336★

NORTHEASTERN ILLINOIS PLANNING COMMISSION - LIBRARY (Plan)†
400 W. Madison St.   Phone: (312) 454-0400
Chicago, IL 60606   Mildred L. Cutberth, Sr.Libn.
Founded: 1958. **Staff:** Prof 1. **Subjects:** Planning, census, transportation,

ecology, noise pollution. **Special Collections:** U.S. and Illinois Census summaries (microfilm and tapes); Chicago Area Hospital and Transportation studies; Northeastern Illinois Planning Commission publications. **Holdings:** 5000 books; 250 periodical titles; 15 VF drawers of planning materials; government documents, newsletters. **Subscriptions:** 50 journals and other serials. **Services:** Interlibrary loans; copying; library open to public for reference use only. **Networks/Consortia:** Member of Metropolitan Chicago Library Assembly.

★9337★

NORTHEASTERN ILLINOIS UNIVERSITY - LIBRARY (Educ)
5500 N. St. Louis Ave.   Phone: (312) 583-4050
Chicago, IL 60625   Melvin R. George, Dir.
Founded: 1961. **Staff:** Prof 30; Other 55. **Subjects:** Education, ethnic studies, pop culture. **Special Collections:** ERIC. **Holdings:** 405,661 books; 43,478 bound periodical volumes; 50,626 archives; 119,319 pamphlets; 477,305 microfiche; 21,952 reels of microfilm. **Subscriptions:** 5187 journals and other serials; 46 newspapers. **Services:** Interlibrary loans; copying; library open to public for reference use only. **Computerized Information Services:** DIALOG; internal database; computerized cataloging and circulation. **Networks/Consortia:** Member of OCLC through ILLINET; CRL; Chicago Academic Library Council (CALC). **Publications:** Annual Report; Curriculum Materials Center Acquisition List. **Special Catalogs:** Departmental notebooks in book form. **Staff:** Sophie K. Black, Assoc.Libn., Pub.Serv.; James Wilson McGregor, Asst.Libn., Tech.Serv.; Ronald Saiet, Assoc.Dir., Lrng.Serv.; Joseph Gregg, Hd., Acq.; Gail Peyton, Inner City Stud.Libn; Albert Jen, Hd., Cat.; Glen Kistner, Hd., Circ.; Bradley Baker, Doc.Libn.; Annette Vilaro, Educ.Ref.Libn.; Evangeline Mistaras, Hd., Ref.; Virginia Reed, Hd., Ser.Serv.

★9338★

NORTHEASTERN LOGGERS ASSOCIATION, INC. - LIBRARY
Box 69
Old Forge, NY 13420
Defunct

★9339★

NORTHEASTERN NEVADA MUSEUM - LIBRARY (Hist)
1515 Idaho St.
Box 503   Phone: (702) 738-3418
Elko, NV 89801   Bevette Moore, Registrar
Founded: 1968. **Staff:** Prof 1. **Subjects:** Northeastern Nevada and Nevada; pioneers, antiques. **Special Collections:** Area newspapers, 1869 to present (235 bound books). **Holdings:** 2000 books; 280 newspapers (cataloged); 3000 photographs and negatives; 250 unpublished manuscripts; area newspapers on microfilm. **Subscriptions:** 10 journals and other serials. **Services:** Copying; library and archives not open to public. **Publications:** Northeastern Nevada Historical Society Quarterly - to members and available in sales shop. **Special Indexes:** Area newspaper index (in progress). **Remarks:** Maintained by Northeastern Nevada Historical Society.

★9340★

NORTHEASTERN OHIO UNIVERSITIES COLLEGE OF MEDICINE - BASIC MEDICAL SCIENCES LIBRARY (Med)
                                                Phone: (216) 325-2511
Rootstown, OH 44272   Karen Brewer, Dir.
Founded: 1976. **Staff:** Prof 5; Other 6. **Subjects:** Basic life sciences, medicine. **Holdings:** 17,180 books; 17,394 bound periodical volumes; 1573 AV items; 10 VF drawers of archival material. **Subscriptions:** 846 journals and other serials. **Services:** Interlibrary loans; SDI; library open to public for reference use only. **Computerized Information Services:** MEDLINE, DIALOG, SDC, BRS, Lithium Library; computerized cataloging and serials. **Networks/Consortia:** Member of OHIONET; NEOMAL; Kentucky-Ohio-Michigan Regional Medical Library Network (KOMRML). **Publications:** Medical Periodicals in Northeastern Ohio, annual; Medical Audiovisuals in Northeast Ohio, annual; Input/Output, monthly. **Staff:** Dick R. Miller, Assoc.Libn.; Judith Warnement, Regional Lib.Coord.; Jean Jarsoz, Ref.Libn.; Monica Unger, Cat.Libn.

★9341★

NORTHEASTERN OKLAHOMA STATE UNIVERSITY - JOHN VAUGHAN LIBRARY/LRC - SPECIAL COLLECTIONS (Hum)
                                                Phone: (918) 456-5511
Tahlequah, OK 74464   Dr. J. Richard Madaus, Dir.
Founded: 1909. **Special Collections:** Cherokee Indian Collection (2400 volumes); E. Edmondson Papers (135 boxes); Government Document Depository (239,912 items). **Services:** Interlibrary loans; copying; library open to public. **Computerized Information Services:** DIALOG, BRS. **Networks/Consortia:** Member of OCLC through AMIGOS Bibliographic Council. **Special Catalogs:** Film catalog (book). **Staff:** Delores Sumner, Native

Amer.Mtls.Spec.; Victoria Sheffler, Archv.Spec.

NORTHEASTERN RESEARCH FOUNDATION, INC. - BIGELOW LABORATORY FOR OCEAN SCIENCES
See: Maine State Department of Marine Resources

★9342★

NORTHEASTERN UNIVERSITY - DANA RESEARCH CENTER - PHYSICS ELECTRICAL ENGINEERING LIBRARY (Sci-Tech)
110 Forsyth St.   Phone: (617) 437-2363
Boston, MA 02115   Anastasija Cakste, Libn., Res.Ref.
Staff: Prof 1. **Subjects:** Electrical engineering, physics, mathematics, electronics, geophysics, astronomy. **Holdings:** 8211 books; 10,112 bound periodical volumes; several hundred preprints. **Subscriptions:** 289 journals and other serials. **Services:** Interlibrary loans; copying; library not open to public. **Computerized Information Services:** DIALOG. **Networks/Consortia:** Member of Boston Library Consortium.

★9343★

NORTHEASTERN UNIVERSITY - LAW SCHOOL LIBRARY (Law)
400 Huntington Ave.   Phone: (617) 437-3338
Boston, MA 02115   Rajinder S. Walia, Law Libn./Prof. of Law
Founded: 1967. **Staff:** Prof 5; Other 5. **Subjects:** Law. **Special Collections:** Sara Ehrmann Collection on Capital Punishment (250 files); international law. **Holdings:** 17,035 books; 82,937 bound periodical volumes; 10,521 microform volume equivalents; records and briefs of the Massachusetts Supreme Judicial Court. **Subscriptions:** 1524 journals and other serials. **Services:** Interlibrary loans; copying; library open to public with written request. **Computerized Information Services:** Internal database; computerized cataloging. **Networks/Consortia:** Member of Microform Consortium. **Publications:** Bibliography, generated from internal database. **Special Catalogs:** Catalog on microfiche, from internal database. **Staff:** Charles L. Field, Asst. Law Libn.; Jeanette Yetman, Tech.Proc.Asst.; Cheryl L. Ade, Asst.Libn./Tech.Serv.; Margaret Cianfarini, Acq./Cat.Libn.

★9344★

NORTHEASTERN UNIVERSITY - MARINE SCIENCE AND MARITIME STUDIES CENTER (Sci-Tech)
East Point   Phone: (617) 581-7370
Nahant, MA 01908   E. Cole, Sec.
Staff: 2. **Subjects:** Marine biology, ocean chemistry. **Holdings:** 750 books; 7000 reprints. **Subscriptions:** 25 journals and other serials. **Services:** Copying; library open to public for reference use only.

★9345★

NORTHEASTERN UNIVERSITY - ROBERT GRAY DODGE LIBRARY (Sci-Tech; Mus)
360 Huntington Ave.   Phone: (617) 437-2350
Boston, MA 02115   Roland H. Moody, Dean
Special Collections: History of Engineering Collection; Louise Hall Tharp-Horace Mann Collection; Glen Grey-Casa Loma Orchestra Collection; Leaf Collection. **Holdings:** Figures not available. **Services:** Interlibrary loans; copying; SDI; library open to public. **Computerized Information Services:** DIALOG, BRS, SDC; internal database; computerized cataloging, acquisitions, serials and circulation. **Networks/Consortia:** Member of Boston Library Consortium; OCLC through NELINET. **Special Catalogs:** Comfiche for graduate research libraries in chemistry, chemical engineering, biology, pharmacy, health sciences, physics, electrical engineering, mathematics, psychology.

★9346★

NORTHEASTERN VERMONT REGIONAL HOSPITAL - INFORMATION CENTER/LIBRARY (Med)
Hospital Dr.   Phone: (802) 748-8141
St. Johnsbury, VT 05819   Eleanor Simons, Libn.
Founded: 1972. **Staff:** Prof 1; Other 1. **Subjects:** Medicine, nursing, and allied health fields. **Holdings:** 802 books; 5 VF drawers of pamphlets. **Subscriptions:** 183 journals and other serials. **Services:** Interlibrary loans; copying; open to the health community and to others with permission. **Networks/Consortia:** Member of North Country Consortium.

★9347★

NORTHERN ALBERTA INSTITUTE OF TECHNOLOGY - LEARNING RESOURCE CENTRE (Bus-Fin; Sci-Tech)
11762 106th St.   Phone: (403) 477-4375
Edmonton, AB, Canada T5G 2R1   Miss Jean Paul, Chf.Libn.
Founded: 1963. **Staff:** Prof 4; Other 16. **Subjects:** Business; pure and applied sciences. **Holdings:** 73,300 books, pamphlets and documents; 2964 bound periodical volumes. **Subscriptions:** 612 journals and other serials.

Services: Interlibrary loans; copying; library open to public for reference use only.

NORTHERN ARIZONA PIONEERS' HISTORICAL SOCIETY LIBRARY AND ARCHIVES
See: Northern Arizona University - Libraries - Special Collections Division

★9348★
NORTHERN ARIZONA UNIVERSITY - LIBRARIES (Educ)†
Box 6022   Phone: (602) 523-2951
Flagstaff, AZ 86011   Robert E. Kemper, Dir.
Staff: Prof 15; Other 33. **Subjects:** Education, Arizoniana, Southwestern Americans. **Holdings:** Figures not available. **Services:** Interlibrary loans; copying; library open to public. **Computerized Information Services:** Online systems; computerized cataloging and circulation. **Networks/Consortia:** Member of OCLC through AMIGOS Bibliographic Council, Inc. **Special Indexes:** Discovery Series (books) 6/year; guides to special subjects.

★9349★
NORTHERN ARIZONA UNIVERSITY - LIBRARIES - SPECIAL COLLECTIONS DIVISION (Hist)†
CU Box 6022   Phone: (602) 523-4730
Flagstaff, AZ 86011   Bill Mullane, Spec.Coll.Libn.
Founded: 1972. **Staff:** Prof 1; Other 4. **Subjects:** Arizona history, Elbert Hubbard, Roycroft Press, Grand Canyon, cameras, radicalism in the U.S., conservatism, Communism, Socialism, Southwest U.S., Navajo Indians. **Special Collections:** George F. Wales Checkers Collection; Emery Kolb Collection of Grand Canyon photographs, motion picture film, and 20th century cameras; Northern Arizona Pioneers' Historical Society Library and Archives; Elbert Hubbard-Roycroft Press Collection; Norman Allderdice Collection (20th century social and political issues). **Holdings:** 11,000 books; 1250 bound periodical volumes; 3000 linear feet of manuscript and archival materials; 3500 pamphlets; 500 oral history tapes; 250,000 photographs; 800 reels of microfilm; 500 motion picture films. **Subscriptions:** 300 journals and other serials; 25 newspapers. **Services:** Interlibrary loans; library open to public. **Computerized Information Services:** Computerized cataloging and serials. **Special Indexes:** Historical Index to the Arizona Champion-Coconino Sun Newspaper of Flagstaff, 1883 to 1894; Spanish Southwest, 1519-1776 and after; A Guide to Spanish Southwest Literature in the NAU Libraries, 1976; Selected Bibliography of Grand Canyon Literature in the NAU Libraries, 1978; Emery Kolb, A Guide to the Kolb Collection in the NAU Libraries, 1980.

NORTHERN CALIFORNIA AMERICAN CIVIL LIBERTIES UNION ARCHIVE
See: California Historical Society - Schubert Hall Library

★9350★
NORTHERN COLLEGE - HAILEYBURY SCHOOL OF MINES - LIBRARY (Sci-Tech)
Latchford St.   Phone: (705) 672-3376
Haileybury, ON, Canada P0J 1K0   Maureen Taeger, Libn.
Founded: 1959. **Staff:** Prof 1; Other 1. **Subjects:** Mining, geology. **Special Collections:** Publications and maps of the Ontario Department of Mines and Geological Survey of Canada; Mining Institutes Transactions (446 items). **Holdings:** 6196 books; 3113 government reports; 6698 maps. **Subscriptions:** 150 journals and other serials; 9 newspapers. **Services:** Interlibrary loans; copying; library open to public.

NORTHERN FOREST RESEARCH CENTRE
See: Canada - Canadian Forestry Service

★9351★
NORTHERN ILLINOIS UNIVERSITY - CENTER FOR BIOPOLITICAL RESEARCH - LIBRARY (Soc Sci)
                                                   Phone: (815) 753-0431
DeKalb, IL 60115   Thomas C. Wiegele, Dir.
Subjects: Evolutionary theory, biology of behavior/ethology, biotechnology, bioethics, biopolicy, philosophy of science. **Holdings:** 500 books. **Subscriptions:** 50 journals and other serials. **Services:** Library open to public by permission.

NORTHERN ILLINOIS UNIVERSITY - CLEARINGHOUSE FOR SOCIOLOGICAL LITERATURE
See: Clearinghouse for Sociological Literature

★9352★
NORTHERN ILLINOIS UNIVERSITY - FARADAY LIBRARY (Sci-Tech)†
Faraday Hall, Rm. 212   Phone: (815) 753-1257
DeKalb, IL 60115   Paul L. Knapp, Sci.Libn.
Founded: 1964. **Staff:** Prof 1; Other 1. **Subjects:** Chemistry, physics. **Holdings:** 16,172 books; 20,388 bound periodical volumes; 320 volumes of bound government documents; 4881 unbound government documents; 323 reels of microfilm; 4038 microfiche; 9551 microcards. **Subscriptions:** 532 journals and other serials. **Services:** Interlibrary loans; copying; library open to public with restrictions.

★9353★
NORTHERN ILLINOIS UNIVERSITY - MUSIC LIBRARY (Mus)
175 Music Bldg.   Phone: (815) 753-1426
DeKalb, IL 60115   Gordon S. Rowley, Music Libn.
Founded: 1974. **Staff:** Prof 1; Other 2. **Subjects:** Music. **Holdings:** 28,000 books and scores; 2100 bound periodical volumes; 18,000 sound recordings; 65 Master's degree theses. **Subscriptions:** 196 journals and other serials. **Services:** Interlibrary loans; copying; library open with full service to Illinois residents; open to others for room use only. **Computerized Information Services:** Computerized cataloging, acquisitions and circulation. **Networks/Consortia:** Member of OCLC.

★9354★
NORTHERN ILLINOIS UNIVERSITY - REGIONAL HISTORY CENTER (Hist)†
268 Swen Parson Hall   Phone: (815) 753-1779
DeKalb, IL 60115   Glen A. Gildemeister, Dir.
Founded: 1978. **Staff:** Prof 3; Other 4. **Subjects:** Northern Illinois history. **Holdings:** 800 books; 1200 linear feet of manuscripts; 200 AV items; 3000 vertical file items. **Services:** Copying; library open to public. **Staff:** Marcia Sommerfeld, Archv.; Robert W. Graham, Field Rep.

★9355★
NORTHERN ILLINOIS UNIVERSITY - SOUTHEAST ASIA COLLECTION (Area-Ethnic)
Founders Memorial Library   Phone: (815) 753-1819
DeKalb, IL 60115   Lee Dutton, Libn.
Founded: 1963. **Staff:** Prof 1; Other 1. **Subjects:** Southeast Asia, including history, art history, economics, politics, sociology, anthropology and linguistics of Thailand, Philippines, Indonesia, Malaysia, Burma, Indochina. **Special Collections:** Thai Collection (8200 volumes in Thai); Philippine American Collection; modern Indonesia microfiche collection; N.P.A.C. holdings for Malaysia, Singapore, Brunei, Indonesia. **Holdings:** 39,000 books; 3230 bound periodical volumes; 38 VF drawers of pamphlets, reports; Southeast Asian newspapers on 1300 reels of microfilm. **Subscriptions:** 2000 journals and other serials; 54 newspapers. **Services:** Interlibrary loans; copying; library open to public with restrictions. **Computerized Information Services:** Computerized cataloging, acquisitions and circulation. **Networks/Consortia:** Member of OCLC; CRL; Southeast Asia Microform Project (SEAM). **Publications:** A Guide to the Southeast Asia Collection, 1972; Newspapers in the Southeast Asia Collection, 1976; Southeast Asia Collection Bibliographic Notes, irregular. **Special Catalogs:** Card catalog of Southeast Asia holdings.

★9356★
NORTHERN ILLINOIS UNIVERSITY - UNIVERSITY ARCHIVES (Hist)†
                                                   Phone: (815) 753-1779
DeKalb, IL 60115   Glen A. Gildemeister, Archv.
Founded: 1964. **Staff:** Prof 1; Other 1. **Special Collections:** Charles Alexander McMurry Papers (3 linear feet and 40 volumes); John W. Cook Papers (8 linear feet). **Holdings:** 765 linear feet of university records; 1455 cubic feet of state and local records; 607 reels of microfilm; 637 reels of phonotapes; 85,000 photographs and negatives; university records; faculty and alumni records. **Services:** Interlibrary loans; copying; library open to public.

★9357★
NORTHERN INDIANA HISTORICAL SOCIETY - FREDERICK ELBEL LIBRARY (Hist)
112 S. Lafayette Blvd.   Phone: (219) 284-9664
South Bend, IN 46601   James Sullivan, Musm.Dir.
Founded: 1895. **Staff:** 1. **Subjects:** Indian history and language; Indiana history; French, Indian, English, and American occupations of South Bend and Saint Joseph County. **Holdings:** 7500 books; 925 pamphlets; 300 boxes of archives (manuscripts, dissertations, documents); 1 filing drawer of clippings; 25 oral history tapes. **Subscriptions:** 25 journals and other serials. **Services:** Copying; library open to public for reference use only. **Publications:** Old Courthouse News, quarterly.

★9358★
NORTHERN KENTUCKY UNIVERSITY - SALMON P. CHASE COLLEGE OF LAW - LIBRARY (Law)
Highland Heights, KY 41076
Phone: (606) 572-5394
Carol B. Allred, Law Lib.Dir.
Founded: 1893. **Staff:** Prof 6; Other 8. **Subjects:** Law. **Special Collections:** Depository for U.S. 6th Circuit Court of Appeals Briefs and Records. **Holdings:** 156,000 volumes; 49,400 volumes in microform. **Subscriptions:** 540 journals and other serials; 6 newspapers. **Services:** Interlibrary loans; copying; library open to public. **Computerized Information Services:** LEXIS. **Networks/Consortia:** Member of OCLC through SOLINET. **Formerly:** Located in Covington, KY. **Staff:** Thomas French, Tech.Serv.Libn.; Claudia Zaher, Rd.Serv.Libn.; Donna Bennett, Rd.Serv.Libn.; Debbie Epstein, Rd.Serv.Libn.; Linda Newman, Cat.Libn.; Carol Bredemeyer, Rd.Serv.Libn.

NORTHERN MICHIGAN HOSPITALS, INC.
See: Burns (Dean C.) Health Sciences Library

★9359★
NORTHERN MINER - LIBRARY (Sci-Tech; Publ)
7 Labatt Ave.
Toronto, ON, Canada M5A 1Z1
Phone: (416) 368-3481
Mrs. M. Murray, Libn.
Staff: 1. **Subjects:** Mines, mineral resources, oil and gas; metallurgy; geology; mineralogy. **Special Collections:** Status files on 20,000 dormant and/or defunct mining companies. **Holdings:** 2000 books. **Subscriptions:** 40 journals and other serials. **Services:** Copying; library open to public. **Publications:** Canadian Mines Handbook; Canadian Oil and Gas Handbook, both annual.

★9360★
NORTHERN MONTANA COLLEGE - LIBRARY (Educ)†
Havre, MT 59501
Phone: (406) 265-7821
Terrence A. Thompson, Dir. of Lib.
Staff: Prof 2; Other 2. **Subjects:** Education, history, literature, industrial arts. **Holdings:** 85,000 books; 9000 bound periodical volumes; 18 VF drawers of pamphlets; 170,000 titles on microfiche. **Subscriptions:** 683 journals. **Services:** Interlibrary loans; copying; library open to public. **Computerized Information Services:** Online systems through Montana State Library. **Networks/Consortia:** Member of Consortium of Academic and Special Libraries in Montana (CASLIM). **Staff:** Elaine Kipp, Ref.Libn.

★9361★
NORTHERN PETROCHEMICAL COMPANY - TECHNICAL CENTER LIBRARY (Sci-Tech)
Morris, IL 60450
Phone: (815) 942-7558
Ingrid M. Voss, Libn.
Founded: 1970. **Staff:** Prof 1; Other 1. **Subjects:** Chemistry, physics, business, government regulations, plastics. **Holdings:** 2000 books; 1550 bound periodical volumes; 6 drawers of patents. **Subscriptions:** 101 journals and other serials. **Services:** Interlibrary loans; copying; library open to public. **Computerized Information Services:** New England Research Application Center (NERAC), SDC; internal database. **Networks/Consortia:** Member of OCLC through ILLINET; Bur Oak Library System.

★9362★
NORTHERN PIGMENT LIMITED - TECHNICAL LIBRARY (Sci-Tech)†
35 Towns Rd.
P.O. Box One, Station N
Etobicoke, ON, Canada M8V 3S5
Phone: (416) 251-1161
W. Nord, V.P., Oper.
Staff: 2. **Subjects:** Magnetism, physical and inorganic chemistry, ferrite processing and properties, electron microscopy, iron oxide pigments. **Special Collections:** Ferrite and electronic ceramics collection; American Society for Testing and Materials X-ray diffraction file inorganic sets 1-20. **Holdings:** 386 books and bound periodical volumes; 100 patents. **Subscriptions:** 20 journals and other serials. **Services:** Library open to public with prior clearance.

NORTHERN PRAIRIE WILDLIFE RESEARCH CENTER LIBRARY
See: U.S. Fish & Wildlife Service

NORTHERN REGION OPERATION INFORMATION SERVICE
See: Canada - National Defence - Northern Region Reference Library

★9363★
NORTHERN RESEARCH & ENGINEERING CORPORATION - LIBRARY (Sci-Tech)
39 Olympia Ave.
Woburn, MA 01801
Phone: (617) 935-9050
Mary Frances O'Brien, Libn.
Staff: Prof 1. **Subjects:** Compressors, turbines, pumps, combustion, aeronautics. **Holdings:** 200 books; 10,100 technical reports. **Subscriptions:**

100 journals and other serials. **Services:** Library not open to public. **Computerized Information Services:** DIALOG.

★9364★
NORTHERN STATES POWER COMPANY - "ASK NSP" TAPE LIBRARY (Energy)
414 Nicollet Mall
Minneapolis, MN 55401
Phone: (612) 330-6000
Mr. Lynn M. Gustafson, Supv.
Staff: Prof 2. **Subjects:** Alternative energy, customer information, electricity, fuels, government, heating and cooling, natural gas, safety, weatherization. **Holdings:** 172 tapes - scripts are available upon request at no cost. **Services:** Energy reference service; library open to public. **Staff:** Marilyn Post, Energy Info.Cons.

NORTHERN STUDIES LIBRARY
See: Mc Gill University

★9365★
NORTHERN TELECOM CANADA, LTD. - BUSINESS SYSTEMS LIBRARY (Info Sci)
304 The East Mall
Islington, ON, Canada M9B 6E4
Phone: (416) 232-2000
Karen J. Ryan, Data Adm.Libn.
Founded: 1978. **Staff:** Prof 1. **Subjects:** In-house systems documentation, software and hardware vendors, computer science. **Special Collections:** Hardware and software vendor and product information; systems management. **Holdings:** 900 books. **Subscriptions:** 55 journals and other serials. **Services:** Interlibrary loans; copying; library not open to public. **Computerized Information Services:** Data Dictionary (internal database). **Special Catalogs:** Software manuals; Data Dictionary/Directory System.

★9366★
NORTHERN TELECOM CANADA, LTD. - LIBRARY & TECHNICAL INFORMATION CENTRE (Sci-Tech)
P.O. Box 6122, Sta. A
Montreal, PQ, Canada H3C 3J4
Phone: (514) 634-3511
Miss M.Y. Pollock, Mgr.
Founded: 1953. **Staff:** 2. **Subjects:** Communication, rubber and plastic technology, analytical chemistry, spectroscopy, electrical and electronics processes and equipment, finance and accounting, administration and personnel, management science, data processing. **Holdings:** 4800 books and bound periodical volumes; 6 VF drawers of internal reports; 5000 specifications. **Subscriptions:** 100 journals and other serials. **Services:** Interlibrary loans; copying; library not open to public. **Computerized Information Services:** SDC. **Publications:** Magazine Perusal, biweekly; Technical Reports and Memos, biweekly; Library Bulletin, monthly - all for internal distribution only. **Special Indexes:** Cumulative index of internal technical reports.

★9367★
NORTHERN TELECOM CANADA, LTD. - NT LIBRARY (Sci-Tech; Bus-Fin)
304 The East Mall
Islington, ON, Canada M9B 6E4
Phone: (416) 232-2000
Eileen Daniel, Libn.
Founded: 1928. **Staff:** Prof 1; Other 1. **Subjects:** Telecommunications, electronics, business and finance, management, industrial relations. **Holdings:** 5000 books; 2000 bound periodical volumes. **Subscriptions:** 750 journals and other serials; 30 newspapers. **Services:** Interlibrary loans; copying; library not open to public. **Computerized Information Services:** DIALOG, SDC, Info Globe, CAN/OLE; computerized cataloging and journal routing.

★9368★
NORTHERN TRUST COMPANY - LIBRARY (Bus-Fin)
50 S. LaSalle St.
Chicago, IL 60675
Phone: (312) 630-6000
Marianne S. Lee, Hd.Libn.
Founded: 1950. **Staff:** Prof 2; Other 2. **Subjects:** Banking, finance, investments, accounting, management. **Special Collections:** Moody's Manuals (1930 to present); Commercial & Financial Chronicle (1947 to present); Central Bank Bulletins (40 countries). **Holdings:** 3000 books; 25 VF drawers of pamphlets. **Subscriptions:** 1000 journals and other serials; 38 newspapers. **Services:** Interlibrary loans; library open to public for reference use only on request through banking or trust officer. **Computerized Information Services:** DIALOG, Dow Jones News Retrieval, New York Times Information Service. **Networks/Consortia:** Member of Metropolitan Chicago Library Assembly; RLG. **Publications:** Library Notes, bimonthly - for internal distribution only. **Staff:** Kathryn M. Camp, Asst.Libn.

★9369★
NORTHERN WESTCHESTER HOSPITAL CENTER - HEALTH SCIENCES LIBRARY (Med)
Mount Kisco, NY 10549
Phone: (914) 666-1259
Nona C. Willoughby, Hd.Libn.
Founded: 1960. **Staff:** Prof 1; Other 1. **Subjects:** Clinical medicine, basic

sciences, nursing. **Holdings:** 2200 books; 1700 bound periodical volumes; 800 cassettes. **Subscriptions:** 134 journals and other serials. **Services:** Interlibrary loans; copying; library open to public. **Computerized Information Services:** MEDLARS. **Networks/Consortia:** Member of Health Information Libraries of Westchester (HILOW); Union Catalog of Medical Periodicals (UCMP).

★9370★
NORTHERN WISCONSIN CENTER FOR THE DEVELOPMENTALLY DISABLED - LIBRARY/INSTRUCTIONAL MATERIALS CENTER (Educ)
E. Park Ave.
Box 340   Phone: (715) 723-5542
Chippewa Falls, WI 54729   Robert Carlsen, Teacher-Libn.
Founded: 1959. **Staff:** Prof 1; Other 1. **Subjects:** Education and recreation of the mentally handicapped; psychology; arts and crafts; medical aspects of the mentally handicapped. **Special Collections:** Educational materials for severely and profoundly mentally retarded; Medical Library for staff; Education of the Retarded collection. **Holdings:** 6035 books; 250 other cataloged items; 4644 AV materials; 4 VF drawers. **Subscriptions:** 68 journals and other serials. **Services:** Interlibrary loans; library open to public. **Networks/Consortia:** Member of Regional Medical Library - Region 3; Regional Developmental Disabilities Information Center; Western Wisconsin Council of Libraries. **Publications:** Bibliography, biennial - to department heads. **Special Catalogs:** Union Catalog; IMC Accession List; Basic Academic Subject Skills Index.

★9371★
NORTHMINSTER UNITED PRESBYTERIAN CHURCH - LIBRARY (Rel-Theol)†
2434 Wilmington Rd.   Phone: (412) 658-9051
New Castle, PA 16105   Helen Sloat, Church Libn.
Subjects: Religion. **Holdings:** 3085 books. **Services:** Library is open to responsible persons.

★9372★
NORTHPORT-EAST NORTHPORT SCHOOL DISTRICT - TEACHERS' PROFESSIONAL LIBRARY (Educ)†
110 Elwood Rd.
Northport, NY 11768   Edwin Sorensen, Hd.
Staff: Prof 1; Other 1. **Subjects:** Education. **Holdings:** 3000 books. **Subscriptions:** 80 journals and other serials. **Services:** Library open to public. **Remarks:** Maintained by Union Free School District 4.

★9373★
NORTHROP CORPORATION - AIRCRAFT DIVISION - LIBRARY SERVICES (Sci-Tech)
One Northrop Ave.   Phone: (213) 970-4136
Hawthorne, CA 90250   John E. Reynolds, Lib.Mgr.
Founded: 1942. **Staff:** Prof 5; Other 7. **Subjects:** Aerospace sciences, materials, aeronautical engineering. **Holdings:** 14,000 books; 1000 bound periodical volumes; 50,000 reports (cataloged); 9000 military specifications and standards; 15,000 military manuals, regulations, handbooks; 275,000 reports on microfiche. **Subscriptions:** 520 journals and other serials. **Services:** Interlibrary loans; library not open to public. **Computerized Information Services:** DIALOG, DTIC, NASA/RECON. **Networks/Consortia:** Member of CLASS. **Publications:** Accessions List - for internal distribution only; Library Guide, subscription list. **Staff:** Jill Napier, Mil.Pubn./Cat.Libn.; Marilyn Greenbaum, Br./Ref.; Carrol Speich, Acq.Libn.; Renee Soiffer, Ref.Libn.

★9374★
NORTHROP CORPORATION - ELECTRO-MECHANICAL DIVISION - TECHNICAL INFORMATION CENTER (Sci-Tech)
500 E. Orangethorpe Ave.   Phone: (714) 871-5000
Anaheim, CA 92801   B.J. Duba, Mgr.
Founded: 1952. **Staff:** 3. **Subjects:** Automatic test equipment; machinery noise monitoring; command control and communications; laser systems; guidance and control; operations systems analysis. **Holdings:** 4900 books; 4600 bound periodical volumes; 25,000 reports (cataloged); vendor catalogs on microfilm. **Subscriptions:** 250 journals and other serials. **Services:** Interlibrary loans; copying (both limited); center not open to public. **Publications:** Accessions List, monthly; Periodical Holdings List, annual.

★9375★
NORTHROP CORPORATION - RESEARCH AND TECHNOLOGY CENTER - LIBRARY SERVICES (Sci-Tech)
One Research Park   Phone: (213) 377-4811
Palos Verdes Peninsula, CA 90274
Founded: 1967. **Staff:** Prof 1; Other 1. **Subjects:** Laser research, solid state electronics, optics, image processing. **Holdings:** 6900 books; 3832 bound

periodical volumes; 5000 technical reports. **Subscriptions:** 267 journals and other serials. **Services:** Interlibrary loans; copying (limited); library not open to public. **Computerized Information Services:** DIALOG. **Publications:** Acquisitions list, monthly; list of current subscriptions, semiannual.

★9376★
NORTHROP CORPORATION - VENTURA DIVISION - TECHNICAL INFORMATION CENTER (Sci-Tech)
1515 Rancho Conejo Blvd.   Phone: (805) 498-3131
Newbury Park, CA 91320   Marjorie Raine, Lib.Asst.Sr.
Founded: 1952. **Staff:** 2. **Subjects:** Target drones. **Holdings:** 6250 books; 700 bound periodical volumes; 200 VF drawers of reports and documents. **Subscriptions:** 150 journals and other serials. **Services:** Interlibrary loans; center not open to public.

NORTHROP (Preston G.) MEMORIAL LIBRARY
See: Southwest Foundation for Research and Education - Preston G. Northrop Memorial Library

★9377★
NORTHROP UNIVERSITY - ALUMNI LIBRARY - SPECIAL COLLECTIONS (Sci-Tech; Hist; Law)†
1155 W. Arbor Vitae St.   Phone: (213) 776-5466
Inglewood, CA 90306   Chere Negaard, Dir., Lib.Serv.
Founded: 1942. **Special Collections:** Aviation history (140,000 items); law library (11,554 volumes); Pacific Technical Information Services. **Services:** Interlibrary loans; copying; library open to industry on a fee basis. **Computerized Information Services:** Computerized serials. **Special Catalogs:** Aviation history (card). **Remarks:** Includes the holdings of the American Institute of Aeronautics and Astronautics - Pacific Aerospace Library.

★9378★
NORTHSIDE HOSPITAL - WOODRUFF HEALTH SCIENCE LIBRARY (Med)
1000 Johnson Ferry Rd., N.E.   Phone: (404) 256-8744
Atlanta, GA 30042   Sharon Cann, Libn.
Founded: 1971. **Staff:** Prof 1; Other 1. **Subjects:** Medicine, nursing, psychiatry, health science. **Holdings:** 700 books; 300 AV items (cataloged); 6 vertical files. **Subscriptions:** 158 journals and other serials. **Services:** Interlibrary loans; copying; library not open to public. **Computerized Information Services:** MEDLINE. **Networks/Consortia:** Member of Atlanta Health Science Libraries Consortium; Georgia Library Information Network (GLIN); Southeastern Regional Medical Library Program (SERMLP).

★9379★
NORTHUMBERLAND COUNTY LAW LIBRARY (Law)
Court House   Phone: (717) 286-0147
Sunbury, PA 17801   Pauline M. Sokalzuk, Law Libn.
Staff: Prof 1. **Subjects:** Law. **Holdings:** 13,200 books and bound periodical volumes. **Subscriptions:** 10 journals and other serials. **Services:** Interlibrary loans; copying; library open to public.

★9380★
NORTHVILLE HISTORICAL SOCIETY - LIBRARY (Hist)
No. 1 Griswold
Box 71   Phone: (313) 348-1845
Northville, MI 48167   Carol L. Butske, Libn.
Staff: 3. **Subjects:** Architecture, historic preservation. **Holdings:** 300 books; archival material. **Services:** Library open to public by appointment.

★9381★
NORTHVILLE REGIONAL PSYCHIATRIC HOSPITAL - PROFESSIONAL LIBRARY (Med)
41001 W. 7 Mile Rd.   Phone: (313) 349-1800
Northville, MI 48167
Founded: 1953. **Subjects:** Medicine, psychiatry, psychology, social service, nursing. **Holdings:** 3057 volumes; 285 cassettes; 100 reprints; magnetic tapes for closed circuit TV. **Subscriptions:** 83 journals and other serials. **Services:** Interlibrary loans; copying; library not open to public. **Networks/Consortia:** Member of Kentucky-Ohio-Michigan Regional Medical Library Network (KOMRML).

★9382★
NORTHWEST ALABAMA COUNCIL OF LOCAL GOVERNMENTS - LIBRARY (Plan)†
Box 2603   Phone: (205) 383-3861
Muscle Shoals, AL 35660   Leon Graham, Exec.Dir.
Founded: 1967. **Staff:** Prof 1; Other 1. **Subjects:** Transportation, energy. **Special Collections:** Regional Data Center for Alabama State Data System

(Census Bureau). **Holdings:** 1500 books and bound periodical volumes; 500 pamphlets (cataloged); 4 VF drawers of clippings; 1 VF drawer of documents; 500 maps. **Subscriptions:** 6 newspapers. **Services:** Copying; library open to public. **Computerized Information Services:** Computerized cataloging. **Remarks:** Library is located at 204 Annapolis Ave., Sheffield, AL 35630.

NORTHWEST ARKANSAS HEALTH EDUCATION CENTER
See: University of Arkansas, Fayetteville - Medical Center

★9383★
NORTHWEST BANCORPORATION - LIBRARY (Bus-Fin)
1200 Northwestern Bank Bldg.   Phone: (612) 372-8263
Minneapolis, MN 55403   Marilyn J. Schlee, Lib.Serv.Off.
Founded: 1952. **Staff:** Prof 1; Other 2. **Subjects:** Banking, business management, economics, personnel and office management, industrial relations, industry studies. **Holdings:** 2000 books; 26 shelves of subject files; 16 shelves of corporate and bank annual reports. **Subscriptions:** 300 journals and other serials. **Services:** Interlibrary loans; library open to public with restrictions. **Computerized Information Services:** NEXIS. **Publications:** Monthly list of magazine articles and new books - for internal distribution only.

★9384★
NORTHWEST BAPTIST THEOLOGICAL COLLEGE AND SEMINARY - LIBRARY (Rel-Theol)
3358 S.E. Marine Dr.   Phone: (604) 433-2475
Vancouver, BC, Canada V5S 3W3   W.B. Badke, Libn.
Staff: Prof 1. **Subjects:** Theology. **Holdings:** 15,000 books. **Subscriptions:** 170 journals and other serials. **Services:** Library open to public at the discretion of the librarian.

★9385★
NORTHWEST BIBLE COLLEGE - J.C. COOKE LIBRARY (Rel-Theol)
11617 106th Ave.   Phone: (403) 452-0808
Edmonton, AB, Canada T5H 0S1   Braden S. Fawcett, Libn.
Founded: 1979. **Staff:** Prof 1; Other 1. **Subjects:** Theology, religion, Christian education, homiletics, church history, pastoral counseling. **Holdings:** 8000 books, clippings, archival material. **Subscriptions:** 20 journals and other serials. **Services:** Copying; library not open to public. **Remarks:** Contains the faculty library known as Hillerud Memorial Library.

★9386★
NORTHWEST BIBLE COLLEGE - LIBRARY (Rel-Theol)
1900 8th Ave., S.E.   Phone: (701) 852-3781
Minot, ND 58701   Clyde R. Root, Hd.Libn.
Founded: 1934. **Staff:** 2. **Subjects:** Bible, religion, theology, Christian education, music, liberal arts. **Special Collections:** Church of God History (Cleveland, Tennessee); Pentecostal and Holiness material. **Holdings:** 32,468 books and bound periodical volumes; 3685 pamphlets; 1829 microforms. **Subscriptions:** 98 journals and other serials. **Services:** Interlibrary loans; copying; library open to public.

★9387★
NORTHWEST CHRISTIAN COLLEGE - LEARNING RESOURCE CENTER (Rel-Theol)
828 E. 11th   Phone: (503) 343-1641
Eugene, OR 97401   Margaret W. Hewitt, Dir.
Founded: 1895. **Staff:** Prof 2; Other 3. **Subjects:** Religion and theology, Church Growth Movement. **Special Collections:** Rare books and Bibles; Disciplina representing Christian Church (Disciples of Christ) Northwest; archives; missionary papers. **Holdings:** 55,000 volumes; 3120 bound periodical volumes; 250 cubic feet of manuscripts and unlisted serials; 472 reels of microfilm. **Subscriptions:** 390 journals and other serials; 6 newspapers. **Services:** Interlibrary loans; copying; library open to public with restrictions on use of special collections. **Networks/Consortia:** Member of OCLC. **Publications:** Friends of the Library Newsletter, bi-annual. **Staff:** Sue M. Rhee, Tech.Serv.; Aulani Mahoe, Lib.Asst.; Leta Hamm, Circ. & Per.; Phillip Gibson, AV.

★9388★
NORTHWEST COLLEGE OF THE ASSEMBLIES OF GOD - HURST LIBRARY (Rel-Theol)†
11102 N.E. 53rd Ave.
Box 579
Kirkland, WA 98033   Phone: (206) 822-8266
                    Ruth Petty, Libn.
Founded: 1949. **Staff:** Prof 2; Other 3. **Subjects:** Religion, social sciences, history, literature. **Special Collections:** Ness Bible Translations Reference Collection; Pentecostal Movement Collection; Kenneth Schlosser Near East Collection. **Holdings:** 49,372 books; 4047 bound periodical volumes; 3962 microfiche; 284 filmstrips; 1749 reels, recordings, kits. **Subscriptions:** 317

journals and other serials; 8 newspapers. **Services:** Interlibrary loans; copying; library open to public for reference use only. **Networks/Consortia:** Member of University of Washington Libraries Resource Sharing Program (UWRSP). **Publications:** Faculty and student manuals. **Special Catalogs:** Catalog to the sermons of Dr. Charles S. Price. **Also Known As:** Assemblies of God Northwest College. **Staff:** Margaret Frye, Asst.Libn.; Anne Schefter, Tech.Serv.Asst.; Dennis Lee, ILL.

★9389★
NORTHWEST COMMUNITY HOSPITAL - MEDICAL LIBRARY (Med)
800 West Central Rd.   Phone: (312) 259-1000
Arlington Heights, IL 60005   Sharon Glinski, Med.Libn.
Staff: Prof 1. **Subjects:** Medicine, nursing. **Holdings:** 800 books; 4000 bound periodical volumes; 4 VF drawers of pamphlets. **Subscriptions:** 300 journals and other serials. **Services:** Interlibrary loans; copying; SDI; library open to public with restrictions. **Computerized Information Services:** MEDLINE. **Networks/Consortia:** Member of Illinois Health Library Consortium.

NORTHWEST FILM STUDY CENTER
See: Portland Art Association

★9390★
NORTHWEST GENERAL HOSPITAL - MEDICAL LIBRARY (Med)
5310 W. Capitol Dr.   Phone: (414) 447-8599
Milwaukee, WI 53216   Coralyn Marks, Lib.Dir.
Staff: Prof 2. **Subjects:** Medicine, nursing. **Holdings:** 925 books; 300 bound periodical volumes. **Subscriptions:** 187 journals and other serials. **Services:** Interlibrary loans; copying; library not open to public. **Networks/Consortia:** Member of Southeastern Wisconsin Health Science Libraries Consortium. **Staff:** Connie Taagen, Med.Libn.

★9391★
NORTHWEST GEORGIA REGIONAL HOSPITAL AT ROME - MEDICAL LIBRARY (Med)†
Redmond Rd.   Phone: (404) 295-6060
Rome, GA 30161   James R. Fletcher, Lib.Ck.
Founded: 1946. **Staff:** 1. **Subjects:** Chest, tuberculosis, psychiatry, psychology, mental retardation, alcoholism. **Holdings:** 916 books; 1003 bound periodical volumes; 659 audiotapes; 4 VF drawers; 13 videotapes. **Subscriptions:** 64 journals and other serials. **Services:** Interlibrary loans; copying; library open to public with legitimate need for medical information. **Publications:** Library Handbook - for internal distribution only.

★9392★
NORTHWEST HOSPITAL - EFFIE M. STOREY LEARNING CENTER (Med)
1550 North 115th   Phone: (206) 364-0500
Seattle, WA 98133   Marilyn R. Carlson, Libn.
Founded: 1975. **Staff:** Prof 2. **Subjects:** Medicine, nursing, management. **Holdings:** 500 books; 100 videotapes; 100 audiotapes; 15 sets of slides. **Subscriptions:** 80 journals and other serials. **Services:** Interlibrary loans; copying; SDI; library not open to public. **Publications:** Current Literature, bimonthly - for internal distribution only. **Special Catalogs:** Audiovisual Resources (booklet). **Staff:** Ivan L. Buck, AV Coord.

★9393★
NORTHWEST HOSPITAL - MEDICAL LIBRARY (Med)
5645 W. Addison St.   Phone: (312) 282-7000
Chicago, IL 60634   Therese Wiedenfeld, Libn.
Founded: 1973. **Staff:** Prof 1; Other 1. **Subjects:** Medicine and allied health sciences. **Holdings:** 750 books; 7200 bound periodical volumes. **Subscriptions:** 204 journals and other serials. **Services:** Interlibrary loans; copying; SDI; library open to relatives of staff and employees. **Networks/Consortia:** Member of Illinois Health Libraries Consortium; ILLINET; Regional Medical Library - Region 3.

★9394★
NORTHWEST INDUSTRIES LTD. - TECHNICAL DATA CONTROL CENTRE (Sci-Tech)
Municipal Airport
Box 517   Phone: (403) 455-3161
Edmonton, AB, Canada T5J 2K5   C.E. "Chuck" Buckley, Supv.
Staff: 6. **Subjects:** Aircraft maintenance, engineering, military and federal specifications. **Holdings:** 300 books; 500 bound periodical volumes; 40,000 military technical manuals; 55,000 specifications on microfiche; 100,000 blueprints and specifications on aperture cards; 25,000 blueprints and masters. **Subscriptions:** 150 journals and other serials; 5 newspapers. **Services:** Library open to public except for classified materials.

★9395★

NORTHWEST MINNESOTA HISTORICAL CENTER - LIBRARY (Hist)
Moorhead State University Library   Phone: (218) 236-2812
Moorhead, MN 56560   Evelyn J. Swenson, Dir.
Founded: 1972. **Staff:** Prof 1; Other 3. **Subjects:** Ethnicity in Northwest Minnesota, social welfare, politics, government, business, church history, oral history, women's organizations. **Special Collections:** Scandinavian ethnic retention; World War II on the Homefront in the Red River Valley of the North; The Depressions in the Red River Valley of the North. **Holdings:** 546 linear feet of local history materials; microfilm; oral history cassettes; slides. **Services:** Copying; research aid; library open to public. **Publications:** Scandinavian Heritage, Guide to the Holdings of the Northwest Minnesota Historical Center. **Remarks:** The center is maintained by Moorhead State University. **Formerly:** Minnesota Historical Society - Northwest Minnesota Historical Center.

★9396★

NORTHWEST MISSOURI STATE UNIVERSITY - HORACE MANN LEARNING CENTER (Educ)
    Phone: (816) 582-7141
Maryville, MO 64468   Nancy C. Hanks, Asst.Prof./Libn.
Staff: Prof 2. **Subjects:** Children's literature. **Holdings:** 14,580 books; 721 item curriculum collection; 50 multi-media kits; 3800 filmstrips; 740 records; 260 tapes; 150 film loops; 2500 slides; 1200 pictures and art prints; 100 transparencies; 55 titles of computer software. **Subscriptions:** 83 journals and other serials. **Services:** Library open to public. **Remarks:** This library serves as the research and resource center for the Elementary Education and the Library Science Departments of the University. **Staff:** Holly Stuart, Libn.

★9397★

NORTHWEST MISSOURI STATE UNIVERSITY - WELLS LIBRARY - SPECIAL COLLECTIONS (Educ; Hist)†
    Phone: (816) 582-7141
Maryville, MO 64468   Charles W. Koch, Dir., Lrng.Rsrcs.
Founded: 1905. **Special Collections:** Missouriana (2300 volumes); Laboratory School Library; university archives (24 drawers). **Services:** Interlibrary loans; copying (fee); library open to public with restrictions. **Computerized Information Services:** Online systems; computerized cataloging. **Networks/Consortia:** Member of OCLC; Northwest Missouri Library Network.

★9398★

NORTHWEST MUNICIPAL CONFERENCE - GOVERNMENT INFORMATION CENTER (Soc Sci)
Mt. Prospect Public Library
10 S. Emerson St.   Phone: (312) 398-6460
Mt. Prospect, IL 60056   Kenneth L. Gross, Lib.Serv.Dir.
Staff: Prof 1; Other 1. **Subjects:** Municipal government, public administration, Illinois rules and regulations. **Holdings:** 6200 books; 400 pamphlets. **Subscriptions:** 20 journals and other serials. **Services:** Interlibrary loans; copying; library open to public. **Networks/Consortia:** Member of ILLINET. **Remarks:** This library is also a partial federal depository.

★9399★

NORTHWEST PULP AND PAPER ASSOCIATION - TECHNICAL INFORMATION CENTER
555 116th Ave., N.E., Suite 266
Bellevue, WA 98004
Founded: 1957. **Subjects:** Environmental regulations, emissions, effluents, pollution expenditures. **Holdings:** 450 books and bound periodical volumes; 200 NCASI reports (cataloged). **Remarks:** Presently inactive.

★9400★

NORTHWEST REGIONAL EDUCATIONAL LABORATORY - CENTER FOR PERFORMANCE ASSESSMENT (Educ)
300 S.W. Sixth Ave.   Phone: (503) 248-6800
Portland, OR 97204   Richard J. Stiggins, Dir.
Staff: Prof 2; Other 1. **Subjects:** Assessment of skills in reading, writing, speaking, listening and other areas of skill performance. **Holdings:** 350 references related to performance assessment. **Services:** Center not open to public. **Publications:** CAPTRENDS, quarterly newsletter - free upon request; monograph series - available upon request. **Special Indexes:** Annotated bibliographies on topics within subject collection. **Formerly:** Its Clearinghouse for Applied Performance Testing. **Staff:** Nancy J. Bridgeford, Prog.Spec.

★9401★

NORTHWEST REGIONAL EDUCATIONAL LABORATORY - INFORMATION CENTER/LIBRARY (Educ)
300 S.W. Sixth Ave.   Phone: (503) 248-6800
Portland, OR 97204   M. Margaret Rogers, Dir.Info.Serv.
Founded: 1966. **Staff:** Prof 2; Other 1. **Subjects:** Educational research, psychology, evaluation, career education, computer applications in education. **Special Collections:** ERIC microfiche collection and special indexes. **Holdings:** 4250 books and bound periodical volumes; 32 VF drawers of pamphlets; 5 shelves of ERIC Clearinghouse Publications. **Subscriptions:** 300 journals and other serials; 10 newspapers. **Services:** Interlibrary loans; copying; SDI; center open to public. **Computerized Information Services:** DIALOG, BRS. **Networks/Consortia:** Member of National Institute of Education Research and Development Exchange; Council for Educational Development and Research.

★9402★

NORTHWEST TERRITORIES - GOVERNMENT LIBRARY (Soc Sci)
Laing No. 1   Phone: (403) 873-7628
Yellowknife, NT, Canada X1A 2L9   G. Anderson, Libn.
Staff: Prof 2; Other 1. **Subjects:** Government documents - Northwest Territories and Canada; the Canadian North. **Special Collections:** Full depository for Northwest Territories and federal government documents; complete Mackenzie Valley Pipeline Inquiry. **Holdings:** 20,100 books; 5000 microfiche. **Subscriptions:** 195 journals and other serials; 30 newspapers. **Services:** Interlibrary loans; copying; library open to public. **Publications:** Acquisitions list, irregular.

★9403★

NORTHWESTERN COLLEGE OF CHIROPRACTIC - LIBRARY (Med)
1834 S. Mississippi River Blvd.   Phone: (612) 690-1735
St. Paul, MN 55116   Cheryl A. Bjerke, Dir.
Founded: 1966. **Staff:** Prof 2; Other 3. **Subjects:** Chiropractic, neurology, roentgenology, orthopedics, nutrition, other medical and basic science subjects. **Special Collections:** Diagnostic Radiologic Health Sciences Learning Laboratory (3300 X rays); archives of chiropractic literature (260 items). **Holdings:** 7200 books; 1205 bound periodical volumes; 16 VF drawers of clippings, reprints, and pamphlets; 983 audiotapes; 70 models; 90 video cassettes; 282 slide sets; 1300 microfiche of chiropractic journals. **Subscriptions:** 275 journals and other serials. **Services:** Interlibrary loans; cassette duplication; library open to public with restrictions. **Computerized Information Services:** DIALOG. **Networks/Consortia:** Member of Twin Cities Biomedical Consortium (TCBC); Chiropractic Library Consortium (CLIBCON). **Special Indexes:** Index of chiropractic periodical articles (card); index of Archives from the Canadian Memorial Chiropractic College. **Staff:** Carol Y. Jones, Libn.

★9404★

NORTHWESTERN CONNECTICUT COMMUNITY COLLEGE - LIBRARY (Educ)
Park Place   Phone: (203) 379-8543
Winsted, CT 06098   Arthur Pethybridge, Dir. of Lib.Serv.
Staff: Prof 3; Other 1. **Subjects:** Deaf education, recreation management. **Special Collections:** Matke Collection (plant morphology; 500 titles); World War I (200 titles). **Holdings:** 45,900 books; 1690 phonograph records; 1612 microforms. **Subscriptions:** 257 journals and other serials; 8 newspapers. **Services:** Interlibrary loans; copying; library open to public. **Networks/Consortia:** Member of Northwest Connecticut Library Group, Inc. **Publications:** Library Handbook, annual; Periodical List, annual. **Staff:** Anne Corbett, Libn.; Andrea Dombrowski, Lib. Aide.

★9405★

NORTHWESTERN MEDICAL CENTER - INFORMATION CENTER (Med)
Fairfield St.   Phone: (802) 524-5911
St. Albans, VT 05478   June C. Wakefield, Info.Ctr.Dir.
Staff: 1. **Subjects:** Medicine, nursing, behavioral science. **Holdings:** 800 books; tapes. **Subscriptions:** 40 journals and other serials. **Services:** Interlibrary loans; library open to public for reference use only.

NORTHWESTERN MEMORIAL HOSPITAL - SCHROEDER MEDICAL LIBRARY
See: Northwestern University - Health Sciences Library

NORTHWESTERN MEMORIAL HOSPITAL - WESLEY-PASSAVANT SCHOOL OF NURSING LIBRARY
See: Northwestern University - Health Sciences Library

★9406★
NORTHWESTERN MUTUAL LIFE INSURANCE COMPANY - LAW LIBRARY
(Law)†
720 E. Wisconsin Ave.   Phone: (414) 271-1444
Milwaukee, WI 53202   Jane Marshall, Law Libn.
Staff: Prof 1; Other 2. **Subjects:** Law - general, tax, insurance. **Special Collections:** All state statutes and tax reports; U.S. and state case law. **Holdings:** 16,500 books. **Subscriptions:** 39 journals and other serials. **Services:** Copying; library open to public for reference use only. **Networks/Consortia:** Member of Library Council of Metropolitan Milwaukee, Inc.

★9407★
NORTHWESTERN MUTUAL LIFE INSURANCE COMPANY - MEDICAL
LIBRARY (Med)†
720 E. Wisconsin Ave.   Phone: (414) 271-1444
Milwaukee, WI 53202   Virginia Murphy, Med.Libn.
Founded: 1929. **Staff:** 1. **Subjects:** Medicine and medical insurance underwriting. **Holdings:** 400 books. **Subscriptions:** 25 journals and other serials. **Services:** Library not open to public.

★9408★
NORTHWESTERN MUTUAL LIFE INSURANCE COMPANY - REFERENCE
LIBRARY (Bus-Fin)†
720 E. Wisconsin Ave.   Phone: (414) 271-1444
Milwaukee, WI 53202   Patricia H. Ehr, Hd.Libn.
Founded: 1951. **Staff:** 4. **Subjects:** Economics, mathematics, history, statistics, investments, real estate, taxes. **Special Collections:** Life insurance; NML publications; NML history. **Holdings:** 14,000 books; 250 bound periodical volumes; 100 insurance company reports; 50 State Insurance Commissioner's annual reports; 40 VF drawers of general reference materials. **Subscriptions:** 1200 journals and other serials; 13 newspapers. **Services:** Interlibrary loans; copying; library open to public by special permission. **Publications:** New Books, periodically. **Remarks:** This library is considered the main company library. **Staff:** Patricia J. Johnson, Asst.Libn.

★9409★
NORTHWESTERN NATIONAL LIFE INSURANCE COMPANY - LIBRARY (Bus-
Fin)
20 Washington Ave., S.   Phone: (612) 372-5606
Minneapolis, MN 55440   Beth O'Connor, Libn.
Founded: 1947. **Staff:** Prof 1; Other 1. **Subjects:** Life and health insurance, law, actuarial science, taxes, business management, vital statistics. **Holdings:** 10,000 books; 200 bound periodical volumes; 20 VF drawers; 6 VF drawers of archives. **Subscriptions:** 125 journals and other serials; 7 newspapers. **Services:** Interlibrary loans; library open to public for reference use only. **Computerized Information Services:** DIALOG, SDC, New York Times Information Service, Dow Jones News Retrieval, WESTLAW.

★9410★
NORTHWESTERN OKLAHOMA STATE UNIVERSITY - LIBRARY (Educ)
    Phone: (405) 327-1700
Alva, OK 73717   Ray D. Lau, Lib.Dir.
Founded: 1897. **Staff:** Prof 4; Other 4. **Subjects:** Education, arts and sciences, Oklahoma history and local history, library science. **Special Collections:** William J. Mellor Collection of Indian artifacts, paintings, sculpture, stereoptican and slides, rare books (1000 items). **Holdings:** 120,000 books and bound periodical volumes; 100,000 government publications; 250,000 items on microfiche. **Subscriptions:** 1200 journals and other serials; 20 newspapers. **Services:** Interlibrary loans; copying; library open to public for reference use only with borrowing permitted for Alva residents. **Staff:** Milton Ream, Cat.; Shirley Thorne, Ref.; Diane Calvin, Govt.Doc.; Shirley Ferguson, Circ.; Kathy Koch, Acq.

NORTHWESTERN SCHOOL OF LAW
See: Lewis and Clark Law School

★9411★
NORTHWESTERN STATE UNIVERSITY OF LOUISIANA - EUGENE P.
WATSON LIBRARY - SHREVEPORT DIVISION (Med)
1800 Warrington Pl.   Phone: (318) 424-1827
Shreveport, LA 71101   Dorcas M.C. McCormick, Div.Hd.
Founded: 1949. **Staff:** Prof 2. **Subjects:** Nursing, education. **Special Collections:** Archive collection of nursing history (100 items). **Holdings:** 8000 books; 2150 bound periodical volumes; pamphlets; VF drawers; 83 periodical titles on microfilm. **Subscriptions:** 185 journals and other serials. **Services:** Interlibrary loans; copying; library open to public. **Staff:** Dixie E.A. Jones, Asst.Libn.

★9412★
NORTHWESTERN UNIVERSITY - ARCHIVES (Hist)
University Library   Phone: (312) 492-3354
Evanston, IL 60201   Patrick M. Quinn, Univ.Archv.
Staff: Prof 2; Other 3. **Subjects:** University history. **Holdings:** 3700 cubic feet of records and papers. **Subscriptions:** 376 University published journals and other serials. **Services:** Copying; library open to public. **Networks/Consortia:** Member of ILLINET; CRL; MIDLNET; RLG; North Suburban Library System. **Publications:** Annual report. **Staff:** Kevin B. Leonard, Asst.Univ.Archv.; Thomas Dorst, Asst.Archv.; William K. Beatty, Archival Assoc.; Margaret Faverty, Archival Proc.

★9413★
NORTHWESTERN UNIVERSITY - DENTAL SCHOOL LIBRARY (Med)
311 E. Chicago Ave.   Phone: (312) 649-8332
Chicago, IL 60611   Minnie Orfanos, Libn.
Founded: 1896. **Staff:** Prof 3; Other 5. **Subjects:** Oral hygiene, operative dentistry, prosthetics, orthodontics, endodontics, dental ethics and jurisprudence, dental office practice, oral surgery, pedodontics, periodontics, cleft palate, forensic dentistry, history of dentistry. **Special Collections:** Rare books on dentistry, in all languages (1390); catalogs of all dental schools in the United States; early anesthesia collection; dental supply catalogs; G.V. Black manuscripts; Eugene W. Skinner manuscripts; Hutchinson Collection; Teuscher and Freeman artifacts. **Holdings:** 55,100 books and bound periodical volumes; 14,589 pamphlets (cataloged); 61 manuscripts; 333 reels of microfilm; 22 moving pictures; 1597 photographs and prints; 7 discs; 345 tapes; 4627 slides. **Subscriptions:** 651 journals and other serials. **Services:** Interlibrary loans; copying; library open to public. **Computerized Information Services:** MEDLINE; computerized cataloging. **Networks/Consortia:** Member of Regional Medical Library - Region 3. **Publications:** Suggested Dental Books and Periodicals for a Non-Dental Library with a Dental Hygiene Curriculum; Dental Books and Journals for a Hospital Library. **Special Catalogs:** Rare Books Catalog. **Remarks:** Library is considered the most comprehensive dental collection in the world; schools organizing dental collections may write for duplicate materials available, and for basic books and periodicals list. A satellite library exists in the Dental Clinic Area and contains 100 reserve books and 35 key dental journals. It is a noncirculating collection. **Staff:** Mary Pace, Ref.Libn.

★9414★
NORTHWESTERN UNIVERSITY - GEOLOGY LIBRARY (Sci-Tech)
Locy Hall, Rm. 101   Phone: (312) 492-5525
Evanston, IL 60201   Janet Ayers, Geology Libn.
Staff: 1. **Subjects:** Geology, geophysics, geochemistry, crystallography, paleontology, oceanography, seismology. **Special Collections:** United States Geological Survey publications; state geological survey publications. **Holdings:** 23,000 books; 2000 pamphlets; 5031 maps. **Subscriptions:** 870 journals and other serials. **Services:** Copying. **Computerized Information Services:** DIALOG, BRS, Chemical Abstracts Service (CAS); computerized cataloging, acquisitions, serials and online public access through Northwestern Online Total Integrated System (NOTIS). **Networks/Consortia:** Member of CRL; ILLINET; RLG; MIDLNET; North Suburban Library System.

★9415★
NORTHWESTERN UNIVERSITY - HEALTH SCIENCES LIBRARY (Med)†
303 E. Chicago Ave.   Phone: (312) 649-8133
Chicago, IL 60611   Cecile E. Kramer, Dir.
Founded: 1859. **Staff:** Prof 8; Other 17. **Subjects:** All basic and clinical medical sciences, nursing, behavioral sciences and allied health subjects. **Special Collections:** History of medicine, medical portraits and illustrations. **Holdings:** 211,782 volumes; 287 slide sets; 129 videotapes; 147 16mm films; 477 audiotapes; 19 models. **Subscriptions:** 1962 journals and other serials. **Services:** Interlibrary loans (fee); copying; SDI; library not open to public. **Computerized Information Services:** DIALOG, BRS, NLM; computerized cataloging and serials. **Networks/Consortia:** Member of Regional Medical Library - Region 3; ILLINET; Metropolitan Chicago Library Assembly; RLG. **Publications:** Library Guide; Automated Literature Searches; brochures. **Remarks:** Contains holdings of the former Northwestern Memorial Hospital libraries. **Staff:** Sophie Price, Hd., Cat.Sect.; Anton Olson, Asst.Cat.; Jacqueline Adams, Hd., Acq.Sect.; Edward Tawyea, Hd., Circ. Media Libn.; Meg Panzarella, Ref.Libn.; Roger Tachuk, Hd., Ref.Sect.; Jean Emery, Ref.Libn.

★9416★
NORTHWESTERN UNIVERSITY - LAW SCHOOL LIBRARY (Law)†
357 E. Chicago Ave.   Phone: (312) 649-8450
Chicago, IL 60611   George S. Grossman, Libn.
Founded: 1859. **Staff:** Prof 10; Other 15. **Subjects:** Law - Anglo-American, comparative, foreign, international, criminal; criminology. **Special Collections:**

Rare Book Collection. **Holdings:** 384,000 books. **Services:** Interlibrary loans. **Publications:** Selected Recent Acquisitions; The Rare Book Collection; The Collections of Foreign and International Law. **Staff:** Elaine E. Teigler, Asst.Libn./Pub.Serv.; Barbara Hycnar, Asst.Libn./Tech.Serv.; Anne Zitkovich, Act.Hd., Cat.Dept.; Carl A. Yirka, Hd., Acq.

★9417★

NORTHWESTERN UNIVERSITY - MAP COLLECTION (Geog-Map)
University Library   Phone: (312) 492-7603
Evanston, IL 60201   Mary Fortney, Map Libn.
Founded: 1948. **Staff:** Prof 1; Other 1. **Subjects:** Maps and charts (mostly contemporary) covering all regions and countries of the world. **Special Collections:** Depository for U.S. Geological Survey topographic maps; Defense Mapping Agency maps and charts; National Ocean Survey aeronautical and nautical charts. **Holdings:** 2013 books and atlases; 163,487 map sheets; 1540 aerial photographs. **Services:** Interlibrary loans; copying; library open to public with restrictions. **Computerized Information Services:** DIALOG, SDC, BRS, New York Times Information Service. **Networks/Consortia:** Member of CRL; ILLINET; MIDLNET; RLG; North Suburban Library System.

★9418★

NORTHWESTERN UNIVERSITY - MATHEMATICS LIBRARY (Sci-Tech)
Lunt Bldg., Rm. 111   Phone: (312) 492-7627
Evanston, IL 60201   Zita Hayward, Lib.Asst.
Staff: 1. **Subjects:** Pure mathematics, statistics. **Holdings:** 23,400 volumes; 9830 reprints. **Subscriptions:** 645 journals and other serials. **Services:** Copying. **Computerized Information Services:** DIALOG, BRS; computerized cataloging, acquisitions and serials through Northwestern Online Total Integrated System (NOTIS). **Networks/Consortia:** Member of CRL; ILLINET; MIDLNET; RLG; North Suburban Library System. **Publications:** Accessions lists. **Special Catalogs:** Reprint collection card catalog.

★9419★

NORTHWESTERN UNIVERSITY - MELVILLE J. HERSKOVITS LIBRARY OF AFRICAN STUDIES (Area-Ethnic)
University Library   Phone: (312) 492-7684
Evanston, IL 60201   Hans E. Panofsky, Cur. of Africana
Founded: 1851. **Staff:** Prof 4; Other 2. **Subjects:** Africa - anthropology, exploration and travel, history, linguistics, literature, bibliography, statistics, geography, sociology, economics. **Special Collections:** Papers of Melville J. Herskovits (70 feet); Dennis Brutus Papers (3 feet); Arabic/Hausa Manuscripts from Kano (3000); G.M. Carter/T. Karis Collection on South African Politics (80 feet); African Studies Association (25 feet); Economic Survey of Liberia Papers (3 feet); Vernon McKay Papers (50 feet); Claude Barnett clipping files (18 feet); A. Abdurahman and Z. Gool Papers (2 feet); Leo Kuper Papers (8 feet); Alex Hepple (5 feet); Gwendolen M. Carter Papers (40 feet); Program of African Studies Records (10 feet). **Holdings:** 118,500 books; 21,650 bound periodical volumes; 1220 feet of vertical files; 7000 pamphlets; 260 posters; 800 phonograph records; 1.1 million feet of tape recordings; 7500 map sheets. **Subscriptions:** 5400 journals and other serials; 102 current African newspapers. **Services:** Interlibrary loans; copying; library open to public with restrictions. **Computerized Information Services:** Computerized cataloging, acquisitions, serials, circulation and online public access catalog through Northwestern Online Total Integrated System (NOTIS). **Networks/Consortia:** Member of CRL; ILLINET; MIDLNET; RLG; North Suburban Library System. **Publications:** Joint Acquisitions List of Africana (JALA), 6/year - by subscription; Annual Cumulation of JALA. **Special Catalogs:** Catalog of the Melville J. Herskovits Library of African Studies, Northwestern University Library and Africana in selected libraries, 1972, 8 volumes; Supplement, 1978, 6 volumes. **Staff:** Daniel A. Britz, Bibliog. of Africana; Maidel Cason, African Doc.Libn.; Mette Shayne, Francophone Africa.

★9420★

NORTHWESTERN UNIVERSITY - MUSIC LIBRARY (Mus)
                                       Phone: (312) 492-3434
Evanston, IL 60201   Don L. Roberts, Hd.
Founded: 1945. **Staff:** Prof 4; Other 5. **Subjects:** Musicology, music theory, church music, music education, 20th century music, ethnomusicology. **Special Collections:** A portion of the Moldenhauer Archive (1000 manuscripts, correspondence, documents, and photographs); Rare Book, Score and Manuscript Collection; Recorded Sound Archive; John Cage "Notations" Collection (manuscript); Ricordi Collection. **Holdings:** 26,726 books and bound periodical volumes; 43,379 music scores (cataloged); 35 VF drawers of pamphlets, catalogs and brochures; 65 VF drawers of sheet music; 4109 microforms; 3519 audiotapes; 23,981 phonograph records. **Subscriptions:** 330 journals and other serials. **Services:** Interlibrary loans; copying; library open to public with restrictions. **Computerized Information Services:** DIALOG, SDC, BRS, New York Times Information Service; computerized

cataloging, acquisitions, serials, circulation and online public access catalog through Northwestern Online Total Integrated System (NOTIS). **Networks/Consortia:** Member of CRL; ILLINET; MIDLNET; RLG; North Suburban Library System. **Publications:** NU Quarter Notes (Music Library newsletter). **Special Indexes:** Song Index. **Staff:** Constance N. Field, Asst. Music Libn.; Karen N. Nagy, Asst. Music Libn.; Richard Griscom, Cat.

★9421★

NORTHWESTERN UNIVERSITY - SEELEY G. MUDD LIBRARY FOR SCIENCE AND ENGINEERING (Sci-Tech)
2233 Sheridan Rd.   Phone: (312) 492-3362
Evanston, IL 60201   Robert Michaelson, Hd.Libn.
Founded: 1977. **Staff:** Prof 4; Other 7. **Subjects:** Engineering, life sciences, chemistry, astronomy, physics, applied mathematics. **Holdings:** 189,000 volumes; 25,000 American Engineering Council (AEC) and NASA reports in hard copy, 81,091 on microcard; 115,545 on microfiche. **Subscriptions:** 1849 journals and other serials; 1000 monographic series. **Services:** Interlibrary loans; copying; library open to public with restrictions. **Computerized Information Services:** DIALOG, BRS, Chemical Abstracts Service; computerized cataloging, acquisitions, serials, circulation and online public access catalog through Northwestern Online Total Integrated System (NOTIS). **Networks/Consortia:** Member of CRL; ILLINET; MIDLNET; RLG; North Suburban Library System. **Publications:** Acquisitions List, monthly. **Staff:** Janet Ayers, Ref. & Coll.Dev.; Joanna Mitchell, Tech.Serv.

★9422★

NORTHWESTERN UNIVERSITY - TRANSPORTATION LIBRARY (Trans)
                                       Phone: (312) 492-5273
Evanston, IL 60201   Mary Roy, Libn.
Founded: 1956. **Staff:** Prof 4; Other 3. **Subjects:** Transportation (nonengineering aspects), police administration and training, traffic safety, control and analysis. **Holdings:** 99,500 books and reports; 27,000 pamphlets and 16,500 corporate annual reports. **Subscriptions:** 3000 journals and other serials. **Services:** Interlibrary loans; copying; library open to public; fees charged for external services. **Computerized Information Services:** DIALOG; computerized cataloging, indexing, serials check-in and online public access catalog through Northwestern Online Total Integrated System (NOTIS). **Networks/Consortia:** Member of Transportation Research Information Services (TRISNET); CRL; ILLINET; MIDLNET; RLG; North Suburban Library System. **Publications:** Current Literature in Traffic and Transportation, monthly; Containerization, basic bibliography, 1965-1968, annual supplements - all available for purchase. **Special Catalogs:** Catalog of the Transportation Center Library, 1973 (book). **Staff:** Ronald Karr, Pub.Serv.Libn.; Nancy Pope, Cat.; Dorothy Ramm, Per./Ref.Libn.

★9423★

NORTHWOOD INSTITUTE - STROSACKER LIBRARY (Bus-Fin)
3225 Cook Rd.   Phone: (517) 631-1600
Midland, MI 48640   Catherine Chen, Hd.Libn.
Staff: Prof 3; Other 5. **Subjects:** Business management, automotive marketing and replacement, accounting, executive secretarial science, advertising, marketing, hotel and restaurant management, fashion, liberal arts. **Special Collections:** Magill Collection; Leland I. Doan Memorial. **Holdings:** 31,473 books; 1752 bound periodical volumes; 24 VF drawers; 100 princeton files, pamphlets. **Subscriptions:** 519 journals and other serials; 9 newspapers. **Services:** Interlibrary loans; copying; library open to public with restrictions. **Staff:** Connie Weaver, Ref.Libn.; Carolyn Wolf, Ref./Per.Libn.

★9424★

NORTHWOOD INSTITUTE OF TEXAS - FREEDOM EDUCATION CENTER (Soc Sci)
Box 58   Phone: (214) 291-7466
Cedar Hill, TX 75104   James R. Bromley, Dir.
Founded: 1963. **Staff:** Prof 1. **Subjects:** Revisionist history, economic education, philosophy of freedom, political philosophy, subversive activity, revolutionary groups. **Holdings:** 12,000 volumes; 112 drawers of subject files; 200 shelf feet of unbound periodicals; Congressional Record, 1948 to present. **Subscriptions:** 183 journals and other serials; 10 newspapers. **Services:** Copying; library open to public. **Publications:** Monthly Letter.

★9425★

NORTHWOOD INSTITUTE OF TEXAS - LIBRARY (Bus-Fin)
Box 58   Phone: (214) 291-1541
Cedar Hill, TX 75104   Carla W. Bryan, Libn.
Founded: 1968. **Staff:** Prof 1. **Subjects:** Automotive marketing, executive secretarial science, fashion merchandising, hotel restaurant management, business management. **Holdings:** 12,500 books; 971 bound periodical volumes; 26 VF drawers of pamphlets and clippings; 392 AV items; 14 phonograph records; 900 microforms. **Subscriptions:** 210 journals and other

serials; 20 newspapers. **Services:** Interlibrary loans; copying; library open to public. **Publications:** Library News Bulletin, bimonthly - campus distribution and on request.

★9426★

NORTHWOOD INSTITUTE OF TEXAS - ROSALIND KRESS HALEY LIBRARY (Soc Sci)

Box 58   Phone: (214) 291-7466
Cedar Hill, TX 75104   JoAnn Seguin, Registrar
Founded: 1976. **Staff:** Prof 1. **Subjects:** Domestic and international communism and Marxism, theory and practice of free enterprise, international politics and history, U.S. Political Studies - figures and events. **Special Collections:** U.S. Congressional Investigations (100 shelf feet of reports); communist activity; organized crime in the U.S.; Bella Dodd Collection (25 shelf feet). **Holdings:** 2000 books; 200 shelf feet of periodicals; 3 VF drawers of articles and clippings; 50 boxes of pamphlets, clippings; 100 tapes; 40 phonograph records; 17 films. **Services:** Library open to public. **Publications:** Report on National Committee for Monetary Reform, semiannual - by subscription.

NORTON AIR FORCE BASE (CA)
See: U.S. Air Force Base - Norton Base Library

NORTON-CHILDREN'S HOSPITALS
See: NKC, Inc.

★9427★

NORTON COMPANY - CHAMBERLAIN LABORATORIES - TECHNICAL LIBRARY (Sci-Tech)

Box 350   Phone: (216) 673-5860
Akron, OH 44309   Jan York, Libn.
Staff: Prof 1. **Subjects:** Engineering-technology, biomedicine, environmental research, chemical engineering. **Holdings:** 4000 books; 35 bound periodical volumes; 6500 U.S. and foreign patents. **Subscriptions:** 80 journals and other serials. **Services:** Interlibrary loans; copying; library not open to public. **Remarks:** Located at 3840 Fishcreek Rd., Stow, OH 44224.

★9428★

NORTON COMPANY - COATED ABRASIVE DIVISION - TECHNICAL LIBRARY (Sci-Tech)

Box 808   Phone: (518) 273-0100
Troy, NY 12181   P.E. Smith, Tech.Info.Spec.
Founded: 1946. **Staff:** Prof 1; Other 1. **Subjects:** Organic chemistry, resins, abrasives. **Holdings:** 2500 books; 1500 bound periodical volumes; 77 VF drawers of company reports; 12 VF drawers of reprints; 7 VF drawers of pamphlets; 45 VF drawers of archives. **Subscriptions:** 70 journals and other serials. **Services:** Interlibrary loans; library open to public by appointment. **Computerized Information Services:** DIALOG. **Networks/Consortia:** Member of Capitol District Library Council for Reference & Research Resources (CDLC). **Special Indexes:** Company reports, 1946-1962 (punched cards).

★9429★

NORTON COMPANY - LIBRARY (Sci-Tech)

One New Bond St.   Phone: (617) 853-1000
Worcester, MA 01606   Joan K. Chaffee, Libn.
Founded: 1909. **Staff:** Prof 1; Other 1. **Subjects:** Abrasives, ceramics, refractories, business management, physics, chemistry, metallurgy, mineralogy, electronics, grinding wheels, polymers. **Holdings:** 5000 books; 3500 bound periodical volumes; 32 VF drawers of pamphlets, unbound reports, documents; microfiche. **Subscriptions:** 184 journals and other serials. **Services:** Interlibrary loans; copying; library open to public on a limited basis. **Computerized Information Services:** DIALOG, New England Research Application Center; internal database. **Publications:** Quarterly listing of acquisitions.

★9430★

NORTON GALLERY AND SCHOOL OF ART - LIBRARY (Art)

1451 S. Olive Ave.   Phone: (305) 832-5194
West Palm Beach, FL 33401   Betty Kletter, Libn.
Staff: Prof 1; Other 1. **Subjects:** Art history, painting, sculpture, biography (artists). **Holdings:** 3800 books; 2000 museum pamphlets; 500 art slides. **Subscriptions:** 15 journals and other serials. **Services:** Interlibrary loans; library open to public for reference use only. **Staff:** Kaye M. Fish, Asst.Libn.

★9431★

NORTON (R.W.) ART GALLERY - REFERENCE-RESEARCH LIBRARY (Art; Hist)

4747 Creswell Ave.   Phone: (318) 865-4201
Shreveport, LA 71106   Jerry M. Bloomer, Libn.
Founded: 1970. **Staff:** 2. **Subjects:** Fine arts, American history, Louisiana and Virginia history, literature, ornithology, bibliography, world history. **Special Collections:** James M. Owens Memorial Collection of Virginiana (500 volumes); rare books, including 15th-18th century atlases; J.J. Audubon's double-elephant folio edition of The Birds of America; ornithological works of James Gould (43 volumes); Charles M. Russell and Frederic Remington Collection (books, catalogs, pamphlets). **Holdings:** 6500 volumes. **Subscriptions:** 105 journals and other serials. **Services:** Copying; library open to public for reference use only. **Remarks:** Maintained by R.W. Norton Art Foundation. **Staff:** Eva W. Moses, Asst.Libn.

★9432★

NORTON RESEARCH CORPORATION (Canada) LTD. - LIBRARY (Sci-Tech)

8001 Daly St.   Phone: (416) 295-4311
Niagara Falls, ON, Canada L2G 6S2   Wende Cournoyea, Exec.Sec.
Founded: 1930. **Staff:** 1. **Subjects:** Technology, abrasives, refractories, high temperature, crystallography, history of the abrasive industry. **Holdings:** 2700 books; 1600 bound periodical volumes; 6650 pamphlets (cataloged); 1700 government publications (cataloged); 300 vendors' catalogs; 150 reels of microfilm; 5500 patents; 400 slides. **Subscriptions:** 25 journals and other serials. **Services:** Interlibrary loans; copying; library open to public for reference use only by request. **Staff:** Dr. J.E. Patchett, Asst.Dir. of Res.

★9433★

NORTON SIMON MUSEUM OF ART AT PASADENA - GALKA E. SCHEYER ARCHIVES (Art)

411 W. Colorado Blvd.   Phone: (213) 449-6840
Pasadena, CA 91105   Sara Campbell, Cur.
Founded: 1961. **Staff:** 1. **Subjects:** Material pertaining to the life and collections of Galka E. Scheyer and ''The Blue Four'' - Paul Klee, Wassily Kandinsky, Lyonel Feininger, and Alexei Jawlensky. **Holdings:** 150 books; 200 brochures and catalogs; letters of Klee, Jawlensky, Kandinsky, Feininger; photographs of artists and collections. **Services:** Use of archives limited to scholars.

★9434★

NORTON SIMON MUSEUM OF ART AT PASADENA - LIBRARY (Art)

411 W. Colorado Blvd.   Phone: (213) 449-6840
Pasadena, CA 91105
Founded: 1924. **Subjects:** Art history. **Special Collections:** The Knoedler Library of auction and exhibition catalogs on microfiche (18th century - 1970). **Holdings:** 50 bound periodical volumes; 6000 exhibition catalogs; auction catalogs; 2000 American, British, French sales catalogs from 1970 to present. **Services:** SDI; library not open to public.

★9435★

NORTON STATE HOSPITAL - PROFESSIONAL LIBRARY (Med)†

Rte. 1   Phone: (913) 877-3301
Norton, KS 67654
Staff: 1. **Subjects:** Mental retardation, psychology, psychiatry, special education, medicine, speech pathology, social work. **Holdings:** 1200 books; 100 bound periodical volumes; related reports and research materials primarily on behavior modification with the trainable, mentally retarded adult. **Subscriptions:** 10 journals and other serials. **Services:** Library open to authorized professionals.

★9436★

NORWALK HOSPITAL - R. GLEN WIGGANS MEMORIAL LIBRARY (Med)†

24 Stevens St.   Phone: (203) 852-2793
Norwalk, CT 06856   Joan Sjostrom, Libn.
Staff: Prof 2. **Subjects:** Medicine and allied health sciences. **Holdings:** 965 books; 5500 bound periodical volumes; 6 indices (cataloged); 6 VF drawers of materials on health sciences. **Subscriptions:** 145 journals and other serials. **Services:** Interlibrary loans; copying; library open to public by appointment. **Computerized Information Services:** Computerized bibliographies and searches. **Networks/Consortia:** Member of Southwestern Connecticut Health Science Library Consortium. **Staff:** Jean Botts, Asst.Libn.

★9437★

NORWALK STATE TECHNICAL COLLEGE - LIBRARY (Sci-Tech)

181 Richards Ave.   Phone: (203) 838-0601
Norwalk, CT 06854   Rita Schara, Libn.
Founded: 1962. **Staff:** Prof 1; Other 1. **Subjects:** Engineering - electrical, chemical, mechanical; computer technology; metallurgy; architectural drafting.

Holdings: 15,000 volumes; 100 bound periodical volumes; 8 VF drawers of pamphlets. **Subscriptions:** 129 journals and other serials; 5 newspapers. **Services:** Interlibrary loans; copying; library open to public for reference use only. **Networks/Consortia:** Member of Southwestern Connecticut Library Council. **Publications:** Newsletter, monthly.

★9438★
NORWEGIAN-AMERICAN HISTORICAL ASSOCIATION - ARCHIVES (Area-Ethnic; Hist)
St. Olaf College   Phone: (507) 663-3221
Northfield, MN 55057   Charlotte Jacobson, Cur. of Archv.
Founded: 1925. **Staff:** Prof 2. **Subjects:** Norwegian-American history and genealogy. **Holdings:** 8000 books; 1500 bound periodical volumes; 500 other volumes; newspapers; scrapbooks; correspondence; clippings; diaries; records; manuscripts. **Subscriptions:** 15 journals and other serials. **Services:** Interlibrary loans; archives open to public. **Staff:** Lloyd Hustvedt, Exec.Sec.

★9439★
NORWEGIAN-AMERICAN HOSPITAL, INC. - SEUFERT MEMORIAL LIBRARY (Med)
1044 N. Francisco Ave.   Phone: (312) 278-8800
Chicago, IL 60622   Estrella P. de la Cruz, Libn.
Founded: 1921. **Staff:** 1. **Subjects:** Medicine, surgery, obstetrics, pediatrics. **Special Collections:** Collection of medical illustrations (loose-leaf). **Holdings:** 811 books; 173 bound periodical volumes; 200 Audio-Digest tapes. **Subscriptions:** 65 journals and other serials. **Services:** Interlibrary loans; library open to retired NAH doctors. **Networks/Consortia:** Member of Regional Medical Library - Region 3.

★9440★
NORWEGIAN-AMERICAN MUSEUM - REFERENCE LIBRARY (Area-Ethnic)
502 W. Water St.   Phone: (319) 382-9681
Decorah, IA 52101   Darrell D. Henning, Cur.
Subjects: Norwegian-American history, genealogy, crafts, antiques. **Special Collections:** Norwegian rosemaling. **Holdings:** 2000 books. **Subscriptions:** 15 journals and other serials. **Services:** Library open to public for reference use only.

NORWEGIAN-AMERICAN MUSEUM/VESTERHEIM GENEALOGICAL CENTER
See: Vesterheim Genealogical Center/Norwegian-American Museum

★9441★
NORWICH-EATON - FILM LIBRARY (Med; Aud-Vis)
P.O. Box 2005   Phone: (519) 442-6361
Paris, ON, Canada N3L 3T8   Nicole Delplace
Subjects: Urology, nutrition, neurology, spasticity, plastic and reconstructive burn therapy, gynecology. **Holdings:** 130 films. **Services:** Library open to public with restrictions. **Special Catalogs:** Directory of Medical Films, Audio Visual & Medical Educational Resources (book). **Remarks:** The library is located at 326 Grand River St., N., Paris, ON N3L 3T8. **Also Known As:** Norwich-Eaton - Division of Morton-Norwich Products, Inc.

★9442★
NORWICH-EATON PHARMACEUTICALS, INC. - LIBRARY (Med)
Box 191   Phone: (607) 335-2678
Norwich, NY 13815   Donald A. Windsor, Leader, Lib./Search Group
Founded: 1947. **Staff:** Prof 5; Other 1. **Subjects:** Pharmacy, medicine, chemistry, pharmacology. **Holdings:** 7000 books; 16,000 bound periodical volumes. **Subscriptions:** 510 journals and other serials. **Services:** Interlibrary loans; library open to serious researchers with permission. **Computerized Information Services:** DIALOG, SDC, NLM. **Networks/Consortia:** Member of South Central Research Library Council (SCRLC). **Formerly:** Morton-Norwich Products, Inc. - Norwich Pharmacal Company - R&D Dept. - Library Information Group. **Staff:** Marcia G. Samer, Info.Sci; Elizabeth A. Nies, Info.Sci.; Cynthia C. Kumatz, Libn.

★9443★
NORWICH HOSPITAL - HEALTH SCIENCES LIBRARY (Med)
Box 508   Phone: (203) 889-7361
Norwich, CT 06360   Emily Court, Libn.
Founded: 1940. **Staff:** Prof 1; Other 1. **Subjects:** Psychiatry, neurology, psychology, general medicine, nursing, occupational therapy, social service. **Holdings:** 4000 books; 5750 bound periodical volumes. **Subscriptions:** 106 journals and other serials. **Services:** Interlibrary loans; library open to public for reference use only. **Networks/Consortia:** Member of Connecticut Association of Health Sciences Libraries. (CAHSL).

★9444★
NOSTALGIA PRESS, INC. - ARCHIVES AND PICTURE LIBRARY (Publ; Pict)
Box 293   Phone: (516) 488-4747
Franklin Square, NY 11010   Martin F. Jackson, Info.Dir.
Founded: 1965. **Staff:** Prof 1; Other 3. **Subjects:** Illustration, humor and satire; advertising (1790 to present). **Special Collections:** Cartoons; posters (1000 original 1890 posters); dime novels; sheet music; advertisements (1790 to present); illustrations. **Holdings:** 10,000 books; 16,000 bound periodical volumes; 100,000 advertising cards; 1000 illustrated newspapers; 1000 boxes of loose picture material. **Subscriptions:** 259 journals and other serials. **Services:** Interlibrary loans (fee); copying; picture rental; library not open to public. **Special Indexes:** Nostalgia Comics; America Card Collector's Catalog; Pioneer Postcards; Burdick Collection.

★9445★
NOTRE DAME COLLEGE - LANE HALL MEMORIAL LIBRARY - SPECIAL COLLECTIONS (Hum)
Box 220   Phone: (306) 732-2080
Wilcox, SK, Canada S0G 5E0   Louis Stoeckle, College Sec.
Staff: 1. **Subjects:** Humanities, life skills. **Special Collections:** Nuremberg Chronicles; Rex Beach Collection. **Holdings:** 14,000 volumes. **Services:** Collections open to public by permission.

NOTRE DAME HOSPITAL
See: Hopital Notre Dame

★9446★
NOTRE DAME HOSPITAL - LIBRARY (Med)†
1405 Edward St.   Phone: (705) 362-4291
Hearst, ON, Canada P0L 1N0   Mary Kellie, Inservice Coord.
Founded: 1960. **Staff:** Prof 1. **Subjects:** Medicine, nursing, paramedicine, hospital administration. **Holdings:** 700 books; 600 bound periodical volumes. **Subscriptions:** 115 journals and other serials. **Services:** Interlibrary loans; copying; library open to public with permission.

★9447★
NOVA - CORPORATE LIBRARY (Energy; Sci-Tech)
205 5th Ave., S.W.   Phone: (403) 231-9327
Calgary, AB, Canada T2P 2V7   M.W. Genoe, Corp.Libn.
Staff: Prof 3; Other 8. **Subjects:** Energy, business administration, engineering, environment. **Special Collections:** Regulatory material. **Holdings:** 5000 books. **Subscriptions:** 500 journals and other serials; 25 newspapers. **Services:** Interlibrary loans; SDI; library open to public with restrictions. **Computerized Information Services:** DIALOG, SDC, CAN/OLE, New York Times Information Service, Info Globe; computerized cataloging and circulation. **Special Indexes:** Indexes to major Canadian regulatory transcripts. **Staff:** Carol Weaver, Coord., Cat. & Indexing; Lois Salmon, Coord., Main Lib.

★9448★
NOVA SCOTIA AGRICULTURAL COLLEGE - LIBRARY (Agri)
Box 550   Phone: (902) 895-1571
Truro, NS, Canada B2N 5E3   B. Sodhi, Libn.
Staff: Prof 1; Other 4. **Subjects:** Agriculture. **Holdings:** 15,500 books; 4550 bound periodical volumes. **Subscriptions:** 320 journals and other serials. **Services:** Interlibrary loans; copying.

★9449★
NOVA SCOTIA - ATTORNEY GENERAL'S LIBRARY (Law)
Provincial Bldg.
P.O. Box 7   Phone: (902) 424-7699
Halifax, NS, Canada B3J 2L6   Margaret Murphy, Libn.
Founded: 1920. **Staff:** Prof 1. **Subjects:** Law. **Holdings:** 7000 volumes. **Subscriptions:** 60 journals and other serials. **Services:** Copying; SDI; library open to public for reference use only. **Special Indexes:** Card index to Nova Scotia Regulations; Opinion File; Memorandum File.

★9450★
NOVA SCOTIA BARRISTERS' SOCIETY - LIBRARY (Law)
Law Courts, 1815 Upper Water St.   Phone: (902) 422-1491
Halifax, NS, Canada B3J 1S7   Linda M. Keddy, Libn.
Founded: 1858. **Staff:** Prof 1. **Subjects:** Law - Canadian, American, British. **Holdings:** 15,000 volumes; 160 volumes of Nova Scotia Supreme Court unreported decisions; 19 volumes of County Court decisions. **Subscriptions:** 90 journals and other serials. **Services:** Interlibrary loans; copying; library not open to public.

★9451★

NOVA SCOTIA COLLEGE OF ART AND DESIGN - LIBRARY (Art)
5163 Duke St.   Phone: (902) 422-7381
Halifax, NS, Canada B3J 3J6   John Murchie, Lib.Dir.
Founded: 1887. **Staff:** Prof 2; Other 5. **Subjects:** Art history, contemporary art, Canadian art, Oriental art, crafts, photography, graphic and environmental design. **Special Collections:** Contemporary art in book form. **Holdings:** 18,000 books; 1200 bound periodical volumes; 85,000 slides. **Subscriptions:** 300 journals and other serials; 4 newspapers. **Services:** Interlibrary loans; copying; library open to public with restrictions. **Computerized Information Services:** DIALOG; computerized cataloging and circulation. **Networks/Consortia:** Member of UTLAS, Inc. **Publications:** Accessions list, Path Finders, irregular. **Staff:** Mary Snyder, Non-Print Libn.; Kit Clark, Cat.; Joyce Stephenson, Circ.

★9452★

NOVA SCOTIA COMMISSION ON DRUG DEPENDENCY - LIBRARY AND INFORMATION CENTRE (Soc Sci)
4th Fl., 5668 South St.   Phone: (902) 424-4270
Halifax, NS, Canada B3J 1A6   Patricia MacNeil, Libn.
Founded: 1973. **Staff:** Prof 1; Other 1. **Subjects:** Drug and alcohol use, pharmacology, sociology, social problems, psychology and psychiatry, highway safety. **Holdings:** 1100 books and documents; 3 drawers of reprints; 2 drawers of pamphlets; 69 films. **Subscriptions:** 70 journals and other serials. **Services:** Interlibrary loans; copying; distribution of pamphlets and commission publications to general public on request; library open to public for reference use only. **Publications:** Acquisition list, bimonthly; newsletter, irregular; staff directory, annual; current news clippings, irregular.

★9453★

NOVA SCOTIA - DEPARTMENT OF CULTURE, RECREATION AND FITNESS - LIBRARY (Rec)
P.O. Box 864   Phone: (902) 424-7734
Halifax, NS, Canada B3J 2V2   Genni Archibald, Lib.Off.
Founded: 1978. **Staff:** Prof 1; Other 1. **Subjects:** Crafts, theatre, music, art and art education, sports, community services. **Special Collections:** Canadian plays. **Holdings:** 13,000 books; 162 bound periodical volumes; 600 slides; 4 VF drawers of clippings. **Subscriptions:** 170 journals and other serials; 5 newspapers. **Services:** Interlibrary loans; mail service; library open to public. **Publications:** Library News - for internal distribution only. **Special Catalogs:** DDS card catalogue.

★9454★

NOVA SCOTIA - DEPARTMENT OF DEVELOPMENT - LIBRARY (Plan)
5151 George St., 8th Fl.
P.O. Box 519   Phone: (902) 424-5807
Halifax, NS, Canada B3J 2R7   Donald Purcell, Libn.
Founded: 1971. **Staff:** Prof 1. **Subjects:** Industrial development, urban planning, statistics, transportation, natural resources, business, economics, forestry, fisheries. **Special Collections:** Nova Scotia Design Institute Library (200 volumes). **Holdings:** 7000 books; 2000 annual reports; 75 manufacturing and trade directories; Statistics Canada reports (complete subscription). **Subscriptions:** 180 journals and other serials. **Services:** Interlibrary loans; copying; library open to public with restrictions on borrowing. **Publications:** Acquisitions list, monthly.

★9455★

NOVA SCOTIA - DEPARTMENT OF EDUCATION - EDUCATION MEDIA SERVICES (Aud-Vis)
5250 Spring Garden Rd.   Phone: (902) 424-5445
Halifax, NS, Canada B3J 1E8   B.F. Hart, Educ. Media Serv.
Founded: 1937. **Staff:** Prof 24. **Subjects:** Education, teacher training. **Holdings:** 7800 films; 850 videotapes. **Services:** Systems design for media-related curriculum materials; educational television production, small format (filmstrip, slide/tape); graphic design; photography; maintenance and repair service for schools; film library service. **Remarks:** Aligned with the Educational Resources Branch of the Department of Education. **Staff:** Audrey B. McSweeney, Libn.

★9456★

NOVA SCOTIA - DEPARTMENT OF LABOUR AND MANPOWER - LIBRARY (Soc Sci)
P.O. Box 697   Phone: (902) 424-4313
Halifax, NS, Canada B3J 2T8   Marie DeYoung, Libn.
Founded: 1970. **Staff:** Prof 1. **Subjects:** Labour, industrial relations, manpower training, economic statistics, public administration. **Holdings:** 1600 books; 40 bound periodical volumes; Conference Board in Canada publications; government documents. **Subscriptions:** 355 journals and other serials. **Services:** Interlibrary loans; copying; library open to public.

Computerized Information Services: CANSIM. **Publications:** Acquisitions list, quarterly - free upon request. **Remarks:** Library is located at 5151 Terminal Road, 6th Floor, Halifax, NS.

★9457★

NOVA SCOTIA - DEPARTMENT OF MINES & ENERGY - LIBRARY (Sci-Tech; Energy)
P.O. Box 1087   Phone: (902) 424-8633
Halifax, NS, Canada B3J 2X1   Valerie Brisco, Res.Asst.
Founded: 1960. **Staff:** Prof 1. **Subjects:** Geoscience, mining, energy, engineering. **Special Collections:** Company assessment reports (3000). **Holdings:** 4000 books; 1000 bound periodical volumes; 500 open file reports; 1000 reprints; 6000 maps. **Subscriptions:** 200 journals and other serials; 11 newspapers. **Services:** Interlibrary loans; copying; library open to public. **Computerized Information Services:** GEOSCAN. **Special Indexes:** Index to open file reports (book); index to company assessment reports (book).

★9458★

NOVA SCOTIA - DEPARTMENT OF SOCIAL SERVICES - LIBRARY (Soc Sci; Plan)
P.O. Box 696   Phone: (902) 424-4383
Halifax, NS, Canada B3J 2T7   Jane Phillips, Libn.
Founded: 1969. **Staff:** Prof 1. **Subjects:** Social services, social planning and research. **Holdings:** 2500 books; 317 bound periodical volumes. **Subscriptions:** 60 journals and other serials. **Services:** Interlibrary loans; library open to public for reference use only.

NOVA SCOTIA DESIGN INSTITUTE LIBRARY
See: Nova Scotia - Department of Development

★9459★

NOVA SCOTIA HOSPITAL - HEALTH SCIENCE LIBRARY (Med)
P.O. Box 1004   Phone: (902) 469-7500
Dartmouth, NS, Canada B2Y 3Z9   Marjorie A. Cox
Staff: 1. **Subjects:** Psychiatry, medicine, psychology, neurology, pre-clinical science. **Special Collections:** Nova Scotia government reports, 1856 to present. **Holdings:** 5500 books; 400 bound periodical volumes; 8000 psychiatric and medical reprints; 450 slides and cassettes; hospital archives. **Subscriptions:** 108 journals and other serials. **Services:** Interlibrary loans; copying; library open to public with restrictions. **Special Indexes:** Index to psychiatric reports and papers published by hospital staff; index to journal articles on special psychiatric and medical subjects.

★9460★

NOVA SCOTIA INSTITUTE OF TECHNOLOGY - LEARNING RESOURCES CENTER (Sci-Tech)
5685 Leeds St.
P.O. Box 2210   Phone: (902) 424-4224
Halifax, NS, Canada B3J 3C4   Nola Brennan, Libn.
Founded: 1972. **Staff:** Prof 1; Other 2. **Subjects:** Engineering, medical and dental technology, trades. **Holdings:** 6750 books; 950 bound periodical volumes; 500 student reports; 30 clippings; 35 school calendars. **Subscriptions:** 110 journals and other serials. **Services:** Interlibrary loans; copying; center open to public with restrictions. **Computerized Information Services:** Online systems (through Nova Scotia Provincial Library). **Special Indexes:** Index to student reports (card).

★9461★

NOVA SCOTIA - LEGISLATIVE LIBRARY (Soc Sci)
Province House   Phone: (902) 424-5932
Halifax, NS, Canada B3J 2P8   Ilga Leja, Legislative Libn.
Founded: 1862. **Staff:** Prof 2; Other 3. **Subjects:** Legislative material (federal, provincial, U.S., Great Britain); political science; history; economics; biography. **Special Collections:** Novascotiana (10,000 volumes). **Holdings:** 65,000 books; 3000 reels of microfilm; 8000 microfiche. **Services:** Interlibrary loans; copying; library open to public. **Publications:** Publications of the Province of Nova Scotia, quarterly and annual - distributed on request; Nova Scotia Royal Commissions and Commissions of Inquiry appointed by the Province of Nova Scotia; Nova Scotia Book of Days, a calendar of the province's history. **Special Indexes:** Index of pictorial material relating to Nova Scotia; index to regulations of the province of Nova Scotia. **Remarks:** Maintained by the Nova Scotia House of Assembly - Office of the Speaker. **Staff:** Jean Sawyer, Asst.Libn.

★9462★
NOVA SCOTIA MUSEUM - LIBRARY (Sci-Tech; Hist)
1747 Summer St.   Phone: (902) 429-4610
Halifax, NS, Canada B3H 3A6   S. Whiteside, Libn.
Founded: 1885. **Staff:** Prof 1; Other 1. **Subjects:** Zoology, botany, social history of Nova Scotia. **Special Collections:** Entomology collection (1000 volumes). **Holdings:** 15,000 titles; pamphlets; slides; slide/tape sets. **Subscriptions:** 140 journals and other serials. **Services:** Interlibrary loans; library open to public for reference use only.

★9463★
NOVA SCOTIA POWER CORPORATION - LIBRARY (Energy)
Box 910   Phone: (902) 424-2928
Halifax, NS, Canada B3J 2W5   Barbara N. MacKenzie, Libn.
Founded: 1972. **Staff:** Prof 1; Other 1. **Subjects:** Engineering, business, data processing. **Holdings:** 3000 books; 450 bound periodical volumes. **Subscriptions:** 380 journals and other serials; 11 newspapers. **Services:** Interlibrary loans; SDI; library open to public by appointment. **Computerized Information Services:** SDC, CAN/OLE, QL Systems, CANSIM, DIALOG, I.P. Sharp Associates Limited; Conference Board of Canada - Applied Economic Research and Information Center (AERIC). **Networks/Consortia:** Member of Nova Scotia On-Line Consortium. **Publications:** Library Acquisitions, irregular - for internal distribution only. **Special Indexes:** C.E.A. Publications Index (computer print-out).

★9464★
NOVA SCOTIA - PROVINCIAL LIBRARY (Info Sci)
5250 Spring Garden Rd.   Phone: (902) 424-5439
Halifax, NS, Canada B3J 1E8   Mrs. Carin Somers, Dir.
Founded: 1952. **Staff:** Prof 10; Other 35. **Subjects:** Bibliography, education, library and information science. **Holdings:** 65,000 books; 1000 bound periodical volumes. **Subscriptions:** 230 journals and other serials. **Services:** Interlibrary loans; copying; reference service to regional and government departmental libraries and educators; library open to librarians and government employees. **Computerized Information Services:** DIALOG, SDC, QL Systems, CAN/OLE; computerized cataloging. **Networks/Consortia:** Member of Nova Scotia On-Line Consortium; UTLAS, Inc. **Publications:** Nova Scotia Regional Public Library Statistics; Nova Scotia Provincial Library Annual Report; Directory of Nova Scotia Libraries, annual - free upon request. **Special Catalogs:** Union Catalog of Monographs and Serials. **Staff:** Lorraine McQueen, Coord., Ref.Serv.; Bertha Higgins, Coord., Tech.Serv.; Elizabeth MacDonald, Coord., Pub.Libs.; Shirley Coulter, Coord., Sch.Libs.

★9465★
NOVA SCOTIA - PUBLIC ARCHIVES OF NOVA SCOTIA (Hist)
6016 University Ave.   Phone: (902) 423-9115
Halifax, NS, Canada B3H 1W4   Phyllis R. Blakeley, Prov.Archv.
Founded: 1929. **Staff:** Prof 12; Other 12. **Subjects:** Novascotiana. **Special Collections:** Akins Library (colonial history, Canadian history, Maritime Provinces). **Holdings:** 40,000 books; 2000 bound periodical volumes; large collection of public records and historical documents; 7400 pictures; 8000 maps; 9000 reels of microfilm. **Subscriptions:** 65 journals and other serials. **Services:** Copying; library open to public. **Special Catalogs:** Akins Library Catalog. **Staff:** Marcia Aronson, Libn.

★9466★
NOVA SCOTIA RESEARCH FOUNDATION CORPORATION - LIBRARY (Sci-Tech)†
100 Fenwick St.
P.O. Box 790   Phone: (902) 424-8670
Dartmouth, NS, Canada B2Y 3Z7   Helen I. Hendry, Libn.
Founded: 1947. **Staff:** Prof 2; Other 1. **Subjects:** Technology, marine biology, chemistry, geosciences, electronics, production management, small business, ocean engineering. **Special Collections:** Canada Patent Office Record, current 17 years. **Holdings:** 5000 books; 800 bound periodical volumes; 1500 unbound periodicals; 2000 government documents, reports, pamphlets. **Subscriptions:** 241 journals and other serials; 6 newspapers. **Services:** Interlibrary loans; copying; library open to serious inquirers. **Publications:** Selected Bibliography on Algae, 1952-1973 - available for purchase.

★9467★
NOVA UNIVERSITY - LAW LIBRARY (Law)
3100 S.W. 9th Ave.   Phone: (305) 522-2300
Fort Lauderdale, FL 33315   Carole Roehrenbeck, Dir.
Staff: Prof 3; Other 8. **Subjects:** Law - state, federal, patent, tax, corporate; legal history. **Special Collections:** Government document depository; United Nations document depository. **Holdings:** 65,000 books; 20,000 microfiche. **Subscriptions:** 11 newspapers. **Services:** Interlibrary loans; copying; library open to public for reference use only. **Staff:** Faye Jones, Ser./Cat.Libn.; Jeanne Underhill, Ref./Pub.Serv.Libn.

★9468★
NOVA UNIVERSITY - OCEANOGRAPHIC CENTER LIBRARY (Sci-Tech)
8000 N. Ocean Dr.   Phone: (305) 475-7487
Dania, FL 33004   James F. Kane, Libn.
Staff: Prof 1. **Subjects:** Physical oceanography, marine biology. **Holdings:** 1700 books; 1634 bound periodical volumes; charts and maps; reprints. **Subscriptions:** 103 journals and other serials. **Services:** Interlibrary loans; copying; library open to public. **Computerized Information Services:** DIALOG; internal database. **Networks/Consortia:** Member of International Association of Marine Science Libraries and Information Centers.

★9469★
NOVATO UNIFIED SCHOOL DISTRICT - INSTRUCTIONAL MATERIALS CENTER (Educ)
1015 7th St.   Phone: (415) 897-4247
Novato, CA 94947   Annette Conklin, Rsrcs.Libn.
Founded: 1965. **Staff:** Prof 1; Other 2. **Subjects:** Education, educational psychology, art. **Special Collections:** Collection of early 20th century California textbooks (150). **Holdings:** 4000 books; 100 resource guides; 650 art prints, 200 sculpture reproductions; 200 microfiche; 25 sound filmstrips; 6 VF drawers of pamphlets. **Subscriptions:** 50 journals and other serials. **Services:** Interlibrary loans; copying; center open to public with restrictions.

★9470★
NOVO LABORATORIES INC. - LIBRARY (Sci-Tech)
59 Danbury Rd.   Phone: (203) 762-7401
Wilton, CT 06897-0608   James W. Fleagle, Info.Spec.
Staff: Prof 1. **Subjects:** Industrial enzymology, diabetes. **Holdings:** 1200 books; 600 bound periodical volumes. **Subscriptions:** 150 journals and other serials; 10 newspapers. **Services:** Interlibrary loans; copying; library open to public by appointment. **Computerized Information Services:** DIALOG, SDC, Institute for Scientific Information (ISI). **Networks/Consortia:** Member of Southwestern Connecticut Library Council.

★9471★
NOVOCOL CHEMICAL MANUFACTURING COMPANY, INC. - LIBRARY (Med; Sci-Tech)†
2921 Atlantic Ave.   Phone: (212) 277-5400
Brooklyn, NY 11207   Elias Epstein, Dir. of Res.
Founded: 1940. **Staff:** Prof 1. **Subjects:** Dentistry, chemistry. **Special Collections:** Complete sets of "Dental Items of Interest" and "Modern Dentistry." **Holdings:** 200 books; 500 bound periodical volumes; 100 unbound dental and chemical journals. **Subscriptions:** 10 journals and other serials. **Services:** Library not open to public.

NOVOTNY LIBRARY OF ECONOMIC HISTORY
See: Syracuse University - George Arents Research Library for Special Collections

NOW
See: National Organization for Women

NPR
See: National Public Radio

NRA
See: National Rifle Association

NRC
See: U.S. Nuclear Regulatory Commission

NSSDC
See: World Data Center A - Rockets & Satellites - National Space Science Data Center (NSSDC)

NTIS
See: U.S. Dept. of Commerce - Natl. Technical Information Service

★9472★
NUCLEAR ASSURANCE CORPORATION - INFORMATION CENTER (Energy)
24 Executive Pk., W.   Phone: (404) 325-4200
Atlanta, GA 30329   Nancy G. Reinhold, Mgr., Info.Ctr.
Founded: 1971. **Staff:** Prof 2; Other 1. **Subjects:** Energy, nuclear fuel cycle. **Holdings:** 1500 books; 350 bound periodical volumes; 30,000 microfiche; 145 notebooks; 2500 slides and photographs. **Subscriptions:** 66 journals and other serials. **Services:** Center not open to public. **Publications:** Acquisitions

list, monthly - for internal distribution only. **Special Indexes:** Indexes of papers and speeches given by company employees, international company government reporting, conference papers. **Staff:** Mary Anne Brown, Asst.

NUCLEAR SAFETY INFORMATION CENTER
See: Oak Ridge National Laboratory

★9473★
NUMAX ELECTRONICS, INC. - LIBRARY
135 Engineers Rd.
Hauppauge, NY 11788
Subjects: Electronics. **Holdings:** Figures not available. **Remarks:** Presently inactive.

★9474★
NUMISMATICS INTERNATIONAL - LIBRARY (Rec)
30 Pleasant St.
Colebrook, NH 03576   Granvyl Hulse, Libn.
Founded: 1964. **Staff:** 1. **Subjects:** Coins, currency. **Holdings:** 1600 books; slide sets; journals and other serials. **Services:** Interlibrary loans (fee); library open to members and other numismatic organizations. **Remarks:** Also maintains a branch library in Wichita, KS, of 600 sales catalogs and price lists.

NUROCK (Dr. E.C.) LIBRARY
See: New Jersey Optometric Association - Dr. E.C. Nurock Library

★9475★
NUS CORPORATION - LIBRARY (Sci-Tech; Energy)
910 Clopper Rd.   Phone: (301) 258-6000
Gaithersburg, MD 20878   Jo Ann Merchant, Hd.Libn.
Founded: 1960. **Staff:** Prof 1; Other 2. **Subjects:** Nuclear engineering, environmental science, energy. **Special Collections:** NTIS reports, 1973 to present (800,000 on microfiche). **Holdings:** 12,000 books; 5000 bound periodical volumes; 2000 NUS reports. **Subscriptions:** 350 journals and other serials. **Services:** Interlibrary loans; copying; library open to public with prior permission. **Computerized Information Services:** DIALOG, SDC. **Networks/Consortia:** Member of Interlibrary Users Association. **Publications:** NUS Library Bulletin. **Formerly:** Located in Rockville, MD.

★9476★
NUS CORPORATION - TECHNICAL LIBRARY (Env-Cons; Sci-Tech)
Parkwest Two
Cliff Mine Rd.   Phone: (412) 788-1080
Pittsburgh, PA 15275   Kathryn E. Marlow, Libn.
Founded: 1964. **Staff:** Prof 1. **Subjects:** Consulting and design. engineering, hazardous waste/waste treatment, nuclear power, environmental protection, pollution. **Holdings:** Figures not available for books; microfiche technical report file; U.S. Geological Survey Water Resources Data for each state; product catalogs; road and topographical maps. **Subscriptions:** 250 journals and other serials; 10 newspapers. **Services:** Interlibrary loans; library not open to public. **Computerized Information Services:** DIALOG, SDC, DOE/RECON. **Publications:** Library Newsletter, monthly - for internal distribution only.

★9477★
NUTLEY HISTORICAL SOCIETY MUSEUM - ALICE J. BICKERS LIBRARY (Hist)*
65 Church St.   Phone: (201) 667-5239
Nutley, NJ 07110   Caroline Evangelista, Cur./Hist.
Founded: 1945. **Staff:** 6. **Subjects:** New Jersey and local history. **Special Collections:** Nutley authors; old account books of Nutley merchants; old costumes; Annie Oakley Collection. **Holdings:** 200 volumes. **Services:** Interlibrary loans; library open to public with restrictions. **Publications:** Annual report, quarterly Bulletins. **Staff:** Jeanne Van Steen, Pres.

★9478★
NUTRILITE PRODUCTS, INC. - RESEARCH LIBRARY (Sci-Tech)
5600 Beach Blvd.   Phone: (714) 521-3900
Buena Park, CA 90620   Jacqueline M. McCoy, Libn.
Founded: 1950. **Staff:** Prof 1. **Subjects:** Biochemistry, nutrition, cosmetics, accounting, law, business management, agriculture. **Holdings:** 6071 books;

700 bound periodical volumes; 12 VF drawers of pamphlets, clippings, pictures. **Subscriptions:** 155 journals and other serials. **Services:** Interlibrary loans; copying; library not open to public.

NUTRITION PLANNING INFORMATION SERVICE
See: Community Systems Foundation

NUTTING MEMORIAL LIBRARY
See: Maine Maritime Academy

★9479★
NYACK COLLEGE - LIBRARY (Rel-Theol)
                                                Phone: (914) 358-1710
Nyack, NY 10960   May K. Leo, Libn.
Founded: 1882. **Staff:** Prof 3; Other 2. **Subjects:** Protestant missions, Bible, theology, cultural anthropology, church history. **Holdings:** 70,000 books and bound periodical volumes; 36 VF drawers of pamphlets. **Subscriptions:** 565 journals and other serials. **Services:** Interlibrary loans; copying; library open to public for reference use only. **Publications:** Acquisition list, bimonthly - to faculty; library manual - to students. **Staff:** F. Ruth Bailey, Asst.Libn./Rd.Serv.; Jeffrey L. Brigham, Asst.Libn./Tech.Serv.

★9480★
NYACK HOSPITAL - MEMORIAL LIBRARY (Med)
N. Midland Ave.   Phone: (914) 358-6200
Nyack, NY 10960   Daniel J. Heenan, Dir.
Staff: Prof 1. **Subjects:** Medicine, nursing. **Holdings:** 1100 books; 1670 bound periodical volumes; 100 audiotapes. **Subscriptions:** 118 journals and other serials. **Services:** Interlibrary loans; copying; library open to public by appointment. **Networks/Consortia:** Member of New York State Interlibrary Loan Network (NYSILL); Health Information Libraries of Westchester (HILOW).

★9481★
NYBERG CARTOGRAPHIC COLLECTION (Geog-Map)
4946 Devonshire Circle   Phone: (612) 474-9011
Shorewood, MN 55331   Nancy Nyberg, Libn.
Founded: 1978. **Staff:** Prof 1. **Subjects:** Maps. **Special Collections:** U.S. and European cities, early world maps, panoramic views; old road maps. **Holdings:** 450 books and maps. **Services:** Library not open to public.

★9482★
NYE COUNTY LAW LIBRARY (Law)
Court House, Box 1271   Phone: (702) 482-6666
Tonopah, NV 89049
Founded: 1905. **Subjects:** Law. **Holdings:** 15,000 volumes. **Services:** Library open to public.

NYE (Russel B.) POPULAR CULTURE COLLECTION
See: Michigan State University - Special Collections Division - Russel B. Nye Popular Culture Collection

★9483★
NYLANDER MUSEUM - LIBRARY (Sci-Tech)†
                                                Phone: (207) 493-4474
Caribou, ME 04736   Clara Piper, Libn.
Founded: 1938. **Staff:** Prof 1. **Subjects:** Geology, botany, conchology, art, antiques, butterflies. **Special Collections:** Papers, correspondence and publications of Olof Nylander (1864-1943), early explorer of Northern Maine. **Holdings:** Books, pamphlets, clippings, documents (figures not available). **Services:** Library open to public for reference use only. **Staff:** Martha Chambers, Cur.